COME VISIT OUR NEW YORK CITY SHO ONLY.)
P9-BYM-235
FOUR COLOR
COMICS
BUY
SELL
WHY YOU SHOULD CALL US BEFORE YOU SELL YOUR COLLECTION OF COMICS, ARTWORK OR MEMORABILIA:
We make it easy! No waiting for payment, No song and dance about grading. We'll come to you: Anywhere, Anytime! FOUR COLOR COMICS takes the risk out of selling. Treat yourself to an honest, straight-forward experience—Sell your collection to us and walk away with more money in your pocket and a smile on your face.
And if you're looking to buy comics, original artwork or memorabilia, give us a call first! We probably already have that elusive issue or object you've been searching for—and at a price you'll like!
CALL ROBERT ROGOVIN!
(212) 675-6990
THE JOKER © 1939, 1998 DC COMICS. ALL RIGHTS RESERVED
NEW YORK SHOWROOM: 115 W. 27th St, NY, NY 10001 TEL: (212) 675-6990, FAX (212) 675-6145
NEW!
Visit our on-line
SEARCHABLE DATABASE!
1000's of Golden and Silver Age comics available without scrolling thru endless listings!
www.fourcolorcomics.com
ORIGINAL COMIC ART
SEARCH COMICS!
MOVIE POSTERS

GET
TOMORROW'S
CLASSICS...
...TODAY!
COMPELLING
STORIES.
UNFORGETTABLE
HEROES.
SPECTACULAR
ARTWORK.
WE'VE GOT
THEM ALL...
EVERY MONTH!
DC
©1998 DC COMICS. ALL RIGHTS RESERVED.

CALL 1-888-COMIC BOOK FOR THE COMICS SHOP NEAREST YOU!

BUYING COMICS

FROM

1900 - 1975

We want to purchase your comic collection, large or small. Highest prices paid. We travel anywhere to buy your collection. We will treat you fairly and make your selling experience an enjoyable one!

CALL TODAY

1-800-974-2999

FOR IMMEDIATE CASH OFFER

VINCENT ZURZOLO Jr.
SENIOR OVERSTREET PRICE GUIDE ADVISOR

424 BEACH 134th St.
BELLE HARBOR, NY. 11694
718-318-2423 fax: 718-318-1257

www.vincentscollectibles.com

BY APPOINTMENT ONLY

Selling the Finest Silver & Golden Age Comic Books
Call for Catalog/Computer Want List Service

COMIC BOOKS

Wanted

1900 through 1956

We are searching for thousands of Goldenage comic books and **Will Pay More** than anyone for what we want **Period!**

Immediate payment

© Marvel Publ.

© D.C. Publ.

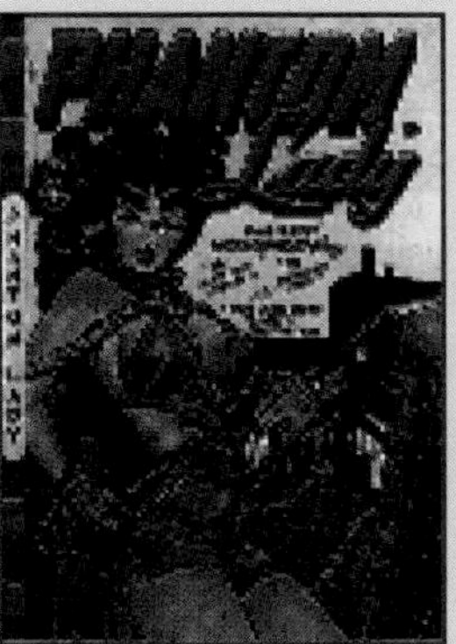
© Fox Publ.

We accept ALL grades!

World's Finest Comics & Collectibles

"The Right Choice"

- **Call -** (800) 225-4189 **Or** (360) 274-9163
- **Fax -** (360) 274-2270 anytime
- **Write -** P.O. Box 340 Castle Rock, Wa 98611
- **Catch us on the Web at -** www.worldsfinestcomics.com

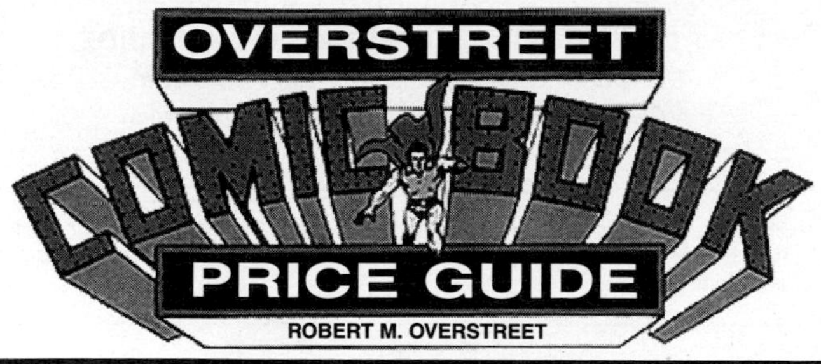

28th Edition

BOOKS FROM 1897 - PRESENT INCLUDED
CATALOGUE & EVALUATION GUIDE - ILLUSTRATED

By
Robert M. Overstreet

SPECIAL CONTRIBUTORS TO THIS EDITION
Murphy Anderson, Arnold T. Blumberg, Scott Braden, Jackie Estrada, Stephen Fishler, M. Thomas Inge, Richard D. Olson, Ph.D., Marc Patten, J. C. Vaughn

SPECIAL ADVISORS TO THIS EDITION
David T. Alexander • Dave Anderson • David J. Anderson, D.D.S. • Jon Berk • Gary M. Carter
John Chruscinski • Gary Colabuono • Larry Curcio • Gary Dolgoff • Joe Dungan
Bruce Ellsworth • Conrad Eschenberg • Richard Evans • Stephen Fishler • Keif Fromm
Philip J. Gaudino • Steve Gentner • Steve Geppi • Michael Goldman • Jamie Graham
Daniel Greenhalgh • Eric Groves • Gary Guzzo • John Grasse • Bruce Hamilton • John Hone
John Hauser • Bill Hughes • Rob Hughes • Joseph Koch • Phil Levine • Joe Mannarino
Rick Manzella • Harry Matetsky • Jon McClure • Matt Nelson • Hugh O'Kennon • Richard Olson
Michael Naiman • James Payette • Ron Pussell • Todd Reznik • "Doc" Robinson • Robert Rogovin
Rory Root • Robert Roter • Chuck Rozanski • Matt Schiffman • Dave Smith • John Snyder
Tony Starks • Terry Stroud • Doug Sulipa • Joel Thingvall • Raymond S. True • Joe Verenault
John Verzyl • Rose Verzyl • Jerry Weist • Mark Wilson • Harley Yee • Vincent Zurzolo, Jr.

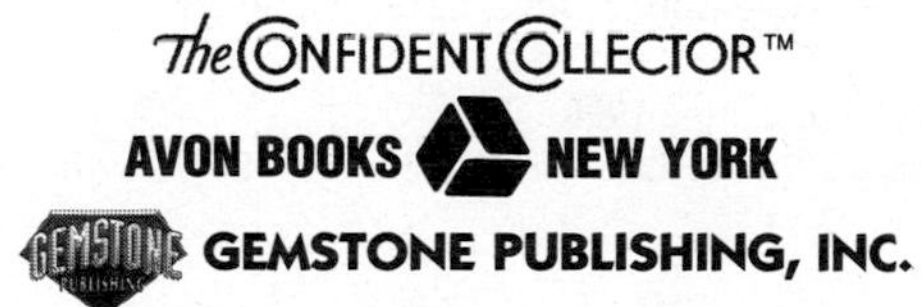
The CONFIDENT COLLECTOR™
AVON BOOKS NEW YORK
GEMSTONE PUBLISHING, INC.

Serious Comic Book Collectors, Also Look For
THE OVERSTREET COMIC BOOK GRADING GUIDE
By Robert M. Overstreet and Gary M. Carter
A Confident Collector Title from Avon Books

If you purchased this book without a cover, you should be aware that this book is stolen property. It was reported as "unsold and destroyed" to the publisher, and neither the author nor the publisher has received any payment for this "stripped book."

Important Notice. All of the information, including valuations, in this book has been compiled from the most reliable sources, and every effort has been made to eliminate errors and questionable data. Nevertheless, the possibility of error always exists in a work of such immense scope. The publisher will not be held responsible for losses which may occur in the purchase, sale, or other transaction of items because of information contained herein. Readers who feel they have discovered errors are invited to *write* and inform us so that the errors may be corrected in subsequent editions.

Front cover art: All Characters are trademarks of DC Comics and are used with permission. Copyright 1998 DC Comics. All rights reserved. Spine art: © DC Comics. © Marvel Entertainment Group

Cover Illustration and logo design by Murphy Anderson.

THE OVERSTREET COMIC BOOK PRICE GUIDE (28th Edition) is an original publication of Gemstone Publishing, Inc. and Avon Books. This edition has never before appeared in book form.

AVON BOOKS
A division of
The Hearst Corporation
1350 Avenue of the Americas
New York, New York 10019

Copyright © 1992, 1993, 1994, 1995, 1996, 1997, 1998 by Gemstone Publishing, Inc.
The Confident Collector and its logo are trademarked properties of Avon Books.
Overstreet is a registered trademark of Gemstone Publishing, Inc.
Published by arrangement with Gemstone Publishing
ISBN: 0-380-80075-6

All rights reserved, which includes the right to reproduce this book or portions thereof in any form whatsoever except as provided by the U.S. Copyright Law. For information address Gemstone Publishing, 1966 Greenspring Drive, Suite 405, Timonium, Maryland 21093.

First Avon Books Trade Printing: June 1998
AVON TRADEMARK REG. U.S. PAT. OFF. AND IN OTHER COUNTRIES, MARCA REGISTRADA, HECHO EN U.S.A.

Printed in the U.S.A.
10 9 8 7 6 5 4 3 2 1

TABLE OF CONTENTS

ACKNOWLEDGEMENTS

Mark Arnold (Harvey data); Larry Bigman (Frazetta-Williamson data); Glenn Bray (Kurtzman data); Gary Carter (DC data); J. B. Clifford Jr. (EC data); Gary Coddington (Superman data); Wilt Conine (Fawcett data); Dr. S. M. Davidson (Cupples & Leon data); Al Dellinges (Kubert data); David Gerstein (Walt Disney Comics data); Kevin Hancer (Tarzan data); Charles Heffelfinger and Jim Ivey (March of Comics listing); R. C. Holland and Ron Pussell (Seduction and Parade of Pleasure data); Grant Irwin (Quality data); Richard Kravitz (Kelly data); Phil Levine (giveaway data); Dan Malan & Charles Heffelfinger (Classic Comics data); Fred Nardelli (Frazetta data); Michelle Nolan (love comics); Mike Nolan (MLJ, Timely, Nedor data); George Olshevsky (Timely data); Richard Olson (LOA & R. F. Outcault data); Scott Pell ('50s data); Greg Robertson (National data); Don Rosa (Late 1940s to 1950s data); Matt Schiffman (Bronze Age data); Frank Scigliano (Little Lulu data); Gene Seger (Buck Rogers data); Rick Sloane (Archie data); David R. Smith, Archivist, Walt Disney Productions (Disney data); Tony Starks (Silver and Bronze Age data); Don and Maggie Thompson (Four Color listing); Mike Tiefenbacher & Jerry Sinkovec (Atlas and National data); Raymond True (Classic Comics data); Jim Vadeboncoeur Jr. (Williamson and Atlas data); Kim Weston (Disney and Barks data); Cat Yronwode (Spirit data); Andrew Zerbe and Gary Behymer (M. E. data).

My appreciation must also be extended to Dave Smith, Bruce Hamilton, Jerry Weist, John Verzyl, James Payette, Robert Rotor, Ron Pussell, Joe Mannarino, Terry Stroud, Conrad Eschenberg, Eric Groves, Jon McClure, Matt Schiffman, Robert Rogovin, Dave Anderson (OK), Gary Colabuono, Rod Dyke, Gary Guzzo, Harley Yee, John Snyder, Doug Supipa, Gary Dolgoff, Tony Starks, Matt Hawkins, Lou Bank, Jeff Mariotte, Donna Sava, Maureen McTigue, Marty Stever, Gale Young, Steve Geppi, Hugh O'Kennon and Don Maris, for their continued support and help; to Stephen Fishler and Marc Patten for their "How to Sell Your Comic Collection"; to Tracey Heft for his article on storage of comic books used in previous editions #25 and 26; to Dr. Richard Olson for grading and Yellow Kid information; to Tom Inge for his "Chronology of the American Comic Book"; to Robert Beerbohm for supplying much needed data on the Platinum Age; to Bill Blackbeard of the San Francisco Academy of Comic Art for his Platinum Age cover photos; to Bill Spicer and Zetta DeVoe (Western Publishing Co.) for their contribution of data; and especially to Bill for his kind permission to reprint portions of his and Jerry Bails' America's Four Color Pastime.

Late in the year, several knowledgeable people pitched in to help with data and pricing: Doug Sulipa sent in a book filled with data and Dave Smith, Jon McClure and Mark Wilson also provided needed data. Thanks is given to Rob Rogovin and Terry Stroud for their year-long help and advice.

Special Credit is due our talented staff for their assistance with this 28th edition; to Benn Ray (Editor), Arnold T. Blumberg (Managing Editor), Mark Huesman (Pricing Coordinator); Brenda Busick (Art Director), J. C. Vaughn (Marketing), and Dave Noah (research and statistical data) for their valuable contributions to this edition and the continuing success of the Annual Price Guide.

Finally, thanks is due to my wife Caroline Overstreet for her inspiration, advice and hard work in getting this reference work to the printer on time. Thanks to all who placed ads in this edition.

Acknowledgement is also due to the following people who generously contributed much needed data for this edition:

Aaasulewihi, Michael
Andreasen, Henrik
Becker, E.F.
Brown, Richard M.
Davis, Howard Leroy
Dinallo, Eric
Fischler, Mark
Fredd, Eliot,
French, Don
Garfunkel, Max
George, David R.,
Grande, John J.
Harms, Terry
Holmes, Corey
Howell, Jr., Jerry
Karon, Robert L.
Lavalier, Mark P.
Ledford, Rob
Linder, Mark
Maris, Don
Mathis, Robert L.
McClure, Jon
McLoughlin, J.P.
Mlachnik, John
Nicastre, Mike
Russell, Joan
Russell, John P.
Saltzman, Mark
Savage, Jr, William W.
Smith, Barry S.
Streenz, Andy
Sulipa, Doug

INTRODUCTION

Congratulations! We at Gemstone welcome you to the hobby of comic books. This book is the most comprehensive reference work available on comics. It is also respected and used by dealers and collectors everywhere. The Overstreet price is the accepted price around the world, and we have not earned this privilege easily. Through hard work, diligence and constant contact with the market for decades, Overstreet has become the most trusted name in comics.

HOW TO USE THIS BOOK

This volume is an accurate, detailed alphabetical list of comic books and their retail values. Comic books are listed by title, regardless of company. Prices listed are shown in Good, Fine and Near Mint condition with many key books priced in an additional Very Fine grade. Comic books that fall in between the grades listed can be priced simply with the following procedure: Very Good is half way between Good and Fine; Very Fine is half way between Fine and Near Mint (unless a VF price is already shown). The older true Mint books usually bring a premium over the Near Mint price. Books in Fair bring 50 to 70% of the Good price. Some books only show a Very Fine price as the highest grade. The author has not been able to determine if these particular books exist in better than Very Fine condition, thus the omission of a Near Mint price. Most comic books are listed in groups, i.e., 11-20, 21-30, 31-50, etc. The prices listed opposite these groupings represent the value of each issue in that group. More detailed information is given for individual comic books. If you are looking for a particular character, consult the first appearance indexes which will help you locate the correct title and issue. This book also contains hundreds of ads covering all aspects of this hobby. Whether you are buying or selling, the advertising sections can be of tremendous benefit to you.

NEW COMIC BOOKS LISTED

New comic books usually enter the listings at their retail cover price. Since new listings have yet to become valuable on the secondary market, the listed cover price only represents what it costs to buy a reading copy at a retail store. These books are not yet collectors items and their value in the collector's market would be nil.

COMIC BOOK VALUES LISTED

All values listed in this book are in U.S. currency and are retail prices based on (but not limited to) reports from our extensive network of experienced advisors which include convention sales, mail order, auctions, unpublished personal sales and stores. Overstreet, with several decades of market experience, has developed a unique and comprehensive system for gathering, documenting, averaging and pricing data on comic books. The end result is a true fair market value for your use. We have earned the reputation for our cautious, conservative approach to pricing comic books. You, the collector, can be assured that the prices listed in this volume are the most accurate and useful in print.

IMPORTANT NOTE: This book is not a dealer's price list, although some dealers may base their prices on the values listed. The true value of any comic book is what you are willing to pay. Prices listed herein are an indication of what collectors (not dealers) would probably pay. For one reason or another, these collectors might want certain books badly, or else need specific issues to complete their runs and so are willing to pay more.

DEALERS POSITION: Dealers are not in a position to pay the full prices listed, but work on a percentage depending largely on the amount of investment required and the quality of material offered. Usually they will pay from 20 to 70% of the list price depending on how long it will take them to sell the collection after making the investment; the higher the demand and better the condition, the more the percentage. Most dealers are faced with expenses such as advertising, travel, telephone and mailing, rent, employee salaries, plus convention costs. These costs all go in before the books are sold. The high demand books usually sell right away but there are many other titles that are difficult to sell due to low demand. Sometimes a dealer will have cost tied up in this type of material for several years before finally moving it. Remember, his position is that of handling, demand, and overhead. Most dealers are victims of these economics.

HOW COMIC BOOKS ARE LISTED

Comic books are listed alphabetically by title. The true title of a comic book can be found listed with the publisher's information, or indicia, usually found at the bottom of the inside front cover. Titles that appear on the front cover can vary from the official title listed inside.

Comic book titles, sequence of issues, dates of first and last issues, publishing companies, origin and special issues are listed when known. Prominent and collectible artists are also pointed out (usually in footnotes). Page counts will always include covers. Most comic books began with a #1, but occasionally many titles began with an odd number. There is a reason for this. Publishers had to register new titles with the post office for 2nd class permits. The registration fee was expensive. To avoid this expense, many publishers would continue the numbering of new titles from old defunct titles. For instance, **Weird Science** #12 (1st issue) was continued from the defunct **Saddle Romances** #11 (the last issue). In doing this, the publishers hoped to avoid having to register new titles. However, the post office would soon discover the new title and force the publisher to pay the registration fee as well as to list the correct number. For instance, the previous title mentioned began with #12 (1st issue). Then #13 through #15 were published. The next issue became #5 after the Post Office correction. Now the sequence of published issues (see the listings) is #12-

15, 5-on. This created a problem in early fandom for the collector because the numbers 12-15 in this title were duplicated.

WHAT COMIC BOOKS ARE LISTED

The Guide lists primarily American comic books due to space limitations. The earliest comic books date back to 1897 and are included in their own section under The Platinum Age. These books basically reprinted newspaper strips and were published in varying sizes, usually with cardboard covers, but sometimes as hardbacks. The format of **Funnies On Parade**, published in 1933 (saddle-stitched), soon became the standard for the modern comic book, although squarebound versions were also published. Most of these formats that appeared on newsstands will be included.

POLICY OF LISTING NEW COMIC BOOKS

The 1980s and '90s have experienced an explosion of publishers with hundreds of new titles appearing in black & white and color. Many of these comics are listed in this book, but not all due to space limitation. We will attempt to list complete information only on those titles that show some collector interest. The selection of titles to include is constantly being monitored by our board of advisors. Please do not contact us to list your new comic books. Listings are determined by the marketplace. However, we are interested in receiving review copies of all new comic books published.

GRADING COMIC BOOKS

GET THE TOOLS

For complete, detailed information on grading and restoration, consult the **Overstreet Comic Book Grading Guide**. Copies are available through all normal distribution channels or can be ordered direct from the publisher by sending $12 plus $2 postage and handling. You can also call Gemstone toll free at 1-888-375-9800.

The Overstreet Comic Book Grading Card, known as the **ONE** and **OWL Card** is also available. This card has two functions. The **ONE Card** (**O**verstreet's **N**umerical **E**quivalent) is used to convert grading condition terms to the new numerical grading system. The **OWL Card** (**O**verstreet's **W**hiteness **L**evel) is used for grading the whiteness of paper. The color scale on the **OWL Card** is simply placed over the interior comic book paper. The paper color is matched with the color on the card to get the **OWL** number. The **ONE/OWL Card** may be ordered direct from the publisher by sending $1.30 per card.

HOW TO GRADE

Before a comic book's true value can be assessed, its condition or state of preservation must be determined. In all comic books, the better the condition the more desirable and valuable the book. Comic books in **MINT** condition will bring several times the price of the same book in **POOR** condition. Therefore it is very important to be able to properly grade your books. Comics should be graded from the inside out, so the following comic book areas should be examined before assigning a final grade.

Check inside pages, inside spine and covers and outside spine and covers for any tears, markings, brittleness, tape, soiling, chunks out or other defects that would affect the grade. After all the above steps have been taken, then the reader can begin to consider an overall grade for his or her book. The grading of a comic book is done by simply looking at the book and describing its condition, which may range from absolutely perfect newsstand condition **MINT** to extremely worn, dirty, and torn **POOR**.

Numerous variables influence the evaluation of a comic book's condition and all must be considered in the final evaluation. As grading is the most subjective aspect of determining a comic's value, it is very important that the grader be careful not to allow wishful thinking to influence what the eyes see. It is also very important to realize that older comics in **MINT** condition are extremely scarce and are rarely advertised for sale; most of the higher grade comics advertised range from **VERY FINE** to **NEAR MINT**.

GRADING DEFINITIONS

Note: This edition uses both the traditional grade abbreviations and the **ONE** number throughout the listings. The **O**verstreet **N**umerical **E**quivalent (**ONE**) spread range is given with each grade.

MINT (MT) (ONE 100-98): Near perfect in every way. Only the most subtle bindery or printing defects are allowed. Cover is flat with no surface wear. Cover inks are bright with high reflectivity and minimal fading. Corners are cut square and sharp. Staples are generally centered, clean with no rust. Cover is generally well centered and firmly secured to interior pages. Paper is supple and fresh. Spine is tight and flat.

NEAR MINT (NM) (ONE 97-90): Nearly perfect with only minor imperfections allowed. This grade should have no corner or impact creases, stress marks should be almost invisible, and bindery tears must be less than 1/16 inch. A couple of very tiny color flecks, or a combination of the above that keeps the book from being perfect, where the overall eye appeal is less than Mint drops the book into this grade. Only the most subtle binding and/or printing defects allowed. Cover is flat with no surface wear. Cover inks are bright with high reflectivity and minimum of fading. Corners are cut square and sharp with ever so slight blunting permitted. Staples are generally centered, clean with no rust. Cover is well centered and firmly secured to interior pages. Paper is supple and like new. Spine is tight and flat.

VERY FINE (VF) (ONE 89-75): An excellent copy with outstanding eye appeal. Sharp, bright and clean with supple pages. Cover is relatively flat with almost no surface wear. Cover inks are generally bright with moderate to high reflectivity. Staples may show some discoloration. Spine may have a couple of almost insignificant transverse stress lines and is almost completely flat. A barely unnoticeable 1/4 inch crease is acceptable, if color is not broken. Pages and covers can be yellowish/tannish (at the least, but not brown and will usually be off-white to white).

FINE (FN) (ONE 74-55): An exceptional, above-average copy that shows minor wear but is still relatively flat and clean with no creasing or other serious defects. Eye appeal is somewhat reduced because of slight surface wear and possibly a very small defect such as a few very slight cross stress marks on spine. A Fine condition

Pr serve & Prot ct

Your comic books with only the best possible preservation supplies

In **3** Easy Steps:

1 **True Archival Quality Mylar® Sleeves**

- Comic Gards™ (4 mil.)
- Ark-Lites™ (1 mil.)
- Time-Loks® (4 mil.)

2 **True Archival Quality Acid-Free Backing Boards**

- Time-X-Tenders™ (42 mil.)
- Thin-X-Tenders™ (24 mil.)
- Life-X-Tenders™ (30 mil.)

3 **True Archival Quality Acid-Free Boxes**

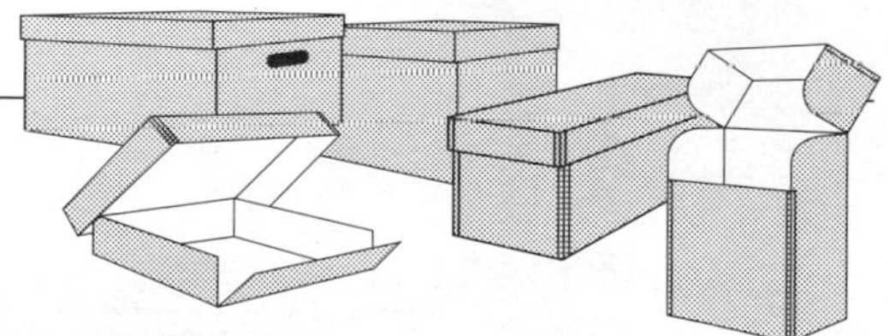

- Acid-Free Corrugated
- Flip top box
- Comic Carton
- Drop Front Shelf Box
- Shoe Box Style

See our FULL CATALOG on the INTERNET!

and sign up for our E-Mail mailing list to receive on-line specials

Feel free to browse and E-Mail us at any time.

INTERNET ADDRESS: http://www.neponset.com/bcemylar **E-MAIL: bcemylar@internetmci.com**

For information about an Internet Site, contact Dan Petipaus at
D&S Associates, 19 Carol Ave, Westwood, MA 02090 , 781-329-1344

Send for your free catalog today and receive a $5.00 merchandise coupon good towards your first order

Bill Cole Enterprises, Inc.

P.O. Box 60, DEPT. 58 , Randolph, MA 02368-0060

(781) 986-2653 FAX (781) 986-2656

Comic-Gards™, Ark-Lites™, Thin-X-Tenders™, Time-X-Tenders™ and Life-X-tenders™ are trademarks of Bill Cole Enterprises, Inc., Time-Loks® is a registered trademark of Bill Cole Enterprises, Inc. Mylar® is a registered trademark of DuPont Co.

New Machinery + Increased Production = LOWER PRICES

on our R-Kival™ Quality Mylar® Sleeves

From Bill Cole Enterprises, the Preservation Professionals℠

Bill Cole Enterprises has just purchased a machine that can more than triple our current production without compromising quality. With this new equipment, we are able to bring our manufacturing costs down and pass the savings along to you!

For over 23 continuous years, longer than any other supplier of comic supplies, BCE has been bringing you the best quality archival and preservation materials available. With our unlimited guarantee — and new lower prices — you can't lose.

R-Kival™

Comic-Gards™ (4 mil Mylar® Sleeves)

CAT #	SIZE with 1½" flap	TO FIT	PRICE PER 50	wt. lbs.	PRICE PER 100	wt. lbs.	PRICE PER 500	wt. lbs.	PRICE PER 1,000	wt. lbs.
57	7" x 10 1/2"	Current Size Comics	$24.00	2	$42.00	4	$181.00	18	$315.00	40
58	7 1/4" x 10 1/2"	Standard Size Comics	25.00	2	44.00	4	190.00	18	330.00	40
61	7 3/4" x 10 1/2"	Silver/Golden Age Size Comics	26.50	2	46.00	4	198.00	19	345.00	42
62	8" 1/4" x 10 1/2"	Super Golden Age Size Comics	27.50	2	48.00	4	207.00	20	360.00	42
63	9" x 11 1/2"	Magazines, Letters	32.00	3	56.00	6	242.00	22	420.00	45

/M = per 1,000 **Arklites™ (1 mil Mylar® Sleeves)** *Measurements may vary ±1/8"*

CAT #	SIZE with 1½" flap	TO FIT	PRICE PER 100	wt. lbs.	PRICE PER 500	wt. lbs.	PRICE PER 1,000	wt. lbs.	PRICE PER 3,000	wt. lbs.	PRICE PER 5,000	wt. lbs.
158	7" x 10 1/2"	Current Size Comics	$28.00	4	$100.00	7	$146.00	11	$127.00/M	33	$110.00/M	55
159	7 3/8" x 10 1/2"	Standard Size Comics	29.00	4	104.00	7	152.00	11	132.00/M	33	114.00/M	55
161	7 5/8" x 10 1/2"	Silver/Golden Age Size Comics	30.00	4	107.00	7	156.00	11	136.00/M	35	118.00/M	55
162	8" x 10 1/2"	Super Golden Age Size Comics	31.00	4	111.00	7	162.00	13	141.00/M	39	122.00/M	65
163	8 7/8" x 11 3/4"	Magazines, Letters	42.00	4	150.00	7	219.00	13	191.00/M	39	165.00/M	65

Everything is in stock for immediate delivery –

We've got what you want, when you want it, and there is no better preservation product anywhere!

Preservation Professionals℠ is a servicemark of BCE, Comic-Gards™ and Arklites™ are a trademarks of Bill Cole Enterprises, Inc. All references to Mylar® refer to archival quality polyester film such as Mylar® type D by Dupont Co.,or equivalent material such as Melinex®516 by ICI Corp.

See Next Page for Ordering Information →

The Final Step in Comic Book Protection!

Now Available R-Kival™ Quality Grey Acid-Free Corrugated Boxes

Exclusively From Bill Cole Enterprises

Same Great Acid Free Properties as our Comic Book Cartons —
(minimum pH of 8.5 with a 3% Calcium Carbonate Buffer Throughout)

These corrugated boxes have a 200lb test bursting strength which means you can stack them as high as you want.

Since you only store your comics in protective sleeves made entirely from Mylar® D – and you only use genuine acid free backing boards to support your comics – Now, don't store them in anything but R-Kival™ quality acid free boxes

OVER TIME, ANY OTHER BOXES CAN RUIN YOUR COMICS

Acid Free Corrugated Cartons

CAT #	SIZE L x W x H	DESCRIPTION	PRICE PER 5	wt. lbs.	PRICE PER 10	wt. lbs.	PRICE PER 25	wt. lbs.	PRICE PER 50	wt. lbs.
C-13	15" x 8" x 11 1/2"	Grey Acid free Corrugated Boxes *fits Current through Silver/Golden Age comics, will hold approx. 120*	$ 47.50	8	$ 90.00	10	$ 212.50	38	$ 400.00	76
C-15	15" x 9" x 12 1/2"	Grey Acid free Corrugated Boxes *fits Super Golden Age Comics and Magazines will hold approx. 95*	51.25	9	97.50	11	231.25	39	437.50	78

Note: *Acid-Free Boxes may only be ordered in increments of 5. Sorry, no mix and match.*

Shipped flat! • Easy assembly does not require glue or tape!

GENERAL SHIPPING AND HANDLING CHART

TOTAL SHIPPING WEIGHT	IF YOUR ZIP CODE BEGINS WITH: 0,1	2,3 or 4	5,6 or 7	8,9	APO, FPO, AK,HI & ALL U.S. TER. via Parcel Post	ALL FOREIGN COUNTRIES via Parcel Post
0-2	6.50	7.50	8.00	8.50	7.00	12.50
3-5	8.00	8.50	9.00	9.75	9.50	14.50
6-10	9.75	11.00	11.50	12.75	16.75	29.25
11-15	11.00	12.75	13.50	15.75	22.00	37.75
16-20	12.75	15.00	16.00	19.50	25.50	48.75
21-25	15.50	16.75	19.50	21.25	28.50	65.50
26-30	16.75	18.75	21.75	24.25	29.00	75.00
31-35	19.25	21.75	24.25	28.50	30.00	84.50
36-40	20.50	22.50	25.75	29.00	33.00	94.50
41-45	21.50	24.75	28.50	32.50	34.00	103.75
46-50	23.00	27.50	30.50	35.75	35.00	116.50

Note: *If weight is above 50 lbs., add together additional amounts. (Example: 60 lbs. in Zip 1 would be $23.00 plus $9.75, or $32.75 total.)*

PAYMENT MUST ACCOMPANY ORDERS

MA residents add 5% sales tax.
24 hour Toll Free Order Line for Mastercard, Visa, or Discover Orders Only

1-800-225-8249

This is a recorded tape and does not relay product information or messages.

24 hour Toll Free FAX Line for ordering only

1-800-FAX-BCE8
(1-800-329-2238)

Bill Cole Enterprises, Inc.
P.O. Box 60, DEPT. 58, Randolph, MA 02368-0060
(781) 986-2653 FAX (781) 986-2656
e-mail: bcemylar@internetmci.com web site: http://www.neponset.com/bcemylar

Preservation Professionals℠ is a servicemark of BCE, R-Kival™ is a trademark of Bill Cole Enterprises, Inc.

comic book appears to have been read a few times and has been handled with moderate care. Compared to a VF, cover inks are beginning to show a significant reduction in reflectivity but it is still a highly collectible and desirable book.

VERY GOOD (VG) (ONE 54-35): The average used comic book. A comic in this grade shows some wear, can have a reading or center crease or a rolled spine, but has not accumulated enough total defects to reduce eye appeal to the point that it is not a desirable copy. Some discoloration, fading and even minor soiling is allowed. As much as a 1/4" triangle can be missing out of the corner or edge. A missing square piece (1/8" by 1/8") is also acceptable. Store stamps, name stamps, arrival dates, initials, etc. have no effect on this grade. Cover and interior pages can have one or two minor tears and folds and the centerfold may be loose or detached. One staple can be loose, but the cover is not completely detached. Common bindery and printing defects do not affect grade. Pages and inside covers may be brown but not brittle. Tape should never be used for comic book repair, however many VG condition comics have minor tape repair.

GOOD (GD) (ONE 34-15): A copy in this grade has all pages and covers, although there may be small pieces missing inside; the largest piece allowed from front or back cover is a 1/2" triangle or a square 1/4" by 1/4". Books in this grade are commonly creased, scuffed, abraded and soiled, but completely readable. Often paper quality is low but not brittle. Cover reflectivity is low and in some cases completely absent. Most collectors consider this the lowest collectible grade because comic books in lesser condition are usually incomplete and/or brittle. This grade can have a moderate accumulation of defects but still maintains its basic structural integrity.

FAIR (FR) (ONE 14-5): A copy in this grade has all pages and most of the covers, centerfold may be missing, if it does not affect the story, but price should be reduced; a book in this condition is soiled, ragged and unattractive. Creases and folds are prevalent and paper quality may be moderately low. Spine may be split up to 2/3 its entire length. Staples may be gone, and/or cover split up to 2/3 its length. Corners are commonly slightly rounded. If coupons are cut from front cover and/or back cover and/or interior pages the book will fall into this grade. Up to 1/12 of front cover may be missing. These books are mostly readable although soiling, staining, tears, markings or chunks missing may interfere with reading the complete story. Very often paper quality is low and may have slight brittleness around the edges but not in the central portion of the pages.

POOR (PR) (ONE 4-1): Most comic books in this grade have been sufficiently degraded to the point that there is no longer any collector value. Copies in this grade typically have pages and/or approximately 1/3 or more of the front cover missing. They may have extremely severe stains, mildew or heavy cover abrasion to the point that cover inks are indistinct/absent. They may have been defaced with paints, varnishes, glues, oil, indelible markers or dyes. Other defects often include severe rips, tears, folding and creasing. Another common defect in this grade is moderate to severe brittleness, often to the point that the comic book literally "falls apart" when examined.

Used by Professional Archivists Worldwide

Life-X-Tenders™

The 3 Layer, Acid-Neutralizing Backing Boards

- The single most important innovation in archival comic storage since the introduction of Mylar® sleeves
- Unique 30 mil thick design has a layer of activated charcoal sandwiched between two sheets of true archival acid-free board
- Absorbs and neutralizes the harmful gases and contaminants comic book paper and inks release as they age
- Retards the aging process and preserves the value of your comics

Mix and Match in increments of 25

CAT.#	SIZE	TO FIT	PRICE	wt. lbs.
726	7" x 10 3/8"	Standard Size Comics	25 @ $24.95	3
724	7 3/8" x 10 3/8"	Silver/Golden Age Size Comics	100 @ $70.00	10
			500 @ $325.00	40
729	7 3/4" x 10 3/8"	Super Golden Age Size Comics	1000 @ $595.00	80

SHIPPING AND HANDLING CHART

Total Ordered	FOR UPS SHIPMENT IF YOUR ZIP CODE BEGINS WITH: 0,1	2,3 or 4	5,6 or 7	8,9
25	8.00	8.50	9.00	9.75
100	9.75	11.00	11.50	12.75
500	20.50	22.50	25.75	29.00
1000	39.75	46.25	52.25	60.00

Call for shipping charges for orders outside the continental U.S.

Put your message in the hands of over 13,000 potential customers for as little as 10¢ each!

Rent the MAILING LIST for the Comic Book & Baseball/Trading Card Industries

All lists are up to date and specifically target Comic Book and Baseball Card Retailers and Dealers. Lists can be customized by state, type of business or other demographics to help you put your advertising message into the hands of potential customers.

Increase your sales with a Direct Marketing campaign

Bill Cole Enterprises, Inc.

P.O. Box 60, DEPT. 58, Randolph, MA 02368-0060
(781) 986-2653 FAX (781) 986-2656
e-mail: bcemylar@internetmci.com
web site: http://www.neponset.com/bcemylar

Life-X-Tenders™ and R-Kival™ are trademarks of Bill Cole Enterprises, Inc. All references to Mylar® refer to archival quality polyester film such as Mylar® type D by Dupont Co., or Melinex® by ICI Corp.

DUST JACKETS

Many of the early strip reprint comics were printed in hardback with dust jackets. Books with dust jackets are worth more. The value can increase from 20 to 50 percent depending on the rarity of book. Usually, the earlier the book, the greater the percentage. Unless noted, prices listed are without dust jackets. The condition of the dust jacket should be graded independently of the book itself.

RESTORED COMICS

Our board of advisors suggests that **professionally restored comic books** are an accepted component of the comic book market, but only if the following criteria are met: 1–Must be professional work. 2–Complete disclosure of the extent and type of restoration. 3–Both parties are informed. 4–Priced accordingly depending on availability and demand. **Note:** A professionally restored book, reasonably priced, while not worth as much as the same book unrestored, will increase in value at the same rate. However, if you pay the unrestored price for a restored book, you would be paying a premium, which of course may not be a good investment.

Initial indications on sales and auction results suggests the following: Unrestored key books in Fine or better condition may prove in the future to be better investments as their availability decreases and should not be restored to an apparent higher grade. Restoration should be concentrated on books in less than Fine condition. **Warning:** Before getting restoration done, seek advice from a professional and avoid doing it yourself.

Many rare and expensive books are being repaired and restored by professionals and amateurs alike. If the book is expensive, there is a strong likelihood that some type of repair, cleaning or restoration has been done. In most cases, after restoration, these books are not actually higher grades but are altered lower grade books. **Note:** Expert restoration is always preferable to amateur work and is sometimes very difficult to spot when grading. In some cases, the work is done so skillfully that it is impossible to spot. Depending upon the extent and type of restoration and the quality of what was done, you will have to decide whether the value has increased or decreased. In many cases we have observed in the market that the value has been increased on certain books that were originally in low grade before restoration where the appearance and structural integrity was greatly improved afterwards. Restoration on higher grade copies may or may not affect value depending on what is done. Of course, when a comic book is graded, everything must be taken into account in the final grade given.

To the novice grading will appear difficult at first, but as experience is gained accuracy will improve. Whenever in doubt (after using ***The Overstreet Comic Book Grading Guide***), consult with a reputable dealer or experienced collector in your area. The following grading information is given to further aid the collector:

SCARCITY OF COMIC BOOKS RELATED TO GRADE

1897-1933 Comics: Most of these books are bound with thick cardboard covers and are very rare to non-existent in VF or better condition. Due to their extreme age, paper browning is very common. Brittleness could be a problem.

1933-1940 Comics: There are many issues from this period that are very scarce in any condition, especially from the early to mid-1930s. Surviving copies of any particular issue range from a handful to several hundred. Near Mint to Mint copies are virtually non-existent with known examples of any particular issue limited to five or fewer copies. Most surviving copies are in FN-VF or less condition. Brittleness or browning of paper is fairly common and could be a problem.

1941-1952 Comics: Surviving comic books would number from less than 100 to several thousand copies of each issue. Near Mint to Mint copies are a little more common but are still relatively scarce with only a dozen or so copies in this grade existing of any particular issue. Exceptions would be recent warehouse finds of most Dell comics (6-100 copies, but usually 30 or less), and Harvey comics (1950s-1970s) surfacing. Due to low paper quality of the late 1940s and 1950s, many comics from this period are rare in Near Mint to Mint condition. Most remaining copies are VF or less. Browning of paper could be a problem.

1953-1959 Comics: As comic book sales continued to drop during the 1950s, production values were lowered resulting in cheaply printed comics. For this reason, high grade copies are extremely rare. Many Atlas and Marvel comics have chipping along the trimmed edges (Marvel chipping) which reduces even more the number of surviving high grade copies.

1960-1979 Comics: Early '60s comics are rare in Near Mint to Mint condition. Most copies of early '60s Marvels and DCs grade no higher than VF. Many early keys in NM or MT exist in numbers less than 10-20 of each. Mid-'60s to late-'70s books in high grade are more common due to the hoarding of comics that began in the mid-'60s.

1980-Present: Comics of today are common in high grade. VF to NM is the standard rather than the exception.

When you consider how few Golden and Silver Age books exist compared to the current market, you will begin to appreciate the true rarity of these early books. In many cases less than 5-10 copies exist of a particular issue in Near Mint to Mint condition, while most of the 1930s books do not exist in this grade at all.

COLLECTING COMIC BOOKS

HOW TO START COLLECTING

New comic books are available in many different kinds of stores. Grocery stores, drug stores, Wal-Mart, K-Mart, book stores, comic book stores and card and comics specialty shops are a few examples. Local flea markets and, of course, comic book conventions in your area are excellent sources for new and old comic books.

Most collectors begin by buying new issues in Mint condition directly off the newsstand or from their local comic store. (Subscription copies are available from several mail-order services, and often the publishers themselves.) Each week new comics appear on the stands that are destined to become true collectors' items. The trick is to locate a store that carries a complete line of comics. In several localities this may be difficult. Most collectors frequent several magazine stands in order not to miss something they want. Even then, it pays to keep in close contact with collectors in other areas. Sooner or later, nearly every collector has to rely upon a friend in Fandom or a dealer to obtain for him an item that is unavailable locally (see ads in this book).

Before you buy any comic to add to your collection, you should carefully inspect its condition. Unlike stamps and coins, defective comics are generally not highly prized. The cover should be properly cut and printed. Remember that every blemish or sign of wear depreciates the beauty and value of your comics.

The serious collector usually buys extra copies of popular titles. He may trade these multiples for items unavailable locally (for example, foreign comics), or he may store the multiples for resale at some future date. Such speculation is, of course, a gamble. Selecting the right investment books is tricky business that requires special knowledge. With experience, the beginner will improve his buying skills. Remember, if you play the new comics market, be prepared to buy and sell fast as values rise and fall rapidly.

COLLECTING IN THE 1990s

Today's comic books offer a wide variety of subjects, art styles and writers to satisfy even the most discriminating fan. Whether it's the latest new hot title or company, or one of many popular titles that have been around for a long time, the comic book fan has a broad range from which to pick. Print runs of many popular titles have dropped over the past few years, creating the possibility of a true rarity occurring when demand outstrips supply. Less "gimmicky" covers are seen these days, but occasionally an eye-catching specialty cover will appear, such as the Superman new costume issue (#123) that glows-in-the-dark. Some cover variants continue to appear as well. "Bad Girl" and horror titles have been popular along with the standard superhero fare. The collector should always stay informed about the new trends developing in this fast-moving market. Since the market fluctuates greatly, and there is a vast array of comics to choose from, it's recommended first and foremost that you collect what you enjoy reading; that way, despite any value changes, you will always maintain a sense of personal satisfaction with your collection.

POLYBAGGED COMICS: It is the official policy of this Guide to grade comics regardless of whether they are still sealed in their polybag or not. Sealed comics in bags are not always in MINT condition and could even be damaged. The value should not suffer as long as the bag (opened) and all of its original manufactured contents are preserved and kept together.

COLLECTING ON A BUDGET: Collectors check out their local newsstand or comic specialty store for the latest arrivals. Hundreds of brand new comic books are displayed each week for the collector, much more than anyone can afford to purchase. Today's reader must be careful and budget his money wisely in choosing what to buy.

COLLECTING ARTISTS: Many collectors enjoy favorite artists and follow their work from issue to issue, title to title, company to company. In recent years, some artists have achieved "star" status. Autograph signings occur at all major comic conventions as well as special promotions with local stores. Fans line up by the hundreds at such events to meet these superstars. Some of the current top artists of new comics are: Todd McFarlane, Alex Ross, Jim Lee, Michael Turner, Marc Silvestri, Rob Liefeld, Chris Bachalo, J. Scott Campbell, Humberto Ramos, and Adam and Andy Kubert. Original artwork from these artists have been bringing record prices at auctions and from dealers' lists.

COLLECTING BY COMPANIES: Some collectors become loyal to a particular company and only collect its titles. It's another way to specialize and collect in a market that expands faster than your pocket book.

COLLECTING #1 ISSUES: For decades, comic enthusiasts have always collected first (#1) issues. This is yet another way to control spending and build an interesting collection for the future. #1 issues have everything going for them--some introduce new characters, while others are under-printed, creating a rarity factor. #1 issues cross many subjects as well as companies, and make for an intriguing collection.

COLLECTING BACK ISSUES

A back issue is any comic currently not available on the stands. Collectors of current titles often want to find the earlier issues in order to complete the run. Thus a back issue collector is born. Comic books have been published and collected for over 100 years. However, the earliest known comic book dealers didn't appear until the late 1930s. But today, there are hundreds of dealers that sell old comic books (See ads in this book).

LOCATING BACK ISSUES: The first place to begin, of course, is with your collector friends who may have unwanted back issues or duplicates for sale. Look in the yellow pages, or call the Comic Shop Locator Service at 1-888-COMIC-BOOK, to see if you have a comic book store available. If you do, they would know of other collectors in your area. Advertising in local papers could get good results. Go to regional markets and look for comic book dealers. There are many trade publications in the hobby that would put you in touch with out-of-town dealers. This Annual Guide has ads buying and selling old comic books. Some dealers publish regular price lists of old comic books for sale. Get on their mailing list.

Putting a quality collection of old comics together takes a lot of time, effort and money. Many old comics are not easy to find. Persistence and luck play a big part in acquiring needed issues. Most quality collections are put together over a long period of time by placing mail orders with dealers and other collectors.

Comics of early vintage are extremely expensive if they are purchased through a regular dealer or collector. Unless you have unlimited funds to invest in your hobby, you will find it necessary to restrict your collecting in certain ways. However you define your collection, you should be careful to set your goals well within affordable limits.

PRESERVATION & STORAGE

PROPER HANDLING OF COMIC BOOKS

Comic books are fragile and easy to damage. Most dealers and collectors hesitate to let anyone personally handle their rare comics. It is common courtesy to ask permission before handling another person's comic book. Most dealers would prefer to remove the comic from its bag and show it to the customer themselves. In this way, if the book is damaged, it would be the dealer's responsibility–not the customer's. Remember, the slightest crease or chip could render an otherwise Mint book to Near Mint or even Very Fine.

Consult the **Overstreet Comic Book Grading Guide** and learn the proper way to hold a comic book. The following steps are provided to aid the novice in the proper handling of comic books: 1. Remove the comic from its protective sleeve or bag very carefully. 2. Gently lay the comic (unopened) in the palm of your hand so that it will stay relatively flat and secure. 3. You can now leaf through the book by carefully rolling or flipping the pages with the thumb and forefinger of your other hand. Caution: Be sure the book always remains relatively flat or slightly rolled. Avoid creating stress points on the covers with your fingers and be particularly cautious in bending covers back too far on Mint books. 4. After examining the book, carefully insert it back into the bag or protective sleeve. Watch corners and edges for folds or tears as you replace the book. Always keep tape completely away while inserting a comic in a bag.

STORAGE OF COMIC BOOKS

Comic books should be protected from the elements as well as the dangers of light, heat, and humidity. This can easily be achieved with proper storage. Improper storage methods will be detrimental to the "health" of your collection, and may even quicken its deterioration.

Comic books should be stored away from direct light sources, especially florescent which contains high levels of ultraviolet (UV) radiation. UV lights are like sunlight, and will quickly fade the cover inks. Tungsten filament lighting is safer than florescent but should still be used at brief intervals. Remember, exposure to light accumulates damage, so store your collection in a cool, dark place away from windows.

Temperatures must also be carefully regulated. Fungus and mold thrives in higher temperatures, so the lower the temperature, the longer the life of your collection.

Atmospheric pollution is another problem associated with long term storage of paper. Sulfuric dioxide which can occur from automobile exhaust will cause paper to turn yellow over a period of time. For this reason, it is best not to store your valuable comics close to a garage. Some of the best preserved comic books known were protected from exposure to the air such as the Gaines EC collection. These books were carefully wrapped in paper at time of publication, and completely sealed from the air. Each package was then sealed in a box and stored in a closet in New York. After over 40 years of storage when the packages were opened, you could instantly catch the odor of fresh newsprint; the paper was snow white and supple, and the cover inks were as brilliant as the day they were printed. This illustrates how important it is to protect your comics from the atmosphere.

Like UV, high relative humidity (rh) can also be damaging to paper. Maintaining a low and stable relative humidity, around 50%, is crucial; varying humidity will only damage your collection.

Care must be taken when choosing materials for storing your comics. Many common items such as plastic bags, boards, and boxes may not be as safe as they seem. Some contain chemicals that will actually help to destroy your collection rather than save it. Always purchase materials designed for long-term storage, such as Mylar type "D" sleeves and acid-free boards and boxes. Polypropylene and polyethylene bags, while safe for temporary storage, should be changed every three to five years.

Comics are best stored vertically in boxes. For shelving, make sure that comics do not come into direct contact with the shelving surface. Use acid-free boards as a buffer between shelves comics. Also, never store comics directly on the floor; elevate them 6-10 inches to allow for flooding. Similarly, never store your collection directly against a wall, particularly an outside wall. Condensation and poor air circulation will encourage mold and fungus growth.

When handling your high grade comics, wash your hands first, eliminating harmful oils from the skin before coming into contact with the books. Lay the comic on a flat surface and slowly turn the pages. This will minimize the stress to the staples and spine. With these guidelines, your collection should enjoy a long life and maintain a reasonable condition and value.

BUYING & SELLING

HOW TO SELL YOUR COMIC COLLECTION

By purchasing this Guide, you have begun the long process necessary to successfully sell your comics. Before you can proceed, however, you must decide what category listed below best describes your collection. As a rule of thumb, the lower cate-

why not start at the top?

VIA is always buying!

Any comic book, in any condition, printed before 1973.

Phone us toll free:
1 888 VIABUYS

Visit our Web site:
www.viabuys.com

25 years of collectibles experience

VIA vintage investment associates

P.O. Box 354 Eastpointe, MI 48021

DIAMOND
INTERNATIONAL GALLERIES

WANTED: GOLDEN AGE

We pay the highest prices!

We'll give you top dollar for your Golden Age comics – in cash! No collection is too large or too small, and no one pays more!

We Pay Attention to You!

Whether you're buying or selling, Diamond International Galleries is dedicated to giving you the best deal, backed by unparalleled customer service from one of the industry's most responsible and knowledgeable staffs!

Send us a list of what you have for a quick reply, or give us a call!
Diamond International Galleries
1966 Greenspring Drive
Suite 401
Timonium, MD 21093
Call John K. Snyder toll free at
(888) 355-9800, ext. 271

Visit us on the Internet
www.diamondgalleries.com

gories will need less detail provided in your inventory list. A collection of key late '30s DCs will require you to list exact titles, numbers, and grades, as well as possible restoration information. If, however, you have 20,000 miscellaneous '80s and '90s comics for sale, a rough list of the number of books and publishers should be enough. The categories are:

1. PLATINUM AGE (1897-1932): The supply is very scarce. More people are becoming interested in these early books due to comics passing their 100th birthday. Moderate interest among average dealers, but high interest with dealers that specialize in this material. A detailed list will be necessary paying attention to brittleness, damage and pages missing. Dealers will pay up to a high percentage of Guide list for key titles.

2. GOLDEN AGE, All Grades (1933 - pre-1956): The most desirable. A detailed inventory will be necessary. Key higher grade books are easier to sell, but lower grades in most titles show the best selling potential, due to the fact that many collectors cannot afford a $20,000 VF book but may be able to afford a GD for only $2,000. Highest demand is for the superhero titles such as **Batman**, **Superman**, **Human Torch**, etc. The percentage of Guide that dealers will pay for your collection will vary depending on condition and contents. A collection of low demand titles will not bring the same percentage as a collection of prime titles.

3. High Grade SILVER AGE (1956-mid 1960s): A detailed inventory will be necessary. There are always investors looking for VF or better books from this period. Dealers will usually pay a high percentage of Guide list for these high grade books. Silver Age below VF will fall into category #4.

4. Low Grade SILVER AGE: Spanning books lower than VF from the late '50s to 1970, this category exhibits the average grade of most collections. Consequently, the supply of this material is much more common than category #2. This means that you could be competing with many other similar collections being offered at the same time. You will have to shop this type of collection to get the best price, and be prepared to sell at a significant discount if you find a willing buyer with good references.

5. MODERN AGE (post-1970): Certain titles from the early 1970s in high grade are showing increasing demand. However, many books from the 1980s to the 1990s are in low demand with the supply for the most part always being of high grade books. These collections are typified by long runs of certain titles and/or publishers. A detailed inventory will not be necessary. Contact local comic stores or buyers first to gauge their level of interest. Dealing with buyers outside your area should be avoided if possible.

IMPORTANT: Many of the 1980s and 1990s books are listed at cover price. This indicates that these books have not established a collector's value. When selling books of this type, the true market value could be 20-50% of cover price or less.

6. BULK (post-1980 in quantities greater than 5,000): These collections usually contain multiple copies of the same issues. It is advisable to price on a per-book basis (2¢ and 20¢ each). Do NOT attempt an inventory list, and only contact buyers who advertise buying in bulk quantity.

You should never deal with a buyer without fully checking their references. For additional verification, consult The Better Business Bureau; the local BBB may be able to help you in establishing a buyer's credibility, as well as assisting in resolving any disputes. **The Overstreet Comic Book Price Guide** and **Comic Book Marketplace** are also recognized authorities. Advertised dealers will likely have a more established reputation.

Potential buyers will be most concerned with the retail value of your entire collection, which may be more or less than Guide depending what you have and their current demand. Some rare early books in VF or NM may bring a price over Guide list while other titles in lower grade may sell for a price under Guide list. Most vintage books, however, will sell for around the Guide price. However, 1980s or 1990s books that list at cover price may only be worth a percentage of that price. You must then decide on what percentage you would be willing to accept for your collection, taking into account how the collection breaks down into fast, moderate and slow moving books. To expect someone to pay full retail is unrealistic. You will have to be flexible in order to close a deal.

Many buyers may want to purchase only certain key or high grade books from your collection, almost always favoring the buyer. While you may be paid a high percentage of retail, you will find that "cherry-picked" collections are much more difficult to sell. Furthermore, the percentage of retail that you will receive for a "cherry-picked" collection will be much lower than if the collection had been left intact. Remember, key issues and/or high grade issues make or break a collection. Selling on consignment, another popular option in today's market, could become a breeding ground for cherry-pickers, so again, always check a dealer's references thoroughly.

Some collectors may choose to sell their comic books on a piecemeal basis, requiring much greater care and detail in preparing an inventory list and grading comics for sale. You will be able to realize a higher percentage of retail by selling your collection this way, but the key books will certainly sell first, leaving a significant portion of the collection unsold. You will need to keep repricing and discounting your books to encourage buyers.

You can advertise your collection in trade publications or through mass mailings. If you sell books through the mail, you must also establish a reasonable return policy, as some books will unquestionably be returned. Check the local post office and/or UPS regarding the various rates and services available for shipping your books. Marketing your books at conventions is another option. As a dealer, you will also incur overhead expenses such as postage, mailing and display supplies, advertising costs, etc.

In all cases, be willing to establish trust with a prospective buyer. By following the procedures outlined here, you will be able to sell your collection successfully, for a fair price, with both parties walking away satisfied. After all, collecting comic books is supposed to be fun; it only becomes a chore if you let it.

WHERE TO BUY AND SELL

Throughout this book you will find the advertisements of many reputable dealers who sell back-issue comics magazines. If you are an inexperienced collector, be sure to compare prices before you buy. When a dealer is selected (ask for references), send him a small order (under $100) first to check out his grading accuracy, promptness in delivery, guarantees of condition advertised, and whether he will accept returns when dissatisfied. Never send cash through the mail. Send money orders or checks for your personal protection. Beware of bargains, as the items advertised sometimes do not exist but are only a fraud to get your money.

The Price Guide is indebted to everyone who placed ads in this volume. Your mentioning this book when dealing with the advertisers would be greatly appreciated.

COMIC BOOK CONVENTIONS

The first comic book conventions, or cons, were originally conceived as the comic book counterpart to science fiction fandom conventions. There were many attempts to form successful national cons, but they were all stillborn. It is interesting that after only three relatively organized years of existence, the first comic con was held. Of course, its magnitude was nowhere near as large as most established cons held today.

What is a comic con? Dealers, collectors, fans, publishers, distributors, manufacturers, whatever they call themselves can be found trading, selling, and buying the adventures of their favorite characters for hours on end. Additionally most cons have guests of honor, usually professionals in the field of comic art, either writers, artists, or editors. The committees put together panels for the con attendees in which the assembled pros talk about certain areas of comics, most of the time fielding questions from the assembled audience. At cons one can usually find displays of various and sundry things, usually toys, thousands of comic books, original art, and more. There can be the showing of movies or videos. Of course there is always the chance to get together with friends at cons and just talk about comics. One also has a good opportunity to make new friends who have similar interests and with whom one can correspond after the con.

It is difficult to describe accurately what goes on at a con. The best way to find out is to go to one and see for yourself. The largest cons are WonderCon (April), Pittsburgh (April), San Diego (July), Chicago (July), and Atlanta (July). For accurate dates and addresses, consult ads in this edition as well as some of the adzines. Please remember when writing for convention information to include a self addressed, stamped envelope for reply.

COVER BAR CODES FOR NEW COMIC BOOKS

Today's comic books are cover-coded for the direct sales (comic shop, newsstand, and foreign markets). They are all first printings, with the special coding being the only difference. The comics sold to the comic shops have to be coded differently, as they are sold on a no-return basis while newsstand comics are not. The Price Guide has not detected any price difference between these versions. Currently, the difference is easily detected by looking at the front cover bar code (a box located at the lower left). The bar code used to be filled in for newsstand sales and left blank or contain a character for comic shop sales. Now, as you can see above, direct sale editions are clearly marked, both versions containing the bar code.

Newsstand

Direct Sales (DC)

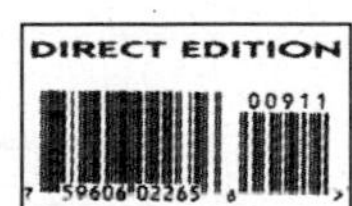

Direct Edition (Marvel)

MARVEL REPRINTS

In recent years Marvel has reprinted some of their comics. There has been confusion in identifying the reprints from the originals, but in 99% of the cases, the reprints have listed "reprint," or "2nd printing," etc. in the indicia, along with a later copyright date in some cases. Some Marvel 2nd printings have a gold logo. The only known exceptions are a few of the movie books such as **Star Wars**, the **Marvel Treasury Editions**, and tie-ins such as **G.I. Joe**. These books were reprinted and not identified as reprints. The **Star Wars** reprints have a large diamond with no date and a blank UPC symbol on the cover. Others had cover variations such as a date missing or different colors. Beginning in mid-1990, all Marvel 2nd printings have a gold logo.

Gold Key and other comics were also sold with a Whitman label. Even though collectors may prefer one label over the other, the Price Guide does not differentiate in the price. Beginning in 1980, all comics produced by Western carried the Whitman label.

COMIC BOOK PUBLISHERS' CODES The following abbreviations are used with the cover reproductions throughout the book for copyright credit purposes. The companies they represent are listed here:

AC-(Americomics)
ACE-Ace Periodicals
ACG-American Comics Group
AJAX-Ajax-Farrell
AP-Archie Publications
ATLAS-Atlas Comics (see below)
AVON-Avon Periodicals
BP-Better Publications
C & L-Cupples & Leon
CC-Charlton Comics
CEN-Centaur Publications
CCG-Columbia Comics Group
CG-Catechetical Guild
CHES-Harry 'A' Chesler
CLDS-Classic Det. Stories
CM-Comics Magazine
DC-DC Comics, Inc.
DEF-Defiant Comics
DELL-Dell Publishing Co.
DH-Dark Horse
DMP-David McKay Publishing
DS-D. S. Publishing Co.
EAS-Eastern Color Printing Co.
EC-E. C. Comics
ECL-Eclipse Comics
ENWIL-Enwil Associates
EP-Elliott Publications
ERB-Edgar Rice Burroughs
FAW-Fawcett Publications
FC-First Comics
FF-Famous Funnies
FH-Fiction House Magazines
FOX-Fox Features Syndicate
GIL-Gilberton
GK-Gold Key
GP-Great Publications
HARV-Harvey Publications
H-B-Hanna-Barbera
HILL-Hillman Periodicals
HOKE-Holyoke Publishing Co.
KING-King Features Syndicate
LEV-Lev Gleason Publications
MAL-Malibu Comics
ME-Magazine Enterprises
MEG-Marvel Ent. Group
MLJ-MLJ Magazines
MS-Mirage Studios
NOVP-Novelty Press
PG-Premier Group
PINE-Pines
PMI-Parents' Magazine Institute
PRIZE-Prize Publications
QUA-Quality Comics Group
REAL-Realistic Comics
RH-Rural Home
S & S-Street and Smith Publishers
SKY-Skywald Publications
STAR-Star Publications
STD-Standard Comics
STJ-St. John Publishing Co.
SUPR-Superior Comics
TC-Tower Comics
TM-Trojan Magazines
TOBY-Toby Press
TOPS-Tops Comics
UFS-United Features Syndicate
VAL-Valiant
VITL-Vital Publications
WDC-The Walt Disney Company
WEST-Western Publishing Co.
WHIT-Whitman Publishing Co.
WHW-William H. Wise
WMG-William M. Gaines (E. C.)
WP-Warren Publishing Co.
YM-Youthful Magazines
Z-D-Ziff-Davis Publishing Co.

TIMELY/MARVEL/ATLAS COMICS

"A Marvel Magazine" and "Marvel Group" was the symbol used between December 1946 and May 1947 (not used on all titles/issues during period). The Timely Comics symbol was used between July 1942 and September 1942 (not on all titles/issues during period). The round "Marvel Comic" symbol was used between February 1949 and June 1950. Early comics code symbol (star and bar) was used between April 1952 and February 1955. The Atlas globe symbol was used between December 1951 and September 1957. The M over C symbol (beginning of Marvel Comics) was used between July 1961 until the price increased to 12 cents on February 1962.

MARVEL/TIMELY/ATLAS PUBLISHERS' ABBREVIATION CODES

ACI-Animirth Comics, Inc.
AMI-Atlas Magazines, Inc.
ANC-Atlas News Co., Inc.
BPC-Bard Publishing Corp.
BFP-Broadcast Features Pubs.
CBS-Crime Bureau Stories
CLDS-Classic Detective Stories
CCC-Comic Combine Corp.
CDS-Current Detective Stories
CFI-Crime Files, Inc.
CmPI-Comedy Publications, Inc.
CmPS-Complete Photo Story
CnPC-Cornell Publishing Corp.
CPC-Chipiden Publishing Corp.
CPI-Crime Publications, Inc.
CPS-Canam Publishing Sales Corp.
CSI-Classics Syndicate, Inc.
DCI-Daring Comics, Inc.
EPC-Euclid Publishing Co.
EPI-Emgee Publications, Inc.
FCI-Fantasy Comics, Inc.
FPI-Foto Parade, Inc.
GPI-Gem Publishing, Inc.
HPC-Hercules Publishing Corp.
IPS-Interstate Publishing Corp.
JPI-Jaygee Publications, Inc.
LBI-Lion Books, Inc.
LCC-Leading Comic Corp.
LMC-Leading Magazine Corp.
MALE-Male Publishing Corp.
MAP-Miss America Publishing Corp.
MCI-Marvel Comics, Inc.
MgPC-Margood Publishing Corp.
MjMC-Marjean Magazine Corp.
MMC-Mutual Magazine Corp.
MPC-Medalion Publishing Corp.
MPI-Manvis Publications, Inc.
NPI-Newsstand Publications, Inc.
NPP-Non-Pareil Publishing Corp.
OCI-Official Comics, Inc.
OMC-Official Magazine Corp.
OPI-Olympia Publications, Inc.
PPI-Postal Publications, Inc.
PrPI-Prime Publications, Inc.
RCM-Red Circle Magazines, Inc.
SAI-Sports Actions, Inc.
SePI-Select Publications, Inc.
SnPC-Snap Publishing Co.
SPC-Select Publishing Co.
SPI-Sphere Publications, Inc.
TCI-Timely Comics, Inc.
TP-Timely Publications
20 CC-20th Century Comics Corp.
USA-U.S.A. Publications, Inc.
VPI-Vista Publications, Inc.
WFP-Western Fiction Publishing
WPI-Warwick Publications, Inc.
YAI-Young Allies, Inc.
ZPC-Zenith Publishing Co., Inc.

GLOSSARY

a-Story art; **a(i)**-Story art inks; **a(p)**-Story art pencils; **a(r)**-Story art reprint.
adult material–Contains story and/or art for "mature" readers. Re: sex, violence, strong language.
adzine-A magazine primarily devoted to the advertising of comic books and collectibles as its first publishing priority as opposed to written articles.
annual-A book that is published yearly.
arrival date-Markings on a comic book cover (usually in pencil) made by either the newsstand dealer or the distributor. These markings denote the date the book was placed on the newsstand. Usually the arrival date is one to two months prior to the cover date.
ashcan-A prepublication facsimile or dummy issue of an intended title usually prepared to show advertisers. Part or all of the pages may be blank or from a different book with a new cover. Black and white ashcans are common.
B&W-Black and white art.
bad girl art (BGA)-A term coined in 1993 to describe an attitude as well as a style of art that portrays women in a sexually implicit way.
Baxter paper–A high quality, white, heavy paper used in the printing of some comic books.
bi-monthly-Published every two months.
bi-weekly-Published every two weeks.
bondage cover-Usually denotes a female in restraints.
brittleness-The final stage of paper deterioration.
c-Cover art; **c(i)**-Cover inks; **c(p)**-Cover pencils; **c(r)**-Cover reprint.
Bronze Age–(1) Non-specific term not in general acceptance by collectors which denotes comics published from approximately 1970 through 1980, (2) Term which describes "the Age" of comic books after the Silver Age.
browning-Paper aging between tanning and brittleness.
cameo-When a character appears briefly.
CCA-Comics Code Authority.
CCA seal-An emblem that was placed on the cover of all CCA approved comics beginning in April-May, 1955.
center crease– (see Subscription Crease)
centerfold-The stapled, four page middle sheet of a comic or magazine.
CFO–Abbreviation for "Centerfold out."
chromium cover–A special Chromium foil used on covers
Church, Edgar collection-A large high grade comic book collection discovered by Mile High Comics in Colorado (over 22,000 books).
classic cover–A cover highly prized by collectors as a prime or matchless example of its kind.
cleaning–A process in which dirt and dust is removed.
color touch–A restoration process by which colored ink is used to hide color flecks, flakes and larger areas
colorist-An artist who paints the color guides for comics. Many modern colorists use computer technology.
comic book dealer–(1) A seller of comic books. (2) One who makes a living buying and selling comic books.
comic book repair-When a tear, loose staple or centerfold has been mended without changing or adding to the original finish of the book. Repair may involve tape, glue or nylon gossamer and is easily detected. It is considered a defect
comic book restoration-Any attempt, whether professional or amateur, to enhance the appearance of a comic book. These procedures may include any or all of the following techniques: recoloring, adding missing paper, stain, ink, dirt, tape removal, whitening, pressing out wrinkles, staple replacement, trimming, re-glossing, etc. Note: Unprofessional work can lower the value of a book. In all cases, except for some simple cleaning procedures, a restored book can never be worth the same as an unrestored book in the same condition.
Comics Code Authority-In 1954 the major publishers joined together and formed a committee which set up guidelines for acceptable comic contents. It was their task to approve the contents of comics before publication.
complete run–All issues of a given title.
con-A Convention or public gathering of fans.
condition–The state of preservation of a comic book.
Cosmic Aeroplane-Refers to a large collection discovered by Cosmic Aeroplane Books.
costumed hero–A costumed crime fighter with "developed" powers instead of "super" powers.
coupon cut–Comic book missing a coupon.
cover loose–Cover is detached from staple or staples
cover trimmed–Cover has been reduced in size through trimming.
crease–A paper fold that occurs in comic books from misuse
crossover–When one character or characters appears briefly in another character's story.
deacidification–The process of reducing acid in paper.
debut-The first time that a character appears anywhere.
defect–Any fault or flaw that detracts from perfection.
Denver collection–A collection of early '40s high grade #1s bought at auction in Pennsylvania by a Denver, Colorado dealer.
die-cut cover–When areas of a cover are precut by a printer to a special shape or to create a desired effect.
distributor painted stripes–Color brushed or sprayed on the edges of comic book stacks as special coding by distributors (not a defect).
double–A duplicate copy.
double cover-An error in the binding process which results in two or more

covers being bound to a single book. Multiple covers are not considered a defect.
drug propaganda story-Where comic makes an editorial stand about drug abuse.
drug use story-Shows the actual use of drugs: shooting, taking a trip, harmful effects, etc.
dust shadow–Usually the fore-edge of a comic cover exposed to the gathering of dust creating a dark stripe.
embossed cover–When a pattern is embossed onto the cover creating a raised area.
eye appeal–A term used to describe the overall appeal of a comic's apparent condition.
fanzine-An amateur fan publication.
file copy-A comic originating from the publisher's file. Not all file copies are in pristine condition. **Note:** An arrival date on the cover of a comic indicates that it is not a file copy though a copyright date may.
first app.-Same as debut.
flashback-When a previous story is being recalled.
foil cover–A thin metallic foil that is hot stamped on comic covers.
four color-A printing process in which the three primary colors plus black are used. Also refers to the Four Color series published by Dell.
foxing-Tiny orange-brown spots on the cover or pages of a comic book caused by mold growth.
G. A.-Golden Age period.
gatefold cover–A double cover folded in itself.
genre–Categories of comic book subject matter grouped as to type.
giveaway–Type of comic book used as a premium for promotional purposes.
Golden Age (G.A.)-The period beginning with **Action** #1 (June, 1938) and ending with World War II in 1945.
good girl art (GGA)-A term coined in 1977 to describe a style of art that portrays women in a sexually implicit way.
headlights-Women's breasts, usually provocative.
hologram cover–True 3-D holograms are prepared and affixed to comic book covers and cards for special effect.
hot stamping–The process of pressing foil, prism paper and inks on cover stock.
i-Art inks.
indicia-Publishers title, issue number, date, copyright and general information statement usually located on the inside front facing pages or inside back cover.
infinity cover-Shows the same scene within a scene repeated into infinity.
inker-Artist that does the inking.
intro-Same as debut.
JLA-Justice League of America.
JLI-Justice League International.
JSA-Justice Society of America.
key issue–An important issue in a run.
Lamont Larson-Refers to a large high grade collection of comics. Many of the books have Lamont or Larson written on the cover.
lenticular covers (aka flicker covers)–Images move when viewed at different angles specially prepared and affixed to cover.
logo-The title of a strip or comic book as it appears on the cover or title page.
LSH-Legion of Super-Heroes.
Marvel chipping-A defect that occurred during the trimming process of 1950s and 1960s Marvels which produced a ragged edge around the comic cover. Usually takes the form of a tiny chip or chips along the right hand edge of the cover.
Mile High-Refers to a large NM-Mint collection of comics originating from Denver, Colorado (Edgar Church collection).
Modern Age–Period from 1980 to the present.
Mylar ™–An inert, very hard, space age plastic used to make high quality protective bags and sleeves used for comic storage. Mylar ™ is a trademark of the DuPont Company.
nd-No date.
nn-No number.
N. Y. Legis. Comm.-New York Legislative Committee to Study the Publication of Comics (1951).
one-shot-When only one issue is published of a title or the title is published on an infrequent or irregular schedule, whether or not as part of a numbered series (such as Dell's Four Color).
origin-When the story of the character's creation is given.
over Guide-When a comic book is priced at a value over Guide list.
p-Art pencils.
painted cover–Cover taken from an actual painting instead of a line drawing.
paper cover–Comic book cover made from the same newsprint as interior pages (self cover). These books are extremely rare in high grade.
pedigree-A book from a famous collection, e.g. Allentown, Larson, Church/Mile High, Denver, San Francisco, Cosmic Aeroplane, etc. Note: Beware of non-pedigree collections being promoted as pedigree books. Only outstanding high grade collections similar to those listed qualify.
penciler-Artist that does the pencils.
photo cover–Made from a photograph instead of a line drawing or painting.
POP-Parade of Pleasure, book about the censorship of comics.
post-Code-Comic books published with the CCA seal.
post-Golden Age-Comic books published between 1945 and 1950.
post-Silver Age-Comic books published from 1969 to present.
Poughkeepsie-Refers to a large collection of Dell Comics' "file copies" believed to have originated from the warehouse of Western Publishing in Poughkeepsie, N.Y.
pre-Code-Comic books published before the CCA seal.
pre-Golden Age-Comic books published prior to **Action** #1 (June, 1938).
pre-hero–A term that describes the issues in a run prior to a superhero entering the run.
pre-Silver Age-Comic books published between 1950 and **Showcase** #4 (1956).
printing defect-A defect caused by the printing process. Examples would include paper wrinkling, miscut edges, misfolded spine, untrimmed pages, off-

registered color, off-centered trimming, misfolded and misbound pages. It should be noted that these are defects that lower the grade of the book.

prism cover–Special reflective foil material with 3-dimensional repeated designs. Used for special effect.

provenance-When the owner of a book is known and is stated for the purpose of authenticating and documenting the history of the book. Example: A book from the Stan Lee or Forrest Ackerman collection would be an example of a value-adding provenance.

quarterly-Published every three months (four times a year).

R or r-Reprint.

rare-10 to 20 copies estimated to exist.

rat chew–Damage caused by gnawing rats or mice.

reprint comics-Comic books that contain newspaper strip reprints.

restoration–The fine art of repairing a comic book to look as close as possible to its original condition.

rice paper-A thin, transparent paper commonly used by restorers to repair tears and replace small pieces on covers and pages of comic books.

rolled spine–A spine condition caused by folding back pages while reading.

S. A.-Silver Age.

saddle stitch–The staple binding of comic books.

S&K-Joe Simon and Jack Kirby (artists).

scarce-20 to 100 copies estimated to exist.

semi-monthly-Published twice a month, as distinguished from bi-weekly.

Silver Age-Officially begins with **Showcase** #4 in 1956 and ends in 1969.

silver proof-A black & white actual size print on thick glossy paper hand painted by an artist to indicate colors to the engraver.

SOTI-Seduction of the Innocent, book about the censorship of comics. Refer to listing in this Guide.

spine-The area representing the folded and stapled part of a comic book.

spine roll-A defect caused by improper storage which results in uneven pages and the shifting or bowing of the spine.

splash panel-A large panel that usually appears at the front of a comic story.

squarebound-A comic book glue-bound with a square spined cover, aka perfect bound.

store stamp–Store name stamped in ink on cover.

stress lines-Light, tiny wrinkles occurring along the spine, projecting from the staples or appearing anywhere on the covers of a comic book.

subscription crease-A center crease caused by the folding of comic books for mailing to subscribers. This is considered a defect.

sun shadow–A darkened strip along the fore-edge of a comic cover caused by prolonged exposure to light, unlike the dust shadow which can often be removed. A serious defect.

superhero–A costumed hero crime fighter with powers beyond those of mortal man.

supervillain–A costumed criminal with powers beyond those of mortal man.

swipe–A panel, sequence, or story obviously stolen or copied from previously published material.

3-D comic-Comic art that is drawn and printed in two mismatched colors, producing a 3-D effect when viewed through special glasses.

3-D effect comic-Comic art that is drawn to appear 3-D, but isn't.

title page–The first page showing the title of a story.

under Guide-When a comic book is priced at a value less than Guide list.

variant cover-a different cover image used on the same issue of a comic title.

very rare-1 to 10 copies estimated to exist.

warehouse copy-Originating from a publisher's warehouse; similar to file copy.

x-over-When one character crosses over into another's strip.

zine-See Fanzine.

COMIC BOOK ARTISTS

COMIC BOOK ARTISTS LISTED: Many of the popular artists are pointed out in the listings. When more than one artist worked on a story, their names are separated by a (/). The first name did the pencil drawings and the second the inks. When two or more artists work on a story, only the most prominent will be noted in some cases. We wish all good artists could be listed, but due to space limitation, only the most popular can. The following list of artists are considered to be either the most collected in the comic field or are historically significant. Artists designated below with an (*) indicate that only their most noted work will be listed. The rest will eventually have all their work shown as the information becomes available. This list could change from year to year as new artists come into prominence.

Adams, Arthur
Adams, Neal
Bachalo, Chris
Bagley, Mark
Baker, Matt
Barks, Carl
Beck, C. C.
*Brunner, Frank
*Buscema, John
Byrne, John
Campbell, J. Scott
Capullo, Greg
*Check, Sid
Cole, Jack
Cole, L. B.
Craig, Johnny
Crandall, Reed
Darrow, Geof
Davis, Jack
Disbrow, Jayson
*Ditko, Steve
Eisner, Will
*Elder, Bill
Evans, George
Everett, Bill
Feldstein, Al
Fine, Lou
Foster, Harold
Fox, Matt
Frazetta, Frank
Gibbons, Dave
*Giffen, Keith
Golden, Michael
Gottfredson, Floyd
*Guardineer, Fred
Gustavson, Paul
*Heath, Russ
Howard, Wayne
*Infantino, Carmine
Ingels, Graham
Jones, Jeff
Kamen, Jack
Kane, Bob
*Kane, Gil
Kelly, Walt
Kieth, Sam
Kinstler, E. R.
Kirby, Jack
Krenkel, Roy
Krigstein, Bernie
Kubert, Adam
Kubert, Andy
*Kubert, Joe
Kurtzman, Harvey
Lapham, Dave
Larsen, Erik
Lee, Jae
Lee, Jim
Liefeld, Rob
Madureira, Joe
Manning, Russ
McFarlane, Todd
McWilliams, Al
Meskin, Mort
Mignola, Mike
Miller, Frank
Moreira, Ruben
*Morisi, Pete
*Newton, Don
Nostrand, Howard
Orlando, Joe
Pakula, Mac
*Palais, Rudy
*Perez, George
Portacio, Whilce
Powell, Bob
Quesada, Joe
Raboy, Mac
Ramos, Humberto
Raymond, Alex
Ravielli, Louis
*Redondo, Nestor
Rogers, Marshall
Ross, Alex
Schomburg, Alex
Sears, Bart
Siegel & Shuster
Silvestri, Marc
Simon & Kirby (S&K)
*Simonson, Walt
Smith, Paul
Stanley, John
*Starlin, Jim
Steranko, Jim
Stevens, Dave
Texeira, Mark
Thibert, Art
Torres, Angelo
Toth, Alex
Turner, Michael
Tuska, George
Ward, Bill
Williamson, Al
Windsor-Smith, Barry
Woggon, Bill
Wolverton, Basil
Wood, Wallace
Wrightson, Bernie
Zeck, Mike

COMIC BOOK ARTISTS & THEIR FIRST WORK

Adams, Neal - (1 pg.) **Archie's Jokebook Mag.** #41, 9/59; (1st on Batman, cvr only) **Detective Comics** #370, 12/67; (1st Warren art) **Creepy** #14

Balent, Jim - Sgt. Rock #393, 10/84

Barks, Carl - (art only) **Donald Duck Four Color** #9, 8/42; (scripts only) **Large Feature Comic** #7, ca. Spring 1942

Broderick, Pat - (cover & art) **Planet of Vampires** #1, 2/75

Brunner, Frank - (fan club sketch) **Creepy** #10, 1965

Buckler, Rich - Flash Gordon #10, 11/67

Burnley, Jack - (cover & art) **NY World's Fair** nn, '40

Buscema, John - (1st at Marvel) **Strange Tales** #150, 11/66

Byrne, John - Nightmare #20, 8/74; (1st at DC) **Untold Legend of the Batman** #1, 7/80; (1st at Marvel) **Giant-Size Dracula** #5, 6/75

Capullo, Greg - (1st on X-Force) **X-Force Annual** #1, '92

Cole, Jack - (1 pg.) **Star Comics** #11, 4/38

Crandall, Reed - Hit Comics #10, 4/41

Davis, Jack - (cartoon) **Tip Top Comics** #32, 12/38

Ditko, Steve - (1st publ.) **Black Magic** V4#3, 11-12/53 (1st drawn story), **Fantastic Fears** #5, 1-2/54

Everett, Bill - Amazing Mystery Funnies V1#2, 9/38

Fine, Lou - (1st cvr) **Wonder Comics** #2, 6/39; **Jumbo Comics** #4, 12/38

Frazetta, Frank - Tally-Ho Comics nn, 12/44

Garney, Ron - G. I. Joe, A Real American Hero #110, 3/91

Giffen, Keith - (1 pg.) **Deadly Hands of Kung-Fu** #17, 11/75; (1st story) **Deadly Hands of Kung-Fu** #22, 4?/76; (tied w/Deadly Hands) **Amazing Adventures** #35, 3/76

Golden, Michael - Marvel Classics Comics #28, '77

Grell, Mike - Adventure Comics #435, 9-10/74

Hamner, Cully - Green Lantern: Mosaic #1, 6/92

Hughes, Adam - Blood of Dracula #1, 11/87

Ingels, Graham art at E.C. - Saddle Justice #4, Sum '48

Jurgens, Dan - Warlord #53, 1/82

Kaluta, Michael - Teen Confessions #59, 12/69

Kelly, Walt - New Comics #1, 12/35

Keown, Dale - Nth Man the Ultimate Ninja #8, 1/90; (1st at Marvel) **Samurai** #13, ?/87; (1st on Hulk) **Incredible Hulk** #367, 3/90

Kieth, Sam - Primer #5, 11?/83

Kirby, Jack - Jumbo Comics #1, 9/38;

Kubert, Adam/Andy/Joe art - Sgt. Rock #422, 7/88

Kurtzman, Harvey - Tip Top Comics #36, 4/39; (1st at E.C.) **Lucky Fights It Through** nn, 1949

Larsen, Erik - Megaton #1, 11/83

Lee, Jae - Marvel Comics Presents #85, '91

Lee, Jim - (1st at Marvel) **Alpha Flight** #51, 10/87; (1st on X-Men) **X-Men** #248?, ?/89; (art on Punisher) **Punisher War Journal** #1, 11/88

Liefeld, Rob - (1st at DC) **Warlord** #131, 9/88; (1st at Marvel) **X-Factor** #40, 4?/89; (1st full story) **Megaton** #8, 8/87; (inside front cover only) **Megaton** #5, 6/86; (art on New Mutants) **New Mutants Annual** #5, '89

Lim, Ron - (art on Silver Surfer) **Silver Surfer Ann.** #1, '88

Matsuda, Jeff - Brigade #0, 9/93

Mayer, Sheldon - New Comics #1, 12/35

McFarlane, Todd - Coyote #11, ?/85; (1st full story) **All Star Squadron** #47, 7/85; (1st on Hulk) **Incredible Hulk** #330, 4/87

Medina, Angel - (pin-up only) **Megaton** #3, 2/86

Mignola, Mike - Marvel Fanfare #15, 5/83

Miller, Frank - (1st on Batman) **DC Special Series** #21, Spr '80; (1st on Daredevil) **Spectacular Spider-Man** #27, 2/79

Newton, Don - Many Ghosts of Dr. Graves #45, 5/74

Perez, George - (1st at DC) **Flash** #289, 9/80; (2 pgs.) **Astonishing Tales** #25, 8/74

Portacio, Whilce - (1st on X-Men) **X-Men** #201, 1/86

Pulido, Brian - Evil Ernie #1, 12/91

Quesada, Joe - (1st on X-Factor) **X-Factor Ann.** #7, '92

Raboy, Mac - (1st cover for Fawcett) **Master Comics** #21, 12/41

Ramos, Humberto - (1st U.S. work) **Hardwire** #15, 6/94
Romita, John - **Daredevil** #12, 1/66
Romita, John Jr. - (1st complete story) **Iron Man** #115, 10/78
Ross, Alex - **The Terminator: The Burning Earth** V2#1, 3/90
Shuster, Joe - (cover) **New Adv. Comics** #16, 6/37
Siegel & Shuster - **New Fun Comics** #6, 10/35
Simon & Kirby - **Blue Bolt** #2, 7/40
Simonson, Walter - **Magnus, Robot Fighter** #10, 5/65
Smith, Paul - (1 pg. pin-up) **King Conan** #7, 9/81; (1st full story) **Marvel Fanfare** #1, 3/82
Steranko, Jim - **Spyman** #1, Sep '66; (1st at Marvel) **Strange Tales** #151, 12/66
Swan, Curt - **Dick Cole** #1, 12-1/48-49
Talbot, Bryan - (1st U.S. work) **Hellblazer Annual** #1, Summer '89
Thomas, Roy - (scripts) **Son of Vulcan** #50, 1/66
Torres, Angelo - **Crime Mysteries** #13, 5/54
Turner, Mike - **Cyberforce Origins-Stryker**, 2/95
Weeks, Lee - **Tales of Terror** #5, 11/85
Weiss, Alan - (illo) **Blue Beetle** #5, 3-4/65
Williamson, Al - (1st at E.C.) **Tales From the Crypt** #31, 9/52; (text illos) **Famous Funnies** #169, 8/48
Windsor-Smith, Barry - **X-Men** #53, 2/69
Wood, Wally - (1st at E.C.) **Saddle Romances** #10, 1-2/50
Wrightson, Bernie - **House of Mystery** #179, 4/68; (1st at Marvel) **Chamber of Darkness** #7, 10/70; (1st cover) **Web of Horror** #3, 4/70; (fan club sketch) **Creepy** #9
Zeck, Mike - (illos) **Barney and Betty Rubble** #11, 2/75

KEY COMICS SOLD IN 1997

The following lists of sales were reported to Gemstone during the year and represent only a small portion of the total amount of important books that have sold.

GOLDEN-ATOM AGE SALES

Allentown (AT), Bethlehem (BH), Big Apple (BA), File (FC), Cosmic Aeroplane (CA), Denver (DEN), Gains (GA), Green River (GR), Larson (LR), Mile High (MH), Mohawk Valley (MV), Pennsylvania (PA), Restored (R), San Francisco (SF), Traded (T), White Mountain (WM); trade (tr)

Action Comics #1FN+(r)	$52,500
Action Comics #1GD+	$37,950
Action #1VG (mostly trade)	$100,000
Action Comics #2VG	$6,727
Action #2GD+ & #3VG+	$11,500
Action Comics #5FR+	$1,725
Action Comics #5VG+	$2,185
Action Comics #10GD	$1,840
Action Comics #21VG+	$1,100
Action Comics #23VG+	$3,300
Action Comics #24VF+(r)	$925
Action Comics #46VF+	$775
Action Comics #86VF+	$425
Action Comics #102VF+	$550
Adventure Comics #38FN	$700
Adventure #40VG+ (CA)	$12,650
Adventure Comics #51FN	$825
Adventure Comics #103FN	$1,265
Advs. Into Terror #43VF+ (WM)	$660
Advs. Into/Unknown #25NM(WM)	$360
Advs. of Rex #1VF+	$977
All American #25VF+ (MH)	$16,100
All American Comics #89NM	$2,127
All American #61FN+	$4,313
All American #100FN+	$1,265
All American #102NM+	$2932
All-Flash #1VF+ (Recil Macon)	$9,900
All-Flash #1FN	$4,000
All Star Comics #1NM (MH)	$48,000
All Star Comics #1VF+	$34,500
All Star #6VG+	$920
All Star #8FN	$7,475
All Star #12VF+ (MH)	$4,888
All Star Comics #20NM+ (MH)	$6,490
All Top #10VF	$700
All Winners #8FN	$550
All Winners #21VF+	$3,852
America's Best #11NM+ (MH)	$1,320
America's Greatest #1FN	$550
Archie Comics #1NM (MH)	$53,000
Atomic Comics #1VF+	$871
Atomic Comics #2VF+	$370
Batman #1VG (r)	$7,500
Batman #1FR	$3,400
Batman #4VG	$980
Batman #5VG+	$1,100
Batman #25VF	$980
Batman #27NM	$1,980
Batman #33NM (MH)	$4,000
Batman #39NM (MH)	$3,600
Batman #43NM (MH)	$3,600
Batman #49NM (MH)	$5,500
Beware #8VF+	$190
Big Book of Fun #1GD	$3,000
Blackhawk #10VF+	$1,096
Blue Beetle #1-5 (MH)	$10,350
Bold Stories nn FN	$450
Boy Commandos #7NM+ (MH)	$2,090
Bulletman #1VG+	$900
Bulletman #5NM+ (MH)	$2,065
Candid Tales nn FN	$450
Captain America #1VF(r)	$11,500
Captain America #53VF+	$1,150
Captain America #74VG	$1,650
Captain America Annual VG	$6,000
Captain Marvel #3FN+	$900
Captain Marvel Jr. #13MT (MH)	$1,650
Captain Marvel Jr. #17FN+	$200
Captain Midnight #1FN	$750
Captain 3D #1NM	$60
Catman #1VF+ (LR)	$4,887
Chilling Tales #13(#1)NM	$690
Comic Calvacade #1NM (MH)	$8,050
Comic Calvacade #5VF+ (MH)	$1,725
Comic Calvacade #8NM (MH)	$1,840
Comic Cavalcade #26FN+ (MH)	$520
Crack Comics #2FN	$635
Crack Comics #27NM (MH)	$1,035
Crime Must Stop #1VF	$575
Crimes By Women #4FN+	$345
Dagar #16FN+	$180
Danger Trail #3GD+	$350
Daredevil Battles Hitler #1GD	$800
Daredevil #1&2NM (MH)	$18,400
Daring Mystery #1NM (DEN)	$17,500
Detective Comics #2FR+	$3,163
Detective Comics #12GD	$780
Detective Comics #32FN	$1,900
Detective Comics #151VF+	$550
Double Comics 1940FN	$980
Detective Comics #4VG	$2,970
Detective Comics #16VG	$1,500
Detective #21VF (r)	$2,100
Detective Comics #27FN	$66,000
Detective Comics #28VG+	$4,600
Detective Comics #34VG+	$1,265

Detective Comics #54VF $1,150
Detective Comics #58FN $1,155
Detective Comics #64VG+ $1,035
Detective Comics #66VF $1,675
Detective Comics #146VF $325
Detective Comics #188NM+ (MH)$2,200
Dollman #8FN $250
Donald Duck Four Color #9FR $300
Eerie Adventures #1VF+ $431
Exciting Comics #9FN $2,300
Famous Crimes #1VF+ $747
Famous Funnies, A Carnival VF+$6,900
Famous Funnies, A Carnival FN+$5,175
Fantastic #2,3,4 $5462
Fantastic Comics #22VF $510
Feature Book #51NM+ (MH) $715
Fight Comics #1VG+ $700
Fighting Yank #4VF $510
Flash Comics #1FN (r) $6,000
Flash Comics #1VG $10,350
Flash Comics #1FR $800
Flash Comics #2VF $5,750
Flash Comics #86VF+ (MH) $7,475
Forbidden Love #1FN+ $295
Four Color #9VG $900
Funnies On Parade #1GD+ $2,000
Funny Man nn VF $575
Funny Picture Stories #1VG $1,030
Gangbusters #11NM+ (MH) $530
Ghost #1VG $113
Great Comics #3FN+ $2,000
Green Hornet #4VF (LR) $635
Green Lantern #1FN+ $9,200
Green Lantern #1FN $6,900
Haunt of Fear #15NM+ (GA) $825
Hickory #1NM $240
Horrific #3VF+ $220
Human Torch #1VG+ $4,400
Human Torch #8VG $450
Human Torch #9VF+ $1,150
Human Torch #9VF+ repair $925
Human Torch #37NM $980
Ibis The Invincible #1FN+ $550
Impact #1NM (GA) $282
Impact #1VF $125
Impact #3NM (GA) $156
Incred. Sci/fiction #30NM+ (GA) $990
Jackpot Comics #4FN+ $900
Jo-Jo #12VF+ $325
Jo-Jo #17VF+ $546
Jungle Comics #124NM $125
Kaanga #1NM $250
Katy Keene Annual #1VF+ $450
Key Comics #1VF+ $285
Killers, The #1FN+ $322
Leading Comics #1FN+ $1,380
Leading Comics #1VG+ $715
Lone Ranger Ice Cream VG+ $2,185
Lover's Lane #1VF+ $135
Mad #1VG $1,500
Mad #20NM+ (WM) $770
Mad #22NM+ (GA) $1,100
Magic Comics 1VG+ $1,000
Master Comics #23FN+ $1,400
March of Comics #4VF(r) $4,025
March of Comics #41VF $2,530
Marvel Comics #1VF (LR) $41,400
Marvel Comics #1FN(r) $12,650
Marvel Mystery #2VF+ (LR) $16,100
Marvel Mystery #3VF+ (LR) $11,500
Marvel Mystery #4FN+ $3,738
Marvel Mystery #4FR $2,500
Marvel Mystery #10VF $5,800
Marvel Mystery #16VF $3,000
Marvel Mystery #27NM $2,500
Marvel Mystery #47FN+ $375
Marvel Mystery Annual VG $6,000
Marvel Tales #115NM+ (WM) $605
Master Comics #1FN+ $2,300
Master Comics #2FN $780
M.D. #1NM (GA) $229
Military Comics #1GD $1,100
Miss Fury #5NM+ $785
More Fun Comics #14(V2#2)VG $4427
More Fun #28VG+ $450
More Fun #55VG+ $3,738
More Fun #55GD $1,450
More Fun #59VG $805
More Fun #68VG+ $380
More Fun #72,74,83,87VF $4,025
More Fun #73FN+ $4,600
More Fun #75NM+ (MH) $8,800
More Fun #101FN(r) $1,500
Motion Pic. Funnies #1 (no-c) $2,500
Movie Comics #1('39)VF $2,200
Mystery Comics #1VF+ $448
Mystery In Space #1VF+ $2,875
Mystery In Space #1FN $1,100
Mystery In Space #2VF+ $1,200
Mystery Men #2FN+ $840
Mystery Men #13NM+ (AT) $1,540
Mystic Comics #1FN $500
National Comics #8FN+ $975
New Book of Comics #2VG+ $2,185
New Fun #1FN (r) $34,000
Nickel Comics#2NM $1,100
Nickel Comics #2NM+ (AT) $1,495
Nickel Comics #8NM (AT) $690
Our Gang Comics #11VF+ $747
Pep Comics #22NM (MH) $47,000
Pep Comics #22VF $12,000
Pep Comics #58NM+ (MH) $550
Peter Panda #2NM $195
Phantom Lady #13VF+ $1,650
Phantom Lady #17VF $4,600
Phantom Lady #17GD $1,450
Phantom Lady #21FN $650
Phantom Lady #23VG $1,700
Planet Comics #42VG+ $95
Plastic Man #17NM+ $690
Police Comics #1VG+ $1,840
Police Comics #5FN+ $525
Popular Teenagers #10NM $185
Psychoanalysis #1NM (GA) $310
Red Ryder #18NM $265
Roy Rogers Four Color #38VF+ $1,400
Samson #6VF+ $345
Sensation Comics #3VF+ $2,530
Sensation Comics #4FN $600
Sensation Comics #26VF $495
Sensation Comics #100VF+ $500
Seven Seas #4FN+ $500
Silver Streak #23FN+ $175
Slave Girl #1FN+ $300
Smash Comics #14VG $525
Spirit #22GD+ $250
Spotlight #3VF $350
Spy Smasher #1FN+ $980
Star Spangled #16NM+ (MH) $4,400
Star Spangled #25NM+ (MH) $3,575
Star Spangled #32NM+ (MH) $1,815
Star Spangled #50NM+ (MH) $1,735
Startling Comics #48VF+ $600
Startling Comics #49VF $1,200
Startling Terror Tales #11FN+ $1,265
Sub-Mariner #1GD $1,500
Sub-Mariner #2FN+ $3,062
Sunny #12FN+ $158
Superboy #1VF+ $6,325
Superboy #1FN+ $5,200
Superboy #1VG+ $1,610
Superman #1FN+(r) $13,500
Superman #3VF+ repair $3,300
Superman #11VF+ $2,640
Superman #14FN+ $2,300
Superman #51VF $370
Superman #69VF $395
Superman #100FN $500
Superman #100GD $1,500
Suspense #14VF+ (WM) $305
Tales From/Crypt #26NM+ (GA) $1,320
Thing #2VG $86
Thrilling Comics #40NM+ (MH) $1,320
Tomahawk #1VF+ $1,782
Uncle Sam Quarterly #1GD $275
USA Comics #1VG $1,500
USA Comics #8VF $974
Vault of Horror #17NM+ (GA) $1,155
Vault of Horror #21NM+ (GA) $990
Vault of Horror #29NM+ (GA) $715
Walt Disney's C&S #34VG $140
Weird Comics #4VF+ $825
Weird Science #6NM (WM) $660
Weird Science #7NM+ (GA) $1,265
Witchcraft #3FN $89
Woman Outlaws #1FN $225
Wonder Comics #1 (AT) $9,775
Wonder Woman #1NM $19,000
Wonder Woman #1VG $3,300
Wonder Woman #5NM+ (MH) $4,840
Wonder Woman #9MT (MH) $4,345
Wonder Woman #17MT (MH) $2,860
Wonder Woman #45VF $525
World of Fantasy #6VF+ (WM) $220
World's Finest #17NM (MH) $4,750
Wow Comics #1GD+ $2,600
Wow Comics #69VF+ $140
Young Allies #1FN $2,400
Youthful Romances #1VF+ $225
Zip Comics #27FN $350
Zoot #10VF $355
Zoot #14VF+ $517

SILVER AGE SALES

Action Comics #242VF	$680
Action Comics #252FN+	$550
Action Comics #252VG	$250
Action Comics #254VF+	$170
Action Comics #267NM	$400
Action Comics #304NM	$58
Adventure Comics #240NM (MV)	$415
Adventure Comics #248VF+ (MV)	$270
Adventure Comics #300NM	$400
Adventure Comics #327NM	$40
All Star Western #10VF+	$120
Amazing Fantasy #15VG+	$3,100
Amazing Fantasy #15FR	$810
Amazing Spider-Man #1VF	$8,000
Amazing Spider-Man #1FR+	$600
Amazing Spider-Man #2VF+	$2,500
Amazing Spider-Man #2FN	$750
Amazing Spider-Man #3GD	$150
Amazing Spider-Man #4VG	$155
Amazing Spider-Man #5FN	$350
Amazing Spider-Man #7GD	$50
Amazing Spider-Man #10FN	$175
Amazing Spider-Man #14NM	$2,588
Amazing Spider-Man #14VF	$950
Amazing Spider-Man #14FN	$500
Amazing Spider-Man #22NM	$280
Amazing Spider-Man #50FN	$100
Amazing Spider-Man #53VF+	$30
Amazing Spider-Man #74NM	$45
Amazing Spider-Man #117NM (WM)	$85
Amazing Spider-Man #238NM	$60
Amazing Spider-Man #300NM	$60
Aquaman #1FN	$275
Atom #1NM	$750
Atom #1VF	$500
Atom #1FN	$250
Avengers #1FN	$495
Avengers #1GD+	$200
Avengers #2VF	$375
Avengers #4VF+	$1,000
Avengers #14NM	$75
Avengers #23NM	$56
Avengers #57NM	$125
Avengers #57NM	$90
Avengers #57NM+	$125
Barbie & Ken #5NM	$315
Batman #100FN	$700
Batman #105VF+	$530
Batman #139VF	$165
Batman #181VF+	$140
Batman #232VF	$75
Batman #234FN	$50
Batman Annual #1NM	$600
Batman Annual #5NM+ (GR)	$525
Betty & Me #1VF+	$120
Beverly Hillbillies #1VF	$98
Blackhawk #164VF+	$65
Brave & the Bold #26NM	$500
Brave & the Bold #28VF+	$5,225
Brave & the Bold #28VF	$2,500
Brave & the Bold #34VG	$250
Brave & the Bold #34VF+	$1,900
Brave & the Bold #34VF+	$1,760
Brave & the Bold #54VF	$200
Captain America #100VG	$30
Challengers/Unknown #2VR+	$1,380
Challengers/Unknown #8NM	$977
Conan #1MT	$195
Conan #1NM	$200
Conan #2NM	$100
Daredevil #1VF+	$1,800
Daredevil #7VF+	$265
Detective #225FN	$1,870
Detective #225VG	$1,450
Detective #235FN+	$360
Eighty Page Giant #7VF	$125
Eighty Page Giant #8VF	$400
Fantastic Four #1VF+(part trade)	$9,000
Fantastic Four #5VG	$450
Fantastic Four #12VF	$1,000
Fantastic Four #48VF+	$660
Fantastic Four #48VF	$500
Fantastic Four Annual #1NM	$750
Fighting American #1FN	$700
Flash #105FN+	$1,150
Flash #105VG	$500
Flash #107FN	$200
Flash #113NM	$550
Flash #123VF+	$1,320
Flash #123GD+	$170
Flash #175NM	$120
Flash Annual #1NM	$400
Giant Size X-Men #1NM	$400
Green Lantern #1FN	$1,400
Green Lantern #2NM	$1,000
Green Lantern #4VF+	$350
Green Lantern #40NM	$500
Green Lantern #45NM	$100
Green Lantern #76NM	$175
Harvey Hits #15VF	$100
Hawkman #4NM	$155
Herbie #1VF	$150
Incredible Hulk #1VG	$1,175
Incredible Hulk #1GD	$450
Incredible Hulk #2NM	$2,500
Incredible Hulk #2FN+	$1,400
Incredible Hulk #3VF	$1,000
Incredible Hulk #6VF+	$1,150
Incredible Hulk #6FN	$475
Incredible Hulk #181VF	$350
Iron Man #1NM	$325
Jetsons #3VF+	$75
Jimmy Olsen #1FN+	$2,475
Jimmy Olsen #3FN	$200
Journey Into Mystery #83VF	$2,900
Journey Into Mystery #99VF	$100
Justice League #1VF	$2,500
Justice League #1VF	$2,000
Justice League #46NM	$100
Lois Lane #1FR	$120
Man From U.N.C.L.E. #1FN+	$78
Marvel Team-Up #1NM	$100
Mystery In Space #53FN	$500
Nick Fury #1NM	$75
Our Army At War #83VF	$1,100
Our Army At War #85VF+	$310
Our Army At War #153NM	$130
Our Fighting Forces #1GD	$120
Phantom Stranger #1NM	$85
Plastic Man #1VF+	$78
Richie Rich #1FN+	$460
Richie Rich #1VG	$285
Rip Hunter #1FN	$150
Rip Hunter #6NM	$110
Sea Devils #1VF	$325
Secret Origins Giant #1VF	$500
Secret Six #1NM	$65
Sgt. Fury #13NM	$300
Showcase #1,2,3,5VG+	$1,610
Showcase #4FN(r)	$3,400
Showcase #9VF & #10VG+	$3,450
Showcase #13VF & #14VG	$3,450
Showcase #15FN	$485
Showcase #19VF+(MV)	$1,640
Showcase #25NM	$300
Showcase #27FN	$220
Showcase #30FN	$200
Showcase #34VF	$1,000
Showcase #40VF	$200
Showcase #45FN	$110
Showcase #74NM	$50
Showcase #77NM	$40
Silver Surfer #1NM	$400
Silver Surfer #1NM	$595
Silver Surfer #2NM	$240
Silver Surfer #4NM	$400
Space Adventures #33NM	$400
Space Ghost #1vg	$59
Spectre #1NM	$140
Star Trek #1VF+	$500
Strange Adventures #100NM	$160
Strange Tales Annual #2NM	$600
Strange Tales #135VF	$100
Sub-Mariner #1NM	$100
Superman #199NM	$250
Superman Annual #1VF	$1,000
SGF Lois Lane #70NM	$250
Tales of Suspense #32NM	$250
Tales of Suspense #39VF	$2,588
Tales of Suspense #39FN	$1,000
Tales of Suspense #57NM	$100
Tales of Suspense #58NM	$250
Tales of Suspense #64NM	$60
Tales to Astonish #27VF	$2,300
Tales to Astonish #35VG	$200
Tales to Astonish #51NM	$100
Wonder Woman #105VF+	$700
Wonder Woman #105VG	$550
Wonder Woman #128NM	$65
World's Finest #88NM	$250
X-Men #1FN+	$1,265
X-Men #2VF	$650
X-Men #2VF	$1,000
X-Men #4NM	$500
X-Men #4FN+	$225
X-Men #7NM	$150
X-Men #14NM	$300
X-Men #14VF+	$148
Young Men #24FN+	$1,200

RUSS COCHRAN'S COMIC ART AUCTION

Russ Cochran's Comic Art Auction, which has been published regularly since 1973, specializes in the finest comic strip art, comic book art, and illustrations by artists such as Frank Frazetta and Carl Barks.

If you collect (or would like to start a collection of) classic strips such as **Krazy Kat**, **Tarzan**, **Flash Gordon**, **Prince Valiant**, **Dick Tracy**, **Terry and the Pirates**, **Gasoline Alley**, **Li'l Abner**, **Pogo**, **Mickey Mouse**, **Donald Duck**, or comic book art from **EC Comics**, then you need to subscribe to this auction!

To subscribe to **Russ Cochran's Comic Art Auction**, send $20.00 (Canada $25.00; other international orders, $30.00) for a four-issue subscription. These fully illustrated catalogs will be sent to you by first class mail prior to each auction. If you're still not sure about subscribing and would like a sample issue from a past auction, send $1.00 to **Gemstone Publishing, P.O. Box 469, West Plains, MO 65775**, or call **Toll Free (800) 322-7978**.

MD residents must ad 5% sales tales; MO residents add 6.225% sales tax; CA residents add 7.25% sales tax (San Diego County residents 7.75%).

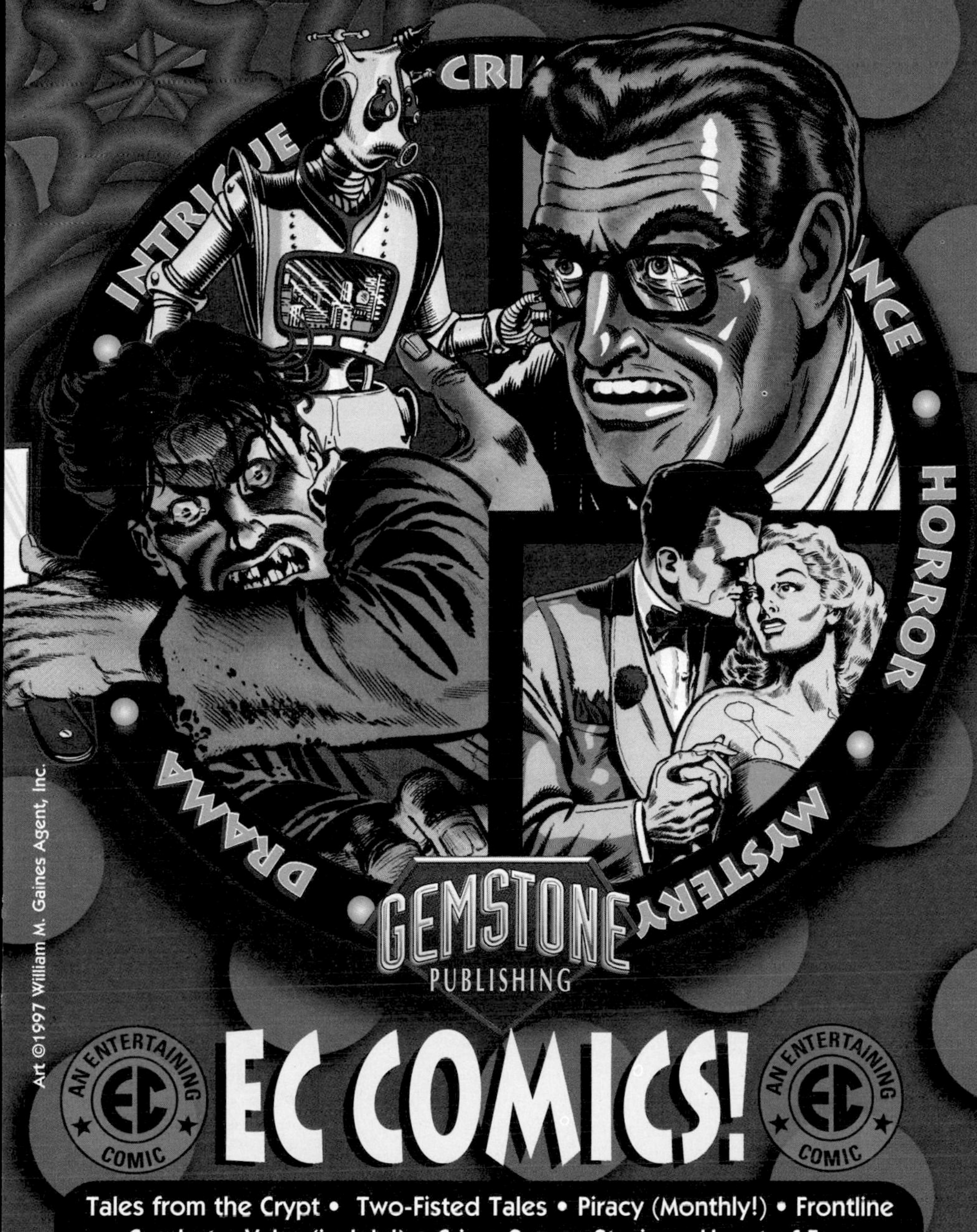

Tales from the Crypt • Two-Fisted Tales • Piracy (Monthly!) • Frontline Combat • Valor (in July!) • Crime SuspenStories • Haunt of Fear Vault of Horror • PANIC

Ask for them in your local comic shop or visit us on the web at

www.gemstonepub.com

Call Toll Free (800) EC-CRYPT for your FREE catalog!

BY ROBERT M. OVERSTREET

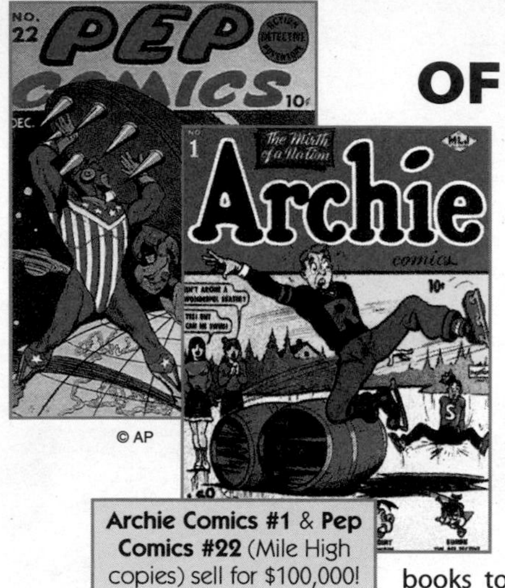

© AP

Archie Comics #1 & **Pep Comics #22** (Mile High copies) sell for $100,000!

A PERIOD OF CORRECTION

Prices stabilized overall in the comic book marketplace during the past year . Substantial gains were confined to specific areas in the collectible hobby which will be explored later. Because of the large price increases that have occurred over the past three years in both Golden Age and Silver Age books, last year's market has to be termed "a period of correction," as prices leveled off with noticeable decreases in the lower grades. With the help of many of our advisors, we have changed the price spreads on most books to reflect last year's correction. The Silver Age was affected the most where Good to Fine copies were being discounted from 20% to 70% off guide list. The new price spread was accomplished in most cases with a slight increase in the Near Mint price and a reduction in the Good and Fine price. Most Silver Age books are now on a 1 to 10 spread, with Golden Age on a 1 to 8 from Good to Near Mint. This means that if good is $10, Near Mint would be $100 for Silver or $80 for Gold. As higher prices are paid for true Near Mint to Mint books, these spreads will probably continue to increase in the future.

Auction house sales for 1997 were mixed but respectable. Early **Action** comics sold for record prices. Golden Age sold better than Silver with restored books still showing price resistance. **Action** #1 remains very strong and is still the number one book! Record sales were occurring in all areas, but mostly in the Golden Age and Bronze Age books. The Mile High copies of **Archie** #1 and **Pep** #22 (Archie's first app.) sold as a set for $100,000!

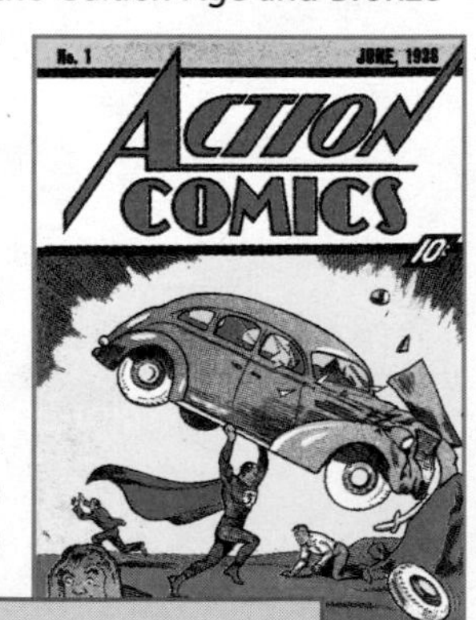

© DC

Action Comics #1 is still the most valuable book!

GOLDEN AGE/ ATOM AGE

The cornerstone of the hobby--collections were surfacing frequently throughout the year. One large collection of high grade Golden Age appeared late in the year, dubbed "The Rockford" collection. Congratulations, Mark! A few issues from this source sold quickly at the San Diego Comicon. Another group of high grade Golden Age books came out and is known as the "Big Apple" collection. Like "The Rockford" collection, these books had beautiful cover gloss and white pages. Demand in this area still outstrips supply. High grade copies continue to be in short supply, far below current demand levels. Most of the mainline titles in less than Fine sold at 70-125% of guide list, indicating the necessity of expanding the spreads as mentioned above. It has been reported to us that dealers who grade their books accurately have much better success in getting guide or better prices. Unfortunately, dealers that are not strict graders (who grade a VG as FN or a VF as NM) will have more difficulty getting their price. These dealers may report the market as slow.

L.B. Cole, Lou Fine, Simon & Kirby and Schomburg cover books continued to be in high demand, as well as World War II Axis or Hitler covers. Fox romance titles and all good girl art comics sold very well at above guide list levels. Demand for Frazetta covers continued to be on the up-swing. More and more collectors are going after the "classic covers" of popular runs. Most late 1940s and 1950s horror, weird, atomic and radio theme books were very popular. With the scheduled comeback of many western TV shows planned, the western genre comic books may be poised to take off in 1998.

© DC

New Fun #1 gets $34,000!!

A LOOK AT SOME OF THE HOTTEST COMIC BOOK TITLES IN 1997

1897-1920s TITLES: Most titles from this period remained very scarce with few reported sales. The supply limitations once again governed the increases shown in this area of collecting.

1930s TITLES: All DC titles such as **Adventure**, **Detective**, **More Fun**, **New Fun**, etc. remained the most popular, followed by most reprint titles. Sales: **Ace Comics** #11 VG(r) $350; **Big Book of Fun** #1 GD $3,000; **Comics On Parade** #11 VG+ $135, #17 VG+ $110; **Famous Funnies** #28 FN+ $250; **Famous Funnies, A Carnival of Comics** VF+ $6,900; **The Funnies** #3 GD $140; **Funnies On Parade** #1 GD+ $2,000; **Magic** #1 VG+ $1,000, GD $475, #2 FR $70, **More Fun** #28 VG+ $450; **New Book of Comics** #2 VG+ $2,185; **New Comics** #2 FR $728; **New Fun** #1 FN(r) $34,000; **Popular Comics** #5 GD $135; **Super Comics** #26 VG $80.

1940s TITLES: The most collected continue to be the superhero titles from all companies. DC is the hottest publisher followed by Timely. Books with covers by L.B. Cole, Schomburg, and Simon and Kirby remained strong. Late 1940s Good-girl art comics were hot. These books have covers by Matt Baker, Jack Kamen, Al Feldstein, Walter Johnson and others. Title examples are **Phantom Lady**, **Rulah**, **Brenda Starr**, **Blue Beetle**, **Jo-Jo**, **All Top**, **Teenage Romances**, etc. All Fox love comics were red hot with increased demand for crime, hor-

Phantom Lady comics are hot!! (#23 shown)

© FOX

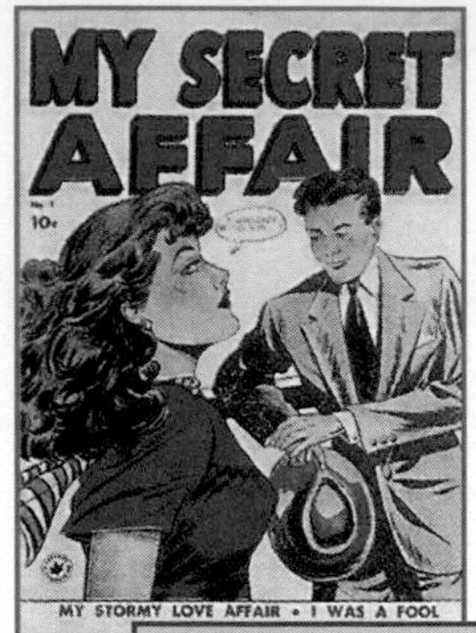

© FOX

Fox romance comics are HOT!!

ror and weird titles. Especially those with covers by L.B. Cole and Ditko. NM copies of most key books were not available for sale.

1950s TITLES: A very hot area! One of the few periods in the hobby where a few hundred dollars still buys a stack of books. Horror, crime, western and love comics ruled this period with many popular companies and titles. The hottest publisher is still Fox. Superhero books from this area are very scarce in high grade and continue to sell very well. The most collected publishers were DC, Atlas, Fox, Charlton, Star (L.B. Cole covers), Ziff Davis, Avon, ACG as well as many of the more obscure publishers such as St. John, Fawcett, Ajax, Superior, Story, Premier, Avon, etc. The Pre-Marvel hero prototype books remained in high demand. Many of comics' most loved artists worked during this time with all their books selling well. Simon & Kirby, L.B. Cole, Matt Baker, Joe Kubert, Al Feldstein, Wally Wood, Steve Ditko, Murphy Anderson, Reed Crandall, Will Eisner, Bob Powell, Matt Fox, Basil Wolverton are just a few of the greats.

GOLDEN AGE/ ATOM AGE REPORT (BY COMPANY)

DC

In higher grade all main-line superhero titles were selling at around 150% - 300% of guide; in lesser grade the books were selling for approximately 75% - 125% of guide. Key scarcer issues were selling at even higher percentages of guide. Best selling titles are **Batman**, **Superman**, **Flash**, **Green Lantern** and their related titles. Small gains were made for offbeat titles. **Wonder Woman** and related titles showed a strong pickup in demand. The Mile High copy of **All Star Comics** #1 changed hands again and sold for $48,000!. Sotheby's 1997 Summer auction again offered a unique run of early issues of **Action Comics** which all went for over-guide prices. A **Detective** #27 in FN67 brought $66,000! An **Action** #1 in GD+ sold for $37,950. A 43-issue group of **Adventure Comics** brought guide list at auction and a 26-issue group of **Sensation** sold for $5,175 or 53% over guide.

Detective Comics #27 in FN67 sells for $66,000!!

© DC

REPORTED SALES: Action Comics #2 VG $6,727, #2 & 3 VG $11,500, #5,11 & 39 FN $6,900, #5VG+ $2,185, FR+ $1,725, #10 GD $1,840, #12 VG+(r) $1,540, #15 GD+ $790, #21 VG+ $1,100, #23 VG+ $3,300, #94 FN+ $115, #102 $550, #115 VG+ $115; **Adventure Comics** #33 VG+(r) $330, #38 FN $700, #40 VG+ $12,650, #42 GD+ $725, #49 GD $155, #51 FN $825, #80

All-American Comics #25 (Mile High copy) brings $16,100!!

© DC

VG $385, #103 FN $1,265, #123 FN $125, #161 VG+$115; **Adventures of Rex, The Wonder Dog** #1 VF+ $977; **All American Comics** #25 VF+ (Mile High) $16,100, #61 FN+ $4,313, #82 VG+ $135, #89 NM $2,127, #90NM $1,380, $100 FN+ $1,265, #102 NM $2,932; **All Flash** #1 VF+(Recil Macon) $9,900, FN $4,000; **All Star Comics** #1 VG+ $2,860, #6 VG+ $920, #7 VG+ $580, #8 FN $7,475, #12 VF+ (Mile High) $4,888, #20 NM+(Mile High) $6,490, #31 FN+ $385, #43 FN+ $410; **Batman** #1 VG(r) $7,500, #2 GD+ $900, #4 GD $500, #16 VF $2,420, #19 FN+ $660, #25 VF $980, #27 NM $1,980, #28 NM+ $1,735, #33 NM (Mile High) $4,000, #43 NM (Mile High) $3,600, #49 NM (Mile High) $5,500, #71 VF+ $495, #92 VF+ $550, #100 FN $700, #105 VF+ $520; **Boy Commandos** #7 NM+ (Mile High) $2,090, #12 NM+ (Mile High) $1,320; **Comic Cavalcade** #24 VG $150, #26 FN+ (Mile High) $520, #34 VF+ $140; **Detective Comics** #2 FR+ $3,163, #4 VG $2,970, #9 VG+(r) $1,460, #12 GD $780, #16 VG $1,500, #28 VG+(r) $4,600, #32 FN $1,900, #34 VG+ $1,265, #35 GD $1,000, GD+ $1,650, #48 VG+ $385, #54 VF $1,150, #58 FN $1,155, #59 FN $550, #64 VG+ $1,035, #66 VF $1,675, #103 VG+ $160, #109 FN $300, #146 VF $325, #151 VF+ $550, #188 NM+ (Mile High) $2,200; **Flash Comics** #1 FN(r) $6,000, VG $10,350, #2 VF $5,750, FN+(r) $1,800, #24 FN $590, #86 VF+ (Mile High) $7,475; **Green Lantern** #1 FN+ $9,200, FN $6,900, #11 VG+ $250, #25 FN+ $330; **Leading** #1 FN+ $1,380, VG+ $715; **More Fun** #9 VG $3,850; #14 (V2#2) VG $4,427, #55VG+ $3738, GD $1450, #57GD $415, #59VG $805, #73FN+ $4600, FR $800, #75 NM+ (Mile High) $8,800, #101 FN(r) $1,500, #127 FN+ $180; **Real Fact** #5 VF+ $1,075; **Sensation** #3 VF+ $2,530, #4FN $600, #26 VG $110, #50 FN+ $250, #61 VG+ $80, #100 VF+ $500, #107 VF(r) $300; **Star Spangled** #16 NM+ (Mile High) $4,400, #25 NM+ (Mile High) $3,575, #32 NM+ (Mile High) $1,815, #50 NM+ (Mile High) $1,735, #65 FN+ $620, #117 FN+ $140; **Superboy** #1 VF+ $6,325, FN+ $5,200, VG+ $1,610; **Superman** #1 FN(r) $13,500, #3VF+(r) $3,300, #4 FN(r) $1,000, #11 VF+ $2,640, #14 FN+ $2,300, #55 VF $420, #69 VF $395, #80 VF $345, #97 FN+ $200, #100 FN $500; **Wonder Woman** #1VG $3,300, #2 GD $350, #5 NM+ (Mile High) $4,840, #9M (Mile High) $4,345, #10VF+ $3,300, #17M (Mile High) $2,860, #25NM+ $1,320, #39 NM+ $770, #43 VF $240, #45 VF $525; **World's Finest** #11 NM $1,650, #16 FN $375, #17 NM (Mile High) $4,750, #54FN+ $180.

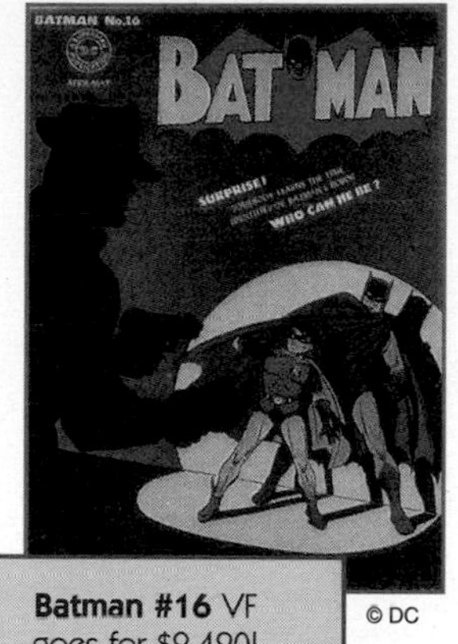

Batman #16 VF goes for $2,420!

© DC

© DC

Green Lantern #1 FN+ sales for $9,200!

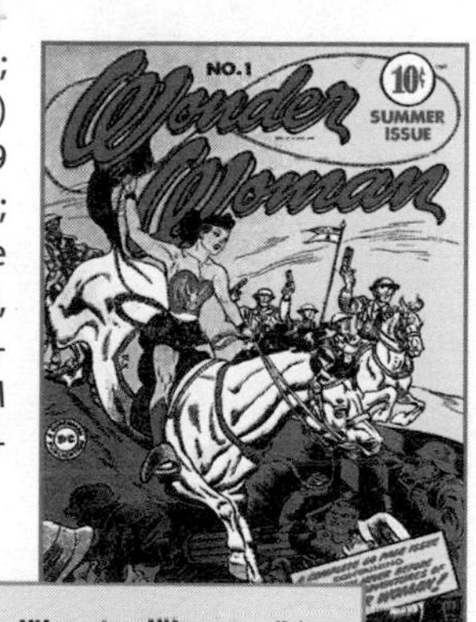

Wonder Woman #1 in VG gets $3,300!

© DC

TIMELY

After years of large gains, prices finally stabilized. High grade copies for most titles sold for around

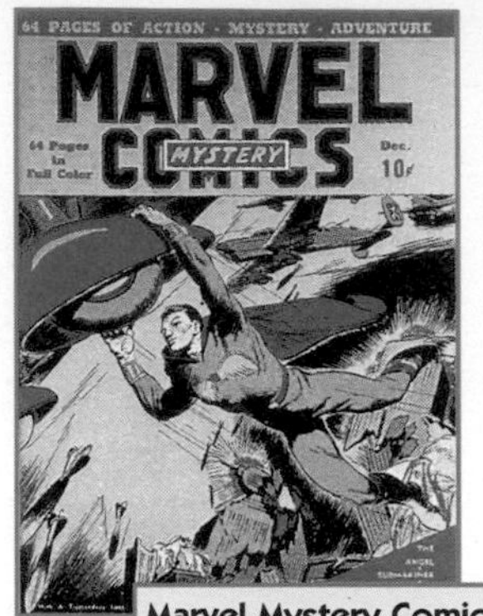

© MEG

Marvel Mystery Comics #2 (Larson copy) sells for $16,100!!

135% - 300% of current guide levels with lesser condition copies selling for approximately 60% - 115% of guide. **Captain America** and related titles are still the most popular. There is also a solid demand **for Human Torch, Sub-Mariner** and their related titles. NM copies of most titles were very scarce with few reported sales. Small gains were made by offbeat titles. Issues with Schomburg covers remained in high demand. A coverless copy of **Motion Picture Funnies Weekly** sold for $2,500.

REPORTED SALES: All Winners #8 FN $550, #21 VF+ $3,852; **America's Greatest** #1 FN $550; **Captain America** #31 GD+ $220, #55 GD $140, #67 VG+ $320, #74 VG $1,650; **Annual** VG $6,000; **Complete Comics** #2 VG $400; **Daring** #10 FN $240; **Human Torch** #1 VG+ $4,400, $3,960, #8 VG $450, #36 VG+ $250, #37 NM $980; **Joker Comics** #1 VG $440; **Kid Comics** #10 VG $145; **Marvel Comics** #1 (Larson copy) VF $41,400, FN(r) $12,650; **Marvel Mystery** #2 (Larson copy) VF+ $16,100, #3 VF+ (Larson copy) $11,500, #4 FN+ $3,738, #11 VG $525, #21 FN $540, #24 VG $240, #36 VG $270, #41 FN $320, #47 FN+ $375; **Miss Fury** #5 NM+ $785; **Mystic** #1 FR $790; **Namora** #1 GD $250; **Sub-Mariner** #1 GD $1,500, #2 GD $600, #7 FN $535, VG $265, #9 VG $375, #19 VG $210, #38 FN+ $470; **USA** #1 VG $1,500; **Young Allies** #1 FN $2,400, #3 VG $410.

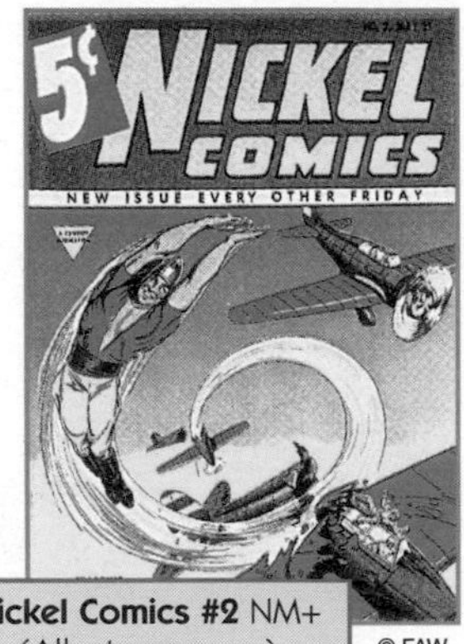

© FAW

Nickel Comics #2 NM+ (Allentown copy) sells for $1,495!

FAWCETT

Compared to DC and Timely, this company's books appear to be under-valued. Sales of **Captain Marvel** and related titles were at approximately 70% - 115% of guide in lesser condition and 135% - 250% of guide for higher grade copies. Good sales were achieved for **Captain Midnight**. Small gains were also made by offbeat titles.

REPORTED SALES: Bulletman #1 VG+ $900, #5 NM+ (Mile High) $2,065; **Captain Marvel** #3 FN+ $900, #19 VG $100, #21, VG+ $155; **Captain Marvel Jr.** #13 MT (Mile High) $1,650; **Captain Midnight** #1 FN $750; **Gift Comics** #4 VG+ $115; **Ibis** #1 FN+ $550; **Master Comics** #2 FN $780, #133 VF+ $200; **Nickel Comics** #2 NM+ (Allentown copy) $1,495, NM $1,100, #8 NM (Allentown copy) $690; **Spy Smasher** #1 FN+ $980, FN+(r) $780, GD $395, #4 VG+ $250; **Whiz** #2 VG $990; **Wow** #1 GD+ $2,600, #69 VF+ $140.

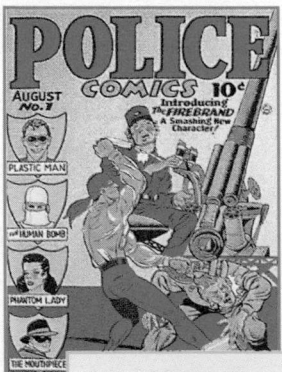

© QUA

Police Comics #1 VG+ sells for $1,840!

QUALITY

Good demand was led by all Lou Fine titles selling at 75% - 135% in lesser condition and 115% - 250% in higher grade. Moderate sales of **Blackhawk** and all related titles were at about 65% - 105% of current guide levels in lesser grade and 90% - 220% of guide in higher grade. Small gains were made by offbeat titles.

REPORTED SALES: Blackhawk #13 VF+(Cosmic Aero.) $550; **Crack Comics** #1 GD $450, #2 FN $635, #27 NM (Mile High) $1,725; **Doll Man** #8FN $250; **Hit Comics** #2 FN+ $780, GD $365, #3 FR $85, #5 GD $510, #58 VF $110; **Military Comics** #1 VG(r) $825, GD $1,100; **Modern Comics** #102 FN+ $160; **National Comics** #8 FN+ $975, #9 VG+ $210, #14 VG+ $220; **Plastic Man** #17 NM+ $690; **Police Comics** #1 VG+ $1,840, #5FN+ $525; **Smash Comics** #14 VG $525; **Zip** #27 FN $350.

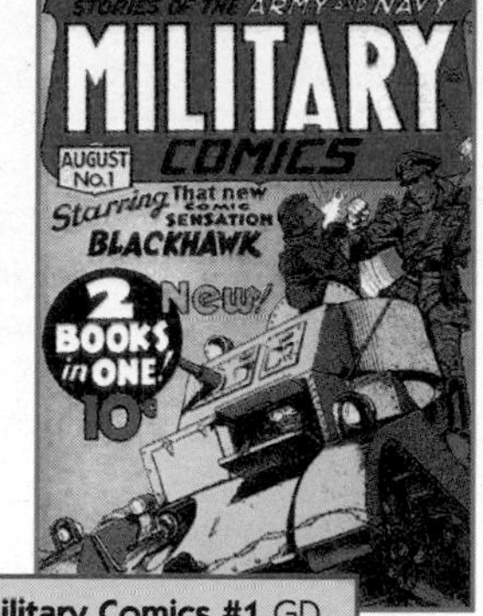

Military Comics #1 GD goes for $1,100!

© QUA

FICTION HOUSE

Continued demand from good-girl art collectors have lead to good sales for this publisher. Most popular is still **Planet** followed by **Jumbo, Jungle, Fight, Rangers** and **Wings**. These titles sell for approximately 75% - 130% of current guide in lesser condition, and 125% - 250% in higher grade. Small gains were made by offbeat titles.

REPORTED SALES: Fight #1 VG+ $700, #31 VG $120; **Jumbo** #2 GD $575, #7 GD+ $550; **Jungle** #110 VF+ $110, #124 NM $125; **Kaanga** #2 NM $250; **Planet Comics** #42 VG+ $95, #54 FN $158, #56 VF+ $305; **Rangers** #36 VF+ $135; **Sheena** #1 GD+ $330, # 9 FN $85; a collection of **Jumbo Comics** (76 books, avg. FN+) sold for $5,750 or 20% over guide and a collection of **Fight Comics** (36 books, avg FN+) sold for $4,025 or 37% over guide.

© FH

Fight Comics #1 in VG+ moves at $700!

FOX

Good sales were realized for this publisher. Largest demand is for all superhero titles at prices 90% - 145% of current guide in lesser grade, and approximately 135% - 300% in higher grade. Fox experienced strong demand for early Lou Fine cover books (see Good Girl Art for late 1940s Issues).

REPORTED SALES: Blue Beetle #1-5 (Mile High) $10,350, #2 GD $110, #5 FN $180; **Fantastic Comics** #2 - 4 $5,462 (111% over guide!); #22 VF $510; **Green Mask** #1 GD $350; **Mystery Men** #2 FN+ $840; **Rex Dexter** #1 VG $240; **Samson** #6 VF+ $345; **Science Comics** #5 VG+ $320; **Weird Comics** #4 VF+ $825; **Wonder Comics** #1 VF (Allentown copy) $9,775; **Wonderworld** #5 & 11 $4,887.

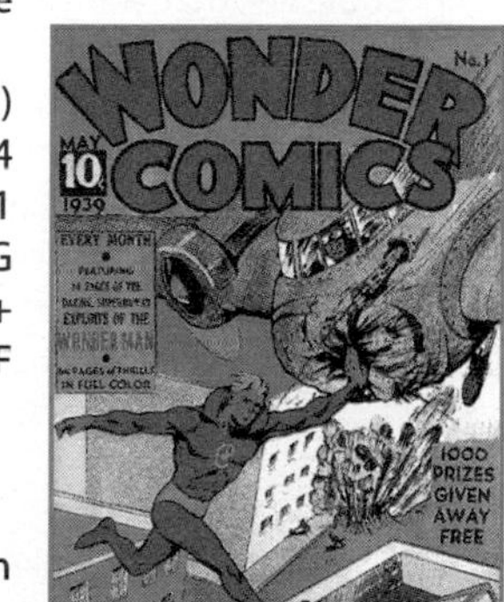

Wonder Comics #1 VF (Allentown copy) goes for $9,775!

© FOX

NEDOR

All issues with Schomburg covers remained strong from the previous year. Prices for these books still remain low when compared to Timelys.

REPORTED SALES: America's Best #8 NM+ (Mile

High) $1,100, #11 NM+ (Mile High) $1,320, #29 NM+ (Mile High) $1,100; **Exciting Comics** #3 VF+ $1,155, #9 FN $2,300; #37 NM $550, #62 VF+ $250; **Fighting Yank** #1 GD $325, #4 VF $510, #25 VF $275; **Startling** #48 VF+ $600, $550, #49 VF $1,200, FN+ $610; **Thrilling** #1 GD $350, #19 VF+ $500, #40 NM+ (Mile High) $1,320, #65 VF+ $350, #80 VF+ $125; **Wonder Comics** ('44) #1 FN $350. #19 VG+ $135.

Exciting Comics #3 VF+ brings $1,155!

© STD

MLJ/ARCHIE

Good demand was seen for the superhero titles of this publisher. Sales were at about 90% - 145% of current guide for lesser conditions, and 125% - 285% in higher grade. The Mile High copies of **Archie** #1 and **Pep** #22 sold as a set for $100,000! Early **Archies** remained scarce in high grade. The late 1940s issues of **Archie**, **Pep**, **Laugh**, **Suzie**, **Wilbur**, etc. had mediocre sales while **Katy Keene** was reported slow.

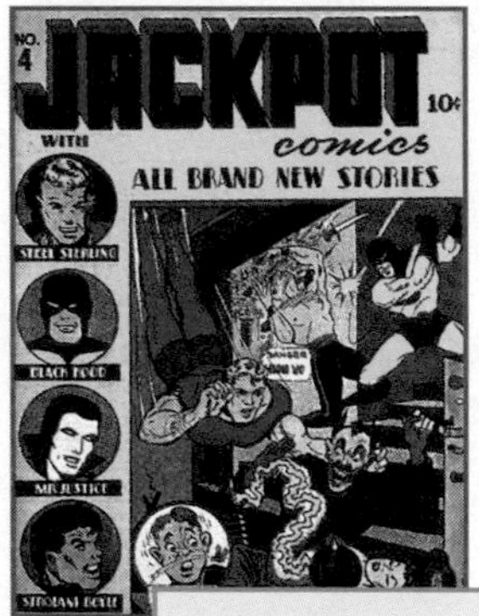

© MLJ

Jackpot Comics #4 FN+ goes for $900!

REPORTED SALES: Archie #10 VG $180; **Betty & Me** #1 VF+ $120; **Jackpot** #4 FN+ $900, $795; **Katy Keene Annual** #1 VF+ $450, GD $70; **Pep Comics** #26 FN $550, #58 NM+ (Mile High) $550; **Top Notch** #8 VG $415, #9 FN(r) $995.

HARVEY

Harvey saw good sales overall, especially for Schomburg covers. Solid sales were seen for **Green Hornet** and **Speed** while **Dick Tracy**, **Terry and the Pirates**, **Joe Palooka**, **Steve Canyon** and **Kerry Drake** remained slow.

REPORTED SALES: Green Hornet #4 VF $635; **Harvey Hits** #15 VF $100.

CENTAUR

Demand for Centaur titles has reached a temporary plateau. Still, this is an interesting publisher that will gain further should Timely prices become too high in relation to Centaur levels. This publisher has become a poor man's Timely. Books are selling at approximately 70% - 100% of guide in lesser condition, and 85% - 235% of guide in higher grade.

REPORTED SALES: Amazing Man #5 FR+ $1,450; **Funny Picture Stories** #1 VG $1,030, #7 VG+(r) $212; a group of **Star Comics** and **Star Ranger** (10 books) sold for $1,380 (25% over guide).

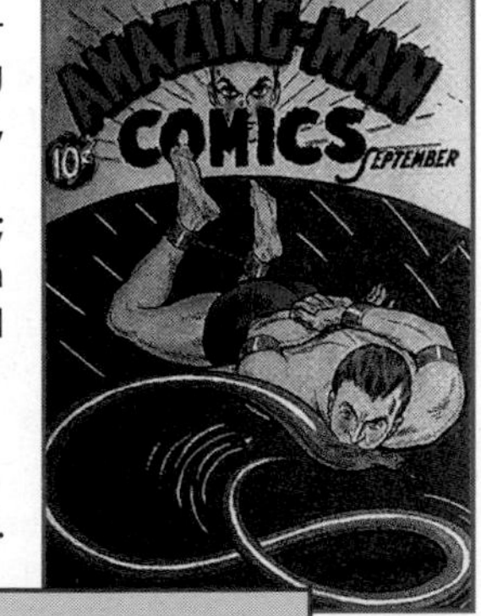

Amazing Man #5 FR+ sells for $1,450!

© CEN

DISNEY

Disney experienced only a moderate demand overall. Most titles were available in the lower grades which justifies the broader spreads for these books. However, high grade copies are quite scarce. Where

are the NM/MT duck one-shots, or the early issues of **Comics & Stories**?
REPORTED SALES: Mickey Mouse Four Color #16 FN $9,500; **Merry Christmas From Mickey Mouse** VF $1,500; **Walt Disney's Comics & Stories** #1 VG $2,300.

LEV GLEASON

Moderate demand was experienced for this company's flagship titles such as **Daredevil, Boy** and **Silver Streak.**
REPORTED SALES: Daredevil #1 & 2 NM $18,400, 1GD $800; **Silver Streak** #6 VG+ $2,400, #23 FN+ $175.

© LEV

Daredevil #1 & #2 bring $18,400 as a set!!

DELLS—DISNEY

The print runs of most of this company's titles were very high. Consequently, many collections that surface contain Dells, and usually they are in low grade. The funny animal Dells are fun to read. Because of the wider price spreads reported in previous years, sales have begun to pick up for low grade copies. Today you can buy a large stack for a small amount of money. Early issues **of Walt Disney's Comics & Stories** remained scarce, especially in high grade. A pick up in demand for **Uncle Scrooge** was noticed and **Mickey Mouse Four Colors** have been reported slow. **Dell Giants** were selling at and below current guide levels.
REPORTED SALES: Four Color #9 VG $900**; March of Comics** #41 GD+ $275; **Mickey Mouse Magazine** #4 FN $200; **Our Gang** #11 VF+ $747.

DELLS—NON-DISNEY

Slow to moderate sales were reported last year by many dealers. However, **Little Lulu** sales were up. **The Four Color** series, with many obscure titles, needed some price adjustments to bring it in line with the current market. Other titles in this run such as **The Andy Griffith Show, Annie Oakley, Beany & Cecil, Bonanza, Crusader Rabbit, Davy Crockett, Gunsmoke, Mister Magoo, Quick Draw McGraw, Rocky & Bullwinkle, The Three Stooges**, etc. enjoyed modest price increases last year. There was renewed interest in **Looney Tunes**, especially #1, due to its historical importance and the perception in the market of being under-valued.
REPORTED SALES: Many of the key titles brought record prices.

STREET & SMITH

Solid demand was seen for **Doc Savage, Shadow** and **Supersnipe.** Books from this company are relatively scarce and sell whenever they turn up.
REPORTED SALES: Bill Barnes #1 FN+ $380; **Shadow** V7 #8 VG+ $115; a group of **Shadow** and **Doc Savage** (6 books) sold for $2,875 (10% over guide).

HOLYOKE-CONTINENTAL

This company's books haven't shown any sign of cooling down! Comic books with

© HOKE

Catman #1 VF+
(Larson copy) brings $4,887!

L.B. Cole covers continued to be hot! **Suspense** #3 (with the classic Schomburg cover) remained very scarce and in high demand. **Catman** and **Terrific Comics** continued to sell for over guide list all year long. A **Captain Aero** #26 with an L.B. Cole cover sold in Chicago for $500.
REPORTED SALES: Captain Aero #3 FN $195; **Catman** #1 VF+ (Larson copy) $4,887; **Terrific** #4 GD $350.

CLASSIC COMICS

Average sales were seen for #1-50 1st editions in most grades. Sales were slow on #51 up with a few exceptions. Rare giveaways and gift boxes would sell for over guide list but they never turn up for sale.
REPORTED SALES: Classic Comics #1 (HRN 28) VF+ $70.

MISC. 1940s

Although sales and demand in this area was still primarily for keys and first issues of superhero titles, there were good gains across the board in higher grade. There are many great books here that will enhance a collection from **Frankenstein** to **Great Comics.**
REPORTED SALES: Big Shot #28 VF+ (Mile High) $360; **Bingo** #1 VF+ $200 (L.B. Cole)**; Bold Stories** (3/50) FN $450; **Candid Tales** nn-FN $450; **Double Comics** 1940 FN $980; **Famous Funnies** #216 NM $1,295 (Frazetta-c); **Feature Book** #52 NM+ (Mile High) $695; **Great Comics** #3 FN+ $2,000, FN $475; **Green Giant** #1GD $920; **Key Comics** #1VF $140; **Liberty Comics** #12 VF $287; **Li'l Abner** #4 VG+ $225; **Movie Comics** #1 ('39) VF $,2200; **OK Comics** #1 VG+ $300; **Punch** #10 VF+ $375; **Red Dragon** #1 GD $125; **Rocket Kelly** #1 VF $150; **The Spirit** #22 FN+ $385.

Great Comics #3 FN+
sells for $2,000!

© GP

1950s TITLES

Very hot area! Compared to prices for Golden Age material, 1950s books are very affordable. The most collected are horror, crime, war, science fiction, western and special art books. Multiples of guide are still being paid for books from pedigree collections (like Mile High, Bethlehem, White Mountain and others).

Adventures Into Terror
#43(#1)(White Mountain)
sells for $550!

© MEG

ATLAS

This publisher's titles are very popular among collectors. Most horror/science fiction titles were selling at and above guide levels with crime titles following close behind. A few titles are**: Adventures Into Terror,**

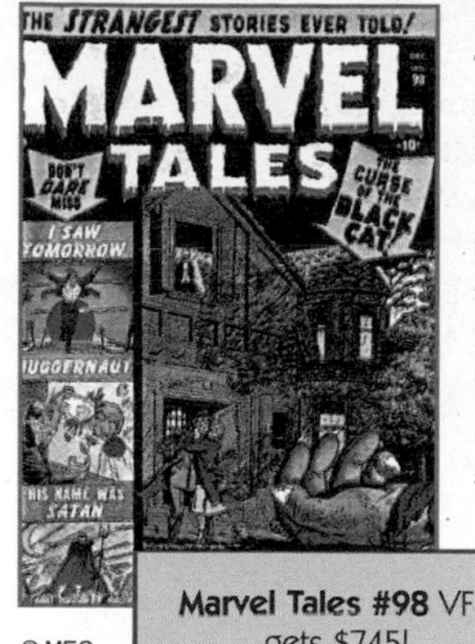

© MEG

Marvel Tales #98 VF+ gets $745!

Journey Into Mystery, Crime Cases, Journey Into Unknown Worlds, Marvel Tales, Menace, Mystery Tales, Spaceman and **Space Squadron**. Whenever high grade pedigree copies were sold, record prices of up to 300% of guide were paid. Some recorded sales are: **Astonishing** #22 VF+ $180; **Journey Into Mystery** #2 VG $200, #7 FN $370; **Strange Tales** #8 VF+ $550.

PACIFIC COMIC EXCHANGE REPORTED THE FOLLOWING PEDIGREE SALES: Adventures Into Terror #43 (#1) (White Mountain) VF+ $660, #25 VF+ $250; **Astonishing** #60 (White Mountain) NM+ $250; **Marvel Tales** #98 VF+ $745, #102 VF+ $715, #117 NM+ $580, #124 NM $470, #159 VF+ $265 (all White Mountain); **Mystic** #1 FN $500, #11 VF+ $250 (White Mountain); **Mystical Tales** #2 NM+ $330 (White Mountain); **Strange Stories of Suspense** #12 VF+ (White Mountain) $210; **Strange Tales** #35 VF (White Mountain) $265; **Suspense** #13 NM $275 (White Mountain); **World of Fantasy** #6 VF+ (White Mountain) $220.

EC

This publisher's line of titles experienced strong demand. Horror and SF titles were selling well at approximately 85% - 140% of guide in lesser condition, and 100 - 250% in higher grade. **Mad** is still the hottest title selling quickly at and above guide list. A few Gaines file copies were sold in auction by PCE (Pacific Comic Exchange) during the year and brought 300% - 400% of NM guide. Christies auction held in December 1997 included Gaines file copy runs which were very hot, selling for 200% to 860 % of guide. The **Panic** run, which guides at $425, sold for $3,680!

Mad #1 in VG brings $1,500!!

© EC

REPORTED SALES (auction): Weird Science ($7,500 guide) - $20,700; **Weird Fantasy** ($6,700 guide) - $17,250; **Crime SuspenStories** ($5,385 guide) - $13,800; **Mad** ($14,745 guide) - $43,700; **Frontline Combat** ($2,200 guide) - $4,830. Pacific Comic Exchange sold the following Gaines file copies: **Haunt of Fear** #15 NM+ $825; **Incredible Science Fiction** #30 NM+ $990; **Tales From The Crypt** #26 NM+ $1,320, #30 NM+ $1,320, #39 NM+ $990; **Vault of Horror** #17 NM+ $1,155, #21 NM+ $990, #29 NM+ $715, #32 NM+ $715; **Weird Science** #7NM+ $1,265.

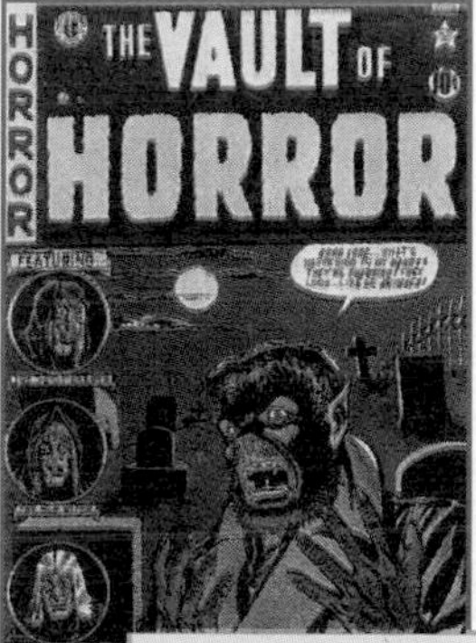

© WMG

Vault of Horror #17 in NM+ goes for $1,155!

REPORTED SALES (other): Crime Patrol #7 VG+ $140, #10 VG+ $105, #15 VG $415; **Crime SuspenStories** #14 VF+ $195; **Dandy** #3 VF+ $140; **Gunfighter** #8 FN+ $140; **Impact** #1 VF $125; **Mad** #1 VG $1,500, GD $520, #2 GD $198, #24 VF $995; **Moon Girl** #3 GD+ $105.

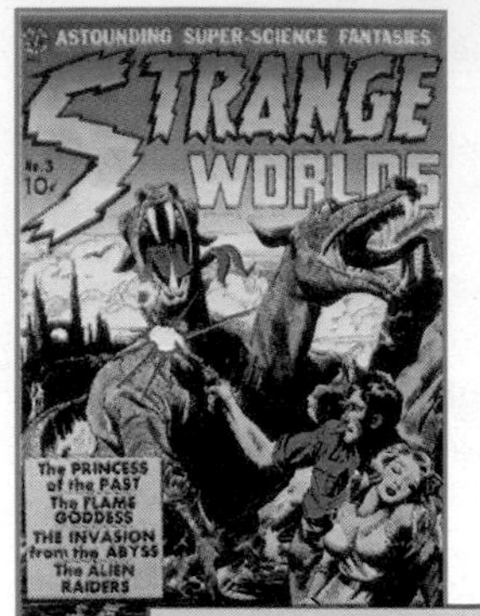

© MEG

Strange Worlds #3 VF+ brings $825!

AVON

Increased demand was reported due mainly to the focus on 1950s crime, horror and science fiction titles. Western and war titles are slower sellers for this publisher.

REPORTED SALES: Eerie #1 ('47) VG+ $690, #1 ('51) VG+ $105; **The Saint** #4 VG $110; **Space Detective** #3 FN+ $140; **Strange Worlds** #3 VF+ $825.

GOLDEN AGE/ ATOM AGE REPORT (BY GENRE)

CRIME

Most crime comics hit the stands in 1948, although **Crime Does Not Pay** began in 1942. All titles enjoyed good sales throughout the year. There are many classic issues with key covers and contents.

REPORTED SALES: Crime & Punishment #3 FN $475; **Crime Must Stop** #1 VF $575; **Crime Mysteries** #4 VG+ $200; **Crime Smashers** #1 VG+ $200; **Danger Trail** #3 GD+ $350; **Exposed** #6 FN $100; **Famous Crimes** #1 VF+ $747; **Gangbusters** #11 NM+ (Mile High) $530, #17 NM+ (Mile High) $840, #20 NM+ (Mile High) $335; **The Killers** #1 VF(r) $399, FN+ $322; **Mister Mystery** #6 VG+(r) $525.

Famous Crimes #1 VF+ sells for $747!

© FOX

GOOD GIRL ART

Still hot, carrying over from the previous year. Fox titles led by **Phantom Lady** were the most popular. Atlas titles also have a strong following. Recognized cover classics experienced strong demand. Sales in all grades are over-guide.

REPORTED SALES: All Top #10 VF $700; **Babe** #1 FN $80; **Brenda Starr Reporter** #1 FN $45; **Crimes By Women** #4 FN+ $345, #7 VG $110, #10 VF $350, #15 VG $110; **Crown** #1 VF+ $200; **Dagar, Desert Hawk** #16 FN+ $180, #19 NM $510, #22 VG+ $85, #23 GD $50; **Giant Comics Edition** #13 FN $185; **Hickory** #1 VF+ $165; **Jo-Jo** #12 VF+ $325, #17 VF+ $546, #25 FN+ $500; **Nellie The Nurse** #9 NM $135; **Oscar Comics** #8 NM $115; **Phantom Lady** #13 VF+ $1,650, #17 VF $4,600, VG(r) $1,450, #21 FN $650, #23VG $1700; Seven Seas #4FN+ $500, GD $180, #5GD $200, $120; **Slave Girl** #1 FN+ $300; **Teen Age Temptations** #4 FN $65; **Venus** #10 FN(r) $150; **Western Bandit Trails** #1 VF $145; **Women Outlaws** #1 FN $225; **Zegra** #10 VF $355; **Zoot** #10 VF $355, #14 VF+ $517.

© AVON

Slave Girl Comics #1 in FN+ goes for $300!

HORROR

Collector demand for pre-code horror comics con-

© STAR

Startling Terror Tales **#11** FN+ sells for $1,265!

tinues to be as healthy as it was a year ago. Cover art drives the sale of these books, with the exception of EC's, which are collected due to superior total content. All L.B. Cole, Ditko and Simon & Kirby books were in very high demand. Any eye-catching, colorful cover sold briskly; the more bizarre, the better. Atlas and DC titles are always favorites, but so were all the other companies' books: Charlton, St. John, Aragon, Key, Comic Media, Ajax, Ziff-Davis, Fawcett, Harvey, Superior and others.

REPORTED SALES: Adventures Into The Unknown #26 (White Mountain) NM+ $470, #29 NM+ $385, #31 NM+ $305 (all sold by PCE); **Beware** #8 VF+ $190; **Chilling Tales** #13 (#1) NM $690; **Eerie Adventures** #1 VF+ $431; **Haunted Thrills** #2 VF $125, #11 FN $90; **Horrific** #3 VF+ $220, VG $210; **The Horrors** #13 FN $112; **Mystical Tales** #1 FN $170; **Nightmare** #12 FN $120; **Startling Terror Tales** #11 FN+ $1,265; **Strange Fantasy** #8 VG $80; **Strange Tales of the Unusual** #1 FN $155; **Tales of Horror** #2 VG $98; **Terrors of the Jungle** #20 FN+ $135.

HUMOROUS/FUNNY ANIMAL

The biggest Funny Animal demand is for Timely and DC titles, although there were small gains for all publishers. Early 1940s issues of **Looney Tunes** and **Walt Disney's Comics & Stories** remained scarce in high grade as in previous years. **Little Lulus** enjoyed increased demand, otherwise most other publishers enjoyed slow to average sales.

REPORTED SALES: Here's Howie #1 FN $98; **It's Gametime** #3 GD $70; **Leave It To Binky** #1 VG $95; **Mighty Mouse** #5 GD $75; **Peter Panda** #2 NM $195; **Sick** #1 VF $98; **Sugar & Spike** #1 GD $165.

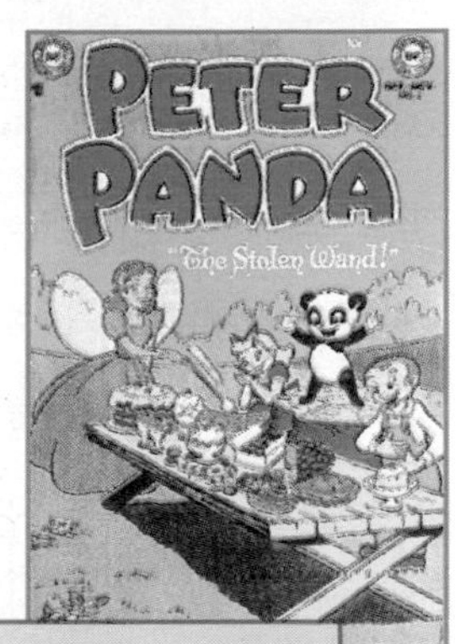

Peter Panda #2 NM sells for $195!

© DC

ROMANCE

Romance is in very strong demand, since one can spend a few hundred dollars in this area and still buy a sizable stack of books. Sales are at and above guide levels. Fox romance books are hot! Sales in all grades were occurring at above guide levels. Some of the most collected artists are Matt Baker, Jack Kamen, L.B. Cole and Simon & Kirby.

REPORTED SALES: Brides In Love #1 VF+ $90; **Forbidden Love** #1 FN+ $295; **Girl Confession** #15 VF+ $82; **Hollywood Secrets** #1 FN $95; **Lover's Lane** #1 VF+ $135; **My Great Love** #1 VF $140; **My Love Affair** #1 VF $150; **My Secret Affair** #1 FN $95; **Personal Love** #27 FN $110; **Popular Teenagers** #10 NM $185, #39 NM $240; **Romantic Secrets** #1 VF $125; **Romantic Story** #10 VF+ $78; **Secret Loves** #2 FN $65; **Youthful Romances** #1 VF+ $225.

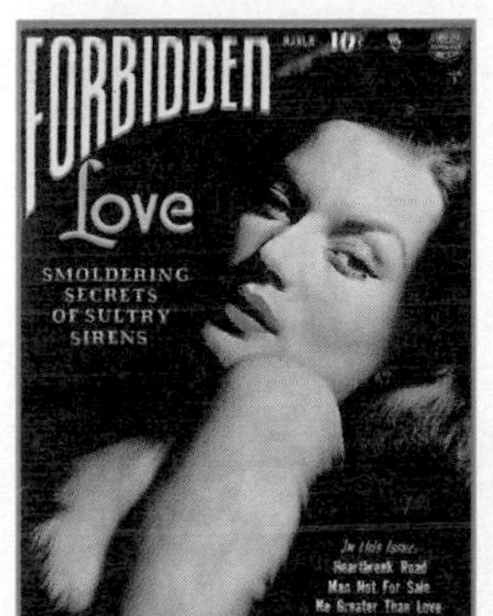

© QUA

Forbidden Love #1 FN+ brings a sultry $295!

SCIENCE FICTION

Good sales and demand for all issues was seen for this genre. EC, DC, Atlas, Charlton, Aragon titles sold very well. There are dozens of good artists in these books: Wally Wood, Al Williamson, Al Feldstein, Basil Wolverton, Murphy Anderson, Russ Heath, Maneely, Bill Everett, etc.

REPORTED SALES: Buster Crabbe #1 VF $245; **Captain Science** #4 VG+ $115; **Crusader From Mars** #1 VG+ $140, #2 VF+ $575; **Forbidden Worlds** #12 NM+ (White Mountain) $660, #62 VF+ $110; **Gorgo** #4 VF+ (White Mountain) $110; **Lars Of Mars** #10 FN $210; **Mysteries of Unexplored Worlds** #19 VF+ (White Mountain) $220; **Mystery In Space** #1 VF+ $2875, FN $1100. Space War #3dNM+ (White Mountain $160, Unknown Worlds #9NM+ (White Mountain) $195.

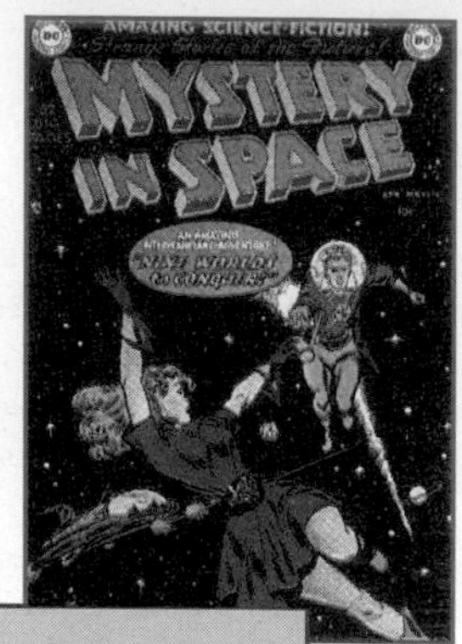

Mystery In Space #1 in VF+ sells for $2,875!!

© DC

TV/MOVIE TIE-INS

Reported sales Dell and Gold Key movie books were slow with discounting observed last year at the major conventions. However the DC TV/movie titles such as **Ozzie and Harriet**, **Jackie Gleason**, **Sgt. Bilko**, etc. are consistent good sellers and difficult to locate in high grade.

REPORTED SALES: Beverly Hillbillies #1 VF $98.

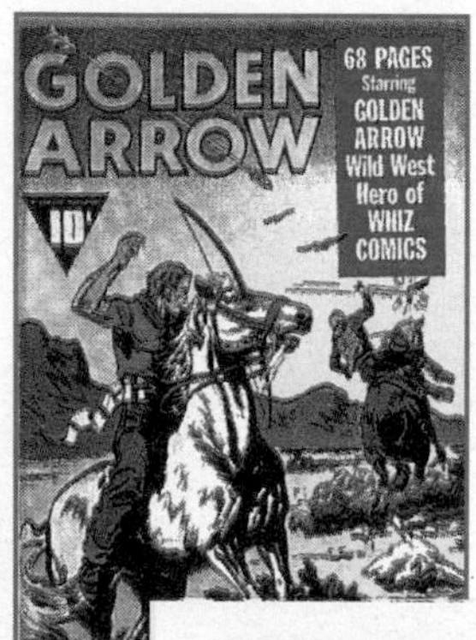

Golden Arrow #1 in VF gets $425!

© FAW

WAR

Led by EC and DC, and followed by Atlas, collector interest remained stable for the year.

REPORTED SALES: Our Army At War #1 GD+ $350; **War Action** #1 VF+ $325.

WESTERNS

Average sales were led by photo cover issues. The top collected companies were Fawcett, DC, Atlas, Fox and Dell.

REPORTED SALES: All Star Western #10 VF+ $120; **Bobby Benson's** #9 FN $75; **Golden Arrow** #1 VF $425; **Roy Rogers Four Color** #38 VF+ $1,400; **Tomahawk** #1 VF+ $1,782.

SILVER AGE

Demand in this area was still quite specialized. Most sales at prices over guide are almost exclusively for high grade books. Currently the most popular title for Marvel is **X-Men**, and for DC it is **Showcase** and key **Brave and the Bold** issues in high grade. Heavy discounting for most Silver Age books in lower grades was seen in published sales lists and at the major shows last year. Our advisory network also reported reduced prices for these books which were reflected last November in the first issue of **THE GUIDE: The Overstreet Comic Book Price Update**.

This price guide was the product of extensive research into the current market and was enthusiastically received by all. With the help of our many advisors there was a lot of discussion in trying to understand the changes that were occurring in the Silver Age market. It was obvious that most books in Fine or less were selling for lower prices than listed in the guide. It was also noted that most books in true Near Mint were selling at and above guide list. To bring the guide back into balance with the market, it was decided to increase spreads from Good to Mint by a factor of 10. This means that a book in Good would list for $10 and in Mint for $100. We hope that the new price decreases will have a positive impact in the lower grade area now that they are much more affordable to collectors. Many years ago when the Good price was reduced on Golden Age books, it spurred the market with Good condition books selling again. Today, Good in Golden Age is still selling well if graded correctly.

Showcase #14 VF+ sold for $6,500!!

© DC

SILVER AGE REPORT (BY COMPANY)

DC

This company's books are perceived in the marketplace to be a little scarcer than Marvel's. However, the large demand for Marvels over the years offset this scarcity. Most titles of this company were being discounted in the lower grades as with Marvel's. Due to this, Silver Age DCs have been placed on a 1 to 10 spread as well. However, high grade copies of most titles were selling at and above guide levels. A VF+ copy of **Showcase** #14 sold for $6,500 late in the year. **Showcase**, **Brave and the Bold**, **Batman**, **Superman** and related titles remained popular; **Wonder Woman** also continued to be hot. There were very strong sales for the DC war titles, led by **Our Army At War**.

REPORTED SALES: Action #242 VF $680, 254 VF+ $170; **Adventure** #300 NM $370; **The Atom** #1 NM $750; **Batman** #105 VF+ $530, **Annual** #1 NM $600; **Blackhawk** #164 VF+ $65; **Brave & The Bold** #26 NM $500, #28 VF $2,500, #34 VF+ $1,900, $1,760, VG $250, #54 VF $200, #84 NM $55, #91 NM $35; **Challengers Of The Unknown** # 2 VF+ $1,380, #8 NM $977; **Flash** #105 FN+ $1,150; **G.I. Combat** #68 FN $55; **Green Lantern** #1 FN $1,400, #2 NM $1,000, #40 NM $500, #45 NM $100, #76 NM $175; **Hawkman** #4 NM $155; **JLA** #1 VF $2,500, $2,000, #29 VF $100, #46 NM $100, #55 NM $70; **Mystery In Space** #2 VF+ $1,200; **Our Army At War** #83 VF $1,100, #85 VF+ $310, #115 VF $75, #153 NM $130; **Phantom Stranger** #1 NM $85; **Plastic Man** #1 VF+ $78; **Secret Six** #1 NM $65, VF $55; **Showcase** #9 VF & 10 VG+ $3,450, #13 VF & 14 VG $3,450, #15 FN $485, #27 FN $220; **Spectre** #1 NM $140; **Strange Adventures** #100 NM $160; **Wonder Woman** #105 VF+ $700, VG $550.

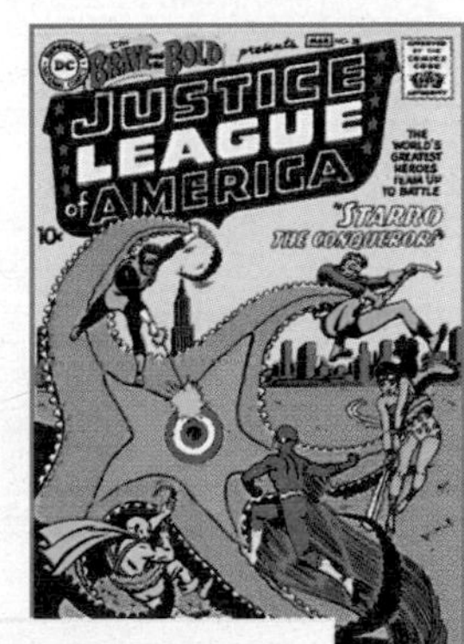

Brave & The Bold #28 in VF sells for $2,500!!

© DC

MARVEL

At year's end this company's stock had dropped below $1. Discounting for the lower grades of most titles was evident in advertised for-sale lists as well as at the major conventions last year. As mentioned earlier, most Marvel comics have been reduced in the lower grades to more accurately reflect the market. However, key issues in VF+ or better condition continued to sell at and above guide list prices. An **Amazing Spider-Man** #14 in NM sold for $2,588 at auction (Sotheby's) while **Tales of Suspense** #39 in VF brought $2,588. A collection of **X-Men** #1-66 in VF+ to NM went for almost double guide list at $17,250! A collection of **Incredible Hulk** #2-6 (most in FN64) sold for $5,175 or 46% over guide list. **Incredible Hulk** #6 in VF+ sold at auction for $1,150 (Exec. Coll. Fall Sale) which is below guide list. Pacific Comic Exchange sold various grades of **Amazing Spider-Man** with NM copies generally going for guide list or above, and GD to FN copies selling at around the new adjusted prices in this edition.

© MEG

Amazing Spider-Man #2 in VF+ gets $2,640!

PACIFIC COMIC EXCHANGE REPORTED SALES: Amazing Fantasy #15 VG+ $3,100, FR $810; **Amazing Spider-Man** #2 VF+ $2,640, FN $750; #4 VG $155, #5 VG $145, #7 GD $75, #14 NM $2,588, VG+ $275, #14 VF+ $950, FN $500, #15 VF+ $500, VG+ $115, #17 FN+ $155, #20 FN+ $100, #32 NM $170, #40 NM $330, #42 VF+ $90, #60 VF+ $30, #69 VF+ $20, #74 NM $45, #96 VF+ $80, #122 NM $145; **Captain America** #100 NM $330, VG $30, GD $10, #111 NM+ $85; **Conan** #24 NM $30; **Daredevil** #1 VG $400, #4 FN $120, #50 NM $38; **Fantastic Four** #3 VG+ $350, #4 FN+ $440, #11 VF $305, #24 VF+ $160, #48 VF+ $660; **Incredible Hulk** #5 VG+ $250, #6 VF+ $1,150, #103 NM $70; **Iron Man** #1 NM+ $415; **Iron Man & Sub-Mariner** #1 NM+ $160; **Silver Surfer** #3 NM $145, #4 NM $440; **Strange Tales** #101 VF+$770; **Tales of Suspense** #43 FN $90, #48 FN+ $110; **X-Men** #1 VG+ $525, $660, #15 VF+ $190, #24 NM $80.

REPORTED SALES (other): Amazing Fantasy #15 VG+ $3,100, FR $810; **Amazing Spider-Man** #1 VF $8,000, FR+ $600, #2 VF+ $2,500, #3 GD $150, #5 FN $350, #7 GD $50, #9 VG $125, #10 FN $175, #14 VF $950, #22 NM $280, #40 VF $300, #50 FN $100, #52 VG $15, #60 VF+ $30, #69 VF+ $20, #74 NM $45, #98 NM $75, #124 NM $35, #135 VF $35, #200 NM $25, #300 NM $60; **Avengers** #1 GD+ $200, #2 VF $375, #4 VF+ $1,000, #5 GD $25, #14 NM $75; **Captain America** #100 VG $30. #117 NM $55; **Conan** #1 NM $200; **Daredevil** #1 VF+ $1,800, #168 NM $40; **Fantastic Four** #1 VF+ $9,000 (part trade), #4 GD $200, #24 VG $15, #48 VF $500, GD $100, #67 NM $100; **Incredible Hulk** #1 FN+ $1,400, VG $1,175, GD $750, $450, #2 NM $2,500, #3 VF $1,000, #4 GD $120, #181 VF $350; **Iron Man** #1 NM $325, #3 NM $75; **Journey Into Mystery** #83 GD $275, #91 VF $100; **Nick Fury** #1 NM $70; **Ringo Kid** #21 NM $75; **Sgt. Fury** #13 NM $300; **Silver Surfer** #1 NM $595, $480, $400, #2 NM $240, #4 NM $400; **Strange Tales** #79 NM $425; **Strange Tales Annual** #2 NM $600; **Sub-Mariner** #1 NM $100;

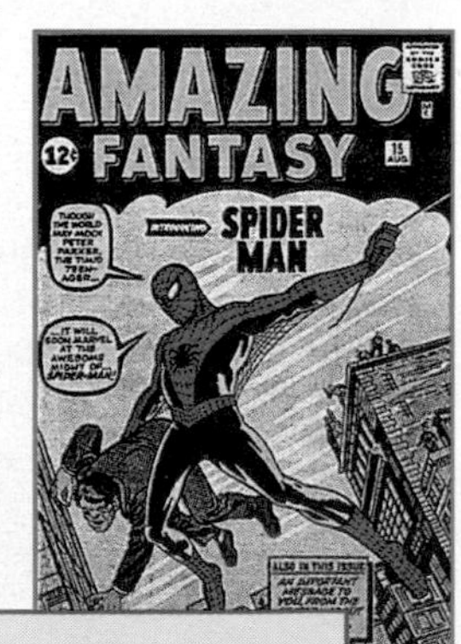

Amazing Fantasy #15 VG+ brings $3,100!

© MEG

© MEG

Fantastic Four #1 VF+ fetches $9,000!!

Tales of Suspense #32 NM $250, #36 NM $150, #39 VF $2,588, #52 VG $30, #57 NM $100, #59 NM $250, #63 GD $15, #64 NM $60; **Tales To Astonish** #27 VF $2,300, #35 VG $200, #44 NM $275, #51 NM $100; **X-Men** #2 VF $1,000, $650, #3 VF $500, #4 NM $500, #5 VG $43, #7 NM $150, #10 NM $250, #11 GD $20, #14 NM $300.

DELL/GOLD KEY/ARCHIE

All issues shifted into a 1 to 11 spread. Reports indicated a pickup in sales for the lower grades, otherwise average sales for most titles. However, most all of the cartoon titles, many of which appeared on TV, were in high demand such as **Astro Boy**, **Atom Ant**, **Augie Doggie**, **Bamm Bamm & Pebbles**, **Deputy Dawg**, **Frankenstein, Jr.**, **George of the Jungle**, **Hanna-Barbera Super TV Heroes**, **Hector Heathcote**, **Hi-Adventure Heroes**, **Linus the Lionhearted**, **Magilla Gorilla**, **Mr. & Mrs. J. Evil Scientist**, and others. All digest comics were selling well including **Golden Comics Digest** and **Mystery Comics Digest**. Other titles on the move are: **Naza**, **Nurses**, **The Outer Limits**, **Private Secretary**, **Thirteen**, and **Toka**.

REPORTED SALES: Doctor Solar #10 FN+ $20, #16 FN+ $15; **Jetsons** #3 VF+ $75, #7 VF+ $90, #11 VF+ $75, #12 VF+ $55, #19 VF+ $60; **Josie** #1 FN $75; **Jughead's Fantasy** #1 FN+ $175; **Korak** #4 VF $27, #29 VF $12, #35 VF $8; **Mighty Samson** #3 VF $16, #6 VF $12; **Peanuts** #2 VF $45, #3 VF $40, #10 VF $35; **Space Family Robinson** #36 VF $20, #41 VF+ $5; **Star Trek** #1 VF+ $500, #7 VF+ $135, #17 NM $75, #49 NM $25, #61 NM $25.

BRONZE AGE REPORT (BY COMPANY)

Hundreds of books from this era have become valuable. Usually, it is not the mainstream titles as you may expect, but the more obscure titles. The most volatile books have been placed in auctions. A **DC 100 Page Super Spectacular** #5 brought $477 at auction late in the year. Since almost all 1970s publishers have books worth noting, the following information will be broken down by publisher.

DC

All DC 52 page to 100 page giants and large format books from this era have become popular. From **Action Comics**, **Adventure Comics**, **Batman**, **Detective** to **World's Finest**, all giant size issues are hot. Probably the hottest title is **DC 100 Page Super Spectacular**, and issue #5 is one of the most valuable Bronze Age books. Other hot books are **Famous First Edition**, **Weird War Tales** #1-10 (a #1 in VF+ sold for $150!), **Limited Collectors' Edition**, **Weird Western Tales**, **Witching Hour**, **Dark Mansion of Forbidden Love** #1-4, **Ghosts**, **Date**

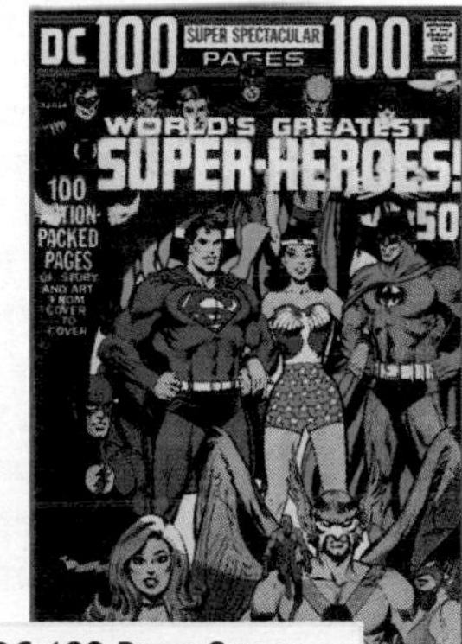

DC 100 Page Super Spectacular is hot! (#6 shown)

© DC

Adventure Comics #431 in NM scares up $45!

© DC

With Debbi, Secrets Of Sinister House, Sinister House of Secret Love, DC Super Special (especially S-13 & the romance issues), **Super DC Giant, Young Love** and **Young Romance**. All digest-size comics are also hot such as **Adventure Digest, The Best of DC** and **DC Blue Ribbon Digest**. Other titles worth noting are: **All Star, All Star Western, Batman Family, Battle Classics, Black Magic, Blitzkrieg, Champion Sports, Doorway To Nightmare, Four Star Battle Tales, G.I. War Tales, Korak, Leave It To Binky, Son of Tarzan, Secret Origins, Sherlock Holmes, Strange Sports Stories, Super Friends, Swing With Scooter, Tarzan, Unknown Soldier, Weird Mystery Tales** and **Windy & Willy**. The title **Hot Wheels**, based on a TV show, showed strong demand.

REPORTED SALES: Adventure #425 NM $22, #431 NM $45, VF+ $20; **All Star Western** #10 VF+ $120; **Batman** #189 NM $90, #232 VF $38, #234 NM $135; **Brave & The Bold** #91 $35; **Champion Sports** #1 NM $14; **DC 100 Page Super Spectacular** #5 GD $120, #20 NM $35; **The Demon** #1 NM $32; **Detective** #440 VF+ $35; **Four Star Battle** #1 VF+ $12; **Green Lantern** #76 NM $175; **Jimmy Olsen** #141 NM $15; **Johnny Thunder** #1 NM $18; **Laurel and Hardy** #1 FN $40; **Legion of Superheroes** #1 NM $22; **Lois Lane** #105 NM $18, #105 NM $26; **Mister Miracle** #1 NM $45; **Phantom Stranger** #23 NM $22; **Prez** #1 VF+ $15; **Rima** #1 NM $15, VF+ $10; **Secrets of Haunted House** #10 NM $18; **Sgt. Rock** #302 NM $30; **Shazam** #8 NM $28; **Super DC Giant** #S-13 GD $38, #S-18 FN $15, #S-25 FN $10; **Super Friends** #1 VF+ $28; **Supergirl** #1 VF+ $15; **Swamp Thing** #7 NM $28; **Tarzan** #207 NM $14; **The Unknown Soldier** #205 NM $18; **Weird War** #1 VF+ $125, VF $75; **Wonder Woman** #211 VF $22; **Young Love** #107 VF $78, #109 VF $60.

MARVEL

Marvel has some of the most valuable books from this period. **Giant Size X-Men** #1, **X-Men** #94, the 35¢ **Star Wars** #1 and **Incredible Hulk** #181. A **Giant Size X-Men** #1 NM sold for $400 and in VF+ for $450. An **X-Men** #94 NM brought $474, $400 and a 35¢ **Star Wars** #1 VF+ sold for $575. All of this company's horror, western and war titles are in demand: **Amazing Adventures, Beware, Chamber of Chills, Chamber of Darkness, Combat Kelly, Creatures on the Loose, Crypt of Shadows, Dead of Night, Fear, Gunslinger, Gunhawks, Mighty Marvel Western, Monsters on the Prowl, Night Rider, Outlaw Kid, Red Wolf, Ringo Kid, Supernatural Thrillers, Tex Dawson, Tomb of Darkness, Tower of Shadows, Uncanny Tales, Vault of Evil, War is Hell, Weird Wonder Tales**, and **Western Kid** & **Western Team-Up**. Other hot titles are: **The Cat, Chili, Harvey, Jungle Action, Ka-Zar, Kull The Conqueror, Laff-A-Lympics, L'il Kids, Shanna, The She-Devil, Son of Satan, Spoof, Spotlight, TV Stars**, most giant-size issues have picked up such as **Marvel Treasury Edition** and some of the **Giant-Size** issues. Some of the love-theme comics from this

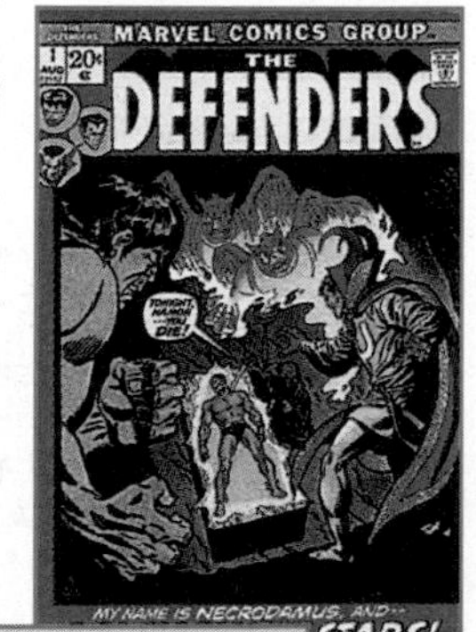

Defenders #1 NM sells for $100!

© MEG

period are scarce and have become hot such as **Night Nurse** and **Our Love Story**. The popularity of **Planet of the Apes** movies has created a large following and the comic book series is also very popular as a result.

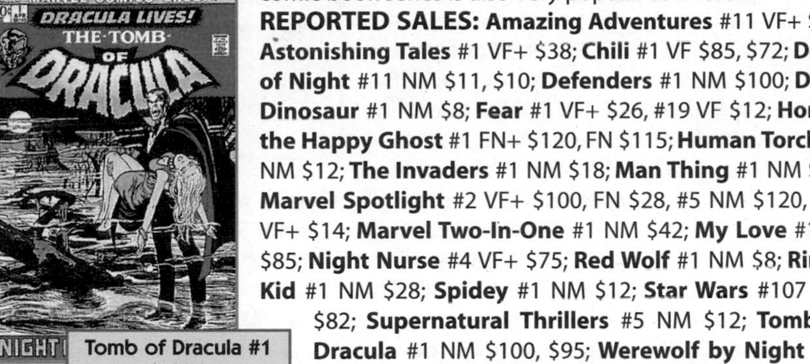

Tomb of Dracula #1 in NM sells for $100!

© MEG

REPORTED SALES: Amazing Adventures #11 VF+ $60; **Astonishing Tales** #1 VF+ $38; **Chili** #1 VF $85, $72; **Dead of Night** #11 NM $11, $10; **Defenders** #1 NM $100; **Devil Dinosaur** #1 NM $8; **Fear** #1 VF+ $26, #19 VF $12; **Homer the Happy Ghost** #1 FN+ $120, FN $115; **Human Torch** #1 NM $12; **The Invaders** #1 NM $18; **Man Thing** #1 NM $18; **Marvel Spotlight** #2 VF+ $100, FN $28, #5 NM $120, #28 VF+ $14; **Marvel Two-In-One** #1 NM $42; **My Love** #1 VF $85; **Night Nurse** #4 VF+ $75; **Red Wolf** #1 NM $8; **Ringo Kid** #1 NM $28; **Spidey** #1 NM $12; **Star Wars** #107 NM $82; **Supernatural Thrillers** #5 NM $12; **Tomb of Dracula** #1 NM $100, $95; **Werewolf by Night** #32 NM $85, VF+ $80; **Where Monsters Dwell** #1 NM $20.

ATLAS

All the Spire Christian titles have increased in demand: **Adam & Eve**, all **Archie** titles, **My Brothers Keeper**, etc.

CHARLTON

This company had poor distribution of their comics compared to the larger companies. Consequently, their books have always been difficult to locate. All the horror, love, war and western theme books are scarce and popular: **Army Attack, Army War Heroes, Attack, Beyond the Grave, Confidential Diary, Creepy Things, Cynthia Doyle, Nurse in Love, David Cassidy, Emergency Doctor, Geronimo Jones, Ghostly Tales, Ghost Manor, Gunfighters, Haunted, Haunted Love, House of Yang, Just Married, Love & Romance, Many Ghosts of Dr. Graves, Marines Attack, Midnight Tales, Monster Hunters, Navy War Heroes, Sarge Snorkel, Scary Tales, Shadows from Beyond, Special War Series, Summer Love, Teen-Age Love, Three Nurses, Valley of the Dinosaurs,** and **Young Doctors**. All of the TV cartoon characters are also hot: **Barney & Betty Rubble, Bullwinkle, Dino, Dudley Do-Right, Flintstones, Great Gazoo, Great Grape Ape, Hanna Barbara Parade, Hong Kong Phooey, Huckleberry Hound, Pebbles & Bamm Bamm, Quick Draw McGraw, Ronald McDonald, Top Cat, War & Attack, War Wings** and **Wild West**. Other titles that have increased in value are: **Drag 'N' Wheels, Grand Prix, Hee Haw, Hi and Lois, Holi-day Surprise, Primus, Vengeance Squad**, and **World of Wheels**.
REPORTED SALE: Underdog #1 VF+ $70.

ARCHIE

Price increases reflect that all of the digest-size issues have become very collectible. A few of the titles are: **Archie Comics Digest, Archie's Double Digest, Jughead with Archie Digest, Jughead Jones Comics Digest**. Other popular titles are: **Archie at Riverdale High, Archie's TV Laugh-Out, Archie's Super-Hero Special, Chilling Adventures in Sorcery, Everything's Archie, Mad House, Reggie's Wise Guy Jokes**, and **Sabrina, the Teen-Age Witch**.
REPORTED SALES: Chilling Advs. in Sorcery (Sabrina) #1 NM $20, #2 FN $8.

DELL/GOLD KEY/WESTERN/WHITMAN

The TV cartoon character books have all increased in value. A few of the more popular titles are: **Addams Family, Amazing Chan & The Chan Clan, Baby Snoots, Banana Splits, Brady Bunch, Close Shaves of Pauline Peril, Fat Albert, Flintstones, Fun-In, Funky Phantom, Funtastic World of Hanna-Barbara, Hair Bear Bunch, Happy Days, Harlem Globetrotters, H.R. Pufnstuf, The Inspector, Lidsville, Magilla Gorilla, Mushmouse & Punkin Puss, Pink Panther, Roman Holidays, Scooby Doo, Secret Squirrel, Smokey Bear, Tasmanian Devil, Wacky Races, Wacky Witch, Wally** and others. Other popular titles are: **Brothers of the Spear, Grimm's Ghost Stories, Little Monsters, Little Stooges, Looney Tunes, Lone Ranger, Mighty Samson, Mystery Comics Digest, Occult Files of Dr. Spektor, Walt Disney Comics Digest, Where's Huddles?, Woodsy Owl, Yosemite Sam** and **Zody, The Mod Rob**.

A good investment book is one that the dealer will guarantee buying back at 40% of the sticker price!

REPORTED SALES: Cave Kids #2 VF+ $15; **Close Shaves of Pauline Peril** #1 VF+ $8, #4 VF+ $5; **Flintstones** #60 VF $20; **Happy Days** #1 VF+ $6; **The Inspector** #1 $7; **Jungle Twins** #1 VF+ $5; **O.G. Whiz** #3 VF+ $25, #5 VF+ $25, #7 VF+ $9; **Pink Panther** #1 VF+ $42; **Super Goof** #2 VF+ $9; **Tarzan** #151 VF+ $17; **Turok** #122 VF $8.50; **Underdog** #1 VF $40, #2 NM $28.

© HARV

Richie Rich titles are popular!

HARVEY

A few of the Harvey titles that are on the move are: **Bunny, Casper Digest, Hot Stuff Creepy Caves, Richie Rich** (most titles), **Sad Sad Sack World, Spooky Haunted House**, and **Super Richie**.

REPORTED SALE: Richie Rich Billions #20 VF $3.50.

SKYWALD

This obscure company published several titles in the 1970s which are scarce today and have increased in demand: **Blazing Six-Guns, Crime Machine, Heap, Sundance Kid**, and **Wild Western Action**.

TOWER

This publisher entered the market in the 1960s with some excellent books drawn by Wally Wood such as **Dynamo, No-Man**, etc. But this company's more obscure titles have become sought-after such as **Jungle Adventures, Teen-In, Tippy's Friends Go-Go & Animal**, and **Tippy Teen**.

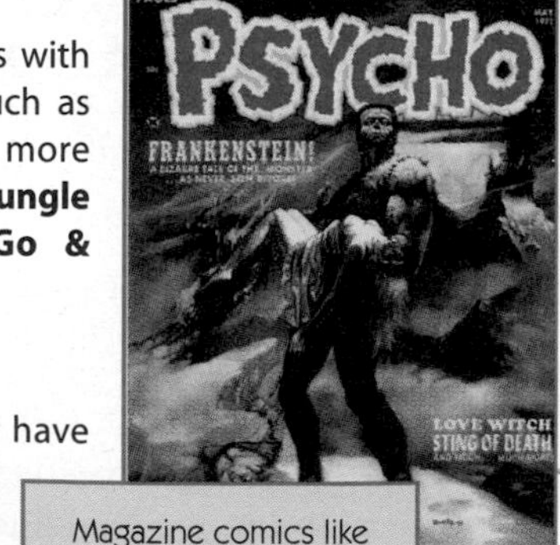

Magazine comics like **Psycho** are on the move! (#3 shown)

© Skywald

MAGAZINE COMICS

All publishers of the magazine-size comics have enjoyed a pick-up in demand. Many publishers were involved such as Atlas/Seaboard, Charlton, Eerie, G&D Publ., Major Mag., Marvel, Skywald, Stanley, Warren, etc. A few of the best selling titles

are: **Blast, Blip, Chilling Tales of Horror, Crazy, Deadly Hands of Kung Fu, Dracula Lives, Emergency, Frenzy, Ghoul Tales, Horror Tales, Laugh-In Magazine, Masters of Terror, Monster Howls, Psycho, Stark Terror, Tales of Voodoo, Vampire Tales, Weird, Weird Worlds** and **Witches Tales.**
REPORTED SALES: Cracked #1 GD $40; **Creepy** #3 VF $20.

MODERN AGE

During the 1980s and early 1990s, comic books were produced in the millions of copies by dozens of companies: Marvel, DC, Image, Dark Horse, Malibu, and Valiant, to name a few. During this time there was a lot of speculation on the latest hot titles in the marketplace which drove up prices. The peak in the market was probably the death of Superman in issue #75, which appeared in 1993. This book sold in the millions of copies, not only in the direct market, but through television marketing and on newsstands. Everybody bought this book speculating that it would be a good investment for the future. Unfortunately, with this and many other books the prices peaked and the market was not able to maintain its momentum, going into a free fall as a result. As investors left the market in 1994 through 1996, sales of new comics went into a decline. Hundreds of comic book stores closed as the market was settling back down to its previous level before the boom.

Over-grading results in over-priced books!

Captain America is in demand!

© MEG

Today, comic book stores are more selective in what they stock. Publishers have reduced titles and are printing fewer copies. The market is going back to the basics. After all, comic books are a form of entertainment and are meant to be read, saved, shared and enjoyed. Second to this, of course, is investment.

CURRENT POPULAR TITLES

MARVEL: Alpha Flight, Captain America, Deadpool, Fantastic Four, Ka-Zar, Human Torch, Maverick, Thunderbolts

DC: Aquaman, Aztek, Flex Mentallo, Hellblazer, Hitman, Impulse, JLA, Kingdom Come, Major Bummer, Nightwing, Preacher, Resurrection Man, The Spectre, Supergirl, Superman, Wonder Woman

IMAGE (and its respective associated studios): Arcanum, Astro City, Curse of Spawn, Darkchylde, Darkness, DV8, Spawn, Witchblade

SLAVE LABOR: Johnny The Homicidal Maniac, Milk & Cheese

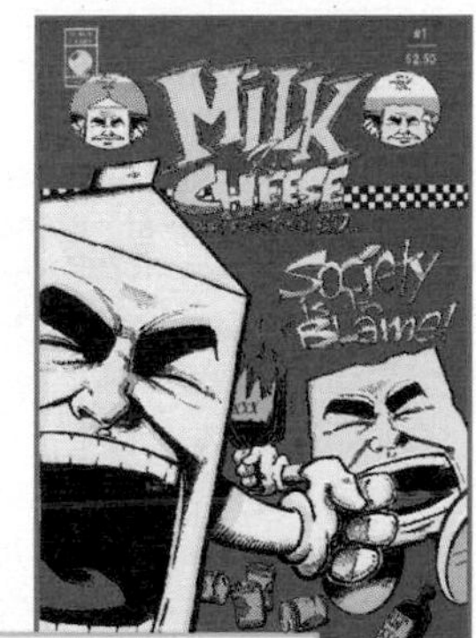

Milk and Cheese #1 is hot!

© Evan Dorkin

CALIBER PRESS: Cave Woman, Creatures of the ID

DARK HORSE: Body Bags, Sin City

SIRIUS: Dawn, Poison Elves

MISC.: Evil Ernie (Chaos!), **I, Lusiphur** (Mulehide), **Madman** (Thundra Press/Dark Horse), **Miracleman** (Eclipse), **Scud** (Fireman Press), **Strangers In Paradise** (Abstract & Homage Studios), **Stray Bullets** (El Capitan), **Too Much Coffee Man** (Adhesive)

Strangers in Paradise is growing in popularity! (Vol. 3 #1 shown)

© Terry Moore

SUMMATION

GOLDEN AGE

Last year saw several Golden Age collections surface, and a few of these were in high grade. The dealers reported no difficulty in getting over-guide list for these books. The superhero books continued to be the most in demand, with VF or better copies remaining scarce as demand continued to outstrip supply. Due in part to the strong price increases for superhero books two years ago, this edition has taken a conservative posture with price increases at this time. The most valuable books were not available in NM condition, and if they were, more record prices would have been set. It is our hope that this conservative edition will encourage an even stronger Golden Age market in 1998.

ATOM AGE

This period of comics has been suggested by Jon Berk, Matt Schiffman, Steve Sibra and others, and is introduced in this edition for the first time. The first atomic bomb was exploded in 1945, ushering in a new era. With World War II also ending in that year, "atomic" theme comic books began to appear in 1946 and are today highly prized. Also after the war, the comics market shifted gears and began moving away from the superhero-themed anthologies to other genres. By 1948, crime, love, western, good-girl art, horror and teen-age comics began cramming the newsstands! With the addition of war, science fiction and comics based on popular television shows beginning in 1950, the consumer had more variety than ever from which to choose. Today, all of these books continue to have a strong demand. The few superhero books still surviving as well as the Fox love, good-girl art, crime and horror books are the most popular, with strong sales last year. The hottest artists are L.B. Cole, Matt Baker, Steve Ditko, Simon & Kirby, Frazetta, Feldstein and Kamen, to name a few.

SILVER AGE

This market has experienced some dramatic changes in recent years due to its volatility which drove prices to higher and higher levels. It was usually the books in VF+ to Mint condition fetching the high prices which drove the market in all the other grades as well. Now that prices for Silver Age books have stabilized in the higher grades, the much larger supply of lower grade books began competing for the consumer dollar. Competing dealers found that they had to discount these books to encourage a sale. For this reason, with the help of our extensive advisory network, this edition has incorporated many price changes to reflect these market changes. There is a high demand for the lower grade books, but the price has to be attractive for them to sell. Some advisors were reporting a slight drop in demand for the expensive keys, although Near Mint copies, for the most part, were not available for sale. If they were, prices at and above guide list would have been paid.

Probably one of the biggest problems in this market is grading. So many books offered for sale are over-graded and therefore over-priced. The consumer should shop around and compare grades/prices before spending their hard-earned money.

If you are buying a book for investment, it might be interesting to find out what the dealer's buy price is for that book. If the book is graded and priced properly, the dealer should give you a guaranteed buy-back price of at least 40% of the sticker price. If his wholesale buying price is less than this, then you know this book may not be a good investment.

BRONZE AGE

This market continues to be on the move! You will note hundreds of price changes that occurred last year. New winners are emerging all the time. Since the majority of books from this period are below $20, they are very affordable to collectors. The direction this market is taking seems to be for whatever is obscure, scarce and rare. These are the comics that were out of the mainstream at the time, being overlooked, missed and neglected. Many of these books have been in the quarter bins for years and were not cared for as the more valuable comics collected in the 1970s were. Now the market has awakened and is seeking out these obscure gems. Our advisors are predicting a banner year for Bronze Age books in 1998!

MODERN AGE

Many comic books published in the last 15 years have shown a decrease in demand compared to the expansion years of the late 1980s and early 1990s. With the lower print runs, there could very well be some winners in the years ahead. As we have always said, new comics are to be enjoyed. Buy to read and to share with friends.

© DC

© AP

© DC

© MEG

© Top Cow

INVESTOR'S DATA

The following tables denote the rate of appreciation of the top Golden Age, Platinum Age, Silver Age and Bronze Age books, as well as selected genres over the past year and the past five years (1993-1998). The retail value for a NM copy of each book (or VF where a Near Mint copy is not known to exist) in 1998 is compared to its value in 1997 and 1993. The rate of return for 1998 over 1997 is given. The place in rank is given for each comic by year, with its corresponding value in highest known grade. Premium books are included in these tables and are denoted with an asterisk(*). These tables can be very useful in forecasting trends in the market place. For instance, the investor might want to know which book is yielding the best dividend from one year to the next, or one might just be interested in seeing how the popularity of books changes from year to year. For instance, *Batman* #1 was in 8th place in 1997 and has increased to 6th place in 1998.

The following tables are meant as a guide to the investor. However, it should be pointed out that trends may change at anytime and that some books can meet market resistance with a slowdown in price increases, while others can develop into real comers from a presently dormant state. In the long run, if the investor sticks to the books that are appreciating steadily each year, he shouldn't go very far wrong.

TOP GOLDEN AGE BOOKS

1998 OVER 1997 GUIDE VALUES

ISSUE NO.	1998 RANK	1998 NM PRICE	1997 RANK	1997 NM PRICE	$ INCR.	% INCR.
Action Comics #1	1	$180,000	1	$160,000	$20,000	13%
Detective Comics #27	2	$160,000	2	$150,000	$10,000	7%
Superman #1	3	$125,000	3	$110,000	$15,000	14%
Marvel Comics #1	4	$108,000	4	$98,000	$10,000	10%
Whiz Comics #2 (#1)	5	$63,000	9	$60,000	$3,000	5%
Batman #1	6	$62,000	8	$60,000	$2,000	3%
All-American Comics #16	7	$60,000	7	$60,000	$0	0%
Captain America Comics #1	8	$56,000	10	$56,000	$0	0%
Flash Comics #1	9	$55,000	11	$50,000	$5,000	10%
Detective Comics #1	10	VF $50,000	5	VF $50,000	$0	0%
More Fun Comics #52	11	$47,000	12	$47,000	$0	0%
New Fun Comics #1	12	VF $37,500	6	VF $37,000	$500	1%
Adventure Comics #40	13	$32,000	13	$32,000	$0	0%
Detective Comics #33	14	$32,000	14	$32,000	$0	0%
More Fun Comics #53	15	$32,000	15	$32,000	$0	0%
All Star Comics #3	16	$30,000	16	$30,000	$0	0%
Detective Comics #38	17	$28,000	18	$28,000	$0	0%
Captain Marvel Adventures #1	18	$27,000	19	$27,000	$0	0%
Green Lantern #1	19	$26,000	21	$25,000	$1,000	4%
All Star Comics #8	20	$24,000	22	$24,000	$0	0%
New York World's Fair 1939	21	$24,000	24	$24,000	$0	0%
Detective Comics #29	22	$23,000	26	$23,000	$0	0%
Detective Comics #31	23	$23,000	27	$23,000	$0	0%
Famous Funnies-Series 1 #1	24	$21,500	28	$21,000	$500	2%
Human Torch #2 (#1)	25	$21,000	29	$21,000	$0	0%
Sensation Comics #1	26	$21,000	32	$20,000	$1,000	5%
Adventure Comics #48	27	$20,000	30	$20,000	$0	0%
Marvel Mystery Comics #2	28	$20,000	35	$19,000	$1,000	5%
Sub-Mariner Comics #1	29	$20,000	33	$20,000	$0	0%
Action Comics #2	30	$19,000	37	$18,000	$1,000	6%
New Fun Comics #6	31	VF $18,000	17	VF $17,500	$500	3%
* Century Of Comics nn	32	VF $17,500	39	VF $17,500	$0	0%
Marvel Mystery Comics #9	33	$17,000	43	$16,000	$1,000	6%
Wonder Woman #1	34	$17,000	42	$16,500	$500	3%
Daring Mystery Comics#1	35	$16,500	40	$16,500	$0	0%
Jumbo Comics #1	36	VF $16,500	34	VF $16,000	$500	3%
New Fun Comics #2	37	VF $16,000	20	VF $15,500	$500	3%
Walt Disney's Comics & Stories #1	38	$16,000	44	$16,000	$0	0%
* Motion Picture Funnies Weekly #1	39	$15,000	45	$15,000	$0	0%
Famous Funnies #1	40	$15,000	47	$14,500	$500	3%

ISSUE NO.	1998 RANK	1998 NM PRICE	1997 RANK	1997 NM PRICE	$ INCR.	% INCR.
Marvel Mystery Comics #5	41	$15,000	51	$14,000	$1,000	7%
New Comics #1	42	VF $15,000	23	VF $14,500	$500	3%
Amazing Man Comics #5	43	$14,500	46	$14,500	$0	0%
Detective Comics #2	44	VF $14,300	25	VF $14,000	$300	2%
Detective Comics #28	45	$14,300	49	$14,000	$300	2%
All Winners #1	46	$14,000	48	$14,000	$0	0%
Wonder Comics #1	47	$13,500	52	$13,500	$0	0%
World's Best Comics #1	48	$13,500	57	$12,500	$1,000	8%
Action Comics #3	49	$13,000	59	$12,000	$1,000	8%
New York World's Fair 1940	50	$13,000	56	$13,000	$0	0%
Wow Comics #1	51	$12,500	58	$12,500	$0	0%
All-American Comics #17	52	$12,000	60	$12,000	$0	0%
All-American Comics #19	53	$12,000	61	$12,000	$0	0%
All Flash #1	54	$12,000	65	$11,500	$500	4%
All Star Comics #1	55	$12,000	62	$12,000	$0	0%
Big Book of Fun Comics #1	56	VF $12,000	31	VF $12,000	$0	0%
Mystic Comics #1	57	$12,000	64	$12,000	$0	0%
More Fun Comics #14	58	VF $11,500	36	VF $11,500	$0	0%
More Fun Comics #55	59	$11,500	66	$11,500	$0	0%
New Book Of Comics #1	60	VF $11,500	38	VF $11,000	$500	5%
* Funnies on Parade nn	61	$11,000	71	$11,000	$0	0%
Action Comics #7	62	$11,000	78	$10,000	$1,000	10%
Adventure Comics #61	63	$11,000	68	$11,000	$0	0%
Adventure Comics #73	64	$11,000	69	$11,000	$0	0%
Batman #2	65	$11,000	73	$10,500	$500	5%
Double Action #2	66	$11,000	70	$11,000	$0	0%
Mickey Mouse Magazine #1	67	$11,000	72	$11,000	$0	0%
Silver Streak #6	68	$11,000	77	$10,500	$500	5%
Big All-American #1	69	$10,800	74	$10,500	$300	3%
Archie Comics #1	70	$10,500	88	$9,000	$1,500	17%
Four Color Ser. 1 (Donald Duck) #4	71	$10,500	75	$10,500	$0	0%
More Fun Comics #73	72	$10,500	76	$10,500	$0	0%
Detective Comics #3	73	VF $10,200	41	VF $10,000	$200	2%
Adventure Comics #72	74	$10,000	79	$10,000	$0	0%
Captain America Comics #2	75	$10,000	80	$10,000	$0	0%
Silver Streak #1	76	$10,000	82	$9,500	$500	5%
Red Raven Comics #1	77	$9,600	84	$9,400	$200	2%
Comics Magazine #1	78	VF $9,500	63	VF $9,000	$500	6%
Looney Tunes and Merrie Melodies #1	79	$9,500	81	$9,500	$0	0%
Superman #2	80	$9,500	85	$9,200	$300	3%
Suspense Comics #3	81	$9,500	90	$9,000	$500	6%
Young Allies Comics #1	82	$9,500	86	$9,200	$300	3%
Mystery Men Comics #1	83	$9,400	83	$9,400	$0	0%
USA Comics #1	84	$9,300	91	$9,000	$300	3%
Action Comics #10	85	$9,000	--	$8,500	$500	6%
Daredevil Comics #1	86	$9,000	92	$8,500	$500	6%
Pep Comics #22	87	$9,000	--	$8,000	$1,000	13%
Planet Comics #1	88	$9,000	89	$9,000	$0	0%
Marvel Mystery Comics #1	89	$8,600	--	$8,400	$200	2%
Four Color Ser. 1 (Mickey Mouse) #16	90	VF $8,500	50	VF $8,500	$0	0%
Captain America Comics #3	91	$8,200	--	$8,000	$200	3%
Green Giant Comics #1	92	$8,200	93	$8,000	$200	3%
More Fun Comics #54	93	$8,200	94	$8,000	$200	3%
All-American Comics #18	94	$8,000	--	$8,000	$0	0%
All-American Comics #25	95	$8,000	--	$8,000	$0	0%
New Fun Comics #3	96	VF $8,000	53	VF $7,800	$200	3%
New Fun Comics #4	97	VF $8,000	54	VF $7,800	$200	3%
New Fun Comics #5	98	VF $8,000	55	VF $7,800	$200	3%
Special Edition Comics #1	99	$8,000	95	$8,000	$0	0%
Military Comics #1	100	$7,800	--	$7,500	$300	4%

TOP 10 PLATINUM AGE BOOKS

1998 OVER 1997 GUIDE VALUES

TITLE/ISSUE#	1998 RANK	1998 VF PRICE	1997 RANK	1997 VF PRICE	$ INCR.	% INCR.
Mickey Mouse Book	1	$10,000	1	$10,000	$0	0%
Yellow Kid in McFadden Flats	2	$7,500	2	$6,500	$1,000	15%
Buster Brown and His Resolutions 1903	3	$4,500	3	$4,500	$0	0%
Dreams of the Rarebit Fiend	4	$3,600	4	$3,500	$100	3%
* Buster Brown's Blue Ribbon #1 1904	5	$3,400	5	$3,400	$0	0%
Little Nemo 1906	6	$3,300	6	$3,000	$300	10%
Little Sammy Sneeze	7	$3,300	7	$3,000	$300	10%
Little Nemo 1909	8	$2,800	8	$2,500	$300	12%
Yellow Kid #1	9	$2,400	9	$2,200	$200	9%
Pore Li'l Mose	10	$2,000	10	$1,800	$200	11%

TOP 10 SILVER AGE BOOKS

1998 OVER 1997 GUIDE VALUES

TITLE/ISSUE#	1998 RANK	1998 NM PRICE	1997 RANK	1997 NM PRICE	$ INCR.	% INCR.
Amazing Fantasy #15	1	$27,000	1	$27,000	$0	0%
Showcase #4	2	$25,000	2	$25,000	$0	0%
Amazing Spider-Man #1	3	$19,000	3	$19,000	$0	0%
Fantastic Four #1	4	$18,400	4	$18,000	$400	2%
Showcase #8	5	$12,500	5	$11,250	$1,250	11%
Incredible Hulk #1	6	$11,000	6	$11,000	$0	0%
X-Men #1	7	$5,500	8	$5,000	$500	10%
Detective Comics #225	8	$5,200	7	$5,000	$200	4%
Flash #105(#1)	9	$5,200	10	$4,800	$400	8%
Brave And The Bold #28	10	$5,000	9	$4,800	$200	4%

TOP 10 BRONZE AGE BOOKS

1998 OVER 1997 GUIDE VALUES

TITLE/ISSUE#	1998 RANK	1998 NM PRICE	1997 RANK	1997 NM PRICE	$ INCR.	% INCR.
Star Wars #1 (35¢ cover price)	1	$490	1	$450	$40	9%
House of Secrets #92	2	$460	2	$435	$25	6%
Incredible Hulk #181	3	$450	3	$400	$50	13%
Giant-Size X-Men #1	4	$440	5	$350	$90	26%
X-Men #94	5	$420	4	$400	$20	5%
DC 100 Page Super Spectacular #5	6	$375	--	$45	$330	733%
X-Men #98 (30¢ cover price)	7	$280	--	$65	$215	331%
X-Men #99 (30¢ cover price)	8	$280	--	$65	$215	331%
Cerebus #1	9	$250	8	$225	$25	11%
Vampirella Annual #1	10	$250	6	$250	$0	0%

TOP 10 HORROR BOOKS

1998 OVER 1997 AND 1993 GUIDE VALUES

TITLE/ISSUE#	1998	1997	% CHANGE '97 TO '98	1993
Vault of Horror #12	$3,600	$3,500	3%	$2,200
Tales of Terror Annual #1	VF $3,200	VF $3,000	7%	$2,200
Journey into Mystery #1	$2,450	$2,300	7%	$900
Strange Tales #1	$2,400	$2,300	4%	$1,000
Crypt of Terror #17	$2,000	$1,900	5%	$1,200
Eerie #1	$2,000	$1,800	11%	$425
Haunt of Fear #15	$2,000	$1,900	5%	$1,100
Crime Patrol #15	$1,800	$1,700	6%	$900
House of Mystery #1	$1,600	$1,550	3%	$600
Tales to Astonish #1	$1,450	$1,400	4%	$600

TOP 10 SCI-FI BOOKS

1998 OVER 1997 AND 1993 GUIDE VALUES

TITLE/ISSUE#	1998	1997	% CHANGE '97 TO '98	1993
Mystery In Space #1	$2,600	$2,500	4%	$1,450
Strange Adventures #1	$2,300	$2,200	5%	$1,300
Showcase (Adam Strange) #17	$2,100	$1,950	8%	$950
Showcase (Space Ranger) #15	$1,650	$1,550	6%	$650
Fawcett Movie (Man From Planet X) #15	$1,600	$1,500	7%	$1,050
Journey Into Unknown Worlds #36	$1,500	$1,400	7%	$650
Strange Adventures #9	$1,400	$1,300	8%	$750
Weird Fantasy #13 (#1)	$1,400	$1,300	8%	$700
Weird Science #12 (#1)	$1,400	$1,300	8%	$725
Weird Science-Fantasy Annual 1952	$1,400	$1,300	8%	$900

TOP 10 WESTERN BOOKS

1998 OVER 1997 AND 1993 GUIDE VALUES

TITLE/ISSUE#	1998	1997	% CHANGE '97 TO '98	1993
Gene Autry Comics #1	$6,500	$5,800	12%	$1,800
Hopalong Cassidy #1	$4,200	$4,000	5%	$1,800
* Lone Ranger Ice Cream 1939	VF $4,000	VF $3,800	5%	VF $1,500
Red Ryder Victory Patrol	$3,400	$3,400	0%	$1,500
Tom Mix Ralston #1	$2,700	$2,500	8%	$1000
Red Ryder Comics #1	$2,400	$2,200	9%	$700
Roy Rogers Four Color #38	$1,800	$1,600	13%	$500
Western Picture Stories #1	$1,250	$1,200	4%	$700
Tomahawk #1	$1,200	$1,150	4%	$575
John Wayne Adventure Comics #1	$1,100	$1,000	10%	$400

Selected samplings from particular genres. Note the proximity of the starting points (prices) of these selected books.

THE OVERSTREET COMIC BOOK HALL OF FAME

For decades, historians, collectors and bibliofiles have tried to identify, list and document all the important, trend-setting comic books of the past century. This interesting topic continues to be debated and discussed by experts everywhere. In an attempt to answer these questions, Overstreet would like to nominate the following books to Overstreet's Hall Of Fame. The author invites your comments and ideas concerning the accuracy of this list for future editions. Remember, only the very top books will be considered for inclusion.

PLATINUM AGE 1897 - 1932

Yellow Kid in McFadden's Flats, The, 1897, Dillingham Co. (1st comic book)

Funny Folk, 1899, E.P. Dutton (2nd comic book)

Vaudeville and Other Things, 1900, Blandiard Co. (3rd comic book)

Blackberries, The, 1901, R.H. Russell (Ties as 4th comic book)

Foxy Grandpa, 1901, F.A. Stokes Co. (Ties as 4th comic book)

Pore Li'l Mose, 1902, Cupples & Leon (1st satire book) (1st Cupples & Leon book)

Alphonse & Gaston & Leon, 1903, Hearst's New York American

Buster Brown and His Resolutions, 1903, F.A. Stokes Co. (1st nationally distr. comic)

Happy Hooligan, 1903, Hearst's New York American (1st comic book app.)

Katzenjammer Kids, 1903, Hearst's New York American (1st comic book app.)

Brown's Blue Ribbon Book of Jokes and Jingles, 1904, Brown Shoe Co. (1st comic book premium)

Dreams of the Rarebit Fiend, 1905, Doffield & Co. (Ties as 1st Winsor McCay book)

Little Sammy Sneeze, 1905, New York Herald Co. (Ties as 1st Winsor McCay book)

Buster Brown, 1906, Cupples & Leon (1st C&L series comic)

Little Nemo, 1906, Doffield & Co. by Winsor McCay

3 Funmakers, 1908, Stokes (1st comic to feature more than one character)

Mutt & Jeff, 1910, Ball Publ. (1st comic book app.)

Comic Monthly, 1922, Embee Dist. Co. (1st monthly newsstand comic)

Funnies, The, 1929, Dell Publ. Co. (1st four-color comic newsstand publ.)

Mickey Mouse Book, 1930, Bibo & Lang (1st Disney licensed book)

Thimble Theatre Starring Popeye, 1931, Sonnet Publ. Co. (1st Popeye book)

Detective Dan, 1933, Humor Publ. Co. (1st comic w/original art & 1st on newsstand)

PRE-GOLDEN AGE 1933 - May, 1938

Funnies On Parade #nn, 1933, Eastern Color (1st GA comic book)

Century Of Comics #nn, 1933, Eastern Color (2nd GA comic book, 1st 100 pgs.)

Famous Funnies-Carnival Of Comics, nn, 1933, Eastern Color, (3rd GA comic book)

Detective Dan, 1933, Humor Publ. Co. (the book that helped bridge the gap between the PA and SA)

Famous Funnies-Series 1, 1934, Eastern Color, (1st 10 cent comic book)

Famous Funnies #1, 7/34, Eastern Color (1st newsstand comic book)

New Fun Comics #1, 2/35, DC (1st DC comic book)

Big Book Of Fun Comics #1, Spr/35, DC, (1st annual in comics)

New Fun Comics #6, 10/35, DC (1st Siegel & Shuster work in comics)

More Fun Comics #14, 10/36, DC (1st Superman prototype at DC, 1st in color)

Detective Comics #1, 3/37, DC (1st issue of title that launched Batman)

GOLDEN AGE June, 1938 - 1945

Action Comics #1, 6/38, DC (1st Superman and Lois Lane)

Funny Pages #V2#10, 9/38, Centaur (1st Arrow, 1st costumed hero)

Jumbo Comics #1, 9/38, Fiction House (1st Sheena, 1st Fiction House comic book)

Movie Comics #1, 4/39, DC (1st movie comic)

New York World's Fair 1939, 4/39, DC (1st published Sandman story)

Detective Comics #27, 5/39, DC (1st Batman)

Wonder Comics #1, 5/39, Fox (1st Wonderman, 1st Superman imitator)

Superman #nn (#1), Summer/39, DC (1st issue, 1st hero to get his own book)

Adventure Comics #40, 7/39, DC (1st conceived Sandman story)

Marvel Comics #1, 10/39, Timely (1st newsstand Sub-Mariner, 1st Human Torch, 1st Marvel comic)

Silver Streak #1, 12/39, Lev Gleason (1st Gleason comic book, 1st Claw)

Flash Comics #1, 1/40, DC (1st Flash, Hawkman, & Johnny Thunder)

Pep Comics #1, 1/40, MLJ/Archie (1st app. Shield, 1st patriotic hero)

Planet Comics #1, 1/40, Fiction House (1st all science fiction comic book)

More Fun Comics #52, 2/40, DC (1st Spectre)

Whiz Comics #2 (#1), 2/40, Fawcett (1st Captain Marvel & Spy Smasher, 1st Fawcett comic book)

Adventure Comics #48, 3/40, DC (1st Hourman)

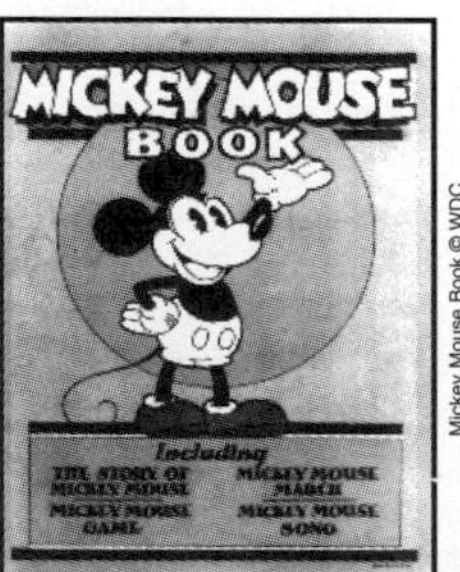

Mickey Mouse Book © WDC

Funnies on Parade © Eastern Color

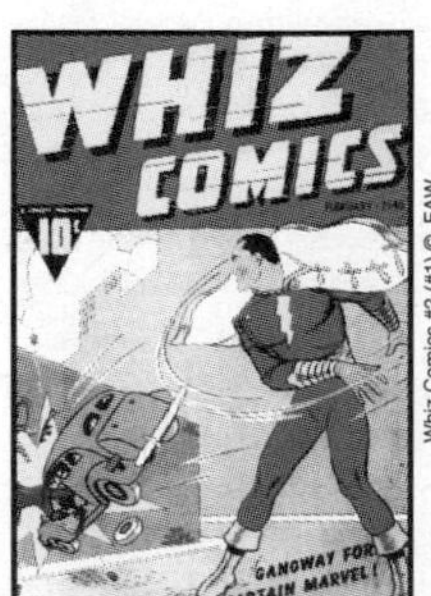

Whiz Comics #2 (#1) © FAW

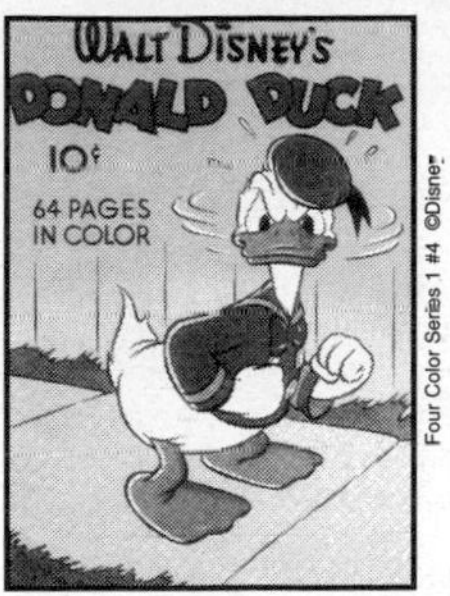

Four Color Series 1 #4 ©Disney

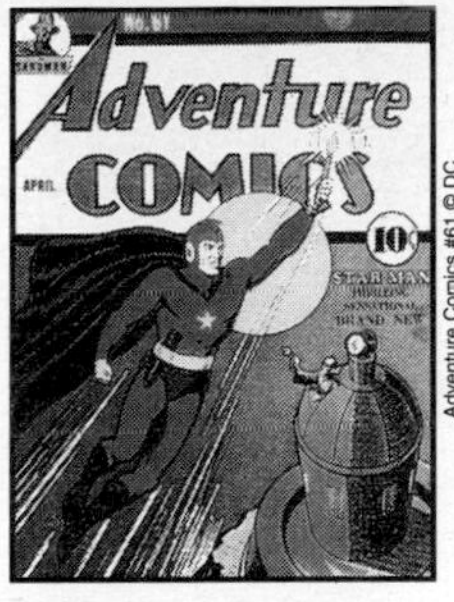

Adventure Comics #61 © DC

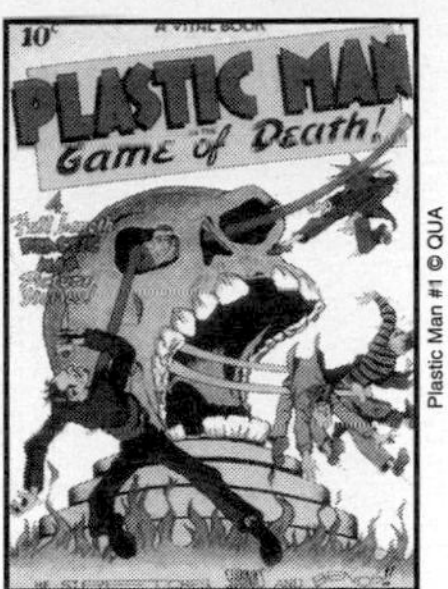

Plastic Man #1 © QUA

More Fun Comics #53, 3/40, DC (Part II of 1st Spectre story)
Four Color Ser. 1 (Donald Duck) #4, 3?/40, (1st four color Donald Duck)
Action Comics #23, 4/40, DC (1st Lex Luthor)
Detective Comics #38, 4/40, DC (1st Robin)
Batman #1, Spring/40, DC (1st issue of DC's 2nd most important character; 1st 2 Joker stories; 1st Catwoman)
More Fun Comics #55, 5/40, DC (1st Dr. Fate)
All American Comics #16, 7/40, DC (1st Green Lantern)
Blue Bolt #3, 7/40, Fox (1st Simon & Kirby story art)
Marvel Mystery Comics #9, 7/40, Timely (1st superhero battle; key battle issue)
Red Raven #1, 8/40, Timely (Early Kirby art)
Special Edition Comics #1, 8/40, Fawcett (1st comic book devoted to Captain Marvel)
Silver Streak #6, 9/40, Lev Gleason (1st Daredevil)
Batman #3, Fall/40, DC (1st Catwoman in costume)
Human Torch #2 (#1), Fall/40, Timely (1st issue of early Marvel star)
Walt Disney's Comics & Stories #1, 10/40, Dell (1st funny animal comic book series)
All American Comics #19, 10/40, DC (1st Atom)
All Star Comics #3, Winter/40-41, DC (1st superhero group)
Adventure Comics #72, 3/41, DC (1st Simon & Kirby Sandman)
Captain America Comics #1, 3/41, Timely (1st Captain America)

Captain Marvel Adventures #1, 3/41, Fawcett (1st issue of Fawcett's top character)
Sub-Mariner Comics #1, Spring/41, Timely (1st issue of Marvel's important character)
Adventure Comics #61, 4/41, DC (1st Starman)
All Flash #1, Summer/41, DC (1st issue of top DC character)
Daredevil #1, 7/41, Lev Gleason (1st issue of top character)
Military Comics #1, 8/41, Quality (1st Blackhawk)
Famous Funnies #100, 10/41, Eastern (1st comic book to reach 100)
Green Lantern #1, Fall/41, DC (1st issue of top DC character)
More Fun Comics #73, 11/41, DC (1st Aquaman)
Pep Comics #22, 12/41, MLJ/Archie (1st Archie)
Four Color Ser. 1 (Mickey Mouse) #16, 1941, (1st comic book devoted to Mickey Mouse)
Looney Tunes #1, Fall/41, Dell (1st Bugs Bunny, Porky Pig & Elmer Fudd in comics)
All Star Comics #8, 12-1/41-42, DC (1st Wonder Woman)
Animal Comics #1, 12-1/41-42, Dell (1st Pogo by Walt Kelly)
Sensation Comics #1, 1/42, DC (1st series to star Wonder Woman)
Crime Does Not Pay #22, 6/42, Gleason (1st Crime comic book series)
Sensation #6, June, 1942, DC, (1st app. Wonder Woman's magic lasso)
Wonder Woman #1, Summer/42, DC (1st issue of top DC character)
Four Color (Donald Duck) #9, 8/42 Dell (1st Barks story/art on Donald Duck)

Archie Comics #1, Winter/42-43, MLJ/ Archie, (1st Teenage comic)
Capt Marvel Adventures #22, 3/43, Fawcett, (Begins Mr. Mind serial)
Plastic Man #1, Summer/43, Quality (1st issue of top Quality character)
Big All-American Comic Book #1, 1944, DC, (1st annual of **All-American Comics**)
More Fun Comics #101, 1/2/45, DC (1st Superboy)
Molly O'Day #1, 2/45, Avon (1st Avon comic)
Terry Toones #38, 11/45, Timely (1st Mighty Mouse)

ATOM AGE 1946 - 1956

Romantic Picture Novelette #1, 1946, ME (one shot)(1st love comic theme)
All Winners #19, Fall/46, Timely (1st All Winners Squad, 1st Marvel group)
All Winners #21, Winter/46-47, Timely (2nd All Winners Squad)
Eerie #1, 1/47, Avon (1st horror comic)
Young Romance Comics #1, 9-10/47, Prize (1st romance series)
Four Color (Uncle Scrooge) #178, 12/47, Dell (1st Uncle Scrooge)
Phantom Lady #17, 4/48, Fox (Classic cover issue–good girl art)
Adventures Into The Unknown #1, Fall/48, ACG (1st horror series)
Moon Girl #5, Winter/48, EC (1st EC horror story)
Casper #1, 9/49, St John (1st Baby Huey)
Crime Patrol #15, 12-1/49-50, EC (1st Crypt Keeper)
War Against Crime #10, 12-1/49-50, EC (1st Vault Keeper)

Batman #3 © DC

Looney Tunes and Merrie Melodies Comics #1 © DELL

Young Romance Comics #1 © PRIZE

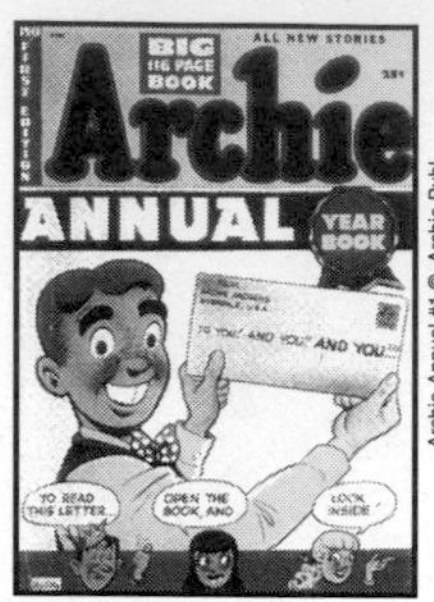

Archie Annual #1 © Archie Publ.

Howdy Doody #1, 1/50, Dell (1st TV comic book)
Archie Annual #1, 1950, Archie (1st **Archie** annual)
Crypt Of Terror #17, 4-5/50, EC (1st issue of Crypt Keeper tales, EC horror)
Haunt Of Fear #15 (#1), 5-6/50, EC (1st issue of EC horror, trend-setting)
Weird Fantasy #13 (#1), 5-6/50, EC (1st issue of EC science fiction, trend-setting)
Weird Science #12 (#1), 5-6/50, EC (1st issue of EC science fiction)
Strange Tales #1, 6/51, Marvel (1st issue of top Marvel title)
Mad #1, 10-11/52, EC (1st satire comic)
Journey Into Mystery #1, 6/52, Marvel (1st issue of top Marvel title)
Little Dot #1, 9/53, Harvey (1st Richie Rich)
Young Men #24, 12/53, Marvel (Revival of Capt. America, Human Torch & Sub-Mariner)
World's Finest Comics #71, 7-8/54, DC (1st Superman/Batman team issue)
Superman's Pal, Jimmy Olsen #1, 9-10/54, DC, (1st issue of top DC title)
My Greatest Adventure #1, 1-2/55, DC (1st issue of top DC fantasy title)
Brave And The Bold #1, 8-9/55, DC (1st issue of top DC showcase title)
Superman #100, 9-10/55, DC (Landmark issue)
Detective Comics #225, 11/55, DC (1st Martian Manhunter)
Tales Of The Unexpected #1, 2-3/56, DC (1st issue of top DC fantasy title)

World's Finest Comics #71 © DC

Sugar & Spike #1 © DC

Showcase #1, 3-4/56, DC (1st issue of top DC showcase title)
Sugar & Spike #1, 4-5/56, DC (1st issue of top title by Sheldon Mayer)
Batman #100, 6/56, DC (Landmark issue)
Detective Comics #233, 7/56, DC (1st Batwoman)

SILVER AGE
Sept, 1956 - 1969

Showcase #4, 9-10/56, DC (1st Silver Age book) (The Flash)
House Of Secrets #1, 11-12/56, DC (1st issue of top DC horror title)
Showcase #6, 1-2/57, DC (1st Silver Age group)(Challengers)
Showcase #9, 7-8/57, DC (1st Lois Lane book)
Superman's Girl Friend, Lois Lane #1, 3-4/58, DC (1st issue of top character)
Adventure Comics #247, 4/58, DC (1st Legion of Superheroes)
Challengers Of The Unknown #1, 4-5/58, DC, (1st issue of 1st Silver Age group)
Showcase #15, 7-8/58, DC (1st Space Ranger)
Showcase #17, 11-12/58, DC (1st Adam Strange)
Tales Of Suspense #1, 1/59, Marvel (1st issue of top fantasy title)
Tales To Astonish #1, 1/59, Marvel (1st issue of top fantasy title)
Flash #105 (#1), 2-3/59, DC (1st issue of top DC title)
Our Army At War #81, 4/59, DC (1st Sgt. Rock)
Action Comics #252, 5/59, DC (1st Supergirl)
Showcase #20, 5-6/59, DC (1st Rip Hunter)

Tales of Suspense #1 © MEG

Action Comics #252 © DC

Double Life Of Private Strong #1, 6/59, Archie (1st Silver Age Shield, 1st Fly)
Mystery In Space #53, 8/59, DC (1st Adam Strange)
Tales Of The Unexpected #40, 8/59, DC (1st Space Ranger in own title)
Adventures of the Fly #1, 8/59, Archie (1st issue of top Archie title)
Showcase #22, 9-10/59, DC (1st Silver Age Green Lantern)
Flash #110, 12-1/59/60, DC (1st Kid Flash)
Brave And The Bold #28, 2/3/60, DC (1st Justice League of America)
Green Lantern #1, 7-8/60, DC (1st issue of top DC character)
Showcase #27, 7-8/60, DC (1st Sea Devils)
Brave And The Bold #31, 8-9/60, DC (1st Cave Carson)
Justice League Of America #1, 10-11/60, DC (1st issue of top DC title)
Showcase #30, 1-2/61, DC (1st Silver Age Aquaman)
Brave And The Bold #34, 2-3/61, DC (1st Silver Age Hawkman)
Amazing Adventures #1, 6/61, Marvel (1st Dr. Droom, the 1st Marvel-Age superhero)
Flash #123, 9/61, DC (1st G.A. Flash in Silver Age)
Showcase #34, 9-10/61, DC (1st Silver Age Atom)
Fantastic Four #1, 11/61, Marvel (1st Fantastic Four)
Amazing Adult Fantasy #7, 12/61, Marvel (1st issue of title that leads to Spider-Man)
Tales To Astonish #27, 1/62, Marvel (1st Antman)

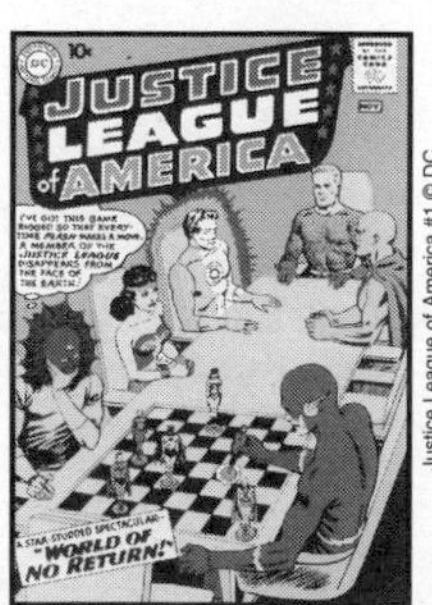

Justice League of America #1 © DC

Avengers #4 © MEG

Daredevil #158 © MEG

Superman: The Wedding Album © DC

Showcase #37, 3-4/62, DC (1st Metal Men)
Fantastic Four #4, 5/62, Marvel (1st Silver Age Sub-Mariner)
Incredible Hulk #1, 5/62, Marvel (1st Hulk)
Mystery In Space #75, 5/62, DC (Early JLA cross-over in Adam Strange story)
Fantastic Four #5, 7/62, Marvel (1st Dr. Doom)
Journey Into Mystery #83, 8/62, Marvel (1st Thor)
Amazing Fantasy #15, 8-9/62, Marvel (1st Spider-Man)
Tales To Astonish #35, 9/62, Marvel (2nd Antman, 1st in cos tume)
Strange Tales #101, 10/62, Marvel (1st S.A. Human Torch solo story)
Amazing Spider-Man #1, 3/63, Marvel (1st Spider-Man in own title)
Tales Of Suspense #39, 3/63, Marvel (1st Iron Man)
Strange Tales #110, 7/63, Marvel (1st Dr. Strange)
Avengers #1, 9/63, Marvel (1st Avengers)
X-Men #1, 9/63, Marvel (1st X Men)
Mystery In Space #87, 11/63, DC (1st Hawkman in title)
Avengers #4, 3/64, Marvel (1st Silver Age Captain America)
Daredevil #1, 4/64, Marvel (1st Daredevil)
Amazing Spider-Man #14, 7/64, Marvel (1st Green Goblin)
Fantastic Four #48, 3/66, Marvel (1st Silver Surfer)
Strange Tales #135, 7/65, Marvel (Origin & 1st app. Nick Fury)
Strange Adventures #205, 10/67, DC (1st Deadman)

BRONZE AGE 1970 - 1979

Detective Comics #400, 6/70, DC (1st Man-Bat)
Star Spangled War Stories #151, 6-7/70, DC (1st Unknown Soldier)
Superman's Pal, Jimmy Olsen #133, 10/70, DC (1st Silver Age Newsboy Legion)
Forever People #1, 2-3/71, DC (1st Forever People)
New Gods #1, 3/71, DC (1st New Gods)
Mister Miracle #1, 3/71, DC (1st Mister Miracle)
Savage Tales #1, 5/71, Marvel (1st Man-Thing)
House of Secrets #92, 6/71, DC (1st app. Swamp Thing by Bernie Wrightson)
Amazing Spider-Man #101, 10/71, Marvel (1st Morbius the Living Vampire)
Marvel Feature #1, 12/71, Marvel (Origin and 1st app. Defenders)
All Star Western #10, 2-3/72, DC (1st Jonah Hex)
Tomb of Dracula #1, 4/72, Marvel (1st app. Dracula)
Marvel Spotlight #2, 6/72, Marvel (1st app. Werewolf by Night)
Marvel Spotlight #5, 8/72, Marvel (Origin and 1st app. new Ghost Rider)
Kamandi: The Last Boy on Earth #1, 10/72, DC (Origin and 1st app. Kamandi)
Iron Man #55, 2/73, Marvel (1st. app. Thanos & Drax the Destroyer)
Amazing Spider-Man #121, 6/73 Marvel (Death of Gwen Stacy)
Amazing Spider-Man #122, 7/73, Marvel (Death of Green Goblin I)
Amazing Spider-Man #129, 2/74, Marvel (1st Punisher)
Marvel Spotlight #12, 10/73, Marvel (1st solo Son of Satan)
Marvel Special Edition #15, 12/73, Marvel (1st Master of Kung Fu)
Amazing Spider-Man #129, 2/74, Marvel (1st Punisher)
Astonishing Tales #25, 8/74, Marvel (1st Deathlok)
Incredible Hulk #181, 11/74, Marvel (1st app. of Wolverine) (story)
Giant Size X-Men #1, Summer/75, Marvel (1st New X-Men; intro Nightcrawler, Storm, Colossus & Thunderbird)
X-Men #94, 8/75, Marvel (New X-Men team begins)
All Star Comics #58, 1-2/76, DC (1st Power Girl)
Marvel Spotlight #32, 2/77, Marvel (1st Spider-Woman)
Black Lightning #1, 4/77, DC (1st Black Lightning)
Cerebus #1, 12/77, Aardvark-Vanaheim (1st app. Cerebus)(B&W)
X-Men #108, 12/77, Marvel (1st important Byrne work)
Daredevil #158, 5/79, Marvel (Frank Miller begins work on Daredevil; his 1st important work)

MODERN AGE 1980 - PRESENT

X-Men #137, 9/80, Marvel (The story that started comicdom's "Death Craze")
Daredevil #169, 2/81, Marvel (1st Elektra)
Detective Comics #327, 5/84, DC (New Batman) (Silver Age/ Modern)
Teenage Mutant Ninja Turtles #1, pre 6/84, Mirage, (1st app. Teenage Mutant Ninja Turtles)
Batman: The Dark Knight #1, 3/86, DC (beginning of Frank Miller's landmark revision of Batman)
Maus, 1986, Pantheon Books (1st comic book to win the Pulitzer Prize) (depicts the horrors of the Holocaust through the eyes of artist Art Spiegelman's father)
The Man of Steel #1, 6/86, DC (beginning of John Byrne's landmark work on Superman)
Crisis on Infinite Earths #1-12, 85/86, DC (1st appearance of revamped Modern Age DC universe) (#7, Death of Supergirl)(#8, Death of the Barry Allen Flash)
Watchmen #1, 10/87, DC (beginning of Alan Moore's revisionist look at superheroes)
Amazing Spider-Man #300, 5/88, Marvel (1st Venom) (full app & story)
Sandman #1, 1/89, DC (1st app. new Sandman)
X-Men #1, 10/91, Marvel (1st comic to reach a print run of 8 million copies)
Youngblood #1, 4/92, Image (1st Image comic)
Spawn #1, 5/92, Image (1st app. Spawn)
Superman (2nd Series) #75, 1/93, DC (Death of Superman) (Huge Media Coverage)
Deathmate Black, 9/93, Valiant/ Image (1st Gen13 story)
Starman #0, 10/94, DC (1st app. of Modern Age Starman)
DC Vs. Marvel #1, 1996, DC (1st issue of landmark company crossover)
Final Night #4, 11/96, DC (Death of former Green Lantern Hal Jordan)
Superman: The Wedding Album, 12/96, DC (Marriage of Clark Kent and Lois Lane)

(First comic book of a genre, publisher, theme or type, etc.)

AVIATION COMIC–Wings Comics #1, 9/40
COMIC BOOK ANNUAL–Big Book of Fun Comics #1, Spr, 1936
COMIC BOOK–Funnies On Parade nn, 1933
COMIC BOOK TO GO INTO ENDLESS REPRINTS–Classic Comics #1, 10/41
COMIC BOOK TO KILL OFF A SUPERHERO–Pep Comics #17, 7/41 (The Comet)
COMIC BOOK WITH METALLIC LOGO–Silver Streak #1, 12/39
COMIC BOOK WITH ORIGINAL MATERIAL–New Fun Comics #1, 2/35
COSTUMED HERO BATTLE COMIC–Marvel Mystery #9, 7/40
COSTUMED HERO COMIC (STRIP)–Ace Comics #11, 2/38 (The Phantom)
COSTUMED HERO COMIC (Original material)–Funny Pages V2/10 9/38 (The Arrow)(3 months after Superman)
COSTUMED HERO SIDEKICK COMIC– Detective Comics #38, 4/40 (Robin)
CRIME–Crime Does Not Pay #22, 6/42
DETECTIVE COMIC–Detective Picture Stories #1, 12/36
DISNEY SINGLE CHARACTER COMIC BOOK–Donald Duck nn, 1938
DISNEY SINGLE CHARACTER COMIC BOOK IN COLOR–Donald Duck 4-Color #4, 3/40
EDUCATIONAL THEME COMIC–Classic Comics #1, 10/41
5 CENT COMIC–Nickel Comics #1, 1938
15 CENT COMIC–New York World's Fair, 1940
FLYING SAUCER COMIC–Spirit Section 9/28/47 (3 months after 1st alleged sighting in Idaho on 6/25/47)
FUNNY ANIMAL SERIES–Walt Disney's Comics & Stories #1, 10/40
FUNNY ANIMAL SINGLE CHARACTER COMIC–Donald Duck nn, 1938
GIVEAWAY COMIC–Funnies on Parade nn, 1933
GOLDEN AGE COMIC–Action Comics #1, 6/38
HEROINE SINGLE THEME COMIC–Sheena, Queen of the Jungle #1, Spr, 1942
HORROR COMIC (ONE SHOT)–Eerie Comics #1, 1/47
HORROR COMIC (SERIES)–Adventures into the Unknown #1, Fall, 1948
JUNGLE COMIC–Jumbo Comics #1, 9/38
LARGE SIZED COMIC–New Fun Comics #1, 2/35
LOVE COMIC (ONE SHOT)–Romantic Picture Novelettes #1, 1946 (Mary Worth strip-r)
LOVE COMIC (SERIES)–Young Romance Comics #1, 10/47
MAGICIAN COMIC–Super Magic Comics #1, 5/41
MAGICIAN COMIC SERIES–Super Magician Comics #2, 9/41
MASKED HERO–Funny Pages #6, 11/36 (The Clock)
MOVIE COMIC–Movie Comics #1, 4/39
NEGRO COMIC–Negro Heroes, Spr, 1947
NEWSSTAND COMIC–Famous Funnies #1, 7/34
#2 IN COMICS–Famous Funnies #2, 8/34
100 PAGE COMIC–Century of Comics nn, 1933
100TH ISSUE–Famous Funnies #100, 11/43
ONE SHOT SERIES–Feature Book nn, 1937
PATRIOTIC HERO COMIC–Pep Comics #1, 1/40 (The Shield)
PROTOTYPE COMIC–The Comics Magazine #1, 5/36 (Superman)
PUBLIC EVENT COMIC–New York World's Fair 1939

All Star Comics #8 © DC

RELIGIOUS THEME SERIES–Topix Comics #1, 11/42
REPRINT COMIC–Funnies on Parade nn, 1933
SATIRE COMIC–Mad #1, 10-11/52
SCIENCE FICTION COMIC–Planet Comics #1, 1/40
SIDEKICK GROUP COMIC–Young Allies #1, Sum, 1941
SILVER AGE ARCHIE COMIC–Double Life of Private Strong #1, 6/59
SILVER AGE COMIC–Showcase #4, 9-10/56
SILVER AGE DC ANNUAL–Superman Annual #1, 10/60
SILVER AGE MARVEL ANNUAL–Strange Tales Annual #1, 1962
SILVER AGE MARVEL COMIC–Fantastic Four #1, 11/61
SINGLE CHARACTER COMIC–Skippy's Own Book of Comics, 1934
SINGLE ORIGINAL CHARACTER COMIC–Superman #1, Sum, 1939
SINGLE STRIP REPRINT CHARACTER COMIC–Mutt and Jeff #1, Sum, 1939
SINGLE THEME COMIC–Detective Picture Stories #1, 12/36
SINGLE THEME COMIC, THE FIRST IMPORTANT–Detective Comics #1, 3/37
SINGLE THEME REPRINT STRIP COMIC–Mutt and Jeff #1, Sum, 1939
SMALL-SIZED COMIC–Little Giant Comics #1, 7/38
SPORTS COMIC–Champion Comics #2, 12/39
SQUAREBOUND COMIC–New Book of Comics #1, 1937
SQUAREBOUND SERIES–World's Best #1, Spr, 1941
SUPER HERO COMIC–Action Comics #1, 6/38 (Superman)
SUPER HERO TEAM–All Star Comics #3, Wint, 1940-41
SUPER HEROINE COMIC–All Star Comics #8, 11-12/41
SUPER HEROINE COMIC SERIES–Sensation Comics #1, 1/42
SUPERMAN IMITATOR–Wonder Comics #1, 5/39 (Wonder Man)
TEEN-AGE COMIC–Pep Comics #22, 12/41
TEEN-AGE COMIC SERIES–Archie Comics #1, Wint, 1942-43
10 CENT COMIC–Famous Funnies Series 1, 3-5/34
3-D COMIC–Mighty Mouse 3-D #1, 9/53
T.V. COMIC–Howdy Doody #1, 1/50
25 CENT COMIC–New York World's Fair, 1939
TRUE LIFE COMIC–Sport Comics #1, 10/40
VILLAIN COVER (FU MANCHU)–Detective Comics #1, 3/37
VILLAIN STORY (FU MANCHU)–Detective Comics #17, 7/38
VILLAIN COVER/STORY (ORIGINAL TO COMICS)– Silver Streak #1, 12/39 (The Claw)
WAR COMIC–War Comics #1, 5/40
WEEKLY COMIC BOOK–The Spirit #1, 6/2/40
WESTERN COMIC–Western Picture Stories #1, 2/37 & Star Ranger #1, 2/37
WESTERN OF ONE CHARACTER–The Lone Ranger Comics nn, 1939
WESTERN RUN OF ONE CHARACTER (GIVEAWAY)–Tom Mix #1, 9/40
WESTERN NEWSSTAND RUN OF ONE CHARACTER–Red Ryder Comics #1, 8/41
WESTERN WITH PHOTO COVER–Roy Rogers Four Color #38, 4/44
X-OVER COMIC–Marvel Mystery #9, 7/40

A CHRONOLOGY OF THE DEVELOPMENT OF THE AMERICAN COMIC BOOK

BY M. THOMAS INGE

Precursors: The facsimile newspaper strip reprint collections constitute the earliest "comic books." The first of these was a collection of Richard Outcault's **Yellow Kid** from the **Hearst New York American** in March 1897. Commercial and promotional reprint collections, usually in cardboard covers, appeared through the 1920s and featured such newspaper strips as **Mutt and Jeff**, **Foxy Grandpa**, **Buster Brown**, and **Barney Google**. During 1922 a reprint magazine, **Comic Monthly**, appeared with each issue devoted to a separate strip, and from 1929 to 1930 George Delacorte published 36 issues of **The Funnies** in tabloid format with original comic pages in color, becoming the first four-color comic newsstand publication.

1933: The Ledger syndicate published a small broadside of their Sunday comics on 7" by 9" plates. Employees of Eastern Color Printing Company in New York, sales manager Harry I. Wildenberg and salesman Max C. Gaines, saw it and figured that two such plates would fit a tabloid page, which would produce a book about 7-1/2" x 10" when folded. Thus 10,000 copies of **Funnies on Parade**, containing 32 pages of Sunday newspaper reprints, was published for Proctor and Gamble to be given away as premiums. Some of the strips included were: **Joe Palooka**, **Mutt and Jeff**, **Hairbreadth Harry**, and **Reg'lar Fellas**. M. C. Gaines was very impressed with this book and convinced Eastern Color that he could sell a lot of them to such big advertisers as Milk-O-Malt, Wheatena, Kinney Shoe Stores, and others to be used as premiums and radio give-aways. So, Eastern Color printed **Famous Funnies: A Carnival of Comics**, and then **Century of Comics**, both as before, containing Sunday newspaper reprints. Mr. Gaines sold these books in quantities of 100,000 to 250,000. Although slightly larger in size than **Famous Funnies**, Humor Publications produced two one-issue magazines, **Detective Dan** and **The Adventures of Detective Ace King**, which contained original comic art and sold for ten cents per copy.

1934: The give-away comics were so successful that Mr. Gaines believed that youngsters would buy comic books for ten cents like the "Big Little Books" coming out at that time. So, early in 1934, Eastern Color ran off 35,000 copies of **Famous Funnies, Series 1**, 64 pages of reprints for Dell Publishing Company to be sold for ten cents in chain stores. Since it sold out promptly on the stands, Eastern Color, in May 1934, issued **Famous Funnies** No. 1 (dated July 1934) which became, with issue No. 2 in July, the first monthly comic magazine. The title continued for over 20 years through 218 issues, reaching a circulation peak of over 400,000 copies a month. At the same time, Mr. Gaines went to the sponsors of Percy Crosby's *Skippy*, which was on the radio, and convinced them to put out a Skippy book, advertise it on the air, and give away a free copy to anyone who bought a tube of Phillip's toothpaste. Thus 500,000 copies of **Skippy's Own Book of Comics** was run off and distributed through drug stores everywhere. This was the first four-color comic book of reprints devoted to a single character.

1935: Major Malcolm Wheeler-Nicholson's National Periodical Publications issued in

February a tabloid-sized comic publication called **New Fun**, which became **More Fun** after the sixth issue and was converted to the normal comic-book size after issue eight. **More Fun** was the first comic book of a standard size to publish original material, and it continued publication until 1949. **Mickey Mouse Magazine** began in the summer, to become **Walt Disney's Comics and Stories** in 1940, and combined original material with reprinted newspaper strips in most issues.

1936: In the wake of the success of **Famous Funnies**, other publishers, in conjunction with the major newspaper strip syndicates, inaugurated more reprint comic books: **Popular Comics** (News Tribune, February), **Tip Top Comics** (United Features, April), **King Comics** (King Features, April), and **The Funnies** (new series, NEA, October). Four issues of **Wow Comics**, from David McKay and Henle Publications, appeared, edited by S. M. Iger and including early art by Will Eisner, Bob Kane, and Alex Raymond. The first non-reprint comic book devoted to a single theme was **Detective Picture Stories** issued in December by The Comics Magazine Company.

1937: The second single theme title, **Western Picture Stories**, came in February from The Comics Magazine Company, and the third was **Detective Comics**, an offshoot of **More Fun**, which began in March to be published to the present. The book's initials, "D.C.," have long served to refer to National Periodical Publications, which was purchased from Major Nicholson by Harry Donenfeld late this year.

1938: "DC" copped a lion's share of the comic book market with the publication of **Action Comics** #1 in June which contained the first appearance of Superman by writer Jerry Siegel and artist Joe Shuster, a discovery of Max C. Gaines. The "man of steel" inaugurated the "Golden Era" in comic book history. Fiction House, a pulp publisher, entered the comic book field in September with **Jumbo Comics**, featuring Sheena, Queen of the Jungle, and appearing in over-sized format for the first eight issues.

1939: The continued success of "DC" was assured in May with the publication of **Detective Comics** #27 containing the first episode of Batman by artist Bob Kane and writer Bill Finger. **Superman Comics** appeared in the summer. Also, during the summer, a black and white premium comic titled **Motion Picture Funnies Weekly** was published to be given away at motion picture theatres. The plan was to issue it weekly and to have continued stories so that the kids would come back week after week not to miss an episode. Four issues were planned but only one came out. This book contains the first appearance and origin of the Sub-Mariner by Bill Everett (8 pages) which was later reprinted in **Marvel Comics**. In November, the first issue of **Marvel Comics** came out, featuring the Human Torch by Carl Burgos and the Sub-Mariner reprint with color added.

1940: The April issue of **Detective Comics** #38 introduced Robin the Boy Wonder as a sidekick to Batman, thus establishing the "Dynamic Duo" and a major precedent for later costumed heroes who would also have boy companions. **Batman Comics** began in the spring. Over 60 different comic book titles were being issued, including **Whiz Comics** begun in February by Fawcett Publications. A creation of writer Bill Parker and artist C. C. Beck, Whiz's Captain Marvel was the only superhero ever to surpass Superman in comic book sales. Drawing on their own popular pulp magazine heroes, Street and Smith Publications introduced **Shadow Comics** in March and **Doc Savage Comics** in May. A second trend was established with the summer appearance of the first issue of **All Star Comics**, which brought several superheroes together in one story and in its third issue that winter would announce the establishment of the Justice Society of America.

1941: Wonder Woman was introduced in the spring issue of **All Star Comics** #8, the creation of psychologist William Moulton Marston and artist Harry Peter. **Captain Marvel Adventures** began this year. By the end of 1941, over 160 titles were being published, including **Captain America** by Jack Kirby and Joe Simon, **Police Comics** with Jack Cole's Plastic Man and later Will Eisner's Spirit, **Military Comics** with Blackhawk by Eisner and Charles Cuidera, **Daredevil Comics** with the original character by Charles Biro, **Air Fighters** with Airboy also by Biro, and **Looney Tunes & Merrie Melodies** with Porky Pig, Bugs Bunny, and Elmer Fudd, reportedly created by Bob Clampett for the Leon Schlesinger Productions animated films and drawn for the comics by Chase Craig. Also, Albert Kanter's Gilberton Company initiated the **Classics Illustrated** series with **The Three Musketeers**.

1942: **Crime Does Not Pay** by editor Charles Biro and publisher Lev Gleason, devoted to factual accounts of criminals' lives, began a different trend in realistic crime stories. **Wonder Woman** appeared in the summer. John Goldwater's character Archie, drawn by Bob Montana, first published in **Pep Comics**, was given his own magazine **Archie Comics**, which has remained popular over 40 years. The first issue of **Animal Comics** contained Walt Kelly's "Albert Takes the Cake," featuring the new character of Pogo. In mid-1942, the undated Dell Four Color title, #9, **Donald Duck Finds Pirate Gold**, appeared with art by Carl Barks and Jack Hannah. Barks, also featured in **Walt Disney's Comics and Stories**, remained the most popular delineator of Donald Duck and later introduced his greatest creation, Uncle Scrooge, in **Christmas on Bear Mountain** (Dell Four Color #178). The fantasy work of George Carlson appeared in the first issue of **Jingle Jangle Comics**, one of the most imaginative titles for children ever to be published.

1945: The first issue of **Real Screen Comics** introduced the Fox and the Crow by James F. Davis, and John Stanley began drawing the **Little Lulu** comic book based on a popular feature in the **Saturday Evening Post** by Marjorie Henderson Buell from 1935 to 1944. Bill Woggon's Katy Keene appears in #5 of **Wilbur Comics** to be followed by appearances in **Laugh, Pep, Suzie** and her own comic book in 1950. The popularity of Dick Briefer's satiric version of the Frankenstein monster, originally drawn for **Prize Comics** in 1941, led to the publication of **Frankenstein Comics** by Prize publications.

1950: The son of Max C. Gaines, William M. Gaines, who earlier had inherited his father's firm Educational Comics (later Entertaining Comics), began publication of a series of well-written and masterfully drawn titles which would establish a "New Trend" in comics magazines: **Crypt of Terror** (later **Tales from the Crypt**, April), **The Vault of Horror** (April), **The Haunt of Fear** (May), **Weird Science** (May), **Weird Fantasy** (May), **Crime SuspenStories** (October), and **Two Fisted Tales** (November), the latter stunningly edited by Harvey Kurtzman.

1952: In October EC published the first number of **Mad** under Kurtzman's creative editorship, thus establishing a style of humor which would inspire other publications and powerfully influence the underground comic book movement of the 1960s.

1953: All Fawcett titles featuring Captain Marvel were ceased after many years of litigation in the courts during which National Periodical Publications claimed that the superhero was an infringement on the copyrighted Superman. In December, Captain America, Human Torch, and Sub-Mariner were revived by Atlas Comics. The first 3-D comic book, **Three Dimension Comics**, featuring **Mighty Mouse** and created by Joe Kubert and Norman Maurer, was issued in September by St. John

Publishing Co.

954: The appearance of Fredric Wertham's book **Seduction of the Innocent** in the spring was the culmination of a continuing war against comic books fought by those who believed they corrupted youth and debased culture. The U. S. Senate Subcommittee on Juvenile Delinquency investigated comic books and in response the major publishers banded together in October to create the Comics Code Authority and adopted, in their own words, "the most stringent code in existence for any communications media." Before the Code took effect, more than 1,000,000,000 issues of comic books were being sold annually.

955: In an effort to avoid the Code, EC launched a "New Direction" series of titles, such as **Impact**, **Valor**, **Aces High**, **Extra, M.D.**, and **Psychoanalysis**, none of which lasted beyond the year. **Mad** was changed into a larger magazine format with #24 in July to escape the Comics Code entirely, and EC closed down its line of comic books altogether.

956: Beginning with the Flash in **Showcase** #4, Julius Schwartz began a popular revival of DC superheroes which would lead to the Silver Age in comic book history.

957: Atlas reduced the number of titles published by two-thirds, with **Journey into Mystery** and **Strange Tales** surviving, while other publishers did the same or went out of business. Atlas would survive as a part of the Marvel Comics Group.

960: After several efforts at new satire magazines (**Trump** and **Humbug**), Harvey Kurtzman, no longer with Gaines, issued in August the first number of another abortive effort, **Help!**, where the early work of underground cartoonists Jay Lynch, Skip Williamson, Gilbert Shelton, and Robert Crumb appeared.

961: Stan Lee edited in November the first **Fantastic Four**, featuring Mr. Fantastic, the Human Torch, the Thing, and the Invisible Girl, and inaugurated an enormously popular line of titles from Marvel Comics featuring a more contemporary style of superhero.

962: Lee introduced **The Amazing Spider-Man** in August, with art by Steve Ditko, **The Hulk** in May and **Thor** in August, the last two produced by Dick Ayers and Jack Kirby.

963: Marvel's **The X-Men**, with art by Jack Kirby, began a successful run in November, but the title would experience a revival and have an even more popular reception in the 1980s.

965: James Warren issued **Creepy**, a larger black and white comic book, outside Comics Code's control, which emulated the EC horror comic line. Warren's **Eerie** began in September and **Vampirella** in September 1969.

967: Robert Crumb's **Zap** #1 appeared, the first underground comic book to achieve wide popularity, although the undergrounds had begun in 1962 with **Adventures of Jesus** by Foolbert Sturgeon (Frank Stack) and 1964 with **God Nose** by Jack Jackson.

970: Editor Roy Thomas at Marvel begins **Conan the Barbarian** based on fiction by Robert E. Howard with art by Barry Smith, and Neal Adams began to draw for DC a series of **Green Lantern/Green Arrow** stories which would deal with relevant social issues such as racism, urban poverty, and drugs.

972: **The Swamp Thing** by Berni Wrightson begins in November from DC.

973: In February, DC revived the original **Captain Marvel** with new art by C. C. Beck and reprints in the first issue of **Shazam** and in October **The Shadow** with scripts by Denny O'Neil and art by Mike Kaluta.

974: DC began publication in the spring of a series of over-sized facsimile reprints of the most valued comic books of the past under the general title of "Famous First Editions," beginning with a reprint of **Action** #1 and including afterwards **Detective Comics** #27, **Sensation Comics** #1, **Whiz Comics** #2, **Batman** #1, **Wonder Woman** #1, **All-Star Comics** #3, **Flash Comics** #1, and **Superman** #1. Mike Friedrich, an independent publisher, released **Star-Reach** with work by Jim Starlin, Neal Adams, and Dick Giordano, with ownership of the characters and stories invested in the creators themselves.

1975: In the first collaborative effort between the two major comic book publishers of the previous decade, Marvel and DC produced together an over-sized comic book version of MGM's **Marvelous Wizard of Oz** in the fall, and then the following year, in an unprecedented crossover, produced **Superman vs. the Amazing Spider-Man**, written by Gerry Conway, drawn by Ross Andru, and inked by Dick Giordano.

1976: Frank Brunner's Howard the Duck, who had appeared earlier in Marvel's **Fear** and **Man-Thing**, was given his own book in January, which because of distribution problems became an overnight collector's item. After decades of litigation, Jerry Siegel and Joe Shuster were given financial recompense and recognition by National Periodical Publications for their creation of Superman, after several friends of the team made a public issue of the case.

1977: Stan Lee's **Spider-Man** was given a second birth, fifteen years after his first, through a highly successful newspaper comic strip, which began syndication on January 3 with art by John Romita. This invasion of the comic strip by comic book characters continued with the appearance on June 6 of Marvel's **Howard the Duck**, with story by Steve Gerber and visuals by Gene Colan. In an unusually successful collaborative effort, Marvel began publication of the comic book adaption of the George Lucas film **Star Wars**, with script by Roy Thomas and art by Howard Chaykin, at least three months before the film was released nationally on May 25. The demand was so great that all six issues of **Star Wars** were reprinted at least seven times, and the installments were reprinted in two volumes of an over-sized Marvel Special Edition and a single paperback volume for the book trade. Dave Sim, with an issue dated December, began self-publication of his **Cerebus the Aardvark**, the success of which would help establish the independent market for non-traditional black-and-white comics.

1978: In an effort to halt declining sales, Warner Communications drastically cut back on the number of DC titles and overhauled its distribution process in June. The interest of the visual media in comic book characters reached a new high with the Hulk, Spider-Man, and Doctor Strange, the subjects of television shows; with various film versions produced of Flash Gordon, Dick Tracy, Popeye, Conan, The Phantom, and Buck Rogers; and with the movement reaching an outlandish peak of publicity with the release of **Superman** in December. Two significant applications of the comic book format to traditional fiction appeared this year: **A Contract with God and Other Tenement Stories** by Will Eisner and **The Silver Surfer** by Stan Lee and Jack Kirby. Eclipse Enterprises published Don McGregor and Paul Gulacy's **Sabre**, the first graphic album produced for the direct sales market, and initiated a policy of paying royalties and granting copyrights to comic book creators. Wendy and Richard Pini's **Elfquest**, a self-publishing project begun this year, eventually became so popular that it achieved bookstore distribution. The magazine **Heavy Metal** brought to American attention the avant-garde comic book work of European artists.

1980: Publication of the November premiere issue of **The New Teen Titans**, with art by George Perez and story by Marv Wolfman, brought back to widespread popularity a title originally published by DC in 1966.

981: Distributor Pacific Comics began publishing titles for direct sales through comic shops with the first issue of Jack Kirby's **Captain Victory and the Galactic Rangers** and offered royalties to artists and writers on the basis of sales. DC would do the same for regular newsstand comics in November (with payments retroactive to July 1981), and Marvel followed suit by the end of the year. The first issue of **Raw**, irregularly published by Art Spiegelman and Francoise Mouly, carried comic book art into new extremes of experimentation and innovation with work by European and American artists. With #158, Frank Miller began to write and draw Marvel's **Daredevil** and brought a vigorous style of violent action to comic book pages.

982: The first slick format comic book in regular size appeared, **Marvel Fanfare** #1, with a March date. Fantagraphics Books began publication in July of **Love and Rockets** by Mario, Gilbert, and Jaime Hernandez and brought a new ethnic sensibility and sophistication in style and content to comic book narratives for adults.

983: More comic book publishers, aside from Marvel and DC, issued more titles than had existed in the past 40 years, most small independent publishers relying on direct sales, such as Americomics, Capital, Eagle, Eclipse, First, Pacific, and Red Circle, and with Archie, Charlton, and Whitman publishing on a limited scale. Frank Miller's mini-series **Ronin** demonstrated a striking use of sword play and martial arts typical of Japanese comic book art, and Howard Chaykin's stylish but controversial **American Flagg** appeared with an October date on its first issue.

984: A publishing, media, film, and merchandising phenomenon began with the first issue of **Teenage Mutant Ninja Turtles** from Mirage Studios by Kevin Eastman and Peter Laird.

1985: Ohio State University's Library of Communication and Graphic Arts hosted the first major exhibition devoted to the comic book May 19 through August 2. In what was billed as an irreversible decision, the Silver Age superheroine Supergirl was killed in the seventh (October) issue of **Crisis on Infinite Earths**, a limited series intended to reorganize and simplify the DC universe on the occasion of their 50th anniversary.

986: In recognition of its twenty-fifth anniversary, Marvel began publishing several new ongoing titles comprising Marvel's "New Universe", a self-contained fictional world. DC attracted extensive publicity and media coverage with its revisions of the character of **Superman** by John Byrne and of **Batman** in the **Dark Knight** series by Frank Miller. **Watchmen**, a limited-series graphic novel by Alan Moore and artist Dave Gibbons, began publication with a September issue from DC and Marvel's **The `Nam**, written by Vietnam veteran Doug Murray and penciled by Michael Golden, began with its December issue. DC issued guidelines in December for labelling their titles either for mature readers or for readers of all ages; in response, many artists and writers publicly objected or threatened to resign.

987: Art Spiegelman's **Maus: A Survivor's Tale** was nominated for the National Book Critics Circle Award in biography, the first comic book to be so honored. A celebration of Superman's fiftieth Birthday began with the opening of an exhibition on his history at the Smithsonian's Museum of American History in Washington, D.C., in June and a symposium on "The Superhero in America" in October.

988: Superman's birthday celebration continued with a public party in New York and a CBS television special in February, a cover story in **Time Magazine** in March (the first comic book character to appear on the cover), and an international exposition in Cleveland in June. With issue number 601 for May 24, **Action Comics** became the first modern weekly comic book, which ceased publication after 42 issues with the December 13 issue. In August, DC initiated a new policy of allowing creators of new characters to retain ownership of them rather than rely solely on work-for-hire.

1989: The fiftieth anniversary of Batman was marked by the release of the film **Batman**, starring Michael Keaton as Bruce Wayne and Jack Nicholson as the Joker; it grossed more money in its opening weekend than any other motion picture in film history to that time.

1990: The publication of a new **Classics Illustrated** series began in January from Berkley/First with adaptations of Poe's **The Raven and Other Poems** by Gahan Wilson, Dickens' **Great Expectations** by Rick Geary, Carroll's **Through the Looking Glass** by Kyle Baker, and Melville's **Moby Dick** by Bill Sienkiewicz, with extensive media attention. The adaptation of characters to film continued with the most successful in terms of popularity and box office receipts being **Teenage Mutant Ninja Turtles** and Warren Beatty's **Dick Tracy**. In November, the engagement of Clark Kent and Lois Lane was announced in **Superman** #50 which brought public fanfare about the planned marriage.

1991: One of the first modern comic books to appear in the former Soviet Union was a Russian version of **Mickey Mouse** published in Moscow on May 16 in a printing of 200,000 copies which were sold out within hours. The first issue of **Bone**, written, drawn, and published by Jeff Smith, appeared with a July cover date. Issue number one of a new series of Marvel's **X-Men**, with story and art by Chris Claremont and Jim Lee, was published in October in five different editions with a print run of eight million copies, the highest number in the history of the comic book. On December 18, Sotheby's of New York held its first auction of comic book material.

1992: In April, Image Comics debuted with **Youngblood** #1, changing the comic book industry by widening the playing field and legitimizing independent comics. Image Comics began publication of the first Todd McFarlane Productions title, **Spawn**, with a May cover date. The opening weekend for **Batman Returns** in June was the biggest in film box office history, bringing in over 46 million dollars, exceeding the record set by **Batman** in 1989, and not to be topped until the release of **Jurassic Park** a year later. At the second Sotheby auction in September, **Action Comics** #1 brought $82,500, a world record for a single comic book sold at auction. In November the death of Superman generated considerable media attention, with **Superman** #75 selling in excess of 4 million copies, the second best-selling issue in comic book history. A record number of over one hundred publishers of comic books and graphic albums issued titles this year.

1993: In April, for the first time since 1987, DC Comics surpassed Marvel in sales, primarily because of interest in the titles devoted to the return of Superman.

1994: Overproduction, changes in marketing practices, and publisher mergers and collapses triggered an apparent crisis in comic book publishing–which some have read as a sign of its influence and presence in American commerce and culture.

1995: **Batman Forever**, released in June with Val Kilmer in the lead role, grossed in its opening weekend over $53 million, the largest return in film box office history, exceeding the similar records set by the first two Batman films in 1989 and 1992. Writer Neil Gaiman decided after seven years to retire his popular and literate version of **Sandman**, the second revival of a Golden Age DC superhero first created in 1939.

1996: The longest-running give-away title ended after #467 of **The Adventures of the Big Boy** in September. In a long anticipated event coordinated between several comic book titles, the ABC television series **Lois & Clark: The New Adventures of Superman**, and the publication of **Superman: The Wedding Album**, Lois Lane and Clark Kent were married in October.

1997: Several Marvel Universe titles (**Fantastic Four**, **Avengers**, **Captain America**, **Iron Man**) ended their long runs and started over with new #1 issues under the umbrella title **Heroes Reborn**, a separate universe under the creative direction of Rob Liefeld and Jim Lee. They later returned, again with new #1s, in the **Heroes Return** crossover. Superman went through a startling metamorphosis at DC, complete with new powers and a new costume, eventually splitting into two beings, Superman Red & Superman Blue. The latest Batman film, **Batman & Robin**, was released to a tepid response, while the movie adaptation of Todd McFarlane's **Spawn** movie was moderately well received.

NEW COMIC BOOKS

This book lists all new comic books at cover price, regardless of their performance in the secondary market. In most cases, new comics are not worth their cover price in the secondary market, and collectors may pay pennies on the dollar for copies of these issues. Nevertheless, since these comics have yet to establish themselves as collectors' items, they are listed at full cover price. It should also be noted that regarding polybagged comics, it is the official policy of **The Overstreet Comic Book Price Guide** to grade comics regardless of whether they are still sealed in their polybag or not. If opened, the polybag and its contents should be preserved separately so that all components of the original package remain together.

FOREIGN COMIC BOOKS

One extremely interesting source of early vintage comics–one which is not necessarily expensive–is the foreign market. Many American newspaper and magazine strips are reprinted abroad (in English and in other languages) months and even years after they appear in the States. By arranging trades with foreign collectors, one can obtain, for practically cover price, substantial runs of American comic book reprints and newspaper strips dating back five, ten, and even twenty or more years. These reprints are often in black and white, and sometimes the reproduction is poor, but this is not always the case. Once interest in foreign-published comics has been piqued, a collector might become interested in original strips from these countries. Many are excellent, with a broader appeal than American comic books.

COMIC BOOK FANDOM

It is possible to discern two distinct and largely unrelated movements in the history of Comics Fandom. The first began about 1953 as a response to the the trend-setting EC lines of comics. The first true comics fanzines of this movement were short-lived. Bob Stewart's **EC FAN BULLETIN** was a hectographed newsletter that ran two issues about six months apart; Jimmy Taurasi's **FANTASY COMICS**, a newsletter devoted to all science-fiction comics of the period, was a monthly that ran for about six months. These were followed by other newsletters such as Mike May's **EC FAN JOURNAL**, and George Jennings' **EC WORLD PRESS.** EC fanzines of a wider and more critical scope appeared somewhat later. Two of the finest were **POTRZEBIE**, from a number of fans, and Ron Parker's **HOOHAH**. Gauging from the response that **POTRZEBIE** received from an EC letter column plug, Ted White estimated the average age of EC fans at 9 to 13, while many were actually in their mid-teens. This was discouraging to many fanzine editors hoping to reach an older audience. Consequently, many gave up their efforts on behalf of Comics Fandom, especially with the demise of the EC groups, and turned to SF (science fiction) fandom with its longer tradition and older membership. While the flourish of fan activity in response to the EC comics was certainly noteworthy, it never developed into a full-fledged, independent, and self-sustaining movement.

The second comics fan movement began in 1960, largely as a response to (and later stimulus for) the reappearance of the costumed hero and the Second Heroic Age of Comics. Most historians date the Second Heroic Age from **Flash** #105, February 1959. The letter departments of Julius Schwartz (editor at National Periodicals), and later those of Stan Lee (Marvel Group) and Bill Harris (Gold Key) were influential in bringing comics readers into Fandom. Sparks were lit among SF fans first, when experienced fan writers, who were part of an established tradition, produced the first in a series of articles on '40s comics–ALL IN COLOR FOR A DIME. The series was introduced in **XERO** #1 (September 1960), a general SF fanzine edited and published by Dick Lupoff.

Meanwhile, outside SF fandom, Jerry Bails and Roy Thomas, two comics fans of long-standing, conceived the first true comics fanzine in response to the Second Heroic Age, **ALTER EGO**, appearing in March 1961. The first issues were widely circulated, and profoundly influenced the comics fan movement, attracting many fans in their twenties and thirties, unlike the earlier EC fan following. Many of these older fans had been collectors for years but were largely unknown to each other. Joined by scores of new, younger fans, this group formed the nucleus of a movement that is still growing and shows every sign of being self-sustaining. Although it has borrowed a few appropriate SF terms, Comics Fandom of the '60s was an independent if fledging movement without the advantages and disadvantages of a longer tradition. What Comics Fandom did derive from SF fans was largely thanks to fanzines produced by so-called double fans, the most notable being **COMIC ART**, edited and published by Don and Maggie Thompson.

The **ROCKET'S BLAST COMIC COLLECTOR** by G.B. Love was the first sucessful adzine in the early 1960s and was instrumental in the early development of the comics market. G.B. remembers beginning his fanzine **THE ROCKET'S BLAST** in late 1961. Only six copies of the first 4 page issue were printed. Soon after Mr. Love had a letter published in **MYSTERY IN SPACE**, telling all about his new fanzine. His circulation began to grow. Buddy Saunders, a well known comic book store owner, designed the first **ROCKET'S BLAST** logo and was an artist on the publication for many years thereafter. With issue #29 he took over **THE COMICOLLECTOR** fanzine from Biljo White and combined it with **ROCKET'S BLAST** to form the **RBCC**. He remembers that the **RBCC** hit its highest circulation of 2,500 around 1971. Many people who wrote, drew or otherwise contributed to the **RBCC** went on to become well known writers, artists, dealers and store-owners in the comics field.

COMIC-RELATED COLLECTIBLES

COLLECTING STRIPS

Collecting newspaper comic strips is somewhat different than collecting comic books, although it can be equally satisfying. Obviously, most strip collectors begin by clipping strips from their local paper, but soon branch out to out-of-town papers. Naturally this can become more expensive and more frustrating, as it is easy to miss out-of-town editions. Consequently, most strip collectors work out trade agreements with collectors in other cities to get the strips they want. This usually means saving local strips for trade purposes only.

Back issues of strips dating back several decades are also occasionally available from dealers. Prices per panel vary greatly depending on the age, condition, and demand for the strip. When the original strips are unavailable, it is sometimes possible to get photostatic copies from collectors, libraries, or newspaper morgues.

COLLECTING ORIGINAL ART

In addition to comic books and strips, some enthusiasts also collect original comic book and strip art. These mostly black and white, inked drawings are usually done on illustration paper at about 30 percent up (30 percent larger than the original printed panels). Because original art is a one-of-a-kind article, it is highly prized and can be difficult to obtain.

Interest in original comic art has increased tremendously in the past few years. One of the reasons more current art is available is that companies now return originals to the artists, who then either sell the work themselves at cons, or through agents and dealers. The best way to find the piece you want is to scour cons and get on as many art dealers' mailing lists as possible. As with any other area of collecting, rarity and demand govern value. Although the masters' works from the Golden and Silver Ages bring fine art prices, most current work is available at moderate prices, with something for everyone at various costs, from Kirby to McFarlane, Ditko to Steve Dillon, Heath to Chris Bachalo. The art is there for fans to seek out.

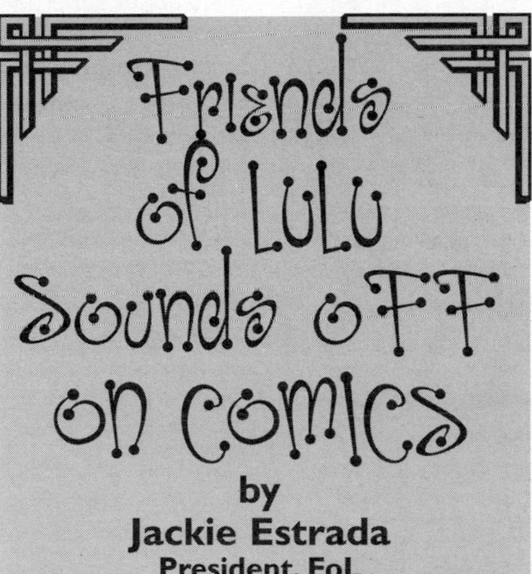

Friends of Lulu Sounds off on Comics
by
Jackie Estrada
President, FoL

Why don't more women and girls read comics, and what can be done about it? Those are questions that we in Friends of Lulu have been exploring.

But before we get to these questions, you may be wondering, "What in the heck is Friends of Lulu? And who's 'Lulu' anyway?"

WHAT IS FRIENDS OF LULU?

Friends of Lulu is an organization devoted to getting more women and girls involved in comics: both as readers and as creators or producers. "Lulu" comes, of course, from Little Lulu, one of the strongest female characters ever to grace the four-color comics pages, and a favorite comic among girls (and lots of boys, too!) for decades.

The organization was incorporated as a nonprofit charity in 1995 and is run by a national board of directors. Membership in FoL is open to males and females, professionals and fans, adults and kids. Nationally, FoL has more than 400 members, and there are regional chapters in several U.S. cities, including New York, Chicago, San Francisco, and Los Angeles.

Here are just a few of the things FoL has done since its founding: (1) put together a catalog (published by Diamond Comic Distributors) of recommended comics and graphic novels that would appeal to readers (especially female readers) who don't normally read comics; (2) produced a booklet for comics retailers titled **How to Get Girls (in Your Store)**; (3) put together programs and conducted portfolio reviews at comic conventions around the country; (4) had booths at all the major comic conventions; (5) handed out the first Lulu Awards; (6) held its first LuluCon conference; (7) produced a regular newsletter for its members; (8) produced buttons, T-shirts, stickers, and other items.

For more on FoL activities, including a listing of

Illustrations by Mary Wilshire

conventions where FoL will have booths in 1998, visit our website: **www.friends-lulu.org**.

SO WHY DON'T MORE WOMEN AND GIRLS READ COMICS?

Back in the late 1940s and early 1950s, females constituted roughly half of comics readership. And why not? Lots of comics were aimed directly at them—romance comics, in particular. The typical newsstand was bulging with comics of every imaginable genre, from funny animals to westerns, from sports to teen humor, from crime and horror to **Classics Illustrated**.

Historians can argue over what happened to the industry over the next two decades: Did comics sales decline because of television? Because of Fredric Wertham's **Seduction of the Innocent**, the Kefauver hearings, and the institution of the Comics Code? Because of competition from an exploding number of choices in entertainment? Because comics companies stuck with an outmoded format, cutting the number of pages periodically to keep from increasing prices? Because newsstand distribution was corrupt and spotty?

Whatever the case (and all these factors may have contributed), comics nearly became extinct in the 1970s. What saved them was the rise of a network of comic book specialty stores, which evolved into what today is called the Direct Market. The great majority of these stores were run by males who were longtime fans and collectors of superhero comics, and their customers tended to be similar. As the direct market became the predominant distribution outlet for comics, publishers targeted their comics more and more to that core audience: the male superhero fan/collector.

The result was that in the 1980s the direct market was essentially a string of boys' clubs across the country, run by variations of "the comic book guy" from *The Simpsons.* As in the Little Lulu comics, the majority of these boys' clubs had an implied sign: "No Girls Allowed."

Why don't more women and girls read comics? The short answer is that today most females are unaware of the existence of comics they might enjoy, and those who become aware of the books are afraid to venture into a comics shop to look for them.

WHAT CAN BE DONE?

The answer is easy, right? Produce more comics and graphic novels that will appeal to female readers (just having *plots* would be a step in the right direction!), and make comics stores more female-friendly.

In practice, of course, it's not that simple. After all, there are already *hundreds* of comics that have strong appeal to a female readership. I'm referring to the sorts of books that are accessible to a typical non-comics reader who happens to like a good story, is intrigued by interesting characters, and appreciates well-done artwork. (Sorry, part 7 of a 15-part crossover series consisting of 20 fight-scene pinup pages doesn't count!) Just to name a few of those reader-friendly comics and graphic novels: **Castle Waiting**, **Concrete**, **Kane**, **Maus**, **Strangers in Paradise**, **Naughty Bits**, **Sandman**, **Love and Rockets**, **Stuck Rubber Baby**, the Paradox "**Big Books**" series, **The Tale of One Bad Rat**, **Twisted**

Sisters, **Bone**, **Milk & Cheese**, **Elfquest**, **The Tick**, **The Simpsons**, **Why I Hate Saturn**, **Gon**, **Too Much Coffeeman**, **Groo**, **Akiko**, **Fairy Tales of Oscar Wilde**, **Our Cancer Year**, **Life of the Party**, **Joy Ride**, **Usagi Yojimbo**, and **Wolff & Byrd, Counselors of the Macabre**.

Most of these books have been nominated for or won Eisner or Harvey Awards. Yet trying to find them in a typical comics shop is haphazard at best. So producing more "female-friendly" titles may not do much good if retailers don't carry them.

So how about making the stores more appealing? Again, easier said than done. Yes, there are some fabulous stores around the country that bring in female customers because they have inviting window displays; a clean, well-laid-out store; a good product mix; a friendly, helpful staff; and promotions designed to cultivate a clientele beyond the core comics fan. The owners make sure that shopping in their stores is an enjoyable experience—and these stores are doing well. However, not every comic shop caters to diversified customers or a customer's diversified interests.

What, then, is the answer? Unfortunately, we don't have any easy solutions. One way in which Friends of Lulu is doing its part is to sponsor trade-show programs and within-industry conferences to look at ways to reach a wider audience, looking at such issues as: How can we get more comics into schools? Libraries? Regular bookstores? How can we get more positive media coverage for comics? How can we get more kids back in the comics-reading habit so they will be more receptive to comics as they get older? How can we help stores widen their customer base?

WHY DOES FRIENDS OF LULU CARE?

Those of us who are active in FoL believe that comics is a rich artform; not only are there a vast number of existing and ongoing titles that could have widespread appeal, but the medium has untapped potential for creative expression. In short, we love comics, we want others to see their value, and we want to see them survive.

To survive, the comics industry needs more women. It needs female readers (statistics show that females spend much more on books than males do and read more as well). The industry also needs women as producers, whether in the form of creators or businesspeople. If we can attract more writers and artists of the caliber of Wendy Pini, Jill Thompson, Carol Lay, Linda Medley, Mary Fleener, Louise Simonson, Donna Barr, Debbie Drechsler, Colleen Doran, Amanda Conner, Trina Robbins and Roberta Gregory; if we can bring in more publishers/editors like Diana Schutz, Karen Berger, Vijaya Iyer, Jenette Kahn, Brownyn Taggart, Sarah Dyer, and Maria Lapham, then the industry can only benefit.

For further information on Friends of Lulu, write to them at:
4657 Cajon Way
San Diego, CA 92115

the worl TOMORR

HOW COMICS OF THE PAST PORTRAYED THE 1990S

by ARNOLD T. BLUMBERG

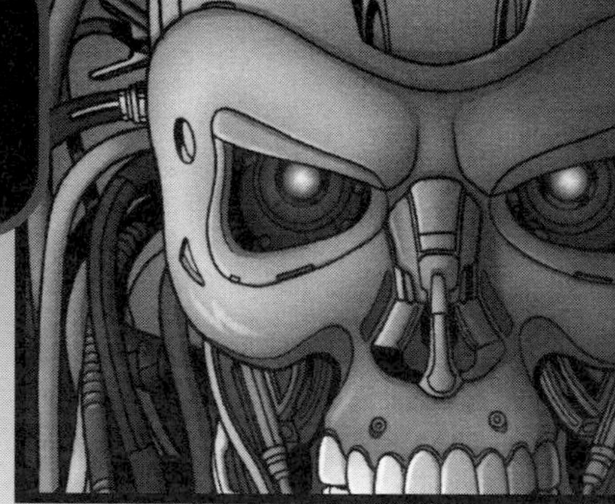

A MATTER OF PERSPECTIVE

In a 1989 *Calvin & Hobbes* comic strip, the two friends are walking through a snow-covered forest when Hobbes observes that a "new decade is coming up."

"Big deal," Calvin responds. "Where are all the flying cars? Where are the moon colonies? You call this the future?? HA! Where are the rocket packs? Where are the disintegration rays? Where are the floating cities?"

"Frankly, I'm not sure people have the brains to manage the technology they've *got*," Hobbes offers.

"I mean, *look* at this! We still have *weather*?! Give me a break!"

So where *are* the flying cars and floating cities? Well, the '90s may not be the '90s we envisioned decades ago, but there are still tech toys and advances aplenty. Look at cell phones, CDs, the internet, cable television—all of these electronic innovations and more have defined the '90s as a high-tech decade, but certainly not the one anyone imagined. Our development has followed an inward rather than an outward path, with subtle but significant improvements in communications, medicine, and entertainment. The future has arrived, but quietly, cautiously, and as a result, anyone dreaming of the '90s as seen in those old pulps—a world of huge-finned rockets, meals in a pill and ringed spires stretching to the heavens—will find themselves disappointed by the reality of 1997.

All artwork ©1998 their respective owners...in this time-line, that is, not including alternate realities...

d of

ow

Thankfully, as we move into the next millennium, we will always have the vision of the '90s we grew up with—it's forever documented in those wonderful four-color flights of fantasy, the comic books of our youth. On the following pages we'll take a look at some memorable examples of the 1990s as seen by comic book writers and artists of the past. Never mind that they missed by a mile at times—they had no idea some of these stories would still be around when the '90s actually arrived—but here they are, ready to be reread and enjoyed as wistful reminders of simpler, more innocent days and the dreams (and nightmares) of the future that filled them.

KINGDOMS TO COME

DC made the most of the future with its many science-fiction anthology series—**Strange Adventures**, **Mystery in Space**—and even with heroes based in times as far-flung as the **Legion of Super-Heroes**' 30th century. But of all the DC characters whose adventures have given us a glimpse of a 1990s that will never be, what better guide could we choose than the Man of Tomorrow himself—Superman.

Perhaps one of the most subtle and intriguing '90s Superman tales was printed as a two part "imaginary story" in **Superman** #423 and **Action Comics** #583. Written by Alan Moore, "Whatever

INVASION OF THE GIANT (AND NOT SO GIANT) ROBOTS!

Begin transmission . . .

If the covers to this year's edition of the guide (both versions) are any indication, robots have always had a powerful and exciting presence in the comic book world. Marauding automatons like those threatening our DC and Quality Comics heroes are robots in the mold of the old pulp and SF periodicals—huge, monstrous machines that seek only to destroy and conquer humanity. In fact, the many "giant robot" comic book covers can trace their stylistic lineage right back to the science fiction anthology magazines that first featured such stories.

But there's much more to robots in comics than just the tin terrors that carry off screaming victims and pummel superheroes into submission—quite a few of the most prominent robots to appear in comics are superheroes themselves. After all, there's plenty of room for robots who are good guys as well as bad, and comic book fans have seen them all.

Here then are our picks (listed alphabetically) for the top ten most intriguing robot characters in the history of comics. Some of your favorites may not be on this list, and you may discover one or two characters you never knew existed. We've also broadened the definition of "robot" for the purposes of this list, including android and cyborg candidates as well. Nevertheless, whether they are on this list or not, the many robotic creations that have graced the comic book pages are a welcome addition, and even if they reside in the past, the present, or the far future, robots in fiction will always reflect the best and worst—not of machine, but of man.

(A special thanks to all who visited our website at www.gemstonepub.com/fan, and gave us their picks for this list.)

Happened to the Man of Tomorrow" was the "last" Earth I Superman story, and wrapped up decades of continuity as DC closed the book on the Silver Age Superman and ushered in a reworked **Man of Steel** (updated for the '80s by John Byrne). With a framing sequence set in August 1997, Moore's story flashes back to the last stand of Superman at the Fortress of Solitude against the now malevolent Mr. Mxyzptlk. Powerless and under another identity, Superman has retired to married life with Lois, and has no regrets about leaving his superhero days behind.

Although this vision of the '90s is not nearly so outlandish as in other stories, it's charming for several reasons. The story was printed in 1986—not so far off—and yet the style of Lois' clothing and apartment looks *Jetson*-esque. It's less a case of the typical overestimation of future technology and more of an affectionate tribute to the earlier stories that gave us a '90s filled with wondrous technology and bizarre apparel. Considering Moore's sense of wit, it's fitting that the end of the Silver Age Superman's reign finds him happy and settled down in a future much like the one his comics portrayed in the '50s and '60s.

Superman wasn't the only DC hero who faced the ultimate challenge in a '90s that would never be. His erstwhile **World's Finest** partner, Batman, fought the Joker in a grim late '90s in the now legendary Frank Miller epic, **The Dark Knight Returns**. Universally regarded as one of the greatest comic book tales of all time, this story also looks forward only about ten years, and yet it is just as charmingly askew as any '90s story written fifty years ago. Not so much a possible future as a collection of the worst fears of the time—a sort of *über-'80s*—this 1990s is a dark place of intense heat waves, violent gangs running amok, and the horror of nuclear war (an intrinsically '80s "Reagan-era" dread) looming on the horizon. Its only concession to readers' expectations of a near-future tale is in the visual depiction of fashion. Incidental characters sport unusual hairstyles, earrings and neckties, particularly

Designation: Anna
Primary Function: Housekeeper
First Activated: **Gen13** #1
Operational Parameters: The Image Universe
Program Log: Although she prefers the term "android," Anna is a robot with some considerable skills and an important task. Employed by John Lynch, she serves as housekeeper for Gen13, and is, in her own words, "programmed and equipped to maintain the security of [their] domicile." Not just your average nanny, she comes loaded for bear with a plethora of weapons, most of which are built into her body. This is a maid for the 21st century—but she probably doesn't do windows.

Designation: Brainiac
Primary Function: Cold, calculating enemy of Superman
First Activated: **Action Comics** #242, (redesign) #544
Operational Parameters: The DC Universe
Program Log: Although he has taken many forms over the decades, his '80s redesign places Brainiac squarely in the middle of the comic book robot population. Sporting a chrome cranium capable of limitless evil, this alien being bent on defeating Superman has given our fearless hero some serious trouble over the years, even masterminding the death of Pete Ross and the final dissolution of the Superman family as we knew it while controlling the dead form of Lex Luthor (in Alan Moore's "last" Superman story anyway—see main article).

Designation: Doctor Doom's Robots
Primary Function: To obey their master without question
First Activated: **Fantastic Four** #5
Operational Parameters: Latveria and beyond, The Marvel Universe
Program Log: Taking many forms and serving the whims of the Fantastic Four's greatest foe, the robots of Victor Von Doom are perfect representations of automatons fulfilling a function regardless of right or wrong—these creatures are not intrinsically evil, they're just programmed that way. From the mindless gun-toting soldiers who regularly patrol Latveria to the sophisticated duplicates of Doom himself, the robots of Doom are ceaseless in their dedication and terrifying

the many news anchors whose reports are woven throughout the story, but these too are more distinctly '80s than anything we wear today.

MARVELS OF THE FUTURE

DC hardly had the comic book monopoly on guessing at the wonders that awaited us at the end of this century. Marvel Comics too has dipped into the '90s from time to time, but rarely with such near-apocalyptic finality as in the tales of Deathlok. A cyborg creation that regularly sparred with the on-board computer in his brain, Deathlok roamed the deserted streets of a decimated New York in 1990, with only his schizoid personality and the occasional gun-toting marauder for company. Spider-Man visited Deathlok's grotesque world from fifteen years in the past (in **Marvel Team-Up** #46), and prayed that this was not what the 1990s truly had to offer. He needn't have worried, because in 1997, New York is still relatively intact, and Spider-Man has faced much greater nightmares than anything in Deathlok's time—like the "Clone Saga."

The Marvel Universe even has an "escape clause" to justify their inaccurate renderings of the future. Other Marvel heroes have

for anyone who dares to stand in their way.

Designation: Machine Man
Primary Function: Steel superhero
First Activated: 2001: A Space Odyssey #8
Operational Parameters: The Marvel Universe
Program Log: A rare incidence of a character appearing in a licensed tie-in series first then moving into the Marvel Universe at large, the career of Machine Man has been a spotty but intriguing one. Introduced as Mr. Machine, Marvel's "misunderstood mechanoid" has enjoyed moderate success as a superhero in a variety of appearances, including a team-up with Spider-Man himself (who always seems to have time to meet everyone sooner or later). With his fast-extending limbs (supply your own joke here) and enhanced sensors, Machine Man is a formidable opponent, but he is also plagued by doubt and confusion. The tragic aspects of the character, a Marvel trademark going back to the Thing and the Silver Surfer, gives Machine Man a strangely ironic human quality.

Designation: The Metal Men
Primary Function: Goofy superhero team
First Activated: Showcase #37
Operational Parameters: The DC Universe
Program Log: Man-like embodiments of Platinum, Gold, Iron, Tin, Mercury, and Lead, taken together are the mighty Metal Men. Actually five metal men and one metal woman (Platinum), the Metal Men were created by Doc Magnus and each fitted with a "responsometer"—fancy technobabble for a near-sentient computer brain that gives the Metal Men the capacity to feel and perform superhuman tasks. Led by Gold, they battled numerous supervillains and their own inventor, when he turned against them, while simultaneously dealing with their own artificial angst.

Designation: Roberta
Primary Function: The Fantastic Four's secretary & receptionist

First Activated: FF #239
Operational Parameters:
New York, The Marvel Universe
Program Log: No list of robots in comics would be complete without a nod to the most tireless secretary in the world. Whether she's fielding calls, screening visitors, or warning the FF of dangerous incursions into the Baxter Building/Four Freedoms Plaza by evil villains bent on worldwide domination, she still manages to keep the business end of things running smoothly.

Designation: The Sentinels
Primary Function:
To destroy mutantkind
First Activated: X-Men #14
Operational Parameters:
The Marvel Universe, Present and Future
Program Log: Finally, some giant robots!!! These marauding monsters chill the bones when they take to the sky to massacre mutants in the name of order. Created to combat the rising "menace" of the mutant population, these huge hulking horrors with the dull glowing eyes have regularly crossed paths with the X-Men and their many offshoots, creating havoc (a bit of a pun, get it?) wherever they trod. Even non-mutant super-heroes like Spider-Man have tussled with the Sentinels over the years, and in a dark future that exists somewhere in the multiverse, the Sentinels succeeded in laying waste to much of the Marvel mutant contingent. With their towering stature and soulless gaze, they live up to the reputation of the classic "giant robot" characters of the pulps, and will continue to inspire Luddite fears in us all.

Designation: Superman's Robot Duplicates
Primary Function:
Stand-ins for the original Man of Steel
First Activated:
(chronologically) Adventure Comics #218
Operational Parameters:
The DC Universe
Program Log: Not just an individual robot, these identical minions of the Man of Tomorrow are loyal and true, accomplishing all the many tasks that even Superman can't complete, either due to a weakness or his inability to be in two places at once (the old George Reeves TV show notwithstanding).

tripped through time and seen versions of the '90s and beyond, including the Fantastic Four (often employing Doctor Doom's distinctive time machine), the Avengers (particularly in battle with their time-traveling nemesis, Kang), and the X-Men (whose convoluted future continuity still plagues X-writers and readers alike), but it was Reed Richards who finally explained why the many trips through Marvel past, present, and future, such as Spider-Man's jaunt into the '90s, did not reflect the true course of time. Reed deduced that time travel resulted in the creation of *alternate* realities, leaving the original time-line unaffected. So although Spidey saw a glimpse of the '90s, it wasn't the "real" future that lay ahead for our hero. If only Superman or Batman had that assurance.

THE WONDER THAT WILL BE?

Other publishers have presented distorted visions of the 1990s, often in the form of licensed TV and movie tie-ins. **Space Family Robinson**, originally published by Gold Key from 1962 to 1969, followed the exploits of a family marooned in space. Later based on the cult '60s series **Lost in Space**, the Robinsons' adventures took place in the late '90s, and although their predicament prevented readers from seeing what Earth was like, a lot could be inferred from the Robinsons themselves. Clearly, the values and beliefs of the "typical" American family were the same. But as with most predictions of the future, strange fashions and advanced technology (ray guns, spacecraft) were always in evidence.

The launch date for the Robinsons' spacecraft, as given in the series, was October 1997. Having just passed that date ourselves, we can testify to the fact that no such missions are underway—we still have a long way to go before we can colonize other planets in our own system, much less those orbiting other stars! This highly exaggerated development of our space program is a reflection of the hope that many held for the future of space exploration. Thirty years ago, we were just starting to reach beyond the confines of our world, sending brave men to visit the moon and return with souvenirs of the journey. It was the dawn of a new age, and it was easy to imagine that we would live in space and spread out among the stars. It was also easy to assume that would be soon, and the '90s seemed plausible enough. No one could have predicted the ways in which the space program would atrophy, and today, we are only just beginning to see the rebirth of those dreams in plans for Mars missions and an international space station. If those

BONUS! A perfect example of comic books missing the mark when predicting the future--look at the date of this bizarre convention! This 1970s Harvey Kurtzman piece was a proposed **Overstreet Comic Book Price Guide** cover, and ran in altered form on the cover of **Overstreet's Advanced Collector** #1 (Sum.'93). Think about this vision of the "future" when visiting the San Diego con this year!

Whether shielding him from Kryptonite o diving deep into the ocean depths on a daring missinn, these mechanical men ir blue do Superman proud. In arguably thei first chronological appearance in Supes career, a double of the Boy o[illegible]teel helps Superboy conceal his identity. The strangest part is that the implied invento of the "sponge rubber" robo[illegible] filled with gears and operated by remote contro is...Jonathan Kent? Those spare tracto parts really came in handy.

Designation: Ultron
Primary Function: Avengers nemesis
First Activated: Avengers #58
Operational Parameters:
The Marvel Universe
Program Log: An undying evil tha serves as the perfect example of the ulti mate nightmare in robotic[illegible] Ultron was created by Hank "Ant-Man" [illegible] and con tinues to plague his "fathe[illegible] and the Avengers through many siniste[illegible] incarna tions. With his polished metal form and skull-like visage, Ultron still stands as one of the Avengers' deadliest enemies, regu larly reincarnating himself in new bodies whenever an old one was destroyed. No doubt there will be Ultrons around to threaten the World's Mightiest Heroes until we run out of numbers.

Designation: Vision
Primary Function: Avenger
First Activated: Avengers #57
Operational Parameters:
The Marvel Universe
Program Log: Strangely enough, anoth er Avenger star follows Ultron on the list but just as Ultron symbolizes the wors robots have to offer, the Vision stands fo the best. Not strictly a robot in the trues sense (he's more of an android[illegible] this rec skinned Avenger with the checkered pas is a devoted servant to the cause of jus tice, and a powerful crus[illegible] for good regardless of his artificia[illegible] composition Throughout much of his career, he was also a rather controversial spouse in ar android/mutant marriage with the Scarle Witch. As one half of one [illegible] the mos memorable Marvel coup[illegible] the Vision struggled with his lack of emotion, echoing similar themes in the character arcs o *Star Trek's* Mr. Spock and [illegible] Commande Data. **. . . End transmission**

dreams do come true, however, they will not be the gleaming, streamlined '90s envisioned in series like **Space Family Robinson**, but a far more conservative and practical future.

The future holds equal potential for hope or harm, and another licensed tie-in series published by Now Comics in the late '80s adapted a popular cult sci-fi film and gave us a glimpse of hell, circa 1997. In **The Terminator**, man's own creations—the computers that ran our defense systems—rebelled and attempted to destroy us, in true Frankenstein fashion, in a nuclear holocaust. The plot hinged on the events of August 1997, in which the sentient computer Skynet launched the missile attack that plunged the world into war. With no one left but a few haggard survivors, the machines rose up and dominated the Earth. Opposed by a small group of rebel humans led by John Connor in 2029, the Terminators and their masters would eventually be thwarted, but thankfully, this version of the 1990s would also prove to be inaccurate. Except for New York City and some portions of Los Angeles, the world has not become a smoking wilderness of ash and twisted metal, and August 1997, like October 1997 after it, passed without incident. Our 1990s were not marked by glorious achievements in space exploration, but neither did it sound the death knell for the human race.

PREDICTION PARADOX

In a medium based on escapist fantasy, it's only natural that comics would explore the promises and pitfalls of the future and attempt to capture something of what the years ahead may hold for us all. It's just as reasonable to expect that more often than not, the talented men and women of the comics, despite their skills and foresight, will get it wrong. Nevertheless, what's more important is that the many versions of the 1990s that we have seen in comics are as much a representation of the present day as they are of the future—more so, in fact, because it's the present that provides the basis for understanding. Whether it's a "grim and gritty" '90s filled with devastated cities and disheartened anti-heroes, or a glorious, gleaming '90s where sprawling metroplexes reach to the stars and the skies are filled with jet-packing citizens and streamlined spaceships—all of these interpretations reflect the times in which they were created, incorporating the hopes and fears of the writers and artists that crafted them.

In **Back to the Future Part III**, Doc Emmett L. Brown, inventor of a car that travels through time, observes that "your future is whatever you make it!" Some of us are so driven to see what awaits us that we make that future today, and the results are some of the exciting stories we've just discussed. The 1990s were not the World of Tomorrow the comics portrayed, but that world is still waiting for us. For as long as comics explore other worlds and adventures, with super-heroes and space travelers carrying the best and worst of humanity to the stars and beyond, they will also give us glimpses of the future and the wonders that future might bring. And more often than not, they'll probably be wrong. But that's as it should be.

After all, we're only human.

BUILT TO LAST

It happened very innocently under darkening skies. Everyday people were getting back on their feet and taking a long, hard look at the world. The weight of the Great Depression was lifting from the land, but the fires of war had been lit in Europe and Asia. It was a time of ominous signs and enormous potential. It was a time of fear and desperation, a time of hope and glory.

IT WAS ALSO A TIME FOR HEROES . . .

Art and DC logo ©1998 DC Comics, from material published by DC except as noted.

Two men in Ohio set the stage for what would become the foundation of an industry so many now love. These pioneers, Jerry Siegel and Joe Shuster, passed up work as newspaper strip cartoonists and instead turned their attention toward a character named Dr. Occult. He appeared in **More Fun** #6 and opened the door for the mystery men that followed, including what would be the duo's greatest creation.

Catching an unsuspecting world off guard, these heroes exploded onto the pages of the four-color comic book. First there was a mild-mannered man-god who could leap tall buildings in a single bound. Then, a creature of the night emerged in the city Gotham, declaring war on those who preyed upon the weak. Others would soon follow. A magical princess with a will of iron and a lasso of gold. A scarlet speedster who used his swiftness to fight the forces of evil, an emerald guardian who used his ring of green to protect the innocent, and still more came. A vengeful spirit risen from the dead to bring the guilty to justice. A doctor who walked the world in darkness only to strike a blow against the corrupt while proving that justice wasn't blind. Still more would follow. Characters created by men to show others the way, to set an example, to represent that which we should strive to achieve. Heroes, though ink on paper, that would eventually take on a life of their own and prove to the world they were here for good, created from the best intentions, made of the right stuff.

This page and next: Superman and Wonder Woman by Alex Ross from **Revelations** (1997), a companion to **Kingdom Come**. DC/Graphitti Designs.

From the beginning, "the right stuff" set these characters apart from their peers in this and every other medium. They latched onto the collective psyche we call popular culture and became American icons. They were dreams, an almost-tangible essence of childhood fantasy, a populist combination of desire for justice and thirst for adventure.

They were heroes. Superman, Batman, Flash, Wonder Woman and others burst upon the scene in the late 1930s, and quickly they carved out a niche with their fans.

Despite the tumultuous changes the world has endured over the past 60 years, these characters have survived,

BY J.C. VAUGHN AND SCOTT BRADEN

basically intact, and thrived. Other superheroes of the Golden Age, and every age since, have disappeared. For whatever reason, they failed to grab the fans, to seize them and find a way into their hearts. These surviving heroes were built to last.

What was it, though, about these heroes that has kept them around for sixty years? What makes these particular characters important today?

"Because they are archetypes, pure and simple," according to writer Mark Waid, writer of DC's **Flash** and **Impulse**, as well as the epic **Kingdom Come**. "Superman, Wonder Woman and Batman are the heroes that all others have sprung from. Tom Peyer has a great quote that 'Kids can tell **Cracked** from **Mad**.' They can always tell the Black Terror from Batman. They can always tell Wonder Man from Superman. It has to do with the fact that the more archetypal you get with your characters, the more simple they are, the wider a range of stories you can tell with them."

"Superman is an archetype, and so is Batman," said Jerry Ordway, contributor to DC's revamped **Superman** in the late '80s and early '90s, as well as the man behind Captain Marvel in **The Power of Shazam!**" They had their roots in the pulps as well as newspaper strips of the time, though. Superman owes a lot to Doc Savage and Philip Wylie's Gladiator, while Batman is Sherlock Holmes and The Shadow. They, like their predecessors, are good concepts and have been published continuously for half a century."

"The good ones are based on very solid myths, whether they're created for the character or from the outside," added Marv Wolfman, writer/editor veteran of both DC and Marvel. "Certain types of legends click, and always have with people. For example, the story of Batman is the eternal struggle for justice. They're very primal characters, and that's the reason they've been popular since the day they have come out. They give writers the ability to tell endless stories since the original essence of the characters stays pure and undiluted," he said.

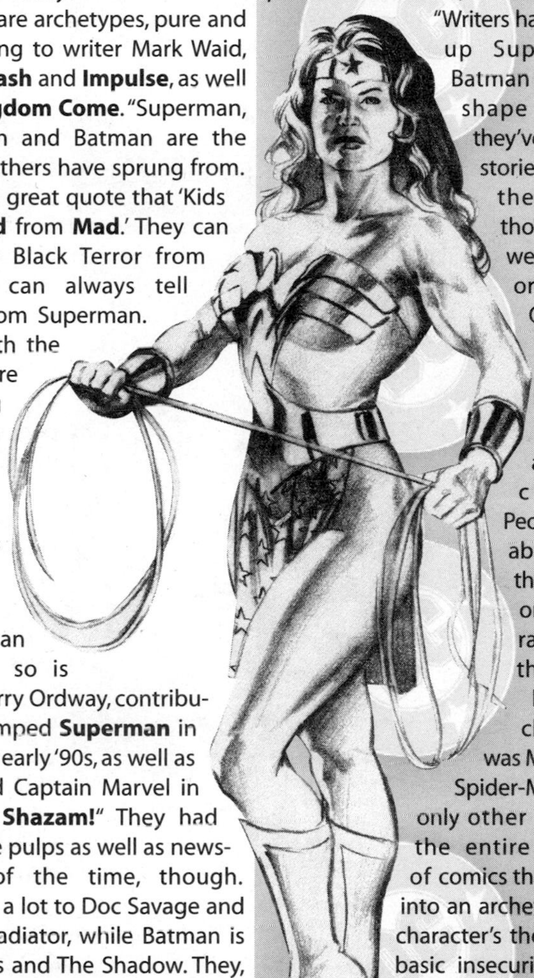

"Writers haven't screwed up Superman and Batman in any way, shape or form as they've created new stories. Very often, the writers on those books just went back to the original myth. On the other hand, character's like Charlton's Blue Beetle are 'also-ran' characters. People can probably catch on to this, but there's only one 'also-ran' character that came far later and just clicked, which was Marvel Comics' Spider-Man. He's the only other character in the entire middle era of comics that has tapped into an archetype with the character's theme of 'man's basic insecurity to do the correct thing.' In other words, no other characters from any other company have lasted nearly as long as Superman, Batman, Wonder Woman or Spider-Man, though there are other characters that are more important, have sold better, etc., etc.," Wolfman concluded.

Waid added, "One of the real appeals of Batman is, as we've proven with the Elseworlds stories, there's not a single setting or single kind of story that can't be told if you're telling it right."

John Byrne's work has been seen in both **Wonder Woman** and the **New Gods**, as well as other DC titles, but it was his six-issue mini-series **The Man of Steel** which had the greatest impact on the DC Universe. The writer/artist's mini-series redefined Superman and served as a successful relaunch for the character. A veteran of the comics industry, Byrne expands on how even the Silver Age incarnations of DC characters were icons within themselves.

A familiar scene from the Batman mythos; this version from "Batman: Year Two" ran in **Detective Comics**.

"The current versions or what remains of the current versions [of the DC heroes] were created in the fifties and early sixties," said Byrne. "These were simpler times demanding simpler heroes, and therefore the heroes were created much more as straight-forward icons. [The Silver Age] Green Lantern is a classic example. Hal Jordan got to be Green Lantern because he was the bravest man on Earth. It was just that simple. That's been stepped on in recent years with rewrites of Hal's origin, but it still gives us a very iconic character."

With the advent of a more sophisticated audience, is the fact a character is an archetype enough to be firmly planted in the public consciousness? Pulp characters of the past such as The Shadow can certainly be considered an archetype, but are they still viable today?

Dick Giordano, a former vice-president at DC Comics, as well as one of the company's most prolific creators, believes that it takes more than just being considered an original hero to reach today's more over-saturated comic reader.

"An important reason is that Superman, Batman, and some of the others are the ones that started it all. Their origins are relatively pure and it's the kind of thing that people can understand and relate to," Giordano said. "But more importantly, with a character like Superman, you have something like a 98% worldwide recognition factor. I'm not sure if it's anything more than just habit in many cases. They are everywhere you look. Even if Superman doesn't sell as many books as the X-Men, he is certainly more recognizable than others in all parts of the world."

Nothing could be a better example of Superman's popularity, the heart and soul of DC Comics, than the response to the "death" of the character several years back. Covered by both newspapers, television, and radio, the huge response to the death of "The Man of Tomorrow" surprised both fans and creators alike.

"One of the things that's true about comic books, for readers as well as creators, is that the biggest dramatic event you're going to have in a character's life is to bump him off," said Walt Simonson, whose noted works include DC's **Manhunter** in the '70s to Marvel's **Thor** in the '80s. "Virtually everytime a comic book character dies, they usually get better...unlike real life. In fact, they've done the famous imaginary story of several issues where [Superman's] poisoned by Kryptonite and shot off into space, so it isn't like Superman hasn't died before. Perhaps the power of the character in the public mind was not fully appreciated, because after all, you've got to remember that the comic was selling okay, but not in huge numbers. And really the only measure that you have, as a creator, of the character's popularity is how the book is selling. So this was really far beyond anything anybody expected."

"People were curious because we were tampering with a huge icon," Ordway said. "There was this feeling that we just shouldn't be doing this...killing him. In hindsight, probably a lot of fans were happy to see us kill him, and liked the way Doomsday looked. And once they bought the books, it no longer became a kid's embarrassment to be caught buying a super-book. **Superman** was fun again, and they hung around."

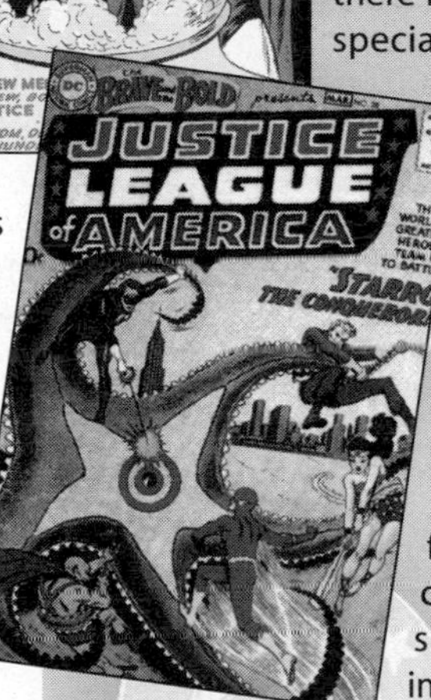

Top: **All Star Comics** #8 (1942) featured the Justice Society of America. Above: **The Brave & The Bold** #28 (1960) featured the first appearance of the Justice League of America.

And though Ordway speaks of the fans, the same can easily be said for many of today's creators. Dan Jurgens might as well be nominated as one of the hardest working men in the comics industry. Writing **Superman** for DC, Jurgens may be best known for his blockbuster DC mini-series **Zero Hour**.

"It's probably more fashionable for big name creators to sit around and bash today's big comic companies, but there is really something special about working on American icons," Jurgens said. "And if that's not the fashionable mode these days, well then I can only plead guilty. Working on these characters, you feel like you're contributing to something more important than on some other books."

THE GOOD FIGHT

Fighting the good fight for the noble cause. Protecting those who could not protect themselves. Once upon a time, these ideals were at the very center of the heroes we admired. Today, these same concepts appear to be few and far between in most comics. Of course, there are always exceptions...notable exceptions.

"I grew up when heroes were heroes," said Len Wein, co-creator of Marvel's Wolverine, the new X-Men, and DC's Swamp Thing. No stranger to the DC characters, Wein edited the massive task that was the **Who's Who in the DC Universe**.

"I grew up on superheroes who had a strict moral code, heroes who taught me a lot about right and wrong and formed my own moral code. So, what I got from those characters was a way to live my life. It's stuff I try to put in my own work and in my heroes when I can."

"Superman is probably the most noble character in comics and perhaps the most powerful," Jurgens added. "There is something incredibly attractive to readers about the ideals he symbolizes. Here's someone with this great, magnificent, colossal power, yet through it all he's just a farm kid. He's Mr. Middle America, a man filled with integrity who stands for all of us."

The original **Justice League of America** #1 (1960) launched the group into its own title.

But the Man of Steel isn't the only denizen in the DC Universe to reach that higher ground. According to Mark Waid, the very essence of most DC heroes stems from characters who want to constantly strive to do the right thing, to help their fellow man.

"The first and second string DC heroes were built to appeal to everything that is good and noble about human beings and reflect that," Waid added. "Whereas the Punisher and almost everything created at Image Comics have a much darker tone and a much darker nature. In the short run, that can be appealing to a range of readers, because every kid at one time or another wants to blow his teacher's head off, whether it's right or wrong. And that certainly appeals to the anger and the rage that most adolescents feel, but once you get to be 19, 20, 21 and you're still that mad, then you're pretty screwed up. So, that has a lot more to do with what the DC heroes were built around. They were built around virtues."

Virtues. Nobility. Morality. Words used to 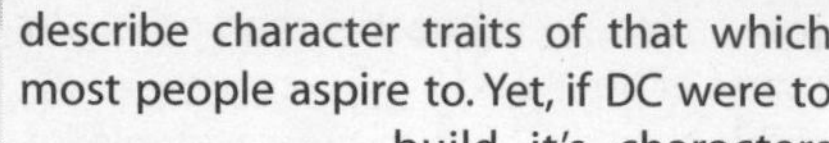 describe character traits of that which most people aspire to. Yet, if DC were to build it's characters on virtue and morality, how could they later release projects that questioned heroics in modern day society as well as promote this age of the grim and gritty? No comic company today has escaped the darkening of some, if not all, of their heroes. This raises the question as to whether DC itself was to blame for starting this movement in mainstream comics with its ambitious and tremendously successful series **The Watchmen** and **Batman: The Dark Knight Returns**.

Critics still characterize those two projects, as well as the current incarnation of DC's Batman character, as the genesis for the grim picture that modern comicdom's heroes have become. If these allegations were true, why would a company change course so drastically and forget everything it once stood for?

Every man's perspective is different from the next. One reader might see the DC heroes as virtuous, while another might look at the same characters as flat and two-dimensional. A creator might explore the idea of heroism and nobility by putting his character in a situation where the character must struggle within himself to find that which is heroic. This, according to Marv Wolfman, is just what **The Dark Knight Returns** and **The Watchmen** do, to the reader's delight.

"I don't believe **The Dark Knight Returns** was a darkening of Batman," Wolfman said. "This was a logical character who was still a hero in the end. What Frank [Miller] did on **Dark Knight** which everybody else misinterpreted was put Batman in a very dark world and had him struggle through until he discovered that he wasn't as dark as that world. That's why he was able to come out of it. Alan Moore did very much the same thing [with **The Watchmen**]. Most of these are very optimistic characters and that's the difference. Writers who came after, who were not nearly as talented as either of those two, misinterpreted and [injected flaws into] these characters, as if you can do it with everyone."

DC Editor and long-time **Batman** scribe Denny O'Neil, who has shepherded the Caped Crusader and his cohorts through both major and minor transitions, said the darkening of Batman or any of the other DC characters on his watch was originally implied by those creators who had come before.

"Batman has an iron-clad code of ethics that he will not, for any reason, violate," said O'Neil. The initial change in Batman he directed with artist Neal Adams redefined and rescued the Batman in the late '60s from the camp trappings which accompanied the very successful, yet slightly embarrassing television show. "I don't think we ever, for one second, abandoned the idea of heroism."

O'Neil said that the whole "Knightfall" storyline that ran in the **Batman** titles not too long ago was set up to once and for all prove that Bruce Wayne's Batman is not as dark as readers were misinterpreting him to be, and that worse alternatives to the current Darknight Detective existed. The storyline, which involved Bruce Wayne having to give up his Batman persona to the younger, more violent Azrael because of a debilitating injury, was to leave no doubt that though the Batman had the appearance of a vigilante, he was all hero. Late in the storyline, though, O'Neil was getting worried that the whole intent of the story had backfired in DC's proverbial face.

"I was never so relieved as [when] three quarters of the way through 'Knightfall' the hate mail started coming in by the sack full," O'Neil remembers. "Azrael [the new Batman] was a character that I had created and fans hated him, and I thought 'Thank God,' because part of 'Knightfall' was an attempt to answer was the very question of a darker knight."

ASHES TO ASHES OR ETERNAL YOUTH?

The second series, beginning with **Justice League** #1 (1987), followed the **Legends** mini-series.

Batman replaced? Superman killed off? The entire DC Universe tipped over, rebooted, shaken and stirred? Given their status in popular culture, why have these heroes been subject to revision and upheaval?

To be fair, there is no one correct answer. The revisions, though, which run the gambit from subtle twists to massive overhauls, have primarily been driven by the desire to keep up with the times or make a character more contemporary. Some of these changes have gone almost unnoticed. Others, like **Showcase** #4 (the first appearance of Barry Allen as The Flash), have marked the start of a particular era in comics.

Creators and fans have many different opinions about the success of, and even the need for, these revisions. Characters which have survived—and at times thrived—have shared the common thread of adaptability in their composition.

"I don't want to offend anybody," said

O'Neil. "I'm in the business of entertaining and yet if I were doing the version of Batman that I personally loved when I was eight years old, there would be like six dozen other old creeps like me who wouldn't miss an issue, but we would have nothing to say to a bright 13-year-old."

"My best guess about this is that the characters that survive are allowed to evolve and to change," O'Neil said. "Sometimes that just happens naturally. Sometimes, as with Green Lantern, you have to kick the process along." Hal Jordan, the Silver Age Green Lantern, was turned into a renegade and replaced in DC's 1994 universe update, **Zero Hour**, only to finally be killed off in 1996's **The Final Night**. Giving evolution that helping kick, though, isn't always met with the warmest of responses.

"Whenever you kick the process along," O'Neil said, "you're taking a chance. You know you're going to alienate a lot of readers. Any change we make we get hammered for."

With other revisions the road is less bumpy. He characterized the revamping of some characters as a logical progression rather than a rejection of what has gone before.

Justice League: A Midsummer's Nightmare #1 (1996) relaunched the team again in a mini-series which brought back the core characters.

"I would like to believe that with Batman we have kept the soul of the character, the essence, intact. What we have is just a mutation of what Bill Finger and Bob Kane started with in 1939. It is the same idea—elaborated, complicated, and refined a lot—58 years worth of a lot—but the character's essence remains the same. That's certainly true of Superman, [and] probably Wonder Woman to a somewhat lesser degree."

The costs of such changes, whether natural or kick started, do not outweigh the needs, O'Neil said.

"It's not a good idea for a company to try to bask in former glories. Eventually, you become like Paul Bunyon or Doc Savage, characters that people have a respect for, but nobody has an interest in reading," he said. "It's very much part of our job to stay as contemporary as we can. The idea of a man obsessed with crime because of his parents' death is perhaps more relevant in 1997 than it was in 1939. We've got to cast that in modern sensibility in terms of the language and props. Even the stories we tell are far more complicated and complex. Characterization was one micron deep in those days. Now, according to [frequent **Batman** writer] Alan Grant, Batman is the most fully characterized character in comics and may be one of the most fully characterized characters in melodramatic fiction.

"We've learned to some degree what works in this medium and what doesn't. Several times in the past ten years there have been wholesale revampings of the DC Universe. In each case I have resisted changing Batman's origin because it's absolutely perfect. It sure ain't broke, and I ain't gonna fix it. But costumes, props, attitudes—that stuff has to be adjusted or you have a small, intensely loyal, and gradually diminishing audience."

Since this discussion of the Golden Age superheroes centers on the cream of the crop, it's probably wise to remember that there were many failures. Indeed, even some of the successes were not as well defined as others. (This is not to say that the characters aren't fun, just that standing next to the likes of Superman, Batman or a handful of others, some superheroes do not appear to be very original.)

Archie Goodwin, a DC editor who previously served as Marvel's first editor of their Epic line, views the rejuvenation process as a chance to invigorate such characters with some fresh ideas. He illustrated the point with Dr. Mid-Nite.

"[We're] working on a **Dr. Mid-Nite** mini-series with Matt Wagner writing and John K. Snyder III illustrating. One of the things that I found very interesting when we first talked about doing this was that I went back and read the Dr. Mid-Nite origin story, and it replicates a lot of the Batman origin. So Dr. Mid-Nite was actually a cool name and a sort of cool costume, but beyond that a lot of it was pretty unoriginal in a lot of ways. So there's a case where reinventing the character, you've got a chance to take something that was not very well thought out and really embellish it, change it, and make it into something pretty cool."

JLA #1 was one of the certified hits of 1997 and returned the team to its sense of greatness.

Goodwin himself brought new life to DC's **Manhunter** in the '70s when he and Walter Simonson revived and changed the character in a short-lived but well-remembered incarnation.

In addition to **Dr. Mid-Nite**, he also commends the current incarnation of **Starman** to both new and old readers. Like many, he has only vague memories of some of the many previous incarnations of the character. The new one, he believes, has finally latched onto something.

"With what James [Robinson] and Tony [Harris] have done with the **Starman** book, they've retroactively made him a very interesting character and certainly awakened my interest," he said. "Actually, through James' fondness and Tony's interpretation of both the Golden Age characters and the characters they create now, they've given me a higher appreciation of the older characters."

Joe Kubert, the illustrator who for generations defined many of DC's classics such as **Hawkman** and **Sgt. Rock** in the same way his sons Adam and Andy defined Marvel's **X-Men**, said that characters had to be updated to have any credibility with the modern audience.

"It seemed to me," he said, "that of the stuff we were doing at the time, the character Hawkman almost had a fairy tale-ish lacing to it. You had to suspend all [disbelief], you had to suspend all normal reactions of reality in order to really believe what was going on in some of the strips. Now I find that the people who are reading the books, despite the fact that superheroes have all kinds of incredible powers, have to [have] some sort of logical explanation for those things.

"Flash Gordon got into this ridiculous looking spaceship and suddenly found himself on the planet Mongo. You have to believe that in order to have a sustained interest in what's going on."

He described today's audience as "just too sophisticated" to accept things which they recognized as totally impossible.

Both DC's **Zero Hour**, and its predecessors, **Crisis on Infinite Earths**, and **Legends**, played parts in major, well-planned universe shake-ups addressing contradictions in then-established continuity.

The previously mentioned **Showcase** #4, the book that started the Silver Age, was part of a less orchestrated—but no less radical—departure from what had gone before. Not all revisions, though, are as distinct. Some, in fact, are far less dramatic.

"In other words," said veteran artist Gil Kane, "Batman is not the same Batman that was introduced in 1939 by Bob Kane, and it isn't the same Batman that was done by Dick Sprang. Sprang's Batman was an entirely different Batman than the early Bob Kane." For readers unfamiliar with Sprang's work, he wasn't a recent revisionist. In fact, he was one of the first artists other than Bob Kane to work on the Dark Knight. His work was a departure from Kane's moody, stylized renderings.

"Dick Sprang's [Batman] wasn't atmospheric, as far as I can see," he said. "It all depended upon puzzles and solutions. It was more a 'How does Batman get out of this trap?' kind of thing, and that atmospheric characterization took second place to the way the editors saw the new material."

JLA: Paradise Lost #1 (1998).

If such subtle changes were being plied on these characters from the beginning, what was there to revise? Jerry Ordway suggested that not all creative or editorial teams have known what to do with some characters.

"Nowadays we talk from time to time about writers and artists who seem to 'inherit' a comic character, and then proceed to trash him," he said. "It's an annoying trend. We'd rather see a Prime [Malibu's take on Captain Marvel] or Supreme [Awesome Entertainment's take on Superman] than see someone try to turn an established character into something he's not. If your version is going to stray so far afield, then you might as well make up a new character and leave the icons alone."

John Byrne took a fundamental approach with Superman. He changed many of the details surrounding the character, but the last son of Krypton himself was basically as he originally was.

"What I did was to say, 'Let's go back to the very beginning, let's ask ourselves what it was that seized the public's attention so much other than the fact that, essentially, he was the first," Byrne said. "It's a little difficult all these years later to realize just what a massive impact Superman had. The character debuted in 1938, and in 1939 they had Superman Day at the World's Fair. That's how big the impact was."

He said that much of Superman's impact was due to his "primal" character. "What kind of barnacles have accumulated that take away from that? How can I get back to it?," he asked. "That was how I stripped away things like Supergirl and Superdog and Superaardvark and all the other stuff.

"With **Wonder Woman**, it's a different approach because I never really followed the book. My real awareness of Wonder Woman when I was a kid reading comic books was based pretty much entirely on her appearances in **Justice League**. **Wonder Woman** was a 'girl's book,' so I didn't buy it," he said.

For his part, Ordway's process of revitalizing Captain Marvel was less radical and more rudimentary.

"That was a conscious effort," he said. "Having worked on **Superman** along with John Byrne when **The Man of Steel** happened, as much as I liked it, it really rubbed a lot people the wrong way. We had to spend several years on Superman, for example, really winning back the core audience of people who always loved Superman, who were just alienated by the change.

"With so many of these character makeovers, creators end up throwing out too much. There's no reason why you can't try to reconcile events." Toward that end, Ordway said he believes in a back-to-basics approach, looking for the character's roots.

"On the regular **Shazam!** title, I'm trying to incorporate as many elements from the mythos as I can. Of course, I'm trying to do them in a different way, but if you read the **Archives** or if you pick up some of the back issues of the '70s series, it's not going to seem that drastically different," he said.

"A character like Sherlock Holmes has been successful for a long time because their creators haven't strayed too far from their initial concepts," Ordway said. "Holmes is the world's greatest detective, and people expect him to solve mysteries. If they portrayed him as a gun-toting action hero, it wouldn't be the character we all know and love."

Like Ordway and Byrne, not everyone believes that enormous distance from the original characters is what's called for. Len Wein questions the motivation for some of the changes.

"The initial concepts of all those characters are so strong that it's hard to kill them," he said. "Maybe that's a better way of phrasing it than whether or not they're still 'viable.' I think, and maybe it's the old fanboy in me speaking, that the industry has changed a lot of things over the past 10 years for sake of change [rather] than the sake of necessity."

JLA: Year One #1 (1998) kicked off a year-long limited series exploring the group's early days.

Wein suggests that the in-breeding in comics—today's narrow fan base becomes tomorrow's narrow base of professionals—plays a negative role in shaping the characters. "Because the bulk of professionals in this business are ex-fans, or still fans, people who've grown up on these books and who've read them their entire lives get to the point where they are now in charge of things, and say, 'I'm so sick of seeing this; I've been seeing this for the last 20 years.' They're changing things without considering the fact that we have audience base that turns over every three of four years [almost] entirely, and what is 'old hat' to us is always new to them."

While some argue over the need or use for changing the characters, others haggle over the methods of change.

Marv Wolfman was the author of **Crisis on Infinite Earths** which erased the old Earth-1, Earth-2, Earth-47 continuity in DC's titles. He considered **Crisis** a labor of love, and is not opposed to updating characters. He believes, though, that the changes must be well thought out.

"When I started reading comics and **The Flash** was started over, it was a brand new Flash. They didn't just replicate what they used to do. The big problem in comics today is that there's been no [break in publication for] the superheroes for people to revitalize them the way they need to be. You can't publish character, a lot of characters, without revamping. A lot of them just are not Superman or Batman. They're not icons that can continue on forever. A lot of them will be canceled and started again with a whole new approach," Wolfman said. "**Flash** was canceled in 1951 and was brought back in 1956, only five years later, which is nothing today. That's a subplot today," he said with a laugh.

Mark Waid is pumping a sense of nobility back into some established characters. He succeeded where several noted others had failed in making Wally West, the current Flash, seem like a hero. At Marvel he rapidly revitalized the moribund **Captain America** by, again, infusing the nobility which made the character something for others to look up to. Some of it may just be timing. Part of it most definitely is the writer.

"I'm not sure that in the '60s or '70s any writer or artist in the world could have made Jay Garrick [the Golden Age Flash] look cool with that hat," Waid said, "or Green Lantern (Alan Scott), with that garish Golden Age costume. By necessity every once in awhile there needs to be some reinventing and some updating." And while some background details might be lost in the revisions, Waid said, it's keeping the characters fresh that counts. "It's a shame that we lose history from time to time, but better for us to keep the characters primal and focused than have them weighed down with stuff."

Waid is also the author behind **Kingdom Come**, DC's Elseworlds epic set in a future where Batman, Superman and their compatriots have retired and been replaced by beings reminiscent of many of today's costumed combatants. "We joked about it being the Image superheroes taking over the DC Universe," Waid said. "The world has been taken over by a bunch of super-creeps who just throw buses at each other and they don't give a crap about the people that they are supposed to be helping. Which, to me, pretty much describes about 94% of the comic books that are being published today."

Not the comics, we should point out, that Waid is writing. And not comics that feature heroes.

Showcase #4 (1956) featured Barry Allen as The Flash and kicked off the Silver Age re-birth of superhero comics.

TOWARD A WELL-LIT HIGHWAY

With the tumult and turmoil in the industry recently—lower sales, increased competition from new media, and several publishers being acquired or going under—is there anything acting as a beacon of hope, promising a brighter future?

There are good signs, and there are more than a few. It may be a cliché, but in bad times there is often greater opportunity than good times. Sometimes all it comes down to is a faith in the material and the willingness to take a stand.

First sign: Things have been bad before. Things have been worse. They've been lots worse.

"There were a lot guys in the business," Joe Kubert said of his early days in comics, "at that time and in the last fifty years who have said 'The business is not going to last another year, another six months...[it's going] down the sewer... everything is going to be wiped out.... We're being attacked by Senate committees and they're saying this is terrible. The books are not selling this month. There's a terrible dip in sales. We're going out of business.' I never felt that way. I have always felt, and feel more strongly today than I ever have, that this business is definitely here to stay.

"If anything, it's going to grow a lot stronger. It's been accepted on a much more legitimate basis than it ever has before, and it's only going to continue in that direction."

Other signs that lend credence to Kubert's thoughts: **RollingStone**, **Spin**, and **Entertainment Weekly** have no problem including comics and comics-related material in their review sections. *Entertainment Tonight*, *E! News Daily*, and other television shows don't hesitate to air spots on popular comic creations. Hollywood, for better or worse, has fully discovered comics as a hotbed of creative ideas. These aspects are not enough to cause us to say "We've arrived in the Promised Land," but they are significant inroads.

Still other signals come from within the industry: James Robinson, author of DC's newest incarnation of **Starman**, is one of the most popular and most insightful writers in comics today. He created **Firearm** for Malibu Comics' Ultraverse, has written **WildC.A.T.S** for Image, created **Leave It To Chance** with Paul Smith for Jim Lee's creator-owned imprint Homage, and penned several creator-owned projects for other publishers. He also wrote DC's **The Golden Age**, an Elseworlds mini-series which featured many of the less-remembered Golden Age heroes in a disturbing, post-World War II story of intrigue. Despite his thoroughly modern and revisionist credentials, though, he finds himself drawn to older characters.

"There was a charm to those old characters," he said, "and a brightness in this weird, dark, shadowy world of the 1940s, that we can look back on and imagine being draped in shadow and [seeing them] through the wartime melancholy."

As new creators are drawn to the characters, so are some of the children of older creators. Adam Kubert, Joe's son, colored the **Adam Strange** mini-series for DC and has made quite a name for himself on Marvel's **X-Men**. The characters are no strangers to him. "I grew up with free DC comics strewn all over the house," he said. "They're definitely relevant today and [DC is] always looking to update their characters, as well as Marvel."

Flash #75 (1993) finally established Wally West as The Flash.

He said that the updates just reflect the current society, "It's reflected in what I do and what every creator does. It's a form of popular culture, and comic books back in the '40s reflect the thinking and what was going on at that time."

Andy Kubert, who illustrated **Adam Strange**, and has since made his mark on **X-Men** with his brother, agrees that the characters remain attractive. "When you see somebody come up, a guy like Chris Bachalo [whose work] has a fresh look to it, or Kelley Jones and what he's doing on **Batman**, that's what excites me."

Comics are gaining acceptance. It may be the multi-media, pop culture icon status of the greats like Batman and Superman. It may be the cutting edge appeal of the independent press. It may even be the fact that they never previously existed in a time when they'd been around for so long and had such protracted exposure to generations of fans and observers.

Everyone knows who Superman is. Folks who have never read a comic book know who Batman is. Others approach the same status. These characters show no signs of fading, and with their strength they can propel superhero comics into the hands of future readers.

Even ghosts of the past may be fanning the flames of future interest in comics. **Superman** writer Roger Stern, one of the architects of the "Death of Superman" storyline, said that while writer Mark Waid was on staff at DC, he unearthed a previously unpublished Siegel and Shuster Superman story from 1940 in which Kryptonite was introduced (5 or 6 years prior to its first appearance in **Superman** #61) and, more surprisingly, Lois Lane discovers Clark Kent and Superman are one and the same...and she remembers it at the conclusion of the story (this didn't happen again until 50 years later in **Action Comics** #662)! Let this one sink in:

"It was written in 1939-1940," Stern said, "about a year and a half, two years into the series, and at that point DC [then National Periodical Publications] was starting to license and market Superman. He was in newspapers, he was on the radio, the animated series was underway, they were starting negotiations which would take forever for the serials. I can see the story showing up and the new editors at DC going, 'Well, this changes everything. We can't allow this. We just sold this character. It's A. We can't give them B.' So it was killed. This would have changed everyone's idea about Superman because it was always 'Clark loves Lois, Lois loves Superman, Lois doesn't know....' It would literally have changed the history of comics as we know it."

It's not hard to see just how radically this story would've changed comics history if it had been published. It's also very easy to see now that many of the "radical" changes some fans have complained about in recent years weren't so radical at all; those changes that just played with elements of the characters, without destroying what went on before. They were glorified tune-ups for the vehicles of adventure, turning onto the access road and headed at high speed toward a well-lit highway. These changes only added to characters who'd already proven that they still had what it took—heroes that were built to last.

"The great thing about Superman is that he's such a strong character. Through all the strange permutations that he's been through over the past almost 60 years, there's still something incredibly appealing about the character that comes through all of his various incarnations. He's someone that you either want to be or want to know or wish was around," Stern added. "Superman is still a character who fights a never-ending battle for truth, justice, and the American way."

*J.C. Vaughn is Gemstone Publishing's Marketing Coordinator and is based out of our Timonium, Maryland headquarters. Scott Braden is Associate Editor of **riot Magazine**. The authors would like to thank Scott Nybakken of DC Comics for his assistance in arranging many of the interviews necessary for this article.*

When you are selling golden and silver age comics,
there is only one clear choice

*Metropolis is the biggest dealer of comic books in the world.

873 Broadway, Suite 201, New York, NY 10003 212-260-4147 Fax:212-260-4304
e-mail: comicbooks@earthlink.net

Buying

Paying up to 150%

1930 - 1964 Wanted

• Why sell to us?

Being a mail order company, we are not dependent on any one local economy to support our business.
Our customer base consists of the entire United States, as well as Canada, Great Britain, Australia, Japan, and many other countries.
Our **large** customer base allows us to buy at much higher prices than any other dealer.

WE PAY MORE BECAUSE WE SELL MORE

• We offer immediate payment.

How fast? For books and collections shipped to us we can send payment to you within 24 hours!
If we travel to you for large valuable collections, payment can be made immediately.

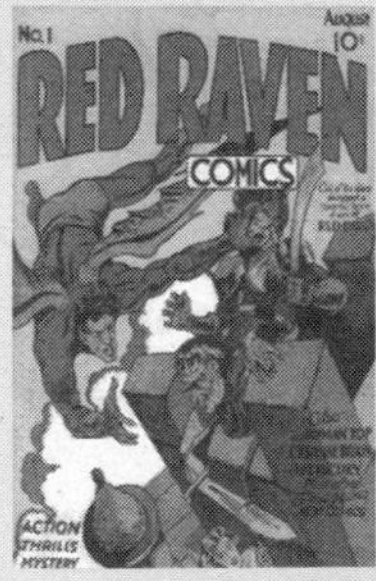

• If you ship your books to us WE pay the cost!

Please call before you ship. This allows us to give you complete and thorough shipping instructions. You can expect a reply the same day we receive your package.

• You are under NO risk or obligation at any time. If you do not except our offer we will return your books at **our** expense.

WORLD'S FINEST COMICS & COLLECTIBLES

P.O. Box 340 Castle Rock, WA 98611

Phone - (360) 274-9163 Fax - (360) 274-2270

Reach us on the Web at: www.worldsfinestcomics.com

COMICS

Of Price Guide Value!

Immediate Payment

• Reputation

We have worked hard to build a reputation of complete customer satisfaction, and welcome any inquiries you might have. We invite you to contact the author of this Price Guide as a reference.

• Expert in accurately grading and pricing

We use the standards written in this Price Guide, and will be happy to go over the grading procedure with you.

• We travel most ANYWHERE

to purchase larger and more valuable collections.

• Don't be afraid to ask questions.

We are aware that selling comic books might be something you have never done before. We are here to help and explain the process to you. That's good business.

• We offer a TOLL FREE number to call

Call and leave a message at any time, day or night at **(800) 225-4189**. Or speak to us directly at **(360) 274-9163**.

• Confidence

We are an advisor to the Overstreet Price Guide and the Overstreet Grading Guide.

WORLD'S FINEST COMICS & COLLECTIBLES

"The Right Choice"

• Dedicated To Customer Service Since 1985 •

E-Mail us at: Mark.Wilson@Worldsfinestcomics.com

Finders Fees Paid!

Here at World's Finest we know the value of a good tip. We're willing to pay well for it!

If you know someone who owns a great collection or even a few choice books, give us a call. It could be worth hundreds or even **thousands** of dollars to you!

• What are we looking for?

Large or small collections of Comic books from the years 1930 through 1960. Important books like **Action Comics**, **Detective Comics**, **Adventure** ,**Superman** **Bat Man**, **Marvel Mystery** , **Capt. America**, and **thousands more!** We want books in any condition but are extremely interested in books of high quality.

• Where to look?

There are still many unknown collections yet to be found. Check at flea markets & garage sales. Run ads in your area's newspapers. Many times, some great books will surface at comic book conventions in your area or even at your local comic book shop. Put your skills to work, it will pay off.

• What's the next step?

Call us! Put us in touch with the owner. If we are successful in buying the books, you can expect a payment of **at least 10%** and possibly as high as 20% of the purchase price. We definitely make it worth your time and effort!

And by the way, **we pay immediately**.

• Call us toll free at (800) 225-4189 and leave a message. We will get right back to you the same day.

During business hours we can be reached directly at **(360) 274-9163.**

World's Finest Comics & Collectibles

"The Right Choice"

COMIC BOOKS
WANTED

1930 through 1956

We are searching for <u>thousands</u> of GOLDENAGE COMIC BOOKS, and WILL PAY MORE than anyone for what we want - Period!

Immediate Payment

© D.C.

© D.C. Publ.

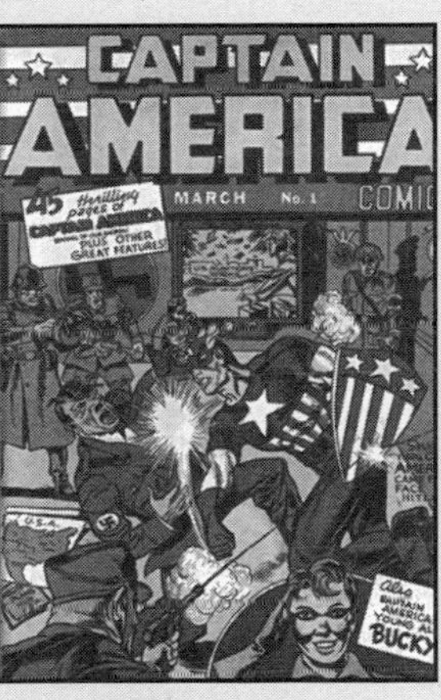

© Fox

We accept ALL grades!

WORLD'S FINEST COMICS & COLLECTIBLES

"The Right Choice"

• **Call** - (360) 274-9163 • **Fax** - (360) 274-2270

P.O. Box 340 Castle Rock, WA 98611

<u>Reach us on the Web at:</u> www.worldsfinestcomics.com

Comic Character Advertising
Wanted

Since the beginning of this century, comic characters have been used to sell a multitude of items and products - from toothpaste to linoleum. Many of these advertisements were in the form of paper posters, cardboard and metal signs, die cut cardboard standees, and cardboard displays.

If you locate any such items Give us a call!

1890 - 1950's only

I collect these items and will pay **top dollar** to get them

Superman
Mickey Mouse
Donald Duck
Popeye
The Yellow Kid

Betty Boop
Snow White
Pinocchio
Bugs Bunny
Captain Marvel

Batman
Porky Pig
Little Nemo
Tom & Jerry
Flash Gordon

1890 - 1950's

As well as **many** others

Any condition

World's Finest Comics & Collectibles

Call - (360) 274-9163 **Fax** - (360) 274-2270

E-Mail us at: Mark.Wilson@Worldsfinestcomics.com

WANTED

I collect and deal in all types of theater posters and displays. My main focus is on **Animation**. Such as: early Disney characters, Superman, Popeye, Betty Boop, Tom & Jerry, Porky Pig, Bugs Bunny, Daffy Duck, and more; also **Classic movies**. Such as: Frankenstein, Dracula, The Mummy, King Kong, The Wolfman, Casablanca, early John Wayne, Gone With The Wind, Charlie Chaplin, The Wizard Of Oz, etc.

Theater Posters & Displays

WE WANT IT!

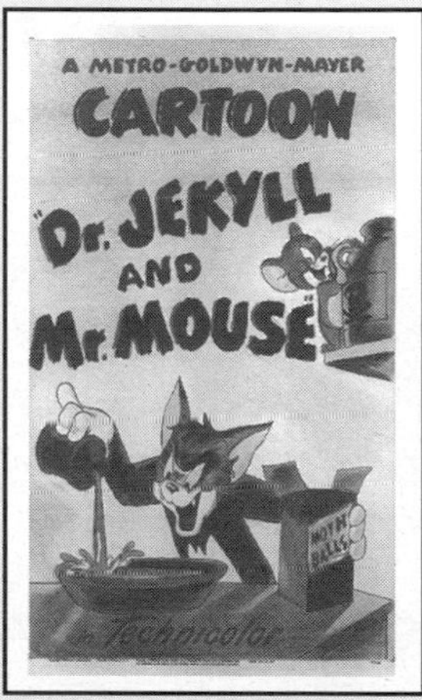

World's Finest Comics & Collectibles

Call - (360) 274-9163 **Fax** - (360) 274-2270

E-Mail us at: Mark.Wilson@Worldsfinestcomics.com

Superman Wanted

© D.C. Publ.

1938 - 1956 only

While I collect and deal in all types of Superman collectibles, my main focus is on the **paper items:** Posters, cardboard standees, cardboard displays, original Sunday proof pages, original art, and comic books.

If you have a truly great Superman piece

we want it!

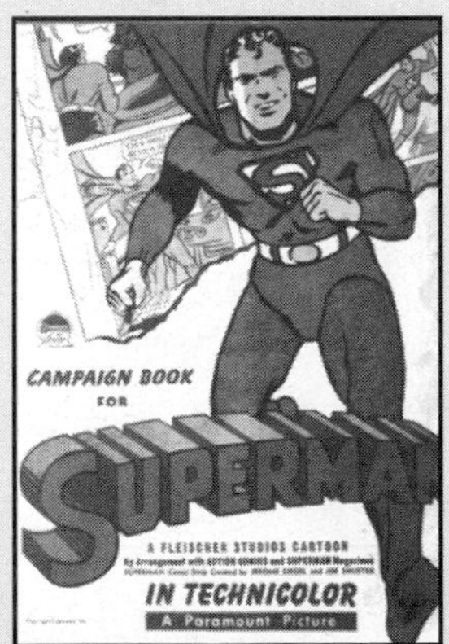

World's Finest Comics & Collectibles

"The Right Choice"

Call - (360) 274-9163 **Fax** - (360) 274-2270

E-Mail us at: Mark.Wilson@Worldsfinestcomics.com

Planning to sell an important Comic Book?

Call Us!

We simply pay more than any other dealer for the items we want

Period!

Following are just a **few** examples of prices **we will pay** Based on the NM+ condition grade.

Action Comics	#1	$165,000.00
	#2	20,000.00
	#3	11,500.00
	#4-6	6,500.00
	#7	8,500.00
Adventure	#40	35,000.00
	#41	4,000.00
	#42	5,000.00
	#44	4,000.00
	#46, 47	3,200.00
Batman	#1	60,000.00
More Fun	#55	10,000.00
	#56 - 60	3,200.00
	#61 - 66	2,500.00
Detective	#27	140,000.00
	#28	14,000.00
	#31	20,000.00
Superman	#1	85,000.00

World's Finest Comics & Collectibles

"The Right Choice"

Call - (360) 274-9163 **Fax** - (360) 274-2270

E-Mail us at: Mark.Wilson@Worldsfinestcomics.com

Why buy from World's Finest?

• ACCURATE GRADING

Our company is considered by many to be among the most conservative graders in the business. We were chosen as an advisor to the Overstreet Grading Guide because of this.

• COMPETITIVE PRICING

We price fairly. Our pricing is based on the Overstreet Guide value, and the price we paid for the book. We cater to the collector first & foremost. Investors generally find our pricing to good to be true.

• GREAT SELECTION

Reach us on the Web at:
www.worldsfinestcomics.com

We spend a great deal of our time tracking down collections. And always seem to come up with many great items. Whether you are searching for a Batman #1 or an X-Men #100, chances are that we will get it in. We deal in all types of comic books from 1900 - 1980. **Also:** Cartoon Posters, Movie Posters, Premiums, Original Art, Superman items, Animation cels, and much more!

• QUARTERLY CATALOG

We consistently put out the best catalog in the business. Not a list, but a **huge** (11" x 14") photo illustrated catalog that averages 80 pages each issue. At a cost of only $3.00 per issue (1st class post paid), it's an incredible bargain!

• ORDER YOUR COPY TODAY •

• FULLY GUARANTEED

We are the safest way to buy: Why? We offer a seven day return privilege, which takes the pressure off. If we made a mistake, give us a call. We're here to talk. If after talking to us you decide not to keep the book you ordered, simply return it for a full refund. Remember: I want you as a customer for many years. It is good business to satisfy your collecting needs.

WORLD'S FINEST COMICS & COLLECTIBLES
"THE RIGHT CHOICE"

Call: (360) 274-9163 **Write:** P.O. Box 340 Castle Rock, WA 98611

E-Mail us at: Mark.Wilson@Worldsfinestcomics.com

IF YOU ARE A COLLECTOR OF

• COMIC BOOKS • MOVIE & CARTOON POSTERS

• ORIGINAL ART • ANIMATION • SUPERMAN ITEMS

AS WELL AS SEVERAL OTHER COMIC CHARACTER ITEMS

THEN THIS CATALOG IS FOR YOU!

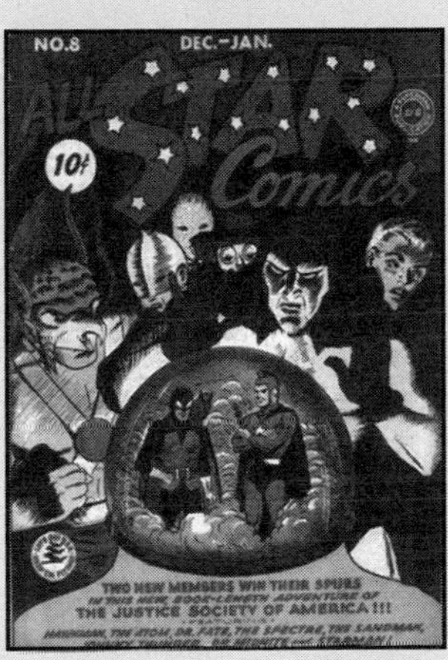

• A FULL 11 X 14"

• 84 PAGES

• PHOTO ILLUSTRATED

LOADED WITH OVER TEN THOUSAND COLLECTIBLES! ALONG WITH A LOOK AT THE MARKET, IMPORTANT COLLECTORS TIPS, AND AN AUCTION SECTION.

• ISSUED FOUR TIMES PER YEAR •

ORDER YOUR COPY TODAY!

"SIMPLY THE BEST CATALOG IN THE BUSINESS"

$3.00 per issue
$11.00 for a 1 year subscription
Sent 1st class
Foreign orders: please add an extra dollar per issue

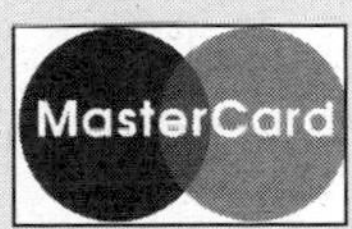

WORLD'S FINEST COMICS & COLLECTIBLES

"The Right Choice"

P.O. Box 340 Castle Rock, WA 98611
• **Call** - (360) 274-9163 • **Fax** - (360) 274-2270
E-Mail us at: Mark.Wilson@Worldsfinestcomics.com
Reach us on the Web at: www.worldsfinestcomics.com

© DIS

COMIC BOOKS WANTED

NO COLLECTION TOO LARGE OR TOO SMALL

NO ONE PAYS MORE!

IF YOU HAVE COMIC BOOKS TO SELL, CONTACT US!

WE WILL TRAVEL TO VIEW LARGE COLLECTIONS

873 Broadway Suite 201,
New York, New York 10003
(212) 260-4147 FAX: (212) 260-4304
By Appointment Only

© MEG

© DC

© DC

- Accurate Grading • Competitive Pricing
- Large Selection Of Golden & Silver age
- Complete Want List Service
- New Approval Policy (Available to Want List Customers Only)

Will ship all books under $5000 to any want list customer without prepayment.

Payment due within 7 days unless other arrangements are made. Time payments possible.

© FAW

© FAW

© MEG

SHOWCASE
© DC

METROPOLIS

873 Broadway Suite 201,
New York, New York 10003
(212) 260-4147 FAX: (212) 260-4304
By Appointment Only

© Marvel

© DC

© DC

© Marvel

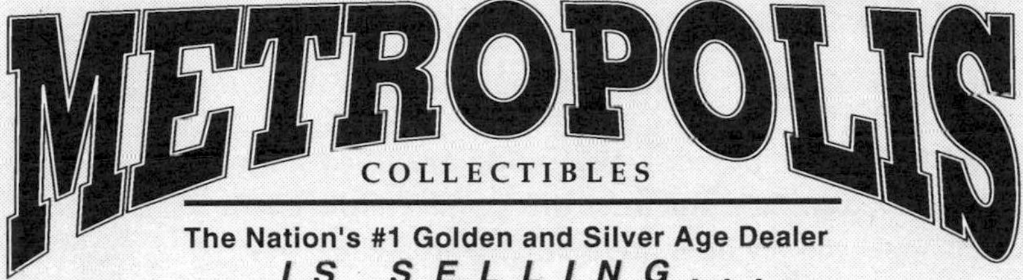

The Nation's #1 Golden and Silver Age Dealer

IS SELLING...

1. Through Our Catalog - We publish a catalog that includes the majority of our present inventory. This means millions of dollars worth of the finest comic books on the market. If you would like to receive this catalog on a regular basis, you can't subscribe to it. If you are on our mailing list and make at least one purchase every 2 years, it will be sent to you free of charge. Please call or fill out the form below to be placed on our mailing list.

2. Through Want Lists - The best way to purchase comics from Metropolis is by having your want list on file with us. Want lists are ideal for both the customer and the dealer. The customer is able to get first shot at all new acquisitions that come into our office, before they get publicly advertised. The dealer is able to sell comics directly to his customer without having to incur the cost of advertising. Year after year, our very best comic books are sold to people who have placed their want lists on file with us. We now have a fully computerized system to handle and coordinate all want lists. All we ask is that you please include both daytime and evening phone numbers and that you periodically advise us when certain books are no longer desired. It is also important to remember that we will send orders on approval to all collectors who have placed at least one order with us in the past year. This way, a collector can actually view the books he or she has ordered before payment is made. If the books meet with the collector's approval, payment must be sent within 7 days. The minimum order using the approval policy is $50. Collectors should be advised that the only books we offer for sale are pre-1969.

3. At Our New Showroom - We keep the majority of our inventory at our showroom. If you're planning to be in the New York area, please give us a call (at least 48 hours in advance) to set up an appointment to visit. We have an elaborate security system and great facilities in which to view merchandise. Our new offices are located at 873 Broadway, Suite 201, New York, NY 10003. Our office phone number is 212-260-4147 and our fax number is 212-260-4304.

4. Through CBG and Comic Book Marketplace ads - The ads we run in these and other fine publications feature the finest comic books on the market. Please remember that everything we sell through the mail is graded accurately and is fully refundable.

IF YOU'RE CONSIDERING MAKING A PURCHASE, PLEASE REMEMBER THESE 5 KEY POINTS!

1. All items we sell are covered by a return privilege.
2. Our grading standards are among the strictest and most precise in the industry.
3. If you are interested in making a large purchase, we do offer extended payment plans.
4. Our regular customers receive their books on approval.
5. There is no other dealer in America who consistently offers such a large and diverse assortment of golden and silver age comics.

Name : ____________________

Address : ____________________

City : ____________ **State:** ______ **Zip :** ____________

Daytime Phone : ____________ **Evening Phone :** ____________

☐ I have silver and or golden age comic books to sell, please call me.
☐ I would like to receive your catalogs, so please place my name on your mailing list.
☐ Enclosed is a copy of my want list containing the titles I collect, the specific issues I need and the minimum grade that I would accept.

873 BROADWAY SUITE 201, NEW YORK, NEW YORK 10003

PHONE: 212•260•4147 FAX: 212•260•4304

Just the Facts.

Fact 1: **Absolutely no other comic dealer buys more golden and silver age comics than we do.**

Although the pages of this guide are filled with other dealers offering to pay "top dollar", the simple truth is that Metropolis spends more money on more quality comic book collections, year in and year out, than any other dealer in the country. We have the funds and the expertise to back up our words. The fact is that we have spent nearly 2 million dollars on rare comic books and movie posters over the last year. If you have books to sell, call us toll-free at 1-800-229-6387. If you know of any comic book or movie poster collections, call us today for a generous finder's fees. All calls will be kept strictly confidential.

Fact 2: **Absolutely no other comic dealer sells more golden and silver books than we do.**

We simply have the best stock of golden and silver age comic books in the country. The thousands of collectors familiar with our strict grading standards and excellent service can attest to this. Chances are, if you want it, we have it.

METROPOLIS COMICS

873 Broadway Suite 201, New York, NY 10003
1-800-229-6387
1-212-260-4147
Fax: 212-260-4304

© 1995 DC COMICS

METROPOLIS

PROUDLY PRESENTS

The Metropolis Appraisal Service

and the best news is.........IT'S ABSOLUTELY FREE!

This service includes the following:
1. Value appraisal: determination of retail value based on all parameters including current desirability of book, relative scarcity, and historical significance.
2. Complete examination of books for all types of restoration.
3. Double grading system to insure greatest accuracy.

•Our staff reflects over forty years of comic evaluation and retail experience. There is not a more knowledgeable staff anywhere in the field of comic collecting.

•For more information on our free appraisal service, give us a phone call today.

•All we ask is that you limit the number of books to be examined to five (5) and that these books be from the period of 1930 to 1968. This is our field of expertise.

METROPOLIS

873 Broadway, Suite 201 New York, NY 10003
Tel: (212) 260-4147 Fax: (212) 260-4304

ART RESTORATION

Matthew Wilson, Conservator

P.O. BOX 881 / KELSO, WA 98626 / (360) 577-0351

FANTASY MASTERPIECES is a business dedicated to the art of paper conservation. It is our philosophy that art restoration should take the *whole* item into account. That means that not only should your item look as good as possible but that it should be made as structurally sound as possible. What good is a restored work of art if it disintegrates two years later? For that reason, I have developed various methods and techniques of paper art restoration unmatched anywhere else.

I am familiar with the construction of 19th & 20th century papers and have worked extensively on the most valuable of the Golden and Silver aged books from Action #1 to Amazing Fantasy #15.

When it comes to your paper art collection, whether it's a Superman #1 or a rare paper document that is priceless to you, why take a risk with anyone else? **FANTASY MASTERPIECES** is the answer.

Before

64 PAGES OF ACTION!
ALL IN FULL COLOR
THE COMPLETE STORY OF THE DARING EXPLOITS OF THE ONE AND ONLY SUPERMAN

After

Our rate is $55.00 per hour. Estimates are free & questions are always welcome. Items to be restored should be worth at least $125.00 in their present condition.

We perform the following services with expert precision:

1) Cleaning
2) Whitening
3) Tape Removal
4) Piece Replacement
5) Repair Tears
6) Spine Roll Removal
7) Deacidification
8) Color Retouching
9) Staple Replacement
10) Page Lightening

OMI OO S W TE

The following prices represent a small sample of the prices that we will pay for your comic books. Other dealers say that they will pay top dollar, but when it really comes down to it, they simply do not. If you have comics to sell, we invite you to contact every comic dealer in the country to get their offers. Then come to us to get your best offer. **Metropolis Comics** is not a store. We are a Golden and Silver Age mail-order comic company. We can afford to pay the highest price for your Golden and Silver Age comics because that is all we sell. If you wish to sell us your comic books, please either ship us the books securely via Registered U.S. Mail or UPS. However, if your collection is too large to ship, kindly send us a detailed list of what you have and we will travel directly to you. The prices below are for NM copies, however, we are interested in **all** grades. Thank You.

Action #1	$170,000
Action #242	$2,000
Adventure #40	$43,000
Adventure #48	$16,000
Adventure #61	$9,000
Adventure #210	$2,800
All-American #16	$55,000
All-American #19	$13,000
All-Star #3	$23,000
Amazing Fantasy #15	$25,000
Amaz.Spiderman #1	$15,000
Amaz.Spiderman #6	$1,200
Arrow #1	$2,200
Atom #1	$1,000
Batman #1	$55,000
Brave & the Bold #28.	$4,800
Brave & the Bold #34	$1,200
Captain America #1	$42,000
Classic Comics #1	$4,000
Detective #1	$82,000
Detective #27	$150,000
Detective #35	$9,000
Detective #38	$23,000
Detective #40	$6,500
Detective #168	$4,200
Detective #225	$4,400
Detec. Picture Stories #1	$2,900
Donald Duck #9	$5,200
Famous Funnies #1	$8,900

Famous Funnies Series #1. paying $16,000 for Very Fine copy!!!

Fantastic Comics #3	$15,000
Fantastic Four #1	$17,000
Fantastic Four #5	$2,200
Flash #105	$6,500
Flash #110	$980
Flash Comics #1	$67,000
Funnies On Parade	$7,000
Funny Pages 2#10	$2,400
Green Hornet #1	$2,200
Green Lantern #1 (GA)	$23,000
Green Lantern #1 (SA)	$3,000
Human Torch #2(#1)	$18,000
Incredible Hulk #1	$10,000
Journey into Myst. #83	$3,700
Justice League #1	$3,000
Jumbo Comics #1	$12,000
March of Comics #4	$3,500
Marvel Comics #1	$70,000
More Fun #52	$60,000
More Fun #53	$20,000
More Fun #54	$8,500
More Fun #55	$16,000
More Fun #73	$13,000
More Fun #101	$7,800
New Comics #1	$10,000
New Fun #1	$34,000
NY World's Fair '39	$16,000
New Fun #6	$22,000
Pep Comics #22	$11,000
Real Fact Comics #5	$1,400
Science Fict. Fanzine	$12,000
Showcase #4	$25,0000
Showcase #8	$8,000
Showcase #13	$4,600
Showcase #22	$6,000
Showcase #34	$1,200
Superboy #1	$7,500
Superman #1	$85,000
Superman #14	$4,000
Suspense Comics #3	$16,0000
Tales of Suspense #1	$1,600
Tales of Suspense #39	$4,000
Tales to Astonish #27	$3,700
Target Comics V1#7	$3,800
Walt Disney C&S #1	$12,000
Weird Fantasy #13(#1)	$900
Whiz #2 (#1)	$40,000
Wonder Woman #1	$13,500
Wow #1 (1936)	$7,500
Young Allies #1	$7,500
X-Men #1	$6,500

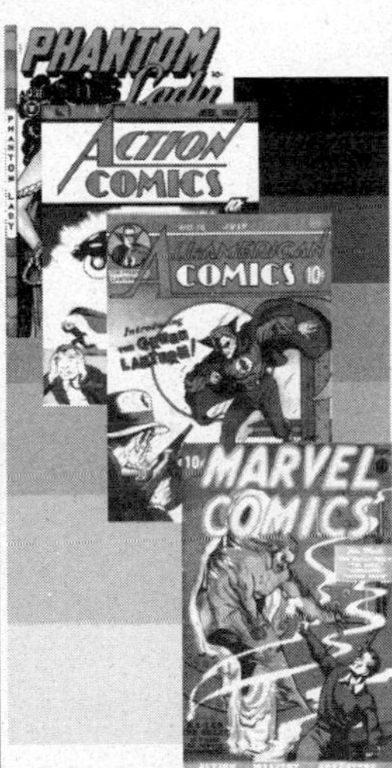

METROPOLIS

873 Broadway
Suite 201
New York, NY 10003
212-260-4147
Fax:212-260-4304

The following is a sample of the books we are purchasing:

Action Comics	#1-300
Adventure Comics	#32-320
All-American Comics	#1-102
All-Flash Quarterly	#1-32
All-Select	#1-11
All-Star Comics	#1-57
All-Winners	#1-21
Amazing Spiderman	#1-50
Amazing Man	#5-26
Amaz. Mystery Funnies	#1-24
Avengers	#1-20
Batman	#1-200
Blackhawk	#9-130
Boy Commandos	#1-32
Brave & the Bold	#1-50
Captain America	#1-78
Captain Marvel Advs.	#1-150
Challengers	#1-25
Classic Comics	#1-169
Comic Cavalcade	#1-63
Daredevil Comics	#1-60
Daredevil (MCG)	#1-15
Daring Mystery	#1-8
Detective Comics	#1-350
Donald Duck 4-Colors	#4-up
Fantastic Four	#1-50
Fight Comics	#1-86
Flash	#105-150
Flash Comics	#1-104
Funny Pages	#6-42
Green Lantern (GA)	#1-32
Green Lantern (SA)	#1-59
Hit Comics	#1-65
Human Torch	#2(#1)-38
Incredible Hulk	#1-6
Journey Into Mystery	#1-125
Jumbo Comics	#1-167
Jungle Comics	#1-163
Justice League	#1-50
Mad	#1-30
Marvel Mystery	#1-92
Military Comics	#1-43
More Fun Comics	#7-127
Mystery in Space	#1-75
Mystic Comics	#1-up
New Adventure	#12-31
New Fun Comics	#1-6
Planet Comics	#1-73
Rangers Comics	#1-69
Sensation Comics	#1-116
Showcase	#1-75
Star-Spangled Comics	#1-130
Strange Tales	#1-145
Sub-Mariner	#1-42
Superboy	#1-110
Superman	#1-175
Tales of Suspense	#1-80
Tales to Astonish	#1-80
USA Comics	#1-17
Wings Comics	#1-124
Whiz Comics	#1-155
Wonder Woman	#1-120
World's Finest	#1-100
X-Men	#1-30

JHV ASSOCIATES
is
BUYING COMICS
1935–1975

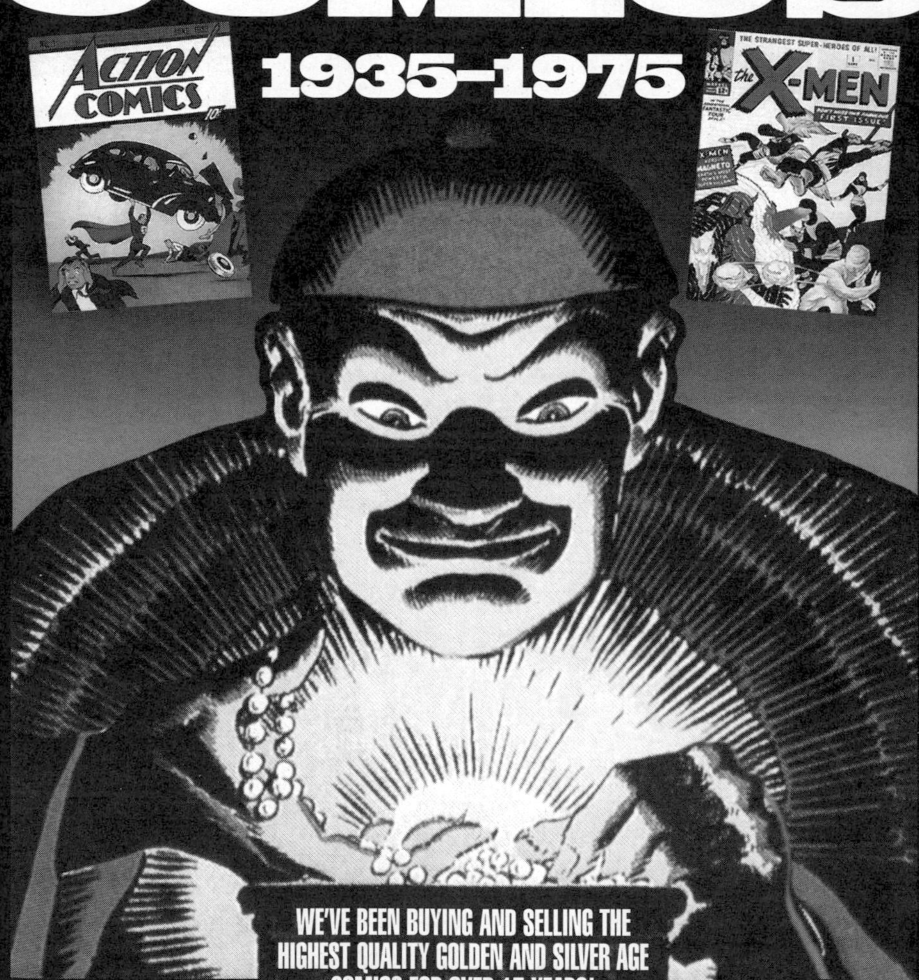

WE'VE BEEN BUYING AND SELLING THE HIGHEST QUALITY GOLDEN AND SILVER AGE COMICS FOR OVER 15 YEARS!

If you are thinking of selling your prized collection...call us!
We'll fly anywhere to meet with you and we guarantee we'll treat you right!

Ask Around (Even Our Competitors)...Our Reputation Can't Be Beat!

P.O.BOX 317, WOODBURY HEIGHTS, NEW JERSEY 08097 TEL: 609-845-4010 FAX: 609-845-3977

THE LARGEST INVENTORY OF GOLDEN AND SILVER AGE COMICS IN THE WORLD

Torch is TM & © 1996 Marvel Characters, Inc. All Rights Reserved & used with permission

METROPOLIS
COLLECTIBLES, INC.

873 Broadway Suite 201 New York, NY 10003 212-260-4147 Fax: 212-260-4304

COME VISIT OUR NEW YORK CITY SHOWROOM! OPEN WEEKDAYS, BY APPOINTMENT ONLY.

SILVER

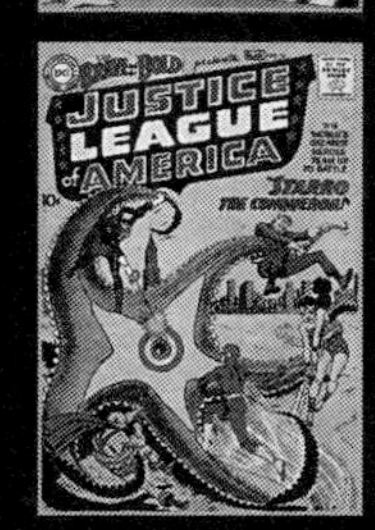

DESIGN: ARNIE SAWYER All artwork: © DC COMICS, © MARVEL ENTERTAINMENT GROUP, INC

WHY YOU SHOULD CALL US BEFORE YOU SELL YOUR COLLECTION OF COMICS, ARTWORK OR MEMORABILIA:

We make it easy! No waiting for payment, No song and dance about grading. We'll come to you; anywhere, anytime! Four Color Comics takes the risk out of selling. Treat yourself to an honest, straight-forward experience—Sell your collection to us and walk away with more money in your pocket and a smile on your face!

1000's of comics on-line!
SEARCHABLE DATABASE!
no more scrolling thru endless listings!

www.fourcolorcomics.com

FOUR COLOR
COMICS

115 West 27th Street, New York, NY 10001
TEL: (212) 675-6990 FAX: (212) 675-6145

COME VISIT OUR NEW YORK CITY SHOWROOM! OPEN WEEKDAYS, BY APPOINTMENT ONLY.

GOLD

DESIGN: ARNIE SAWYER All artwork : © DC COMICS, © MARVEL ENTERTAINMENT GROUP, INC

BUY, SELL & TRADE!!

WHY YOU SHOULD BUY FROM US:
We always have a great selection of high-grade Silver and Golden age books on hand! Plus artwork and memorabilia, too! We work hard, everyday, to give you the service, quality and attention to detail that you deserve. Our grading is strictly by Overstreet, and your satisfaction is guaranteed–or we'll give you your money back! Mail in your want list or CALL US TODAY!

FOUR COLOR COMICS

115 West 27th Street, New York, NY 10001
TEL: (212) 675-6990 FAX: (212) 675-6145

DID YOU TURN INTO A
MONSTER
THE LAST TIME YOU RECEIVED
A MAIL ORDER?
If this looks familiar, treat yourself to honest grading and fair pricing by buying your Silver and Golden Age comics from us!
At FOUR COLOR COMICS, we specialize in treating the customer right and we unconditionally guarantee every book we sell!
DESIGN: ARNIE SAWYER All artwork: © DC COMICS, © MARVEL ENTERTAINMENT GROUP, INC
Fantastic Four
10¢
FEATURING "THE THING!" "MR. FANTASTIC!" "HUMAN TORCH!" "INVISIBLE GIRL!" TOGETHER FOR THE FIRST TIME IN ONE MIGHTY MAGAZINE!
FOUR COLOR
COMICS
NY SHOWROOM (By Appointment Only): 115 West 27th St, New York, NY 10001 (212) 675-6990 Fax:(212) 675-6145
IF YOU'VE GOT BOOKS TO SELL, CALL IMMEDIATELY: (212) 675-6990

1000's
of comics on-line!
SEARCHABLE DATABASE!
no more scrolling thru endless listings!

JUST IMAGINE!

one of the world's most amazing inventories of Golden and Silver Age comic books—in grades from strict Near Mint to collectible reading copies, single books and complete runs...

24 HOURS A DAY
7 DAYS A WEEK
and 365 DAYS A YEAR!!

All in a completely searchable database so you can locate a specific copy of the book you need without painfully scrolling through hundreds of titles and thousands of listings!!

File Edit View Bookmarks Options Directory Win
Netscape: four color comics
Back Forward Home Reload Images Open Print Find Stop

FAN FORUM
FOUR COLOR COMICS
COMPANY INFO.
SEARCH COMICS!

Detective Comics
Action Comics

DESIGN: ARNIE SAWYER All artwork: © DC COMICS, © MARVEL ENTERTAINMENT GROUP, INC

FOUR COLOR COMICS

NY SHOWROOM: 115 West 27th St, New York, NY 10001 (212) 675-6990 Fax:(212) 675-6145

www.fourcolorcomics.com

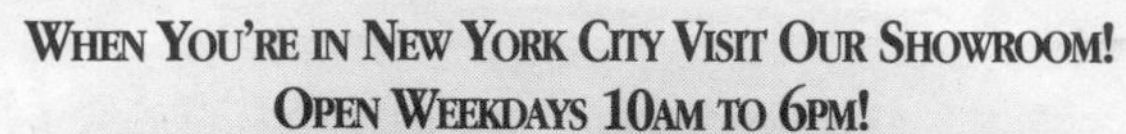

FOUR COLOR COMICS

Send us your want list today!

115 West 27th St.
New York, NY 10001

Tel: (212) 675-6990 • Fax: (212) 675-6145
Keybooks@aol.com
www.fourColorComics.com

FOUR COLOR
COMICS
BUYING PRE-1955 POSTERS
I buy, sell, and collect movie posters and theater displays. I can and will pay you the highest price for your poster or collection of posters. Call me before you sell.
Of particular interest:
EARLY DISNEY
UNIVERSAL HORROR
1950'S SCIENCE-FICTION
1930'S POSTERS
115 West 27th St.
New York, NY 10001
Tel: (212) 675-6990
Fax: (212) 675-6145
Keybooks@aol.com
www.fourColorComics.com

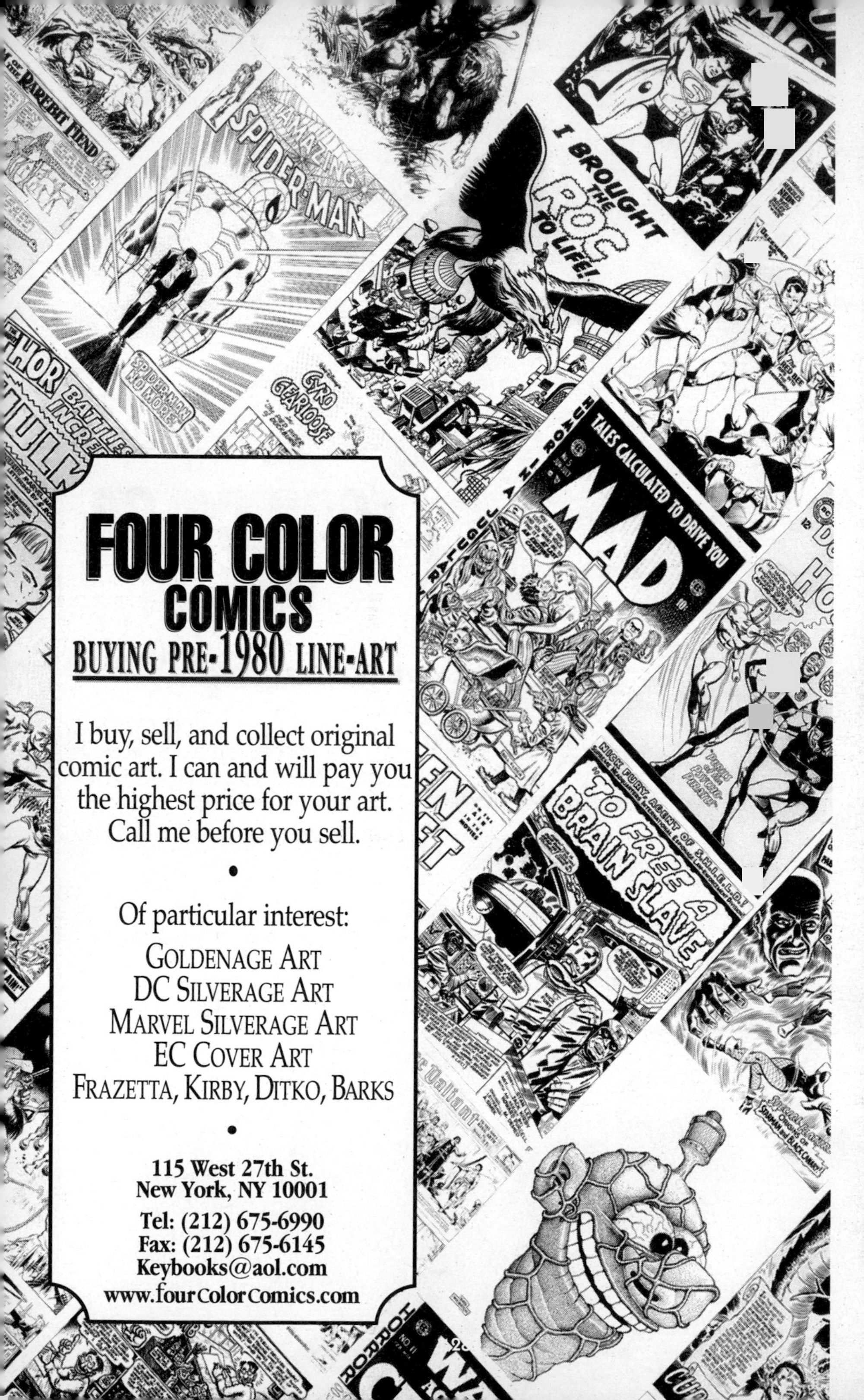
FOUR COLOR
COMICS
BUYING PRE-1980 LINE-ART
I buy, sell, and collect original comic art. I can and will pay you the highest price for your art. Call me before you sell.
Of particular interest:
GOLDENAGE ART
DC SILVERAGE ART
MARVEL SILVERAGE ART
EC COVER ART
FRAZETTA, KIRBY, DITKO, BARKS
115 West 27th St.
New York, NY 10001
Tel: (212) 675-6990
Fax: (212) 675-6145
Keybooks@aol.com
www.fourColorComics.com
SPIDER-MAN
I BROUGHT THE ROC TO LIFE!
TALES CALCULATED TO DRIVE YOU MAD
TO FREE A BRAIN SLAVE
GYRO GEARLOOSE
RAREBIT FIEND
THOR BATTLES THE INCREDIBLE HULK

FOUR COLOR COMICS

Many of you may not be aware of how generously we pay for books.. So we thought we'd show you.

• BUYING • BUYING •

SILVER AGE	VF	NM
Adventure 210	1,600	3,000
Adventure 247	2,000	4,000
Amazing Fantasy 15	9,000	18,000
Amazing Spiderman 1	5,500	16,000
Avengers	1,000	2,000
Batman 100	1,000	2,500
Brave & the Bold 28	2,000	4,500
Fantastic Four 1	5,500	15,000
Flash 105	2,500	6,500
Green Lantern 1	1,250	3,000
Incredible Hulk 1	3,500	8,500
JLA 1	1,500	3,000
MAD 1	2,500	5,000
Showcase 4	8,000	20,000
Showcase 6	2,000	3,500
Showcase 8	4,500	9,500
Showcase 9	2,800	6,000
Strange Tales 1	1,500	2,500
Sup's Girlfriend Lois 1	1,300	2,500
Sup's Pal Jimmy 1	2,500	6,000
Tales of Suspense 1	900	1,750
Tales of Suspense 39	1,750	3,500
Tales to Astonish 1	800	1,500
Tales of the Unexpected	750	1,500
X-Men 1	2,000	6,500

GOLDEN AGE	VF	NM
Action 1	90,000	175,000
Adventure 40	18,000	40,000
All American16	35,000	55,000
All American 19	7,500	14,000
All Select 1	3,500	7,500
All Star 3	20,000	38,000
All Star 8	50,000	25,000
Batman 1	35,000	65,000
Captain America 1	25,000	45,000
Captain Marvel 1	10,000	18,000
Detective 1	45,000	75,000
Detective 27	90,000	160,000
Detective 33	20,000	35,000
Detective 38	15,000	25,000
Flash 1	40,000	70,000
Green Lantern 1	15,000	25,000
Human Torch 1	10,000	18,000
Marvel Comics 1	45,000	75,000
More Fun 52	38,000	65,000
New Comics 1	7,000	11,000
Sensation 1	12,000	20,000
Superman 1	55,000	90,000
WDisney C & S 1	8,500	14,000
Whiz 1	9,000	35,000
Young Allies	4,500	7,500

OPEN WEEKDAYS, 10 AM TO 5 PM: BY APPOINTMENT ONLY

CALL ROBERT ROGOVIN (212) 675-6990

NEW YORK SHOWROOM:

115 W. 27th St, NY, NY 10001 TEL: (212) 675-6990 FAX: (212) 675-6145

Visit our on-line **SEARCHABLE DATABASE!**

1000's of Golden and Silver Age comics available without scrolling thru endless listings!

www.fourcolorcomics.com

TOP DOLLAR PAID! WE PAY THE MOST!

CALL ME TOLL-FREE 800-462-4905

Tired of hearing these type of statements only to be offered less than you really wanted for your most prized golden age or silver age comic books?

NOTE: CALL ONLY WITH PRE 1963 BOOKS

Whether you're selling a new found collection or just a few comic books from your personal collection, my cash offer for your 1933 to 1963 books will be based on current OVERSTREET PRICE GUIDE information.

ATTENTION ADVANCED COLLECTORS:

I can and have paid TOP DOLLAR for ultra high grade books or pedigrees ie. Mile Highs, Allentowns, San Francisco, Chicago, etc... If you're selling, I'm buying. Please call me Toll-Free.

BEFORE YOU SETTLE FOR LESS FOR YOUR 1933-1963 BOOKS, PLEASE CALL OR WRITE FOR MY CASH OFFER.

FRANK SIMMONS

1876 FULTON AVE., SACRAMENTO, CALIFORNIA 95825

PHONE#: (916) 676-3122

Golden Age

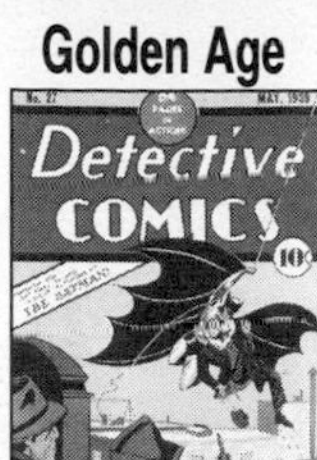

WANT LIST COMICS

WE FILL WANT LISTS

Silver Age

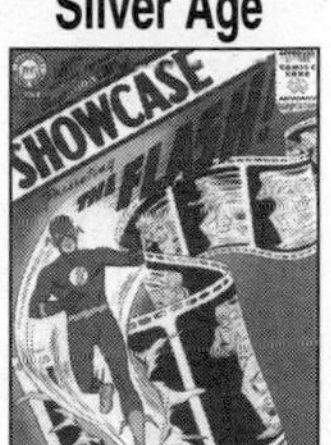

ATTENTION: INVESTORS AND COLLECTORS

Can't find those missing comic books **yet?** Are these books priced **TOO high** or are they just **IMPOSSIBLE** to find? Have local stores and conventions not produced what you want? **(Have you sent us a want list yet?)**

WHAT ARE YOU WAITING FOR?

"The **Batman #1** you sold me was in the **nicest, unrestored condition** I've ever seen!", **Bob Overstreet, author "The Official Overstreet Comic Book Price Guide."**

"I'm glad that you have a **great selection** of **Golden Age** and **Silver Age** comics in stock. You have been able to constantly find books to fill some very tough missing holes in my collection. I also appreciate your **consistent, tight** grading and **fair** prices!"

Dan Hampton, Las Cruces, NM

These are just two of the **many** satisfied customers that have bought books from us in the past. Over the years, we have developed a **very strong return customer base** because we **ACCURATELY** price, grade, and describe books (in detail) over the phone and through the mail. If a book is restored, we will tell you **up front** so you won't be **UNpleasantly** surprised or deceived. In the past few years, we have acquired nearly **EVERY** major **Golden Age** and **Silver Age** book **more than once** for our many want list clients. These include books like **Action 1, Detective 1, Detective 27, Marvel 1, Superman 1** and more recent gems like **AF 15, FF 1, Hulk 1, Flash 105** and **Showcase 4, 8, 22. OUR SPECIALTY IS GOLDEN AGE AND SILVER AGE BOOKS (1933 - 1969)**, but we do carry some issues up to 1984. Please check out our **great selection** of old books!

We don't claim that we can fill every list all the time, but if any company can accomplish this, it **would certainly** be us! We can say this with **much confidence** because we travel to the **majority** of the 50 states and Canada plus attend many of the major comic book conventions (San Diego, Chicago, Detroit, etc.) to uncover books **you would not** have the opportunity to find. When we are not on the road, we spend **MANY** hours on the phone locating books from our **long** list of past and present comic sources we've developed over the **25 years** we have been dealing in comic books. When sending your want list, **please** include a self-addressed stamped envelope if possible, **your phone number,** and a good time to reach you. We **DON'T** send out catalogs, so **please** ask for **specific** books and **conditions** desired. We will contact you **when** we find the items you've requested. **Phone calls are also welcomed. WE WILL GLADLY SUGGEST AND PERSONALLY PUT TOGETHER COMIC BOOK INVESTMENT PORTFOLIOS FOR BIG AND SMALL INVESTORS. OUR ADVICE IS ALWAYS FREE!**

SAVE YOURSELF ALL THE HASSLE AND LET US DO THE LOOKING FOR YOU!

CALL, FAX, OR MAIL US YOUR WANT LIST!

YOU *HAVE NOTHING TO LOSE AND EVERTHING ON YOUR WANT LIST TO GAIN!!*

Competitive pricing always. Accurate grading. Friendly, courteous service. **Interest free time payments/layaways possible.** Visa, Mastercard and American Express accepted for total payment **OR** down payment on books. Seven day money back guarantee before a sale is considered final. No collect calls please.

Our office/warehouse # is:

1-918-299-0440

Call us anytime between 1 pm and 8 pm, CST
Please ask for our private FAX #

WANT LIST COMICS

BOX 701932
TULSA, OK 74170-1932

Senior Advisor to the Overstreet Comic Price Guide
CBG Customer Service Award
References gladly provided!

BUYING!

Consider The Following:

■Willing to pay up to 200% of Overstreet Price Guide(or more depending upon current market conditions). Do not settle for less.

■ Buying all comics 1900-1970 in all grades!Whether one book or 10,000. I can pay instantly!

■ Having been involved in collecting/selling for 22 years, I have built my reputation on courteous, professional service (I do not believe in high pressure transactions-I do believe in the seller being fully informed!) Please ask questions

■ Advisor to Overstreet.

■ Finders fee paid for information leading to purchase. I will travel to view large collections.

SELLING - TRADING

●Accurate Grading & Pricing
●Dependable, Reputable Service
●Large Selection of Golden Age & Silver Age Marvel & DC
●Constantly Acquiring New Collections
●Satisfaction Guaranteed
●Send $2.00 For Catalog Or Peruse Our Catalog At http://www.a-1comics.com

A-1 Comics

Brian Peets - Owner
5800 Madison Ave.
Sacramento, CA 95841
(916)331-9203 Fax(916)331-2141

"Serving The West Since 1974"

COMIC BOOKS WANTED!

generous finder's fees

free appraisals

we travel to you

P.O. Box 354 Eastpointe, MI 48021

Toll Free: 888-VIA-BUYS

vintage
investment
associates

VIA Sells

Spiderman #1 NM
"Bethlehem Copy"

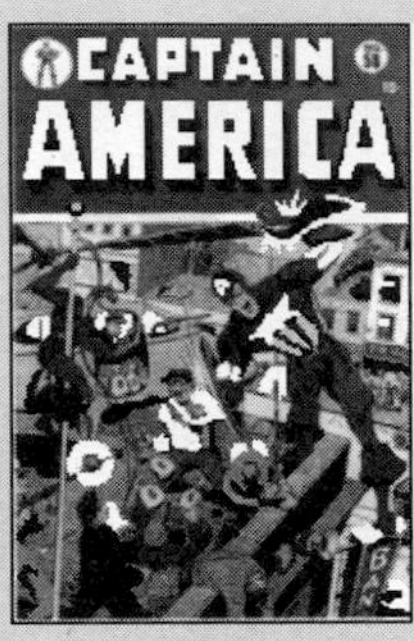

Capt. America #58 NM
"D Collection"

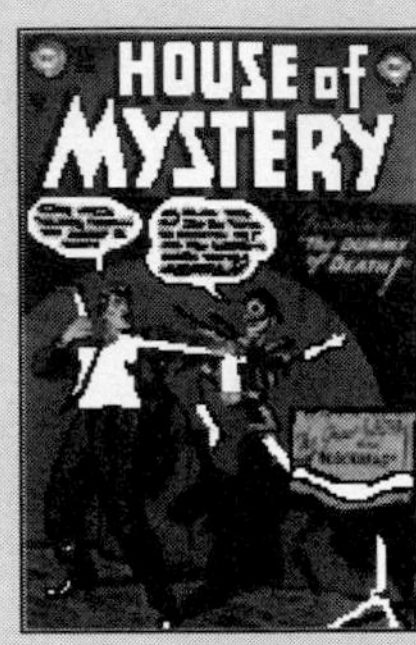

House of Mystery #3 NM
"Aurora Collection"

- **Visit our Web site - www.viabuys.com for a complete listing of books.**
- **Phone toll free: 1- 888- VIABUYS**
  P.O. Box 354 Eastpointe, MI 48021
- **Credit cards accepted**
  Layaway plans offered

VIA Buys

Three locations nation wide

Absolute top dollar paid

Immediate cash payment

We travel to you

Phone toll free: 1- 888- VIABUYS

This is what I ask myself every time I hear of a significant collection being sold for less money than I would pay, and I wasn't contacted. You have nothing to lose and everything to gain by contacting me. I have purchased many of the major collections over the years. We are serious about buying your comics and paying you the most for them.

If you have comics or related items for sale, please call or send a list for my quote. Remember, no collection is too large or small, even if it's $200,000 or more.

These are some of the high prices I will pay for comics. Percentages stated will be paid for any grade unless otherwise noted, and are based on the Overstreet Guide.

—JAMES F. PAYETTE

Action #2–20	85%
Action #21–200	65%
Action #1 (Mint)	125%
Adventure #247	75%
All American #16 (Mint)	150%
All Star #8	70%
Amazing Man	70%
Amazing Mystery Funnies	70%
The Arrow	70%
Batman #2–100	60%
Batman #1 (Mint)	150%
Bob Steele	70%
Detective #1–26	85%
Detective #28–100	60%
Detective #27 (Mint)	125%
Green Lantern #1 (Mint)	150%
Jackie Gleason #1–12	70%
Keen Detective Funnies	70%
Ken Maynard	70%
More Fun #7–51	75%
New Adventure #12–31	80%
New Comics #1–11	70%
New Fun #1–6	70%
Sunset Carson	70%
Superman #1 (Mint)	150%
Whip Wilson	70%

We are also paying 70% of Guide for the following:

All Winners
Andy Devine
Captain America (1st)
Congo Bill
Detective Eye
Detective Picture Stories
Funny Pages
Funny Picture Stories
Hangman
Jumbo 1–10
Mystery Men
Marvel Mystery
Tim McCoy
Wonder Comics (Fox 1 & 2)

BUYING & SELLING GOLDEN AND SILVER AGE COMICS SINCE 1975

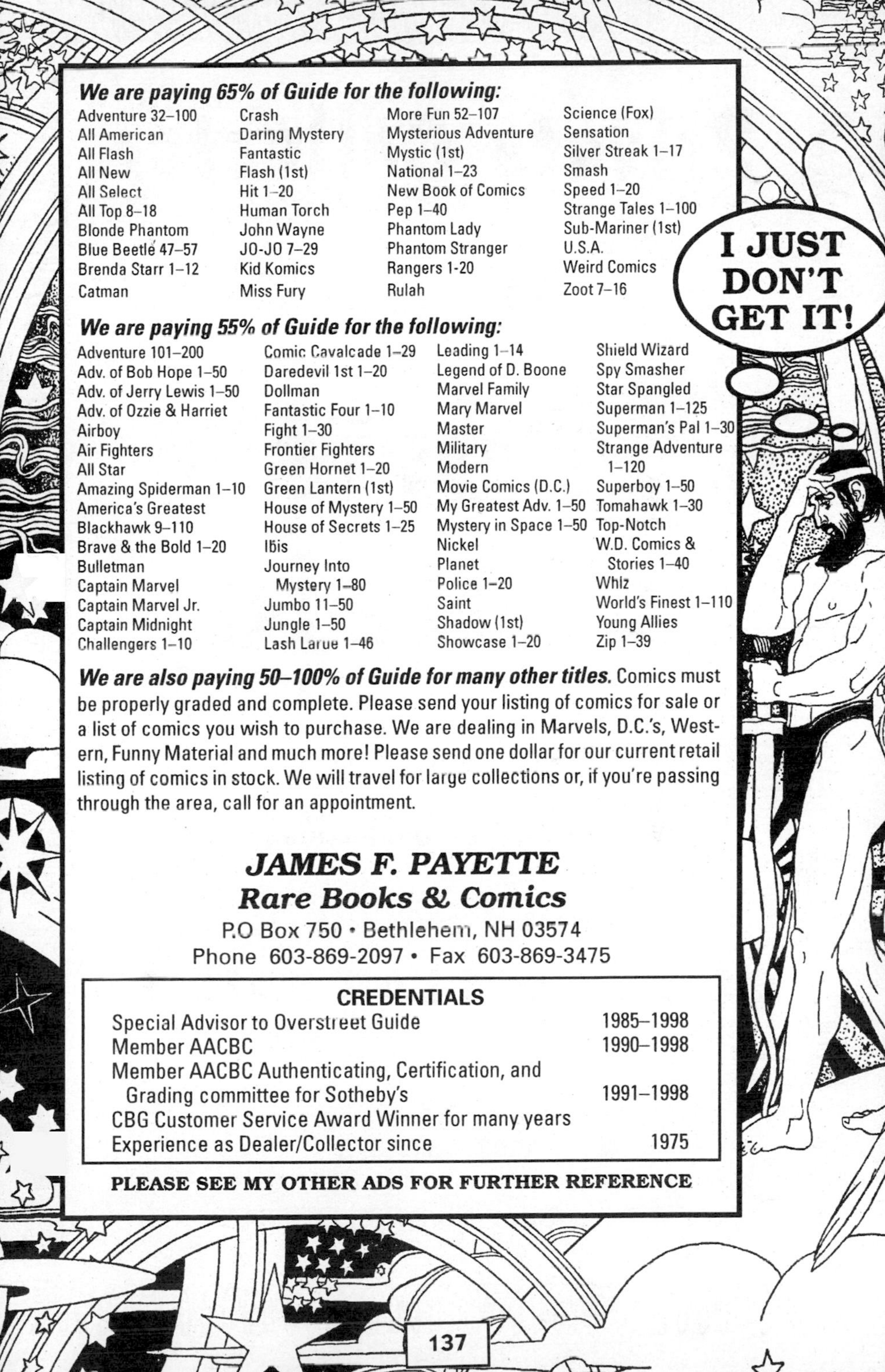
We are paying 65% of Guide for the following:
Adventure 32–100
All American
All Flash
All New
All Select
All Top 8–18
Blonde Phantom
Blue Beetle 47–57
Brenda Starr 1–12
Catman
Crash
Daring Mystery
Fantastic
Flash (1st)
Hit 1–20
Human Torch
John Wayne
JO-JO 7–29
Kid Komics
Miss Fury
More Fun 52–107
Mysterious Adventure
Mystic (1st)
National 1–23
New Book of Comics
Pep 1–40
Phantom Lady
Phantom Stranger
Rangers 1-20
Rulah
Science (Fox)
Sensation
Silver Streak 1–17
Smash
Speed 1–20
Strange Tales 1–100
Sub-Mariner (1st)
U.S.A.
Weird Comics
Zoot 7–16
I JUST DON'T GET IT!
We are paying 55% of Guide for the following:
Adventure 101–200
Adv. of Bob Hope 1–50
Adv. of Jerry Lewis 1–50
Adv. of Ozzie & Harriet
Airboy
Air Fighters
All Star
Amazing Spiderman 1–10
America's Greatest
Blackhawk 9–110
Brave & the Bold 1–20
Bulletman
Captain Marvel
Captain Marvel Jr.
Captain Midnight
Challengers 1–10
Comic Cavalcade 1–29
Daredevil 1st 1–20
Dollman
Fantastic Four 1–10
Fight 1–30
Frontier Fighters
Green Hornet 1–20
Green Lantern (1st)
House of Mystery 1–50
House of Secrets 1–25
Ibis
Journey Into Mystery 1–80
Jumbo 11–50
Jungle 1–50
Lash Larue 1–46
Leading 1–14
Legend of D. Boone
Marvel Family
Mary Marvel
Master
Military
Modern
Movie Comics (D.C.)
My Greatest Adv. 1–50
Mystery in Space 1–50
Nickel
Planet
Police 1–20
Saint
Shadow (1st)
Showcase 1–20
Shield Wizard
Spy Smasher
Star Spangled
Superman 1–125
Superman's Pal 1–30
Strange Adventure 1–120
Superboy 1–50
Tomahawk 1–30
Top-Notch
W.D. Comics & Stories 1–40
Whiz
World's Finest 1–110
Young Allies
Zip 1–39
We are also paying 50–100% of Guide for many other titles. Comics must be properly graded and complete. Please send your listing of comics for sale or a list of comics you wish to purchase. We are dealing in Marvels, D.C.'s, Western, Funny Material and much more! Please send one dollar for our current retail listing of comics in stock. We will travel for large collections or, if you're passing through the area, call for an appointment.
JAMES F. PAYETTE
Rare Books & Comics
P.O Box 750 • Bethlehem, NH 03574
Phone 603-869-2097 • Fax 603-869-3475
CREDENTIALS
Special Advisor to Overstreet Guide 1985–1998
Member AACBC 1990–1998
Member AACBC Authenticating, Certification, and Grading committee for Sotheby's 1991–1998
CBG Customer Service Award Winner for many years
Experience as Dealer/Collector since 1975
PLEASE SEE MY OTHER ADS FOR FURTHER REFERENCE

Private Collector

seeking original

Boris Vallejo

Oil paintings for
Savage Sword of Conan Magazines

$$ TOP DOLLAR PAID $$

Daniel Greenhalgh
(203) 484-4579

67 Gail Drive, Northford, CT 06472

SHOWCASE NEW ENGLAND

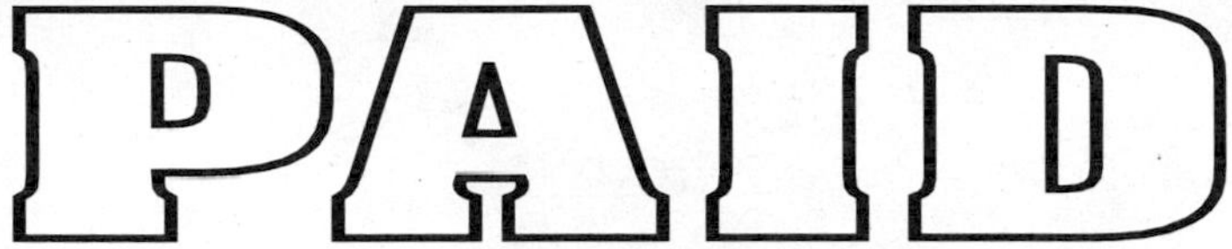

$400,000
PAID
in Canada, 1997

We pay amounts from

$1,000 to $50,000

EVERY WEEK

for books we need.

BOOKS SHOWN BY APPOINTMENT ONLY • WEEKDAYS 9:30 a.m. - 5:30 p.m. E.S.T.
CALL DANIEL GREENHALGH TODAY

CBG Customer Service Award Winner 1994, 1995, 1996, 1997
Member AACBC Authenticity, Certification, & Grading Committee
(Christie's Auction) 1994, 1995, 1996, 1997 (Sotheby's Auction) 1995, 1996, 1997, 1998
Special Advisor to Overstreet Annual 1994, 1995, 1996, 1997, 1998

67 GAIL DRIVE • NORTHFORD, CT 06472 • (203) 484-4579 • FAX (203) 484-4837

6517 Westheimer
(at Hillcroft)
Houston, Texas 77057
(713) 780-0675

2204-D FM 1960 W.
(at Kuykendahl)
Houston, Texas 77090
(281) 444-9763

fax (713) 780-2366

www.bedrockcity.com

Shazam © 1997 D.C. Comics

BELIEVE IT OR NOT!

Albuquerque	**Houston**	**New Orleans**	**Birmingham**
Indianapolis	**Nashville**	**Chicago**	**Jackson**
Omaha	**Cincinnati**	**Kansas City**	**San Antonio**
Dallas	**Little Rock**	**Shreveport**	**Denver**
Louisville	**Sioux Falls**	**Des Moines**	**Memphis**
St. Louis	**El Paso**	**Minneapolis**	**Wichita**

WE ARE **JUST A 1 DAY DRIVE** (OR LESS) FROM YOU!!

We are a one day drive from you and will **gladly** travel to you if have quality **PRE-1965** comic books to sell. Although many dealers "claim" they will fly to you, the simple truth is that most will ask you to **mail** some if not all of your books for their personal inspection and grading. We realize that many people are uncomfortable with this and so **we'll make it easy for you** by coming to your town and meeting you **personally**. We have actually driven to towns like **Jasper, AR, Lone Tree, IA** and **Grand Forks, ND** to purchase books and collections for our clients. We will pay you **CASH** on the spot, **no** time payments, **no** I.O.U.'s, **no** promises, **no** "cherry picking" books from your collection and **no** "we'll take it on consignment" options. All you need to do is **call us (preferred)**, FAX, or mail us a list of what you have and tell us **when** we can come to you. **It's just that simple!**

In the past few years, we have purchased books in **ALL** grades (some for **WORLD RECORD PRICES**) like **Action 1, Detective 27, Marvel 1, Superman 1, Captain America 1, All American 16, New Fun 2,** and **Batman 1** plus every "key" **Marvel** and **DC Silver Age** issue imaginable! Many of our purchases have come in **DIRECT COMPETITION** with other dealers who advertise in this guide. We don't mind the competition because we at WANT LIST COMICS can be **EXTREMELY COMPETITIVE** when we purchase individual books or collections. Often times, it's not who has **(or claims to have)** the most money that counts, it's who **has** the most established customers **looking anxiously** for comic books to buy. Because we have **many** want list customers waiting in line for books we purchase (*please note our other ads in this guide) we can usually expect a quick return on our money invested and therefore justify buying books at **very, very** high percentages of current Overstreet. We have purchased **some books at OVER 250% Guide** because of customer demand!

Give us a chance to make an offer **IN PERSON** before shipping your books to someplace you've never been before. **Don't** deal with a fast talking voice on the phone . . . **don't** spend money on postage and worry about your books arriving with damage or loss to their destination . . . **don't** let someone talk you into something you really don't want to do. **YOU DON'T HAVE TO!** If you need references of people we've bought books from in the past · · **no problem** · · we'll get you in contact with them and you can check us out. **We want to provide you with many good reasons for doing business with us. Please give us that opportunity!**

WE PAY GENEROUS FINDER'S FEES FOR ANY INFORMATION LEADING TO THE PURCHASE OF INDIVIDUAL BOOKS OR COLLECTIONS

FOR A QUICK REPLY CALL, FAX, OR WRITE US AT:

Our office/warehouse # is:

1-918-299-0440

Call us anytime between 1 pm and 8 pm, CST

Please ask for our private FAX #

WANT LIST COMICS

BOX 701932

TULSA, OK 74170-1932

Senior Advisor to the Overstreet Comic Price Guide

CBG Customer Service Award

References gladly provided!

SELLING

SERVING CLIENTS
WORLDWIDE OVER 14 YEARS

HARD TO FIND BOOKS
ACCURATE GRADING
COMPETITIVE PRICING
PROMPT, PROFESSIONAL SERVICE
SPECIALIZING IN GOLDEN & SILVER AGE
WANT LIST

OVER 14 YEARS EXPERIENCE SELLING
SENIOR ADVISOR TO
OVERSTREET PRICE GUIDE
PROMPT, PROFESSIONAL SERVICE
SPECIALIZING IN GOLDEN AND SILVER AGE

CALL, WRITE OR FAX:

HARLEY YEE

P.O. BOX 51758
LIVONIA, MI 48151-5758
PHONE: 800.731.1029 OR 734.421.7921
FAX: 734.421.7928

CALL OR WRITE FOR A FREE CATALOG

©Batman & Robin DC Publications

BUYING

I WILL TRAVEL ANYWHERE TO VIEW YOUR COLLECTION

HIGHEST PRICES PAID
IMMEDIATE CASH
NO COLLECTION TOO BIG OR TOO SMALL
COMPLETE CUSTOMER SATISFACTION
EXPERIENCED, PROFESSIONAL SERVICE
SENIOR ADVISOR TO OVERSTREET PRICE GUIDE

OVER 14 YEAR EXPERIENCE BUYING
SENIOR ADVISOR TO
OVERSTREET PRICE GUIDE
PROMPT, PROFESSIONAL SERVICE
SPECIALIZING IN GOLDEN AND SILVER AGE

CALL, WRITE OR FAX:

HARLEY YEE

P.O. BOX 51758
LIVONIA, MI 48151-5758
PHONE: 800.731.1029 OR 734.421.7921
FAX: 734.421.7928

CALL OR WRITE FOR A FREE CATALOG

©Batman & Robin DC Publications

The World's Leading Auction House for Comics

Sotheby's Founded 1744

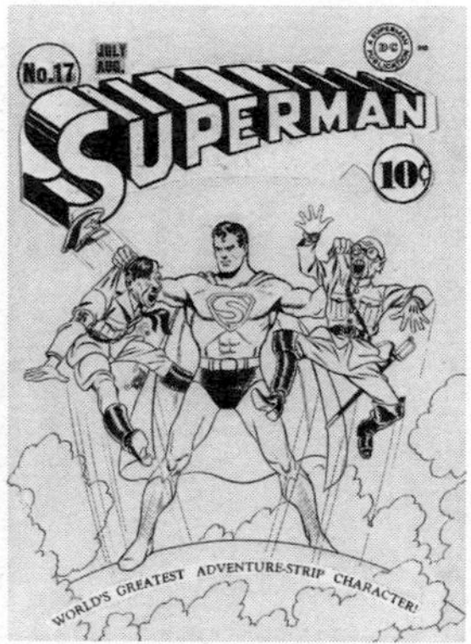

Fred Ray, original art for cover of Superman No. 17, July 1942, sold at auction for $36,800

Each season Sotheby's offers the most comprehensive selection of Comic Books and original Comic Art at auction. With over ten million dollars in sales from our first seven auctions, we look forward to representing clients with important property in our upcoming spring 1998 auction. Sotheby's catalogues have become invaluable reference sources. Besides savoring each year's selection of historic treasures, collectors always know that if they decide to consign important property it will receive first class treatment worthy of its value.

Highlights and record-breaking prices from our past sales include:

Bob Kane, original art for second Batman daily, October 1943, sold for $29,000

Action Comics No. 1, June 1938, Very Fine copy, sold at auction for $82,500

Robert Crumb, cover artwork for "R. Crumb's Fritz the Cat," sold for $56,350

Jack Kirby/Don Heck, original cover recreation to Tales of Suspense No. 39 with 13-page original story for Iron Man, sold at auction for $46,000

Frank Frazetta, painting for Vampirella No. 1, 1969, sold at auction for $77,000

Marvel Comics No. 1, from the Lamont Larson collection, sold for $41,400

Action Comics No. 1, unrestored copy in good-32, sold at auction for $37,950

Highlights already consigned for our spring 1998 auction include:

Curt Swan, original twice up cover for Action Comics No. 319. Auction estimate: $3,000–5,000

The Lamont Larson copies of Fantastic Comics Nos. 3, 4. Wonderworld Nos. 7, 11, 13, with Weird Comics Nos. 2, 3. Auction estimate: $3,000–5,000

All-Star Comics Nos. 1, 2, 3, 4, & 6, unrestored copies in F-. Auction estimate: $4,000–6,000

Near complete runs of Weird Tales, Terror Tales, Horror Stories, and many Spicy Pulp titles from the collection of Fred Cook.

For more information, please call Jerry Weist at (212) 606-7862, home office (718) 789-5542; or Dana Hawkes or Peter Staller at (212) 606-7910. To purchase an illus-trated catalogue, call (203) 847-0465 or fax (203) 849-0223. To inquire about consigning important property call Jerry Weist (212) 606-7862, or Dana Hawkes or Peter Staller at (212) 606-7910. http://www.sothebys.com

Sotheby's
1334 York Avenue
New York, NY 10021

© SOTHEBY'S, INC. 1997 WILLIAM F. RUPRECHT, PRINCIPAL AUCTIONEER, #0794917

SOTHEBY'S

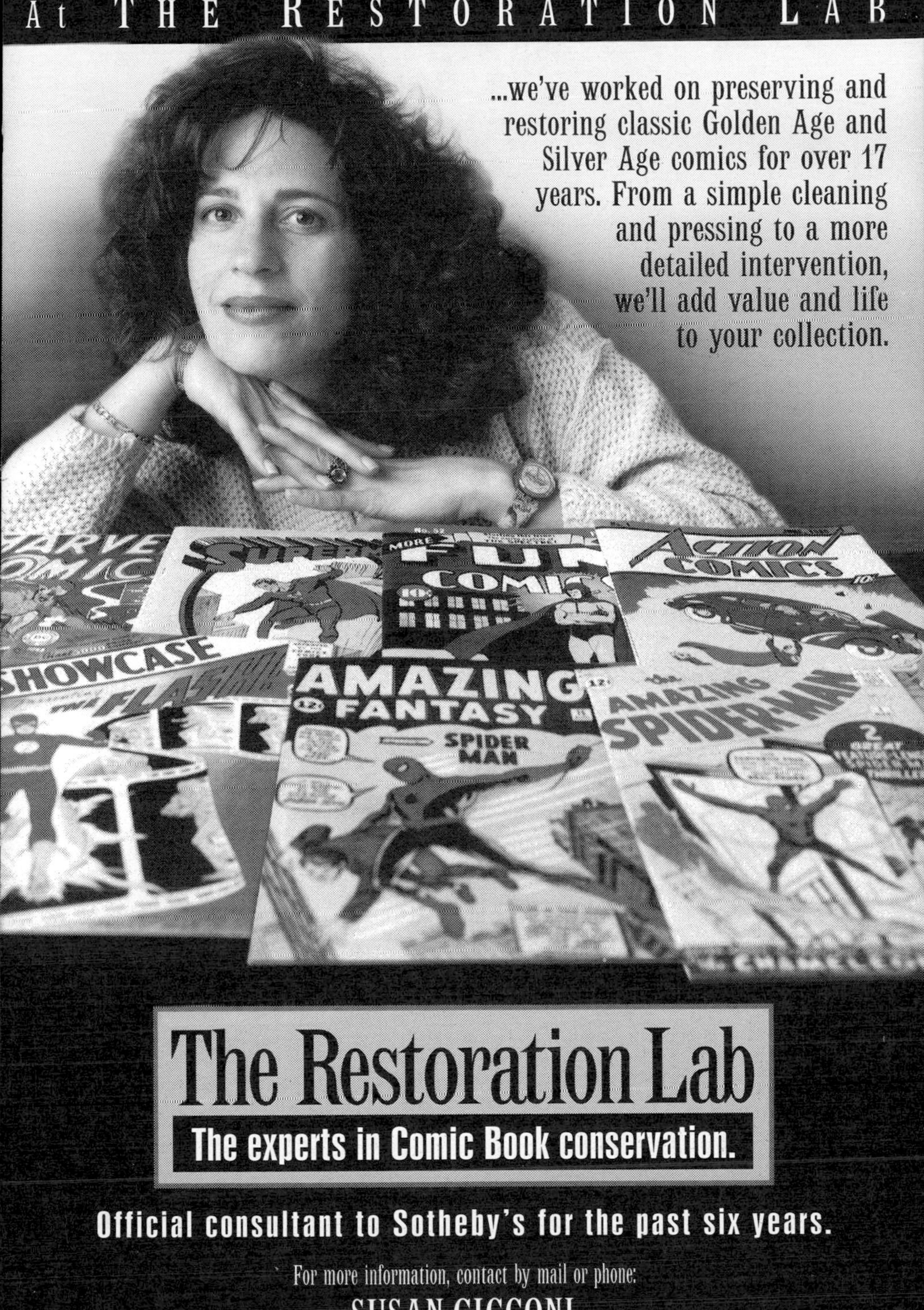

At THE RESTORATION LAB
...we've worked on preserving and restoring classic Golden Age and Silver Age comics for over 17 years. From a simple cleaning and pressing to a more detailed intervention, we'll add value and life to your collection.
ACTION COMICS
SHOWCASE
AMAZING FANTASY
SPIDER MAN
The Restoration Lab
The experts in Comic Book conservation.
Official consultant to Sotheby's for the past six years.
For more information, contact by mail or phone:
SUSAN CICCONI,
P.O. Box 632, New Town Branch, Boston, MA 02258 TELEPHONE: (617) 924-4297 FAX: (617) 924-5580

COLLECTORS ASSEMBLE!

OUR NAME HAS CHANGED, BUT OUR REPUTATION REMAINS THE SAME

I ONLY COLLECT BOOKS WITH COFFINS ON THE COVER.

MYSTERIOUS ADVENTURES

MY GAWD, I'M HOT FOR BOUNCING BOY!

Adventure COMICS

JUST DON'T BEND 'EM!!

GREAT INK REFLECTIVITY!

FLASH

SPACE ADVENTURES

I WON'T USE VF-NM! LET'S HAVE A DEBATE.

Drew Friedman © 1996

To Sell Books | **To Buy Books**

(Buying books from 1933 to 1966)

Scott Whaley
507 Carlisle Drive
Alexandria, VA 22301-2709
phone/fax
(800) 344-9111

Marnin Rosenberg
P.O. Box 222047
Great Neck, NY 11022-9998
phone/fax
(516) 466-8147

Overstreet Advisors • CBG Customer Service Award • Members A.C.C.

Visit our website at: www.collectorsassemble.com

Who Can You TRUST?

Have you been searching through this guide and asking yourself "Who can I trust to sell my collection to?" and "Who can I trust to buy **GUARANTEED UNRESTORED BOOKS** from?" *The answer is clear!*

At Collectors Assemble, (previously known as Marnin Rosenberg and Scott Whaley), we've been buying and selling books through the pages of the Comics Buyer's Guide (CBG) since 1973, and never, we repeat, **NEVER** has that publication received a complaint about us! We've also advertised in various other major comic publications including Overstreet, with the same **SPOTLESS REPUTATION.**

Just how many othcr dealers in these pages can boast that claim along with such longevity? We believe in ourselves and you can too!

COLLECTORS ASSEMBLE!

Drew Friedman © 1996

To Sell Books | **To Buy Books**

(Buying books from 1933 to 1966)

Scott Whaley
507 Carlisle Drive
Alexandria, VA 22301-2709
phone/fax
(800) 344-9111

Marnin Rosenberg
P.O. Box 222047
Great Neck, NY 11022-9998
phone/fax
(516) 466-8147

Overstreet Advisors • CBG Customer Service Award • Members A.C.C.

Visit our website at: www.collectorsassemble.com

COMIC-CON INTERNATIONAL:
SAN DIEGO '98

JOIN US IN SAN DIEGO ON AUGUST 13-16, 1998

THE LARGEST
CONVENTION OF ITS TYPE
IN THE UNITED STATES

•Japanese Animation • Films • Gaming •
•Nighttime Programming • Masquerade •
•Parties, Parties and more parties•

SPECIAL GUESTS SO FAR

Naoko Takeuchi (Sailor Moon) • James Robinson (Starman) • Wendy Pini (Elfquest) • Tom Batiuk (Funky Winkerbean) • Michael Kaluta (fantasy artist) • Terry Moore (Strangers in Paradise) • Joe Simon (Golden Age) • Mark Crilley (Akiko) • Eddie Campbell (Bachhus) • Paul S. Newman (Golden Age) • Chris Ware (Acme Novelty Library)•

SAN DIEGO COMIC CON INTERNATIONAL

FOR MORE INFORMATION:
Comic-Con International: San Diego
P.O. Box 128458
San Diego, CA 92112
619-491-2475; Fax: 619-544-0743
Exhibitors or retailers interested in Comic Book Expo (August 11-12) call 619-544-9555. Comic-Con International is a non-profit corporation dedicated to creating awareness of and appreciation for comic art.

BUYING!

Consider The Following:

■Willing to pay up to 200% of Overstreet Price Guide(or more depending upon current market conditions). Do not settle for less.

■ Buying all comics 1900-1970 in all grades!Whether one book or 10,000. I can pay instantly!

■ Having been involved in collecting/selling for 22 years, I have built my reputation on courteous, professional service (I do not believe in high pressure transactions-I do believe in the seller being fully informed!) Please ask questions

■ Advisor to Overstreet.

■ Finders fee paid for information leading to purchase. I will travel to view large collections.

SELLING - TRADING

●Accurate Grading & Pricing
●Dependable, Reputable Service
●Large Selection of Golden Age & Silver Age Marvel & DC
●Constantly Acquiring New Collections
●Satisfaction Guaranteed
●Send $2.00 For Catalog Or Peruse Our Catalog At http://www.a-1comics.com

A-1 Comics

Brian Peets - Owner
5800 Madison Ave.
Sacramento, CA 95841
(916)331-9203 Fax(916)331-2141

"Serving The West Since 1974"

BUYING ALL COMICS

with 10 and 12¢ cover prices

TOP PRICES PAID!

IMMEDIATE CASH PAYMENT

Stop Throwing Away Those Old Comic Books!

I'm always paying top dollar for any pre-1966 comic. No matter what title or condition, whether you have one comic or a warehouse full.

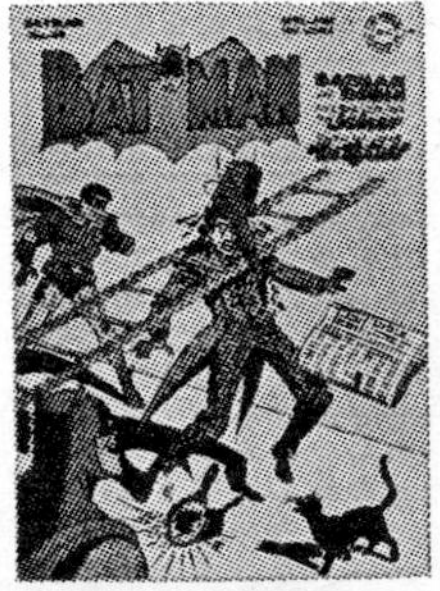

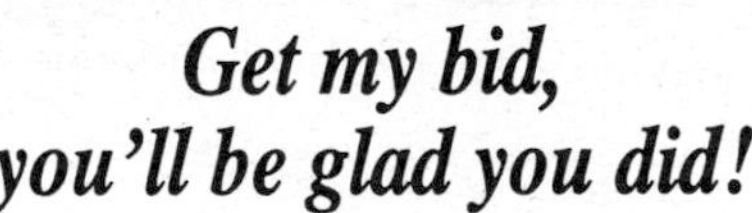
Get my bid, you'll be glad you did!

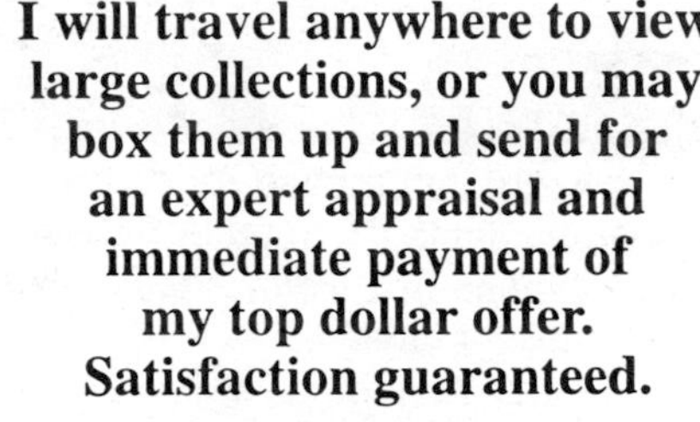
I will travel anywhere to view large collections, or you may box them up and send for an expert appraisal and immediate payment of my top dollar offer. Satisfaction guaranteed.

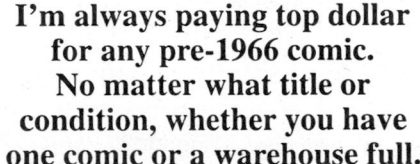

For a Quick Reply Send a List of What You Have or Call

1-608-277-8750

or Fax

1-608-277-8775

or Write

Jef Hinds

P.O. Box 44803
Madison, WI 53744-4803

Insurance & Estate Appraisal Service, Strictly Confidential.
Pictured comics are for sale. Please call for details.

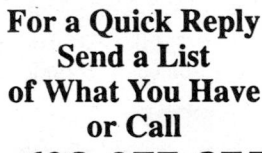

Human Torch, All Winners, Hulk, Spider Man, Captain America © Marvel • All Star, Batman, Superman © DC

OUR SPECIALTIES SINCE 1976...

BUYING OUT STORES WAREHOUSES, PUBLISHERS REMAINDERS, COLLECTIONS

GOT A FEW HUNDRED THOUSAND BOOKS? A **MILLION** BOOKS? WE ARE LOOKING FOR **LARGE LOTS** OF COMICS AND RELATED MATERIALS (Sci-Fi, Games, Cards, Records, etc.. etc.). **SMALLER STOCKS & COLLECTIONS** APPRECIATED AS WELL. **LOVE GOLD & SILVER AGE COMICS – WILL PAY FINDER'S FEE.**

THE MORE, THE MERRIER
WILL FLY, SWIM, SKATEBOARD
ANYWHERE IN THE WORLD

SUPPLYING DEALERS & INVESTORS STOCKING NEW STORES

THE MOST EXTENSIVE BACK ISSUE WHOLESALE LIST IN THE WORLD – BY FAR, WE HAVE BEEN SUPPLYING DEALERS IN THE U.S. & ABROAD FOR YEARS. OUR LISTS INCLUDE BACK-ISSUE LISTINGS, LOTS, COLLECTIONS, ETC. **OPENING A STORE? LOOKING FOR INVENTORY?** WE HAVE PROVIDED THE INITIAL STOCKS FOR DOZENS OF STORES OPENING IN THE LAST DECADE.

OVERSEAS ACCOUNTS A SPECIALTY

THE ENDLESS DEALER'S ONLY CONVENTION

OUR WAREHOUSE IS OPEN TO DEALERS BY INVITATION OR APPOINTMENT ONLY. IT'S A COMIC BOOK SUPERMARKET: OVER 400,000 PRICED, UNADVERTISED COMICS (IN ALPHA NUMERICAL ORDER) AVAILABLE AT ALL TIMES. WHEN YOU'RE IN TOWN GIVE US A CALL.

JOSEPH KOCH
208 41ST ST., BROOKLYN, NY 11232
718-768-8571

our PASSION since 1962...

CELEBRATING COMICS
GOING STRONG & BETTER THAN EVER

The one catalogue, you **MUST** have, the largest comic, horror, fantasy,contest, questionnaire, feature filled catalogue in the world ***BY FAR***

THE AVALANCHE OF WONDER

Larger than the *New York Daily News*, the *Wall Street Journal*, your Hometown Paper!!. Over 200 000 DIFFERENT items; A 200 page *COMIC/ FANTASY/ FILM* spectacle without peer — *nothing else even comes close*

Gold & Silver Age, Mags & Fanzines, Undergrounds, Archies, Famous Monsters, British & other foreign publications, Trade Paperbacks & Graphic Novels, British Annuals, Westerns, Movie/ TV publications - tons of illos, info: just about the only comprehensive back issue comic/ horror/ fantasy catalogue at large today

OUR BOOKS FOR A BUCK (*AND LESS*) INSERT ALONE HAS MORE LISTINGS (15 000) THAN 90% OF THE CATALOGS PUBLISHED TODAY

70% of the comics published since 1981 have appeared in our Books for A Buck supplement in the last year - all with further discount programs!

WE TRADE

the following are worth $1.00 each against selected parts of our catalog:

all Archies, Digests, Barbie, Simpsons,Cracked, Sick, Babylon 5, Star Trek, Star Wars, Heavy Metal, all adult comics, all Warren magazines, Mad, RBCC, Sonic the Hedgehog, Spawn, Nemo, Beavis, Ren, Comic Book Marketplace, Hanna Barbera, Phantom, all pre-1980 Monster Magazines & magazine sized comics, and just about all pre-1980 comics, most comics by Alan Moore, Gaiman, Miller, Miyazaki, Drawn & Quarterly, Fantagraphics, Moebius, Los Bros Hernandez,Teri S Woods, R Gregory,Spiegelman, most TV/Movie Adaptation comics, most books of the last six months, more

TRADE INFO ACCOMPANIES ALL CATALOG REQUESTS - SEE NEXT PAGE

SPECIAL COMIC FAN & FAN CLUB ALERT

Special discounts are available for comic clubs and zine publishers; we are looking databases, capsule comic reviews, expressions of enthusiasm, art work to be published in our catalog; check out our catalog or our website for more details

ORIGINAL ART . . . Kirby, Crumb,

Kurtzman, Ditko, Kubert, Eisner, Frazetta, complete stories always wanted; spectacular selection always available; specify your interest with your catalog request (see next page) or write, phone or fax directly to our ORIGINAL ART department attention Peter Koch, PO Box 283, Leonia, NJ 07605 phone: 201-585-2765, fax 201-585-5096 .

Joseph Koch "The Avalanche"

206 41st St, Brooklyn, NY 11232 (718) 768-8571

our speciality since 1985 . . . .

SUPPLYING EVERYBODY —
DEALERS, COLLECTORS & READERS

GET THE WHOLE STORY: 1000's of bagged sets, complete story arcs, an unbelievable selection of complete stories, complete series - 1968 on

THE AVALANCHE OF WONDER

BACK ISSUE SUBSCRIPTION SERVICE

the most amazing system for collecting comics ever devised; comics at 10-50% of guide and less; see the Avalanche for the different programs available

CATALOG ON DISK, UPDATES ON LINE

for now, our catalog is too massive to put on line, but it is available on disk; info accompanies all catalog requests; e mail us (jkcom@mail.idt.net) and we will direct you to our website of updates;

STOCK 1000 000 COMICS WITHOUT A RACK

Stop turning away back issue requests! The following stores have our computer and entire inventory at their fingertips for 24 hour delivery. In addition they offer spectacular selections of **Video Games, Magic & Games, Sports Cards, & YO YOS (yesss!!!)**

DRAGONS DEN AT CROSS COUNTY, Yonkers, NY 10704 (914)-376-3336

MANHATTAN COMICS, 228 W 23rd St NY NY 10011 (212)-243-9349

this back issue support is available to a **limited** number of outlets; please inquire for terms and availability

DEALERS, COLLECTORS - LET US PRODUCE YOUR CATALOG

We can also **produce** a professional catalog (or collection presentation) to your specification from dbase & foxpro compatible databases; send SASE for details

who else could offer these Instant collection specials?

10 000 different comics $7 000
15 000 different comics $11 000
25 000 different comics $25 000 PLUS SHIPPING

send $7.50 (refundable with your first order) for **2 pounds of catalogues & FREEBIES ($20.00 retail value) via US PRIORITY**; $10.00 for US PRIORITY mailing **plus annual subscription**; Canada & Mexico $10.00 and $15.00, **OVERSEAS AIR MAIL** $15.00 and $20.00 respectively; **TRADE, BACK ISSUE SUBSCRIPTION, ORDER BY DISK, AND ON-LINE INFO WILL ACCOMPANY ALL CATALOG REQUESTS**

Joseph Koch "The Avalanche"

206 41st St, Brooklyn, NY 11232 FAX (718)-768-8571

Classic Conservations

Matt Nelson
Conservator of Ephemera

My professional method of paper restoration includes using only chemicals and adhesives that are safe for your comic book. The methods used in restoring your comics are tried and true and are used by most of the respected conservators in the field.

In addition to preserving comics, I am an avid collector as well. I too have experienced the anticipation and anxiety of waiting for a book to be restored and thus understand the needs of you, the collector. I treat every comic as if it were mine and will always try to finish it within a <u>reasonable</u> period of time.

I promise to deliver excellent performance quickly and at minimum cost to you. If you have any comics that need reviving, give me a call.

Visit my website: http://members.aol.com/spectre52/comic.htm

504 - 639 - 0621

Rates are $30.00 per hour.
Estimates are free. If you have questions, call me!

Classic Conservations
P.O. Box 2335
Slidell, La 70459

CHICAGO

IF YOU'RE SELLING COMICS - CALL ME. NO ONE PAYS MORE!

Your call to PCR will put you in contact with Gary Colabuono, one of the most trusted and respected experts in the comic-book field. Whether you're selling a single comic book or an entire collection, PCR is the place for top dollar.

We specialize in Golden-Age and Silver-Age comics from 1933-1968.

Over 20 years experience.

Appraisals available for insurance coverage and claims.

Gary Colabuono
POP CULTURE RESOURCES, INC.
P. O. Box 117
Elk Grove Village, Illinois 60009

Call Toll Free: (800) 344-6060

Fax: (847) 806-1158

OVER 45,000 DIFFERENT COMICS IN STOCK

BUY – SELL with
Marty Hay or I'll
SMASH YA!!!
Enclose 1 stamp each for Buying or Selling List!

Copyright © 1994 Marvel Entertainment Group. All rights reserved.

I PAY BIG CASH FOR QUALITY COMICS

FAST CASH SINGLE BOOKS AND LARGE COLLECTIONS. I WANT ALL EARLY MARVELS, SILVER-AGE DC'S. GOLDEN AGE, DISNEY POSTERS & MISC. ANY CONDITION. 50% TO 400% OF GUIDE FOR ITEMS NEEDED! WHY TAKE LESS FOR YOUR VALUED COLLECTIBLES? I SELL QUALITY COMICS AT REASONABLE PRICES. **SEND YOUR LIST FOR FAST CASH OFFER!!! NO RECENT COMICS PLEASE!**

SAMPLE BUYING PRICES (SUBJECT TO INCREASE)

FLASH #105 ....UP TO $8,000 FOR TOP QUALITY
BRAVE & BOLD #1-43,50,61 ....N-MINTS ARE WORTH 110%-300%
JUSTICE LEAGUE #1....PERFECTION CAN BE WORTH $7,000
SHOWCASE #1-45,55,60. ....CHOICE ISSUES 110%-300% PAID
OUR ARMY AT WAR #81 ....CASH PERHAPS TO $1,600
CAPT. AMERICA #1-78....VG OR BETTER 75%-125% OFFERED
MORE FUN #1-107....VG OR BETTER 70%-150% PAID
ACTION #1-252 ....VG OR BETTER 65%-150% PAID
DETECTIVE #1-233 ....VG OR BETTER 70%-150% PAID
SUSPENSE COMICS ....ANY CONDITION UP TO 10X GUIDE (#3)

"BIG CASH FOR OTHER DC, TIMELYS, OTHER GOLD OR SILVER AGE."

SERVING FANDOM FOR OVER 27 YEARS

MARTY HAY

P.O. BOX 359
329 E. MAIN
SPRINGERVILLE, AZ 85938
WORK (520) 333-2222
HOME (520) 333-2255

SERVING FANDOM FOR OVER 27 YEARS

I WILL PAY MORE THAN ANY BUYING PRICES OFFERED IN THIS GUIDE!

NOT JUST ANOTHER AD OF RHETORIC!

You see many ads stating *"top dollar paid... I'm the best... I'm only a collector...",* but many of these are just so much RHETORIC. ***You will receive the BEST OFFER FROM US!***

HONESTY! INTEGRITY! EXPERIENCE!

Dealing & collecting Golden/Silver Age Comics since 1975!

Here are some of the high prices we are paying for comics in near mint to mint condition!

Action #1	$200,000	Marvel Comics #1	$ 85,000
All American #16	90,000	More Fun #52	125,000
All Star #3	35,000	More Fun #55	15,000
All Star #8	30,000	Mystery Men #1	9,500
Amazing Man #5	17,000	Phantom Lady #17	4,000
All Winners #1	18,000	Science #1 (Fox)	4,500
Batman #1	90,000	Sensation #1	20,000
Captain America #1	60,000	Sub-Mariner #1	18,000
Detective #1	80,000	Superman #1	165,000
Detective #27	190,000	W.D. Comics & Stories #1	16,000
Fantastic #1	3,500	Wonder Woman #1	20,000
Flash #1	125,000	Wonderworld #3	7,000
Green Lantern #1	38,000	Young Allies #1	9,000

JAMES F. PAYETTE
Rare Books & Comics

P.O Box 750 • Bethlehem, NH 03574
Phone 603-869-2097 • Fax 603-869-3475

CREDENTIALS

Special Advisor to Overstreet Guide	1985–1998
Member AACBC	1990–1998
Member AACBC Authenticating, Certification, and Grading committee for Sotheby's	1991–1998
CBG Customer Service Award Winner for many years	
Experience as Dealer/Collector since	1975

PLEASE SEE MY OTHER ADS FOR FURTHER REFERENCE

Selling

Serving Clients
Worldwide Over 14 Years

Hard to Find Books
Accurate Grading
Competitive Pricing
Prompt, Professional Service
Specializing in Golden & Silver Age
Want List

Call, Write or Fax:

Harley Yee

P.O. Box 51758
Livonia, MI 48151-5758
Phone: 800.731.1029 or 734.421.7921
Fax: 734.421.7928

©Better Publications

I Will Travel Anywhere
to View Your Collection

Highest Prices Paid
Immediate Cash
No Collection Too Big or Too Small
Complete Customer Satisfaction
Experienced, Professional Service

Buying

Call, Write or Fax:

Harley Yee

P.O. Box 51758
Livonia, MI 48151-5758
Phone: 800.731.1029 or 734.421.7921
Fax: 734.421.7928

©Better Publications

COMIC BOOKS FOR SALE

Thousands of Golden Age, Marvels, Silver Age, E.C.'s,
Disneys as well as BLB's, Sunday Pages,
TV Guides, and Mystery and Detective Magazines

Send one dollar (refundable with first order) to:

SAMUEL FRAZER
P.O. BOX 144
OLD BETHPAGE, NY 11804
(516)694-4835
e-mail: sfrazer457@aol.com
website:http//members.aol.com/sfrazer457/index.html
for catalog number 29

TOP PRICES PAID FOR YOUR COMICS AND RELATED ITEMS
LET ME KNOW WHAT YOU HAVE

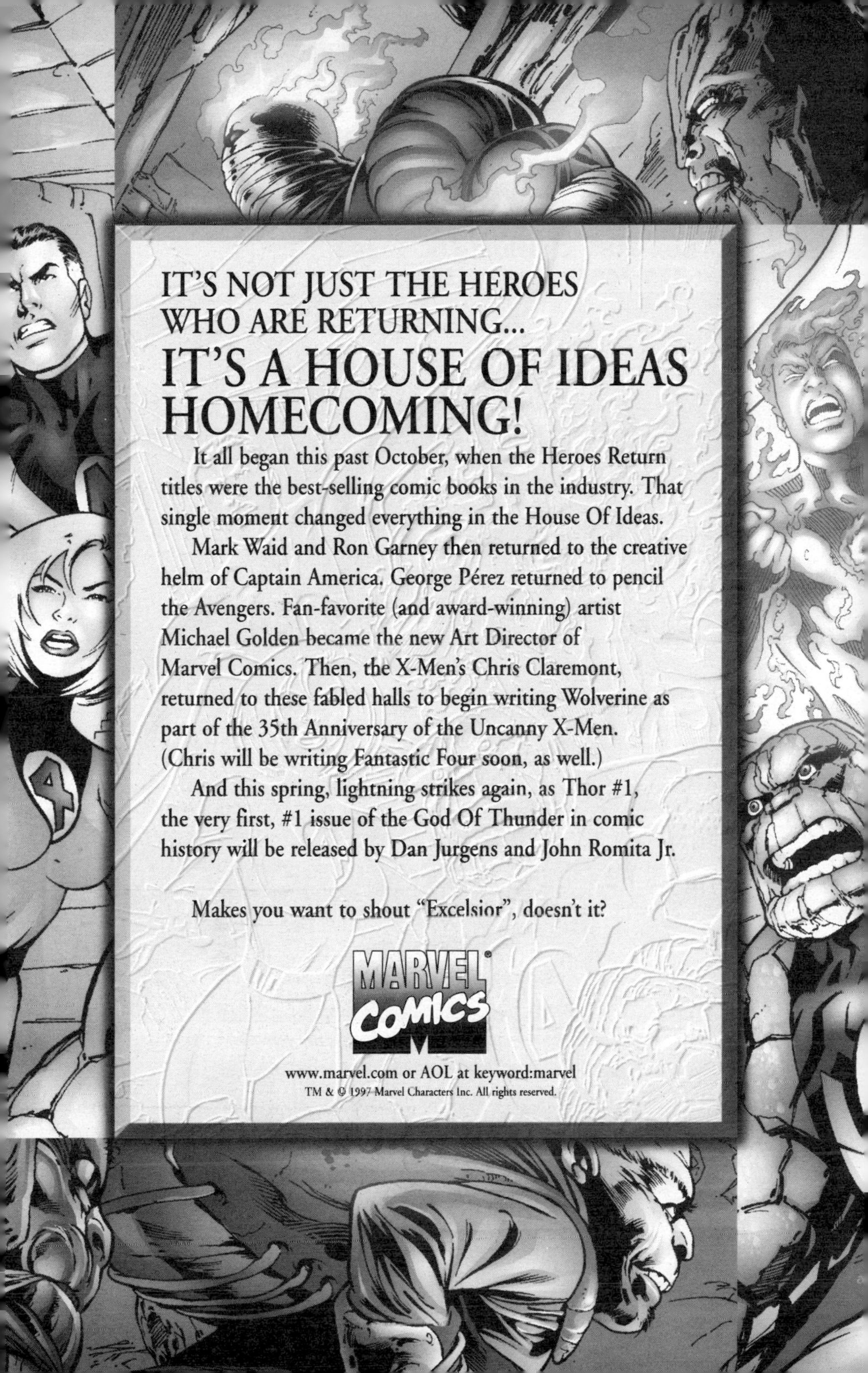
IT'S NOT JUST THE HEROES
WHO ARE RETURNING...
IT'S A HOUSE OF IDEAS
HOMECOMING!
It all began this past October, when the Heroes Return titles were the best-selling comic books in the industry. That single moment changed everything in the House Of Ideas.
Mark Waid and Ron Garney then returned to the creative helm of Captain America. George Pérez returned to pencil the Avengers. Fan-favorite (and award-winning) artist Michael Golden became the new Art Director of Marvel Comics. Then, the X-Men's Chris Claremont, returned to these fabled halls to begin writing Wolverine as part of the 35th Anniversary of the Uncanny X-Men. (Chris will be writing Fantastic Four soon, as well.)
And this spring, lightning strikes again, as Thor #1, the very first, #1 issue of the God Of Thunder in comic history will be released by Dan Jurgens and John Romita Jr.
Makes you want to shout "Excelsior", doesn't it?
MARVEL COMICS
www.marvel.com or AOL at keyword:marvel
TM & © 1997 Marvel Characters Inc. All rights reserved.

Comic Collecting Supplies

Polypropylene Bags

High Clarity, 100% Virgin Material, 2 Mil Comic Bags, Made in USA, Pre-packed in 100-count Color-Coded Bags

CURRENT 6 7/8" X 10 1/2 W/1 1/4" Flap		REGULAR 7 1/8" X 10 1/2" W/1 1/4" Flap		SILVER/GOLD/MAGAZINE S-7 3/8" X 10 1/2"; G-7 3/4" X 10 1/2"; M-8 3/4" X 11" W 1 1/2" Flap	
1,000	$28.00	1,000	$28.00	1,000	$45.00
2,000-9,000	$27.00	2,000-9,000	$27.00	2,000-9,000	$43.00
10,000-24,000	$25.00	10,000-24,000	$25.00	10,000-24,000	$39.00

Backing Boards

Pure White All The Way Through, 100% Virgin Material, 24 Mil Thick, Loose 1,000's or Pre-packed in 100-count Color-Coded Corrugated Collection Boxes.

CURRENT 6 3/4" X 10 1/2" Loose/100 Packs		REGULAR 7" X 10 1/2" Loose/100 Packs		SILVER/GOLD/MAGAZINE S-7 1/4" X 10 1/2"; G-7 5/8" X 10 1/2"; M-8 1/2" X 11"; Loose/100 Shrink-wrapped	
1,000	$42.00/47.00	1,000	$42.00/47.00	1,000	$56.00/61.00
2,000-9,000	$40.00/45.00	2,000-9,000	$40.00/45.00	2,000-9,000	$54.00/59.00
10,000-24,000	$37.00-42,00	10,000-24,000	$37.00/42.00	10,000-24,000	$48.00/53.00

Comic Storage Boxes

Boxes made of 275# Test, Double-Walled Cardboard. All White Outside. Easy Assembly & Storage. Designed With Extra Strength At The Handles And On The Bottom.

LARGE COMIC BOX 26" X 7 3/4" X 11 1/2" Holds over 300		SMALL COMIC BOX 16" X 7 3/4" X 11 1/2" Holds over 200		MAGAZINE BOX 15 1/2" X 9" X 11 1/2" Holds over 100	
1-9	$3.95	1-9	$3.50	1-9	$3.95
10-49	$2.50	10-49	$2.00	10-49	$2.75
50up	$2.25	50up	$1.75	50up	$2.50

Buyer pays only exact shipping costs. Inquire for shipping costs & larger quantity rates. Mix & match bags, boards & boxes to gain best rate. MasterCard, VISA, AMEX and Discover accepted. Checks for COD must be pre-approved. All orders shipped within 24 hours. NC residents add 6% tax or Tax #

Visit our HUGE Retail Store!

Old & New Comic Books • Complete Gaming Section
Magic & CCG's • Toys • Trading Cards
Much, Much More!

located at: Midwood Corners Shopping Center
1306 The Plaza, Charlotte, NC

We Are The Proud Sponsors Of The
HEROES CONVENTION
July 3-5, 1998

Dealers & Publishers: Contact us for Set-up Rates & Info!
P.O. Box 9181, Charlotte, NC 28299
704-375-7463 • fax 704-375-7464 • www.heroesonline.com

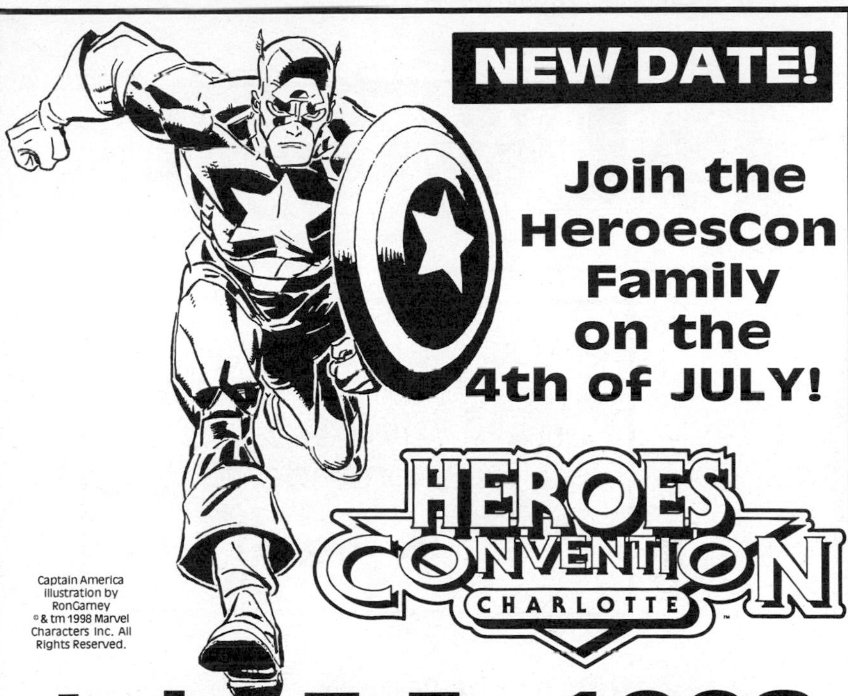
NEW DATE!
Join the
HeroesCon
Family
on the
4th of JULY!
HEROES
CONVENTION
CHARLOTTE
™

Captain America
illustration by
RonGarney
© & tm 1998 Marvel
Characters Inc. All
Rights Reserved.

July 3-5, 1998

Charlotte Convention Center
501 South College Street
Comic Books•Toys•Gaming
Original Art•Workshops•Exhibits

just a few of the confirmed guests include...
Mike Allred•Adam Hughes•Gil Kane
George Perez•Joe Quesada•Joe Simon
Jeff Smith•Charles Vess
Matt Wagner•Mark Waid•Mike Wieringo
...with hundreds more to be announced!!!

Host Hotel
The Westin Hotel
222 East Third Street
HeroesCon Rate $89
704-377-1500 or 1-800-WESTIN1

Show Hours
Friday Noon-7pm•Saturday 10am-6pm
Sunday 11am-6pm
Admission
$10 per day•$20 Three-day Pass

Sponsored By:
HEROES AREN'T HARD TO FIND
P.O. Box 9181 Charlotte NC 28299
704-375-7463 • fax 704-375-7464

Visit us on the Web...
www.heroesonline.com

Always

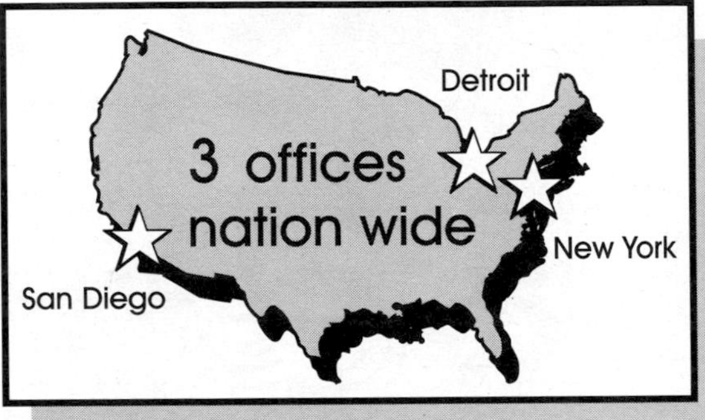

Rob Ronin, President
11956 Bernardo Plaza Dr. #537
San Diego, CA 92128
Tel: **619-451-9408** FAX: 619-451-9531

Jason Ewert, Vice President
P.O. Box 354
Eastpointe, MI 48021
Tel: **810-773-7828** FAX: 810-445-3962

Tom Brulato, Vice President
70 East Ridgewood Ave.
Ridgewood, NJ 07450
Tel: **201-689-1480** FAX: 201-689-1490

Toll Free:
888-VIABUYS

Buying

Past Purchases:

1997:
Bethlehem DC collection $135,000
1996:
Silver Age collection $45,000
1995:
Action 1 .... $55,000
1993:
Marvel collection $180,000
1990:
Golden Age collection $140,000

Web site: www.viabuys.com
E-Mail: help@viabuys.com

Toll Free: 888-VIABUYS

25 years
collectibles
experience

JOHN NICHOLS'

BEAR MOUNTAIN ENTERPRISES
P.O. BOX 616
Victoria, Virginia 23974
Phone: (804) 696-2925
Fax: (804) 696-1675 (24 hrs.)
e-mail: jnichols@msinets.com

BARKS FANS: For nearly 20 years Bear Mountain has offered these services:

•THE BARKS QUICKLIST: Costs $1 ($2 overseas air). It's a Barks supermarket! Old comics, lithos, reprints, Barks Library, Albums, etc. For 2 decades, Bear Mountain has made thousands of Barks fans around the world happy. Send for your Quicklist today, and find out why! (Call or fax for a FREE copy.) Not even Old Demontooth is more reliable than Bear Mountain!

•WE BUY DUCKS: We buy all issues of Barks comics, from one book to 1,000 books. Whatever you have in Barks oldies or new material like lithos, etc., WE WANT IT. We've handled some of the world's best collections of Barks comics, and we'll buy yours too, no matter how small or how large. Since we supply thousands of fans with their Ducks, we need to buy like crazy. **If you've got ducks, we want 'em**! References on request.

•CARL BARKS ART: We sell both new and back issues of BARKS LITHOS and the new Disney BARKS SERIGRAPHS. (Nearly 1,000 sold worldwide!). Send $2 ($4 overseas air) for a brochure of the current Disney Barks serigraph. This includes the Quicklist also. (We ship Barks serigraphs 2-day UPS overseas.) We carry the mini lithos, regular large lithos, and the Disney serigraphs. We are always buying back issues of large and mini lithos.

•BARKS STARTER PAK: Send $20 and we'll send you: The Barks Quicklist, the current Barks Serigraph color brochure, 4 copies of our fanzine "The Barks Collector," and 10 different Uncle Scrooge reprints, including "Only a Poor Old Man." Over $40 value total! Overseas: Make it $28 air or $23 surface.

**BARKS COMICS.
PERIOD.**

Spawn

Divine Right

Gen 13

Witchblade

Savage Dragon

A Touch Of Silver

THERE'S NEVER BEEN ANYTHING LIKE US BEFORE!

image®
COMICS

Kiss

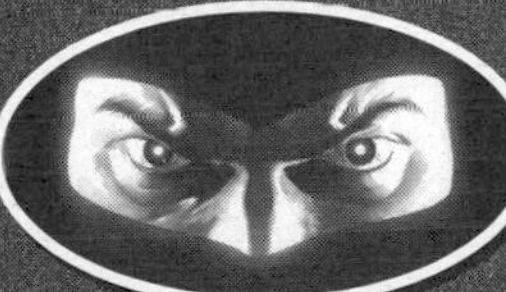
Astro City

The Maxx

The Tenth

Danger Girl

Mage

All characters are trademark™ and copyright © their respective owners. 1998.

10590 West Cortez Circle #28, Franklin WI 53132
PHONE (414) 427-4962 (e-mail jimhaack@mail.execpc.com)

WEB SITE >> http://www.web-galaxy.com/jhcollect/

SELLING

Specializing in Golden & Silver Age Comics.
Also Pulps, Premiums, Old Toys, Barbies, Magazines

FREE CATALOG call , write, e-mail for a copy, or view our online catalog above, featuring 100's of full color covers!

BUYING

All PRE-1970 Comics. Including Super Hero, Horror, Crime, Romance, Sci-Fi, Adventure. **IMMEDIATE CASH** available.

Send a list or the comics for my offer. Shipping reimbursed whether or not I buy them . Will travel for large collections.

Let us introduce you to an exciting source for those hard-to-find Character Collectibles you want to add to your collection . . . Hake's mail & phone bid auctions.

Hake's
FREE CATALOG OFFER
Write or Call—
just specify offer #356
to receive your introductory
auction catalog
FREE!
(A $7.50 value.)
ILLUSTRATION BY BILL NELSON

Five times a year, Hake's publishes a catalog of 3200+ items available for sale by mail & phone bid auction. All items are fully photo illustrated (many in color) and thoroughly described in careful detail. Each catalogue contains 1000 or more quality character collectibles.

Forget about the frustrating waste of time, energy and dollars scouring those endless toy shows and flea markets. Enjoy the ease and convenience of shopping from the privacy and comfort of your home or office. Simply submit your advance bids by mail or phone. On auction days, you can check on the current status of your bids by telephone.

You Can Buy from Hake's with confidence because . . .

- All items are original—NO reproductions.
- No hidden buyer's premium or credit card surcharges.
- In keeping with Hake's 30 year reputation for fair and honest dealing, the accuracy of each item's description is satisfaction guaranteed.
- We take extreme care and pride in the packing and shipping of your valued collectibles—so you can receive your delicate items in a safe and timely manner.

Don't miss that special addition to your collection! Call or write today—for your FREE sample catalog for Hake's current or next auction. **Specify offer #356.**

Hake's Americana & Collectibles

POB 1444 • York, PA 17405

Phone 717-848-1333 • FAX 717-852-0344

Hake's is a major buyer of character and personality collectibles. One quality item or an entire collection. Hake's also accepts high grade consignments. Contact us for details.

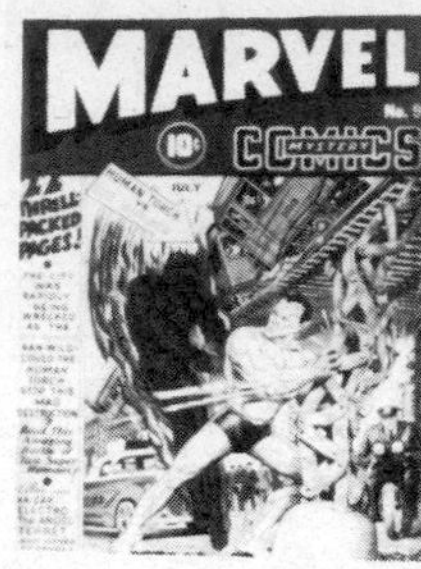

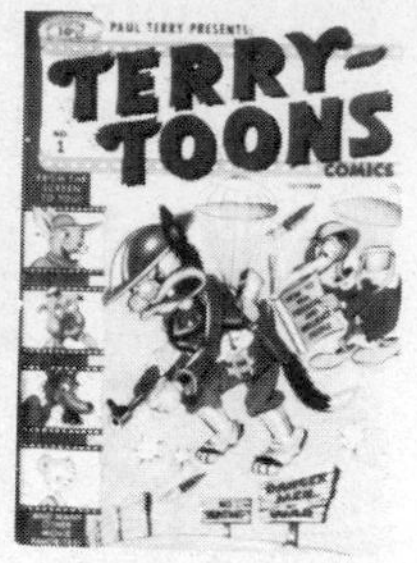

BUYING

COMIC BOOKS & RELATED ITEMS

Actively seeking:

Large collections

Big-ticket books

Childhood troves

Back inventories

Low grade & high grade

(published before 1975)

please call or write:

AVALON

COMICS & COLLECTIBLES

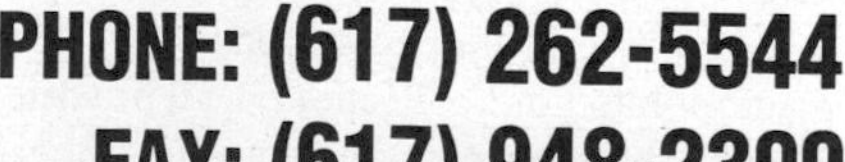

PHONE: (617) 262-5544

FAX: (617) 948-2300

P.O. Box 234
Boston, MA 02123

AVALON

In our seven years we have gained one of the best reputations in the business, for:

Grading
Plain dealing
Fairness to beginners
Choice selection
Super service

And we have consistently issued one of the best catalogs in the business!

68 jam-packed pages
150 photographs

Featuring over 15,000 comic books from 1933-1975, and choice memorabilia from 1880-1980.

Character & personality items
Vintage Superman collectibles
Disneyana
Cowboy & Western items
Movie posters
Antique advertising
Premiums, Pulps
Big Little books
Cardboard & Hardcover books
& much, much more!

Please sign up to receive our catalogs!

Send your name, address and $2. (in the U.S. and Canada, $3. foreign) to get our current and next catalogs, or send $5. to receive our current and next three catalogs ($7. foreign).

Avalon Comics
P.O. Box 234
Boston, MA 02123

PHONE: (617) 262-5544
FAX: (617) 948-2300

Larry Curcio, proprietor
Overstreet Senior Advisor 1994-1996
Comic's Buyers Guide Customer Service Award Winner 1990-1996

ARCHANGELS©

Fine Vintage Collectibles

The Very Best in Vintage Golden-Age and Silver-Age Comic Books

Always Buying and Selling.

Specializing in High Quality, Investment Grade Collectibles.

Rob Hughes

1116 - 8th Street • Suite #106
Manhattan Beach, CA 90266
310-335-1359 • 619-297-0549 Fax
www.archangels.com
sales @ archangels.com

Senior Advisor to Overstreet Price Guide.

- Over 20 Years Experience-

COMIC COLLECTOR/DEALER

WANTS YOUR COMICS!

Paying up to 100% or more of Guide for many comics of interest.

▼ POINTS TO CONSIDER ▼

1. I have over 20 years experience in comic fandom. I have bought many of the major collections over the years and purchased them against competing bidders.
2. Consigning your comics to an auction does not always let you realize your collection's potential. Many collectors and dealers end up purchasing a large portion of these comics well below market value. Plus the fact that you do not receive your money in a timely manner. Selling to us would assure you of immediate payment.
3. Being a collector/dealer allows me the ability to buy your entire collection and pay you the most for it. We will figure individual demand items at a high percentage and adjust the percentage on lesser items. The end result is maximizing your value.
4. You have nothing to lose by contacting me. ***Why miss out on your best offer?***

***Give us a try!* CALL 603-869-2097 TODAY!**

JAMES F. PAYETTE

Rare Books & Comics

P.O Box 750 • Bethlehem, NH 03574
Phone 603-869-2097 • Fax 603-869-3475

CREDENTIALS

Special Advisor to Overstreet Guide	1985–1998
Member AACBC	1990–1998
Member AACBC Authenticating, Certification, and Grading committee for Sotheby's	1991–1998
CBG Customer Service Award Winner for many years	
Experience as Dealer/Collector since	1975

PLEASE SEE MY OTHER ADS FOR FURTHER REFERENCE

PACIFIC COMIC EXCHANGE, INC.

SELLERS: Please contact The Exchange if you would like to *consign* these or other books at full market value. All books should be graded according to CGSA standards.

Call for our free catalog!

CGSA	M	NM/M	++ + NM --	VFN/NM	++ + VFN --	FN/VFN	+ FN --	VG/FN	+ VG	G/VG	G	Fr/G	Fr	Pr
	100 - 91	90	88.85.80.75	70	68.65.63.60.55	50	45.40.35	30	25.20	15	10	8	6	3
OVERSTREET -	100	99	98.96.94.92	90	88.86.84.82.78	73	70.65.60	55	50.45	35	25	18	10	3

© DC

Action Comics 1

© DC

Detective Comics 27

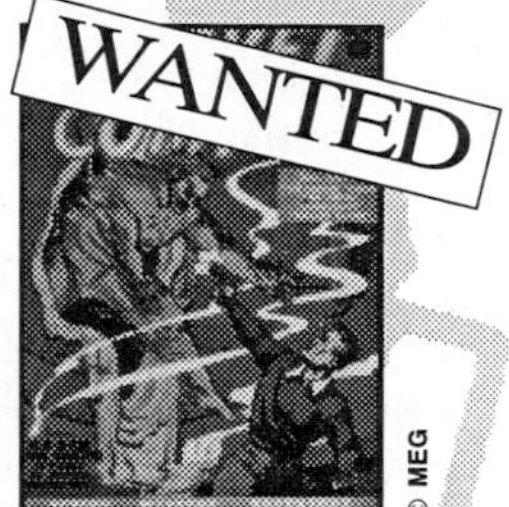

© MEG

Marvel Comics 1

	G 10	VG 20	FN 40	VFN 60	NM 80	NM/M 90
Action Comics 1	$25,000	$50,000	$80,000	$130,000	$260,000	$450,000
Detective Comics 27	$22,000	$45,000	$75,000	$115,000	$225,000	$375,000
Marvel Comics 1	$15,000	$25,000	$45,000	$65,000	$130,000	$260,000

Wanted Immediately in VFN 60 - NM/M 90

	VFN 60	NM 80	NM/M 90
Action Comics 1	$130,000	$260,000	$450,000
Adventure Comics 40	$30,000	$60,000	$100,000
Adventure Comics 210	$2,000	$5,000	$7,500
Adventure Comics 247	$2,500	$6,000	$10,000
All Star Comics 3	$30,000	$60,000	$120,000
All Star Comics 8	$25,000	$50,000	$75,000
All-American Comics 16	$50,000	$100,000	$175,000
Amazing Fantasy 15	———	$25,000	$50,000
Amazing Spider-Man 1	———	$20,000	$35,000
Batman 1	$40,000	$80,000	$130,000
Batman 100	$1,200	$3,000	$6,000
Captain America 1	$35,000	$70,000	$110,000
Detective Comics 1	$75,000	$150,000	$225,000
Detective Comics 27	$115,000	$225,000	$375,000
Detective Comics 33	$25,000	$50,000	$100,000
Detective Comics 38	$25,000	$50,000	$100,000
Fantastic Four 1	———	$20,000	$40,000
Flash Comics 1	$40,000	$80,000	$140,000
Flash Comics 104	$5,000	$10,000	$20,000
Green Lantern 1 (SA)	$1,500	$4,000	$7,500
Green Lantern 1 (GA)	$15,000	$30,000	$60,000
Incredible Hulk 1	$5,000	$12,000	$25,000
Jimmy Olsen 1	$3,500	$10,000	$15,000
Journey Into Mystery 83	———	$6,000	$12,000
Justice League 1	$1,500	$5,500	$10,000
Lois Lane 1	$2,000	$4,500	$8,500
Marvel Comics 1	$65,000	$130,000	$260,000
More Fun Comics 52	$50,000	$100,000	$150,000
More Fun Comics 55	$10,000	$20,000	$40,000
Sensation Comics 1	$13,000	$25,000	$50,000
Showcase 4	$18,000	$35,000	$70,000
Showcase 22	$2,000	$8,000	$12,000
Sub-Mariner Comics 1	$12,000	$25,000	$50,000
Superman 1	$75,000	$125,000	$250,000
Superman 100	$1,500	$3,500	$6,000
Suspense Comics 3	$7,000	$14,000	$21,000
Wonder Woman 1	$12,000	$30,000	$60,000
X-Men 1	———	$6,000	$12,000

Visit our web site at www.pcei.com

Corporate Office:
337 S. Robertson Blvd. Ste 203, Beverly Hills, CA 90211
Tel: (310) 836-7234 (PCEI), Fax: (310) 836-7127

Shipping Address:
P.O. Box 34849 Los Angeles, CA 90034
E-Mail: sales@pcei.com, www.pcei.com

CGSA, PCE, and the PCE logo are Trademarks of the PACIFIC COMIC EXCHANGE, INC.
Copyright © 1998 by PACIFIC COMIC EXCHANGE, INC. All rights reserved.

PCE PACIFIC COMIC EXCHANGE, INC

P.O. BOX 34849, Los Angeles, CA 90034 ◆ Tel: (310) 836-7234 ◆ Fax: (310) 836-7127 ◆ E-Mail: sales@pcei.com

Instructions: The following books are currently listed on the Exchange and are available for sale at the prices specified. Prices are subject to change without notice. All orders are subject to a 10% buyers commission.

PgQ: Page Quality (0.0 - 3.0: White; 3.3: Near White; 3.5: Off-White; 4: Beige or Cream, 4.5-6.5: Light to Dark Tan).

The grade listed is the **CGSA** grade (see diagram below). Call for our free catalog or visit our web site at **www.pcei.com**

CGSA M	NM/M	NM	VFN/NM	VFN	FN/VFN	FN	VG/FN	VG	G/VG	G	Fr	Pr
100.99.98.97.96.95.94.93.92.91	90	88.85.80.75	70	65.60.55	50	45.40.35	30	25.20	15	10	6	3
OVERSTREET - 100	99	98,96,94,92	90	86,82,78	73	70,65,60	55	50,45	35	25	10	3

DC Adventure Comics 78
Mile High / S & K Cover
NM+ 85 (1.0) $7,000

DC All Star Comics 3
Origin/1stApp J.S.A.
FN/VF 50 (3.5) $19,500

MVL Amazing Fantasy 15
Origin/1stApp Spider-Man
VF++ 68 (3.5) $19,500

FWCT America's Greatest 1
Mile High/White Pages
NM+ 85 (2.0) $8,000

DC Batman 1
Origin Batman/1stApp Joker
VG+ 25 (3.3) $17,500

DC Batman 5
1stApp Batmobile W/Bat-Head
NM- 75 (3.3) $7,500

DC Batman 100
VF- 55 (5.0) $1,650

FWCT Bulletman 3
Mile High
NM/M 90 (3.0) $3,000

TIM Captain America 3
Murphy Anderson Copy
FN+ 45 (5.5) $4,750

FWCT Capt. Marvel Adv. 1
Captain Marvel By Jack Kirby
VG+ 25 (4.5) $6,500

DC Detective Comics 1
Mod. Restored (Scarce)
M aFN 35 (5.0) $22,500

DC Detective Comics 27
Mod. Restored / 1st App Batman
M aVG/FN 30 (4.5) $45,000

DC Detective Comics 38
Origin/1stApp Robin
VG 20 (4.5) $6,000

MVL Fantastic Four 1
White Mountain Copy
NM+ 85 (2.0) $50,000

DC Flash Comics 1
Origin/1stApp Flash
VG+ 25 (5.0) $15,000

MVL Incredible Hulk 1
Origin/1stApp Hulk
VF- 55 (4.5) $6,250

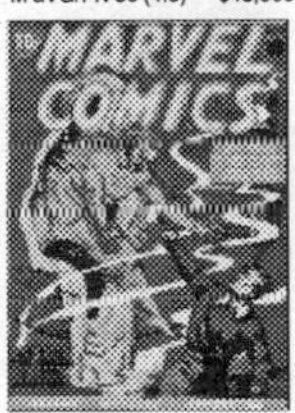

TIM Marvel Comics 1
Larson Copy / Origin Sub-Mariner
VF 60 (3.5) $70,000

DC More Fun Comics 52
Mod. Restored By S. Cicconne
M aVFN 60 (4.0) $17,500

DC New Book of Comics 2
Mile High
NM 80 (2.0) $12,000

DC NewYork World's Fair 1939
1st Publ App Sandman
VG 20 (5.5) $3,600

DC Sensation Comics 2
Etta Candy Begins
VF/NM 70 (3.5) $5,000

DC Showcase 4
Origin/1st App SA Flash
NM 80 (4.5) $40,000

DC Star Spangled Comics 17
Mile High / Double Cover
dVF/NM 70 (1.0) $4,825

DC Superman 1
Moderate Restoration
M aVG/FN 30 (6.5) $22,000

DC Wonder Woman 1
Best known Copy / Origin W.W.
NM++ 88 (3.0) $75,000

CGSA, PCE, and the PCE logo are Trademarks of the PACIFIC COMIC EXCHANGE, INC. Copyright © 1990-1998 by PACIFIC COMIC EXCHANGE, INC. All rights reserved.

Sold.

That is all you will be able to say when you are dealing with Harley Yee. My prices paid out are among the highest. You are always able to receive cash immediately. There is no collection that is too small because I will travel anywhere to view your collection.

I have over 14 years experience and I'm also a senior advisor to the *Overstreet Price Guide.* You will always receive prompt, professional service. I specialize in the Golden and Silver Age.

HARLEY YEE

P.O. Box 51758
Livonia, MI 48151-5758
voice: 800.731.1029 or 734.421.7921
fax: 734.421.7928

Call or write for a free catalog.

WANTED!
PRIME COMICS AND ART

Frazetta

Photos courtesy of Christie's

GOLDEN AGE

GOLD & SILVER AGE ART

Comics and Stories has been a leader in Comic Character Collectibles for over 20 years. As exclusive consultants, we inaugurated and conducted six record setting Comic Collectible sales at **Christie's**, the world renowned auction house. Agents of Frank Frazetta, Mort Drucker and Carmine Infantino for the sale of original art, advisors to the Overstreet Price Guide and authors of the definitive features on high end transactions in the field, we have an unparalleled record of honesty and integrity. **Whether securing consignments for inclusion at auction or buying material outright,** we have consistently attained record prices for prime collectibles.

Currently accepting consignments!
Call us before parting with any of your treasures.

Key Wants:

•Comics Books - Gold and silver age 1933-1965
•Comic Art - Shuster to Kirby
•**Comic Strip art** - McCay to Foster to Schulz

122 West End Avenue • Ridgewood • NJ • 07450 • 201-652-1305
Fax: 201-445-3371 • **(By Appointment Only)**

COMICS & TOYS OF THE 20th Century

WANTED>>
GOLDEN AGE SILVER AGE MODERN BULK

WE SPECIALIZE IN
60's MARVEL & GOLDEN AGE

BUYING & SELLING
G.I. JOE, BARBIE, STAR WARS, JAMES BOND, MARILYN MONROE, KING KONG, ELVIS, BEATLES, KISS, BUCK ROGERS, ORIGINAL ART, PULPS, MOVIE POSTERS, BIG LITTLE BOOKS, TOYS, BASE BALL & MARVEL STUFF!

COMIC BOX PRODUCTIONS
c/o
MICHAEL CARBONARO
67-53 WOODHAVEN BLVD. REGO PARK, NY 11374

718-459-1781
FAX 718-4[illegible]-2[illegible]

WHERE THE SUPERHEROES MEET

Top Artists

Top Dealers

Top Publishers

@ St. Paul Church NYC>> 59th St. & 9th Ave.

>>June.6th++Sep.11th-12th++Nov.13th-14th<<

718-275-1567

www.digdomdes.com/bigapple

Looking for these Goldenage Gems?

We specialize in Pre-'65 Comics
Golden Age: Mainstream, Rare/Esoteric
Precode: Horror, Good-Girl, Crime, Romance
Non-Pictured Gerber's "8","9","10"s
Silver Age: High Grade & Keys only

Original Art from the 1880's through Today
Comic, Strip, Illustration, Fantasy, Pulp

CONTACT US FIRST
BUY/SELL/TRADE

PUT US TO WORK FOR YOU!
WANT LISTS FILLED

Ken Danker

Toll Free: (888) 504-3024
email: monster@collzone.com
3050 Five Forks Trickum Rd.
Suite 110-203
Lilburn, GA 30047

Cliff Wiener

(561) 488-1874
Fax: (954) 741-1022
10695 Lake Oak Way
Boca Raton, FL 33498

Website: http://www.collzone.com/monster
ALL Comics and Art are PICTURED Online!

COSMIC COMIX INC

SPECIALIZING IN INVESTMENT QUALITY COLLECTABLES

1544 S.W. 23rd TERR.
DEERFIELD BCH., FL 33442

(954) 426-1210

OPEN MON - FRI
10AM - 6PM EST
ASK FOR MARK

WANTED

Strict Overstreet Grading
Telephone Orders Only
Checks or Money Orders
5 Day Return Policy

BUY - SELL - TRADE

COSMIC COMIX INC. ONLY BUYS AND SELLS THE HIGHEST QUALITY, PRE-1966, UNRESTORED BOOKS, IN FINE OR BETTER CONDITION. 40 YEARS OF COLLECTING EXPERIENCE INSURES ACCURATE AND STRICT GRADING, ALONG WITH MY 1 YEAR WARRANTY AGAINST UNDETECTED RESTORATION FOUND.

CALL TODAY!!!

WE DEAL IN QUALITY NOT QUANTITY PEDIGREE AND HIGH GRADE BOOKS.

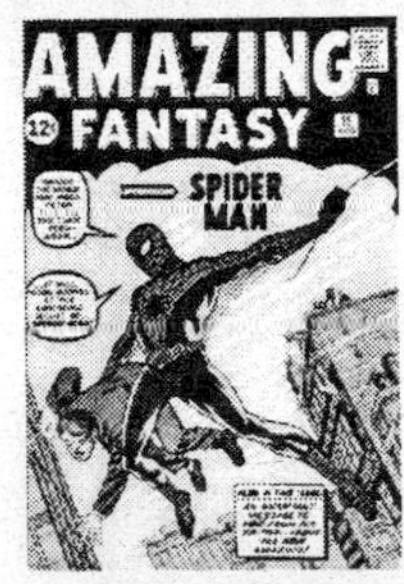

MONEY BACK GUARANTEE

BUYING/SELLING
COMIC BOOKS & ORIGINAL ART
$$ TOP DOLLAR PAID $$

Golden Age and Silver Age comic books and original art

I have been a collector since 1959. I am an accurate grader, and I know how you want to be treated.

I will **Buy** both small and large collections. Send your list today for a prompt reply, **and remember** - before you sell, contact me.
Also, please send me your **want list.**

CONRAD ESCHENBERG
RT. 1, BOX 204-A
COLD SPRING, NY 10516
PHONE/FAX: (914) 265-2649
E-MAIL: COMICART@PCREALM.NET
INTERNET SITE:
WWW.COMICSNART.PCREALM.NET

ABSOLUTE TOP DOLLAR FOR DITKO & KIRBY ORIGINAL ART!!!!!!!!!!

		FAIR	GOOD	V. GOOD
WANTED:	ACTION #1	14,000	25,000	48,000
	DETECTIVE #27	12,000	21,000	44,000

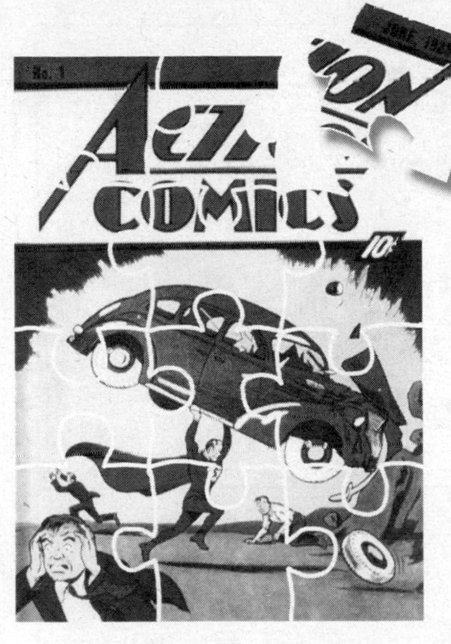

Renaissance Restoration Lab

Over the years restoration has changed from cut-and-paste work to a highly skilled profession requiring thorough knowledge of chemicals and materials. Choosing a restorer has become increasingly difficult: technology has improved and comic book buyers have become more concerned about the long term effects of certain procedures.

Renaissance Restoration Lab is a partnership between an experienced artist-restorer and a chemical engineer, dedicated to modern archival restoration technologies. We are commited to providing restoration of exceptional quality at a fair price.

With each book restored we provide a restoration certificate and disclosure sheet detailing each process and compound used to rejuvenate your prized collectable. This is your guarantee of the quality and completeness of the restoration, and it provides valuable insurance for future evaluation.

Now you will not have to compromise on quality or peace-of-mind to get a fair price. If you have questions or concerns, please feel free to call.

Chris Friesen
Artist-Restorer

Peter Birkemoe
Chemist-Conservator

* Website coming soon—call for details *

81 Riverwood Parkway, Toronto, Ontario, Canada, M8Y 4E4 Ph: (416) 231-1272
email: birkemoe@interlog.com

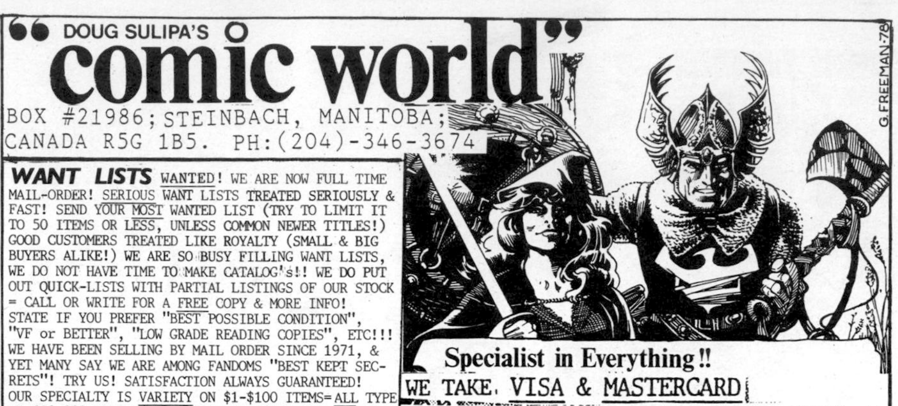

"DOUG SULIPA'S comic world"
BOX #21986; STEINBACH, MANITOBA; CANADA R5G 1B5. PH:(204)-346-3674
G.FREEMAN-78
WANT LISTS WANTED! WE ARE NOW FULL TIME MAIL-ORDER! SERIOUS WANT LISTS TREATED SERIOUSLY & FAST! SEND YOUR MOST WANTED LIST (TRY TO LIMIT IT TO 50 ITEMS OR LESS, UNLESS COMMON NEWER TITLES!) GOOD CUSTOMERS TREATED LIKE ROYALTY (SMALL & BIG BUYERS ALIKE!) WE ARE SO BUSY FILLING WANT LISTS, WE DO NOT HAVE TIME TO MAKE CATALOG's!! WE DO PUT OUT QUICK-LISTS WITH PARTIAL LISTINGS OF OUR STOCK = CALL OR WRITE FOR A FREE COPY & MORE INFO! STATE IF YOU PREFER "BEST POSSIBLE CONDITION", "VF or BETTER", "LOW GRADE READING COPIES", ETC!!! WE HAVE BEEN SELLING BY MAIL ORDER SINCE 1971, & YET MANY SAY WE ARE AMONG FANDOMS "BEST KEPT SECRETS"! TRY US! SATISFACTION ALWAYS GUARANTEED! OUR SPECIALTY IS VARIETY ON $1-$100 ITEMS= ALL TYPE >> 600,000 POUNDS OF INVENTORY, ALL TYPES ARE IN OUR VERY TIGHTLY PACKED 7,000 SQ.FT WAREHOUSE!
Specialist in Everything!!
WE TAKE VISA & MASTERCARD
>> IN MAIL ORDER BUSINESS SINCE 1971! <<

COMPETIONISTS ALERT! WE LUV YA! OUR NEWEST SPECIALTY IS CHARACTER/PERSONALITY/SUBJECT SEARCH's! SO YOU THINK YOU HAVE IT ALL! WELL THEN YOU HAVEN'T DEALT WITH US! ALONG WITH OUR H-U-G-E VARIETY WE ALSO HAVE CANADIAN & BILINGUAL (FRENCH & ENGLISH) VARIATIONS, THAT NO ONE ELSE HAS! We have searched for Covers/Appearances with Spiderman, Shazam,W.Woman,Bruce Lee,M.Monroe,Baseball/Golf/Chess/Xmas/etc-THEMES,KISS(have mostly mags),JFK,Royalty,Beatles, Monkees,Elvis,Travola,F.Fawcett,Star Trek/Wars,Lesbian,Nazi,UFO,Shadow,REH,HPL,ERB,Gretzky,Bradbury,POTA & MORE! (Our greatest STRENGH is in Mags,Canadian Editions,Odd books,Fanzines,etc!) Most items we have are from 1960-1996! A list of what you have, or at less a detailed general description of what you don't need HELPS a LOT!

>>> ONE MILLION COMICS & RELATED ITEMS IN STOCK (1960-1996) We have about 95% of ALL comics printed from 1960-96! We specialize in UNDER $100 items! (But have a GOOD selection of over $100 items)! We have Comics,Digests,Mags, Fanzines,Treasury's,Kids books,British,Foreign,Canadian,Graphic Novels,Paperbacks,Cards,Games,etc! OUR INVENTORY INCLUDES; (400,000 MARVEL)(300,000 DC)(150,000 ALTERNATES 60's-90's)(15,000 DELL 1950 up)(25,000 GOLD KEY)(7,000 DISNEY,all companies)(3,000 HANNA BARBERA,all companies)(25,000 HARVEY)(20,000 CHARLTON)(25,000 ARCHIE), PLUS Warren,ACG,CLASSICS Sr/Jr,Tower,Dennis Menace,King,Spire Christian,Treasure Chest,Fawcett & Misc Westerns,MAD,SICK ,Cracked,Skywald,Adult Cartoon (pre-1980, NO XXX),IPC/British,Capt Canuck,Gladstone,Atlas/Seaboard,TRIB comics, Red Circle/JC,Star,Help,Heavy Metal,National Lampoon,& more! SEND THOSE SERIOUS WANT LISTS!

>>> 100,000 RECORDS; Most Standard issue LP's from 1970-90 in stock, Good Selection 1950-69)(Most $20 & under)

>>> SPORTS CARDS; All 71/2-89/90 OPC HOCKEY in stock!(Good selection of 51-69,& 90's inserts)! BASEBALL= Most 1965-89 OPC in stock! (Good selection of other 80's Stars & 90's inserts)! Most 58-72 CFL! NFL= Selection of 70's & 80's Stars & 90's inserts! BASKETBALL= 90's inserts! Lots of 1970-90 Magazines & some older! NO SETS/WAX!

>>> NON-SPORT CARDS; Decent selection of 50's-80's Singles (Most G-EX), including lots of 1975-1990 SCARCER OPC VERSIONS of Topps cards! Good selection of sets/Inserts of 1990-1994! NO Wax/Foil boxes!

>>> COLLECTIBLE CARD GAMES; SINGLES ONLY! From MAGIC (Unlimited/Revised/4th/Arabian/Dark,Fallen,Ice,Home,Legends, Antiquities,Chronicles), MARVEL OVERPOWER(1st 3 series),JYHAD,Illuminati,Star Trek TNG(1st Series=Ltd/UnL,STARWAR

>>> SCIENCE FICTION/FANTASY/HORROR = 50,000 Paperback/Digests 1940-1990! VINTAGE PAPERBACKS = 200,000 IN STOCK! (75% of ALL-TYPES PRINTED from 1940-1970; 50% of all 71-80; 25% of ALL 81-90) VINTAGE HARDCOVERS (50,000 ALL-TYPE 1900-1995) 150,000 MAGAZINES; ALL-TYPE 1940-1996 (Especially 1960 up, & SOME older); (50,000 COMIC/RELATED)(15,000 SF/F/HORROR), (10,000 SPORT)(10,000 MUSIC),(10,000 CAR/HOT ROD/HARLEY/CAR),(10,000 PLAYBOY/PENTHOUSE/MENS ADV/ADULT, no XXX), PLUS = LIFE,LOOK,POST,TIME, MACLEANS,EBONY,NAT GEO,(5,000 TV/MOVIE),TV GUIDES,ESQUIRE,FASHION,TEEN,KIDS,MODELING(AIR,RAIL,etc), RPG, AIRCRAFT,MILITARY,READERS DIGEST, CORONET,SCANDAL(Digest,Mag,Tabloid),Beckett,Price Guides,Hobby,NEWS,Popular Mech,Mech Ill,Womens,Western,True Crime,UFO,PULPS,Digests, Humor,Parody,Political,Science,Mystery,Fanzines,Video Game,Newspapers,KISS,B.LEE,BEATLES,ELVIS,JFK,STAR WAR/TREK,PERSONALITIES & MORE!

BUYING (BUYING ONE OF EACH, IF YOU HAVE MORE, LET US KNOW FIRST! RUNS PREFERED! BUYING "G" to "NM" UNLESS o/w Stated! If ONLY the title is listed, we want all! PERCENTAGES (50% etc) LISTED, are the % of Overstreet ANNUAL Guide we pay for STRICTLY Graded by condition comics! If you grade badly, we will NOT return, we will RE-GRADE & send appropriate amount! (We are VERY fair!) NO BRITTLE & INCOMPLETE ACCEPTED! YOU MUST CALL FIRST & GET AN AUTHORIZATION NUMBER TO SEND! Parcels w/o Authorization #'s = Returned Un-Opened! WRAP EXTRA WELL & INSURE! We do NOT pay postage! CALL FIRST, in case we get too many, or swamped with stuff!

DC COMICS; ACTION (#334,347,360,373,400,402-413,437,443=50%);ADVENTURE (#381-431,491-503=50%);ALL STAR WESTERN (#1-9,11=50%)(#10=75%) BATMAN (#155,169,171,176,179,181,182,185,187,189,190,193,197,198,200,203,208,213,218,219,222,223,228,232-242,254-262=50%);BATMAN FAMILY(50%); BINKY(#72-76,82=50%)(#77-81=100%);BINKYS BUDDIES(50%);BLACK MAGIC(73/5)(60%);BRAVE&BOLD(#97-102,197=50%);ALL STAR COMICS(76/8)(#60-74=50%); DARK MANSION FORBIDDEN LOVE (#1=100%)(#2-4=75%);DC 100 PAGE SUPER SPECTACULAR (#4-13=100%)(#14-18,20-22 FN-NM ONLY=50%);DC SPECIAL (#2,3= 100%;#4-15=50%);DATE WITH DEBBI (#2-13=50%)(#1,14-17=75%);DEBBI'S DATES(#1,4,6=75%)(#2,3,5,7-11=50%);DETECTIVE (#301,327,328,359,369,371, 377,395,397,400,402,404,407,408,410,414-424,437-445=50%);DOORWAY TO NIGHTMARE (#2-5=50%);FALLING IN LOVE (#100-124,134-143=50%)(#125-133= 100%);FLASH (#160,169,173,178,187,196,200,201,205,208-213,215,216=50%)(#214=100%);FOX & CROW(#81-112=50%);FOUR STAR BATTLE(50%);FROM BEYOND THE UNKNOWN (#1,7-17=75%)(REST 50%);GHOSTS (#1=100%)(#2-5=75%)(#6-40=50%);(GI COMBAT (#91,114,138-160=50%);GIRLS LOVE STORIES (#100-160, 171-180=50%)(#161-170=75%);GIRLS ROMANCE (#100-160=50%);HEART THROBS (#100-132,143-146=50%)(#133-142=75%);HOUSE OF MYSTERY (174-259=50%); HOUSE OF SECRETS (#81-120,140=50%);INFERIOR FIVE(50%);JIMMY OLSEN (#94,104,113,122,131,136-150=50%);JOHNNY THUNDER(50%);JUSTICE LEAGUE OF AMERICA (#73-160 50%);LARRY HARMONS LAUREL & HARDY(1972 DIGEST OR COMIC=100%);LEAVE IT TO BINKY(#61-71 =50%);LOIS LANE (#68,70,71,77,89,93,104, 105,112-123=50%);OUR ARMY AT WAR(#81-260=50%);OUR FIGHTING FORCES(#95,99,100,123-137=50%);PHANTOM STRANGER (#1-20=50%);PLOP(#2,3,6-9,12,13, 16,19-24=50%);PREZ (#3,4=50%);SECRET HEARTS(#100-149=50%, GIANTS=75%);SECRETS HAUNTED HOUSE(1975)(#1-5=50%);SGT ROCK (#302-320=25%);STRANGE ADVENTURES(#217-244=50%, GIANTS=75%);SHAZAM(73/8)(PAY 25%; 100pgs=75%);SUPER DC GIANT (#13,18,19=100%)(#17,21=150%)(#14-16,20,22-26=50%); SUGAR & SPIKE(#96-98=50%; #61-95=35%);SUPERBOY (#129,138,147,156,165,174,177-208=50%; #185=100%);SUPERMAN (#183,187,193,197,202,207,212,217, 222,227,232,239,241-247,250,252 ,272,278,284=50%;#245,252=100%);SUPERMAN FAMILY (#164-169=75%;#170-176=50%);SWING WITH SCOOTER (#1-5,9,20, 32-35=75%;REST=50%);THREE MOUSEKETEERS(70/71=75%);TEEN BEAT/BEAM (#1,2=50%);TOMAHAWK (#100-135=35%;#136-140=50%);UNEXPECTED(#105-162=35%, EXCEPT #116,119,121,126-136,157-162=50%);WANTED(72/3)(50%);WEIRD MYSTERY(#1-10=50%);WEIRD WESTERN (#12,14,16-19=35%);WEIRD WAR (#1=100%;#2-10 =75%;#11-40,64,68=50%);WELCOME BACK KOTTER(#3-10=50%);WITCHING HOUR (#1-21,38=50%; #22-37=35%);WONDERWOMAN (#171-217=50%);WORLDS FINEST(#161, 170,179,188,197,200-205,323=50%);YOUNG LOVE(#71-106,115-126=50%;#107-114=100%;OTHER GIANTS=75%)(YOUNG ROMANCE #154,163-196,205-208=50%; #197-204=100%;OTHER GIANTS=75%);IN THE DAYS OF THE MOB (#1=50%);LIMITED COLLECTORS EDITION (#NN[C-20]=150%;#24,33,42=75%;#23,25,28,29,32,34, 37,48,55,F-5=50%); MARVEL (PAYING 50% FOR ANY 1968-1975 CARTOON,WESTERN,(REPRINT HORROR-ONLY!),LOVE,TEEN ,SPOOF,B&W MAG,WAR(EXCEPT SG.FURY TITLES!)(PAY 100% FOR MARVEL HANNA BARBERA #2 up ONLY,1977-79);(PAY 50% for EERIE[PUBLISHER],STANLEY Pub,SKYWALD B&W Mags)(PAY 35%, [OR 50% FOR #1's/GIANTS] FOR; ANY HANNA-BARBERA Gold Key/Charlton, or TV Cartoon(same), OR ANY NON-SUPERHERO 1960's ARCHIE/HARVEY/CHARLTON(esp.TV,Love, Teen,Western,War,Cartoon), ANY G or VG (NON-DELL) 10 cent Comic Worth $10 OR LESS IN CONDITION, OR TOWER (TEEN titles ONLY)! ALSO BUYING; MARVEL/DC(60's/70's BOOKS,FANZINES),ADULT CARTOON COMICS(50's-70's),CHAIN-STORE POSTERS(Pre-1985),FANZINES(Pre-1978)MORE! SEND $1 for BUY LIST!

phone (800) 278-9691, (718) 721-9691 fax (718) 728-9691

www.silveragecomics.com/e-mail gus@silveragecomics.com

Take charge with ComicBase™

The ultimate software for the serious collector

ComicBase Master Edition combines a powerful collection management system with a thorough interactive comic book encyclopedia and guide.

■ View descriptions, with sample cover art, for over 3,300 titles ranging from classic favorites like *Adventure Comics* and *Fantastic Four* to current critically-acclaimed independents.

Captain America (Vol. 1)
When World War II began, Steve Rogers attempted to enlist in the army, but was turned away because he was considered too frail. Wanting to help any way he could, he offered to serve as a human guinea pig for the experimental Super Soldier Serum. The formula worked, transforming this former 98-pound weakling into the powerhouse known as Captain America.
A star of the Golden Age of comics, Captain America joined the Silver Age when he was revived in The Avengers #4. He soon became the leader of that team, as well as co-starring with Iron Man in Tales of Suspense. Following issue #99, Tales of Suspense spun Iron Man off into a new title, and changed its name to Captain America.
Marvel
1969-1996

■ Use the annually updated pricing information on over 70,000 individual issues to evaluate your collection. Check any issue's value history with graphs based on pricing data for the past *four years*. You can even import your own information and records from any major database or spreadsheet, including Microsoft Excel™.

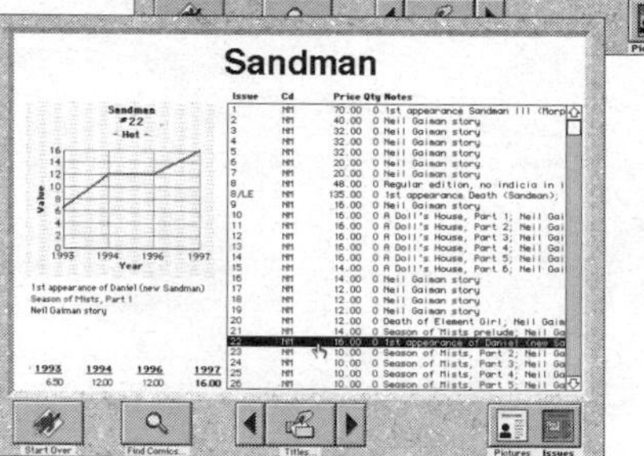

Sandman

■ Search for first appearances, origin stories, deaths, multipart storylines, and other special issues, and work by well-known artists and writers, with just the click of a button.

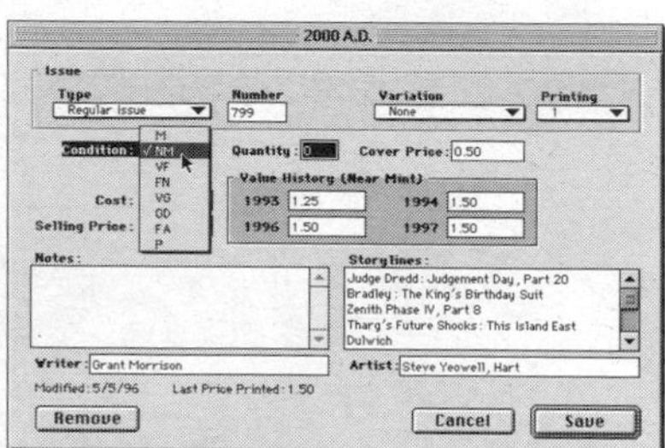

2000 A.D.
Remove
Cancel
Save

■ Track your comics, their condition, value, what you paid for them, and what you expect to sell them for, using an intelligent design that lets you enter a comic's information with just a few keystrokes. ComicBase™ also prints title reports, price lists, issue checklists, price labels and much more.

■ Use Hypertext links to explore the connections between titles. Enjoy video clips of featured comic-book related movies, too!

Bubblegum Crisis- Grand Mal

All this and more for only $89! (Reg. $129)
Call Human Computing at (408) 266-6883.
Mention code OY-8 for special $89 price.

Visit our web site: **<www.human-computing.com>**

Mac OS
PowerPC

Macintosh
✓ 68020 or later processor
✓ System 7 and 8 MB of RAM
✓ Hard drive
✓ CD-ROM drive

Windows 95
✓ 80486 or later processor
✓ Windows 95 and 10 MB of RAM
✓ Hard drive
✓ CD-ROM drive

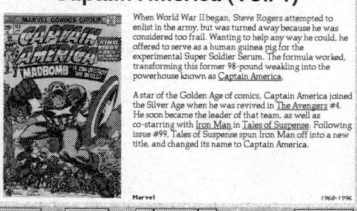

ComicBase is a trademark of Human Computing. Microsoft Excel and Windows 95 are trademarks of Microsoft Corp., Inc. Macintosh and PowerPC are trademarks of Apple Computer. Comic artwork and characters are ™ and © their respective owners. Tales from the Crypt also ® William M. Gaines, Agent

Super Sales Catalog Only $2.00

Contains everything from Superheroes to Ducks! Includes Westerns, Independents, Combat, Space, Magazines, and much, much more.

MOST COMPLETE LISTING NEXT TO OVERSTREET'S!

Covers virtually every issue printed in the last 20 - 30 years and all available for sale in three different grades.

Order your catalog today!

Individual titles of interest sent FREE with a SASE.

Dealer Inquiries welcome!

Also available, complete inventory lists of pre-1968 books:

Super-hero, Adventure, etc. * Western
Classics Illustrated * Movie and T.V.
Funny Animal, Archie, Disney, etc.

EACH LIST ONLY $1.00 OR ALL FIVE FOR $2.00.

One list may be requested FREE when ordering Super Sales Catalog. Lists for **Independents, Non-sport Cards, Magazines, and Star Trek** will be sent free upon request with your catalog or list order.

WE SPECIALIZE IN BUYING ENTIRE COLLECTIONS.

We pay up to 100% of Overstreet for selected issues. Please write or call for our buying list and terms, or with any questions you may have.

Collectors Ink

932-A W. 8th Ave. ☆ Chico, CA ☆ 95926

(530) 345-0958 ☆ Tues.-Sat. 11-5:30

e-mail: collink@cmc.net

in association with

THE PENNY RANCH

SERVING THE COLLECTING COMMUNITY SINCE 1967

• TRH Gallery •

Vintage & Contemporary Comic Art
Bought-Sold-Appraised

- Comic Book Art
- Comic Strip Art
- Animation Art
- Pulp/Science Fiction Art

Tom Horvitz, owner of TRH Gallery, is one of the country's leading comic art dealers. He's an active member of the Antique Appraisal Association of America, and continues to be one of the country's only specialists in the field of comic art truly qualified to render professional appraisals. Whatever the reason, personal, institutional donations, estate, or insurance, TRH Gallery offers you the most qualified, accurate, and professional appraisals for all your important vintage and contemporary comic art.

TRH Gallery

18324 Clark Street #223
Tarzana, CA 91356
Phone: 818-757-0747/Fax: 818-757-0859
Website: TRHGALLERY.COM
E-mail: TRHGALLERY@EARTHLINK.NET

Marvel
DC Comics
Acclaim
Caliber
Dark Horse
Image
More Comics
Magazines
Books
Apparel
Art
Games
International
Novelties
Sports
Star Trek
Star Wars
Trading Cards
Video
Adults
Backlists
Supplies

www.westfield.com

For nearly 20 years Westfield has been making it easy for comics fans to order all their favorite titles. Now, through the Internet, we've increased our selection of merchandise to thousands each month.

So, check us out on the Internet or call us for a free catalogue. We're looking forward to serving you!

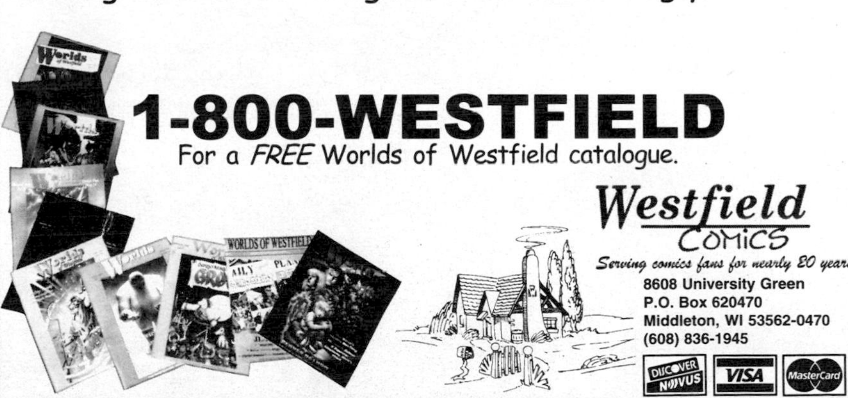

1-800-WESTFIELD

For a *FREE* Worlds of Westfield catalogue.

Westfield Comics

Serving comics fans for nearly 20 years.

8608 University Green
P.O. Box 620470
Middleton, WI 53562-0470
(608) 836-1945

DISCOVER NOVUS VISA MasterCard

NEVER THE SAME OLD CUD.
www.topcow.com

WITCHBLADE™, TALES OF THE WITCHBLADE™, The DARKNESS® & TALES OF THE DARKNESS® their logos are ®,™ & © 1998 TOP COW Productions Inc. ASCENSION™ its logo™ & © 1998 David Finch and Matthew Banning. SPIRIT OF THE TAO™ its logo™ & © 1998 Billy Tan, Duy Truong and Hoai Truong. All Artwork © 1998 TOP COW Productions Inc. All Rights Reserved.

Executive Collectibles Gallery

Auctioneers & Appraisers of Fine Vintage Comics, Original Comic Art, & Animation

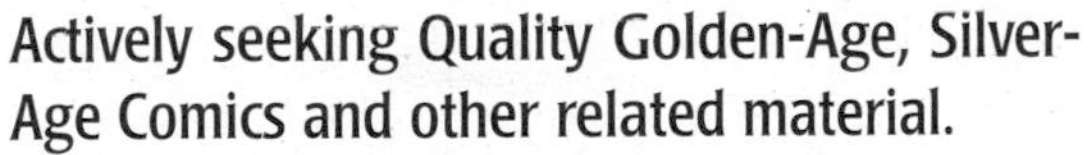

Actively seeking Quality Golden-Age, Silver-Age Comics and other related material.

When it comes time to sell your comics (one book or an entire collection), nobody will get you more for it than Executive Collectibles Gallery. Our unparalleled knowledge, experience, and integrity means more money in your pocket.

Always Purchasing:

Comic Books:
Platinum, Golden, and Silver-Age (1900-1970)

Movie Posters:
Animation, Comedy, Epic, Horror, Mystery, Western (1920-1970)

Related Material:
Original Comic Book Artwork, Production Cels, Pulps, Lithographs, Etc... (1920-Present)

3419 Via Lido #604
Newport Beach, CA 92663
(714) 955-0601 • (714) 955-0607 fax
www.execcollect.com

We hold several major auctions each year and are always seeking quality Golden and Silver-Age comics and related material for consignment or purchase. Call us for details about our next major auction event!

CANADA'S FINEST
IN PREMIUM QUALITY GOLDEN & SILVER AGE COMIC BOOKS

Try us once and you'll be hooked!

19 Harrison Court • Toronto • CANADA • L1N 6E2
tel:905•666•0011 fax:905•839•0330

Nick Catros Steve Quinnell

Mail order/Want list specialists
GRADE GUARANTEED

VISA

TOP DOLLAR PAID FOR ALL COLLECTIONS

COMING IN JUNE 1998...

THE
NEXT
COMIC

HEAVEN

AUCTION

OVER 5,000 GOLDEN AND SILVER
AGE COMIC BOOKS WILL BE OFFERED

Comic Heaven
John and Nanette Verzyl
P.O. Box 900
Big Sandy, TX 75755
1-903-636-5555

COMIC HEAVEN

IS

BUYING

- Timely's
- Golden Age DC's
- MLJ/Fox/Quality
- "Mile High" Copies (Church Collection)
- 1950's Atlas Comics
- E.C.'s
- 1950's Horror
- Most Other Brands and Titles from the Golden and Silver Age

Specializing In Large Silver and Golden Age Collections

Comic Heaven
John and Nanette Verzyl
P.O. Box 900
Big Sandy, TX 75755
1-903-636-5555

COMIC HEAVEN

IS

BUYING

Selling Your Collection?

Contact Us First

Highest Prices Paid

We Do The Work

You Get The Cash!!!!

Specializing In Large Silver and Golden Age Collections

Comic Heaven
John and Nanette Verzyl
P.O. Box 900
Big Sandy, TX 75755
1-903-636-5555

YOU CAN GET OUR AUCTION CATALOG

ABSOLUTELY

FREE

JUST CALL

1-903-636-5555

ANY TIME

OR WRITE TO:

COMIC HEAVEN

P.O. BOX 900

BIG SANDY, TX 75755

Comic Heaven
John and Nanette Verzyl
P.O. Box 900
Big Sandy, TX 75755
1-903-636-5555

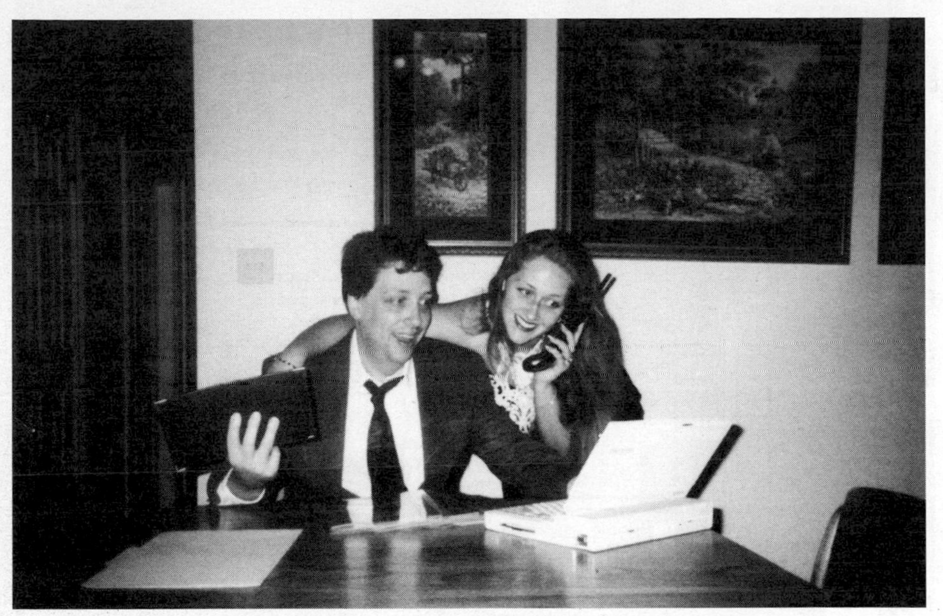

JOHN VERZYL AND DAUGHTER ROSE, "HARD AT WORK."

John Verzyl started collecting comic books in 1965, and within ten years he had amassed thousands of Golden and Silver Age comic books. In 1979, with his wife Nanette, he opened "COMIC HEAVEN," a retail store devoted entirely to the buying and selling of comic books.

Over the years, John Verzyl has come to be recognized as an authority in the field of comic books. He has served as an advisor to the "Overstreet Price Guide." Thousands of his "mint" comics were photographed for Ernst Gerber's newly-released "Photo-Journal Guide To Comic Books." His tables and displays at the annual San Diego Comic Convention draw customers from all over the country.

The first COMIC HEAVEN AUCTION was held in 1987, and today his Auction Catalogs are mailed out to more than ten thousand interested collectors and dealers.

Comic Heaven
John and Nanette Verzyl
P.O. Box 900
Big Sandy, TX 75755
1-903-636-5555

E. Gerber Products, Inc.
PO Box 906 Minden, NV 89423

Orders: 800-79-MYLAR
Information: 702-883-4100
24 hr. Fax: 702-883-4179

1 mil Mylar D ®. Standard sleeve sealed on 3 sides with a 1"+ flap which can be tucked in or taped closed. The least expensive of all Mylar products.

Cat#	Size	Description	Price per: 100	500	3000	(1000) Bundle
700M	7 x 10 3/4	Current Comics	$18	$85	$136 /1000	$98
725M	7 1/4 x 10 3/4	Standard Comics	20	86	138 /1000	109
775M	7 3/4 x 10 3/4	Silver/Gold Comics	21	87	140 /1000	121
800M	8 x 10 3/4	Gold Age Comics	22	88	141 /1000	127
825M	8 1/4 x 10 3/4	Super Gold Age Comics	22	90	143 /1000	132

2 mil Mylar D®. Sealed on 3 sides with a 1"+ flap. Easier to handle than the 1 mil sleeves. Flaps can be folded over & taped or tucked inside. Most practical & economical solution for most collections.

Cat#	Size	Description	Price per: 50	200	1000	(500) Bundle
700M2	7 x 10 3/4	Current Comics	$12	$38	$152	$68
725M2	7 1/4 x 10 3/4	Standard Comics	13	41	167	74
775M2	7 3/4 x 10 3/4	Silver/Gold Comics	13	43	168	78
800M2	8 x 11 1/2	Gold Age Comics	14	46	193	83
825M2	8 1/4 x 11 1/2	Super Gold Age Comics	16	53	213	85
875M2	8 3/4 x 11 1/2	Large Comics, Mags & Letter	17	58	228	89

4 mil Mylar®. The classic design of 2 flaps which open& receive your collectible like lips. New improved (patent pending) design with one top edge slightly higher than the other. Easier to open the flaps for collection insertion. (more than 20 million sold world wide).

Cat#	Size	Description	Price per: 10	50	200	1000	(500) Bundle
700S	7 x 10 3/4	Current Comics	$7	$21	$72	$305	$138
725S	7 1/4 x 10 3/4	Standard Comics	7	22	75	316	144
775S	7 3/4 x 10 3/4	Silver/Gold Comics	8	24	81	322	150
800S	8 x 11 1/2	Gold Age Comics	9	26	85	339	155
825S	8 1/4 x 11 1/2	Super Gold Age Comics	10	29	94	379	161
875S	8 3/4 x 11 1/2	Large Comics, Mags & Letter	11	31	102	409	173

Glass vault enclosure with a UV TOPS sleeve, held together by air pressure and 'hook & loop' fasteners. No screws, simple to open & close. Air tight, the optimum & ultimate protection for Comic Book sizes

Cat#	Fits Tops! Size	Description	Visible Framed Size	Price per: 1	10	50
725DC	725T	Standard Comics	6 7/8 x 10	$22	$201	$861
775DC	775T	Silver/Gold Comics	7 1/4 x 10 1/4	23	203	891
825DC	825T	Gold Age Comics	7 3/4 x 10 3/8	24	205	918

MOTOR CITY COMICS

BUYING:

- Top Prices Paid !!!
- We Always Pay 60%-200% of Guide for pre-1970 Comics
- We Will Travel Anywhere to View Large Collections
- Senior Advisor to the Overstreet Price Guide

GOLD & SILVER AGE COMICS

NOW OPEN
Come Visit Our New Warehouse
by appointment only

& SELLING:

- Large Selection of Gold & Silver Age
- Accurate Grading
- Competitive Pricing
- Want List Service

FREE
CATALOGS
Call or Write for Your Copy

MOTOR CITY COMICS
19785 W. 12 MILE RD. • SUITE 231 • SOUTHFIELD, MI 48076
PHONE: (248) 426-8059 • FAX: (248) 426-8064

Top of the Line
Preservation And
Storage Supplies

...At The Lowest Prices

E. Gerber
PRODUCTS, INC.

TM A revolution in design. 4 mil Mylar® D with patent pending beaded top opening edges. These prevent snagging your collectibles on those sharp Mylar edges. At the same time, they provide a way for the plastic "C" clip (Slip-Locks) to slide on effectively sealing your collectible 99% air tight.

Cat#	Size	Description	Price per: 10	50	200	1000	(500) Bundle
700T	7 x 10 3/4	Current Comics	$8	$24	$79	320	$144
725T	7 1/4 x 10 3/4	Standard Comics	8.25	25	83	331	150
775T	7 3/4 x 10 3/4	Silver/Gold Comics	8.50	26	85	338	155
800T	8 x 11 1/2	Gold Age Comics	9	27	88	355	161
825T	8 1/4 x 11 1/2	Super Gold Age Comics	9.50	30	99	398	167
875T	8 3/4 x 11 1/2	Large Comics, Mags & Letter	10	32	105	417	178
SL	Slip-Lock	matches width of sleeve opening	6	17	58	228	

TM
- Extra thick, 42 mil, genuine acid-free, virgin wood, cellular fiber.
- Meets strict U.S. Gov't standards for archival storage.
- 3% calcium carbonate buffer throughout, maintains ph of 8.0+.
- White on both sides.
- The highest quality backing board available anywhere.

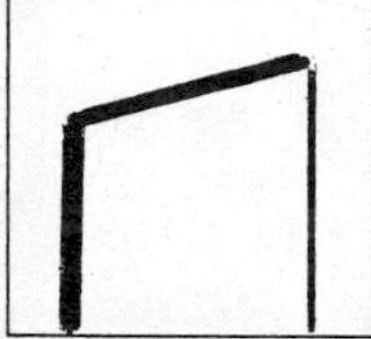

Cat#	Size	Description	Price per: 50	200	1000	(500) Bundle
658FB	6 5/8 x 10 1/4	Current Comics	$12	$41	$167	$75
678FB	6 7/8 x 10 1/4	Standard Comics	12	42	170	77
725FB	7 1/4 x 10 1/4	Silver/Gold Comics	13	44	175	78
750FB	7 1/2 x 10 3/8	Gold Age Comics	14	46	183	81
775FB	7 3/4 x 10 3/8	Super Gold Age Comics	15	52	205	83
825FB	8 1/4 x 10 3/4	Large Comics, Mags & Letter	15	52	205	85

ACID FREE BOXES

Cat#	Size	Description	Price per: 5	20	40
Acid-Free, corrugated box. All white. Shipped flat.					
20	15 x 8 x 11 1/2	Current to Gold Age Comics	$25	$94	$150
Acid-Free, Lignin free, Double wall corrugated box. Light tan, one piece. Shipped flat.					
22	15 x 8 x 11 1/2	Current to Gold Age Comics	$54	$200	$320
Acid-Free, 3% alkaline buffered throughout. 200 lb. grey corrugated. Shipped flat.					
13	15 x 8 1/2 x 11 1/2	Silver/Gold Comics	$41	$150	$265
15	15 x 9 1/4 x 12 1/2	Super Gold/Magazines	46	166	299

E. Gerber Products, Inc.
PO Box 906 Minden NV 89423

Mylar® Trademark of DuPont Co.
All other trademarks (TM) E. Gerber Products, Inc.

VISA®

Shipping & Handling:
Customers:
Add 15% of total order
Add 45% for Canada
Add 70% for Foreign

Retailers: Be sure to look for the line of E. Gerber Collecting Supplies in issues of *PREVIEW.*

We are pleased to announce:
Diamond Comic Distributors carry all our products which are available to Comic Book Specialty Shops.

The American Comic Book: 1897-1932
IN THE BEGINNING:
THE PLATINUM AGE

J. C. Vaughn

For most of the time since comics fandom became organized, many collectors have thought of the period dubbed the "Golden Age" (June 1938 to 1945) as the true beginning of the American comic book. Even though that date is wrong by a third of a century, it's easy to see how it came to be misconstrued--a little comic book called **Action Comics #1** had something to do with it.

The first appearance of Superman in that historic issue not only kicked off an amazing era, but it warped perceptions about what came before and obscured many of the crucial comics and characters that paved the way for the Last Son of Krypton and his peers. After all, who could stand up to the Man of Steel? But to ignore the comics that were published before little Kal-El became Clark Kent is to turn our backs on a rich tapestry of popular culture dating back to shortly before the turn of the century.

Now, as the 20th century draws to a close, we find ourselves in a unique position. Within the confines of a century, it might make sense to consider a collection of a particular era a "complete" body of work. When viewed from the next century, though--even just a few years into the new millennium--that same collection suddenly seems very incomplete.

GIMBLE BROTHERS, PHILADELPHIA

FAMOUS COMICS In Book Form

Each book contains 48 pages of the latest and most humorous drawings of the world's foremost and cleverest cartoonists. These cartoons printed in the daily newspapers are the favorites of millions of people, young and old, and are now published in permanent book form.

BRINGING UP FATHER, First Series, By George McManus

BRINGING UP FATHER, Second Series, By George McManus

BRINGING UP FATHER, Third Series, By George McManus

BRINGING UP FATHER, Fourth Series, By George McManus

PERCY AND FERDIE, By H. A. MacGill

REG'LAR FELLERS, By Gene Byrnes

The Toonerville Trolley and Other Picture Stories, By Fontaine Fox

MUTT AND JEFF, Book No. 6, By Bud Fisher

MUTT AND JEFF, Book No. 7, By Bud Fisher

MUTT AND JEFF, Book No. 8, By Bud Fisher

KEEPING UP WITH THE JONESES, First Series, By "Pop" Momand

KEEPING UP WITH THE JONESES, Second Series, By "Pop" Momand

Size, 10 x 10 inches. Heavy Cardboard Covers with Design in Colors.
Price, per volume, 25 cents. Postage, each, 8 cents

MERRY BOOKS TO AMUSE

Hans and Fritz
Nippy's Pop
Lady Bountiful
Hawkshaw, the Detective
13¼x10¼ inches, 28 pages.
Each, 25 cents
Postage, each, 8 cents

'Smatter, Pop
The Newlyweds and Their Baby
The Funny Larks of Hans and Fritz
[illegible] inches, 52 pages, in colors throughout.
Each, 50 Cents.
Postage, each, 8 cents

BUSTER BROWN BOOKS

The Children's Favorite Character

No more popular character has ever been conceived than "Buster Brown." His funny pranks and adventures with his wonderful Dog, Tige, have caused endless amusement and entertainment for young and old.

Buster Brown in Foreign Lands
Buster Brown the Busybody
Buster Brown on His Travels
Buster Brown, His Dog Tige, and Their Jolly Times
Buster Brown's Amusing Capers
Buster Brown's Latest Frolics

Bound in strong board covers, with original design in colors. Illustrated in colors. Size 11x16 inches. Price, per volume, 50 cents. Postage, each, 8 cents.

The cover and a page from **Gimbel Brothers' Catalog** (circa 1920). Big department stores offered comics such as **Bringing Up Father** and **Mutt & Jeff** to their customers in the early days of the medium.
©Gimbels

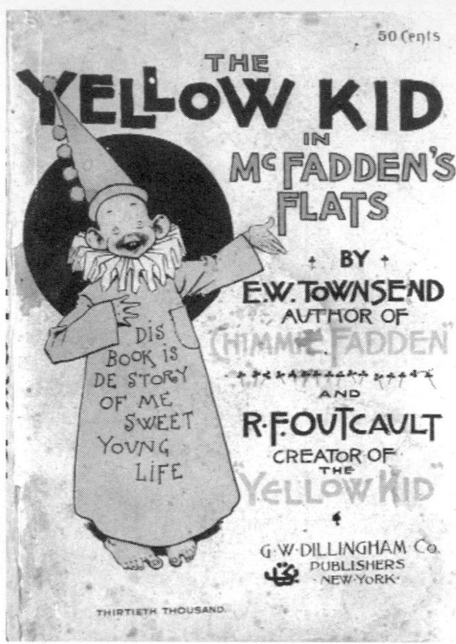

The Yellow Kid in McFadden's Flats (1897) was the first comic book. © G. W. Dillingham

To better understand, think of collecting baseball cards only from 1974 to the present, records from September of 1943 to August of 1944, paintings only from May 1857, or some other arbitrarily limited niche. Sooner or later, someone is going to ask, "Why didn't you collect the rest?" A good question, but until recently, the full importance and scope of the Platinum Age of comics had barely been determined, and now it can be placed in its proper historical context as the first chapter in the story of the American comic book.

Comic books from the "Platinum Age" (1897 to 1932) have been increasing in value throughout the 1990s as collectors expanded their want lists in shrewd anticipation of this new post-millennial viewpoint. Many of the going prices have risen steadily, particularly since the 100 Year Anniversary of Richard Outcault's **The Yellow Kid** in 1995.

More and more often, though, serious collectors are expanding their awareness of the Platinum Age not just as a new arena for investment, but as a definitive period of comics history and a reflection of the times in which the comic book was first created.

The comics of the Platinum Age were the logical extension of the daily comic strips which had themselves rapidly become popular with adult audiences of the day. In fact, most of the early comics were volumes collecting the newspaper strips in one publication and featuring characters like **Little Nemo**, **Mutt & Jeff**, and **Little Orphan Annie**.

The price of these comics was generally around 50¢, a price which clearly suggests these books were aimed at adults rather than children. In the 1920s the price dropped to 25¢, still well above the disposable income level of most children (comic book prices would not reach that height again until the mid-

Little Nemo in Slumberland
© Duffield & Co.

1970s). This is not to say that adults weren't passing these comics on to their children--rather it is clear from this evidence that comics of this sort were intended for adult consumers, and were probably enjoyed by a great many adult readers as well as young ones.

The production values, too, indicate the early comics were not targeted at children. The dimensions of the first comics were larger, up to twice as large as current comics. They often came with thick cover stock (the aforementioned cardboard covers) and high quality paper interiors. Once they began appearing in color, the four-color reproduction on many of these comic books was, for its time, state-of-the-art.

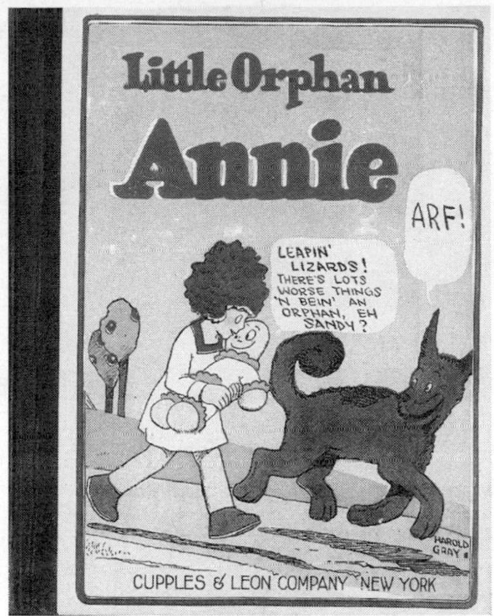

Little Orphan Annie
© C&L

In the years prior to the end of the Platinum Age in 1933 (marked by the debut of the 10¢ 32-page giveaway **Funnies on Parade**), comic books moved rapidly from products which stood on their own to marketing tools for other products; from straightforward reprints of comic strips to books featuring original material and stories; from regional successes to national sensations.

These early books set the stage for everything that was to follow and represent the true beginning of the American comic book. As collectors begin developing a more holistic approach to collecting comics and related items from the 20th century, the comics of the Platinum Age can not help but attract the attention they deserve.

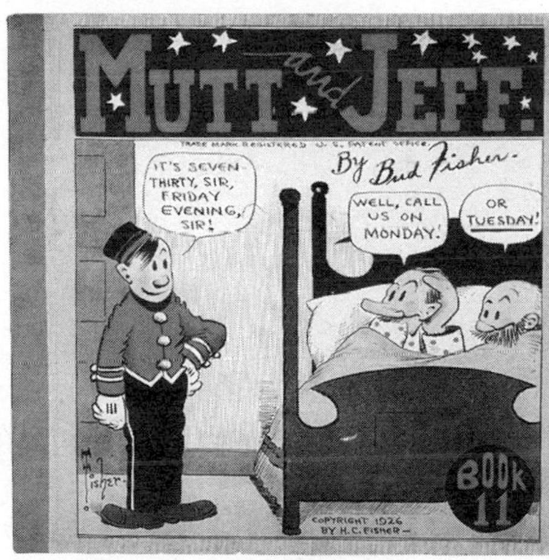

Mutt & Jeff #11
© C&L

Readers looking for more information about the Platinum Age can find key books listed in "The Overstreet Comic Book Hall of Fame" in this edition, a thorough listing of comics and prices in the Platinum Age pricing section, also in this edition, and in Robert L. Beerbohm's article, "The American Comic Book: 1897-1932," originally printed in the 27th edition of ***The Overstreet Comic Book Price Guide*** *and on our website at* ***www.gemstonepub.com****.*

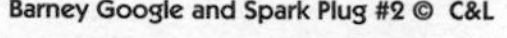
Barney Google and Spark Plug #2 © C&L

Bringing Up Father #1 © C&L

Bringing Up Father #9 © C&L

GD25 FN65 VF82

ADVENTURES OF HAWKSHAW (See Hawkshaw The Detective)
1917 (9-3/4x13-1/2", 48 pgs., Color & two-tone)
The Saalfield Publishing Co.

nn-By Gus Mager (only 24 pgs. of strips, reverse of each pg. is blank) 40.00 160.00 280.00

ADVENTURES OF MICKEY MOUSE, THE
Book I, 1931 - Book II, 1932 (5-1/2"x8-1/2", 32 pgs.)
David McKay Co., Inc.

Book I-First Disney book, by strict definition (1st printing-50,000 copies)(see Mickey Mouse Book by Bibo & Lang). Illustrated text refers to Clarabelle Cow as "Carolyn" and Horace Horsecollar as "Henry". The name "Donald Duck" appears with a non-costumed generic duck on back cover & inside, not in the context of the character that later debuted in the Wise Little Hen.
Hardback w/characters on back-c 71.00 284.00 500.00
Softcover w/characters on back-c 36.00 144.00 250.00
Version without characters on back-c 43.00 172.00 300.00
Book II-Less common than Book I. Character development brought into conformity with the Mickey Mouse cartoon shorts and syndicated strips. Captain Church Mouse, Tanglefoot, Peg-Leg Pete and Pluto appear with Mickey & Minnie 18.00 72.00 125.00

ADVENTURES OF SLIM AND SPUD, THE
1924 (3-3/4x 9-3/4", 104 pgs., B&W strip reprints)
Prairie Farmer Publ. Co.

nn 40.00 160.00 280.00

ADVENTURES OF WILLIE GREEN, THE
1915 (50¢, 8-1/2X16", B&W, soft-c)
Frank M. Acton Co.

Book 1-By Harris Brown; strip-r 40.00 160.00 280.00

AIN'T IT A GRAND & GLORIOUS FEELING? (Also see Mr. & Mrs.)
1922 (9x9-3/4", 52 pgs., stiff cardboard-c)
Whitman Publishing Co.

nn-1921 daily strip-r; B&W, color-c; Briggs-a 40.00 160.00 280.00
nn-(9x9-1/2", 28pgs., stiff cardboard-c)-Sunday strip-r in color (inside front-c says "More of the Married Life of Mr. & Mrs".) 29.00 116.00 200.00

ALL THE FUNNY FOLKS
1926 (11-1/2x8-1/2", 112 pgs., color, hard-c)
World Press Today, Inc.

nn-Barney Google, Spark Plug, Jiggs & Maggie, Tillie The Toiler, Happy Hooligan, Hans & Fritz, Toots & Casper, etc. 86.00 344.00 600.00

ALONG THE FIRING LINE WITH ROGER BEAN
1916 (6x17", 66 pgs., B&W, hard-c)
Chas. B. Jackson

3-By Chic Jackson (1915 daily strips) 49.00 196.00 340.00

ALPHONSE & GASTON & LEON
1903 (15x10", Sunday strip reprints in color)
Hearst's New York American & Journal

nn-By Fred Opper 129.00 516.00 900.00

ANGELIC ANGELINA
1909 (11-1/2x17", 30 pgs., 2 colors)
Cupples & Leon Company

nn-By Munson Paddock 40.00 160.00 280.00

BANANA OIL
1924 (52 pgs., B&W)
MS Publ. Co.

nn-Milt Gross-a; not reprints 50.00 200.00 350.00

BARNEY GOOGLE AND SPARK PLUG (See Comic Monthly & Giant Comic Album)
1923 - No. 6, 1928 (52 pgs., B&W, daily strip-r)
Cupples & Leon Co.

1-By Billy DeBeck 50.00 200.00 350.00
2-6 40.00 160.00 280.00
NOTE: *Started in 1918 as newspaper strip; Spark Plug began 1922, 1923.*

GD25 FN65 VF82

BLACKBERRIES, THE
1901 (9"x12", color, hard-c)
R. H. Russell

nn-By E. W. Kemble 100.00 400.00 700.00

BOBBY THATCHER & TREASURE CAVE
1932 (7x9", 86 pgs., B&W, hard-c)
Altemus Co.

nn-Reprints; Storm-a 23.00 92.00 160.00

BOBBY THATCHER'S ROMANCE
1931 (7x8-3/4")
The Bell Syndicate/Henry Altemus Co.

nn-By Storm 23.00 92.00 160.00

BRINGING UP FATHER
1917 (16-1/2x5-1/2", 100 pgs., B&W, cardboard-c)
Star Co. (King Features)

nn-(Rare)-Daily strip reprints by George McManus (no price on-c) 121.00 484.00 850.00

BRINGING UP FATHER
1919 - No. 26, 1934 (10x10", 52 pgs., B&W, stiff cardboard-c) (No. 22 is 9-1/4x9-1/2")
Cupples & Leon Co.

1-Daily strip-r by George McManus in all 82.00 328.00 575.00
2-10 40.00 160.00 280.00
11-26 (Scarcer) 48.00 192.00 335.00
The Big Book 1(1926)-Thick book (hardcover); 10-1/4x10-1/4", 142 pgs. 118.00 472.00 825.00
The Big Book 2(1929) 93.00 372.00 650.00
NOTE: *The Big Books contain 3 regular issues rebound and probably w/dust jackets.*

BUDDY TUCKER & HIS FRIENDS (Also see Buster Brown)
1906 (11x17", color)
Cupples & Leon Co.

nn-1905 Sunday strip-r by R. F. Outcault 111.00 444.00 775.00

BUDDY TUCKER VISITS THE HOUSE THAT JACK BUILT
1907
Cupples & Leon Co.

nn 34.00 136.00 240.00

BUFFALO BILL'S PICTURE STORIES
1909 (Soft cardboard cover)
Street & Smith Publications

nn 43.00 172.00 300.00

BUGHOUSE FABLES
1921 (10¢, 4x4-1/2", 48 pgs.)
Embee Distributing Co. (King Features)

1-Barney Google 32.00 128.00 225.00

BUG MOVIES
1931 (52 pgs., B&W)
Dell Publishing Co.

nn-Not reprints; Stookie Allen-a 26.00 104.00 185.00

BUSTER BROWN (Also see Brown's Blue Ribbon Book of Jokes and Jingles & Buddy Tucker & His Friends)
1903 - 1916 (Daily strip-r in color)
Frederick A. Stokes Co.

(1)...& His Resolutions (1903, 11-1/4x16", 66 pgs.) by R. F. Outcault (Rare)-1st nationally distributed comic. Distr. through Sears & Roebuck(Rare) 643.00 2572.00 4500.00
(2)...His Dog Tige & Their Troubles (1904, 11-1/4x16-1/4", 66 pgs.)(Rare) 243.00 972.00 1700.00
(3)...Pranks (1905, 11-1/4x16-3/8", 66 pgs.)(Rare) 200.00 800.00 1400.00
(4)...Antics (1906, 11x16-3/8", 66 pgs.)(Rare) 200.00 800.00 1400.00
(5)...And Company (1906, 11x16-1/2", 66 pgs.)(Scarce) 164.00 656.00 1150.00

Buster Brown's Amusing Capers © C&L

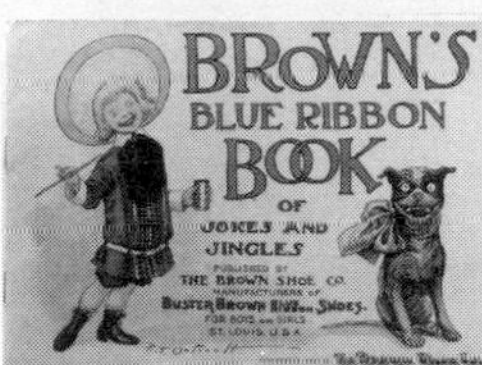

Buster Brown's Blue Ribbon Book of Jokes and Jingles-Book 2 © Brown Shoe Co.

Buster Brown's Book of Jokes and Jingles-Book 3 © Brown Shoe Co.

GD25 FN65 VF82

(6)...Mary Jane & Tige (1906, 11-1/4x16, 66 pgs.)(Scarce) 164.00 656.00 1150.00
(7) Collection of Buster Brown Comics (1908)(Scarce) 136.00 544.00 950.00
(8)...Up to Date (1910, 10-1/8x15-3/4", 66 pgs.)(Rare) 136.00 544.00 950.00
(9)... Fun And Nonsense (1911, 10-1/8x15-3/4", 62 pgs.) 136.00 544.00 950.00
(10)...The Fun Maker (1912, 10-1/8x15-3/4", 66 pgs.)(Rare)-Yellow Kid (4 pgs.) 136.00 544.00 950.00
(11)...At Home (1913, 10-1/8x15-3/4", 56 pgs.)
(12)...The Little Rogue (1916, 10-1/8x15-3/4", 62 pgs.) (Rare) 121.00 484.00 850.00
(13)...And Tige Here Again 114.00 456.00 800.00
(14)...The Real Buster Brown 114.00 456.00 800.00
NOTE: *Rarely found in fine or mint condition.*

BUSTER BROWN
1904 - 1912 (3x5" to 5x7"; sizes vary)(Advertising premium booklets)
Various Publishers

The Brown Shoe Company, St. Louis, USA
Set of five books (5x7", 16 pgs., color)

Brown's Blue Ribbon Book of Jokes and Jingles Book 1 (nn, 1904)-By R. F. Outcault; Buster Brown & Tige, Little Tommy Tucker, Jack & Jill, Little Boy Blue, Dainty Jane; The Yellow Kid app. on back-c (1st comic book premium) 486.00 1944.00 3400.00
Buster Brown's Blue Ribbon Book of Jokes and Jingles Book 2 (1905)-Original color art by Outcault 200.00 800.00 1400.00
Buster's Book of Jokes & Jingles Book 3 (1909)-r/Blue Ribbon post cards not signed by R.F. Outcault 200.00 800.00 1400.00
Buster's Book of Instructive Jokes and Jingles Book 4 (1910)-Original color art not signed by R.F. Outcault 200.00 800.00 1400.00
...Book of Travels nn (1912, 3x5")-Original color art not signed by Outcault 86.00 344.00 600.00
NOTE: *Estimated 5 to 6 known copies exist of books #1-4.*

The Buster Brown Bread Company

"Buster Brown" Bread Book of Rhymes, The nn (1904, 4x6", 12 pgs.)-Original color art not signed by R.F. Outcault 121.00 484.00 850.00

The Buster Brown Stocking Company

Buster Brown Drawing Book, The nn (nd, 5x6", 20 pgs.)-B&W reproductions of 1903 R.F. Outcault art to trace 61.00 244.00 425.00

Collins Baking Company

Buster Brown Drawing Book nn (1904, 3x5", 12 pgs.)-Original B&W art to trace not signed by R.F. Outcault 61.00 244.00 425.00

C. H. Morton, St. Albans, VT

Merry Antics of Buster Brown, Buddy Tucker & Tige nn (nd, 3-1/2x5-1/2", 16 pgs.)-Original B&W art by R.F. Outcault 61.00 244.00 425.00

Frederick A. Stokes Co.

...Abroad (1904, 8x10-1/4, 86 pgs., B&W, hard-c)-R. F. Outcault-a (Rare) 136.00 544.00 950.00
...Abroad (1904, B&W, 67 pgs.)-R. F. Outcault-a 136.00 544.00 950.00
...My Resolutions (1906, 10x8", B&W, 68 pgs.)-R.F. Outcault-a (Rare) 164.00 656.00 1150.00

Ivan Frank & Company

Buster Brown nn (1904, 3x5", 12 pgs.)-B&W repros of R. F. Outcault Sunday pages (First premium to actually reproduce Sunday comic pages – may be first premium comic book?) 61.00 244.00 425.00

Pond's Extract

Buster Brown's Experiences With Pond's Extract nn (1904, 4-1/2x6-3/4", 28 pgs.)-Original color art by R.F. Outcault 121.00 484.00 850.00

Ringen Stove Company

Quick Meal Steel Ranges nn (nd, 3x5", 16 pgs.)-Original B&W art not signed by R.F. Outcault 57.00 228.00 400.00

Saalfield Company Muslin Books

(1)...Goes Fishing (1907, 6-7/8x6-1/8", 24 pgs., color)-r/1905 Sunday comics page by Outcault(Rare) 29.00 116.00 200.00
(2)...Plays Indian (1907, 6-7/8x6-1/8", 24 pgs., color)-r/1905 Sunday comics page by Outcault(Rare) 21.00 84.00 150.00
(3)...Plays Cowboy (1907, 6-7/8x6-1/8", 24 pgs., color)-r/1905 Sunday comics page by Outcault(Rare) 21.00 84.00 150.00
(4)...And The Donkey (1907, 6-7/8x6-1/8", 24 pgs., color)-r/1905 Sunday comics page by Outcault (Rare) 21.00 84.00 150.00

No Publisher Listed

The Drawing Book nn (1906, 3-9/16x5", 8 pgs.)-Original B&W art to trace not signed by R.F. Outcault 55.00 220.00 400.00

BUSTER BROWN
1906 - 1917 (11x17", color, strip-r)
Cupples & Leon Co./N. Y. Herald Co.
(By R. F. Outcault)

GD25 FN65 VF82

(1A)...His Dog Tige & Their Jolly Times (1906, 11x16, 46 pgs.) 200.00 800.00 1400.00
(1B)...His Dog Tige And Their Jolly Times (1906, 11-3/8x16-5/8", 68 pgs.)
(2)...Latest Frolics (1906, 11-3/8x16-5/8", 66 pgs.) 118.00 472.00 825.00
(3)...Amusing Capers (1908, 58 pgs.) 89.00 355.00 625.00
(4)...The Busy Body (1909, 11-3/8x16-5/8", 62 pgs.)
(5)...On His Travels (1910, 11x16", 46 pgs.) 89.00 356.00 625.00
(6)...Happy Days (1911, 11-3/8x16-5/8", 58 pgs.) 89.00 356.00 625.00
(7)...In Foreign Lands (1912) 89.00 356.00 625.00
(8)...And His Pets (1913, 11x16", 46 pgs.) 89.00 356.00 625.00
(9)...Funny Tricks (1914, 11-3/8x16-5/8", 58 pgs.)
(10)...And the Cat (1917) 89.00 356.00 625.00
NOTE: *Rarely found in fine or mint condition.*

BUSTER BROWN NUGGETS
1907 (1905, 7-1/2x6-1/2", 36 pgs., color, strip-r, hard-c)(By R. F. Outcault)
Cupples & Leon Co./N.Y.Herald Co.

(1) Buster Brown Goes Fishing 32.00 128.00 225.00
(2) Buster Brown Goes Swimming 32.00 128.00 225.00
(3) Buster Brown Plays Indian 32.00 128.00 225.00
(4) Buster Brown Goes Shooting 32.00 128.00 225.00
(5) Buster Brown Plays Cowboy 32.00 128.00 225.00
(6) Buster Brown On Uncle Jack's Farm 32.00 128.00 225.00
(7) Buster Brown Tige And The Bull 32.00 128.00 225.00
(8) Buster Brown And Uncle Buster 32.00 128.00 225.00
(9) Buddy Tucker Meets Alice in Wonderland 32.00 128.00 225.00
(10) Buddy Tucker Visits The House That Jack Built 32.00 128.00 225.00

BUSTER BROWN'S AUTOBIOGRAPHY
1907 (B&W, 10x8", 71 pgs.) (16 color plates & 36 B&W illos)
Frederick A. Stokes Co.

nn 50.00 200.00 350.00

BUTTONS & FATTY IN THE FUNNIES
nd (1927)(10-1/4"x15-1/2", 28pg., color)
Whitman Publishing Co.

W936-Signed "M.E.B.", probably Merrill Blosser; strips in color copyright The Brooklyn Daily Eagle; thought to be one of the first two western Publ. Co. books (very rare) 57.00 228.00 400.00

CHARLIE CHAPLIN
1917 (9x16", B&W, large size soft-c)
Essanay/M. A. Donohue & Co.

Series 1, #315-Comic Capers (9-3/4x15-3/4")-18pgs. by Segar; Series 1, #316-In the Movies 200.00 800.00 1400.00
Series 1, #317-Up in the Air, #318-In the Army 200.00 800.00 1400.00
Funny Stunts-(12-1/2x16-3/8", color) 164.00 656.00 1150.00
NOTE: *All contain **Segar** -a; pre-Thimble Theatre.*

CHASING THE BLUES
1912 (7-1/2x10", 52 pgs., B&W, hard-c)
Doubleday Page

nn-by Rube Goldberg 111.00 444.00 775.00

CLANCY THE COP

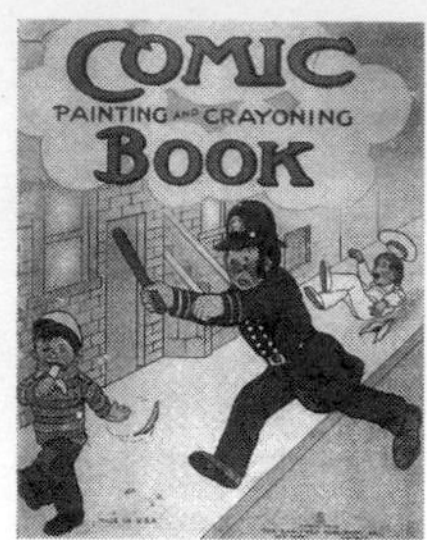

Comic Painting and Crayoning Book
© Saalfield Publ.

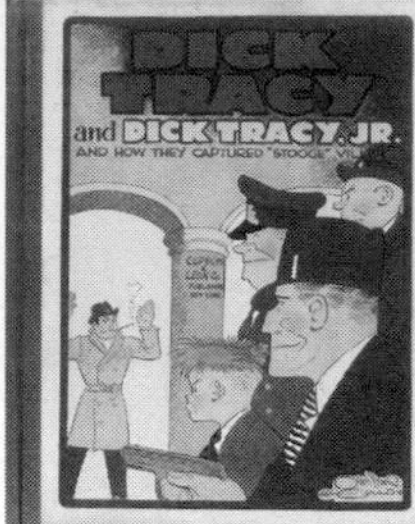

Dick Tracy & Dick Tracy Jr.
And How They Captured "Stooge" Viller
© C&L

Foxy Grandpa: The Latest Larks of...
© Frederick A. Stokes

GD25 FN65 VF82

1930 - No. 2, 1931 (10x10", 52 pgs., B&W, cardboard-c) (not-r)
Dell Publishing Co.

1,2-Vep-a 40.00 160.00 280.00

CLIFFORD MCBRIDE'S IMMORTAL NAPOLEON & UNCLE ELBY
1932 (12x17"; soft-c cartoon book)
The Castle Press

nn-Intro. by Don Herod 36.00 144.00 250.00

COMIC MONTHLY
Jan, 1922 - No. 12, Dec, 1922 (10¢, 8-1/2"x9", 28 pgs., 2-color covers) (1st monthly newsstand comic publication) (Reprints 1921 B&W dailies)
Embee Dist. Co.

1-Polly & Her Pals 157.00 628.00 1100.00
2-Mike & Ike by Rube Goldberg 79.00 316.00 550.00
3-S'Matter, Pop? 50.00 200.00 350.00
4-Barney Google 79.00 316.00 550.00
5-Tillie the Toiler 44.00 176.00 310.00
6-12: 6-Indoor Sports. 7-Little Jimmy. 8-Toots and Casper. 9,10-Foolish Questions. 11-Barney Google & Spark Plug in the Abadaba Handicap. 12-Polly & Her Pals 40.00 160.00 280.00

COMIC PAINTING AND CRAYONING BOOK
1917 (10x13-1/2", 32 pgs.) (No price on-c)
Saalfield Publ. Co.

nn-Tidy Teddy by F. M. Follett, Clarence the Cop, Mr. & Mrs. Butt-In; regular comic stories to read or color 36.00 144.00 250.00

DAFFYDILS
1911 (6x8", 52 pgs., B&W, hard-c)
Cupples & Leon Co.

nn-By Tad 37.00 148.00 260.00

DEADWOOD GULCH
1931 (52 pgs., B&W)
Dell Publishing Co.

nn-By Charles "Boody" Rogers 24.00 96.00 165.00

DICK TRACY & DICK TRACY JR. CAUGHT THE RACKETEERS, HOW
1933 (7x8-1/2", 88pgs., hard-c) (See Treasure Box of Famous Comics)
Cupples & Leon Co.

2-(Numbered on pg. 84)-Continuation of Stooge Viller book (daily strip reprints from 8/3/33 thru 11/8/33)(Rarer than #1) 79.00 316.00 550.00
With dust jacket... 118.00 472.00 825.00

DICK TRACY & DICK TRACY JR. AND HOW THEY CAPTURED "STOOGE" VILLER
1933 (7x8-1/2", 100 pgs., hard-c, one-shot)
Reprints 1932 & 1933 Dick Tracy daily strips
Cupples & Leon Co.

nn(No.1)-1st app. of "Stooge" Viller 45.00 180.00 315.00
with dust jacket... 79.00 316.00 550.00

DOINGS OF THE DOO DADS, THE
1922 (50¢, 7-3/4x7-3/4", 34 pgs, B&W, red & white-c, square binding)
Detroit News (Universal Feat. & Specialty Co.)

nn-Reprints 1921 newspaper strip "Text & Pictures" given away as prize in the Detroit News Doo Dads contest; by Arch Dale 39.00 156.00 275.00

DOLLY DIMPLES & BOBBY BOONCE'
1933
Cupples & Leon Co.

nn 21.00 84.00 150.00

DREAMS OF THE RAREBIT FIEND
1905
Doffield & Co.?

nn-By Winsor McCay (Very Rare) (Three copies known to exist)
Estimated value.... 514.00 2056.00 3600.00

GD25 FN65 VF82

FELIX
1931 (6-1/2"x8-1/4", 52 pgs., color, hard-c w/dust jacket)
Henry Altemus Company

1-3-Sunday strip reprints of Felix the Cat by Otto Messmer. Book No. 2 r/1931 Sunday panels mostly two to a page in a continuity format oddly arranged so each tier of panels reads across two pages, then drops to the next tier. (Books 1 & 3 have not been documented.)(Rare)
Each 82.00 328.00 575.00
With dust jacket 129.00 516.00 900.00

FELIX THE CAT BOOK
1927 (8"x15-3/4", 52 pgs, half in color-half in B&W)
McLoughlin Bros.

nn-Reprints 23 Sunday strips by Otto Messmer from 1926 & 1927, every other one in color, two pages per strip. (Rare) 171.00 684.00 1200.00
260-Reissued (1931), reformatted to 9-1/2"x10-1/4" (same color plates, but one strip per every three pages), retitled ("Book" dropped from title) and abridged (only eight strips repeated from first issue, 28 pgs.).(Rare) 79.00 316.00 550.00

FOXY GRANDPA (Also see The Funnies, 1st series)
1901 - 1916 (Strip-r in color, hard-c)
N. Y. Herald/Frederick A. Stokes Co./M. A. Donahue & Co./Bunny Publ. (L. R. Hammersly Co.)

1901-9x15" in color-N. Y. Herald 136.00 544.00 950.00
1902- "Latest Larks of...", 32 pgs., 9-1/2x15-1/2" 96.00 384.00 675.00
1902- "The Many Advs. of...", 9x12", 148 pgs. (Hammersly) 104.00 416.00 725.00
1903- "Latest Advs.", 9x15", 24 pgs., Hammersly Co. 96.00 384.00 675.00
1903- "...'s New Advs.", 10x15", 32 pgs., Stokes 96.00 384.00 675.00
1904- "Up to Date", 10x15", 28 pgs., Stokes 96.00 384.00 675.00
1905- "& Flip Flaps", 9-1/2x15-1/2", 52 pgs. 96.00 384.00 675.00
1905- "The Latest Advs. of", 9x15", 28, 52, & 66 pgs, M.A. Donohue Co.; re-issue of 1902 issue 71.00 284.00 500.00
1905- "Merry Pranks of", 9-1/2x15-1/2", 52 pgs., Donahue 71.00 284.00 500.00
1905- "Latest Larks of", 9-1/2x15-1/2", 52 pgs., Donahue; re-issue of 1902 issue 71.00 284.00 500.00
1905- "Latest Larks of", 9-1/2x15-1/2", 24 pg. edition, Donahue; re-issue of 1902 issue 71.00 284.00 500.00
1906- "Frolics", 10x15", 30 pgs., Stokes 71.00 284.00 500.00
1907 71.00 284.00 500.00
1908?- "Triumphs", 10x15" 71.00 284.00 500.00
1908?- "...& Little Brother", 10x15" 71.00 284.00 500.00
1911- "Latest Tricks", r-1910,1911 Sundays-Stokes Co. 71.00 284.00 500.00
1914-(9-1/2x15-1/2", 24 pgs.)-6 color cartoons/page, Bunny Publ. 64.00 256.00 450.00
1916- "Merry Book", 10x15", Stokes 64.00 256.00 450.00

FOXY GRANDPA SPARKLETS SERIES
1908 (6-1/2x7-3/4"; 24 pgs., color)
M. A. Donahue & Co.

"... Rides the Goat", "...& His Boys", "...Playing Ball", "...Fun on the Farm", "...Fancy Shooting", "...Show the Boys Up Sports",... "Plays Santa Claus" each.... 75.00 300.00 525.00
900- "Playing Ball"; Bunny illos; 8 pgs., linen like pgs., no date 61.00 244.00 425.00

FUNNIES, THE (Also see Comic Cuts)
1929 - No. 36, 10/18/30 (10¢; 5¢ No. 22 on) (16 pgs.)
Full tabloid size in color; not reprints; published every Saturday
Dell Publishing Co.

1-My Big Brudder, Johnathan, Jazzbo & Jim, Foxy Grandpa, Sniffy, Jimmy Jams & other strips begin; first four-color comic newsstand publication; also contains magic, puzzles & stories 107.00 428.00 750.00

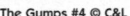

The Gumps #4 © C&L

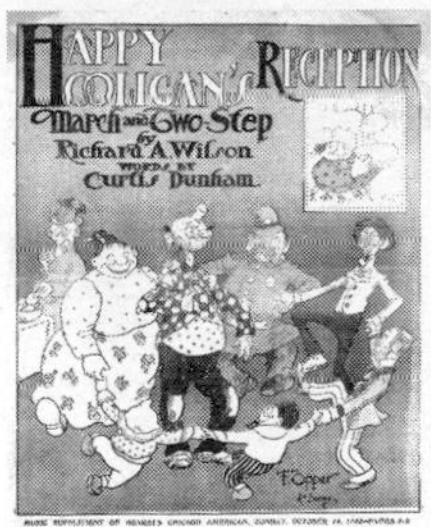

Happy Hooligan © Frederick A. Stokes

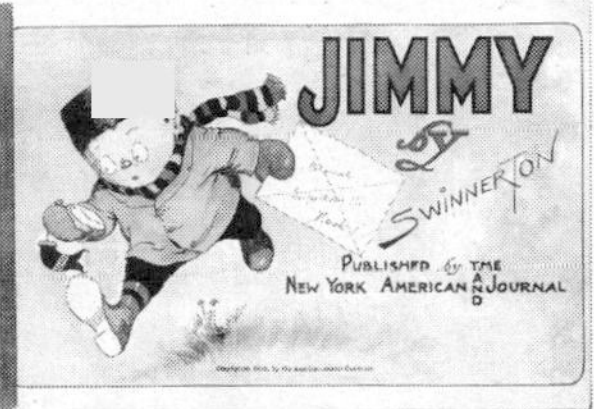

Jimmy nn © NY American & Journal

GD25 FN65 VF82

2-21 (1930, 30¢) 39.00 156.00 275.00
22(nn-7/12/30-5¢) 31.00 124.00 220.00
23(nn-7/19/30-5¢), 24(nn-7/26/30-5¢), 25(nn-8/2/30), 26(nn-8/9/30), 27(nn-8/16/30), 28(nn-8/23/30), 29(nn-8/30/30), 30(nn-9/6/30), 31(nn-9/13/30), 32(nn-9/20/30), 33(nn-9/27/30), 34(nn-10/4/30), 35(nn-10/11/30), 36(nn, no date-10/18/30) each.... 31.00 124.00 220.00

FUNNY FOLK
1899 (12"x16-1/2", half in color-half in B&W, hard-c) (Reprints cartoons from Puck)
E. P. Dutton
nn 186.00 744.00 1300.00

GASOLINE ALLEY (Also see Popular Comics & Super Comics)
1929 (7x8-3/4", B&W daily strip-r, hard-c)
Reilly & Lee Publishers
nn-By King (96 pgs.) 43.00 172.00 300.00

GUMPS, THE
No. 1, 1918 - No. 6, 1921; 1924 - No. 8, 1931 (10x10", 52 pgs., B&W)
Landfield-Kupfer/Cupples & Leon No. 2
Book No. 1(1918)(Rare)-cardboard-c, 5-1/4x13-1/3", 64 pgs., daily strip-r by Sidney Smith 121.00 484.00 850.00
Book No.2(1918)-(Rare); 5-1/4x13-1/3"; paper cover; 36 pgs. daily strip reprints by Sidney Smith 86.00 344.00 600.00
Book No. 3-6 (Rare) 54.00 216.00 375.00
nn(1924)-By Sidney Smith 57.00 228.00 400.00
2,3 37.00 148.00 260.00
4-7 31.00 124.00 220.00
8-(10x14"); 36 pgs.; B&W; National Arts Co. 31.00 124.00 220.00

GUMPS, ANDY AND MIN, THE
nd (1920s)(Giveaway, 5-1/2"x14", 20 pgs., B&W, soft-c)
Landfield-Kupfer Printing Co., Chicago/Morrison Hotel
nn-Strip-r by Sidney Smith; art & logo embossed on cover w/hotel restaurant menu on back-c or a hotel promo ad; 4 diff. issues known 24.00 96.00 165.00

HANS UND FRITZ
1929 (10x13-1/2", 28 pgs., B&W)
The Saalfield Publishing Co.
193-(Rare)-By R. Dirks; contains 1916 Sunday strip reprints of Katzenjammer Kids & Hawkshaw the Detective 100.00 400.00 700.00
...The Funny Larks Of 2(1929) 79.00 316.00 550.00

HAPPY HOOLIGAN (See Alphonse...)
1903 (18 pgs., Sunday strip reprints in color)
Hearst's New York American-Journal
Book 1-By Fred Opper 121.00 484.00 850.00
50 Pg. Edition(1903)-10x15" in color 125.00 500.00 875.00

HAPPY HOOLIGAN (Handy...) (See The Travels of...)
1908 (10x15", 32 pgs, color, cardboard-c)
Frederick A. Stokes Co.
nn 79.00 316.00 550.00

HAPPY HOOLIGAN (Story of...)
No. 281, 1932 (9-1/2x12", 16 pgs., soft-c)
McLoughlin Bros.
281-Three-color text, pictures on heavy paper 41.00 164.00 290.00

HAROLD TEEN (Adventures of...)
1929-31 (52 pgs., cardboard-c)
Cupples & Leon Co.
nn-B&W daily strip reprints by Carl Ed 40.00 160.00 280.00

HAWKSHAW THE DETECTIVE (See Advs. of..., Hans Und Fritz & Okay)
1917 (10-1/2x13-1/2", 24 pgs., B&W Sunday strip-r)
The Saalfield Publishing Co.
nn-By Gus Mager 40.00 160.00 280.00

HENRY
1935 (25¢, soft-c)
David McKay Co.
Book 1-By Carl Anderson 46.00 184.00 325.00

HOME, SWEET HOME
1925 (10-1/4x10")
M.S. Publishing Co.
nn-By Tuthill 32.00 128.00 225.00

IT HAPPENS IN THE BEST FAMILIES
1920 (52 pgs., B&W Sunday strip-r)
Powers Photo Engraving Co.
nn-By Briggs 26.00 104.00 185.00
Special Railroad Edition (30¢)-r/strips from 1914-1920 24.00 96.00 165.00

JIMMY (James Swinnorton)
1905 (10x15", 40 pgs., color)
N. Y. American & Journal
nn 86.00 344.00 600.00

JOE PALOOKA
1933 (52 pgs., B&W daily strip-r)
Cupples & Leon Co.
nn-(Scarce)-by Fisher 111.00 444.00 775.00

JUST KIDS
No. 283, 1932 (9-1/2x12", 16 pgs., paper-c)
McLoughlin Bros.
283-Three-color text, pictures on heavy paper 20.00 80.00 140.00

KATZENJAMMER KIDS, THE (Also see Hans Und Fritz)
1903 (10x15-1/4", 50 pgs., color)
New York American & Journal (By Rudolph Dirks; strip 1st appeared in 1898)
1903 (Rare) 214.00 856.00 1500.00
1905 121.00 484.00 850.00
1905-A Series of Comic Pictures, 10x15", 40 pgs. in color 121.00 484.00 850.00
1905-Tricks of...(10x15) 121.00 484.00 850.00
1906-Stokes-10x16", 32 pgs. in color 111.00 444.00 775.00
1910-The Komical...(10x15) 75.00 300.00 525.00
1921-Embee Dist. Co., 10x16", 20 pgs. in color 61.00 244.00 425.00

KEEPING UP WITH THE JONESES
1920 - No. 2, 1921 (9-1/4x9-1/4", 52 pgs., B&W daily strip-r)
Cupples & Leon Co.
1,2-By Pop Momand 34.00 136.00 240.00

LADY BOUNTIFUL
1917 (10-1/4x13-1/2", 24 pgs., B&W, cardboard-c)
Saalfield Publ. Co./Press Publ. Co.
nn-By Gene Carr; 2 panels per page 34.00 136.00 240.00

LIFE'S LITTLE JOKES
No date (1924) (52 pgs., B&W)
M.S. Publ. Co.
nn-By Rube Goldberg 54.00 216.00 375.00

LILY OF THE ALLEY IN THE FUNNIES
No date (1927) (10-1/4x15-1/2"; 28 pgs., color)
Whitman Publishing Co.(one of their first two books)
W936 - By T. Burke (Rare) 49.00 196.00 340.00

LITTLE ANNIE ROONEY
1935 (25¢, soft-c)
David McKay Co.
Book 1 43.00 172.00 300.00

LITTLE JOHNNY & THE TEDDY BEARS

Little Nemo © Doffield & Co.

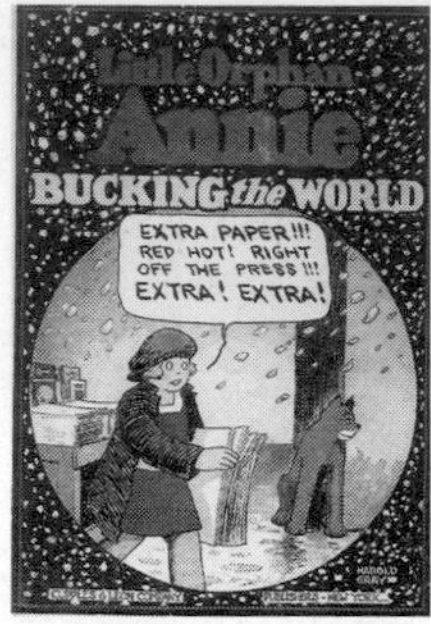

Little Orphan Annie #4 © C&L

Mutt & Jeff Book 2 © C&L

	GD25	FN65	VF82

1907 (10x14", 32 pgs., color)
Reilly & Britton Co.

nn-By J. R. Bray	43.00	172.00	300.00

LITTLE NEMO (...in Slumberland)
1906, 1909 (Sunday strip-r in color, cardboard covers)
Doffield & Co.(1906)/Cupples & Leon Co.(1909)

1906-11x16-1/2" by Winsor McCay; 30 pgs. (Rare)	471.00	1884.00	3300.00
1909-10x14" by Winsor McCay (Rare)	400.00	1200.00	2800.00

LITTLE ORPHAN ANNIE (See Treasure Box of Famous Comics)
1926 - 1934 (7x8-3/4", 100 pgs., B&W daily strip-r, hard-c)
Cupples & Leon Co.

1(1926)-Little Orphan Annie	50.00	200.00	350.00
1(1926)-softback (see Treasure Box...)			
2('27)-In the Circus	36.00	144.00	250.00
2('28)-softback (36 pgs.)	30.00	120.00	210.00
3('28)-The Haunted House	36.00	144.00	250.00
3('28)-softback (36 pgs.)	30.00	120.00	210.00
4('29)-Bucking the World	36.00	144.00	250.00
5('30)-Never Say Die	30.00	120.00	210.00
6('31)-Shipwrecked	30.00	120.00	210.00
7('32)-A Willing Helper	24.00	96.00	170.00
8('33)-In Cosmic City	24.00	96.00	170.00
9('34)-Uncle Dan	30.00	120.00	210.00

NOTE: *Each book reprints dailies from the previous year.*

LITTLE SAMMY SNEEZE
1905 (11x16-1/2", 28 pgs., color)
New York Herald Co.

nn-By Winsor McCay (Rare)	471.00	1884.00	3300.00

NOTE: *Rarely found in fine to mint condition.*

MAUD
1906 (10x15-1/2", 32 pgs., color, cardboard-c)
Frederick A. Stokes Co.

nn-By Fred Opper	64.00	256.00	445.00

MICKEY MOUSE BOOK
1930-1931 (9"x12", stapled-c, 20 pgs., 4 printings)
Bibo & Lang

nn-First Disney licensed publication (a magazine; see first book, Adventures of Mickey Mouse.) Contains story of how Mickey met Walt and got his name; contains games, cartoons & song "Mickey Mouse (You Cute Little Feller)," written by Irving Bibo. Minnie, Clarabelle Cow, Horace Horsecollar & caricature of Walt shaking hands with Mickey appear. Two Win Smith Mickey strips from 4/15/30 and 4/17/30 appear on page 8 & back-c of some printings. **Variations known:** Words "Printed in U.S.A." on front cover; Xmas-New Year greeting & Dec. 27, 1930 printed on inside front-c. All other printings have blank inside covers. some covers reinked with brown ink during printing. Art by Albert Barbelle, imitating Ub Iwerks. Total circulation all printings: 97,938 copies.

1st-4th printings (complete)	1430.00	6500.00	10,000.00

(Estimated up to 75 total copies exist)

NOTE: Identification of first printing has not been conclusively proven. Most copies are missing pages 9 & 10 which had a puzzle to be cut out. *Rare variations add 10%. Puzzle (pages 9 and 10) cut out or missing, subtract 60% to 75%.*

MICKEY MOUSE COMIC
1931 - No. 4, 1934 (10"x9-3/4", 52 pgs., cardboard-c) (Later reprints exist)
David McKay Co.

1(1931)-Reprints Floyd Gottfredson daily strips in black & white from 1930 & 1931, including the famous two week sequence in which Mickey tries to commit suicide	214.00	856.00	1500.00
2(1932)-1st app. of Pluto reprinted from 7/8/31 daily. All pgs. from 1931	164.00	656.00	1150.00
3(1933)-Reprints 1932 & 1933 Sunday pages in color, one strip per page, including the "Lair of Wolf Barker" continuity pencilled by Gottfredson and inked by Al Taliaferro & Ted Thwaites. First app. Mickey's nephews, Morty & Ferdie, one identified by name of Mortimer Fieldmouse, not to be confused with Uncle Mortimer Mouse who is introduced in the Wolf Barker story	214.00	856.00	1500.00
4(1934)-1931 dailies, include the only known reprint of the infamous strip of 2/4/31 where the villainous Kat Nipp snips off the end of Mickey's tail with a pair of scissors	121.00	484.00	850.00

MILITARY WILLY
1907 (7x9-1/2", 14 pgs., every other page in color, stapled)
J. I. Austen Co.

nn-By F. R. Morgan	40.00	160.00	280.00

MISCHIEVOUS MONKS OF CROCODILE ISLE, THE
1908 (8-1/2x11-1/2", 12 pgs., 4 pgs. in color)
J. I. Austen Co., Chicago

nn-By F. R. Morgan; reads longwise	43.00	172.00	300.00

MR. & MRS. (Also see Ain't It A Grand and Glorious Feeling?)
1922 (9x9-1/2", 52 & 28 pgs., cardboard-c)
Whitman Publishing Co.

nn-By Briggs (B&W, 52 pgs.)	31.00	124.00	220.00
nn-28 pgs.-(9x9-1/2")-Sunday strips-r in color	36.00	144.00	250.00

MONKEY SHINES OF MARSELEEN
1909 (11-1/2x17", 28 pgs. in two colors)
Cupples & Leon Co.

nn-By Norman E. Jennett	34.00	136.00	240.00

MOON MULLINS
1927 - 1933 (52 pgs., B&W daily strip-r)
Cupples & Leon Co.

Series 1('27)-By Willard	54.00	216.00	375.00
Series 2('28), Series 3('29), Series 4('30)	38.00	152.00	265.00
Series 5('31), 6('32), 7('33)	34.00	136.00	240.00
Big Book 1('30)-B&W	45.00	180.00	315.00

MUTT & JEFF (...Cartoon, The)
1910 - No. 5, 1916 (5-3/4x15-1/2", B&W, hard-c)
Ball Publications

1(1910)(68 pgs., 50¢)	164.00	656.00	1150.00
2,3: 2(1911, 68 pgs.)-Opium den panels; Jeff smokes opium (pipe dreams). 3(1912, 68 pgs.)	89.00	356.00	625.00
4(1915)(68 pgs., 50¢)(Rare)	89.00	356.00	625.00
5(1916)(68 pgs.)(Rare)-Photos of Fisher, 1st pg.	118.00	472.00	825.00

NOTE: *Mutt & Jeff first appeared in newspapers in 1908. Cover variations exist showing Mutt & Jeff reading various newspapers; i.e., The Oregon Journal, The American, and The Detroit News. Reprinting of each issue began soon after publication. No. 5 may not have been reprinted. Values listed include the reprints.*

MUTT & JEFF
No. 6, 1919 - No. 22, 1933? (9-1/2x9-1/2", 52 pgs., B&W dailies, stiff-c)
Cupples & Leon Co.

6-22-By Bud Fisher	54.00	216.00	375.00

NOTE: *Later issues are somewhat rarer.*

nn(1920)-(Advs. of...) 16x11"; 20 pgs.; reprints 1919 Sunday strips	89.00	356.00	625.00
Big Book nn(1926, 144 pgs., hardcovers)	111.00	444.00	775.00
w/dust jacket	186.00	744.00	1300.00
Big Book 1(1928)-Thick book (hardcovers)	111.00	444.00	775.00
w/dust jacket (rare)	179.00	716.00	1250.00
Big Book 2(1929)-Thick book (hardcovers)	111.00	444.00	775.00
w/dust jacket (rare)	179.00	716.00	1250.00

NOTE: *The Big Books contain three previous issues rebound.*

MUTT & JEFF
1921 (9x15")

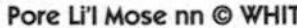
Pore Li'l Mose nn © WHIT

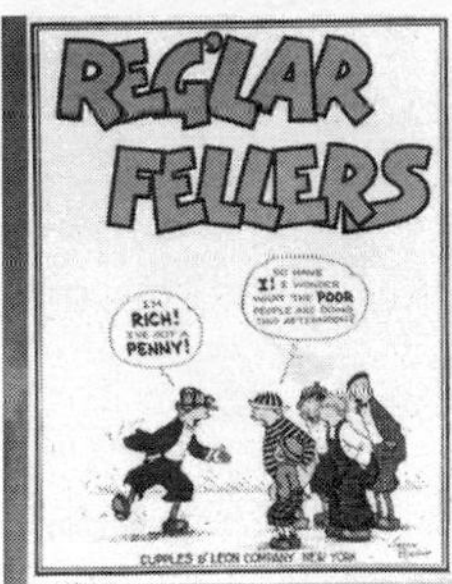

Reg'lar Fellers #1 © C&L

Smitty (Treasure Box of Famous Comics) © C&L

	GD25	FN65	VF82
Embee Publ. Co.			
nn-Sunday strips in color (Rare)	136.00	544.00	950.00
NEBBS, THE			
1928 (52 pgs., B&W daily strip-r)			
Cupples & Leon Co.			
nn-By Sol Hess; Carlson-a	40.00	160.00	280.00
NEWLYWEDS			
1907; 1917 (cardboard-c)			
Saalfield Publ. Co.			
...& Their Baby' by McManus; Saalfield, (1907, 13x10", 52 pgs.); daily strips in full color	96.00	384.00	675.00
...& Their Baby's Comic Pictures, The, by McManus, Saalfield, (1917, 14x10", 22 pgs, oblong, cardboard-c); reprints 'Newlyweds' (Baby Snookums stips) mainly from 1916; blue cover; says for painting & crayoning, but some pages in color. (Scarce)	70.00	280.00	485.00
NIPPY'S POP			
1917 (10-1/2x13-1/2", B&W, Sunday strip-r)			
The Saalfield Publishing Co.			
nn-32 pgs.	34.00	136.00	240.00
OH, MAN (A Bully Collection of Those Inimitable Humor Cartoons)			
1919 (8-1/2x13")			
P.F. Volland & Co.			
nn-By Briggs	34.00	136.00	240.00
OH SKIN-NAY!			
1913 (8-1/2x13")			
P.F. Volland & Co.			
nn-The Days Of Real Sport by Briggs	34.00	136.00	240.00
ON THE LINKS			
Dec, 1926 (9x10", 48 pgs.)			
Associated Feature Service			
nn-Daily strip-r	21.00	84.00	150.00
OUTBURSTS OF EVERETT TRUE			
1921 (32 pgs., B&W)			
Saalfield Publ. Co.			
1907 (2-panel strips reprint)	34.00	136.00	235.00
PECKS BAD BOY			
1906 - 1908 (11-1/4x15-3/4", strip-r)			
Thompson of Chicago (by Walt McDougal)			
...& Cousin Cynthia(1907)-In color	54.00	216.00	375.00
...& His Chums (1908)-Hardcover; in full color; 16 pgs.	54.00	216.00	375.00
Advs. of...And His Country Cousins (1906)-In color, 18 pgs., oblong	54.00	216.00	375.00
Advs. of...in Pictures (1908)-In color; Stanton & Van V. Liet Co.	54.00	216.00	375.00
PERCY & FERDIE			
1921 (10x10", 52 pgs., B&W dailies, cardboard-c)			
Cupples & Leon Co.			
nn-By H. A. MacGill (Rare)	54.00	216.00	375.00
PETER RABBIT			
1922 - 1923 (9-1/4x6-1/4", paper-c)			
John H. Eggers Co. The House of Little Books Publishers			
B1-B4-(Rare)-(Set of 4 books which came in a cardboard box)-Each book reprints half of a Sunday page per page and contains 8 B&W and 2 color pages; by Harrison Cady each....	43.00	172.00	300.00
Box only	57.00	228.00	400.00
PINK LAFFIN			
1922 (9x12")(Strip-r)			
Whitman Publishing Co.			
...the Lighter Side of Life, ...He Tells 'Em, ...and His Family, ...Knockouts; Ray Gleason-a (All rare) each...	26.00	104.00	180.00
PORE LI'L MOSE			
1902 (10-1/2x15", 30 pgs., color)			
New York Herald Publ. by Grand Union Tea			
Cupples & Leon Co.			
nn-By R. F. Outcault; 1 pg. strips about early Negroes	286.00	1144.00	2000.00
REG'LAR FELLERS (See All-American Comics, Popular Comics & Treasure Box of Famous Comics)			
1921 - 1929			
Cupples & Leon Co./MS Publishng Co.			
1(1921)-52 pgs. B&W dailies (Cupples & Leon, 10x10")	39.00	156.00	275.00
1925, 48 pgs. B&W dailies (MS Publ.)	36.00	144.00	250.00
Hardcover (1929, 96 pgs.)-B&W reprints	49.00	196.00	340.00
ROGER BEAN, R. G. (Regular Guy)			
1915 - No. 5, 1917 (4-3/4x16", 34 pgs., B&W, cardboard-c)			
(No. 1 & 4 bound on side, No. 3 bound at top)			
The Indiana News Co.			
1-By Chic Jackson (48 pgs.)(Scarce)	39.00	156.00	275.00
2-5 (Scarce)	26.00	104.00	185.00
SILK HAT HARRY'S DIVORCE SUIT			
1912 (5-3/4x15-1/2", B&W)			
M. A. Donoghue & Co.			
Newspaper-r by Tad (Thomas Dorgan)	24.00	96.00	170.00
SKEEZIX (Also see Gasoline Alley)			
1925 - 1928 (Strip-r, soft covers) (pictures & text)			
Reilly & Lee Co.			
...and Uncle Walt (1924)-Origin	26.00	104.00	180.00
...and Pal (1925)	21.00	84.00	150.00
...at the Circus (1926)	21.00	84.00	150.00
...& Uncle Walt (1927)	21.00	84.00	150.00
...Out West (1928)	21.00	84.00	150.00
Hardback Editions...	34.00	136.00	235.00
SKIPPY			
Circa 1920s (10x8", 16 pgs., color/B&W cartoons)			
No publisher listed			
nn-By Percy Crosby	79.00	316.00	550.00
S'MATTER POP?			
1917 (10x14", 44 pgs., B&W, cardboard-c)			
Saalfield Publ. Co.			
nn-By Charlie Payne; in full color; pages printed on one side	37.00	148.00	260.00
SMITTY (See Treasure Box of Famous Comics)			
1928 - 1933 (9-1/2x9-1/2", 52 pgs., B&W strip-r, cardboard-c)			
Cupples & Leon Co.			
1928-(96 pgs. 7x8-3/4")	41.00	164.00	290.00
1929-At the Ball Game, 1930-The Flying Office Boy, 1931-The Jockey, 1932-In the North Woods each...	31.00	124.00	220.00
1933-At Military School	31.00	124.00	220.00
Hardback Editions-(7x8-1/4", 100 pgs.)(Rare)-With dust jacket each...	40.00	160.00	280.00
STRANGE AS IT SEEMS			
1932 (64 pgs., B&W, square binding)			
Blue-Star Publishing Co.			
1-Newspaper-r	32.00	128.00	225.00

NOTE: *Published with and without No. 1 and price on cover.*

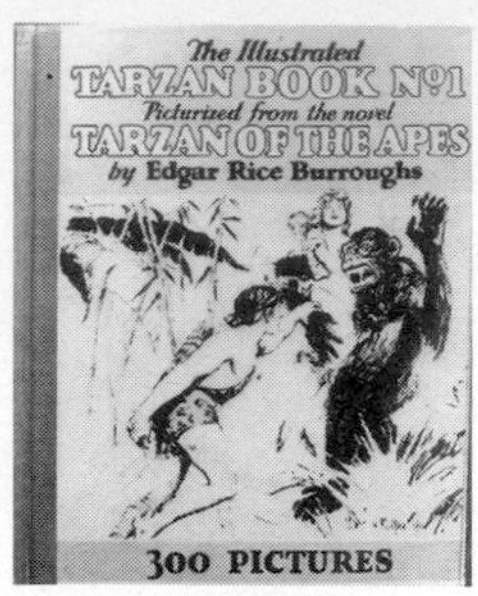

Tarzan Book
© Grosset & Dunlap

TILLIE THE TOILER
BY RUSS WESTOVER
BOOK 5
CUPPLES AND LEON COMPANY - PUBLISHERS - NEW YORK

Tillie The Toiler #5 © C&L

Toonerville Trolley #1
© C&L

	GD25	FN65	VF82
Ex-Lax giveaway(1936, B&W, 24 pgs., 5x7")-McNaught Synd.	11.00	44.00	75.00

TAILSPIN TOMMY STORY & PICTURE BOOK
No. 266, 1931? (nd) (10-1/2x10", color strip-r)
McLoughlin Bros.

	GD25	FN65	VF82
266-By Forrest	34.00	136.00	240.00

TAILSPIN TOMMY (Also see Famous Feature Stories & The Funnies)
1932 (100 pgs., hard-c)
Cupples & Leon Co.

	GD25	FN65	VF82
nn-(Rare)-B&W strip reprints from 1930 by Hal Forrest & Glenn Claffin	39.00	156.00	275.00

TARZAN BOOK (The Illustrated...)
1929 (7x9", 80 pgs.)
Grosset & Dunlap

	GD25	FN65	VF82
1(Rare)-Contains 1st B&W Tarzan newspaper comics from 1929. Cloth reinforced spine & dust jacket (50¢); Foster-c			
with dust jacket...	82.00	328.00	575.00
without dust jacket...	33.00	132.00	230.00
2nd Printing(1934, 25¢, 76 pgs.)-4 Foster pgs. dropped; paper spine, circle in lower right cover with 25¢ price. The 25¢ is barely visible on some copies	31.00	124.00	220.00
1967-House of Greystoke reprint-7x10", using the complete 300 illustrations/text from the 1929 edition minus the original indicia, foreword, etc. Initial version bound in gold paper & sold for $5.00. Officially titled **Burroughs Biblophile #2**. A very few additional copies were bound in heavier blue paper. Gold binding...	2.25	6.75	18.00
Blue binding...	2.50	7.50	24.00

TARZAN OF THE APES TO COLOR
No. 988, 1933 (10-3/4x15-1/4", 24 pgs)(Coloring book)
Saalfield Publishing Co.

	GD25	FN65	VF82
988-(Very Rare)-Contains 1929 daily reprints with some new art by Hal Foster. Two panels blown up large on each page with one at the top of opposing pages on every other double-page spread. Believed to be the only time these panels appeared in color. Most color panels are reproduced a second time in b&w to be colored	229.00	916.00	1600.00

THIMBLE THEATRE STARRING POPEYE
1931 - No. 2, 1932 (25¢, B&W, 52 pgs.)(Rare)
Sonnet Publishing Co.

	GD25	FN65	VF82
1-Daily strip serial-r in both by Segar	157.00	628.00	1100.00
2	136.00	544.00	950.00

NOTE: *The very first Popeye reprint book. Popeye first entered Thimble Theatre in 1929.*

3 FUNMAKERS, THE
1908 (10x15", 64 pgs., color) (1904-06 Sunday strip-r)
Stokes and Company

	GD25	FN65	VF82
nn-Maude, Katzenjammer Kids, Happy Hooligan	100.00	400.00	700.00

"TIGE" HIS STORY
1905 (10x8", 63 pgs., B&W) (63 illos.)
Frederick A. Stokes Co.

	GD25	FN65	VF82
nn	77.00	308.00	535.00

TILLIE THE TOILER
1925 - No. 8, 1933 (52 pgs., B&W, daily strip-r)
Cupples & Leon Co.

	GD25	FN65	VF82
nn (#1)	46.00	184.00	325.00
2-8	34.00	136.00	240.00

NOTE: *First strip appearance was January, 1921.*

TOM SAWYER & HUCK FINN
1925 (10-3/4x10", 52 pgs, stiff covers)(Sunday strips in color)
Stoll & Edwards Co.

	GD25	FN65	VF82
nn-By Dwiggins; 1923, 1924-r	34.00	136.00	240.00

TOONERVILLE TROLLEY
1921 (52 pgs., B&W, daily strip-r)
Cupples & Leon Co.

	GD25	FN65	VF82
1-By Fontaine Fox	43.00	172.00	300.00

TRAVELS OF HAPPY HOOLIGAN, THE
1906 (10-1/4x15-3/4", 32 pgs., cardboard covers)
Frederick A. Stokes Co.

	GD25	FN65	VF82
nn-Contains reprints from 1905	60.00	240.00	420.00

TREASURE BOX OF FAMOUS COMICS
Mid 1930's (6-7/8x8-1/2", 36 pgs, soft covers)(Boxed set of 5 books)
Cupples & Leon Co.

	GD25	FN65	VF82
Little Orphan Annie (1926)	20.00	80.00	140.00
Reg'lar Fellers (1928)	17.00	68.00	120.00
Smitty (1928)	17.00	68.00	120.00
Harold Teen (1931)	17.00	68.00	120.00
How Dick Tracy & Dick Tracy Jr. Caught The Racketeers (1933)	25.00	100.00	175.00
Softcover set of five books in box	157.00	628.00	1100.00
Box only	50.00	200.00	350.00

NOTE: *Dates shown are copyright dates; all books actually came out in 1934 or later. The softcovers are abbreviated versions of the hardcover editions listed under each character.*

TRIALS OF LULU AND LEANDER, THE
1906 (10x16", 32 pgs. in color)
William A. Stokes Co.

	GD25	FN65	VF82
nn-By F. M. Howarth	36.00	144.00	250.00

TROUBLE OF BRINGING UP FATHER, THE
1921 (9x15", Sunday-r in color)
Embee Publ. Co.

	GD25	FN65	VF82
nn-(Rare)	71.00	284.00	500.00

VAUDEVILLE AND OTHER THINGS
1900 (10-1/2x13", 18+ pgs., color)
Isaac H. Blandiard Co.

	GD25	FN65	VF82
nn-By Bunny	69.00	276.00	480.00

WILLIE WESTINGHOUSE EDISON SMITH THE BOY INVENTOR
1906 (10x16", 36 pgs. in color)
William A. Stokes Co.

	GD25	FN65	VF82
nn-By Frank Crane	61.00	244.00	425.00

WINNIE WINKLE
1930 - No. 4, 1933 (52 pgs., B&W daily strip-r)
Cupples & Leon Co.

	GD25	FN65	VF82
1	36.00	144.00	250.00
2-4	24.00	96.00	170.00

YELLOW KID, THE (Magazine)(becomes The Yellow Kid Book #10 on)
Mar. 20, 1897 - #9, July 17, 1897 (5¢, B&W w/color covers, 52p., stapled)
Howard Ainslee & Co., N.Y.

	GD25	FN65	VF82
1-R.F. Outcault Yellow kid on-c only #1-6. The same Yellow Kid color ad app. on back-c #1-6 (advertising the New York Sunday Journal)	600.00	2400.00	-
2 (4/3/97)	325.00	1300.00	-
3-6 (#6, 6/5/97)	238.00	950.00	-
7-9 (Yellow Kid not on-c)	100.00	400.00	-

NOTE: Richard Outcault's Yellow Kid from the Hearst New York American represents the very first successful comic strip in America. Eventually the first prototype comic books appeared reprinting these early strips. This magazine is listed here due to historical importance but is not a comic book.

YELLOW KID IN MCFADDEN'S FLATS, THE
1897 (50¢, 5 1/2x7 1/2", 196 pgs., B&W, squarebound)
G. W. Dillingham Company, New York

	GD25	FN65	VF82
nn-The first "comic" book; E. W. Townsend narrative w/R. F. Outcault Sunday comic page art-r & some original drawings	4200.00	7500.00	-

THE GOLDEN AGE & BEYOND: THE MODERN COMIC BOOK

Richard D. Olson, Ph.D.

By the early 1930s the era of cardboard covered comics was over. With the appearance of **Detective Dan** in 1933, the stage was set for the new frontier to emerge. This experimental one shot comic book retained the format of the old era but was the first book to include completely original material since **The Funnies** of 1929. Today, historians consider this to be the book that bridged the gap of the two eras--Platinum and Modern. However, with another format change, the birth of the modern American comic book occurred in 1933, with the publication of Harry I. Wildenberg and Max Gaines' **Funnies on Parade.** It had a small print run of 10,000, and was only 32 pages. Just another experimental format at the time of its issue for reprinting newspaper comics, it rapidly became the seminal model of comic books for the next 50 years! The reasons the new format proved to be so successful included the total use of color, packaging a variety of characters in one book, and the cost--it was free, a premium given out by Proctor and Gamble.

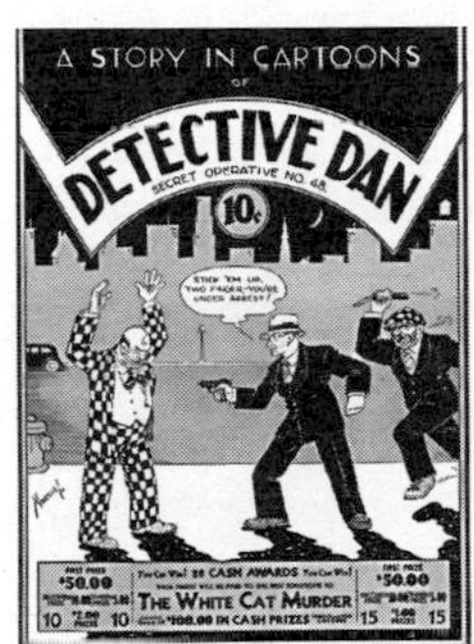

Detective Dan Secret Op.48
© Humor Publ. Co.

The great success of **Funnies on Parade** quickly led Gaines to publish additional giveaway books in the same format, including **A Century of Comics**, **A Carnival of Comics**, and **Skippy's Own Book of Comics**. After several of these comic magazine premiums were successfully produced and distributed, Max Gaines stickered 10¢ on several dozen copies of the latest premium, titled **Famous Funnies**, as a test, and talked a couple newsstands into trying this experiment out. The copies sold out over the weekend and the newsies asked for more. George Janosik, the president of Eastern Color, then called on George Delacorte to go into a possible partnership. The latter publisher had already tried out a weekly comics publication a few years earlier, however, and together they went to American News in early 1933 with a proposal which was promptly turned down. They then interested a few chain stores into buying 35,000 copies of what became known as **Famous Funnies, Series 1,** with a 10¢ price on the cover.

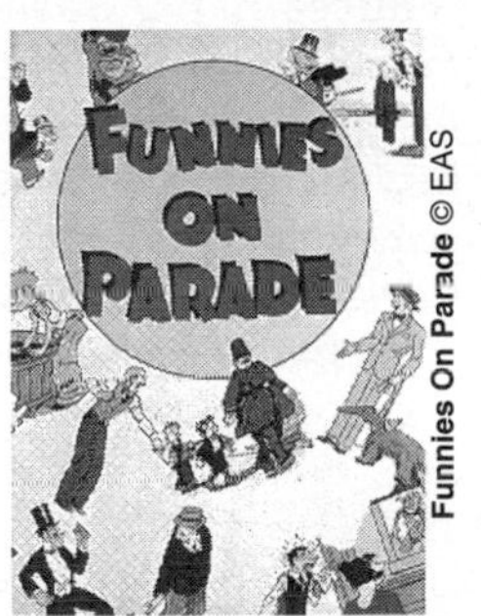

Funnies On Parade © EAS

In early 1934, while riding the train, another Eastern Color employee named Harold A. Moore read an account from a prominent New York newspaper that indicated they owed much of their circulation success to their comics section. Mr. Moore went back to American News with the article in hand. He succeeded in acquiring a print order of 200,000 for a proposed monthly comics magazine. In May of 1934, **Famous Funnies** #1 (with a July cover date) hit the newsstands with Steven A. Douglass as its only editor until it ceased publication some 20 years later. It was a 64-page version of the 32-page giveaways, and more importantly, it sold for a dime! The first issue lost $4,150.60. Delacorte got cold feet and sold back his interest to Eastern, even though the 7th issue cleared a profit of $2,664.25. The second issue was published in September and came out monthly through July 1955, ending with issue #218. **Famous Funnies** also began carrying some original material, apparently as early as the second issue.

After Max Gaines did a successful half-million copy promo with a **Skippy** premium for Philips Dental that was given away during the Skippy radio program, he convinced Delacorte to try a new title called **Popular Comics** in late 1935. Packaged by Gaines and his youthful assistant Sheldon Mayer, it became the 2nd continuing series of the modern newsstand comic books as we know them today. The first modern comic book to contain only original material after the still-born **Detective Dan**, however, was **New Fun Comics** #1, published by National in February 1935. **New Fun Comics**, a large tabloid, became **More Fun Comics** with issue #7, and adopted the modern format with issue #9. **New Fun Comics** #6 is now famous for introducing Siegel and Shuster's Dr. Occult, later to become the first superhero.

New Fun Comics #1 © DC

And the race was on! New publishers entered the arena with a variety of titles, and the comic book market exploded. DC published **Detective Comics** #1 in March 1937, and **Action Comics** #1 in June 1938. Centaur, Fiction House, Timely, and Lev Gleason were all publishing their own titles before 1940. Within a year, MLJ, Fawcett, Fox, and Dell, had also joined the market, as well as numerous smaller companies. The comic book had become an integral part of society.

Over the years, the comic book down-sized, reduced paper quality, printed more ads, and increased its cover price, but it has survived. There have been several developmental periods that collectors now recognize: (1) Platinum Age, 1897-1932, beginning with the **Yellow Kid** and consisting mostly of all-reprint comics, representing the transformation of newspaper comic strips into repackaged forms; (2) Golden Age, June, 1938-1945, following the superhero through WW II; (3) Atomic Age 1946-1956; (4) Silver Age, (September)1956-1969, showcasing a clear change in content and themes, including the Marvel books; (5) Post Silver Age or Bronze Age, 1970-1979, where sales decrease as comics stagnate; and (6) Modern Age, 1980-Present, in which DC and Marvel are challenged by the Independents, while all are threatened by overproduction.

A final few notes of personal interest. First, many of the early comic artists and writers toiled in virtual anonymity. One of the great changes in the field is that today there are annual awards and everyone in the production line is recognized in each issue. Second, as in so many hobbies, condition is king! The prices of all comic books have to reflect the marketplace, and the marketplace issues the greatest premiums on the most perfect books. Third, enjoy the books you collect. I have a run of **Green Arrow** that has little investment potential, but I really like the scripts and art. Collecting comics can be and is a great hobby... enjoy.

additional material by Robert L. Beerbohm

Abbott and Costello #3 © STJ

Absolute Vertigo © DC

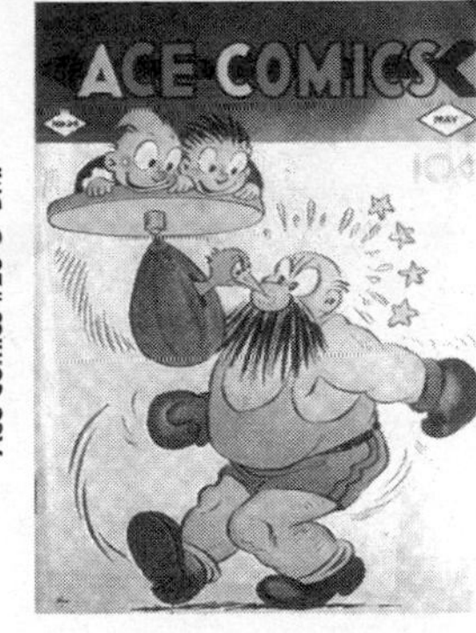

Ace Comics #26 © DMP

The correct title listing for each comic book can be determined by consulting the indicia (publication data) on the beginning interior pages of the comic. The official title is determined by those words of the title in capital letters only, and not by what is on the cover.

Titles are listed in this book as if they were one word, ignoring spaces, hyphens, and apostrophes, to make finding titles easier. Comic books listed should be assumed to be in color unless noted "B&W".

Comic publishers are invited to send us sample copies for possible inclusion in future guides.

Near Mint is the highest value listed in this price guide. True mint books from the 1970s and 1990s do exist, so the Near Mint value listed should be interpreted as a Mint value for those books.

A-1 (See A-One)

AARON STRIPS
Apr, 1997 - Present ($2.95, B&W)
Image Comics

	GD25	FN65	NM94
1-4 -Reprints Adventures of Aaron			2.95

ABBIE AN' SLATS (...With Becky No. 1-4) (See Comics On Parade, Fight for Love, Giant Comics Edition 2, Giant Comics Editions #1, Sparkler Comics, Tip Topper, Treasury of Comics, & United Comics)
1940; March, 1948 - No. 4, Aug, 1948 (Reprints)
United Features Syndicate

	GD25	FN65	NM94
Single Series 25 ('40)	31.00	94.00	250.00
Single Series 28	26.00	80.00	210.00
1 (1948)	14.00	41.00	110.00
2-4: 3-r/Sparkler #68-72	7.85	23.50	55.00

ABBOTT AND COSTELLO (...Comics)(See Giant Comics Editions #1 & Treasury of Comics)
Feb, 1948 - No. 40, Sept, 1956 (Mort Drucker-a in most issues)
St. John Publishing Co.

	GD25	FN65	NM94
1	42.00	125.00	375.00
2	21.00	64.00	170.00
3-9 (#8, 8/49; #9, 2/50)	14.00	41.00	110.00
10-Son of Sinbad story by Kubert (new)	17.50	53.00	140.00
11,13-20 (#11, 10/50; #13, 8/51; #15, 12/52)	9.50	28.00	75.00
12-Movie issue	11.30	34.00	90.00
21-30: 28-r/#8. 30-Painted-c	8.50	26.00	60.00
31-40: 33,38-Reprints	6.50	19.50	45.00
3-D #1 (11/53, 25¢)-Infinity-c	29.00	88.00	235.00

ABBOTT AND COSTELLO (TV)
Feb, 1968 - No. 22, Aug, 1971 (Hanna-Barbera)
Charlton Comics

	GD25	FN65	NM94
1	6.00	18.00	60.00
2	3.00	9.00	30.00
3-10	2.60	7.80	26.00
11-22	2.35	7.00	19.00

ABC (See America's Best TV Comics)

ABOMINATIONS (See Hulk)
Dec, 1996 - No. 3, Feb, 1997 (1.50, limited series)
Marvel Comics

	GD25	FN65	NM94
1-3-Future Hulk stoyline			1.50

ABRAHAM LINCOLN LIFE STORY (See Dell Giants)

ABSENT-MINDED PROFESSOR, THE
Apr, 1961 (Disney)
Dell Publishing Co.

	GD25	FN65	NM94
Four Color #1199-Movie, photo-c	6.40	19.00	70.00

ABSOLUTE VERTIGO
Winter, 1995 (99¢, mature)
DC Comics (Vertigo)

	GD25	FN65	NM94
nn-1st app. Preacher. Previews upcoming titles including Jonah Hex: Riders of the Worm, The Invisibles (King Mob), The Eaters, Ghostdancing & Preacher	1.85	5.50	15.00

ABYSS, THE (Movie)
June, 1989 - No. 2, July, 1989 ($2.25, limited series)
Dark Horse Comics

	GD25	FN65	NM94
1,2-Adaptation of film; Kaluta & Moebius-a		.90	2.25

ACCLAIM ADVENTURE ZONE
1997 ($4.50, digest size)
Acclaim Books

	GD25	FN65	NM94
1-Short stories of Turok, Troublemakers, Ninjak and others			4.50

ACE COMICS
Apr, 1937 - No. 151, Oct-Nov, 1949 (All contain some newspaper strip reprints)
David McKay Publications

	GD25	FN65	NM94
1-Jungle Jim by Alex Raymond, Blondie, Ripley's Believe It Or Not, Krazy Kat begin (1st app. of each)	250.00	750.00	2500.00
2	77.00	231.00	700.00
3-5	52.00	156.00	465.00
6-10	38.00	114.00	340.00
11-The Phantom begins (1st app., 2/38) (in brown costume)	54.00	162.00	490.00
12-20	33.00	98.00	260.00
21-25,27-30	29.00	86.00	230.00
26-Origin & 1st app. Prince Valiant (5/39); begins series?	71.00	213.00	640.00
31-40: 37-Krazy Kat ends	20.00	60.00	160.00
41-60	15.50	47.00	125.00
61-64,66-76-(7/43; last 68 pgs.)	14.00	41.00	110.00
65-(8/42)-Flag-c	14.50	43.00	115.00
77-84 (3/44; all 60 pgs.)	11.30	34.00	90.00
85-99 (52 pgs.)	9.50	28.00	75.00
100 (7/45; last 52 pgs.)	10.50	32.00	85.00
101-134: 128-(11/47)-Brick Bradford begins. 134-Last Prince Valiant (all 36 pgs.)	7.85	23.50	55.00
135-151: 135-(6/48)-Lone Ranger begins	7.15	21.50	50.00

ACE KELLY (See Tops Comics & Tops In Humor)

ACE KING (See Adventures of Detective...)

ACES
Apr, 1988 - No. 5, Dec, 1988 ($2.95, B&W, magazine)
Acme Press (Eclipse Comics)

	GD25	FN65	NM94
1-5		1.20	3.00

ACES HIGH
Mar-Apr, 1955 - No. 5, Nov-Dec, 1955
E.C. Comics

	GD25	FN65	NM94
1-Not approved by code	18.00	54.00	145.00
2	11.30	34.00	90.00
3-5	9.50	28.00	75.00

NOTE: *All have stories by* ***Davis, Evans, Krigstein,*** *and* ***Wood. Evans*** *c-1-5.*

ACTION ADVENTURE (War) (Formerly Real Adventure)
V1#2, June, 1955 - No. 4, Oct, 1955
Gillmor Magazines

	GD25	FN65	NM94
V1#2-4	4.00	11.00	22.00

ACTION COMICS (...Weekly #601-642) (Also see The Comics Magazine #1, More Fun #14-17 & Special Edition)
6/38 - No. 583, 9/86; No. 584, 1/87 - Present
National Periodical Publ./Detective Comics/DC Comics

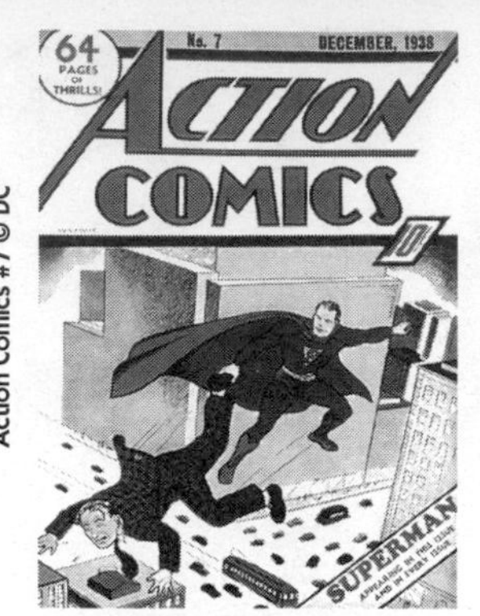

Action Comics #7 © DC

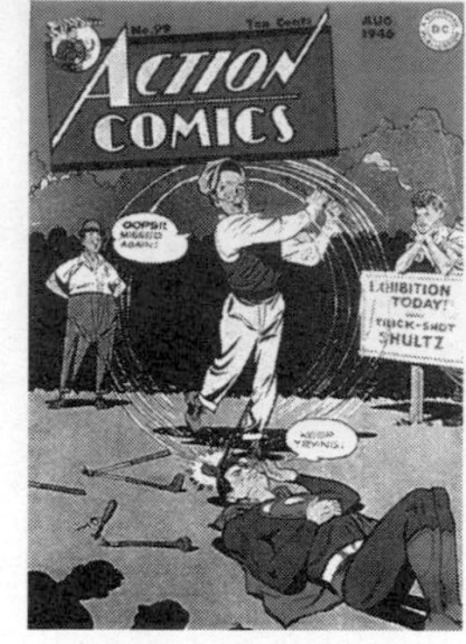

Action Comics #99 © DC

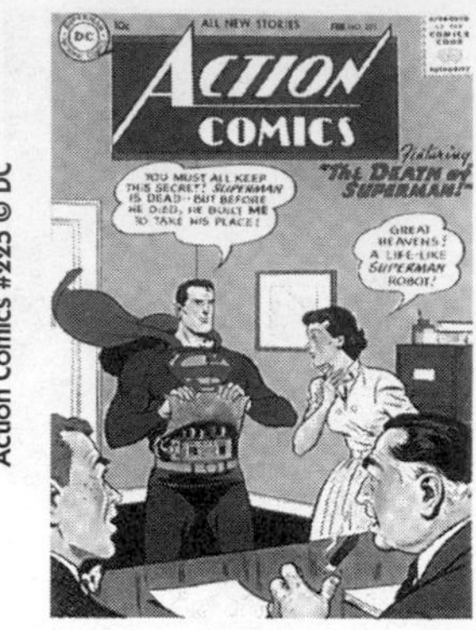

Action Comics #225 © DC

GD25 FN65 VF82 NM94

1-Origin & 1st app. Superman by Siegel & Shuster, Marco Polo, Tex Thompson, Pep Morgan, Chuck Dawson & Scoop Scanlon; 1st app. Zatara & Lois Lane; Superman story missing 4 pgs. which were included when reprinted in Superman #1; Clark Kent works for Daily Star; story continued in #2 30,000.00 70,000.00 105,000.00 180,000.00

(Estimated up to 75+ total copies exist, 1 in NM/Mint)

(Issues 1 through 10 are all scarce to rare)

1-Reprint, Oversize 13-1/2x10". **WARNING:** This comic is an exact reprint of the original except for its size. DC published it in 1974 with a second cover titling it as a Famous First Edition. There have been many reported cases of the outer cover being removed and the interior sold as the original edition. The reprint with the new outer cover removed is practically worthless. See Famous First Edition for value.

GD25 FN65 NM94

1(1976,1983)-Giveaway; paper cover, 16pgs. in color; reprints complete Superman story from #1 ('38) 2.00 6.00 16.00
1(1987 Nestle Quik giveaway; 1988, 50¢) 2.00 5.00
1(1993)-Came w/Reign of Superman packs 1.50
2 1727.00 5200.00 19,000.00
3 (Scarce)-Superman apps. in costume in only one panel 1180.00 3540.00 13,000.00
4-6: 6-1st Jimmy Olsen (called office boy) 750.00 2250.00 7500.00
7-2nd Superman cover 1000.00 3000.00 11,000.00
8,9 580.00 1680.00 5800.00
10-3rd Superman cover by Siegel & Shuster 900.00 2700.00 9000.00
11,14: 14-Clip Carson begins, ends #41; Zatara-c 290.00 810.00 2900.00
12-Has 1 pg. Batman ad for Det. #27 (5/39); Zatara sci-fi cover 300.00 900.00 3000.00
13-Guardineer Superman-c; last Scoop Scanlon 470.00 1410.00 4700.00
15-Guardineer Superman-c 420.00 1260.00 4200.00
16 233.00 700.00 2100.00
17-Superman cover; last Marco Polo 330.00 990.00 3300.00
18-Origin 3 Aces; 1st X-Ray Vision? 233.00 700.00 2100.00
19-Superman covers begin; has full pg. ad for New York World's Fair 1939 290.00 810.00 2900.00
20-The 'S' left off Superman's chest; Clark Kent works at 'Daily Star' 280.00 840.00 2800.00
21-Has 2 ads for More Fun #52 (1st Spectre) 211.00 633.00 1900.00
22,24,25: 24-Kent at Daily Planet. 25-Last app. Gargantua T. Potts, Tex Thompson's sidekick 189.00 567.00 1700.00
23-1st app. Luthor (w/red hair) & Black Pirate; Black Pirate by Moldoff; 1st mention of The Daily Planet (4/40)-Has 1 panel ad for Spectre in More Fun 500.00 1500.00 5000.00
26-28,30 161.00 483.00 1450.00
29-1st Lois Lane-c (10/40) 189.00 567.00 1700.00
31,32: 32-Intro/1st app. Krypto Ray Gun in Superman story by Burnley 100.00 300.00 900.00
33-Origin Mr. America; Superman by Burnley; has half page ad for All Star Comics #3 121.00 363.00 1100.00
34-40: 37-Origin Congo Bill. 40-(9/41)-Intro/1st app. Star Spangled Kid & Stripesy 100.00 300.00 900.00
41 93.00 279.00 840.00
42-1st app./origin Vigilante; Bob Daley becomes Fat Man; origin Mr. America's magic flying carpet; The Queen Bee & Luthor app; Black Pirate ends; not in #41 133.00 400.00 1200.00
43-46,48-50: 44-Fat Man's i.d. revealed to Mr. America. 45-1st app. Stuff (Vigilante's oriental sidekick) 93.00 279.00 840.00
47-1st Luthor cover in comics (4/42) 133.00 400.00 1200.00
51-1st app. The Prankster 93.00 279.00 840.00
52-Fat Man & Mr. America become the Ameri-commandos; origin Vigilante retold 97.00 291.00 875.00
53-60: 56-Last Fat Man. 57-2nd Lois Lane-c in Action (3rd anywhere, 2/43). 59-Kubert Vigilante begins?, ends #70. 60-First app. Lois Lane as Superwoman 61.00 183.00 550.00
61-63,65-70: 63-Last 3 Aces 56.00 168.00 500.00
64-Intro Toyman 63.00 189.00 570.00
71-79: 74-Last Mr. America 52.00 156.00 470.00
80-2nd app. & 1st Mr. Mxyztplk-c (1/45) 78.00 234.00 700.00
81-90: 83-Intro Hocus & Pocus 53.00 159.00 475.00
91-99: 93-X-Mas-c. 99-1st small logo (8/46) 50.00 150.00 450.00
100 106.00 318.00 950.00
101-Nuclear explosion-c 106.00 318.00 950.00
102-120: 105,117-X-Mas-c 47.00 141.00 425.00
121-126,128-140: 135,136,138-Zatara by Kubert 43.00 129.00 390.00
127-Vigilante by Kubert; Tommy Tomorrow begins (12/48, see Real Fact #6) 52.00 156.00 465.00
141-157,159-161: 151-Luthor/Mr. Mxyztplk/Prankster team-up. 156-Lois Lane as Super Woman. 160- Last 52 pgs. 41.00 123.00 365.00
158-Origin Superman retold 97.00 291.00 875.00
162-180: 168,176-Used in **POP**, pg. 90 36.00 108.00 300.00
181-201: 191-Intro. Janu in Congo Bill. 198-Last Vigilante. 201-Last pre-code issue 36.00 108.00 290.00
202-220: 212-(1/56)-Includes 1956 Superman calendar that is part of story. 27.00 82.00 275.00
221-240: 221-1st S.A. issue. 224-1st Golden Gorilla story. 228-(5/57)-Kongorilla in Congo Bill story (Congorilla try-out) 21.00 63.00 210.00
241,243-251: 241-Batman x-over. 248-Origin/1st app. Congorilla; Congo Bill renamed Congorilla. 251-Last Tommy Tomorrow 17.00 51.00 170.00
242-Origin & 1st app. Brainiac (7/58); 1st mention of Shrunken City of Kandor 96.00 288.00 1150.00
252-Origin & 1st app. Supergirl (5/59); intro new Metallo 113.00 339.00 1350.00
253-2nd app. Supergirl 33.00 100.00 370.00
254-1st meeting of Bizarro & Superman-c/story 24.50 74.00 245.00
255-1st Bizarro Lois Lane-c/story & both Bizarros leave Earth to make Bizarro World 18.00 54.00 180.00
256-261: 259-Red Kryptonite used. 261-1st X-Kryptonite which gave Streaky his powers; last Congorilla in Action; origin & 1st app. Streaky The Super Cat 11.00 33.00 110.00
262,264-266,268-270 10.00 30.00 100.00
263-Origin Bizarro World 12.50 38.00 125.00
267(8/60)-3rd Legion app; 1st app. Chameleon Boy, Colossal Boy, & Invisible Kid, 1st app. of Supergirl as Superwoman. 33.00 100.00 370.00
271-275,277-282: 274-Lois Lane as Superwoman; 282-Last 10¢ issue 7.50 22.50 75.00
276(5/61)-6th Legion app; 1st app. Brainiac 5, Phantom Girl, Triplicate Girl, Bouncing Boy, Sun Boy, & Shrinking Violet; Supergirl joins Legion 16.50 50.00 165.00
283(12/61)-Legion of Super-Villains app. 1st 12¢ 8.50 25.50 85.00
284(1/62)-Mon-el app. 8.50 25.50 85.00
285(2/62)-12th Legion app; Brainiac 5 cameo; Supergirl's existence revealed to world; JFK & Jackie cameos 8.50 25.50 85.00
286(3/62)-Legion of Super Villains app. 5.50 16.50 55.00
287(4/62)-14th Legion app.(cameo) 5.50 16.50 55.00
288-Mon-el app.; r-origin Supergirl 5.50 16.50 55.00
289(6/62)-16th Legion app. (Adult); Lightning Man & Saturn Woman's marriage 1st revealed 5.50 16.50 55.00
290(7/62)-17th Legion app. (cameo); Phantom Girl app. 290-1st Supergirl emergency squad 5.50 16.50 55.00
291,292,294-299: 291-1st meeting Supergirl & Mr. Mxyzptlk. 292-2nd app. Superhorse (see Adv. #293). 297-Mon-el app. 298-Legion cameo 5.55 16.50 55.00
293-Origin Comet (Superhorse) 8.50 25.50 85.00
300-(5/63) 5.50 16.50 55.00
301-303,305-308,310-320: 306-Brainiac 5, Mon-el app. 307-Saturn Girl app. 314-r-origin Supergirl; J.L.A. x-over. 317-Death of Nor-Kan of Kandor. 319-Shrinking Violet app. 2.50 7.50 24.00
304-Origin & 1st app. Black Flame (9/63) 3.20 9.60 32.00
309-(2/64)-Legion app.; Batman & Robin-c & cameo; JFK app. (he died 11/22/63; on stands same time as death?) 3.20 9.60 32.00
321-333,335-339: 336-Origin Akvar (Flamebird) 2.25 6.75 18.00

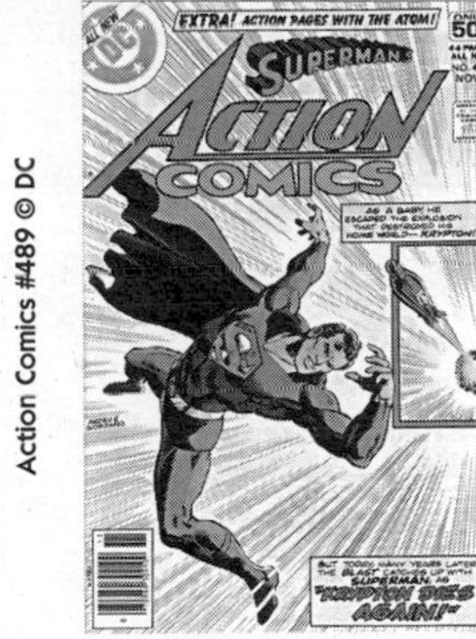

Action Comics #489 © DC

Action Comics #674 © DC

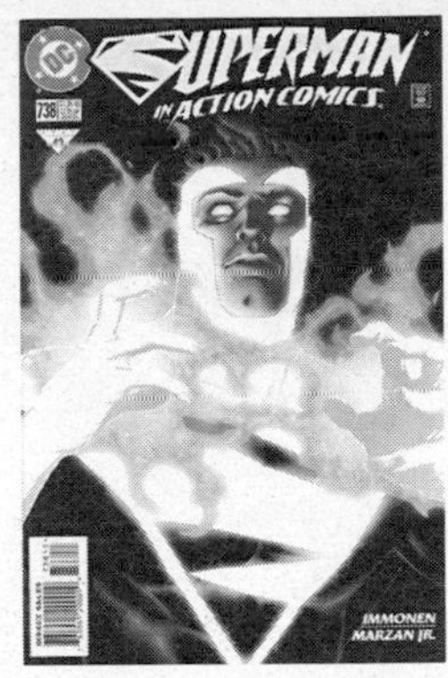

Action Comics #738 © DC

GD25 FN65 NM94

334-Giant G-20; origin Supergirl, Streaky, Superhorse & Legion (all-r) 5.00 15.00 50.00
340-Origin, 1st app. of the Parasite 2.00 6.00 16.00
341-346,348-359: 344-Batman x-over. 350-Batman, Green Arrow & Green Lantern app. in Supergirl back-up story 1.60 4.85 13.00
347,360-Giant Supergirl G-33,G-45; 347-Origin Comet-r plus 3 Bizarro stories. 360-Legion-r; r/origin Supergirl 3.50 10.50 35.00
361-372,374-380: 361-2nd app. Parasite. 365-Legion app. 370-New facts about Superman's origin. 376-Last Supergirl in Action. 377-Legion begins. 1.25 3.75 10.00
373-Giant Supergirl G-57; Legion-r 3.00 9.00 30.00
381-399,401,402: 392-Last Legion in Action; Saturn Girl gets new costume. 393-402-All Superman issues 1.00 3.00 8.00
400 1.85 5.50 15.00
403-413: All 52 pg. issues. 411-Origin Eclipso-(r). 413-Metamorpho begins, ends #418 1.50 4.50 12.00
414-424: 419-Intro. Human Target. 421-Intro Capt. Strong; Green Arrow begins. 422,423-Origin Human Target 1.00 2.80 7.00
425-Neal Adams-a(p); The Atom begins 1.85 5.50 15.00
426-431,433-436,438,439 1.60 4.00
432-1st S.A. Toyman app (2/74). 2.40 6.00
437,443-(100 pg. giants) 2.25 6.75 18.00
440-1st Grell-a on Green Arrow 1.00 2.80 7.00
441-Grell-a on Green Arrow continues 1.60 4.00
442,444-499: 449-(68 pgs.). 454-Last Atom. 458-Last Green Arrow. 484-Earth II Superman & Lois Lane wed; 40th anniversary issue (6/78). 487,488-(44 pgs.). 487-Origin & 1st app. Microwave Man; origin Atom retold 1.20 3.00
500-($1.00, 68 pgs.)-Infinity-c; Superman life story; shows Legion statues in museum 1.60 4.00
501-551,554-582: 511-514-Airwave II solo stories. 513-The Atom begins. 517-Aquaman begins; ends #541. 521-1st app. The Vixen. 532,536-New Teen Titans cameo. 535,536-Omega Men app. 544-(Mando paper, 68 pgs.)-Origins new Luthor & Brainiac; Omega Men cameo. 544-Shuster-a (pin-up); article by Siegel. 546-J.L.A., New Teen Titans app. 551-Starfire becomes Red-Star .80 2.00
552,553-Animal Man-c & app. (2/84 & 3/84) 1.20 3.00
583-Alan Moore scripts; last Earth 1 Superman story (cont'd from Superman #423) 1.60 4.00
584-Byrne-a begins; New Teen Titans app. .80 2.00
585-599: 586-Legends x-over. 596-Millennium x-over; Spectre app. 598-1st app. Checkmate 1.75
600-($2.50, 84 pgs., 5/88) 2.00 5.00
601-642-Weekly issues ($1.50, 52 pgs.): 601-Re-intro The Secret Six. 611-614-: Catwoman stories (new costume in #611). 613-618-Nightwing stories .70 1.75
643-Superman & monthly issues begin again; Perez-c/a/scripts begin; swipes cover to Superman #1 .70 1.75
644-649,651-661,663-666,668-673,675-679: 645-1st app. Maxima. 654-Part 3 of Batman storyline. 655-Free extra 8 pgs. 660-Death of Lex Luthor. 661-Begin $1.00-c. 675-Deathstroke cameo. 679-Last $1.00 issue .70 1.75
650-($1.50, 52 pgs.)-Lobo cameo (last panel) 1.60 4.00
662-Clark Kent reveals i.d. to Lois Lane; story continued in Superman #53 2.60 5.00
667-($1.75, 52 pgs.) .80 2.00
674-Supergirl logo & c/story (reintro) 1.20 3.00
680-682 .70 1.75
683-Doomsday cameo 1.20 3.00
683-2nd & 3rd printings 1.25
684-Doomsday battle issue 1.20 3.00
685,686-Funeral for a Friend issues; Supergirl app. 1.00 2.50
685-2nd & 3rd printings 1.25
687-($1.95)-Collector's Edition with die-cut-c .90 2.25
687-($1.50)-Newsstand Edition with mini-poster .70 1.75
688-694,696-699,701-703-($1.50): 688-Guy Gardner-c/story. 697-Bizarro-c/story. 703-(9/94)-Zero Hour 1.50
695-($2.50)-Collector's Edition w/embossed foil-c 1.00 2.50
700-($2.95, 68 pgs.)-Fall of Metropolis Pt 1; Pete Ross marries Lana Lang; Curt Swan & Murphy Anderson inks 1.20 3.00
700-Platinum 2.00 5.00
700-Gold 5.50 15.00
0,704-709: 0-(10/94). 704-(11/94) 1.50
710-719,721-744: 710-Begin $1.95-c. 714-Joker app. 718-Batman-c/app. 721-Mr. Mxyzptlk app. 723-Brainiac as Superman; Dave Johnson-c.727-Final Night x-over. 732-New powers. 733-New costume, Ray app. 738-Immonen-s/a(p) begins. 741-Legion app. .80 2.00
720-Lois breaks off engagement w/Clark 1.20 3.00
720-2nd print. .80 2.00
Annual 1(1987)-Art Adams-c/a(p); Batman app. 1.20 3.00
Annual 2(1989, $1.75, 68 pgs.)-Perez-c/a(i) .80 2.00
Annual 3(1991, $2.00, 68 pgs.)-Armageddon 2001 .80 2.00
Annual 4(1992, $2.50, 68 pgs.)-Eclipso vs. Shazam 1.00 2.50
Annual 5(1993, $2.50, 68 pgs.)-Bloodlines; 1st app. Loose Cannon. 1.00 2.50
Annual 6(1994, $2.95)-Elseworlds story 1.20 3.00
Annual 7(1995, $3.95)-Year One story 1.60 4.00
Annual 8(1996, $2.95)-Legends of the Dead Earth story 1.20 3.00
Annual 9(1997, $3.95)-Pulp Heroes story 1.60 4.00
Theater Giveaway (1947, 32 pgs., 6-1/2 x 8-1/4", nn)-Vigilante story based on Columbia Vigilante serial; no Superman-c or story 58.00 174.00 525.00

NOTE: ***Supergirl's*** *origin in 262, 280, 285, 291, 305, 309.* ***N. Adams*** *c-356, 358, 359, 361-364, 366, 367, 370-374, 377-379i, 398-400, 402, 404-406, 419p, 466, 468, 473i, 485.* ***Aparo*** *a-642.* ***Austin*** *c/a-682i.* ***Baily*** *a-24, 25.* ***Burnley*** *a-28-33; c-48?, 53-55, 58, 59?, 60-63, 65, 66p, 67p, 70p, 71p, 79p, 82p, 84-86p, 90-92p, 93p?, 94p, 107p, 108p.* ***Byrne*** *a-584-598p, 599i, 600p; c-584-591, 596-600.* ***Ditko*** *a-642.* ***Giffen*** *a-560, 563, 565, 577, 579; c-539, 560, 563, 565, 577, 579.* ***Grell*** *a-440-442, 444-446, 450-452, 456-458; c-456.* ***Guardineer*** *a-24, 25; c-8, 11, 12, 14-16, 18. 25.* ***Guice*** *a(p)-676-681, 683-698, 700; c-683, 685, 686, 687(direct), 688-693i, 694-696, 697i, 698-700.* ***Infantino*** *a-642.* ***Kaluta*** *c-613.* ***Bob Kane's*** *Clip Carson-14-41.* ***Gil Kane*** *a-443r, 493r, 539-541, 544-546, 551-554, 601-605, 642; c-535p, 540, 541, 544p, 545-549, 551-554, 580, 627.* ***Kirby*** *c-638.* ***Meskin*** *a-42-121(most).* ***Mignola*** *a-600, Annual 2; c-c-614.* ***Moldoff*** *a-23-25, 443r.* ***Mooney*** *a-667p.* ***Mortimer*** *c-153, 154, 159-172, 174, 178-181, 184, 186-189, 191-193, 196, 200, 206.* ***Orlando*** *a-617p; c-621.* ***Perez*** *a-600i, 643-652p, Annual 2p; c-529p, 602, 643-651, Annual 2p.* ***Quesada*** *c-Annual 4p.* ***Fred Ray*** *c-34, 36-46, 50-52.* ***Siegel & Shuster*** *a-1-27.* ***Paul Smith*** *c-608.* ***Starlin*** *a-509; c-631.* ***Leonard Starr*** *a-597i(part),* ***Staton*** *a-525p, 526p, 531p, 535p, 536p.* ***Swan/Moldoff*** *c-281, 286, 287, 293, 298, 331.* ***Thibert*** *c-670, 677p, 678-681, 684.* ***Toth*** *a-406, 407, 413, 431; c-616.* ***Tuska*** *a-486p, 550.* ***Williamson*** *a-568i.* ***Zeck*** *c-Annual 5*

ACTION FORCE (Also see G.I. Joe European Missions)
Mar, 1987 - No. 40?, 1988 ($1.00, weekly, magazine)
Marvel Comics Ltd. (British)

1-40: British G.I. Joe series. 3-w/poster insert 1.00

ACTION GIRL
Oct, 1994 - Present ($2.50/$2.75, B&W)
Slave Labor Graphics

1-3 1.00 2.50
4-13: 4-Begin $2.75-c 1.10 2.75
1-6 ($2.75, 2nd printings): All read 2nd Print in indicia. 1-(2/96). 2-(10/95). 3-(2/96). 4-(7/96). 5-(2/97). 6-(9/97) 1.10 2.75
1-4 ($2.75, 3rd printings): All read 3rd Print in indicia. 1.10 2.75

ACTION PLANET COMICS
1996 - Present ($3.95, B&W, 44 pgs.)
Action Planet

1-3: 1-Intro Monster Man by Mike Manley & other stories 1.60 4.00

ACTUAL CONFESSIONS (Formerly Love Adventures)
No. 13, Oct, 1952 - No. 14, Dec, 1952
Atlas Comics (MPI)

13,14 4.00 11.50 23.00

ACTUAL ROMANCES (Becomes True Secrets #3 on?)
Oct, 1949 - No. 2, Jan, 1950 (52 pgs.)

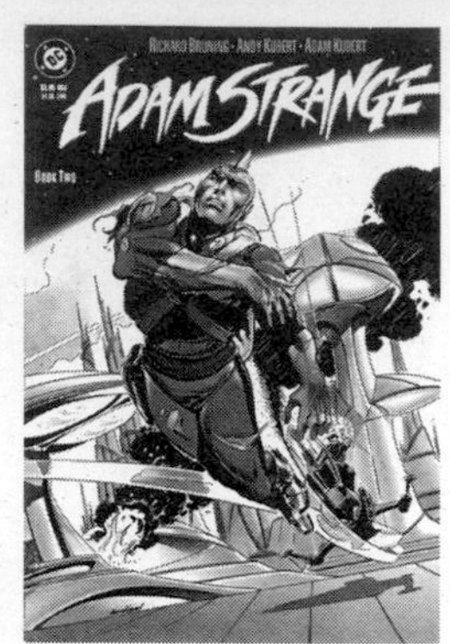

Adam Strange Book Two © DC

Adventure Comics #39 © DC

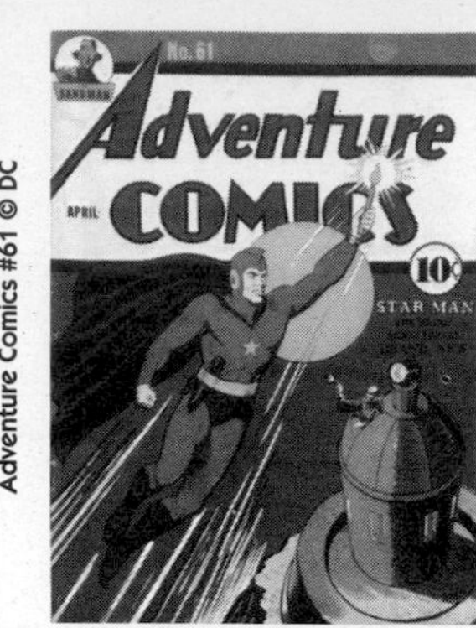

Adventure Comics #61 © DC

GD25 FN65 NM94 | GD25 FN65 NM94

Marvel Comics (IPS)

1 8.30 25.00 58.00
2-Photo-c 5.70 17.00 34.00

ADAM AND EVE
1975,1978 (35¢/49¢)
Spire Christian Comics (Fleming H. Revell Co.)

nn-By Al Hartley 1.60 4.00

ADAM STRANGE (Also see Green Lantern #132, Mystery In Space #53 & Showcase #17)
1990 - No. 3, 1990 ($3.95, 52 pgs, limited series, squarebound)
DC Comics

Book One - Three: Andy & Adam Kubert-c/a 1.60 4.00

ADAM-12 (TV)
Dec, 1973 - No. 10, Feb, 1976 (Photo-c)
Gold Key

1 5.50 16.50 60.00
2-10 1.80 5.50 20.00

ADDAM OMEGA
Feb, 1997 - Present ($2.95. B&W)
Antarctic Press

1-4 2.95

ADDAMS FAMILY (TV cartoon)
Oct, 1974 - No. 3, Apr, 1975 (Hanna-Barbera)
Gold Key

1 8.00 23.00 85.00
2,3 4.00 12.00 45.00

ADLAI STEVENSON
Dec, 1966
Dell Publishing Co.

12-007-612-Life story; photo-c 2.25 6.75 25.00

ADOLESCENT RADIOACTIVE BLACK BELT HAMSTERS (See Clint)
1986 - No. 9, Jan, 1988 ($1.50, B&W)
Comic Castle/Eclipse Comics

1-9: 1st & 2nd printings exist 1.00
1-Limited Edition 1.20 3.00
1-In 3-D (7/86) .75 1.80
2-4 ($2.50) 1.00 2.50
Massacre The Japanese Invasion #1 (8/89, $2.00) .80 2.00

ADULT TALES OF TERROR ILLUSTRATED (See Terror Illustrated)

ADVANCED DUNGEONS & DRAGONS (Also see TSR Worlds)
Dec, 1988 - No. 36, Dec, 1991 (Newsstand #1 is Holiday, 1988-89) ($1.25/$1.50/$1.75)
DC Comics

1-Based on TSR role playing game .80 2.00
2-24 1.50
25-36: 25-$1.75-c begins .70 1.75
Annual 1 (1990, $3.95, 68 pgs.) 1.60 4.00

ADVENTURE BOUND
Aug, 1949
Dell Publishing Co.

Four Color 239 4.25 13.00 48.00

ADVENTURE COMICS (Formerly New Adventure)(...Presents Dial H For Hero #479-490)
No. 32, 11/38 - No. 490, 2/82; No. 491, 9/82 - No. 503, 9/83
National Periodical Publications/DC Comics

32-Anchors Aweigh (ends #52), Barry O'Neil (ends #60, not in #33), Captain Desmo (ends #47), Dale Daring (ends #47), Federal Men (ends #70), The Golden Dragon (ends #36), Rusty & His Pals (ends #52) by Bob Kane, Todd Hunter (ends #38) and Tom Brent (ends #39) begin
466.00 1400.00 3000.00
33-38: 37-Cover used on Double Action #2 216.00 650.00 1400.00
39(6/39):-Jack Wood begins, ends #42; 1st mention of Marijuana in comics
216.00 650.00 1400.00

GD25 FN65 VF82 NM94

40-(Rare, 7/39, on stands 6/10/39)-The Sandman begins by Bert Christman (who died in WWII); believed to be 1st conceived story (see N.Y. World's Fair for 1st published app.); Socko Strong begins, ends #54
2900.00 8700.00 18,850.00 32,000.00

GD25 FN65 NM94

41 390.00 1170.00 3900.00
42,44-Sandman-c by Flessel. 44-Opium story 500.00 1500.00 5000.00
43,45 240.00 720.00 2400.00
46,47-Sandman covers by Flessel. 47-Steve Conrad Adventurer begins, ends #76 350.00 1050.00 3500.00

GD25 FN65 VF82 NM94

48-Intro & 1st app. The Hourman by Bernard Bailey; Baily-c (Hourman c-48,50,52-59) 1818.00 5455.00 10,908.00 20,000.00
(Estimated up to 80 total copies exist, 5 in NM/Mint)

GD25 FN65 NM94

49,50: 50-Cotton Carver by Jack Lehti begins, ends #64
195.00 585.00 1750.00
51,60-Sandman-c: 51-Sandman-c by Flessel. 240.00 720.00 2200.00
52-59: 53-1st app. Jimmy "Minuteman" Martin & the Minutemen of America in Hourman; ends #78. 58-Paul Kirk Manhunter begins (1st app.), ends #72
167.00 500.00 1500.00

GD25 FN65 VF82 NM94

61-1st app. Starman by Jack Burnley (4/41); Starman c-61-72; Starman by Burnley in #61-80 1100.00 3335.00 6675.00 11,000.00
(Estimated up to 100+ total copies exist, 7 in NM/Mint)

GD25 FN65 NM94

62-65,67,68,70: 67-Origin & 1st app. The Mist. 70-Last Federal Men
144.00 433.00 1300.00
66-Origin/1st app. Shining Knight (9/41) 178.00 534.00 1600.00
69-1st app. Sandy the Golden Boy (Sandman's sidekick) by Paul Norris (in a Bob Kane style); Sandman dons new costume 156.00 468.00 1400.00
71-Jimmy Martin becomes costume aide to the Hourman; 1st app.Hourman's Miracle Ray machine 133.00 400.00 1200.00

GD25 FN65 VF82 NM94

72-1st Simon & Kirby Sandman (3/42, 1st DC work)
910.00 2730.00 5460.00 10,000.00
(Estimated up to 100+ total copies exist, 8 in NM/Mint)
73-Origin Manhunter by Simon & Kirby; begin new series; Manhunter-c
1000.00 3000.00 6500.00 11,000.00
(Estimated up to 100+ total copies exist, 7 in NM/Mint)

GD25 FN65 NM94

74-80: 74-Thorndyke replaces Jimmy, Hourman's assistant; new Sandman-c begin by S&K. 75-Thor app. by Kirby; 1st Kirby Thor (see Tales of the Unexpected #16). 77-Origin Genius Jones; Mist story. 79-Manhunter-c. 80-Last S&K Manhunter & Burnley Starman 156.00 468.00 1400.00
81-90: 83-Last Hourman. 84-Mike Gibbs begins, ends #102
100.00 300.00 900.00
91-Last Simon & Kirby Sandman 83.00 250.00 750.00
92-99,101,102: 92-Last Manhunter. 102-Last Starman, Sandman, & Genius Jones; most-S&K-c (Genius Jones cont'd in More Fun #108)
81.00 243.00 725.00
100-S&K-c 106.00 318.00 950.00
103-Aquaman, Green Arrow, Johnny Quick & Superboy all move over from More Fun Comics #107; 8th app. Superboy; Superboy-c begin; 1st small logo (4/46) 233.00 700.00 2100.00
104 83.00 250.00 750.00
105-110 58.00 174.00 525.00

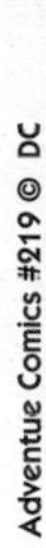

Adventure Comics #219 © DC

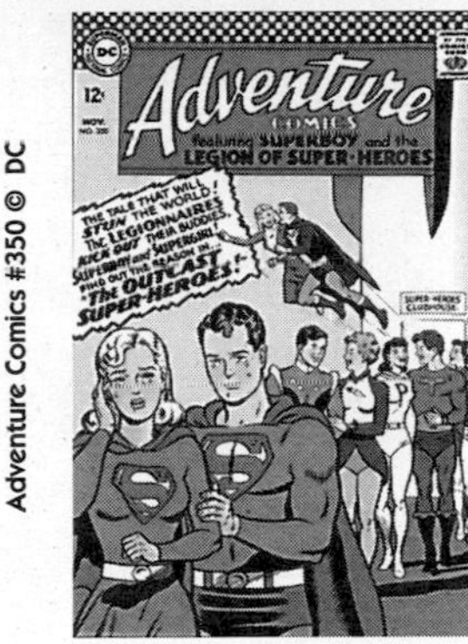

Adventure Comics #350 © DC

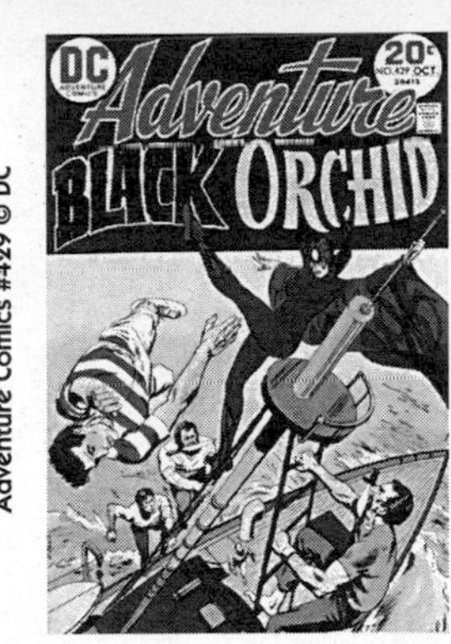

Adventure Comics #429 © DC

GD25 FN65 NM94

111-120: 113-X-Mas-c 54.00 162.00 485.00
121-126,128-130: 128-1st meeting Superboy & Lois Lane
48.00 144.00 430.00
127-Brief origin Shining Knight retold 50.00 150.00 450.00
131-141,143-149: 132-Shining Knight 1st return to King Arthur time; origin aide Sir Butch 40.00 120.00 360.00
142-Origin Shining Knight & Johnny Quick retold 44.00 133.00 400.00
150,151,153,155,157,159,161,163-All have 6 pg. Shining Knight stories by Frank Frazetta. 159-Origin Johnny Quick 44.00 133.00 400.00
152,154,156,158,160,162,164-169: 166-Last Shining Knight. 168-Last 52 pg. issue 36.00 108.00 300.00
170-180 36.00 107.00 285.00
181-199: 189-B&W and color illo in **POP** 34.00 102.00 280.00
200 (5/54) 38.00 114.00 420.00
201-208: 207-Last Johnny Quick (not in 205) 27.00 82.00 275.00
209-Last pre-code issue; origin Speedy 29.00 87.00 290.00

GD25 FN65 VF82 NM94

210-1st app. Krypto (Superdog)-c/story (3/55)
223.00 670.00 1560.00 2900.00

GD25 FN65 NM94

211-213,215-220: 220-Krypto app. 24.00 72.00 240.00
214-2nd app. Krypto 33.00 100.00 370.00
221-246: 229-1st S.A. issue. 237-1st Intergalactic Vigilante Squadron (6/57)
20.50 62.00 205.00

GD25 FN65 VF82 NM94

247(4/58)-1st Legion of Super Heroes app.; 1st app. Cosmic Boy, Lightning Boy (later Lightning Lad in #267), & Saturn Girl (origin)
300.00 900.00 2100.00 4200.00

GD25 FN65 NM94

248-252,254,255-Green Arrow in all: 255-Intro. Red Kryptonite in Superboy (used in #252 but with no effect) 16.00 48.00 160.00
253-1st meeting of Superboy & Robin; Green Arrow by Kirby in #250-255 (also see World's Finest #96-99) 22.00 66.00 220.00
256-Origin Green Arrow by Kirby 46.00 138.00 560.00
257-259: 258-Green Arrow x-over in Superboy 13.00 39.00 130.00
260-1st Silver-Age origin Aquaman (5/59) 51.00 153.00 610.00
261-265,268,270: 262-Origin Speedy in Green Arrow. 270-Congorilla begins, ends #281,283 10.50 32.00 105.00
266-(11/59)-Origin & 1st app. Aquagirl (tryout, not same as later character)
11.50 34.00 115.00
267(12/59)-2nd Legion of Super Heroes; Lightning Boy now called Lightning Lad; new costumes for Legion 64.00 192.00 770.00
269-Intro. Aqualad (2/60); last Green Arrow (not in #206)
21.00 63.00 210.00
271-Origin Luthor retold 23.00 69.00 230.00
272-274,277-280: 279-Intro White Kryptonite in Superboy. 280-1st meeting Superboy-Lori Lemaris 10.00 30.00 100.00
275-Origin Superman-Batman team retold (see World's Finest #94)
18.50 55.00 185.00
276-(9/60) Re-intro Metallo (3rd app?); story similar to Superboy #49
8.50 25.50 85.00
281,284,287-289: 281-Last Congorilla. 284-Last Aquaman in Adv. 287,288-Intro Dev-Em, the Knave from Krypton. 287-1st Bizarro Perry White & J. Olsen. 288-Bizarro-c. 289-Legion cameo (statues) 8.50 25.50 85.00
282(3/61)-5th Legion app; intro/origin Star Boy 16.00 48.00 160.00
283-Intro. The Phantom Zone 16.00 48.00 160.00
285-1st Tales of the Bizarro World-c/story (ends #299) in Adv. (see Action #255) 14.00 42.00 140.00
286-1st Bizarro Mxyzptlk; Bizarro-c 12.00 36.00 120.00
290(11/61)-8th Legion app; origin Sunboy in Legion (last 10¢ issue)
16.00 48.00 160.00
291,292,295-298: 291-1st 12¢ ish, (12/61). 292-1st Bizarro Lana Lang & Lucy Lane. 295-Bizarro-c; 1st Bizarro Titano 6.50 19.50 65.00
293(2/62)-13th Legion app; Mon-el & Legion Super Pets (1st app./origin) app. (1st Superhorse). 1st Bizarro Luthor & Kandor 10.50 32.00 105.00
294-1st Bizarro Marilyn Monroe, Pres. Kennedy. 10.00 30.00 100.00
299-1st Gold Kryptonite (8/62) 7.00 21.00 70.00
300-Tales of the Legion of Super-Heroes series begins (9/62); Mon-el leaves Phantom Zone (temporarily), joins Legion 31.00 93.00 350.00
301-Origin Bouncing Boy 11.50 34.00 115.00
302-305: 303-1st app. Matter Eater Lad. 304-Death of Lightning Lad in Legion
7.50 22.50 75.00
306-310: 306-Intro. Legion of Substitute Heroes. 307-1st app. Element Lad in Legion. 308-1st app. Lightning Lass in Legion 6.50 19.50 65.00
311-320: 312-Lightning Lad back in Legion. 315-Last new Superboy story; Colossal Boy app. 316-Origins & powers of Legion given. 317-Intro. Dream Girl in Legion; Lightning Lass becomes Light Lass; Hall of Fame series begins. 320-Dev-Em 2nd app. 5.00 15.00 50.00
321-Intro Time Trapper 4.00 12.00 40.00
322-330: 327-Intro/1st app. Lone Wolf in Legion. 329-Intro The Bizarro Legionnaires 3.50 10.50 35.00
331-340: 337-Chlorophyll Kid & Night Girl app. 340-Intro Computo in Legion
2.50 7.50 25.00
341-Triplicate Girl becomes Duo Damsel 2.25 6.75 18.00
342-345,347,350,351: 345-Last Hall of Fame; returns in 356,371. 351-1st app. White Witch 1.50 4.50 12.00
346,348,349: 346-1st app. Karate Kid, Princess Projectra, Ferro Lad, & Nemesis Kid. 348-Origin Sunboy; intro Dr. Regulus in Legion. 349-Intro Universo & Rond Vidar 1.50 4.50 12.00
352,354-360: 355-Insect Queen joins Legion (4/67) 1.10 3.30 9.00
353-Death of Ferro Lad in Legion 1.50 4.50 12.00
361-364,366,368-370: 369-Intro Mordru in Legion 1.00 3.00 8.00
365,367,371,372: 365-Intro Shadow Lass; lists origins & powers of L.S.H. 367-New Legion headquarters. 371-Intro. Chemical King. 372-Timber Wolf & Chemical King join. 374-Article on comics fandom 1.00 3.00 8.00
373,374,376-380: Last Legion in Adventure 1.00 2.80 7.00
375-Intro Quantum Queen & The Wanderers 1.00 2.80 7.00
381-Supergirl begins; 1st full length Supergirl story & her 1st solo book (6/69)
4.50 13.50 45.00
382-389,391-400: 399-Unpubbed G.A. Black Canary story. 400-New costume for Supergirl 1.25 3.75 10.00
390-Giant Supergirl G-69 2.50 7.50 25.00
401,402,404-408 2.40 6.00
403-68pg. Giant G-81; Legion-r/#304,305,308,312 2.50 7.50 25.00
409,410,411-(52 pgs.) 1.25 3.75 10.00
412-(52 pgs.) Reprints origin & 1st app. of Animal Man from Strange Adventures #180 1.75 5.25 14.00
413,418,419: 413-Hawkman by Kubert r/B&B #44; G.A. Robotman-r/Det. #178; Zatanna by Morrow 1.50 4.50 12.00
414-(52 pgs.) Reprints 2nd Animal Man/Strange Advs. #184
1.50 4.50 12.00
415,420-(52 pgs.)Animal Man reprints from Strange Adventures #190 (origin recap) & #195 1.50 4.50 12.00
416-Giant DC-100 Page Super Spect. #10; GA-r; r/1st app. Black Canary from Flash #86; no Zatanna (see DC 100 Page... for price) - -
417-(52 pgs.) Morrow Vigilante; Frazetta Shining Knight-r/Adv. #161; origin The Enchantress; no Zatanna 1.50 4.50 12.00
421-424,427: Last Supergirl in Adventure. 418-Previously unpublished Dr. Mid-Nite story from 1948; No Zatanna. 427-Last Vigilante. 1.20 3.00
425-New look, content change to adventure; Kaluta-c; Toth-a, origin Capt. Fear
1.50 4.50 12.00
426-1st Adventurers Club. 1.00 3.00 8.00
428-Origin/1st app. Black Orchid (c/story, 6-7/73) 2.80 8.40 28.00
429,430-Black Orchid-c/stories 1.50 4.50 12.00
431-Spectre by Aparo begins, ends #440. 3.00 9.00 30.00
432-440-Spectre app. 433-437-Cover title is Weird Adv. Comics. 436-Last 20¢ issue. 440-New Spectre origin. 1.50 4.50 12.00
441,442,444,448-458: 441-452-Aquaman app. 450-Weather Wizard app. in

Adventure Comics #466 © DC

Adventures in the DC Universe #7 © DC

Adventures Into Terror #43(#1) © MEG

GD25 FN65 NM94

Aquaman story. 449-451-Martian Manhunter app. 453-458-Superboy app.
453-Intro Mighty Girl. 457,458-Eclipso app. 1.20 3.00
443,445-447: 443-Re-intro Clay Face. 445-447-The Creeper app. 446-Flag-c 2.40 6.00
459,460: 459-New Gods/Darkseid storyline concludes from New Gods #19 (#459 is dated 9-10/78) without missing a month. 459-Flash (ends #466), Deadman (ends #466), Wonder Woman (ends #464), Green Lantern (ends #460). 460-Aquaman (ends #478) 1.25 3.75 10.00
461,462: 461-Justice Society begins; ends 466. 461,462-Death Earth II Batman (both $1.00, 68 pgs.) 1.25 3.75 10.00
463-466($1.00 size, 68 pgs.): 2.00 5.00
467-Starman by Ditko & Plastic Man begins; 1st app. Prince Gavyn (Starman). 2.40 6.00
468-470,479: 469,470-Origin Starman. 479-Dial 'H' For Hero begins, ends #490 1.20 3.00
471-478: 478-Last Starman & Plastic Man. 1.00 2.50
480-490: 488,489-Deathstroke-c/cameos. .80 2.00
491-499: 491-100pg. Digest size begins; r/Legion of Super Heroes/Adv. #247, 267; Spectre, Aquaman, Superboy, S&K Sandman, Black Canary-r & new Shazam by Newton begin. 492,495,496,499-S&K Sandman-r/Adventure in all. 493-Challengers of the Unknown begins by Tuska w/brief origin. 493-495, 497-499-G.A. Captain Marvel-r. 494-499-Spectre-r/Spectre 1-3, 5-7. 496-Capt. Marvel Jr. new-s, Cockrum-a. 498-Mary Marvel new-s. Plastic Man-r begin; origin Bouncing Boy-r/ #301. 1.10 3.30 9.00
500-503: 500-Legion-r (Digest size, 148 pgs.). 501-503: G.A.-r 1.00 2.80 7.00

NOTE: *Bizarro covers-285, 286, 288, 294, 295, 329. Vigilante app.-420, 426, 427.* **N. Adams** *a(r)-495i-498i; c-365-369, 371-373, 375-379, 381-383.* **Aparo** *a-431-433, 434i, 435, 436, 437i, 438i, 439-452, 503r; c-431-452.* **Austin** *a-449i 451i.* **Bernard Baily** *c-48, 50, 52-59.* **Bolland** *c-475.* **Burnley** *c-61-72, 116-120p.* **Chaykin** *a-438.* **Ditko** *a-467-478p; c-467p.* **Creig Flessel** *c-32, 33, 40, 42, 44, 46, 47, 51, 60.* **Giffen** *c-491p-494p, 500p.* **Grell** *a-435-437, 440.* **Guardineer** *c-34, 35, 45.* **Infantino** *a-416r.* **Kaluta** *c-425.* **Bob Kane** *a-38.* **G. Kane** *a-414r, 425; c-496-499, 537.* **Kirby** *a-250-256.* **Kubert** *a-413.* **Meskin** *a-81,127.* **Moldoff** *a-494i; c-49.* **Morrow** *a-413-415, 417, 422, 502r, 503r.* **Netzer/Nasser** *a-449-451.* **Newton** *a-459-461, 464-466, 491p, 492p.* **Paul Norris** *a-69.* **Orlando** *a-457p, 458p.* **Perez** *c-484-486, 490p.* **Simon/Kirby** *a-503r; c-73-97, 100-102.* **Starlin** *c-471.* **Staton** *a-445-447i, 456-458p, 459, 460, 461p-465p, 466,467p-478p, 502p(r); c-458, 461(back).* **Toth** *a-418, 419, 425, 431, 495p-497p.* **Tuska** *a-494p.*

ADVENTURE COMICS
No date (early 1940s) (Paper-c, 32 pgs.)
IGA

Two diff.issues; Super-Mystery-r from 1941 20.00 60.00 160.00

ADVENTURE IN DISNEYLAND
May, 1955 (Giveaway, soft-c., 16 pgs)
Walt Disney Productions (Dist. by Richfield Oil)

nn 8.50 26.00 60.00

ADVENTURE INTO MYSTERY
May, 1956 - No. 8, July, 1957
Atlas Comics (BFP No. 1/OPI No. 2-8)

	GD25	FN65	NM94
1-Powell s/f-a; Forte-a; Everett-c	30.00	90.00	240.00
2-Flying Saucer story	17.00	51.00	132.00
3,6-Everett-c	14.00	42.00	110.00
4-Williamson-a, 4 pgs; Powell-a	15.00	45.00	120.00
5-Everett-c/a, Orlando-a	15.00	45.00	120.00
7-Torres-a; Everett-c	15.00	45.00	120.00
8-Moriera, Sale, Torres, Woodbridge-a, Severin-c	14.00	42.00	110.00

ADVENTURE IS MY CAREER
1945 (44 pgs.)
U.S. Coast Guard Academy/Street & Smith

nn-Simon, Milt Gross-a 15.50 47.00 125.00

ADVENTURERS, THE
Aug, 1986 - No. 10, 1987? ($1.50, B&W)
V2#1, 1987 - V2#9, 1988; V3#1, Oct, 1989 - V3#6, 1990
Aircel Comics/Adventure Publ.

	GD25	FN65	NM94
1-Peter Hsu-a		1.20	3.00
1-Cover variant, limited ed.		2.00	5.00
1-2nd print (1986); 1st app. Elf Warrior		.80	2.00
2,3		.80	2.00
0 (#4, 12/86)-Origin		.80	2.00
5-10			1.60
Book II, regular & limited ed. #1			1.60
Book II, #2,3,0,4-9			1.60
Book III, #1 (10/89, $2.25)-Regular & limited-c		.90	2.25
Book III, #2-6		.90	2.25

ADVENTURES (No. 2 Spectacular... on cover)
Nov, 1949 - No. 2, Feb, 1950 (No. 1 ...in Romance on cover)
St. John Publishing Co. (Slightly large size)

1(Scarce); Bolle, Starr-a(2) 21.00 62.00 165.00
2(Scarce)-Slave Girl; China Bombshell app.; Bolle, L. Starr-a 34.00 103.00 275.00

ADVENTURES FOR BOYS
Dec, 1954
Bailey Enterprises

nn-Comics, text, & photos 5.00 15.00 30.00

ADVENTURES IN PARADISE (TV)
Feb-Apr, 1962
Dell Publishing Co.

Four Color#1301 3.60 11.00 40.00

ADVENTURES IN ROMANCE (See Adventures)

ADVENTURES IN SCIENCE (See Classics Illustrated Special Issue)

ADVENTURES IN THE DC UNIVERSE
Apr, 1997 - Present ($1.75)
DC Comics

1-Animated style in all: JLA-c/app .80 2.00
2-8: 2-Flash app. 3-Wonder Woman. 4-Green Lantern. 6-Aquaman. 7-Shazam Family. 8-Blue Beetle & Booster Gold. 1.75
9-13: 9-Flash, begin $1.95-c. 10-Legion. 11-Green Lantern & Wonder Woman. 12-JLA. 13-Impulse 1.95
Annual 1(1997, $3.95)-Dr. Fate, Impulse, Rose & Thorn, Superboy, Mister Miracle app. 3.95

ADVENTURES IN 3-D
Nov, 1953 - No. 2, Jan, 1954 (25¢)
Harvey Publications

1-Nostrand, Powell-a, 2-Powell-a 15.00 45.00 120.00

ADVENTURES INTO DARKNESS (See Seduction of the Innocent 3-D)
No. 5, Aug, 1952 - No. 14, 1954
Better-Standard Publications/Visual Editions

	GD25	FN65	NM94
5-Katz-c/a; Toth-a(p)	23.00	70.00	185.00
6-Tuska, Katz-a	14.00	41.00	110.00
7-Katz-c/a	15.00	45.00	120.00
8,9-Toth-a(p)	16.00	49.00	130.00
10,11-Jack Katz-a	12.00	38.00	100.00
12-Toth-a?; lingerie panels	12.00	38.00	100.00
13-Toth-a(p); Cannibalism story cited by T. E. Murphy articles	15.50	47.00	125.00
14	10.00	30.00	80.00

NOTE: **Fawcette** *a-13.* **Moriera** *a-5.* **Sekowsky** *a-10, 11, 13(2).*

ADVENTURES INTO TERROR (Formerly Joker Comics)
No. 43, Nov, 1950 - No. 31, May, 1954
Marvel/Atlas Comics (CDS)

	GD25	FN65	NM94
43(#1)	50.00	150.00	425.00
44(#2, 2/51)-Sol Brodsky-c	39.00	118.00	290.00
3(4/51), 4	21.00	64.00	160.00

Adventures Into Weird Worlds #1 © MEG

Adventures of Baron Munchausen #1 © Columbia Pictures

Adventures of Bob Hope #3 © DC

	GD25	FN65	NM94
5-Wolverton-c panel/Mystic #6; Rico-c panel also; Atom Bomb story	26.00	77.00	190.00
6,8: 8-Wolverton text illo r-/Marvel Tales #104	20.00	60.00	150.00
7-Wolverton-a "Where Monsters Dwell", 6 pgs.; Tuska-c; Maneely-c panels	45.00	130.00	350.00
9,10,12-Krigstein-a. 9-Decapitation panels	18.00	54.00	130.00
11,13-20	14.00	43.00	110.00
21-24,26-31	13.00	39.00	95.00
25-Matt Fox-a	17.00	51.00	130.00

NOTE: ***Ayers*** *a-21.* ***Colan*** *a-3, 5, 14, 21, 24, 25, 28, 29; c-27.* ***Colletta*** *a-30.* ***Everett*** *c-13, 21, 25.* ***Fass*** *a-28, 29.* ***Forte*** *a-28.* ***Heath*** *a-43, 44, 4-6, 22, 24, 26; c-43, 9, 11.* ***Lazarus*** *a-7.* ***Maneely*** *a-7(3 pg.), 10, 11, 21., 22 c-15, 29.* ***Don Rico*** *a-4, 5(3 pg.).* ***Sekowsky*** *a-43, 3, 4.* ***Sinnott*** *a-8, 9, 11, 28.* ***Tuska*** *a-14; c-7.*

ADVENTURES INTO THE UNKNOWN
Fall, 1948 - No. 174, Aug, 1967 (No. 1-33: 52 pgs.)
American Comics Group

(1st continuous series horror comic; see Eerie #1)

	GD25	FN65	NM94
1-Guardineer-a; adapt. of 'Castle of Otranto' by Horace Walpole.	139.00	417.00	1250.00
2	58.00	174.00	520.00
3-Feldstein-a (9 pgs)	58.00	174.00	520.00
4,5: 5-'Spirit Of Frankenstein' series begins, ends #12 (except #11)	31.00	92.00	245.00
6-10	24.00	71.00	190.00
11-16,18-20: 13-Starr-a	19.00	56.00	150.00
17-Story similar to movie 'The Thing'	23.00	69.00	185.00
21-26,28-30	15.50	47.00	125.00
27-Williamson/Krenkel-a (8 pgs.)	20.00	60.00	160.00
31-50: 38-Atom bomb panels	12.00	38.00	100.00
51-(1/54)-(3-D effect-c/story)-Only white cover	26.00	80.00	210.00
52-58: (3-D effect-c/stories with black covers). 52-E.C. swipe/Haunt Of Fear #14	25.00	75.00	200.00
59-3-D effect story only; new logo	20.00	60.00	160.00
60-Woodesque-a by Landau	8.75	26.25	65.00
61-Last pre-code issue (1-2/55)	8.75	26.25	65.00
62-70	4.50	13.50	45.00
71-90	3.20	9.60	32.00
91,96(#95 on inside),107,116-All have Williamson-a	4.50	13.50	45.00
92-95,97-99,101-106,108-115,117-127: 109-113,118-Whitney painted-c	3.00	9.00	30.00
100	3.20	9.60	32.00
128-Williamson/Krenkel/Torres-a(r)/Forbidden Worlds #63; last 10¢ issue	3.00	9.00	30.00
129-152	2.60	7.80	26.00
153, 157-Magic Agent app.	2.50	7.50	24.00
154-Nemesis series begins (origin), ends #170	3.00	9.00	30.00
155,156,158-167,169-174: 169-Nemesis battles Hitler	2.50	7.50	22.00
168-Ditko-a(p)	3.00	9.00	30.00

NOTE: *"Spirit of Frankenstein" series in 5, 6, 8-10, 12, 16.* ***Buscema*** *a-100, 106, 108-110, 158r, 165r.* ***Cameron*** *a-34.* ***Craig*** *a-152, 160.* ***Goode*** *a-45, 47, 60.* ***Landau*** *a-51, 59-63.* ***Lazarus*** *a-34, 48, 51, 52, 56, 58, 79, 87; c-31-56, 58.* ***Reinman*** *a-102, 111, 112, 115-118, 124, 130, 137, 141, 145, 164.* ***Whitney*** *c-12-30, 57, 59-on (most.)* ***Torres/Williamson*** *a-116.*

ADVENTURES INTO WEIRD WORLDS
Jan, 1952 - No. 30, June, 1954
Marvel/Atlas Comics (ACI)

	GD25	FN65	NM94
1-Atom bomb panels	42.00	130.00	360.00
2-Sci/fic stories (2); one by Maneely	30.00	90.00	220.00
3-10: 7-Tongue ripped out. 10-Krigstein, Everett-a	20.00	60.00	150.00
11-21: 21-Hitler in Hell story	16.00	47.00	120.00
22-26: 24-Man holds hypo & splits in two	13.50	41.00	100.00
27-Matt Fox end of world story-a; severed head-c	29.00	86.00	220.00
28-Atom bomb story; decapitation panels	16.00	47.00	120.00
29,30	11.00	33.00	80.00

NOTE: ***Ayers*** *a-8, 26.* ***Everett*** *a-4, 5; c-6, 8, 10-13, 18, 19, 22, 24, 25; a-4, 25.* ***Fass*** *a-7.* ***Forte*** *a-21, 24.* ***Al Hartley*** *a-2.* ***Heath*** *a-1, 4, 17, 22; c-7, 9, 20.* ***Maneely*** *a-2, 3, 11, 20, 22, 23, 25; c-1, 3, 22, 25-27, 29.* ***Reinman*** *a-24, 28.* ***Rico*** *a-13.* ***Robinson*** *a-13.* ***Sinnott*** *a-25, 30.* ***Tuska*** *a-1, 2, 12, 15.* ***Whitney*** *a-7.* ***Wildey*** *a-28. Bondage c-22.*

ADVENTURES IN WONDERLAND
April, 1955 - No. 5, Feb, 1956 (Jr. Readers Guild)
Lev Gleason Publications

	GD25	FN65	NM94
1-Maurer-a	7.15	21.50	50.00
2-4	5.00	15.00	30.00
5-Christmas issue	5.70	17.00	35.00

ADVENTURES OF AARON
Mar, 1997 - Present (2.95, B&W)
Image Comics

	GD25	FN65	NM94
1,2,100(#3)			2.95

ADVENTURES OF ALAN LADD, THE
Oct-Nov, 1949 - No. 9, Feb-Mar, 1951 (All 52 pgs.)
National Periodical Publications

	GD25	FN65	NM94
1-Photo-c	81.00	243.00	725.00
2-Photo-c	43.00	129.00	390.00
3-6: Last photo-c	36.00	107.00	285.00
7-9	28.00	84.00	225.00

NOTE: ***Dan Barry*** *a-1.* ***Moreira*** *a-3-7.*

ADVENTURES OF ALICE
1945 (Also see Alice in Wonderland & ...at Monkey Island)
Civil Service Publ./Pentagon Publishing Co.

	GD25	FN65	NM94
1	8.75	26.25	65.00
2-Through the Magic Looking Glass	7.85	23.50	55.00

ADVENTURES OF BARON MUNCHAUSEN, THE
July, 1989 - No. 4, Oct, 1989 ($1.75, limited series)
Now Comics

	GD25	FN65	NM94
1-4: Movie adaptation		.70	1.80

ADVENTURES OF BAYOU BILLY, THE
Sept, 1989 - No. 5, June, 1990 ($1.00)
Archie Comics

	GD25	FN65	NM94
1-5: Esposito-c/a(i). 5-Kelley Jones-c			1.00

ADVENTURES OF BOB HOPE, THE (Also see True Comics #59)
Feb-Mar, 1950 - No. 109, Feb-Mar, 1968 (#1-10: 52pgs.)
National Periodical Publications

	GD25	FN65	NM94
1-Photo-c	128.00	384.00	1150.00
2-Photo-c	63.00	189.00	570.00
3,4-Photo-c	38.00	113.00	340.00
5-10	36.00	107.00	285.00
11-20	19.50	58.00	155.00
21-31 (2-3/55; last precode)	12.00	38.00	100.00
32-40	8.50	25.50	85.00
41-50	7.00	21.00	70.00
51-70	5.00	15.00	50.00
71-93,96-105	2.60	7.80	26.00
94-Aquaman cameo	3.00	9.00	30.00
95-1st app. Super-Hip & 1st monster issue (11/65)	3.50	10.50	35.00
106-109-All monster-c/stories by N. Adams-c/a	4.20	12.60	42.00

NOTE: *Buzzy in #34. Kitty Karr of Hollywood in #15, 17-20, 23, 28. Liz in #26, 109. Miss Beverly Hills of Hollywood in #7, 8, 10, 13, 14. Miss Melody Lane of Broadway in #15. Rusty in #23, 25. Tommy in #24. No 2nd feature in #2-4, 6, 8, 11, 12, 28-108.*

ADVENTURES OF CAPTAIN AMERICA
Sept, 1991 - No. 4, Jan, 1992 ($4.95, 52 pgs., squarebound, limited series)
Marvel Comics

	GD25	FN65	NM94
1-4: 1-Embossed-c; Fabian Nicieza scripts; Kevin Maguire-c/a(p) begins, ends #3. 2-4-Austin-c/a(i)		2.00	5.00

ADVENTURES OF CYCLOPS AND PHOENIX (Also See Askani'son & The

Adventures of Dean Martin and Jerry Lewis #17 © DC

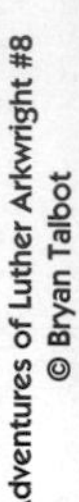
Adventures of Luther Arkwright #8 © Bryan Talbot

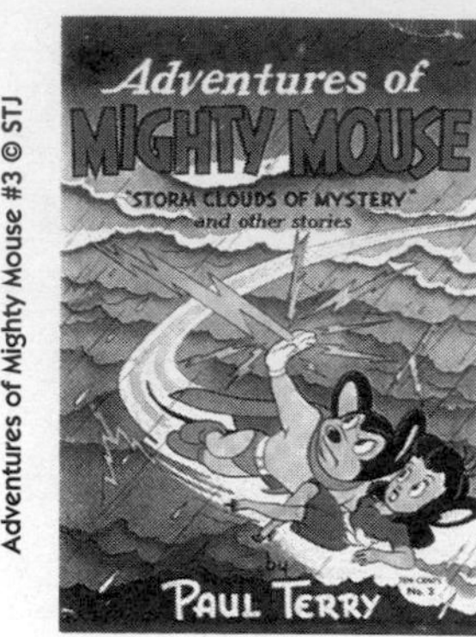

Adventures of Mighty Mouse #3 © STJ

Further Adventures of Cyclops And Phoenix)
May, 1994 - No. 4, Aug, 1994 ($2.95, limited series)
Marvel Comics

	GD25	FN65	NM94
1-Characters from X-Men		1.20	3.00
2-4		1.20	3.00
Trade paperback ($14.95)-reprints #1-4			15.00

ADVENTURES OF DEAN MARTIN AND JERRY LEWIS, THE
(The Adventures of Jerry Lewis #41 on) (See Movie Love #12)
July-Aug, 1952 - No. 40, Oct, 1957
National Periodical Publications

	GD25	FN65	NM94
1	75.00	225.00	675.00
2-3 pg origin on how they became a team	38.00	113.00	340.00
3-10: 3- I Love Lucy text featurette	19.00	56.00	150.00
11-19: Last precode (2/55)	12.00	36.00	95.00
20-30	7.50	22.50	75.00
31-40	5.50	16.50	55.00

ADVENTURES OF DETECTIVE ACE KING, THE (See Detective Dan)
No date (1933) (36 pgs., 9-1/2x12") (10¢, B&W, one-shot) (paper-c)
Humor Publ. Corp.

	GD25	FN65	VF82
Book 1-Along with Detective Dan, the first comic w/original art & the first of a single theme.; Not reprints; Ace King by Martin Nadle (The American Sherlock Holmes). A Dick Tracy look-alike	200.00	600.00	1200.00

ADVENTURES OF FELIX THE CAT, THE
May, 1992 ($1.25)
Harvey Comics

	GD25	FN65	NM94
1-Messmer-r			1.25

ADVENTURES OF FORD FAIRLANE, THE
May, 1990 - No. 4, Aug, 1990 ($1.50, limited series, mature)
DC Comics

	GD25	FN65	NM94
1-4: Movie tie-in; Don Heck inks			1.50

ADVENTURES OF G. I. JOE
1969 (3-1/4x7") (20 & 16 pgs.)
Giveaways

First Series: 1-Danger of the Depths. 2-Perilous Rescue. 3-Secret Mission to Spy Island. 4-Mysterious Explosion. 5-Fantastic Free Fall. 6-Eight Ropes of Danger. 7-Mouth of Doom. 8-Hidden Missile Discovery. 9-Space Walk Mystery. 10-Fight for Survival. 11-The Shark's Surprise.
Second Series: 2-Flying Space Adventure. 4-White Tiger Hunt. 7-Capture of the Pygmy Gorilla. 12-Secret of the Mummy's Tomb.
Third Series: Reprinted surviving titles of First Series. Fourth Series: 13-Adventure Team Headquarters. 14-Search For the Stolen Idol.

	GD25	FN65	NM94
each....		2.00	5.00

ADVENTURES OF HOMER COBB, THE
Sept, 1947 (Oversized)
Say/Bart Prod. (Publ. in the U.S., but printed in Canada)

	GD25	FN65	NM94
1-(Scarce)-Feldstein-c/a	24.00	71.00	190.00

ADVENTURES OF HOMER GHOST (See Homer The Happy Ghost)
June, 1957 - No. 2, Aug, 1957
Atlas Comics

	GD25	FN65	NM94
V1#1,2	3.50	10.50	35.00

ADVENTURES OF JERRY LEWIS, THE (Adventures of Dean Martin & Jerry Lewis No. 1-40)(See Super DC Giant)
No. 41, Nov, 1957 - No. 124, May-June, 1971
National Periodical Publications

	GD25	FN65	NM94
41	5.50	16.50	55.00
42-60	5.00	15.00	50.00
61-80: 68,74-Photo-c	3.50	10.50	35.00
81-91,93-96,98-100: 89-Bob Hope app.	2.50	7.50	22.00
92-Superman cameo	3.40	10.20	34.00
97-Batman/Robin/Joker-c/story; Riddler & Penguin app; Dick Sprang-c.	4.50	13.50	45.00
101,103,104-Neal Adams-c/a	3.80	11.40	38.00
102-Beatles app.; Neal Adams c/a	5.50	16.50	55.00
105-Superman x-over	3.20	9.60	32.00
106-111,113-116	2.00	6.00	16.00
112-Flash x-over	3.20	9.60	32.00
117-Wonder Woman x-over	2.50	7.50	20.00
118-124	1.25	3.75	10.00

ADVENTURES OF JO-JOY, THE (See Jo-Joy)

ADVENTURES OF LUTHER ARKWRIGHT, THE
Oct, 1987 - No. 9, Jan, 1989 ($2.00, B&W)
V2, #1, Mar, 1990 - V2#9, 1990 ($1.95, B&W)
Valkyrie Press/Dark Horse Comics

	GD25	FN65	NM94
1-9: 1-Alan Moore intro.		.80	2.00
V2#1-9 (Dark Horse): Reprints 1st series; new-c		.80	2.00
TPB (1997, $14.95) r/#1-9 w/Michael Moorcock intro.			15.00

ADVENTURES OF MARGARET O'BRIEN, THE
1947 (20 pgs. in color, slick-c, regular size) (Premium)
Bambury Fashions (Clothes)

	GD25	FN65	NM94
In "The Big City" movie adaptation (scarce)	17.00	51.00	135.00

ADVENTURES OF MIGHTY MOUSE (Mighty Mouse Adventures No. 1)
No. 2, Jan, 1952 - No. 18, May, 1955
St. John Publishing Co.

	GD25	FN65	NM94
2	21.00	64.00	170.00
3-5	10.50	32.00	85.00
6-18	8.50	26.00	60.00

ADVENTURES OF MIGHTY MOUSE (2nd Series)
(Two No. 144's; formerly Paul Terry's Comics; No. 129-137 have nn's)
(Becomes Mighty Mouse No. 161 on)
No. 126, Aug, 1955 - No. 160, Oct, 1963
St. John/Pines/Dell/Gold Key

	GD25	FN65	NM94
126(8/55), 127(10/55), 128(11/55)-St. John	6.85	21.00	48.00
nn(129, 4/56)-144(8/59)-Pines	4.00	12.00	40.00
144(10-12/59)-155(7-9/62) Dell	2.90	8.70	32.00
156(10/62)-160(10/63) Gold Key	2.90	8.70	32.00

NOTE: *Early issues titled "Paul Terry's Adventures of ...."*

ADVENTURES OF MIGHTY MOUSE (Formerly Mighty Mouse)
No. 166, Mar, 1979 - No. 172, Jan, 1980
Gold Key

	GD25	FN65	NM94
166-172		1.60	4.00

ADVS. OF MR. FROG & MISS MOUSE (See Dell Junior Treasury No. 4)

ADVENTURES OF OZZIE AND HARRIET, THE (Radio)
Oct-Nov, 1949 - No. 5, June-July, 1950
National Periodical Publications

	GD25	FN65	NM94
1-Photo-c	75.00	225.00	675.00
2	40.00	120.00	360.00
3-5	36.00	108.00	290.00

ADVENTURES OF PATORUZU
Aug, 1946 - Winter, 1946
Green Publishing Co.

	GD25	FN65	NM94
nn's-Contains Animal Crackers reprints	4.15	12.50	25.00

ADVENTURES OF PINKY LEE, THE (TV)
July, 1955 - No. 5, Dec, 1955
Atlas Comics

	GD25	FN65	NM94
1	22.00	66.00	175.00
2-5	14.00	41.00	110.00

ADVENTURES OF PIPSQUEAK, THE (Formerly Pat the Brat)

Adventures of Rex The Wonder Dog #5 © DC

Adventures of Superman #514 © DC

Adventures of the Fly #3 © AP

No. 34, Sept, 1959 - No. 39, July, 1960
Archie Publications (Radio Comics)

	GD25	FN65	NM94
34	3.00	9.00	30.00
35-39	2.50	7.50	20.00

ADVENTURES OF QUAKE & QUISP, THE (See Quaker Oats "Plenty of Glutton")

ADVENTURES OF REX THE WONDER DOG, THE (Rex...No. 1)
Jan-Feb, 1952 - No. 45, May-June, 1959; No. 46, Nov-Dec, 1959
National Periodical Publications

	GD25	FN65	NM94
1-(Scarce)-Toth-c/a	92.00	276.00	825.00
2-(Scarce)-Toth-c/a	46.00	138.00	410.00
3-(Scarce)-Toth-a	36.00	108.00	320.00
4,5	29.00	86.00	230.00
6-10	21.00	64.00	170.00
11-Atom bomb-c/story	23.00	69.00	185.00
12-19: 19-Last precode (1-2/55)	12.00	36.00	95.00
20-46	7.00	21.00	70.00

NOTE: ***Infantino, Gil Kane** art in 5-19 (most)*

ADVENTURES OF ROBIN HOOD, THE (Formerly Robin Hood)
No. 7, 9/57 - No. 8, 11/57 (Based on Richard Greene TV Show)
Magazine Enterprises (Sussex Publ. Co.)

	GD25	FN65	NM94
7,8-Richard Greene photo-c. 7-Powell-a	13.00	39.00	105.00

ADVENTURES OF ROBIN HOOD, THE
Mar, 1974 - No. 7, Jan, 1975 (Disney cartoon) (36 pgs.)
Gold Key

	GD25	FN65	NM94
1(90291-403)-Part-r of $1.50 editions		2.00	5.00
2-7: 1-7 are part-r		1.20	3.00

ADVENTURES OF SNAKE PLISSKEN
Jan, 1997 ($2.50, one-shot)
Marvel Comics

	GD25	FN65	NM94
1: Based on Escape From L.A. movie; Brereton-c		1.00	2.50

ADVENTURES OF SPIDER-MAN, THE (TV cartoon)
Apr, 1996 - No. 12,Mar,1997 (99¢)
Marvel Comics

	GD25	FN65	NM94
1-12: Based on animated television show.			1.00

ADVENTURES OF STUBBY, SANTA'S SMALLEST REINDEER, THE
nd (early 1940s) (Giveaway, 12 pgs.)
W. T. Grant Co.

	GD25	FN65	NM94
nn	4.00	11.00	22.00

ADVENTURES OF SUPERBOY, THE (See Superboy, 2nd Series)

ADVENTURES OF SUPERMAN (Formerly Superman)
No. 424, Jan, 1987 - No. 499, Feb, 1993; No. 500, Early June, 1993 - Present
DC Comics

	GD25	FN65	NM94
424		.90	2.25
425-449: 426-Legends x-over. 432-1st app. Jose Delgado who becomes Gangbuster in #434. 436-Byrne scripts begin. 436,437-Millennium x-over. 438-New Brainiac app. 440-Batman app. 449-Invasion		.80	2.00
450-462: 457-Perez plots		.70	1.75
463-Superman/Flash race; cover swipe/Superman #199		1.60	4.00
464-Lobo-c & app. (pre-dates Lobo #1)		1.20	3.00
465-479,481-491: 467-Part 2 of Batman story. 473-Hal Jordan, Guy Gardner x-over. 477-Legion app. 491-Last $1.00-c			1.25
480-($1.75, 52 pgs.)		.80	2.00
492-495: 495-Forever People-c/story; Darkseid app.			1.50
496-Doomsday cameo		1.20	3.00
496,497-2nd printings			1.25
497-Doomsday battle issue		1.20	3.00
498,499-Funeral for a Friend; Supergirl app.		.80	2.00
498-2nd & 3rd printings			1.25
500-($2.95, 68 pgs.)-Collector's edition w/card		1.30	3.25
500-($2.50, 68 pgs.)-Regular edition w/different-c		1.10	2.75
500-Platinum edition	2.50	7.50	25.00
501-($1.95)-Collector's edition with die-cut-c		.80	2.00
501-($1.50)-Regular edition w/mini-poster & diff.-c			1.50
502-517: 502-Supergirl-c/story. 508-Challengers of the Unknown app. 510-Bizarro-c/story. 517-(9/94)-Zero Hour			1.50
505-($2.50)-Holo-grafx foil-c edition		1.00	2.50
0,518-523: 0-(10/94). 518-(11/94)			1.50
524-557: 524-Begin $1.95-c. 527-Return of Alpha Centurion from Zero Hour. 533-Impulse c/app. 535-Luthor-c/app. 536-Brainiac app. 537-Parasite app. 540-Final Night x-over. 541 Superboy-c/app.;Lois and Clark honeymoon 545-New powers. 546-New costume. 551-Cyborg app.		.80	2.00
550-($3.50)-Double sized		1.40	3.50
Annual 1 (1987, $1.25, 52 pgs.)-Starlin-c & scripts			1.50
Annual 2,3 (1990, 1991, $2.00, 68 pgs.): 2-Byrne-c/a(i); Legion '90 (Lobo) app. 3-Armageddon 2001 x-over		.90	2.25
Annual 4,5 (1992, 1993, $2.50, 68 pgs.): 4-Guy Gardner/Lobo-c/story; Eclipso storyline; Quesada-c(p). 5-Bloodlines storyline		1.10	2.75
Annual 6 (1994, $2.95, 68 pgs.)-Elseworlds story		1.20	3.00
Annual 7 (1995, $3.95)-Year One story		1.60	4.00
Annual 8 (1996, $2.95)-Legends of the Dead Earth story		1.20	3.00
Annual 9 (1997, $3.95)-Pulp Heroes story		1.60	3.95

NOTE: ***Erik Larsen** a-431.*

ADVENTURES OF THE BIG BOY
1956 - No. 466, 1996? (Giveaway) (East & West editions of early issues)
Timely Comics/Webs Adv. Corp./Illus. Features

	GD25	FN65	NM94
1-Everett-a	50.00	150.00	600.00
2-Everett-a	21.00	63.00	210.00
3-5	7.50	22.50	75.00
6-10: 6-Sci/fic issue	4.00	12.00	40.00
11-20	2.50	7.50	20.00
21-30	1.50	4.50	12.00
31-50		2.40	6.00
51-100		1.20	3.00
101-150		.80	2.00
151-240			1.00
241-466: 266-Superman x-over. 417-(1992)			.20
1-50 ('76-'84,Paragon Prod.)			.20
Summer, 1959 issue, large size	2.50	7.50	25.00

NOTE: No. 467 was completed but never published.

ADVENTURES OF THE DOVER BOYS
September, 1950 - No. 2, 1950 (No month given)
Archie Comics (Close-up)

	GD25	FN65	NM94
1,2	7.15	21.50	50.00

ADVENTURES OF THE FLY (The Fly #1-6; Fly Man No. 32-39; See The Double Life of Private Strong, The Fly, Laugh Comics & Mighty Crusaders)
Aug, 1959 - No. 30, Oct, 1964; No. 31, May, 1965
Archie Publications/Radio Comics

	GD25	FN65	NM94
1-Shield app.; origin The Fly; S&K-c/a	43.00	130.00	520.00
2-Williamson, S&K-a	28.00	84.00	280.00
3-Origin retold; Davis, Powell-a	22.00	66.00	220.00
4-Neal Adams-a(p)(1 panel); S&K-c; Powell-a; 2 pg. Shield story	11.50	34.00	115.00
5-10: 7-1st S.A. app. Black Hood (7/60). 8-1st S.A. app. Shield (9/60). 9-Shield app. 9-1st app. Cat Girl. 10-Black Hood app.	8.00	24.00	80.00
11-13,15-20: 13-1st app. Fly Girl w/o costume. 16-Last 10¢ issue. 20-Origin Fly Girl retold	5.00	15.00	50.00
14-Origin & 1st app. Fly Girl in costume	6.50	19.50	65.00
21-30: 23-Jaguar cameo. 27-29-Black Hood 1 pg. strips. 30-Comet x-over (1st S.A. app.) in Fly Girl	3.20	9.60	32.00
31-Black Hood, Shield, Comet app.	3.50	10.50	35.00

NOTE: ***Simon** c-2-4. **Tuska** a-1. Cover title to #31 is Flyman; Advs. of the Fly inside.*

ADVENTURES OF THE JAGUAR, THE (See Blue Ribbon Comics, Laugh Comics & Mighty Crusaders)

Adventures of the Mask #4 © DH

Adventures of the X-Men #6 © MEG

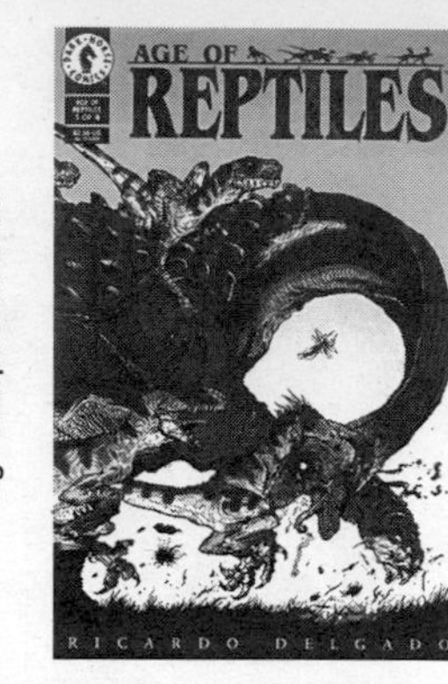

Age of Reptiles #1 © DH

	GD25	FN65	NM94
Sept, 1961 - No. 15, Nov, 1963			
Archie Publications (Radio Comics)			
1-Origin Jaguar (1st app?) by J. Rosenberger	16.50	50.00	165.00
2,3: 3-Last 10¢ issue	8.50	25.50	85.00
4-6-Catgirl app. (#4's-c is same as splash pg.)	6.50	19.50	65.00
7-10	5.00	15.00	50.00
11-15: 13,14-Catgirl, Black Hood app. in both	4.00	12.00	40.00

ADVENTURES OF THE MASK (TV cartoon)
Jan, 1996 - No. 12, Dec, 1996 ($2.50)
Dark Horse Comics

	GD25	FN65	NM94
1-12: Based on animated series		1.00	2.50

ADVENTURES OF THE NEW MEN (Formerly Newmen #1-21)
No. 22, Nov, 1996 - No. 23, March, 1997 ($2.50)
Maximum Press

	GD25	FN65	NM94
22,23-Sprouse-c/a		1.00	2.50

ADVENTURES OF THE OUTSIDERS, THE (Formerly Batman & The Outsiders; also see The Outsiders)
No. 33, May, 1986 - No. 46, June, 1987
DC Comics

	GD25	FN65	NM94
33-46: 39-45-r/Outsiders #1-7 by Aparo			1.00

ADVENTURES OF THE SUPER MARIO BROTHERS (Also see Super Mario Bros.)
1990 - No. 9?, 1990? ($1.50)
Valiant

	GD25	FN65	NM94
V2#1-9			1.50

ADVENTURES OF THE THING, THE (Also see The Thing)
Apr, 1992 - No. 4, July, 1992, ($1.25, limited series)
Marvel Comics

	GD25	FN65	NM94
1-4: 1-r/Marvel Two-In-One #50 by Byrne; Kieth-c. 2-4-r/Marvel Two-In-One #80,51 & 77; 2-Ghost Rider-c/story. 3-Miller-r			1.25

ADVENTURES OF THE X-MEN, THE (TV cartoon)
Apr, 1996 - No. 12, Mar, 1997 (99¢)
Marvel Comics

	GD25	FN65	NM94
1-12: Based on television show.			1.00

ADVENTURES OF TINKER BELL (See Tinker Bell, 4-Color No. 896 & 982)

ADVENTURES OF TOM SAWYER (See Dell Junior Treasury No. 10)

ADVENTURES OF YOUNG DR. MASTERS, THE
Aug, 1964 - No. 2, Nov, 1964
Archie Comics (Radio Comics)

	GD25	FN65	NM94
1	1.50	4.50	12.00
2	1.00	3.00	8.00

ADVENTURES ON OTHER WORLDS (See Showcase #17 & 18)

ADVENTURES ON THE PLANET OF THE APES
Oct, 1975 - No. 11, Dec, 1976
Marvel Comics Group

	GD25	FN65	NM94
1-Planet of the Apes-r in color; Starlin-c	1.00	3.00	8.00
2-5		1.60	4.00
6-11 (scarce)		2.40	6.00

NOTE: ***Alcala** a-6-11r. **Buckler** c-2p. **Nasser** c-7. **Starlin** c-6. **Tuska** a-1-5r.*

ADVENTURES WITH SANTA CLAUS
No date (early 50's) (9-3/4x 6-3/4", 24 pgs., giveaway, paper-c)
Promotional Publ. Co. (Murphy's Store)

	GD25	FN65	NM94
nn-Contains 8 pgs. ads	4.00	12.00	24.00
16 pg. version	4.00	12.00	24.00

AFRICA
1955
Magazine Enterprises

	GD25	FN65	NM94
1(A-1 #137)-Cave Girl, Thun'da; Powell-c/a(4)	18.00	54.00	145.00

AFRICAN LION (Disney movie)
Nov, 1955
Dell Publishing Co.

	GD25	FN65	NM94
Four Color #665	4.50	13.50	50.00

AFTER DARK
No. 6, May, 1955 - No. 8, Sept, 1955
Sterling Comics

	GD25	FN65	NM94
6-8-Sekowsky-a in all	6.50	19.50	45.00

AGAINST BLACKSHARD 3-D (Also see SoulQuest)
August, 1986 ($2.25)
Sirius Comics

	GD25	FN65	NM94
1		.90	2.25

AGENT LIBERTY SPECIAL (See Superman, 2nd Series)
1992 ($2.00, 52 pgs, one-shot)
DC Comics

	GD25	FN65	NM94
1-1st solo adventure; Guice-c/a(i)		.80	2.00

AGENT THREE-ZERO
Sept, 1993 ($3.95, 52 pgs.)
Galaxinovels, Inc.

	GD25	FN65	NM94
1-Polybagged with card & mini-poster; Platt-c/a(1st work)		1.60	4.00

AGENT THREE–ZERO: THE BLUE SULTANS QUEST/ BLUE SULTAN–GALAXI FACT FILES
1994 ($2.95, color w/text-no comics, limited series)
Galaxi Novels

	GD25	FN65	NM94
1-($2.95)-Flip book w/Blue Sultan		1.20	3.00
1-($3.95)-Polybagged w/trading card; flip book w/Blue Sultan.		1.60	4.00
1-($5.95)-Platinum embossed edition; flip book w/ Blue Sultan		2.40	6.00

AGENTS OF LAW (Also see Comic's Greatest World)
Mar, 1995 - No.6, Sept, 1995 ($2.50)
Dark Horse Comics

	GD25	FN65	NM94
1-6: 5-Predator app. 6-Predator app.; death of Law		1.00	2.50

AGE OF APOCALYPSE: THE CHOSEN
Apr, 1995 ($2.50, one-shot)
Marvel Comics

	GD25	FN65	NM94
1-Wraparound-c		1.00	2.50

AGE OF HEROES, THE
1996 - Present ($2.95, B&W)
Halloween Comics/Image Comics #3 on

	GD25	FN65	NM94
1-4: James Hudnall scripts; John Ridgway-c/a		1.20	3.00
...Special ($4.95) r/#1,2			4.95

AGE OF INNOCENCE: THE REBIRTH OF IRON MAN
Feb, 1996 ($2.50, one-shot)
Marvel Comics

	GD25	FN65	NM94
1-New origin of Tony Stark		1.00	2.50

AGE OF REPTILES
Nov, 1993 - No. 4, Feb, 1994 ($2.50, limited series)
Dark Horse Comics

	GD25	FN65	NM94
1-4: Delgado-c/a/scripts in all		1.00	2.50

AGE OF REPTILES: THE HUNT
May, 1996 - No. 5, Sept, 1996 ($2.95, limited series)
Dark Horse Comics

	GD25	FN65	NM94
1-5: Delgado-c/a/scripts in all; wraparound-c		1.20	3.00

AGGIE MACK

Airboy #17 © ECL

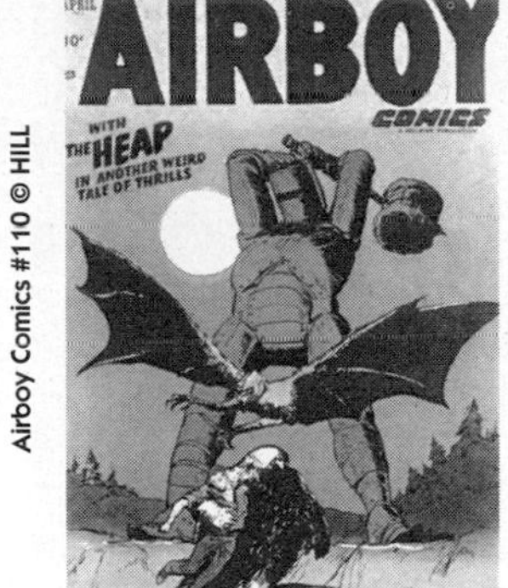

Airboy Comics #110 © HILL

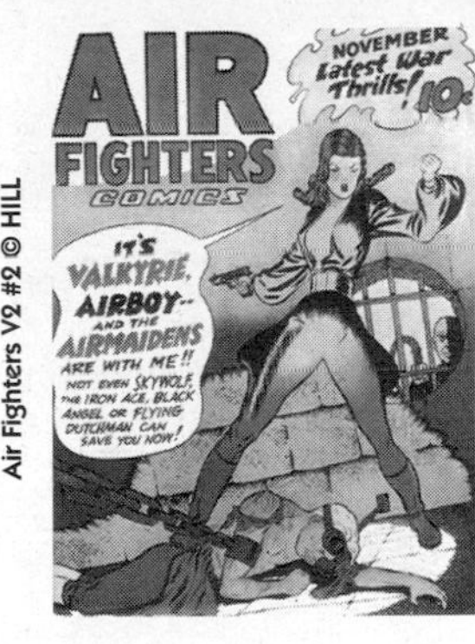

Air Fighters V2 #2 © HILL

GD25 FN65 NM94

Jan, 1948 - No. 8, Aug, 1949
Four Star Comics Corp./Superior Comics Ltd.

1-Feldstein-a, "Johnny Prep" 23.00 69.00 185.00
2,3-Kamen-c 12.00 36.00 95.00
4-Feldstein "Johnny Prep"; Kamen-c 16.00 49.00 130.00
5-8-Kamen-c/a 13.00 39.00 105.00

AGGIE MACK
Apr - Jun, 1962
Dell Publishing Co.

Four Color #1335 2.75 8.00 30.00

AIR ACE (Formerly Bill Barnes No. 1-12)
V2#1, Jan, 1944 - V3#8(No. 20), Feb-Mar, 1947
Street & Smith Publications

V2#1 19.00 56.00 150.00
V2#2-12: 7-Powell-a 8.75 26.25 70.00
V3#1-6 7.85 23.50 55.00
V3#7-Powell bondage-c/a; all atomic issue 15.50 47.00 125.00
V3#8 (V5#8 on-c)-Powell-c/a 8.75 26.25 65.00

AIRBOY (Also see Airmaidens, Skywolf, Target: Airboy & Valkyrie)
July, 1986 - No. 50, Oct, 1989 (#1-8, 50¢, 20 pgs., bi-weekly; #9-on, 36pgs.; #34-on monthly)
Eclipse Comics

1 1.00
2-4,6-8: 2-1st Marisa; Skywolf gets new costume. 3-The Heap begins 1.00
5-Valkyrie returns; Dave Stevens-c 1.00
9-32: 9-Begin $1.25-c; Skywolf begins. 11-Origin of G.A. Airboy & his plane Birdie. 28-Mr. Monster vs. The Heap. 1.25
33-41: 33-Begin $1.75-c. 38-40-The Heap-r by Infantino. 41-r/1st app. Valkyrie from Air Fighters 1.75
42-49: 42-Begin $1.95-c. 46,47-part-r/Air Fighters. 48-Black Angel-r/A.F .80 2.00
50 ($4.95, 52 pgs.)-Kubert-c 2.00 5.00

NOTE: ***Evans*** c-21. ***Gulacy*** c-7, 20. ***Spiegle*** a-34, 35, 37. ***Ken Steacy*** painted c-17, 33.

AIRBOY COMICS (Air Fighters Comics No. 1-22)
V2#11, Dec, 1945 - V10#4, May, 1953 (No V3#3)
Hillman Periodicals

V2#11 56.00 168.00 500.00
12-Valkyrie app. 36.00 108.00 320.00
V3#1,2(no #3) 31.00 94.00 250.00
4-The Heap app. in Skywolf 28.00 84.00 225.00
5-8,10,11: 6-Valkyrie app. 23.00 69.00 185.00
9-Origin The Heap 28.00 84.00 225.00
12-Skywolf & Airboy x-over; Valkyrie app. 32.00 96.00 255.00
V4#1-Iron Lady app. 27.00 81.00 215.00
2,3,12: 2-Rackman begins 19.00 56.00 150.00
4-Simon & Kirby-c 21.00 64.00 170.00
5-11-All S&K-a 20.00 60.00 160.00
V5#1-4,6-11: 4-Infantino Heap. 10-Origin The Heap 13.00 39.00 105.00
5-Skull-c. 15.00 45.00 120.00
12-Krigstein-a(p) 15.50 47.00 125.00
V6#1-3,5-12: 6,8-Origin The Heap 13.00 39.00 105.00
4-Origin retold 17.00 51.00 135.00
V7#1-12: 7,8,10-Origin The Heap 13.00 39.00 105.00
V8#1-3,5-12 12.00 36.00 95.00
4-Krigstein-a 12.00 38.00 100.00
V9#1-4,6-12: 2-Valkyrie app. 7-One pg. Frazetta ad 9.50 28.00 75.00
5(#100) 10.50 32.00 85.00
V10#1-4 8.75 26.25 70.00

NOTE: ***Barry*** *a-V2#3, 7.* ***Bolle*** *a-V4#12.* ***McWilliams*** *a-V3#7, 9.* ***Powell*** *a-V7#2, 3, V8#1, 6.* ***Starr*** *a-V5#1, 12.* ***Dick Wood*** *a-V4#12. Bondage-c V5#8.*

AIRBOY MEETS THE PROWLER
Aug, 1987 ($1.95, one-shot)
Eclipse Comics

1-John Snyder, III-c/a 1.95

AIRBOY-MR. MONSTER SPECIAL
Aug, 1987 ($1.75, one-shot)
Eclipse Comics

1 1.80

AIRBOY VERSUS THE AIR MAIDENS
July, 1988 ($1.95)
Eclipse Comics

1 1.95

AIR FIGHTERS CLASSICS
Nov, 1987 - No. 6, May, 1989 ($3.95, 68 pgs., B&W)
Eclipse Comics

1-6: Reprints G.A. Air Fighters #2-7. 1-Origin Airboy 1.60 4.00

AIR FIGHTERS COMICS (Airboy Comics #23 (V2#11) on)
Nov, 1941; No. 2, Nov, 1942 - V2#10, Fall, 1945
Hillman Periodicals

V1#1-(Produced by Funnies, Inc.); Black Commander only app. 167.00 500.00 1500.00
2(11/42)-(Produced by Quality artists & Biro for Hillman); Origin & 1st app. Airboy & Iron Ace; Black Angel (1st app.), Flying Dutchman & Skywolf (1st app.) begin; Fuje-a; Biro-c/a 240.00 720.00 2400.00
3-Origin/1st app. The Heap; origin Skywolf 128.00 384.00 1150.00
4 89.00 267.00 800.00
5,6 69.00 207.00 620.00
7-12 57.00 171.00 515.00
V2#1,3-9: 5-Flag-c; Fuje-a. 7-Valkyrie app. 52.00 156.00 465.00
2-Skywolf by Giunta; Flying Dutchman by Fuje; 1st meeting Valkyrie & Airboy (she worked for the Nazis in beginning); 1st app. Valkyrie (11/43) 69.00 207.00 625.00
10-Origin The Heap & Skywolf 57.00 171.00 515.00

NOTE: ***Fuje*** *a-V1#2, 5, 7, V2#2, 3, 5, 7-9.* ***Giunta*** *a-V2#2, 3, 7, 9.*

AIRFIGHTERS MEET SGT. STRIKE SPECIAL, THE
Jan, 1988 ($1.95, one-shot, stiff-c)
Eclipse Comics

1-Airboy, Valkyrie, Skywolf app. .80 2.00

AIR FORCES (See American Air Forces)

AIRMAIDENS SPECIAL
August, 1987 ($1.75, one-shot, Baxter paper)
Eclipse Comics

1-Marisa becomes La Lupina (origin) .70 1.80

AIR POWER (CBS TV & the U.S. Air Force Presents)
1956 (5-1/4x7-1/4", 32 pgs., giveaway, soft-c)
Prudential Insurance Co.

nn-Toth-a? Based on 'You Are There' TV program by Walter Cronkite 8.50 26.00 60.00

AIR RAIDERS
Nov, 1987 - No. 5, Mar, 1988 ($1.00)
Marvel Comics (Star Comics)/Marvel Comics #3 on

1-5 .80 2.00

AIRTIGHT GARAGE, THE
July, 1993 - No. 4, Oct, 1993 ($2.50, limited series)
Marvel Comics (Epic Comics)

1-4: Moebius-c/a/scripts 1.00 2.50

AIR WAR STORIES
Sept-Nov, 1964 - No. 8, Aug, 1966
Dell Publishing Co.

Akiko on the Planet Smoo #19 © Mark Crilley

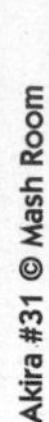
Akira #31 © Mash Room

Al Capp's Wolf Gal #1 © TOBY

GD25 FN65 NM94

1-Painted-c; Glanzman-c/a begins 2.60 7.80 26.00
2-8: 2-Painted-c (all painted?) 1.60 5.00 16.00

AKIKO ON THE PLANET SMOO
Dec, 1995 - Present ($3.95/$2.50, B&W)
Sirius

1-($3.95)-Crilley-c/a/scripts; gatefold-c 1.10 3.30 9.00
1-16: Crilley-c/a/scripts 2.00 5.00
2 1.60 4.00
3-10 1.20 3.00
11-22 1.00 2.50
Hardcover V1#1 (12/95, $19.95, B&W, 40 pgs.) 2.50 7.50 20.00

AKIRA
Sept, 1988 - No. 38, Dec, 1995 ($3.50/$3.95/$6.95, deluxe, 68 pgs.)
Marvel Comics (Epic Comics)

1 1.50 4.50 12.00
1,2-2nd printings (1989, $3.95) 1.60 4.00
2-5 2.00 5.00
6-16 1.80 4.50
17-33: 17-$3.95-c begins 1.60 4.00
34-38: 34-(1994)-$6.95-c begins. 35-37: 35-(1995). 37-Texieira back-up, Gibbons, Williams pin-ups. 38-Moebius, Allred, Pratt, Toth, Romita, Van Fleet, O'Neill, Madureira pin-ups. 1.00 2.80 7.00

ALADDIN & HIS WONDERFUL LAMP (See Dell Jr Treasury #2)

ALAN LADD (See The Adventures of...)

ALARMING ADVENTURES
Oct, 1962 - No. 3, Feb, 1963
Harvey Publications

1-Crandall/Williamson-a 6.00 18.00 60.00
2,3: 2-Williamson/Crandall-a 3.50 10.50 35.00
NOTE: ***Bailey*** *a-1, 3.* ***Crandall*** *a-1p, 2i.* ***Powell*** *a-2(2).* ***Severin*** *c-1-3.* ***Torres*** *a-2?* ***Tuska*** *a-1.* ***Williamson*** *a-1i, 2p.*

ALARMING TALES
Sept, 1957 - No. 6, Nov, 1958
Harvey Publications (Western Tales)

1-Kirby-c/a(4); Kamandi prototype story by Kirby 16.00 49.00 130.00
2-Kirby-a(4) 14.00 41.00 110.00
3,4-Kirby-a. 4-Powell, Wildey-a 8.75 26.25 70.00
5-Kirby/Williamson-a; Wildey-a; Severin-c 10.00 30.00 80.00
6-Williamson-a?; Severin-c 8.75 26.25 65.00

ALBEDO
Apr, 1985 - No. 14, Spring, 1989 (B&W)
Thoughts And Images

0-Yellow cover; 50 copies 1.85 5.50 15.00
0-White cover, 450 copies 1.25 3.75 10.00
0-Blue, 1st printing, 500 copies 2.00 5.00
0-Blue, 2nd printing, 1000 copies 1.60 4.00
0-3rd printing .80 1.20
0-4th printing .80 1.20
1-Dark red; 1st app. Usagi Yojimbo 2.00 5.00
1-Bright red 1.60 4.00
2 1.20 3.00
3-14 .80 1.20

ALBEDO ANTHROPOMORPHICS
Spring, 1994
Antartic Press

V3#1-Steve Gallacci-c/a .80 2.00

ALBERTO (See The Crusaders)

ALBERT THE ALLIGATOR & POGO POSSUM
No. 105, Apr, 1946; No. 148, May, 1947
Dell Publishing Co.

Four Color #105 (#1)-Kelly-c/a 61.00 184.00 675.00
Four Color #148 (#2)-Kelly-c/a 55.00 164.00 600.00

ALBINO SPIDER OF DAJETTE, THE
Jan, 1997 - Present ($2.95, mature)
Verotik

1,2-Danzig-s 2.95

ALBUM OF CRIME (See Fox Giants)

ALBUM OF LOVE (See Fox Giants)

AL CAPP'S DOGPATCH (Also see Mammy Yokum)
No. 71, June, 1949 - No. 4, Dec, 1949
Toby Press

71(#1)-Reprints from Tip Top #112-114 21.00 62.00 165.00
2-4: 4-Reprints from Li'l Abner #73 14.00 41.00 110.00

AL CAPP'S SHMOO (Also see Oxydol-Dreft & Washable Jones & Shmoo)
July, 1949 - No. 5, Apr, 1950 (None by Al Capp)
Toby Press

1 30.00 90.00 240.00
2-5: 3-Sci-fi trip to moon. 4-X-Mas-c; origin/1st app. Super-Shmoo 21.00 64.00 170.00

AL CAPP'S WOLF GAL
1951 - No. 2, 1952
Toby Press

1,2-Edited-r from Li'l Abner #63,64 28.00 84.00 225.00

ALEXANDER THE GREAT (Movie)
No. 688, May, 1956
Dell Publishing Co.

Four Color 688-Buscema-a; photo-c 6.00 19.00 68.00

ALF (TV) (See Star Comics Digest)
Mar, 1988 - No. 50, Feb, 1992 ($1.00)
Marvel Comics

1-49: 1-Photo-c. 22-X-Men parody 1.00
50-($1.75, 52 pgs.)-Final issue; photo-c .70 1.75
Annual 1-3: 2-Sienkiewicz-c .70 1.75
...Comics Digest 1 (1988)-Reprints Alf #1,2 1.50
Holiday Special 1 (1988, $1.75, 68 pgs.) .70 1.75
Holiday Special 2 (Winter, 1989, $2.00, 68 pgs.) .80 2.00
Spring Special 1 (Spr/89, $1.75, 68 pgs.) .70 1.75

ALFRED HARVEY'S BLACK CAT
1995 ($3.50, B&W/color)
Lorne-Harvey Productions

1-Origin by Mark Evanier & Murphy Anderson; contains history of Alfred Harvey & Harvey Publications; 5 pg. B&W Sad Sack story; Hildebrandts-c 1.40 3.50

ALGIE
Dec, 1953 - No. 3, 1954
Timor Publ. Co.

1-Teenage 4.15 12.50 25.00
1-Misprint exists w/Secret Mysteries #19 inside 5.00 15.00 30.00
2,3 3.60 9.00 18.00
Accepted Reprint #2(nd) 2.40 6.00 12.00
Super Reprint #15 2.00 5.00 10.00

ALIAS:
July, 1990 - No. 5, Nov, 1990 ($1.75)
Now Comics

1-5: 1-Sienkiewicz-c .70 1.80

ALICE (New Adventures in Wonderland)
No. 10, 7-8/51 - No. 2, 11-12/51

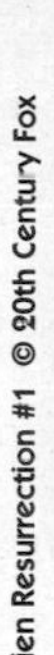
Alien Legion #18 © MEG

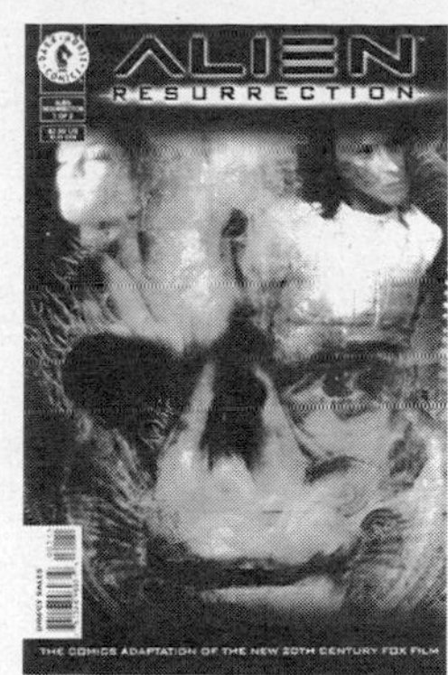

Alien Resurrection #1 © 20th Century Fox

Aliens: Alchemy #1 © 20th Century Fox

GD25 FN65 NM94

Ziff-Davis Publ. Co.
10-Painted-c; Berg-a 17.00 51.00 135.00
11-Dave Berg-a 8.75 26.25 70.00
2-Dave Berg-a 8.50 26.00 60.00

ALICE AT MONKEY ISLAND (See The Adventures of Alice)
No. 3, 1946
Pentagon Publ. Co. (Civil Service)
3 6.50 19.50 45.00

ALICE IN BLUNDERLAND
1952 (Paper cover, 16 pgs. in color)
Industrial Services
nn-Facts about big government waste and inefficiency
10.50 32.00 84.00

ALICE IN WONDERLAND (Disney; see Advs. of Alice, Dell Jr. Treasury #1, The Dreamery, Movie Comics, Walt Disney Showcase #22, and World's Greatest Stories)
No. 24, 1940; No. 331, 1951; No. 341, July, 1951
Dell Publishing Co.
Single Series 24 (#1)(1940) 36.00 108.00 300.00
Four Color 331, 341-"Unbirthday Party w/... 13.00 40.00 145.00

ALICE IN WONDERLAND
1965; 1982
Western Printing Company/Whitman Publ. Co.
Meets Santa Claus(1950s), nd, 16 pgs. 2.50 7.50 22.00
Rexall Giveaway(1965, 16 pgs., 5x7-1/4) Western Printing (TV, Hanna-Barbera)
2.50 7.50 20.00
Wonder Bakery Giveaway(16 pgs, color, nn, nd) (Continental Baking Company, 1969) 2.50 7.50 20.00
1-(Whitman; 1982)-r/4-Color #331 1.20

ALICE IN WONDERLAND MEETS SANTA
nd (6-5/8x9-11/16", 16 pgs., giveaway, paper-c)
No publisher
nn 8.75 26.25 65.00

ALIEN ENCOUNTERS (Replaces Alien Worlds)
June, 1985 - No. 14, Aug, 1987 ($1.75, Baxter paper, mature readers)
Eclipse Comics
1-14: Nudity, strong language in all. 9-Snyder-a .70 1.75

ALIEN LEGION (See Epic & Marvel Graphic Novel #25)
Apr, 1984 - No. 20, Sept, 1987 ($2.00/$1.50)
Marvel Comics (Epic Comics)
1-High quality paper .80 2.00
2-20: 2-$1.50-c 1.50

ALIEN LEGION (2nd Series)
Aug, 1987 (indicia) (10/87 on-c) - No. 18, Aug, 1990 ($1.25)
Marvel Comics (Epic Comics)
V2#1-6 1.25
7-18: 7-Begin $1.50-c 1.50

ALIEN LEGION: BINARY DEEP
1993 ($3.50, one-shot, 52 pgs.)
Marvel Comics (Epic Comics)
nn-With bound-in trading card 1.40 3.50

ALIEN LEGION: JUGGER GRIMROD
Aug, 1992 ($5.95, one-shot, 52 pgs.)
Marvel Comics (Epic Comics)
Book One 2.40 6.00

ALIEN LEGION: ONE PLANET AT A TIME
May, 1993 - Book 3, July, 1993 ($4.95, squarebound, 52 pgs.)

GD25 FN65 NM94

Marvel Comics (Epic Comics)
Book 1-3: Hoang Nguyen-a 2.00 5.00

ALIEN LEGION: ON THE EDGE (The... #2 & 3)
Nov, 1990 - No. 3, Jan, 1991 ($4.50, limited series, 52 pgs.)
Marvel Comics (Epic Comics)
1-3 1.80 4.50

ALIEN LEGION: TENNANTS OF HELL
1991 - No. 2, 1991 ($4.50, squarebound, 52 pgs.)
Marvel Comics (Epic Comics)
Book 1,2-Stroman-c/a(p) 1.80 4.50

ALIEN NATION (Movie)
Dec, 1988 ($2.50; 68 pgs.)
DC Comics
1-Adaptation of film; painted-c 1.00 2.50

ALIEN RESURRECTION (Movie)
Oct, 1997 - No. 2, Nov, 1997 ($2.50, limited series)
Dark Horse Comics
1,2-Adaptation of film; Dave McKean-c 1.00 2.50

ALIENS, THE (Captain Johner and...)(Also see Magnus Robot Fighter...)
Sept-Dec, 1967; No. 2, May, 1982
Gold Key
1-Reprints from Magnus #1,3,4,6-10; Russ Manning-a in all
1.85 5.50 15.00
2-Same contents as #1 2.00 5.00

ALIENS (Movie) (See Alien: The Illustrated..., Dark Horse Comics & Dark Horse Presents #24)
May, 1988 - No. 6, July, 1989 ($1.95, B&W, limited series)
Dark Horse Comics
1-Based on movie sequel;1st app. Aliens in comics 1.85 5.50 15.00
1-2nd printing .80 2.00
1-3rd - 6th printings; 4th w/new inside front-c 1.50
2 1.00 2.80 7.00
2-2nd printing 1.50
2-3rd printing w/new inside front-c 1.50
3 1.60 4.00
4 1.20 3.00
5,6 1.20 3.00
3-6-2nd printings 1.50
Mini Comic #1 (2/89, 4x6")-Was included with Aliens Portfolio
1.60 4.00
Collection 1 ($10.95,)-r/#1-6 plus Dark Horse Presents #24 plus new-a
1.25 3.75 10.00
Collection 1-2nd printing (1991, $11.95)-Printed on higher quality paper than 1st print; Dorman painted-c 1.50 4.50 12.00
Hardcover ('90, $24.95, B&W)-r/1-6, DHP #24 2.50 7.50 25.00
Platinum Edition (See Dark Horse Presents: Aliens Platinum Edition)

ALIENS (Movie)
V2#1, Aug, 1989 - No. 4, 1990 ($2.25, limited series)
Dark Horse Comics
V2#1-Adapts sequel 1.60 4.00
1-2nd printing (1990, $2.25) .90 2.25
2-4 .90 2.25

ALIENS: ALCHEMY
Oct, 1997 - No. 3, Dec, 1997 ($2.95, limited series)
Dark Horse Comics
1-3-Corben-c/a, Arcudi-s 1.20 2.95

ALIENS: BERSERKERS
Jan, 1995 - No. 4, Apr, 1995 ($2.50, limited series)

Aliens: Earth Angel #1 © 20th Century Fox

Aliens: Music of the Spears #1 © 20th Century Fox

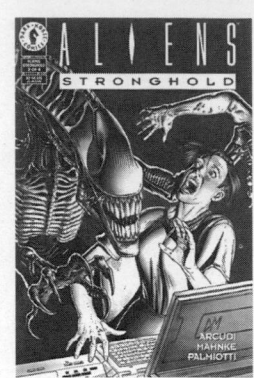

Aliens: Stronghold #2 © 20th Century Fox

	GD25	FN65	NM94

Dark Horse Comics

	GD25	FN65	NM94
1-4		1.00	2.50

ALIENS: COLONIAL MARINES
Jan, 1993 - No. 10, July, 1994 ($2.50, limited series)
Dark Horse Comics

	GD25	FN65	NM94
1-10		1.00	2.50

ALIENS: EARTH ANGEL
Aug, 1994 ($2.95, one-shot)
Dark Horse Comics

	GD25	FN65	NM94
1-Byrne-a/story; wraparound-c		1.20	2.95

ALIENS: EARTH WAR
June, 1990 - No. 4, Oct, 1990 ($2.50, limited series)
Dark Horse Comics

	GD25	FN65	NM94
1-All have Sam Kieth-a & Bolton painted-c		1.60	4.00
1-2nd printing		1.00	2.50
2		1.40	3.50
3,4		1.00	2.50

ALIENS: GENOCIDE
Nov, 1991 - No. 4, Feb, 1992 ($2.50, limited series)
Dark Horse Comics

	GD25	FN65	NM94
1-4-Arthur Suydam painted-c. 4-Wraparound-c, poster		1.00	2.50

ALIENS: HAVOC
June, 1997 - No. 2, July, 1997 ($2.95, limited series)
Dark Horse Comics

	GD25	FN65	NM94
1,2: Schultz-s, Kent Williams-c, 40 artists including Art Adams, Kelley Jones, Duncan Fegredo, Kevin Nowlan			2.95

ALIENS: HIVE
Feb, 1992 - No. 4, May, 1992 ($2.50, limited series)
Dark Horse Comics

	GD25	FN65	NM94
1-4: Kelley Jones-c/a in all		1.00	2.50

ALIENS: LABYRINTH
Sept, 1993 - No. 4, Jan, 1994 ($2.50, limited series)
Dark Horse Comics

	GD25	FN65	NM94
1-4: 1-Painted-c		1.00	2.50

ALIENS: LOVESICK
Dec, 1996 ($2.95, one-shot)
Dark Horse Comics

	GD25	FN65	NM94
1			2.95

ALIENS: MONDO HEAT
Feb, 1996 ($2.50, one-shot)
Dark Horse Comics

	GD25	FN65	NM94
nn-Sequel to Mondo Pest		1.00	2.50

ALIENS: MONDO PEST
Apr, 1995 ($2.95, one-shot, 44 pgs.)
Dark Horse Comics

	GD25	FN65	NM94
nn-Reprints Dark Horse Comics #22-24			2.95

ALIENS: MUSIC OF THE SPEARS
Jan, 1994 - No. 4, Apr, 1994 ($2.50, limited series)
Dark Horse Comics

	GD25	FN65	NM94
1-4		1.00	2.50

ALIENS: PIG
Mar, 1997 ($2.95, one-shot)
Dark Horse Comics

	GD25	FN65	NM94
1			2.95

ALIENS/PREDATOR: THE DEADLIEST OF SPECIES
July, 1993 - No. 12, Aug, 1995 ($2.50, limited series)
Dark Horse Comics

	GD25	FN65	NM94
1-Bolton painted-c; Guice-a(p)		1.60	4.00
1-Embossed foil platinum edition	1.25	3.75	10.00
2-12: Bolton painted-c. 2,3-Guice-a(p)		1.00	2.50

ALIENS: PURGE
Aug, 1997 ($2.95, one-shot)
Dark Horse Comics

	GD25	FN65	NM94
nn-Hester-a			2.95

ALIENS: ROGUE
Apr, 1993 - No. 4, July, 1993 ($2.50, limited series)
Dark Horse Comics

	GD25	FN65	NM94
1-4: Painted-c		1.00	2.50

ALIENS: SACRIFICE
May, 1993 ($4.95, one-shot, 52 pgs.)
Dark Horse Comics

	GD25	FN65	NM94
nn-Peter Milligan scripts; painted-c/a		2.00	5.00

ALIENS: SALVATION
Nov, 1993 ($4.95, one-shot, 52 pgs.)
Dark Horse Comics

	GD25	FN65	NM94
nn-Mike Mignola-c/a(p); Dave Gibbons script		2.00	5.00

ALIENS: SPECIAL
June, 1997 ($2.50, one-shot)
Dark Horse Comics

	GD25	FN65	NM94
1		1.00	2.50

ALIENS: STRONGHOLD
May, 1994 - No. 4, Sept, 1994 ($2.50, limited series)
Dark Horse Comics

	GD25	FN65	NM94
1-4		1.00	2.50

ALIENS VS. PREDATOR (See Dark Horse Presents #36)
June, 1990 - No. 4, Dec, 1990 ($2.50, limited series)
Dark Horse Comics

	GD25	FN65	NM94
1-Painted-c		2.00	5.00
1-2nd printing		1.00	2.50
0-(7/90, $1.95, B&W)-r/Dark Horse Pres. #34-36	1.00	2.80	7.00
2,3		1.60	4.00
4-Dave Dorman painted-c		1.00	2.50

ALIENS VS. PREDATOR: BOOTY
Jan, 1996 ($2.50, one-shot)
Dark Horse Comics

	GD25	FN65	NM94
nn-painted-c		1.00	2.50

ALIENS VS. PREDATOR: DUEL
Mar, 1995 - No. 2, Apr, 1995 ($2.50, limited series)
Dark Horse Comics

	GD25	FN65	NM94
1,2		1.00	2.50

ALIENS VS. PREDATOR: WAR
No. 0, May, 1995 - No. 4, Aug, 1995 ($2.50, limited series)
Dark Horse Comics

	GD25	FN65	NM94
0-4: Corben painted-c		1.00	2.50

ALIEN TERROR (See 3-D Alien Terror)

ALIEN: THE ILLUSTRATED STORY (Also see Aliens)
1980 ($3.95, soft-c, 8X11")
Heavy Metal Books

	GD25	FN65	NM94
nn-Movie adaptation; Simonson-a		1.60	4.00

ALIEN³ (Movie)
June, 1992 - No. 3, July, 1992 ($2.50, limited series)
Dark Horse Comics

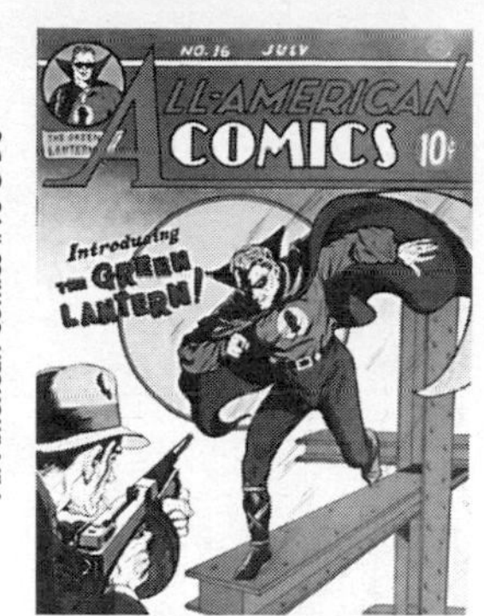

All-American Comics #16 © DC

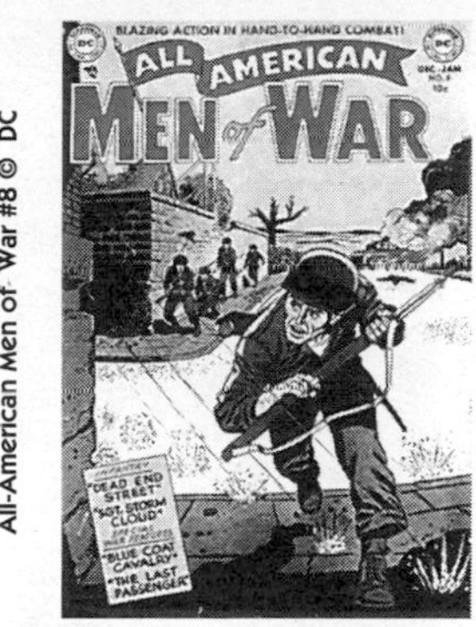

All-American Men of War #8 © DC

All-American Western #103 © DC

GD25 FN65 NM94

1-3: Adapts 3rd movie; Suydam painted-c 1.00 2.50

ALIEN WORLDS (Also see Eclipse Graphic Album #22)
Dec, 1982 - No. 9, Jan, 1985
Pacific Comics/Eclipse

1 1.50
2-9: 2,4-Dave Stevens-c/a 1.00
3-D No. 1-Art Adams 1st published art 1.20 3.00

ALISTER THE SLAYER
Oct, 1995 ($2.50)
Midnight Press

1-Boris-c 1.00 2.50

ALL-AMERICAN COMICS (...Western #103-126, ...Men of War #127 on; also see The Big All-American Comic Book)
April, 1939 - No. 102, Oct, 1948
All-American/National Periodical Publications

1-Hop Harrigan (1st app.), Scribbly by Mayer (1st app.), Toonerville Folks, Ben Webster, Spot Savage, Mutt & Jeff, Red White & Blue (1st app.), Adv. in the Unknown, Tippie, Reg'lar Fellers, Skippy, Bobby Thatcher, Mystery Men of Mars, Daiseybelle, Wiley of West Point begin 830.00 2500.00 5300.00
2-Ripley's Believe It or Not begins, ends #24 230.00 700.00 1500.00
3-5: 5-The American Way begins, ends #10 165.00 500.00 1100.00
6,7: 6-Last Spot Savage; Popsicle Pete begins, ends #26, 28. 7-Last Bobby Thatcher 140.00 425.00 900.00
8-The Ultra Man begins & 1st-c app. 210.00 625.00 1300.00
9,10: 10-X-Mas-c 130.00 400.00 840.00
11-15: 11-Ultra Man-c. 12-Last Toonerville Folks. 15-Last Tippie & Reg'lar Fellars; Ultra Man-c 125.00 375.00 775.00

GD25 FN65 VF82 NM94

16-(Rare)-Origin/1st app. Green Lantern by Sheldon Moldoff (c/a)(7/40) & begin series; appears in costume on-c & only one panel inside; created by Martin Nodell. Inspired in 1940 by a switchman's green lantern that would give trains the go ahead to proceed.
6500.00 19,500.00 38,000.00 60,000.00
(Estimated up to 35+ total copies exist, 3 in NM/Mint)

GD25 FN65 NM94

17-2nd Green Lantern 1090.00 3270.00 12,000.00
18-N.Y. World's Fair-c/story 800.00 2400.00 8,000.00

GD25 FN65 VF82 NM94

19-Origin/1st app. The Atom (10/40); last Ultra Man
1090.00 3270.00 7085.00 12,000.00
(Estimated up to 80 total copies exist, 5 in NM/Mint)

GD25 FN65 NM94

20-Atom dons costume; Ma Hunkle becomes Red Tornado (1st app.)(1st DC costumed heroine, before Wonder Woman, 11/40); Rescue on Mars begins, ends #25; 1 pg. origin Green Lantern 330.00 990.00 3300.00
21-23: 21-Last Wiley of West Point & Skippy. 23-Last Daiseybelle; 3 Idiots begin, end #82 217.00 650.00 1950.00
24-Sisty & Dinky become the Cyclone Kids; Ben Webster ends; origin Dr. Mid-Nite & Sargon, The Sorcerer in text with app. 245.00 735.00 2450.00

GD25 FN65 VF82 NM94

25-Origin & 1st story app. Dr. Mid-Nite by Stan Asch; Hop Harrigan becomes Guardian Angel; last Adventure in the Unknown
800.00 2400.00 4800.00 8000.00
(Estimated up to 120 total copies exist, 6 in NM/Mint)

GD25 FN65 NM94

26-Origin/1st story app. Sargon, the Sorcerer 290.00 870.00 2900.00
27: #27-32 are misnumbered in indicia with correct No. appearing on-c. Intro. Doiby Dickles, Green Lantern's sidekick 310.00 930.00 3100.00
28-Hop Harrigan gives up costumed i.d. 128.00 384.00 1150.00
29,30 128.00 384.00 1150.00
31-40: 35-Doiby learns Green Lantern's i.d. 97.00 291.00 875.00
41-50: 50-Sargon ends 83.00 264.00 750.00

GD25 FN65 NM94

51-60: 59-Scribbly & the Red Tornado ends 72.00 216.00 650.00
61-Origin/1st app. Solomon Grundy (11/44) 350.00 1050.00 3500.00
62-70: 70-Kubert Sargon; intro Sargon's helper, Maximillian O'Leary
67.00 201.00 600.00
71-88: 71-Last Red White & Blue. 72-Black Pirate begins (not in #74-82); last Atom. 73-Winky, Blinky & Noddy begins, ends #82. 79,83-Mutt & Jeff-c.
58.00 174.00 525.00
89-Origin & 1st app. Harlequin 81.00 243.00 725.00
90-99: 90-Origin/1st app. Icicle. 99-Last Hop Harrigan
69.00 207.00 625.00
100-1st app. Johnny Thunder by Alex Toth (8/48); western theme begins (Scarce) 133.00 400.00 1200.00
101-Last Mutt & Jeff (Scarce) 100.00 300.00 900.00
102-Last Green Lantern, Black Pirate & Dr. Mid-Nite (Scarce)
167.00 500.00 1500.00

NOTE: *No Atom in 47, 62-69.* ***Kinstler*** *Black Pirate-89.* ***Stan Aschmeier*** *a (Dr. Mid-Nite) 25-84; c-7.* ***Mayer*** *c-1, 2(part), 6, 10.* ***Moldoff*** *c-16-23.* ***Nodell*** *c-31.* ***Paul Reinman*** *a (Green Lantern)-53-55p, 56-84, 87; (Black Pirate)-83-88, 90; c-52, 55-76, 78, 80, 81, 87.* ***Toth*** *a-88, 92, 96, 98-102; c(p)-92, 96-102. Scribbly by* ***Mayer*** *in #1-59. Ultra Man by* ***Mayer*** *in #8-19.*

ALL-AMERICAN MEN OF WAR (Previously All-American Western)
No. 127, Aug-Sept, 1952 - No. 117, Sept-Oct, 1966
National Periodical Publications

127 (#1, 1952) 86.00 258.00 775.00
128 (1952) 56.00 167.00 500.00
2(12-1/'52-53)-5 46.00 137.00 410.00
6-10 36.00 107.00 285.00
11-18: Last precode (2/55) 33.00 98.00 260.00
19-28 23.00 68.00 180.00
29,30,32-Wood-a 24.00 71.00 190.00
31,33-40: 38-1st S.A. issue 19.50 58.00 155.00
41-50 12.50 38.00 125.00
51-66 9.00 27.00 90.00
67-1st Gunner & Sarge by Andru & Esposito 26.00 78.00 260.00
68-70 9.50 28.50 95.00
71-80 6.00 18.00 60.00
81,83-88: 88-Last 10¢ issue 5.50 16.50 55.00
82-Johnny Cloud begins(1st app.), ends #111,114,115,117
10.50 32.00 105.00
89-100 3.80 11.40 38.00
101-117: 112-Balloon Buster series begins, ends #114,116. 117-Johnny Cloud-c & 3-part story 3.00 9.00 30.00

NOTE: ***Colan*** *a-112.* ***Drucker*** *a-47, 65, 71, 74, 77.* ***Grandenetti*** *c(p)-127, 128, 2-17(most).* ***Heath*** *a-27, 32, 47, 71, 95, 111, 112; c-85, 91, 94-96, 100, 101, 112, others?* ***Kirby*** *a-29.* ***Krigstein*** *a-128('52), 2, 3, 5.* ***Kubert*** *a-29, 36, 38, 41, 43, 47, 49, 50, 52, 53, 55, 56, 60, 63, 65, 69, 71-73, 102, 103, 105, 106, 108, 114; c-41, 77, 102, 103, 105, 106, 108, 114, others? Tank Killer in 69, 71, 76 by* ***Kubert.*** ***P. Reinman*** *c-55, 57, 61, 62, 71, 72, 74-76, 80.*

ALL-AMERICAN SPORTS
Oct, 1967
Charlton Comics

1 2.25 6.75 18.00

ALL-AMERICAN WESTERN (Formerly All-American Comics; Becomes All-American Men of War)
No. 103, Nov, 1948 - No. 126, June-July, 1952 (103-121: 52 pgs.)
National Periodical Publications

103-Johnny Thunder & his horse Black Lightning continues by Toth, ends #126; Foley of The Fighting 5th, Minstrel Maverick, & Overland Coach begin; Captain Tootsie by Beck; mentioned in Love and Death
41.00 123.00 365.00
104-Kubert-a 31.00 94.00 250.00
105,107-Kubert-a 26.00 80.00 210.00
106,108-110,112: 112-Kurtzman's "Pot-Shot Pete" (1 pg.)
19.50 58.00 155.00
111,114-116-Kubert-a 21.00 64.00 170.00
113-Intro. Swift Deer, J. Thunder's new sidekick (4-5/50); classic Toth-c;

Allegra #3 © Aegis Entertainment

All-Flash #5 © DC

All Good nn © STJ

	GD25	FN65	NM94
Kubert-a	23.00	69.00	185.00
117-126: 121-Kubert-a; bondage-c	15.50	47.00	125.00

NOTE: ***G. Kane** c(p)-119, 120, 123. **Kubert** a-103-105, 107, 111, 112(1 pg.), 113-116, 121. **Toth** a 103-126; c(p)-103-116, 121, 122, 124-126. Some copies of #125 have #12 on-c.*

ALL COMICS
1945
Chicago Nite Life News

	GD25	FN65	NM94
1	10.00	30.00	80.00

ALLEGRA
Aug, 1996 - No. 4, Dec, 1996 ($2.50)
Image Comics (Wildstorm Productions)

	GD25	FN65	NM94
1-4		1.00	2.50

ALLEY OOP (See The Comics, The Funnies, Red Ryder and Super Book #9)
No. 3, 1942
Dell Publishing Co.

	GD25	FN65	NM94
Four Color 3 (#1)	44.00	132.00	485.00

ALLEY OOP
Nov, 1955 - No. 3, Mar, 1956 (Newspaper reprints)
Argo Publ.

	GD25	FN65	NM94
1	14.00	41.00	110.00
2,3	9.50	28.00	75.00

ALLEY OOP
12-2/62-63 - No. 2, 9-11/63
Dell Publishing Co.

	GD25	FN65	NM94
1,2	4.00	12.00	45.00

ALLEY OOP
No. 10, 1947 - No. 18, Oct, 1949
Standard Comics

	GD25	FN65	NM94
10	19.00	56.00	150.00
11-18: 17,18-Schomburg-c	14.50	43.00	115.00

ALL-FAMOUS CRIME (Formerly Law Against Crime #1-3; becomes All-Famous Police Cases #6 on)
No. 4, 2/50 - No. 5, 5/50; No. 8, 5/51 - No. 10, 11/51
Star Publications

	GD25	FN65	NM94
4 (#1-1st series)-Formerly Law-Crime	18.00	54.00	145.00
5 (#2)	12.00	36.00	95.00
8 (#3-2nd series)	11.30	34.00	90.00
9 (#4)-Used in **SOTI**, illo- "The wish to hurt or kill couples in lovers' lanes is a not uncommon perversion;" L.B. Cole-c/a(r)/Law-Crime #3	22.00	66.00	175.00
10 (#5)-Becomes All-Famous Police Cases #6	10.50	32.00	85.00

NOTE: *All have **L.B. Cole** covers.*

ALL FAMOUS CRIME STORIES (See Fox Giants)

ALL-FAMOUS POLICE CASES (Formerly All Famous Crime #10 [#5])
No. 6, Feb, 1952 - No. 16, Sept, 1954
Star Publications

	GD25	FN65	NM94
6	12.00	36.00	95.00
7,8: 7-Baker story; . 8-Marijuana story	10.50	32.00	85.00
9-16	9.50	28.00	75.00

NOTE: ***L. B. Cole** c-all; a-15, 1pg. **Hollingsworth** a-15.*

ALL-FLASH (...Quarterly No. 1-5)
Summer, 1941 - No. 32, Dec-Jan, 1947-48
National Periodical Publications/All-American

	GD25	FN65	VF82	NM94
1-Origin The Flash retold by E. E. Hibbard; Hibbard c-1-10,12-14,16,31p.	1100.00	3300.00	6600.00	12,000.00

(Estimated up to 200 total copies exist, 11 in NM/Mint)

	GD25	FN65	NM94
2-Origin recap	240.00	720.00	2300.00
3,4	133.00	400.00	1200.00
5-Winky, Blinky & Noddy begins (1st app.), ends #32	95.00	285.00	850.00
6-10	81.00	243.00	725.00
11-13: 12-Origin/1st The Thinker. 13-The King app.	69.00	207.00	625.00
14-Green Lantern cameo	81.00	243.00	725.00
15-20: 18-Mutt & Jeff begins, ends #22	61.00	183.00	550.00
21-31	50.00	150.00	450.00
32-Origin/1st app. The Fiddler; 1st Star Sapphire	78.00	234.00	700.00

NOTE: *Book length stories in 2-13, 16. Bondage c-31, 32. **Martin Nodell** c-15, 17-28.*

ALL FOR LOVE (Young Love V3#5-on)
Apr-May, 1957 - V3#4, Dec-Jan, 1959-60
Prize Publications

	GD25	FN65	NM94
V1#1	5.25	15.75	52.00
2-6: 5-Orlando-c	3.00	9.00	30.00
V2#1-5(1/59), 5(3/59)	2.50	7.50	20.00
V3#1(5/59), 1(7/59)-4: 2-Powell-a	1.60	4.85	13.00

ALL FUNNY COMICS
Winter, 1943-44 - No. 23, May-June, 1948
Tilsam Publ./National Periodical Publications (Detective)

	GD25	FN65	NM94
1-Genius Jones (1st app.), Buzzy (1st app., ends #4), Dover & Clover (see More Fun #93) begin; Bailey-a	42.00	125.00	375.00
2	20.00	60.00	160.00
3-10	12.00	36.00	95.00
11-13,15,18,19-Genius Jones app.	11.30	34.00	90.00
14,17,20-23	8.50	26.00	60.00
16-DC Super Heroes app.	28.00	83.00	220.00

ALL GOOD
Oct, 1949 (50¢, 260 pgs.)
St. John Publishing Co.

	GD25	FN65	NM94
nn-(8 St. John comics bound together)	51.00	153.00	460.00

NOTE: *Also see Li'l Audrey Yearbook & Treasury of Comics.*

ALL GOOD COMICS (See Fox Giants)
No.1, Spring, 1946 (36 pgs.)
Fox Features Syndicate

	GD25	FN65	NM94
1-Joy Family, Dick Transom, Rick Evans, One Round Hogan	16.00	49.00	130.00

ALL GREAT (See Fox Giants)
1946 (36 pgs.)
Fox Feature Syndicate

	GD25	FN65	NM94
1-Crazy House, Bertie Benson Boy Detective, Gussie the Gob	16.00	49.00	130.00

ALL GREAT
nd (1945?) (132 pgs.)
William H. Wise & Co.

	GD25	FN65	NM94
nn-Capt. Jack Terry, Joan Mason, Girl Reporter, Baron Doomsday; Torture scenes	31.00	94.00	250.00

ALL GREAT COMICS (Formerly Phantom Lady #13? Dagar, Desert Hawk No. 14 on)
No. 14, Oct, 1947 - No. 13, Dec, 1947 (Newspaper strip reprints)
Fox Features Syndicate

	GD25	FN65	NM94
14(#12)-Brenda Starr & Texas Slim-r (Scarce)	42.00	125.00	350.00
13-Origin Dagar, Desert Hawk; Brenda Starr (all-r); Kamen-c; Dagar covers begin	40.00	120.00	325.00

ALL-GREAT CONFESSIONS (See Fox Giants)

ALL GREAT CRIME STORIES (See Fox Giants)

ALL GREAT JUNGLE ADVENTURES (See Fox Giants)

ALL HALLOW'S EVE
1991 ($4.95, 52 pgs.)
Innovation Publishing

Alliance #1 © Aegis Entertainment

All New Collectors' Edition C-56 © DC

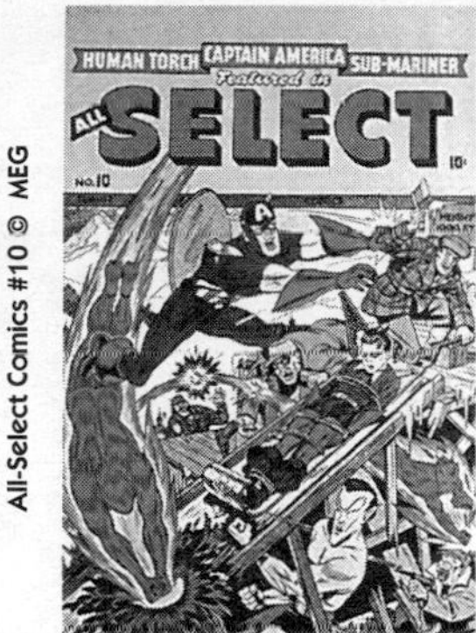

All-Select Comics #10 © MEG

GD25 FN65 NM94

1-Painted-c/a — 2.00 5.00

ALL HERO COMICS
Mar, 1943 (100 pgs., cardboard-c)
Fawcett Publications

1-Capt. Marvel Jr., Capt. Midnight, Golden Arrow, Ibis the Invincible, Spy Smasher, Lance O'Casey; 1st Banshee O'Brien; Raboy-c — 128.00 384.00 1150.00

ALL HUMOR COMICS
Spring, 1946 - No. 17, December, 1949
Quality Comics Group

1 — 15.00 45.00 120.00
2-Atomic Tot story; Gustavson-a — 8.50 26.00 60.00
3-9: 3-Intro Kelly Poole who is cover feature #3 on. 5-1st app. Hickory? 8-Gustavson-a — 5.00 15.00 30.00
10-17 — 4.00 11.00 22.00

ALLIANCE, THE
Aug, 1995 - No. 3, Nov, 1995 ($2.50)
Image Comics (Shadowline Ink)

1-3: 2-(9/95) — 1.00 2.50

ALL LOVE (...Romances No. 26)(Formerly Ernie Comics)
No. 26, May, 1949 - No. 32, May, 1950
Ace Periodicals (Current Books)

26 (No. 1)-Ernie, Lily Belle app. — 6.85 21.00 48.00
27-L. B. Cole-a — 8.75 26.25 70.00
28-32 — 4.15 12.50 25.00

ALL-NEGRO COMICS
June, 1947 (15¢)
All-Negro Comics

1 (Rare) — 250.00 750.00 2500.00
NOTE: *Seldom found in fine or mint condition; many copies have brown pages.*

ALL-NEW COLLECTORS' EDITION (Formerly Limited ...)
Jan, 1978 - Vol. 8, No. C-62, 1979 (No. 54-58: 76 pgs.)
DC Comics, Inc.

C-53-Rudolph the Red-Nosed Reindeer — 3.50 10.50 35.00
C-54-Superman Vs. Wonder Woman — 1.50 4.50 12.00
C-55-Superboy & the Legion of Super-Heroes; marriage of Lightning Lad & Saturn Girl — 2.25 6.75 18.00
C-56-Superman Vs. Muhammad Ali: story & wraparound N. Adams-c/a — 2.50 7.50 24.00
C-58-Superman Vs. Shazam — 1.60 4.85 13.00
C-60-Rudolph's Summer Fun(8/78) — 3.00 9.00 30.00
C-61-See Famous First Edition
C-62-Superman the Movie (68 pgs.; 1979)-Photo-c from movie plus photos inside (also see DC Special Series #25) — 1.00 3.00 8.00
NOTE: ***Buckler** a-C-58; c-C-58*

ALL-NEW COMICS (...Short Story Comics No. 1-3)
Jan, 1943 - No. 14, Nov, 1946; No. 15, Mar-Apr, 1947 (10 x 13-1/2")
Family Comics (Harvey Publications)

1-Steve Case, Crime Rover, Johnny Rebel, Kayo Kane, The Echo, Night Hawk, Ray O'Light, Detective Shane begin (all 1st app.?); Red Blazer on cover only; Sultan-a — 211.00 633.00 1900.00
2-Origin Scarlet Phantom by Kubert — 78.00 234.00 700.00
3 — 58.00 174.00 525.00
4,5 — 50.00 150.00 450.00
6-The Boy Heroes & Red Blazer (text story) begin, end #12; Black Cat app.; intro. Sparky in Red Blazer — 51.00 153.00 460.00
7-Kubert, Powell-a; Black Cat & Zebra app. — 51.00 153.00 460.00
8,9: 8-Shock Gibson app.; Kubert, Powell-a; Schomburg bondage-c. 9-Black Cat app.; Kubert-a — 51.00 153.00 460.00
10-12: 10-The Zebra app. (from Green Hornet Comics); Kubert-a(3). 11-Girl Commandos, Man In Black app. 12-Kubert-a — 44.00 133.00 400.00
13-Stuntman by Simon & Kirby; Green Hornet, Joe Palooka, Flying Fool app.; Green Hornet-c — 47.00 142.00 425.00
14-The Green Hornet & The Man in Black Called Fate by Powell, Joe Palooka app.; J. Palooka-c by Ham Fisher — 44.00 133.00 400.00
15-(Rare)-Small size (5-1/2x8-1/2"; B&W; 32 pgs.). Distributed to mail subscribers only. Black Cat and Joe Palooka app. Estimated value....$250-350
NOTE: *Also see Boy Explorers No. 2, Flash Gordon No. 5, and Stuntman No. 3.* ***Powell** a-11.* ***Schomburg** c-5, 7-11. Captain Red Blazer & Spark on c-5-11 (w/Boy Heroes #12).*

ALL NEW COMICS
Oct, 1993 (Giveaway, no cover price, 16 pgs.) (Hanna-Barbera)
Harvey Comics

1-Flintstones, Scooby Doo, Jetsons, Yogi Bear & Wacky Races previews for upcoming Harvey's new Hanna-Barbera line-up — 1.00
NOTE: Material previewed in Harvey giveaway was eventually published by Archie.

ALL-OUT WAR
Sept-Oct, 1979 - No. 6, Aug, 1980 ($1.00, 68 pgs.)
DC Comics

1-6: 1-The Viking Commando(origin), Force Three(origin), & Black Eagle Squadron begin — 1.60 4.00
NOTE: ***Ayers** a(p)-1-6.* ***Elias** r-2.* ***Evans** a-1-6.* ***Kubert** c-16.*

ALL PICTURE ADVENTURE MAGAZINE
Oct, 1952 - No. 2, Nov, 1952 (100 pg. Giants, 25¢, squarebound)
St. John Publishing Co.

1-War comics — 20.00 60.00 160.00
2-Horror-crime comics — 31.00 94.00 250.00
NOTE: *Above books contain three St. John comics rebound; variations possible.* ***Baker** art known in both.*

ALL PICTURE ALL TRUE LOVE STORY
October, 1952 (100 pgs., 25¢)
St. John Publishing Co.

1-Canteen Kate by Matt Baker — 40.00 120.00 325.00

ALL-PICTURE COMEDY CARNIVAL
October, 1952 (100 pgs., 25¢)(Contains 4 rebound comics)
St. John Publishing Co.

1-Contents can vary; Baker-a — 36.00 108.00 300.00

ALL REAL CONFESSION MAGAZINE (See Fox Giants)

ALL ROMANCES (Mr. Risk No. 7 on)
Aug, 1949 - No. 6, June, 1950
A. A. Wyn (Ace Periodicals)

1 — 6.85 21.00 48.00
2 — 4.00 11.00 22.00
3-6 — 3.60 9.00 18.00

ALL-SELECT COMICS (Blonde Phantom No. 12 on)
Fall, 1943 - No. 11, Fall, 1946
Timely Comics (Daring Comics)

1-Capt. America (by Rico #1), Human Torch, Sub-Mariner begin; Black Widow story (4 pgs.); Classic Schomburg-c — 700.00 2100.00 7000.00
2-Red Skull app. — 240.00 720.00 2300.00
3-The Whizzer begins — 167.00 500.00 1500.00
4,5-Last Sub-Mariner — 111.00 333.00 1000.00
6-9: 6-The Destroyer app. 8-No Whizzer — 94.00 283.00 850.00
10-The Destroyer & Sub-Mariner app.; last Capt. America & Human Torch issue — 94.00 283.00 850.00
11-1st app. Blonde Phantom; Miss America app.; all Blonde Phantom-c by Shores — 178.00 534.00 1600.00
NOTE: ***Schomburg** c-1-10.* ***Sekowsky** a-7. #7 & 8 show 1944 in indicia, but should be 1945.*

ALL SPORTS COMICS (Formerly Real Sports Comics; becomes All Time Sports Comics No. 4 on)
No. 2, Dec-Jan, 1948-49; No. 3, Feb-Mar, 1949

All Star Comics #9 © DC

All-Star Squadron #47 © DC

All Star Western #66 © DC

GD25 FN65 NM94

Hillman Periodicals

2-Krigstein-a(p), Powell, Starr-a 28.00 84.00 225.00
3-Mort Lawrence-a 19.00 56.00 150.00

ALL STAR COMICS (All Star Western No. 58 on)
Sum, '40 - No. 57, Feb-Mar, '51; No. 58, Jan-Feb, '76 -No. 74, Sept-Oct, '78
National Periodical Publ./All-American/DC Comics

GD25 FN65 VF82 NM94

1-The Flash (#1 by E.E. Hibbard), Hawkman(by Shelly), Hourman(by Bernard Baily), The Sandman(by Creig Flessel), The Spectre(by Baily), Biff Bronson, Red White & Blue(ends #2) begin; Ultra Man's only app. (#1-3 are quarterly; #4 begins bi-monthly issues) 1100.00 3300.00 6600.00 12,000.00
(Estimated up to 200+ total copies exist, 6 in NM/Mint)

GD25 FN65 NM94

2-Green Lantern (by Martin Nodell), Johnny Thunder begin; Green Lantern figure swipe from the cover of All-American Comics #16; Flash figure swipe from the cover of Flash Comics #8; Moldoff/Bailey-c (cut & paste-c.) 450.00 1350.00 4500.00

GD25 FN65 VF82 NM94

3-Origin & 1st app. The Justice Society of America (Win/40); Dr. Fate & The Atom begin, Red Tornado cameo 2700.00 8100.00 17,550.00 30,000.00
(Estimated up to 150+ total copies exist, 6 in NM/Mint)

3-Reprint, Oversize 13-1/2x10". **WARNING:** This comic is an exact reprint of the original except for its size. DC published it in 1974 with a second cover titling it as a Famous First Edition. There have been many reported cases of the outer cover being removed and the interior sold as the original edition. The reprint with the new outer cover removed is practically worthless. See Famous First Edition for value.

GD25 FN65 NM94

4-1st adventure for J.S.A. 430.00 1290.00 4300.00
5-1st app. Shiera Sanders as Hawkgirl (1st costumed super-heroine, 6-7/41) 390.00 1170.00 3900.00
6-Johnny Thunder joins JSA 240.00 720.00 2400.00
7-Batman, Superman, Flash cameo; last Hourman; Doiby Dickles app. 280.00 840.00 2800.00

GD25 FN65 VF82 NM94

8-Origin & 1st app. Wonder Woman (12-1/41-42)(added as 9 pgs. making book 76 pgs.; origin cont'd in Sensation #1; see W.W. #1 for more detailed origin); Dr. Fate dons new helmet; Hop Harrigan text stories & Starman begin; Shiera app.; Hop Harrigan JSA guest; Starman & Dr. Mid-Nite become members 2182.00 6545.00 14,183.00 24,000.00
(Estimated up to 150 total copies exist, 6 in NM/Mint)

GD25 FN65 NM94

9,10: 9-JSA's girlfriends cameo; Shiera app.; J. Edgar Hoover of FBI made associate member of JSA. 10-Flash, Green Lantern cameo; Sandman new costume 250.00 750.00 2250.00
11-Wonder Woman begins; Spectre cameo; Shiera app. Classic Moldoff Hawkman-c 256.00 768.00 2300.00
12-Wonder Woman becomes JSA Secretary 233.00 700.00 2100.00
13-15: Sandman w/Sandy in #14 & 15. 15-Origin & 1st app. Brain Wave; Shiera app. 211.00 633.00 1900.00
16-20: 19-Sandman w/Sandy. 20-Dr. Fate & Sandman cameo 156.00 468.00 1400.00
21-23: 21-Spectre & Atom cameo; Dr. Fate by Kubert; Dr. Fate, Sandman end. 22-Last Hop Harrigan; Flag-c. 23-Origin/1st app. Psycho Pirate; last Spectre & Starman 139.00 417.00 1250.00
24-Flash & Green Lantern cameo; Mr. Terrific only app.; Wildcat, JSA guest; Kubert Hawkman begins 139.00 417.00 1250.00
25-27: 25-Flash & Green Lantern start again. 26-Robot-c. 27-Wildcat, JSA guest (#24-26: only All-American imprint) 117.00 351.00 1050.00
28-32 106.00 318.00 950.00
33-Solomon Grundy & Doiby Dickles app; classic Solomon Grundy cover. Last Solomon Grundy G.A. app. 244.00 732.00 2200.00
34,35-Johnny Thunder cameo in both 100.00 300.00 900.00
36-Batman & Superman JSA guests 244.00 732.00 2200.00
37-Johnny Thunder cameo; origin & 1st app. Injustice Society; last Kubert Hawkman 133.00 400.00 1200.00

GD25 FN65 NM94

38-Black Canary begins; JSA Death issue 156.00 468.00 1400.00
39,40: 39-Last Johnny Thunder 94.00 282.00 850.00
41-Black Canary joins JSA; Injustice Society app. (2nd app.?) 94.00 282.00 850.00
42-Atom & the Hawkman don new costumes 94.00 282.00 850.00
43-49,51-56: 43-New logo. 55-Sci/Fi story 94.00 282.00 850.00
50-Frazetta art, 3 pgs. 106.00 318.00 950.00
57-Kubert-a, 6 pgs. (Scarce); last app. G.A. Green Lantern, Flash & Dr.Mid-Nite 122.00 366.00 1100.00
V12 #58-(1976) JSA (Flash, Hawkman, Dr. Mid-Nite, Wildcat, Dr. Fate, Green Lantern, Star Spangled Kid, & Robin) app.; intro Power Girl. 1.00 3.00 8.00
V12 #59-68,70-74(1976-78) 2.00 5.00
V12 #69-1st Modern app. Huntress (Wonder Woman villain)(see Sensation) 1.25 3.75 10.00

NOTE: *No Atom-27, 36; no Dr. Fate-13; no Flash-8, 9, 11-23; no Green Lantern-8, 9,11-23; Hawkman in 1-57 (only one to app. in all 57 issues); no Johnny Thunder-5, 36; no Wonder Woman-9, 10, 23. Book length stories in 4-9, 11-14, 18-22, 25, 26, 29, 30, 32-36, 42, 43. Johnny Peril in #42-46, 48, 49, 51, 52,54-57.* ***Baily*** *a-1-10, 12, 13, 14i, 15-20.* ***Burnley*** *Starman-8-13; c-12, 13.* ***Grell*** *c-58.* ***E.E. Hibbard*** *c-3, 4, 6-10.* ***Infantino*** *c-40.* ***Kubert*** *Hawkman-24-30, 33-37.* ***Lampert/Baily/Flessel*** *c-1, 2.* ***Moldoff*** *Hawkman-3-23; c-11.* ***Mart Nodell*** *c-25i, 26i, 27-32.* ***Purcell*** *c-5.* ***Simon & Kirby*** *Sandman 14-17, 19.* ***Staton*** *a-66-74p. c-74p.* ***Toth*** *a-37(2), 38(2), 40, 41; c-38, 41.* ***Wood*** *a-58i-63i, 64, 65; c-63i, 64, 65. Issues 1-7, 9-16 are 68 pgs.; #8 is 76 pgs.; #17-19 are 60 pgs.; #20-57 are 52 pgs.*

ALL STAR INDEX, THE
Feb, 1987 ($2.00, Baxter paper)
Independent Comics Group (Eclipse)

1 2.00 5.00

ALL-STAR SQUADRON (See Justice League of America #193)
Sept, 1981 - No. 67, Mar, 1987
DC Comics

1-Original Atom, Hawkman, Dr. Mid-Nite, Robotman (origin), Plastic Man, Johnny Quick, Liberty Belle, Shining Knight begin .80 2.00
2-24: 4, 7-Spectre app. 5-Danette Reilly becomes new Firebrand. 8-Re-intro Steel, the Indestructable Man. 12-Origin G.A. Hawkman retold. 23-Origin/1st app. The Amazing Man. 24-Batman app. 1.00
25-1st app. Infinity, Inc. (9/83) 1.00
26-Origin Infinity, Inc. (2nd app.); Robin app. 1.00
27-46,48,49: 27-Dr. Fate vs. The Spectre. 30-35-Spectre app. 33-Origin Freedom Fighters of Earth-X. 36,37-Superman vs. Capt. Marvel; Ordway-c. 41-Origin Starman 1.00
47-Origin Dr. Fate; McFarlane-a (1st full story)/part-c (7/85) 1.60 4.00
50-Double size; Crisis x-over 1.00
51-67: 51-56-Crisis x-over. 61-Origin Liberty Belle. 62-Origin The Shining Knight. 63-Origin Robotman. 65-Origin Johnny Quick. 66-Origin Tarantula 1.00
Annual 1-3: 1(11/82)-Retells origin of G.A. Atom, Guardian & Wildcat; Jerry Ordway's 1st pencils for DC.(1st work was inking Carmine Infantino in House of Mystery #94) 2(11/83)-Infinity, Inc. app. 3(9/84) 1.00

NOTE: ***Buckler*** *a-1-5; c-1, 3-5, 51.* ***Kubert*** *c-2, 7-18. JLA app. in 14, 15. JSA app. in 4, 14, 15, 19, 27, 28.*

ALL-STAR STORY OF THE DODGERS, THE
Apr, 1979 ($1.00)
Stadium Communications

1 1.00

ALL STAR WESTERN (Formerly All Star Comics No. 1-57)
No. 58, Apr-May, 1951 - No. 119, June-July, 1961
National Periodical Publications

58-Trigger Twins (ends #116), Strong Bow, The Roving Ranger & Don Caballero begin 36.00 108.00 325.00
59,60: Last 52 pgs. 19.50 58.00 155.00
61-66: 61-64-Toth-a 16.00 49.00 130.00
67-Johnny Thunder begins; Gil Kane-a 19.50 58.00 155.00
68-81: Last precode (2-3/55) 8.75 26.25 68.00

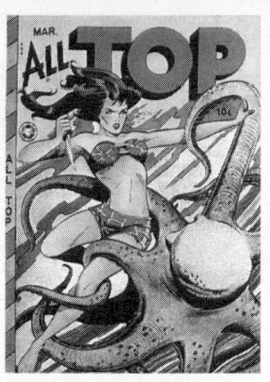

All Top Comics #16 © FOX

All True Romance Illustrated #6 © MEG

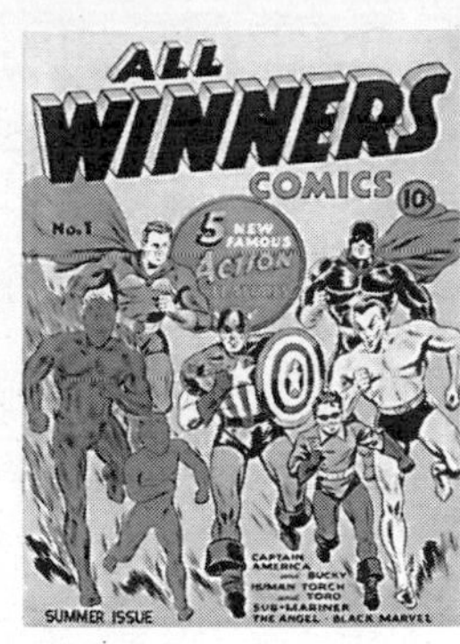

All Winners #1 © MEG

	GD25	FN65	NM94
82-98: 97-1st S.A. issue	8.75	26.25	62.00
99-Frazetta-r/Jimmy Wakely #4	8.75	26.25	68.00
100	8.75	26.25	68.00
101-107,109-116,118,119	6.50	19.50	45.00
108-Origin J. Thunder; J. Thunder logo begins	16.00	49.00	130.00
117-Origin Super Chie	9.50	28.00	75.00

NOTE: ***Gil Kane** c(p)-58, 59, 61, 63, 64, 68, 69, 70-95(most), 97-199(most). **Infantino** art in most issues. Madame .44 app.-#117-119.*

ALL-STAR WESTERN (Weird Western Tales No. 12 on)
Aug-Sept, 1970 - No. 11, Apr-May, 1972
National Periodical Publications

	GD25	FN65	NM94
1-Pow-Wow Smith-r; Infantino-a	2.50	7.50	25.00
2-6: 2-Outlaw begins; El Diablo by Morrow begins; has cameos by Williamson, Torres, Kane, Giordano & Phil Seuling. 3-Origin El Diablo. 5-Last Outlaw issue. 6-Billy the Kid begins, ends #8	1.25	3.75	10.00
7-9-(52 pgs.) 9-Frazetta-a, 3pgs.(r)	1.50	4.50	12.00
10-(52 pgs.) Jonah Hex begins (1st app., 2-3/72)	18.50	55.00	185.00
11-(52 pgs.) 2nd app. Jonah Hex	9.00	27.00	90.00

NOTE: ***Neal Adams** c-2-5; **Aparo** a-5. **G. Kane** a-3, 4, 6, 8. **Kubert** a-4r, 7-9r. **Morrow** a-2-4, 10, 11. No. 7-11 have 52 pgs..*

ALL SURPRISE (Becomes Jeanie #13 on) (Funny animal)
Fall, 1943 - No. 12, Winter, 1946-47
Timely/Marvel (CPC)

	GD25	FN65	NM94
1-Super Rabbit, Gandy & Sourpuss begin	22.00	66.00	175.00
2	10.00	30.00	80.00
3-10,12	8.50	26.00	60.00
11-Kurtzman "Pigtales" art	9.50	28.00	75.00

ALL TEEN (Formerly All Winners; All Winners & Teen Comics No. 21 on)
No. 20, January, 1947
Marvel Comics (WFP)

	GD25	FN65	NM94
20-Georgie, Mitzi, Patsy Walker, Willie app.; Syd Shores-c	7.15	21.50	50.00

ALL-TIME SPORTS COMICS (Formerly All Sports Comics)
V2No. 4, Apr-May, 1949 - V2No. 7, Oct-Nov, 1949 (All 52 pgs.)
Hillman Periodicals

	GD25	FN65	NM94
V2#4	18.00	54.00	145.00
5-7: 5-(V1#5 inside)-Powell-a; Ty Cobb sty. 7 Krigstein-p; Walter Johnson & Knute Rockne sty	13.00	39.00	105.00

ALL TOP
1944 (132 pgs.)
William H. Wise Co.

	GD25	FN65	NM94
Capt. V, Merciless the Sorceress, Red Robbins, One Round Hogan, Mike the M.P., Snooky, Pussy Katnip app.	24.00	73.00	195.00

ALL TOP COMICS (My Experience No. 19 on)
1945; No. 2, Sum, 1946 - No. 18, Mar, 1949; 1957 - 1959
Fox Features Synd./Green Publ./Norlen Mag.

	GD25	FN65	NM94
1-Cosmo Cat & Flash Rabbit begin (1st app.)	17.00	51.00	135.00
2 (#1-7 are funny animal)	8.50	26.00	60.00
3-7	6.50	19.50	45.00
8-Blue Beetle, Phantom Lady, & Rulah, Jungle Goddess begin (11/47); Kamen-c	175.00	525.00	1500.00
9-Kamen-c	93.00	280.00	800.00
10-Kamen bondage-c	100.00	300.00	850.00
11-13,15-17: 15-No Blue Beetle	80.00	240.00	700.00
14-No Blue Beetle; used in **SOTI**, illo- "Corpses of colored people strung up by their wrists"	94.00	282.00	850.00
18-Dagar, Jo-Jo app; no Phantom Lady or Blue Beetle	55.00	160.00	465.00
6(1957-Green Publ.)-Patoruzu the Indian; Cosmo Cat on cover only	3.60	9.00	18.00
6(1958-Literary Ent.)-Muggy Doo; Cosmo Cat on cover only	3.60	9.00	18.00
6(1959-Norlen)-Atomic Mouse; Cosmo Cat on cover only	3.60	9.00	18.00
6(1959)-Little Eva	3.60	9.00	18.00
6(Cornell)-Supermouse on-c	3.60	9.00	18.00

NOTE: *Jo-Jo by **Kamen**-12,18.*

ALL TRUE ALL PICTURE POLICE CASES
Oct, 1952 - No. 2, Nov, 1952 (100 pgs.)
St. John Publishing Co.

	GD25	FN65	NM94
1-Three rebound St. John crime comics	40.00	120.00	285.00
2-Three comics rebound	29.00	86.00	200.00

NOTE: *Contents may vary.*

ALL-TRUE CRIME (...Cases No. 26-35; formerly Official True Crime Cases)
No. 26, Feb, 1948 - No. 52, Sept, 1952
Marvel/Atlas Comics(OFI #26,27/CFI #28,29/LCC #30-46/LMC #47-52)

	GD25	FN65	NM94
26(#1)-Syd Shores-c	23.00	68.00	180.00
27(4/48)-Electric chair-c	15.50	47.00	125.00
28-41,43-48,50-52: 35-37-Photo-c	7.15	21.50	50.00
42,49-Krigstein-a. 49-Used in **POP**, Pg 79	8.50	26.00	60.00

NOTE: ***Robinson** a-47, 50. **Shores** c-26. **Tuska** a-48(3).*

ALL-TRUE DETECTIVE CASES (Kit Carson No. 5 on)
Feb-Mar, 1954 - No. 4, Aug-Sept, 1954
Avon Periodicals

	GD25	FN65	NM94
1	19.50	58.00	155.00
2-Wood-a	16.00	49.00	130.00
3-Kinstler-c	8.50	26.00	60.00
4-r/Gangsters And Gun Molls #2; Kamen-a	14.00	41.00	110.00
nn(100 pgs.)-7 pg. Kubert-a, Kinstler back-c	30.00	90.00	240.00

ALL TRUE ROMANCE (...Illustrated No. 3)
3/51 - No. 20, 12/54; No. 22, 3/55 - No. 30?, 7/57; No. 3(#31), 9/57; No. 4(#32), 11/57; No. 33, 2/58 - No. 34, 3/58
Artful Publ. #1-3/Harwell(Comic Media) #4-20?/Ajax-Farrell(Excellent Publ.) No. 22 on/Four Star Comic Corp.

	GD25	FN65	NM94
1 (3/51)	11.30	34.00	90.00
2 (10/51; 11/51 on-c)	5.70	17.00	40.00
3(12/51) - #5(5/52)	5.35	16.00	32.00
6-Wood-a, 9 pgs. (exceptional)	12.00	36.00	100.00
7-10	4.25	13.00	27.00
11-13,16-19 (2/54)	4.00	10.00	20.00
14-Marijuana story	4.00	12.00	24.00
20,22: Last precode issue (Ajax, 3/55)	3.20	8.00	16.00
23-27,29,30	2.60	6.50	13.00
28 (9/56)-L. B. Cole, Disbrow-a	6.50	19.50	45.00
3,4,33,34 (Farrell, '57- '58)	2.00	5.00	10.00

ALL WESTERN WINNERS (Formerly All Winners; becomes Western Winners with No. 5; see Two-Gun Kid No. 5)
No. 2, Winter, 1948-49 - No. 4, April, 1949
Marvel Comics(CDS)

	GD25	FN65	NM94
2-Black Rider (origin & 1st app.) & his horse Satan, Kid Colt & his horse Steel, & Two-Gun Kid & his horse Cyclone begin; Shores c-2-4	57.00	171.00	510.00
3-Anti-Wertham editorial	33.00	98.00	260.00
4-Black Rider i.d. revealed; Heath, Shores-a	33.00	98.00	260.00

ALL WINNERS COMICS (All Teen #20)
Summer, 1941 - No. 19, Fall, 1946; No. 21, Winter, 1946-47
(No #20) (No. 21 continued from Young Allies No. 20)
USA No. 1-7/WFP No. 10-19/YAI No. 21

	GD25	FN65	VF82	NM94
1-The Angel & Black Marvel only app.; Capt. America by Simon & Kirby, Human Torch & Sub-Mariner begin (#1 was advertised as All Aces); 1st app. All-Winners Squad in text story by Stan Lee				

Alpha Flight #130 © MEG

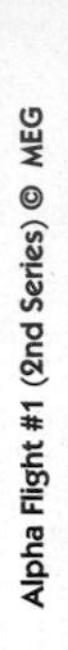
Alpha Flight #1 (2nd Series) © MEG

Alpha Korps #1 © Diversity

GD25 FN65 NM94

1273.00 3820.00 8275.00 14,000.00

GD25 FN65 NM94

2-The Destroyer & The Whizzer begin; Simon & Kirby Captain America
370.00 1110.00 3700.00
3 233.00 700.00 2100.00
4-Classic War-c by Al Avison 256.00 768.00 2300.00
5 150.00 450.00 1350.00
6-The Black Avenger only app.; no Whizzer story; Hitler, Hirohito & Mussolini-c 167.00 500.00 1500.00
7-10 133.00 400.00 1200.00
11,13-18: 11-1st Atlas globe on-c (Winter, 1943-44; also see Human Torch #14). 14-16-No Human Torch 106.00 318.00 950.00
12-Red Skull story; last Destroyer; no Whizzer story
122.00 366.00 1100.00
19-(Scarce)-1st story app. & origin All Winners Squad (Capt. America & Bucky, Human Torch & Toro, Sub-Mariner, Whizzer, & Miss America; r-in Fantasy Masterpieces #10 290.00 870.00 2900.00
21-(Scarce)-All Winners Squad; bondage-c 260.00 780.00 2600.00

NOTE: ***Everett*** *Sub-Mariner-1, 3, 4;* ***Burgos*** *Torch-1, 3, 4.* ***Schomburg*** *c-1, 7-18.* ***Shores*** *c-19p, 21.*

(2nd Series - August, 1948, Marvel Comics (CDS))
(Becomes All Western Winners with No. 2)

1-The Blonde Phantom, Capt. America, Human Torch, & Sub-Mariner app.
189.00 567.00 1700.00

ALL YOUR COMICS (See Fox Giants)
Spring, 1946 (36 pgs.)
Fox Feature Syndicate (R. W. Voight)

1-Red Robbins, Merciless the Sorceress app. 12.00 38.00 100.00

ALMANAC OF CRIME (See Fox Giants)

AL OF FBI (See Little Al of the FBI)

ALPHA AND OMEGA
1978 (49¢)
Spire Christian Comics (Fleming H. Revell)

nn 1.00

ALPHA CENTURION (See Superman, 2nd Series & Zero Hour)
1996 ($2.95, one-shot)
DC Comics

1 1.20 3.00

ALPHA FLIGHT (See X-Men #120,121 & X-Men/Alpha Flight)
Aug, 1983 - No. 130, Mar, 1994 (#52-on are direct sales only)
Marvel Comics Group

1-Byrne-a begins (52pgs.)-Wolverine & Nightcrawler cameo
.80 2.00
2-12: 2-Vindicator becomes Guardian; origin Marrina & Alpha Flight. 3-Concludes origin Alpha Flight. 6-Origin Shaman. 7-Origin Snowbird. 10,11-Origin Sasquatch. 12-(52 pgs.)-Death of Guardian 1.50
13-Wolverine app. 1.00 2.50
14-16,18-28: 16-Wolverine cameo. 20-New headquarters. 25-Return of Guardian. 28-Last Byrne issue 1.25
17-X-Men x-over (70% reprinted from X-Men #109); Wolverine cameo
.80 2.00
29-32,35-49: 39-47,49-Portacio-a(i) 1.00
33,34: 33-X-Men (Wolverine) app. 34-Origin Wolverine 1.00 2.50
50-Double size; Portacio-a(i) 1.25
51-Jim Lee's 1st work at Marvel (10/87); Wolverine cameo; 1st Jim Lee Wolverine; Portacio-a(i) 1.20 3.00
52,53-Wolverine app.; Lee-a on Wolverine; Portacio-a(i); 53-Lee/Portacio-a
.80 2.00
54,63,64-No Jim Lee-a; 54-Portacio-a(i) 1.00
55-62-Jim Lee-a(p) 1.50
65-74,76-86: 65-Begin $1.50-c. 71-Intro The Sorcerer (villain). 74-Wolverine, Spider-Man & The Avengers app. 89-Original Guardian returns
1.25
75-Double size ($1.95, 52 pgs.) .80 2.00
87-90-Wolverine 4 part story w/Jim Lee covers .80 2.00
91-99,101-104: 91-Dr. Doom app. 94-F.F. x-over. 99-Galactus, Avengers app. 102-Intro Weapon Omega. 104-Last $1.50-c 1.50
100-($2.00, 52 pgs.)-Avengers & Galactus app. .80 2.00
105,107-119,121-129: 107-X-Factor x-over. 110-112-Infinity War x-overs. 110, 111-Wolverine app. (brief). 111-Thanos cameo 1.50
106-Northstar revelation issue .80 2.00
106-2nd printing (direct sale only) 1.25
120-($2.25)-Polybagged w/Paranormal Registration Act poster
.90 2.25
130-($2.25, 52 pgs.) .90 2.25
Annual 1 (9/86, $1.25) 1.25
Annual 2(12/87, $1.25) 1.25
Special V2#1(6/92, $2.50, 52 pgs.)-Wolverine-c/story 1.00 2.50

NOTE: ***Austin*** *c-1i, 2i, 53i.* ***Byrne*** *c-81, 82.* ***Guice*** *c-85, 91-99.* ***Jim Lee*** *a(p)-51, 53, 55-62, 64; c-53, 87-90.* ***Mignola*** *a-29-32p.* ***Whilce Portacio*** *a(i)-39-47, 49-54.*

ALPHA FLIGHT (2nd Series)
Aug, 1997 - Present ($1.99)
Marvel Comics

1-($2.99)-Wraparound cover 1.60 4.00
2,3: 2-Variant-c 3.25
4-8 1.99

ALPHA FLIGHT: IN THE BEGINNING
July, 1997 ($1.95, one-shot)
Marvel Comics

Minus 1-Flashback/ Wolverine 1.95

ALPHA FLIGHT SPECIAL
July, 1991 - No. 4, Oct, 1991 ($1.50, limited series)
Marvel Comics

1-3: Reprints Flight #97-99 w/covers 1.50
4 ($2.00, 52 pgs.)-Reprints Alpha Flight #100 .80 2.00

ALPHA KORPS
Sept, 1996 ($2.50)
Diversity Comics

1-Origin/1st app. Alpha Korps 1.00 2.50

ALPHA WAVE
Mar, 1987 ($1.75, 36pgs.)
Darkline Comics

1 1.50

ALTER EGO
May, 1986 - No. 4, Nov, 1986 (Mini-series)
First Comics

1-4 1.40

ALVIN (TV) (See Four Color Comics No. 1042)
Oct-Dec, 1962 - No. 28, Oct, 1973
Dell Publishing Co.

12-021-212 (#1) 8.00 25.00 90.00
2 4.50 13.50 50.00
3-10 3.60 11.00 40.00
11-28 2.75 8.00 30.00
Alvin For President (10/64) 1.80 5.50 20.00
...& His Pals in Merry Christmas with Clyde Crashcup & Leonardo 1 (02-120-402)-(12-2/64), reprinted in 1966 (12-023-604)
4.50 13.50 50.00

ALVIN & THE CHIPMUNKS
July, 1992 - No. 5, May, 1994
Harvey Comics

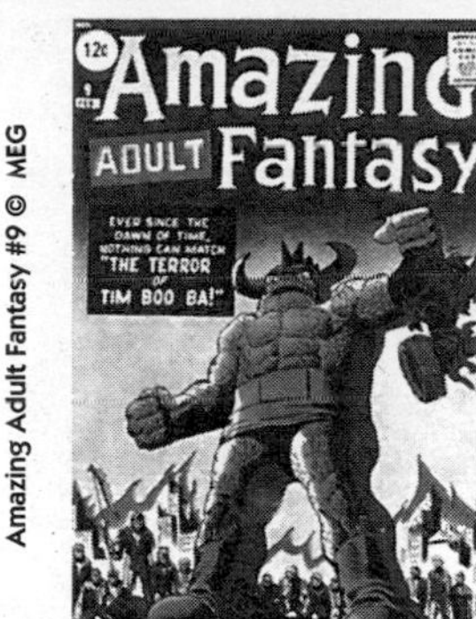

Amazing Adult Fantasy #9 © MEG

Amazing Adventures #4 © MEG

Amazing Adventures #2 © MEG

GD25 FN65 NM94

1-5 1.25

AMALGAM AGE OF COMICS, THE: THE DC COMICS COLLECTION
1996 ($12.95, trade paperback)
DC Comics

nn-r/Amazon, Assassins, Doctor Strangefate, JLX, Legends of the Dark Claw, & Super Soldier 13.00

AMANDA AND GUNN
Apr, 1997 - No. 4, Oct, 1997 ($2.95, B&W, limited series)
Image Comics

1-4 2.95

AMAZING ADULT FANTASY (Formerly Amazing Adventures #1-6; becomes Amazing Fantasy #15)
No. 7, Dec, 1961 - No. 14, July, 1962
Marvel Comics Group (AMI)

7-Ditko-c/a begins, ends #14 48.00 144.00 575.00
8-Last 10¢ issue 43.00 130.00 475.00
9-13: 12-1st app. Mailbag. 13-Anti-communist sty 38.00 115.00 420.00
14-Prototype issue (Professor X) 43.00 127.00 465.00

AMAZING ADVENTURE FUNNIES (Fantoman No. 2 on)
June, 1940 - No. 2, Sept. 1940
Centaur Publications

1-The Fantom of the Fair by Gustavson (r/Amaz. Mystery Funnies V2#7,V2#8), The Arrow, Skyrocket Steele From the Year X by Everett (r/AMF #2); Burgos-a 156.00 468.00 1400.00
2-Reprints; Published after Fantoman #2 100.00 300.00 900.00
NOTE: ***Burgos** a-1(2). **Everett** a-1(3). **Gustavson** a-1(5), 2(3). **Pinajian** a-2.*

AMAZING ADVENTURES (Also see Boy Cowboy & Science Comics)
1950; No. 1, Nov, 1950 - No. 6, Fall, 1952 (Painted covers)
Ziff-Davis Publ. Co.

1950 (no month given) (8-1/2x11) (8 pgs.) Has the front & back cover plus Schomburg story used in Amazing Advs. #1 (Sent to subscribers of Z-D s/f magazines & ordered through mail for 10¢. Used to test market) Estimated value... 280.00
1-Wood, Schomburg, Anderson, Whitney-a 56.00 168.00 500.00
2-5: 2-Schomburg-a. 2,4,5-Anderson-a. 3,5-Starr-a 27.00 81.00 215.00
6-Krigstein-a 29.00 88.00 235.00

AMAZING ADVENTURES (Becomes Amazing Adult Fantasy #7 on)
June, 1961 - No. 6, Nov, 1961
Atlas Comics (AMI)/Marvel Comics No. 3 on

1-Origin Dr. Droom (1st Marvel-Age Superhero) by Kirby; Kirby/Ditko-a (5 pgs.) Ditko & Kirby-a in all; Kirby monster c-1-6 96.00 288.00 1150.00
2 41.00 123.00 480.00
3-6: 6-Last Dr. Droom 37.00 111.00 410.00

AMAZING ADVENTURES
Aug, 1970 - No. 39, Nov, 1976
Marvel Comics Group

1-Inhumans by Kirby(p) & Black Widow (1st app. in Tales of Suspense #52) double feature begins 3.50 10.50 35.00
2-4: 2-F.F. brief app. 4-Last Kirby Inhumans 1.50 4.50 12.00
5-8: Neal Adams-a(p); 8-Last Black Widow 2.50 7.50 20.00
9,10: Magneto app. 10-Last Inhumans (origin-r by Kirby) 1.25 3.75 10.00
11-New Beast begins(1st app. in mutated form; origin in flashback); X-Men cameo in flashback (#11-17 are X-Men tie-ins) 6.50 19.50 65.00
12-17: 13-Brotherhood of Evil Mutants x-over from X-Men. 15-X-Men app. 17-Last Beast (origin); X-Men app. 1.75 5.25 14.00
18-War of the Worlds begins (5/73); 1st app. Killraven; Neal Adams-a(p) 1.75 5.25 14.00
19-35,38,39: 35-Giffen's first published story (art), along with Deadly Hands of Kung-Fu #22 (3/76) 2.00 5.00
36,37-(Regular 25¢ edition)(7-8/76) 2.00 5.00
36,37-(30¢-c, limited distribution) 2.50 7.50 20.00
NOTE: ***N. Adams** c-6-8. **Buscema** a-1p, 2p. **Colan** a-3-5p, 26p. **Ditko** a-24r. **Everett** a(i)3-5, 7-9. **Giffen** a-35i, 38p. **G. Kane** c-11, 25p, 29p. **Ploog** a-12i. **Russell** a-27-32, 34-37, 39; c-28, 30-32, 33i, 34, 35, 37, 39i. **Starlling** a-17. **Starlin** c-15p, 16, 17, 27. **Sutton** a-11-15p.*

AMAZING ADVENTURES
Dec, 1979 - No. 14, Jan, 1981
Marvel Comics Group

V2#1-Reprints story/X-Men #1 & 38 (origins) 1.20 3.00
2-14: 2-6-Early X-Men-r. 7,8-Origin Iceman .80 2.00
NOTE: ***Byrne** c-6p, 9p. **Kirby** a-1-14r; c-7, 9. **Steranko** a-12r. **Tuska** a-7-9.*

AMAZING ADVENTURES
July, 1988 ($4.95, squarebound, one-shot, 80 pgs.)
Marvel Comics

1-Anthology; Austin, Golden-a 2.00 5.00

AMAZING ADVENTURES OF CAPTAIN CARVEL AND HIS CARVEL CRUSADERS, THE (See Carvel Comics)

AMAZING CHAN & THE CHAN CLAN, THE (TV)
May, 1973 - No. 4, Feb, 1974 (Hanna-Barbera)
Gold Key

1-Warren Tufts-a in all 2.25 6.75 18.00
2-4 1.25 3.75 10.00

AMAZING COMICS (Complete Comics No. 2)
Fall, 1944
Timely Comics (EPC)

1-The Destroyer, The Whizzer, The Young Allies (by Sekowsky), Sergeant Dix; Schomburg-c 156.00 468.00 1400.00

AMAZING DETECTIVE CASES (Formerly Suspense No. 2?)
No. 3, Nov, 1950 - No. 14, Sept, 1952
Marvel/Atlas Comics (CCC)

3 19.50 58.00 155.00
4-6 12.00 36.00 95.00
7-10 10.00 30.00 80.00
11,14: 11-(3/52)-Changes to horror 13.00 39.00 105.00
12-Krigstein-a 12.00 36.00 95.00
13-(Scarce)-Everett-a; electrocution-c/story 17.50 53.00 140.00
NOTE: ***Colan** a-9. **Maneely** c-13. **Sekowsky** a-12. **Sinnott** a-13. **Tuska** a-10.*

AMAZING FANTASY (Formerly Amazing Adult Fantasy #7-14)
#15, Aug, 1962 (Sept, 1962 shown in indicia); #16, Dec, 1995 - #18, Feb, 1996
Marvel Comics Group (AMI) GD25 FN65 VF82 NM94

15-Origin/1st app. of Spider-Man by Ditko (11 pgs.); 1st app. Aunt May & Uncle Ben; Kirby/Ditko-c 1100.00 3300.00 11,000.00 27,000.00

GD25 FN65 NM94

16-18 ($3.95): Kurt Busiek scripts; painted-c/a 1.60 4.00

AMAZING GHOST STORIES (Formerly Nightmare)
No. 14, Oct, 1954 - No. 16, Feb, 1955
St. John Publishing Co.

14-Pit & the Pendulum story by Kinstler; Baker-c 22.00 66.00 175.00
15-r/Weird Thrillers #5; Baker-c, Powell-a 15.00 45.00 120.00
16-Kubert reprints of Weird Thrillers #4; Baker-c; Roussos, Tuska-a; Kinstler-a (1 pg.) 15.50 47.00 125.00

AMAZING HIGH ADVENTURE
8/84; No. 2, 10/85; No. 3, 10/86 - No. 5, 1987 ($2.00)
Marvel Comics

1-5: 3,4-Baxter paper .80 2.00
NOTE: ***Bissette** a-4. **Bolton** c/a-4. **Severin** a-1, 3. **Paul Smith** a-2. **Williamson** a-2i.*

AMAZING-MAN COMICS (Formerly Motion Picture Funnies Weekly?)
(Also see Stars And Stripes Comics)
No. 5, Sept, 1939 - No. 26, Jan, 1942

Amazing Man Comics #12 © CEN

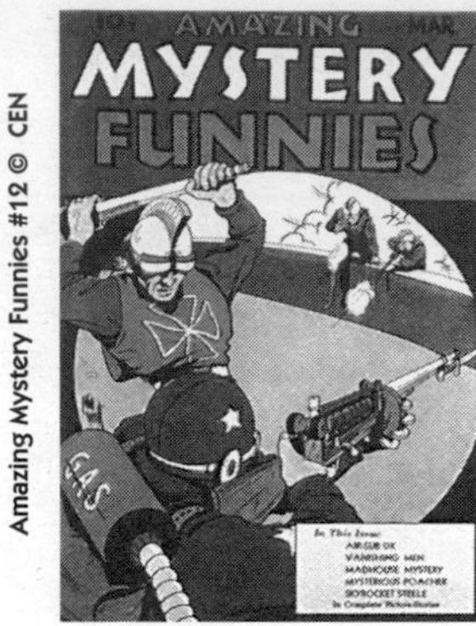

Amazing Mystery Funnies #12 © CEN

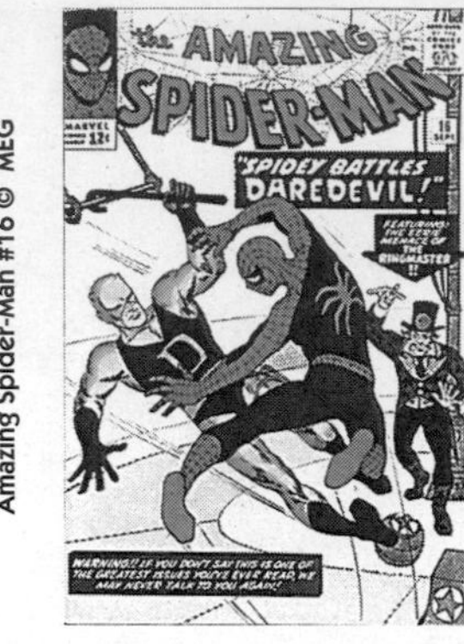

Amazing Spider-Man #16 © MEG

Centaur Publications

	GD25	FN65	VF82	NM94
5(#1)(Rare)-Origin/1st app. A-Man the Amazing Man by Bill Everett; The Cat-Man by Tarpe Mills (also #8), Mighty Man by Filchock, Minimidget & sidekick Ritty, & The Iron Skull by Burgos begins	1318.00	3955.00	8567.00	14,500.00

(Estimated up to 60 total copies exist, 3 in NM/Mint)

	GD25	FN65	NM94
6-Origin The Amazing Man retold; The Shark begins; Ivy Menace by Tarpe Mills app.	260.00	780.00	2600.00
7-Magician From Mars begins; ends #11	172.00	516.00	1550.00
8-Cat-Man dresses as woman	121.00	363.00	1100.00
9-Magician From Mars battles the 'Elemental Monster,' swiped into The Spectre in More Fun #54 & 55	121.00	363.00	1100.00
10,11: 11-Zardi, the Eternal Man begins; ends #16; Amazing Man dons costume; last Everett issue	106.00	318.00	950.00
12,13	92.00	276.00	825.00
14-Reef Kinkaid, Rocke Wayburn (ends #20), & Dr. Hypno (ends #21) begin; no Zardi or Chuck Hardy	78.00	234.00	700.00
15,17-20: 15-Zardi returns; no Rocke Wayburn. 17-Dr. Hypno returns; no Zardi	64.00	192.00	575.00
16-Mighty Man's powers of super strength & ability to shrink & grow explained; Rocke Wayburn returns; no Dr. Hypno; Al Avison (a character) begins, ends #18 (a tribute to the famed artist)	67.00	200.00	600.00
21-Origin Dash Dartwell (drug-use story); origin & only app. T.N.T.	64.00	192.00	575.00
22-Dash Dartwell, the Human Meteor & The Voice app; last Iron Skull & The Shark; Silver Streak app.	61.00	183.00	550.00
23-Two Amazing Man stories; intro/origin Tommy the Amazing Kid; The Marksman only app.	64.00	192.00	575.00
24-King of Darkness, Nightshade, & Blue Lady begin; end #26; 1st app. Super-Ann	61.00	183.00	550.00
25,26 (Scarce): Meteor Martin by Wolverton in both; 26-Electric Ray app.	94.00	282.00	850.00

NOTE: ***Everett*** *a-5-11; c-5-11.* ***Gilman*** *a-14-20.* ***Giunta/Mirando*** *a-7-10.* ***Sam Glanzman*** *a-14-16, 18-21, 23.* ***Louis Glanzman*** *a-6, 9-11, 14-21; c-13-19, 21.* ***Robert Golden*** *a-9.* ***Gustavson*** *a-6; c-22, 23.* ***Lubbers*** *a-14-21.* ***Simon*** *a-10.* ***Frank Thomas*** *a-6, 9-11, 14, 15, 17-21.*

AMAZING MYSTERIES (Formerly Sub-Mariner Comics No. 31)
No. 32, May, 1949 - No. 35, Jan, 1950 (1st Marvel Horror Comic)
Marvel Comics (CCC)

	GD25	FN65	NM94
32-The Witness app.	70.00	205.00	575.00
33-Horror format	26.00	79.00	190.00
34,35: Changes to Crime. 34,35-Photo-c	15.00	45.00	110.00

AMAZING MYSTERY FUNNIES
Aug, 1938 - No. 24, Sept, 1940 (All 52 pgs.)
Centaur Publications

	GD25	FN65	NM94
V1#1-Everett-c(1st); Dick Kent Adv. story; Skyrocket Steele in the Year X on cover only	260.00	780.00	2600.00
2-Everett 1st-a (Skyrocket Steele)	144.00	432.00	1300.00
3	75.00	225.00	675.00
3(#4, 12/38)-nn on cover, #3 on inside; bondage-c	67.00	200.00	600.00
V2#1-4,6: 2-Drug use story. 3-Air-Sub DX begins by Burgos. 4-Dan Hastings, Hastings, Sand Hog begins (ends #5). 6-Last Skyrocket Steele	61.00	183.00	550.00
5-Classic Everett-c	75.00	225.00	675.00
7 (Scarce)-Intro. The Fantom of the Fair & begins; Everett, Gustavson, Burgos-a	260.00	780.00	2600.00
8-Origin & 1st app. Speed Centaur	106.00	318.00	950.00
9-11: 11-Self portrait and biog. of Everett; Jon Linton begins; early Robot cover (11/39)	61.00	183.00	550.00
12 (Scarce)-1st Space Patrol; Wolverton-a (12/39); new costume Phantom of the Fair	156.00	468.00	1400.00
V3#1(#17, 1/40)-Intro. Bullet; Tippy Taylor serial begins, ends #24 (continued in The Arrow #2)	61.00	183.00	550.00
18,20: 18-Fantom of the Fair by Gustavson	58.00	174.00	525.00
19,21-24: Space Patrol by Wolverton in all	82.00	246.00	735.00

NOTE: ***Burgos a-****V2#3-9.* ***Eisner*** *a-V1#2, 3(2).* ***Everett*** *a-V1#2-4, V2#1, 3-6; c-V1#1-4,V2#3, 5, 18.* ***Filchock*** *a-V2#9.* ***Flessel*** *a-V2#6.* ***Guardineer*** *a-V1#4, V2#4-6;* ***Gustavson*** *a-V2#4, 5, 9-12, V3#1, 18, 19; c-V2#7, 9, 12, V3#1, 21, 22;* ***McWilliams*** *a-V2#9, 10.* ***TarpeMills*** *a-V2#2, 4-6, 9-12, V3#1.* ***Leo Morey****(Pulp artist) c-V2#10; text illo-V2#11.* ***FrankThomas*** *a-6-V2#11.* ***Webster*** *a-V2#4.*

AMAZING SAINTS
1974 (39¢)
Logos International

nn-True story of Phil Saint .40

AMAZING SCARLET SPIDER
Nov, 1995 - No. 4, Jan, 1996 ($1.95, limited series)
Marvel Comics

1-4: Replaces "Amazing Spider-Man" for four issues .80 2.00

AMAZING SPIDER-MAN, THE (See All Detergent Comics, Amazing Fantasy, America's Best TV Comics, Aurora, Deadly Foes of Spider-Man, Fireside Book Series, Giant-Size Spider-Man, Giant Size Super-Heroes Featuring..., Marvel Collectors Item Classics, Marvel Fanfare, Marvel Graphic Novel, Marvel Spec. Ed., Marvel Tales, Marvel Team-Up, Marvel Treasury Ed., Nothing Can Stop the Juggernaut, Official Marvel Index To..., Power Record Comics, Spectacular..., Spider-Man, Spider-Man Digest, Spider-Man Saga, Spider-Man 2099, Spider-Man Vs. Wolverine, Spidey Super Stories, Strange Tales Annual #2, Superman Vs. ..., Try-Out Winner Book, Web of Spider- Man & Within Our Reach)

AMAZING SPIDER-MAN, THE
March, 1963 - Present
Marvel Comics Group

	GD25	FN65	VF82	NM94
1-Retells origin by Steve Ditko; 1st Fantastic Four x-over (ties w/F.F. #12 as first Marvel x-over); intro. John Jameson & The Chameleon; Spider-Man's 2nd app.; Kirby/Ditko-c; Ditko-c/a #1-38	700.00	2100.00	7000.00	19,000.00

	GD25	FN65	NM94
1-Reprint from the Golden Record Comic set	10.00	30.00	100.00
with record (1966)	30.00	90.00	200.00
2-1st app. the Vulture & the Terrible Tinkerer	214.00	642.00	2900.00
3-1st full-length story; Human Torch cameo; intro. & 1st app. Doc Octopus;	154.00	461.00	2000.00
4-Origin & 1st app. The Sandman (see Strange Tales #115 for 2nd app.); Intro. Betty Brant & Liz Allen	138.00	414.00	1650.00
5-Dr. Doom app.	120.00	360.00	1450.00
6-1st app. Lizard	96.00	288.00	1150.00
7,8,10: 7-Vs. The Vulture; 1st monthly issue. 8-Fantastic Four app. in back-up story by Kirby/Ditko. 10-1st app. Big Man & The Enforcers	66.00	198.00	790.00
9-Origin & 1st app. Electro (2/64)	73.00	219.00	870.00
11,12: 11-1st app. Bennett Brant. 12-Doc Octopus unmasks Spider-Man-c/story	40.00	120.00	470.00
13-1st app. Mysterio	52.00	156.00	625.00

	GD25	FN65	VF82	NM94
14-(7/64)-1st app. The Green Goblin (c/story)(Norman Osborn); Hulk x-over	125.00	375.00	750.00	1500.00

	GD25	FN65	NM94
15-1st app. Kraven the Hunter; 1st mention of Mary Jane Watson (not shown)	47.00	141.00	570.00
16-Spider-Man battles Daredevil (1st x-over 9/64); still in old yellow costume	33.00	100.00	370.00
17-2nd app. Green Goblin (c/story); Human Torch x-over (also in #18 & #21)	47.00	141.00	570.00
18-1st app. Ned Leeds who later becomes Hobgoblin; Fantastic Four back-up story; 3rd app. Sandman	33.00	100.00	370.00
19-Sandman app.	30.00	90.00	300.00
20-Origin & 1st app. The Scorpion	32.00	96.00	360.00
21-2nd app. The Beetle (see Strange Tales #123)	24.00	72.00	240.00
22-1st app. Princess Python	22.00	66.00	220.00

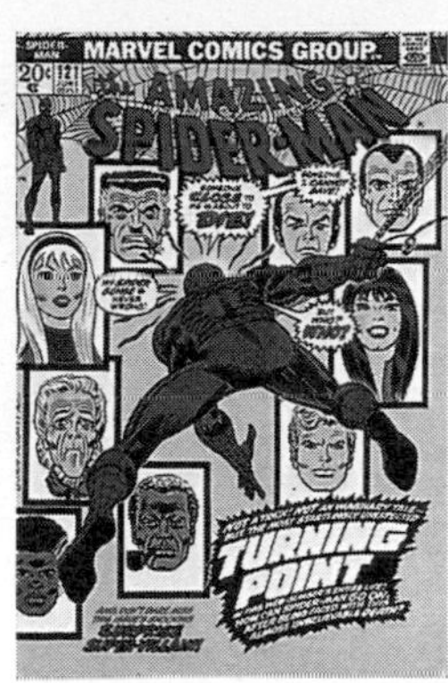

Amazing Spider-Man #121 © MEG

Amazing Spider-Man #185 © MEG

Amazing Spider-Man #201 © MEG

	GD25	FN65	NM94
23-3rd app. The Green Goblin-c/story; Norman Osborn app.	31.00	93.00	330.00
24	19.00	57.00	190.00
25-(6/65)-1st app. Mary Jane Watson (cameo; face not shown); 1st app. Spencer Smythe; Norman Osborn app.	24.00	72.00	240.00
26-4th app. The Green Goblin-c/story; 1st app. Crime Master; dies in #27	26.00	78.00	260.00
27-5th app. The Green Goblin-c/story; Norman Osborn app.	24.50	74.00	245.00
28-Origin & 1st app. Molten Man (9/65, scarcer in high grade)	32.00	95.00	350.00
29,30	15.00	45.00	150.00
31-38: 31-1st app. Harry Osborn who later becomes 2nd Green Goblin, Gwen Stacy & Prof. Warren. 34-2nd app. Kraven the Hunter. 36-1st app. Looter. 37-Intro. Norman Osborn. 38-(7/66)-2nd app. Mary Jane Watson (cameo; face not shown); last Ditko issue	15.00	45.00	150.00
39-The Green Goblin-c/story; Green Goblin's i.d. revealed as Norman Osborn; Romita-a begins (8/66; see Daredevil #16 for 1st Romita-a on Spider-Man)	19.50	58.00	195.00
40-1st told origin The Green Goblin-c/story	29.00	87.00	290.00
41-1st app. Rhino	14.00	42.00	140.00
42-(11/66)-3rd app. Mary Jane Watson (cameo in last 2 panels); 1st time face is shown	12.50	38.00	125.00
43-49: 44,45-2nd & 3rd app. The Lizard. 46-Intro. Shocker. 47-M. J. Watson & Peter Parker 1st date. 47-Green Goblin cameo; Harry & Norman Osborn app. 47,49-3rd & 4th app. Kraven the Hunter	8.50	25.50	85.00
50-1st app. Kingpin (7/67)	35.00	105.00	385.00
51-2nd app. Kingpin	14.50	44.00	145.00
52-60: 52-1st app. Joe Robertson & 3rd app. Kingpin. 56-1st app. Capt. George Stacy. 57,58-Ka-Zar app. 59-1st app. Brainwasher (alias Kingpin); 1st-c app. M. J. Watson	6.50	19.50	65.00
61-74: 67-1st app. Randy Robertson. 69-Kingpin-c. 69,70-Kingpin app. 73-1st app. Silvermane. 74-Last 12¢ issue	4.40	13.20	44.00
75-89,91-93,95,99: 78,79-1st app. The Prowler. 83-1st app. Schemer & Vanessa (Kingpin's wife). 84,85-Kingpin-c/story. 86-Re-intro & origin Black Widow in new costume. 93-1st app. Arthur Stacy	3.60	10.80	36.00
90-Death of Capt. Stacey	4.50	13.50	45.00
94-Origin retold	6.00	18.00	60.00
96-98-Green Goblin app. (97,98-Green Goblin-c); drug books not approved by CCA	7.50	22.50	75.00
100-Anniversary issue (9/71); Green Goblin cameo (2 pgs.)	16.00	48.00	160.00
101-1st app. Morbius the Living Vampire; Wizard cameo; last 15¢ issue (10/71)	13.00	39.00	130.00
101-Silver ink 2nd printing (9/92, $1.75)		.80	2.00
102-Origin & 2nd app. Morbius (25¢, 52 pgs.)	9.00	27.00	90.00
103-118: 104,111-Kraven the Hunter-c/stories. 108-1st app. Sha-Shan. 109-Dr. Strange-c/story (6/72). 110-1st app. Gibbon. 113-1st app. Hammerhead. 116-118-reprints story from Spectacular Spider-Man Mag. in color with some changes	2.50	7.50	24.00
119,120-Spider-Man vs. Hulk (4 & 5/73)	3.80	11.40	38.00
121-Death of Gwen Stacy (6/73) (killed by Green Goblin) (reprinted in Marvel Tales #98 & 192)	9.50	28.50	95.00
122-Death of The Green Goblin-c/story (7/73) (reprinted in Marvel Tales #99 & 192)	12.00	36.00	120.00
123,125-128: 123-Cage app. 125-Man-Wolf origin. 127-1st mention of Harry Osborn becoming Green Goblin	2.25	6.75	18.00
124-1st app. Man-Wolf (9/73)	3.00	9.00	30.00
129-1st app. Jackal & The Punisher (2/74)	12.50	38.00	125.00
130-133,138-141,152-158,160: 131-Last 20¢ issue. 139-1st app. Grizzly. 140-1st app. Glory Grant.	1.10	3.30	9.00
134-(7/74); 1st app. Tarantula; Harry Osborn discovers Spider-Man's ID; Punisher cameo	2.60	7.80	26.00
135-2nd full Punisher app. (8/74)	4.50	13.50	45.00
136-Reappearance of The Green Goblin (Harry Osborn; Norman Osborn's son)	3.50	10.50	35.00
137-Green Goblin-c/story (2nd Harry Osborn)	3.50	10.50	35.00
142,143-Gwen Stacy clone cameos: 143-1st app. Cyclone	2.50	7.50	20.00
144-Full app. of Gwen Stacy clone	1.85	5.50	15.00
145,146-Gwen Stacy clone storyline continues	1.85	5.50	15.00
147-Spider-Man learns Gwen Stacy is clone	1.85	5.50	15.00
148-Jackal revealed	2.50	7.50	22.00
149-Spider-Man clone story begins, clone dies (?); origin of Jackal	3.50	10.50	35.00
150-Spider-Man decides he is not the clone	1.25	3.75	10.00
151-Spider-Man disposes of clone body	1.10	3.30	9.00
159-(Regular 25¢ edition); last 25¢ issue(8/76)	1.00	3.00	8.00
159-(30¢-c, limited distribution)	3.20	9.60	32.00
161-Nightcrawler app. from X-Men; Punisher cameo; Wolverine & Colossus app.	1.10	3.30	9.00
162-Punisher, Nightcrawler app.; 1st Jigsaw	1.10	3.30	9.00
163-173,181-190: 167-1st app. Will O' The Wisp. 169-Clone story recapped. 171-Nova app. 181-Origin retold; gives life history of Spidey; Punisher cameo in flashback (1 panel). 182-(7/78)-Peter proposes to Mary Jane for 1st time, but she refuses		2.40	6.00
174,175-Punisher app.	1.50	4.50	12.00
176-180-Green Goblin app	1.60	4.85	13.00
191-193,195-199,203-208,210-219: 193-Peter & Mary Jane break up. 196-Faked death of Aunt May. 203-2nd app. Dazzler. 209-1st app. Calypso (Kraven's girlfriend). 210-1st app. Madame Web. 212-1st app. Hydro Man; origin Sandman		2.00	5.00
194-1st app. Black Cat	1.50	4.50	12.00
200-Giant origin issue (1/80)	2.25	6.25	18.00
201,202-Punisher app.	1.25	3.75	10.00
209-Origin & 1st app. Calypso (10/80)		2.40	6.00
220-237: 225-(2/82)-Foolkiller-c/story. 226,227-Black Cat returns. 236-Tarantula dies. 234-Free 16 pg. insert "Marvel Guide to Collecting Comics". 235-Origin Will-'O-The-Wisp		1.60	4.00
238-(3/83)-1st app. Hobgoblin (Ned Leeds); came with skin "Tattooz" decal. **Note:** The same decal appears in the more common Fantastic Four #252 which is being removed & placed in this issue as incentive to increase value (Value listed is with or without tattooz)	6.00	18.00	60.00
239-2nd app. Hobgoblin & 1st battle w/Spidey	3.00	9.00	30.00
240-243,246-248: 241-Origin The Vulture. 243-Reintro Mary Jane Watson after 4 year absence		1.60	4.00
244-3rd app. Hobgoblin (cameo)	1.00	3.00	8.00
245-(10/83)-4th app. Hobgoblin (cameo); Lefty Donovan gains powers of Hobgoblin & battles Spider-Man	1.25	3.75	10.00
249-251: 3 part Hobgoblin/Spider-Man battle. 249-Retells origin & death of 1st Green Goblin. 251-Last old costume	1.00	3.00	8.00
252-Spider-Man dons new black costume (5/84); ties with Marvel Team-Up #141 & Spectacular Spider-Man #90 for 1st new costume (See Marvel S-H Secret Wars #8)	2.50	7.50	20.00
253-1st app. The Rose		2.00	5.00
254		1.60	4.00
255,263,264,266-273,277-280,282,283: 277-Vess back-up art. 279-Jack O'Lantern-c/story. 282-X-Factor x-over		1.40	3.50
256-1st app. Puma		2.00	5.00
257-Hobgoblin cameo; 2nd app. Puma; M. J. Watson reveals she knows Spidey's i.d.		2.00	5.00
258-Hobgoblin app. (minor)		1.80	4.50
259-Full Hobgoblin app.; Spidey back to old costume; origin Mary Jane Watson	1.00	3.00	8.00
260-Hobgoblin app.		2.40	6.00
261-Hobgoblin-c/story; painted-c by Vess	1.00	2.80	7.00
262-Spider-Man unmasked; photo-c		2.00	5.00
265-1st app. Silver Sable (6/85)		2.40	6.00

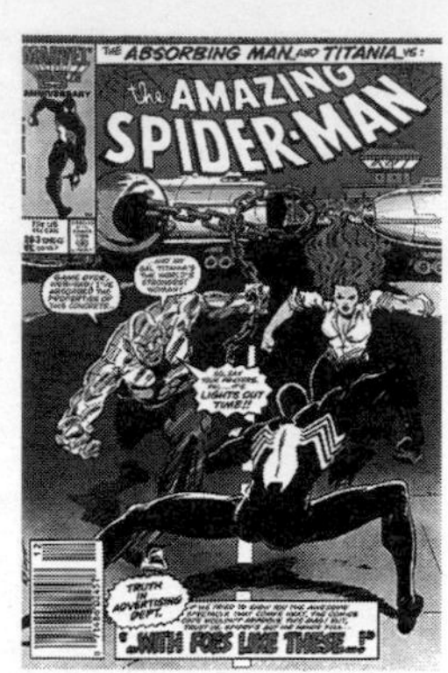

Amazing Spider-Man #283 © MEG

Amazing Spider-Man #393 © MEG

Amazing Spider-Man Annual #28 © MEG

GD25 FN65 NM94

265-Silver ink 2nd printing ($1.25) 1.00 2.50
274-Zarathos (The Spirit of Vengeance) app. (3/86) 1.20 3.00
275-($1.25, 52 pgs.)-Hobgoblin-c/story; origin-r by Ditko 1.00 3.00 7.50
276-Hobgoblin app. 2.40 6.00
281-Hobgoblin battles Jack O'Lantern 1.00 2.60 6.50
284-Punisher cameo; Gang War story begins; Hobgoblin-c/story 1.00 2.60 6.50
285-Punisher app.; minor Hobgoblin app. 1.00 2.80 7.00
286,287: 286-Hobgoblin-c & app. (minor). 287-Hobgoblin app. (minor) 1.80 4.50
288-Full Hobgoblin app.; last Gang War 2.00 5.00
289-(6/87, $1.25, 52 pgs.)-Hobgoblin's i.d. revealed as Ned Leeds; death of Ned Leeds; Macendale (Jack O'Lantern) becomes new Hobgoblin (1st app.) 2.25 6.75 18.00
290-292: 290-Peter proposes to Mary Jane. 292-She accepts; leads into Amazing Spider-Man Annual #21 1.20 3.00
293,294-Part 2 & 5 of Kraven story from Web of Spider-Man. 294-Death of Kraven 2.00 5.00
295-297 1.20 3.00
298-Todd McFarlane-c/a begins (3/88); 1st app. Eddie Brock who becomes Venom; (cameo on last pg.) 3.00 9.00 30.00
299-1st app. Venom with costume (cameo) 2.25 6.75 18.00
300 ($1.50, 52 pgs.; 25th Anniversary)-1st full Venom app.; last black costume (5/88) 6.50 19.50 65.00
301-305: 301 ($1.00 issues begin). 304-1st bi-weekly issue 1.25 3.75 10.00
306-311,313,314: 306-Swipes-c from Action #1. 315-317-Venom app. 1.00 2.80 7.00
312-Hobgoblin battles Green Goblin 1.85 5.50 15.00
315-317-Venom app. 1.85 5.50 15.00
318-323,325: 319-Bi-weekly begins again 2.00 5.00
324-Sabretooth app.; McFarlane cover only 1.00 3.00 8.00
326,327,329: 327-Cosmic Spidey continues from Spectacular Spider-Man (no McFarlane-c/a) 1.00 2.50
328-Hulk x-over; last McFarlane issue 1.00 2.80 7.00
330,331-Punisher app. 331-Minor Venom app. 1.20 3.00
332,333-Venom-c/story 2.00 5.00
334-336,338-343: 341-Tarantula app. 1.00 2.50
337-Hobgoblin app. 1.20 3.00
344-1st app. Cletus Kasady (Carnage) 1.00 2.80 7.00
345-1st full app. Cletus Kasady; Venom cameo on last pg. 1.00 3.00 8.00
346,347-Venom app. 1.80 4.50
348,349,351-359: 348-Avengers x-over. 351,352-Nova of New Warriors app. 353-Darkhawk app.; brief Punisher app. 354-Punisher cameo & Nova, Night Thrasher (New Warriors), Darkhawk & Moon Knight app. 357,358-Punisher, Darkhawk, Moon Knight, Night Thrasher, Nova x-over. 358-3 part gatefold-c; last $1.00-c. 360-Carnage cameo .80 2.00
350-($1.50, 52pgs.)-Origin retold; Spidey vs. Dr. Doom; pin-ups; Uncle Ben app. 1.00 2.50
360-Carnage cameo 1.20 3.00
361-Intro Carnage (the Spawn of Venom); begin 3 part story; recap of how Spidey's alien costume became Venom 1.00 2.80 7.00
361-($1.25)-2nd printing; silver-c .80 2.00
362,363-Carnage & Venom-c/story 1.60 4.00
362-2nd printing 1.50
364,366-374,376-387: 364-The Shocker app. (old villain). 366-Peter's parents-c/story. 369-Harry Osborn back-up (Gr. Goblin II). 373-Venom back-up. 374-Venom-c/story. 376-Cardiac app. 378-Maximum Carnage part 3. 381,382-Hulk app. 383-The Jury app. 384-Venom/carnage app. 387-New costume Vulture .70 1.75
365-($3.95, 84 pgs.)-30th anniversary issue w/silver hologram on-c; Spidey/Venom/Carnage pull-out poster; contains 5 pg. preview of Spider-Man 2099 (1st app.); Spidey's origin retold; Lizard app.; reintro Peter's parents in Stan Lee 3 pg. text w/illo (story continues thru #370). 1.20 3.00
365-Second printing; gold hologram on-c .80 2.00
375-($3.95, 68 pgs.)-Holo-grafx foil-c; vs. Venom story; ties into Venom: Lethal Protector #1; Pat Olliffe-a. 1.20 3.00
388-($2.25, 68 pgs.)-Newsstand edition; Venom back-up & Cardiac & chance back-up .90 2.25
388-($2.95, 68 pgs.)-Collector's edition w/foil-c 1.20 3.00
389-396,398,399,401-420: 389-$1.50-c begins; bound-in trading card sheet; Green Goblin app. 394-Power & Responsibility Pt. 2. 396-Daredevil-c & app. 403-Carnage app. 406-1st New Doc Octopus. 407-Human Torch, Silver Sable, Sandman app. 409-Kaine, Rhino app. 410-Carnage app. 414-The Rose app. 415-Onslaught story; Spidey vs. Sentinels. 416-Epilogue to Onslaught; Garney-a(p); Williamson-a(i) 1.50
390-($2.95)-Collector's edition polybagged w/16 pg. insert of new animated Spidey TV show plus animation cel 1.20 3.00
394-($2.95, 48 pgs.)-Deluxe edition; flip book w/Birth of a Spider-Man Pt. 2; silver foil both-c 1.20 3.00
397-($2.25)-Flip book w/Ultimate Spider-Man .90 2.25
400-($2.95)-Death of Aunt May 1.20 3.00
400-($3.95)-Death of Aunt May; embossed double-c 1.60 4.00
400-Collector's Edition; white-c 1.00 2.80 7.00
421-424, -1 (7/97)($1.95-c) 1.95
425-($2.99)-48 pgs., wraparound-c 2.99
426,428-433: 426-Begin $1.99-c 1.99
427-($2.25) Return of Dr. Octopus; double gatefold-c 2.25
Annual 1 (1964, 72 pgs.)-Origin Spider-Man; 1st app. Sinister Six (Dr. Octopus, Electro, Kraven the Hunter, Mysterio, Sandman, Vulture) (41 pg. story); plus gallery of Spidey foes 50.00 150.00 600.00
Annual 2 (1965, 25¢, 72 pgs.)-Reprints from #1,2,5 plus new Doctor Strange story 25.00 75.00 250.00
Special 3 (11/66, 25¢, 72 pgs.)-Avengers & Hulk x-over; Doctor Octopus-r from #11,12; Romita-a 9.00 27.00 90.00
Special 4 (11/67, 25¢, 68 pgs.)-Spidey battles Human Torch (new 41 pg. story) 8.50 25.50 85.00
Special 5 (11/68, 25¢, 68 pgs.)-New 40 pg. Red Skull story; 1st app. Peter Parker's parents; last annual with new-a 8.00 24 00 80.00
Special 6 (11/69, 25¢, 68 pgs.)-Reprints 41 pg. Sinister Six story from annual #1 plus 2 Kirby/Ditko stories (r) 3.00 9.00 30.00
Special 7 (12/70, 25¢, 68 pgs.)-All-r(#1,2) 3.00 9.00 30.00
Special 8 (12/71)-All-r 3.00 9.00 30.00
King Size 9 ('73)-Reprints Spectacular Spider-Man (mag.) #2; 40 pg. Green Goblin-c/story (re-edited from 58 pgs.) 2.80 8.40 28.00
Annual 10 (1976)-Origin Human Fly (vs. Spidey); new-a begins 1.75 5.25 14.00
Annual 11,12: 11 (1977). 12 (1978)-Spider-Man vs. Hulk-r/#119,120 1.25 3.75 10.00
Annual 13 (1979)-Byrne/Austin-a (new) 1.25 3.75 10.00
Annual 14 (1980)-Miller-c/a(p), 40pgs. 1.50 4.50 12.00
Annual 15 (1981)-Miller-c/a(p); Punisher app. 1.50 4.50 12.00
Annual 16-20: 16 (1982)-Origin/1st app. new Capt. Marvel (female heroine). 17 (1983). 18 (1984). 19 (1985). 20 (1986)-Origin Iron Man of 2020 1.00 2.80 7.00
Annual 21 (1987)-Special wedding issue; newsstand & direct sale versions exist & are worth same 1.25 3.75 10.00
Annual 22 (1988, $1.75, 68 pgs.)-1st app. Speedball; Evolutionary War x-over; Daredevil app. 2.40 6.00
Annual 23 (1989, $2.00, 68 pgs.)-Atlantis Attacks; origin Spider-Man retold; She-Hulk app.; Byrne-c; Liefeld-a(p), 23 pgs. 1.60 4.00
Annual 24 (1990, $2.00, 68 pgs.)-Ant-Man app. 1.20 3.00
Annual 25 (1991, $2.00, 68 pgs.)-3 pg. origin recap; Iron Man app.; 1st Venom solo story; Ditko-a (6 pgs.) 2.00 5.00
Annual 26 (1992, $2.25, 68 pgs.)-New Warriors-c/story; Venom solo story cont'd in Spectacular Spider-Man Annual #12 1.60 4.00

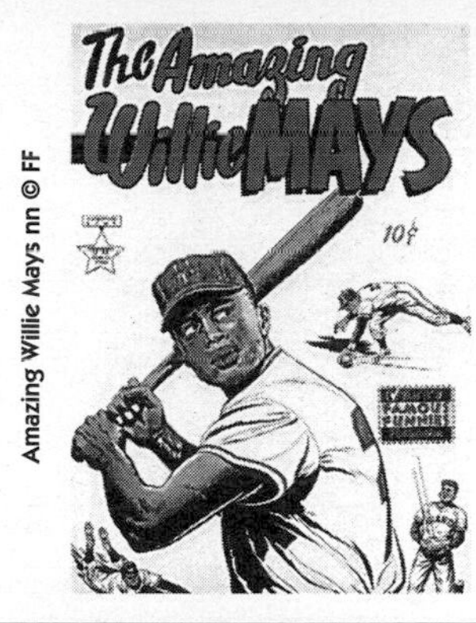

Amazing Willie Mays nn © FF

Amazing X-Men #2 © MEG

Amazon Woman #1 (1st Series) © FantaCo

GD25 FN65 NM94

Annual 27 (1993, $2.95, 68 pgs.)-Bagged w/card; 1st app. Annex 1.20 3.00
Annual 28 (1994, $2.95, 68 pgs.)-Carnage-c/story; Rhino & Cloak and Dagger back-ups 1.20 3.00
'96 Special-($2.95, 64 pgs.)-"Blast From The Past"- 1.20 3.00
'97 Special-($2.99)-Wraparound-c,Sundown app. 2.99
Super Special 1 (4/95, $3.95)-Flip Book 1.60 4.00
...: Skating on Thin Ice 1(1990, $1.25, Canadian)-McFarlane-c; anti-drug issue 2.00 5.00
...: Skating on Thin Ice 1 (2/93, $1.50, American) 1.10 3.30 9.00
...: Double Trouble 2 (1990, $1.25, Canadian) 2.40 6.00
...: Double Trouble 2 (2/93, $1.50, American) .80 2.00
...: Hit and Run 3 (1990, $1.25, Canadian)-Ghost Rider-c/story 1.00 3.00 8.00
...: Hit and Run 3 (2/93, $1.50, American) .80 2.00
... : Carnage (6/93, $6.95)-r/ASM #344,345,359-363 1.00 2.80 7.00
...: Chaos in Calgary 4 (Canadian; part of 5 part series) 1.75 5.25 14.00
...: Chaos in Calgary 4 (2/93, $1.50, American) .80 2.00
...: Deadball 5 (1993, $1.60, Canadian)-Green Goblin-c/story; features Montreal Expos 2.00 6.00 16.00
Note: Prices listed above are for English Canadian editions. French editions are worth double.
...: Soul of the Hunter nn (8/92, $5.95, 52 pgs.)-Zeck-c/a(p) 2.40 6.00
Parallel Lives (1990, $8.95, 68pgs.)-Graphic novel 1.10 3.30 9.00
Aim Toothpaste Giveaway (36 pgs., reg. size)-1 pg. origin recap; Green Goblin-c/story 1.00 3.00 8.00
Aim Toothpaste Giveaway (16 pgs., reg. size)-Dr. Octopus app. 1.00 3.00 8.00
All Detergent Giveaway (1979, 36 pgs.), nn-Origin-r 1.25 3.75 10.00
GiveawayY-Acme & Dingo Children's Boots (1980)-Spider-Woman app. 1.25 3.75 10.00
Amazing Spider-Man nn (1990, 6-1/8x9", 28 pgs.)-Shan-Lon giveaway; r/ Amazing Spider-Man #303 w/McFarlane-c/a 2.00 5.00
...& Power Pack (1984, nn)(Nat'l Committee for Prevention of Child Abuse (two versions, mail offer & store giveaway)-Mooney-a; Byrne-c
Mail offer 1.25 3.75 10.00
Store giveaway 1.20 3.00
...& The Hulk (Special Edition)(6/8/80; 20 pgs.)-Supplement to Chicago Tribune (giveaway) 1.25 3.75 10.00
...& The Incredible Hulk (1981, 1982; 36 pgs.)-Sanger Harris supplement to Dallas Times, Dallas Herald, Denver Post, Kansas City Star, Tulsa World; Foley's supplement to Houston Chronicle (1982, 16 pgs.)-"Great Rodeo Robbery"; The Jones Store-giveaway (1983, 16 pgs.) 2.25 6.75 18.00
...and the New Mutants Featuring Skids nn (National Committee for Prevention of Child Abuse/K-Mart giveaway)-Williams-c(i) 1.20 3.00
...Captain America, The Incredible Hulk, & Spider-Woman (1981) (7-11 Stores giveaway; 36 pgs.) 1.00 2.80 7.00
...: Christmas in Dallas (1983) (Supplement to Dallas Times Herald) giveaway 1.00 2.80 7.00
..., Fire-Star, And Ice-Man at the Dallas Ballet Nutcracker (1983; supplement to Dallas Times Herald)-Mooney-p 1.00 3.00 8.00
Giveaway-Esquire & Eye Magazines (2/69)-Miniature-Still attached 8.00 24.00 80.00
..., Storm & Powerman (1982; 20 pgs.)(American Cancer Society) giveaway 2.40 6.00
...Vs. The Hulk (Special Edition; 1979, 20 pgs.)(Supplement to Columbus Dispatch)-Giveaway 1.00 3.00 8.00
...Vs. The Prodigy (Giveaway, 16 pgs. in color (1976, 5x6-1/2")-Sex education; (1 million printed; 35-50¢) 1.75 5.25 14.00
NOTE: ***Austin*** *a(i)-248, 335, 337, Annual 13; c(i)-188, 241, 242, 248, 331, 334, 343, Annual 25.* ***J. Buscema*** *a(p)-72, 73, 76-81, 84, 85.* ***Byrne*** *a-189p, 190p, 206p, Annual 3r, 6r, 7r, 13p; c-189p, 268, 296, Annual 12.* ***Ditko*** *a-1-38, Annual 1, Special 3(r), 2, 24(2); c-1i, 2-38.* ***Guice*** *c/a-Annual 18i.* ***Gil Kane*** *a(p)-89-105, 120-124, 150, Annual 10, 12i, 24p; c-90p, 96, 98, 99, 101-105p, 129p, 131p, 132p, 137-140p, 143p, 148p, 149p, 151p, 153p, 160p, 161p, Annual 10p, 24.* ***Kirby*** *a-8.* ***Erik Larsen*** *a-324, 327, 329-350; c-327, 329-350, 354i, Annual 25.* ***McFarlane*** *a-298p, 299p, 300-303, 304-323p, 325p, 328; c-298-325, 328.* ***Miller*** *c-218, 219.* ***Mooney*** *a-65i, 67-82i, 84-88i, 173i, 178i, 189i, 190i, 192i, 193i, 196-202i, 207i, 211-219i, 221i, 222i, 226i, 227i, 229-233i, Annual 11i, 17i.* ***Nasser*** *c-228p.* ***Nebres*** *a-Annual 24i.* ***Russell*** *c-357i.* ***Simonson*** *c-222, 337i.* ***Starlin*** *a-113i, 114i, 187p.* ***Williamson*** *a-365i.*

AMAZING WILLIE MAYS, THE
No date (Sept, 1954)
Famous Funnies Publ.
nn 58.00 174.00 525.00

AMAZING WORLD OF SUPERMAN (See Superman)

AMAZING X-MEN
Mar, 1995 - No.4, July, 1995 ($1.95, limited series)
Marvel Comics
1-Age of Apocalypse .80 2.00
2-4 .80 2.00

AMAZON
Mar, 1989 - No. 3, May, 1989 ($1.95, limited series)
Comico
1-3: Ecological theme .90 2.25

AMAZON (Also see Marvel Versus DC #3 & DC Versus Marvel #4)
Apr, 1996 ($1.95, one-shot)
DC Comics (Amalgam)
1-John Byrne-c/a/scripts .80 2.00

AMAZON ATTACK 3-D
Sept, 1990 ($3.95, 28 pgs.)
The 3-D Zone
1-Chaykin-a 1.60 4.00

AMAZON WOMAN (1st Series)
Summer, 1994 - No. 2, Fall, 1994 ($2.95, B&W, limited series, mature)
FantaCo
1,2: Tom Simonton-c/a/scripts 1.20 3.00

AMAZON WOMAN (2nd Series)
Feb, 1996 - No. 4, May, 1996 ($2.95, B&W, limited series, mature)
FantaCo
1-4: Tom Simonton-a/scripts 1.20 3.00

AMAZON WOMAN: INVADERS OF TERROR
1996 ($5.95, B&W, one-shot, mature)
FantaCo
nn-Tom Simonton-a/scripts 2.40 6.00

AMBUSH (See Zane Grey, Four Color 314)

AMBUSH BUG (Also see Son of...)
June, 1985 - No. 4, Sept, 1985 (75¢, limited series)
DC Comics
1-4: Giffen-c/a in all 1.00
Nothing Special 1 (9/92, $2.50, 68pg.)-Giffen-c/a 1.00 2.50
Stocking Stuffer (2/86, $1.25)-Giffen-c/a 1.25

AMERICA AT WAR - THE BEST OF DC WAR COMICS (See Fireside Book Series)

AMERICA IN ACTION
1942; Winter, 1945 (36 pgs.)
Dell(Imp. Publ. Co.)/Mayflower House Publ.
1942-Dell-(68 pgs.) 14.00 41.00 110.00
1-(1945)-Has 3 adaptations from American history; Kiefer, Schrotter & Webb-a 9.50 28.00 75.00

AMERICA MENACED!
1950 (Paper-c)
Vital Publications

American: Lost in America #4 © DH

American Splendor: Music Comics #3 © DH

America's Best Comics #3 © Nedor

nn-Anti-communism estimated value... 200.00

AMERICAN, THE
July, 1987 - No. 8, 1989 ($1.50/$1.75, B&W)
Dark Horse Comics

1-8: ($1.50) 1.50
Collection ($5.95, B&W)-Reprints 2.40 6.00
Special 1 (1990, $2.25, B&W) .90 2.25

AMERICAN AIR FORCES, THE (See A-1 Comics)
Sept-Oct, 1944 - No. 4, 1945; No. 5, 1951 - No. 12, 1954
William H. Wise(Flying Cadet Publ. Co./Hasan(No.1)/Life's Romances/ Magazine Ent. No. 5 on)

1-Article by Zack Mosley, creator of Smilin' Jack 11.30 34.00 90.00
2-4 7.50 22.50 52.00
NOTE: *All part comic, part magazine. Art by* ***Whitney, Chas. Quinlan, H. C. Kiefer****, and* ***Tony Dipreta****.*
5(A-1 45)(Formerly Jet Powers), 6(A-1 54), 7(A-1 58), 8(A-1 65), 9(A-1 67), 10(A-1 74), 11(A-1 79), 12(A-1 91) 5.70 17.00 34.00
NOTE: ***Powell*** *c/a-5-12.*

AMERICAN COMICS
1940's
Theatre Giveaways (Liberty Theatre, Grand Rapids, Mich. known)

Many possible combinations. "Golden Age" superhero comics with new cover added and given away at theaters. Following known: Superman #59, Capt. Marvel #20, Capt. Marvel Jr. #5, Action #33, Classics Comics #8, Whiz #39. Value would vary with book and should be 70-80 percent of the original.

AMERICAN FLAGG! (See First Comics Graphic Novel 3,9,12,21 & Howard Chaykin's..)
Oct, 1983 - No. 50, Mar, 1988
First Comics

1-Chaykin-c/a begins .80 2.00
2-50: 21-27-Alan Moore scripts. 31-Origin Bob Violence 1.00
Special 1 (11/86)-Introduces Chaykin's Time[2] 1.50

AMERICAN FREAK: A TALE OF THE UN-MEN
Feb, 1994 - No. 5, June, 1994 ($1.95, limited series, mature readers)
DC Comics (Vertigo)

1-5 .80 2.00

AMERICAN GRAPHICS
No. 1, 1954; No. 2, 1957 (25¢)
Henry Stewart

1-The Maid of the Mist, The Last of the Eries (Indian Legends of Niagara) (sold at Niagara Falls) 7.85 23.50 55.00
2-Victory at Niagara & Laura Secord (Heroine of the War of 1812) 5.70 17.00 35.00

AMERICAN INDIAN, THE (See Picture Progress)

AMERICAN LIBRARY
1943 - No. 6, 1944 (15¢, 68 pgs., B&W, text & pictures)
David McKay Publications

nn (#1)-Thirty Seconds Over Tokyo (movie) 29.00 86.00 230.00
nn (#2)-Guadalcanal Diary; painted-c (only 10¢) 23.00 68.00 180.00
3-6: 3-Look to the Mountain. 4-Case of the Crooked Candle (Perry Mason). 5-Duel in the Sun. 6-Wingate's Raiders 10.00 30.00 80.00

AMERICAN: LOST IN AMERICA, THE
July, 1992 - No. 4, Oct, 1992 ($2.50, limited series)
Dark Horse Comics

1-4: 1-Dorman painted-c. 2-Joe Phillips painted-c. 3-Mignola-c. 4-Jim Lee-c. 1.00 2.50

AMERICAN SPLENDOR: COMIC-CON COMICS
Aug, 1996 ($2.95, B&W, one-shot)
Dark Horse Comics

GD25 FN65 NM94

1-H. Pekar script 1.20 3.00

AMERICAN SPLENDOR: MUSIC COMICS
Nov, 1997 ($2.95, B&W, one-shot)
Dark Horse Comics

nn-H. Pekar-s/Sacco-a; r/Villiage Voice jazz strips 1.20 3.00

AMERICAN SPLENDOR: ON THE JOB
May, 1997 ($2.95, B&W, one-shot)
Dark Horse Comics

1-H. Pekar script 2.95

AMERICAN SPLENDOR SPECIAL: A STEP OUT OF THE NEST
Aug, 1994 ($2.95, B&W, one-shot)
Dark Horse Comics

1-H. Pekar script 1.20 3.00

AMERICAN SPLENDOR: WINDFALL
Sept, 1995 - No. 2, 1995 ($3.95, B&W, limited series)
Dark Horse Comics

1,2-Pekar script 1.60 4.00

AMERICAN TAIL: FIEVEL GOES WEST, AN
Early Jan, 1992 - No. 3, Early Feb, 1992 ($1.00, limited series)
Marvel Comics

1-Adapts Universal animated movie; Wildman-a 1.00

AMERICA'S BEST COMICS
Feb, 1942; No. 2, Sept, 1942 - No. 31, July, 1949 (New logo with #9)
Nedor/Better/Standard Publications

1-The Woman in Red, Black Terror, Captain Future, Doc Strange, The Liberator, & Don Davis, Secret Ace begin 178.00 534.00 1600.00
2-Origin The American Eagle; The Woman in Red ends 69.00 207.00 625.00
3-Pyroman begins (11/42, 1st app.; also see Startling Comics #18, 12/42) 54.00 162.00 490.00
4-6: 5-Last Capt. Future (not in #4); Lone Eagle app. 6-American Crusader app. 42.00 126.00 380.00
7-Hitler, Mussolini & Hirohito-c 52.00 156.00 465.00
8-Last Liberator 39.00 117.00 345.00
9-The Fighting Yank begins; The Ghost app. 47.00 141.00 415.00
10-21: 10-Flag-c. 11-Hirohito & Tojo-c. (10/44) 14-American Eagle ends. 21-Infinity-c. 36.00 108.00 300.00
22-Capt. Future app. 34.00 103.00 275.00
23-Miss Masque begins; last Doc Strange 39.00 117.00 345.00
24-Miss Masque bondage-c 37.00 110.00 330.00
25-Last Fighting Yank; Sea Eagle app. 33.00 98.00 260.00
26-31: 26-The Phantom Detective & The Silver Knight app.; Frazetta text illo & some panels in Miss Masque. 27,28-Commando Cubs. 27-Doc Strange. 28-Tuska Black Terror. 29-Last Pyroman 33.00 98.00 260.00
NOTE: *American Eagle not in 3, 8, 9, 13. Fighting Yank not in 10, 12. Liberator not in 2, 6, 7. Pyroman not in 9, 11, 14-16, 23, 25-27.* ***Schomburg (Xela)*** *c-5, 7-31. Bondage c-18, 24.*

AMERICA'S BEST TV COMICS (TV)
1967 (25¢, 68 pgs.)
American Broadcasting Company (Produced by Marvel Comics)

1-Spider-Man, Fantastic Four (by Kirby/Ayers), Casper, King Kong, George of the Jungle, Journey to the Center of the Earth stories (promotes new TV cartoon show) 9.00 27.00 90.00

AMERICA'S BIGGEST COMICS BOOK
1944 (196 pgs., one-shot)
William H. Wise

1-The Grim Reaper, The Silver Knight, Zudo, the Jungle Boy, Commando Cubs, Thunderhoof app. 36.00 108.00 290.00

AMERICA'S FUNNIEST COMICS
1944 - No. 2, 1944 (15¢, 80 pgs.)

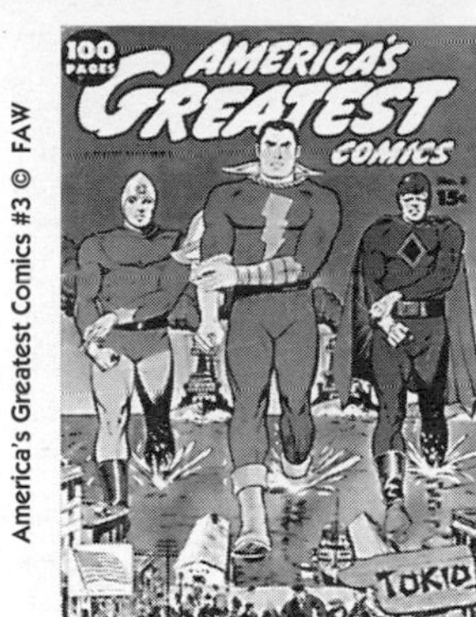

America's Greatest Comics #3 © FAW

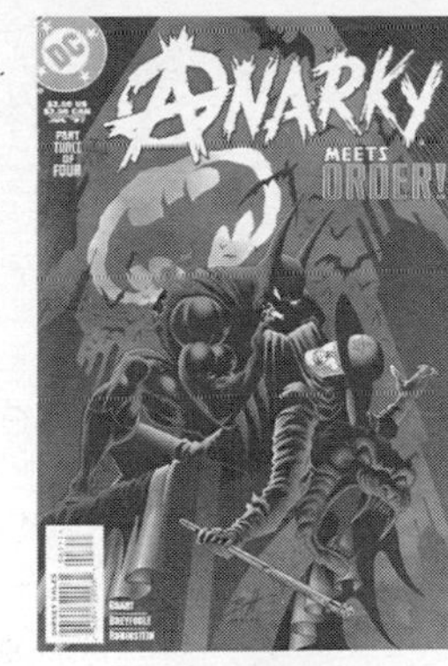

Anarky #3 © DC

Angela/Glory Rage of Angels #1 © Todd McFarlane

GD25 FN65 NM94

William H. Wise
nn(#1), 2 23.00 68.00 180.00

AMERICA'S GREATEST COMICS
May?, 1941 - No. 8, Summer, 1943 (15¢, 100 pgs., soft cardboard-c)
Fawcett Publications
1-Bulletman, Spy Smasher, Capt. Marvel, Minute Man & Mr. Scarlet begin; Classic Mac Raboy-c. 1st time that Fawcett's major super-heroes appear together as a group on a cover. Fawcett's 1st squarebound comic. 233.00 700.00 2100.00
2 117.00 350.00 1050.00
3 83.00 250.00 750.00
4,5: 4-Commando Yank begins; Golden Arrow, Ibis the Invincible & Spy Smasher cameo in Captain Marvel 64.00 192.00 575.00
6,7: 7-Balbo the Boy Magician app.; Captain Marvel, Bulletman cameo in Mr. Scarlet 58.00 174.00 525.00
8-Capt. Marvel Jr. & Golden Arrow app.; Spy Smasher x-over in Capt. Midnight; no Minute Man or Commando Yank 58.00 174.00 525.00

AMERICA'S SWEETHEART SUNNY (See Sunny, ...)

AMERICA VS. THE JUSTICE SOCIETY
Jan, 1985 - No. 4, Apr, 1985 ($1.00, limited series)
DC Comics
1-Double size; Alcala-a(i) in all 1.20 3.00
2-4: 3,4-Spectre cameo .80 2.00

AMERICOMICS
April, 1983 - No. 6, Mar, 1984 ($2.00, Baxter paper/slick paper)
Americomics
1-Intro/origin The Shade; Intro. The Slayer, Captain Freedom and The Liberty Corps; Perez-c .80 2.00
1,2-2nd printings ($2.00) .80 2.00
2-6: 2-Messenger app. & 1st app. Tara on Jungle Island. 3-New & old Blue Beetle battle. 4-Origin Dragonfly & Shade. 5-Origin Commando D. 6-Origin the Scarlet Scorpion .80 2.00
Special 1 (8/83, $2.00)-Sentinels of Justice (Blue Beetle, Captain Atom, Nightshade & The Question) .80 2.00

AMETHYST
Jan, 1985 - No. 16, Aug, 1986 (75¢)
DC Comics
1-16: 8-Fire Jade's i.d. revealed 1.00
Special 1 (10/86, $1.25) 1.25

AMETHYST
Nov, 1987 - No. 4, Feb, 1988 ($1.25, limited series)
DC Comics
1-4 1.25

AMETHYST, PRINCESS OF GEMWORLD
May, 1983 - No. 12, Apr, 1984 (Maxi-series)
DC Comics
1-(60¢) 1.00
1,2-(35¢): Comic book tested in Austin & Kansas City 2.40 6.00
2-12: Perez-c(p) #6-11 1.00
Annual 1(9/84) 1.25
NOTE: *Perez c-4i, 5-11p.*

AMY RACECAR COLOR SPECIAL (See Stray Bullets)
July, 1997 ($2.95, one-shot)
El Capitán Books
1-David Laphan-a/scripts 1.20 3.00

ANARCHO DICTATOR OF DEATH (See Comics Novel)

ANARKY (See Batman)
May, 1997 - No. 4, Aug, 1997 ($2.50, limited series)
DC Comics
1-4 1.00 2.50

ANCHORS ANDREWS (The Saltwater Daffy)
Jan, 1953 - No. 4, July, 1953 (Anchors the Saltwater... No. 4)
St. John Publishing Co.
1-Canteen Kate by Matt Baker (9 pgs.) 15.50 47.00 125.00
2-4 5.35 16.00 32.00

ANDY & WOODY (See March of Comics No. 40, 55, 76)

ANDY BURNETT (TV, Disney)
Dec, 1957
Dell Publishing Co.
Four Color 865-Photo-c 9.00 27.00 100.00

ANDY COMICS (Formerly Scream Comics; becomes Ernie Comics)
No. 20, June, 1948 - No. 21, Aug, 1948
Current Publications (Ace Magazines)
20,21: Archie-type comic 5.70 17.00 34.00

ANDY DEVINE WESTERN
Dec, 1950 - No. 2, 1951
Fawcett Publications
1 47.00 141.00 415.00
2 36.00 108.00 310.00

ANDY GRIFFITH SHOW, THE (TV)(1st show aired 10/3/60)
#1252, Jan-Mar, 1962 - #1341, Apr-Jun, 1962
Dell Publishing Co.
Four Color 1252(#1), 1341-Photo-c 27.00 82.00 300.00

ANDY HARDY COMICS (See Movie Comics #3 by Fiction House)
April, 1952 - No. 6, Sept-Nov, 1954
Dell Publishing Co.
Four Color 389(#1) 2.75 8.00 30.00
Four Color 447,480,515,5,6 2.25 6.75 25.00
...& the New Automatic Gas Clothes Dryer (1952, 5x7-1/4", 16 pgs.) Bendix Giveaway (soft-c) 2.35 7.00 26.00

ANDY PANDA (Also see Crackajack Funnies #39, The Funnies, New Funnies & Walter Lantz...)
1943 - No. 56, Nov-Jan, 1961-62 (Walter Lantz)
Dell Publishing Co.
Four Color 25(#1, 1943) 44.00 132.00 485.00
Four Color 54(1944) 27.00 82.00 300.00
Four Color 85(1945) 14.00 42.00 155.00
Four Color 130(1946),154,198 9.00 27.00 100.00
Four Color 216,240,258,280,297 6.00 19.00 68.00
Four Color 326,345,358 3.50 11.00 38.00
Four Color 383,409 2.75 8.00 30.00
16(11-1/52-53) - 30 1.20 3.60 12.00
31-56 .80 2.40 8.00
(See March of Comics #5, 22, 79, & Super Book #4, 15, 27.)

ANGEL
Aug, 1954 - No. 16, Nov-Jan, 1958-59
Dell Publishing Co.
Four Color 576(#1, 8/54) 2.25 6.75 25.00
2(5-7/55) - 16 1.50 4.50 12.00

ANGELA
Dec, 1994 - No. 3, Feb, 1995 ($2.95, limited series)
Image Comics (Todd McFarlane Productions)
1-Gaiman scripts & Capullo-c/a in all; Spawn app. 1.50 4.50 12.00
2,3 1.25 3.75 10.00
Special Edition (1995)-Pirate Spawn-c 2.50 7.50 25.00
Special Edition (1995)-Angela-c 3.00 9.00 30.00

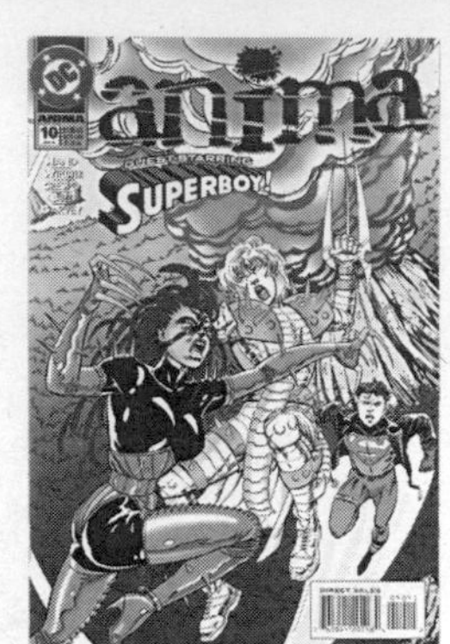

Anima #10 © DC

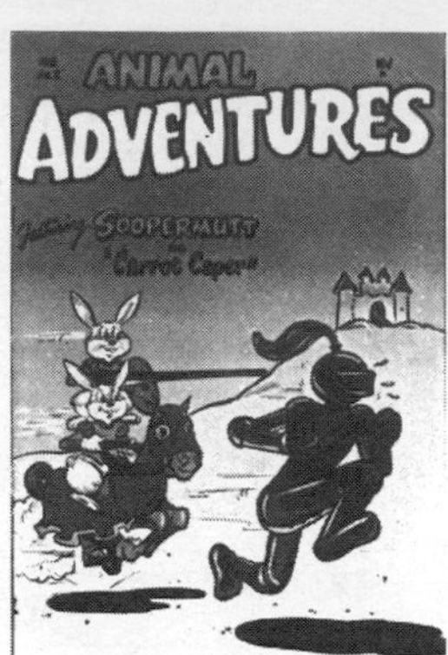

Animal Adventures #2 © MEG

Animal Man #75 © DC

GD25 FN65 NM94

Trade paperback ($9.95, 1995) reprints #1-3 & Special Ed. w/additional pin-ups. 10.00

ANGELA/GLORY: RAGE OF ANGELS (See Glory/Angela: Rage of Angels)
Mar, 1996 ($2.50, one-shot)
Image Comics (Todd McFarlane Productions)

1-Liefeld-c/Cruz-a(p); Darkchylde preview flip book 1.20 3.00

ANGEL AND THE APE (Meet Angel No. 7) (See Limited Collector's Edition C-34 & Showcase No. 77)
Nov-Dec, 1968 - No. 6, Sept-Oct, 1969
National Periodical Publications

1-(11-12/68)-Not Wood-a 3.50 10.50 35.00
2-6-Wood inks in all 2.50 7.50 20.00

ANGEL AND THE APE (2nd Series)
Mar, 1991 - No. 4, June, 1991 ($1.00, limited series)
DC Comics

1-4 1.00

ANGEL FIRE
June, 1997 - No. 3, Oct, 1997 ($2.95, limited series)
Crusade Comics

1-3: 1-(3 variant covers). 3-B&W 2.95

ANGEL LOVE
Aug, 1986 - No. 8, Mar, 1987 (75¢, limited series)
DC Comics

1-8 1.00
Special 1 (1987, $1.25, 52 pgs.) 1.25

ANGEL OF LIGHT, THE (See The Crusaders)

ANIMA
Mar, 1994 - No. 15, July, 1995 ($1.75/$1.95/$2.25)
DC Comics

1-6 .70 1.75
7-(9/94)-Begin $1.95-c; Zero Hour x-over .80 2.00
0,8-14: 0-(10/94). 8-(11/94) .80 2.00
15-Begin $2.25-c 2.25

ANIMAL ADVENTURES
Dec, 1953 - No. 3, May?, 1954
Timor Publications/Accepted Publications (reprints)

1-Funny animal 4.25 13.00 26.00
2,3: 2-Featuring Soopermutt (2/54) 3.20 8.00 16.00
1-3 (reprints, nd) 1.60 4.00 8.00

ANIMAL ANTICS (Movie Town... No. 24 on)
Mar-Apr, 1946 - No. 23, Nov-Dec, 1949 (All 52 pgs.?)
National Periodical Publications

1-Raccoon Kids begins by Otto Feur; some-c by Grossman; Seaman Sy Wheeler by Kelly in some issues 38.00 113.00 340.00
2 21.00 64.00 170.00
3-10: 10-Post-c/a 13.00 39.00 105.00
11-23: 14,15,18,19-Post-a 8.75 26.25 70.00

ANIMAL COMICS
Dec-Jan, 1941-42 - No. 30, Dec-Jan, 1947-48
Dell Publishing Co.

1-1st Pogo app. by Walt Kelly (Dan Noonan art in most issues) 88.00 264.00 875.00
2-Uncle Wiggily begins 44.00 132.00 440.00
3,5 32.00 96.00 320.00
4,6,7-No Pogo 19.00 57.00 190.00
8-10 23.00 69.00 230.00
11-15 14.00 42.00 140.00
16-20 9.50 28.50 95.00
21-30: 25-30- "Jigger" by John Stanley 7.00 21.00 70.00

NOTE: ***Dan Noonan** a-18-30. **Gollub** art in most later issues; c-29, 30. **Kelly** c-7-26.*

ANIMAL CRACKERS (Also see Adventures of Patoruzu)
1946; No. 31, July, 1950; No. 9, 1959
Green Publ. Co./Norlen/Fox Feat.(Hero Books)

1-Super Cat begins (1st app.) 12.00 36.00 95.00
2 7.15 21.50 50.00
3-10 (Exist?) 4.00 11.00 22.00
31(Fox)-Formerly My Love Secret 5.35 16.00 32.00
9(1959-Norlen)-Infinity-c 3.00 7.50 15.00
nn, nd ('50s), no publ.; infinity-c 3.00 7.50 15.00

ANIMAL FABLES
July-Aug, 1946 - No. 7, Nov-Dec, 1947
E. C. Comics (Fables Publ. Co.)

1-Freddy Firefly (clone of Human Torch), Korky Kangaroo, Petey Pig, Danny Demon begin 33.00 98.00 260.00
2-Aesop Fables begin 21.00 62.00 165.00
3-6 17.50 53.00 140.00
7-Origin Moon Girl 47.00 141.00 425.00

ANIMAL FAIR (Fawcett's...)
Mar, 1946 - No. 11, Feb, 1947
Fawcett Publications

1 20.00 60.00 160.00
2 9.50 28.00 75.00
3-6 7.50 22.50 52.00
7-11 5.70 17.00 38.00

ANIMAL FUN
1953 (25¢, came w/glasses)
Premier Magazines

1-(3-D)-Ziggy Pig, Silly Seal, Billy & Buggy Bear 29.00 86.00 230.00

ANIMAL MAN (See Action Comics #552, 553, DC Comics Presents #77, 78, Secret Origins #39, Strange Adventures #180 & Wonder Woman #267, 268)
Sept, 1988 - No. 89, Nov, 1995 ($1.25/$1.50/$1.75/$1.95/$2.25, mature)
DC Comics (Vertigo imprint #57 on)

1-Grant Morrison scripts begin, ends #26 2.00 5.00
2-Superman cameo 1.20 3.00
3,4 .80 2.00
5-10: 6-Invasion tie-in. 9-Manhunter-c/story 1.50
11-26: 11-Begin $1.50-c; 24-Arkham Asylum story; Bizarro Superman app. 25-Inferior Five app. 26-Morrison apps. in story; part photo-c (of Morrison?) 1.50
27-49,51-55,57-59: 41-Begin $1.75-c, end #59 1.50
50-($2.95, 52 pgs.)-Last issue w/Veitch scripts .80 2.00
56-($3.50, 68 pgs.) 1.40 3.50
60-82: 60-Begin $1.95-c. 68-Photo-c. 71-Sutton-a(i) .80 2.00
83-89: 83-Begin $2.25-c .90 2.25
Annual 1 (1993, $3.95, 68 pgs.)-Bolland-c; Children's Crusade Pt. 3 1.60 4.00

NOTE: ***Bolland** c-1-63.*

ANIMAL MYSTIC (See Dark One...)
1993 - No. 4, 1995 ($2.95?/$3.50, B&W)
Cry For Dawn/Sirius

1 3.50 10.50 35.00
1-Alternate 6.50 19.50 65.00
1-2nd printing 1.00 3.00 8.00
2 3.20 9.60 32.00
2,3-2nd prints (Sirius) 2.20 5.50
3 1.75 5.25 14.00
4-Color poster insert 2.40 6.00
TPB ($14.95) r/ 14.95

ANIMAL MYSTIC WATER WARS

Animaniacs #23 © Warner Bros.

Annie #1 © Tribune Co. Synd.

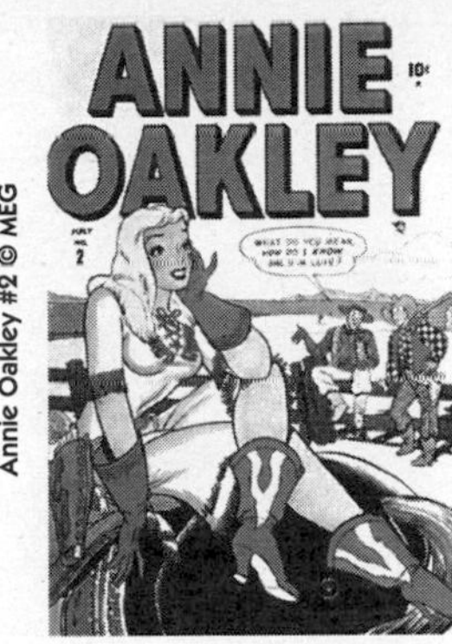

Annie Oakley #2 © MEG

GD25 FN65 NM94

1996/1997 ($2.95, limited series)
Sirius

1-3-Dark One-c/a/scripts 1.20 3.00

ANIMAL WORLD, THE (Movie)
No. 713, Aug, 1956
Dell Publishing Co.

Four Color 713 2.75 8.00 30.00

ANIMANIACS (TV)
May, 1995 - Present ($1.50/$1.75)
DC Comics

1-12 1.50
13-31: 13-Manga issue. 19-X-Files parody; Miran Kim-c; Adlard-a (4 pgs.) 26-E.C. parody-c 1.75
32-36: 32-Begin $1.95-c 1.95
A Christmas Special (12/94, $1.50, "1" on-c) 1.50

ANIMATED COMICS
No date given (Summer, 1947?)
E. C. Comics

1 (Rare) 58.00 174.00 520.00

ANIMATED FUNNY COMIC TUNES (See Funny Tunes)

ANIMATED MOVIE-TUNES (Movie Tunes No. 3)
Fall, 1945 - No. 2, Sum, 1946
Margood Publishing Corp. (Timely)

1,2-Super Rabbit, Ziggy Pig & Silly Seal 15.50 47.00 125.00

ANIMAX
Dec, 1986 - No. 4, June, 1987
Marvel Comics (Star Comics)

1-4: Based on toys .80 2.00

ANNE RICE'S THE MUMMY OR RAMSES THE DAMNED
Oct, 1990 - No. 12, 1991 ($2.50, high quality, limited series)
Millennium Publications

1-12: Adapts novel; Mooney-p in all 1.00 2.50

ANNETTE (Disney, TV)
No. 905, May, 1958; No. 1100, May, 1960 (Mickey Mouse Club)
Dell Publishing Co.

Four Color 905-Annette Funicello photo-c 26.00 77.00 280.00
Four Color 1100-...'s Life Story (Movie); A. Funicello photo-c 21.00 62.00 225.00

ANNEX
Aug, 1994 - No. 4, Nov, 1994 ($1.75)
Marvel Comics

1-4: 1-Spider-Man app. .70 1.75

ANNIE
Oct, 1982 - No. 2, Nov, 1982 (60¢)
Marvel Comics Group

1,2-Movie adaptation 1.00
Treasury Edition ($2.00, tabloid size) .80 2.00

ANNIE OAKLEY (See Tessie The Typist #19, Two-Gun Kid & Wild Western)
Spring, 1948 - No. 4, 11/48; No. 5, 6/55 - No. 11, 6/56
Marvel/Atlas Comics(MPI No. 1-4/CDS No. 5 on)

1 (1st Series, 1948)-Hedy Devine app. 36.00 108.00 300.00
2 (7/48, 52 pgs.)-Kurtzman-a, "Hey Look", 1 pg; Intro. Lana; Hedy Devine app; Captain Tootsie by Beck 22.00 66.00 175.00
3,4 18.00 54.00 145.00
5 (2nd Series, 1955)-Reinman-a ; Maneely-c 12.00 38.00 100.00
6-9: 6,8-Woodbridge-a. 9-Williamson-a (4 pgs.) 9.50 28.00 75.00
10,11: 11-Severin-c 8.75 26.25 65.00

GD25 FN65 NM94

ANNIE OAKLEY AND TAGG (TV)
1953 - No. 18, Jan-Mar, 1959; July, 1965 (Gail Davis photo-c #3 on)
Dell Publishing Co./Gold Key

Four Color 438 (#1) 14.00 41.00 150.00
Four Color 481,575 (#2,3) 8.00 23.00 85.00
4(7-9/55)-10 6.40 19.00 70.00
11-18(1-3/59) 5.50 16.50 60.00
1(7/65-Gold Key)-Photo-c (c-r/#6) 4.00 12.00 45.00
NOTE: ***Manning** a-13. Photo back c-4, 9, 11.*

ANOTHER WORLD (See Strange Stories From...)

ANTARCTIC PRESS JAM 1996
Dec, 1996 ($2.95, one-shot)
Antarctic Press

1 2.95

ANTHRO (See Showcase #74)
July-Aug, 1968 - No. 6, July-Aug, 1969
National Periodical Publications

1-(7-8/68)-Howie Post-a in all 4.20 12.60 42.00
2-6: 6-Wood-c/a (inks) 2.50 7.50 25.00

ANTONY AND CLEOPATRA (See Ideal, a Classical Comic)

ANYTHING GOES
Oct, 1986 - No. 6, 1987 ($2.00, #1-5 color & B&W/#6 B&W, limited series)
Fantagraphics Books

1-Flaming Carrot app. (1st in color?); G. Kane-c .80 2.00
2-6: 2-Miller-c(p); Alan Moore scripts; early Sam Kieth-a (2 pgs.). 3-Capt. Jack, Cerebus app.; Cerebus-c by N. Adams. 4-Perez-c. 5-2nd color Teenage Mutant Ninja Turtles app. .80 2.00

A-1
1992 - No. 4, 1993 ($5.95, limited series, mature)
Marvel Comics (Epic Comics)

1-4: 3-Bisley-c 2.40 6.00

A-1 COMICS (A-1 appears on covers No. 1-17 only)(See individual title listings.)
(1st two issues not numbered.)
1944 - No. 139, Sept-Oct, 1955 (No #2)
Life's Romances Publ. No. 1/Compix/Magazine Ent.

(See Individual Alphabetical listings for prices)

nn-Kerry Drake, Johnny Devildog, Rocky, Streamer Kelly (slightly large size)
9-Texas Slim (all)
11-Teena; Ogden Whitney-c
12,15-Teena
13-Guns of Fact & Fiction (1948). Used in **SOTI**, pg. 19; Ingels & Johnny Craig-a
16-Vacation Comics; The Pixies, Tom Tom, Flying Fredd, & Koko & Kola
18,20-Jimmy Durante; photo covers
19-Tim Holt #3; photo-c
22-Dick Powell (1949)-Photo-c
23-Cowboys and Indians #6; Doc Holiday-c/story
25-Fibber McGee & Molly (1949) (Radio)
26-Trail Colt #2-Ingels-c
28-Christmas-(Koko & Kola #6) ("50)
30-Jet Powers #1-Powell-a
32-Jet Powers #2
33-Muggsy Mouse #1('51)
35-Jet Powers #3-Williamson/Evans-a
37-Ghost Rider #5-Frazetta-c (1951)
1-Dotty Dripple (1 pg.), Mr. Ex, Bush Berry, Rocky, Lew Loyal (20 pgs.)
2-8,10-Texas Slim & Dirty Dalton, The Corsair, Teddy Rich, Dotty Dripple, Inca Dinca, Tommy Tinker, Little Mexico & Tugboat Tim, The Masquerader & others. 7-Corsair-c/s. 8-Intro. Rodeo Ryan
14-Tim Holt Western Adventures #1 (1948)
17-Tim Holt #2; photo-c; last issue to carry A-1 on cover (9-10/48)
21-Joan of Arc (1949)-Movie adaptation; Ingrid Bergman photo-covers & interior photos; Whitney-a
24-Trail Colt #1-Frazetta-r in-Manhunt #13; Ingels-c; L. B. Cole-a
27-Ghost Rider #1(1950)-Origin
29-Ghost Rider #2-Frazetta-c (1950)
31-Ghost Rider #3-Frazetta-c & origin ('51)
34-Ghost Rider #4-Frazetta-c (1951)
36-Muggsy Mouse #2; Racist-c
38-Jet Powers #4-Williamson/Wood-a

A-1 Comics #64 © ME

Apparition #1 © Caliber

Approved Comics #11 © STJ

39-Muggsy Mouse #3
41-Cowboys 'N' Indians #7 (1951)
43-Dogface Dooley #2
45-American Air Forces #5-Powell-c/a
47-Thun'da, King of the Congo #1-Frazetta-c/a('52)
50-Danger Is Their Business #11 ('52)-Powell-a
53-Dogface Dooley #4
55-U.S. Marines #5-Powell-a
56-Thun'da #2-Powell-c/a
58-American Air Forces #7-Powell-a
60-The U.S. Marines #6-Powell-a
62-Starr Flagg, Undercover Girl #5 (#1) reprinted from A-1 #24
65-American Air Forces #8-Powell-a
67-American Air Forces #9-Powell-a
69-Ghost Rider #9(10/52)
71-Ghost Rider #10(12/52)-Vs. Frankenstein
74-American Air Forces #10-Powell-a
76-Best of the West #7
78-Thun'da #4-Powell-c/a
80-Ghost Rider #12(6/52)-One-eyed Devil-c
83-Thun'da #5-Powell-c/a
84-Ghost Rider #13(7-8/53)
86-Thun'da #6-Powell-c/a
88-Bobby Benson's B-Bar-B Riders #20
90-Red Hawk #11(1953)-Powell-c/a
91-American Air Forces #12-Powell-a
93-Great Western #8('54)-Origin The Ghost Rider; Powell-a
95-Muggsy Mouse #4
96-Cave Girl #12, with Thun'da; Powell-c/a
99-Muggsy Mouse #5
101-White Indian #12-Frazetta-a(r)
101-Dream Book of Romance #6 (4-6/54); Marlon Brando photo-c; Powell, Bolle, Guardineer-a
105-Great Western #9-Ghost Rider app.; Powell-a, 6 pgs.; Bolle-c
107-Hot Dog #1
108-Red Fox #15 (1954)-L.B. Cole c/a; Powell-a
110-Dream Book of Romance #8 (10/54)-Movie photo-c
112-Ghost Rider #14 ('54)
114-Dream Book of Love #2-Guardineer, Bolle-a; Piper Laurie, Victor Mature photo-c
118-Undercover Girl #7-Powell-c
120-Badmen of the West #2
121-Mysteries of Scotland Yard #1; reprinted from Manhunt (5 stories)
124-Dream Book of Romance #8 (10-11/54)
126-I'm a Cop #2-Powell-a
128-I'm a Cop #3-Powell-a
130-Strongman #1-Powell-a (2-3/55)
132-Strongman #2
134-Strongman #3
136-Hot Dog #4
138-The Avenger #4-Powell-c/a

40-Dogface Dooley #1('51)
42-Best of the West #1-Powell-a
44-Ghost Rider #6
46-Best of the West #2
48-Cowboys 'N' Indians #8
49-Dogface Dooley #3
51-Ghost Rider #7 ('52)
52-Best of the West #3
54-American Air Forces #6(8/52)-Powell-a
57-Ghost Rider #8
59-Best of the West #4
61-Space Ace #5(1953)-Guardineer-a
63-Manhunt #13-Frazetta
64-Dogface Dooley #5
66-Best of the West #5
68-U.S. Marines #7-Powell-a
70-Best of the West #6
72-U.S. Marines #8-Powell-a(3)
73-Thun'da #3-Powell-c/a
75-Ghost Rider #11(3/52)
77-Manhunt #14
79-American Air Forces #11-Powell-a
81-Best of the West #8
82-Cave Girl #11(1953)-Powell-c/a; origin (#1)
85-Best of the West #9
87-Best of the West #10(9-10/53)
89-Home Run #3-Powell-a; Stan Musial photo-c
92-Dream Book of Romance #5-Photo-c; Guardineer-a
94-White Indian #11-Frazetta-a(r); Powell-c
97-Best of the West #11
98-Undercover Girl #6-Powell-c
100-Badmen of the West #1-Meskin-a(?)
103-Best of the West #12-Powell-a
104-White Indian #13-Frazetta-a(r) ('54)
106-Dream Book of Love #1 (6-7/54) -Powell, Bolle-a; Montgomery Clift, Donna Reed photo-c
109-Dream Book of Romance #7 (7-8/54). Powell-a; movie photo-c
111-I'm a Cop #1 ('54); drug mention story; Powell-a
113-Great Western #10; Powell-a
115-Hot Dog #3
116-Cave Girl #13-Powell-c/a
117-White Indian #14
119-Straight Arrow's Fury #1 (origin); Fred Meagher-c/a
122-Black Phantom #1 (11/54)
123-Dream Book of Love #3 (10-11/54)-Movie photo-c
125-Cave Girl #14-Powell-c/a
127-Great Western #11('54)-Powell-a
129-The Avenger #1('55)-Powell-c
131-The Avenger #2('55)-Powell-c/a
133-The Avenger #3-Powell-c/a
135-White Indian #15
137-Africa #1-Powell-c/a(4)
139-Strongman #4-Powell-a

NOTE: ***Bolle*** *a-110. Photo-c-17-22, 89, 92, 101, 106, 109, 110, 114, 123, 124.*

APACHE
1951
Fiction House Magazines

	GD25	FN65	NM94
1	16.00	49.00	130.00
I.W. Reprint No. 1-r/#1 above	3.20	8.00	16.00

APACHE HUNTER
1954 (18 pgs. in color) (promo copy) (saddle stitched)
Creative Pictorials

	GD25	FN65	NM94
nn-Severin, Heath stories	14.00	41.00	110.00

APACHE KID (Formerly Reno Browne; Western Gunfighters #20 on)
(Also see Two-Gun Western & Wild Western)
No. 53, 12/50 - No. 10, 1/52; No. 11, 12/54 - No. 19, 4/56
Marvel/Atlas Comics(MPC No. 53-10/CPS No. 11 on)

	GD25	FN65	NM94
53(#1)-Apache Kid & his horse Nightwind (origin), Red Hawkins by Syd Shores begins	26.00	80.00	210.00
2(2/51)	12.00	38.00	100.00
3-5	8.75	26.25	65.00
6-10 (1951-52): 7-Russ Heath-a	7.15	21.50	50.00
11-19 (1954-56)	5.70	17.00	40.00

NOTE: ***Heath*** *a-7. c-11, 13.* ***Maneely*** *a-53; c-53(#1), 12, 14-16.* ***Powell*** *a-14.* ***Severin*** *c-17.*

APACHE MASSACRE (See Chief Victorio's...)

APACHE TRAIL
Sept, 1957 - No. 4, June, 1958
Steinway/America's Best

	GD25	FN65	NM94
1	8.50	26.00	60.00
2-4: 2-Tuska-a	5.70	17.00	35.00

APPARITION
1995 ($3.95, 52 pgs., B&W)
Caliber Comics

	GD25	FN65	NM94
1 ($3.95)		1.60	4.00
1 ($2.95)		1.20	3.00
Visitations		1.60	4.00

APPLESEED
Sept, 1988 - Book 4, Vol. 4, Aug, 1991 ($2.50/$2.75/$3.50, 52/68 pgs, B&W)
Eclipse Comics

	GD25	FN65	NM94
Book One, Vol. 1 ($2.50)		1.20	3.00
Book One, Vol. 2-5: 5-(1/89, $2.75 cover)		1.20	3.00
Book Two, Vol. 1(2/89) -5(7/89): Art Adams-c		1.20	3.00
Book Three, Vol. 1(8/89) -4 ($2.75)		1.20	3.00
Book Three, Vol. 5 ($3.50)		1.20	3.00
Book Four, Vol. 1 (1/91) - 4 (8/91) ($3.50, 68 pgs.)		1.20	3.00

APPLESEED DATABOOK
Apr, 1994 - No. 2, May, 1994 ($3.50, B&W, limited series)
Dark Horse Comics

	GD25	FN65	NM94
1,2: 1-Flip book format		1.40	3.50

APPROVED COMICS
March, 1954 - No. 12, Aug, 1954 (All painted-c)
St. John Publishing Co. (Most have no c-price)

	GD25	FN65	NM94
1-The Hawk #5-r	8.50	26.00	60.00
2-Invisible Boy (3/54)-Origin; Saunders-c	13.00	39.00	105.00
3-Wild Boy of the Congo #11-r (4/54)	8.50	26.00	60.00
4,5: 4-Kid Cowboy-r. 5-Fly Boy-r	8.50	26.00	60.00
6-Daring Adv.-r (5/54); Krigstein-a(2); Baker-c	9.50	28.00	75.00
7-The Hawk #6-r	8.50	26.00	60.00
8-Crime on the Run (6/54); Powell-a; Saunders-c	8.50	26.00	60.00
9-Western Bandit Trails #3-r, with new-c; Baker-c/a	9.50	28.00	75.00
11-Fightin' Marines #3-r (8/54); Canteen Kate app; Baker-c/a	10.00	30.00	80.00

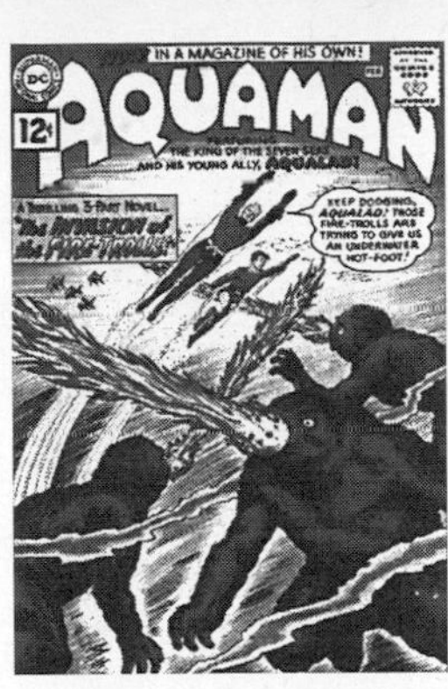

Aquaman #1 (1st Series) © DC

Aquaman #33 (3rd Series) © DC

Arak/Son of Thunder #30 © DC

	GD25	FN65	NM94
12-North West Mounties #4-r(8/54); new Baker-c	10.00	30.00	80.00

AQUAMAN (See Adventure #260, Brave & the Bold, DC Comics Presents #5, DC Special #28, DC Special Series #1, DC Super Stars #7, Detective, Justice League of America, More Fun #73, Showcase #30-33, Super DC Giant, Super Friends, and World's Finest Comics)

AQUAMAN (1st Series)
Jan-Feb, 1962 - #56, Mar-Apr, 1971; #57, Aug-Sept,1977 - #63, Aug-Sept, 1978
National Periodical Publications/DC Comics

	GD25	FN65	NM94
1-(1-2/62)-Intro. Quisp	57.00	171.00	625.00
2	26.00	78.00	260.00
3-5	14.00	42.00	145.00
6-10: 9-Sea Devils app.	9.00	27.00	95.00
11-20: 11-1st app. Mera. 18-Aquaman weds Mera; JLA cameo	8.00	24.00	80.00
21-32: 23-Birth of Aquababy. 26-Huntress app.(3-4/66). 29-1st app. Ocean Master, Aquaman's step-brother. 30-Batman & Superman-c & cameo	4.50	13.50	45.00
33-1st app. Aqua-Girl (see Adventure #266)	5.00	15.00	50.00
34-40: 40-Jim Aparo's 1st DC work (8/68)	2.50	7.50	25.00
41-47,49	1.85	5.50	15.00
48-Origin reprinted	2.25	6.75	18.00
50-52-Deadman by Neal Adams	4.00	12.00	40.00
53-56('71): 56-1st app. Crusader	1.00	2.80	7.00
57('77)-63: 58-Origin retold		2.00	5.00

NOTE: ***Aparo** a-40-45, 46p, 47-59; c-58-63. **Nick Cardy** c-1-39. **Newton** a-60-63.*

AQUAMAN (1st limited series)
Feb, 1986 - No. 4, May, 1986 (75¢, limited series)
DC Comics

	GD25	FN65	NM94
1-New costume; 1st app. Nuada of Thierna Na Oge.		.80	2.00
2-4: 3-Retelling of Aquaman & Ocean Master's origins.		.80	2.00
Special 1 (1988, $1.50, 52 pgs.)		.80	2.00

NOTE: ***Craig Hamilton** c/a-1-4p. **Russell** c-2-4i.*

AQUAMAN (2nd limited series)
June, 1989 - No. 5, Oct, 1989 ($1.00, limited series)
DC Comics

	GD25	FN65	NM94
1-5: Giffen plots/breakdowns; Swan-a(p).			1.25
Special 1 (Legend of..., $2.00, 1989, 52 pgs.)-Giffen plots/breakdowns; Swan-a(p).		.80	2.00

AQUAMAN (2nd Series)
Dec, 1991 - No. 13, Dec, 1992 ($1.00/$1.25)
DC Comics

	GD25	FN65	NM94
1-5			1.25
6-13: 6-Begin $1.25-c. 9-Sea Devils app.			1.50

AQUAMAN (3rd Series)(Also see Atlantis Chronicles)
Aug, 1994 - Present ($1.50/$1.75)
DC Comics

	GD25	FN65	NM94
1-(8/94)-Peter David scripts begin; reintro Dolphin	1.10	3.30	9.00
2-(9/94)-Aquaman loses hand	1.25	3.75	10.00
0-(10/94)-Aquaman replaces lost hand w/hook.	1.10	3.30	9.00
3-8: 3-(11/94)-Superboy-c/app. 4-Lobo app. 6-Deep Six app.	1.00		2.50
9-38: 9-Begin $1.75-c. 10-Green Lantern app. 11-Reintro Mera. 15-Reintro Kordax. 16-vs. JLA. 18-Reintro Ocean Master & Atlan (Aquaman's father). 19-Reintro Garth (Aqualad). 23-Ist app. Deep Blue (Neptune Perkins & Tsunami's daughter). 23,24-Neptune Perkins, Nuada, Tsunami, Arion, Power Girl, & The Sea Devils app. 26-Final Night. 28-Martian Manhunter-c/app. 29-Black Manta-c/app. 32-Swamp Thing-c/app. 37-Genesis x-over.		.80	2.00
39-43: 39-Begin $195-c.			1.95
Annual 1 (1995, $3.50)-Year One story		1.40	3.50
Annual 2 (1996, $2.95)-Legends of the Dead Earth story		1.20	3.00
Annual 3 (1997, $3.95)-Pulp Heroes story			3.95

NOTE: ***Mignola** c-6. **Simonson** c-15.*

AQUAMAN: TIME & TIDE (3rd limited series) (Also see Atlantis Chronicles)
Dec, 1993 - No. 4, Mar, 1994 ($1.50, limited series)
DC Comics

	GD25	FN65	NM94
1-4: Peter David scripts; origin retold.		1.20	3.00
Trade paperback ($9.95)			10.00

AQUANAUTS (TV)
May - July, 1961
Dell Publishing Co.

	GD25	FN65	NM94
Four Color 1197-Photo-c	5.75	17.00	63.00

ARABIAN NIGHTS (See Cinema Comics Herald)

ARACHNOPHOBIA (Movie)
1990 ($5.95, 68 pg. graphic novel)
Hollywood Comics (Disney Comics)

	GD25	FN65	NM94
nn-Adaptation of film; Spiegle-a		2.40	6.00
Comic edition ($2.95, 68 pgs.)		1.20	3.00

ARAKNIS
1995 - No. 4, 1996 ($2.50, limited series)
Mushroom Comics

	GD25	FN65	NM94
1,2		1.20	3.00
3,4: 3-w/pin-ups		1.00	2.50

ARAKNIS
No. 0, Apr, 1996 - No. 4, 1997 ($2.95/$2.50)
Mushroom Comics/Morningstar Productions #3 on

	GD25	FN65	NM94
0-(4/96, $2.95)		1.20	3.00
0-Special Edition		2.00	5.00
1-4: 1-Ongoing series (5/96)		1.00	2.50
1-Special Edition; polybagged w/certificate		3.75	10.00

ARAKNIS: RETRIBUTION
May, 1997- No. 4 ($2.50, limited series)
Morningstar Productions

	GD25	FN65	NM94
1,2-Ortiz Brothers-s/a		1.00	2.50

ARAK/SON OF THUNDER (See Warlord #48)
Sept, 1981 - No. 50, Nov, 1985
DC Comics

	GD25	FN65	NM94
1-50: 1-Origin; 1st app. Angelica, Princess of White Cathay. 3-Intro Valda, The Iron Maiden. 12-Origin Valda. 20-Origin Angelica. 24,50-(52 pgs.)			1.00
Annual 1(10/84)			1.00

ARCANA (Also see Books of Magic limited & ongoing series and Mister E)
1994 ($3.95, 68 pgs., annual)
DC Comics (Vertigo)

	GD25	FN65	NM94
1-Bolton painted-c; Children's Crusade/Tim Hunter story		1.60	4.00

ARCANUM
Apr, 1997 - Present ($2.50)
Image Comics (Top Cow Productions)

	GD25	FN65	NM94
1-Brandon Peterson-s/a(p);		1.60	4.00
2-7		1.00	2.50

ARCHANGEL (See Uncanny X-Men, X-Factor & X-Men)
Feb, 1996 ($2.50, B&W, one-shot)
Marvel Comics

	GD25	FN65	NM94
1-Milligan story		1.00	2.50

ARCHER & ARMSTRONG
July (June inside), 1992 - No. 25, Sept, 1994 ($2.50)
Valiant

	GD25	FN65	NM94
0-(7/92)-B. Smith-c/a; Reese-i assists		1.20	3.00
0-(Gold Logo)		2.40	6.00

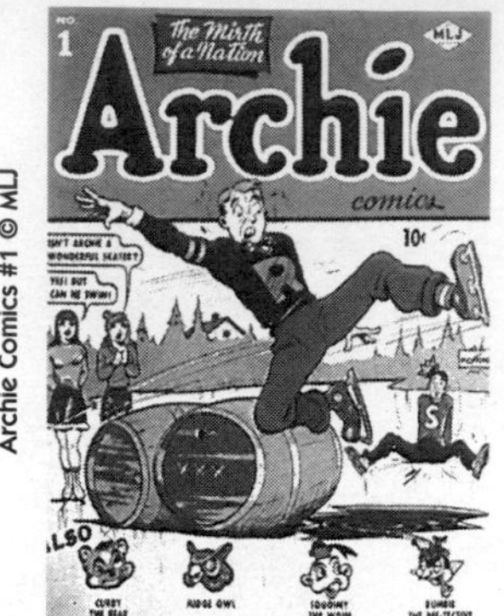

Archie Comics #1 © MLJ

Archie Comics #408 © Archie Publ.

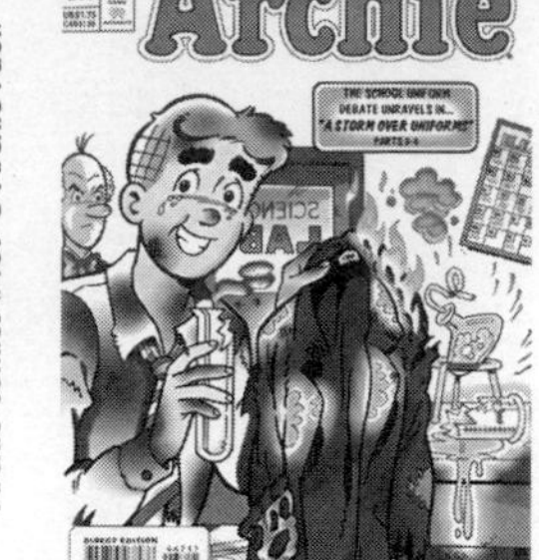

Archie Comics #467 © Archie Publ.

GD25 FN65 NM94

1-(8/92)-Origin & 1st app. Archer; Miller-c; B. Smith/Layton-a 1.00 2.50
2-7: 2-2nd app. Turok(c/story); Smith/Layton-a; Simonson-c. 3,4-Smith-c&a(p) & scripts 1.00 2.50
8-($4.50, 52 pgs.)-Combined with Eternal Warrior #8; B. Smith-c/a & scripts; 1st app. Ivar the Time Walker 1.80 4.50
9-25: 10-2nd app. Ivar. 10,11-B. Smith-c. 21,22-Shadowman app. 22-w/bound-in trading card. 25-Eternal Warrior app. 1.00 2.50

ARCHIE AMERICANA SERIES, BEST OF THE SIXTIES
1995 ($9.95, trade paperback)
Archie Publications

V3-r/strips from Archie #167; Betty & Veronica #67,101,105,135,138,142,156; Laugh #162; Life w/Archie #78, 84; Jughead #154; Pep #219,225,229; introduction by Frankie Avalon. 1.25 3.75 10.00

ARCHIE AND BIG ETHEL
1982 (69¢)
Spire Christian Comics (Fleming H. Revell Co.)

nn 1.60 4.00

ARCHIE & FRIENDS
Dec, 1992 - Present ($1.25/$1.50/$1.75, quarterly/bi-monthly)
Archie Comics

1-13 1.25
14-26: 14-Begin $1.50-c 1.50
27-31: 27-Begin $1.75-c 1.75

ARCHIE AND ME (See Archie Giant Series Mag. #578, 591, 603, 616, 626)
Oct, 1964 - No. 161, Feb, 1987
Archie Publications

1 14.00 42.00 140.00
2 7.00 21.00 70.00
3-5 3.50 10.50 35.00
6-10 1.80 5.40 18.00
11-20 1.40 4.15 11.00
21-30: 26-X-Mas-c 1.00 3.00 8.00
31-63: 43-63-(All Giants) 2.00 5.00
64-100-(Regular size) 1.40 3.50
101-161 .80 2.00

ARCHIE AND MR. WEATHERBEE
1980 (59¢)
Spire Christian Comics (Fleming H. Revell Co.)

nn 1.60 4.00

ARCHIE...ARCHIE ANDREWS, WHERE ARE YOU? (...Comics Digest #9, 10; ...Comics Digest Mag. No. 11 on)
Feb, 1977 - Present (Digest size, 160-128 pgs., quarterly)
Archie Publications

1 1.25 3.75 10.00
2,3,5,7-9-N. Adams-a; 8-r-/origin The Fly by S&K. 9-Steel Sterling-r 1.00 3.00 8.00
4,6,10 ($1.00/$1.50): 17-Katy Keene story 2.40 6.00
11-20 2.00 5.00
21-50 1.60 4.00
61-112 .80 2.00
113-117: 113-Begin $1.89-c 1.89

ARCHIE AS PUREHEART THE POWERFUL (Also see Archie Giant Series #142, Jughead as Captain Hero, Life With Archie & Little Archie)
Sept, 1966 - No. 6, Nov, 1967
Archie Publications (Radio Comics)

1-Super hero parody 6.50 19.50 65.00
2 4.50 13.50 45.00
3-6 3.20 9.60 32.00

NOTE: *Evilheart cameos in all. Title: Archie As Pureheart the Powerful #1-3; ...As Capt. Pureheart-#4-6.*

GD25 FN65 NM94

ARCHIE AT RIVERDALE HIGH (See Archie Giant Series Magazine #573, 586, 604 & Riverdale High)
Aug, 1972 - No. 113, Feb, 1987
Archie Publications

1 4.20 12.60 42.00
2 2.50 7.50 22.00
3-5 1.85 5.50 15.00
6-10 1.10 3.30 9.00
11-30 2.00 5.00
31-50 1.60 4.00
51-80 1.20 3.00
81-114: 96-Anti-smoking issue .80 2.00

ARCHIE COMICS (Also see Christmas & Archie, Everything's..., Explorers of the Unknown, Jackpot, Little..., Oxydol-Dreft, Pep, Riverdale High, Teenage Mutant Ninja Turtles Adventures & To Riverdale and Back Again)

ARCHIE COMICS (Archie #114 on; 1st Teen-age comic; Radio show aired 6/2/45 by NBC)
Winter, 1942-43 - No. 19, 3-4/46; No. 20, 5-6/46 - Present
MLJ Magazines No. 1-19/Archie Publ.No. 20 on

GD25 FN65 VF82 NM94
1 (Scarce)-Jughead, Veronica app.; 1st app. Mrs. Andrews 955.00 2865.00 5730.00 10,500.00
(Estimated up to 50+ total copies exist, 5 in NM/Mint)

GD25 FN65 NM94
2 240.00 720.00 2300.00
3 (60 pgs.)(scarce) 189.00 567.00 1700.00
4,5: 4-Article about Archie radio series 100.00 300.00 900.00
6-10: 6-X-Mas-c. 7-1st definitive love triangle story 72.00 216.00 650.00
11-20: 15,17,18-Dotty & Ditto by Woggon. 16-Woggon-a 48.00 144.00 430.00
21-30: 23-Betty & Veronica by Woggon. 25-Woggon-a. 30-Coach Piffle app., a Coach Kleets prototype. 34-Pre-Dilton try-out (named Dilbert) 34.00 103.00 275.00
31-40 19.00 56.00 150.00
41-50 12.00 38.00 100.00
51-60: (1954) 51-Katy Keene app. 8.75 26.25 70.00
61-70 (1954): 65-70, Katy Keene app. 7.85 23.50 55.00
71-80: 72-74-Katy Keene app. 4.50 13.50 45.00
81-99: 94-1st Coach Kleets 3.50 10.50 35.00
100 4.50 13.50 45.00
101-130 (1962) 2.50 7.50 20.00
131-160 1.50 4.50 12.00
161-200 1.00 3.00 8.00
201-240 2.00 5.00
241-282 1.60 4.00
283-Cover/story plugs "International Children's Appeal" which was a fraudulent charity, according to TV's 20/20 news program broadcast July 20, 1979 2.00 5.00
284-350: 300-Anniversary issue. 1.20 3.00
351-466: 393-Infinity-c; 1st comic book printed on recycled paper. 423-Dan DeCarlo-c .80 2.00
467-472: 467-Begin $1.75-c; "A Storm Over Uniforms" x-over parts 3,4 1.75
Annual 1('50)-116 pgs. (Scarce) 144.00 432.00 1300.00
Annual 2('51) 72.00 216.00 650.00
Annual 3('52) 44.00 132.00 400.00
Annual 4,5(1953-54) 33.00 98.00 260.00
Annual 6-10(1955-59) 17.50 53.00 140.00
Annual 11-15(1960-65) 5.50 16.50 55.00
Annual 16-20(1966-70) 2.50 7.50 20.00
Annual 21-26(1971-75) 1.25 3.75 10.00
Annual Digest 27('75)-30 1.50 4.50 12.00
31-40 (...Magazine #35 on) 1.10 3.30 9.00
41-65 ('94) 1.60 4.00

Archie Comics Digest #122 © Archie Publ.

Archie Giant Series #9 © Archie Publ.

Archie Giant Series #10 © Archie Publ.

GD25 FN65 NM94

...All-Star Specials(Winter '75, $1.25)-6 remaindered Archie comics rebound in each; titles: "The World of Giant Comics", "Giant Grab Bag of Comics", "Triple Giant Comics" & "Giant Spec. Comics 2.25 6.75 18.00
...And His Friends Help Raise Literacy Awareness In Mississippi nn (3/94)-Giveaway 1.20 3.00
...And the History of Electronics nn (5/90, 36 pgs.)-Radio Shack giveaway; Howard Bender-c/a 1.60 4.00
Mini-Comics (1970-Fairmont Potato Chips Giveaway-Miniature)(8 issues-nn's., 8 pgs. each) 1.50 4.50 12.00
Official Boy Scout Outfitter (1946, 9-1/2x6-1/2, 16 pgs.)-B. R. Baker Co. (Scarce) 39.00 117.00 350.00
Shoe Store giveaway (1948, Feb?) 13.00 39.00 105.00
Special Edition-Christmas With Archie 1(1/75)-Treasury (rare) 3.00 9.00 30.00
...Vacation Special 1 (Summer 1994, $2.00, 52 pgs. plus poster) .80 2.00

NOTE: ***Al Fagly*** *c-17-35.* ***Bob Montana*** *c-38, 41-50, 58, Annual 1-4.* ***Bill Woggon*** *c-53, 54.*

ARCHIE COMICS DIGEST (...Magazine No. 37-95)
Aug, 1973 - Present (Small size, 160-128 pgs.)
Archie Publications

1	6.00	18.00	60.00
2	3.00	9.00	30.00
3-5	2.50	7.50	20.00
6-10	1.50	4.50	12.00
11-33: 32,33-The Fly-r by S&K	1.00	2.80	7.00
34-60		2.00	5.00
61-100		1.20	3.00
101-140: 36-Katy Keene story		.70	1.75
141-151			1.79
152-155-($1.95)			1.95

NOTE: ***Neal Adams*** *a-1, 2, 4, 5, 19-21, 24, 25, 27, 29, 31, 33. X-mas c-88, 94, 100, 106.*

ARCHIE COMICS PRESENTS: THE LOVE SHOWDOWN COLLECTION
1994 ($4.95, squarebound)
Archie Publications
nn-r/Archie #429, Betty #19, Betty & Veronica #82, & Veronica #39 1.00 2.00 5.00

ARCHIE GETS A JOB
1977
Spire Christian Comics (Fleming H. Revell Co.)
nn 1.60 4.00

ARCHIE GIANT SERIES MAGAZINE
1954 - No. 632, July, 1992 (No No. 36-135, no No. 252-451)(#1 not code approved)
Archie Publications

1-Archie's Christmas Stocking 100.00 300.00 900.00
2-Archie's Christmas Stocking('55) 61.00 183.00 550.00
3-6-Archie's Christmas Stocking('56- '59) 42.00 126.00 375.00
7-10: 7-Katy Keene Holiday Fun(9/60); Bill Woggon-c. 8-Betty & Veronica Summer Fun(10/60). 9-The World of Jughead (12/60). 10-Archie's Christmas Stocking(1/61) 31.00 94.00 250.00
11,13,16,18: 11-Betty & Veronica Spectacular (6/61). 13-Betty & Veronica Summer Fun (10/61). 16-Betty & Veronica Spectacular (6/62). 18-Betty & Veronica Summer Fun (10/62) 22.00 66.00 175.00
12,14,15,17,19,20: 12-Katy Keene Holiday Fun (9/61). 14-The World of Jughead (12/61). 15-Archie's Christmas Stocking (1/62). 17-Archie's Jokes (9/62); Katy Keene app. 19-The World of Jughead (12/62). 20-Archie's Christmas Stocking (1/63) 11.50 34.50 115.00
21,23,26,28: 21-Betty & Veronica Spectacular (6/63). 23-Betty & Veronica Summer Fun (10/63). 26-Betty & Veronica Spectacular (6/64). 28-Betty & Veronica Summer Fun (9/64) 8.50 25.50 85.00
22,24,25,27,29,30: 22-Archie's Jokes (9/63). 24-The World of Jughead (12/63). 25-Archie's Christmas Stocking (1/64). 27-Archie's Jokes (8/64). 29-Around the World with Archie (10/64). 30-The World of Jughead (12/64) 6.00 18.00 60.00
31-35,136-141: 31-Archie's Christmas Stocking (1/65). 32-Betty & Veronica Spectacular (6/65). 33-Archie's Jokes (8/65). 34-Betty & Veronica Summer Fun (9/65). 35-Around the World with Archie (10/65). 136-The World of Jughead (12/65). 137-Archie's Christmas Stocking (1/66). 138-Betty & Veronica Spectacular (6/66). 139-Archie's Jokes (6/66). 140-Betty & Veronica Summer Fun (8/66). 141-Around the World with Archie (9/66) 4.50 13.50 45.00
142-Archie's Super-Hero Special (10/66)-Origin Capt. Pureheart, Capt. Hero, and Evilheart 4.00 12.00 40.00
143-160: 143-The World of Jughead (12/66). 144-Archie's Christmas Stocking (1/67). 145-Betty & Veronica Spectacular (6/67). 146-Archie's Jokes (6/67). 147-Betty & Veronica Summer Fun (8/67) 148-World of Archie (9/67). 149-World of Jughead (10/67). 150-Archie's Christmas Stocking (1/68). 151-World of Archie (2/68). 152-World of Jughead (2/68). 153-Betty & Veronica Spectacular (6/68). 154-Archie Jokes (6/68). 155-Betty & VeronicaSummer Fun (8/68). 156-World of Archie (10/68). 157-World of Jughead (12/68). 158-Archie's Christmas Stocking (1/69). 159-Betty & Veronica Christmas Spectacular (1/69). 160-World of Archie (2/69) 1.80 5.50 18.00
161-200: 161-World of Jughead (2/69). 162-Betty & Veronica Spectacular (6/69). 163-Archie's Jokes(8/69). 164-Betty & Veronica Summer Fun (9/69). 165-World of Archie (9/69). 166-World of Jughead (9/69). 167-Archie's Christmas Stocking (1/70). 168-Betty & Veronica Christmas Spect. (1/70). 169-Archie's Christmas Love-In (1/70). 170-Jughead's Eat-Out Comic Book Mag. (12/69). 171-World of Archie (2/70). 172-World of Jughead (2/70). 173-Betty & Veronica Spectacular (6/70). 174-Archie's Jokes (8/70). 175-Betty & Veronica Summer Fun (9/70). 176-Li'l Jinx Giant Laugh-Out (8/70). 177-World of Archie (9/70). 178-World of Jughead (9/70). 179-Archie's Christmas Stocking (1/71). 180-Betty & Veronica Christmas Spect. (1/71). 181-Archie's Christmas Love-In (1/71). 182-World of Archie (2/71). 183-World of Jughead (2/71). 184-Betty & Veronica Spectacular (6/71). 185-Li'l Jinx Giant Laugh-Out (6/71). 186-Archie's Jokes (8/71). 187-Betty & Veronica Summer Fun (9/71). 188-World of Archie (9/71). 189-World of Jughead (9/71). 190-Archie's Christmas Stocking (12/71). 191-Betty & Veronica Christmas Spectacular (2/72). 192-Archie's Christmas Love-In (1/72). 193-World of Archie (3/72). 194-World of Jughead (4/72). 195-Li'l Jinx Christmas Bag (1/72). 196-Sabrina's Christmas Magic (1/72). 197-Betty & Veronica Spectacular (6/72). 198-Archie's Jokes (8/72). 199-Betty & Veronica Summer Fun (9/72). 200-World of Archie (10/72) 1.50 4.50 12.00
201-251: 201-Betty & Veronica Spectacular (10/72). 202-World of Jughead (11/72). 203-Archie's Christmas Stocking (12/72). 204-Betty & Veronica Christmas Spectacular (2/73). 205-Archie's Christmas Love-In (1/73). 206-Li'l Jinx Christmas Bag (12/72). 207-Sabrina's Christmas Magic (12/72). 208-World of Archie (3/73). 209-World of Jughead (4/73). 210-Betty & Veronica Spectacular (6/73). 211-Archie's Jokes (8/73). 212-Betty & Veronica Summer Fun (9/73). 213-World of Archie (10/73). 214-Betty & Veronica Spectacular (10/73). 215-World of Jughead (11/73). 216-Archie's Christmas Stocking (12/73). 217-Betty & Veronica Christmas Spectacular (2/74). 218-Archie's Christmas Love-In (1/74). 219-Li'l Jinx Christmas Bag (12/73). 220-Sabrina's Christmas Magic (12/73). 221-Betty & Veronica Spectacular (Advertised as World of Archie) (6/74). 222-Archie's Jokes (advertised as World of Jughead) (8/74). 223-Li'l Jinx (8/74). 224-Betty & Veronica Summer Fun (9/74). 225-World of Archie (9/74). 226-Betty & Veronica Spectacular (10/74). 227-World of Jughead (10/74). 228-Archie's Christmas Stocking (12/74). 229-Betty & Veronica Christmas Spectacular (12/74). 230-Archie's Christmas Love-In (1/75). 231-Sabrina's Christmas Magic (1/75). 232-World of Archie (3/75). 233-World of Jughead (4/75). 234-Betty & Veronica Spectacular (6/75). 235-Archie's Jokes (8/75). 236-Betty & Veronica Summer Fun (9/75). 237-World of Archie (9/75) 238-Betty & Veronica Spectacular (10/75). 239-World of Jughead (10/75). 240-Archie's Christmas Stocking (12/75). 241-Betty & Veronica Christmas Spectacular (12/75). 242-Archie's Christmas Love-In (1/76). 243-Sabrina's Christmas Magic (1/76). 244-World of Archie (3/76). 245-World of Jughead (4/76). 246-Betty & Veronica Spectacular (6/76). 247-Archie's Jokes (8/76). 248-Betty &

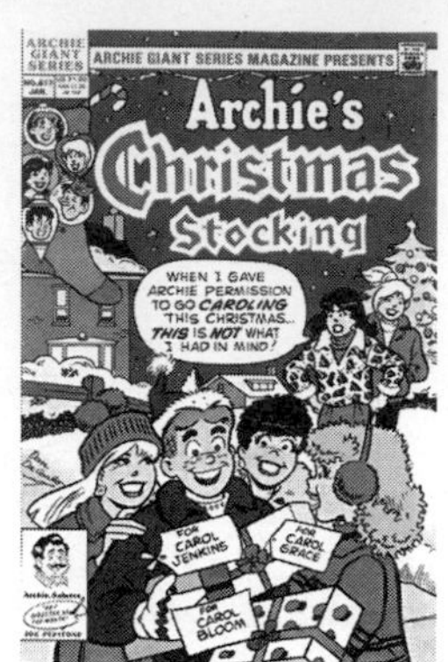

Archie Giant Series #617 © Archie Publ.

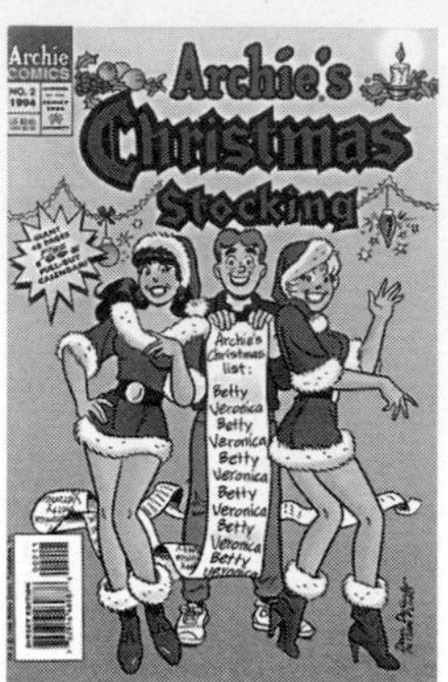

Archie's Christmas Stocking #2 © Archie Publ.

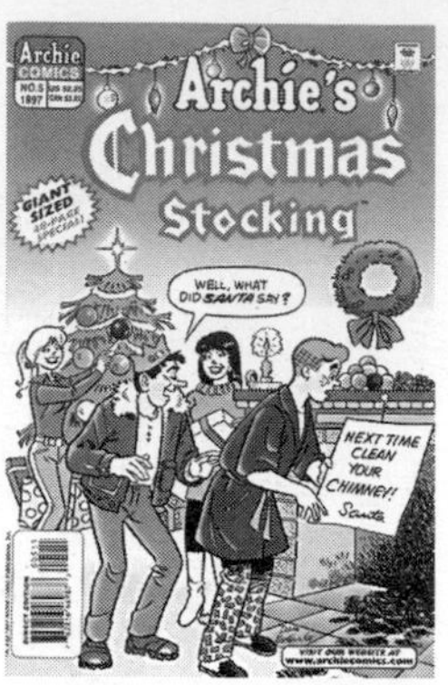

Archie's Christmas Stocking #5 © Archie Publ.

GD25 FN65 NM94

Veronica Summer Fun (9/76). 249-World of Archie (9/76). 250-Betty & Veronica Spectacular (10/76). 251-World of Jughead each.... 2.40 6.00

452-500: 452-Archie's Christmas Stocking (12/76). 453-Betty & Veronica Christmas Spectacular (12/76). 454-Archie's Christmas Love-In (1/77). 455-Sabrina's Christmas Magic (1/77). 456-World of Archie (3/77). 457-World of Jughead (4/77). 458-Betty & Veronica Spectacular (6/77). 459-Archie's Jokes (8/77)-Shows 8/76 in error. 460-Betty & Veronica Summer Fun (9/77). 461-World of Archie (9/77). 462-Betty & Veronica Spectacular (10/77). 463-World of Jughead (10/77). 464-Archie's Christmas Stocking (12/77). 465-Betty & Veronica Christmas Spectacular (12/77). 466-Archie's Christmas Love-In (1/78). 467-Sabrina's Christmas Magic (1/78). 468-World of Archie (2/78). 469-World of Jughead (2/78). 470-Betty & Veronica Spectacular(6/78). 471-Archie's Jokes (8/78). 472-Betty & Veronica Summer Fun (9/78). 473-World of Archie (9/78). 474-Betty & Veronica Spectacular (10/78). 475-World of Jughead (10/78). 476-Archie's Christmas Stocking (12/78). 477-Betty & Veronica Christmas Spectacular (12/78). 478-Archie's Christmas Love-In (1/79). 479-Sabrina Christmas Magic (1/79). 480-The World of Archie (3/79). 481-World of Jughead (4/79). 482-Betty & Veronica Spectacular (6/79). 483-Archie's Jokes (8/79). 484-Betty & Veronica Summer Fun(9/79). 485-The World of Archie (9/79). 486-Betty & Veronica Spectacular(10/79). 487-The World of Jughead (10/79). 488-Archie's Christmas Stocking (12/79). 489-Betty & Veronica Christmas Spectacular (1/80). 490-Archie's Christmas Love-in (1/80). 491-Sabrina's Christmas Magic (1/80).492-The World of Archie (2/80). 493-The World of Jughead (4/80). 494-Betty & Veronica Spectacular (6/80). 495-Archie's Jokes (8/80). 496-Betty & Veronica Summer Fun (9/80). 497-The World of Archie (9/80). 498-Betty & Veronica Spectacular (10/80). 499-The World of Jughead (10/80). 500-Archie's Christmas Stocking (12/80) each... 1.60 4.00

501-550: 501-Betty & Veronica Christmas Spectacular (12/80). 502-Archie's Christmas Love-in (1/81). 503-Sabrina Christmas Magic (1/81). 504-The World of Archie (3/81). 505-The World of Jughead (4/81). 506-Betty & Veronica Spectacular (6/81). 507-Archie's Jokes (8/81). 508-Betty & Veronica Summer Fun (9/81). 509-The World of Archie (9/81). 510-Betty & Vernonica Spectacular (9/81). 511-The World of Jughead (10/81). 512-Archie's Christmas Stocking (12/81). 513-Betty & Veronica Christmas Spectacular (12/81). 514-Archie's Christmas Love-in (1/82). 515-Sabrina's Christmas Magic (1/82). 516-The World of Archie (3/82). 517-The World of Jughead (4/82). 518-Betty & Veronica Spectacular (6/82). 519-Archie's Jokes (8/82). 520-Betty & Veronica Summer Fun (9/82). 521-The World of Archie (9/82). 522-Betty & Veronica Spectacular (10/82). 523-The World of Jughead (10/82). 524-Archie's Christmas Stocking (1/83). 525-Betty and Veronica Christmas Spectacular (1/83). 526-Betty and Veronica Spectacular (5/83). 527-Little Archie (8/83). 528-Josie and the Pussycats (8/83). 529-Betty and Veronica Summer Fun (8/83). 530-Betty and Veronica Spectacular (9/83). 531-The World of Jughead (9/83). 532-The World of Archie (10/83). 533-Space Pirates by Frank Bolling (10/83). 534-Little Archie (1/84). 535-Archie's Christmas Stocking (1/84). 536-Betty and Veronica Christmas Spectacular (1/84). 537-Betty and Veronica Spectacular (6/84). 538-Little Archie (8/84). 539-Betty and Veronica Summer Fun (8/84). 540-Josie and the Pussycats (8/84). 541-Betty and Veronica Spectacular (9/84). 542-The World of Jughead (9/84). 543-The World of Archie (10/84). 544-Sabrina the Teen-Age Witch (10/84). 545-Little Archie (12/84). 546-Archie's Christmas Stocking (12/84). 547-Betty and Veronica Christmas Spectacular (12/84). 548-? 549-Little Archie. 550-Betty and Veronica Summer Fun each... 1.20 3.00

551-600: 551-Josie and the Pussycats. 552-Betty and Veronica Spectacular. 553-The World of Jughead. 554-The World of Archie. 555-Betty's Diary. 556-Little Archie (1/86). 557-Archie's Christmas Stocking (1/86). 558-Betty & Veronica Christmas Spectacular (1/86). 559-Betty & Veronica Spectacular. 560-Little Archie. 561-Betty & Veronica Summer Fun. 562-Josie and the Pussycats. 563-Betty & Veronica Spectacular. 564-World of Jughead. 565-World of Archie. 566-Little Archie. 567-Archie's Christmas Stocking. 568-Betty & Veronica Christmas Spectacular. 569-Betty & Veronica Spring Spectacular. 570-Little Archie. 571-Josie & the Pussycats. 572-Betty & Veronica Summer Fun. 573-Archie At Riverdale High. 574-World of Archie. 575-Betty & Veronica Spectacular. 576-Pep. 577-World of Jughead. 578-Archie And Me. 579-Archie's Christmas Stocking. 580-Betty and Veronica Christmas Spectacular. 581-Little Archie Christmas Special. 582-Betty & Veronica Spring Spectacular. 583-Little Archie. 584-Josie and the Pussycats. 585-Betty & Veronica Summer Fun. 586-Archie At Riverdale High. 587-The World of Archie (10/88); 1st app. Explorers of the Unknown. 588-Betty & Veronica Spectacular. 589-Pep (10/88). 590-The World of Jughead. 591-Archie & Me. 592-Archie's Christmas Stocking. 593-Betty & Veronica Christmas Spectacular. 594-Little Archie. 595-Betty & Veronica Spring Spectacular. 596-Little Archie. 597-Josie and the Pussycats. 598-Betty & Veronica Summer Fun. 599-The World of Archie (10/89); 2nd app. Explorers of the Unknown. 600-Betty and Veronica Spectacular each.... 1.00 2.50

601-632: 601-Pep. 602-The World of Jughead. 603-Archie and Me. 604-Archie at Riverdale High. 605-Archie's Christmas Stocking. 606-Betty and Veronica Christmas Spectacular. 607-Little Archie. 608-Betty and Veronica Spectacular. 609-Little Archie. 610-Josie and the Pussycats. 611-Betty and Veronica Summer Fun. 612-The World of Archie. 613-Betty and Veronica Spectacular. 614-Pep (10/90). 615-Veronica's Summer Special. 616-Archie and Me. 617-Archie's Christmas Stocking. 618-Betty & Veronica Christmas Spectacular. 619-Little Archie. 620-Betty and Veronica Spectacular. 621-Betty and Veronica Summer Fun. 622-Josie & the Pussycats; not published. 623-Betty and Veronica Spectacular. 624-Pep Comics. 625-Veronica's Summer Special. 626-Archie and Me. 627-World of Archie. 628-Archie's Pals 'n' Gals Holiday Special. 629-Betty & Veronica Christmas Spectacular. 630-Archie's Christmas Stocking. 631-Archie's Pals 'n' Gals. 632-Betty & Veronica spectacular each.... .80 2.00

ARCHIE MEETS THE PUNISHER (Same contents as The Punisher Meets Archie)
Aug, 1994 ($2.95, 52 pgs., one-shot)
Marvel Comics & Archie Comics Publications

1-Batton Lash story, J. Buscema-a on Punisher, S. Goldberg-a on Archie 1.20 3.00

ARCHIE'S ACTIVITY COMICS DIGEST MAGAZINE
1985 - No. 4? (Annual, 128 pgs., digest size)
Archie Enterprises

1 2.40 6.00
3-4 2.00 5.00

ARCHIE'S CAR
1979 (49¢)
Spire Christian Comics (Fleming H. Revell co.)

nn 1.60 4.00

ARCHIE'S CHRISTMAS LOVE-IN (See Archie Giant Series Mag. No. 169, 181,192, 205, 218, 230, 242, 454, 466, 478, 490, 502, 514)

ARCHIE'S CHRISTMAS STOCKING (See Archie Giant Series Mag. No. 1-6,10, 15, 20, 25, 31, 137, 144, 150, 158, 167, 179, 190, 203, 216, 228, 240, 452, 464, 476, 488, 500, 512, 524, 535, 546, 557, 567, 579, 592, 605, 617, 630)

ARCHIE'S CHRISTMAS STOCKING
1993 -Present ($2.00, 52 pgs.)(Bound-in calendar poster in all)
Archie Comics

1-5: 1-Dan DeCarlo-c/a 1.20 3.00

ARCHIE'S CLEAN SLATE
1973 (35/49¢)
Spire Christian Comics (Fleming H. Revell Co.)

1(Some issues have nn) 1.60 4.00

ARCHIE'S DATE BOOK
1981
Spire Christian comics (Fleming H. Revell co.)

Archie's Double Digest #66 © Archie Publ.

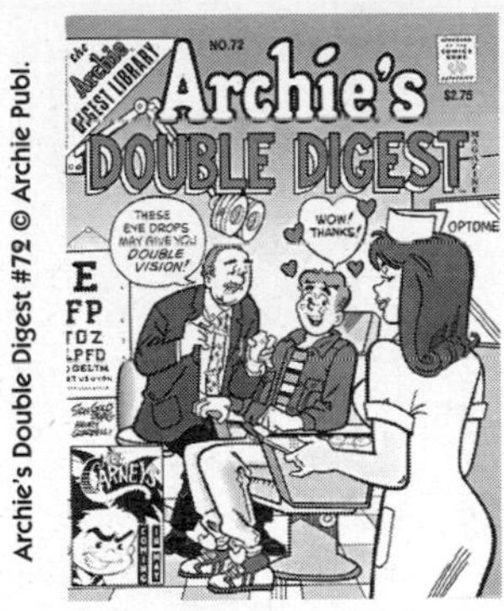

Archie's Double Digest #72 © Archie Publ.

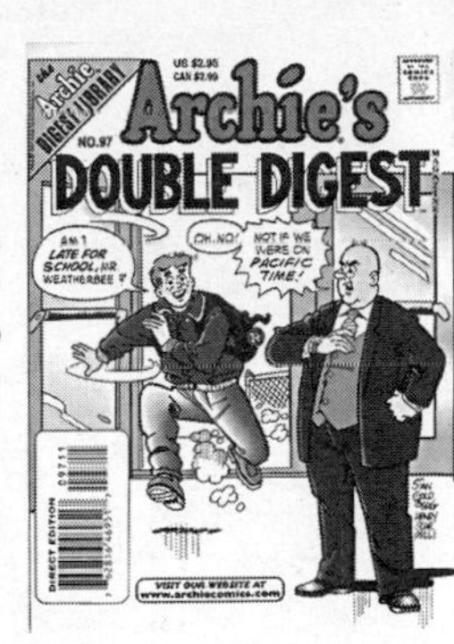

Archie's Double Digest #97 © Archie Publ.

	GD25	FN65	NM94
nn		1.60	4.00

ARCHIE'S DOUBLE DIGEST QUARTERLY MAGAZINE
1981 - Present ($1.95/$2.75/$2.95, 256pgs.) (A.D.D. Magazine No. 10 on)
Archie Comics

	GD25	FN65	NM94
1	1.50	4.50	12.00
2-10; 6-Katy Keene story.	1.10	3.30	9.00
11-30: 29-Pureheart story	1.00	2.80	7.00
31-50		2.00	5.00
51-105		1.20	3.00

ARCHIE'S FAMILY ALBUM
1978 (39¢, 36 pgs.)
Spire Christian Comics (Fleming H. Revell Co.)

	GD25	FN65	NM94
nn		1.60	4.00

ARCHIE'S FESTIVAL
1980 (49¢)
Spire Christian Comics (Fleming H. Revell Co.)

	GD25	FN65	NM94
nn		1.60	4.00

ARCHIE'S GIRLS, BETTY AND VERONICA (Becomes Betty & Veronica)(Also see Veronica)
1950 - No. 347, Apr, 1987
Archie Publications (Close-Up)

	GD25	FN65	NM94
1	131.00	393.00	1175.00
2	63.00	189.00	565.00
3-5	38.00	113.00	340.00
6-10: 6-Dan DeCarlo's 1st Archie work; Betty's 1st ponytail. 10-Katy Keene app. (2 pgs.)	33.00	100.00	265.00
11-20: 11,13,14,17-19-Katy Keene app. 17-Last pre-code issue (3/55). 20-Debbie's Diary (2 pgs.)	24.00	71.00	190.00
21-30: 27,30-Katy Keene app.	16.00	49.00	130.00
31-50: 44-Elvis Presley 1 pg. photo & bio. 45-Fabian 1 pg. photo & bio. 46-Bobby Darin 1 pg. photo & bio	10.00	30.00	80.00
51-74: 73-Sci-fi-c	6.00	18.00	60.00
75-Betty & Veronica sell souls to Devil	10.50	32.00	105.00
76-99: Bobby Rydell 1 pg. illustrated bio	3.00	9.00	30.00
100	4.00	12.00	40.00
101-117,119,120: 119-Last Superteen story	2.25	6.75	18.00
118-Origin Superteen (see Betty & Me #3)	2.50	7.50	24.00
121-140	1.50	4.50	12.00
141-180	1.10	3.30	9.00
181-220		2.40	6.00
221-299		1.60	4.00
300-Anniversary issue		2.00	5.00
301-347		.80	2.00
Annual 1 (1953)	75.00	225.00	675.00
Annual 2(1954)	36.00	108.00	315.00
Annual 3-5 (1955-1957)	29.00	86.00	230.00
Annual 6-8 (1958-1960)	19.00	56.00	150.00

ARCHIE SHOE-STORE GIVEAWAY
1944-49 (12-15 pgs. of games, puzzles, stories like Superman-Tim books, No nos. - came out monthly)
Archie Publications

	GD25	FN65	NM94
(1944-47)-issues	10.50	32.00	85.00
2/48-Peggy Lee photo-c	8.75	26.25	65.00
3/48-Marylee Robb photo-c	8.50	26.00	60.00
4/48-Gloria De Haven photo-c	8.50	26.00	60.00
5/48,6/48,7/48	8.50	26.00	60.00
8/48-Story on Shirley Temple	8.75	26.25	65.00
10/48-Archie as Wolf on cover	8.75	26.25	70.00
5/49-Kathleen Hughes photo-c	6.50	19.50	45.00
7/49	6.50	19.50	45.00
8/49-Archie photo-c from radio show	10.00	30.00	80.00
10/49-Gloria Mann photo-c from radio show	8.75	26.25	65.00
11/49,12/49	6.50	19.50	45.00

ARCHIE'S HOLIDAY FUN DIGEST
1997 - Present ($1.75/$1.95, annual)
Archie Comics

	GD25	FN65	NM94
1,2-Christmas stories			1.95

ARCHIE'S JOKEBOOK COMICS DIGEST ANNUAL (See Jokebook...)

ARCHIE'S JOKE BOOK MAGAZINE (See Joke Book ...)
1953 - No. 3, Sum, 1954; No. 15, Fall, 1954 - No. 288, 11/82
Archie Publications

	GD25	FN65	NM94
1953-One Shot (#1)	69.00	207.00	625.00
2	38.00	113.00	340.00
3 (no #4-14)	32.00	96.00	255.00
15-20: 15-Formerly Archie's Rival Reggie #14; last pre-code issue (Fall/54). 15-17-Katy Keene app.	19.00	56.00	150.00
21-30	10.50	32.00	85.00
31-40,42,43: 43-story about guitarist Duane Eddy	7.85	23.50	55.00
41-1st professional comic work by Neal Adams (9/59), 1 pg.	18.00	54.00	145.00
44-47-N. Adams-a in all, 1-3 pgs.	9.50	28.00	75.00
48-Four pgs. N. Adams-a	10.00	30.00	80.00
49-60 (1962)	2.00	6.00	20.00
61-80	1.20	3.60	12.00
81-100	1.10	3.30	9.00
101-140	1.00	2.80	7.00
141-200		2.00	5.00
201-288		1.20	3.00
Drug Store Giveaway (No. 39 w/new-c)	4.00	10.00	20.00

ARCHIE'S JOKES (See Archie Giant Series Mag. No. 17, 22, 27, 33, 139, 146, 154, 163, 174, 186, 198, 211, 222, 235, 247, 459, 471, 483, 495, 519)

ARCHIE'S LOVE SCENE
1973 (35¢/49¢)
Spire Christian Comics (Fleming H. Revell Co.)

	GD25	FN65	NM94
1(Some copies have nn)		1.60	4.00

ARCHIE'S MADHOUSE (Madhouse Ma-ad No. 67 on)
Sept, 1959 - No. 66, Feb, 1969
Archie Publications

	GD25	FN65	NM94
1-Archie begins	21.00	63.00	210.00
2	10.50	32.00	105.00
3-5	7.00	21.00	70.00
6-10	5.00	15.00	50.00
11-17 (Last w/regular characters)	3.20	9.60	32.00
18-21,23-30 (New format): 25-1st app. Captain Sprocket (4/63)	2.50	7.50	20.00
22-1st app. Sabrina, the Teen-age Witch (10/62)	9.50	28.50	95.00
31-34,36-40: 34-Bordered-c begin.	1.50	4.50	12.00
35-Beatles cameo	2.25	6.75	18.00
41-66: 43-Mighty Crusaders cameo. 44-Swipes Mad #4 (Super-Duperman) in "Bird Monsters From Outer Space"	1.00	3.00	8.00
Annual 1 (1962-63)	5.50	16.50	55.00
Annual 2 (1964)	3.40	10.20	34.00
Annual 3 (1965)-Origin Sabrina the Teen-Age Witch	2.50	7.50	24.00
Annual 4-6('66-69)(Becomes Madhouse Ma-ad Annual #7 on)	1.75	5.25	14.00

NOTE: *Cover title to 61-65 is "Madhouse" and to 66 is "Madhouse Ma-ad Jokes".*

ARCHIE'S MECHANICS
Sept, 1954 - No. 3, 1955
Archie Publications

	GD25	FN65	NM94
1-(15¢; 52 pgs.)	67.00	200.00	600.00
2-(10¢)-Last pre-code issue	41.00	123.00	365.00
3-(10¢)	38.00	114.00	300.00

Archie's Pal Jughead #2 © Archie Publ.

Archie's Pal Jughead #57 © Archie Publ.

Archie's RC Racers #3 © Archie Publ.

ARCHIE'S ONE WAY
1972 (35/49¢, 36 pgs.)
Spire Christian Comics (Fleming H. Revell Co.)

	GD25	FN65	NM94
nn		1.60	4.00

ARCHIE'S PAL, JUGHEAD (Jughead No. 122 on)
1949 - No. 126, Nov, 1965
Archie Publications

	GD25	FN65	NM94
1 (1949)-1st app. Moose (see Pep #33)	97.00	291.00	875.00
2 (1950)	50.00	150.00	450.00
3-5	34.00	103.00	275.00
6-10: 7-Suzie app.	23.00	69.00	185.00
11-20	14.50	43.00	115.00
21-30: 23-25,28-30-Katy Keene app. 28-Debbie's Diary app.	9.50	28.00	75.00
31-50	4.00	12.00	40.00
51-70	2.50	7.50	25.00
71-100	1.40	4.20	14.00
101-126	1.25	3.75	10.00
Annual 1 (1953, 25¢)	46.00	138.00	415.00
Annual 2 (1954, 25¢)-Last pre-code issue	33.00	98.00	260.00
Annual 3-5 (1955-57, 25¢)	23.00	68.00	180.00
Annual 6-8 (1958-60, 25¢)	14.00	41.00	110.00

ARCHIE'S PAL JUGHEAD COMICS (Formerly Jughead #1-45)
No. 46, June, 1993 - Present ($1.25/$1.50/$1.75)
Archie Comic Publications

	GD25	FN65	NM94
46-64			1.25
65-99			1.50
100-108- ($1.75): 100-"A Storm Over Uniforms" x-over part 1,2			1.75

ARCHIE'S PALS 'N' GALS (Also see Archie Giant Series Magazine #628)
1952-53 - No. 6, 1957-58; No. 7, 1958 - No. 224, Sept, 1991
Archie Publications

	GD25	FN65	NM94
1-(116 pgs., 25¢)	58.00	174.00	525.00
2(Annual)('54, 25¢)	35.00	105.00	285.00
3-5(Annual, '55-57, 25¢): 3-Last pre-code issue	25.00	75.00	200.00
6-10('58-'60)	14.50	43.00	115.00
11-20: 12-Harry Belafonte 2 pg. photo & bio	6.50	19.50	45.00
21-28,30-40	2.20	6.60	22.00
29-Beatles satire	4.20	12.60	42.00
41-60	1.50	4.50	12.00
61-80	1.10	3.30	9.00
81-110		2.40	6.00
111-140		1.60	4.00
141-180		1.20	3.00
181-224: Later issues $1.00 cover. 197-G. Colan-a			2.00

ARCHIE'S PALS 'N' GALS DOUBLE DIGEST MAGAZINE
Nov, 1992 - Present ($2.50/$2.75/$2.95)
Archie Comic Publications

	GD25	FN65	NM94
1-3: 1-Capt. Hero story; Pureheart app. 2-Superduck story; Little Jinx in all		2.00	5.00
4-29: 4-Begin $2.75-c.		1.40	3.50
30-35-($2.95)			2.95

ARCHIE'S PARABLES
1973, 1975 (39/49¢, 36 pgs.)
Spire Christian Comics (Fleming H. Revell Co.)

	GD25	FN65	NM94
nn-By Al Hartley		1.60	4.00

ARCHIE'S R/C RACERS
Sept, 1989 - No. 10, Mar, 1991 (.95-$1)
Archie Comics

	GD25	FN65	NM94
1		1.20	3.00
2-10: Radio contol cars		.80	2.00

ARCHIE'S RIVAL REGGIE (Reggie & Archie's Joke Book #15 on)
1950 - No. 14, Aug, 1954
Archie Publications

	GD25	FN65	NM94
1-Reggie 1st app. in Jackpot Comics #5	61.00	183.00	550.00
2	34.00	103.00	275.00
3-5	24.00	71.00	190.00
6-10	17.00	51.00	135.00
11-14: Katy Keene in No. 10-14, 1-2 pgs.	12.00	38.00	100.00

ARCHIE'S RIVERDALE HIGH (See Riverdale High)

ARCHIE'S ROLLER COASTER
1981 (69¢)
Spire Christian Comics (Fleming H. Revell Co.)

	GD25	FN65	NM94
nn		1.60	4.00

ARCHIE'S SOMETHING ELSE
1975 (39/49¢, 36 pgs.)
Spire Christian Comics (Fleming H. Revell Co.)

	GD25	FN65	NM94
nn		1.60	4.00

ARCHIE'S SONSHINE
1973, 1974 (39/49¢, 36 pgs.)
Spire Christian Comics (Fleming H. Revell Co.)

	GD25	FN65	NM94
nn		1.60	4.00

ARCHIE'S SPORTS SCENE
1983
Spire Christian Comics (Fleming H. Revell Co.)

	GD25	FN65	NM94
nn		1.60	4.00

ARCHIE'S SPRING BREAK
1996 ($2.00, 48 pgs.)
Archie Comics

	GD25	FN65	NM94
1-Dan DeCarlo-c		.80	2.00

ARCHIE'S STORY & GAME COMICS DIGEST MAGAZINE
Nov, 1986 - Present ($1.25/$1.35/$1.50/$1.95, 128 pgs., digest-size)
Archie Enterprises

	GD25	FN65	NM94
1 1.	1.10	3.30	9.00
2-10		2.40	6.00
11-20		1.60	4.00
21-38		1.00	2.50
39-42-($1.95)			1.95

ARCHIE'S SUPER HERO SPECIAL (See Archie Giant Series Mag. No. 142)

ARCHIE'S SUPER HERO SPECIAL (...Comics Digest Mag. 2)
Jan, 1979 - No. 2, Aug, 1979 (95¢, 148 pgs.)
Archie Publications (Red Circle)

	GD25	FN65	NM94
1-Simon & Kirby r-/Double Life of Pvt. Strong #1,2; Black Hood, The Fly, Jaguar, The Web app.	1.25	3.75	10.00
2-Contains contents to the never published Black Hood #1; origin Black Hood; N. Adams, Wood, McWilliams, Morrow, S&K-a(r); N. Adams-c. The Shield, The Fly, Jaguar, Hangman, Steel Sterling, The Web, The Fox-r	1.00	2.80	7.00

ARCHIE'S SUPER TEENS
1994 - No. 3, 1994 ($2.00, 52 pgs.)
Archie Comic Publications, Inc.

	GD25	FN65	NM94
1-3: 1-Staton/Esposito-c/a; pull-out poster. 2-Fred Hembeck script; Bret Blevins/Terry Austin-a		.80	2.00

ARCHIE'S TV LAUGH-OUT
Dec, 1969 - No. 106, Apr, 1986
Archie Publications

	GD25	FN65	NM94
1	4.50	13.50	45.00
2	2.50	7.50	20.00
3-5	1.50	4.50	12.00

Archie 3000 #9 © Archie Publ.

Armageddon 2001 #2 © DC

Armorines #6 © Voyager Comm.

	GD25	FN65	NM94
6-10	1.00	3.00	8.00
11-20		2.40	6.00
21-50		1.60	4.00
51-106			2.00

ARCHIE'S VACATION SPECIAL
Winter, 1994? - Present ($2.00, annually)
Archie Publications

	GD25	FN65	NM94
1-5		.80	2.00

ARCHIE'S WORLD
1973, 1976 (39/49¢)
Spire Christian Comics (Fleming H. Revell Co.)

	GD25	FN65	NM94
nn		1.60	4.00

ARCHIE 3000
May, 1989 - No. 16, July, 1991 (75¢/95¢/$1.00)
Archie Comics

	GD25	FN65	NM94
1-		1.20	3.00
2-16: 6-Begin $1.00-c, X-Mas-c		.80	2.00

ARCOMICS PREMIERE
July, 1993 ($2.95)
Arcomics

	GD25	FN65	NM94
1-1st lenticular-c on a comic (flicker-c)		1.20	3.00

AREA 88
May 26, 1987 - No. 42, 1989 ($1.50/$1.75, B&W)
Eclipse Comics/VIZ Comics #37 on

	GD25	FN65	NM94
1-36: 1,2-2nd printings exist			1.50
37-42: 37-Begin $1.75-c		.70	1.80

ARENA (Also see Marvel Graphic Novel)
Jan, 1990 ($1.50, 7x10-1/8", 20 pgs.)
Alchemy Studios

	GD25	FN65	NM94
1-Science fiction			1.50
1-Signed & numbered ed. (500 copies)		1.20	2.95

ARGUS (See Flash, 2nd Series) (Also see Showcase '95 #1,2)
Apr, 1995 - No. 6, Oct, 1995 ($1.50, limited series)
DC Comics

	GD25	FN65	NM94
1-3			1.50
4-6: 4-Begin $1.75-c		.70	1.75

ARIANE AND BLUEBEARD (See Night Music #8)

ARIEL & SEBASTIAN (See Cartoon Tales & The Little Mermaid)

ARION, LORD OF ATLANTIS (Also see Warlord #55)
Nov, 1982 - No. 35, Sept, 1985
DC Comics

	GD25	FN65	NM94
1-35: 1-Story cont'd from Warlord #62			1.00
Special #1 (11/85)			1.00

ARION THE IMMORTAL (Also see Showcase '95 #7)
July, 1992 - No. 6, Dec, 1992 ($1.50, limited series)
DC Comics

	GD25	FN65	NM94
1-6: 4-Gustovich-a(i)			1.50

ARISTOCATS (See Movie Comics & Walt Disney Showcase No. 16)

ARISTOKITTENS, THE (...Meet Jiminy Cricket No. 1)(Disney)
Oct, 1971 - No. 9, Oct, 1975
Gold Key

	GD25	FN65	NM94
1	1.80	5.50	20.00
2-9: 6-52 pgs.	1.10	3.30	12.00

ARIZONA KID, THE (Also see The Comics & Wild Western)
Mar, 1951 - No. 6, Jan, 1952
Marvel/Atlas Comics(CSI)

	GD25	FN65	NM94
1	17.50	53.00	140.00
2-4: 2-Heath-a(3)	8.75	26.25	70.00
5,6	8.75	26.25	65.00

NOTE: ***Heath*** *a-1-3; c-1-3.* ***Maneely*** *c-4-6.* ***Morisi*** *a-4-6.* ***Sinnott*** *a-6.*

ARK, THE (See The Crusaders)

ARKAGA
Sept, 1997 - Present ($2.95)
Image Comics

	GD25	FN65	NM94
1-Jorgensen-s/a		1.20	3.00

ARMAGEDDON: ALIEN AGENDA
Nov, 1991 - No. 4, Feb, 1992 ($1.00, limited series)
DC Comics

	GD25	FN65	NM94
1-4			1.00

ARMAGEDDON FACTOR, THE
1987 - No. 2, 1987; No. 3, 1990 ($1.95)
AC Comics

	GD25	FN65	NM94
1,2: Sentinels of Justice, Dragonfly, Femforce		.80	2.00
3-($3.95, color)-Almost all AC characters app.		1.60	4.00

ARMAGEDDON: INFERNO
Apr, 1992 - No. 4, July, 1992 ($1.00, limited series)
DC Comics

	GD25	FN65	NM94
1-4: Many DC heroes app. 3-A. Adams/Austin-a			1.00

ARMAGEDDON 2001
May, 1991 - No. 2, Oct, 1991 ($2.00, squarebound, 68 pgs.)
DC Comics

	GD25	FN65	NM94
1-Features many DC heroes; intro Waverider		1.00	2.50
1-2nd & 3rd printings; 3rd has silver ink-c		.70	1.75
2		1.00	2.50

ARMATURE
Nov, 1996 - No. 2, ($2.95, limited series)
Olyoptics

	GD25	FN65	NM94
1,2-Steve Oliff-c/s/a; Maxx app.		1.20	3.00

ARMED & DANGEROUS
Apr, 1996 - No.4, July, 1996 ($2.95, B&W, limited series)
Acclaim Comics (Armada)

	GD25	FN65	NM94
1-4-Bob Hall-c/a & scripts		1.20	3.00
Special 1 (8/96, $2.95, B&W)-Hall-c/a & scripts.		1.20	3.00

ARMED & DANGEROUS HELL'S SLAUGHTERHOUSE
Oct, 1996 - No. 4, Jan, 1997 ($2.95, B&W, limited series)
Acclaim Comics (Armada)

	GD25	FN65	NM94
1-4: Hall-c/a/scripts.		1.20	3.00

ARMOR (AND THE SILVER STREAK)
Sept, 1985 - No.7, Mar, 1986 ($2.00)
Continuity Comics

	GD25	FN65	NM94
1-7: 1-Intro/origin Armor & the Silver Streak; Neal Adams-c/a. 7-Origin Armor; Nebres-i		.80	2.00

ARMORED TROOPER VOTOMS (Manga)
July, 1996 ($2.95)
CPM Comics

	GD25	FN65	NM94
1		1.20	3.00

ARMORINES (See X-O Manowar #25)
June, 1994 - No. 12, June, 1995 ($2.25)
Valiant

	GD25	FN65	NM94
1-12: 7-Wraparound-c. 12-Byrne-c/swipe (X-Men, 1st Series #138)		.90	2.25

ARMY AND NAVY COMICS (Supersnipe No. 6 on)
May, 1941 - No. 5, July, 1942

Army of Darkness #1 © DH

Arrow #3 © CEN

Artemis: Requiem #3 © DC

GD25 FN65 NM94

Street & Smith Publications
1-Cap Fury & Nick Carter 40.00 120.00 365.00
2-Cap Fury & Nick Carter 25.00 75.00 200.00
3,4 17.00 51.00 135.00
5-Supersnipe app.; see Shadow V2#3 for 1st app.; Story of Douglas MacArthur; George Marcoux-c/a 40.00 120.00 360.00

ARMY ATTACK
July, 1964 - No. 4, Feb, 1965; V2#38, July, 1965 - No. 47, Feb, 1967
Charlton Comics
V1#1 3.00 9.00 30.00
2-4(2/65) 1.85 5.50 15.00
V2#38(7/65)-47 (formerly U.S. Air Force #1-37) 1.85 5.50 15.00
NOTE: ***Glanzman*** *a-1-3.* ***Montes/Bache*** *a-44.*

ARMY AT WAR (Also see Our Army at War & Cancelled Comic Cavalcade)
Oct-Nov, 1978
DC Comics
1-Kubert-c 1.60 4.00

ARMY OF DARKNESS (Movie)
Nov, 1992 - No. 2, Dec, 1992; No. 3, Oct, 1993 ($2.50, limited series)
Dark Horse Comics
1-3-Bolton painted-c/a 1.00 2.50

ARMY SURPLUS KOMIKZ FEATURING CUTEY BUNNY
1982 - No. 5, 1985 ($1.50, B&W)
Army Surplus Komikz/Eclipse Comics No. 5
1-Cutey Bunny begins .80 2.00
2-5: 5-JLA/X-Men/Batman parody 1.50

ARMY WAR HEROES (Also see Iron Corporal)
Dec, 1963 - No. 38, June, 1970
Charlton Comics
1 3.00 9.00 30.00
2-10 2.50 7.50 20.00
11-30: 22-Origin & 1st app. Iron Corporal series by Glanzman. 24-Intro. Archer & Corp. Jack series 1.85 5.50 15.00
31-38: 1.25 3.75 10.00
Modern Comics Reprint 36 ('78) 1.60 4.00
NOTE: ***Montes/Bache*** *a-1, 16, 17, 21, 23-25, 27-30.*

AROUND THE BLOCK WITH DUNC & LOO (See Dunc and Loo)

AROUND THE WORLD IN 80 DAYS (Movie) (See A Golden Picture Classic)
Feb, 1957
Dell Publishing Co.
Four Color 784-Photo-c 5.75 17.00 63.00

AROUND THE WORLD UNDER THE SEA (See Movie Classics)

AROUND THE WORLD WITH ARCHIE (See Archie Giant Series Mag. #29, 35, 141)

AROUND THE WORLD WITH HUCKLEBERRY & HIS FRIENDS (See Dell Giant No. 44)

ARRGH! (Satire)
Dec, 1974 - No. 5, Sept, 1975 (25¢)
Marvel Comics Group
1 1.50 4.50 12.00
2-5 1.10 3.30 9.00
NOTE ***Alcala*** *a-2; c-3.* ***Everett*** *a-1r, 2r.* ***Maneely*** *a-4r.* ***Sekowsky*** *a-1p.* ***Sutton*** *a-1, 2.*

ARROW, THE (See Funny Pages)
Oct, 1940 - No. 2, Nov, 1940; No. 3, Oct, 1941
Centaur Publications
1-The Arrow begins(r/Funny Pages) 233.00 700.00 2100.00
2,3: 2-Tippy Taylor serial continues from Amazing Mystery Funnies #24. 3-Origin Dash Dartwell, the Human Meteor; origin The Rainbow-r; bondage-c 97.00 291.00 875.00

NOTE: ***Gustavson*** *a-1, 2; c-3.*

ARROWHEAD (See Black Rider and Wild Western)
April, 1954 - No. 4, Nov, 1954
Atlas Comics (CPS)
1-Arrowhead & his horse Eagle begin 12.00 36.00 95.00
2-4: 4-Forte-a 8.50 26.00 60.00
NOTE: ***Heath*** *c-3.* ***Jack Katz*** *a-3.* ***Maneely*** *c-2.* ***Pakula*** *a-2.* ***Sinnott*** *a-1-4; c-1.*

ARSENAL SPECIAL (See New Titans, Showcase '94 #7 & Showcase '95 #8)
1996 ($2.95, one-shot)
DC Comics
1 1.20 3.00

ARTBABE
May, 1997 - Present ($2.95, B&W)
Fantagraphics Books
1 2.95

ARTEMIS: REQUIEM (Also see Wonder Woman, 2nd Series #90)
June, 1996 - No. 6, Nov, 1996 ($1.75, limited series)
DC Comics
1-6: Messner-Loebs scripts & Ed Benes-c/a in all. 1,2-Wonder Woman app. .70 1.75

ART OF ZEN INTERGALACTIC NINJA, THE
1994 - No. 2, 1994 ($2.95)
Entity Comics
1,2 1.20 3.00

ARZACH (See Moebius...)
1996 ($6.95, one-shot)
Dark Horse Comics
nn-Moebius-c/a/scripts 1.00 2.80 7.00

ASCENSION
Oct, 1997 - Present ($2.50)
Image Comics (Top Cow Productions)
1-David Finch-s/a(p)/Batt-s/a(i) 1.20 3.00
2,3 1.00 2.50

ASH
Nov, 1994 - No. 6, Dec, 1995; No. 0, May, 1996 ($2.50/$3.00)
Event Comics
0-(5/96, $3.00)-Present foil logo-c; w/pin-ups 1.20 3.00
0-(5/96, $3.00)-Future foil logo-c; w/pin-ups 1.20 3.00
0-Present Blue Foil logo-c (1000) 8.00
0-Future Blue Foil logo-c (1000) 8.00
0-Present Silver Prism logo-c (500) 18.00
0-Future Silver Prism logo-c (500) 18.00
0-Present Red Prism logo-c (250) 27.00
0-Future Red Prism logo-c (250) 27.00
0-Present Gold Hologram logo-c (1000) 15.00
0-Future Gold Hologram logo-c (1000) 15.00
1-Quesada-p/story; Palmiotti-i/story: Barry Windsor-Smith pin-up 2.15 6.50 11.00
2-Mignola Hellboy pin-up 1.65 4.20 7.00
3,4: 3-Big Guy pin-up by Geoff Darrow. 4-Jim Lee pin-up 1.30 3.25 5.00
4-Fahrenheit Gold 2.40 7.20 12.00
4-Fahrenheit Red 2.85 8.50 15.00
4-Fahrenheit White 4.30 13.00 21.00
5, 6-Double-c w/Hildebrandt Bros.-a, Quesada & Palmiotti. 6-Texiera-c 1.60 3.00
5-Fahrenheit Gold (2000) 8.00
5-Fahrenheit Red (1000) 12.00
5-Fahrenheit White (500) 20.00

Ash: Cinder & Smoke #6 © Quesada & Palmiotti

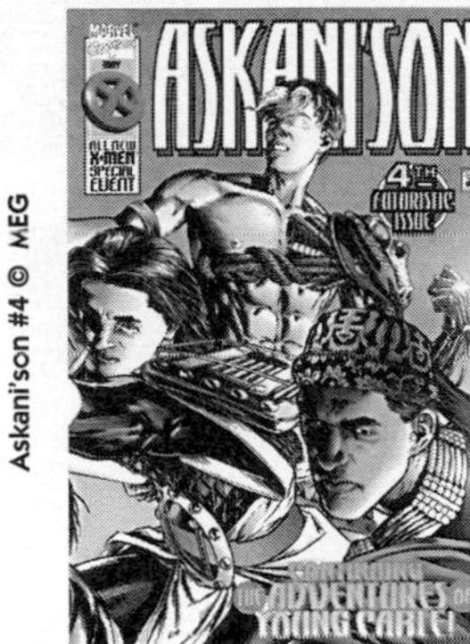

Askani'son #4 © MEG

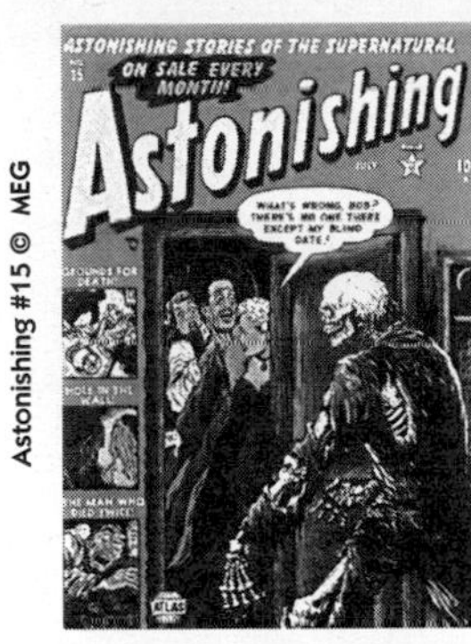

Astonishing #15 © MEG

GD25 FN65 NM94

6-Fahrenheit Gold (2000) 8.00
6-Fahrenheit Red (1000) 12.00
6-Fahrenheit White (500) 20.00
6-Fahrenheit White (500)-Texiera-c 20.00
Volume 1 (1996, $14.95, TPB)-r/#1-5, intro by James Robinson. 11.00

ASH: CINDER & SMOKE
May, 1997 - No. 6, Oct, 1997($2.95, limited series)
Event Comics
1-6:Ramos-a/Waid, Augustyn-s in all
2-6-variant covers by Ramos and Quesada 2.95

ASH: FILES
Mar, 1997 ($2.95, one-shot)
Event Comics
1-Comics w/text 2.95

ASH: FIRE WITHIN, THE
Sept, 1996 - No. 3 ($2.95, limited series)
Event Comics
1-3:Quesada & Palmiotti-c/s/a 2.95

ASH/ 22 BRIDES
Dec, 1996 - No. 2, Apr, 1997 ($2.95, limited series)
Event Comics
1,2:Nicieza-s/Ramos-c/a 2.95

ASKANI'SON (See Adventures of Cyclops & Phoenix limited series)
Jan, 1996 - No. 4, May, 1996 ($2.95, limited series)
Marvel Comics
1-4: Story cont'd from Advs. of Cyclops & Phoenix; Lobdell/Loeb story; Gene Ha-c/a(p) 1.20 3.00
TPB (1997, $12.99) r/#1-4; Gene Ha painted-c 12.99

ASSASSINETTE
1994 - No.7, 1995? ($2.50, B&W)
Pocket Change Comics
1-7: 1-Silver foil-c 1.00 2.50

ASSASSINETTE HARDCORE
1995 - No.2, 1995 ($2.50, B&W, limited series)
Pocket Change Comics
1,2 1.00 2.50

ASSASSINS
Apr, 1996 ($1.95)
DC Comics (Amalgam)
1 2.00

ASSASSINS, INC.
1987 - No. 2, 1987 ($1.95)
Silverline Comics
1,2 .80 2.00

ASTER
Oct, 1994 - No. 4, 1995 ($2.95)
Entity Comics
0-4: 1,3,4-Foil Logo. 2-Foil-c. 3-Variant-c exists. 1.20 3.00

ASTER: THE LAST CELESTIAL KNIGHT
1995 - No. 3, 1996 ($2.50)
Entity Comics
1-3 2.50

ASTONISHING (Formerly Marvel Boy No. 1, 2)
No. 3, Apr, 1951 - No. 63, Aug, 1957
Marvel/Atlas Comics(20CC)
3-Marvel Boy continues; 3-5-Marvel Boy-c 80.00 240.00 675.00
4-6-Last Marvel Boy; 4-Stan Lee app. 51.00 155.00 450.00
7-10: 7-Maneely s/f story. 10-Sinnott s/f story 23.00 69.00 175.00
11,12,15,17,20 20.00 60.00 155.00
13,14,16,18,19-Krigstein-a. 18-Jack The Ripper sty 21.00 64.00 165.00
21,22,24 18.00 54.00 135.00
23-E.C. swipe "The Hole In The Wall" from Vault Of Horror #16 19.00 56.00 145.00
25,29: 25-Crandall-a. 29-Decapitation-c 16.00 47.00 120.00
26-28 14.00 43.00 110.00
30-Tentacled eyeball story 18.00 54.00 135.00
31-37-Last pre-code issue 13.00 39.00 100.00
38-43,46,48-52,56,58,59,61 10.00 30.00 75.00
44,45,47,53-55,57,60: 44-Crandall swipe/Weird Fantasy #22. 45,47-Krigstein-a. 53-Ditko-a. 54-Torres-a, 55-Crandall, Torres-a. 57-Williamson/Krenkel-a (4 pgs.). 60-Williamson/Mayo-a (4 pgs.) 11.50 34.00 85.00
62,63: 62-Torres, Powell-a. 63-Woodbridge-a 10.00 30.00 70.00

NOTE: ***Ayers*** *a-16.* ***Berg*** *a-36, 53, 56.* ***Cameron*** *a-50.* ***Gene Colan*** *a-12, 20, 29, 56.* ***Ditko*** *a-53.* ***Drucker*** *a-41, 62.* ***Everett*** *a-3-6(3), 6, 10, 12, 37, 47, 48, 58; c-3-5, 13,15, 16, 18, 29, 47, 49, 51, 53-55, 57, 59-63.* ***Fass*** *a-11, 34.* ***Forte*** *a-53, 58, 60.* ***Fuje*** *a-11.* ***Heath*** *a-8, 29; c-8, 9, 19, 22, 25, 26.* ***Kirby*** *a-56.* ***Lawrence*** *a-28, 37, 38, 42.* ***Maneely*** *a-7(2); c-7, 31, 33, 34, 56.* ***Moldoff*** *a-33.* ***Morisi*** *a-10, 60.* ***Morrow*** *a-52, 61.* ***Orlando*** *a-47, 58, 61.* ***Pakula*** *a-10.* ***Powell*** *a-43, 44, 48.* ***Ravielli*** *a-28.* ***Reinman*** *a-32, 34, 38.* ***Robinson*** *a-20.* ***J. Romita*** *a-7, 18, 24, 43, 57,61.* ***Roussos*** *a-55.* ***Sale*** *a-28, 38, 59; c-32.* ***Sekowsky*** *a-13.* ***Severin*** *c-46.* ***Shores*** *a-16, 60.* ***Sinnott*** *a-11, 30.* ***Whitney*** *a-13.* ***Ed Win*** *a-20. Canadian reprints exist.*

ASTONISHING TALES (See Ka-Zar)
Aug, 1970 - No. 36, July, 1976 (#1-7: 15¢; #8: 25¢)
Marvel Comics Group
1-Ka-Zar (by Kirby(p) #1,2; by B. Smith #3-6) & Dr. Doom (by Wood #1-4; by Tuska #5,6; by Colan #7,8) double feature begins; Kraven the Hunter-c/story; Nixon cameo 3.40 10.20 34.00
2-Kraven the Hunter-c/story; Kirby, Wood-a 1.85 5.50 15.00
3-6: B. Smith-p; Wood-a-#3,4. 5,6-Red Skull 2-part story 2.50 7.50 22.00
7-12: 7,8: 8-(25¢, 52 pgs.)-Last Dr. Doom. 9-Lorna-r/Lorna #14. 10-B. Smith/Sal Buscema-a. 11-Origin Ka-Zar & Zabu. 12-Man-Thing by Neal Adams (apps. #13 also) 1.50 4.50 12.00
13-20: 14-Jann of the Jungle-r (1950s). 19-Starlin-a(p). 20-Last Ka-Zar. 2.00 5.00
21-24: 21-(12/73)-It! the Living Colossus begins, ends #24 (see Supernatural Thrillers #1). 23,24-Fin Fang Foom app. 1.10 3.30 9.00
25-1st app. Deathlok the Demolisher; full length stories begin, end #36; Perez's 1st work, 2 pgs. (8/74) 2.50 7.50 20.00
26-28,30 2.40 6.00
29-r/origin/1st app. Guardians of the Galaxy from Marvel Super-Heroes #18 plus-c w/4 pgs. omitted; no Deathlok story 2.40 6.00
31-34: 31-Watcher-r/Silver Surfer #3 2.00 5.00
35,36-(Regular 25¢ edition)(5,7/76) 2.00 5.00
35,36-(30¢-c, low distribution) 2.50 7.50 20.00

NOTE: ***Buckler*** *a-13i, 16p, 25, 26p, 27p, 28, 29p-36p; c-13, 25p, 26-30, 32-35p, 36.* ***John Buscema*** *a-9, 12p-14p, 16p; c-4-6p, 12p.* ***Colan*** *a-7p, 8p.* ***Ditko*** *a-21r.* ***Everett*** *a-6i.* ***G. Kane*** *a-11p, 15p; c-9, 10p, 11p, 14, 15p, 21p.* ***McWilliams*** *a-30i.* ***Starlin*** *a-19p; c-16p.* ***Sutton & Trimpe*** *a-8.* ***Tuska*** *a-5p, 6p, 8p.* ***Wood*** *a-1-4.* ***Wrightson*** *c-31i.*

ASTONISHING X-MEN
Mar, 1995 - No.4, July, 1995 ($1.95, limited series)
Marvel Comics
1-Age of Apocalypse 1.20 3.00
2-4 .80 2.00

ASTRO BOY (TV) (See March of Comics #285 & The Original...)
August, 1965 (12¢)
Gold Key
1(10151-508)-Scarce;1st app. Astro Boy in comics 39.00 116.00 425.00

ASTRO CITY (See Kurt Busiek's Astro City)

ASTRO COMICS

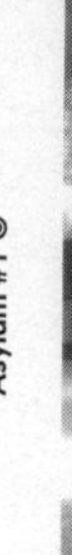

Asylum #1 ©

Atom #3 © DC

Atoman #2 © Spark Publ.

1969 - 1979 (Giveaway)
American Airlines (Harvey)

nn-Harvey's Casper, Spooky, Hot Stuff, Stumbo the Giant, Little Audrey, Little Lotta, & Richie Rich reprints. 1970-r/Richie Rich #97. 1973-r/Richie Rich #122. 1977-r/Richie Rich & Casper #20. 1979-r/Richie Rich & Casper #30 (scarce) 1.50 4.50 12.00

ASYLUM
1993 ($2.50)
Millennium Publications

1-4: 1-Bolton-c/a; Russell 2-pg. illos 1.00 2.50

ASYLUM
Dec, 1995 - No. 11, Jan, 1997 ($2.95/$2.99, anthology) (#1-6 are flip books)
Maximum Press

1-10: 1-Warchild by Art Adams, Beanworld, Avengelyne, Battlestar Galactica. 2-Intro Mike Deodato's Deathkiss; Cybrid story begins, ends #5. 4-1st app.Christian; painted Battlestar Galactica story begins. 5-Intro Black Seed (formerly Black Flag) by Dan Fraga; B&W Christian story. 6-Intro Bionix (Six Million Dollar Man & the Bionic Woman). 7-Begin $2.99-c; Don Simpson's Megaton Man; Black Seed pinup. 8-B&W-a. 9- Foot Soldiers & Kid Supreme. 10-Lady Supreme by Terry Moore-c/app. 1.20 3.00

ATARI FORCE
1982 - No. 5, 1983; Jan, 1984 - No. 20, Aug, 1985 (Mando paper)
DC Comics

1-3 (1982, 5X7", 52 pgs.)-Given away with Atari games 1.20 3.00
4,5 (1982-1983, 52 pgs.)-Given away with Atari games (scarcer) 2.40 6.00
1-20: 1-(1/84)-Intro Tempest, Packrat, Babe, Morphea, & Dart 1.00
Special 1 (4/86) 1.00
NOTE: ***Byrne*** *c-Special 1i.* ***Giffen*** *a-12p, 13i.* ***Rogers*** *a-18p, Special 1p.*

A-TEAM, THE (TV)
Mar, 1984 - No. 3, May, 1984
Marvel Comics Group

1-3 .80 2.00
1,2 (Whitman bagged set) 1.60 4.00

ATLANTIS CHRONICLES, THE (Also see Aquaman, 3rd Series & Aquaman: Time & Tide)
Mar, 1990 - No. 7, Sept, 1990 ($2.95, limited series, 52 pgs.)
DC Comics

1-7: 1-Peter David scripts. 7-True origin of Aquaman; nudity panels 1.30 3.25

ATLANTIS, THE LOST CONTINENT
May, 1961
Dell Publishing Co.

Four Color #1188-Movie, photo-c 9.00 27.00 100.00

ATLAS (See 1st Issue Special)

ATLAS
Feb, 1994 - No. 4, 1994 ($2.50, limited series)
Dark Horse Comics

1-4 1.00 2.50

ATOM, THE (See Action #425, All-American #19, Brave & the Bold, D.C. Special Series #1, Detective, Flash Comics #80, Power Of The Atom, Showcase #34 -36 , Super Friends, Sword of The Atom, Teen Titans & World's Finest)

ATOM, THE (...& the Hawkman No. 39 on)
June-July, 1962 - No. 38, Aug-Sept, 1968
National Periodical Publ.

1-(6-7/62)-Intro Plant-Master; 1st app. Maya 63.00 188.00 750.00
2 30.00 90.00 300.00
3-1st Time Pool story; 1st app. Chronos (origin) 19.00 57.00 190.00
4,5: 4-Snapper Carr x-over 15.00 45.00 150.00
6,8-10: 8-Justice League, Dr. Light app. 10.00 30.00 100.00
7-Hawkman x-over (6-7/63; 1st Atom & Hawkman team-up); 1st app. Hawkman since Brave & the Bold tryouts 26.00 78.00 260.00
11-15: 13-Chronos-c/story 7.00 21.00 70.00
16-20: 19-Zatanna x-over 5.00 15.00 50.00
21-28,30: 28-Chronos-c/story 4.00 12.00 40.00
29-1st solo Golden Age Atom x-over in S.A. 14.00 42.00 140.00
31-35,37,38: 31-Hawkman x-over. 37-Intro. Major Mynah; Hawkman cameo 4.00 12.00 40.00
36-G.A. Atom x-over 5.00 15.00 50.00
NOTE: ***Anderson*** *a-1-11i, 13i; c-inks-1-25, 31-35, 37.* ***Sid Greene*** *a-8i-37i.* ***Gil Kane*** *a-1p-37p; c-1p-28p, 29, 33p, 34.* ***George Roussos*** *38i* ***Mike Sekowsky*** *38p Time Pool stories also in 6, 9,12, 17, 21, 27, 35.*

ATOM ,THE (See Tangent Comics/ The Atom)

ATOM AGE (See Classics Illustrated Special Issue)

ATOM-AGE COMBAT
June, 1952 - No. 5, Apr, 1953; Feb, 1958
St. John Publishing Co.

1-Buck Vinson in all 40.00 120.00 320.00
2-Flying saucer story 24.00 71.00 175.00
3,5: 3-Mayo-a (6 pgs.). 5-Flying saucer-c/story 19.00 56.00 140.00
4 (Scarce) 24.00 71.00 170.00
1(2/58-St. John) 16.00 47.00 110.00

ATOM-AGE COMBAT
Nov, 1958 - No. 3, Mar, 1959
Fago Magazines

1-All have Dick Ayers-c/a 21.00 64.00 165.00
2,3: 2-A-Bomb explosion-c 16.00 47.00 120.00

ATOMAN
Feb, 1946 - No. 2, April, 1946
Spark Publications

1-Origin & 1st app. Atoman; Robinson/Meskin-a; Kidcrusaders, Wild Bill Hickok, Marvin the Great app. 43.00 129.00 385.00
2-Robinson/Meskin-a; Robinson c-1,2 36.00 108.00 285.00

ATOM & HAWKMAN, THE (Formerly The Atom)
No. 39, Oct-Nov, 1968 - No. 45, Oct-Nov, 1969
National Periodical Publications

39-45: 40-41- Kubert/Anderson-a. 43-(7/69)-Last 12¢ issue; 1st app. Gentleman Ghost, origin in #44. 44-(9/69)-1st 15¢ issue 3.00 9.00 30.00
NOTE: ***M. Anderson*** *a-39, 40i, 41i, 43, 44.* ***Sid Greene*** *a-40i-45i.* ***Kubert*** *a-40p, 41p; c-39-45.*

ATOM ANT (TV) (See Golden Comics Digest #2)
January, 1966 (12¢)
Gold Key

1(10170-601)-Hanna-Barbera character 27.00 82.00 300.00

ATOM ANT & SECRET SQUIRREL
Nov, 1995 - Present ($1.50, bi-monthly)
Archie Publications

1-12-Hanna-Barbera characters 1.50

ATOMIC AGE
Nov, 1990 - No. 4, Feb, 1991 ($4.50, limited series, squarebound, 52 pgs.)
Marvel Comics (Epic Comics)

1-4: Williamson-a(i) 1.80 4.50

ATOMIC ATTACK (True War Stories; formerly Attack, first series)
No. 5, Jan, 1953 - No. 8, Oct, 1953 (1st story is sci/fi in all issues)
Youthful Magazines

5-Atomic bomb-c; science fiction stories in all 31.00 94.00 250.00
6-8 19.00 56.00 150.00

ATOMIC BOMB

Atomic Comics #3 © Green Publ. Co.

Atom Special #1 © DC

Attack #3 © YM

GD25 FN65 NM94

1945 (36 pgs.)
Jay Burtis Publications
1-Airmale & Stampy 36.00 108.00 315.00

ATOMIC BUNNY (Formerly Atomic Rabbit)
No. 12, Aug, 1958 - No. 19, Dec, 1959
Charlton Comics
12 9.50 28.00 75.00
13-19 5.70 17.00 40.00

ATOMIC COMICS
Jan, 1946 (Reprints, one-shot)
Daniels Publications (Canadian)
1-Rocketman, Yankee Boy, Master Key app. 25.00 75.00 200.00

ATOMIC COMICS
Jan, 1946 - No. 4, July-Aug, 1946 (#1-4 were printed w/o cover gloss)
Green Publishing Co.
1-Radio Squad by Siegel & Shuster; Barry O'Neal app.; Fang Gow cover-r/ Detective Comics (Classic-c) 111.00 333.00 1000.00
2-Inspector Dayton; Kid Kane by Matt Baker; Lucky Wings, Congo King, Prop Powers (only app.) begin 50.00 150.00 450.00
3,4: 3-Zero Ghost Detective app.; Baker-a(2) each; 4-Baker-c 36.00 108.00 300.00

ATOMIC KNIGHTS (See Strange Adventures #117)

ATOMIC MOUSE (TV, Movies) (See Blue Bird, Funny Animals, Giant Comics Edition & Wotalife Comics)
3/53 - No. 54, 6/63; No. 1, 12/84; V2#10, 9/85 - No. 13, ?/86
Capitol Stories/Charlton Comics
1-Origin & 1st app.; Al Fago-c/a in all? 26.00 80.00 210.00
2 9.50 28.00 75.00
3-10: 5-Timmy The Timid Ghost app.; see Zoo Funnies 8.50 26.00 60.00
11-13,16-25 5.00 15.00 30.00
14,15-Hoppy The Marvel Bunny app. 6.50 19.50 45.00
26-(68 pgs.) 8.75 26.25 65.00
27-40: 36,37-Atom The Cat app. 4.15 12.50 25.00
41-54 2.80 7.00 14.00
1 (1984) 1.60 4.00
V2#10 (10/85) -13-Fago-r. #12(1/86) 1.20 3.00

ATOMIC RABBIT (Atomic Bunny #12 on; see Giant Comics #3 & Wotalife)
Aug, 1955 - No. 11, Mar, 1958
Charlton Comics
1-Origin & 1st app.; Al Fago-c/a in all? 23.00 69.00 185.00
2 8.75 26.25 70.00
3-10 6.50 19.50 45.00
11-(68 pgs.) 8.75 26.25 70.00

ATOMIC SPY CASES
Mar-Apr, 1950 (Painted-c)
Avon Periodicals
1-No Wood-a; A-bomb blast panels; Fass-a 26.00 77.00 190.00

ATOMIC THUNDERBOLT, THE
Feb, 1946 (one-shot)
Regor Company
1-Intro. Atomic Thunderbolt & Mr. Murdo 41.00 123.00 365.00

ATOMIC WAR!
Nov, 1952 - No. 4, Apr, 1953
Ace Periodicals (Junior Books)
1-Atomic bomb-c 75.00 225.00 650.00
2,3: 3-Atomic bomb-c 50.00 150.00 430.00
4-Used in **POP**, pg. 96 & illo. 50.00 150.00 430.00

GD25 FN65 NM94

ATOMIK ANGELS
May, 1996 - Present ($2.50)
Crusade Comics
1-3: 1-Freefall from Gen 13 app 1.20 3.00
1-Variant-c 1.60 4.00
Intrep-Edition (2/96, B&W, giveaway at launch party)-Previews Atomik Angels #1; includes Billy Tucci interview. 1.60 4.00

ATOM SPECIAL (See Atom & Justice League of America)
1993/1995 ($2.50/$2.95)
DC Comics
1-(1993, $2.50, 68 pgs.)-Dillon-c/a. 1.00 2.50
2-(1995, $2.95)-Dillon-c/a. 1.20 3.00

ATOM THE CAT (Formerly Tom Cat; see Giant Comics #3)
No. 9, Oct, 1957 - No. 17, Aug, 1959
Charlton Comics
9 7.15 21.50 50.00
10,13-17 4.25 13.00 28.00
11,12: 11(64pgs)-Atomic Mouse app. 12(100 pgs.) 8.75 26.25 65.00

ATTACK
May, 1952 - No. 4, Nov, 1952; No. 5, Jan, 1953 - No. 5, Sept, 1953
Youthful Mag./Trojan No. 5 on
1-(1st series)-Extreme violence 21.00 62.00 165.00
2,3-Both Harrison-c/a; bondage, whipping 10.00 30.00 80.00
4-Krenkel-a (7 pgs.); Harrison-a (becomes Atomic Attack #5 on) 10.50 32.00 85.00
5-(#1, Trojan, 2nd series) 8.75 26.25 65.00
6-8 (#2-4), 5 6.00 18.00 42.00

ATTACK
No. 54, 1958 - No. 60, Nov, 1959
Charlton Comics
54 (25¢, 100 pgs.) 8.50 26.00 60.00
55-60 3.60 9.00 18.00

ATTACK!
1962 - No. 15, 3/75; No. 16, 8/79 - No. 48, 10/84
Charlton Comics
nn(#1)-('62) Special Edition 2.50 7.50 25.00
2('63), 3(Fall, '64) 2.25 6.75 18.00
V4#3(10/66), 4(10/67)-(Formerly Special War Series #2; becomes Attack At Sea V4#5) 1.50 4.50 12.00
1(9/71) 1.50 4.50 12.00
2-15(3/75): 4-American Eagle app. 1.00 3.00 8.00
16(8/79) - 48: 48(10/84)-Wood-r; S&K-c 1.20 3.00
Modern Comics 13('78)-r 1.20 3.00

ATTACK!
1975 (39¢/49¢, 36 pgs.)
Spire Christian Comics (Fleming H. Revell Co.)
nn 1.60 4.00

ATTACK AT SEA (Formerly Attack!, 1967)
V4#5, Oct, 1968
Charlton Comics
V4#5 1.75 5.25 14.00

ATTACK ON PLANET MARS (See Strange Worlds #18)
1951
Avon Periodicals
nn-Infantino, Fawcette, Kubert & Wood-a; adaptation of Tarrano the Conqueror by Ray Cummings 62.00 190.00 525.00

ATTITUDE LAD
Apr, 1994 - No. 3, Nov, 1994 ($2.95, B&W, limited series)

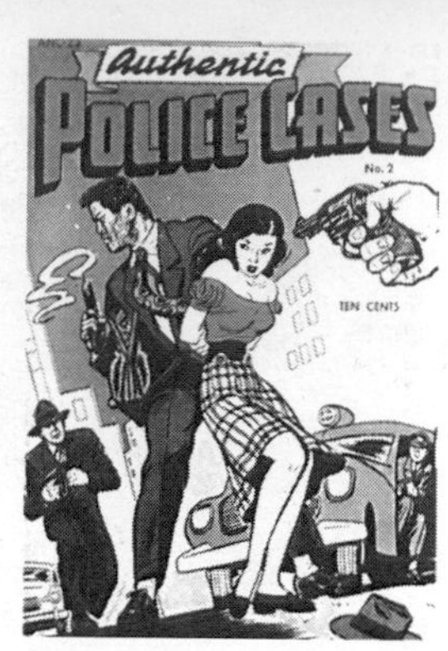

Authentic Police Cases #2 © STJ

Autumn #2 © Caliber

Avengelyne: Deadly Sins #2 © Rob Liefeld

Slave Labor Graphics
1-3 1.20 3.00

AUDREY & MELVIN (Formerly Little...)(See Little Audrey & Melvin)
No. 62, Sept, 1974
Harvey Publications
62 2.40 6.00

AUGIE DOGGIE (TV) (See Hanna-Barbera Band Wagon, Quick-Draw McGraw, Spotlight #2, Top Cat & Whitman Comic Books)
October, 1963 (12¢)
Gold Key
1-Hanna-Barbera character 16.00 47.00 170.00

AURORA COMIC SCENES INSTRUCTION BOOKLET
1974 (6-1/4x9-3/4," 8 pgs., slick paper) (Included with superhero model kits)
Aurora Plastics Co.
181-140-Tarzan; Neal Adams-a 2.25 6.75 18.00
182-140-Spider-Man. 2.50 7.50 25.00
183-140-Tonto(Gil Kane art). 184-140-Hulk. 185-140-Superman. 186-140-Superboy. 187-140-Batman. 188-140-The Lone Ranger(1974-by Gil Kane). 192-140-Captain America(1975). 193-140-Robin 2.00 6.00 16.00

AUTHENTIC POLICE CASES
2/48 - No. 6, 11/48; No. 7, 5/50 - No. 38, 3/55
St. John Publishing Co.
1-Hale the Magician by Tuska begins 33.00 99.00 240.00
2-Lady Satan, Johnny Rebel app. 20.00 60.00 140.00
3-Veiled Avenger app.; blood drainage story plus 2 Lucky Coyne stories; used in **SOTI**, illo. from Red Seal #16 39.00 118.00 285.00
4,5: 4-Masked Black Jack app. 5-Late 1930s Jack Cole-a(r); transvestism story 21.00 64.00 150.00
6-Matt Baker-c; used in **SOTI**, illo- "An invitation to learning", r-in Fugitives From Justice #3; Jack Cole-a; also used by the N.Y. Legis. Comm. 40.00 120.00 300.00
7,8,10-14: 7-Jack Cole-a; Matt Baker-a begins #8, ends #?; Vic Flint in #10-14. 10-12-Baker-a(2 each) 17.00 49.00 120.00
9-No Vic Flint 13.00 39.00 90.00
15-Drug-c/story; Vic Flint app.; Baker-c 17.00 49.00 120.00
16,18,20,21,23: Baker-a(i) 10.00 30.00 70.00
17,19,22-Baker-c 11.00 33.00 80.00
24-28 (All 100 pgs.): 26-Transvestism 19.00 56.00 140.00
29-32 6.00 18.00 40.00
33-38: 33-Transvestism; Baker-c. 34-Baker-c; r/#95. 35-Baker-c/a(2); r/#10 36-r/#11; Vic Flint strip-r; Baker-c/a(2) unsigned. 37-Baker-c; r/#17. 38-Baker-c/a; r/#18 9.00 27.00 60.00
NOTE: ***Matt Baker*** *c-6-16, 17, 19, 22, 27, 29, 31-38; a-13, 16. Bondage c-1, 3.*

AUTUMN
1995 - No. 3, 1995 ($2.95, B&W)
Caliber Comics
1-3 1.20 3.00

AUTUMN ADVENTURES (Walt Disney's...)
Autumn, 1990; No. 2, Autumn, 1991 ($2.95, 68 pgs.)
Disney Comics
1-Donald Duck-r(2) by Barks, Pluto-r, & new-a 1.30 3.25
2-D. Duck-r by Barks; new Super Goof story 1.30 3.25

AVATAR
Feb, 1991 - No. 3, Apr, 1991 ($5.95, limited series, 100 pgs.)
DC Comics
1-3: Based on TSR's Forgotten Realms 2.40 6.00

AVENGEBLADE
July, 1996 - No. 2, Aug, 1996 ($2.99, limited series)
Maximum Press

1,2: Bad Girls parody 1.20 3.00

AVENGELYNE
May, 1995 - No. 3, July, 1995 ($2.50/$3.50, limited series)
Maximum Press
1/2 1.85 5.50 15.00
1-Newstand ($2.50)-Photo-c; poster insert 2.00 5.00
1-Direct Market ($3.50)-Chromium-c; poster 1.00 3.00 8.00
1-Glossy edition 2.50 7.50 25.00
1-Gold 2.50 7.50 20.00
2-3: 2-Polybagged w/card 1.60 4.00
3-Variant-c; Deodato pin-up 2.00 5.00
...Swimsuit (8/95, $2.95)-Pin-ups/photos. 3-Variant-c exist (2 photo, 1 Liefeld-a) 1.20 3.00
...Swimsuit (1/96, $3.50, 2nd printing)-photo-c 1.40 3.50
Trade paperback (12/95, $9.95) 10.00

AVENGELYNE
V2#1, Apr, 1996 - Present ($2.95/$2.50)
Maximum Press
V2#1-Four covers exist (2 photo-c). 2.00 5.00
V2#2-Three covers exist (1 photo-c); flip book w/Darkchylde 4.50 12.00
V2#0, 3-14: 0-(10/96).3-Flip book w/Priest preview. 4-Cybrid app; w/Darkchylde/Avengelyne poster. 5-Flip book w/Blindside. 6-Divinity-c/app. 1.20 3.00

AVENGELYNE: ARMAGEDDON
Dec, 1996 - No. 3, Feb, 1997 ($2.99, limited series)
Maximum Press
1-3-Scott Clark-a(p) 1.20 3.00

AVENGELYNE: DEADLY SINS
Feb, 1996 - No. 2, Mar, 1996 ($2.95, limited series)
Maximum Press
1,2: 1-Two-c exist (1 photo, 1 Liefeld-a). 2-Liefeld-c; Pop Mhan-a(p). 1.20 3.00

AVENGELYNE/GLORY
Sept, 1995 ($3.95, one-shot)
Maximum Press
1-Chromium-c 1.20 3.00
1-Variant-c 1.20 3.00

AVENGELYNE/GLORY: GODYSSEY, THE (See Glory/...)
Sept, 1996 ($2.99, one-shot)
Maximum Press
1-Two covers (1 photo) 1.20 3.00

AVENGELYNE/GLORY SWIMSUIT SPECIAL
June, 1996 ($2.95)
Maximum Press
1-Pin-ups & photos of Avengelyne and Glory; photo-c (variant illos-c. also exists) 1.20 3.00

AVENGELYNE/POWER
Nov, 1995 - No.3, Jan, 1996 ($2.95, limited series)
Maximum Press
1-3: 1,2-Liefeld-c. 3-Three variant-c. exist (1 photo-c) 1.00 2.50
1-Variant-c 1.40 3.50

AVENGELYNE • PROPHET
May, 1996 ($2.95, unfinished limited series)
Maximum Press
1-Liefeld-c/a(p) 1.20 3.00

AVENGELYNE/ WARRIOR NUN AREALA (See Warrior Nun/...)
Nov, 1996 ($2.99, one-shot)
Maximum Press

Avengers #23 © MEG

Avengers #223 © MEG

Avengers #376 © MEG

GD25 FN65 NM94

1 — 1.20 3.00

AVENGER, THE (See A-1 Comics)
Feb-Mar, 1955 - No. 4, Aug-Sept, 1955
Magazine Enterprises

1(A-1 #129)-Origin 33.00 100.00 265.00
2(A-1 #131), 3(A-1 #133), 4(A-1 #138) 21.00 64.00 170.00
IW Reprint #9('64)-Reprints #1 (new cover) 4.00 12.00 24.00
NOTE: ***Powell*** *a-2-4; c-1-4.*

AVENGERS, THE (See Giant-Size..., Kree/Skrull War Starring..., Marvel Graphic Novel #27, Marvel Super Action, Marvel Super Heroes('66), Marvel Treasury Ed., Marvel Triple Action, Solo Avengers, Tales Of Suspense #49, West Coast Avengers & X-Men Vs....)

AVENGERS, THE (The Mighty Avengers on cover only #63-69)
Sept, 1963 - No. 402, Sept, 1996
Marvel Comics Group

GD25 FN65 VF82 NM94

1-Origin & 1st app. The Avengers (Thor, Iron Man, Hulk, Ant-Man, Wasp); Loki app. 176.00 528.00 1232.00 2300.00

GD25 FN65 NM94

2-Hulk leaves Avengers 52.00 156.00 620.00
3-1st Sub-Mariner x-over (outside the F.F.); Hulk & Sub-Mariner team-up & battle Avengers; Spider-Man cameo (1/64) 35.00 105.00 385.00
4-Revival of Captain America who joins the Avengers; 1st Silver Age app. of Captain America & Bucky (3/64) 125.00 375.00 1500.00
4-Reprint from the Golden Record Comic set 7.50 22.50 75.00
With Record (1966) 11.00 33.00 110.00
5-Hulk app. 22.50 68.00 225.00
6-8: 6-Intro/1st app. original Zemo & his Masters of Evil. 8-Intro Kang 18.00 54.00 180.00
9-Intro Wonder Man who dies in same story 18.50 55.00 185.00
10-Intro/1st app. Immortus; early Hercules app. (11/64) 15.50 47.00 155.00
11-Spider-Man-c & x-over (12/64) 18.50 55.00 185.00
12-15: 15-Death of original Zemo 11.50 34.00 115.00
16-New Avengers line-up (Hawkeye, Quicksilver, Scarlet Witch join; Thor, Iron Man, Giant-Man, Wasp leave) 12.50 38.00 125.00
17-19: 19-Intro/1st app. Swordsman; origin Hawkeye (8/65) 8.50 25.50 85.00
20-22: Wood inks 5.50 16.50 55.00
23-30: 25-Dr. Doom-c/story. 28-Giant-Man becomes Goliath (5/66) 4.00 12.00 40.00
31-40 2.50 7.50 25.00
41-52,54-56: 43,44-1st app. Red Guardian. 46-Ant-Man returns (re-intro, 11/67) 47-Magneto-c/story. 48-Origin/1st app. new Black Knight (1/68). 52-Black Panther joins; 1st app. The Grim Reaper. 54-1st app. new Masters of Evil. 56-Zemo app; story explains how Capt. America became imprisioned in ice during WWII, only to be rescued in Avengers #4 2.25 6.75 22.00
53-X-Men app. 3.50 10.50 35.00
57-1st app. S.A. Vision (10/68) 6.50 19.50 65.00
58-Origin The Vision 4.00 12.00 40.00
59-67: 59-Intro. Yellowjacket. 60-Wasp & Yellowjacket wed. 63-Goliath becomes Yellowjacket; Hawkeye becomes the new Goliath. 65-Last 12¢ issue. 66,67-B. Smith-a 2.50 7.50 20.00
68-70: 70-Nighthawk on cover 1.25 3.75 10.00
71-1st app. The Invaders (12/69); 1st app. Nighthawk; Black Knight joins 2.60 7.80 26.00
72-82,84-86,88-91: 80-Intro. Red Wolf (9/70). 82-Daredevil app. 88-Written by Harlan Ellison 1.25 3.75 10.00
83-Intro. The Liberators (Wasp, Valkyrie, Scarlet Witch, Medusa & the Black Widow) 2.25 6.75 18.00
87-Origin The Black Panther 2.50 7.50 22.00
92-Last 15¢ issue; Neal Adams-c 2.00 6.00 16.00
93-(52 pgs.)-Neal Adams-c/a 5.00 15.00 50.00
94-96-Neal Adams-c/a 3.00 9.00 30.00
97-G.A. Capt. America, Sub-Mariner, Human Torch, Patriot, Vision, Blazing Skull, Fin, Angel, & new Capt. Marvel x-over 1.60 4.85 13.00
98,99: 98-Goliath becomes Hawkeye; Smith c/a(i). 99-Smith-c, Smith/Sutton-a 2.25 6.75 18.00
100-(6/72)-Smith-c/a; featuring everyone who was an Avenger 6.00 18.00 60.00
101-106,108,109: 101-Harlan Ellison scripts 1.10 3.30 9.00
107-Starlin-a(p) 1.25 3.75 10.00
110,111-X-Men app. 2.50 7.50 20.00
112-1st app. Mantis 1.50 4.50 12.00
113-124,126-130: 116-118-Defenders/Silver Surfer app. 123-Origin Mantis 1.00 2.80 7.00
125-Thanos-c & brief app. 1.85 5.50 15.00
131-140: 134,135-True origin Vision. 136-Ploog-r/Amazing Advs. #12 2.40 6.00
141-145,147,148,150-163: 144-Origin & 1st app. Hellcat. 150-Kirby-a(r); new line-up: Capt. America, Scarlet Witch, Iron Man, Wasp, Yellowjacket, Vision & The Beast. 151-Wonder Man returns w/new costume 1.60 4.00
146,149-(Regular 25¢ edition)(4,7/76) 1.60 4.00
146,149-(30¢-c, limited distribution) 2.00 6.00 16.00
164-166: Byrne-a 2.00 5.00
167-191: 168-Guardians of the Galaxy app. 174-Thanos cameo. 176-Starhawk app. 181-191-Byrne-a. 181-New line-up: Capt. America, Scarlet Witch, Iron Man, Wasp, Vision, Beast & The Falcon. 183-Ms. Marvel joins. 185-Origin Quicksilver & Scarlet Witch 1.20 3.00
192-213,215-262: 195-1st Taskmaster. 200-(10/80, 52 pgs.)-Ms. Marvel leaves. 211-New line-up: Capt. America, Iron Man, Tigra, Thor, Wasp & Yellowjacket. 213-Yellowjacket leaves. 215,216-Silver Surfer app. 216-Tigra leaves. 217-Yellowjacket & Wasp return. 221-Hawkeye & She-Hulk join. 227-Capt. Marvel (female) joins; origins of Ant-Man, Wasp, Giant-Man, Goliath, Yellowjacket, & Avengers. 230-Yellowjacket quits. 231-Iron Man leaves. 232-Starfox (Eros) joins. 234-Origin Quicksilver, Scarlet Witch. 236-New logo. 238-Origin Blackout. 239-Avengers app. on David Letterman show. 240-Spider-Woman revived. 250-($1.00, 52 pgs.) .90 2.25
214-Ghost Rider-c/story 1.20 3.00
263-1st app. X-Factor (1/86)(story continues in Fantastic Four #286) 1.60 4.00
264-299: 272-Alpha Flight app. 291-$1.00 issues begin. 297-Black Knight, She-Hulk & Thor resign. 298-Inferno tie-in .80 2.00
300 (2/89, $1.75, 68 pgs.)-Thor joins; Simonson-a .80 2.00
301-304,306-325,327,329-343: 302-Re-intro Quasar. 314-318-Spider-Man x-over. 320-324-Alpha Flight app. (320-cameo). 327-2nd app. Rage. 341, 342-New Warriors app. 343-Last $1.00-c 1.50
305-Byrne scripts begin .80 2.00
326-1st app. Rage (11/90) 1.60 4.00
328-Origin Rage 1.20 3.00
344-346,348,349,351-359,361,362,364,365,367: 365-Contains coupon for Hunt for Magneto contest 1.50
347-($1.75, 56 pgs.) .80 2.00
350-($2.50, 68 pgs.)-Double gatefold-c showing-c to #1; r/#53 w/cover in flip book format; vs. The Starjammers 1.00 2.50
360-($2.95, 52 pgs.)-Embossed all-foil-c; 30th ann. 1.40 3.50
363-($2.95, 52 pgs.)-All silver foil-c 1.00 2.50
366-($3.95, 68 pgs.)-Embossed all gold foil-c 1.60 4.00
368-Bloodties part 1; Avengers/X-Men x-over 1.50
369-($2.95)-Foil embossed-c; Bloodties part 5 1.20 3.00
370-373 1.50
374,376-399: 374-$1.50-c begins; bound-in trading card sheet. 380-Deodato-a. 390,391-"The Crossing." 395-Death of "old" Tony Stark; wraparound-c. 1.50
375-($2.00, 52 pgs.)-Regular ed.; Thunderstrike returns; leads into Malibu Comics' Black September. .80 2.00
375-($2.50, 52 pgs.)-Collector's ed. w/bound-in poster; leads into Malibu Comics' Black September. 1.00 2.50

Avengers #7 (2nd Series) © MEG

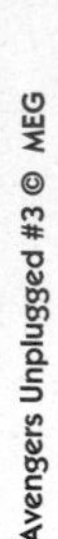
Avengers Unplugged #3 © MEG

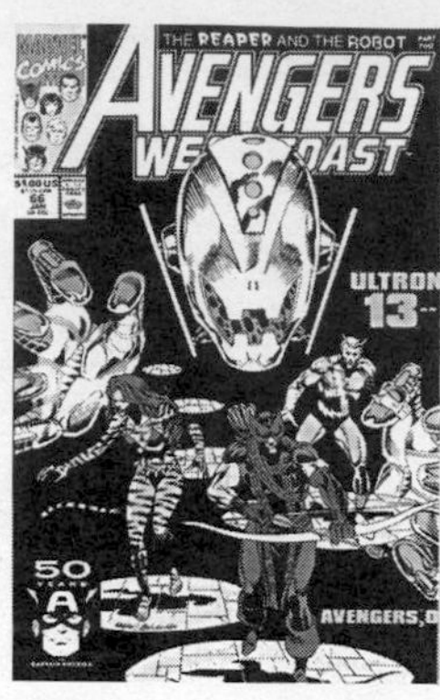

Avengers West Coast #66 © MEG

GD25 FN65 NM94

400-Waid script 1.60 4.00
401,402: Waid-s; 402-Deodato breakdowns; cont'd in X-Men #56 & Onslaught: Marvel Universe. 1.00 2.50
Special 1(9/67, 25¢, 68 pgs.)-New-a; original & new Avengers team-up 5.00 15.00 50.00
Special 2(9/68, 25¢, 68 pgs.)-New-a; original vs. new Avengers 2.50 7.50 24.00
Special 3(9/69, 25¢, 68 pgs.)-r/Avengers #4 plus 3 Capt. America stories by Kirby (art); origin Red Skull 2.50 7.50 20.00
Special 4(1/71, 25¢, 68 pgs.)-Kirby-r/Avengers #5,6 1.25 3.75 10.00
Special 5(1/72)-Spider-Man x-over 1.10 3.30 9.00
Annual 6(11/76) 2.40 6.00
Annual 7(11/77)-Starlin-c/a; Warlock dies; Thanos app. 1.50 4.50 12.00
Annual 8(1978)-Dr. Strange, Ms. Marvel app. 1.80 4.50
Annual 9(1979)-Newton-a(p) 1.40 3.50
Annual 10(1981)-Golden-p; X-Men cameo; 1st app. Rogue & Madelyne Pryor 2.50 7.50 20.00
Annual 11-16: 11(1982)-Vs. The Defenders. 12(1983). 13(1984). 14(1985). 15(1986). 16(1987) 1.40 3.50
Annual 17(1988)-Evolutionary War x-over 1.60 4.00
Annual 18(1989, $2.00, 68 pgs.)-Atlantis Attacks 1.20 3.00
Annual 19,20(1990, 1991)(both $2.00, 68 pgs.) 1.00 2.50
Annual 21(1992, $2.25, 68 pgs.) .90 2.25
Annual 22(1993, $2.95, 68 pgs.)-Bagged w/card 1.20 3.00
Annual 23(1994, $2.95, 68 pgs.) 1.20 3.00
Marvel Double Feature...Avengers/Giant-Man #379 ($2.50, 52 pgs.)-Same as Avengers #379 w/Giant-Man flip book 1.00 2.50
The Yesterday Quest ($6.95)-r/#181,182,185-187 1.00 2.80 7.00

NOTE: **Austin** *c(i)-157, 167, 168, 170-177, 181, 183-188, 198-201, Annual 8.* **John Buscema** *a-41-44p, 46p, 47p, 49, 50, 51-62p, 74-77, 79-85, 87-91, 97, 105p, 121p, 124p,125p, 152, 153p, 255-279p, 281-302p; c-41-66, 68-71, 73-91, 97-99, 178, 256-259p, 261-279p, 281-302p.* **Byrne** *a-164-166p, 181-191p, 233p, Annual 13i, 14p; c-186-190p, 233p, 260, 305p; scripts-305-312.* **Colan** *a(p)-63-65, 111, 206-208, 210, 211; c(p)-65, 206-208, 210, 211.* **Ditko** *a-Annual 13.* **Guice** *a-Annual 12p.* **Don Heck** *a-9-15, 17-40, 157.* **Kane** *c-37p, 159p.* **Kane/Everett** *c-97.* **Kirby** *a-1-8p, Special 3r, 4r(p); c-1-30, 148, 151-158; layouts-14-16.* **Ron Lim** *c(p)-335-341.* **Miller** *c-193p.* **Mooney** *a-86i, 179p, 180p.* **Nebres** *a-178i; c-179i.* **Newton** *a-204p, Annual 9p.* **Perez** *a(p)-141, 143, 144, 148, 150, 154, 155, 160, 161, 162, 167,168, 170, 171, 194-196, 198-202, Annual 6, 8; c(p)-160-162, 164-166, 170-174, 181,183-185, 191, 192, 194-201, 379-382, Annual 8.* **Starlin** *c-121, 135.* **Staton** *a-127-134i.* **Tuska** *a-47i,48i, 51i, 53i, 54i, 106p, 107p, 135p, 137-140p, 163p. Guardians of the Galaxy app. in #167, 168, 170, 173, 175, 181.*

AVENGERS, THE (2nd Series)
V2#1, Nov, 1996 - No. 13, Nov, 1997 ($2.95/$1.95/$1.99) (Produced by Extreme Studios)
Marvel Comics

1-($2.95)-Heroes Reborn begins; intro new team (Captain America, Swordsman, Scarlet Witch, Vision, Thor, Hellcat & Hawkeye); 1st app. Avengers Island; Loki & Enchantress app.; Rob Liefeld-p & plot; Chap Yaep-p; Jim Valentino scripts; variant-c exists 1.60 4.00
1-($1.95)-Variant-c 1.00 2.80 7.00
2,3: 2-Begin $1.95-c; Jeph Loeb scripts begin, Kang app. .80 2.00
4-9: 4-Hulk-c/app. 5-Thor/Hulk battle 1.95
10, 11: 10-Begin-$1.99-c 1.99
12-($2.99) "Heroes Reunited"-pt. 2 2.99
13-"World War 3"-pt. 2, x-over w/Image 1.99

AVENGERS, THE (TV)(Also see Steed and Mrs. Peel)
Nov, 1968 ("John Steed & Emma Peel" cover title) (15¢)
Gold Key

1-Photo-c 21.00 62.00 225.00

AVENGERS COLLECTOR'S EDITION, THE
1993 (Ordered through mail w/candy wrapper, 20 pgs.)
Marvel Comics

1-Contains 4 bound-in trading cards .80 2.00

AVENGERS LOG, THE
Feb, 1994 ($1.95)
Marvel Comics

1-Gives history of all members; Perez-c .80 2.00

AVENGERS SPOTLIGHT (Formerly Solo Avengers #1-20)
No. 21, Aug, 1989 - No. 40, Jan, 1991 (75¢/$1.00)
Marvel Comics

21 (75¢)-Byrne-c/a 1.00
22-40 ($1.00): 26-Acts of Vengeance story. 31-34-U.S. Agent series. 36-Heck-i. 37-Mortimer-i. 40-The Black Knight app. 1.00

AVENGERS STRIKEFILE
Jan, 1994 ($1.75, one-shot)
Marvel Comics

1 .70 1.75

AVENGERS: THE CROSSING
July, 1995 ($4.95, one-shot)
Marvel Comics

1-Deodato-c/a; 1st app. Thor's new costume 2.00 5.00

AVENGERS: THE LEGEND
Oct, 1996 ($3.95, one-shot)
Marvel Comics

1-Tribute issue 1.60 4.00

AVENGERS: THE TERMINATRIX OBJECTIVE
Sept, 1993 - No. 4, Dec, 1993 ($1.25, limited series)
Marvel Comics

1 ($2.50)-Holo-grafx foil-c 1.00 2.50
2-4-Old vs. current Avengers 1.25

AVENGERS: TIMESLIDE
Feb, 1996 ($4.95, one-shot)
Marvel Comics

1-Foil-c 2.00 5.00

AVENGERS/ULTRAFORCE (See Ultraforce/Avengers)
Oct, 1995 ($3.95, one-shot)
Marvel Comics

1-Wraparound foil-c by Perez 1.60 4.00

AVENGERS UNPLUGGED
Oct, 1995 - No. 6, Aug, 1996 (99¢, bi-monthly)
Marvel Comics

1-6 1.00

AVENGERS WEST COAST (Formerly West Coast Avengers)
No. 48, Sept, 1989 - No. 102, Jan, 1994 ($1.00/$1.25)
Marvel Comics

48,49: 48-Byrne-c/a & scripts continue thru #57 1.10
50-Re-intro original Human Torch 1.50
51-74,76-99,101,102: 54-Cover swipe/F.F. #1. 70-Spider-Woman app. 78-Last $1.00-c. 79-Dr. Strange x-over. 84-Origin Spider-Woman retold; Spider-Man app. (also in #85,86). 87,88-Wolverine-c/story. 93-95-Darkhawk app. 101-X-Men x-over 1.25
75-($1.50, 52 pgs.)-Fantastic Four x-over 1.50
100-($3.95, 68 pgs.)-Embossed all red foil-c 1.60 4.00
Annual 8 (1993, $2.95, 68 pgs.)-Bagged w/card 1.20 3.00

AVIATION ADVENTURES AND MODEL BUILDING
No. 16, Dec, 1946 - No. 17, Feb, 1947 (True Aviation Advs. ...No. 15)
Parents' Magazine Institute

16,17-Half comics and half pictures 5.70 17.00 38.00

AVIATION CADETS
1943
Street & Smith Publications

Axa #2 © Eclipse

Aztek: The Ultimate Man #10 © DC

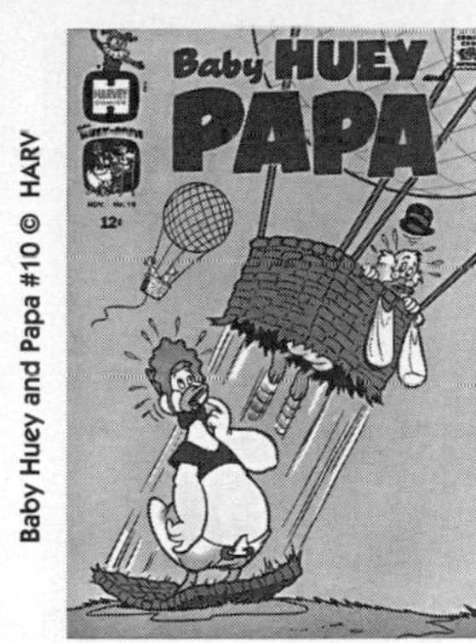

Baby Huey and Papa #10 © HARV

	GD25	FN65	NM94
nn	12.00	38.00	100.00

A-V IN 3-D
Dec, 1984 ($2.00, 28 pgs. w/glasses)
Aardvark-Vanaheim

	GD25	FN65	NM94
1-Cerebus, Flaming Carrot, Normalman & Ms. Tree		.80	2.00

AWAKENING, THE
Oct, 1997 - No. 4 ($2.95, B&W, limited series)
Image Comics

	GD25	FN65	NM94
1-Stephen Blue-s/c/a			2.95

AWFUL OSCAR (Formerly & becomes Oscar Comics with No. 13)
No. 11, June, 1949 - No. 12, Aug, 1949
Marvel Comics

	GD25	FN65	NM94
11,12	6.50	19.50	45.00

AWKWARD UNIVERSE
12/95 ($9.95, graphic novel)
Slave Labor Graphics

	GD25	FN65	NM94
nn			10.00

AXA
Apr, 1987 - No. 2, Aug, 1987 ($1.75)
Eclipse Comics

	GD25	FN65	NM94
1,2		.70	1.80

AXEL PRESSBUTTON (Pressbutton No. 5; see Laser Eraser &...)
Nov, 1984 - No. 6, July, 1985 ($1.50/$1.75, Baxter paper)
Eclipse Comics

	GD25	FN65	NM94
1-6: Reprints Warrior (British mag.). 1-Bolland-c; origin Laser Eraser & Pressbutton		.70	1.80

AXIS ALPHA
Feb, 1994 ($2.50, one-shot)
Axis Comics

	GD25	FN65	NM94
V1-Previews Axis titles including, Tribe, Dethgrip, B.E.A.S.T.I.E.S. & more; Pitt app. in Tribe story.		1.00	2.50

AZRAEL (Also see Batman; Sword of Azrael)
Feb, 1995 - Present ($1.95)
DC Comics

	GD25	FN65	NM94
1-Dennis O'Neil scripts begin		2.00	5.00
2,3		1.60	4.00
4-40: 5,6-Ras Al Ghul app. 13-Nightwing-c/app. 15-Contagion Pt. 5 (Pt. 4 on-c). 16-Contagion Pt. 10. 22-Batman-c/app. 23, 27-Batman app. 27,28-Joker app. 35-Hitman app. 36-Batman, Bane app.		.80	2.00
Annual 1 (1995, $3.95)-Year One story		1.60	4.00
Annual 2 (1996, $2.95)-Legends of the Dead Earth story		1.20	3.00
Annual 3 (1997, $3.95)-Pulp Heroes story			3.95
Plus (12/96, $2.95)-Question-c/app.			2.95

AZRAEL/ ASH)
1997 ($4.95, one-shot)
DC Comics

	GD25	FN65	NM94
1-O'Neil-s/Quesada, Palmiotti-a-			4.95

AZTEC ACE
Mar, 1984 - No. 15, Sept, 1985 ($2.25/$1.50/$1.75, Baxter paper)
Eclipse Comics

	GD25	FN65	NM94
1-$2.25-c (52 pgs.)		.90	2.30
2,3: 2-Begin $1.50-c & 36 pgs.			1.50
4-15: ($1.75/$1.50-c)		.70	1.80

NOTE: ***N. Redondo** a-1i-8i, 10i. c-6-8i.*

AZTEK: THE ULTIMATE MAN
Aug, 1996 - No. 10, May 1997 ($1.75)
DC Comics

	GD25	FN65	NM94
1-1st app. Aztek & Synth; Grant Morrison & Mark Millar scripts in all.		1.60	4.00
2-9: 2-Green Lantern app. 3-1st app. Death-Doll. 4-Intro The Lizard King. 5-Origin. 6-Joker app.; Batman cameo. 7-Batman app. 8-Luthor app. 9-vs. Parasite-c/app.		.80	2.00
10-JLA-c/app.		1.20	3.00

NOTE: ***Breyfogle** c-5p. **N. Steven Harris** a-1-5p. **Porter** c-1p. **Wieringo** c-2p.*

BABE (...Darling of the Hills, later issues)(See Big Shot and Sparky Watts)
June-July, 1948 - No. 11, Apr-May, 1950
Prize/Headline/Feature

	GD25	FN65	NM94
1-Boody Rogers-a	15.00	45.00	120.00
2-Boody Rogers-a	9.50	28.00	75.00
3-11-All by Boody Rogers	8.75	26.25	65.00

BABE
July, 1994 - No. 4, Jan, 1994 ($2.50, limited series)
Dark Horse Comics (Legend)

	GD25	FN65	NM94
1-4: John Byrne-c/a/scripts; ProtoTykes back-up story		1.00	2.50

BABE RUTH SPORTS COMICS (Becomes Rags Rabbit #11 on?)
April, 1949 - No. 11, Feb, 1951
Harvey Publications

	GD25	FN65	NM94
1-Powell-a	33.00	98.00	260.00
2-Powell-a	23.00	68.00	180.00
3-11: Powell-a in most	19.00	56.00	150.00

NOTE: *Baseball c-2-4, 9. Basketball c-1, 6. Football c-5. Yogi Berra c/story-8. Joe DiMaggio c/story-3. Bob Feller c/story-4. Stan Musial c-9.*

BABES IN TOYLAND (Disney, Movie) (See Golden Pix Story Book ST-3)
No. 1282, Feb-Apr, 1962
Dell Publishing Co.

	GD25	FN65	NM94
Four Color 1282-Annette Funicello photo-c	11.00	34.00	125.00

BABES OF BROADWAY
May, 1996 ($2.95, one-shot)
Broadway Comics

	GD25	FN65	NM94
1-Pin-ups of Broadway Comics' female characters; Alan Davis, Michael Kaluta, J. G. Jones, Alan Weiss, Guy Davis & others-a; Giordano-c.		1.20	3.00

BABE 2
Mar, 1995 - No. 2, May, 1995 ($2.50, limited series)
Dark Horse Comics (Legend)

	GD25	FN65	NM94
1,2: John Byrne-c/a/scripts		1.00	2.50

BABY ANGEL X
1995 ($2.95, B&W, mature)
Brainstorm Comics

	GD25	FN65	NM94
1-3		1.20	3.00
1-3-Gold ($5.00)		2.00	5.00

BABY HUEY
No. 100, Oct, 1990 - No. 101, Nov, 1990; No. 1, Oct, 1991 - No. 9, June, 1994 ($1.00/$1.25/$1.50, quarterly)
Harvey Comics

	GD25	FN65	NM94
100,101,1,2 ($1.00): 1-Cover says "Big Baby Huey"		1.20	3.00
3-9 ($1.25-$1.50)		.80	2.00

BABY HUEY AND PAPA (See Paramount Animated...)
May, 1962 - No. 33, Jan, 1968 (Also see Casper The Friendly Ghost)
Harvey Publications

	GD25	FN65	NM94
1	15.00	45.00	150.00
2	6.50	19.50	65.00
3-5	4.50	13.50	45.00
6-10	2.20	6.60	22.00
11-20	1.85	5.50	15.00
21-33	1.50	4.50	12.00

Backlash #3 © Aegis Entertainment

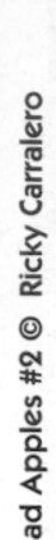
Bad Apples #2 © Ricky Carralero

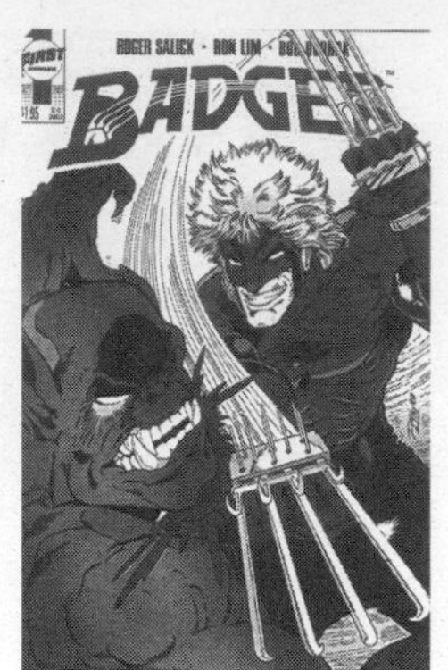
Badger #51 © Mike Baron

BABY HUEY DIGEST
June, 1992 (Digest-size, one-shot)
Harvey Publications

	GD25	FN65	NM94
1-Reprints		1.60	4.00

BABY HUEY DUCKLAND
Nov, 1962 - No. 15, Nov, 1966 (25¢ Giants, 68 pgs.)
Harvey Publications

	GD25	FN65	NM94
1	11.00	33.00	110.00
2-5	4.50	13.50	45.00
6-15	2.10	6.30	21.00

BABY HUEY, THE BABY GIANT (Also see Big Baby Huey, Casper, Harvey Hits #22, Harvey Comics Hits #60, & Paramount Animated Comics)
9/56 - #97, 10/71; #98, 10/72; #99, 10/80; #100, 10/90 - #102?
Harvey Publications

	GD25	FN65	NM94
1-Infinity-c	35.00	105.00	350.00
2	17.00	51.00	170.00
3-Baby Huey takes anti-pep pills	11.00	33.00	110.00
4,5	8.50	25.50	85.00
6-10	4.50	13.50	45.00
11-20	3.50	10.50	35.00
21-40	2.20	6.60	22.00
41-60	1.85	5.50	15.00
61-79 (12/67)	1.50	4.50	12.00
80(12/68) - 95-All 68 pg. Giants	2.00	6.00	16.00
96,97-Both 52 pg. Giants	1.50	4.50	12.00
98-99: Regular size		2.40	6.00
100-102 ($1.00)		1.20	3.00

BABYLON 5 (TV)
Jan, 1995 - No. 11, Dec, 1995 ($1.95/$2.50)
DC Comics

	GD25	FN65	NM94
1	1.00	3.00	8.00
2		2.40	6.00
3-6		2.00	5.00
7-11: 7-Begin $2.50-c		1.20	3.00

BABY SNOOTS (Also see March of Comics #359, 371, 396, 401, 419, 431,443, 450, 462, 474, 485)
Aug, 1970 - No. 22, Nov, 1975
Gold Key

	GD25	FN65	NM94
1	2.25	6.75	18.00
2-11	1.00	3.00	8.00
12-22: 22-Titled Snoots, the Forgetful Elefink		2.00	5.00

BACCHUS
1988 - No. 2, Aug, 1988 ($1.95, B&W)
Harrier Comics (New Wave)

	GD25	FN65	NM94
1,2: Eddie Campbell-c/a/scripts.		.80	2.00

BACHELOR FATHER (TV)
No. 1332, 4-6/62 - No. 2, 1962
Dell Publishing Co.

	GD25	FN65	NM94
Four Color 1332 (#1), 2-Written by Stanley	7.00	22.00	80.00

BACHELOR'S DIARY
1949 (15¢)
Avon Periodicals

	GD25	FN65	NM94
1(Scarce)-King Features panel cartoons & text-r; pin-up, girl wrestling photos; similar to Sideshow	33.00	100.00	265.00

BACK DOWN THE LINE
1991 (Mature adults, 8-1/2 x 11", 52 pgs.)
Eclipse Books

	GD25	FN65	NM94
nn (Soft-c, $8.95)-Bolton-c/a	1.10	3.30	9.00
nn (Limited Hard-c, $29.95)	3.00	9.00	30.00

BACKLASH (Also see The Kindred)
Nov,1994 - No. 32, May, 1997 ($1.95/$2.50)
Image Comics (WildStorm Productions)

	GD25	FN65	NM94
1-Double-c; variant-double-c		1.20	3.00
2-6:5-Intro Mindscape; 2 pinups		.90	2.25
7,9-32: 7-Begin $2.50-c. 19-Fire From Heaven Pt 2. 20-Fire From Heaven Pt 10. 31-WildC.A.T.S app.		.90	2.25
8-($1.95, newsstand)-Wildstorm Rising Pt. 8		.80	2.00
8-($2.50, direct market)-Wildstorm Rising Pt. 8		1.00	2.50
25-($3.95)-Double-size			3.95

BACKLASH/SPIDER-MAN
Aug, 1996 - No. 2, Sept, 1996 ($2.50, limited series)
Image Comics (Wildstorm Productions)

	GD25	FN65	NM94
1,2: Pike (villain from WildC.A.T.S) & Venom app.		1.00	2.50

BACK TO THE FUTURE (Movie, TV cartoon)
Nov, 1991 - No. 4, June, 1992 ($1.25)
Harvey Comics

	GD25	FN65	NM94
1-4: 1,2-Gil Kane-c; based on animated cartoon			1.25
Special nn (1991, 20 pgs.)-Brunner-c; given away at Universal Studios in Florida			1.00

BACK TO THE FUTURE: FORWARD TO THE FUTURE
Oct, 1992 - No. 3, Feb, 1993 ($1.50, limited series)
Harvey Comics

	GD25	FN65	NM94
1-3			1.50

BAD APPLES
1997- No. 2 ($2.95, B&W, limited series)
High Impact Entertainment

	GD25	FN65	NM94
1,2			2.95

BAD COMPANY
Aug, 1988 - No. 19?, 1990 ($1.50/$1.75, high quality paper)
Quality Comics/Fleetway Quality #15 on

	GD25	FN65	NM94
1-15: 5,6-Guice-c			1.50
16-19: ($1.75-c)		.70	1.75

BAD EGGS, THE
June, 1995 - No. 8, Jan, 1997 ($2.95, limited series)
Acclaim Comics (Armada)

	GD25	FN65	NM94
1-8: Layton scripts; Perlin-a. 5-William Shatner app.		1.20	3.00

BADGE OF JUSTICE
No. 22, 1/55 - No. 23, 3/55; 4/55 - No. 4, 10/55
Charlton Comics

	GD25	FN65	NM94
22(1/55)	7.85	23.50	55.00
23(3/55), 1	5.70	17.00	35.00
2-4	4.15	12.50	25.00

BADGER, THE
Dec, 1983 - No. 70, Apr, 1991; V2#1, Spring, 1991
Capital Comics(#1-4)/First Comics

	GD25	FN65	NM94
1-4			1.50
5			1.50
6-49			1.00
50-($3.95, 52 pgs.)		1.60	4.00
51-70: 52-54-Tim Vigil-c/a		.80	2.00
V2#1 (Spring, 1991, $4.95)		2.00	5.00

BADGER, THE
V3#78, May, 1997 - Present ($2.95, B&W)
Image Comics

	GD25	FN65	NM94
78-Cover lists #1, Baron-s			2.95
79/#2, 80/#3, 81(indicia lists #80)/#4,82-84/#5-7			2.95

BADGER GOES BERSERK

Badrock and Company #2 © Extreme

Baffling Mysteries #6 © ACE

Ballistic Imagery #1 © Top Cow

GD25 FN65 NM94

Sept, 1989 - No. 4, Dec, 1989 ($1.95, limited series, Baxter paper)
First Comics
1-4: 2-Paul Chadwick-c/a(2pgs.) .80 2.00

BADGER: SHATTERED MIRROR
July, 1994 - No. Oct, 1994 ($2.50, limited series)
Dark Horse Comics
1-4 1.00 2.50

BADGER: ZEN POP FUNNY-ANIMAL VERSION
July, 1994 - No. 2, Aug, 1994 ($2.50, limited series)
Dark Horse Comics
1,2 1.00 2.50

BAD GIRLS OF BLACKOUT
July, 1995 ($3.50)
Blackout Comics
1 1.40 3.50
Annual 1 (1995, $3.50) 1.40 3.50
Annual 1 Commemorative (1995, $9.95) 1.25 3.75 10.00

BADLANDS
May, 1990 ($3.00, glossy stock, mature)
Vortex Comics
1-Chaykin-c 1.20 3.00

BADLANDS
July, 1991 - No. 6, Dec, 1991 ($2.25, B&W, limited series, mature)
Dark Horse Comics
1-6: 1-John F. Kennedy-c .90 2.30

BADMEN OF THE WEST
1951 (Giant) (132 pgs., painted-c)
Avon Periodicals
1-Contains rebound copies of Jesse James, King of the Bad Men of Deadwood, Badmen of Tombstone; other combinations possible. Issues with Kubert-a... 29.00 86.00 230.00

BADMEN OF THE WEST! (See A-1 Comics)
1953 - No. 3, 1954
Magazine Enterprises
1(A-1 100)-Meskin-a? 19.50 58.00 155.00
2(A-1 120), 3: 2-Larsen-a 12.00 36.00 95.00

BADMEN OF TOMBSTONE
1950
Avon Periodicals
nn 11.30 34.00 90.00

BADROCK (Also see Youngblood)
Mar, 1995 - No. 2, Jan, 1996 ($1.75/$2.50)
Image Comics (Extreme Studios)
1-Variant-c (3) .70 1.75
2-Liefeld-c/a & story; Savage Dragon app, flipbook w/Grifter/Badrock #2; variant-c exist 1.00 2.50
Annual 1(1995,$2.95)-Arthur Adams-c 1.20 3.00
Annual 1 Commemorative ($9.95)-Print run of 3,000 1.25 3.75 10.00
.../Wolverine (6/96, $4.95, squarebound)-Sauron app; pin-ups; variant-c exists 2.00 5.00
.../Wolverine (6/96)-Special Comicon Edition; variant-c exists 2.00 5.00

BADROCK AND COMPANY (Also see Youngblood)
Sept, 1994 - No.6, Feb, 1995 ($2.50, limited series)
Image Comics (Extreme Studios)
1-6 : 6-Indicia reads "October 1994"; story cont'd in Shadowhawk #17 1.00 2.50

BAFFLING MYSTERIES (Formerly Indian Braves No. 1-4; Heroes of the Wild Frontier No. 26-on)
No. 5, Nov, 1951 - No. 26, Oct, 1955
Periodical House (Ace Magazines)
5 26.00 79.00 200.00
6-24: 8-Woodish-a by Cameron. 10-E.C. Crypt Keeper swipe on-c. 24-Last pre-code issue 16.00 47.00 115.00
25-Reprints; surrealistic-c 13.00 39.00 95.00
26-Reprints 11.00 33.00 80.00
NOTE: ***Cameron*** *a-8, 10, 16-18, 20-22.* ***Colan*** *a-5, 11, 25r/5.* ***Sekowsky*** *a-5, 6, 22. Bondage c-20, 23. Reprints in 18(1), 19(1), 24(3).*

BALBO (See Master Comics #33 & Mighty Midget Comics)

BALDER THE BRAVE
Nov, 1985 - No. 4, 1986 (Limited series)
Marvel Comics Group
1-4: Simonson-c/a; character from Thor 1.00

BALLAD OF HALO JONES, THE
Sept, 1987 - No. 12, Aug, 1988 ($1.25/$1.50)
Quality Comics
1-12: Alan Moore scripts in all 1.50

BALLISTIC (Also See Cyberforce)
Sept, 1995 - No. 3, Dec, 1995 ($2.50, limited series)
Image Comics (Top Cow Productions)
1-3: Wetworks app, Turner-c/a 1.60 4.00

BALLISTIC ACTION
May, 1996 ($2.95, one-shot)
Image Comics (Top Cow Productions)
1-Pin-ups of Top Cow characters participating in outdoor sports. 1.20 3.00

BALLISTIC IMAGERY
Jan, 1996 ($2.50, anthology, one-shot)
Image Comics (Top Cow Productions)
1-Cyberforce app. 1.00 2.50

BALLISTIC/ WOLVERINE
Feb, 1997 ($2.95, one-shot)
Image Comics (Top Cow Productions)
1-Devil's Reign pt. 4; Witchblade cameo (1 page) 2.95

BALOO & LITTLE BRITCHES (Disney)
Apr, 1968
Gold Key
1-From the Jungle Book 2.25 6.75 24.00

BALTIMORE COLTS
1950 (Giveaway)
American Visuals Corp.
nn-Eisner-c 42.00 126.00 375.00

BAMBI (Disney) (See Movie Classics, Movie Comics, and Walt Disney Showcase No. 31)
No. 12, 1942; No. 30, 1943; No. 186, Apr, 1948
Dell Publishing Co.
Four Color 12-Walt Disney's... 49.00 146.00 535.00
Four Color 30-Bambi's Children (1943) 49.00 146.00 535.00
Four Color 186-Walt Disney's...; reprinted as Movie Classic Bambi #3 (1956) 15.00 45.00 165.00

BAMBI (Disney)
1941, 1942, 1984
K. K. Publications (Giveaways)/Whitman Publ. Co.

Barbie #45 © MEG

Barb Wire #7 © DH

The Barker #3 © QUA

1941-Horlick's Malted Milk & various toy stores; text & pictures; most copies mailed out with store stickers on-c 23.00 69.00 185.00
1942-Same as 4-Color #12, but no price (Same as '41 issue?) (Scarce) 36.00 108.00 300.00
1-(Whitman, 1984; 60¢)-r/4-Color #186 1.60 4.00

BAMBI (Disney)
1942 (50¢, 7"x8-1/2", 32pg, hard-c w/dust jacket)
Grosset & Dunlap
nn-Given away w/a copy of Thumper for a $2.00, 2-yr. subscription to WDC&S in 1942 (Xmas offer). Book only 15.50 47.00 125.00
w/dust jacket 25.00 75.00 200.00

BAMM BAMM & PEBBLES FLINTSTONE (TV)
Oct, 1964 (Hanna-Barbera)
Gold Key
1 6.40 19.00 70.00

BANANA SPLITS, THE (TV) (See Golden Comics Digest & March of Comics No. 364)
June, 1969 - No. 8, Oct, 1971 (Hanna-Barbera)
Gold Key
1-Photo-c 8.00 23.00 85.00
2-8 4.00 12.00 45.00

BAND WAGON (See Hanna-Barbera Band Wagon)

BANDY MAN, THE
1996 ($2.95, B&W, one-shot)
Caliber
1-Stephan Petrucha scripts; Jill Thompson-a; Miran Kim-c 1.20 3.00

BANG-UP COMICS
Dec, 1941 - No. 3, June, 1942
Progressive Publishers
1-Cosmo Mann & Lady Fairplay begin; Buzz Balmer by Rick Yager in all (origin #1) 72.00 216.00 650.00
2,3 39.00 117.00 350.00

BANNER COMICS (Becomes Captain Courageous No. 6)
No. 3, Sept, 1941 - No. 5, Jan, 1942
Ace Magazines
3-Captain Courageous (1st app.) & Lone Warrior & Sidekick Dicky begin; Jim Mooney-c 83.00 250.00 750.00
4,5: 4-Flag-c 53.00 159.00 475.00

BARABBAS
Aug, 1986 - No. 2, Nov, 1986 ($1.50, B&W, limited series)
Slave Labor Graphics
1,2 1.50

BARBARIANS, THE
June, 1975
Atlas Comics/Seaboard Periodicals
1-Origin, only app. Andrax; Iron Jaw app. 1.20 3.00

BARBIE
Jan, 1991 - No. 66, Apr, 1996 ($1.00/$1.25/$1.50)
Marvel Comics
1-Polybagged w/Barbie Pink Card; Romita-c 2.40 6.00
2-66 1.20 3.00

BARBIE & KEN
May-July, 1962 - No. 5, Nov-Jan, 1963-64
Dell Publishing Co.
01-053-207(#1)-Based on Mattel toy dolls 33.00 98.00 360.00
2-4 24.00 72.00 265.00
5 (Rare) 28.00 85.00 310.00

BARBIE FASHION
Jan, 1991 - No. 63, Jan, 1996 ($1.00/$1.25/$1.50)
Marvel Comics
1-Polybagged w/doorknob hanger 2.00 5.00
2-63-($1.25): 4-Contains preview to Sweet XVI. 14-Begin $1.25-c 1.20 3.00

BARBI TWINS, THE
1995 ($2.50/$5.00)
Topps Comics
1-Razor app. 1.00 2.50
Swimsuit Art Calendar ($5.00)-art by Linsner, Bradstreet, Hughes; Julie Bell-c 2.00 5.00

BARB WIRE (See Comics' Greatest World)
Apr, 1994 - No. 9, Feb, 1995 ($2.00/$2.50)
Dark Horse Comics
1-4: 1-Foil logo .80 2.00
5-9-($2.50) 1.00 2.50
Trade paperback (1996, $8.95)-r/#2,3,5,6 w/Pamela Anderson bio. 9.00

BARB WIRE: ACE OF SPADES
May, 1996 - No. 4, Sept, 1996 ($2.95, limited series)
Dark Horse Comics
1-4: Chris Warner-c/a(p)/scripts; Tim Bradstreet-c/a(i) in all 1.20 3.00

BARB WIRE COMICS MAGAZINE SPECIAL
May, 1996 ($3.50, B&W, magazine, one-shot)
Dark Horse Comics
nn-Adaptation of film; photo-c; poster insert. 1.40 3.50

BARB WIRE MOVIE SPECIAL
May, 1996 ($3.95, one-shot)
Dark Horse Comics
nn-Adaptation of film; photo-c; 1st app. new look 1.60 4.00

BARKER, THE (Also see National Comics #42)
Autumn, 1946 - No. 15, Dec, 1949
Quality Comics Group/Comic Magazine
1 15.00 45.00 120.00
2 8.50 26.00 60.00
3-10 5.70 17.00 40.00
11-14 4.25 13.00 26.00
15-Jack Cole-a(p) 5.70 17.00 34.00
NOTE: ***Jack Cole*** *art in some issues.*

BARNABY
1945 (25¢,102 pgs., digest size)
Civil Service Publications Inc.
V1#1-r/Crocket Johnson strips from 1942 2.40 6.00 12.00

BARNEY AND BETTY RUBBLE (TV) (Flintstones' Neighbors)
Jan, 1973 - No. 23, Dec, 1976 (Hanna-Barbera)
Charlton Comics
1 2.80 8.40 28.00
2-10 1.75 5.25 14.00
11-23: 11(2/75)-1st Mike Zeck-a (illos) 1.10 3.30 9.00

BARNEY BAXTER (Also see Magic Comics)
1938 - No. 2, 1956
David McKay/Dell Publishing Co./Argo
Feature Books 15(McKay-1938) 25.00 74.00 270.00
Four Color 20(1942) 24.00 71.00 260.00
4,5 10.00 30.00 110.00
1,2 (1956-Argo) 4.50 13.50 50.00

BARNEY BEAR ...

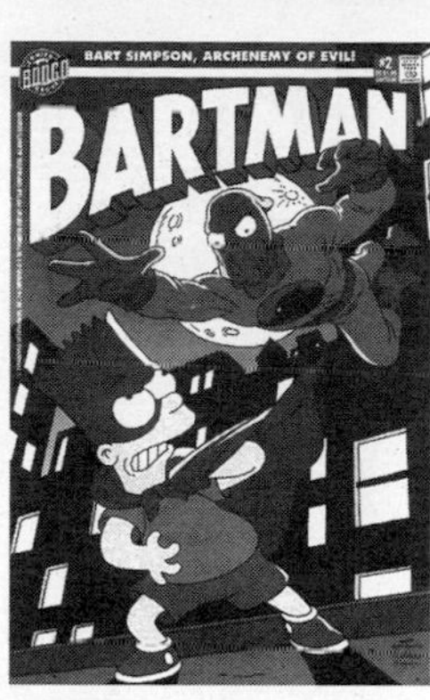

Bartman #2 © Matt Groening

Baseball's Greatest Heroes #2 © Magnum

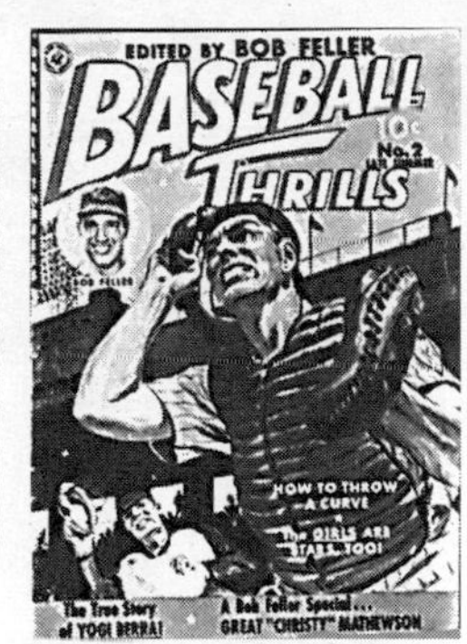

Baseball Thrills #2 © Ziff-Davis Publ.

GD25 FN65 NM94

1977-1981
Spire Christian Comics (Fleming H. Revell Co.)

...Home Plate nn-(1979, 49¢), ...Lost and Found nn-(1979, 49¢), Out of The Woods nn-(1980, 49¢), Sunday School Picnic nn-(1981, 69¢, The Swamp Gang!-(1977, 39¢) 1.20 3.00

BARNEY GOOGLE & SNUFFY SMITH
1942 - 1943; April, 1964
Dell Publishing Co./Gold Key

Four Color 19(1942) 35.00 104.00 380.00
Four Color 40(1944) 20.00 60.00 220.00
Large Feature Comic 11(1943) 21.00 64.00 235.00
1(10113-404)-Gold Key (4/64) 3.00 9.00 32.00

BARNEY GOOGLE & SNUFFY SMITH
June, 1951 - No. 4, Feb, 1952 (Reprints)
Toby Press

1 10.00 30.00 80.00
2,3 6.50 19.50 45.00
4-Kurtzman-a "Pot Shot Pete", 5 pgs.; reprints John Wayne #5 10.00 30.00 80.00

BARNEY GOOGLE AND SNUFFY SMITH
Mar, 1970 - No. 6, Jan, 1971
Charlton Comics

1 2.25 6.75 18.00
2-6 1.50 4.50 12.00

BARNYARD COMICS (Dizzy Duck No. 32 on)
June, 1944 - No. 31, Sept, 1950; No. 10, 1957
Nedor/Polo Mag./Standard(Animated Cartoons)

1 (nn, 52 pgs.)-Funny animal 15.00 45.00 120.00
2 (52 pgs.) 8.50 26.00 60.00
3-5 5.70 17.00 38.00
6-12,16 5.00 15.00 30.00
13-15,17,21,23,26,27,29-All contain Frazetta text illos 5.70 17.00 38.00
18-20,22,24,25-All contain Frazetta-a & text illos 8.75 26.25 70.00
28,30,31 3.60 9.00 18.00
10 (1957)(Exist?) 2.00 5.00 10.00

BARRY M. GOLDWATER
Mar, 1965 (Complete life story)
Dell Publishing Co.

12-055-503-Photo-c 2.25 6.75 26.00

BARRY WINDSOR-SMITH: STORYTELLER
Oct, 1996 - Present ($4.95, oversize)
Dark Horse Comics

1-9: 1-Intro Young Gods, Paradox Man & the Freebooters; Barry Smith-c/a/scripts 2.00 5.00

BAR SINISTER (Also see Shaman's Tears)
Jun, 1995 - No. 4, Sept, 1995 ($2.50, limited series)
Acclaim Comics (Windjammer)

1-4: Mike Grell-c/a/scripts 1.00 2.50

BARTMAN (Also see Simpson's Comics & Radioactive Man)
1993 - No. 6, 1994 ($1.95/$2.25)
Bongo Comics

1-($2.95)-Foil-c; bound-in jumbo Bartman poster 1.30 3.25
2 .80 2.00
3-6: 3-$2.25-c begins; w/trading card .90 2.25

BASEBALL COMICS
Spring, 1949 (Reprinted later as a Spirit section)
Will Eisner Productions

1-Will Eisner-c/a 58.00 174.00 525.00

BASEBALL COMICS
1991 ($3.95, coated stock)
Kitchen Sink Press

1-r/1949 ish. by Eisner; contains trading cards 1.60 4.00

BASEBALL HEROES
1952 (one-shot)
Fawcett Publications

nn (Scarce)-Babe Ruth photo-c; baseball's Hall of Fame biographies 62.00 186.00 560.00

BASEBALL'S GREATEST HEROES
Dec, 1991 - No. 2, May, 1992 ($1.75)
Magnum Comics

1-Mickey Mantle #1; photo-c; Sinnott-a(p) .70 1.75
2-Brooks Robinson #1; photo-c; Sinnott-a(i) .70 1.75

BASEBALL THRILLS
No. 10, Sum, 1951 - No. 3, Sum, 1952 (Saunders painted-c No.1,2)
Ziff-Davis Publ. Co.

10(#1)-Bob Feller, Musial, Newcombe & Boudreau stories 35.00 105.00 280.00
2-Powell-a(2)(Late Sum, '51); Feller, Berra & Mathewson stories 24.00 71.00 190.00
3-Kinstler-c/a; Joe DiMaggio story 24.00 71.00 190.00

BASEBALL THRILLS 3-D
May, 1990 ($2.95, w/glasses)
The 3-D Zone

1-New L.B. Cole-c; life stories of Ty Cobb & Ted Williams 1.20 3.00

BASICALLY STRANGE (Magazine)
Dec, 1982 ($1.95, B&W)
John C. Comics (Archie Comics Group)

1-(21,000 printed; all but 1,000 destroyed; pgs. out of sequence) 1.20 3.00
1-Wood, Toth-a; Corben-c; reprints & new art .80 2.00

BASIC HISTORY OF AMERICA ILLUSTRATED
1976 (B&W) (Soft-c $1.50; Hard-c $4.50)
Pendulum Press

07-1999-America Becomes a World Power 1890-1920. 07-2251-The Industrial Era 1865-1915. 07-226x-Before the Civil War 1830-1860. 07-2278-Americans Move Westward 1800-1850. 07-2286-The Civil War 1850-1876; Redondo-a. 07-2294-The Fight for Freedom 1750-1783. 07-2308-The New World 1500-1750. 07-2316-Problems of the NewNation 1800-1830. 07-2324-Roaring Twenties and the Great Depression 1920-1940. 07-2332-The United States Emerges 1783-1800. 07-2340-America Today 1945-1976. 07-2359-World War II 1940-1945

BASIL (...the Royal Cat)
Jan, 1953 - No. 4, Sept, 1953
St. John Publishing Co.

1-Funny animal 4.15 12.50 25.00
2-4 3.20 8.00 16.00
I.W. Reprint 1 1.40 3.50 7.00

BASIL WOLVERTON'S FANTASTIC FABLES
Oct, 1993 - No. 2, Dec, 1993 ($2.50, B&W, limited series)
Dark Horse Comics

1,2-Wolverton-c/a(r) 1.00 2.50

BASIL WOLVERTON'S GATEWAY TO HORROR
June, 1988 ($1.75, B&W, one-shot)
Dark Horse Comics

1-Wolverton-r .70 1.80

BASIL WOLVERTON'S PLANET OF TERROR
Oct, 1987 ($1.75, B&W, one-shot)

Batman #1 © DC

Batman #28 © DC

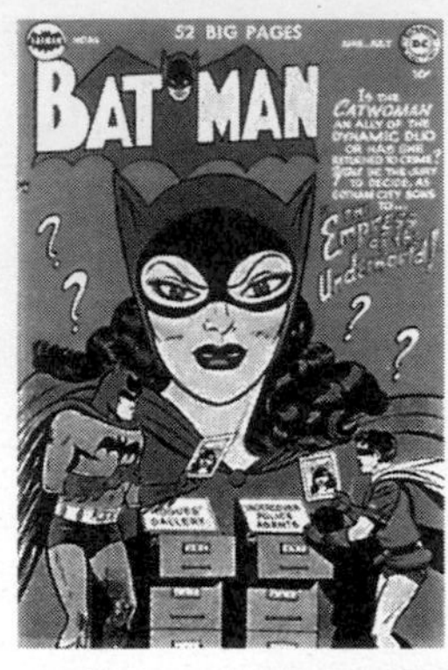

Batman #65 © DC

GD25 FN65 NM94

Dark Horse Comics

1-Wolverton-r; Alan Moore-c .70 1.80

BATGIRL ADVENTURES (See Batman Adventures, The)
1998 ($2.95, one-shot) (Based on animated series)
DC Comics

1-Harley Quinn and Poison Ivy app.; Timm-c 1.20 3.00

BATGIRL SPECIAL (See Teen Titans #50)
1988 ($1.50, one-shot, 52 pgs)
DC Comics

1 2.00 5.00

NOTE: ***Mignola*** *c-1.*

BAT LASH (See DC Special Series #16, Showcase #76, Weird Western Tales)
Oct-Nov, 1968 - No. 7, Oct-Nov, 1969 (All 12¢ issues)
National Periodical Publications

1-(10-11/68)-2nd app. Bat Lash 1.75 5.25 14.00
2-7 1.00 3.00 8.00

BATMAN (See Arkham Asylum, Aurora, The Best of DC #2, Blind Justice, The Brave & the Bold, Cosmic Odyssey, DC 100-Page Super Spec. #14,20, DC Special, DC Special Series, Detective, Dynamic Classics, 80-Page Giants, Gotham By Gaslight, Gotham Nights, Greatest Batman Stories Ever Told, Greatest Joker Stories Ever Told, Heroes Against Hunger, The Joker, Justice League of America #250, Justice League Int., Legends of the Dark Knight, Limited Coll. Ed., Man-Bat, Power Record Comics, Real Fact #5, Saga of Ra's Al Ghul, Shadow of the..., Star Spangled, Super Friends, 3-D Batman, Untold Legend of..., Wanted... & World's Finest Comics)

BATMAN
Spring, 1940 - Present (#1-5 were quarterly)
National Periodical Publ./Detective Comics/DC Comics

GD25 FN65 VF82 NM94

1-Origin The Batman reprinted (2 pgs.) from Det. #33 w/splash from #35 by Bob Kane; see Detective #33 for 1st origin; 1st app. Joker (2 stories intended for 2 separate issues of Det. Comics which would have been 1st & 2nd app.); splash pg. to 2nd Joker story is similar to cover of Det. #40 (story intended for #40); 1st app. The Cat (Catwoman)(1st villainess in comics); has Batman story (w/Hugo Strange) without Robin originally planned for Det. #38; mentions location (Manhattan) where Batman lives (see Det. #31). This book was created entirely from the inventory of Det. Comics; 1st Batman/Robin pin-up on back-c; has text piece & photo of Bob Kane
5,167.00 15,500.00 33,580.00 62,000.00
(Estimated up to 250+ total copies exist, 16 in NM/Mint)

1-Reprint, oversize 13-1/2x10". **WARNING**: This comic is an exact duplicate reprint of the original except for its size. DC published it in 1974 with a second cover titling it as a Famous First Edition. There have been many reported cases of the outer cover being removed and the interior sold as the original edition. The reprint with the new outer cover removed is practically worthless. See Famous First Edition for value.

GD25 FN65 NM94

2-2nd app. The Joker; 2nd app. Catwoman (out of costume) in Joker story; 1st time called Catwoman
NOTE: A 15¢-c for Canadian distr. exists.
1000.00 3000.00 11,000.00
3-3rd app Catwoman (1st in costume & 1st costumed villainess); 1st Puppet Master app. 700.00 2100.00 7000.00
4-3rd app. The Joker (see Det. #45 for 4th); 1st mention of Gotham City in a Batman comic (on newspaper)(Win/40) 580.00 1740.00 5800.00
5-1st app. the Batmobile with its bat-head front 420.00 1260.00 4200.00
6,7: 7-Bullseye-c 350.00 1050.00 3500.00
8-Infinity-c. 300.00 900.00 3000.00
9-10:9-1st Batman x-mas story; Burnley-c. 10-Catwoman story (gets new costume) 270.00 810.00 2700.00
11-Classic Joker-c by Ray/Robinson (3rd Joker-c, 6-7/42); Joker & Penguin app. 520.00 1560.00 5200.00
12,15: 15-New costume Catwoman 210.00 630.00 2100.00
13-Jerry Siegel (Superman's co-creator) appears in a Batman story. 240.00 720.00 2400.00
14-2nd Penguin-c; Penguin app. (12-1/42-43) 230.00 690.00 2300.00
16-Intro/origin Alfred (4-5/43); cover is a reverse of #9 cover by Burnley; 1st small logo 435.00 1305.00 4350.00
17,19,20: 17-Penguin app. 20-1st Batmobile-c (12-1/43-44) 156.00 468.00 1400.00
18-Hitler, Hirohito, Mussolini-c. 194.00 582.00 1750.00
21,22,24,26,28-30: 21-1st skinny Alfred in Batman (2-3/44). 21,30-Penguin app. 22-1st Alfred solo-c/story (Alfred solo stories in 22-32,36); Catwoman & The Cavalier app. 117.00 350.00 1050.00
23-Joker-c/story 167.00 500.00 1500.00
25-Only Joker/Penguin team-up; 1st team-up between two major villains 172.00 516.00 1550.00
27-Burnley Christmas-c; Penguin app. 156.00 468.00 1400.00
31,32,34-36,39: 32-Origin Robin retold. 35-Catwoman story (in new costume w/o cat head mask). 36-Penguin app. 89.00 267.00 800.00
33-Christmas-c 100.00 300.00 900.00
37,40,44-Joker-c/stories 111.00 333.00 1000.00
38-Penguin-c/story 94.00 282.00 850.00
41,45,46: 41-Penguin app. 45-Christmas-c/story; Catwoman story; Vicki Vale app. (1st app?) 67.00 200.00 600.00
42,43: 42-2nd Catwoman-c (1st in Batman)(8-9/47); Catwoman story also. 43-Penguin-c/story 82.00 246.00 740.00
47-1st detailed origin The Batman (6-7/48); 1st Bat-signal-c this title (see Detective #108); Batman tracks down his parent's killer and reveals i.d. to him 250.00 750.00 2500.00
48-1000 Secrets of the Batcave; r-in #203; Penguin story 83.00 250.00 750.00
49-Joker-c/story; 1st app. Mad Hatter; Vicki Vale app. 133.00 400.00 1200.00
50-Two-Face impostor app. 72.00 216.00 650.00
51,54,56,57,59: 57-Centerfold is a 1950 calendar. 59-1st app. Deadshot; Batman in the future-c/story 63.00 189.00 570.00
52,55-Joker-c/stories 78.00 234.00 700.00
53,58,60,61: 58-Penguin-c. 61-Origin Batman Plane II 69.00 207.00 625.00
62-Origin Catwoman; Catwoman-c 89.00 267.00 800.00
63,80-Joker stories. 63-Flying saucer story(2-3/51) 58.00 174.00 520.00
64,67,70-72,74-77,79: 72-Last 52 pg. issue. 74-Used in **POP**, Pg. 90. 79-Vicki Vale in "The Bride of Batman" 50.00 150.00 450.00
65,69,84-Catwoman-c/stories. 84-Two-Face app. 56.00 168.00 500.00
66,73-Joker-c/stories. 66-Pre-2nd Batman & Robin team try-out. 73-Vicki Vale story 65.00 195.00 585.00
68,81-Two-Face-c/stories 52.00 156.00 470.00
78-(8-9/53)-Roh Kar, The Man Hunter from Mars story-the 1st lawman of Mars to come to Earth (green skinned) 63.00 189.00 570.00
82,83,85-89: 86-Intro Batmarine (Batman's submarine). 89-Last pre-code issue 49.00 147.00 440.00
90,91,93-99: 97-2nd app. Bat-Hound-c/story; Joker app. 99-(4/56)-Last S.A. Penguin app. 40.00 120.00 355.00
92-1st app. Bat-Hound-c/story 50.00 150.00 450.00
100-(6/56) 211.00 633.00 1900.00
101-(8/56)-Clark Kent x-over who protects Batman's i.d. (3rd story) 43.00 130.00 390.00
102-104,106-109: 103-1st S.A. issue; 3rd Bat-Hound-c/story 31.00 93.00 350.00
105-1st Batwoman in Batman (2nd anywhere) 39.00 117.00 440.00
110-Joker story 31.00 93.00 350.00
111-120: 112-1st app. Signalman (super villain). 113-1st app. Fatman; Batman meets his counterpart on Planet X w/a chest plate similar to S.A. Batman's design (yellow oval w/black design inside). 29.00 87.00 290.00
121- Origin/1st app. of Mr. Zero (Mr. Freeze). 31.00 93.00 350.00
122,124-126,128,130: 124-2nd app. Signal Man. 126-Batwoman-c/story. 128-Batwoman cameo. 130-Lex Luthor app. 19.50 58.00 195.00
123,127: 123-Joker story; Bat-Hound app. 127-(10/59)-Batman vs. Thor the Thunder God-c/story; Joker story; Superman cameo

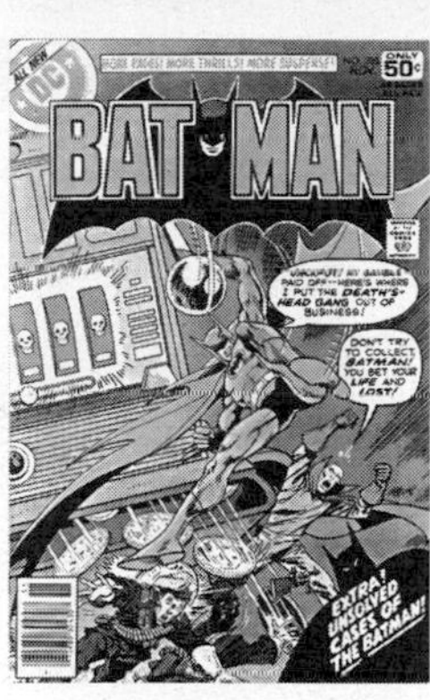

Batman #305 © DC

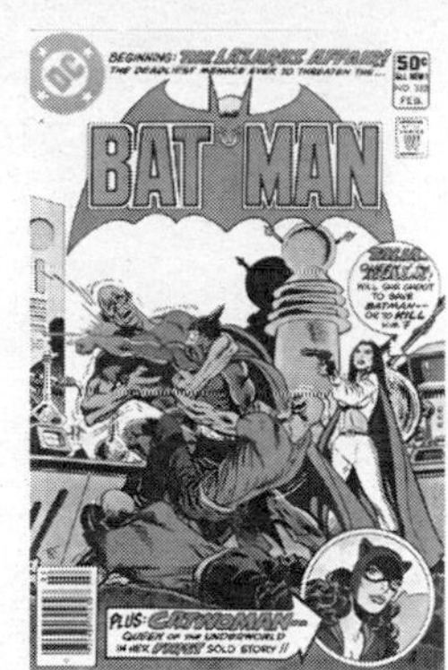

Batman #332 © DC

Batman #348 © DC

GD25 FN65 NM94

22.50 68.00 225.00

129-Origin Robin retold; bondage-c; Batwoman-c/story (reprinted in Batman Family #8) 24.00 72.00 240.00

131-135,137-139,141-143: 131-Intro 2nd Batman & Robin series (see #66; also in #135,145,154,159,163). 133-1st Bat-Mite in Batman (3rd app. anywhere). 134-Origin The Dummy. 139-Intro 1st original Bat-Girl; only app. Signalman as the Blue Bowman. 141-2nd app. original Bat-Girl. 143-(10/61)-Last 10¢ issue 15.50 47.00 155.00

136-Joker-c/story 18.00 54.00 180.00

140,144-Joker stories. 140-Batwoman-c/story; Superman cameo. 144-(12/61)-3rd app. original Bat-Girl; 1st 12¢ issue 15.00 45.00 150.00

145,148-Joker-c/stories 16.00 48.00 160.00

146,147,149,150 11.50 34.00 115.00

151,152,153,154,156-158,160-162,164-168,170: 152-Joker story. 153-4th app. original Bat-Girl. 156-Ant-Man/Robin team-up (6/63). 163-Original Bat-Girl as Batwoman II. 164-New Batmobile (6/64); new look & Mystery Analysts series begins 9.00 27.00 90.00

155-1st S.A. app. The Penguin (5/63) 31.00 93.00 320.00

159,163-Joker-c/stories. 159-5th app. original Bat-Girl. 163-7th app. original Bat-Girl & only app. as Batwoman II (last app. until Tales of the Teen Titans #50) 11.00 33.00 110.00

169-2nd SA Penguin app. 13.50 41.00 135.00

171-1st Riddler app.(5/65) since Dec. 1948 39.00 117.00 425.00

172-175,177,178,180,184 5.50 16.50 55.00

176-(80-Pg. Giant G-17); Joker-c/story; Penguin app. in strip-r; Catwoman reprint 7.00 21.00 70.00

179-2nd app. Silver Age Riddler 12.50 38.00 125.00

181-Batman & Robin poster insert; intro. Poison Ivy. 12.00 36.00 120.00

182,187-(80 Pg. Giants G-24, G-30); Joker-c/stories 6.00 18.00 60.00

183-2nd app. Poison Ivy 8.50 25.50 85.00

185-(80 Pg. Giant G-27) 8.00 24.00 60.00

186-Joker-c/story 4.50 13.50 45.00

188,191,192,194-196,199 2.80 7.60 28.00

189-1st S.A. app. Scarecrow; retells origin of G.A. Scarecrow from World's Finest #3(1st app.) 6.00 18.00 60.00

190-Penguin app. 3.80 11.40 38.00

193-(80-Pg. Giant G-37) 4.50 13.50 45.00

197-4th S.A. Catwoman app. cont'd from Det. #369; 1st new Batgirl app. in Batman (5th anywhere) 5.50 16.50 55.00

198-(80-Pg. Giant G-43); Joker-c/story-r/World's Finest #61; Catwoman-r/ Det. #211; Penguin-r; origin-r/#47 7.00 21.00 70.00

200-(3/68)-Joker cameo; retells origin of Batman & Robin; 1st Neal Adams work this title (cover only) 12.00 36.00 120.00

201-Joker story 3.00 9.00 30.00

202,204-207,209,210 2.25 6.75 18.00

203-(80 Pg. Giant G-49); r/#48, 61, & Det. 185; Batcave Blueprints 4.00 12.00 40.00

208-(80 Pg. Giant G-55); New origin Batman by Gil Kane plus 3 G.A. Batman reprints w/Catwoman, Vicki Vale & Batwoman 4.00 12.00 40.00

211,212,214-217: 212-Last 12¢ issue. 214-Alfred given a new last name- "Pennyworth" (see Detective #96). 2.00 6.00 16.00

213-(80-Pg. Giant G-61); 30th anniversary issue (7-8/69); origin Alfred (r/Batman #16), Joker(r/Det. #168), Clayface; new origin Robin with new facts 5.50 16.50 55.00

218-(80-Pg. Giant G-67) 3.60 10.80 36.00

219-Neal Adams-a 3.60 10.80 36.00

220,221,224-227,229-231 1.75 5.25 14.00

222-Beatles take-off; art lesson by Joe Kubert 2.80 8.40 28.00

223,228,233-(80-Pg. Giants G-73,G-79,G-85) 2.80 8.40 28.00

232-N. Adams-a. Intro/1st app. Ras Al Ghul; origin Batman & Robin retold. 7.50 22.50 75.00

234-(9/71)-Two-Face app.; (see World's Finest #173); N. Adams-a; 52 pg. issues begin, end #242 10.00 30.00 100.00

235,236,239-242: 239-XMas-c. 241-Reprint/#5 2.00 6.00 16.00

GD25 FN65 NM94

237-N. Adams-a. G.A. Batman-r/Det. #37; 1st app. The Reaper; Wrightson/Ellison plots 4.20 12.60 42.00

238-DC-8 100 Page Super Spec.; G.A. Atom, Sargon (r/Sensation #57), Plastic Man (r/Police #14) stories; Doom Patrol origin-r; Batman, Legion, Aquaman-r; N. Adams wraparound-c. (see DC 100 Page Supec. #8 for price) -

243-245-Neal Adams-a 3.00 9.00 30.00

246-250,252,253: 246-Scarecrow app. 253-Shadow-c & app. 2.00 6.00 16.00

251-(9/73)-N. Adams-c/a; Joker-c/story 4.80 14.40 48.00

254,256-259,261-All 100 pg. editions; part-r: 254-(2/74)-Man-Bat-c & app. 256-Catwoman app. 258-Joker & Penguin app.; The Cavalier-r. 259-Shadow-c/app. 2.25 6.75 18.00

255-(100 pgs.)-N. Adams-c/a; tells of Bruce Wayne's father who wore bat costume & fought crime (r/Det. #235); r/story Batman #22 3.20 9.60 32.00

260-Joker-c/story (100 pgs.) 3.80 11.40 38.00

262 (68pgs.) 2.00 6.00 16.00

263-285,287-290,292,293,295-299: 266-Catwoman back to old costume 1.00 3.00 8.00

286,291,294: 294-Joker-c/stories 1.50 4.50 12.00

300-Double-size 1.75 5.25 14.00

301-(7/78)-320,322-331,333-352: 304-(44 pgs.). 306-3rd app. Black Spider. 308-Mr. Freeze app. 310-1st modern app. The Gentleman Ghost in Batman; Kubert-c. 311-Batgirl-c/story; Batgirl reteams w/Batman. 313-2nd app. Calendar Man. 313,314,346-Two-Face-c/stories. 316-Robin returns. 318-Intro Firebug. 319-2nd modern age app. The Gentleman Ghost; Kubert-c. 322-324-Catwoman (Selina Kyle) app. 322,323-Cat-Man cameos (1st In Batman, 1 panel each). 323-1st meeting Catwoman & Cat-Man. 324-1st full app. Cat-Man this title. 344-Poison Ivy app. 345-1st app. new Dr. Death. 345,346,351-7 pg. Catwoman back-ups 1.25 3.75 10.00

321,353,359-Joker-c/stories. 1.25 3.75 10.00

332-Catwoman's 1st solo. 1.00 3.00 8.00

354-356,358,360-365,369,370: 358-1st app. Killer Croc. 361-1st app Harvey Bullock 2.40 6.00

357-1st app. Jason Todd (3/83); see Det. 524 1.00 3.00 8.00

366-Jason Todd 1st in Robin costume; Joker-c/story 1.00 3.00 8.00

368-1st new Robin in costume (Jason Todd) 2.00 5.00

371-399,401-403: 371-Cat-Man-c/story; brief origin Cat-Man (cont'd in Det. #538). 386,387-Intro Black Mask (villain). 380-391-Catwoman app. 398-Catwoman & Two-Face app. 401-2nd app. Magpie (see Man of Steel #3 for 1st). 403-Joker cameo .80 2.00

NOTE: *Most issues between 397 & 432 were reprinted in 1989 and sold in multi-packs. Some are not identified as reprints but have newer ads copyrighted after cover dates. 2nd and 3rd printings exist.*

400 ($1.50, 68pgs.)-Dark Knight special; intro by Stephen King; Art Adams/ Austin-a 1.85 5.50 15.00

404-Miller scripts begin (end 407); Year 1; 1st modern app. Catwoman (2/87) 2.40 6.00

405-407: 407-Year 1 ends (See Det. Comics for Year 2) 1.60 4.00

408-410: New Origin Jason Todd (Robin) 1.20 3.00

411-416,421-425: 411-Two-face app. 412-Origin/1st app. Mime. 414-Starlin scripts begin, end #429. 416-Nightwing-c/story. 423-McFarlane-c .80 2.00

417-420: "Ten Nights of the Beast" storyline 2.40 6.00

426-($1.50, 52 pgs.)- "A Death In The Family" storyline begins, ends #429 1.10 3.30 9.00

427- "A Death In The Family" part 2. 1.10 3.30 9.00

428-Death of Robin (Jason Todd) 2.00 5.00

429-Joker-c/story; Superman app. 2.00 5.00

430-432 .80 2.00

433-435-Many Deaths of the Batman story by John Byrne-c/scripts .80 2.00

436-Year 3 begins (ends #439); origin original Robin retold by Nightwing

Batman #512 © DC

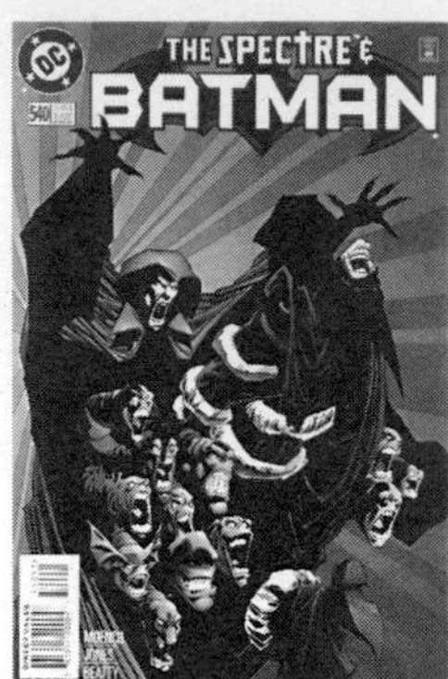

Batman #540 © DC

Batman Arkham Asylum © DC

GD25 FN65 NM94

(Dick Grayson); 1st app. Timothy Drake (8/89) 1.20 3.00
436-2nd printing 1.00
437-439: 437-Origin Robin continued .80 2.00
440,441: "A Lonely Place of Dying" Parts 1 & 3 1.25
442-1st app. Timothy Drake in Robin costume 1.00 2.50
443-456,458,459,462-464: 445-447-Batman goes to Russia. 448,449-The Penguin Affair Pts 1 & 3. 450-Origin Joker. 450,451-Joker-c/stories. 452-454-Dark Knight Dark City storyline; Riddler app. 455-Alan Grant scripts begin, ends #466, 470. 464-Last solo Batman story; free 16 pg. preview of Impact Comics line 1.50
457-Timothy Drake officially becomes Robin & dons new costume 1.20 3.00
457-Direct sale edition (has #000 in indicia) 1.00 2.50
460,461-Two part Catwoman story .80 2.00
465-487: 465-Robin returns to action with Batman. 470-War of the Gods x-over. 475,476-Return of Scarface-c/story. 476-Last $1.00-c. 477,478-Photo-c 1.50
488-Cont'd from Batman: Sword of Azrael #4; Azrael-c & app. 2.40 6.00
489-Bane-c/story; 1st app. Azrael in Bat-costume 1.60 4.00
490-Riddler-c/story; Azrael & Bane app. 1.20 3.00
491,492: 491-Knightfall lead-in; Joker-c/story; Azrael & Bane app.; Kelley Jones-c begin. 492-Knightfall part 1; Bane app. 1.20 3.00
492-Platinum edition (promo copy) 1.00 2.80 7.00
493-Knightfall Pt. 3 1.00 2.50
494-Knightfall Pt. 5; Joker-c & app. .80 2.00
495,496: 495-Knightfall Pt. 7; brief Bane & Joker apps. 496-Knightfall Pt. 9; Joker-c/story; Bane cameo .80 2.00
497-(Late 7/93)-Knightfall Pt. 11; Bane breaks Batman's back; B&W outer-c; Aparo-a(p); Giordano-a(i) 1.20 3.00
497-499: 497-2nd printing. 497-Newsstand edition w/o outer cover. 498-Knightfall part 15; Bane & Catwoman-c & app. (see Showcase 93 #7 & 8) 499-Knightfall Pt. 17; Bane app. .80 2.00
500-($2.50, 68 pgs.)-Knightfall Pt. 19; Azrael in new Bat-costume; Bane-c/story 1.00 2.50
500-($3.95, 68 pgs.)-Collector's Edition w/die-cut double-c w/foil by Joe Quesada & 2 bound-in post cards 1.80 4.50
501-508,510,511: 501-Begin $1.50-c. 501-508-Knightquest. 503,504-Catwoman app. 507-Ballistic app.; Jim Balent-a(p). 510-KnightsEnd Pt. 7. 511-(9/94)-Zero Hour; Batgirl-c/story 1.75
509-($2.50, 52 pgs.)-KnightsEnd Pt. 1 1.00 2.50
0,512-514,516-520: 0-(10/94)-Origin retold. 512-(11/94)-Dick Grayson assumes Batman role 1.75
515-($2.50)-Kelley Jones-a begins; all black embossed-c; Troika Pt. 1 1.20 3.00
521-534,536-549: 521-Begin $1.95-c, return of Alfred, 522-Swamp Thing app. 525-Mr. Freeze app. 527,528-Two Face app. 529-Contagion Pt. 6. 530-532-Deadman app. 533-Legacy prelude. 534-Legacy Pt. 5. 536-Final Night x-over; Man-Bat-c/app. 540,541-Spectre-c-app. 544-546-Joker & The Demon. 548,549-Penguin-c/app. .80 2.00
530-532 ($2.50)-Enhanced edition; glow-in-the-dark-c. 1.10 2.75
535-(10/96, $2.95)-1st app. The Ogre 1.20 3.00
535-(10/96, $3.95)-1st app. The Ogre; variant, cardboard, foldout-c 1.60 4.00
550-($3.50)-Collector's Ed., includes 4 collector cards; intro. Chase, return of Clayface; Kelley Jones-c 3.50
550-($2.95)-Standard Ed.; Williams & Gray-c 2.95
551-553: 551-Ragman app. 1.95
Annual 1 (8-10/61)-Swan-c 50.00 150.00 600.00
Annual 2 27.50 82.50 275.00
Annual 3(Summer, '62)-Joker-c/story 28.00 85.00 285.00
Annual 4,5 12.50 38.00 125.00
Annual 6,7(7/64, 25¢, 80 pgs.) 9.50 28.50 95.00
Annual V5#8(1982)-Painted-c 1.80 4.50
Annual 9,10,12: 9(7/85). 10(1986). 12(1988, $1.50) 1.20 3.00

GD25 FN65 NM94

Annual 11(1987, $1.25)-Penguin-c/story; Alan Moore scripts 1.60 4.00
Annual 13(1989, $1.75, 68 pgs.)-Gives history of Bruce Wayne, Dick Grayson, Jason Todd, Alfred, Comm. Gordon, Barbara Gordon (Batgirl) & Vicki Vale; Morrow-i .90 2.25
Annual 14(1990, $2.00, 68 pgs.)-Origin Two-Face .90 2.25
Annual 15(1991, $2.00, 68 pgs.)-Armageddon 2001 x-over; Joker app.; .90 2.25
Annual 15(2nd printing) .80 2.00
Annual 16(1992, $2.50, 68 pgs.)-Joker-c/s; Kieth-c 1.00 2.50
Annual 17(1993, $2.50, 68 pgs.)-Azrael in Bat-costume; intro Ballistic 1.00 2.50
Annual 18(1994, $2.95) 1.20 3.00
Annual 19(1995, $3.95)-Year One story; retells Scarecrow's origin 1.60 4.00
Annual 20(1996, $2.95)-Legends of the Dead Earth story; Moench script; Giarrano-a. 1.20 3.00
Annual 21(1997, $3.95)-Pulp Heroes story 3.95
Special 1 (4/84)-Mike W. Barr story; Golden-c/a 1.00 2.00 5.00
Pizza Hut giveaway(12/77)-exact-r of #122,123; Joker-c/story 1.20 3.00
Prell Shampoo giveaway(1966, 16 pgs.)- "The Joker's Practical Jokes" (6-7/8x3-3/8") 2.80 8.40 28.00

NOTE: ***Art Adams*** *a-400p.* ***Neal Adams*** *c-200, 203, 210, 217, 219-222, 224-227, 229, 230, 232, 234, 236-241, 243-246, 251, 255, Annual 14.* ***Aparo*** *a-414-420, 426-435, 440-448, 450, 451, 480-483, 486-491, 494-500; c-414-416, 481, 482, 463i, 486, 487i.* ***Bolland*** *a-400; c-445-447.* ***Burnley*** *a-10, 12-18, 20, 22, 25, 27; c-9, 15, 16, 27, 28p, 40p, 42p.* ***Byrne*** *c-401, 433-435, 533-535, Annual 11.* ***Travis Charest*** *c-488-490p.* ***Colan*** *a-340p, 343-345p, 348-351p, 373p, 383p; c-343p, 345p, 350p.* ***J. Cole*** *a-238r.* ***Cowan*** *a-Annual 10p.* ***Golden*** *a-295p, 303p, 484, 485.* ***Alan Grant*** *scripts-455-466, 470, 474-476, 479, 480, Annual 16(part).* ***Grell*** *a-287, 288p, 289p, 290; c-287-290.* ***Infantino/Anderson*** *c-167, 173, 175, 181, 186, 191, 192, 194, 195, 198, 199.* ***Kelley Jones*** *a-513-519, 521-525, 527; c-491-499, 500(newsstand), 501-510, 513.* ***Kaluta*** *c-242, 248, 253, Annual 12.* ***G. Kane/Anderson*** *c-178-180.* ***Bob Kane*** *a-1, 2, 5; c-1-5, 7, 17.* ***G. Kane*** *a-(r)-254, 255, 259, 261, 353i.* ***Kubert*** *a-238r, 400; c-310, 319p, 327, 328, 344.* ***McFarlane*** *c-423.* ***Mignola*** *c-426-429, 452-454, Annual 18.* ***Moldoff*** *c-101-140.* ***Moldoff/Giella*** *a-164-175, 177-181, 183, 184, 186.* ***Moldoff/Greene*** *a-169, 172-174, 177-179, 181, 184.* ***Mooney*** *a-255r.* ***Morrow*** *a-Annual 13i.* ***Newton*** *a-305, 306, 328p, 331p, 332p, 337p, 338p, 346p, 352-357p, 360-372p, 374-378p; c-374p, 378p.* ***Nino*** *a-Annual 9.* ***Irv Novick*** *c-201, 202.* ***Perez*** *a-400; c-436-442.* ***Fred Ray*** *c-8, 10; w/****Robinson****-11.* ***Robinson/Roussos*** *a-12-17, 20, 22, 24, 25, 27, 28, 31, 33, 37.* ***Robinson*** *a-12, 14, 18, 22-32,34, 36, 37, 255r, 260r, 261r; c-6, 8, 10, 12-15, 18, 21, 24, 26, 30, 37, 39.* ***Simonson*** *a-300p, 312p, 321p; c-300p, 312p, 366, 413i.* ***P. Smith*** *a-Annual 9.* ***Dick Sprang*** *c-19, 20, 22, 23, 25, 29, 31-36, 38, 51, 55, 66, 73, 76.* ***Starlin*** *c/a-402.* ***Staton*** *a-334.* ***Sutton*** *a-400.* ***Wrightson*** *a-265i, 400; c-320r. Bat-Hound app. in 92, 97, 103, 123, 125, 133, 156, 158. Bat-Mite app. in 133, 136, 144, 146, 158, 161. Batwoman app. in 105, 116, 122, 125, 128, 129, 131, 133, 139, 140, 141, 144, 145, 150, 151, 153, 154, 157, 159, 162, 163.* ***Zeck*** *c-417-420. Catwoman back-ups in 332, 345, 346, 348-351. Joker app. in 1, 2, 4, 5, 7-9, 11-13, 19, 20, 23, 25, 28, 32 & many more. Robin solo back-up stories in 337-339, 341-343.*

BATMAN (Books and trade paperbacks)

...: A LONELY PLACE OF DYING (1990, $3.95, 132 pgs.)-r/Batman #440-442 & New Titans #60,61; Perez-c 1.60 4.00
...AND DRACULA: RED RAIN nn (1991, $24.95)-Hard-c.; Elseworlds storyline 3.00 9.00 30.00
...AND DRACULA: Red Rain nn (1992, $9.95)-SC 1.25 3.75 10.00
ARKHAM ASYLUM Hard-c (1989, $24.95) 2.50 7.50 25.00
ARKHAM ASYLUM Soft-c ($14.95) 1.85 5.50 15.00
BIRTH OF THE DEMON Hard-c (1992, $24.95)-Origin of Ras al Ghul 2.50 7.50 25.00
BIRTH OF THE DEMON Soft-c (1993, $12.95) 1.60 4.85 13.00
BLIND JUSTICE nn (1992, $7.50)-r/Det. #598-600 1.00 3.00 7.50
BRIDE OF THE DEMON Hard-c (1990, $19.95) 2.50 7.50 20.00
BRIDE OF THE DEMON Soft-c ($12.95) 1.60 4.85 13.00
...: CASTLE OF THE BAT ($5.95)-Elseworlds story 2.40 6.00
...: COLLECTED LEGENDS OF THE DARK KNIGHT nn (1994, $12.95)-r/Legends of the Dark Knight #32-34,38,42,43 1.60 4.85 13.00
...: DARK JOKER-THE WILD (1993, $9.95)-Elseworlds story 1.25 3.75 10.00
...DARK KNIGHT DYNASTY nn (1997, $24.95)-Hard-c.; 3 Elseworlds stories;

Batman Plus #1 © DC

Batman: Poison Ivy © DC

Batman/Spawn: War Devil © DC/ Todd McFarlane

GD25 FN65 NM94

Barr-s/ S. Hampton painted-a, Gary Frank, McDaniel-a(p) 24.95
...DEADMAN: DEATH AND GLORY nn (1996, $24.95)-Hard-c.; Robinson-s/ Estes-c/a 2.50 7.50 25.00
...DEADMAN: DEATH AND GLORY ($12.95)-SC 1.60 4.85 13.00
DEATH IN THE FAMILY (1988, $3.95, trade paperback)-r/Batman #426-429 by Aparo 2.00 5.00
DEATH IN THE FAMILY: (2nd - 5th printings) 1.60 4.00
DIGITAL JUSTICE nn (1990, $24.95, Hard-c.)-Computer generated art 2.50 7.50 25.00
... FACES (1995, $9.95, TPB) 1.25 3.75 10.00
...GOTHIC (1992, $12.95, TPB)-r/Legends of the Dark Knight #6-10 1.60 4.85 13.00
GREATEST BATMAN STORIES Hard-c ($24.95) 3.50 10.50 35.00
GREATEST BATMAN STORIES Soft-c ($15.95) 2.00 6.00 16.00
GREATEST BATMAN STORIES Vol. 2 (1992, $16.95)2.15 6.50 17.00
GREATEST JOKER STORIES Hard-c ($19.95) 2.50 7.50 20.00
GREATEST JOKER STORIES Soft-c ($14.95) 1.85 5.50 15.00
GREATEST JOKER STORIES (Stacked Deck...Expanded Edition) (1992, $29.95)-Longmeadow Press Publ. 3.00 9.00 30.00
... LEGACY-(1996,17.95) reprints Legacy 6.75 18.00
...: THE MANY DEATHS OF THE BATMAN (1992, $3.95, 84 pgs.)-r/Batman #433-435 w/new Byrne-c 1.60 4.00
...: THE MOVIES (1997, $19.95)-r/movie adaptions of Batman, Batman Returns, Batman Forever, Batman and Robin 19.95
...: PREY (1992, $12.95)-Gulacy/Austin-a 1.60 4.85 13.00
SHAMAN (1993, $12.95)-r/Legends/D.K. #1-5 1.60 4.85 13.00
...: SON OF THE DEMON Hard-c (9/87, $14.95 4.00 12.00 40.00
...: SON OF THE DEMON limited signed & numbered Hard-c (1,700) 5.00 15.00 50.00
...: SON OF THE DEMON Soft-c w/new-c ($8.95) 1.10 3.30 9.00
...: SON OF THE DEMON Soft-c (1989, $9.95, 2nd printing - 4th printing) 1.25 3.75 10.00
...: TALES OF THE DEMON (1991, $17.95, 212 pgs.)-Intro by Sam Hamm; reprints by N. Adams(3) & Golden; contains Saga of Ra's Al Ghul #1 2.25 6.75 18.00
...: TEN NIGHTS OF THE BEAST (1994, $5.95)-r/Batman #417-420 2.40 6.00
...:THE LAST ANGEL (1994, $12.95, TPB) 1.60 4.85 13.00
...: VENOM (1993, $9.95, TPB)-r/Legends of the Dark Knight #16-20; embossed-c 1.25 3.75 10.00
YEAR ONE Hard-c (1988, $12.95) 1.60 4.85 13.00
YEAR ONE (1988, $9.95, TPB)-r/Batman #404-407 by Miller; intro by Miller 1.25 3.75 10.00
YEAR ONE (TPB, 2nd & 3rd printings) 1.25 3.75 10.00
YEAR TWO (1990, $9.95, TPB)-r/Det. 575-578 by McFarlane; wraparound-c 1.25 3.75 10.00

BATMAN (one-shots)
BATMAN AND OTHER DC CLASSICS 1 (1989, giveaway)-DC Comics/Diamond Comic Distributors; Batman origin-r/Batman #47, Camelot 3000-r by Bolland, Justice League-r('87), New Teen Titans-r by Perez. 1.00
... & ROBIN (1997, $5.95)-Movie adaption 5.95
... :BANE (1997, $4.95)-Dixon-s/Burchett-a; Stelfreeze-c; cover interlocks w/Batman:(Batgirl, Mr. Freeze, Poison Ivy) 4.95
... :BATGIRL (1997, $4.95)-Puckett-s/Haley,Kesel-a; Stelfreeze-c; cover interlocks w/Batman:(Bane, Mr. Freeze, Poison Ivy) 4.95
... : BLACKGATE (1/97, $3.95) Dixon-s 3.95
.../CAPTAIN AMERICA (1996, $5.95, DC/Marvel) Elseworlds story; Byrne-c/s/a 5.95
... : CATWOMAN DEFIANT nn (1992, $4.95, prestige format)-Milligan scripts; cover interlocks w/Batman: Penguin Triumphant; special foil logo. 2.00 5.00
... FOREVER (1995, $5.95, direct market) 2.40 6.00
... FOREVER (1995, $3.95, newsstand) 1.60 4.00
BROTHERHOOD OF THE BAT (1995, $5.95)-Elseworlds story. 2.40 6.00
... : DARK ALLEGIANCES (1996, $5.95)-Elseworlds story, Chaykin-c/a. 2.40 6.00
... : DARK KNIGHT GALLERY (1995, $3.50)-Pin-ups by Pratt, Balent, & others. 1.40 3.50
...:DEATH OF INNOCENTS (12/96, $3.95)-O'Neil-s/ Staton-a(p) 3.95
.../DEMON (1996, $4.95)-Alan Grant scripts 2.00 5.00
FULL CIRCLE nn (1991, $5.95, stiff-c, 68 pgs.)-Sequel to Batman: Year Two 2.40 6.00
...GALLERY, The 1 (1992, $2.95)-Pin-ups by Miller, N. Adams & others 1.20 3.00
...GOTHAM BY GASLIGHT (1989, $3.95) 1.60 4.00
.../GREEN ARROW: THE POISON TOMORROW nn (1992, $5.95, squarebound, 68 pgs.)-Netzer-c/a 2.40 6.00
HOLY TERROR nn (1991, $4.95, 52 pgs.) Elseworlds story 2.00 5.00
.../HOUDINI: THE DEVIL'S WORKSHOP (1993, $5.95) 2.40 6.00
...: IN DARKEST KNIGHT nn (1994, $4.95, 52 pgs.)-Elseworlds story; Batman w/Green Lantern's ring. 2.00 5.00
...:JUDGE DREDD: JUDGEMENT ON GOTHAM nn (1991, $5.95, 68 pgs.)-Grant/Wagner scripts; Simon Bisley-c/a 2.40 6.00
...:JUDGE DREDD: JUDGEMENT ON GOTHAM nn (2nd printing) 2.40 6.00
...:JUDGE DREDD: THE ULTIMATE RIDDLE (1995, $4.95) 2.00 5.00
...:JUDGE DREDD: VENDETTA IN GOTHAM (1993, $5.95) 2.40 6.00
...: KNIGHTGALLERY (1995, $3.50)-Elseworlds sketchbook. 1.40 3.50
...: MASK OF THE PHANTASM ($2.95)-Movie adaptation 1.20 3.00
...: MASK OF THE PHANTASM ($4.95)-Movie adaptation 2.00 5.00
...: MASTER OF THE FUTURE nn (1991, $5.95, 68 pgs.)-Elseworlds storyline; sequel to Gotham By Gaslight; embossed-c 2.40 6.00
...: MITEFALL (1995, $4.95)-Alan Grant script, Kevin O'Neill-a 2.00 5.00
... : MR. FREEZE (1997, $4.95)-Dini-s/Buckingham-a; Stelfreeze-c; cover interlocks w/Batman:(Bane, Batgirl, Poison Ivy) 4.95
...: PENGUIN TRIUMPHANT nn (1992, $4.95)-Staton-a(p); special foil logo 2.00 5.00
.../PHANTOM STRANGER nn (1997, $4.95) nn-Grant-s/Ransom-a 4.95
... : PLUS (2/97, $2.95) Arsenal-c/app. 1.20 3.00
... : POISON IVY (1997, $4.95)-J.F. Moore-s/Apthorp-a; Stelfreeze-c; cover interlocks w/Batman:(Bane, Batgirl, Mr. Freeze) 4.95
.../PUNISHER: LAKE OF FIRE (1994, $4.95, DC/Marvel) 2.00 5.00
...RETURNS MOVIE SPECIAL (1992, $3.95) 1.60 4.00
...RETURNS MOVIE PRESTIGE (1992, $5.95, squarebound)-Dorman painted-c 2.40 6.00
...:RIDDLER-THE RIDDLE FACTORY (1995, $4.95)-Matt Wagner scripts 2.00 5.00
...: SCAR OF THE BAT nn (1996, $4.95)-Elseworlds story; Max Allan Collins script; Barreto-a. 2.00 5.00
...: SEDUCTION OF THE GUN nn (1992, $2.50, 68 pgs.) 1.00 2.50
.../SPAWN: WAR DEVIL nn (1994, $4.95, 52 pgs.) 2.00 5.00
.../SPIDER-MAN (1997, $4.95) Dematteis-s/Nolan & Kesel-a 4.95
...: THE BLUE, THE GREY, & THE BAT nn (1992, $5.95, 68 pgs.)-Weiss/Lopez-a 2.40 6.00
...: THE KILLING JOKE (1988, deluxe 52 pgs., mature readers)-Bolland-c/a; Alan Moore scripts. 1.25 3.75 10.00
...: THE KILLING JOKE (2nd thru 8th printings) 1.40 3.50
...: THE OFFICIAL COMIC ADAPTATION OF THE WARNER BROS. MOTION PICTURE (1989, $2.50, regular format, 68 pgs.)-Ordway-c. 1.20 3.00
...: THE OFFICIAL COMIC ADAPTATION OF THE WARNER BROS. MOTION PICTURE (1989, $4.95, prestige format, 68 pgs.)-same interiors but different-c than regular format. 2.00 5.00

Batman and Robin Adventures #25 © DC

Batman And The Outsiders #11 © DC

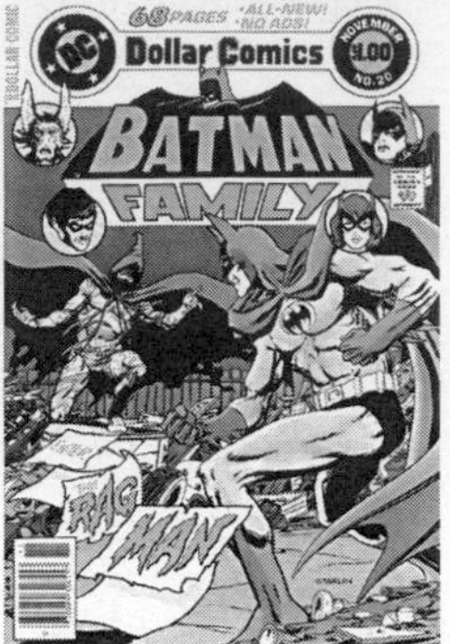

Batman Family #20 © DC

GD25 FN65 NM94

...: TWO-FACE-CRIME AND PUNISHMENT-(1995, $4.95)-Scott McDaniel-a 2.00 5.00
...: VENGEANCE OF BANE SPECIAL 1 (1992, $2.50, 68 pgs.)-Origin & 1st app. Bane (see Batman #491) 1.25 3.75 10.00
...: VENGEANCE OF BANE SPECIAL 1 (2nd printing) 1.00 2.50
....:VENGEANCE OF BANE II nn (1995, $3.95)-sequel 1.60 4.00
...Vs. THE INCREDIBLE HULK (1995, $3.95)-r/DC Special Series #27 1.60 4.00

BATMAN (Kellogg's Poptarts comics)
1966 (Set of 6) (16 pgs.)
National Periodical Publications

"The Man in the Iron Mask", "The Penguin's Fowl Play", "The Joker's Happy Victims", "The Catwoman's Catnapping Caper", "The Mad Hatter's Hat Crimes", "The Case of the Batman II"
each.... 2.50 7.50 25.00

NOTE: *All above were folded and placed in Poptarts boxes.* ***Infantino*** *art on Catwoman and Joker issues.*

BATMAN ADVENTURES, THE (TV)
Oct, 1992 - No. 36, Oct, 1995 ($1.25/$1.50) (Based on animated series)
DC Comics

1-Penguin-c/story 1.60 4.00
1 ($1.95, Silver Edition)-2nd printing .90 2.25
2-6,8-19: 2,12-Catwoman-c/story. 3-Joker-c/story. 5-Scarecrow-c/story. 10-Riddler-c/story. 11-Man-Bat-c/story. 12-Batgirl & Catwoman-c/story. 16-Joker-c/story; begin $1.50-c. 18-Batgirl-c/story. 19-Scarecrow-c/story. 1.00 2.50
7-Special edition polybagged with Man-Bat trading card 2.40 6.00
20-24,26-32: 26-Batgirl app. 1.75
25-($2.50, 52 pgs.)-Superman app. 1.00 2.50
33-36: 33-Begin $1.75-c .70 1.75
Mad Love nn (2/94, $3.95, 68 pgs.)-Joker-c/story 1.60 4.00
The Collected Adventures Vol. 1 (1993, $5.95) 2.40 6.00
The Collected Adventures Vol. 2 (1994, $5.95) 2.40 6.00
Annual 1 (1994, $2.95) 1.20 3.00
Annual 2 (1995, $3.50)-Demon-c/story; Ras al Ghul app. 1.40 3.50
Holiday Special 1 (1995, $2.95) 1.20 3.00

BATMAN ADVENTURES, THE: THE LOST YEARS (TV)
Jan, 1998 - No. 5 ($1.95) (Based on animated series)
DC Comics

1-5-Leads into Fall '97's new animated episodes 1.95

BATMAN/ALIENS
Mar, 1997 - No. 2, Apr, 1997 ($4.95, limited series)
DC Comics/Dark Horse Comics

1,2: Wrightson-c/a. 2.00 5.00

BATMAN AND ROBIN ADVENTURES (TV)
Nov, 1995 - No. 25, Dec, 1997 ($1.75) (Based on animated series)
DC Comics

1-Dini-s. 1.00 2.50
2-24: 2-4-Dini script. 4-Penguin-c/story. 5-Joker-c/story; Poison Ivy, Harley Quinn-c/app. 9-Batgirl & Talia-c/story. 10-Ra's Al Ghul-c/story 11-Man-Bat app. 12-Bane-c/app. 13-Scarecrow-c/app. 15 Deadman-c/app. 16-Catwoman-c/app. 18-Joker-c/app. 24-Poison Ivy app. .70 1.75
25-($2.95, 48 pgs.) 2.95
Annual 1(11/96, $2.95) Phantasm-c/app. 1.20 3.00
Annual 2(11/97, $3.95) Zatara and Zatanna-c/app. 3.95

BATMAN AND SUPERMAN ADVENTURES: WORLD'S FINEST
1997 ($6.95, square-bound, one-shot) (Based on animated series)
DC Comics

1-Adaption of animated crossover episode; Dini-s/Timm-c. 6.95

BATMAN AND THE OUTSIDERS (The Adventures of the Outsiders#33 on)
(Also see Brave & The Bold #200 & The Outsiders) (Replaces The Brave and the Bold)
Aug, 1983 - No. 32, Apr, 1986 (Mando paper #5 on)
DC Comics

1-Batman, Halo, Geo-Force, Katana, Metamorpho & Black Lightning begin. 1.00 2.50
2-32: 5-New Teen Titans x-over. 9-Halo begins. 11,12-Origin Katana. 18-More facts about Metamorpho's origin. 28-31-Lookers origin. 32-Team disbands 1.00
Annual 1 (9/84)-Miller/Aparo-c; Aparo-i 1.00
Annual 2 (9/85)-Metamorpho & Sapphire Stagg wed; Aparo-c 1.00

NOTE: ***Aparo*** *a-1-9, 11-13p, 16-20; c-1-4, 5i, 6-21.* ***B. Kane*** *a-3r.* ***Layton*** *a-19i, 20i.* ***Lopez*** *a-3p.* ***Perez*** *c-5p.* ***B. Willingham*** *a-14p.*

BATMAN: BLACK & WHITE
June, 1996 - No. 4, Sept, 1996 ($2.95, B&W, limited series)
DC Comics

1-4: 1-Stories by McKeever, Timm, Kubert, Chaykin, Goodwin; Jim Lee-c; Allred inside front-c; Moebius inside back-c. 2-Stories by Simonson, Corben, Bisley & Gaiman; Miller-c. 3-Stories by M. Wagner, Janson, Sienkiewicz, O'Neil & Kristiansen; B. Smith-c; Russell inside front-c; Silvestri inside back-c. 4-Stories by Bolland, Goodwin & Gianni, Strnad & Nowlan, O'Neil & Stelfreeze; Toth-c; Neal Adams & Alex Ross pinups 1.60 4.00

BATMAN: CATWOMAN DEFIANT (See Batman one-shots)

BATMAN CHRONICLES, THE
Summer, 1995 - Present ($2.95, quarterly)
DC Comics

1-3,5-11: 1-Dixon/Grant/Moench script. 2-Bolland-c. 5-Oracle Year One story, Chaykin-c. 6-Kaluta-c; Ra's Al Ghul story. 7-Superman-c/app. 11-Elseworlds; Paul Pope-s/a 1.20 3.00
4-Hitman story by Garth Ennis, Contagion tie-in; Balent-c 2.40 6.00
...Gallery (3/97, $3.50) Pin-ups 1.40 3.50
Gauntlet, The (1997, $4.95, one-shot) 4.95

BATMAN FAMILY, THE
Sept-Oct, 1975 - No. 20, Oct-Nov, 1978 (#1-4, 17-on: 68 pgs.)
(Combined with Detective Comics with No. 481)
National Periodical Publications/DC Comics

1-Origin/2nd app. Batgirl-Robin team-up (The Dynamite Duo); reprints plus one new story begins; N. Adams-a(r); r/1st app. Man-Bat from Det. #400 1.50 4.50 12.00
2-5: 2-r/Det. #369. 3-Batgirl & Robin learn each's i.d.; r/Batwoman app. from Batman #105. 8-r/Batwoman app. 4-r/1st Fatman app. from Batman #113. 5-r/1st Bat-Hound app. from Batman #92 1.00 2.80 7.00
6,9-Joker's daughter on cover (1st app?) 1.50 4.50 12.00
7,8,14-16: 14-Batwoman app. 15-3rd app. Killer Moth. 16-Bat-Girl cameo (last app. in costume until New Teen Titans #47) 1.00 2.80 7.00
10-1st revival Batwoman; Cavalier app.; 2nd app. Killer Moth. 1.50 4.50 12.00
11-13-Rogers-a(p): 11-New stories begin; Man-Bat begins. 13-Batwoman cameo 1.25 3.75 10.00
17-20: 17-($1.00 size)-Batman, Huntress begin; Batwoman & Catwoman 1st meet. 18-20: Huntress by Staton in all. 20-Origin Ragman retold 1.25 3.75 10.00

NOTE: ***Aparo*** *a-17; c-11-16.* ***Austin*** *a-12i.* ***Chaykin*** *a-14p.* ***Michael Golden*** *a-15-17,18-20p.* ***Grell*** *a-1; c-1.* ***Gil Kane*** *a-2r.* ***Kaluta*** *c-17, 19.* ***Newton*** *a-13.* ***Robinson*** *a-1r, 3i(r), 9r.* ***Russell*** *a-18i, 19i.* ***Starlin*** *a-17; c-18, 20.*

BATMAN: GCPD
Aug, 1996 - No. 4, Nov, 1996 ($2.25, limited series)
DC Comics

1-4: Features Jim Gordon; Aparo/Sienkiewicz-a 2.25

BATMAN: GORDON'S LAW
Dec, 1996 - No. 3, Feb, 1997 ($1.95, limited series)
DC Comics

Batman/Grendel #1 © DC

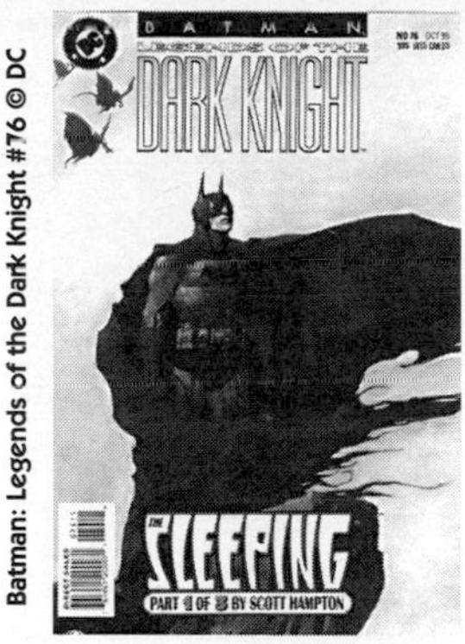

Batman: Legends of the Dark Knight #76 © DC

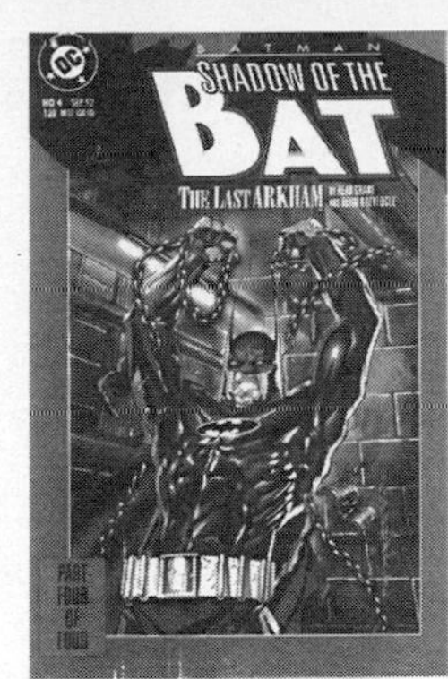

Batman: Shadow of the Bat #4 © DC

GD25 FN65 NM94

1-3: Dixon-s/Janson-c/a 1.95

BATMAN: GOTHAM NIGHTS II (Also see Gotham Nights)
Mar, 1995 - No. 4, June, 1995 ($1.95, limited series)
DC Comics

1-4 .80 2.00

BATMAN/GRENDEL (1st limited series)
1993 - No. 2, 1993 ($4.95, limited series, squarebound; 52 pgs.)
DC Comics

1,2: Batman vs. Hunter Rose. 1-Devil's Riddle; Matt Wagner-c/a/scripts. 2-Devil's Masque; Matt Wagner-c/a/scripts 2.40 6.00

BATMAN/GRENDEL (2nd limited series)
June, 1996 - No. 2, July, 1996 ($4.95, limited series, squarebound)
DC Comics

1,2: Batman vs. Grendel Prime. 1-Devil's Bones; Matt Wagner-c/a/scripts. 2.00 5.00

BATMAN: KNIGHTGALLERY (See Batman one-shots)

BATMAN: LEGENDS OF THE DARK KNIGHT (Legends of the Dark...#1-36)
Nov, 1989 - Present ($1.50/$1.75/$1.95)
DC Comics

1- "Shaman" begins, ends #5; outer cover has four different color variations, all worth same 1.20 3.00
2 .80 2.00
3-5 .80 2.00
6-10- "Gothic" by Grant Morrison (scripts) .80 2.00
11-15,17,18: 11-15-Gulacy/Austin-a. 14-Catwoman app. 18-Last $1.50-c .80 2.00
16-Intro drug Bane uses; begin Venom story 1.60 4.00
19-49,51-63: 38-Bat-Mite-c/story. 46-49-Catwoman app. w/Heath-c/a. 51-Ragman app.; Joe Kubert-c. 59,60-Knightquest x-over. 62,63-KnightsEnd Pt. 4 & 10 .80 2.00
50-($3.95, 68 pgs.)-Bolland embossed gold foil-c; Joker-c/story; pin-ups by Chaykin, Simonson, Williamson, Kaluta, Russell, others 1.60 4.00
64,0,65-99: 64-(9/94)-Begin $1.95-c. 0-(10/94)-Quesada/Palmiotti-c; various artists on story. 71-73-James Robinson-s, J. Watkiss-c/a. 74,75-Ted McKeever-c/a/s. 76-78-Scott Hampton-c/a/s. 81-Card insert. 83,84-Ellis-s. 85-Robinson-s. 91-93-Ennis-s. 94-Michael T. Gilbert-s/a. .80 2.00
100-($3.95) Alex Ross painted-c; gallery by various 3.95
101-105: 101-Ezquerra-a. 102-104-Robinson-s 1.95
Annual 1 (1991, $3.95, 68 pgs.)-Joker app. 1.60 4.00
Annual 2 (1992, $3.50, 68 pgs.)-Netzer-c/a 1.40 3.50
Annual 3 (1993, $3.50, 68 pgs.)-New Batman (Azrael) app. 1.40 3.50
Annual 4 (1994, $3.50, 68 pgs.)-Elseworlds story 1.40 3.50
Annual 5 (1995, $3.95, 68 pgs.) 1.60 4.00
Annual 6 (1996, $2.95)-Legend of the Dead Earth story 1.20 3.00
Halloween Special 1 (12/93, $6.95, 84 pgs.)-Embossed & foil stamped-c 1.00 2.80 7.00
Batman Madness-...Halloween Special (1994, $4.95) 2.00 5.00
Batman Ghosts-...Halloween Special (1995, $4.95) 2.00 5.00

NOTE: ***Aparo** a-Annual 1. **Chaykin** scripts-24-26. **Giffen** a-Annual 1. **Golden** a-Annual 1. **Alan Grant** scripts-38, 52, 53. **Gil Kane** c/a-24-26. **Mignola** a-54; c-54, 62. **Morrow** a-Annual 3i. **Quesada** a-Annual 1. **James Robinson** scripts- 71-73. **Russell** c/a-42, 43. **Sears** a-21, 23; c-21, 23. **Zeck** a-69, 70; c-69, 70.*

BATMAN-LEGENDS OF THE DARK KNIGHT: JAZZ
Apr, 1995 - No. 3, June, 1995 ($2.50, limited series)
DC Comics

1-3 1.00 2.50

BATMAN: MANBAT
Oct, 1995 - No. 3, Dec, 1995 ($4.95, limited series)
DC Comics (Elseworlds)

1-3-Delano-script; Bolton-a. 2.00 5.00

TPB-(1997, $14.95) r#1-3 14.95

BATMAN: MITEFALL (See Batman one-shots)

BATMAN MINIATURE (See Batman Kellogg's)

BATMAN: PENGUIN TRIUMPHANT (See Batman one-shots)

BATMAN/PREDATOR III: BLOOD TIES
Nov, 1997 - No. 4 ($1.95, limited series)
DC Comics/Dark Horse Comics

1-4: Dixon-s/Damaggio-c/a 1.95

BATMAN RECORD COMIC
1966 (one-shot)
National Periodical Publications

1-With record (still sealed) 12.50 38.00 125.00
Comic only 7.00 21.00 70.00

BATMAN RETURNS MOVIE SPECIAL (See Batman one-shots)

BATMAN: RIDDLER-THE RIDDLE FACTORY (See Batman one-shots)

BATMAN: RUN, RIDDLER, RUN
1992 - Book 3, 1992 ($4.95, limited series)
DC Comics

Book 1-3: Mark Badger-a & plot 2.00 5.00

BATMAN: SCAR OF THE BAT (See Batman one-shots)

BATMAN: SECRET FILES
Oct, 1997 ($4.95)
DC Comics

1-New origin-s and profiles 4.95

BATMAN: SHADOW OF THE BAT
June, 1992 - Present ($1.50/$1.75/$1.95)
DC Comics

1-The Last Arkham-c/story begins; Alan Grant scripts in all 1.20 3.00
1-($2.50)-Deluxe edition polybagged w/poster, pop-up & book mark 1.60 4.00
2-7: 4-The Last Arkham ends. 7-Last $1.50-c 1.50
8-28: 14,15-Staton-a(p). 16-18-Knightfall tie-ins. 19-28-Knightquest tie-ins w/Azrael as Batman. 19,20-Painted-c. 25-Silver ink-c; anniversary issue .70 1.75
29-($2.95, 52 pgs.)-KnightsEnd Pt. 2 1.20 3.00
30,31,0,32-73: 30-KnightsEnd Pt. 8. 31-(9.94)-Begin $1.95-c; Zero Hour. 0-(10/94). 32-(11/94). 33-Robin-c. 35-Troika-Pt.2. 44-Cat-Man & Catwoman-c. 48-Contagion Pt. 1; card insert. 49-Contagion Pt.7. 56,57-Poison Ivy-c/app. 62-Two-Face app. 69,70-Fate app. .80 2.00
35-($2.95)-Variant embossed-c 1.20 3.00
Annual 1 (1993, $3.50, 68 pgs.) 1.40 3.50
Annual 2 (1994, $3.95, 68 pgs.) 1.60 4.00
Annual 3 (1995, $3.95)-Year One story; Poison Ivy app. 1.60 4.00
Annual 4 (1996, $2.95)-Legends of the Dead Earth story; Starman cameo 1.20 3.00
Annual 5 (1997, $3.95)-Pulp Heroes story; Poison Ivy app. 3.95

BATMAN-SPAWN: WAR DEVIL (See Batman one-shots)

BATMAN SPECTACULAR (See DC Special Series No. 15)

BATMAN: SWORD OF AZRAEL (Also see Azrael & Batman #488,489)
Oct, 1992 - No. 4, Jan, 1993 ($1.75, limited series)
DC Comics

1-Wraparound gatefold-c; Quesada-c/a(p) in all; 1st app. Azrael 1.25 3.75 10.00
2-4: 4-Cont'd in Batman #488 1.00 2.80 7.00
Silver Edition 1-4 (1993, $1.95)-Reprints #1-4 .80 2.00
Trade Paperback (1993, $9.95)-Reprints #1-4 1.25 3.75 10.00
Trade Paperback Gold Edition 1.85 5.50 15.00

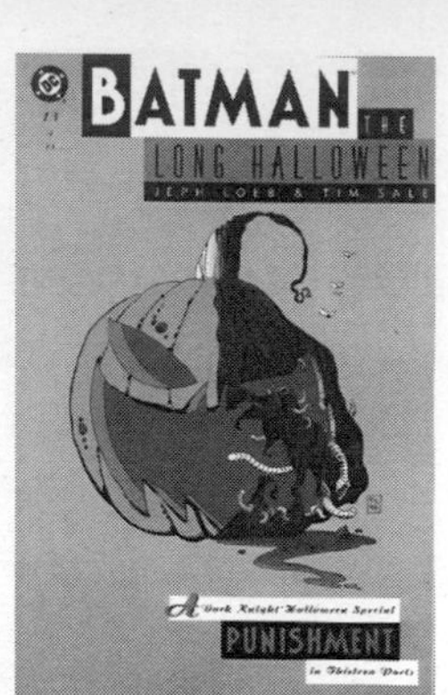

Batman: The Long Halloween #13 © DC

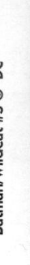

Batman/Wildcat #3 © DC

Battle #2 © MEG

	GD25	FN65	NM94

BATMAN: THE CULT
1988 - No. 4, Nov, 1988 ($3.50, deluxe limited series)
DC Comics

	GD25	FN65	NM94
1-Wrightson-a/painted-c in all		1.60	4.00
2-4		1.40	3.50
Trade Paperback ('91, $14.95)-New Wrightson-c	1.85	5.50	15.00

BATMAN: THE DARK KNIGHT
Mar, 1986 - No. 4, 1986 ($2.95, squarebound, limited series)
DC Comics

	GD25	FN65	NM94
1-Miller story & c/a(p); set in the future	2.25	6.75	18.00
1-2nd & 3rd printings		1.20	3.00
2-Carrie Kelly becomes 1st female Robin	1.25	3.75	10.00
2-2nd & 3rd printings		1.20	3.00
3-Death of Joker; Superman app.	1.00	3.00	7.50
3-2nd printing		1.20	3.00
4-Death of Alfred; Superman app.		2.00	5.00
Hard-c, signed & numbered edition ($40.00)(4000 copies)			250.00
Hard-c, trade edition	4.00	12.00	40.00
Soft-c, trade edition (1st printing only)	1.25	3.75	10.00
Soft-c, trade edition (2nd thru 8th printings)	1.00	3.00	7.50
10th Anniv. Slipcase set ('96, $100.00): Signed & numbered hard-c edition (10,000 copies), sketchbook, copy of script for #1, 2 colorprints			80.00
10th Anniv. Hard-c ('96, $45.00)			45.00
10th Anniv. Soft-c ('97, $14.95)			14.95

NOTE: *The #2 second printings can be identified by matching the grey background colors on the inside front cover and facing page. The inside front cover of the second printing has a dark grey background which does not match the lighter grey of the facing page. On the true 1st printings, the backgrounds are both light grey. All other issues are clearly marked.*

BATMAN: THE KILLING JOKE (See Batman one-shots)

BATMAN: THE LONG HALLOWEEN
Oct, 1996 - No. 13, Oct, 1997 ($2.95, limited series)
DC Comics

	GD25	FN65	NM94
1-($4.95)-Loeb-s/Sale-c/a in all	1.50	4.50	12.00
2-5($2.95): 2-Solomon Grundy-c/app. 3-Joker-c/app., Catwoman, Poison Ivy app.	1.00	3.00	8.00
6-10: 6-Poison Ivy-c. 7-Riddler-c/app.		1.80	4.50
11,12			2.95
13-($4.95, 48 pgs.)-Killer revealed			4.95

BATMAN: THE OFFICIAL COMIC ADAPTATION OF THE WARNER BROS. MOTION PICTURE (See Batman one-shots)

BATMAN: THE ULTIMATE EVIL
1995 ($5.95, limited series, prestige format)
DC Comics

	GD25	FN65	NM94
1,2-Barrett, Jr. adaptation of Vachss novel.		2.40	6.00

BATMAN 3-D (Also see 3-D Batman)
1990 ($9.95, w/glasses, 8-1/8x10-3/4")
DC Comics

	GD25	FN65	NM94
nn-Byrne-a/scripts; Riddler, Joker, Penguin & Two-Face app. plus r/1953 3-D Batman; pin-ups by many artists	1.25	3.75	10.00

BATMAN: TWO-FACE-CRIME AND PUNISHMENT (See Batman one-shots)

BATMAN: TWO-FACE STRIKES TWICE
1993 - No. 2, 1993 ($4.95, 52 pgs.)
DC Comics

	GD25	FN65	NM94
1,2-Flip book format w/Staton-a (G.A. side)		2.00	5.00

BATMAN VERSUS PREDATOR
1991 - No. 3, 1992 ($4.95/$1.95, limited series) (1st DC/Dark Horse x-over)
DC Comics/Dark Horse Comics

	GD25	FN65	NM94
1 (Prestige format, $4.95)-1 & 3 contain 8 Batman/Predator trading cards; Andy & Adam Kubert-a; Suydam painted-c		2.20	5.50
1 (Regular format, $1.95)-No trading cards		1.00	2.50
2-(Prestige)-Extra pin-ups inside; Suydam-c		2.00	5.00
2-(Regular)-w/o cards		1.00	2.50
3-(Prestige)-Suydam-c		2.00	5.00
3-(Regular)-w/o cards		1.00	2.50
TPB (1993, $5.95, 132 pgs.)-r/#1-3 w/new introductions & forward plus new wraparound-c by Gibbons		2.40	6.00

BATMAN VERSUS PREDATOR II: BLOODMATCH
Late 1994 - No. 4, 1995 ($2.50, limited series)
DC Comics

	GD25	FN65	NM94
1-4-Huntress app.; Moench scripts; Gulacy-a		1.00	2.50
TPB (1995, $6.95)-r/#1-4	1.00	2.80	7.00

BATMAN VS. THE INCREDIBLE HULK (See DC Special Series No. 27)

BATMAN/ WILDCAT
Apr, 1997 - No.3, June, 1997 ($2.25, mini-series)
DC Comics

	GD25	FN65	NM94
1-3: Dixon/Smith-s: 1-Killer Croc app.			2.25

BAT MASTERSON (TV) (Also see Tim Holt #28)
Aug-Oct, 1959; Feb-Apr, 1960 - No. 9, Nov-Jan, 1961-62
Dell Publishing Co.

	GD25	FN65	NM94
Four Color 1013 (#1) (8-10/59)	11.00	34.00	125.00
2-9: Gene Barry photo-c on all. 2-Two different back-c exist	5.50	16.50	60.00

BATS (See Tales Calculated to Drive You Bats)

BATS, CATS & CADILLACS
Oct, 1990 - No. 2, Nov, 1990 ($1.75)
Now Comics

	GD25	FN65	NM94
1,2: 1-Gustovich-a(i); Snyder-c		.70	1.80

BAT-THING
June, 1997 ($1.95, one-shot)
DC Comics (Amalgam)

	GD25	FN65	NM94
1-Hama-s/Damaggio & Sienkiewicz-a			1.95

BATTLE
Mar, 1951 - No. 70, June, 1960
Marvel/Atlas Comics(FPI No. 1-62/Male No. 63 on)

	GD25	FN65	NM94
1	24.00	71.00	175.00
2	11.00	33.00	80.00
3-10: 4-1st Buck Pvt. O'Toole. 10-Pakula-a	8.35	25.00	55.00
11-20: 11-Check-a	6.35	19.00	40.00
21,23-Krigstein-a	8.00	24.00	50.00
22,24-36: 32-Tuska-a. 36-Everett-a	5.35	16.00	32.00
37-Kubert-a (Last precode, 2/55)	5.70	17.00	38.00
38-40,42-48	4.25	13.00	26.00
41-Kubert/Moskowitz-a	5.70	17.00	38.00
49-Davis-a	5.70	17.00	38.00
50-54,56-58	4.25	13.00	26.00
55-Williamson-a (5 pgs.)	5.70	17.00	40.00
59-Torres-a	5.35	16.00	32.00
60-62: 60,62-Combat Kelly app. 61-Combat Casey app.	4.00	12.00	24.00
63-Ditko-a	7.15	21.50	50.00
64-66-Kirby-a. 66-Davis-a; has story of Fidel Castro in pre-Communism days (an admiring profile)	8.50	26.00	60.00
67,68: 67-Williamson/Crandall-a (4 pgs.); Kirby, Davis-a. 68-Kirby/Williamson-a (4 pgs.); Kirby/Ditko-a	8.75	26.25	65.00
69,70: 69-Kirby-a. 70-Kirby/Ditko-a	7.85	23.50	55.00

NOTE: ***Andru** a-37. **Berg** a-38, 14, 60-62. **Colan** a-33, 55. **Everett** a-36, 50, 70; c-56, 57. **Heath** a-6, 9, 13, 31, 69; c-6, 9, 12, 26, 35, 37. **Kirby** c-64-69. **Maneely** a-4, 6, 31, 61; c-4, 33, 59, 61. **Orlando** a-47. **Powell** a-53, 55. **Reinman** a-8, 9, 26, 32. **Robinson** a-9, 39. **Romita** a-26. **Severin** a-28, 32-34, 66-69; c-36, 55. **Sinnott** a-33, 37. **Woodbridge** a-52, 55.*

BATTLE ACTION

Battle Cry #11 © Stanmor Publ.

Battlefield #4 © MEG

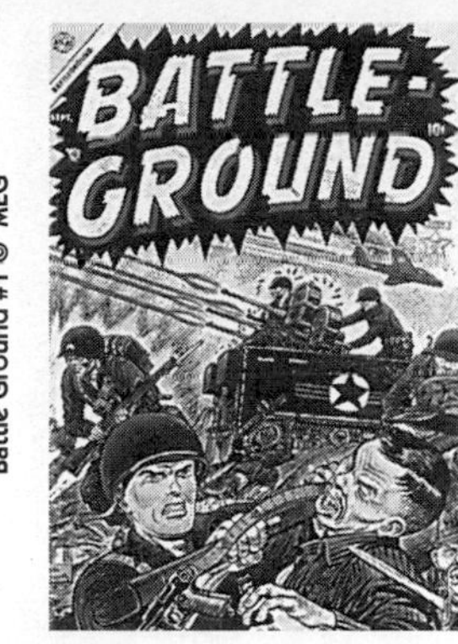

Battle Ground #1 © MEG

Feb, 1952 - No. 12, 5/53; No. 13, 11/54 - No. 30, 8/57
Atlas Comics (NPI)

	GD25	FN65	NM94
1-Pakula-a	19.00	58.00	140.00
2	10.00	30.00	65.00
3,4,6,7,9,10: 6-Robinson-c/a. 7-Partial nudity	5.70	17.00	38.00
5-Used in **POP**, pg. 93,94	6.00	18.00	42.00
8-Krigstein-a	6.50	19.50	45.00
11-15 (Last precode, 2/55)	5.70	17.00	38.00
16-26,28,29	5.35	16.00	32.00
27,30-Torres-a	5.35	16.00	32.00

NOTE: *Battle Brady app. 5-7, 10-12.* ***Berg*** *a-3.* ***Check*** *a-11.* ***Everett*** *a-7; c-13, 25.* ***Heath*** *a-3, 8, 18; c-3,15, 18, 21.* ***Maneely*** *a-1; c-5.* ***Reinman*** *a-1.* ***Robinson*** *a-6, 7; c-6.* ***Shores*** *a-7(2).* ***Sinnott*** *a-3.* ***Woodbridge*** *a-28, 30.*

BATTLE ATTACK
Oct, 1952 - No. 8, Dec, 1955
Stanmor Publications

	GD25	FN65	NM94
1	7.85	23.50	55.00
2	5.00	15.00	30.00
3-8: 3-Hollingsworth-a	4.00	10.00	20.00

BATTLE BEASTS
Feb, 1988 - No. 4, 1988 ($1.50/$1.75, B&W/color)
Blackthorne Publishing

	GD25	FN65	NM94
1-3 (B&W)-Based on Hasbro toys			1.50
4 ($1.75, color)		.75	1.80

BATTLE BRADY (Formerly Men in Action No. 1-9; see 3-D Action)
No. 10, Jan, 1953 - No. 14, June, 1953
Atlas Comics (IPC)

	GD25	FN65	NM94
10: 10-12-Syd Shores-c	10.50	32.00	85.00
11-Used in **POP**, pg. 95 plus B&W & color illos	7.85	23.50	55.00
12-14	5.70	17.00	40.00

BATTLE CLASSICS (See Cancelled Comic Cavalcade)
Sept-Oct, 1978 (44 pgs.)
DC Comics

	GD25	FN65	NM94
1-Kubert-r; new Kubert-c		1.60	4.00

BATTLE CRY
1952 (May) - No. 20, Sept, 1955
Stanmor Publications

	GD25	FN65	NM94
1	10.00	30.00	70.00
2	5.70	17.00	35.00
3,5-10: 8-Pvt. Ike begins, ends #13,17	4.00	11.00	22.00
4-Classic E.C. swipe	5.35	16.00	32.00
11-20	3.60	9.00	18.00

NOTE: ***Hollingsworth*** *a-9; c-20.*

BATTLEFIELD (War Adventures on the...)
April, 1952 - No. 11, May, 1953
Atlas Comics (ACI)

	GD25	FN65	NM94
1-Pakula, Reinman-a	16.00	47.00	120.00
2-5: 2-Heath, Maneely, Pakula, Reinman-a	8.35	25.00	55.00
6-11	5.70	17.00	35.00

NOTE: ***Colan*** *a-11.* ***Everett*** *a-8.* ***Heath*** *a-1, 2, 5p; c-2, 8, 9, 11.* ***Ravielli*** *a-11.*

BATTLEFIELD ACTION (Formerly Foreign Intrigues)
No. 16, Nov, 1957 - No. 62, 2-3/66; No. 63, 7/80 - No. 89, 11/84
Charlton Comics

	GD25	FN65	NM94
V2#16	4.25	13.00	28.00
17,20-30	3.00	7.50	15.00
18,19-Check-a (2 stories in #18)	3.60	9.00	18.00
31-62(1966)	1.50	4.50	12.00
63-89(1983-84)		1.20	3.00

NOTE: ***Montes/Bache*** *a-43, 55, 62.* ***Glanzman*** *a-87r.*

BATTLE FIRE
Apr, 1955 - No. 7, 1955
Aragon Magazine/Stanmor Publications

	GD25	FN65	NM94
1	6.70	20.00	40.00
2	4.00	11.00	22.00
3-7	2.80	7.00	14.00

BATTLE FOR A THREE DIMENSIONAL WORLD
May, 1983 (20 pgs., slick paper w/stiff-c, $3.00)
3D Cosmic Publications

	GD25	FN65	NM94
nn-Kirby c/a in 3-D; shows history of 3-D		1.20	3.00

BATTLEFORCE
Nov, 1987 - No. 2?, 1988 ($1.75, color/B&W)
Blackthorne Publishing

	GD25	FN65	NM94
1,2: Based on game. 1-In color. 2-B&W		.70	1.75

BATTLE FOR INDEPENDENTS, THE (Also See Cyblade/Shi & Shi/Cyblade: The Battle For Independents)
1995 ($29.95)
Image Comics (Top Cow Productions)/Crusade Comics

	GD25	FN65	NM94
nn-boxed set of all editions of Shi/Cyblade & Cyblade/Shi plus new variant.	4.00	12.00	40.00

BATTLE FOR THE PLANET OF THE APES (See Power Record Comics)

BATTLEFRONT
June, 1952 - No. 48, Aug, 1957
Atlas Comics (PPI)

	GD25	FN65	NM94
1-Heath-c	21.00	64.00	160.00
2-Robinson-a(4)	10.00	30.00	75.00
3-5-Robinson-a(4) in each	9.00	27.00	60.00
6-10: Combat Kelly in No. 6-10	7.15	21.50	50.00
11-22,24-28: 14,16-Battle Brady app. 22-Teddy Roosevelt & His Rough Riders story. 28-Last pre-code (2/55)	5.70	17.00	35.00
23,43-Check-a	5.70	17.00	40.00
29-39,41,44-47	4.25	13.00	28.00
40,42-Williamson-a	6.50	19.50	45.00
48-Crandall-a	5.70	17.00	35.00

NOTE: ***Ayers*** *a-19, 32.* ***Berg*** *a-44.* ***Colan*** *a-21, 22, 32, 33, 40.* ***Drucker*** *a-28, 29.* ***Everett*** *a-44.* ***Heath*** *c-23, 26, 27, 29, 32.* ***Maneely*** *a-22, 23; c-2, 13, 22, 35.* ***Morisi*** *a-42.* ***Morrow*** *a-41.* ***Orlando*** *a-47.* ***Powell*** *a-19, 21, 25, 29, 32, 40, 47.* ***Robinson*** *a-1-4, 5(4); c-4, 5.* ***Robert Sale*** *a-19.* ***Severin*** *a-32; c-40.* ***Woodbridge*** *a-45, 46.*

BATTLEFRONT
No. 5, June, 1952
Standard Comics

	GD25	FN65	NM94
5-Toth-a	11.30	34.00	90.00

BATTLE GROUND
Sept, 1954 - No. 20, Aug, 1957
Atlas Comics (OMC)

	GD25	FN65	NM94
1	15.00	45.00	120.00
2-Jack Katz-a	8.50	26.00	60.00
3,4-Last precode (3/55)	5.70	17.00	40.00
5-8,10	5.70	17.00	35.00
9,11,13,18: 9-Krigstein-a. 11,13,18-Williamson-a in each	7.15	21.50	50.00
12,15-17,19,20	5.35	16.00	32.00
14-Kirby-a	7.15	21.50	50.00

NOTE: ***Ayers*** *a-13.* ***Colan*** *a-11, 13.* ***Drucker*** *a-7, 12, 13, 20.* ***Heath*** *c-2, 5, 13.* ***Maneely*** *a-19; c-1, 19.* ***Orlando*** *a-17.* ***Pakula*** *a-11.* ***Severin*** *a-5, 12, 19. c-20.* ***Tuska*** *a-11.*

BATTLE HEROES
Sept, 1966 - No. 2, Nov, 1966 (25¢)
Stanley Publications

	GD25	FN65	NM94
1,2		2.40	6.00

BATTLE OF THE BULGE (See Movie Classics)

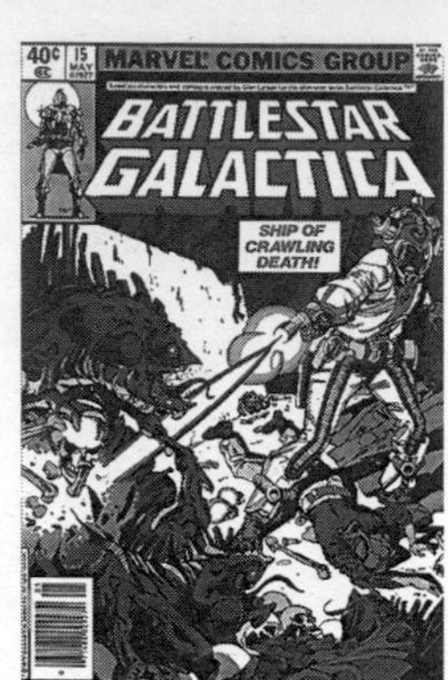

Battlestar Galactica #15 © Universal Studios

Battle Stories #6 © FAW

Battle Tide II #2 © MEG

BATTLE OF THE PLANETS (TV)
6/79 - No. 10, 12/80 (Based on syndicated cartoon by Sandy Frank)
Gold Key/Whitman No. 6 on

	GD25	FN65	NM94
1,6-10: Mortimer a-1-4,7-10	1.00	1.60	7.00
2-5		1.60	4.00

BATTLE REPORT
Aug, 1952 - No. 6, June, 1953
Ajax/Farrell Publications

	GD25	FN65	NM94
1	6.50	19.50	45.00
2-6	4.25	13.00	28.00

BATTLE SQUADRON
April, 1955 - No. 5, Dec, 1955
Stanmor Publications

	GD25	FN65	NM94
1	5.70	17.00	35.00
2-5: 3-Iwo Jima & flag-c	4.00	10.00	20.00

BATTLESTAR GALACTICA (TV) (Also see Marvel Comics Super Special #8)
Mar, 1979 - No. 23, Jan, 1981
Marvel Comics Group

	GD25	FN65	NM94
1: 1-5 adapt TV episodes		2.20	5.50
2-23: 1-3-Partial-r		1.30	3.25

NOTE: ***Austin*** *c-9i, 10i.* ***Golden*** *c-18.* ***Simonson*** *a(p)-4, 5, 11-13, 15-20, 22, 23; c(p)-4, 5,11-17, 19, 20, 22, 23.*

BATTLESTAR GALACTICA (TV) (Also see Asylum)
July, 1995 - No.4, Nov, 1995 ($2.50, limited series)
Maximum Press

	GD25	FN65	NM94
1-4: Continuation of TV series		1.30	3.25
Trade paperback (12/95, $12.95)-reprints series			13.00

BATTLESTAR GALACTICA: APOLLO'S JOURNEY (TV)
Apr, 1996 - No. 3, June, 1996 ($2.95, limited series)
Maximum Press

	GD25	FN65	NM94
1-3: Richard Hatch scripts		1.20	3.00

BATTLESTAR GALACTICA: JOURNEY'S END (TV)
Aug, 1996 - No. 4, Nov, 1996 ($2.99, limited series)
Maximum Press

	GD25	FN65	NM94
1-4-Continuation of the T.V. series		1.20	3.00

BATTLESTAR GALACTICA: SPECIAL EDITION (TV)
Jan, 1997 ($2.99, one-shot)
Maximum Press

	GD25	FN65	NM94
1-Fully painted; Scalf-c/s/a; r/Asylum			2.99

BATTLESTAR GALACTICA: STARBUCK (TV)
Dec, 1995 - No. 3, Mar, 1996 ($2.50, limited series)
Maximum Press

	GD25	FN65	NM94
1-3		1.00	2.50

BATTLESTAR GALACTICA: THE COMPENDIUM (TV)
Feb, 1997 ($2.99, one-shot)
Maximum Press

	GD25	FN65	NM94
1			2.99

BATTLESTAR GALACTICA: THE ENEMY WITHIN (TV)
Nov, 1995 - No. 3, Feb, 1996 ($2.50, limited series)
Maximum Press

	GD25	FN65	NM94
1-3: 3-Indicia reads Feb, 1995 in error.		1.00	2.50

BATTLESTONE (Also see Brigade & Youngblood)
Nov, 1994 - No. 2, Dec, 1994 ($2.50, limited series)
Image Comics (Extreme Studios)

	GD25	FN65	NM94
1,2-Liefeld plots		1.00	2.50

BATTLE STORIES (See XMas Comics)
Jan, 1952 - No. 11, Sept, 1953
Fawcett Publications

	GD25	FN65	NM94
1-Evans-a	10.00	30.00	80.00
2	5.70	17.00	40.00
3-11	5.00	15.00	30.00

BATTLE STORIES
1963 - 1964
Super Comics

	GD25	FN65	NM94
Reprints #10-12,15-18: 10-r/U.S Tank Commandos #? 11-r/? 11, 12,17-r/Monty Hall #?; 13-Kintsler-a (1pg).15-r/American Air Forces #7 by Powell; Bolle-r. 18-U.S. Fighting Air Force #?		2.00	5.00

BATTLETECH (See Blackthorne 3-D Series #41 for 3-D issue)
Oct, 1987 - No. 6, 1988 ($1.75/$2.00)
Blackthorne Publishing\

	GD25	FN65	NM94
1-6: Based on game. 1-Color. 2-Begin B&W		.70	1.75
Annual 1 ($4.50, B&W)		1.80	4.50

BATTLETECH
Feb, 1995 ($2.95)
Malibu Comics

	GD25	FN65	NM94
0		1.20	3.00

BATTLETECH FALLOUT
Dec, 1994 - No. 4, Mar, 1995 ($2.95)
Malibu Comics

	GD25	FN65	NM94
1-Two editions exist; normal logo and gold version w/foil logo stamped "Gold Limited Edition		1.20	3.00
1-Full-c holographic limited edition		2.40	6.00
2-4		1.20	3.00

BATTLETIDE (Death's Head II & Killpower...)
Dec, 1992 - No. 4, Mar, 1993 ($1.75, mini-series)
Marvel Comics UK, Ltd.

	GD25	FN65	NM94
1-4: Wolverine, Psylocke, Dark Angel app.		.70	1.75

BATTLETIDE II (Death's Head II & Killpower...)
Aug, 1993 - No. 4, Nov, 1993 ($1.75, mini-series)
Marvel Comics UK, Ltd.

	GD25	FN65	NM94
1-($2.95)-Foil embossed logo		1.20	3.00
2-4: 2-Hulk-c/story		.70	1.75

BATTLEZONES: DREAM TEAM 2 (See Dream Team)
Mar, 1996 ($3.95)
Malibu Comics (Ultraverse)

	GD25	FN65	NM94
1-pin-ups between Marvel & Malibu characters by Mike Wieringo, Phil Jimenez, Mike McKone, Cully Hamner, Gary Frank & others			4.00

BAYWATCH COMIC STORIES (TV) (Magazine)
May, 1996 - No. 4, 1997 ($4.95) (Photo-c on all)
Acclaim Comics (Armada)

	GD25	FN65	NM94
1-4: Photo comics based on TV show		2.00	5.00

BEACH BLANKET BINGO (See Movie Classics)

BEAGLE BOYS, THE (Walt Disney)(See The Phantom Blot)
11/64; No. 2, 11/65; No. 3, 8/66 - No. 47, 2/79 (See WDC&S #134)
Gold Key

	GD25	FN65	NM94
1	2.25	6.75	25.00
2-5	1.10	3.30	12.00
6-10	.80	2.40	8.00
11-20: 11,14,19-r		2.00	5.00
21-47: 27-r		1.00	2.50

BEAGLE BOYS VERSUS UNCLE SCROOGE
Mar, 1979 - No. 12, Feb, 1980
Gold Key

	GD25	FN65	NM94
1	.80	2.40	8.00

Beast #1 © MEG

Beavis and Butt-head #7 © MTV

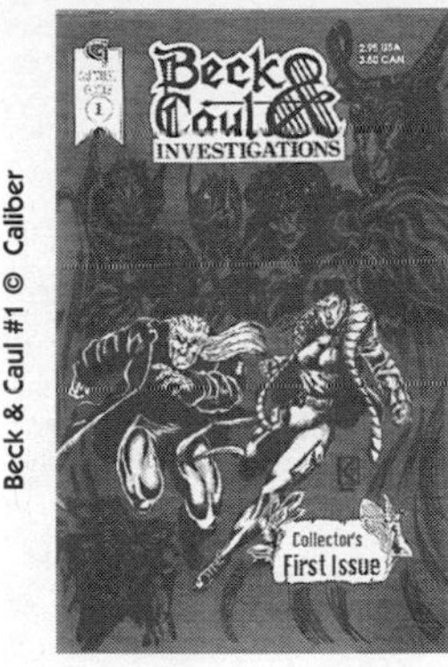

Beck & Caul #1 © Caliber

GD25 FN65 NM94

2-12: 9-r — 1.60 4.00

BEANBAGS
Winter, 1951 - No. 2, Spring, 1952
Ziff-Davis Publ. Co. (Approved Comics)

	GD25	FN65	NM94
1,2	7.85	23.50	55.00

BEANIE THE MEANIE
1958 - No. 3, May, 1959
Fago Publications

	GD25	FN65	NM94
1-3	4.00	11.00	22.00

BEANY AND CECIL (TV) (Bob Clampett's...)
Jan, 1952 - 1955; July-Sept, 1962 - No. 5, July-Sept, 1963
Dell Publishing Co.

	GD25	FN65	NM94
Four Color 368	25.00	75.00	275.00
Four Color 414,448,477,530,570,635(1/55)	16.00	47.00	170.00
01-057-209 (#1)	14.00	41.00	150.00
2-5	9.00	27.00	100.00

BEAR COUNTRY (Disney)
No. 758, Dec, 1956
Dell Publishing Co.

	GD25	FN65	NM94
Four Color 758-Movie	4.50	13.50	50.00

BEAST (See X-Men)
May, 1997 - No. 3, 1997 ($2.50, mini-series
Marvel Comics

	GD25	FN65	NM94
1-3-Giffen-s/Nocon-a		1.00	2.50

B.E.A.S.T.I.E.S. (Also see Axis Alpha)
Apr, 1994 ($1.95)
Axis Comics

	GD25	FN65	NM94
1-Javier Saltares-c/a/scripts		.80	2.00

BEATLES, THE (See Girls' Romances #109, Go-Go, Heart Throbs #101, Herbie #5, Howard the Duck Mag. #4, Laugh #166, Marvel Comics Super Special #4, My LittleMargie #54, Not Brand Echh, Strange Tales #130, Summer Love, Superman's Pal Jimmy Olsen #79, Teen Confessions #37, Tippy's Friends & Tippy Teen)

BEATLES, THE (Life Story)
Sept-Nov, 1964 (35¢)
Dell Publishing Co.

	GD25	FN65	NM94
1-(Scarce)-Stories with color photo pin-ups	41.00	123.00	500.00

BEATLES EXPERIENCE, THE
Mar, 1991 - No. 8, 1991 ($2.50, B&W, limited series)
Revolutionary Comics

	GD25	FN65	NM94
1-8: 1-Gold logo		1.00	2.50

BEATLES YELLOW SUBMARINE (See Movie Comics under Yellow...)

BEAUTIFUL PEOPLE
Apr, 1994 ($4.95, 8-1/2x11", one-shot)
Slave Labor Graphics

	GD25	FN65	NM94
nn		2.00	5.00

BEAUTIFUL STORIES FOR UGLY CHILDREN
1989 - No. 30, 1991 ($2.00/$2.50, B&W, mature)
DC Comics (Piranha Press)

	GD25	FN65	NM94
V1-11		.80	2.00
12-30: 12-$2.50-c begins		1.00	2.50
A Cotton Candy Autopsy ($12.95, B&W)-Reprints 1st two volumes			13.00

BEAUTY AND THE BEAST, THE
Jan, 1985 - No. 4, Apr, 1985 (limited series)
Marvel Comics Group

	GD25	FN65	NM94
1-4: Dazzler & the Beast from X-Men			1.50

BEAUTY AND THE BEAST (Graphic novel)(Also see Cartoon Tales & Disney's New Adventures of...)
1992
Disney Comics

	GD25	FN65	NM94
nn-($4.95, prestige edition)-Adapts animated film		2.00	5.00
nn-($2.50, newsstand edition)		1.00	2.50

BEAUTY AND THE BEAST
Sept., 1992 - No. 2, 1992 ($1.50, limited series)
Disney Comics

	GD25	FN65	NM94
1		.80	2.00
2			1.50

BEAUTY AND THE BEAST: PORTRAIT OF LOVE (TV)
May, 1989 - No. 2, Mar, 1990 ($5.95, 60 pgs., squarebound)
First Comics

	GD25	FN65	NM94
1,2: 1-Based on TV show, Wendy Pini-a/scripts. 2-...: Night of Beauty; by Wendy Pini		2.40	6.00

BEAVER VALLEY (Movie)(Disney)
No. 625, Apr, 1955
Dell Publishing Co.

	GD25	FN65	NM94
Four Color 625	5.50	16.50	60.00

BEAVIS AND BUTTHEAD (MTV's...)(TV cartoon)
Mar, 1994 - No. 28, June, 1996 ($1.95)
Marvel Comics

	GD25	FN65	NM94
1-Silver ink-c. 1, 2-Punisher & Devil Dinosaur app.		1.20	3.00
1-2nd printing		.80	2.00
2,3: 2-Wolverine app. 3-Man-Thing, Spider-Man, Venom, Carnage, Mary Jane & Stan Lee cameos; John Romita, Sr. art (2 pgs.)		1.00	2.50
4-28: 5-War Machine, Thor, Loki, Hulk, Captain America & Rhino cameos. 6-Psylocke, Polaris, Daredevil & Bullseye app. 7-Ghost Rider & Sub-Mariner app. 8-Quasar & Eon app.9-Prowler & Nightwatch app. 11-Black Widow app. 12-Thunderstrike & Bloodaxe app. 13-Night Thrasher app. 14-Spider-Man 2099 app. 15-Warlock app. 16-X-Factor app. 25-Juggernaut app.		.80	2.00

BECK & CAUL INVESTIGATIONS
Jan, 1994 - No. 5, 1995? ($2.95, B&W)
Gauntlet Comics (Caliber)

	GD25	FN65	NM94
1-5		1.20	3.00
Special 1 ($4.95)		2.00	5.00

BEDKNOBS AND BROOMSTICKS (See Walt Disney Showcase No. 6 & 50)

BEDLAM!
Sept, 1985 - No. 2, Sept, 1985 (B&W-r in color)
Eclipse Comics

	GD25	FN65	NM94
1,2: Bissette-a		.70	1.80

BEDTIME STORY (See Cinema Comics Herald)

BEELZELVIS
Feb, 1994 ($2.95, B&W, one-shot)
Slave Labor Graphics

	GD25	FN65	NM94
1		1.20	3.00

BEEP BEEP, THE ROAD RUNNER (TV)(See Daffy & Kite Fun Book)
July, 1958 - No. 14, Aug-Oct, 1962; Oct, 1966 - No. 105, 1983
Dell Publishing Co./Gold Key No. 1-88/Whitman No. 89 on

	GD25	FN65	NM94
Four Color 918 (#1, 7/58)	8.00	25.00	90.00
Four Color 1008,1046 (11-1/59-60)	4.00	12.00	45.00
4(2-4/60)-14(Dell)	3.00	10.00	36.00
1(10/66, Gold Key)	3.00	10.00	36.00
2-5	2.25	6.75	26.00
6-14 (1962)	1.65	5.00	18.00
15-18,20-40	1.30	4.00	13.00
19-With pull-out poster	2.25	6.75	26.00

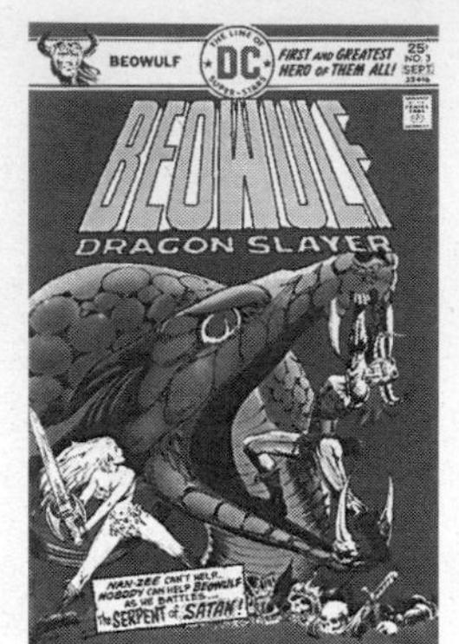

Beowulf #3 © DC

Berni Wrightson, Master of the Macabre #5 © Berni Wrightson

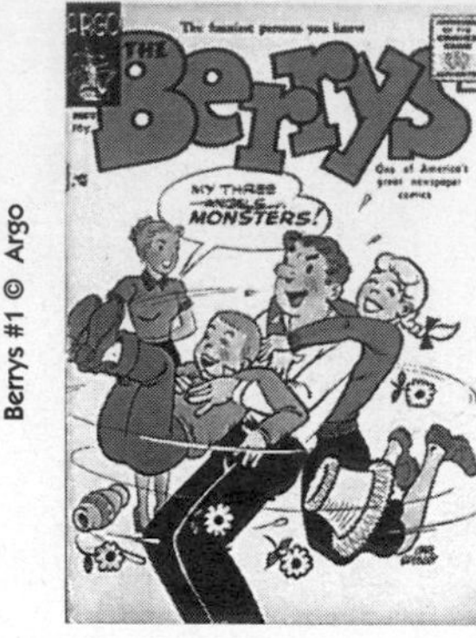

Berrys #1 © Argo

	GD25	FN65	NM94
41-50	1.10	3.30	9.00
51-70		2.40	6.00
71-88		1.20	3.00
89-105		1.60	4.00

NOTE: *See March of Comics #351, 353, 375, 387, 397, 416, 430, 442, 455. #5, 8-10, 35, 53, 59-62, 68-r; 96-102, 104 are 1/3-r.*

BEETLE BAILEY (See Comics Reading Library, Giant Comic Album & Sarge Snorkel)
#459, 5/53 - #38, 5-7/62; #39, 11/62 - #53, 5/66; #54, 8/66 - #65, 12/67; #67, 2/69 - #119, 11/76; #120, 4/78 - #132, 4/80
Dell Publishing Co./Gold Key #39-53/King #54-66/Charlton #67-119/ Gold Key #120-131/Whitman #132

	GD25	FN65	NM94
Four Color 469 (#1)-By Mort Walker	9.00	27.00	100.00
Four Color 521,552,622	4.50	13.50	50.00
5(2-4/56)-10(5-7/57)	3.60	11.00	40.00
11-20(4-5/59)	2.75	8.00	30.00
21-38(5-7/62)	1.65	5.00	18.00
39-53(5/66)	1.00	3.00	9.00
54-65	1.25	3.75	10.00
67-99 (No. 66 publ. overseas only?)	1.00	3.00	8.00
100	1.25	3.75	10.00
101-119		2.40	6.00
120-132		1.20	3.00
Bold Detergent Giveaway('69)-same as regular issue (#67) minus price		1.20	3.00
Cerebral Palsy Assn. Giveaway V2#71('69)-V2#73; (#1), 1/70 (Charlton)		1.20	3.00
Red Cross Giveaway-(1969, 5x7", 16 pgs., paper-c		1.20	3.00

BEETLE BAILEY
V2#1, Sept, 1992 - V2#9, Aug, 1994 ($1.25/$1.50)
Harvey Comics

	GD25	FN65	NM94
V2#1-4			1.25
5-9-($1.50)			1.50
Big Book 1(11/92),2(5/93)(Both $1.95, 52 pgs.)		.80	2.00
Giant Size V2#1(10/92),2(3/93)(Both $2.25,68 pgs.)		.90	2.25

BEETLEJUICE (TV)
Oct, 1991 ($1.25)
Harvey Comics

	GD25	FN65	NM94
1			1.25

BEETLEJUICE CRIMEBUSTERS ON THE HAUNT
Sept, 1992 - No. 3, Jan, 1993 ($1.50, limited series)
Harvey Comics

	GD25	FN65	NM94
1-3			1.50

BEE 29, THE BOMBARDIER
Feb, 1945
Neal Publications

	GD25	FN65	NM94
1-(Funny animal)	16.00	49.00	130.00

BEHIND PRISON BARS
1952
Realistic Comics (Avon)

	GD25	FN65	NM94
1-Kinstler-c	23.00	68.00	180.00

BEHOLD THE HANDMAID
1954 (Religious) (25¢ with a 20¢ sticker price)
George Pflaum

	GD25	FN65	NM94
nn	3.20	8.00	16.00

BELIEVE IT OR NOT (See Ripley's...)

BEN AND ME (Disney)
No. 539, Mar, 1954
Dell Publishing Co.

	GD25	FN65	NM94
Four Color 539	3.00	9.00	32.00

BEN BOWIE AND HIS MOUNTAIN MEN
1952 - No. 17, Nov-Jan, 1958-59
Dell Publishing Co.

	GD25	FN65	NM94
Four Color 443 (#1)	5.50	16.50	60.00
Four Color 513,557,599,626,657	2.75	8.00	30.00
7(5-7/56)-11: 11-Intro/origin Yellow Hair	2.75	8.00	30.00
12-17	2.25	6.75	24.00

BEN CASEY (TV)
June-July, 1962 - No. 10, June-Aug, 1965 (Photo-c)
Dell Publishing Co.

	GD25	FN65	NM94
12-063-207 (#1)	3.60	11.00	40.00
2(10/62)-10: 4-Marijuana & heroin use story	2.75	8.00	30.00

BEN CASEY FILM STORY (TV)
Nov, 1962 (25¢) (Photo-c)
Gold Key

	GD25	FN65	NM94
30009-211-All photos	5.50	16.50	70.00

BENEATH THE PLANET OF THE APES (See Movie Comics & Power Record Comics)

BEN FRANKLIN (See Kite Fun Book)

BEN HUR
No. 1052, Nov, 1959
Dell Publishing Co.

	GD25	FN65	NM94
Four Color 1052-Movie, Manning-a	9.00	27.00	100.00

BEN ISRAEL
1974 (39¢)
Logos International

	GD25	FN65	NM94
nn			1.00

BEOWULF (Also see First Comics Graphic Novel #1)
Apr-May, 1975 - No. 6, Feb-Mar, 1976
National Periodical Publications

	GD25	FN65	NM94
1-6: 5-Flying saucer-c/story		1.20	3.00

BERLIN
Apr, 1996 - Present ($2.50, B&W)
Black Eye Productions

	GD25	FN65	NM94
1-3: Jason Lutes-c/a/scripts.		1.00	2.50

BERNI WRIGHTSON, MASTER OF THE MACABRE
July, 1983 - No. 5, Nov, 1984 ($1.50, Baxter paper)
Pacific Comics/Eclipse Comics No. 5

	GD25	FN65	NM94
1-5: Wrightson-c/a(r). 4-Jeff Jones-r (11 pgs.)			1.50

BERRYS, THE (Also see Funny World)
May, 1956
Argo Publ.

	GD25	FN65	NM94
1-Reprints daily & Sunday strips & daily Animal Antics by Ed Nofziger	5.00	15.00	30.00

BERZERKERS (See Youngblood V1#2)
Aug, 1995 - No. 3, Oct, 1995 ($2.50, limited series)
Image Comics (Extreme Studios)

	GD25	FN65	NM94
1-3: Beau Smith scripts, Fraga-a		1.00	2.50

BEST COMICS
Nov, 1939 - No. 4, Feb, 1940 (Large size, reads sideways)
Better Publications

	GD25	FN65	NM94
1-(Scarce)-Red Mask begins(1st app.) & c/s-all	61.00	183.00	550.00
2-4: 4-Cannibalism story	39.00	117.00	350.00

BEST FROM BOY'S LIFE, THE
Oct, 1957 - No. 5, Oct, 1958 (35¢)
Gilberton Company

Best of DC #1 © DC

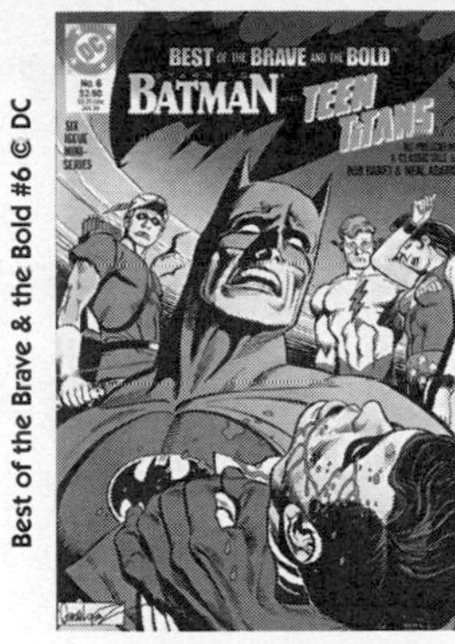

Best of the Brave & the Bold #6 © DC

Best Romance #5 © STD

	GD25	FN65	NM94
1-Space Conquerors & Kam of the Ancient Ones begin, end #5	8.50	26.00	60.00
2,3,5	5.35	16.00	32.00
4-L.B. Cole-a	5.70	17.00	40.00

BEST LOVE (Formerly Sub-Mariner Comics No. 32)
No. 33, Aug, 1949 - No. 36, April, 1950 (Photo-c 33-36)
Marvel Comics (MPI)

	GD25	FN65	NM94
33-Kubert-a	8.75	26.25	65.00
34	5.35	16.00	32.00
35,36-Everett-a	6.00	18.00	42.00

BEST OF BUGS BUNNY, THE
Oct, 1966 - No. 2, Oct, 1968
Gold Key

	GD25	FN65	NM94
1,2-Giants	3.60	11.00	40.00

BEST OF DC, THE (Blue Ribbon Digest) (See Limited Coll. Ed. C-52)
Sept-Oct, 1979 - No. 71, Apr, 1986 (100-148 pgs; mostly reprints)
DC Comics

	GD25	FN65	NM94
1-10: 1-Superman, w/"Death of Superman"-r. 2-Batman 40th Ann. Special. 3-Superfriends. 4 Rudolph. 5-Best of 1979. 6,8-Superman. 7-Superboy. 9-Batman, Creeper app. 10-Secret Origins of Super Villains		1.20	3.00
11-20: 11-The Year's Best Stories. 12-Superman Time and Space Stories. 13-Best of DC Comics Presents. 14-Origins of Batman Villains. 15-Superboy 16-Superman Anniv. 17-Supergirl. 18-Teen Titans new-s., Adams, Kane-a; Perez-c. 19-Superman. 20-World's Finest		1.20	3.00
21-27: 21-Justice Society. 22-Christmas. 23-(148 pgs.)-Best of 1981. 24 Legion, new story and 16 pgs. new costumes. 25-Superman. 26-Brave & Bold. 27-Superman vs. Luthor		2.00	5.00
28,29: 28-Binky, Sugar & Spike app. 29-Sugar & Spike, 3 new stories; new Stanley & his Monster story		2.00	5.00
30-36,38,40: 30-Detective Comics. 31-JLA. 32-Superman. 33-Secret origins of Legion Heroes and Villains. 34-Metal Men; has #497 on-c from Adv. Comics. 35-The Year's Best Comics Stories(148 pgs.). 36-Superman vs. Kryptonite. 38-Superman. 40-World of Krypton		2.00	5.00
37,39: 37-"Funny Stuff", Mayer-a. 39-Binky		2.00	5.00
41,43,45,47,49,53,55,58,60,63,65,68,70: 41-Sugar & Spike new stories with Mayer-a. 43,49,55-Funny Stuff. 45,53,70-Binky. 47,58,65,68-Sugar & Spike. 60-Plop!; Wood-c(r) & Aragonés-r (5/85). 63-Plop!; Wrightson-a(r)	1.00	2.80	7.00
42,44,46,48,50-52,54,56,57,59,61,62,64,66,67,69,71: 42,56-Superman vs. Aliens. 44,57,67-Superboy & LSH. 46-Jimmy Olsen. 48-Superman Team-ups 50-Year's best Superman. 51-Batman Family. 52 Best of 1984. 54,56,59-Superman. 61-(148 pgs.)Year's best. 62-Best of Batman 1985. 69-Year's best Team stories. 71-Year's best	1.00	2.80	7.00

NOTE: ***N. Adams*** *a-2r, 14r, 18r, 26, 51.* ***Aparo*** *a-9, 14, 26, 30; c-9, 14, 26.* ***Austin*** *a-51i.* ***Buckler*** *a-40p; c-16, 22.* ***Giffen*** *a-50, 52; c-33p.* ***Grell*** *a-33p.* ***Grossman*** *a-37.* ***Heath*** *a-26.* ***Infantino*** *a-10r, 18.* ***Kaluta*** *a-40.* ***G. Kane*** *a-10r, 18r; c-40, 44.* ***Kubert*** *a-10r, 21, 26.* ***Layton*** *a-21.* ***S. Mayer*** *c-29, 37, 41, 43, 47; a-28, 29, 37, 41, 43, 47, 58, 65, 68.* ***Moldoff*** *c-64p.* ***Morrow*** *a-40; c-40.* ***W. Mortimer*** *a-39p.* ***Newton*** *a-5, 51.* ***Perez*** *a-24, 50p; c-18, 21, 23.* ***Rogers*** *a-14, 51p.* ***Simonson*** *a-11r.* ***Spiegle*** *a-52.* ***Starlin*** *a-51.* ***Staton*** *a-5, 21.* ***Tuska*** *a-24.* ***Wolverton*** *a-60.* ***Wood*** *a-60, 63; c-60, 63.* ***Wrightson*** *a-60. New art in #14, 18, 24.*

BEST OF DENNIS THE MENACE, THE
Summer, 1959 - No. 5, Spring, 1961 (100 pgs.)
Hallden/Fawcett Publications

	GD25	FN65	NM94
1-All reprints; Wiseman-a	5.50	16.50	55.00
2-5	3.50	10.50	35.00

BEST OF DONALD DUCK, THE
Nov, 1965 (12¢, 36 pgs.)(Lists 2nd printing in indicia)
Gold Key

	GD25	FN65	NM94
1-Reprints Four Color #223 by Barks	6.00	18.00	65.00

BEST OF DONALD DUCK & UNCLE SCROOGE, THE
Nov, 1964 - No. 2, Sept, 1967 (25¢ Giants)
Gold Key

	GD25	FN65	NM94
1(30022-411)('64)-Reprints 4-Color #189 & 408 by Carl Barks; cover of F.C. #189 redrawn by Barks	6.40	19.00	70.00
2(30022-709)('67)-Reprints 4-Color #256 & "Seven Cities of Cibola" & U.S. #8 by Barks	6.40	19.00	70.00

BEST OF HORROR AND SCIENCE FICTION COMICS
1987 ($2.00)
Bruce Webster

	GD25	FN65	NM94
1-Wolverton, Frazetta, Powell, Ditko-r		.80	2.00

BEST OF MARMADUKE, THE
1960
Charlton Comics

	GD25	FN65	NM94
1-Brad Anderson's strip reprints	2.50	7.50	22.00

BEST OF MS. TREE, THE
1987 - No. 4, 1988 ($2.00, B&W, limited series)
Pyramid Comics

	GD25	FN65	NM94
1-4		.80	2.00

BEST OF THE BRAVE AND THE BOLD, THE (See Super DC Giant)
Oct, 1988 - No. 6, Jan, 1989 ($2.50, limited series)
DC Comics

	GD25	FN65	NM94
1-6: Neal Adams-r, Kubert-r & Heath-r in all		1.00	2.50

BEST OF THE WEST (See A-1 Comics)
1951 - No. 12, April-June, 1954
Magazine Enterprises

	GD25	FN65	NM94
1(A-1 42)-Ghost Rider, Durango Kid, Straight Arrow, Bobby Benson begin	36.00	108.00	295.00
2(A-1 46)	17.00	51.00	135.00
3(A-1 52), 4(A-1 59), 5(A-1 66)	15.00	45.00	120.00
6(A-1 70), 7(A-1 76), 8(A-1 81), 9(A-1 85), 10(A-1 87), 11(A-1 97), 12(A-1 103)	10.50	32.00	85.00

NOTE: ***Bolle*** *a-9.* ***Borth*** *a-12.* ***Guardineer*** *a-5, 12.* ***Powell*** *a-1, 12.*

BEST OF UNCLE SCROOGE & DONALD DUCK, THE
Nov, 1966 (25¢)
Gold Key

	GD25	FN65	NM94
1(30030-611)-Reprints part 4-Color #159 & 456 & Uncle Scrooge #6,7 by Carl Barks	6.40	19.00	70.00

BEST OF WALT DISNEY COMICS, THE
1974 ($1.50, 52 pgs.) (Walt Disney)
(8-1/2x11" cardboard covers; 32,000 printed of each)
Western Publishing Co.

	GD25	FN65	NM94
96170-Reprints 1st two stories less 1 pg. each from 4-Color #62	2.25	6.75	25.00
96171-Reprints Mickey Mouse and the Bat Bandit of Inferno Gulch from 1934 (strips) by Gottfredson	2.25	6.75	25.00
96172-r/Uncle Scrooge #386 & two other stories	2.25	6.75	25.00
96173-Reprints "Ghost of the Grotto" (from 4-Color #159) & "Christmas on Bear Mountain" (from 4-Color #178)	2.25	6.75	25.00

BEST ROMANCE
No. 5, Feb-Mar, 1952 - No. 7, Aug, 1952
Standard Comics (Visual Editions)

	GD25	FN65	NM94
5-Toth-a; photo-c	8.75	26.25	70.00
6,7-Photo-c	4.15	12.50	25.00

BEST SELLER COMICS (See Tailspin Tommy)

BEST WESTERN (Formerly Terry Toons? or Miss America Magazine V7#24(#57)?; Western Outlaws & Sheriffs No. 60 on)
No. 58, June, 1949 - No. 59, Aug, 1949
Marvel Comics (IPC)

	GD25	FN65	NM94
58,59-Black Rider, Kid Colt, Two-Gun Kid app.; both have Syd Shores-c	16.00	49.00	130.00

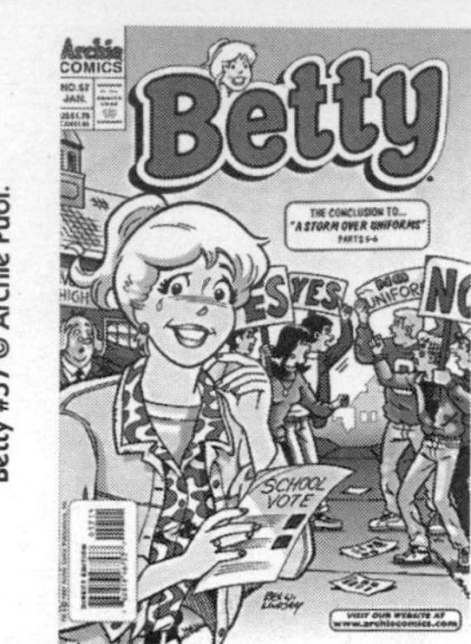

Betty #57 © Archie Publ.

Beverly Hillbillies #5 © DELL

Beware #13 (#1) © TM

	GD25	FN65	NM94

BETTIE PAGE COMICS
Mar, 1996 ($3.95)
Dark Horse Comics

	GD25	FN65	NM94
1-Dave Stevens-c; Bret Blevins & Russ Heath-a; Jaime Hernandez pin-up		1.60	4.00

BETTIE PAGE COMICS: SPICY ADVENTURE
Jan, 1997 ($2.95, one-shot, mature)
Dark Horse Comics

	GD25	FN65	NM94
nn-Silke-c/s/a			2.95

BETTY (See Pep Comics #22 for 1st app.)
Sept, 1992 - Present ($1.25/$1.50/$1.75)
Archie Comics

	GD25	FN65	NM94
1-24			1.25
25-56			1.50
57-64: 57-Begin $1.75-c; "A Storm Over Uniforms" x-over part 5,6			1.75

BETTY AND HER STEADY (Going Steady with Betty No. 1)
No. 2, Mar-Apr, 1950
Avon Periodicals

	GD25	FN65	NM94
2	7.85	23.50	55.00

BETTY AND ME
Aug, 1965 - No. 200, Aug, 1992
Archie Publications

	GD25	FN65	NM94
1	8.50	25.50	85.00
2	4.20	12.60	42.00
3-5: 3-Origin Superteen. Superteen in new costume #4-7; dons new helmet in #5, ends #8 (see Archie's Girls #118)	2.50	7.50	25.00
6-10	1.40	4.20	14.00
11-20	1.20	3.60	12.00
21-30	1.10	3.30	9.00
31-35		2.40	6.00
36-55 (52 pgs.)	1.10	3.30	9.00
56-100		1.60	4.00
101-150		1.20	3.00
151-200: Later issues $1.00 cover		.80	2.00

BETTY AND VERONICA (Also see Archie's Girls...)
June, 1987 - Present (75¢ /$1.25/$1.50/$1.75)
Archie Enterprises

	GD25	FN65	NM94
1		1.60	4.00
2-10		1.20	3.00
11-130		.80	2.00
Summer Fun 1 (1994, $2.00, 52 pgs. plus poster)		.80	2.00

BETTY & VERONICA ANNUAL DIGEST (...Digest Magazine #1-4, 44 on; ...Comics Digest Mag. #5-43)
Nov, 1980 - Present ($1.00/$1.50/$1.75/$1.95, digest size)
Archie Publications

	GD25	FN65	NM94
1	1.50	4.50	12.00
2-10: 2(11/81-Katy Keene story), 3(8/82)		2.40	6.00
11-30		1.60	4.00
31-98		.80	2.00

BETTY & VERONICA ANNUAL DIGEST MAGAZINE
Sept, 1989 - Present ($1.50/$1.75/$1.79, 128 pgs.)
Archie Comics

	GD25	FN65	NM94
1		1.60	4.00
2-17: 9-Neon ink logo. 16-Begin $1.79-c		1.20	3.00

BETTY & VERONICA CHRISTMAS SPECTACULAR (See Archie Giant Series Magazine #159, 168, 180, 191, 204, 217, 229, 241, 453, 465, 477, 489, 501, 513, 525, 536, 547, 558, 568, 580, 593, 606, 618)

BETTY & VERONICA DOUBLE DIGEST MAGAZINE
1987 - Present ($2.25/$2.75/$1.50/$2.79/$2.95, digest size, 256 pgs.)(...Digest #12 on)
Archie Enterprises

	GD25	FN65	NM94
1	1.00	3.00	8.00
2-10		2.00	5.00
11-25: 5,17-Xmas-c. 16-Capt. Hero story		1.40	3.50
26-72		1.20	3.00

BETTY & VERONICA SPECTACULAR (See Archie Giant Series Mag. #11, 16, 21, 26, 32, 138, 145, 153, 162, 173, 184, 197, 201, 210, 214, 221, 226, 234, 238, 246, 250, 458, 462, 470, 482, 486, 494, 498, 506, 510, 518, 522, 526, 530, 537, 552, 559, 563, 569, 575, 582, 588, 600, 608, 613, 620, 623, and Betty & Veronica)

BETTY AND VERONICA SPECTACULAR
Oct, 1992 - Present ($1.25/$1.50/$1.75)
Archie Comics

	GD25	FN65	NM94
1		1.20	3.00
2-10: 1-Dan DeCarlo-c/a		.80	2.00
11-34			1.75

BETTY & VERONICA SPRING SPECTACULAR (See Archie Giant Series Magazine #569, 582, 595)

BETTY & VERONICA SUMMER FUN (See Archie Giant Series Mag. #8, 13, 18, 23, 28, 34, 140, 147, 155, 164, 175, 187, 199, 212, 224, 236, 248, 460, 484, 496, 508, 520, 529, 539, 550, 561, 572, 585, 598, 611, 621)
1994 - Present ($2.00)
Archie Comics

	GD25	FN65	NM94
1-4		.80	2.00

BETTY BOOP'S BIG BREAK
1990 ($5.95, 52 pgs.)
First Publishing

	GD25	FN65	NM94
nn-By Joshua Quagmire; 60th anniversary ish.		2.40	6.00

BETTY PAGE 3-D COMICS
1991 ($3.95, "7-1/2x10-1/4," 28pgs, no glasses)
The 3-D Zone

	GD25	FN65	NM94
1-Photo inside covers; back-c nudity		1.60	4.00

BETTY'S DIARY (See Archie Giant Series Magazine No. 555)
April, 1986 - No. 40, Apr, 1991 (#1:65¢; 75¢/95¢)
Archie Enterprises

	GD25	FN65	NM94
1		1.60	4.00
2-10		1.20	3.00
11-40		.80	2.00

BETTY'S DIGEST
Nov, 1996 - Present ($1.75/$1.79)
Archie Enterprises

	GD25	FN65	NM94
1,2			1.79

BEVERLY HILLBILLIES (TV)
4-6/63 - No. 18, 8/67; No. 19, 10/69; No. 20, 10/70; No. 21, Oct, 1971
Dell Publishing Co.

	GD25	FN65	NM94
1-Photo-c	14.00	42.00	155.00
2-Photo-c	8.00	23.00	85.00
3-9: All have photo covers	5.00	15.00	55.00
10: No photo cover	3.00	9.00	35.00
11-21: All have photo covers. 18-Last 12¢ issue	4.00	12.00	45.00

NOTE: *#1-9, 11-21 are photo covers. #19 reprints cover to #1, but not insides.*

BEWARE (Formerly Fantastic; Chilling Tales No. 13 on)
No. 10, June, 1952 - No. 12, Oct, 1952
Youthful Magazines

	GD25	FN65	NM94
10-E.A. Poe's Pit & the Pendulum adaptation by Wildey; Harrison/Bache-a; atom bomb and shrunken head-c	36.00	107.00	275.00
11-Harrison-a; Ambrose Bierce adapt.	25.00	75.00	185.00
12-Used in **SOTI**, pg. 388; Harrison-a	25.00	75.00	185.00

BEWARE

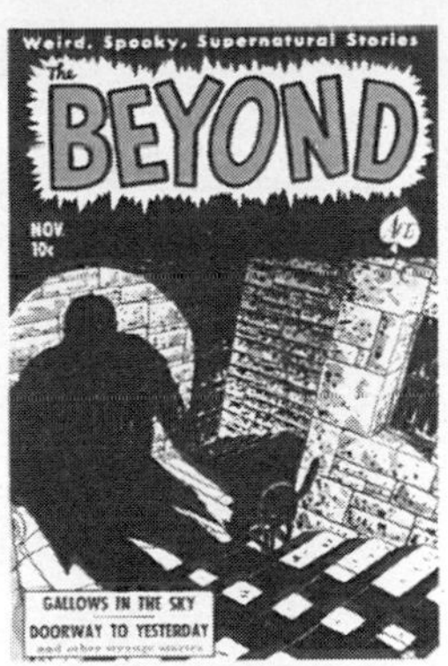

Beyond #7 © ACE

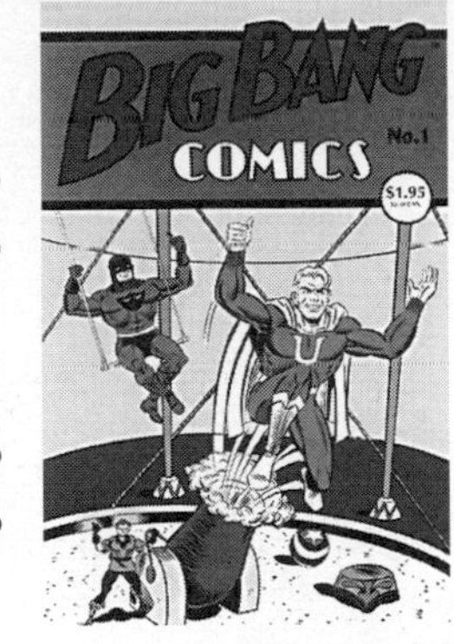

Big Bang Comics #1 © Big Bang Comics

Big Blown Baby #3 © Bill Wray

GD25 FN65 NM94

No. 13, 1/53 - No. 16, 7/53; No. 5, 9/53 - No. 15, 5/55
Trojan Magazines/Merit Publ. No. ?

13(#1)-Harrison-a 36.00 108.00 290.00
14(#2, 3/53)-Krenkel/Harrison-c; dismemberment, severed head panels 25.00 75.00 190.00
15,16(#3, 5/53; #4, 7/53)-Harrison-a 19.00 56.00 140.00
5,9,12,13 19.00 56.00 140.00
6-Ill. in **SOTI**- "Children are first shocked and then desensitized by all this brutality." Corpse on cover swipe/V.O.H. #26; girl on cover swipe/Advs. Into Darkness #10 40.00 120.00 300.00
7,8-Check-a 19.00 58.00 145.00
10-Frazetta/Check-c; Disbrow, Check-a 45.00 130.00 365.00
11-Disbrow-a; heart torn out, blood drainage 21.00 64.00 165.00
14,15: 14-Myron Fass-c. 15-Harrison-a 16.00 47.00 120.00

NOTE: ***Fass*** *a-5, 6, 8; c-6, 11, 14.* ***Forte*** *a-8.* ***Hollingsworth*** *a-15(#3), 16(#4), 9; c-16(#4), 8, 9.* ***Kiefer*** *a-16(#4), 5, 6, 10.*

BEWARE (Becomes Tomb of Darkness No. 9 on)
Mar, 1973 - No. 8, May, 1974 (All reprints)
Marvel Comics Group

1-Everett-c; Sinnott-r ('54) 1.25 3.75 10.00
2-8: 2-Forte, Colan-r. 6-Tuska-a. 7-Torres-r/Mystical Tales #7 1.00 3.00 8.00

NOTE: ***Infantino*** *a-4r.* ***Gil Kane*** *c-4.* ***Wildey*** *a-7r.*

BEWARE TERROR TALES
May, 1952 - No. 8, July, 1953
Fawcett Publications

1-E.C. art swipe/Haunt of Fear #5 & Vault of Horror #26 36.00 107.00 275.00
2 21.00 64.00 165.00
3-8: 8-Tothish-a 17.00 51.00 130.00

NOTE: ***Andru*** *a-2.* ***Bernard Bailey*** *a-1; c-1-5.* ***Powell*** *a-1, 2, 8.* ***Sekowsky*** *a-2.*

BEWARE THE CREEPER (See Adventure, Best of the Brave & the Bold, Brave & the Bold, 1st Issue Special, Flash #318-323, Showcase #73, World's Finest #249)
May-June, 1968 - No. 6, Mar-Apr, 1969 (All 12¢ issues)
National Periodical Publications

1-(5-6/68)-Classic Ditko-c; Ditko-a in all 6.50 19.50 65.00
2-6: 2-5-Ditko-c. 6-Gil Kane-c 4.20 12.60 42.00

BEWITCHED (TV)
4-6/65 - No. 11, 10/67; No. 12, 10/68 - No. 13, 1/69; No. 14, 10/69
Dell Publishing Co.

1-Photo-c 13.00 38.00 140.00
2-No photo-c 6.40 19.00 70.00
3-13-All have photo-c 4.50 13.50 50.00
14-No photo-c 3.00 9.00 32.00

BEYOND, THE
Nov, 1950 - No. 30, Jan, 1955
Ace Magazines

1-Bakerish-a(p) 32.00 96.00 240.00
2-Bakerish-a(p) 20.00 60.00 150.00
3-10: 10-Woodish-a by Cameron 12.00 36.00 90.00
11-20: 18-Used in **POP**, pgs. 81,82 10.00 30.00 70.00
21-26,28-30 10.00 30.00 65.00
27-Used in **SOTI**, pg. 111 10.00 30.00 75.00

NOTE: ***Cameron*** *a-10, 11p, 12p, 15, 16, 21-27, 30; c-20.* ***Colan*** *a-6, 13, 17.* ***Sekowsky*** *a-2, 3, 5, 7, 11, 14, 27r. No. 1 was to appear as Challenge of the Unknown No. 7.*

BEYOND THE GRAVE
July, 1975 - No. 6, June, 1976; No. 7, Jan, 1983 - No. 17, Oct, 1984
Charlton Comics

1-Ditko-a (6 pgs.); Sutton painted-c 1.50 4.50 12.00
2-6: 2-5-Ditko-a; Ditko c-2,3,6 1.00 3.00 8.00

GD25 FN65 NM94

7-17: ('83-'84) Reprints. 13-Aparo-c(r). 15-Sutton-c 2.00 5.00
Modern Comics Reprint 2('78) 3.00

BIBLE TALES FOR YOUNG FOLK (...Young People No. 3-5)
Aug, 1953 - No. 5, Mar, 1954
Atlas Comics (OMC)

1 19.00 56.00 150.00
2-Everett, Krigstein-a 14.00 41.00 110.00
3-5: 4-Robinson-c 10.00 30.00 80.00

BIG (Movie)
Mar, 1989 ($2.00)
Hit Comics (Dark Horse Comics)

1-Adaptaiton of film; Paul Chadwick-c .80 2.00

BIG ALL-AMERICAN COMIC BOOK, THE (See All-American Comics)
1944 (132 pgs., one-shot) (Early DC Annual)
All-American/National Per.l Publ.

GD25 FN65 VF82 NM94

1-Wonder Woman, Green Lantern, Flash, The Atom, Wildcat, Scribbly, The Whip, Ghost Patrol, Hawkman by Kubert (1st on Hawkman), Hop Harrigan, Johnny Thunder, Little Boy Blue, Mr. Terrific, Mutt & Jeff app.; Sargon on cover only; cover by Kubert/Hibbard/Mayer/others 900.00 2700.00 6600.00 10,800.00
(Estimated up to 80+ total copies exist, 6 in NM/Mint)

BIG BABY HUEY (Also see Baby Huey)
Oct, 1991 - No. 4, Mar, 1992 ($1.00, quarterly)
Harvey Comics

GD25 FN65 NM94

1-4 .80 2.00

BIG BANG COMICS (Becomes Big Bang #4)
Spring, 1994 - No. 4, Feb, 1995 ($1.95, limited series)
Caliber Press

0-4: 0-Alex Ross-c. .80 2.00

BIG BANG COMICS
V2#1, May, 1996 - Present ($1.95/$2.50/$2.95)
Image Comics (Highbrow Entertainment)

V2#1-Mighty Man app. .80 2.00
2-4: 2-Begin $2.50-c., S.A. Shadowhawk app. 1.00 2.50
5-16: 5-Begin $2.95-c. 6-Curt Swan/Murphy Anderson-c. 7-Begin B&W 12-Savage Dragon-c/app. 15-Bissette-c 1.20 3.00

BIG BLOWN BABY (Also see Dark Horse Presents)
Aug, 1996 - No. 4, Nov, 1996 ($2.95, limited series, mature)
Dark Horse Comics

1-4: Bill Wray-c/a/scripts 1.20 3.00

BIG BOOK OF CONSPIRACIES, THE
1995 ($12.95, B&W, trade paperback)
DC Comics (Paradox Press)

nn-Doug Moench-s/art by various 13.00

BIG BOOK OF DEATH, THE
1994 ($12.95, B&W, trade paperback)
DC Comics (Paradox Press)

nn 13.00

BIG BOOK OF FREAKS, THE
1996 ($14.95, B&W, trade paperback)
DC Comics (Paradox Press)

nn 15.00

BIG BOOK OF FUN COMICS (See New Book of Comics)
Spring, 1936 (Large size, 52 pgs.)(1st comic book annual & DC annual)
National Periodical Publications

GD25 FN65 VF82

1 (Very rare)-r/New Fun #1-5 2000.00 6000.00 12,000.00
(Estimated up to 15 total copies exist, none in NM/Mint)

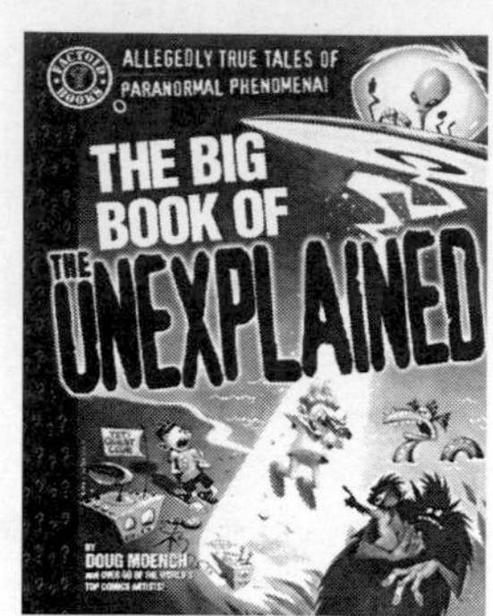

Big Book of the Unexplained © DC

Big Chief Wahoo #1 © EAS

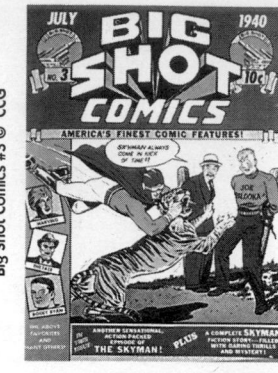

Big Shot Comics #3 © CCG

GD25 FN65 NM94

BIG BOOK OF HOAXES, THE
1996 ($14.95, B&W, trade paperback)
DC Comics (Paradox Press)

	GD25	FN65	NM94
nn			15.00

BIG BOOK OF LITTLE CRIMINALS, THE
1996 ($14.95, B&W, trade paperback)
DC Comics (Paradox Press)

nn 15.00

BIG BOOK OF LOSERS, THE
1997 ($14.95, B&W, trade paperback)
DC Comics (Paradox Press)

nn 15.00

BIG BOOK OF MARTYRS, THE
1997 ($14.95, B&W, trade paperback)
DC Comics (Paradox Press)

nn 15.00

BIG BOOK OF SCANDAL, THE
1997 ($14.95, B&W, trade paperback)
DC Comics (Paradox Press)

nn-Jonathan Vankin-s/art by various 15.00

BIG BOOK OF THUGS, THE
1997 ($14.95, B&W, trade paperback)
DC Comics (Paradox Press)

nn-Joel Rose-s/art by various 15.00

BIG BOOK OF UNEXPLAINED, THE
1997 ($14.95, B&W, trade paperback)
DC Comics (Paradox Press)

nn-Doug Moench-s/art by various 15.00

BIG BOOK OF URBAN LEGENDS, THE
1994 ($12.95, B&W, trade paperback)
DC Comics (Paradox Press)

nn 13.00

BIG BOOK OF WEIRDOS, THE
1995 ($12.95, B&W, trade paperback)
DC Comics (Paradox Press)

nn 13.00

BIG BOOK ROMANCES
Feb, 1950 (no date given) (148 pgs.)
Fawcett Publications

1-Contains remaindered Fawcett romance comics - several combinations possible 29.00 86.00 230.00

BIG BOY (See Adventures of the Big Boy)

BIG BRUISERS
July, 1996 ($3.50, one-shot)
Image Comics (Wildstorm Productions)

1-Features Maul from WildC.A.T.S, Impact from Cyberforce & Badrock from Youngblood; wraparound-c 1.40 3.50

BIG CHIEF WAHOO
July, 1942 - No. 7, Wint., 1943/44?(no yr. given)(Quarterly)
Eastern Color Printing/George Dougherty (distr. by Fawcett)

1-Newspaper-r (on sale 6/15/42) 36.00 108.00 290.00
2-Steve Roper app. 18.00 54.00 145.00
3-5: 4-Chief is holding a Katy Keene comic 13.00 39.00 105.00
6-7 8.75 26.25 70.00
NOTE: *Kerry Drake in some issues.*

BIG CIRCUS, THE (Movie)
No. 1036, Sept-Nov, 1959
Dell Publishing Co.

Four Color 1036-Photo-c 5.50 16.50 60.00

BIG COUNTRY, THE (Movie)
No. 946, Oct, 1958
Dell Publishing Co.

Four Color 946-Photo-c 6.40 19.00 70.00

BIG DADDY ROTH (Magazine)
Oct-Nov, 1964 - No. 4, Apr-May, 1965 (35¢)
Millar Publications

1-Toth-a 14.00 42.00 140.00
2-4-Toth-a 10.50 32.00 105.00

BIG GUY AND RUSTY THE BOY ROBOT, THE (Also See Madman Comics #6,7 & Martha Washington Stranded In Space)
July, 1995 - No. 2, Aug, 1995 ($4.95, oversize, limited series)
Dark Horse (Legend)

1,2-Frank Miller scripts & Geoff Darrow-c/a 1.00 2.80 7.00
Trade paperback (10/96, $14.95)-r/1,2 w/cover gallery 15.00

BIG HERO ADVENTURES (See Jigsaw)

BIG JIM'S P.A.C.K.
No date (1975) (16 pgs.)
Mattel, Inc. (Marvel Comics)

nn-Giveaway with Big Jim doll; Buscema/Sinnott-c/a 2.50 7.50 20.00

BIG JON & SPARKIE (Radio)(Formerly Sparkie, Radio Pixie)
No. 4, Sept-Oct, 1952 (Painted-c)
Ziff-Davis Publ. Co.

4-Based on children's radio program 14.50 43.00 115.00

BIG LAND, THE (Movie)
No. 812, July, 1957
Dell Publishing Co.

Four Color 812-Alan Ladd photo-c 9.00 27.00 100.00

BIG RED (See Movie Comics)

BIG SHOT COMICS
May, 1940 - No. 104, Aug, 1949
Columbia Comics Group

1-Intro. Skyman; The Face (1st app.; Tony Trent), The Cloak (Spy Master), Marvelo, Monarch of Magicians, Joe Palooka, Charlie Chan, Tom Kerry, Dixie Dugan, Rocky Ryan begin; Charlie Chan moves over from Feature Comics #31 (4/40). 156.00 468.00 1400.00
2 61.00 183.00 550.00
3-The Cloak called Spy Chief; Skyman-c 50.00 150.00 450.00
4,5 40.00 120.00 360.00
6-10: 8-Christmas-c 36.00 108.00 300.00
11-14: 14-Origin & 1st app. Sparky Watts (6/41) 34.00 101.00 270.00
15-Origin The Cloak 36.00 108.00 300.00
16-20 25.00 75.00 200.00
21-27,29,30: 24-Tojo-c. 29-Intro. Capt. Yank; Bo (a dog) newspaper strip-r by Frank Beck begin, ends #104. 30-X-Mas-c 21.00 62.00 165.00
28-Hitler, Tojo & Mussolini-c 28.00 83.00 220.00
31,33-40 15.00 45.00 120.00
32-Vic Jordan newspaper strip reprints begin, ends #52; Hitler, Tojo & Mussolini-c 19.00 56.00 150.00
41-50: 42-No Skyman. 43,46-Hitler-c. 50-Origin The Face retold 12.00 36.00 95.00
51-60 9.50 28.00 75.00
61-70: 63 on-Tony Trent, the Face 8.50 26.00 60.00
71-80: 73-The Face cameo. 74-(2/47)-Mickey Finn begins. 74,80-The Face app. in Tony Trent. 78-Last Charlie Chan strip-r 7.85 23.50 55.00
81-90: 85-Tony Trent marries Babs Walsh. 86-Valentines-c 6.50 19.50 45.00

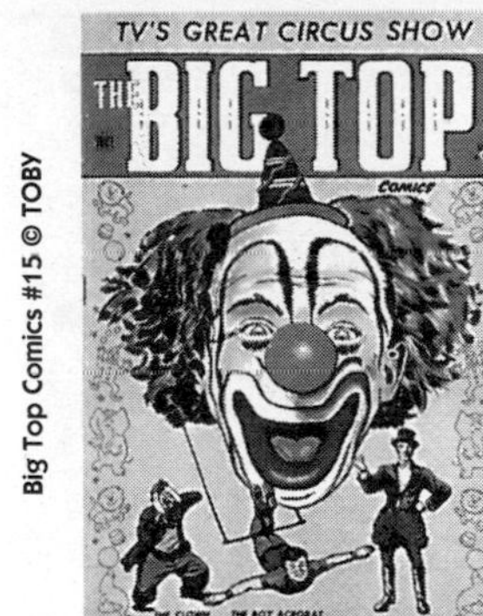

Big Top Comics #15 © TOBY

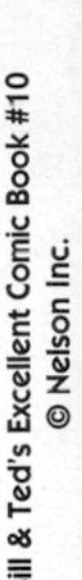

Bill & Ted's Excellent Comic Book #10 © Nelson Inc.

Bill the Clown #1 © Troy Nixey

GD25 FN65 NM94

91-99,101-104: 69-94-Skyman in Outer Space. 96-Xmas-c 5.70 17.00 38.00
100 7.15 21.50 50.00

NOTE: ***Mart Bailey** art on "The Face" No. 1-104. **Guardineer** a-5. Sparky Watts by **Boody Rogers**-No. 14-42, 77-104, (by others No. 43-76). Others than Tony Trent wear "The Face" mask in No. 46-63, 93. Skyman by **Ogden Whitney**-No. 1, 2, 4, 12-37, 49, 70-101. Skyman covers-No. 1, 3, 7-12, 14, 16, 20, 27, 89, 95, 100.*

BIG TEX
June, 1953
Toby Press

1-Contains (3) John Wayne stories-r with name changed to Big Tex 7.15 21.50 50.00

BIG-3
Fall, 1940 - No. 7, Jan, 1942
Fox Features Syndicate

1-Blue Beetle, The Flame, & Samson begin 167.00 500.00 1500.00
2 72.00 216.00 650.00
3-5 50.00 150.00 450.00
6,7: 6-Last Samson. 7-V-Man app. 42.00 126.00 375.00

BIG TOP COMICS, THE (TV's Great Circus Show)
1951 - No. 2, 1951 (No month)
Toby Press

1,2 6.85 21.00 48.00

BIG TOWN (Radio/TV) (Also see Movie Comics, 1946)
Jan, 1951 - No. 50, Mar-Apr, 1958 (No. 1-9: 52pgs.)
National Periodical Publications

1-Dan Barry-a begins 50.00 150.00 450.00
2 28.00 84.00 225.00
3-10 15.50 47.00 125.00
11-20 10.50 32.00 85.00
21-31: Last pre-code (1-2/55) 8.75 26.25 65.00
32-50 6.50 19.50 45.00

BIG VALLEY, THE (TV)
June, 1966 - No. 5, Oct, 1967; No. 6, Oct, 1969
Dell Publishing Co.

1: Photo-c #1-5 3.00 11.00 40.00
2-6: 6-Reprints #1 2.00 6.00 22.00

BIKER MICE FROM MARS (TV)
Nov, 1993 - No. 3, Jan, 1994 ($1.50, limited series)
Marvel Comics

1-3: 1-Intro Vinnie, Modo & Throttle. 2-Origin 1.50

BILL & TED'S BOGUS JOURNEY
Sept, 1991 ($2.95, squarebound, 84 pgs.)
Marvel Comics

1-Adapts movie sequel 1.20 3.00

"BILL AND TED'S EXCELLENT ADVENTURE" MOVIE ADAPTATION
1989 (No cover price)
DC Comics

nn-Torres-a. 1.00

BILL & TED'S EXCELLENT COMIC BOOK (Movie)
Dec, 1991 - No. 12, 1992 ($1.00/$1.25)
Marvel Comics

1,2: 2-Last $1.00-c 1.00
3-12 1.25

BILL BARNES COMICS (...America's Air Ace Comics No. 2 on)
(Becomes Air Ace V2#1 on; also see Shadow Comics)
Oct, 1940(No. month given) - No. 12, Oct, 1943
Street & Smith Publications

1-23 pgs.-comics; Rocket Rooney begins 61.00 183.00 550.00
2-Barnes as The Phantom Flyer app.; Tuska-a 36.00 108.00 300.00
3-5 28.00 84.00 225.00
6-12 24.00 73.00 195.00

BILL BATTLE, THE ONE MAN ARMY (Also see Master Comics No. 133)
Oct, 1952 - No. 4, Apr, 1953 (All photo-c)
Fawcett Publications

1 8.75 26.25 65.00
2 5.70 17.00 38.00
3,4 5.00 15.00 30.00

BILL BLACK'S FUN COMICS
Dec, 1982 - No. 4, Mar, 1983 ($1.75, Baxter paper)(1st AC comic)
Paragon #1-3/Americomics #4

1-Intro. Capt. Paragon, Phantom Lady & Commando D (#1-3 are B&W fanzines; 8-1/2x11") .80 2.00
2-4: 4-($2.00, color)-Origin Nightfall (formerly Phantom Lady); Nightveil app. .80 2.00

BILL BOYD WESTERN (Movie star; see Hopalong Cassidy & Western Hero)
Feb, 1950 - No. 23, June, 1952 (1-3,7,11,14-on: 36 pgs.)
Fawcett Publications

1-Bill Boyd & his horse Midnite begin; photo front/back-c 41.00 123.00 370.00
2-Painted-c 23.00 69.00 185.00
3-Photo-c begin, end #23; last photo back-c 17.50 53.00 140.00
4-6(52 pgs.) 14.00 41.00 110.00
7,11(36 pgs.) 10.50 32.00 85.00
8-10,12,13(52 pgs.) 11.30 34.00 90.00
14-22 10.00 30.00 80.00
23-Last issue 11.30 34.00 90.00

BILL BUMLIN (See Treasury of Comics No. 3)

BILL ELLIOTT (See Wild Bill Elliott)

BILLI 99
Sept, 1991 - No. 4, 1991 ($3.50, B&W, limited series, 52 pgs.)
Dark Horse Comics

1-4: Tim Sale-c/a 1.40 3.50

BILL STERN'S SPORTS BOOK
Spring-Summer, 1951 - V2#2, Winter, 1952
Ziff-Davis Publ. Co.(Approved Comics)

V1#10-(1951) 15.50 47.00 125.00
2-(Sum/52; reg. size) 12.00 36.00 95.00
V2#2-(1952, 96 pgs.)-Krigstein, Kinstler-a 15.50 47.00 125.00

BILL THE BULL: ONE SHOT, ONE BOURBON, ONE BEER
Dec, 1994 ($2.95, B&W, mature)
Boneyard Press

1 1.20 3.00

BILL THE CLOWN
Feb, 1992 ($2.50, one-shot)
Slave Labor Graphics

1 1.00 2.50
1-(2nd printing, 4/93, $2.95) 1.20 3.00
Comedy Isn't Pretty 1 (11/92, $2.50) 1.00 2.50
Death & Clown White 1 (9/93, $2.95) 1.20 3.00

BILLY AND BUGGY BEAR (See Animal Fun)
1958; 1964
I.W. Enterprises/Super

I.W. Reprint #1, #7('58)-All Surprise Comics #?(Same issue-r for both) 2.00 5.00
Super Reprint #10(1964) 2.00 5.00

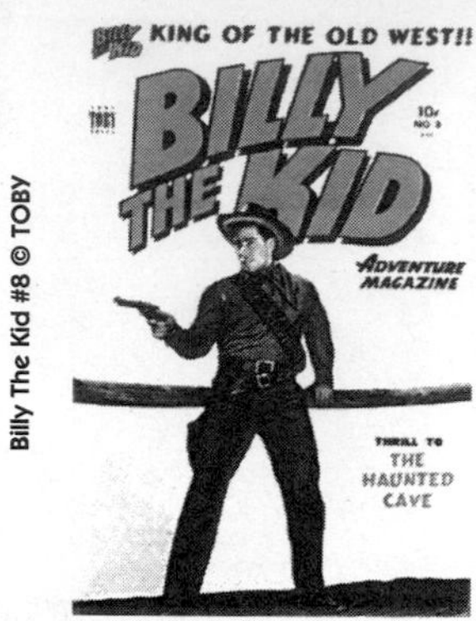

Billy The Kid #8 © TOBY

Bingo, The Monkey Doodle Boy #1 © STJ

Birds of Prey: Batgirl #1 © DC

BILLY BUCKSKIN WESTERN (2-Gun Western No. 4)
Nov, 1955 - No. 3, Mar, 1956
Atlas Comics (IMC No. 1/MgPC No. 2,3)

	GD25	FN65	NM94
1-Mort Drucker-a; Maneely-c/a	10.50	32.00	85.00
2-Mort Drucker-a	8.50	26.00	60.00
3-Williamson, Drucker-a	8.75	26.25	65.00

BILLY BUNNY (Black Cobra No. 6 on)
Feb-Mar, 1954 - No. 5, Oct-Nov, 1954
Excellent Publications

	GD25	FN65	NM94
1	5.70	17.00	35.00
2	4.00	10.00	20.00
3-5	3.20	8.00	16.00

BILLY BUNNY'S CHRISTMAS FROLICS
1952 (25¢ Giant, 100 pgs.)
Farrell Publications

	GD25	FN65	NM94
1	15.00	45.00	120.00

BILLY COLE
May, 1994 - No. 4, Aug, 1994 ($2.75, B&W, limited series)
Cult Press

	GD25	FN65	NM94
1-4		1.10	2.75

BILLY MAKE BELIEVE
No. 14, 1939
United Features Syndicate

	GD25	FN65	NM94
Single Series 14	23.00	69.00	185.00

BILLY NGUYEN, PRIVATE EYE
V2#1, 1990 ($2.50)
Caliber Press

	GD25	FN65	NM94
V2#1		1.00	2.50

BILLY THE KID (Formerly The Masked Raider; also see Doc Savage Comics & Return of the Outlaw)
No. 9, Nov, 1957 - No. 121, Dec, 1976; No. 122, Sept, 1977 - No. 123, Oct, 1977; No. 124, Feb, 1978 - No. 153, Mar, 1983
Charlton Publ. Co.

	GD25	FN65	NM94
9	8.50	26.00	60.00
10,12,14,17-19: 12-2 pg Check-sty	5.35	16.00	32.00
11-(68 pgs.)-Origin & 1st app. The Ghost Train	5.70	17.00	38.00
13-Williamson/Torres-a	5.70	17.00	40.00
15-Origin; 2 pgs. Williamson-a	5.70	17.00	40.00
16-Williamson-a, 2 pgs.	5.70	17.00	38.00
20-26-Severin-a(3-4 each)	5.70	17.00	40.00
27-30	2.50	7.50	22.00
31-40	2.00	6.00	16.00
41-60	1.50	4.50	12.00
61-80: 66-Bounty Hunter series begins. Not in #79,82,84-863	1.00	3.00	8.00
81-100,101-123: 87-Last Bounty Hunter. 111-Origin The Ghost Train. 117-Gunsmith & Co., The Cheyenne Kid app.		2.00	5.00
124(2/78)-153		1.20	3.00
Modern Comics 109 (1977 reprint)		1.20	3.00

NOTE: ***Severin** a(r)-121-129, 134; c-23, 25. **Sutton** a-111.*

BILLY THE KID ADVENTURE MAGAZINE
Oct, 1950 - No. 30, 1955
Toby Press

	GD25	FN65	NM94
1-Williamson/Frazetta-a (2 pgs) r/from John Wayne Adventure Comics #2; photo-c	26.00	80.00	210.00
2-Photo-c	8.50	26.00	60.00
3-Williamson/Frazetta "The Claws of Death", 4 pgs. plus Williamson art	29.00	86.00	230.00
4,5,7,8,10: 4,7-Photo-c	5.70	17.00	40.00
6-Frazetta assist on "Nightmare"; photo-c	12.00	36.00	95.00
9-Kurtzman Pot-Shot Pete; photo-c	9.50	28.00	75.00
11,12,15-20: 11-Photo-c	5.70	17.00	35.00
13-Kurtzman-r/John Wayne #12 (Genius)	5.70	17.00	40.00
14-Williamson/Frazetta; r-of #1 (2 pgs.)	8.50	26.00	60.00
21,23-30	4.25	13.00	28.00
22-Williamson/Frazetta-r(1pg.)/#1; photo-c	5.70	17.00	35.00

BILLY THE KID AND OSCAR (Also see Fawcett's Funny Animals)
Winter, 1945 - No. 3, Summer, 1946 (Funny animal)
Fawcett Publications

	GD25	FN65	NM94
1	11.30	34.00	90.00
2,3	8.50	26.00	60.00

BILLY WEST (Bill West No. 9,10)
1949 - No. 9, Feb, 1951; No. 10, Feb, 1952
Standard Comics (Visual Editions)

	GD25	FN65	NM94
1	8.75	26.25	70.00
2	5.70	17.00	35.00
3-10: 7,8-Schomburg-c	4.15	12.50	25.00

NOTE: ***Celardo** a-1-6, 9; c-1-3. **Moreira** a-3. **Roussos** a-2.*

BING CROSBY (See Feature Films)

BINGO (...Comics) (H. C. Blackerby)
1945 (Reprints National material)
Howard Publ.

	GD25	FN65	NM94
1-L. B. Cole opium-c	22.00	66.00	175.00

BINGO, THE MONKEY DOODLE BOY
Aug, 1951; Oct, 1953
St. John Publishing Co.

	GD25	FN65	NM94
1(8/51)-By Eric Peters	5.00	15.00	30.00
1(10/53)	4.00	12.00	24.00

BINKY (Formerly Leave It to...)
No. 72, 4-5/70 - No. 81, 10-11/71; No. 82, Summer/77
National Periodical Publ./DC Comics

	GD25	FN65	NM94
72-76	1.50	4.50	12.00
77-79: (68pgs.). 77-Bobby Sherman 1pg. story w/photo. 78-1 pg. sty on Barry Williams of Brady Bunch. 79-Osmonds 1pg. story	2.60	7.80	26.00
80,81 (52pgs.)-Sweat Pain story	2.25	6.75	18.00
82 (1977, one-shot)	1.00	3.00	8.00

BINKY'S BUDDIES
Jan-Feb, 1969 - No. 12, Nov-Dec, 1970
National Periodical Publications

	GD25	FN65	NM94
1	2.80	8.40	28.00
2-12	1.50	4.50	12.00

BIONEERS
Aug, 1994 ($2.75)
Mirage Publishing

	GD25	FN65	NM94
1-w/bound-in trading card		1.10	2.75

BIONIC WOMAN, THE (TV)
Oct, 1977 - No. 5, June, 1978
Charlton Publications

	GD25	FN65	NM94
1		2.40	6.00
2-5		1.60	4.00

BIRDS OF PREY: BATGIRL (See Black Canary/Oracle: Birds of Prey)
Feb,1998 ($2.95, one-shot)
DC Comics

	GD25	FN65	NM94
1-Dixon-s/Frank-c			2.95

BIRDS OF PREY: MANHUNT (See Black Canary/Oracle: Birds of Prey)
Sept, 1996 - No. 4, Dec, 1996 ($1.95, limited series)
DC Comics

1-4: Features Black Canary, Oracle, Huntress, & Catwoman; Chuck Dixon

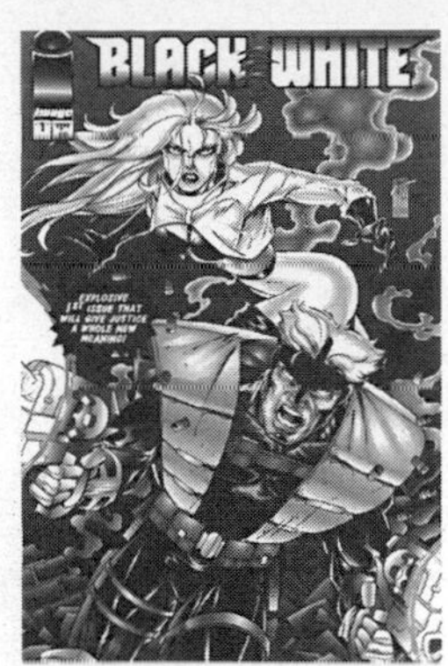

Black Cat Comics #6 © HARV

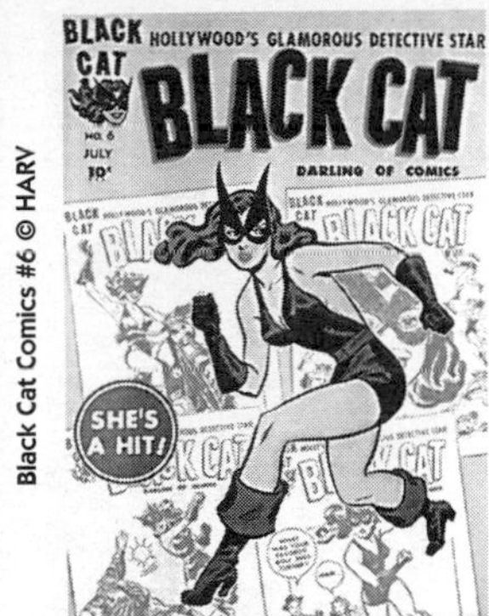

GD25 FN65 NM94

scripts; Gary Frank-c on all. 1-Catwoman cameo only .80 2.00
NOTE: *Gary Frank c-1-4. Matt Haley a-1-4p. Wade Von Grawbadger a-1i.*

BIRDS OF PREY: REVOLUTION (See Black Canary/Oracle: Birds of Prey)
1997 ($2.95, one-shot)
DC Comics
1-Frank-c/Dixon-s 1.20 3.00

BIRDS OF PREY: WOLVES (See Black Canary/Oracle: Birds of Prey)
1997 ($2.95, one-shot)
DC Comics
1-Dixon-s/Giordano & Faucher-a 1.20 3.00

BIRTH OF THE DEFIANT UNIVERSE, THE
May, 1993 (Giveaway)
Defiant Comics
nn-contains promotional artwork & text; limited print run of 1000 copies.
1.25 3.75 10.00

BISHOP (See Uncanny X-Men & X-Men)
Dec, 1994 - No.4, Mar, 1995 ($2.95, limited series)
Marvel Comics
1-4: Foil-c 1.20 3.00

BISHOP: XAVIER SECURITY ENFORCER
Jan, 1998 - No.3, Mar, 1998 ($2.50, limited series)
Marvel Comics
1-4: Foil-c 1.00 2.50

BIZARRE ADVENTURES (Formerly Marvel Preview)
No. 25, 3/81 - No. 34, 2/83 (#25-33: Magazine-$1.50)
Marvel Comics Group
25-Lethal Ladies. 26-King Kull 1.60 4.00
27-Phoenix, Iceman & Nightcrawler app. 28-The Unlikely Heroes; Elektra by Miller; Neal Adams-a 2.00 5.00
29-Horror. 30-Tomorrow. 31-After The Violence Stops; new Hangman story; Miller-a. 32-Gods. 33-Horror; photo-c 1.60 4.00
34 ($2.00, Baxter paper, comic size)-Son of Santa; Christmas special; Howard the Duck by Paul Smith 1.60 4.00
NOTE: *Alcala a-27i. Austin a-25i, 28i. J. Buscema a-27p, 29, 30p; c-26. Byrne a-31 (2 pg.). Golden a-25p, 28p. Perez a-27p. Rogers a-25p. Simonson a-29; c-29. Paul Smith a-34.*

BLACK AND WHITE (See Large Feature Comic, Series I)

BLACK & WHITE (Also see Codename: Black & White)
Oct,1994 - No. 3, Jan,1995 ($1.95, limited series)
Image Comics (Extreme Studios)
1-3: Thibert-c/story .80 2.00

BLACK & WHITE MAGIC
1991 ($2.95, 98 pgs., B&W w/30 pgs. color, squarebound)
Innovation Publishing
1-Contains rebound comics w/covers removed; contents may vary
1.20 2.95

BLACKBALL COMICS
Mar, 1994 ($3.00)
Blackball Comics
1-Trencher-c/story by Giffen; John Pain by O'Neill 1.20 3.00

BLACKBEARD'S GHOST (See Movie Comics)

BLACK BEAUTY (See Son of Black Beauty)
No. 440, Dec, 1952
Dell Publishing Co.
Four Color 440 2.78 8.00 30.00

BLACK CANARY (See All Star Comics #38, Flash Comics #86, Justice League of America #75 & World's Finest #244)
Nov, 1991 - No. 4, Feb, 1992 ($1.75, limited series)
DC Comics
1-4 .70 1.75

BLACK CANARY
Jan, 1993 - No. 12, Dec, 1993 ($1.75)
DC Comics
1-12: 8-The Ray-c/story. 9,10-Huntress-c/story .70 1.75

BLACK CANARY/ORACLE: BIRDS OF PREY (Also see Showcase '96 #3)
1996 ($3.95, one-shot)
DC Comics
1-Chuck Dixon scripts & Gary Frank-c/a. 1.80 4.50

BLACK CAT COMICS (...Western #16-19; ...Mystery #30 on)
(See All-New #7,9, The Original Black Cat, Pocket & Speed Comics)
June-July, 1946 - No. 29, June, 1951
Harvey Publications (Home Comics)
1-Kubert-a; Joe Simon c-1-3 50.00 150.00 445.00
2-Kubert-a 29.00 86.00 230.00
3,4: 4-The Red Demons begin (The Demon #4 & 5)
23.00 68.00 180.00
5,6,7: 5,6-The Scarlet Arrow app. in ea. by Powell; S&K-a in both. 6-Origin Red Demon. 7-Vagabond Prince by S&K plus 1 more story
29.00 86.00 230.00
8-S&K-a; Kerry Drake begins, ends #13 25.00 75.00 200.00
9-Origin Stuntman (r/Stuntman #1) 31.00 94.00 250.00
10-20: 14,15,17-Mary Worth app. plus Invisible Scarlet O'Neil-#15,20,24
19.00 56.00 150.00
21-26 15.50 47.00 125.00
27,28: 27-Used in **SOTI**, pg. 193; X-Mas-c; 2 pg. John Wayne story. 28-Intro. Kit, Black Cat's new sidekick 17.50 53.00 140.00
29-Black Cat bondage-c; Black Cat stories 16.00 49.00 130.00

BLACK CAT MYSTERY (Formerly Black Cat; ...Western Mystery #54; ...Western #55,56;...Mystery #57; ...Mystic #58-62; Black Cat #63-65)
No. 30, Aug, 1951 - No. 65, Apr, 1963
Harvey Publications
30-Black Cat on cover only 20.00 60.00 150.00
31,32,34,37,38,40 14.00 43.00 110.00
33-Used in **POP**, pg. 89; electrocution-c 15.00 45.00 115.00
35-Atomic disaster cover/story 17.00 51.00 130.00
36,39-Used in **SOTI**: #36-Pgs. 270,271; #39-Pgs. 386-388
20.00 60.00 150.00
41-43 14.00 43.00 110.00
44-Eyes, ears, tongue cut out; Nostrand-a 15.00 45.00 115.00
45-Classic "Colorama" by Powell; Nostrand-a 24.00 71.00 175.00
46-49,51-Nostrand-a in all 15.00 45.00 115.00
50-Check-a; Warren Kremer?-c showing a man's face burning away
36.00 107.00 260.00
52,53 (r/#34 & 35) 10.00 30.00 75.00
54-Two Black Cat stories (2/55, last pre-code) 13.50 41.00 95.00
55,56-Black Cat app. 10.00 30.00 75.00
57(7/56)-Kirby-c 8.75 26.25 65.00
58-60-Kirby-a(4). 58,59-Kirby-c. 60,61-Simon-c 13.00 39.00 95.00
61-Nostrand-a; "Colorama" r/#45 11.00 33.00 80.00
62(3/58)-E.C. story swipe 9.00 27.00 60.00
63-Giant(10/62); Reprints; Black Cat app.; origin Black Kitten
11.50 34.00 85.00
64-Giant(1/63); Reprints; Black Cat app. 11.50 34.00 85.00
65-Giant(4/63); Reprints; Black Cat app.; 1 pg. Powell-a
11.50 34.00 85.00
NOTE: *Kremer a-37, 39, 43; c-36, 37, 47. Meskin a-51. Palais a-30, 31(2), 32(2), 33-35, 37-40. Powell a-32-35, 36(2), 40, 41, 43-53, 57. Simon c-63-65. Sparling a-44. Bondage c-32, 34, 43.*

BLACK COBRA (Bride's Diary No. 4 on) (See Captain Flight #8)
No. 1, 10-11/54; No. 6(No. 2), 12-1/54-55; No. 3, 2-3/55
Ajax/Farrell Publications(Excellent Publ.)

Black Condor #12 © DC

Blackball Comics #1 © Blackball Comics

Blackhawk #81 © QUA

	GD25	FN65	NM94
1-Re-intro Black Cobra & The Cobra Kid (costumed heroes)	23.00	68.00	180.00
6(#2)-Formerly Billy Bunny	14.00	41.00	110.00
3-(Pre-code)-Torpedoman app.	12.00	38.00	100.00

BLACK CONDOR (Also see Crack Comics, Freedom Fighters & Showcase '94 #10,11)
June, 1992 - No. 12, May, 1993 ($1.25)
DC Comics

	GD25	FN65	NM94
1-12: 1-10,12-Heath-c. 9,10-The Ray app. 12-Batman-c/scripts			1.25

BLACK CROSS SPECIAL (See Dark Horse Presents)
Jan, 1988 ($1.75, B&W, one-shot)(Reprints & new-a)
Dark Horse Comics

	GD25	FN65	NM94
1-1st & 2nd print; 2nd has 2pgs new-a		.70	1.75

BLACK CROSS: DIRTY WORK (See Dark Horse Presents)
Apr, 1997 ($2.95, one-shot)
Dark Horse Comics

	GD25	FN65	NM94
1-Chris Warner-c/s/a			2.95

BLACK DIAMOND
May, 1983 - No. 5, 1984 (no month)($2.00-$1.75, Baxter paper)
Americomics

	GD25	FN65	NM94
1-3-Movie adapt.; 1-Colt back-up begins		1.00	2.50
4,5			1.50

NOTE: ***Bill Black*** *a-1i; c-1.* ***Gulacy*** *c-2-5. Sybil Danning photo back-c-1.*

BLACK DIAMOND WESTERN (Formerly Desperado No. 1-8)
No. 9, Mar, 1949 - No. 60, Feb, 1956 (No. 9-28: 52 pgs.)
Lev Gleason Publications

	GD25	FN65	NM94
9-Black Diamond & his horse Reliapon begin; origin & 1st app. Black Diamond	16.00	49.00	130.00
10	8.50	26.00	60.00
11-15	6.50	19.50	45.00
16-28(11/49-11/51)-Wolverton's Bing Bang Buster	8.50	26.00	60.00
29-40: 31-One pg. Frazetta anti-drug ad	5.00	15.00	30.00
41-50,53-59	4.15	12.50	25.00
51-3-D effect-c/story	10.00	30.00	80.00
52-3-D effect story	9.50	28.00	75.00
60-Last issue	5.00	15.00	30.00

NOTE: ***Biro*** *c-9-35?.* ***Fass*** *a-58, c-54-56, 58.* ***Guardineer*** *a-9, 15, 18.* ***Kida*** *a-9.* ***Maurer*** *a-10.* ***Ed Moore*** *a-16.* ***Morisi*** *a-55.* ***Tuska*** *a-10, 48.*

BLACK DRAGON, THE
May, 1985 - No. 6, Oct, 1985 (Limited series, Baxter paper, mature)
Marvel Comics (Epic Comics)

	GD25	FN65	NM94
1-Chris Claremont story & John Bolton-c/a in all.		.80	2.00
2-6			1.00

BLACK DRAGON, THE
Apr, 1996 ($17.95, B&W, trade paperback)
Dark Horse Comics

	GD25	FN65	NM94
nn-Reprints Epic Comics limited series; intro by Anne McCaffrey			18.00

BLACK FLAG (See Asylum #5)
Jan, 1995 - No.4, 1995; No. 0, July, 1995 ($2.50, B&W) (No. 0 in color)
Maximum Press

	GD25	FN65	NM94
0-4: 0-(7/95)-Liefeld/Fraga-c. 1-(1/95). 2,4-Variant covers exist.		1.20	3.00
Preview Edition (6/94, $1.95, B&W)-Fraga/McFarlane-c.		.80	2.00

NOTE: ***Fraga*** *a-0-4, Preview Edition; c-1-4.* ***Liefeld/Fraga*** *c-0.* ***McFarlane/Fraga*** *c-Preview Edition.*

BLACK FURY (Becomes Wild West No. 58) (See Blue Bird)
May, 1955 - No. 57, Mar-Apr, 1966 (Horse stories)
Charlton Comics Group

	GD25	FN65	NM94
1	5.70	17.00	35.00
2	3.20	8.00	16.00
3-10	2.40	6.00	12.00
11-15,19,20	1.60	4.00	8.00
16-18-Ditko-a	5.70	17.00	35.00
21-30		2.40	6.00
31-57		1.60	4.00

BLACK GOLD
1945? (8 pgs. in color)
Esso Service Station (Giveaway)

	GD25	FN65	NM94
nn-Reprints from True Comics	5.00	15.00	30.00

BLACK GOLIATH
Feb, 1976 - No. 5, Nov, 1976
Marvel Comics Group

	GD25	FN65	NM94
1: 1-3-Tuska-a(p)		2.40	6.00
2-5		1.60	4.00

BLACKHAWK (Formerly Uncle Sam #1-8; see Military & Modern Comics)
No. 9, Winter, 1944 - No. 243, 10-11/68; No. 244, 1-2/76 - No. 250, 1-2/77; No. 251, 10/82 - No. 273, 11/84
Comic Magazines(Quality)No. 9-107(12/56); National Periodical Publications No. 108(1/57)-250; DC Comics No. 251 on

	GD25	FN65	NM94
9 (1944)	250.00	750.00	2500.00
10 (1946)	89.00	267.00	800.00
11-15: 14-Ward-a; 13,14-Fear app.	58.00	174.00	525.00
16-20: 20-Ward Blackhawk	47.00	141.00	425.00
21-30	36.00	108.00	325.00
31-40: 31-Chop Chop by Jack Cole	29.00	86.00	230.00
41-49,51-60	23.00	68.00	180.00
50-1st Killer Shark; origin in text	24.00	73.00	195.00
61,62: 61-Used in **POP**, pg. 91. 62-Used in **POP**, pg. 92 & color illo	20.00	60.00	160.00
63-70,72-80: 65-H-Bomb explosion panel. 66-B&W & color illos **POP**. 70-Return of Killer Shark; atomic explosion panel. 75-Intro. Blackie the Hawk	19.00	56.00	150.00
71-Origin retold; flying saucer-c; A-Bomb panels	22.00	66.00	175.00
81-86: Last precode (3/55)	17.50	53.00	140.00
87-92,94-99,101-107: 105-1st S.A. issue	14.00	41.00	110.00
93-Origin in text	14.50	43.00	115.00
100	17.50	53.00	140.00
108-1st DC issue (1/57); re-intro. Blackie, the Hawk, their mascot; not in #115	38.00	114.00	420.00
109-117: 117-(10/57)-Mr. Freeze app.	14.00	42.00	140.00
118-(11/57)-Frazetta-r/Jimmy Wakely #4 (3 pgs.)	15.00	45.00	150.00
119-130 (11/58)	9.50	28.50	95.00
131-140 (2/59): 133-Intro. Lady Blackhawk	7.00	21.00	70.00
141-150,152-163,165,166: 143-Kurtzman-r/Jimmy Wakely #4. 150-(7/60)-King Condor returns. 166-Last 10¢ issue	5.00	15.00	50.00
151-Lady Blackhawk receives & loses super powers	5.50	16.50	55.00
164-Origin retold	5.00	15.00	50.00
167-180	2.50	7.50	20.00
181-190	2.00	6.00	16.00
191-196,199-202,204-210: 196-Combat Diary series begins.	1.50	4.50	12.00
197-New look for Blackhawks	2.00	6.00	16.00
198-Origin retold	1.75	5.25	14.00
203-Origin Chop Chop (12/64)	1.75	5.25	14.00
211-243(1968): 228-Batman, Green Lantern, Superman, The Flash cameos. 230-Blackhawks become superheroes. 242-Return to old costumes	1.10	3.30	9.00
244 ('76) -250: 250-Chuck dies		1.60	4.00
251-273: 251-Origin retold; Black Knights return. 252-Intro Domino. 253-Part origin Hendrickson. 258-Blackhawk's Island destroyed. 259-Part origin Chop-Chop. 265-273 (75¢ cover price)			1.50

Black Hood #1 © DC

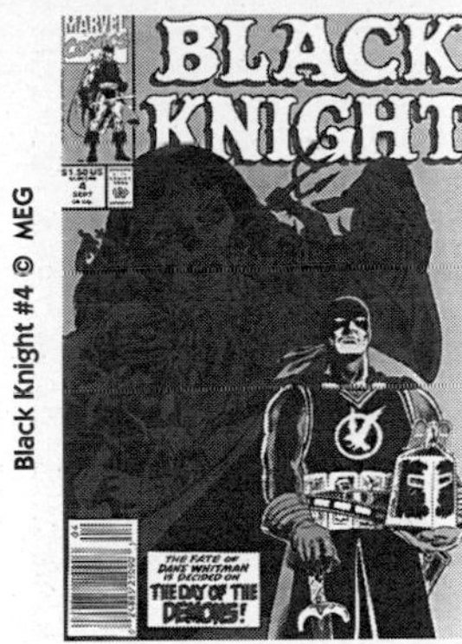

Black Knight #4 © MEG

Black Lightning #2 © DC

NOTE: ***Chaykin*** *a-260; c-257-260, 262.* ***Crandall*** *a-10, 11, 13, 16?, 18-20, 22-26, 30-33, 35p, 36(2), 37, 38?, 39-44, 46-50, 52-58, 60, 63, 64, 66, 67; c-14-20, 22-63(most except #28-33, 36, 37, 39).* ***Evans*** *a-244, 245,246i, 248-250i.* ***G. Kane*** *c-263, 264.* ***Kubert*** *c-244, 245.* ***Newton*** *a-266p.* ***Severin*** *a-257.* ***Spiegle*** *a-261-267, 269-273; c-265-272.* ***Toth*** *a-260p.* ***Ward*** *a-16-27(Chop Chop, 8pgs. ea.); pencilled stories-No. 17-63(approx.).* ***Wildey*** *a-268. Chop Chop solo stories in #10-95?*

BLACKHAWK
Mar, 1988 - No. 3, May, 1988 ($2.95, limited series, mature)
DC Comics

	GD25	FN65	NM94
1-3: Chaykin painted-c/a/scripts		1.20	3.00

BLACKHAWK
Mar, 1989 - No. 16, Aug, 1990 ($1.50, mature)
DC Comics

	GD25	FN65	NM94
1-6,8-16: 16-Crandall-c swipe			1.50
7-($2.50, 52 pgs.)-Story-r/Military #1		1.00	2.50
Annual 1 (1989, $2.95, 68 pgs.)-Recaps origin of Blackhawk, Lady Blackhawk, and others		1.20	3.00
Special 1 (1992, $3.50, 68 pgs.)-Mature readers		1.40	3.50

BLACKHAWK INDIAN TOMAHAWK WAR, THE
1951 (Also see Fighting Indians of the Wild West)
Avon Periodicals

	GD25	FN65	NM94
nn-Kinstler-c; Kit West story	14.00	41.00	110.00

BLACK HEART ASSASSIN
Jan, 1994 ($2.95)
Iguana Comics

	GD25	FN65	NM94
1		1.20	3.00

BLACK HOLE (See Walt Disney Showcase #54) (Disney, movie)
Mar, 1980 - No. 4, Sept, 1980
Whitman Publishing Co.

	GD25	FN65	NM94
11295(#1)-4: 1-Photo-c; Spiegle-a. 1,2-Movie adaptation. 2-4-Spiegle-a. 3-McWilliams-a; photo-c. 3,4-New stories			1.00

BLACK HOOD, THE (See Blue Ribbon, Flyman & Mighty Comics)
June, 1983 - No. 3, Oct, 1983 (Printed on Mandell paper)
Red Circle Comics (Archie)

	GD25	FN65	NM94
1-Morrow, McWilliams, Wildey-a; Toth-c			1.50
2,3: MLJ's The Fox by Toth-c/a. 3-Morrow-a			1.00

(Also see Archie's Super-Hero Special Digest #2)

BLACK HOOD
Dec, 1991 - No. 12, Dec, 1992 ($1.00)
DC Comics (Impact Comics)

	GD25	FN65	NM94
1-12: 11-Intro The Fox. 12-Origin Black Hood			1.00
Annual 1 (1992, $2.50, 68 pgs.)-w/Trading card		1.00	2.50

BLACK HOOD COMICS (Formerly Hangman #2-8; Laugh Comics #20 on; also see Black Swan, Jackpot, Roly Poly & Top-Notch #9)
No. 9, Winter, 1943-44 - No. 19, Summer, 1946 (on radio in 1943)
MLJ Magazines

	GD25	FN65	NM94
9-The Hangman & The Boy Buddies cont'd	81.00	243.00	725.00
10-Hangman & Dusty, the Boy Detective app.	45.00	135.00	405.00
11-Dusty app.; no Hangman	36.00	108.00	300.00
12-18: 14-Kinstler blood-c. 17-Hal Foster swipe from Prince Valiant; 1st issue with "An Archie Magazine" on-c	34.00	103.00	275.00
19-I.D. exposed	40.00	120.00	360.00

NOTE: *Hangman by* ***Fuje*** *in 9, 10.* ***Kinstler*** *a-15, c-14-16.*

BLACK JACK (Rocky Lane's...; formerly Jim Bowie)
No. 20, Nov, 1957 - No. 30, Nov, 1959
Charlton Comics

	GD25	FN65	NM94
20	7.15	21.50	50.00
21,27,29,30	4.25	13.00	28.00
22-(68 pgs.)	5.70	17.00	38.00
23-Williamson/Torres-a	5.70	17.00	40.00
24-26,28-Ditko-a	7.15	21.50	50.00

BLACK KNIGHT, THE
May, 1953; 1963
Toby Press

	GD25	FN65	NM94
1-Bondage-c	17.50	53.00	140.00
Super Reprint No. 11 (1963)-Reprints 1953 issue	3.60	9.00	18.00

BLACK KNIGHT, THE (Also see The Avengers #48, Marvel Super Heroes & Tales To Astonish #52)
May, 1955 - No. 5, April, 1956
Atlas Comics (MgPC)

	GD25	FN65	NM94
1-Origin Crusader; Maneely-c/a	67.00	200.00	600.00
2-Maneely-c/a(4)	50.00	150.00	450.00
3-5: 4-Maneely-c/a. 5-Maneely-c, Shores-a	39.00	117.00	350.00

BLACK KNIGHT (Also see Avengers & Ultraforce)
June, 1990 - No. 4, Sept, 1990 ($1.50, limited series)
Marvel Comics

	GD25	FN65	NM94
1-4: 1-Original Black Knight returns			1.50

NOTE: ***Buckler*** *c-1-4p*

BLACK KNIGHT: EXODUS
Dec, 1996 ($2.50, one-shot)
Marvel Comics

	GD25	FN65	NM94
1-Raab-s; Apocalypse-c/app.		1.00	2.50

BLACK LAMB, THE
Nov, 1996 - No, 6, Apr, 1997 ($2.50, limited series)
DC Comics (Helix)

	GD25	FN65	NM94
1-6: Tim Truman-c/a/scripts		1.00	2.50

BLACK LIGHTNING (See The Brave & The Bold, Cancelled Comic Cavalcade, DC Comics Presents #16, Detective #490 and World's Finest #257)
Apr, 1977 - No. 11, Sept-Oct, 1978
National Periodical Publications/DC Comics

	GD25	FN65	NM94
1,11		2.00	5.00
2-01: 4-Intro Cyclotronic Man. 11-The Ray app.		1.40	3.50

NOTE: ***Buckler*** *c-1-3p, 6-11p. #11 is 44 pgs.*

BLACK LIGHTNING (2nd Series)
Feb, 1995 - No. 13, Feb, 1996 ($1.95/$2.25)
DC Comics

	GD25	FN65	NM94
1-5-Tony Isabella scripts begin, ends #8		.80	2.00
6-13; 6-Begin $2.25-c. 13-Batman-c/app.		.90	2.25

BLACK MAGIC (...Magazine) (Becomes Cool Cat V8#6 on)
10-11/50 - V4#1, 6-7/53: V4#2, 9-10/53 - V5#3, 11-12/54; V6#1, 9-10/57 - V7#2, 11-12/58: V7#3, 7-8/60 - V8#5, 11-12/61
(V1#1-5, 52pgs.; V1#6-V3#3, 44pgs.)
Crestwood Publ. V1#1-4,V6#1-V7#5/Headline V1#5-V5#3,V7#6-V8#5

	GD25	FN65	NM94
V1#1-S&K-a, 10 pgs.; Meskin-a(2)	78.00	234.00	700.00
2-S&K-a, 17 pgs.; Meskin-a	40.00	120.00	325.00
3-6(8-9/51)-S&K, Roussos, Meskin-a	36.00	107.00	275.00
V2#1(10-11/51),4,5,7(#13),9(#15),12(#18)-S&K-a	26.00	77.00	190.00
2,3,6,8,10,11(#17)	17.00	49.00	120.00
V3#1(#19, 12/52) - 6(#24, 5/53)-S&K-a	19.00	58.00	140.00
V4#1(#25, 6-7/53), 2(#26, 9-10/53)-S&K-a(3-4)	21.00	62.00	150.00
3(#27, 11-12/53)-S&K-a; Ditko-a (2nd published-a); also see Captain 3-D, Daring Love #1, Strange Fantasy #9, & Fantastic Fears #5 (Fant. Fears was 1st drawn, but not 1st publ.)	40.00	120.00	290.00
4(#28)-Eyes ripped out/story-S&K, Ditko-a	29.00	86.00	200.00
5(#29, 3-4/54)-S&K, Ditko-a	22.00	66.00	160.00
6(#30, 5-6/54)-S&K, Powell?-a	17.00	49.00	120.00
V5#1(#31, 7-8/54 - 3(#33, 11-12/54)-S&K-a	13.50	41.00	95.00
V6#1(#34, 9-10/57), 2(#35, 11-12/57)	7.50	22.50	50.00
3(1-2/58) - 6(7-8/58)	7.50	22.50	50.00

Black Orchid Annual #1 © DC

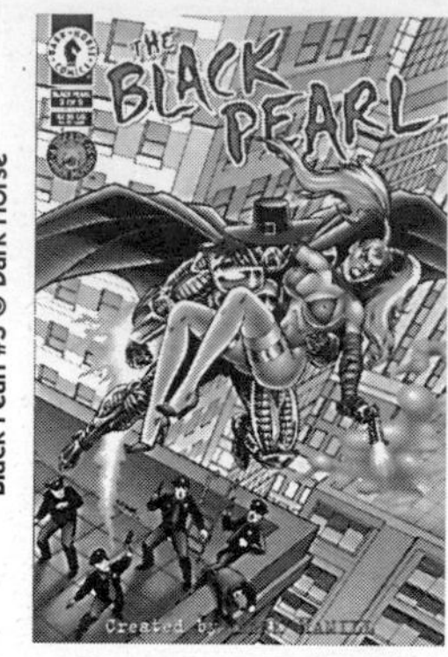

Black Pearl #3 © Dark Horse

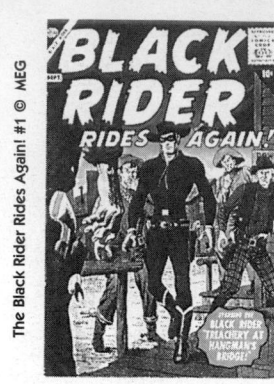

The Black Rider Rides Again! #1 © MEG

	GD25	FN65	NM94
V7#1(9-10/58) - 3(7-8/60)	5.70	17.00	40.00
4(9-10/60), 5(11-12/60)-Torres-a	7.50	22.50	50.00
6(1-2/61)-Powell-a(2)	5.70	17.00	40.00
V8#1(3-4/61)-Powell-c/a	5.70	17.00	40.00
2(5-6/61)-E.C. story swipe/W.F. #22; Ditko, Powell-a	7.50	22.50	50.00
3(7-8/61)-E.C. story swipe/W.F. #22; Powell-a(2)	7.50	22.50	50.00
4(9-10/61)-Powell-a(5)	5.70	17.00	40.00
5-E.C. story swipe/W.S.F. #28; Powell-a(3)	7.50	22.50	50.00

NOTE: ***Bernard Baily** a-V4#6?, V5#3(2). **Grandenetti** a-V2#3, 11. **Kirby** c-V1#1-6, V2#1-12, V3#1-6, V4#1, 2, 4-6, V5#1-3. **McWilliams** a-V3#2i. **Meskin** a-V1#1(2), 2, 3, 4(2), 5(2), 6, V2/1, 2, 3(2), 4(3), 5, 6(2), 7-9, 11, 12i, V3#1(2), 5, 6, V5#1(2), 2. **Orlando** a-V6#1, 4, V7#2; c-V6/1-6. **Powell** a-V5#1?. **Roussos** a-V1#3-5, 6(2), V2#3(2), 4, 5(2), 6, 8, 9, 10(2), 11, 12p, V3#1(2), 2i, 5, V5#2. **Simon** a-V2#12, V3#2, V7#5? c-V4#3?, V7#3?, 4, 5?, 6?, V8#1-5. **Simon & Kirby** a-V1#1, 2(2), 3-6, V2#1, 4, 5, 7, 9, 12, V3#1-6, V4#1(3), 2(4), 3(2), 4(2), 5, 6, V5#1-3; c-V2#1. **Leonard Starr** a-V1#1. **Tuska** a-V6#3, 4. **Woodbridge** a-V7#4.*

BLACK MAGIC
Oct-Nov, 1973 - No. 9, Apr-May, 1975
National Periodical Publications

	GD25	FN65	NM94
1-S&K reprints	2.50	7.50	20.00
2-9-S&K reprints	1.00	3.00	8.00

BLACK MAGIC
Apr, 1990 - No. 4, Oct, 1990 ($2.75, B&W, mini-series, 52pgs.)
Eclipse International

	GD25	FN65	NM94
1-($3.50, 68pgs.)-Japanese manga		1.40	3.50
2-4 ($2.75)		1.10	2.80

BLACKMAIL TERROR (See Harvey Comics Library)

BLACK MASK
1993 - No. 3, 1994 ($4.95, limited series, 52 pgs.)
DC Comics

	GD25	FN65	NM94
1-3		2.00	5.00

BLACK OPS
Jan, 1996 - No. 5, May, 1996 ($2.50, limited series)
Image Comics (Wildstorm Productions)

	GD25	FN65	NM94
1-5		1.00	2.50

BLACK ORCHID (See Adventure Comics #428 & Phantom Stranger)
Holiday, 1988-89 - No. 3, 1989 ($3.50, limited series, prestige format)
DC Comics

	GD25	FN65	NM94
Book 1,3: Neil Gaiman scripts & McKean-a in all		2.00	5.00
Book 2-Arkham Asylum story; Batman app.		2.00	5.00

BLACK ORCHID
Sept, 1993 - No. 22, June, 1995 ($1.95/$2.25)
DC Comics

	GD25	FN65	NM94
1-20: Dave McKean-c all issues		.80	2.00
1-Platinum Edition	1.50	4.50	12.00
21,22		.90	2.25
Annual 1 (1993, $3.95, 68 pgs.)-Children's Crusade		1.60	4.00

BLACKOUTS (See Broadway Hollywood...)

BLACK PANTHER, THE (Also see Avengers #52, Fantastic Four #52, Jungle Action & Marvel Premiere #51-53)
Jan, 1977 - No. 15, May, 1979
Marvel Comics Group

	GD25	FN65	NM94
1	1.50	4.50	12.00
2-12		2.40	6.00
13-15: 14,15-Avengers x-over		1.60	4.00

NOTE: ***J. Buscema** c-15p. **Kirby** c/a & scripts-1-12. **Layton** c-13i.*

BLACK PANTHER
July, 1988 - No. 4, Oct, 1988 ($1.25)
Marvel Comics Group

	GD25	FN65	NM94
1-4			1.25

BLACK PANTHER: PANTHER'S PREY
1991 - No. 4, 1991 ($4.95, squarebound, limited series, 52 pgs.)
Marvel Comics

	GD25	FN65	NM94
1-4		2.00	5.00

BLACK PEARL, THE
Sept, 1996 - No. 5, Jan, 1997 ($2.95, limited series)
Dark Horse Comics

	GD25	FN65	NM94
1-5: Mark Hamill scripts		1.20	3.00

BLACK PHANTOM (See Tim Holt #25, 38)
Nov, 1954 (one-shot) (Female outlaw)
Magazine Enterprises

	GD25	FN65	NM94
1 (A-1 #122)-The Ghost Rider story plus 3 Black Phantom stories; Headlight-c/a	32.00	96.00	255.00

BLACK PHANTOM
1989 - No. 3, 1990 ($2.50, B&W; #2 color)(Reprints & new-a)
AC Comics

	GD25	FN65	NM94
1,2: 1-Ayers-r, Bolle-r/B.P. #1. 2-Redmask-r		1.00	2.50
3 ($2.75, B&W)-B.P., Redmask-r & new-a		1.10	2.75

BLACK PHANTOM, RETURN OF THE (See Wisco)

BLACK RIDER (Western Winners #1-7; Western Tales of Black Rider #28-31; Gunsmoke Western #32 on)(See All Western Winners, Best Western, Kid Colt, Outlaw Kid, Rex Hart, Two-Gun Kid, Two-Gun Western, Western Gunfighters, Western Winners, & Wild Western)
No. 8, 3/50 - No. 18, 1/52; No. 19, 11/53 - No. 27, 3/55
Marvel/Atlas Comics(CDS No. 8-17/CPS No. 19 on)

	GD25	FN65	NM94
8 (#1)-Black Rider & his horse Satan begin; 36 pgs; Stan Lee photo-c as Black Rider)	36.00	108.00	300.00
9-52 pgs. begin, end #14	17.50	53.00	140.00
10-Origin Black Rider	21.00	64.00	170.00
11-14: 14-Last 52pgs.	12.00	38.00	100.00
15-19: 19-Two-Gun Kid app.	10.50	32.00	85.00
20-Classic-c; Two-Gun Kid app.	12.00	36.00	95.00
21-27: 21-23-Two-Gun Kid app. 24,25-Arrowhead app. 26-Kid Colt app. 27-Last issue; last precode. Kid Colt app. The Spider (a villain) burns to death	9.50	28.00	75.00

NOTE: ***Ayers** c-22. **Jack Keller** a-15, 26, 27. **Maneely** a-14; c-16, 17, 25, 27. **Syd Shores** a-19, 21, 22, 23(3), 24(3), 25-27; c-19, 21, 23. **Sinnott** a-24, 25. **Tuska** a-12, 19-21.*

BLACK RIDER RIDES AGAIN!, THE
Sept, 1957
Atlas Comics (CPS)

	GD25	FN65	NM94
1-Kirby-a(3); Powell-a; Severin-c	19.00	56.00	150.00

BLACK SEPTEMBER (Also see Avengers/Ultraforce, Ultraforce (1st series) #10 & Ultraforce/Avengers)
1995 ($1.50, one-shot)
Malibu Comics (Ultraverse)

	GD25	FN65	NM94
Infinity-Intro to the newUltraverse; variant-c exists.			1.50

BLACKSTONE (See Super Magician Comics & Wisco Giveaways)

BLACKSTONE, MASTER MAGICIAN COMICS
Mar-Apr, 1946 - No. 3, July-Aug, 1946
Vital Publications/Street & Smith Publ.

	GD25	FN65	NM94
1	22.00	66.00	175.00
2,3	16.00	49.00	130.00

BLACKSTONE, THE MAGICIAN (...Detective on cover only #3 & 4)
No. 2, May, 1948 - No. 4, Sept, 1948 (No #1)(Cont'd from E.C. #1?)
Marvel Comics (CnPC)

	GD25	FN65	NM94
2-The Blonde Phantom begins, ends #4	47.00	141.00	425.00
3,4: 3-Blonde Phantom by Sekowsky	36.00	108.00	285.00

BLACKSTONE, THE MAGICIAN DETECTIVE FIGHTS CRIME

The Black Terror #16 © Pub. Ent. Ltd.

Blackwulf #3 © MEG

Blade: The Vampire Hunter #3 © MEG

	GD25	FN65	NM94
Fall, 1947			
E. C. Comics			
1-1st app. Happy Houlihans	38.00	113.00	340.00

BLACK SWAN COMICS
1945
MLJ Magazines (Pershing Square Publ. Co.)

	GD25	FN65	NM94
1-The Black Hood reprints from Black Hood No. 14; Bill Woggon-a; Suzie app.	18.00	54.00	145.00

BLACK TARANTULA (See Feature Presentations No. 5)

BLACK TERROR (See America's Best Comics & Exciting Comics)
Winter, 1942-43 - No. 27, June, 1949
Better Publications/Standard

	GD25	FN65	NM94
1-Black Terror, Crime Crusader begin	217.00	651.00	1950.00
2	78.00	234.00	700.00
3	56.00	168.00	500.00
4,5	47.00	141.00	425.00
6-10: 7-The Ghost app.	42.00	126.00	375.00
11-20: 20-The Scarab app.	36.00	108.00	300.00
21-Miss Masque app.	36.00	108.00	325.00
22-Part Frazetta-a on one Black Terror story	36.00	108.00	300.00
23,25-27	36.00	108.00	290.00
24-Frazetta-a (1/4 pg.)	36.00	108.00	300.00

*NOTE: **Schomburg** (Xela) c-2-27; bondage c-2, 17, 24. **Meskin** a-27. **Moreira** a-27. **Robinson/Meskin** a-23, 24(3), 25, 26. **Roussos/Mayo** a-24. **Tuska** a-26, 27.*

BLACK TERROR, THE (Also see Total Eclipse)
Oct, 1989 - No. 3, June, 1990 ($4.95, 52 pgs., squarebound, limited series)
Eclipse Comics

	GD25	FN65	NM94
1-3: Beau Smith & Chuck Dixon scripts; Dan Brereton painted-c/a		2.00	5.00

BLACKTHORNE 3-D SERIES
May, 1985 - No. 80, 1989 ($2.25/$2.50)
Blackthorne Publishing Co.

	GD25	FN65	NM94
1-Sheena in 3-D #1. D. Stevens-c/retouched-a		1.00	2.50
2-10: 2-MerlinRealm in 3-D #1. 3-3-D Heroes #1. Goldyn in 3-D #1. 5-Bizarre 3-D Zone #1. 6-Salimba in 3-D #1. 7-Twisted Tales in 3-D #1. 8-Dick Tracy in 3-D #1. 9-Salimba in 3-D #2. 10-Gumby in 3-D #1		1.00	2.50
11-20: 11-Betty Boop in 3-D #1. 12-Hamster Vice in 3-D #1. 13-Little Nemo in 3-D #1. 14-Gumby in 3-D #2. 15-Hamster Vice #6 in 3-D. 16-Laffin' Gas #6 in 3-D. 17-Gumby in 3-D #3. 18-Bullwinkle and Rocky in 3-D #1. 19-The Flintstones in 3-D #1. 20-G.I. Joe in 3-D #1		1.00	2.50
21-30: 21-Gumby in 3-D #4. 22-The Flintstones in 3-D #2. 23-Laurel & Hardy in 3-D #1. 24-Bozo the Clown in 3-D #1. 25-The Transformers in 3-D #1. 26-G.I. Joe in 3-D #2. 27-Bravestarr in 3-D #1. 28- Gumby in 3-D #5. 29-The Transformers in 3-D #2. 30-Star Wars in 3-D #1		1.00	2.50
31-40: 31-The California Raisins in 3-D #1. 32-Richie Rich & Casper in 3-D #1. 33-Gumby in 3-D #6. 34-Laurel & Hardy in 3-D #2. 35-G.I. Joe in 3-D #3. 36-The Flintstones in 3-D #3. 37-The Transformers in 3-D #3. 38-Gumby in 3-D #7. 39-G.I. Joe in 3-D #4. 40-Bravestarr in 3-D #2		1.00	2.50
41-50: 41-Battletech in 3-D #1. 42-The Flintstones in 3-D #4. 43-Underdog in 3-D #1 44-The California Raisins in 3-D #2. 45-Red Heat in 3-D #1 (movie adapt.). 46-The California Raisins in 3-D #3. 47. 48-Star Wars in 3-D #2,3. 49-Rambo in 3-D #1. 49-Sad Sack in 3-D #1. 50-Bullwinkle For President in 3-D #1		1.00	2.50
51-60: 51-Kull in 3-D #1. 52-G.I. Joe in 3-D #5. 53-Red Sonja in 3-D #1. 54-Bozo in 3-D #2. 55-Waxwork in 3-D #1 (movie adapt.). 56. 57-Casper in 3-D #1. 58-Baby Huey in 3-D #1. 59-Little Dot in 3-D #1. 60-Solomon Kane in 3-D #1		1.00	2.50
61-70: 61-Werewolf in 3-D #1. 62-G.I. Joe in 3-D Annual #1. 63-The California Raisins in 3-D #4. 64-To Die For in 3-D #1. 65-Capt. Holo in 3-D #1. 66-Playful Little Audrey in 3-D #1. 67-Kull in 3-D #2. 68. 69-The California Raisins in 3-D#5. 70-Wendy in 3-D #1		1.00	2.50
71-80: 71. 72-Sports Hall of Shame #1. 73. 74-The Noid in 3-D #1. 75-Moonwalker in 3-D #1 (Michael Jackson movie adapt.). 76-79. 80-The Noid in 3-D #2		1.00	2.50

BLACKWULF
June, 1994 - No. 10, Mar, 1995 ($1.50)
Marvel Comics

	GD25	FN65	NM94
1-($2.50)-Embossed-c; Angel Medina-a		1.00	2.50
2-10			1.50

BLADE OF THE IMMORTAL (Manga)
June, 1996 - Present ($2.95, B&W, limited series)
Dark Horse Comics

	GD25	FN65	NM94
1-10: 2-#1 on cover in error		1.20	3.00
11-($3.95, 48 pgs.)			3.95
12-16:12-Begin Dreamsong			2.95

BLADE RUNNER (Movie)
Oct, 1982 - No. 2, Nov, 1982
Marvel Comics Group

	GD25	FN65	NM94
1,2-r/Marvel Super Special #22; 1-Williamson-c/a. 2-Williamson-a			.75

BLADESMEN UNDERSEA
1994 ($3.50, B&W)
Blue Comet Press

	GD25	FN65	NM94
1-Polybagged w/trading card		1.40	3.50

BLADE: THE VAMPIRE-HUNTER
July, 1994 - No. 10, Apr, 1995 ($1.95)
Marvel Comics

	GD25	FN65	NM94
1-($2.95)-Foil-c		1.20	3.00
2-10		.80	2.00

BLAST (Satire Magazine)
Feb, 1971 - No. 2, May, 1971
G & D Publications

	GD25	FN65	NM94
1-Wrightson & Kaluta-a	4.50	13.50	45.00
2-Kaluta-a	3.00	9.00	30.00

BLASTERS SPECIAL
1989 ($2.00, one-shot)
DC Comics

	GD25	FN65	NM94
1-Peter David scripts; Invasion spin-off		.80	2.00

BLAST-OFF (Three Rocketeers)
Oct, 1965 (12¢)
Harvey Publications (Fun Day Funnies)

	GD25	FN65	NM94
1-Kirby/Williamson-a(2); Williamson/Crandall-a; Williamson/Torres/Krenkel-a; Kirby/Simon-c	3.50	10.50	35.00

BLAZE
Aug, 1994 - No. 12, July, 1995 ($1.95)
Marvel Comics

	GD25	FN65	NM94
1-($2.95)-Foil embossed-c		1.20	3.00
2-12: 2-Man-Thing-c/story		.80	2.00

BLAZE CARSON (Rex Hart #6 on)(See Kid Colt, Tex Taylor, Wild Western, Wisco)
Sept, 1948 - No. 5, June, 1949
Marvel Comics (USA)

	GD25	FN65	NM94
1: 1,2-Shores-c	20.00	60.00	160.00
2,4,5: 4-Two-Gun Kid app. 5-Tex Taylor app.	15.00	45.00	120.00
3-Used by N.Y. State Legis. Comm. (injury to eye splash); Tex Morgan app.	16.00	49.00	130.00

BLAZE: LEGACY OF BLOOD (See Ghost Rider & Ghost Rider/Blaze)
Dec, 1993 - No. 4, Mar, 1994 ($1.75, limited series)

Blazing Comics #1 © ENWIL

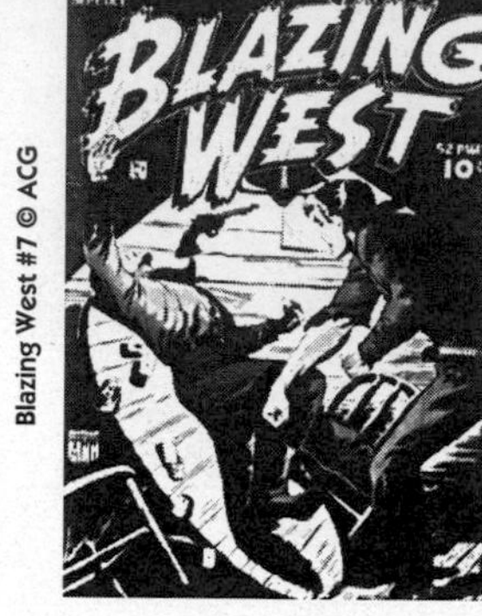

Blazing West #7 © ACG

Blitzkrieg #4 © DC

GD25 FN65 NM94

Marvel Comics (Midnight Sons imprint)
1-4 .70 1.75

BLAZE THE WONDER COLLIE (Formerly Molly Manton's Romances #1?)
No. 2, Oct, 1949 - No. 3, Feb, 1950 (Both have photo-c)
Marvel Comics(SePI)
2(#1), 3-(Scarce) 19.00 56.00 150.00

BLAZING BATTLE TALES
July, 1975
Seaboard Periodicals (Atlas)
1-Intro. Sgt. Hawk & the Sky Demon; Severin, McWilliams, Sparling-a; Thorne-c 1.20 3.00

BLAZING COMBAT (Magazine)
Oct, 1965 - No. 4, July, 1966 (35¢, B&W)
Warren Publishing Co.
1-Frazetta painted-c on all 14.00 42.00 140.00
2 2.80 8.40 28.00
3,4: 4-Frazetta half pg. ad 2.50 7.50 20.00
...Anthology (reprints from No. 1-4) 4.00 12.00 40.00
NOTE: *Above has art by* ***Colan, Crandall, Evans, Morrow, Orlando, Severin, Torres, Toth, Williamson,*** *and* ***Wood.***

BLAZING COMBAT: WORLD WAR I AND WORLD WAR II
Mar, 1994 ($3.75, B&W)
Apple Press
1,2: 1-r/Colan, Toth, Goodwin, Severin, Wood-a. 2-r/Crandall, Evans, Severin, Torres, Williamson-a 1.50 3.75

BLAZING COMICS
6/44 - #3, 9/44; #4, 2/45; #5, 3/45; #5(V2#2), 3/55 - #6(V2#3), 1955?
Enwil Associates/Rural Home
1-The Green Turtle, Red Hawk, Black Buccaneer begin; origin Jun-Gal 39.00 117.00 350.00
2-5: 3-Briefer-a. 5-(V2#2 inside) 26.00 80.00 210.00
5(3/55, V2#2-inside)-Black Buccaneer-c, 6(V2#3-inside, 1955)-Indian/Japanese-c 9.50 28.00 75.00
NOTE: *No. 5 & 6 contain remaindered comics rebound and the contents can vary. Cloak & Daggar, Will Rogers, Superman 64, Star Spangled 130, Kaanga known. Value would be half of contents.*

BLAZING SIXGUNS
Dec, 1952
Avon Periodicals
1-Kinstler-c/a; Larsen/Alascia-a(2), Tuska?-a; Jesse James, Kit Carson, Wild Bill Hickok app. 11.30 34.00 90.00

BLAZING SIXGUNS
1964
I.W./Super Comics
I.W. Reprint #1,8,9: 1-r/Wild Bill Hickok #26, Western True Crime #? & Blazing Sixguns #1 by Avon; Kinstler-c. 8-r/Blazing Western #?; Kinstler-c. 9-r/Blazing Western #1; Ditko-r; Kintsler-c reprinted from Dalton Boys #1. 1.25 3.75 10.00
Super Reprint #10,11,15,16: 10,11-r/The Rider #2,1. 15-r/Silver Kid Western #?. 16-r/Buffalo Bill #?; Wildey-r; Severin-c. 17(1964)-r/Western True Crime #? 1.25 3.75 10.00
12-Reprints Bullseye #3; S&K-a 2.50 7.50 25.00
18-r/Straight Arrow #? by Powell; Severin-c 1.50 4.50 12.00

BLAZING SIX-GUNS (Also see Sundance Kid)
Feb, 1971 - No. 2, Apr, 1971 (52 pgs.)
Skywald Comics
1-The Red Mask, Sundance Kid begin, Avon's Geronimo reprint by Kinstler; Wyatt Earp app. 1.00 3.00 8.00
2-Wild Bill Hickok, Jesse James, Kit Carson-r plus M.E. Red Mask-r 2.00 5.00

GD25 FN65 NM94

BLAZING WEST (Also see The Hooded Horseman)
Fall, 1948 - No. 22, Mar-Apr, 1952
American Comics Group (B&I Publ./Michel Publ.)
1-Origin & 1st app. Injun Jones, Tenderfoot & Buffalo Belle; Texas Tim & Ranger begins, ends #13 16.00 49.00 130.00
2,3 8.75 26.25 65.00
4-Origin & 1st app. Little Lobo; Starr-a 6.50 19.50 45.00
5-10: 5-Starr-a 5.70 17.00 40.00
11-13 5.00 15.00 30.00
14-Origin & 1st app. The Hooded Horseman 8.75 26.25 70.00
15-22: 15,16,18,19-Starr-a 6.50 19.50 45.00

BLAZING WESTERN
Jan, 1954 - No. 5, Sept, 1954
Timor Publications
1-Ditko-a (1st Western-a?); text story by Bruce Hamilton 11.30 34.00 90.00
2-4 5.35 16.00 32.00
5-Disbrow-a 5.70 17.00 38.00

BLEAT
Aug, 1995 ($2.95)
Slave Labor Graphics
1 1.20 3.00

BLESSED PIUS X
No date (Text/comics, 32 pgs., paper-c)
Catechetical Guild (Giveaway)
nn 3.60 9.00 18.00

BLIND JUSTICE (Also see Batman: Blind Justice)
1989 (Giveaway, squarebound)
DC Comics/Diamond Comic Distributors
nn-Contains Detective #598-600 by Batman movie writer Sam Hamm, w/covers; published same time as originals? .80 2.00

BLINDSIDE
Aug, 1996 ($2.50)
Image Comics (Extreme Studios)
1-Variant-c exists 1.20 2.50

BLIP
2/1983 - 1983 (Marvel video game mag. in color comic format)
Marvel Comics Group
1-1st app. Donkey Kong & Mario Bros. in comics, 6pgs. comics; photo-c 2.40 6.00
2-Spider-Man photo-c; 6pgs. Spider-Man comics w/Green Goblin 1.00 2.80 7.00
3,4,6 1.40 3.50
5-E.T., Indiana Jones; Rocky-c 1.60 4.00
7-6pgs. Hulk comics; Pacman & Donkey Kong Jr. Hints 2.00 5.00

BLISS ALLEY
July, 1997 - Present ($2.95, B&W)
Image Comics
1,2-Messner-Loebs-s/a 2.95

BLITZKRIEG
Jan-Feb, 1976 - No. 5, Sept-Oct, 1976
National Periodical Publications
1-Kubert-c on all 3.50 10.50 35.00
2-5 2.50 7.50 20.00

BLONDE PHANTOM (Formerly All-Select #1-11; Lovers #23 on)(Also see Blackstone, Marvel Mystery, Millie The Model #2, Sub-Mariner Comics #25 & Sun Girl)
No. 12, Winter, 1946-47 - No. 22, Mar, 1949

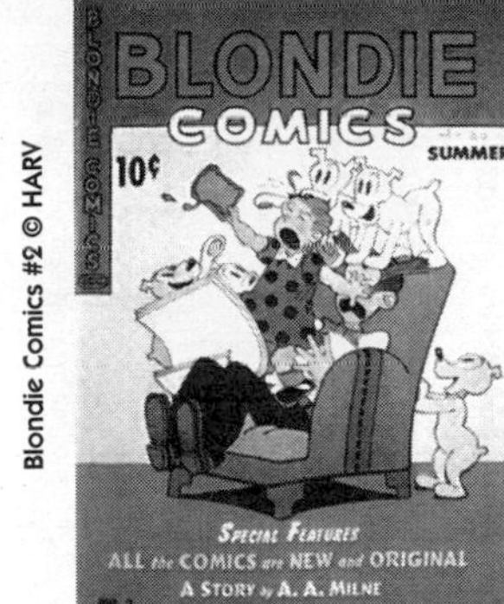

Blondie Comics #2 © HARV

Bloodbath #2 © DC

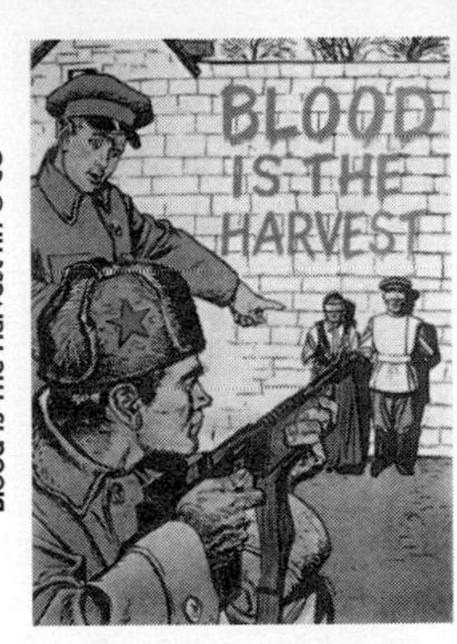

Blood Is The Harvest nn © CG

GD25 FN65 NM94

Marvel Comics (MPC)
12-Miss America begins, ends #14 111.00 333.00 1000.00
13-Sub-Mariner begins (not in #16) 70.00 210.00 630.00
14,15: 15-Kurtzman's "Hey Look" 64.00 192.00 575.00
16-Captain America with Bucky story by Rico(p), 6 pgs.; Kurtzman's "Hey Look" (1 pg.) 89.00 267.00 800.00
17-22: 22-Anti Wertham editorial 61.00 183.00 550.00
NOTE: ***Shores** c-12-18.*

BLONDIE (See Ace Comics, Comics Reading Libraries, Dagwood, Daisy & Her Pups, Eat Right to Work..., King & Magic Comics)
1942 - 1946
David McKay Publications
Feature Books 12 (Rare) 67.00 200.00 600.00
Feature Books 27-29,31,34(1940) 15.00 45.00 120.00
Feature Books 36,38,40,42,43,45,47 14.00 41.00 110.00
...1944 (Hard-c, 1938, B&W, 128 pgs.)-1944 daily strip-r 11.30 34.00 90.00

BLONDIE & DAGWOOD FAMILY
Oct, 1963 - No. 4, Dec, 1965 (68 pgs.)
Harvey Publications (King Features Synd.)
1 1.60 4.80 16.00
2-4 1.00 3.00 10.00

BLONDIE COMICS (...Monthly No. 16-141)
Spring, 1947 - No. 163, Nov, 1965; No. 164, Aug, 1966 - No. 175, Dec, 1967; No. 177, Feb, 1969 - No. 222, Nov, 1976
David McKay #1-15/Harvey #16-163/King #164-175/Charlton #177 on
1 19.00 56.00 150.00
2 8.75 26.25 70.00
3-5 7.15 21.50 50.00
6-10 5.70 17.00 38.00
11-15 4.25 13.00 28.00
16-(3/50; 1st Harvey issue) 5.70 17.00 36.00
17-20: 20-(3/51)-Becomes Daisy & Her Pups #21 & Chamber of Chills #21 2.60 7.80 26.00
21-30 1.80 5.40 18.00
31-50 1.50 4.50 15.00
51-80 1.20 3.60 12.00
81-124,126-130 1.00 3.00 10.00
125 (80 pgs.) 1.80 5.40 18.00
131-136,138,139 .80 2.40 8.00
137,140-(80 pgs.) 1.80 5.40 18.00
141-147,149-154,156,160,164-167 1.00 3.00 10.00
148,155,157-159,161-163 are 68 pgs. 2.00 6.00 16.00
168-175,177-222 (no #176) .50 1.50 5.00
Blondie, Dagwood & Daisy 1(100 pgs., 1953) 15.00 45.00 120.00
1950 Giveaway 4.00 10.00 20.00
1962,1964 Giveaway .80 2.40 8.00
N. Y. State Dept. of Mental Hygiene Giveaway-('50, '56, '61) Regular size (Diff. issues) 16 pgs.; no # 1.80 4.50 9.00

BLOOD
Feb, 1988 - No. 4, Apr, 1988 ($3.25, mature)
Marvel Comics (Epic Comics)
1-4: DeMatteis scripts & Kent Williams-c/a 1.40 3.50

BLOOD AND GLORY (Punisher & Captain America)
Oct, 1992 - No. 3, Dec, 1992 ($5.95, limited series)
Marvel Comics
1-3: 1-Embossed wraparound-c 2.40 6.00

BLOOD & ROSES: FUTURE PAST TENSE (Bob Hickey's...)
Dec, 1993 ($2.25)
Sky Comics
1-Silver ink logo .90 2.25

BLOOD & ROSES: SEARCH FOR THE TIME-STONE (Bob Hickey's...)
Apr, 1994 ($2.50)
Sky Comics
1 1.00 2.50

BLOOD AND SHADOWS
1996 - Book 4, 1996 ($5.95, squarebound, limited series, mature)
DC Comics (Vertigo)
Books 1-4: Joe R. Lansdale scripts; Mark A. Nelson-c/a. 2.40 6.00

BLOOD: A TALE
Nov, 1996 - No. 4, Feb, 1997 ($2.95, limited series)
DC Comics (Vertigo)
1-4: Reprints Epic series w/new-c; DeMatteis scripts; Kent Williams-c/a 1.20 3.00

BLOODBATH
Early Dec, 1993 - No. 2, Late Dec, 1993 ($3.50, limited series, 68 pgs.)
DC Comics
1-Neon ink-c; Superman app.: 1-New Batman-c & app. 1.40 3.50
2-Hitman 2nd app. 1.25 3.75 10.00

BLOODFIRE
June, 1993 - No. 12, May, 1994 ($2.95)
Lightning Comics
1-($3.50)-Foil-c; 1st app. Bloodfire 1.40 3.50
2-12: 2-Origin; contracts HIV virus via transfusion. 5-Polybagged w/card & collectors warning on bag. 12-(5/94) 1.20 3.00
0-(Indicia reads June 1994, MAY on-c, $3.50) 1.40 3.50
.../Hellina 1 (7/95, $3.00) 1.20 3.00
.../Hellina 1 (7/95, $9.95)-Nude edition; Deodato-c 1.25 3.75 10.00
.../Hellina (8/95, $9.95)-Commemorative edition 1.25 3.75 10.00

BLOOD IS THE HARVEST
1950 (32 pgs., paper-c)
Catechetical Guild
(Scarce)-Anti-communism (13 known copies) 86.00 258.00 775.00
Black & white version (5 known copies), saddle stitched 34.00 103.00 275.00
Untrimmed version (only one known copy); estimated value-$600
NOTE: *In 1979 nine copies of the color version surfaced from the old Guild's files plus the five black & white copies.*

BLOODLINES: A TALE FROM THE HEART OF AFRICA (See Tales From the Heart of Africa)
1992 ($5.95, 52 pgs.)
Marvel Comics (Epic Comics)
1-Story cont'd from Tales From... 2.40 6.00

BLOOD OF DRACULA
Nov, 1987 - No. 20?, 1990 ($1.75/$1.95, B&W)($2.25 #14,16 on)
Apple Comics
1-13: 6-Begin $1.95-c. 10-Chadwick-c .80 2.00
14,16-20 ($2.25): 14,16-19-Lost Frankenstein pgs. by Wrightson .90 2.25
15-Contains stereo flexidisc ($3.75) 1.50 3.75

BLOOD OF THE INNOCENT (See Warp Graphics Annual)
1/7/86 - No. 4, 1/28/86 (Weekly mini-series, mature)
WaRP Graphics
1-4 .80 2.00

BLOODPACK
Mar, 1995 - No. 4, June,1995 ($1.50, limited series)

Bloodseed #1 © MEG

Bloodstrike #10 © Rob Liefeld

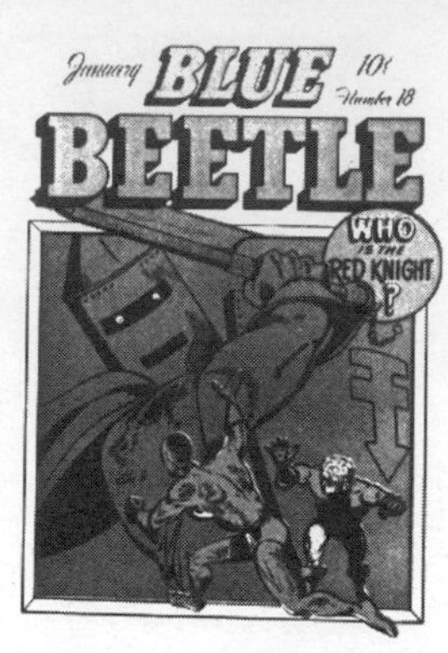

Blue Beetle #18 © FOX

GD25 FN65 NM94

DC Comics
1-4 — 1.50

BLOODPOOL
Aug, 1995 - No. 4, Nov, 1995 ($2.50, limited series)
Image Comics (Extreme Studios)
1-4: Jo Duffy scripts in all — 1.00 2.50
Special (3/96, $2.50)-Jo Duffy scripts — 1.00 2.50
Trade Paperback (1996, $12.95)-r/#1-4 — 13.00

BLOOD REIGN SAGA
1996 ($3.00, B&W, mature)
London Night Studios
1-"Encore Edition" — 1.20 3.00

BLOODSCENT
Oct, 1988 ($2.00, one-shot, Baxter paper)
Comico
1-Colan-p — .80 2.00

BLOODSEED
Oct, 1993 - No. 2, Nov, 1993 ($1.95, limited series)
Marvel Comics (Frontier Comics)
1,2: Sharp/Cam Smith-a — .80 2.00

BLOODSHOT (See Eternal Warrior #4 & Rai #0)
Nov, 1992 - No. 51, Aug, 1996 ($2.25/$2.50)
Valiant/Acclaim Comics (Valiant)
1-($3.50)-Chromium embossed-c by B. Smith w/poster — 1.40 3.50
2-($2.50) — 1.00 2.50
3-5,8-14: 3-$2.25-c begins; cont'd in Hard Corps #5. 4-Eternal Warrior-c/story. 5-Rai & Eternal Warrior app. 14-(3/94)-Reese-c(i) — .90 2.25
6-1st app. Ninjak (out of costume) — 1.20 3.00
7-1st app. Ninjak in costume — 1.40 3.50
0-(3/94, $3.50)-Wraparound chromium-c by Quesada(p); origin — 1.40 3.50
0-Gold variant — 2.40 6.00
15-49: 15-(4/94). 16-w/bound-in trading card — .90 2.25
50,51: 50-$2.50-c begins. 51-Bloodshot dies? — 1.00 2.50
Yearbook 1 (1994, $3.95) — 1.60 4.00
Special 1 (3/94, $5.95)-Zeck-c/a(p) — 2.40 6.00

BLOODSHOT (Volume Two)
July, 1997 - Present ($2.50)
Acclaim Comics (Valiant)
1-10: 1-Two covers. 5-Copycat-c. X-O Manowar-c/app — 1.00 2.50

BLOODSTRIKE (See Supreme V2#3)
1993 - No. 22, May, 1995; No. 25, May, 1994 ($1.95/$2.50)
Image Comics (Extreme Studios)
1-12, 25: Liefeld layouts in early issues. 1-Blood Brothers prelude. 2-1st app. Lethal. 5-1st app. Noble. 9-Black and White part 6 by Art Thibert; Liefeld pin-up. 9,10-Have coupon #3 & 7 for Extreme Prejudice #0. 10-(4/94). 11-(7/94). 25-(5/94) -Liefeld/Fraga-c — .80 2.00
13-22: 13-$2.50-c begins. 16:Platt-c; Prophet app. 17-19-polybagged w/card — 1.00 2.50
NOTE: ***Giffen*** *story/layouts-4-6.* ***Jae Lee*** *c-7, 8.* ***Rob Liefeld*** *layouts-1-3.* ***Art Thibert*** *c-6i.*

BLOODSTRIKE ASSASSIN
June, 1995 - No. 3, Aug, 1995; No. 0, Oct, 1995 ($2.50, limited series)
Image Comics (Extreme Studios)
0-3: 3-(8/95)-Quesada-c. 0-(10/95)-Battlestone app — 1.00 2.50

BLOOD SWORD, THE
Aug, 1988 - No. 44? 1991 ($1.50/$1.95, 68 pgs.)
Jademan Comics

GD25 FN65 NM94

1-8 ($1.50)-Kung Fu stories — 1.50
9-44: ($1.95) — .80 2.00

BLOOD SWORD DYNASTY
1989 -No. 30, 1991? ($1.25, 36 pgs.)
Jademan Comics
1-30: Ties into Blood Sword — 1.30

BLOOD SYNDICATE
Apr, 1993 - No. 35, Feb, 1996 ($1.50/$1.75/$2.50/$3.50)
DC Comics (Milestone)
1-($2.95)-Collector's Edition; polybagged with poster, trading card, & acid-free backing board (direct sale only) — 1.20 3.00
1-9,11-17: 8-Intro Kwai. 15-Byrne-c. 16-Worlds Collide Pt. 6; Superman-c/app. 17-Worlds Collide Pt. 13 — 1.50
10-($2.50, 52 pgs.)-Simonson-c — 1.00 2.50
18-27: 18-Begin $1.75-c — .70 1.75
25-($2.95, 52 pgs.) — 1.20 3.00
28, 30-32: 28-Begin $2.50-c. 30-Long Hot Summer x-over — 1.00 2.50
29, 33-34: 29-(99¢); Long Hot Summer x-over — 1.00
35-Kwai disappears — 1.40 3.50

BLOODWULF
Feb, 1995 - No. 4, May, 1995 ($2.50, limited series)
Image Comics (Extreme Studios)
1-4: 1-Liefeld-c w/4 diferent captions & alternate-c. — 1.00 2.50
Summer Special (8/95, $2.50)-Jeff Johnson-c/a; Supreme app; story takes place between Legend of Supreme #3 & Supreme #23. — 1.00 2.50

BLOODY MARY
Oct, 1996 - No. 4, Jan, 1997 ($2.25, limited series)
DC Comics (Helix)
1-4: Garth Ennis scripts; Ezquerra-c/a in all — .90 2.25

BLOODY MARY: LADY LIBERTY
Sept, 1997 - No. 4, Dec, 1997 ($2.50, limited series)
DC Comics (Helix)
1-4: Garth Ennis scripts; Ezquerra-c/a in all — 1.00 2.50

BLUEBEARD
Nov, 1993 - No. 3, Mar, 1994 ($2.95, B&W, limited series)
Slave Labor Graphics
1-3: James Robinson scripts. 2-(12/93) — 3.00
Trade paperback (6/94, $9.95) — 9.95
Trade paperback (2nd printing, 7/96, $12.95)-New-c — 12.95

BLUE BEETLE, THE (Also see All Top, Big-3, Mystery Men & Weekly Comic Magazine)
Winter, 1939-40 - No. 57, 7/48; No. 58, 4/50 - No. 60, 8/50
Fox Publ. No. 1-11, 31-60; Holyoke No. 12-30
1-Reprints from Mystery Men 1-5; Blue Beetle origin; Yarko the Great-r/from Wonder/Wonderworld 2-5 all by Eisner; Master Magician app.; (Blue Beetle in 4 different costumes) — 340.00 1020.00 3400.00
2-K-51-r by Powell/Wonderworld 8,9 — 117.00 350.00 1050.00
3-Simon-c — 83.00 250.00 750.00
4-Marijuana drug mention story — 56.00 168.00 500.00
5-Zanzibar The Magician by Tuska — 50.00 150.00 450.00
6-Dynamite Thor begins (1st); origin Blue Beetle — 47.00 141.00 425.00
7,8-Dynamo app. in both. 8-Last Thor — 44.00 132.00 400.00
9-12: 9,10-The Blackbird & The Gorilla app. in both. 10-Bondage/hypo-c 11(2/42)-The Gladiator app. 12(6/42)-The Black Fury app. — 40.00 120.00 360.00
13-V-Man begins (1st app.), ends #18; Kubert-a — 47.00 141.00 425.00
14,15-Kubert-a in both. 14-Intro. side-kick (c/text only), Sparky (called Spunky #17-19) — 41.00 123.00 370.00
16-18: 17-Brodsky-c — 36.00 108.00 290.00

Blue Beetle #58 © FOX

Blue Beetle #8 © DC

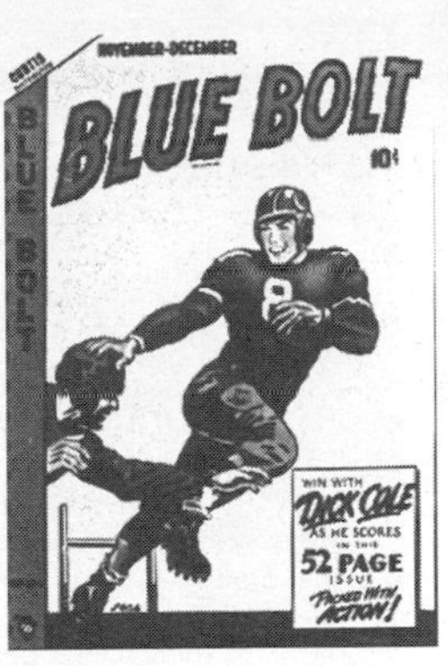

Blue Bolt V9 #6 © NOVP

GD25 FN65 NM94

19-Kubert-a 36.00 108.00 300.00
20-Origin/1st app. Tiger Squadron; Arabian Nights begin
36.00 108.00 325.00
21-26: 24-Intro. & only app. The Halo. 26-General Patton story & photo
26.00 80.00 210.00
27-Tamaa, Jungle Prince app. 24.00 71.00 190.00
28-30(2/44) 22.00 66.00 175.00
31(6/44), 33,34,36-40: 34-38-"The Threat from Saturn" serial.
20.00 60.00 160.00
32-Hitler-c 26.00 80.00 210.00
35-Extreme violence 24.00 71.00 190.00
41-45 17.50 53.00 140.00
46-The Puppeteer app. 20.00 60.00 160.00
47-Kamen & Baker-a begin 93.00 281.00 800.00
48-50 76.00 230.00 650.00
51,53 64.00 190.00 550.00
52-Kamen bondage-c; true crime stories begin 96.00 290.00 825.00
54-Used in **SOTI**. Illo, "Children call these 'headlights' comics"
109.00 330.00 900.00
55-57: 56-Used in **SOTI**, pg. 145. 57(7/48)-Last Kamen issue; becomes Western Killers? 62.00 187.00 525.00
58(4/50)-60-No Kamen-a 13.50 41.00 95.00
NOTE: ***Kamen** a-47-51, 53, 55-57; c-47, 49-52. **Powell** a-4(2). Bondage-c 9-12, 46, 52.*

BLUE BEETLE (Formerly The Thing; becomes Mr. Muscles No. 22 on)
(See Charlton Bullseye & Space Adventures)
No. 18, Feb, 1955 - No. 21, Aug, 1955
Charlton Comics

18,19-(Pre-1944-r). 18-Last pre-code issue. 19-Bouncer, Rocket Kelly-r
15.00 45.00 120.00
20-Joan Mason by Kamen 19.00 56.00 150.00
21-New material 13.00 39.00 105.00

BLUE BEETLE (Unusual Tales #1-49; Ghostly Tales #55 on)(See Captain Atom & Charlton Bullseye)
V2#1, June, 1964 - V2#5, Mar-Apr, 1965; V3#50, July, 1965 - V3#54, Feb-Mar, 1966; #1, June, 1967 - #5, Nov, 1968
Charlton Comics

V2#1-Origin/1st S.A. app. Dan Garrett-Blue Beetle 5.25 15.75 52.00
2-5: 5-Weiss illo; 1st published-a? 3.80 11.40 38.00
V3#50-54-Formerly Unusual Tales 3.80 11.40 38.00
1(1967)-Question series begins by Ditko 8.50 25.50 85.00
2-Origin Ted Kord-Blue Beetle (see Capt. Atom #83 for 1st Ted Kord Blue Beetle); Dan Garrett x-over 3.20 9.60 32.00
3-5 (All Ditko-c/a in #1-5) 2.70 8.00 27.00
1,3(Modern Comics-1977)-Reprints 1.00
NOTE: *#6 only appeared in the fanzine 'The Charlton Portfolio.'*

BLUE BEETLE (Also see Americomics, Crisis On Infinite Earths, Justice League & Showcase '94 #2-4)
June, 1986 - No. 24, May, 1988
DC Comics

1-Origin retold; intro. Firefist 1.00
2-24: 2-Origin Firefist. 5-7-The Question app. 11-14-New Teen Titans x-over. 20-Justice League app. 20,21-Millennium tie-ins 1.00

BLUEBERRY (See Lt. Blueberry & Marshal Blueberry)
1989 - No. 5, 1990 ($12.95/$14.95, graphic novel)
Marvel Comics (Epic Comics)

1,3,4,5-($12.95)-Moebius-a in all 1.60 4.85 13.00
2-($14.95) 1.85 5.50 15.00

BLUE BIRD COMICS
Late 1940's - 1964 (Giveaway)
Various Shoe Stores/Charlton Comics

nn(1947-50)(36 pgs.)-Several issues; Human Torch, Sub-Mariner app. in some
10.00 30.00 80.00
1959-Li'l Genius, Timmy the Timid Ghost, Wild Bill Hickok (All #1)
1.25 3.75 10.00
1959-(6 titles; all #2) Black Fury #1,4,5, Freddy #4, Li'l Genius, Timmy the Timid Ghost #4, Masked Raider #4, Wild Bill Hickok (Charlton)
1.25 3.75 10.00
1959-(#5) Masked Raider #21 1.25 3.75 10.00
1960-(6 titles)(All #4) Black Fury #8,9, Masked Raider, Freddy #8,9, Timmy the Timid Ghost #9, Li'l Genius #7,9 (Charlt.) 1.25 3.75 10.00
1961,1962-(All #10's) Atomic Mouse #12,13,16, Black Fury #11,12, Freddy, Li'l Genius, Masked Raider, Six Gun Heroes, Texas Rangers in Action, Timmy the Ghost, Wild Bill Hickok, Wyatt Earp #3,11-13,16-18 (Charlton)
1.00 3.00 8.00
1963-Texas Rangers #17 (Charlton) 2.00 5.00
1964-Mysteries of Unexplored Worlds #18, Teenage Hotrodders #18, War Heroes #18 (Charlton) 1.00 2.80 7.00
1965-War Heroes #18 1.20 3.00
NOTE: *More than one issue of each character could have been published each year. Numbering is sporadic.*

BLUE BIRD CHILDREN'S MAGAZINE, THE
V1#2, 1957 - No. 10 1958 (16 pgs., soft-c, regular size)
Graphic Information Service

V1#2-10: Pat, Pete & Blue Bird app. 1.60 4.00

BLUE BOLT
June, 1940 - No. 101 (V10#2), Sept-Oct, 1949
Funnies, Inc. No. 1/Novelty Press/Premium Group of Comics

V1#1-Origin Blue Bolt by Joe Simon, Sub-Zero Man, White Rider & Super Horse, Dick Cole, Wonder Boy & Sgt. Spook (1st app. of each)
240.00 720.00 2200.00
2-Simon & Kirby's 1st art & 1st super-hero (Blue Bolt)
111.00 333.00 1000.00
3-1 pg. Space Hawk by Wolverton; 2nd S&K-a on Blue Bolt (same cover date as Red Raven #1); 1st time S&K names app. in a comic; Simon-c
94.00 282.00 850.00
4,5-S&K-a in each; 5-Everett-a begins on Sub-Zero
89.00 267.00 800.00
6,8-10-S&K-a 81.00 243.00 725.00
7-S&K-c/a 89.00 267.00 800.00
11,12: 11-Robot-c 83.00 250.00 750.00
V2#1-Origin Dick Cole & The Twister; Twister x-over in Dick Cole, Sub-Zero, & Blue Bolt; origin Simba Karno who battles Dick Cole thru V2#5 & becomes main supporting character V2#6 on; battle-c 28.00 84.00 225.00
2-Origin The Twister retold in text 21.00 64.00 170.00
3-5: 5-Intro. Freezum 19.00 56.00 150.00
6-Origin Sgt. Spook retold 15.00 45.00 120.00
7-12: 7-Lois Blake becomes Blue Bolt's costume aide; last Twister. 12-Text-sty by Mickey Spillaine 12.00 38.00 100.00
V3#1-3 10.00 30.00 80.00
4-12: 4-Blue Bolt abandons costume 8.50 26.00 60.00
V4#1-Hitler, Tojo, Mussolini-c 12.00 36.00 95.00
V4#2-12: 3-Shows V4#3 on-c, V4#4 inside (9-10/43). 5-Infinity-c. 8-Last Sub-Zero 7.15 21.50 50.00
V5#1-8, V6#1-3,5-10, V7#1-12 6.50 19.50 45.00
V6#4-Racist cover 7.15 21.50 50.00
V8#1-6,8-12, V9#1-5,7,8 5.70 17.00 40.00
V8#7,V9#6,9-L. B. Cole-c 12.00 36.00 95.00
V10#1(#100) 5.70 17.00 40.00
V10#2(#101)-Last Dick Cole, Blue Bolt 5.70 17.00 40.00
NOTE: ***Everett** c-V1#4, 11, V2#1, 2. **Gustavson** a-V1#1-12, V2#1-7. **Kiefer** c-V3#1. **Rico** a-V6#10, V7#4. Blue Bolt not in V9#8.*

BLUE BOLT (Becomes Ghostly Weird Stories #120 on; continuation of Novelty Blue Bolt) (...Weird Tales of Terror #111,...Weird Tales #112-119)
No. 102, Nov-Dec, 1949 - No. 119, May-June, 1953

Blue Bolt #115 © STAR

Blue Devil #3 © DC

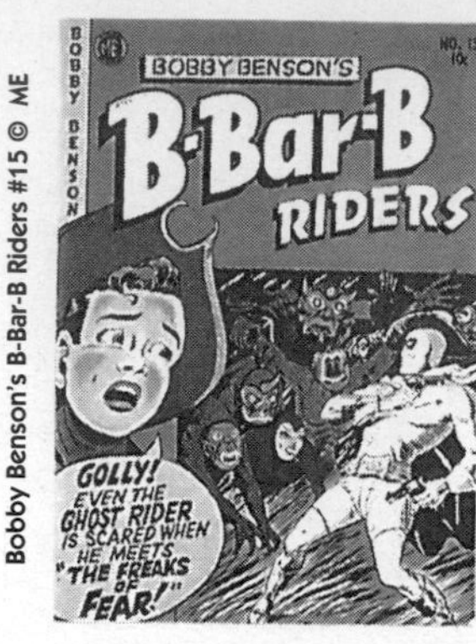

Bobby Benson's B-Bar-B Riders #15 © ME

GD25 FN65 NM94

Star Publications
102-The Chameleon, & Target app. 26.00 77.00 190.00
103,104-The Chameleon app. 104-Last Target 24.00 73.00 180.00
105-Origin Blue Bolt (from #1) retold by Simon; Chameleon & Target app.; opium den story 40.00 120.00 325.00
106-Blue Bolt by S&K begins; Spacehawk reprints from Target by Wolverton begin, ends #110; Sub-Zero begins; ends #109 40.00 120.00 300.00
107-110: 108-Last S&K Blue Bolt reprint. 109-Wolverton-c(r)/inside Spacehawk splash. 110-Target app. 399.00 118.00 290.00
111,112: 111-Red Rocket & The Mask-r; last Blue Bolt; 1pg. L. B. Cole-a 112-Last Torpedo Man app. 36.00 109.00 270.00
113-Wolverton's Spacehawk-r/Target V3#7 39.00 116.00 290.00
114,116: 116-Jungle Jo-r 36.00 109.00 270.00
115-Sgt. Spook app. 39.00 116.00 290.00
117-Jo-Jo & Blue Bolt-r 37.00 111.00 280.00
118-"White Spirit" by Wood 39.00 116.00 290.00
119-Disbrow/Cole-c; Jungle Jo-r 37.00 111.00 280.00
Accepted Reprint #103(1957?, nd) 7.85 23.50 55.00
NOTE: ***L. B. Cole*** *c-102-108, 110 on.* ***Disbrow*** *a-112(2), 113(3), 114(2), 115(2), 116-118.* ***Hollingsworth*** *a-117.* ***Palais*** *a-112r. Sci/Fi c-105-110. Horror c-111.*

BLUE BULLETEER, THE (Also see Femforce Special)
1989 ($2.25, B&W, one-shot)
AC Comics
1-Origin by Bill Black; Bill Ward-a 1.00 2.50

BLUE BULLETEER (Also see Femforce Special)
1996 ($5.95, B&W, one-shot)
AC Comics
1-Photo-c 2.40 6.00

BLUE CIRCLE COMICS (Also see Roly Poly Comic Book)
June, 1944 - No. 5, Mar, 1945; No. 6, 1950s
Enwil Associates/Rural Home
1-The Blue Circle begins (1st app.); origin & 1st app. Steel Fist 19.00 56.00 150.00
2,3: 3-Hitler parody-c 14.00 41.00 110.00
4-6: 5-Last Steel Fist. 6-(1950s)-Colossal Features-r 8.50 26.00 60.00

BLUE DEVIL (See Fury of Firestorm #24, Underworld Unleashed, Starman #38)
June, 1984 - No. 31, Dec, 1986 (75¢/$1.25)
DC Comics
1-30: 4-Origin Nebiros. 7-Gil Kane-a. 8-Giffen-a. 17-19-Crisis x-over 1.00
31-($1.25, 52 pgs.) 1.25
Annual 1 (11/85)-Team-ups w/Black Orchid, Creeper, Demon, Madame Xanadu, Man-Bat & Phantom Stranger 1.25

BLUE PHANTOM, THE
June-Aug, 1962
Dell Publishing Co.
1(01-066-208)-by Fred Fredericks 2.25 6.75 24.00

BLUE RIBBON COMICS (...Mystery Comics No. 9-18)
Nov, 1939 - No. 22, Mar, 1942 (1st MLJ series)
MLJ Magazines
1-Dan Hastings, Richy the Amazing Boy, Rang-A-Tang the Wonder Dog begin (1st app. of each); Little Nemo app. (not by W. McCay); Jack Cole-a(3) 250.00 750.00 2500.00
2-Bob Phantom, Silver Fox (both in #3), Rang-A-Tang Club & Cpl. Collins begin (1st app. of each); Jack Cole-a 100.00 300.00 900.00
3-J. Cole-a 69.00 207.00 625.00
4-Doc Strong, The Green Falcon, & Hercules begin (1st app. each); origin & 1st app. The Fox & Ty-Gor, Son of the Tiger 75.00 225.00 675.00
5-8: 8-Last Hercules; 6,7-Biro, Meskin-a. 7-Fox app. on-c 53.00 159.00 475.00
9-(Scarce)-Origin & 1st app. Mr. Justice (2/41) 222.00 667.00 2000.00
10-13: 12-Last Doc Strong. 13-Inferno, the Flame Breather begins, ends #19; Devil-c 81.00 243.00 725.00
14,15,17,18: 15-Last Green Falcon 69.00 207.00 625.00
16-Origin & 1st app. Captain Flag (9/41) 139.00 417.00 1250.00
19-22: 20-Last Ty-Gor. 22-Origin Mr. Justice retold 69.00 207.00 625.00
NOTE: ***Biro*** *c-3-5; a-2 (Cpl. Collins & Scoop Cody).* ***S. Cooper*** *c-9-17. 20-22 contain "Tales From the Witch's Cauldron" (same strip as "Stories of the Black Witch" in Zip Comics). Mr. Justice c-9-18. Captain Flag c-16(w/Mr. Justice), 19-22.*

BLUE RIBBON COMICS (Becomes Teen-Age Diary Secrets #4)(See Heckle & Jeckle)
Feb, 1949 - No. 6, Aug, 1949
Blue Ribbon (St. John)
1,3-Heckle & Jeckle 7.15 21.50 50.00
2(4/49)-Diary Secrets; Baker-c 15.00 45.00 120.00
4(6/49)-Teen-Age Diary Secrets; Baker c/a(2) 15.50 47.00 125.00
5(8/49)-Teen-Age Diary Secrets; Oversize; photo-c; Baker-a(2)- Continues as Teen-Age Diary Secrets 20.00 60.00 160.00
6-Dinky Duck(8/49) 4.00 10.00 20.00

BLUE-RIBBON COMICS
Nov, 1983 - No. 14, Dec, 1984
Red Circle Prod./Archie Ent. No. 5 on
1-S&K-r/Advs. of the Fly #1,2; Williamson/Torres-r/Fly #2; Ditko-c 1.00
2-14: 3-Origin Steel Sterling. 5-S&K Shield-r. 6,7-The Fox app. 8-Toth centerspread. 8,11-Black Hood. 12-Thunder Agents. 13-Thunder Bunny. 14-Web & Jaguar 1.00
NOTE: ***N. Adams*** *a(r)-8.* ***Buckler*** *a-4i.* ***Nino*** *a-2i.* ***McWilliams*** *a-8.* ***Morrow*** *a-8.*

BLUE STREAK (See Holyoke One-Shot No. 8)

BLYTHE (Marge's)
No. 1072, Jan-Mar, 1960
Dell Publishing Co.
Four Color 1072 4.50 13.50 50.00

B-MAN (See Double-Dare Adventures)

BO (Tom Cat #4 on) (Also see Big Shot #29 & Dixie Dugan)
June, 1955 - No. 3, Oct, 1955 (A dog)
Charlton Comics Group
1-3: Newspaper reprints by Frank Beck 6.00 18.00 42.00

BOATNIKS, THE (See Walt Disney Showcase No. 1)

BOB & BETTY & SANTA'S WISHING WHISTLE
1941 (Christmas giveaway, 12 pgs.)
Sears Roebuck & Co.
nn 8.50 26.00 60.00

BOBBY BENSON'S B-BAR-B RIDERS (Radio) (See Best of The West, The Lemonade Kid & Model Fun)
May-June, 1950 - No. 20, May-June, 1953
Magazine Enterprises
1-The Lemonade Kid begins; Powell-a (Scarce) 36.00 108.00 325.00
2 13.00 39.00 105.00
3-5: 4,5-Lemonade Kid-c (#4-Spider-c) 10.00 30.00 80.00
6-8,10 8.75 26.25 70.00
9,11,13-Frazetta-c; Ghost Rider in #13-15 by Ayers-a. 13-Ghost Rider-c 26.00 80.00 210.00
12,17-20: 20-(A-1 #88) 8.75 26.25 65.00
14-Decapitation/Bondage-c & story; horror-c 15.00 45.00 120.00
15-Ghost Rider-c 12.00 36.00 95.00
16-Photo-c 10.00 30.00 80.00
...in the Tunnel of Gold-(1936, 5-1/4x8"; 100 pgs.) Radio giveaway by

GD25 FN65 NM94

Bob Steele Western #1 © FAW

Bodycount #1 © Mirage Studios

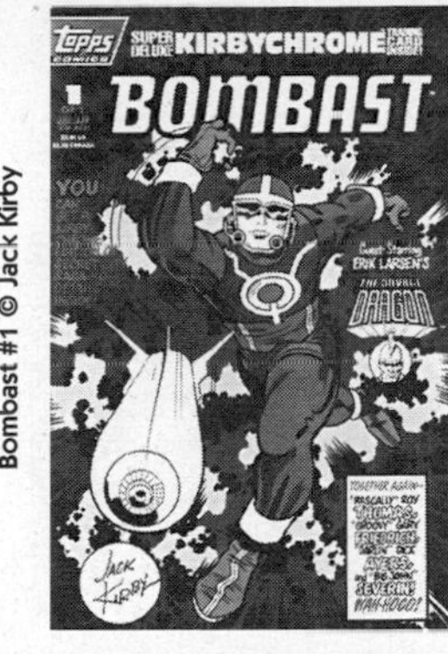

Bombast #1 © Jack Kirby

GD25 FN65 NM94

Hecker-H.O. Company(H.O. Oats); contains 22 color pgs. of comics, rest in novel form 9.15 27.50 55.00
...And The Lost Herd-same as above 9.15 27.50 55.00
NOTE: *Ayers a-13-15, 20. Powell a-1-12(4 ea.), 13(3), 14-16(Red Hawk only); c-1-8,1 0, 12. Lemonade Kid in most 1-13.*

BOBBY COMICS
May, 1946
Universal Phoenix Features
1-By S. M. Iger 6.50 19.50 45.00

BOBBY SHELBY COMICS
1949
Shelby Cycle Co./Harvey Publications
nn 3.20 8.00 16.00

BOBBY SHERMAN (TV)
Feb, 1972 - No. 7, Oct, 1972
Charlton Comics
1-Based on TV show "Getting Together" 3.00 9.00 30.00
2-7: 4-Photo-c 2.50 7.50 20.00

BOB COLT (Movie star)(See XMas Comics)
Nov, 1950 - No. 10, May, 1952
Fawcett Publications
1-Bob Colt, his horse Buckskin & sidekick Pablo begin; photo front/back-c begin 36.00 108.00 320.00
2 24.00 71.00 190.00
3-5 19.00 56.00 150.00
6-Flying Saucer story 16.00 49.00 130.00
7-10: 9-Last photo back-c 15.00 45.00 120.00

BOB HOPE (See Adventures of... & Calling All Boys #12)

BOB MARLEY, TALE OF THE TUFF GONG (Music star)
Aug, 1994 - No, 3, Nov, 1994 ($5.95, limited series)
Marvel Comics
1-3 2.40 6.00

BOB POWELL'S TIMELESS TALES
March, 1989 ($2.00, B&W)
Eclipse Comics
1-Powell-r/Black Cat #5 (Scarlet Arrow), 9 & Race for the Moon #1 .80 2.00

BOB SCULLY, TWO-FISTED HICK DETECTIVE
No date (1930's) (36 pgs., 9-1/2x12", B&W, paper cover)
Humor Publ. Co.
nn-By Howard Dell; not reprints 8.75 26.25 70.00

BOB SON OF BATTLE
No. 729, Nov, 1956
Dell Publishing Co.
Four Color 729 2.75 8.00 30.00

BOB STEELE WESTERN (Movie star)
Dec, 1950 - No. 10, June, 1952; 1990
Fawcett Publications/AC Comics
1-Bob Steele & his horse Bullet begin; photo front/back-c begin 47.00 141.00 420.00
2 26.00 80.00 210.00
3-5: 4-Last photo back-c 20.00 60.00 160.00
6-10: 10-Last photo-c 15.50 47.00 125.00
1 (1990, $2.75, B&W)-Bob Steele & Rocky Lane reprints; photo-c & inside covers 1.10 2.75

BOB SWIFT (Boy Sportsman)
May, 1951 - No. 5, Jan, 1952
Fawcett Publications
1 7.15 21.50 50.00
2-5: Saunders painted-c #1-5 4.25 13.00 28.00

BOB, THE GALACTIC BUM
Feb, 1995 - No. 4, June, 1995 ($1.95, limited series)
DC Comics
1-4: 1-Lobo app. .80 2.00

BODY BAGS
Sept, 1996 - No. 4, Jan, 1997 ($2.95, mini-series, mature)(1st Blanc Noir series)
Dark Horse Comics (Blanc Noir)
1-Jason Pearson-c/a/scripts in all. 1-Intro Clownface & Panda. 1.25 3.75 10.00
2 1.60 4.85 13.00
3,4 1.00 2.60 6.50

BODYCOUNT (Also see Casey Jones & Raphael)
Mar, 1996 - No. 4, July, 1996 ($2.50, limited series)
Image Comics (Highbrow Entertainment)
1-4: Kevin Eastman-a(p)/scripts; Simon Bisley-c/a(i); Turtles app. 1.00 2.50

BOLD ADVENTURES
Oct, 1983 - No. 3, June, 1984 ($1.50)
Pacific Comics
1-Time Force, Anaconda, & The Weirdling begin 1.50
2,3: 2-Soldiers of Fortune begins. 3-Spitfire 1.50
NOTE: *Kaluta c-3. Nebres a-1-3. Nino a-2, 3. Severin a-3.*

BOLD STORIES (Also see Candid Tales & It Rhymes With Lust)
Mar, 1950 - July, 1950 (Digest size, 144 pgs.)
Kirby Publishing Co.
Mar issue (Very Rare) - Contains "The Ogre of Paris" by Wood 100.00 300.00 900.00
May issue (Very Rare) - Contains "The Cobra's Kiss" by Graham Ingels (21 pgs.) 86.00 258.00 775.00
July issue (Very Rare) - Contains "The Ogre of Paris" by Wood 75.00 225.00 675.00

BOLT AND STAR FORCE SIX
1984 ($1.75)
Americomics
1-Origin Bolt & Star Force Six .80 2.00
Special 1 (1984, $2.00, 52pgs., B&W) .80 2.00

BOMBARDIER (See Bee 29, the Bombardier & Cinema Comics Herald)

BOMBAST
1993 ($2.95, one-shot) (Created by Jack Kirby)
Topps Comics
1-Polybagged w/Kirbychrome trading card; Savage Dragon app.; Kirby-c; has coupon for Amberchrome Secret City Saga #0 1.20 3.00

BOMBA THE JUNGLE BOY (TV)
Sept-Oct, 1967 - No. 7, Sept-Oct, 1968 (12¢)
National Periodical Publications
1-Intro. Bomba; Infantino/Anderson-c 2.15 6.50 17.00
2-7 1.25 3.75 10.00

BOMBER COMICS
Mar, 1944 - No. 4, Winter, 1944-45
Elliot Publ. Co./Melverne Herald/Farrell/Sunrise Times
1-Wonder Boy, & Kismet, Man of Fate begin 44.00 132.00 400.00
2-4: 2-4-Have Classics Comics ad to HRN 20. 4-Hitler, Tojo & Mussolini-c; Sensation Comics #13-c/swipe 30.00 90.00 240.00

BONANZA (TV)
June-Aug, 1960 - No. 37, Aug, 1970 (All Photo-c)
Dell/Gold Key

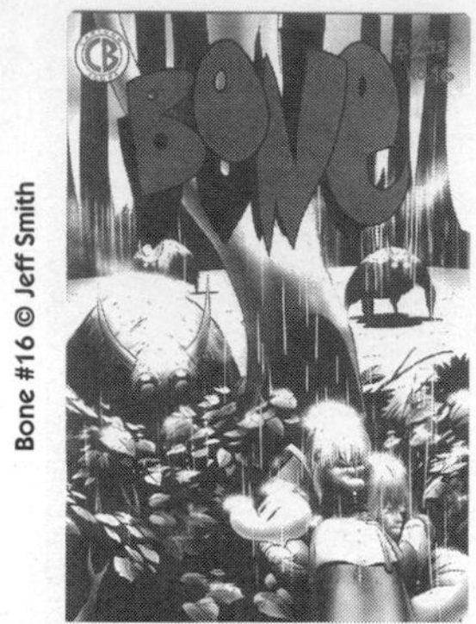

Bone #16 © Jeff Smith

Boof #2 © Todd McFarlane

Books of Magic #28 © DC

	GD25	FN65	NM94
Four Color 1110 (6-8/60)	34.00	102.00	375.00
Four Color 1221,1283, & #01070-207, 01070-210	16.00	49.00	180.00
1(12/62-Gold Key)	16.00	49.00	180.00
2	8.00	25.00	90.00
3-10	7.00	20.00	75.00
11-20	5.50	16.50	60.00
21-37: 29-Reprints	4.50	13.50	50.00

BONE
July, 1991 - Present ($2.95, B&W)
Cartoon Books/Image Comics #21 on

	GD25	FN65	NM94
1-Jeff Smith-c/a in all	10.00	30.00	100.00
1-2nd printing	1.50	4.50	12.00
1-3rd thru 5th printings		1.60	4.00
2-1st printing	6.00	18.00	60.00
2-2nd & 3rd printings		2.00	5.00
3-1st printing	5.00	15.00	50.00
3-2nd thru 4th printings		1.60	4.00
4,5	2.50	7.50	20.00
6-8	1.25	3.75	10.00
9,10	1.00	2.80	7.00
11,12		1.20	3.00
13-20		1.00	2.50
13 1/2	1.00	3.00	8.00
13 1/2 (Gold)	1.25	3.75	10.00
21,22: 21-1st Image issue ($2.95)		1.00	2.50
23-29		1.20	3.00
1-24-($2.95): 1-Image reprints begin w/new-c. 2-Allred pin-up.		1.20	3.00
Holiday Special (1993, giveaway)		1.20	3.00
Sourcebook-San Diego Edition	1.00	2.80	7.00
Complete Bone Adventures Vol 1 (1993, $12.95, r/#1-6)	1.60	4.85	13.00
Complete Bone Adventures Vol 2 (1994, $12.95, r/#7-12)	1.60	4.85	13.00
Volume 1-($19.95, hard-c)-"Out From Boneville"			20.00
Volume 1-($12.95, soft-c)			13.00
Volume 2-($22.95, hard-c)-"The Great Cow Race"			23.00
Volume 2-($14.95, soft-c)			15.00
Volume 3-($24.95, hard-c)-"Eyes of the Storm"			25.00
Volume 3-($16.95, soft-c)			17.00
Volume 4-($24.95, hard-c)-"The Dragonslayer"			25.00

NOTE: *Printings not listed sell for cover price.*

BONGO (See Story Hour Series)

BONGO & LUMPJAW (Disney, see Walt Disney Showcase #3)
No. 706, June, 1956; No. 886, Mar, 1958
Dell Publishing Co.

	GD25	FN65	NM94
Four Color 706 (#1)	4.00	12.00	45.00
Four Color 886	3.00	9.00	35.00

BON VOYAGE (See Movie Classics)

BOOF
July, 1994 - No. 6, Dec, 1994 ($1.95)
Image Comics (Todd McFarlane Productions)

	GD25	FN65	NM94
1-6		.80	2.00

BOOF AND THE BRUISE CREW
July, 1994 - No. 6, Dec, 1994 ($1.95)
Image Comics (Todd McFarlane Productions)

	GD25	FN65	NM94
1-6		.80	2.00

BOOK AND RECORD SET (See Power Record Comics)

BOOK OF ALL COMICS
1945 (196 pgs.)(Inside f/c has Green Publ. blacked out)
William H. Wise

	GD25	FN65	NM94
nn-Green Mask, Puppeteer & The Bouncer	31.00	94.00	250.00

BOOK OF BALLADS AND SAGAS, THE
Oct, 1995 - Present ($2.95/$3.50/$3.25, B&W)
Green Man Press

	GD25	FN65	NM94
1,2: 1-Vess-c/a; Gaiman story.		1.20	3.00
3-($3.50)		1.40	3.50
4-($3.25)			3.25

BOOK OF COMICS, THE
No date (1944) (25¢, 132 pgs.)
William H. Wise

	GD25	FN65	NM94
nn-Captain V app.	31.00	94.00	250.00

BOOK OF FATE, THE (See Fate)
Feb, 1997 - Present ($2.25/$2.50)
DC Comics

	GD25	FN65	NM94
1-7: 4-Two-Face-c/app. 6-Convergence		.90	2.25
8-11: 8-Begin 2.50-c. 11-Sentinel app.		1.00	2.50

BOOK OF LOVE (See Fox Giants)

BOOK OF NIGHT, THE
July, 1987 - No. 3, 1987 ($1.75, B&W)
Dark Horse Comics

	GD25	FN65	NM94
1-3: Reprints from Epic Illustrated; Vess-a		.75	1.80

BOOK OF THE DEAD
Dec, 1993 - No. 4, Mar, 1994 ($1.75, limited series, 52 pgs.)
Marvel Comics

	GD25	FN65	NM94
1-4: 1-Ploog Frankenstein & Morrow Man-Thing-r begin; Wrightson-r/Chamber of Darkness #7. 2-Morrow new painted-c; Chaykin/Morrow Man-Thing; Krigstein-r/Uncanny Tales #54; r/Fear #10. 3-r/Astonishing Tales #10 & Starlin Man-Thing. 3,4-Painted-c		1.20	3.00

BOOKS OF FAERIE, THE
Mar, 1997 - No. 3, May,1997 ($2.50, limited series)
DC Comics (Vertigo)

	GD25	FN65	NM94
1-3-Gross-a		1.00	2.50

BOOKS OF MAGIC
1990 - No. 4, 1991 ($3.95, 52 pgs., limited series, mature)
DC Comics

	GD25	FN65	NM94
1-Bolton painted-c/a; Phantom Stranger app.; Gaiman scripts in all	1.05	3.15	8.50
2,3: 2-John Constantine, Dr. Fate, Spectre, Deadman app. 3-Dr. Occult app.; minor Sandman app.		2.10	5.25
4-Early Death-c/app. (early 1991)		2.50	6.25
Trade paperback-($19.95)-Reprints limited series			20.00

BOOKS OF MAGIC
May, 1994 - Present ($1.95, mature)
DC Comics (Vertigo)

	GD25	FN65	NM94
1-Charles Vess-c		1.60	4.00
1-Platinum	1.00	3.00	8.00
2,3		1.60	4.00
4-Death app.		2.00	5.00
5-14; Charles Vess-c		1.00	2.50
15-45: 15-$2.50-c begins. 22-Kaluta-c. 25-Death-c/app; Bachalo-c		1.00	2.50
Bindings (1995, $12.95, trade paperback)-r/#1-4			13.00
Reckonings (1997, $12.95, trade paperback)-r/#14-20			13.00
Summonings (1996, $17.50, trade paperback)-r/#5-13, Vertigo Rave #1			17.50

BOONDOGGLE
Mar, 1995 - No. 4 ($2.95, B&W)

Booster Gold #22 © DC

Box Office Poison #3 © Alex Robinson

Boy Comics #9 © LEV

Knight Press

	GD25	FN65	NM94
1-4: Stegelin-c/a/scripts		1.20	3.00

BOONDOGGLE
Jan, 1997 - Present ($2.95, B&W)
Caliber Press

	GD25	FN65	NM94
1,2: Stegelin-c/a/scripts		1.20	3.00

BOOSTER GOLD (See Justice League #4)
Feb, 1986 - No. 25, Feb, 1988 (75¢)
DC Comics

	GD25	FN65	NM94
1-25: 4-Rose & Thorn app. 6-Origin. 6,7,23-Superman app. 8,9-LSH app. 22-JLI app. 24,25-Millennium tie-ins			1.00

NOTE: ***Austin** c-22i. **Byrne** c-23i.*

BOOTS AND HER BUDDIES
No. 5, 9/48 - No. 9, 9/49; 12/55 - No. 3, 1956
Standard Comics/Visual Editions/Argo (NEA Service)

	GD25	FN65	NM94
5-Strip-r	12.00	36.00	100.00
6,8	8.75	26.25	65.00
7-(Scarce)-Spanking panels(3)	12.00	36.00	95.00
9-(Scarce)-Frazetta-a (2 pgs.)	21.00	64.00	170.00
1-3(Argo-1955-56)-Reprints	4.25	13.00	28.00

BOOTS & SADDLES (TV)
No. 919, July, 1958; No. 1029, Sept, 1959; No. 1116, Aug, 1960
Dell Publishing Co.

	GD25	FN65	NM94
Four Color 919 (#1)-Photo-c	7.00	22.00	80.00
Four Color 1029, 1116-Photo-c	4.50	13.50	50.00

BORDERLINE
June, 1992 ($2.25, B&W)
Friction Press

	GD25	FN65	NM94
0-Ashcan edition; 1st app. of Cliff Broadway		.80	2.00
1-Painted-c		1.20	3.00
1-Special Edition (bagged w/ photo, S&N)		1.60	4.00

BORDER PATROL
May-June, 1951 - No. 3, Sept-Oct, 1951
P. L. Publishing Co.

	GD25	FN65	NM94
1	8.75	26.25	70.00
2,3	7.15	21.50	50.00

BORDER WORLDS (Also see Megaton Man)
7/86 - No. 7, 1987; V2#1, 1990 - No. 4, 1990 ($1.95-$2.00, B&W, mature)
Kitchen Sink Press

	GD25	FN65	NM94
1-7: ($1.95)-Donald Simpson-c/a/scripts		.80	2.00
V2#1-4 ($2.00)-Donald Simpson-c/a/scripts		.80	2.00

BORIS KARLOFF TALES OF MYSTERY (TV) (...Thriller No. 1,2)
No. 3, April, 1963 - No. 97, Feb, 1980
Gold Key

	GD25	FN65	NM94
3-8,10-(Two #5's, 10/63,11/63): 5-(10/63)-11 pgs. Toth-a. 10-Orlando-a	2.50	7.50	20.00
9-Wood-a	2.50	7.50	24.00
11-Williamson-a, 8 pgs.; Orlando-a, 5 pgs.	2.50	7.50	24.00
12-Torres, McWilliams-a; Orlando-a(2)	2.25	6.75	18.00
13,14,16-20	1.75	5.75	14.00
15-Crandall	2.00	6.00	16.00
21-Jeff Jones-a(3 pgs.) "The Screaming Skull"	2.00	6.00	16.00
22-30: 23-Reprint; photo-c	1.25	3.75	10.00
31-50: 36-Weiss-a	1.00	2.80	7.00
51-74: 74-Origin & 1st app. Taurus		2.00	5.00
75-79,87-97: 90-r/Torres, McWilliams-a/#12; Morrow-c		1.20	3.00
80-86-(52 pgs.)		2.00	5.00
Story Digest 1(7/70-Gold Key)-All text	2.50	7.50	20.00

(See Mystery Comics Digest No. 2, 5, 8, 11, 14, 17, 20, 23, 26)

NOTE: ***Bolle** a-51-54, 56, 58, 59. **McWilliams** a-12, 14, 18, 19, 72, 80, 81, 93. **Orlando** a-11-15, 21. Reprints: 78, 81-86, 88, 90, 92, 95, 97.*

BORIS KARLOFF THRILLER (TV) (Becomes Boris Karloff Tales...)
Oct, 1962 - No. 2, Jan, 1963 (80 pgs.)
Gold Key

	GD25	FN65	NM94
1-Photo-c	5.00	15.00	55.00
2	3.60	11.00	40.00

BORIS THE BEAR INSTANT COLOR CLASSICS
July, 1987 - No. 3, 1987 ($1.75/$1.95)
Dark Horse Comics

	GD25	FN65	NM94
1-3		.80	2.00

BORN AGAIN
1978 (39¢)
Spire Christian Comics (Fleming H. Revell Co.)

	GD25	FN65	NM94
nn-Watergate, Nixon, etc.			1.00

BOUNCER, THE (Formerly Green Mask #9)
1944 - No. 14, Jan, 1945
Fox Features Syndicate

	GD25	FN65	NM94
nn(1944, #10?)	20.00	60.00	160.00
11(#1)(9/44)-Origin; Rocket Kelly, One Round Hogan app.	16.00	49.00	130.00
12-14: 14-Reprints no # issue	12.00	38.00	100.00

BOUNTY GUNS (See Luke Short's..., Four Color 739)

BOX OFFICE POISON
1996 - Present ($2.95, B&W)
Antarctic Press

	GD25	FN65	NM94
1-7-Alex Robinson-s/a in all			2.95
...Super Special 0 (5/97, $4.95)			4.95

BOY AND HIS 'BOT, A
Jan, 1987 ($1.95)
Now Comics

	GD25	FN65	NM94
1-A Holiday Special		.80	2.00

BOY AND THE PIRATES, THE (Movie)
No. 1117, Aug, 1960
Dell Publishing Co.

	GD25	FN65	NM94
Four Color 1117-Photo-c	5.50	16.50	60.00

BOY COMICS (Captain Battle No. 1 & 2; Boy Illustories No. 43-108)
(Stories by Charles Biro)(Also see Squeeks)
No. 3, Apr, 1942 - No. 119, Mar, 1956
Lev Gleason Publications (Comic House)

	GD25	FN65	NM94
3(No.1)-Origin Crimebuster, Bombshell & Young Robin Hood; Yankee Longago, Case 1001-1008, Swoop Storm, & Boy Movies begin; 1st app. Iron Jaw; Crimebuster's pet monkey Squeeks begins	240.00	720.00	2200.00
4-Hitler, Tojo, Mussolini-c	94.00	282.00	850.00
5	71.00	213.00	640.00
6-Origin Iron Jaw; origin & death of Iron Jaw's son; Little Dynamite begins, ends #39; 1st Iron Jaw-c	178.00	534.00	1600.00
7-Flag & Hitler, Tojo, Mussolini-c	64.00	192.00	575.00
8-Death of Iron Jaw; Iron Jaw-c	71.00	213.00	640.00
9-Iron Jaw-c	64.00	192.00	575.00
10-Return of Iron Jaw; classic Biro-c; Iron Jaw-c	94.00	282.00	850.00
11-Classic Iron Jaw-c	60.00	180.00	540.00
12,13	44.00	132.00	400.00
14-Iron Jaw-c	47.00	141.00	420.00
15-Death of Iron Jaw	58.00	174.00	520.00
16,18-20	29.00	88.00	235.00
17-Flag-c	33.00	100.00	265.00

21-29,31,32-(All 68 pgs.). 28-Yankee Longago ends. 32-Swoop Storm

Boy Commandos #35 © DC

Boy Explorers Comics #1 © HARV

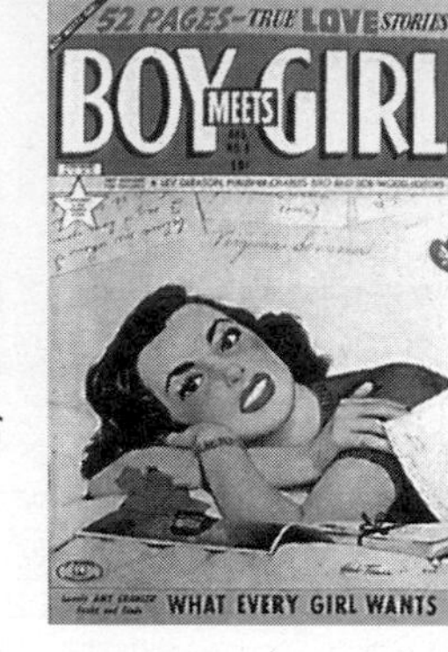

Boy Meets Girl #4 © LEV

	GD25	FN65	NM94
& Young Robin Hood end	20.00	60.00	160.00
30-(68 pgs.)-Origin Crimebuster retold	29.00	86.00	230.00
33-40: 34-Crimebuster story(2); suicide-c/story	14.50	43.00	115.00
41-50	12.00	38.00	100.00
51-59: 57-Dilly Duncan begins, ends #71	11.30	34.00	90.00
60-Iron Jaw returns	12.00	38.00	100.00
61-Origin Crimebuster & Iron Jaw retold	14.50	43.00	115.00
62-Death of Iron Jaw explained	13.00	39.00	105.00
63-73: 63-McWilliams-a. 73-Frazetta 1-pg. ad	9.50	28.00	75.00
74-88: 80-1st app. Rocky X of the Rocketeers; becomes "Rocky X" #101; Iron Jaw, Sniffer & the Deadly Dozen in 80-118	8.50	26.00	60.00
89-92-The Claw serial app. in all	8.75	26.25	65.00
93-Claw cameo; Rocky X by Sid Check	8.50	26.00	60.00
94-97,99	7.85	23.50	55.00
98-Rocky X by Sid Check	8.50	26.00	60.00
100	8.50	26.00	60.00
101-107,109,111,119: 111-Crimebuster becomes Chuck Chandler. 119-Last Crimebuster	6.50	19.50	45.00
108,110,112-118-Kubert-a	7.85	23.50	55.00

(See Giant Boy Book of Comics)

NOTE: *Boy Movies in 3-5,40,41. Iron Jaw app.-3, 4, 6, 8, 10, 11, 13-15; returns-60-62, 68, 69, 72-79, 81-118.* ***Biro*** *c-all.* ***Briefer*** *a-5, 13, 14, 16-20 among others.* ***Fuje*** *a-55, 18 pgs.* ***Palais*** *a-14, 16, 17, 19, 20 among others.*

BOY COMMANDOS (See Detective #64 & World's Finest Comics #8)
Winter, 1942-43 - No. 36, Nov-Dec, 1949
National Periodical Publications

	GD25	FN65	NM94
1-Origin Liberty Belle; The Sandman & The Newsboy Legion x-over in Boy Commandos; S&K-a, 48 pgs.; S&K cameo? (classic-c)	430.00	1290.00	4300.00
2-Last Liberty Belle; Hitler-c; S&K-a, 46 pgs.	122.00	366.00	1100.00
3-S&K-a, 45 pgs.	83.00	250.00	750.00
4-6: 6-S&K-a	60.00	180.00	540.00
7-10	41.00	123.00	365.00
11-Infinity-c	30.00	90.00	240.00
12-16,18-19-More S&K	23.00	69.00	185.00
17,20-Sci/fi-c/stories	25.00	75.00	200.00
21,22,24,25: 22-Judy Canova x-over. 24-1st costumed superhero satire-c. (11-12/47).	17.50	53.00	140.00
23-S&K-c/a(all)	21.00	64.00	170.00
26-Flying Saucer story (3-4/48)-4th of this theme	19.00	56.00	150.00
27,28,30: 30-Cleveland Indians story	17.00	51.00	135.00
29-S&K story (1)	19.00	56.00	150.00
31-35: 32-Dale Evans app. on-c & in story. 34-Intro. Wolf, their mascot	16.00	49.00	130.00
36-Intro The Atomobile c/sci-fi story (Scarce)	26.00	80.00	210.00

NOTE: *Most issues signed by* ***Simon & Kirby*** *are not by them.* ***S&K*** *c-1-9, 13, 14, 17, 21, 23, 24, 30-32.* ***Feller*** *c-30.*

BOY COMMANDOS
Sept-Oct, 1973 - No. 2, Nov-Dec, 1973 (G.A. S&K reprints)
National Periodical Publications

	GD25	FN65	NM94
1,2: 1-Reprints story from Boy Commandos #1 plus-c & Detective #66 by S&K. 2-Infantino/Orlando-c		2.40	6.00

BOY COWBOY (Also see Amazing Adventures & Science Comics)
1950 (8 pgs. in color)
Ziff-Davis Publ. Co.

	GD25	FN65	NM94
nn-Sent to subscribers of Ziff-Davis mags. & ordered through mail for 10¢; used to test market for Kid Cowboy Estimated value			150.00

BOY DETECTIVE
May-June, 1951 - No. 4, May, 1952
Avon Periodicals

	GD25	FN65	NM94
1	14.00	41.00	110.00
2,3: 3-Kinstler-c	8.75	26.25	65.00
4-Kinstler-c	12.00	36.00	95.00

BOY EXPLORERS COMICS (Terry and The Pirates No. 3 on)
May-June, 1946 - No. 2, Sept-Oct, 1946
Family Comics (Harvey Publications)

	GD25	FN65	NM94
1-Intro The Explorers, Duke of Broadway, Calamity Jane & Danny Dixon... Cadet; S&K-c/a, 24 pgs.	49.00	147.00	440.00
2-(Scarce)-Small size (5-1/2x8-1/2"; B&W; 32 pgs.) Distributed to mail subscribers only; S&K-a Estimated value			$250.00-$400.00

(Also see All New No. 15, Flash Gordon No. 5, and Stuntman No. 3)

BOY ILLUSTORIES (See Boy Comics)

BOY LOVES GIRL (Boy Meets Girl No. 1-24)
No. 25, July, 1952 - No. 57, June, 1956
Lev Gleason Publications

	GD25	FN65	NM94
25(#1)	5.70	17.00	35.00
26,27,29-33: 30-33-Serial, 'Loves of My Life	4.00	10.00	20.00
34-42: 39-Lingerie panels	3.60	9.00	18.00
28-Drug propaganda story	4.15	12.50	25.00
43-Toth-a	5.70	17.00	35.00
44-50: 50-Last pre-code (2/55)	2.80	7.00	14.00
51-57: 57-Ann Brewster-a	2.00	5.00	10.00

BOY MEETS GIRL (Boy Loves Girl No. 25 on)
Feb, 1950 - No. 24, June, 1952 (No. 1-17: 52 pgs.)
Lev Gleason Publications

	GD25	FN65	NM94
1-Guardineer-a	6.50	19.50	45.00
2	4.15	12.50	25.00
3-10	4.00	11.00	22.00
11-24	3.60	9.00	18.00

NOTE: ***Briefer*** *a-24.* ***Fuje*** *c-3,7. Painted-c 1-17. Photo-c 19-21, 23.*

BOYS' AND GIRLS' MARCH OF COMICS (See March of Comics)

BOYS' RANCH (Also see Western Tales & Witches' Western Tales)
Oct, 1950 - No. 6, Aug, 1951 (No.1-3, 52 pgs.; No. 4-6, 36 pgs.)
Harvey Publications

	GD25	FN65	NM94
1-S&K-c/a(3)	50.00	150.00	450.00
2-S&K-c/a(3)	36.00	108.00	325.00
3-S&K-c/a(2); Meskin-a	36.00	108.00	290.00
4-S&K-c/a, 5 pgs.	31.00	94.00	250.00
5,6-S&K-c, splashes & centerspread only; Meskin-a	17.50	53.00	140.00
Shoe Store Giveaway #5,6 (Identical to regular issues except S&K centerfold replaced with ad)	16.00	49.00	130.00

BOZO (Larry Harmon's Bozo, the World's Most Famous Clown)
1992 ($6.95, 68 pgs.)
Innovation Publishing

	GD25	FN65	NM94
1-Reprints Four Color #285(#1)	1.00	2.80	7.00

BOZO THE CLOWN (TV) (Bozo No. 7 on)
July, 1950 - No. 4, Oct-Dec, 1963
Dell Publishing Co.

	GD25	FN65	NM94
Four Color 285(#1)	16.00	49.00	180.00
2(7-9/51)-7(10-12/52)	10.00	30.00	110.00
Four Color 464,508,551,594(10/54)	8.00	25.00	90.00
1(nn, 5-7/62) - 4(1963)	4.50	13.50	50.00
Giveaway-1961, 16 pgs., 3-1/2x7-1/4", Apsco Products	2.75	8.00	30.00

BOZZ CHRONICLES, THE
Dec, 1985 - No. 6, 1986 (Limited series, mature)
Marvel Comics (Epic Comics)

	GD25	FN65	NM94
1-6-Logan/Wolverine look alike in 19th century. Wrightsonish-a		1.00	2.50

BRADY BUNCH, THE (TV)(See Kite Fun Book and Binky #78)
Feb, 1970 - No. 2, May, 1970

Brainbanx #3 © Elaine Lee & Jason Temujin Minor

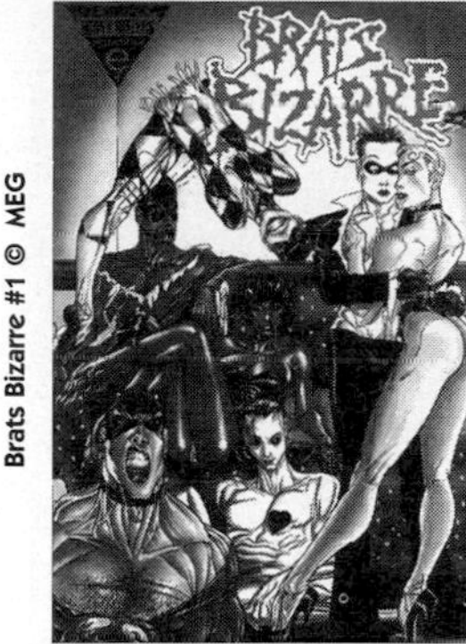

Brats Bizarre #1 © MEG

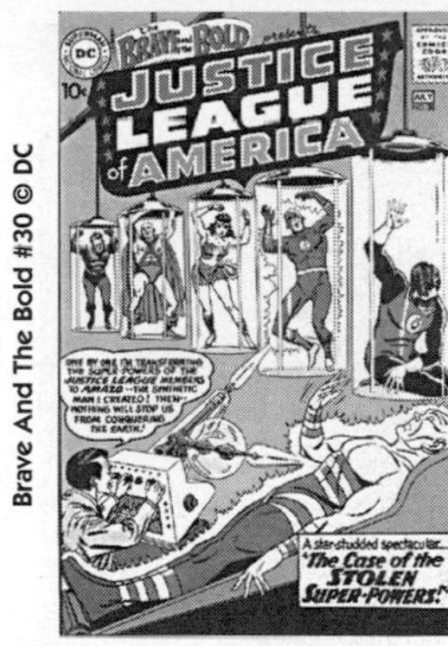

Brave And The Bold #30 © DC

GD25 FN65 NM94

Dell Publishing Co.

	GD25	FN65	NM94
1	8.00	23.00	85.00
2	5.50	16.50	60.00

BRAIN, THE
Sept, 1956 - No. 7, 1958
Sussex Publ. Co./Magazine Enterprises

	GD25	FN65	NM94
1-Dan DeCarlo-a in all including reprints	5.70	17.00	40.00
2,3	4.00	11.00	22.00
4-7	3.20	8.00	16.00
I.W. Reprints #1-4,8-10('63),14: 2-Reprints Sussex #2 with new cover added	1.70	4.25	8.00
Super Reprint #17,18(nd)	1.70	4.25	8.00

BRAINBANX
Mar, 1997 - No. 6, Aug, 1997 ($2.50, limited series)
DC Comics (Helix)

	GD25	FN65	NM94
1-6: Elaine Lee-s/Temujin-a		1.00	2.50

BRAIN BOY
Apr-June, 1962 - No. 6, Sept-Nov, 1963 (Painted c-#1-6)
Dell Publishing Co.

	GD25	FN65	NM94
Four Color 1330(#1)-Gil Kane-a; origin	12.00	37.00	135.00
2(7-9/62),3-6: 4-Origin retold	7.00	20.00	75.00

BRAM STOKER'S BURIAL OF THE RATS (Movie)
Apr, 1995 - No.3, June, 1995 ($2.50)
Roger Corman's Cosmic Comics

	GD25	FN65	NM94
1-3: Adaptation of film; Jerry Prosser scripts		1.00	2.50

BRAM STOKER'S DRACULA (Movie)(Also see Dracula: Vlad the Impaler)
Oct, 1992 - No. 4, Jan, 1993 ($2.95, limited series, polybagged)
Topps Comics

	GD25	FN65	NM94
1-Adaptation of film begins; Mignola-c/a in all; 4 trading cards & poster; photo scenes of movie		1.20	3.00
1-2nd printing		1.20	3.00
1-Crimson foil edition (limited to 500)	1.25	3.75	10.00
2-Bound-in poster & cards		1.20	3.00
3,4: 4 trading cards in both. 3-Contains coupon to win 1 of 500 crimson foil-c edition of #1. 4-Contains coupon to win 1 of 500 uncut sheets of all 16 trading cards		1.20	3.00
3,4-Without coupon		1.20	3.00

BRAND ECHH (See Not Brand Echh)

BRAND OF EMPIRE (See Luke Short's...Four Color 771)

BRASS
Aug, 1996 - No. 3, May, 1997 ($2.50, limited series)
Image Comics (Wildstorm Productions)

	GD25	FN65	NM94
1-($4.50) Folio Ed.; oversized		1.80	4.50
1-3: Wiesenfeld-s/Bennett-a. 3-Grunge & Roxy(Gen 13) cameo		1.00	2.50

BRATPACK/MAXIMORTAL SUPER SPECIAL
1996 ($2.95, B&W, limited series)
King Hell Press

	GD25	FN65	NM94
1,2: Veitch-s/a			2.95

BRATS BIZARRE
1994 - No. 4, 1994 ($2.50, limited series)
Marvel Comics (Epic Comics/Heavy Hitters)

	GD25	FN65	NM94
1-4: All w/bound-in trading cards		1.00	2.50

BRAVADOS, THE (See Wild Western Action)
Aug, 1971 (52 pgs., one-shot)
Skywald Publ. Corp.

	GD25	FN65	NM94
1-Red Mask, The Durango Kid, Billy Nevada-r	1.00	2.80	7.00

BRAVE AND THE BOLD, THE (See Best Of... & Super DC Giant) (Replaced by Batman & The Outsiders)
Aug-Sept, 1955 - No. 200, July, 1983
National Periodical Publications/DC Comics

	GD25	FN65	NM94
1-Viking Prince by Kubert, Silent Knight, Golden Gladiator begin; part Kubert-c	208.00	624.00	2600.00
2	96.00	288.00	1150.00
3,4	52.00	156.00	600.00
5-Robin Hood begins (4-5/56, 1st DC app.), ends #15; see Robin Hood Tales #7	53.00	159.00	640.00
6-10: 6-Robin Hood by Kubert; last Golden Gladiator app.; Silent Knight; no Viking Prince. 8-1st S.A. issue	39.00	117.00	430.00
11-22,24: 12,14-Robin Hood-c. 18,21-23-Grey tone-c. 22-Last Silent Knight. 24-Last Viking Prince by Kubert (2nd solo book)	33.00	100.00	325.00
23-Viking Prince origin by Kubert; 1st B&B single theme issue & 1st Viking Prince solo book	39.00	117.00	430.00
25-1st app. Suicide Squad (8-9/59)	34.00	102.00	340.00
26,27-Suicide Squad	30.00	90.00	300.00

	GD25	FN65	VF82	NM94
28-(2-3/60)-Justice League intro./1st app.; origin/1st app. Snapper Carr	358.00	1075.00	2688.00	5000.00
29-Justice League (4-5/60)-2nd app.	170.00	510.00	1190.00	2200.00
30-Justice League (6-7/60)-3rd app.	150.00	450.00	1050.00	1800.00

	GD25	FN65	NM94
31-1st app. Cave Carson (8-9/60); scarce in high grade; 1st try-out series	31.00	93.00	310.00
32,33-Cave Carson	21.00	63.00	210.00

	GD25	FN65	VF82	NM94
34-Origin/1st app. Silver-Age Hawkman, Hawkgirl & Byth by Kubert (2-3/61); 1st S.A. Hawkman tryout series; all predate Hawkman #1	150.00	450.00	1050.00	1800.00

	GD25	FN65	NM94
35-Hawkman by Kubert (4-5/61)-2nd app.	44.00	132.00	485.00
36-Hawkman by Kubert; origin & 1st app. Shadow Thief (6-7/61)-3rd app.	36.00	108.00	410.00
37-Suicide Squad (2nd tryout series)	25.00	75.00	250.00
38,39-Suicide Squad. 38-Last 10¢ issue	22.00	66.00	220.00
40,41-Cave Carson Inside Earth (2nd try-out series). 40-Kubert-a. 41-Meskin-a	15.00	45.00	150.00
42-Hawkman by Kubert (2nd tryout series)	28.00	84.00	285.00
43-Hawkman by Kubert; more detailed origin	33.00	100.00	330.00
44-Hawkman by Kubert; grey-tone-c	24.00	72.00	240.00
45-49-Strange Sports Stories by Infantino	6.00	18.00	60.00
50-The Green Arrow & Manhunter From Mars (10-11/63); 1st Manhunter x-over outside of Detective (pre-dates House of Mystery #143); team-ups begin	17.00	51.00	170.00
51-Aquaman & Hawkman (12-1/63-64); pre-dates Hawkman #1	24.00	72.00	240.00
52-(2-3/64)-3 Battle Stars; Sgt. Rock, Haunted Tank, Johnny Cloud, & Mlle. Marie team-up for 1st time by Kubert (c/a)	14.00	42.00	140.00
53-Atom & The Flash by Toth	7.00	21.00	70.00
54-Kid Flash, Robin & Aqualad; 1st app./origin Teen Titans (6-7/64)	26.00	78.00	260.00
55-Metal Men & The Atom	4.50	13.50	45.00
56-The Flash & Manhunter From Mars	4.50	13.50	45.00
57-Origin & 1st app. Metamorpho (12-1/64-65)	14.00	42.00	140.00
58-2nd app. Metamorpho by Fradon	7.00	21.00	70.00
59-Batman & Green Lantern; 1st Batman team-up in Brave and the Bold	9.00	27.00	90.00
60-Teen Titans (2nd app.)-1st app. new Wonder Girl (Donna Troy), who joins Titans (6-7/65)	8.00	24.00	80.00
61-Origin Starman & Black Canary by Anderson	11.00	33.00	110.00
62-Origin Starman & Black Canary cont'd. 62-1st S.A. app. Wildcat (10-11/65); 1st S.A. app. of G.A. Huntress	9.00	27.00	90.00
63-Supergirl & Wonder Woman	4.00	12.00	40.00
64-Batman Versus Eclipso (see H.O.S. #61)	6.00	18.00	60.00
65-Flash & Doom Patrol (4-5/66)	2.50	7.50	22.00

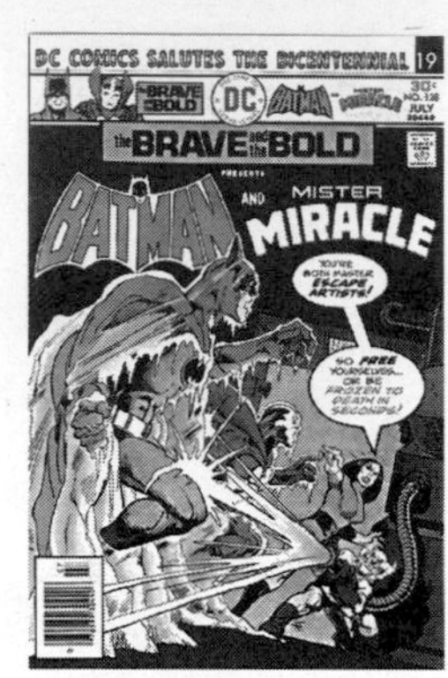

Brave And The Bold #128 © DC

Brave And The Bold #167 © DC

Brave And The Bold #198 © DC

GD25 FN65 NM94

66-Metamorpho & Metal Men (6-7/66) 2.50 7.50 22.00

67-Batman & The Flash by Infantino; Batman team-ups begin, end #200 (8-9/66) 4.20 12.60 42.00

68-Batman/Metamorpho/Joker/Riddler/Penguin-c/story; Batman as Bat-Hulk (Hulk parody) 6.00 18.00 60.00

69-Batman & Green Lantern 3.00 9.00 30.00

70-Batman & Hawkman; Craig-a(p) 3.00 9.00 30.00

71-Batman & Green Arrow 3.00 9.00 30.00

72-Spectre & Flash (6-7/67); 4th app. The Spectre; predates Spectre #1 3.50 10.50 35.00

73-Aquaman & The Atom 2.70 8.10 27.00

74-Batman & Metal Men 2.70 8.10 27.00

75-Batman & The Spectre (12-1/67-68); 6th app. Spectre; came out between Spectre #1 & #2 3.00 9.00 30.00

76-Batman & Plastic Man (2-3/68); came out between Plastic Man #8 & #9 2.70 8.10 27.00

77-Batman & The Atom 2.70 8.10 27.00

78-Batman, Wonder Woman & Batgirl 2.70 8.10 27.00

79-Batman & Deadman by Neal Adams (8-9/68); early Deadman app. 5.00 15.00 50.00

80-Batman & Creeper (10-11/68); N. Adams-a; early app. The Creeper; came out between Creeper #3 & #4 4.00 12.00 40.00

81-Batman & Flash; N. Adams-a 4.00 12.00 40.00

82-Batman & Aquaman; N. Adams-a; origin Ocean Master retold (2-3/69) 4.50 13.50 45.00

83-Batman & Teen Titans; N. Adams-a (4-5/69); last 12¢ issue 5.00 15.00 50.00

84-Batman (G.A., 1st S.A. app.) & Sgt. Rock; N. Adams-a 4.00 12.00 40.00

85-Batman & Green Arrow; 1st new costume for Green Arrow by Neal Adams (8-9/69) 4.00 12.00 40.00

86-Batman & Deadman (10-11/69); N. Adams-a; story concludes from Strange Adventures #216 (1-2/69) 4.00 12.00 40.00

87-Batman & Wonder Woman 2.50 7.50 24.00

88-Batman & Wildcat 2.50 7.50 24.00

89-Batman & Phantom Stranger (4-5/70); early Phantom Stranger app. (came out between Phantom Stranger #6 & 7 2.50 7.50 24.00

90-Batman & Adam Strange 2.50 7.50 24.00

91-Batman & Black Canary (8-9/70) 2.50 7.50 24.00

92-Batman; intro the Bat Squad 2.50 7.50 24.00

93-Batman-House of Mystery; N. Adams-a 4.00 12.00 40.00

94-Batman-Teen Titans 1.85 5.50 15.00

95-Batman & Plastic Man 1.75 5.25 14.00

96-Batman & Sgt. Rock 1.85 5.50 15.00

97-Batman & Wildcat; 52 pg. issues begin, end #102; reprints origin & 1st app. Deadman from Strange Advs. #205 1.85 5.50 15.00

98-Batman & Phantom Stranger; 1st Jim Aparo Batman-a? 1.85 5.50 15.00

99-Batman & Flash 1.85 5.50 15.00

100-(2-3/72, 25¢, 52 pgs.)-Batman-Gr. Lantern-Gr. Arrow-Black Canary-Robin; Deadman-r by Adams/Str. Advs. #210 3.80 11.40 38.00

101-Batman & Metamorpho; Kubert Viking Prince 1.00 3.00 8.00

102-Batman-Teen Titans; N. Adams-a(p) 1.50 4.50 12.00

103-110: Batman team-ups: 103-Metal Men. 104-Deadman. 105-Wonder Woman. 106-Green Arrow. 107-Black Canary. 108-Sgt. Rock. 109-Demon. 110-Wildcat 2.40 6.00

111-Batman/Joker-c/story 1.40 4.15 11.00

112-117: All 100 pgs.; Batman team-ups: 112-Mr. Miracle. 113-Metal Men; reprints origin/1st Hawkman from Brave and the Bold #34; r/origin Multi-Man/Challengers #14. 114-Aquaman. 115-Atom; r/origin Viking Prince from #23; r/Dr. Fate/Hourman/Solomon Grundy/Green Lantern from Showcase #55. 116-Spectre. 117-Sgt. Rock; last 100 pg. issue 1.50 4.50 12.00

118-Batman/Wildcat/Joker-c/story 1.50 4.50 12.00

119-128,132-140: Batman team-ups: 119-Man-Bat. 120-Kamandi(68 pgs.). 121-Metal Men. 122-Swamp Thing. 123-Plastic Man/Metamorpho. 124-Sgt. Rock. 125-Flash. 126-Aquaman. 127-Wildcat. 128-Mr. Miracle. 132-Kung-Fu Fighter. 133-Deadman. 134-Green Lantern. 135-Metal Men. 136-Metal Men/Green Arrow. 137-Demon. 138-Mr. Miracle. 139-Hawkman. 140-Wonder Woman 2.00 5.00

129,130-Batman/Green Arrow/Atom parts 1 & 2; Joker & Two Face-c/stories 1.50 4.50 12.00

131-Batman & Wonder Woman vs. Catwoman-c/sty 1.00 2.80 7.00

141-Batman/Black Canary vs. Joker-c/story 1.50 4.50 12.00

142-190,192-195,198,199: Batman team-ups: 142-Aquaman. 143-Creeper; origin Human Target (44 pgs.). 144-Green Arrow; origin Human Target part 2 (44 pgs.).145-Phantom Stranger. 146-G.A. Batman/Unknown Soldier. 147-Supergirl.148-Plastic Man; X-Mas-c. 149-Teen Titans. 150-Anniversary issue; Superman. 151-Flash. 152-Atom. 153-Red Tornado. 154-Metamorpho. 155-Green Lantern. 156-Dr. Fate. 157-Batman vs. Kamandi (ties into Kamandi #59). 158-Wonder Woman. 159-Ra's Al Ghul. 160-Supergirl. 161-Adam Strange. 162-G.A. Batman/Sgt. Rock. 163-Black Lightning. 164-Hawkman. 165-Man-Bat. 166-Black Canary; Nemesis (intro) back-up story begins, ends #192; Penguin-c/story. 167-G.A. Batman/Blackhawk; origin Nemesis. 168-Green Arrow. 169-Zatanna. 170-Nemesis. 171-Scalphunter. 172-Firestorm. 173-Guardians of the Universe. 174-Green Lantern. 175-Lois Lane. 176-Swamp Thing. 177-Elongated Man. 178-Creeper. 179-Legion. 180-Spectre. 181-Hawk & Dove. 182-G.A. Robin; G.A. Starman app.; 1st modern app. G.A. Batwoman. 183-Riddler. 184-Huntress. 185-Green Arrow. 186-Hawkman. 187-Metal Men. ,188,189-Rose & the Thorn. 190-Adam Strange. 192-Superboy vs. Mr. I.Q. 193-Nemesis. 194-Flash. 195-I... Vampire. 198-Karate Kid. 199-Batman vs. The Spectre 1.40 3.50

191-Batman/Joker-c/story; Nemesis app. 1.00 3.00 8.00

196-Ragman; origin Ragman retold. 2.40 6.00

197-Catwoman; Earth II Batman & Catwoman marry; 2nd modern app. of G.A. Batwoman 1.00 3.00 8.00

200-Double-sized (64 pgs.); printed on Mando paper; Earth One & Earth Two Batman app. in separate stories; intro/1st app. Batman & The Outsiders 1.10 3.30 9.00

NOTE: ***Neal Adams*** *a-79-86, 93, 100r, 102; c-75, 76, 79-86, 88-90, 93, 95, 99, 100r.* ***M. Anderson*** *a-115r; c-72i, 96i.* ***Andru/Esposito*** *c-25-27.* ***Aparo*** *a-98, 100-102, 104-125, 126i, 127-136, 138-145, 147, 148i, 149-152, 154, 155, 157-162, 168-170, 173-178, 180-182, 184, 186i-189i, 191i-193i, 195, 196, 200; c-105-109, 111-136, 137i, 138-175, 177, 180-184, 186-200.* ***Austin*** *a-166i.* ***Bernard Baily*** *c-32, 33, 58.* ***Buckler*** *a-185, 186p; c-137, 178p, 185p, 186p.* ***Giordano*** *a-143, 144.* ***Infantino*** *a-67p, 72p, 97r, 98r, 115r, 172p, 183p, 190p, 194p; c-45-49, 67p, 69p, 70p, 72p, 96p, 98r.* ***Kaluta*** *c-176.* ***Kane*** *a-115r; c-59, 64.* ***Kubert*** *&/or* ***Heath*** *a-1-24; reprints-101, 113, 115, 117.* ***Kubert*** *a-99r; c-22-24, 34-36, 40, 42-44, 52.* ***Mooney*** *a-114r.* ***Mortimer*** *a-64, 69.* ***Newton*** *a-153p, 156p, 165p.* ***Irv Novick*** *c-1(part), 2-21.* ***Fred Ray*** *a-78r.* ***Roussos*** *a-50, 76i, 114r.* ***Staton*** *148p. 52 pgs.-97, 100; 68 pgs.-120; 100 pgs.-112-117.*

BRAVE AND THE BOLD, THE
Dec, 1991 - No. 6, June, 1992 ($1.75, limited series)
DC Comics

1-6: Green Arrow, The Butcher, The Question in all; Grell scripts in all. .70 1.75

NOTE: ***Grell*** *c-3, 4-6.*

BRAVE AND THE BOLD SPECIAL, THE (See DC Special Series No. 8)

BRAVE EAGLE (TV)
No. 705, June, 1956 - No. 929, July, 1958
Dell Publishing Co.

Four Color 705 (#1)-Photo-c 5.50 16.50 60.00

Four Color 770, 816, 879 (2/58), 929-All photo-c 2.75 8.00 30.00

BRAVE ONE, THE (Movie)
No. 773, Mar, 1957
Dell Publishing Co.

Four Color 773-Photo-c 4.50 13.50 50.00

BRAVURA
1995 (mail-in offer)
Malibu Comics (Bravura)

'Breed #6 © Jim Starlin

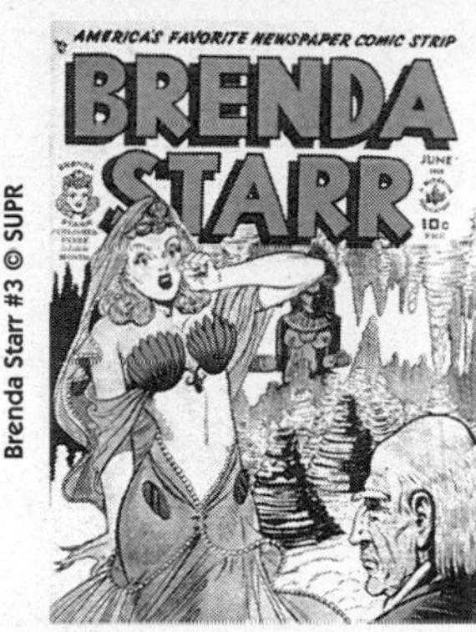

Brenda Starr #3 © SUPR

Brigade #3 (limited series) © Rob Liefeld

GD25 FN65 NM94

0-wraparound holographic-c; short stories and promo pin-ups of Chaykin's Power &Glory, Gil Kane's & Steven Grant's Edge, Starlin's Breed, & Simonson's Star Slammers. 2.00 5.00

BREAKNECK BLVD.
No. 0, Feb, 1994 - No. 2, Nov, 1994; Vol. 2#1, Jul, 1995 - Present ($2.50/$2.95, B&W)
MotioN Comics/Slave Labor Graphics Vol. 2

0-2: 0-Perez/Giordano-c 1.00 2.50
V2#1-6: 6-(12/96) 1.20 3.00

BREAK-THRU (Also see Exiles V1#4)
Dec, 1993 - No. 2, Jan, 1994 ($2.50, 44 pgs.)
Malibu Comics (Ultraverse)

1,2-Perez-c/a(p); has x-overs in Ultraverse titles 1.00 2.50

BREATHTAKER
1990 - No. 4, 1990 ($4.95, 52 pgs., prestige format, mature)
DC Comics

Book 1-4: Mark Wheatley-painted-c/a & scripts; Marc Hempel-a 2.00 5.00

'BREED
Jan, 1994 - No. 6, 1994 ($2.50, limited series)
Malibu Comics (Bravura)

1-(48 pgs.)-Origin & 1st app. of 'Breed by Starlin; contains Bravura stamps; spot varnish-c 1.00 2.50
2-6: 2-5-contains Bravura stamps. 6-Death of Rachel 1.00 2.50
...:Book of Genesis (1994, $12.95) reprints #1-6 12.95

'BREED II
Nov, 1994 - No. 6, Apr, 1995 ($2.95, limited series)
Malibu Comics (Bravura)

1-6: Starlin-c/a/scripts in all. 1-Gold edition 1.20 3.00

BREEZE LAWSON, SKY SHERIFF (See Sky Sheriff)

BRENDA LEE STORY, THE
Sept, 1962
Dell Publishing Co.

01 078 200 7.00 22.00 80.00

BRENDA STARR (Also see All Great)
No. 13, 9/47; No. 14, 3/48; V2#3, 6/48 - V2#12, 12/49
Four Star Comics Corp./Superior Comics Ltd.

V1#13-By Dale Messick 68.00 206.00 565.00
14-Kamen bondage-c 71.00 215.00 585.00
V2#3-Baker-a? 60.00 180.00 490.00
4-Used in **SOTI**, pg. 21; Kamen bondage-c 70.00 210.00 575.00
5-10 56.00 168.00 460.00
11,12 (Scarce) 59.00 178.00 485.00
NOTE: *Newspaper reprints plus original material through #6. All original #7 on.*

BRENDA STARR (...Reporter)(Young Lovers No. 16 on?)
No. 13, June, 1955 - No. 15, Oct, 1955
Charlton Comics

13-15-Newspaper-r 30.00 90.00 240.00

BRENDA STARR REPORTER
Oct, 1963
Dell Publishing Co.

1 14.00 44.00 160.00

BRER RABBIT (See Kite Fun Book, Walt Disney Showcase #28 and Wheaties)
No. 129, 1946; No. 208, Jan, 1949; No. 693, 1956 (Disney)
Dell Publishing Co.

Four Color 129 (#1)-Adapted from Disney movie "Song of the South" 26.00 79.00 290.00
Four Color 208 (1/49) 11.00 32.00 115.00
Four Color 693-Part-r 129 8.00 25.00 90.00

BRER RABBIT IN "ICE CREAM FOR THE PARTY"
1955 (5x7-1/4", 16 pgs., soft-c) (Walt Disney) (Premium)
American Dairy Association

nn-(Scarce) 35.00 105.00 280.00

BRIAN BOLLAND'S BLACK BOOK
July, 1985 (one-shot)
Eclipse Comics

1-British B&W-r in color 1.50

BRICK BRADFORD (Also see Ace Comics & King Comics)
No. 5, July, 1948 - No. 8, July, 1949 (Ritt & Grey reprints)
King Features Syndicate/Standard

5 15.00 45.00 120.00
6-Robot-c (by Schomburg?). 20.00 60.00 160.00
7-Schomburg-c. 8-Says #7 inside, #8 on-c 12.00 36.00 95.00

BRIDE'S DIARY (Formerly Black Cobra No. 3)
No. 4, May, 1955 - No. 10, Aug, 1956
Ajax/Farrell Publ.

4 (#1) 5.70 17.00 34.00
5-8 4.00 11.00 22.00
9,10-Disbrow-a 5.70 17.00 34.00

BRIDES IN LOVE (Hollywood Romances & Summer Love No. 46 on)
Aug, 1956 - No. 45, Feb, 1965
Charlton Comics

1 7.15 21.50 50.00
2 4.25 13.00 28.00
3-10 2.50 7.50 20.00
11-20 1.50 4.50 12.00
21-45 1.00 2.80 7.00

BRIDES ROMANCES
Nov, 1953 - No. 23, Dec, 1956
Quality Comics Group

1 8.75 26.25 70.00
2 5.35 16.00 32.00
3-10: Last precode (3/55) 4.15 12.50 25.00
11-14,16,17,19-22 3.60 9.00 18.00
15-Baker-a(p)?; Colan-a 4.00 10.00 20.00
18-Baker-a 4.25 13.00 28.00
23-Baker-c/a 5.70 17.00 40.00

BRIDE'S SECRETS
Apr-May, 1954 - No. 19, May, 1958
Ajax/Farrell(Excellent Publ.)/Four-Star Comic

1 8.50 26.00 60.00
2 5.00 15.00 30.00
3-6: Last precode (3/55) 4.00 11.00 22.00
7-11,13-19: 18-Hollingsworth-a 4.00 10.00 20.00
12-Disbrow-a 4.00 12.00 24.00

BRIDE-TO-BE ROMANCES (See True...)

BRIGADE
Aug, 1992 - No. 4, 1993 ($1.95, limited series)
Image Comics (Extreme Studios)

1-Liefeld part plots/scripts in all, Liefeld-c(p); contains 2 Brigade trading cards; 1st app. Genocide 1.20 3.00
1-Gold foil stamped logo edition 1.00 3.00 8.00
2-Contains coupon for Image Comics #0 & 2 trading cards 1.20 3.00
2-With coupon missing .80 2.00
3-Contains 2 bound-in trading cards; 1st Birds of Prey .80 2.00
4-Flip book format featuring Youngblood #5 .80 2.00

Brinke of Eternity #1 © Brinke Stevens

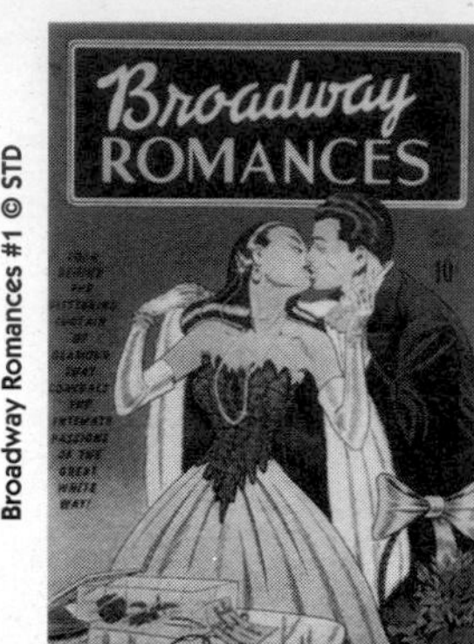

Broadway Romances #1 © STD

Bruce Lee #2 © MAL

BRIGADE
V2#1, May, 1993 - V2#22, July, 1995 ($1.95/$2.50)
Image Comics (Extreme Studios)

V2#1-Gatefold-c; Liefeld co-plots; Blood Brothers part 1; Bloodstrike app.; 1st app. Boone & Hacker .80 2.00
2-10, 13, 14: 2-(6/93, V2#1 on inside)-Foil merricote-c (newsstand ed. w/out foil-c exists). 3-1st app. Roman; Perez-c(i); Liefeld scripts. 6-1st app. Coral & Worlok. 6-8-Thibert-c(i). 8-Liefeld scripts;Black and White part 5 by Art Thibert. 8,9-Coupons#2 & 6 for Extreme Prejudice #0 bound-in. 9-(4/94). 10-(6/94). .80 2.00
0-(9/93)-Liefeld scripts; 1st app. Warcry; Youngblood & Wildcats app.; Thibert-c(i) 1.20 3.00
11,12,15-22: 11-(8/94, $2.50) WildC.A.T.S app. 16-Polybagged w/ trading card. 19-Glory app. 20 (Regular-c.)-Troll, Supreme, Shadowhawk, Glory, Vanguard, & Roman form new team. 22-"Supreme Apocalypse" Pt. 4; Marv Wolfman scripts; polybagged w/ trading card 1.00 2.50
20-(Variant-c. by Quesada & Palmiotti)-Troll, Supreme, Shadowhawk, Glory, Vanguard, & Roman form new team. 1.20 3.00
Sourcebook 1 (8/94, $2.95) 1.20 3.00

BRIGAND, THE (See Fawcett Movie Comics No. 18)

BRINGING UP FATHER
No. 9, 1942 - No. 37, 1944
Dell Publishing Co.

Large Feature Comic 9 17.00 52.00 190.00
Four Color 37 17.00 52.00 190.00

BRING ON THE BAD GUYS (See Fireside Book Series)

BRINKE OF DESTRUCTION
Dec, 1995 - Jan, 1997($2.95)
High-Top and Brinke Stevens

1-3: 1-Boris-c. 2-Julie Bell-c. 3-Garris-c 1.20 3.00
Holiday Special ($6.99)-Comic w/audio tape 2.80 7.00

BRINKE OF DISASTER
1996 ($2.25, B&W, one-shot)
Revenge Entertainment Group

nn-Photo-c .90 2.25

BRINKE OF ETERNITY
Apr, 1994 ($2.75, one-shot)
Chaos! Comics

1 .80 2.00
1-Signed Edition 1.20 3.00

BROADWAY HOLLYWOOD BLACKOUTS
Mar-Apr, 1954 - No. 3, July-Aug, 1954
Stanhall

1 8.75 26.25 65.00
2,3 6.00 18.00 42.00

BROADWAY ROMANCES
January, 1950 - No. 5, Sept, 1950
Quality Comics Group

1-Ward-c/a (9 pgs.); Gustavson-a 26.00 80.00 210.00
2-Ward-a (9 pgs.); photo-c 20.00 60.00 160.00
3-5: All-Photo-c 8.75 26.25 65.00

BROKEN ARROW (TV)
No. 855, Oct, 1957 - No. 947, Nov, 1958
Dell Publishing Co.

Four Color 855 (#1)-Photo-c 5.00 15.00 54.00
Four Color 947-Photo-c 4.00 12.00 45.00

BROKEN CROSS, THE (See The Crusaders)

BRONCHO BILL (See Comics On Parade, Sparkler & Tip Top Comics)

GD25 FN65 NM94

1939 - 1940; No. 5, 1?/48 - No. 16, 8?/50
United Features Syndicate/Standard(Visual Editions) No. 5-on

Single Series 2 ('39) 40.00 120.00 360.00
Single Series 19 ('40)(#2 on cvr) 36.00 108.00 300.00
5 9.50 28.00 75.00
6(4/48)-10(4/49) 5.70 17.00 40.00
11(6/49)-16 5.00 15.00 30.00
NOTE: ***Schomburg*** *c-6, 7, 9-13, 16.*

BROOKLYN DREAMS
1994, ($4.95, B&W, limited series, mature)
DC Comics (Paradox Press)

1-4 2.00 5.00

BROOKS ROBINSON (See Baseball's Greatest Heroes #2)

BROTHER BILLY THE PAIN FROM PLAINS
1979 (68pgs.)
Marvel Comics Group

1-B&W comics, satire, Jimmy Carter-c & x-over w/Brother Billy peanut jokes. Joey Adams-a (scarce) 2.00 6.00 16.00

BROTHER POWER, THE GEEK (See Saga of Swamp Thing Annual & Vertigo Visions)
Sept-Oct, 1968 - No. 2, Nov-Dec, 1968
National Periodical Publications

1-Origin; Simon-c(i?) 4.50 13.50 45.00
2 2.50 7.50 25.00

BROTHERS, HANG IN THERE, THE
1979 (49¢)
Spire Christian Comics (Fleming H. Revell Co.)

nn 1.00

BROTHERS OF THE SPEAR (Also see Tarzan)
June, 1972 - No. 17, Feb, 1976; No. 18, May, 1982
Gold Key/Whitman No. 18

1 2.50 7.50 24.00
2-Painted-c begin, end #17 1.25 3.75 10.00
3-10 2.40 6.00
11-17: 12-Line drawn-c. 13-17-Spiegle-a 1.60 4.00
18-r/#2; Leopard Girl-r 1.60 4.00

BROTHERS, THE CULT ESCAPE, THE
1980 (49¢)
Spire Christian Comics (Fleming H. Revell Co.)

nn 1.00

BROWNIES (See New Funnies)
No. 192, July, 1948 - No. 605, Dec, 1954
Dell Publishing Co.

Four Color 192(#1)-Kelly-a 11.00 33.00 120.00
Four Color 244(9/49), 293 (9/50)-Last Kelly c/a 10.00 30.00 110.00
Four Color 337(7-8/51), 365(12-1/51-52), 398(5/52) 3.00 10.00 36.00
Four Color 436(11/52), 482(7/53), 522(12/53), 605 3.00 9.00 32.00

BRUCE GENTRY
Jan, 1948 - No. 8, July, 1949
Better/Standard/Four Star Publ./Superior No. 3

1-Ray Bailey strip reprints begin, end #3; E. C. emblem appears as a monogram on stationery in story; negligee panels 40.00 120.00 290.00
2,3 30.00 90.00 210.00
4-8 21.00 62.00 150.00
NOTE: ***Kamenish*** *a-2-7; c-1-8.*

BRUCE LEE
July, 1994 - No. 6, Dec, 1994 ($2.95, 36 pgs.)
Malibu Comics

Brute & Babe #2 © Ominous Press

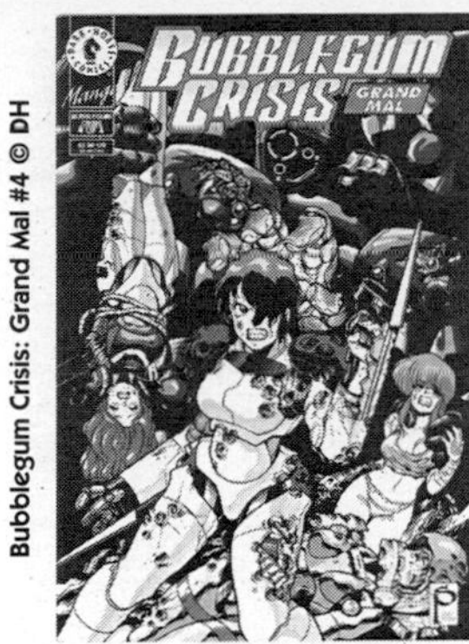

Bubblegum Crisis: Grand Mal #4 © DH

Buck Rogers #3 © TSR

GD25 FN65 NM94

1-6: 1-(44 pgs.)-Mortal Kombat preview, 1st app. in comics. 2,6-(36 pgs.) 1.00

BRUCE JONES' OUTER EDGE
1993 ($2.50, B&W, one-shot)
Innovation

1-Bruce Jones-c/a/script 1.00 2.50

BRUCE WAYNE: AGENT OF S.H.I.E.L.D. (Also see Marvel Versus DC #3 & DC Versus Marvel #4)
Apr, 1996 ($1.95, one-shot)
Marvel Comics (Amalgam)

1-Chuck Dixon scripts & Cary Nord-c/a. .80 2.00

BRU-HEAD: AMERICA'S FAVORITE BLOCKHEAD
Mar, 1994 - No. 4, 1994 ($2.50, B&W, limited series)
Schism Comics

1 1.00 2.50

BRUISER
Feb, 1994 ($2.45)
Anthem Publications

1 1.00 2.45

BRUTE, THE
Feb, 1975 - No. 3, July, 1975
Seaboard Publ. (Atlas)

1,2: 1-Origin & 1st app; Sekowsky-a(p). 2-Sekowsky-a(p) 1.20 3.00
3-Brunner/Starlin/Weiss-a(p) 1.60 4.00

BRUTE & BABE
July, 1994 - No. 2, Aug, 1994
Ominous Press

1-($3.95, 8 tablets plus-c)-"...It Begins..."; tablet format 1.60 4.00
2-($2.50, 36 pgs.)-"Mael's Rage" 1.00 2.50
2-(40 pgs.)-Stiff additional variant-c 1.00 2.50

BRUTE FORCE
Aug, 1990 - No. 4, Nov, 1990 ($1.00, limited series)
Marvel Comics

1-4: Animal super-heroes 1.00

BUBBLEGUM CRISIS: GRAND MAL
Mar, 1994 - No. 4, June, 1994 ($2.50, limited series)
Dark Horse Comics

1-4-Japanese manga 1.00 2.50

BUCCANEER
No date (1963)
I. W. Enterprises

I.W. Reprint #1(r-/Quality #20), #8(r-/#23): Crandall-a in each 2.50 7.50 22.00

BUCCANEERS (Formerly Kid Eternity)
No. 19, Jan, 1950 - No. 27, May, 1951 (No. 24-27: 52 pgs.)
Quality Comics Group

19-Captain Daring, Black Roger, Eric Falcon & Spanish Main begin; Crandall-a 44.00 132.00 360.00
20,23-Crandall-a 32.00 96.00 230.00
21-Crandall-c/a 40.00 120.00 290.00
22-Bondage-c 26.00 77.00 190.00
24-26: 24-Adam Peril, U.S.N. begins. 25-Origin & 1st app. Corsair Queen. 26-last Spanish Main 21.00 64.00 160.00
27-Crandall-c/a 34.00 101.00 240.00
Super Reprint #12 (1964)-Crandall-r/#21 2.50 7.50 24.00

BUCCANEERS, THE (TV)
No. 800, 1957
Dell Publishing Co.

Four Color 800-Photo-c 6.40 19.00 70.00

BUCKAROO BANZAI (Movie)
Dec, 1984 - No. 2, Feb, 1985
Marvel Comics Group

1,2-Movie adaptation; r/Marvel Super Special #33 1.00

BUCK DUCK
June, 1953 - No. 4, Dec, 1953
Atlas Comics (ANC)

1-Funny animal stories in all 10.00 30.00 80.00
2-4: 2-Ed Win-a(5) 5.35 16.00 32.00

BUCK JONES (Also see Crackajack Funnies, Famous Feature Stories, Master Comics #7 & Wow Comics #1, 1936)
No. 299, Oct, 1950 - No. 850, Oct, 1957 (All Painted-c)
Dell Publishing Co.

Four Color 299(#1)-Buck Jones & his horse Silver-B begin; painted back-c begins, ends #5 11.00 34.00 125.00
2(4-6/51) 6.00 18.00 65.00
3-8(10-12/52) 5.00 15.00 55.00
Four Color 460,500,546,589 4.50 13.50 50.00
Four Color 652,733,850 2.75 8.00 30.00

BUCK ROGERS (In the 25th Century)
1933 (6x8", 36 pgs)
Kelloggs Corn Flakes Giveaway

370A-By Phil Nowlan & Dick Calkins; 1st Buck Rogers radio premium & 1st app. in comics (tells origin) (Reissued in 1995) 60.00 250.00 425.00

BUCK ROGERS (Also see Famous Funnies, Pure Oil Comics, Salerno Carnival of Comics, 24 Pages of Comics, & Vicks Comics)
Winter, 1940-41 - No. 6, Sept, 1943
Famous Funnies

1-Sunday strip reprints by Rick Yager; begins with strip #190; Calkins-c 260.00 780.00 2600.00
2 (7/41)-Calkins-c 106.00 318.00 950.00
3 (12/41), 4 (7/42) 89.00 267.00 800.00
5-Story continues with Famous Funnies No. 80; Buck Rogers, Sky Roads 78.00 234.00 700.00
6-Reprints of 1939 dailies; contains B.R. story "Crater of Doom" (2 pgs.) by Calkins not-r from Famous Funnies 78.00 234.00 700.00

BUCK ROGERS
No. 100, Jan, 1951 - No. 9, May-June, 1951
Toby Press

100(#7)-All strip-r begin 23.00 68.00 180.00
101(#8), 9-All Anderson-a(1947-49-r/dailies) 19.00 56.00 150.00

BUCK ROGERS (...in the 25th Century No. 5 on) (TV)
Oct, 1964; No. 2, July, 1979 - No. 16, May, 1982 (No #10)
Gold Key/Whitman No. 7 on

1(10128-410, 12¢)-1st S.A. app. Buck Rogers & 1st new B. R. in comics since 1933 giveaway; painted-c; back-c pin-up 3.60 11.00 40.00
2(7/79)-6: 3,4,6-Movie adaptation; painted-c 1.20 4.00
7-11 (Whitman) 2.40 6.00
12-16 1.20 3.00
Giant Movie Edition 11296(64pp, Whitman, $1.50), reprints GK #2-4 minus cover; tabloid size .80 2.00
Giant Movie Edition 02489(Western/Marvel, $1.50), reprints GK #2-4 minus cover 1.50 4.50 12.00

NOTE: ***Bolle** a-2p,3p, Movie Ed.(p).* ***McWilliams** a-2i,3i, 5-11, Movie Ed.(i). Painted c-1-9,11-13.*

BUCK ROGERS (Comics Module)
1990 - No. 10, 1991 ($2.95, 44 pgs.)
TSR, Inc.

Buffalo Bill #3 © YM

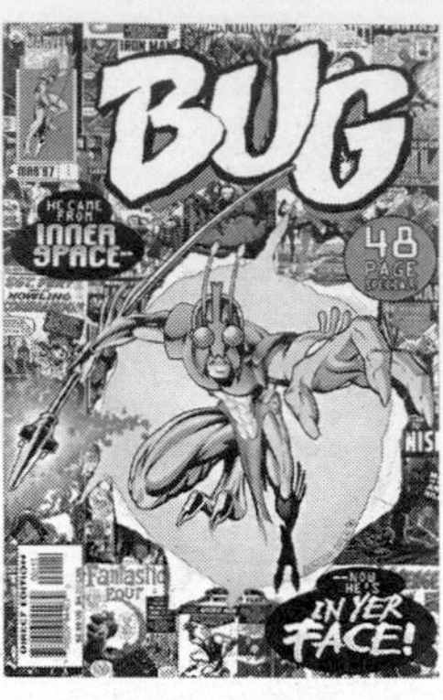

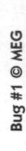

Bug #1 © MEG

Bugs Bunny #88 © Warner Bros.

GD25 FN65 NM94 GD25 FN65 NM94

1-5 (1990): 1-Begin origin in 3 parts. 2-Indicia says #1. 2,3-Black Barney back-up story. 4-All Black Barney issue; B. B.-c. 5-Indicia says #6; Black Barney-c & lead story; Buck Rogers back-up story. 1.20 3.00
6-10 (1991): 10-Flip book (72 pgs.) 1.20 3.00

BUCKSKIN (TV)
No. 1011, July, 1959 - No. 1107, June-Aug, 1960
Dell Publishing Co.

Four Color 1011 (#1)-Photo-c 6.40 19.00 70.00
Four Color 1107-Photo-c 5.50 16.50 60.00

BUCKY O'HARE (Funny Animal)
1988 ($5.95, graphic novel)
Continuity Comics

1-Michael Golden-c/a(r); r/serial-Echo of Futurepast #1-6. 2.40 6.00
Deluxe Hardcover ($40, 52pg, 8x11") 40.00

BUCKY O'HARE
Jan, 1991 - No. 5, 1991 ($2.00)
Continuity Comics

1-6: 1-Michael Golden-c/a .80 2.00

BUDDIES IN THE U.S. ARMY
Nov, 1952 - No. 2, 1953
Avon Periodicals

1-Lawrence-c 9.50 28.00 75.00
2-Mort Lawrence-c/a 7.15 21.50 50.00

BUFFALO BEE (TV)
No. 957, Nov, 1958 - No. 1061, Dec-Feb, 1959-60
Dell Publishing Co.

Four Color 957 (#1) 9.00 27.00 100.00
Four Color 1002 (8-10/59), 1061 6.00 18.00 65.00

BUFFALO BILL (See Frontier Fighters, Super Western Comics &Western Action Thrillers)
No. 2, Oct, 1950 - No. 9, Dec, 1951
Youthful Magazines

2-Annie Oakley story 10.00 30.00 70.00
3-9: 2-4-Walter Johnson-c/a. 9-Wildey-a 6.70 20.00 45.00

BUFFALO BILL CODY (See Cody of the Pony Express)

BUFFALO BILL, JR. (TV) (See Western Roundup)
Jan, 1956 - No. 13, Aug-Oct, 1959; 1965 (All photo-c)
Dell Publishing Co./Gold Key

Four Color 673 (#1) 5.75 17.00 63.00
Four Color 742,766,798,828,856(11/57) 4.00 12.00 45.00
7(2-4/58)-13 3.00 10.00 36.00
1(6/65, Gold Key)-Photo-c(r/F.C. #798); photo-b/c 3.00 10.00 36.00

BUFFALO BILL PICTURE STORIES
June-July, 1949 - No. 2, Aug-Sept, 1949
Street & Smith Publications

1,2-Wildey, Powell-a in each 9.50 28.00 75.00

BUG
Mar, 1997 ($2.99, one-shot)
Marvel Comics

1-Micronauts character 2.99

BUGALOOS (TV)
Sept, 1971 - No. 4, Feb, 1972
Charlton Comics

1 2.50 7.50 20.00
2-4 1.75 5.25 14.00

NOTE: *No. 3(1/72) went on sale late in 1972 (after No. 4) with the 1/73 issues.*

BUGHOUSE (Satire)
Mar-Apr, 1954 - No. 4, Sept-Oct, 1954
Ajax/Farrell (Excellent Publ.)

V1#1 14.00 41.00 110.00
2-4 8.75 26.25 65.00

BUGS BUNNY (See The Best of..., Camp Comics, Comic Album #2, 6, 10, 14, Dell Giant #28, 32, 46, Dynabrite, Golden Comics Digest #1, 3, 5, 6, 8, 10, 14, 15, 17, 21, 26, 30, 34, 39, 42, 47, Kite Fun Book, Large Feature Comic #8, Looney Tunes and Merry Melodies, March of Comics #44, 59, 75, 83, 97, 115, 132, 149, 160, 179, 188, 201, 220, 231, 245, 259, 273, 287, 301, 315, 329, 343, 363, 367, 380, 392, 403, 415, 428, 440, 452, 464, 476, 487, Porky Pig, Puffed Wheat, Story Hour Series #802, Super Book #14, 26 and Whitman Comic Books)

BUGS BUNNY (See Dell Giants for annuals)
1942 - No. 245, 1983
Dell Publishing Co./Gold Key No. 86-218/Whitman No. 219 on

Large Feature Comic 8(1942)-(Rarely found in fine-mint condition) 100.00 300.00 1100.00
Four Color 33 ('43) 100.00 300.00 1100.00
Four Color 51 33.00 98.00 360.00
Four Color 88 18.00 55.00 200.00
Four Color 123('46),142,164 14.00 41.00 150.00
Four Color 187,200,217,233 9.00 27.00 100.00
Four Color 250-Used in **SOTI**, pg. 309 11.00 33.00 120.00
Four Color 266,274,281,289,298('50) 8.00 25.00 90.00
Four Color 307,317(#1),327(#2),338,347,355,366,376,393 7.00 20.00 75.00
Four Color 407,420,432(10/52) 5.50 16.50 60.00
Four Color 498(9/53),585(9/54), 647(9/55) 4.50 13.50 50.00
Four Color 724(9/56),838(9/57),1064(12/59) 3.60 11.00 40.00
28(12-1/52-53)-30 3.00 10.00 36.00
31-50 2.25 6.75 26.00
51-85(7-9/62) 2.00 6.00 16.00
86(10/62)-88-Bugs Bunny's Showtime-(25¢, 80pgs.) 4.50 13.50 50.00
89-100 1.50 4.50 12.00
101-120 1.10 3.30 9.00
121-140 1.00 2.80 7.00
141-170 2.00 5.00
171-218 1.20 3.00
219-245: 229-Swipe of Barks story/WDC&S #223 1.60 4.00

NOTE: *Reprints-100, 102, 104, 123, 143, 144, 147, 167, 173, 175-177, 179-185, 187, 190.*

...Comic-Go-Round 11196-(224 pgs.)($1.95)(Golden Press, 1979) 1.20 3.00
...Winter Fun 1(12/67-Gold Key)-Giant 2.50 7.50 28.00

BUGS BUNNY (Puffed Rice Giveaway)
1949 (32 pgs. each, 3-1/8x6-7/8")
Quaker Cereals

A1-Traps the Counterfeiters, A2-Aboard Mystery Submarine, A3- Rocket to the Moon, A4-Lion Tamer, A5-Rescues the Beautiful Princess, B1-Buried Treasure, B2-Outwits the Smugglers, B3-Joins the Marines, B4-Meets the Dwarf Ghost, B5-Finds Aladdin's Lamp, C1-Lost in the Frozen North, C2-Secret Agent, C3-Captured by Cannibals, C4-Fights the Man from Mars, C5-And the Haunted Cave
each.... 5.70 17.00 40.00

BUGS BUNNY (3-D)
1953 (Pocket size) (15 titles)
Cheerios Giveaway

each.... 6.85 21.00 48.00

BUGS BUNNY
June, 1990 - No. 3, Aug, 1990 ($1.00, limited series)
DC Comics

1-3: Daffy Duck, Elmer Fudd, others app. 1.00

BUGS BUNNY (...Monthly on-c)
1993 - No. 3, 1994? ($1.95)
DC Comics

1-3-Bugs, Porky Pig, Daffy, Road Runner .80 2.00

Bulletman #5 © FAW

Bullets and Bracelets #1 © MEG

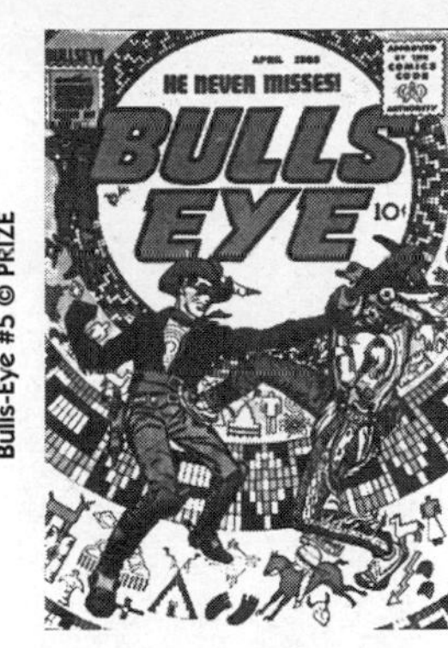

Bulls-Eye #5 © PRIZE

	GD25	FN65	NM94

BUGS BUNNY & PORKY PIG
Sept, 1965 (Paper-c, giant, 100 pgs.)
Gold Key

	GD25	FN65	NM94
1(30025-509)	7.00	20.00	75.00

BUGS BUNNY'S ALBUM (See Bugs Bunny, Four Color No. 498,585,647,724)

BUGS BUNNY LIFE STORY ALBUM (See Bugs Bunny, Four Color No. 838)

BUGS BUNNY MERRY CHRISTMAS (See Bugs Bunny, Four Color No. 1064)

BULLET CROW, FOWL OF FORTUNE
Mar, 1987 - No. 2, Apr, 1987 ($2.00, B&W, limited series)
Eclipse Comics

	GD25	FN65	NM94
1,2-The Comic Reader-r & new-a		.80	2.00

BULLETMAN (See Fawcett Miniatures, Master Comics, Mighty Midget Comics, Nickel Comics & XMas Comics)
Sum, 1941 - #12, 2/12/43; #14, Spr, 1946 - #16, Fall, 1946 (No #13)
Fawcett Publications

	GD25	FN65	NM94
1-Silver metallic-c	270.00	810.00	2700.00
2-Classic Raboy-c	122.00	366.00	1100.00
3,5-Classic Raboy-c each	89.00	267.00	800.00
4	78.00	234.00	700.00
6-10: 7-Ghost Stories told by night watchman of cemetery begins; Eisnerish-a; hidden message "Chic Stone is a jerk"	64.00	192.00	575.00
11,12,14-16 (nn 13)	50.00	150.00	450.00
Well Known Comics (1942)-Paper-c, glued binding; printed in red (Bestmaid/Samuel Lowe giveaway)	12.00	36.00	95.00

NOTE: ***Mac Raboy** c-1-3, 5, 6, 10. "Bulletman the Flying Detective" on cover #8 on.*

BULLETS AND BRACELETS (Also see Marvel Versus DC #3 & DC Versus Marvel #4)
Apr, 1996 ($1.95)
Marvel Comics (Amalgam)

	GD25	FN65	NM94
1-John Ostrander script & Gary Frank-c/a		.80	2.00

BULLS-EYE (Cody of The Pony Express No. 8 on)
7-8/54 - No. 5, 3-4/55; No. 6, 6/55; No. 7, 8/55
Mainline No. 1-5/Charlton No. 6,7

	GD25	FN65	NM94
1-S&K-c, 2 pgs.-a	42.00	120.00	375.00
2-S&K-c/a	36.00	108.00	325.00
3-5-S&K-c/a(2 each). 4-Last pre-code issue (1-2/55). 5-Censored issue with tomahawks removed in battle scene	31.00	94.00	250.00
6-S&K-c/a	24.00	71.00	190.00
7-S&K-c/a(3)	31.00	94.00	250.00
Great Scott Shoe Store giveaway-Reprints #2 with new cover	16.00	49.00	130.00

BULLS-EYE COMICS (Formerly Komik Pages #10; becomes Kayo #12)
No. 11, 1944
Harry 'A' Chesler

	GD25	FN65	NM94
11-Origin K-9, Green Knight's sidekick, Lance; The Green Knight, Lady Satan, Yankee Doodle Jones app.	33.00	98.00	260.00

BULLWHIP GRIFFIN (See Movie Comics)

BULLWINKLE (...and Rocky No. 20 on; See March of Comics #233 and Rocky & Bullwinkle)(TV) (Jay Ward)
3-5/62 - #11, 4/74; #12, 6/76 - #19, 3/78; #20, 4/79 - #25, 2/80
Dell Publishing/Gold Key

	GD25	FN65	NM94
Four Color 1270 (3-5/62)	18.00	55.00	200.00
01-090-209 (Dell, 7-9/62)	14.00	44.00	160.00
1(11/62, Gold Key)	12.00	37.00	135.00
2(2/63)	7.00	22.00	80.00
3(4/72)-11(4/74-Gold Key)	4.50	13.50	50.00
12(6/76)-Reprints	2.25	6.75	18.00
13(9/76), 14-New stories	2.25	6.75	18.00
15-25	1.25	3.75	10.00
Mother Moose Nursery Pomes 01-530-207 (5-7/62, Dell)	16.00	49.00	180.00

NOTE: *Reprints: 6, 7, 20-24.*

BULLWINKLE (...& Rocky No. 2 on)(TV)
July, 1970 - No. 7, July, 1971
Charlton Comics

	GD25	FN65	NM94
1	4.00	12.00	40.00
2-7	3.00	9.00	30.00

BULLWINKLE AND ROCKY
Nov, 1987 - No. 9, Mar, 1989
Star Comics/Marvel Comics No. 3 on

	GD25	FN65	NM94
1-9: 3,5,8-Dudley Do-Right app. 4-Reagan-c		1.60	4.00

BUMMER
June, 1995 ($3.50, B&W, mature)
Fantagraphics Books

	GD25	FN65	NM94
1		1.40	3.50

BUNNY (Also see Rock Happening)
Dec, 1966 - No. 20, Dec, 1971; No. 21, Nov, 1976
Harvey Publications

	GD25	FN65	NM94
1-68 pg. Giants begin	4.50	13.50	45.00
2-10	2.80	8.40	28.00
11-18: 18-Last 68 pg. Giant	2.50	7.50	22.00
19-21-52 pg. Giants: 21-Fruitman app.	2.25	6.75	18.00

BURKE'S LAW (TV)
1-3/64; No. 2, 5-7/64; No. 3, 3-5/65 (All have Gene Barry photo-c)
Dell Publishing Co.

	GD25	FN65	NM94
1-Photo-c	4.00	12.00	45.00
2,3-Photo-c	3.00	9.00	35.00

BURNING ROMANCES (See Fox Giants)

BUSTER BEAR
Dec, 1953 - No. 10, June, 1955
Quality Comics Group (Arnold Publ.)

	GD25	FN65	NM94
1-Funny animal	6.50	19.50	45.00
2	4.00	11.00	22.00
3-10	3.60	9.00	18.00
I.W. Reprint #9,10 (Super on inside)	1.40	3.50	7.00

BUSTER BROWN COMICS (Radio)(Also see My Dog Tige)
1945 - No. 43, 1959 (No. 5: paper-c)
Brown Shoe Co

	GD25	FN65	NM94
nn, nd (#1,scarce)-Featuring Smilin' Ed McConnell & the Buster Brown gang "Midnight" the cat, "Squeaky" the mouse & "Froggy" the Gremlin; covers mention diff. shoe stores. Contains adventure stories	56.00	168.00	500.00
2	17.00	51.00	135.00
3,5-10	8.75	26.25	70.00
4 (Rare)-Low print run due to paper shortage	14.00	41.00	110.00
11-20	6.50	19.50	45.00
21-24,26-28	5.35	16.00	32.00
25,33-37,40,41-Crandall-a in all	8.75	26.25	65.00
29-32-"Interplanetary Police Vs. the Space Siren" by Crandall (pencils only #29)	8.75	26.25	65.00
38,39,42,43	5.35	16.00	32.00
...Goes to Mars (2/58-Western Printing), slick-c, 20 pgs., reg. size	8.75	26.25	70.00
...In "Buster Makes the Team!" (1959-Custom Comics)	5.70	17.00	40.00
...In The Jet Age ('50s), slick-c, 20 pgs., 5x7-1/4"	8.75	26.25	65.00
...Of the Safety Patrol ('60-Custom Comics)	4.00	12.00	24.00
...Out of This World ('59-Custom Comics)	5.70	17.00	40.00
...Safety Coloring Book ('58, 16 pgs.)-Slick paper	5.70	17.00	35.00

The Butcher #1 © DC

Buzzy #17 © DC

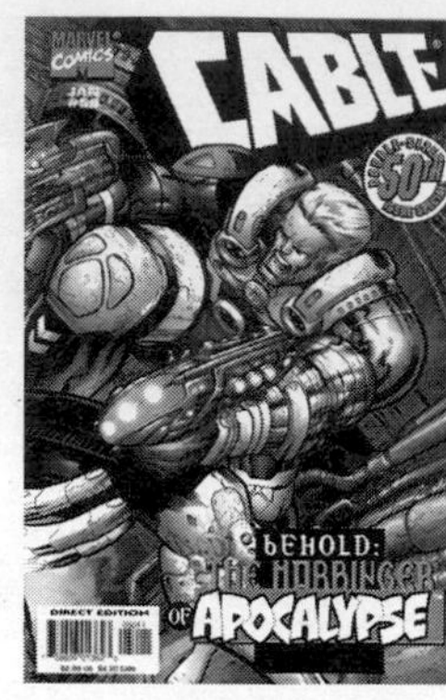

Cable #50 © MEG

BUSTER BUNNY
Nov, 1949 - No. 16, Oct, 1953
Standard Comics(Animated Cartoons)/Pines

	GD25	FN65	NM94
1-Frazetta 1 pg. text illo.	6.50	19.50	45.00
2	4.00	11.00	22.00
3-16: 15-Racist-c	3.20	8.00	16.00

BUSTER CRABBE (TV)
Nov, 1951 - No. 12, 1953
Famous Funnies Publ.

	GD25	FN65	NM94
1-1st app.(?) Frazetta anti-drug ad; text story about Buster Crabbe & Billy the Kid	28.00	83.00	220.00
2-Williamson/Evans-c; text story about Wild Bill Hickok & Pecos Bill	29.00	86.00	230.00
3-Williamson/Evans-c/a	33.00	98.00	260.00
4-Frazetta-c/a, 1pg.; bondage-c	36.00	108.00	320.00
5-Frazetta-c; Williamson/Krenkel/Orlando-a, 11pgs. (per Mr. Williamson)	89.00	267.00	800.00
6,8	14.00	41.00	110.00
7-Frazetta one pg. ad	15.00	45.00	120.00
9-One pg. Frazetta Boy Scouts ad (1st?)	12.00	38.00	100.00
10-12	8.75	26.25	65.00

NOTE: Eastern Color sold 3 dozen each NM file copies of #s 9-12 a few years ago.

BUSTER CRABBE (The Amazing Adventures of...)(Movie star)
Dec, 1953 - No. 4, June, 1954
Lev Gleason Publications

	GD25	FN65	NM94
1,4: 1-Photo-c. 4-Flash Gordon-c	17.50	53.00	140.00
2,3-Toth-a	16.00	49.00	130.00

BUTCH CASSIDY
June, 1971 - No. 3, Oct, 1971 (52 pgs.)
Skywald Comics

	GD25	FN65	NM94
1-Red Mask reprint, retitled Maverick; Bolle-a	1.00	3.00	8.00
2,3: 2-Whip Wilson-r. 3-Dead Canyon Days reprint/Crack Western No. 63; Sundance Kid app.; Crandall-a		2.40	6.00

BUTCH CASSIDY (...& the Wild Bunch)
1951
Avon Periodicals

	GD25	FN65	NM94
1-Kinstler-c/a	14.00	41.00	110.00

NOTE: ***Reinman*** *story; Issue number on inside spine.*

BUTCH CASSIDY (See Fun-In No. 11 & Western Adventure Comics)

BUTCHER, THE (Also see Brave and the Bold, 2nd Series))
May, 1990 - No. 5, Sept, 1990 ($1.50, mature)
DC Comics

	GD25	FN65	NM94
1-5: 1-No indicia inside			1.50

BUZ SAWYER (Sweeney No. 4 on)
June, 1948 - No. 3, 1949
Standard Comics

	GD25	FN65	NM94
1-Roy Crane-a	17.50	53.00	140.00
2-Intro his pal Sweeney	10.00	30.00	80.00
3	8.75	26.25	65.00

BUZ SAWYER'S PAL, ROSCOE SWEENEY (See Sweeney)

BUZZ BUZZ COMICS MAGAZINE
May, 1996 ($4.95, B&W, over-sized magazine)
Horse Press

	GD25	FN65	NM94
1-Paul Pope-c/a/scripts; Moebius-a		2.00	5.00

BUZZY (See All Funny Comics)
Winter, 1944-45 - No. 75, 1-2/57; No. 76, 10/57; No. 77, 10/58
National Periodical Publications/Detective Comics

	GD25	FN65	NM94
1 (52 pgs. begin); "America's favorite teenster"	23.00	69.00	185.00
2 (Spr, 1945)	10.50	32.00	85.00
3-5	7.85	23.50	55.00
6-10	5.70	17.00	35.00
11-20	5.00	15.00	30.00
21-30	4.00	11.00	22.00
31,35-38	3.60	9.00	18.00
32-34,39-Last 52 pgs. Scribbly story by Mayer in each (these four stories were done for Scribbly #14 which was delayed for a year)	4.00	11.00	22.00
40-77: 62-Last precode (2/55)	3.20	8.00	16.00

BUZZY THE CROW (See Harvey Comics Hits #60 & 62, Harvey Hits #18 & Paramount Animated Comics #1)

BY BIZARRE HANDS
Apr, 1994 - No. 3, June, 1994 ($2.50, B&W, limited series, mature)
Dark Horse Comics

	GD25	FN65	NM94
1-3: Lansdale stories		1.00	2.50

CABBOT: BLOODHUNTER (Also see Bloodstrike & Bloodstrike: Assassin)
Jan, 1997 ($2.50, one-shot)
Maximum Press

	GD25	FN65	NM94
1-Rick Veitch-a/script; Platt-c; Thor, Chapel & Prophet cameos		1.00	2.50

CABLE (See Ghost Rider &..., & New Mutants #87)
May, 1993 - Present ($3.50/$1.95/$1.50)
Marvel Comics

	GD25	FN65	NM94
1-($3.50, 52 pgs.)-Gold foil & embossed-c; Thibert a-1-4p; c-1-3; Liefeld-a assist #4		2.00	5.00
2-15: 3-Extra 16 pg. X-Men/Avengers ann. preview. 4-Liefeld-a assist; last Thibert-a(p). 6-8-Reveals that Baby Nathan is Cable; gives background on Stryfe. 9-Omega Red-c/story. 11-Bound-in trading card sheet		.80	2.00
16-Newsstand edition		1.20	3.00
16-Enhanced edition	1.00	2.80	7.00
17-20-($1.95)-Deluxe edition, 20-w/bound in '95 Fleer Ultra cards		.80	2.00
17-20-($1.50)-Standard edition			1.50
21-24, 26-44, -1(7/97): 21-Begin $1.95-c; return from Age of Apocalyse. 24-Grizzly dies. 28-vs. Sugarman; Mr. Sinister app. 30-X-Man-c/app.; Exodus app. 31-vs. X-Man. 32-Post app. 33-Post-c/app; Mandarin app (flashback); includes "Onslaught Update". 34-Onslaught x-over; Hulk-c/app.; Apocalypse app (cont'd in Hulk #444). 35-Onslaught x-over; Apocalypse vs. Cable. 36-w/card insert. 38-Weapon X-c/app; Psycho Man & Micronauts app. 40-Scott Clark-a(p). 41-Bishop-c/app.		.80	2.00
25 ($3.95)-Foil gatefold-c		1.60	4.00
45-49,51-53: 45-Begin $1.99-c; Operation Zero Tolerance			1.99
50-($2.99) Double sized w/wraparound-c			2.99
.../X-Force '96 ($2.95) Wraparound-c			2.95

CABLE - BLOOD AND METAL (Also see New Mutants #87 & X-Force #8)
Oct, 1992 - No. 2, Nov, 1992 ($2.50, limited series, 52 pgs.)
Marvel Comics

	GD25	FN65	NM94
1-Fabian Nicieza scripts; John Romita, Jr.-c/a in both; Cable vs. Stryfe; 2nd app. of The Wild Pack (becomes The Six Pack); wraparound-c.		1.40	3.50
2-Prelude to X-Cutioner's Song		1.00	2.50

CADET GRAY OF WEST POINT (See Dell Giants)

CADILLACS & DINOSAURS (TV)
Nov, 1990 - No. 6, Apr, 1991 ($2.50, limited series, coated paper)
Marvel Comics (Epic Comics)

	GD25	FN65	NM94
1-6: r/Xenozoic Tales in color w/new-c		1.00	2.50
...In 3-D #1 (7/92, $3.95, Kitchen Sink)-With glasses		1.60	4.00

CADILLACS AND DINOSAURS (TV)
V2#1, Feb, 1994 - V2#6, July, 1994 ($2.50, limited series)

Caffeine #5 © Jim Hill

Cage #1 © MEG

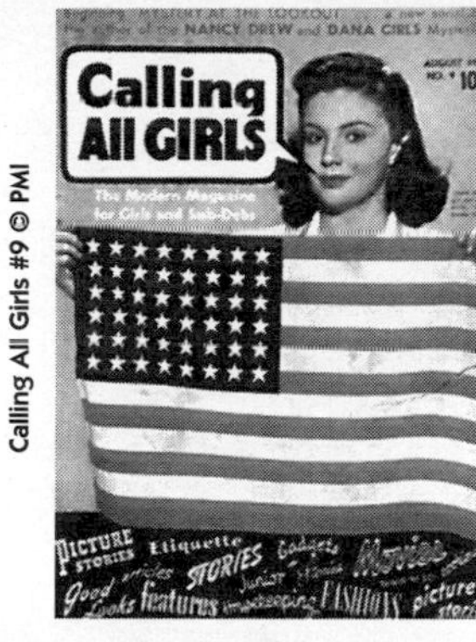

Calling All Girls #9 © PMI

	GD25	FN65	NM94

Topps Comics

	GD25	FN65	NM94
V2#1-($2.95)-Collector's edition w/Stout-c & bound-in poster; Buckler-a; foil stamped logo; Giordano-a in all		1.20	3.00
V2#1-Newsstand edition w/Giordano-c		1.00	2.50
2,3-Collector's editions w/Stout-c & posters		1.00	2.50
2,3-Newsstand ed. w/Giordano-c; w/o posters		1.00	2.50
4-6-Collectors edition; Kieth-c		1.00	2.50
4-6-Newsstand edition		1.00	2.50

CAFFEINE
Jan, 1996 - Present ($2.95, B&W)
Slave Labor Graphics

	GD25	FN65	NM94
1-8		1.20	3.00

CAGE (Also see Hero for Hire, Power Man & Punisher)
Apr, 1992 - No. 20, Nov, 1993 ($1.25)
Marvel Comics

	GD25	FN65	NM94
1-($1.50)-Has extra color on-c			1.50
2-11,13-20: 3-Punisher-c & minor app. 9-Rhino-c/story; Hulk cameo. 10-Rhino & Hulk-c/story			1.25
12-($1.75, 52 pgs.)-Iron Fist app.		.70	1.75

CAGED HEAT 3000 (Movie)
Nov, 1995 - No. 3, Jan, 1996 ($2.50, limited series)
Roger Corman's Cosmic Comics

	GD25	FN65	NM94
1-3: Adaptation of film		1.00	2.50

CAGES
1991 - No. 10, May, 1996 ($3.50/$3.95/$4.95, limited series)
Tundra Publishing

	GD25	FN65	NM94
1-Dave McKean-c/a in all	1.50	4.50	12.00
2-Misprint exists	1.00	3.00	8.00
3-9: 5-$3.95-c begins		1.60	4.00
10-($4.95)		2.00	5.00

CAIN'S HUNDRED (TV)
May-July, 1962 - No. 2, Sept-Nov, 1962
Dell Publishing Co.

	GD25	FN65	NM94
nn(01-094-207)	1.75	5.25	14.00
2	1.25	3.75	10.00

CAIN/VAMPIRELLA FLIP BOOK
Oct, 1994 ($6.95, one-shot, squarebound)
Harris Comics

	GD25	FN65	NM94
nn-contains Cain #3 & #4; flip book is r/Vampirella story from 1993 Creepy Fearbook.	1.00	3.00	7.50

CALIBER PRESENTS
Jan, 1989 - No. 24, 1991 ($1.95/$2.50, B&W, 52 pgs.)
Caliber Press

	GD25	FN65	NM94
1-Anthology; 1st app. The Crow; Tim Vigil-c/a	6.00	18.00	60.00
2-Deadworld story; Tim Vigil-a		2.00	5.00
3-14: 9-Begin $2.50-c		1.20	3.00
15-24 ($3.50, 68 pgs.)		1.40	3.50

CALIBER PRESENTS: CINDERELLA ON FIRE
1994 ($2.95, B&W, mature)
Caliber Press

	GD25	FN65	NM94
1		1.20	3.00

CALIBER SPOTLIGHT
May, 1995 ($2.95, B&W)
Caliber Press

	GD25	FN65	NM94
1-Kabuki app		1.40	3.50

CALIBRATIONS
1996 - Present (99¢, anthology)
Caliber

	GD25	FN65	NM94
1,2: 1-Jill Thompson-c/a. 1,2-Atmospherics by Warren Ellis			1.00

CALIFORNIA GIRLS
June, 1987 - No. 8, May, 1988 ($2.00, 40 pgs, B&W)
Eclipse Comics

	GD25	FN65	NM94
1-8: All contain color paper dolls		.80	2.00

CALL FROM CHRIST
1952 (Giveaway, 36 pgs.)
Catechetical Educational Society

	GD25	FN65	NM94
nn	2.00	5.00	10.00

CALLING ALL BOYS (Tex Granger No. 18 on)
Jan, 1946 - No. 17, May, 1948 (Photo c-1-5,7,8)
Parents' Magazine Institute

	GD25	FN65	NM94
1	8.75	26.25	65.00
2-Contains Roy Rogers article	4.25	13.00	28.00
3-7,9,11,14-17: 6-Painted-c. 11-Rin Tin Tin photo on-c; Tex Granger begins. 14-J. Edgar Hoover photo on-c. 15-Tex Granger-c begin	4.00	10.00	20.00
8-Milton Caniff story	5.70	17.00	35.00
10-Gary Cooper photo on-c	5.35	16.00	32.00
12-Bob Hope photo on-c	7.15	21.50	50.00
13-Bing Crosby photo on-c	5.70	17.00	40.00

CALLING ALL GIRLS
Sept, 1941 - No. 89, Sept, 1949 (Part magazine, part comic)
Parents' Magazine Institute

	GD25	FN65	NM94
1	10.00	30.00	80.00
2-Photo-c	5.70	17.00	40.00
3-Shirley Temple photo-c	6.85	21.00	48.00
4-10: 4,5,7,9-Photo-c. 9-Flag-c	4.00	12.00	24.00
11-Tina Thayer photo-c; Mickey Rooney photo-b/c; B&W photo inside of Gary Cooper as Lou Gehrig in "Pride of Yankees"	4.00	11.00	22.00
12-20	4.00	11.00	20.00
21-39,41-43(10-11/45)-Last issue with comics	3.00	7.50	15.00
40-Liz Taylor photo-c	7.85	23.50	55.00
44-51(7/46)-Last comic book size issue	2.80	7.00	14.00
52-89	2.00	5.00	10.00

NOTE: ***Jack Sparling*** *art in many issues; becomes a girls' magazine "Senior Prom" with #90.*

CALLING ALL KIDS (Also see True Comics)
Dec-Jan, 1945-46 - No. 26, Aug, 1949
Parents' Magazine Institute

	GD25	FN65	NM94
1-Funny animal	8.50	26.00	60.00
2	4.25	13.00	28.00
3-10	2.80	7.00	14.00
11-26	2.00	5.00	10.00

CALVIN (See Li'l Kids)

CALVIN & THE COLONEL (TV)
No. 1354, Apr-June, 1962 - No. 2, July-Sept, 1962
Dell Publishing Co.

	GD25	FN65	NM94
Four Color 1354(#1)	7.00	22.00	80.00
2	4.50	13.50	50.00

CAMBION
Dec, 1995 - No. 2, Feb, 1996 ($2.95, B&W)
Slave Labor Graphics

	GD25	FN65	NM94
1,2		1.20	3.00

CAMELOT 3000
12/82 - #11, 7/84; #12, 4/85 (Direct sales, maxi series, Mando paper)
DC Comics

	GD25	FN65	NM94
1-12: 1-Mike Barr scripts & Brian Bolland-c/a begin. 5-Intro Knights of New Camelot		1.00	2.50

NOTE: ***Austin*** *a-7i-12i.* ***Bolland*** *a-1-12p; c-1-12.*

Camp Candy #2 © DIC

Candy #46 © QUA

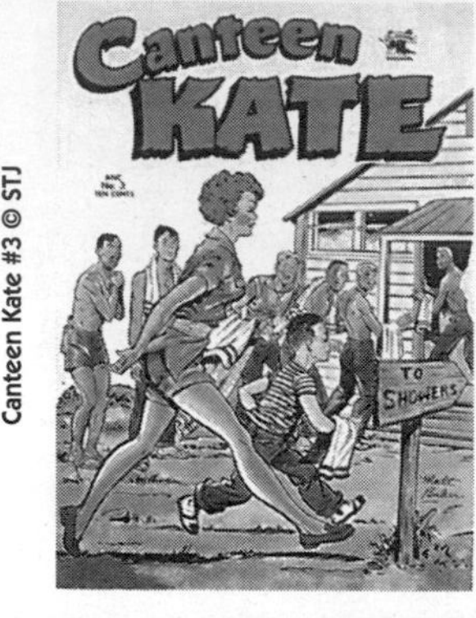

Canteen Kate #3 © STJ

	GD25	FN65	NM94

CAMERA COMICS
July, 1944 - No. 9, Summer, 1946
U.S. Camera Publishing Corp./ME

nn (7/44)	18.00	54.00	145.00
nn (9/44)	15.00	45.00	120.00
1(10/44)-The Grey Comet	15.00	45.00	120.00
2	10.00	30.00	80.00
3-Nazi WW II-c; photos	8.75	26.25	70.00
4-9: All half photos	8.75	26.25	65.00

CAMP CANDY (TV)
May, 1990 - No. 6, Oct, 1990 ($1.00, limited series)
Marvel Comics

1-6: Post-c/a(p); featuring John Candy		.80	2.00

CAMP COMICS
Feb, 1942 - No. 3, April, 1942 (All have photo-c)
Dell Publishing Co.

1- "Seaman Sy Wheeler" by Kelly, 7 pgs.; Bugs Bunny app.; Mark Twain adaptation	39.00	117.00	390.00
2-Kelly-a, 12 pgs.; Bugs Bunny app.	28.50	86.00	285.00
3-(Scarce)-Dave Berg & Walt Kelly-a	39.00	117.00	390.00

CAMP RUNAMUCK (TV)
Apr, 1966
Dell Publishing Co.

1-Photo-c	2.50	7.50	22.00

CAMPUS LOVES
Dec, 1949 - No. 5, Aug, 1950
Quality Comics Group (Comic Magazines)

1-Ward-c/a (9 pgs.)	25.00	75.00	180.00
2-Ward-c/a	19.00	58.00	140.00
3-5: 5-Spanking panels (2)	10.00	30.00	65.00

NOTE: ***Gustavson*** *a-1-5. Photo c-3-5.*

CAMPUS ROMANCE (...Romances on cover)
Sept-Oct, 1949 - No. 3, Feb-Mar, 1950
Avon Periodicals/Realistic

1-Walter Johnson-a; c-/Avon paperback #348	20.00	60.00	140.00
2-Grandenetti-a; c-/Avon paperback #151; spanking panel	14.00	43.00	100.00
3-c-/Avon paperback #201	14.00	43.00	100.00
Realistic reprint	5.70	17.00	40.00

CANADA DRY PREMIUMS (See Swamp Fox, The & Terry & The Pirates)

CANCELLED COMIC CAVALCADE
Summer, 1978 - No. 2, Fall, 1978 (8-1/2x11", B&W)
(Xeroxed pgs. on one side only w/blue cover and taped spine)
DC Comics, Inc.

1-(412 pgs.) Contains xeroxed copies of art for: Black Lightning #12, cover to #13; Claw #13, 14; The Deserter #1; Doorway to Nightmare #6; Firestorm #6; The Green Team #2,3.
2-(532 pgs.) Contains xeroxed copies of art for: Kamandi #60 (including Omac), #61; Prez #5; Shade #9 (including The Odd Man); Showcase #105 (Deadman), 106 (The Creeper); The Vixen #1; and covers to Army at War #2, Battle Classics #3, Demand Classics #1 & 2, Dynamic Classics #3, Mr. Miracle #26, Ragman #6, Weird Mystery #25 & 26, & Western Classics #1 & 2. (Rare) (One set sold in 1989 for $1,200.00)

NOTE: *In June, 1978, DC cancelled several of their titles. For copyright purposes, the unpublished original art for these titles was xeroxed, bound in the above books, published and distributed. Only 35 copies were made.*

CANDID TALES (Also see Bold Stories & It Rhymes With Lust)
April, 1950; June, 1950 (Digest size) (144 pgs.) (Full color)
Kirby Publishing Co.

nn-(Scarce) Contains Wood female pirate story, 15 pgs., and 14 pgs. in June issue; Powell-a	72.00	216.00	650.00

NOTE: *Another version exists with Dr. Kilmore by Wood; no female pirate story.*

	GD25	FN65	NM94

CANDY
Fall, 1944 - No. 3, Spring, 1945
William H. Wise & Co.

1-Two Scoop Scuttle stories by Wolverton	30.00	90.00	240.00
2,3-Scoop Scuttle by Wolverton, 2-4 pgs.	24.00	71.00	190.00

CANDY (Teen-age)(Also see Police Comics #37)
Autumn, 1947 - No. 64, July, 1956
Quality Comics Group (Comic Magazines)

1-Gustavson-a	16.00	49.00	130.00
2-Gustavson-a	8.75	26.25	65.00
3-10	5.70	17.00	40.00
11-30	4.15	12.50	25.00
31-63	4.00	12.00	24.00
64-Ward-c(p)?	4.00	12.00	24.00
Super Reprint No. 2,10,12,16,17,18('63- '64):17-Candy #12	2.00	5.00	10.00

NOTE: ***Jack Cole*** *1-2 pg. art in many issues.*

CANNON (See Heroes, Inc. Presents Cannon)

CANNONBALL COMICS
Feb, 1945 - No. 2, Mar, 1945
Rural Home Publishing Co.

1-The Crash Kid, Thunderbrand, The Captive Prince & Crime Crusader begin; skull-c	56.00	168.00	500.00
2-Devil-c	47.00	141.00	425.00

CANTEEN KATE (See All Picture All True Love Story & Fightin' Marines)
June, 1952 - No. 3, Nov, 1952
St. John Publishing Co.

1-Matt Baker-c/a	40.00	120.00	350.00
2-Matt Baker-c/a	39.00	118.00	290.00
3-(Rare)-Used in **POP**, pg. 75; Baker-c/a	40.00	120.00	350.00

CAP'N CRUNCH COMICS (See Quaker Oats)
1963; 1965 (16 pgs.; miniature giveaways; 2-1/2x6-1/2")
Quaker Oats Co.

(1963 titles)- "The Picture Pirates", "The Fountain of Youth", "I'm Dreaming of a Wide Isthmus". (1965 titles)- "Bewitched, Betwitched, & Betweaked", "Seadog Meets the Witch Doctor" (another 1965 title suspected)	3.80	11.40	38.00

CAP'N QUICK & A FOOZLE (Also see Eclipse Mag. & Monthly)
July, 1984 - No. 3, Nov, 1985 ($1.50, color, Baxter paper)
Eclipse Comics

1-3-Rogers-c/a			1.50

CAPTAIN ACTION (Toy)
Oct-Nov, 1968 - No. 5, June-July, 1969 (Based on Ideal toy)
National Periodical Publications

1-Origin; Wood-a; Superman-c app.	8.00	24.00	80.00
2,3,5-Kane/Wood-a	5.00	15.00	50.00
4	3.80	11.40	38.00
...& Action Boy('67)-Ideal Toy Co. giveaway (1st app. Captain Action)	8.00	24.00	80.00

CAPTAIN AERO COMICS (Samson No. 1-6; also see Veri Best Sure Fire &Veri Best Sure Shot Comics)
V1#7(#1), Dec, 1941 - V2#4(#10), Jan, 1943; V3#9(#11), Sept, 1943 - V4#3(#17), Oct, 1944; #21, Dec, 1944 - #26, Aug, 1946 (No #18-20)
Holyoke Publishing Co.

V1#7(#1)-Flag-Man & Solar, Master of Magic, Captain Aero, Cap Stone, Adventurer begin	122.00	366.00	1100.00
8(#2)-Pals of Freedom app.	61.00	183.00	550.00
9(#3)-Alias X begins; Pals of Freedom app.	61.00	183.00	550.00
10(#4)-Origin The Gargoyle; Kubert-a	61.00	183.00	550.00

Captain America #230 © MEG

Captain America #370 © MEG

Captain America #431 © MEG

GD25 FN65 NM94

11,12(#5,6)-Kubert-a; Miss Victory in #6 50.00 150.00 450.00
V2#1,2(#7,8): 8-Origin The Red Cross; Miss Victory app.; Brodsky-c(i)
30.00 90.00 240.00
3(#9)-Miss Victory app. 24.00 71.00 190.00
4(#10)-Miss Victory app. 19.00 56.00 150.00
V3#9 - V3#13(#11-15): 11,15-Miss Victory app. 15.50 47.00 125.00
V4#2(#16) 14.00 41.00 110.00
V4#3(#17), 21-24-L. B. Cole covers. 22-Intro/origin Mighty Mite.
25 25.00 75.00 200.00
26--L. B. Cole S/F-c; Palais-a(2) 44.00 132.00 400.00
NOTE: ***L.B. Cole** c-17. **Hollingsworth** a-23. **Infantino** a-23, 26. **Schomburg** c-15, 16.*

CAPTAIN AMERICA (See Adventures of..., All-Select, All Winners, Aurora, Avengers #4, Blood and Glory, Captain Britain 16-20, Giant-Size..., The Invaders, Marvel Double Feature, Marvel Fanfare, Marvel Mystery, Marvel Super-Action, Marvel Super Heroes V2#3, Marvel Team-Up, Marvel Treasury Special, Power Record Comics, USA Comics, Young Allies & Young Men)

CAPTAIN AMERICA (Formerly Tales of Suspense #1-99) (Captain America and the Falcon #134-223 & Steve Rogers: Captain America #444-454 appears on cover only)
No. 100, Apr, 1968 - No. 454, Aug, 1996
Marvel Comics Group

100-Flashback on Cap's revival with Avengers & Sub-Mariner; story continued from Tales of Suspense #99; Kirby-c/a begins 25.00 75.00 250.00
101-The Sleeper-c/story; Red Skull app. 5.00 15.00 50.00
102-108: 102-Sleeper-c/s. 103,104-Red Skull-c/sty 3.00 9.00 30.00
109-Origin Capt. America retold 4.50 13.50 45.00
110,111,113-Classic Steranko-c/a: 110-Rick becomes Cap's partner; Hulk x-over; 1st app. Viper. 111-Death of Steve Rogers. 113-Cap's funeral
4.50 13.50 45.00
112-Origin retold; last Kirby-c/a 2.80 8.40 28.00
114-116,118-120: 115-Last 12¢ issue 2.25 6.75 18.00
117-1st app. The Falcon (9/69) 4.50 13.50 45.00
121-140: 121-Retells origin. 133-The Falcon becomes Cap's partner; origin Modok. 137,138-Spider-Man x-over. 140-Origin Grey Gargoyle retold
1.10 3.30 9.00
141,142,144-153,155-171,176-179: 142-Last 15¢ issue. 144-New costume Falcon. 153-1st app. (cameo) Jack Monroe. 155-Origin; redrawn w/Falcon added; origin J. Monroe. 158-Cap's strength increased. 160-1st app. Solarr. 164-1st app. Nightshade. 176-End of Capt. America 2.40 6.00
143-(52 pgs). 1.25 3.75 10.00
154-1st full app. Jack Monroe (Nomad)(10/72) 2.40 6.00
172-175: X-Men x-over 1.50 4.50 12.00
180-Intro/origin of Nomad (Steve Rogers) 1.00 2.80 7.00
181-Intro/origin new Cap. 2.40 6.00
182,184-192,194-197,199(7/76): 186-True origin The Falcon 1.60 4.00
183-Death of new Cap; Nomad becomes Cap 2.40 6.00
193,200: 193-Kirby-a returns 2.40 6.00
198-(Regular 25¢ edition)(6/76) 1.60 4.00
198-(30¢-c, limited distribution) 2.00 6.00 16.00
201-240,242-246: 215-Retells Cap's origin. 216-r/story from Strange Tales #114. 217-1st app. Marvel Man (later Quasar). 229-Marvel Man app. 230-Battles Hulk-c/story cont'd in Hulk #232. 233-Death of Sharon Carter. 234,235-Daredevil x-over; 235(7/79)-Miller-a(p). 244,245-Miller-c. 1.20 3.00
241-Punisher app.; Miller-c. 1.00 3.00 8.00
241-2nd print .80 2.00
247-255-Byrne-a. 255-Origin; Miller-c. 1.40 3.50
256-281,284,285,289-322,324-326,329-331: 264-Old X-Men cameo in flash-back. 265,266-Nick Fury & Spider-Man app. 267-1st app. Everyman. 269-1st Team America. 279-(3/83)-Contains Tattooz skin decals. 281-1950s Bucky returns. 284-Patriot (Jack Mace) app. 285-Death of Patriot. 298-Origin Red Skull .80 2.00
282-Bucky becomes new Nomad (Jack Monroe) 1.60 4.00
282-Silver ink 2nd print ($1.75) w/original date (6/83) .70 1.75
283-2nd app. Nomad 1.20 3.00

GD25 FN65 NM94

286-288-Deathlok app. 1.00 2.50
323-1st app. new Super Patriot (see Nick Fury) 1.60 4.00
327-Captain America battles Super Patriot 1.20 3.00
328-Origin & 1st app. D-Man 1.00 2.50
332-Old Cap resigns 2.00 5.00
333-Intro & origin new Captain (Super Patriot) 1.20 3.00
334-340: 339-Fall of the Mutants tie-in 1.20 3.00
341-343,345-349 1.50
344-($1.50, 52 pgs.)-Ronald Reagan cameo .80 2.00
350-($1.75, 68 pgs.)-Return of Steve Rogers (original Cap) to original costume
1.20 3.00
351-354: 351-Nick Fury app. 354-1st app. U.S. Agent (6/89, see Avengers West Coast) 1.50
355-382,384-396: 373-Bullseye app. 375-Daredevil app. 386-U.S. Agent app. 387-389-Red Skull back-up stories. 396-Last $1.00-c. 396,397-1st app. all new Jack O'Lantern 1.50
383-($2.00, 68 pgs.)-50th anniversary issue; Red Skull story; Jim Lee-c(i)
1.20 3.00
397-399,401-424,426: 402-Begin 6 part Man-Wolf story w/Wolverine in #403-407. 405-410-New Jack O'Lantern app. in back-up story. 406-Cable & Shatterstar cameo. 407-Capwolf vs. Cable-c/story. 408-Infinity War x-over; Falcon solo back-up. 423-Vs. Namor-c/story 1.25
400-($2.25, 84 pgs.)-Flip book format w/double gatefold-c; r/Avengers #4 plus-c; contains cover pin-ups. 1.00 2.50
425-($2.95, 52 pgs.)-Embossed Foil-c edition; Fighting Chance Pt. 1
1.20 3.00
425-($1.75, 52 pgs.)-Regular edition .75 1.80
427-443,446,447,449-454: 427-Begin $1.50-c; bound-in trading card sheet. 449-Thor app. 450-"Man Without A Country" storyline begins, ends #453; Bill Clinton app; variant-c exists. 451-1st app.Cap's new costume. 452-Machinesmith app. 453-Cap gets old costume back; Bill Clinton app. 1.50
444-Mark Waid scripts & Ron Garney-c/a(p) begins, ends #454; Avengers app.
2.00 5.00
445-Sharon Carter & Red Skull return. 1.00 2.50
448-($2.95, double-sized issue)-Waid script & Garney-c/a; Red Skull dies?
1.40 3.50
Special 1(1/71)-Origin retold 2.50 7.50 24.00
Special 2(1/72) Colan r/Not Brand Echh; all-r 1.50 4.50 12.00
Annual 3,4('76,'77, 52 pgs.)-Kirby-c/a(new); 4-Magneto-c/story (34 pgs.)
1.00 2.80 7.00
Annual 5-7: (52 pgs.)('81-'83) 1.00 2.50
Annual 8(9/86)-Wolverine-c/story 1.85 5.50 15.00
Annual 9(1990, $2.00, 68 pgs.)-Nomad back-up 1.20 3.00
Annual 10(1991, $2.00, 68 pgs.)-Origin retold (2 pgs.) .80 2.00
Annual 11(1992, $2.25, 68 pgs.)-Falcon solo story .90 2.25
Annual 12(1993, $2.95, 68 pgs.)-Bagged w/card 1.20 3.00
Annual 13(1994, $2.95, 68 pgs.)-Red Skull-c/story 1.20 3.00
...ASHCAN EDITION ('95, 75¢) .75
...: DEATHLOK LIVES! nn(10/93, $4.95)-r/#286-288 2.00 5.00
...DRUG WAR 1-(1994, $2.00, 52 pgs.)-New Warriors app. .80 2.00
...MEDUSA EFFECT 1 (1994, $2.95, 68 pgs.)-Origin Baron Zemo 1.20 3.00
...OPERATION REBIRTH (1996, $9.95)-r/#445-448 1.25 3.75 10.00
...STREETS OF POISON ($15.95)-r/#372-378 2.00 6.00 16.00
...: THE MOVIE SPECIAL nn (5/92, $3.50, 52 pgs.)-Adapts movie; printed on coated stock; The Red Skull app. 1.20 3.00
...& THE CAMPBELL KIDS (1980, 36pg. giveaway, Campbell's Soup/U.S. Dept. of Energy) 1.00 3.00 8.00
...GOES TO WAR AGAINST DRUGS (1990, no #, giveaway)-Distributed to direct sales shops; 2nd printing exists 1.60 4.00
...MEETS THE ASTHMA MONSTER (1987, no #, giveaway, Your Physician and Glaxo, Inc.) 2.40 6.00
...VS. ASTHMA MONSTER (1990, no #, giveaway, Your Physician & Allen & Hanbury's) 1.60 4.00
NOTE: ***Austin** c-225i, 239i, 246i. **Buscema** a-115p, 217p; c-136p, 217, 297. **Byrne** c-223(part), 238, 239, 247p-254p, 290, 291, 313p; a-247-254p, 255, 313p, 350. **Colan** a(p)-116-137, 256,*

Captain America V2 #13 © MEG

Captain America V3 #1 © MEG

Captain America Comics #21 © MEG

GD25 FN65 NM94

Annual 5; c(p)-116-123, 126, 129. ***Everett*** *a-136i, 137i; c-126i.* ***Garney*** *a(p)-444-454.* ***Gil Kane*** *a-145p; c-147p, 149p, 150p, 170p, 172-174, 180, 181p, 183-190p, 215, 216, 220, 221.* ***Kirby*** *a(p)-100-109, 112, 193-214, 216, Special 1, 2(layouts), Annual 3, 4; c-100-109, 112, 126p, 193-214.* ***Ron Lim*** *a(p)-366, 368-378, 380-386; c-366p, 368-378p, 379, 380-393p.* ***Miller*** *c-241p, 244p, 245p, 255p, Annual 5.* ***Mooney*** *a-149i.* ***Morrow*** *a-144.* ***Perez*** *c-243p, 246p.* ***Robbins*** *c(p)-183-187, 189-192, 225.* ***Roussos*** *a-140i, 168i.* ***Starlin/Sinnott*** *c-162.* ***Sutton*** *a-244i.* ***Tuska*** *a-112i, 215p, Special 2.* ***Waid*** *scripts-444-454.* ***Williamson*** *a-313i.* ***Wood*** *a-127i.* ***Zeck*** *a-263-289; c-300.*

CAPTAIN AMERICA (Volume Two)
V2#1, Nov, 1996 - No. 13, Nov, 1997($2.95/$1.95) (Produced by Extreme Studios)
Marvel Comics

1-($2.95)-Heroes Reborn begins; Rob Liefeld-c/a; Jeph Loeb scripts; reintro Nick Fury 2.00 5.00
1-($2.95)-(Variant-c)-Liefeld-c/a 2.00 5.00
1-(7/96, $2.95)-(Exclusive Comicon Edition)-Liefeld-c/a 2.80 7.00
2-9-($1.95): 5-Two covers. 6-Cable-c/app. .80 2.00
10, 11: 10-Begin-$1.99-c 1.99
12-($2.99) "Heroes Reunited"-pt. 4 2.99
13-"World War 3"-pt. 4, x-over w/Image 1.99

CAPTAIN AMERICA (Volume Three)
Jan, 1998 - Present ($2.99/$1.99)
Marvel Comics

1-($2.99) Mark Waid-s/Ron Garney-a 2.99
2-4-($1.99): 2-Two covers 1.99

CAPTAIN AMERICA COMICS
Mar, 1941 - No. 75, Jan, 1950; No. 76, 5/54 - No. 78, 9/54
(No. 74 & 75 titled Capt. America's Weird Tales)
Timely/Marvel Comics (TCI 1-20/CmPS 21-68/MjMC 69-75/Atlas Comics (PrPI 76-78)

GD25 FN65 VF82 NM94
1-Origin & 1st app. Captain America & Bucky by S&K; Hurricane, Tuk the Caveboy begin by S&K; 1st app. Red Skull; Hitler-c (by Simon?); intro of the "Capt. America Sentinels of Liberty Club" (advertised on inside front-c.); indicia reads Vol. 2, Number 1 4,667.00 14,000.00 30,335.00 56,000.00
(Estimated up to 180 total copies exist, 8 in NM/Mint)

GD25 FN65 NM94
2-S&K Hurricane; Tuk by Avison (Kirby splash); classic Hitler-c 910.00 2730.00 10,000.00
3-Classic Red Skull-c & app; Stan Lee's 1st text (1st work for Marvel) 820.00 2460.00 8200.00
4-1st full pg. panel in comics 490.00 1470.00 4900.00
5 460.00 1380.00 4600.00
6-Origin Father Time; Tuk the Caveboy ends 410.00 1230.00 4100.00
7-Red Skull app.; classic-c 460.00 1380.00 4600.00
8-10-Last S&K issue, (S&K centerfold #6-10) 330.00 990.00 3300.00
11-Last Hurricane, Headline Hunter; Al Avison Captain America begins, ends #20; Avison-c(p) 290.00 870.00 2900.00
12-The Imp begins, ends #16; last Father Time 270.00 810.00 2700.00
13-Origin The Secret Stamp; classic-c 290.00 870.00 2900.00
14,15 270.00 810.00 2700.00
16-Red Skull unmasks Cap; Red Skull-c 320.00 960.00 3200.00
17-The Fighting Fool only app. 240.00 720.00 2200.00
18-classic-c 240.00 720.00 2200.00
19-Human Torch begins #19 189.00 567.00 1700.00
20-Sub-Mariner app.; no H. Torch 189.00 567.00 1700.00
21-25: 25-Cap drinks liquid opium 178.00 534.00 1600.00
26-30: 27-Last Secret Stamp; last 68 pg. issue. 28-60 pg. issues begin. 167.00 500.00 1500.00
31-35,38-40: 34-Centerfold poster of Cap 144.00 432.00 1300.00
36-Classic Hitler-c 222.00 667.00 2000.00
37-Red Skull app. 178.00 534.00 1600.00
41-47: 41-Last Jap War-c. 46-German Holocaust-c. 47-Last German War-c 128.00 384.00 1150.00
48-58,60 106.00 318.00 950.00

GD25 FN65 NM94

59-Origin retold 240.00 720.00 2300.00
61-Red Skull-c/story 200.00 600.00 1800.00
62,64,65: 65-Kurtzman's "Hey Look" 128.00 384.00 1150.00
63-Intro/origin Asbestos Lady 133.00 400.00 1200.00
66-Bucky is shot; Golden Girl teams up with Captain America & learns his i.d; origin Golden Girl 139.00 417.00 1250.00
67-Captain America/Golden Girl team-up; Mxyztplk swipe; last Toro in Human Torch 128.00 384.00 1150.00
68,70-Sub-Mariner/Namora, and Captain America/Golden Girl team-up in each. 70-Science fiction-c/story 128.00 384.00 1150.00
69,71-73: 69-Human Torch/Sun Girl team-up. 71-Anti Wertham editorial; The Witness, Bucky app. 128.00 384.00 1150.00
74-(Scarce)(1949)-Titled "Captain America's Weird Tales"; Red Skull-c & app.; classic-c 350.00 1050.00 3500.00
75(2/50)-Titled "C.A.'s Weird Tales"; no C.A. app.; horror cover/stories 133.00 400.00 1200.00
76-78(1954): Human Torch/Toro stories; all have communist-c/stories 86.00 258.00 775.00
132-Pg. Issue (B&W-1942)(Canadian)-Has blank inside-c and back-c; contains Marvel Mystery #33 & Capt. America #18 w/cover from Capt. America #22; same contents as Marvel Mystery annual 2000.00 6000.00 12000.00
Shoestore Giveaway #77 47.00 141.00 425.00

NOTE: ***Crandall*** *a-2i, 3i, 9i, 10i.* ***Kirby*** *c-8p.* ***Rico*** *c-69-71.* ***Romita*** *c-77, 78.* ***Schomburg*** *c-3, 4, 26-29, 31, 33, 37-39, 41, 42, 45-54, 58.* ***Sekowsky*** *c-55, 56.* ***Shores*** *c-1, 2, 5-7, 11i, 20-25, 30, 32, 34, 35, 40, 57, 59-67.* ***S&K*** *c-1, 2, 5-7, 9, 10. Bondage c-3, 7, 15, 16, 34, 38.*

CAPTAIN AMERICA/NICK FURY: BLOOD TRUCE
Feb, 1995 ($5.95, one-shot, squarebound)
Marvel Comics

nn-Chaykin story 2.40 6.00

CAPTAIN AMERICA, SENTINEL OF LIBERTY (See Fireside Book Series)

CAPTAIN AMERICA SPECIAL EDITION
Feb, 1984 - No. 2, Mar, 1984 ($2.00, Baxter paper)
Marvel Comics Group

1-Steranko-c/a(r) in both 1.20 3.00
2-Reprints the scarce Our Love Story #5 1.60 4.00

CAPTAIN AMERICA: THE LEGEND
Sept, 1996 ($3.95, one-shot)
Marvel Comics

1-Tribute issue; wraparound-c 1.60 4.00

CAPTAIN AND THE KIDS, THE (See Famous Comics Cartoon Books)

CAPTAIN AND THE KIDS, THE (See Comics on Parade, Katzenjammer Kids, Okay Comics & Sparkler Comics)
1938 -12/39; Sum, 1947 - No. 32, 1955; Four Color No. 881, Feb, 1958
United Features Syndicate/Dell Publ. Co.

Single Series 1(1938) 72.00 216.00 650.00
Single Series 1(Reprint)(12/39- "Reprint" on-c) 39.00 117.00 350.00
1(Summer, 1947-UFS)-Katzenjammer Kids 10.50 32.00 85.00
2 6.85 21.00 48.00
3-10 5.70 17.00 35.00
11-20 4.00 12.00 24.00
21-32(1955) 4.00 10.00 20.00
50th Anniversary issue-(1948)-Contains a 2 pg. history of the strip, including an account of the famous Supreme Court decision allowing both Pulitzer & Hearst to run the same strip under different names 7.15 21.50 50.00
Special Summer issue, Fall issue (1948) 5.70 17.00 35.00
Four Color 881 (Dell) 2.75 8.00 30.00

CAPTAIN ATOM
1950 - No. 7, 1951 (5¢, 5x7-1/4", 52 pgs.)
Nationwide Publishers

1-Sci/fic 28.00 83.00 220.00

Captain Atom #2 © DC

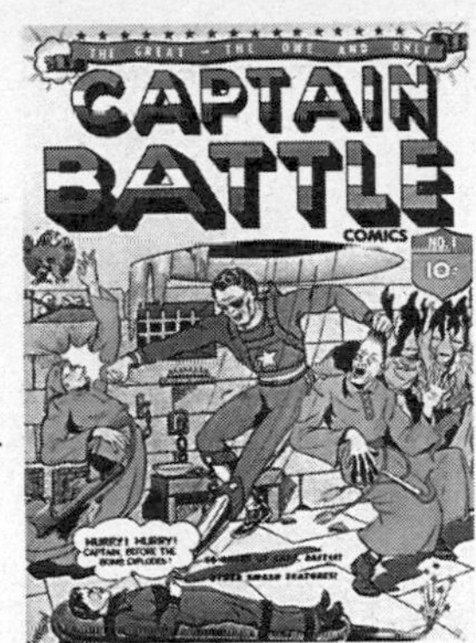

Captain Battle #1 © LEV

Captain Easy nn © NEA Services

GD25 FN65 NM94

2-7 15.00 45.00 120.00
...- Secret of the Columbian Jungle (16 pgs. in color, paper-c, 3-3/4x5-1/8")-
Fireside Marshmallow giveaway 4.15 12.50 25.00

CAPTAIN ATOM (Formerly Strange Sus. Stories #77)(Also see Space Adv.)
V2#78, Dec, 1965 - V2#89, Dec, 1967
Charlton Comics

V2#78-Origin retold; Bache-a (3 pgs.) 6.50 19.50 65.00
79-82: 79-1st app. Dr. Spectro; 3 pg. Ditko cut & paste /Space Adventures #24. 82-Intro. Nightshade (9/66) 4.20 12.60 42.00
83-86: Ted Kord Blue Beetle in all. 83-(11/66)-1st app. Ted Kord. 84-1st app. new Captain Atom 3.80 11.40 38.00
87-89: Nightshade by Aparo in all 3.80 11.40 38.00
83-85(Modern Comics-1977)-reprints 1.00
NOTE: ***Aparo** a-87-89. **Ditko** c/a(p) 78-89. #90 only published in fanzine 'The Charlton Bullseye' #1, 2.*

CAPTAIN ATOM (Also see Americomics & Crisis On Infinite Earths)
Mar, 1987 - No. 57, Sept, 1991 (Direct sales only #35 on)
DC Comics

1-(44 pgs.)-Origin/1st app. with new costume .80 2.00
2-41,43-49: 5-Firestorm x-over. 6-Intro. new Dr. Spectro. 11-Millennium tie-in 14-Nightshade app. 16-Justice League app. 17-$1.00-c begins; Swamp Thing app. 20-Blue Beetle x-over. 24,25-Invasion tie-in 1.00
42 1.20 3.00
50-($2.00, 52 pgs.) .80 2.00
51-57: 57-War of the Gods x-over 1.00
Annual 1 (1988, $1.25)-Intro Major Force 1.50
Annual 2 (1988, $1.50) 1.50

CAPTAIN BATTLE (Boy Comics #3 on) (See Silver Streak Comics)
Summer, 1941 - No. 2, Fall, 1941
New Friday Publ./Comic House

1-Origin Blackout by Rico; Captain Battle begins (1st appeared in Silver Streak #10, 5/41) 94.00 282.00 850.00
2 67.00 200.00 600.00

CAPTAIN BATTLE (2nd Series)
No. 3, Wint, 1942-43 - No. 5, Sum, 1943 (#3: 52pgs., nd)(#5: 68pgs.)
Magazine Press/Picture Scoop No. 5

3-Origin Silver Streak-r/SS#3; origin Lance Hale-r/Silver Streak; Simon-a(r) 56.00 168.00 500.00
4,5: 5-Origin Blackout retold 39.00 117.00 350.00

CAPTAIN BATTLE, JR.
Fall, 1943 - No. 2, Winter, 1943-44
Comic House (Lev Gleason)

1-The Claw vs. The Ghost 83.00 250.00 750.00
2-Wolverton's Scoop Scuttle; Don Rico-c/a; The Green Claw story is reprinted from Silver Streak #6 67.00 200.00 600.00

CAPTAIN BEN DIX
1943 (Small size)
Bendix Aviation Corporation

nn 6.70 20.00 40.00

CAPTAIN BRITAIN (Also see Marvel Team-Up No. 65, 66)
Oct. 13, 1976 - No. 39, July 6, 1977 (Weekly)
Marvel Comics International

1-Origin; with Capt. Britain's face mask inside 1.00 3.00 8.00
2-Origin, part II; Capt. Britain's Boomerang inside 1.60 4.00
3-8: 3,8-Vs. Bank Robbers. 4-7-Vs. Hurricane 1.20 3.00
9-11: Vs. Dr. Synne .80 2.00
12-27: (scarce)-12,13-Vs. Dr. Synne. 14,15-Vs. Mastermind. 16-20-With Capt. America; 17 misprinted & color section reprinted in #18. 21-23,25,26-With Capt. America. 24-With C.B.'s Jet Plane inside. 27-Origin retold 1.50 4.50 12.00

GD25 FN65 NM94

28-32,36-39: 28-32-Vs. Lord Hawk. 36-Star Sceptre. 37-39-Vs. Highwayman & Munipulator 1.50
33-35-More on origin .70 1.80
Annual (1978, Hardback, 64 pgs.)-Reprints #1-7 with pin-ups of Marvel characters 2.40 6.00
Summer Special (1980, 52 pgs.)-Reprints .80 2.00
NOTE: *No. 1, 2, & 24 are rarer in mint due to inserts. Distributed in Great Britain only. Nick Fury-r by **Steranko** in 1-20, 24-31, 35-37. Fantastic Four-r by **J. Buscema** in all. New **Buscema**-a in 24-30. Story from No. 39 continues in Super Spider-Man (British weekly) No. 231-247. Following cancellation of his series, new Captain Britain stories appeared in "Super Spider-Man" (British weekly) No. 231-247. Captain Britain stories which appear in Super-Spider-Man No 248-253 are reprints of Marvel Team-Up No. 65&66. Capt. Britain strips also appeared in Hulk Comic (weekly) 1, 3-30, 42-55, 57-60, in Marvel Superheroes (monthly) 377-388, in Daredevils (monthly) 1-11, Mighty World of Marvel (monthly) 7-16 & Captain Britain (monthly) 1-14. Issues 1-23 have B&W & color, paper-c, & are 32 pgs. Issues 24 on are all B&W w/glossy-c & are 36 pgs.*

CAPTAIN CANUCK
7/75 - No. 4, 7/77; No. 4, 7-8/79 - No. 14, 3-4/81
Comely Comix (Canada) (All distr. in U. S.)

1-1st app. Bluefox 1.60 4.00
2-1st app. Dr. Walker, Redcoat & Kebec 1.20 3.00
3(5-7/76)-1st app. Heather 1.20 3.00
4(1st printing-2/77)-10x14-1/2"; (5.00); B&W; 300 copies serially numbered and signed with one certificate of authenticity 8.50 25.50 85.00
4(2nd printing-7/77)-11x17", B&W; only 15 copies printed; signed by creator Richard Comely, serially #'d and two certificates of authenticity inserted; orange cardboard covers (Very Rare) 12.00 36.00 120.00
4-14: 4(7-8/79)-1st app. Tom Evans & Mr. Gold; origin The Catman. 5-Origin Capt. Canuck's powers; 1st app. Earth Patrol & Chaos Corps. 8-Jonn 'The Final Chapter'. 9-1st World Beyond. 11-1st 'Charlots of Fire' story .80 2.00
Summer Special 1(7-9/80, 95¢, 64 pgs.) .80 2.00
NOTE: *30,000 copies of No. 2 were destroyed in Winnipeg.*

CAPTAIN CARROT AND HIS AMAZING ZOO CREW (Also see New Teen Titans & Oz-Wonderland War)
Mar, 1982 - No. 20, Nov, 1983
DC Comics

1-20: 1-Superman app. 3-Re-intro Dodo & The Frog. 9-Re-intro Three Mouseketeers, the Terrific Whatzit. 10,11- Pig Iron reverts back to Peter Porkchops. 20-The Changeling app. 1.00

CAPTAIN CARVEL AND HIS CARVEL CRUSADERS (See Carvel Comics)

CAPTAIN CONFEDERACY
Nov, 1991 - No. 4, Feb, 1992 ($1.95)
Marvel Comics (Epic Comics)

1-4: All new stories .80 2.00

CAPTAIN COURAGEOUS COMICS (Banner #3-5; see Four Favorites #5)
No. 6, March, 1942
Periodical House (Ace Magazines)

6-Origin & 1st app. The Sword; Lone Warrior, Capt. Courageous app.; Capt. moves to Four Favorites #5 in May 61.00 183.00 550.00

CAPT'N CRUNCH COMICS (See Cap'n...)

CAPTAIN DAVY JONES
No. 598, Nov, 1954
Dell Publishing Co.

Four Color 598 3.60 11.00 40.00

CAPTAIN EASY (See The Funnies & Red Ryder #3-32)
1939 - No. 17, Sept, 1949; April, 1956
Hawley/Dell Publ./Standard(Visual Editions)/Argo

nn-Hawley(1939)-Contains reprints from The Funnies & 1938 Sunday strips by Roy Crane 72.00 216.00 650.00
Four Color 24 (1943) 38.00 115.00 420.00
Four Color 111(6/46) 13.00 40.00 145.00

Captain Flight Comics #5 © Four Star

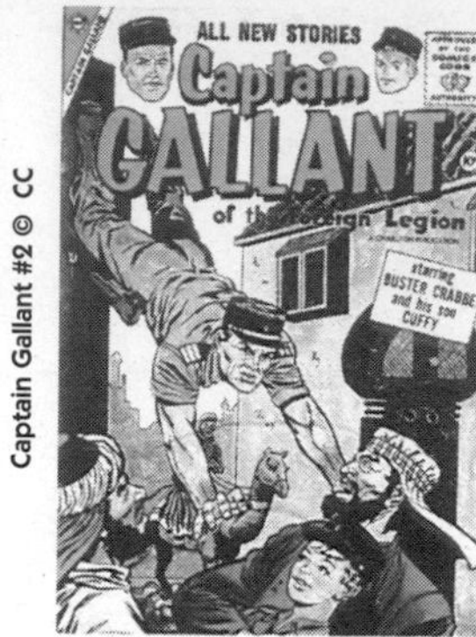

Captain Gallant #2 © CC

Captain Johner & the Aliens #2 © WEST

GD25 FN65 NM94

10(Standard-10/47) 9.50 28.00 75.00
11-17: All contain 1930s & '40s strip-r 7.85 23.50 55.00
Argo 1(4/56)-Reprints 5.70 17.00 40.00
NOTE: ***Schomburg*** *c-13, 16.*

CAPTAIN EASY & WASH TUBBS (See Famous Comics Cartoon Books)

CAPTAIN ELECTRON
Aug, 1986 ($2.25)
Brick Computer Science Institute

1-Disbrow-a .90 2.25

CAPTAIN EO 3-D (Disney)
July, 1987 (Eclipse 3-D Special #18, $3.50, Baxter)
Eclipse Comics

1-Adapts 3-D movie 1.40 3.50
1-2-D limited edition 2.00 5.00
1-Large size (11x17", 8/87)-Sold only at Disney Theme parks ($6.95) 1.00 2.80 7.00

CAPTAIN FEARLESS COMICS (Also see Holyoke One-Shot #6, Old Glory Comics & Silver Streak #1)
August, 1941 - No. 2, Sept, 1941
Helnit Publishing Co. (Holyoke Publishing Co.)

1-Origin Mr. Miracle, Alias X, Captain Fearless, Citizen Smith Son of the Unknown Soldier; Miss Victory (1st app.) begins (1st patriotic heroine? before Wonder Woman) 63.00 189.00 570.00
2-Grit Grady, Captain Stone app. 40.00 120.00 360.00

CAPTAIN FLAG (See Blue Ribbon Comics #16)

CAPTAIN FLASH
Nov, 1954 - No. 4, July, 1955
Sterling Comics

1-Origin; Sekowsky-a; Tomboy (female super hero) begins; only pre-code issue; atomic rocket-c 33.00 98.00 260.00
2-4: 4-Flying saucer invasion-c 19.00 56.00 150.00

CAPTAIN FLEET (Action Packed Tales of the Sea)
Fall, 1952
Ziff-Davis Publishing Co.

1-Painted-c 13.00 39.00 95.00

CAPTAIN FLIGHT COMICS
Mar, 1944 - No. 10, Dec, 1945; No. 11, Feb-Mar, 1947
Four Star Publications

nn 33.00 98.00 260.00
2-4: 4-Rock Raymond begins, ends #7 16.00 49.00 130.00
5-Bondage, classic torture-c; Red Rocket begins; the Grenade app. (scarce) 44.00 132.00 400.00
6 15.00 45.00 120.00
7-10: 7-L. B. Cole covers begin, end #11. 8-Yankee Girl begins; intro. Black Cobra & Cobra Kid & begins. 9-Torpedoman app.; last Yankee Girl; Kinstler-a. 10-Deep Sea Dawson, Zoom of the Jungle, Rock Raymond, Red Rocket, & Black Cobra app; bondage-c 34.00 103.00 275.00
11-Torpedoman, Blue Flame (Human Torch clone) app.; last Black Cobra, Red Rocket; classic L. B. Cole-c 42.00 126.00 375.00

CAPTAIN FORTUNE PRESENTS
1955 - 1959 (Giveaway, 3-1/4x6-7/8", 16 pgs.)
Vital Publications

"Davy Crockett in Episodes of the Creek War", "Davy Crockett at the Alamo", "In Sherwood Forest Tells Strange Tales of Robin Hood" ('57), "Meets Bolivar the Liberator" ('59), "Tells How Buffalo Bill Fights the Dog Soldiers" ('57), "Young Davy Crockett" 1.80 4.50 9.00

CAPTAIN GALLANT (...of the Foreign Legion) (TV) (Texas Rangers in Action No. 5 on?)
1955; No. 2, Jan, 1956 - No. 4, Sept, 1956
Charlton Comics

Heinz Foods Premium (#1?)(1955; regular size)-U.S. Pictorial; contains Buster Crabbe photos; Don Heck-a 1.80 4.50 9.00
Non-Heinz version (same as above except pictures of show replaces ads) (#1)-Buster Crabbe photo on-c; full page Buster Crabbe photo inside front-c 8.50 26.00 60.00
2-4: Buster Crabbe in all 7.15 21.50 50.00

CAPTAIN GLORY
Apr, 1993 ($2.95) (Created by Jack Kirby)
Topps Comics

1-Polybagged w/Kirbychrome trading card; Ditko-a & Kirby-c; has coupon for Amberchrome Secret City Saga #0 1.20 3.00

CAPTAIN HERO (See Jughead as...)

CAPTAIN HERO COMICS DIGEST MAGAZINE
Sept, 1981
Archie Publications

1-Reprints of Jughead as Super-Guy 1.00

CAPTAIN HOBBY COMICS
Feb, 1948 (Canadian)
Export Publication Ent. Ltd. (Dist. in U.S. by Kable News Co.)

1 5.70 17.00 35.00

CAPT. HOLO IN 3-D (See Blackthorne 3-D Series #65)

CAPTAIN HOOK & PETER PAN (Movie)(Disney)
No. 446, Jan, 1953
Dell Publishing Co.

Four Color 446 8.00 25.00 90.00

CAPTAIN JET (Fantastic Fears No. 7 on)
May, 1952 - No. 5, Jan, 1953
Four Star Publ./Farrell/Comic Media

1-Bakerish-a 15.00 45.00 120.00
2 8.75 26.25 70.00
3-5,6(?) 7.85 23.50 55.00

CAPTAIN JOHNER & THE ALIENS
May, 1995 - No. 2, May, 1995 ($2.95, limited series, shipped in same month)
Valiant

1,2: Reprints Magnus Robot Fighter 4000 A.D. back-up stories; new Paul Smith-c 1.20 3.00

CAPTAIN JUSTICE (TV)
Mar, 1988 - No. 2, Apr, 1988 (limited series)
Marvel Comics

1,2-Based on True Colors television series. 1.25

CAPTAIN KANGAROO (TV)
No. 721, Aug, 1956 - No. 872, Jan, 1958
Dell Publishing Co.

Four Color 721 (#1)-Photo-c 13.00 40.00 145.00
Four Color 780, 872-Photo-c 11.00 34.00 125.00

CAPTAIN KIDD (Formerly Dagar; My Secret Story #26 on)(Also see Comic Comics & Fantastic Comics)
No. 24, June, 1949 - No. 25, Aug, 1949
Fox Feature Syndicate

24,25: 24-Features Blackbeard the Pirate 12.00 36.00 90.00

CAPTAIN MARVEL (See All Hero, All-New Collectors' Ed., America's Greatest, Fawcett Miniature, Gift, Legends, Limited Collectors' Ed., Marvel Family, Master No. 21, Mighty Midget Comics, Shazam, Special Edition Comics, Whiz, Wisco, World's Finest #253 and XMas Comics)

CAPTAIN MARVEL (Becomes ...Presents the Terrible 5 No. 5)
April, 1966 - No. 4, Nov, 1966 (25¢ Giants)
M. F. Enterprises

Captain Marvel #15 © MEG

Captain Marvel Adventures #16 © FAW

Captain Marvel Adventures #67 © FAW

GD25 FN65 NM94

nn-(#1 on pg. 5)-Origin; created by Carl Burgos 1.85 5.50 15.00
2-4: 3-(#3 on pg. 4)-Fights the Bat 1.00 3.00 8.00

CAPTAIN MARVEL (Marvel's Space-Born Super-Hero! Captain Marvel #1-6; see Giant-Size..., Life Of..., Marvel Graphic Novel #1, Marvel Spotlight V2#1 & Marvel Super-Heroes #12)
May, 1968 - No. 19, Dec, 1969; No. 20, June, 1970 - No. 21, Aug, 1970; No. 22, Sept, 1972 - No. 62, May, 1979
Marvel Comics Group

1 6.00 18.00 60.00
2-Super Skrull-c/story 1.85 5.50 15.00
3-5: 4-Captain Marvel battles Sub-Mariner 1.25 3.75 10.00
6-11: 11-Capt. Marvel given great power by Zo the Ruler; Smith/Trimpe-c; Death of Una 1.10 3.30 9.00
12-24: 14-Capt. Marvel vs. Iron Man; last 12¢ issue. 16,17-New costume. 21-Capt. Marvel battles Hulk; last 15¢ issue 2.40 6.00
25-Starlin-c/a begins; Starlin's 1st Thanos saga begins (3/73), ends #34; Thanos cameo (5 panels) 1.50 4.50 12.00
26-Minor Thanos app. (see Iron Man #55); 1st Thanos-c 1.75 5.25 14.00
27,28-1st & 2nd full app. Thanos. 28-Thanos-c/s 1.25 3.75 10.00
29,30-Thanos cameos. 29-C.M. gains more powers 1.00 3.00 8.00
31,32: Thanos app. 31-Last 20¢ issue. 32-Thanos-c 1.25 3.75 10.00
33-Thanos-c & app.; Capt. Marvel battles Thanos; 1st origin Thanos 1.50 4.50 12.00
34-1st app. Nitro; C.M. contracts cancer which eventually kills him; last Starlin-c/a 1.00 2.80 7.00
35,37-40,42,44,46-56,58-62: 39-Origin Watcher. 49-Starlin & Weiss-p assists. 58-Thanos cameo 1.50
36-Reprints origin/1st app. Capt. Marvel from Marvel Super-Heroes #12; Starlin-a (3 pgs.) 2.40 6.00
41,43-Wrightson part inks; #43-c(i). 2.40 6.00
45-(Regular 25¢ edition)(7/76) 1.50
45-(30¢-c, limited distribution) 2.40 6.00
57-Thanos appears in flashback 2.40 6.00

NOTE: *Alcala a-35.* ***Austin*** *a-46i, 49-53i; c-52i.* ***Buscema*** *a-18p-21p.* ***Colan*** *a(p)-1-4; c(p)-1-4, 8, 9.* ***Heck*** *a-5-10p, 16p.* ***Gil Kane*** *a-17-21p; c-17-24p, 37p, 53.* ***McWilliams*** *a-40i. #25-34 were reprinted in The Life of Captain Marvel.*

CAPTAIN MARVEL
Nov, 1989 ($1.50, one-shot, 52 pgs.)
Marvel Comics

1-Super-hero from Avengers; new powers 1.50

CAPTAIN MARVEL
Feb, 1994 ($1.75, 52 pgs.)
Marvel Comics

1-(Indicia reads Vol 2 #2)-Minor Captain America app. .70 1.75

CAPTAIN MARVEL
Dec, 1995 - No. 6, May, 1996 ($2.95/$1.95)
Marvel Comics

1 ($2.95)-Advs. of Mar-Vell's son begins; Fabian Nicieza scripts; foil-c 1.00 3.00
2-6: 2-Begin $1.95-c .80 2.00

CAPTAIN MARVEL ADVENTURES (See Special Edition Comics for pre #1)
1941 (March) - No. 150, Nov, 1953 (#1 on stands 1/16/41)
Fawcett Publications

GD25 FN65 VF82 NM94

nn(#1)-Captain Marvel & Sivana by Jack Kirby. The cover was printed on unstable paper stock and is rarely found in Fine or Mint condition; blank bank inside-c 2300.00 6900.00 14,950.00 27,000.00
(Estimated up to 140 total copies exist, 2 in NM/Mint)

GD25 FN65 NM94

2-(Advertised as #3, which was counting Special Edition Comics as the real #1); Tuska-a 320.00 960.00 3200.00
3-Metallic silver-c 211.00 633.00 1900.00
4-Three Lt. Marvels app. 139.00 417.00 1250.00
5 106.00 318.00 950.00
6-10: 9-1st Otto Binder scripts on Capt. Marvel 83.00 250.00 750.00
11-15: 12-Capt. Marvel joins the Army. 13-Two pg. Capt. Marvel pin-up. 15-Comic cards on back-c begin, end #26 69.00 207.00 625.00
16,17: 17-Painted-c 64.00 192.00 575.00
18-Origin & 1st app. Mary Marvel & Marvel Family (12/11/42); painted-c; Mary Marvel by Marcus Swayze 150.00 450.00 1350.00
19-Mary Marvel x-over; Christmas-c 53.00 159.00 475.00
20,21-Attached to the cover, each has a miniature comic just like the Mighty Midget Comics #11, except that each has a full color promo ad on the back cover. Most copies were circulated without the miniature comic. These issues with miniatures attached are very rare, and should not be mistaken for copies with the similar Mighty Midget glued in its place. The Mighty Midgets had blank back covers except for a small victory stamp seal. Only the Capt. Marvel and Captain Marvel Jr. No. 11 miniatures have been positively documented as having been affixed tothese covers. Each miniature was only partially glued by its back cover to the Captain Marvel comic making it easy to see if it's the genuine miniature rather than a Mighty Midget.
with comic attached.... 290.00 870.00 2900.00
20-Without miniature 50.00 150.00 450.00
21-Without miniature; Hitler-c 64.00 192.00 575.00
22-Mr. Mind serial begins; 1st app. Mr. Mind 71.00 213.00 640.00
23-25 47.00 141.00 425.00
26-30: 26-Flag-c. 29-1st Mr. Mind-c & 1st app. (his voice was heard over the radio before now)(11/43) 40.00 120.00 360.00
31-35: 35-Origin Radar (5/44, see Master #50) 36.00 108.00 325.00
36-40: 37-Mary Marvel x-over 35.00 105.00 280.00
41-46: 42-Christmas-c. 43-Capt. Marvel 1st meets Uncle Marvel (1st app.); Mary Batson cameo. 46-Mr. Mind serial ends 28.00 84.00 225.00
47-50 25.00 75.00 200.00
51-53,55-60: 51-63-Bi-weekly issues. 52-Origin & 1st app. Sivana Jr.; Capt. Marvel Jr. x-over 21.00 64.00 170.00
54-Special oversize 68 pg. issue 22.00 66.00 175.00
61-The Cult of the Curse serial begins 25.00 75.00 200.00
62-66-Serial ends; Mary Marvel x-over in #65. 66-Atomic War-c. 21.00 64.00 170.00
67-77,79: 69-Billy Batson's Christmas; Uncle Marvel, Mary Marvel, Capt. Marvel Jr. x-over. 71-Three Lt. Marvels app. 79-Origin Mr. Tawny 19.50 58.00 155.00
78-Origin Mr. Atom 22.00 66.00 175.00
80-Origin Capt. Marvel retold 36.00 108.00 315.00
81-84,86-90: 81,90-Mr. Atom app. 82-Infinity-c. 86-Mr. Tawny app. 18.00 54.00 145.00
85-Freedom Train issue 23.00 68.00 180.00
91-99: 96-Mr. Tawny app. 18.00 54.00 145.00
100-Origin retold; silver metallic-c 35.00 105.00 280.00
101-115,117-120 17.50 53.00 140.00
116-Flying Saucer issue (1/51) 19.00 56.00 150.00
121-Origin retold 23.00 69.00 185.00
122-137,139-149: 141-Pre-code horror story "The Hideous Head-Hunter". 142-used in **POP**, pgs. 92,96 17.00 51.00 135.00
138-Flying Saucer issue (11/52) 19.50 58.00 155.00
150-(Low distribution) 24.00 71.00 190.00
Bond Bread Giveaways-(24 pgs.; pocket size-7-1/4x3-1/2"; paper cover): "...& the Stolen City" ('48), "The Boy Who Never Heard of Capt. Marvel", "Meets the Weatherman" -(1950)(reprint) each.... 26.00 77.00 185.00
...Well Known Comics (1944; 12 pgs.; 8-1/2x10-1/2")-printed in red & in blue; soft-c; glued binding)-Bestmaid/Samuel Lowe Co. giveaway 15.00 45.00 120.00

NOTE: ***Swayze*** *a-12, 14, 15, 18, 19, 40; c-12, 15, 19.*

CAPTAIN MARVEL ADVENTURES
1945 (6x8", full color, paper-c)
Fawcett Publications (Wheaties Giveaway)

nn- "Captain Marvel & the Threads of Life" plus 2 other stories (32 pgs.) 44.00 132.00 400.00

NOTE: *All copies were taped at each corner to a box of Wheaties and are never found in Fine or*

Captain Marvel, Jr. #22 © FAW

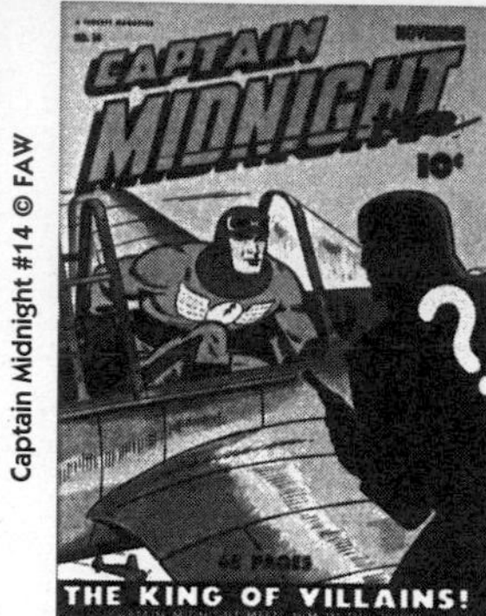

Captain Midnight #14 © FAW

Captain Savage and His Leatherneck Raiders #4 © MEG

GD25 FN65 NM94

Mint condition. Prices listed for each grade include tape.

CAPTAIN MARVEL AND THE GOOD HUMOR MAN (Movie)
1950
Fawcett Publications nn-Partial photo-c w/Jack Carson & the Captain Marvel Club Boys 37.00 110.00 330.00

CAPTAIN MARVEL AND THE LTS. OF SAFETY
1950 - 1951 (3 issues - no No.'s)
Ebasco Services/Fawcett Publications

	GD25	FN65	VF82
"Danger Flies a Kite" ('50, scarce), "Danger Takes to Climbing" ('50), "Danger Smashes Street Lights" ('51)	106.00	318.00	850.00

CAPTAIN MARVEL COMIC STORY PAINT BOOK (See Comic Story...)

CAPTAIN MARVEL, JR. (See Fawcett Miniatures, Marvel Family, Master Comics, Mighty Midget Comics, Shazam & Whiz Comics)

CAPTAIN MARVEL, JR.
Nov, 1942 - No. 119, June, 1953 (No #34)
Fawcett Publications

	GD25	FN65	NM94
1-Origin Capt. Marvel Jr. retold (Whiz No. 25); Capt. Nazi app. Classic Raboy-c	430.00	1290.00	4300.00
2-Vs. Capt. Nazi; origin Capt. Nippon	155.00	467.00	1400.00
3	83.00	250.00	750.00
4-Classic Raboy-c	89.00	267.00	800.00
5-Vs. Capt. Nazi	78.00	234.00	700.00
6-10: 8-Vs. Capt. Nazi. 9-Flag-c. 10-Hitler-c	58.00	174.00	525.00
11,12,15-Capt. Nazi app.	50.00	150.00	450.00
13,14,16-20: 13-Hitler-c. 14-X-Mas-c. 16-Capt. Marvel & Sivana x-over. 19-Capt. Nazi & Capt. Nippon app.	44.00	132.00	400.00
21-30: 25-Flag-c	36.00	108.00	300.00
31-33,36-40: 37-Infinity-c	24.00	71.00	190.00
35-#34 on inside; cover shows origin of Sivana Jr. which is not on inside. Evidently the cover to #35 was printed out of sequence and bound with contents to #34	24.00	71.00	190.00
41-70: 53-Atomic Bomb-c/story	17.50	53.00	140.00
71-99,101-104: 104-Used in **POP**, pg. 89	12.00	38.00	100.00
100	15.00	45.00	120.00
105-114,116-118: 116-Vampira, Queen of Terror app. 119-Electric chair-c	12.00	36.00	95.00
115-Injury to eye-c; Eyeball story w/injury-to-eye panels	17.50	53.00	140.00
119-Electric chair-c	15.00	45.00	120.00
...Well Known Comics (1944; 12 pgs.; 8-1/2x10-1/2")(Printed in blue; paper-c, glued binding)-Bestmaid/Samuel Lowe Co. giveaway	10.00	30.00	80.00

NOTE: ***Mac Raboy** c-1-28, 30-32, 57, 59 among others.*

CAPTAIN MARVEL PRESENTS THE TERRIBLE FIVE
Aug, 1966; V2#5, Sept, 1967 (No #2-4) (25¢)
M. F. Enterprises

	GD25	FN65	NM94
1	1.50	4.50	12.00
V2#5-(Formerly Captain Marvel)		2.40	6.00

CAPTAIN MARVEL'S FUN BOOK
1944 (1/2" thick) (cardboard covers)
Samuel Lowe Co.

	GD25	FN65	NM94
nn-Puzzles, games, magic, etc.; infinity-c	28.00	84.00	225.00

CAPTAIN MARVEL SPECIAL EDITION (See Special Edition)

CAPTAIN MARVEL STORY BOOK
Summer, 1946 - No. 4, Summer?, 1948
Fawcett Publications

	GD25	FN65	NM94
1-Half text	47.00	141.00	420.00
2-4	35.00	105.00	280.00

CAPTAIN MARVEL THRILL BOOK (Large-Size)
1941 (B&W w/color-c)
Fawcett Publications

	GD25	FN65	VF82
1-Reprints from Whiz #8,10, & Special Edition #1 (Rare)	250.00	750.00	2500.00

NOTE: *Rarely found in Fine or Mint condition.*

CAPTAIN MIDNIGHT (TV, radio, films) (See The Funnies & Popular Comics) (Becomes Sweethearts No. 68 on)
Sept, 1942 - No. 67, Fall, 1948 (#1-14: 68 pgs.)
Fawcett Publications

	GD25	FN65	NM94
1-Origin Captain Midnight; Captain Marvel cameo on cover	233.00	700.00	2100.00
2	106.00	318.00	950.00
3-5	78.00	234.00	700.00
6-10: 9-Raboy-c. 10-Raboy Flag-c	56.00	168.00	500.00
11-20: 11,17,18-Raboy-c	40.00	120.00	360.00
21-30	34.00	103.00	275.00
31-40	24.00	71.00	190.00
41-59,61-67: 50-Sci/fi theme begins?	19.00	56.00	150.00
60-Flying Saucer issue (2/48)-3rd of this theme; see Shadow Comics V7#10 & Boy Commandos #26	26.00	80.00	210.00

CAPTAIN NICE (TV)
Nov, 1967 (one-shot)
Gold Key

	GD25	FN65	NM94
1(10211-711)-Photo-c	6.00	18.00	65.00

CAPTAIN N: THE GAME MASTER (TV)
1990 - No. 6? ($1.95, thick stock, coated-c)
Valiant Comics

	GD25	FN65	NM94
1-6: 4-6-Layton-c		.80	2.00

CAPTAIN PARAGON (See Bill Black's Fun Comics)
Dec, 1983 - No. 4, 1985
Americomics

	GD25	FN65	NM94
1-4: 1-Intro/1st app. Ms. Victory			1.50

CAPTAIN PARAGON AND THE SENTINELS OF JUSTICE
April, 1985 - No. 6, 1986 ($1.75)
AC Comics

	GD25	FN65	NM94
1-6: 1-Capt. Paragon, Commando D., Nightveil, Scarlet Scorpion, Stardust & Atoman begin		.75	1.80

CAPTAIN PLANET AND THE PLANETEERS (TV cartoon)
Oct, 1991 - No. 12, Oct, 1992 ($1.00/$1.25)
Marvel Comics

	GD25	FN65	NM94
1-N. Adams painted-c		1.20	3.00
2-12: 3-Romita-c		.80	2.00

CAPTAIN POWER AND THE SOLDIERS OF THE FUTURE (TV)
Aug, 1988 - No. 2, 1988 ($2.00)
Continuity Comics

	GD25	FN65	NM94
1,2: 1-Neal Adams-c/layouts/inks; variant-c exists.		.80	2.00

CAPTAIN PUREHEART (See Archie as...)

CAPTAIN ROCKET
Nov, 1951
P. L. Publ. (Canada)

	GD25	FN65	NM94
1	36.00	107.00	265.00

CAPT. SAVAGE AND HIS LEATHERNECK RAIDERS (...And His Battlefield Raiders #9 on)
Jan, 1968 - No. 19, Mar, 1970 (See Sgt. Fury No. 10)
Marvel Comics Group (Animated Timely Features)

	GD25	FN65	NM94
1-Sgt. Fury & Howlers cameo	1.85	5.50	15.00
2,7,11: 2-Origin Hydra. 1-5,7-Ayers/Shores-a. 7-Pre-"Thing" Ben Grimm story	1.25	3.75	10.00
3-6,8-10,12-19	1.00	3.00	8.00

BERNIE WRIGHTSON'S
CAPTAIN STERNN
RUNNING OUT OF TIME

Captain Sternn #4 © KSP

A Fawcett Publication
Captain VIDEO
"FAMOUS STAR OF THE DUMONT TELEVISION NETWORK"
10¢
THE MISSILES OF DOOM!

Captain Video #5 © FAW

Cardinal Mindszenty nn © CG

GD25 FN65 NM94

CAPTAIN SCIENCE (Fantastic No. 8 on)
Nov, 1950 - No. 7, Dec, 1951
Youthful Magazines

1-Wood-a; origin; 2 pg. text w/ photos of George Pal's "Destination Moon." 68.00 206.00 575.00
2 39.00 118.00 290.00
3,6,7; 3,6-Bondage c-swipes/Wings #94,91 36.00 107.00 260.00
4,5-Wood/Orlando-c/a(2) each 68.00 206.00 565.00

NOTE: ***Fass** a-4. Bondage c-3, 6, 7.*

CAPTAIN SILVER'S LOG OF SEA HOUND (See Sea Hound)

CAPTAIN SINBAD (Movie Adaptation) (See Fantastic Voyages of... & Movie Comics)

CAPTAIN STERNN: RUNNING OUT OF TIME
Sept, 1993 - No. 5, 1994 ($4.95, limited series, coated stock, 52 pgs.)
Kitchen Sink Press

1-5: Berni Wrightson-c/a/scripts 2.00 5.00
1-Gold ink variant 1.25 3.75 10.00

CAPTAIN STEVE SAVAGE (...& His Jet Fighters, No. 2-13)
1950 - No. 8, 1/53; No. 5, 9-10/54 - No. 13, 5-6/56
Avon Periodicals

nn(1st series)-Wood art, 22 pgs. (titled "...Over Korea") 36.00 107.00 250.00
1(4/51)-Reprints nn issue (Canadian) 15.00 45.00 105.00
2-Kamen-a 10.00 30.00 60.00
3-11 (#6, 9-10/54, last precode) 5.70 17.00 35.00
12-Wood-a (6 pgs.) 10.00 30.00 70.00
13-Check, Lawrence-a 7.50 26.25 45.00

NOTE: ***Kinstler** c-2-5, 7-9, 11. **Lawrence** a-8. **Ravielli** a-5, 9.*

5(9-10/54-2nd series)(Formerly Sensational Police Cases) 5.70 17.00 38.00
6-Reprints nn issue; Wood-a 8.50 26.00 60.00
7-13: 9,10-Kinstler-c. 10-r/cover #2 (1st series). 13-r/cover #8 (1st series) 4.00 12.00 24.00

CAPTAIN STONE (See Holyoke One-Shot No. 10)

CAPT. STORM (Also see G. I. Combat #138)
May-June, 1964 - No. 18, Mar-Apr, 1967 (Grey tone c-8)
National Periodical Publications

1-Origin 3.00 9.00 30.00
2-18: 3,6,13-Kubert-a. 4-Colan-a. 12-Kubert-c 2.50 7.50 20.00

CAPTAIN 3-D (Super hero)
December, 1953 (25¢, came with 2 pairs of glasses)
Harvey Publications

1-Kirby/Ditko-a (Ditko's 3rd published work tied with Strange Fantasy #9, see also Daring Love #1 & Black Magic V4 #3); shows cover in 3-D on inside; Kirby/Meskin-c 8.50 26.00 60.00

CAPTAIN THUNDER AND BLUE BOLT
Sept, 1987 - No. 10, 1988 ($1.95)
Hero Comics

1-10: 1-Origin Blue Bolt. 3-Origin Capt. Thunder. 6-1st app. Wicket. 8-Champions x-over .80 2.00

CAPTAIN TOOTSIE & THE SECRET LEGION (Advs. of...)(Also see Monte Hale #30,39 & Real Western Hero)
Oct, 1950 - No. 2, Dec, 1950
Toby Press

1-Not Beck-a; both have sci/fi covers 22.00 66.00 175.00
2-The Rocketeer Patrol app.; not Beck-a 14.00 41.00 110.00

CAPTAIN TRIUMPH (See Crack Comics #27)

CAPTAIN VENTURE & THE LAND BENEATH THE SEA (See Space Family Robinson)
Oct, 1968 - No. 2, Oct, 1969)
Gold Key

1,2: 1-r/Space Family Robinson serial; Spiegle-a in both 3.00 9.00 35.00

CAPTAIN VICTORY AND THE GALACTIC RANGERS
11/81 - #13, 1/84 ($1.00, direct sales, 36-48 pgs.) (Created by Jack Kirby)
Pacific Comics

1-13: 1-1st app. Mr. Mind. 3-N. Adams-a 1.00
Special 1-(10/83)-Kirby c/a(p) 1.00

NOTE: ***Conrad** a-10, 11. **Ditko** a-6. **Kirby** a-1-3p; c-1-13.*

CAPTAIN VIDEO (TV) (See XMas Comics)
Feb, 1951 - No. 6, Dec, 1951 (No. 1,5,6-36pgs.; 2-4, 52pgs.) (All photo-c)
Fawcett Publications

1-George Evans-a(2) 93.00 281.00 800.00
2-Used in **SOTI**, pg. 382 62.00 187.00 525.00
3-6-All Evans-a except #5 mostly Evans 52.00 157.00 440.00

NOTE: *Minor **Williamson** assists on most issues. Photo c-1, 5, 6; painted c-2-4.*

CAPTAIN WILLIE SCHULTZ (Also see Fightin' Army)
No. 76, Oct, 1985 - No. 77, Jan, 1986
Charlton Comics

76,77 1.00

CAPTAIN WIZARD COMICS (See Meteor, Red Band & Three Ring Comics)
1946
Rural Home

1-Capt. Wizard dons new costume; Impossible Man, Race Wilkins app. 21.00 64.00 170.00

CARDINAL MINDSZENTY (The Truth Behind the Trial of...)
1949 (24 pgs., paper cover)
Catechetical Guild Education Society

nn-Anti-communism 5.70 17.00 35.00
Press Proof-(Very Rare)-(Full color, 7-1/2x11-3/4", untrimmed)
Only two known copies 150.00
Preview Copy (B&W, stapled), 18 pgs.; contains first 13 pgs. of Cardinal Mindszenty and was sent out as an advance promotion.
Only one known copy 150.00 - 200.00

NOTE: *Regular edition also printed in French. There was also a movie released in 1949 called "Guilty of Treason" which is a fact-based account of the trial and imprisonment of Cardinal Mindszenty by the Communist regime in Hungary.*

CARE BEARS (TV, Movie)(See Star Comics Magazine)
Nov, 1985 - No. 20, Jan, 1989 ($1.00 #11 on)
Star Comics/Marvel Comics No. 15 on

1-20: Post-a begins. 13-Madballs app. 1.00 2.50

CAREER GIRL ROMANCES (Formerly Three Nurses)
June, 1964 - No. 78, Dec, 1973
Charlton Comics

V4#24-31,33-50 1.60 4.00
32-Elvis Presley, Hermans Hermits, Johnny Rivers line drawn-c 8.50 25.50 85.00
51-78 .80 2.00

CAR 54, WHERE ARE YOU? (TV)
Mar-May, 1962 - No. 7, Sept-Nov, 1963; 1964 - 1965 (All photo-c)
Dell Publishing Co.

Four Color 1257(#1, 3-5/62) 6.40 19.00 70.00
2(6-8/62)-7 3.00 9.00 35.00
2,3(10-12/64), 4(1-3/65)-Reprints #2,3,&4 of 1st series 2.25 6.75 25.00

CARL BARKS LIBRARY OF WALT DISNEY'S GYRO GEARLOOSE COMICS AND FILLERS IN COLOR, THE
1993 ($7.95, 8-1/2x11", limited series, 52 pgs.)

Carneys #1 © Archie Publ.

Cartoon Network Presents #4 © H-B

Casey-Crime Photographer #4 © MEG

GD25 FN65 NM94

Gladstone

1-6: Carl Barks reprints 1.25 3.75 10.00

CARL BARKS LIBRARY OF WALT DISNEY'S COMICS AND STORIES IN COLOR, THE
Jan, 1992 - No. 51, Mar, 1996 ($8.95, 8-1/2x11", 60 pgs.)(51 ish. series)
Gladstone

1,2,6,8-51: 1-Barks Donald Duck-r/WDC&S #31-35; 2-r/#36,38-41; 6-r/#57-61; 8-r/#67-71; 9-r/#72-76; 10-r/#77-81; 11-r/#82-86; 12-r/#87-91; 13-r/#92-96; 14-r/#97-101; 15-r/#102-106; 16-r/#107-111; 17-r/#112,114,117,124,125; 18-r/#126-130; 19-r/#131,132(2),133,134; 20-r/#135-139; 21-r/#140-144; 22-r/#145-149; 23-r/#150-154; 24-r/#155-159; 25-r/#160-164; 26-r/#165-169; 27-r/#170-174;28-r/#175-179; 29-r/#180-184; 30-r/#185-189; 31-r/#190-194; 32-r/#195-199;33-r/#200-204; 34-r/#205-209; 35-r/#210-214; 36-r/#215-219; 37-r/#220-224; 38-r/#225-229; 39-r/#230-234; 40-r/#235-239; 41-r/#240-244; 42r/#245-249; 43-r/#250-254; 44-50; All contain one Heroes & Villains trading card each 1.25 3.75 10.00
3,4,7: 3-r/#42-46. 4-r/#47-51. 7-r/#62-66. 1.85 5.50 15.00
5-r/#52-56 2.50 7.50 20.00

CARL BARKS LIBRARY OF WALT DISNEY'S DONALD DUCK ADVENTURES IN COLOR, THE
1994 - Present ($7.95/$9.95, 44-68pgs., 8-1/2"x11")(25 issue series)
(all contain one Donald Duck trading card each)
Gladstone

1-16-Carl Barks-r: 1-r/FC #9; 2-r/FC #29; 3-r/FC #62; 4-r/FC #108; 5-r/FC #147 & #79(Mickey Mouse); 6-r/MOC #4, Cheerios "Atom Bomb," D.D. Tells About Kites; 7-r/FC #159. 8-r/FC #178 & 189. 9-r/FC #199 & 203; 10-r/FC 223 & 238; 11-r/Christmas Parade #1 & 2; 12-r/FC #296; 13-r/FC #263; 14-r/MOC #20 & 41; 15-r/FC 275 & 282; 16-r/FC #291&300; 17-r/FC #308 & 318; 18-r/Vac. Parade #1 & Summer Fun #2; 19-r/FC #328 & 367 1.50 4.50 12.00

CARL BARKS LIBRARY OF WALT DISNEY'S DONALD DUCK CHRISTMAS STORIES IN COLOR, THE
1992 ($7.95, 44pgs., one-shot)
Gladstone

nn-Reprints Firestone giveaways 1945-1949 1.85 5.50 15.00

CARL BARKS LIBRARY OF WALT DISNEY'S UNCLE SCROOGE COMICS ONE PAGERS IN COLOR, THE
1992 - No. 2, 1993 ($8.95, limited series, 60 pgs., 8-1/2x11")
Gladstone

1-Carl Barks one pg. reprints 2.50 7.50 25.00
2-Carl Barks one pg. reprints 1.85 5.50 15.00

CARNAGE: IT'S A WONDERFUL LIFE
Oct, 1996 ($1.95, one-shot)
Marvel Comics

1-David Quinn scripts .80 2.00

CARNAGE: MIND BOMB
Feb, 1996 ($2.95, one-shot)
Marvel Comics

1-Warren Ellis script; Kyle Hotz-a 1.20 3.00

CARNATION MALTED MILK GIVEAWAYS (See Wisco)

CARNEYS, THE
Summer, 1994 ($2.00, 52 pgs)
Archie Comics

1-Bound-in pull-out poster .80 2.00

CARNIVAL COMICS (Formerly Kayo #12; becomes Red Seal Comics #14)
1945
Harry 'A' Chesler/Pershing Square Publ. Co.

nn (#13)-Guardineer-a 12.00 38.00 100.00

GD25 FN65 NM94

CARNIVAL OF COMICS
1954 (Giveaway)
Fleet-Air Shoes

nn-Contains a comic bound with new cover; several combinations possible; Charlton's Eh! known 2.40 6.00 12.00

CAROLINE KENNEDY
1961 (one-shot)
Charlton Comics

nn-Interior photo covers of Kennedy family 8.00 24.00 80.00

CAROUSEL COMICS
V1#8, April, 1948
F. E. Howard, Toronto

V1#8 5.35 16.00 32.00

CARTOON KIDS
1957 (no month)
Atlas Comics (CPS)

1-Maneely-c/a; Dexter The Demon, Willie The Wise-Guy, Little Zelda app. 7.15 21.50 50.00

CARTOON NETWORK PRESENTS
Aug, 1997 - Present ($1.75)
DC Comics

1-4: 1-Dexter's Lab. 2-Space Ghost 1.75
1-Platinum Edition 1.75
5-12: 5-Begin $1.95-c 1.95

CARTOON TALES (Disney's...)
No date (1992) ($2.95, 6-5/8x9-1/2", 52 pgs.)
W.D. Publications (Disney)

nn-Ariel & Sebastian - Serpent Teen 1.20 3.00
nn-Beauty and the Beast - A Tale of Enchantment 1.20 3.00
nn-Darkwing Duck - Just Us Justice Ducks 1.20 3.00
nn-101 Dalmations - Canine Classics 1.20 3.00
nn-Tale Spin - Surprise in the Skies 1.20 3.00
nn-Uncle Scrooge - Blast to the Past 1.20 3.00

CARVEL COMICS (Amazing Advs. of Capt. Carvel)
1975 - No. 5, 1976 (25¢; #3-5: 35¢) (#4,5: 3-1/4x5")
Carvel Corp. (Ice Cream)

1-3 1.00
4,5(1976)-Baseball theme 2.40 6.00

CAR WARRIORS
June, 1991 - No. 4, Sept, 1991 ($2.25, limited series)
Marvel Comics (Epic Comics)

1-4: 1-Says April in indicia .90 2.25

CASE OF THE SHOPLIFTER'S SHOE (See Perry Mason, Feature Book No.50)

CASE OF THE WASTED WATER, THE
1972? (Giveaway)
Rheem Water Heating

nn-Neal Adams-a 3.20 9.60 32.00

CASE OF THE WINKING BUDDHA, THE
1950 (132 pgs.; 25¢; B&W; 5-1/2x7-5-1/2x8")
St. John Publ. Co.

nn-Charles Raab-a; reprinted in Authentic Police Cases No. 25 21.00 64.00 170.00

CASEY-CRIME PHOTOGRAPHER (Two-Gun Western No. 5 on)(Radio)
Aug, 1949 - No. 4, Feb, 1950
Marvel Comics (BFP)

1-Photo-c; 52 pgs. 15.50 47.00 125.00
2-4: Photo-c 10.00 30.00 80.00

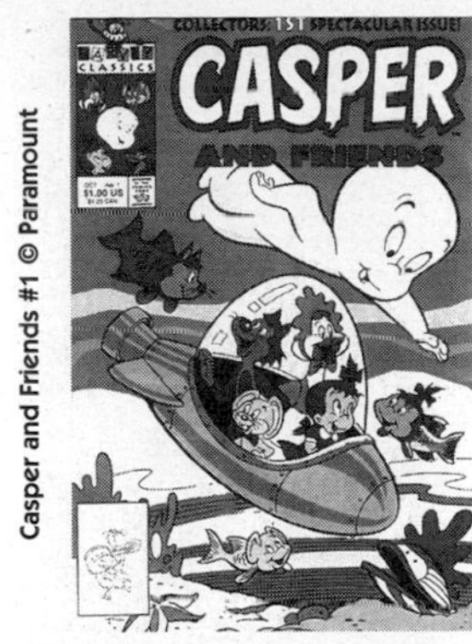

Casper and Friends #1 © Paramount

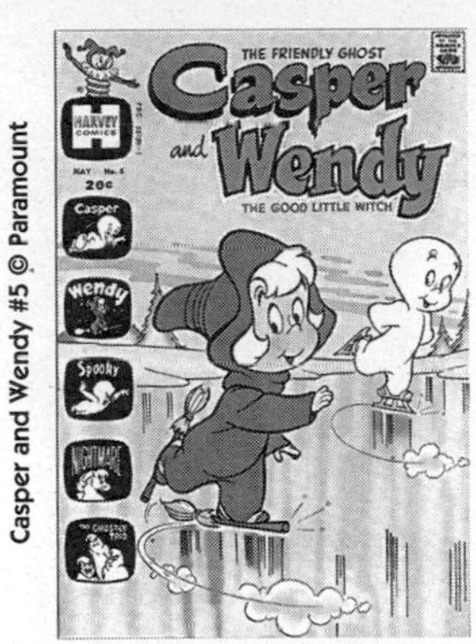

Casper and Wendy #5 © Paramount

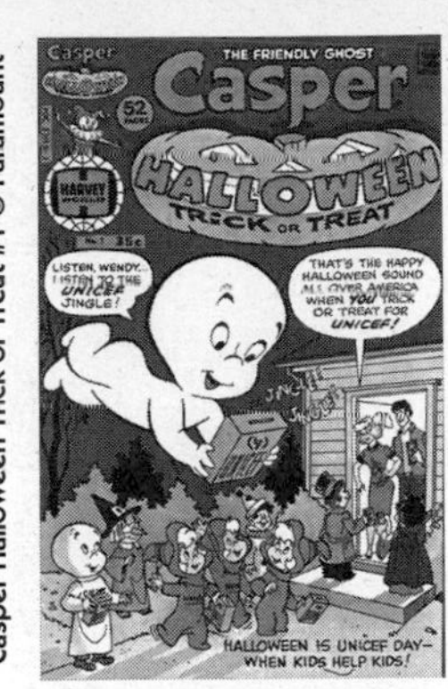

Casper Halloween Trick or Treat #1 © Paramount

GD25 FN65 NM94

CASEY JONES (TV)
No. 915, July, 1958
Dell Publishing Co.
Four Color 915-Alan Hale photo-c 4.50 13.50 50.00

CASEY JONES & RAPHAEL (See Bodycount)
Oct, 1994 ($2.75, unfinished limited series)
Mirage Studios
1-Bisley-c; Eastman story & pencils 1.10 2.75

CASEY JONES: NORTH BY DOWNEAST
June, 1994? - No. 2, July, 1994 ($2.75, limited series)
Mirage Studios
1,2-Rick Veitch script & pencils; Kevin Eastman story & inks 1.10 2.75

CASPER ADVENTURE DIGEST
V2#1, Oct, 1992 - V2#8, Apr, 1994 ($1.75/$1.95, digest-size)
Harvey Comics
V2#1: Casper, Richie Rich, Spooky, Wendy 1.20 3.00
2-8 .80 2.00

CASPER AND...
Nov, 1987 - No. 12, June, 1990 (.75/$1.00, all reprints)
Harvey Comics
1-Ghostly Trio 1.20 3.00
2-12: 2-Spooky; begin $1.00-c. 3-Wendy. 4-Nightmare. 5-Ghostly Trio. 6-Spooky. 7-Wendy. 8-Hot Stuff. 9-Baby Huey. 10-Wendy.11-Ghostly Trio. 12-Spooky .80 2.00

CASPER AND FRIENDS
Oct, 1991 - No. 5, July, 1992 ($1.00/$1.25)
Harvey Comics
1-Nightmare, Ghostly Trio, Wendy, Spooky 1.20 3.00
2-5 .80 2.00

CASPER AND FRIENDS MAGAZINE
Mar/Apr, 1997 - Present ($3.99)
Marvel Comics
1-3 1.60 4.00

CASPER AND NIGHTMARE (See Harvey Hits# 37, 45, 52, 56, 59, 62, 65, 68,71, 75)

CASPER AND NIGHTMARE (Nightmare & Casper No. 1-5)
No. 6, 11/64 - No. 44, 10/73; No. 45, 6/74 - No. 46, 8/74 (25¢)
Harvey Publications
6: 68 pg. Giants begin, ends #32 3.20 9.60 32.00
7-10 2.20 6.60 22.00
11-20 1.85 5.50 15.00
21-37: 33-37-(52 pg. Giants) 1.25 3.75 10.00
38-46 2.40 6.00
NOTE: *Many issues contain reprints.*

CASPER AND SPOOKY (See Harvey Hits No. 20)
Oct, 1972 - No. 7, Oct, 1973
Harvey Publications
1 2.25 6.75 18.00
2-7 1.00 3.00 8.00

CASPER AND THE GHOSTLY TRIO
Nov, 1972 - No. 7, Nov, 1973; No. 8, Aug, 1990 - No. 10, Dec, 1990
Harvey Publications
1 2.25 6.75 18.00
2-7 1.00 3.00 8.00
8-10 2.00 5.00

CASPER AND WENDY
Sept, 1972 - No. 8, Nov, 1973
Harvey Publications
1: 52 pg. Giant 2.50 7.50 20.00
2-8 1.00 3.00 8.00

CASPER BIG BOOK
V2#1, Aug, 1992 - No. 3, May, 1993 ($1.95, 52 pgs.)
Harvey Comics
V2#1-Spooky app. 1.20 3.00
2,3 .80 2.00

CASPER CAT (See Dopey Duck)
1958; 1963
I. W. Enterprises/Super
1,7:1-Wacky Duck #?.7-Reprint, Super No. 14('63) 2.40 6.00

CASPER DIGEST (...Magazine #?; ...Halloween Digest #8, 10)
Oct, 1986 - No. 18, Jan, 1991 ($1.25/$1.75, digest-size)
Harvey Publications
1 2.00 5.00
2-18: 11-Valentine-c. 18-Halloween-c 1.20 3.00

CASPER DIGEST (...Magazine #? on)
V2#1, Sept, 1991 - V2#14, Nov, 1994 ($1.75/$1.95, digest-size)
Harvey Comics
V2#1 1.20 3.00
2-14 .80 2.00

CASPER DIGEST STORIES
Feb, 1980 - No. 4, Nov, 1980 (95¢, 132 pgs., digest size)
Harvey Publications
1 1.00 3.00 8.00
2-4 2.00 5.00

CASPER DIGEST WINNERS
Apr, 1980 - No. 3, Sept, 1980 (95¢, 132 pgs., digest size)
Harvey Publications
1 1.00 3.00 8.00
2,3 2.00 5.00

CASPER ENCHANTED TALES DIGEST
May, 1992 - No. 10, Oct, 1994 ($1.75, digest-size, 98 pgs.)
Harvey Comics
1-Casper, Spooky, Wendy stories 1.20 3.00
2-10 .80 2.00

CASPER GHOSTLAND
May, 1992 ($1.25)
Harvey Comics
1 .80 2.00

CASPER GIANT SIZE
Oct, 1992 - No. 4, Nov, 1993 ($2.25, 68 pgs.)
Harvey Comics
V2#1-4-Casper, Wendy, Spooky stories 1.20 3.00

CASPER HALLOWEEN TRICK OR TREAT
Jan, 1976 (52 pgs.)
Harvey Publications
1 1.85 5.50 15.00

CASPER IN SPACE (Formerly Casper Spaceship)
No. 6, June, 1973 - No. 8, Oct, 1973
Harvey Publications
6-8 1.00 2.80 7.00

CASPER'S GHOSTLAND
Winter, 1958-59 - No. 97, 12/77; No. 98, 12/79 (25¢)
Harvey Publications
1-84 pgs. begin, ends #10 19.00 56.00 150.00

Casper The Friendly Ghost #21 © Paramount

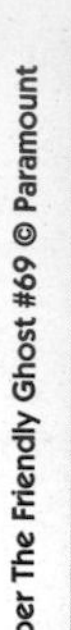
Casper The Friendly Ghost #69 © Paramount

The Cat #1 © MEG

	GD25	FN65	NM94
2	10.00	30.00	80.00
3-10	5.50	16.50	55.00
11-20: 11-68 pgs. begin, ends #61. 13-X-Mas-c	4.20	12.60	42.00
21-40	3.20	9.60	32.00
41-61	1.85	5.50	15.00
62-77: 62-52 pgs. begin	1.00	3.00	8.00
78-98: 94-X-Mas-c		1.60	4.00

NOTE: *Most issues contain reprints w/new stories.*

CASPER SPACESHIP (Casper in Space No. 6 on)
Aug, 1972 - No. 5, April, 1973
Harvey Publications

	GD25	FN65	NM94
1: 52 pg. Giant	2.25	6.75	18.00
2-5	1.00	3.00	8.00

CASPER SPECIAL
nd (Dec, 1990) (Giveaway with $1.00 cover)
Target Stores (Harvey)

	GD25	FN65	NM94
Three issues-Given away with Casper video		1.20	3.00

CASPER STRANGE GHOST STORIES
October, 1974 - No. 14, Jan, 1977 (All 52 pgs.)
Harvey Publications

	GD25	FN65	NM94
1	1.50	4.50	12.00
2-14	1.00	3.00	8.00

CASPER, THE FRIENDLY GHOST (See America's Best TV Comics, Famous TV Funday Funnies, The Friendly Ghost..., Nightmare &..., Richie Rich and..., Tastee-Freez, Treasury of Comics, Wendy the Good Little Witch & Wendy Witch World)

CASPER, THE FRIENDLY GHOST (Becomes Harvey Comics Hits No. 61 (No. 6), and then continued with Harvey issue No. 7)(1st Series)
Sept, 1949 - No. 5, Aug, 1951
St. John Publishing Co.

	GD25	FN65	NM94
1(1949)-Origin & 1st app. Baby Huey & Herman the Mouse (1st time the name Casper app. in any media, even films)	128.00	384.00	1150.00
2,3 (2/50 & 8/50)	56.00	168.00	500.00
4,5 (3/51 & 8/51)	42.00	126.00	380.00

CASPER, THE FRIENDLY GHOST (Paramount Picture Star...)(2nd Series)
No. 7, Dec, 1952 - No. 70, July, 1958
Harvey Publications (Family Comics)
Note: No. 6 is Harvey Comics Hits No. 61 (10/52)

	GD25	FN65	NM94
7-Baby Huey begins, ends #9	28.00	84.00	280.00
8,9	15.50	47.00	155.00
10-Spooky begins (1st app., 6/53), ends #70?	17.00	51.00	170.00
11-18: Alfred Harvey app. in story	9.00	27.00	90.00
19-1st app. Nightmare (4/54)	11.50	35.00	115.00
20-Wendy the Witch begins (1st app., 5/54)	15.00	45.00	150.00
21-30: 24-Infinity-c	7.00	21.00	70.00
31-40	4.80	14.40	48.00
41-50	3.80	11.40	38.00
51-70 (Continues as Friendly Ghost... 8/58)	3.50	10.50	35.00
American Dental Association (Giveaways):			
...'s Dental Health Activity Book-1977		1.40	3.50
...Presents Space Age Dentistry-1972		1.60	4.00
..., His Den, & Their Dentist Fight the Tooth Demons-1974		1.60	4.00

CASPER THE FRIENDLY GHOST (Formerly The Friendly Ghost...)(3rd Series)
No. 254, July, 1990 - No. 260, Jan, 1991 ($1.00)
Harvey Comics

	GD25	FN65	NM94
254-260		.80	2.00

CASPER THE FRIENDLY GHOST (4th Series)
Mar, 1991 - No. 28, Nov, 1994 ($1.00/$1.25/$1.50)
Harvey Comics

	GD25	FN65	NM94
1-Casper becomes Mighty Ghost; Spooky & Wendy app.		1.20	3.00
2-10: 7,8-Post-a		.80	2.00
11-28-($1.50)			1.50

CASPER T.V. SHOWTIME
Jan, 1980 - No. 5, Oct, 1980
Harvey Comics

	GD25	FN65	NM94
1		2.40	6.00
2-5		1.60	4.00

CASSETTE BOOKS
(Classics Illustrated)
1984 (48 pgs, b&w comic with cassette tape)
Cassette Book Co./I.P.S. Publ.

NOTE: *This series was illegal. The artwork was illegally obtained, and the Classics Illustrated copyright owner, Twin Circle Publ. sued to get an injunction to prevent the continued sale of this series. Many C.I. collectors obtained copies before the 1987 injunction, but now they are already scarce. Here again the market is just developing, but sealed mint copies of com ic and tape should be worth at least $25.*
1001 (Cl#1-A2)New-PC 1002(Cl#3-A2)Cl-PC 1003(Cl#13-A2)Cl-PC 1004(Cl#25)Cl-LDC 1005(Cl#10-A2)New-PC 1006(Cl#64)Cl-LDC

CASTILIAN (See Movie Classics)

CASUAL HEROES
Apr, 1996 ($2.25, unfinished limited series
Image Comics (Motown Machineworks)

	GD25	FN65	NM94
1-Steve Rude-c		.90	2.25

CAT, T.H.E. (TV) (See T.H.E. Cat)

CAT, THE (See Movie Classics)

CAT, THE
Nov, 1972 - No. 4, June, 1973
Marvel Comics Group

	GD25	FN65	NM94
1-Origin & 1st app. The Cat (who later becomes Tigra); Mooney-a(i); Wood-c(i)/a(i)	2.25	6.75	18.00
2,3: 2-Marie Severin/Mooney-a. 3-Everett inks	1.25	3.75	10.00
4-Starlin/Weiss-a(p)	1.50	4.50	12.00

CATALYST: AGENTS OF CHANGE (Also see Comics' Greatest World)
Feb, 1994 - No.7, Nov, 1994 ($2.00, limited series)
Dark Horse Comics

	GD25	FN65	NM94
1-7: 1-Foil stamped logo		.80	2.00

CAT & MOUSE
Dec, 1988 ($1.75, color w/part B&W)
EF Graphics (Silverline)

	GD25	FN65	NM94
1-1st printing (12/88, 32 pgs.)		.70	1.75
1-2nd printing (5/89, 36 pgs.)		.70	1.75

CATFIGHT: DREAM INTO ACTION (Also see Hellina/Catfight)
Mar, 1996 ($2.75, B&W, one-shot)
Lightning Comics

	GD25	FN65	NM94
1-Creed app.			2.75
1 Nude A & Nude B ($9.95)-Polybagged			10.00
1 Commemorative ($5.95)-Polybagged			6.00

CATFIGHT: DREAM WARRIOR (Also see Hellina/Catfight)
June, 1995 ($2.75, B&W, one-shot)
Insomnia Press

	GD25	FN65	NM94
1-Hellina cameo		1.10	2.75

CAT FROM OUTER SPACE (See Walt Disney Showcase #46)

CATHOLIC COMICS (See Heroes All Catholic...)
June, 1946 - V3#10, July, 1949
Catholic Publications

	GD25	FN65	NM94
1	22.00	66.00	175.00
2	12.00	36.00	95.00
3-13(7/47)	10.00	30.00	80.00

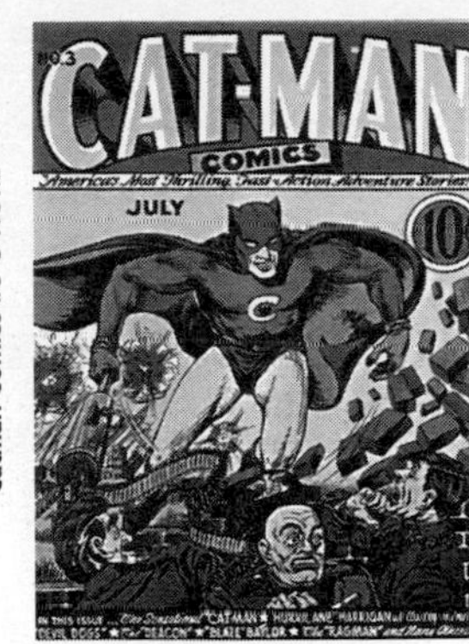

Catman Comics #3 © HOKE

Catwoman #52 © DC

Cave Girl #1 © AC

GD25 FN65 NM94

V2#1-10 7.15 21.50 50.00
V3#1-10: Reprints 10-part Treasure Island serial from Target V2#2-11 (see Key Comics #5) 7.85 23.50 55.00

CATHOLIC PICTORIAL
1947
Catholic Guild
1-Toth-a(2) (Rare) 33.00 98.00 260.00

CATMAN COMICS (Formerly Crash Comics No. 1-5)
5/41 - No. 17, 1/43; No. 18, 7/43 - No. 22, 12/43; No. 23, 3/44 - No. 26, 11/44; No. 27, 4/45 - No. 30, 12/45; No. 31, 6/46 - No. 32, 8/46
Holyoke Publishing Co./Continental Magazines V2#12, 7/44 on
1(V1#6)-Origin The Deacon & Sidekick Mickey, Dr. Diamond & Rag-Man; The Black Widow app.; The Catman by Chas. Quinlan & Blaze Baylor begin 250.00 750.00 2500.00
2(V1#7) 89.00 267.00 800.00
3(V1#8), 4(V1#9): 3-The Pied Piper begins 67.00 200.00 600.00
5(V2#10)-Origin Kitten; The Hood begins (c-redated), 6,7(V2#11,12) 53.00 159.00 475.00
8(V2#13,3/42)-Origin Little Leaders; Volton by Kubert begins (his 1st comic book work) 67.00 200.00 600.00
9,10(V2#14,15): 10-Origin Blackout retold; Phantom Falcon begins 42.00 126.00 380.00
11 (V3#1)-Kubert-a 42.00 126.00 380.00
12 (V3#2) - 15, 17, 18(V3#8, 7/43) 39.00 117.00 350.00
16 (V3#5)-Hitler, Tojo, Mussolini, Stalin-c 47.00 141.00 425.00
19 (V2#6)-Hitler, Tojo, Mussolini-c 47.00 141.00 425.00
20 (V2#7): 20-Hitler-c 47.00 141.00 425.00
21- 23 (V2#10, 3/44) 36.00 108.00 300.00
nn(V3#13, 5/44)-Rico-a; Schomburg bondage-c 35.00 105.00 280.00
nn(V2#12, 7/44) 35.00 105.00 280.00
nn(V3#1, 9/44)-Origin The Golden Archer; Leatherface app. 35.00 105.00 280.00
nn(V3#2, 11/44)-L. B. Cole-c 53.00 159.00 475.00
27-Origin Kitten retold; L. B. Cole Flag-c 58.00 174.00 525.00
28-Catman learns Kitten's I.D.; Dr. Macabre, Deacon app.; L. B. Cole c/a 61.00 183.00 550.00
29-32-L. B. Cole-c; bondage-#30 53.00 159.00 475.00
NOTE: *Fuje a-11, 29(3), 30.* ***Palais*** *a-11, 29(2), 30(2), 32; c-25(7/44).* ***Rico*** *a-11(2).*

CAT TALES (3-D)
Apr, 1989 ($2.95)
Eternity Comics
1-Felix the Cat-r in 3-D 1.20 3.00

CATWOMAN (Also see Action Comics Weekly #611, Batman #404-407, Detective Comics, & Superman's Girlfriend Lois Lane #70, 71)
Feb, 1989 - No. 4, May, 1989 ($1.50, limited series, mature)
DC Comics
1 1.20 3.00
2 .80 2.00
3,4: 3-Batman cameo. 4-Batman app. .80 2.00
Her Sister's Keeper (1991, $9.95, trade paperback)-r/#1-4 1.25 3.75 10.00

CATWOMAN (Also see Showcase '93, Showcase '95 #4, & Batman #404-407)
Aug, 1993 - Present ($1.50/$1.95)
DC Comics
1-($1.95)-Embossed-c; Bane app.; Balent c-1-10; a-1-10p 1.00 2.80 7.00
2,3: 3-Bane flashback cameo 1.60 4.00
0,4-11, 13-20, 26-35: 4-Brief Bane app. 6,7-Knightquest tie-ins; new Batman (Azrael) app. 8-1st app. Zephyr. 13-KnightsEnd Aftermath. 14-(9/94)-Zero Hour. 0-(10/94)-Origin retold 1.00 2.50
12-KnightsEnd pt. 6. 1.00 2.80 7.00
21-24, 26-30, 33-49: 21-$1.95-c begins. 28,29-Penguin cameo app. 36-Legacy pt. 2. 38,39-Year Two; Batman, Joker, Penguin & Two-Face app. 46-Two-Face app. .80 2.00
25-($2.95)-Robin app. 1.20 3.00
31, 32: 31-Contagion pt. 4 (Reads pt. 5 on-c). 32-Contagion pt. 9. 1.20 3.00
50-($2.95, 48 pgs.)-New armored costume 1.20 3.00
50-($2.95, 48 pgs.)-Collector's Ed.w/metallic ink-c 1.20 3.00
51-56: 51-Huntress-c/app 1.95
Annual 1 (1994, $2.95, 68 pgs.)-Elseworlds story; Batman app.; no Balent-a 1.20 3.00
Annual 2 (1995, $3.95)-Year One story 1.60 4.00
Annual 3 (1996, $2.95)-Legends of the Dead Earth story 1.20 3.00
Annual 4 (1997, $3.95)-Pulp Heroes story 3.95
...Plus 1 (11/97, $2.95) Screamqueen (Scare Tactics) app. 2.95
TPB ($9.95) r/#15-19, Balent-c 3.75 10.00

CATWOMAN/VAMPIRELLA: THE FURIES
Feb, 1997 ($4.95, squarebound, one-shot, 46 pgs.)(1st DC/Harris x-over)
DC Comics/Harris Publications
nn-Reintro Pantha; Chuck Dixon scripts; Jim Balent-c/a 2.00 5.00

CAUGHT
Aug, 1956 - No. 5, Apr, 1957
Atlas Comics (VPI)
1 15.00 45.00 120.00
2,4: 4-Maneely-a (4 pgs.) 8.50 26.00 60.00
3-Maneely, Pakula, Torres-a 8.50 26.00 60.00
5-Crandall, Krigstein-a 8.75 26.25 70.00
NOTE: ***Drucker*** *a-2.* ***Heck*** *a-4.* ***Severin*** *c-1, 2, 4, 5.* ***Shores*** *a-4.*

CAVALIER COMICS
1945; 1952 (Early DC reprints)
A. W. Nugent Publ. Co.
2(1945)-Speed Saunders, Fang Gow 15.50 47.00 125.00
2(1952) 8.50 26.00 60.00

CAVE GIRL (Also see Africa)
No. 11, 1953 - No. 14, 1954
Magazine Enterprises
11(A-1 82)-Origin; all Cave Girl stories 40.00 120.00 315.00
12(A-1 96), 13(A-1 116), 14(A-1 125)-Thunda by Powell in each 29.00 86.00 210.00
NOTE: ***Powell*** *c/a in all.*

CAVE GIRL
1988 ($2.95, 44 pgs.) (16 pgs. of color, rest B&W)
AC Comics
1-Powell-r/Cave Girl #11; Nyoka photo back-c from movie; Powell/Bill Black-c; Special Limited Edition on-c 1.20 3.00

CAVE KIDS (TV)
Feb, 1963 - No. 16, Mar, 1967 (Hanna-Barbera)
Gold Key
1 5.50 16.50 60.00
2-5 2.75 8.00 30.00
6-16: 7,12-Pebbles & Bamm Bamm app. 1.80 5.50 20.00

CAVEWOMAN
Jan, 1994 - No. 6, 1995 ($2.95)
Basement Comics
1 5.00 15.00 50.00
2 3.00 9.00 30.00
3-6 2.50 7.50 20.00

CAVEWOMAN MEETS EXPLORERS
1997 ($2.95, B&W, one-shot)
Basement Comics

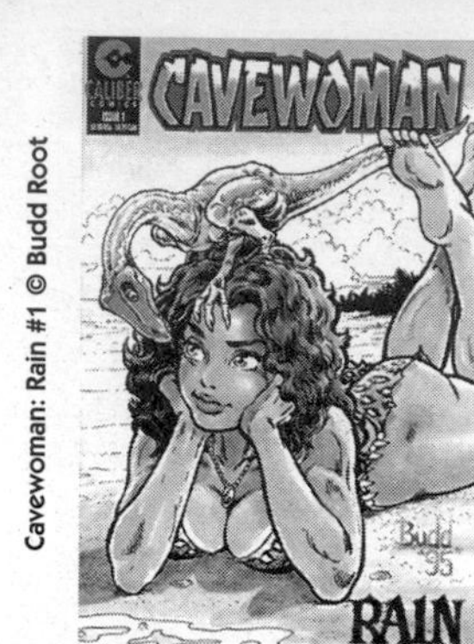

Cavewoman: Rain #1 © Budd Root

Cerebus #179 © Dave Sim

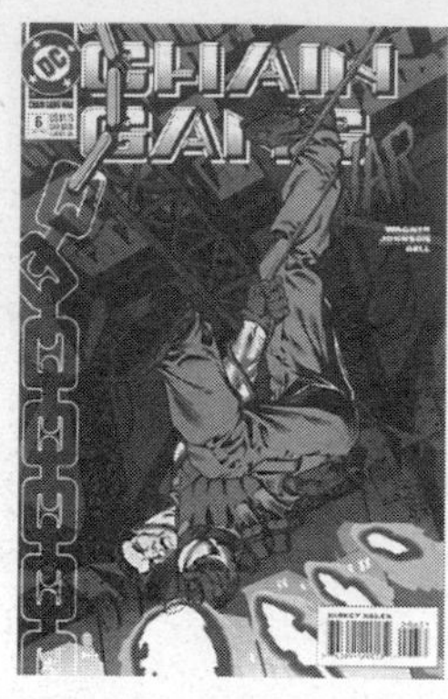
Chain Gang War #6 © DC

GD25 FN65 NM94

1 — 1.20 3.00

CAVEWOMAN: RAIN
1996 - Present ($2.95)
Caliber

1 — 1.20 3.00
2 — 2.00 5.00
3,4 — 1.40 3.50
5-7 — 2.95

CELESTINE (See Violator Vs. Badrock #1)
May, 1996 - No. 2, June, 1996 ($2.50, limited series)
Image Comics (Extreme Studios)

1,2: Warren Ellis scripts — 1.00 2.50

CENTURION OF ANCIENT ROME, THE
1958 (no month listed) (B&W, 36 pgs.)
Zondervan Publishing House

(Rare) All by Jay Disbrow — 28.00 84.00 225.00

CENTURIONS (TV)
June, 1987 - No. 4, Sept, 1987 (75¢, limited series)
DC Comics

1-4 — 1.00

CENTURY: DISTANT SONS
Feb, 1996 ($2.95, one-shot)
Marvel Comics

1-Wraparound-c — 1.20 3.00

CENTURY OF COMICS
1933 (100 pgs.) (Probably the 3rd comic book)
Eastern Color Printing Co.

Bought by Wheatena, Milk-O-Malt, John Wanamaker, Kinney Shoe Stores, & others to be used as premiums and radio giveaways. No publisher listed.

GD25 FN65 VF82
nn-Mutt & Jeff, Joe Palooka, etc. reprints — 3400.00 10,200.00 17,500.00
(Estimated up to 20 total copies exist, none in NM-Mint)

CEREBUS BI-WEEKLY
Dec. 2, 1988 - No. 26, Nov. 11, 1989 ($1.25, B&W)
Aardvark-Vanaheim

GD25 FN65 NM94
Reprints Cerebus The Aardvark#1-26
1-16, 18, 19, 21-26: — .80 2.00
17-Hepcats app. — 1.85 5.50 15.00
20-Milk & Cheese app. — 2.50 7.50 20.00

CEREBUS: CHURCH & STATE
Feb, 1991 - No. 30, Apr, 1992 ($2.00, B&W, bi-weekly)
Aardvark-Vanaheim

1-30: r/Cerebus #51-80 — 1.00 2.50

CEREBUS: HIGH SOCIETY
Feb, 1990 - No. 25, 1991 ($1.70, B&W)
Aardvark-Vanaheim

1-25: r/Cerebus #26-50 — .90 2.25

CEREBUS JAM
Apr, 1985
Aardvark-Vanaheim

1-Eisner, Austin, Dave Sim-a (Cerebus vs. Spirit) — 2.00 5.00

CEREBUS THE AARDVARK (See A-V in 3-D, Nucleus, Power Comics)
Dec, 1977 - Present ($1.70/$2.00/$2.25, B&W)
Aardvark-Vanaheim

0 — 1.20 3.00
0-Gold — 2.50 7.50 25.00
1-1st app. Cerebus; 2000 print run; most copies poorly printed — 25.00 75.00 250.00

Note: *There is a counterfeit version known to exist. It can be distinguished from the original in the following ways: inside cover is glossy instead of flat, black background on the front cover is blotted or spotty. Reports show that a counterfeit #2 also exists.*

2-Dave Sim art in all — 7.00 21.00 70.00
3-Origin Red Sophia — 6.00 18.00 60.00
4-Origin Elrod the Albino — 4.00 12.00 40.00
5,6 — 3.50 10.50 35.00
7-10 — 2.50 7.50 25.00
11,12: 11-Origin The Cockroach — 2.50 7.50 20.00
13-15: 14-Origin Lord Julius — 1.25 3.75 10.00
16-20 — 2.40 6.00
21-B. Smith letter in letter column — 3.50 10.50 35.00
22-Low distribution; no cover price — 1.60 4.85 13.00
23-30: 23-Preview of Wandering Star by Teri S. Wood. 26-High Society begins, ends #50 — 2.40 6.00
31-Origin Moonroach — 1.00 3.00 8.00
32-40 — 2.00 5.00
41-50,52: 52-Church & State begins, ends #111; Cutey Bunny app. — 1.60 4.00
51-Cutey Bunny app. — 1.25 3.75 10.00
53-Intro. Wolveroach (cameo) — 2.00 5.00
54-1st full Wolveroach story — 2.40 6.00
55,56-Wolveroach app.; Normalman back-ups by Valentino — 2.00 5.00
57-79: 61,62: Flaming Carrot app. 65-Gerhard begins — 1.00 2.50
80-224: 104-Flaming Carrot app. 112/113-Double issue. 114-Jaka's Story begins, ends #136. 137-$2.25-c begins. 139-Melmoth begins, ends #150. 175-($2.25, 44 pgs). 151-Mothers & Daughters begins, ends #200 201-Guys storyline begins; Eddie Campbell's Bacchus app. 220-Rick's Story begins — .90 2.25
151-153-2nd printings — .90 2.25
Free Cerebus (Giveaway, 1991-92?, 36 pgs.)-All-r — 1.00

CHAIN GANG WAR
July, 1993 - No. 12, June, 1994 ($1.75)
DC Comics

1-($2.50)-Embossed silver foil-c, Dave Johnson-c/a — 1.00 2.50
2-4,6-12: 3-Deathstroke app. 4-Brief Deathstroke app. 6-New Batman (Azrael) cameo. 11-New Batman-c/story. 12-New Batman app. — .70 1.75
5-($2.50)-Foil embossed-c; Deathstroke app; new Batman cameo (1 panel). — 1.00 2.50

CHAINS OF CHAOS
Nov, 1994 - No. 3, Jan, 1995 ($2.95, limited series)
Harris Comics

1-3-Re-Intro of The Rook w/ Vampirella — 1.20 3.00

CHALLENGE OF THE UNKNOWN (Formerly Love Experiences)
No. 6, Sept, 1950 (See Web Of Mystery No. 19)
Ace Magazines

6- "Villa of the Vampire" used in N.Y. Joint Legislative Comm. Publ; Sekowsky-a — 21.00 64.00 170.00

CHALLENGER, THE
1945 - No. 4, Oct-Dec, 1946
Interfaith Publications/T.C. Comics

nn; nd; 32 pgs.; Origin the Challenger Club; Anti-Fascist with funny animal filler — 28.00 83.00 220.00
2-4: Kubert-a; 4-Fuje-a — 23.00 68.00 180.00

CHALLENGERS OF THE FANTASTIC
June 1997 ($1.95, one-shot)
Marvel Comics (Amalgam)

1-Karl Kesel-s/Tom Grummett-a — 1.95

Challengers of the Unknown #63 © DC

Chamber Of Chills #19 © HARV

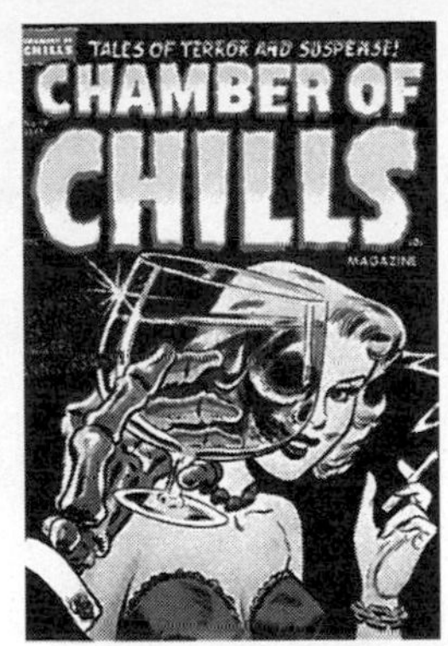

Champion Comics #10 © HARV

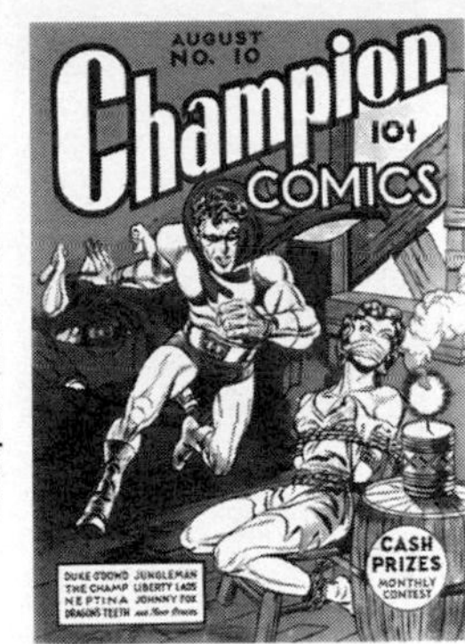

GD25 FN65 NM94

CHALLENGERS OF THE UNKNOWN (See Showcase #6, 7, 11, 12, Super DC Giant, and Super Team Family)
4-5/58 - No. 77, 12-1/70-71; No. 78, 2/73 - No. 80, 6-7/73; No. 81, 6-7/77 - No. 87, 6-7/78
National Per. Publ./DC Comics

1-(4-5/58)-Kirby/Stein-a(2); Kirby-c 200.00 600.00 2100.00
2-Kirby/Stein-a(2) 78.00 233.00 770.00
3-Kirby/Stein-a(2) 67.00 200.00 660.00
4-8-Kirby/Wood-a plus cover to #8 60.00 180.00 530.00
9,10 34.00 101.00 260.00
11-15: 11-Grey tone-c. 14-Origin/1st app. Multi-Man (villain) 23.00 69.00 175.00
16-22: 18-Intro. Cosmo, the Challengers Spacepet. 22-Last 10¢ issue 15.00 45.00 150.00
23-30 8.00 24.00 80.00
31-Retells origin of the Challengers 8.50 25.50 85.00
32-40 4.00 12.00 40.00
41-60: 43-New look begins. 48-Doom Patrol app. 49-Intro. Challenger Corps. 51-Sea Devils app. 55-Death of Red Ryan. 60-Red Ryan returns 2.50 7.50 20.00
61-68: 64,65-Kirby origin-r, parts 1 & 2. 66-New logo. 68-Last 12¢ issue. 1.10 3.30 9.00
69-73,75-80: 69-1st app. Corinna 2.00 5.00
74-Deadman by Tuska/Adams; 1 pg. Wrightson-a 1.85 5.50 15.00
81,83-87: 83-87-Swamp Thing app. 2.40 6.00
82-Swamp Thing begins, c/s 1.10 3.30 9.00
NOTE: ***N. Adams** c-67, 68, 70, 72, 74i, 81i. **Buckler** c-83-86p. **Giffen** a-83-87p. **Kirby** a-75-80r; c-75, 77, 78. **Kubert** c-64, 66, 69, 76, 79. **Nasser** c/a-81p, 82p. **Tuska** a-73. **Wood** r-76.*

CHALLENGERS OF THE UNKNOWN
Mar, 1991 - No. 8, Oct, 1991 ($1.75, limited series)
DC Comics

1-Jeph Loeb scripts & Tim Sale-a in all (1st work together); Bolland-c .80 2.00
2-8: 2-Superman app. 3-Dr. Fate app. 6-G. Kane-c(p). 7-Steranko-c/swipe by Art Adams .70 1.75
NOTE: ***Art Adams** c-7. **Bolland** c-1. **Hempel** c-5. **Gil Kane** c-6p. **Sale** a-1-8; c-2, 3, 8. **Wagner** c-4.*

CHALLENGERS OF THE UNKNOWN
Feb, 1997 - Present ($2.25)
DC Comics

1-15: 1-Intro new team; John Paul Leon-c/a(p) begins .90 2.25

CHALLENGE TO THE WORLD
1951 (10¢, 36 pgs.)
Catechetical Guild

nn 3.60 9.00 18.00

CHAMBER OF CHILLS (Formerly Blondie Comics #20; ...of Clues No. 27 on)
No. 21, June, 1951 - No. 26, Dec, 1954
Harvey Publications/Witches Tales

21 (#1) 33.00 98.00 260.00
22,24 (#2,3) 19.50 58.00 155.00
23 (#4)-Excessive violence; eyes torn out 22.00 66.00 175.00
5(2/52)-Decapitation, acid in face scene 22.00 66.00 175.00
6-Woman melted alive 21.00 62.00 165.00
7-Used in **SOTI**, pg. 389; decapitation/severed head panels 20.00 60.00 160.00
8-10: 8-Decapitation panels 15.50 47.00 125.00
11,12,14 11.30 34.00 90.00
13,15-24-Nostrand-a in all. 13,21-Decapitation panels. 18-Atom bomb panels. 20-Nostrand-c 18.00 54.00 135.00
25,26 10.00 30.00 75.00
NOTE: *About half the issues contain bondage, torture, sadism, perversion, gore, cannibalism, eyes ripped out, acid in face, etc. **Elias** c-4-11, 14-19, 21-26. **Kremer** a-12, 17. **Palais** a-21(1), 23. **Nostrand/Powell** a-13, 15, 16. **Powell** a-21, 23, 24('51), 5-8, 11, 13, 18-21, 23-25. Bondage-c-21, 24('51), 7. 25-r/#5; 26-r/#9.*

CHAMBER OF CHILLS
Nov, 1972 - No. 25, Nov, 1976
Marvel Comics Group

1-Harlan Ellison adaptation 1.85 5.50 15.00
2-25 1.00 2.80 7.00
NOTE: ***Adkins** a-1i, 2i. **Brunner** a-2-4; c-4. **Chaykin** a-4. **Ditko** r-14, 16, 19, 23, 24. **Everett** a-3i, 11r,21r. **Heath** a-1r. **Gil Kane** c-2p. **Powell** a-13r. **Russell** a-1p, 2p. **Williamson/Mayo** a-13r. **Robert E. Howard** horror story adaptation-2, 3.*

CHAMBER OF CLUES (Formerly Chamber of Chills)
No. 27, Feb, 1955 - No. 28, April, 1955
Harvey Publications

27-Kerry Drake-r/#19; Powell-a; last pre-code 8.75 26.25 65.00
28-Kerry Drake 5.70 17.00 40.00

CHAMBER OF DARKNESS (Monsters on the Prowl #9 on)
Oct, 1969 - No. 8, Dec, 1970
Marvel Comics Group

1-Buscema-a(p) 4.00 12.00 40.00
2,3: 2-Neal Adams scripts. 3-Smith, Buscema-a 2.50 7.50 20.00
4-A Conanesque tryout by Smith (4/70); reprinted in Conan #16; Marie Severin/Everett-c 5.00 15.00 50.00
5,8: 5-H.P. Lovecraft adaptation 1.85 5.50 15.00
6 1.25 3.75 10.00
7-Wrightson-c/a, 7pgs. (his 1st work at Marvel); Wrightson draws himself in 1st & last panels; Kirby/Ditko-r 1.85 5.50 15.00
1-(1/72; 25¢ Special) 1.85 5.50 15.00
NOTE: ***Adkins/Everett** a-8. **Buscema** a-Special 1r. **Craig** a-5. **Ditko** a-6-8r. **Heck** a-1, 2, 8, Special 1r. **Kirby** a(p)-4, 5, 7r. **Kirby/Everett** c-5. **Severin/Everett** c-6. **Shores** a-2, 3i, Special 1r. **Sutton** a-1, 2i, 4, 7, Special 1r. **Wrightson** c-7, 8.*

CHAMP COMICS (Formerly Champion No. 1-10)
No. 11, Oct, 1940 - No. 29, March, 1944
Worth Publ. Co./Champ Publ./Family Comics(Harvey Publ.)

11-Human Meteor cont'd. from Champion 69.00 207.00 625.00
12-17,20: 14,15-Crandall-c. 20-The Green Ghost app. 50.00 150.00 450.00
18,19-Simon-c. 19-The Wasp app. 64.00 192.00 575.00
21-29: 22-The White Mask app. 23-Flag-c 40.00 120.00 360.00

CHAMPION (See Gene Autry's...)

CHAMPION COMICS (Formerly Speed Comics #1?; Champ Comics No. 11 on)
No. 2, Dec, 1939 - No. 10, Aug, 1940 (no No.1)
Worth Publ. Co.(Harvey Publications)

2-The Champ, The Blazing Scarab, Neptina, Liberty Lads, Jungleman, Bill Handy, Swingtime Sweetie begin 111.00 333.00 1000.00
3-7: 7-The Human Meteor begins? 60.00 180.00 535.00
8-10: 8-Simon-c. 9-1st S&K-c (1st collaboration together). 10-Bondage-c by Kirby 106.00 318.00 950.00

CHAMPIONS, THE
Oct, 1975 - No. 17, Jan, 1978
Marvel Comics Group

1-Origin & 1st app. The Champions (The Angel, Black Widow, Ghost Rider, Hercules, Iceman); Venus x-over 1.25 3.75 10.00
2-4,8-14,16,17: 2,3-Venus x-over. 11-14,17-Byrne-a. 2.40 6.00
5-7-(Regular 25¢ edition)(4-8/76) 2.40 6.00
5-7-(30¢-c, limited distribution) 2.50 7.50 24.00
15-(Regular 30¢ edition)(9/77)-Byrne-a 2.40 6.00
15-(35¢-c, limited distribution) 2.50 7.50 24.00
NOTE: ***Buckler/Adkins** c-3. **Byrne** a-11-15, 17. **Kane/Adkins** c-1. **Kane/Layton** c-11. **Tuska** a-3p, 4p, 6p, 7p. Ghost Rider c-1-4, 7, 8, 10, 14, 16, 17 (4, 10, 14 are more prominent).*

CHAMPIONS (Game)
June, 1986 - No. 6, Feb, 1987 (limited series)
Eclipse Comics

Chaos Effect Omega © VAL

Chaos! Quarterly #3 © Chaos! Comics

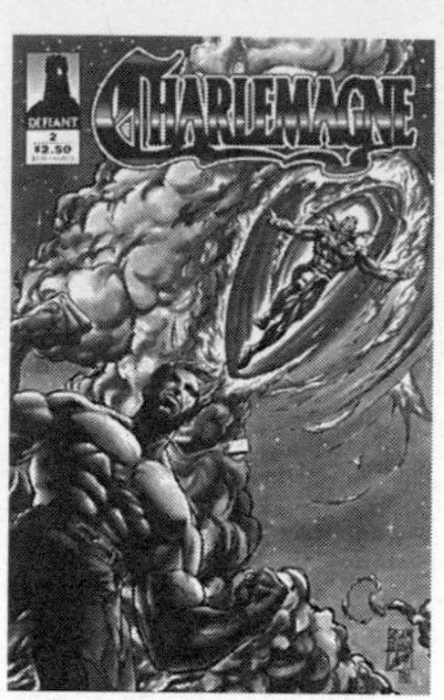

Charlemagne #2 © EEP

GD25 FN65 NM94

1-6: 1-Intro Flare; based on game. 5-Origin Flare 1.50

CHAMPIONS (Also see The League of Champions)
Sept, 1987 - No. 12, 1989 ($1.95)
Hero Comics

1-12: 1-Intro The Marksman & The Rose. 14-Origin Malice .80 2.00
Annual 1(1988, $2.75, 52pgs.)-Origin of Giant 1.10 2.75

CHAMPION SPORTS
Oct-Nov, 1973 - No. 3, Feb-Mar, 1974
National Periodical Publications

1 2.50 7.50 20.00
2,3 1.25 3.75 10.00

CHAOS (See The Crusaders)

CHAOS! BIBLE
Nov, 1995 ($3.30, one-shot)
Chaos! Comics

1-Profiles of characters & creators 1.40 3.50

CHAOS EFFECT, THE
1994
Valiant

Alpha (Giveaway w/trading card checklist) 1.00
Alpha-Gold variant 2.00 5.00
Omega (11/94, $2.25) .90 2.25
Omega-Gold variant 2.00 5.00
Epilogue Pt. 1, 2 (12/94, 1/95; $2.95) 1.20 3.00

CHAOS! GALLERY
Aug, 1997 ($2.95, one-shot)
Chaos! Comics

1-Pin-ups of characters 2.95

CHAOS! QUARTERLY
Oct, 1995 -No. 3, May, 1996 ($4.95, quarterly)
Chaos! Comics

1-3: 1-anthology; Lady Death-c by Julie Bell. 2-Boris "Lady Demon"-c. 2.00 5.00
1-Premium Edition (7,500) 35.00

CHAPEL (Also see Youngblood & Youngblood Strikefile #1-3)
No. 1 Feb, 1995 - No. 2, Mar, 1995 ($2.50, limited series)
Image Comics (Extreme Studios)

1,2 1.00 2.50

CHAPEL (Also see Youngblood & Youngblood Strikefile #1-3)
V2 #1, Aug, 1995 - No. 7, Apr, 1996 ($2.50)
Image Comics (Extreme Studios)

V2#1-7: 4-Babewatch x-over. 5-vs. Spawn. 7-Shadowhawk-c/app; Shadowhunt x-over 1.00 2.50
#1-Quesada & Palmiotti variant-c 1.20 3.00

CHAPEL (Also see Youngblood & Youngblood Strikefile #1-3)
Sept, 1997 ($2.99, one-shot)
Awesome Entertainment

1 2.99

CHARLEMAGNE (Also see War Dancer)
Mar, 1994 - No. 5, July, 1994 ($2.50)
Defiant Comics

1/2 (Hero Illustrated giveaway)-Adam Pollina-c/a.
1-(3/94, $3.50, 52 pgs.)-Adam Pollina-c/a. 1.40 3.50
2,3,5: Adam Pollina-c/a. 2-War Dancer app. 5-Pre-Schism issue. 1.00 2.50
4-($3.25, 52 pgs.) 1.30 3.25

CHARLIE CHAN (See Big Shot Comics, Columbia Comics, Feature Comics & The New Advs. of...)

CHARLIE CHAN (The Adventures of...) (Zaza The Mystic No. 10 on) (TV)
6-7/48 - No. 5, 2-3/49; No.6, 6/55 - No. 9, 3/56
Crestwood(Prize) No. 1-5; Charlton No. 6(6/55) on

1-S&K-c, 2 pgs.; Infantino-a 58.00 174.00 525.00
2-5-S&K-c: 3-S&K-c/a 39.00 117.00 350.00
6 (6/55-Charlton)-S&K-c 26.00 80.00 210.00
7-9 12.00 38.00 100.00

CHARLIE CHAN
Oct-Dec, 1965 - No. 2, Mar, 1966
Dell Publishing Co.

1-Springer-a 3.00 9.00 35.00
2 2.00 6.00 22.00

CHARLIE McCARTHY (See Edgar Bergen Presents...)
No. 171, Nov, 1947 - No. 571, July, 1954 (See True Comics #14)
Dell Publishing Co.

Four Color 171 23.00 68.00 250.00
Four Color 196-Part photo-c; photo back-c 16.00 47.00 170.00
1(3-5/49)-Part photo-c; photo back-c 14.00 44.00 160.00
2-9(7/52; #5,6-52 pgs.) 6.40 19.00 70.00
Four Color 445,478,527,571 4.50 13.50 50.00

CHARLTON BULLSEYE
1975 - No. 5, 1976 ($1.50, B&W, bi-monthly, magazine format)
CPL/Gang Publications

1: 1 & 2 are last Capt. Atom by Ditko/Byrne intended for the never published Capt. Atom #90; Nightshade app.; Jeff Jones-a 2.50 7.50 20.00
2-Part 2 Capt. Atom story by Ditko/Byrne 1.85 5.50 15.00
3-Wrong Country by Sanho Kim 1.25 3.75 10.00
4-Doomsday + 1 by John Byrne 1.50 4.50 12.00
5-Doomsday + 1 by Byrne, The Question by Toth; Neal Adams back-c; Toth-c 2.50 7.50 20.00

CHARLTON BULLSEYE
June, 1981 - No. 10, Dec, 1982; Nov, 1986
Charlton Publications

1-Blue Beetle, The Question app.; 1st app. Rocket Rabbit 1.20 3.00
2-10: 2-1st app. Neil The Horse; Rocket Rabbit app. 6-Origin & 1st app. Thunderbunny .80 2.00
Special 1(11/86) (Half in B&W) 1.20 3.00
Special 2-Atomic Mouse app. (1987) .80 2.00

CHARLTON CLASSICS
Apr, 1980 - No. 9, Aug, 1981
Charlton Comics

1 1.60 4.00
2-9 1.00 2.50

CHARLTON CLASSICS LIBRARY (1776)
V10 No.1, Mar, 1973 (one-shot)
Charlton Comics

1776 (title) - Adaptation of the film musical "1776"; given away at movie theatres 1.00 3.00 8.00

CHARLTON PREMIERE (Formerly Marine War Heroes)
V1#19, July, 1967; V2#1, Sept, 1967 - No. 4, May, 1968
Charlton Comics

V1#19-Marine War Heroes. V2#1-Trio; intro. Shape. Tyro Team. & Spookman. 2-Children of Doom. 3-Sinistro Boy Fiend; Blue Beetle & Peacemaker x-over. 4-Unlikely Tales; Aparo, Ditko-a 1.75 5.25 14.00

CHARLTON SPORT LIBRARY - PROFESSIONAL FOOTBALL
Winter, 1969-70 (Jan. on cover) (68 pgs.)
Charlton Comics

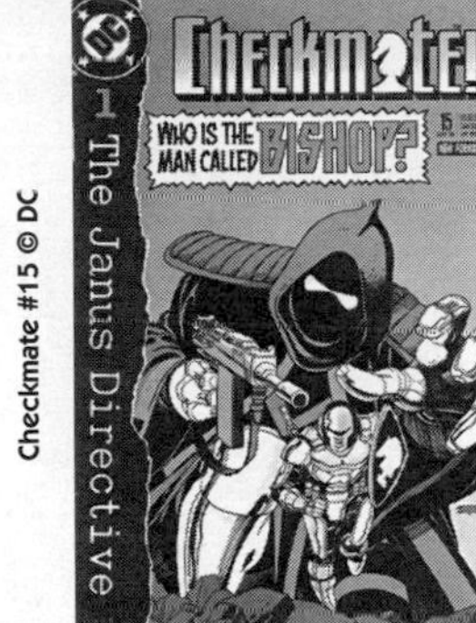

Checkmate #15 © DC

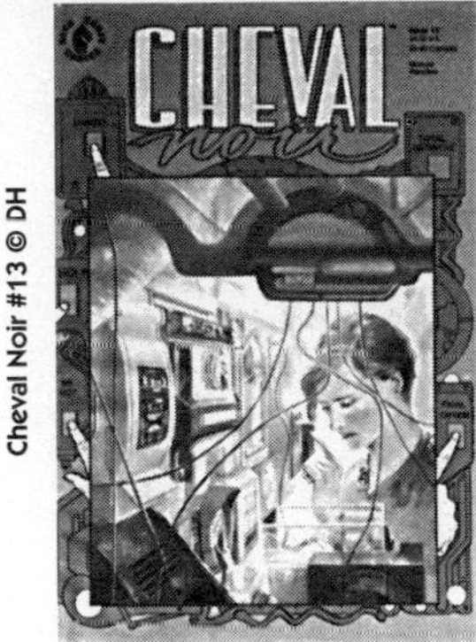

Cheval Noir #13 © DH

Cheyenne #24 © DELL

	GD25	FN65	NM94
1	2.50	7.50	24.00

CHASSIS
1996 - Present ($2.95)
Millenium Publications

	GD25	FN65	NM94
1,2: 1-Adam Hughes-c			2.95

CHASTITY: THEATER OF PAIN
Feb, 1997 - No. 3, June, 1997 ($2.95, limited series)
Chaos! Comics

	GD25	FN65	NM94
1-3-Pulido-s/Justiniano-c/a			2.95

CHECKMATE (TV)
Oct, 1962 - No. 2, Dec, 1962
Gold Key

	GD25	FN65	NM94
1,2-Photo-c	4.00	12.00	45.00

CHECKMATE! (See Action Comics #598)
Apr, 1988 - No. 33, Jan, 1991 ($1.25)
DC Comics

	GD25	FN65	NM94
1-12			1.25
13-33: $1.50/$2.00, new format			1.50

NOTE: ***Gil Kane*** *c-2, 4, 7, 8, 10, 11, 15-19.*

CHEERIOS PREMIUMS (Disney)
1947 (16 titles, pocket size, 32 pgs.)
Walt Disney Productions

	GD25	FN65	NM94
Set "W"			
W1-Donald Duck & the Pirates	6.50	19.50	45.00
W2-Bucky Bug & the Cannibal King	4.00	11.00	22.00
W3-Pluto Joins the F.B.I.	4.00	11.00	22.00
W4-Mickey Mouse & the Haunted House	5.00	15.00	30.00
Set "X"			
X1-Donald Duck, Counter Spy	6.50	19.50	45.00
X2-Goofy Lost in the Desert	4.00	10.00	20.00
X3-Br'er Rabbit Outwits Br'er Fox	4.00	10.00	20.00
X4-Mickey Mouse at the Rodeo	5.00	15.00	30.00
Set "Y"			
Y1-Donald Duck's Atom Bomb by Carl Barks. Disney has banned reprinting this book	78.00	234.00	700.00
Y2-Br'er Rabbit's Secret	4.00	10.00	20.00
Y3-Dumbo & the Circus Mystery	4.25	13.00	28.00
Y4-Mickey Mouse Meets the Wizard	5.00	15.00	30.00
Set "Z"			
Z1-Donald Duck Pilots a Jet Plane (not by Barks)	6.50	19.50	45.00
Z2-Pluto Turns Sleuth Hound	4.00	10.00	20.00
Z3-The Seven Dwarfs & the Enchanted Mtn.	4.25	13.00	28.00
Z4-Mickey Mouse's Secret Room	5.00	15.00	30.00

CHEERIOS 3-D GIVEAWAYS (Disney)
1954 (24 titles, pocket size) (Glasses were cut-outs on boxes)
Walt Disney Productions

	GD25	FN65	NM94
Glasses only...	5.70	17.00	40.00
(Set 1) 1-Donald Duck & Uncle Scrooge, the Firefighters 2-Mickey Mouse & Goofy, Pirate Plunder 3-Donald Duck's Nephews, the Fabulous Inventors 4-Mickey Mouse, Secret of the Ming Vase 5-Donald Duck with Huey, Dewey, & Louie; ...the Seafarers (title on 2nd page) 6-Mickey Mouse, Moaning Mountain 7-Donald Duck, Apache Gold 8-Mickey Mouse, Flight to Nowhere (per book)	7.15	21.50	50.00
(Set 2) 1-Donald Duck, Treasure of Timbuktu 2-Mickey Mouse & Pluto, Operation China 3-Donald Duck in the Magic Cows 4-Mickey Mouse & Goofy, Kid Kokonut 5-Donald Duck, Mystery Ship 6-Mickey Mouse, Phantom Sheriff 7-Donald Duck, Circus Adventures 8-Mickey Mouse, Arctic Explorers (per book)	7.15	21.50	50.00
(Set 3) 1-Donald Duck & Witch Hazel 2-Mickey Mouse in Darkest Africa 3-Donald Duck & Uncle Scrooge, Timber Trouble 4-Mickey Mouse, Rajah's Rescue 5-Donald Duck in Robot Reporter 6-Mickey Mouse, Slumbering Sleuth 7-Donald Duck in the Foreign Legion 8-Mickey Mouse, Airwalking Wonder (per book)....	7.15	21.50	50.00

CHERYL BLOSSOM
Sept, 1995 - No. 3, Nov, 1995 ($1.50, limited series)
Archie Publications

	GD25	FN65	NM94
1-3			1.50
Special 1 (1995, $2.00)		.80	2.00
Special 2 (1995, $2.00)		.80	2.00

CHERYL BLOSSOM
July, 1996 - Present ($1.50/$1.75)
Archie Publications

	GD25	FN65	NM94
1-7: Dan DeCarlo-c/a			1.50
8-14: 8-Begin $1.75-c			1.75

CHESTY AND COPTIE (Disney)
1946 (Giveaway, 4pgs.)
Los Angeles Community Chest

	GD25	FN65	NM94
nn-(One known copy) by Floyd Gottfredson	83.00	250.00	745.00

CHESTY AND HIS HELPERS (Disney)
1943 (Giveaway, 12 pgs., 5-1/2x7-1/4")
Los Angeles War Chest

	GD25	FN65	NM94
nn-Chesty & Coptie	56.00	168.00	500.00

CHESTY SANCHEZ
Nov, 1995 ($2.95, B&W)
Antarctic Press

	GD25	FN65	NM94
1		1.20	3.00

CHEVAL NOIR
1989 - No. 48, Nov, 1993 ($3.50, B&W, 68 pgs.)
Dark Horse Comics

	GD25	FN65	NM94
1-8,10 ($3.50): 6-Moebius poster insert		1.40	3.50
9,11,13,15,17,20,22 ($4.50, 84 pgs.)		1.80	4.50
12,18,19,21,23,25,26 ($3.95): 12-Geary-a; Mignola-c. 26-Moebius-a begins		1.60	4.00
14 ($4.95, 76 pgs.)(7 pgs. color)		2.00	5.00
16,24 ($3.75): 16-19-Contain trading cards		1.50	3.75
27-48 ($2.95): 33-Snyder III-c		1.20	3.00

NOTE: ***Bolland*** *a-2, 6, 7, 13, 14.* ***Bolton*** *a-2, 4, 45; c-4, 20.* ***Chadwick*** *c-13.* ***Dorman*** *painted c-16.* ***Geary*** *a-13, 14.* ***Kelley Jones*** *c-27.* ***Kaluta*** *a-6; c-6, 18.* ***Moebius*** *c-5, 9, 26.* ***Dave Stevens*** *c-1, 7.* ***Sutton*** *painted c-36.*

CHEYENNE (TV)
No. 734, Oct, 1956 - No. 25, Dec-Jan, 1961-62
Dell Publishing Co.

	GD25	FN65	NM94
Four Color 734(#1)-Clint Walker photo-c	16.00	47.00	170.00
Four Color 772,803: Clint Walker photo-c	7.00	20.00	75.00
4(8-10/57) - 12: 4-9-Clint Walker photo-c. 10-12-Ty Hardin photo-c	4.50	13.50	50.00
13-25 (All Clint Walker photo-c)	4.50	13.50	50.00

CHEYENNE AUTUMN (See Movie Classics)

CHEYENNE KID (Formerly Wild Frontier No. 1-7)
No. 8, July, 1957 - No. 99, Nov, 1973

Chiaroscuro (The Private Lives of Leonardo da Vinci) #2 © DC

Chiller #2 © MEG

Chilling Tales #13 © YM

Charlton Comics

	GD25	FN65	NM94
8 (#1)	5.70	17.00	35.00
9,15-19	4.00	10.00	20.00
10-Williamson/Torres-a(3); Ditko-c	7.85	23.50	55.00
11,12-Williamson/Torres-a(2) ea.; 11-(68 pgs.)-Cheyenne Kid meets Geronimo	8.50	26.00	60.00
13-Williamson/Torres-a (5 pgs.)	5.70	17.00	35.00
14-Williamson-a (5 pgs.?)	5.70	17.00	35.00
20-22,24,25-Severin c/a(3) each	2.50	7.50	22.00
23,27-29	1.25	3.75	10.00
26,30-Severin-a	2.00	6.00	16.00
31-59	1.25	3.75	10.00
60-80: 66-Wander by Aparo begins, ends #87	1.00	2.80	7.00
81-99: . Apache Red begins #88, origin in #89		2.00	5.00
Modern Comics Reprint 87,89(1978)		1.20	3.00

CHIAROSCURO (THE PRIVATE LIVES OF LEONARDO DA VINCI)
July, 1995 - No. 10, Apr, 1996 ($2.50, limited series, mature)
DC Comics (Vertigo)

	GD25	FN65	NM94
1-10		1.00	2.50

CHICAGO MAIL ORDER (See C-M-O Comics)

CHI-CHIAN
1997 - No. 6 ($2.95, limited series)
Sirius Entertainment

	GD25	FN65	NM94
1-3-Voltaire-s/a			2.95

CHIEF, THE (Indian Chief No. 3 on)
No. 290, Aug, 1950 - No. 2, Apr-June, 1951
Dell Publishing Co.

	GD25	FN65	NM94
Four Color 290(#1), 2	4.50	13.50	50.00

CHIEF CRAZY HORSE (See Wild Bill Hickok #21)
1950 (Also see Fighting Indians of the Wild West!)
Avon Periodicals

	GD25	FN65	NM94
nn-Fawcette-c	16.00	49.00	130.00

CHIEF VICTORIO'S APACHE MASSACRE (See Fight Indians of/Wild West!)
1951
Avon Periodicals

	GD25	FN65	NM94
nn-Williamson/Frazetta-a (7 pgs.); Larsen-a; Kinstler-c	39.00	118.00	280.00

CHILDHOOD'S END
Oct, 1997 - Present ($2.95, B&W)
Image Comics

	GD25	FN65	NM94
1-Bourne-s/Calafiore-a			2.95

CHILDREN OF FIRE
Nov, 1987 - No. 3, 1988 ($2.00, limited series)
Fantagor Press

	GD25	FN65	NM94
1-3: by Richard Corben		.80	2.00

CHILDREN OF THE VOYAGER (See Marvel Frontier Comics Unlimited)
Sept, 1993 - No. 4, Dec, 1993 ($1.95, limited series)
Marvel Frontier Comics

	GD25	FN65	NM94
1-($2.95)-Embossed glow-in-the-dark-c		1.20	3.00
2-4			1.50

CHILDREN'S BIG BOOK
1945 (25¢, stiff-c, 68 pgs.)
Dorene Publ. Co.

	GD25	FN65	NM94
nn-Comics & fairy tales; David Icove-a	8.75	26.25	65.00

CHILDREN'S CRUSADE, THE
Dec, 1993 - No. 2, Jan, 1994 ($3.95, limited series, mature)
DC Comics (Vertigo)

	GD25	FN65	NM94
1,2-Neil Gaiman scripts & Chris Bachalo-a; framing issues for Children's Crusade x-over		1.60	4.00

CHILD'S PLAY: THE SERIES (Movie)
May, 1991 - #3, 1991 ($2.50, 28pgs.)
Innovation Publishing

	GD25	FN65	NM94
1-3		1.00	2.50

CHILD'S PLAY 2 THE OFFICIAL MOVIE ADAPTATION (Movie)
1990 - No. 3, 1990 ($2.50, bi-weekly limited series, high quality)
Innovation Publishing

	GD25	FN65	NM94
1-3: Adapts movie sequel		1.00	2.50

CHILI (Millie's Rival)
5/69 - No. 17, 9/70; No. 18, 8/72 - No. 26, 12/73
Marvel Comics Group

	GD25	FN65	NM94
1	4.00	12.00	40.00
2-5	2.50	7.50	20.00
6-17	1.50	4.50	12.00
18-26	1.10	3.30	9.00
Special 1(12/71)	2.50	7.50	24.00

CHILLER
Nov, 1993 - No. 2, Dec, 1993 ($7.95, limited series, 68 pgs.)
Marvel Comics (Epic Comics)

	GD25	FN65	NM94
1,2	1.00	3.00	8.00

CHILLING ADVENTURES IN SORCERY (...as Told by Sabrina #1, 2)
(Red Circle Sorcery No. 6 on)
9/72 - No. 2, 10/72; No. 3, 10/73 - No. 5, 2/74
Archie Publications (Red Circle Productions)

	GD25	FN65	NM94
1-Sabrina cameo	1.85	5.50	15.00
2-Sabrina cameo	1.10	3.30	9.00
3-5: Morrow-c/a, all		2.40	6.00

CHILLING TALES (Formerly Beware)
No. 13, Dec, 1952 - No. 17, Oct, 1953
Youthful Magazines

	GD25	FN65	NM94
13(No.1)-Harrison-a; Matt Fox-c/a	40.00	120.00	325.00
14-Harrison-a	26.00	79.00	200.00
15-Has #14 on-c; Matt Fox-c; Harrison-a	33.00	100.00	250.00
16-Poe adapt.-'Metzengerstein'; Rudyard Kipling adapt.- 'Mark of the Beast,' by Kiefer; bondage-c	22.00	66.00	170.00
17-Matt Fox-c; Sir Walter Scott & Poe adapt.	29.00	86.00	220.00

CHILLING TALES OF HORROR (Magazine)
V1#1, 6/69 - V1#7, 12/70; V2#2, 2/71 - V2#5, 10/71 (50¢, B&W, 52 pgs.)
Stanley Publications

	GD25	FN65	NM94
V1#1	4.00	12.00	40.00
2-7: 7-Cameron-a	2.80	8.40	28.00
V2#2,3,5: 2-Spirit of Frankenstein-r/Adventures into the Unknown #16	2.50	7.50	24.00
V2#4-r/9 pg. Feldstein-a from Adventures into the Unknown #3	2.80	8.40	28.00

NOTE: *Two issues of V2#2 exist, Feb, 1971 and April, 1971.*

CHILLY WILLY
No. 740, Oct, 1956 - No. 1281, Apr-June, 1962 (Walter Lantz)
Dell Publishing Co.

	GD25	FN65	NM94
Four Color 740 (#1)	3.60	11.00	40.00
Four Color 852 (2/58),967 (2/59),1017 (9/59), 1074 (2-4/60),1122 (8/60), 1177 (4-6/61), 1212 (7-9/61), 1281	2.75	8.00	30.00

CHINA BOY (See Wisco)

CHIP 'N' DALE (Walt Disney)(See Walt Disney's C&S #204)
Nov, 1953 - No. 30, June-Aug, 1962; Sept, 1967 - No. 83, 1982
Dell Publishing Co./Gold Key/Whitman No. 65 on

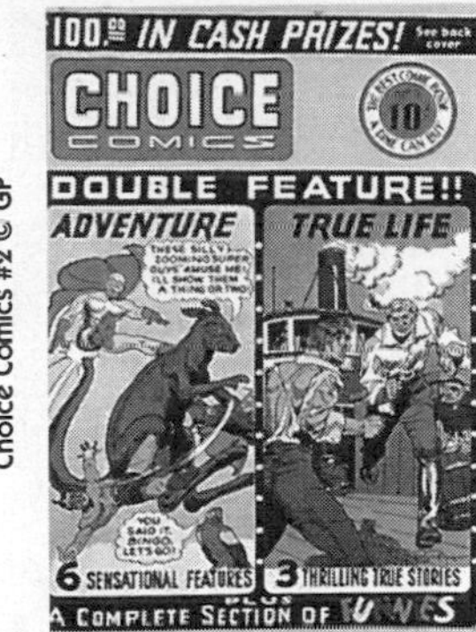

Choice Comics #2 © GP

Christmas Coloring Fun nn © H. Burnside

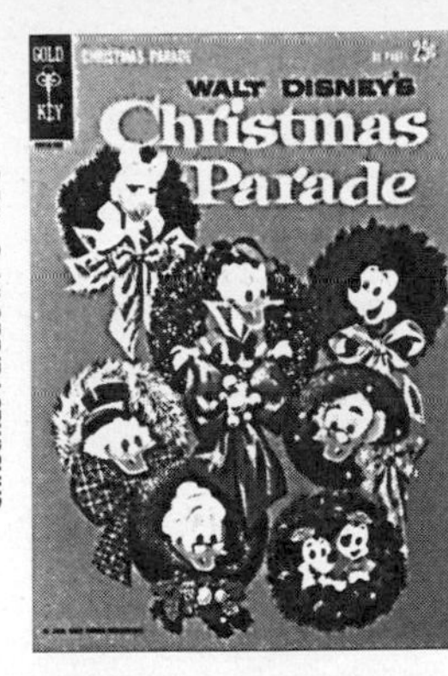

Christmas Parade #1 © WDC

GD25 FN65 NM94

Four Color 517(#1) 7.00 22.00 80.00
Four Color 581,636 4.50 13.50 50.00
4(12/55-2/56)-10 3.60 11.00 40.00
11-30 2.75 8.00 30.00
1(Gold Key, 1967)-Reprints 1.65 5.00 18.00
2-10 1.00 3.00 8.00
11-20 1.40 3.50
21-83 1.50
NOTE: *All Gold Key/Whitman issues have reprints except No. 32-35, 38-41, 45-47. No. 23-28, 30-42, 45-47, 49 have new covers.*

CHIP 'N DALE RESCUE RANGERS
June, 1990 - No. 19, Dec, 1991 ($1.50)
Disney Comics
1-19: New stories; 1,2-Origin 1.50

CHITTY CHITTY BANG BANG (See Movie Comics)

CHOICE COMICS
Dec, 1941 - No. 3, Feb, 1942
Great Publications
1-Origin Secret Circle; Atlas the Mighty app.; Zomba, Jungle Fight, Kangaroo Man, & Fire Eater begin 111.00 333.00 1000.00
2 61.00 183.00 550.00
3-Double feature; Features movie "The Lost City" (classic cover); continued from Great Comics #3 89.00 267.00 800.00

CHOO CHOO CHARLIE
Dec, 1969
Gold Key
1-John Stanley-a (scarce) 9.00 26.00 95.00

CHRISTIAN HEROES OF TODAY
1964 (36 pgs.)
David C. Cook
nn 1.60 4.00

CHRISTMAS (Also see A-1 Comics)
No. 28, 1950
Magazine Enterprises
A-1 28 4.25 13.00 28.00

CHRISTMAS ADVENTURE, A (See Classics Comics Giveaways, 12/69)

CHRISTMAS ADVENTURE, THE
1963 (16 pgs.)
S. Rose (H. L. Green Giveaway)
nn 2.40 6.00

CHRISTMAS ALBUM (See March of Comics No. 312)

CHRISTMAS & ARCHIE
Jan, 1975 ($1.00, 68 pgs., 10-1/4x13-1/4")
Archie Comics
1 3.00 9.00 30.00

CHRISTMAS AT THE ROTUNDA (Titled Ford Rotunda Christmas Book 1957 on) (Regular size)
1954 - 1961 (Given away every Christmas at one location)
Ford Motor Co. (Western Printing)
1954-56 issues (nn's) 5.00 15.00 30.00
1957-61 issues (nn's) 4.00 12.00 24.00

CHRISTMAS BELLS (See March of Comics No. 297)

CHRISTMAS CARNIVAL
1952 (25¢, one-shot, 100 pgs.)
Ziff-Davis Publ. Co./St. John Publ. Co. No. 2
nn 23.00 69.00 185.00
2-Reprints Ziff-Davis issue plus-c 14.00 41.00 110.00

GD25 FN65 NM94

CHRISTMAS CAROL, A (See March of Comics No. 33)

CHRISTMAS CAROL, A
No date (1942-43) (Giveaway, 32 pgs., 8-1/4x10-3/4", paper cover)
Sears Roebuck & Co.
nn-Comics & coloring book 14.00 41.00 110.00

CHRISTMAS CAROL, A
1940s ? (Christmas giveaway, 20 pgs.)
Sears Roebuck & Co.
nn-Comic book & animated coloring book 12.00 36.00 95.00

CHRISTMAS CAROLS
1959? (16 pgs.)
Hot Shoppes Giveaway
nn 3.60 9.00 18.00

CHRISTMAS COLORING FUN
1964 (20 pgs., slick-c, B&W)
H. Burnside
nn 1.00 3.00 8.00

CHRISTMAS DREAM, A
1950 (Kinney Shoe Store Giveaway, 16 pgs.)
Promotional Publishing Co.
nn 3.60 9.00 18.00

CHRISTMAS DREAM, A
1952? (Giveaway, paper cover, 16 pgs.)
J. J. Newberry Co.
nn 3.60 9.00 18.00

CHRISTMAS DREAM, A
1952 (Giveaway, 16 pgs., paper cover)
Promotional Publ. Co.
nn 3.60 9.00 18.00

CHRISTMAS EVE, A (See March of Comics No. 212)

CHRISTMAS FUN AROUND THE WORLD
No date (early 50's) (16 pgs., paper cover)
No publisher
nn 4.00 10.00 20.00

CHRISTMAS IN DISNEYLAND (See Dell Giants)

CHRISTMAS JOURNEY THROUGH SPACE
1960
Promotional Publiching Co.
nn-Reprints 1954 issue Jolly Christmas Book with new slick cover 4.15 12.50 25.00

CHRISTMAS ON THE MOON
1958 (Giveaway, 20 pgs., slick cover)
W. T. Grant Co.
nn 7.15 21.50 50.00

CHRISTMAS PARADE (See Dell Giant No. 26, Dell Giants, March of Comics No. 284, Walt Disney Christmas Parade & Walt Disney's...)

CHRISTMAS PARADE (Walt Disney's)
Jan, 1963 (no month) - No. 9, Jan, 1972 (#1,5: 80 pgs.; #2-4,7-9: 36 pgs.)
Gold Key
1 (30018-301)-Giant 7.00 22.00 80.00
2-6: 2-r/F.C. #367 by Barks. 3-r/F.C. #178 by Barks. 4-r/F.C. #203 by Barks. 5-r/Christ. Parade #1 (Dell) by Barks; giant. 6-r/Christmas Parade #2 (Dell) by Barks (64 pgs.); giant 5.50 16.50 60.00
7,9: 7-Pull-out poster 2.75 8.00 30.00
8-r/F.C. #367 by Barks; pull-out poster 5.50 16.50 60.00

CHRISTMAS PARTY (See March of Comics No. 256)

Chroma-Tick #8 © Ben Edlund

Chromium Man #4 © Triumphant

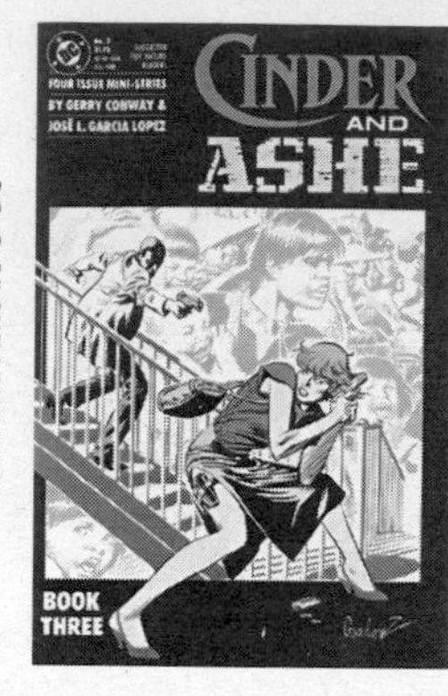

Cinder and Ashe #3 © DC

CHRISTMAS PLAY BOOK
1946 (Giveaway, 16 pgs., paper cover)
Gould-Stoner Co.

	GD25	FN65	NM94
nn	5.00	15.00	30.00

CHRISTMAS ROUNDUP
1960
Promotional Publishing Co.

	GD25	FN65	NM94
nn-Marv Levy-c/a	1.10	3.30	9.00

CHRISTMAS STORIES
No. 959, 1951; No. 1062, 1959?
Dell Publishing Co.

	GD25	FN65	NM94
Four Color #959 (Walt Scott's Little People 1951-56 strip-r.)	3.00	9.00	35.00
Four Color #1062 (Walt Scott's Little People strip-r	3.00	9.00	35.00

CHRISTMAS STORY (See March of Comics No. 326)

CHRISTMAS STORY BOOK (See Woolworth's Christmas Story Book)

CHRISTMAS STORY CUT-OUT BOOK, THE
No. 393, 1951 (15¢, 36 pgs.)
Catechetical Guild

	GD25	FN65	NM94
393-Half text & half comics	4.15	12.50	25.00

CHRISTMAS TREASURY, A (See Dell Giants & March of Comics No. 227)

CHRISTMAS USA (Through 300 Years) (Also see Uncle Sam's...)
1956 (Giveaway)
Promotional Publ. Co.

	GD25	FN65	NM94
nn-Marv Levy-c/a	1.80	4.50	9.00

CHRISTMAS WITH ARCHIE
1973, 1974 (49¢, 52 pgs.)
Spire Christian Comics (Fleming H. Revell Co.)

	GD25	FN65	NM94
nn		1.60	4.00

CHRISTMAS WITH MOTHER GOOSE
No. 90, Nov, 1945 - No. 253, Nov, 1949
Dell Publishing Co.

	GD25	FN65	NM94
Four Color 90 (#1)-Kelly-a	16.00	49.00	180.00
Four Color 126 ('46), 172 (11/47)-By Walt Kelly	13.00	38.00	140.00
Four Color 201 (10/48), 253-By Walt Kelly	11.00	33.00	120.00

CHRISTMAS WITH SANTA (See March of Comics No. 92)

CHRISTMAS WITH SNOW WHITE AND THE SEVEN DWARFS
1953 (16 pgs., paper-c)
Kobackers Giftstore of Buffalo, N.Y.

	GD25	FN65	NM94
nn	4.25	13.00	28.00

CHRISTMAS WITH THE SUPER-HEROES (See Limited Collectors' Edition)
1988; No. 2, 1989 ($2.95)
DC Comics

	GD25	FN65	NM94
1,2: 1-(100 pgs.)-All reprints; N. Adams-r, Byrne-c; Batman, Superman, JLA, LSH Christmas stories; r-Miller's 1st Batman/DC Special Series #21. 2-(68 pgs.)-Superman by Chadwick; Batman, Wonder Woman, Deadman, Gr. Lantern, Flash app.; Morrow-a; Enemy Ace by Byrne; all new-a		1.40	3.50

CHRISTOPHERS, THE
1951 (Giveaway, 36 pgs.) (Some copies have 15¢ sticker)
Catechetical Guild

	GD25	FN65	NM94
nn-Stalin as Satan in Hell	20.00	60.00	160.00

CHROMA-TICK, THE (...Special Edition, #1,2) (Also see The Tick)
Feb, 1992 - No. 8, Nov, 1993 ($3.95/$3.50, 44 pgs.)
New England Comics Press

	GD25	FN65	NM94
1,2-Includes serially numbered trading card set		2.00	5.00
3-8 ($3.50, 36 pgs.): 6-Bound-in card		1.40	3.50

CHROME
1986 - No. 3, 1986 ($1.50, limited series)
Hot Comics

	GD25	FN65	NM94
1-3			1.50

CHROMIUM MAN, THE
Aug, 1993 - No.10, May, 1994 ($2.50)
Triumphant Comics

	GD25	FN65	NM94
1-1st app. Mr. Death; all serially numbered		1.00	2.50
2-10: 2-1st app. Prince Vandal. 3-1st app. Candi, Breaker & Coil. 4,5-Triumphant Unleashed x-over. 8,9-(3/94). 10-(5/94)		1.00	2.50
0-(4/94)-Four color-c		1.00	2.50
0-All pink-c & all blue-c; no cover price		1.00	2.50

CHROMIUM MAN: VIOLENT PAST, THE
Jan, 1994 - No. 2, Jan, 1994 ($2.50, limited series)
Triumphant Comics

	GD25	FN65	NM94
1,2-Serially numbered to 22,000 each		1.00	2.50

CHRONICLES OF CORUM, THE (Also see Corum...)
Jan, 1987 - No. 12, Nov, 1988 ($1.75/$1.95, deluxe series)
First Comics

	GD25	FN65	NM94
1-12: Adapts Michael Moorcock's novel		.80	2.00

CHRONOWAR (Manga)
Aug, 1996 - No. 9, Apr, 1997 ($2.95, limited series)
Dark Horse Comics

	GD25	FN65	NM94
1-9		1.20	3.00

CHUCKLE, THE GIGGLY BOOK OF COMIC ANIMALS
1945 (132 pgs., one-shot)
R. B. Leffingwell Co.

	GD25	FN65	NM94
1-Funny animal	15.50	47.00	125.00

CHUCK NORRIS (TV)
Jan, 1987 - No. 4, July, 1987
Marvel Comics (Star Comics)

	GD25	FN65	NM94
1-3: Ditko-a		1.20	3.00
4-No Ditko-a (scarce)		2.00	5.00

CHUCK WAGON (See Sheriff Bob Dixon's...)

CICERO'S CAT
July-Aug, 1959 - No. 2, Sept-Oct, 1959
Dell Publishing Co.

	GD25	FN65	NM94
1,2-Cat from Mutt & Jeff	3.00	9.00	35.00

CIMARRON STRIP (TV)
Jan, 1968
Dell Publishing Co.

	GD25	FN65	NM94
1-Stuart Whitman photo-c	2.70	8.10	30.00

CINDER AND ASHE
May, 1988 - No. 4, Aug, 1988 ($1.75, limited series)
DC Comics

	GD25	FN65	NM94
1-4: Mature readers		.70	1.75

CINDERELLA (Disney) (See Movie Comics)
No. 272, Apr, 1950 - No. 786, Apr, 1957
Dell Publishing Co.

	GD25	FN65	NM94
Four Color 272	9.00	27.00	100.00
Four Color 786-Partial-r 272	5.50	16.50	60.00

CINDERELLA
Apr, 1982
Whitman Publishing Co.

Cinderella Love #25 © STJ

Cisco Kid #4 © DELL

ClanDestine #7 © MEG

GD25 FN65 NM94

nn-Reprints 4-Color #272 1.00

CINDERELLA IN "FAIREST OF THE FAIR"
1955 (5x7-1/4", 16 pgs., soft-c) (Walt Disney)
American Dairy Association (Premium)
nn 8.75 26.25 65.00

CINDERELLA LOVE
No. 10, 1950; No. 11, 4-5/51; No. 12, 9/51; No. 4, 10-11/51 - No. 11, Fall, 1952; No. 12, 10/53 - No. 15, 8/54; No. 25, 12/54 - No. 29, 10/55 (No #16-24)
Ziff-Davis/St. John Publ. Co. No. 12 on
10(#1)(1st Series, 1950)-Painted-c 9.50 28.00 75.00
11(#2, 4-5/51)-Crandall-a; Saunders painted-c 7.15 21.50 50.00
12(#3, 9/51)-Photo-c 5.70 17.00 35.00
4-8: 4,6,7-Photo-c 4.25 13.00 28.00
9-Kinstler-a; photo-c 5.70 17.00 40.00
10,11(Fall/'52), 14: 10,11-Photo-c. 14-Baker-a 5.70 17.00 35.00
12(St. John-10/53)-#13:13-Painted-c. 4.15 12.50 25.00
15 (8/54)-Matt Baker-c 5.70 17.00 40.00
25(2nd Series)(Formerly Romantic Marriage) 4.15 12.50 25.00
26-Baker-c; last precode (2/55) 5.70 17.00 40.00
27,29-Matt Baker-c 5.70 17.00 40.00
28 4.00 10.00 20.00

CINDY COMICS (...Smith No. 39, 40; Crime Can't Win No. 41 on)(Formerly Krazy Komics) (See Junior Miss & Teen Comics)
No. 27, Fall, 1947 - No. 40, July, 1950
Timely Comics
27-Kurtzman-a, 3 pgs: Margie, Oscar begin 15.00 45.00 120.00
28-31-Kurtzman-a 8.75 26.25 70.00
32-40: 33-Georgie story; anti-Wertham editorial 5.70 17.00 40.00
NOTE: *Kurtzman's "Hey Look"-#27(3), 29(2), 30(2), 31; "Giggles 'n' Grins"-28.*

CINEMA COMICS HERALD
1941 - 1943 (4-pg. movie "trailers", paper-c, 7-1/2x10-1/2")(Giveaway)
Paramount Pictures/Universal/RKO/20th Century Fox/Republic
"Mr. Bug Goes to Town" (1941) 6.50 19.50 45.00
"Bedtime Story" 5.00 15.00 30.00
"Lady For A Night", John Wayne, Joan Blondell (1942) 10.00 30.00 80.00
"Reap The Wild Wind" (1942) 7.15 21.50 50.00
"Thunder Birds" (1942) 6.50 19.50 45.00
"They All Kissed the Bride" 6.50 19.50 45.00
"Arabian Nights" (nd) 6.50 19.50 45.00
"Bombardie" (1943) 6.50 19.50 45.00
"Crash Dive" (1943)-Tyrone Power 6.50 19.50 45.00
NOTE: *The 1941-42 issues contain line art with color photos. 1943 issues are line art.*

CIRCUS (...the Comic Riot)
June, 1938 - No. 3, Aug, 1938
Globe Syndicate
1-(Scarce)-Spacehawks (2 pgs.), & Disk Eyes by Wolverton (2 pgs.), Pewee Throttle by Cole (2nd comic book work; see Star Comics V1#11), Beau Gus, Ken Craig & The Lords of Crillon, Jack Hinton by Eisner, Van Bragger by Kane 750.00 2250.00 4600.00
2,3-(Scarce)-Eisner, Cole, Wolverton, Bob Kane-a in each 383.00 1150.00 2400.00

CIRCUS BOY (TV) (See Movie Classics)
No. 759, Dec, 1956 - No. 813, July, 1957
Dell Publishing Co.
Four Color 759 (#1)-The Monkees' Mickey Dolenz photo-c 10.00 30.00 110.00
Four Color 785 (4/57),813-Mickey Dolenz photo-c 10.00 30.00 110.00

CIRCUS COMICS
1945 - No. 2, June, 1945; Winter, 1948-49
Farm Women's Publishing Co./D. S. Publ.
1-Funny animal 8.75 26.25 70.00
2 6.50 19.50 45.00
1(1948)-D.S. Publ.; 2 pgs. Frazetta 20.00 60.00 160.00

CIRCUS OF FUN COMICS
1945 - No. 3, Dec, 1947 (A book of games & puzzles)
A. W. Nugent Publishing Co.
1 10.00 30.00 80.00
2,3 7.15 21.50 50.00

CISCO KID, THE (TV)
July, 1950 - No. 41, Oct-Dec, 1958
Dell Publishing Co.
Four Color 292(#1)-Cisco Kid, his horse Diablo, & sidekick Pancho & his horse Loco begin; painted-c begin 20.00 60.00 220.00
2(1/51)-5 9.00 27.00 100.00
6-10 7.00 22.00 80.00
11-20 6.40 19.00 70.00
21-36-Last painted-c 4.50 13.50 50.00
37-41: All photo-c 9.00 27.00 100.00
NOTE: ***Buscema** a-40. **Ernest Nordli** painted c-5-16, 20, 35.*

CISCO KID COMICS
Winter, 1944 (one-shot)
Bernard Bailey/Swappers Quarterly
1-Illustrated Stories of the Operas: Faust; Funnyman by Giunta; Cisco Kid (1st app.) & Superbaby begin; Giunta-c 36.00 108.00 300.00

CITIZEN SMITH (See Holyoke One-Shot No. 9)

CITY OF THE LIVING DEAD (See Fantastic Tales No. 1)
1952
Avon Periodicals
nn-Hollingsworth-c/a 36.00 1071.00 270.00

CITY SURGEON (Blake Harper...)
August, 1963
Gold Key
1(10075-308)-Painted-c 3.00 9.00 30.00

CIVIL WAR MUSKET, THE (Kadets of America Handbook)
1960 (25¢, half-size, 36 pgs.)
Custom Comics, Inc.
nn 2.50 7.50 20.00

CLAIRE VOYANT (Also see Keen Teens)
1946 - No. 4, 1947 (Sparling strip reprints)
Leader Publ./Standard/Pentagon Publ.
nn 48.00 144.00 400.00
2,4: 2-Kamen-c. 4-Kamen bondage-c 40.00 120.00 325.00
3-Kamen bridal-c; contents mentioned in Love and Death, a book by Gershom Legman(1949) referenced by Dr. Wertham in **SOTI** 45.00 135.00 385.00

CLAIRE VOYANTE
June, 1996 ($3.50, B&W)
Lightning Comics
1-Cleary-c 1.40 3.50
1-($9.95)-Platinum Edition 10.00
1-($9.95)-Nude A 10.00
1-($9.95)-Nude B 10.00

CLANDESTINE (Also see Marvel Comics Presents & X-Men: ClanDestine)
Oct, 1994 - No.12, Sept, 1995 ($2.95/$2.50)
Marvel Comics
1-($2.95)-Alan Davis-c/a(p)/scripts & Mark Farmer-c/a(i) begin, ends #8; Modok app.; Silver Surfer cameo; gold foil-c 1.20 3.00
2-12: 2-Wraparound-c. 2,3-Silver Surfer app. 5-Origin of ClanDestine.

Clash #2 © Tom Veitch & Adam Kubert

Classic Comics #1 © GIL

Classic Comics #2 © GIL

GD25 FN65 NM94

6-Capt. America, Hulk, Spider-Man, Thing & Thor-c; Spider-Man cameo. 7-Spider-Man-c/app; Punisher cameo. 8-Invaders & Dr. Strange app. 9-12-Modok app. 10-Captain Britain-c/app. 11-Sub-Mariner app — 1.00 — 2.50

Preview (10/94, $1.50) — 1.50

CLASH
1991 - No. 3, 1991 ($4.95, limited series, 52 pgs.)
DC Comics

Book One - Three: Adam Kubert-c/a — 2.00 — 5.00

CLASSIC COMICS/ILLUSTRATED - INTRODUCTION
by Dan Malan

Further revisions have been made to help in understanding the **Classics** section. **Classics** reprint editions prior to 1963 had either incorrect dates or no dates listed. Those reprint editions should be identified only by the highest number on the reorder list (HRN). Past price guides listed what were calculated to be approximately correct dates, but many people found it confusing for the price guide to list a date not listed in the comic itself.

We have also attempted to clear up confusion about edition variations, such as color, printer, etc. Such variations will be identified by letters. Editions will now be determined by three categories. Original edition variations will be Edition 1A, 1B, etc. All reprint editions prior to 1963 will be identified by HRN only. All reprint editions from 9/63 on will be identified by the correct date listed in the comic.

We have also included new information on four recent reprintings of **Classics** not previously listed. From 1968-1976 Twin Circle, the Catholic newspaper, serialized over 100 **Classics** titles. That list can be found under non-series items at the end of this section. In 1972 twelve **Classics** were reissued as **Now Age Books Illustrated**. They are listed under **Pendulum Illustrated Classics**. In 1982, 20 **Classics** were reissued, adapted for teaching English as a second language. They are listed under **Regents Illustrated Classics**. Then in 1984, six **Classics** were reissued with cassette tapes. See the listing under **Cassette Books**.

UNDERSTANDING CLASSICS ILLUSTRATED
by Dan Malan

Since **Classics Illustrated** is the most complicated comic book series, with all its reprint editions and variations, with changes in covers and artwork, with a variety of means of identifying editions, and with the most extensive worldwide distribution of any comic-book series; therefore this introductory section is provided to assist you in gaining expertise about this series.

THE HISTORY OF CLASSICS

The **Classics** series was the brain child of Albert L. Kanter, who saw in the new comic-book medium a means of introducing children to the great classics of literature. In October of 1941 his Gilberton Co. began the **Classic Comics** series with **The Three Musketeers**, with 64 pages of storyline. In those early years, the struggling series saw irregular schedules and numerous printers, not to mention variable art quality and liberal story adaptations. With No.13 the page total was reduced to 56 (except for No. 33, originally scheduled to be No. 9), and with No. 15 the coming-next ad on the outside back cover moved inside. In 1945 the Jerry Iger Shop began producing all new CC titles, beginning with No. 23. In 1947 the search for a classier logo resulted in **Classics Illustrated**, beginning with No. 35, **Last Days of Pompeii**. With No. 45 the page total dropped again to 48, which was to become the standard.

Two new developments in 1951 had a profound effect upon the success of the series. One was the introduction of painted covers, instead of the old line drawn covers, beginning with No. 81, **The Odyssey**. The second was the switch to the major national distributor Curtis. They raised the cover price from 10 to 15 cents, making it the highest priced comic-book, but it did not slow the growth of the series, because they were marketed as books, not comics. Because of this higher quality image, **Classics** flourished during the fifties while other comic series were reeling from outside attacks. They diversified with their new **Juniors**, **Specials**, and **World Around Us** series.

Classics artwork can be divided into three distinct periods. The pre-Iger era (1941-44) was mentioned above for its variable art quality. The Iger era (1945-53) was a major improvement in art quality and adaptations. It came to be dominated by artists Henry Kiefer and Alex Blum, together accounting for some 50 titles. Their styles gave the first real personality to the series. The EC era (1954-62) resulted from the demise of the EC horror series, when many of their artists made the major switch to classical art.

But several factors brought the production of new CI titles to a complete halt in 1962. Gilberton lost its 2nd class mailing permit. External factors like television, cheap paperback books, and Cliff Notes were all eating away at their market. Production halted with No.167, **Faust**, even though many more titles were already in the works. Many of those found their way into foreign series, and are very desirable to collectors. In 1967, **Classics Illustrated** was sold to Patrick Frawley and his Catholic publication, Twin Circle. They issued two new titles in 1969 as part of an attempted revival, but succumbed to major distribution problems in 1971. In 1988, the trio: First Publishing, Berkley Press, and Classics Media Group acquired the u se rights for the old CI series art, logo, and name from the Frawley Group. So far they have used only the name in the new series, but do have plans to reprint the old CI.

One of the unique aspects of the **Classics Illustrated** (CI) series was the proliferation of reprint variations. Some titles had as many as 25 editions. Reprinting began in 1943. Some **Classic Comics** (CC) reprints (r) had the logo format revised to a banner logo, and added a motto under the banner. In 1947 CC titles changed to the CI logo, but kept their line drawn covers (LDC). In 1948, Nos. 13, 18, 29 and 41 received second covers (LDC2), replacing covers considered too violent, and reprints of Nos. 13-44 had pages reduced to 48, except for No. 26, which had 48 pages to begin with.

Starting in the mid-1950s, 70 of the 80 LDC titles were reissued with new painted covers (PC). Thirty of them also received new interior artwork (A2). The new artwork was generally higher quality with larger art panels and more faithful but abbreviated storylines. Later on, there were 29 second painted covers (PC2), mostly by Twin Circle. Altogether there were 199 interior art variations (169 (O)s and 30 A2 editions) and 272 different covers (169 (O)s, four LDC2s, 70 new PCs of LDC (O)s, and 29 PC2s). It is mildly astounding to realize that there are nearly 1400 different editions in the U.S. CI series.

FOREIGN CLASSICS ILLUSTRATED

If U.S. Classics variations are mildly astounding, the veritable plethora of foreign CI variations will boggle your imagination. While we still anticipate additional discoveries, we presently know about series in 25 languages and 27 countries. There were 250 new CI titles in foreign series, and nearly 400 new foreign covers of U.S. titles. The 1400 U.S. CI editions pale in comparison to the 4000 plus foreign editions. The very nature of CI lent itself to flourishing as an international series. Worldwide, they published over one billion copies! The first foreign CI series consisted of six Canadian Classic Comic reprints in 1946.

The following chart shows when CI series first began in each country:
1946: Canada. 1947: Australia. 1948: Brazil/The Netherlands. 1950: Italy. 1951: Greece/Japan/Hong Kong(?)/England/Argentina/Mexico. 1952: West Germany. 1954: Norway. 1955: New Zealand/South Africa. 1956: Denmark/Sweden/Iceland. 1957: Finland/France. 1962: Singapore(?). 1964: India (8 languages). 1971: Ireland (Gaelic). 1973: Belgium(?) /Philippines(?) & Malaysia(?).

Significant among the early series were Brazil and Greece. In 1950, Brazil was the first country to begin doing its own new titles. They issued nearly 80 new CI titles by Brazilian authors. In Greece in 1951 they actually had debates in parliament about the effects of Classics Illustrated on Greek culture, leading to the inclusion of 88 new Greek History & Mythology titles in the CI series.

But by far the most important foreign CI development was the joint European series which began in 1956 in 10 countries simultaneously. By 1960, CI had the largest European distribution of any American publication, not just comics! So when all the problems came up with U.S. distribution, they literally moved the CI operation to Europe in 1962, and continued producing new titles in all four CI series. Many of them were adapted and drawn in the U.S., the most famous of which was the British CI #158A. Dr. No, drawn by Norman Nodel. Unfortunately, the British CI series ended in late 1963, which limited the European CI titles available in English to 15. Altogether there were 82 new CI art titles in the joint European series, which ran until 1976.

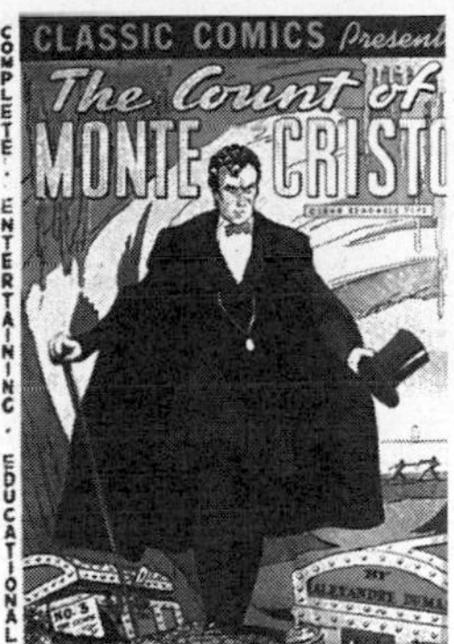

Classic Comics #3 © GIL

Classic Comics #4 © GIL

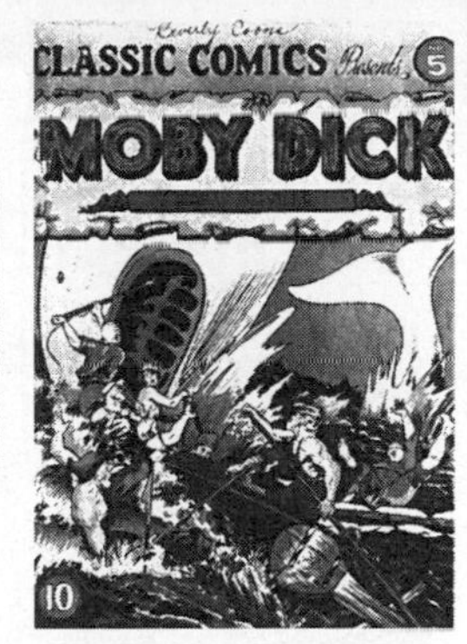

Classic Comics #5 © GIL

IDENTIFYING CLASSICS EDITIONS

HRN: This is the highest number on the reorder list. It should be listed in ( ) after the title number. It is crucial to understanding various CI editions.

ORIGINALS (O): This is the all-important First Edition. To determine (O)s,there is one primary rule and two secondary rules (with exceptions):

Rule No. 1: All (O)s and only (O)s have coming-next ads for the next number. **Exceptions**: No. 14(15) (reprint) has an ad on the last inside text page only. No. 14(0) also has a full-page outside back cover ad (also rule 2). Nos.55(75) and 57(75) have coming-next ads. (Rules 2 and 3 apply here). Nos. 168(0) and 169(0) do not have coming-next ads. No.168 was never reprinted; No. 169(0) has HRN (166). No. 169(169) is the only reprint.

Rule No. 2: On nos.1-80, all (O)s and only (O)s list 10c on the front cover. **Exceptions**: Reprint variations of Nos. 37(62), 39(71), and 46(62) list 10c on the front cover. (Rules 1 and 3 apply here.)

Rule No. 3: All (O)s have HRN close to that title No. **Exceptions**: Some reprints also have HRNs close to that title number: a few CC(r)s, 58(62), 60(62), 149(149), 152(149) 153(149), and title nos. in the 160's. (Rules 1 and 2 apply here.)

DATES: Many reprint editions list either an incorrect date or no date. Since Gilberton apparently kept track of CI editions by HRN, they often left the (O) date on reprints. Often, someone with a CI collection for sale will swear that all their copies are originals. That is why we are so detailed in pointing out how to identify original editions. Except for original editions, which should have a coming-next ad, etc., all CI dates prior to 1963 are incorrect! So you want to go by HRN only if it is (165) or below, and go by listed date if it is 1963 or later. There are a few (167) editions with incorrect dates. They could be listed either as (167) or (62/3), which is meant to indicate that they were issued sometime between late 1962 and early 1963.

COVERS: A change from CC to LDC indicates a logo change, not a cover change; while a change from LDC to LDC2, LDC to PC, or from PC to PC2 does indicate a new cover. New PCs can be identified by HRN, and PC2s can be identified by HRN and date. Several covers had color changes, particularly from purple to blue.

Notes: If you see 15 cents in Canada on a front cover, it does not necessarily indicate a Canadian edition. Editions with an HRN between 44 and 75, with 15 cents on the cover are Canadian. Check the publisher's address. An HRN listing two numbers with a / between them indicates that there are two different reorder lists in the front and back covers. Official Twin Circle editions have a full-page back cover ad for their TC magazine, with no CI reorder list. Any CI with just a Twin Circle sticker on the front is not an official TC edition.

TIPS ON LISTING CLASSICS FOR SALE

It may be easy to just list Edition 17, but Classics collectors keep track of CI editions in terms of HRN and/or date, (O) or (r), CC or LDC, PC or PC2, A1 or A2, soft or stiff cover, etc. Try to help them out. For originals, just list (0), unless there are variations such as color (Nos. 10 and 61), printer (Nos. 18-22), HRN (Nos. 95, 108, 160), etc. For reprints, just list HRN if its (165) or below. Above that, list HRN and date. Also, please list type of logo/cover/art for the convenience of buyers. They will appreciate it.

CLASSIC COMICS (Also see Best from Boys Life, Cassette Books, Famous Stories, Fast Fiction, Golden Picture Classics, King Classics, Marvel Classics Comics, Pendulum Illustrated Classics, Picture Parade, Picture Progress, Regents Ill. Classics, Spitfire, Stories by Famous Authors, Superior Stories, and World Around Us.)

CLASSIC COMICS (Classics Illustrated No. 35 on)
10/41 - No. 34, 2/47; No. 35, 3/47 - No. 169, Spring 1969
(Reprint Editions of almost all titles 5/43 - Spring 1971)
(Painted Covers (0)s No. 81 on, and (r)s of most Nos. 1-80)
Elliot Publishing #1-3 (1941-1942)/Gilberton Publications #4-167 (1942-1967)/
Twin Circle Pub. (Frawley) #168-169 (1968-1971)

Abbreviations:
A–Art; C or c–Cover; CC–Classic Comics; CI–Classics Ill.;
Ed–Edition; LDC–Line Drawn Cover; PC–Painted Cover; r–Reprint

1. The Three Musketeers

Ed	HRN	Date	Details	A	C	GD25	FN65	NM94
1	–	10/41	Date listed-1941; Elliot Pub; 68 pgs.	1	1	420.00	1260.00	4200.00
2	10	–	10¢ price removed on all (r)s; Elliot Pub; CC-r	1	1	30.00	90.00	240.00
3	15	–	Long Isl. Ind. Ed.; CC-r	1	1	21.00	64.00	170.00
4	18/20		Sunrise Times Ed.; CC-r	1	1	14.50	43.00	115.00
5	21	–	Richmond Courier Ed.; CC-r	1	1	13.00	39.00	105.00
6	28	1946	CC-r	1	1	10.00	30.00	80.00
7	36	–	LDC-r	1	1	5.70	17.00	38.00
8	60	–	LDC-r	1	1	4.25	13.00	26.00
9	64	–	LDC-r	1	1	3.60	9.00	18.00
10	78	–	C-price 15¢;LDC-r	1	1	3.20	8.00	16.00
11	93	–	LDC-r	1	1	3.20	8.00	16.00
12	114	–	Last LDC-r	1	1	2.40	6.00	12.00
13	134	–	New-c; old-a; 64 pg. PC-r	1	2	2.40	6.00	12.00
14	143	–	Old-a; PC-r; 64 pg.	1	2	2.00	5.00	10.00
15	150	–	New-a; PC-r; Evans/Crandall-a	2	2	2.40	6.00	12.00
16	149	–	PC-r	2	2	1.00	2.00	5.00
17	167	–	PC-r	2	2	1.00	2.00	5.00
18	167	4/64	PC-r	2	2	1.00	2.00	5.00
19	167	1/65	PC-r	2	2	1.00	2.00	5.00
20	167	3/66	PC-r	2	2	1.00	2.00	5.00
21	166	11/67	PC-r	2	2	1.00	2.00	5.00
22	166	Spr/69	C-price 25¢ ; stiff-c; PC-r	2	2	1.00	2.00	5.00
23	169	Spr/71	PC-r; stiff-c	2	2	1.00	2.00	5.00

2. Ivanhoe

Ed	HRN	Date	Details	A	C	GD25	FN65	NM94
1	(O)	12/41?	Date listed-1941; Elliot Pub; 68 pgs.	1	1	189.00	567.00	1700.00
2	10	–	Price & 'Presents' removed; Elliot Pub; CC-r	1	1	25.00	75.00	200.00
3	15	–	Long Isl. Ind. ed.; CC-r	1	1	17.00	51.00	135.00
4	18/20		Sunrise Times ed.; CC-r	1	1	14.50	43.00	115.00
5	21	–	Richmond Courier ed.; CC-r	1	1	13.00	39.00	105.00
6	28	1946	Last 'Comics'-r	1	1	10.00	30.00	80.00
7	36	–	1st LDC-r	1	1	5.70	17.00	40.00
8	60	–	LDC-r	1	1	4.15	12.50	25.00
9	64	–	LDC-r	1	1	4.00	10.00	20.00
10	78	–	C-price 15¢; LDC-r	1	1	3.20	8.00	16.00
11	89	–	LDC-r	1	1	2.80	7.00	14.00
12	106	–	LDC-r	1	1	2.40	6.00	12.00
13	121	–	Last LDC-r	1	1	2.40	6.00	12.00
14	136	–	New-c&a; PC-r	2	2	2.80	7.00	14.00
15	142	–	PC-r	2	2	1.00	2.00	5.00
16	153	–	PC-r	2	2	1.00	2.00	5.00
17	149	–	PC-r	2	2	1.00	2.00	5.00
18	167	–	PC-r	2	2	1.00	2.00	5.00
19	167	5/64	PC-r	2	2	1.00	2.00	5.00
20	167	1/65	PC-r	2	2	1.00	2.00	5.00
21	167	3/66	PC-r	2	2	1.00	2.00	5.00

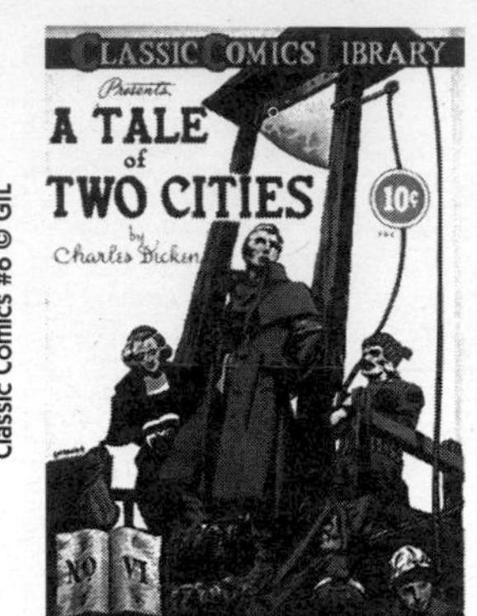

Classic Comics #6 © GIL

Classic Comics #7 © GIL

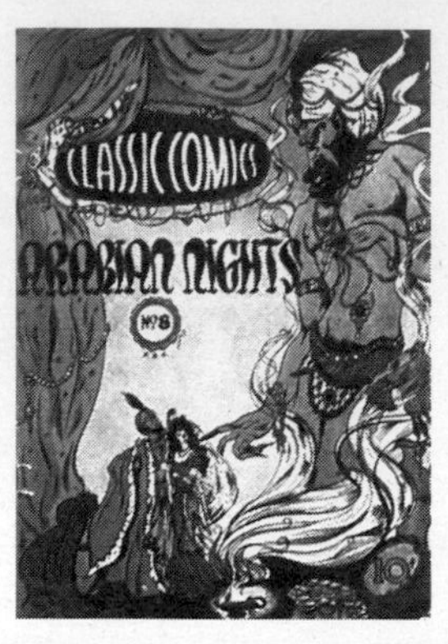

Classic Comics #8 © GIL

Ed	HRN	Date	Details	A	C	GD25	FN65	NM94
22A	166	9/67	PC-r	2	2	1.00	2.00	5.00
22B	166	–	Center ad for Children's Digest & Young Miss; rare; PC-r	2	2	8.75	26.25	65.00
23	166	R/68	C-Price 25¢; PC-r	2	2	1.00	2.00	5.00
24	169	Win/69	Stiff-c	2	2	1.00	2.00	5.00
25	169	Win/71	PC-r; stiff-c	2	2	1.00	2.00	5.00

3. The Count of Monte Cristo

Ed	HRN	Date	Details	A	C	GD25	FN65	NM94
1	(O)	3/42	Elliot Pub; 68 pgs.	1	1	122.00	366.00	1100.00
2	10	–	Conray Prods; CC-r	1	1	23.00	68.00	180.00
3	15	–	Long Isl. Ind. ed.; CC-r	1	1	17.50	53.00	140.00
4	18/20		Sunrise Times ed.; CC-r	1	1	15.50	47.00	125.00
5	20	–	Sunrise Times ed.; CC-r	1	1	14.00	41.00	110.00
6	21	–	Richmond Courier ed.; CC-r	1	1	13.00	39.00	105.00
7	28	1946	CC-r; new Banner logo	1	1	10.00	30.00	80.00
8	36	–	1st LDC-r	1	1	5.70	17.00	40.00
9	60	–	LDC-r	1	1	4.15	12.50	25.00
10	62	–	LDC-r	1	1	5.00	15.00	30.00
11	71	–	LDC-r	1	1	3.60	9.00	18.00
12	87	–	C-price 15¢; LDC-r	1	1	3.20	8.00	16.00
13	113	–	LDC-r	1	1	2.40	6.00	12.00
14	135	–	New-c&a; PC-r; Cameron-a	2	2	2.40	6.00	12.00
15	143	–	PC-r	2	2	1.00	2.00	5.00
16	153	–	PC-r	2	2	1.00	2.00	5.00
17	161	–	PC-r	2	2	1.00	2.00	5.00
18	167	–	PC-r	2	2	1.00	2.00	5.00
19	167	7/64	PC-r	2	2	1.00	2.00	5.00
20	167	7/65	PC-r	2	2	1.00	2.00	5.00
21	167	7/66	PC-r	2	2	1.00	2.00	5.00
22	166	R/68	C-price 25¢; PC-r	2	2	1.00	2.00	5.00
23	169	–	Win/69 Stiff-c; PC-r	2	2	1.00	2.00	5.00

4. The Last of the Mohicans

Ed	HRN	Date	Details	A	C	GD25	FN65	NM94
1	(O)	8/42	Date listed-1942; Gilberton #4(0) on; 68 pgs.	1	1	103.00	309.00	925.00
2	12	–	Elliot Pub; CC-r	1	1	23.00	68.00	180.00
3	15	–	Long Isl. Ind. ed.; CC-r	1	1	17.50	53.00	140.00
4	20	–	Long Isl. Ind. ed.; CC-r; banner logo	1	1	15.00	45.00	120.00
5	21	–	Queens Home News ed.; CC-r	1	1	14.00	41.00	110.00
6	28	1946	Last CC-r; new	1	1	10.00	30.00	80.00
7	36	–	1st LDC-r	1	1	5.70	17.00	40.00
8	60	–	LDC-r	1	1	4.15	12.50	25.00
9	64	–	LDC-r	1	1	3.60	9.00	18.00
10	78	–	C-price 15¢; LDC-r	1	1	3.20	8.00	16.00
11	89	–	LDC-r	1	1	2.80	7.00	14.00
12	117	–	Last LDC-r	1	1	2.40	6.00	12.00
13	135	–	New-c; PC-r	1	2	2.40	6.00	12.00
14	141	–	PC-r	1	2	2.00	5.00	10.00
15	150	–	New-a; PC-r; Severin, L.B. Cole-a	2	2	2.80	7.00	14.00
16	161	–	PC-r	2	2	1.00	2.00	5.00
17	167	–	PC-r	2	2	1.00	2.00	5.00
18	167	6/64	PC-r	2	2	1.00	2.00	5.00
19	167	8/65	PC-r	2	2	1.00	2.00	5.00
20	167	8/66	PC-r	2	2	1.00	2.00	5.00
21	166	R/67	C-price 25¢; PC-r	2	2	1.00	2.00	5.00
22	169	Spr/69	Stiff-c; PC-r	2	2	1.00	2.00	5.00

5. Moby Dick

Ed	HRN	Date	Details	A	C	GD25	FN65	NM94
1A	(O)	9/42	Date listed-1942; Gilberton; 68 pgs.	1	1	128.00	384.00	1150.00
1B			inside-c, rare free promo			189.00	567.00	1700.00
2	10	–	Conray Prods; Pg. 64 changed from 105 title list to letter from Editor; CC-r	1	1	24.00	71.00	190.00
3	15	–	Long Isl. Ind. ed.; Pg. 64 changed from Letter to the Editor to Ill. poem-Concord Hymn; CC-r	1	1	20.00	60.00	160.00
4	18/20	–	Sunrise Times ed.; CC-r	1	1	15.50	47.00	125.00
5	20	–	Sunrise Times ed.; CC-r	1	1	15.00	45.00	120.00
6	21	–	Sunrise Times ed.; CC-r	1	1	14.00	41.00	110.00
7	28	1946	CC-r; new banner logo	1	1	11.30	34.00	90.00
8	36	–	1st LDC-r	1	1	6.00	18.00	42.00
9	60	–	LDC-r	1	1	4.15	12.50	25.00
10	62	–	LDC-r	1	1	5.00	15.00	30.00
11	71	–	LDC-r	1	1	4.00	10.00	20.00
12	87	–	C-price 15¢; LDC-r	1	1	3.60	9.00	18.00
13	118	–	LDC-r	1	1	2.80	7.00	14.00
14	131	–	New c&a; PC-r	2	2	3.20	8.00	16.00
15	138	–	PC-r	2	2	1.00	2.00	5.00
16	148	–	PC-r	2	2	1.00	2.00	5.00
17	158	–	PC-r	2	2	1.00	2.00	5.00
18	167	–	PC-r	2	2	1.00	2.00	5.00
19	167	6/64	PC-r	2	2	1.00	2.00	5.00
20	167	7/65	PC-r	2	2	1.00	2.00	5.00
21	167	3/66	PC-r	2	2	1.00	2.00	5.00
22	166	9/67	PC-r	2	2	1.00	2.00	5.00
23	166	Win/69	New-c & c-price 25¢; Stiff-c; PC-r	2	3	2.40	6.00	12.00
24	169	Win/71	PC-r	2	3	2.00	5.00	10.00

6. A Tale of Two Cities

Ed	HRN	Date	Details	A	C	GD25	FN65	NM94
1	(O)	10/42	Date listed-1942; 68 pgs. Zeckerberg c/a	1	1	100.00	300.00	900.00
2	14	–	Elliot Pub; CC-r	1	1	21.00	64.00	170.00
3	18	–	Long Isl. Ind. ed.; CC-r	1	1	17.00	51.00	135.00
4	20	–	Sunrise Times ed.; CC-r	1	1	15.00	45.00	120.00
5	28	1946	Last CC-r; new banner logo	1	1	10.00	30.00	80.00
6	51	–	1st LDC-r	1	1	5.70	17.00	38.00
7	64	–	LDC-r	1	1	4.00	11.00	22.00
8	78	–	C-price 15¢; LDC-r	1	1	3.60	9.00	18.00
9	89	–	LDC-r	1	1	2.40	6.00	12.00
10	117	–	LDC-r	1	1	2.40	6.00	12.00
11	132	–	New-c&a; PC-r;	2	2	2.80	7.00	14.00

Classic Comics #9 © GIL

Classic Comics #10 © GIL

Classic Comics #11 © GIL

Ed	HRN	Date	Details	A	C	GD25	FN65	NM94
			Joe Orlando-a					
12	140	–	PC-r	2	2	1.00	2.00	5.00
13	147	–	PC-r	2	2	1.00	2.00	5.00
14	152	–	PC-r; very rare	2	2	14.50	43.00	115.00
15	153	–	PC-r	2	2	1.00	2.00	5.00
16	149	–	PC-r	2	2	1.00	2.00	5.00
17	167	–	PC-r	2	2	1.00	2.00	5.00
18	167	6/64	PC-r	2	2	1.00	2.00	5.00
19	167	8/65	PC-r	2	2	1.00	2.00	5.00
20	166	5/67	PC-r	2	2	1.00	2.00	5.00
21	166	Fall/68	New-c & 25¢; PC-r	2	3	2.80	7.00	14.00
22	169	Sum/70	Stiff-c; PC-r	2	3	2.40	6.00	12.00

7. Robin Hood

Ed	HRN	Date	Details	A	C	GD25	FN65	NM94
1	(O)	12/42	Date listed-1942; first Gift Box ad-bc; 68 pgs.	1	1	75.00	225.00	675.00
2	12	–	Elliot Pub; CC-r	1	1	21.00	62.00	165.00
3	18	–	Long Isl. Ind. ed.; CC-r	1	1	15.50	47.00	125.00
4	20	–	Nassau Bulletin ed.; CC-r	1	1	14.50	43.00	115.00
5	22	–	Queens Cty. Times ed.; CC-r	1	1	13.00	39.00	105.00
6	28	–	CC-r	1	1	10.00	30.00	80.00
7	51	–	LDC-r	1	1	5.70	17.00	38.00
8	64	–	LDC-r	1	1	4.00	11.00	22.00
9	78	–	LDC-r	1	1	3.20	8.00	16.00
10	97	–	LDC-r	1	1	2.80	7.00	14.00
11	106	–	LDC-r	1	1	2.40	6.00	12.00
12	121	–	LDC-r	1	1	2.40	6.00	12.00
13	129	–	New-c; PC-r	1	2	2.80	7.00	14.00
14	136	–	New-a; PC-r	2	2	2.80	7.00	14.00
15	143	–	PC-r	2	2	1.00	2.00	5.00
16	153	–	PC-r	2	2	1.00	2.00	5.00
17	164	–	PC-r	2	2	1.00	2.00	5.00
18	167	–	PC-r	2	2	1.00	2.00	5.00
19	167	6/64	PC-r	2	2	1.20	2.40	6.00
20	167	5/65	PC-r	2	2	1.00	2.00	5.00
21	167	7/66	PC-r	2	2	1.00	2.00	5.00
22	166	12/67	PC-r	2	2	1.20	2.40	6.00
23	169	Sum/69	Stiff-c; c-price 25¢; PC-r	2	2	1.00	2.00	5.00

8. Arabian Nights

Ed	HRN	Date	Details	A	C	GD25	FN65	NM94
1	(O)	2/43	Original; 68 pgs. Lilian Chestney-c/a	1	1	133.00	400.00	1200.00
2	17	–	Long Isl. ed.; pg. 64 changed from Gift Box ad to Letter from British Medical Worker; CC-r	1	1	48.00	144.00	430.00
3	20	–	Nassau Bulletin; Pg. 64 changed from letter to article-Three Men Named Smith; CC-r	1	1	38.00	113.00	340.00
4A	28	1946	CC-r; new banner logo, slick-c	1	1	28.00	83.00	220.00
4B	28	1946	Same, but w/stiff-c	1	1	28.00	83.00	220.00
5	51	–	LDC-r	1	1	19.00	56.00	150.00
6	64	–	LDC-r	1	1	15.50	47.00	125.00
7	78	–	LDC-r	1	1	14.50	43.00	115.00
8	164	–	New-c&a; PC-r	2	2	13.00	39.00	105.00

9. Les Miserables

Ed	HRN	Date	Details	A	C	GD25	FN65	NM94
1A	(O)	3/43	Original; slick paper cover; 68 pgs.	1	1	72.00	216.00	650.00
1B	(O)	3/43	Original; rough, pulp type-c; 68 pgs.	1	1	94.00	282.00	850.00
2	14	–	Elliot Pub; CC-r	1	1	23.00	68.00	180.00
3	18	3/44	Nassau Bul. Pg. 64 changed from Gift Box ad to Bill of Rights article; CC-r	1	1	18.00	54.00	145.00
4	20	–	Richmond Courier ed.; CC-r	1	1	15.00	45.00	120.00
5	28	1946	Gilberton; pgs. 60-64 rearranged/ illos added; CC-r	1	1	10.50	32.00	85.00
6	51	–	LDC-r	1	1	5.70	17.00	40.00
7	71	–	LDC-r	1	1	5.00	15.00	30.00
8	87	–	C-price 15¢; LDC-r	1	1	4.15	12.50	25.00
9	161	–	New-c&a; PC-r	2	2	4.25	13.00	26.00
10	167	9/63	PC-r	2	2	1.25	3.75	10.00
11	167	12/65	PC-r	2	2	1.25	3.75	10.00
12	166	R/1968	New-c & price 25¢; PC-r	2	3	2.00	6.00	16.00

10. Robinson Crusoe (Used in **SOTI**, pg. 142)

Ed	HRN	Date	Details	A	C	GD25	FN65	NM94
1A	(O)	4/43	Original; Violet-c; 68 pgs; Zuckerberg c/a	1	1	64.00	192.00	575.00
1B	(O)	4/43	Original; blue-grey-c, 68 pgs.	1	1	72.00	216.00	650.00
2A	14	–	Elliot Pub; violet-c; 68 pgs; CC-r	1	1	24.00	71.00	190.00
2B	14	–	Elliot Pub; blue-grey-c; CC-r	1	1	21.00	64.00	170.00
3	18	–	Nassau Bul. Pg. 64 changed from Gift Box ad to Bill of Rights article; CC-r	1	1	15.50	47.00	125.00
4	20	–	Queens Home News ed.; CC-r	1	1	14.00	41.00	110.00
5	28	1946	Gilberton; pg. 64 changes from Bill of Rights to WWII article-One Leg Shot Away; last CC-r	1	1	10.00	30.00	80.00
6	51	–	LDC-r	1	1	5.70	17.00	38.00
7	64	–	LDC-r	1	1	4.15	12.50	25.00
8	78	–	C-price 15¢; LDC-r	1	1	3.60	9.00	18.00
9	97	–	LDC-r	1	1	3.00	7.50	15.00
10	114	–	LDC-r	1	1	2.40	6.00	12.00
11	130	–	New-c; PC-r	1	2	2.80	7.00	14.00
12	140	–	New-a; PC-r	2	2	2.80	7.00	14.00
13	153	–	PC-r	2	2	1.00	2.00	5.00
14	164	–	PC-r	2	2	1.00	2.00	5.00
15	167	–	PC-r	2	2	1.00	2.00	5.00
16	167	7/64	PC-r	2	2	1.10	3.30	9.00
17	167	5/65	PC-r	2	2	1.10	3.30	9.00
18	167	6/66	PC-r	2	2	1.00	2.00	5.00
19	166	Fall/68	C-price 25¢; PC-r	2	2	1.00	2.00	5.00
20	166	R/68	(No Twin Circle ad)	2	2	1.20	2.40	6.00
21	169	Sm/70	Stiff-c; PC-r	2	2	1.20	2.40	6.00

11. Don Quixote

Ed	HRN	Date	Details	A	C	GD25	FN65	NM94
1	10	5/43	First (O) with HRN	1	1	69.00	207.00	625.00

Classic Comics #12 © GIL

Classic Comics #13 © GIL

Classic Comics #14 © GIL

Ed	HRN	Date	Details	A	C	GD25	FN65	NM94
			list; 68 pgs.					
2	18	–	Nassau Bulletin ed.; CC-r	1	1	20.00	60.00	160.00
3	21	–	Queens Home News ed.; CC-r	1	1	15.50	47.00	125.00
4	28	–	CC-r	1	1	10.50	32.00	85.00
5	110	–	New-PC; PC-r	1	2	4.00	11.00	22.00
6	156	–	Pgs. reduced 68 to 52; PC-r	1	2	2.40	6.00	12.00
7	165	–	PC-r	1	2	1.40	3.50	7.00
8	167	1/64	PC-r	1	2	1.00	3.00	8.00
9	167	11/65	PC-r	1	2	1.00	2.80	7.00
10	166	R/1968	New-c & price 25¢; PC-r	1	3	2.25	6.75	18.00

12. Rip Van Winkle and the Headless Horseman

Ed	HRN	Date	Details	A	C	GD25	FN65	NM94
1	11	6/43	Original; 68 pgs.	1	1	67.00	200.00	600.00
2	15	–	Long Isl. Ind. ed.; CC-r	1	1	19.50	58.00	155.00
3	20	–	Long Isl. Ind. ed.;	1	1	15.00	45.00	120.00
4	22	–	Queens Cty. Times ed.; CC-r	1	1	13.00	39.00	105.00
5	28	–	CC-r	1	1	10.00	30.00	80.00
6	60	–	1st LDC-r	1	1	5.35	16.00	32.00
7	62	–	LDC-r	1	1	4.00	11.00	22.00
8	71	–	LDC-r	1	1	3.20	8.00	16.00
9	89	–	C-price 15¢; LDC-r	1	1	2.80	7.00	14.00
10	118	–	LDC-r	1	1	2.40	6.00	12.00
11	132	–	New-c; PC-r	1	2	2.80	7.00	14.00
12	150	–	New-a; PC-r	2	2	2.80	7.00	14.00
13	158	–	PC-r	2	2	1.00	2.00	5.00
14	167	–	PC-r	2	2	1.00	2.00	5.00
15	167	12/63	PC-r	2	2	1.00	2.00	5.00
16	167	4/65	PC-r	2	2	1.20	2.40	6.00
17	167	4/66	PC-r	2	2	1.00	2.00	5.00
18	166	R/1968	New-c&price 25¢; PC-r; stiff-c	2	3	2.40	6.00	12.00
19	169	Sm/70	PC-r; stiff-c	2	3	2.00	5.00	10.00

13. Dr. Jekyll and Mr. Hyde (Used in **SOTI**, pg. 143)(1st horror comic?)

Ed	HRN	Date	Details	A	C	GD25	FN65	NM94
1	12	8/43	Original 60 pgs.	1	1	97.00	291.00	875.00
2	15	–	Long Isl. Ind. ed.; CC-r	1	1	28.00	83.00	220.00
3	20	–	Long Isl. Ind. ed.; CC-r	1	1	19.00	56.00	150.00
4	28	–	No c-price; CC-r	1	1	14.50	43.00	115.00
5	60	–	New-c; Pgs. reduced from 60 to 52; H.C. Kiefer-c; LDC-r	1	2	5.70	17.00	34.00
6	62	–	LDC-r	1	2	4.25	13.00	26.00
7	71	–	LDC-r	1	2	4.00	10.00	20.00
8	87	–	Date returns (erroneous); LDC-r	1	2	3.60	9.00	18.00
9	112	–	New-c&a; PC-r; Cameron-a	2	3	4.00	11.00	22.00
10	153	–	PC-r	2	3	1.00	2.00	5.00
11	161	–	PC-r	2	3	1.00	2.00	5.00
12	167	–	PC-r	2	3	1.00	2.00	5.00
13	167	8/64	PC-r	2	3	1.00	2.00	5.00
14	167	11/65	PC-r	2	3	1.00	2.00	5.00
15	166	R/68	C-price 25¢; PC-r	2	3	1.20	2.40	6.00
16	169	Wn/69	PC-r; stiff-c	2	3	1.00	2.00	5.00

14. Westward Ho!

Ed	HRN	Date	Details	A	C	GD25	FN65	NM94
1	13	9/43	Original; last outside bc coming-next ad; 60 pgs.	1	1	161.00	483.00	1450.00
2	15	–	Long Isl. Ind. ed.; CC-r	1	1	50.00	150.00	450.00
3	21	–	Queens Home News; Pg. 56 changed from coming-next ad to Three Men Named Smith; CC-r	1	1	36.00	108.00	320.00
4	28	1946	Gilberton; Pg. 56 changed again to WWII article-Speaking for America; last CC-r	1	1	31.00	94.00	250.00
5	53	–	Pgs. reduced from 60 to 52; LDC-r	1	1	29.00	86.00	230.00

15. Uncle Tom's Cabin (Used in **SOTI**, pgs. 102, 103)

Ed	HRN	Date	Details	A	C	GD25	FN65	NM94
1	14	11/43	Original; Outside-bc ad: 2 Gift Boxes; 60 pgs.; color var. on-c; green trunk,root on left & brown trunk, root on left	1	1	58.00	174.00	525.00
2	15	–	Long Isl. Ind. listed- bottom inside-fc; also Gilberton listed bottom-pg. 1; CC-r; green root vs. brown root var. occurs again	1	1	21.00	64.00	170.00
3	21	–	Nassau Bulletin ed.; CC-r	1	1	17.00	51.00	135.00
4	28	–	No c-price; CC-r	1	1	10.50	32.00	85.00
5	53	–	Pgs. reduced 60 to 52; LDC-r	1	1	5.70	17.00	36.00
6	71	–	LDC-r	1	1	4.15	12.50	25.00
7	89	–	C-price 15¢; LDC-r	1	1	4.00	12.00	24.00
8	117	–	New-c/lettering changes; PC-r	1	2	2.80	7.00	14.00
9	128	–	'Picture Progress' promo; PC-r	1	2	1.60	4.00	8.00
10	137	–	PC-r	1	2	1.00	2.00	5.00
11	146	–	PC-r	1	2	1.00	2.00	5.00
12	154	–	PC-r	1	2	1.00	2.00	5.00
13	161	–	PC-r	1	2	1.00	2.00	5.00
14	167	–	PC-r	1	2	1.00	2.00	5.00
15	167	6/64	PC-r	1	2	1.00	2.00	5.00
16	167	5/65	PC-r	1	2	1.00	2.00	5.00
17	166	5/67	PC-r	1	2	1.00	2.00	5.00
18	166	Wn/69	New-stiff-c; PC-r	1	3	2.00	5.00	10.00
19	169	Sm/70	PC-r; stiff-c	1	3	2.00	5.00	10.00

16. Gullivers Travels

Ed	HRN	Date	Details	A	C	GD25	FN65	NM94
1	15	12/43	Original-Lilian Chestney c/a; 60 pgs.	1	1	58.00	174.00	525.00
2	18/20	–	Price deleted; Queens Home News ed; CC-r	1	1	19.00	56.00	150.00
3	22	–	Queens Cty. Times ed.; CC-r	1	1	15.00	45.00	120.00
4	28	–	CC-r	1	1	10.00	30.00	80.00
5	60	–	Pgs. reduced to	1	1	5.00	15.00	30.00

NO. 15 CLASSIC COMICS
UNCLE TOM'S CABIN
10¢

Classic Comics #15 © GIL

Classic Comics #16 © GIL

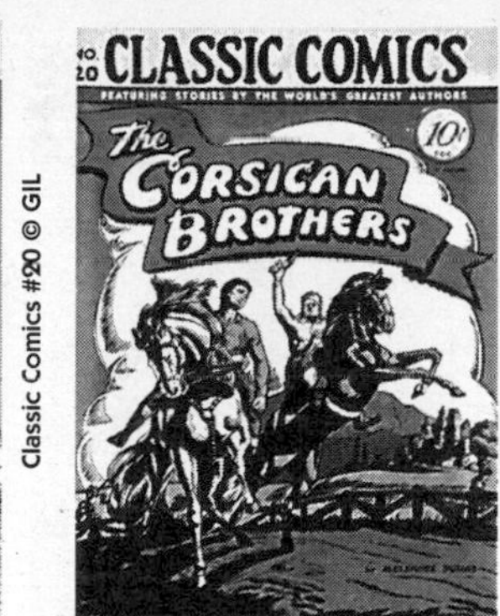

Classic Comics #20 © GIL

Ed	HRN	Date	Details	A	C	GD25	FN65	NM94
			48; LDC-r					
6	62	–	LDC-r	1	1	4.00	11.00	22.00
7	78	–	C-price 15¢; LDC-r	1	1	3.60	9.00	18.00
8	89	–	LDC-r	1	1	2.80	7.00	14.00
9	155	–	New-c; PC-r	1	2	2.80	7.00	14.00
10	165	–	PC-r	1	2	1.00	2.00	5.00
11	167	5/64	PC-r	1	2	1.00	2.00	5.00
12	167	11/65	PC-r	1	2	1.00	2.00	5.00
13	166	R/1968	C-price 25¢; PC-r	1	2	1.00	2.00	5.00
14	169	Wn/69	PC-r; stiff-c	1	2	1.00	2.00	5.00

17. The Deerslayer

Ed	HRN	Date	Details	A	C	GD25	FN65	NM94
1	16	1/44	Original; Outside-bc ad: 3 Gift Boxes; 60 pgs.	1	1	51.00	153.00	460.00
2A	18	–	Queens Cty Times (inside-fc); CC-r	1	1	19.50	58.00	155.00
2B	18	–	Gilberton (bottom-pg. 1); CC-r; Scarce	1	1	29.00	86.00	230.00
3	22	–	Queens Cty. Times ed.; CC-r	1	1	15.50	47.00	125.00
4	28	–	CC-r	1	1	10.50	32.00	85.00
5	60	–	Pgs.reduced to 52; LDC-r	1	1	5.70	17.00	35.00
6	64	–	LDC-r	1	1	4.00	10.00	20.00
7	85	–	C-price 15¢; LDC-r	1	1	2.80	7.00	14.00
8	118	–	LDC-r	1	1	2.40	6.00	12.00
9	132	–	LDC-r	1	1	2.40	6.00	12.00
10	167	11/66	Last LDC-r	1	1	2.00	5.00	10.00
11	166	R/1968	New-c & price 25¢; PC-r	1	2	3.20	8.00	16.00
12	169	Spr/71	Stiff-c; letters from parents & educators; PC-r	1	2	2.00	5.00	10.00

18. The Hunchback of Notre Dame

Ed	HRN	Date	Details	A	C	GD25	FN65	NM94
1A	17	3/44	Orig.; Gilberton ed; 60 pgs.	1	1	69.00	207.00	625.00
1B	17	3/44	Orig.; Island Pub. Ed.; 60 pgs.	1	1	61.00	183.00	550.00
2	18/20	–	Queens Home News ed.; CC-r	1	1	21.00	64.00	170.00
3	22	–	Queens Cty. Times ed.; CC-r	1	1	16.00	49.00	130.00
4	28	–	CC-r	1	1	14.00	41.00	110.00
5	60	–	New-c; 8pgs. deleted; Kiefer-c; LDC-r	1	2	5.35	16.00	32.00
6	62	–	LDC-r	1	2	4.00	10.00	20.00
7	78	–	C-price 15¢; LDC-r	1	2	3.60	9.00	18.00
8A	89	–	H.C.Kiefer on bottom right-fc; LDC-r	1	2	3.20	8.00	16.00
8B	89	–	Name omitted; LDC-r	1	2	4.00	12.00	24.00
9	118	–	LDC-r	1	2	2.80	7.00	14.00
10	140	–	New-c; PC-r	1	3	4.00	11.00	22.00
11	146	–	PC-r	1	3	3.20	8.00	16.00
12	158	–	New-c&a; PC-r; Evans/Crandall-a	2	4	3.60	9.00	18.00
13	165	–	PC-r	2	4	1.20	2.40	6.00
14	167	9/63	PC-r	2	4	1.20	2.40	6.00
15	167	10/64	PC-r	2	4	1.20	2.40	6.00
16	167	4/66	PC-r	2	4	1.00	2.00	5.00
17	166	R/1968	New price 25¢; PC-r	2	4	1.00	2.00	5.00
18	169	Sp/70	Stiff-c; PC-r	2	4	1.00	2.00	5.00

19. Huckleberry Finn

Ed	HRN	Date	Details	A	C	GD25	FN65	NM94
1A	18	4/44	Orig.; Gilberton ed.; 60 pgs.	1	1	43.00	129.00	385.00
1B	18	4/44	Orig.; Island Pub.; 60 pgs.	1	1	47.00	141.00	420.00
2	18	–	Nassau Bulletin ed.; fc-price 15¢-Canada; no coming-next ad; CC-r	1	1	20.00	60.00	160.00
3	22	–	Queens City Times ed.; CC-r	1	1	15.00	45.00	120.00
4	28	–	CC-r	1	1	10.00	30.00	80.00
5	60	–	Pgs. reduced to 48; LDC-r	1	1	5.00	15.00	30.00
6	62	–	LDC-r	1	1	4.00	11.00	22.00
7	78	–	LDC-r	1	1	3.20	8.00	16.00
8	89	–	LDC-r	1	1	2.80	7.00	14.00
9	117	–	LDC-r	1	1	2.40	6.00	12.00
10	131	–	New-c&a; PC-r	2	2	2.40	6.00	12.00
11	140	–	PC-r	2	2	1.00	2.00	5.00
12	150	–	PC-r	2	2	1.00	2.00	5.00
13	158	–	PC-r	2	2	1.00	2.00	5.00
14	165	–	PC-r (scarce)	2	2	2.40	6.00	12.00
15	167	–	PC-r	2	2	1.00	2.00	5.00
16	167	6/64	PC-r	2	2	1.00	2.00	5.00
17	167	6/65	PC-r	2	2	1.00	2.00	5.00
18	167	10/65	PC-r	2	2	1.00	2.00	5.00
19	166	9/67	PC-r	2	2	1.00	2.00	5.00
20	166	Win/69	C-price 25¢; PC-r; stiff-c	2	2	1.00	2.00	5.00
21	169	Sm/70	PC-r; stiff-c	2	2	1.00	2.00	5.00

20. The Corsican Brothers

Ed	HRN	Date	Details	A	C	GD25	FN65	NM94
1A	20	6/44	Orig.; Gilberton ed.; bc-ad: 4 Gift Boxes; 60 pgs.	1	1	38.00	113.00	340.00
1B	20	6/44	Orig.; Courier ed.; 60 pgs.	1	1	36.00	108.00	315.00
1C	20	6/44	Orig.; Long Island Ind. ed.; 60 pgs.	1	1	36.00	108.00	315.00
2	22	–	Queens Cty. Times ed.; white logo banner; CC-r	1	1	17.00	51.00	135.00
3	28	–	CC-r	1	1	15.00	45.00	120.00
4	60	–	CI logo; no price; 48 pgs.; LDC-r	1	1	13.00	39.00	105.00
5A	62	–	LDC-r; Classics Ill. logo at top of pgs.	1	1	10.50	32.00	85.00
5B	62	–	w/o logo at top of pg. (scarcer)	1	1	12.00	36.00	95.00
6	78	–	C-price 15¢; LDC-r	1	1	10.00	30.00	80.00
7	97	–	LDC-r	1	1	8.75	26.25	70.00

21. 3 Famous Mysteries ("The Sign of the 4", "The Murders in the Rue Morgue", "The Flayed Hand")

Ed	HRN	Date	Details	A	C	GD25	FN65	NM94
1A	21	7/44	Orig.; Gilberton ed.; 60 pgs.	1	1	78.00	234.00	700.00
1B	21	7/44	Orig. Island Pub. Co.; 60 pgs.	1	1	83.00	250.00	735.00
1C	21	7/44	Original; Courier Ed.; 60 pgs.	1	1	70.00	210.00	630.00

Classic Comics #22 © GIL

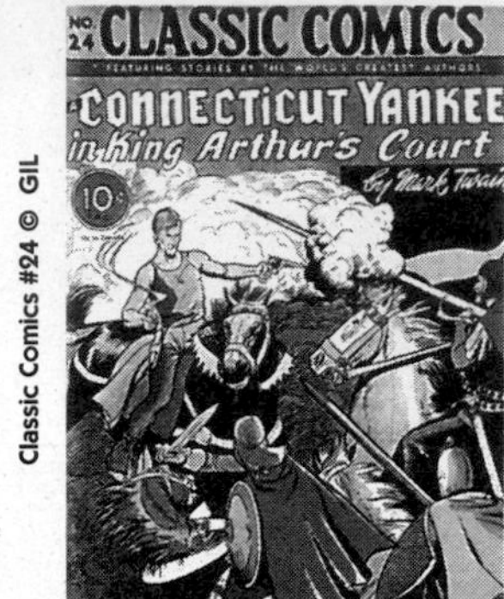

Classic Comics #24 © GIL

Classic Comics #26 © GIL

Ed	HRN	Date	Details	A	C	GD25	FN65	NM94
2	22	–	Nassau Bulletin ed.; CC-r	1	1	31.00	94.00	245.00
3	30	–	CC-r	1	1	24.00	73.00	195.00
4	62	–	LDC-r; 8 pgs. deleted; LDC-r	1	1	19.00	56.00	150.00
5	70	–	LDC-r	1	1	17.00	51.00	135.00
6	85	–	C-price 15¢; LDC-r	1	1	15.00	45.00	120.00
7	114	–	New-c; PC-r	1	2	15.00	45.00	120.00

22. The Pathfinder

Ed	HRN	Date	Details	A	C	GD25	FN65	NM94
1A	22	10/44	Orig.; No printer listed; ownership statement inside fc lists Gilberton & date; 60 pgs.	1	1	36.00	108.00	325.00
1B	22	10/44	Orig.; Island Pub. ed.; 60 pgs.	1	1	35.00	105.00	280.00
1C	22	10/44	Orig.; Queens Cty Times ed. 60 pgs.	1	1	35.00	105.00	280.00
2	30	–	C-price removed; CC-r	1	1	10.50	32.00	85.00
3	60	–	Pgs. reduced to 52; LDC-r	1	1	4.15	12.50	25.00
4	70	–	LDC-r	1	1	4.00	10.00	20.00
5	85	–	C-price 15¢; LDC-r	1	1	3.20	8.00	16.00
6	118	–	LDC-r	1	1	2.80	7.00	14.00
7	132	–	LDC-r	1	1	2.40	6.00	12.00
8	146	–	LDC-r	1	1	2.40	6.00	12.00
9	167	11/63	New-c; PC-r	1	2	4.00	11.00	22.00
10	167	12/65	PC-r	1	2	2.80	7.00	14.00
11	166	8/67	PC-r	1	2	2.80	7.00	14.00

23. Oliver Twist (1st Classic produced by the Iger Shop)

Ed	HRN	Date	Details	A	C	GD25	FN65	NM94
1	23	7/45	Original; 60 pgs.	1	1	36.00	108.00	295.00
2A	30	–	Printers Union logo on bottom left-fc same as 23(Orig.) (very rare); CC-r	1	1	26.00	80.00	210.00
2B	30	–	Union logo omitted; CC-r	1	1	10.00	30.00	80.00
3	60	–	Pgs. reduced to 48; LDC-r	1	1	4.25	13.00	28.00
4	62	–	LDC-r	1	1	4.00	11.00	22.00
5	71	–	LDC-r	1	1	3.60	9.00	18.00
6	85	–	C-price 15¢; LDC-r	1	1	3.20	8.00	16.00
7	94	–	LDC-r	1	1	2.60	6.50	13.00
8	118	–	LDC-r	1	1	2.60	6.50	13.00
9	136	–	New-PC, old-a; PC-r	1	2	2.60	6.50	13.00
10	150	–	Old-a; PC-r	1	2	2.00	5.00	10.00
11	164	–	Old-a; PC-r	1	2	3.00	7.50	15.00
12	164	–	New-a; PC-r; Evans/Crandall-a	2	2	4.00	11.00	22.00
13	167	–	PC-r	2	2	2.40	6.00	12.00
14	167	8/64	PC-r	2	2	1.00	2.00	5.00
15	167	12/65	PC-r	2	2	1.00	2.00	5.00
16	166	R/1968	New 25¢; PC-r	2	2	1.00	2.00	5.00
17	169	Win/69	Stiff-c; PC-r	2	2	1.00	2.00	5.00

24. A Connecticut Yankee in King Arthur's Court

Ed	HRN	Date	Details	A	C	GD25	FN65	NM94
1	9/45	–	Original	1	1	33.00	98.00	260.00
2	30	–	No price circle; CC-r	1	1	9.50	28.00	75.00
3	60	–	8 pgs. deleted; LDC-r	1	1	4.15	12.50	25.00
4	62	–	LDC-r	1	1	4.00	11.00	22.00
5	71	–	LDC-r	1	1	3.60	9.00	18.00
6	87	–	C-price 15¢; LDC-r	1	1	3.20	8.00	16.00
7	121	–	LDC-r	1	1	2.80	7.00	14.00
8	140	–	New-c&a; PC-r	2	2	3.20	8.00	16.00
9	153	–	PC-r	2	2	1.00	2.00	5.00
10	164	–	PC-r	2	2	1.00	2.00	5.00
11	167	–	PC-r	2	2	1.00	2.00	5.00
12	167	7/64	PC-r	2	2	1.00	2.00	5.00
13	167	6/66	PC-r	2	2	1.00	2.00	5.00
14	166	R/1968	C-price 25¢; PC-r	2	2	1.00	2.00	5.00
15	169	Spr/71	PC-r; stiff-c	2	2	1.00	2.00	5.00

25. Two Years Before the Mast

Ed	HRN	Date	Details	A	C	GD25	FN65	NM94
1	10/45	–	Original; Webb/Heames-a&c	1	1	33.00	98.00	260.00
2	30	–	Price circle blank; CC-r	1	1	10.00	30.00	80.00
3	60	–	8 pgs. deleted; LDC-r	1	1	4.15	12.50	25.00
4	62	–	LDC-r	1	1	4.00	11.00	22.00
5	71	–	LDC-r	1	1	3.20	8.00	16.00
6	85	–	C-price 15¢; LDC-r	1	1	2.80	7.00	14.00
7	114	–	LDC-r	1	1	2.40	6.00	12.00
8	156	–	3 pgs. replaced by fillers; new-c; PC-r	1	2	3.20	8.00	16.00
9	167	12/63	PC-r	1	2	1.00	2.00	5.00
10	167	12/65	PC-r	1	2	1.00	2.00	5.00
11	166	9/67	PC-r	1	2	1.00	2.00	5.00
12	169	Win/69	C-price 25¢; stiff-c PC-r	1	2	1.00	2.00	5.00

26. Frankenstein (2nd horror comic?)

Ed	HRN	Date	Details	A	C	GD25	FN65	NM94
1	26	12/45	Orig.; Webb/Brewster a&c; 52 pgs.	1	1	78.00	234.00	700.00
2A	30	–	Price circle blank; no indicia; CC-r	1	1	23.00	69.00	185.00
2B	30	–	With indicia; scarce; CC-r	1	1	28.00	83.00	220.00
3	60	–	LDC-r	1	1	6.85	21.00	48.00
4	62	–	LDC-r	1	1	10.00	30.00	80.00
5	71	–	LDC-r	1	1	5.00	15.00	30.00
6A	82	–	C-price 15¢; soft-c LDC-r	1	1	4.15	12.50	25.00
6B	82	–	Stiff-c; LDC-r	1	1	5.35	16.00	32.00
7	117	–	LDC-r	1	1	3.20	8.00	16.00
8	146	–	New Saunders-c; PC-r	1	2	3.60	9.00	18.00
9	152	–	Scarce; PC-r	1	2	5.35	16.00	32.00
10	153	–	PC-r	1	2	1.00	2.00	5.00
11	160	–	PC-r	1	2	1.00	2.00	5.00
12	165	–	PC-r	1	2	1.00	2.00	5.00
13	167	–	PC-r	1	2	1.00	2.00	5.00
14	167	6/64	PC-r	1	2	1.00	2.00	5.00
15	167	6/65	PC-r	1	2	1.00	2.00	5.00
16	167	10/65	PC-r	1	2	1.00	2.00	5.00
17	166	9/67	PC-r	1	2	1.00	2.00	5.00
18	169	Fall/69	C-price 25¢; stiff-c PC-r	1	2	1.00	2.00	5.00
19	169	Spr/71	PC-r; stiff-c	1	2	1.00	2.00	5.00

27. The Adventures of Marco Polo

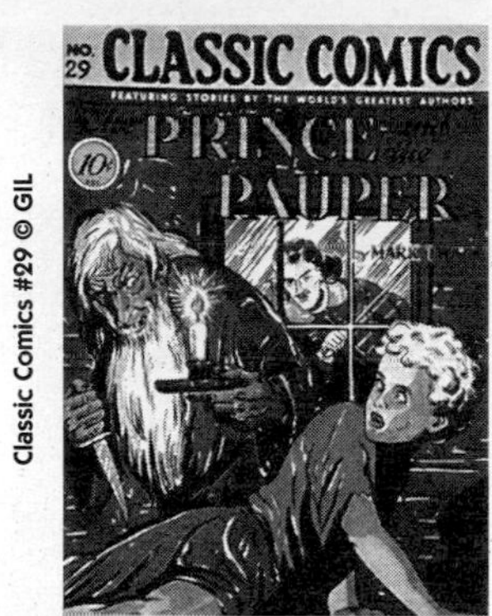

Classic Comics #29 © GIL

Classic Comics #31 © GIL

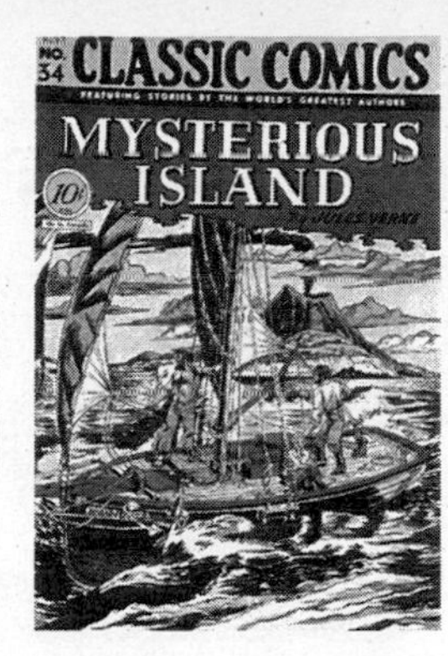

Classic Comics #34 © GIL

Ed	HRN	Date	Details	A	C	GD25	FN65	NM94
1	4/46	–	Original	1	1	35.00	105.00	280.00
2	30	–	Last 'Comics' reprint; CC-r	1	1	10.00	30.00	80.00
3	70	–	8 pgs. deleted; no c-price; LDC-r	1	1	4.00	10.50	23.00
4	87	–	C-price 15¢; LDC-r	1	1	3.20	8.00	16.00
5	117	–	LDC-r	1	1	2.40	6.00	12.00
6	154	–	New-c; PC-r	1	2	2.40	6.00	12.00
7	165	–	PC-r	1	2	1.00	2.00	5.00
8	167	4/64	PC-r	1	2	1.00	2.00	5.00
9	167	6/66	PC-r	1	2	1.00	2.00	5.00
10	169	Spr/69	New price 25¢; stiff-c; PC-r	1	2	1.00	2.00	5.00

28. Michael Strogoff

Ed	HRN	Date	Details	A	C	GD25	FN65	NM94
1	6/46	–	Original	1	1	36.00	108.00	290.00
2	51	–	8 pgs. cut; LDC-r	1	1	10.00	30.00	80.00
3	115	–	New-c; PC-r	1	2	4.00	10.00	20.00
4	155	–	PC-r	1	2	1.80	4.50	9.00
5	167	11/63	PC-r	1	2	1.80	4.50	9.00
6	167	7/66	PC-r	1	2	1.80	4.50	9.00
7	169	Sm/69	C-price 25¢; stiff-c PC-r	1	3	2.20	5.50	11.00

29. The Prince and the Pauper

Ed	HRN	Date	Details	A	C	GD25	FN65	NM94
1	7/46	–	Orig.; "Horror"-c	1	1	47.00	141.00	420.00
2	60	–	8 pgs. cut; new-c by Kiefer; LDC-r	1	2	4.25	13.00	28.00
3	62	–	LDC-r	1	2	4.00	11.50	23.00
4	71	–	LDC-r	1	2	3.20	8.00	16.00
5	93	–	LDC-r	1	2	2.80	7.00	14.00
6	114	–	LDC-r	1	2	2.40	6.00	12.00
7	128	–	New-c; PC-r	1	3	2.40	6.00	12.00
8	138	–	PC-r	1	3	1.00	2.00	5.00
9	150	–	PC-r	1	3	1.00	2.00	5.00
10	164	–	PC-r	1	3	1.00	2.00	5.00
11	167	–	PC-r	1	3	1.00	2.00	5.00
12	167	7/64	PC-r	1	3	1.00	2.00	5.00
13	167	11/65	PC-r	1	3	1.00	2.00	5.00
14	166	R/68	C-price 25¢; PC-r	1	3	1.00	2.00	5.00
15	169	Sm/70	PC-r; stiff-c	1	3	1.00	2.00	5.00

30. The Moonstone

Ed	HRN	Date	Details	A	C	GD25	FN65	NM94
1	9/46	–	Original; Rico-c/a	1	1	35.00	108.00	280.00
2	60	–	LDC-r; 8pgs. cut	1	1	5.70	17.00	36.00
3	70	–	LDC-r	1	1	5.00	15.00	30.00
4	155	–	New L.B. Cole-c; PC-r	1	2	5.35	16.00	32.00
5	165	–	PC-r; L.B. Cole-c	1	2	3.20	8.00	16.00
6	167	1/64	PC-r; L.B. Cole-c	1	2	1.50	3.00	8.00
7	167	9/65	PC-r; L.B. Cole-c	1	2	1.20	2.40	6.00
8	166	R/1968	C-price 25¢; PC-r	1	2	1.00	2.00	5.00

31. The Black Arrow

Ed	HRN	Date	Details	A	C	GD25	FN65	NM94
1	10/46	–	Original	1	1	26.00	80.00	210.00
2	51	–	CI logo; LDC-r 8pgs. deleted	1	1	4.25	13.00	28.00
3	64	–	LDC-r	1	1	3.20	8.00	16.00
4	87	–	C-price 15¢; LDC-r	1	1	2.80	7.00	14.00
5	108	–	LDC-r	1	1	2.40	6.00	12.00
6	125	–	LDC-r	1	1	2.00	5.00	10.00
7	131	–	New-c; PC-r	1	2	2.80	7.00	14.00
8	140	–	PC-r	1	2	1.00	2.00	5.00
9	148	–	PC-r	1	2	1.00	2.00	5.00
10	161	–	PC-r	1	2	1.00	2.00	5.00
11	167	–	PC-r	1	2	1.00	2.00	5.00
12	167	7/64	PC-r	1	2	1.20	2.40	6.00
13	167	11/65	PC-r	1	2	1.00	2.00	5.00
14	166	R/1968	C-price 25¢; PC-r	1	2	1.00	2.00	5.00

32. Lorna Doone

Ed	HRN	Date	Details	A	C	GD25	FN65	NM94
1	12/46	–	Original; Matt Baker c&a	1	1	33.00	98.00	260.00
2	53/64	–	8 pgs. deleted; LDC-r	1	1	5.70	17.00	36.00
3	85	–	C-price 15¢; LDC-r; Baker c&a	1	1	4.25	13.00	28.00
4	118	–	LDC-r	1	1	3.20	8.00	16.00
5	138	–	New-c; old-c becomes new title pg.; PC-r	1	2	3.20	8.00	16.00
6	150	–	PC-r	1	2	1.00	2.00	5.00
7	165	–	PC-r	1	2	1.00	2.00	5.00
8	167	1/64	PC-r	1	2	1.50	3.00	8.00
9	167	11/65	PC-r	1	2	1.50	3.00	8.00
10	166	R/1968	New-c; PC-r	1	3	3.20	8.00	16.00

33. The Adventures of Sherlock Holmes

Ed	HRN	Date	Details	A	C	GD25	FN65	NM94
1	33	1/47	Original; Kiefer-c; contains Study in Scarlet & Hound of the Baskervilles; 68 pgs.	1	1	100.00	300.00	900.00
2	53	–	"A Study in Scarlet" (17 pgs.) deleted; LDC-r	1	1	36.00	108.00	315.00
3	71	–	LDC-r	1	1	29.00	88.00	235.00
4A	89	–	C-price 15¢; LDC-r	1	1	23.00	69.00	185.00
4B	89	–	Kiefer's name omitted from c	1	1	25.00	75.00	200.00

34. Mysterious Island (Last "Classic Comic")

Ed	HRN	Date	Details	A	C	GD25	FN65	NM94
1	2/47	–	Original; Webb/ Heames-c/a	1	1	35.00	105.00	280.00
2	60	–	8 pgs. deleted; LDC-r	1	1	5.00	15.00	30.00
3	62	–	LDC-r	1	1	4.00	11.00	22.00
4	71	–	LDC-r	1	1	5.00	15.00	30.00
5	78	–	C-price 15¢ in circle; LDC-r	1	1	3.60	9.00	18.00
6	92	–	LDC-r	1	1	3.20	8.00	16.00
7	117	–	LDC-r	1	1	2.60	6.50	13.00
8	140	–	New-c; PC-r	1	2	2.60	6.50	13.00
9	156	–	PC-r	1	2	1.00	2.00	5.00
10	167	10/63	PC-r	1	2	1.00	2.00	5.00
11	167	5/64	PC-r	1	2	1.00	2.00	5.00
12	167	6/66	PC-r	1	2	1.00	2.00	5.00
13	166	R/1968	C-price 25¢; PC-r	1	2	1.00	2.00	5.00

35. Last Days of Pompeii (First "Classics Illustrated")

Ed	HRN	Date	Details	A	C	GD25	FN65	NM94
1	–	3/47	Original; LDC; Kiefer-c/a	1	1	36.00	108.00	285.00
2	161	–	New c&a; 15¢; PC-r; Kirby/Ayers-a	2	2	4.00	12.00	24.00
3	167	1/64	PC-r	2	2	2.40	6.00	12.00

Classics Illustrated #37 © GIL

Classics Illustrated #39 © GIL

Classics Illustrated #45 © GIL

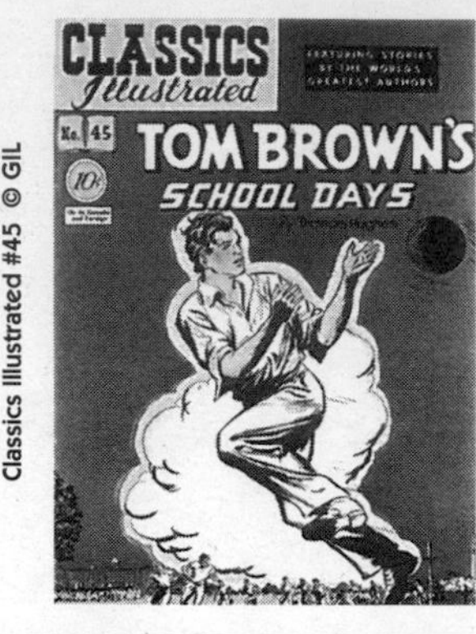

Ed	HRN	Date	Details	A	C	GD25	FN65	NM94
4	167	7/66	PC-r	2	2	2.40	6.00	12.00
5	169	Spr/70	New price 25¢; stiff-c; PC-r	2	2	2.40	6.00	12.00

36. Typee

Ed	HRN	Date	Details	A	C	GD25	FN65	NM94
1	4/47	–	Original	1	1	18.00	54.00	145.00
2	64	–	No c-price; 8 pg. ed.; LDC-r	1	1	5.35	16.00	32.00
3	155	–	New-c; PC-r	1	2	2.80	7.00	14.00
4	167	9/63	PC-r	1	2	1.40	2.80	7.00
5	167	7/65	PC-r	1	2	1.40	2.80	7.00
6	169	Sm/69	C-price 25¢; stiff-c PC-r	1	2	1.40	2.80	7.00

37. The Pioneers

Ed	HRN	Date	Details	A	C	GD25	FN65	NM94
1	37	5/47	Original; Palais-c/a	1	1	13.00	39.00	105.00
2A	62	–	8 pgs. cut; LDC-r; price circle blank	1	1	4.00	11.00	22.00
2B	62	–	10¢; LDC-r;	1	1	21.00	62.00	165.00
3	70	–	LDC-r	1	1	2.80	7.00	14.00
4	92	–	15¢; LDC-r	1	1	2.40	6.00	12.00
5	118	–	LDC-r	1	1	2.00	5.00	10.00
6	131	–	LDC-r	1	1	2.00	5.00	10.00
7	132	–	LDC-r	1	1	2.00	5.00	10.00
8	153	–	LDC-r	1	1	1.80	4.50	9.00
9	167	5/64	LDC-r	1	1	1.40	2.80	7.00
10	167	6/66	LDC-r	1	1	1.40	2.80	7.00
11	166	R/1968	New-c; 25¢; PC-r	1	2	3.20	8.00	16.00

38. Adventures of Cellini

Ed	HRN	Date	Details	A	C	GD25	FN65	NM94
1	6/47	–	Original; Froehlich c/a	1	1	23.00	69.00	185.00
2	164	–	New-c&a; PC-r	2	2	2.80	7.00	14.00
3	167	12/63	PC-r	2	2	1.50	3.00	8.00
4	167	7/66	PC-r	2	2	1.50	3.00	8.00
5	169	Spr/70	Stiff-c; new price 25¢; PC-r	2	2	1.60	3.30	9.00

39. Jane Eyre

Ed	HRN	Date	Details	A	C	GD25	FN65	NM94
1	7/47	–	Original	1	1	23.00	68.00	180.00
2	60	–	No c-price; 8 pgs. cut; LDC-r	1	1	4.25	13.00	28.00
3	62	–	LDC-r	1	1	4.00	11.50	23.00
4	71	–	LDC-r; c-price 10¢	1	1	4.00	10.00	20.00
5	92	–	C-price 15¢; LDC-r	1	1	3.20	8.00	16.00
6	118	–	LDC-r	1	1	2.80	7.00	14.00
7	142	–	New-c; old-a; PC-r	1	2	3.60	9.00	18.00
8	154	–	Old-a; PC-r	1	2	3.00	7.50	15.00
9	165	–	New-a; PC-r	2	2	3.40	8.50	17.00
10	167	12/63	PC-r	2	2	3.20	8.00	16.00
11	167	4/65	PC-r	2	2	2.80	7.00	14.00
12	167	8/66	PC-r	2	2	2.80	7.00	14.00
13	166	R/1968	New-c; PC-r	2	3	5.70	17.00	38.00

40. Mysteries ("The Pit and the Pendulum", "The Advs. of Hans Pfall" & "The Fall of the House of Usher")

Ed	HRN	Date	Details	A	C	GD25	FN65	NM94
1	8/47	–	Original; Kiefer-c/a, Froehlich, Griffiths-a	1	1	56.00	168.00	500.00
2	62	–	LDC-r; 8pgs. cut	1	1	23.00	69.00	185.00
3	75	–	LDC-r	1	1	20.00	60.00	160.00
4	92	–	C-price 15¢; LDC-r	1	1	15.50	47.00	125.00

41. Twenty Years After

Ed	HRN	Date	Details	A	C	GD25	FN65	NM94
1	9/47	–	Original; 'horror'-c	1	1	37.00	112.00	335.00
2	62	–	New-c; no c-price 8 pgs. cut; LDC-r; Kiefer-c	1	2	5.00	15.00	30.00
3	78	–	C-price 15¢; LDC-r	1	2	4.00	11.00	22.00
4	156	–	New-c; PC-r	1	3	2.80	7.00	14.00
5	167	12/63	PC-r	1	3	1.20	2.40	6.00
6	167	11/66	PC-r	1	3	1.20	2.40	6.00
7	169	Spr/70	New price 25¢; stiff-c; PC-r	1	3	1.20	2.40	6.00

42. Swiss Family Robinson

Ed	HRN	Date	Details	A	C	GD25	FN65	NM94
1	42	10/47	Orig.; Kiefer-c&a;	1	1	17.00	51.00	135.00
2A	62	–	8 pgs. cut; outside bc: Gift Box ad; LDC-r	1	1	4.25	13.00	28.00
2B	62	–	8 pgs. cut; outside-bc: Reorder list; scarce; LDC-r	1	1	7.50	22.50	52.00
3	75	–	LDC-r	1	1	3.60	9.00	18.00
4	93	–	LDC-r	1	1	3.20	8.00	16.00
5	117	–	LDC-r	1	1	2.80	7.00	14.00
6	131	–	New-c; old-a; PC-r	1	2	2.80	7.00	14.00
7	137	–	Old-a; PC-r	1	2	2.00	5.00	10.00
8	141	–	Old-a; PC-r	1	2	2.00	5.00	10.00
9	152	–	New-a; PC-r	2	2	2.80	7.00	14.00
10	158	–	PC-r	2	2	1.00	2.00	5.00
11	165	–	PC-r	2	2	2.40	6.00	12.00
12	167	12/63	PC-r	2	2	1.80	4.50	9.00
13	167	4/65	PC-r	2	2	1.20	2.40	6.00
14	167	5/66	PC-r	2	2	1.20	2.40	6.00
15	166	11/67	PC-r	2	2	1.00	2.00	5.00
16	169	Spr/69	PC-r; stiff-c	2	2	1.00	2.00	5.00

43. Great Expectations (Used in **SOTI**, pg. 311)

Ed	HRN	Date	Details	A	C	GD25	FN65	NM94
1	11/47	–	Original; Kiefer-a/c	1	1	75.00	225.00	675.00
2	62	–	No c-price; 8 pgs. cut; LDC-r	1	1	43.00	129.00	385.00

44. Mysteries of Paris (Used in **SOTI**, pg. 323)

Ed	HRN	Date	Details	A	C	GD25	FN65	NM94
1A	44	12/47	Original; 56 pgs.; Kiefer-c/a	1	1	56.00	168.00	500.00
1B	44	12/47	Orig.; printed on white/heavier paper; (rare)	1	1	61.00	183.00	550.00
2A	62	–	8 pgs. cut; outside-bc: Gift Box ad; LDC-r	1	1	23.00	69.00	185.00
2B	62	–	8 pgs. cut; outside-bc: reorder list; LDC-r	1	1	23.00	69.00	185.00
3	78	–	C-price 15¢; LDC-r	1	1	20.00	60.00	160.00

45. Tom Brown's School Days

Ed	HRN	Date	Details	A	C	GD25	FN65	NM94
1	44	1/48	Original; 1st 48pg. issue	1	1	10.50	32.00	85.00
2	64	–	No c-price; LDC-r	1	1	5.00	15.00	30.00
3	161	–	New-c&a; PC-r	2	2	2.80	7.00	14.00
4	167	2/64	PC-r	2	2	1.50	3.00	8.00
5	167	8/66	PC-r	2	2	1.50	3.00	8.00
6	166	R/1968	C-price 25¢; PC-r	2	2	1.50	3.00	8.00

Classics Illustrated #47 © GIL

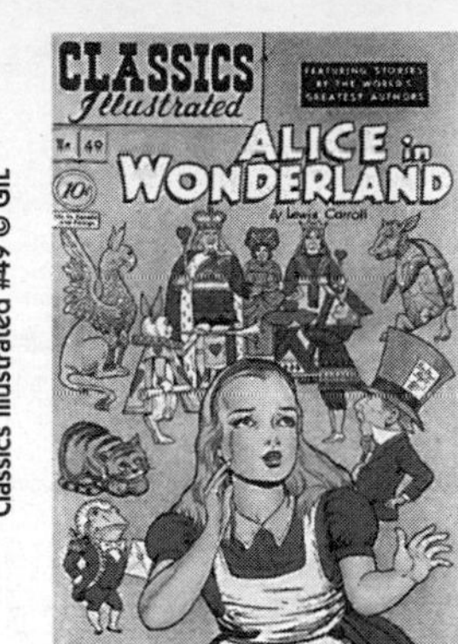

Classics Illustrated #49 © GIL

Classics Illustrated #51 © GIL

46. Kidnapped

Ed	HRN	Date	Details	A	C	GD25	FN65	NM94
1	47	4/48	Original; Webb-c/a	1	1	10.00	30.00	80.00
2A	62	–	Price circle blank; LDC-r	1	1	4.00	12.00	24.00
2B	62	–	C-price 10¢; rare; LDC-r	1	1	23.00	68.00	180.00
3	78	–	C-price 15¢; LDC-r	1	1	3.60	9.00	18.00
4	87	–	LDC-r	1	1	2.80	7.00	14.00
5	118	–	LDC-r	1	1	2.40	6.00	12.00
6	131	–	New-c; PC-r	1	2	2.40	6.00	12.00
7	140	–	PC-r	1	2	1.00	2.00	5.00
8	150	–	PC-r	1	2	1.00	2.00	5.00
9	164	–	Reduced pg.width; PC-r	1	2	1.00	2.00	5.00
10	167	–	PC-r	1	2	1.00	2.00	5.00
11	167	3/64	PC-r	1	2	1.00	2.00	5.00
12	167	6/65	PC-r	1	2	1.00	2.00	5.00
13	167	12/65	PC-r	1	2	1.00	2.00	5.00
14	166	9/67	PC-r	1	2	1.00	2.00	5.00
15	166	Win/69	New price 25¢; PC-r; stiff-c	1	2	1.00	2.00	5.00
16	169	Sm/70	PC-r; stiff-c	1	2	1.00	2.00	5.00

47. Twenty Thousand Leagues Under the Sea

Ed	HRN	Date	Details	A	C	GD25	FN65	NM94
1	47	5/48	Orig.; Kiefer-a&c;	1	1	10.00	30.00	80.00
2	64	–	No c-price; LDC-r	1	1	4.00	12.00	24.00
3	78	–	C-price 15¢; LDC-r	1	1	3.20	8.00	16.00
4	94	–	LDC-r	1	1	2.80	7.00	14.00
5	118	–	LDC-r	1	1	2.40	6.00	12.00
6	128	–	New-c; PC-r	1	2	2.40	6.00	10.00
7	133	–	PC-r	1	2	1.80	4.50	9.00
8	140	–	PC-r	1	2	1.00	2.00	5.00
9	148	–	PC-r	1	2	1.00	2.00	5.00
10	156	–	PC-r	1	2	1.00	2.00	5.00
11	165	–	PC-r	1	2	1.00	2.00	5.00
12	167	–	PC-r	1	2	1.00	2.00	5.00
13	167	3/64	PC-r	1	2	1.00	2.00	5.00
14	167	8/65	PC-r	1	2	1.00	2.00	5.00
15	167	10/66	PC-r	1	2	1.00	2.00	5.00
16	166	R/1968	C-price 25¢; new-c PC-r	1	3	2.00	5.00	10.00
17	169	Spr/70	Stiff-c; PC-r	1	3	2.40	6.00	12.00

48. David Copperfield

Ed	HRN	Date	Details	A	C	GD25	FN65	NM94
1	47	6/48	Original; Kiefer-c/a	1	1	10.00	30.00	80.00
2	64	–	Price circle replaced by motif of boy reading; LDC-r	1	1	4.00	12.00	24.00
3	87	–	C-price 15¢; LDC-r	1	1	2.80	7.00	14.00
4	121	–	New-c; PC-r	1	2	2.00	5.00	10.00
5	130	–	PC-r	1	2	1.50	3.00	6.00
6	140	–	PC-r	1	2	1.50	3.00	6.00
7	148	–	PC-r	1	2	1.50	3.00	6.00
8	156	–	PC-r	1	2	1.50	3.00	6.00
9	167	–	PC-r	1	2	1.00	2.00	5.00
10	167	4/64	PC-r	1	2	1.00	2.00	5.00
11	167	6/65	PC-r	1	2	1.00	2.00	5.00
12	166	5/67	PC-r	1	2	1.00	2.00	5.00
13	166	R/67	PC-r; C-price 25¢	1	2	2.00	5.00	10.00
14	166	Spr/69	C-price 25¢; stiff-c PC-r	1	2	1.00	2.00	5.00
15	169	Win/69	Stiff-c; PC-r	1	2	1.00	2.00	5.00

49. Alice in Wonderland

Ed	HRN	Date	Details	A	C	GD25	FN65	NM94
1	47	7/48	Original; 1st Blum a & c	1	1	14.50	43.00	115.00
2	64	–	No c-price; LDC-r	1	1	5.35	16.00	32.00
3A	85	–	C-price 15¢; soft-c LDC-r	1	1	4.25	13.00	26.00
3B	85	–	Stiff-c; LDC-r	1	1	5.00	15.00	30.00
4	155	–	New PC, similar to orig.; PC-r	1	2	4.25	13.00	26.00
5	165	–	PC-r	1	2	4.00	10.00	20.00
6	167	3/64	PC-r	1	2	3.20	8.00	16.00
7	167	6/66	PC-r	1	2	3.20	8.00	16.00
8A	166	Fall/68	New-c; soft-c; 25¢ c-price; PC-r	1	3	4.25	13.00	26.00
8B	166	Fall/68	New-c; stiff-c; 25¢ c-price; PC-r	1	3	6.85	21.00	48.00

50. Adventures of Tom Sawyer (Used in **SOTI**, pg. 37)

Ed	HRN	Date	Details	A	C	GD25	FN65	NM94
1A	51	8/48	Orig.; Aldo Rubano a&c	1	1	11.30	34.00	90.00
1B	51	9/48	Orig.; Rubano c&a	1	1	11.30	34.00	90.00
1C	51	9/48	Orig.; outside-bc: blue & yellow only; rare	1	1	17.00	51.00	135.00
2	64	–	No c-price; LDC-r	1	1	4.00	10.00	20.00
3	78	–	C-price 15¢; LDC-r	1	1	2.80	7.00	14.00
4	94	–	LDC-r	1	1	2.40	6.00	12.00
5	117	–	LDC-r	1	1	2.00	5.00	10.00
6	132	–	LDC-r	1	1	2.00	5.00	10.00
7	140	–	New-c; PC-r	1	2	2.40	6.00	12.00
8	150	–	PC-r	1	2	1.60	4.00	8.00
9	164	–	New-a; PC-r	2	2	2.80	7.00	14.00
10	167	–	PC-r	2	2	1.60	4.00	8.00
11	167	1/65	PC-r	2	2	1.00	2.00	5.00
12	167	5/66	PC-r	2	2	1.00	2.00	5.00
13	166	12/67	PC-r	2	2	1.00	2.00	5.00
14	169	Fall/69	C-price 25¢; stiff-c; PC-r	2	2	1.00	2.00	5.00
15	169	Win/71	PC-r	2	2	1.00	2.00	5.00

51. The Spy

Ed	HRN	Date	Details	A	C	GD25	FN65	NM94
1A	51	9/48	Original; inside-bc illo: Christmas Carol	1	1	9.50	28.00	75.00
1B	51	9/48	Original; inside-bc illo: Man in Iron Mask	1	1	9.50	28.00	75.00
1C	51	8/48	Original; outside-bc: full color	1	1	9.50	28.00	75.00
1D	51	8/48	Original; outside-bc: blue & yellow only; scarce	1	1	13.00	39.00	105.00
2	89	–	C-price 15¢; LDC-r	1	1	3.60	9.00	18.00
3	121	–	LDC-r	1	1	2.80	7.00	14.00
4	139	–	New-c; PC-r	1	2	2.40	6.00	12.00
5	156	–	PC-r	1	2	1.00	2.00	5.00
6	167	11/63	PC-r	1	2	1.00	2.00	5.00
7	167	7/66	PC-r	1	2	1.00	2.00	5.00
8A	166	Win/69	C-price 25¢; soft-c; scarce; PC-r	1	2	2.00	6.00	16.00
8B	166	Win/69	C-price 25¢; stiff-c; PC-r	1	2	1.00	2.00	5.00

52. The House of the Seven Gables

Classics Illustrated #55 © GIL

Classics Illustrated #56 © GIL

Classics Illustrated #57 © GIL

Ed	HRN	Date	Details	A	C	GD25	FN65	NM94
1	53	10/48	Orig.; Griffiths a&c	1	1	9.50	28.00	75.00
2	89	–	C-price 15¢; LDC-r	1	1	3.60	9.00	18.00
3	121	–	LDC-r	1	1	2.80	7.00	14.00
4	142	–	New-c&a; PC-r; Woodbridge-a	2	2	3.20	8.00	16.00
5	156	–	PC-r	2	2	1.00	2.00	5.00
6	165	–	PC-r	2	2	1.00	2.00	5.00
7	167	5/64	PC-r	2	2	1.50	3.00	8.00
8	167	3/66	PC-r	2	2	1.00	2.00	5.00
9	166	R/1968	C-price 25¢; PC-r	2	2	1.00	2.00	5.00
10	169	Spr/70	Stiff-c; PC-r	2	2	1.00	2.00	5.00

53. A Christmas Carol

Ed	HRN	Date	Details	A	C	GD25	FN65	NM94
1	53	11/48	Original & only ed; Kiefer-c/a	1	1	12.00	36.00	95.00

54. Man in the Iron Mask

Ed	HRN	Date	Details	A	C	GD25	FN65	NM94
1	55	12/48	Original; Froehlich-a, Kiefer-c	1	1	8.75	26.25	70.00
2	93	–	C-price 15¢; LDC-r	1	1	4.00	11.00	22.00
3A	111	–	(O) logo lettering; scarce; LDC-r	1	1	5.00	15.00	30.00
3B	111	–	New logo as PC; LDC-r	1	1	4.00	10.00	20.00
4	142	–	New-c&a; PC-r	2	2	2.80	7.00	14.00
5	154	–	PC-r	2	2	1.00	2.00	5.00
6	165	–	PC-r	2	2	1.00	2.00	5.00
7	167	5/64	PC-r	2	2	1.00	2.00	5.00
8	167	4/66	PC-r	2	2	1.00	2.00	5.00
9A	166	Win/69	C-price 25¢; soft-c PC-r	2	2	2.25	6.75	18.00
9B	166	Win/69	Stiff-c	2	2	1.00	2.00	5.00

55. Silas Marner (Used in **SOTI**, pgs. 311, 312)

Ed	HRN	Date	Details	A	C	GD25	FN65	NM94
1	55	1/49	Original-Kiefer-c	1	1	9.50	28.00	75.00
2	75	–	Price circle blank; 'Coming Next' ad; LDC-r	1	1	4.00	12.00	24.00
3	97	–	LDC-r	1	1	2.80	7.00	14.00
4	121	–	New-c; PC-r	1	2	2.40	6.00	12.00
5	130	–	PC-r	1	2	1.00	2.00	5.00
6	140	–	PC-r	1	2	1.00	2.00	5.00
7	154	–	PC-r	1	2	1.00	2.00	5.00
8	165	–	PC-r	1	2	1.00	2.00	5.00
9	167	2/64	PC-r	1	2	1.00	2.00	5.00
10	167	6/65	PC-r	1	2	1.00	2.00	5.00
11	166	5/67	PC-r	1	2	1.00	2.00	5.00
12A	166	Win/69	C-price 25¢; soft-c PC-r	1	2	2.25	6.75	18.00
12B	166	Win/69	C-price 25¢; stiff-c PC-r	1	2	1.00	2.00	5.00

56. The Toilers of the Sea

Ed	HRN	Date	Details	A	C	GD25	FN65	NM94
1	55	2/49	Original; A.M. Froehlich-c/a	1	1	20.00	60.00	140.00
2	165	–	New-c&a; PC-r; Angelo Torres-a	2	2	4.25	13.00	28.00
3	167	3/64	PC-r	2	2	2.00	6.00	16.00
4	167	10/66	PC-r	2	2	1.75	5.25	14.00

57. The Song of Hiawatha

Ed	HRN	Date	Details	A	C	GD25	FN65	NM94
1	55	3/49	Original; Alex Blum-c/a	1	1	9.50	28.00	75.00
2	75	–	No c-price w/15¢ sticker; 'Coming Next' ad; LDC-r	1	1	4.00	12.00	24.00
3	94	–	C-price 15¢; LDC-r	1	1	3.60	9.00	18.00
4	118	–	LDC-r	1	1	2.80	7.00	14.00
5	134	–	New-c; PC-r	1	2	2.40	6.00	12.00
6	139	–	PC-r	1	2	1.00	2.00	5.00
7	154	–	PC-r	1	2	1.00	2.00	5.00
8	167	–	Has orig.date; PC-r	1	2	1.00	2.00	5.00
9	167	9/64	PC-r	1	2	1.00	2.00	5.00
10	167	10/65	PC-r	1	2	1.00	2.00	5.00
11	166	F/1968	C-price 25¢; PC-r	1	2	1.00	2.00	5.00

58. The Prairie

Ed	HRN	Date	Details	A	C	GD25	FN65	NM94
1	60	4/49	Original; Palais c/a	1	1	9.50	28.00	75.00
2A	62	–	No c-price; no coming-next ad; LDC-r	1	1	5.70	17.00	38.00
2B	62		10¢ (rare)	1	1	14.00	41.00	110.00
3	78	–	C-price 15¢ in dbl. circle; LDC-r	1	1	3.60	9.00	18.00
4	114	–	LDC-r	1	1	2.80	7.00	14.00
5	131	–	LDC-r	1	1	2.40	6.00	12.00
6	132	–	LDC-r	1	1	2.40	6.00	12.00
7	146	–	New-c; PC-r	1	2	2.40	6.00	12.00
8	155	–	PC-r	1	2	1.00	2.00	5.00
9	167	5/64	PC-r	1	2	1.00	2.00	5.00
10	167	4/66	PC-r	1	2	1.00	2.00	5.00
11	169	Sm/69	New price 25¢; stiff-c; PC-r	1	2	1.00	2.00	5.00

59. Wuthering Heights

Ed	HRN	Date	Details	A	C	GD25	FN65	NM94
1	60	5/49	Original; Kiefer-c/a	1	1	10.50	32.00	85.00
2	85	–	C-price 15¢; LDC-r	1	1	4.25	13.00	28.00
3	156	–	New-c; PC-r	1	2	3.20	8.00	16.00
4	167	1/64	PC-r	1	2	1.40	2.80	7.00
5	167	10/66	PC-r	1	2	1.40	2.80	7.00
6	169	Sm/69	C-price 25¢; stiff-c; PC-r	1	2	1.20	2.40	6.00

60. Black Beauty

Ed	HRN	Date	Details	A	C	GD25	FN65	NM94
1	62	6/49	Original; Froehlich-c/a	1	1	10.00	30.00	80.00
2	62	–	No c-price; no coming-next ad; LDC-r (rare)	1	1	12.00	38.00	100.00
3	85	–	C-price 15¢; LDC-r	1	1	4.00	11.00	22.00
4	158	–	New L.B. Cole-c/a; PC-r	2	2	4.15	12.50	25.00
5	167	2/64	PC-r	2	2	2.40	6.00	12.00
6	167	3/66	PC-r	2	2	2.40	6.00	12.00
7	166	R/1968	New-c&price, 25¢; PC-r	2	3	6.00	18.00	42.00

61. The Woman in White

Ed	HRN	Date	Details	A	C	GD25	FN65	NM94
1A	62	7/49	Original; Blum-c/a fc-purple; bc: top illos light blue	1	1	10.50	32.00	85.00
1B	62	7/49	Original; Blum-c/a fc-pink; bc: top illos light violet	1	1	10.50	32.00	85.00
2	156	–	New-c; PC-r	1	2	3.60	9.00	18.00

Classics Illustrated #64 © GIL

Classics Illustrated #65 © GIL

Classics Illustrated #68 © GIL

Ed	HRN	Date	Details	A	C	GD25	FN65	NM94
3	167	1/64	PC-r	1	2	2.80	7.00	14.00
4	166	R/1968	C-price 25¢; PC-r	1	2	2.80	7.00	14.00

62. Western Stories ("The Luck of Roaring Camp" and "The Outcasts of Poker Flat")

Ed	HRN	Date	Details	A	C	GD25	FN65	NM94
1	62	8/49	Original; Kiefer-c/a	1	1	8.75	26.25	70.00
2	89	–	C-price 15¢; LDC-r	1	1	4.00	11.00	22.00
3	121	–	LDC-r	1	1	3.20	8.00	16.00
4	137	–	New-c; PC-r	1	2	2.40	6.00	12.00
5	152	–	PC-r	1	2	1.50	3.00	6.00
6	167	10/63	PC-r	1	2	1.50	3.00	6.00
7	167	6/64	PC-r	1	2	1.00	2.00	5.00
8	167	11/66	PC-r	1	2	1.00	2.00	5.00
9	166	R/1968	New-c&price 25¢; PC-r	1	3	3.00	6.00	16.00

63. The Man Without a Country

Ed	HRN	Date	Details	A	C	GD25	FN65	NM94
1	62	9/49	Original; Kiefer-c/a	1	1	9.50	28.00	75.00
2	78	–	C-price 15¢ in double circle; LDC-r	1	1	4.00	11.00	22.00
3	156	–	New-c, old-a; PC-r	1	2	3.20	8.00	18.00
4	165	–	New-a & text pgs.; PC-r; A. Torres-a	2	2	2.80	7.00	14.00
5	167	3/64	PC-r	2	2	1.00	2.00	5.00
6	167	8/66	PC-r	2	2	1.00	2.00	5.00
7	169	Sm/69	New price 25¢; stiff-c; PC-r	2	2	1.00	2.00	5.00

64. Treasure Island

Ed	HRN	Date	Details	A	C	GD25	FN65	NM94
1	62	10/49	Original; Blum-c/a	1	1	9.50	28.00	75.00
2A	82	–	C-price 15¢; soft-c LDC-r	1	1	4.00	10.00	20.00
2B	82	–	Stiff-c; LDC-r	1	1	4.00	11.00	22.00
3	117	–	LDC-r	1	1	3.20	8.00	16.00
4	131	–	New-c; PC-r	1	2	2.40	6.00	12.00
5	138	–	PC-r	1	2	1.00	2.00	5.00
6	146	–	PC-r	1	2	1.00	2.00	5.00
7	158	–	PC-r	1	2	1.00	2.00	5.00
8	165	–	PC-r	1	2	1.00	2.00	5.00
9	167	–	PC-r	1	2	1.00	2.00	5.00
10	167	6/64	PC-r	1	2	1.00	2.00	5.00
11	167	12/65	PC-r	1	2	1.00	2.00	5.00
12A	166	10/67	PC-r	1	2	1.10	3.30	9.00
12B	166	10/67	w/Grit ad stapled in book	1	2	9.50	28.00	75.00
13	169	Spr/69	New price 25¢; stiff-c; PC-r	1	2		2.40	6.00
14	–	1989	Long John Silver's Seafood Shoppes; $1.95, First/Berkley Publ.; Blum-r	1	2		.80	2.00

65. Benjamin Franklin

Ed	HRN	Date	Details	A	C	GD25	FN65	NM94
1	64	11/49	Original; Kiefer-c; Iger Shop-a	1	1	9.50	28.00	75.00
2	131	–	New-c; PC-r	1	2	3.20	8.00	16.00
3	154	–	PC-r	1	2	1.20	2.40	6.00
4	167	2/64	PC-r	1	2	1.20	2.40	6.00
5	167	4/66	PC-r	1	2	1.20	2.40	6.00
6	169	Fall/69	New price 25¢; stiff-c; PC-r	1	2	1.25	2.80	7.00

66. The Cloister and the Hearth

Ed	HRN	Date	Details	A	C	GD25	FN65	NM94
1	67	12/49	Original & only ed; Kiefer-a & c	1	1	21.00	62.00	165.00

67. The Scottish Chiefs

Ed	HRN	Date	Details	A	C	GD25	FN65	NM94
1	67	1/50	Original; Blum-a&c	1	1	8.75	26.25	65.00
2	85	–	C-price 15¢; LDC-r	1	1	4.00	11.00	22.00
3	118	–	LDC-r	1	1	3.20	8.00	16.00
4	136	–	New-c; PC-r	1	2	2.80	7.00	14.00
5	154	–	PC-r	1	2	1.60	4.00	8.00
6	167	11/63	PC-r	1	2	1.90	3.75	10.00
7	167	8/65	PC-r	1	2	1.50	3.00	8.00

68. Julius Caesar (Used in **SOTI**, pgs. 36, 37)

Ed	HRN	Date	Details	A	C	GD25	FN65	NM94
1	70	2/50	Original; Kiefer-c/a	1	1	10.00	30.00	60.00
2	85	–	C-price 15¢; LDC-r	1	1	4.00	10.00	20.00
3	108	–	LDC-r	1	1	3.20	8.00	16.00
4	156	–	New L.B. Cole-c; PC-r	1	2	3.60	9.00	18.00
5	165	–	New-a by Evans, Crandall; PC-r	2	2	3.60	9.00	18.00
6	167	2/64	PC-r	2	2	1.00	2.00	5.00
7	167	10/65	Tarzan books inside cover; PC-r	2	2	1.20	2.40	6.00
8	166	R/1967	PC-r	2	2	1.00	2.00	5.00
9	169	Win/69	PC-r; stiff-c	2	2	1.00	2.00	5.00

69. Around the World in 80 Days

Ed	HRN	Date	Details	A	C	GD25	FN65	NM94
1	70	3/50	Original; Kiefer-c/a	1	1	8.50	26.00	60.00
2	87	–	C-price 15¢; LDC-r	1	1	4.00	10.00	20.00
3	125	–	LDC-r	1	1	3.20	8.00	16.00
4	136	–	New-c; PC-r	1	2	2.60	6.50	13.00
5	146	–	PC-r	1	2	1.00	2.00	5.00
6	152	–	PC-r	1	2	1.00	2.00	5.00
7	164	–	PC-r	1	2	1.00	2.00	5.00
8	167	–	PC-r	1	2	1.00	2.00	5.00
9	167	7/64	PC-r	1	2	1.00	2.00	5.00
10	167	11/65	PC-r	1	2	1.00	2.00	5.00
11	166	7/67	PC-r	1	2	1.00	2.00	5.00
12	169	Spr/69	C-price 25¢; stiff-c; PC-r	1	2	1.00	2.00	5.00

70. The Pilot

Ed	HRN	Date	Details	A	C	GD25	FN65	NM94
1	71	4/50	Original; Blum-c/a	1	1	7.85	23.50	55.00
2	92	–	C-price 15¢; LDC-r	1	1	4.00	11.00	22.00
3	125	–	LDC-r	1	1	3.20	8.00	16.00
4	156	–	New-c; PC-r	1	2	3.20	8.00	16.00
5	167	2/64	PC-r	1	2	2.40	6.00	12.00
6	167	5/66	PC-r	1	2	1.80	4.50	9.00

71. The Man Who Laughs

Ed	HRN	Date	Details	A	C	GD25	FN65	NM94
1	71	5/50	Original; Blum-c/a	1	1	13.00	39.00	105.00
2	165	–	New-c&a; PC-r	2	2	7.85	23.50	55.00
3	167	4/64	PC-r	2	2	7.50	22.50	52.00

72. The Oregon Trail

Ed	HRN	Date	Details	A	C	GD25	FN65	NM94
1	73	6/50	Original; Kiefer-c/a	1	1	7.85	23.50	55.00
2	89	–	C-price 15¢; LDC-r	1	1	4.00	11.00	22.00
3	121	–	LDC-r	1	1	3.20	8.00	16.00
4	131	–	New-c; PC-r	1	2	3.00	7.50	15.00
5	140	–	PC-r	1	2	1.50	3.00	6.00
6	150	–	PC-r	1	2	1.00	2.00	5.00

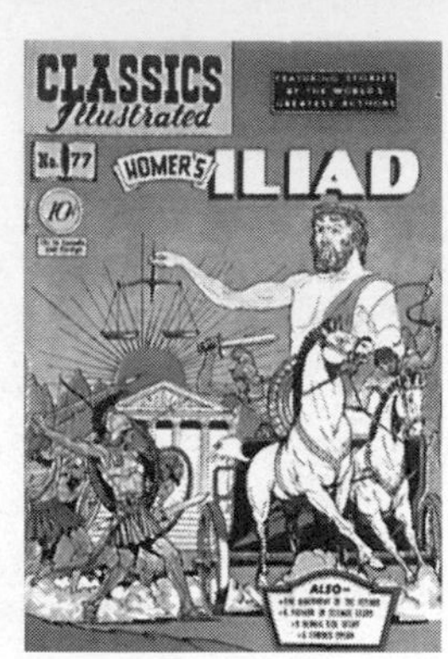

Classics Illustrated #77 © GIL

Classics Illustrated #79 © GIL

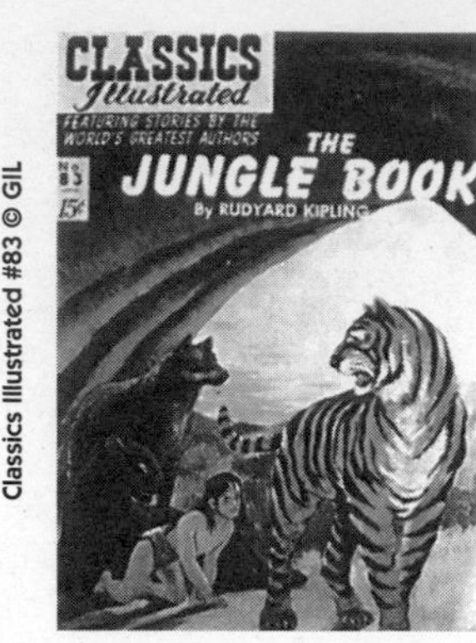

Classics Illustrated #83 © GIL

Ed	HRN	Date	Details	A	C	GD25	FN65	NM94
7	164	–	PC-r	1	2	1.00	2.00	5.00
8	167	–	PC-r	1	2	1.00	2.00	5.00
9	167	8/64	PC-r	1	2	1.00	2.00	5.00
10	167	10/65	PC-r	1	2	1.00	2.00	5.00
11	166	R/1968	C-price 25¢; PC-r	1	2	1.00	2.00	5.00

73. The Black Tulip

Ed	HRN	Date	Details	A	C	GD25	FN65	NM94
1	75	7/50	1st & only ed.; Alex Blum-c/a	1	1	26.00	80.00	210.00

74. Mr. Midshipman Easy

Ed	HRN	Date	Details	A	C	GD25	FN65	NM94
1	75	8/50	1st & only edition	1	1	25.00	75.00	200.00

75. The Lady of the Lake

Ed	HRN	Date	Details	A	C	GD25	FN65	NM94
1	75	9/50	Original; Kiefer-c/a	1	1	7.85	23.50	55.00
2	85	–	C-price 15¢; LDC-r	1	1	4.00	12.00	24.00
3	118	–	LDC-r	1	1	3.60	9.00	18.00
4	139	–	New-c; PC-r	1	2	2.60	6.50	13.00
5	154	–	PC-r	1	2	1.00	2.00	5.00
6	165	–	PC-r	1	2	1.00	2.00	5.00
7	167	4/64	PC-r	1	2	1.00	2.00	5.00
8	167	5/66	PC-r	1	2	1.00	2.00	5.00
9	169	Spr/69	New price 25¢; stiff-c; PC-r	1	2	1.00	2.00	5.00

76. The Prisoner of Zenda

Ed	HRN	Date	Details	A	C	GD25	FN65	NM94
1	75	10/50	Original; Kiefer-c/a	1	1	7.15	21.50	50.00
2	85	–	C-price 15¢; LDC-r	1	1	4.00	11.00	22.00
3	111	–	LDC-r	1	1	3.20	8.00	16.00
4	128	–	New-c; PC-r	1	2	2.80	7.00	14.00
5	152	–	PC-r	1	2	1.00	2.00	5.00
6	165	–	PC-r	1	2	1.00	2.00	5.00
7	167	4/64	PC-r	1	2	1.00	2.00	5.00
8	167	9/66	PC-r	1	2	1.00	2.00	5.00
9	169	Fall/69	New price 25¢; stiff-c; PC-r	1	2	1.20	2.40	6.00

77. The Iliad

Ed	HRN	Date	Details	A	C	GD25	FN65	NM94
1	78	11/50	Original; Blum-c/a	1	1	7.85	23.50	55.00
2	87	–	C-price 15¢; LDC-r	1	1	4.00	12.00	24.00
3	121	–	LDC-r	1	1	3.20	8.00	16.00
4	139	–	New-c; PC-r	1	2	2.40	6.00	12.00
5	150	–	PC-r	1	2	1.00	2.00	5.00
6	165	–	PC-r	1	2	1.00	2.00	5.00
7	167	10/63	PC-r	1	2	1.00	2.00	5.00
8	167	7/64	PC-r	1	2	1.00	2.00	5.00
9	167	5/66	PC-r	1	2	1.00	2.00	5.00
10	166	R/1968	C-price 25¢; PC-r	1	2	1.00	2.00	5.00

78. Joan of Arc

Ed	HRN	Date	Details	A	C	GD25	FN65	NM94
1	78	12/50	Original; Kiefer-c/a	1	1	7.15	21.50	50.00
2	87	–	C-price 15¢; LDC-r	1	1	4.00	11.00	22.00
3	113	–	LDC-r	1	1	3.20	8.00	16.00
4	128	–	New-c; PC-r	1	2	2.80	7.00	14.00
5	140	–	PC-r	1	2	1.00	2.00	5.00
6	150	–	PC-r	1	2	1.00	2.00	5.00
7	159	–	PC-r	1	2	1.00	2.00	5.00
8	167	–	PC-r	1	2	1.00	2.00	5.00
9	167	12/63	PC-r	1	2	1.00	2.00	5.00
10	167	6/65	PC-r	1	2	1.00	2.00	5.00
11	166	6/67	PC-r	1	2	1.00	2.00	5.00
12	166	Win/69	New-c&price, 25¢; PC-r; stiff-c	1	3	3.00	6.00	16.00

79. Cyrano de Bergerac

Ed	HRN	Date	Details	A	C	GD25	FN65	NM94
1	78	1/51	Orig.; movie promo inside front-c; Blum-c/a	1	1	7.15	21.50	50.00
2	85	–	C-price 15¢; LDC-r	1	1	4.00	11.00	22.00
3	118	–	LDC-r	1	1	3.20	8.00	16.00
4	133	–	New-c; PC-r	1	2	3.00	7.50	15.00
5	156	–	PC-r	1	2	2.00	5.00	10.00
6	167	8/64	PC-r	1	2	2.00	5.00	10.00

80. White Fang (Last line drawn cover)

Ed	HRN	Date	Details	A	C	GD25	FN65	NM94
1	79	2/51	Orig.; Blum-c/a	1	1	7.15	21.50	50.00
2	87	–	C-price 15¢; LDC-r	1	1	4.00	12.00	24.00
3	125	–	LDC-r	1	1	3.20	8.00	16.00
4	132	–	New-c; PC-r	1	2	2.40	6.00	12.00
5	140	–	PC-r	1	2	1.00	2.00	5.00
6	153	–	PC-r	1	2	1.00	2.00	5.00
7	167	–	PC-r	1	2	1.00	2.00	5.00
8	167	9/64	PC-r	1	2	1.00	2.00	5.00
9	167	7/65	PC-r	1	2	1.00	2.00	5.00
10	166	6/67	PC-r	1	2	1.00	2.00	5.00
11	169	Fall/69	New price 25¢; PC-r; stiff-c	1	2	1.00	2.00	5.00

81. The Odyssey (1st painted cover)

Ed	HRN	Date	Details	A	C	GD25	FN65	NM94
1	82	3/51	First 15¢ Original; Blum-c	1	1	6.85	21.00	48.00
2	167	8/64	PC-r	1	1	1.25	3.75	10.00
3	167	10/66	PC-r	1	1	1.25	3.75	10.00
4	169	Spr/69	New, stiff-c; PC-r	1	2	1.85	5.50	15.00

82. The Master of Ballantrae

Ed	HRN	Date	Details	A	C	GD25	FN65	NM94
1	82	4/51	Original; Blum-c	1	1	5.35	16.00	32.00
2	167	8/64	PC-r	1	1	2.80	7.00	14.00
3	166	Fall/68	New, stiff-c; PC-r	1	2	2.80	7.00	14.00

83. The Jungle Book

Ed	HRN	Date	Details	A	C	GD25	FN65	NM94
1	85	5/51	Original; Blum-c Bossert/Blum-a	1	1	5.00	15.00	30.00
2	110	–	PC-r	1	1	1.40	3.50	7.00
3	125	–	PC-r	1	1	1.00	2.00	5.00
4	134	–	PC-r	1	1	1.00	2.00	5.00
5	142	–	PC-r	1	1	1.00	2.00	5.00
6	150	–	PC-r	1	1	1.00	2.00	5.00
7	159	–	PC-r	1	1	1.00	2.00	5.00
8	167	–	PC-r	1	1	1.00	2.00	5.00
9	167	3/65	PC-r	1	1	1.00	2.00	5.00
10	167	11/65	PC-r	1	1	1.00	2.00	5.00
11	167	5/66	PC-r	1	1	1.00	2.00	5.00
12	166	R/1968	New c&a; stiff-c; PC-r	2	2	1.85	5.50	15.00

84. The Gold Bug and Other Stories ("The Gold Bug", "The Tell-Tale Heart", "The Cask of Amontillado")

Ed	HRN	Date	Details	A	C	GD25	FN65	NM94
1	85	6/51	Original; Blum-c/a; Palais, Laverly-a	1	1	8.75	26.25	65.00
2	167	7/64	PC-r	1	1	8.50	26.00	60.00

85. The Sea Wolf

Ed	HRN	Date	Details	A	C	GD25	FN65	NM94
1	85	7/51	Original; Blum-c/a	1	1	4.00	10.00	20.00

Classics Illustrated #87 © GIL

Classics Illustrated #91 © GIL

Classics Illustrated #97 © GIL

Ed	HRN	Date	Details	A	C	GD25	FN65	NM94
2	121	–	PC-r	1	1		1.60	4.00
3	132	–	PC-r	1	1		1.60	4.00
4	141	–	PC-r	1	1		1.60	4.00
5	161	–	PC-r	1	1		1.60	4.00
6	167	2/64	PC-r	1	1		2.00	5.00
7	167	11/65	PC-r	1	1		1.60	4.00
8	169	Fall/69	New price 25¢; stiff-c; PC-r	1	1		1.60	4.00

86. Under Two Flags

Ed	HRN	Date	Details	A	C	GD25	FN65	NM94
1	87	8/51	Original; first delBourgo-a	1	1	4.00	10.00	20.00
2	117	–	PC-r	1	1		1.60	4.00
3	139	–	PC-r	1	1		1.60	4.00
4	158	–	PC-r	1	1		1.60	4.00
5	167	2/64	PC-r	1	1		1.60	4.00
6	167	8/66	PC-r	1	1		1.60	4.00
7	169	Sm/69	New price 25¢; stiff-c; PC-r	1	1		1.60	4.00

87. A Midsummer Nights Dream

Ed	HRN	Date	Details	A	C	GD25	FN65	NM94
1	87	9/51	Original; Blum c/a	1	1	4.00	11.00	22.00
2	161	–	PC-r	1	1	1.00	2.00	5.00
3	167	4/64	PC-r	1	1		1.60	4.00
4	167	5/66	PC-r	1	1		1.60	4.00
5	169	Sm/69	New price 25¢; stiff-c; PC-r	1	1		1.60	4.00

88. Men of Iron

Ed	HRN	Date	Details	A	C	GD25	FN65	NM94
1	89	10/51	Original	1	1	4.00	12.00	24.00
2	154	–	PC-r	1	1	1.00	2.00	5.00
3	167	1/64	PC-r	1	1	1.00	2.00	5.00
4	166	R/1968	C-price 25¢; PC-r	1	1	1.00	2.00	5.00

89. Crime and Punishment (Cover illo. in **POP**)

Ed	HRN	Date	Details	A	C	GD25	FN65	NM94
1	89	11/51	Original; Palais-a	1	1	4.25	13.00	26.00
2	152	–	PC-r	1	1		1.60	4.00
3	167	4/64	PC-r	1	1		1.60	4.00
4	167	5/66	PC-r	1	1		1.60	4.00
5	169	Fall/69	New price 25¢ stiff-c; PC-r	1	1		1.60	4.00

90. Green Mansions

Ed	HRN	Date	Details	A	C	GD25	FN65	NM94
1	89	12/51	Original; Blum-c/a	1	1	4.00	12.00	24.00
2	148	–	New L.B. Cole-c; PC-r	1	2	2.00	5.00	10.00
3	165	–	PC-r	1	2		1.60	4.00
4	167	4/64	PC-r	1	2		1.60	4.00
5	167	9/66	PC-r	1	2		1.60	4.00
6	169	Sm/69	New price 25¢; stiff-c; PC-r	1	2		1.60	4.00

91. The Call of the Wild

Ed	HRN	Date	Details	A	C	GD25	FN65	NM94
1	92	1/52	Orig.; delBourgo-a	1	1	4.00	11.00	22.00
2	112	–	PC-r	1	1	1.00	2.00	5.00
3	125	–	'Picture Progress' on back-c; PC-r	1	1		1.60	4.00
4	134	–	PC-r	1	1		1.60	4.00
5	143	–	PC-r	1	1		1.60	4.00
6	165	–	PC-r	1	1		1.60	4.00
7	167	–	PC-r	1	1		1.60	4.00
8	167	4/65	PC-r	1	1		1.60	4.00
9	167	3/66	PC-r	1	1		1.60	4.00
10	166	11/67	PC-r	1	1		1.60	4.00
11	169	Spr/70	New price 25¢; stiff-c; PC-r	1	1		1.60	4.00

92. The Courtship of Miles Standish

Ed	HRN	Date	Details	A	C	GD25	FN65	NM94
1	92	2/52	Original; Blum-c/a	1	1	4.00	11.00	22.00
2	165	–	PC-r	1	1		1.60	4.00
3	167	3/64	PC-r	1	1		1.60	4.00
4	166	5/67	PC-r	1	1		1.60	4.00
5	169	Win/69	New price 25¢ stiff-c; PC-r	1	1		1.60	4.00

93. Pudd'nhead Wilson

Ed	HRN	Date	Details	A	C	GD25	FN65	NM94
1	94	3/52	Orig.; Kiefer-c/a;	1	1	4.00	12.00	24.00
2	165	–	New-c; PC-r	1	2	1.80	4.50	9.00
3	167	3/64	PC-r	1	2	1.40	3.50	7.00
4	166	R/1968	New price 25¢; soft-c; PC-r	1	2	1.40	3.50	7.00

94. David Balfour

Ed	HRN	Date	Details	A	C	GD25	FN65	NM94
1	94	4/52	Original; Palais-a	1	1	4.00	12.00	24.00
2	167	5/64	PC-r	1	1	1.25	3.75	10.00
3	166	R/1968	C-price 25¢; PC-r	1	1	1.25	3.75	10.00

95. All Quiet on the Western Front

Ed	HRN	Date	Details	A	C	GD25	FN65	NM94
1A	96	5/52	Orig.; del Bourgo-a	1	1	8.75	26.25	70.00
1B	99	5/52	Orig.; del Bourgo-a	1	1	7.50	22.50	52.00
2	167	10/64	PC-r	1	1	1.85	5.50	15.00
3	167	11/66	PC-r	1	1	1.85	5.50	15.00

96. Daniel Boone

Ed	HRN	Date	Details	A	C	GD25	FN65	NM94
1	97	6/52	Original; Blum-a	1	1	4.00	10.00	20.00
2	117	–	PC-r	1	1		1.60	4.00
3	128	–	PC-r	1	1		1.60	4.00
4	132	–	PC-r	1	1		1.60	4.00
5	134	–	"Story of Jesus" on back-c; PC-r	1	1		1.60	4.00
6	158	–	PC-r	1	1		1.60	4.00
7	167	1/64	PC-r	1	1		1.60	4.00
8	167	5/65	PC-r	1	1		1.60	4.00
9	167	11/66	PC-r	1	1		1.60	4.00
10	166	Win/69	New-c; price 25¢; PC-r; stiff-c	1	2	1.25	3.75	10.00

97. King Solomon's Mines

Ed	HRN	Date	Details	A	C	GD25	FN65	NM94
1	96	7/52	Orig.; Kiefer-a	1	1	4.00	10.00	20.00
2	118	–	PC-r	1	1	1.50	3.50	7.00
3	131	–	PC-r	1	1		1.60	4.00
4	141	–	PC-r	1	1		1.60	4.00
5	158	–	PC-r	1	1		1.60	4.00
6	167	2/64	PC-r	1	1		1.60	4.00
7	167	9/65	PC-r	1	1		1.60	4.00
8	169	Sm/69	New price 25¢; stiff-c; PC-r	1	1		2.00	5.00

98. The Red Badge of Courage

Ed	HRN	Date	Details	A	C	GD25	FN65	NM94
1	98	8/52	Original	1	1	4.00	11.00	22.00
2	118	–	PC-r	1	1		1.60	4.00
3	132	–	PC-r	1	1		1.60	4.00
4	142	–	PC-r	1	1		1.60	4.00
5	152	–	PC-r	1	1		1.60	4.00

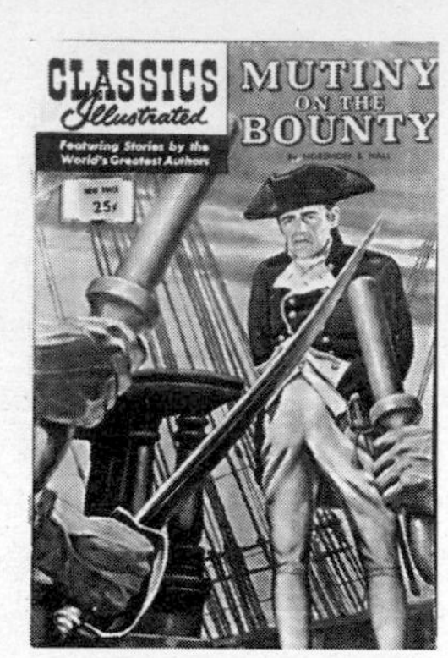

Classics Illustrated #100 © GIL

Classics Illustrated #102 © GIL

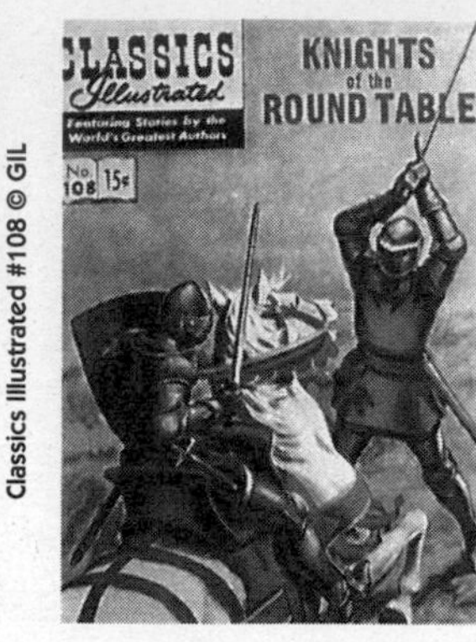

Classics Illustrated #108 © GIL

Ed	HRN	Date	Details	A	C	GD25	FN65	NM94
6	161	–	PC-r	1	1		1.60	4.00
7	167	–	Has orig.date; PC-r	1	1		1.60	4.00
8	167	9/64	PC-r	1	1		1.60	4.00
9	167	10/65	PC-r	1	1		1.60	4.00
10	166	R/1968	New-c&price 25¢; PC-r; stiff-c	1	2	1.75	5.25	14.00

99. Hamlet (Used in **POP**, pg. 102)

Ed	HRN	Date	Details	A	C	GD25	FN65	NM94
1	98	9/52	Original; Blum-a	1	1	4.00	12.00	24.00
2	121	–	PC-r	1	1		1.60	4.00
3	141	–	PC-r	1	1		1.60	4.00
4	158	–	PC-r	1	1		1.60	4.00
5	167	–	Has orig.date; PC-r	1	1		1.60	4.00
6	167	7/65	PC-r	1	1		1.60	4.00
7	166	4/67	PC-r	1	1		1.60	4.00
8	169	Spr/69	New-c&price 25¢; PC-r; stiff-c	1	2	1.50	4.50	12.00

100. Mutiny on the Bounty

Ed	HRN	Date	Details	A	C	GD25	FN65	NM94
1	100	10/52	Original	1	1	4.00	10.00	20.00
2	117	–	PC-r	1	1		1.60	4.00
3	132	–	PC-r	1	1		1.60	4.00
4	142	–	PC-r	1	1		1.60	4.00
5	155	–	PC-r	1	1		1.60	4.00
6	167	–	Has orig. date;PC-r	1	1		1.60	4.00
7	167	5/64	PC-r	1	1		1.60	4.00
8	167	3/66	PC-r	1	1		1.60	4.00
9	169	Spr/70	PC-r; stiff-c	1	1		1.60	4.00

101. William Tell

Ed	HRN	Date	Details	A	C	GD25	FN65	NM94
1	101	11/52	Original; Kiefer-c delBourgo-a	1	1	4.00	10.00	20.00
2	118	–	PC-r	1	1		1.60	4.00
3	141	–	PC-r	1	1		1.60	4.00
4	158	–	PC-r	1	1		1.60	4.00
5	167	–	Has orig.date; PC-r	1	1		1.60	4.00
6	167	11/64	PC-r	1	1		1.60	4.00
7	166	4/67	PC-r	1	1		1.60	4.00
8	169	Win/69	New price 25¢; stiff-c; PC-r	1	1		1.60	4.00

102. The White Company

Ed	HRN	Date	Details	A	C	GD25	FN65	NM94
1	101	12/52	Original; Blum-a	1	1	6.85	21.00	48.00
2	165	–	PC-r	1	1	2.25	6.75	18.00
3	167	4/64	PC-r	1	1	2.25	6.75	18.00

103. Men Against the Sea

Ed	HRN	Date	Details	A	C	GD25	FN65	NM94
1	104	1/53	Original; Kiefer-c; Palais-a	1	1	4.00	12.00	24.00
2	114	–	PC-r	1	1	2.80	7.00	14.00
3	131	–	New-c; PC-r	1	2	2.00	5.00	10.00
4	158	–	PC-r	1	2	2.00	5.00	10.00
5	149	–	White reorder list; came after HRN-158; PC-r	1	2	4.00	11.00	22.00
6	167	3/64	PC-r	1	2	1.00	3.00	8.00

104. Bring 'Em Back Alive

Ed	HRN	Date	Details	A	C	GD25	FN65	NM94
1	105	2/53	Original; Kiefer-c/a	1	1	3.60	9.00	18.00
2	118	–	PC-r	1	1		1.60	4.00
3	133	–	PC-r	1	1		1.60	4.00
4	150	–	PC-r	1	1		1.60	4.00
5	158	–	PC-r	1	1		1.60	4.00
6	167	10/63	PC-r	1	1		1.60	4.00
7	167	9/65	PC-r	1	1		1.60	4.00
8	169	Win/69	New price 25¢; stiff-c; PC-r	1	1		1.60	4.00

105. From the Earth to the Moon

Ed	HRN	Date	Details	A	C	GD25	FN65	NM94
1	106	3/53	Original; Blum-a	1	1	3.60	9.00	18.00
2	118	–	PC-r	1	1		1.60	4.00
3	132	–	PC-r	1	1		1.60	4.00
4	141	–	PC-r	1	1		1.60	4.00
5	146	–	PC-r	1	1		1.60	4.00
6	156	–	PC-r	1	1		1.60	4.00
7	167	–	Has orig. date; PC-r	1	1		1.60	4.00
8	167	5/64	PC-r	1	1		1.60	4.00
9	167	5/65	PC-r	1	1		1.60	4.00
10A	166	10/67	PC-r	1	1		1.60	4.00
10B	166	10/67	w/Grit ad stapled in book	1	1	8.75	26.25	70.00
11	169	Sm/69	New price 25¢; stiff-c; PC-r	1	1		1.60	4.00
12	169	Spr/71	PC-r	1	1		1.60	4.00

106. Buffalo Bill

Ed	HRN	Date	Details	A	C	GD25	FN65	NM94
1	107	4/53	Orig.; delBourgo-a	1	1	3.60	9.00	18.00
2	118	–	PC-r	1	1		1.60	4.00
3	132	–	PC-r	1	1		1.60	4.00
4	142	–	PC-r	1	1		1.60	4.00
5	161	–	PC-r	1	1		1.60	4.00
6	167	3/64	PC-r	1	1		1.60	4.00
7	166	7/67	PC-r	1	1		1.60	4.00
8	169	Fall/69	PC-r; stiff-c	1	1		1.60	4.00

107. King of the Khyber Rifles

Ed	HRN	Date	Details	A	C	GD25	FN65	NM94
1	108	5/53	Original	1	1	4.00	10.00	20.00
2	118	–	PC-r	1	1		1.60	4.00
3	146	–	PC-r	1	1		1.60	4.00
4	158	–	PC-r	1	1		1.60	4.00
5	167	–	Has orig.date; PC-r	1	1		1.60	4.00
6	167	–	PC-r	1	1		1.60	4.00
7	167	10/66	PC-r	1	1		1.60	4.00

108. Knights of the Round Table

Ed	HRN	Date	Details	A	C	GD25	FN65	NM94
1A	108	6/53	Original; Blum-a	1	1	4.00	12.00	24.00
1B	109	6/53	Original; scarce	1	1	5.70	17.00	34.00
2	117	–	PC-r	1	1		1.60	4.00
3	165	–	PC-r	1	1		1.60	4.00
4	167	4/64	PC-r	1	1		1.60	4.00
5	166	4/67	PC-r	1	1		1.60	4.00
6	169	Sm/69	New price 25¢; stiff-c; PC-r	1	1		1.60	4.00

109. Pitcairn's Island

Ed	HRN	Date	Details	A	C	GD25	FN65	NM94
1	110	7/53	Original; Palais-a	1	1	4.00	12.00	24.00
2	165	–	PC-r	1	1	1.00	2.80	7.00
3	167	3/64	PC-r	1	1	1.00	2.80	7.00
4	166	6/67	PC-r	1	1	1.00	2.80	7.00

110. A Study in Scarlet

Ed	HRN	Date	Details	A	C	GD25	FN65	NM94
1	111	8/53	Original	1	1	8.75	26.25	70.00

Classics Illustrated #118 © GIL

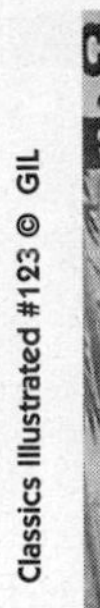
Classics Illustrated #123 © GIL

Classics Illustrated #124 © GIL

Ed	HRN	Date	Details	A	C	GD25	FN65	NM94
2	165	–	PC-r	1	1	7.85	23.50	55.00

111. The Talisman

Ed	HRN	Date	Details	A	C	GD25	FN65	NM94
1	112	9/53	Original; last H.C. Kiefer-a	1	1	4.00	11.00	22.00
2	165	–	PC-r	1	1	1.00	2.00	5.00
3	167	5/64	PC-r	1	1	1.00	2.00	5.00
4	166	Fall/68	C-price 25¢; PC-r	1	1	1.00	2.00	5.00

112. Adventures of Kit Carson

Ed	HRN	Date	Details	A	C	GD25	FN65	NM94
1	113	10/53	Original; Palais-a	1	1	4.00	11.00	22.00
2	129	–	PC-r	1	1		1.60	4.00
3	141	–	PC-r	1	1		1.60	4.00
4	152	–	PC-r	1	1		1.60	4.00
5	161	–	PC-r	1	1		1.60	4.00
6	167	–	PC-r	1	1		1.60	4.00
7	167	2/65	PC-r	1	1		1.60	4.00
8	167	5/66	PC-r	1	1		1.60	4.00
9	166	Win/69	New-c&price 25¢; PC-r; stiff-c	1	2	1.25	3.75	10.00

113. The Forty-Five Guardsmen

Ed	HRN	Date	Details	A	C	GD25	FN65	NM94
1	114	11/53	Orig.; delBourgo-a	1	1	6.00	18.00	42.00
2	166	7/67	PC-r	1	1	2.50	7.50	22.00

114. The Red Rover

Ed	HRN	Date	Details	A	C	GD25	FN65	NM94
1	115	12/53	Original	1	1	6.00	18.00	42.00
2	166	7/67	PC-r	1	1	2.50	7.50	22.00

115. How I Found Livingstone

Ed	HRN	Date	Details	A	C	GD25	FN65	NM94
1	116	1/54	Original	1	1	7.50	22.50	52.00
2	167	1/67	PC-r	1	1	3.20	9.60	32.00

116. The Bottle Imp

Ed	HRN	Date	Details	A	C	GD25	FN65	NM94
1	117	2/54	Orig.; Cameron-a	1	1	7.50	22.50	52.00
2	167	1/67	PC-r	1	1	3.20	9.60	32.00

117. Captains Courageous

Ed	HRN	Date	Details	A	C	GD25	FN65	NM94
1	118	3/54	Orig.; Costanza-a	1	1	6.50	19.50	45.00
2	167	2/67	PC-r	1	1	2.00	6.00	16.00
3	169	Fall/69	New price 25¢; stiff-c; PC-r	1	1	2.00	6.00	16.00

118. Rob Roy

Ed	HRN	Date	Details	A	C	GD25	FN65	NM94
1	119	4/54	Original; Rudy & Walter Palais-a	1	1	7.50	22.50	52.00
2	167	2/67	PC-r	1	1	3.20	9.60	32.00

119. Soldiers of Fortune

Ed	HRN	Date	Details	A	C	GD25	FN65	NM94
1	120	5/54	Original Schaffenberger-a	1	1	5.70	17.00	38.00
2	166	3/67	PC-r	1	1	1.85	5.50	15.00
3	169	Spr/70	New price 25¢; stiff-c; PC-r	1	1	1.85	5.50	15.00

120. The Hurricane

Ed	HRN	Date	Details	A	C	GD25	FN65	NM94
1	121	6/54	Orig.; Cameron-a	1	1	5.70	17.00	38.00
2	166	3/67	PC-r	1	1	2.50	7.50	24.00

121. Wild Bill Hickok

Ed	HRN	Date	Details	A	C	GD25	FN65	NM94
1	122	7/54	Original	1	1	3.00	7.50	15.00
2	132	–	PC-r	1	1		1.60	4.00
3	141	–	PC-r	1	1		1.60	4.00
4	154	–	PC-r	1	1		1.60	4.00
5	167	–	PC-r	1	1		1.60	4.00
6	167	8/64	PC-r	1	1		1.60	4.00
7	166	4/67	PC-r	1	1		1.60	4.00
8	169	Win/69	PC-r; stiff-c	1	1		1.60	4.00

122. The Mutineers

Ed	HRN	Date	Details	A	C	GD25	FN65	NM94
1	123	9/54	Original	1	1	4.00	11.00	22.00
2	136	–	PC-r	1	1		1.60	4.00
3	146	–	PC-r	1	1		1.60	4.00
4	158	–	PC-r	1	1		1.60	4.00
5	167	11/63	PC-r	1	1		1.60	4.00
6	167	3/65	PC-r	1	1		1.60	4.00
7	166	8/67	PC-r	1	1		1.60	4.00

123. Fang and Claw

Ed	HRN	Date	Details	A	C	GD25	FN65	NM94
1	124	11/54	Original	1	1	4.00	11.00	22.00
2	133	–	PC-r	1	1		1.60	4.00
3	143	–	PC-r	1	1		1.60	4.00
4	154	–	PC-r	1	1		1.60	4.00
5	167	–	Has orig.date; PC-r	1	1		1.60	4.00
6	167	9/65	PC-r	1	1		1.60	4.00

124. The War of the Worlds

Ed	HRN	Date	Details	A	C	GD25	FN65	NM94
1	125	1/55	Original; Cameron-c/a	1	1	5.00	15.00	30.00
2	131	–	PC-r	1	1	1.40	3.50	7.00
3	141	–	PC-r	1	1	1.40	3.50	7.00
4	148	–	PC-r	1	1	1.40	3.50	7.00
5	156	–	PC-r	1	1	1.40	3.50	7.00
6	165	–	PC-r	1	1	1.80	4.50	9.00
7	167	–	PC-r	1	1	1.40	3.50	7.00
8	167	11/64	PC-r	1	1	1.00	3.00	8.00
9	167	11/65	PC-r	1	1	1.00	2.80	7.00
10	166	R/1968	C-price 25¢; PC-r	1	1	1.00	2.80	7.00
11	169	Sm/70	PC-r; stiff-c	1	1	1.00	2.80	7.00

125. The Ox Bow Incident

Ed	HRN	Date	Details	A	C	GD25	FN65	NM94
1	3/55	–	Original; Picture Progress replaces reorder list	1	1	3.00	7.50	15.00
2	143	–	PC-r	1	1		1.60	4.00
3	152	–	PC-r	1	1		1.60	4.00
4	149	–	PC-r	1	1		1.60	4.00
5	167	–	PC-r	1	1		1.60	4.00
6	167	11/64	PC-r	1	1		1.60	4.00
7	166	4/67	PC-r	1	1		1.60	4.00
8	169	Win/69	New price 25¢; stiff-c; PC-r	1	1		1.60	4.00

126. The Downfall

Ed	HRN	Date	Details	A	C	GD25	FN65	NM94
1	5/55	–	Orig.; 'Picture Progress' replaces reorder list; Cameron-c/a	1	1	4.00	11.00	22.00
2	167	8/64	PC-r	1	1	1.00	3.00	8.00
3	166	R/1968	C-price 25¢; PC-r	1	1	1.00	3.00	8.00

127. The King of the Mountains

Ed	HRN	Date	Details	A	C	GD25	FN65	NM94
1	128	7/55	Original	1	1	4.00	11.00	22.00

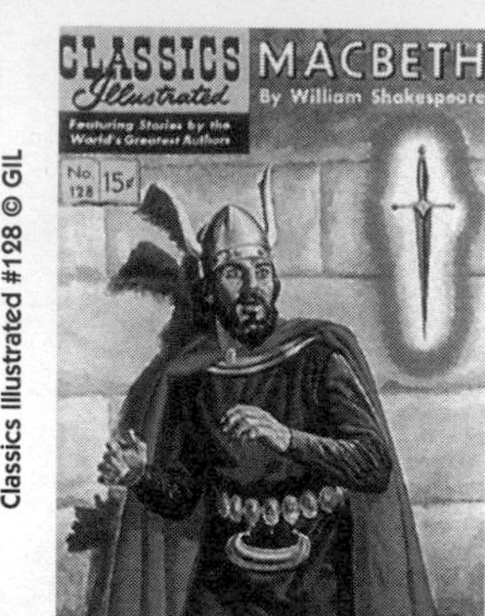

Classics Illustrated #128 © GIL

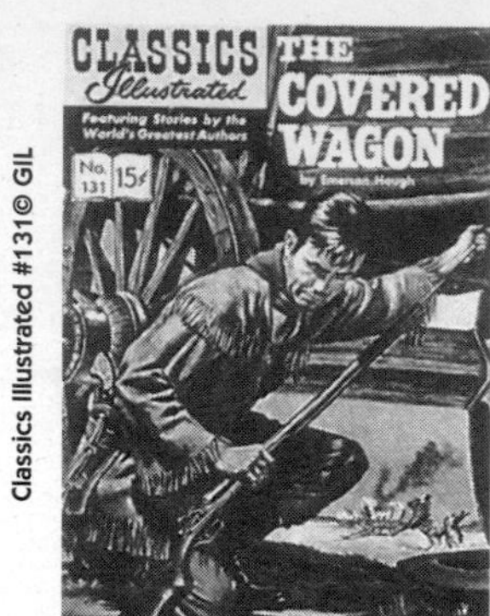

Classics Illustrated #131© GIL

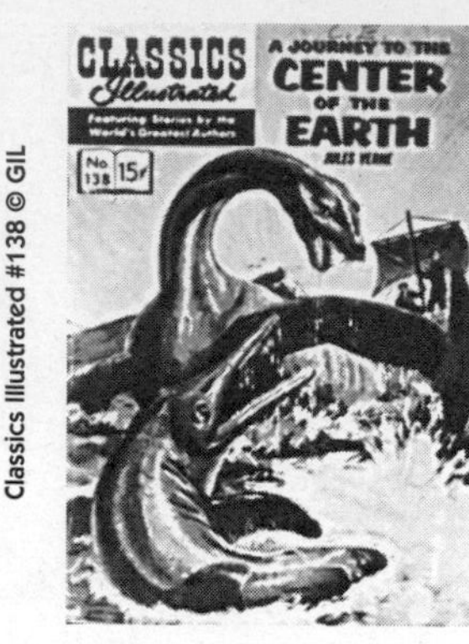

Classics Illustrated #138 © GIL

Ed	HRN	Date	Details	A	C	GD25	FN65	NM94
2	167	6/64	PC-r	1	1	1.00	3.00	8.00
3	166	F/1968	C-price 25¢; PC-r	1	1	1.00	3.00	8.00

128. Macbeth (Used in **POP**, pg. 102)

Ed	HRN	Date	Details	A	C	GD25	FN65	NM94
1	128	9/55	Orig.; last Blum-a	1	1	4.00	12.00	24.00
2	143	–	PC-r	1	1		1.60	4.00
3	158	–	PC-r	1	1		1.60	4.00
4	167	–	PC-r	1	1		1.60	4.00
5	167	6/64	PC-r	1	1		1.60	4.00
6	166	4/67	PC-r	1	1		1.60	4.00
7	166	R/1968	C-Price 25¢; PC-r	1	1		1.60	4.00
8	169	Spr/70	Stiff-c; PC-r	1	1		1.60	4.00

129. Davy Crockett

Ed	HRN	Date	Details	A	C	GD25	FN65	NM94
1	129	11/55	Orig.; Cameron-a	1	1	8.75	26.25	65.00
2	167	9/66	PC-r	1	1	7.85	23.50	55.00

130. Caesar's Conquests

Ed	HRN	Date	Details	A	C	GD25	FN65	NM94
1	130	1/56	Original; Orlando-a	1	1	5.00	15.00	30.00
2	142	–	PC-r	1	1	1.00	2.00	5.00
3	152	–	PC-r	1	1	1.00	2.00	5.00
4	149	–	PC-r	1	1	1.00	2.00	5.00
5	167	–	PC-r	1	1	1.00	2.00	5.00
6	167	10/64	PC-r	1	1	1.00	2.00	5.00
7	167	4/66	PC-r	1	1	1.00	2.00	5.00

131. The Covered Wagon

Ed	HRN	Date	Details	A	C	GD25	FN65	NM94
1	131	3/56	Original	1	1	3.00	7.50	15.00
2	143	–	PC-r	1	1		1.60	4.00
3	152	–	PC-r	1	1		1.60	4.00
4	158	–	PC-r	1	1		1.60	4.00
5	167	–	PC-r	1	1		1.60	4.00
6	167	11/64	PC-r	1	1		1.60	4.00
7	167	4/66	PC-r	1	1		1.60	4.00
8	169	Win/69	New price 25¢; stiff-c; PC-r	1	1		1.60	4.00

132. The Dark Frigate

Ed	HRN	Date	Details	A	C	GD25	FN65	NM94
1	132	5/56	Original	1	1	4.00	12.00	24.00
2	150	–	PC-r	1	1	1.40	3.50	7.00
3	167	1/64	PC-r	1	1	1.00	2.80	7.00
4	166	5/67	PC-r	1	1	1.00	2.80	7.00

133. The Time Machine

Ed	HRN	Date	Details	A	C	GD25	FN65	NM94
1	132	7/56	Orig.; Cameron-a	1	1	5.00	15.00	30.00
2	142	–	PC-r	1	1	1.40	3.50	7.00
3	152	–	PC-r	1	1	1.40	3.50	7.00
4	158	–	PC-r	1	1	1.40	3.50	7.00
5	167	–	PC-r	1	1	1.40	3.50	7.00
6	167	6/64	PC-r	1	1	1.10	3.30	9.00
7	167	3/66	PC-r	1	1	1.00	2.80	7.00
8	166	12/67	PC-r	1	1	1.00	2.80	7.00
9	169	Win/71	New price 25¢; stiff-c; PC-r	1	1	1.00	2.80	7.00

134. Romeo and Juliet

Ed	HRN	Date	Details	A	C	GD25	FN65	NM94
1	134	9/56	Original; Evans-a	1	1	4.00	12.00	24.00
2	161	–	PC-r	1	1		1.60	4.00
3	167	9/63	PC-r	1	1		1.60	4.00
4	167	5/65	PC-r	1	1		1.60	4.00
5	166	6/67	PC-r	1	1		1.60	4.00
6	166	Win/69	New c&price 25¢; stiff-c; PC-r	1	2	2.25	6.75	18.00

135. Waterloo

Ed	HRN	Date	Details	A	C	GD25	FN65	NM94
1	135	11/56	Orig.; G. Ingels-a	1	1	4.00	11.00	22.00
2	153	–	PC-r	1	1		1.60	4.00
3	167	–	PC-r	1	1		1.60	4.00
4	167	9/64	PC-r	1	1		2.00	5.00
5	166	R/1968	C-price 25¢; PC-r	1	1		1.60	4.00

136. Lord Jim

Ed	HRN	Date	Details	A	C	GD25	FN65	NM94
1	136	1/57	Original; Evans-a	1	1	4.00	11.00	22.00
2	165	–	PC-r	1	1		1.60	4.00
3	167	3/64	PC-r	1	1		1.60	4.00
4	167	9/66	PC-r	1	1		1.60	4.00
5	169	Sm/69	New price 25 ¢; stiff-c; PC-r	1	1		1.60	4.00

137. The Little Savage

Ed	HRN	Date	Details	A	C	GD25	FN65	NM94
1	136	3/57	Original; Evans-a	1	1	4.00	11.00	22.00
2	148	–	PC-r	1	1		1.60	4.00
3	156	–	PC-r	1	1		1.60	4.00
4	167	–	PC-r	1	1		1.60	4.00
5	167	10/64	PC-r	1	1		2.00	5.00
6	166	8/67	PC-r	1	1		1.60	4.00
7	169	Spr/70	New price 25¢; stiff-c; PC-r	1	1		1.60	4.00

138. A Journey to the Center of the Earth

Ed	HRN	Date	Details	A	C	GD25	FN65	NM94
1	136	5/57	Original	1	1	5.70	17.00	35.00
2	146	–	PC-r	1	1	1.00	2.00	5.00
3	156	–	PC-r	1	1	1.00	2.00	5.00
4	158	–	PC-r	1	1	1.00	2.00	5.00
5	167	–	PC-r	1	1	1.00	2.00	5.00
6	167	6/64	PC-r	1	1	1.00	2.80	7.00
7	167	4/66	PC-r	1	1	1.00	2.80	7.00
8	166	R/68	C-price 25¢; PC-r	1	1		2.00	5.00

139. In the Reign of Terror

Ed	HRN	Date	Details	A	C	GD25	FN65	NM94
1	139	7/57	Original; Evans-a	1	1	3.00	7.50	15.00
2	154	–	PC-r	1	1		1.60	4.00
3	167	–	Has orig.date; PC-r	1	1		1.60	4.00
4	167	7/64	PC-r	1	1		2.00	5.00
5	166	R/1968	C-price 25¢; PC-r	1	1		1.60	4.00

140. On Jungle Trails

Ed	HRN	Date	Details	A	C	GD25	FN65	NM94
1	140	9/57	Original	1	1	3.00	7.50	15.00
2	150	–	PC-r	1	1		1.60	4.00
3	160	–	PC-r	1	1		1.60	4.00
4	167	9/63	PC-r	1	1		2.00	5.00
5	167	9/65	PC-r	1	1		1.60	4.00

141. Castle Dangerous

Ed	HRN	Date	Details	A	C	GD25	FN65	NM94
1	141	11/57	Original	1	1	5.00	15.00	30.00
2	152	–	PC-r	1	1		2.40	6.00
3	167	–	PC-r	1	1		2.40	6.00
4	166	7/67	PC-r	1	1		2.40	6.00

142. Abraham Lincoln

Ed	HRN	Date	Details	A	C	GD25	FN65	NM94
1	142	1/58	Original	1	1	5.00	15.00	30.00
2	154	–	PC-r	1	1		1.60	4.00
3	158	–	PC-r	1	1		1.60	4.00
4	167	10/63	PC-r	1	1		2.00	5.00

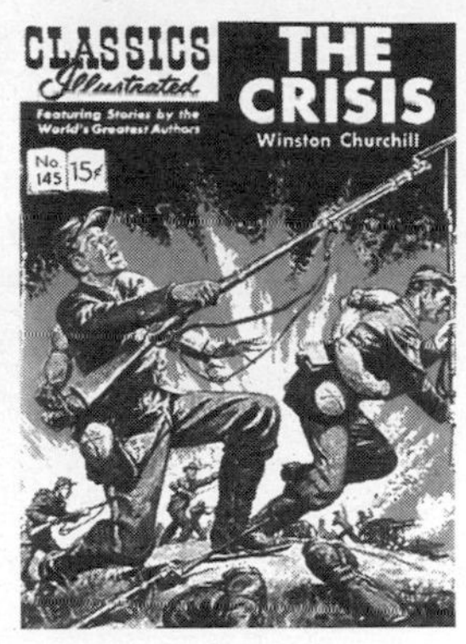

Classics Illustrated #145 © GIL

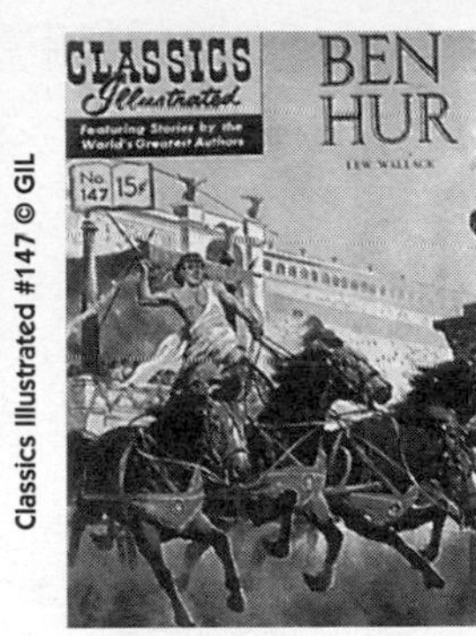

Classics Illustrated #147 © GIL

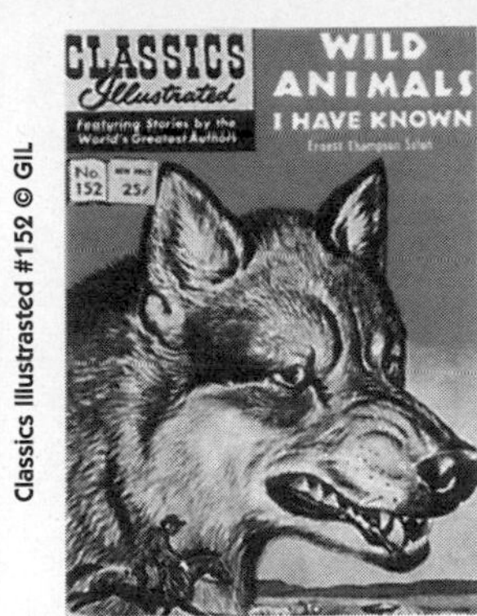

Classics Illustrated #152 © GIL

Ed	HRN	Date	Details	A	C	GD25	FN65	NM94
5	167	7/65	PC-r	1	1		1.60	4.00
6	166	11/67	PC-r	1	1		1.60	4.00
7	169	Fall/69	New price 25¢; stiff-c; PC-r	1	1		1.60	4.00

143. Kim

Ed	HRN	Date	Details	A	C	GD25	FN65	NM94
1	143	3/58	Original; Orlando-a	1	1	4.00	11.00	22.00
2	165	–	PC-r	1	1		1.60	4.00
3	167	11/63	PC-r	1	1		2.00	5.00
4	167	8/65	PC-r	1	1		1.60	4.00
5	169	Win/69	New price 25¢; stiff-c; PC-r	1	1		1.60	4.00

144. The First Men in the Moon

Ed	HRN	Date	Details	A	C	GD25	FN65	NM94
1	143	5/58	Original; Woodbridge/Williamson/Torres-a	1	1	4.00	12.00	24.00
2	152	–	(Rare)-PC-r	1	1	5.70	17.00	38.00
3	153	–	PC-r	1	1	1.00	2.00	5.00
4	161	–	PC-r	1	1	1.00	2.00	5.00
5	167	–	PC-r	1	1	1.00	2.00	5.00
6	167	12/65	PC-r	1	1	1.00	2.00	5.00
7	166	Fall/68	New-c&price 25¢; PC-r; stiff-c	1	2	1.50	4.50	12.00
8	169	Win/69	Stiff-c; PC-r	1	2	1.25	3.75	10.00

145. The Crisis

Ed	HRN	Date	Details	A	C	GD25	FN65	NM94
1	143	7/58	Original; Evans-a	1	1	4.00	11.00	22.00
2	156	–	PC-r	1	1		1.60	4.00
3	167	10/63	PC-r	1	1		2.00	5.00
4	167	3/65	PC-r	1	1		1.60	4.00
5	166	R/68	C-price 25¢; PC-r	1	1		1.60	4.00

146. With Fire and Sword

Ed	HRN	Date	Details	A	C	GD25	FN65	NM94
1	143	9/58	Original; Woodbridge-a	1	1	5.00	15.00	30.00
2	156	–	PC-r	1	1	1.00	2.80	7.00
3	167	11/63	PC-r	1	1	1.00	3.00	8.00
4	167	3/65	PC-r	1	1	1.00	2.80	7.00

147. Ben-Hur

Ed	HRN	Date	Details	A	C	GD25	FN65	NM94
1	147	11/58	Original; Orlando-a	1	1	4.00	11.00	22.00
2	152	–	Scarce; PC-r	1	1	4.25	13.00	26.00
3	153	–	PC-r	1	1	1.00	2.00	5.00
4	158	–	PC-r	1	1		1.60	4.00
5	167	–	Orig.date; but PC-r	1	1		1.60	4.00
6	167	2/65	PC-r	1	1		1.60	4.00
7	167	9/66	PC-r	1	1		1.60	4.00
8A	166	Fall/68	New-c&price 25¢; PC-r; soft-c	1	2	2.00	6.00	16.00
8B	166	Fall/68	New-c&price 25¢; PC-r; stiff-c; scarce	1	2	2.80	8.40	28.00

148. The Buccaneer

Ed	HRN	Date	Details	A	C	GD25	FN65	NM94
1	148	1/59	Orig.; Evans/Jenny-a; Saunders-c	1	1	4.00	11.00	22.00
2	568	–	Juniors list only PC-r	1	1	1.60	4.00	8.00
3	167	–	PC-r	1	1		1.60	4.00
4	167	9/65	PC-r	1	1		1.60	4.00
5	169	Sm/69	New price 25¢; PC-r; stiff-c	1	1		1.60	4.00

149. Off on a Comet

Ed	HRN	Date	Details	A	C	GD25	FN65	NM94
1	149	3/59	Orig.;G.McCann-a; blue reorder list	1	1	4.00	11.00	22.00
2	155	–	PC-r	1	1		1.60	4.00
3	149	–	PC-r; white reorder list; no coming-next ad	1	1		1.60	4.00
4	167	12/63	PC-r	1	1		2.00	5.00
5	167	2/65	PC-r	1	1		2.00	5.00
6	167	10/66	PC-r	1	1		1.60	4.00
7	166	Fall/68	New-c & price 25¢; PC-r	1	2	1.75	5.25	14.00

150. The Virginian

Ed	HRN	Date	Details	A	C	GD25	FN65	NM94
1	150	5/59	Original	1	1	5.70	17.00	36.00
2	164	–	PC-r	1	1	1.75	5.25	14.00
3	167	10/63	PC-r	1	1	2.25	6.75	18.00
4	167	12/65	PC-r	1	1	1.75	5.25	14.00

151. Won By the Sword

Ed	HRN	Date	Details	A	C	GD25	FN65	NM94
1	150	7/59	Original	1	1	5.00	15.00	30.00
2	164	–	PC-r	1	1	1.40	4.15	11.00
3	167	10/63	PC-r	1	1	1.50	4.50	12.00
4	166	7/67	PC-r	1	1	1.25	3.75	10.00

152. Wild Animals I Have Known

Ed	HRN	Date	Details	A	C	GD25	FN65	NM94
1	152	9/59	Orig.; L.B. Cole c/a	1	1	5.70	17.00	36.00
2A	149	–	PC-r; white reorder list; no coming-next ad; IBC: Jr. list #572	1	1	1.00	2.00	5.00
2B	149	–	PC-r; inside-bc: Jr. list to #555	1	1	1.40	3.50	7.00
2C	149	–	PC-r; inside-bc: has World Around Us ad; scarce	1	1	3.20	8.00	16.00
3	167	9/63	PC-r	1	1		1.60	4.00
4	167	8/65	PC-r	1	1		1.60	4.00
5	169	Fall/69	New price 25¢; stiff-c; PC-r	1	1		1.60	4.00

153. The Invisible Man

Ed	HRN	Date	Details	A	C	GD25	FN65	NM94
1	153	11/59	Original	1	1	5.70	17.00	36.00
2A	149	–	PC-r; white reorder list; no coming-next ad; inside-bc: Jr. list to #572	1	1	1.00	2.00	5.00
2B	149	–	PC-r; inside-bc: Jr. list to #555	1	1	1.40	3.50	7.00
3	167	–	PC-r	1	1		1.60	4.00
4	167	2/65	PC-r	1	1		1.60	4.00
5	167	9/66	PC-r	1	1		1.60	4.00
6	166	Win/69	New price 25¢; PC-r; stiff-c	1	1		1.60	4.00
7	169	Spr/71	Stiff-c; letters spelling 'Invisible Man' are 'solid' not 'invisible;' PC-r	1	1		1.60	4.00

154. The Conspiracy of Pontiac

Ed	HRN	Date	Details	A	C	GD25	FN65	NM94
1	154	1/60	Original	1	1	3.60	10.80	36.00
2	167	11/63	PC-r	1	1	1.50	4.50	12.00
3	167	7/64	PC-r	1	1	1.50	4.50	12.00

Classics Illustrated #163 © GIL

Classics Illustrated #165 © GIL

Classics Illustrated #169 © GIL

Ed	HRN	Date	Details	A	C	GD25	FN65	NM94
4	166	12/67	PC-r	1	1	1.50	4.50	12.00

155. The Lion of the North

Ed	HRN	Date	Details	A	C	GD25	FN65	NM94
1	154	3/60	Original	1	1	3.00	9.00	30.00
2	167	1/64	PC-r	1	1	1.25	3.75	10.00
3	166	R/1967	C-price 25¢; PC-r	1	1	1.10	3.30	9.00

156. The Conquest of Mexico

Ed	HRN	Date	Details	A	C	GD25	FN65	NM94
1	156	5/60	Orig.; Bruno Premiani-c/a	1	1	3.00	9.00	30.00
2	167	1/64	PC-r	1	1	1.00	2.80	7.00
3	166	8/67	PC-r	1	1	1.00	2.80	7.00
4	169	Spr/70	New price 25¢; stiff-c; PC-r	1	1		2.00	5.00

157. Lives of the Hunted

Ed	HRN	Date	Details	A	C	GD25	FN65	NM94
1	156	7/60	Orig.; L.B. Cole-c	1	1	3.60	10.80	36.00
2	167	2/64	PC-r	1	1	1.50	4.50	12.00
3	166	10/67	PC-r	1	1	1.50	4.50	12.00

158. The Conspirators

Ed	HRN	Date	Details	A	C	GD25	FN65	NM94
1	156	9/60	Original	1	1	3.20	9.60	32.00
2	167	7/64	PC-r	1	1	1.50	4.50	12.00
3	166	10/67	PC-r	1	1	1.50	4.50	12.00

159. The Octopus

Ed	HRN	Date	Details	A	C	GD25	FN65	NM94
1	159	11/60	Orig.; Gray Morrow-a; L.B. Cole-c	1	1	3.20	9.60	32.00
2	167	2/64	PC-r	1	1	1.25	3.75	10.00
3	166	R/1967	C-price 25¢; PC-r	1	1	1.25	3.75	10.00

160. The Food of the Gods

Ed	HRN	Date	Details	A	C	GD25	FN65	NM94
1A	159	1/61	Original	1	1	3.60	10.80	36.00
1B	160	1/61	Original; same, except for HRN	1	1	3.30	9.90	33.00
2	167	1/64	PC-r	1	1	1.40	4.15	11.00
3	166	6/67	PC-r	1	1	1.40	4.15	11.00

161. Cleopatra

Ed	HRN	Date	Details	A	C	GD25	FN65	NM94
1	161	3/61	Original	1	1	3.60	10.80	36.00
2	167	1/64	PC-r	1	1	1.75	5.25	14.00
3	166	8/67	PC-r	1	1	1.75	5.25	14.00

162. Robur the Conqueror

Ed	HRN	Date	Details	A	C	GD25	FN65	NM94
1	162	5/61	Original	1	1	3.50	10.50	35.00
2	167	7/64	PC-r	1	1	1.50	4.50	12.00
3	166	8/67	PC-r	1	1	1.50	4.50	12.00

163. Master of the World

Ed	HRN	Date	Details	A	C	GD25	FN65	NM94
1	163	7/61	Original; Gray Morrow-a	1	1	3.20	9.60	32.00
2	167	1/65	PC-r	1	1	1.50	4.50	12.00
3	166	R/1968	C-price 25¢; PC-r	1	1	1.50	4.50	12.00

164. The Cossack Chief

Ed	HRN	Date	Details	A	C	GD25	FN65	NM94
1	164	(1961)	Orig.; nd(10/61?)	1	1	3.00	9.00	30.00
2	167	4/65	PC-r	1	1	1.50	4.50	12.00
3	166	Fall/68	C-price 25¢; PC-r	1	1	1.50	4.50	12.00

165. The Queen's Necklace

Ed	HRN	Date	Details	A	C	GD25	FN65	NM94
1	164	1/62	Original; Morrow-a	1	1	3.20	9.60	32.00
2	167	4/65	PC-r	1	1	1.50	4.50	12.00
3	166	Fall/68	C-price 25¢; PC-r	1	1	1.50	4.50	12.00

166. Tigers and Traitors

Ed	HRN	Date	Details	A	C	GD25	FN65	NM94
1	165	5/62	Original	1	1	5.80	17.50	58.00
2	167	2/64	PC-r	1	1	2.50	7.50	20.00
3	167	11/66	PC-r	1	1	2.50	7.50	20.00

167. Faust

Ed	HRN	Date	Details	A	C	GD25	FN65	NM94
1	165	8/62	Original	1	1	8.50	25.50	85.00
2	167	2/64	PC-r	1	1	3.50	10.50	35.00
3	166	6/67	PC-r	1	1	3.50	10.50	35.00

168. In Freedom's Cause

Ed	HRN	Date	Details	A	C	GD25	FN65	NM94
1	169	Win/69	Original; Evans/ Crandall-a; stiff-c; 25¢; no coming-next ad;	1	1	9.50	28.50	95.00

169. Negro Americans The Early Years

Ed	HRN	Date	Details	A	C	GD25	FN65	NM94
1	166	Spr/69	Orig. & last issue; 25¢; Stiff-c; no coming-next ad; other sources indicate publication date of 5/69	1	1	7.50	22.50	75.00
2	169	Spr/69	Stiff-c	1	1	4.20	12.60	42.00

NOTE: *Many other titles were prepared or planned but were only issued in British/European series.*

CLASSIC PUNISHER (Also see Punisher)
Dec, 1989 ($4.95, B&W, deluxe format, 68 pgs.)
Marvel Comics

1-Reprints Marvel Super Action #1 & Marvel Preview #2 plus new story 2.00 5.00

CLASSICS GIVEAWAYS (Arranged in chronological order)

12/41–Walter Theatre Enterprises (Huntington, WV) giveaway containing #2 (orig.) w/new generic-c (only 1 known copy) 106.00 319.00 850.00

1942–Double Comics containing CC#1 (orig.) (diff. cover) (not actually a giveaway) (very rare) (also see Double Comics) (only one known copy) 194.00 582.00 1750.00

12/42–Saks 34th St. Giveaway containing CC#7 (orig.) (diff. cover) (very rare; only 6 known copies) 686.00 2057.00 4800.00

2/43–American Comics containing CC#8 (orig.) (Liberty Theatre giveaway) (different cover) (only one known copy) (see American Comics) 137.00 400.00 1200.00

12/44–Robin Hood Flour Co. Giveaway - #7-CC(R) (diff. cover) (rare) (edition probably 5 [22]) 288.00 862.00 2300.00

NOTE: How are above editions determined without CC covers? 1942 is dated 1942, and CC#1-first reprint did not come out until 5/43. 12/42 and 2/43 are determined by blue note at bottom of first text page only in original edition. 12/44 is estimated from page width each reprint edition had progressively slightly smaller page width.

1951–Shelter Thru the Ages (C.I. Educational Series) (actually Giveaway by the Ruberoid Co.) (16 pgs.) (contains original artwork by H. C. Kiefer) (there are 5 diff. back cover ad variations: "Ranch" house ad, "Igloo" ad, "Doll House" ad, "Tree House" ad & blank)(scarce) 72.00 216.00 650.00

1952–George Daynor Biography Giveaway (CC logo) (partly comic book/ pictures/newspaper articles) (story of man who built Palace Depression out of junkyard swamp in NJ) (64 pgs.)(very rare; only 3 known copies, one missing-bc) 857.00 2571.00 6000.00

1953–Westinghouse/Dreams of a Man (C.I. Educational Series) (Westinghouse bio./Westinghouse Co. giveaway) (contains original artwork by H. C. Kiefer) (16 pgs.) (also French/Spanish/Italian versions)

Classics Illustrated: Hamlet © Twin Circle Pub.

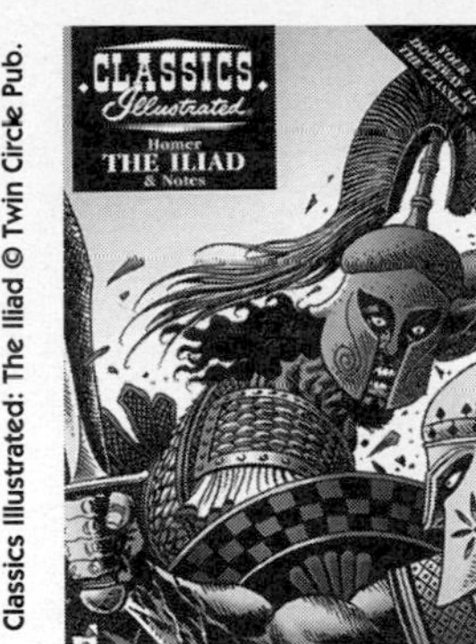

Classics Illustrated: The Iliad © Twin Circle Pub.

Classics Illustrated Junior #502 © GIL

GD25 FN65 NM94

(scarce) 72.00 216.00 650.00

NOTE: Reproductions of 1951, 1952, and 1953 exist with color photocopy covers and black & white photocopy interior ("W.C.N. Reprint") 2.00 5.00 10.00

1951-53–Coward Shoe Giveaways (all editions very rare); 2 variations of back-c ad exist:

With back-c photo ad: 5 (87), 12 (89), 22 (85), 32 (85),49 (85), 69 (87), 72 (no HRN), 80 (0), 91 (0), 92 (0), 96 (0), 98 (0), 100 (0), 101 (0), 103-105 (all Os) 36.00 108.00 325.00

With back-c cartoon ad: 106-109 (all 0s), 110 (111), 112 (0) 42.00 126.00 375.00

1956–Ben Franklin 5-10 Store Giveaway (#65-PC with back cover ad) (scarce) 34.00 103.00 275.00

1956–Ben Franklin Insurance Co. Giveaway (#65-PC with diff. back cover ad) (very rare) 65.00 195.00 585.00

11/56–Sealtest Co. Edition - #4 (135) (identical to regular edition except for Sealtest logo printed, not stamped, on front cover) (only two copies known to exist) 36.00 108.00 325.00

1958–Get-Well Giveaway containing #15-CI (new cartoon-type cover)(Pressman Pharmacy) (only one copy known to exist) 36.00 108.00 290.00

1967-68–Twin Circle Giveaway Editions - all HRN 166, with back cover ad for National Catholic Press.

2(R68), 4(R67), 10(R68), 13(R68) 2.80 8.40 28.00
48(R67), 128(R68), 535(576-R68) 3.20 9.60 32.00
16(R68), 68(R67) 4.50 13.50 45.00

12/69–Christmas Giveaway ("A Christmas Adventure") (reprints Picture Parade #4-1953, new cover) (4 ad variations)

Stacy's Dept. Store 2.50 7.50 22.00
Anne & Hope Store 5.00 15.00 50.00
Gibson's Dept. Store (rare) 5.00 15.00 50.00
"Merry Christmas" & blank ad space 2.50 7.50 22.00

CLASSICS ILLUSTRATED
Feb, 1990 - No. 27, July?, 1991 ($3.75/$3.95, 52 pgs.)
First Publishing/Berkley Publishing

1-17: 1-Gahan Wilson-c/a. 4-Sienkiewicz painted-c/a. 6-Russell scripts/ layouts. 7-Spiegle-a. 9-Ploog-c/a. 16-Staton-a 1.50 3.75

18-27: 18-Gahan Wilson-c/a; begin $3.95-c. 20-Geary-a. 26-Aesop's Fables (6/91). 26,27-Direct sale only 1.60 4.00

CLASSICS ILLUSTRATED
Feb, 1997 - Present ($4.99, digest-size) (Each book contains study notes)
Acclaim Books/Twin Circle PublishingCo.

A Christmas Carol-(12/97) 5.00
A Connecticut Yankee in King Arthur's Court-(5/97) 5.00
All Quiet on the Western Front-(1/98) 5.00
A Midsummer's Night Dream-(4/97) 5.00
Around the World in 80 Days-(1/98) 5.00
A Tale of Two Cities-(2/97)-Joe Orlando-r 5.00
Captains Courageous-(11/97) 5.00
Crime and Punishment (3/97) 5.00
Dr. Jekyll and Mr. Hyde-(10/97) 5.00
Don Quixote-(12/97) 5.00
Frankenstein-(10/97) 5.00
Great Expectations-(4/97) 5.00
Hamlet-(3/97) 5.00
Huckleberry Finn-(3/97) 5.00
Jane Eyre-(2/97) 5.00
Kidnapped-(1/98) 5.00
Les Miserables-(5/97) 5.00
Lord Jim-(9/97) 5.00
Macbeth-(5/97) 5.00
Moby Dick-(4/97) 5.00
Oliver Twist-(5/97) 5.00
Robinson Crusoe-(9/97) 5.00
Romeo & Juliet-(2/97) 5.00
Silas Marner-(11/97) 5.00
The Call of the Wild-(9/97) 5.00
The Count of Monte Cristo-(1/98) 5.00
The House of the Seven Gables-(9/97) 5.00
The Iliad-(12/97) 5.00
The Invisible Man-(10/97) 5.00
The Last of the Mohicans-(12/97) 5.00
The Master of Ballantrae-(11/97) 5.00
The Odyssey-(3/97) 5.00
The Prince and the Pauper-(4/97) 5.00
The Red Badge Of Courage-(9/97) 5.00
Tom Sawyer-(2/97) 5.00
Wuthering Heights-(11/97) 5.00

NOTE: *Stories reprinted from the original Gilberton Classic Comics and Classics Illustrated.*

CLASSICS ILLUSTRATED GIANTS
Oct, 1949 (One-Shots - "OS")
Gilberton Publications

These Giant Editions, all with new Kiefer front and back covers, were advertised from 10/49 to 2/52. They were 50¢ on the newsstand and 60¢ by mail. They are actually fourclassics in one volume. All the stories are reprints of the Classics Illustrated Series. NOTE: There were also British hardback Adventure & Indian Giants in 1952, with the same covers but different contents: Adventure - 2, 7, 10; Indian - 17, 22, 37, 58. They are also rare.

"An Illustrated Library of Great Adventure Stories" - reprints of No. 6,7,8,10 (Rare); Kiefer-c 111.00 333.00 1000.00

"An Illustrated Library of Exciting Mystery Stories" - reprints of No. 30,21,40, 13 (Rare) 122.00 366.00 1100.00

"An Illustrated Library of Great Indian Stories" - reprints of No. 4,17,22,37 (Rare) 111.00 333.00 1000.00

INTRODUCTION TO CLASSICS ILLUSTRATED JUNIOR

Collectors of Juniors can be put into one of two categories those who want any copy of each title, and those who want all the originals. Those seeking every original and reprint edition are a limited group, primarily because Juniors have no changes in art or covers to spark interest, and because reprints are so low in value it is difficult to get dealers to look for specific reprint editions.

In recent years it has become apparent that most serious Classics collectors seek Junior originals. Those seeking reprints seek them for low cost. This has made the previous note about the comparative market value of reprints inadequate. Most dealers report difficulty in moving reprints for more than $2-$4 for mint copies. Some may be worth $5-$7, just because of the popularity of the title, such as Snow White, Sleeping Beauty, and Wizard of Oz. Others may be worth $5-$7, because of the scarcity of particular title nos., such as 514, 560, 562, 575 & 576. Three particular reprint editions are worth even more. For the 535-Twin Circle edition, see Giveaways. There are also reprint editions of 501 and 503 which have a full-page bc ad for the very rare Junior record. Those may sell as high as $10-$15 in mint. Original editions of 557 and 558 also have that ad.

There are no reprint editions of 577. The only edition, from 1969, is a 25 cent stiff-cover edition with no ad for the next issue. All other original editions have coming-next ad. But 577, like C.I. #168, was prepared in 1962 but not issued. Copies of 577 can be found in 1963 British/European series, which then continued with dozens of additional new Junior titles.

PRICES LISTED BELOW ARE FOR ORIGINAL EDITIONS, WHICH HAVE AN AD FOR THE NEXT ISSUE.

CLASSICS ILLUSTRATED JUNIOR
Oct, 1953 - Spring, 1971
Famous Authors Ltd. (Gilberton Publications)

501-Snow White & the Seven Dwarfs; Alex Blum-a 8.50 26.00 60.00
502-The Ugly Duckling 5.70 17.00 38.00
503-Cinderella 4.00 11.00 22.00
504-512: 504-The Pied Piper. 505-The Sleeping Beauty. 506-The Three Little

Classics Illustrated Special Issue #132A © GIL

Classics Illustrated Special Issue #165A © GIL

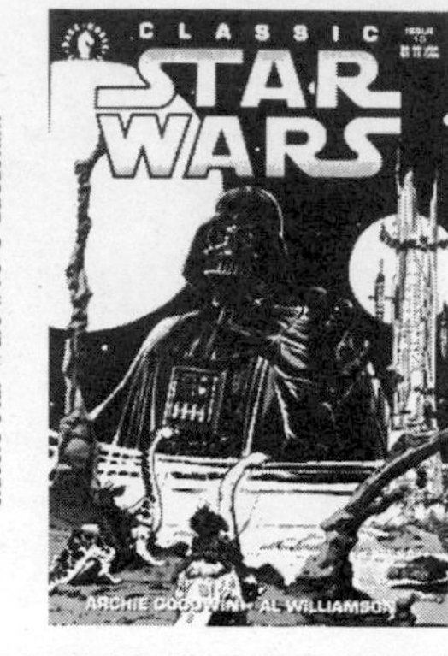

Classic Star Wars #10 © Lucasfilm

GD25 FN65 NM94

Pigs. 507-Jack & the Beanstalk. 508-Goldilocks & the Three Bears. 509-Beauty and the Beast. 510-Little Red Riding Hood. 511-Puss-N Boots. 512-Rumpelstiltskin 3.00 7.50 15.00
513-Pinocchio 4.00 11.00 22.00
514-The Steadfast Tin Soldier 5.35 16.00 32.00
515-Johnny Appleseed 3.00 7.50 15.00
516-Aladdin and His Lamp 4.00 11.00 22.00
517-519: 517-The Emperor's New Clothes. 518-The Golden Goose. 519-Paul Bunyan 3.00 7.50 15.00
520-Thumbelina 4.00 11.00 22.00
521-King of the Golden River 3.00 7.50 15.00
522-524,527,528,530: 522-The Nightingale. 523-The Gallant Tailor. 524-The Wild Swans. 527-The Golden-Haired Giant. 528-The Penny Prince. 530-The Golden Bird 2.40 6.00 12.00
525,526,529: 525-The Little Mermaid. 526-The Frog Prince. 529-The Magic Servants 2.60 6.50 13.00
531-Rapunzel 3.00 7.50 15.00
532-534: 532-The Dancing Princesses. 533-The Magic Fountain. 534-The Golden Touch 2.40 6.00 12.00
535-The Wizard of Oz 5.00 15.00 30.00
536,537: 536-The Chimney Sweep. 537-The Three Fairies. 2.80 7.00 14.00
538-Silly Hans 2.40 6.00 12.00
539-The Enchanted Fish 4.00 11.00 22.00
540-The Tinder-Box 4.00 11.00 22.00
541-Snow White & Rose Red 3.00 7.50 15.00
542-The Donkey's Tale 3.00 7.50 15.00
543-The House in the Woods 2.40 6.00 12.00
544-The Golden Fleece 5.00 15.00 30.00
545-The Glass Mountain 3.00 7.50 15.00
546-The Elves & the Shoemaker 3.00 7.50 15.00
547-The Wishing Table 2.80 7.00 14.00
548-551: 548-The Magic Pitcher. 549-Simple Kate. 550-The Singing Donkey. 551-The Queen Bee 2.40 6.00 12.00
552-The Three Little Dwarfs 3.00 7.50 15.00
553,556: 553-King Thrushbeard. 556-The Elf Mound 2.40 6.00 12.00
554,555: 554-The Enchanted Deer. 555-The Three Golden Apples 2.40 6.00 12.00
557-Silly Willy 4.00 10.50 21.00
558-The Magic Dish; L.B. Cole-c; soft and stiff-c exist on original 4.25 13.00 26.00
559-The Japanese Lantern; 1 pg. Ingels-a; L.B. Cole-c 4.25 13.00 26.00
560-The Doll Princess; L.B. Cole-c 4.25 13.00 28.00
561-Hans Humdrum; L.B. Cole-c 3.00 7.50 15.00
562-The Enchanted Pony; L.B. Cole-c 4.25 13.00 28.00
563-570: 563-The Wishing Well; L.B. Cole-c. 564-The Salt Mountain; L.B.Cole-c. 565-The Silly Princess; L.B. Cole-c. 566-Clumsy Hans; L.B. Cole-c. 567-The Bearskin Soldier; L.B. Cole-c. 568-The Happy Hedgehog; L.B. Cole-c. 569-The Three Giants. 570-The Pearl Princess 2.40 6.00 12.00
571-574: 571-How Fire Came to the Indians. 572-The Drummer Boy. 573-The Crystal Ball. 574-Brightboots 3.00 7.50 15.00
575-The Fearless Prince 3.60 9.00 18.00
576-The Princess Who Saw Everything 4.25 13.00 26.00
577-The Runaway Dumpling 5.35 16.00 32.00

NOTE: *Prices are for original editions. Last reprint - Spring, 1971.* ***Costanza & Shaffenberger*** *art in many issues.*

CLASSICS ILLUSTRATED SPECIAL ISSUE
Dec, 1955 - July, 1962 (35¢, 100 pgs.)
Gilberton Co. (Came out semi-annually)

129-The Story of Jesus (titled ...Special Edition) "Jesus on Mountain" cover 7.15 21.50 50.00
"Three Camels" cover (12/58) 8.75 26.25 70.00
"Mountain" cover (no date)-Has checklist on inside b/c to HRN #161 & different testimonial on back-c 6.50 19.50 45.00
"Mountain" cover (1968 re-issue; has white 50¢ circle) 5.70 17.00 36.00
132A-The Story of America (6/56); Cameron-a 5.70 17.00 38.00
135A-The Ten Commandments(12/56) 5.70 17.00 36.00
138A-Adventures in Science(6/57); HRN to 137 5.00 15.00 30.00
138A-(6/57)-2nd version w/HRN to 149 4.00 12.00 24.00
138A-(12/61)-3rd version w/HRN to 149 5.00 15.00 30.00
141A-The Rough Rider (Teddy Roosevelt)(12/57); Evans-a 5.70 17.00 36.00
144A-Blazing the Trails West(6/58)- 73 pgs. of Crandall/Evans plus Severin-a 5.70 17.00 36.00
147A-Crossing the Rockies(12/58)-Crandall/Evans-a 5.70 17.00 36.00
150A-Royal Canadian Police(6/59)-Ingels, Sid Check-a 5.70 17.00 36.00
153A-Men, Guns & Cattle(12/59)-Evans-a (26 pgs.); Kinstler-a 5.70 17.00 36.00
156A-The Atomic Age(6/60)-Crandall/Evans, Torres-a 5.70 17.00 36.00
159A-Rockets, Jets and Missiles(12/60)-Evans, Morrow-a 5.70 17.00 36.00
162A-War Between the States(6/61)-Kirby & Crandall/Evans-a; Ingels-a 10.50 32.00 85.00
165A-To the Stars(12/61)-Torres, Crandall/Evans, Kirby-a 5.70 17.00 36.00
166A-World War II('62)-Torres, Crandall/Evans, Kirby-a 8.50 26.00 60.00
167A-Prehistoric World(7/62)-Torres & Crandall/Evans-a; two versions exist (HRN to 165 & HRN to 167) 8.50 26.00 60.00
nn Special Issue-The United Nations (1964; 50¢; scarce); this is actually part of the European Special Series, which cont'd on after the U.S. series stopped issuing new titles in 1962. This English edition was prepared specifically for sale at the U.N. It was printed in Norway 28.00 83.00 220.00

NOTE: *There was another U.S. Special Issue prepared in 1962 with artwork by* ***Torres*** *entitled World War I. Unfortunately, it was never issued in any English-language edition. It was issued in 1964 in West Germany, The Netherlands, and some Scandanavian countries, with another edition in 1974 with a new cover.*

CLASSICS LIBRARY (See King Classics)

CLASSIC STAR WARS (Also see Star Wars)
Aug, 1992 - No. 20, June, 1994 ($2.50)
Dark Horse Comics

1-19: Star Wars strip-r by Williamson; Williamson redrew portions of the panels to fit comic book format; Williamson c-1-5,7,9,10,14,15,20: 8-Polybagged w/ Star Wars Galaxy trading card. 8,17-M. Schultz-c. 13-Yeates-c. 19-Evans-c 1.20 3.00
20-($3.50, 52 pgs.)-Polybagged w/trading card 1.40 3.50
Trade paperback ($29.95, slip-cased)-Reprints all movie adaptations 30.00

CLASSIC STAR WARS: A NEW HOPE
June, 1994 - No. 2, July, 1994 ($3.95, limited series)
Dark Horse Comics

1-r/Star Wars #1-3, 7-9 pubbed Marvel Comics 1.60 4.00
2-r/Star Wars #4-6, 10-12 pubbed Marvel Comics 1.60 4.00

CLASSIC STAR WARS: HAN SOLO AT STARS' END
Mar, 1997 - No.3, May, 1997 ($2.95, limited series)
Dark Horse Comics

1-3: r/strips by Alfredo Alcala 2.95

CLASSIC STAR WARS: RETURN OF THE JEDI
Oct, 1994 - No.2, Nov, 1994 ($3.50, limited series)
Dark Horse Comics

1,2: 1-r/1983-84 Marvel Comics series; polybagged with w/trading card 1.40 3.50

Claw the Unconquered #2 © DC

Clive Barker's Nightbreed #8 © Morgan Creek

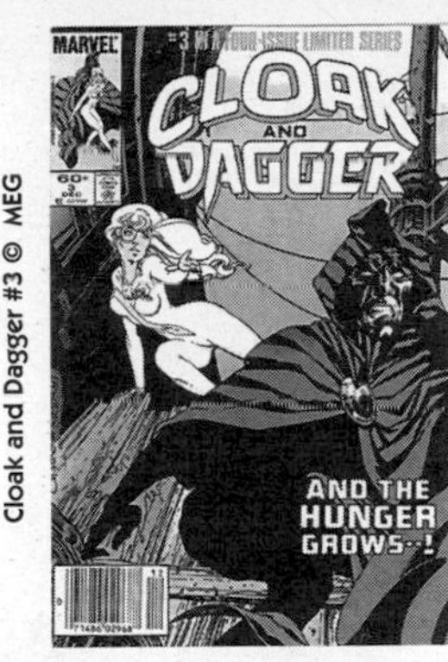

Cloak and Dagger #3 © MEG

CLASSIC STAR WARS: THE EARLY ADVENTURES
Aug, 1994 - No. 9, Apr, 1995 ($2.50, limited series)
Dark Horse Comics

	GD25	FN65	NM94
1-9		1.00	2.50

CLASSIC STAR WARS: THE EMPIRE STRIKES BACK
Aug, 1994 - No. 2, Sept, 1994 ($3.95, limited series)
Dark Horse Comics

	GD25	FN65	NM94
1-r/Star Wars #39-44 pubbed by Marvel Comics		1.60	4.00

CLASSIC X-MEN (Becomes X-Men Classic #46 on)
Sept, 1986 - No. 45, Mar, 1990
Marvel Comics Group

	GD25	FN65	NM94
1-Begins r of New X-Men		1.60	4.00
2-4		.90	2.25
5-9		.80	2.00
10-Sabretooth app.		1.10	2.75
11-15: 11-1st origin of Magneto in back-up story		.70	1.75
16,18-20			1.50
17-Wolverine-c		1.10	2.75
21-25,27-30: 27-r/X-Men #121; $1.25-c begins			1.50
26-r/X-Men #120; Wolverine-c/app.		1.10	2.75
31-38,40-42,44,45: 35-r/X-Men #129			1.50
39-New Jim Lee back-up story (2nd-a on X-Men)		1.20	3.00
43-Byrne-c/a(r); $1.75, double-size		.70	1.75

NOTE: ***Art Adams*** *c(p)-1-10, 12-16, 18, 19, 25.* ***Austin*** *c-19i.* ***Bolton*** *back up stories in 1-28 at least.* ***Williamson*** *c-12-14i.*

CLAW (See Capt. Battle, Jr. Daredevil Comics & Silver Streak Comics)

CLAW THE UNCONQUERED (See Cancelled Comic Cavalcade)
5-6/75 - No. 9, 9-10/76; No. 10, 4-5/78 - No. 12, 8-9/78
National Periodical Publications/DC Comics

	GD25	FN65	NM94
1,3,9:-1st app. Claw. 3-Nudity panel. 9-Origin		1.60	4.00
2,4-8,10-12		1.20	3.00

NOTE: ***Giffen*** *a-8-12p.* ***Kubert*** *c-10-12.* ***Layton*** *a-9i, 12i.*

CLAY CODY, GUNSLINGER
Fall, 1957
Pines Comics

	GD25	FN65	NM94
1-Painted-c	4.25	13.00	28.00

CLEAN FUN, STARRING "SHOOGAFOOTS JONES"
1944 (10¢, B&W, oversized covers, 24 pgs.)
Specialty Book Co.

	GD25	FN65	NM94
nn-Humorous situations involving Negroes in the Deep South			
White cover issue...	7.15	21.50	50.00
Dark grey cover issue...	8.50	26.00	60.00

CLEMENTINA THE FLYING PIG (See Dell Jr. Treasury)

CLEOPATRA (See Ideal, a Classical Comic No. 1)

CLIFF MERRITT SETS THE RECORD STRAIGHT
Giveaway (2 different issues)
Brotherhood of Railroad Trainsmen

	GD25	FN65	NM94
...and the Very Candid Candidate by Al Williamson		1.20	3.00
...Sets the Record Straight by Al Williamson (2 different-c: one by Williamson, the other by McWilliams)		1.20	3.00

CLIMAX! (Mystery)
July, 1955 - No. 2, Sept, 1955
Gillmor Magazines

	GD25	FN65	NM94
1,2	11.50	34.00	80.00

CLINT (Also see Adolescent Radioactive Black Belt Hamsters)
Sept, 1986 - No. 2, Jan, 1987 ($1.50, B&W)
Eclipse Comics

	GD25	FN65	NM94
1,2			1.50

CLINT & MAC (TV, Disney)
No. 889, Mar, 1958
Dell Publishing Co.

	GD25	FN65	NM94
Four Color 889-Alex Toth-a, photo-c	12.00	35.00	130.00

CLIVE BARKER'S BOOK OF THE DAMNED: A HELLRAISER COMPANION
Oct, 1991 - No. 3, Nov, 1992 ($4.95, semi-annual, 52 pgs.)
Marvel Comics (Epic Comics)

	GD25	FN65	NM94
Volume 1-3: 1-Simon Bisley-c. 2-(4/92). 3-(11/92)-McKean-a (1 pg.)		2.00	5.00

CLIVE BARKER'S HELLRAISER (Also see Epic, Hellraiser Nightbreed –Jihad, Revelations, Son of Celluloid, Tapping the Vein & Weaveworld)
1989 - No. 20, 1993 ($4.95, mature readers, quarterly, 68 pgs.)
Marvel Comics (Epic Comics)

	GD25	FN65	NM94
Book 1-Based on Hellraiser & Hellbound movies; Bolton-c/a; Spiegle & Wrightson-a (graphic album)		2.00	5.00
Book 2-4,14-16,18,19		2.00	5.00
Book 5-9 ($5.95): 7-Bolton-a. 8-Morrow-a		2.40	6.00
Book 10,11,13($4.50, 52 pgs.): 10-Foil-c. 11-Guice-p		1.80	4.50
Book 12-Sam Kieth-a		1.80	4.50
Book 17-Alex Ross-a, 34 pgs.	1.25	3.75	10.00
Book 20-By Gaiman/McKean	1.10	3.30	9.00
...Dark Holiday Special ('92, $4.95)-Conrad-a		2.00	5.00
...Spring Slaughter 1 ('94, $6.95, 52 pgs.)-Painted-c	1.00	2.80	7.00
...Summer Special 1 ('92, $5.95, 68 pgs.)		2.40	6.00

CLIVE BARKER'S NIGHTBREED (Also see Epic)
Apr, 1990 - No. 24, Feb, 1993 ($1.95/$2.25/$2.50, mature readers)
Marvel Comics (Epic Comics)

	GD25	FN65	NM94
1: 1-4-Adapt horror movie		.80	2.00
2-19: 5-New stories & $2.25-c begin; Guice-a(p)		.90	2.25
20-24: 20-Begin $2.50-c		1.00	2.50

CLIVE BARKER'S THE HARROWERS
Dec, 1993 - No. 9, May, 1994 ($2.50)
Marvel Comics (Epic Comics)

	GD25	FN65	NM94
1-($2.95)-Glow-in-the-dark-c; Colan-c/a in all		1.20	3.00
2-9		1.00	2.50

NOTE: ***Colan*** *a(p)-1-6; c-1-3, 4p, 5p.* ***Williamson*** *a(i)-2, 4, 5(part).*

CLOAK AND DAGGER
Fall, 1952
Ziff-Davis Publishing Co.

	GD25	FN65	NM94
1-Saunders painted-c	21.00	64.00	160.00

CLOAK AND DAGGER (Also see Marvel Fanfare)
Oct, 1983 - No. 4, Jan, 1984 (Mini-series)(See Spectacular Spider-Man #64)
Marvel Comics Group

	GD25	FN65	NM94
1-4-Austin-c/a(i) in all. 4-Origin			1.50

CLOAK AND DAGGER (Also see Marvel Graphic Novel #34, Mutant Misadventures Of... & Strange Tales, 2nd Series)
July, 1985 - No. 11, Jan, 1987
Marvel Comics Group

	GD25	FN65	NM94
1			1.50
2-8,10,11			1.00
9-Art Adams-p		.80	2.00
...And Power Pack (1990, $7.95, 68 pgs.)	1.00	3.00	8.00

NOTE: ***Mignola*** *c-7, 8.*

CLOBBERIN' TIME
Sept, 1995 ($1.95) (Based on card game)
Marvel Comics

	GD25	FN65	NM94
nn-Overpower game guide; Ben Grimm story		.80	2.00

CLONEZONE SPECIAL
1989 ($2.00, B&W)

Clutching Hand #1 © ACG

Codename: Firearm #0 © MAL

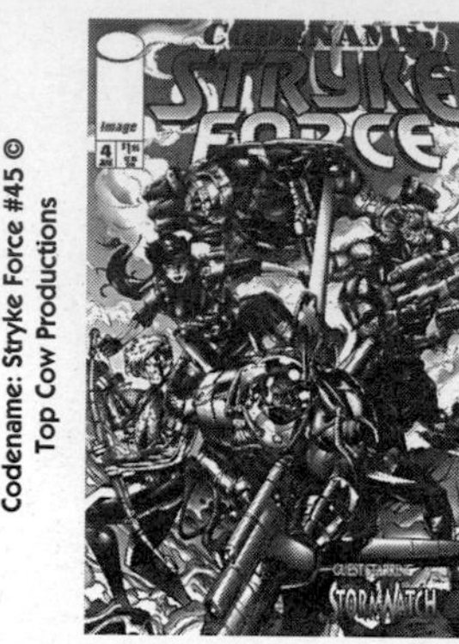

Codename: Stryke Force #45 © Top Cow Productions

Dark Horse Comics/First Comics

	GD25	FN65	NM94
1-Back-up series from Badger & Nexus		.80	2.00

CLOSE ENCOUNTERS (See Marvel Comics Super Special & Marvel Special Edition)

CLOSE SHAVES OF PAULINE PERIL, THE (TV?)
June, 1970 - No. 4, March, 1971 (Jay Ward?)
Gold Key

	GD25	FN65	NM94
1	2.50	7.50	20.00
2-4	1.50	4.50	12.00

CLOWN COMICS (No. 1 titled Clown Comic Book)
1945 - No. 3, Win, 1946
Clown Comics/Home Comics/Harvey Publ.

	GD25	FN65	NM94
nn (#1)	8.50	26.00	60.00
2,3	5.70	17.00	38.00

CLUBHOUSE RASCALS (#1 titled ...Presents?)
June, 1956 - No. 2, Oct, 1956 (Also see Three Rascals)
Sussex Publ. Co. (Magazine Enterprises)

	GD25	FN65	NM94
1,2: The Brain app.	4.25	13.00	28.00

CLUB "16"
June, 1948 - No. 4, Dec, 1948
Famous Funnies

	GD25	FN65	NM94
1-Teen-age humor	8.75	26.25	70.00
2-4	5.70	17.00	38.00

CLUE COMICS (Real Clue Crime V2#4 on)
Jan, 1943 - No. 15(V2#3), May, 1947
Hillman Periodicals

	GD25	FN65	NM94
1-Origin The Boy King, Nightmare, Micro-Face, Twilight, & Zippo	83.00	250.00	750.00
2	39.00	117.00	350.00
3-5	30.00	90.00	240.00
6,8,9: 8-Palais-c/a(2)	22.00	66.00	175.00
7-Classic torture-c	34.00	101.00	270.00
10-Origin/1st app. The Gun Master & begin series; content changes to crime	22.00	66.00	175.00
11	15.50	47.00	125.00
12-Origin Rackman; McWilliams-a, Guardineer-a(2)	20.00	60.00	160.00
V2#1-Nightmare new origin; Iron Lady app.; Simon & Kirby-a	36.00	108.00	325.00
V2#2-S&K-a(2)-Bondage/torture-c; man attacks & kills people with electric iron. Infantino-a	36.00	108.00	325.00
V2#3-S&K-a(3)	36.00	108.00	325.00

CLUELESS SPRING SPECIAL (TV)
May, 1997 ($3.99, magazine sized, one-shot)
Marvel Comics

	GD25	FN65	NM94
1-Photo-c from TV show		1.60	4.00

CLUTCHING HAND, THE
July-Aug, 1954
American Comics Group

	GD25	FN65	NM94
1	26.00	80.00	210.00

CLYDE BEATTY COMICS (Also see Crackajack Funnies)
October, 1953 (84 pgs.)
Commodore Productions & Artists, Inc.

	GD25	FN65	NM94
1-Photo front/back-c; movie scenes and comics	22.00	66.00	175.00
...African Jungle Book('56)-Richfield Oil Co. 16 pg. giveaway, soft-c	8.75	26.25	70.00

CLYDE CRASHCUP (TV)
Aug-Oct, 1963 - No. 5, Sept-Nov, 1964
Dell Publishing Co.

	GD25	FN65	NM94
1-All written by John Stanley	11.00	33.00	120.00
2-5	10.00	30.00	110.00

C-M-O COMICS
1942 - No. 2, 1942 (68 pgs., full color)
Chicago Mail Order Co.(Centaur)

	GD25	FN65	NM94
1-Invisible Terror, Super Ann, & Plymo the Rubber Man app. (all Centaur costume heroes)	69.00	207.00	625.00
2-Invisible Terror, Super Ann app.	44.00	132.00	400.00

COBALT BLUE (Also see Power Comics)
Sept, 1989 - No. 2, Oct, 1989 ($1.95, 28 pgs.)
Innovation Publishing

	GD25	FN65	NM94
1,2-Gustovich-c/a/scripts		.80	2.00
The Graphic Novel ($6.95, color, 52 pgs.)-r/1,2	1.00	2.80	7.00

COCOMALT BIG BOOK OF COMICS
1938 (Regular size, full color, 52 pgs.)
Harry 'A' Chesler (Cocomalt Premium)

	GD25	FN65	NM94
1-(Scarce)-Biro-c/a; Little Nemo by Winsor McCay Jr., Dan Hastings; Jack Cole, Guardineer, Gustavson, Bob Wood-a	189.00	567.00	1700.00

CODE NAME: ASSASSIN (See 1st Issue Special)

CODENAME: DANGER
Aug, 1985 - No. 4, May, 1986 ($1.50)
Lodestone Publishing

	GD25	FN65	NM94
1-4			1.50

CODENAME DOUBLE IMPACT
1997 ($2.95, B&W)
High Impact Entertainment

	GD25	FN65	NM94
1,2			2.95

CODENAME: FIREARM (Also see Firearm)
June, 1995 - No. 5, Sept, 1995 ($2.95, bimonthly limited series)
Malibu Comics (Ultraverse)

	GD25	FN65	NM94
0-5: 0-2-Alec Swan back-up story by James Robinson		1.20	3.00

NOTE: *Perez c-0.*

CODENAME: GENETIX
Jan, 1993 - No. 4, May, 1993 ($1.75, limited series)
Marvel Comics UK

	GD25	FN65	NM94
1-4: Wolverine in all		.70	1.75

CODENAME SPITFIRE (Formerly Spitfire And The Troubleshooters)
No. 10, July, 1987 - No. 13, Oct, 1987
Marvel Comics Group

	GD25	FN65	NM94
10-13: 10-Rogers-c/a			1.00

CODENAME: STRYKE FORCE (Also See Cyberforce V1#4 & Cyberforce/Stryke Force: Opposing Forces)
Jan, 1994 - No. 15, Sept, 1995 ($1.95/$2.25)
Image Comics (Top Cow Productions)

	GD25	FN65	NM94
0		1.00	2.50
1-12-Silvestri stories, Peterson-a. 1-wraparound-c. 4-Stormwatch app.		.80	2.00
1-Gold	1.25	3.75	10.00
1-Blue	2.50	7.50	20.00
13-15: 13-$2.25-c begins. 15-Story continues in Cyberforce/Stryke Force: Opposing Forces.		.90	2.25

CODE NAME: TOMAHAWK
Sept, 1986 ($1.75, high quality paper)
Fantasy General Comics

	GD25	FN65	NM94
1-Sci/fi		.70	1.75

CODE OF HONOR
Feb, 1997 - No. 4, May, 1997 ($5.95, limited series)
Marvel Comics

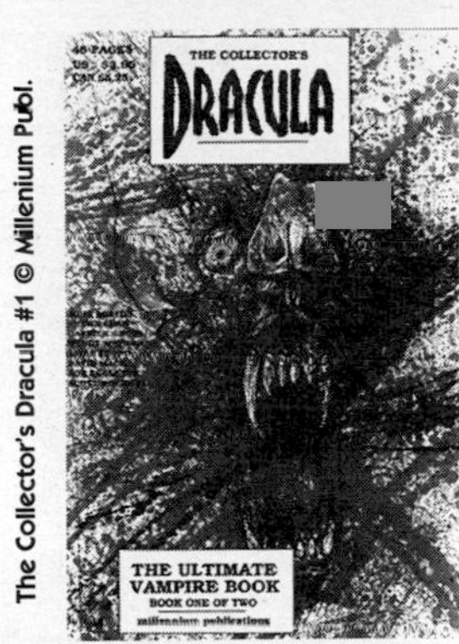

The Collector's Dracula #1 © Millenium Publ.

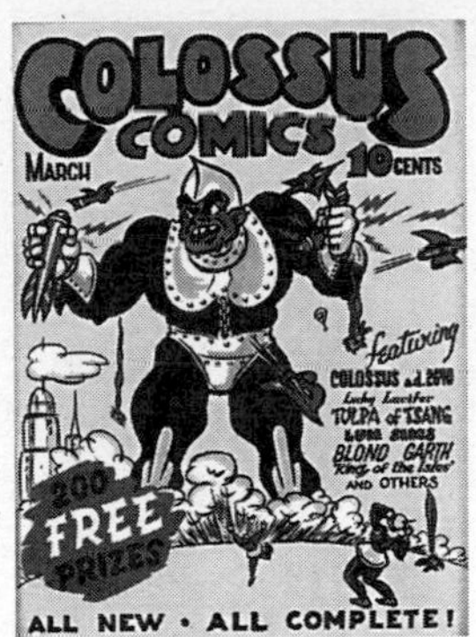

Colossus Comics #1 © Sun Publ.

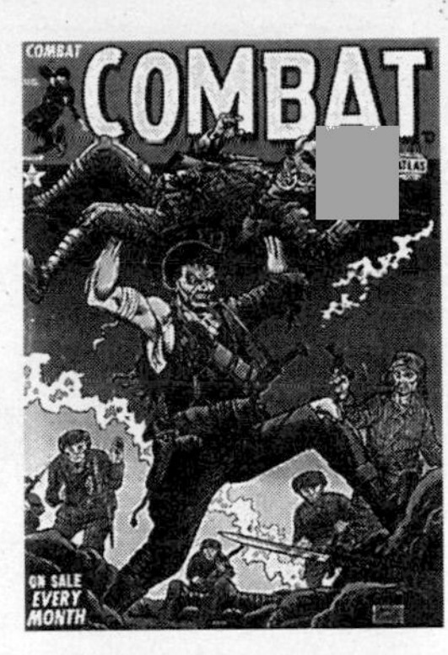

Combat #3 © ATLAS

GD25 FN65 NM94

1-4-Fully painted by various; Dixon-s 5.95

CODY OF THE PONY EXPRESS (See Colossal Features Magazine)
Sept, 1950 - No. 3, Jan, 1951 (See Women Outlaws)
Fox Features Syndicate
1-3 (Actually #3-5). 1-Painted-c 10.00 30.00 80.00

CODY OF THE PONY EXPRESS (Buffalo Bill...) (Outlaws of the West #11 on; Formerly Bullseye)
No. 8, Oct, 1955; No. 9, Jan, 1956; No. 10, June, 1956
Charlton Comics
8-Bullseye on splash pg; not S&K-a 5.70 17.00 40.00
9,10: Buffalo Bill app. in all 4.25 13.00 26.00

CODY STARBUCK (1st app. in Star Reach #1)
July, 1978 (2nd printing exists)
Star Reach Productions
nn-Howard Chaykin-c/a .80 2.00
NOTE: *Both printings say First Printing. True first printing is on lower-grade paper, somewhat off-register, and snow in snow sequence has green tint.*

CO-ED ROMANCES
November, 1951
P. L. Publishing Co.
1 5.35 16.00 32.00

COFFEE WORLD
Oct, 1995 ($1.50, B&W, anthology)
World Comics
1-Shannon Wheeler's Too Much Coffee Man story
1.50

COLLECTORS DRACULA, THE
1994 - No. 2, 1994 ($3.95, color/B&W, 52 pgs., limited series)
Millennium Publications
1-Bolton-a (7 pgs.) 1.60 4.00

COLLECTORS ITEM CLASSICS (See Marvel Collectors Item Classics)

COLORS IN BLACK
Mar, 1995 - No. 4, June, 1995 ($2.95, limited series)
Dark Horse Comics
1-4 1.20 3.00

COLOSSAL FEATURES MAGAZINE (Formerly I Loved) (See Cody of the Pony Express)
No. 33, 5/50 - No. 34, 7/50; No. 3, 9/50 (Based on Columbia serial)
Fox Features Syndicate
33,34: Cody of the Pony Express begins. 33-Painted-c. 34-Photo-c
10.00 30.00 75.00
3-Authentic criminal cases 10.00 30.00 75.00

COLOSSAL SHOW, THE (TV)
Oct, 1969
Gold Key
1 4.00 12.00 40.00

COLOSSUS (See X-Men)
Oct, 1997 ($2.99, 48 pgs., one-shot)
Marvel Comics
1-Raab-s/Hitch & Nealy-a, wraparound-c 2.99

COLOSSUS COMICS (See Green Giant & Motion Picture Funnies Weekly)
March, 1940
Sun Publications (Funnies, Inc.?)
1-(Scarce)-Tulpa of Tsang(hero); Colossus app. 289.00 867.00 2600.00
NOTE: *Cover by artist that drew Colossus in Green Giant Comics.*

COLOUR OF MAGIC, THE (Terry Pratchett's...)
1991 - No. 4, 1991 ($2.50, limited series)
Innovation Publishing
1-4: Adapts 1st novel of the Discworld series 1.00 2.50

COLT .45 (TV)
No. 924, 8/58 - No. 1058, 11-1/59-60; No. 4, 2-4/60 - No. 9, 5-7/61
Dell Publishing Co.
Four Color 924(#1)-Wayde Preston photo-c on all 9.00 27.00 100.00
Four Color 1004,1058, #4,5,7-9: 1004-Photo-b/c 7.00 20.00 75.00
6-Toth-a 8.00 23.00 85.00

COLUMBIA COMICS
1943
William H. Wise Co.
1-Joe Palooka, Charlie Chan, Capt. Yank, Sparky Watts, Dixie Dugan app.
23.00 68.00 180.00

COLUMBUS
Sept, 1992 ($2.50, B&W, one-shot)
Dark Horse Comics
1-Yeates painted-c 1.00 2.50

COMANCHE (See Four Color No. 1350)

COMANCHEROS, THE
No. 1300, Mar-May, 1962
Dell Publishing Co.
Four Color 1300-Movie, John Wayne photo-c 14.00 44.00 160.00

COMBAT
June, 1952 - No. 11, April, 1953
Atlas Comics (ANC)
1 16.00 49.00 130.00
2-Heath-c/a 8.50 26.00 60.00
3,5-9,11: 9-Robert Q. Sale-a 5.70 17.00 40.00
4-Krigstein-a 7.15 21.50 50.00
10-B&W and color illos. in **POP** 6.50 19.50 45.00
NOTE: *Combat Casey in 7-11.* ***Heath*** *c-1, 2, 9.* ***Maneely*** *a-1; c-3.* ***Pakula*** *a-1.* ***Reinman*** *a-1.*

COMBAT
Oct-Nov, 1961 - No. 40, Oct, 1973 (No #9)
Dell Publishing Co.
1 3.60 10.80 40.00
2,3,5: 2.20 6.60 24.00
4-John F. Kennedy c/story (P.T. 109) 2.75 8.00 30.00
6,7,8(4-6/63), 8(7-9/63) 1.80 5.50 20.00
10-26 1.50 4.50 15.00
27-40(reprints #1-14). 30-r/#4 1.30 4.00 12.00
NOTE: ***Glanzman*** *c/a-1-27, 28-40r.*

COMBAT CASEY (Formerly War Combat)
No. 6, Jan, 1953 - No. 34, July, 1957
Atlas Comics (SAI)
6 (Indicia shows 1/52 in error) 10.00 30.00 80.00
7-Spanking panel 8.75 26.25 65.00
8-Used in **POP**, pg. 94 5.70 17.00 40.00
9 5.70 17.00 35.00
10,13-19-Violent art by R. Q. Sale; Battle Brady x-over #10
8.50 26.00 60.00
11,12,20-Last Precode (2/55) 5.70 17.00 35.00
21-34 5.00 15.00 30.00
NOTE: ***Everett*** *a-6.* ***Heath*** *c-10, 17, 19, 30.* ***Maneely*** *c-6, 8.* ***Powell*** *a-29(5), 30(5), 34.* ***Severin*** *c-26, 33.*

COMBAT KELLY
Nov, 1951 - No. 44, Aug, 1957
Atlas Comics (SPI)
1-1st app. Combat Kelly; Heath-a 20.00 60.00 160.00
2 9.50 28.00 75.00

Combat Kelly #22 © ATLAS

The Comet #8 © Archie Publ.

Comic Album #12 © DELL

	GD25	FN65	NM94
3-10	7.15	21.50	50.00
11-Used in **POP**, pgs. 94,95 plus color illo.	5.70	17.00	40.00
12-Color illo. in **POP**	5.70	17.00	40.00
13-16	5.00	15.00	30.00
17-Violent art by R. Q. Sale; Combat Casey app.	8.50	26.00	60.00
18-20,22-44: 18-Battle Brady app. 28-Last precode (1/55). 38-Green Berets story (8/56)	5.00	15.00	30.00
21-Transvestism-c	5.70	17.00	40.00

NOTE: ***Berg** a-8, 12-14, 16, 17, 19-23, 25, 26, 28, 31-36, 42-44; c-2. **Colan** a-42. **Heath** a-4; c-31. **Lawrence** a-23. **Maneely** a-4(2), 6, 7(3), 8; c-4, 5, 7, 8, 10, 25. **R.Q. Sale** a-17, 25. **Severin** c-41, 42. **Whitney** a-5.*

COMBAT KELLY (...and the Deadly Dozen)
June, 1972 - No. 9, Oct, 1973
Marvel Comics Group

1-Intro & origin new Combat Kelly; Ayers/Mooney-a; Severin-c (20¢)	1.50	4.50	12.00
2-8	1.00	3.00	8.00
9-Death of the Deadly Dozen	1.25	3.75	10.00

COMBINED OPERATIONS (See The Story of the Commandos)

COMEBACK (See Zane Grey 4-Color 357)

COMEDY CARNIVAL
no date (1950's) (100 pgs.)
St. John Publishing Co.

nn-Contains rebound St. John comics	28.00	84.00	225.00

COMEDY COMICS (1st Series) (Daring Mystery #1-8) (Becomes Margie Comics #35 on)
No. 9, April, 1942 - No. 34, Fall, 1946
Timely Comics (TCI 9,10)

9-(Scarce)-The Fin by Everett, Capt. Dash, Citizen V, & The Silver Scorn app.; Wolverton-a; 1st app. Comedy Kid; satire on Hitler & Stalin; The Fin, Citizen V & Silver Scorn cont. from Daring Mystery	233.00	700.00	2100.00
10-(Scarce)-Origin The Fourth Musketeer, Victory Boys; Monstro, the Mighty app.	167.00	500.00	1500.00
11-Vagabond, Stuporman app.	40.00	120.00	360.00
12,13	12.00	36.00	95.00
14-Origin/1st app. Super Rabbit (3/43) plus-c	40.00	120.00	360.00
15-20	10.00	30.00	80.00
21-32	8.50	26.00	60.00
33-Kurtzman-a (5 pgs.)	9.50	28.00	75.00
34-Intro Margie; Wolverton-a (5 pgs.)	15.00	45.00	120.00

COMEDY COMICS (2nd Series)
May, 1948 - No. 10, Jan, 1950
Marvel Comics (ACI)

1-Hedy, Tessie, Millie begin; Kurtzman's "Hey Look" (he draws himself)	26.00	80.00	210.00
2	9.50	28.00	75.00
3,4-Kurtzman's "Hey Look" (?&3)	11.30	34.00	90.00
5-10	5.70	17.00	40.00

COMET, THE (See The Mighty Crusaders & Pep Comics #1)
Oct, 1983 - No. 2, Dec, 1983
Red Circle Comics (Archie)

1,2: 1-Re-intro & origin The Comet; The American Shield begins. 2-Origin continues			1.00

COMET, THE
July, 1991 - No. 18, Dec, 1992 ($1.00/$1.25)
DC Comics (Impact Comics)

1-13: 4-Black Hood app. 6-Re-intro Hangman. 8-Web x-over. 10-Contains Crusaders trading card. 13-Last $1.00-c			1.00
14-18: 14-Origin. Netzer(Nasser) c(p)-11,14-17			1.25
Annual 1 (1992, $2.50, 68 pgs.)-Contains Impact trading card; Shield back-up story		1.00	2.50

COMET MAN, THE (Movie)
Feb, 1987 - No. 6, July, 1987 (limited series)
Marvel Comics Group

1-3,5,6: 3-Hulk app. 5-Fantastic 4 app.			1.50
4-She Hulk shower scene c/s. Fantastic 4 app.		1.20	3.00

NOTE: ***Kelley Jones** a-1-6p.*

COMIC ALBUM (Also see Disney Comic Album)
Mar-May, 1958 - No. 18, June-Aug, 1962
Dell Publishing Co.

1-Donald Duck	7.00	22.00	80.00
2-Bugs Bunny	3.60	11.00	40.00
3-Donald Duck	5.50	16.50	60.00
4-6,8-10: 4-Tom & Jerry. 5-Woody Woodpecker. 6,10-Bugs Bunny. 8-Tom & Jerry. 9-Woody Woodpecker	2.75	8.00	30.00
7,11: 7-Popeye (9-11/59). 11-Popeye (9-11/60)	3.60	11.00	40.00
12-14: 12-Tom & Jerry. 13-Woody Woodpecker. 14-Bugs Bunny	2.75	8.00	30.00
15-Popeye	3.60	11.00	40.00
16-Flintstones (12-2/61-62)-3rd app.	6.40	19.00	70.00
17-Space Mouse (3rd app.)	3.60	11.00	40.00
18-Three Stooges; photo-c	6.40	19.00	70.00

COMIC BOOK (Also see Comics From Weatherbird)
1954 (Giveaway)
American Juniors Shoe

Contains a comic rebound with new cover. Several combinations possible. Contents determines price.

COMIC BOOK
1995 ($6.95, oversize)
Marvel Comics

1-Spumco characters by John K.	1.00	2.80	7.00

COMIC BOOK MAGAZINE
1940 - 1943 (Similar to Spirit Sections)(7-3/4x10-3/4"; full color; 16-24 pgs. ea.)
Chicago Tribune & other newspapers

1940 issues	5.70	17.50	35.00
1941, 1942 issues	4.25	13.00	28.00
1943 issues	4.00	12.00	24.00

NOTE: *Published weekly. Texas Slim, Kit Carson, Spooky, Josie, Nuts & Jolts, Lew Loyal, Brenda Starr, Daniel Boone, Captain Storm, Rocky, Smokey Stover, Tiny Tim, Little Joe, Fu Manchu appear among others. Early issues had photo stories with pictures from the movies; later issues had comic art.*

COMIC BOOKS (Series 1)
1950 (16 pgs.; 5-1/4x8-1/2"; full color; bound at top; paper cover)
Metropolitan Printing Co. (Giveaway)

1-Boots and Saddles; intro The Masked Marshal	5.00	15.00	30.00
1-The Green Jet; Green Lama by Raboy	25.00	75.00	200.00
1-My Pal Dizzy (Teen-age)	2.80	7.00	14.00
1-New World; origin Atomaster (costumed hero)	7.85	23.50	55.00
1-Talullah (Teen-age)	2.80	7.00	14.00

COMIC CAPERS
Fall, 1944 - No. 6, Summer, 1946
Red Circle Mag./Marvel Comics

1-Super Rabbit, The Creeper, Silly Seal, Ziggy Pig, Sharpy Fox begin	19.00	56.00	150.00
2	9.50	28.00	75.00
3-6	8.50	26.00	60.00

COMIC CAVALCADE
Winter, 1942-43 - No. 63, June-July, 1954
(Contents change with No. 30, Dec-Jan, 1948-49 on)

Comic Cavalcade #16 © DC

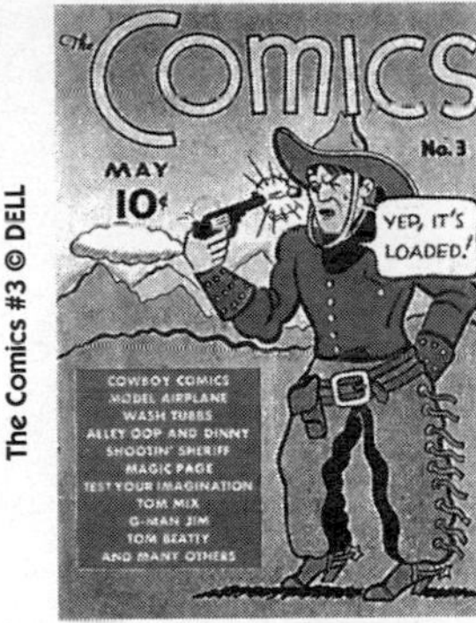

The Comics #3 © DELL

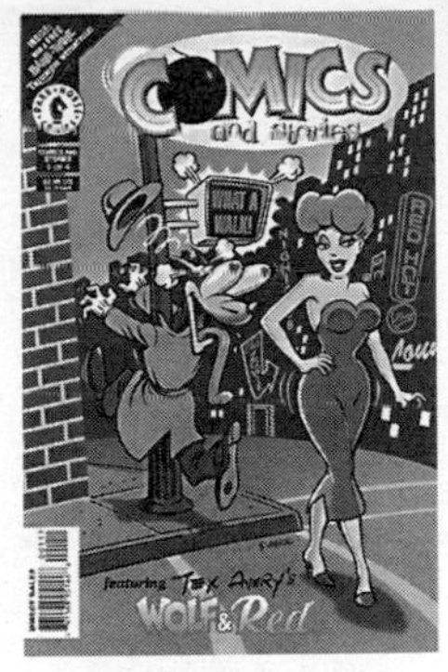

Comics and Stories #1 © DH

All-American/National Periodical Publications

	GD25	FN65	VF82	NM94
1-The Flash, Green Lantern, Wonder Woman, Wildcat, The Black Pirate by Moldoff (also #2), Ghost Patrol, and Red White & Blue begin; Scribbly app.; Minute Movie	800.00	2400.00	4800.00	8000.00

(Estimated up to 175 total copies exist, 6 in NM/Mint)

	GD25	FN65	NM94
2-Mutt & Jeff begin; last Ghost Patrol & Black Pirate; Minute Movies	189.00	567.00	1700.00
3-Hop Harrigan & Sargon, the Sorcerer begin; The King app.	139.00	417.00	1250.00
4,5: 4-The Gay Ghost, The King, Scribbly, & Red Tornado app. 5-Christmas-c. 5-Prints ad for Jr. JSA membership kit that includes "The Minute Man Answers The Call"	117.00	350.00	1050.00
6-10: 7-Red Tornado & Black Pirate app.; last Scribbly. 9-Fat & Slat app.; X-Mas-c	89.00	267.00	800.00
11,12,14-20: 12-Last Red White & Blue. 15-Johnny Peril begins (1st app., 6-7/46), ends #29. 19-Christmas-c	75.00	225.00	675.00
13-Solomon Grundy app.; X-Mas-c	117.00	350.00	1050.00
21-23: 23-Harry Lampert-c (Toth swipes)	75.00	225.00	675.00
24-Solomon Grundy x-over in Green Lantern	86.00	258.00	775.00
25-28: 25-Black Canary app.; X-Mas-c. 26-28-Johnny Peril app. 28-Last Mutt & Jeff	58.00	174.00	525.00
29-(10-11/48)-Last Flash, Wonder Woman, Green Lantern & Johnny Peril; Wonder Woman invents "Thinking Machine"; 1st computer in comics?; Leave It to Binky story (early app.)	67.00	200.00	600.00
30-(12-1/48-49)-The Fox & the Crow, Dodo & the Frog & Nutsy Squirrel begin	36.00	108.00	320.00
31-35	20.00	60.00	160.00
36-49	14.00	41.00	110.00
50-62(Scarce)	17.50	53.00	140.00
63(Rare)	29.00	86.00	230.00
Giveaway (1944, 8 pgs., paper-c, in color)-One Hundred Years of Co-operation-r/Comic Cavalcade #9	61.00	183.00	550.00
Giveaway (1945, 16 pgs., paper-c, in color)-Movie "Tomorrow The World" (Nazi theme); r/Comic Cavalcade #10	83.00	250.00	750.00
Giveaway (c. 1944-45; 8 pgs, paper-c, in color)-The Twain Shall Meet-r/Comic Cavalcade #8	72.00	216.00	650.00

NOTE: ***Grossman** a-30-63. **E.E. Hibbard** c-(Flash only)-1-4, 7-14, 16-19, 21. **Sheldon Mayer** a(2-3)-40-63. **Moulson** c(G.L.)-7, 15. **Nodell** c(G.L.)-9. **H.G. Peter** c(W. Woman only)-1, 3-21, 24. **Post** a-31, 36. **Purcell** c(G.L.)-2-5, 10. **Reinman** a(Green Lantern)-4-6, 8, 9, 13, 15-21; c(Gr. Lantern)-6, 8, 19. **Toth** a(Green Lantern)-26-28; c-27. Atom app.-22, 23.*

COMIC COMICS
Apr, 1946 - No. 10, Feb, 1947
Fawcett Publications

	GD25	FN65	NM94
1-Captain Kidd; Nutty Comics #1 in indicia	9.50	28.00	75.00
2-10-Wolverton-a, 4 pgs. each. 5-Captain Kidd app. Mystic Moot by Wolverton in #2-10?	10.50	32.00	85.00

COMIC CUTS (Also see The Funnies)
5/19/34 - 7/28/34 (5¢, 24 pgs.) (Tabloid size in full color)
(Not reprints; published weekly; created for newsstand sale)
H. L. Baker Co., Inc.

	GD25	FN65	NM94
V1#1 - V1#7(6/30/34), V1#8(7/14/34), V1#9(7/28/34)-Idle Jack strips	8.50	26.00	60.00

COMIC LAND
March, 1946
Fact and Fiction Publ.

	GD25	FN65	NM94
1-Sandusky & the Senator, Sam Stupor, Sleuth, Marvin the Great, Sir Passer, Phineas Gruff app.; Irv Tirman & Perry Williams art	10.00	30.00	80.00

COMICO CHRISTMAS SPECIAL
Dec, 1988 ($2.50, 44pgs.)
Comico

	GD25	FN65	NM94
1-Rude/Williamson-a; Dave Stevens-c		1.00	2.50

COMICO PRIMER (See Primer)

COMIC PAGES (Formerly Funny Picture Stories)
V3#4, July, 1939 - V3#6, Dec, 1939
Centaur Publications

	GD25	FN65	NM94
V3#4-Bob Wood-a	58.00	174.00	525.00
5,6: 6-Schwab-c	44.00	132.00	400.00

COMICS (See All Good)

COMICS, THE
Mar, 1937 - No. 11, Nov, 1938 (Newspaper strip-r; bi-monthly)
Dell Publishing Co.

	GD25	FN65	NM94
1-1st app. Tom Mix in comics; Wash Tubbs, Tom Beatty, Myra North, Arizona Kid, Erik Noble & International Spy w/Doctor Doom begin	139.00	417.00	1250.00
2	67.00	200.00	600.00
3-11: 3-Alley Oop begins	53.00	159.00	475.00

COMICS AND STORIES (See Walt Disney's.Comics and Stories)

COMICS & STORIES (Also see Wolf & Red)
Apr, 1996 - No. 3, June, 1996 ($2.95, limited series) (Created by Tex Avery)
Dark Horse Comics

	GD25	FN65	NM94
1-3: Wolf & Red app; reads Comics and Stories on-c. 1-Terry Moore-a. 2-Reed Waller-a.		1.20	3.00

COMICS CALENDAR, THE (The 1946...)
1946 (25¢, 116 pgs.)(Stapled at top)
True Comics Press (ordered through the mail)

	GD25	FN65	NM94
nn-(Rare) Has a "strip" story for every day of the year in color	33.00	100.00	265.00

COMICS DIGEST (Pocket size)
Winter, 1942-43 (B&W, 100 pgs)
Parents' Magazine Institute

	GD25	FN65	NM94
1-Reprints from True Comics (non-fiction World War II stories)	7.85	23.50	55.00

COMIC SELECTIONS (Shoe store giveaway)
1944-46 (Reprints from Calling All Girls, True Comics, True Aviation, & Real Heroes)
Parents' Magazine Press

	GD25	FN65	NM94
1	4.00	10.00	20.00
2-5	3.20	8.00	16.00

COMICS EXPRESS
Nov, 1989 - No. 2, Jan, 1990 ($2.95, B&W, 68pgs.)
Eclipse Comics

	GD25	FN65	NM94
1,2: Collection of strip-r; 2(12/89-c, 1/90 inside)		1.20	3.00

COMICS FOR KIDS
1945 (no month); No. 2, Sum, 1945 (Funny animal)
London Publishing Co./Timely

	GD25	FN65	NM94
1,2-Puffy Pig, Sharpy Fox	10.00	30.00	80.00

COMICS FROM WEATHER BIRD (Also see Comic Book, Edward's Shoes, Free Comics to You & Weather Bird)
1954 - 1957 (Giveaway)
Weather Bird Shoes
Contains a comic bound with new cover. Many combinations possible. Contents would determine price. Some issues do not contain complete comics, but only parts of comics.Value equals 40 to 60 percent of contents.

COMICS' GREATEST WORLD
June, 1993 - V4#4, Sept, 1993 ($1.00, weekly, limited series)
Dark Horse Comics

Arcadia (Week 1)

	GD25	FN65	NM94
V1#1,2,4: 1-X: Frank Miller-c. 2-Pit Bulls. 4-Monster.			1.00

Comics Greatest World V1#3 © DH

Comics On Parade #29 © UFS

Comics On Parade #38 © UFS

GD25 FN65 NM94

1-B&W Press Proof Edition (1500 copies) 1.50 4.50 12.00
1-Silver-c; distr. retailer bonus w/print & cards 1.25 3.75 10.00
3-Ghost, Dorman-c; Hughes-a 2.00 5.00
Retailer's Premium Embossed Silver Foil Logo-r/V1#1-4.
1.50 4.50 12.00
Golden City (Week 2)
V2#1-4: 1-Rebel; Ordway-c. 2-Mecha; Dave Johnson-c. 3-Titan; Walt Simonson-c. 4-Catalyst; Perez-c. 1.00
1-Gold-c; distr. retailer bonus w/print & cards. 1.00 3.00 8.00
Retailer's Premium Embossed Gold Foil Logo-r/V2#1-4.
1.25 3.75 10.00
Steel Harbor (Week 3)
V3#1-Barb Wire; Dorman-c; Gulacy-a(p) 2.00 5.00
2-4: 2-The Machine; Mignola-c. 3-Wolfgang; Warner-c. 4-Motorhead
1.00
1-Silver-c; distr. retailer bonus w/print & cards 1.25 3.75 10.00
Retailer's Premium Embossed Red Foil Logo-r/V3#1-4.
1.50 4.50 12.00
Vortex (Week 4)
V4#1-4: 1-Division 13; Dorman-c. 2-Hero Zero; Art Adams-c. 3-King Tiger; Chadwick-a(p); Darrow-c. 4-Vortex; Miller-c. 1.00
1-Gold-c; distr. retailer bonus w/print & cards. 1.00 3.00 8.00
Retailer's Premium Embossed Blue Foil Logo-r/V4#1-4.
1.25 3.75 10.00

COMICS' GREATEST WORLD: OUT OF THE VORTEX (See Out of The Vortex)

COMICS HITS (See Harvey Comics Hits)

COMICS MAGAZINE, THE (...Funny Pages #3)(Funny Pages #6 on)
May, 1936 - No. 5, Sept, 1936 (Paper covers)
Comics Magazine Co. (1st Comics Mag./Centaur Publ.)

GD25 FN65 VF82

1-1st app. Dr. Mystic (a.k.a. Dr. Occult) by Siegel & Shuster (the 1st app. of a Superman prototype in comics). Dr. Mystic is not in costume but later appears in costume as a more pronounced prototype in More Fun #14-17. (1st episode of "The Koth and the Seven"; continues in More Fun #14; originally scheduled for publication at DC). 1 pg. Kelly-a; Sheldon Mayer-a
950.00 2850.00 9500.00
(Estimated up to 10 total copies exist)

GD25 FN65 NM94

2-Federal Agent (a.k.a. Federal Men) by Siegel & Shuster; 1 pg. Kelly-a
200.00 600.00 1800.00
3-5 156.00 468.00 1400.00

COMICS NOVEL (Anarcho, Dictator of Death)
1947
Fawcett Publications

1-All Radar; 51 pg anti-fascism story 24.00 71.00 190.00

COMICS ON PARADE (No. 30 on are a continuation of Single Series)
Apr, 1938 - No. 104, Feb, 1955
United Features Syndicate

1-Tarzan by Foster; Captain & the Kids, Little Mary Mixup, Abbie & Slats, Ella Cinders, Broncho Bill, Li'l Abner begin 280.00 840.00 2800.00
2 (Tarzan & others app. on-c of #1-3,17) 111.00 333.00 1000.00
3 89.00 267.00 800.00
4,5 67.00 200.00 600.00
6-10 44.00 132.00 400.00
11-16,18-20 36.00 108.00 325.00
17-Tarzan-c 42.00 126.00 375.00
21-29: 22-Son of Tarzan begins. 22,24,28-Tailspin Tommy-c. 29-Last Tarzan issue 31.00 94.00 250.00
30-Li'l Abner 20.00 60.00 160.00
31-The Captain & the Kids 14.00 41.00 110.00
32-Nancy & Fritzi Ritz 11.30 34.00 90.00
33-Li'l Abner 16.00 49.00 130.00

GD25 FN65 NM94

34-The Captain & the Kids (10/41) 14.00 41.00 110.00
35-Nancy & Fritzi Ritz 11.30 34.00 90.00
36-Li'l Abner 16.00 49.00 130.00
37-The Captain & the Kids (6/42) 14.00 41.00 110.00
38-Nancy & Fritzi Ritz; infinity-c 11.30 34.00 90.00
39-Li'l Abner 16.00 49.00 130.00
40-The Captain & the Kids (3/43) 14.00 41.00 110.00
41-Nancy & Fritzi Ritz 8.75 26.25 70.00
42-Li'l Abner 16.00 49.00 130.00
43-The Captain & the Kids 14.00 41.00 110.00
44-Nancy & Fritzi Ritz (3/44) 8.75 26.25 70.00
45-Li'l Abner 14.00 41.00 110.00
46-The Captain & the Kids 11.30 34.00 90.00
47-Nancy & Fritzi Ritz 8.75 26.25 70.00
48-Li'l Abner (3/45) 14.00 41.00 110.00
49-The Captain & the Kids 11.30 34.00 90.00
50-Nancy & Fritzi Ritz 8.75 26.25 70.00
51-Li'l Abner 11.30 34.00 90.00
52-The Captain & the Kids (3/46) 8.50 26.00 60.00
53-Nancy & Fritzi Ritz 8.50 26.00 60.00
54-Li'l Abner 11.30 34.00 90.00
55-Nancy & Fritzi Ritz 8.50 26.00 60.00
56-The Captain & the Kids (r/Sparkler) 8.50 26.00 60.00
57-Nancy & Fritzi Ritz 8.50 26.00 60.00
58-Li'l Abner; continues as Li'l Abner #61? 11.30 34.00 90.00
59-The Captain & the Kids 6.85 21.00 48.00
60-70-Nancy & Fritzi Ritz 6.85 21.00 48.00
71-76-Nancy only 5.70 17.00 35.00
77-99,101-104-Nancy & Sluggo 5.70 17.00 35.00
100-Nancy & Sluggo 6.50 19.50 45.00
Special Issue, 7/46; Summer, 1948 - The Captain & the Kids app.
5.70 17.00 35.00
NOTE: Bound Volume (Very Rare) includes No. 1-12; bound by publisher in pictorial comic boards & distributed at the 1939 World's Fair and through mail order from ads in comic books (also see Tip Top) 222.00 667.00 2000.00
NOTE: *Li'l Abner reprinted from Tip Top.*

COMICS READING LIBRARIES (Educational Series)
1973, 1977, 1979 (36 pgs. in color) (Giveaways)
King Features (Charlton Publ.)

R-01-Tiger, Quincy 2.00 5.00
R-02-Beetle Bailey, Blondie & Popeye 1.00 3.00 8.00
R-03-Blondie, Beetle Bailey 2.00 5.00
R-04-Tim Tyler's Luck, Felix the Cat 1.85 5.50 15.00
R-05-Quincy, Henry 2.00 5.00
R-06-The Phantom, Mandrake 1.85 5.50 15.00
1977 reprint(R-04) 1.00 3.00 8.00
R-07-Popeye, Little King 1.25 3.75 10.00
R-08-Prince Valiant(Foster), Flash Gordon 2.25 6.75 18.00
1977 reprint 1.50 4.50 12.00
R-09-Hagar the Horrible, Boner's Ark 1.00 3.00 8.00
R-10-Redeye, Tiger 2.00 5.00
R-11-Blondie, Hi & Lois 2.00 5.00
R-12-Popeye-Swee'pea, Brutus 1.25 3.75 10.00
R-13-Beetle Bailey, Little King 2.00 5.00
R-14-Quincy-Hamlet 2.00 5.00
R-15-The Phantom, The Genius 1.50 4.50 12.00
R-16-Flash Gordon, Mandrake 2.25 6.75 18.00
1977 reprint 1.25 3.75 10.00
Other 1977 editions.... 2.00 5.00
1979 editions(68pgs.) 2.00 5.00
NOTE: *Above giveaways available with purchase of $45.00 in merchandise. Used as a reading skills aid for small children.*

COMICS REVUE
June, 1947 - No. 5, Jan, 1948

Commander Battle and the Atomic Sub #1 © ACG

Complete Love Magazine V26 #3 © ACE

Conan Classic #4 © MEG

GD25 FN65 NM94

St. John Publ. Co. (United Features Synd.)

	GD25	FN65	NM94
1-Ella Cinders & Blackie	8.75	26.25	65.00
2-Hap Hopper (7/47)	6.50	19.50	45.00
3-Iron Vic (8/47)	5.70	17.00	40.00
4-Ella Cinders (9/47)	6.50	19.50	45.00
5-Gordo No. 1 (1/48)	5.70	17.00	40.00

COMIC STORY PAINT BOOK
1943 (Large size, 68 pgs.)
Samuel Lowe Co.

1055-Captain Marvel & a Captain Marvel Jr. story to read & color; 3 panels in color per pg. (reprints) 60.00 180.00 600.00

COMIX BOOK
1974 - No. 5, 1976 ($1.00, B&W, magazine)
Marvel Comics Group/Krupp Comics Works No. 4,5

	GD25	FN65	NM94
1-Underground comic artists; 2 pgs. Wolverton-a	2.50	7.50	24.00
2-Wolverton-a (1 pg.)	2.25	6.75	18.00
3-Low distribution (3/75)	2.50	7.50	24.00
4(2/76), 4(5/76), 5	1.50	4.50	12.00

NOTE: *Print run No. 1-3: 200-250M; No. 4&5: 10M each.*

COMIX INTERNATIONAL
July, 1974 - No. 5, Spring, 1977 (Full color)
Warren Magazines

	GD25	FN65	NM94
1-Low distribution; all Corben story remainders from Warren	7.50	22.50	75.00
2-Wood, Wrightson-r	2.50	7.50	25.00
3-5: 4-(printing without Corben story). 4-Crandall-a. 5-Spirit story	2.50	7.50	20.00
4-printing w/Corben story	2.50	7.50	25.00

NOTE: *No. 4 had two printings with extra **Corben** story in one. No. 3 may also have a variation. No. 3 has two Jeff Jones reprints from Vampirella.*

COMMANDER BATTLE AND THE ATOMIC SUB
July-Aug, 1954 - No. 7, Aug-Sept, 1955
American Comics Group (Titan Publ. Co.)

	GD25	FN65	NM94
1 (3-D effect)-Moldoff flying saucer-c	40.00	120.00	325.00
2,4-7: 2-Moldoff-c. 4-(1-2/55)-Last pre-code; Landau-a. 5-3-D effect story (2 pgs.). 6,7-Landau-a. 7-Flying saucer-c	26.00	77.00	190.00
3-H-Bomb-c; Atomic Sub becomes Atomic Spaceship	27.00	81.00	200.00

COMMANDMENTS OF GOD
1954, 1958
Catechetical Guild

300-Same contents in both editions; diff-c 2.00 5.00 10.00

COMMANDO ADVENTURES
June, 1957 - No. 2, Aug, 1957
Atlas Comics (MMC)

1,2-Severin-c. 2-Drucker-a? 6.85 21.00 48.00

COMMANDO YANK (See The Mighty Midget Comics & Wow Comics)

COMPLETE BOOK OF COMICS AND FUNNIES
1944 (25¢, one-shot, 196 pgs.)
William H. Wise & Co.

1-Origin Brad Spencer, Wonderman; The Magnet, The Silver Knight by Kinstler, & Zudo the Jungle Boy app. 35.00 105.00 280.00

COMPLETE BOOK OF TRUE CRIME COMICS
No date (Mid 1940's) (25¢, 132 pgs.)
William H. Wise & Co.

nn-Contains Crime Does Not Pay rebound (includes #22) 81.00 243.00 700.00

COMPLETE COMICS (Formerly Amazing Comics No. 1)
No. 2, Winter, 1944-45
Timely Comics (EPC)

2-The Destroyer, The Whizzer, The Young Allies & Sergeant Dix; Schomburg-c 122.00 366.00 1100.00

COMPLETE LOVE MAGAZINE (Formerly a pulp with same title)
V26#2, May-June, 1951 - V32#4(#191), Sept, 1956
Ace Periodicals (Periodical House)

	GD25	FN65	NM94
V26#2-Painted-c (52 pgs.)	4.25	13.00	28.00
V26#3-6(2/52), V27#1(4/52)-6(1/53)	4.00	10.00	20.00
V28#1(3/53), V28#2(5/53), V29#3(7/53)-6(12/53)	3.20	8.00	16.00
V30#1(2/54), V30#1(#176, 4/54),2,4-6(#181, 1/55)	3.20	8.00	16.00
V30#3(#178)-Rock Hudson photo-c	4.00	12.00	24.00
V31#1(#182, 3/55)-Last precode	3.20	8.00	16.00
V31#2(5/55)-6(#187, 1/56)	2.00	5.00	10.00
V32#1(#188, 3/56)-4(#191, 9/56)	2.00	5.00	10.00

NOTE: *(34 total issues). Photo-c V27#5-on. Painted-c V26#3.*

COMPLETE MYSTERY (True Complete Mystery No. 5 on)
Aug, 1948 - No. 4, Feb, 1949 (Full length stories)
Marvel Comics (PrPI)

	GD25	FN65	NM94
1-Seven Dead Men	40.00	120.00	315.00
2-Jigsaw of Doom!	39.00	118.00	285.00
3-Fear in the Night; Burgos-c/a (28 pgs.)	39.00	118.00	285.00
4-A Squealer Dies Fast	39.00	118.00	285.00

COMPLETE ROMANCE
1949
Avon Periodicals

1-(Scarce)-Reprinted as Women to Love 34.00 103.00 250.00

COMPLIMENTARY COMICS
No date (1950's) (Giveaway)
Sales Promotion Publ.

1-Strongman by Powell, 3 stories 5.70 17.00 38.00

CONAN (See Chamber of Darkness #4, Giant-Size..., Handbook of..., King Conan, Marvel Graphic Novel #19, 28, Marvel Treasury Ed., Power Record Comics, Robert E. Howard's..., Savage Sword of Conan, and Savage Tales)

CONAN
Aug, 1995 - No. 11, June, 1996 ($2.95)
Marvel Comics

1-11: 4-Malibu Comic's Rune app. 1.20 3.00

CONAN CLASSIC
June, 1994 - No. 11, Apr, 1995 ($1.50)
Marvel Comics

1-11: 1-r/Conan #1 by B. Smith, r/covers w/changes. 2-11-r/Conan #2-11 by Smith 1.50
2-Bound w/cover to Conan The Adventurer #2 by mistake 1.50

CONAN SAGA, THE
June, 1987 - No. 97, Apr, 1995 ($2.00/$2.25, B&W, magazine)
Marvel Comics

1-Barry Smith-r 1-9,11; new Barry Smith-c 1-9 .80 2.00
2-27: 13,15-Boris-c. 17-Adams-r. 18,25-Chaykin-r. 22-r/Giant-Size Conan 1,2 .80 2.00
28-97 ($2.25): 31-Red Sonja-r by N. Adams/SSOC #1; 1 pg. Jeff Jones-r. 32-Newspaper strip-r begin by Buscema. 33-Smith/Conrad-a. 39-r/Kull #1('71) by Andru/Wood. 44-Swipes-c/Savage Tales #1. 57-Brunner-r/SSOC #30. 66-r/Conan Annual #2 by Buscema. 79-r/Conan #43-45 w/Red Sonja. 85-Based on Conan #57-63 .90 2.25

NOTE: ***J. Buscema** r-32-on; c-86. **Chaykin** r-34. **Chiodo** painted c-63, 65, 66, 82. **G. Colan** a-47p. **Jusko** painted c-64, 83. **Kaluta** c-84. **Nino** a-37. **Ploog** a-50. **N. Redondo** painted c-48, 50, 51, 53, 57, 62. **Simonson** r-50-54, 56. **B. Smith** r-51. **Starlin** c-34. **Williamson** r-50i.*

CONAN THE ADVENTURER
June, 1994 - No. 14, July, 1995 ($1.50)

Conan The Adventurer #4 © MEG

Conan The Barbarian #241 © MEG

Concrete: Killer Smile #1 © DH

GD25 FN65 NM94

Marvel Comics
1-($2.50)-Embossed foil-c; Kayaran-a 1.00 2.50
2-14 1.50
2-Contents are Conan Classics #2 by mistake 1.50

CONAN THE BARBARIAN
Oct, 1970 - No. 275, Dec, 1993
Marvel Comics
1-Origin/1st app. Conan (in comics) by Barry Smith; Kull app.; #1-9 are 15¢ issues 19.00 57.00 190.00
2 7.00 21.00 70.00
3-(Low distribution in some areas) 12.00 36.00 120.00
4,5 5.00 15.00 50.00
6-9: 8-Hidden panel message, pg. 14 3.20 9.60 32.00
10,11 (25¢ giants): 10-Black Knight-r; Kull story by Severin 4.20 12.60 42.00
12,13: 12-Wrightson-c(i) 2.50 7.50 20.00
14,15-Elric app. 3.20 9.60 32.00
16,19,20: 16-Conan-r/Savage Tales #1 2.25 6.75 18.00
17,18-No Barry Smith-a 1.10 3.30 9.00
21,22: 22-Has reprint from #1 1.85 5.50 15.00
23-1st app. Red Sonja (2/73) 2.50 7.50 24.00
24-1st full Red Sonja story; last Smith-a 2.50 7.50 20.00
25-John Buscema-c/a begins 2.40 6.00
26-30 1.60 4.00
31-36,38-40 1.20 3.00
37-Neal Adams-c/a; last 20¢ issue; contains pull-out subscription form 1.25 3.75 10.00
41-57,59,60: 44,45-N. Adams-i(Crusty Bunkers). 45-Adams-c. 48-Origin retold. 59-Origin Belit 1.60 4.00
58-2nd Belit app. (see Giant-Size Conan #1) 2.00 5.00
61-99: 68-Red Sonja story cont'd from Marvel Feature #7. 84-Intro. Zula. 85-Origin Zula. 87-r/Savage Sword of Conan #3 in color 1.20 3.00
100-(52 pg. Giant)-Death of Belit 1.20 3.00
101-114,116-199: 116-r/Power Record Comic PR31 1.25
115-Double size 1.50
200,250 ($1.50): 200-(52 pgs.). 250-(60 pgs.) 1.50
201-249,251,252: 232-Young Conan storyline begins; Conan is born. 244-Return of Zula. 252-Last $1.00-c 1.25
253-274: 262-Adapted from R.E. Howard story 1.25
275-($2.50, 68 pgs.)-Final issue; painted-c 1.00 2.50
King Size 1(1973, 35¢)-Smith-r/#2,4; Smith-c 1.25 3.75 10.00
Annual 2(1976, 50¢)-New full length story 1.40 3.50
Annual 3(1978)-Chaykin/N. Adams-r/SSOC #2 .80 2.00
Annual 4-6: 4(1978)-New full length story. 5(1979)-New full length Buscema story & part-c, 6(1981)-Kane-c/a 1.50
Annual 7-12: 7(1982)-Based on novel "Conan of the Isles" (new-a). 8(1984). 9(1984), 10(1986). 11(1986). 12(1987) 1.25
Special Edition 1 (Red Nails) 1.40 3.50

NOTE: ***Arthur Adams*** *c-248, 249.* ***Neal Adams*** *a-116r(i); c-49i.* ***Austin*** *a-125, 126; c-125i, 126i.* ***Brunner*** *c-17i. c-40.* ***Buscema*** *a-25-36p, 38, 39, 41-56p, 58-63p, 65-67p, 68, 70-78p, 84-86p, 88-91p, 93-126p, 136p, 140, 141-144p, 146-158p, 159, 161, 162, 163p, 165-185p, 187-190p, Annual 2(3pgs.). 3-5p, 7p; c(p)-26, 36, 44, 46, 52, 56, 58, 59, 64, 65, 72, 78-80, 83-91, 93-103, 105-126, 136-151, 155-159, 161, 162, 168, 169, 171, 172, 174, 175, 178-185, 188, 189, Annual 4, 5, 7.* ***Chaykin*** *a-79-83.* ***Golden*** *c-152.* ***Kaluta*** *c-167.* ***Gil Kane*** *a-12p, 17p, 18p, 127-130, 131-134p; c-12p, 17p, 18p, 23, 25, 27-32, 34, 35, 38, 39, 41-43, 45-51, 53-55, 57, 60-63, 65-71, 73p, 76p, 127-134.* ***Jim Lee*** *c-242.* ***McFarlane*** *c-241p.* ***Ploog*** *a-57.* ***Russell*** *a-21; c-251i.* ***Simonson*** *c-135.* ***B. Smith*** *a-1-11p, 12, 13-15p, 16, 19-21, 23, 24; c-1-11, 13-16, 19-24p.* ***Starlin*** *a-64.* ***Wood*** *a-47r. Issue Nos. 3-5, 7-9, 11, 16-18, 21, 23, 25, 27-30, 35, 37, 38, 42, 45, 52, 57, 58, 65, 69-71, 73, 79-83, 99, 100, 104, 114, Annual 2 have original Robert E. Howard stories adapted. Issues #32-34 adapted from Norvell Page's novel* ***Flame Winds****.*

CONAN THE BARBARIAN (Volume 2)
July, 1997 - No. 3, Oct, 1997 ($2.50, limited series)
Marvel Comics
1-3-Castellini-a 1.00 2.50

GD25 FN65 NM94

CONAN THE BARBARIAN MOVIE SPECIAL (Movie)
Oct, 1982 - No. 2, Nov, 1982
Marvel Comics Group
1,2-Movie adaptation; Buscema-a 1.00

CONAN THE BARBARIAN: THE USURPER
Dec, 1997 - No. 3 ($2.50, limited series)
Marvel Comics
1-3-Dixon-s 1.00 2.50

CONAN THE DESTROYER (Movie)
Jan, 1985 - No. 2, Mar, 1985
Marvel Comics Group
1,2-r/Marvel Super Special 1.00

CONAN THE KING (Formerly King Conan)
No. 20, Jan, 1984 - No. 55, Nov, 1989
Marvel Comics Group
20-55: 48-55 ($1.50) 1.50
NOTE: ***Kaluta*** *c-20-23, 24i, 26, 27, 30, 50, 52.* ***Williamson*** *a-37i; c-37i, 38i.*

CONAN THE SAVAGE
Aug, 1995 - No. 10, May, 1996 ($2.95, B&W, Magazine)
Marvel Comics
1-10: 1-Bisley-c. 4-vs. Malibu Comic's Rune. 5,10-Brereton-c 1.20 3.00

CONAN VS. RUNE (Also See Conan #4)
Nov, 1995 ($2.95, one-shot)
Marvel Comics
1-Barry Smith-c/a/scripts 1.20 3.00

CONCRETE (Also see Dark Horse Presents & Within Our Reach)
March, 1987 - No. 10, Nov, 1988 ($1.50, B&W)
Dark Horse Comics
1-Paul Chadwick-c/a in all 2.00 5.00
1-2nd print 1.50
2 1.20 3.00
3-Origin .80 2.00
4-10 1.50
A New Life 1 (1989, $2.95, B&W)-r/#3,4 plus new-a (11 pgs.) 1.20 3.00
Celebrates Earth Day 1990 ($3.50, 52 pgs.) 1.40 3.50
Color Special 1 (2/89, $2.95, 44 pgs.)-r/1st two Concrete apps. from Dark Horse Presents #1,2 plus new-a 1.20 3.00
Land And Sea 1 (2/89, $2.95, B&W)-r/#1,2 1.20 3.00
Odd Jobs 1 (7/90, $3.50)-r/5,6 plus new-a 1.40 3.50

CONCRETE: ECLECTICA
Apr, 1993 - No. 2, May, 1993 ($2.95, limited series)
Dark Horse Comics
1,2 1.20 3.00

CONCRETE: FRAGILE CREATURE
June, 1991 - No. 4, Feb, 1992 ($2.50, limited series)
Dark Horse Comics
1-4 1.00 2.50

CONCRETE: KILLER SMILE
July, 1994 - No. 4, Oct, 1994 ($2.95, limited series)
Dark Horse Comics (Legend)
1-4: 1st Concrete limited series under Legend Imprint 1.20 3.00

CONCRETE: THINK LIKE A MOUNTAIN
Mar, 1996 - No. 6, Aug, 1996 ($2.95, limited series)
Dark Horse Comics (Legend)
1-6: Chadwick-a/scripts & Darrow-c in all 1.20 3.00

CONDORMAN (Walt Disney)

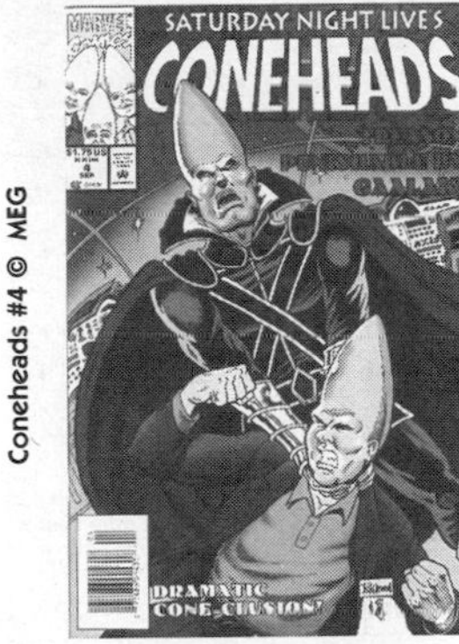

Coneheads #4 © MEG

Congorilla #1 © DC

Contact Comics #3 © Aviation Press

Oct, 1981 - No. 3, Jan, 1982
Whitman Publishing

	GD25	FN65	NM94
1-3: 1,2-Movie adaptation; photo-c			1.00

CONEHEADS
June, 1994 - No. 4, 1994 ($1.75, limited series)
Marvel Comics

	GD25	FN65	NM94
1-4		.70	1.75

CONFESSIONS ILLUSTRATED (Magazine)
Jan-Feb, 1956 - No. 2, Spring, 1956
E. C. Comics

	GD25	FN65	NM94
1-Craig, Kamen, Wood, Orlando-a	12.00	38.00	100.00
2-Craig, Crandall, Kamen, Orlando-a	10.50	32.00	85.00

CONFESSIONS OF LOVE
Apr, 1950 - No. 2, July, 1950 (25¢, 7-1/4x5-1/4", 132 pgs.)
Artful Publ.

	GD25	FN65	NM94
1-Bakerish-a	24.00	71.00	175.00
2-Art & text; Bakerish-a	12.00	36.00	95.00

CONFESSIONS OF LOVE (Formerly Startling Terror Tales #10; becomes Confessions of Romance No. 7 on)
No. 11, 7/52 - No. 14, 1/53; No. 4, 3/53- No. 6, 8/53
Star Publications

	GD25	FN65	NM94
11-13: 12,13-Disbrow-a	10.00	30.00	80.00
14,5,6	7.85	23.50	55.00
4-Disbrow-a	8.75	26.25	65.00

NOTE: *All have* ***L. B. Cole*** *covers.*

CONFESSIONS OF ROMANCE (Formerly Confessions of Love)
No. 7, Nov, 1953 - No. 11, Nov, 1954
Star Publications

	GD25	FN65	NM94
7	10.00	30.00	80.00
8	7.85	23.50	55.00
9-Wood-a	10.00	30.00	80.00
10,11-Disbrow-a	8.75	26.25	65.00

NOTE: *All have* ***L. B. Cole*** *covers.*

CONFESSIONS OF THE LOVELORN (Formerly Lovelorn)
No. 52, Aug, 1954 - No. 114, June-July, 1960
American Comics Group (Regis Publ./Best Synd. Features)

	GD25	FN65	NM94
52 (3-D effect)	24.00	73.00	180.00
53,55	5.70	17.00	40.00
54 (3-D effect)	24.00	73.00	180.00
56-Anti-communist propaganda story, 10 pgs; last pre-code (2/55)	7.85	26.25	55.00
57-90	4.15	12.50	25.00
91-Williamson-a	6.50	19.50	45.00
92-99,101-114	4.00	12.00	20.00
100	4.15	12.50	25.00

NOTE: ***Whitney*** *a-most issues; c-52, 53. Painted c-106, 107.*

CONFIDENTIAL DIARY (Formerly High School Confidential Diary; Three Nurses #18 on)
No. 12, May, 1962 - No. 17, Mar, 1963
Charlton Comics

	GD25	FN65	NM94
12-17	1.85	5.50	15.00

CONGO BILL (See Action Comics & More Fun Comics #56)
Aug-Sept, 1954 - No. 7, Aug-Sept, 1955
National Periodical Publication

	GD25	FN65	VF82
1 (Scarce)	83.00	249.00	670.00
2,7 (Scarce)	65.00	195.00	525.00
3-6 (Scarce). 4-Last pre-code issue	59.00	177.00	475.00

NOTE: *(Rarely found in fine to mint condition.)* ***Nick Cardy*** *c-1-7.*

CONGORILLA (Also see Actions Comics #224)
Nov, 1992 - No. 4, Feb, 1993 ($1.75, limited series)
DC Comics

	GD25	FN65	NM94
1-4: 1,2-Brian Bolland-c		.70	1.75

CONNECTICUT YANKEE, A (See King Classics)

CONQUEROR, THE
No., 690, Mar, 1956
Dell Publishing Co.

	GD25	FN65	NM94
Four Color 690-Movie, John Wayne photo-c	14.00	44.00	160.00

CONQUEROR COMICS
Winter, 1945
Albrecht Publishing Co.

	GD25	FN65	NM94
nn	14.00	41.00	110.00

CONQUEROR OF THE BARREN EARTH (See The Warlord #63)
Feb, 1985 - No. 4, May, 1985 (Limited series)
DC Comics

	GD25	FN65	NM94
1-4: Back-up series from Warlord			1.00

CONQUEST
1953 (6¢)
Store Comics

	GD25	FN65	NM94
1-Richard the Lion Hearted, Beowulf, Swamp Fox	4.15	12.50	25.00

CONQUEST
Spring, 1955
Famous Funnies

	GD25	FN65	NM94
1-Crandall-a, 1 pg.; contains contents of 1953 ish.	4.00	11.00	22.00

CONSTRUCT
1996 - No. 6, 1997 ($2.95, B&W, limited series)
Caliber (New Worlds)

	GD25	FN65	NM94
1-6: Paul Jenkins scripts		1.20	3.00

CONTACT COMICS
July, 1944 - No. 12, May, 1946
Aviation Press

	GD25	FN65	NM94
nn-Black Venus, Flamingo, Golden Eagle, Tommy Tomahawk begin	36.00	108.00	325.00
2-5: 3-Last Flamingo. 3,4-Black Venus by L. B. Cole. 5-The Phantom Flyer app.	31.00	92.00	245.00
6,11-Kurtzman's Black Venus; 11-Last Golden Eagle, last Tommy Tomahawk; Feldstein-a	34.00	101.00	270.00
7-10	27.00	81.00	215.00
12-Sky Rangers, Air Kids, Ace Diamond app.	28.00	84.00	225.00

NOTE: ***L. B. Cole*** *a-3, 9; c-1-12.* ***Giunta*** *a-3.* ***Hollingsworth*** *a-5, 7, 10.* ***Palais*** *a-11, 12.*

CONTEMPORARY MOTIVATORS
1977 - 1978 ($1.45, 5-3/8x8", 31 pgs., B&W)
Pendelum Press

14-3002 The Caine Mutiny; 14-3010 Banner in the Sky; 14-3029 God Is My Co-Pilot;14-3037 Guadalcanal Diary, 14-3045 Hiroshima; 14 3053 Hot Rod; 14-3061 Just Dial a Number; 14-307x Star Wars; 14-3088 The Diary of Anne Frank; 14-3096 Lost Horizon — 1.50

NOTE: *Also see Now Age Illustrated. Above may have been distributed the same.*

CONTEST OF CHAMPIONS (See Marvel Super-Hero...)

CONTRACTORS
June, 1987 ($2.00, B&W, one-shot)
Eclipse Comics

	GD25	FN65	NM94
1-Funny animal		.80	2.00

CONVOCATIONS: A MAGIC THE GATHERING GALLERY
Jan, 1996 ($2.50, one-shot)
Acclaim Comics (Armada)

1-pin-ups by various artists including Kaluta, Vess, and Dringenberg.

"Cookie" #12 © ACG

Cops: The Job #1 © MEG

Cosmo Cat #3 © FOX

GD25 FN65 NM94

1.00 2.50

COO COO COMICS (...the Bird Brain No. 57 on)
Oct, 1942 - No. 62, Apr, 1952
Nedor Publ. Co./Standard (Animated Cartoons)

- 1-Origin/1st app. Super Mouse & begin series (cloned from Superman); the first funny animal super hero series (see Looney Tunes #5 for 1st funny animal super hero) 24.00 71.00 190.00
- 2 10.50 32.00 85.00
- 3-10: 10-(3/44) 6.50 19.50 45.00
- 11-33: 33-1 pg. Ingels-a 5.35 16.00 32.00
- 34-40,43-46,48-Text illos by Frazetta in all. 36-Super Mouse covers begin 7.15 21.50 50.00
- 41-Frazetta-a (6-pg. story & 3 text illos) 13.00 39.00 105.00
- 42,47-Frazetta-a & text illos. 8.75 26.25 70.00
- 49-(1/50)-3-D effect story; Frazetta text illo 8.50 26.00 60.00
- 50,51-3-D effect-c only. 50-Frazetta text illo 7.85 23.50 55.00
- 52-62: 56-Last Supermouse? 4.15 12.50 25.00

"COOKIE" (Also see Topsy-Turvy)
Apr, 1946 - No. 55, Aug-Sept, 1955
Michel Publ./American Comics Group(Regis Publ.)

- 1-Teen-age humor 17.50 53.00 140.00
- 2 8.75 26.25 70.00
- 3-10 6.50 19.50 45.00
- 11-20 5.70 17.00 35.00
- 21-23,26,28-30 4.25 13.00 26.00
- 24,25,27-Starlett O'Hara stories 5.00 15.00 30.00
- 31-34,37-50,52-55 4.00 12.00 24.00
- 35,36-Starlett O'Hara stories 4.25 13.00 26.00
- 51-(10-11/54) 8pg. TrueVision 3-D effect story 6.50 19.50 45.00

COOL CAT (Formerly Black Magic)
V8#6, Mar-Apr, 1962 - V9#2, July-Aug, 1962
Prize Publications

- V8#6, nn(V9#1, 5-6/62), V9#2 4.00 12.00 24.00

COOL WORLD (Movie)
Apr, 1992 - No. 4, Sept, 1992 ($1.75, limited series)
DC Comics

- 1-4: Prequel to animated/live action movie by Ralph Bakshi. 1-Bakshi-c. Bill Wray inks in all .70 1.75
- Movie Adaptation nn ('92, $3.50, 68pg.)-Bakshi-c 1.40 3.50

COPPER CANYON (See Fawcett Movie Comics)

COPS (TV)
Aug, 1988 - No. 15, Aug, 1989 ($1.00)
DC Comics

- 1 ($1.50, 52 pgs.)-Based on Hasbro Toys 1.50
- 2-15: 14-Orlando-c(p) 1.00

COPS: THE JOB
June, 1992 - No. 4, Sept, 1992 ($1.25, limited series)
Marvel Comics

- 1-4: All have Jusko scripts & Golden-c 1.25

CORBEN SPECIAL, A
May, 1984 (one-shot)
Pacific Comics

- 1-Corben-c/a; E.A. Poe adaptation .80 2.00

CORKY & WHITE SHADOW (Disney, TV)
No. 707, May, 1956 (Mickey Mouse Club)
Dell Publishing Co.

- Four Color 707-Photo-c 6.40 19.00 70.00

CORLISS ARCHER (See Meet Corliss Archer)

GD25 FN65 NM94

CORMAC MAC ART (Robert E. Howard's...)
1990 - No. 4, 1990 ($1.95, B&W, mini-series)
Dark Horse Comics

- 1-4: All have Bolton painted-c; Howard adapts. .80 2.00

CORPORAL RUSTY DUGAN (See Holyoke One-Shot #2)

CORPSES OF DR. SACOTTI, THE (See Ideal a Classical Comic)

CORSAIR, THE (See A-1 Comics No. 5, 7, 10)

CORTEZ AND THE FALL OF THE AZTECS
1993 ($2.95, B&W, limited series)
Tome Press

- 1,2 1.20 3.00

CORUM: THE BULL AND THE SPEAR (See Chronicles Of Corum)
Jan, 1989 - No. 4, July, 1989 ($1.95)
First Comics

- 1-4: Adapts Michael Moorcock's novel .80 2.00

COSMIC BOOK, THE
Dec, 1986 - No. 1, 1987 ($1.95)
Ace Comics

- 1-(44pgs.)-Wood, Toth-a .80 2.00
- 2-(B&W) 1.60

COSMIC BOY (Also see The Legion of Super-Heroes)
Dec, 1986 - No. 4, Mar, 1987 (limited series)
DC Comics

- 1-4: Legends tie-ins all issues 1.00

COSMIC ODYSSEY
1988 - No. 4, 1988 ($3.50, limited series, squarebound)
DC Comics

- 1-4: Reintro. New Gods into DC continuity; Superman, Batman, Green Lantern (John Stewart) app; Starlin scripts, Mignola-c/a in all. 2-Darkseid merges Demon & Jason Blood (seperated in Demon limited series #4); John Stewart responsible for the death of a star system. 1.40 3.50
- Trade paperback-r/#1-4. 19.95

COSMIC POWERS
Mar, 1994 - No. 6, Aug, 1994 ($2.50, limited series)
Marvel Comics

- 1-6: 1-Ron Lim-c/a(p). 1,2-Thanos app. 2-Terrax. 3-Ganymede & Jack of Hearts app. 1.00 2.50

COSMIC POWERS UNLIMITED
May, 1995 - No. 4, Feb, 1996 ($3.95, quarterly)
Marvel Comics

- 1-4 1.60 4.00

COSMO CAT (Becomes Sunny #11 on; also see All Top & Wotalife Comics)
July-Aug, 1946 - No. 10, Oct, 1947; 1957; 1959
Fox Publications/Green Publ. Co./Norlen Mag.

- 1 23.00 68.00 180.00
- 2 11.30 34.00 90.00
- 3-Origin (11-12/46) 15.00 45.00 120.00
- 4-10 7.15 21.50 50.00
- 2-4(1957-Green Publ. Co.) 4.00 12.00 24.00
- 2-4(1959-Norlen Mag.) 3.60 9.00 18.00
- I.W. Reprint #1 2.00 5.00 10.00

COSMO THE MERRY MARTIAN
Sept, 1958 - No. 6, Oct, 1959
Archie Publications (Radio Comics)

- 1-Bob White-a in all 12.00 36.00 95.00
- 2-6 8.75 26.25 65.00

COTTON WOODS

Count Duckula #9 © MEG

Coven #3 © Awesome Ent.

Cowboy Love #2 © FAW

	GD25	FN65	NM94
No. 837, Sept, 1957			
Dell Publishing Co.			
Four Color 837	2.75	8.00	30.00
COUGAR, THE (Cougar No. 2)			
April, 1975 - No. 2, July, 1975			
Seaboard Periodicals (Atlas)			
1,2: 1-Adkins-a(p). 2-Origin; Buckler-c(p)		1.20	3.00
COUNTDOWN (See Movie Classics)			
COUNT DUCKULA (TV)			
Nov, 1988 - No. 15, Jan, 1991 ($1.00)			
Marvel Comics			
1-7,9-15: Dangermouse back-ups.		.80	2.00
8-Geraldo Rivera photo-c/& app.; Sienkiewicz-a(i)		2.00	5.00
COUNT OF MONTE CRISTO, THE			
No. 794, May, 1957			
Dell Publishing Co.			
Four Color 794-Movie, Buscema-a	8.00	25.00	90.00
COURAGE COMICS			
1945			
J. Edward Slavin			
1,2,77	7.85	23.50	55.00
COURTSHIP OF EDDIE'S FATHER (TV)			
Jan, 1970 - No. 2, May, 1970			
Dell Publishing Co.			
1,2-Bill Bixby photo-c	2.70	8.10	30.00
COVEN			
Aug, 1997 - Present ($2.50)			
Awesome Entertainment			
1-Loeb-s/Churchill-a, two covers			2.50
2,3: 3-Wraparound-c & flip book preview of ReGex			2.50
COVERED WAGONS, HO (Disney, TV)			
No. 814, June, 1957 (Donald Duck)			
Dell Publishing Co.			
Four Color 814-Mickey Mouse app.	4.50	13.50	50.00
COWBOY ACTION (Formerly Western Thrillers No. 1-4; Becomes Quick-Trigger Western No. 12 on)			
No. 5, March, 1955 - No. 11, March, 1956			
Atlas Comics (ACI)			
5	9.50	28.00	75.00
6-10: 6-8-Heath-c	7.15	21.50	50.00
11-Williamson-a (4 pgs.); Baker-a	8.50	26.00	60.00
NOTE: ***Ayers** a-8. **Drucker** a-6. **Maneely** c/a-5, 6. **Severin** c-10. **Shores** a-7.*			
COWBOY COMICS (Star Ranger #12, Stories #14)(Star Ranger Funnies #15)			
No. 13, July, 1938 - No. 14, Aug, 1938			
Centaur Publishing Co.			
13-(Rare)-Ace and Deuce, Lyin Lou, Air Patrol, Aces High, Lee Trent, Trouble Hunters begin	100.00	300.00	900.00
14-Filchock-c	72.00	216.00	650.00
NOTE: ***Guardineer** a-13, 14. **Gustavson** a-13, 14.*			
COWBOY IN AFRICA (TV)			
Mar, 1968			
Gold Key			
1(10219-803)-Chuck Connors photo-c	3.00	9.00	35.00
COWBOY LOVE (Becomes Range Busters?)			
7/49 - V2#10, 6/50; No. 11, 1951; No. 28, 2/55 - No. 31, 8/55			
Fawcett Publications/Charlton Comics No. 28 on			
V1#1-Rocky Lane photo back-c	15.00	45.00	120.00
2	5.70	17.00	35.00
V1#3,4,6 (12/49)	5.00	15.00	30.00
5-Bill Boyd photo back-c (11/49)	5.70	17.00	40.00
V2#7-Williamson/Evans-a	7.85	23.50	55.00
V2#8-11	4.15	12.50	25.00
V1#28 (Charlton)-Last precode (2/55) (Formerly Romantic Story?)	4.15	12.50	25.00
V1#29-31 (Charlton; becomes Sweetheart Diary #32 on)	4.00	11.00	22.00
NOTE: ***Powell** a-10. **Marcus Swayze** a-2, 3. Photo c-1-11. No. 1-3, 5-7, 9, 10 are 52 pgs.*			
COWBOY ROMANCES (Young Men No. 4 on)			
Oct, 1949 - No. 3, Mar, 1950 (All photo-c & 52 pgs.)			
Marvel Comics (IPC)			
1-Photo-c	17.50	53.00	140.00
2-William Holden, Mona Freeman "Streets of Laredo" photo-c	11.30	34.00	90.00
3-Photo-c	9.50	28.00	75.00
COWBOYS 'N' INJUNS (...and Indians No. 6 on)			
1946 - No. 5, 1947; No. 6, 1949 - No. 8, 1952			
Com No. 1-5/Magazine Enterprises No. 6 on			
1	8.75	26.25	65.00
2-5-All funny animal western	5.70	17.00	40.00
6(A-1 23)-Half violent, half funny; Ayers-a	7.85	23.50	55.00
7(A-1 41, 1950), 8(A-1 48)-All funny	5.70	17.00	40.00
I.W. Reprint No. 1,7 (Reprinted in Canada by Superior, No. 7)	1.25	3.75	10.00
Super Reprint #10 (1963)	1.25	3.75	10.00
COWBOY WESTERN COMICS (TV)(Formerly Jack In The Box; Becomes Space Western No. 40-45 & Wild Bill Hickok & Jingles No. 68 on; title:Cowboy Western Heroes No. 47 & 48; Cowboy Western No. 49 on)			
No. 17, 7/48 - No. 39, 8/52; No. 46, 10/53; No. 47, 12/53; No. 48, Spr, '54; No. 49, 5-6/54 - No. 67, 3/58 (nn 40-45)			
Charlton (Capitol Stories)			
17-Jesse James, Annie Oakley, Wild Bill Hickok begin; Texas Rangers app.	15.00	45.00	120.00
18,19-Orlando-c/a. 18-Paul Bunyan begins. 19-Wyatt Earp story	8.75	26.25	70.00
20-25: 21-Buffalo Bill story. 22-Texas Rangers-c/story. 24-Joel McCrea photo-c & adaptation from movie "Three Faces West". 25-James Craig photo-c & adaptation from movie "Northwest Stampede"	8.50	26.00	60.00
26-George Montgomery photo-c and adaptation from movie "Indian Scout"; 1 pg. bio on Will Rogers	9.50	28.00	75.00
27-Sunset Carson photo-c & adapts movie "Sunset Carson Rides Again" plus 1 other Sunset Carson story	50.00	150.00	450.00
28-Sunset Carson line drawn-c; adapts movies "Battling Marshal" & "Fighting Mustangs" starring Sunset Carson	28.00	84.00	225.00
29-Sunset Carson line drawn-c; adapts movies "Rio Grande" with Sunset Carson & "Winchester '73" w/James Stewart plus 5 pg. life history of Sunset Carson featuring Tom Mix	28.00	84.00	225.00
30-Sunset Carson photo-c; adapts movie "Deadline" starring Sunset Carson plus 1 other Sunset Carson story	50.00	150.00	450.00
31-34,38,39,47-50 (no #40-45): 50-Golden Arrow, Rocky Lane & Blackjack (r?) stories	6.50	19.50	45.00
35,36-Sunset Carson-c/stories (2 in each). 35-Inside front-c photo of Sunset Carson plus photo on-c	28.00	84.00	225.00
37-Sunset Carson stories (2)	17.50	53.00	140.00
46-(Formerly Space Western)-Space western story	16.00	49.00	130.00
51-57,59-66: 51-Golden Arrow(r?) & Monte Hale-r renamed Rusty Hall. 53,54-Tom Mix-r. 55-Monte Hale story(r?). 66-Young Eagle story. 67-Wild Bill Hickok and Jingles-c/story	5.00	15.00	30.00
58-(1/56, 15¢, 68 pgs.)-Wild Bill Hickok, Annie Oakley & Jesse James stories; Forgione-a	5.70	17.00	35.00
67-(15¢, 68 pgs.)-Williamson/Torres-a, 5 pgs.	8.50	26.00	60.00

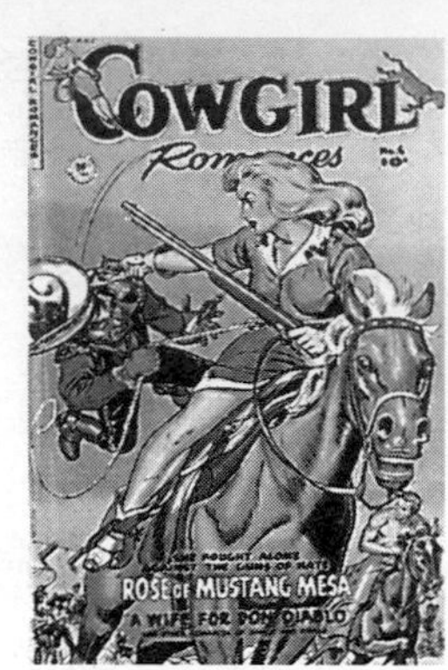

Cowgirl Romances #6 © FH

Crackajack Funnies #40 © DELL

Crack Comics #52 © QUA

GD25 FN65 NM94

NOTE: *Many issues trimmed 1" shorter.* ***Maneely*** *a-67(5). Inside front/back photo c-29.*

COWGIRL ROMANCES (Young Men No. 4 on)
No. 28, Jan, 1950 (52 pgs.)
Marvel Comics (CCC)

28(#1)-Photo-c 16.00 49.00 130.00

COWGIRL ROMANCES
1950 - No. 12, Winter, 1952-53 (No. 1-3: 52 pgs.)
Fiction House Magazines

1-Kamen-a 26.00 80.00 210.00
2 13.00 39.00 105.00
3-5: 5-12-Whitman-c (most) 12.00 36.00 95.00
6-9,11,12 10.50 32.00 85.00
10-Frazetta?/Williamson?-a; Kamen?/Baker-a; r/Mitzi story from Movie Comics #4 w/all new dialogue 26.00 80.00 210.00

COW PUNCHER (...Comics)
Jan, 1947; No. 2, Sept, 1947 - No. 7, 1949
Avon Periodicals

1-Clint Cortland, Texas Ranger, Kit West, Pioneer Queen begin; Kubert-a; Alabam stories begin 36.00 107.00 260.00
2-Kubert, Kamen/Feldstein-a; Kamen-c 29.00 86.00 210.00
3-5,7: 3-Kiefer story 19.00 58.00 140.00
6-Opium drug mention story; bondage, headlight-c; Reinman-a 25.00 75.00 180.00

COWPUNCHER
1953 (nn) (Reprints Avon's No. 2)
Realistic Publications

nn-Kubert-a 10.00 30.00 65.00

COWSILLS, THE (See Harvey Pop Comics)

COYOTE
June, 1983 - No. 16, Mar, 1986
Marvel Comics (Epic Comics)

1-10,15: 7-10-Ditko-a .80 2.00
11-1st McFarlane-a. 2.40 6.00
12-14,16: 12-14-McFarlane-a. 16-Reagan c app. 1.60 4.00

CRACKAJACK FUNNIES (Giveaway)
1937 (Full size, soft-c, full color, 32 pgs.)(Before No. 1?)
Malto-Meal

nn-Features Dan Dunn, G-Man, Speed Bolton, Freckles, Buck Jones, Clyde Beatty, The Nebbs, Major Hoople, Wash Tubbs 83.00 250.00 750.00

CRACKAJACK FUNNIES (Also see The Owl)
June, 1938 - No. 43, Jan, 1942
Dell Publishing Co.

1-Dan Dunn, Freckles, Myra North, Wash Tubbs, Apple Mary, The Nebbs, Don Winslow, Tom Mix, Buck Jones, Major Hoople, Clyde Beatty, Boots begin 200.00 600.00 1800.00
2 83.00 250.00 750.00
3 58.00 174.00 525.00
4 44.00 132.00 400.00
5-Nude woman on cover 47.00 141.00 425.00
6-8,10: 8-Speed Bolton begins (1st app.) 36.00 108.00 315.00
9-(3/39)-Red Ryder strip-r begin by Harman; 1st app. in comics & 1st cover app. 106.00 318.00 950.00
11-14 36.00 108.00 300.00
15-Tarzan text feature begins by Burroughs (9/39); not in #26,35 36.00 108.00 325.00
16-24: 18-Stratosphere Jim begins (1st app., 12/39). 23-Ellery Queen begins plus-c (1st comic book app., 5/40) 28.00 83.00 220.00
25-The Owl begins (1st app., 7/40); in new costume #26 by Frank Thomas (also see Popular Comics #72) 58.00 174.00 525.00
26-30: 28-Part Owl-c 42.00 126.00 375.00

GD25 FN65 NM94

31-Owl covers begin, end #42 40.00 120.00 360.00
32-Origin Owl Girl 47.00 141.00 425.00
33-38: 36-Last Tarzan issue. 37-Cyclone & Midge begin (1st app.) 36.00 108.00 290.00
39-Andy Panda begins (intro/1st app., 9/41) 40.00 120.00 360.00
40-42: 42-Last Owl-c. 35.00 105.00 280.00
43-Terry & the Pirates-r 30.00 90.00 240.00
NOTE: ***McWilliams*** *art in most issues.*

CRACK COMICS (Crack Western No. 63 on)
May, 1940 - No. 62, Sept, 1949
Quality Comics Group

1-Origin & 1st app. The Black Condor by Lou Fine, Madame Fatal, Red Torpedo, Rock Bradden & The Space Legion; The Clock, Alias the Spider (by Gustavson), Wizard Wells, & Ned Brant begin; Powell-a; Note: Madame Fatal is a man dressed as a woman 380.00 1140.00 3800.00
2 178.00 534.00 1600.00
3 117.00 350.00 1050.00
4 106.00 318.00 950.00
5-10: 5-Molly The Model begins. 10-Tor, the Magic Master begins 81.00 243.00 725.00
11-20: 13-1 pg. J. Cole-a. 18-1st app. Spitfire? 75.00 225.00 625.00
21-24: 23-Pen Miller begins; continued from National Comics #22. 24-Last Fine Black Condor 53.00 159.00 475.00
25,26: 26-Flag-c 44.00 132.00 400.00
27-(1/43)-Intro & origin Captain Triumph by Alfred Andriola (Kerry Drake artist) & begin series 81.00 243.00 725.00
28-30 36.00 108.00 315.00
31-39: 31-Last Black Condor 23.00 68.00 180.00
40-46 15.50 47.00 125.00
47-57,59,60-Capt. Triumph by Crandall 17.50 53.00 140.00
58,61,62-Last Captain Triumph 11.30 34.00 90.00
NOTE: *Black Condor by* ***Fine****: No. 1, 2, 4-6, 8, 10-24; by* ***Sultan****: No. 3, 7; by* ***Fugitani****: No. 9.* ***Cole*** *a-34.* ***Crandall*** *a-61(unsigned); c-48, 49, 51-61.* ***Guardineer*** *a-17.* ***Gustavson*** *a-1, 13, 17.* ***McWilliams*** *a-15-27. Black Condor c-2, 4, 6, 8, 10, 12, 14, 16, 18, 20-26. Capt. Triumph c-27-62. The Clock c-1, 3, 5, 7, 9, 11, 13, 15, 17, 19.*

CRACKED (Magazine) (Satire) (Also see The 3-D Zone #19)
Feb-Mar, 1958 - Present
Major Magazines(#1-212)/Globe Communications(#213 on)

1-One pg. Williamson-a 12.00 36.00 120.00
2-1st Shut-Ups & Bonus Cut-Outs 5.00 15.00 50.00
3-6 3.00 9.00 30.00
7-10: 7-Reprints 1st 6 covers on-c 2.50 7.50 24.00
11-12, 13(nn,3/60), 14-17, 18(nn,2/61), 19,20 2.50 7.50 22.00
21-27(11/62), 27(No.28, 2/63; mis-#d), 29(5/63) 2.25 6.75 18.00
31-60 2.00 6.00 16.00
61-98,100 1.50 4.50 12.00
99-Alfred E. Neuman on-c 2.80 8.40 28.00
101-150: 131-Bill Ward-a 1.10 3.30 9.00
151-200: 234-Don Martin-a begins ($1.75 #? on) 2.40 6.00
201-300 1.60 4.00
301-341 1.00 2.50
Biggest... (Winter, 1977) 1.50 4.50 12.00
Biggest, Greatest... nn('65) 2.60 7.80 26.00
Biggest, Greatest... 2('66) - #12('76) 2.00 6.00 16.00
...Blockbuster 1,2 ('88) 2.40 6.00
...Digest 1(Fall, '86, 148 pgs.) - #5 2.40 6.00
...Collectors' Edition 4 ('73; formerly ...Special) 1.10 3.30 9.00
5-70: 23-Ward-a 2.00 5.00
71-84: 83-Elvis, Batman parodies 1.60 4.00
...Party Pack 1,2('88) 1.60 4.00
...Shut-Ups (2/72-'72; Cracked Spec. #3) 1,2 1.00 2.80 7.00
...Special 3('73; formerly Cracked Shut-Ups; ...Collectors' Edition#4 on) 1.00 3.00 8.00
Extra Special... 1('76), 2('76) 1.60 4.00

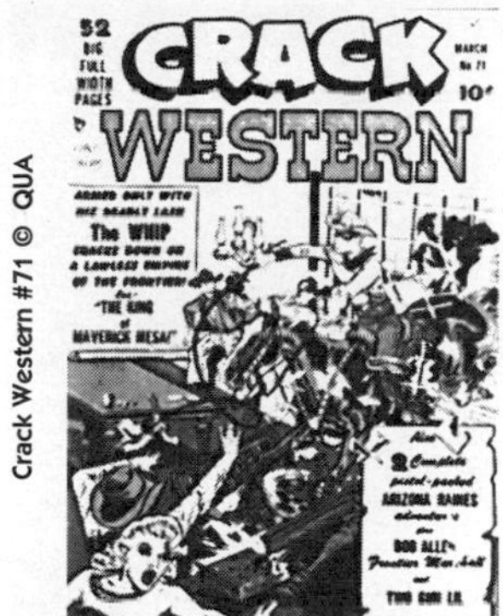

Crack Western #71 © QUA

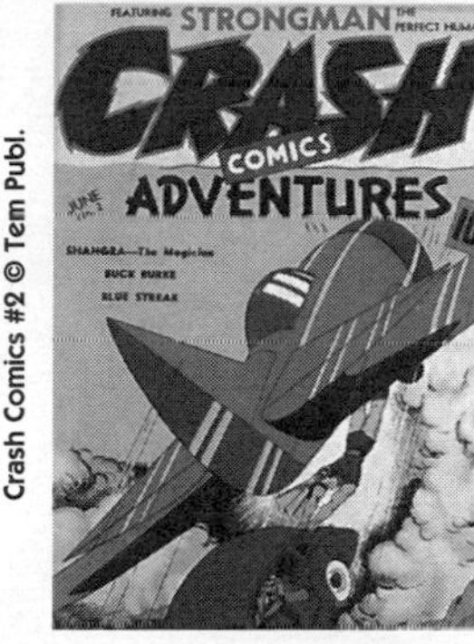

Crash Comics #2 © Tem Publ.

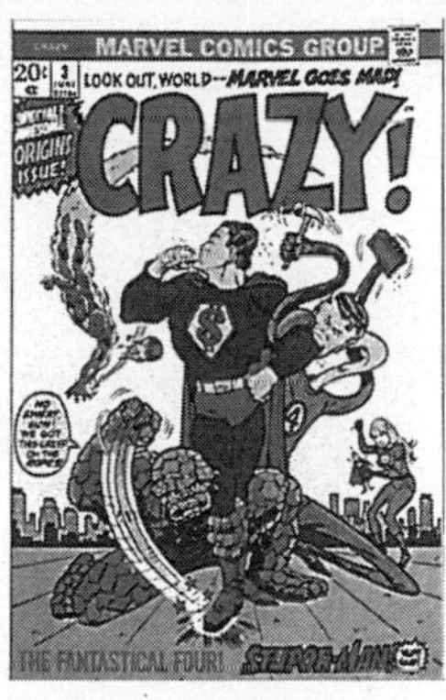

Crazy #3 © MEG

GD25 FN65 NM94

Giant... nn('65) 3.00 9.00 30.00
Giant... 2('66)-12('76), nn(9/77)-48('87) 2.25 6.75 18.00
King Sized... 1('67) 3.50 10.50 35.00
King Sized... 2('68)-11('77) 2.50 7.50 22.00
King Sized... 12-22 (Sum/'86) 2.40 6.00
Super... 1('68) 3.00 9.00 30.00
Super... 2('69)-24('88) 2.50 7.50 22.00
Super... 1('87, 100 pgs.)-Severin & Elder-a 2.40 6.00

NOTE: ***Burgos** a-1-10. **Colan** a-257. **Davis** a-5, 11-17, 24, 40, 80; c-12-14, 16. **Elder** a-5, 6, 10-13; c-10. **Everett** a-1-10, 23-25, 61; c-1. **Heath** a-1-3, 6, 13, 14, 17, 110; c-6. **Jaffee** a-5, 6. **Don Martin** c-235, 244, 247, 259, 261, 264. **Morrow** a-8-10. **Reinman** a-1-4. **Severin** c/a-in most all issues. **Shores** a-3-7. **Torres** a-7-10. **Ward** a-22-24, 27, 35, 40, 143, 144, 149, 150, 152, 153, 156. **Williamson** a-1 (1 pg.). **Wolverton** a-10 (2 pgs.), Giant nn('65). **Wood** a-27, 35, 40. Alfred E. Neuman c-177, 200, 202. Batman c-234, 248, 249, 256. Captain America c-256. Christmas c-234, 243. Spider-Man c-260. Star Trek c-127, 169, 207, 228. Star Wars c-145, 146, 148, 149, 152, 155, 173, 174, 199. Superman c-183, 233. #144, 146 have free full-color pre-glued stickers. #145, 147, 155, 163 have free full-color postcards. #123, 137, 154, 157 have free iron-ons.*

CRACKED MONSTER PARTY
July, 1988 - No. 26, 1990?
Globe Communications

1 1.25 3.75 10.00
2-10 2.40 6.00
11-26 1.60 4.00

CRACKED'S FOR MONSTERS ONLY
Sept, 1969 - No. 9, Sept, 1969
Major Magazines

1 2.50 7.50 20.00
2-9 1.25 3.75 10.00

CRACKED SPACED OUT
Fall, 1993 - No. 4, 1994?
Globe Communications

1-4 .80 2.00

CRACK WESTERN (Formerly Crack Comics; Jonesy No. 85 on)
No. 63, Nov, 1949 - No. 84, May, 1953 (36 pgs., 63-68,74-on)
Quality Comics Group

63(#1)-Ward-c; Two-Gun Lil (origin & 1st app.)(ends #84), Arizona Ames, his horse Thunder (with sidekick Spurs & his horse Calico), Frontier Marshal (ends #70), & Dead Canyon Days (ends #69) begin; Crandall-a 19.00 56.00 150.00
64,65: 64-Ward-c. Crandall-a in both. 14.00 41.00 110.00
66,68-Photo-c. 66-Arizona Ames becomes A. Raines (ends #84) 12.00 36.00 95.00
67-Randolph Scott photo-c; Crandall-a 14.00 41.00 110.00
69(52pgs.)-Crandall-a 12.00 36.00 95.00
70(52pgs.)-The Whip (origin & 1st app.) & his horse Diablo begin (ends #84); Crandall-a 12.00 36.00 95.00
71(52pgs.)-Frontier Marshal becomes Bob Allen F. Marshal (ends #84); Crandall-c/a 14.00 41.00 110.00
72(52pgs.)-Tim Holt photo-c 11.30 34.00 90.00
73(52pgs.)-Photo-c 8.50 26.00 60.00
74-76,78,79,81,83-Crandall-c. 83-Crandall-a(p) 10.00 30.00 80.00
77,80,82 7.15 21.50 50.00
84-Crandall-c/a 11.30 34.00 90.00

NOTE: ***Crandall** c-71p, 74-81, 83p(w/**Cuidera**-i).*

CRASH COMICS (Catman Comics No. 6 on)
May, 1940 - No. 5, Nov, 1940
Tem Publishing Co.

1-The Blue Streak, Strongman (origin), The Perfect Human, Shangra begin (1st app. of each); Kirby-a 200.00 600.00 2200.00
2-Simon & Kirby-a 117.00 350.00 1050.00
3,5-Simon & Kirby-a 106.00 318.00 950.00
4-Origin & 1st app. The Catman; S&K-a 211.00 633.00 1900.00

NOTE: *Solar Legion by **Kirby** No. 1-5 (5 pgs. each). Strongman c-1-4. Catman c-5.*

GD25 FN65 NM94

CRASH DIVE (See Cinema Comics Herald)

CRASH RYAN (Also see Dark Horse Presents #44)
Oct, 1984 - No. 4, Jan, 1985 (Baxter paper, limited series)
Marvel Comics (Epic Comics)

1-4 1.50

CRAZY (Also see This Magazine is Crazy)
Dec, 1953 - No. 7, July, 1954
Atlas Comics (CSI)

1-Everett-c/a 20.00 60.00 160.00
2 15.00 45.00 120.00
3-7: 4-I Love Lucy satire. 5-Satire on censorship 12.00 38.00 100.00

NOTE: ***Ayers** a-5. **Berg** a-1, 2. **Burgos** c-5, 6. **Drucker** a-6. **Everett** a-1-4. **Al Hartley** a-4. **Heath** a-3, 7; c-7. **Maneely** a-1-7, c-3, 4. **Post** a-3-6. Funny monster c-1-4.*

CRAZY (Satire)
Feb, 1973 - No. 3, June, 1973
Marvel Comics Group

1-Not Brand Echh-r; Beatles cameo (r) 1.85 5.50 15.00
2,3-Not Brand Echh-r 1.25 3.75 10.00

CRAZY MAGAZINE (Satire)
Oct, 1973 - No. 94, Apr, 1983 (40-90¢, B&W magazine)
(#1, 44 pgs; #2-90, reg. issues, 52 pgs; #92-95, 68 pgs)'
Marvel Comics Group

1-Wolverton(1 pg.), Bode-a; 3 pg. photo story of Neal Adams & Dick Giordano; Harlan Ellison story; TV Kung Fu sty. 2.50 7.50 25.00
2-"Live & Let Die" c/s; 8pgs; Adams/Buscema-a; McCloud w5 pgs. Adams-a; Kurtzman's "Hey Look" 2 pg.-r 2.50 7.50 20.00
3-5: 3-"High Plains Drifter" w/Clint Eastwood c/s; Waltons app; Drucker, Reese-a. 4-Shaft-c/s; Ploog-a; Nixon 3 pg. app; Freas-a. 5-Michael Crichton's "Westworld" c/s; Nixon app. 1.85 5.50 15.00
6,7,18: 6-Excorcist c/s; Nixon app. 7-TV's Kung Fu c/s; Nixon app.; Ploog & Freas-a. 18-Six Million Dollar Man/Bionic Woman c/s; Welcome Back Kotter story 1.50 4.50 12.00
8-10: 8-Serpico c/s; Casper parody; TV's Police Story. 9-Joker cameo; Chinatown story; Eisner s/a begins; Has 1st 8 covers on-c. 10-Playboy Bunny-c; M. Severin-a; LeeMarrs-a begins; "Deathwish" story 1.25 3.75 10.00
11-17,19: 11-Towering Inferno. 12-Rhoda. 13-"Tommy" the Who Rock Opera. 14-Mandingo. 15-Jaws story. 16-Santa/Xmas-c; "Good Times" TV story; Jaws. 17-Bi-Centennial ish; Baretta; Woody Allen. 19-King Kong c/s; Reagan, J. Carter, Howard the Duck cameos, "Lavern & Shirley" 1.00 3.00 8.00
20,27: 20-Bi-Centennial-c; Space 1999 sty; Superheroes song sheet, 4pgs. 27-Charlies Angels/Travolta/Fonz-c; Bionic Woman sty 1.25 3.75 10.00
21-23,25,26,28-30: 21-Starskey & Hutch. 22-Mount Rushmore/J. Carter-c; TV's Barney Miller; Superheroes spoof. 23-Santa/Xmas-c; "Happy Days" sty; "Omen" sty. 25-J. Carter-c/s; Grandenetti-a begins; TV's Alice; Logans Run. 26-TV Stars-c; Mary Hartman, King Kong. 28-Donny & Marie Osmond-c/s; Marathon Man. 29-Travolta/Kotter-c; "One Day at a Time", Gong Show. 30-1977, 84 pgs. w/bonus; Jaws, Baretta, King Kong, Happy Days 1.00 3.00 8.00
24-Charlies Angels 1.50 4.50 12.00
31,33-35,38,40: 31-"Rocky"-c/s; TV game shows. 33-Peter Benchley's "Deep". 34-J. Carter-c; TV's "Fish". 35-Xmas-c with Fonz/Six Million Dollar Man/Wonder Woman/Darth Vader/Travolta, TV's "Mash" & "Family Matters". 38-Close Encounters of the Third Kind-c/s. 40-"Three's Company-c/s 2.40 6.00
32-Star Wars/Darth Vader-c/s; "Black Sunday" 1.85 5.50 15.00
36,42,47,49: 36-Farrah Fawcett/Six Million Dollar Man-c; TV's Nancy Drew & Hardy Boys; 1st app. Howard The Duck in Crazy, 2 pgs. 42-84 pgs. w/bonus; TV Hulk/Spider-Man-c; Mash, Gong Show, One Day at a Time, Disco, Alice. 47-Battlestar Galactica xmas-c; movie "Foul Play". 49-1979, 84 pgs. w/bonus; Mork & Mindy-c; Jaws, Saturday Night Fever, Three's Company

Crazyman #3 © Continuity Assoc.

Creatures On The Loose #23 © MEG

The Creech #1 © Greg Capullo

1.00 3.00 8.00
37-1978, 84 pgs. w/bonus. Darth Vader-c; Barney Miller, Laverne & Shirley, Good Times, Rocky, Donny & Marie Osmond, Bionic Woman 1.50 4.50 12.00
39,44: 39-Saturday Night Fever-c/s. 44-"Grease"-c w/Travolta/O. Newton-John 1.25 3.75 10.00
41-Kiss-c & 1pg. photos; Disaster movies, TV's "Family", Annie Hall 2.50 7.50 20.00
43,45,46,48,51: 43-Jaws-c; Saturday Night Fever; Stallone's "Fist".43-E.C. swipe from Mad #131 45-Travolta/O. Newton-John/J. Carter-c; Eight is Enough. 46-TV Hulk-c/s; Punk Rock. 48-"Wiz"-c, Battlestar Galactica-s. 51-Grease/Mork & Mindy/D&M Osmond-c, Mork & Mindy-sty. "Boys from Brazil" 2.40 6.00
50,58: 50-Superman movie-c/sty, Playboy Mag., TV Hulk, Fonz; Howard the Duck, 1 pg. 58-1980, 84 pgs. w/32 pg. color comic bonus insert-Full reprint of Crazy Comic #1, Battlestar Galactica, Charlie's Angels, Starsky & Hutch 1.50 4.50 12.00
52,59,60,64: 52-1979, 84 pgs. w/bonus. Marlon Brando-c; TV Hulk, Grease. Kiss, 1 pg. photos. 59-Santa Ptd-c by Larkin; "Alien", "Moonraker", Rocky-2, Howard the Duck, 1 pg. 60-Star Trek w/Muppets-c; Star Trek sty; 1st app/origin Teen Hulk; Severin-a. 64-84 pgs. w/bonus Monopoly game satire. "Empire Strikes Back", 8 pgs,.One Day at a Time. 1.25 3.75 10.00
53,54,65,67-70: 53-"Animal House"-c/sty; TV's "Vegas", Howard the Duck, 1 pg. 54-Love at First Bite-c/sty, Fantasy Island sty, Howard the Duck 1 pg. 65-(Has #66 on-c, Aug/'80). "Black Hole" w/Janson-a; Kirby Wood/Severin-a(r), 5 pgs. Howard the Duck, 3 pgs.; Broderick-a; Buck Rogers, Mr. Rogers. 67-84 pgs. w/bonus; TV's Kung Fu, Excorcist; Ploog-a(r). 68-American Gigalo, Dukes of Hazard, Teen Hulk; Howard the Duck, 3 pgs. Broderick-a; Monster sty/5 pg. Ditko-a(r). 69-Obnoxio the Clown-c/sty; Stephen King's "Shining", Teen Hulk, Richie Rich, Howard the Duck, 3pgs; Broderick-a. 70-84 pgs. Towering Inferno, Daytime TV; Trina Robbins-a 2.40 6.00
55-57,61,63: 55-84 pgs. w/bonus; Love Boat, Mork & Mindy, Fonz, TV Hulk. 56-Mork/Rocky/J. Carter-c; China Syndrome. 57-TV Hulk with Miss Piggy-c, Dracula, Taxi, Muppets. 61-1980, 84 pgs. Adams-a(r), McCloud, Pro wrestling, Casper, TV's Police Story. 63-Apocalypse Now-Coppola's cult movie; 3rd app. Teen Hulk, Howard the Duck, 3 pgs. 1.00 3.00 8.00
62-Kiss Ptd-c & 2 pg. app; Quincy, 2nd app. Teen Hulk 2.50 7.50 20.00
66-Sept/'80, Empire Strikes Back-c/sty; Teen Hulk by Severin, Howard the Duck, 3pgs. by Broderick 1.25 3.75 10.00
71,72,75-77,79: 71-Blues Brothers parody, Teen Hulk, Superheroes parody, WKRP in Cincinnati, Howard the Duck, 3pgs. by Broderick. 72-Jackie Gleason/Smokey & the Bandit II-c/sty, Shogun, Teen Hulk. Howard the Duck, 3pgs. by Broderick. 75-Flash Gordon movie c/sty; Teen Hulk, Cat in the Hat, Howard the Duck 3pgs. by Broderick. 76-84 pgs. w/bonus; Monster-sty w/ Crandall-a(r), Monster-stys(2) w/Kirby-a(r), 5pgs. ea; Mash, TV Hulk, Chinatown. 77-Popeye movie/R. Williams-c/sty; Teen Hulk, Love Boat, Howard the Duck 3 pgs. 79-84 pgs. w/bonus color stickers; has new material; "9 to 5" w/Dolly Parton, Teen Hulk, Magnum P.I., Monster-sty w/5pgs, Ditko-a(r), "Rat" w/Sutton-a(r), Everett-a, 4 pgs.(r) 2.40 6.00
73,74,78,80: 73-84 pgs. w/bonus Hulk/Spiderman Finger Puppets-c & bonus; "Live & Let Die, Jaws, Fantasy Island. 74-Dallas/"Who Shot JR"-c/sty; Elephant Man, Howard the Duck 3pgs. by Broderick. 78-Clint Eastwood-c/sty; Teen Hulk, Superheroes parody, Lou Grant. 80-Star Wars, 2 pg. app; "Howling", TV's "Greatest American Hero" 1.00 3.00 8.00
81,84,86,87,89: 81-.Superman Movie II-c/sty; Wolverine cameo, Mash, Teen Hulk. 84-American Werewolf in London, Johnny Carson app; Teen Hulk. 86-Time Bandits-c/sty; Private Benjamin. 87-Rubix Cube-c; Hill Street Blues, "Ragtime", Origin Obnoxio the Clown; Teen Hulk. 89-Burt Reynolds "Sharkeys Machine", Teen Hulk 2.40 6.00
82-X-Men-c w/new Byrne-a, 84 pgs. w/new material; Fantasy Island, Teen Hulk, "For Your Eyes Only", Spiderman/Human Torch-r by Kirby/Ditko; Sutton-a(r); Rogers-a; Hunchback of Notre Dame, 5 pgs. 1.85 5.50 15.00
83-Raiders of the Lost Ark-c/sty; Hart to Hart; Reese-a; Teen Hulk 1.25 3.75 10.00
85,88: 85-84 pgs; Escape from New York, Teen Hulk; Kirby-a(r), 5 pgs, Posiedon Adventure, Flintstones, Sesame Street. 88-84 pgs. w/bonus Dr. Strange Game; some new material; Jeffersons, X-Men/Wolverine, 10 pgs.; Byrne-a; Apocalypse Now, Teen Hulk 1.00 3.00 8.00
90-94: 90-Conan-c/sty; M. Severin-a; Teen Hulk. 91-84 pgs, some new material; Bladerunner-c/sty, "Deathwish-II, Teen Hulk, Black Knight, 10 pgs.-'50s-r w/Maneely-a. 92-Wrath of Khan Star Trek-c/sty; Jonnie & Chachi, Teen Hulk. 93-"E.T."-c/sty, Teen Hulk, Archie Bunkers Place, Dr. Doom Game. 94-Poltergeist, Smurfs, Teen Hulk, Casper, Avengers parody-8pgs. Adams-a. 1.50 4.50 12.00
Crazy Summer Special #1 (Sum, '75, 100 pgs.)-Nixon, TV Kung Fu, Babe Ruth, Joe Namath, Waltons, McCloud, Chariots of the Gods 1.50 4.50 12.00

NOTE: ***N. Adams*** *a-2, 61r, 94p.* ***Austin*** *a-82i.* ***Buscema*** *a-2, 82.* ***Byrne*** *c-82p.* ***Nick Cardy*** *c-7, 8, 10, 12-16, Super Special 1.* ***Crandall*** *a-76r.* ***Ditko*** *a-68r, 79r, 82r.* ***Drucker*** *a-3.* ***Eisner*** *a-9-16.* ***Kelly Freas*** *c-1-6, 9, 11; a-7.* ***Kirby/Wood*** *a-66r.* ***Ploog*** *a-1, 4, 7, 67r, 73r.* ***Rogers*** *a-82.* ***Sparling*** *a-92.* ***Wood*** *a-65r. Howard the Duck in 36, 50, 51, 53, 54, 59, 63, 65, 66, 68, 69, 71, 72, 74, 75, 77. Hulk in 46, c-42, 46, 57, 73. Star Wars in 32, 66; c-37.*

CRAZYMAN
Apr, 1992 - No. 5, 1992 ($2.50, high quality paper)
Continuity Comics

1-($3.95, 52 pgs.)-Embossed-c; N. Adams part-i 1.60 4.00
2-5 ($2.50): 2-N. Adams/Bolland-c 1.00 2.50

CRAZYMAN
V2#1, May, 1993 - No. 4, Jan, 1994 ($2.50, high quality paper)
Continuity Comics

V2#1-($2.50)-Entire book is die-cut 1.00 2.50
2-4: 2-(12/93)-Adams-c(p) & part scripts. 3-(12/93). 4-Indicia says #3, Jan. 1993 1.00 2.50

CRAZY, MAN, CRAZY (Magazine) (Becomes This Magazine is...?)
(Formerly From Here to Insanity)
V2#1, Dec, 1955 - V2#2, June, 1956 Humor Magazines (Charlton)

V2#1,V2#2-Satire; Wolverton-a, 3 pgs. 10.00 30.00 80.00

CREATURE, THE (See Movie Classics)

CREATURES OF THE ID
1990-? ($2.95, B&W)
Caliber Press

1-?; 1-Frank Einstein (Madman) app.; Allred-a 5.00 15.00 50.00

CREATURES ON THE LOOSE (Formerly Tower of Shadows No. 1-9)(See Kull)
No. 10, March, 1971 - No. 37, Sept, 1975 (New-a & reprints)
Marvel Comics Group

10-(15¢)-1st King Kull story; see Kull the Conqueror; Wrightson-a 3.20 9.60 32.00
11-15 1.25 3.75 10.00
29,31-37: 16-Origin Warrior of Mars (begins? ends #21). 21,22-Steranko-c. 22-29-Thongor-c/stories. 1.00 2.80 7.00
30-Manwolf begins 1.10 3.30 9.00

NOTE: ***Crandall*** *a-13.* ***Ditko*** *r-15, 17, 18, 20, 22, 24, 27, 28.* ***Everett*** *a-16i(new).* ***Matt Fox*** *r-21i.* ***Howard*** *a-26i.* ***Gil Kane*** *a-16p, 17p, 19i; c-16, 17, 19, 20, 25, 29, 33p, 35p, 36p.* ***Kirby*** *a-10r, 16(2)r, 17r, 19r.* ***Morrow*** *a-20, 21.* ***Perez*** *a-33-37; c-34p.* ***Sinnott*** *r-21.* ***Sutton*** *c-10.* ***Tuska*** *a-31p, 32p.*

CREECH, THE
Oct, 1997 - No. 3, Jan, 1998 ($1.95/$2.50, limited series)
Image Comics

1-Capullo-s/c/a(p) 1.95
2,3-($2.50) 2.50

CREED
Dec, 1994 - No. 2, Jan, 1995 ($2.50, B&W)

Creed #1 © Trent Kaniuga

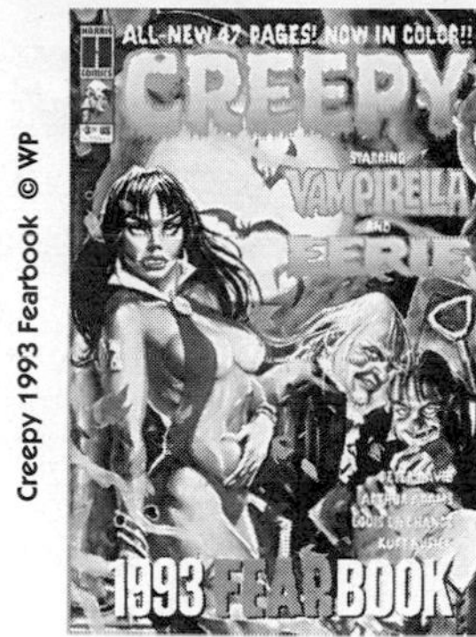

Creepy 1993 Fearbook © WP

Crime and Punishment #37 © LEV

	GD25	FN65	NM94
Hall of Heroes Comics			
1	1.85	5.50	15.00
2	1.50	4.50	12.00

CREED
June, 1995 - Present ($2.75/$3.00, B&W/color)
Lightning Comics

	GD25	FN65	NM94
1-($2.75)		1.60	4.00
1-($3.00, color)		1.80	4.50
1-($9.95)-Commemorative Edition	1.25	3.75	10.00
1-Twin Variant Edition (1250? print run)	1.25	3.75	10.00
1-Special Edition; polybagged w/certificate		1.60	4.00
1 Gold Collectors Edition; polybagged w/certificate		1.20	3.00
2,3-($3.00, color)-Butt Naked Edition & regular-c		1.20	3.00
3-($9.95)-Commemorative Edition; polybagged w/certificate & card	1.25	3.75	10.00

CREED: CRANIAL DISORDER
Oct, 1996 ($3.00, one-shot)
Lightning Comics

	GD25	FN65	NM94
1-3-Two covers		1.20	3.00
1-($5.95)-Platinum Edition		2.40	6.00
2,3-($9.95)Ltd.l Edition	1.25	3.75	10.00

CREED/TEENAGE MUTANT NINJA TURTLES
May, 1996 ($3.00, one-shot)
Lightning Comics

	GD25	FN65	NM94
1-Kaniuga-a(p)/scripts; Laird-c; variant-c exists		1.20	3.00
1-($9.95)-Platinum Edition	1.25	3.75	10.00
1-Special Edition; polybagged w/certificate		2.00	5.00

CREEPER, THE (See Beware..., Showcase #73 & 1st Issue Special #7)
Dec, 1997 - Present ($2.50)
DC Comics

	GD25	FN65	NM94
1-3-Kaminski-s/Martinbrough-a(p)		1.00	2.50

CREEPSVILLE
V2#1, Winter, 1995 ($4.95)
Laughing Reindeer Press

	GD25	FN65	NM94
V2#1-Comics w/text		2.00	5.00

CREEPY (See Warren Presents)
1964 - No. 145, Feb, 1983; No. 146, 1985 (B&W, magazine)
Warren Publishing Co./Harris Publ. #146

	GD25	FN65	NM94
1-Frazetta-a (his last story in comics?); Jack Davis-c; 1st Warren all comics magazine	8.00	24.00	90.00
2: 2-Frazetta-c & 1 pg. strip	4.00	12.00	45.00
3-13: 3-7,9-11-Frazetta-c. 7-Frazetta 1 pg. strip. 9-Creepy fan club sketch by Wrightson (1st published-a); has 1/2 pg. anti-smoking strip by Frazetta. 10-Brunner fan club sketch (1st published work)	2.25	6.75	20.00
14-Neal Adams 1st Warren work	2.50	7.50	24.00
15-20: 15-17-Frazetta-c	1.75	5.25	16.00
21-30: 27-Frazett-c	2.25	6.75	18.00
31,33-37,39-47,49	1.50	4.50	22.00
32-Frazetta-c; Harlan Ellison sty	3.60	10.80	36.00
38 (scarce)	3.00	9.00	30.00
48,55,65-(1973, 1974, 1975 Annuals) #55 & 65 contain an 8 pg. slick comic insert.	1.50	4.50	22.00
50-Vampirella-c	1.50	4.50	22.00
51,54,56-64: All contain an 8 pg. slick comic insert in middle	2.25	6.75	18.00
52,53,66-112,114-140: 93-Sports issue. 96-Aliens issue. 102-All monster issue. 121-All Severin-r issue. 125-All N. Adams-r issue. 137-All Williamson-r issue. 139-All Toth-r issue	1.00	3.00	8.00
113-All Wrightson-r issue	1.25	3.75	10.00
141-145 (low dist.) 144-Giant, $2.25; Frazetta-c	1.85	5.50	15.00
146 ($2.95)-1st from Harris; resurrection issue	5.00	15.00	40.00
Year Book 1968, 1969	3.00	9.00	30.00
Year Book 1970-Neal Adams, Ditko-a(r)	3.00	9.00	30.00
Annual 1971,1972	3.00	9.00	30.00
1993 Fearbook ($3.95)-Harris Publ. Vampirella app.	3.00	9.00	30.00

NOTE: *All issues contain many good artists works:* ***Neal Adams, Brunner, Corben, Craig (Taycee), Crandall, Ditko, Evans, Frazetta, Heath, Jeff Jones, Krenkel, McWilliams, Morrow, Nino, Orlando, Ploog, Severin, Torres, Toth, Williamson, Wood, & Wrightson****; covers by* ***Crandall, Davis, Frazetta, Morrow, San Julian, Todd/Bode****; Otto Binder's "Adam Link" stories in No. 2, 4, 6, 8, 9, 12, 13, 15 with* ***Orlando*** *art.* ***Frazetta*** *c-2-7, 9-11, 15-17, 27, 32, 83r, 89r, 91r.* ***E.A. Poe*** *adaptations in 66, 69, 70.*

CREEPY THINGS
July, 1975 - No. 6, June, 1976
Charlton Comics

	GD25	FN65	NM94
1	1.26	3.75	10.00
2-6: Ditko-a in 3,5. Sutton c-3,4		2.00	5.00
Modern Comics Reprint 2-6(1977)		1.60	4.00

CRIME AND JUSTICE (Rookie Cop? No. 27 on)
March, 1951 - No. 26, Sept, 1955
Capitol Stories/Charlton Comics

	GD25	FN65	NM94
1	26.00	75.00	180.00
2	8.35	25.00	55.00
3-8,10-13: 6-Negligee panels	7.00	21.00	45.00
9-Classic story "Comics Vs. Crime"	17.00	49.00	120.00
14-Color illos in **POP**; gory story of man who beheads women	12.00	36.00	90.00
15-17,19-26; 15-Negligee panels	5.00	15.00	30.00
18-Ditko-a	19.00	55.00	140.00

NOTE: ***Alascia*** *c-20.* ***Ayers*** *a-17.* ***Shuster*** *a-19-21; c-19. Bondage c-11, 12.*

CRIME AND PUNISHMENT (Title inspired by 1935 film)
April, 1948 - No. 74, Aug, 1955
Lev Gleason Publications

	GD25	FN65	NM94
1-Mr. Crime app. on-c	25.00	75.00	180.00
2	13.00	39.00	90.00
3-Used in **SOTI**, pg. 112; injury-to-eye panel; Fuje-a	17.00	49.00	120.00
4,5	10.00	30.00	65.00
6-10	0.70	26.00	55.00
11-20	7.50	22.50	48.00
21-30	5.70	17.00	38.00
31-38,40-44,46: 46-One pg. Frazetta-a	5.00	15.00	30.00
39-Drug mention story "The 5 Dopes"	8.35	25.00	50.00
45- "Hophead Killer" drug story	8.35	25.00	50.00
47-57,60-65,70-74:	5.00	15.00	30.00
58-Used in **POP**, pg. 79	5.35	16.00	32.00
59-Used in **SOTI**, illo "What comic-book America stands for"	23.00	69.00	160.00
66-Toth-c/a(4); 3-D effect issue (3/54); 1st "Deep Dimension" process	31.00	94.00	220.00
67- "Monkey on His Back" heroin story; 3-D effect issue	25.00	75.00	175.00
68-3-D effect issue; Toth-c (7/54)	23.00	69.00	160.00
69- "The Hot Rod Gang" dope crazy kids	9.15	27.00	55.00

NOTE: ***Biro*** *c-most.* ***Everett*** *a-31.* ***Fuje*** *a-3, 4, 12, 13, 17, 18, 20, 26, 27.* ***Guardineer*** *a-2-4, 10, 14, 17, 18, 20, 26-28, 32, 38-44.* ***Kinstler*** *c-69.* ***McWilliams*** *a-41, 48, 49.* ***Tuska*** *a-28, 30, 51, 64, 70.*

CRIME AND PUNISHMENT: MARSHALL LAW TAKES MANHATTAN
1989 ($4.95, 52 pgs., direct sales only, mature readers)
Marvel Comics (Epic Comics)

	GD25	FN65	NM94
nn-Graphic album featuring Marshall Law		2.00	5.00

CRIME CAN'T WIN (Formerly Cindy Smith)
No. 41, 9/50 - No. 43, 2/51; No. 4, 4/51 - No. 12, 9/53
Marvel/Atlas Comics (TCI 41/CCC 42,43,4-12)

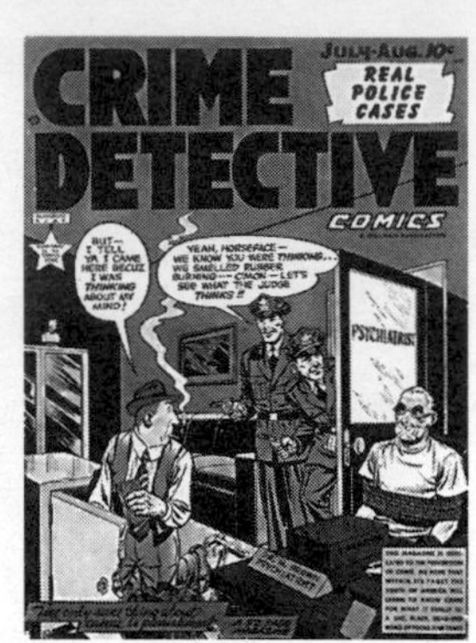

Crime Detective Comics #9 © HILL

Crime Does Not Pay #26 © LEV

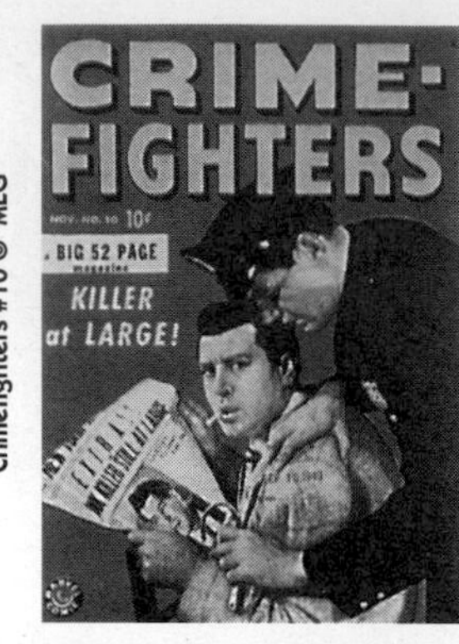

Crimefighters #10 © MEG

	GD25	FN65	NM94
41(#1)	20.00	60.00	150.00
42(#2)	11.50	34.00	85.00
43(#3)-Horror story	13.00	39.00	95.00
4(4/51),5-12: 10-Possible use in **SOTI**, pg. 161	9.00	27.00	60.00

NOTE: ***Robinson** a-9-11. **Tuska** a-43.*

CRIME CASES COMICS (Formerly Willie Comics)
No. 24, 8/50 - No. 27, 3/51; No. 5, 5/51 - No. 12, 7/52
Marvel/Atlas Comics(CnPC No.24-8/MJMC No.9-12)

	GD25	FN65	NM94
24 (#1, 52 pgs.)-True police cases	12.00	36.00	90.00
25-27(#2-4): 27-Morisi-a	9.00	27.00	60.00
5-12: 11-Robinson-a. 12-Tuska-a	7.15	21.50	50.00

CRIME CLINIC
No. 10, July-Aug, 1951 - No. 5, Summer, 1952
Ziff-Davis Publishing Co.

	GD25	FN65	NM94
10(#1)-Painted-c; origin Dr. Tom Rogers	21.00	62.00	150.00
11(#2),4,5: 4,5-Painted-c	14.00	43.00	105.00
3-Used in **SOTI**, pg. 18	16.00	47.00	115.00

NOTE: *All have painted covers by **Saunders**. **Starr** a-10.*

CRIME CLINIC
May, 1995 - No. 2, Oct, 1995 ($2.95, B&W, limited series)
Slave Labor Graphics

	GD25	FN65	NM94
1,2		1.20	3.00

CRIME DETECTIVE COMICS
Mar-Apr, 1948 - V3#8, May-June, 1953
Hillman Periodicals

	GD25	FN65	NM94
V1#1-The Invisible 6, costumed villains app; Fuje-c/a, 15 pgs.	20.00	60.00	150.00
2,5: 5-Krigstein-a	8.50	26.00	60.00
3,4,6,7,10-12: 6-McWilliams-a	7.15	21.50	50.00
8-Kirbyish-a by McCann	7.15	21.50	50.00
9-Used in **SOTI**, pg. 16 & "Caricature of the author in a position comic book publishers wish he were in permanently" illo.	29.00	86.00	210.00
V2#1,4,7-Krigstein-a: 1-Tuska-a	7.85	23.50	55.00
2,3,5,6,8-12 (1-2/52)	5.35	16.00	32.00
V3#1-Drug use-c	5.70	17.00	35.00
2-8	4.25	13.00	28.00

NOTE: ***Briefer** a-11, V3#1. **Kinstlerish**-a by **McCann**-V2#7, V3#2. **Powell** a-10, 11. **Starr** a-10.*

CRIME DETECTOR
Jan, 1954 - No. 5, Sept, 1954
Timor Publications

	GD25	FN65	NM94
1	13.00	39.00	95.00
2	7.15	21.50	50.00
3,4	6.50	19.50	45.00
5-Disbrow-a (classic)	13.50	41.00	105.00

CRIME DOES NOT PAY (Formerly Silver Streak Comics No. 1-21)
No. 22, June, 1942 - No. 147, July, 1955 (1st crime comic)
Comic House/Lev Gleason/Golfing (Title inspired by film)

	GD25	FN65	NM94
22(23 on cover, 22 on indicia)-Origin The War Eagle & only app.; Chip Gardner begins; #22 was rebound in Complete Book of True Crime (Scarce)	167.00	500.00	1500.00
23 (Scarce)	100.00	300.00	900.00
24-Intro. & 1st app. Mr. Crime (Scarce)	75.00	225.00	675.00
25-30	44.00	132.00	400.00
31-40	29.00	86.00	230.00
41-Origin & 1st app. Officer Common Sense	20.00	60.00	160.00
42-Electrocution-c	24.00	71.00	190.00
43-46,48-50: 44,45,50 are 68 pg. issues	12.00	38.00	100.00
47-Electric chair-c	23.00	68.00	180.00
51-70: 63,64-Possible use in **SOTI**, pg. 306. 63-Contains Biro & Gleason's self censorship code of 12 listed restrictions (5/48)	11.30	34.00	90.00
71-99: 87-Chip Gardner begins, ends #100	8.75	26.25	70.00
100	9.50	28.00	75.00
101-104,107-110: 102-Chip Gardner app	7.15	21.50	50.00
105-Used in **POP**, pg. 84	8.50	26.00	60.00
106,114-Frazetta-a, 1 pg.	7.15	21.50	50.00
111-Used in **POP**, pgs. 80 & 81; injury-to-eye sty illo	7.15	21.50	50.00
112,113,115-130	5.70	17.00	35.00
131-140	4.25	13.00	28.00
141,142-Last pre-code issue; Kubert-a(1)	7.15	21.50	50.00
143,147-Kubert-a, one story each	7.15	21.50	50.00
144-146	4.25	13.00	28.00
1(Golfing-1945)	5.70	17.00	35.00
The Best of...(1944, 128 pgs.)-Series contains 4 rebound issues	67.00	200.00	600.00
...1945 issue	50.00	150.00	450.00
...1946-48 issues	37.00	110.00	330.00
...1949-50 issues	36.00	108.00	285.00
...1951-53 issues	28.00	84.00	225.00

NOTE: *Many issues contain violent covers and stories. Who Dunnit by **Guardineer**-39-42, 44-105, 108-110; Chip Gardner by **Bob Fujitani (Fuje)**-88-103. **Alderman** a-29, 41-44, 49. **Dan Barry** a-75. **Biro** c-1-76, 122, 142. **Briefer** a-29(2), 30, 31, 33, 37, 39. **G. Colan** a-105. **Fuje** c-88, 89, 91-94, 96, 98, 99, 102, 103. **Guardineer** a-57, 71. **Kubert** c-143. **Landau** a-118. **Maurer** a-29, 39, 41, 42. **McWilliams** a-91, 93, 95, 100-103. **Palais** a-30, 33, 37, 39, 41-43, 44(2), 46, 49. **Powell** a-146, 147. **Tuska** a-48, 50(2), 51, 52, 56, 57(2), 60-64, 66, 67, 71. Painted c-87-102. Bondage c-43, 62, 98.*

CRIME EXPOSED
June, 1948; Dec, 1950 - No. 14, June, 1952
Marvel Comics (PPI)/Marvel Atlas Comics (PrPI)

	GD25	FN65	NM94
1(6/48)	25.00	75.00	180.00
1(12/50)	15.00	45.00	110.00
2	10.00	30.00	70.00
3-9,11,14	8.35	25.00	55.00
10-Used in **POP**, pg. 81	8.50	26.00	60.00
12-Krigstein & Robinson-a	8.50	26.00	60.00
13-Used in **POP**, pg. 81; Krigstein-a	10.00	30.00	70.00

NOTE: ***Maneely** c-8. **Robinson** a-11, 12. **Tuska** a-3, 4.*

CRIMEFIGHTERS
Apr, 1948 - No. 10, Nov, 1949
Marvel Comics (CmPS 1-3/CCC 4-10)

	GD25	FN65	NM94
1-Some copies are undated & could be reprints	20.00	60.00	150.00
2,3: 3-Morphine addict story	10.00	30.00	70.00
4-10: 6-Anti-Wertham editorial. 9,10-Photo-c	8.50	26.00	60.00

CRIME FIGHTERS (...Always Win)
No. 11, Sept, 1954 - No. 13, Jan, 1955
Atlas Comics (CnPC)

	GD25	FN65	NM94
11-13: 11-Maneely-a,13-Pakula, Reinman, Severin-a	8.75	26.25	65.00

CRIME-FIGHTING DETECTIVE (Shock Detective Cases No. 20 on; formerly Criminals on the Run)
No. 11, Apr-May, 1950 - No. 19, June, 1952 (Based on true crime cases)
Star Publications

	GD25	FN65	NM94
11-L. B. Cole-c/a (2 pgs.); L. B. Cole-c on all	12.00	36.00	95.00
12,13,15-19: 17-Young King Cole & Dr. Doom app.	8.75	26.25	70.00
14-L. B. Cole-c/a, r/Law-Crime #2	10.50	32.00	85.00

CRIME FILES
No. 5, Sept, 1952 - No. 6, Nov, 1952
Standard Comics

	GD25	FN65	NM94
5-1pg. Alex Toth-a; used in **SOTI**, pg. 4 (text)	20.00	60.00	150.00
6-Sekowsky-a	10.00	30.00	75.00

CRIME ILLUSTRATED (Magazine)
Nov-Dec, 1955 - No. 2, Spring, 1956 (25¢, Adult Suspense Stories on-c)
E. C. Comics

	GD25	FN65	NM94
1-Ingels & Crandall-a	11.30	34.00	90.00

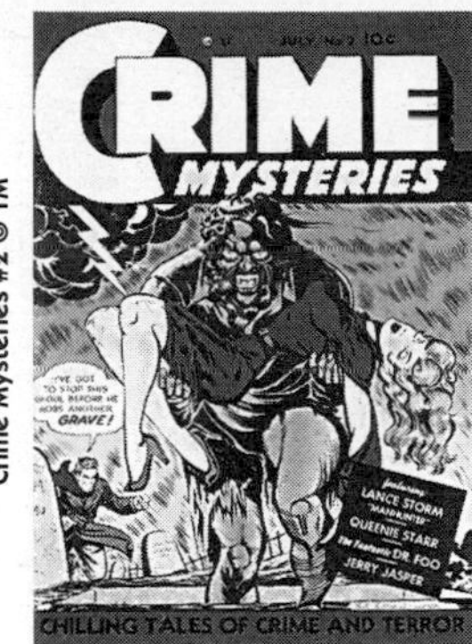

Crime Mysteries #2 © TM

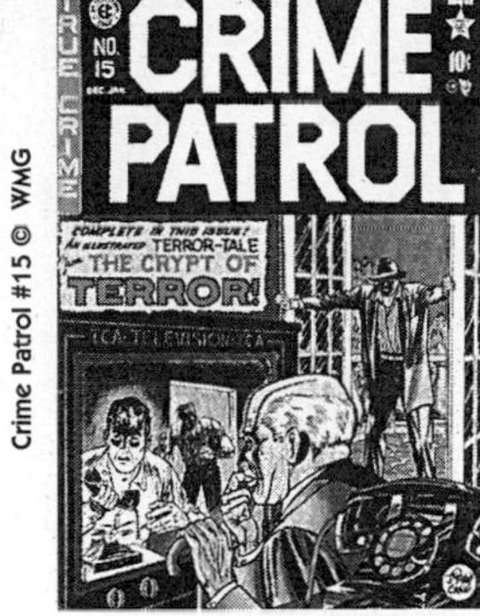

Crime Patrol #15 © WMG

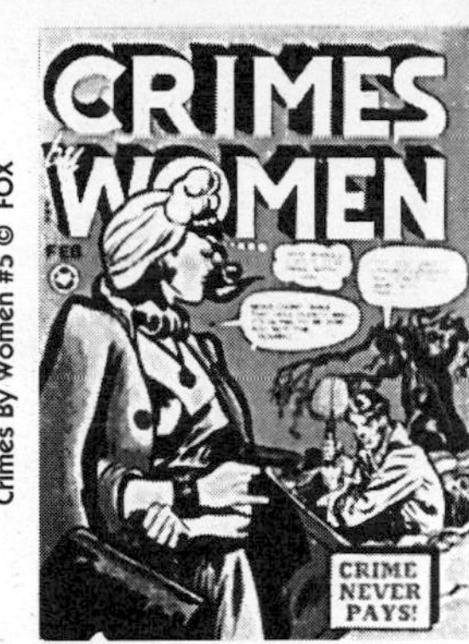

Crimes By Women #5 © FOX

	GD25	FN65	NM94
2-Ingels & Crandall-a	9.50	28.00	75.00

NOTE: **Craig** a-2. **Crandall** a-1, 2; c-2. **Evans** a-1. **Davis** a-2. **Ingels** a-1, 2. **Krigstein/Crandall** a-1. **Orlando** a-1, 2; c-1.

CRIME INCORPORATED (Formerly Crimes Incorporated)
No. 2, Aug, 1950; No. 3, Aug, 1951
Fox Features Syndicate

	GD25	FN65	NM94
2	20.00	60.00	150.00
3(1951)-Hollingsworth-a	14.00	43.00	110.00

CRIME MACHINE (Magazine)
Feb, 1971 - No. 2, May, 1971 (B&W)
Skywald Publications

	GD25	FN65	NM94
1-Kubert-a(2)(r)(Avon)	4.50	13.50	45.00
2-Torres, Wildey-a; violent-c/a	3.00	9.00	30.00

CRIME MUST LOSE! (Formerly Sports Action?)
No. 4, Oct, 1950 - No. 12, April, 1952
Sports Action (Atlas Comics)

	GD25	FN65	NM94
4-Ann Brewster-a in all; c-used in N.Y. Legis. Comm. documents	14.00	43.00	105.00
5-10,12: 9-Robinson-a	10.00	30.00	65.00
11-Used in **POP**, pg. 89	10.00	30.00	70.00

CRIME MUST PAY THE PENALTY (Formerly Four Favorites; Penalty #47, 48)
No. 33, Feb, 1948; No. 2, June, 1948 - No. 48, Jan, 1956
Ace Magazines (Current Books)

	GD25	FN65	NM94
33(#1, 2/48)-Becomes Four Teeners #34?	24.00	73.00	185.00
2(6/48)-Extreme violence; Palais-a?	16.00	47.00	120.00
3- "Frisco Mary" story used in Senate Investigation report, pg. 7	10.50	32.00	85.00
4,8-Transvestism stories	11.30	34.00	90.00
5-7,9,10	7.15	21.50	50.00
11-20-Drug story "Dealers in White Death"	6.50	19.50	45.00
21-32,34-40,42-48	5.35	16.00	32.00
33(7/53)- "Dell Fabry-Junk King" drug story; mentioned in Love and Death	7.15	21.50	50.00
41-reprints "Dealers in White Death"	7.15	21.50	50.00

NOTE: **Cameron** a-29-31, 34, 35, 39-41. **Colan** a-20, 31. **Kremer** a-3, 37r. **Larsen** a-32. **Palais** a-5?,37.

CRIME MUST STOP
October, 1952 (52 pgs.)
Hillman Periodicals

	GD25	FN65	NM94
V1#1(Scarce)-Similar to Monster Crime; Mort Lawrence, Krigstein-a	50.00	150.00	425.00

CRIME MYSTERIES (Secret Mysteries #16 on; combined with Crime Smashers #7 on)
May, 1952 - No. 15, Sept, 1954
Ribage Publishing Corp. (Trojan Magazines)

	GD25	FN65	NM94
1-Transvestism story; crime & terror stories begin	40.00	120.00	350.00
2-Marijuana story (7/52)	32.00	96.00	230.00
3-One pg. Frazetta-a	26.00	77.00	180.00
4-Cover shows girl in bondage having her blood drained; 1 pg. Frazetta-a	39.00	118.00	300.00
5-10	20.00	60.00	150.00
11,12,14	19.00	56.00	140.00
13-(5/54)-Angelo Torres 1st comic work (inks over Check's pencils); Check-a	24.00	71.00	180.00
15-Acid in face-c	29.00	86.00	210.00

NOTE: **Fass** a-13; c-4, 10. **Hollingsworth** a-10-13, 15; c-2, 12, 13, 15. **Kiefer** a-4. **Woodbridge** a-13? Bondage-c-1, 8, 12.

CRIME ON THE RUN (See Approved Comics #8)

CRIME ON THE WATERFRONT (Formerly Famous Gangsters)
No. 4, May, 1952 (Painted cover)
Realistic Publications

	GD25	FN65	NM94
4	24.00	73.00	180.00

CRIME PATROL (Formerly International #1-5; International Crime Patrol #6; becomes Crypt of Terror #17 on)
No. 7, Summer, 1948 - No. 16, Feb-Mar, 1950
E. C. Comics

	GD25	FN65	NM94
7-Intro. Captain Crime	50.00	150.00	420.00
8-14: 12-Ingels-a	44.00	132.00	360.00
15-Intro. of Crypt Keeper (inspired by Witches Tales radio show) & Crypt of Terror (see Tales From the Crypt #33 for origin); used by N.Y. Legis. Comm.; last pg. Feldstein-a	212.00	638.00	1800.00
16-2nd Crypt Keeper app.; Roussos-a	138.00	412.00	1150.00

NOTE: **Craig** c/a in most issues. **Feldstein** a-9-16. **Kiefer** a-8, 10, 11. **Moldoff** a-7.

CRIME PHOTOGRAPHER (See Casey...)

CRIME REPORTER
Aug, 1948 - No. 3, Dec, 1948 (Indicia shows Oct.)
St. John Publ. Co.

	GD25	FN65	NM94
1-Drug club story	40.00	120.00	300.00
2-Used in **SOTI**: illo- "Children told me what the man was going to do with the red-hot poker;" r/Dynamic #17 with editing; Baker-c; Tuska-a	58.00	174.00	485.00
3-Baker-c; Tuska-a	31.00	92.00	220.00

CRIMES BY WOMEN
June, 1948 - No. 15, Aug, 1951; 1954 (True crime cases)
Fox Features Syndicate

	GD25	FN65	NM94
1-True story of Bonnie Parker	100.00	300.00	840.00
2,3: 3-Used in **SOTI**, pg. 234	53.00	159.00	440.00
4,5,7-9,11-15: 8-Used in **POP**.14-Spanking panel r/from All Famous Crime Stories (1949) (Fox Giant)	48.00	146.00	390.00
6-Classic girl fight-c; acid-in-face panel	53.00	159.00	425.00
10-Used in **SOTI**, pg. 72; girl fight-c	45.00	136.00	365.00
54(M.S. Publ.-'54)-Reprint; (formerly My Love Secret)	22.00	66.00	155.00

CRIMES INCORPORATED (Formerly My Past)
No. 12, June, 1950 (Crime Incorporated No. 2 on)
Fox Features Syndicate

	GD25	FN65	NM94
12	10.50	32.00	85.00

CRIMES INCORPORATED (See Fox Giants)

CRIME SMASHER (See Whiz #76)
Summer, 1948 (one-shot)
Fawcett Publications

	GD25	FN65	NM94
1-Formerly Spy Smasher	39.00	118.00	280.00

CRIME SMASHERS (Becomes Secret Mysteries No. 16 on)
Oct, 1950 - No. 15, Mar, 1953
Ribage Publishing Corp.(Trojan Magazines)

	GD25	FN65	NM94
1-Used in **SOTI**, pg. 19,20, & illo "A girl raped and murdered;" Sally the Sleuth begins	62.00	187.00	525.00
2-Kubert-c	36.00	107.00	260.00
3,4	26.00	79.00	190.00
5-Wood-a	34.00	103.00	250.00
6,8-11	20.00	60.00	145.00
7-Female heroin junkie story	21.00	62.00	150.00
12-Injury to eye panel; 1 pg. Frazetta-a	21.00	64.00	155.00
13-Used in **POP**, pgs. 79,80; 1 pg. Frazetta-a	21.00	64.00	155.00
14,15	18.00	54.00	130.00

NOTE: **Hollingsworth** a-14. **Kiefer** a-15. Bondage c-7, 9.

CRIME SUSPENSTORIES (Formerly Vault of Horror No. 12-14)
No. 15, Oct-Nov, 1950 - No. 27, Feb-Mar, 1955
E. C. Comics

15-Identical to #1 in content; #1 printed on outside front cover. #15 (formerly "The Vault of Horror") printed and blackened out on inside front cover with Vol. 1, No. 1 printed over it.

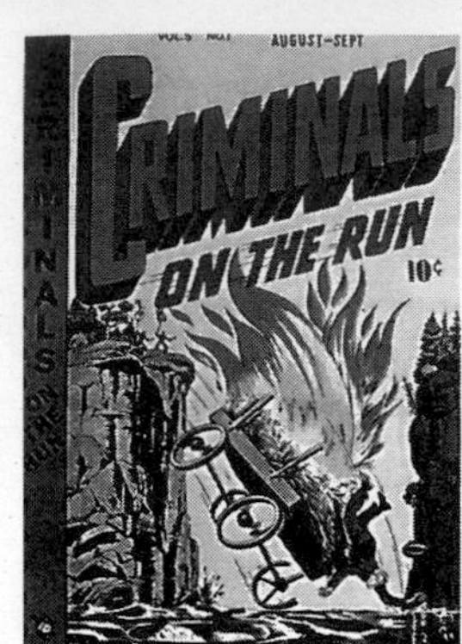

Criminals on the Run V5 #1 © NOVP

Crisis On Infinite Earths #8 © DC

Critters #23 © Fantagraphics Books

GD25 FN65 NM94

Evidently, several of No. 15 were printed before a decision was made not to drop the Vault of Horror and Haunt of Fear series. The print run was stopped on No. 15 and continued on No. 1. All of No. 15 were changed as described above.99 119.00 356.00 1000.00
1 94.00 281.00 775.00
2 49.00 146.00 400.00
3-5: 3-Poe adaptation. 3-Old Witch stories begin 38.00 114.00 275.00
6-10 30.00 90.00 220.00
11,12,14,15: 15-The Old Witch guest stars 23.00 69.00 165.00
13,16-Williamson-a 26.00 77.00 185.00
17-Williamson/Frazetta-a (6 pgs.) 28.00 84.00 200.00
18,19: 19-Used in **SOTI**, pg. 235 19.00 58.00 140.00
20-Cover used in **SOTI**, illo "Cover of a children's comic book" 26.00 77.00 185.00
21,24-27: 24- "Food For Thought" similar to "Cave In" in Amazing Detective Cases #13 (1952) 13.50 41.00 95.00
22,23-Used in Senate investigation on juvenile delinquency. 22-Ax decapitation-c 20.00 60.00 140.00
NOTE: ***Craig*** *a-1-21; c-1-18, 20-22.* ***Crandall*** *a-18-26.* ***Davis*** *a-4, 5, 7, 9-12, 20.* ***Elder*** *a-17,18.* ***Evans*** *a-15, 19, 21, 23, 25, 27; c-23, 24.* ***Feldstein*** *c-19.* ***Ingels*** *a-1-12, 14, 15, 27.* ***Kamen*** *a-2, 4-18, 20-27; c-25-27.* ***Krigstein*** *a-22, 24, 25, 27.* ***Kurtzman*** *a-1, 3.* ***Orlando*** *a-16, 22, 24, 26.* ***Wood*** *a-1, 3. Issues No. 11-15 have E. C. "quickie" stories. No. 25 contains the famous "Are You a Red Dupe?" editorial. Ray Bradbury adaptations-15, 17.*

CRIME SUSPENSTORIES
Nov, 1992 - Present ($1.50/$2.00/$2.50)
Russ Cochran/Gemstone Publishing
1-3: 1,2-r/Crime SuspenStories #1,2 1.50
4-15-($2.00) .80 2.00
16-23-($2.50) 1.00 2.50

CRIMINALS ON THE RUN (Formerly Young King Cole)
(Crime Fighting Detective No. 11 on)
V4#1, Aug-Sept, 1948 - #10, Dec-Jan, 1949-50
Premium Group (Novelty Press)
V4#1-Young King Cole continues 23.00 69.00 170.00
2-6: 6-Dr. Doom app. 19.00 56.00 140.00
7-Classic "Fish in the Face" c by L. B. Cole 40.00 120.00 315.00
V5#1,2 (#8,9): 9-L. B. Cole-c 17.00 49.00 120.00
10-L. B. Cole-c 17.00 49.00 120.00
NOTE: *Most issues have* ***L. B. Cole*** *covers.* ***McWilliams*** *a-V4#6, 7, V5#2; c-V4#5.*

CRIMSON AVENGER, THE (See Detective Comics #20 for 1st app.)(Also see Leading Comics #1 & World's Best/Finest Comics)
June, 1988 - No. 4, Sept, 1988 ($1.00, limited series)
DC Comics
1-4 .50 1.00

CRIMSON NUN
May, 1997 - No. 4, Nov, 1997 ($2.95, limited series)
Antarctic Press
1-4 2.95

CRIMSON PLAGUE
June, 1997 - Present ($2.95, limited series)
Event Comics
1 George Perez-a 1.60 4.00

CRISIS ON INFINITE EARTHS (Also see Official... Index)
Apr, 1985 - No. 12, Mar, 1986 (maxi-series)
DC Comics
1-1st DC app. Blue Beetle & Detective Karp from Charlton; Perez-c on all 2.40 6.00
2-7, 9-11: 6-Intro Charlton's Capt. Atom, Nightshade, Question, Judomaster, Peacemaker & Thunderbolt into DC Universe. 7-Double size; death of Supergirl 9-Intro. Charlton's Ghost into DC Universe. 10-Intro. Charlton's Banshee, Dr. Spectro, Image, Punch & Jewellee into DC Universe; Starman (Prince Gavyn) dies. 2.40 6.00
8-Death of the Flash (Barry Allen) 1.00 3.00 8.00

GD25 FN65 NM94

12-(52 pgs.)-Deaths of Dove, Kole, Lori Lemaris, Sunburst, G.A. Robin & Huntress; Kid Flash becomes new Flash; 3rd & final DC app. of the 3 Lt. Marvels; Green Fury gets new look (becomes Green Flame in Infinity, Inc. #32) 2.40 6.00

CRITICAL MASS (See A Shadowline Saga: Critical Mass)

CRITTERS (Also see Usagi Yojimbo Summer Special)
1986 - No. 50, 1990 ($1.70/$2.00, B&W)
Fantagraphics Books
1-Cutey Bunny, Usagi Yojimbo app. 1.00 2.50
2-11: 3,6,7,10,11-Usagi Yojimbo app. 11-Christmas Special (68 pgs.); Usagi Yojimbo .80 2.00
12-22,24-49: 14,38-Usagi Yojimbo app. 22-Watchmen parody; two diff. covers exist .70 1.75
23-With Alan Moore Flexi-disc ($3.95) 1.60 4.00
50 ($4.95, 84 pgs.)-Neil the Horse, Capt. Jack, Sam & Max & Usagi Yojimbo app.; Quagmire, Shaw-a 2.00 5.00
Special 1 (1/88, $2.00) .80 2.00

CROSLEY'S HOUSE OF FUN (Also see Tee and Vee Crosley...)
1950 (Giveaway, paper cover, 32 pgs.)
Crosley Div. AVCO Mfg. Corp.
nn-Strips revolve around Crosley appliances 4.25 13.00 26.00

CROSS
No. 0, Oct, 1995 - No. 6, Apr, 1995 ($2.95, limited series, mature)
Dark Horse Comics
0-6: Darrow-c & Vachss scripts in all 1.20 3.00

CROSS AND THE SWITCHBLADE, THE
1972 (35-49¢)
Spire Christian Comics (Fleming H. Revell Co.)
1-Some issues have nn 1.00

CROSSFIRE
1973 (39/49¢)
Spire Christian Comics (Fleming H. Revell Co.)
nn 1.00

CROSSFIRE (Also see DNAgents)
5/84 - No. 17, 3/86; No. 18, 1/87 - No. 26, 2/88 ($1.50, Baxter paper)
Eclipse Comics
1-17: 1-DNAgents x-over; Spiegle-c/a begins. 12-Dave Stevens-c. 12,13-Death of Marilyn Monroe. 1.50
18-26-(B&W) .70 1.80

CROSSFIRE AND RAINBOW (Also see DNAgents)
June, 1986 - No. 4, Sept, 1986 ($1.25, deluxe format)
Eclipse Comics
1-3: Spiegle-a 1.30
4-Dave Stevens-c .80 2.00

CROSSING THE ROCKIES (See Classics Illustrated Special Issue)

CROSSROADS
July, 1988 - No. 5, Nov, 1988 ($3.25, limited series, deluxe format)
First Comics
1-5 1.20 3.25

CROW, THE (Also see Caliber Presents)
Feb, 1989 - No. 4, 1989 ($1.95, B&W, limited series)
Caliber Press
1-James O'Barr-c/a/scripts 7.50 22.50 75.00
1-3-2nd printing 1.50 4.50 12.00
2,4 4.00 12.00 40.00
2-3rd printing 1.25 3.75 10.00
3 4.20 12.60 42.00

The Crow: City Of Angels #1 © James O'Barr

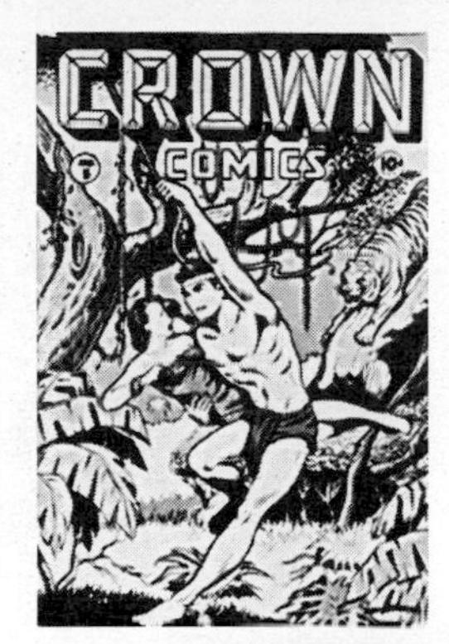

Crown Comics #5 © Golfing/McCombs Pub.

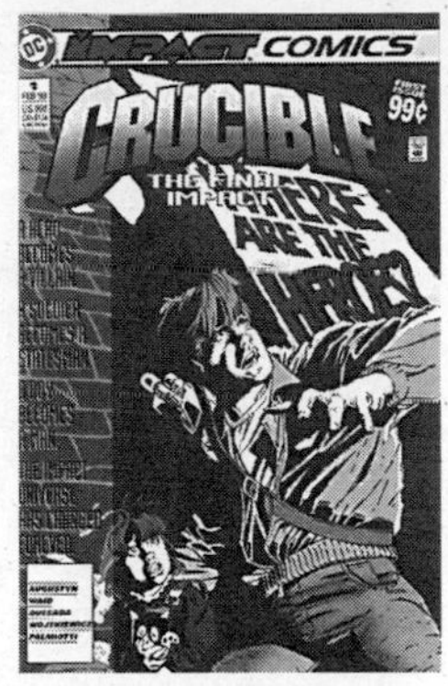

Crucible #1 © DC

CROW, THE
Jan, 1992 - No. 3, 1992 ($4.95, B&W, 68 pgs.)
Tundra Publishing, Ltd.

	GD25	FN65	NM94
1-3: 1-r/#1,2 of Caliber series. 2-r/#3 of Caliber series w/new material. 3-All new material	1.50	4.50	12.00

CROW, THE
Jan, 1996 - No. 3, Mar, 1996 ($2.95, B&W, limited series)
Kitchen Sink Press

	GD25	FN65	NM94
1-3: James O'Barr-c/scripts		1.20	3.00

CROW, THE: CITY OF ANGELS (Movie)
July, 1996 - No. 3, Sept, 1996 ($2.95, limited series)
Kitchen Sink Press

	GD25	FN65	NM94
1-3: Adaptation of film; two-c (photo & illos.). 1-Vincent Perez interview		1.20	3.00

CROW, THE: FLESH AND BLOOD
May, 1996 - No. 3, July, 1996 ($2.95, limited series)
Kitchen Sink Press

	GD25	FN65	NM94
1-3: O'Barr-c		1.20	3.00

CROW, THE: WAKING NIGHTMARES
Jan, 1997 - No.4 ($2.95, B&W, limited series)
Kitchen Sink Press

	GD25	FN65	NM94
1-Miran Kim-c		1.20	3.00

CROW, THE: WILD JUSTICE
Oct, 1996 - No.3, Dec, 1996 ($2.95, B&W, limited series)
Kitchen Sink Press

	GD25	FN65	NM94
1-Prosser-s/Adlard-a		1.20	3.00

CROWN COMICS
Winter, 1944-45; No. 2, Sum, 1945 - No. 19, July, 1949
Golfing/McCombs Publ.

	GD25	FN65	NM94
1- "The Oblong Box" E.A. Poe adaptation	30.00	90.00	220.00
2,3-Baker-a; 3-Voodah by Baker	19.00	56.00	140.00
4-6-Baker-c/a; Voodah app. #4,5	20.00	60.00	150.00
7-Feldstein, Baker, Kamen-a; Baker-c	19.00	56.00	140.00
8-Baker-a; Voodah app.	17.00	51.00	125.00
9-11,13-19: Voodah in #10-19. 13-New logo	10.00	30.00	70.00
12-Master Marvin by Feldstein, Starr-a; Voodah-c	10.00	30.00	75.00

NOTE: ***Bolle** a-11, 13-16, 18, 19; c-11p, 15. **Powell** a-19. **Starr** a-11-13; c-11i.*

CRUCIBLE
Feb, 1993 - No. 6, July, 1993 ($1.25, limited series)
DC Comics (Impact Comics)

	GD25	FN65	NM94
1-(99¢)-Quesada-c(p) & layouts begin; neon ink-c			1.00
2-6: 2-Last Quesada-c. 4-Last Quesada layouts			1.25

CRUSADER FROM MARS (See Tops in Adventure)
Jan-Mar, 1952 - No. 2, Fall, 1952 (Painted-c)
Ziff-Davis Publ. Co.

	GD25	FN65	NM94
1-Cover is dated Spring	59.00	178.00	500.00
2-Bondage-c	48.00	144.00	400.00

CRUSADER RABBIT (TV)
No. 735, Oct, 1956 - No. 805, May, 1957
Dell Publishing Co.

	GD25	FN65	NM94
Four Color 735 (#1)	30.00	89.00	325.00
Four Color 805	23.00	68.00	250.00

CRUSADERS, THE (Religious)
1974 - Vol. 16, 1985 (39/69¢, 36 pgs.)
Chick Publications

	GD25	FN65	NM94
Vol.1-Operation Bucharest ('74). Vol.2-The Broken Cross ('74). Vol.3-Scarface ('74). Vol.4-Exorcists ('75). Vol.5-Chaos ('75)			1.00
Vol.6-Primal Man? ('76)-(Disputes evolution theory). Vol.7-The Ark-(claims proof of existence, destroyed by Bolsheviks). Vol.8-The Gift-(Life story of Christ). Vol.9-Angel of Light-(Story of the Devil). Vol.10-Spellbound?-(Tells how rock music is Satanical & produced by witches). 11-Sabotage?. 12-Alberto. 13-Double Cross. 14-The Godfathers. (No. 6-14 low in distribution; loaded in religious propaganda.). 15-The Force. 16-The Four Horsemen			1.00

CRUSADERS (Southern Knights No. 2 on)
1982 (B&W, magazine size)
Guild Publications

	GD25	FN65	NM94
1-1st app. Southern Knights		1.20	3.00

CRUSADERS, THE (Also see Black Hood, The Jaguar, The Comet, The Fly, Legend of the Shield, The Mighty... & The Web)
May, 1992 - No. 8, Dec, 1992 ($1.00/$1.25)
DC Comics (Impact Comics)

	GD25	FN65	NM94
1-Contains 3 Impact trading cards			1.25
2-8			1.00

CRUSH, THE
Jan, 1996 - No. 5, July, 1996 ($2.25, limited series)
Image Comics (Motown Machineworks)

	GD25	FN65	NM94
1-5: Baron scripts			2.25

CRY FOR DAWN
1989 - No. 9 ($2.25, B&W, mature)
Cry For Dawn Pub.

	GD25	FN65	NM94
1	19.00	57.00	190.00
1-2nd printing	8.00	24.00	80.00
1-3rd printing	6.50	19.50	65.00
2	11.50	34.00	115.00
2-2nd printing	3.00	9.00	30.00
3	8.00	24.00	80.00
4-6	4.00	12.00	40.00
5-2nd printing	1.00	3.00	8.00
7-9	2.50	7.50	20.00
4-9-Signed & numbered editions	4.00	12.00	40.00
...Calendar (1993)			47.00

CRYIN' LION COMICS
Fall, 1944 - No. 3, Spring, 1945
William H. Wise Co.

	GD25	FN65	NM94
1-Funny animal	12.00	36.00	95.00
2-Hitler app.	9.50	28.00	75.00
3	8.50	26.00	60.00

CRYPT
Aug, 1995 - No.2, Oct. 1995 ($2.50, limited series)
Image Comics (Extreme Studios)

	GD25	FN65	NM94
1,2-Prophet app.		1.00	2.50

CRYPTIC WRITINGS OF MEGADETH
Sept, 1997 - Present ($2.95, quarterly)
Chaos! Comics

	GD25	FN65	NM94
1,2-Stories based on song lyrics by Dave Mustaine			2.95

CRYPT OF DAWN (see Dawn)
1996 ($2.95, B&W, limited series)
Sirius

	GD25	FN65	NM94
1,2-Linsner-c/s; anthology.	1.25	3.75	10.00
Ltd. Edition	1.85	5.50	15.00

CRYPT OF SHADOWS
Jan, 1973 - No. 21, Nov, 1975 (#1-9 are 20¢)
Marvel Comics Group

	GD25	FN65	NM94
1-Wolverton-r/Advs. Into Terror #7	1.25	3.75	10.00

Crypt of Shadows #2 © MEG

Curse of Spawn #3 © Todd McFarlane

Cyberforce #6 © Top Cow

	GD25	FN65	NM94
2-21: 2-Starlin/Everett-c	1.00	2.80	7.00

NOTE: ***Briefer*** *a-2r.* ***Ditko*** *a-13r, 18-20r.* ***Everett*** *a-6, 14r; c-2i.* ***Heath*** *a-1r.* ***Gil Kane*** *c-1, 6.* ***Mort Lawrence*** *a-1r, 8r.* ***Maneely*** *a-2r.* ***Moldoff*** *a-8.* ***Powell*** *a-12r, 14r.* ***Tuska*** *a-2r.*

CRYPT OF TERROR (Formerly Crime Patrol; Tales From the Crypt No. 20 on)
No. 17, Apr-May, 1950 - No. 19, Aug-Sept, 1950
E. C. Comics

	GD25	FN65	NM94
17-1st New Trend to hit stands	238.00	712.00	2000.00
18,19	138.00	412.00	1150.00

NOTE: ***Craig*** *c/a-17-19.* ***Feldstein*** *a-17-19.* ***Ingels*** *a-19.* ***Kurtzman*** *a-18.* ***Wood*** *a-18. Canadian reprints known; see Table of Contents.*

CUD
Aug, 1992 - No. 8, Dec, 1994 ($2.25/$2.50/$2.75, B&W, mature)
Fantagraphics Books

	GD25	FN65	NM94
1($2.25)-Terry LaBan scripts & art in all		1.00	2.50
2-7 ($2.50): 6-1st Eno & Plum		1.10	2.75
8 ($2.75)		1.20	3.00

CUD COMICS
Jan, 1995 - Present ($2.95, B&W)
Dark Horse Comics

	GD25	FN65	NM94
1-8: Terry LaBan-c/a/scripts. 5-Nudity; marijuana story		1.20	3.00
Eno and Plum TPB (1997, $12.95) r/#1-4, DHP #93-95			12.95

CUPID
Dec, 1949 - No. 2, Mar, 1950
Marvel Comics (U.S.A.)

	GD25	FN65	NM94
1-Photo-c	11.00	33.00	80.00
2-Betty Page ('50s pin-up queen) photo-c; Powell-a (see My Love #4)	24.00	73.00	180.00

CURIO
1930's(?) (Tabloid size, 16-20 pgs.)
Harry 'A' Chesler

	GD25	FN65	NM94
nn	15.00	45.00	120.00

CURLY KAYOE COMICS (Boxing)
1946 - No. 8, 1950; Jan, 1958
United Features Syndicate/Dell Publ. Co.

	GD25	FN65	NM94
1 (1946)-Strip-r (Fritzi Ritz); biography of Sam Leff, Kayoe's artist	14.00	41.00	110.00
2	7.85	23.50	55.00
3-8	5.70	17.00	40.00
United Presents...(Fall, 1948)	5.00	15.00	30.00
Four Color 871 (Dell, 1/58)	1.80	5.50	20.00

CURSE OF DREADWOLF
Sept, 1994 ($2.75, B&W)
Lightning Comics

	GD25	FN65	NM94
1		1.10	2.75

CURSE OF RUNE (Becomes Rune, 2nd Series)
May, 1995 - No. 4, Aug, 1995 ($2.50, limited series)
Malibu Comics (Ultraverse)

	GD25	FN65	NM94
1-4: 1-Two covers form one image		1.00	2.50

CURSE OF THE SPAWN
Sept, 1996 - Present ($1.95)
Image Comics (Todd McFarlane Productions)

	GD25	FN65	NM94
1-Dwayne Turner-a(p)	1.25	3.75	10.00
2-3		1.60	4.00
4-14: 12-Movie photo-c of Melinda Clarke (Priest)			1.95

CURSE OF THE WEIRD
Dec, 1993 - No. 4, Mar, 1994 ($1.25, limited series)(Pre-code horror-r)
Marvel Comics

	GD25	FN65	NM94
1-4: 1,3,4-Wolverton-r(1-Eye of Doom; 3-Where Monsters Dwell; 4-The End of the World). 2-Orlando-r. 4-Zombie-r by Everett; painted-c		.80	2.00

NOTE: ***Briefer*** *r-2.* ***Jack Davis*** *a-4r.* ***Ditko*** *a-1r, 2r, 4r; c-1r.* ***Everett*** *r-1.* ***Heath*** *r-1-3.* ***Kubert*** *r-3.* ***Wolverton*** *a-1r, 3r, 4r.*

CUSTER'S LAST FIGHT
1950
Avon Periodicals

	GD25	FN65	NM94
nn-Partial reprint of Cowpuncher #1	14.00	41.00	110.00

CUTEY BUNNY (See Army Surplus Komikz Featuring...)

CUTIE PIE
May, 1955 - No. 3, Dec, 1955; No. 4, Feb, 1956; No. 5, Aug, 1956
Junior Reader's Guild (Lev Gleason)

	GD25	FN65	NM94
1	5.00	15.00	30.00
2-5: 4-Misdated 2/55	3.60	9.00	18.00

CUTTING EDGE
Dec, 1995 ($2.95)
Marvel Comics

	GD25	FN65	NM94
1-Hulk-c/story; Messner-Loebs scripts		1.20	3.00

CYBERCITY
Sept, 1995- Present ($2.95, bi-monthly)
CPM Comics

	GD25	FN65	NM94
Part One #1,2; Part Two #1,2; Part Three #1,2		1.20	3.00

CYBERELLA
Sept, 1996 - No. 12, Aug, 1997 ($2.25/$2.50)(1st Helix series)
DC Comics (Helix)

	GD25	FN65	NM94
1-5: Chaykin-s & Cameron-a in all. 1,2-Chaykin-c. 3-5-Cameron-c			2.25
6-12: 6-Begin $2.50-c			2.50

CYBERFORCE
Oct, 1992 - No. 4, 1993; No. 0, Sept, 1993 ($1.95, limited series)
Image Comics (Top Cow Productions)

	GD25	FN65	NM94
1-Silvestri-c/a in all; coupon for Image Comics #0; 1st Top Cow Productions title.	1.00	2.80	7.00
1-With coupon missing		.80	2.00
2-4: 2-(3/93). 3-Pitt-c/story. 4-Codename: Stryke Force back-up (1st app.); foil-c		.80	2.00
0-(9/93)-Walt Simonson-c/a/scripts		1.00	2.50

CYBERFORCE
V2#1, Nov, 1993 - Present ($1.95)
Image Comics (Top Cow Productions)/Top Cow Comics No. 28 on

	GD25	FN65	NM94
V2#1-24: 1-7-Marc Silvestri/Keith Williams-c/a. 8-McFarlane-c/a. 10-Painted variant-c exists. 18-Variant-c exists. 23-Velocity-c.		.80	2.00
1-3: 1-Gold Logo-c. 2-Silver embossed-c. 3-Gold embossed-c		3.75	10.00
1-(99¢, 3/96, 2nd printing)			1.00
25-($3.95)-Wraparound, foil-c		1.60	4.00
26-35: 26-Begin $2.50-c. 28-(11/96)-1st Top Cow Comics issue; Quesada & Palmiotti's Gabriel app.		1.00	2.50
27-Quesada & Palmiotti's Ash app.		1.20	3.00
Annual 1 (3/95, $2.50)		1.00	2.50
Annual 2 (8/96, $2.95)		1.20	3.00

NOTE: *Annuals read Volume One in the indica.*

CYBERFORCE ORIGINS
Jan, 1995 - No. 3, Nov, 1995 ($2.50)
Image Comics (Top Cow Productions)

	GD25	FN65	NM94
1-Cyblade (1/95)	1.00	2.80	7.00
1-Cyblade (3/96, 99¢, 2nd printing)			1.00
2-Stryker (2/95)-1st Mike Turner-a		1.00	2.50
3-Impact		1.00	2.50

CYBERFORCE/STRYKEFORCE: OPPOSING FORCES (See Codename: Stryke Force #15)

Cyberforce Universe Sourcebook #1 © Top Cow

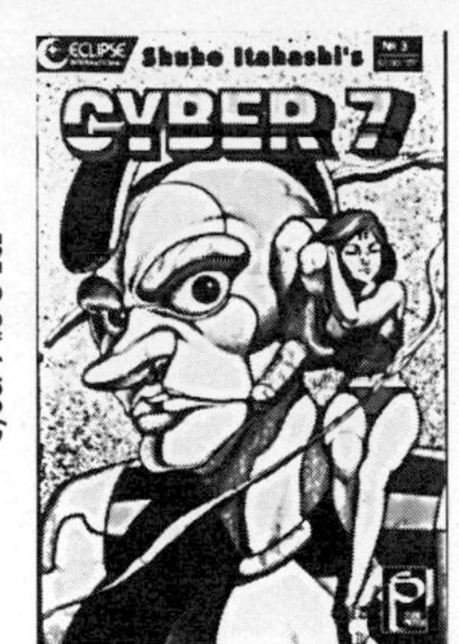

Cyber 7 #3 © ECL

Cyclone Comics #2 © Bilbara Publ

	GD25	FN65	NM94
Sept, 1995 - No.2, Oct, 1995 ($2.50, limited series)			
Image Comics (Top Cow Productions)			
1,2: 2-Stryker disbands Strykeforce.		1.00	2.50
CYBERFORCE UNIVERSE SOURCEBOOK			
Aug, 1994/Feb, 1995 ($2.50)			
Image Comics (Top Cow Productions)			
1-Silvestri-c (8/94)		1.00	2.50
2-Silvestri-c (2/95)		1.00	2.50
CYBERFROG			
June, 1994 - No. 2, Dec, 1994 ($2.50, B&W, limited series)			
Hall of Heroes			
1,2		1.00	2.50
CYBERFROG			
Feb, 1996 - No. 3, Apr, 1996 ($2.95)			
Harris Comics			
0-3: Van Sciver-c/a/scripts. 2-Variant-c exists	1.25	3.75	10.00
CYBERFROG: RESERVOIR FROG			
Sept, 1996 - No. 2, Oct, 1996 ($2.95, limited series)			
Harris Comics			
1,2: Van Sciver-c/a/scripts; wraparound-c		1.20	3.00
CYBERFROG: 3RD ANNIVERSARY SPECIAL			
Jan, 1997 - Present ($2.50, B&W, limited series)			
Harris Comics			
1,2		1.00	2.50
CYBERFROG VS. CREED			
July, 1997 - Present ($2.95, B&W, limited series)			
Harris Comics			
1			2.95
CYBERNARY (See Deathblow #1)			
Nov, 1995 - No.5, Mar, 1996 ($2.50, limited series)			
Image Comics (Wildstorm Productions)			
1-5		1.00	2.50
CYBERPUNK			
Sept, 1989 - No. 2, Oct, 1989 ($1.95, limited series, 28 pgs.)			
Book 2, #1, May, 1990 - No. 2, 1990 ($2.25, 28 pgs.)			
Innovation Publishing			
1,2-Both have Ken Steacy painted-c (Adults)		.80	2.00
Book 2, #1,2		.90	2.30
CYBERPUNK: THE SERAPHIM FILES			
Nov, 1990 - No. 2, Dec, 1990 ($2.50, 28 pgs., mature)			
Innovation Publishing			
1,2: 1-Painted-c; story cont'd from Seraphim		1.00	2.50
CYBERPUNX			
Mar, 1996 ($2.50)			
Image Comics (Extreme Studios)			
1		1.00	2.50
CYBERRAD			
1991 - No. 7, 1992 ($2.00)(Direct sale & newsstand-c variations)			
V2#1 - V2#5, 1993? ($2.50/$2.00)			
Continuity Comics			
1-7: 5-Glow-in-the-dark-c by N. Adams (direct sale only). 6-Contains 4 pg. fold-out poster; N. Adams layouts		.80	2.00
V2#1-($2.95, direct sale ed.)-Die-cut-c w/B&W hologram on-c; Neal Adams sketches		1.20	3.00
V2#1-($2.50, newsstand ed.)-Without sketches		1.00	2.50
V2#2-5: 2-N. Adams-c		.80	2.00
CYBERRAD DEATHWATCH 2000 (Becomes CyberRad w/#2, 7/93)			
Apr, 1993 - No. 2, 1993? ($2.50)			
Continuity Comics			
1,2: 1-Bagged w/2 cards; Adams-c & layouts & plots. 2-Bagged w/card; Adams scripts		1.00	2.50
CYBER 7			
Mar, 1989 - #7, Sept, 1989; V2#1, Oct, 1989 - #10, 1990 ($2.00, B&W)			
Eclipse Comics			
1-7: Stories translated from Japanese		.80	2.00
Book Two, #1-10		.80	2.00
CYBLADE/ GHOST RIDER			
Jan 1997 ($2.95, one-shot)			
Marvel Comics /Top Cow Productions			
1-Devil's Reign pt. 2			2.95
CYBLADE/SHI (Also see Battle For The Independents & Shi/Cyblade: The Battle For The Independents)			
1995 ($2.95, one-shot)			
Image Comics (Top Cow Productions)			
San Diego Preview	3.00	9.00	30.00
1-($2.95)-1st app. Witchblade	2.50	7.50	20.00
1-($2.95)-variant-c; Tucci-a	2.50	7.50	20.00
CYBRID			
July, 1995; No. 0, Jan, 1997 ($2.95/$3.50)			
Maximum Press			
1-(7/95)		1.20	3.00
0-(1/97)-Liefeld-a/script; story cont'd in Avengelyne #4		1.40	3.50
CYCLONE COMICS (Also see Whirlwind Comics)			
June, 1940 - No. 5, Nov, 1940			
Bilbara Publishing Co.			
1-Origin Tornado Tom; Volton (the human generator), Tornado Tom, Kingdom of the Moon, Mister Q begin (1st app. of each)	106.00	318.00	950.00
2,3	53.00	159.00	480.00
4,5	44.00	132.00	400.00
CYCLOPS: RETRIBUTION			
1994 ($5.95, trade paperback)			
Marvel Comics			
nn-r/Marvel Comics Presents #17-24		2.60	6.00
CYNDER			
1995 - No. 3, 1996 ($2.50, B&W)			
Immortelle Studios			
1-3: 2-Tucci centerfold		1.00	2.50
Annual 1-(5/96, $2.95, color)		1.20	3.00
CYNDER (Series 2)			
1996 - No.2, 1996 ($2.95, color)			
Immortelle Studios			
1,2		1.00	2.50
CYNDER/NIRA X			
1996 ($2.95, one-shot)			
Immortelle Studios			
1-w/centerfold		1.20	3.00
1-Hughes variant-c.		1.20	3.00
1 (Gold)-Hughes-c.	1.25	3.75	10.00
CYNTHIA DOYLE, NURSE IN LOVE (Formerly Sweetheart Diary)			
No. 66, Oct, 1962 - No. 74, Feb, 1964			
Charlton Publications			
66-74	1.50	4.50	12.00
DAEMONSTORM			

Daffy Duck #22 © Warner Bros.

Dagar #19 © FOX

Daily Bugle #1 © MEG

	GD25	FN65	NM94
1997 ($3.95, one-shot)			
Caliber Comics			
1-McFarland-c			3.95

DAEMONSTORM: STORMWALKER
1997 ($3.95, B&W, one-shot)
Caliber Comics

	GD25	FN65	NM94
nn			3.95

DAFFY (Daffy Duck No. 18 on)(See Looney Tunes)
#457, 3/53 - #30, 7-9/62; #31, 10-12/62 - #145, 1983 (No #132,133)
Dell Publishing Co./Gold Key No. 31-127/Whitman No. 128 on

	GD25	FN65	NM94
Four Color 457(#1)-Elmer Fudd x-overs begin	8.00	25.00	90.00
Four Color 536,615('55)	4.00	12.00	45.00
4(1-3/56)-11('57)	2.50	7.50	27.00
12-19(1958-59)	1.65	5.00	18.00
20-40(1960-64)	1.50	4.50	12.00
41-60(1964-68)	1.10	3.30	9.00
61-90(1969-74)-Road Runner in most		2.40	6.00
91-131,134-145(1974-83)		1.20	3.00
Mini-Comic 1 (1976; 3-1/4x6-1/2")		1.60	4.00

NOTE: *Reprint issues-No.41-46, 48, 50, 53-55, 58, 59, 65, 67, 69, 73, 81, 96, 103-108; 136-142, 144, 145(1/3-2/3-r). (See March of Comics No. 277, 288, 303, 313, 331, 347, 357,375, 387, 397, 402, 413, 425, 437, 460).*

DAFFY TUNES COMICS
June, 1947; No. 12, Aug, 1947
Four-Star Publications

	GD25	FN65	NM94
nn	6.50	19.50	45.00
12-Al Fago-c/a; funny animal	5.70	17.00	38.00

DAGAR, DESERT HAWK (Captain Kidd No. 24 on; formerly All Great)
No. 14, Feb, 1948 - No. 23, Apr, 1949 (No #17,18)
Fox Features Syndicate

	GD25	FN65	NM94
14-Tangi & Safari Cary begin; Good bondage-c/a	62.00	187.00	525.00
15,16-E. Good-a; 15-Bondage-c	40.00	120.00	310.00
19,20,22: 19-Used in **SOTI**, pg. 180 (Tangi)	37.00	111.00	270.00
21- "Bombs & Bums Away" panel in "Flood of Death" story used in **SOTI**	40.00	120.00	290.00
23-Bondage-c	39.00	118.00	290.00

NOTE: *Tangi by **Kamen**-14-16, 19, 20; c-20, 21.*

DAGAR THE INVINCIBLE (Tales of Sword & Sorcery...) (Also see Dan Curtis Giveaways & Gold Key Spotlight)
Oct, 1972 - No. 18, Dec, 1976; No. 19, Apr, 1982
Gold Key

	GD25	FN65	NM94
1-Origin; intro. Villains Olstellon & Scor	2.25	6.75	18.00
2-5: 3-Intro. Graylin, Dagar's woman; Jarn x-over		2.40	6.00
6-1st Dark Gods story		2.00	5.00
7-10: 9-Intro. Torgus. 10-1st Three Witches story		2.00	5.00
11-18: 13-Durak & Torgus x-over; story continues in Dr. Spektor #15. 14-Dagar's origin retold. 18-Origin retold		1.60	4.00
19-Origin-r/#18		1.60	4.00

NOTE: *Durak app. in 7, 12, 13. Tragg app. in 5, 11.*

DAGWOOD (Chic Young's) (Also see Blondie Comics)
Sept, 1950 - No. 140, Nov, 1965
Harvey Publications

	GD25	FN65	NM94
1	9.00	27.00	90.00
2	4.50	13.50	45.00
3-10	3.60	10.80	36.00
11-20	2.70	8.10	27.00
21-30	2.50	7.50	22.00
31-50	2.25	6.75	18.00
51-70	2.00	6.00	16.00
71-100	1.50	4.50	12.00
101-128,130,135	1.00	3.00	8.00
129,131-134,136-140-All are 68-pg. issues	1.50	4.50	12.00

NOTE: *Popeye and other one page strips appeared in early issues.*

DAGWOOD SPLITS THE ATOM (Also see Topix V8#4)
1949 (Science comic with King Features characters) (Giveaway)
King Features Syndicate

	GD25	FN65	NM94
nn-Half comic, half text; Popeye, Olive Oyl, Henry, Mandrake, Little King, Katzenjammer Kids app.	4.00	12.00	36.00

DAI KAMIKAZE!
June, 1987 - No. 12, Aug, 1988 ($1.75)
Now Comics

	GD25	FN65	NM94
1-12: 1-1st app. Speed Racer; 2nd print exists		.70	1.80

DAILY BUGLE (See Spider-Man)
Dec, 1996 - No. 3, Feb, 1997 ($2.50, B&W, limited series)
Marvel Comics

	GD25	FN65	NM94
1-3-Paul Grist-s		1.00	2.50

DAISY AND DONALD (See Walt Disney Showcase No. 8)
May, 1973 - No. 59, 1984 (no No. 48)
Gold Key/Whitman No. 42 on

	GD25	FN65	NM94
1-Barks-r/WDC&S #280,308	2.00	6.00	16.00
2-5: 4-Barks-r/WDC&S #224	1.00	3.00	8.00
6-10		2.00	5.00
11-20		1.60	4.00
21-46,49,50: 32-r/WDC&S #308. 50-r/#3		1.20	3.00
47-8-(12/80)-Only distr. in Whitman 3-pack	3.00	9.00	35.00
51-Barks-r/4-Color #1150		1.20	3.00
52-59: 52-r/#2. 55-r/#5			1.50

DAISY & HER PUPS (Blondie's Dogs)(Formerly Blondie Comics #20)
No. 21, 7/51 - No. 27, 7/52; No. 8, 9/52 - No. 18, 5/54
Harvey Publications

	GD25	FN65	NM94
21 (#1)-Blondie's dog Daisy and her 5 pups led by Elmer begin. Rags Rabbit app	1.50	4.50	15.00
22-27 (#2-7): 26,27 have No. 6 & 7 on cover but No. 26 & 27 on inside. 23,25-The Little King app. 24-Bringing Up Father by McManus app. 25-27-Rags Rabbit app.	1.20	3.60	12.00
8-18: 8,9-Rags Rabbit app. 8,17-The Little King app. 11-The Flop Family Swan begins. 22-Cookie app. 11-Felix The Cat app. by 17,18-Popeye app.	1.00	3.00	10.00

DAISY COMICS
Dec, 1936 (5-1/4x7-1/2")
Eastern Color Printing Co.

	GD25	FN65	NM94
nn-Joe Palooka, Buck Rogers (2 pgs. from Famous Funnies No. 18), Napoleon Flying to Fame, Butty & Fally	28.00	83.00	220.00

DAISY DUCK & UNCLE SCROOGE PICNIC TIME (See Dell Giant #33)

DAISY DUCK & UNCLE SCROOGE SHOW BOAT (See Dell Giant #55)

DAISY DUCK'S DIARY (See Dynabrite Comics, & Walt Disney's C&S #298)
No. 600, Nov, 1954 - No. 1247, Dec-Fef, 1961-62 (Disney)
Dell Publishing Co.

	GD25	FN65	NM94
Four Color 600 (#1)	5.50	16.50	60.00
Four Color 659, 743 (11/56)	4.50	13.50	50.00
Four Color 858 (11/57), 948 (11/58), 1247 (12-2/61-62)	3.60	11.00	40.00
Four Color 1055 (11-1/59-60), 1150 (12-1/60-61)-By Carl Barks)	9.00	27.00	100.00

DAISY HANDBOOK
1946; No. 2, 1948 (10¢, pocket-size, 132 pgs.)
Daisy Manufacturing Co.

	GD25	FN65	NM94
1-Buck Rogers, Red Ryder; Wolverton-a(2 pgs.)	34.00	103.00	275.00
2-Captain Marvel & Ibis the Invincible, Red Ryder, Boy Commandos & Robotman; Wolverton-a (2 pgs.); contains 8 pg. color catalog			

Dale Evans #20 © DC

Damage #4 © DC

Dances With Demons #2 © MEG

GD25 FN65 NM94

34.00 103.00 275.00

DAISY LOW OF THE GIRL SCOUTS
1954, 1965 (16 pgs., paper-c)
Girl Scouts of America

1954-Story of Juliette Gordon Low 4.00 10.00 20.00
1965 1.00 3.00 8.00

DAISY MAE (See Oxydol-Dreft)

DAISY'S RED RYDER GUN BOOK
1955 (25¢, pocket-size, 132 pgs.)
Daisy Manufacturing Co.

nn-Boy Commandos, Red Ryder; 1pg. Wolverton-a
22.00 66.00 175.00

DAKKON BLACKBLADE ON THE WORLD OF MAGIC: THE GATHERING
June, 1996 ($5.95, one-shot)
Acclaim Comics (Armada)

1-Jerry Prosser scripts; Rags Morales-c/a. 2.40 6.00

DAKOTA LIL (See Fawcett Movie Comics)

DAKOTA NORTH
June, 1986 - No. 5, Feb, 1987
Marvel Comics Group

1-5 1.00

DAKTARI (Ivan Tors) (TV)
July, 1967 - No. 3, Oct, 1968; No. 4, Sept, 1969 (All have photo-c)
Dell Publishing Co.

1 2.00 6.00 22.00
2-4 1.85 5.50 15.00

DALE EVANS COMICS (Also see Queen of the West...)
Sept-Oct, 1948 - No. 24, July-Aug, 1952 (No. 1-19: 52 pgs.)
National Periodical Publications

1-Dale Evans & her horse Buttermilk begin; Sierra Smith begins by Alex Toth
83.00 250.00 750.00
2-Alex Toth-a 39.00 117.00 350.00
3-11-Alex Toth-a 26.00 80.00 210.00
12-24: 12-Target-c 12.00 36.00 95.00
NOTE: *Photo-c-1, 2, 4-14.*

DALGODA
Aug, 1984 - No. 8, Feb, 1986 (High quality paper)
Fantagraphics Books

1-($2.25); Fujitake-c/a in all .90 2.25
2-8-($1.50). 2,3-Debut Grimwood's Daughter. 8-Alan Moore story 1.50

DALTON BOYS, THE
1951
Avon Periodicals

1-(Number on spine)-Kinstler-c 14.00 43.00 100.00

DAMAGE
Apr, 1994 - No. 20, Jan, 1996 ($1.75/$1.95)
DC Comics

1-4 .70 1.75
5,6,0,7-12: 5-Begin $1.95-c. 6-(9/94)-Zero Hour. 0-(10/94). 7-(11/94)
.80 2.00
13-20: 13-Begin $2.25-c. 14-Ray app. .90 2.25

DAMAGE CONTROL (See Marvel Comics Presents #19)
5/89 - No. 4, 8/89; V2#1, 12/89 - No. 4, 2/90 ($1.00)
V3#1, 6/91 - No. 4, 9/91 ($1.25, all are limited series)
Marvel Comics

V1#1-4,V2#1,3: V1#4-Wolverine app. 1.00
V2#2,4-Punisher app. 1.00
V3#1-4: 1-Spider-Man app. 2-New Warriors app. 3,4-Silver Surfer app. 4-Infinity Guantlet parody 1.25

DAMNED
June, 1997 - No. 4, Sept, 1997 ($2.50, limited series)
Image Comics (Homage Comics)

1-4-Steven Grant-s/Mike Zeck-c/a in all 1.60 4.00

DANCES WITH DEMONS (See Marvel Frontier Comics Unlimited)
Sept, 1993 - No. 4, Dec, 1993 ($1.95, limited series)
Marvel Frontier Comics

1-($2.95)-Foil embossed-c 1.20 3.00
2-4 .80 2.00

DAN CURTIS GIVEAWAYS
1974 (3x6", 24 pgs., reprints)
Western Publishing Co.

1-Dark Shadows, 2-Star Trek, 3-The Twilight Zone, 4-Ripley's Believe It or Not!, 5-Turok, Son of Stone (partial-r/Turok #78), 6-Star Trek, 7-The Occult Files of Dr. Spektor, 8-Dagar the Invincible, 9-Grimm's Ghost Stories
Set... 3.00 9.00 30.00

DANDEE
1947
Four Star Publications

nn 5.70 17.00 35.00

DAN DUNN (See Crackajack Funnies, Detective Dan, Famous Feature Stories & Red Ryder)

DANDY COMICS (Also see Happy Jack Howard)
Spring, 1947 - No. 7, Spring, 1948
E. C. Comics

1-Funny animal; Vince Fago-a in all; Dandy in all 28.00 83.00 220.00
2 21.00 62.00 165.00
3-7: 3-Intro Handy Andy who is c-feature #3 on 15.00 45.00 120.00

DANGER
Jan, 1953 - No. 11, Aug, 1954
Comic Media/Allen Hardy Assoc.

1-Heck-c/a 12.00 36.00 95.00
2,3,5,7,9-11: 7.15 21.50 50.00
6- "Narcotics" story; begin spy theme 7.85 23.50 55.00
4-Marijuana cover/story 8.75 26.25 65.00
8-Bondage/torture/headlights panels 9.50 28.00 75.00
NOTE: ***Morisi** a-2, 5, 6(3), 10; c-2. Contains some reprints from Danger & Dynamite.*

DANGER (Jim Bowie No. 15 on) (Formerly Comic Media title)
No. 12, June, 1955 - No. 14, Oct, 1955
Charlton Comics Group

12(#1) 6.50 19.50 45.00
13,14: 14-r/#12 5.70 17.00 35.00

DANGER
1964
Super Comics

Super Reprint #10-12 (Black Dwarf; #10-r/Great Comics #1 by Novack. #11-r/Johnny Danger #1. #12-r/Red Seal #14), #15-r/Spy Cases #26. #16-Unpublished Chesler material (Yankee Girl), #17-r/Scoop #8 (Capt. Courage & Enchanted Dagger), #18(nd)-r/Guns Against Gangsters #5 (Gun-Master, Annie Oakley, The Chameleon; L.B. Cole-r)
1.25 3.75 10.00

DANGER AND ADVENTURE (Formerly This Magazine Is Haunted; Robin Hood and His Merry Men No. 28 on)
No. 22, Feb, 1955 - No. 27, Feb, 1956
Charlton Comics

22-Ibis the Invincible-c/story; Nyoka app.; last pre-code issue; Ditko-a in all
8.75 26.25 70.00
23-Lance O'Casey-c/story; Nyoka app. 8.75 26.25 70.00
24-27: 24-Mike Danger & Johnny Adventure begin 5.70 17.00 40.00

Danger Trail #2 © DC

Daredevil #11 © MEG

Daredevil #50 © MEG

GD25 FN65 NM94 GD25 FN65 NM94

DANGER IS OUR BUSINESS!
1953(Dec.) - No. 10, June, 1955
Toby Press

1-Captain Comet by Williamson/Frazetta-a, 6 pgs. (science fiction)
40.00 120.00 310.00
2 10.00 30.00 70.00
3-10 8.50 26.00 60.00
I.W. Reprint #9('64)-Williamson/Frazetta-r/#1; Kinstler-c
6.50 19.50 65.00

DANGER IS THEIR BUSINESS (Also see A-1 Comic)
No. 50, 1952
Magazine Enterprises

A-1 50-Powell-a 10.00 30.00 80.00

DANGER MAN (TV)
No. 1231, Sept-Nov, 1961
Dell Publishing Co.

Four Color 1231-Patrick McGoohan photo-c 10.00 30.00 110.00

DANGER TRAIL (Also see Showcase #50, 51)
July-Aug, 1950 - No. 5, Mar-Apr, 1951 (52 pgs.)
National Periodical Publications

1-King Faraday begins, ends #4; Toth-a in all 92.00 276.00 825.00
2 67.00 200.00 600.00
3-(Rare) one of the rarest early '50s DCs 92.00 276.00 825.00
4,5: 5-Johnny Peril-c/story (moves to Sensation Comics #107); new logo
56.00 168.00 500.00

DANGER TRAIL
Apr, 1993 - No. 4, July, 1993 ($1.50, limited series)
DC Comics

1-4: Gulacy-c on all 1.50

DANGER UNLIMITED (See San Diego Comic Con Comics #2 & Torch of Liberty Special)
Feb, 1994 - No. 4, May, 1994 ($2.00, limited series)
Dark Horse Comics (Legend)

1-4: Byrne-c/a/scripts in all; origin stories of both original team (Doc Danger, Thermal, Miss Mirage, & Hunk) & future team (Thermal, Belebet, & Caucus). 1-Intro Torch of Liberty & Golgotha (cameo) in back-up story. 4-Hellboy & Torch of Liberty cameo in lead story .80 2.00
Trade paperback (1995, $14.95)-r/#1-4; includes last pg. originally cut from #4
15.00

DAN HASTINGS (See Syndicate Features)

DANIEL BOONE (See The Exploits of..., Fighting... Frontier Scout...,The Legends of... & March of Comics No. 306)
No. 1163, Mar-May, 1961
Dell Publishing Co.

Four Color 1163-Marsh-a 4.50 13.50 50.00

DANIEL BOONE (TV) (See March of Comics No. 306)
Jan, 1965 - No. 15, Apr, 1969 (All have Fess Parker photo-c)
Gold Key

1 7.00 22.00 80.00
2 3.60 11.00 40.00
3-5 2.75 8.00 30.00
6-15 1.80 5.50 20.00

DAN'L BOONE
Sept, 1955 - No. 8, Sept, 1957
Sussex Publ. Co.

1 12.00 38.00 100.00
2 7.85 23.50 55.00
3-8 5.70 17.00 40.00

DANNY BLAZE (...Firefighter) (Nature Boy No. 3 on)
Aug, 1955 - No. 2, Oct, 1955
Charlton Comics

1,2 5.70 17.00 40.00

DANNY DINGLE (See Sparkler Comics)
No. 17, 1940
United Features Syndicate

Single Series 17 19.50 58.00 155.00

DANNY KAYE'S BAND FUN BOOK
1959 (Giveaway)
H & A Selmer

nn 5.70 17.00 35.00

DANNY THOMAS SHOW, THE (TV)
No. 1180, Apr-June, 1961 - No. 1249, Dec-Feb, 1961-62
Dell Publishing Co.

Four Color 1180-Toth-a, photo-c 14.00 42.00 153.00
Four Color 1249-Manning-a, photo-c 14.00 42.00 153.00

DARBY O'GILL & THE LITTLE PEOPLE (Movie)(See Movie Comics)
1959 (Disney)
Dell Publishing Co.

Four Color 1024-Toth-a; photo-c. 9.00 27.00 100.00

DAREDEVIL (...& the Black Widow #92-107 on-c only; see Giant-Size...,Marvel Advs., Marvel Graphic Novel #24, Marvel Super Heroes, '66 & Spider-Man &...)
Apr, 1964 - Present
Marvel Comics Group

GD25 FN65 VF82 NM94
1-Origin/1st app. Daredevil; reprinted in Marvel Super Heroes #1 (1966); death of Battling Murdock; intro Foggy Nelson & Karen Page; Everett-c/a
154.00 462.00 924.00 1850.00

GD25 FN65 NM94
2-Fantastic Four cameo; 2nd app. Electro (Spidey villain); Thing guest star;
42.00 126.00 520.00
3-Origin & 1st app. The Owl (villain) 31.50 95.00 350.00
4 31.00 93.00 320.00
5-Minor costume change; Wood-a begins 21.50 65.00 215.00
6,8-10: 8-Origin/1st app. Stilt-Man 15.50 47.00 155.00
7-Daredevil battles Sub-Mariner & dons new red costume (4/65)
25.00 75.00 250.00
11-15: 12-Romita's 1st work at Marvel; 1st app. Plunderer; Ka-Zar app. 13-Facts about Ka-Zar's origin; Kirby-a 7.50 22.50 75.00
16,17-Spider-Man x-over. 16-1st Romita-a on Spider-Man (5/66)
9.00 27.00 90.00
18-20: 18-Origin & 1st app. Gladiator 5.40 16.20 54.00
21-26,28-30: 24-Ka-Zar app. 3.80 11.40 38.00
27-Spider-Man x-over 4.00 12.00 40.00
31-40: 38-Fantastic Four x-over; cont'd in F.F. #73. 39-1st Exterminator (later becomes Death-Stalker) 2.60 7.80 26.00
41-49: 41-Death Mike Murdock. 42-1st app. Jester. 43-Daredevil battles Captain America; origin partially retold. 45-Statue of Liberty photo-c
2.25 6.25 18.00
50-52-B. Smith-a 2.50 7.50 20.00
53-Origin retold; last 12¢ issue 2.50 7.50 20.00
54-56,58-60: 54-Spider-Man cameo. 56-1st app. Death's Head (9/69); story cont'd in #57 (not same as new Death's Head) 1.40 4.15 11.00
57-Reveals i.d. to Karen Page; Death's Head app. 1.50 4.50 12.00
61-70,72-80,82-99: 79-Stan Lee cameo. 83-B. Smith layouts/Weiss-p. 87-Electro-c/story 1.10 3.30 9.00
71-Spider-Man x-over 1.85 5.50 15.00
81-Oversize issue; Black Widow begins (11/71). 2.50 7.50 20.00
100-Origin retold 2.25 6.75 18.00
101-104,106,108-113,115-120: 113-1st app. Deathstalker (cameo)
2.00 5.00

Daredevil #200 © MEG

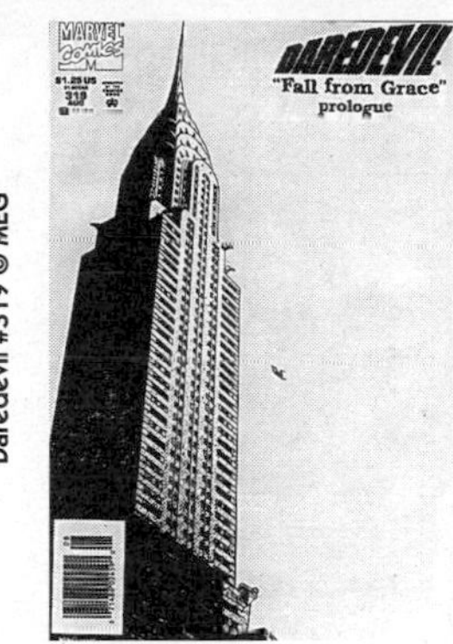

Daredevil #319 © MEG

Daredevil Annual #10 © MEG

GD25 FN65 NM94

105-Origin Moondragon by Starlin (12/73); Thanos cameo in flashback (early app.) 1.50 4.50 12.00
107-Starlin-c; Thanos cameo 2.00 5.00
114-1st full app. Deathstalker 2.00 5.00
121-130,133-137: 124-1st app. Copperhead; Black Widow leaves. 126-1st new Torpedo 1.40 3.50
131-Origin/1st app. new Bullseye (see Nick Fury #15) 2.25 6.75 18.00
132-Bullseye app. 1.40 3.50
138-Ghost Rider-c/story; Death's Head is reincarnated; Byrne-a 1.00 2.80 7.00
139-147-149-157: 142-Nova cameo. 146-Bullseye app. 150-1st app. Paladin. 151-Reveals i.d. to Heather Glenn. 155-Black Widow returns. 156-The 1960s Daredevil app. 1.00 2.50
148-(Regular 30¢ edition)(9/77) 1.00 2.50
148-(35¢-c, limited distribution) 1.25 3.75 10.00
158-Frank Miller art begins (5/79); origin/death of Deathstalker (see Captain America #235 & Spectacular Spider-Man #27 3.00 9.00 30.00
159 2.25 6.75 18.00
160,161 1.00 3.00 8.00
162-Ditko-a; no Miller-a 1.20 3.00
163,164: 163-Hulk cameo. 164-Origin retold 1.00 3.00 8.00
165-167,170 1.00 3.00 8.00
168-Origin/1st app. Elektra 3.80 11.40 38.00
169-Elektra app. 1.00 3.00 8.00
171-175: 174,175-Elektra app. 2.40 6.00
176-180-Elektra app. 178-Cage app. 179-Anti-smoking issue mentioned in the Congressional Record 2.00 5.00
181-(52 pgs.)-Death of Elektra; Punisher cameo out of costume 1.25 3.75 10.00
182-184-Punisher app. by Miller (drug issues) 1.60 4.00
185-191: 187-New Black Widow. 189-Death of Stick. 190-($1.00, 52 pgs.)-Elektra returns, part origin. 191-Last Miller Daredevil 1.00 2.50
192-195,197-210: 197,200-Bullseye app. 208-Harlan Ellison scripts borrowed from Avengers TV episode "House that Jack Built" 1.50
196-Wolverine app. 1.00 3.00 7.50
211-225: 219-Miller-c/script 1.25
226-Frank Miller plots begin .80 2.00
227-Miller scripts begin 1.20 3.00
228-233-Last Miller scripts .80 2.00
234-237,239,240,242-247 1.25
238-Mutant Massacre; Sabretooth app. 1.60 4.00
241-Todd McFarlane-a(p) .80 2.00
248,249-Wolverine app. 1.60 4.00
250,251,253,258: 250-1st app. Bullet. 258-Intro The Bengal (a villain) 1.25
252-(52 pgs.); Fall of the Mutants 1.20 3.00
254-Origin & 1st app. Typhoid Mary (5/88) 1.00 3.00 7.50
255-2nd app. Typhoid Mary 1.60 4.00
256-3rd app. Typhoid Mary 1.20 3.00
257-Punisher app. (x-over w/Punisher #10) 2.00 5.00
259,260-Typhoid Mary app. 260-(52 pgs.) 1.20 3.00
261-291,294,296-299: 270-1st app. Black Heart. 272-Intro Shotgun (villain). 282-Silver Surfer app. (cameo in #281). 283-Capt. America app. 297-Typhoid Mary app.; Kingpin storyline begins. 299-Last $1.00-c 1.25
292,293,295: 293-Punisher app. 292-D. G. Chichester scripts begin. 295-Ghost Rider app. .80 2.00
300-($2.00, 52 pgs.)-Kingpin story ends 1.00 2.50
301-318: 301-303-Re-intro the Owl. 304-Garney-c/a. 305,306-Spider-Man-c. 309-Punisher-c.; Terror app. 310-Calypso-c. 1.25
319-Prologue to Fall From Grace; Elektra returns 1.60 4.00
319-2nd printing w/black-c 1.25
320-Fall From Grace Pt 1 1.60 4.00

GD25 FN65 NM94

321-Fall From Grace regular ed.; Pt 2; new costume; Venom app. .80 2.00
321-($2.00)-Wraparound Glow-in-the-dark-c ed. 1.20 3.00
322-Fall From Grace Pt 3; Eddie Brock app. 1.20 3.00
323,324-Fall From Grace Pt. 4 & 5: 323-Vs. Venom-c/story. 324-Morbius-c/story .70 1.75
325-($2.50, 52 pgs.)-Fall From Grace ends; contains bound-in poster 1.00 2.50
326,327: 326-New logo 1.25
328-343: 328-$1.50-c begins; bound-in trading card sheet. 330-Gambit app. 1.50
344-349, 351-353: 344-Begin $1.95-c. 348-1st Cary Nord art in DD (1/96); "Dec" on-c. 353-Karl Kesel scripts; Nord-c/a begins; Mr. Hyde-c/app. .80 2.00
350-($2.95)-Double-sized 1.20 3.00
350-($3.50)-Double-sized; gold ink-c 1.40 3.50
354-368: Kesel scripts, Nord-c/a in all. 354-$1.50-c begins. 355-Larry Hama layouts; Pyro app. 358-Mysterio-c/app. 359-Absorbing Man cameo 360-Absorbing Man-c/app. 361-Black Widow-c/app. 363-Gene Colan-a(p) begins 1.50
364, 365, -1(7/97): 364-Begin $1.95-c .80 2.00
366-372: 366-Begin $1.99-c. 368-Omega Red-c/app. 372-Ghost Rider-c/app. 1.99
Special 1(9/67, 25¢, 68 pgs.)-New art/story 2.50 7.50 24.00
Special 2,3: 2(2/71, 25¢, 52 pgs.)-Entire book has Powell/Wood-r; Wood-c. 3(1/72)-Reprints 1.00 2.80 7.00
Annual 4(10/76) 2.40 6.00
Annual 4(#5)(1989, $2.00, 68 pgs.)-Atlantis Attacks 1.20 3.00
Annual 6(1990, $2.00, 68 pgs.)-Sutton-a .80 2.00
Annual 7(1991, $2.00, 68 pgs.)-Guice-a (7 pgs.) .80 2.00
Annual 8(1992, $2.25, 68 pgs.)-Deathlok-c/story .90 2.25
Annual 9(1993, $2.95, 68 pgs.)-Polybagged w/card 1.20 3.00
Annual 10(1994, $2.95, 68 pgs.) 1.20 3.00
.../DEADPOOL- (Annual '97, $2.99)-Wraparound-c 2.99
.../PUNISHER TPB (1988, $4.95)-r/D.D. #182-184 2.00 5.00
.../PUNISHER TPB, 2nd & 3rd printings 2.00 5.00
...:FALL FROM GRACE TPB ($19.95)-r #319-325 20.00
...VS. VAPORA 1(Engineering Show Giveaway, 1993, 16 pg.)–Intro Vapora 1.20 3.00

NOTE: ***Art Adams*** *c-238p, 239.* ***Austin*** *a-191i; c-151i, 200i.* ***John Buscema*** *a-136, 137p, 234p, 235p; c-86p, 136i, 137p, 142, 219.* ***Byrne*** *c-200p, 201, 203, 223.* ***Capullo*** *a-286p.* ***Colan*** *a(p)-20-49, 53-82, 84-98, 100, 110, 112, 124, 153, 154, 156, 157, Spec. 1p; c(p)-20-42, 44-49, 53-60, 71, 92, 98, 138, 153, 154, 156, 157, Annual 1.* ***Craig*** *a-50i, 52i.* ***Ditko*** *a-162, 234p, 235p, 264p; c-162.* ***Everett*** *c/a-1; inks-21, 83.* ***Garney*** *c/a-304.* ***Gil Kane*** *a-141p, 146-148p, 151p; c(p)-85, 90, 91, 93, 94, 115, 116, 119, 120, 125-128, 133, 139, 147, 152.* ***Kirby*** *c-2-4, 5p, 12p, 13p, 43, 136p.* ***Layton*** *c-202.* ***Miller*** *scripts-168-182, 183(part), 184-191, 219, 227-233; a-158-161p, 163-184p, 191p; c-158-161p, 163-184p, 185-189, 190p, 191.* ***Orlando*** *a-2-4p.* ***Powell*** *a-9p, 11p, Special 1r, 2r.* ***Simonson*** *c-199, 236p.* ***B. Smith*** *a-236p; c-51p, 52p.* ***Starlin*** *a-105p.* ***Steranko*** *c-44i.* ***Tuska*** *a-39i, 145p.* ***Williamson*** *a(i)-237, 239, 240, 243, 248-257, 259-282, 283(part), 284, 285, 287, 288(part), 289(part), 293-300; c(i)-237, 243, 244, 248-257, 259-263, 265-278, 280-289, Annual 8.* ***Wood*** *a-5-8, 9i, 10, 11i, Spec. 2i; c-5i, 6-11, 164i.*

DAREDEVIL COMICS (See Silver Streak Comics)
July, 1941 - No. 134, Sept, 1956 (Charles Biro stories)
Lev Gleason Publications (Funnies, Inc. No. 1)

GD25 FN65 VF82 NM94

1-No. 1 titled "Daredevil Battles Hitler"; The Silver Streak, Lance Hale, Cloud Curtis, Dickey Dean, Pirate Prince team up w/Daredevil and battle Hitler; Daredevil battles the Claw; Origin of Hitler feature story. Hitler photo app. on-c 900.00 2700.00 5400.00 9000.00
(Estimated up to 215 total copies exist, 12 in NM/Mint)

GD25 FN65 NM94

2-London, Pat Patriot (by Reed Crandall), Nightro, Real American No. 1 (by Briefer #2-11), Dickie Dean, Pirate Prince, & Times Square begin; intro. & only app. The Pioneer, Champion of America 240.00 720.00 2400.00
3-Origin of 13 156.00 468.00 1400.00
4 133.00 400.00 1200.00

Daredevil Comics #9 © LEV

Daring Comics #11 © TCI

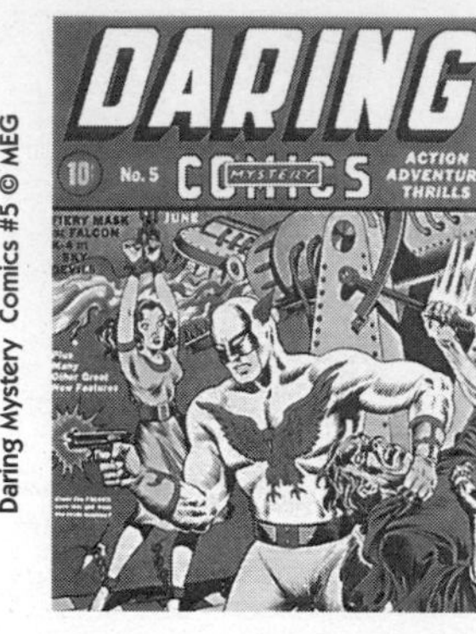

Daring Mystery Comics #5 © MEG

GD25 FN65 NM94

5-Intro. Sniffer & Jinx; Ghost vs. Claw begins by Bob Wood, ends #20
106.00 318.00 950.00
6-(#7 in indicia) 89.00 267.00 800.00
7-10: 8-Nightro ends 75.00 225.00 675.00
11-London, Pat Patriot end; classic bondage/torture-c
81.00 243.00 725.00
12-Origin of The Claw; Scoop Scuttle by Wolverton begins (2-4 pgs.), ends #22, not in #21 117.00 350.00 1050.00
13-Intro. of Little Wise Guys (10/42) 100.00 300.00 900.00
14 53.00 159.00 475.00
15-Death of Meatball 77.00 231.00 685.00
16,17 48.00 144.00 430.00
18-New origin of Daredevil (not same as Silver Streak #6)
105.00 315.00 940.00
19,20 41.00 123.00 370.00
21-Reprints cover of Silver Streak #6 (on inside) plus intro. of The Claw from Silver Streak #1 69.00 207.00 625.00
22-30: 27-Bondage/torture-c 34.00 101.00 270.00
31-Death of The Claw 64.00 192.00 575.00
32-37,39,41: 35-Two Daredevil stories begin, end #68 (35-41 are 64 pgs.)
23.00 69.00 185.00
38-Origin Daredevil retold from #18 36.00 108.00 315.00
42-50: 42-Intro. Kilroy in Daredevil; 1 panel Steranko-a
19.00 56.00 150.00
51-69-Last Daredevil issue (12/50) 12.00 38.00 100.00
70-Little Wise Guys take over book; McWilliams-a; Hot Rock Flanagan begins, ends #80 10.00 30.00 80.00
71-79,81: 79-Daredevil returns 8.75 26.25 65.00
80-Daredevil x-over 8.75 26.25 70.00
82,90-One pg. Frazetta ad in both 8.75 26.25 65.00
83-89,91-99,101-134 7.85 23.50 55.00
100 8.75 26.25 65.00

NOTE: ***Wolverton's*** *Scoop Scuttle-12-20, 22.* ***Biro*** *c/a-all?* ***Bolle*** *a-125.* ***Maurer*** *a-75.* ***McWilliams*** *a-73, 75, 79, 80.*

DAREDEVIL/ BATMAN
1997 ($5.99, one-shot)
Marvel Comics/ DC Comics

nn-McDaniel-c/a 5.99

DAREDEVIL/ SHI (See Shi/ Daredevil)
Feb,1997 ($2.95, limited series)
Marvel Comics/ Crusade Comics

1- 2.95

DAREDEVIL THE MAN WITHOUT FEAR
Oct, 1993 - No. 5, Feb, 1994 ($2.95, limited series)(foil embossed covers)
Marvel Comics

1-5: Miller scripts; Romita, Jr./Williamson-c/a 1.60 4.00
Hardcover 100.00
Trade paperback 20.00

DARING ADVENTURES (Also see Approved Comics)
Nov, 1953 (25¢, 3-D, came w/glasses)
St. John Publishing Co.

1 (3-D)-Reprints lead story from Son of Sinbad #1 by Kubert
35.00 105.00 245.00

DARING ADVENTURES
1963 - 1964
I.W. Enterprises/Super Comics

I. W. Reprint #8-r/Fight Comics #53; Matt Baker-a 4.20 12.60 42.00
I.W. Reprint #9-r/Blue Bolt #115; Disbrow-a(3) 4.20 12.60 42.00
Super Reprint #10,11('63)-r/Dynamic #24,16; 11-Marijuana story; Yankee Boy app.; Mac Raboy-a 2.50 7.50 22.00
Super Reprint #12('64)-Phantom Lady from Fox (r/#14 only? w/splash pg. omitted); Matt Baker-a 10.50 32.00 105.00
Super Reprint #15('64)-r/Hooded Menace #1 6.50 19.50 65.00
Super Reprint #16('64)-r/Dynamic #12 2.25 6.75 18.00
Super Reprint #17('64)-r/Green Lama #3 by Raboy 3.20 9.60 32.00
Super Reprint #18-Origin Atlas from unpublished Atlas Comics #1
2.50 7.50 24.00

DARING COMICS (Formerly Daring Mystery) (Jeanie Comics No. 13 on)
No. 9, Fall, 1944 - No. 12, Fall, 1945
Timely Comics (HPC)

9-Human Torch, Toro & Sub-Mariner begin 94.00 282.00 850.00
10-The Angel only app. 81.00 243.00 725.00
11,12-The Destroyer app. 81.00 243.00 725.00

NOTE: ***Schomburg*** *c-9-11.* ***Sekowsky*** *c-12? Human Torch, Toro & Sub-Mariner c-9-12.*

DARING CONFESSIONS (Formerly Youthful Hearts)
No. 4, 11/52 - No. 7, 5/53; No. 8, 10/53
Youthful Magazines

4-Doug Wildey-a; Tony Curtis story 10.00 30.00 75.00
5-8: 5-Ray Anthony photo on-c. 6,8-Wildey-a 8.35 25.00 55.00

DARING LOVE (Radiant Love No. 2 on)
Sept-Oct, 1953
Gilmor Magazines

1–Steve Ditko's 1st published work (1st drawn was Fantastic Fears #5)(Also See Black Magic #27)(scarce) 29.00 86.00 230.00

DARING LOVE (Formerly Youthful Romances)
No. 15, 12/52; No. 16, 2/53-c, 4/53-Indicia; No. 17-4/53-c & indicia
Ribage/Pix

15 8.70 26.00 55.00
16,17: 17-Photo-c 7.00 21.00 45.00

NOTE: ***Colletta*** *a-15.* ***Wildey*** *a-17.*

DARING LOVE STORIES (See Fox Giants)

DARING MYSTERY COMICS (Comedy Comics No. 9 on; title changed to Daring Comics with No. 9)
1/40 - No. 5, 6/40; No. 6, 9/40; No. 7, 4/41 - No. 8, 1/42
Timely Comics (TPI 1-6/TCI 7,8) GD25 FN65 VF82 NM94

1-Origin The Fiery Mask (1st app.) by Joe Simon; Monako, Prince of Magic (1st app.), John Steele, Soldier of Fortune (1st app.), Doc Doyle (1st app.) begin; Flash Foster & Barney Mullen, Sea Rover only app; bondage-c
1500.00 4500.00 9750.00 16,500.00
(Estimated up to 60 total copies exist, 5 in NM/Mint)

GD25 FN65 NM94

2-(Rare)-Origin The Phantom Bullet (1st & only app.); The Laughing Mask & Mr. E only app.; Trojak the Tiger Man begins, ends #6; Zephyr Jones & K-4 & His Sky Devils app., also #4 600.00 1800.00 6000.00
3-The Phantom Reporter, Dale of FBI, Breeze Barton, Captain Strong & Marvex the Super-Robot only app.; The Purple Mask begins
360.00 1080.00 3600.00
4-Last Purple Mask; Whirlwind Carter begins; Dan Gorman, G-Man app.
245.00 735.00 2200.00
5-The Falcon begins (1st app.); The Fiery Mask, Little Hercules app. by Sagendorf in the Segar style; bondage-c 245.00 735.00 2200.00
6-Origin & only app. Marvel Boy by S&K; Flying Flame, Dynaman, & Stuporman only app.; The Fiery Mask by S&K; S&K-c
300.00 900.00 3000.00
7-Origin The Blue Diamond, Captain Daring by S&K, The Fin by Everett, The Challenger, The Silver Scorn & The Thunderer by Burgos; Mr. Millions app
250.00 750.00 2500.00
8-Origin Citizen V; Last Fin, Silver Scorn, Capt. Daring by Borth, Blue Diamond & The Thunderer; Kirby & part solo Simon-c; Rudy the Robot only app.; Citizen V, Fin & Silver Scorn continue in Comedy #9
217.00 651.00 1950.00

NOTE: ***Schomburg*** *c-1-4, 7.* ***Simon*** *a-2, 3, 5. Cover features: 1-Fiery Mask; 2-Phantom Bullet; 3-Purple Mask; 4-G-Man; 5-The Falcon; 6-Marvel Boy; 7, 8-Multiple characters.*

Dark Angel #14 © MEG

Darkchylde The Diary #1 © Randy Queen

Darker Image #1 © Aegis Entertainment

DARING NEW ADVENTURES OF SUPERGIRL, THE
Nov, 1982 - No. 13, Nov, 1983 (Supergirl No. 14 on)
DC Comics

	GD25	FN65	NM94
1-Origin retold; Lois Lane back-ups in #2-12			1.50
2-13: 8,9-Doom Patrol app. 13-New costume; flag-c			1.00

NOTE: ***Buckler** c-1p, 2p. **Giffen** c-3p, 4p. **Gil Kane** c-6, ,8, 9, 11-13.*

DARK, THE
Nov, 1990 - No. 4, Feb, 1993; V2#1, May, 1993 - V2#7, Apr?, 1994 ($1.95)
Continum Comics

	GD25	FN65	NM94
1-($2.00)-Bright-p; Panosian, Hanna-i; Stroman-c		.80	2.00
2-(1/92, $2.25)-Stroman-c/a(p)		.90	2.25
3,4-($2.50): 4-Perez-c & part-i		1.00	2.50
V2#1-Red foil Bart Sears-c		.80	2.00
V2#1-Red non-foil variant-c		.80	2.00
V2#1-2nd printing w/blue foil Bart Sears-c		.80	2.00
V2#2-6: 2-Stroman/Bryant-a. 3-Perez-c(i). 3-6-Foil-c. 4-Perez-c & part-i; bound-in trading cards. 5,6-(2,3/94)-Perez-c(i)		.80	2.00
V2#7-(B&W)-Perez-c(i)		.80	2.00
Convention Book 1 (Fall/94, $2.00)-Perez-c		.80	2.00
Convention Book 2 (10/94, $2.00)-Perez-c(i)		.80	2.00

DARK ANGEL (Formerly Hell's Angel)
No. 6, Dec, 1992 - No. 16, Dec, 1993 ($1.75)
Marvel Comics UK, Ltd.

	GD25	FN65	NM94
6-8,13-16: 6-Excalibur-c/story. 8-Psylocke app.		.70	1.75
9-12-Wolverine/X-Men app.		1.20	3.00

DARKCHYLDE
June, 1996 - Present ($2.95/ $2.50)
Maximum Press #1-3/ Image Comics #4 on

	GD25	FN65	NM94
1-Randy Queen-c/a/scripts; "Roses" cover	1.60	4.85	13.00
1-American Entertainment Edition-wraparound-c	1.60	4.85	13.00
1-"Fashion magazine-style" variant-c	1.60	4.85	13.00
1-Special Comicon Edition (contents of #1) Winged devil variant-c	1.60	4.85	13.00
1-($2.50)-Remastered Ed.-wraparound-c		2.00	5.00
2-	1.50	4.50	12.00
2-Spiderweb and Moon variant-c	1.50	4.50	12.00
3	1.00	3.00	8.00
3-"Kalvin Clein" variant-c by Drew	1.00	3.00	8.00
4-($2.50)		2.00	5.00
5		1.00	2.50

DARKCHYLDE THE DIARY
June, 1997 ($2.50, one-shot)
Image Comics

	GD25	FN65	NM94
1-Queen-c/s/ art by various			2.50
1-Variant-c			2.50

DARK CLAW ADVENTURES
June, 1997 ($1.95, one-shot)
DC Comics (Amalgam)

	GD25	FN65	NM94
1-Templeton-c/s/a & Burchett-a			2.95

DARK CRYSTAL, THE (Movie)
April, 1983 - No. 2, May, 1983
Marvel Comics Group

	GD25	FN65	NM94
1,2-Adaptation of film		.50	1.00

DARK DOMINION
Oct, 1993 - No. 10, July, 1994 ($2.50)
Defiant

	GD25	FN65	NM94
1-9-Len Wein scripts begin. 4-Free extra 16 pgs. 7-9-J.G. Jones-c/a		1.00	2.50
10-Pre-Schism issue; Shooter/Wein script; John Ridgway-a		1.00	2.50

DARKER IMAGE (Also see Deathblow, The Maxx, & Bloodwulf)
Mar, 1993 ($1.95, one-shot)
Image Comics

	GD25	FN65	NM94
1-The Maxx by Sam Kieth begins; Bloodwulf by Rob Liefeld & Deathblow by Jim Lee begin (both 1st app.); polybagged w/1 of 3 cards by Kieth, Lee or Liefeld		1.00	2.50
1-B&W interior pgs. w/silver foil logo	1.25	3.75	10.00

DARKEWOOD
1987 - No. 5, 1988 ($2.00, 28pgs, limited series)
Aircel Publishing

	GD25	FN65	NM94
1-5		.80	2.00

DARK FANTASIES
1994 - No. 6, 1995 ($2.95)
Dark Fantasy

	GD25	FN65	NM94
1-Test print Run (3,000)-Linsner-c	1.00	3.00	8.00
1-Linsner-c		2.00	5.00
2-4 (Deluxe): 4-($3.95)		1.60	4.00
2-4 (Regular)		1.20	3.00
5,6 (Deluxe; $3.95)		1.60	4.00
5,6 (Regular; $3.50)		1.40	3.50

DARK GUARD
Oct, 1993 - No. 4, Jan, 1994 ($1.75)
Marvel Comics UK

	GD25	FN65	NM94
1-($2.95)-Foil stamped-c		1.20	3.00
2-4		.70	1.75

DARKHAWK
Mar, 1991 - No. 50, Apr, 1995 ($1.00/$1.25/$1.50)
Marvel Comics

	GD25	FN65	NM94
1-Origin/1st app. Darkhawk; Hobgoblin cameo			1.50
2-14: 2-Spider-Man & Hobgoblin app. 3-Spider-Man & Hobgoblin app. 6-Capt. America & Daredevil x-over. 9-Punisher app. 11-Last $1.00-c. 11,12-Tombstone app. 13,14-Venom-c/story			1.50
15-24,26-38: 19-Spider-Man & Brotherhood of Evil Mutants-c/story. 20-Spider-Man app. 22-Ghost Rider-c/story. 23-Origin begins, ends #25. 27-New Warriors-c/story. 35-Begin 3 part Venom story			1.25
25-($2.95, 52 pgs.)-Red holo-grafx foil-c w/double gatefold poster; origin of Darkhawk armor revealed		1.20	3.00
39-49: 39-Begin $1.50-c; bound-in trading card sheet			1.50
50-($2.50, 52 pgs)		1.00	2.50
Annual 1 (1992, $2.25, 68 pgs.)-Vs. Iron Man		.90	2.25
Annual 2 (1993, $2.95, 68 pgs.)-Polybagged w/card		1.20	3.00
Annual 3 (1994, $2.95)		1.20	3.00

DARKHOLD: PAGES FROM THE BOOK OF SINS (See Midnight Sons Unlimited)
Oct, 1992 - No. 16, Jan, 1994 ($1.75)
Marvel Comics (Midnight Sons imprint #15 on)

	GD25	FN65	NM94
1-($2.75, 52 pgs.)-Polybagged w/poster by Andy & Adam Kubert; part 4 of Rise of the Midnight Sons storyline		1.10	2.75
2-10,12-16: 3-Reintro Modred the Mystic (see Marvel Chillers #1). 4-Sabertooth-c/sty. 5-Punisher & Ghost Rider app. 15-Spot varnish-c. 15,16-Siege of Darkness part 4&12		.70	1.75
11-($2.25)-Outer-c is a Darkhold envelope made of black parchment w/gold ink		.90	2.25

DARK HORSE CLASSICS
1992 ($3.95, B&W, 52 pgs.)
Dark Horse Comics

	GD25	FN65	NM94
nn's: The Last of the Mohicans. 20,000 Leagues Under the Sea		1.60	4.00

DARK HORSE CLASSICS
May, 1996 ($2.95, one-shot)

Dark Horse Comics #22 © DH

Dark Horse Presents #80 © DH

Darkman #3 © MEG

GD25 FN65 NM94

Dark Horse Comics
1-r/Predator: Jungle Tales 1.20 3.00

DARK HORSE CLASSICS- ALIENS VERSUS PREDATOR
Feb, 1997 - No. 6, July, 1997 ($2.95, mini-series)
Dark Horse Comics
1-6: r/Aliens Versus Predator 1.20 3.00

DARK HORSE CLASSICS- STAR WARS: DARK EMPIRE
Mar, 1997 - No. 5 ($2.95, mini-series)
Dark Horse Comics
1-5: r/Star Wars: Dark Empire 1.20 3.00

DARK HORSE COMICS
Aug, 1992 - No. 25, Sept, 1994 ($2.50)
Dark Horse Comics
1-Dorman double gategold painted-c; Predator, Robocop, Timecop (3-part) & Renegade stories begin; 1st app. of Timecop 1.20 3.00
2-6,11-25: 2-Mignola-c. 3-Begin 3-part Aliens story; Aliens-c. 4-Predator-c. 6-Begin 4 part Robocop story. 12-Begin 2-part Aliens & 3-part Predator stories. 13-Thing From Another World begins w/Nino-a(i). 15-Begin 2-part Aliens: Cargo story. 16-Begin 3-part Predator story. 17-Begin 3-part Star Wars: Droids story & 3-part Aliens: Alien story; Droids-c. 19-Begin 2-part X story; X cover 1.00 2.50
7-Begin Star Wars: Tales of the Jedi 3-part story 2.40 6.00
8-1st app. X and begins; begin 4-part James Bond 1.60 4.00
9,10: 9-Star Wars ends. 10-X ends; Begin 3-part Predator & Godzilla stories 1.20 3.00
NOTE: ***Art Adams*** *c-11.*

DARK HORSE DOWN UNDER
June, 1994 - No. 3, Oct, 1994 ($2.50, B&W, limited series)
Dark Horse Comics
1-3 1.00 2.50

DARK HORSE MONSTERS
Feb, 1997 ($2.95, one-shot)
Dark Horse Comics
1-reprints 2.95

DARK HORSE PRESENTS
July, 1986 - Present ($1.50/$1.75/$1.95/$2.25/$2.50/$2.95, B&W)
Dark Horse Comics
1-1st app. Concrete by Paul Chadwick 1.25 3.75 10.00
1-2nd printing (1988, $1.50) 1.00 2.50
1-Silver ink 3rd printing (1992, $2.25)-Says 2nd printing inside .90 2.25
2-Concrete app. 1.60 4.00
3-Concrete app. 1.20 3.00
4,5-Concrete app. 1.00 2.50
6-10: 6,8,10-Concrete app. 10-1st app. The Mask 1.00 2.50
11-19,21-23: 11-19,21-Mask stories. 12,14,16,18,22-Concrete app. 15(2/88) 17-All Roachmill issue .80 2.00
20-($2.95, 68 pgs.)-Concrete, Flaming Carrot, Mask 1.00 2.50
24-Origin Aliens-c/story (11/88); Mr. Monster app. 2.25 6.75 18.00
25-31,33: 28-($2.95, 52 pgs.)-Concrete app.; Mr. Monster story (homage to Graham Ingels). 33-($2.25, 44 pgs.) 1.00 2.50
32-($3.50, 68 pgs.)-Annual; Concrete, American 1.60 4.00
34-Aliens-c/story 1.20 3.00
35-Predator-c/story; begin $1.95-c 1.20 3.00
36-1st Aliens Vs. Predator story; painted-c 2.40 6.00
36-Same as above, but line drawn-c 2.00 5.00
37-39,41,44,45,47-50: 38-Concrete. 44-Crash Ryan. 48-50-Contain 2 trading cards. 50-S/F story by Perez .80 2.00
40-($2.95, 52 pgs.)-1st Argosy story 1.20 3.00
42,43-Aliens-c/stories 2.00 5.00
46-Prequel to new Predator II mini-series 1.20 3.00
51-53-Sin City by Frank Miller, parts 2-4; 51,53-Miller-c 1.60 4.00
54-The Next Men begins(1st app.) by Byrne(9/91); Miller-a 1.60 4.00
55-2nd app. The Next Men; parts 5 & 6 of Sin City by Miller; Homocide by Morrow in both. 54-Morrow-c; begin $2.25-c. 55-Miller-c 1.20 3.00
56-($3.95, 68 pg. annual)-2-part prologue to Aliens: Genocide; part 7 of Sin City by Miller; Next Men by Byrne 1.20 3.00
57-($3.50, 52 pgs.)-Part 8 of Sin City by Miller; Next Men by Byrne; Byrne & Miller-c; Alien Fire story; swipes cover to Daredevil #1 1.20 3.00
58-66,68-79,81-84-($2.25): 58,59-Part 9,10 Sin City by Miller; Alien Fire stories. 60,61-Part 11,12 Sin City by Miller. 62-Last Sin City (entire book by Miller, c/a;52 pgs.). 64-Dr. Giggles begins (1st app.), ends #66; Boris the Bear story. 66-New Concrete-c/story by Chadwick. 71-Begin 3 part Dominque story by Jim Balent; Balent-c. 72-(3/93)-Begin 3-part Eudaemon (1st app.) story by Nelson. .90 2.25
67-($3.95, 68 pgs.)-Begin 3-part prelude to Predator: Race War mini-series; Oscar Wilde adapt. by Russell 1.60 4.00
80-Art Adams-c/a (Monkeyman & O'Brien) 2.40 6.00
85-87,92-99,101-108: 85-Begin $2.50-c. 92, 93, 95-Too Much Coffee Man. 101-Aliens c/a by Wrightson, story by Paul Pope. 103-Kirby gatefold-c. 106-Big Blown Baby by Bill Wray. 107-Mignola-c/a 1.00 2.50
88-91-Hellboy by Mignola. 2.40 6.00
100-1-Intro Lance Blastoff by Miller; Milk & Cheese by Evan Dorkin. 2.00 5.00
100-2-Hellboy-c by Wrightson; Hellboy story by Mignola; includes Roberta Gregory & Paul Pope stories 1.40 3.50
100-3-Darrow-c, Concrete by Chadwick; Pekar story 1.00 2.50
100-4-Gibbons-c: Miller story, Geary story/a 1.00 2.50
100-5-Allred-c, Adams, Dorkin, Pope 1.00 2.50
109-125: 109-Begin $2.95-c; Paul Pope-c. 110-Ed Brubaker-a/scripts. 114-Flip books begin; Lance Blastoff by Miller; Star Slammers by Simonson. 115-Miller-c. 117-Aliens-c/app. 118-Evan Dorkin-c/a. 119-Monkeyman & O'Brien. 121-Jack Zero. 122-Lords of Misrue 123-Imago. 124-Predator. 125-Nocturnals 1.20 3.00
126-($3.95, 48 pgs.)-Flip book: Nocturnals, Starship Troopers 3.95
...Aliens Platinum Edition (1992)-r/DHP #24,43,43,56 & Special 1.25 3.75 10.00
...Fifth Anniversary Special nn (4/91, $9.95)-Part 1 of Sin City by Frank Miller (c/a); Aliens, Aliens vs. Predator, Concrete, Roachmill, Give Me Liberty & The American stories 1.25 3.75 10.00
The One Trick Rip-off (1997, $12.95, TPB)-r/stories from #101-112 13.00
NOTE: ***Geary*** *a-59, 60.* ***Miller*** *a-Special, 51-53, 55-62; c-59-62, 100-1; c-51, 53, 55, 59-62, 100-1.* ***Moebius*** *a-63; c-63, 70.* ***Vess*** *a-78; c-75, 78.*

DARK KNIGHT (See Batman: The Dark Knight & Legends of the...)

DARKLON THE MYSTIC (Also see Eerie Magazine #79,80)
Oct, 1983 (one-shot)
Pacific Comics
1-Starlin-c/a(r) 1.50

DARKMAN (Movie)
Sept, 1990; Oct, 1990 - No. 3, Dec, 1990 ($1.50)
Marvel Comics
1 (9/90, $2.25, B&W mag., 68 pgs.)-Adaptation of film .90 2.25
1-3: Reprints B&W magazine 1.50

DARKMAN
V2#1, Apr, 1993 -No. 6, Sept, 1993 ($2.95, limited series)
Marvel Comics
V2#1 ($3.95, 52 pgs.) 1.60 4.00
2-6 1.20 3.00

DARK MANSION OF FORBIDDEN LOVE, THE (Becomes Forbidden Tales of Dark Mansion No. 5 on)

Dark Mysteries #1 © Merit

Darkness #9 © Top Cow

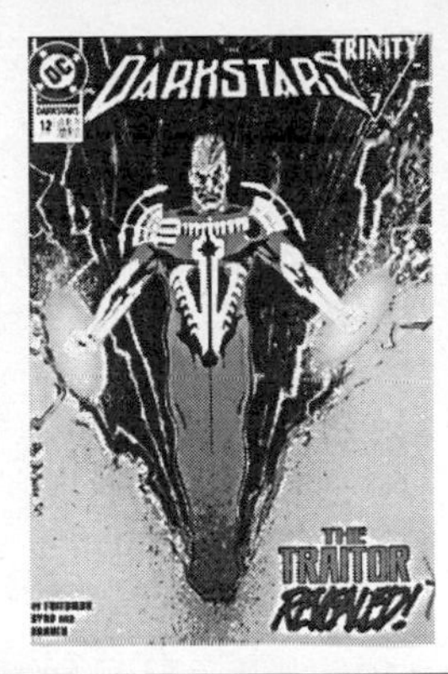

Darkstars #12 © DC

	GD25	FN65	NM94

Sept-Oct, 1971 - No. 4, Mar-Apr, 1972 (52 pgs.)
National Periodical Publications

1	11.00	33.00	110.00
2-4: 2-Adams-c. 3-Jeff Jones-c	3.00	9.00	30.00

DARK MYSTERIES (Thrilling Tales of Horror & Suspense)
June-July, 1951 - No. 25?, 1955
"Master" - "Merit" Publications

1-Wood-c/a (8 pgs.)	75.00	225.00	650.00
2-Wood/Harrison-c/a (8 pgs.)	51.00	153.00	440.00
3-9: 7-Dismemberment, hypo blood drainage stys	26.00	77.00	200.00
10-Cannibalism story; witch burning-c	27.00	81.00	210.00
11-13,15-18: 11-Severed head panels. 13-Dismemberment-c/story. 17-The Old Gravedigger host	20.00	60.00	155.00
14-Several E.C. Craig swipes	21.00	62.00	160.00
19-Injury-to-eye panel; E.C. swipe; torture-c	26.00	79.00	200.00
20-Female bondage, blood drainage story	24.00	71.00	180.00
21,22-Last pre-code issue, misdated 3/54 instead of 3/55	14.00	43.00	110.00
23-25 (#25-Exist?)	12.00	36.00	85.00

NOTE: ***Cameron** a-1, 2. **Myron Fass** c/a-21. **Harrison** a-3, 7; c-3. **Hollingsworth** a-7-17, 20, 21, 23. **Wildey** a-5. Woodish art by **Fleishman**-9; c-10, 14-17. Bondage c-10, 18, 19.*

DARKNESS, THE (See Witchblade #10)
Dec, 1996 - Present ($2.50)
Image Comics (Top Cow Productions)

Special Preview Edition-(B&W)-Ennis script; Silvestri-a(p)	2.25	6.75	18.00
0	2.00	6.00	16.00
0-Gold Edition	2.50	7.50	22.00
1/2	2.00	6.00	16.00
1/2-Christmas-c	3.00	9.00	30.00
1-Ennis-s/Silvestri-a	1.25	3.75	10.00
1-Black variant-c	1.50	4.50	12.00
1-Platinum variant-c	3.00	9.00	30.00
2	1.10	3.30	9.00
3		2.40	6.00
4, 5		1.80	4.50
6-10: 9,10-Witchblade "Family Ties" x-over pt. 2,3		1.00	2.50
...Collected Editions #1 ($4.95, trade paperback) r/1,2			4.95
...Collected Editions #2 ($4.95, trade paperback) r/3,4			4.95

DARK ONE'S THIRD EYE
1996 ($4.95, squarebound, one-shot)
Sirius Entertainment

nn-Dark One-a; pinups		2.00	5.00

DARKSEID VS. GALACTUS: THE HUNGER
1995 ($4.95, one-shot) (1st DC/Marvel x-over by John Byrne)
DC Comics

nn-John Byrne-c/a/scripts		2.00	5.00

DARK SHADOWS
Oct, 1957 - No. 3, May, 1958
Steinway Comic Publications (Ajax)(America's Best)

1	12.00	38.00	100.00
2,3	9.50	28.00	75.00

DARK SHADOWS (TV) (See Dan Curtis Giveaways)
Mar, 1969 - No. 35, Feb, 1976 (Photo-c: 1-7)
Gold Key

1(30039-903)-With pull-out poster (25¢)	21.00	64.00	235.00
1-With poster missing	8.00	23.00	85.00
2	7.00	22.00	80.00
3-With pull-out poster	10.00	30.00	110.00
3-With poster missing	5.50	16.50	60.00
4-7: 7-Last photo-c	6.40	19.00	70.00
8-10	5.00	15.00	55.00
11-20	4.00	12.00	45.00
21-35: 30-Last painted-c	3.00	9.00	35.00
Story Digest 1 (6/70)-Photo-c	8.00	25.00	90.00

DARK SHADOWS (TV) (See Nightmare on Elm Street)
June, 1992 - No. 4, Spring, 1993 ($2.50, limited series, coated stock)
Innovation Publishing

1-Based on 1991 NBC TV mini-series; painted-c		1.20	4.00
2-4		1.00	3.00

DARK SHADOWS: BOOK TWO
1993 - No. 4, July, 1993 ($2.50, limited series)
Innovation Publishing

1-4-Painted-c. 4-Maggie Thompson scripts		1.20	3.00

DARK SHADOWS: BOOK THREE
Nov, 1993 ($2.50)
Innovation Publishing

1-(Whole #9)		1.20	3.00

DARKSIDE
Oct, 1996 ($2.99, one-shot)
Maximum Press

1-Avengelyne-c/app.			2.99

DARKSTARS, THE
Oct, 1992 - No. 38, Jan, 1996 ($1.75/$1.95)
DC Comics

1-1st app. The Darkstars		.80	2.00
2-21: 5-Hawkman & Hawkwoman app. 18-20-Flash app.		.70	1.75
22-24: 22-Begin $1.95-c. 24-(9/94)-Zero Hour		.80	2.00
0,25-30: 0-(10/94). 25-(11/94). 30-Green Lantern app.		.80	2.00
31-38: 31-...vs, Darkseid. 32-Green Lantern app.		.90	2.25

NOTE: ***Travis Charest** a(p)-4-7; c(p)-2-5; c-6-11. **Stroman** a-1-3; c-1.*

DARK TOWN
1995 ($3.95, magazine-size, quarterly)
Mad Monkey Press

1-Kaja Blackley scripts; Vanessa Chong-a		1.60	4.00

DARKWING DUCK (TV cartoon) (Also see Cartoon Tales)
Nov, 1991 - No. 4, Feb, 1992 ($1.50, limited series)
Disney Comics

1-4: Adapts hour-long premiere TV episode			1.50

DARLING LOVE
Oct-Nov, 1949 - No. 11, 1952 (no month) (52 pgs.)(All photo-c?)
Close Up/Archie Publ. (A Darling Magazine)

1-Photo-c	10.50	32.00	85.00
2-Photo-c	7.85	23.50	55.00
3-8,10,11: 3-6-photo-c	5.70	17.00	40.00
9-Krigstein-a	7.15	21.50	50.00

DARLING ROMANCE
Sept-Oct, 1949 - No. 7, 1951 (All photo-c)
Close Up (MLJ Publications)

1-(52 pgs.)-Photo-c	17.50	53.00	140.00
2	7.85	23.50	55.00
3-7	6.50	19.50	45.00

DARQUE RAZOR
Aug, 1997 - Present ($2.25/$3.00, limited series)
London Night Studios

1/2			2.25

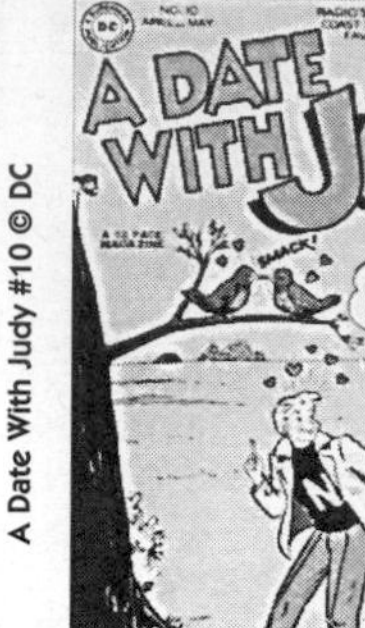

A Date With Judy #10 © DC

Davy Crockett #3 © CC

Dawn #4 © Joseph Michael Linsner

	GD25	FN65	NM94
1-($3.00)			3.00
1-($10.00) Nude Edition	1.25	3.75	10.00

DART (Also see Freak Force & Savage Dragon)
Feb, 1996 - No. 3, May, 1996 ($2.50, limited series)
Image Comics (Highbrow Entertainment)

	GD25	FN65	NM94
1-3		1.00	2.50

DASTARDLY & MUTTLEY (See Fun-In No. 1-4, 6 and Kite Fun Book)

DATE WITH DANGER
No. 5, Dec, 1952 - No. 6, Feb, 1953
Standard Comics

	GD25	FN65	NM94
5,6-Secret agent stories	5.70	17.00	40.00

DATE WITH DEBBI (Also see Debbi's Dates)
Jan-Feb, 1969 - No. 17, Sept-Oct, 1971; No. 18, Oct-Nov, 1972
National Periodical Publications

	GD25	FN65	NM94
1-Teenage	3.50	10.50	35.00
2-5	1.75	5.25	14.00
6-17: 14,15-68 pgs. 14-1 pg. story on Jack Wild. 15-Marlo Thomas/"That Girl" sty. 17-52 pgs; James Taylor sty.	1.50	4.50	12.00
18-Last issue	1.60	4.85	13.00

DATE WITH JUDY, A (Radio/TV, and 1948 movie)
Oct-Nov, 1947 - No. 79, Oct-Nov, 1960 (No. 1-25: 52 pgs.)
National Periodical Publications

	GD25	FN65	NM94
1-Teenage	24.00	71.00	190.00
2	11.30	34.00	90.00
3-10	8.75	26.25	70.00
11-20	5.70	17.00	40.00
21-40	5.35	16.00	32.00
41-45: 45-Last pre-code (2-3/55)	4.25	13.00	28.00
46-79: 79-Drucker-c/a	4.00	11.00	22.00

DATE WITH MILLIE, A (Life With Millie No. 8 on)(Teenage)
Oct, 1956 - No. 7, Aug, 1957; Oct, 1959 - No. 7, Oct, 1960
Atlas/Marvel Comics (MPC)

	GD25	FN65	NM94
1(10/56)-(1st Series)-Dan DeCarlo-a in #1-7	19.00	56.00	150.00
2	9.50	28.00	75.00
3-7	7.15	21.50	50.00
1(10/59)-(2nd Series)	9.50	28.00	75.00
2-7	7.15	21.50	50.00

DATE WITH PATSY, A (Also see Patsy Walker)
Sept, 1957 (One-shot)
Atlas Comics

	GD25	FN65	NM94
1-Starring Patsy Walker	8.75	26.25	65.00

DAVID AND GOLIATH (Movie)
No. 1205, July, 1961
Dell Publishing Co.

	GD25	FN65	NM94
Four Color 1205-Photo-c	5.50	16.50	60.00

DAVID CASSIDY (TV)(See Partridge Family, Swing With Scooter #33 & Time For Love #30)
Feb, 1972 - No. 14, Sept, 1973
Charlton Comics

	GD25	FN65	NM94
1	3.50	10.50	35.00
2-4,6,8,10-13	2.25	6.75	18.00
5,7,9,14-Photo-c	2.50	7.50	24.00

DAVID LADD'S LIFE STORY (See Movie Classics)

DAVY CROCKETT (See Dell Giants, Fightin..., Frontier Fighters, It's Game Time, Power Record Comics, Western Tales & Wild Frontier)

DAVY CROCKETT (Frontier Fighter...)
1951
Avon Periodicals

	GD25	FN65	NM94
nn-Tuska?, Reinman-a; Fawcette-c	14.00	41.00	110.00

DAVY CROCKETT (...King of the Wild Frontier No. 1,2)(TV)
5/55 - No. 671, 12/55; No. 1, 12/63; No. 2, 11/69 (Walt Disney)
Dell Publishing Co./Gold Key

	GD25	FN65	NM94
Four Color 631(#1)-Fess Parker photo-c	16.00	48.00	175.00
Four Color 639-Photo-c	13.00	38.00	140.00
Four Color 664,671(Marsh-a)-Photo-c	12.00	35.00	130.00
1(12/63-Gold Key)-Fess Parker photo-c; reprints	12.00	35.00	130.00
2(11/69)-Fess Parker photo-c; reprints	3.60	11.00	40.00
...Christmas Book (no date, 16 pgs., paper-c)-Sears giveaway	5.70	17.00	35.00
...In the Raid at Piney Creek (1955, 16 pgs., 5x7-1/4")-American Motors giveaway; slick, photo-c	6.50	19.50	45.00
...Safety Trails (1955, 16pgs, 3-1/4x7")-Cities Service giveaway	6.50	19.50	45.00

DAVY CROCKETT (...Frontier Fighter #1,2; Kid Montana #9 on)
Aug, 1955 - No. 8, Jan, 1957
Charlton Comics

	GD25	FN65	NM94
1	7.15	21.50	50.00
2	5.00	15.00	30.00
3-8	4.00	11.00	22.00
Hunting With... nn ('55, 16 pgs.)-Ben Franklin Store giveaway (Publ.-S. Rose)	4.25	13.00	28.00

DAWN
June, 1995 - No. 6, 1996 ($2.95)
Sirius Entertainment

	GD25	FN65	NM94
1/2-w/certificate	2.50	7.50	20.00
1/2-Variant-c	3.50	10.50	35.00
1-Linsner-c/a	1.85	5.50	15.00
1-Black Light Edition	2.50	7.50	25.00
1-White Trash Edition	4.00	12.00	40.00
1-Look Sharp Edition	6.00	18.00	60.00
2-4: Linsner-c/a	1.25	3.75	10.00
2-Variant-c	3.50	10.50	35.00
3-Limited Edition	4.00	12.00	40.00
4-6-Vibrato-c		2.00	5.00
4, 5-Limited Edition	2.50	7.50	25.00

DAYDREAMERS (See Generation X)
Aug, 1997 - No. 3, Oct, 1997 ($2.50, limited series)
Marvel Comics

	GD25	FN65	NM94
1-3-Franklin Richards, Howard the Duck, Man-Thing app.		1.00	2.50

DAYS OF THE MOB (See In the Days of the Mob)

DAZEY'S DIARY
June-Aug, 1962
Dell Publishing Co.

	GD25	FN65	NM94
01-174-208: Bill Woggon-c/a	2.75	8.00	30.00

DAZZLER, THE (Also see Marvel Graphic Novel & X-Men #130)
Mar, 1981 - No. 42, Mar, 1986
Marvel Comics Group

	GD25	FN65	NM94
1,2-X-Men app.		1.00	2.50
3-21: 10,11-Galactus app. 21-Double size; photo-c.			1.00
22 (12/82)-vs. Rogue Battle-c/sty		2.00	5.00
23,26: 23-Rogue/Mystique 1 pg. app. 26-Jusko-c		.80	2.00
24,28: 24-Full app. Rogue w/Powerman (Iron Fist). 28-Full app. Rogue; Mystique app.		1.60	4.00
25,29-32,34-37,39			1.00

27,33,38,40: 27-Rogue app. 33-Michael Jackson thriller swipe-c/sty.38-

DC Comics Presents #27 © DC

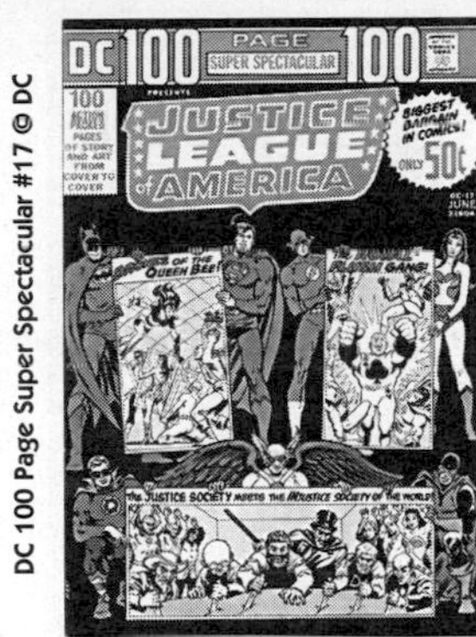

DC 100 Page Super Spectacular #17 © DC

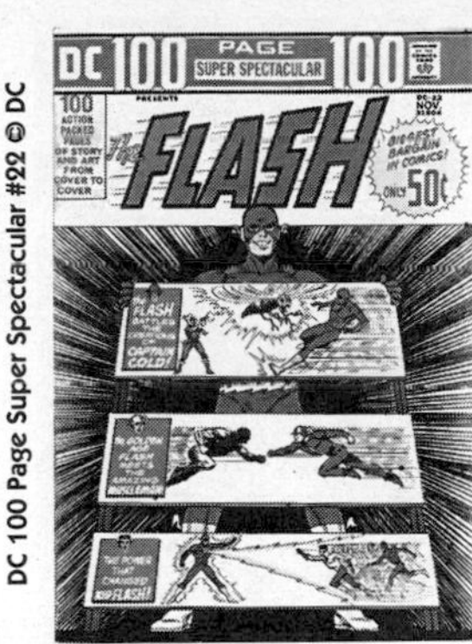

DC 100 Page Super Spectacular #22 © DC

GD25 FN65 NM94

Wolverine-c/app.; X-Men app. 40-Secret Wars II 1.20 3.00
41- 1.60 4.00
42-Beast-c/sty 2.00 5.00
NOTE: *No. 1 distributed only through comic shops.* **Alcala** *a-1i, 2i.* **Chadwick** *a-38-42p; c(p)-39, 41, 42.* **Guice** *a-38i, 42i; c-38, 40.*

DC CHALLENGE
Nov, 1985 - No. 12, Oct, 1986 ($1.25, maxi-series)
DC Comics

1-11: 1-Colan-a. 2,8-Batman-c/app. 4-Gil Kane-c/a 1.25
12-($2.00)-Ordway-c .80 2.00
NOTE: *Batman app. in 1-4, 6-12. Joker app. in 7.* **Giffen** *c/a-11.* **Infantino** *a-3.* **Ordway** *c-12.* **Swan/Austin** *c-10.*

DC COMICS PRESENTS
July-Aug, 1978 - No. 97, Sept, 1986 (Superman team-ups in all)
DC Comics

1-4th & final Superman/Flash race 1.00 2.80 7.00
2-10: 2-4th & final Superman/Flash race. 4-Metal Men. 9-Wonder Woman 2.00 5.00
11,12,14-26,30-32,38-40,43-46,48,50,51,53-71,73-76,79-84: 19-Batgirl. 31,58-Robin.. 43,80-Legion of Super Heroes. .82-Adam Strange. 83-Batman & Outsiders. 1.20 3.00
13,27-29,33-37,42,47,49,52,86-96: 13-Legion of Super Heroes. 35-Man-Bat. 42,47-Sandman. 52-Doom Patrol. 86-88-Crisis x-over. 88-Creeper 1.60 4.00
26-(10/80)-Green Lantern; intro Cyborg, Starfire, Raven (1st app. New Teen Titans in 16 pg. preview); Starlin-c/a; Sargon the Sorcerer back-up 1.75 5.25 14.00
41,72,77,78,97: 41-Superman/Joker-c/story. 72-Joker/Phantom Stranger-c/story.77,78-Animal Man app. (77-cover app. also) 2.40 6.00
85-Swamp Thing; Alan Moore scripts 1.00 3.00 8.00
Annual 1,4: 1(9/82)-G.A. Superman. 4(10/85)-Superwoman 1.20 3.00
2,3: 2(7/83)-Intro/origin Superwoman. 3(9/84)-Shazam. 1.60 4.00
NOTE: **Adkins** *a-2, 54; c-2.* **Buckler** *a-33, 34; c-30, 33, 34.* **Giffen** *a-39; c-59.* **Gil Kane** *a-28, 35, Annual 3; c-48p, 56, 58, 60, 62, 64, 68, Annual 2, 3.* **Kirby** *c/a-84.* **Kubert** *c/a-66.* **Morrow** *c/a-65.* **Newton** *c/a-54p.* **Orlando** *c-53i.* **Perez** *a-26p, 61p; c-38, 61, 94.* **Starlin** *a-26-29p, 36p, 37p; c-26-29, 36, 37, 93.* **Toth** *a-84.* **Williamson** *i-79, 85, 87.*

DC GRAPHIC NOVEL (Also see DC Science Fiction...)
Nov, 1983 - No. 7, 1986 ($5.95, 68 pgs.)
DC Comics

1-3,5,7: 1-Star Raiders. 2-Warlords; not from regular Warlord series. 3-The Medusa Chain; Ernie Colon story/a. 5-Me and Joe Priest; Chaykin-c. 7-Space Clusters; Nino-c/a. 1.10 3.30 9.00
4-The Hunger Dogs by Kirby; Darkseid kills Himon from Mister Miracle & destroys New Genesis 2.50 7.50 20.00
6-Metalzoic; Sienkiewicz-c ($6.95) 1.10 3.30 9.00

DC/MARVEL: ALL ACCESS (Also see DC Versus Marvel & Marvel Versus DC)
1996 - No. 4, 1997 ($2.95, limited series)
DC Comics

1-4: 1-Superman & Spider-Man app. 2-Robin & Jubilee app. 3-Dr. Strange & Batman-c/app., X-Men , JLA app. 4-X-Men vs. JLA-c/app. rebirth of Amalgam 1.20 3.00

DC 100 PAGE SUPER SPECTACULAR
(Title is 100 Page... No. 14 on)(Square bound) (Reprints, 50¢)
No. 4, Summer, 1971 - No. 13, 6/72; No. 14, 2/73 - No. 22, 11/73 (No #1-3)
National Periodical Publications

4-Weird Mystery Tales; Johnny Peril & Phantom Stranger; cover & splashes by Wrightson; origin Jungle Boy of Jupiter 10.00 30.00 100.00
5-Love Stories; Wood inks (7 pgs.)(scarcer) 34.00 102.00 375.00
6- "World's Greatest Super-Heroes"; JLA, JSA, Spectre, Johnny Quick, Vigilante & Hawkman; contains unpublished Wildcat story; N. Adams wrap-around-c; r/JLA #21,22 4.50 13.50 90.00
7,10:7-(see Superman #245). 10-(see Adv. #416) 2.50 7.50 24.00
8,9,11: 8-(See Batman #238)9-(See Our Army at War #242). 11-(See Flash #214). 3.50 10.50 35.00
12,13: 12-(see Superboy #185). 13-(See Superman #252) 2.50 7.50 24.00
14-Batman-r/Detective #31,32,156; Atom-r/Showcase#34 2.50 7.50 24.00
15-22: 15-r/2nd Boy Commandos/Det. #65. 17-JSA-r/All Star #37 (10-11/47, 38 pgs.), Sandman-r/Adv. #65 (8/41), JLA #23 (11/63) & JLA #43 (3/66). 20-Batman-r/Det. #66,68, Spectre; origin Two-Face. 21-r/Brave & the Bold #54. 22-r/All-Flash #13. 1.85 5.50 15.00
NOTE: **Anderson** *r-11, 14, 18i, 22.* **B. Baily** *r-18, 20.* **Burnley** *r-18, 20.* **Crandall** *r-14p, 20.* **Drucker** *r-4.* **Grandenetti** *a-22(2)r.* **Heath** *a-22r.* **Infantino** *r-17, 20, 22.* **G. Kane** *r-18.* **Kubert** *r-6, 7, 16, 17; c-16, 19.* **Manning** *a-19r.* **Meskin** *r-4, 22.* **Mooney** *r-15, 21.* **Toth** *r-17, 20.*

DC SCIENCE FICTION GRAPHIC NOVEL
1985 - No. 7, 1987 ($5.95)
DC Comics

SF1-SF7: SF1-Hell on Earth by Robert Bloch; Giffen-p. SF2-Nightwings by Robert Silverberg; G. Colan-p. SF3-Frost & Fire by Bradbury. SF4-Merchants of Venus. SF5-Demon With A Glass Hand by Ellison; M. Rogers-a. SF6-The Magic Goes Away by Niven. SF7-Sandkings by George R.R. Martin 1.00 3.00 8.00

DC SILVER AGE CLASSICS
1992 ($1.00, all reprints)
DC Comics

...Action Comics #252; r/1st Supergirl; Adventure Comics #247; r/1st Legion of S.H....The Brave and the Bold #28; r/1st JLA; Detective Comics #225; r/1st Martian Manhunter; Detective Comics #327; r/1st new look Batman; Green Lantern #76; r/Green Lantern/Gr. Arrow; House of Secrets #92; r/1st Swamp Thing; Showcase #4; r/1st S.A. Flash; Showcase #22; r/1st S.A. Green Lantern; Sugar and Spike #99; 2 unpublished stories 1.00

DC SPECIAL (Also see Super DC...)
10-12/68 - No. 15, 11-12/71; No. 16, Spr/75 - No. 29, 8-9/77
National Periodical Publications

1-All Infantino issue; Flash, Batman, Adam Strange-r; begin 68 pg. issues, end #21 3.00 9.00 30.00
2-Teen humor. 5.00 15.00 50.00
3 3.00 9.00 30.00
4-13: 5-All Kubert issue; Viking Prince, Sgt. Rock-r. 7-(see Superman #245). 8-(see Batman #238). 9-(see Our Army at War $242). 10-(see Adventure #416). 11-(see Flash #214). 12-(see Superboy #185).12-Viking Prince; Kubert-c/a(r/B&B almost entirely) 13-(see Superman #252).**Note:** #7-13 are part of each respective title's numbering and are priced here only 2.25 6.75 18.00
14,15: 15-G.A. Plastic Man origin-r/Police #1; origin Woozy by Cole; 14,15-(52 pgs.) 2.25 6.75 18.00
16-29: 16-Super Heroes Battle Super Gorillas; r/Capt. Storm #1, 1st Johnny Cloud/All-Amer. Men of War #82. 17-Early S.A. Green Lantern-r. 22-Origin Robin Hood. 26-Enemy Ace on-c only. 27-Captain Comet story. 28-Earth Shattering Disaster Stories; Legion of Super-Heroes story. 29-The Untold Origin of the Justice Society 1.00 3.00 8.00
NOTE: **N. Adams** *c-3, 4, 6, 11, 29.* **Grell** *a-20; c-17, 20.* **Heath** *a-12r.* **G. Kane** *a-6p, 13r, 17r, 19-21r.* **Kubert** *a-6r, 12r, 22.* **Meskin** *a-10.* **Moreira** *a-10.* **Staton** *a-29p.* **Toth** *a-13, 20r. #1-15: 25¢; 16-27: 50¢; 28, 29: 60¢. #1-13, 16-21: 68 pgs.; 14, 15: 52 pgs.; 25-27: oversized.*

DC SPECIAL BLUE-RIBBON DIGEST
Mar-Apr, 1980 - No. 24, Aug, 1982
DC Comics

1-5: 1-Legion reprints. 2-Flash. 3-Justice Society. 4-Green Lantern 5-Secret Origins; new Zatara and Zatanna 1.60 4.00
6-10: 6-Ghosts. 7-Sgt. Rock's Prize Battle Tales. 8-Legion. 9-Secret Origins. 10-Warlord-"The Deimus Saga"-Grell-s/c/a 1.60 4.00
11-15: 11-Justice League. 12-Haunted Tank; reprints 1st app. 13-Strange Sports Stories. 14-UFO Invaders; Adam Strange app. 15-Secret Origins of Super Villains; JLA app. 2.40 6.00
16-19: 16-Green Lantern/Green Arrow-r; all Adams-a. 17-Ghosts. 18-Sgt. Rock;

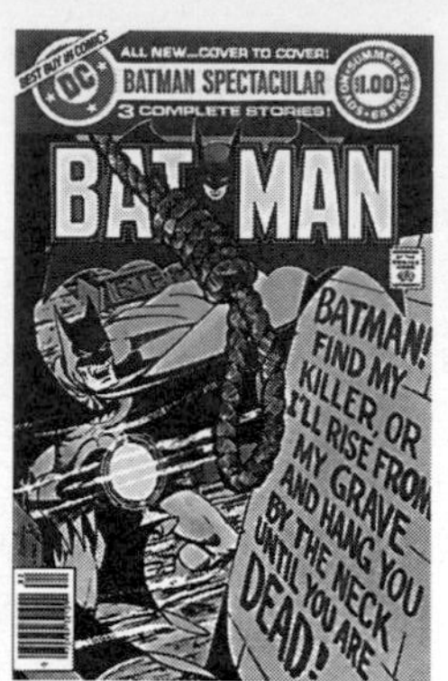

DC Special Series #15 © DC

DC Super-Stars #13 © DC

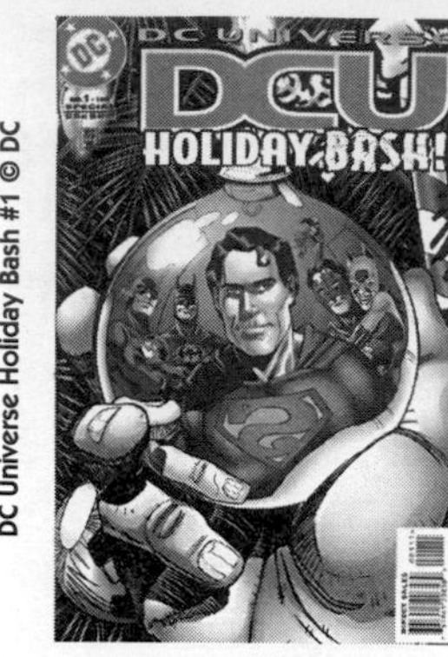

DC Universe Holiday Bash #1 © DC

GD25 FN65 NM94

Kubert front & back-c. 19-Doom Patrol; new Perez-c 2.40 6.00
20-Dark Mansion of Forbidden Love (scarce) 2.50 7.50 20.00
21-24: 21-Our Army at War. 22-Secret Origins. 23-Green Arrow, w/new 7 pg. story. 24-House of Mystery; new Kubert wraparound-c 2.40 6.00

NOTE: ***N. Adams** a-16(6)r, 17r, 23r; c-16. **Aparo** a-6r, 24r; c-23. **Grell** a-8, 10; c-10. **Heath** a-14. **Infantino** a-15r. **Kaluta** a-17r. **Gil Kane** a-15r, 22r. **Kirby** a-23r. **Kubert** a-3, 18r, 21r; c-7, 12, 14, 17, 18, 21, 24. **Morrow** a-24r. **Orlando** a-17r, 22r; c-1, 20. **Toth** a-21r, 24r. **Wood** a-3, 17r, 24r. **Wrightson** a-16r, 17r, 24r.*

DC SPECIAL SERIES
9/77 - No. 16, Fall, 1978; No. 17, 8/79 - No. 27, Fall, 1981
(No. 19, 23, 24 - digest size, 100 pgs.; No. 25-27 - over-sized)
National Periodical Publications/DC Comics

1-"5-Star Super-Hero Spectacular 1997"; Batman, Atom, Flash, Green Lantern, Aquaman, in solo stories, Kobra app.; N. Adams-c. 2.40 6.00
2(#1)-"The Original Swamp Thing Saga 1977"-r/Swamp Thing #1&2 by Wrightson; new Wrightson wraparound-c. 2.40 6.00
3,4,6-9: 3-Sgt Rock. 4-Unexpected. 6-Secret Society of Super Villains, Jones-a. 7-Ghosts Special. 8-Brave and Bold w/ new Batman, Deadman & Sgt Rock team-up. 9-Wonder Woman; Ditko-a (11 pgs.) 2.40 6.00
5-"Superman Spectacular 1977"-(84 pg, $1.00)-Superman vs. Brainiac & Lex Luthor, new 63 pg. story 2.40 6.00
10-"Secret Origins of Superheroes Special 1978"-(52. pgs)-Dr. Fate, Lightray & Black Canary-c/new origin stories; Staton, Newton-a 2.40 6.00
11-"Flash Spectacular 1978"-(84 pgs.) Flash, Kid Flash, GA Flash & Johnny Quick vs. Grodd; Wood-i on Kid Flash chapter 2.40 6.00
12-"Secrets of Haunted House Special Spring 1978" 2.40 6.00
13-"Sgt. Rock Special Spring 1978", 50 pgs new story 2.40 6.00
14,17,20-"Original Swamp Thing Saga", Wrightson-a: 14-Sum '78, r/#3,4. 17-Sum '79 r/#5-7. 20-Jan/Feb '80, r/#8-10 2.40 6.00
15-"Batman Spectacular Summer 1978", Ra's Al Ghul-app.; Golden-a. Rogers-a/front & back-c 2.40 6.00
16-"Jonah Hex Spectacular Fall 1978"; death of Jonah Hex, Heath-a; Bat Lash and Scalphunter stories 2.50 7.50 25.00
18,19-Digest size: 18-"Sgt. Rock's Prize Battle Tales Fall 1979". 19-"Secret Origins of Super-Heroes Fall 1979"; origins Wonder Woman (new-a),r/Robin, Batman-Superman team, Aquaman, Hawkman and others 2.40 6.00
21-"Superstar Holiday Special Spring 1980", Frank Miller-a in "Batman--Wanted Dead or Alive" (1st Batman story); Jonah Hex, Sgt. Rock, Superboy &LSH and House of Mystery/Witching Hour-c/stories 1.50 4.50 12.00
22-"G.I. Combat Sept. 1980", Kubert-c. Haunted Tank-s 2.40 6.00
23,24-Digest size: 23-World's Finest-r. 24-Flash 1.00 2.80 7.00
V5#25-($2.95)-"Superman II, the Adventure Continues Summer 1981"; photos from movie & photo-c (see All-New Coll. Ed. C-62)1.25 3.75 10.00
26-($2.50)-"Superman and His Incredible Fortress of Solitude Summer 1981" 1.25 3.75 10.00
27-($2.50)-"Batman vs. The Incredible Hulk Fall 1981" 1.85 5.50 15.00

NOTE: ***Aparo** c-8. **Heath** a-12i, 16. **Infantino** a-19r. **Kubert** c-13, 19r. **Nasser/Netzer** a-1, 10i, 15. **Newton** a-10. **Nino** a-4, 7. **Starlin** c-12. **Staton** a-1. **Tuska** a-19r. #25 & 26. were advertised as All-New Collectors' Edition C-63, C-64. #26 was originally planned as All-New Collectors' Ed. C-30?; has C-630 & A.N.C.E. on cover.*

DC SPOTLIGHT
1985 (50th anniversary special) (giveaway)
DC Comics

1-Includes profiles on Batman:The Dark Knight & Watchmen. 1.20 3.00

DC SUPER-STARS
March, 1976 - No. 18, Winter, 1978 (No.3-18: 52 pgs.)
National Periodical Publications/DC Comics

1-(68 pgs.)-Re-intro Teen Titans (predates T. T. #44 (11/76); tryout iss.) plus r/Teen Titans; W.W. as girl was original Wonder Girl 1.10 3.30 9.00
2-7,9,11,12,16,18: 2,4-6,8-Adam Strange; 2-(68 pgs.)-r/1st Adam Strange/Hawkman team-up from Mystery in Space #90 plus Atomic Knights origin-r. 3-Legion issue. 4-r/Tales/Unexpected #45 2.40 6.00
8-r/1st Space Ranger from Showcase #15, Adam Strange-r/Mystery in Space #89 & Star Rovers-r/M.I.S. #80 1.10 3.30 9.00
10-Strange Sports Stories; Batman/Joker-c/story 1.10 3.30 9.00
13-15: 13-Sergio Aragones Special. 15-Sgt. Rock 1.10 3.30 9.00
17-Secret Origins of Super-Heroes (origin of The Huntress); origin Green Arrow by Grell; Legion app.; Earth II Batman & Catwoman marry (1st revealed; also see B&B #197 & Superman Family #211) 1.10 3.30 9.00

NOTE: ***M. Anderson** r-2, 4, 6. **Aparo** c-7, 14, 18. **Austin** a-11i. **Buckler** a-14p; c-10. **Grell** a-17. **G. Kane** a-1r, 10r. **Kubert** c-15. **Layton** c/a-16i, 17i. **Mooney** a-4r, 6r. **Morrow** c/a-11r. **Nasser** a-11. **Newton** c/a-16p. **Staton** a-17; c-17. No. 10, 12-18 contain all new material; the rest are reprints. #1 contains new and reprint material.*

DC UNIVERSE HOLIDAY BASH
1997 ($3.95, one-shot)
DC Comics

1-Christmas stories by various 3.95

DC UNIVERSE: TRINITY
Aug, 1993 - No. 2, Sept, 1993 ($2.95, 52 pgs, limited series)
DC Comics

1,2-Foil-c; Green Lantern, Darkstars, Legion app. 1.20 3.00

DC VERSUS MARVEL (See Marvel Versus DC) (Also see Amazon, Assassins, Bruce Wayne: Agent of S.H.I. E. L.D., Bullets & Bracelets, Doctor Strangefate, JLX, Legend of the Dark Claw, Magneto & The Magnetic Men, Speed Demon, Spider-Boy, Super Soldier, X-Patrol)
No. 1, 1996, No. 4, 1996 ($3.95, limited series)
DC Comics

1,4: 1-Marz script, Jurgens-a(p); 1st app. of Access. 1.60 4.00
.../Marvel Versus DC ($12.95, trade paperback) r/1-4 12.95

D-DAY (Also see Special War Series)
Sum/63; No. 2, Fall/64; No. 4, 9/66; No. 5, 10/67; No. 6, 11/68
Charlton Comics (no No. 3)

1(1963)-Montes/Bache-c 2.50 7.50 24.00
2(Fall,'64)-Wood-a(4) 2.50 7.50 20.00
4-6('66-'68)-Montes/Bache-a #5 1.75 5.25 14.00

DEAD AIR
July, 1989 ($5.95, graphic novel)
Slave Labor Graphics

nn-Mike Allred's 1st published work 2.40 6.00

DEAD END CRIME STORIES
April, 1949 (52 pgs.)
Kirby Publishing Co.

nn-(Scarce)-Powell, Roussos-a; painted-c 43.00 128.00 350.00

DEAD-EYE WESTERN COMICS
Nov-Dec, 1948 - V3#1, Apr-May, 1953
Hillman Periodicals

V1#1-(52 pgs.)-Krigstein, Roussos-a 14.00 41.00 110.00
V1#2,3-(52 pgs.) 7.85 23.50 55.00
V1#4-12-(52 pgs.) 5.35 16.00 32.00
V2#1,2,5-8,10-12: 1-7-(52 pgs.) 4.15 12.50 25.00
3,4-Krigstein-a 5.70 17.00 40.00
9-One pg. Frazetta ad 4.15 12.50 25.00
V3#1 4.00 11.00 22.00

NOTE: ***Briefer** a-V1#8. Kinstleresque stories by **McCann**-12, V2#1, 2, V3#1. **McWilliams** a-V1#5. **Ed Moore** a-V1#4.*

DEADFACE: DOING THE ISLANDS WITH BACCHUS
July, 1991 - No. 3, Sept, 1991 ($2.95, B&W,limited series, 52 pgs.)
Dark Horse Comics

1-3: By Eddie Campbell 1.20 3.00

DEADFACE: EARTH, WATER, AIR, AND FIRE

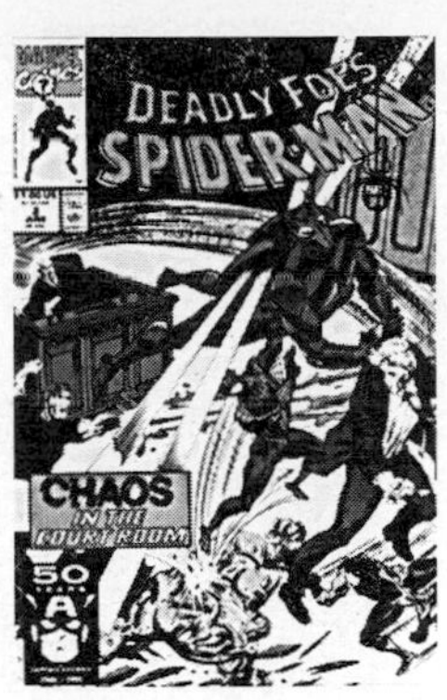

Deadly Foes of Spider-Man #2 © MEG

Deadman #3 © DC

Dead of Night #8 © MEG

GD25 FN65 NM94

July, 1992 - No. 4, Oct, 1992 ($2.50, B&W, limited series; British-r)
Dark Horse Comics

1-4: By Eddie Campbell 1.00 2.50

DEAD IN THE WEST
Oct, 1993 - No. 2, Mar, 1994 ($3.95, B&W, 52 pgs.)
Dark Horse Comics

1,2-Timothy Truman-c 1.60 4.00

DEADLIEST HEROES OF KUNG FU (Magazine)
Summer, 1975 (B&W)(76 pgs.)
Marvel Comics Group

1 -Bruce Lee vs. Carradine painted-c; TV Kung Fu, 4pgs. photos/article; Enter the Dragon, 24 pgs. photos/article w/ Bruce Lee; Bruce Lee photo pinup 1.85 5.50 15.00

DEADLINE USA
Apr, 1992 - No. 8, Nov, 1992 ($3.95, B&W, 52 pgs.)
Dark Horse Comics

1-8: Johnny Nemo w/Milligan scripts in all 1.60 4.00

DEADLY DUO, THE
Nov, 1994 - No. 3, Jan, 1995 ($2.50, limited series)
Image Comics (Highbrow Entertainment)

1-3: 1-lst app. of Kill Cat 1.00 2.50

DEADLY DUO, THE
June, 1995 - No. 4, Oct, 1995 ($2.50, limited series)
Image Comics (Highbrow Entertainment)

1-4: 1-Spawn app. 2-Savage Dragon app. 3-Gen 13 app. 1.00 2.50

DEADLY FOES OF SPIDER-MAN (See Lethal Foes of...)
May, 1991 - No. 4, Aug, 1991 ($1.00, limited series)
Marvel Comics

1-4: 1-Punisher, Kingpin, Rhino app. 1.00

DEADLY HANDS OF KUNG FU, THE (See Master of Kung Fu)
April, 1974 - No. 33, Feb, 1977 (75¢) (B&W, magazine)
Marvel Comics Group

1(V1#4 listed in error)-Origin Sons of the Tiger; Shang-Chi, Master of Kung Fu begins (ties w/Master of Kung Fu #17 as 3rd app. Shang-Chi); Bruce Lee painted-c by Neal Adams; 2pg. memorial photo pinup w/8 pgs. photos/articles; TV Kung Fu, 9 pgs. photos/articles; 15 pgs. Starlin-a. 2.50 7.50 24.00

2-Adams painted-c; 1st time origin of Shang Chi, 34 pgs. by Starlin. TV Kung Fu, 6 pgs. ph/a w/2 pg. pinup. Bruce Lee, 11 pgs. ph/a 2.50 7.50 20.00

3,4,7,10: 3-Adams painted-c; Gulacy-a. Enter the Dragon, photos/articles, 8 pgs. 4-TV Kung Fu painted-c by Neal Adams; TV Kung Fu 7 pg. article/art; Fu Manchu; Enter the Dragon, 10 pg. photos/article w/Bruce Lee. 7-Bruce Lee painted-c & 9 pgs. photos/articles-Return of Dragon plus 1 pg. photo pinup. 10-(3/75)-Ironfist painted-c & 34 pg. sty-Early app. 1.85 5.50 15.00

5,6: 5-1st app. Manchurian, 6 pgs. Gulacy-a. TV Kung Fu, 4 pg. article; re books w/Barry Smith-a. Capt. America-sty, 10 pgs. Kirby-a(r). 6-Bruce Lee photos/article, 6 pgs.; 15 pgs. early Perez-a 1.50 4.50 12.00

8,9,11: 9-Ironfist, 2 pg. Preview pinup; Nebres-a. 11-Billy Jack painted-c by Adams; 17 pgs. photos/article 1.10 3.30 9.00

12,13: 12-James Bond painted-c by Adams; 14 pg. photos/article. 13-16 pgs. early perez-a; Piers Anthony, 7 pgs. photos/article 1.00 2.80 7.00

14-Classic Bruce Lee painted-c by Adams. Lee pinup by Chaykin. Lee 16 pg. photos/article w/2 pgs. Green Hornet TV 3.00 9.00 30.00

15,19: 15-Sum, '75 Giant Annual #1. 20pgs. Starlin-a. Bruce Lee photo pinup & 3 pg photos/article re book; Manthing app. Ironfist-c/sty; Gulacy 18pgs.-a. 19-Ironfist painted-c & series begins. 1st White Tiger 1.50 4.50 12.00

GD25 FN65 NM94

16,18,20: 16-1st app. Corpse Rider, a Samurai w/Sanho Kim-a. 20-Chuck Norris painted-c & 16 pgs. interview w/photos/article; Bruce Lee vs. C. Norris pinup by Ken Barr. Origin The White Tiger, Perez-a 1.10 3.30 9.00

17-Bruce Lee painted-c by Adams; interview w/R. Clouse, director Enter Dragon 7 pgs. w/B. Lee app. 1st Giffen-a (1pg. 11/75) 2.00 6.00 16.00

21-Bruce Lee 1pg. photos/article 1.00 2.80 7.00

22,30-32: 22-1st app. Jack of Hearts (cameo). 1st Giffen sty-a (along w/Amazing Adv. #35, 3/76). 30-Swordquest-c/sty & conclusion; Jack of Hearts app. 31-Jack of Hearts app; Staton-a. 32-1st Daughters of the Dragon -c/sty, 21 pgs. M. Rogers-a/Claremont-sty; Ironfist pinup 1.10 3.30 9.00

23-26,29: 23-1st full app. Jack of Hearts. 24-Ironfist-c & centerfold pinup. early Zeck-a; Shang Chi pinup; 6 pgs. Piers Anthony text sty w/Perez/Austin-a; Jack of Hearts app. early Giffen-a. 25-1st app. Shimuru, "Samurai", 20 pgs. Mantlo-sty/Broderick-a; "Swordquest"-c & begins 17 pg. sty by Sanho Kim; 11 pg. photos/article; partly Bruce Lee. 26-Bruce Lee painted-c & pinup; 16 pgs. interviews w/Kwon & Clouse; talk about B. Lee re filming of B. Lee legend. 29-Ironfist vs. Shang Chi battle-c/sty; Jack of Hearts app. 1.50 4.50 12.00

27 1.00 3.00 8.00

28-All Bruce Lee Special Issue; (1st time in comics). Bruce Lee painted-c by Ken Barr & pinup. 36 pgs. comics chronicaling Bruce Lee's life; 15 pgs. B. Lee photos/article (Rare in high grade) 3.50 10.50 35.00

33-Shang Chi-c/sty; Classic Daughters of the Dragon, 21 pgs. M. Rogers-a/Claremont-sty with Nudity; Bob Wall interview, photos/article, 14 pgs. 1.25 3.75 10.00

...Special Album Edition 1(Summer, '74)-Iron Fist-c/story (early app., 3rd?); 10 pgs. Adams-i; Shang Chi/Fu Manchu, 10 pgs.; Sons of Tiger, 11 pgs.; TV Kung Fu, 6 pgs. photos/article 1.50 4.50 12.00

NOTE: ***Bruce Lee:*** *1-7, 14, 15, 17, 25, 26, 28.* ***Kung Fu (TV):*** *1, 2, 4.* ***Jack of Hearts:*** *22, 23, 29-33.* ***Shang Chi Master of Kung Fu:*** *1-9, 11-18, 29, 31, 33.* ***Sons of Tiger:*** *1, 3, 4, 6-14, 16-19.* ***Swordquest:*** *25-27, 29-33.* ***White Tiger:*** *19-24, 26, 27, 29-33.* ***N. Adams*** *a-1i(part), 27i; c-1, 2-4, 11, 12, 14, 17.* ***Giffen*** *a-22p, 24p.* ***G. Kane*** *a-23p.* ***Kirby*** *a-5r.* ***Nasser*** *a-27p, 28.* ***Perez*** *a(p)-6-14, 16, 17, 19, 21.* ***Rogers*** *a-26, 32, 33.* ***Starlin*** *a-1, 2r, 15r.* ***Staton*** *a-28p, 31, 32.*

DEADMAN (See The Brave and the Bold & Phantom Stranger #39)
May, 1985 - No. 7, Nov, 1985 ($1.75, Baxter paper)
DC Comics

1-Deadman-r by Infantino, N. Adams in all .70 1.75
2-7: 5-Batman-c/story-r/Str. Advs. 7-Batman-r .70 1.75

DEADMAN
Mar, 1986 - No. 4, June, 1986 (75¢, limited series)
DC Comics

1-4: Lopez-c/a. 4-Byrne-c(p) 1.00

DEADMAN: EXORCISM
1992 - No. 2, 1992 ($4.95, limited series, 52 pgs.)
DC Comics

1,2: Kelley Jones-c/a in all. 2.00 5.00

DEADMAN: LOVE AFTER DEATH
1989 - No. 2, 1990 ($3.95, 52 pgs., limited series, mature)
DC Comics

Book One, Two: Kelley Jones-c/a in all. 1-contains nudity. 1.60 4.00

DEAD OF NIGHT
Dec, 1973 - No. 11, Aug, 1975
Marvel Comics Group

1-Horror reprints 1.25 3.75 10.00
2-11: 11-Intro Scarecrow; Kane/Wrightson-c 1.00 2.80 7.00

NOTE: ***Ditko*** *r-7, 10.* ***Everett*** *c-2.* ***Sinnott*** *r-1.*

DEADPOOL (See New Mutants #98)
Aug, 1994 - No. 4, Nov, 1994 ($2.50, limited series)
Marvel Comics

Deadpool #11 © MEG

Deathblow #16 © Aegis Entertainment

Deathlok #3 (mini-series) © MEG

GD25 FN65 NM94

1: Mark Waid's 1st Marvel work; Ian Churchill-c/a 1.60 4.00
2--4 1.20 3.00

DEADPOOL: THE CIRCLE CHASE (See New Mutants #98)
Aug, 1993 - No. 4, Nov, 1993 ($2.00, limited series)
Marvel Comics

1-($2.50)-Embossed-c 1.00 2.50
2-4 .80 2.00

DEADPOOL
Jan, 1997 - Present ($2.95/$1.95/$1.99)
Marvel Comics

1-($2.95)-Wraparound-c 2.40 6.00
2-Begin-$1.95-c. 1.60 4.00
3 1.20 3.00
4-6, -1(7/97): 4-Hulk-c/app. 2.00
7-10,12: 7-Begin $1.99-c. 1.99
11-($3.99)-Deadpool replaces Spider-Man from Amazing Spider-Man #47; Kraven, Gwen Stacy app. 3.99

DEADSHOT (See Batman #59, Detective Comics #474, & Showcase '93 #8)
Nov, 1988 - No. 4, Feb, 1989 ($1.00, limited series)
DC Comics

1-4 1.00

DEAD WHO WALK, THE (See Strange Mysteries, Super Reprint #15, 16)
1952 (one-shot)
Realistic Comics

nn 41.00 124.00 340.00

DEADWORLD (Also see The Realm)
Dec, 1986 - No. 28? ($1.50/$1.95/#15-28: $2.50, B&W, mature)
Arrow Comics/Caliber Comics

1 1.50
2 .80 2.00
3,4 1.50
5-11: Graphic covers 1.50
5-11: Tame covers .70 1.75
12-28: Graphic covers, 12-28: Tame covers .70 1.75
...Archives 1 (1992, $2.50) 1.00 2.50

DEAN MARTIN & JERRY LEWIS (See Adventures of...)

DEAR BEATRICE FAIRFAX
No. 5, Nov, 1950 - No. 9, Sept, 1951 (Vern Greene art)
Best/Standard Comics (King Features)

5-All have Schomburg air brush-c 6.50 19.50 45.00
6-9 5.00 15.00 30.00

DEAR HEART (Formerly Lonely Heart)
No. 15, July, 1956 - No. 16, Sept, 1956
Ajax

15,16 4.25 13.00 28.00

DEAR LONELY HEART (...Illustrated No. 1-6)
Mar, 1951; No. 2, Oct, 1951 - No. 8, Oct, 1952
Artful Publications

1 11.30 34.00 90.00
2 5.70 17.00 40.00
3-Matt Baker Jungle Girl story 12.00 36.00 95.00
4-8 5.70 17.00 35.00

DEAR LONELY HEARTS (Lonely Heart #9 on)
Aug, 1953 - No. 8, Oct, 1954
Harwell Publ./Mystery Publ. Co. (Comic Media)

1 5.70 17.00 40.00
2-8 4.00 11.00 22.00

DEARLY BELOVED
Fall, 1952
Ziff-Davis Publishing Co.

1-Photo-c 11.30 34.00 90.00

DEAR NANCY PARKER
June, 1963 - No. 2, Sept, 1963
Gold Key

1,2-Painted-c 1.80 5.40 18.00

DEATHBLOW (Also see Darker Image)
May (Apr. inside), 1993 - No. 29, Aug, 1996 ($1.75/$1.95/$2.50)
Image Comics (Wildstorm Productions)

0-(8/96, $2.95, 32 pgs.)-r/Darker Image w/new story & art; Jim Lee & Trevor Scott-a; new Jim Lee-c 1.20 3.00
1-($2.50)-Red foil stamped logo on black varnish-c; Jim Lee-c/a; flip-book side has Cybernary -c/story (#2 also) 1.20 3.00
1-($1.95)-Newsstand version w/o foil-c & varnish .80 2.00
2,4: 2-(8/93)-Lee-a; with bound-in poster. 4-Jim Lee-c. .70 1.75
2-($1.75)-Newsstand version w/o poster .70 1.75
3 1.60 4.00
5-9: Jim Lee-c in all. 5-Begin $1.95-c .80 2.00
5-Alternate Portacio-c (Forms larger picture when combined with alternate-c for Gen 13 #5, Kindred #3, Stormwatch #10, Team 7 #1, Union #0, Wetworks #2 & WildC.A.T.S # 11) 1.25 3.75 10.00
10-14,15,19-29: 10-Begin $2.50-c. 13-W/pinup poster by Tim Sale & Jim Lee. 17-Variant "Chicago Comicon" edition exists. 20,21-Gen 13 app. 23-Backlash-c/app. 24,25-Grifter-c/app; Gen 13 & Dane from Wetworks app. 28-Deathblow dies. 29-Memorial issue 1.00 2.50
16 ($1.95, Newsstand)-Wildstorm Rising Pt. 6 .80 2.00
16 ($2.50, Direct Market)-Wildstorm Rising Pt. 6 1.00 2.50

DEATHBLOW/WOLVERINE
Sept, 1996 - No. 2, Feb, 1997 ($2.50, limited series)
Image Comics (Wildstorm Productions)/ Marvel Comics

1,2: Wiesenfeld-s/Bennett-a 1.00 2.50

DEATHDEALER
July, 1995 - Present ($5.95)
Verotik

1-Frazetta-c; Bisley-a 1.00 3.00 8.00
1-2nd print 1.00 2.80 7.00
2,3-($6.95)-Frazetta-c; embossed logo 1.00 2.80 7.00
4-($6.95)-Frazetta-c; Suydam-a 6.95

DEATHLOK (Also see Astonishing Tales #25)
July, 1990 - No. 4, Oct, 1990 ($3.95, limited series, 52 pgs.)
Marvel Comics

1-4: 1,2-Guice-a(p). 3,4-Denys Cowan-a, c-4 1.60 4.00

DEATHLOK
July, 1991 - No. 34, Apr, 1994 ($1.75)
Marvel Comics

1-Silver ink cover; Denys Cowan-c/a(p) begins .80 2.00
2-5: 2-Forge (X-Men) app. 3-Vs. Dr. Doom. 5-X-Men & F.F. x-over 1.00 2.50
6-10: 6,7-Punisher x-over. 9,10-Ghost Rider-c/story .70 1.75
11-18,20-24,26-34: 16-Infinity War x-over. 17-Jae Lee-c. 22-Black Panther app. 27-Siege app. .70 1.75
19-($2.25)-Foil-c .90 2.25
25-($2.95, 52 pgs.)-Holo-grafx foil-c 1.20 3.00
Annual 1 (1992, $2.25, 68 pgs.)-Guice-p; Quesada-c(p) 1.00 2.50
Annual 2 (1993, $2.95, 68 pgs.)-Bagged w/card; intro Tracer 1.20 3.00

NOTE: *Denys Cowan a(p)-9-13, 15, Annual 1; c-9-12, 13p, 14. Guice/Cowan c-8.*

DEATHLOK SPECIAL
May, 1991 - No. 4, Late-June, 1991 ($2.00, bi-weekly limited series)

Death of Hari Kari #0 © Blackout

Death's Head II #1 © MEG

Deathstroke The Terminator #30 © DC

GD25 FN65 NM94

Marvel Comics
1-4: r/1-4(1990) w/new Guice-c #1,2; Cowan c-3,4 .80 2.00
1-2nd printing w/white-c .80 2.00

DEATHMARK
Dec, 1994 ($2.95, B&W)
Lightning Comics
1 1.20 3.00

DEATHMATE
Sept, 1993 - Epilogue (#6), Feb, 1994 ($2.95/$4.95, limited series)
Valiant (Prologue/Yellow/Blue)/Image Comics (Black/Red/Epilogue)
Preview-(7/93, 8 pgs.) 1.00
Prologue (#1)–Silver foil; Jim Lee/Layton-c; B. Smith/Lee-a; Liefeld-a(p) 1.00 2.50
Prologue–Special gold foil ed. of silver ed. 1.00 2.80 7.00
Black (#2)-(9/93, $4.95, 52 pgs.)-Silvestri/Jim Lee-c; pencils by Peterson/Silvestri/Capullo/Jim Lee/Portacio; 1st story app. Gen 13 telling their rebellion against the Troika (see WildC.A.T.S. Trilogy) 2.20 5.50
Black-Special gold foil edition 1.50 4.50 12.00
Yellow (#3)-(10/93, $4.95, 52 pgs)-Yellow foil-c; Indicia says Prologue Sept 1993 by mistake; 3rd app. Ninjak; Thibert-c(i) 1.40 3.50
Yellow-Special gold foil edition 1.00 2.80 7.00
Blue (#4)-(10/93, $4.95, 52 pgs.)-Thibert blue foil-c(i); Reese-a(i) 1.80 4.50
Blue-Special gold foil edition 1.00 2.80 7.00
Red (#5) 1.40 3.50
Epilogue (#6)-(2/94, $2.95)-Silver foil Quesada/Silvestri-c; Silvestri-a(p) 1.20 3.00

DEATH METAL
Jan, 1994 - No. 4, Apr, 1994 ($1.95, limited series)
Marvel Comics UK
1-4: 1-Silver ink-c. Alpha Flight app. .80 2.00

DEATH METAL VS. GENETIX
Dec, 1993 - No. 2, Jan, 1994 (Limited series)
Marvel Comics UK
1-($2.95)-Polybagged w/2 trading cards 1.20 3.00
2-($2.50)-Polybagged w/2 trading cards 1.00 2.50

DEATH OF CAPTAIN MARVEL (See Marvel Graphic Novel #1)

DEATH OF HARI KARI
1997 ($2.95, limited series)
Blackout Comics
0-Regular Edition 2.95
0-($9.95)-"Super Sexy Parody Cover" 9.95
0-($14.95)-"3-D Parody Cover" 14.95

DEATH OF LADY VAMPRE
1995 ($2.95, bi-monthly)
Blackout Comics
1-Mignola, Colan flip-c 1.20 3.00

DEATH OF MR. MONSTER, THE (See Mr. Monster #8)

DEATH OF SUPERMAN (See Superman, 2nd Series)

DEATH RACE 2020
Apr, 1995 - No. 8, Nov, 1995 ($2.50)
Roger Corman's Cosmic Comics
1-8: Sequel to the Movie 1.00 2.50

DEATH RATTLE (Formerly an Underground)
V2#1, 10/85 - No. 18, 1988, 1994 ($1.95, Baxter paper, mature)
Kitchen Sink Press
V2#1-7,9-18: 1-Corben-c. 2-Unpubbed Spirit story by Eisner. 5-Robot Woman-r by Wolverton. 6-B&W issues begin. 10-Savage World-r by by Williamson/Torres/ Krenkel/Frazetta from Witzend #1. 16-Wolverton Spacehawk-r .80 2.00
8-(12/86)-1st app. Mark Schultz's Xenozoic Tales/Cadillacs & Dinosaurs 1.20 3.00
8-(1994)-r plus interview w/Mark Schultz .80 2.00

GD25 FN65 VF82 NM94

DEATH'S HEAD (See Daredevil #56, Dragon's Claws #5 & Incomplete...)
Dec, 1988 - No. 10, Sept, 1989 ($1.75)
Marvel Comics
1-Dragon's Claws spin-off 1.20 3.00
2-Fantastic Four app.; Dragon's Claws x-over .80 2.00
3,4 .80 2.00
5-10: 8-Dr. Who app. 9-F. F. x-over; Simonson-c(p) .80 2.00
...Gold 1 (1/94, $3.95, 68 pgs.)-Gold foil-c 1.60 4.00

DEATH'S HEAD II (Also see Battletide)
Mar, 1992 - No. 4, June (May inside), 1992 ($1.75, color, limited series)
Marvel Comics UK, Ltd.
1 .80 2.00
1,2-Silver ink 2nd printiings .70 1.75
2-4: 2-Fantastic Four app. 4-Punisher, Spider-Man , Daredevil, Dr. Strange, Capt. America & Wolverine in the year 2020 .80 2.00

DEATH'S HEAD II (Also see Battletide)
Dec, 1992 - Present ($1.75/$1.95)
Marvel Comics UK, Ltd.
V2#1-5: 1-Gatefold-c. 1-4-X-Men app. .70 1.75
6-13,15,16 ($1.95): 15-Capt. America & Wolverine app. .80 2.00
14-($2.95)-Foil flip-c w/Death's Head II Gold #0 1.20 3.00

DEATH'S HEAD II & THE ORIGIN OF DIE CUT
Aug, 1993 - No. 2, Sept, 1993 (limited series)
Marvel Comics UK, Ltd.
1-($2.95)-Embossed-c 1.20 3.00
2 ($1.75) .70 1.75

DEATHSTROKE: THE TERMINATOR (Deathstroke: The Hunted #0-47; Deathstroke #48-60) (Also see Marvel & DC Present, New Teen Titans #2, New Titans, Showcase '93 #7,9 & Tales of the Teen Titans #42-44)
Aug, 1991 - No. 60, June, 1996 ($1.75/$1.95/$2.25)
DC Comics
1-New Titans spin-off; Mike Zeck c-1-28 1.20 3.00
1-Gold ink 2nd printing ($1.75) .80 2.00
2 1.20 3.00
3-5 .80 2.00
6-37: 6,8-Batman cameo. 7,9-Batman-c/story. 9-1st new Vigilante (female) in cameo. 10-1st full app. new Vigilante; Perez-i. 13-Vs. Justice League; Team Titans cameo on last pg. 14-Total Chaos, part 1; Team Titans-c/story cont'd in New Titans #90. 15-Total Chaos, part 4 .70 1.75
38-40: 38-Begin $1.95-c. 40-(9/94) .80 2.00
0 (10/94)-Begin Deathstroke, The Hunted, ends #47. .80 2.00
41 (11/94) - 47 .80 2.00
48,49,51-60: 48-Begin 2.25-c. .90 2.25
50 ($3.50) 1.40 3.50
Annual 1,2 (1992, 1993, $3.50, 68 pgs.): 1-Nightwing & Vigilante app.; minor Eclipso app. 2-Bloodlines Deathstorm; 1st app. Gunfire. 1.40 3.50
Annual 3 (1994, $3.95, 68 pgs.)-Elseworlds story 1.60 4.00
Annual 4 (1995, $3.95)-Year One story 1.60 4.00
NOTE: ***Golden** a-12. **Perez** a-11i. **Zeck** c-Annual 1, 2.*

DEATH: THE HIGH COST OF LIVING (See Sandman #8) (Also see the Books of Magic limited & ongoing series)
Mar, 1993 - No. 3, May, 1993 ($1.95, limited series)
DC Comics (Vertigo)
1-Bachalo/Buckingham-a; Dave McKean-c; Neil Gaiman scripts in all 1.25 3.75 10.00

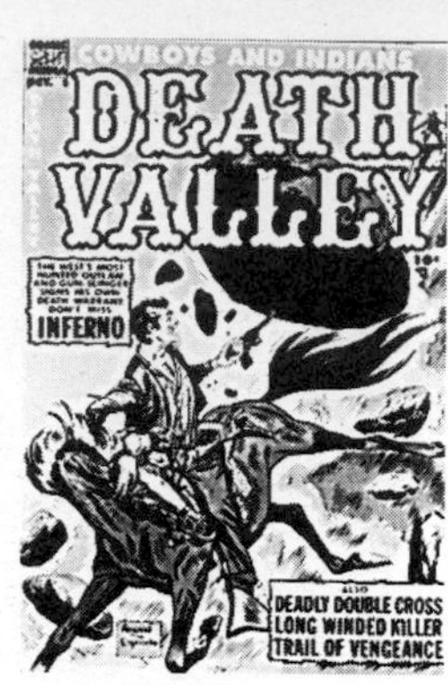

Death Valley #1 © Comic Media

Deathwish #1 © DC

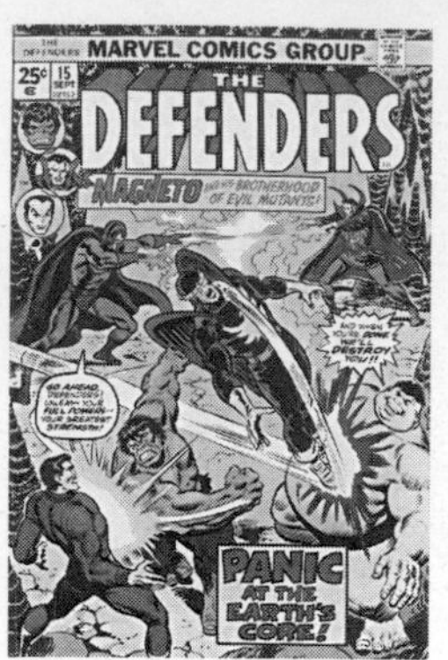

Defenders #15 © MEG

GD25 FN65 VF82 NM94

1-Platinum edition 4.00 12.00 40.00
2 1.00 3.00 8.00
3-Pgs. 19 & 20 had wrong placement 2.00 5.00
3-Corrected version w/pgs. 19 & 20 facing each other; has no-c price plus has ads for Sebastion O & The Geek added 2.00 5.00
Hardcover (1994, $19.95)-r/#1-3 & Death Talks About Life; intro. by Tori Amos. 20.00
Trade paperback (6/94, $12.95, Titan Books)-r/#1-3 & Death Talks About Life; prism-c 13.00

DEATH: THE TIME OF YOUR LIFE (See Sandman #8)
Apr, 1996 - No. 3, July, 1996 ($2.95, limited series)
DC Comics (Vertigo)

1-3: Neil Gaiman story & Bachalo/Buckingham-a; Dave McKean-c. 2-(5/96). 1.20 3.00
Hardcover (1997, $19.95)-r/#1-3 w/3 new pages & gallery art by various 19.95
Trade paperback (1997, $12.95)-r/#1-3 & Visions of Death gallery; Intro. by Claire Danes 12.95

DEATH 3
Sept, 1993 - No. 4, Dec, 1993 ($1.75, limited series)
Marvel Comics UK

1-($2.95)-Embossed-c 1.20 3.00
2-4 .70 1.75

DEATH VALLEY (Cowboys and Indians)
Oct, 1953 - No. 6, Aug, 1954
Comic Media

1-Billy the Kid; Morisi-a; Andru/Esposito-c/a 7.15 21.50 50.00
2-Don Heck-c 5.00 15.00 30.00
3-6: 3,5-Morisi-a. 5-Discount-a 4.15 12.50 25.00

DEATH VALLEY (Becomes Frontier Scout, Daniel Boone No.10-13)
No. 7, 6/55 - No. 9, 10/55 (Cont'd from Comic Media series)
Charlton Comics

7-9: 8-Wolverton-a (half pg.) 4.25 13.00 28.00

DEATHWISH
Dec, 1994 - No. 4, Mar, 1995 (2.50, limited series)
DC Comics (Milestone Media)

1-4 1.00 2.50

DEATH WRECK
Jan, 1994 - No. 4, Apr, 1994 ($1.95, limited series)
Marvel Comics UK

1-4: 1-Metallic ink logo; Death's Head II app. .80 2.00

DEBBIE DEAN, CAREER GIRL
April, 1945 - No. 2, July, 1945
Civil Service Publ.

1,2-Newspaper reprints by Bert Whitman 10.50 32.00 85.00

DEBBI'S DATES (Also see Date With Debbi)
Apr-May, 1969 - No. 11, Dec-Jan, 1970-71
National Periodical Publications

1 3.50 10.50 35.00
2,3,5,7-11 1.75 5.25 14.00
4-Neal Adams text illo 2.50 7.50 24.00
6-Superman cameo 3.50 10.50 35.00

DECADE OF DARK HORSE, A
July, 1996 - No. 4, Oct, 1996 ($2.95, B&W/color, limited series)
Dark Horse Comics

1-4: 1-Sin City-c/story by Miller; Grendel by Wagner; Predator. 2-Star Wars wraparound-c. 3-Aliens-c/story; Nexus, Mask stories 1.20 3.00

DEEP, THE (Movie)
Nov, 1977
Marvel Comics Group

1-Infantino-c/a 1.50

DEEP DARK FANTASIES
Oct, 1995 ($4.50/$4.95, B&W)
Dark Fantasy Productions

1-($4.50)-Clive Barker-c, anthology 1.80 4.50
1-($4.95)-Red foil logo-c 2.00 5.00

DEFCON 4
Feb, 1996 - No. 4, Sept, 1996 ($2.50, limited series)
Image Comics (Wildstorm Productions)

1/2 1.10 3.30 9.00
1/2 Gold-(1000 printed) 1.75 5.25 14.00
1-Main Cover by Mat Broome & Edwin Rosell 1.80 4.50
1-Hordes of Cymulants variant-c by Michael Golden 2.40 6.00
1-Backs to the Wall variant-c by Humberto Ramos & Alex Garner 2.40 6.00
1-Defcon 4-Way variant-c by Jim Lee 1.25 3.75 10.00
2-4 1.00 2.50

DEFENDERS, THE (TV)
Sept-Nov, 1962 - No. 2, Feb-Apr, 1963
Dell Publishing Co.

12-176-211(#1), 12-176-304(#2) 2.25 6.75 26.00

DEFENDERS, THE (Also see Giant-Size..., Marvel Feature, Marvel Treasury Edition, Secret Defenders & Sub-Mariner #34, 35; The New...#140-on)
Aug, 1972 - No. 152, Feb, 1986
Marvel Comics Group

1-The Hulk, Doctor Strange, Sub-Mariner begin 5.50 16.50 55.00
2-Silver Surfer x-over 2.50 7.50 25.00
3-5: 3-Silver Surfer x-over. 4-Valkyrie joins 2.25 6.75 18.00
6-9: 6,8-Silver Surfer x-over. 9-Avengers app. 1.60 4.85 13.00
10-Hulk vs. Thor battle; Avengers app. 2.25 6.75 18.00
11-14: 11-Silver Surfer x-over. 12-Last 20¢ issue 2.40 6.00
15,16-Magneto & Brotherhood of Evil Mutants app. from X-Men 1.10 3.30 9.00
17-20: 17-Power Man x-over (11/74) 2.00 5.00
21-25: 24,25-Son of Satan app. 1.60 4.00
26-29-Guardians of the Galaxy app. (#26 is 8/75; pre-dates Marvel Presents #3): 28-1st full app. Starhawk (cameo #27). 29-Starhawk joins Guardians 2.40 6.00
30-35,37,39-50: 31,32-Origin Nighthawk. 35-Intro New Red Guardian. 44-Hellcat joins. 45-Dr. Strange leaves. 47-49-Early Moon Knight app. (5/77) 1.20 3.00
36,38-(Regular 25¢ edition) 1.20 3.00
36,38-(30¢-c, limited distribution) 1.50 4.50 12.00
51-60: 53-1st app. Lunatik (cameo, Lobo lookalike). 55-Origin Red Guardian; Lunatik cameo. 56-1st full Lunatik story 1.00 2.50
61-75: 61-Lunatik & Spider-Man app. 70-73-Lunatik (origin #71). 73-75-Foolkiller II app. (Greg Salinger). 74-Nighthawk resigns .80 2.00
76-95,97-124,126-149,151: 77-Origin Omega. 78-Original Defenders return thru #101. 94-1st Gargoyle. 100-(52 pgs.)-Hellcat (Patsy Walker) revealed as Satan's daughter. 101-Silver Surfer-c & app. 104-The Beast joins. 105-Son of Satan joins. 106-Death of Nighthawk. 120,121-Son of Satan-c/stories. 122-Final app. Son of Satan (2 pgs.). 129-New Mutants cameo (3/84, early x-over) .70 1.75
96-Ghost Rider app. 1.20 3.00
125,150,152: 125-(52 pgs.)-Intro new Defenders. 150-(52 pgs.)-Origin Cloud. 152-(52 pgs.)-Ties in with X-Factor & Secret Wars II 1.00 2.50
Annual 1 (1976, 52 pgs.)-New book-length story 1.20 3.00

NOTE: **Art Adams** *c-142p.* **Austin** *a-53i; c-65i, 119i, 145i.* **Frank Bolle** *a-7i, 10i, 11i.* **Buckler** *c(p)-34, 38, 76, 77, 79-86, 90, 91.* **J. Buscema** *c-66.* **Giffen** *a-42-49p, 50, 51-54p.* **Golden** *a-53p, 54p; c-94, 96.* **Guice** *c-129.* **G. Kane** *c(p)-13, 16, 18, 19, 21-26, 31-33, 35-37, 40, 41, 52, 55.* **Kirby** *c-42-45.* **Mooney** *a-3i, 31-34i, 62i, 63i, 85i.* **Nasser** *c-88p.* **Perez** *c(p)-51, 53, 54.*

Dell Giant - Bugs Bunny Vacation Funnies #7
© Warner Bros.

Dell Giant - Christmas Parade #7 © WDC

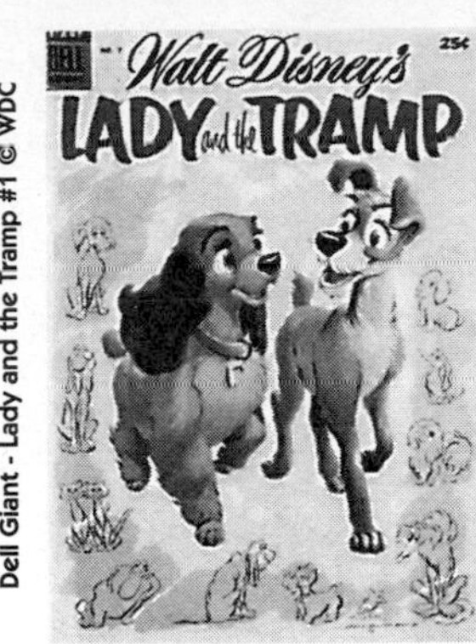

Dell Giant - Lady and the Tramp #1 © WDC

Rogers c-98. Starlin c-110. Tuska a-57p. Silver Surfer in No. 2, 3, 6, 8-11, 92, 98-101, 107, 112-115, 122-125.

DEFENDERS OF DYNATRON CITY
Feb, 1992 - No. 6, July, 1992 ($1.25, limited series)
Marvel Comics

1-6-Lucasarts characters. 2-Origin 1.25

DEFENDERS OF THE EARTH (TV)
Jan, 1987 - No. 5, Sept, 1987
Marvel Comics (Star Comics)

1-5: The Phantom, Mandrake The Magician, Flash Gordon begin. 3-Origin Phantom. 4-Origin Mandrake 2.00

DEFINITIVE DIRECTORY OF THE DC UNIVERSE, THE (See Who's Who...)

DELECTA OF THE PLANETS (See Don Fortune & Fawcett Miniatures)

DELLA VISION (...The Television Queen) (Patty Powers #4 on)
April, 1955 - No. 3, Aug, 1955
Atlas Comics

	GD25	FN65	NM94
1-Al Hartley-c	11.30	34.00	90.00
2,3	8.75	26.25	65.00

DELL GIANT COMICS

Dell Publishing began to release square bound comics in 1949 with a 132-page issue called Christmas Parade #1. The covers were of a heavier stock to accommodate the increased number of pages. The books proved profitable at 25 cents, but the average number of pages was quickly reduced to 100. Ten years later they were converted to a numbering system similar to the Four Color Comics, for greater ease in distribution and the page counts cut back to mostly 84 pages. The label "Dell Giant" began to appear on the covers in 1954. Because of the size of the books and the heavier, less pliant cover stock, they are rarely found in high grade condition, and with the exception of a small quantity of copies released from Western Publishing's warehouse–are almost never found in near mint.

	GD25	FN65	VF82	NM94
Abraham Lincoln Life Story 1(3/58)	5.50	16.50	39.00	100.00
Bugs Bunny Christmas Funnies 1(11/50, 116pp)	14.50	43.50	102.00	260.00
...Christmas Funnies 2(11/51, 116pp)	9.50	28.50	67.00	170.00
...Christmas Funnies 3-5(11/52-11/54,)-Becomes Christmas Party #6	8.50	25.50	60.00	155.00
...Christmas Funnies 7-9(12/56-12/58)	8.00	24.00	56.00	140.00
...Christmas Party 6(11/55)-Formerly Bugs Bunny Christmas Funnies	6.50	19.50	46.00	115.00
...County Fair 1(9/57)	9.50	28.50	67.00	170.00
...Halloween Parade 1(10/53)	9.00	27.00	63.00	160.00
...Halloween Parade 2(10/54)-Trick 'N' Treat Halloween Fun #3 on	8.00	24.00	56.00	140.00
...Trick 'N' Treat Halloween Fun 3,4(10/55-10/56)-Formerly Halloween Parade #2	8.50	25.50	60.00	150.00
...Vacation Funnies 1(7/51, 112pp)	14.50	43.50	102.00	260.00
...Vacation Funnies 2('52)	11.50	34.50	81.00	210.00
...Vacation Funnies 3-5('53-'55)	8.50	25.50	60.00	155.00
...Vacation Funnies 6-9('54-6/59)	8.00	24.00	56.00	140.00
Cadet Gray of West Point 1(4/58)-Williamson-a, 10pgs.; Buscema-a; photo-c	4.50	13.50	32.00	85.00
Christmas In Disneyland 1(12/57)-Barks-a, 18 pgs.	21.00	63.00	147.00	380.00
Christmas Parade 1(11/49)(132 pgs.)(1st Dell Giant)-Donald Duck (25pgs. by Barks, r-in G.K. Christmas Parade #5); Mickey Mouse & other film oriented stories; Cinderella (prior to movie), 7 Dwarfs, Bambi & Thumper, So Dear To My Heart, Flying Mouse, Dumbo, Cookieland & others	47.00	141.00	329.00	850.00
Christmas Parade 2('50)-Donald Duck (132 pgs.)(25 pgs. by Barks, r-in G.K. Christmas Parade #6). Mickey, Pluto, Chip & Dale, etc. Contents shift to a holiday expansion of W.D. C&S type format	36.00	108.00	252.00	650.00
Christmas Parade 3-7('51-'55, #3-116pgs; #4-7, 100 pgs.)	10.50	31.50	74.00	190.00
Christmas Parade 8(12/56)-Barks-a, 8 pgs.	18.00	54.00	126.00	320.00
Christmas Parade 9(12/58)-Barks-a, 20 pgs.	21.00	63.00	147.00	380.00
Christmas Treasury, A 1(11/54)	7.00	21.00	49.00	125.00
Davy Crockett, King Of The Wild Frontier 1(9/55)-Fess Parker photo-c; Marsh-a	14.00	42.00	98.00	250.00
Disneyland Birthday Party 1(10/58)-Barks-a, 16 pgs. r-by Gladstone	21.00	63.00	147.00	380.00
Donald and Mickey In Disneyland 1(5/58)	9.50	28.50	67.00	170.00
Donald Duck Beach Party 1(7/54)-Has an Uncle Scrooge story (not by Barks) that prefigures the later rivalry with Flinthoart Glomgold and tells of Scrooge's wild rivalry with another millionaire	12.00	36.00	84.00	220.00
...Beach Party 2(1955)-Lady & Tramp	9.00	27.00	63.00	160.00
...Beach Party 3-5(1956-58)	9.00	27.00	63.00	160.00
...Beach Party 6(8/59, 84pp)-Stapled	6.00	18.00	42.00	110.00
Donald Duck Fun Book 1,2(1953 & 10/54)-Games, puzzles, comics & cut-outs (very rare in unused condition)(most copies commonly have defaced interior pgs.)	30.50	91.50	214.00	550.00
Donald Duck In Disneyland 1(9/55)-1st Disneyland Dell Giant	11.00	33.00	77.00	195.00
Golden West Rodeo Treasury 1(10/57)	7.00	21.00	49.00	125.00
Huey, Dewey and Louie Back To School 1(9/58)	7.00	21.00	49.00	130.00
Lady and The Tramp 1(6/55)	15.00	45.00	105.00	270.00
Life Stories of American Presidents 1(11/57)-Buscema-a	4.00	12.00	28.00	70.00
Lone Ranger Golden West 3(8/55)-Formerly Lone Ranger Western Treasury	14.50	43.50	102.00	260.00
Lone Ranger Movie Story nn(3/56)-Origin Lone Ranger in text; Clayton Moore photo-c	27.00	81.00	189.00	490.00
...Western Treasury 1(9/53)-Origin Lone Ranger, Silver, & Tonto; painted cover	15.50	46.50	109.00	280.00
...Western Treasury 2(8/54)-Becomes Lone Ranger Golden West #3	9.50	28.50	67.00	175.00
Marge's Little Lulu & Alvin Story Telling Time 1(3/59)-r/#2,5,3,11,30,10,21,17,8, 14,16; Stanley-a	11.00	33.00	77.00	195.00
...& Her Friends 4(3/56)-Tripp-a	9.00	27.00	63.00	165.00
...& Her Special Friends 3(3/55)-Tripp-a	11.00	33.00	77.00	200.00
...& Tubby At Summer Camp 5(10/57)-Tripp-a	9.00	27.00	63.00	165.00
...& Tubby At Summer Camp 2(10/58)-Tripp-a	9.00	27.00	63.00	165.00
...& Tubby Halloween Fun 6(10/57)-Tripp-a	9.00	27.00	63.00	165.00
...& Tubby Halloween Fun 2(10/58)-Tripp-a	9.00	27.00	63.00	165.00
...& Tubby In Alaska 1(7/59)-Tripp-a	9.00	27.00	63.00	165.00
...On Vacation 1(7/54)-r/4C-110,14,4C-146,5,4C-97,4,4C-158,3,1;Stanley-a	20.00	60.00	140.00	360.00
...& Tubby Annual 1(3/53)-r/4C-165,4C-74,4C-146,4C-97,4C-158, 4C-139, 4C-131; Stanley-a (1st Lulu Dell Gnt)	24.50	73.50	172.00	435.00
...& Tubby Annual 2('54)-r/4C-139,6,4C-115,4C-74,5,4C-97,3,4C-146,18; Stanley-a	21.50	64.50	151.00	390.00
Marge's Tubby & His Clubhouse Pals 1(10/56)-1st app. Gran'pa Feeb;1st app. Janie; written by Stanley; Tripp-a	10.50	31.50	74.00	190.00
Mickey Mouse Almanac 1(12/57)-Barks-a, 8pgs.	21.50	64.50	151.00	390.00

...Birthday Party 1(9/53)-r/entire 48pgs. of Gottfredson's "Mickey Mouse in Love Trouble" from WDC&S 36-39. Quality equal to original. Also reprints one story each from 4-Color 27, 29, & 181 plus 6 panels of highlights in the

Dell Giant - Silly Symphonies #9 © WDC

Dell Giant - Vacation Parade #1 © WDC

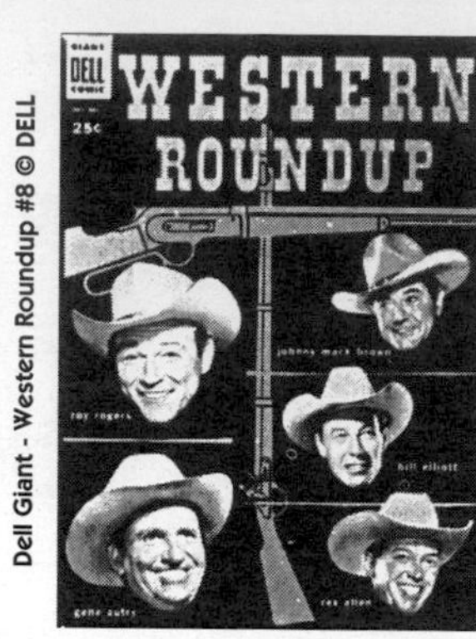

Dell Giant - Western Roundup #8 © DELL

GD25 FN65 NM94

career of Mickey Mouse 26.00 78.00 182.00 470.00
...Club Parade 1(12/55)-r/4-Color 16 with some death trap scenes redrawn by Paul Murry & recolored with night turned into day; quality less than original 21.00 63.00 147.00 380.00
...In Fantasy Land 1(5/57) 10.50 31.50 74.00 190.00
...In Frontier Land 1(5/56)-Mickey Mouse Club issue 10.50 31.00 74.00 190.00
...Summer Fun 1(8/58)-Mobile cut-outs on back-c; becomes Summer Fun with #2 10.50 31.00 74.00 190.00
Moses & The Ten Commandments 1(8/57)-Not based on movie; Dell's adaptation; Sekowsky-a 4.50 13.50 32.00 80.00
Nancy & Sluggo Travel Time 1(9/58) 6.00 18.00 42.00 105.00
Peter Pan Treasure Chest 1(1/53, 212pp)-Disney; contains 54-page movie adaptation & other P. Pan stories; plus Donald & Mickey stories w/P. Pan; a 32-page retelling of "D. Duck Finds Pirate Gold" with yellow beak, called "Capt. Hook & the Buried Treasure" 83.50 250.00 585.00 1500.00
Picnic Party 6,7(7/55-6/56)(Formerly Vacation Parade)-UncleScrooge, Mickey & Donald 9.00 27.00 63.00 160.00
Picnic Party 8(7/57)-Barks-a, 6pgs 18.00 54.00 126.00 320.00
Pogo Parade 1(9/53)-Kelly-a(r-/Pogo from Animal Comics in this order: #11,13,21,14,27,16,23,9,18,15,17) 23.50 70.50 165.00 425.00
Raggedy Ann & Andy 1(2/55) 13.50 39.00 91.00 235.00
Santa Claus Funnies 1(11/52)-Dan Noonan -A Christmas Carol adaptation 7.00 21.00 49.00 125.00
Silly Symphonies 1(9/52)-Redrawing of Gotfredson's Mickey Mouse strip of "The Brave Little Tailor;" 2 Good Housekeeping pages (from 1943); Lady and the Two Siamese Cats, three years before "Lady & the Tramp;" a retelling of Donald Duck's first app. in "The Wise Little Hen" & other stories based on 1930's Silly Symphony cartoons 23.50 70.50 165.00 425.00
Silly Symphonies 2(9/53)-M. Mouse in "The Sorcerer's Apprentice", 2 Good Housekeeping pages (from 1944); The Pelican & the Snipe, Elmer Elephant, Peculiar Penguins, Little Hiawatha, & others 21.00 63.00 147.00 380.00
Silly Symphonies 3(2/54)-r/Mickey & The Beanstalk (4-Color #157, 39pgs.), Little Minnehaha, Pablo, The Flying Gauchito, Pluto, & Bongo, & 2 Good Housekeeping pages (1944) 18.00 54.00 126.00 320.00
Silly Symphonies 4(8/54)-r/Dumbo (4-Color 234), Morris The Midget Moose, The Country Cousin, Bongo, & Clara Cluck 18.00 54.00 126.00 320.00
Silly Symphonies 5(2/55)-r/Cinderella (4-Color 272), Bucky Bug, Pluto, Little Hiawatha, The 7 Dwarfs & Dumbo, Pinocchio 14.50 43.50 102.00 260.00
Silly Symphonies 6(8/55)-r/Pinocchio(WDC&S 63), The 7 Dwarfs & Thumper (WDC&S 45), M. Mouse "Adventures With Robin Hood" (40 pgs.), Johnny Appleseed, Pluto & Peter Pan, & Bucky Bug; Cut-out on back-c 14.50 43.50 102.00 260.00
Silly Symphonies 7(2/57)-r/Reluctant Dragon, Ugly Duckling, M. Mouse & Peter Pan, Jiminy Cricket, Peter & The Wolf, Brer Rabbit, Bucky Bug; Cut-out on back-c 14.50 43.50 102.00 260.00
Silly Symphonies 8(2/58)-r/Thumper Meets The 7 Dwarfs (4-Color #19), Jiminy Cricket, Niok, Brer Rabbit; Cut-out on back-c 14.50 43.50 102.00 260.00
Silly Symphonies 9(2/59)-r/Paul Bunyan, Humphrey Bear, Jiminy Cricket, The Social Lion, Goliath II; cut-out on back-c 13.50 40.50 95.00 235.00
Sleeping Beauty 1(4/59) 23.50 70.50 165.00 425.00
Summer Fun 2(8/59, 84pp, stapled binding)(Formerly Mickey Mouse...)-Barks-a(2), 24 pgs. 21.00 63.00 147.00 380.00
Tarzan's Jungle Annual 1(8/52)-Lex Barker photo on-c of #1,2 10.50 31.50 74.00 190.00
...Annual 2(8/53) 8.00 24.00 56.00 145.00
...Annual 3-7('54-9/58)(two No. 5s)-Manning-a-No. 3,5-7; Marsh-a in No. 1-7 plus painted-c 1-7 6.50 19.50 46.00 120.00
Tom And Jerry Back To School 1(9/56) 11.50 34.50 81.00 205.00
...Picnic Time 1(7/58) 8.50 25.50 60.00 155.00
...Summer Fun 1(7/54)-Droopy written by Barks 13.50 40.50 95.00 240.00
...Summer Fun 2-4(7/55-7/57) 6.00 18.00 42.00 105.00
...Toy Fair 1(6/58) 8.50 25.50 60.00 155.00
...Winter Carnival 1(12/52)-Droopy written by Barks 18.00 54.00 126.00 320.00
...Winter Carnival 2(12/53)-Droopy written by Barks 15.00 45.00 105.00 265.00
...Winter Fun 3(12/54) 6.00 18.00 42.00 105.00
...Winter Fun 4-7(12/55-11/58) 5.00 15.00 35.00 90.00
Treasury of Dogs, A 1(10/56) 4.50 13.50 32.00 85.00
Treasury of Horses, A (9/55) 4.50 13.50 32.00 85.00
Uncle Scrooge Goes To Disneyland 1(8/57p)-Barks-a, 20pgs.r-by Gladstone 21.00 63.00 147.00 380.00
Vacation In Disneyland 1(8/58) 9.50 28.50 67.00 170.00
Vacation Parade 1(7/50, 132pp)-Donald Duck & Mickey Mouse; Barks-a, 55 pgs. 66.50 200.00 466.00 1200.00
Vacation Parade 2(7/51,116pp) 23.50 70.50 165.00 425.00
Vacation Parade 3-5(7/52-7/54)-Becomes Picnic Party No. 6 on. #4-Robin Hood Advs. 11.50 34.50 81.00 210.00
Western Roundup 1(6/52)-Photo-c; Gene Autry, Roy Rogers, Johnny Mack Brown, Rex Allen, & Bill Elliott begin; photo back-c begin, end No. 14,16,18 19.00 57.00 133.00 340.00
Western Roundup 2(2/53)-Photo-c 11.00 33.00 77.00 200.00
Western Roundup 3-5(7-9/53 - 1-3/54)-Photo-c 9.00 27.00 63.00 160.00
Western Roundup 6-10(4-6/54 - 4-6/55)-Photo-c 8.50 25.50 60.00 150.00
Western Roundup 11-13,16,17-Photo-c; Manning-a. 11-Flying A's Range Rider, Dale Evans begin 7.50 22.50 53.00 135.00
Western Roundup 14,15,25(1-3/59)-Photo-c 7.50 22.50 53.00 135.00
Western Roundup 18-Toth-a; last photo-c; Gene Autry ends 8.00 24.00 56.00 140.00
Western Roundup 19-24-Manning-a. 19-Buffalo Bill Jr. begins (7-9/57; early app.). 19,20,22-Toth-a. 21-Rex Allen, Johnny Mack Brown end. 22-Jace Pearson's Texas Rangers, Rin Tin Tin, Tales of Wells Fargo (2nd app., 4-6/58) & Wagon Train (2nd app.) begin 6.50 19.50 46.00 120.00
Woody Woodpecker Back To School 1(10/52) 8.50 25.50 670.00 150.00
...Back To School 2-4,6('53-10/57)-County Fair No. 5 6.00 18.00 42.00 105.00
...County Fair 5(9/56)-Formerly Back To School 6.00 18.00 42.00 105.00
...County Fair 2(11/58) 5.00 15.00 35.00 90.00

DELL GIANTS (Consecutive numbering)
No. 21, Sept, 1959 - No. 55, Sept, 1961 (Most 84 pgs., 25¢)
Dell Publishing Co.

21-(#1)-M.G.M.'s Tom & Jerry Picnic Time (84pp, stapled binding)-Painted-c 9.50 28.50 67.00 170.00
22-Huey, Dewey & Louie Back to School (Disney; 10/59, 84pp, square binding begins) 7.00 21.00 49.00 130.00
23-Marge's Little Lulu & Tubby Halloween Fun (10/59)-Tripp-a 9.00 27.00 63.00 160.00
24-Woody Woodpecker's Family Fun (11/59)(Walter Lantz) 7.00 21.00 49.00 125.00
25-Tarzan's Jungle World(11/59)-Marsh-a; painted-c 9.00 27.00 63.00 160.00
26-Christmas Parade(Disney; 12/59)-Barks-a, 16pgs.; Barks draws himself on wanted poster pg. 13 18.00 54.00 126.00 320.00
27-Man in Space r-/4-Color 716,866, & 954 (100 pgs., 35¢)(Disney)(TV)

Dell Giant #33 © WDC

Demolition Man #4 © Warner Bros.

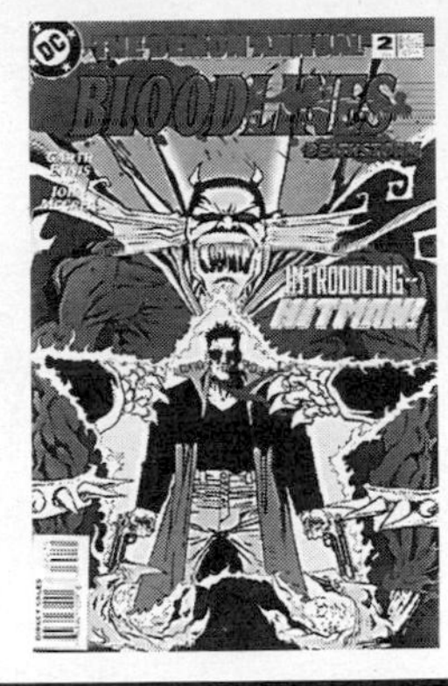

Demon Annual #2 © DC

GD25 FN65 NM94

8.50 25.50 60.00 155.00
28-Bugs Bunny's Winter Fun (2/60) 8.50 25.50 60.00 155.00
29-Marge's Little Lulu & Tubby in Hawaii (4/60)-Tripp-a
9.00 27.00 63.00 160.00
30-Disneyland USA(Disney; 6/60) 8.00 24.00 56.00 140.00
31-Huckleberry Hound Summer Fun (7/60)(TV)(HannaBarbera)-Yogi Bear & Pixie & Dixie app. 11.50 34.50 81.00 205.00
32-Bugs Bunny Beach Party 5.50 16.50 39.00 95.00
33-Daisy Duck & Uncle Scrooge Picnic Time (Disney; 9/60)
8.00 24.00 56.00 140.00
34-Nancy & Sluggo Summer Camp (8/60)
6.00 18.00 42.00 110.00
35-Huey, Dewey & Louie Back to School (Disney; 10/60)-1st app. Daisy Duck's Nieces, April, May & June 9.00 27.00 63.00 160.00
36-Marge's Little Lulu & Witch Hazel Halloween Fun (10/60)-Tripp-a
9.00 27.00 63.00 160.00
37-Tarzan, King of the Jungle (11/60)-Marsh-a; painted-c
8.00 24.00 56.00 145.00
38-Uncle Donald & His Nephews Family Fun (Disney; 11/60)-Cover painting based on a pencil sketch by Barks 11.50 34.50 81.00 205.00
39-Walt Disney's Merry Christmas (Disney; 12/60)-Cover painting based on a pencil sketch by Barks 11.50 34.50 81.00 205.00
40-Woody Woodpecker Christmas Parade (12/60)(Walter Lantz)
5.50 16.50 39.00 95.00
41-Yogi Bear's Winter Sports (12/60)(TV)(Hanna-Barbera)-Huckleberry Hound & Top Cat app. 11.00 33.00 77.00 200.00
42-Marge's Little Lulu & Tubby in Australia (4/61)
9.00 27.00 63.00 160.00
43-Mighty Mouse in Outer Space (5/61) 17.00 51.00 119.00 305.00
44-Around the World with Huckleberry and His Friends (7/61)(TV)(Hanna-Barbera)-Yogi Bear app. 11.00 33.00 77.00 200.00
45-Nancy & Sluggo Summer Camp (8/61)
5.50 16.50 39.00 95.00
46-Bugs Bunny Beach Party (8/61) 5.50 16.50 39.00 95.00
47-Mickey & Donald in Vacationland (Disney; 8/61)
7.00 21.00 49.00 130.00
48-The Flintstones (No. 1)(Bedrock Bedlam)(7/61)(TV)(Hanna-Barbera)
15.50 46.50 109.00 275.00
49-Huey, Dewey & Louie Back to School (Disney; 9/61)
7.00 21.00 49.00 130.00
50-Marge's Little Lulu & Witch Hazel Trick 'N' Treat (10/61)
9.00 27.00 63.00 160.00
51-Tarzan, King of the Jungle by Jesse Marsh (11/61)-Painted-c
6.50 19.50 46.00 115.00
52-Uncle Donald & His Nephews Dude Ranch (Disney; 11/61)
6.00 18.00 42.00 110.00
53-Donald Duck Merry Christmas (Disney; 12/61)
6.00 18.00 42.00 110.00
54-Woody Woodpecker's Christmas Party (12/61)-Issued after No. 55
6.00 18.00 42.00 110.00
55-Daisy Duck & Uncle Scrooge Showboat (Disney; 9/61)
7.00 21.00 49.00 130.00
NOTE: All issues printed with & without ad on back cover.

DELL JUNIOR TREASURY
June, 1955 - No. 10, Oct, 1957 (15¢) (All painted-c)
Dell Publishing Co.

	GD25	FN65	NM94
1-Alice in Wonderland; r/4-Color #331 (52 pgs.)	9.00	26.00	95.00
2-Aladdin & the Wonderful Lamp	5.50	16.50	60.00
3-Gulliver's Travels (1/56)	4.50	13.50	50.00
4-Adventures of Mr. Frog & Miss Mouse	5.00	15.00	55.00
5-The Wizard of Oz (7/56)	5.50	16.50	60.00
6-Heidi (10/56)	4.50	13.50	50.00
7-Santa and the Angel	4.50	13.50	50.00
8-Raggedy Ann and the Camel with the Wrinkled Knees	4.50	13.50	50.00
9-Clementina the Flying Pig	4.50	13.50	50.00
10-Adventures of Tom Sawyer	4.50	13.50	50.00

GD25 FN65 NM94

DEMOLITION MAN
Nov, 1993 - No. 4, Feb, 1994 ($1.75, color, limited series)
DC Comics
1-4-Movie adaptation .70 1.75

DEMON, THE (See Detective Comics No. 482-485)
Aug-Sept, 1972 - V3#16, Jan, 1974
National Periodical Publications
1-Origin; Kirby-c/a in all 1.50 4.50 12.00
2-5 2.40 6.00
6-16 1.60 4.00

DEMON, THE (1st limited series)(Also see Cosmic Odyssey #2)
Nov, 1986 - No. 4, Feb, 1987 (75¢, limited series)(#2 has #4 of 4 on-c)
DC Comics
1-4: Matt Wagner-a(p) & scripts in all. 4-Demon & Jason Blood become seperate entities. 1.00

DEMON, THE (2nd Series)
July, 1990 - No. 57, May, 1995 ($1.50/$1.75/$1.95)
DC Comics
1-Grant scripts begin, ends #39: 1-4-Painted-c .70 1.80
2-18,20-27: 3,8-Batman app. (cameo #4). 12-Bisley painted-c. 12-15,21-Lobo app. (1 pg. cameo #11). 23-Robin app. 1.60
19-($2.50, 44 pgs.)-Lobo poster stapled inside 1.00 2.50
28-42,46,47: 28-Superman-c/story; begin $1.75-c. 29-Superman app. 31,33-39-Lobo app. 40-Garth Ennis scripts begin. 46-48 Return of The Haunted Tank-c/s. .70 1.75
43-45-Hitman app. 1.75 5.25 14.00
48,49,51: 48-Begin $1.95-c. 51-(9/94) .80 2.00
50 ($2.95, 52 pgs.) 1.20 3.00
0,52-57: 0-(10/94) .80 2.00
Annual 1 (1992, $3.00, 68 pgs.)-Eclipso-c/story 1.20 3.00
Annual 2 (1993, $3.50, 68 pgs.)-1st app. of Hitman 1.85 5.50 15.00
NOTE: ***Alan Grant** scripts in #1-16, 20, 21, 23-25, 30-39, Annual 1. **Wagner** a/scripts-22.*

DEMON DREAMS
Feb, 1984 - No. 2, May, 1984
Pacific Comics
1,2-Mostly r-/Heavy Metal 1.50

DEMONGATE
May, 1996 - Present ($2.50, B&W)
Sirius Entertainment
1-10-Bao Lin Hum/Steve Blevins-s/a 1.00 2.50

DEMON GUN
June, 1996 - No. 3, Jan, 1997 ($2.95, B&W, limited series)
Crusade Entertainment
1-3: Gary Cohn scripts in all. 2-(10/96) 1.20 3.00

DEMON-HUNTER
Sept, 1975
Seaboard Periodicals (Atlas)
1-Origin; Buckler-c/a 1.20 3.00

DEMONIQUE
1994 - No. 4, 1995 ($3.00, B&W, limited series)
London Night Studios
1-4 1.20 3.00

DEMONIQUE
No. 0, Aug, 1996 - Present ($3.00, mature)
London Night Studios

Dennis The Menace #20 © KFS

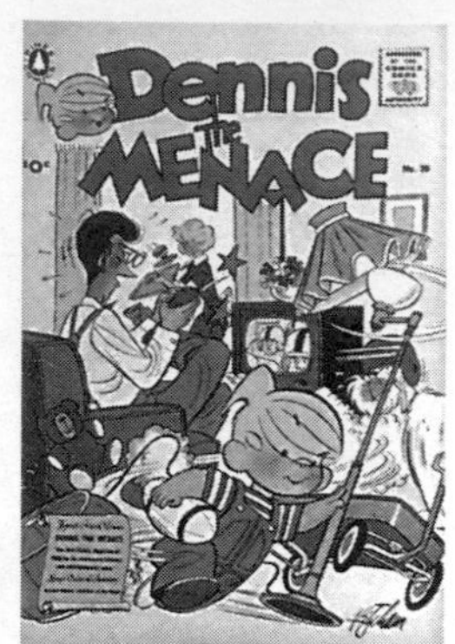

Dennis The Menace #40 © KFS

Dennis The Menace #7 © KFS

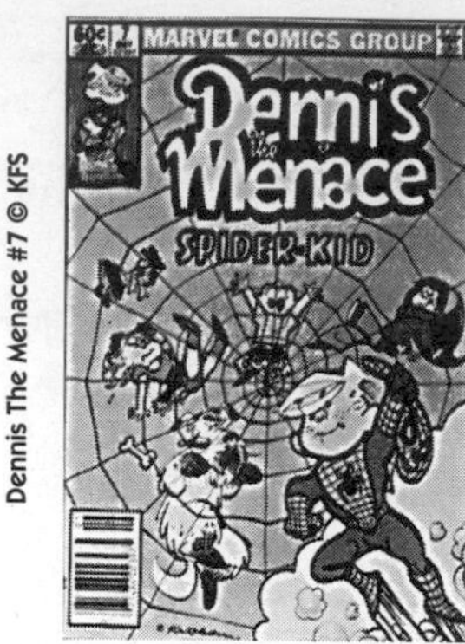

0,1, 1/2 (8/97) 1.20 3.00
1,1/2 (8/97)-($6.00)-Nude Edition 2.40 6.00

DEMON KNIGHT: A GRIMJACK GRAPHIC NOVEL
1990 ($8.95, 52 pgs.)
First Publishing

nn-Flint Henry-a 1.10 3.30 9.00

DENNIS THE MENACE (TV with 1959 issues) (Becomes ...Fun Fest Series; See The Best of... & The Very Best of...)(...Fun Fest on-c only to #156-166)
8/53 - #14, 1/56; #15, 3/56 - #31, 11/58; #32, 1/59 - #166, 11/79
Standard Comics/Pines No.15-31/Hallden (Fawcett) No.32 on

1-1st app. Dennis, Mr. & Mrs. Wilson, Ruff & Dennis' mom & dad; Wiseman-a, written by Fred Toole-most issues 46.00 138.00 410.00
2 23.00 69.00 185.00
3-10: 8-Last pre-code issue 13.00 39.00 105.00
11-20 10.00 30.00 80.00
21-30: 22-1st app. Margaret w/blonde hair 7.85 23.50 55.00
31-40: 31-1st app. Joey. 37-A-Bomb blast panel. 39-1st app. Gina (11/59) 5.35 16.00 32.00
41-60 2.50 7.50 20.00
61-90 1.50 4.50 12.00
91-166 2.40 6.00
...& Dirt('59,'68)-Soil Conservation giveaway; r-# 36; Wiseman-c/a 2.40 6.00
...Away We Go('70)-Caladayl giveaway 2.40 6.00
...Coping with Family Stress-giveaway 1.60 4.00
...Takes a Poke at Poison('61)-Food & Drug Assn. giveaway; Wiseman-c/a 2.40 6.00
...Takes a Poke at Poison-Revised 1/66, 11/70, 1972, 1974, 1977, 1981 1.60 4.00

NOTE: ***Wiseman*** *c/a-1-46, 53, 68, 69.*

DENNIS THE MENACE (Giants) (No. 1 titled Giant Vacation Special; becomes Dennis the Menace Bonus Magazine No. 76 on)
(#1-8,18,23,25,30,38: 100 pgs.; rest to #41: 84 pgs.; #42-75: 68 pgs.)
Summer, 1955 - No. 75, Dec, 1969
Standard/Pines/Hallden(Fawcett)

nn-Giant Vacation Special(Summ/55-Standard) 15.00 45.00 120.00
nn-Christmas issue (Winter '55) 12.00 38.00 100.00
2-Giant Vacation Special (Summer '56-Pines)
3-Giant Christmas issue (Winter '56-Pines)
4-Giant Vacation Special (Summer '57-Pines)
5-Giant Christmas issue (Winter '57-Pines)
6-In Hawaii (Giant Vacation Special)(Summer '58-Pines)
6-In Hawaii (Summer '59-Hallden)-2nd printing; says 3rd large printing on-c
6-In Hawaii (Summer '60)-3rd printing; says 4th large printing on-c
6-In Hawaii (Summer '62)-4th printing; says 5th large printing on-c
6-Giant Christmas issue (Winter '58)
each.... 9.50 28.00 75.00
7-In Hollywood (Winter '59-Hallden)
7-In Hollywood (Summer '61)-2nd printing
8-In Mexico (Winter '60, 100 pgs.-Hallden/Fawcett)
8-In Mexico (Summer '62, 2nd printing)
9-Goes to Camp (Summer '61, 84 pgs.)-1st CCA approved issue
9-Goes to Camp (Summer '62)-2nd printing
10-X-Mas issue (Winter '61)
11-Giant Christmas issue (Winter '62)
12-Triple Feature (Winter '62)
each.... 5.50 16.50 55.00
13-Best of Dennis the Menace (Spring '63)-Reprints
14-And His Dog Ruff (Summer '63)
15-In Washington, D.C. (Summer '63)
16-Goes to Camp (Summer '63)-Reprints No. 9
17-& His Pal Joey (Winter '63)
18-In Hawaii (Reprints No. 6)
19-Giant Christmas issue (Winter '63)
20-Spring Special (Spring '64)
each.... 2.50 7.50 25.00
21-40: 30-r/#6 2.00 6.00 16.00
41-75: 68-Partial-r/#6 1.25 3.75 10.00

NOTE: ***Wiseman*** *c/a-1-8, 12, 14, 15, 17, 20, 22, 27, 28, 31, 35, 36, 41, 49.*

DENNIS THE MENACE
Nov, 1981 - No. 13, Nov, 1982
Marvel Comics Group

1-New-a 2.40 6.00
2-13: 2-New art. 3-Part-r. 4,5-r. 5-X-Mas-c & issue. 7-Spider Kid-c/sty 1.60 4.00

NOTE: ***Hank Ketcham*** *c-most; a-3, 12.* ***Wiseman*** *a-4, 5.*

DENNIS THE MENACE AND HIS DOG RUFF
Summer, 1961
Hallden/Fawcett

1-Wiseman-c/a 4.00 12.00 40.00

DENNIS THE MENACE AND HIS FRIENDS
1969; No. 5, Jan, 1970 - No. 46, April, 1980 (All reprints)
Fawcett Publications

Dennis the Menace & Joey No. 2 (7/69) 1.50 4.50 12.00
Dennis the Menace & Ruff No. 2 (9/69) 1.25 3.75 10.00
Dennis the Menace & Mr. Wilson No. 1 (10/69) 2.50 7.50 20.00
Dennis & Margaret No. 1 (Winter '69) 2.50 7.50 20.00
5-20: 5-Dennis the Menace & Margaret. 6-...& Joey. 7-...& Ruff. 8-...& Mr. Wilson 1.00 2.80 7.00
21-37 2.00 5.00
38-46 (Digest size, 148 pgs., 4/78, 95¢) 2.40 6.00

NOTE: *Titles rotate every four issues, beginning with No. 5.*

DENNIS THE MENACE AND HIS PAL JOEY
Summer, 1961 (10¢) (See Dennis the Menace Giants No. 45)
Fawcett Publications

1-Wiseman-c/a 4.00 12.00 40.00

DENNIS THE MENACE AND THE BIBLE KIDS
1977 (36 pgs.)
Word Books

1-10: 1-Jesus. 2-Joseph. 3-David. 4-The Bible Girls. 5-Moses. 6-More About Jesus. 7-The Lord's Prayer. 8-Stories Jesus told. 9-Paul, God's Traveller. 10-In the Beginning 1.60 4.00

NOTE: ***Ketcham*** *c/a in all.*

DENNIS THE MENACE BIG BONUS SERIES
No. 10, Feb, 1980 - No. 11, Apr, 1980
Fawcett Publications

10,11 1.20 3.00

DENNIS THE MENACE BONUS MAGAZINE (Formerly Dennis the Menace Giants Nos. 1-75)
No. 76, 1/70 - No. 194, 10/79; (No. 76-124: 68 pgs.; No. 125-163: 52 pgs.; No. 164 on: 36 pgs.)
Fawcett Publications

76-90 2.40 6.00
91-110 2.00 5.00
111-150 1.60 4.00
151-194: 166-Indicia printed backwards 1.20 13.00

DENNIS THE MENACE COMICS DIGEST
April, 1982 - No. 3, Aug, 1982 ($1.25, digest-size)
Marvel Comics Group

1-3-Reprints 1.00 3.00 8.00

NOTE: ***Ketcham*** *c-all.* ***Wiseman*** *a-all. A few thousand #1's were published with a DC emblem on cover.*

DENNIS THE MENACE FUN BOOK

Destiny: A Chronicle of Deaths Foretold #2 © DC

Destroyer V2 #1 © MEG

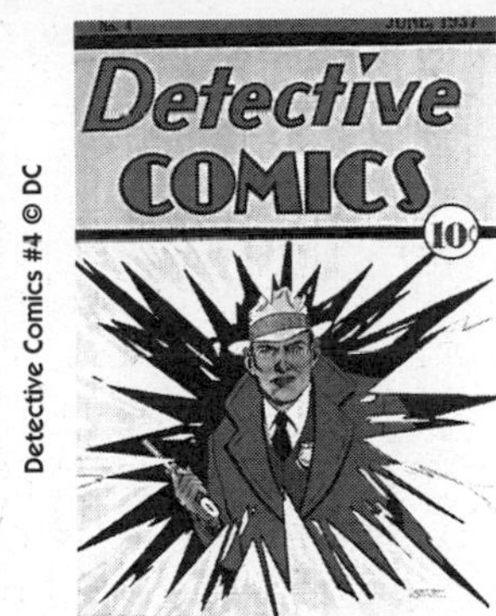

Detective Comics #4 © DC

1960 (100 pgs.)
Fawcett Publications/Standard Comics

	GD25	FN65	NM94
1-Part Wiseman-a	5.50	16.50	55.00

DENNIS THE MENACE FUN FEST SERIES (Formerly Dennis the Menace #166)
No. 16, Jan, 1980 - No. 17, Mar, 1980 (40¢)
Hallden (Fawcett)

	GD25	FN65	NM94
16,17-By Hank Ketcham		1.20	3.00

DENNIS THE MENACE POCKET FULL OF FUN!
Spring, 1969 - No. 50, March, 1980 (196 pgs.) (Digest size)
Fawcett Publications (Hallden)

	GD25	FN65	NM94
1-Reprints in all issues	3.00	9.00	30.00
2-10	2.50	7.50	20.00
11-20	1.50	4.50	12.00
21-28	1.00	3.00	8.00
29-50: 35,40,46-Sunday strip-r		2.00	5.00

NOTE: *No. 1-28 are 196 pgs.; No. 29-36: 164 pgs.; No. 37: 148 pgs.; No. 38 on: 132 pgs. No. 8, 11, 15, 21, 25, 29 all contain strip reprints.*

DENNIS THE MENACE TELEVISION SPECIAL
Summer, 1961 - No. 2, Spring, 1962 (Giant)
Fawcett Publications (Hallden Div.)

	GD25	FN65	NM94
1	5.00	15.00	50.00
2	2.80	8.40	28.00

DENNIS THE MENACE TRIPLE FEATURE
Winter, 1961 (Giant)
Fawcett Publications

	GD25	FN65	NM94
1-Wiseman-c/a	5.00	15.00	50.00

DEPUTY, THE (TV)
No. 1077, Feb-Apr, 1960 - No. 1225, Oct-Dec, 1961 (all-Henry Fonda photo-c)
Dell Publishing Co.

	GD25	FN65	NM94
Four Color 1077 (#1)-Buscema-a	12.00	35.00	130.00
Four Color 1130 (9-11/60)-Buscema-a,1225	9.00	27.00	100.00

DEPUTY DAWG (TV) (Also see New Terrytoons)
Oct-Dec, 1961 - No. 1299, 1962; No. 1, Aug, 1965
Dell Publishing Co./Gold Key

	GD25	FN65	NM94
Four Color 1238,1299	10.00	30.00	110.00
1(10164-508)(8/65)-Gold Key	9.00	27.00	100.00

DEPUTY DAWG PRESENTS DINKY DUCK AND HASHIMOTO-SAN (TV)
August, 1965
Gold Key

	GD25	FN65	NM94
1(10159-508)	8.00	25.00	90.00

DESERT GOLD (See Zane Grey 4-Color 467)

DESIGN FOR SURVIVAL (Gen. Thomas S. Power's...)
1968 (36 pgs. in color) (25¢)
American Security Council Press

	GD25	FN65	NM94
nn-Propaganda against the Threat of Communism-Aircraft cover; H-Bomb panel	2.50	7.50	20.00
Twin Circle Edition-Cover shows panels from inside	1.50	4.50	12.00

DESPERADO (Becomes Black Diamond Western No. 9 on)
June, 1948 - No. 8, Feb, 1949 (All 52 pgs.)
Lev Gleason Publications

	GD25	FN65	NM94
1-Biro-c on all; contains inside photo-c of Charles Biro, Lev Gleason & Bob Wood	10.00	30.00	80.00
2	5.70	17.00	40.00
3-Story with over 20 killings	6.50	19.50	45.00
4-8	5.00	15.00	30.00

NOTE: ***Barry** a-2. **Fuje** a-4, 8. **Guardineer** a-5-7. **Kida** a-3-7. **Ed Moore** a-4, 6.*

DESPERADOES
Sept, 1997 - Present ($2.50/$2.95)
Image Comics (Homage Comics)

	GD25	FN65	NM94
1-Mariotte-s/Cassaday-c/a		1.00	2.50
2,3-($2.95)			2.95

DESTINATION MOON (See Fawcett Movie Comics, Space Adventures #20, 23, & Strange Adventures #1)

DESTINY: A CHRONICLE OF DEATHS FORETOLD (See Sandman)
1997 - No.3 ($5.95, limited series)
DC Comics (Vertigo)

	GD25	FN65	NM94
1-3-Kwitney-s in all: 1-Williams & Zulli-a, Williams painted-c. 2-Williams & Scott Hampton-painted-c/a. 3-Williams & Guay-a			5.95

DESTROY!!
1986 ($4.95, B&W, magazine-size, one-shot)
Eclipse Comics

	GD25	FN65	NM94
1		2.00	5.00
3-D Special 1-r-/#1 ($2.50)		1.00	2.50

DESTROYER, THE
Nov, 1989 - No. 9, June, 1990 ($2.25, B&W, magazine, 52 pgs.)
Marvel Comics

	GD25	FN65	NM94
1-Based on Remo Williams movie, paperbacks		.90	2.25
2-9: 2-Williamson part inks. 4-Ditko-a		.90	2.25

DESTROYER, THE
V2#1, March, 1991 ($1.95, 52 pgs.)
V3#1, Dec, 1991 - No. 4, Mar, 1992 ($1.95, mini-series)
Marvel Comics

	GD25	FN65	NM94
V2#1,V3#1-4: Based on Remo Williams paperbacks. V3#1-4-Simonson-c. 3-Morrow-a		.80	2.00

DESTROYER, THE (Also see Solar, Man of the Atom)
Apr, 1995 ($2.95, color, one-shot)
Valiant

	GD25	FN65	NM94
0-Indicia indicates #1		1.20	3.00

DESTROYER DUCK
Feb, 1982 - No. 7, May, 1984 (#2-7: Baxter paper) ($1.50)
Eclipse Comics

	GD25	FN65	NM94
1-Origin Destroyer Duck; 1st app. Groo		2.40	6.00
2-7: 2-Starling back-up begins			1.25

NOTE: ***Neal Adams** c-1i. **Kirby** c/a-1-5p. **Miller** c-7.*

DESTRUCTOR, THE
February, 1975 - No. 4, Aug, 1975
Atlas/Seaboard

	GD25	FN65	NM94
1-Origin; Ditko/Wood-a; Wood-c(i)		1.60	4.00
2-4: 2-Ditko/Wood-a. 3,4-Ditko-a(p)		1.20	3.00

DETECTIVE COMICS (Also see Batman, Batman:Shadow of the Bat & Special Edition)
Mar, 1937 - Present
National Periodical Publications/DC Comics

	GD25	FN65	VF82
1-(Scarce)-Slam Bradley & Spy by Siegel & Shuster, Speed Saunders by Guardineer, Flat Foot Flannigan by Gustavson, Cosmo, the Phantom of Disguise, Buck Marshall, Bruce Nelson begin; Chin Lung in 'Claws of the Red Dragon' serial begins; Vincent Sullivan-c.	8,333.00	25,000.00	50,000.00
(Estimated up to 30 total copies exist, 1 in NM/Mint)			
2 (Rare)-Creig Flessel-c begin; new logo	2333.00	6999.00	14,300.00
3 (Rare)	1666.00	5000.00	10,200.00

	GD25	FN65	NM94
4,5: 5-Larry Steele begins	1033.00	3099.00	6400.00
6,7,9,10	750.00	2250.00	4600.00
8-Mister Chang-c; classic-c	1133.00	3399.00	7000.00
11-17,19: 17-1st app. Fu Manchu in Det.	566.00	1700.00	3500.00

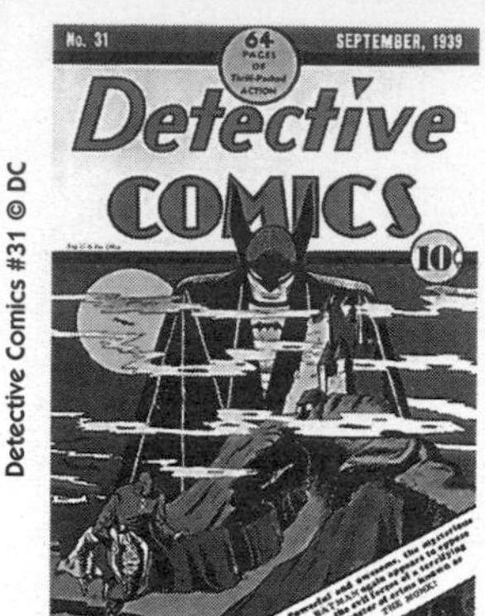

Detective Comics #31 © DC

Detective Comics #45 © DC

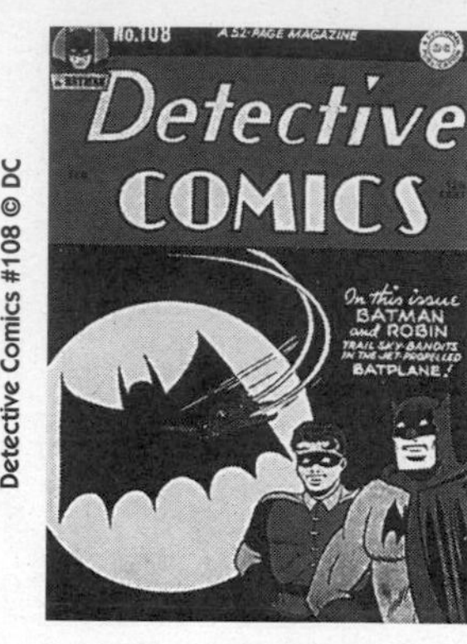

Detective Comics #108 © DC

GD25 FN65 NM94 — **GD25 FN65 NM94**

18-Fu Manchu-c; last Flessel-c 950.00 2850.00 5800.00
20-The Crimson Avenger begins (1st app.) 866.00 2600.00 5300.00
21,23-25 450.00 1350.00 2800.00
22-1st & only Crimson Avenger-c (12/38) 583.00 1749.00 3600.00
26 400.00 1200.00 2450.00

GD25 FN65 VF82 NM94

27-The Bat-Man & Commissioner Gordon begin (1st app.), created by Bill Finger & Bob Kane (5/39); Batman-c (1st)(by Kane). Bat-Man's secret identity revealed as Bruce Wayne in 6pg. sty. Signed Rob't Kane (also see Det. plcture Stories #5)
25,000.00 65,000.00 100,000.00 160,000.00
(Estimated up to 50+ total copies exist, 1 in NM/Mint)

27-Reprint, Oversize 13-1/2x10". WARNING: This comic is an exact duplicate reprint of the original except for its size. DC published it in 1974 with a second cover titling it as Famous First Edition. There have been many reported cases of the outer cover being removed and the interior sold as the original edition. The reprint with the new outer cover removed is practically worthless; see Famous First Edition for value.

GD25 FN65 NM94

27(1984)-Oreo Cookies giveaway (32 pgs., paper-c, r-/Det. 27, 38 & Batman No. 1 (1st Joker) 2.80 8.40 28.00
28-2nd app. The Batman (6 pg. story); non-Bat-Man-c; signed Rob't Kane
1300.00 3900.00 14,300.00

GD25 FN65 VF82 NM94

29-1st app. Doctor Death-c/story, Batman's 1st name villain. 1st 2 part story (10 pgs.). 2nd Batman-c by Kane 2100.00 6300.00 13,650.00 23,000.00
(Estimated up to 75+ total copies exist, 6 in NM/Mint)

GD25 FN65 NM94

30-Dr. Death app. Story concludes from issue #29. Classic Batman splash panel. 520.00 1560.00 5200.00

GD25 FN65 VF82 NM94

31-Classic Batman over castle-c; 1st app. The Monk & 1st Julie Madison (Bruce Wayne's 1st love interest); 1st Batplane (Bat-Gyro) and Batarang; 2nd 2-part Batman adventure. Gardner Fox takes over script from Bill Finger. 1st men tion of Locale (New York City) where Batman lives
2100.00 6300.00 13,650.00 23,000.00
(Estimated up to 75+ total copies exist, 6 in NM/Mint)
32-Batman story concludes from issue #31. 1st app. Dala (Monk's assistant). Batman uses gun for 1st time to slay The Monk and Dala. This was the 1st time a costumed hero used a gun in comic books. 1st Batman head logo on cover

GD25 FN65 NM94

500.00 1500.00 5000.00

GD25 FN65 VF82 NM94

33-Origin The Batman (2 pgs.)(1st told origin); Batman gun holster-c; Batman w/smoking gun panel at end of story. Batman story now 12 pgs. Classic Batman-c 2900.00 8700.00 18,850.00 32,000.00
(Estimated up to 75+ total copies exist, 7 in NM/Mint)

GD25 FN65 NM94

34-2nd Crimson Avenger-c by Creig Flessel and last non Batman-c. Story from issue #32 x-over as Bruce Wayne sees Julie Madison off to America from Paris. Classic Batman splash panel used later in Batman #1 for origin story. Steve Malone begins 400.00 1200.00 4000.00
35-Classic Batman hypodermic needle-c that reflects story in issue #34. Classic Batman with smoking .45 automatic splash panel. Last time a costumed hero used a gun in comic books. Batman-c begin 720.00 2160.00 7200.00
36-Batman-c that reflects adventure in issue #35. Origin/1st app. of Dr. Hugo Strange (1st major villain, 2/40). 1st finned-gloves worn by Batman
520.00 1560.00 5200.00
37-Last solo Golden-Age Batman adventure in Detective Comics. Panel at end of story reflects solo Batman adventure in Batman #1 that was originally planned for Detective #38. Cliff Crosby begins
520.00 1560.00 5200.00

GD25 FN65 VF82 NM94

38-Origin/1st app. Robin the Boy Wonder (4/40); Batman and Robin-c begin; cover by Kane & Robinson taken from splash pg.
2545.00 7635.00 16,542.00 28,000.00
(Estimated up to 85+ total copies exist, 9 in NM/Mint)

GD25 FN65 NM94

39-Opium story 460.00 1380.00 4600.00
40-Origin & 1st app. Clay Face (Basil Karlo); 1st Joker cover app. (6/40); Joker story intended for this issue was used in Batman #1 instead; cover is similar to splash pg. in 2nd Joker story in Batman #1 580.00 1740.00 5800.00
41-Robin's 1st solo 270.00 810.00 2700.00
42-44: 44-Crimson Avenger-new costume 194.00 582.00 1750.00
45-1st Joker story in Det. (3rd book app. & 4th story app. over all, 11/40)
270.00 810.00 2700.00
46-50: 46-Death of Hugo Strange. 48-1st time car called Batmobile (2/41); Gotham City 1st mention in Det. (1st mentioned in Wow #1; also see Batman #4). 49-Last Clay Face 172.00 516.00 1550.00
51-57 120.00 360.00 1075.00
58-1st Penguin app. (12/41); last Speed Saunders; Fred Ray-c
320.00 960.00 3200.00
59-Last Steve Malone; 2nd Penguin; Wing becomes Crimson Avenger's aide
139.00 417.00 1250.00
60-Intro. Air Wave; Joker app. (2nd in Det.) 139.00 417.00 1250.00
61,63: 63-Last Cliff Crosby; 1st app. Mr. Baffle 122.00 366.00 1100.00
62-Joker-c/story (2nd Joker-c, 4/42) 189.00 567.00 1700.00
64-Origin & 1st app. Boy Commandos by Simon & Kirby (6/42); Joker app.
320.00 960.00 3200.00
65-1st Boy Commandos-c (S&K-a on Boy Commandos & Ray/Robinson-a on Batman & Robin on-c; 4 artists on one-c) 240.00 720.00 2350.00
66-Origin & 1st app. Two-Face 280.00 840.00 2800.00
67-1st Penguin-c (9/42) 178.00 533.00 1600.00
68-Two-Face-c/story; 1st Two-Face-c 139.00 417.00 1250.00
69-Joker-c/story 139.00 417.00 1250.00
70 94.00 282.00 850.00
71-Joker-c/story 107.00 321.00 965.00
72,74,75: 74-1st Tweedledum & Tweedledee plus-c; S&K-a
86.00 258.00 775.00
73-Scarecrow-c/story (1st Scarecrow-c) 100.00 300.00 900.00
76-Newsboy Legion & The Sandman x-over in Boy Commandos; S&K-a; Joker-c/story 139.00 417.00 1250.00
77-79: All S&K-a 94.00 282.00 850.00
80-Two-Face app.; S&K-a 102.00 306.00 915.00
81,82,84,86-90: 81-1st Cavalier-c & app. 89-Last Crimson Avenger; 2nd Cavalier-c & app. 75.00 225.00 675.00
83-1st "skinny" Alfred (2/44)(see Batman #21; last S&K Boy Commandos. (also #92,128); most issues #84 on signed S&K are not by them
83.00 250.00 750.00
85-Joker-c/story; last Spy; Kirby/Klech Boy Commandos
97.00 291.00 875.00
91,102-Joker-c/story 92.00 276.00 825.00
92-98: 96-Alfred's last name 'Beagle' revealed, later changed to 'Pennyworth' in #214 64.00 192.00 575.00
99-Penguin-c 97.00 291.00 875.00
100 (6/45) 100.00 300.00 900.00
101,103-108,110-113,115-117,119: 108-1st Bat-signal-c (2/46). 114-1st small logo (8/46) 61.00 183.00 550.00
109,114,118-Joker-c/stories 83.00 250.00 750.00
120-Penquin-c (white-c, rare above fine) 133.00 400.00 1200.00
121,123,125,127,129,130 58.00 174.00 525.00
122-1st Catwoman-c (4/47) 106.00 318.00 950.00
124,128-Joker-c/stories 78.00 234.00 700.00
126-Penguin-c 81.00 243.00 725.00
131-136,139: 135-Frankenstein-c/story 50.00 150.00 450.00
137-Joker-c/story; last Air Wave 64.00 192.00 575.00
138-Origin Robotman (see Star Spangled #7 for 1st app.); series ends #202
94.00 282.00 850.00
140-The Riddler-c/story (1st app., 10/48) 380.00 1140.00 3800.00
141,143-148,150: 150-Last Boy Commandos 50.00 150.00 450.00
142-2nd Riddler-c/story 94.00 282.00 850.00

Detective Comics #163 © DC

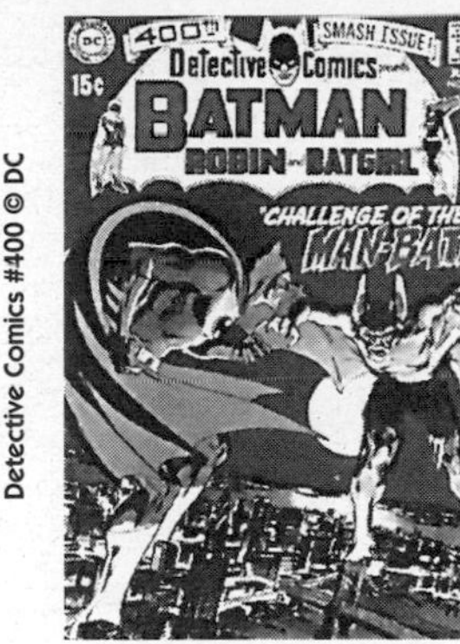

Detective Comics #400 © DC

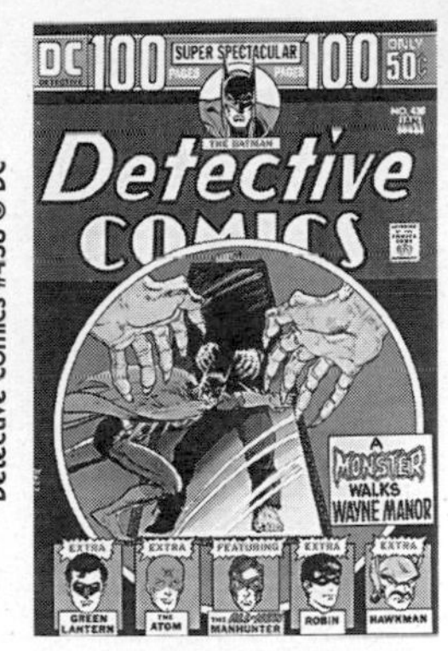

Detective Comics #438 © DC

GD25 FN65 NM94

149-Joker-c/story 69.00 207.00 625.00
151-Origin & 1st app. Pow Wow Smith, Indian lawman (9/49) & begins series 61.00 183.00 550.00
152,154,155,157-160: 152-Last Slam Bradley 50.00 150.00 450.00
153-1st app. Roy Raymond TV Detective (11/49) ; origin The Human Fly 57.00 171.00 510.00
156(2/50)-The new classic Batmobile 69.00 207.00 625.00
161-167,169,170,172-176: Last 52 pg. issue 48.00 144.00 430.00
168-Origin the Joker 300.00 900.00 3000.00
171-Penguin-c 75.00 225.00 675.00
177-179,181-186,188,189,191,192,194-199,201,202,204,206-210,212,214-216: 184-1st app. Fire Fly. 185-Secret of Batman's utility belt. 187-Two-Face app. 202-Last Robotman & Pow Wow Smith. 215-1st app. of Batmen of all Nations. 216-Last precode (2/55) 42.00 126.00 380.00
180,193-Joker-c/story 46.00 138.00 410.00
187-Two-Face-c/story 46.00 138.00 410.00
190-Origin Batman retold 61.00 183.00 550.00
200 (10/53) 58.00 174.00 520.00
203,211-Catwoman-c/stories 46.00 138.00 410.00
205-Origin Batcave 58.00 174.00 520.00
213-Origin & 1st app. Mirror Man 50.00 150.00 450.00
217-224: 218-Batman Jr. & Robin Sr. app. 31.00 93.00 325.00

GD25 FN65 VF82 NM94

225-(11/55)-1st app. Martian Manhunter, John Jones; later changed to J'onn J'onzz; origin begins; also see Batman #78 347.00 1041.00 2429.00 5200.00

GD25 FN65 NM94

226-Origin Martian Manhunter cont'd (2nd app.) 105.00 315.00 1260.00
227-229: Martian Manhunter stories in all 40.00 120.00 470.00
230-1st app. Mad Hatter; brief recap origin of Martian Manhunter 41.00 123.00 495.00
231-Brief origin recap Martian Manhunter 31.00 93.00 320.00
232,234,237-240: 232-Batwoman app. 239-Early DC grey tone-c 30.00 90.00 300.00
233-Origin & 1st app. Batwoman (7/56) 96.00 288.00 1150.00
235-Origin Batman & his costume; tells how Bruce Wayne's father (Thomas Wayne) wore Bat costume & fought crime (reprinted in Batman #255) 46.00 138.00 560.00
236-1st S.A. issue; J'onn J'onzz talks to parents and Mars-1st since being stranded on Earth; 1st app. Bat-Tank? 31.00 93.00 350.00
241-260: 246-Intro. Diane Meade, John Jones' girl. 249-Batwoman-c/app. 253-1st app. The Terrible Trio. 254-Bat-Hound-c/story. 257-Intro. & 1st app. Whirly Bats. 259-1st app. The Calendar Man 25.00 75.00 250.00
261-J. Jones tie-in to sci/fi movie "Incredible Shrinking Man" 18.50 55.00 185.00
262-264,266,269,270: 261-1st app. Dr. Double X. 262-Origin Jackal 18.50 55.00 185.00
265-Batman's origin retold with new facts 29.00 88.00 295.00
267-Origin & 1st app. Bat-Mite (5/59) 25.00 76.00 255.00
268,271-Manhunter origin recap 18.00 54.00 180.00
272,274-280: 276-2nd app. Bat-Mite 14.50 44.00 145.00
273-J'onn J'onzz i.d. revealed for 1st time 15.50 47.00 155.00
281-292, 294-297: 286,292-Batwoman-c/app. 287-Origin J'onn J'onzz retold. 289-Bat-Mite-c/story. 292-Last Roy Raymond. 297-Last 10¢ issue (11/61) 11.50 34.00 115.00
293-(7/61)-Aquaman begins (pre #1); ends #300 12.00 36.00 120.00
298-(12/61)-1st modern Clayface (Matt Hagen) 22.00 66.00 220.00
299,300: 300-(2/62)-Aquaman ends 8.50 25.50 85.00
301-(3/62)-J'onn J'onzz returns to Mars (1st since stranded on Earth 6 years before) 8.50 25.50 85.00
302-326,329,330: 302,311,318,321-Batwoman-c/app. 311-Intro. Zook in John Jones; 1st app. Cat-Man. 318,325-Cat-Man-c/story (2nd & 3rd app.); also 1st & 2nd app. Batwoman as the Cat-Woman. 321-2nd Terrible Trio. 322-Bat-Girl's 1st/only app. in Det. (6th in all); Batman cameo in J'onn J'onzz (only hero to app. in series). 326-Last J'onn J'onzz, story cont'd in H.O.M. #143; intro. Idol-Head of Diabolu 6.50 19.50 65.00
327-(5/64)-Elongated Man begins, ends #383; 1st new look Batman with new costume; Infantino/Giella new look-a begins; Batman with gun 10.50 32.00 105.00
328-Death of Alfred; Bob Kane biog, 2 pgs. 9.00 27.00 90.00
331,333-340,342-358,360-364,366-368,370: 334-1st app. The Outsider. 345-Intro Block Buster. 347-"What If" theme story (1/66). 351-Elongated Man new costume. 355-Zatanna x-over in Elongated Man. 356-Alfred brought back in Batman, 1st SA app.? 359-1st app. Killer Moth. 362,364-S.A. Riddler app. (early). 363-2nd app. new Batgirl. 370-1st Neal Adams-a on Batman (cover only, 12/67) 4.00 12.00 40.00
332,341,365-Joker-c/stories 4.80 14.40 48.00
359-Intro/origin new Batgirl-c/story (1/67) 9.50 28.50 95.00
369(11/67)-N. Adams-a (Elongated Man); 3rd app. S.A. Catwoman (cameo; leads into Batman #197); 4th app. new Batgirl 5.00 15.00 50.00
371-1st new Batmobile from TV show (1/68) 4.50 13.50 45.00
372-386,389,390: 375-New Batmobile-c. 377-S.A. Riddler app. 3.00 9.00 30.00
387-r/1st Batman story from #27 (30th anniversary, 5/69); Joker-c 4.00 12.00 40.00
388-Joker-c/story; last 12¢ issue 3.00 9.00 30.00
391-394,396,398,399,401,403,405,406,409: 392-1st app. Jason Bard. 401-2nd Batgirl/Robin team-up 1.50 4.50 12.00
395,397,402,404,407,408,410-Neal Adams-a. 404-Tribute to Enemy Ace 2.50 7.50 24.00
400-(6/70)-Origin & 1st app. Man-Bat; 1st Batgirl/Robin team-up (cont'd in #401); Neal Adams-a 4.50 13.50 45.00
411-413: 413-Last 15¢ issue 1.60 4.85 13.00
414-424: All-25¢, 52 pgs. 418-Creeper x-over. 424-Last Batgirl. 2.50 7.50 20.00
425-436: 426,430,436-Elongated Man app. 428,434-Hawkman begins, ends #467 1.25 3.75 10.00
437-New Manhunter begins (10-11/73, 1st app.) by Simonson, ends #443 2.00 6.00 16.00
438-445 (All 100 Page Super Spectaculars): 438-Kubert Hawkman-r. 439-Origin Manhunter. 440-G.A. Manhunter(Adv. #79) by S&K, Hawkman, Dollman, Gr. Lantern; Toth-a. 441-G.A. Plastic Man, Batman, Ibis-r. 442-G.A. Newsboy Legion, Bl. Canary, Elongated Man, Dr. Fate-r. 443-Origin The Creeper-r; death of Manhunter; G.A. Green Lantern, Spectre-r; Batman-r/Batman #18. 444-G.A. Kid Eternity-r. 445-G.A. Dr. Midnite-r 3.00 9.00 30.00
446-460: 457-Origin retold & updated 1.05 3.15 8.50
461-465,469,470,480: 480-(44 pgs.). 463-1st app. Black Spider. 464-2nd app. Black Spider 1.00 2.80 7.00
466-468,471-474,478,479-Rogers-a in all: 466-1st app. Signalman since Batman #139. 469-Intro/origin Dr. Phosphorous. 470,471-1st modern app. Hugo Strange. 474-1st app. new Deadshot. 478-1st app. 3rd Clayface (Preston Payne). 479-(44 pgs.)-Clayface app. 1.85 5.50 15.00
475,476-Joker-c/stories; Rogers-a 2.50 7.50 25.00
477-Neal Adams-a(r); Rogers-a (3 pgs.) 2.25 6.75 18.00
481-(Combined with Batman Family, 12-1/78-79, begin $1.00, 68 pg. issues, ends #495); 481-495-Batgirl, Robin solo stories 1.50 4.50 12.00
482-Starlin/Russell, Golden-a; The Demon begins (origin-r), ends #485 (by Ditko #483-485) 1.00 3.00 7.50
483-40th Anniversary issue; origin retold; Newton Batman begins 1.25 3.75 10.00
484-499: 484-Origin Robin. 485-Death of Batwoman. 487-The Odd Man by Ditko. 489-Robin/Batgirl team-up. 490-Black Lightning begins. 491-(#492 on inside) 2.00 5.00
500-($1.50, 52 pgs.)-Batman/Deadman team-up; new Hawkman story by Joe Kubert; incorrectly says 500th anniv. of Det. 1.40 4.15 11.00
501-503,505-523: 512-2nd app. new Dr. Death. 519-Last Batgirl. 521-Green Arrow series begins. 523-Solomon Grundy app. 2.00 5.00
504-Joker-c/story 1.00 2.80 7.00

Detective Comics #677 © DC

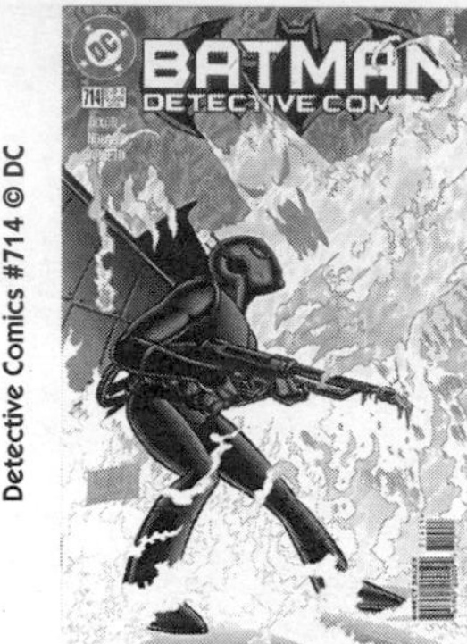

Detective Comics #714 © DC

Detective Comics Annual #10 © DC

GD25 FN65 NM94

524-2nd app. Jason Todd (cameo)(3/83) 1.40 3.50
525-3rd app. Jason Todd (See Batman #357) 1.60 4.00
526-Batman's 500th app. in Detective Comics ($1.50, 68 pgs.); Death of Jason Todd's parents, Joker-c/story (55 pgs.); Bob Kane pin-up 1.50 4.50 12.00
527-531,533,534,536-568,571,573: 538-Cat-Man-c/story cont'd from Batman #371. 542-Jason Todd quits as Robin (becomes Robin again #547). 549, 550-Alan Moore scripts (Gr. Arrow). 554-1st new Black Canary (9/85). 566-Batman villains profiled. 567-Harlan Ellison scripts 1.20 3.00
532,569,570-Joker-c/stories 2.00 5.00
535-Intro new Robin (Jason Todd)-1st appeared in Batman 1.20 3.00
572-(3/87, $1.25, 60 pgs.)-50th Anniv. of Det. Comics 1.20 3.00
574-Origin Batman & Jason Todd retold 1.20 3.00
575-Year 2 begins, ends #578 1.00 3.00 8.00
576-578: McFarlane-c/a. 578-Clay Face app. 2.40 6.00
579-597,601-610: 579-New bat wing logo. 583-1st app. villains Scarface & Vintriloquist. 589-595-(52 pgs.)-Each contain free 16 pg. Batman stories. 604-607-Mudpack storyline; 604,607-Contain Batman mini-posters. 610-Faked death of Penguin; artists names app. on tombstone on-c 1.50
598-($2.95, 84 pgs.)- "Blind Justice" storyline begins by Batman movie writer Sam Hamm, ends #600 1.20 3.00
599 1.00 2.50
600-(5/89, $2.95, 84 pgs.)-50th Anniv. of Batman in Det.; 1 pg. Neal Adams pin-up, among other artists 1.60 4.00
611-626,628-658: 612-1st new look Cat-Man; Catwoman app. 615- "The Penguin Affair" part 2 (See Batman #448,449). 617-Joker-c/story. 624-1st new Catwoman (w/death) & 1st new Batwoman. 626-Batman's 600th app. in Det. 642-Return of Scarface, part 2. 644-Last $1.00-c. 652,653-Huntress-c/story w/new costume plus Travis Charest-c on both 1.50
627-($2.95, 84 pgs.)-Batman's 601st app. in Det.; reprints 1st story/#27 plus 3 versions (2 new) of same story 1.20 3.00
659,660: 659-Knightfall part 2; Kelley Jones-c. 660-Knightfall part 4; Bane-c by Sam Kieth 1.20 3.00
661-664: 661-Knightfall part 6; brief Joker & Riddler app. 662-Knightfall part 8; Riddler app.; Sam Kieth-c. 663-Knightfall part 10; Kelley Jones-c. 664-Knightfall part 12; Bane-c/story; Joker app.; continued in Showcase 93 #7 & 8; Jones-c 1.20 3.00
665,666-Knightfall parts 16 & 18; 666-Bane-c/story .80 2.00
667,668: 667-Knightquest: The Crusade & new Batman begins (1st app. in Batman #500) .70 1.75
669-675: 669-Begin $1.50-c; Knightquest, cont'd in Robin #1. 671,673-Joker app. .70 1.75
675-($2.95)-Collectors edition w/foil-c 1.20 3.00
676-($2.50, 52 pgs.)-KnightsEnd Pt. 3 1.00 2.50
677,678: 677-KnightsEnd Pt. 9. 678-(9/94)-Zero Hour tie-in. 1.50
0,679-684: 0-(10/94). 679-(11/94). 682-Troika Pt. 3 1.50
682-($2.50) Embossed-c Troika Pt. 3 1.00 2.50
686-699,701-718: 686-Begin $1.95-c. 693,694-Poison Ivy-c/app. 695-Contagion Pt. 2; Catwoman, Penguin app. 696-Contagion Pt. 8. 698-Two-Face-c/app. 701-Legacy Pt. 6; Batman vs. Bane-c/app. 702-Legacy Epilogue. 703-Final Night x-over. 705-707-Riddler-app. 714,715-Martian Manhunter-app. .80 2.00
700-($4.95, Collectors Edition)-Legacy Pt. 1; Ra's Al Ghul-c/app; Talia & Bane app; book displayed at shops in envelope 2.00 5.00
700-($2.95, Regular Edition)-Different-c 1.20 3.00
Annual 1 (1988, $1.50) 2.00 5.00
Annual 2 (1989, $2.00, 68 pgs.) 1.20 3.00
Annual 3 (1990, $2.00, 68 pgs.) .80 2.00
Annual 4 (1991, $2.00, 68 pgs.)-Painted-c .80 2.00
Annual 5 (1992, $2.50, 68 pgs.)-Joker-c/story (54 pgs.) continued in Robin Annual #1; Sam Kieth-c; Eclipso app. 1.00 2.50
Annual 6 (1993, $2.50, 68 pgs.)-Azrael as Batman in new costume; intro Geist the Twilight Man; Bloodlines storyline 1.00 2.50
Annual 7 (1994, $2.95, 68 pgs.)-Elseworlds story 1.20 3.00
Annual 8 (1995, $3.95, 68 pgs.)-Year One story 1.60 4.00
Annual 9 (1996, $2.95)-Legends of the Dead Earth story 1.20 3.00
Annual 10 (1997, $3.95)-Pulp Heroes story 3.95

NOTE: **Neal Adams** *c-370, 372, 383, 385, 389, 391, 392, 394-422, 439.* **Aparo** *a-437, 438, 444-446, 500, 625-632p, 638-643p; c-430, 437, 440-446, 448, 468-470, 480, 484(back), 492-502,508, 509, 515, 518-522, 641.* **Austin** *a(i)-450, 451, 463-468, 471-476; c(i)-474-476, 478.* **Baily** *a-443r.* **Buckler** *a-434, 446p, 479p; c(p)-467, 482, 505-507, 511, 513-516, 518.* **Burnley** *a(Batman)-65, 75, 78, 83, 100, 103, 125; c-62i, 63i, 64, 73i, 78, 83p, 96p, 103p, 105p, 106, 108, 121p, 123p, 125p.* **Chaykin** *a-441.* **Colan** *a(p)-510, 512, 517, 523, 528-538, 540-546, 555-567; c(p)-510, 512, 528, 530-535, 537, 538, 540, 541, 543-545, 556-558, 560-564.* **J. Craig** *a-488.* **Ditko** *a-443r, 483-485, 487.* **Golden** *a-482p; c-625, 626, 628-631, 633, 644-646.* **Alan Grant** *scripts-584-597, 601-621, 641, 642, Annual 5.* **Grell** *a-445, 455, 463p, 464p; c-455.* **Guardineer** *c-23, 24, 26, 28, 30, 32.* **Gustavson** *a-441r.* **Infantino** *a-442(2)r, 500, 572.* **Infantino/Anderson** *c-333, 337-340, 343, 344, 347, 351, 352, 359, 361-368, 371.* **Kelley Jones** *c-651, 657i, 658i, 659, 661, 663-675.* **Kaluta** *c-423, 424, 426-428, 431, 434, 438, 484, 486, 572.* **Bob Kane** *a-Most early issues #27 on, 297r, 356r, 438-440r, 442r, 443r.* **Kane/Robinson** *c-33.* **Gil Kane** *a(p)-368, 370-374, 384, 385, 388-407, 438r, 439r, 520.* **Kane/Anderson** *c-369.* **Sam Kieth** *c-654-656 (657, 658 w/***Kelley Jones***), 660, 662, Annual #5.* **Kubert** *a-438r, 439r, 500; c-348, 350.* **McFarlane** *c/a(p)-576-578.* **Meskin** *a-420r.* **Mignola** *c-583.* **Moldoff** *c-233-354, 259, 266, 267, 275, 287, 289, 290, 297, 300.* **Moldoff/Giella** *a-328, 330, 332, 334, 336, 338, 340, 342, 344, 346, 348, 350, 352, 354, 356.* **Mooney** *a-444r.* **Moreira** *a-153-300, 419r, 444r, 445r.* **Nasser/Netzer** *a-654, 655, 657, 658.* **Newton** *a(p)-480, 481, 483-499, 501-509, 511, 513-516, 518-520, 524, 526, 539; c-526p.* **Irv Novick** *c-375-377.* **Robbins** *a-426p, 429p.* **Robinson** *a-part: 66, 68, 71-73; all: 74-76, 79, 80; c-62, 64, 66, 68-74, 76, 79, 82, 86, 88, 442r, 443r.* **Rogers** *a-466-468, 471-479p, 481p; c-471p, 472p, 473, 474-479p.* **Roussos** *Airwave-76-105(most); c(i)-71, 72, 74-76, 79, 107.* **Russell** *a-481i, 482i.* **Simon/Kirby** *a-440r, 442r.* **Simonson** *a-437-443, 450, 469, 470, 500.* **Dick Sprang** *c-77, 82, 84, 85, 87, 89-93, 95-100, 102, 103i, 104i, 106, 108, 114, 117, 118, 122, 123, 128, 129, 131, 133, 135, 141, 148, 149, 168, 622-624.* **Starlin** *a-481p, 482p; c-503, 504, 567p.* **Starr** *a-444r.* **Toth** *a-442; r-414, 416, 418, 424, 440-441, 443, 444.* **Tuska** *a-486p, 490p.* **Matt Wagner** *c-647-649.* **Wrightson** *c-425.*

DETECTIVE DAN, SECRET OP. 48 (Also see Advs. of Detective Ace King)
1933 (10¢, 10x13", 36 pgs., B&W, one-shot) (3 color, cardboard-c)
Humor Publ. Co. (Norman Marsh)

GD FN VF

nn-By Norman Marsh, 1st comic w/ original-a; 1st newsstand-c; Dick Tracy look-alike; forerunner of Dan Dunn. (Title and Wu Fang character inspired Detective #1 four years later.) (1st comic of a single theme) 1400.00 4200.00 5500.00

DETECTIVE EYE (See Keen Detective Funnies)
Nov, 1940 - No. 2, Dec, 1940
Centaur Publications

GD FN NM

1-Air Man (see Keen Detective) & The Eye Sees begins; The Masked Marvel & Dean Denton app. 178.00 534.00 1600.00
2-Origin Don Rance and the Mysticape; Binder-a; Frank Thomas-c 111.00 333.00 1000.00

DETECTIVE PICTURE STORIES (Keen Detective Funnies No. 8 on?)
Dec, 1936 - No. 5, Apr, 1937 (1st comic of a single theme)
Comics Magazine Company

1 (all issues are very scarce) 550.00 1650.00 3400.00
2-The Clock app. (1/37, early app.) 233.00 699.00 1500.00
3,4: 4-Eisner-a 150.00 450.00 950.00
5-The Clock-c/story (4/37); 1st detective/adventure art by Bob Kane; Bruce Wayne prototype app. 166.00 500.00 1050.00

DETECTIVES, THE (TV)
No. 1168, Mar-May, 1961 - No. 1240, Oct-Dec, 1961
Dell Publishing Co.

Four Color 1168 (#1)-Robert Taylor photo-c 9.00 27.00 100.00
Four Color 1219-Robert Taylor, Adam West photo-c 7.00 22.00 80.00
Four Color 1240-Tufts-a; Robert Taylor photo-c 7.00 22.00 80.00

DETECTIVES, INC. (See Eclipse Graphic Album Series)
Apr, 1985 - #2, Apr, 1985 ($1.75, both w/April dates)
Eclipse Comics

1,2: 2-Nudity .70 1.80

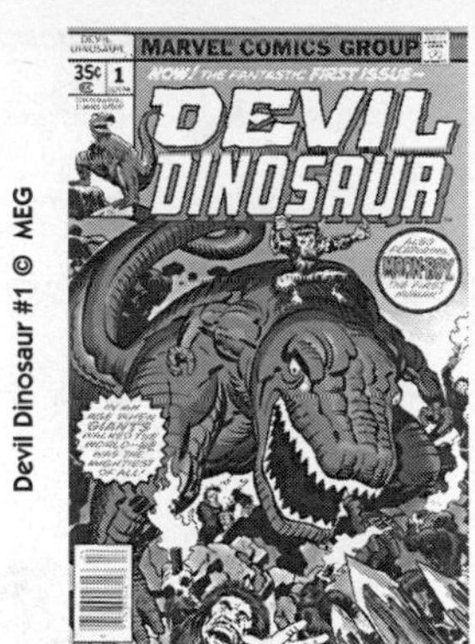

Devil Dinosaur #1 © MEG

Devil Kids Starring Hot Stuff #1 © HARV

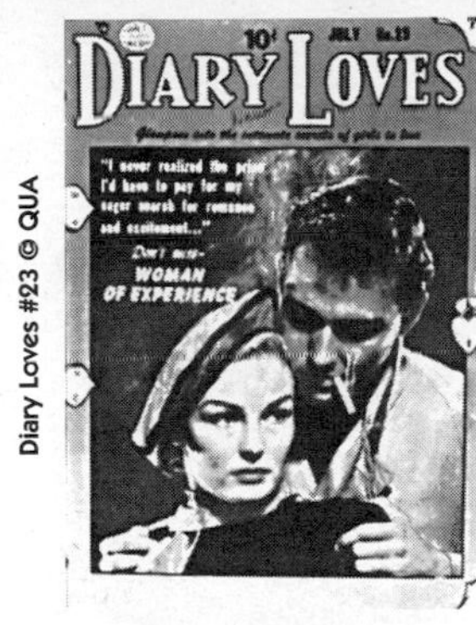

Diary Loves #23 © QUA

DETENTION COMICS
Oct, 1996 ($3.50, 56 pgs., one-shot)
DC Comics

	GD25	FN65	NM94
1-Robin story by Dennis O'Neil & Norm Breyfogle; Superboy story by Ron Marz & Ron Lim; Warrior story by Ruben Diaz & Joe Phillips; Phillips-c		1.40	3.50

DETONATOR
Dec, 1994 - No. 2, 1995 ($2.95, limited series)
Chaos! Comics

	GD25	FN65	NM94
1,2-Brian Pulido scripts; Steven Hughes-a		1.20	3.00

DEVIL CHEF
July, 1994 ($2.50, B&W, one-shot)
Dark Horse Comics

	GD25	FN65	NM94
nn		1.00	2.50

DEVIL DINOSAUR
Apr, 1978 - No. 9, Dec, 1978
Marvel Comics Group

	GD25	FN65	NM94
1-Kirby/Royer-a in all; all have Kirby-c	1.00	3.00	8.00
2,3,8,9: 8-Dinoriders-c/sty		1.60	4.00
4-7-UFO/sci. fic		2.00	5.00

DEVIL DINOSAUR SPRING FLING
June, 1997 ($2.99. one-shot)
Marvel Comics

	GD25	FN65	NM94
1-(48pgs.) Moon-Boy-c/app.			2.99

DEVIL-DOG DUGAN (Tales of the Marines No. 4 on)
July, 1956 - No. 3, Nov, 1956
Atlas Comics (OPI)

	GD25	FN65	NM94
1-Severin-c	8.75	26.25	65.00
2-Iron Mike McGraw x-over; Severin-c	5.70	17.00	40.00
3	5.00	15.00	30.00

DEVIL DOGS
1942
Street & Smith Publishers

	GD25	FN65	NM94
1-Boy Rangers, U.S. Marines	22.00	66.00	175.00

DEVLIN (See Avengelyne/Glory)
Apr, 1996 ($2.50, one-shot)
Maximum Press

	GD25	FN65	NM94
1-Avengelyne app.		1.00	2.50

DEVILINA (Magazine)
Feb, 1975 - No. 2, May, 1975 (B&W)
Atlas/Seaboard

	GD25	FN65	NM94
1-Reese-a	1.10	3.30	9.00
2	1.85	5.50	15.00

DEVIL KIDS STARRING HOT STUFF
July, 1962 - No. 107, Oct, 1981 (Giant-Size #41-55)
Harvey Publications (Illustrated Humor)

	GD25	FN65	NM94
1 (12¢ cover price #1-#41-9/69)	12.50	38.00	125.00
2	6.00	18.00	60.00
3-10 (1/64)	4.50	13.50	45.00
11-20	2.50	7.50	22.00
21-30	2.25	6.75	18.00
31-40: 40-(6/69)	1.75	5.50	14.00
41-50: All 68 pg. Giants	2.00	6.00	16.00
51-55: All 52 pg. Giants	1.75	5.50	14.00
56-70	1.00	2.80	7.00
71-90		1.60	4.00
91-107		1.20	3.00

DEVILMAN
June, 1995 - Present ($2.95, mature)
Verotik

	GD25	FN65	NM94
1-3: Go Nagai story and art. 3-Bisley-c		1.20	3.00

DEXTER COMICS
Summer, 1948 - No. 5, July, 1949
Dearfield Publ.

	GD25	FN65	NM94
1-Teen-age humor	6.50	19.50	45.00
2-Junie Prom app.	5.35	16.00	32.00
3-5	4.00	12.00	24.00

DEXTER THE DEMON (Formerly Melvin The Monster)(See Cartoon Kids & Peter the Little Pest)
No. 7, Sept, 1957
Atlas Comics (HPC)

	GD25	FN65	NM94
7	4.25	13.00	28.00

DHAMPIRE: STILLBORN
1996 ($5.95, one-shot, mature)
DC Comics (Vertigo)

	GD25	FN65	NM94
1-Nancy Collins script; Paul Lee-c/a		2.40	6.00

DIARY CONFESSIONS (Formerly Ideal Romance)
No. 9, May, 1955 - No. 14, Apr, 1955
Stanmor/Key Publ.(Medal Comics)

	GD25	FN65	NM94
9	5.35	16.00	32.00
10-14	4.00	11.00	22.00

DIARY LOVES (Formerly Love Diary #1; G. I. Sweethearts #32 on)
No. 2, Nov, 1949 - No. 31, April, 1953
Quality Comics Group

	GD25	FN65	NM94
2-Ward-c/a, 9 pgs.	12.00	36.00	95.00
3 (1/50)-Photo-c begin, end #27?	4.25	13.00	28.00
4-Crandall-a	6.00	18.00	42.00
5-7,10	4.00	10.00	20.00
8,9-Ward-a 6,8 pgs. 8-Gustavson-a	8.50	26.00	60.00
11,13,14,17-20	4.00	10.00	20.00
12,15,16-Ward-a 9,7,8 pgs.	7.85	23.50	55.00
21-Ward-a, 7 pgs.	6.00	18.00	42.00
22-31: 31-Whitney-a	2.60	6.50	13.00

NOTE: *Photo c-3-10, 12-27.*

DIARY OF HORROR
December, 1952
Avon Periodicals

	GD25	FN65	NM94
1-Hollingsworth-c/a; bondage-c	31.00	92.00	225.00

DIARY SECRETS (Formerly Teen-Age Diary Secrets)
No. 10, Feb, 1952 - No. 30, Sept, 1955
St. John Publishing Co.

	GD25	FN65	NM94
10-Baker-c/a most issues	12.00	36.00	90.00
11-16,18,19	10.00	30.00	65.00
17,20: Kubert-r/Hollywood Confessions #1. 17-r/Teen Age Romances #9	10.00	30.00	65.00
21-30: 22,27-Signed stories by Estrada. 28-Last precode (3/55)	6.35	19.00	40.00

(See Giant Comics Edition for Annual)

DIATOM
Apr, 1995 ($4.95, unfinished limited series)
Photographics

	GD25	FN65	NM94
1-Photo/computer-a		2.00	5.00

DICK COLE (Sport Thrills No. 11 on)(See Blue Bolt & Four Most #1)
Dec-Jan, 1948-49 - No. 10, June-July, 1950
Curtis Publ./Star Publications

	GD25	FN65	NM94
1-Sgt. Spook; L. B. Cole-c; McWilliams-a; Curt Swan's 1st work	21.00	64.00	170.00

Dick Tracy #24 © Tribune Media Services

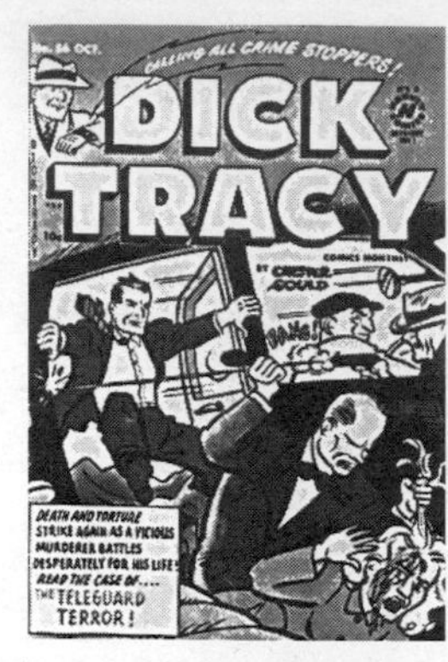

Dick Tracy #56 © Tribune Media Services

Dick Tracy #105 © Tribune Media Services

	GD25	FN65	NM94
2,5	10.00	30.00	80.00
3,4,6-10: All-L.B. Cole-c. 10-Joe Louis story	12.00	36.00	95.00
Accepted Reprint #7(V1#6 on-c)(1950's)-Reprints #7; L.B. Cole-c	5.70	17.00	38.00
Accepted Reprint #9(nd)-(Reprints #9 & #8-c)	5.70	17.00	38.00

NOTE: ***L. B. Cole** c-1, 3, 4, 6-10. **Al McWilliams** a-6. Dick Cole in 1-9. Baseball c-10. Basketball c-9. Football c-8.*

DICKIE DARE
1941 - No. 4, 1942 (#3 on sale 6/15/42)
Eastern Color Printing Co.

	GD25	FN65	NM94
1-Caniff-a, Everett-c	34.00	101.00	270.00
2	21.00	64.00	170.00
3,4-Half Scorchy Smith by Noel Sickles who was very influential in Milton Caniff's development	24.00	71.00	190.00

DICK POWELL (Also see A-1 Comics)
No. 22, 1949 (one shot)
Magazine Enterprises

	GD25	FN65	NM94
A-1 22-Photo-c	24.00	71.00	170.00

DICK QUICK, ACE REPORTER (See Picture News #10)

DICKS
1997 - No. 4, 1997 ($2.95, B&W)
Caliber Comics

	GD25	FN65	NM94
1-4-Ennis-s/McCrea-c/a; r/Fleetway		1.80	4.50

DICK'S ADVENTURES
No. 245, Sept, 1949
Dell Publishing Co.

	GD25	FN65	NM94
Four Color 245	4.50	13.50	50.00

DICK TRACY (See Famous Feature Stories, Harvey Comics Library, Limited Collectors' Ed., Mammoth Comics, Merry Christmas, The Original..., Popular Comics, Super Book No. 1, 7, 13, 25, Super Comics & Tastee-Freez)

DICK TRACY
May, 1937 - Jan, 1938
David McKay Publications

	GD25	FN65	NM94
Feature Books nn - 100 pgs., partially reprinted as 4-Color No. 1 (appeared before Large Feature Comics, 1st Dick Tracy comic book) (Very Rare-three known copies) Estimated Value....	600.00	1800.00	6000.00
Feature Books 4 - Reprints nn ish. w/new-c	110.00	330.00	1100.00
Feature Books 6,9	80.00	240.00	800.00

DICK TRACY (...Monthly #1-24)
1939 - No. 24, Dec, 1949
Dell Publishing Co.

	GD25	FN65	NM94
Large Feature Comic 1 (1939) -Dick Tracy Meets The Blank	118.00	355.00	1300.00
Large Feature Comic 4,8	59.00	177.00	650.00
Large Feature Comic 11,13,15	68.00	205.00	750.00

	GD25	FN65	VF82	NM94
Four Color 1(1939)('35-r)	590.00	1775.00	3540.00	6500.00

(Estimated up to 75+ total copies exist, 5 in NM/Mint)

	GD25	FN65	NM94
Four Color 6(1940)('37-r)-(Scarce)	134.00	400.00	1470.00
Four Color 8(1940)('38-'39-r)	67.00	200.00	735.00
Large Feature Comic 3(1941, Series II)	58.00	175.00	640.00
Four Color 21('41)('38-r)	57.00	170.00	625.00
Four Color 34('43)('39-'40-r)	39.00	116.00	425.00
Four Color 56('44)('40-r)	31.00	83.00	340.00
Four Color 96('46)('40-r)	22.00	67.00	245.00
Four Color 133('47)('40-'41-r)	19.00	57.00	210.00
Four Color 163('47)('41-r)	15.00	45.00	165.00
Four Color 215('48)-Titled "Sparkle Plenty", Tracy-r	9.00	27.00	100.00
1(1/48)('34-r)	36.00	107.00	390.00
2,3	19.00	57.00	210.00
4-10	18.00	55.00	200.00
11-18: 13-Bondage-c	12.00	37.00	135.00
19-1st app. Sparkle Plenty, B.O. Plenty & Gravel Gertie in a 3-pg. strip not by Gould	13.00	40.00	145.00
20-1st app. Sam Catchem; c/a not by Gould	10.00	30.00	110.00
21-24-Only 2 pg. Gould-a in each	10.00	30.00	110.00

NOTE: *No. 19-24 have a 2 pg. biography of a famous villain illustrated by **Gould**: 19-Little Face; 20-Flattop; 21-Breathless Mahoney; 22-Measles; 23-Itchy; 24-The Brow.*

DICK TRACY (Continued from Dell series)(...Comics Monthly #25-140)
No. 25, Mar, 1950 - No. 145, April, 1961
Harvey Publications

	GD25	FN65	NM94
25-Flat Top-c/story (also #26,27)	16.50	49.50	165.00
26-28,30: 28-Bondage-c. 28,29-The Brow-c/stories	11.50	34.50	115.00
29-1st app. Gravel Gertie in a Gould-r	15.50	46.50	155.00
31,32,34,35,37-40: 40-Intro/origin 2-way wrist radio (6/51)	10.50	31.50	105.00
33- "Measles the Teen-Age Dope Pusher"	11.50	34.50	115.00
36-1st app. B.O. Plenty in a Gould-r	11.50	34.50	115.00
41-50	8.50	25.50	85.00
51-56,58-80: 51-2pgs Powell-a	7.50	22.50	75.00
57-1st app. Sam Catchem in a Gould-r	9.50	28.50	95.00
81-99,101-140	5.80	17.40	58.00
100	6.50	19.50	65.00
141-145 (25¢)(titled "Dick Tracy")	5.80	17.40	58.00

NOTE: ***Powell** a(1-2pgs.)-43, 44, 104, 108, 109, 145. No. 110-120, 141-145 are all reprints from earlier issues.*

DICK TRACY
12/84 - No. 24, 6/89 (1-12: $5.95; 13-24: $6.95, B&W, 76 pgs.)
Blackthorne Publishing

	GD25	FN65	NM94
1-3-1st printings; hard-c ed. ($14.95)	1.85	5.50	15.00
1-3-1st printings; squarebound. thick-c		2.40	6.00
1-3-2nd printings, 1986; hard-c ed.	1.85	5.50	15.00
1-3-2nd printings, 1986; squarebound, thick-c		2.40	6.00
4-8-Hardcover ed. ($14.95)	1.85	5.50	15.00
4-12: Squarebound, thick-c		2.40	6.00
13-24 ($6.95): 21,22-Regular-c & stapled	1.00	2.80	7.00

NOTE: **Gould** daily & Sunday strip-r in all. 1-12 r-12/31/45-4/5/49; 13-24 r-7/13/41-2/20/44.

DICK TRACY (Disney)
1990 - No. 3, 1990 (color) (Book 3 adapts 1990 movie)
WD Publications

	GD25	FN65	NM94
Book One ($3.95, 52pgs.)-Kyle Baker-c/a		1.60	4.00
Book Two, Three ($5.95, 68pgs.)-Direct sale		2.40	6.00
Book Two, Three ($2.95, 68pgs.)-Newsstand		1.20	3.00

DICK TRACY ADVENTURES
May, 1991 ($4.95, 76 pgs.)
Gladstone Publishing

	GD25	FN65	NM94
1-Reprints strips 2/1/42-4/18/42		2.00	5.00

DICK TRACY, EXPLOITS OF
1946 ($1.00, hard-c strip reprints)
Rosdon Books, Inc.

	GD25	FN65	NM94
1-Reprints the near complete case of "The Brow" from 6/12/44 to 9/24/44 (story starts a few weeks late)	22.00	66.00	175.00
with dust jacket...	36.00	108.00	300.00

DICK TRACY GIVEAWAYS
1939 - 1958; 1990

	GD25	FN65	NM94
Buster Brown Shoes Giveaway (1940s?, 36 pgs. in color); 1938-39-r by Gould	29.00	88.00	235.00
Gillmore Giveaway (See Superbook)			
...Hatful of Fun (No date, 1950-52, 32pgs.; 8-1/2x10")-Dick Tracy hat promotion; Dick Tracy games, magic tricks. Miller Bros. premium	14.00	41.00	110.00

Die Cut #4 © MEG

Dilton's Strange Science #3 © Archie

Ding Dong #3 © Compix

GD25 FN65 NM94

Motorola Giveaway (1953)-Reprints Harvey Comics Library #2; "The Case of the Sparkle Plenty TV Mystery" 5.00 15.00 30.00
Original Dick Tracy by Chester Gould, The (Aug, 1990, 16 pgs., 5-1/2x8-1/2")-Gladstone Publ.; Bread Giveaway 2.50 7.50 20.00
Popped Wheat Giveaway (1947, 16 pgs. in color)-1940-r; Sig Feuchtwanger Publ.; Gould-a 2.00 5.00 10.00
...Presents the Family Fun Book; Tip Top Bread Giveaway, no date or number (1940, Fawcett Publ., 16 pgs. in color)-Spy Smasher, Ibis, Lance O'Casey app. 50.00 50.00 450.00
Same as above but without app. of heroes & Dick Tracy on cover only 9.50 28.00 75.00
Service Station Giveaway (1958, 16 pgs. in color)(regular size, slick cover)-Harvey Info. Press 3.60 9.00 18.00
Shoe Store Giveaway (Weatherbird)(1939, 16 pgs.)-Gould-a 12.00 36.00 95.00

DICK TRACY MONTHLY/WEEKLY
May, 1986 - No. 99, 1989 ($2.00, B&W) (Becomes Weekly #26 on)
Blackthorne Publishing
1-99: Gould-r. 30,31-Mr. Crime app. .80 2.00
NOTE: *#1-10 reprint strips 3/10/40-7/13/41; #10(pg.8)-51 reprint strips 4/6/49-12/31/55; #52-99 reprint strips 12/26/56-4/26/64.*

DICK TRACY SHEDS LIGHT ON THE MOLE
1949 (16 pgs.) (Ray-O-Vac Flashlights giveaway)
Western Printing Co.
nn-Not by Gould 5.70 17.00 40.00

DICK TRACY SPECIAL
Jan, 1988 - No. 3, Aug. (no month), 1989 ($2.95, B&W)
Blackthorne Publishing
1-3: 1-Origin D. Tracy; 4/strips 10/12/31-3/30/32 1.20 3.00

DICK TRACY: THE EARLY YEARS
Aug, 1987 - No. 4, Aug (no month) 1989 ($6.95, B&W, 76 pgs.)
Blackthorne Publishing
1-3: 1-4-r/strips 10/12/31(1st daily)-8/31/32 & Sunday strips 6/12/32-8/28/32; Big Boy apps. in #1-3 1.00 2.80 7.00
4 ($2.95, 52pgs.) 1.20 3.00

DICK TRACY UNPRINTED STORIES
Sept, 1987 - No. 4, June, 1988 ($2.95, B&W)
Blackthorne Publishing
1-4: Reprints strips 1/1/56-12/25/56 1.20 3.00

DICK TURPIN (See Legend of Young...)

DICK WINGATE OF THE U.S. NAVY
1951; 1953 (no month)
Superior Publ./Toby Press
nn-U.S. Navy giveaway 2.40 6.00 12.00
1(1953, Toby)-Reprints nn issue? (same-c) 4.00 10.00 20.00

DIE-CUT
Nov, 1993 - No. 4, Feb, 1994 ($1.75, limited series)
Marvel Comics UK, Ltd
1-($2.50)-Die-cut-c; The Beast app. 1.00 2.50
2-4 .70 1.75

DIE-CUT VS. G-FORCE
Nov, 1993 - No. 2, Dec, 1993 ($2.75, limited series)
Marvel Comics UK, Ltd
1,2-($2.75)-Gold foil-c on both 1.10 2.75

DIE, MONSTER, DIE (See Movie Classics)

DIESEL
Apr, 1997 - Present ($2.95)
Antarctic Press
1 2.95

DIG 'EM
1973 (2-3/8x6", 16 pgs.)
Kellogg's Sugar Smacks Giveaway
nn-4 different issues 2.00 5.00

DIGITEK
Dec, 1992 - No. 4, Mar, 1993 ($1.95/$2.25, mini-series)
Marvel Comics UK, Ltd
1,2 ($1.95) .80 2.00
3,4 ($2.25): 3-Deathlock-c/story .90 2.25

DILLY (Dilly Duncan from Daredevil Comics; see Boy Comics #57)
May, 1953 - No. 3, Sept, 1953
Lev Gleason Publications
1-Teenage; Biro-c 5.00 15.00 30.00
2,3-Biro-c 4.00 10.00 20.00

DILTON'S STRANGE SCIENCE (See Pep Comics #78)
May, 1989 - No. 5, May, 1990 (75¢/$1.00)
Archie Comics
1-5 1.00

DIME COMICS
1945; 1951
Newsbook Publ. Corp.
1-Silver Streak-c/story; L. B. Cole-c 38.00 113.00 340.00
1(1951), 5 4.00 10.00 20.00

DINGBATS (See 1st Issue Special)

DING DONG
Summer?, 1946 - No. 5, 1947 (52 pgs.)
Compix/Magazine Enterprises
1-Funny animal 15.00 45.00 120.00
2 (9/46) 8.50 26.00 60.00
3 (Wint '46-'47) - 5 7.15 21.50 50.00

DINKY DUCK (Paul Terry's...) (See Blue Ribbon, Giant Comics Edition #5A & New Terrytoons)
Nov, 1951 - No. 16, Sept, 1955; No. 16, Fall, 1956; No. 17, May, 1957 - No. 19, Summer, 1958
St. John Publishing Co./Pines No. 16 on
1-Funny animal 8.75 26.25 70.00
2 5.70 17.00 35.00
3-10 4.00 11.00 22.00
11-16(9/55) 3.20 8.00 16.00
16(Fall,'56) - 19 2.40 6.00 12.00

DINKY DUCK & HASHIMOTO-SAN (See Deputy Dawg Presents...)

DINO (TV)(The Flintstones)
Aug, 1973 - No. 20, Jan, 1977 (Hanna-Barbera)
Charlton Publications
1 2.50 7.50 20.00
2-10 1.50 4.50 12.00
11-20 1.10 3.30 9.00

DINO ISLAND
Feb, 1994 - No. 2, Mar, 1994 ($2.75, limited series)
Mirage Studios
1,2-By Jim Lawson 1.10 2.75

DINO RIDERS
Feb, 1989 - No. 3, 1989 ($1.00)
Marvel Comics
1-3: Based on toys 1.00

DINOSAUR REX

Dinosaurs For Hire #11 © Tom Mason

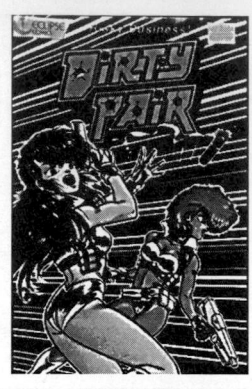

Dirty Pair #2 © ECL

Disney Action Club #1 © WDC

GD25 FN65 NM94

1986 - No. 3, 1986 ($2.00, limited series)
Upshot Graphics (Fantagraphics Books)

1-3 .80 2.00

DINOSAURS, A CELEBRATION
Oct, 1992 - No. 4, Oct, 1992 ($4.95, limited series, 52 pgs.)
Marvel Comics (Epic Comics)

1-4: 2-Bolton painted-c 2.00 5.00

DINOSAURS ATTACK! THE GRAPHIC NOVEL
1991 - Book 3, 1992 ($3.95, limited series, coated stock, stiff-c)
Eclipse Comics

Book One - Three: Based on Topps trading cards 1.60 4.00

DINOSAURS FOR HIRE
Feb, 1993 - No. 12, Feb, 1994 ($1.95/$2.50)
Malibu Comics

1-Flip book .80 2.00
2-12: 8-($2.50)-Bagged w/Skycap; Staton-c. 10-Flip book 1.00 2.50

DINOSAURS GRAPHIC NOVEL (TV)
1992 - No. 2, 1993 ($2.95, 52 pgs.)
Disney Comics

1,2-Staton-a; based on Dinosaurs TV show 1.20 3.00

DINOSAURUS
No. 1120, Aug, 1960
Dell Publishing Co.

Four Color 1120-Movie, painted-c 6.40 19.00 70.00

DIPPY DUCK
October, 1957
Atlas Comics (OPI)

1-Maneely-a; code approved 6.50 19.50 45.00

DIRECTORY TO A NONEXISTENT UNIVERSE
Dec, 1987 ($2.00, B&W)
Eclipse Comics

1 .80 2.00

DIRTY DOZEN (See Movie Classics)

DIRTY PAIR (Manga)
Dec, 1988 - No. 4, Apr, 1989 ($2.00, B&W, limited series)
Eclipse Comics

1-4: Japanese manga with original stories .80 2.00

DIRTY PAIR: FATAL BUT NOT SERIOUS (Manga)
July, 1995 - No. 5, Nov, 1995 ($2.95, limited series)
Dark Horse Comics

1-5 1.20 3.00

DIRTY PAIR: SIM HELL (Manga)
May, 1993 - No. 4, Aug, 1993 ($2.50, B&W, limited series)
Dark Horse Comics

1-4 1.00 2.50

DIRTY PAIR II (Manga)
June, 1989 - No. 5, Mar, 1990 ($2.00, B&W, limited series)
Eclipse Comics

1-5: 3-Cover is misnumbered as #1 .80 2.00

DIRTY PAIR III, THE (A Plague of Angels) (Manga)
Aug, 1990 - No. 5, Aug, 1991 ($2.00, B&W, limited series)
Eclipse Comics

1,2 .80 2.00
3-5: ($2.25) .90 2.25

DISHMAN
Sept, 1988 ($2.50, B&W, 52 pgs.)
Eclipse Comics

1 1.00 2.50

DISNEY AFTERNOON, THE (TV)
Nov, 1994 - No. 10?, Aug, 1995 ($1.50)
Marvel Comics

1-10: 3-w/bound-in Power Ranger Barcode Card 1.00 2.50

DISNEY COMIC ALBUM
1990(no month, year) - No. 8, 1991 ($6.95/$7.95)
Disney Comics

1,2 ($6.95): 1-Donald Duck and Gyro Gearloose by Barks(r). 2-Uncle Scrooge by Barks(r); Jr. Woodchucks app. 1.00 2.80 7.00
3-8: 3-Donald Duck-r/F.C. 308 by Barks; begin $7.95-c. 4-Mickey Mouse Meets the Phantom Blot; r/M.M Club Parade(censored 1956 version of story). 5-Chip `n' Dale Rescue Rangers; new-a. 6-Uncle Scrooge. 7-Donald Duck in Too Many Pets; Barks-r(4) including F.C. #29. 8-Super Goof; r/S.G. #1, D.D. #102 1.00 3.00 8.00

DISNEY COMIC HITS
Oct, 1995 - Present ($1.50/$2.50)
Marvel Comics

1-9,11-15: 4-Toy Story. 6-Aladdin. 7-Pocahontas. 13-Aladdin and the Forty Thieves 1.00 2.50
10-(7/96, $2.50)-The Hunchback of Notre Dame (Same story in Disney's The Hunchback of Notre Dame) 1.40 3.50

DISNEY COMICS
June, 1990
Disney Comics

Boxed set of #1 issues includes Donald Duck Advs., Ducktales, Chip 'n Dale Rescue Rangers, Roger Rabbit, Mickey Mouse Advs. & Goofy Advs.; limited to 10,000 sets 1.10 3.30 9.00

DISNEYLAND BIRTHDAY PARTY (Also see Dell Giants)
Aug, 1985 ($2.50)
Gladstone Publishing Co.

1-Reprints Dell Giant with new-photo-c 1.50 4.50 12.00
...Comics Digest #1-(Digest) 1.25 3.75 10.00

DISNEYLAND MAGAZINE
Feb. 15, 1972 - ? (10-1/4"x12-5/8", 20 pgs, weekly)
Fawcett Publications

1-One or two page painted art features on Dumbo, Snow White, Lady & the Tramp, the Aristocats, Brer Rabbit, Peter Pan, Cinderella, Jungle Book, Alice & Pinocchio. Most standard characters app. 2.50 7.50 20.00

DISNEYLAND, USA (See Dell Giant No. 30)

DISNEY MOVIE BOOK
1990 ($7.95, 8-1/2"x11", 52 pgs.)(w/pull-out poster)
Walt Disney Productions (Gladstone)

1-Roger Rabbit in Tummy Trouble; from the cartoon film strips adapted to the comic format. Ron Dias-c 1.50 4.50 12.00

DISNEY'S ACTION CLUB
1997 - Present ($4.50, digest size)
Acclaim Books

1-4: 1-Hercules. 4-Mighty Ducks 4.50

DISNEY'S ALADDIN (Movie)
Oct, 1994 - No. 11, 1995 ($1.50)
Marvel Comics

1-11 1.00 2.50

DISNEY'S BEAUTY AND THE BEAST (Movie)
Sept, 1994 - No. 13, 1995 ($1.50)
Marvel Comics

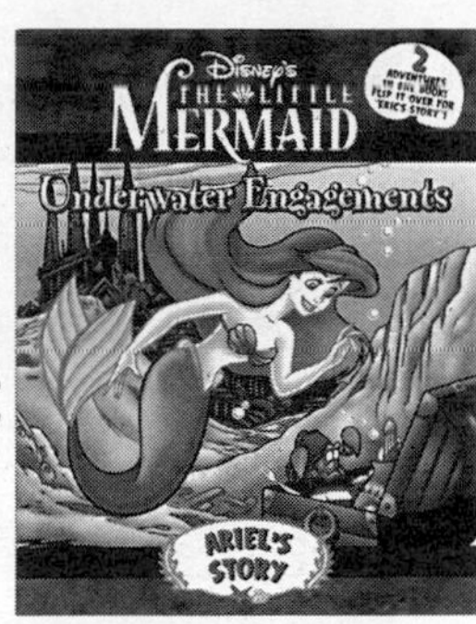

Disney's The Little Mermaid: Underwater Engagements #1 © WDC

A Distant Soil #21 © Colleen Doran

Division 13 #1 © DH

	GD25	FN65	NM94
1-13		1.00	2.50

DISNEY'S BEAUTY AND THE BEAST HOLIDAY SPECIAL
1997 ($4.50, digest size, one-shot)
Acclaim Books

1-Based on The Enchanted Christmas video			4.50

DISNEY'S COLOSSAL COMICS COLLECTION
1991 - No. 10, 1993 ($1.95, digest-size, 96/132 pgs.)
Disney Comics

1-10: Ducktales, Talespin, Chip 'n Dale's Rescue Rangers. 4-r/Darkwing Duck #1-4. 6-Goofy begins. 8-Little Mermaid		1.20	3.00

DISNEY'S COMICS IN 3-D
1992 ($2.95, w/glasses, polybagged)
Disney Comics

1-Infinity-c; Barks, Rosa, Gottfredson-r		1.60	4.00

DISNEY'S ENCHANTING STORIES
1997 - Present ($4.50, digest size)
Acclaim Books

1-5: 1-Hercules. 2-Pocahontas			1.50

DISNEY'S NEW ADVENTURES OF BEAUTY AND THE BEAST (Also see Beauty and the Beast & Disney's Beauty and the Beast)
1992 - No. 2, 1992 ($1.50, limited series)
Disney Comics

1,2-New stories based on movie		1.00	2.50

DISNEY'S POCAHONTAS (Movie)
1995 ($4.95, one-shot)
Marvel Comics

1-Movie adaptation		2.40	6.00

DISNEY'S TALESPIN LIMITED SERIES: "TAKE OFF" (TV) (See Talespin)
Jan, 1991 - No. 4, Apr, 1991 ($1.50, limited series, 52 pgs.)
W. D. Publications (Disney Comics)

1-4: Based on animated series; 4 part origin		.80	2.00

DISNEY'S THE LION KING (Movie)
July, 1994 - No. 2, July, 1994 ($1.50, limited series)
Marvel Comics

1,2: 2-part movie adaptation		1.00	2.50
1-($2.50, 52 pgs.)-Complete story		1.40	3.50

DISNEY'S THE LITTLE MERMAID (Movie)
Sept, 1994 - No. 12, 1995 ($1.50)
Marvel Comics

1-12		1.00	2.50

DISNEY'S THE LITTLE MERMAID LIMITED SERIES (Movie)
Feb, 1992 - No. 4, May, 1992 ($1.50, limited series)
Disney Comics

1-4: Peter David scripts		1.00	2.50

DISNEY'S THE LITTLE MERMAID: UNDERWATER ENGAGEMENTS
1997 ($4.50, digest size)
Acclaim Books

1-Flip book			4.50

DISNEY'S THE HUNCHBACK OF NOTRE DAME (Movie)(See Disney's Comic Hits #10)
July, 1996 ($4.95, squarebound, one-shot)
Marvel Comics

1-Movie adaptation.		2.40	6.00

NOTE: *A different edition of this series was sold at Wal-Mart stores with new covers depicting scenes from the 1989 feature film. Inside contents and price were identical.*

DISNEY'S THE THREE MUSKETEERS (Movie)
Jan, 1994 - No. 2, Feb, 1994 ($1.50, limited series)
Marvel Comics

	GD25	FN65	NM94
1,2-Morrow-c; Spiegle-a; Movie adaptation		.80	2.00

DISNEY'S TOY STORY (Movie)
Dec, 1995 ($4.95, one-shot)
Marvel Comics

nn-Adaptation of film		2.40	6.00

DISTANT SOIL, A (1st Series)
Dec, 1983 - No. 9, Mar 1986 ($1.50, B&W)
WaRP Graphics

1-9			1.50

NOTE: Second printings exist of #1, 2, 3 & 6.

DISTANT SOIL, A
Mar, 1989 ($12.95, trade paperback)
Donning (Star Blaze)

nn-new material			13.00

DISTANT SOIL, A (2nd Series)
June, 1991 - Present ($1.75/$2.50/$2.95, B&W)
Aria Press/Image Comics (Highbrow Entertainment) #15 on

1-8		1.00	2.50
9-12: 9-$2.50-c begins		1.00	2.50
13-21: 13-$2.95-c begins. 14-Sketchbook. 15-(8/96)-1st Image issue.		1.20	3.00
The Gathering ('97, $18.95,TPB) r/#1-13; intro. Neil Gaiman			18.95

NOTE: Four separate printings exist for #1 and are clearly marked. Second printings exist of #2-4 and are also clearly marked.

DISTANT SOIL, A: IMMIGRANT SONG
Aug, 1987 ($6.95, trade paperback)
Donning (Star Blaze)

nn-new material			7.00

DIVER DAN (TV)
Feb-Apr, 1962 - No. 2, June-Aug, 1962
Dell Publishing Co.

Four Color 1254(#1), 2	4.50	13.50	50.00

DIVINE RIGHT
Sept, 1997 - Present ($2.50)
Image Comics (WildStorm Productions)

1-Jim Lee-s/a(p); two covers by Lee & Charest		1.20	3.00
1-($3.50)-Voyager Pack w/Stormwatch preview			3.50
2,3: 2: Two covers by Lee. 3-Fairchild & Lynch app.			2.50

DIVISION 13 (See Comic's Greatest World)
Sept, 1994 - Jan, 1995 ($2.50, color)
Dark Horse Comics

1-4: Giffen story in all. 1-Art Adams-c		1.00	2.50

DIXIE DUGAN (See Big Shot, Columbia Comics & Feature Funnies)
July, 1942 - No. 13, 1949 (Strip reprints in all)
McNaught Syndicate/Columbia/Publication Ent.

1-Joe Palooka x-over by Ham Fisher	24.00	71.00	190.00
2	13.00	39.00	105.00
3	9.50	28.00	75.00
4,5(1945-46)-Bo strip-r	7.15	21.50	50.00
6-13(1/47-49): 6-Paperdoll cut-outs	5.70	17.00	38.00

DIXIE DUGAN
V3#1, Nov, 1951 - V4#4, Feb, 1954
Prize Publications (Headline)

V3#1	6.50	19.50	45.00
2-4	5.00	15.00	30.00
V4#1-4(#5-8)	4.00	12.00	24.00

DNAgents #22 © ECL

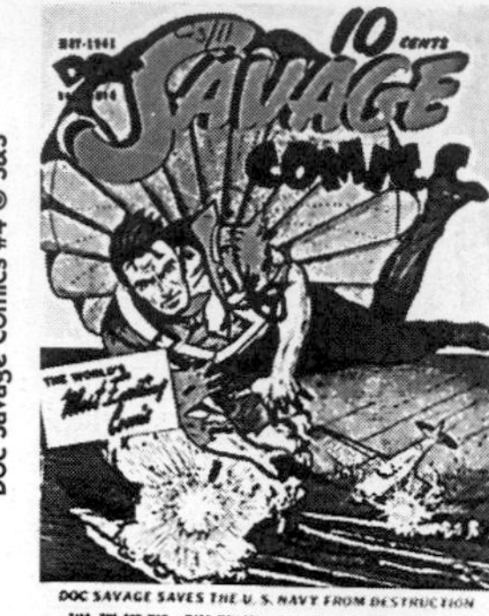

Doc Savage Comics #4 © S&S

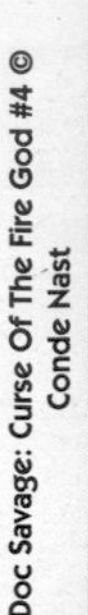
Doc Savage: Curse Of The Fire God #4 © Conde Nast

DIZZY DAMES
Sept-Oct, 1952 - No. 6, July-Aug, 1953
American Comics Group (B&M Distr. Co.)

	GD25	FN65	NM94
1-Whitney-c	8.75	26.25	65.00
2	5.70	17.00	38.00
3-6	5.00	15.00	30.00

DIZZY DON COMICS
1942 - No. 22, Oct, 1946; No. 3, Apr, 1947 (Most B&W)
F. E. Howard Publications/Dizzy Don Ent. Ltd (Canada)

	GD25	FN65	NM94
1 (B&W)	8.50	26.00	60.00
2 (B&W)	5.00	15.00	30.00
4-21 (B&W)	4.25	13.00	28.00
22-Full color, 52 pgs.	8.50	26.00	60.00
3 (4/47)-Full color, 52 pgs.	7.15	21.50	50.00

DIZZY DUCK (Formerly Barnyard Comics)
No. 32, Nov, 1950 - No. 39, Mar, 1952
Standard Comics

	GD25	FN65	NM94
32-Funny animal	7.15	21.50	50.00
33-39	4.15	12.50	25.00

DNAGENTS (The New DNAgents V2/1 on)(Also see Surge)
March, 1983 - No. 24, July, 1985 ($1.50, Baxter paper)
Eclipse Comics

	GD25	FN65	NM94
1-10: 1-Origin. 4-Amber app. 9-Spiegle-a			1.50
11-24: 18-Infinity-c. 24-Dave Stevens-c			1.50

DOBERMAN (See Sgt. Bilko's Private...)

DOBIE GILLIS (See The Many Loves of...)

DOC CARTER VD COMICS
1949 (16 pgs. in color) (Paper-c)
Health Publications Institute, Raleigh, N. C. (Giveaway)

	GD25	FN65	NM94
nn	17.00	51.00	135.00

DOC CHAOS: THE STRANGE ATTRACTOR
Apr, 1990 - #3, 1990 ($3.00, 32 pgs.)
Vortex Comics

	GD25	FN65	NM94
1-3: The Lust For Order		1.20	3.00

DOC SAMSON (Also see Incredible Hulk)
Jan, 1996 - No. 4, Apr, 1996 ($1.95, limited series)
Marvel Comics

	GD25	FN65	NM94
1-4: 1-Hulk c/app. 2-She-Hulk-c/app. 3-Punisher-c/app. 4-Polaris-c/app.		.80	2.00

DOC SAVAGE
Nov, 1966
Gold Key

	GD25	FN65	NM94
1-Adaptation of the Thousand-Headed Man; James Bama c-r/1964 Doc Savage paperback	9.00	26.00	95.00

DOC SAVAGE (Also see Giant-Size...)
Oct, 1972 - No. 8, Jan, 1974
Marvel Comics Group

	GD25	FN65	NM94
1	1.25	3.75	10.00
2,3-Steranko-c	1.00	2.80	7.00
4-8		2.00	5.00

NOTE: ***Gil Kane** c-5, 6. **Mooney** a-1i. No. 1, 2 adapts pulp story "The Man of Bronze"; No. 3, 4 adapts "Death in Silver"; No. 5, 6 adapts "The Monsters"; No. 7, 8 adapts "The Brand of The Werewolf".*

DOC SAVAGE (Magazine)
Aug, 1975 - No. 8, Spring, 1977 ($1.00, B&W)
Marvel Comics Group

	GD25	FN65	NM94
1-Cover from movie poster; Ron Ely photo-c	1.00	2.80	7.00
2-8: 1,3-Buscema-a. 5-Adams-a(1 pg.), Rogers-a(1 pg)		1.60	4.00

DOC SAVAGE
Nov, 1987 - No. 4, Feb, 1988 ($1.75, limited series)
DC Comics

	GD25	FN65	NM94
1-4		.70	1.75

DOC SAVAGE
Nov, 1988 - No. 24, Oct, 1990 ($1.75/$2.00: #13-24)
DC Comics

	GD25	FN65	NM94
1-24		.80	2.00
Annual 1 (1989, $3.50, 68 pgs.)		1.40	3.50

DOC SAVAGE COMICS (Also see Shadow Comics)
May, 1940 - No. 20, Oct, 1943 (1st app. in Doc Savage pulp, 3/33)
Street & Smith Publications

	GD25	FN65	NM94
1-Doc Savage, Cap Fury, Danny Garrett, Mark Mallory, The Whisperer, Captain Death, Billy the Kid, Sheriff Pete & Treasure Island begin; Norgil, the Magician app.	380.00	1140.00	3800.00
2-Origin & 1st app. Ajax, the Sun Man; Danny Garrett, The Whisperer end	122.00	366.00	1100.00
3	97.00	291.00	875.00
4-Treasure Island ends; Tuska-a	81.00	243.00	725.00
5-Origin & 1st app. Astron, the Crocodile Queen, not in #9 & 11; Norgi the Magician app.	61.00	183.00	550.00
6-10: 6-Cap Fury ends; origin & only app. Red Falcon in Astron story. 8-Mark Mallory ends; Charlie McCarthy app. on-c plus true life story. 9-Supersnipe app. 10-Origin & only app. The Thunderbolt	50.00	150.00	450.00
11,12	43.00	129.00	385.00
V2#1-8(#13-20): 16-The Pulp Hero, The Avenger app.; Fanny Brice story. 17-Sun Man ends; Nick Carter begins; Duffy's Tavern part photo-c & story. 18-Huckleberry Finn part-c/story. 19-Henny Youngman part photo-c & life story. 20-Only all funny-c w/Huckleberry Finn	43.00	129.00	385.00

DOC SAVAGE: CURSE OF THE FIRE GOD
Sept, 1995 - No, 4, Dec, 1995 ($2.95, limited series)
Dark Horse Comics

	GD25	FN65	NM94
1-4		1.20	3.00

DOC SAVAGE: THE MAN OF BRONZE
1991 - No. 4, 1991 ($2.50, limited series)
Millennium Publications

	GD25	FN65	NM94
1-4: 1-Bronze logo		1.00	2.50
...: The Manual of Bronze 1 ($2.50, B&W, color, one-shot)-Unpublished proposed Doc Savage strip in color, B&W strip-r		1.00	2.50

DOC SAVAGE: THE MAN OF BRONZE, DOOM DYNASTY
1992 (Says 1991) - No. 2, 1992 ($2.50, limited series)
Millennium Publications

	GD25	FN65	NM94
1,2		1.00	2.50

DOC SAVAGE: THE MAN OF BRONZE - REPEL
1992 ($2.50)
Innovation Publishing

	GD25	FN65	NM94
1-Dave Dorman painted-c		1.00	2.50

DOC SAVAGE: THE MAN OF BRONZE THE DEVIL'S THOUGHTS
1992 (Says 1991) - No. 2, 1992 ($2.50, limited series)
Millennium Publications

	GD25	FN65	NM94
1,2		1.00	2.50

DOC STEARN...MR. MONSTER (See Mr. Monster)

DR. ANTHONY KING, HOLLYWOOD LOVE DOCTOR
1952(Jan) - No. 3, May, 1953; No. 4, May, 1954
Minoan Publishing Corp./Harvey Publications No. 4

	GD25	FN65	NM94
1	10.00	30.00	70.00
2-4: 4-Powell-a	6.70	20.00	40.00

DR. ANTHONY'S LOVE CLINIC (See Mr. Anthony's...)

Dr. Fate #10 © DC

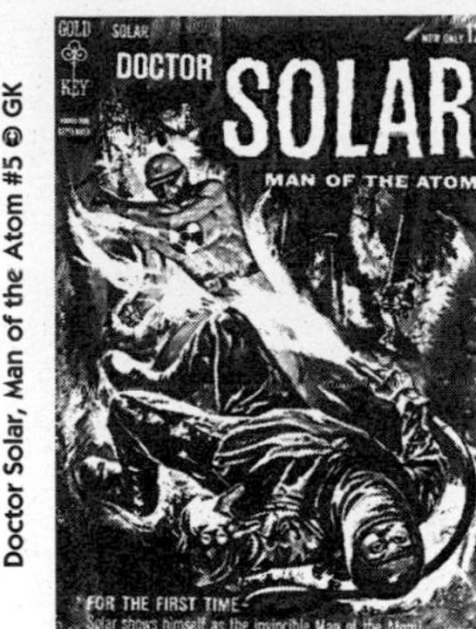

Doctor Solar, Man of the Atom #5 © GK

Doctor Strange #169(#1) © MEG

GD25 FN65 NM94

DR. BOBBS
No. 212, Jan, 1949
Dell Publishing Co.

	GD25	FN65	NM94
Four Color 212	3.00	10.00	36.00

DOCTOR BOOGIE
1987 ($1.75)
Media Arts Publishing

	GD25	FN65	NM94
1-Airbrush waparound-c; Nick Cuti-i		.70	1.80

DOCTOR CHAOS
Nov, 1993 - No. 6, Mar, 1994 ($2.50)
Triumphant Comics

	GD25	FN65	NM94
1-6: 1,2-Triumphant Unleashed x-over. 2-1st app. War Dancer in pin-up. 3-Intro The Cry		1.00	2.50

DOCTOR CYBORG
1996 - Present ($2.95, B&W)
Attention! Publishing

	GD25	FN65	NM94
1,2		1.20	3.00

DR. DOOM'S REVENGE
1989 (Came w/computer game from Paragon Software)
Marvel Comics

	GD25	FN65	NM94
V1#1-Spider-Man & Captain America fight Dr. Doom			1.00

DR. FATE (See 1st Issue Special, The Immortal..., Justice League, More Fun #55, & Showcase)

DOCTOR FATE
July, 1987 - No. 4, Oct, 1987 ($1.50, limited series, Baxter paper)
DC Comics

	GD25	FN65	NM94
1-4: Giffen-c/a in all			1.50

DOCTOR FATE
Winter, 1988-'89 - No. 41, June, 1992 ($1.25/$1.50 #5 on)
DC Comics

	GD25	FN65	NM94
1-31: 15-Justice League app. 25-1st new Dr. Fate		.75	1.50
32-41: 32-Begin $1.75-c. 36-Original Dr. returns		.70	1.75
Annual 1(1989, $2.95, 68 pgs.)-Sutton-a		1.20	3.00

DR. FU MANCHU (See The Mask of...)
1964
I.W. Enterprises

	GD25	FN65	NM94
1-r/Avon's "Mask of Dr. Fu Manchu"; Wood-a	6.50	19.50	65.00

DR. GIGGLES (See Dark Horse Presents #64-66)
Oct, 1992 - No. 2, Oct, 1992 ($2.50, limited series)
Dark Horse Comics

	GD25	FN65	NM94
1,2-Based on movie		1.00	2.50

DOCTOR GRAVES (Formerly The Many Ghosts of...)
No. 73, Sept, 1985 - No. 75, Jan, 1986
Charlton Comics

	GD25	FN65	NM94
73-75			1.00

DR. JEKYLL AND MR. HYDE (See A Star Presentation & Supernatural Thrillers #4)

DR. KILDARE (TV)
No. 1337, 4-6/62 - No. 9, 4-6/65 (All Richard Chamberlain photo-c)
Dell Publishing Co.

	GD25	FN65	NM94
Four Color 1337(#1, 1962)	8.00	25.00	90.00
2-9	5.00	15.00	55.00

DR. MASTERS (See The Adventures of Young...)

DOCTOR SOLAR, MAN OF THE ATOM (Also see The Occult Files of Dr. Spektor #14 & Solar)
10/62 - No. 27, 4/69; No. 28, 4/81 - No. 31, 3/82 (1-27 have painted-c)
Gold Key/Whitman No. 28 on

GD25 FN65 NM94

	GD25	FN65	NM94
1-(#10000-210)-Origin/1st app. Dr. Solar (1st original Gold Key character)	18.00	55.00	200.00
2-Prof. Harbinger begins	7.00	20.00	75.00
3,4	4.50	13.50	50.00
5-Intro. Man of the Atom in costume	5.00	15.00	55.00
6-10	2.75	8.00	30.00
11-14,16-20	1.80	5.50	20.00
15-Origin retold	2.25	6.75	25.00
21-27	1.85	5.50	15.00
28-31: 29-Magnus Robot Fighter begins. 31-The Sentinel app.	1.00	3.00	8.00

NOTE: ***Frank Bolle** a-6-19, 29-31; c-29i, 30i. **Bob Fugitani** a-1-5. **Spiegle** a-29-31. **Al McWilliams** a-20-23.*

DOCTOR SOLAR, MAN OF THE ATOM
1990 - No. 2, 1991 ($7.95, card stock-c, high quality, 96 pgs.)
Valiant Comics

	GD25	FN65	NM94
1,2: Reprints Gold Key series	1.00	3.00	8.00

DOCTOR SPEKTOR (See The Occult Files of..., & Spine-Tingling Tales)

DOCTOR STRANGE (Formerly Strange Tales #1-168) (Also see The Defenders, Giant-Size..., Marvel Fanfare, Marvel Graphic Novel, Marvel Premiere, Marvel Treasury Edition & Strange Tales, 2nd Series)
No. 169, 6/68 - No. 183, 11/69; 6/74 - No. 81, 2/87
Marvel Comics Group

	GD25	FN65	NM94
169(#1)-Origin retold; panel swipe/M.D. #1-c	11.00	33.00	110.00
170-176	3.00	9.00	30.00
177-New costume	3.00	9.00	30.00
178-183: 178-Black Knight app. 179-Spider-Man story-r. 180-Photo montage-c. 181-Brunner-c(part-i)	2.50	7.50	25.00
1(6/74, 2nd series)-Brunner-c/a	3.20	9.60	32.00
2	1.85	5.50	15.00
3-5	1.00	2.80	7.00
6-10		1.60	4.00
11-20: 14-Dracula app.		1.20	3.00
21-26: 21-Origin-r/Doctor Strange #169		1.00	2.50
27-77,79-81: 31-Sub-Mariner-c/story. 56-Origin retold. 58-Re-intro Hannibal King (cameo). 59-Hannibal King full app. 59-62-Dracula app. (Darkhold storyline). 61,62-Doctor Strange, Blade, Hannibal King & Frank Drake team-up to battle Dracula. 62-Death of Dracula & Lilith		.80	2.00
78-New costume		1.00	2.50
Annual 1(1976, 52 pgs.)-New Russell-a (35 pgs.)		1.60	4.00
.../Silver Dagger Special Edition 1 (3/83, $2.50)-r/#1,2,4,5; Wrightson-c		1.00	2.50
...What Is It That Disturbs You, Stephen? #1 (10/97, $5.99, 48 pgs.) Russell-a/Andreyko & Russell-s, retelling of Annual #1 story			5.99

NOTE: ***Adkins** a-169, 170, 171i; c-169-171, 172i, 173. **Adams** a-4i. **Austin** a(i)-48-60, 66, 68, 70, 73; c(i)-38, 47-53, 55, 58-60, 70. **Brunner** a-1-5p; c-1-6, 22, 28-30, 33. **Colan** a(p)-172-178, 180-183, 6-18, 36-45, 47; c(p)-172, 174-183, 11-21, 23, 27, 35, 36, 47. **Ditko** a-179r, 3r. **Everett** c-183i. **Golden** a-46p, 55p; c-42-44, 46, 55p. **G. Kane** c(p)-8-10. **Miller** c-46p. **Nebres** a-20, 22, 23, 24i, 26i, 32i; c-32i, 34. **Rogers** a-48-53p; c-47p-53p. **Russell** a-34i, 46i, Annual 1. **B. Smith** c-179. **Paul Smith** a-54p, 56p, 65, 66p, 68p, 69, 71-73; c-56, 65, 66, 68, 71. **Starlin** a-23p, 26; c-25, 26. **Sutton** a-27-29p, 31i, 33, 34p. Painted c-62, 63.*

DOCTOR STRANGE CLASSICS
Mar, 1984 - No. 4, June, 1984 ($1.50 cover price; Baxter paper)
Marvel Comics Group

	GD25	FN65	NM94
1-4: Ditko-r; Byrne-c. 4-New Golden pin-up		.80	2.00

NOTE: ***Byrne** c-1i, 2-4.*

DOCTOR STRANGEFATE (See Marvel Versus DC #3 & DC Versus Marvel #4)
Apr, 1996 ($1.95)
DC Comics (Amalgam)

	GD25	FN65	NM94
1-Ron Marz script w/Jose Garcia-Lopez-(p) & Kevin Nowlan-(i). Access & Charles Xavier app.		.80	2.00

DOCTOR STRANGE MASTER OF THE MYSTIC ARTS (See Fireside Book Series)

Doctor Strange Sorcerer Supreme #75 © MEG

Dr. Weird Special #1 © Big Bang Comics

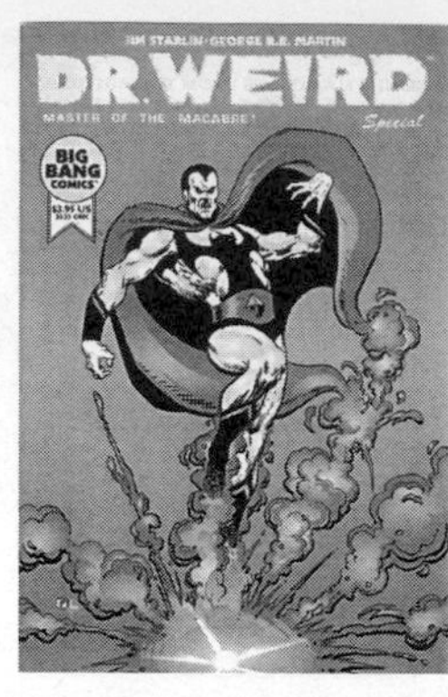

Dog's O'War #1 © William Tucci

GD25 FN65 NM94

DOCTOR STRANGE, SORCERER SUPREME
Nov, 1988 - No. 90, June, 1996 ($1.25/$1.50/$1.75/$1.95, direct sales only, Mando paper)
Marvel Comics (Midnight Sons imprint #60 on)

1 ($1.25) 1.20 3.00
2-9,12-14,16-27,29,30 ($1.50): 3-New Defenders app. 5-Guice-96c/a begins. 14-18-Morbius story line. 26-Werewolf by Night app. 1.50
10-Re-intro Morbius w/new costume (11/89) .80 2.00
11-Hobgoblin app. 1.60 4.00
15-Unauthorized Amy Grant photo-c 1.20 3.00
28-Ghost Rider story cont'd from G.R. #12; same book published at same time as Doctor Strange/Ghost Rider Special #1 (4/91) 1.20 3.00
31-36-Infinity Gauntlet x-overs: 31-Silver Surfer app. 33-Thanos-c & cameo. 36-Warlock app. 1.20 3.00
37-49,51-64: 37-Silver Surfer app. 38-Begin $1.75-c. 40-Daredevil x-over. 41-Wolverine-c/story. 42-47-Infinity War x-overs. 47-Gamora app. 52,53-Morbius-c/stories. 60,61-Siege of Darkness pt. 7 & 15. 60-Spot varnish-c. 61-New Doctor Strange begins (cameo, 1st app.). 62-Dr. Doom & Morbius app. .70 1.75
50-($2.95, 52 pgs.)-Holo-grafx foil-c; Hulk, Ghost Rider & Silver Surfer app.; leads into new Secret Defenders series 1.20 3.00
65-74, 76-90: 65-Begin $1.95-c; bound-in card sheet. 72-Silver ink-c. 80-82-Ellis story. 84-DeMatteis story begins. 87-Death of Baron Mordo. .80 2.00
75 ($2.50) 1.00 2.50
75 ($3.50)-Foil-c 1.40 3.50
Annual 2 ('92, $2.25, 68 pgs.)-Return of Defenders .90 2.25
Annual 3 ('93, $2.95, 68 pgs.)-Polybagged w/card 1.20 3.00
Annual 4 ('94, $2.95) 1.20 3.00
.../Ghost Rider Special 1 (4/91, $1.50)-Same book as D.S.S.S. #28 .80 2.00
...Vs. Dracula 1 (3/94, $1.75, 52 pgs.)-r/Tomb of Dracula #44 & Dr. Strange #14 .70 1.75

NOTE: ***Colan** c/a-19. **Golden** c-28. **Guice** a-5-16, 18, 20-24; c-5-12, 20-24. See 1st series for Annual #1.*

DR. TOM BRENT, YOUNG INTERN
Feb, 1963 - No. 5, Oct, 1963
Charlton Publications

1 1.10 3.30 9.00
2-5 2.00 5.00

DR. TOMORROW
Sept, 1997 - Present ($2.50)
Acclaim Comics (Valiant)

1-7: 1-Mignola-c 1.00 2.50

DR. VOLTZ (See Mighty Midget Comics)

DR. WEIRD
1994 ($2.95, B&W)
Big Bang Comics

1,2: 1-Frank Brunner-c 1.60 4.00

DR. WEIRD SPECIAL
Feb, 1994 ($3.95, B&W, 68 pgs.)
Big Bang Comics

1-Origin-r by Starlin; Starlin-c. 1.60 4.00

DOCTOR WHO (Also see Marvel Premiere #57-60)
Oct, 1984 - No. 23, Aug, 1986 ($1.50, color, direct sales, Baxter paper)
Marvel Comics Group

1-23-British-r. 1.50

DR. WHO & THE DALEKS (See Movie Classics)

DR. WONDER
June, 1996 - Present ($2.95, B&W)
Old Town Publishing

1-5: 1-Intro & origin of Dr. Wonder; Dick Ayers-c/a; Irwin Hasen-a; contains profiles of the artists 1.20 3.00

GD25 FN65 NM94

DOCTOR ZERO
Apr, 1988 - No. 8, Aug, 1989 ($1.25/$1.50)
Marvel Comics (Epic Comics)

1-8: 1-Sienkiewicz-c. 6,7-Spiegle-a 1.50

NOTE: ***Sienkiewicz** a-3i, 4i; c-1. **Spiegle** a-6, 7.*

DO-DO (Funny Animal Circus Stories)
1950 - No. 7, 1951 (5¢, 5x7-1/4" Miniature)
Nation Wide Publishers

1 (52 pgs.) 14.50 43.00 115.00
2-7 8.50 26.00 60.00

DODO & THE FROG, THE (Formerly Funny Stuff; also see It's Game Time #2)
No. 80, 9-10/54 - No. 88, 1-2/56; No. 89, 8-9/56; No. 90, 10-11/56; No. 91, 9/57; No. 92, 11/57 (See Comic Cavalcade)
National Periodical Publications

80-1st app. Doodles Duck by Sheldon Mayer 17.50 53.00 140.00
81-91: Doodles Duck by Mayer in #81,83-90 11.30 34.00 90.00
92-(Scarce)-Doodles Duck by S. Mayer 15.00 45.00 120.00

DOGFACE DOOLEY
1951 - No. 5, 1953
Magazine Enterprises

1(A-1 40) 5.70 17.00 35.00
2(A-1 43), 3(A-1 49), 4(A-1 53), 5(A-1 64) 4.25 13.00 26.00
I.W. Reprint #1('64), Super Reprint #17 2.40 6.00 12.00

DOG MOON
1996 ($6.95, one-shot)
DC Comics (Vertigo)

1-Robert Hunter-scripts; Tim Truman-c/a. 1.00 2.80 7.00

DOG OF FLANDERS, A
No. 1088, Mar, 1960
Dell Publishing Co.

Four Color 1088-Movie, photo-c 3.60 11.00 40.00

DOGPATCH (See Al Capp's... & Mammy Yokum)

DOGS OF WAR (Also see Warriors of Plasm)
Apr, 1994 - No. 5, Aug, 1994 ($2.50)
Defiant

1-5 1.00 2.50

DOGS-O-WAR
June, 1996 - No. 3, Jan, 1997 ($2.95, B&W, limited series)
Crusade Comics

1-3: 1,2-Photo-c 1.20 3.00

DOLLFACE & HER GANG (Betty Betz'...)
No. 309, Jan, 1951
Dell Publishing Co.

Four Color 309 4.50 13.50 50.00

DOLLMAN (Movie)
Sept, 1991 - No. 4, Dec, 1991 ($2.50, limited series)
Eternity Comics

1-4: Adaptation of film 1.00 2.50

DOLL MAN QUARTERLY, THE (Doll Man #17 on; also see Feature Comics #27 & Freedom Fighters)
Fall, 1941 - No. 7, Fall, '43; No. 8, Spring, '46 - No. 47, Oct, 1953
Quality Comics Group

1-Dollman (by Cassone), Justin Wright begin 240.00 720.00 2400.00
2-The Dragon begins; Crandall-a(5) 100.00 300.00 900.00

Doll Man Quarterly #35 © QUA

Dolls #1 © Sirius

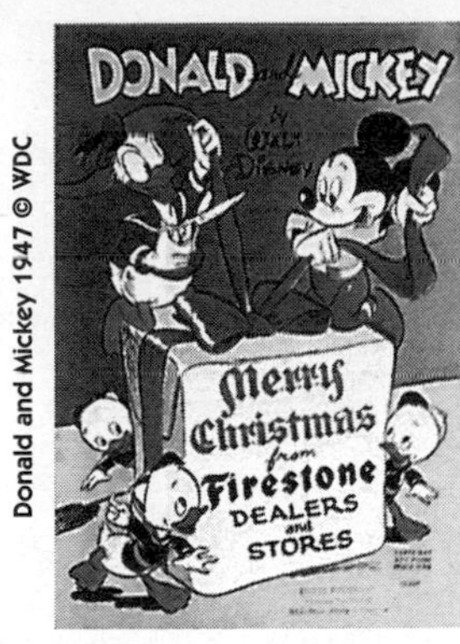

Donald and Mickey 1947 © WDC

GD25 FN65 NM94

3,4 72.00 216.00 650.00
5-Crandall-a 56.00 168.00 500.00
6,7(1943) 42.00 126.00 375.00
8(1946)-1st app. Torchy by Bill Ward 100.00 300.00 900.00
9 42.00 126.00 375.00
10-20 33.00 98.00 260.00
21-30: 28-Vs. The Flame 28.00 83.00 220.00
31-36,38,40: 31-(12/50)-Intro Elmo, the wonder dog (Dollman's faithful dog). 32-34-Jeb Rivers app.; 34 by Crandall(p) 22.00 66.00 175.00
37-Origin & 1st app. Dollgirl; Dollgirl bondage-c 33.00 98.00 260.00
39- "Narcotics...the Death Drug" c-/story 23.00 68.00 180.00
41-47 16.00 49.00 130.00
Super Reprint #11('64, r/#20),15(r/#23),17(r/#28): 15,17-Torchy app.; Andru/Esposito-c 2.60 7.80 26.00

NOTE: ***Ward*** *Torchy in 8, 9, 11, 12, 14-24, 26, 27; by Fox-#30, 35-47.* ***Crandall*** *a-2, 5, 10, 13 & Super #11, 17, 18.* ***Crandall/Cuidera*** *c-40-42.* ***Guardineer*** *a-3. Bondage c-27, 37, 38, 39.*

DOLLS
June, 1996 ($2.95, B&W, one-shot)
Sirius
1 1.20 3.00

DOLLY
No. 10, July-Aug, 1951 (Funny animal)
Ziff-Davis Publ. Co.
10-Painted-c 5.00 15.00 30.00

DOLLY DILL
1945
Marvel Comics/Newsstand Publ.
1 12.00 36.00 95.00

DOMINION (Manga)
Dec, 1990 - No. 6., July, 1990 ($2.00, B&W, limited series)
Eclipse Comics
1-6 .80 2.00

DOMINION: CONFLICT 1 (Manga)
Mar, 1996 - Present ($2.95, B&W, limited series)
Dark Horse Comics
1-5: Shirow-c/a/scripts 1.20 3.00

DOMINIQUE: KILLZONE
May, 1995 ($2.95, B&W)
Caliber Comics
1 1.20 3.00

DOMINO (See X-Force)
Jan, 1997 - No. 3, Mar,, 1997 ($1.95, limited series)
Marvel Comics
1-3: 2-Deathstrike-c/app. 1.95

DOMINO CHANCE
May-June, 1982 - No. 9, May, 1985 (B&W)
Chance Enterprises
1 1.20 3.00
1-Reprint, May, 1985 1.00 2.50
2-6,9 1.00
7-1st app. Gizmo, 2 pgs. .80 2.00
8-1st full Gizmo story 1.20 3.00

DONALD AND MICKEY IN DISNEYLAND (See Dell Giants)

DONALD AND MICKEY MERRY CHRISTMAS (Formerly Famous Gang Book Of Comics)
1943 - 1949 (Giveaway, 20 pgs.) Put out each Christmas; 1943 issue titled "Firestone Presents Comics" (Disney)
K. K. Publ./Firestone Tire & Rubber Co.
1943-Donald Duck-r/WDC&S #32 by Carl Barks 59.00 177.00 650.00

GD25 FN65 NM94

1944-Donald Duck-r/WDC&S #35 by Barks 59.00 177.00 650.00
1945- "Donald Duck's Best Christmas", 8 pgs. Carl Barks; intro. & 1st app. Grandma Duck in comic books 80.00 240.00 875.00
1946-Donald Duck in "Santa's Stormy Visit", 8 pgs. Carl Barks 64.00 192.00 700.00
1947-Donald Duck in "Three Good Little Ducks", 8 pgs. Carl Barks 55.00 165.00 600.00
1948-Donald Duck in "Toyland", 8 pgs. Carl Barks 55.00 165.00 600.00
1949-Donald Duck in "New Toys", 8 pgs. Barks 55.00 165.00 600.00

DONALD AND SCROOGE
1992 ($8.95, squarebound, 100 pgs.)
Disney Comics
nn-Don Rosa reprint special; r/U.S., D.D. Advs. 1.25 3.75 10.00
1-3 (1992, $1.50)-r/D.D. Advs. (Disney) #1,22,24 & U.S. #261-263,269 .80 2.00

DONALD AND THE WHEEL (Disney)
No. 1190, Nov, 1961
Dell Publishing Co.
Four Color 1190-Movie, Barks-c 6.40 19.00 70.00

DONALD DUCK (See Adventures of Mickey Mouse, Cheerios, Donald & Mickey, Ducktales, Dynabrite Comics, Gladstone Comic Album, Mickey & Donald, Mickey Mouse Mag., Story Hour Series, Uncle Scrooge, Walt Disney's Comics & Stories, W. D.'s Donald Duck, Wheaties & Whitman Comic Books, Wise Little Hen, The)

DONALD DUCK
1935, 1936 (All pages on heavy linen-like finish cover stock in color;1st book ever devoted to Donald Duck; see Advs. of Mickey Mouse for 1st app.) (9-1/2x13")
Whitman Publishing Co./Grosset & Dunlap/K.K.
978(1935)-16 pgs.; Illustrated text story book 222.00 667.00 2000.00
nn(1936)-36 pgs.plus hard cover & dust jacket. Story completely rewritten with B&W illos added. Mickey appears and his nephews are named Morty & Monty
Book only 222.00 667.00 2000.00
Dust jacket only.... 56.00 168.00 500.00

DONALD DUCK (Walt Disney's) (10¢)
1938 (8-1/2x11-1/2", B&W, cardboard-c)(Has D. Duck with bubble pipe on-c)
Whitman/K.K. Publications GD25 FN65 VF82 NM94
nn-The first Donald Duck & Walt Disney comic book; 1936 & 1937 Sunday strip-r(in B&W); same format as the Feature Books; 1st strips with Huey, Dewey & Louie from 10/17/37 250.00 750.00 1500.00 2250.00

DONALD DUCK (Walt Disney's...#262 on; see 4-Color listings for titles & Four Color No. 1109 for origin story)
1940 - No. 84, Sept-Nov, 1962; No. 85, Dec, 1962 - No. 245, 1984; No. 246, Oct, 1986 - No. 279, May, 1990; No. 280, Sept, 1993 - Present
Dell Publishing Co./Gold Key #85-216/Whitman #217-245/ Gladstone #246 on GD25 FN65 VF82 NM94
Four Color 4(1940)-Daily 1939 strip-r by Al Taliaferro 808.00 2423.00 5656.00 10,500.00
(Estimated up to 175 total copies exist, 9 in NM/Mint)
Large Feature Comic 16(1/41?)-1940 Sunday strips-r in B&W 308.00 923.00 2155.00 4000.00
Large Feature Comic 20('41)-Comic Paint Book, r-single panels from Large Feature #16 at top of each pg. to color; daily strip-r across bottom of each pg. 385.00 1154.00 2695.00 5000.00
Four Color 9('42)- "Finds Pirate Gold"; 64 pgs. by Carl Barks & Jack Hannah (pgs. 1,2,5,12-40 are by Barks, his 1st Donald Duck comic book art work; © 8/17/42) 577.00 1730.00 4039.00 7500.00
(Estimated up to 270 total copies exist, 18 in NM/Mint)
Four Color 29(9/43)- "Mummy's Ring" by Barks; reprinted in Uncle Scrooge & Donald Duck #1('65), W. D. Comics Digest #44('73) & Donald Duck Advs. #14 477.00 1430.00 3340.00 6200.00
(Estimated up to 300 total copies exist, 14 in NM/Mint)
GD25 FN65 NM94

Donald Duck #26 © WDC

Donald Duck #246 © WDC

Donald Duck Album #1 © WDC

GD25 FN65 NM94

Four Color 62(1/45)- "Frozen Gold"; 52 pgs. by Barks, reprinted in The Best of W.D. Comics & Donald Duck Advs. #4 154.00 462.00 2000.00
Four Color 108(1946)- "Terror of the River"; 52 pgs. by Carl Barks; reprinted in Gladstone Comic Album #2 112.00 335.00 1450.00
Four Color 147(5/47)-in "Volcano Valley" by Barks 77.00 231.00 1000.00
Four Color 159(8/47)-in "The Ghost of the Grotto";52 pgs. by Carl Barks; reprinted in Best of Uncle Scrooge & Donald Duck #1 ('66) & The Best of W.D. Comics & D.D. Advs. #9; two Barks stories 62.00 185.00 800.00
Four Color 178(12/47)-1st app. Uncle Scrooge by Carl Barks; reprinted in Gold Key Christmas Parade #3 & The Best of Walt Disney Comics 92.00 277.00 1200.00
Four Color 189(6/48)-by Carl Barks; reprinted in Best of Donald Duck & Uncle Scrooge #1('64) & D.D. Advs. #19 58.00 173.00 750.00
Four Color 199(10/48)-by Carl Barks; mentioned in Love and Death; r/in Gladstone Comic Album #5 64.00 190.00 825.00
Four Color 203(12/48)-by Barks; reprinted as Gold Key Christmas Parade #4 43.00 129.00 560.00
Four Color 223(4/49)-by Barks; reprinted as Best of Donald Duck #1 & Donald Duck Advs. #3 62.00 185.00 800.00
Four Color 238(8/49)-in "Voodoo Hoodoo" by Barks 43.00 129.00 560.00
Four Color 256(12/49)-by Barks; reprinted in Best of Donald Duck & Uncle Scrooge #2('67), Gladstone Comic Album #16 & W.D. Comics Digest 44('73) 33.00 99.00 425.00
Four Color 263(2/50)-Two Barks stories; r-in D.D. #278 31.00 92.00 400.00
Four Color 275(5/50), 282(7/50), 291(9/50), 300(11/50)-All by Carl Barks; 275, 282 reprinted in W.D. Comics Digest #44('73). #275 r/in Gladstone Comic Album #10. #291 r/in D. Duck Advs. #16 29.00 87.00 375.00
Four Color 308(1/51), 318(3/51)-by Barks; #318-reprinted in W.D. Comics Digest #34 & D.D. Advs. #2,19 25.00 75.00 325.00
Four Color 328(5/51)-by Carl Barks 27.00 81.00 350.00
Four Color 339(7-8/51), 379-2nd Uncle Scrooge-c; art not by Barks. 6.00 18.00 60.00
Four Color 348(9-10/51), 356,394-Barks-c only 15.00 45.00 160.00
Four Color 367(1-2/52)-by Barks; reprinted as Gold Key Christmas Parade #2 & #8 25.00 75.00 320.00
Four Color 408(7-8/52), 422(9-10/52)-All by Carl Barks. #408-r-in Best of Donald Duck & Uncle Scrooge #1('64) & Gladstone Comic Album #13 25.00 75.00 320.00
26(11-12/52)-In "Trick or Treat" (Barks-a, 36pgs.) 1st story r-in Walt Disney Digest #16 & Gladstone C.A. #23 25.00 76.00 330.00
27-30-Barks-c only 10.00 30.00 110.00
31-44,47-50 4.50 13.50 50.00
45-Barks-a (6 pgs.) 11.00 34.00 125.00
46- "Secret of Hondorica" by Barks, 24 pgs.; reprinted in Donald Duck #98 & 154 18.00 55.00 200.00
51-Barks-a,1/2 pg. 4.50 13.50 50.00
52- "Lost Peg-Leg Mine" by Barks, 10 pgs. 12.00 35.00 130.00
53,55-59 3.60 11.00 40.00
54- "Forbidden Valley" by Barks, 26 pgs. (10¢ & 15¢ versions exist) 12.00 37.00 135.00
60- "Donald Duck & the Titanic Ants" by Barks, 20 pgs. plus 6 more pgs. 12.00 37.00 135.00
61-67,69,70 3.00 9.00 32.00
68-Barks-a, 5 pgs. 9.00 29.00 105.00
71-Barks-r, 1/2 pg. 3.00 9.00 32.00
72-78,80,82-97,99,100: 96-Donald Duck Album 3.00 9.00 32.00
79,81-Barks-a, 1pg. 3.00 9.00 32.00
98-Reprints #46 (Barks) 3.00 9.00 32.00
101-133: 102-Super Goof. 112-1st Moby Duck 1.80 5.50 20.00
134-Barks-r/#52 & WDC&S 194 1.80 5.50 20.00
135-Barks-r/WDC&S 198, 19 pgs. 1.80 5.50 20.00
136-153,155,156,158 1.70 5.00 12.00
154-Barks-r(#46) 1.85 5.50 15.00
157,159,160,164: 157-Barks-r(#45). 159-Reprints/WDC&S #192 (10 pgs.). 160-Barks-r(#26). 164-Barks-r(#79) 1.70 5.00 12.00
161-163,165-173,175-187,189-191: 187-Barks r/#68. 1.30 3.25 8.00
174,188: 174-r/4-Color #394. 1.65 4.20 10.00
192-Barks-r(40 pgs.) from Donald Duck #60 & WDC&S #226,234 (52 pgs.) 1.65 4.20 10.00
193-200,202-207,209-211,213-218: 217 has 216 on-c 2.00 5.00
201,208,212: 201-Barks-r/Christmas Parade #26, 16pgs. 208-Barks-r/#60 (6 pgs.). 212-Barks-r/WDC&S #130 2.00 5.00
219-Barks-r/WDC&S #106,107, 10 pgs. ea. 2.00 5.00
220,221,223-227,231-245 1.60 4.00
222-(8-12/80)-Only distr. in Whitman 3-pack 7.50 22.50 75.00
228-230: 228-Barks-r/F.C. #275. 229-Barks-r/F.C. #282. 230-Barks-r/ #52 & WDC&S #194 2.00 5.00
246-(1st Gladstone issue)-Barks-r/FC #422 1.85 5.50 15.00
247-249,251: 248,249-Barks-r/DD #54 & 26. 251-Barks-r/1945 Firestone 1.65 4.20 10.00
250-($1.50, 68 pgs.)-Barks-r/4-Color #9 1.70 5.00 12.00
252-279: 254-Barks-r/FC #328. 256-Barks-r/FC #147. 257-($1.50, 52 pgs.)-Barks-r/Vacaction Parade #1. 261-Barks-r/FC #300. 275-Kelly-r/FC #92. 278-($1.95, 68 pgs.)-Rosa-a; Barks-r/FC #263. 279-($1.95, 68 pgs.)-Rosa-c; Barks-r/MOC #4 2.00 5.00
280, 286: 280 (#1, 2nd Series). 286-Rosa-a. 2.00 5.00
281,282,284 1.60 4.00
283,285,287-294: 283-Don Rosa-a, part-c & scripts .80 2.00
286 ($2.95, 68 pgs.)-Happy Birthday, Donald 1.20 3.00
295-301: 295-Begin $1.50-c 2.00
302-304: 302-Begin $1.95-c 2.00
Mini-Comic #1(1976)-(3-1/4x6-1/2"); r/D.D. #150 1.00

NOTE: ***Carl Barks** wrote all issues he illustrated, but #117, 126, 138 contain his script only. Issues 4-Color #189, 199, 203, 223, 238, 256, 263, 275, 282, 308, 348, 356, 367, 394, 408, 422, 26-30, 35, 44, 46, 52, 55, 57, 60, 65, 70-73, 77-80, 83, 101, 103, 105, 106, 111, 126, 246r, 266r, 268r, 271r, 275r, 278r(F.C. 263) all have **Barks** covers. **Barks** r-263-267, 269-278-282, 284, 285. #96 titled "Comic Album", #99-"Christmas Album". New art issues (not reprints)-106-46, 148-63, 167, 169, 170, 172, 173, 175, 178, 179, 196, 209, 223, 225, 236. **Taliaferro** daily newspaper strips #258-260, 264, 284, 285; Sunday strips #247, 280-283.*

DONALD DUCK
1944 (Christmas giveaway, paper-c, 16 pgs.)(2 versions)
K. K. Publications
nn-Kelly cover reprint 65.00 195.00 650.00

DONALD DUCK ALBUM (See Comic Album No. 1,3 & Duck Album)
5-7/59 - F.C. No. 1239, 10-12/61; 1962; 8/63 - No. 2, Oct, 1963
Dell Publishing Co./Gold Key
Four Color 995 (#1) 4.50 13.50 50.00
Four Color 1182, 01204-207 (1962-Dell) 3.60 11.00 40.00
Four Color 1099,1140,1239-Barks-c 5.50 16.50 60.00
1(8/63-Gold Key)-Barks-c 4.50 13.50 50.00
2(10/63) 3.60 11.00 40.00

DONALD DUCK AND THE BOYS (Also see Story Hour Series)
1948 (5-1/4x5-1/2", 100pgs., hard-c; art & text)
Whitman Publishing Co.
845-(49) new illos by Barks based on his Donald Duck 10-pager in WDC&S #74, Expanded text not written by Barks; Cover not by Barks 48.00 143.00 475.00
(Prices vary widely on this book)

DONALD DUCK AND THE CHRISTMAS CAROL
1960 (A Little Golden Book, 6-3/8"x7-5/8", 28 pgs.)
Whitman Publishing Co.
nn-Story book pencilled by Carl Barks with the intended title "Uncle Scrooge's Christmas Carol." Finished art adapted by Norman McGary. (Rare)-Reprinted in Uncle Scrooge in Color. 75.00

DONALD DUCK AND THE RED FEATHER

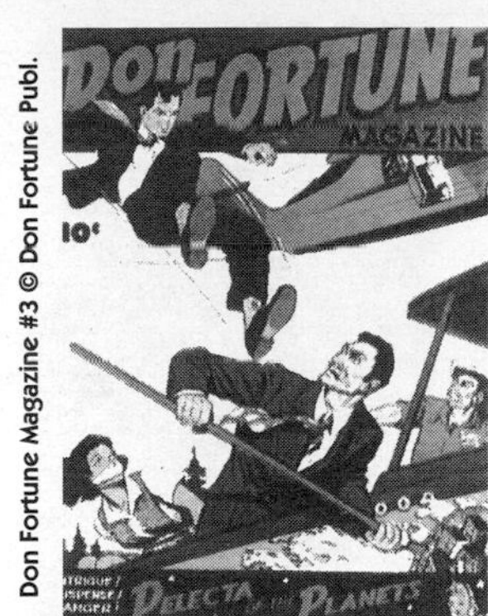

Don Fortune Magazine #3 © Don Fortune Publ.

Donna Mia #0 © Avatar Press

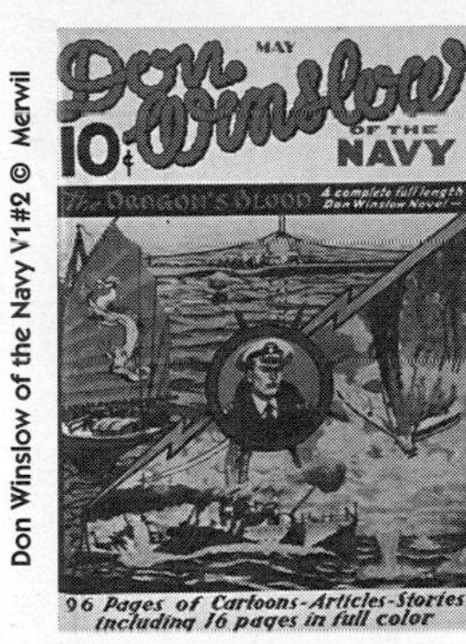

Don Winslow of the Navy V1#2 © Merwil

	GD25	FN65	NM94
1948 (8-1/2x11", 4 pgs., B&W) Red Feather Giveaway			
nn	12.00	36.00	95.00

DONALD DUCK BEACH PARTY (Also see Dell Giants)
Sept, 1965 (12¢)
Gold Key

1(#10158-509)-Barks-r/WDC&S #45; painted-c	5.00	15.00	55.00

DONALD DUCK BOOK (See Story Hour Series)

DONALD DUCK COMIC PAINT BOOK
No. 20, 1941 (B&W)
Dell Publishing Co.

Large Feature Comic 20	417.00	1250.00	5200.00

DONALD DUCK COMICS DIGEST
Nov, 1986 - No. 5, July, 1987 ($1.25/$1.50, 96 pgs.)
Gladstone Publishing

1,3: 1-Barks-c/a-r		2.00	5.00
2,4,5: 4,5-$1.50-c		1.20	3.00

DONALD DUCK FUN BOOK (See Dell Giants)

DONALD DUCK IN DISNEYLAND (See Dell Giants)

DONALD DUCK IN "THE LITTERBUG"
1963 (5x7-1/4", 16 pgs., soft-c) (Disney giveaway)
Keep America Beautiful

nn	3.00	9.00	30.00

DONALD DUCK MARCH OF COMICS (See March of Comics #4,20,41,56,69,263)

DONALD DUCK MERRY CHRISTMAS (See Dell Giant No. 53)

DONALD DUCK PICNIC PARTY (See Picnic Party listed under Dell Giants)

DONALD DUCK "PLOTTING PICNICKERS" (Also see Ludwig Von Drake & Mickey Mouse)
1962 (3-1/4x7", soft-c, 16 pgs.) (Disney)
Fritos Giveaway

nn	4.50	13.50	45.00

DONALD DUCK'S SURPRISE PARTY
1948 (16 pgs.) (Giveaway for Icy Frost Twins Ice Cream Bars)
Walt Disney Productions

nn-(Rare)-Kelly-c/a	233.00	700.00	2100.00

DONALD DUCK TELLS ABOUT KITES (See Kite Fun Book)

DONALD DUCK, THIS IS YOUR LIFE (Disney, TV)
No. 1109, Aug-Oct, 1960
Dell Publishing Co.

Four Color 1109-Gyro flashback to WDC&S #141; origin Donald Duck (1st told)	14.00	41.00	150.00

DONALD DUCK XMAS ALBUM (See regular Donald Duck No. 99)

DONALD IN MATHMAGIC LAND (Disney)
No. 1051, Oct-Dec, 1959 - No. 1198, May-July, 1961
Dell Publishing Co.

Four Color 1051 (#1)-Movie	8.00	25.00	90.00
Four Color 1198-Reprint of above	5.50	16.50	60.00

DONATELLO, TEENAGE MUTANT NINJA TURTLE
Aug, 1986 ($1.50, B&W, one-shot, 44 pgs.)
Mirage Studios

1		1.20	3.00

DONDI
No. 1176, Mar-May, 1961 - No. 1276, Dec, 1961
Dell Publishing Co.

Four Color 1176 (#1)-Movie; origin, photo-c	3.60	11.00	40.00
Four Color 1276	1.80	5.50	20.00

DON FORTUNE MAGAZINE
Aug, 1946 - No. 6, Feb, 1947
Don Fortune Publishing Co.

1-Delecta of the Planets by C. C. Beck in all	16.00	49.00	130.00
2	10.00	30.00	80.00
3-6: 3-Bondage-c	8.50	26.00	60.00

DONNA MATRIX
Aug, 1993 ($2.95, 52 pgs.)
Reactor, Inc.

1-Computer generated-c/a by Mike Saenz; 3-D effects		1.20	3.00

DONNA MIA
Oct, 1995 - No. 2, Sept, 1996 ($3.95/$4.95, limited series, mature)
Dark Fantasy Productions

1,2-($4.95): 1-Kaluta-c-red foil; fold-out centerfold. 2-Kaluta blue foil-c; nudity		2.00	5.00
1,2-($3.95): Kaluta-c on both. 2-Nudity		1.60	4.00

DONNA MIA
Jan, 1997 - Present ($3.00/$3.95, B&W, mature)
Avatar Press

1, 0(10/97)-($3.00)		1.20	3.00
1-($5.00)-Nude Edition		2.00	5.00
2-4-($3.95)		1.60	4.00
2-($4.95)-Foil Edition		2.00	5.00

DONNA MIA GIANT SIZE
May, 1997 - Present ($3.95, B&W, limited series, mature)
Avatar Press

1,2			3.95

DON NEWCOMBE
1950 (Baseball)
Fawcett Publications

nn-Photo-c	35.00	105.00	280.00
0-14: 0-r/Bizarre Heroes #1(1990). 1,2-Megaton Man-c/story		1.20	3.00

DON SIMPSON'S BIZARRE HEROES (Also see Megaton Man)
May, 1990 - Present ($2.50/$2.95, B&W)
Fiasco Comics

1-10		1.00	2.50
0,11-17: 0-Begin $2.95-c; r/Bizarre Heroes #1. 17-(9/96)-Indicia also reads Megaton Man #0; intro Megaton Man and the Fiascoverse to new readers		1.20	3.00

DON'T GIVE UP THE SHIP
No. 1049, Aug, 1959
Dell Publishing Co.

Four Color 1049-Movie, Jerry Lewis photo-c	6.40	19.00	70.00

DON WINSLOW OF THE NAVY
Apr, 1937 - No. 2, May, 1937 (96 pgs.)(A pulp/comic book cross; stapled spine)
Merwil Publishing Co.

	GD25	FN65	VF82
V1#1-Has 16 pgs. comics in color. Captain Colorful & Jupiter Jones by Sheldon Mayer; complete Don Winslow novel	567.00	1700.00	3600.00
2-Sheldon Mayer-a	100.00	300.00	850.00

DON WINSLOW OF THE NAVY (See Crackajack Funnies, Famous Feature Stories, Popular Comics & Super Book #5,6)
No. 2, Nov, 1939 - No. 22, 1941
Dell Publishing Co.

Four Color 2 (#1)-Rare	116.00	348.00	1275.00
Four Color 22	28.00	85.00	310.00

DON WINSLOW OF THE NAVY (See TV Teens; Movie, Radio, TV)

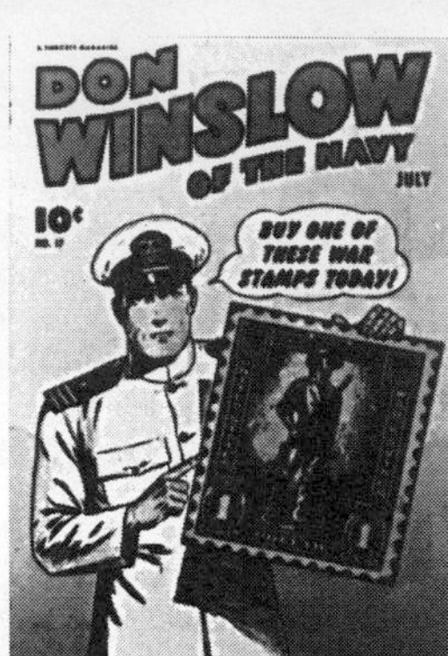

Don Winslow of the Navy #17 © FAW

Doom Patrol #26 © DC

Doom 2099 #20 © MEG

 GD25 FN65 NM94

(Fightin' Navy No. 74 on)
2/43 - #64, 12/48; #65, 1/51 - #69, 9/51; #70, 3/55 - #73, 9/55
Fawcett Publications/Charlton No. 70 on

	GD25	FN65	NM94
1-(68 pgs.)-Captain Marvel on cover	87.00	261.00	780.00
2	42.00	126.00	375.00
3	34.00	101.00	270.00
4-6: 6-Flag-c	25.00	75.00	200.00
7-10: 8-Last 68 pg. issue?	17.50	53.00	140.00
11-20	14.00	41.00	110.00
21-40	8.75	26.25	70.00
41-64: 51,60-Singapore Sal (villain) app. 64-(12/48)	8.50	26.00	60.00
65(1/51)-Flying Saucer attack; photo-c	9.50	28.00	75.00
66 - 69(9/51): All photo-c. 66-sci-fi story	9.50	28.00	75.00
70(3/55)-73: 70-73 r-/#26,58 & 59	7.15	21.50	50.00

DOOM FORCE SPECIAL
July, 1992 ($2.95, 68 pgs., one-shot, mature) (X-Force parody)
DC Comics

1-Grant Morrison scripts; Simonson, Steacy, & others-a; Giffen/Mignola-c. 1.20 3.00

DOOM PATROL, THE (Formerly My Greatest Adventure No. 1-85; see Brave and the Bold, DC Special Blue Ribbon Digest 19, Official... Index & Showcase No. 94-96)
No. 86, 3/64 - No. 121, 9-10/68; No. 122, 2/73 - No. 124, 6-7/73
National Periodical Publications

86-1 pg. origin (#86-121 are 12¢ issues) 9.00 27.00 90.00
87-99: 88-Origin The Chief. 91-Intro. Mento. 99-Intro. Beast Boy (later becomes the Changeling in New Teen Titans 6.50 19.50 65.00
100-Origin Beast Boy; Robot-Maniac series begins (12/65) 7.00 21.00 70.00
101-110: 102-Challengers of the Unknown app. 105-Robot-Maniac series ends. 106-Negative Man begins (origin) 3.00 9.00 30.00
111-120 2.50 7.50 20.00
121-Death of Doom Patrol; Orlando-c. 6.50 19.50 65.00
122-124: All reprints 1.00 3.00 8.00

DOOM PATROL
Oct, 1987 - No, 87, Feb, 1995 (75¢/$1.00/$1.50/$1.75/$1.95, new format)
DC Comics (Vertigo imprint #64 on)

1-75¢-c begins. .80 2.00
2-18: 3-1st app. Lodestone. 4-1st app. Karma. 8,15,16-Art Adams-c(i). 10-$1.00-c begins. 18-Invasion tie-in. 1.00
19-(2/89)-Grant Morrison scripts begin, ends #63; 1st app Crazy Jane; $1.50-c & new format begins. 1.60 4.00
20-25 1.00 2.50
26-30: 29-Superman app. 30-Night Breed fold-out 1.20 3.00
31-40: 35-1st app. of Flex Mentallo (cameo). 36-1st full app. of Flex Mentallo. 39-World Without End preview. .80 2.00
41-49,51-56,58-60: 42-Origin of Flex Mentallo. .80 2.00
50,57 ($2.50, 52 pgs.) 1.00 2.50
61-65: 61-$1.75-c begins; photo-c. 63-(1/93). .80 2.00
66-87: 66-$1.95-c begins. 70-Photo-c. 73-Death cameo (2 panels). .80 2.00
...And Suicide Squad 1 (3/88, $1.50, 52 pgs.)-Wraparound-c .65 1.60
Annual 1 (1988, $1.50, 52 pgs.) .65 1.60
Annual 2 (1994, $3.95, 68 pgs.)-Children's Crusade tie-in. 1.60 4.00
NOTE: ***Simon Bisley*** *painted c-26-48, 55-58.* ***Bolland*** *c-64, 75.* ***Dringenberg*** *a-42(p).* ***Steacy*** *a-53.*

DOOM PATROL (See Tangent Comics/ Doom Patrol)

DOOMSDAY
1995 ($3.95, one-shot)
DC Comics

1-Year One story by Jurgens, L. Simonson, Ordway, and Gil Kane; Darkseid, Superman app. 1.60 4.00

DOOMSDAY + 1 (Also see Charlton Bullseye)
July, 1975 - No. 6, June, 1976; No. 7, June, 1978 - No. 12, May, 1979
Charlton Comics

1: #1-5 are 25¢ issues 1.50 4.50 12.00
2-6: 4-Intro Lor. 5-Ditko-a(1 pg.) 6-Begin 30¢ issues 2.40 6.00
V3#7-12 (reprints #1-6) 1.20 3.00
5 (Modern Comics reprint, 1977) 1.20 3.00
NOTE: ***Byrne*** *c/a-1-12; Painted covers-2-7.*

DOOMSDAY SQUAD, THE
Aug, 1986 - No. 7, 1987 ($2.00)
Fantagraphics Books

1-7: Byrne-a in all. 1-3-New Byrne-c. 3-Usagi Yojimbo app. (1st in color).4-N Adams-c. 5-7-Gil Kane-c .80 2.00

DOOM'S IV
July, 1994 - No.4, Oct, 1994 ($2.50, limited series)
Image Comics (Extreme Studios)

1-4-Liefeld story 1.00 2.50
1,2-Two alternate Liefeld-c each, 4 covers form 1 picture 2.00 5.00

DOOM 2099 (See Marvel Comics Presents #118 & 2099: World of Tomorrow)
Jan, 1993 - No. 44, Aug, 1996 ($1.25/$1.50/$1.95)
Marvel Comics

1-($1.75)-Metallic foil stamped-c .80 2.00
1-2nd printing .70 1.75
2-16: 14-Ron Lim-c(p) 1.25
17-24, 26-28: 17-Begin $1.50-c; bound-in trading card sheet 1.50
25 ($2.25, 52 pgs.) 1.30 3.25
25 ($2.95, 52pgs.) Foil embossed cover 1.20 3.00
29-44: 29-Begin $2.95-c. 40-Namor & Doctor Strange app. 41-Daredevil app., Namor-c/app. 44-Intro The Emissary; story contin'd in 2099: World of Tomorrow. .80 2.00
29 ($3.50)-acetate-c. 1.40 3.50

DOORWAY TO NIGHTMARE (See Cancelled Comic Cavalcade)
Jan-Feb, 1978 - No. 5, Sept-Oct, 1978
DC Comics

1-5-Madame Xanadu in all. 4-Craig-a 1.60 4.00
NOTE: ***Kaluta*** *covers on all. Merged into The Unexpected with No. 190.*

DOPEY DUCK COMICS (Wacky Duck No. 3) (See Super Funnies)
Fall, 1945 - No. 2, Apr, 1946
Timely Comics (NPP)

1,2-Casper Cat, Krazy Krow 15.00 45.00 120.00

DORK
June, 1993 - No. 3, 1995 ($2.50/$2.75, B&W, mature)
Slave Labor

1-3: Evan Dorkin-c/a/scripts in all. 3-$2.75-c 1.10 2.75
1,2-(2nd printing, $2.75): 1-(8/95). 2-(1/96)-Reads 2nd Print on bottom inside-c 1.10 2.75

DOROTHY LAMOUR (Formerly Jungle Lil)(Stage, screen, radio)
No. 2, June, 1950 - No. 3, Aug, 1950
Fox Features Syndicate

2,3-Wood-a(3) each, photo-c 21.00 64.00 160.00

DOT AND DASH AND THE LUCKY JINGLE PIGGIE
1942 (Christmas giveaway, 12 pgs.)
Sears Roebuck Co.

nn-Contains a war stamp album and a punch out Jingle Piggie bank 5.70 17.00 40.00

Double Comics 1941 © DC

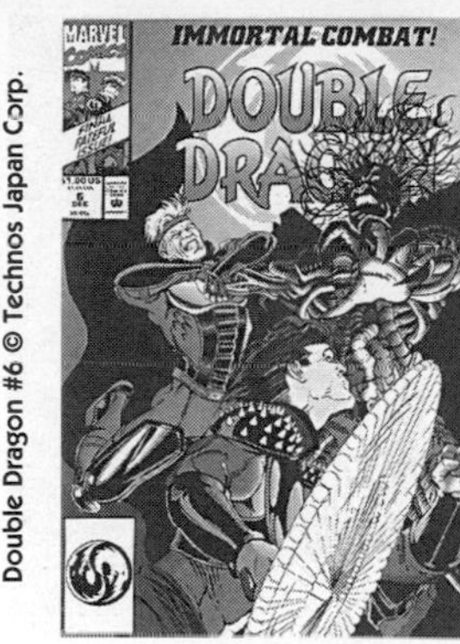

Double Dragon #6 © Technos Japan Corp.

Double Life of Private Strong #2 © MLJ

GD25 FN65 NM94

DOT DOTLAND (Formerly Little Dot Dotland)
No. 62, Sept, 1974 - No. 63, Nov, 1974
Harvey Publications

62,63 .80 2.00

DOTTY (...& Her Boy Friends)(Formerly Four Teeners; Glamorous Romances No. 41 on)
No. 35, June, 1948 - No. 40, May, 1949
Ace Magazines (A. A. Wyn)

35-Teen-age 5.70 17.00 35.00
36,38-40 3.60 9.00 18.00
37-Transvestism story 4.00 10.00 20.00

DOTTY DRIPPLE (Horace & Dotty Dripple No. 25 on)
1946 - No. 24, June, 1952 (Also see A-1 No. 3-8, 10)
Magazine Ent.(Life's Romances)/Harvey No. 3 on

A-1 #1 (1pg. D. Dripple; Mr. Ex, Bush Berry, Rocky, Lew Loyal (20 pgs.)
8.75 26.25 70.00
1 (nd) (10¢) 4.15 12.50 25.00
2 2.40 6.00 12.00
3-10: 3,4-Powell-a 1.60 4.00 8.00
11-24 1.20 3.00 6.00

DOTTY DRIPPLE AND TAFFY
No. 646, Sept, 1955 - No. 903, May, 1958
Dell Publishing Co.

Four Color 646 (#1) 2.75 8.00 30.00
Four Color 691,718,746,801,903 1.80 5.50 20.00

DOUBLE ACTION COMICS
No. 2, Jan, 1940 (68 pgs., B&W)
National Periodical Publications

2-Contains original stories(?); pre-hero DC contents; same cover as Adventure No. 37. (six known copies) (not an ashcan)
Estimated value.... 11,000.00

NOTE: *The cover to this book was probably reprinted from Adventure #37. #1 exists as an ash can copy with B&W cover; contains a coverless comic on inside with 1st & last page missing.*

DOUBLE COMICS
1940 - 1944 (132 pgs.)
Elliot Publications

1940 issues; Masked Marvel-c & The Mad Mong vs. The White Flash covers known 172.00 516.00 1550.00
1941 issues; Tornado Tim-c, Nordac-c, & Green Light covers known
122.00 366.00 1100.00
1942 issues 94.00 282.00 850.00
1943,1944 issues 75.00 225.00 675.00

NOTE: *Double Comics consisted of an almost endless combination of pairs of remaindered, unsold issues of comics representing most publishers and usually mixed publishers in the same book; e.g., a Captain America with a Silver Streak, or a Feature with a Detective, etc., could appear inside the same cover. The actual contents would have to determine its price. Prices listed are for average contents. Any containing rare origin or first issues are worth much more. Covers also vary in same year. Value would be approximately 50 percent of contents.*

DOUBLE-CROSS (See The Crusaders)

DOUBLE-DARE ADVENTURES
Dec, 1966 - No. 2, Mar, 1967 (35¢/25¢, 68 pgs.)
Harvey Publications

1-Origin Bee-Man, Glowing Gladiator, & Magic-Master; Simon/Kirby-a (last S&K art as a team?) 4.00 12.00 40.00
2-Williamson/Crandall-a; r/Alarming Adv. #3('63) 3.00 9.00 30.00

NOTE: ***Powell** a-1. **Simon/Sparling** c-1, 2.*

DOUBLE DRAGON
July, 1991 - No. 6, Dec, 1991 ($1.00, limited series)
Marvel Comics

1-6: Based on video game. 2-Art Adams-c 1.00

GD25 FN65 NM94

DOUBLE EDGE
Alpha, 1995; Omega, 1995 ($4.95, limited series)
Marvel Comics

Alpha ($4.95)- Punisher story, Nick Fury app. 2.00 5.00
Omega ($4.95)-Punisher, Daredevil, Ghost Rider app. Death of Nick Fury
2.00 5.00

DOUBLE IMPACT (Double Impact Blondage #3 & Double Impact Buttshots #6 on cover only)
Mar, 1995 - No. 7, 1996 ($3.95/$2.95/$3.00)
High Impact Studios

0 (1997, $2.95) 1.20 3.00
0 ($9.95)-Nude Edition 1.25 3.75 10.00
1 (Chromium-c.)-Intro Jazz & China. 1.60 4.00
1 (Rainbow-c.) 1.50 4.50 12.00
2-7 (Regular-c.): 4-variant-c. w/no logo exists. 5-fold out back-c. 6-3 variant-c exist. 7-Intro Nikki Blade. 1.20 3.00
2 ($9.95) Nude-c;.polybagged & signed 1.25 3.75 10.00
2,3 (Nude-c.) (limited to 5000) 1.25 3.75 10.00
3-"Blondage" variant-c 2.40 6.00
3-($14.95) "Blondage Deluxe"; polybagged & signed 1.85 5.50 15.00
4-"Bad Boy Arizona" variant-c 2.40 6.00
7-Gold (1,000 copies); gold foil logo 2.40 6.00
San Diego Special ('95, limited to 5000) 1.25 3.75 10.00
San Diego Special ('96, limited to 1000) 2.40 6.00
San Diego Special Nude Ed. ('96, limited to 1000) 1.85 5.50 15.00

DOUBLE IMPACT
V2#1, 1996 - Present ($3.00)
High Impact Studios

V2#1-3-Wraparound-c. 3-Three-c 1.20 3.00
1-($4.00)-Deluxe Edition; wraparound-foil-c 1.20 3.00
1-Wraparound, prism, foil-c 2.00 5.00
1-Gold foil logo 1.20 3.00
1-($14.95) Swedish Erotica 1.85 5.50 15.00
1-Variant-c 1.20 3.00
2-($10.00)-Nude Ed.; suicide-c 1.25 3.75 10.00

DOUBLE IMPACT/HELLINA (See Hellina/Double Impact)
Mar, 1996 ($3.00, one-shot)
High Impact Studios

1 1.20 3.00
1-($9.95) Nude Edition 1.25 3.75 10.00

DOUBLE LIFE OF PRIVATE STRONG, THE
June, 1959 - No. 2, Aug, 1959
Archie Publications/Radio Comics

1-Origin & re-intro The Shield; Simon & Kirby-c/a, their re-entry into the super-hero genre; intro./1st app. The Fly; 1st S.A. super-hero for Archie Publ.
48.00 144.00 575.00
2-S&K-c/a; Tuska-a; The Fly app. (2nd or 3rd?) 32.00 96.00 320.00

DOUBLE TALK (Also see Two-Faces)
No date (1962?) (32 pgs., full color, slick-c)
Christian Anti-Communism Crusade (Giveaway)
Feature Publications

nn-Sickle with blood-c 7.00 21.00 70.00

DOUBLE TROUBLE
Nov, 1957 - No. 2, Jan-Feb, 1958
St. John Publishing Co.

1,2: Tuffy & Snuffy by Frank Johnson; dubbed "World's Funniest Kids"
4.25 13.00 28.00

DOUBLE TROUBLE WITH GOOBER
No. 417, Aug, 1952 - No. 556, May, 1954
Dell Publishing Co.

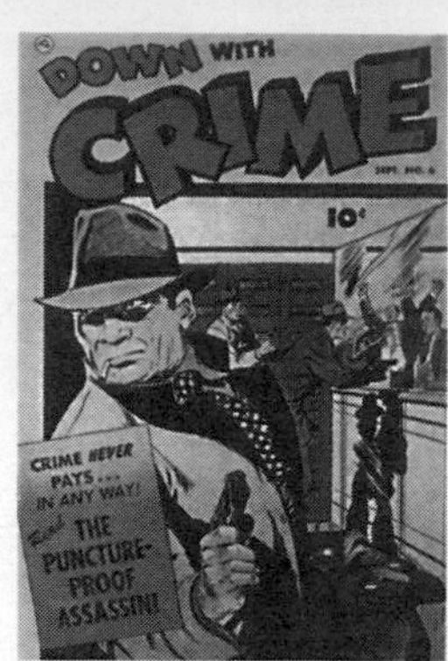

Down With Crime #6 © FAW

Dracula Chronicles #3 © Topps

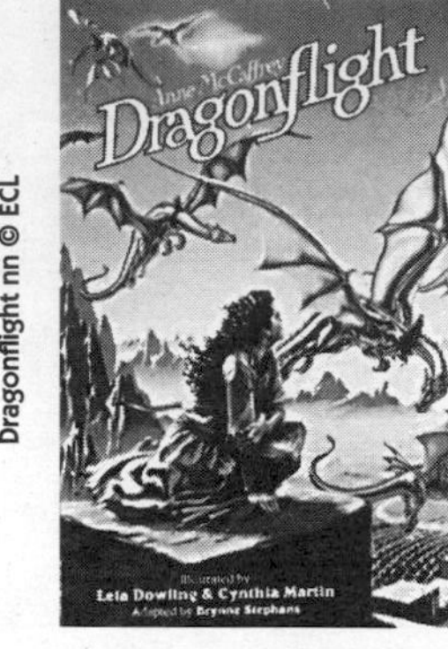

Dragonflight nn © ECL

	GD25	FN65	NM94
Four Color 417	2.25	6.75	25.00
Four Color 471,516,556	1.85	5.50	15.00

DOUBLE UP
1941 (Pocket size, 200 pgs.)
Elliott Publications

	GD25	FN65	NM94
1-Contains rebound copies of digest sized issues of Pocket Comics, Speed Comics, & Spitfire Comics	63.00	189.00	565.00

DOVER & CLOVER (See All Funny & More Fun Comics #93)

DOVER BOYS (See Adventures of the...)

DOVER THE BIRD
Spring, 1955
Famous Funnies Publishing Co.

	GD25	FN65	NM94
1-Funny animal; code approved	4.25	13.00	28.00

DOWN WITH CRIME
Nov, 1952 - No. 7, Nov, 1953
Fawcett Publications

	GD25	FN65	NM94
1	23.00	68.00	180.00
2,4,5: 2,4-Powell-a in each. 5-Bondage-c	11.30	34.00	90.00
3-Used in **POP**, pg. 106; "H is for Heroin" drug story	12.00	36.00	95.00
6,7: 6-Used in **POP**, pg. 80	8.75	26.25	70.00

DO YOU BELIEVE IN NIGHTMARES?
Nov, 1957 - No. 2, Jan, 1958
St. John Publishing Co.

	GD25	FN65	NM94
1-Mostly Ditko-c/a	39.00	116.00	280.00
2-Ayers-a	21.00	62.00	150.00

D.P. 7
Nov, 1986 - No. 32, June, 1989 (26 on: $1.50)
Marvel Comics Group (New Universe)

	GD25	FN65	NM94
1-20			1.25
21-32		.80	2.00
Annual #1 (11/87)-Intro. The Witness			1.25

NOTE: ***Williamson*** *a-9i, 11i; c-9i.*

DRACULA (See Bram Stoker's Dracula, Giant-Size..., Little Dracula, Marvel Graphic Novel, Requiem for Dracula, Spider-Man Vs...., Tomb of... & Wedding of...; also see Movie Classics under Universal Presents as well as Dracula)

DRACULA (See Movie Classics for #1)(Also see Frankenstein & Werewolf)
No. 2, 11/66 - No. 4, 3/67; No. 6, 7/72 - No. 8, 7/73 (No #5)
Dell Publishing Co.

	GD25	FN65	NM94
2-Origin & 1st app. Dracula (11/66) (super hero)	2.25	6.75	24.00
3,4: 4-Intro. Fleeta ('67)	1.75	5.25	14.00
6-('72)-r/#2 w/origin	1.50	4.50	12.00
7,8-r/#3, #4	1.25	3.75	10.00

DRACULA (Magazine)
1979 (120 pgs., full color)
Warren Publishing Co.

	GD25	FN65	NM94
Book 1-Maroto art; Spanish material translated into English	3.50	10.50	35.00

DRACULA CHRONICLES
Apr, 1995 - No. 3, June, 1995 ($2.50, limited series)
Topps Comics

	GD25	FN65	NM94
1-3-Linsner-c		1.00	2.50

DRACULA LIVES! (Magazine)(Also see Tomb of Dracula)
1973(no month) - No. 13, July, 1975 (75¢, B&W)(76 pgs.)
Marvel Comics Group

	GD25	FN65	NM94
1-Buris painted-c	3.00	9.00	30.00
2 (7/73)-1st time origin Dracula; Adams, Starlin-a	2.50	7.50	22.00
3-1st app. Robert E. Howard's Soloman Kane; Adams-c/a	2.50	7.50	20.00
4,5: 4-Ploog-a. 5(V2#1)-Bram Stoker's Classic Dracula adapt. begins	2.00	6.00	16.00
6-9: 6-8-Bram Stoker adapt. 9-Bondage-c	1.75	5.25	14.00
10 (1/75)-16 pg. Lilith solo (1st?)	2.50	7.50	20.00
11-13: 11-21 pg. Lilith solo sty. 12-31 pg. Dracula sty	1.75	5.25	14.00
Annual 1(Summer, 1975, $1.25, 92 pgs.)-Morrow painted-c; 6 Dracula stys. 25 pgs. Adams-a(r)	2.25	6.75	18.00

NOTE: ***N. Adams*** *a-2, 3i, 10i, Annual 1r(2, 3i).* ***Alcala*** *a-9.* ***Buscema*** *a-3p, 6p, Annual 1p.* ***Colan*** *a(p)-1, 2, 5, 6, 8.* ***Evans*** *a-7.* ***Gulacy*** *a-9.* ***Heath*** *a-1r, 13.* ***Pakula*** *a-6r. Sutton a-13.* ***Weiss*** *r-Annual 1p. 4* ***Dracula*** *stories each in 1, 609; 3* ***Dracula*** *stories each in 2, 4, 5,, 13.*

DRACULA: RETURN OF THE IMPALER
July, 1993 - No. 4, Oct, 1994 ($2.95, limited series)
Slave Labor Graphics

	GD25	FN65	NM94
1-4		1.20	3.00

DRACULA VERSUS ZORRO
Oct, 1993 - No. 2, Nov, 1993 ($2.95, limited series)
Topps Comics

	GD25	FN65	NM94
1,2: 1-Spot varnish & red foil-c. 2-Polybagged w/16 pg. Zorro #0		1.20	3.00

DRACULA: VLAD THE IMPALER (Also see Bram Stoker's Dracula)
Feb, 1993 - No. 3, Apr, 1993 ($2.95, limited series)
Topps Comics

	GD25	FN65	NM94
1-3-Polybagged with 3 trading cards each; Maroto-c/a		1.20	3.00

DRAFT, THE
1988 ($3.50, one-shot, squarebound)
Marvel Comics

	GD25	FN65	NM94
1-Sequel to "The Pitt"		1.40	3.50

DRAG 'N' WHEELS (Formerly Top Eliminator)
No. 30, Sept, 1968 - No. 59, May, 1973
Charlton Comics

	GD25	FN65	NM94
30	3.00	9.00	30.00
31-40-Scot Jackson begins	2.50	7.50	24.00
41-50	2.25	6.75	18.00
51-59: Scot Jackson	1.25	3.75	10.00
Modern Comics Reprint 58('78)		2.40	6.00

DRAGON, THE (Also see The Savage Dragon)
Mar, 1996 - No. 5, July, 1996 (99¢, limited series)
Image Comics (Highbrow Entertainment)

	GD25	FN65	NM94
1-5: Reprints Savage Dragon limited series w/new story & art. 5-Youngblood app; includes 5 pg. Savage Dragon story from 1984			1.00

DRAGON, THE: BLOOD & GUTS (Also see The Savage Dragon)
Mar, 1995 - No. 3, May, 1995 ($2.50, limited series)
Image Comics (Highbrow Entertainment)

	GD25	FN65	NM94
1-3: Jason Pearson-c/a/scripts		1.00	2.50

DRAGON CHIANG
1991 ($3.95, B&W, squarebound, 52 pgs.)
Eclipse Books

	GD25	FN65	NM94
nn -Timothy Truman-c/a(p)		1.60	4.00

DRAGONFLIGHT
Feb, 1991 - No. 3, 1991 ($4.95, 52 pgs.)
Eclipse Books

	GD25	FN65	NM94
Book One - Three: Adapts 1968 novel		2.00	5.00

DRAGONFLY (See Americomics #4)
Sum, 1985 - No. 8, 1986 ($1.75/$1.95)
Americomics

	GD25	FN65	NM94
1		1.20	3.00

Dragon Lines: Way of the Warrior #2 © MEG

Dragon Strike #1 © MEG

Dreadstar #46 © Jim Starlin

	GD25	FN65	NM94
2-8		.80	2.00

DRAGONFORCE
1988 - No. 13, 1989 ($2.00)
Aircel Publishing

	GD25	FN65	NM94
1-Dale Keown-c/a/scripts in #1-12		1.60	4.00
2-13: 13-No Keown-a		.80	2.00
...Chronicles Book 1-5 ($2.95, B&W, 60 pgs.): Dale Keown-r/Dragonring & Dragonforce		1.20	3.00

DRAGONHEART (Movie)
May, 1996 - No. 2, June, 1996 ($2.95/$4.95, limited series)
Topps Comics

	GD25	FN65	NM94
1-($2.95, 24 pgs.)-Adaptation of the film; Hildebrandt Bros-c; Lim-a.		1.20	3.00
2-($4.95, 64 pgs.)		2.00	5.00

DRAGONLANCE (Also see TSR Worlds)
Dec, 1988 - No. 34, Sept, 1991 ($1.25/$1.50, Mando paper)
DC Comics

	GD25	FN65	NM94
1-Based on TSR game		.80	2.00
2			1.50
3-15: 6-Begin $1.50-c			1.50
16-34: 25-Begin $1.75-c. 30-32-Kaluta-c		.70	1.80
Annual 1 (1990, $2.95, 68 pgs.)		1.20	3.00

DRAGON LINES
May, 1993 - No. 4, Aug, 1993 ($1.95, limited series)
Marvel Comics (Epic Comics/Heavy Hitters)

	GD25	FN65	NM94
1-($2.50)-Embossed-c; Ron Lim-c/a in all		1.00	2.50
2-4		.80	2.00

DRAGON LINES: WAY OF THE WARRIOR
Nov, 1993 - No. 2, Jan, 1994 ($2.25, limited series)
Marvel Comics (Epic Comics/ Heavy Hitters)

	GD25	FN65	NM94
1,2-Ron Lim-c/a(p)		.90	2.25

DRAGONQUEST
Dec, 1986 - No. 3, 1987 ($1.50, B&W, 28 pgs.)
Silverwolf Comics

	GD25	FN65	NM94
1-3-Tim Vigil-c/a in all			1.50

DRAGONRING
1986 - V2#15, 1988 ($1.70/$2.00, B&W/color)
Aircel Publishing

	GD25	FN65	NM94
1		.80	2.00
2-6: 6-Last B&W issue		.80	2.00
V2#1-($2.00, color)		.80	2.00
2-15		.70	1.80

DRAGON'S CLAWS
July, 1988 - No. 10, Apr, 1989 ($1.25/$1.50/$1.75, British)
Marvel Comics UK, Ltd.

	GD25	FN65	NM94
1-4: 2-Begin $1.50-c. 3-Death's Head 1 pg. strip on back-c (1st app.). 4-Silhouette of Death's Head on last pg.			1.50
5-1st full app. new Death's Head; begin $1.75-c		.70	1.75
6-10		.70	1.75

DRAGONSLAYER (Movie)
October, 1981 - No. 2, Nov, 1981
Marvel Comics Group

	GD25	FN65	NM94
1,2-Paramount Disney movie adaptation			1.00

DRAGON'S STAR 2
1994 ($2.95, B&W)
Caliber Press

	GD25	FN65	NM94
1		1.20	3.00

DRAGON STRIKE
Feb, 1994 ($1.25)
Marvel Comics

	GD25	FN65	NM94
1-Based on TSR role playing game			1.25

DRAGOON WELLS MASSACRE
No. 815, June, 1957
Dell Publishing Co.

	GD25	FN65	NM94
Four Color 815-Movie, photo-c	7.00	22.00	80.00

DRAGSTRIP HOTRODDERS (World of Wheels No. 17 on)
Sum, 1963; No. 2, Jan, 1965 - No. 16, Aug, 1967
Charlton Comics

	GD25	FN65	NM94
1	3.60	10.80	36.00
2-5	2.50	7.50	24.00
6-16	2.25	6.75	18.00

DRAKUUN
Feb, 1997 - Present ($2.95, B&W, limited series, manga)
Dark Horse Comics

	GD25	FN65	NM94
1-6- Johji Manabe-s/a in all. Rise of the Dragon Princess.			2.95
..7-12-Revenge of Gustav.			2.95

DRAMA
June, 1994 ($2.95, mature)
Sirius

	GD25	FN65	NM94
1-1st full color Dawn app. in comics	2.50	7.50	25.00
1-Limited edition (1400 copies); signed & numbered; fingerprint authenticity	6.00	18.00	60.00

NOTE: *Dawn's 1st full color app. was a pin-up in Amazing Heroes' Swimsuit Special #5.*

DRAMA OF AMERICA, THE
1973 ($1.95, 224 pgs.)
Action Text

	GD25	FN65	NM94
1- "Students' Supplement to History"		1.20	3.00

DREADLANDS (Also see Epic)
1992 - No. 4, 1992 ($3.95, limited series, 52 pgs.)
Marvel Comics (Epic Comics)

	GD25	FN65	NM94
1-4: Stiff-c		1.60	4.00

DREADSTAR
Nov, 1982 - No. 64, Mar, 1991
Marvel Comics (Epic Comics)/First Comics No. 27 on

	GD25	FN65	NM94
1-5,8-64: 1-Starlin-a begins		.80	2.00
6,7-1st app. Interstellar Toybox; 8pgs. ea.; Wrightson-a		1.20	3.00
Annual 1 (12/83)-r/The Price		1.20	3.00

DREADSTAR
Apr, 1994 - No.6, Jan, 1995 ($2.50, limited series)
Malibu Comics (Bravura)

	GD25	FN65	NM94
1-6-Peter David scripts: 1,2-Starlin-c		1.00	2.50

NOTE: *Issues 1-6 contain Bravura stamps.*

DREADSTAR AND COMPANY
July, 1985 - No. 6, Dec, 1985
Marvel Comics (Epic Comics)

	GD25	FN65	NM94
1-6: 1,3,6-New Starlin-a: 2-New Wrightson-c; reprints of Dreadstar series.			1.00

DREAM ANGEL
No. 0, Fall, 1996 - No. 1, Winter, 1997 ($2.95, B&W, limited series)
Angel Entertainment

	GD25	FN65	NM94
0,1: Deodato Studios-c		1.20	3.00
0,1-($5.95) Deluxe Ed.; foil-c		2.40	6.00
0,1-($10.00) Nude-c	1.25	3.75	10.00
0,1-($10.00) Deodato Studios Nude-c	1.25	3.75	10.00

The Dreaming #17 © DC

Dreamwalker #5 © Jenni Gregory

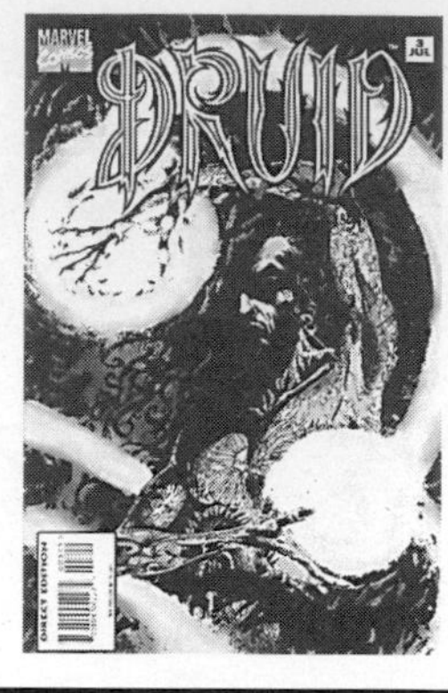

Druid #3 © MEG

GD25 FN65 NM94

DREAM ANGEL: THE QUANTUM DREAMER
No. 0, Winter, 1997 - No. 2, Spring, 1997 ($2.95, B&W, limited series)
Angel Entertainment

0-2 — 1.20 3.00

DREAM BOOK OF LOVE (Also see A-1 Comics)
No. 106, June-July, 1954 - No. 123, Oct-Nov, 1954
Magazine Enterprises

A-1 106 (#1)-Powell, Bolle-a; Montgomery Clift, Donna Reed photo-c — 8.75 26.25 65.00
A-1-114 (#2)-Guardineer, Bolle-a; Piper Laurie, Victor Mature photo-c — 7.85 23.50 55.00
A-1 123 (#3)-Movie photo-c — 6.50 19.50 45.00

DREAM BOOK OF ROMANCE (Also see A-1 Comics)
No. 92, 1954 - No. 124, Oct-Nov, 1954
Magazine Enterprises

A-1 92 (#5)-Guardineer-a; photo-c — 8.50 26.00 60.00
A-1 101 (#6)(4-6/54)-Marlon Brando photo-c; Powell, Bolle, Guardineer0a — 14.50 43.00 115.00
A-1 109 (#7)(7-8/54)-Powell-a; movie photo-c — 6.50 19.50 45.00
A-1 110 (#8)(1/54)-Movie photo-c — 6.50 19.50 45.00
A-1 124 (#8)(10-11/54) — 6.50 19.50 45.00

DREAMERY, THE
Dec, 1986 - No. 14, Feb, 1989 ($2.00, B&W, Baxter paper)
Eclipse Comics

1-14: 2-7-Alice In Wonderland adapt. — .80 2.00

DREAMING, THE (See Sandman, 2nd Series)
June, 1996 - Present ($2.50)
DC Comics (Vertigo)

1-McKean-c on all.; LaBan scripts & Snejbjerg-a — 1.40 3.50
2-20: 2,3-LaBan scripts & Snejbjerg-a. 4-7-Hogan scripts; Parkhouse-a. 8-Zulli-a. 9-11-Talbot-s/Taylor-a(p) — 1.00 2.50
...Beyond The Shores of Night TPB ('97, $19.95) r/#1-8 — 19.95

DREAM OF LOVE
1958 (Reprints)
I. W. Enterprises

1,2,8: 1-r/Dream Book of Love #1; Bob Powell-a. 2-r/Grest Lovers Romances #10. 8-Great Lover's Romances #1; also contains 2 Jon Juan stories by Siegel & Schomburg; Kinstler-c. — 2.00 5.00 10.00
9-Kinstler-c; 1pg. John Wayne interview & Frazetta illo from John Wayne Adv. Comics #2 — 1.60 4.00 8.00

DREAM TEAM (See Battlezones: Dream Team 2)
July, 1995 ($4.95, one-shot)
Malibu Comics (Ultraverse)

1-Pin-ups teaming up Marvel & Ultraverse characters by various artists including Allred, Hamner, Romita, Darrow, Balent, Quesada & Palmiotti. — 2.00 5.00

DREAMWALKER
Dec, 1996 - Present ($2.95, B&W)
Caliber Comics (Tapestry)

1-5-Jenni Gregory-c/s/a — 2.95

DRIFT FENCE (See Zane Grey 4-Color 270)

DRIFT MARLO
May-July, 1962 - No. 2, Oct-Dec, 1962
Dell Publishing Co.

01-232-207(#1), 2(12-232-212) — 2.75 8.00 30.00

DRISCOLL'S BOOK OF PIRATES
1934 (B&W, hardcover; 124 pgs, 7x9")
David McKay Publ. (Not reprints)

nn-By Montford Amory — 17.50 53.00 140.00

DROIDS (Also see Dark Horse Comics)
April, 1986 - No. 8, June, 1987 (Based on Saturday morning cartoon)
Marvel Comics (Star Comics)

1-R2D2 & C-3PO from Star Wars app. in all — 1.50 4.50 12.00
2-8 — 1.10 3.30 9.00
NOTE: *Romita* a-3p. *Williamson* a-2i, 5i, 7i, 8i. *Sinnott* a-3i.

DROOPY (see Tom & Jerry #60)

DROOPY (Tex Avery's...)
Oct, 1995 - No. 3, Dec, 1995 ($2.50, limited series)
Dark Horse Comics

1-3: Characters created by Tex Avery; painted-c — 2.50

DROPSIE AVENUE: THE NEIGHBORHOOD
June, 1995 ($15.95/$24.95, B&W)
Kitchen Sink Press

nn-Will Eisner (softcover) — 2.00 6.00 16.00
nn-Will Eisner (hardcover) — 2.50 7.50 25.00

DROWNED GIRL, THE
1990 ($5.95, 52 pgs, mature)
DC Comics (Piranha Press)

nn — 2.40 6.00

DRUG WARS
1989 ($1.95)
Pioneer Comics

1-Grell-c — .80 2.00

DRUID
May, 1995 - No. 4, Aug, 1995 ($2.50, limited series)
Marvel Comics

1-4: Warren Ellis scripts. — 1.00 2.50

DRUM BEAT
No. 610, Jan, 1955
Dell Publishing Co.

Four Color 610-Movie, Alan Ladd photo-c — 9.00 27.00 100.00

DRUMS OF DOOM
1937 (25¢)(Indian)(Text w/color illos.)
United Features Syndicate

nn-By Lt. F.A. Methot; Golden Thunder app.; Tip Top Comics ad in comic; nice-c — 25.00 75.00 200.00

DRUNKEN FIST
Aug, 1988 - Present? ($1.50/$1.95, 68 pgs.)
Jademan Comics

1-8-($1.50) — 1.50
9-44-($1.95) — .80 2.00

DUCK ALBUM (See Donald Duck Album)
No. 353, Oct, 1951 - No. 840, Sept, 1957
Dell Publishing Co.

Four Color 353 (#1)-Barks-c; 1st Uncle Scrooge-c (also appears on back-c). — 7.00 22.00 80.00
Four Color 450-Barks-c — 5.50 16.50 60.00
Four Color 492,531,560,586,611,649,686 — 4.50 13.50 50.00
Four Color 726,782,840 — 4.50 13.50 50.00

DUCKMAN
Sept, 1990 ($1.95, B&W, one-shot)
Dark Horse Comics

1-Story & art by Everett Peck — .80 2.00

DUCKMAN
Nov, 1994 - No. 5, May, 1995; No. 0, Feb, 1996 ($2.50, bi-monthly)

Ducktales #1 © WDC

Dumbo Weekly #7 © WDC

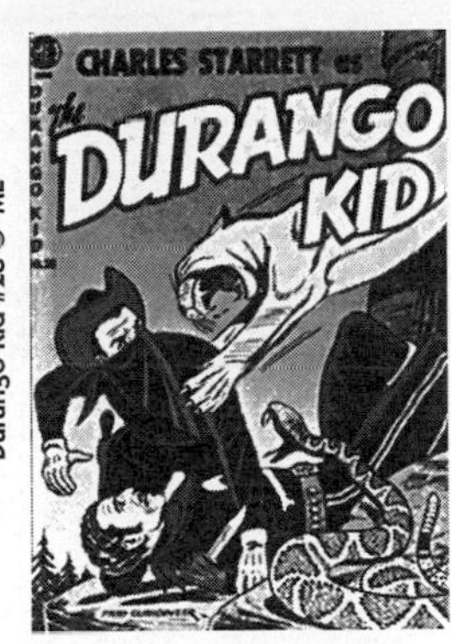

Durango Kid #28 © ME

GD25 FN65 NM94

Topps Comics
0 (2/96, $2.95, B&W)-r/Duckman #1 from Dark Horse Comics. 1.20 3.00
1-5: 1-w/ coupon #A for Duckman trading card. 2-w/Duckman 1st season episode guide 1.00 2.50

DUCKMAN: THE MOB FROG SAGA
Nov, 1994 - No. 3, Feb, 1995 ($2.50, limited series)
Topps Comics
1-3: 1-w/coupon #B for Duckman tradiing card, S. Shaw!-c 1.00 2.50

DUCKTALES
Oct, 1988 - No. 13, May, 1990 (1,2,9-11: $1.50; 3-8: 95¢)
Gladstone Publishing
1-Barks-r 2.40 6.00
2,10,11: Barks-r 1.60 4.00
3-9:4-6,9-Barks-r. 7-Barks-r(1 pg.) 1.60 4.00
12,13 ($1.95, 68 pgs.)-Barks-r; 12-r/F.C. #495 2.00 5.00

DUCKTALES
June, 1990 - No. 18, Nov, 1991 ($1.50)
Disney Comics
1-All new stories 1.10 2.75
2-18 .65 1.60
The Movie nn (1990, $7.95, 68 pgs.)-Graphic novel adapting animated movie 1.00 3.00 8.00

DUDLEY (Teen-age)
Nov-Dec, 1949 - No. 3, Mar-Apr, 1950
Feature/Prize Publications
1-By Boody Rogers 12.00 38.00 100.00
2,3 8.75 26.25 65.00

DUDLEY DO-RIGHT (TV)
Aug, 1970 - No. 7, Aug, 1971 (Jay Ward)
Charlton Comics
1 7.50 22.50 75.00
2-7 5.00 15.00 50.00

DUKE OF THE K-9 PATROL
Apr, 1963
Gold Key
1 (10052-304) 2.75 8.00 30.00

DUMBO (Disney; see Movie Comics, & Walt Disney Showcase #12)
No. 17, 1941 - No. 668, Jan, 1958
Dell Publishing Co.
Four Color 17 (#1)-Mickey Mouse, Donald Duck, Pluto app. 157.00 470.00 1725.00
Large Feature Comic 19 ('41)-Part-r 4-Color 17 227.00 682.00 2500.00
Four Color 234 ('49) 9.00 27.00 100.00
Four Color 668 (12/55)-1st of two printings. Dumbo on-c with starry sky. Reprints Four Color 234? same-c as 234 7.00 22.00 80.00
Four Color 668 (1/58)-2nd printing. Same cover altered with Timothy Mouse added. Same contents as above 5.50 16.50 60.00

DUMBO (Walt Disney's..., The Flying Elephant)
1941 (K.K. Publ. Giveaway)
Weatherbird Shoes/Ernest Kern Co.(Detroit)
nn-16 pgs., 9x10" (Rare) 36.00 108.00 325.00
nn-52 pgs., 5-1/2x8-1/2", slick cover in color; B&W interior; half text, half reprints 4-Color No. 17 22.00 66.00 175.00

DUMBO COMIC PAINT BOOK (See Dumbo, Large Feature Comic No. 19)

DUMBO WEEKLY
1942 (Premium supplied by Diamond D-X Gas Stations)
Walt Disney Productions
1 40.00 120.00 360.00
2-16 14.00 41.00 110.00
Binder only 290.00
NOTE: *A cover and binder came separate at gas stations. Came with membership card.*

DUNC AND LOO (#1-3 titled "Around the Block with Dunc and Loo")
Oct-Dec, 1961 - No. 8, Oct-Dec, 1963
Dell Publishing Co.
1 8.00 25.00 90.00
2 5.00 15.00 55.00
3-8 3.60 11.00 40.00
NOTE: *Written by* ***John Stanley; Bill Williams*** *art.*

DUNE (Movie)
Apr, 1985 - No. 3, June, 1985
Marvel Comics
1-3-r/Marvel Super Special; movie adaptation 1.00

DUNG BOYS, THE
1996 - No. 3, 1996 ($2.95, B&W, limited series)
Kitchen Sink Press
1-3 1.20 3.00

DURANGO KID, THE (Also see Best of the West, Great Western & White Indian) (Charles Starrett starred in Columbia's Durango Kid movies)
Oct-Nov, 1949 - No. 41, Oct-Nov, 1955 (All 36 pgs.)
Magazine Enterprises
1-Charles Starrett photo-c; Durango Kid & his horse Raider begin; Dan Brand & Tipi (origin) begin by Frazetta & continue through #16 58.00 174.00 525.00
2-Starrett photo-c. 30.00 90.00 240.00
3-5-All have Starrett photo-c. 29.00 86.00 230.00
6-10: 7-Atomic weapon-c/story 15.00 45.00 120.00
11-16-Last Frazetta issue 10.00 30.00 80.00
17-Origin Durango Kid 14.50 43.00 115.00
18-Fred Meagher-a on Dan Brand begins 8.75 26.25 65.00
19-30: 19-Guardineer-c/a(3) begins, end #41. 23-Intro. The Red Scorpion 8.75 26.25 65.00
31-Red Scorpion returns 8.50 26.00 60.00
32-41 Bollo/Frazettaish-a (Dan Brand; true in later issues?) 8.50 26.00 60.00
NOTE: *#6, 8, 14, 15 contain* ***Frazetta*** *art not reprinted in White Indian.* ***Ayers*** *c-18.* ***Guardineer*** *a(3)-19-41; c-19-41.* ***Fred Meagher*** *a-18-29 at least.*

DURANGO KID, THE
1990 - #2, 1990 ($2.50, half-color)
AC Comics
1-Starrett photo front/back-c; Guardineer-r 1.00 2.50
2-($2.75, B&W)-Starrett photo-c; White Indian-r by Frazetta; Guardineer-r (50th anniversary of films) 1.10 2.75

DUSTY STAR
Apr, 1997 - Present ($2.95, B&W)
Image Comics (Desperado Studios)
0,1-Pruett-s/Robinson-a 3.95

DV8 (See Gen 13)
Aug, 1996 - Present ($2.50)
Image Comics (Wildstorm Productions)
1/2 1.25 3.75 10.00
1-Warren Ellis scripts & Humberto Ramos-c/a(p) 2.00 5.00
NOTE: *Seven variant-c exist based on the seven deadly sins*
1-Jim Lee variant-c 2.40 6.00
1-Each of the six variant-c not by Jim Lee 1.80 4.50
2-4: 3-No Ramos-a 1.80 4.50
5-13 1.00 2.50
Rave-(7/96, $1.75)-Ramos-c; pinups & interviews 1.80 4.50

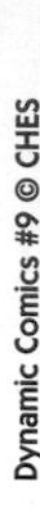
Dynamic Comics #9 © CHES

Dynamo #3 © TC

Elarthworm Jim #2 © MEG

GD25 FN65 NM94

DV8 VS. BLACK OPS
Oct, 1997 - No. 3 ($2.50, limited series)
Image Comics (Wildstorm Productions)

1-Bury-s/Norton-a — 1.00 2.50

DWIGHT D. EISENHOWER
December, 1969
Dell Publishing Co.

01-237-912 - Life story — 1.80 5.50 20.00

DYNABRITE COMICS
1978 - 1979 (69¢, 10x7-1/8", 48 pgs., cardboard-c)
(Blank inside covers)
Whitman Publishing Co.

11350 - Walt Disney's Mickey Mouse & the Beanstalk (4-C 157). 11350-1 - Mickey Mouse Album (4-C 1057,1151,1246). 11351 - Mickey Mouse & His Sky Adventure (4-C 214, 343). 11352 - Donald Duck (4-C 408, Donald Duck 45,52)-Barks-a. 11352-1 - Donald Duck (4-C 318, 10 pg. Barks/WDC&S 125,128)-Barks-c(r). 11353 - Daisy Duck's Diary (4-C 1055,1150) Barks-a. 11354 - Goofy: A Gaggle of Giggles. 11354-1 - Super Goof Meets Super Thief. 11355 - Uncle Scrooge (Barks-a/U.S. 12,33). 11355-1 - Uncle Scrooge (Barks-a/U.S. 13,16) - Barks-c(r). 11356 - (?). 11357 - Star Trek (r/-Star Trek 33,41). 11358 - Star Trek (r/-Star Trek 34,36). 11359 - Bugs Bunny-r. 11360 - Winnie the Pooh Fun and Fantasy (Disney-r). 11361 - Gyro Gearloose & the Disney Ducks (r/4-C 1047,1184)-Barks-c(r)
each.... — 1.00

DYNAMIC ADVENTURES
No. 8, 1964 - No. 9, 1964
I. W. Enterprises

8-Kayo Kirby-r by Baker?/Fight Comics 53. — 2.00 6.00 16.00
9-Reprints Avon's "Escape From Devil's Island"; Kinstler-c — 2.25 6.75 18.00
nn (no date)-Reprints Risks Unlimited with Rip Carson, Senorita Rio; r/Fight #53 — 2.00 6.00 16.00

DYNAMIC CLASSICS (See Cancelled Comic Cavalcade)
Sept-Oct, 1978 (44 pgs.)
DC Comics

1-Neal Adams Batman, Simonson Manhunter-r — 1.60 4.00

DYNAMIC COMICS (No #4-7)
Oct, 1941 - No. 3, Feb, 1942; No. 8, 1944 - No. 25, May, 1948
Harry 'A' Chesler

1-Origin Major Victory by Charles Sultan (reprinted in Major Victory #1), Dynamic Man & Hale the Magician; The Black Cobra only app.; Major Victory & Dynamic Man begin — 133.00 400.00 1200.00
2-Origin Dynamic Boy & Lady Satan; intro. The Green Knight & sidekick Lance Cooper — 61.00 183.00 550.00
3 — 50.00 150.00 450.00
8-Dan Hastings, The Echo, The Master Key, Yankee Boy begin; Yankee Doodle Jones app.; hypo story — 50.00 150.00 450.00
9-Mr. E begins; Mac Raboy-c — 53.00 159.00 475.00
10 — 39.00 117.00 350.00
11-15: 15-The Sky Chief app. — 36.00 108.00 300.00
16-Marijuana story — 36.00 108.00 310.00
17(1/46)-Illustrated in **SOTI**, "The children told me what the man was going to do with the hot poker," but Wertham saw this in Crime Reporter #2 — 44.00 132.00 400.00
18,19,21,22,24,25 — 28.00 83.00 220.00
20-Bare-breasted woman-c — 39.00 117.00 350.00
23-Yankee Girl app. — 28.00 83.00 220.00
I.W. Reprint #1,8('64): 1-r/#23. 8-Exist? — 2.50 7.50 20.00

NOTE: ***Kinstler** c-IW #1. **Tuska** art in many issues, #3, 9, 11, 12, 16, 19. Bondage c-16.*

DYNAMITE (Becomes Johnny Dynamite No. 10 on)
May, 1953 - No. 9, Sept, 1954
Comic Media/Allen Hardy Publ.

1-Pete Morisi-a; Don Heck-c; r-as Danger #6 — 14.00 41.00 110.00
2 — 8.50 26.00 60.00
3-Marijuana story; Johnny Dynamite (1st app.) begins by Pete Morisi(c/a); Heck text-a; man shot in face at close range — 9.50 28.00 75.00
4-Injury-to-eye, prostitution; Morisi-c/a — 10.50 32.00 85.00
5-9-Morisi-c/a in all. 7-Prostitute story plus reprints — 7.85 23.50 55.00

DYNAMO (Also see Tales of Thunder & T.H.U.N.D.E.R. Agents)
Aug, 1966 - No. 4, June, 1967 (25¢)
Tower Comics

1-Crandall/Wood, Ditko/Wood-a; Weed series begins; NoMan & Lightning cameos; Wood-c/a — 4.80 14.40 48.00
2-4: Wood-c/a in all — 3.20 9.60 32.00

NOTE: ***Adkins/Wood** a-2. **Ditko** a-4?. **Tuska** a-2, 3.*

DYNAMO JOE (Also see First Adventures & Mars)
May, 1986 - No. 15, Jan, 1988 (#12-15: $1.75)
First Comics

1-15: 4-Cargonauts begin — 1.50
Special 1(1/87)-Mostly-r/Mars — 1.50

DYNOMUTT (TV)(See Scooby-Doo (3rd series))
Nov, 1977 - No. 6, Sept, 1978 (Hanna-Barbera)
Marvel Comics Group

1-The Blue Falcon, Scooby Doo in all — 1.25 3.75 10.00
2-6: — 1.10 3.30 9.00

EAGLE, THE (1st Series) (See Science Comics & Weird Comics #8)
July, 1941 - No. 4, Jan, 1942
Fox Features Syndicate

1-The Eagle begins; Rex Dexter of Mars app. by Briefer; all issues feature German war covers — 156.00 468.00 1400.00
2-The Spider Queen begins (origin) — 72.00 216.00 650.00
3,4: 3-Joe Spook begins (origin) — 58.00 174.00 525.00

EAGLE (2nd Series)
Feb-Mar, 1945 - No. 2, Apr-May, 1945
Rural Home Publ.

1-Aviation stories — 28.00 83.00 220.00
2-Lucky Aces — 17.50 53.00 140.00

NOTE: ***L. B. Cole** c/a in each.*

EAGLE
Sept, 1986 - No. 26?, 1989 ($1.50/1.75/1.95, B&W)
Crystal Comics/Apple Comics #17 on

1 — .80 2.00
1-Signed and limited — 1.10 2.75
2-26: 12-Double size origin issue ($2.50) — 1.50

EAGLES DARE
Aug, 1994 - Present? ($1.95, B&W, limited series)
Aager comics, Inc.

1,2 — .80 2.00

EARTH MAN ON VENUS (An...) (Also see Strange Planets)
1951
Avon Periodicals

nn-Wood-a (26 pgs.); Fawcette-c — 100.00 300.00 850.00

EARTHWORM JIM (TV, cartoon)
Dec, 1995 - No. 3?, Feb, 1996 ($2.25)
Marvel Comics

1-3: Based on video game and toys — .90 2.25

EASTER BONNET SHOP (See March of Comics No. 29)

EASTER WITH MOTHER GOOSE
No. 103, 1946 - No. 220, Mar, 1949
Dell Publishing Co.

Four Color 103 (#1)-Walt Kelly-a — 17.00 52.00 190.00
Four Color 140 ('47)-Kelly-a — 14.00 42.00 155.00

East Meets West #1 © Innovative Corp.

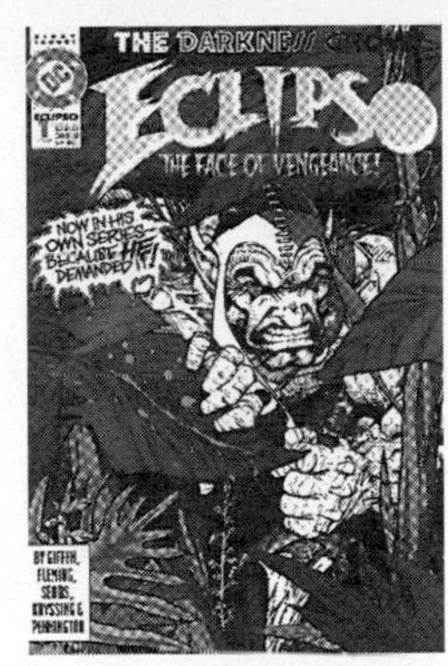

Eclipso #1 © DC

Eclipso #11 © DC

	GD25	FN65	NM94
Four Color 185 ('48),220-Kelly-a	12.00	35.00	130.00

EAST MEETS WEST
Apr, 1990 - No. 2, 1990 ($2.50, limited series, mature)
Innovation Publishing

1,2: 1-Stevens part-i; Redondo-c(i). 2-Stevens-c(i); 1st app. Cheech & Chong in comics 1.00 2.50

EAT RIGHT TO WORK AND WIN
1942 (16 pgs.) (Giveaway)
Swift & Company

Blondie, Henry, Flash Gordon by Alex Raymond, Toots & Casper, Thimble Theatre(Popeye), Tillie the Toiler, The Phantom, The Little King, & Bringing up Father - original strips just for this book -(in daily strip form which shows what foods we should eat and why) 30.00 90.00 240.00

E. C. CLASSIC REPRINTS
May, 1973 - No. 12, 1976 (E. C. Comics reprinted in color minus ads)
East Coast Comix Co.

1-The Crypt of Terror #1 (Tales from the Crypt #46) 2.40 6.00
2-Weird Science #15('52) 1.60 4.00
3-12: 3-Shock SuspenStories #12. 4-Haunt of Fear #12. 5-Weird Fantasy #13 ('52). 6-Crime SuspenStories #25. 7-Vault of Horror #26. 8-Shock SuspenStories #6. 9-Two-Fisted Tales #34. 10-Haunt of Fear #23. 11-Weird Science #12(#1). 12-Shock SuspenStories #2 1.20 3.00

EC CLASSICS
Aug, 1985 - No. 12, 1986? (High quality paper; each-r 8 stories in color)
Russ Cochran (#2-12 were resolicited in 1990)($4.95, 56 pgs., 8x11")

1-12: 1-Tales From the Crypt. 2-Weird Science. 3-Two-Fisted Tales. 4-Shock SuspenStories. 5-Weird Fantasy. 6-Vault of Horror. 7-Weird Science-Fantasy (r/23,24). 8-Crime SuspensStories. 9-Haunt of Fear. 10-Panic (r/1,2). 11-Tales From the Crypt (r/23,24). 12-Weird Science (r/20,22) 2.00 5.00

ECHO OF FUTUREPAST
May, 1984 - No. 9, Jan, 1986 ($2.95, color, 52 pgs.)
Pacific Comics/Continuity Comics

1-9: Neal Adams-c/a in all? 1.20 3.00

NOTE: ***N. Adams*** *a-1-6,7i,9i; c-1-3, 5p,7i,8,9i.* ***Golden*** *a-1-6 (Bucky O'Hare); c-6.* ***Toth*** *a-6,7.*

ECLIPSE GRAPHIC ALBUM SERIES
Oct, 1978 - 1989 (8-1/2x11") (B&W #1-5)
Eclipse Comics

	GD25	FN65	NM94
1-Sabre (10/78, B&W, 1st print.); Gulacy-a; 1st direct sale graphic novel	1.00	3.00	8.00
1-Sabre (2nd printing, 1/79)	1.00	3.00	8.00
1-Sabre (3rd printing, $5.95)		2.40	6.00
2-Night Music (11/79, B&W)-Russell-a		2.00	5.00
3-Detectives, Inc. (5/80, B&W)-Rogers-a	1.00	2.80	7.00
4-Stewart The Rat (1980, B&W)-G. Colan-a	1.00	2.80	7.00
5-The Price (10/81, B&W)-Starlin-a	1.50	4.50	12.00
6-I Am Coyote (11/84, color)-Hogers-c/a	1.00	3.00	8.00
7-The Rocketeer (9/85, color)-Dave Stevens-a (r/chapters 1-5)(see Pacific Presents & Starslayer); has 7 pgs. new-a	1.00	3.00	8.00
7-The Rocketeer (2nd print, $7.95)	1.00	3.00	8.00
7-The Rocketeer (3rd print, 1991, $8.95)	1.10	3.30	9.00
7-The Rocketeer, signed & limited HC	6.00	18.00	60.00
7-The Rocketeer, hard-c (1986, $19.95)	2.50	7.50	20.00
7-The Rocketeer, unsigned HC (3rd, $32.95)	3.30	10.00	33.00
8-Zorro In Old California ('86, color)	1.00	3.00	8.00
8-Hardcover	1.50	4.50	12.00
9-Sacred And The Profane ('86)-Steacy-a	2.00	6.00	16.00
9-Hardcover ($24.95)	2.50	7.50	25.00
10-Somerset Holmes ('86, $15.95)-Adults, soft-c	2.00	6.00	16.00
10-Hardcover ($24.95)	2.50	7.50	25.00
11-Floyd Farland, Citizen of the Future ('87, $3.95, B&W)		1.60	4.00
12-Silverheels ('87, $8.95, color)	1.10	3.30	9.00
12-Hardcover ($14.95)	1.85	5.50	15.00
12-Hardcover, signed & #'d ($24.95)	2.50	7.50	25.00
13-The Sisterhood of Steel ('87, $9.95, color)	1.25	3.75	10.00
14-Samurai, Son of Death ('87, $4.95, B&W)		2.00	5.00
14-Samurai, Son of Death ($3.95, 2nd printing)		1.60	4.00
15-Twisted Tales (11/87, color)-Dave Stevens-c		1.60	4.00
16-See Airfighters Classics #1		1.60	4.00
17-Valkyrie, Prisoner of the Past ('88, $3.95, color)		1.60	4.00
18-See Airfighters Classics #2		1.60	4.00
19-Scout: The Four Monsters ('88, $14.95, color)-r/Scout #1-7; soft-c	1.85	5.50	15.00
20-See Airfighters Classics #3		1.60	4.00
21-XYR-Multiple ending comic ('88, $3.95, B&W)		1.60	4.00
22-Alien Worlds #1 (5/88, $3.95, 52 pgs.)-Nudity		1.60	4.00
23-See Airfighters Classics #4		1.60	4.00
24-Heartbreak ($4.95, B&W)		2.00	5.00
25-Alex Toth's Zorro Vol. 1 ($10.95, B&W)	1.40	4.15	11.00
26-Alex Toth's Zorro Vol. 2 ($10.95, B&W)	1.40	4.15	11.00
27-Fast Fiction (She) ($5.95, B&W)		2.40	6.00
28-Miracleman Book I ($5.95)		2.40	6.00
29-Real Love: The Best of the Simon and Kirby Romance Comics (10/88, $12.95)	1.60	4.85	13.00
30-Brought To Light; Alan Moore scripts (1989)	1.40	4.15	11.00
30-Limited hardcover ed. ($29.95)	3.00	9.00	30.00
31-Pigeons From Hell by R. E. Howard (11/88)	1.00	3.00	8.00
31-Signed & Limited Edition ($29.95)	3.00	9.00	30.00

ECLIPSE MAGAZINE (Becomes Eclipse Monthly)
May, 1981 - No. 8, Jan, 1983 ($2.95, B&W, magazine)
Eclipse Publishing

1-8: 1-1st app. Cap'n Quick and a Foozle by Rogers, Ms. Tree by Beatty, and Dope by Trina Robbins. 2-1st app. I Am Coyote by Rogers. 7-1st app. Masked Man by Boyer 1.20 3.00

NOTE: ***Colan*** *a-3, 5, 8.* ***Golden*** *c/a-2.* ***Gulacy*** *a-6, c-1, 6.* ***Kaluta*** *c/a-5.* ***Mayerik*** *a-2, 3.* ***Rogers*** *a-1-8.* ***Starlin*** *a-1.* ***Sutton*** *a-6.*

ECLIPSE MONTHLY
Aug, 1983 - No. 10, July, 1984 (Baxter paper; 1-3, 52 pgs., $2.00)
Eclipse Comics

1-3: ($2.00)-Cap'n Quick and a Foozle by Rogers, Static by Ditko, Dope by Trina Robbins, Rio by Doug Wildey, The Masked Man by Boyer begin. 3-Ragamuffins begins .80 2.00
4-10: 4-8-$1.50-c. 9,10-$1.75-c .70 1.80

NOTE: ***Boyer*** *c-6.* ***Ditko*** *a-1-3.* ***Rogers*** *a-1-4; c-2, 4, 7.* ***Wildey*** *a-1, 2, 5, 9, 10; c-5, 10.*

ECLIPSO (See Brave and the Bold #64, House of Secrets #61 & Phantom Stranger, 1987)
Nov, 1992 - No. 18, Apr, 1994 ($1.25)
DC Comics

1-14: 1-Giffen plots/breakdowns begin. 10-Darkseid app. 1.25
15-18: 15-Begin $1.50-c; Creeper in #3-6,9,11-13. 18-Spectre-c/s 1.50
Annual 1 (1993, $2.50, 68 pgs.)-Intro Prism 1.00 2.50

ECLIPSO: THE DARKNESS WITHIN
July, 1992 - No. 2, Oct, 1992 ($2.50, 68 pgs.)
DC Comics

1-With purple gem attached to-c 1.00 2.50
1-Without gem; Superman, Creeper app. 1.00 2.50
2-Concludes Eclipso storyline from annuals 1.00 2.50

E. C. 3-D CLASSICS (See Three Dimensional...)

ECTOKID (See Razorline)
Sept, 1993 - No. 9, May, 1994 ($1.75/$1.95)
Marvel Comics

1-($2.50)-Foil embossed-c; created by C. Barker 1.00 2.50

Eden Matrix #1 © Adhesive Comics

Eerie #13 © AVON

Eerie #14 © AVON

GD25 FN65 NM94

2-8: 2-Origin. 5-Saint Sinner x-over .70 1.75
9-Begin $1.95-c .80 2.00
...: Unleashed! 1 (10/94, $2.95, 52 pgs.) 1.20 3.00

EDDIE CAMPBELL'S BACCHUS
May, 1995 - Present ($2.95, B&W)
Eddie Campbell Comics

1-29: 1-Cerebus app. 9-Alex Ross back-c. 1.20 3.00
1-2nd printing (5/97) 2.95

EDDIE STANKY (Baseball Hero)
1951 (New York Giants)
Fawcett Publications

nn-Photo-c 26.00 80.00 210.00

EDEN MATRIX, THE
1994 ($2.95)
Adhesive Comics

1,2-Two variant-c; alternate-c on inside back-c 1.20 3.00

EDGAR BERGEN PRESENTS CHARLIE McCARTHY
No. 764, 1938 (36 pgs.; 15x10-1/2"; in color)
Whitman Publishing Co. (Charlie McCarthy Co.)

764 61.00 183.00 550.00

EDGAR RICE BURROUGHS' TARZAN: A TALE OF MUGAMBI
1995 ($2.95, one-shot)
Dark Horse Comics

1 1.20 3.00

EDGAR RICE BURROUGHS' TARZAN: IN THE LAND THAT TIME FORGOT AND THE POOL OF TIME
1996 ($12.95, trade paperback)
Dark Horse Comics

nn-r/Russ Manning-a 13.00

EDGAR RICE BURROUGHS' TARZAN: THE LOST ADVENTURE
Jan, 1995 - No. 4, Apr, 1995 ($2.95, B&W, limited series)
Dark Horse Comics

1-4: ERB's last Tarzan story, adapted by Joe Lansdale 1.20 3.00
Hardcover (12/95, $19.95) 20.00
Limited Edition Hardcover ($99.95)-signed & numbered 100.00

EDGAR RICE BURROUGHS' TARZAN: THE RETURN OF TARZAN
May, 1997 - No. 3, July, 1997 ($2.95, limited series)
Dark Horse Comics

1-3: 2.95

EDGE
July, 1994 - No. 3, Apr, 1995 ($2.50, unfinished limited series)
Malibu Comics (Bravura)

1-3-S. Grant-story & Gil Kane-c/a; w/Bravura stamp 1.00 2.50

EDGE OF CHAOS
July, 1983 - No. 3, Jan, 1984 (Limited series)
Pacific Comics

1-3-Morrow c/a; all contain nudity .80 2.00

EDWARD'S SHOES GIVEAWAY
1954 (Has clown on cover)
Edward's Shoe Store

Contains comic with new cover. Many combinations possible. Contents determines price, 50-60 percent of original. (Similar to Comics From Weatherbird & Free Comics to You)

ED WHEELAN'S JOKE BOOK STARRING FAT & SLAT (See Fat & Slat)

EERIE (Strange Worlds No. 18 on)
No. 1, Jan, 1947; No. 1, May-June, 1951 - No. 17, Aug-Sept, 1954
Avon Periodicals

GD25 FN65 NM94

1(1947)-1st horror comic; Kubert, Fugitani-a; bondage-c
225.00 675.00 2000.00
1(1951)-Reprints story from 1947 #1 45.00 136.00 400.00
2-Wood-c/a; bondage-c 53.00 159.00 450.00
3-Wood-c; Kubert, Wood/Orlando-a 53.00 159.00 450.00
4,5-Wood-c 43.00 130.00 360.00
6,8,13,14: 8-Kinstler-a; bondage-c; Phantom Witch Doctor story
24.00 71.00 175.00
7-Wood/Orlando-c; Kubert-a 39.00 116.00 280.00
9-Kubert-a; Check-c 27.00 81.00 200.00
10,11: 10-Kinstler-a. 11-Kinstlerish-a by McCann 21.00 64.00 160.00
12-Dracula story from novel, 25 pgs. 28.00 84.00 200.00
15-Reprints No. 1('51)minus-c(bondage) 17.00 49.00 120.00
16-Wood-a r-/No. 2 19.00 56.00 130.00
17-Wood/Orlando & Kubert-a; reprints #3 minus inside & outside Wood-c
24.00 71.00 165.00

NOTE: ***Hollingsworth*** *a-9-11; c-10, 11.*

EERIE
1964
I. W. Enterprises

I.W. Reprint #1('64)-Wood-c(r); r-story/Spook #1 2.60 7.80 26.00
I.W. Reprint #2,6,8: 8-Dr. Drew by Grandenetti from Ghost #9
2.50 7.50 20.00
I.W. Reprint #9-r/Tales of Terror #1(Toby); Wood-c 2.80 8.40 28.00

EERIE (Magazine)(See Warren Presents)
No. 1, Sept, 1965; No. 2, Mar, 1966 - No. 139, Feb, 1983
Warren Publishing Co.

1-24 pgs., black & white, small size (5-1/4x7-1/4"), low distribution; cover from inside back cover of Creepy No. 2; stories reprinted from Creepy No. 7, 8. At least three different versions exist.

First Printing - B&W, 5-1/4" wide x 7-1/4" high, evenly trimmed. On page 18, panel 5, in the upper left-hand corner, the large rear view of a bald headed man blends into solid black and is unrecognizable. Overall printing quality is poor. 25.00 75.00 250.00

Second Printing - B&W, 5-1/4x7-1/4", with uneven, untrimmed edges (if one of these were trimmed evenly, the size would be less than as indicated). The figure of the bald headed man on page 18, panel 5 is clear and discernible. The staples have a 1/4" blue stripe.
9.50 28.50 95.00

Other unauthorized reproductions for comparison's sake would be practically worthless. One known version was probably shot off a first printing copy with some loss of detail; the finer lines tend to disappear in this version which can be determined by looking at the lower right-hand corner of page one, first story. The roof of the house is shaded with straight lines. These lines are sharp and distinct on original, but broken on this version.

NOTE: ***The Overstreet Comic Book Price Guide*** *recommends that, before buying a 1st issue, you consult an expert.*

2-Frazetta-c (also #3,5,7,8) 6.00 18.00 60.00
3-Frazetta-c & half pg. ad (rerun in #4) 4.60 13.80 46.00
4-10: 4-Frazetta-a (1/2 pg. ad). 5,7,8-Frazetta-c. 9-Headlight-c
2.50 7.50 22.00
11-16,18-20 2.25 6.75 18.00
17 (scarce) 7.50 22.50 75.00
21,22,24,25: 25-Steranko-c 2.50 7.50 24.00
23-Frazetta-c 3.60 10.80 36.00
26-30 2.00 6.00 16.00
31-38,40,43-45 2.50 7.50 20.00
39,41: 39-1st Dax. 41 (scarce) 2.50 7.50 24.00
42,51-('73 & '74 Annuals). 51-Color poster insert 2.50 7.50 24.00
46-50,52,53: 46-Dracula series by Sutton begins 1.00 3.00 8.00
54,55-Color Spirit story by Eisner, reprints sections 12/21/47 & 6/16/46
1.85 5.50 15.00
56-60,62,68,69,72,77: All have an 8 pg. slick color insert., 60-Summer Giant (9/74, $1.25) 1.50 4.50 12.00
61,63-67,70,71,73-76,78: 78-The Mummy-r 1.25 3.75 10.00
79,80-Origin Darklon the Mystic by Starlin (1st app.) 1.50 4.50 12.00
81,83-94,96-129: 84-All sports issue 1.10 3.30 9.00
82-1st app. The Rook 2.50 7.50 20.00

Eightball #18 © Fantagraphics

80 Page Giant #8 © DC

El Diablo #3 © DC

GD25 FN65 NM94

95-The Rook & Vampirella team-up 1.25 3.75 10.00
130-Vampirella-c/story 1.25 3.75 10.00
131-139 (lower distr.) 1.50 4.50 12.00
Year Book 1970, 1971-Reprints in both 3.00 9.00 30.00
Year Book 1972-Reprints 3.00 9.00 30.00

NOTE: *The above books contain art by many good artists:* ***N. Adams, Brunner, Corben, Craig (Taycee), Crandall, Ditko, Eisner, Evans, Jeff Jones, Krenkel, McWilliams, Morrow, Orlando, Ploog, Severin, Starlin, Torres, Toth, Williamson, Wood,*** *and* ***Wrightson****; covers by* ***Bode', Corben, Davis, Frazetta, Morrow,*** *and* ***Orlando. Frazetta*** *c-2, 3, 7, 8, 23. Annuals from 1973-on are included in regular numbering. 1970-74 Annuals are complete reprints. Annuals from 1975-on are in the format of the regular issues.*

EERIE ADVENTURES (Also see Weird Adventures)
Winter, 1951 (Painted-c)
Ziff-Davis Publ. Co.

1-Powell-a(2), McCann-a; used in **SOTI**; bondage-c; Krigstein back-c
31.00 92.00 235.00

NOTE: *Title dropped due to similarity to Avon's Eerie & legal action.*

EERIE TALES (Magazine)
1959 (Black & White)
Hastings Associates

1-Williamson, Torres, Tuska-a, Powell(2), & Morrow(2)-a
8.50 26.00 60.00

EERIE TALES
1963-1964
Super Comics

Super Reprint No. 10,11,12,18: 10('63)-r/Spook #27. Purple Claw in #11,12 ('63); #12-r/Avon's Eerie #1('51)-Kida-r 1.75 5.25 14.00
15-Wolverton-a, Spacehawk-r/Blue Bolt Weird Tales #113; Disbrow-a
3.60 10.80 36.00

EGBERT
Spring, 1946 - No. 20, 1950
Arnold Publications/Quality Comics Group

1-Funny animal; intro Egbert & The Count 15.50 47.00 125.00
2 8.75 26.25 65.00
3-10 5.70 17.00 35.00
11-20 4.00 12.00 24.00

EGYPT
Aug, 1995 - No.7, Feb, 1996 ($2.50, limited series, mature)
DC Comics (Vertigo)

1-7: Milligan scripts in all. 1.00 2.50

EH! (...Dig This Crazy Comic) (From Here to Insanity No. 8 on)
Dec, 1953 - No. 7, Nov-Dec, 1954 (Satire)
Charlton Comics

1-Davisish-c/a by Ayers, Woodish-a by Giordano; Atomic Mouse app.
24.00 71.00 190.00
2-Ayers-c/a 15.00 45.00 120.00
3,5,7 12.00 38.00 100.00
4,6: Sexual innuendo-c. 6-Ayers-a 14.00 41.00 110.00

EIGHTBALL
Oct, 1989 - Present ($2.75/$2.95/$3.95, semi-annually, mature)
Fantagraphics Books

1 ($2.95) 1.25 3.75 10.00
2-7 ($2.75) 1.00 2.80 7.00
8 ($2.95) 2.00 5.00
9,10,11,13-15 ($2.95) 1.20 3.00
12 ($2.75) 1.10 2.75
16-18 ($3.95): 17-(8/96) 1.60 4.00

EIGHTH WONDER, THE
Nov, 1997 ($2.95, one-shot)
Dark Horse Comics

nn-Reprints stories from Dark Horse Presents #85-87 2.95

EIGHT IS ENOUGH KITE FUN BOOK (See Kite Fun Book)

80 PAGE GIANT (...Magazine No. 2-15)
8/64 - No. 15, 10/65; No. 16, 11/65 - No. 89, 7/71 (25¢)(All reprints)
National Periodical Publications (#1-56: 84 pgs.; #57-89: 68 pgs.)

1-Superman Annual; originally planned as Superman Annual #9 (8/64)
35.00 105.00 450.00
2-Jimmy Olsen 19.00 57.00 260.00
3,4: 3-Lois Lane. 4-Flash-G.A.-r; Infantino-a 14.50 43.75 195.00
5-Batman; has Sunday newspaper strip; Catwoman-r; Batman's Life Story-r (25th anniversary special) 14.50 43.75 195.00
6-Superman 11.50 35.00 170.00
7-Sgt. Rock's Prize Battle Tales; Kubert-c/a 12.50 37.50 175.00
8-More Secret Origins-origins of JLA, Aquaman, Robin, Atom, & Superman; Infantino-a 28.00 85.00 380.00
9-11: 9-Flash (r/Flash #106,117,123 & Showcase #14); Infantino-a. 10-Superboy. 11-Superman; all Luthor issue 11.25 33.75 155.00
12-Batman; has Sunday newspaper strip 11.25 33.75 155.00
13,14: 13-Jimmy Olsen. 14-Lois Lane 11.25 33.75 155.00
15-Superman and Batman; Joker-c/story 11.25 33.75 155.00

Continued as part of regular series under each title in which that particular book came out, a Giant being published instead of the regular size. Issues No. 16 to No. 89 are listed for your information. See individual titles for prices.

16-JLA #39 (11/65), 17-Batman #176, 18-Superman #183, 19-Our Army at War #164, 20-Action #334, 21-Flash #160, 22-Superboy #129, 23-Superman #187, 24-Batman #182, 25-Jimmy Olsen #95, 26-Lois Lane #68, 27-Batman #185, 28-World's Finest #161, 29-JLA #48, 30-Batman #187, 31-Superman #193, 32-Our Army at War #177, 33-Action #347, 34-Flash #169, 35-Superboy #138, 36-Superman #197, 37-Batman #193, 38-Jimmy Olsen #104, 39-Lois Lane #77, 40-World's Finest #170, 41-JLA #58, 42-Superman #202, 43-Batman #198, 44-Our Army at War #190, 45-Action #360, 46-Flash #178, 47-Superboy #147, 48-Superman #207, 49-Batman #203, 50-Jimmy Olsen #113, 51-Lois Lane #86, 52-World's Finest #179, 53-JLA #67, 54-Superman #212, 55-Batman #208, 56-Our Army at War #203, 57-Action #373, 58-Flash #187, 59-Superboy #156, 60-Superman #217, 61-Batman #213, 62-Jimmy Olsen #122, 63-Lois Lane #95, 64-World's Finest #188, 65-JLA #76, 66-Superman #222, 67-Batman #218, 68-Our Army at War #216, 69-Adventure #390, 70-Flash #196, 71-Superboy #165, 72-Superman #227, 73-Batman #223, 74-Jimmy Olsen #131, 75-Lois Lane #104, 76-World's Finest #197, 77-JLA #85, 78-Superman #232, 79-Batman #228, 80-Our Army at War #229, 81-Adventure #403, 82-Flash #205, 83-Superboy #174, 84-Superman #239, 85-Batman #233, 86-Jimmy Olsen #140, 87-Lois Lane #113, 88-World's Finest #206, 89-JLA #93.

87TH PRECINCT (TV)
Apr-June, 1962 - No. 2, July-Sept, 1962
Dell Publishing Co.

Four Color 1309(#1)-Krigstein-a 9.00 27.00 100.00
2 7.00 22.00 80.00

EL BOMBO COMICS
1946
Standard Comics/Frances M. McQueeny

nn(1946) 8.75 26.25 70.00
1(no date) 8.75 26.25 70.00

EL CID
No. 1259, 1961
Dell Publishing Co.

Four Color 1259-Movie, photo-c 6.40 19.00 70.00

EL DIABLO (See All-Star Western #2 & Weird Western Tales #12)
Aug, 1989 - No. 16, Jan, 1991 ($1.50-$1.75, color)
DC Comics

1 ($2.50, 52pgs.)-Masked hero 1.00 2.50
2-6 ($1.50) 1.50
7-11: 7-Begin $1.75-c .70 1.80
12-16: 12-Begin $2.00-c .80 2.00

EL DORADO (See Movie Classics)

ELECTRIC UNDERTOW (See Strikeforce Morituri: Electric Undertow)

ELECTRIC WARRIOR

Elektra #3 © MEG

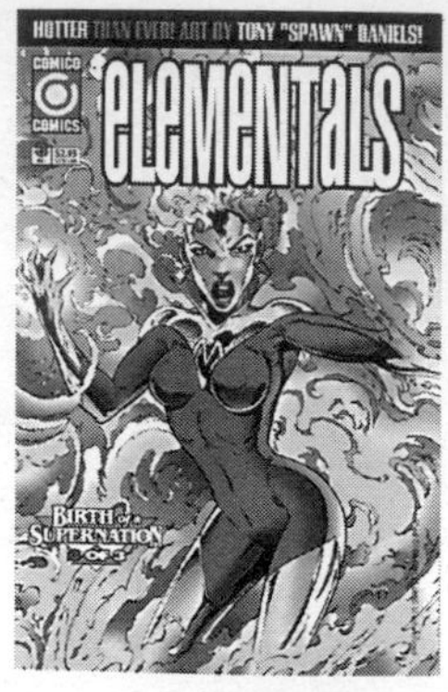

Elementals #3 © Comico

Elflord (Cuts Loose) #1 © Warp Graphics

GD25 FN65 NM94

May, 1986 - No. 18, Oct, 1987 ($1.50, Baxter paper)
DC Comics

1-18 1.50

ELEKTRA (Also see Daredevil #319-325)
Mar, 1995 - No. 4, June, 1995 ($2.95, limited series)
Marvel Comics

1-4-Embossed-c; Scott McDaniel-a 1.60 4.00

ELEKTRA (Also see Daredevil)
Nov, 1996 - Present ($1.95)
Marvel Comics

1-Peter Milligan scripts; Deodato-c/a 1.60 4.00
1-Variant-c 2.40 6.00
2 1.00 2.50
3-8, -1(7/97): Dr. Strange-c/app. .80 2.00
9-14: 9-Begin $1.99-c. 10-Logan-c/app. 1.99

ELEKTRA: ASSASSIN (Also see Daredevil)
Aug, 1986 - No. 8, June, 1987 (Limited series, mature)
Marvel Comics (Epic Comics)

1-Miller scripts in all; Sienkiewicz-c/a. 2.40 6.00
2 1.80 4.50
3-7 1.40 3.50
8 2.20 5.50
Signed & numbered hardcover (Graphittii Designs, $39.95, 2000 print run)-reprints 1-8 50.00

ELEKTRA LIVES AGAIN (Also see Daredevil)
1990 ($24.95, oversize, hardcover, 76 pgs.)(Produced by Graphitti Designs)
Marvel Comics (Epic Comics)

nn-Frank Miller-c/a/scripts; Lynn Varley painted-a; Matt Murdock & Bullseye app.; Elektra dies 25.00

ELEKTRA MEGAZINE
Nov, 1996 - No. 2, Dec, 1996 ($3.95, 96 pgs., reprints, limited series)
Marvel Comics

1,2: Reprints Frank Miller's Elektra stories in Daredevil 1.60 4.00

ELEKTRA SAGA, THE
Feb, 1984 - No. 4, June, 1984 ($2.00, limited series, Baxter paper)
Marvel Comics Group

1-4-r/Daredevil 168-190; Miller-c/a 1.20 3.00

ELEMENTALS, THE (See The Justice Machine & Morningstar Spec.)
June, 1984 - No. 29, Sept, 1988; V2#1, Mar, 1989 - No. 28, 1994? ($1.50/$2.50, Baxter paper); V3#1, Dec, 1995 - Present ($2.95)
Comico The Comic Co.

1-Willingham-c/a, 1-8 1.20 3.00
2 .80 2.00
3-10: 9-Bissette-a(p). 10-Photo-c .80 2.00
11-29 1.50
V2#1-28: 1-3-$1.95-c. 4-Begin $2.50-c. 16-1st app. Strike Force America. 18-Prelude to Avalon mini-series. 37-Prequel to Strike Force America series .80 2.00
V3#1,2: 1-Daniel-a(p), bagged w/gaming card. .80 2.00
Lingerie (5/96, $2.95) 1.20 3.00
Special 1 (3/86)-Willingham-a(p) .70 1.75
Special 2 (1/89, $1.95) .80 2.00

ELEMENTALS: GHOST OF A CHANCE
Dec, 1995 ($5.95, graphic novel)
Comico

nn-Ross-c. 2.40 6.00

ELEMENTALS: HOW THE WAR WAS WON
June, 1996 - No. 2, Aug, 1996 ($2.95, limited series)
Comico

1,2-Tony Daniel-a 2.95
1-Variant-c; no logo 2.95

ELEMENTALS: SEX SPECIAL
May, 1997 - Present ($2.95, limited series)
Comico

1-Tony Daniel, Jeff Moy-a 2.95
2-Robb Phipps, Adam McDaniel-a 2.95

ELEMENTALS: SWIMSUIT SPECTACULAR 1996
June, 1996 ($2.95, one-shot)
Comico

1-pin-ups by various 2.95
1-Variant-c; no logo 2.95

ELEMENTALS: THE VAMPIRE'S REVENGE
June, 1996 - No. 2 Aug, 1996($2.95, limited series)
Comico

1,2-Willingham-s 2.95
1-Variant-c; no logo 2.95

ELEVEN OR ONE
Apr, 1995 ($2.95)
Sirius

1-Linsner-c/a 1.00 3.00 8.00
1-(6/96) 2nd printing 1.20 3.00

ELFLORD
1986 - No. 30, 1989 ($1.70, B&W); V2#1- V2#30, 1995 ($2.00)
Aircel Publishing

1 .80 2.00
1,2-2nd printings 1.50
2,3 .80 2.00
4-6: Last B&W issue 1.60
V2#1-Color-a begins .80 2.00
2-20 1.60
21-Double size ($4.95) 2.00 5.00
22-30: 22-New cast. 25-Begin B&W, $1.95-c .70 1.75

ELFLORD
Jan, 1997-No.4, Apr, 1997 ($2.95, B&W, mini-series)
Warp Graphics

1 4 2.95

ELFLORD (CUTS LOOSE) (Vol. 2)
Sept, 1997 - Present ($2.95, B&W, mini-series)
Warp Graphics

1-3 2.95

ELFLORD: DRAGON'S EYE
1993 ($2.50, B&W)
Night Wynd Enterprises

1 1.00 2.50

ELFLORD: THE RETURN
1996 ($6.95, magazine size)
Mad Monkey Press

1 7.00

ELFQUEST (Also see Fantasy Quarterly & Warp Graphics Annual)
No. 2, Aug, 1978 - No. 21, Feb, 1985 (All magazine size)
No. 1, Apr, 1979
Warp Graphics, Inc.
NOTE: ***Elfquest*** was originally published as one of the stories in **Fantasy Quarterly** #1. When the publisher went out of business, the creative team, Wendy and Richard Pini, formed WaRP Graphics and continued the series, beginning with **Elfquest** #2. **Elfquest** #1, which reprinted the story from **Fantasy Quarterly**, was published about the same time **Elfquest** #4 was released.

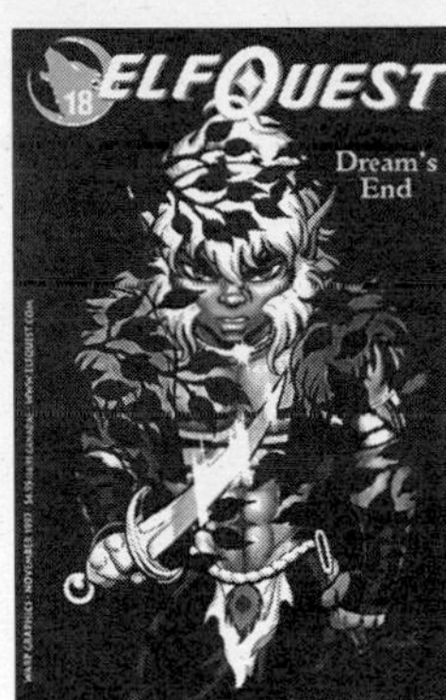

Elfquest: V2 #18 © Richard & Wendy Pini

Elfquest: Hidden Years #6 © Richard & Wendy Pini

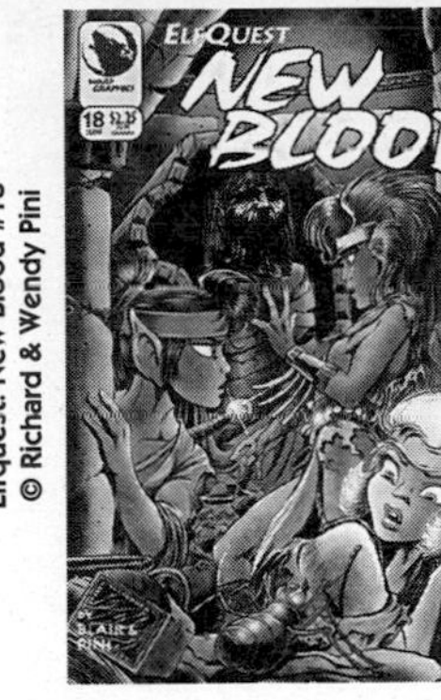

Elfquest: New Blood #18 © Richard & Wendy Pini

	GD25	FN65	NM94

Thereafter, most issues were reprinted as demand warranted, until Marvel announced it would reprint the entire series under its Epic imprint (Aug., 1985).

	GD25	FN65	NM94
1(4/79)-Reprints Elfquest story from Fantasy Quarterly No. 1			
1st printing ($1.00-c)	2.50	7.50	25.00
2nd printing ($1.25-c)	1.25	3.75	10.00
3rd printings ($1.50-c)		1.60	4.00
4th printing; different-c ($1.50-c)			1.50
2(8/78)-5: 1st printings ($1.00-c)	2.00	6.00	16.00
2nd printings ($1.25-c)		2.00	5.00
3rd & 4th printings ($1.50-c)(all 4th prints 1989)		1.20	3.00
6-9: 1st printings ($1.25-c)	1.00	2.80	7.00
2nd printings ($1.50-c)		1.60	4.00
3rd printings ($1.50-c)		.80	2.00
10-14: ($1.50-c); 16-8pg. preview of A Distant Soil		2.00	5.00
10-14: 2nd printings ($1.50)			1.50
15-21 (only one printing)		2.00	5.00

ELFQUEST
Aug, 1985 - No. 32, Mar, 1988
Marvel Comics (Epic Comics)

	GD25	FN65	NM94
1-Reprints in color the Elfquest epic by Warp Graphics		1.20	3.00
2-32			1.50

ELFQUEST
1989 - No. 4, 1989 ($1.50, B&W)
Warp Graphics

	GD25	FN65	NM94
1-4: Reprints original Elfquest series			1.50

ELFQUEST (Volume 2)
V2#1, May, 1996 - Present ($4.95, B&W)
Warp Graphics

	GD25	FN65	NM94
V2#1-18: 1,3,5,8,10,12,13,18-Wendy Pini-c		2.00	5.00

ELFQUEST: BLOOD OF TEN CHIEFS
July, 1993 - No. 20, Sept, 1995 ($2.00/$2.50)
Warp Graphics

	GD25	FN65	NM94
1-15-By Richard & Wendy Pini		.90	2.25
16-20: 16-Begin $2.50-c		1.00	2.50

ELFQUEST:HIDDEN YEARS
May, 1992 - No. 29, Mar, 1996 ($2.00/$2.25)
Warp Graphics

	GD25	FN65	NM94
1-7-		.90	2.25
8-29: 8-Begin $2.25-c		1.00	2.50

ELFQUEST:JINK
Nov, 1994 - No. 12, Feb, 1996 ($2.25/$2.50)
Warp Graphics

	GD25	FN65	NM94
1-3-W. Pini and John Byrne collaborate on Back-c		.90	2.25
4-12: 4-Begin $2.50-c		1.00	2.50

ELFQUEST: KAHVI
Oct, 1995 - No. 6, Mar, 1996 ($2.25, B&W)
Warp Graphics

	GD25	FN65	NM94
1-6		.90	2.25

ELFQUEST: KINGS CROSS
Nov, 1997 - No. 2 ($2.95, B&W, limited series)
Warp Graphics

	GD25	FN65	NM94
1,2			2.95

ELFQUEST: KINGS OF THE BROKEN WHEEL
June, 1990 - No. 9, Feb, 1992 ($2.00, B&W) (3rd Elfquest saga)
Warp Graphics

	GD25	FN65	NM94
1-9: By Richard & Wendy Pini; 1-Color insert		.80	2.00
1-2nd printing		.80	2.00

ELFQUEST: METAMORPHOSIS
Apr, 1996 ($2.95, B&W, one-shot)
Warp Graphics

	GD25	FN65	NM94
1		1.20	3.00

ELFQUEST: NEW BLOOD (...Summer Special on-c #1 only)
Aug, 1992 - No. 35, Jan, 1996 ($2.00/$2.25/$2.50, color/B&W, bi-monthly)
WaRP Graphics

	GD25	FN65	NM94
1-($3.95, 68 pgs.)-Byrne-a/scripts (16 pgs.)		1.60	4.00
2-17: Barry Blair-a in all		.90	2.25
18-26,35: 18-Begin $2.25-c		.90	2.25
27-34: 27 begin $2.50-c.		1.00	2.50

ELFQUEST: SHARDS
Aug, 1994 - No. 16, Mar, 1996 ($2.25/$2.50)
Warp Graphics

	GD25	FN65	NM94
1-8		.90	2.25
9-16:9-Begin $2.50-c		1.00	2.50

ELFQUEST: SIEGE AT BLUE MOUNTAIN
Mar, 1987 - No. 8, Dec, 1988 ($1.75/$1.95, B&W, limited series)
WaRP Graphics/Apple Comics

	GD25	FN65	NM94
1-Staton-a(i) in all; 2nd Elfquest saga		2.00	5.00
1-2nd printing		.80	2.00
2		1.20	3.00
2,3-2nd printings		.70	1.75
3-8		.80	2.00

ELFQUEST: THE REBELS
Nov, 1994 - No. 12, Mar, 1996 ($2.25/$2.50, B&W/color)
Warp Graphics

	GD25	FN65	NM94
1-3		.90	2.25
4-12: 4-Begin $2.50-c		1.00	2.50

ELFQUEST: TWO-SPEAR
Oct, 1995 - No. 5, Feb, 1996 ($2.25, B&W)
Warp Graphics

	GD25	FN65	NM94
1-5		.90	2.25

ELFQUEST: WAVE DANCERS
Dec, 1993 - No. 6, Mar, 1996 ($2.00/$2.25)
Warp Graphics

	GD25	FN65	NM94
1,2: 1-Foil-c & poster		1.00	2.50
3-6: 3-Begin 2.25-c		.90	2.25
Special 1 ($2.95)		1.20	3.00

ELFQUEST: WORLDPOOL
July, 1997 ($2.95, B&W, one-shot)
Warp Graphics

	GD25	FN65	NM94
1 Richard Pini-s/Barry Blair-a			2.95

ELF-THING
March, 1987 ($1.50, B&W, one-shot)
Eclipse Comics

	GD25	FN65	NM94
1			1.50

ELIMINATOR (Also see The Solution #16 & The Night Man #16)
Apr, 1995 - No. 3, July, 1995 ($2.95/$2.50, limited series)
Malibu Comics (Ultraverse)

	GD25	FN65	NM94
0-Mike Zeck-a in all		1.20	3.00
1-3-($2.50): 1-1st app. Siren		1.00	2.50
1-($3.95)-Black cover edition		1.60	4.00

ELIMINATOR FULL COLOR SPECIAL
Oct, 1991 ($2.95, one-shot)
Eternity Comics

	GD25	FN65	NM94
1-Dave Dorman painted-c		1.20	3.00

ELLA CINDERS (See Comics On Parade, Comics Revue #1,4, Famous Comics Cartoon

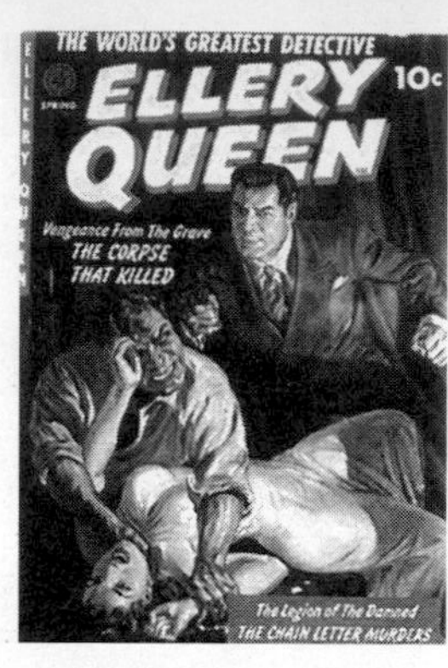

Ellery Queen #1 © Z-D

Elric, Stormbringer #7 © Michael Moorcock

Elseworld's Finest #2 © DC

GD25 FN65 NM94

Book, Giant Comics Editions, Sparkler Comics, Tip Top & Treasury of Comics)

ELLA CINDERS
1938 - 1940
United Features Syndicate

Single Series 3(1938) 35.00 105.00 285.00
Single Series 21(#2 on-c, #21 on inside), 28('40) 30.00 90.00 240.00

ELLA CINDERS
Mar, 1948 - No. 5, Mar, 1949
United Features Syndicate

1-(#2 on cover) 10.50 32.00 85.00
2 7.15 21.50 50.00
3-5 5.70 17.00 35.00

ELLERY QUEEN
May, 1949 - No. 4, Nov, 1949
Superior Comics Ltd.

1-Kamen-c; L.B. Cole-a; r-in Haunted Thrills 40.00 120.00 350.00
2-4: 3-Drug use stories(2) 34.00 101.00 250.00
NOTE: *Iger shop art in all issues.*

ELLERY QUEEN (TV)
1-3/52 (Spring on-c) - No. 2, Summer/52 (Saunders painted-c)
Ziff-Davis Publishing Co.

1-Saunders-c 40.00 120.00 300.00
2-Saunders bondage, torture-c 34.00 101.00 240.00

ELLERY QUEEN (Also see Crackajack Funnies No. 23)
No. 1165, Mar-May, 1961 - No.1289, Apr, 1962
Dell Publishing Co.

Four Color 1165 (#1)- 10.00 30.00 110.00
Four Color 1243 (11-1/61-61), 1289 8.00 25.00 90.00

ELMER FUDD (Also see Camp Comics, Daffy, Looney Tunes #1 & Super Book #10, 22)
No. 470, May, 1953 - No. 1293, Mar-May, 1962
Dell Publishing Co.

Four Color 470 (#1) 3.60 11.00 40.00
Four Color 558,628,689('56) 2.75 8.00 30.00
Four Color 725,783,841,888,938,977,1032,1081,1131,1171,1222,1293('62) 1.80 5.50 20.00

ELMO COMICS
Jan, 1948 (Daily strip-r)
St. John Publishing Co.

1-By Cecil Jensen 8.50 26.00 60.00

ELONGATED MAN (See Flash #112 & Justice League of America #105)
Jan, 1992 - No. 4, Apr, 1992 ($1.00, limited series)
DC Comics

1-4: 3-The Flash app. 1.00

ELRIC (Of Melnibone)(See First Comics Graphic Novel #6 & Marvel Graphic Novel #2)
Apr, 1983 - No. 6, Apr, 1984 ($1.50, Baxter paper)
Pacific Comics

1-6: Russell-c/a(i) in all 1.50

ELRIC
1996 ($2.95, one-shot)
Topps Comics

0--One Life: Russell-c/a; adapts Neil Gaiman's short story "One Life--Furnished in Early Moorcock." 1.20 3.00

ELRIC, SAILOR ON THE SEAS OF FATE
June, 1985 - No. 7, June, 1986 ($1.75, limited series)
First Comics

1-7: Adapts Michael Moorcock's novel .80 2.00

ELRIC, STORMBRINGER
1997 - No. 7, 1997($2.95, limited series)
Dark Horse Comics/Topps Comics

1-7: Russell-c/s/a; adapts Michael Moorcock's novel 2.95

ELRIC: THE BANE OF THE BLACK SWORD
Aug, 1988 - No. 6, June, 1989 ($1.75/$1.95, limited series)
First Comics

1-4: Adapts Michael Moorcock's novel .80 2.00

ELRIC: THE VANISHING TOWER
Aug, 1987 - No. 6, June, 1988 ($1.75, limited series)
First Comics

1-6: Adapts Michael Moorcock's novel .70 1.80

ELRIC: WEIRD OF THE WHITE WOLF
Oct, 1986 - No. 5, June, 1987 ($1.75, limited series)
First Comics

1-5: Adapts Michael Moorcock's novel .70 1.80

EL SALVADOR - A HOUSE DIVIDED
March, 1989 ($2.50, B&W, Baxter paper, stiff-c, 52 pgs.)
Eclipse Comics

1-Gives history of El Salvador 1.00 2.50

ELSEWHERE PRINCE, THE (Moebius' Airtight Garage)
May, 1990 - No. 6, Oct, 1990 ($1.95, limited series)
Marvel Comics (Epic Comics)

1-6: Moebius scripts & back-up-a in all .80 2.00

ELSEWORLD'S FINEST
1997-No. 2, 1997 ($4.95, limited series)
DC Comics

1,2: Elseworld's story-Superman & Batman in the 1920's 4.95

ELSIE THE COW
Oct-Nov, 1949 - No. 3, July-Aug, 1950
D. S. Publishing Co.

1-(36 pgs.) 20.00 60.00 160.00
2,3 15.00 45.00 120.00
Borden Milk Giveaway-(16 pgs., nn) (3 ishs, 1957) 11.30 34.00 90.00
Elsie's Fun Book(1950; Borden Milk) 11.30 34.00 90.00
Everyday Birthday Fun With... (1957; 20 pgs.)(100th Anniversary); Kubert-a 11.30 34.00 90.00

ELSON'S PRESENTS
1981 (100 pgs., no cover price)
DC Comics

Series 1-6: Repackaged 1981 DC comics; Superman, Action, Flash, DC Comics Presents & Batman known. Series I has a Batman/Joker-c. Series 3-New Teen Titans #3('81) 1.20 3.00

ELVEN (Also see Prime)
Oct, 1994 - No. 4, Feb, 1995 ($2.50, limited series)
Malibu Comics (Ultraverse)

0 ($2.95)-Prime app. 1.20 3.00
1-4: 2,4-Prime app. 3-Primevil app. 1.00 2.50
1-Limited Foil Edition- no price on cover 1.20 3.00

ELVIRA MISTRESS OF THE DARK
Oct, 1988 ($2.00, B&W, magazine size)
Marvel Comics

1-Movie adaptation 1.60 4.00

ELVIRA MISTRESS OF THE DARK
May, 1993 - Present ($2.50, B&W)
Claypool Comics (Eclipse)

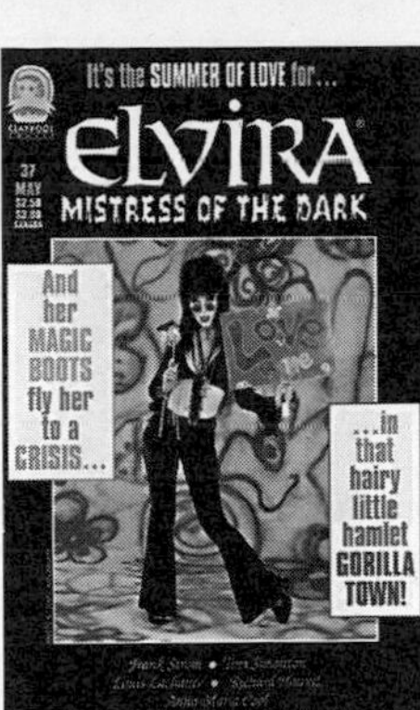

Elvira Mistress of the Dark #37 © Queen "B" Prod.

Embrace: Hunger of the Flesh #3 © Everette Hartsoe

Enemy #1 © DH

GD25 FN65 NM94

1-54-Photo-c: 1-Austin-a(i). 1-6-Spiegle-a 1.00 2.50

ELVIRA'S HOUSE OF MYSTERY
Jan, 1986 - No. 11, Jan, 1987
DC Comics

1-($1.50) 1.50
2-11: 9-Photo-c. 11-Dave Stevens-c 1.25
Special 1 (3/87, $1.25) 1.25

ELVIS MANDIBLE, THE
1990 ($3.50, 52 pgs., B&W, mature)
DC Comics (Piranha Press)

nn 1.40 3.50

ELVIS PRESLEY (See Career Girl Romances #32, Go-Go, Howard Chaykin's American Flagg #10, Humbug #8, I Love You #60 & Young Lovers #18)

E-MAN
Oct, 1973 - No. 10, Sept, 1975 (Painted-c No. 7-10)
Charlton Comics

1-Origin & 1st app. E-Man; Staton c/a in all 1.75 5.25 14.00
2-4: 2,4-Ditko-a. 3-Howard-a 2.40 6.00
5-Miss Liberty Belle app. by Ditko 2.00 5.00
6-10: Early Byrne-a in all (#6 is 1/75). 8-Full-length story; Nova begins as E-Man's partner 1.00 3.00 8.00
1-4,9,10(Modern Comics reprints, '77) 1.60 4.00

NOTE: *Killjoy app.-No. 2, 4. Liberty Belle app.-No. 5. Rog 2000 app.-No. 6, 7, 9, 10. Travis app.-No. 3.* ***Tom Sutton*** *a-1.*

E-MAN (Also see Michael Mauser & The Original E-Man)
Apr, 1983 - No. 25, Aug, 1985 ($1.00/$1.25, direct sales only)
First Comics

1-25: 2-X-Men satire. 3-X-Men/Phoenix satire. 6-Origin retold. 8-Cutey Bunny app. 10-Origin Nova Kane. 24-Origin Michael Mauser 1.00

NOTE: ***Staton*** *a-1-5, 6-25p; c-1-25.*

E-MAN
Sept, 1989 ($2.75, one-shot, no ads, high quality paper)
Comico

1-Staton-c/a; Michael Mauser story 1.10 2.80

E-MAN
V4#1, Jan, 1990 - No. 3, Mar, 1990 ($2.50, limited series)
Comico

1-3: Staton-c/a 1.00 2.50

E-MAN
Oct, 1993 ($2.75)
Alpha Productions

V5#1-Staton-c/a; 20th anniversary issue 1.10 2.75

E-MAN RETURNS
1994 ($2.75, B&W)
Alpha Productions

1-Joe Staton-c/a(p) 1.10 2.75

EMBRACE
Nov, 1996 ($3.00)
London Night Studios

1-Photo-c(Carmen Electra) 1.20 3.00
1-($5.00)-NC-17 Edition 2.00 5.00

EMBRACE: HUNGER OF THE FLESH
July, 1997 - Present ($3.00, limited series)
London Night Studios

1-3 1.20 3.00
1-3-($6.00)-Nude Edition 2.40 6.00

EMERALD DAWN
1991 ($4.95, trade paperback)
DC Comics

nn-Reprints Green Lantern: Emerald Dawn #1-6 2.00 5.00

EMERALD DAWN II (See Green Lantern...)

EMERGENCY (Magazine)
June, 1976 - No. 4, Jan, 1977 (B&W)
Charlton Comics

1-Neal Adams-c/a; Heath, Austin-a 1.00 3.00 8.00
2-4: 2-N. Adams-c. 3-N. Adams-a. 4-Alcala-a 1.60 4.00

EMERGENCY (TV)
June, 1976 - No. 4, Dec, 1976
Charlton Comics

1-Staton-c; Byrne-a 1.00 3.00 8.00
2-4: 2-Staton-c 2.00 5.00

EMERGENCY DOCTOR
Summer, 1963 (one-shot)
Charlton Comics

1 2.50 7.50 20.00

EMIL & THE DETECTIVES (See Movie Comics)

EMMA PEEL & JOHN STEED (See The Avengers)

EMPEROR'S NEW CLOTHES, THE
1950 (10¢, 68 pgs., 1/2 size, oblong)
Dell Publishing Co.

nn - (Surprise Books series) 2.00 6.00 16.00

EMPIRE STRIKES BACK, THE (See Marvel Comics Super Special #16 & Marvel Special Edition)

EMPTY LOVE STORIES
Nov, 1994 - Present ($2.95, B&W)
Slave Labor Graphics

1,2: Steve Darnall scripts in all. 1-Alex Ross-c. 2-(8/96)-Mike Allred-c 1.20 3.00

ENCHANTED
1997 - No. 3 ($2.50, B&W, limited series)
Sirius Entertainment

1-3-Robert Chang-s/a 2.50

ENCHANTED APPLES OF OZ, THE (See First Comics Graphic Novel #5)

ENCHANTER
Apr, 1987 - No. 3, Aug. 1987 ($2.00, B&W, limited series)
Eclipse Comics

1-3 .80 2.00

ENCHANTING LOVE
Oct, 1949 - No. 6, July, 1950 (All 52 pgs.)
Kirby Publishing Co.

1-Photo-c 9.50 28.00 75.00
2-Photo-c; Powell-a 5.70 17.00 40.00
3,4,6: 3-Jimmy Stewart photo-c 5.70 17.00 35.00
5-Ingels-a, 9 pgs.; photo-c 11.30 34.00 90.00

ENCHANTMENT VISUALETTES (Magazine)
Dec, 1949 - No. 5, Apr, 1950 (Painted c-1)
World Editions

1-Contains two romance comic strips each 12.00 36.00 95.00
2 8.75 26.25 70.00
3-5 8.50 26.00 60.00

ENEMY
May, 1994 - No. 5, Sept, 1994 ($2.50, limited series)
Dark Horse Comics

1-5 1.00 2.50

Enigma #2 © Peter Milligan & Duncan Fegredo

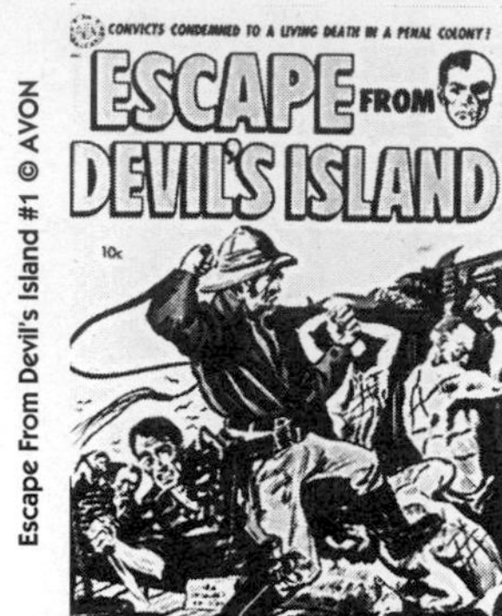

Escape From Devil's Island #1 © AVON

ESPers V3 #1 © James D. Hudnall

	GD25	FN65	NM94

ENEMY ACE SPECIAL (Also see Our Army at War #151, Showcase #57, 58 & Star Spangled War Stories #138)
1990 ($1.00, one-shot)
DC Comics

	GD25	FN65	NM94
1-Kubert-r/Our Army #151,153; c-r/Showcase 57		1.20	3.00

ENIGMA
Mar, 1993 - No. 8, Oct, 1993 ($2.50, limited series)
DC Comics (Vertigo)

	GD25	FN65	NM94
1-8: Milligan scripts		1.00	2.50
Trade paperback ($19.95)-reprints			20.00

ENSIGN O'TOOLE (TV)
Aug-Oct, 1963 - No. 2, 1964
Dell Publishing Co.

	GD25	FN65	NM94
1,2	1.65	5.00	18.00

ENSIGN PULVER (See Movie Classics)

EPIC
1992 - Book 4, 1992 ($4.95, limited series, 52 pgs.)
Marvel Comics (Epic Comics)

	GD25	FN65	NM94
Book One-Four: 2-Dorman painted-c		2.00	5.00

NOTE: *Alien Legion in #3. Cholly & Flytrap by* ***Burden****(scripts) &* ***Suydam****(art) in 3, 4. Dinosaurs in #4. Dreadlands in #1. Hellraiser in #1. Nightbreed in #2. Sleeze Brothers in #2. Stalkers in #1-4. Wild Cards in #1-4.*

EPIC ILLUSTRATED (Magazine)
Spring, 1980 - No. 36, Feb, 1986 ($2.00/$2.50, B&W/color, mature)
Marvel Comics Group

	GD25	FN65	NM94
1-Frazetta-c		1.60	4.00
2-18: 12-Wolverton Spacehawk-r edited & recolored w/article on him. 13-Bladerunner preview by Williamson. 14-Elric of Melnibone by Russell; Revenge of the Jedi preview. 15-Vallejo-c & interview; 1st Dreadstar story (cont'd in Dreadstar #1). 16-B. Smith-c/a(2).		1.60	4.00
19-30: 20-The Sacred & the Profane begins by Ken Steacy. 26-Galactus series begins; Cerebus the Aardvark story by Dave Sim27-Groo. 28-Cerebus app.		2.40	6.00
31-33,35,36	1.10	3.30	9.00
34	2.00	6.00	16.00

NOTE: ***N. Adams*** *a-7; c-6.* ***Austin*** *a-15-20i.* ***Bode*** *a-19, 23, 27r.* ***Bolton*** *a-7, 10-12, 15, 18, 22-25; c-10, 18, 22, 23.* ***Boris*** *c/a-15.* ***Brunner*** *c-12.* ***Buscema*** *a-1p, 9p, 11-13p.* ***Byrne/Austin*** *a-26-34.* ***Chaykin*** *a-2; c-8.* ***Conrad*** *a-2-5, 7-9, 25-34; c-17.* ***Corben*** *a-15; c-2.* ***Frazetta*** *c-1.* ***Golden*** *a-3r.* ***Gulacy*** *c/a-3.* ***Jeff Jones*** *c-25.* ***Kaluta*** *a-17r, 21, 24r, 26; c-4, 28.* ***Nebres*** *a-1.* ***Reese*** *a-12.* ***Russell*** *a-2-4, 9, 14, 33; c-14.* ***Simonson*** *a-17.* ***B. Smith*** *c/a-7, 16.* ***Starlin*** *a-1-9, 14, 15, 34.* ***Steranko*** *c-19.* ***Williamson*** *a-13, 27, 34.* ***Wrightson*** *a-13p, 22, 25, 27, 34; c-30.*

EPIC LITE
Sept, 1991 ($3.95, 52 pgs., one-shot)
Marvel Comics (Epic Comics)

	GD25	FN65	NM94
1-Bob the Alien, Normalman by Valentino		1.60	4.00

EPICURUS THE SAGE
Vol. 1, 1991 - Vol. 2, 1991 ($9.95, 8-1/8x10-7/8")
DC Comics (Piranha Press)

	GD25	FN65	NM94
Volume 1,2-Sam Kieth-c/a	1.25	3.75	10.00

EPSILON WAVE
Oct, 1985 - V2#2, 1987 ($1.50/$1.25/$1.75)
Independent Comics/Elite Comics No. 5 on

	GD25	FN65	NM94
1-4: 1-3-($1.50)-Seadragon app. 4-$1.25-c			1.50
5-8: 5-8-$1.75-c. 6-Seadragon app.		.70	1.75
V2#1,2 (B&W)			1.60

ERADICATOR
Aug, 1996 - No. 3, Oct, 1996 ($1.75, limited series)
DC Comics

	GD25	FN65	NM94
1-3: Superman app.			1.75

ERNIE COMICS (Formerly Andy Comics #21; All Love Romances #26 on)
No. 22, Sept, 1948 - No. 25, Mar, 1949
Current Books/Ace Periodicals

	GD25	FN65	NM94
nn (9/48,11/48; #22,23)-Teenage humor	5.70	17.00	35.00
24,25	4.15	12.50	25.00

ESCAPADE IN FLORENCE (See Movie Comics)

ESCAPE FROM DEVIL'S ISLAND
1952
Avon Periodicals

	GD25	FN65	NM94
1-Kinstler-c; r/as Dynamic Adventures #9	31.00	94.00	230.00

ESCAPE FROM FEAR
1956, 1962, 1969 (Giveaway, 8 pgs. full color) (On birth control)
Planned Parenthood of America

	GD25	FN65	NM94
1956 edition	8.75	26.25	65.00
1962 edition	4.50	13.50	45.00
1969 edition	2.50	7.50	22.00

ESCAPE FROM THE PLANET OF THE APES (See Power Record Comics)

ESCAPE TO WITCH MOUNTAIN (See Walt Disney Showcase No. 29)

ESPERS
July, 1986 - No. 5, Apr, 1987 ($1.25/$1.75, Mando paper)
Eclipse Comics

	GD25	FN65	NM94
1-3 ($1.25)-James Hudnall story & David Lloyd-a.			1.30
4,5 ($1.75)		.70	1.80

ESPERS
V2#1, 1996 - No. 6 ($2.95, B&W)(1st Halloween Comics series)
Halloween Comics

	GD25	FN65	NM94
V2#1-6: James D. Hudnall scripts.		1.20	3.00

ESPERS
V3#1, 1997 - Present ($2.95, B&W, limited series)
Image Comics

	GD25	FN65	NM94
V3#1-4: James D. Hudnall scripts.			2.95

ESPIONAGE (TV)
May-July, 1964 - No. 2, Aug-Oct, 1964
Dell Publishing Co.

	GD25	FN65	NM94
1,2	1.80	5.50	20.00

ESSENTIAL SPIDER-MAN (Vol. 2)
1997 ($12.95,B&W reprints)
Marvel Comics

	GD25	FN65	NM94
V2-Reprints Amazing Spider-Man #21-43, Annual #2,3			12.95

ESSENTIAL VERTIGO: THE SANDMAN
Aug, 1996 - Present ($1.95, reprints)
DC Comics (Vertigo)

	GD25	FN65	NM94
1-13,15-21: Reprints Sandman, 2nd series		.80	2.00
.14-($2.95)		1.20	3.00

ESSENTIAL VERTIGO: SWAMP THING
Nov, 1996 - Present ($1.95/$2.25,B&W, reprints)
DC Comics

	GD25	FN65	NM94
1-9: Reprints Alan Moore's Swamp Thing stories		.80	2.00
10,11,13-18-($2.25)		.90	2.25
12-($3.50) r/Annual #2		1.40	3.50

ETC
1989 - No. 5, 1990 ($4.50, 60 pgs., limited series, mature)
DC Comics (Piranha Press)

	GD25	FN65	NM94
Book 1-5: Conrad scripts/layouts in all		1.80	4.50

ETERNAL BIBLE, THE
1946 (Large size) (16 pgs. in color)
Authentic Publications

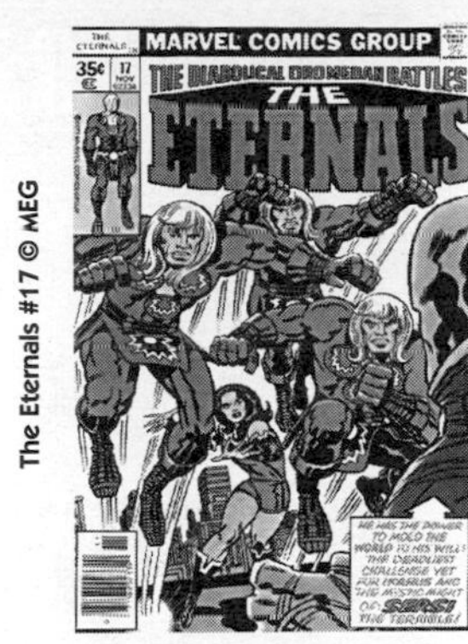

The Eternals #17 © MEG

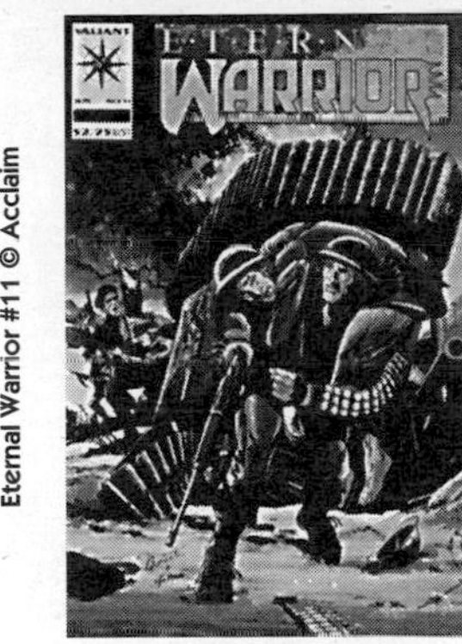

Eternal Warrior #11 © Acclaim

Everything Happens to Harvey #4 © DC

	GD25	FN65	NM94
1	10.50	32.00	85.00

ETERNALS, THE
July, 1976 - No. 19, Jan, 1978
Marvel Comics Group

	GD25	FN65	NM94
1-(Regular 25¢ edition)-Origin & 1st app. Eternals		2.40	6.00
1-(30¢-c, limited distribution)	2.50	7.50	24.00
2-(Regular 25¢ edition)-1st app. Ajak & The Celestials		1.20	3.00
2-(30¢-c, limited distribution)	1.50	4.50	12.00
3-19: 14,15-Cosmic powered Hulk-c/story		1.20	3.00
Annual 1(10/77)		1.20	3.00

NOTE: ***Kirby** c/a(p) in all.*

ETERNALS, THE
Oct, 1985 - No. 12, Sept, 1986 (Maxi-series, mando paper)
Marvel Comics Group

	GD25	FN65	NM94
1,12 ($1.25, 52 pgs.): 12-Williamson-a(i)			1.25
2-11-(75¢)			1.00

ETERNALS: THE HEROD FACTOR
Nov, 1991 ($2.50, 68 pgs.)
Marvel Comics

	GD25	FN65	NM94
1		1.00	2.50

ETERNAL WARRIOR (See Solar #10 & 11)
Aug, 1992 - No. 50, Mar, 1996 ($2.25/$2.50)
Valiant/Acclaim Comics (Valiant)

	GD25	FN65	NM94
1-Unity x-over; Miller-c; origin Eternal Warrior & Aram (Armstrong)		1.20	3.00
1-Gold logo		2.00	5.00
1-Gold foil logo		2.40	6.00
2-8: 2-Unity x-over; Simonson-c. 3-Archer & Armstrong x-over. 4-1st app. Bloodshot (last pg. cameo); see Rai #0 for 1st full app.; Cowan-c. 5-2nd full app. Bloodshot (12/92; see Rai #0). 6,7: 6-2nd app. Master Darque. 8-Flip book w/Archer & Armstrong #8		.80	2.00
9-25,27-37: 9-1st Book of Geomancer. 14-16-Bloodshot app. 18-Doctor Mirage cameo. 19-Doctor Mirage app. 22-W/bound-in trading card. 25-Archer & Armstrong app.; cont'd from A&A #25		.80	2.00
26-($2.75, 44 pgs.)-Flip book w/Archer & Armstrong		1.10	2.75
35-50: 35-Double-c; $2.50-c begins. 50-Geomancer app.		1.00	2.50
Special 1 (2/96, $2.50)-Art Holcomb script		1.00	2.50
Yearbook 1 (1993, $3.95), 2(1994, $3.95)		1.60	4.00

ETERNAL WARRIORS: BLACKWORKS
Mar, 1998 ($3.50, one-shot)
Acclaim Comics (Valiant Heroes)

	GD25	FN65	NM94
1			3.50

ETERNAL WARRIORS: DIGITAL ALCHEMY
Vol. 2, Sept, 1997 ($3.95, one-shot, 64 pgs.)
Acclaim Comics (Valiant Heroes)

	GD25	FN65	NM94
Vol. 2-Holcomb-s/Eaglesham-a(p)			3.95

ETERNAL WARRIORS: FIST AND STEEL
May, 1996 - No. 2, June, 1996 ($2.50, limited series)
Acclaim Comics (Valiant)

	GD25	FN65	NM94
1,2: Geomancer app. in both. 1-Indicia reads "June." 2-Bo Hampton-a		1.00	2.50

ETERNAL WARRIORS: TIME AND TREACHERY
Vol. 1, June, 1997 ($3.95, one-shot, 48 pgs.)
Acclaim Comics (Valiant Heroes)

	GD25	FN65	NM94
Vol. 1-Reintro Aram, Archer, Ivar the Timewalker, & Gilad the Warmaster; 1st app. Shalla Redburn; Art Holcomb script		1.60	4.00

ETERNITY SMITH
Sept, 1986 - No. 5, May, 1987 ($1.25/$1.50, 36 pgs.)
Renegade Press

	GD25	FN65	NM94
1 ($1.25)-1st app. Eternity Smith			1.30
2-5 ($1.50): 5-Death of Jasmine			1.50

ETERNITY SMITH
Sept, 1987 - No. 9, 1988 ($1.95)
Hero Comics

	GD25	FN65	NM94
V2#1-9: 8-Indigo begins		.80	2.00

ETTA KETT
No. 11, Dec, 1948 - No. 14, Sept, 1949
King Features Syndicate/Standard

	GD25	FN65	NM94
11-Teenage	7.15	21.50	50.00
12-14	5.35	16.00	32.00

EUDAEMON, THE (See Dark Horse Presents #72-74)
Aug, 1993 - No. 3, Nov, 1993 ($2.50, limited series)
Dark Horse Comics

	GD25	FN65	NM94
1-3: Nelson-a, painted-c & scripts		1.00	2.50

EUROPA AND THE PIRATE TWINS
Oct, 1996 - No. 4, ($2.50, B&W, limited series)
Powder Monkey Productions

	GD25	FN65	NM94
1,2: Two covers		1.20	3.00

EVANGELINE (Also see Primer)
1984 - #2, 6/84; V2#1, 5/87 - V2#12, Mar, 1989 (Baxter paper)
Comico/First Comics V2#1 on/Lodestone Publ.

	GD25	FN65	NM94
1,2, V2#1 (5/87) - 12		.80	2.00
Special #1 (1986, $2.00)-Lodestone Publ.		.80	2.00

EVA THE IMP
1957 - No. 2, Nov, 1957
Red Top Comic/Decker

	GD25	FN65	NM94
1,2	3.20	8.00	16.00

EVEL KNIEVEL
1974 (Giveaway, 20 pgs.)
Marvel Comics Group (Ideal Toy Corp.)

	GD25	FN65	NM94
nn-Contains photo on inside back-c	2.50	7.50	20.00

EVERYBODY'S COMICS (See Fox Giants)

EVERYMAN, THE
Nov, 1991 ($4.50, one-shot, 52 pgs.)
Marvel Comics (Epic Comics)

	GD25	FN65	NM94
1-Mike Allred-a	1.00	2.80	7.00

EVERYTHING HAPPENS TO HARVEY
Sept-Oct, 1953 - No. 7, Sept-Oct, 1954
National Periodical Publications

	GD25	FN65	NM94
1	20.00	60.00	160.00
2	11.30	34.00	90.00
3-7	8.75	26.25	70.00

EVERYTHING'S ARCHIE
May, 1969 - No. 157, Sept, 1991 (Giant issues No. 1-20)
Archie Publications

	GD25	FN65	NM94
1	6.00	18.00	60.00
2	4.00	12.00	40.00
3-5	3.00	9.00	30.00
6-10	2.50	7.50	20.00
11-20	1.50	4.50	12.00
21-30	1.00	3.00	8.00
31-50		2.40	6.00
51-100		1.60	4.00
101-157: 142,148-Gene Colan-a		.80	2.00

EVERYTHING'S DUCKY (Movie)
No. 1251, 1961

Evil Ernie: Destroyer #1 © Chaos!

Excalibur #99 © MEG

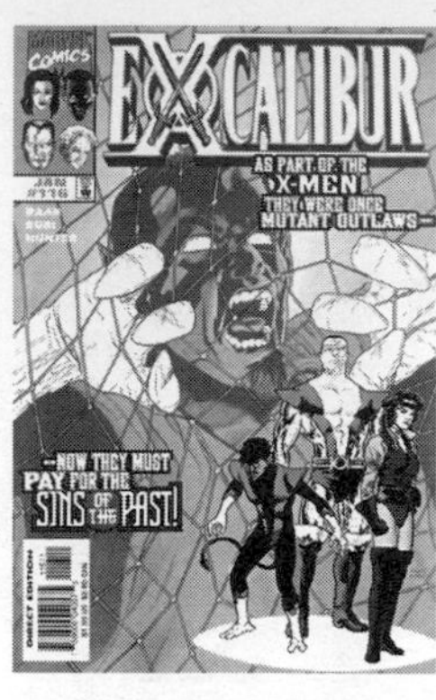

Excalibur #116 © MEG

GD25 FN65 NM94

Dell Publishing Co.
Four Color 1251 3.60 11.00 40.00

EVIL ERNIE
Dec, 1991 - No. 5, 1992 ($2.50, B&W, limited series)
Eternity Comics
1-1st app. Lady Death by Steven Hughes (12,000 print run); Lady Death app. in all issues 7.50 22.50 75.00
2,3: 2-1st Lady Death-c. 2,3-(7,000 print run) 5.00 15.00 50.00
4-(8,000 print run) 3.50 10.50 35.00
5 2.50 7.50 25.00
Special Edition 1 4.00 12.00 40.00
Youth Gone Wild! ($9.95, trade paperback)-r/#1-5 1.25 3.75 10.00
Youth Gone Wild! Director's Cut ($4.95)-Limited to 15,000 copies, shows the making of the comic 2.00 5.00

EVIL ERNIE: BADDEST BATTLES
Jan, 1997 ($1.50, one-shot)
Chaos! Comics
1-Pin-ups 1.50
1-Variant-c 2.00

EVIL ERNIE: DESTROYER
Oct, 1997 - No. 9 ($2.95, limited series)
Chaos! Comics
Preview ($2.50) 1.00 2.50
1-3-Flip cover 2.95

EVIL ERNIE: THE RESURRECTION
1993 - No. 4, 1994 (Limited series)
Chaos! Comics
1 2.25 6.75 18.00
1A-Gold 5.00 15.00 50.00
2-4 1.50 4.50 12.00

EVIL ERNIE: REVENGE
Oct, 1994 - No.4, Feb, 1995 ($2.95, limited series)
Chaos! Comics
1: 1-Glow-in-the-dark-c; Lady Death app. 1-3-flip book w. Kilzone Preview (series of 3) 1.00 3.00 8.00
1-Commemorative-(4000 print run) 2.50 7.50 20.00
2-4 1.00 3.00 8.00
Trade paperback (10/95, $12.95) 13.00

EVIL ERNIE: STRAIGHT TO HELL
Oct, 1995 - No. 5, May, 1996 ($2.95, limited series)
Chaos! Comics
1-5: 1-fold-out-c 1.60 4.00
1-($19.95) Chromium Ed. 2.50 7.50 25.00
3-Chastity Chase Cover-(4000 print run) 2.50 7.50 25.00
Special Edition (10,000) 3.00 9.00 30.00

EVIL ERNIE VS. THE MOVIE MONSTERS
Mar, 1997 ($2.95, one-shot)
Chaos! Comics
1 1.20 3.00
1-Variant-"Chaos-Scope•Terror Vision" card stock-c 2.00 5.00

EVIL ERNIE VS. THE SUPER HEROES
Aug, 1995 ($2.95, one-shot)
Chaos! Comics
1-Lady Death poster 1.20 3.00
1-Foil-c variant (limited to 10,000) 3.00 9.00 30.00
1-Limited Edition (1000) 2.50 7.50 25.00

EWOKS (TV) (See Star Comics Magazine)
June, 1985 - No. 15?, Sept, 1987 (75¢/$1.00 #14 on) (Star Wars)
Marvel Comics (Star Comics)
1,10: 10-Williamson-a (From Star Wars) 1.00 3.00 8.00
2-9,11-15 2.40 6.00

EXCALIBUR (Also see Marvel Comics Presents #31)
Apr, 1988; Oct, 1988 - Present ($1.50/$1.75)
Marvel Comics
Special Edition nn (The Sword is Drawn)(4/88, $3.25)-1st Excalibur comic 1.00 2.60 6.50
Special Edition nn (4/88)-no price on-c (scarce) 1.50 4.50 12.00
Special Edition nn (2nd print, 10/88, $3.50) .80 2.00
Special Edition nn (3rd print, 12/89, 4.50) .80 2.00
...The Sword is Drawn (Apr, 1992, $4.95) 1.20 3.00
1($1.50, 10/88)-X-Men spin-off; Nightcrawler, Shadowcat(Kitty Pryde), Capt. Britain, Phoenix & Meggan begin 2.00 5.00
2 1.00 2.50
3,4 .80 2.00
5-10 .80 2.00
11-15: 10,11-Rogers/Austin-a .80 2.00
16-23: 19-Austin-i. 21-Intro Crusader X. 22-Iron Man x-over 1.50
24-40,42-49,51-70,72-74,76: 32-($1.50). 24-John Byrne app. in story; $1.75-c begins. 26-Ron Lim-c/a. 27-B. Smith-a(p). 37-Dr. Doom & Iron Man app. 49-Neal Adams c-swipe. 52,57-X-Men (Cyclops, Wolverine) app. 53-Spider-Man-c/story. 58-X-Men (Wolverine, Gambit, Cyclops, etc.)-c/story. 61-Phoenix returns. 68-Starjammers-c/story 1.50
41-X-Men (Wolverine) app.; Cable cameo .80 2.00
50-($2.75, 56 pgs.)-New logo 1.10 2.75
71-($3.95, 52 pgs.)-Hologram on-c; 30th anniversary 1.60 4.00
75-($3.50, 52 pgs.)-Holo-grafx foil-c 1.60 4.00
75-($2.25, 52 pgs.)-Regular edition .90 2.25
77-81,83-86: 77-Begin $1.95-c; bound-in trading card sheet. 83-86-Deluxe edition. 86-1st app. Pete Wisdom .80 2.00
82-($2.50)-Newsstand edition 1.00 2.50
82-($3.50)-Enhanced edition 1.40 3.50
83-86-($1.50)-Standard edition 1.50
87-89,91-99,101-110, -1(7/97): 87-Return from Age of Apocalypse. 92-Colossus-c/app. 94-Days of Future Tense 95-X-Man-c/app. 96-Sebastian Shaw & the Hellfire Club app. 99-Onslaught app. 101-Onslaught tie-in. 102-w/card insert. 103-Last Warren Ellis scripts; Belasco app. 109-Spiral-c/app. .80 2.00
90-($2.95)-double-sized 1.20 3.00
100-($2.95)-Onslaught tie-in; wraparound-c 1.40 3.50
111-119: 111-Begin $1.99-c, wraparound-c 1.99
Annual 1 (1993, $2.95)-1st app. Khaos 1.20 3.00
Annual 2 (1994, $2.95, 68 pgs.)-X-Men & Psylocke app. 1.20 3.00
...Air Apparent nn (12/91, $4.95)-Simonson-c 1.60 4.00
...Mojo Mayhem nn (12/89, $4.50)-Art Adams/Austin-c/a 1.60 4.00
...: The Possession nn (7/91, $2.95, 52 pgs.) 1.00 2.50
...: XX Crossing (7/92, 5/92-inside, $2.50)-vs. The X-Men .80 2.00

EXCITING COMICS
Apr, 1940 - No. 69, Sept, 1949
Nedor/Better Publications/Standard Comics
1-Origin & 1st app. The Mask, Jim Hatfield, Sgt. Bill King, Dan Williams begin; early Robot-c (see Smash #1) 280.00 840.00 2800.00
2-The Sphinx begins; The Masked Rider app.; Son of the Gods begins, ends #8 122.00 366.00 1100.00
3-Robot-c 83.00 250.00 750.00
4,5 56.00 168.00 500.00
6-Robot-c 67.00 200.00 600.00
7,8 44.00 132.00 400.00
9-Origin/1st app. of The Black Terror & sidekick Tim, begin series (5/41) (Black Terror c-9-52,54,55) 640.00 1920.00 6400.00
10-2nd app. Black Terror 200.00 600.00 1800.00

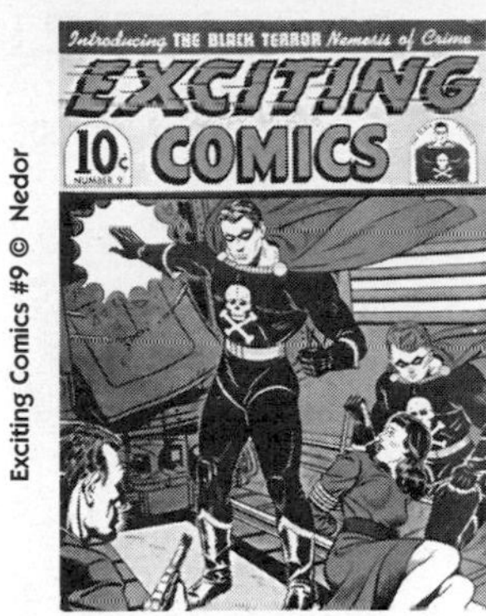

Exciting Comics #9 © Nedor

Ex-Mutants #18 © MAL

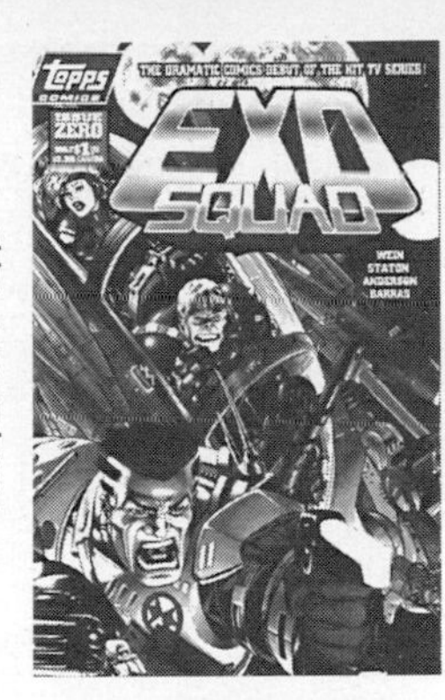

Exosquad #0 © Topps

	GD25	FN65	NM94
11	100.00	300.00	900.00
12,13	67.00	200.00	600.00
14-Last Sphinx, Dan Williams	44.00	132.00	400.00
15-The Liberator begins (origin)	47.00	141.00	425.00
16-20: 20-The Mask ends	36.00	108.00	325.00
21,23-27	35.00	105.00	280.00
22-Origin The Eaglet; The American Eagle begins	40.00	120.00	360.00
28-30: 28-Schomburg-c begin. 28-Crime Crusader begins, ends #58	41.00	123.00	370.00
31-38: 35-Liberator ends, not in 31-33	36.00	108.00	325.00
39-Origin Kara, Jungle Princess	44.00	132.00	400.00
40-50: 42-The Scarab begins. 45-Schomburg Robot-c. 49-Last Kara, Jungle Princess. 50-Last American Eagle	42.00	126.00	375.00
51-Miss Masque begins (1st app.)	47.00	141.00	420.00
52-54: Miss Masque ends. 53-Miss Masque-c	38.00	113.00	340.00
55-58: 55-Judy of the Jungle begins (origin), ends #69; 1 pg. Ingels-a; Judy of the Jungle c-56-66. 56-58: All airbrush-c	42.00	126.00	375.00
59-Frazetta art in Caniff style; signed Frank Frazeta (one t), 9 pgs.	42.00	126.00	375.00
60-66: 60-Rick Howard, the Mystery Rider begins. 66-Robinson/Meskin-a	36.00	108.00	325.00
67-69-All western covers	14.50	43.00	115.00

NOTE: ***Schomburg (Xela)*** *c-28-68; airbrush c-57-66. Black Terror by* ***R. Moreira****-#65.* ***Roussos*** *a-62. Bondage-c 9, 12, 13, 20, 23, 25, 30, 59.*

EXCITING ROMANCES
1949 (nd); No. 2, Spring, 1950 - No. 5, 10/50; No. 6 (1951, nd); No. 7, 9/51 - No. 14, 1/53
Fawcett Publications

	GD25	FN65	NM94
1(1949)	10.00	30.00	80.00
2,4,5-(1950)	6.00	18.00	42.00
3-Wood-a	10.00	30.00	80.00
6-14	5.35	16.00	32.00

NOTE: ***Powell*** *a-8-10.* ***Marcus Swayze*** *a-5, 6, 9. Photo c-1-7, 10-12.*

EXCITING ROMANCE STORIES (See Fox Giants)

EXCITING WAR (Korean War)
No. 5, Sept, 1952 - No. 8, May, 1953; No. 9, Nov, 1953
Standard Comics (Better Publ.)

	GD25	FN65	NM94
5	6.70	20.00	42.00
6,7,9	4.00	12.00	24.00
8-Toth-a	6.70	20.00	42.00

EXCITING X-PATROL
June, 1997 ($1.95, one-shot)
Marvel Comics (Amalgam)

	GD25	FN65	NM94
1-Barbara Kesel-s/ Bryan Hitch-a			1.95

EXILES (Also see Break-Thru)
Aug, 1993 - No. 4, Nov, 1993 ($1.95)
Malibu Comics (Ultraverse)

	GD25	FN65	NM94
1,2,4: 1,2-Bagged copies of each exist. 2-Gustovich-c. 4-Team dies; story cont'd in Break-Thru #1		.80	2.00
3-($2.50, 40 pgs.)-Rune flip-c/story by B. Smith (3 pgs.)		1.00	2.50
1-Holographic-c edition	1.00	3.00	8.00

EXILES (All New, The) (2nd Series) (Also see Black September)
Sept, 1995 - V2#11, Aug, 1996 ($1.50)
Malibu Comics (Ultraverse)

	GD25	FN65	NM94
Infinity (9/95, $1.50)-Intro new team including Marvel's Juggernaut & Reaper.			1.50
Infinity (2000 signed)	1.25	3.75	10.00
V2#1 (2000 signed)	1.25	3.75	10.00
V2#1-4,6-11: 1-(10/95, 64 pgs.)-Reprint of Ultraforce V2#1 follows lead story. 2-1st app. Hellblade. 8-Intro Maxis. 11-Vs. Maxis; Ripfire app.; cont'd in Ultraforce #12			1.50
V2#5-($2.50) Juggernaut returns to the Marvel Universe.		1.00	2.50

EXILES VS THE X-MEN
Oct, 1995 (one-shot)
Malibu Comics (Ultraverse)

	GD25	FN65	NM94
0-Limited Super Premium Edition; signed w/certificate; gold foil logo	1.25	3.75	10.00
0-Limited Premium Edition	1.85	5.50	15.00

EX-MUTANTS
Nov, 1992 - No. 18, Apr, 1994 ($1.95/$2.25/$2.50)
Malibu Comics

	GD25	FN65	NM94
1-10		.80	2.00
11-14 ($2.25): 11-Polybagged w/Skycap		.90	2.25
15-18 ($2.50)		1.00	2.50

EXORCISTS (See The Crusaders)

EXOSQUAD (TV)
No. 0, Jan, 1994 ($1.25)
Topps Comics

	GD25	FN65	NM94
0-($1.00, 20 pgs.)-1st app.; Staton-a(p); wraparound-c			1.00

EXOTIC ROMANCES (Formerly True War Romances)
No. 22, Oct, 1955 - No. 31, Nov, 1956
Quality Comics Group (Comic Magazines)

	GD25	FN65	NM94
22	7.15	21.50	50.00
23-26,29	4.15	12.50	25.00
27,31-Baker-c/a	8.50	26.00	60.00
28,30-Baker-a	7.15	21.50	50.00

EXPLOITS OF DANIEL BOONE
Nov, 1955 - No. 6, Oct, 1956
Quality Comics Group

	GD25	FN65	NM94
1-All have Cuidera-c(i)	22.00	66.00	175.00
2	14.00	41.00	110.00
3-6	11.30	34.00	90.00

EXPLOITS OF DICK TRACY (See Dick Tracy)

EXPLORER JOE
Winter, 1951 - No. 2, Oct-Nov, 1952
Ziff-Davis Comic Group (Approved Comics)

	GD25	FN65	NM94
1-2: Saunders painted covers; 2-Krigstein-a	9.50	28.00	75.00

EXPLORERS OF THE UNKNOWN (See Archie Giant Series #587, 599)
June, 1990 - No. 6, Apr, 1991 ($1.00)
Archie Comics

	GD25	FN65	NM94
1-6: Featuring Archie and the gang			1.00

EXPOSED (...True Crime Cases; ...Cases in the Crusade Against Crime #5-9)
Mar-Apr, 1948 - No. 9, July-Aug, 1949
D. S. Publishing Co.

	GD25	FN65	NM94
1	16.00	49.00	130.00
2-Giggling killer story with excessive blood; two injury-to-eye panels; electrocution panel	19.00	56.00	150.00
3,8,9	8.50	26.00	60.00
4-Orlando-a	8.75	26.25	65.00
5-Breeze Lawson, Sky Sheriff by E. Good	8.50	26.00	60.00
6-Ingels-a; used in **SOTI**, illo. "How to prepare an alibi"	30.00	90.00	240.00
7-Illo. in **SOTI**, "Diagram for housebreakers;" used by N.Y. Legis. Committee	30.00	90.00	240.00

EXTRA!
Mar-Apr, 1955 - No. 5, Nov-Dec, 1955
E. C. Comics

	GD25	FN65	NM94
1-Not code approved	15.00	45.00	120.00
2-5	10.00	30.00	80.00

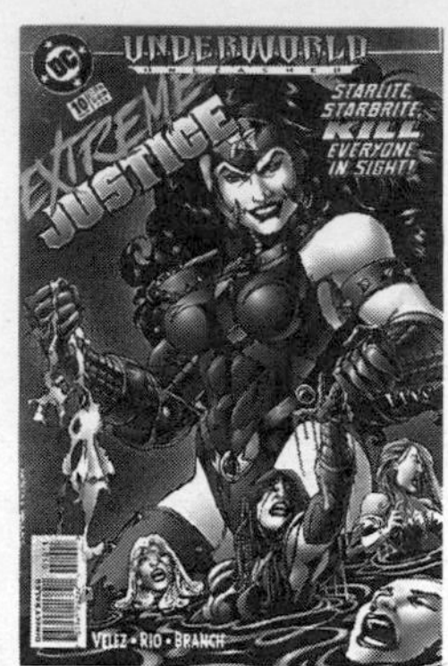

Extreme Justice #10 © DC

Fairy Tale Parade #2 © DELL

Falcon #1 © MEG

GD25 FN65 NM94

NOTE: ***Craig, Crandall, Severin** art in all.*

EXTRA COMICS
1948 (25¢, 3 comics in one)
Magazine Enterprises

1-Giant; consisting of rebound ME comics. Two versions known; (1)-Funnyman by Siegel & Shuster, Space Ace, Undercover Girl, Red Fox by L.B. Cole, Trail Colt & (2)-All Funnyman — 42.00 126.00 375.00

EXTREME
Aug, 1993 (Giveaway)
Image Comics (Extreme Studios)

0 — .80 2.00

EXTREME DESTROYER
Jan, 1996 ($2.50)
Image Comics (Extreme Studios)

Prologue 1-Polybagged w/card; Liefeld-c — 1.00 2.50
Epilogue 1-Liefeld-c — 1.00 2.50

EXTREME JUSTICE
Jan, 1995 - No. 18, July, 1996 ($1.50/$1.75)
DC Comics

1-5 — 1.50
6-18: 6-Begin $1.75-c — .90 2.25

EXTREMELY YOUNGBLOOD
Sept, 1996 ($3.50, one-shot)
Image Comics (Extreme Studios)

1 — 1.40 3.50

EXTREME SACRIFICE
Jan, 1995 ($2.50, limited series)
Image Comics (Extreme Studios)

Prelude (#1)-Liefeld wraparound-c; polybagged w/ trading card — 1.00 2.50
Epilogue (#2)-Liefeld wraparound-c; polybagged w/trading card — 1.00 2.50
Trade paperback (6/95, $16.95)-Platt-a — 17.00

EXTREME SUPER CHRISTMAS SPECIAL
Dec, 1994 ($2.95, one-shot)
Image Comics (Extreme Studios)

1 — 1.20 3.00

EXTREMIST, THE
Sept, 1993 - No. 4, Dec, 1993 ($1.95, limited series)
DC Comics (Vertigo)

1-4-Peter Milligan scripts; McKeever-c/a — 1.00 2.50
1-Platinum Edition — 1.25 3.75 10.00

EYE OF THE STORM
Dec, 1994 - No. 7, June, 1995? ($2.95)
Rival Productions

1-7: Computer generated comic — 1.20 3.00

FACE
Jan, 1995 ($4.95, one-shot)
DC Comics (Vertigo)

1 — 2.00 5.00

FACE, THE (Tony Trent, the Face No. 3 on) (See Big Shot Comics)
1941 - No. 2, 1941?
Columbia Comics Group

1-The Face; Mart Bailey-c — 71.00 213.00 640.00
2-Bailey-c — 42.00 126.00 380.00

FACTOR X
Mar, 1995 - No. 4, July, 1995 ($1.95, limited series)
Marvel Comics

1-Age of Apocalypse — 1.20 3.00
2-4 — .80 2.00

FACULTY FUNNIES
June, 1989 - No. 5, May, 1990 (75¢/95¢ #2 on)
Archie Comics

1-5: 1,2-The Awesome Four app. — 1.00

FAFHRD AND THE GREY MOUSER (Also see Sword of Sorcery & Wonder Woman #202)
Oct, 1990 - No. 4, 1991 ($4.50, 52 pgs., squarebound)
Marvel Comics

1-4: Mignola/Williamson-a; Chaykin scripts — 1.80 4.50

FAIRY TALE PARADE (See Famous Fairy Tales)
June-July, 1942 - No. 121, Oct, 1946 (Most all by Walt Kelly)
Dell Publishing Co.

1-Kelly-a begins — 118.00 355.00 1300.00
2(8-9/42) — 50.00 150.00 550.00
3-5 (10-11/42 - 2-4/43) — 35.00 104.00 380.00
6-9 (5-7/43 - 11-1/43-44) — 26.00 79.00 290.00
Four Color 50('44),69('45), 87('45) — 24.00 71.00 260.00
Four Color 104,114('46)-Last Kelly issue — 17.00 52.00 190.00
Four Color 121('46)-Not by Kelly — 10.00 30.00 110.00

*NOTE: #1-9, 4-Color #50, 69 have **Kelly** c/a; 4-Color #87, 104, 114-**Kelly** art only. #9 has a redrawn version of The Reluctant Dragon. This series contains all the classic fairy tales from Jack In The Beanstalk to Cinderella.*

FAIRY TALES
No. 10, Apr-May, 1951 - No. 11, June-July, 1951
Ziff-Davis Publ. Co. (Approved Comics)

10,11-Painted-c — 14.00 41.00 110.00

FAITH
July, 1997 - Present ($2.95, B&W)
Lightning Entertainment

1 — 2.95

FAITHFUL
Nov, 1949 - No. 2, Feb, 1950 (52 pgs.)
Marvel Comics/Lovers' Magazine

1,2-Photo-c — 7.15 21.50 50.00

FALCON (See Marvel Premiere #49)(Also see Avengers #181 & Captain America #117 & 133)
Nov, 1983 - No. 4, Feb, 1984 (Mini-series)
Marvel Comics Group

1-4: 1-Paul Smith-c/a(p). 2-Paul Smith-c — 1.00

FALLEN ANGEL ON THE WORLD OF MAGIC: THE GATHERING
May, 1996 ($5.95, one-shot)
Acclaim (Armada)

1-Nancy Collins story. — 2.40 6.00

FALLEN ANGELS
April, 1987 - No. 8, Nov, 1987 (Limited series)
Marvel Comics Group

1 — .80 2.00
2-8 — 1.40

FALLING IN LOVE
Sept-Oct, 1955 - No. 143, Oct-Nov, 1973
Arleigh Publ. Co./National Periodical Publications

1 — 31.00 94.00 250.00
2 — 15.00 45.00 120.00
3-10 — 8.75 26.25 70.00
11-20 — 7.15 21.50 50.00

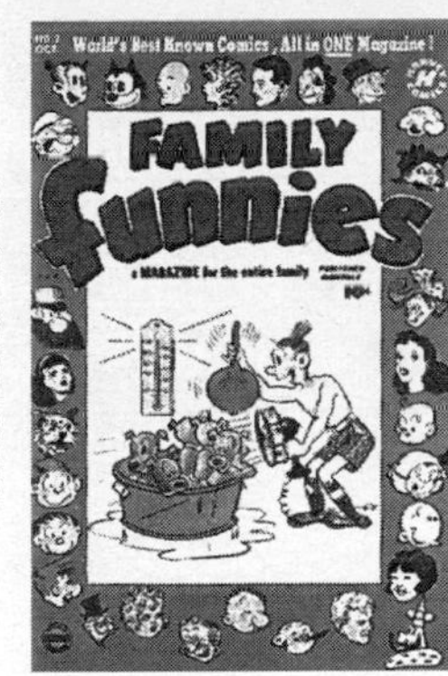

Famous Funnies #2 © KFS

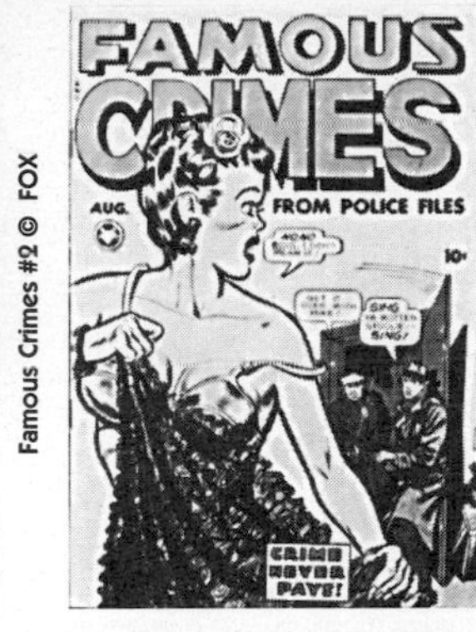

Famous Crimes #2 © FOX

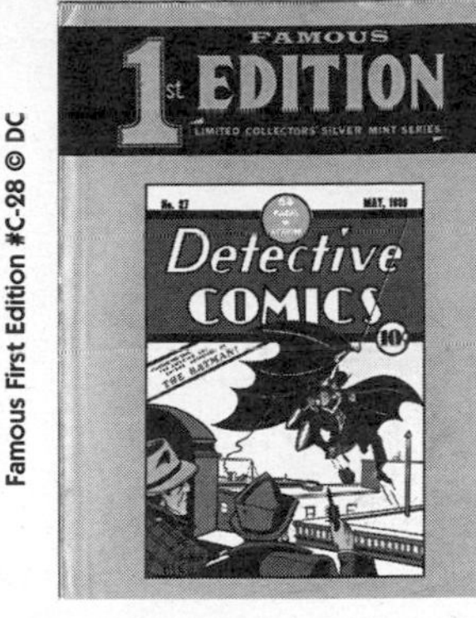

Famous First Edition #C-28 © DC

	GD25	FN65	NM94
21-40	5.70	17.00	35.00
41-47: 47-Last 10¢ issue?	4.25	13.00	26.00
48-70	2.25	6.75	18.00
71-99,108: 108-Wood-a (4 pgs., 7/69)	1.75	5.25	14.00
100	2.50	7.50	25.00
101-107,109-124,134-143	1.00	3.00	8.00
125-133: 52 pgs.	2.50	7.50	20.00

NOTE: *Colan c/a-75, 81. 52 pgs.-#125-133.*

FALL OF THE HOUSE OF USHER, THE (See A Corben Special & Spirit section 8/22/48)

FALL OF THE ROMAN EMPIRE (See Movie Comics)

FAMILY AFFAIR (TV)
Feb, 1970 - No. 4, Oct, 1970 (25¢)
Gold Key

	GD25	FN65	NM94
1-With pull-out poster; photo-c	3.00	10.00	36.00
1-With poster missing	1.30	3.90	14.00
2-4: 3,4-Photo-c	1.65	5.00	18.00

FAMILY FUNNIES
No. 9, Aug-Sept, 1946
Parents' Magazine Institute

	GD25	FN65	NM94
9	4.00	11.00	22.00

FAMILY FUNNIES (Tiny Tot Funnies No. 9)
Sept, 1950 - No. 8, Apr, 1951
Harvey Publications

	GD25	FN65	NM94
1-Mandrake (has over 30 King Feature strips)	5.70	17.00	40.00
2-Flash Gordon, 1 pg.	4.25	13.00	28.00
3-8: 4,5,7-Flash Gordon, 1 pg.	4.15	12.50	25.00
1(Black & white)	2.40	6.00	12.00

FAMILY MAN
1995 - No. 3, 1995 ($4.95, B&W, digest-size, limited series)
DC Comics (Paradox Press)

	GD25	FN65	NM94
1-3		2.00	5.00

FAMOUS AUTHORS ILLUSTRATED (See Stories by...)

FAMOUS COMICS (Also see Favorite Comics)
No date; Mid 1930's (24 pgs., paper-c)
Zain-Eppy/United Features Syndicate

	GD25	FN65	NM94
nn-Reprinted from 1933 & 1934 newspaper strips in color; Joe Palooka, Hairbreadth Harry, Napoleon, The Nebbs, etc. (Many different versions known)	36.00	108.00	320.00

FAMOUS COMICS
1934 (100 pgs., daily newspaper-r)
(3-1/2x8-1/2"; paper cover) (came in a box)
King Features Syndicate (Whitman Publ. Co.)

	GD25	FN65	NM94
684(#1)-Little Jimmy, Katzenjammer Kids, & Barney Google	29.00	86.00	230.00
684(#2)-Polly, Little Jimmy, Katzenjammer Kids	29.00	86.00	230.00
684(#3)-Little Annie Rooney, Polly and her Pals, Katzenjammer Kids	29.00	86.00	230.00
....Box price....	27.00	81.00	215.00

FAMOUS COMICS CARTOON BOOKS
1934 (8x7-1/4", 72 pgs., B&W hard-c, daily strip-r)
Whitman Publishing Co.

	GD25	FN65	NM94
1200-The Captain & the Kids (1st app?); Dirks reprints credited to Bernard Dibble	24.00	71.00	190.00
1202-Captain Easy (1st app?) & Wash Tubbs by Roy Crane; 2 slightly different versions of cover exist	29.00	86.00	230.00
1203-Ella Cinders (1st app?)	23.00	69.00	185.00
1204-Freckles & His Friends (1st app?)	21.00	62.00	165.00

NOTE: *Called Famous Funnies Cartoon Books inside.*

FAMOUS CRIMES
June, 1948 - No. 19, Sept, 1950; No. 20, Aug, 1951; No. 51, 52, 1953
Fox Features Syndicate/M.S. Dist. No. 51,52

	GD25	FN65	NM94
1-Blue Beetle app. & crime story-r/Phantom Lady #16	40.00	120.00	325.00
2-Has woman dissolved in acid; lingerie-c/panels	31.00	94.00	240.00
3-Injury-to-eye story used in **SOTI**, pg. 112; has two electrocution stories	39.00	118.00	300.00
4-6	15.00	45.00	115.00
7- "Tarzan, the Wyoming Killer" used in **SOTI**, pg. 44; drug trial/possession story	33.00	99.00	245.00
8-20: 17-Morisi-a	12.00	36.00	90.00
51(nd, 1953)	12.00	36.00	90.00
52	6.70	20.00	40.00

FAMOUS FAIRY TALES
1942; 1943 (32 pgs.); 1944 (16 pgs.) (Giveaway, soft-c)
K. K. Publ. Co.

	GD25	FN65	NM94
1942-Kelly-a	36.00	108.00	300.00
1943-r-/Fairy Tale Parade No. 2,3; Kelly-a	28.00	84.00	225.00
1944-Kelly-a	25.00	75.00	200.00

FAMOUS FEATURE STORIES
1938 (7-1/2x11", 68 pgs.)
Dell Publishing Co.

	GD25	FN65	NM94
1-Tarzan, Terry & the Pirates, King of the Royal Mtd., Buck Jones, Dick Tracy, Smilin' Jack, Dan Dunn, Don Winslow, G-Man, Tailspin Tommy, Mutt & Jeff, Little Orphan Annie reprints - all illustrated text	58.00	174.00	525.00

FAMOUS FIRST EDITION (See Limited Collectors' Edition)
($1.00, 10x13-1/2", 72 pgs.) (No.6-8, 68 pgs.)
1974 - No. 8, Aug-Sept, 1975; C-61, 1979
National Periodical Publications/DC Comics

	GD25	FN65	NM94
C-26-Action Comics #1; gold ink outer-c	2.50	7.50	20.00
C-28-Detective #27; silver ink outer-c	5.00	15.00	50.00
C-28-Hardbound edition	20.00	60.00	200.00
C-30-Sensation #1(1974); bronze ink outer-c	2.50	7.50	20.00
F-4-Whiz Comics #2(#1)(10-11/74)-Cover not identical to original (dropped "Gangway for Captain Marvel" from cover); gold ink on outer-c	2.50	7.50	20.00
F-5-Batman #1(F-6 inside); silver ink on outer-c	4.00	12.00	40.00
V2#F-6-Wonder Woman #1	2.50	7.50	20.00
F-7-All-Star Comics #3	1.20	3.60	12.00
F-8-Flash Comics #1(8-9/75)	1.20	3.60	12.00
V8#C-61-Superman #1(1979, $2.00)	1.20	3.60	12.00
Hardbound editions (w/dust jackets $5.00 extra) (Lyle Stuart, Inc.) C-26,C-30,F-4,F-6 known	15.00	45.00	150.00

Warning: The above books are almost **exact** reprints of the originals that they represent except for the Giant-Size format. None of the originals are Giant-Size. The first five issues and C-61 were printed with two covers. Reprint information can be found on the outside cover, but not on the inside cover which was reprinted exactly like the original (inside and out).

FAMOUS FUNNIES
1933 - No. 218, July, 1955
Eastern Color

	GD25	FN65	VF82	NM94
A Carnival of Comics (probably the second comic book), 36 pgs., no date given, no publisher, no number; contains strip reprints of The Bungle Family, Dixie Dugan, Hairbreadth Harry, Joe Palooka, Keeping Up With the Jones, Mutt & Jeff, Reg'lar Fellers, S'Matter Pop, Strange As It Seems, and others. This book was sold by M. C. Gaines to Wheatena, Milk-O-Malt, John Wanamaker, Kinney Shoe Stores, & others to be given away as premiums and radio give-aways (1933).	680.00	2040.00	4420.00	7500.00

(Estimated up to 50 total copies exist, 2 in NM/Mint)

Series 1-(Very rare)(nd-early 1934)(68 pgs.) No publisher given (Eastern Color PrintingCo.); sold in chain stores for 10¢. 35,000 print run. Contains Sunday strip reprints of Mutt & Jeff, Reg'lar Fellers, Nipper, Hairbreadth Harry, Strange As It Seems, Joe Palooka, Dixie Dugan, The Nebbs, Keeping Up With the Jones, and others. Inside front and back covers and pages 1-16 of Famous Funnies Series 1, #s 49-64 reprinted from **Famous Funnies**, **A Carnival of Comics**, and most of pages 17-48 reprinted from **Funnies on Parade**. This was the first comic book sold.

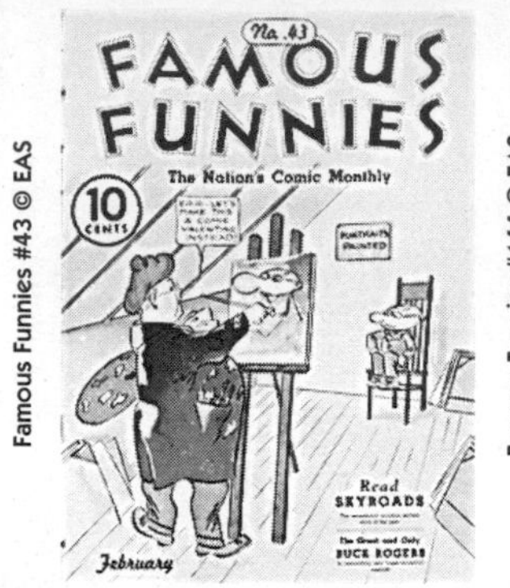

Famous Funnies #43 © EAS

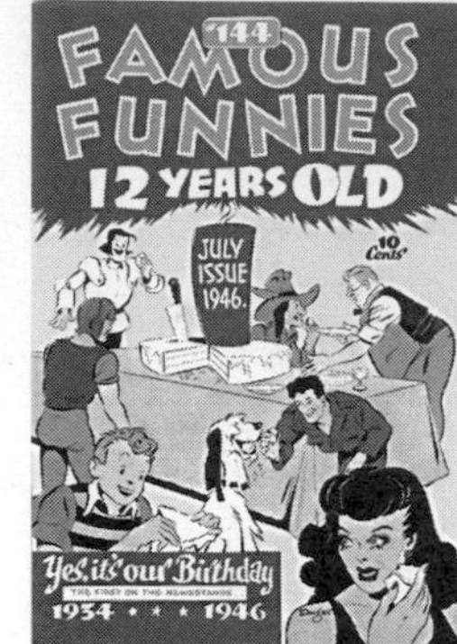

Famous Funnies #144 © EAS

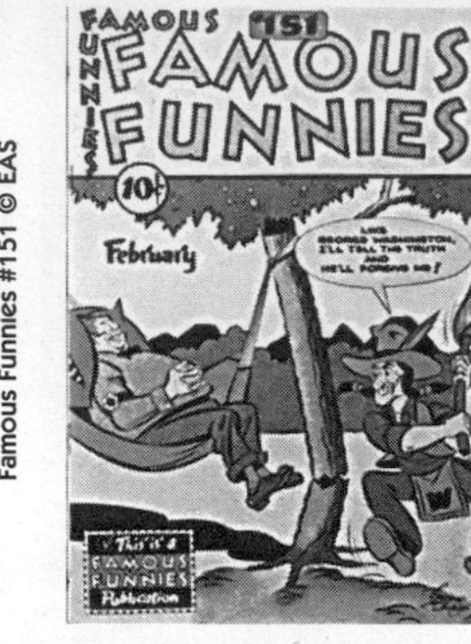

Famous Funnies #151 © EAS

GD25 FN65 NM94

3000.00 9000.00 15,000.00 21,500.00
(Estimated up to 12 copies exist, 1 in NM/Mint)

No. 1 (Rare)(7/34-on stands 5/34) - Eastern Color Printing Co. First monthly newsstand comic book. Contains Sunday strip reprints of Toonerville Folks, Mutt & Jeff, Hairbreadth Harry, S'Matter Pop, Nipper, Dixie Dugan, The Bungle Family, Connie, Ben Webster, Tailspin Tommy, The Nebbs, Joe Palooka, & others. 2415.00 7250.00 10,865.00 15,000.00
(Estimated up to 30 total copies exist, 2 in NM/Mint)

	GD25	FN65	VF82
2 (Rare, 9/34)	450.00	1350.00	2800.00
3-Buck Rogers Sunday strip-r by Rick Yager begins, ends #218; not in #191-208; 1st comic book app. of Buck Rogers; the number of the 1st strip reprinted is pg. 190, Series No. 1	583.00	1750.00	3600.00
4	183.00	550.00	1150.00
5-1st Christmas-c on a newsstand comic	150.00	450.00	940.00
6-10	108.00	324.00	675.00

	GD25	FN65	NM94
11,12,18-Four pgs. of Buck Rogers in each issue, completes stories in Buck Rogers #1 which lacks these pages. 18-Two pgs. of Buck Rogers reprinted in Daisy Comics #1	95.00	287.00	600.00
13-17,19,20: 14-Has two Buck Rogers panels missing. 17-2nd Christmas-c on a newsstand comic (12/35)	73.00	219.00	460.00
21,23-30: 27-(10/36)-War on Crime begins (4 pgs.); 1st true crime in comics (reprints); part photo-c. 29-X-Mas-c (12/36)	52.00	157.00	325.00
22-Four pgs. of Buck Rogers needed to complete stories in Buck Rogers #1	56.00	170.00	350.00
31,33,34,36,37,39,40: 33-Careers of Baby Face Nelson & John Dillinger traced	40.00	120.00	250.00
32-(3/37) 1st app. the Phantom Magician (costume hero) in Advs. of Patsy	43.00	130.00	270.00
35-Two pgs. Buck Rogers omitted in Buck Rogers #2	43.00	130.00	270.00
38-Full color portrait of Buck Rogers	39.00	117.00	260.00
41-60: 41,53-X-Mas-c. 55-Last bottom panel, pg. 4 in Buck Rogers redrawn in Buck Rogers #3	28.00	84.00	175.00
61,63,64,66,67,69,70	15.50	47.00	125.00
62,65,68-Two pgs. Kirby-a "Lightnin' & the Lone Rider". 65-X-Mas-c	19.00	56.00	150.00
71,73,77-80: 77-X-Mas-c. 80-(3/41)-Buck Rogers story continues from Buck Rogers #5	12.00	36.00	95.00
72-Speed Spaulding begins by Marvin Bradley (artist), ends #88. This series was written by Edwin Balmer & Philip Wylie (later appeared as film & book "When Worlds Collide")	12.00	38.00	100.00
74-76-Two pgs. Kirby-a in all	12.00	36.00	95.00
81-Origin & 1st app. Invisible Scarlet O'Neil (4/41); strip begins #82, ends #167; 1st non-funny-c (Scarlet O'Neil)	8.75	26.25	70.00
82-Buck Rogers-c	12.00	36.00	95.00
83-87,90: 86-Connie vs. Monsters on the Moon-c (sci/fi). 87 has last Buck Rogers full page-r. 90-Bondage-c	8.75	26.25	70.00
88-Buck Rogers in "Moon's End" by Calkins, 2 pgs.(not reprints). Beginning with #88, all Buck Rogers pgs. have rearranged panels	9.50	28.00	75.00
89-Origin & 1st app. Fearless Flint, the Flint Man	9.50	28.00	75.00
91-93,95,96,98-99,101,103-110: 105-Series 2 begins (Strip Page #1)	8.75	26.25	65.00
94-Buck Rogers in "Solar Holocaust" by Calkins, 3 pgs.(not reprints)	8.75	26.25	65.00
97-War Bond promotion, Buck Rogers by Calkins, 2 pgs.(not reprints)	8.75	26.25	65.00
100	8.75	26.25	65.00
102-Chief Wahoo vs. Hitler,Tojo & Mussolini-c (1/43)	14.50	43.00	115.00
111-130 (5/45): 113-X-Mas-c	6.50	19.50	45.00
131-150 (1/47): 137-Strip page No. 110 omitted	5.35	16.00	32.00
151-162,164-168	4.25	13.00	28.00
163-St. Valentine's Day-c	5.70	17.00	35.00
169,170-Two text illos. by Williamson, his 1st comic book work	8.50	26.00	60.00
171-180: 171-Strip pgs. 227,229,230, Series 2 omitted. 172-Strip Pg. 232 omitted	4.25	13.00	26.00
181-190: Buck Rogers ends with start of strip pg. 302, Series 2. 190-Oaky Doaks-c/story	4.25	13.00	26.00
191-197,199,201,203,206-208: No Buck Rogers. 191-Barney Carr, Space detective begins, ends #192.	4.00	12.00	24.00
198,202,205-One pg. Frazetta ads; no B. Rogers	4.25	13.00	26.00
200-Frazetta 1 pg. ad	4.25	13.00	26.00
204-Used in **POP**, pg. 79,99; war-c begin, end #208	4.25	13.00	28.00
209-Buck Rogers begins (12/53) with strip pg. 480, Series 2; Frazetta-c	67.00	200.00	600.00
210-216: Frazetta-c. 211-Buck Rogers ads by Anderson begins, ends #217. #215-Contains B. Rogers strip pg. 515-518, series 2 followed by pgs. 179-181, Series 3	67.00	200.00	600.00
217,218-B. Rogers ends with pg. 199, Series 3. 218-Wee Three-c/story	4.25	13.00	26.00

NOTE: ***Rick Yager*** *did the Buck Rogers Sunday strips reprinted in Famous Funnies. The Sundays were formerly done by Russ Keaton and Lt. Dick Calkins did the dailies, but would sometimes assist Yager on a panel or two from time to time. Strip No. 169 is Yager's first full Buck Rogers page. Yager did the strip until 1958 when* ***Murphy Anderson*** *took over.* ***Tuska*** *art from 4/26/59 - 1965. Virtually every panel was rewritten for Famous Funnies. Not iden#tical to the original Sunday page. The Buck Rogers reprints run continuously through Famous Funnies issue No. 190 (Strip No. 302) with no break in story line. The story line has no continuity after No. 190. The Buck Rogers newspaper strips came out in four series: Series 1, 3/30/30 - 9/21/41 (No. 1 - 600); Series 2, 9/28/41 -10/21/51 (No. 1 -525)(Strip No. 110-1/2 (1/2 pg.) published in only a few newspapers); Series 3, 10/28/51 -2/9/58 (No. 100-428)(No No.1-99); Series 4, 2/16/58 - 6/13/65 (No numbers, dates only).* ***Everett*** *c-85, 86.* ***Moulton*** *a-100. Chief Wahoo c-93, 97, 102, 116, 136, 139, 151. Dickie Dare c-83, 88. Fearless Flint c-89. Invisible Scarlet O'Neil c-81, 87, 95, 121(part), 132. Scorchy Smith c-84, 90.*

FAMOUS FUNNIES
1964
Super Comics

	GD25	FN65	NM94
Super Reprint Nos. 15-18:17-r/Double Trouble #1. 18-Space Comics #?	1.50	4.50	12.00

FAMOUS GANG BOOK OF COMICS (Becomes Donald & Mickey Merry Christmas 1943 on)
Dec, 1942 (Christmas giveaway, 32 pgs., paper-c)
Firestone Tire & Rubber Co.

	GD25	FN65	NM94
nn-(Rare)-Porky Pig, Bugs Bunny, Mary Jane & Sniffles, Elmer Fudd; r/Looney Tunes	60.00	180.00	600.00

FAMOUS GANGSTERS (Crime on the Waterfront No. 4)
Apr, 1951 - No. 3, Feb, 1952
Avon Periodicals/Realistic No. 3

	GD25	FN65	NM94
1-Capone, Dillinger; c-/Avon paperback #329	30.00	90.00	220.00
2-Dillinger Machine Gun Killer; Wood-c/a (1 pg.); r/Saint #7 & retitled "Mike Strong"	30.00	90.00	220.00
3-Lucky Luciano & Murder, Inc; c-/Avon paperback #66	30.00	90.00	220.00

FAMOUS INDIAN TRIBES
July-Sept, 1962; No. 2, July, 1972
Dell Publishing Co.

	GD25	FN65	NM94
12-264-209(#1) (The Sioux)	.90	1.80	10.00
2(7/72)-Reprints above		.80	2.00

FAMOUS STARS
Nov-Dec, 1950 - No. 6, Spring, 1952 (All have photo-c)
Ziff-Davis Publ. Co.

	GD25	FN65	NM94
1-Shelley Winters, Susan Peters, Ava Gardner, Shirley Temple; Jimmy Stewart & Shelley Winters photo-c; Whitney-a	26.00	77.00	190.00
2-Betty Hutton, Bing Crosby, Colleen Townsend, Gloria Swanson; Betty Hutton photo-c; Everett-a(2)	18.00	54.00	130.00
3-Farley Granger, Judy Garland's ordeal, Alan Ladd; Farley Granger & Judy Garland photo-c; Whitney-a	17.00	49.00	120.00

Fantastic Comics #3 © FOX

Fantastic Force #2 © MEG

Fantastic Four #1 © MEG

GD25 FN65 NM94

4-Al Jolson, Bob Mitchum, Ella Raines, Richard Conte, Vic Damone; Bob Mitchum photo-c; Crandall-a, 6pgs. 15.00 45.00 110.00
5-Liz Taylor, Betty Grable, Esther Williams, George Brent, Mario Lanza; Liz Taylor photo-c; Krigstein-a 20.00 60.00 150.00
6-Gene Kelly, Hedy Lamarr, June Allyson, William Boyd, Janet Leigh, Gary Cooper; Gene Kelly photo-c 13.50 41.00 95.00

FAMOUS STORIES (...Book No. 2)
1942 - No. 2, 1942
Dell Publishing Co.

1,2: 1-Treasure Island. 2-Tom Sawyer 24.00 73.00 195.00

FAMOUS TV FUNDAY FUNNIES
Sept, 1961
Harvey Publications

1-Casper the Ghost 3.20 9.60 32.00

FAMOUS WESTERN BADMEN (Formerly Redskin)
No. 13, Dec, 1952 - No. 15, Apr, 1953
Youthful Magazines

13-Redskin story 9.50 28.00 75.00
14,15: 15-The Dalton Boys story 7.15 21.50 50.00

FANGS OF THE WIDOW
Sept, 1995 - Present ($3.00, B&W)
London Night Studios/Ground Zero #5 on

1-9: 5-1st Ground Zero issue 1.20 3.00
1-Platinum 1.20 3.00

FANTASTIC (Formerly Captain Science; Beware No. 10 on)
No. 8, Feb, 1952 - No. 9, Apr, 1952
Youthful Magazines

8-Capt. Science by Harrison; decapitation, shrunken head panels 30.00 90.00 220.00
9-Harrison-a 21.00 64.00 160.00

FANTASTIC ADVENTURES
1963 - 1964 (Reprints)
Super Comics

9,10,12,15,16,18: 9-r/? 10-r/He-Man #2(Toby). 11-Disbrow-a. 12-Unpublished Chesler material? 15-r/Spook #23. 16-r/Dark Shadows #2(Steinway); Briefer-a. 18-r/Superior Stories #1 2.00 6.00 16.00
11-Wood-a; r/Blue Bolt #118 3.00 9.00 30.00
17-Baker-a(2) r/Seven Seas #6 3.00 9.00 30.00

FANTASTIC COMICS
Dec, 1939 - No. 23, Nov, 1941
Fox Features Syndicate

1-Intro/origin Samson; Stardust, The Super Wizard, Sub Saunders (by Kiefer), Space Smith, Capt. Kidd begin 350.00 1050.00 3500.00
2-Powell text illos 167.00 500.00 1500.00
3-Classic Lou Fine Robot-c; Powell text illos 470.00 1410.00 4700.00
4,5: Last Lou Fine-c 139.00 417.00 1250.00
6,7-Simon-c 106.00 318.00 950.00
8-10: 10-Intro/origin David, Samson's aide 75.00 225.00 675.00
11-17,19,20,22: 16-Stardust ends 64.00 192.00 575.00
18-1st app. Black Fury & sidekick Chuck; ends #23 67.00 200.00 600.00
21,23: 21-The Banshee begins(origin); ends #23; Hitler-c. 22-Likeness of Hitler as furnace on cover. 23-Origin The Gladiator 67.00 200.00 600.00

*NOTE: **Lou Fine** c-1-5. **Tuska** a-3-5, 8. Bondage c-6, 8, 9. Issue #11 has indicia to Mystery Men Comics #15. All issues feature Samson covers.*

FANTASTIC COMICS (Fantastic Fears #1-9; Becomes Samson #12)
No. 10, Nov-Dec, 1954 - No. 11, Jan-Feb, 1955
Ajax/Farrell Publ.

10 (#1) 12.00 38.00 100.00

GD25 FN65 NM94

11-Robot-c 15.00 45.00 120.00

FANTASTIC FABLES
Feb, 1987 ($1.50, 28 pgs., B&W)
Silverwolf Comics

1-Tim Vigil-a (6 pgs.) 1.50

FANTASTIC FEARS (Formerly Captain Jet) (Fantastic Comics #10 on)
No. 7, May, 1953 - No. 9, Sept-Oct, 1954
Ajax/Farrell Publ.

7(#1, 5/53)-Tales of Stalking Terror 32.00 96.00 240.00
8(#2, 7/53) 20.00 60.00 150.00
3,4 14.00 43.00 110.00
5-(1-2/54)-Ditko story (1st drawn) is written by Bruce Hamilton; r-in Weird V2#8 (1st pro work for Ditko but Daring Love #1 was published 1st) 62.00 188.00 525.00
6-Decapitation-girl's head w/paper cutter (classic) 38.00 114.00 280.00
7(5-6/54), 9(9-10/54) 14.00 43.00 110.00
8(7-8/54)-Contains story intended for Jo-Jo; name changed to Kaza; decapitation story 17.00 4900 120.00

FANTASTIC FORCE
Nov, 1994 - No. 18, Apr, 1996 ($1.75)
Marvel Comics

1-($2.50)-Foil wraparound-c; intro Fantastic Force w/Huntara, Delvor, Psi-Lord & Vibraxas 1.00 2.50
2-18: 13-She-Hulk app. .70 1.75

FANTASTIC FOUR (See America's Best TV..., Fireside Book Series, Giant-Size..., Giant Size Super-Stars, Marvel Collectors Item Classics, Marvel Milestone Edition, Marvel's Greatest, Marvel Treasury Edition, Marvel Triple Action, Official Marvel Index to... & Power Record Comics)

FANTASTIC FOUR
Nov, 1961 - No. 416, Sept, 1996 (Created by Stan Lee & Jack Kirby)
Marvel Comics Group

GD25 FN65 VF82 NM94

1-Origin & 1st app. The Fantastic Four (Reed Richards: Mr. Fantastic, Johnny Storm: The Human Torch, Sue Storm: The Invisible Girl, & Ben Grimm: The Thing–Marvel's 1st super-hero group since the G.A.; 1st app. S.A. Human Torch); origin/1st app. The Mole Man. 750.00 2250.00 7500.00 18,400.00

GD25 FN65 NM94

1-Golden Record Comic Set Reprint (1966)-cover not identical to original 16.00 48.00 160.00
with Golden Record 24.00 72.00 240.00
2-Vs. The Skrulls (last 10¢ issue) 243.00 730.00 3400.00
3-Fantastic Four don costumes & establish Headquarters; brief 1pg. origin; intro The Fantasti-Car; Human Torch drawn w/two left hands on-c 177.00 531.00 2300.00

GD25 FN65 VF82 NM94

4-1st S. A. Sub-Mariner app. (5/62) 208.00 624.00 1456.00 2700.00
5-Origin & 1st app. Doctor Doom 223.00 669.00 1561.00 2900.00

GD25 FN65 NM94

6-Sub-Mariner, Dr. Doom team up; 1st Marvel villain team-up (2nd S.A. Sub-Mariner app. 125.00 375.00 1500.00
7-10: 7-1st app. Kurrgo. 8-1st app. Puppet-Master & Alicia Masters. 9-3rd Sub-Mariner app. 10-Stan Lee (1st app. in comics?) & Jack Kirby app. in story 64.00 192.00 770.00
11-Origin/1st app. The Impossible Man (2/63) 54.00 162.00 650.00
12-Fantantic Four Vs. The Hulk (1st meeting); 1st Hulk x-over & ties w/Amazing Spider-Man #1 as 1st Marvel x-over; (3/63) 88.00 263.00 1050.00
13-Intro. The Watcher; 1st app. The Red Ghost 41.00 123.00 470.00
14-19: 14-Sub-Mariner x-over. 15-1st app. Mad Thinker. 16-1st Ant-Man x-over (7/63); Wasp cameo. 18-Origin/1st app. The Super Skrull. 19-Intro. Rama-Tut; Stan Lee & Jack Kirby cameo 29.00 87.00 290.00
20-Origin/1st app. The Molecule Man 31.00 93.00 310.00
21-Intro. The Hate Monger; 1st Sgt. Fury x-over (12/63)

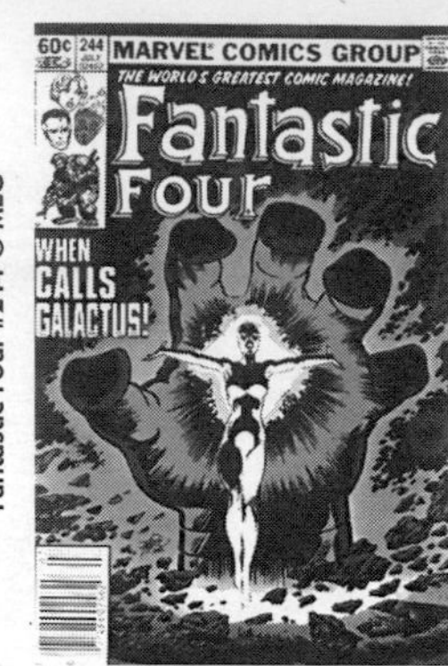

Fantastic Four #244 © MEG

Fantastic Four #307 © MEG

Fantastic Four #413 © MEG

	GD25	FN65	NM94
	21.00	63.00	210.00
22-24: 22-Sue Storm gains more powers	14.00	42.00	140.00
25,26-The Hulk vs. The Thing (their 1st battle). 25-3rd Avengers x-over (1st time w/Capt. America)(cameo, 4/64); 2nd S.A. app. Cap (takes place between Avengers #4 & 5. 26-4th Avengers x-over	35.00	105.00	390.00
27-1st Doctor Strange x-over (6/64)	16.00	48.00	160.00
28-Early X-Men x-over (7/64); same date as X-Men #6	23.00	69.00	230.00
29,30: 30-Intro. Diablo	10.50	32.00	105.00
31-40: 31-Early Avengers x-over (10/64). 33-1st app. Attuma; part photo-c. 35-Intro/1st app. Dragon Man. 36-Intro/1st app. Madam Medusa & the Frightful Four (Sandman, Wizard, Paste Pot Pete). 39-Wood inks on Daredevil (early x-over)	9.00	27.00	90.00
41-44,47: 41-43-Frightful Four app. 44-Intro. Gorgon.	6.00	18.00	60.00
45,46: 45-Intro/1st app. The Inhumans (c/story, 12/65); also see Incredible Hulk Special #1 & Thor #146, & 147. 46-1st Black Bolt-c (Kirby) & 1st full app.	6.50	19.50	65.00
48-Partial origin/1st app. The Silver Surfer & Galactus (3/66) by Lee & Kirby; Galactus cameo in last panel; 1st of 3 part story.	71.00	213.00	850.00
49-2nd app. Silver Surfer & Galactus	24.00	72.00	240.00
50-Silver Surfer battles Galactus	26.00	78.00	260.00
51,54: 54-Inhumans cameo	4.80	14.40	48.00
52-1st app. The Black Panther (7/66)	9.50	28.50	95.00
53-Origin & 2nd app. The Black Panther	8.50	25.50	85.00
55-Thing battles Silver Surfer; 4th app. Silver Surfer	8.00	24.00	80.00
56-60: Silver Surfer x-over. 59,60-Inhumans cameos	5.50	16.50	55.00
61-65,68-70: 61-Silver Surfer cameo; Sandman-c/s	4.20	12.60	42.00
66-Begin 2 part origin of Him (Warlock); does not app. (9/67)	9.50	28.50	95.00
67-Origin/1st app. Him (Warlock); 1 pg. cameo; see Thor #165,166 for 1st full app.	10.50	32.00	105.00
71,73,78-80: 73-Spider-Man, D.D., Thor x-over; cont'd from Daredevil #38	3.50	10.50	35.00
72-Silver Surfer-c/story (pre-dates Silver Surfer #1)	4.20	12.60	42.00
74-77: Silver Surfer app.(#77 is same date/S.S. #1)	4.00	12.00	40.00
81-88: 81-Crystal joins & dons costume. 82,83-Inhumans app. 84-87-Dr. Doom app. 88-Last 12¢ issue	2.50	7.50	25.00
89-99,101: 94-Intro. Agatha Harkness.	2.50	7.50	20.00
100 (7/70)	7.50	22.50	75.00
102,103: Fantastic Four vs. Sub-Mariner	2.50	7.50	22.00
104-111: 104-Magneto-c/story. 108-Last Kirby issue (not in #103-107). 110-reg. version w/green faces	1.50	4.50	12.00
110-Variant-c w/flesh faces color. Common version shows green faces.	2.50	7.50	24.00
112-Hulk Vs. Thing (7/71)	4.80	14.40	48.00
113-115: 115-Last 15¢ issue	1.40	4.15	11.00
116-120: 116-(52 pgs.)	1.00	3.00	7.50
121-123-Silver Surfer-c/stories. 122,123-Galactus	1.50	4.50	12.00
124,125,127,129-149: 129-Intro. Thundra. 130-Sue leaves F.F. 131-Quicksilver app. 132-Medusa joins. 133-Thundra Vs. Thing. 142-Kirbyish-a by Buckler begins. 143-Dr. Doom-c/story. 147-Sub-Mariner		2.40	6.00
126-Origin F.F. retold; cover swipe of F.F. #1	1.00	3.00	8.00
128-Four pg. insert of F.F. Friends & Foes	1.00	3.00	8.00
150-Crystal & Quicksilver's wedding	1.10	3.30	9.00
151-154,158-160: 151-Origin Thundra. 159-Medusa leaves; Sue rejoins		2.00	5.00
155-157: Silver Surfer in all	1.00	2.80	7.00
161-168,172,174-180: 164-The Crusader (old Marvel Boy) revived (origin #165); 1st app.Frankie Raye. 168-170-Cage app. 176-Re-intro Impossible Man; Marvel artists app. 180-r/#101 by Kirby		1.40	3.50
169-171,173-(Regular 25¢ edition)(4-6/75,8/75)		1.40	3.50

	GD25	FN65	NM94
169-171,173-(30¢-c, limited distribution)	1.75	5.25	14.00
181-199: 189-G.A. Human Torch app. & origin retold. 190,191-Fantastic Four break up		1.20	3.00
200-(11/78, 52 pgs.)-F.F. re-united vs. Dr. Doom		1.40	3.50
201-208,219,222-231: 207-Human Torch vs. Spider-Man-c/story. 211-1st app. Terrax		.80	2.00
209-216,218,220,221-Byrne-a. 209-1st Herbie the Robot. 220-Brief origin		1.00	2.50
217-Dazzler app. by Byrne		1.20	3.00
232-Byrne-a begins		1.20	3.00
233-235,237-249,251-260: All Byrne-a. 238-Origin Frankie Raye. 244-Frankie Raye becomes Nova, Herald of Galactus. 252-Reads sideways; Annihilus app.; contains skin "Tattooz" decals		1.20	3.00
236-20th Anniversary issue(11/81, 68 pgs., $1.00)-Brief origin F.F.; Byrne-c/a(p); new Kirby-a(p)		1.20	3.00
250-(52 pgs)-Spider-Man x-over; Byrne-a; Skrulls impersonate New X-Men		1.20	3.00
261-285: 261-Silver Surfer. 262-Origin Galactus; Byrne writes & draws himself into story. 264-Swipes-c of F.F. #1. 274-Spider-Man's alien costume app. (4th app., 1/85, 2 pgs.)		1.00	2.50
286-2nd app. X-Factor continued from Avengers #263; story continues in X-Factor #1		1.20	3.00
287-295: 292-Nick Fury app. 293-Last Byrne-a		.80	2.00
296-($1.50)-Barry Smith-c/a; Thing rejoins		1.20	3.00
297-318,320-330: 300-Johnny Storm & Alicia Masters wed. 306-New team begins (9/87). 311-Re-intro The Black Panther. 312-X-Factor x-over. 327-Mr. Fantastic & Invisible Girl return		.80	2.00
319-Double size		1.00	2.50
331-346,351-357,359,360: 334-Simonson-c/scripts begin. 337-Simonson-a begins. 342-Spider-Man cameo. 356-F.F. vs. The New Warriors; Paul Ryan-c/a begins. 360-Last $1.00-c			1.50
347-Ghost Rider, Wolverine, Spider-Man, Hulk-c/stories thru #349; Arthur Adams-c/a(p) in each		1.20	3.00
347-Gold 2nd printing		.80	2.00
348,349		.90	2.25
348-Gold 2nd printing			1.50
350-($1.50, 52 pgs.)-Dr. Doom app.		1.20	3.00
358-(11/91, $2.25, 88 pgs.)-30th anniversary issue; gives history of F.F.; die cut-c; Art Adams back-up story-a		.90	2.25
361-368,370,372-374,376-380,382-386: 362-Spider-Man app. 367-Wolverine app. (brief). 370-Infinity War x-over; Thanos & Magus app. 374-Secret Defenders (Ghost Rider, Hulk, Wolverine) x-over			1.50
369-Infinity War x-over; Thanos app.		1.00	2.50
371-All white embossed-c ($2.00)		1.60	4.00
371-All red 2nd printing ($2.00)		1.00	2.50
375-($2.95, 52 pgs.)-Holo-grafx foil-c; ann. issue		1.20	3.00
381-Death of Reed Richards (Mister Fantastic) & Dr. Doom		1.20	3.00
387-Newsstand ed. ($1.25)			1.25
387-($2.95)-Collector's Ed. w/Die-cut foil-c		1.20	3.00
388-393, 395-397: 388-Begin $1.50-c; bound-in trading card sheet			1.50
394 ($2.95)-Polybagged w/16 pg. Marvel Action Hour book and acetate print; pink logo		1.20	3.00
398,399-Rainbow Foil-c		1.00	2.50
400-Rainbow-Foil-c		1.40	3.50
401-415: 401,402-Atlantis Rising. 407,408-Return of Reed Richards. 411-Inhumans app. 414-Galactus vs. Hyperstorm. 415-Onslaught tie-in; X-Men app.			1.50
416-($2.50)-Onslaught tie-in; Dr. Doom app.; wraparound-c		1.00	2.50
Annual 1('63)-Origin F.F.; Ditko-i	43.00	129.00	525.00
Annual 2('64)-Dr. Doom origin & c/story	25.00	75.00	300.00
Annual 3('65)-Reed & Sue wed; r/#6,11	12.00	36.00	120.00
Special 4(11/66)-G.A. Torch x-over (1st S.A. app.) & origin retold; r/#25,26			

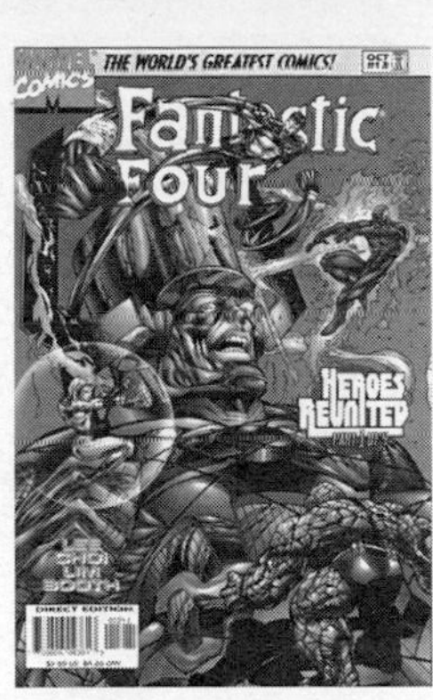

Fantastic Four V2 #12 © MEG

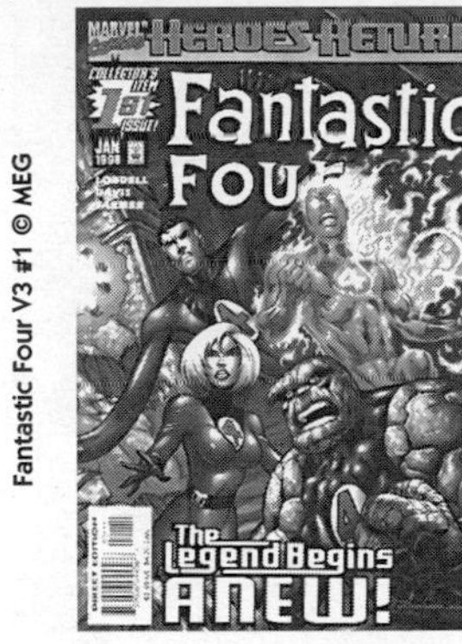

Fantastic Four V3 #1 © MEG

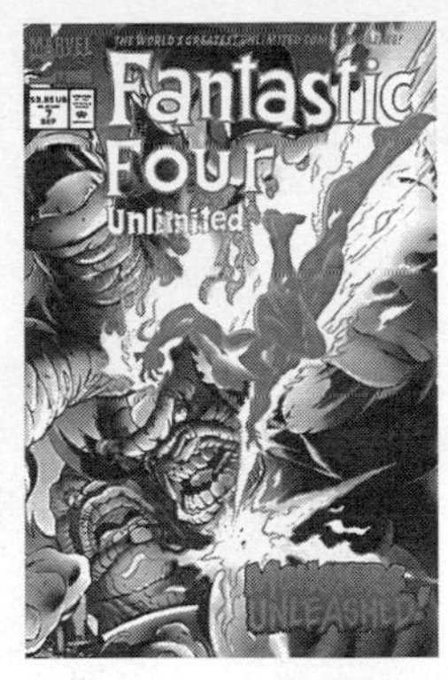

Fantastic Four Unlimited #7 © MEG

GD25 FN65 NM94

(Hulk vs. Thing); Torch vs. Torch battle 7.00 21.00 70.00
Special 5(11/67)-New art; Intro. Psycho-Man; early Black Panther, Inhumans & Silver Surfer (1st solo story) app. 9.00 27.00 90.00
Special 6(11/68)-Intro. Annihilus; birth of Franklin Richards; new 48 pg. movie length epic; last non-reprint annual 4.50 13.50 45.00
Special 7(11/69)-r/F.F. #1-5; Marvel staff photos 2.20 6.60 22.00
Special 8-10: All reprints. 8(12/70)-F.F. vs. Sub-Mariner plus gallery of F.F. foes. 9(12/71). 10('73) 1.50 4.50 12.00
Annual 11-14: 11(1976)-New art begins again. 12(1978). 13(1978). 14(1979) 2.00 5.00
Annual 15-21: 15(1980). 16(1981). 17(1983)-Byrne-c/a. 18(1984). 19(1985). 20(1987). 21(1988)-Evolutionary War x-over 1.20 3.00
Annual 22-24 (1989-91, $2.00, 68 pgs.): 22-Atlantis Attacks x-over; Sub-Mariner & The Avengers app.; Buckler-a. 23-Byrne-c; Guice-p. 24-2 pg. origin recap of Fantastic Four; Guardians of the Galaxy x-over 1.00 2.50
Annual 25(1992, $2.25, 68 pgs.)-Moondragon story .90 2.25
Annual 26,27('93,'94, $2.95, 68 pgs.). 26-Bagged w/card 1.20 3.00
Special Edition 1(5/84)-r/Annual #1; Byrne-c/a 1.00 2.50
....: Monsters Unleashed nn (1992, $5.95)-r/F.F. #347-349 w/new Arthur Adams-c 2.40 6.00
....: Nobody Gets Out Alive (1994, $15.95) TPB r/ #387-392 2.00 6.00 16.00
Giveaway (nn, 1981, 32pgs., Young Model Builders Club) .80 2.00

NOTE: ***Arthur Adams** c/a-347-349p. **Austin** c(i)-232-236, 238, 240-242, 250i, 286i. **Buckler** c-168. **John Buscema** a(p)-107, 108(w/**Kirby** & **Romita**),109-130, 132, 134-141, 160, 173-175, 202, 296-309p, Annual 11, 13; c(p)-107-122, 124-129, 133-139, 202, Annual 12p, Special 10. **Byrne** a-209-218p, 220p, 221p, 232-265, 266i, 267-273, 274-293p, Annual 17, 19; c-211-214p, 220p, 232-236p, 237, 238p, 239, 240-242p, 243-249, 250p, 251-267, 269-277, 278-281p, 283p, 284, 285, 286p, 288-293, Annual 17, 18. **Ditko** a-13i, 14i(w/**Kirby**-p), Annual 16. **G. Kane** c-150p, 160p. **Kirby** a-1-102p, 108, 180r, 189r, 236p, Special 1-10; c-1-101, 164, 167, 171-177, 180, 181, 190, 200, Annual 11, Special 1-7, 9. **Marcos** a-Annual 14i. **Mooney** a-118i, 152i. **Perez** a(p)-164-167, 170-172, 176-178, 184-188, 191p, 192p. Annual 14p, 15p; c(p)-183-188, 191, 192, 194-197. **Simonson** a-337-341, 343, 344p, 345p, 346, 350p, 352-354; c-212, 334-341, 342p, 343-346, 350, 353, 354. **Steranko** c-130-132p. **Williamson** c-357i.*

FANTASTIC FOUR (Volume Two)
V2#1, Nov, 1996 - No. 13, Nov, 1997 ($2.95/$1.95/$1.99)(Produced by Wildstorm Productions)
Marvel Comics

1-($2.95)-Reintro Fantastic Four; Jim Lee-c/a; Brandon Choi scripts; Mole Man app. 2.00 5.00
1-($2.95)-Variant-c 1.00 3.00 8.00
2-Begin $1.95-c; Namor-c/app. 1.60 4.00
3-9: 3-Avengers-c/app. 4-Two covers; Dr. Doom cameo 1.20 3.00
10,11,13: All $1.99-c. 13-"World War 3"-pt. 1, x-over w/Image 1.99
12-($2.99) "Heroes Reunited"-pt. 1 2.99

FANTASTIC FOUR (Volume Three)
V3#1, Jan, 1998 - Present ($2.99/$1.99)
Marvel Comics

1-($2.99)-Heroes Return; Lobdell-s/Davis & Farmer-a 2.99
2-4-($1.95): 2-Two covers 1.99

FANTASTIC FOUR: ATLANTIS RISING
June, 1995 - No. 2, July, 1995 ($3.95, limited series)
Marvel Comics

1,2: Acetate-c 1.60 4.00
Collector's Preview (5/95, $2.25, 52 pgs.) .90 2.25

FANTASTIC FOUR INDEX (See Official...)

FANTASTIC FOUR ROAST
May, 1982 (75¢, one-shot, direct sales)
Marvel Comics Group

1-Celebrates 20th anniversary of F.F.#1; X-Men, Ghost Rider & many others cameo; Golden, Miller, Buscema, Rogers, Byrne, Anderson art; Hembeck/Austin-c 1.60 4.00

FANTASTIC FOUR: THE LEGEND
Oct, 1996 ($3.95, one-shot)
Marvel Comics

1-Tribute issue 1.60 4.00

FANTASTIC FOUR 2099
Jan, 1996 - No. 8, Aug, 1996 ($3.95/$1.95)
Marvel Comics

1-($3.95)-Chromium-c; X-Nation preview 1.60 4.00
2-8: 4-Spider-Man 2099-c/app. 5-Doctor Strange app. 7-Thibert-c .80 2.00

NOTE: ***Williamson** a-1i; c-1i.*

FANTASTIC FOUR UNLIMITED
Mar, 1993 - No. 12, Dec, 1995 ($3.95, 68 pgs.)
Marvel Comics

1-12: 1-Black Panther app. 4-Thing vs. Hulk. 5-Vs. The Frightful Four. 6-Vs. Namor. 7, 9-12-Wraparound-c 1.60 4.00

FANTASTIC FOUR UNPLUGGED
Sept, 1995 - No. 6, Aug 1996 (99¢, bi-monthly)
Marvel Comics

1-6 1.00

FANTASTIC FOUR VS. X-MEN
Feb, 1987 - No. 4, June, 1987 (Limited series)
Marvel Comics

1 1.20 3.00
2-4: 4-Austin-a(i) .80 2.00

FANTASTIC GIANTS (Formerly Konga #1-23)
V2#24, Sept, 1966 (25¢, 68 pgs.)
Charlton Comics

V2#24-Special Ditko issue; origin Konga & Gorgo reprinted plus two new Ditko stories 5.50 16.50 55.00

FANTASTIC TALES
1958 (no date) (Reprint, one-shot)
I. W. Enterprises

1-Reprints Avon's "City of the Living Dead" 2.60 7.80 26.00

FANTASTIC VOYAGE (See Movie Comics)
Aug, 1969 - No. 2, Dec, 1969
Gold Key

1,2 (TV) 3.00 9.00 33.00

FANTASTIC VOYAGES OF SINDBAD, THE
Oct, 1965 - No. 2, June, 1967
Gold Key

1,2-Painted-c 3.60 11.00 40.00

FANTASTIC WORLDS
No. 5, Sept, 1952 - No. 7, Jan, 1953
Standard Comics

5-Toth, Anderson-a 30.00 90.00 220.00
6-Toth-c/a 25.00 75.00 185.00
7 16.00 47.00 115.00

FANTASY FEATURES
1987 - No. 2, 1987 ($1.75)
Americomics

1,2 .70 1.80

FANTASY MASTERPIECES (Marvel Super Heroes No. 12 on)
Feb, 1966 - No. 11, Oct, 1967; V2#1, Dec, 1979 - No. 14, Jan, 1981
Marvel Comics Group

1-Photo of Stan Lee (12¢-c #1,2) 6.00 18.00 60.00
2-r/1st Fin Fang Foom from Strange Tales #89 3.00 9.00 30.00

Fantoman #2 © CEN

Fate #22 © DC

Fatman, the Human Flying Saucer #1 © Milson Publ. Co.

GD25 FN65 NM94

3-8: 3-G.A. Capt. America-r begin, end #11; 1st 25¢ Giant; Colan-r. 3-6-Kirby-c (p). 4-Kirby-c(p)(i). 7-Begin G.A. Sub-Mariner, Torch-r/M. Mystery. 8-Torch battles the Sub-Mariner-r/Marvel Mystery #9 3.00 9.00 30.00
9-Origin Human Torch-r/Marvel Comics #1 3.60 10.80 36.00
10,11: 10-r/origin & 1st app. All Winners Squad from All Winners #19. 11-r/origin of Toro (H.T. #1) & Black Knight #1 3.00 9.00 30.00
V2#1(12/79, 75¢, 52 pgs.)-r/origin Silver Surfer from Silver Surfer #1 with editing plus reprints cover; J. Buscema-a 1.20 3.00
2-14-Reprints Silver Surfer #2-14 w/covers .80 2.00

NOTE: ***Buscema** c-V2#7-9(in part). **Ditko** r-1-3, 7, 9. **Everett** r-1,7-9. **Matt Fox** r-9i. **Kirby** r-1-11; c(p)-3, 4i, 5, 6. **Starlin** r-8-13. Some direct sale V2#14's had a 50¢ cover price. #3-11 contain Capt. America-r/Capt. America #3-10. #7-11 contain G.A.Human Torch & Sub-Mariner-r.*

FANTASY QUARTERLY (Also see Elfquest)
Spring, 1978 (B&W) (2nd printing exist?)
Independent Publishers Syndicate

1-1st app. Elfquest; Dave Sim-a (6 pgs.) 4.00 12.00 40.00

FANTOMAN (Formerly Amazing Adventure Funnies)
No. 2, Aug, 1940 - No. 4, Dec, 1940
Centaur Publications

2-The Fantom of the Fair, The Arrow, Little Dynamite-r begin; origin The Ermine by Filchock; Fantoman app. in 2-4; Burgos, J. Cole, Ernst, Gustavson-a 106.00 318.00 950.00
3,4: Gustavson-r. 4-Red Blaze story 89.00 267.00 800.00

FAREWELL MOONSHADOW (See Moonshadow)
Jan, 1997 ($7.95, one-shot)
DC Comics (Vertigo)

nn-DeMatteis-s/Muth-c/a 7.95

FARGO KID (Formerly Justice Traps the Guilty)(See Feature Comics #47
V11#3(#1), June-July, 1958 - V11#5, Oct-Nov, 1958
Prize Publications

V11#3(#1)-Origin Fargo Kid, Severin-c/a; Williamson-a(2); Heath-a 15.50 47.00 125.00
V11#4,5-Severin-c/a 10.00 30.00 80.00

FARMER'S DAUGHTER, THE
Feb-Mar, 1954 - No. 3, June-July, 1954; No. 4, Oct, 1954
Stanhall Publ./Trojan Magazines

1-Lingerie, nudity panel 15.50 47.00 125.00
2-4(Stanhall) 10.00 30.00 80.00

FASHION IN ACTION
Aug, 1986 - Feb, 1987 (Baxter paper)
Eclipse Comics

Summer Special 1 ($1.75)-Snyder III-c/a .70 1.80
Winter Special 1 (2/87, $2.00)-Snyder III-c/a .80 2.00

FASTEST GUN ALIVE, THE (Movie)
No. 741, Sept, 1956 (one-shot)
Dell Publishing Co.

Four Color 741-Photo-c 6.40 19.00 70.00

FAST FICTION (...Action) (Stories by Famous Authors Illustrated #6 on)
Oct, 1949 - No. 5, Mar, 1950 (All have Kiefer-c)(48 pgs.)
Seaboard Publ./Famous Authors Ill.

1-Scarlet Pimpernel; Jim Lavery-c/a 31.00 94.00 250.00
2-Captain Blood; H. C. Kiefer-c/a 29.00 86.00 230.00
3-She, by Rider Haggard; Vincent Napoli-a 36.00 108.00 310.00
4-(1/50, 52 pgs.)-The 39 Steps; Lavery-c/a 23.00 68.00 180.00
5-Beau Geste; Kiefer-c/a 23.00 68.00 180.00

NOTE: ***Kiefer** a-2, 5; c-2, 3,5. **Lavery** c/a-1, 4. **Napoli** a-3.*

FAST FORWARD
1992 - No. 3, 1993 ($4.95, 68 pgs.)
DC Comics (Piranha Press)

1-3: 1-Morrison scripts; McKean-c/a. 3-Sam Kieth-a 2.00 5.00

FAST WILLIE JACKSON
Oct, 1976 - No. 7, 1977
Fitzgerald Periodicals, Inc.

1-7 1.00

FAT ALBERT (...& the Cosby Kids) (TV)
Mar, 1974 - No. 29, Feb, 1979
Gold Key

1 1.80 5.50 20.00
2-10 1.25 3.75 10.00
11-29 1.00 3.00 8.00

FATALE (Also see Powers That Be #1 & Shadow State #1,2)
Jan, 1996 - No. 6, Aug, 1996 ($2.50)
Broadway Comics

1-6: J.G. Jones-c/a in all 1.00 2.50
Preview Edition 1 (11/95, B&W) 1.00 2.50

FAT AND SLAT (Ed Wheelan) (Becomes Gunfighter No. 5 on)
Summer, 1947 - No. 4, Spring, 1948
E. C. Comics

1-Intro/origin Voltage, Man of Lightning; "Comics" McCormick, the World's No. 1 Comic Book Fan begins, ends #4 26.00 80.00 210.00
2-4: 4-Comics McCormick-c feature 19.00 56.00 150.00

FAT AND SLAT JOKE BOOK
Summer, 1944 (52 pgs., one-shot)
All-American Comics (William H. Wise)

nn-by Ed Wheelan 21.00 64.00 170.00

FATE (See Hand of Fate & Thrill-O-Rama)

FATE
Oct, 1994 - No. 22, Sept, 1996 ($1.95/$2.25)
DC Comics

0-7 .80 2.00
8-22: 8-Begin $2.25-c. 12-Alan Scott (Sentinel) app. 14-Zatanna app. 21-Phantom Stranger app. 22-Spectre app. .90 2.25

FATHER & SON
July, 1995 ($2.75, B&W, limited series)
Kitchen Sink

1-Jeff NIcholson-s/a 1.10 2.75

FATHER OF CHARITY
No date (32 pgs.; paper cover)
Catechetical Guild Giveaway

nn 1.25 3.75 10.00

FATHOM
May, 1987 - No. 3, July, 1987 ($1.50, limited series)
Comico

1-3 1.50

FATIMA...CHALLENGE TO THE WORLD
1951, 36 pgs. (15¢)
Catechetical Guild

nn (not same as 'Challenge to the World') 2.40 6.00 12.00

FATMAN, THE HUMAN FLYING SAUCER
April, 1967 - No. 3, Aug-Sept, 1967 (68 pgs.)
Lightning Comics(Milson Publ. Co.) (Written by Otto Binder)

1-Origin/1st app. Fatman & Tinman by Beck 4.50 13.50 45.00
2-C. C. Beck-a 3.00 9.00 30.00
3-(Scarce)-Beck-a 5.00 15.00 50.00

FAULTLINES

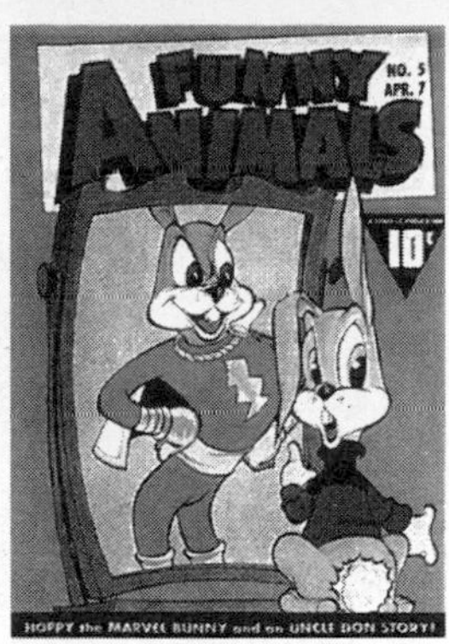

Fawcett Funny Animals #5 © FAW

The F.B.I. #1 © DELL

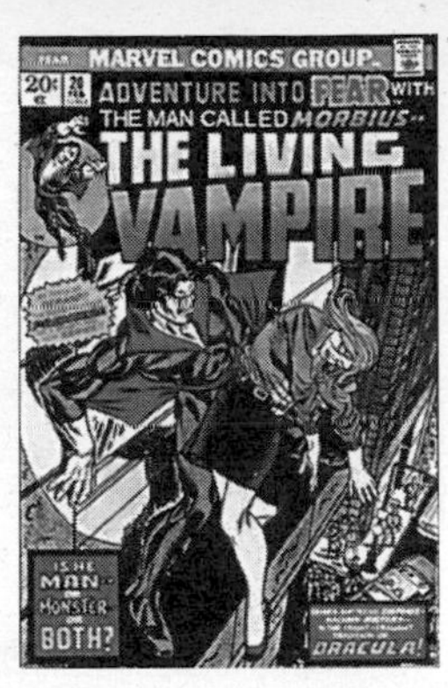

Fear #20 © MEG

GD25 FN65 NM94

May, 1997 - No. 6, Oct, 1997 ($2.50, limited series)
DC Comics (Vertigo)

1-6-Lee Marrs-s/Bill Koeb-a in all 1.00 2.50

FAUNTLEROY COMICS (Super Duck Presents...)
1950; No. 2, 1951; No. 3, 1952
Close-Up/Archie Publications

1-Super Duck-c/stories by Al Fagaly in all 7.15 21.50 50.00
2,3 5.00 15.00 30.00

FAUST
1989 - No 11, 1995 ($2.00/$2.25, B&W, mature themes)
Northstar Publishing/Rebel Studios #7 on

1-Decapitation-c; Tim Vigil-c/a in all; Begin $2.00-c 4.20 12.60 42.00
1-2nd printing 1.25 3.75 10.00
1-3rd printing 1.20 3.00
2 3.00 9.00 30.00
2-2nd & 3rd printings 1.20 3.00
3-Begin $2.25-c 2.50 7.50 20.00
3-2nd printing 1.20 3.00
4 1.10 3.30 9.00
5-10: 7-Begin Rebel Studios series 1.00 2.80 7.00
11-($2.25) .90 2.25

FAVORITE COMICS (Also see Famous Comics)
1934 (36 pgs.)
Grocery Store Giveaway (Diff. Corp.) (detergent)

Book 1-The Nebbs, Strange As It Seems, Napoleon, Joe Palooka, Dixie Dugan, S'Matter Pop, Hairbreadth Harry, etc. reprints 61.00 183.00 550.00
Book 2,3 42.00 126.00 375.00

FAWCETT MINIATURES (See Mighty Midget)
1946 (3-3/4x5", 12-24 pgs.) (Wheaties giveaways)
Fawcett Publications

Captain Marvel "And the Horn of Plenty"; Bulletman story
10.50 32.00 85.00
Captain Marvel "& the Raiders From Space"; Golden Arrow story
10.50 32.00 85.00
Captain Marvel Jr. "The Case of the Poison Press!" Bulletman story
10.50 32.00 85.00
Delecta of the Planets; C. C. Beck art; B&W inside; 12 pgs.; 3 printing variations (coloring) exist 19.00 56.00 150.00

FAWCETT MOTION PICTURE COMICS (See Motion Picture Comics)

FAWCETT MOVIE COMIC
1949 - No. 20, Dec, 1952 (All photo-c)
Fawcett Publications

nn- "Dakota Lil"; George Montgomery & Rod Cameron (1949)
27.00 81.00 215.00
nn- "Copper Canyon"; Ray Milland & Hedy Lamarr (1950)
21.00 62.00 165.00
nn- "Destination Moon" (1950) 68.00 206.00 575.00
nn- "Montana"; Errol Flynn & Alexis Smith (1950) 21.00 62.00 165.00
nn- "Pioneer Marshal"; Monte Hale (1950) 21.00 62.00 165.00
nn- "Powder River Rustlers"; Rocky Lane (1950) 31.00 94.00 250.00
nn- "Singing Guns"; Vaughn Monroe, Ella Raines & Walter Brennan (1950)
18.00 54.00 145.00
7- "Gunmen of Abilene"; Rocky Lane; Bob Powell-a (1950)
23.00 69.00 185.00
8- "King of the Bullwhip"; Lash LaRue; Bob Powell-a (1950)
35.00 105.00 280.00
9- "The Old Frontier"; Monte Hale; Bob Powell-a(2/51; mis-dated 2/50)
22.00 66.00 175.00
10- "The Missourians"; Monte Hale (4/51) 22.00 66.00 175.00
11- "The Thundering Trail"; Lash LaRue (6/51) 29.00 86.00 230.00
12- "Rustlers on Horseback"; Rocky Lane (8/51) 23.00 69.00 185.00
13- "Warpath"; Edmond O'Brien & Forrest Tucker (10/51)
15.00 45.00 120.00
14- "Last Outpost"; Ronald Reagan (12/51) 36.00 108.00 290.00
15-(Scarce)- "The Man From Planet X"; Robert Clark; Schaffenberger-a (2/52)
187.00 562.00 1600.00
16- "10 Tall Men"; Burt Lancaster 12.00 36.00 95.00
17- "Rose of Cimarron"; Jack Buetel & Mala Powers 9.50 28.00 75.00
18- "The Brigand"; Anthony Dexter & Anthony Quinn; Schaffenberger-a
9.50 28.00 75.00
19- "Carbine Williams"; James Stewart; Costanza-a; James Stewart photo-c
10.50 32.00 85.00
20- "Ivanhoe"; Robert Taylor & Liz Taylor photo-c 15.50 47.00 125.00

FAWCETT'S FUNNY ANIMALS (No. 1-26, 80-on titled "Funny Animals"; becomes Li'l Tomboy No. 92 on?)
12/42 - #79, 4/53; #80, 6/53 - #83, 12?/53; #84, 4/54 - #91, 2/56
Fawcett Publications/Charlton Comics No. 84 on

1-Capt. Marvel on cover; intro. Hoppy The Captain Marvel Bunny, cloned from Capt. Marvel; Billy the Kid & Willie the Worm begin
47.00 141.00 425.00
2-Xmas-c 26.00 80.00 210.00
3-5: 3-Spirit of '43-c 16.00 49.00 130.00
6,7,9,10 10.50 32.00 85.00
8-Flag-c 11.30 34.00 90.00
11-20: 14-Cover is a 1944 calendar 8.75 26.25 65.00
21-40: 25-Xmas-c. 26-St. Valentines Day-c 5.70 17.00 40.00
41-87,90,91 5.00 15.00 30.00
87-89(10-54-2/55)-Merry Mailman ish (TV/Radio)-part photo-c
5.70 17.00 40.00

NOTE: *Marvel Bunny in all issues to at least No. 68 (not in 49-54).*

FAZE ONE FAZERS
1986 - No. 4, Sept, 1986 (Limited series)
Americomics (AC Comics)

..1-4 1.50

F.B.I., THE
Apr-June, 1965
Dell Publishing Co.

1-Sinnott-a 2.25 6.75 18.00

F.B.I. STORY, THE (Movie)
No. 1069, Jan-Mar, 1960
Dell Publishing Co.

Four Color 1069-Toth-a; James Stewart photo-c 10.00 30.00 110.00

FEAR (Adventure into...)
Nov, 1970 - No. 31, Dec, 1975
Marvel Comics Group

1-Fantasy & Sci-Fi-r in early issues; Giant size 2.50 7.50 20.00
2-6: All Giant size 1.75 5.25 14.00
7-9 1.10 3.30 9.00
10-Man-Thing begins (10/72, early app.), ends #19; see Savage Tales #1 for 1st app.; Chaykin/Morrow-c/a 2.50 7.50 20.00
11,12: 11-N. Adams-c. 12-Starlin/Buckler-a 1.00 3.00 8.00
13,14,16-18: 17-Origin/1st app. Wundarr 2.40 6.00
15-1st full-length Man-Thing story (8/73) 1.00 3.00 8.00
19-Intro. Howard the Duck; Val Mayerik-a (12/73) 2.50 7.50 20.00
20-Morbius, the Living Vampire begins, ends #31; has history recap of Morbius with X-Men & Spider-Man 2.50 7.50 24.00
21-23,25 2.00 5.00
24-Blade-c/sty 1.85 5.50 15.00
26-31 1.60 4.00

NOTE: ***Bolle** a-13i. **Brunner** c-15-17. **Buckler** a-11p, 12i. **Chaykin** a-10i. **Colan** a-23r. **Craig** a-10p. **Ditko** a-6-8r. **Evans** a-30. **Everett** a-9, 10i, 21r. **Gulacy** a-20p. **Heath** a-12r. **Heck** a-8r, 13r. **Gil Kane** a-21p; c(p)-20, 21, 23-28, 31. **Kirby** a-8r, 9r. **Maneely** a-24r. **Mooney** a-11i, 26r.*

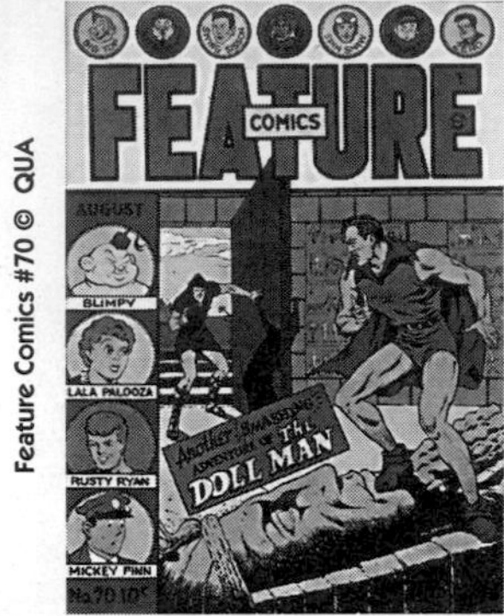

Feature Comics #70 © QUA

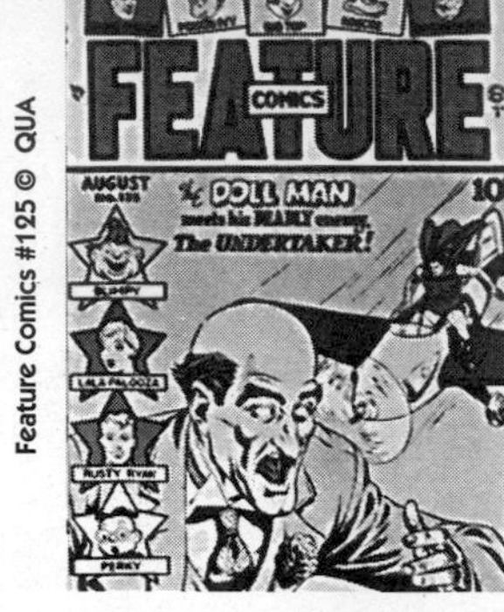

Feature Comics #125 © QUA

Feature Presentation #5 (#1) © FOX

*Morrow a-11i. **Paul Reinman** a-14r. **Robbins** a(p)-25-27, 31. **Russell** a-23p, 24p. **Severin** c-8. **Starlin** c-12p.*

FEARBOOK
April, 1986 ($1.75, one-shot, mature)
Eclipse Comics

..1-Scholastic Mag- r; Bissette-a .90 1.80

FEAR IN THE NIGHT (See Complete Mystery No. 3)

FEARLESS FAGAN
No. 441, Dec, 1952 (one-shot)
Dell Publishing co.

Four Color 441 3.00 9.00 35.00

FEATURE BOOK (Dell) (See Large Feature Comic)

FEATURE BOOKS (Newspaper-r, early issues)
May, 1937 - No. 57, 1948 (B&W) (Full color, 68 pgs. begin #26 on)
David McKay Publications

Note: See individual alphabetical listings for prices

nn-Popeye & the Jeep (#1, 100 pgs.); reprinted as Feature Books #3(Very Rare; only 3 known copies, 1-VF, 2-in low grade)
nn-Dick Tracy (#1)-Reprinted as Feature Book #4 (100 pgs.) & in part as 4-Color #1 (Rare, less than 10 known copies)

NOTE: *Above books were advertised together with different covers from Feat. Books #3 & 4.*

1-King of the Royal Mtd. (#1)
3-Popeye (7/37) by Segar;
4-Dick Tracy (8/37)-Same as nn issue but a new cover added
6-Dick Tracy (10/37)
8-Secret Agent X-9 (12/37) -Not by Raymond
9-Dick Tracy (1/38)
11-Little Annie Rooney (#1, 3/38)
13-Inspector Wade (5/38)
15-Barney Baxter (#1) (7/38)
17-Gangbusters (#1, 9/38) (1st app.)
20-Phantom (#1, 12/38)
22-Phantom
24-Lone Ranger (1941)
26-Prince Valiant (1941)-Hal Foster -c/a; newspaper strips reprinted, pgs. 1-28,30-63; color & 68 pg. issues begin; Foster cover is only original comic book artwork by him
36('43),38,40('44),42,43, 45,47-Blondie
39-Phantom
46-Mandrake in the Fire World-(58 pgs.)
48-Maltese Falcon by Dashiell Hammett('46)
51,54-Rip Kirby; Raymond-c/s; origin-#51
53,56,57-Phantom
2-Popeye (6/37) by Segar same as nn issue but a new cover added
5-Popeye (9/37) by Segar
7-Little Orphan Annie (#1, 11/37) (Rare)-Reprints strips from 12/31/34 to 7/17/35
10-Popeye (2/38)
12-Blondie (#1) (4/38) (Rare)
14-Popeye (6/38) by Segar
16-Red Eagle (8/38)
18,19-Mandrake
21-Lone Ranger
23-Mandrake
25-Flash Gordon (#1)-Reprints not by Raymond
27-29,31,34-Blondie
30-Katzenjammer Kids (#1, 1942)
32,35,41,44-Katzenjammer Kids
33(nn)-Romance of Flying; World War II photos
37-Katzenjammer Kids; has photo & biog. of Harold H.Knerr(1883-1949) who took over strip from Rudolph Dirks in 1914
49,50-Perry Mason; based on Gardner novels
52,55-Mandrake

NOTE: *All Feature Books through #25 are over-sized 8-1/2x11-3/8" comics with color covers and black and white interiors. The covers are rough, heavy stock. The page counts, including covers, are as follows: nn, #3, 4-100 pgs.; #1, 2-52 pgs.; #5-25 are all 76 pgs. #33 was found in bound set from publisher.*

FEATURE COMICS (Formerly Feature Funnies)
No. 21, June, 1939 - No. 144, May, 1950
Quality Comics Group

21-The Clock, Jane Arden & Mickey Finn continue from Feature Funnies 47.00 141.00 420.00
22-26: 23-Charlie Chan begins (8/39, 1st app.) 36.00 108.00 300.00
26-(nn, nd)-Cover in one color, (10¢, 36 pgs.; issue No. blanked out. Two variations exist, each contain half of the regular #26) 11.30 34.00 90.00
27-(Rare)-Origin/1st app. Doll Man by Eisner (scripts) & Lou Fine (art); Doll Man begins, ends #139 280.00 840.00 2800.00
28-2nd app. Doll Man by Lou Fine 128.00 384.00 1150.00
29,30: 30-1st Doll Man-c 75.00 225.00 675.00
31-Last Clock & Charlie Chan issue (4/40); Charlie Chan moves to Big Shot #1 following month (5/40) 60.00 180.00 540.00
32-37: 32-Rusty Ryan & Samar begin. 34-Captain Fortune app. 37-Last Fine Doll Man 43.00 126.00 385.00

Note: *A 15¢ Canadian version of Feature Comics #37, made in the US, exists.*

38-41: 38-Origin the Ace of Space. 39-Origin The Destroying Demon, ends #40; X-Mas-c. 40-Bruce Blackburn in costume 36.00 108.00 310.00
42,43,45-50: 42-USA, the Spirit of Old Glory begins. 46-Intro. Boyville Brigadiers in Rusty Ryan. 47-Fargo Kid begins. 48-USA ends 27.00 81.00 215.00
44-Doll Man by Crandall begins, ends #63; Crandall-a(2) 36.00 108.00 315.00
51-60: 56-Marijuana story in Swing Sisson strip. 57-Spider Widow begins. 60-Raven begins, ends #71 20.00 60.00 160.00
61-68 (5/43) 18.00 54.00 145.00
69,70-Phantom Lady x-over in Spider Widow 20.00 60.00 160.00
71-80,100: 71-Phantom Lady x-over. 72-Spider Widow ends 14.00 41.00 110.00
81-99 12.00 36.00 95.00
101-144: 139-Last Doll Man & last Doll Man-c. 140-Intro. Stuntman Stetson (Stuntman Stetson c-140-144) 8.75 26.25 70.00

NOTE: ***Celardo** a-37-43. **Crandall** a-44-60, 62, 63-on(most). **Gustavson** a-(Rusty Ryan)- 32-134. **Powell** a-34, 64-73. The Clock c-25, 28, 29. Doll Man c-30, 32, 34, 36, 38, 40, 42, 44, 46, 48, 50, 52, 54, 56, 58, 60, 62, 64, 66, 68, 70, 72, 74, 77-139. Joe Palooka c-21, 24, 27.*

FEATURE FILMS
Mar-Apr, 1950 - No. 4, Sept-Oct, 1950 (All photo-c)
National Periodical Publications

1- "Captain China" with John Payne, Gail Russell, Lon Chaney & Edgar Bergen 59.00 178.00 500.00
2- "Riding High" with Bing Crosby 62.00 187.00 525.00
3- "The Eagle & the Hawk" with John Payne, Rhonda Fleming & D. O'Keefe 59.00 178.00 500.00
4- "Fancy Pants"; Bob Hope & Lucille Ball 62.00 187.00 525.00

FEATURE FUNNIES (Feature Comics No. 21 on)
Oct, 1937 - No. 20, May, 1939
Harry 'A' Chesler

1(V9#1-indicia)-Joe Palooka, Mickey Finn (1st app.), The Bungles, Jane Arden, Dixie Dugan (1st app.), Big Top, Ned Brant, Strange As It Seems, & Off the Record strip reprints begin 316.00 950.00 2000.00
2-The Hawk app. (11/37); Goldberg-c 145.00 437.00 900.00
3-Hawks of Seas begins by Eisner, ends #12; The Clock begins; Christmas-c 112.00 337.00 700.00
4,5 83.00 250.00 525.00
6-12: 11-Archie O'Toole by Bud Thomas begins, ends #22 62.00 187.00 400.00
13-Espionage, Starring Black X begins by Eisner, ends #20 70.00 210.00 450.00
14-20 50.00 150.00 325.00

NOTE: *Joe Palooka covers 1, 6, 9, 12, 15, 18.*

FEATURE PRESENTATION, A (Feature Presentations Magazine #6)
(Formerly Women in Love) (Also see Startling Terror Tales #11)
No. 5, April, 1950
Fox Features Syndicate

5(#1)-Black Tarantula 37.00 111.00 270.00

FEATURE PRESENTATIONS MAGAZINE (Formerly A Feature Presentation #5; becomes Feature Stories Magazine #3 on)
No. 6, July, 1950
Fox Features Syndicate

Felicia Hardy, The Black Cat #3 © MEG

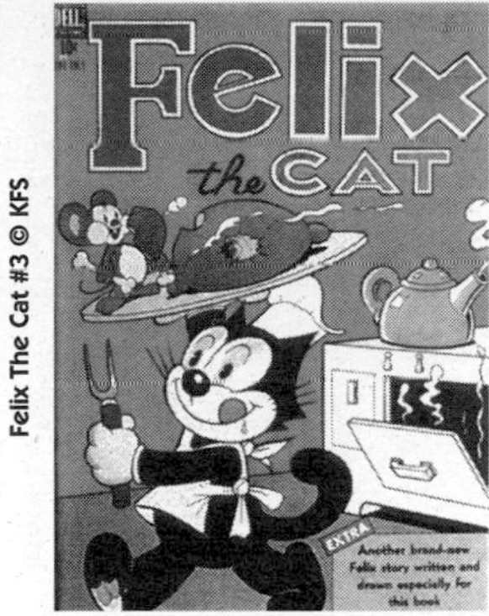

Felix The Cat #3 © KFS

Femforce #32 © AC

	GD25	FN65	NM94
6(#2)-Moby Dick; Wood-c	26.00	79.00	190.00

FEATURE STORIES MAGAZINE (Formerly Feature Presentations Mag. #6)
No. 3, Aug, 1950 - No. 4, Oct, 1950
Fox Features Syndicate

	GD25	FN65	NM94
3-Jungle Lil, Zegra stories; bondage-c	27.00	81.00	200.00
4	21.00	64.00	160.00

FEDERAL MEN COMICS (See Adventure Comics #32, The Comics Magazine, New Adventure Comics, New Book of Comics, New Comics & Star Spangled Comics #91)
No. 2, 1945 (DC reprints from 1930's)
Gerard Publ. Co.

	GD25	FN65	NM94
2-Siegel & Shuster-a; cover redrawn from Detective #9; spanking panel	28.00	84.00	225.00

FELICIA HARDY: THE BLACK CAT
July, 1994 - No. 4, Oct, 1994 ($1.50, limited series)
Marvel Comics

	GD25	FN65	NM94
1-4: 1,4-Spider-Man app.			1.50

FELIX'S NEPHEWS INKY & DINKY
Sept, 1957 - No. 7, Oct, 1958
Harvey Publications

	GD25	FN65	NM94
1-Cover shows Inky's left eye with 2 pupils	7.15	21.50	50.00
2-7	4.00	11.00	22.00

NOTE: ***Messmer** art in 1-6. **Oriolo** a-1-7.*

FELIX THE CAT (See Cat Tales 3-D, The Funnies, March of Comics #24,36, 51, New Funnies & Popular Comics)
1943 - No. 118, Nov, 1961; Sept-Nov, 1962 - No. 12, July-Sept, 1965
Dell Publ. No. 1-19/Toby No. 20-61/Harvey No. 62-118/Dell No. 1-12

	GD25	FN65	NM94
Four Color 15	65.00	194.00	710.00
Four Color 46('44)	38.00	115.00	420.00
Four Color 77('45)	36.00	107.00	390.00
Four Color 119('46)-All new stories begin	30.00	89.00	325.00
Four Color 135('46)	22.00	65.00	240.00
Four Color 162(9/47)	16.00	49.00	180.00
1(2-3/48)(Dell)	24.00	71.00	260.00
2	13.00	38.00	140.00
3-5	10.00	30.00	110.00
6-19(2-3/51-Dell)	7.00	22.00	80.00
20-30,32,33,36,38-61(6/55)-All Messmer issues.(Toby): 28-(2/52)-Some copies have #29 on cover, #28 on inside (Rare in high grade)	18.00	54.00	200.00
31,34,35-No Messmer-a; Messmer-c only 31,34	5.90	17.70	65.00
37-(100 pgs., 25 ¢, 1/15/53, X-Mas-c, Toby; daily & Sunday-r (rare)	40.00	120.00	440.00
62(8/55)-100 (Harvey)	2.90	8.70	32.00
101-118(11/61): 101-117-Reprints. 118-All new-a	2.00	6.00	22.00
12-269-211(#1, 9-11/62)(Dell)-No Messmer	3.30	9.90	36.00
2-12(7-9/65)(Dell, TV)-No Messmer	2.50	7.50	27.00
3-D Comic Book 1(1953-One Shot, 25¢)-w/glasses	34.00	103.00	275.00
Summer Annual nn ('53, 25¢, 100 pgs., Toby)-Daily & Sunday-r	38.00	113.00	375.00
Winter Annual 2 ('54, 25¢, 100 pgs., Toby)-Daily & Sunday-r	38.00	113.00	375.00

(Special note: Despite the covers on Toby 37 and the Summer Annual above proclaiming "all new stories," they were actually reformatted newspaper strips)

NOTE: ***Otto Messmer** went to work for Universal Film as an animater in 1915 and then worked for the Pat Sullivan animation studio in 1916. He created a black cat in the cartoon short, Feline Follies in 1919 that became known as Felix in the early 1920s. The Felix Sunday strip began Aug. 14, 1923 and continued until Sept. 19, 1943 whjen **Messmer** took the character to Dell (Western Publishing) and began doing Felix comic books, first adapting strips to the comic format. The first all new Felix comic was Four Color #119 in 1946 (#4 in the Dell run). The daily Felix was begun on May 9, 1927 by another artist, but by the following year, **Messmer** did it too. King Features took the daily away from **Messmer** in 1954 and he began to do some of his most dynamic art for Toby Press. The daily was continued by **Joe Oriolo** who drew it until it was discontinued Jan. 9, 1967. **Oriolo** was **Messmer's** assistant for many years and inked some of **Messmer's** pencils through the Toby run, as well as doing some of the stories by himself. Though **Messmer** continued to work for Harvey, his contirubitons were limited, and no all **Messmer** stories appeared after the Toby run until some early Toby reprints were published in the 1990s Harvey revival of the title. 4-Color No. 15, 46, 77 and the Toby Annuals are all daily or Sunday newspaper reprints from the 1930's-1940's drawn by **Otto Messmer**. #101-r/#64; 102-r/#65; 103-r/#67; 104-117-r/#68-81. **Messmer**-a in all Dell/Toby/Harvey issues except #31, 34, 35, 97, 98, 100, 118. **Oriolo** a-20, 31-on.*

FELIX THE CAT (Also see The Nine Lives of...)
Sept, 1991 - No. 7, Jan, 1993 ($1.25/$1.50, bi-monthly)
Harvey Comics/Gladstone

	GD25	FN65	NM94
1: 1950s-r/Toby issues by Messmer begins. 1-Inky and Dinky back-up story (produced by Gladstone)		1.20	3.00
2-7, Big Book V2#1 (9/92, $1.95, 52 pgs.)		.80	2.00

FELIX THE CAT AND FRIENDS
1992 - No. 4, 1992 ($1.95)
Felix Comics

	GD25	FN65	NM94
1-Contains Felix trading cards		1.20	3.00
2-4		.80	2.00

FELIX THE CAT & HIS FRIENDS (Pat Sullivan's...)
Dec, 1953 - No. 3, 1954 (Indicia title for #2&3 as listed)
Toby Press

	GD25	FN65	NM94
1 (Indicia title, "Felix and His Friends," #1 only)	24.00	71.00	190.00
2-3	15.00	45.00	120.00

FELIX THE CAT DIGEST MAGAZINE
July, 1992 ($1.75, digest-size, 98 pgs.)
Harvey Comics

	GD25	FN65	NM94
1-Felix, Richie Rich stories		1.60	4.00

FELIX THE CAT KEEPS ON WALKIN'
1991 ($15.95, 8-1/2"x11", 132 pgs.)
Hamilton Comics

	GD25	FN65	NM94
nn-Reprints 15 Toby Press Felix the Cat and Felix and His Friends stories in new computer color	2.00	6.00	16.00

FEM FANTASTIQUE
Aug, 1988 ($1.95, B&W)
AC Comics

	GD25	FN65	NM94
V2#1-By Bill Black; Betty Page pin-up		.80	2.00

FEMFORCE (Also see Untold Origin of the Femforce)
Apr, 1985 - Present (1.75/1.95/2.25/2.75/2.95, B&W #16-56)
Americomics

	GD25	FN65	NM94
1-Black-a in most; Nightveil, Ms. Victory begin	1.25	3.75	10.00
2		1.60	4.00
3-30: 12-15-$1.95-c. 16-19-2.25-c. 20-Begin $2.50-c, 44 pgs. 25-Origin/1st app. new Ms. Victory. 28-Colt leaves. 29,30-Camilla-r by Mayo from Jungle Comics		1.20	3.00
31-35,37-49,51-87: 31-Begin $2.75-c. 44-Contains mini-comic insert, Catman & Kitten #0. 51-Photo-c from movie. 57-Begin color issues.64-Re-intro Black Phantom.		1.20	3.00
36 (2.95, 52 pgs.)		1.20	3.00
50 (2.95, 52 pgs.)-Contains flexi-disc; origin retold; most AC characters app.		1.20	3.00
88-99: 88-Begin $2.95-c. 95-Photo-c		1.20	3.00
100-($3.95)			3.95
100-($6.90)-Polybagged			6.90
101-105-($4.95)			4.95
Special 1 (Fall, '84)(B&W, 52pgs.)-1st app. Ms. Victory, She-Cat, Blue Bulleteer, Rio Rita & Lady Luger		.80	2.00
Bad Girl Backlash-(12/95, $5.00)		2.00	5.00
Frightbook 1 ('92, $2.95, B&W)-Halloween special		1.20	3.00
In the House of Horror 1 ('89, 2.50, B&W)		1.00	2.50
Night of the Demon 1 ('90, 2.75, B&W)		1.10	2.75

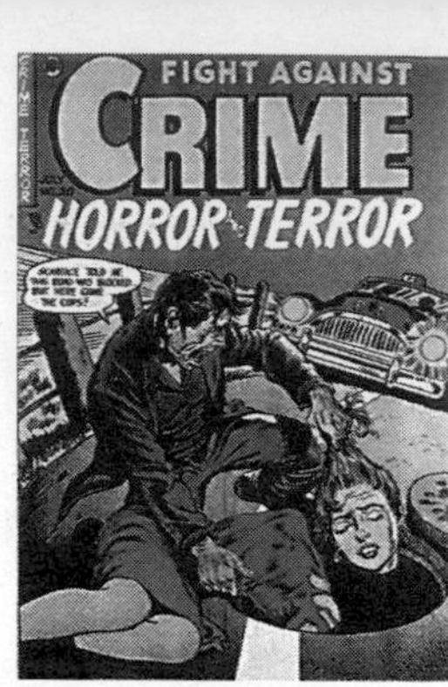

Fight Against Crime #20 © Story Comics

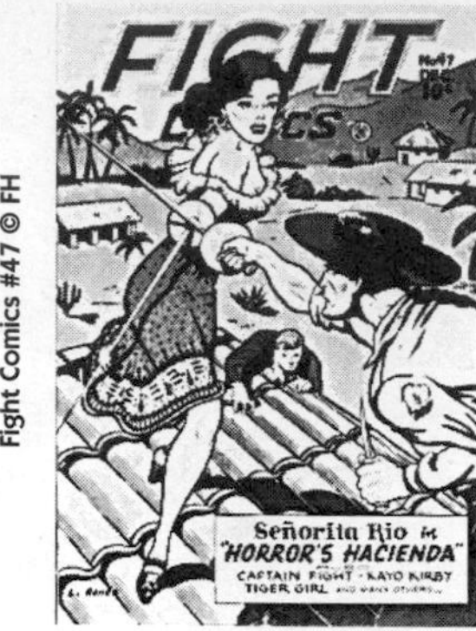

Fight Comics #47 © FH

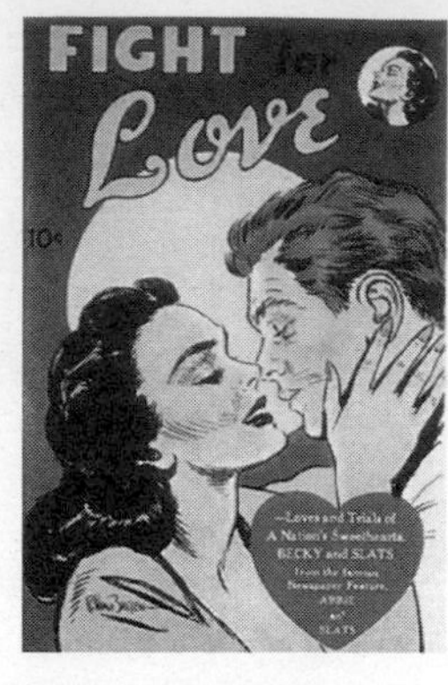

Fight For Love nn © UFS

	GD25	FN65	NM94
Out of the Asylum Special 1 ('87, B&W, $1.95)		.80	2.00
Pin-Up Portfolio		.80	2.00

FEMFORCE UP CLOSE
Apr, 1992 - No. 4, 1993 ($2.75, quarterly)
AC Comics

	GD25	FN65	NM94
1-4: 1-Stars Nightveil; inside f/c photo from Femforce movie. 2-Stars Stardust. 3-Stars Dragonfly. 4-Stars She-Cat		1.10	2.75

FERDINAND THE BULL (See Mickey Mouse Magazine V4#3)
1938 (10¢, large size, some color w/rest B&W)
Dell Publishing Co.

	GD25	FN65	NM94
nn	15.50	47.00	125.00

FERRET
Sept, 1992; May, 1993 - No. 10, Feb, 1994 ($1.95)
Malibu Comics

	GD25	FN65	NM94
1-(1992, one-shot)		.80	2.00
1-($2.50)-Completely die-cut cover		1.00	2.50
2-4-($2.50)-Collector's Edition w/poster		1.00	2.50
2-4-($1.95)-Newsstand Edition w/different-c		.80	2.00
5-8-($2.25): 5-Polybagged w/Skycap		.90	2.25
9,10: 9-Begin $2.50-c		1.00	2.50

FEUD
July, 1993 - No. 4, Oct, 1993 ($1.95, limited series)
Marvel Comics (Epic Comics/Heavy Hitters)

	GD25	FN65	NM94
1-($2.50)-Embossed-c		1.00	2.50
2-4		.80	2.00

FIBBER McGEE & MOLLY (Radio)(Also see A-1 Comics)
No. 25, 1949 (one-shot)
Magazine Enterprises

	GD25	FN65	NM94
A-1 25	8.30	25.00	58.00

55 DAYS AT PEKING (See Movie Comics)

FICTION ILLUSTRATED
1976
Byron Press Publ.

	GD25	FN65	NM94
1,3: 1-Schlomo Raven; Sutton-a. 3-Chandler; new Steranko-a	1.25	3.75	10.00
2 (128 pgs.)-Starfawn; Stephen Fabian-a	1.00	3.00	8.00

FIGHT AGAINST CRIME (Fight Against the Guilty #22, 23)
May, 1951 - No. 21, Sept, 1954
Story Comics

	GD25	FN65	NM94
1-True crime stories #1-4	25.00	75.00	190.00
2	13.00	39.00	95.00
3,5: 5-Frazetta-a, 1 pg.; content change to horror & suspense	10.00	30.00	70.00
4-Drug story "Hopped Up Killers"	10.00	30.00	75.00
6,7: 6-Used in **POP**, pgs. 83,84	10.00	30.00	65.00
8-Last crime format issue	9.00	27.00	60.00

NOTE: *No. 9-21 contain violent, gruesome stories with blood, dismemberment, decapitation, E.C. style plot twists and several E.C. swipes. Bondage c-4, 6, 18, 19.*

	GD25	FN65	NM94
9-11,13	23.00	69.00	170.00
12-Morphine drug story "The Big Dope"	24.00	73.00	180.00
14-Tothish art by Ross Andru; electrocution-c	23.00	69.00	170.00
15-B&W & color illos in **POP**	22.00	66.00	165.00
16-E.C. story swipe/Haunt of Fear #19; Tothish-a by Ross Andru; bondage-c	24.00	73.00	185.00
17-Wildey E.C. swipe/Shock SuspenStories #9; knife through neck-c (1/54)	24.00	73.00	185.00
18,19: 19-Bondage/torture-c	22.00	66.00	175.00
20-Decapitation cover; contains hanging, ax murder, blood & violence	39.00	118.00	295.00
21-E.C. swipe	19.00	56.00	140.00

NOTE: ***Cameron** a-4, 5, 8. **Hollingsworth** a-3-7, 9, 10, 13. **Wildey** a-6, 15, 16.*

FIGHT AGAINST THE GUILTY (Formerly Fight Against Crime)
No. 22, Dec, 1954 - No. 23, Mar, 1955
Story Comics

	GD25	FN65	NM94
22-Tothish-a by Ross Andru; Ditko-a; E.C. story swipe; electrocution-c (Last pre-code)	19.00	56.00	150.00
23-Hollingsworth-a	14.50	43.00	115.00

FIGHT COMICS
Jan, 1940 - No. 83, 11/52; No. 84, Wint, 1952-53; No. 85, Spring, 1953; No. 86, Summer, 1954
Fiction House Magazines

	GD25	FN65	NM94
1-Origin Spy Fighter, Starring Saber; Jack Dempsey life story; Shark Brodie & Chip Collins begin; Fine-c; Eisner-a	222.00	667.00	2000.00
2-Joe Louis life story; Fine/Eisner-c	94.00	282.00	850.00
3-Rip Regan, the Power Man begins (3/40)	67.00	200.00	600.00
4,5: 4-Fine-c	56.00	168.00	500.00
6-10: 6,7-Powell-c	42.00	126.00	375.00
11-14: Rip Regan ends	36.00	108.00	325.00
15-1st app. Super American plus-c (10/41)	50.00	150.00	450.00
16-Captain Fight begins (12/41); Spy Fighter ends	50.00	150.00	450.00
17,18: Super American ends	39.00	117.00	350.00
19-Captain Fight ends; Senorita Rio begins (6/42, origin & 1st app.); Rip Carson, Chute Trooper begins	39.00	117.00	350.00
20	35.00	105.00	280.00
21-30	24.00	71.00	190.00
31,33-50: 31-Decapitation-c. 44-Capt. Fight returns. 48-Used in Love and Death by Legman. 49-Jungle-c begin, end #81	20.00	60.00	160.00
32-Tiger Girl begins (6/44, 1st app.?)	22.00	66.00	175.00
51-Origin Tiger Girl; Patsy Pin-Up app.	34.00	101.00	270.00
52-60,62-64-Last Baker issue	15.00	45.00	120.00
61-Origin Tiger Girl retold	20.00	60.00	160.00
65-78: 78-Used in **POP**, pg. 99	14.00	41.00	110.00
79-The Space Rangers app.	14.00	41.00	110.00
80-85: 81-Last jungle-c. 82-85-War-c/stories	12.00	36.00	95.00
86-Two Tigerman stories by Evans-r/Rangers Comics #40,41; Moreira-r/ Rangers Comics #45	12.00	36.00	95.00

NOTE: *Bondage covers, Lingerie, headlights panels are common. Captain Fight by **Kamen**-51-66. Kayo Kirby by **Baker**-#43-64, 67(not by Baker). Senorita Rio by **Kamen**-#57-64; by **Grandenetti**-#65, 66. Tiger Girl by **Baker**-#36-60, 62-64; **Eisner** c-1-3, 5, 10, 11. **Kamen** a-54?, 57? **Tuska** a-1, 5, 8, 10, 21, 29, 34. **Whitman** c-73-84. **Zolnerwich** c-16, 17, 22. Power Man c-5, 6, 9. Super American c-15-17. Tiger Girl c-49-81.*

FIGHT FOR FREEDOM
1949, 1951 (Giveaway, 16 pgs.)
National Association of Mfgrs./General Comics

	GD25	FN65	NM94
nn-Dan Barry-c/a; used in **POP**, pg. 102	5.70	17.00	35.00

FIGHT FOR LOVE
1952 (no month)
United Features Syndicate

	GD25	FN65	NM94
nn-Abbie & Slats newspaper-r	8.50	26.00	60.00

FIGHTING AIR FORCE (See United States Fighting Air Force)

FIGHTIN' AIR FORCE (Formerly Sherlock Holmes?; Never Again? War and Attack #54 on)
No. 3, Feb, 1956 - No. 53, Feb-Mar, 1966
Charlton Comics

	GD25	FN65	NM94
V1#3	5.70	17.00	35.00
4-10	4.00	10.00	20.00
11(3/58, 68 pgs.)	4.00	12.00	24.00
12 (100 pgs.)	4.25	13.00	28.00
13-30: 13,24-Glanzman-a. 24-Glanzman-c	2.25	6.75	18.00
31-50: 50-American Eagle begins	1.75	5.25	14.00
51-53	1.25	3.75	10.00

Fightin' Army #17 © CC

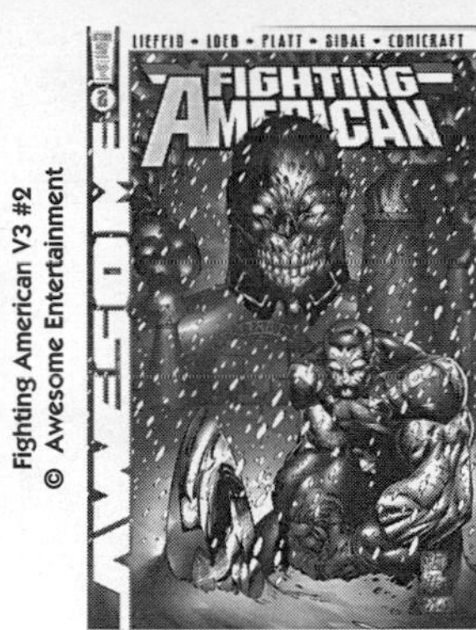

Fighting American V3 #2 © Awesome Entertainment

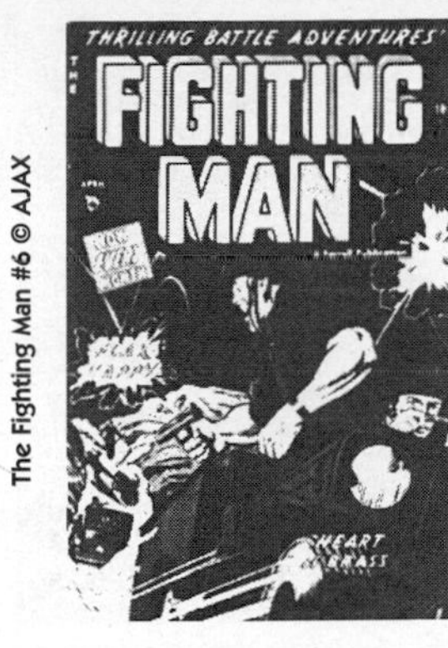

The Fighting Man #6 © AJAX

FIGHTIN' ARMY (Formerly Soldier and Marine Comics) (See Captain Willy Schultz)
No. 16, 1/56 - No. 127, 12/76; No. 128, 9/77 - No. 172, 11/84
Charlton Comics

	GD25	FN65	NM94
16	5.70	17.00	35.00
17-19,21-23,25-30	3.60	9.00	18.00
20-Ditko-a	5.00	15.00	30.00
24 (3/58, 68 pgs.)	4.00	11.00	22.00
31-45	2.00	6.00	16.00
46-60	1.50	4.50	12.00
61-80: 75-92-The Lonely War of Willy Schultz		2.00	5.00
81-100: 89,90,92-Ditko-a; Devil Brigade in #79,82,83	1.00	3.00	8.00
101-127		2.40	6.00
128-140		1.60	4.00
141-172		1.20	3.00
108(Modern Comics-1977)-Reprint		1.60	4.00

NOTE: *Aparo c-154.* ***Montes/Bache*** *a-48, 49, 51, 69, 75, 76, 170r.*

FIGHTING AMERICAN
Apr-May, 1954 - No. 7, Apr-May, 1955
Headline Publications/Prize (Crestwood)

	GD25	FN65	NM94
1-Origin & 1st app. Fighting American & Speedboy (Capt. America & Bucky clones); S&K-c/a(3); 1st super hero satire series	139.00	417.00	1250.00
2-S&K-a(3)	67.00	200.00	600.00
3,4-S&K-a(3)	53.00	159.00	480.00
5-S&K-a(2); Kirby/?-a	53.00	159.00	480.00
6-Origin-r (4 pgs.) plus 2 pgs. by S&K	51.00	153.00	460.00
7-Kirby-a	46.00	138.00	410.00

NOTE: ***Simon*** *&* ***Kirby*** *covers on all. 6 is last pre-code issue.*

FIGHTING AMERICAN
Oct, 1966 (25¢)
Harvey Publications

	GD25	FN65	NM94
1-Origin Fighting American & Speedboy by S&K-r; S&K-c/a(3); 1 pg. Neal Adams ad	3.00	9.00	30.00

FIGHTING AMERICAN
Feb, 1994 - No. 6, 1994 ($1.50, limited series)
DC Comics

	GD25	FN65	NM94
1-6			1.50

FIGHTING AMERICAN (Vol. 3)
Aug, 1997 - Present (25¢)
Awesome Entertainment

	GD25	FN65	NM94
1-Four covers by Liefeld, Churchill, Platt, McGuiness		1.00	2.50
1-Platinum Edition		1.00	2.50
2,3		1.00	2.50

FIGHTING CARAVANS (See Zane Grey 4-Color 632)

FIGHTING DANIEL BOONE
1953
Avon Periodicals

	GD25	FN65	NM94
nn-Kinstler-c/a, 22 pgs.	17.00	49.00	120.00
I.W. Reprint #1-Reprints #1 above; Kinstler-c/a; Lawrence/Alascia-a	1.75	5.25	14.00

FIGHTING DAVY CROCKETT (Formerly Kit Carson)
No. 9, Oct-Nov, 1955
Avon Periodicals

	GD25	FN65	NM94
9-Kinstler-c	8.50	26.00	60.00

FIGHTIN' FIVE, THE (Fightin' 5 #40 on?; formerly Space War) (Also see The Peacemaker)
July, 1964 - No. 41, Jan, 1967; No. 42, Oct, 1981 - No. 49, Dec, 1982
Charlton Comics

	GD25	FN65	NM94
V2#28-Origin & 1st app. Fightin' Five	3.50	10.50	35.00
29-39,41	2.25	6.75	18.00
40-Peacemaker begins (1st app.)	3.50	10.50	35.00
42-49: Reprints		1.60	4.00

FIGHTING FRONTS!
Aug, 1952 - No. 5, Jan, 1953
Harvey Publications

	GD25	FN65	NM94
1	6.50	19.50	45.00
2-Extreme violence; Nostrand/Powell-a	7.85	23.50	55.00
3-5: 3-Powell-a	4.00	12.00	24.00

FIGHTING INDIAN STORIES (See Midget Comics)

FIGHTING INDIANS OF THE WILD WEST!
Mar, 1952 - No. 2, Nov, 1952
Avon Periodicals

	GD25	FN65	NM94
1-Geronimo, Chief Crazy Horse, Chief Victorio, Black Hawk begin; Larsen-a; McCann-a(2)	11.30	34.00	90.00
2-Kinstler-c & inside-c only; Larsen, McCann-a	8.50	26.00	60.00
100 Pg. Annual (1952, 25¢)-Contains three comics rebound; Geronimo, Chief Crazy Horse, Chief Victorio; Kinstler-c	26.00	77.00	180.00

FIGHTING LEATHERNECKS
Feb, 1952 - No. 6, Dec, 1952
Toby Press

	GD25	FN65	NM94
1- "Duke's Diary"; full pg. pin-ups by Sparling	10.00	30.00	80.00
2- "Duke's Diary"	8.50	26.00	60.00
3-5- "Gil's Gals"; full pg. pin-ups	8.50	26.00	60.00
6-(Same as No. 3-5?)	5.70	17.00	40.00

FIGHTING MAN, THE (War)
May, 1952 - No. 8, July, 1953
Ajax/Farrell Publications(Excellent Publ.)

	GD25	FN65	NM94
1	8.75	26.25	65.00
2	5.00	15.00	30.00
3-8	4.15	12.50	25.00
Annual 1 (1952, 25¢, 100 pgs.)	19.00	58.00	140.00

FIGHTIN' MARINES (Formerly The Texan; also see Approved Comics)
No. 15, 8/51 - No. 12, 3/53; No. 14, 5/55 - No. 132, 11/76;
No. 133, 10/77 - No. 176, 9/84 (No #13?) (Korean war #1-3)
St. John(Approved Comics)/Charlton Comics No. 14 on

	GD25	FN65	NM94
15(#1)-Matt Baker c/a "Leatherneck Jack"; slightly large size; Fightin' Texan No. 16 & 17?	33.00	100.00	265.00
2-1st Canteen Kate by Baker; slightly large size; partial Baker-c	35.00	105.00	280.00
3-9,11-Canteen Kate by Baker; Baker c-#2,3,5-11; 4-Partial Baker-c	17.50	53.00	140.00
10-Matt Baker-c	7.15	21.50	50.00
12-No Baker-a; Last St. John issue?	4.00	10.00	20.00
14 (5/55; 1st Charlton issue; formerly?)-Canteen Kate by Baker; all stories reprinted from #2	13.00	39.00	105.00
15-Baker-c	6.00	18.00	42.00
16,18-20-Not Baker-c	4.00	10.00	20.00
17-Canteen Kate by Baker	9.50	28.00	75.00
21-24	4.00	10.00	20.00
25-(68 pgs.)(3/58)-Check-a?	5.70	17.00	40.00
26-(100 pgs.)(8/58)-Check-a(5)	8.50	26.00	60.00
27-50	1.50	4.50	12.00
51-81,83-100: 78-Shotgun Harker & the Chicken series begin	1.00	3.00	8.00
82-(100 pgs.)	2.50	7.50	25.00
83-100		2.40	6.00
101-122: 122-Pilot issue for "War" title (Fightin' Marines Presents War)		1.60	4.00
123-176		1.20	3.00
120(Modern Comics reprint, 1977)		1.20	3.00

Fighting Yank #8 © Nedor

Fight the Enemy #3 © TC

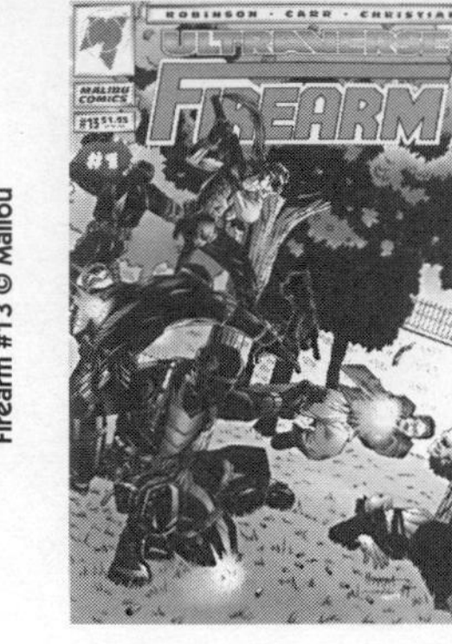

Firearm #13 © Malibu

GD25 FN65 NM94

NOTE: *No. 14 & 16 (CC) reprint St. John issues; No. 16 reprints St. John insignia on cover.* ***Colan*** *a-3, 7.* ***Glanzman*** *c/a-92, 94.* ***Montes/Bache*** *a-48, 53, 55, 64, 65, 72-74, 77-83, 176r.*

FIGHTING MARSHAL OF THE WILD WEST (See The Hawk)

FIGHTIN' NAVY (Formerly Don Winslow)
No. 74, 1/56 - No. 125, 4-5/66; No. 126, 8/83 - No. 133, 10/84
Charlton Comics

	GD25	FN65	NM94
74	3.00	9.00	30.00
75-81	2.00	6.00	20.00
82-Sam Glanzman-a	1.40	4.15	16.00
83-100	1.50	4.50	12.00
101-105,106-125('66)	1.00	2.80	10.00
126-133 (1984)		1.20	3.00

NOTE: ***Montes/Bache*** *a-109.* ***Glanzman*** *a-82, 131r.*

FIGHTING PRINCE OF DONEGAL, THE (See Movie Comics)

FIGHTIN' TEXAN (Formerly The Texan & Fightin' Marines?)
No. 16, Sept, 1952 - No. 17, Dec, 1952
St. John Publishing Co.

	GD25	FN65	NM94
16,17: Tuska-a each. 17-Cameron-c/a	5.70	17.00	40.00

FIGHTING UNDERSEA COMMANDOS (See Undersea Fighting...)
May, 1952 - No. 5, April, 1953 (U.S. Navy frogmen)
Avon Periodicals

	GD25	FN65	NM94
1-Cover title is Undersea Fighting... #1 only	8.75	26.25	70.00
2	6.50	19.50	45.00
3-5: 1,3-Ravielli-c. 4-Kinstler-c	5.70	17.00	40.00

FIGHTING WAR STORIES
Aug, 1952 - No. 5, 1953
Men's Publications/Story Comics

	GD25	FN65	NM94
1	7.15	21.50	50.00
2-5	4.25	13.00	28.00

FIGHTING YANK (See America's Best Comics & Startling Comics)
Sept, 1942 - No. 29, Aug, 1949
Nedor/Better Publ./Standard

	GD25	FN65	NM94
1-The Fighting Yank begins; Mystico, the Wonder Man app; bondage-c	167.00	500.00	1500.00
2	72.00	216.00	650.00
3,4: 4-Schomburg-c begin	56.00	168.00	500.00
5-10: 7-Grim Reaper app. 8,10-Bondage/torture-c	43.00	129.00	385.00
11-20: 11-The Oracle app. 12-Hirohito bondage-c. 15-Bondage/torture-c. 18-The American Eagle app.	36.00	108.00	320.00
21,23,24: 21-Kara, Jungle Princess app. 24-Miss Masque app.	36.00	108.00	300.00
22-Miss Masque-c/story	40.00	120.00	360.00
25-Robinson/Meskin-a; strangulation, lingerie panel; The Cavalier app.	40.00	120.00	360.00
26-29: All-Robinson/Meskin-a. 28-One pg. Williamson-a	36.00	108.00	300.00

NOTE: ***Schomburg (Xela)*** *c-4-29; airbrush-c 28, 29. Bondage c-1, 4, 8, 10, 11, 12, 15, 17.*

FIGHTMAN
June, 1993 ($2.00, one-shot, 52 pgs.)
Marvel Comics

	GD25	FN65	NM94
1		.80	2.00

FIGHT THE ENEMY
Aug, 1966 - No. 3, Mar, 1967 (25¢, 68 pgs.)
Tower Comics

	GD25	FN65	NM94
1-Lucky 7 & Mike Manly begin	2.50	7.50	21.00
2-Boris Vallejo, McWilliams-a	2.15	6.50	17.00
3-Wood-a (1/2 pg.); McWilliams, Bolle-a	2.15	6.50	17.00

FILM FUNNIES
Nov, 1949 - No. 2, Feb, 1950 (52 pgs.)
Marvel Comics (CPC)

	GD25	FN65	NM94
1-Krazy Krow, Wacky Duck	15.00	45.00	120.00
2-Wacky Duck	11.30	34.00	90.00

FILM STARS ROMANCES
Jan-Feb, 1950 - No. 3, May-June, 1950 (True life stories of movie stars)
Star Publications

	GD25	FN65	NM94
1-Rudy Valentino & Gregory Peck stories; L. B. Cole-c; lingerie panels	38.00	114.00	280.00
2-Liz Taylor/Robert Taylor photo-c & true life story	31.00	94.00	230.00
3-Douglas Fairbanks story; photo-c	21.00	64.00	150.00

FINAL CYCLE, THE
July, 1987 - No. 4, 1988 (Limited series)
Dragon's Teeth Productions

	GD25	FN65	NM94
1-4		.80	2.00

FINAL NIGHT, THE (See DC related titles and Parallax: Emerald Night)
Nov, 1996 - No. 4, Nov, 1996 ($1.95, weekly limited series)
DC Comics

	GD25	FN65	NM94
1-3: Kesel-s/Immonen-a(p) in all.		1.20	3.00
4-Parallax's final acts		2.00	5.00
TPB-(1998, $12.95) r/#1-4, Parallax: Emerald Night #1, and preview			12.95

FIRE
1993 - No. 2, 1993 ($2.95, B&W, limited series, 52 pgs.)
Caliber Press

	GD25	FN65	NM94
1,2-Photo-c		1.20	3.00

FIRE AND BLAST
1952 (Giveaway, 16 pgs., paper-c)
National Fire Protection Assoc.

	GD25	FN65	NM94
nn-Mart Baily A-Bomb-c; about fire prevention	13.00	39.00	105.00

FIREARM (Also see Codename: Firearm, Freex #15, Night Man #4 & Prime #10)
Sept, 1993 - No. 18, Mar, 1995 ($1.95/$2.50)
Malibu Comics (Ultraverse)

	GD25	FN65	NM94
0 ($14.95)-Came w/ video containing 1st half of story (comic contains 2nd half); 1st app. Duet	1.85	5.25	15.00
1,3-6: 1-James Robinson scripts begin; Cully Hamner-a; Howard Chaykin-c; 1st app Alec Swan. 3-Intro The Sportsmen; Chaykin-c. 4-Break-Thru x-over; Chaykin-c. 5-1st app. Ellen (Swan's girlfriend); 2 pg. origin of Prime. 6-Prime app. (story cont'd in Prime #10); Brereton-c		.80	2.00
1-($2.50)-Newsstand edition polybagged w/card		1.00	2.50
1-Ultra Limited silver foil-c		2.00	5.00
2 ($2.50, 44 pgs.)-Hardcase app.;Chaykin-c; Rune flip-c/story by B. Smith (3 pgs.)		1.00	2.50
7-10,12-17: 12-The Rafferty Saga begins, ends #18; 1st app. Rafferty 15-Night Man & Freex app. 17-Swan marries Ellen		.80	2.00
11-($3.50, 68 pgs.)-Flip book w/Ultraverse Premiere #5		1.40	3.50
18-Death of Rafferty; Chaykin-c		1.00	2.50

NOTE: ***Brereton*** *c-6.* ***Chaykin*** *c-1-4, 14, 16, 18.* ***Hamner*** *a-1-4.* ***Herrera*** *a-12.* ***James Robinson*** *scripts-0-18.*

FIRE BALL XL5 (See Steve Zodiac & The ...)

FIREBRAND (Also see Showcase '96 #4)
Feb, 1996 - No. 9, Oct, 1996 ($1.75)
DC Comics

	GD25	FN65	NM94
1-9: Brian Augustyn scripts; Velluto-c/a in all. 9-Daredevil #319-c/swipe			1.75

FIRE CHIEF AND THE SAFE OL' FIREFLY, THE
1952 (16 pgs.) (Safety brochure given away at schools)
National Board of Fire Underwriters (produced by American Visuals Corp.) (Eisner)

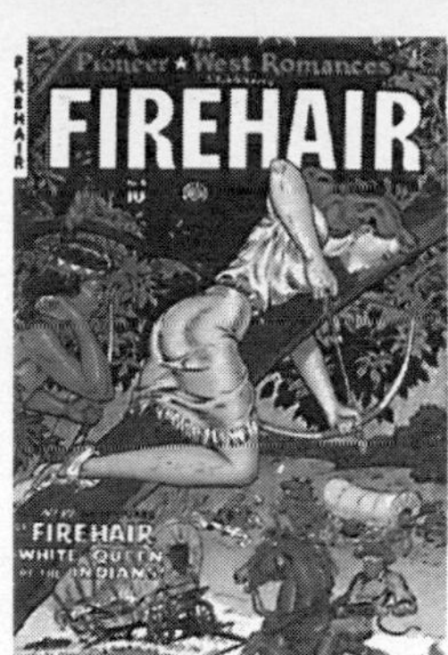

Firehair Comics #6 © FH

Fireside Book Series - Son of Origins of Marvel Comics © MEG

Firestorm, The Nuclear Man #92 © DC

GD25 FN65 NM94

nn-(Rare) Eisner-c/a 44.00 132.00 400.00

FIRE FROM HEAVEN
Mar, 1996 ($2.50)
Image Comics (WildStorm Productions)

1,2-Moore-s 1.00 2.50

FIREHAIR COMICS (Formerly Pioneer West Romances #3-6; also see Rangers Comics)
Winter/48-49; No. 2, Wint/49-50; No. 7, Spr/51 - No. 11, Spr/52
Fiction House Magazines (Flying Stories)

1-Origin Firehair 49.00 147.00 440.00
2 24.00 71.00 190.00
7-11 15.50 47.00 125.00
I.W. Reprint 8-(nd)-Kinstler-c; reprints Rangers #57; Dr. Drew story by Grandenetti 2.50 7.50 22.00

FIRESTAR
Mar, 1986 - No. 4, June, 1986 (75¢)(From Spider-Man TV series)
Marvel Comics Group

1-X-Men & New Mutants app. 1.20 3.00
2-Wolverine-c (not real Wolverine?); Art Adams-a(p) 2.00 5.00
3,4: 3-Art Adams/Sienkiewicz-c. 4-B. Smith-c .80 2.00

FIRESIDE BOOK SERIES
1974 - 1980 (130-260pgs.), Square bound, color
Simon and Schuster

Amazing Spider-Man, The, 1979, 130pgs., $3.95, Bob Larkin-c
Hardcover 6.00 18.00 60.00
Softcover 4.00 12.00 40.00
America At War–The Best of DC War Comics, 1979, $6.95, 260pgs, Joe Kubert-c.
Hardcover 6.00 18.00 60.00
Softcover 4.00 12.00 40.00
Bring On The Bad Guys (origins of the Marvel Comics Villains, 1976, $6.95, 260pgs.); Romita-c
Hardcover 6.00 18.00 60.00
Softcover 4.00 12.00 40.00
Captain America, Sentinel of Liberty, 1979, 130pgs., $12.95
Hardcover 5.00 15.00 50.00
Doctor Strange Master of the Mystic Arts, 1980, 130pgs.
Hardcover 6.00 18.00 60.00
Softcover 4.00 12.00 40.00
Fantastic Four, The, 1979, 130pgs.
Hardcover 5.00 15.00 50.00
Softcover 3.00 9.00 30.00
Heart Throbs–The Best of DC Romance Comics, 1979, 260pgs., $6.,95
Hardcover 12.50 38.00 125.00
Softcover 7.50 22.50 75.00
Marvel's Greatest Superhero Battles, 1978, 260pgs., $6.95, Romita-c
Hardcover 9.00 27.00 90.00
Softcover 5.00 15.00 50.00
Origins of Marvel Comics, 1974, 260pgs., $5.95. Reprints covers & origins of key Marvel books & characters
Hardcover 5.00 15.00 50.00
Softcover 3.00 9.00 30.00
Silver Surfer, The, 1978, 130pgs., $4.95, Norem-c
Hardcover 3.00 9.00 60.00
Softcover 4.00 12.00 40.00
Son of Origins of Marvel Comics, 1975, 260pgs., $6.95, Romita-c. Reprints many covers & origins of Marvel characters
Hardcover 5.00 15.00 50.00
Softcover 3.00 9.00 30.00
Superhero Women, The–Featuring the fabulous females of Marvel Comics, 1977, 260pgs., $6.95, Romita-c
Hardcover 7.50 22.50 75.00
Softcover 4.50 13.50 45.00
Note: Prices listed are for 1st printings. Later printings are worth 30% less.

FIRESTONE (See Donald And Mickey Merry Christmas)

FIRESTORM (See Cancelled Comic Cavalcade, DC Comics Presents, Flash #289, The Fury of... & Justice League of America #179)
March, 1978 - No. 5, Oct-Nov, 1978
DC Comics

1,5: 1-Origin & 1st app. 2.40 6.00
2-4: 2-Origin Multiplex. 3-Origin & 1st app. Killer Frost. 4-1st app. Hyena 1.60 4.00

FIRESTORM, THE NUCLEAR MAN (Formerly Fury of Firestorm)
No. 65, Nov, 1987 - No. 100, Aug, 1990
DC Comics

65-99: 66-1st app. Zuggernaut; Firestorm vs. Green Lantern. 71-Death of Capt. X. 67,68-Millennium tie-ins. 83-1st new look 1.00
100-($2.95, 68 pgs.) 1.20 3.00
Annual 5 (10/87)-1st app. new Firestorm 1.25

FIRST ADVENTURES
Dec, 1985 - No. 5, Apr, 1986 ($1.25)
First Comics

..1-5: Blaze Barlow, Whisper & Dynamo Joe in all 1.30

FIRST AMERICANS, THE
No. 843, Sept, 1957
Dell Publishing Co.

Four Color 843-Marsh-a 8.00 25.00 90.00

FIRST CHRISTMAS, THE (3-D)
1953 (25¢, 8-1/4x10-1/4", oversize)(Came w/glasses)
Fiction House Magazines (Real Adv. Publ. Co.)

nn-(Scarce)-Kelly Freas painted-c; Biblical theme, birth of Christ; Nativity-c 28.00 84.00 225.00

FIRST COMICS GRAPHIC NOVEL
Jan, 1984 - No. 20? (52pgs./176 pgs., high quality paper)
First Comics

1-Beowulf ($5.95) 2.40 6.00
1-2nd printing ($6.95) 1.00 2.80 7.00
2-Time Beavers ($5.95) 2.40 6.00
3($11.95, 100 pgs.)-American Flagg! Hard Times (2nd printing exists) 1.50 4.50 12.00
4-Nexus ($6.95)-r/B&W 1-3 1.10 3.30 9.00
5-The Enchanted Apples of Oz ($7.95, 52 pgs.)-Intro by Harlan Ellison (1986) 1.00 3.0 8.00
6-Elric of Melnibone ($14.95, 176 pgs.)-Reprints with new color 1.85 5.50 15.00
7-The Secret Island Of Oz ($7.95) 1.00 3.00 8.00
8-Teenage Mutant Ninja Turtles Book I ($9.95, 132 pgs.)-r/TMNT #1-3 in color w/12 pgs. new-a; origin 1.25 3.75 10.00
9-Time 2: The Epiphany by Chaykin (11/86, $7.95, 52pgs. - indicia says #8) 1.00 3.00 8.00
10-Teenage Mutant Ninja Turtles Book II ($9.95)-r/TMNT #4-6 in color 1.25 3.75 10.00
11-Sailor On The Sea of Fate ($14.95) 1.85 5.50 15.00
nn-Time 2: The Satisfaction of Black Mariah (9/87) 1.00 3.00 8.00
12-American Flagg! Southern Comfort (10/87, $11.95) 1.50 4.50 12.00
13-The Ice King Of Oz ($7.95) 1.00 3.00 8.00
14-Teenage Mutant Ninja Turtles Book III ($9.95)-r/TMNT #7,8 in color plus new 12 pg. story 1.25 3.75 10.00
15-Hex Breaker: Badger ($7.95, 68 pgs.) 1.00 3.00 8.00
16-The Forgotten Forest of Oz ($8.95) 1.10 3.30 9.00
17-Mazinger (68 pgs., $8.95) 1.10 3.30 9.00
18-Teenage Mutant Ninja Turtles Book IV ($9.95)-r/TMNT #10,11 plus 3 pg. fold-out 1.25 3.75 10.00
19-The Original Nexus Graphic Novel ($7.95, 104 pgs.)-Reprints First Comics

First Love Illustrated #21 © HARV

The Flame #3 © FOX

Flaming Carrot #25 © Bob Burden

GD25 FN65 NM94

Graphic Novel #4 ($7.95) 1.00 3.00 8.00
20-American Flagg!: State of the Union; r/A.F. 7-9 ($11.95, 96 pgs.) 1.50 4.50 12.00
NOTE: *Most or all issues have been reprinted.*

1ST FOLIO (The Joe Kubert School Presents...)
Mar, 1984 ($1.50, one-shot)
Pacific Comics
1-Joe Kubert-c/a(2 pgs.); Adam & Andy Kubert-a 1.50

1ST ISSUE SPECIAL
Apr, 1975 - No. 13, Apr, 1976 (Try out series)
National Periodical Publications
1,5,6: 1-Intro. Atlas; Kirby-c/a/script. 5-Manhunter; Kirby-c/a/script. 6-Dingbats 2.00 5.00
2,7,9,12: 2-Green Team (see Cancelled.Comic Cavalcade). 7-The Creeper by Ditko (c/a). 9-Dr. Fate; Kubert-c. 12-Origin/1st app. "Blue" Starman (2nd app. in Starman, 2nd Series #3); Kubert-c. 2.40 6.00
3,4,10,11: 3-Metamorpho by Ramona Fraden. .4-Lady Cop. 10-The Outsiders. 11-Code Name: Assassin; Grell-c. 1.20 4.00
8,13: 8-Origin/1st app. The Warlord; Grell-c/a (11/75). 13-Return of the New Gods; Darkseid app.; 1st new costume Orion; predates New Gods #12 by more than a year 1.25 3.75 10.00

FIRST KISS
Dec, 1957 - No. 40, Jan, 1965
Charlton Comics
V1#1 3.00 9.00 30.00
V1#2-10 2.50 7.50 20.00
11-40 1.25 3.75 10.00

FIRST LOVE ILLUSTRATED
2/49 - No. 9, 6/50; No. 10, 1/51 - No. 86, 3/58; No. 87, 9/58 - No. 88, 11/58; No. 89, 11/62, No. 90, 2/63
Harvey Publications(Home Comics)(True Love)
1-Powell-a(2) 12.00 38.00 100.00
2-Powell-a 7.15 21.50 50.00
3-"Was I Too Fat To Be Loved" story 7.15 21.50 50.00
4-10 5.00 15.00 30.00
11-30: 13-"I Joined a Teen-age Sex Club" story. 30-Lingerie panel 4.00 11.00 22.00
31-34,37,39-49: 49-Last pre-code (2/55) 3.20 8.00 16.00
35-Used in **SOTI**, illo "The title of this comic book is First Love" 14.00 43.00 110.00
36-Communism story, "Love Slaves" 4.15 12.50 25.00
38-Nostrand-a 5.35 16.00 32.00
50-90 1.85 5.50 15.00
NOTE: ***Disbrow*** *a-13.* ***Orlando*** *c-87.* ***Powell*** *a-1, 3-5, 7, 10, 11, 13-17, 19-24, 26-29, 33,35-41, 43, 45, 46, 50, 54, 55, 57, 58, 61-63, 65, 71-73, 76, 79r, 82, 84, 88.*

FIRSTMAN
June, 1997 ($2.50)
Image Comics
1 Snyder-s/ Andy Smith-a 1.00 2.50

FIRST MEN IN THE MOON (See Movie Comics)

FIRST ROMANCE MAGAZINE
8/49 - #6, 6/50; #7, 6/51 - #50, 2/58; #51, 9/58 - #52, 11/58
Home Comics(Harvey Publ.)/True Love
1 10.50 32.00 85.00
2 6.50 19.50 45.00
3-5 5.70 17.00 35.00
6-10 4.25 13.00 28.00
11-20 4.00 10.00 20.00
21-27,29-32: 32-Last pre-code issue (2/55) 3.20 8.00 16.00
28-Nostrand-a(Powell swipe) 4.25 13.00 28.00
33-52 2.60 6.50 13.00

GD25 FN65 NM94

NOTE: ***Powell*** *a-1-5, 8-10, 14, 18, 20-22, 24, 25, 28, 36, 46, 48, 51.*

FIRST TRIP TO THE MOON (See Space Adventures No. 20)

FISH POLICE (Inspector Gill of the...#2, 3)
Dec, 1985 - No. 11, Nov, 1987 ($1.50, B&W)
V2#5, April, 1988 - V2#17, May, 1989 ($1.75, color)
No. 18, Aug, 1989 - No. 26, Dec, 1990 ($2.25, B&W)
Fishwrap Productions/Comico V2#5-17/Apple Comics #18 on
1-11 1.50
1(5/86),2-2nd print 1.50
V2#5-17-(Color): V2#5-11. 12-17, new-a 1.25 2.50
18-26 ($2.25-c, B&W) 18-Origin Inspector Gill 1.00 2.00
Special 1($2.50, 7/87, Comico) 1.25 2.50
Graphic Novel: The Hairball Saga (r/1-4, color) 1.60 4.00

FISH POLICE
V2#1, Oct, 1992 - No. 6, Mar, 1993 ($1.25)
Marvel Comics
V2#1-6: 1-Hairballs Saga begins; r/#1 (1985) 1.25

5-STAR SUPER-HERO SPECTACULAR (See DC Special Series No. 1)

FLAME, THE (See Big 3 & Wonderworld Comics)
Summer, 1940 - No. 8, Jan, 1942 (#1,2: 68 pgs; #3-8: 44 pgs.)
Fox Features Syndicate
1-Flame stories reprinted from Wonderworld #5-9; origin The Flame; Lou Fine-a (36 pgs.), r/Wonderworld #3,10 250.00 750.00 2500.00
2-Fine-a(2); Wing Turner by Tuska 108.00 324.00 975.00
3-8: 3-Powell-a 72.00 216.00 650.00

FLAME, THE (Formerly Lone Eagle)
No. 5, Dec-Jan, 1954-55 - No. 3, April-May, 1955
Ajax/Farrell Publications (Excellent Publ.)
5(#1)-1st app. new Flame 34.00 103.00 275.00
2,3 23.00 68.00 180.00

FLAMING CARROT (...Comics #6? on; see Anything Goes, Cerebus, Teenage Mutant Ninja Turtles/Flaming Carrot Crossover & Visions)
5/84 - No. 5, 1/85; No. 6, 3/85 - Present? ($1.70/$2.00, B&W)
Aardvark-Vanaheim/Renegade Press #6-17/Dark Horse #18 on
1-Bob Burden story/art 4.00 12.00 40.00
2 2.50 7.50 20.00
3 1.75 5.25 14.00
4-6 1.25 3.75 10.00
7-9 1.00 2.80 7.00
10-12 2.00 5.00
13-15 1.20 3.00
15-Variant without cover price 2.00 5.00
16-20: 18-1st Dark Horse issue 1.20 3.00
21-23,25: 25-Contains trading cards; TMNT app. .80 2.00
24-(2.50, 52 pgs.)-10th anniversary issue 1.00 2.50
26-28: 26-Begin $2.25-c. 26,27-Teenage Mutant Ninja Turtles x-over. 27-Todd McFarlane-c .90 2.25
29,31-(2.50-c) 1.00 2.50
Annual 1(1/97, $5.00) 2.00 5.00
... :The Wild Shall Wild Remain (1997, $17.95, TPB) r/#4-11 17.95

FLAMING CARROT COMICS (Also see Junior Carrot Patrol)
Summer-Fall, 1981 ($1.95, one shot) (Large size, 8-1/2x11")
Killian Barracks Press
1-Bob Burden-c/a/scripts; serially numbered to 6500 5.00 15.00 50.00

FLAMING LOVE
Dec, 1949 - No. 6, Oct, 1950 (Photo covers #2-6) (52 pgs.)
Quality Comics Group (Comic Magazines)
1-Ward-c/a (9 pgs.) 31.00 94.00 230.00

Flare #5 © Hero Comics

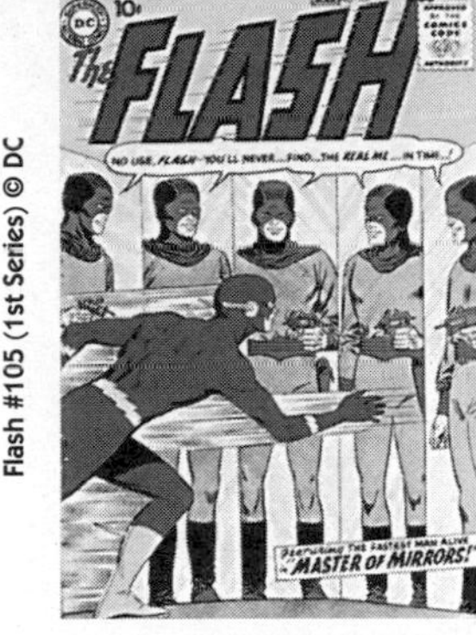

Flash #105 (1st Series) © DC

Flash #237 (1st Series) © DC

GD25 FN65 NM94

2 — 13.00 39.00 95.00
3-Ward-a (9 pgs.); Crandall-a — 22.00 66.00 160.00
4-6: 4-Gustavson-a — 11.50 34.00 85.00

FLAMING WESTERN ROMANCES (Formerly Target Western Romances)
No. 3, Mar-Apr, 1950
Star Publications

3-Robert Taylor, Arlene Dahl photo on-c with biographies inside; L. B. Cole-c — 31.00 94.00 250.00

FLARE (Also see Champions for 1st app. & League of Champions)
Nov, 1988 - No. 3, Jan, 1989 ($2.75, color, 52 pgs)
V2#1, Nov, 1990 - No. 7, Nov, 1991 ($2.95/$3.50, color, mature, 52 pgs.)
V2#8, Oct, 1992 - No. 16, Feb, 1994 ($3.50/$3.95, B&W, mature, 36 pgs.)
Hero Comics/Hero Graphics Vol. 2 on

1-3 — 1.10 2.75
V2#1-3,16 ($2.95) — 1.20 3.00
V2#4-6,8-10: 4-Begin $3.50-c. 5-Eternity Smith returns. 6-Intro The Tigress — 1.40 3.50
V2#7,11-15 ($3.95) — 1.60 4.00
Annual 1(1992, $4.50, B&W, 52 pgs.)-Champions-r — 1.80 4.50

FLARE ADVENTURES
Feb, 1992 - No. 12, 1993? ($3.50/$3.95)
Hero Graphics

1 (90¢, color, 20 pgs.) — .90
2-7 ($3.50)-Flip books w/Champions Classics — 1.40 3.50
8-12 ($3.95)-Flip books w/Champions Classics — 1.60 4.00

FLASH, THE (See Adventure, The Brave and the Bold, Crisis On Infinite Earths, DC Comics Presents, DC Special, DC Special Series, DC Super-Stars, Green Lantern, Justice League of America, Showcase, Super Team Family, & World's Finest)

FLASH, THE (1st Series)(Formerly Flash Comics)(See Showcase #4,8,13,14)
(Also see Justice League of America)
No. 105, Feb-Mar, 1959 - No. 350, Oct, 1985
National Periodical Publ./DC

GD25 FN65 VF82 NM94

105-(2-3/59)-Origin Flash(retold), & Mirror Master (1st app.) — 333.00 1000.00 2500.00 5200.00

GD25 FN65 NM94

106-Origin Grodd & Pied Piper; Flash's 1st visit to Gorilla City; begin Grodd the Super Gorilla trilogy (Scarce) — 117.00 350.00 1400.00
107-Grodd trilogy, part 2 — 63.00 189.00 750.00
108-Grodd trilogy ends — 54.00 162.00 650.00
109-2nd app. Mirror Master — 41.00 123.00 480.00
110-Intro/origin The Weather Wizard & Kid Flash who later becomes Flash in Crisis On Infinite Earths #12; begin Kid Flash trilogy, ends #112 (also in #114,116,118) — 100.00 300.00 1200.00
111-2nd Kid Flash tryout; Cloud Creatures — 31.00 93.00 350.00
112-Origin & 1st app. Elongated Man (4-5/60); also apps. in #115,119,130 — 37.00 111.00 410.00
113-Origin & 1st app. Trickster — 31.00 93.00 350.00
114-Captain Cold app. (see Showcase #8) — 26.00 78.00 260.00
115,116,118-120: 119 Elongated Man marries Sue Dearborn. 120-Flash & Kid Flash team-up for 1st time — 20.00 60.00 200.00
117-Origin & 1st app. Capt. Boomerang; 1st & only S.A. app. Winky Blinky & Noddy — 27.00 81.00 270.00
121,122: 122-Origin & 1st app. The Top — 15.00 45.00 150.00
123-(9/61)-Re-intro. Golden Age Flash; origins of both Flashes; 1st mention of an Earth II where DC G. A. heroes live — 100.00 300.00 1200.00
124-Last 10¢ issue — 12.50 38.00 125.00
125-128,130: 127-Return of Grodd-c/story. 128-Origin & 1st app. Abra Kadabra — 12.00 36.00 120.00
129-2nd G.A. Flash x-over; J.S.A. cameo in flashback (1st S.A. app. G.A. Green Lantern, Hawkman, Atom, Black Canary & Dr. Mid-Nite) — 28.00 84.00 280.00
131-136,138,140: 130-(7/62)-1st Gauntlet of Super-Villains (Mirror Master, Capt. Cold, The Top, Capt. Boomerang & Trickster). 131-Early Green Lantern x-over (9/62). 135-1st app. of Kid Flash's yellow costume (3/63). 136-1st Dexter Miles. 140-Origin & 1st app. Heat Wave — 12.00 36.00 120.00
137-G.A. Flash x-over; J.S.A. cameo (1st S.A. app.)(1st real app. since 2-3/51); 1st S.A. app. Vandal Savage & Johnny Thunder; JSA team decides to re-form — 40.00 120.00 400.00
139-Origin & 1st app. Prof. Zoom — 13.00 39.00 130.00
141-150: 142-Trickster app. — 8.50 25.50 85.00
151-Engagement of Barry Allen & Iris West; G.A. Flash vs. The Shade. — 10.50 32.00 105.00
152-159 — 6.00 18.00 60.00
160-(80-Pg. Giant G-21); G.A. Flash & Johnny Quick-r — 8.50 25.50 85.00
161-168,170: 165 Silver Age Flash weds Iris West. 167-New facts about Flash's origin. 168-Green Lantern-c/story. 170-Dr. Mid-Nite, Dr. Fate, G.A. Flash x-over — 5.50 16.50 55.00
169-(80-Pg. Giant G-34)-New facts about origin — 8.50 25.50 85.00
171-174,176,177,179,180: 171-JLA, Green Lantern, Atom flashbacks. 173-G.A. Flash x-over. 174-Barry Allen reveals I.D. to wife. 179-(5/68)-Flash travels to Earth -Prime and meets DC editor Julie Schwartz; 1st unnamed app. Earth-Prime (See Justice League of America #123 for 1st named app. & 3rd app. overall) — 5.00 15.00 50.00
175-2nd Superman/Flash race (12/67) (See Superman #199 & World's Finest #198,199); JLA cameo; gold kryptonite used (on J'onn J'onzz impersonating Superman) — 13.00 39.00 130.00
178-(80-Pg. Giant G-46) — 7.00 21.00 70.00
181-186,188-195,197-200: 186-Re-intro. Sargon — 3.00 9.00 30.00
187,196: (68-Pg. Giants G-58, G-70) — 4.80 14.40 48.00
201-204,206-210: 201-New G.A. Flash story. 208-52 pg. begins, end #213, 215,216. 206-Elongated Man begins — 1.85 5.50 15.00
205-(68-Pg. Giant G-82) — 3.20 9.60 32.00
211-213,216,220: 211-G.A. Flash origin-r/#104. 213-Reprints #137. 220-1st app. Turtle since Showcase 4 — 1.85 5.50 15.00
214-DC 100 Page Super Spectacular DC-11; origin Metal Men-r/Showcase #37; never before pubbed G.A. Flash story. (see DC 100 pg. Super Spec. #11 for price) — - - -
215 (52 pgs.)-Flash-r/Showcase #4; G.A. Flash x-over, reprinted in #216 — 2.50 7.50 24.00
217-219: Neal Adams-a in all. 217-Green Lantern/Green Arrow series begins (9/72); 2nd G.L. & G.A. team-up series (see Green Lantern #76). 219-Last Green Arrow — 2.50 7.50 20.00
221-225,227,228,230,231,233: 222-G. Lantern x-over. 228-(7-8/74)-Flash writer Cary Bates travels to Earth-One & meets Flash, Iris Allen & Trickster; 2nd unnamed app. Earth-Prime (See Justice League of America #123 for 1st named app. & 3rd app. overall) — 1.00 3.00 8.00
226-Neal Adams-p — 1.25 3.75 10.00
229,232-(100 pg. issues)-G.A. Flash-r & new-a — 2.50 7.50 24.00
234-288,290: 235-Green Lantern x-over. 243-Death of The Top. 245-Origin The Floronic Man in Green Lantern back-up, ends #246. 246-Last Green Lantern 256-Death of The Top retold. 250-Intro Golden Glider. 265-267-(44 pgs.). 267-Origin of Flash's uniform. 270-Intro The Clown. 275,276-Iris West Allen dies. 286-Intro/origin Rainbow Raider — 1.40 3.50
289-1st Perez DC art (Firestorm); new Firestorm back-up series begins (9/80), ends #304 — 2.40 6.00
291-299,301-305: 291-1st app. Saber-Tooth (villain). 295-Gorilla Grodd-c/story. 298-Intro/origin new Shade. 301-Atomic bomb-c. 303-The Top returns. 304-Intro/origin Colonel Computron; 305-G.A. Flash x-over — 1.20 3.00
300-(52 pgs.)-Origin Flash retold; 25th ann. issue — 2.00 5.00
306-Dr. Fate by Giffen begins, ends #313 — 1.20 3.00
307-349: 307-313-Giffen-a. 309-Origin Flash retold. 318-323-Creeper back-ups. 323,324-Two part Flash vs. Flash story. 324-Death of Reverse Flash (Prof. Zoom). 328-Iris West Allen's death retold. 344-Origin Kid Flash — 1.00 2.50
350-Double size ($1.25) — 2.00 5.00

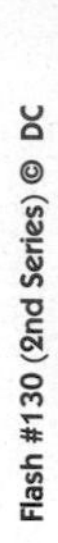
Flash #80 (2nd Series) © DC

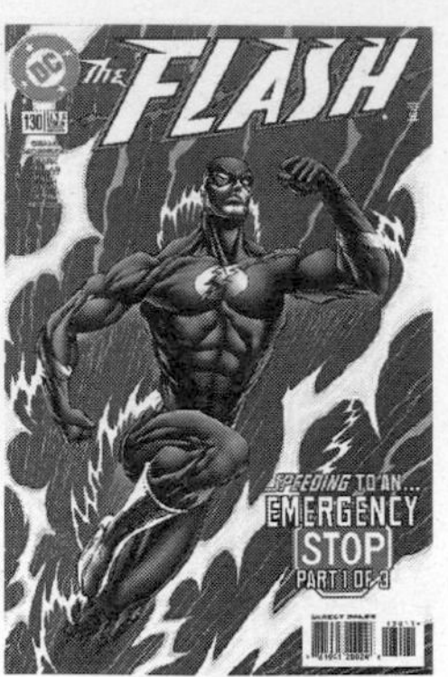

Flash #130 (2nd Series) © DC

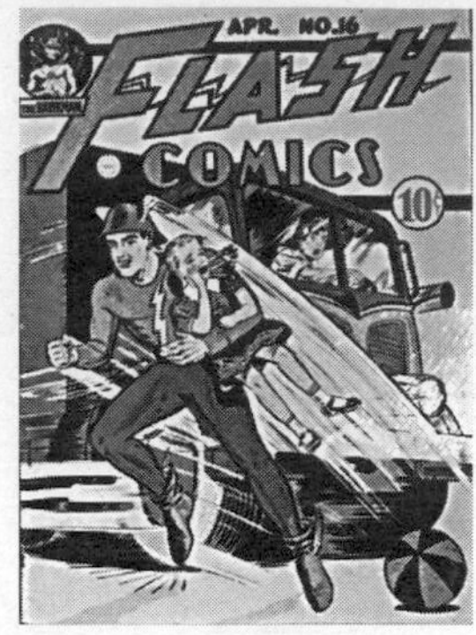

Flash Comics #16 © DC

	GD25	FN65	NM94

Annual 1(10-12/63, 84 pgs.)-Origin Elongated Man & Kid Flash-r; origin Grodd; G.A. Flash-r 36.00 108.00 395.00

NOTE: ***N. Adams*** *c-194, 195, 203, 204, 206-208, 211, 213, 215, 226p, 246.* ***M. Anderson*** *a(i)-195, 200-204, 206-208.* ***Austin*** *a-233i, 234i, 246i.* ***Buckler*** *a-271p, 272p; c(p)-247-250, 252, 253p, 255, 256p, 258, 262, 265-267, 269-271.* ***Giffen*** *a-306-313p; c-310p, 315.* ***Giordano*** *a-226i.* ***Sid Greene*** *a-167-174i, 229i(r).* ***Grell*** *a-237p, 238p, 240-243p; c-236.* ***Heck*** *a-198p.* ***Infantino/Anderson*** *a-135. c-135, 165, 170-174, 192, 200, 201, 328-330.* ***Infantino/Giella*** *c-105-112, 163, 164, 166-168.* ***G. Kane*** *a-195p, 197-199p, 229r, 232r; c-197-199, 312p.* ***Kubert*** *a-108p, 215i(r); c-189-191.* ***Lopez*** *c-272.* ***Meskin*** *a-229r, 232r.* ***Perez*** *a-289-293p; c-293.* ***Starlin*** *a-294-296p.* ***Staton*** *c-263p, 264p. Green Lantern x-over-131, 143, 168, 171, 191.*

FLASH (2nd Series)(See Crisis on Infinite Earths #12)(Also see Justice League Europe)
June, 1987 - Present (75¢/$1.00/$1.50/$1.75)
DC Comics

1-Guice-c/a begins; New Teen Titans app. 1.60 4.00
2,3: 3-Intro. Kilgore 1.00 2.50
4-10: 5-Intro. Speed McGee. 7-1st app. Blue Trinity. 8,9-Millennium tie-ins. 9-1st app. The Chunk 1.00 2.50
11-65: 12-Free extra 16 pg. Dr. Light story. 19-Free extra 16 pg. Flash story. 28-Capt. Cold app. 29-New Phantom Lady app. 40-Dr. Alchemy app. 50-($1.75, 52 pgs.). 62-Flash: Year One begins, ends #65. 65-Last $1.00-c .80 2.00
66-78,80-84: 66-Aquaman app. 69,70-Green Lantern app. 70-Gorilla Grodd story ends. 73-Re-intro Barry Allen & begin saga (Barry Allen revealed as Reverse Flash in #78). 76-Re-intro of Max Mercury (Quality Comic's Quicksilver). 80-Regular ed. 81,82-Nightwing & Starfire app. 84-Razer app. .80 2.00
79-($2.50, 68 pgs.)-Barry Allen saga ends 1.10 2.75
80-($2.50)-Foil-c edition 1.10 2.75
0,85-91,93,101: 85-Begin $1.50-c. 94-Zero Hour. 95-"Terminal Velocity" begins, ends #100. 96,98,99-Kobra app. 97-Origin Max Mercury; Chillblaine app. 1.20 3.00
92-1st Impulse 1.25 3.75 10.00
100 ($2.50)-Newstand edition; Kobra & JLA app. 1.20 3.00
100 ($3.50)-Foil-c edition; Kobra & JLA app. 1.60 4.00
102-131: 102-Mongul app.; begin-$1.75-c. 105-Mirror Master app. 107-Shazam app. 108-"Dead Heat" begins; 1st app. Savitar. 109-"Dead Heat" Pt. 2 (cont'd in Impulse #10). 110-"Dead Heat" Pt. 4 (cont'd in Impulse #11). 111-"Dead Heat" finale; Savitar disappears into the Speed Force; John Fox cameo (2nd app.). 112-"Race Against Time" begins, ends #118; re-intro John Fox; intro new Chillblaine. 113-Tornado Twins app. 119-Final Night x-over 127-129-Rogue's Gallery & Neron. 128,129-JLA-app. 130-Morrison & Millar-s begin .80 2.00
132-136: 132-Begin $1.95-c 1.95
Annual 1 (1987, $1.25) .80 2.00
Annual 2, 3: 2-(1988, $1.50) 3-(1989, $1.75, 68 pgs.)-Gives history of G.A., S.A., & Modern Age Flash in text. .70 1.75
Annual 4 (1991, $2.00, 68 pgs.)-Armaggedon 2001 .80 2.00
Annual 5 (1992, $2.50, 68 pgs.)-Eclipso-c/story 1.00 2.50
Annual 6 (1993, $2.50, 68 pgs.) 1.00 2.50
Annual 7 (1994, $2.95)-Elseworlds story 1.20 3.00
Annual 8 (1995, $3.50)-Year One story 1.40 3.50
Annual 9 (1996, $2.95)-Legends of the Dead Earth story; J.H. Williams-a(p); Mick Gray-a(i) 1.20 3.00
Annual 10 (1997, $3.95)-Pulp Heroes stories 3.95
...Plus 1 (1/1997, $2.95)-Nightwing-c/app. 2.95
...Secret Files 1 (11/97, $4.95, one-shot) Origin-s & pin-ups 4.95
Special 1 (1990, $2.95, 84 pgs.)-50th anniversary issue; Kubert-c; 1st Flash story by Mark Waid; 1st app. John Fox (27th Century Flash). 1.20 3.00
TV Special 1 (1991, $3.95, 76 pgs.)-Photo-c plus behind the scenes photos of TV show; Saltares-a, Byrne scripts 1.60 4.00
Terminal Velocity (1996, $12.95, TPB)-r/#95-100.
The Return of Barry Allen (1996, $12.95, TPB)-r/#74-79. 13.00

NOTE: ***Guice*** *a-1-9p, 11p, Annual 1p; c-1-9p, Annual 1p.* ***Perez*** *c-15-17, Annual 2i.* ***Travest Charest*** *c/a-Annual 5p.*

	GD25	FN65	NM94

FLASH, THE (See Tangent Comics/ The Flash)

FLASH COMICS (Whiz Comics No. 2 on)
Jan, 1940 (12 pgs., B&W, regular size)
(Not distributed to newsstands; printed for in-house use)
Fawcett Publications

NOTE*: **Whiz Comics** #2 was preceded by two books, **Flash Comics** and **Thrill Comics**, both dated Jan, 1940, (12 pgs, B&W, regular size) and were not distributed. These two books are identical except for the title, and were sent out to major distributors as ad copies to promote sales. It is believed that the complete 68 page issue of Fawcett's **Flash** and **Thrill Comics** #1 was finished and ready for publication with the January date. Since DC Comics was also about to publish a book with the same date and title, Fawcett hurriedly printed up the black and white version of **Flash Comics** to secure copyright before DC The inside covers are blank, with the covers and inside pages printed on a high quality uncoated paper stock.The eight page origin story of Captain Thunder is composed of pages 1-7 and 13 of the Captain Marvel story essentially as they appeared in the first issue of **Whiz Comics**. The balloon dialogue on page thirteen was relettered to tie the story into the end of page seven in **Flash** and **Thrill Comics** to produce a shorter version of the origin story for copyright purposes. Obviously, DC acquired the copyright and Fawcett dropped **Flash** as well as **Thrill** and came out with **Whiz Comics** a month later. Fawcett never used the cover to **Flash** and **Thrill** #1, designing a new cover for **Whiz Comics**. Fawcett also must have discovered that Captain Thunder had already been used by another publisher (Captain Terry Thunder by Fiction House). All references to Captain Thunder were relettered to Captain Marvel before appearing in **Whiz**.*

1 (nn on-c, #1 on inside)-Origin & 1st app. Captain Thunder. Eight copies of Flash and three copies of Thrill exist. All 3 copies of Thrill sold in 1986 for between $4,000-$10,000 each. A NM copy of Thrill sold in 1987 for $12,000. A vg copy of Thrill sold in 1987 for $9000 cash; another copy sold in 1987 for $2000 cash, $10,000 trade; cover by Leo O'Mealia

FLASH COMICS (The Flash No. 105 on) (Also see All-Flash)
Jan, 1940 - No. 104, Feb, 1949
National Periodical Publications/All-American

	GD25	FN65	VF82	NM94
1-The Flash (origin/1st app.) by Harry Lampert, Hawkman (origin/1st app.) by Gardner Fox, The Whip, & Johnny Thunder (origin/1st app.) by Stan Asch; Cliff Cornwall by Moldoff, Flash Picture Novelets (later Minute Movies w/#12) begin; Moldoff (Shelly) cover; 1st app. Shiera Sanders who later becomes Hawkgirl, #24; reprinted in Famous First Edition (on sale 11/10/39); The Flash-c	5000.00	15,000.00	30,000.00	55,000.00

(Estimated up to 75+ total copies exist, 7 in NM/Mint)

1-Reprint, Oversize 13-1/2x10". **WARNING:** This comic is an exact reprint of the original except for its size. DC published it in 1974 with a second cover titling it as a Famous First Edition. There have been many reported cases of the outer cover being removed and the interior sold as the original edition. The reprint with the new outer cover removed is practically worthless. See Famous First Edition for value.

	GD25	FN65	NM94
2-Rod Rian begins, ends #11; Hawkman-c	580.00	1740.00	5800.00
3-King Standish begins (1st app.), ends #41 (called The King #16-37,39-41); E.E. Hibbard-a begins on Flash	440.00	1320.00	4400.00
4-Moldoff (Shelly) Hawkman begins; The Whip-c	350.00	1050.00	3500.00
5-The King-c	300.00	900.00	3000.00
6-2nd Flash-c (alternates w/Hawkman #6 on)	400.00	1200.00	4000.00
7-2nd Hawkman-c; 1st Moldoff Hawkman-c	350.00	1050.00	3500.00
8-New logo begins	239.00	717.00	2150.00
9,10: 9-Classic Moldoff Hawkman-c; 10-Classic Moldoff Flash-c	255.00	765.00	2550.00
11-13,15-20: 12-Les Watts begins; "Sparks" #16 on. 17-Last Cliff Cornwall	156.00	468.00	1400.00
14-classic-c	189.00	567.00	1700.00
21-23	133.00	400.00	1200.00
24-Shiera becomes Hawkgirl (12/41); see All-Star Comics #5 for 1st app.	167.00	500.00	1500.00
25-28,30: 28-Last Les Sparks.	94.00	282.00	850.00
29-Ghost Patrol begins (origin/1st app.), ends #104.	106.00	318.00	950.00
31-40: 33-Origin Shade	83.00	250.00	750.00
41-50	75.00	225.00	675.00
51-61: 59-Last Minute Movies. 61-Last Moldoff Hawkman	67.00	200.00	600.00

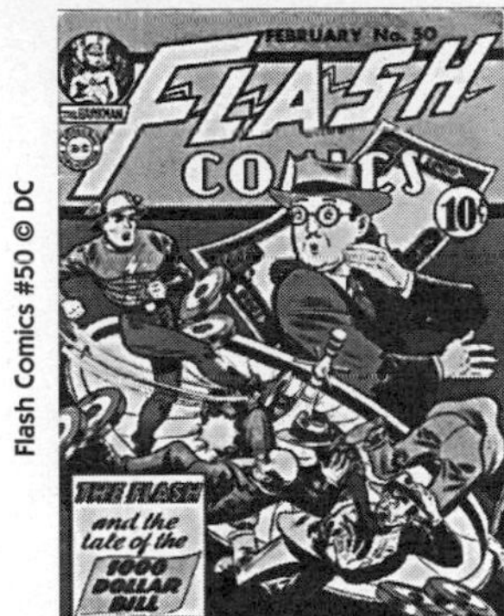

Flash Comics #50 © DC

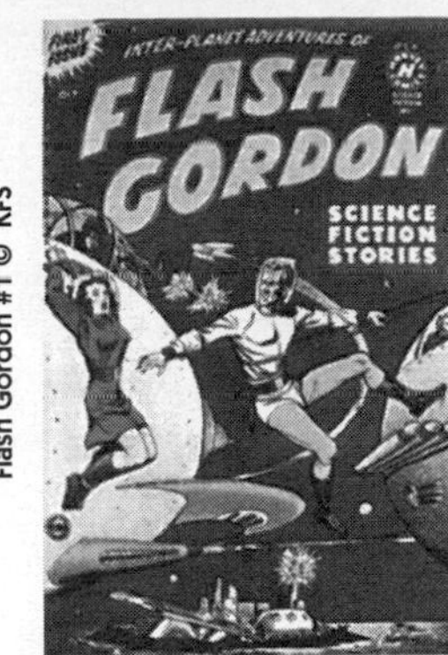

Flash Gordon #1 © KFS

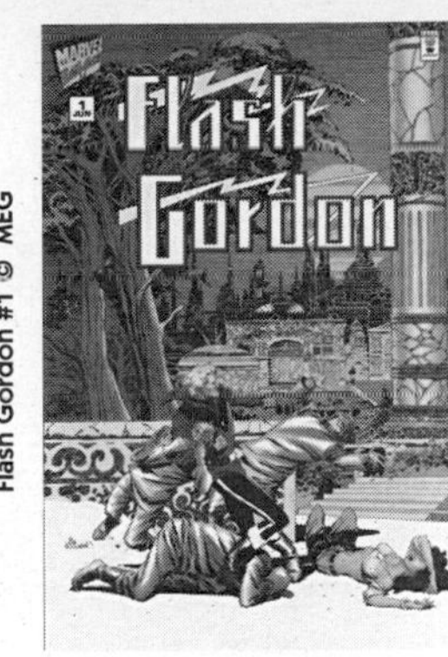

Flash Gordon #1 © MEG

GD25 FN65 NM94

62-Hawkman by Kubert begins 83.00 250.00 750.00
63-70: 66-68-Hop Harrigan in all. 70-Mutt & Jeff app.
64.00 192.00 575.00
71-85: 80-Atom begins, ends #104 64.00 192.00 575.00
86-Intro. The Black Canary in Johnny Thunder (8/47); see All-Star #38.
200.00 600.00 1800.00
87,88,90: 88-Origin Ghost. 97.00 291.00 875.00
89-Intro villain The Thorn 108.00 324.00 975.00
91,93-99: 98-Atom & Hawkman don new costumes
108.00 324.00 975.00
92-1st solo Black Canary plus-c; rare in Mint due to black ink smearing on white-c 240.00 720.00 2400.00
100 (10/48),103(Scarce)-52 pgs. each 240.00 720.00 2300.00
101,102(Scarce) 200.00 600.00 1800.00
104-Origin The Flash retold (Scarce) 570.00 1710.00 5700.00

NOTE: ***Irwin Hasen** a-Wheaties Giveaway. c-97, Wheaties Giveaway. **E.E. Hibbard** c-6, 12, 20, 24, 26, 28, 30, 44, 46, 48, 50, 62, 66, 68, 69, 72, 74, 76, 78, 80, 82. **Infantino** a-86p, 90, 93-95, 99-104; c-90, 92, 93, 97, 99, 101, 103. **Kinstler** a-87, 89(Hawkman); c-87. **Chet Kozlak** c-77, 79, 81. **Krigstein** a-94. **Kubert** a-62-76, 83, 85, 86, 88-104; c-63, 65, 67, 70, 71, 73, 75, 83, 85, 86, 88, 89, 91, 94, 96, 98, 100, 104. **Moldoff** a-3; c-3, 7-11, 13-17, plus odd #'s 19-61. **Martin Naydell** c-52, 54, 56, 58, 60, 64, 84.*

FLASH COMICS
1946 (6-1/2x8-1/4", 32 pgs.)
National Periodical Publications (Wheaties Giveaway)

nn-Johnny Thunder, Ghost Patrol, The Flash & Kubert Hawkman app.; Irwin Hasen-c/a 350.00 1050.00 -

NOTE: *All known copies were taped to Wheaties boxes and are never found in mint condition. Copies with light tape residue bring the listed prices in all grades*

FLASH DIGEST, THE (See DC Special Series #24)

FLASH GORDON (See Defenders Of The Earth, Eat Right to Work..., Giant Comic Album, King Classics, King Comics, March of Comics #118, 133, 142, The Phantom #18, Street Comix & Wow Comics, 1st series)

FLASH GORDON
No. 25, 1941; No. 10, 1943 - No. 512, Nov, 1953
Dell Publishing Co.

Feature Books 25 (#1)(1941))-r-not by Raymond 64.00 191.00 700.00
Four Color 10(1943)-by Alex Raymond; reprints "The Ice Kingdom"
73.00 218.00 800.00
Four Color 84(1945)-by Alex Raymond; reprints "The Fiery Desert"
34.00 102.00 375.00
Four Color 173,190: 190-Bondage-c 12.00 37.00 135.00
Four Color 204,247 9.00 29.00 105.00
Four Color 424-Painted-c 8.00 23.00 85.00
2(5-7/53-Dell)-Painted-c; Evans-a? 4.50 13.50 50.00
Four Color 512-Painted-c 4.50 13.50 50.00
Macy's Giveaway(1943)-(Rare)-20 pgs.; not by Raymond
50.00 150.00 450.00

FLASH GORDON (See Tiny Tot Funnies)
Oct, 1950 - No. 4, April, 1951
Harvey Publications

1-Alex Raymond-a; bondage-c; reprints strips from 7/14/40 to 12/8/40
21.00 64.00 170.00
2-Alex Raymond-a; r/strips 12/15/40-4/27/41 15.50 47.00 125.00
3,4-Alex Raymond-a; 3-bondage-c; r/strips 5/4/41-9/21/41. 4-r/strips 10/24/37-3/27/38 14.00 41.00 110.00
5-(Rare)-Small size-5-1/2x8-1/2"; B&W; 32 pgs.; Distributed to some mail subscribers only. Estimated value $200.00–$300.00
(Also see All-New No. 15, Boy Explorers No. 2, and Stuntman No. 3)

FLASH GORDON
1951 (16 pgs. in color, regular size, paper-c)
Harvey Comics (Gordon Bread giveaway)

1,2: 1-r/strips 10/24/37 - 2/6/38. 2-r/strips 7/14/40 - 10/6/40; Reprints by Raymond each.... 1.50 4.50 10.00
NOTE: *Most copies have brittle edges.*

FLASH GORDON
June, 1965
Gold Key

1 (1947 reprint)-Painted-c 3.60 11.00 40.00

FLASH GORDON (Also see Comics Reading Libraries)
9/66 - #11, 12/67; #12, 2/69 - #18, 1/70; #19, 10-11/78 - #37, 3/82
(Painted covers No. 19-30, 34)
King #1-11/Charlton #12-18/Gold Key #19-23/Whitman #28 on

1-1st S.A. app Flash Gordon; Williamson c/a(2); E.C. swipe/Incredible S.F. #32; Mandrake story 3.50 10.50 35.00
1-8: 1-Army giveaway(1968)("Complimentary" on cover)(Same as regular #1 minus Mandrake story & back-c). 2-Bolle, Gil Kane-c; Mandrake story. 3-Williamson-c. 4-Secret Agent X-9 begins, Williamson-c/a(3). 5-Williamson-c/a(2). 6,8-Crandall-a. 7-Raboy-a (last in comics?). 8-Secret Agent X-9-r
2.50 7.50 20.00
9,10-Raymond-r. 10-Buckler's 1st pro work (11/67) 2.25 6.75 18.00
11-Crandall-a 1.60 4.85 13.00
12-Crandall-c/a 1.85 5.50 15.00
13-Jeff Jones-a (15 pgs.) 2.25 6.75 18.00
14-17: 17-Brick Bradford story 1.05 3.15 8.50
18-Kaluta-a (3rd pro work?)(see Teen Confessions) 1.25 3.75 10.00
19(9/78, G.K.), 20-26 1.60 4.00
27-30 (10/80) (scarce) 2.40 6.00
30-37: 30 (7/81; re-issue). 31-33: Movie adaptation; Williamson-a. 34-37: Movie adaptation 1.60 4.00

NOTE: ***Aparo** a-8. **Bolle** a-21, 22. **Boyette** a-14-18. **Briggs** c-10. **Buckler** a-10. **Crandall** c-6. **Estrada** a-3. **Gene Fawcette** a-29, 30, 34, 37. **McWilliams** a-31-33, 36.*

FLASH GORDON
June, 1988 - No. 9, Holiday, 1988-'89 ($1.25, mini-series)
DC Comics

1-9: 1,5-Painted-c 1.25

FLASH GORDON
June, 1995 - No. 2, July, 1995 ($2.95, limited series)
Marvel Comics

1,2: Schultz scripts; Williamson-a 1.20 3.00

FLASH GORDON THE MOVIE
1980 (8-1/4 x 11", $1.95, 68 pgs.)
Western Publishing Co.

11294-Williamson-c/a; adapts movie .80 2.00
13743-Hardback edition 2.00 5.00

FLASH/ GREEN LANTERN: FASTER FRIENDS (See Green Lantern/Flash...)
1997 ($4.95, continuation of Green Lantern/Flash:Faster Friends #1))
DC Comics

2-Waid/Augustyn-s 4.95

FLASH SPECTACULAR, THE (See DC Special Series No. 11)

FLAT-TOP
11/53 - No. 3, 5/54; No. 4, 3/55 - No. 7, 9/55
Mazie Comics/Harvey Publ.(Magazine Publ.) No. 4 on

1-Teenage; Flat-Top, Mazie, Mortie & Stevie begin 4.25 13.00 28.00
2,3 3.20 8.00 16.00
4-7 2.40 6.00 12.00

FLESH & BLOOD
Dec, 1995 ($2.95, B&W, mature)
Brainstorm Comics

1-Balent-c; foil-c. 1.20 3.00

FLESH AND BONES
June, 1986 - No. 4, Dec, 1986 (Limited series)

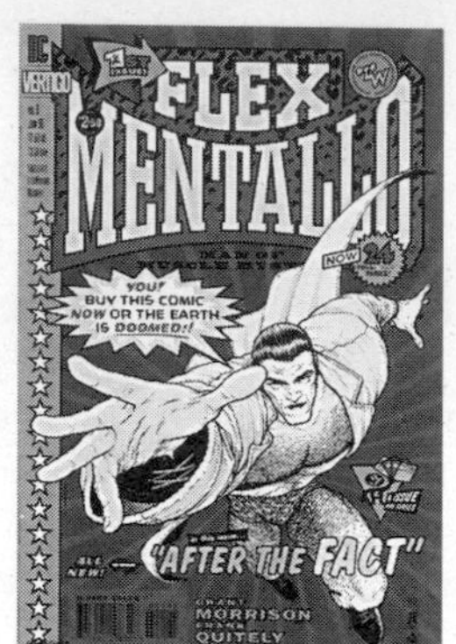

Flex Mentallo #1 © DC

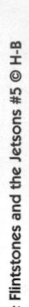

The Flintstones and the Jetsons #5 © H-B

Flippity & Flop #16 © DC

	GD25	FN65	NM94

Upshot Graphics (Fantagraphics Books)

	GD25	FN65	NM94
1-Dalgoda by Fujitake in all		1.00	2.50
2-4 Alan Moore scripts (r) in all		.80	2.00

FLESH CRAWLERS
Aug, 1993 - No. 2, Jan, 1995 ($2.50, B&W, limited series, mature)
Kitchen Sink Press

	GD25	FN65	NM94
1,2		1.00	2.50

FLEX MENTALLO (Man of Muscle Mystery) (See Doom Patrol, 2nd Series)
June, 1996 - No. 4, Sept, 1996 ($2.50, limited series, mature)
DC Comics (Vertigo)

	GD25	FN65	NM94
1: Grant Morrison scripts & Frank Quitely-c/a. in all		2.00	5.00
2-4		1.40	3.50

FLINTSTONE KIDS, THE (TV) (See Star Comics Digest)
Aug, 1987 - No. 11, Apr, 1989
Star Comics/Marvel Comics #5 on

	GD25	FN65	NM94
1-11		.80	2.00

FLINTSTONES, THE (TV)(See Dell Giant #48 for No. 1)
No. 2, Nov-Dec, 1961 - No. 60, Sept, 1970 (Hanna-Barbera)
Dell Publ. Co./Gold Key No. 7 (10/62) on

	GD25	FN65	NM94
2-2nd app. (TV show debuted on 9/30/60)	8.00	25.00	90.00
3-6(7-8/62): 2-5: 15¢. 6-Begin 12¢ issues	6.00	18.00	65.00
7 (10/62; 1st GK)	5.00	15.00	55.00
8-10: Mr. & Mrs. J. Evil Scientist begin?	4.00	12.00	45.00
11-1st app. Pebbles (6/63)	7.00	22.00	80.00
12-15,17-20	3.00	9.00	35.00
16-1st app. Bamm-Bamm (1/64)	6.40	19.00	70.00
21-23,25-30	3.00	9.00	32.00
24-1st app. The Grusomes	4.50	13.50	50.00
31-33,35-40: 31-Xmas-c. 33-Meet Frankenstein & Dracula. 39-Reprints	2.75	8.00	30.00
34-1st app. The Great Gazoo	4.50	13.50	50.00
41-60: 45-Last 12¢ issue	2.50	7.50	28.00
At N. Y. World's Fair('64)-J.W. Books(25¢)-1st printing; no date on-c (29¢ version exists, 2nd print?)	4.00	12.00	45.00
At N. Y. World's Fair (1965 on-c; re-issue). NOTE: Warehouse find in 1984	1.00	2.80	7.00
Bigger & Boulder 1(#30013-211) (Gold Key Giant, 11/62, 25¢, 84 pgs.)	7.00	22.00	80.00
Bigger & Boulder 2-(1966, 25¢)-Reprints B&B No. 1	6.00	18.00	65.00
...With Pebbles & Bamm Bamm (100 pgs., G.K.)-30028-511 (paper-c, 25¢) (11/65)	6.40	19.00	70.00

NOTE: *(See Comic Album #16, Bamm-Bamm & Pebbles Flintstone, Dell Giant 48, Golden Comics Digest, March of Comics #229, 243, 271, 289, 299, 317, 327, 341, Pebbles Flintstone, Top Comics #2-4, and Whitman Comic Books.)*

FLINTSTONES, THE (TV)(...& Pebbles)
Nov, 1970 - No. 50, Feb, 1977 (Hanna-Barbera)
Charlton Comics

	GD25	FN65	NM94
1	5.00	15.00	50.00
2	3.00	9.00	30.00
3-7,9,10	2.50	7.50	20.00
8- "Flintstones Summer Vacation" (Summer, 1971, 52 pgs.)	5.00	15.00	50.00
11-36,38-41,43-50: 36-Mike Zeck illos (early work).	1.85	5.50	15.00
37,42: 37-Byrne text illos (early work; see Nightmare #20). 42-Byrne-a (2 pgs.)	2.50	7.50	22.00

(Also see Barney & Betty Rubble, Dino, The Great Gazoo, & Pebbles & Bamm-Bamm)

FLINTSTONES, THE (TV)(See Yogi Bear, 3rd series)
October, 1977 - No. 9, Feb, 1979 (Hanna-Barbera)
Marvel Comics Group

	GD25	FN65	NM94
1	1.25	3.75	10.00
2,3,5-9: Yogi Bear app. 4-The Jetsons app.	1.10	3.30	9.00
4-The Jetsons app.	1.85	5.50	15.00

FLINTSTONES, THE (TV)
Sept, 1992 - No. 13, June, 1994 ($1.25/$1.50) (Hanna-Barbera)
Harvey Comics

	GD25	FN65	NM94
V2#1-13: 5-Begin $1.50-c		.80	2.00
...Big Book 1,2 (11/92, 3/93; both $1.95, 52 pgs.)		1.20	3.00
...Giant Size 1-3 (10/92, 4/93, 11/93; $2.25, 68 pgs.)		1.20	3.00

FLINTSTONES, THE (TV)
Sept, 1995 - No. 22, June, 1997 ($1.50)
Archie Publications

	GD25	FN65	NM94
1-22		.80	2.00

FLINTSTONES AND THE JETSONS, THE (TV)
Aug, 1997 - Present ($1.75)
DC Comics

	GD25	FN65	NM94
1-4			1.75
5-7: 5-Begin $1.95-c			1.95

FLINTSTONES CHRISTMAS PARTY, THE (See The Funtastic World of Hanna-Barbera No. 1)

FLIP
April, 1954 - No. 2, June, 1954 (Satire)
Harvey Publications

	GD25	FN65	NM94
1,2-Nostrand-a each. 2-Powell-a	18.00	54.00	145.00

FLIPPER (TV)
Apr, 1966 - No. 3, Nov, 1967 (All have photo-c)
Gold Key

	GD25	FN65	NM94
1	4.50	13.50	50.00
2,3	3.00	9.00	35.00

FLIPPITY & FLOP
12-1/51-52 - No. 46, 8-10/59; No. 47, 9-11/60
National Periodical Publ. (Signal Publ. Co.)

	GD25	FN65	NM94
1-Sam dog & his pets Flippity The Bird and Flop The Cat begin; Twiddle and Twaddle begin	23.00	68.00	180.00
2	12.00	38.00	100.00
3-5	10.00	30.00	80.00
6-10	8.75	26.25	70.00
11-20: 20-Last precode (3/55)	8.30	25.00	58.00
21-47	6.85	21.00	48.00

FLOATERS
Sept, 1993 - No. 5, Jan, 1994 ($2.50, B&W, limited series)
Dark Horse Comics

	GD25	FN65	NM94
1-5		1.00	2.50

FLOOD RELIEF
Jan, 1994 (36 pgs.)(Ordered thru mail w/$5.00 to Red Cross)
Malibu Comics (Ultraverse)

	GD25	FN65	NM94
1-Hardcase, Prime & Prototype app.		2.00	5.00

FLOYD FARLAND (See Eclipse Graphic Album Series #11)

FLY, THE (Also see Adventures of..., Blue Ribbon Comics & Flyman)
May, 1983 - No. 9, Oct, 1984
Archie Enterprises, Inc.

	GD25	FN65	NM94
1-9: 1-Mr. Justice app; origin Shield. 2-Flygirl app.			1.00

NOTE: ***Buckler** a-1, 2. **Ditko** a-2-9; c-4-8p. **Nebres** c-3, 4, 5i, 6, 7i. **Steranko** c-1, 2.*

FLY, THE
Aug, 1991 - No. 17, Dec, 1992 ($1.00)
Impact Comics (DC)

	GD25	FN65	NM94
1-17: 4-Vs. The Black Hood. 9-Trading card inside			1.00
Annual 1 ('92, $2.50, 68 pgs.)-Impact trading card		1.00	2.50

The Flying A's Range Rider #18 © DELL

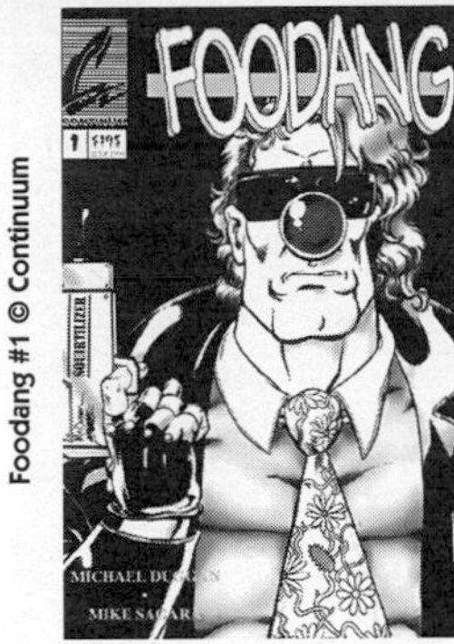

Foodang #1 © Continuum

Foolkiller #1 © MEG

GD25 FN65 NM94

FLYBOY (Flying Cadets)(Also see Approved Comics)
Spring, 1952 - No. 4, 1953
Ziff-Davis Publ. Co. (Approved)

	GD25	FN65	NM94
1-Saunders painted-c	14.00	43.00	110.00
2-(10-11/52)-Saunders painted-c	10.00	30.00	80.00
3,4-Saunders painted-c	8.50	26.00	60.00

FLYING ACES (Aviation stories)
July, 1955 - No. 5, Mar, 1956
Key Publications

	GD25	FN65	NM94
1	4.25	13.00	28.00
2-5: 2-Trapani-a	4.00	10.00	20.00

FLYING A'S RANGE RIDER, THE (TV) (See Western Roundup under Dell Giants)
#404, 6-7/52; #2, June-Aug, 1953 - #24, Aug, 1959 (All photo-c)
Dell Publishing Co.

	GD25	FN65	NM94
Four Color 404(#1)-Titled "The Range Rider"	10.00	30.00	110.00
2	6.00	18.00	65.00
3-10	4.50	13.50	50.00
11-16,18-24	4.00	12.00	45.00
17-Toth-a	5.25	16.00	58.00

FLYING CADET (WW II Plane Photos)
Jan, 1943 - V2#8, 1947 (Half photos, half comics)
Flying Cadet Publishing Co.

	GD25	FN65	NM94
V1#1-Painted-c	10.50	32.00	85.00
2	5.70	17.00	40.00
3-9 (Two #6's, Sept. & Oct.): 5,6a,6b-Photo-c	5.70	17.00	35.00
V2#1-7(#10-16)	4.25	13.00	28.00
8(#17)-Bare-breasted woman-c	13.00	39.00	105.00

FLYIN' JENNY
1946 - No. 2, 1947 (1945 strip-r)
Pentagon Publ. Co./Leader Enterprises #2

	GD25	FN65	NM94
nn-Marcus Swayze strip-r (entire insides)	11.00	33.00	80.00
2-Baker-c; Swayze strip reprints	12.00	36.00	90.00

FLYING MODELS
V61#3, May, 1954 (5¢, 16 pgs.)
H-K Publ. (Health-Knowledge Publs.)

	GD25	FN65	NM94
V61#3 (Rare)	6.50	19.50	45.00

FLYING NUN (TV)
Feb, 1968 - No. 4, Nov, 1968
Dell Publishing Co.

	GD25	FN65	NM94
1-Sally Field photo-c	3.60	11.00	40.00
2-4: 2-Sally Field photo-c	2.25	6.75	25.00

FLYING NURSES (See Sue & Sally Smith...)

FLYING SAUCERS
1950; 1952; 1953
Avon Periodicals/Realistic

	GD25	FN65	NM94
1(1950)-Wood-a, 21 pgs.; Fawcette-c	62.00	187.00	550.00
nn(1952)-Cover altered plus 2 pgs. of Wood-a not in original	40.00	120.00	325.00
nn(1953)-Reprints above	31.00	94.00	225.00

FLYING SAUCERS (Comics)
April, 1967 - No. 4, Nov, 1967; No. 5, Oct, 1969
Dell Publishing Co.

	GD25	FN65	NM94
1	2.50	7.50	24.00
2-5	1.85	5.50	15.00

FLY MAN (Formerly Adventures of The Fly; Mighty Comics #40 on)
No. 32, July, 1965 - No. 39, Sept, 1966 (Also see Mighty Crusaders)
Mighty Comics Group (Radio Comics) (Archie)

	GD25	FN65	NM94
32,33-Comet, Shield, Black Hood, The Fly & Flygirl x-over. 33-Re-intro Wizard, Hangman (1st S.A. appearances)	3.00	9.00	30.00
34-36: 34-Shield begins. 35-Origin Black Hood. 36-Hangman x-over in Shield; re-intro. & origin of Web (1st S.A. app.)	2.50	7.50	20.00
37-39: 37-Hangman, Wizard x-over in Flyman; last Shield issue. 38-Web story. 39-Steel Sterling story (1st S.A. app.)	2.50	7.50	20.00

FOES
1989 - No. 3, 1989 ($1.95, limited series)
Ram Comics

	GD25	FN65	NM94
1-3		.80	2.00

FOLLOW THE SUN (TV)
May-July, 1962 - No. 2, Sept-Nov, 1962 (Photo-c)
Dell Publishing Co.

	GD25	FN65	NM94
01-280-207(No.1), 12-280-211(No.2)	3.60	11.00	40.00

FOODANG
July, 1994 ($1.95, B&W, bi-monthly)
Continum Comics

	GD25	FN65	NM94
1		.80	2.00

FOODINI (TV)(The Great...; see Jingle Dingle & Pinhead &...)
March, 1950 - No. 5, 1950 (All have 52 pgs.)
Continental Publications (Holyoke)

	GD25	FN65	NM94
1-Based on TV puppet show (very early TV comic)	14.00	41.00	110.00
2-Jingle Dingle begins	8.50	26.00	60.00
3-5: 4-(8/50)	6.50	19.50	45.00

FOOEY (Magazine) (Satire)
Feb, 1961 - No. 4, May, 1961
Scoff Publishing Co.

	GD25	FN65	NM94
1	5.35	16.00	32.00
2-4	4.00	11.00	22.00

FOOFUR (TV)
Aug, 1987 - No. 6, June, 1988
Marvel Comics (Star Comics)/Marvel Comics No. 5 on

	GD25	FN65	NM94
1-6			1.00

FOOLKILLER (Also see The Amazing Spider-Man #225, The Defenders #73 Man-Thing #3 & Omega the Unknown #8)
Oct, 1990 - No. 10, Oct, 1991 ($1.75, limited series)
Marvel Comics

	GD25	FN65	NM94
1-10: 1-Origin 3rd Foolkiller; Greg Salinger app; DeZuniga-a(i) in 1-4. 8-Spider-Man x-over		.70	1.75

FOOTBALL THRILLS (See Tops In Adventure)
Fall-Winter, 1951-52 - No. 2, Fall, 1952 (Edited by "Red" Grange)
Ziff-Davis Publ. Co.

	GD25	FN65	NM94
1-Powell a(2); Saunders painted-c; Red Grange, Jim Thorpe stories	24.00	71.00	190.00
2-Saunders painted-c	15.50	47.00	125.00

FOOT SOLDIERS, THE
Jan, 1996 - No. 4, Apr, 1996 ($2.95, limited series)
Dark Horse Comics

	GD25	FN65	NM94
1-4: Jim Krueger story & Michael Avon Oeming-a. in all. 1-Alex Ross-c. 4-John K. Snyder, III-c.		1.20	3.00

FOOT SOLDIERS, THE (Volume Two)
Sept, 1997 - Present ($2.95, limited series)
Image Comics

	GD25	FN65	NM94
1,2: 1-Yeowell-a. 2-McDaniel, Hester, Sienkiewicz, Giffen-a			2.95

FOR A NIGHT OF LOVE
1951
Avon Periodicals

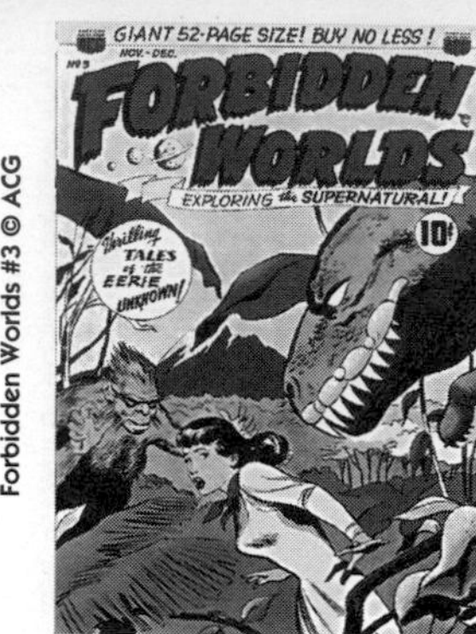

Forbidden Worlds #3 © ACG

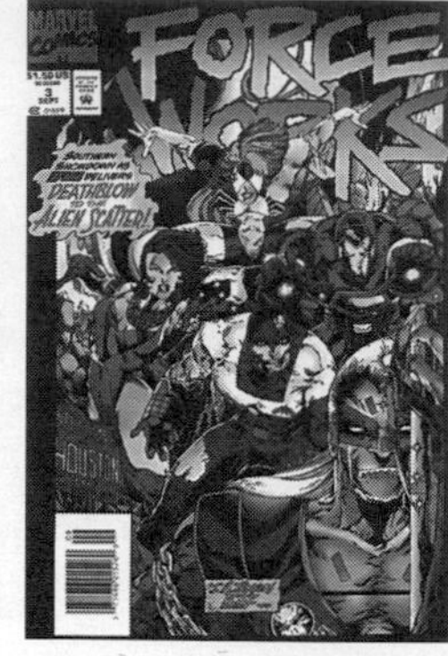

Force Works #3 © MEG

Forever People #7 © DC

GD25 FN65 NM94

nn-Two stories adapted from the works of Emile Zola; Astarita, Ravielli-a;
Kinstler-c 24.00 73.00 180.00

FORBIDDEN KNOWLEDGE: ADVENTURE BEYOND THE DOORWAY TO SOULS WITH RADICAL DREAMER (Also see Radical Dreamer)
1996 ($3.50, B&W, one-shot, 48 pgs.)
Mark's Giant Economy Size Comics

nn-Max Wrighter app.; Wheatley-c/a/script; painted infinity-c 1.40 3.50

FORBIDDEN LOVE
Mar, 1950 - No. 4, Sept, 1950 (52 pgs.)
Quality Comics Group

1-(Scarce)-Classic photo-c; Crandall-a 59.00 178.00 500.00
2,3-(Scarce)-Photo-c 29.00 86.00 210.00
4-(Scarce)-Ward/Cuidera-a; photo-c 33.00 99.00 240.00

FORBIDDEN LOVE (See Dark Mansion of...)

FORBIDDEN PLANET
May, 1992 - No. 4, 1992 ($2.50, limited series)
Innovation Publishing

1-4: Adapts movie; painted-c 1.00 2.50

FORBIDDEN TALES OF DARK MANSION (Formerly Dark Mansion of Forbidden Love #1-4)
No. 5, May-June, 1972 - No. 15, Feb-Mar, 1974
National Periodical Publications

5-(52 pgs.) 2.50 7.50 20.00
6-15: 13-Kane/Howard-a 1.50 4.50 12.00

NOTE: ***N. Adams*** *c-9.* ***Alcala*** *a-9-11, 13.* ***Chaykin*** *a-7,15.* ***Evans*** *a-14.* ***Heck*** *a-5.* ***Kaluta*** *a-7i, 8-12; c-7, 8, 13.* ***G. Kane*** *a-13.* ***Kirby*** *a-6.* ***Nino*** *a-8, 12, 15.* ***Redondo*** *a-14.*

FORBIDDEN WORLDS
7-8/51 - No. 34, 10-11/54; No. 35, 8/55 - No. 145, 8/67
(No. 1-5: 52 pgs.; No. 6-8: 44 pgs.)
American Comics Group

1-Williamson/Frazetta-a (10 pgs.) 112.00 338.00 950.00
2 56.00 168.00 470.00
3-Williamson/Orlando-a (7 pgs.); Wood (2 panels); Frazetta (1 panel)
58.00 176.00 480.00
4 31.00 94.00 230.00
5-Krenkel/Williamson-a (8 pgs.) 45.00 136.00 375.00
6-Harrison/Williamson-a (8 pgs.) 40.00 120.00 320.00
7,8,10: 7-1st monthly issue 24.00 71.00 170.00
9-A-Bomb explosion story 26.00 79.00 190.00
11-20 17.00 49.00 120.00
21-33: 24-E.C. swipe by Landau 11.50 34.00 80.00
34(10-11/54)(Scarce)(becomes Young Heroes #35 on)-Last pre-code issue;
A-Bomb explosion story 11.50 34.00 80.00
35(8/55)-Scarce 10.00 30.00 65.00
36-62 7.50 22.50 45.00
63,69,76,78-Williamson-a in all; w/Krenkel #69 8.35 25.00 50.00
64,66-68,70-72,74,75,77,79-85,87-90 6.35 19.00 38.00
65- "There's a New Moon Tonight" listed in #114 as holding 1st record fan
mail response 7.50 22.50 45.00
73-1st app. Herbie by Ogden Whitney 29.00 88.00 235.00
86-Flying saucer-c by Schaffenberger 5.70 17.00 40.00
91-93,95-100 2.50 7.50 24.00
94-Herbie app. 6.00 18.00 60.00
101-109,111-113,115,117-120 2.50 7.50 20.00
110,114,116-Herbie app. 114-1st Herbie-c; contains list of editor's top 20 ACG
stories. 116-Herbie goes to Hell 4.00 12.00 40.00
121-124: 124-Magic Agent app. 2.50 7.50 22.00
125-Magic Agent app.; intro. & origin Magicman series, ends #141
3.00 9.00 30.00
126-130 2.50 7.50 22.00
131-139: 133-Origin/1st app. Dragonia in Magicman (1-2/66); returns in #138.
136-Nemesis x-over in Magicman 2.50 7.50 20.00
140-Mark Midnight app. by Ditko 2.50 7.50 24.00
141-145 1.75 5.25 14.00

NOTE: ***Buscema*** *a-75, 79, 81, 82, 140r.* ***Cameron*** *a-5.* ***Disbrow*** *a-10.* ***Ditko*** *a-137p, 138, 140.* ***Landau*** *a-24, 27-29, 31-34, 48, 86r, 96, 143-45.* ***Lazarus*** *a-18, 23, 24, 57.* ***Moldoff*** *a-27, 31, 139r.* ***Reinman*** *a-93.* ***Whitney*** *a-115, 116, 137; c-40, 46, 57, 60, 68, 78, 79, 90, 93, 94, 100, 102, 103, 106-108, 114, 129.*

FORCE, THE (See The Crusaders)

FORCE OF BUDDHA'S PALM THE
Aug, 1988 - No. 46, June, 1992? ($1.50/$1.95, 68 pgs.)
Jademan Comics

1-8 ($1.50)-Kung Fu stories 1.50
9-46 ($1.95) .80 2.00

FORCE WORKS
July, 1994 - No. 22, Apr, 1996 ($1.50)
Marvel Comics

1-($3.95)-Fold-out pop-up-c; Iron Man, Wonder Man, Spider-Woman,U.S.
Agent & Scarlet Witch (new costume) 1.60 4.00
2-11, 13-22: 5-Blue logo version & pink logo version. 9-Intro Dreamguard.
13-Avengers app. 1.50
5 Pink logo ($2.95)-polybagged w/ 16pg. Marvel Action Hour Preview & acetate
print 1.20 3.00
12 ($2.50)-Flip book w/War Machine. 1.00 2.50

FORD ROTUNDA CHRISTMAS BOOK (See Christmas at the Rotunda)

FOREIGN INTRIGUES (Formerly Johnny Dynamite; becomes Battlefield Action #16 on)
No. 13, 1956 - No. 15, Aug, 1956
Charlton Comics

13-15-Johnny Dynamite continues 5.35 16.00 32.00

FOREMOST BOYS (See 4Most)

FOREST FIRE (Also see Smokey The Bear)
1949 (dated-1950) (16 pgs., paper-c)
American Forestry Assn.(Commerical Comics)

nn-Intro/1st app. Smokey The Forest Fire Preventing Bear; created by Rudy
Wendelein; Wendelein/Sparling-a; 'Carter Oil Co.' on back-c of original
15.00 45.00 120.00

FOR ETERNITY
July, 1997 - Present ($2.95, B&W)
Antarctic Press

1-3 2.95

FOREVER DARLING (Movie)
No. 681, Feb, 1956
Dell Publishing Co.

Four Color 681-w/Lucille Ball & Desi Arnaz; photo-c 10.00 30.00 110.00

FOREVER PEOPLE, THE
Feb-Mar, 1971 - No. 11, Oct-Nov, 1972 (Fourth World)
National Periodical Publications

1-1st app. Forever People; Superman x-over; Kirby-c/a begins; 1st full app.
Darkseid (3rd anywhere, 3 weeks before New Gods #1); Darkseid storyline
begins, ends #8(app. in 1-4,6,8; cameos in 5,11) 4.00 12.00 40.00
2-5: 4-G.A. reprints begin, end #9 2.50 7.50 24.00
6-11: 9,10-Deadman app. 1.50 4.50 12.00

NOTE: ***Kirby*** *c/a(p)-1-11; #4-9 contain Sandman reprints from Adventure #85, 84, 75, 80, 77, 74 in that order. #1-3, 10-11 are 36pgs; #4-9 are 52pgs.*

FOREVER PEOPLE
Feb, 1988 - No. 6, July, 1988 ($1.25, limited series)
DC Comics

1-6 1.25

FOR GIRLS ONLY

Four Color (Series 1) #3 © NY News Synd.

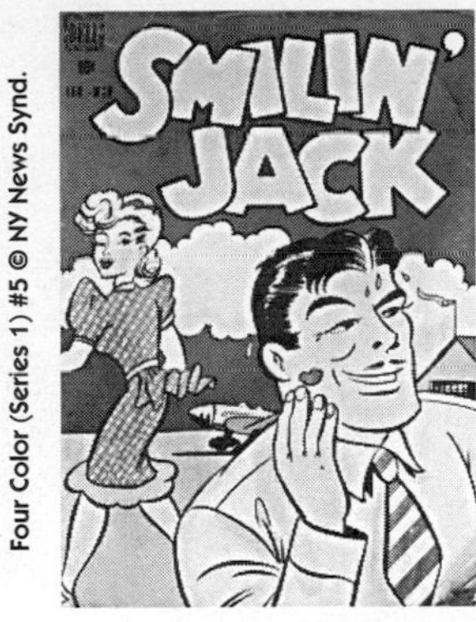

Four Color (Series 1) #5 © NY News Synd.

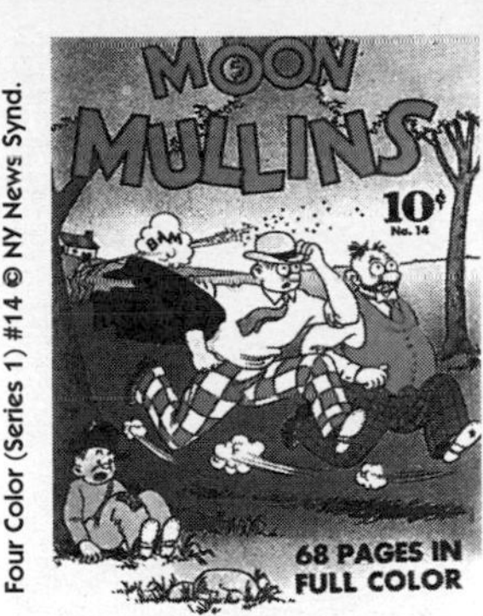

Four Color (Series 1) #14 © NY News Synd.

GD25 FN65 NM94

Nov, 1953 (100 pgs., digest size)
Bernard Bailey Enterprises

1-Half comic book, half magazine 11.50 34.00 80.00

FORGOTTEN FOREST OF OZ, THE (See First Comics Graphic Novel #16)

FORGOTTEN REALMS (Also see Avatar & TSR Worlds)
Sept, 1989 - No. 25, Sept, 1991 ($1.50/$1.75)
DC Comics

1-Based on TSR role-playing game .80 2.00
2,3 .80 2.00
4-10 .75 1.80
11-15 1.50
16-25: 16-Begin $1.75-c. 18-Avatar story .75 1.80
Annual 1 (1990, $2.95, 68 pgs.) 1.20 3.00

FORGOTTEN STORY BEHIND NORTH BEACH, THE
No date (8 pgs., paper-c)
Catechetical Guild

nn 2.40 6.00 12.00

FORLORN RIVER (See Zane Grey Four Color 395)

FOR LOVERS ONLY (Formerly Hollywood Romances)
No. 60, Aug, 1971 - No. 87, Nov, 1976
Charlton Comics

60-87: 73-Spanking scene-c/story 1.20

40 BIG PAGES OF MICKEY MOUSE
No. 945, Jan, 1936 (10-1/4x12-1/2", 44 pgs., cardboard-c)
Whitman Publishing Co.

945-Reprints Mickey Mouse Magazine #1, but with a different cover; ads were eliminated and some illustrated stories had expanded text. The book is 3/4" shorter than Mickey Mouse Mag. #1, but the reprints are the same size (Rare) 140.00 420.00 1200.00

48 FAMOUS AMERICANS
1947 (Giveaway) (Half-size in color)
J. C. Penney Co. (Cpr. Edwin H. Stroh)

nn-Simon & Kirby-a 9.50 28.00 75.00

FOR YOUR EYES ONLY (See James Bond...)

FOUR COLOR
Sept?, 1939 - No. 1354, Apr-June, 1962 (Series I are all 68 pgs.)
Dell Publishing Co.

NOTE: *Four Color only appears on issues #19-25, 1-99,101. Dell Publishing Co. filed these as Series I, #1-25, and Series II, #1-1354. Issues beginning with #710? were printed with and without ads on back cover. Issues without ads are worth more.*

SERIES I: GD25 FN65 VF82 NM94
1(nn)-Dick Tracy 590.00 1775.00 3540.00 6500.00
(Estimated up to 115 total copies exist, 5 in NM/Mint)
GD25 FN65 NM94
2(nn)-Don Winslow of the Navy (#1) (Rare) (11/39?)
116.00 348.00 1275.00
3(nn)-Myra North (1/40?) 68.00 205.00 750.00
GD25 FN65 VF82 NM94
4-Donald Duck by Al Taliaferro (1940)(Disney)(3/40?)
808.00 2423.00 5656.00 10,500.00
(Prices vary widely on this book)
GD25 FN65 NM94
5-Smilin' Jack (#1) (5/40?) 54.00 162.00 595.00
6-Dick Tracy (Scarce) 134.00 400.00 1470.00
7-Gang Busters 33.00 98.00 360.00
8-Dick Tracy 67.00 200.00 735.00
9-Terry and the Pirates-r/Super #9-29 54.00 161.00 590.00
10-Smilin' Jack 49.00 146.00 535.00
11-Smitty (#1) 34.00 101.00 370.00
12-Little Orphan Annie; reprints strips from 12/19/37 to 6/4/38
45.00 135.00 495.00
13-Walt Disney's Reluctant Dragon('41)-Contains 2 pgs. of photos from film; 2 pg. foreword to Fantasia by Leopold Stokowski; Donald Duck, Goofy, Baby Weems & Mickey Mouse (as the Sorcerer's Apprentice) app. (Disney) 147.00 443.00 1625.00
14-Moon Mullins (#1) 33.00 98.00 360.00
15-Tillie the Toiler (#1) 32.00 95.00 360.00
GD25 FN65 VF82
16-Mickey Mouse (#1) (Disney) by Gottfredson 654.00 1961.00 8500.00
GD25 FN65 NM94
17-Walt Disney's Dumbo, the Flying Elephant (#1)(1941)-Mickey Mouse, Donald Duck, & Pluto app. (Disney) 157.00 470.00 1725.00
18-Jiggs and Maggie (#1)(1936-38-r) 36.00 100.00 400.00
19-Barney Google and Snuffy Smith (#1)-(1st issue with Four Color on the cover) 35.00 104.00 380.00
20-Tiny Tim 27.00 80.00 295.00
21-Dick Tracy 57.00 170.50 625.00
22-Don Winslow 28.00 85.00 310.00
23-Gang Busters 26.00 77.00 280.00
24-Captain Easy 38.00 115.00 420.00
25-Popeye (1942) 66.00 197.00 720.00

SERIES II:
1-Little Joe (1942) 42.00 125.00 460.00
2-Harold Teen 24.00 71.00 260.00
3-Alley Oop (#1) 44.00 132.00 485.00
4-Smilin' Jack 40.00 121.00 445.00
5-Raggedy Ann and Andy (#1) 46.00 139.00 510.00
6-Smitty 20.00 60.00 220.00
7-Smokey Stover (#1) 30.00 90.00 330.00
8-Tillie the Toiler 21.00 63.00 230.00
GD25 FN65 VF82 NM94
9-Donald Duck Finds Pirate Gold, by Carl Barks & Jack Hannah (Disney) (© 8/17/42) 577.00 1730.00 4039.00 7500.00
GD25 FN65 NM94
10-Flash Gordon by Alex Raymond; reprinted from "The Ice Kingdom"
73.00 218.00 800.00
11-Wash Tubbs 27.00 80.00 295.00
12-Walt Disney's Bambi (#1) 49.00 146.00 535.00
13-Mr. District Attorney (#1)-See The Funnies #35 for 1st app.
27.00 82.00 300.00
14-Smilin' Jack 32.00 97.00 355.00
15-Felix the Cat (#1) 65.00 194.00 710.00
16-Porky Pig (#1)(1942)- "Secret of the Haunted House"
72.00 215.00 790.00
17-Popeye 48.00 143.50 535.00
18-Little Orphan Annie's Junior Commandos; Flag-c; reprints strips from 6/14/42 to 11/21/42 36.00 107.00 390.00
19-Walt Disney's Thumper Meets the Seven Dwarfs (Disney); reprinted in Silly Symphonies 51.00 153.00 560.00
20-Barney Baxter 24.00 71.00 260.00
21-Oswald the Rabbit (#1)(1943) 46.00 139.00 510.00
22-Tillie the Toiler 16.00 49.00 180.00
23-Raggedy Ann and Andy 35.00 104.00 380.00
24-Gang Busters 26.00 77.00 280.00
25-Andy Panda (#1) (Walter Lantz) 44.00 132.00 485.00
26-Popeye 48.00 143.00 535.00
27-Walt Disney's Mickey Mouse and the Seven Colored Terror
77.00 232.00 850.00
28-Wash Tubbs 20.00 59.00 215.00
GD25 FN65 VF82 NM94
29-Donald Duck and the Mummy's Ring, by Carl Barks (Disney) (9/43)
477.00 1430.00 3340.00 6200.00

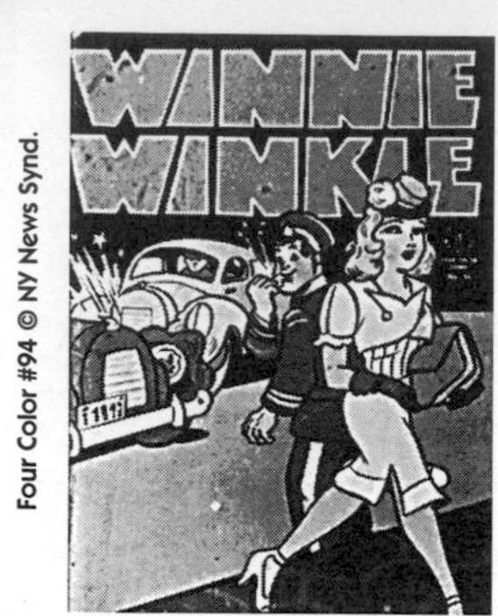

Four Color #94 © NY News Synd.

Four Color #111 © Nea Service

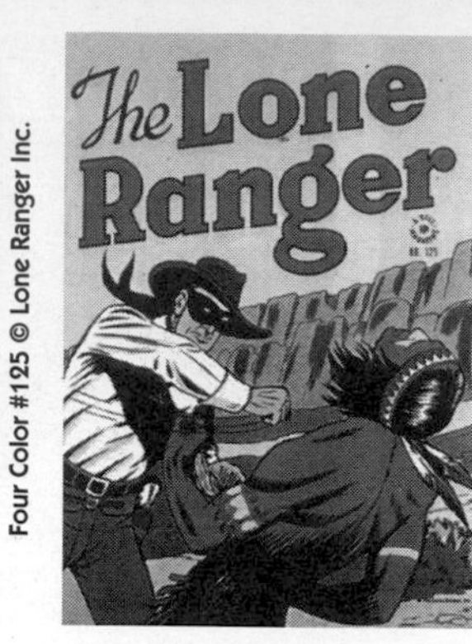

Four Color #125 © Lone Ranger Inc.

	GD25	FN65	NM94
30-Bambi's Children (1943)-Disney	49.00	146.00	535.00
31-Moon Mullins	17.00	50.00	185.00
32-Smitty	14.00	44.00	160.00
33-Bugs Bunny "Public Nuisance #1"	100.00	300.00	1100.00
34-Dick Tracy	39.00	116.00	425.00
35-Smokey Stover	16.00	47.00	170.00
36-Smilin' Jack	21.00	64.00	235.00
37-Bringing Up Father	17.00	52.00	190.00
38-Roy Rogers (#1, © 4/44)-1st western comic with photo-c	164.00	490.00	1800.00
39-Oswald the Rabbit (1944)	33.00	98.00	360.00
40-Barney Google and Snuffy Smith	20.00	60.00	220.00
41-Mother Goose and Nursery Rhyme Comics (#1)-All by Walt Kelly	21.00	63.00	230.00
42-Tiny Tim (1934-r)	16.00	47.00	170.00
43-Popeye (1938-'42-r)	30.00	89.00	325.00
44-Terry and the Pirates (1938-r)	37.00	112.00	410.00
45-Raggedy Ann	28.00	85.00	310.00
46-Felix the Cat and the Haunted Castle	38.00	115.00	420.00
47-Gene Autry (copyright 6/16/44)	37.00	112.00	410.00
48-Porky Pig of the Mounties by Carl Barks (7/44)	91.00	273.00	1000.00
49-Snow White and the Seven Dwarfs (Disney)	56.00	169.00	620.00
50-Fairy Tale Parade-Walt Kelly art (1944)	24.00	71.00	260.00
51-Bugs Bunny Finds the Lost Treasure	33.00	98.00	360.00
52-Little Orphan Annie; reprints strips from 6/18/38 to 11/19/38	28.00	85.00	310.00
53-Wash Tubbs	14.00	44.00	160.00
54-Andy Panda	27.00	82.00	300.00
55-Tillie the Toiler	12.00	37.00	135.00
56-Dick Tracy	31.00	83.00	340.00
57-Gene Autry	34.00	102.00	375.00
58-Smilin' Jack	21.00	64.00	235.00
59-Mother Goose and Nursery Rhyme Comics-Kelly-c/a	18.00	53.00	195.00
60-Tiny Folks Funnies	13.00	40.00	145.00
61-Santa Claus Funnies(11/44)-Kelly art	22.00	67.00	245.00
62-Donald Duck in Frozen Gold, by Carl Barks (Disney) (1/45)	154.00	462.00	2000.00
63-Roy Rogers; color photo-all 4 covers	43.00	130.00	475.00
64-Smokey Stover	11.00	34.00	125.00
65-Smitty	11.00	34.00	125.00
66-Gene Autry	34.00	102.00	375.00
67-Oswald the Rabbit	16.00	48.00	175.00
68-Mother Goose and Nursery Rhyme Comics, by Walt Kelly	18.00	53.00	195.00
69-Fairy Tale Parade, by Walt Kelly	24.00	71.00	260.00
70-Popeye and Wimpy	24.00	72.00	265.00
71-Walt Disney's Three Caballeros, by Walt Kelly (© 4/45)-(Disney)	75.00	225.00	825.00
72-Raggedy Ann	24.00	71.00	260.00
73-The Gumps (#1)	11.00	33.00	120.00
74-Marge's Little Lulu (#1)	91.00	273.00	1000.00
75-Gene Autry and the Wildcat	27.00	82.00	300.00
76-Little Orphan Annie; reprints strips from 2/28/40 to 6/24/40	23.00	70.00	255.00
77-Felix the Cat	36.00	107.00	390.00
78-Porky Pig and the Bandit Twins	22.00	65.00	240.00
79-Walt Disney's Mickey Mouse in The Riddle of the Red Hat by Carl Barks (8/45)	95.00	286.00	1050.00
80-Smilin' Jack	14.00	42.00	155.00
81-Moon Mullins	9.00	27.00	100.00
82-Lone Ranger	39.00	116.00	425.00
83-Gene Autry in Outlaw Trail	27.00	82.00	300.00
84-Flash Gordon by Alex Raymond-Reprints from "The Fiery Desert"	34.00	102.00	375.00
85-Andy Panda and the Mad Dog Mystery	14.00	42.00	155.00
86-Roy Rogers; photo-c	32.00	95.00	350.00
87-Fairy Tale Parade by Walt Kelly; Dan Noonan-c	24.00	71.00	260.00
88-Bugs Bunny's Great Adventure (Sci/fi)	18.00	55.00	200.00
89-Tillie the Toiler	12.00	37.00	130.00
90-Christmas with Mother Goose by Walt Kelly (11/45)	16.00	49.00	180.00
91-Santa Claus Funnies by Walt Kelly (11/45)	16.00	49.00	180.00
92-Walt Disney's The Wonderful Adventures Of Pinocchio (1945); Donald Duck by Kelly, 16 pgs. (Disney)	55.00	164.00	600.00
93-Gene Autry in The Bandit of Black Rock	24.00	71.00	260.00
94-Winnie Winkle (1945)	11.00	33.00	120.00
95-Roy Rogers Comics; photo-c	32.00	95.00	350.00
96-Dick Tracy	22.00	67.00	245.00
97-Marge's Little Lulu (1946)	43.00	128.00	470.00
98-Lone Ranger, The	28.00	85.00	310.00
99-Smitty	9.00	29.00	105.00
100-Gene Autry Comics; photo-c	24.00	71.00	260.00
101-Terry and the Pirates	25.00	74.00	270.00

NOTE: No. 101 is last issue to carry "Four Color" logo on cover; all issues beginning with No. 100 are marked "...O. S." (One Shot) which can be found in the bottom left-hand panel on the first page; the numbers following "O. S." relate to the year/month issued.

	GD25	FN65	NM94
102-Oswald the Rabbit-Walt Kelly art, 1 pg.	14.00	41.00	150.00
103-Easter with Mother Goose by Walt Kelly	17.00	52.00	190.00
104-Fairy Tale Parade by Walt Kelly	17.00	52.00	190.00
105-Albert the Alligator and Pogo Possum (#1) by Kelly (4/46)	61.00	184.00	675.00
106-Tillie the Toiler	9.00	27.00	100.00
107-Little Orphan Annie; reprints strips from 11/16/42 to 3/24/43	19.00	58.00	215.00
108-Donald Duck in The Terror of the River, by Carl Barks (Disney) (© 4/16/46)	112.00	335.00	1450.00
109-Roy Rogers Comics; photo-c	23.00	70.00	255.00
110-Marge's Little Lulu	31.00	92.00	335.00
111-Captain Easy	13.00	40.00	145.00
112-Porky Pig's Adventure in Gopher Gulch	13.00	38.00	140.00
113-Popeye; all new Popeye stories begin	12.00	35.00	130.00
114-Fairy Tale Parade by Walt Kelly	17.00	52.00	190.00
115-Marge's Little Lulu	31.00	92.00	335.00
116-Mickey Mouse and the House of Many Mysteries (Disney)	21.00	64.00	235.00
117-Roy Rogers Comics; photo-c	16.00	49.00	180.00
118-Lone Ranger, The	28.00	85.00	310.00
119-Felix the Cat; all new Felix stories begin	30.00	89.00	325.00
120-Marge's Little Lulu	26.00	79.00	290.00
121-Fairy Tale Parade-(not Kelly)	10.00	30.00	110.00
122-Henry (#1) (10/46)	12.00	35.00	130.00
123-Bugs Bunny's Dangerous Venture	14.00	41.00	150.00
124-Roy Rogers Comics; photo-c	16.00	49.00	180.00
125-Lone Ranger, The	19.00	57.00	210.00
126-Christmas with Mother Goose by Walt Kelly (1946)	13.00	38.00	140.00
127-Popeye	12.00	35.00	130.00
128-Santa Claus Funnies- "Santa & the Angel" by Gollub; "A Mouse in the House" by Kelly	13.00	38.00	140.00
129-Walt Disney's Uncle Remus and His Tales of Brer Rabbit (#1) (1946)-Adapted from Disney movie "Song of the South"	26.00	79.00	290.00
130-Andy Panda (Walter Lantz)	9.00	27.00	100.00
131-Marge's Little Lulu	26.00	79.00	290.00
132-Tillie the Toiler (1947)	9.00	27.00	100.00
133-Dick Tracy	19.00	57.00	210.00
134-Tarzan and the Devil Ogre; Marsh-c/a	59.00	177.00	650.00

Four Color #198 © Walter Lantz

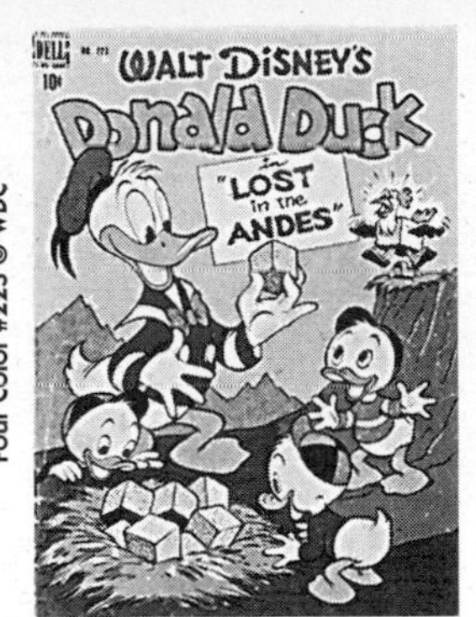

Four Color #223 © WDC

Four Color #226 © Warner Bros.

	GD25	FN65	NM94
135-Felix the Cat	22.00	65.00	240.00
136-Lone Ranger, The	19.00	57.00	210.00
137-Roy Rogers Comics; photo-c	16.00	49.00	180.00
138-Smitty	8.00	25.00	90.00
139-Marge's Little Lulu (1947)	25.00	74.00	270.00
140-Easter with Mother Goose by Walt Kelly	14.00	42.00	155.00
141-Mickey Mouse and the Submarine Pirates (Disney)	18.00	55.00	200.00
142-Bugs Bunny and the Haunted Mountain	14.00	41.00	150.00
143-Oswald the Rabbit & the Prehistoric Egg	8.00	25.00	90.00
144-Roy Rogers Comics (1947)-Photo-c	16.00	49.00	180.00
145-Popeye	12.00	35.00	130.00
146-Marge's Little Lulu	25.00	74.00	270.00
147-Donald Duck in Volcano Valley, by Carl Barks (Disney) (5/47)	77.00	231.00	1000.00
148-Albert the Alligator and Pogo Possum by Walt Kelly (5/47)	55.00	164.00	600.00
149-Smilin' Jack	9.00	27.00	100.00
150-Tillie the Toiler (6/47)	8.00	25.00	90.00
151-Lone Ranger, The	16.00	47.00	170.00
152-Little Orphan Annie; reprints strips from 1/2/44 to 5/6/44	13.00	38.00	140.00
153-Roy Rogers Comics; photo-c	14.00	42.00	155.00
154-Walter Lantz Andy Panda	9.00	27.00	100.00
155-Henry (7/47)	7.00	22.00	80.00
156-Porky Pig and the Phantom	9.00	27.00	100.00
157-Mickey Mouse & the Beanstalk (Disney)	18.00	55.00	200.00
158-Marge's Little Lulu	25.00	74.00	270.00
159-Donald Duck in the Ghost of the Grotto, by Carl Barks (Disney) (8/47)	62.00	185.00	800.00
160-Roy Rogers Comics; photo-c	14.00	42.00	155.00
161-Tarzan and the Fires Of Tohr; Marsh-c/a	50.00	150.00	550.00
162-Felix the Cat (9/47)	16.00	49.00	180.00
163-Dick Tracy	15.00	45.00	165.00
164-Bugs Bunny Finds the Frozen Kingdom	14.00	41.00	150.00
165-Marge's Little Lulu	25.00	74.00	270.00
166-Roy Rogers Comics (52 pgs.)-Photo-c	14.00	42.00	155.00
167-Lone Ranger, The	16.00	47.00	170.00
168-Popeye (10/47)	12.00	35.00	130.00
169-Woody Woodpecker (#1)- "Manhunter in the North"; drug use story	13.00	40.00	145.00
170-Mickey Mouse on Spook's Island (11/47)(Disney)-reprinted in Mickey Mouse #103	14.00	44.00	160.00
171-Charlie McCarthy (#1) and the Twenty Thieves	23.00	68.00	250.00
172-Christmas with Mother Goose by Walt Kelly (11/47)	13.00	38.00	140.00
173-Flash Gordon	12.00	37.00	135.00
174-Winnie Winkle	6.40	19.00	70.00
175-Santa Claus Funnies by Walt Kelly (1947)	13.00	38.00	140.00
176-Tillie the Toiler (12/47)	8.00	25.00	90.00
177-Roy Rogers Comics-(36 pgs.); Photo-c	14.00	42.00	155.00
178-Donald Duck "Christmas on Bear Mountain" by Carl Barks; 1st app. Uncle Scrooge (Disney)(12/47)	92.00	277.00	1200.00
179-Uncle Wiggily (#1)-Walt Kelly-c	14.00	44.00	160.00
180-Ozark Ike (#1)	9.00	27.00	100.00
181-Walt Disney's Mickey Mouse in Jungle Magic	14.00	44.00	160.00
182-Porky Pig in Never-Never Land (2/48)	9.00	27.00	100.00
183-Oswald the Rabbit (Lantz)	8.00	25.00	90.00
184-Tillie the Toiler	8.00	25.00	90.00
185-Easter with Mother Goose by Walt Kelly (1948)	12.00	35.00	130.00
186-Walt Disney's Bambi (4/48)-Reprinted as Movie Classic Bambi #3 (1956)	15.00	45.00	165.00
187-Bugs Bunny and the Dreadful Dragon	9.00	27.00	100.00
188-Woody Woodpecker (Lantz, 5/48)	9.00	27.00	100.00

	GD25	FN65	NM94
189-Donald Duck in The Old Castle's Secret, by Carl Barks (Disney) (6/48)	58.00	173.00	750.00
190-Flash Gordon ('48)	12.00	37.00	135.00
191-Porky Pig to the Rescue	9.00	27.00	100.00
192-The Brownies (#1)-by Walt Kelly (7/48)	11.00	33.00	120.00
193-M.G.M. Presents Tom and Jerry (#1)(1948)	13.00	38.00	140.00
194-Mickey Mouse in The World Under the Sea (Disney)-Reprinted in Mickey Mouse #101	14.00	44.00	160.00
195-Tillie the Toiler	5.50	16.50	60.00
196-Charlie McCarthy in The Haunted Hide-Out; part photo-c	16.00	47.00	170.00
197-Spirit of the Border (#1) (Zane Grey) (1948)	11.00	32.00	115.00
198-Andy Panda	9.00	27.00	100.00
199-Donald Duck in Sheriff of Bullet Valley, by Carl Barks; Barks draws himself on wanted poster, last page; used in Love & Death (Disney) (10/48)	64.00	190.00	825.00
200-Bugs Bunny, Super Sleuth (10/48)	9.00	27.00	100.00
201-Christmas with Mother Goose by W. Kelly	11.00	33.00	120.00
202-Woody Woodpecker	5.75	17.00	63.00
203-Donald Duck in the Golden Christmas Tree, by Carl Barks (Disney) (12/48)	43.00	129.00	560.00
204-Flash Gordon (12/48)	9.00	29.00	105.00
205-Santa Claus Funnies by Walt Kelly	12.00	35.00	130.00
206-Little Orphan Annie; reprints strips from 11/10/40 to 1/11/41	7.00	20.00	75.00
207-King of the Royal Mounted (#1) (12/48)	14.00	41.00	150.00
208-Brer Rabbit Does It Again (Disney) (1/49)	11.00	32.00	115.00
209-Harold Teen	3.60	11.00	40.00
210-Tippie and Cap Stubbs	3.60	11.00	40.00
211-Little Beaver (#1)	7.00	20.00	75.00
212-Dr. Bobbs	3.00	10.00	36.00
213-Tillie the Toiler	5.50	16.50	60.00
214-Mickey Mouse and His Sky Adventure (2/49)(Disney)-Reprinted in Mickey Mouse #105	13.00	38.00	140.00
215-Sparkle Plenty (Dick Tracy-r by Gould)	9.00	27.00	100.00
216-Andy Panda and the Police Pup (Lantz)	6.00	19.00	68.00
217-Bugs Bunny in Court Jester	9.00	27.00	100.00
218-3 Little Pigs and the Wonderful Magic Lamp (Disney) (3/49)(#1)	11.00	33.00	120.00
219-Swee'pe	8.00	25.00	90.00
220-Easter with Mother Goose by Walt Kelly	12.00	35.00	130.00
221-Uncle Wiggily-Walt Kelly cover in part	9.00	27.00	100.00
222-West of the Pecos (Zane Grey)	5.50	16.50	60.00
223-Donald Duck "Lost in the Andes" by Carl Barks (Disney-4/49) (square egg story)	62.00	185.00	800.00
224-Little Iodine (#1), by Hatlo (4/49)	8.00	25.00	90.00
225-Oswald the Rabbit (Lantz)	4.50	13.50	50.00
226-Porky Pig and Spoofy, the Spook	7.00	22.00	80.00
227-Seven Dwarfs (Disney)	10.00	30.00	110.00
228-Mark of Zorro, The (#1) (1949)	20.00	60.00	220.00
229-Smokey Stover	4.50	13.50	50.00
230-Sunset Pass (Zane Grey)	5.50	16.50	60.00
231-Mickey Mouse and the Rajah's Treasure (Disney)	13.00	38.00	140.00
232-Woody Woodpecker (Lantz, 6/49)	5.75	17.00	63.00
233-Bugs Bunny, Sleepwalking Sleuth	9.00	27.00	100.00
234-Dumbo in Sky Voyage (Disney)	9.00	27.00	100.00
235-Tiny Tim	3.60	11.00	40.00
236-Heritage of the Desert (Zane Grey) (1949)	5.50	16.50	60.00
237-Tillie the Toiler	5.50	16.50	60.00
238-Donald Duck in Voodoo Hoodoo, by Carl Barks (Disney) (8/49)	43.00	129.00	560.00
239-Adventure Bound (8/49)	4.25	13.00	48.00
240-Andy Panda (Lantz)	6.00	19.00	68.00

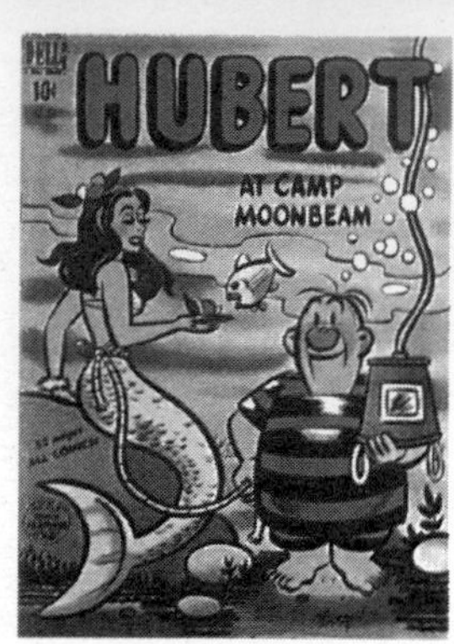

Four Color #251 © KFS

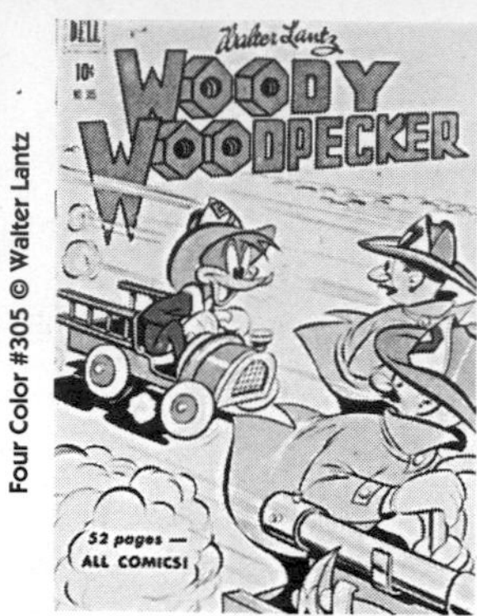

Four Color #305 © Walter Lantz

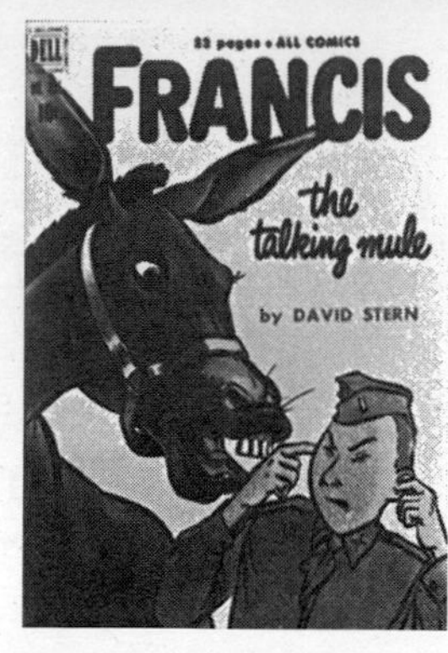

Four Color #335 © UFS

	GD25	FN65	NM94
241-Porky Pig, Mighty Hunter	7.00	22.00	80.00
242-Tippie and Cap Stubbs	2.75	8.00	30.00
243-Thumper Follows His Nose (Disney)	9.00	27.00	100.00
244-The Brownies by Walt Kelly	10.00	30.00	110.00
245-Dick's Adventures (9/49)	4.50	13.50	50.00
246-Thunder Mountain (Zane Grey)	3.60	11.00	40.00
247-Flash Gordon	9.00	29.00	105.00
248-Mickey Mouse and the Black Sorcerer (Disney)	13.00	38.00	140.00
249-Woody Woodpecker in the "Globetrotter" (10/49)	5.75	17.00	63.00
250-Bugs Bunny in Diamond Daze; used in **SOTI**, pg. 309	11.00	33.00	120.00
251-Hubert at Camp Moonbeam	3.60	11.00	40.00
252-Pinocchio (Disney)-not by Kelly; origin	9.00	27.00	100.00
253-Christmas with Mother Goose by W. Kelly	11.00	33.00	120.00
254-Santa Claus Funnies by Walt Kelly; Pogo & Albert story by Kelly (11/49)	12.00	35.00	130.00
255-The Ranger (Zane Grey) (1949)	3.60	11.00	40.00
256-Donald Duck in "Luck of the North" by Carl Barks (Disney) (12/49)-Shows #257 on inside	33.00	99.00	425.00
257-Little Iodine	6.40	19.00	70.00
258-Andy Panda and the Balloon Race (Lantz)	6.00	19.00	68.00
259-Santa and the Angel (Gollub art-condensed from #128) & Santa at the Zoo (12/49)-two books in one	3.60	11.00	40.00
260-Porky Pig, Hero of the Wild West (12/49)	7.00	22.00	80.00
261-Mickey Mouse and the Missing Key (Disney)	13.00	38.00	140.00
262-Raggedy Ann and Andy	6.40	19.00	70.00
263-Donald Duck in "Land of the Totem Poles" by Carl Barks (Disney) (2/50)-Has two Barks stories	31.00	92.00	400.00
264-Woody Woodpecker in the Magic Lantern (Lantz)	5.75	17.00	63.00
265-King of the Royal Mounted (Zane Grey)	7.00	22.00	80.00
266-Bugs Bunny on the "Isle of Hercules" (2/50)-Reprinted in Best of Bugs Bunny #1	8.00	25.00	90.00
267-Little Beaver; Harmon-c/a	3.50	11.00	38.00
268-Mickey Mouse's Surprise Visitor (1950) (Disney)	12.00	35.00	130.00
269-Johnny Mack Brown (#1)-Photo-c	21.00	62.00	225.00
270-Drift Fence (Zane Grey) (3/50)	3.60	11.00	40.00
271-Porky Pig in Phantom of the Plains	7.00	22.00	80.00
272-Cinderella (Disney) (4/50)	9.00	27.00	100.00
273-Oswald the Rabbit (Lantz)	4.50	13.50	50.00
274-Bugs Bunny, Hare-brained Reporter	8.00	25.00	90.00
275-Donald Duck in "Ancient Persia" by Carl Barks (Disney) (5/50)	29.00	87.00	375.00
276-Uncle Wiggily	7.00	22.00	80.00
277-Porky Pig in Desert Adventure (5/50)	7.00	22.00	80.00
278-Bill Elliott Comics (#1)-Photo-c	12.00	35.00	130.00
279-Mickey Mouse and Pluto Battle the Giant Ants (Disney); reprinted in Mickey Mouse #102 & 245	9.00	27.00	100.00
280-Andy Panda in The Isle Of Mechanical Men (Lantz)	6.00	19.00	68.00
281-Bugs Bunny in The Great Circus Mystery	8.00	25.00	90.00
282-Donald Duck and the Pixilated Parrot by Carl Barks (Disney) (© 5/23/50)	29.00	87.00	375.00
283-King of the Royal Mounted (7/50)	7.00	22.00	80.00
284-Porky Pig in The Kingdom of Nowhere	7.00	22.00	80.00
285-Bozo the Clown & His Minikin Circus (#1) (TV)	16.00	49.00	180.00
286-Mickey Mouse in The Uninvited Guest (Disney	9.00	27.00	100.00
287-Gene Autry's Champion in The Ghost Of Black Mountain; photo-c	8.00	25.00	90.00
288-Woody Woodpecker in Klondike Gold (Lantz)	5.75	17.00	63.00
289-Bugs Bunny in "Indian Trouble"	8.00	25.00	90.00
290-The Chief (#1) (8/50)	4.50	13.50	50.00

	GD25	FN65	NM94
291-Donald Duck in "The Magic Hourglass" by Carl Barks (Disney) (9/50)	29.00	87.00	375.00
292-The Cisco Kid Comics (#1)	20.00	60.00	220.00
293-The Brownies-Kelly-c/a	10.00	30.00	110.00
294-Little Beaver	3.50	11.00	38.00
295-Porky Pig in President Porky (9/50)	7.00	22.00	80.00
296-Mickey Mouse in Private Eye for Hire (Disney)	9.00	27.00	100.00
297-Andy Panda in The Haunted Inn (Lantz, 10/50)	6.00	19.00	68.00
298-Bugs Bunny in Sheik for a Day	8.00	25.00	90.00
299-Buck Jones & the Iron Horse Trail (#1)	11.00	34.00	125.00
300-Donald Duck in "Big-Top Bedlam" by Carl Barks (Disney) (11/50)	29.00	87.00	375.00
301-The Mysterious Rider (Zane Grey)	3.60	11.00	40.00
302-Santa Claus Funnies (11/50)	3.60	11.00	40.00
303-Porky Pig in The Land of the Monstrous Flies	4.50	13.50	50.00
304-Mickey Mouse in Tom-Tom Island (Disney) (12/50)	7.00	22.00	80.00
305-Woody Woodpecker (Lantz)	3.00	10.00	36.00
306-Raggedy Ann	4.50	13.50	50.00
307-Bugs Bunny in Lumber Jack Rabbit	7.00	20.00	75.00
308-Donald Duck in "Dangerous Disguise" by Carl Barks (Disney) (1/51)	25.00	75.00	325.00
309-Betty Betz' Dollface and Her Gang (1951)	4.50	13.50	50.00
310-King of the Royal Mounted (1/51)	5.50	16.50	60.00
311-Porky Pig in Midget Horses of Hidden Valley	4.50	13.50	50.00
312-Tonto (#1)	9.00	27.00	100.00
313-Mickey Mouse in The Mystery of the Double-Cross Ranch (#1) (Disney) (2/51)	7.00	22.00	80.00

Note: Beginning with the above comic in 1951 Dell/Western began adding #1 in small print on the covers of several long running titles with the evident intention of switching these titles to their own monthly numbers, but when the conversions were made, there was no connection. It is thought that the post office may have stepped in and decreed the sequences should commence as though the first four colors printed had each begun with number one, or the first issues sold by subscription. Since the regular series' numbers don't correctly match to the numbers of earlier issues published, it's not known whether or not the numbering was in error.

	GD25	FN65	NM94
314-Ambush (Zane Grey)	3.60	11.00	40.00
315-Oswald the Rabbit (Lantz)	3.60	11.00	40.00
316-Rex Allen (#1)-Photo-c; Marsh-a	13.00	38.00	140.00
317-Bugs Bunny in Hair Today Gone Tomorrow (#1)	7.00	20.00	75.00
318-Donald Duck in "No Such Varmint" by Carl Barks (#1)-Indicia shows #317 (Disney, © 1/23/51)	25.00	75.00	325.00
319-Gene Autry's Champion; painted-c	3.60	11.00	40.00
320-Uncle Wiggily (#1)	7.00	22.00	80.00
321-Little Scouts (#1) (3/51)	2.75	8.00	30.00
322-Porky Pig in Roaring Rockets (#1 on-c)	4.50	13.50	50.00
323-Susie Q. Smith (#1) (3/51)	3.00	9.00	35.00
324-I Met a Handsome Cowboy (3/51)	8.00	25.00	90.00
325-Mickey Mouse in The Haunted Castle (#2) (Disney) (4/51)	7.00	22.00	80.00
326-Andy Panda (#1) (Lantz)	3.50	11.00	38.00
327-Bugs Bunny and the Rajah's Treasure (#2)	7.00	20.00	75.00
328-Donald Duck in Old California (#2) by Carl Barks-Peyote drug use issue (Disney) (5/51)	27.00	81.00	350.00
329-Roy Roger's Trigger (#1)(5/51)-Photo-c	10.00	30.00	110.00
330-Porky Pig Meets the Bristled Bruiser (#2)	4.50	13.50	50.00
331-Alice in Wonderland (Disney) (1951)	13.00	40.00	145.00
332-Little Beaver	3.50	11.00	38.00
333-Wilderness Trek (Zane Grey) (5/51)	3.60	11.00	40.00
334-Mickey Mouse and Yukon Gold (Disney) (6/51)	7.00	22.00	80.00
335-Francis the Famous Talking Mule (#1, 6/51)-1st Dell non animated movie comic (all issues based on movie)	7.00	22.00	80.00
336-Woody Woodpecker (Lantz)	3.00	10.00	36.00

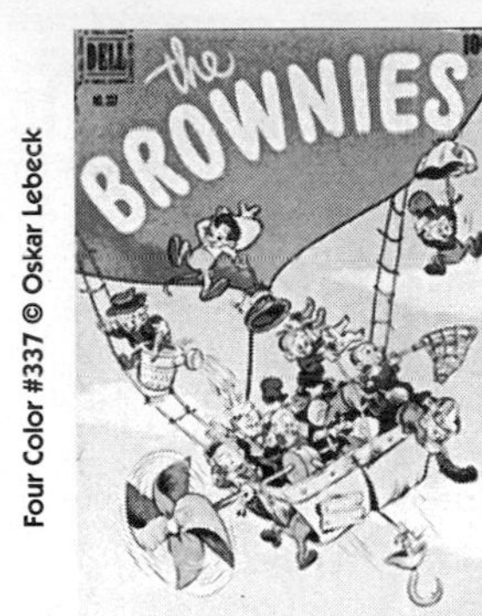

Four Color #337 © Oskar Lebeck

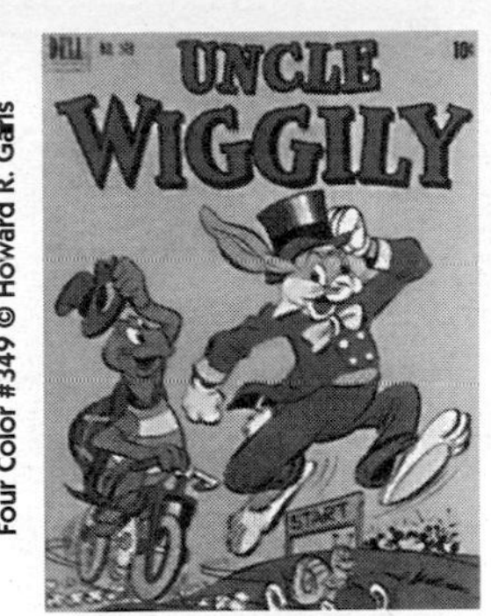

Four Color #349 © Howard R. Garis

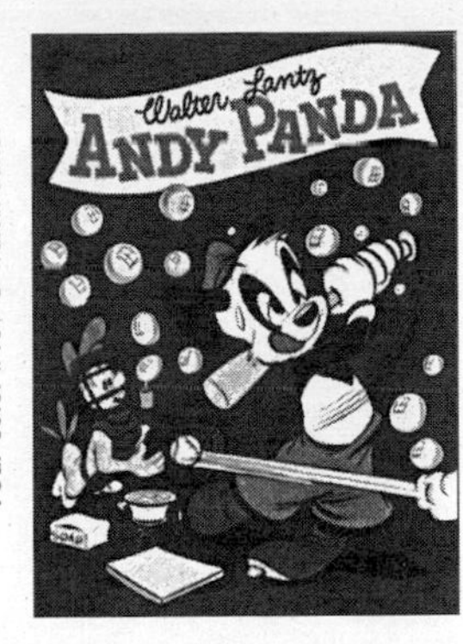

Four Color #409 © Walter Lantz

	GD25	FN65	NM94
337-The Brownies-not by Walt Kelly	3.00	10.00	36.00
338-Bugs Bunny and the Rocking Horse Thieves	7.00	20.00	75.00
339-Donald Duck and the Magic Fountain-not by Carl Barks (Disney) (7-8/51)	6.00	18.00	60.00
340-King of the Royal Mounted (7/51)	5.50	16.50	60.00
341-Unbirthday Party with Alice in Wonderland (Disney) (7/51)	13.00	40.00	145.00
342-Porky Pig the Lucky Peppermint Mine; r/in Porky Pig #3	3.60	11.00	40.00
343-Mickey Mouse in The Ruby Eye of Homar-Guy-Am (Disney)-Reprinted in Mickey Mouse #104	5.50	16.50	60.00
344-Sergeant Preston from Challenge of The Yukon (#1) (TV)	11.00	33.00	120.00
345-Andy Panda in Scotland Yard (8-10/51) (Lantz)	3.50	11.00	38.00
346-Hideout (Zane Grey)	3.60	11.00	40.00
347-Bugs Bunny the Frigid Hare (8-9/51)	7.00	20.00	75.00
348-Donald Duck "The Crocodile Collector"; Barks-c only (Disney) (9-10/51)	15.00	45.00	160.00
349-Uncle Wiggily	5.50	16.50	60.00
350-Woody Woodpecker (Lantz)	3.00	10.00	36.00
351-Porky Pig & the Grand Canyon Giant (9-10/51)	3.60	11.00	40.00
352-Mickey Mouse in The Mystery of Painted Valley (Disney)	5.50	16.50	60.00
353-Duck Album (#1)-Barks-c (Disney)	7.00	22.00	80.00
354-Raggedy Ann & Andy	4.50	13.50	50.00
355-Bugs Bunny Hot-Rod Hare	7.00	20.00	75.00
356-Donald Duck in "Rags to Riches"; Barks-c only	15.00	45.00	160.00
357-Comeback (Zane Grey)	2.75	8.00	30.00
358-Andy Panda (Lantz) (11-1/52)	3.50	11.00	38.00
359-Frosty the Snowman (#1)	7.00	22.00	80.00
360-Porky Pig in Tree of Fortune (11-12/51)	3.60	11.00	40.00
361-Santa Claus Funnies	3.60	11.00	40.00
362-Mickey Mouse and the Smuggled Diamonds (Disney)	5.50	16.50	60.00
363-King of the Royal Mounted	4.50	13.50	50.00
364-Woody Woodpecker (Lantz)	3.00	9.00	34.00
365-The Brownies-not by Kelly	3.00	10.00	36.00
366-Bugs Bunny Uncle Buckskin Comes to Town (12-1/52)	7.00	20.00	75.00
367-Donald Duck in "A Christmas for Shacktown" by Carl Barks (Disney) (1-2/52)	25.00	75.00	320.00
368-Bob Clampett's Beany and Cecil (#1)	25.00	75.00	275.00
369-The Lone Ranger's Famous Horse Hi-Yo Silver (#1); Silver's origin	8.00	25.00	90.00
370-Porky Pig in Trouble in the Big Trees	3.60	11.00	40.00
371-Mickey Mouse in The Inca Idol Case (1952) (Disney)	5.50	16.50	60.00
372-Riders of the Purple Sage (Zane Grey)	2.75	8.00	30.00
373-Sergeant Preston (TV)	6.40	19.00	70.00
374-Woody Woodpecker (Lantz)	3.00	9.00	34.00
375-John Carter of Mars (E. R. Burroughs)-Jesse Marsh-a; origin	23.00	68.00	250.00
376-Bugs Bunny, "The Magic Sneeze"	7.00	20.00	75.00
377-Susie Q. Smith	2.75	8.00	30.00
378-Tom Corbett, Space Cadet (#1) (TV)-McWilliams-a	16.00	48.00	175.00
379-Donald Duck in "Southern Hospitality"; Not by Barks (Disney)	6.00	18.00	60.00
380-Raggedy Ann & Andy	4.50	13.50	50.00
381-Marge's Tubby (#1)	17.00	52.00	190.00
382-Snow White and the Seven Dwarfs (Disney)-origin; partial reprint of 4-Color #49 (Movie)	10.00	30.00	110.00
383-Andy Panda (Lantz)	2.75	8.00	30.00
384-King of the Royal Mounted (3/52)(Zane Grey)	4.50	13.50	50.00

	GD25	FN65	NM94
385-Porky Pig in The Isle of Missing Ships (3-4/52)	3.60	11.00	40.00
386-Uncle Scrooge (#1)-by Carl Barks (Disney) in "Only a Poor Old Man" (3/52)	86.00	259.00	950.00
387-Mickey Mouse in High Tibet (Disney) (4-5/52)	5.50	16.50	60.00
388-Oswald the Rabbit (Lantz)	3.60	11.00	40.00
389-Andy Hardy Comics (#1)	2.75	8.00	30.00
390-Woody Woodpecker (Lantz)	3.00	9.00	34.00
391-Uncle Wiggily	5.50	16.50	60.00
392-Hi-Yo Silver	4.00	12.00	45.00
393-Bugs Bunny	7.00	20.00	75.00
394-Donald Duck in Malayalaya-Barks-c only (Disney)	15.00	45.00	160.00
395-Forlorn River(Zane Grey)-First Nevada (5/52)	2.75	8.00	30.00
396-Tales of the Texas Rangers(#1)(TV)-Photo-c	10.00	30.00	110.00
397-Sergeant Preston of the Yukon (TV) (5/52)	6.40	19.00	70.00
398-The Brownies-not by Kelly	3.00	10.00	36.00
399-Porky Pig in The Lost Gold Mine	3.60	11.00	40.00
400-Tom Corbett, Space Cadet (TV)-McWilliams-c/a	9.00	27.00	100.00
401-Mickey Mouse and Goofy's Mechanical Wizard (Disney) (6-7/52)	3.60	11.00	40.00
402-Mary Jane and Sniffles	7.00	22.00	80.00
403-Li'l Bad Wolf (Disney) (6/52)(#1)	6.40	19.00	70.00
404-The Range Rider (#1) (TV)-Photo-c	10.00	30.00	110.00
405-Woody Woodpecker (Lantz) (6-7/52)	3.00	9.00	34.00
406-Tweety and Sylvester (#1)	7.00	22.00	80.00
407-Bugs Bunny, Foreign-Legion Hare	5.50	16.50	60.00
408-Donald Duck and the Golden Helmet by Carl Barks (Disney) (7-8/52)	25.00	75.00	320.00
409-Andy Panda (7-9/52)	2.75	8.00	30.00
410-Porky Pig in The Water Wizard (7/52)	3.60	11.00	40.00
411-Mickey Mouse and the Old Sea Dog (Disney) (8-9/52)	3.60	11.00	40.00
412-Nevada (Zane Grey)	2.75	8.00	30.00
413-Robin Hood (Disney-Movie) (8/52)-Photo-c (1st Disney movie four color book)	10.00	30.00	110.00
414-Bob Clampett's Beany and Cecil (TV)	16.00	47.00	170.00
415-Rootie Kazootie (#1) (TV)	10.00	30.00	110.00
416-Woody Woodpecker (Lantz)	3.00	9.00	34.00
417-Double Trouble with Goober (#1) (8/52)	2.25	6.75	25.00
418-Rusty Riley, a Boy, a Horse, and a Dog (#1)-Frank Godwin-a (strip reprints) (8/52)	3.60	11.00	40.00
419-Sergeant Preston (TV)	6.40	19.00	70.00
420-Bugs Bunny in The Mysterious Buckaroo (8-9/52)	5.50	16.50	60.00
421-Tom Corbett, Space Cadet(TV)-McWilliams-a	9.00	27.00	100.00
422-Donald Duck and the Gilded Man, by Carl Barks (Disney) (9-10/52) (#423 on inside)	25.00	75.00	320.00
423-Rhubarb, Owner of the Brooklyn Ball Club (The Millionaire Cat) (#1)-Painted cover	4.50	13.50	50.00
424-Flash Gordon-Test Flight in Space (9/52)	8.00	23.00	85.00
425-Zorro, the Return of	11.00	34.00	125.00
426-Porky Pig in The Scalawag Leprechaun	3.60	11.00	40.00
427-Mickey Mouse and the Wonderful Whizzix (Disney) (10-11/52)-Reprinted in Mickey Mouse #100	3.60	11.00	40.00
428-Uncle Wiggily	3.60	11.00	40.00
429-Pluto in "Why Dogs Leave Home" (Disney) (10/52)(#1)	8.00	23.00	85.00
430-Marge's Tubby, the Shadow of a Man-Eater	10.00	30.00	110.00
431-Woody Woodpecker (10/52) (Lantz)	3.00	9.00	34.00
432-Bugs Bunny and the Rabbit Olympics	5.50	16.50	60.00
433-Wildfire (Zane Grey) (11-1/52-53)	2.75	8.00	30.00
434-Rin Tin Tin "In Dark Danger" (#1) (TV) (11/52)-Photo-c	14.00	41.00	150.00

Four Color #471 © KFS

Four Color #504 © KFS

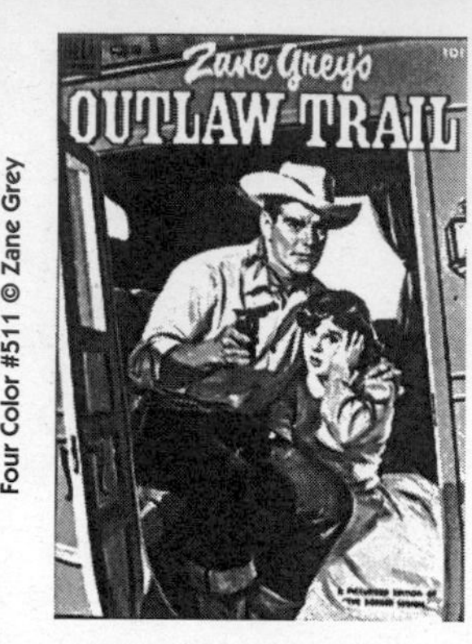

Four Color #511 © Zane Grey

	GD25	FN65	NM94
435-Frosty the Snowman (11/52)	3.60	11.00	40.00
436-The Brownies-not by Kelly (11/52)	3.00	9.00	32.00
437-John Carter of Mars (E. R. Burroughs)-Marsh-a	14.00	44.00	160.00
438-Annie Oakley (#1) (TV)	14.00	41.00	150.00
439-Little Hiawatha (Disney) (12/52)j(#1)	4.50	13.50	50.00
440-Black Beauty (12/52)	2.75	8.00	30.00
441-Fearless Fagan	3.00	9.00	35.00
442-Peter Pan (Disney) (Movie)	8.00	25.00	90.00
443-Ben Bowie and His Mountain Men (#1)	5.50	16.50	60.00
444-Marge's Tubby	10.00	30.00	110.00
445-Charlie McCarthy	4.50	13.50	50.00
446-Captain Hook and Peter Pan (Disney)(Movie)(1/53)	8.00	25.00	90.00
447-Andy Hardy Comics	2.25	6.75	25.00
448-Bob Clampett's Beany and Cecil (TV)	16.00	47.00	170.00
449-Tappan's Burro (Zane Grey) (2-4/53)	2.75	8.00	30.00
450-Duck Album; Barks-c (Disney)	5.50	16.50	60.00
451-Rusty Riley-Frank Godwin-a (strip-r) (2/53)	2.75	8.00	35.00
452-Raggedy Ann & Andy (1953)	4.50	13.50	50.00
453-Susie Q. Smith (2/53)	2.75	8.00	30.00
454-Krazy Kat Comics; not by Herriman	3.00	9.00	35.00
455-Johnny Mack Brown Comics(3/53)-Photo-c	5.50	16.50	60.00
456-Uncle Scrooge Back to the Klondike (#2) by Barks (3/53) (Disney)	57.00	170.00	625.00
457-Daffy (#1)	8.00	25.00	90.00
458-Oswald the Rabbit (Lantz)	2.75	8.00	30.00
459-Rootie Kazootie (TV)	6.40	19.00	70.00
460-Buck Jones (4/53)	4.50	13.50	50.00
461-Marge's Tubby	9.00	26.00	95.00
462-Little Scouts	1.35	4.00	15.00
463-Petunia (4/53)	3.00	9.00	35.00
464-Bozo (4/53)	8.00	25.00	90.00
465-Francis the Famous Talking Mule	4.50	13.50	50.00
466-Rhubarb, the Millionaire Cat; painted-c	3.60	11.00	40.00
467-Desert Gold (Zane Grey) (5-7/53)	2.75	8.00	30.00
468-Goofy (#1) (Disney)	11.00	34.00	125.00
469-Beetle Bailey (#1) (5/53	9.00	27.00	100.00
470-Elmer Fudd	3.60	11.00	40.00
471-Double Trouble with Goober	1.85	5.50	15.00
472-Wild Bill Elliott (6/53)-Photo-c	3.60	11.00	40.00
473-Li'l Bad Wolf (Disney) (6/53)(#2)	3.60	11.00	40.00
474-Mary Jane and Sniffles	6.40	19.00	70.00
475-M.G.M.'s The Two Mouseketeers (#1)	6.40	19.00	70.00
476-Rin Tin Tin (TV)-Photo-c	7.00	22.00	80.00
477-Bob Clampett's Beany and Cecil (TV)	16.00	47.00	170.00
478-Charlie McCarthy	4.50	13.50	50.00
479-Queen of the West Dale Evans (#1)-Photo-c	20.00	60.00	220.00
480-Andy Hardy Comics	2.25	6.75	25.00
481-Annie Oakley And Tagg (TV)	8.00	23.00	85.00
482-Brownies-not by Kelly	3.00	9.00	32.00
483-Little Beaver (7/53)	2.75	8.00	30.00
484-River Feud (Zane Grey) (8-10/53)	2.75	8.00	30.00
485-The Little People-Walt Scott (#1)	5.50	16.50	60.00
486-Rusty Riley-Frank Godwin strip-r	2.75	8.00	30.00
487-Mowgli, the Jungle Book (Rudyard Kipling's)	4.50	13.50	50.00
488-John Carter of Mars (Burroughs)-Marsh-a; painted-c	14.00	48.00	160.00
489-Tweety and Sylvester	3.00	9.00	35.00
490-Jungle Jim (#1)	5.50	16.50	60.00
491-Silvertip (#1) (Max Brand)-Kinstler-a (8/53)	7.00	22.00	80.00
492-Duck Album (Disney)	4.50	13.50	50.00
493-Johnny Mack Brown; photo-c	5.50	16.50	60.00
494-The Little King (#1)	9.00	27.00	100.00
495-Uncle Scrooge (#3) (Disney)-by Carl Barks (9/53)	43.00	130.00	475.00
496-The Green Hornet; painted-c	23.00	68.00	250.00
497-Zorro (Sword of...)-Kinstler-a	12.00	37.00	135.00
498-Bugs Bunny's Album (9/53)	4.50	13.50	50.00
499-M.G.M.'s Spike and Tyke (#1) (9/53)	2.75	8.00	30.00
500-Buck Jones	4.50	13.50	50.00
501-Francis the Famous Talking Mule	3.60	11.00	40.00
502-Rootie Kazootie (TV)	6.40	19.00	70.00
503-Uncle Wiggily (10/53)	3.60	11.00	40.00
504-Krazy Kat; not by Herriman	3.00	9.00	35.00
505-The Sword and the Rose (Disney) (10/53)(Movie)-Photo-c	8.00	25.00	90.00
506-The Little Scouts	1.35	4.00	15.00
507-Oswald the Rabbit (Lantz)	2.75	8.00	30.00
508-Bozo (10/53)	8.00	25.00	90.00
509-Pluto (Disney) (10/53)	4.50	13.50	50.00
510-Son of Black Beauty	2.75	8.00	30.00
511-Outlaw Trail (Zane Grey)-Kinstler-a	3.60	11.00	40.00
512-Flash Gordon (11/53)	4.50	13.50	50.00
513-Ben Bowie and His Mountain Men	2.75	8.00	30.00
514-Frosty the Snowman (11/53)	3.60	11.00	40.00
515-Andy Hardy	2.25	6.75	25.00
516-Double Trouble With Goober	1.85	5.50	15.00
517-Chip 'N' Dale (#1) (Disney)	7.00	22.00	80.00
518-Rivets (11/53)	2.25	6.75	25.00
519-Steve Canyon (#1)-Not by Milton Caniff	8.00	25.00	90.00
520-Wild Bill Elliott-Photo-c	3.60	11.00	40.00
521-Beetle Bailey (12/53)	4.50	13.50	50.00
522-The Brownies	3.00	9.00	32.00
523-Rin Tin Tin (TV)-Photo-c (12/53)	7.00	22.00	80.00
524-Tweety and Sylvester	3.00	9.00	35.00
525-Santa Claus Funnies	3.60	11.00	40.00
526-Napoleon	1.80	5.50	20.00
527-Charlie McCarthy	4.50	13.50	50.00
528-Queen of the West Dale Evans; photo-c	9.00	27.00	100.00
529-Little Beaver	2.75	8.00	30.00
530-Bob Clampett's Beany and Cecil (TV) (1/54)	16.00	51.00	170.00
531-Duck Album (Disney)	4.50	13.50	50.00
532-The Rustlers (Zane Grey) (2-4/54)	2.75	8.00	30.00
533-Raggedy Ann and Andy	4.50	13.50	50.00
534-Western Marshal(Ernest Haycox's)-Kinstler-a	4.50	13.50	50.00
535-I Love Lucy (#1) (TV) (2/54)-Photo-c	48.00	143.00	525.00
536-Daffy (3/54)	4.00	12.00	45.00
537-Stormy, the Thoroughbred... (Disney-Movie) on top 2/3 of each page; Pluto story on bottom 1/3 of each page (2/54)	2.75	8.00	30.00
538-The Mask of Zorro; Kinstler-a	12.00	37.00	135.00
539-Ben and Me (Disney) (3/54)	3.00	9.00	32.00
540-Knights of the Round Table (3/54) (Movie)-Photo-c	6.40	19.00	70.00
541-Johnny Mack Brown; photo-c	5.50	16.50	60.00
542-Super Circus Featuring Mary Hartline (TV) (3/54)	6.40	19.00	70.00
543-Uncle Wiggily (3/54)	3.60	11.00	40.00
544-Rob Roy (Disney-Movie)-Manning-a; photo-c	7.00	22.00	80.00
545-The Wonderful Adventures of Pinocchio-Partial reprint of 4-Color #92 (Disney-Movie)	6.40	19.00	70.00
546-Buck Jones	4.50	13.50	50.00
547-Francis the Famous Talking Mule	3.60	11.00	40.00
548-Krazy Kat; not by Herriman (4/54)	2.75	8.00	30.00
549-Oswald the Rabbit (Lantz)	2.75	8.00	30.00
550-The Little Scouts	1.35	4.00	15.00
551-Bozo (4/54)	8.00	25.00	90.00
552-Beetle Bailey	4.50	13.50	50.00
553-Susie Q. Smith	2.75	8.00	30.00

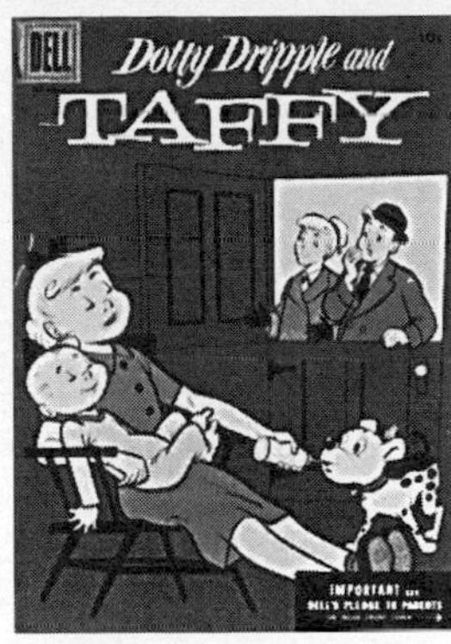

Four Color #646 © ME

Four Color #648 © DELL

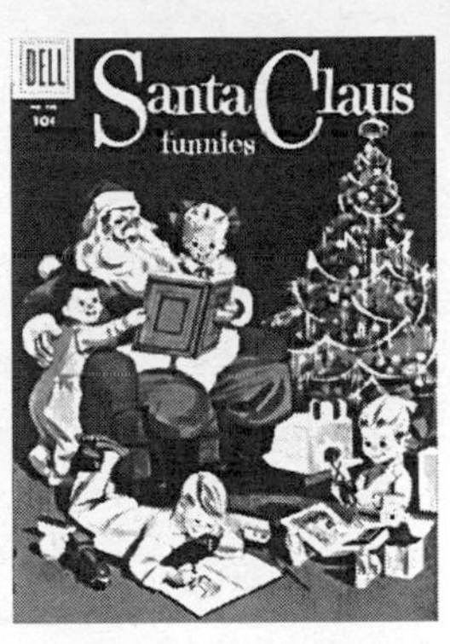

Four Color #666 © WHIT

	GD25	FN65	NM94
554-Rusty Riley (Frank Godwin strip-r)	2.75	8.00	30.00
555-Range War (Zane Grey)	2.75	8.00	30.00
556-Double Trouble With Goober (5/54)	1.85	5.50	15.00
557-Ben Bowie and His Mountain Men	2.75	8.00	30.00
558-Elmer Fudd (5/54)	2.75	8.00	30.00
559-I Love Lucy (#2) (TV)-Photo-c	30.00	89.00	325.00
560-Duck Album (Disney) (5/54)	4.50	13.50	50.00
561-Mr. Magoo (5/54)	11.00	33.00	120.00
562-Goofy (Disney)(#2)	6.40	19.00	70.00
563-Rhubarb, the Millionaire Cat (6/54)	3.60	11.00	40.00
564-Li'l Bad Wolf (Disney)(#3)	3.60	11.00	40.00
565-Jungle Jim	2.75	8.00	30.00
566-Son of Black Beauty	2.75	8.00	30.00
567-Prince Valiant (#1)-By Bob Fuje (Movie)-Photo-c	10.00	30.00	110.00
568-Gypsy Colt (Movie) (6/54)	3.60	11.00	40.00
569-Priscilla's Pop	2.75	8.00	30.00
570-Bob Clampett's Beany and Cecil (TV)	16.00	47.00	170.00
571-Charlie McCarthy	4.50	13.50	50.00
572-Silvertip (Max Brand) (7/54); Kinstler-a	3.60	11.00	40.00
573-The Little People by Walt Scott	3.00	9.00	35.00
574-The Hand of Zorro; Kinstler-a	12.00	38.00	135.00
575-Annie Oakley and Tagg (TV)-Photo-c	8.00	23.00	85.00
576-Angel (#1) (8/54)	2.25	6.75	25.00
577-M.G.M.'s Spike and Tyke	1.80	5.50	20.00
578-Steve Canyon (8/54)	4.50	13.50	50.00
579-Francis the Famous Talking Mule	3.60	11.00	40.00
580-Six Gun Ranch (Luke Short-8/54)	2.75	8.00	30.00
581-Chip 'N' Dale (#2) (Disney)	4.50	13.50	50.00
582-Mowgli Jungle Book (Kipling) (8/54)	3.60	11.00	40.00
583-The Lost Wagon Train (Zane Grey)	2.75	8.00	30.00
584-Johnny Mack Brown-Photo-c	5.50	16.50	60.00
585-Bugs Bunny's Album	4.50	13.50	50.00
586-Duck Album (Disney)	4.50	13.50	50.00
587-The Little Scouts	1.35	4.00	15.00
588-King Richard and the Crusaders (Movie) (10/54) Matt Baker-a; photo-c	9.00	27.00	100.00
589-Buck Jones	4.50	13.50	50.00
590-Hansel and Gretel; partial photo-c	5.50	16.50	60.00
591-Western Marshal(Ernest Haycox's)-Kinstler-a	4.50	13.50	50.00
592-Super Circus (TV)	5.50	16.50	60.00
593-Oswald the Rabbit (Lantz)	2.75	8.00	30.00
594-Bozo (10/54)	8.00	25.00	90.00
595-Pluto (Disney)	2.75	8.00	30.00
596-Turok, Son of Stone (#1)	57.00	170.00	625.00
597-The Little King	4.50	13.50	50.00
598-Captain Davy Jones	3.60	11.00	40.00
599-Ben Bowie and His Mountain Men	2.75	8.00	30.00
600-Daisy Duck's Diary (#1) (Disney) (11/54)	5.50	16.50	60.00
601-Frosty the Snowman	3.60	11.00	40.00
602-Mr. Magoo and Gerald McBoing-Boing	11.00	33.00	120.00
603-M.G.M.'s The Two Mouseketeers	3.60	11.00	40.00
604-Shadow on the Trail (Zane Grey)	2.75	8.00	30.00
605-The Brownies-not by Kelly (12/54)	3.00	9.00	32.00
606-Sir Lancelot (not TV)	6.40	19.00	70.00
607-Santa Claus Funnies	3.60	11.00	40.00
608-Silvertip- "Valley of Vanishing Men" (Max Brand)-Kinstler-a	3.60	11.00	40.00
609-The Littlest Outlaw (Disney-Movie) (1/55)-Photo-c	5.50	16.50	60.00
610-Drum Beat (Movie); Alan Ladd photo-c	9.00	27.00	100.00
611-Duck Album (Disney)	4.50	13.50	50.00
612-Little Beaver (1/55)	2.75	8.00	30.00
613-Western Marshal (Ernest Haycox's) (2/55)-Kinstler-a	4.50	13.50	50.00
614-20,000 Leagues Under the Sea (Disney) (Movie) (2/55)-Painted-c	9.00	27.00	100.00
615-Daffy	4.00	12.00	45.00
616-To the Last Man (Zane Grey)	2.75	8.00	30.00
617-The Quest of Zorro	11.00	34.00	125.00
618-Johnny Mack Brown; photo-c	5.50	16.50	60.00
619-Krazy Kat; not by Herriman	2.75	8.00	30.00
620-Mowgli Jungle Book (Kipling)	3.60	11.00	40.00
621-Francis the Famous Talking Mule (4/55)	2.75	8.00	30.00
622-Beetle Bailey	4.50	13.50	50.00
623-Oswald the Rabbit (Lantz)	1.80	5.50	20.00
624-Treasure Island(Disney-Movie)(4/55)-Photo-c	9.00	27.00	90.00
625-Beaver Valley (Disney-Movie)	5.50	16.50	60.00
626-Ben Bowie and His Mountain Men	2.75	8.00	30.00
627-Goofy (Disney) (5/55)	6.40	19.00	70.00
628-Elmer Fudd	2.75	8.00	30.00
629-Lady and the Tramp with Jock (Disney)	5.50	16.50	60.00
630-Priscilla's Pop	2.75	8.00	30.00
631-Davy Crockett, Indian Fighter (#1) (Disney) (5/55) (TV)-Fess Parker photo-c	16.00	48.00	175.00
632-Fighting Caravans (Zane Grey)	2.75	8.00	30.00
633-The Little People by Walt Scott (6/55)	3.00	9.00	35.00
634-Lady and the Tramp Album (Disney) (6/55)	3.65	11.00	40.00
635-Bob Clampett's Beany and Cecil (TV)	16.00	47.00	170.00
636-Chip 'N' Dale (Disney)	4.50	13.50	50.00
637-Silvertip (Max Brand)-Kinstler-a	3.60	11.00	40.00
638-M.G.M.'s Spike and Tyke (8/55)	1.80	5.50	20.00
639-Davy Crockett at the Alamo (Disney) (7/55) (TV)-Fess Parker photo-c	13.00	38.00	140.00
640-Western Marshal(Ernest Haycox's)-Kinstler-a	4.50	13.50	50.00
641-Steve Canyon (1955)-by Caniff	4.50	13.50	50.00
642-M.G.M.'s The Two Mouseketeers	3.60	11.00	40.00
643-Wild Bill Elliott; photo-c	2.75	8.00	30.00
644-Sir Walter Raleigh (5/55)-Based on movie "The Virgin Queen"; photo-c	5.50	16.50	60.00
645-Johnny Mack Brown; photo-c	5.50	16.50	60.00
646-Dotty Dripple and Taffy (#1)	2.75	8.00	30.00
647-Bugs Bunny's Album (9/55)	4.50	13.50	50.00
648-Jace Pearson of the Texas Rangers (TV)-Photo-c	4.50	13.50	50.00
649-Duck Album (Disney)	4.50	13.50	50.00
650-Prince Valiant; by Bob Fuje	5.50	16.50	60.00
651-King Colt (Luke Short) (9/55)-Kinstler-a	2.75	8.00	30.00
652-Buck Jones	2.75	8.00	30.00
653-Smokey the Bear (#1) (10/55)	9.00	27.00	100.00
654-Pluto (Disney)	2.75	8.00	30.00
655-Francis the Famous Talking Mule	2.75	8.00	30.00
656-Turok, Son of Stone (#2) (10/55)	34.00	102.00	375.00
657-Ben Bowie and His Mountain Men	2.75	8.00	30.00
658-Goofy (Disney)	6.40	19.00	70.00
659-Daisy Duck's Diary (Disney)(#2)	4.50	13.50	50.00
660-Little Beaver	2.75	8.00	30.00
661-Frosty the Snowman	3.60	11.00	40.00
662-Zoo Parade (TV)-Marlin Perkins (11/55)	4.00	12.00	45.00
663-Winky Dink (TV)	7.00	22.00	80.00
664-Davy Crockett in the Great Keelboat Race (TV) (Disney) (11/55)-Fess Parker photo-c	12.00	35.00	130.00
665-The African Lion (Disney-Movie) (11/55)	4.50	13.50	50.00
666-Santa Claus Funnies	3.60	11.00	40.00
667-Silvertip and the Stolen Stallion (Max Brand) (12/55)-Kinstler-a	3.60	11.00	40.00
668-Dumbo (Disney) (12/55)-First of two printings. Dumbo on cover with starry sky. Reprints 4-Color #234?; same-c as #234	7.00	22.00	80.00

Four Color #719 © KFS

Four Color #732 © Grosset & Dunlap

Four Color #749 © WDC

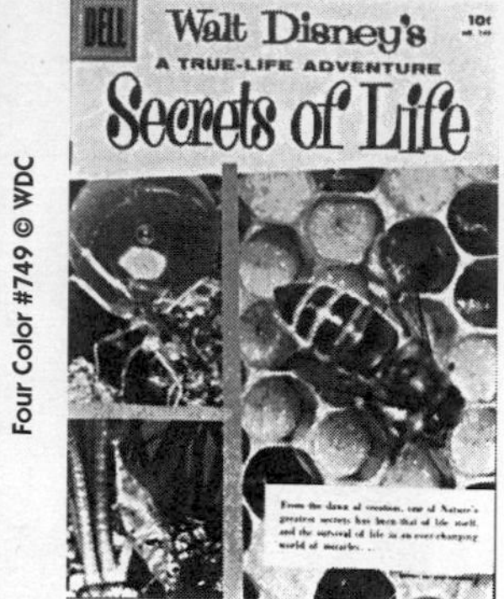

	GD25	FN65	NM94
668-Dumbo (Disney) (1/58)-Second printing. Same cover altered, with Timothy Mouse added. Same contents as above	5.50	16.50	60.00
669-Robin Hood (Disney-Movie) (12/55)-Reprints #413 plus-c; photo-c	4.50	13.50	50.00
670-M.G.M's Mouse Musketeers (#1) (1/56)-Formerly the Two Mouseketeers	2.75	8.00	30.00
671-Davy Crockett and the River Pirates (TV) (Disney) (12/55)-Jesse Marsh-a; Fess Parker photo-c	12.00	35.00	130.00
672-Quentin Durward (1/56) (Movie)-Photo-c	5.50	16.50	60.00
673-Buffalo Bill, Jr. (#1) (TV)-James Arness photo-c	5.75	17.00	63.00
674-The Little Rascals (#1) (TV)	6.40	19.00	70.00
675-Steve Donovan, Western Marshal (#1) (TV)-Kinstler-a; photo-c	7.00	22.00	80.00
676-Will-Yum!	1.80	5.50	20.00
677-Little King	4.50	13.50	50.00
678-The Last Hunt (Movie)-Photo-c	6.40	19.00	70.00
679-Gunsmoke (#1) (TV)-Photo-c	14.00	41.00	150.00
680-Out Our Way with the Worry Wart (2/56)	1.80	5.50	20.00
681-Forever Darling (Movie) with Lucille Ball & Desi Arnaz (2/56)-; photo-c	10.00	30.00	110.00
682-When Knighthood Was in Flower (Disney-Movie)-Reprint of #505; Renamed the Sword & the Rose for the novel; photo-c	6.40	19.00	70.00
683-Hi and Lois (3/56)	2.25	6.75	25.00
684-Helen of Troy (Movie)-Buscema-a; photo-c	10.00	30.00	110.00
685-Johnny Mack Brown; photo-c	5.50	16.50	60.00
686-Duck Album (Disney)	4.50	13.50	50.00
687-The Indian Fighter (Movie)-Kirk Douglas photo-c	7.00	22.00	80.00
688-Alexander the Great (Movie) (5/56)-Buscema-a; photo-c	6.00	19.00	68.00
689-Elmer Fudd (3/56)	2.75	8.00	30.00
690-The Conqueror (Movie) - John Wayne photo-c	14.00	44.00	160.00
691-Dotty Dripple and Taffy	1.80	5.50	20.00
692-The Little People-Walt Scott	3.00	9.00	35.00
693-Song of the South (Disney) (1956)-Partial reprint of #129	8.00	25.00	90.00
694-Super Circus (TV)-Photo-c	5.50	16.50	60.00
695-Little Beaver	2.75	8.00	30.00
696-Krazy Kat; not by Herriman (4/56)	2.75	8.00	30.00
697-Oswald the Rabbit (Lantz)	1.80	5.50	20.00
698-Francis the Famous Talking Mule (4/56)	2.75	8.00	30.00
699-Prince Valiant-by Bob Fuje	5.50	16.50	60.00
700-Water Birds and the Olympic Elk (Disney-Movie) (4/56)	4.50	13.50	50.00
701-Jiminy Cricket (#1) (Disney) (5/56)	8.00	25.00	90.00
702-The Goofy Success Story (Disney)	6.40	19.00	70.00
703-Scamp (#1) (Disney)	8.00	25.00	90.00
704-Priscilla's Pop (5/56)	2.75	8.00	30.00
705-Brave Eagle (#1) (TV)-Photo-c	5.50	16.50	60.00
706-Bongo and Lumpjaw (Disney) (6/56)	4.00	12.00	45.00
707-Corky and White Shadow (Disney) (5/56)-Mickey Mouse Club (TV); photo-c	6.40	19.00	70.00
708-Smokey the Bear	4.50	13.50	50.00
709-The Searchers (Movie) - John Wayne photo-c	24.00	71.00	260.00
710-Francis the Famous Talking Mule	2.75	8.00	30.00
711-M.G.M's Mouse Musketeers	1.80	5.50	20.00
712-The Great Locomotive Chase (Disney-Movie) (9/56)-Photo-c	6.40	19.00	70.00
713-The Animal World (Movie) (8/56)	2.75	8.00	30.00
714-Spin and Marty (#1) (TV) (Disney)-Mickey Mouse Club (6/56); photo-c	10.00	30.00	110.00
715-Timmy (8/56)	2.75	8.00	30.00
716-Man in Space (Disney)(A science feature from Tomorrowland)	8.00	25.00	90.00
717-Moby Dick (Movie)-Gregory Peck photo-c	8.00	25.00	90.00

	GD25	FN65	NM94
718-Dotty Dripple and Taffy	1.80	5.50	20.00
719-Prince Valiant; by Bob Fuje (8/56)	5.50	16.50	60.00
720-Gunsmoke (TV)-James Arness photo-c	6.40	19.00	70.00
721-Captain Kangaroo (TV)-Photo-c	13.00	40.00	145.00
722-Johnny Mack Brown-Photo-c	5.50	16.50	60.00
723-Santiago (Movie)-Kinstler-a (9/56); Alan Ladd photo-c	10.00	30.00	110.00
724-Bugs Bunny's Album	3.60	11.00	40.00
725-Elmer Fudd (9/56)	1.80	5.50	20.00
726-Duck Album (Disney) (9/56)	4.50	13.50	50.00
727-The Nature of Things (TV) (Disney)-Jesse Marsh-a	4.50	13.50	50.00
728-M.G.M's Mouse Musketeers	1.80	5.50	20.00
729-Bob Son of Battle (11/56)	2.75	8.00	30.00
730-Smokey Stover	3.50	11.00	38.00
731-Silvertip and The Fighting Four (Max Brand)-Kinstler-a	3.60	11.00	40.00
732-Zorro, the Challenge of (10/56)	11.00	34.00	125.00
733-Buck Jones	2.75	8.00	30.00
734-Cheyenne (#1) (TV) (10/56)-Clint Walker photo-c	16.00	47.00	170.00
735-Crusader Rabbit (#1) (TV)	30.00	89.00	325.00
736-Pluto (Disney)	2.75	8.00	30.00
737-Steve Canyon-Caniff-a	4.50	13.50	50.00
738-Westward Ho, the Wagons (Disney-Movie)-Fess Parker photo-c	7.00	22.00	80.00
739-Bounty Guns (Luke Short)-Drucker-a	2.75	8.00	30.00
740-Chilly Willy (#1) (Walter Lantz)	3.60	11.00	40.00
741-The Fastest Gun Alive (Movie)(9/56)-Photo-c	6.40	19.00	70.00
742-Buffalo Bill, Jr. (TV)-Photo-c	4.00	12.00	45.00
743-Daisy Duck's Diary (Disney) (11/56)	4.50	13.50	50.00
744-Little Beaver	2.75	8.00	30.00
745-Francis the Famous Talking Mule	2.75	8.00	30.00
746-Dotty Dripple and Taffy	1.80	5.50	20.00
747-Goofy (Disney)	6.40	19.00	70.00
748-Frosty the Snowman (11/56)	3.00	9.00	35.00
749-Secrets of Life (Disney-Movie)-Photo-c	3.60	11.00	40.00
750-The Great Cat Family (Disney-TV/Movie)-Pinocchio & Alice app.	5.50	16.50	60.00
751-Our Miss Brooks (TV)-Photo-c	7.00	22.00	80.00
752-Mandrake, the Magician	9.00	27.00	100.00
753-Walt Scott's Little People (11/56)	3.00	9.00	35.00
754-Smokey the Bear	4.50	13.50	50.00
755-The Littlest Snowman (12/56)	3.00	10.00	36.00
756-Santa Claus Funnies	3.60	11.00	40.00
757-The True Story of Jesse James (Movie)-Photo-c	9.00	27.00	100.00
758-Bear Country (Disney-Movie)	4.50	13.50	50.00
759-Circus Boy (TV)-The Monkees' Mickey Dolenz photo-c (12/56)	10.00	30.00	110.00
760-The Hardy Boys (#1) (TV) (Disney)-Mickey Mouse Club; photo-c	10.00	30.00	110.00
761-Howdy Doody (TV) (1/57)	9.00	26.00	95.00
762-The Sharkfighters (Movie) (1/57); Buscema-a; photo-c	7.00	22.00	80.00
763-Grandma Duck's Farm Friends (#1) (Disney)	6.40	19.00	70.00
764-M.G.M's Mouse Musketeers	1.80	5.50	20.00
765-Will-Yum!	1.80	5.50	20.00
766-Buffalo Bill, Jr. (TV)-Photo-c	4.00	12.00	45.00
767-Spin and Marty (TV) (Disney)-Mickey Mouse Club (2/57)	9.00	27.00	100.00
768-Steve Donovan, Western Marshal (TV)-Kinstler-a; photo-c	5.50	16.50	60.00
769-Gunsmoke (TV)-James Arness photo-c	6.40	19.00	70.00

Four Color #796 © DELL

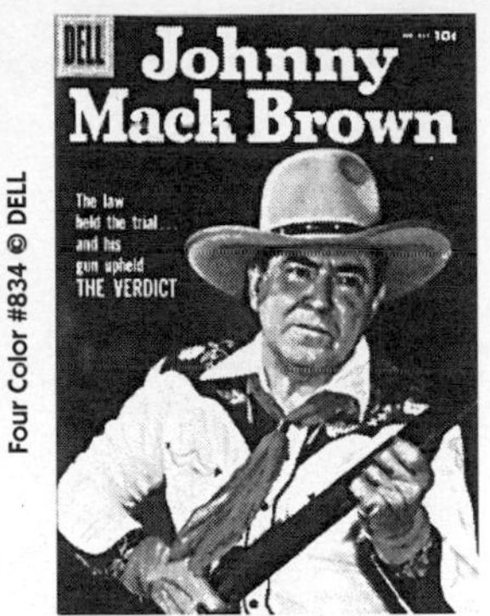

Four Color #834 © DELL

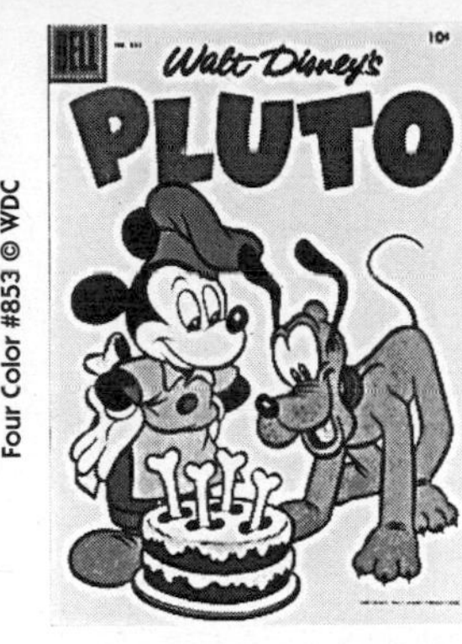

Four Color #853 © WDC

	GD25	FN65	NM94
770-Brave Eagle (TV)-Photo-c	2.75	8.00	30.00
771-Brand of Empire (Luke Short)(3/57)-Drucker-a	2.75	8.00	30.00
772-Cheyenne (TV)-Clint Walker photo-c	7.00	20.00	75.00
773-The Brave One (Movie)-Photo-c	4.50	13.50	50.00
774-Hi and Lois (3/57)	1.80	5.50	20.00
775-Sir Lancelot and Brian (TV)-Buscema-a; photo-c	7.00	22.00	80.00
776-Johnny Mack Brown; photo-c	5.50	16.50	60.00
777-Scamp (Disney) (3/57)	5.50	16.50	60.00
778-The Little Rascals (TV)	3.60	11.00	40.00
779-Lee Hunter, Indian Fighter (3/57)	3.60	11.00	40.00
780-Captain Kangaroo (TV)-Photo-c	11.00	34.00	125.00
781-Fury (#1) (TV) (3/57)-Photo-c	7.00	22.00	80.00
782-Duck Album (Disney)	4.50	13.50	50.00
783-Elmer Fudd	1.80	5.50	20.00
784-Around the World in 80 Days (Movie) (2/57)-Photo-c	5.75	17.00	63.00
785-Circus Boy (TV) (4/57)-The Monkees' Mickey Dolenz photo-c	10.00	30.00	110.00
786-Cinderella (Disney) (3/57)-Partial-r of #272	5.50	16.50	60.00
787-Little Hiawatha (Disney) (4/57)(#2)	3.60	11.00	40.00
788-Prince Valiant; by Bob Fuje	5.50	16.50	60.00
789-Silvertip-Valley Thieves (Max Brand) (4/57)-Kinstler-a	3.60	11.00	40.00
790-The Wings of Eagles (Movie) (John Wayne)-Toth-a; John Wayne photo-c; 10 & 15¢ editions exist	14.00	44.00	160.00
791-The 77th Bengal Lancers (TV)-Photo-c	6.40	19.00	70.00
792-Oswald the Rabbit (Lantz)	1.80	5.50	20.00
793-Morty Meekle	1.80	5.50	20.00
794-The Count of Monte Cristo (5/57) (Movie)-Buscema-a	8.00	25.00	90.00
795-Jiminy Cricket (Disney)(#2)	5.50	16.50	60.00
796-Ludwig Bemelman's Madeleine and Genevieve	2.75	8.00	30.00
797-Gunsmoke (TV)-Photo-c	6.40	19.00	70.00
798-Buffalo Bill, Jr. (TV)-Photo-c	4.00	12.00	45.00
799-Priscilla's Pop	2.75	8.00	30.00
800-The Buccaneers (TV)-Photo-c	6.40	19.00	70.00
801-Dotty Dripple and Taffy	1.80	5.50	20.00
802-Goofy (Disney) (5/57)	6.40	19.00	70.00
803-Cheyenne (TV)-Clint Walker photo-c	7.00	20.00	75.00
804-Steve Canyon-Caniff-a (1957)	4.50	13.50	50.00
805-Crusader Rabbit (TV)	23.00	68.00	250.00
806-Scamp (Disney) (6/57)	5.50	16.50	60.00
807-Savage Range (Luke Short)-Drucker-a	2.75	8.00	30.00
808-Spin and Marty (TV)(Disney)-Mickey Mouse Club; photo-c	9.00	27.00	100.00
809-The Little People (Walt Scott)	3.00	9.00	35.00
810-Francis the Famous Talking Mule	2.25	6.75	25.00
811-Howdy Doody (TV) (7/57)	9.00	26.00	95.00
812-The Big Land (Movie); Alan Ladd photo-c	9.00	27.00	100.00
813-Circus Boy (TV)-The Monkees' Mickey Dolenz photo-c	10.00	30.00	110.00
814-Covered Wagons, Ho! (Disney)-Donald Duck (TV) (6/57); Mickey Mouse app.	4.50	13.50	50.00
815-Dragoon Wells Massacre (Movie)-photo-c	7.00	22.00	80.00
816-Brave Eagle (TV)-photo-c	2.75	8.00	30.00
817-Little Beaver	2.75	8.00	30.00
818-Smokey the Bear (6/57)	4.50	13.50	50.00
819-Mickey Mouse in Magicland (Disney) (7/57)	3.00	9.00	35.00
820-The Oklahoman (Movie)-Photo-c	9.00	27.00	100.00
821-Wringle Wrangle (Disney)-Based on movie "Westward Ho, the Wagons"; Marsh-a; Fess Parker photo-c	7.00	22.00	80.00
822-Paul Revere's Ride with Johnny Tremain (TV) (Disney)-Toth-a	9.00	27.00	100.00
823-Timmy	1.80	5.50	20.00
824-The Pride and the Passion (Movie) (8/57)-Frank Sinatra & Cary Grant photo-c	8.00	25.00	90.00
825-The Little Rascals (TV)	3.60	11.00	40.00
826-Spin and Marty and Annette (TV) (Disney)-Mickey Mouse Club; Annette Funicello photo-c	23.00	68.00	250.00
827-Smokey Stover (8/57)	3.50	11.00	38.00
828-Buffalo Bill, Jr. (TV)-Photo-c	4.00	12.00	45.00
829-Tales of the Pony Express (TV) (8/57)-Painted-c	3.60	11.00	40.00
830-The Hardy Boys (TV) (Disney)-Mickey Mouse Club (8/57); photo-c	9.00	27.00	100.00
831-No Sleep 'Til Dawn (Movie)-Karl Malden photo-c	5.50	16.50	60.00
832-Lolly and Pepper (#1)	2.75	8.00	30.00
833-Scamp (Disney) (9/57)	5.50	16.50	60.00
834-Johnny Mack Brown; photo-c	5.50	16.50	60.00
835-Silvertip-The False Rider (Max Brand)	3.60	11.00	40.00
836-Man in Flight (Disney) (TV) (9/57)	6.40	19.00	70.00
837-All-American Athlete Cotton Woods	2.75	8.00	30.00
838-Bugs Bunny's Life Story Album (9/57)	3.60	11.00	40.00
839-The Vigilantes (Movie)	6.40	19.00	70.00
840-Duck Album (Disney) (9/57)	4.50	13.50	50.00
841-Elmer Fudd	1.80	5.50	20.00
842-The Nature of Things (Disney-Movie) ('57)-Jesse Marsh-a (TV series)	4.50	13.50	50.00
843-The First Americans (Disney) (TV)-Marsh-a	8.00	25.00	90.00
844-Gunsmoke (TV)-Photo-c	6.40	19.00	70.00
845-The Land Unknown (Movie)-Alex Toth-a	11.00	34.00	125.00
846-Gun Glory (Movie)-by Alex Toth; photo-c	9.00	27.00	100.00
847-Perri (squirrels) (Disney-Movie)-Two different covers published	4.50	13.50	50.00
848-Marauder's Moon (Luke Short)	3.60	11.00	40.00
849-Prince Valiant; by Bob Fuje	5.50	16.50	60.00
850-Buck Jones	2.75	8.00	30.00
851-The Story of Mankind (Movie) (1/58)-Hedy Lamarr & Vincent Price photo-c	6.40	19.00	70.00
852-Chilly Willy (2/58) (Lantz)	2.75	8.00	30.00
853-Pluto (Disney) (10/57)	2.75	8.00	30.00
854-The Hunchback of Notre Dame (Movie)-Photo-c	12.00	35.00	130.00
855-Broken Arrow (TV)-Photo-c	5.00	15.00	54.00
856-Buffalo Bill, Jr. (TV)-Photo-c	4.00	12.00	45.00
857-The Goofy Adventure Story (Disney) (11/57)	6.40	19.00	70.00
858-Daisy Duck's Diary (Disney) (11/57)	3.60	11.00	40.00
859-Topper and Neil (TV) (11/57)	3.60	11.00	40.00
860-Wyatt Earp (#1) (TV)-Manning-a; photo-c	10.00	30.00	110.00
861-Frosty the Snowman	3.00	9.00	35.00
862-The Truth About Mother Goose (Disney-Movie) (11/57)	6.40	19.00	70.00
863-Francis the Famous Talking Mule	2.25	6.75	25.00
864-The Littlest Snowman	3.00	10.00	36.00
865-Andy Burnett (TV) (Disney) (12/57)-Photo-c	9.00	27.00	100.00
866-Mars and Beyond (Disney-TV)(A science feature from Tomorrowland)	8.00	25.00	90.00
867-Santa Claus Funnies	3.60	11.00	40.00
868-The Little People (12/57)	3.00	9.00	35.00
869-Old Yeller (Disney-Movie)-Photo-c	4.50	13.50	50.00
870-Little Beaver (1/58)	2.75	8.00	30.00
871-Curly Kayoe	1.80	5.50	20.00
872-Captain Kangaroo (TV)-Photo-c	11.00	34.00	125.00
873-Grandma Duck's Farm Friends (Disney)	4.50	13.50	50.00
874-Old Ironsides (Disney-Movie with Johnny Tremain) (1/58)	5.50	16.50	60.00
875-Trumpets West (Luke Short) (2/58)	2.75	8.00	30.00
876-Tales of Wells Fargo (#1)(TV)(2/58)-Photo-c	9.00	27.00	100.00
877-Frontier Doctor with Rex Allen (TV)-Alex Toth-a; Rex Allen photo-c			

Four Color #918 © Warner Bros.

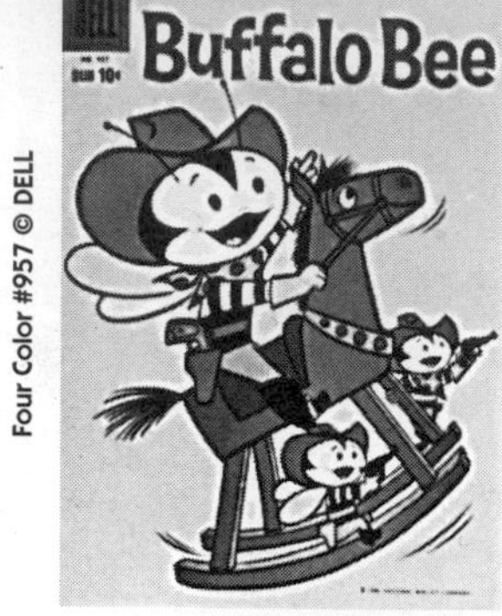

Four Color #957 © DELL

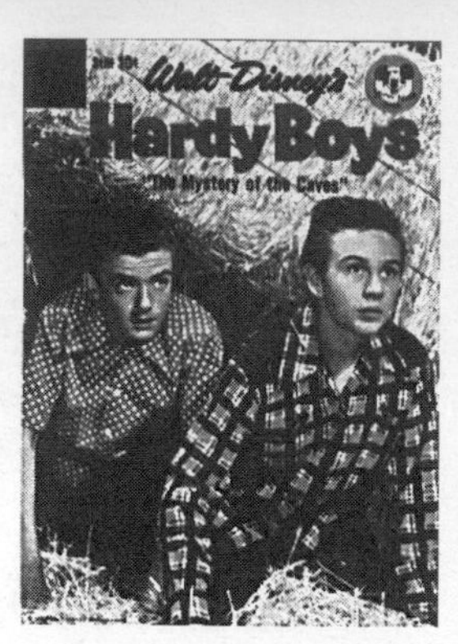

Walt Disney's
Hardy Boys
"The Mystery of the Caves"

Four Color #964 © WDC

	GD25	FN65	NM94
	9.00	27.00	100.00
878-Peanuts (#1)-Schulz-c only (2/58)	14.00	41.00	150.00
879-Brave Eagle (TV) (2/58)-Photo-c	2.75	8.00	30.00
880-Steve Donovan, Western Marshal-Drucker-a (TV)-Photo-c	3.60	11.00	40.00
881-The Captain and the Kids (2/58)	2.75	8.00	30.00
882-Zorro (Disney)-1st Disney issue; by Alex Toth (TV) (2/58); photo-c	16.00	49.00	180.00
883-The Little Rascals (TV)	3.60	11.00	40.00
884-Hawkeye and the Last of the Mohicans (TV) (3/58); photo-c	6.40	19.00	70.00
885-Fury (TV) (3/58)-Photo-c	5.50	16.50	60.00
886-Bongo and Lumpjaw (Disney) (3/58)	3.00	9.00	35.00
887-The Hardy Boys (Disney) (TV)-Mickey Mouse Club (1/58)-Photo-c	9.00	27.00	100.00
888-Elmer Fudd (3/58)	1.80	5.50	20.00
889-Clint and Mac (Disney) (TV) (3/58)-Alex Toth-a; photo-c	12.00	35.00	130.00
890-Wyatt Earp (TV)-by Russ Manning; photo-c	7.00	20.00	75.00
891-Light in the Forest (Disney-Movie) (3/58)-Fess Parker photo-c	7.30	22.00	80.00
892-Maverick (#1) (TV) (4/58)-James Garner photo-c	25.00	75.00	275.00
893-Jim Bowie (TV)-Photo-c	4.50	13.50	50.00
894-Oswald the Rabbit (Lantz)	1.80	5.50	20.00
895-Wagon Train (#1) (TV) (3/58)-Photo-c	11.00	33.00	120.00
896-The Adventures of Tinker Bell (Disney)	7.00	22.00	80.00
897-Jiminy Cricket (Disney)	5.50	16.50	60.00
898-Silvertip (Max Brand)-Kinstler-a (5/58)	3.60	11.00	40.00
899-Goofy (Disney) (5/58)	3.60	11.00	40.00
900-Prince Valiant; by Bob Fuje	5.50	16.50	60.00
901-Little Hiawatha (Disney)	3.60	11.00	40.00
902-Will-Yum!	1.80	5.50	20.00
903-Dotty Dripple and Taffy	1.80	5.50	20.00
904-Lee Hunter, Indian Fighter	2.75	8.00	30.00
905-Annette (Disney) (TV) (5/58)-Mickey Mouse Club; Annette Funicello photo-c	26.00	77.00	280.00
906-Francis the Famous Talking Mule	2.25	6.75	25.00
907-Sugarfoot (#1) (TV)Toth-a; photo-c	12.00	37.00	135.00
908-The Little People and the Giant-Walt Scott (5/58)	3.00	9.00	35.00
909-Smitty	1.80	5.50	20.00
910-The Vikings (Movie)-Buscema-a; Kirk Douglas photo-c	8.00	25.00	90.00
911-The Gray Ghost (TV)-Photo-c	8.00	25.00	90.00
912-Leave It to Beaver (#1) (TV)-Photo-c	17.00	52.00	190.00
913-The Left-Handed Gun (Movie) (7/58); Paul Newman photo-c	10.00	30.00	110.00
914-No Time for Sergeants (Movie)-Andy Griffith photo-c; Toth-a	9.00	27.00	100.00
915-Casey Jones (TV)-Alan Hale photo-c	4.50	13.50	50.00
916-Red Ryder Ranch Comics (7/58)	2.75	8.00	30.00
917-The Life of Riley (TV)-Photo-c	11.00	33.00	120.00
918-Beep Beep, the Roadrunner (#1) (7/58)-Published with two different back covers	8.00	25.00	90.00
919-Boots and Saddles (#1) (TV)-Photo-c	7.00	22.00	80.00
920-Zorro (Disney) (TV) (6/58)Toth-a; photo-c	11.00	34.00	125.00
921-Wyatt Earp (TV)-Manning-a; photo-c	7.00	20.00	75.00
922-Johnny Mack Brown by Russ Manning; photo-c	6.40	19.00	70.00
923-Timmy	1.80	5.50	20.00
924-Colt .45 (#1) (TV) (8/58)-W. Preston photo-c	9.00	27.00	100.00
925-Last of the Fast Guns (Movie) (8/58)-Photo-c	6.40	19.00	70.00
926-Peter Pan (Disney)-Reprint of #442	3.60	11.00	40.00
927-Top Gun (Luke Short) Buscema-a	2.75	8.00	30.00
928-Sea Hunt (#1) (9/58) (TV)-Lloyd Bridges photo-c	11.00	33.00	120.00
929-Brave Eagle (TV)-Photo-c	2.75	8.00	30.00
930-Maverick (TV) (7/58)-James Garner photo-c	10.00	30.00	110.00
931-Have Gun, Will Travel (#1) (TV)-Photo-c	13.00	38.00	140.00
932-Smokey the Bear (His Life Story)	4.50	13.50	50.00
933-Zorro (Disney, 9/58) (TV)-Alex Toth-a; photo-c	11.00	34.00	125.00
934-Restless Gun (#1) (TV)-Photo-c	10.00	30.00	110.00
935-King of the Royal Mounted	2.75	8.00	30.00
936-The Little Rascals (TV)	3.60	11.00	40.00
937-Ruff and Reddy (#1) (9/58) (TV) (1st Hanna-Barbera comic book)	11.00	33.00	120.00
938-Elmer Fudd (9/58)	1.80	5.50	20.00
939-Steve Canyon - not by Caniff	4.50	13.50	50.00
940-Lolly and Pepper (10/58)	1.80	5.50	20.00
941-Pluto (Disney) (10/58)	2.75	8.00	30.00
942-Pony Express (TV)	3.60	11.00	40.00
943-White Wilderness (Disney-Movie) (10/58)	5.50	16.50	60.00
944-The 7th Voyage of Sinbad (Movie) (9/58)-Buscema-a; photo-c	12.00	35.00	130.00
945-Maverick (TV)-James Garner/Jack Kelly photo-c	10.00	30.00	110.00
946-The Big Country (Movie)-Photo-c	6.40	19.00	70.00
947-Broken Arrow (TV)-Photo-c (11/58)	4.00	12.00	45.00
948-Daisy Duck's Diary (Disney) (11/58)	3.60	11.00	40.00
949-High Adventure(Lowell Thomas')(TV)-Photo-c	5.50	13.50	50.00
950-Frosty the Snowman	3.00	9.00	35.00
951-The Lennon Sisters Life Story (TV)-Toth-a, 32 pgs.; photo-c	13.00	40.00	145.00
952-Goofy (Disney) (11/58)	3.60	11.00	40.00
953-Francis the Famous Talking Mule	2.25	6.75	25.00
954-Man in Space-Satellites (TV)	6.40	19.00	70.00
955-Hi and Lois (11/58)	1.80	5.50	20.00
956-Ricky Nelson (#1) (TV)-Photo-c	18.00	55.00	200.00
957-Buffalo Bee (#1) (TV)	9.00	27.00	100.00
958-Santa Claus Funnies	3.00	9.00	35.00
959-Christmas Stories-(Walt Scott's Little People) (1951-56 strip reprints)	3.00	9.00	35.00
960-Zorro (Disney) (TV) (12/58)-Toth art; photo-c	11.00	34.00	125.00
961-Jace Pearson's Tales of the Texas Rangers (TV)-Spiegle-a; photo-c	4.00	12.00	45.00
962-Maverick (TV) (1/59)-James Garner/Jack Kelly photo-c	10.00	30.00	110.00
963-Johnny Mack Brown; photo-c	5.50	16.50	60.00
964-The Hardy Boys (TV) (Disney) (1/59)-Mickey Mouse Club; photo-c	9.00	27.00	100.00
965-Grandma Duck's Farm Friends (Disney)(1/59)	3.60	11.00	40.00
966-Tonka (starring Sal Mineo; Disney-Movie)-Photo-c	7.00	22.00	80.00
967-Chilly Willy (2/59) (Lantz)	2.75	8.00	30.00
968-Tales of Wells Fargo (TV)-Photo-c	8.00	25.00	90.00
969-Peanuts (2/59)	10.00	30.00	110.00
970-Lawman (#1) (TV)-Photo-c	12.00	36.00	130.00
971-Wagon Train (TV)-Photo-c	6.00	18.00	65.00
972-Tom Thumb (Movie)-George Pal (1/59)	9.00	27.00	100.00
973-Sleeping Beauty and the Prince(Disney)(5/59)	11.00	33.00	120.00
974-The Little Rascals (TV) (3/59)	3.60	11.00	40.00
975-Fury (TV)-Photo-c	5.50	16.50	60.00
976-Zorro (Disney) (TV)-Toth-a; photo-c	11.00	34.00	125.00
977-Elmer Fudd (3/59)	1.80	5.50	20.00
978-Lolly and Pepper	1.80	5.50	20.00
979-Oswald the Rabbit (Lantz)	1.80	5.50	20.00
980-Maverick (TV) (4-6/59)-James Garner/Jack Kelly photo-c	10.00	30.00	110.00

Four Color #1003 © WDC

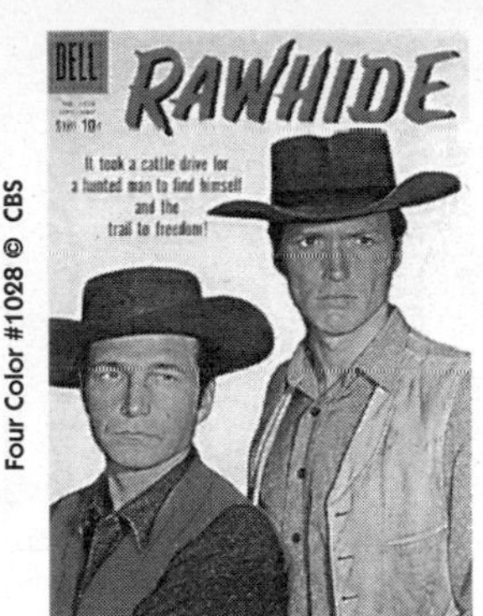

Four Color #1028 © CBS

Four Color #1042 © DELL

	GD25	FN65	NM94
981-Ruff and Reddy (TV) (Hanna-Barbera)	7.00	22.00	80.00
982-The New Adventures of Tinker Bell (TV) (Disney)	7.00	22.00	80.00
983-Have Gun, Will Travel (TV) (4-6/59)-Photo-c	8.00	25.00	90.00
984-Sleeping Beauty's Fairy Godmothers (Disney)	8.00	25.00	90.00
985-Shaggy Dog (Disney-Movie)-Photo-all four covers; Annette on back-c(5/59)	6.40	19.00	70.00
986-Restless Gun (TV)-Photo-c	7.00	22.00	80.00
987-Goofy (Disney) (7/59)	3.60	11.00	40.00
988-Little Hiawatha (Disney)	3.60	11.00	40.00
989-Jiminy Cricket (Disney) (5-7/59)	5.50	16.50	60.00
990-Huckleberry Hound (#1)(TV)(Hanna-Barbera); 1st app. Huck, Yogi Bear, & Pixie & Dixie & Mr. Jinx	10.00	30.00	110.00
991-Francis the Famous Talking Mule	2.25	6.75	25.00
992-Sugarfoot (TV)-Toth-a; photo-c	11.00	34.00	125.00
993-Jim Bowie (TV)-Photo-c	4.50	13.50	50.00
994-Sea Hunt (TV)-Lloyd Bridges photo-c	8.00	25.00	85.00
995-Donald Duck Album (Disney) (5-7/59)(#1)	4.50	13.50	50.00
996-Nevada (Zane Grey)	2.75	8.00	30.00
997-Walt Disney Presents-Tales of Texas John Slaughter (#1) (TV) (Disney)-Photo-c; photo of W. Disney inside-c	6.40	19.00	70.00
998-Ricky Nelson (TV)-Photo-c	18.00	55.00	200.00
999-Leave It to Beaver (TV)-Photo-c	14.00	44.00	160.00
1000-The Gray Ghost (TV) (6-8/59)-Photo-c	8.00	25.00	90.00
1001-Lowell Thomas' High Adventure (TV) (8-10/59)-Photo-c	4.50	13.50	50.00
1002-Buffalo Bee (TV)	6.00	18.00	65.00
1003-Zorro (TV) (Disney)-Toth-a; photo-c	11.00	34.00	125.00
1004-Colt .45 (TV) (6-8/59)-Photo-c	7.00	20.00	75.00
1005-Maverick (TV)-James Garner/Jack Kelly photo-c	10.00	30.00	110.00
1006-Hercules (Movie)-Buscema-a; photo-c	9.00	27.00	100.00
1007-John Paul Jones (Movie)-Robert Stack photo-c	5.00	15.00	50.00
1008-Beep Beep, the Road Runner (7-9/59)	4.00	12.00	45.00
1009-The Rifleman (#1) (TV)-Photo-c	22.00	65.00	240.00
1010-Grandma Duck's Farm Friends (Disney)-by Carl Barks	12.00	37.00	135.00
1011-Buckskin (#1) (TV)-Photo-c	6.40	19.00	70.00
1012-Last Train from Gun Hill (Movie) (7/59)-Photo-c	8.00	24.00	90.00
1013-Bat Masterson (#1) (TV) (8/59)-Gene Barry photo-c	11.00	34.00	125.00
1014-The Lennon Sisters (TV)-Toth-a; photo-c	13.00	40.00	145.00
1015-Peanuts-Schulz-c	10.00	30.00	110.00
1016-Smokey the Bear Nature Stories	2.75	8.00	30.00
1017-Chilly Willy (Lantz)	2.75	8.00	30.00
1018-Rio Bravo (Movie)(6/59)-John Wayne; Toth-a; John Wayne, Dean Martin & Ricky Nelson photo-c	18.00	55.00	200.00
1019-Wagon Train (TV)-Photo-c	6.00	18.00	65.00
1020-Jungle Jim-McWilliams-a	2.25	6.75	25.00
1021-Jace Pearson's Tales of the Texas Rangers (TV)-Photo-c	4.00	12.00	45.00
1022-Timmy	1.80	5.50	20.00
1023-Tales of Wells Fargo (TV)-Photo-c	8.00	25.00	90.00
1024-Darby O'Gill and the Little People (Disney-Movie)-Toth-a; photo-c	9.00	27.00	100.00
1025-Vacation in Disneyland (8-10/59)-Carl Barks-a(24pgs.) (Disney)	18.00	55.00	200.00
1026-Spin and Marty (TV) (Disney) (9-11/59)-Mickey Mouse Club; photo-c	7.00	20.00	75.00
1027-The Texan (#1)(TV)-Photo-c	8.00	25.00	90.00
1028-Rawhide (#1) (TV) (9-11/59)-Clint Eastwood photo-c; Tufts-a	22.00	65.00	240.00
1029-Boots and Saddles (TV) (9/59)-Photo-c	4.50	13.50	50.00
1030-Spanky and Alfalfa, the Little Rascals (TV)	3.60	11.00	40.00

	GD25	FN65	NM94
1031-Fury (TV)-Photo-c	5.50	16.50	60.00
1032-Elmer Fudd	1.80	5.50	20.00
1033-Steve Canyon-not by Caniff; photo-c	4.50	13.50	50.00
1034-Nancy and Sluggo Summer Camp (9-11/59)	2.75	8.00	30.00
1035-Lawman (TV)-Photo-c	6.40	19.00	70.00
1036-The Big Circus (Movie)-Photo-c	5.50	16.50	60.00
1037-Zorro (Disney) (TV)-Tufts-a; Annette Funicello photo-c	14.00	44.00	160.00
1038-Ruff and Reddy (TV)(Hanna-Barbera)(1959)	7.00	22.00	80.00
1039-Pluto (Disney) (11-1/60)	2.75	8.00	30.00
1040-Quick Draw McGraw (#1) (TV) (Hanna-Barbera) (12-2/60)	11.00	34.00	125.00
1041-Sea Hunt (TV) (10-12/59)-Toth-a; Lloyd Bridges photo-c	8.00	25.00	90.00
1042-The Three Chipmunks (Alvin, Simon & Theodore) (#1) (TV) (10-12/59)	4.50	13.50	50.00
1043-The Three Stooges (#1)-Photo-c	18.00	55.00	200.00
1044-Have Gun, Will Travel (TV)-Photo-c	8.00	25.00	90.00
1045-Restless Gun (TV)-Photo-c	7.00	22.00	80.00
1046-Beep Beep, the Road Runner (11-1/60)	4.00	12.00	45.00
1047-Gyro Gearloose (#1) (Disney)-All Barks-c/a	18.00	55.00	200.00
1048-The Horse Soldiers (Movie) (John Wayne)-Sekowsky-a; painted cover featuring John Wayne	13.00	38.00	140.00
1049-Don't Give Up the Ship (Movie) (8/59)-Jerry Lewis photo-c	6.40	19.00	70.00
1050-Huckleberry Hound (TV) (Hanna-Barbera) (10-12/59)	7.00	22.00	80.00
1051-Donald in Mathmagic Land (Disney-Movie)	8.00	25.00	90.00
1052-Ben-Hur (Movie) (11/59)-Manning-a	9.00	27.00	100.00
1053-Goofy (Disney) (11-1/60)	3.60	11.00	40.00
1054-Huckleberry Hound Winter Fun (TV) (Hanna-Barbera) (12/59)	7.00	22.00	80.00
1055-Daisy Duck's Diary (Disney)-by Carl Barks (11-1/60)	9.00	27.00	100.00
1056-Yellowstone Kelly (Movie)-Clint Walker photo-c	5.00	15.00	54.00
1057-Mickey Mouse Album (Disney)	2.75	8.00	30.00
1058-Colt .45 (TV)-Photo-c	7.00	20.00	75.00
1059-Sugarfoot (TV)-Photo-c	8.00	25.00	90.00
1060-Journey to the Center of the Earth (Movie)-Pat Boone & James Mason photo-c	11.00	33.00	120.00
1061-Buffalo Bee (TV)	6.00	18.00	65.00
1062-Christmas Stories (Walt Scott's Little People strip-r)	3.00	9.00	35.00
1063-Santa Claus Funnies	3.00	9.00	35.00
1064-Bugs Bunny's Merry Christmas (12/59)	3.60	11.00	40.00
1065-Frosty the Snowman	3.00	9.00	35.00
1066-77 Sunset Strip (#1) (TV)-Toth-a (1-3/60)-Efrem Zimbalist, Jr. & Edd "Kookie" Byrnes photo-c	11.00	33.00	120.00
1067-Yogi Bear (#1) (TV) (Hanna-Barbera)	10.00	30.00	110.00
1068-Francis the Famous Talking Mule	2.25	6.75	25.00
1069-The FBI Story (Movie)-Toth-a; James Stewart photo on c	10.00	30.00	110.00
1070-Solomon and Sheba (Movie)-Sekowsky-a; photo-c	9.00	27.00	100.00
1071-The Real McCoys (#1) (TV) (1-3/60)-Toth-a; Walter Brennan photo-c	9.00	27.00	100.00
1072-Blythe (Marge's)	4.50	13.50	50.00
1073-Grandma Duck's Farm Friends-Barks-c/a (Disney)	12.00	37.00	135.00
1074-Chilly Willy (Lantz)	2.75	8.00	30.00
1075-Tales of Wells Fargo (TV)-Photo-c	8.00	25.00	90.00
1076-The Rebel (#1) (TV)-Sekowsky-a; photo-c	10.00	30.00	110.00
1077-The Deputy (#1) (TV)-Buscema-a; Henry Fonda photo-c	12.00	35.00	130.00

Four Color #1072 © DELL

Four Color #1078 © DELL

Four Color #1085 © Loew's Inc.

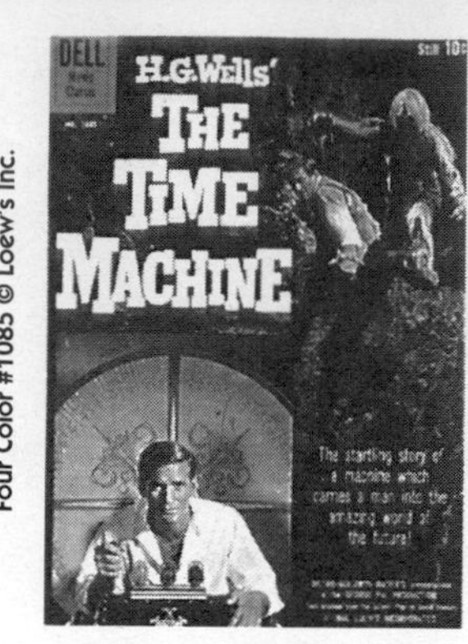

	GD25	FN65	NM94
1078-The Three Stooges (2-4/60)-Photo-c	10.00	30.00	110.00
1079-The Little Rascals (TV) (Spanky & Alfalfa)	3.60	11.00	40.00
1080-Fury (TV) (2-4/60)-Photo-c	5.50	16.50	60.00
1081-Elmer Fudd	1.80	5.50	20.00
1082-Spin and Marty (Disney) (TV)-Photo-c	7.00	20.00	75.00
1083-Men into Space (TV)-Anderson-a; photo-c	4.50	13.50	50.00
1084-Speedy Gonzales	2.75	8.00	30.00
1085-The Time Machine (H.G. Wells) (Movie) (3/60)-Alex Toth-a; Rod Taylor photo-c	14.00	44.00	160.00
1086-Lolly and Pepper	1.80	5.50	20.00
1087-Peter Gunn (TV)-Photo-c	9.00	27.00	100.00
1088-A Dog of Flanders (Movie)-Photo-c	3.60	11.00	40.00
1089-Restless Gun (TV)-Photo-c	7.00	22.00	80.00
1090-Francis the Famous Talking Mule	2.25	6.75	25.00
1091-Jacky's Diary (4-6/60)	3.60	11.00	40.00
1092-Toby Tyler (Disney-Movie)-Photo-c	5.50	16.50	60.00
1093-MacKenzie's Raiders (Movie/TV)-Richard Carlson photo-c from TV show	5.50	16.50	60.00
1094-Goofy (Disney)	3.60	11.00	40.00
1095-Gyro Gearloose (Disney)-All Barks-c/a	10.00	30.00	110.00
1096-The Texan (TV)-Rory Calhoun photo-c	7.00	22.00	80.00
1097-Rawhide (TV)-Manning-a; Clint Eastwood photo-c	14.00	41.00	150.00
1098-Sugarfoot (TV)-Photo-c	8.00	25.00	90.00
1099-Donald Duck Album (Disney) (5-7/60)-Barks-c	5.50	16.50	60.00
1100-Annette's Life Story (Disney-Movie) (5/60)-Annette Funicello photo-c	21.00	62.00	225.00
1101-Robert Louis Stevenson's Kidnapped (Disney-Movie) (5/60); photo-c	5.50	16.50	60.00
1102-Wanted: Dead or Alive (#1) (TV) (5-7/60); Steve McQueen photo-c	12.00	37.00	135.00
1103-Leave It to Beaver (TV)-Photo-c	14.00	44.00	160.00
1104-Yogi Bear Goes to College (TV) (Hanna-Barbera) (6-8/60)	7.00	20.00	75.00
1105-Gale Storm (Oh! Susanna) (TV)-Toth-a; photo-c	12.00	35.00	130.00
1106-77 Sunset Strip(TV)(6-8/60)-Toth-a; photo-c	9.00	27.00	100.00
1107-Buckskin (TV)-Photo-c	5.50	16.50	60.00
1108-The Troubleshooters (TV)-Keenan Wynn photo-c	4.50	13.50	50.00
1109-This Is Your Life, Donald Duck (Disney) (TV) (8-10/60)-Gyro flashback to WDC&S #141; origin Donald Duck (1st told)	14.00	41.00	150.00
1110-Bonanza (#1) (TV) (6-8/60)-Photo-c	34.00	102.00	375.00
1111-Shotgun Slade (TV)-Photo-c	5.50	16.50	60.00
1112-Pixie and Dixie and Mr. Jinks (#1) (TV) (Hanna-Barbera) (7-9/60)	6.40	19.00	70.00
1113-Tales of Wells Fargo (TV)-Photo-c	8.00	25.00	90.00
1114-Huckleberry Finn (Movie) (7/60)-Photo-c	4.50	13.50	50.00
1115-Ricky Nelson (TV)-Manning-a; photo-c	14.00	41.00	150.00
1116-Boots and Saddles (TV) (8/60)-Photo-c	4.50	13.50	50.00
1117-Boy and the Pirates (Movie)-Photo-c	5.50	16.50	60.00
1118-The Sword and the Dragon (Movie) (6/60)-Photo-c	7.00	22.00	80.00
1119-Smokey the Bear Nature Stories	2.75	8.00	30.00
1120-Dinosaurus (Movie)-Painted-c	6.40	19.00	70.00
1121-Hercules Unchained (Movie) (8/60)-Crandall/Evans-a	9.00	27.00	100.00
1122-Chilly Willy (Lantz)	2.75	8.00	30.00
1123-Tombstone Territory (TV)-Photo-c	9.00	27.00	100.00
1124-Whirlybirds (#1) (TV)-Photo-c	8.00	25.00	90.00
1125-Laramie (#1) (TV)-Photo-c; G. Kane/Heath-a	9.00	27.00	100.00
1126-Sundance (TV) (8-10/60)-Earl Holliman photo-c	5.50	16.50	60.00
1127-The Three Stooges-Photo-c (8-10/60)	10.00	30.00	110.00

	GD25	FN65	NM94
1128-Rocky and His Friends (#1) (TV) (Jay Ward) (8-10/60)	36.00	109.00	400.00
1129-Pollyanna (Disney-Movie)-Hayley Mills photo-c	7.00	22.00	80.00
1130-The Deputy (TV)-Buscema-a; Henry Fonda photo-c	9.00	27.00	100.00
1131-Elmer Fudd (9-11/60)	1.80	5.50	20.00
1132-Space Mouse (Lantz) (8-10/60)	3.60	11.00	40.00
1133-Fury (TV)-Photo-c	5.50	16.50	60.00
1134-Real McCoys (TV)-Toth-a; photo-c	9.00	27.00	100.00
1135-M.G.M.'s Mouse Musketeers (9-11/60)	1.80	5.50	20.00
1136-Jungle Cat (Disney-Movie)-Photo-c	5.50	16.50	60.00
1137-The Little Rascals (TV)	3.60	11.00	40.00
1138-The Rebel (TV)-Photo-c	8.00	25.00	90.00
1139-Spartacus (Movie) (11/60)-Buscema-a; Kirk Douglas photo-c	12.00	35.00	130.00
1140-Donald Duck Album (Disney)-Barks-c	5.50	16.50	60.00
1141-Huckleberry Hound for President (TV) (Hanna-Barbera) (10/60)	7.00	22.00	80.00
1142-Johnny Ringo (TV)-Photo-c	6.40	19.00	70.00
1143-Pluto (Disney) (11-1/61)	2.75	8.00	30.00
1144-The Story of Ruth (Movie)-Photo-c	9.00	27.00	100.00
1145-The Lost World (Movie)-Gil Kane-a; photo-c; 1 pg. Conan Doyle biography by Torres	10.00	30.00	110.00
1146-Restless Gun (TV)-Photo-c; Wildey-a	7.00	22.00	80.00
1147-Sugarfoot (TV)-Photo-c	8.00	25.00	90.00
1148-I Aim at the Stars-the Wernher Von Braun Story (Movie) (11-1/61)-Photo-c	6.40	19.00	70.00
1149-Goofy (Disney) (11-1/61)	3.60	11.00	40.00
1150-Daisy Duck's Diary (Disney) (12-1/61) by Carl Barks	9.00	27.00	100.00
1151-Mickey Mouse Album (Disney) (11-1/61)	2.75	8.00	30.00
1152-Rocky and His Friends (TV) (Jay Ward) (12-2/61)	23.00	68.00	250.00
1153-Frosty the Snowman	3.00	9.00	35.00
1154-Santa Claus Funnies	3.00	9.00	35.00
1155-North to Alaska (Movie)-John Wayne photo-c	16.00	47.00	170.00
1156-Walt Disney Swiss Family Robinson (Movie) (12/60)-Photo-c	6.40	19.00	70.00
1157-Master of the World (Movie) (7/61)	4.50	13.50	50.00
1158-Three Worlds of Gulliver (2 issues exist with different covers) (Movie)-Photo-c	5.50	16.50	60.00
1159-77 Sunset Strip (TV)-Toth-a; photo-c	9.00	27.00	100.00
1160-Rawhide (TV)-Clint Eastwood photo-c	14.00	41.00	150.00
1161-Grandma Duck's Farm Friends (Disney) by Carl Barks (2-4/61)	12.00	37.00	135.00
1162-Yogi Bear Joins the Marines (TV) (Hanna-Barbera) (5-7/61)	7.00	20.00	75.00
1163-Daniel Boone (3-5/61); Marsh-a	4.50	13.50	50.00
1164-Wanted: Dead or Alive (TV)-Steve McQueen photo-c	9.00	27.00	100.00
1165-Ellery Queen (#1) (3-5/61)	10.00	30.00	110.00
1166-Rocky and His Friends (TV) (Jay Ward)	23.00	68.00	250.00
1167-Tales of Wells Fargo (TV)-Photo-c	7.00	22.00	80.00
1168-The Detectives (TV)-Robert Taylor photo-c	9.00	27.00	100.00
1169-New Adventures of Sherlock Holmes	14.00	44.00	160.00
1170-The Three Stooges (3-5/61)-Photo-c	10.00	30.00	110.00
1171-Elmer Fudd	1.80	5.50	20.00
1172-Fury (TV)-Photo-c	5.50	16.50	60.00
1173-The Twilight Zone (#1) (TV) (5/61)-Crandall/Evans-c/a; Crandall tribute to Ingles	18.00	55.00	200.00
1174-The Little Rascals (TV)	2.75	8.00	30.00
1175-M.G.M.'s Mouse Musketeers (3-5/61)	1.80	5.50	20.00
1176-Dondi (Movie)-Origin; photo-c	3.60	11.00	40.00

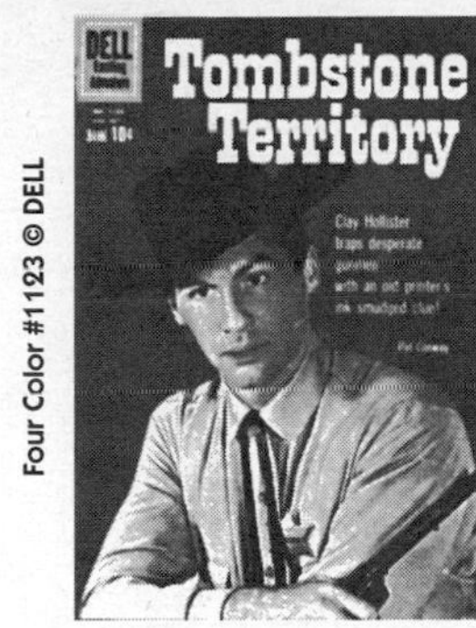

Four Color #1123 © DELL

Four Color #1157 © Alta Vista

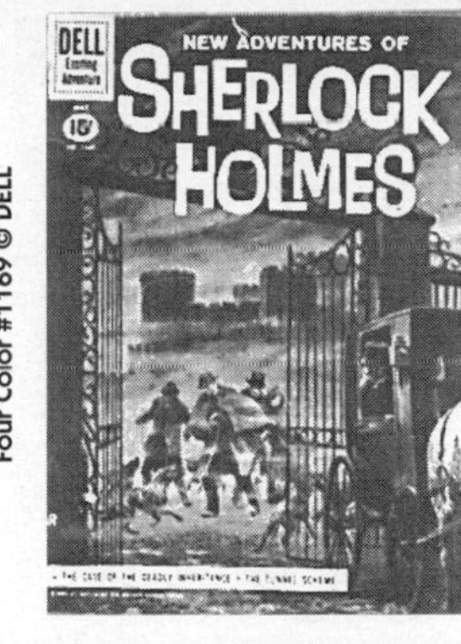

Four Color #1169 © DELL

	GD25	FN65	NM94
1177-Chilly Willy (Lantz) (4-6/61)	2.75	8.00	30.00
1178-Ten Who Dared (Disney-Movie) (12/60)-Painted-c; cast member photo on back-c	6.40	19.00	70.00
1179-The Swamp Fox (TV) (Disney)-Leslie Nielson photo-c	8.00	25.00	90.00
1180-The Danny Thomas Show (TV)-Toth-a; photo-c	14.00	42.00	153.00
1181-Texas John Slaughter (TV) (Disney) (4-6/61)-Photo-c	6.40	19.00	70.00
1182-Donald Duck Album (Disney) (5-7/61)	3.60	11.00	40.00
1183-101 Dalmatians (Disney-Movie) (3/61)	9.00	27.00	100.00
1184-Gyro Gearloose; All Barks-c/a (Disney) (5-7/61) Two variations exist	10.00	30.00	110.00
1185-Sweetie Pie	2.75	8.00	30.00
1186-Yak Yak (#1) by Jack Davis (2 versions - one minus 3-pg. Davis-c/a)	7.00	22.00	80.00
1187-The Three Stooges (6-8/61)-Photo-c	10.00	30.00	110.00
1188-Atlantis, the Lost Continent (Movie) (5/61)-Photo-c	9.00	27.00	100.00
1189-Greyfriars Bobby (Disney-Movie) (11/61)-Photo-c (scarce)	6.40	19.00	70.00
1190-Donald and the Wheel (Disney-Movie) (11/61); Barks-c	6.40	19.00	70.00
1191-Leave It to Beaver (TV)-Photo-c	14.00	44.00	160.00
1192-Ricky Nelson (TV)-Manning-a; photo-c	14.00	41.00	150.00
1193-The Real McCoys (TV) (6-8/61)-Photo-c	8.00	25.00	90.00
1194-Pepe (Movie) (4/61)-Photo-c	1.80	5.50	20.00
1195-National Velvet (#1) (TV)-Photo-c	5.50	16.50	60.00
1196-Pixie and Dixie and Mr. Jinks (TV) (Hanna-Barbera) (7-9/61)	4.50	13.50	50.00
1197-The Aquanauts (TV) (5-7/61)-Photo-c	5.75	17.00	63.00
1198-Donald in Mathmagic Land (Disney-Movie)-Reprint of #1051	5.50	16.50	60.00
1199-The Absent-Minded Professor (Disney-Movie) (4/61)-Photo-c	6.40	19.00	70.00
1200-Hennessey (TV) (8-10/61)-Gil Kane-a; photo-c	5.50	16.50	60.00
1201-Goofy (Disney) (8-10/61)	3.60	11.00	40.00
1202-Rawhide (TV)-Clint Eastwood photo-c	14.00	41.00	150.00
1203-Pinocchio (Disney) (3/62)	4.50	13.50	50.00
1204-Scamp (Disney)	3.00	9.00	35.00
1205-David and Goliath (Movie) (7/61)-Photo-c	5.50	16.50	60.00
1206-Lolly and Pepper (9-11/61)	1.80	5.50	20.00
1207-The Rebel (TV)-Sekowsky-a; photo-c	8.00	25.00	90.00
1208-Rocky and His Friends (Jay Ward) (TV)	23.00	68.00	250.00
1209-Sugarfoot (TV)-Photo-c (10-12/61)	8.00	25.00	90.00
1210-The Parent Trap (Disney-Movie) (8/61)-Hayley Mills photo-c	8.00	25.00	90.00
1211-77 Sunset Strip (TV)-Manning-a; photo-c	8.00	25.00	90.00
1212-Chilly Willy (Lantz) (7-9/61)	2.75	8.00	30.00
1213-Mysterious Island (Movie)-Photo-c	8.00	25.00	90.00
1214-Smokey the Bear	2.75	8.00	30.00
1215-Tales of Wells Fargo (TV) (10-12/61)-Photo-c	7.00	22.00	80.00
1216-Whirlybirds (TV)-Photo-c	7.00	22.00	80.00
1218-Fury (TV)-Photo-c	5.50	16.50	60.00
1219-The Detectives (TV)-Robert Taylor & Adam West photo-c	7.00	22.00	80.00
1220-Gunslinger (TV)-Photo-c	8.00	25.00	90.00
1221-Bonanza (TV) (9-11/61)-Photo-c	16.00	49.00	180.00
1222-Elmer Fudd (9-11/61)	1.80	5.50	20.00
1223-Laramie (TV)-Gil Kane-a; photo-c	5.50	16.50	60.00
1224-The Little Rascals (TV) (10-12/61)	2.75	8.00	30.00
1225-The Deputy (TV)-Henry Fonda photo-c	9.00	27.00	100.00
1226-Nikki, Wild Dog of the North (Disney-Movie) (9/61)-Photo-c	4.50	13.50	60.00
1227-Morgan the Pirate (Movie)-Photo-c	7.00	22.00	80.00
1229-Thief of Baghdad (Movie)-Crandall/Evans-a; photo-c	5.50	16.50	60.00
1230-Voyage to the Bottom of the Sea (#1) (Movie)-Photo insert on-c	9.00	27.00	100.00
1231-Danger Man (TV) (9-11/61)-Patrick McGoohan photo-c	10.00	30.00	110.00
1232-On the Double (Movie)	3.60	11.00	40.00
1233-Tammy Tell Me True (Movie) (1961)	5.50	16.50	60.00
1234-The Phantom Planet (Movie) (1961)	6.40	19.00	70.00
1235-Mister Magoo (#1) (12-2/62)	9.00	27.00	100.00
1235-Mister Magoo (3-5/65) 2nd printing; reprint of 12-2/62 issue	5.50	16.50	60.00
1236-King of Kings (Movie)-Photo-c	7.00	22.00	80.00
1237-The Untouchables (#1) (TV)-Not by Toth; photo-c	22.00	65.00	240.00
1238-Deputy Dawg (TV)	10.00	30.00	110.00
1239-Donald Duck Album (Disney) (10-12/61)-Barks-c	5.50	16.50	60.00
1240-The Detectives (TV)-Tufts-a; Robert Taylor photo-c	7.00	22.00	80.00
1241-Sweetie Pie	2.75	8.00	30.00
1242-King Leonardo and His Short Subjects (#1) (TV) (11-1/62)	13.00	38.00	140.00
1243-Ellery Queen	8.00	25.00	90.00
1244-Space Mouse (Lantz) (11-1/62)	3.60	11.00	40.00
1245-New Adventures of Sherlock Holmes	14.00	44.00	160.00
1246-Mickey Mouse Album (Disney)	2.75	8.00	30.00
1247-Daisy Duck's Diary (Disney) (12-2/62)	3.60	11.00	40.00
1248-Pluto (Disney)	2.75	8.00	30.00
1249-The Danny Thomas Show (TV)-Manning-a; photo-c	14.00	42.00	153.00
1250-The Four Horsemen of the Apocalypse (Movie)-Photo-c	6.40	19.00	70.00
1251-Everything's Ducky (Movie) (1961)	3.60	11.00	40.00
1252-The Andy Griffith Show (TV)-Photo-c; 1st show aired 10/3/60	27.00	82.00	300.00
1253-Space Man (#1) (1-3/62)	6.40	19.00	70.00
1254- "Diver Dan" (#1) (TV) (2-4/62)-Photo-c	4.50	13.50	50.00
1255-The Wonders of Aladdin (Movie) (1961)	5.75	17.00	63.00
1256-Kona, Monarch of Monster Isle (#1) (2-4/62)-Glanzman-a	5.50	16.50	60.00
1257-Car 54, Where Are You? (#1) (TV) (3-5/62)-Photo-c	6.40	19.00	70.00
1258-The Frogmen (#1)-Evans-a	6.40	19.00	70.00
1259-El Cid (Movie) (1961)-Photo-c	6.40	19.00	70.00
1260-The Horsemasters (TV, Movie) (Disney) (12-2/62)-Annette Funicello photo-c	11.00	33.00	120.00
1261-Rawhide (TV)-Clint Eastwood photo-c	14.00	41.00	150.00
1262-The Rebel (TV)-Photo-c	8.00	25.00	90.00
1263-77 Sunset Strip (TV) (12-2/62)-Manning-a; photo-c	8.00	25.00	90.00
1264-Pixie and Dixie and Mr. Jinks (TV) (Hanna-Barbera)	4.50	13.50	50.00
1265-The Real McCoys (TV)-Photo-c	8.00	25.00	90.00
1266-M.G.M.'s Spike and Tyke (12-2/62)	1.65	5.00	18.00
1267-Gyro Gearloose; Barks-c/a, 4 pgs. (Disney) (12-2/62)	7.00	20.00	75.00
1268-Oswald the Rabbit (Lantz)	1.80	5.50	20.00
1269-Rawhide (TV)-Clint Eastwood photo-c	14.00	41.00	150.00
1270-Bullwinkle and Rocky (#1) (TV) (Jay Ward) (3-5/62)	18.00	55.00	200.00
1271-Yogi Bear Birthday Party (TV) (Hanna-Barbera) (11/61)	4.50	13.50	50.00

Four Color #1328 © DELL

The Four Horsemen of the Apocalypse © DELL

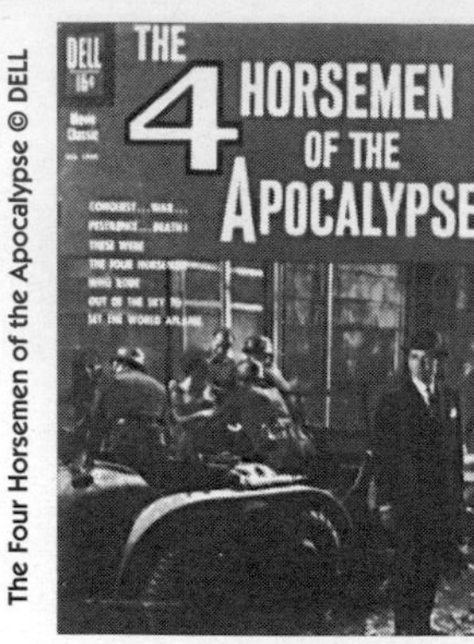

4Most V8 #1 © NOVP

	GD25	FN65	NM94
1272-Frosty the Snowman	3.00	9.00	35.00
1273-Hans Brinker (Disney-Movie)-Photo-c (2/62)	5.50	16.50	60.00
1274-Santa Claus Funnies (12/61)	3.00	9.00	35.00
1275-Rocky and His Friends (TV) (Jay Ward)	23.00	68.00	250.00
1276-Dondi	1.80	5.50	20.00
1278-King Leonardo and His Short Subjects (TV)	13.00	38.00	140.00
1279-Grandma Duck's Farm Friends (Disney)	3.60	11.00	40.00
1280-Hennessey (TV)-Photo-c	5.50	16.50	60.00
1281-Chilly Willy (Lantz) (4-6/62)	2.75	8.00	30.00
1282-Babes in Toyland (Disney-Movie) (1/62); Annette Funicello photo-c	11.00	34.00	125.00
1283-Bonanza (TV) (2-4/62)-Photo-c	16.00	49.00	180.00
1284-Laramie (TV)-Heath-a; photo-c	5.50	16.50	60.00
1285-Leave It to Beaver (TV)-Photo-c	14.00	44.00	160.00
1286-The Untouchables (TV)-Photo-c	16.00	47.00	170.00
1287-Man from Wells Fargo (TV)-Photo-c	4.50	13.50	50.00
1288-Twilight Zone (TV) (4/62)-Crandall/Evans-c/a	11.00	32.00	115.00
1289-Ellery Queen	8.00	25.00	90.00
1290-M.G.M.'s Mouse Musketeers	1.80	5.50	20.00
1291-77 Sunset Strip (TV)-Manning-a; photo-c	8.00	25.00	90.00
1293-Elmer Fudd (3-5/62)	1.80	5.50	20.00
1294-Ripcord (TV)	6.40	19.00	70.00
1295-Mister Ed, the Talking Horse (#1) (TV) (3-5/62)-Photo-c	12.00	35.00	130.00
1296-Fury (TV) (3-5/62)-Photo-c	5.50	16.50	60.00
1297-Spanky, Alfalfa and the Little Rascals (TV)	2.75	8.00	30.00
1298-The Hathaways (TV)-Photo-c	3.60	11.00	40.00
1299-Deputy Dawg (TV)	10.00	30.00	110.00
1300-The Comancheros (Movie) (1961)-John Wayne photo-c	14.00	44.00	160.00
1301-Adventures in Paradise (TV) (2-4/62)	3.60	11.00	40.00
1302-Johnny Jason, Teen Reporter (2-4/62)	2.75	8.00	30.00
1303-Lad: A Dog (Movie)-Photo-c	2.75	8.00	30.00
1304-Nellie the Nurse (3-5/62)-Stanley-a	6.40	19.00	70.00
1305-Mister Magoo (3-5/62)	9.00	27.00	100.00
1306-Target: The Corruptors (#1) (TV) (3-5/62)-Photo-c	4.50	13.50	50.00
1307-Margie (TV) (3-5/62)	3.60	11.00	40.00
1308-Tales of the Wizard of Oz (TV) (3-5/62)	10.00	30.00	110.00
1309-87th Precinct (#1) (TV) (4-6/62)-Krigstein-a; photo-c	9.00	27.00	100.00
1310-Huck and Yogi Winter Sports (TV) (Hanna-Barbera) (3/62)	7.00	22.00	80.00
1311-Rocky and His Friends (TV) (Jay Ward)	23.00	68.00	250.00
1312-National Velvet (TV)-Photo-c	2.75	8.00	30.00
1313-Moon Pilot (Disney-Movie)-Photo-c	6.40	19.00	70.00
1328-The Underwater City (Movie) (1961)-Evans-a; photo-c	6.40	19.00	70.00
1329-See Gyro Gearloose #01329-207			
1330-Brain Boy (#1)-Gil Kane-a	12.00	37.00	135.00
1332-Bachelor Father (TV)	7.00	22.00	80.00
1333-Short Ribs (4-6/62)	4.50	13.50	50.00
1335-Aggie Mack (4-6/62)	2.75	8.00	30.00
1336-On Stage; not by Leonard Starr	3.60	11.00	40.00
1337-Dr. Kildare (#1) (TV) (4-6/62)-Photo-c	8.00	25.00	90.00
1341-The Andy Griffith Show (TV) (4-6/62)-Photo-c	27.00	82.00	300.00
1348-Yak Yak (#2)-Jack Davis-c/a	7.00	22.00	80.00
1349-Yogi Bear Visits the U.N. (TV) (Hanna-Barbera) (1/62)-Photo-c	9.00	27.00	100.00
1350-Comanche (Disney-Movie)(1962)-Reprints 4-Color #966 (title change from "Tonka" to "Comanche") (4-6/62)-Sal Mineo photo-c	4.50	13.50	50.00
1354-Calvin & the Colonel (#1) (TV) (4-6/62)	7.00	22.00	80.00

NOTE: *Missing numbers probably do not exist.*

4-D MONKEY, THE (Adventures of... #? on)
1988 - No. 11, 1990 ($1.80/$2.00, 52 pgs.)
Leung's Publications

	GD25	FN65	NM94
1-Karate Pig, Ninja Flounder & 4-D Monkey (48 pgs., centerfold is a Christmas card)		.75	1.80
2-4 (52 pgs.)		.75	1.80
5-11 ($2.00-c)		.80	2.00

FOUR FAVORITES (Crime Must Pay the Penalty No. 33 on)
Sept, 1941 - No. 32, Dec, 1947
Ace Magazines

	GD25	FN65	NM94
1-Vulcan, Lash Lightning (formerly Flash Lightning in Sure-Fire), Magno the Magnetic Man & The Raven begin; flag-c	106.00	318.00	950.00
2-The Black Ace only app.	42.00	126.00	380.00
3-Last Vulcan	36.00	108.00	325.00
4,5: 4-The Raven & Vulcan end; Unknown Soldier begins (see Our Flag), ends #28. 5-Captain Courageous begins (5/42), ends #28 (moves over from Captain Courageous #6); not in #6	36.00	108.00	290.00
6-8: 6-The Flag app.; Mr. Risk begins (7/42)	31.00	94.00	250.00
9-Kurtzman-a (Lash Lightning);	36.00	108.00	290.00
10-Classic Kurtzman-c/a (Magno & Davey)	38.00	113.00	340.00
11-Kurtzman-a; Hitler, Mussolini, Hirohito-c; L.B. Cole-a; Unknown Soldier by Kurtzman	38.00	113.00	340.00
12-L.B. Cole-a	25.00	75.00	200.00
13-20: 18,20-Palais-c/a	20.00	60.00	160.00
21-No Unknown Soldier; The Unknown app.	15.00	45.00	120.00
22-26: 22-Captain Courageous drops costume. 23-Unknown Soldier drops costume. 25-29-HapHazard app. 26-Last Magno	15.00	45.00	120.00
27-32: 30-Funny-c begin (teen humor), end #32	10.00	30.00	80.00

NOTE: ***Dave Berg** c-5. **Jim Mooney** a-6; c-1-3. **Palais** a-18-20; c-18-25. Torture chamber c-5.*

FOUR HORSEMEN, THE (See The Crusaders)

FOUR HORSEMEN OF THE APOCALYPSE, THE (Movie)
No. 1250, Jan-Mar, 1962 (one-shot)
Dell Publishing co.

	GD25	FN65	NM94
Four Color 1250-Photo-c	6.40	19.00	70.00

4MOST (Foremost Boys No. 32-40; becomes Thrilling Crime Cases #41 on)
Winter, 1941-42 - V8#5(#36), 9-10/49; #37, 11-12/49 - #40, 4-5/50
Novelty Publications/Star Publications No. 37-on

	GD25	FN65	NM94
V1#1-The Target by Sid Greene, The Cadet & Dick Cole begin with origins retold; produced by Funnies Inc.; quarterly issues begin, end V6#3	94.00	283.00	850.00
2-Last Target (Spr/42)	39.00	117.00	350.00
3-Dan'l Flannel begins; flag-c	36.00	107.00	285.00
4-1pg. Dr. Seuss (signed) (Aut/42)	30.00	90.00	240.00
V2#1-3	8.75	26.25	70.00
4-Hitler, Tojo & Mussolini app. as pumpkins on-c	12.00	38.00	100.00
V3#1-4	8.75	26.25	65.00
V4#1-4: 2-Walter Johnson-c	7.15	21.50	50.00
V5#1-4: 1-The Target & Targeteers app.	5.70	17.00	40.00
V6#1-4: 1-White Rider & Super Horse begin	5.70	17.00	40.00
5-L. B. Cole-c	12.00	38.00	100.00
V7#1,3,5, V8#1, 37	5.70	17.00	40.00
2,4,6-L. B. Cole-c. 6-Last Dick Cole	12.00	38.00	100.00
V8#2,3,5-L. B. Cole-c/a	14.00	41.00	110.00
4-L. B. Cole-a	8.75	26.25	70.00
38-40: 38-Johnny Weismuller (Tarzan) life story & Jim Braddock (boxer) life story. 38-40-L.B. Cole-c. 40-Last White Rider	11.30	34.00	90.00
Accepted Reprint 38-40 (nd): 40-r/Johnny Weismuller life story; all have L.B. Cole-c	6.50	19.50	45.00

FOUR-STAR BATTLE TALES
Feb-Mar, 1973 - No. 5, Nov-Dec, 1973
National Periodical Publications

Fox and the Crow #78 © DC

Fox Giant - Love Problems © FOX

Foxhole #1 © Mainline

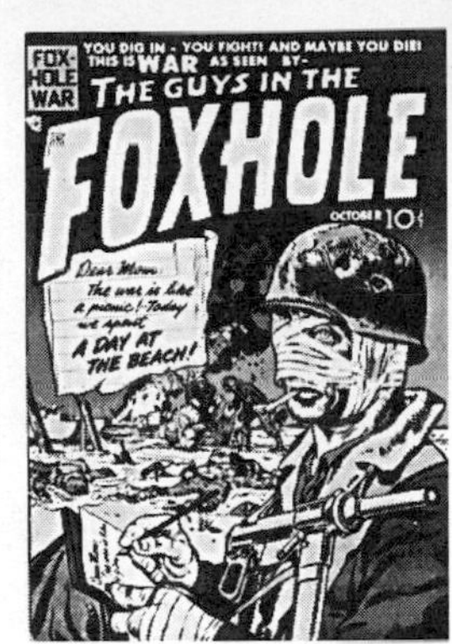

	GD25	FN65	NM94
1-reprints begin	2.50	7.50	20.00
2-5	1.50	4.50	12.00

NOTE: ***Drucker** r-1, 3-5. **Heath** r-2, 5; c-1. **Krigstein** r-5. **Kubert** r-4; c-2.*

FOUR STAR SPECTACULAR
Mar-Apr, 1976 - No. 6, Jan-Feb, 1977
National Periodical Publications

	GD25	FN65	NM94
1		2.40	6.00
2-6: Reprints in all. 2-Infinity cover		1.60	4.00

NOTE: *All contain DC Superhero reprints. #1 has 68 pgs.; #2-6, 52 pgs.. #1, 4-Hawkman app.; #2-Kid Flash app.; #3-Green Lantern app; #2, 4, 5-Wonder Woman, Superboy app; #5-Green Arrow, Vigilante app; #6-Blackhawk G.A.-r.*

FOUR TEENERS (Formerly Crime Must Pay The Penalty; Dotty No. 35 on)
No. 34, April, 1948 (52 pgs.)
A. A. Wyn

	GD25	FN65	NM94
34-Teen-age comic; Dotty app.; Curly & Jerry continue from Four Favorites	5.00	15.00	30.00

FOURTH WORLD GALLERY, THE (Jack Kirby's...)
1996 (9/96) ($3.50, one shot)
DC Comics

	GD25	FN65	NM94
nn-Pin-ups of Jack Kirby's Fourth World characters (New Gods, Forever People & Mister Miracle) by John Byrne, Rick Burchett, Dan Jurgens, Walt Simonson & others		1.40	3.50

FOX AND THE CROW (Stanley & His Monster No. 109 on) (See Comic Cavalcade & Real Screen Comics)
Dec-Jan, 1951-52 - No. 108, Feb-Mar, 1968
National Periodical Publications

	GD25	FN65	NM94
1	83.00	250.00	750.00
2(Scarce)	41.00	123.00	370.00
3-5	29.00	86.00	230.00
6-10	21.00	62.00	165.00
11-20	14.50	43.00	115.00
21-40: 22-Last precode issue (2/55)	9.50	28.00	75.00
41-60	7.15	21.50	50.00
61-80	5.70	17.00	34.00
81-94: 94-(11/65)-The Brat Finks begin	2.50	7.50	25.00
95-Stanley & His Monster begins(origin)(1st app?)	2.80	8.40	28.00
96-99,101-108	1.50	4.50	12.00
100 (10-11/66)	1.85	5.50	15.00

NOTE: *Many covers by **Mort Drucker.***

FOX AND THE HOUND, THE (Disney)(Movie)
Aug, 1981 - No. 3, Oct, 1981
Whitman Publishing Co.

	GD25	FN65	NM94
11292(#1),2,3-Based on animated movie			1.00

FOXFIRE (See The Phoenix Resurrection)
Feb, 1996 - No. 4, May, 1996 ($1.50)
Malibu Comics (Ultraverse)

	GD25	FN65	NM94
1-4: Sludge, Ultraforce app. 4-Punisher app.			1.50

FOX GIANTS
1944 - 1950 (25¢, 132 - 196 pgs.)
Fox Features Syndicate

	GD25	FN65	NM94
Album of Crime nn(1949, 132p)	36.00	108.00	300.00
Album of Love nn(1949, 132p)	34.00	101.00	270.00
All Famous Crime Stories nn('49, 132p)	36.00	108.00	300.00
All Good Comics 1(1944, 132p)(R.W. Voigt)-The Bouncer, Purple Tigress, Rick Evans, Puppeteer, Green Mask; Infinity-c	33.00	100.00	265.00
All Great nn(1944, 132p)-Capt. Jack Terry, Rick Evans, Jaguar Man	33.00	100.00	265.00
All Great nn(Chicago Nite Life News)(1945, 132p)-Green Mask, Bouncer, Puppeteer, Rick Evans, Rocket Kelly	36.00	107.00	285.00
All-Great Confessions nn(1949, 132p)	31.00	94.00	250.00
All Great Crime Stories nn('49, 132p)	36.00	108.00	300.00
All Great Jungle Adventures nn('49, 132p)	40.00	120.00	360.00
All Real Confession Magazine 3 (3/49, 132p)	31.00	94.00	250.00
All Real Confession Magazine 4 (4/49, 132p)	31.00	94.00	250.00
All Your Comics 1(1944, 132p)-The Puppeteer, Red Robbins, & Merciless the Sorcerer	34.00	103.00	275.00
Almanac Of Crime nn(1948, 148p)-Phantom Lady	39.00	117.00	350.00
Almanac Of Crime 1(1950, 132p)	36.00	108.00	300.00
Book Of Love nn(1950, 132p)	30.00	90.00	240.00
Burning Romances 1(1949, 132p)	36.00	107.00	285.00
Crimes Incorporated nn(1950, 132p)	34.00	103.00	275.00
Daring Love Stories nn(1950, 132p)	30.00	90.00	240.00
Everybody's Comics 1(1944, 50¢, 196p)-The Green Mask, The Puppeteer, The Bouncer, Rocket Kelly, Rick Evans	36.00	108.00	300.00
Everybody's Comics 1(1946, 196p)-Green Lama, The Puppeteer	29.00	88.00	235.00
Everybody's Comics 1(1946, 196p)-Same as 1945 Ribtickler	23.00	68.00	180.00
Everybody's Comics nn(1947, 132p)-Jo-Jo, Purple Tigress, Cosmo Cat, Bronze Man	29.00	86.00	230.00
Exciting Romance Stories nn(1949, 132p)	30.00	90.00	240.00
Famous Love nn(1950, 132p)	30.00	90.00	240.00
Intimate Confessions nn(1950, 132p)	30.00	90.00	240.00
Journal Of Crime nn(1949, 132p)	36.00	108.00	300.00
Love Problems nn(1949, 132p)	31.00	94.00	250.00
Love Thrills nn(1950, 132p)	31.00	94.00	250.00
March of Crime nn('48, 132p)-Female w/rifle-c	34.00	103.00	275.00
March of Crime nn('49, 132p)-Cop w/pistol-c	34.00	103.00	275.00
March of Crime nn(1949, 132p)-Coffin & man w/machine-gun-c	34.00	103.00	275.00
Revealing Love Stories nn(1950, 132p)	30.00	90.00	240.00
Ribtickler nn(1945, 50¢, 196p)-Chicago Nite Life News; Marvel Mutt, Cosmo Cat, Flash Rabbit, The Nebbs app.	28.00	83.00	220.00
Romantic Thrills nn(1950, 132p)	30.00	90.00	240.00
Secret Love nn(1949, 132p)	30.00	90.00	240.00
Secret Love Stories nn(1949, 132p)	30.00	90.00	240.00
Strange Love nn(1950, 132p)-Photo-c	36.00	107.00	285.00
Sweetheart Scandals nn(1950, 132p)	30.00	90.00	240.00
Teen-Age Love nn(1950, 132p)	30.00	90.00	240.00
Throbbing Love nn(1950, 132p)-Photo-c; used in **POP**, pg. 107	36.00	107.00	285.00
Truth About Crime nn(1949, 132p)	36.00	108.00	300.00
Variety Comics 1(1946, 132p)-Blue Beetle, Jungle Jo	30.00	90.00	240.00
Variety Comics nn(1950, 132p)-Jungle Jo, My Secret Affair(w/Harrison/Wood-a), Crimes by Women & My Story	29.00	86.00	230.00
Western Roundup nn('50, 132p)-Hoot Gibson; Cody of the Pony Express app.	33.00	100.00	265.00

NOTE: *Each of the above usually contain four remaindered Fox books minus covers. Since these missing covers often had the first page of the first story, most Giants therefore are incomplete. Approximate values are listed. Books with appearances of Phantom Lady, Rulah, Jo-Jo, etc. could bring more.*

FOXHOLE (Becomes Never Again #8?)
9-10/54 - No. 4, 3-4/55; No. 5, 7/55 - No. 7, 3/56
Mainline/Charlton Comics No. 5 on

	GD25	FN65	NM94
1-Classic Kirby-c	27.00	81.00	215.00
2-Kirby-c/a(2); Kirby scripts based on his war time experiences	19.50	58.00	155.00
3-5-Kirby-c only	10.50	32.00	85.00
6-Kirby-c/a(2)	17.50	53.00	140.00
7	5.00	15.00	30.00
Super Reprints #10-12,15-18: 10-r/? 11,12,18-r/Foxhole #1,2,3. 15,16-r/United States Marines #5,8. 17-r/Monty Hall #?	1.10	3.30	9.00

NOTE: ***Kirby** a(r)-Super #11, 12. **Powell** a(r)-Super #15, 16. Stories by actual veterans.*

FOX KIDS FUNHOUSE (TV)

Frank #1 © HARV

Frankenstein Comics #8 © PRIZE

FRANKENSTEIN
NOW LET ME TELL YOU ABOUT HOW I BECAME A KING...

Frankie #4 © MgPC

	GD25	FN65	NM94

1997 - Present ($4.50, digest size)
Acclaim Books

1-The Tlck			4.50

FOXY FAGAN COMICS
Dec, 1946 - No. 7, Summer, 1948
Dearfield Publishing Co.

1-Foxy Fagan & Little Buck begin	10.00	30.00	80.00
2	5.70	17.00	40.00
3-7: 6-Rocket ship-c	5.35	16.00	32.00

FRACTURED FAIRY TALES (TV)
Oct, 1962 (Jay Ward)
Gold Key

1 (10022-210)-From Bullwinkle TV show	9.00	27.00	100.00

FRAGGLE ROCK (TV)
Apr, 1985 - No. 8, Sept, 1986; V2#1, Apr, 1988 - No. 6, Sept, 1988
Marvel Comics (Star Comics)/Marvel V2#1 on

1-8 (75¢)		1.20	3.00
V2#1-6-($1.00): Reprints 1st series			1.50

FRANCIS, BROTHER OF THE UNIVERSE
1980 (75¢, 52 pgs., one-shot)
Marvel Comics Group

nn-Buscema/Marie Severin-a; story of Francis Bernadone celebrating his 800th birthday in 1982		.80	2.00

FRANCIS THE FAMOUS TALKING MULE (All based on movie)
No. 335 (#1), June, 1951 - No. 1090, March, 1960
Dell Publishing Co.

Four Color 335 (#1)	7.00	22.00	80.00
Four Color 465	4.50	13.50	50.00
Four Color 501,547,579	3.60	11.00	40.00
Four Color 621,655,698,710,745	2.75	8.00	30.00
Four Color 810,863,906,953,991,1068,1090	2.25	6.75	25.00

FRANK
Apr (Mar inside), 1994 - No. 4, 1994 ($1.75/$2.50, limited series)
Nemesis Comics (Harvey)

1-4-($2.50, direct sale): 1-Foil-c Edition		1.00	2.50
1-4-($1.75)-Newsstand Editions; Cowan-a in all		.70	1.75

FRANK
Sept, 1996 - Present ($2.95, B&W)
Fantagraphics Books

1-Woodring-c/a/scripts		1.20	3.00

FRANK BUCK (Formerly My True Love)
No. 70, May, 1950 - No. 3, Sept, 1950
Fox Features Syndicate

70-Wood a(p)(3 stories)-Photo-c	30.00	90.00	220.00
71-Wood-a (9 pgs.); photo/painted-c	15.00	45.00	110.00
3: 3-Photo/painted-c	11.50	34.00	85.00

NOTE: *Based on "Bring 'Em Back Alive" TV show.*

FRANKENSTEIN (See Dracula, Movie Classics & Werewolf)
Aug-Oct, 1964; No. 2, Sept, 1966 - No. 4, Mar, 1967
Dell Publishing Co.

1(12-283-410)(1964)	3.60	11.00	42.00
2-Intro. & origin super-hero character (9/66)	2.25	6.75	25.00
3,4	1.30	3.90	14.00

FRANKENSTEIN (The Monster of...; also see Monsters Unleashed #2, Power Record Comics, Psycho & Silver Surfer #7)
Jan, 1973 - No. 18, Sept, 1975
Marvel Comics Group

1-Ploog-c/a begins, ends #6	3.00	9.00	30.00
2-5	2.50	7.50	20.00
6,7,10: 7-Dracula cameo	1.25	3.75	10.00
8,9-Dracula c/sty. 9-Death of Drucula	2.60	7.80	26.00
11-18	1.00	2.80	7.00

NOTE: ***Adkins** c-17i. **Buscema** a-7-10p. **Ditko** a-12r. **G. Kane** c-15p. **Orlando** a-8r. **Ploog** a-1-3, 4p, 5p, 6; c-1-6. **Wrightson** c-18i.*

FRANKENSTEIN COMICS (Also See Prize Comics)
Sum, 1945 - V5#5(#33), Oct-Nov, 1954
Prize Publications (Crestwood/Feature)

1-Frankenstein begins by Dick Briefer (origin); Frank Sinatra parody	83.00	250.00	750.00
2	42.00	126.00	375.00
3-5	33.00	98.00	260.00
6-10: 7-S&K a(r)/Headline Comics. 8(7-8/47)-Superman satire	28.00	84.00	225.00
11-17(1-2/49)-11-Boris Karloff parody-c/story. 17-Last humor issue	24.00	71.00	190.00
18(3/52)-New origin, horror series begins	33.00	100.00	265.00
19,20(V3#4, 8-9/52)	20.00	60.00	160.00
21(V3#5), 22(V3#6)	17.50	53.00	140.00
23(V4#1) - #28(V4#6)	17.50	53.00	140.00
29(V5#1) - #33(V5#5)	17.50	53.00	140.00

NOTE: ***Briefer** c/a-all. **Meskin** a-21, 29.*

FRANKENSTEIN/DRACULA WAR, THE
Feb, 1995 - No. 3, May, 1995 ($2.50, limited series)
Topps Comics

1-3		1.00	2.50

FRANKENSTEIN, JR. (...& the Impossibles) (TV)
Jan, 1966 (Hanna-Barbera)
Gold Key

1-Super hero (scarce)	8.00	25.00	90.00

FRANKENSTEIN: OR THE MODERN PROMETHEUS
1994 ($2.95, one-shot)
Caliber Press

1		1.20	3.00

FRANK FRAZETTA'S THUN'DA TALES
1987 ($2.00, one-shot)
Fantagraphics Books

1-Frazetta-r		.80	2.00

FRANK FRAZETTA'S UNTAMED LOVE (Also see Untamed Love)
Nov, 1987 ($2.00, one-shot)
Fantagraphics Books

..1-Frazetta-r from 1950's romance comics		.80	2.00

FRANKIE COMICS (...& Lana No. 13-15) (Formerly Movie Tunes; becomes Frankie Fuddle No. 16 on)
No. 4, Wint, 1946-47 - No. 15, June, 1949
Marvel Comics (MgPC)

4-Mitzi, Margie, Daisy app.	10.00	30.00	80.00
5-9	6.50	19.50	45.00
10-15: 13-Anti-Wertham editorial	5.70	17.00	35.00

FRANKIE DOODLE (See Sparkler, both series)
No. 7, 1939
United Features Syndicate

Single Series 7	26.00	77.00	205.00

FRANKIE FUDDLE (Formerly Frankie & Lana)
No. 16, Aug, 1949 - No. 17, Nov, 1949
Marvel Comics

16,17	5.70	17.00	35.00

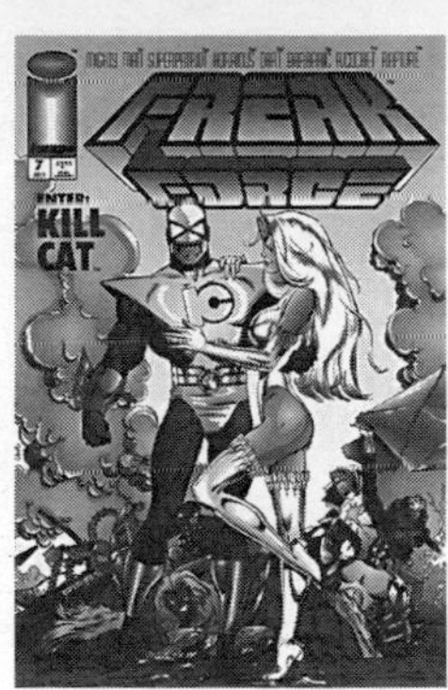
Freak Force #7 © Erik Larsen

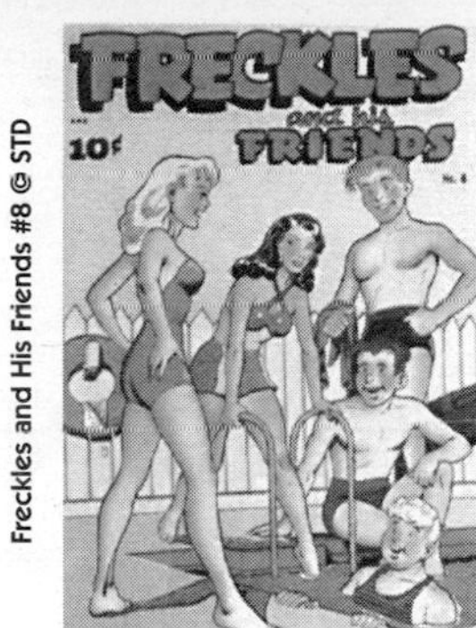
Freckles and His Friends #8 © STD

Freex #5 © Malibu

	GD25	FN65	NM94

FRANK LUTHER'S SILLY PILLY COMICS (See Jingle Dingle...)
1950 (10¢)
Children's Comics (Maltex Cereal)

	GD25	FN65	NM94
1-Characters from radio, records, & TV	5.00	15.00	30.00

FRANK MERRIWELL AT YALE (Speed Demons No. 5 on?)
June, 1955 - No. 4, Jan, 1956 (Also see Shadow Comics)
Charlton Comics

	GD25	FN65	NM94
1	4.25	13.00	28.00
2-4	4.00	11.00	22.00

FRANTIC (Magazine) (See Ratfink & Zany)
Oct, 1958 - V2#2, Apr, 1959 (Satire)
Pierce Publishing Co.

	GD25	FN65	NM94
V1#1,2	5.70	17.00	35.00
V2#1,2: 1-Burgos-a, Severin-c/a; Powell-a?	4.15	12.50	25.00

FREAK FORCE (Also see Savage Dragon)
Dec, 1993 - No. 18, July, 1995 ($1.95/$2.50)
Image Comics (Highbrow Entertainment)

	GD25	FN65	NM94
1-7-Superpatriot & Mighty Man in all; Erik Larsen scripts in all. 4-Vanguard app.		.80	2.00
8-18: 8-Begin $2.50-c. 9-Cyberforce-c & app.		1.00	2.50

FREAK FORCE (Also see Savage Dragon)
Apr, 1997 - No. 3, July, 1997 ($2.95)
Image Comics

	GD25	FN65	NM94
1-3-Larsen-s			2.95

FRECKLES AND HIS FRIENDS (See Crackajack Funnies, Famous Comics Cartoon Book, Honeybee Birdwhistle... & Red Ryder)

FRECKLES AND HIS FRIENDS
No. 5, 11/47 - No. 12, 8/49; 11/55 - No. 4, 6/56
Standard Comics/Argo

	GD25	FN65	NM94
5-Reprints	5.70	17.00	40.00
6-12-Reprints. 7-9-Airbrush-c (by Schomburg?). 11-Lingerie panels	4.25	13.00	26.00

NOTE: *Some copies of No. 8 & 9 contain a printing oddity. The negatives were elongated in the engraving process, probably to conform to page dimensions on the filler pages. Those pages only look normal when viewed at a 45 degree angle.*

	GD25	FN65	NM94
1(Argo,'55)-Reprints (NEA Service)	4.25	13.00	28.00
2-4	4.00	10.00	20.00

FREDDY (Formerly My Little Margie's Boy Friends) (Also see Blue Bird)
V2#12, June, 1958 - No. 47, Feb, 1965
Charlton Comics

	GD25	FN65	NM94
V2#12	2.50	7.50	22.00
13-15	1.85	5.50	15.00
16-47	1.25	3.75	10.00
Schiff's Shoes Presents... #1 (1959)-Giveaway		2.00	5.00

FREDDY
May-July, 1963 - No. 3, Oct-Dec, 1964
Dell Publishing Co.

	GD25	FN65	NM94
1	2.50	7.50	20.00
2,3	1.50	4.50	12.00

FREDDY KRUEGER'S A NIGHTMARE ON ELM STREET
Oct, 1989 - No. 2, Dec, 1989 ($2.25, B&W, movie adaptation)
Marvel Comics

	GD25	FN65	NM94
1,2: Origin Freddy Krueger; Buckler/Alcala-a		.90	2.30

FREDDY'S DEAD: THE FINAL NIGHTMARE
Oct, 1991 - No. 3, Dec 1991 ($2.50, color mini-series, adapts movie)
Innovation Publishing

	GD25	FN65	NM94
..1-3: Dismukes (film poster artist) painted-c		1.00	2.50

FRED HEMBECK DESTROYS THE MARVEL UNIVERSE
July, 1989 ($1.50, one-shot)
Marvel Comics

	GD25	FN65	NM94
1-Punisher app.; Staton-i (5 pgs.)			1.50

FRED HEMBECK SELLS THE MARVEL UNIVERSE
Oct, 1990 ($1.25, one-shot)
Marvel Comics

	GD25	FN65	NM94
1-Punisher, Wolverine parodies; Hembeck/Austin-c			1.25

FREE COMICS TO YOU FROM... (name of shoe store) (Has clown on cover & another with a rabbit) (Like comics from Weather Bird & Edward's Shoes)
Circa 1956, 1960-61
Shoe Store Giveaway

Contains a comic bound with new cover - several combinations possible; some Harvey titles known. Contents determines price.

FREEDOM AGENT (Also see John Steele)
Apr, 1963 (12¢)
Gold Key

	GD25	FN65	NM94
1 (10054-304)-Painted-c	2.50	7.50	28.00

FREEDOM FIGHTERS (See Justice League of America #107,108)
Mar-Apr, 1976 - No. 15, July-Aug, 1978
National Periodical Publications/DC Comics

	GD25	FN65	NM94
1-Uncle Sam, The Ray, Black Condor, Doll Man, Human Bomb, & Phantom Lady begin (all former Quality characters)		2.40	6.00
2-9: 4,5-Wonder Woman x-over. 7-1st app. Crusaders		1.60	4.00
10-15: 10-Origin Doll Man; Cat-Man-c/story (4th app; 1st revival since Det. #325). 11-Origin The Ray. 12-Origin Firebrand. 13-Origin Black Condor. 14-Batgirl & Batwoman app. 15-Batgirl & Batwoman app.; origin Phantom Lady		2.00	5.00

NOTE: ***Buckler** c-5-11p, 13p, 14p.*

FREEDOM TRAIN
1948 (Giveaway)
Street & Smith Publications

	GD25	FN65	NM94
nn-Powell-c w/mailer	15.00	45.00	120.00

FREEX
July, 1993 - No. 18, Mar, 1995 ($1.95)
Malibu Comics (Ultraverse)

	GD25	FN65	NM94
1-3,5-14,16-18: 1-Polybagged w/trading card. 2-Some were polybagged w/card. 6-Nightman-c/story. 7-2 pg. origin Hardcase by Zeck. 17-Rune app.		.80	2.00
1-Holographic-c edition	1.00	3.00	8.00
1-Ultra 5,000 limited silver ink-c		2.00	5.00
4-($2.50, 48 pgs.)-Rune flip-c/story by B. Smith (3 pgs.); 3 pg. Night Man preview		1.00	2.50
15 ($3.50)-w/Ultraverse Premiere #9 flip book; Alec Swan & Rafferty app.		1.40	3.50
Giant Size 1 (1994, $2.50)-Prime app.		1.00	2.50

NOTE: ***Simonson** c-1.*

FRENZY (Magazine) (Satire)
Apr, 1958 - No. 6, Mar, 1959
Picture Magazine

	GD25	FN65	NM94
1	7.15	21.50	50.00
2-6	5.35	16.00	32.00

FRIDAY FOSTER
October, 1972
Dell Publishing Co.

	GD25	FN65	NM94
1	1.80	5.50	20.00

FRIENDLY GHOST, CASPER, THE (Becomes Casper... #254 on)
Aug, 1958 - No. 224, Oct, 1982; No. 225, Oct, 1986 - No. 253, June, 1990
Harvey Publications

	GD25	FN65	NM94
1-Infinity-c	22.00	67.00	220.00

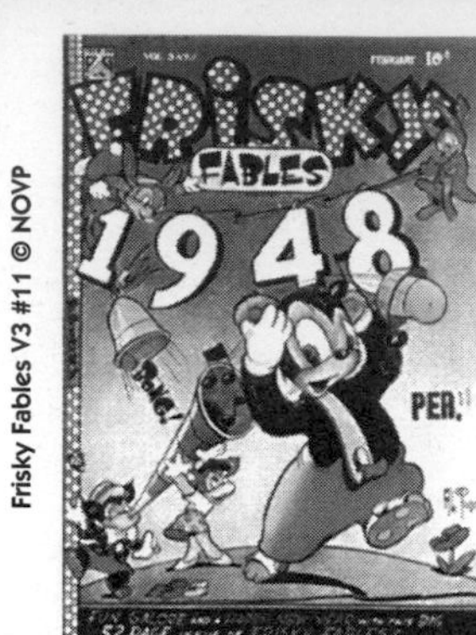

Frisky Fables V3 #11 © NOVP

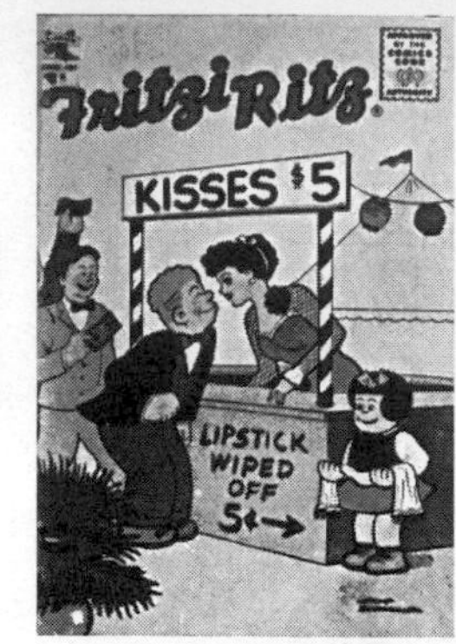

Fritzi Ritz nn © UFS

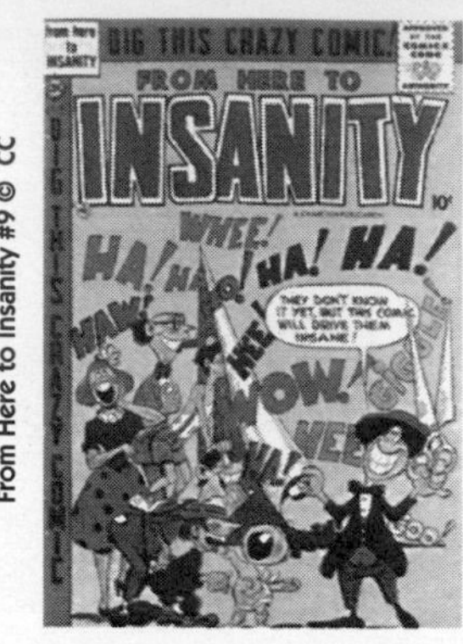

From Here to Insanity #9 © CC

	GD25	FN65	NM94
2	10.00	30.00	100.00
3-10: 6-X-Mas-c	5.00	15.00	50.00
11-20: 18-X-Mas-c	3.50	10.50	35.00
21-30	2.00	6.00	20.00
31-50	1.75	5.25	14.00
51-100: 54-X-Mas-c	1.50	4.50	12.00
101-159	1.10	3.30	9.00
160-163: All 52 pg. Giants	1.10	3.30	9.00
164-200		2.00	5.00
201-237: 173,179,185-Cub Scout Specials. 230-X-mas-c. 232-Valentine's-c		1.60	4.00
238-253: 238-Begin $1.00-c. 238,244-Halloween-c. 243-Last new material		.80	2.00
American Dental Assoc. giveaway-Small size (1967, 16 pgs.)	2.50	7.50	20.00

FRIENDS OF MAXX (Also see Maxx)
Apr, 1996 ($2.95)
Image Comics (I Before E)

	GD25	FN65	NM94
1-Featuring Dude Japan; Sam Kieth-c/a/scripts		1.20	3.00

FRIGHT
June, 1975 (Aug on inside)
Atlas/Seaboard Periodicals

	GD25	FN65	NM94
1-Origin The Son of Dracula; Frank Thorne-c/a		1.20	3.00

FRIGHT NIGHT
Oct, 1988 - No. 22, 1990 ($1.75)
Now Comics

	GD25	FN65	NM94
..1-22: 1-3 Adapts movie. 8, 9-Evil Ed horror photo-c from movie		.70	1.75

FRIGHT NIGHT II
1989 ($3.95, 52 pgs.)
Now Comics

	GD25	FN65	NM94
..1-Adapts movie sequel		1.60	4.00

FRISKY ANIMALS (Formerly Frisky Fables; Super Cat #56 on)
No. 44, Jan, 1951 - No. 55, Sept, 1953
Star Publications

	GD25	FN65	NM94
44-Super Cat; L.B. Cole	16.00	49.00	130.00
45-Classic L. B. Cole-c	24.00	71.00	190.00
46-51,53-55: Super Cat. 54-Super Cat-c begin	15.00	45.00	120.00
52-L. B. Cole-c/a, 3 1/2 pgs.; X-Mas-c	16.00	49.00	130.00

NOTE: *All have* **L. B. Cole**-*c. No. 47-No Super Cat.* **Disbrow** *a-49, 52.* **Fago** *a-51.*

FRISKY ANIMALS ON PARADE (Formerly Parade Comics; becomes Superspook)
Sept, 1957 - No. 3, Dec-Jan, 1957-1958
Ajax-Farrell Publ. (Four Star Comic Corp.)

	GD25	FN65	NM94
1-L. B. Cole-c	14.00	41.00	110.00
2-No L. B. Cole-c	6.00	18.00	42.00
3-L. B. Cole-c	11.30	34.00	90.00

FRISKY FABLES (Frisky Animals No. 44 on)
Spring, 1945 - No. 43, Oct, 1950
Premium Group/Novelty Publ./Star Publ. V5#4 on

	GD25	FN65	NM94
V1#1-Funny animal; Al Fago-c/a #1-38	15.50	47.00	125.00
2,3(Fall & Winter, 1945)	7.85	23.50	55.00
V2#1(#4, 4/46) - 9,11,12(#15, 3/47): 4-Flag-c	5.70	17.00	40.00
10-Christmas-c	6.50	19.50	45.00
V3#1(#16, 4/47) - 12(#27, 3/48): 4-Flag-c. 7,9-Infinity-c. 10-X-Mas-c	5.35	16.00	32.00
V4#1(#28, 4/48) - 7(#34, 2-3/49)	5.35	16.00	32.00
V5#1(#35, 4-5/49) - 4(#38, 10-11/49)	5.35	16.00	32.00
39-43-L. B. Cole-c; 40-X-mas-c	16.00	49.00	130.00
Accepted Reprint No. 43 (nd); L.B. Cole-c	5.70	17.00	40.00

FRITZI RITZ (See Comics On Parade, Single Series #5, 1(reprint), Tip Top & United Comics)

FRITZI RITZ (United Comics No. 8-26)
Fall, 1948 - No. 7, 1949; No. 27, 3-4/53 - No. 36, 9-10/54; No. 42, 1/55; No. 43, 6/56 - No. 55, 9-11/57; No. 56, 12-2/57-58 - No. 59, 9-11/58
United Features Synd./St. John No. 37?-55/Dell No. 56 on

	GD25	FN65	NM94
nn(1948)-Special Fall issue; by Ernie Bushmiller	11.30	34.00	90.00
2	6.50	19.50	45.00
3-7(1949): 6-Abbie & Slats app.	5.70	17.00	35.00
27-29(1953): 29-Five pg. Abbie & Slats; 1 pg. Mamie by Russell Patterson	4.25	13.00	26.00
30-59: 31-Peanuts by Schulz (1st app.?, 11-12/53). 36-1 pg. Mamie by Patterson	4.00	12.00	24.00

NOTE: *Abbie & Slats in #6,7, 27-31. Li'l Abner in #33, 35, 36. Peanuts in #31, 43, 58, 59.*

FROGMAN COMICS
Jan-Feb, 1952 - No. 11, May, 1953
Hillman Periodicals

	GD25	FN65	NM94
1	9.50	28.00	75.00
2	5.70	17.00	38.00
3,4,6-11: 4-Meskin-a	5.00	15.00	30.00
5-Krigstein-a	5.70	17.00	40.00

FROGMEN, THE
No. 1258, Feb-Apr, 1962 - No. 11, Nov-Jan, 1964-65 (Painted-c)
Dell Publishing Co.

	GD25	FN65	NM94
Four Color 1258(#1)-Evans-a	6.40	19.00	70.00
2,3-Evans-a; part Frazetta inks in #2,3	4.50	13.50	50.00
4,6-11	2.25	6.75	25.00
5-Toth-a	3.00	9.00	35.00

FROM BEYOND THE UNKNOWN
10-11/69 - No. 25, 11-12/73 (No. 7-11: 64 pgs.; No. 12-17: 52 pgs.)
National Periodical Publications

	GD25	FN65	NM94
1	3.50	10.50	35.00
2-10	1.85	5.50	15.00
7-11: 7-Intro Col. Glenn Merrit	2.25	6.75	18.00
12-17:13-Wood-a(i)(r)	1.75	5.25	14.00
18-25: Star Rovers-r begin #18,19. Space Museum in #23-25	1.25	3.75	10.00

NOTE: **N. Adams** *c-3, 6, 8, 9.* **Anderson** *c-2, 4, 5, 10, 11i, 15-17, 22; reprints-3, 4, 6-8, 10, 11, 13-16, 24, 25.* **Infantino** *r-1-5, 7-19, 23-25; c-11p.* **Kaluta** *c-18, 19.* **Gil Kane** *a-9r.* **Kubert** *c-1, 7, 12-14.* **Toth** *a-2r.* **Wood** *a-13i. Photo c-22.*

FROM DUSK TILL DAWN (Movie)
1996 ($4.95, one-shot)
Big Entertainment

	GD25	FN65	NM94
nn-Adaptation of the film; Brereton-c		2.00	5.00
nn-($9.95)Deluxe Ed. w/ new material	1.25	3.75	10.00

FROM HERE TO INSANITY (Satire) (Formerly Eh! #1-7)
(See Frantic & Frenzy)
No. 8, Feb, 1955 - V3#1, 1956
Charlton Comics

	GD25	FN65	NM94
8	11.30	34.00	90.00
9	9.50	28.00	75.00
10-Ditko-c/a (3 pgs.)	16.00	49.00	130.00
11,12-All Kirby except 4 pgs.	23.00	68.00	180.00
V3#1(1956)-Ward-c/a(2) (signed McCartney); 5 pgs. Wolverton-a; 3 pgs. Ditko-a; magazine format (cover says "Crazy, Man, Crazy" and becomes Crazy, Man, Crazy with V2#2)	34.00	103.00	275.00

FROM THE PIT
1994 ($4.95, one-shot, mature)
Fantagor Press

	GD25	FN65	NM94
1-R. Corben-a; HP Lovecraft back-up story		2.00	5.00

FRONTIER DAYS

Frontier Fighters #7 © DC

Fugitives From Justice #1 © STJ

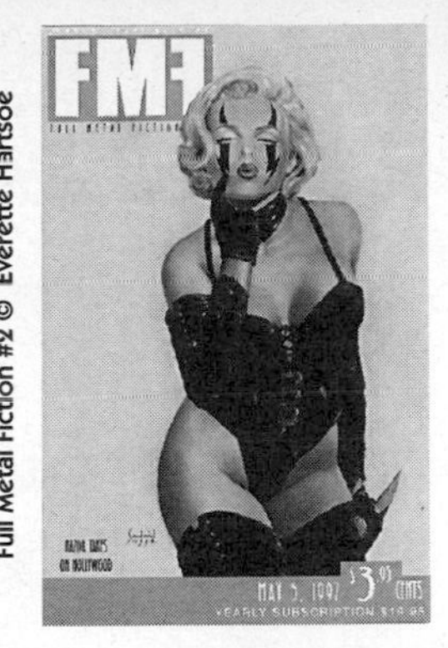

Full Metal Fiction #2 © Everette Hartsoe

	GD25	FN65	NM94

1956 (Giveaway)
Robin Hood Shoe Store (Brown Shoe)

	GD25	FN65	NM94
1	3.20	8.00	16.00

FRONTIER DOCTOR (TV)
No. 877, Feb, 1958 (one-shot)
Dell Publishing Co.

	GD25	FN65	NM94
Four Color 877-Toth-a, Rex Allen photo-c	9.00	27.00	100.00

FRONTIER FIGHTERS
Sept-Oct, 1955 - No. 8, Nov-Dec, 1956
National Periodical Publications

	GD25	FN65	NM94
1-Davy Crockett, Buffalo Bill (by Kubert), Kit Carson begin (Scarce)	50.00	150.00	420.00
2	40.00	120.00	300.00
3-8	36.00	107.00	260.00

NOTE: *Buffalo Bill by **Kubert** in all.*

FRONTIER ROMANCES
Nov-Dec, 1949 - No. 2, Feb-Mar, 1950 (Painted-c)
Avon Periodicals/I. W.

	GD25	FN65	NM94
1-Used in **SOTI**, pg. 180(General reference) & illo. "Erotic spanking in a western comic book"	43.00	128.00	350.00
2 (Scarce)-Woodish-a by Stallman	33.00	99.00	240.00
I.W. Reprint #1-Reprints Avon's #1	3.20	9.60	32.00
I.W. Reprint #9-Reprints ?	2.50	7.50	20.00

FRONTIER SCOUT: DAN'L BOONE (Formerly Death Valley; The Masked Raider No. 14 on)
No. 10, Jan, 1956 - No. 13, Aug, 1956; V2#14, Mar, 1965
Charlton Comics

	GD25	FN65	NM94
10	8.50	26.00	60.00
11-13(1956)	5.35	16.00	32.00
V2#14(3/65)	4.00	10.00	20.00

FRONTIER TRAIL (The Rider No. 1-5)
No. 6, May, 1958
Ajax/Farrell Publ.

	GD25	FN65	NM94
6	4.25	13.00	26.00

FRONTIER WESTERN
Feb, 1956 - No. 10, Aug, 1957
Atlas Comics (PrPI)

	GD25	FN65	NM94
1	16.00	47.00	120.00
2,3,6-Williamson-a, 4 pgs. each	11.00	33.00	80.00
4,7,9,10: 10-Check-a	6.50	19.50	45.00
5-Crandall, Baker, Davis-a; Williamson text illos	10.00	30.00	65.00
8-Crandall, Morrow, & Wildey-a	6.50	19.50	45.00

NOTE: ***Baker** a-9. **Colan** a-2, 6. **Drucker** a-3, 4. **Heath** c-5. **Maneely** c/a-2, 7, 9. **Maurera** a-2. **Romita** a-7. **Severin** c-6, 8, 10. **Tuska** a-2. **Wildey** a-5, 8. Ringo Kid in No. 4.*

FRONTLINE COMBAT
July-Aug, 1951 - No. 15, Jan, 1954
E. C. Comics

	GD25	FN65	NM94
1-Severin/Kurtzman-a	52.00	156.00	465.00
2	37.00	111.00	260.00
3	26.00	79.00	190.00
4-Used in **SOTI**, pg. 257; contains "Airburst" by Kurtzman which is his personal all-time favorite story	24.00	71.00	170.00
5	20.00	60.00	150.00
6-10	17.00	49.00	120.00
11-15	12.00	36.00	90.00

NOTE: ***Davis** a-in all; c-11, 12. **Evans** a-10-15. **Heath** a-1. **Kubert** a-14. **Kurtzman** a-1-5; c-1-9. **Severin** a-5-7, 9, 13, 15. **Severin/Elder** a-2-11; c-10. **Toth** a-8, 12. **Wood** a-1-4, 6-10, 12-15; c-13-15. Special issues: No. 7 (Iwo Jima), No. 9 (Civil War), No. 12 (Air Force).*
(Canadian reprints known; see Table of Contents.)

FRONTLINE COMBAT
Aug, 1995 - Present ($2.50)
Russ Cochran/Gemstone Publishing

	GD25	FN65	NM94
1-4		.80	2.00
5-12		1.00	2.50

FRONT PAGE COMIC BOOK
1945
Front Page Comics (Harvey)

	GD25	FN65	NM94
1-Kubert-a; intro. & 1st app. Man in Black by Powell; Fuje-c	34.00	103.00	250.00

FROST AND FIRE (See DC Science Fiction Graphic Novel)

FROSTY THE SNOWMAN
No. 359, Nov, 1951 - No. 1272, Dec-Feb?/1961-62
Dell Publishing Co.

	GD25	FN65	NM94
Four Color 359 (#1)	7.00	22.00	80.00
Four Color 435	3.60	11.00	40.00
Four Color 514,601,661	3.60	11.00	40.00
Four Color 748,861,950,1065,1153,1272	3.00	9.00	35.00

FRUITMAN SPECIAL
Dec, 1969 (68 pgs.)
Harvey Publications

	GD25	FN65	NM94
1-Funny super hero	2.00	6.00	20.00

F-TROOP (TV)
Aug, 1966 - No. 7, Aug, 1967 (All have photo-c)
Dell Publishing Co.

	GD25	FN65	NM94
1	8.00	23.00	85.00
2-7	4.50	13.50	50.00

FUGITIVES FROM JUSTICE
Feb, 1952 - No. 5, Oct, 1952
St. John Publishing Co.

	GD25	FN65	NM94
1	16.00	47.00	120.00
2-Matt Baker-r/Northwest Mounties #2; Vic Flint strip reprints begin	17.00	51.00	125.00
3-Reprints panel from Authentic Police Cases that was used in **SOTI** with changes; Tuska-a	17.00	51.00	120.00
4	7.15	21.50	50.00
5-Last Vic Flint-r; bondage-c	10.00	30.00	60.00

FUGITOID
1985 (B&W, magazine size, one-shot)
Mirage Studios

	GD25	FN65	NM94
1-Ties into Teenage Mutant Ninja Turtles #5		1.20	3.00

FULL COLOR COMICS
1946
Fox Features Syndicate

	GD25	FN65	NM94
nn	9.50	28.00	75.00

FULL METAL FICTION
Mar, 1997 - Present ($3.95, B&W, mature)
London Night Studios

	GD25	FN65	NM94
1-4-Anthology: 1-Razor			3.95

FULL OF FUN
Aug, 1957 - No. 2, Nov, 1957; 1964
Red Top (Decker Publ.)(Farrell)/I. W. Enterprises

	GD25	FN65	NM94
1(1957)-Funny animal; Dave Berg-a	5.35	16.00	32.00
2-Reprints Bingo, the Monkey Doodle Boy	4.00	11.00	22.00
8-I.W. Reprint('64)	1.00	3.00	8.00

FUN AT CHRISTMAS (See March of Comics No. 138)

FUN CLUB COMICS (See Interstate Theatres...)

FUN COMICS (Formerly Holiday Comics #1-8; Mighty Bear #13 on)

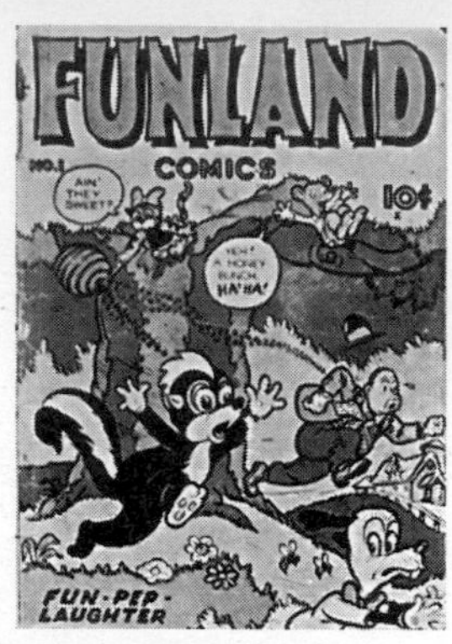

Funland Comics #1 © Croyden Publ.

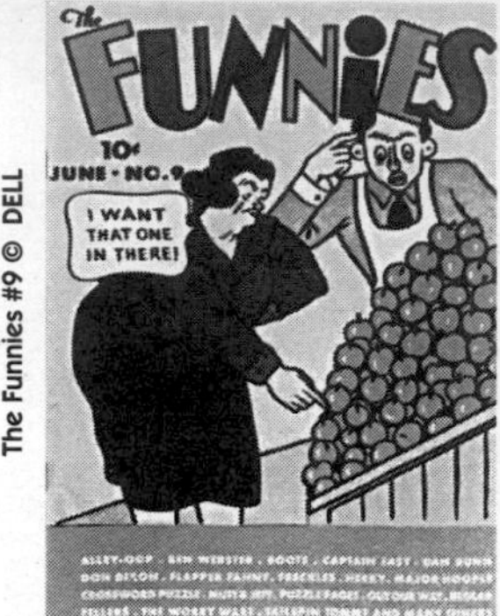

The Funnies #9 © DELL

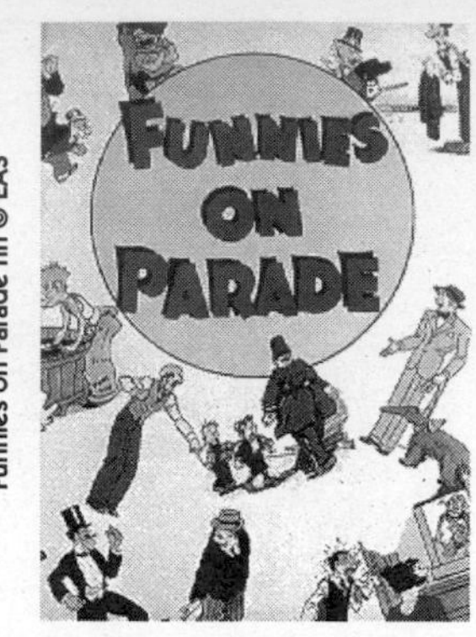

Funnies on Parade nn © EAS

GD25 FN65 NM94

No. 9, Jan, 1953 - No. 12, Oct, 1953
Star Publications

9-(25¢ Giant)-L. B. Cole X-Mas-c; X-Mas issue 16.00 49.00 130.00
10-12-L. B. Cole-c. 12-Mighty Bear-c/story 14.00 41.00 110.00

FUNDAY FUNNIES (See Famous TV..., and Harvey Hits No. 35,40)

FUN-IN (TV)(Hanna-Barbera)
Feb, 1970 - No. 10, Jan, 1972; No. 11, 4/74 - No. 15, 12/74
Gold Key

1-Dastardly & Muttley in Their Flying Machines; Perils of Penelope Pitstop in #1-4; It's the Wolf in all 4.50 13.50 50.00
2-4,6-Cattanooga Cats in 2-4 2.25 6.75 26.00
5,7-Motormouse & Autocat, Dastardly & Muttley in both; It's the Wolf in #7 2.75 8.00 30.00
8,10-The Harlem Globetrotters, Dastardly & Muttley in #10 2.25 6.75 24.00
9-Where's Huddles?, Dastardly & Muttley, Motormouse & Autocat app. 2.75 8.00 30.00
11-15: 11-Butch Cassidy. 12,15-Speed Buggy. 13-Hair Bear Bunch. 14-Inch High Private Eye 1.65 5.00 18.00

FUNKY PHANTOM, THE (TV)
Mar, 1972 - No. 13, Mar, 1975 (Hanna-Barbera)
Gold Key

1 3.60 11.00 40.00
2-5 1.80 5.50 20.00
6-13 1.40 4.20 14.00

FUNLAND
No date (1940s) (25¢)
Ziff-Davis (Approved Comics)

nn-Contains games, puzzles, cut-outs, etc. 12.00 36.00 95.00

FUNLAND COMICS
1945
Croyden Publishers

1-Funny animal 12.00 36.00 95.00

FUNNIES, THE (New Funnies No. 65 on)
Oct, 1936 - No. 64, May, 1942
Dell Publishing Co.

1-Tailspin Tommy, Mutt & Jeff, Alley Oop (1st app?), Capt. Easy (1st app.), Don Dixon begin 325.00 975.00 2150.00
2-Scribbly by Mayer begins (1st app.) 137.00 412.00 875.00
3 110.00 330.00 660.00
4,5: 4-Christmas-c 83.00 249.00 540.00
6-10 62.00 187.00 400.00
11-20: 16-Christmas-c 56.00 170.00 360.00
21-29: 25-Crime Busters by McWilliams(4pgs.) 44.00 132.00 275.00
30-John Carter of Mars (origin/1st app.) begins by Edgar Rice Burroughs; Warner Bros.' Bosko-c (4/39) 92.00 276.00 825.00
31-44: 33-John Coleman Burroughs art begins on John Carter. 34-Last funny-c. 35-(9/39)-Mr. District Attorney begins; based on radio show 56.00 168.00 500.00
45-Origin/1st app. Phantasmo, the Master of the World (Dell's 1st super-hero, 7/40) & his sidekick Whizzer McGee 50.00 150.00 450.00
46-50: 46-The Black Knight begins, ends #62 36.00 108.00 325.00
51-56-Last ERB John Carter of Mars 36.00 108.00 300.00
57-Intro. & origin Captain Midnight (7/41) 133.00 400.00 1200.00
58-60: 58-Captain Midnight-c begin, end #63 56.00 168.00 500.00
61-Andy Panda begins by Walter Lantz 50.00 150.00 450.00
62,63: 63-Last Captain Midnight-c; bondage-c 50.00 150.00 450.00
64-Format change; Oswald the Rabbit, Felix the Cat, Li'l Eight Ball app.; origin & 1st app. Woody Woodpecker in Oswald; last Capt. Midnight; Oswald, Andy Panda, Li'l Eight Ball-c 78.00 234.00 700.00

NOTE: ***Mayer** c-26, 48. **McWilliams** art in many issues on "Rex King of the Deep". Alley Oop c-17, 20. Captain Midnight c-57(i/2), 58-63. John Carter c-35-37, 40. Phantasmo c-45-56, 57(1/2), 58-61(part). Rex King c-38, 39, 42. Tailspin Tommy c-41.*

FUNNIES ANNUAL, THE
1959 ($1.00, approx. 7x10", B&W; tabloid-size)
Avon Periodicals

1-(Rare)-Features the best newspaper comic strips of the year: Archie, Snuffy Smith, Beetle Bailey, Henry, Blondie, Steve Canyon, Buz Sawyer, The Little King, Hi & Lois, Popeye, & others. Also has a chronological history of the comics from 2000 B.C. to 1959. 36.00 108.00 325.00

FUNNIES ON PARADE (Premium)
1933 (Probably the 1st comic book) (36 pgs., slick cover)
No date or publisher listed
Eastern Color Printing Co.

GD25 FN65 VF82 NM94

nn-Contains Sunday page reprints of Mutt & Jeff, Joe Palooka, Hairbreadth Harry, Reg'lar Fellers, Skippy, & others (10,000 print run). This book was printed for Proctor & Gamble to be given away & came out before Famous Funnies or Century of Comics. 1111.00 3333.00 6667.00 11,000.00
(Estimated up to 50 total copies exist, 3 in NM/Mint)

FUNNY ANIMALS (See Fawcett's Funny Animals)
Sept, 1984 - No. 2, Nov, 1984
Charlton Comics

GD25 FN65 NM94

1,2-Atomic Mouse-r 1.00

FUNNYBONE (... The Laugh-Book of Comical Comics)
1944 (25¢, 132 pgs.)
La Salle Publishing Co.

nn 23.00 68.00 180.00

FUNNY BOOK (...Magazine for Young Folks) (Hocus Pocus No. 9)
Dec, 1942 - No. 9, Aug-Sept, 1946 (Comics, stories, puzzles, games)
Parents' Magazine Press (Funny Book Publishing Corp.)

1-Funny animal; Alice In Wonderland app. 11.30 34.00 90.00
2-Gulliver in Giant-Land 6.50 19.50 45.00
3-9: 4-Advs. of Robin Hood. 9-Hocus-Pocus strip 5.35 16.00 32.00

FUNNY COMICS
1955 (7¢, 5x7", 36 pgs.)
Modern Store Publ.

1-Funny animal 1.60 4.00 8.00

FUNNY COMIC TUNES (See Funny Tunes)

FUNNY FABLES
Aug, 1957 - V2#2, Nov, 1957
Decker Publications (Red Top Comics)

V1#1 4.00 12.00 24.00
V2#1,2 3.20 8.00 16.00

FUNNY FILMS (Features funny animal characters from films)
Sept-Oct, 1949 - No. 29, May-June, 1954 (No. 1-4: 52 pgs.)
American Comics Group(Michel Publ./Titan Publ.)

1-Puss An' Boots, Blunderbunny begin 15.50 47.00 125.00
2 8.75 26.25 65.00
3-10: 3-X-Mas-c 5.70 17.00 40.00
11-20 5.00 15.00 30.00
21-29 4.00 10.50 21.00

FUNNY FOLKS (Hollywood... on cover only No. 16-26; becomes Hollywood Funny Folks No. 27 on)
April-May, 1946 - No. 26, June-July, 1950 (52 pgs., #16 on)
National Periodical Publications

1-Nutsy Squirrel begins (1st app.) by Rube Grossman 36.00 108.00 290.00
2 16.00 49.00 130.00
3-5: 4-1st Nutsy Squirrel-c 12.00 36.00 95.00
6-10: 6,9-Nutsy Squirrel-c begin 8.75 26.25 70.00

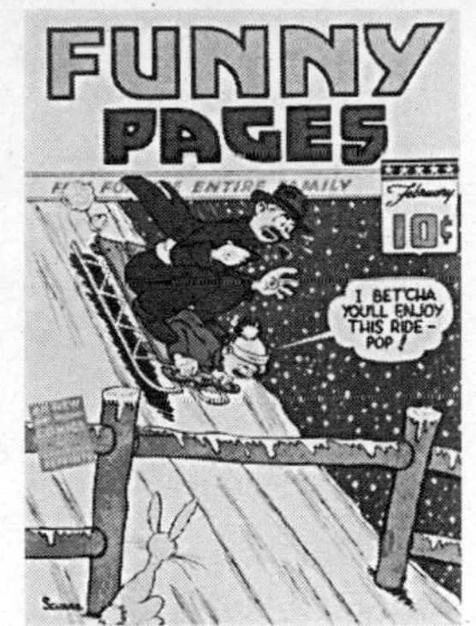

Funny Pages V3 #1 © CHES

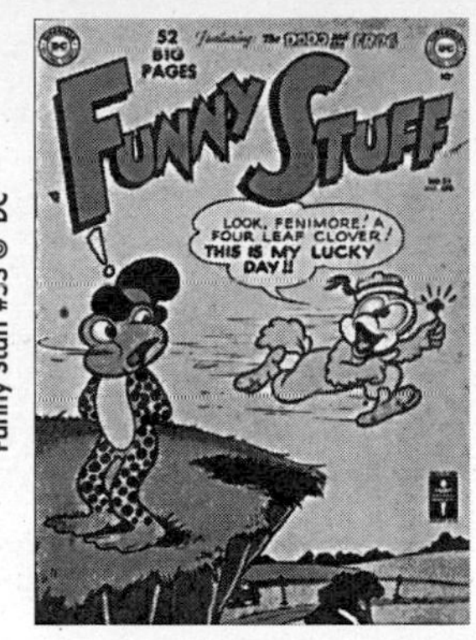

Funny Stuff #53 © DC

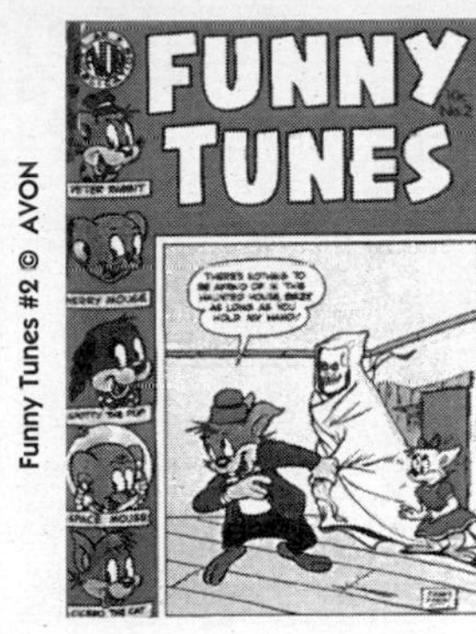

Funny Tunes #2 © AVON

	GD25	FN65	NM94
11-26: 16-Begin 52 pg. issues (10-11/48)	8.50	26.00	60.00

NOTE: ***Sheldon Mayer** a-in some issues. **Post** a-18. Christmas c-12.*

FUNNY FROLICS
Summer, 1945 - No. 5, Dec, 1946
Timely/Marvel Comics (SPI)

	GD25	FN65	NM94
1-Sharpy Fox, Puffy Pig, Krazy Krow	17.00	51.00	135.00
2	8.75	26.25	70.00
3,4	7.15	21.50	50.00
5-Kurtzman-a	8.50	26.00	60.00

FUNNY FUNNIES
April, 1943 (68 pgs.)
Nedor Publishing Co.

	GD25	FN65	NM94
1-Funny animals; Peter Porker app.	15.50	47.00	125.00

FUNNYMAN (Also see Cisco Kid Comics & Extra Comics)
Dec, 1947; No. 1, Jan, 1948 - No. 6, Aug, 1948
Magazine Enterprises

nn(12/47)-Prepublication B&W undistributed copy by Siegel & Shuster-(5-3/4x8"), 16 pgs.; Sold at auction in 1997 for $575.00

	GD25	FN65	NM94
1-Siegel & Shuster-a in all; Dick Ayers 1st pro work (as assistant) on 1st few issues	34.00	103.00	275.00
2	22.00	66.00	175.00
3-6	19.00	56.00	150.00

FUNNY MOVIES (See 3-D Funny Movies)

FUNNY PAGES (Formerly The Comics Magazine)
No. 6, Nov, 1936 - No. 42, Oct, 1940
Comics Magazine Co./Ultem Publ.(Chesler)/Centaur Publications

	GD25	FN65	NM94
V1#6 (nn, nd)-The Clock begins (2 pgs., 1st app.), ends #11; The Clock is the 1st masked comic book hero	139.00	417.00	1250.00
(Estimated up to 10 total copies exist; prices vary widely on this book)			
7-11	58.00	174.00	525.00
V2#1 (9/37)(V2#2 on-c; V2#1 in indicia)	39.00	117.00	350.00
V2#2 (10/37)(V2#3 on-c; V2#2 in indicia)	39.00	117.00	350.00
3(11/37)-5	39.00	117.00	350.00
6(1st Centaur, 3/38)	70.00	210.00	630.00
7-9	47.00	141.00	420.00
10(Scarce, 9/38)-1st app. of The Arrow by Gustavson (Blue costume)	211.00	633.00	1900.00
11,12	85.00	255.00	765.00
V3#1-6: 6,8-Last funny covers	83.00	250.00	740.00
7-1st Arrow-c (9/39)	144.00	432.00	1300.00
8,9: 9-Tarpe Mills jungle-c	84.00	252.00	765.00
10-2nd Arrow-c	117.00	350.00	1050.00
V4#1(1/40, Arrow-c)-(Rare)-The Owl & The Phantom Rider app.; origin Mantoka, Maker of Magic by Jack Cole. Mad Ming begins, ends #42; Tarpe Mills-a	144.00	432.00	1300.00
35-Classic Arrow-c	133.00	400.00	1200.00
36-38-Mad Ming-c	83.00	250.00	740.00
39-42-Arrow-c. 42-Last Arrow	106.00	318.00	950.00

NOTE: ***Biro** c-V2#9. **Burgos** c-V3#10. **Jack Cole** a-V2#3, 7, 8, 10, 11, V3#2, 6, 9, 10, V4#1, 37; c-V3#2, 4. **Eisner** a-V1#7, 8?, 10. **Ken Ernst** a-V1#7, 8. **Everett** a-V2#11 (illos). **Filchock** c-V2#10, V3#6. **Gill Fox** a-V2#11. **Sid Greene** a-39. **Guardineer** a-V2#2, 3, 5. **Gustavson** a-V2#5, 11, 12, V3#1-10, 35, 38-42; c-V3#7, 35, 39-42. **Bob Kane** a-V3#1. **McWilliams** a-V2#12, V3#1, 3-6. **Tarpe Mills** a-V3#8-10, V4#1; c-V3#9. **Ed Moore Jr.** a-V2#12. **Schwab** c-V3#1. **Bob Wood** a-V2#2, 3, 8, 11, V3#6, 9, 10; c-V2#6, 7. Arrow c-V3#7, 10, V4#1, 35, 40-42.*

FUNNY PICTURE STORIES (Comic Pages V3#4 on)
Nov, 1936 - V3#3, May, 1939
Comics Magazine Co./Centaur Publications

	GD25	FN65	NM94
V1#1-The Clock begins (c-feature)(see Funny Pages for 1st app.)	240.00	720.00	2400.00
2	83.00	250.00	740.00
3-9: 4-Eisner-a; X-Mas-c. 7-Racial humor-c	58.00	174.00	525.00
V2#1 (9/37; V1#10 on-c; V2#1 in indicia)-Jack Strand begins	39.00	117.00	350.00
2 (10/37; V1#11 on-c; V2#2 in indicia)	39.00	117.00	350.00
3-5: 4-Xmas-c	36.00	108.00	310.00
6-(1st Centaur, 3/38)	64.00	192.00	575.00
7-11	36.00	108.00	310.00
V3#1-3	36.00	108.00	290.00
Laundry giveaway (16-20 pgs., 1930s)-slick-c	24.00	71.00	190.00

NOTE: ***Biro** c-V2#1, 8, 9, 11. **Guardineer** a-V1#11; c-V2#6, V3#5. **Bob Wood** c/a-V1#11, V2#2; c-V2#3, 5.*

FUNNY STUFF (Becomes The Dodo & the Frog No. 80)
Summer, 1944 - No. 79, July-Aug, 1954 (#1-7 are quarterly)
All-American/National Periodical Publications No. 7 on

	GD25	FN65	NM94
1-The Three Mouseketeers (ends #28) & The "Terrific Whatzit" begin; Sheldon Mayer-a	78.00	234.00	700.00
2-Sheldon Mayer-a	37.00	110.00	330.00
3-5: 3-Flash parody. 5-All Mayer-a/scripts issue	26.00	80.00	210.00
6-10 10-(6/46)	17.50	53.00	140.00
11-17,19,20: 20-1st Dodo & the Frog-c (4/47)	13.00	39.00	105.00
18-The Dodo & the Frog (2/47, 1st app?) begin?; X-Mas-c	23.00	69.00	185.00
21,23-30: 24-Infinity-c	8.75	26.25	70.00
22-Superman cameo	36.00	108.00	300.00
31-79: 70-1st Bo Bunny by Mayer & begins	7.50	22.50	52.00

NOTE: ***Mayer** a-1-8, 55, ,57, 58, 61, 62, 64, 65, 68, 70, 72, 74-79; c-2, 5, 6, 8.*

FUNNY STUFF
1946 (6-1/2x8-1/4")
National Periodical Publications (Wheaties Giveaway)

	GD25	FN65	NM94
nn-(Scarce)-Dodo & the Frog, Three Mouseketeers, etc.; came taped to Wheaties box; never found in better than fine	83.00	250.00	–

FUNNY STUFF STOCKING STUFFER
Mar, 1985 ($1.25, 52 pgs.)
DC Comics

	GD25	FN65	NM94
1-Almost every DC funny animal featured			1.25

FUNNY 3-D
December, 1953 (25¢, came with 2 pair of glasses)
Harvey Publications

	GD25	FN65	NM94
1-Shows cover in 3-D on inside	9.50	28.00	75.00

FUNNY TUNES (Animated Funny Comic Tunes No. 16-22; Funny Comic Tunes No. 23, on covers only; formerly Krazy Komics #15; Oscar No. 24 on)
No. 16, Summer, 1944 - No. 23, Fall, 1946
U.S.A. Comics Magazine Corp. (Timely)

	GD25	FN65	NM94
16-Silly Seal, Ziggy Pig, Krazy Krow begin	10.00	30.00	80.00
17 (Fall/44)-Becomes Gay Comics #18 on?	8.50	26.00	60.00
18-22: 21-Super Rabbit app.	6.50	19.50	45.00
23-Kurtzman-a	8.50	26.00	60.00

FUNNY TUNES (Becomes Space Comics #4 on)
July, 1953 - No. 3, Dec-Jan, 1953-54
Avon Periodicals

	GD25	FN65	NM94
1-Space Mouse, Peter Rabbit, Merry Mouse, Spotty the Pup, Cicero the Cat begin; all continue in Space Comics	7.85	23.50	55.00
2,3	5.70	17.00	35.00

FUNNY WORLD
1947 - No. 3, 1948
Marbak Press

	GD25	FN65	NM94
1-The Berrys, The Toodles & other strip-r begin	6.50	19.50	45.00
2,3	5.70	17.00	35.00

FUNTASTIC WORLD OF HANNA-BARBERA, THE (TV)
Dec, 1977 - No. 3, June, 1978 ($1.25, oversized)
Marvel Comics Group

The Further Adventures Of Cyclops And Phoenix #1 © MEG

Fury Of Firestorm #24 © DC

Gabby #11 (#1) © QUA

1-3: 1-The Flintstones Christmas Party(12/77). 2-Yogi Bear's Easter Parade(3/78). 3-Laff-a-lympics(6/78) 3.00 9.00 30.00

FUN TIME
Spring, 1953; No. 2, Sum, 1953; No. 3(nn), Fall, 1953; No. 4, Wint, 1953-54
Ace Periodicals

1-(25¢, 100 pgs.)-Funny animal 7.15 21.50 50.00
2-4 (All 25¢, 100 pgs.) 10.00 30.00 80.00

FUN WITH SANTA CLAUS (See March of Comics No. 11, 108, 325)

FURTHER ADVENTURES OF CYCLOPS AND PHOENIX (Also see Adventures of Cyclops and Phoenix, Uncanny X-Men & X-Men)
June, 1996 - No. 4, Sept, 1996 ($1.95, limited series)
Marvel Comics

1-4: Origin of Mr. Sinister; Peter Milligan scripts; John Paul Leon-c/a(p). 2-4-Apocalypse app. .80 2.00
Trade Paperback (1997, $14.99) r/1-4 14.99

FURTHER ADVENTURES OF INDIANA JONES, THE (Movie) (Also see Indiana Jones and the Last Crusade & Indiana Jones and the Temple of Doom)
Jan, 1983 - No. 34, Mar, 1986
Marvel Comics Group

1-34: 1-Byrne/Austin-a; Austin-c. 2-Byrne/Austin-c/a 1.00
NOTE: ***Austin*** *a-1i, 2i, 6i, 9i; c-1, 2i, 6i, 9i.* ***Byrne*** *a-1p, 2p; c-2p.* ***Chaykin*** *a-6p; c-6p, 8p-10p.* ***Ditko*** *a-21p, 25-28, 34.* ***Golden*** *c-24, 25.* ***Simonson*** *c-9. Painted c-14.*

FURTHER ADVENTURES OF NYOKA, THE JUNGLE GIRL, THE (See Nyoka)
1988 - No. 5, 1989 ($1.95, color; $2.25/$2.50, B&W)
AC Comics

1,2 ($1.95)-Bill Black-a plus reprints .80 2.00
3,4 ($2.25, B&W); 3-Photo-c. 4-Krigstein-r .90 2.30
5 ($2.50, B&W)-Reprints plus movie photos 1.00 2.50

FURY (Straight Arrow's Horse...) (See A-1 No. 119)

FURY (TV) (See March Of Comics #200)
No. 781, Mar, 1957 - Nov, 1962 (All photo-c)
Dell Publishing Co./Gold Key

Four Color 781 7.00 22.00 80.00
Four Color 885,975,1031,1080,1133,1172,1218,1296, 01292-208(#1-'62) 5.50 16.50 60.00
10020-211(11/62-G.K.) 5.50 16.50 60.00

FURY
May, 1994 ($2.95, one-shot)
Marvel Comics

1-Ironman, Red Skull, FF, Hatemonger, Logan, Scorpio app.; Origin Nick Fury 1.20 3.00

FURY OF FIRESTORM, THE (Becomes Firestorm The Nuclear Man #65 on) (Also see Firestorm)
June, 1982 - No. 64, Oct, 1987 (75¢ on)
DC Comics

1-Intro The Black Bison; brief origin .80 2.00
2-64: 4-JLA x-over. 17-1st app. Firehawk. 21-Death of Killer Frost. 22-Origin. 23-Intro. Byte. 24-(6/84)-1st app. Blue Devil & Bug (origin); origin Byte. 34-1st app./origin Killer Frost II. 39-Weasel's i.d. revealed 41,42-Crisis x-over. 48-Intro. Moonbow. 53-Origin/1st app. Silver Shade. 55,56-Legends x-over. 58-1st app./origin Parasite 1.00
61-Test cover variant; Superman logo 2.50 7.50 25.00
Annual 1-4: 1(1983), 2(1984), 3(1985), 4(1986) 1.25
NOTE: ***Colan*** *a-19p, Annual 4p.* ***Giffen*** *a-Annual 4p.* ***Gil Kane*** *c-30.* ***Nino*** *a-37.* ***Tuska*** *a-(p)-17, 18, 32, 45.*

FURY OF HELLINA (Also see Hellina)
Jan, 1995 ($2.75, B&W)
Lightning Comics

1 1.10 2.75

FURY OF SHIELD
Apr, 1995 - No. 4, July, 1995 ($2.50/$1.95, limited series)
Marvel Comics

1 ($2.50)-Foil-c 1.00 2.50
2-4: 4-Bagged w/ decoder .80 2.00

FUSION
Jan, 1987 - No. 17, Oct, 1989 ($2.00, B&W, Baxter paper)
Eclipse Comics

1-17: 11-The Weasel Patrol begins (1st app.?) 1.00 2.00

FUTURE COMICS
June, 1940 - No. 4, Sept, 1940
David McKay Publications

1-(6/40, 64 pgs.)-Origin The Phantom (4 pgs.); The Lone Ranger (8 pgs.) & Saturn Against the Earth (4 pgs.) begin 208.00 625.00 1850.00
2 100.00 300.00 900.00
3,4 83.00 250.00 750.00

FUTURETECH
Jan, 1996 - Present ($2.50, limited series)
Mushroom Comics

1-Flipbook w/SWARM 1.00 2.50

FUTURE WORLD COMICS
Summer, 1946 - No. 2, Fall, 1946
George W. Dougherty

1,2: H. C. Kiefer-c 20.00 60.00 150.00

FUTURE WORLD COMIX (Warren Presents...)
Sept, 1978
Warren Publications

1-Corben-a; Todd-c 1.00 3.00 8.00

FUTURIANS, THE (See Marvel Graphic Novel #9)
Sept, 1985 - No. 3, 1985 ($1.50)
Lodestone Publishing/Eternity Comics

1-3: Indicia title "Dave Cockrum's..." 1.50
Graphic Novel 1 ($9.95, Eternity)-r/#1-3, plus never published #4 issue 1.25 3.75 10.00

FUTURIANS, THE (See Marvel Graphic Novel #9)
Aug, 1995 ($2.95, one-shot)
Aardwolf

1-Dave Cockrum 1.20 3.00

G-8 (See G-Eight)

GABBY (Formerly Ken Shannon) (Teen humor)
No. 11, July, 1953; No. 2, Sept, 1953 - No. 9, Sept, 1954
Quality Comics Group

11(#1)(7/53) 6.00 18.00 42.00
2 4.25 13.00 26.00
3-9 3.60 9.00 18.00

GABBY GOB (See Harvey Hits No. 85, 90, 94, 97, 100, 103, 106, 109)

GABBY HAYES ADVENTURE COMICS
Dec, 1953
Toby Press

1-Photo-c 12.00 36.00 95.00

GABBY HAYES WESTERN (Movie star) (See Monte Hale, Real Western Hero & Western Hero)
Nov, 1948 - No. 50, Jan, 1953; No. 51, Dec, 1954 - No. 59, Jan, 1957
Fawcett Publications/Charlton Comics No. 51 on

1-Gabby & his horse Corker begin; photo front/back-c begin 44.00 132.00 400.00

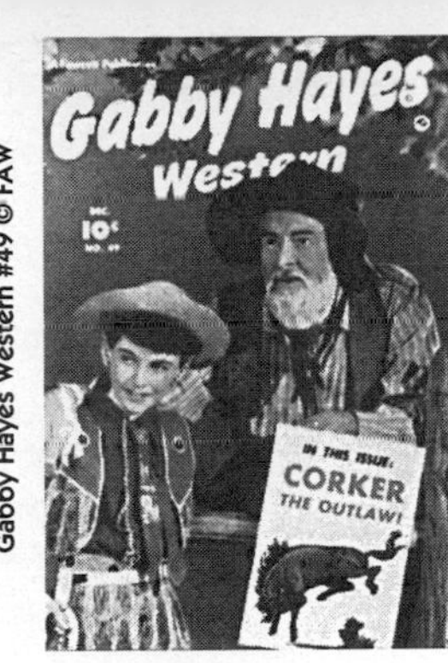

Gabby Hayes Western #49 © FAW

Gameboy #1 © Nintendo

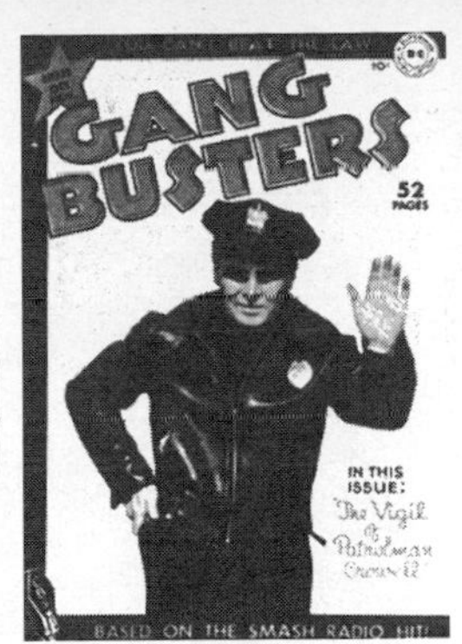

Gang Busters #12 © DC

	GD25	FN65	NM94
2	21.00	62.00	165.00
3-5	14.00	41.00	110.00
6-10: 9-Young Falcon begins	12.00	36.00	90.00
11-20: 19-Last photo back-c	8.75	26.25	70.00
21-49: 20,22,24,26,28,29-(52 pgs.)	7.15	21.50	50.00
50-(1/53)-Last Fawcett issue; last photo-c?	8.50	26.00	60.00
51-(12/54)-1st Charlton issue; photo-c	8.50	26.00	60.00
52-59(1955-57): 53,55-Photo-c. 58-Swayze-a	5.00	15.00	30.00
Quaker Oats Giveaway nn's(#1-5, 1951, 2-1/2x7") (Kagran Corp.)-...In Tracks of Guilt, ...In the Fence Post Mystery, ...In the Accidental Sherlock, ... In the Frame-Up, ...In the Double Cross Brand known	8.75	26.25	65.00

GAGS
July, 1937 - V3#10, Oct, 1944 (13-3/4x10-3/4")
United Features Synd./Triangle Publ. No. 9 on

	GD25	FN65	NM94
1(7/37)-52 pgs.; 20 pgs. Grin & Bear It, Fellow Citizen	5.70	17.00	35.00
V1#9 (36 pgs.) (7/42)	4.00	11.00	22.00
V3#10	3.60	9.00	18.00

GALACTIC GUARDIANS
July, 1994 - No. 4, Oct, 1994 ($1.50, limited series)
Marvel Comics

	GD25	FN65	NM94
1-4			1.50

GALACTIC WAR COMIX (Warren Presents... on cover)
December, 1978
Warren Publications

	GD25	FN65	NM94
nn-Wood, Williamson-r	1.00	3.00	8.00

GALLANT MEN, THE (TV)
Oct, 1963 (Photo-c)
Gold Key

	GD25	FN65	NM94
1(1008-310)-Manning-a	2.00	6.00	16.00

GALLEGHER, BOY REPORTER (Disney, TV)
May, 1965
Gold Key

	GD25	FN65	NM94
1(10149-505)-Photo-c	1.50	4.50	12.00

GAMBIT (See X-Men #266 & X-Men Annual #14)
Dec, 1993 - No. 4, Mar, 1994 ($2.00, limited series)
Marvel Comics

	GD25	FN65	NM94
1-($2.50)-Lee Weeks-c/a in all; gold foil stamped-c.		2.00	5.00
1 (Gold)	1.85	5.50	15.00
2-4		1.20	3.00

GAMBIT
Sept, 1997 - No. 4, Dec, 1997 ($2.50, limited series)
Marvel Comics

	GD25	FN65	NM94
1-4-Janson-a/ Mackie & Kavanagh-s		1.00	2.50

GAMBIT AND THE X-TERNALS
Mar, 1995 - No. 4, July, 1995 ($1.95, limited series)
Marvel Comics

	GD25	FN65	NM94
1-Age of Apocalyse		1.20	3.00
2-4		.80	2.00

GAMEBOY
1990 - No. 6? ($1.95, coated-c)
Valiant

	GD25	FN65	NM94
1-6: 3,4,6-Layton-c. 4-Morrow-a. 5-Layton-c(i)		.80	2.00

GAMMARAUDERS
Jan, 1989 - No. 10, Dec, 1989 ($1.25/$1.50/$2.00)
DC Comics

	GD25	FN65	NM94
1-10-Based on TSR game		.80	2.00

GAMERA
Aug, 1996 - No. 4, Nov, 1996 ($2.95, limited series)
Dark Horse Comics

	GD25	FN65	NM94
1-4		1.20	3.00

GAMORRA SWIMSUIT SPECIAL
June, 1996 ($2.50, one-shot)
Image Comics (Wildstorm Productions)

	GD25	FN65	NM94
1-Campbell wraparound-c; pinups		1.00	2.50

GANDY GOOSE (Movies/TV)(See All Surprise, Giant Comics Edition #5A &10, Paul Terry's Comics & Terry-Toons)
Mar, 1953 - No. 5, Nov, 1953; No. 5, Fall, 1956 - No. 6, Sum/58
St. John Publ. Co./Pines No. 5,6

	GD25	FN65	NM94
1-All St. John issues are pre-code	8.50	26.00	60.00
2	4.25	13.00	28.00
3-5(1953)(St. John)	4.00	12.00	24.00
5,6(1956-58)(Pines)-CBS Televison Presents...	3.60	9.00	18.00

GANG BUSTERS (See Popular Comics #38)
1938 - 1943
David McKay/Dell Publishing Co.

	GD25	FN65	NM94
Feature Books 17(McKay)('38)-1st app.	48.00	144.00	525.00
Large Feature Comic 10('39)-(Scarce)	48.00	144.00	525.00
Large Feature Comic 17('41)	29.00	87.00	315.00
Four Color 7(1940)	33.00	98.00	360.00
Four Color 23,24('42-43)	26.00	77.00	280.00

GANG BUSTERS (Radio/TV)(Gangbusters #14 on)
Dec-Jan, 1947-48 - No. 67, Dec-Jan, 1958-59 (No. 1-23: 52 pgs.)
National Periodical Publications

	GD25	FN65	NM94
1	70.00	210.00	630.00
2	34.00	103.00	275.00
3-5	24.00	71.00	190.00
6-10: 9-Dan Barry-a. 9,10-Photo-c	19.00	56.00	150.00
11-13-Photo-c	15.50	47.00	125.00
14,17-Frazetta-a, 8 pgs. each. 14-Photo-c	33.00	98.00	260.00
15,16,18-20	12.00	36.00	90.00
21-25,27-30	10.00	30.00	80.00
26-Kirby-a	11.30	34.00	90.00
31-44: 44-Last Pre-code (2-3/55)	8.75	26.25	70.00
45-67	7.85	23.50	55.00

NOTE: ***Barry*** *a-6, 8, 10.* ***Drucker*** *a-51.* ***Moreira*** *a-48, 50, 59.* ***Roussos*** *a-8.*

GANGSTERS AND GUN MOLLS
Sept, 1951 - No. 4, June, 1952 (Painted c-1-3)
Avon Periodical/Realistic Comics

	GD25	FN65	NM94
1-Wood-a, 1 pg; c-/Avon paperback #292	40.00	120.00	320.00
2-Check-a, 8 pgs.; Kamen-a; Bonnie Parker story	30.00	90.00	220.00
3-Marijuana mentioned; used in **POP**, pg. 84,85	27.00	81.00	200.00
4-Syd Shores-c	22.00	66.00	165.00

GANGSTERS CAN'T WIN
Feb-Mar, 1948 - No. 9, June-July, 1949 (All 52 pgs?)
D. S. Publishing Co.

	GD25	FN65	NM94
1-True crime stories	26.00	77.00	190.00
2	11.30	34.00	90.00
3-6: 4-Acid in face story	10.00	30.00	75.00
7-9	8.50	26.00	60.00

NOTE: ***Ingles*** *a-5, 6.* ***McWilliams*** *a-5, 7.* ***Reinman*** *c-6.*

GANG WORLD
No. 5, Nov, 1952 - No. 6, Jan, 1953
Standard Comics

	GD25	FN65	NM94
5-Bondage-c	14.00	43.00	110.00

G-8 and His Battle Aces #1 © GK

Gemini Blood #2 © DC

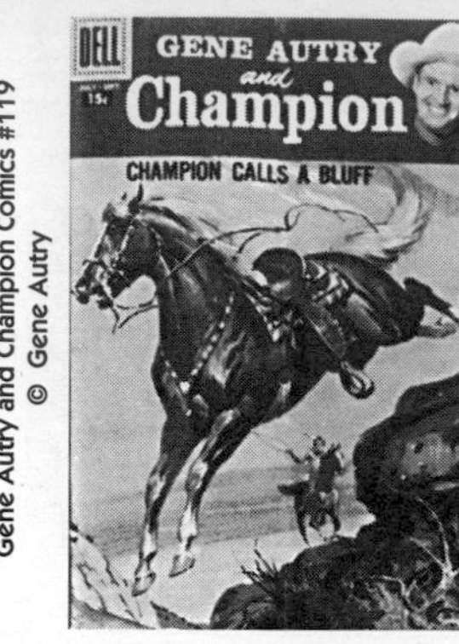

Gene Autry and Champion Comics #119 © Gene Autry

GD25 FN65 NM94

6 — 11.50 34.00 85.00

GARGOYLE (See The Defenders #94)
June, 1985 - No. 4, Sept, 1985 (75¢, limited series)
Marvel Comics Group

1-4: 1-Wrightson-c; character from Defenders — 1.00

GARGOYLES (TV cartoon)
Feb, 1995 - No. 17, June, 1996 ($2.50)
Marvel Comics

1-17: Based on animated series — 1.00 2.50

GARRISON'S GORILLAS (TV)
Jan, 1968 - No. 4, Oct, 1968; No. 5, Oct, 1969 (Photo-c)
Dell Publishing Co.

1 — 3.20 9.60 35.00
2-5: 5-Reprints #1 — 2.10 6.20 23.00

GASOLINE ALLEY (Top Love Stories No. 3 on?)
Sept-Oct, 1950 - No. 2, Dec, 1950 (Newspaper-r)
Star Publications

1-Contains 1 pg. intro. history of the strip (The Life of Skeezix); reprints 15 scenes of highlights from 1921-1935, plus an adventure from 1935 and 1936 strips; a 2-pg. filler is included on the life of the creator Frank King, with photo of the cartoonist. — 17.00 51.00 135.00
2-(1936-37 reprints)-L. B. Cole-c — 19.50 58.00 155.00
(See Super Book No. 21)

GASP!
Mar, 1967 - No. 4, Aug, 1967 (12¢)
American Comics Group

1 — 2.50 7.50 25.00
2-4 — 1.85 5.50 15.00

GAY COMICS (Honeymoon No. 41)
Mar, 1944 (no month); No. 18, Fall, 1944 - No. 40, Oct, 1949
Timely Comics/USA Comic Mag. Co. No. 18-24

1-Wolverton's Powerhouse Pepper; Tessie the Typist begins; 1st app. Willie (one shot) — 36.00 108.00 320.00
18-(Formerly Funny Tunes #17?)-Wolverton-a — 21.00 64.00 170.00
19-29: Wolverton-a in all. 21,24-6 pg., 7 pg. Powerhouse Pepper; additional 2 pg. story in 24). 23-7 pg Wolverton story & 2 two pg stories(total of 11pgs.). 24,29-Kurtzman-a (24-"Hey Look"(2)) — 16.00 49.00 130.00
30,33,36,37-Kurtzman's "Hey Look" — 7.85 23.50 55.00
31-Kurtzman's "Hey Look" (1), Giggles 'N' Grins (1-1/2) — 7.85 23.50 55.00
32,35,38-40: 35-Nellie The Nurse begins? — 5.70 17.00 40.00
34-Three Kurtzman's "Hey Look" — 8.50 26.00 60.00

GAY COMICS (Also see Smile, Tickle, & Whee Comics)
1955 (7¢, 5x7-1/4", 52 pgs.)
Modern Store Publ.

1 — 1.60 4.00

GAY PURR-EE (See Movie Comics)

GEEK, THE (See Brother Power... & Vertigo Visions)

G-8 AND HIS BATTLE ACES
Oct, 1966
Gold Key

1 (10184-610)-Painted-c — 2.80 8.40 28.00

G-8 AND HIS BATTLE ACES
1991 ($1.50, one-shot)
Blazing Comics

1-Glanzman-a; Truman-c — 1.50
NOTE: *Flip book format with "The Spider's Web" #1 on other side w/***Glanzman***-a,* **Truman***-c.*

GEM COMICS
Apr, 1945 (52 pgs, Bondage-c)
Spotlight Publishers

1-Little Mohee, Steve Strong app. — 21.00 64.00 170.00

GEMINI BLOOD
Sept, 1996 - No. 9, May, 1997 ($2.25, limited series)
DC Comics (Helix)

1-9:5-Simonson-c — .90 2.25

GENE AUTRY (See March of Comics No. 25, 28, 39, 54, 78, 90, 104, 120, 135, 150 & Western Roundup under Dell Giants)

GENE AUTRY COMICS (Movie, Radio star; singing cowboy)
(Dell takes over with No. 11)
1941 (On sale 12/31/41) - No. 10, 1943 (68 pgs.)
Fawcett Publications

1 (Rare)-Gene Autry & his horse Champion begin — 650.00 1950.00 6500.00
2-(1942) — 111.00 333.00 1000.00
3-5: 3-(11/1/42) — 78.00 234.00 700.00
6-10 — 64.00 192.00 575.00

GENE AUTRY COMICS (...& Champion No. 102 on)
No. 11, 1943 - No. 121, Jan-Mar, 1959 (TV - later issues)
Dell Publishing Co.

11 (1943, 60 pgs.)-Continuation of Fawcett series; photo back-c — 50.00 150.00 550.00
12 (2/44, 60 pgs.) — 46.00 137.00 500.00
Four Color 47(1944, 60 pgs.) — 37.00 112.00 410.00
Four Color 57(11/44),66('45)(52 pgs. each) — 34.00 102.00 375.00
Four Color 75,83('45, 36 pgs. each) — 27.00 82.00 300.00
Four Color 93,100('45-46, 36 pgs. each): 100-Photo-c — 24.00 71.00 260.00
1(5-6/46, 52 pgs.) — 38.00 115.00 420.00
2(7-8/46)-Photo-c begin, end #111 — 21.00 63.00 230.00
3-5: 4-Intro Flapjack Hobbs — 15.00 45.00 165.00
6-10 — 12.00 35.00 130.00
11-20: 20-Panhandle Pete begins — 10.00 30.00 110.00
21-29(36pgs.) — 8.00 23.00 85.00
30-40(52pgs.) — 6.40 19.00 70.00
41-56(52pgs.) — 5.00 15.00 55.00
57-66(36pgs.): 58-X-mas-c — 3.60 11.00 40.00
67-80(52pgs.) — 3.60 11.00 40.00
81-90(52pgs.): 82-X-mas-c. 87-Blank inside-c — 3.00 9.00 32.00
91-99(36pgs. No. 91-on). 94-X-mas-c — 2.25 6.75 24.00
100 — 2.75 8.00 30.00
101-111-Last Gene Autry photo-c — 2.25 6.75 24.00
112-121-All Champion painted-c, most by Savitt — 1.80 5.50 20.00
...Adventure Comics And Play-Fun Book ('47)-32 pgs., 8x6-1/2"; games, comics, magic (Pillsbury premium) — 20.00 60.00 220.00
Quaker Oats Giveaway(1950)-2-1/2x6-3/4"; 5 different versions; "Death Card Gang", "Phantoms of the Cave", "Riddle of Laughing Mtn.", "Secret of Lost Valley", "Bond of the Broken Arrow" (came in wrapper) each... — 8.00 25.00 90.00
3-D Giveaway(1953)-Pocket-size; 5 different — 9.00 26.00 95.00
NOTE: *Photo back covers 4-18, 20-45, 48-65.* **Manning** *a-118.* **Jesse Marsh** *art: 4-Color No. 66, 75, 93, 100, No. 1-25, 27-37, 39, 40.*

GENE AUTRY'S CHAMPION (TV)
No. 287, 8/50; No. 319, 2/51; No. 3, 8-10/51 - No. 19, 8-10/55
Dell Publishing Co.

Four Color 287(#1)('50, 52pgs.)-Photo-c — 8.00 25.00 90.00
Four Color 319(#2, '51), 3: 2-Painted-c begin, most by Sam Savitt — 3.60 11.00 40.00
4-19: 19-Last painted-c — 2.75 8.00 30.00

GENE AUTRY TIM (Formerly Tim) (Becomes Tim in Space)

Generation X #2 © MEG

Genesis #4 © DC

Gen 13 #13A © Aegis Entertainment

1950 (Half-size) (B&W Giveaway)
Tim Stores

	GD25	FN65	NM94
nn-Several issues (All Scarce)	9.50	28.00	75.00

GENE DOGS
Oct, 1993 - No. 4, Jan, 1994 ($1.75, limited series)
Marvel Comics UK

	GD25	FN65	NM94
1-($2.75)-Polybagged w/4 trading cards		1.10	2.75
2-4: 2-Vs. Genetix		.70	1.75

GENERAL DOUGLAS MACARTHUR
1951
Fox Features Syndicate

	GD25	FN65	NM94
nn-True life story	15.50	47.00	125.00

GENERIC COMIC, THE
Apr, 1984 (one-shot)
Marvel Comics Group

	GD25	FN65	NM94
1		.80	2.00

GENERATION HEX
June, 1997 ($1.95, one-shot)
DC Comics (Amalgam)

	GD25	FN65	NM94
1-Milligan-s/ Pollina & Morales-a			1.95

GENERATION NEXT
Mar, 1995 - No. 4, June, 1995 ($1.95, limited series)
Marvel Comics

	GD25	FN65	NM94
1-Age of Apocalypse; Scott Lobdell scripts & Chris Bachalo-c/a		2.00	5.00
2-4		1.20	3.00

GENERATION X (See Gen 13/ Generation X)
Oct, 1994 - Present ($1.50/$1.95/$1.99)
Marvel Comics

	GD25	FN65	NM94
Collectors Preview ($1.75)		.80	2.00
"Ashcan" Edition			1.00
1/2 (San Diego giveaway)	1.00	2.80	7.00
1-($3.95)-Wraparound chromium-c; Scott Lobdell scripts & Chris Bachalo-a begins.	1.00	2.80	7.00
2-($1.95)-Deluxe edition, Bachalo-a		1.20	3.00
3,4-($1.95)-Deluxe Edition; Bachalo-a		1.20	3.00
2-4-Standard Edition; Bachalo-a		.80	2.00
5-24, 26-28, -1(7/97): 5-Returns from "Age of Apocalypse," begin $1.95-c. 6-Bachalo-a(p) ends, returns #17. 7-Roger Cruz-a(p). 10-Omega Red-c/app. 13,14-Bishop-app. 17-Stan Lee app. (Stan Lee scripts own dialogue); Bachalo/Buckingham-a; Onslaught update. 18-Toad cameo. 20-Franklin Richards app; Howard the Duck cameo. 21-Howard the Duck app. 22-Nightmare app.		.80	2.00
25-($2.99)-Wraparound-c. Black Tom, Howard the Duck app.			2.99
29-35: 29-Begin $1.99-c, "Operation Zero Tolerance"			1.99
'95 Special-($3.95)		1.60	4.00
'96 Special-($2.95)-Wraparound-c; Jeff Johnson-c/a			3.00
'97 Special-($2.99)-Wraparound-c;			2.99

GENERATION X/ GEN 13 (Also see Gen 13/ Generation X)
1997 ($3.99, one-shot)
Image Comics (Wildstorm Publications)

	GD25	FN65	NM94
1-Robinson-s/Larroca-a(p)			4.95

GENE RODDENBERRY'S LOST UNIVERSE
Apr, 1995 - No. 6, Dec, 1995 ($1.95)
Tekno Comix

	GD25	FN65	NM94
0 (11/95, $2.25)		.90	2.25
1-3-w/ bound-in game piece & trading card		.80	2.00
4-6: 4-bound-in trading card		.80	2.00

GENE RODDENBERRY'S XANDER IN LOST UNIVERSE
Dec, 1995 - No. 8, July, 1996 ($2.25)
Tekno Comix

	GD25	FN65	NM94
1-8: 1-5-Jae Lee-c. 4-Polybagged. 8-Includes Pt. 5 of The Big Bang x-over.		.90	2.25

GENESIS (See DC related titles)
Oct, 1997 - No. 4, Oct, 1997 ($1.95, weekly limited series)
DC Comics

	GD25	FN65	NM94
1-4: Byrne-s/Wagner-a(p) in all.			1.95

GENETIX
Oct, 1993 - No. 6, Mar, 1994 ($1.75, limited series)
Marvel Comics UK

	GD25	FN65	NM94
1-($2.75)-Polybagged w/4 cards; Dark Guard app.		1.10	2.75
2-6: 2-Intro Tektos. 4-Vs. Gene Dogs		.70	1.75

GENSAGA
1995 ($2.50/$6.75, one-shot)
Entity Comics

	GD25	FN65	NM94
1		1.00	2.50
1 ($6.75)-bagged w/PC Game	1.00	2.70	6.75

GEN 13 (Also see Wild C.A.T.S. #1 & Deathmate Black #2)
Feb, 1994 - No. 5, July 1994 ($1.95, limited series)
Image Comics (Wildstorm Productions)

	GD25	FN65	NM94
0 (8/95, $2.50)-Ch. 1 w/Jim Lee-p; Ch.4 w/Charest-p		2.00	5.00
1/2	2.25	6.75	18.00
1-($2.50)-Created by Jim Lee	2.50	7.50	25.00
1-2nd printing		1.60	4.00
2-($2.50)	2.50	7.50	20.00
3-Pitt-c & story	1.50	4.50	12.00
4-Pitt-c & story; wraparound-c	1.25	3.75	10.00
5		2.40	6.00
5-Alternate Portacio-c; see Deathblow #5	1.50	4.50	12.00
...Collected Edition ('94, $12.95)-r/#1-5	1.00	2.80	7.00
...Rave ($1.50, 3/95)-wraparound-c		.80	2.00

NOTE: *Issues 1-4 contain coupons redeemable for ashcan edition of Gen 13 #0. Price listed is for complete books.*

GEN 13
Mar, 1995 - Present ($2.50)
Image Comics (Wildstorm Productions)

	GD25	FN65	NM94
1-A (Charge)-Campbell/Gardner-c		2.40	6.00
1-B (Thumbs Up)-Campbell/Gardner-c		2.40	6.00
1-C (Lil' GEN 13)-Art Adams-c	1.50	4.50	12.00
1-D (Barbari-GEN)-Simon Bisley-c	1.50	4.50	12.00
1-E (Your Friendly Neighborhood Grunge)-John Cleary-c	1.50	4.50	12.00
1-F (GEN 13 Goes Madison Ave.)-Michael Golden-c	1.50	4.50	12.00
1-G (Lin-GEN-re)-Michael Lopez-c	1.85	5.50	15.00
1-H (GEN-et Jackson)-Jason Pearson-c	1.85	5.50	15.00
1-I (That's the way we became GEN 13)-Campbell/Gibson-c	1.50	4.50	12.00
1-J (All Dolled Up)-Campbell/McWeeney-c	1.50	4.50	12.00
1-K (Verti-GEN)-Joe Dunn-c	1.50	4.50	12.00
1-L (Picto-Fiction)	1.75	5.25	14.00
1-M (Do it Yourself Cover)	1.50	4.50	12.00
1-"3-D" Edition ('97, $4.95)-w/glasses			4.95
2 ($1.95, Newsstand)-WildStorm Rising Pt. 4; bound-in card		.80	2.00
2-12: 2-($2.50, Direct Market)-WildStorm Rising Pt. 4, bound-in card. 6,7-Jim Lee-c/a(p). 9-Ramos-a. 10-Fire From Heaven Pt. 3. 11-Fire From Heaven Pt. 9		1.20	3.00
11-($4.95)-Special European Tour Edition; chromium-c		7.50	20.00
13A,13B,13C-($1.30, 13 pgs.): 13A-Archie & Friends app. 13B-Bone-c/app.;			

Gen 13 #25 © Aegis Entertainment

Gen 13 Interactive #2 © Aegis Entertainment

Georgie #12 © TCI

GD25 FN65 NM94

Teenage Mutant Ninja Turtles, Madman, Spawn & Jim Lee app. 1.30
14-24: 20-Last Campbell-a 1.00 2.50
25-($3.50)-Two covers by Campbell and Charest 3.50
25-($3.50)-Voyager Pack w/Danger Girl preview 3.50
Annual 1 (1997, $2.95) Ellis-s/ Dillon-c/a. 2.95
...European Vacation ($6.95, trade paperback) r/6,7 6.95
...Lost in Paradise ($6.95, trade paperback) r/3-5 6.95
...#13 A,B&C Collected Edition ($6.95, TPB) r/#13A,B&C 6.95
Variant Collection-Four editions (all 13 variants w/Chromium variant-limited, signed) 25.00 75.00 250.00

GEN 13 BOOTLEG
Nov, 1996 - Present ($2.50)
Image Comics (Wildstorm Publications)

1-13: 1,2-Alan Davis-a. 5,6-Terry Moore-s. 7-Robinson-s/Scott Hampton-a. 8-10-Adam Warren-s/a. 11,12-Lopresti-s/a & Simonson-s 13-Wieringo-s/a 1.00 2.50
1-Variant-c 1.00 2.50

GEN 13/ GENERATION X (Also see Generation X / Gen 13)
July, 1997 ($2.95, one-shot)
Image Comics (Wildstorm Publications)

1-Choi-s/ Art Adams-p/Garner-i. Variant covers by Adams/Garner and Campbell/McWeeney 2.95
1-($4.95) 3-D Edition w/glasses; Campbell-c 4.95

GEN 13 INTERACTIVE
Oct, 1997 - No. 3 ($2.50, limited series)
Image Comics (Wildstorm Publications)

1,2-Internet voting used to determine storyline 2.50

GEN 13/ MAXX
Dec, 1995 ($3.50, one-shot)
Image Comics (Wildstorm Publications)

1-Wm. Messner-Loebs story, 1st Tomm Coker-c/a. 3.50

GEN 13: ORDINARY HEROES
Feb, 1996 - No. 2, July, 1996 ($2.50, limited series)
Image Comics (Wildstorm Publications)

1-Adam Hughes-c/a/scripts 1.20 3.00

GEN 13 3-D SPECIAL
1997 ($4.95, one-shot)
Image Comics (Wildstorm Publications)

1-Art Adams-s/a(p) 4.95

GEN 13: THE UNREAL WORLD
July, 1996 ($2.95, one-shot)
Image Comics (Wildstorm Productions)

1-Humberto Ramos-c/a 2.95

GEN 13: 'ZINE
Dec, 1996 ($1.95, B&W, digest size)
Image Comics (Wildstorm Productions)

1-Campbell/Garner-c 1.95

GENTLE BEN (TV)
Feb, 1968 - No. 5, Oct, 1969 (All photo-c)
Dell Publishing Co.

1 2.50 7.50 25.00
2-5: 5-Reprints #1 1.40 4.20 14.00

GEOMANCER (Also see Eternal Warrior: Fist & Steel)
Nov, 1994 - No. 8, June, 1995 ($3.75/$2.25)
Valiant

1 ($3.75)-Chromium wraparound-c; Eternal Warrior app. 1.50 3.75
2-8 .90 2.25

GD25 FN65 NM94

GEORGE OF THE JUNGLE (TV)(See America's Best TV Comics)
Feb, 1969 - No. 2, Oct, 1969 (Jay Ward)
Gold Key

1 11.00 33.00 120.00
2 7.00 22.00 80.00

GEORGE PAL'S PUPPETOONS
Dec, 1945 - No. 18, Dec, 1947; No. 19, 1950
Fawcett Publications

1-Captain Marvel-c 36.00 108.00 295.00
2 19.00 56.00 150.00
3-10 12.00 36.00 90.00
11-19 9.50 28.00 75.00

GEORGIE COMICS (...& Judy Comics #20-35?; see All Teen & Teen Comics)
Spring, 1945 - No. 39, Oct, 1952 (#1-3 are quarterly)
Timely Comics/GPI No. 1-34

1-Dave Berg-a 17.50 53.00 140.00
2 8.75 26.25 65.00
3-5,7,8 7.15 21.50 50.00
6-Georgie visits Timely Comics 8.75 26.25 70.00
9,10-Kurtzman's "Hey Look" (1 & ?); Margie app. 8.50 26.00 60.00
11,12: 11-Margie, Millie app. 5.70 17.00 35.00
13-Kurtzman's "Hey Look", 3 pgs. 7.15 21.50 50.00
14-Wolverton-a(1 pg.); Kurtzman's "Hey Look" 8.50 26.00 60.00
15,16,18-20 5.00 15.00 30.00
17,29-Kurtzman's "Hey Look", 1 pg. 6.50 19.50 45.00
21-24,27,28,30-39: 21-Anti-Wertham editorial 4.15 12.50 25.00
25-Painted-c by classic pin-up artist Peter Driben 7.15 21.50 50.00
26-Logo design swipe from Archie Comics 5.00 15.00 30.00

GERALD McBOING-BOING AND THE NEARSIGHTED MR. MAGOO (TV)
(Mr. Magoo No. 6 on)
Aug-Oct, 1952 - No. 5, Aug-Oct, 1953
Dell Publishing Co.

1 8.00 25.00 90.00
2-5 6.40 19.00 70.00

GERONIMO (See Fighting Indians of the Wild West!)
1950 - No. 4, Feb, 1952
Avon Periodicals

1-Indian Fighter; Maneely-a; Texas Rangers-r/Cowpuncher #1; Fawcette-c 14.00 43.00 110.00
2-On the Warpath; Kit West app.; Kinstler-c/a 10.00 30.00 65.00
3-And His Apache Murderers; Kinstler-c/a(2); Kit West-r/Cowpuncher #6 10.00 30.00 65.00
4-Savage Raids of; Kinstler-c & inside front-c; Kinstlerish-a by McCann(3) 8.35 25.00 55.00

GERONIMO JONES
Sept, 1971 - No. 9, Jan, 1973
Charlton Comics

1 1.25 3.75 10.00
2-9 2.00 5.00
Modern Comics Reprint #7('78) 1.40 3.50

GETALONG GANG, THE (TV)
May, 1985 - No. 6, Mar, 1986
Marvel Comics (Star Comics)

1-6: Saturday morning TV stars .80 2.00

GET LOST
Feb-Mar, 1954 - No. 3, June-July, 1954 (Satire)
Mikeross Publications/New Comics

1-Andru/Esposito-a in all? 22.00 66.00 175.00
2-Andru/Esposito-c; has 4 pg. E.C. parody featuring "The Sewer Keeper"

Get Smart #5 © DELL

Ghost Special #1 © DH

Ghost Manor #19 © CC

	GD25	FN65	NM94
	15.50	47.00	125.00
3-John Wayne 'Hondo' parody	12.00	36.00	95.00
1,2 (10,12/87-New Comics)-B&W r-original			1.00

GET SMART (TV)
June, 1966 - No. 8, Sept, 1967 (All have Don Adams photo-c)
Dell Publishing Co.

	GD25	FN65	NM94
1	8.00	25.00	90.00
2-Ditko-a	5.00	15.00	55.00
3-8: 3-Ditko-a(p)	4.50	13.50	50.00

GHOST (...Comics #9)
1951(Winter) - No. 11, Summer, 1954
Fiction House Magazines

	GD25	FN65	NM94
1-Most covers by Whitman	55.00	165.00	465.00
2-Ghost Gallery & Werewolf Hunter stories	29.00	86.00	210.00
3-9: 3,6,7,9-Bondage-c. 9-Abel, Discount-a	24.00	73.00	180.00
10,11-Dr. Drew by Grandenetti in each, reprinted from Rangers; 11-Evans-r/Rangers #39; Grandenetti-r/Rangers #49	29.00	86.00	210.00

GHOST (See Comic's Greatest World)
Apr, 1995 - Present ($2.50)
Dark Horse Comics

	GD25	FN65	NM94
1-Adam Hughes-a	1.00	3.00	8.00
2,3-Hughes-a		1.60	4.00
4-24: 4-Barb Wire app. 5,6-Hughes-c. 12-Ghost/Hellboy preview. 15,21-X app. 18,19-Barb Wire app.		1.00	2.50
25-($3.50)-48 pgs. special		1.40	3.50
26-31: 26-Begin $2.95-c. 29-Flip book w/Timecop			2.95
Special 1 (7/94, $3.95, 48 pgs.)	1.00	2.80	7.00
...Nocturnes (1996, $9.95, trade paperback)-r/#1-3 & 5			10.00
...Stories (1995, $9.95, trade paperback)-r/Early Ghost app.			10.00

GHOST AND THE SHADOW
Dec, 1995 ($2.95, one-shot)
Dark Horse Comics

	GD25	FN65	NM94
1-Moench scripts		1.20	3.00

GHOST/HELLBOY
May, 1996 - No. 2, June, 1996 ($2.50, limited series)
Dark Horse Comics

	GD25	FN65	NM94
1,2: Mike Mignola-c/scripts & breakdowns; Scott Benefiel finished-a		1.00	2.50

GHOST BREAKERS (Also see Racket Squad in Action, Red Dragon & (CC) Sherlock Holmes Comics)
Sept, 1948 - No. 2, Dec, 1948 (52 pgs.)
Street & Smith Publications

	GD25	FN65	NM94
1-Powell-c/a(3); Dr. Neff (magician) app.	37.00	111.00	270.00
2-Powell-c/a(2); Maneely-a	29.00	86.00	210.00

GHOSTBUSTERS (TV) (Also, see Real...and Slimer)
Feb, 1987 - No. 6, Aug, 1987 ($1.25)
First Comics

	GD25	FN65	NM94
1-6: Based on new animated TV series			1.30

GHOSTBUSTERS II
Oct, 1989 - No. 3, Dec, 1989 ($1.95, mini-series)
Now Comics

	GD25	FN65	NM94
1-3: Movie Adaptation		.80	2.00

GHOST CASTLE (See Tales of...)

GHOSTDANCING
Mar, 1995 - No. 6, Sept, 1995 ($1.95, limited series)
DC Comics (Vertigo)

	GD25	FN65	NM94
1-6: Case-c/a		.80	2.00

GHOST IN THE SHELL (Manga)
Mar, 1995 - No. 8, Oct, 1995 ($3.95, B&W/color, limited series)
Dark Horse Comics

	GD25	FN65	NM94
1	2.50	7.50	25.00
2	2.80	8.40	28.00
3	1.85	5.50	15.00
4-8	1.25	3.75	10.00

GHOSTLY HAUNTS (Formerly Ghost Manor)
#20, 9/71 - #53, 12/76; #54, 9/77 - #55, 10/77; #56, 1/78 - #58, 4/78
Charlton Comics

	GD25	FN65	NM94
20	1.25	3.75	10.00
21-40: 27-Dr. Graves x-over. 32-New logo. 33-Back to old logo. 39-Origin & 1st app. Destiny Fox	1.00	3.00	8.00
41-58:		2.40	6.00
40,41(Modern Comics-r, 1977, 1978)		1.20	3.00

NOTE: ***Ditko** a-22-25, 27, 28, 31-34, 36-41, 43-48, 50, 52, 54, 56r; c-22-27, 30, 33-37, 47, 54, 56. **Glanzman** a-20. **Howard** a-27, 30, 35, 42. **Newton** c/a-42. **Staton** a-35; c-28, 46. **Sutton** c-33, 37, 39, 41.*

GHOSTLY TALES (Formerly Blue Beetle No. 50-54)
No. 55, 4-5/66 - No. 124, 12/76; No. 125, 9/77 - No. 169, 10/84
Charlton Comics

	GD25	FN65	NM94
55-Intro. & origin Dr. Graves	2.50	7.50	24.00
56-70-Dr. Graves ends	1.50	4.50	12.00
71-100	1.00	3.00	8.00
101-124: 107-Sutton, Wood-a. 114-Newton-a		2.40	6.00
125-169		1.60	4.00

NOTE: ***Aparo** a-65, 66, 68, 72, 141r, 142r; c-71, 72, 74-76, 81, 146r. **Ditko** a-55-58, 60, 61, 67, 69-73, 75-90, 92-95, 97, 99-118, 120-122, 125r, 126r, 131-133r, 136-141r, 143r, 144r, 152, 155, 161, 163; c-67, 69, 73, 77, 78, 83, 84, 86-90, 92-97, 99, 102, 109, 111, 118, 120-122, 125, 131-133, 163. **Glanzman** a-167. **Howard** a-95, 98, 99, 117; c-98, 107, 120, 121, 161. **Morisi** a-83, 84, 86. **Newton** a-114; c-115(painted). **Palais** a-61. **Staton** a-161; c-117. **Sutton** a-107, 112-114; c-100, 106, 110, 113(painted). **Wood** a-107.*

GHOSTLY WEIRD STORIES (Formerly Blue Bolt Weird)
No. 120, Sept, 1953 - No. 124, Sept, 1954
Star Publications

	GD25	FN65	NM94
120-Jo-Jo-r	29.00	86.00	210.00
121-124: 121-Jo-Jo-r. 122-The Mask-r/Capt. Flight #5; Rulah-r; has 1pg. story 'Death and the Devil Pills'-r/Western Outlaws #17. 123-Jo-Jo; Disbrow-a(2). 124-Torpedo Man	24.00	73.00	180.00

NOTE: ***Disbrow** a-120-124. **L. B. Cole** covers-all issues (#122 is a sci-fi cover).*

GHOST MANOR (Ghostly Haunts No. 20 on)
July, 1968 - No. 19, July, 1971
Charlton Comics

	GD25	FN65	NM94
1	2.50	7.50	20.00
2-5	1.50	4.50	12.00
6-12,17: 17-Morisi-a	1.10	3.30	9.00
13-16,18,19-Ditko-a; c-15,18,19	1.50	4.50	12.00

GHOST MANOR (2nd Series)
Oct, 1971 - No. 32, Dec, 1976; No. 33, Sept, 1977 - No. 77, 11/84
Charlton Comics

	GD25	FN65	NM94
1	2.50	7.50	20.00
2-7,9,10	1.25	3.75	10.00
8-Wood-a	1.50	4.50	12.00
11-17		2.40	6.00
18-30: 18-Newton's 1st pro art. 19-20-Newton-a. 22-Newton-c/a. 21-E-Man, Blue Beetle, Capt. Atom cameos. 28-Nudity panels	1.10	3.30	9.00
31-56: 40-Torture & drug use.		2.40	6.00
57-Wood, Ditko, Howard-a	1.00	3.00	8.00
58-77: 77-Aparo-r/Space Adventures V3#60 (Paul Mann		1.60	4.00
19(Modern Comics reprint, 1977)		1.20	3.00

NOTE: ***Ditko** a-4, 8, 10, 11(2), 13, 14, 18, 20-22, 24-26, 28, 29, 31, 37r, 38r, 40r, 42-44r, 46r, 47, 51r, 52r, 54r, 57, 60, 62(4), 64r, 71; c-2-7, 9-11, 14-16, 28, 31, 37, 38, 42, 43, 46, 47, 51, 52, 60, 62, 64. **Howard** a-4, 8, 19-21, 57. **Newton** a-18-20, 22, 64; c-22. **Sutton** a-19;c-8, 18.*

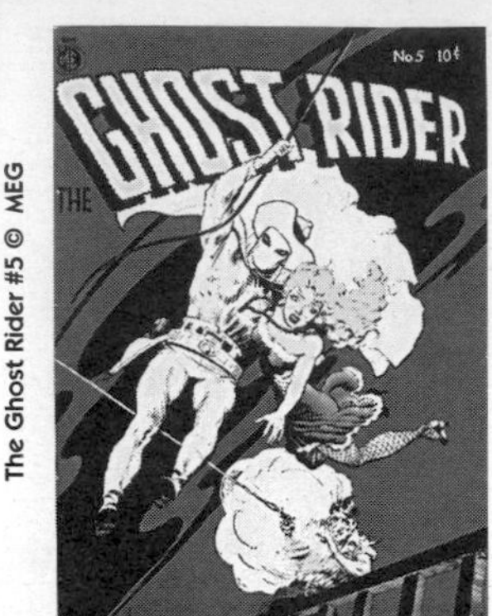

The Ghost Rider #5 © MEG

Ghost Rider #7 © MEG

Ghost Rider V2 #92 © MEG

GD25 FN65 NM94

GHOST RIDER (See A-1 Comics, Best of the West, Black Phantom, Bobby Benson, Great Western, Red Mask & Tim Holt)
1950 - No. 14, 1954
Magazine Enterprises
NOTE: *The character was inspired by Vaughn Monroe's "Ghost Riders in the Sky", and Disney's movie "The Headless Horseman".*

1(A-1 #27)-Origin Ghost Rider 54.00 162.00 490.00
2-5: 2(A-1 #29), 3(A-1 #31), 4(A-1 #34), 5(A-1 #37)-All Frazetta-c only 49.00 147.00 440.00
6,7: 6(A-1 #44)-Loco weed story, 7(A-1 #51) 21.00 64.00 170.00
8,9: 8(A-1 #57)-Drug use story, 9(A-1 #69) 19.00 56.00 150.00
10(A-1 #71)-Vs. Frankenstein 19.00 56.00 150.00
11-14: 11(A-1 #75). 12(A-1 #80)-Bondage-c; one-eyed Devil-c. 13(A-1 #84). 14(A-1 #112) 15.50 47.00 125.00
NOTE: ***Dick Ayers** art in all; c-1, 6-14.*

GHOST RIDER, THE (See Night Rider & Western Gunfighters)
Feb, 1967 - No. 7, Nov, 1967 (Western hero)(12¢)
Marvel Comics Group

1-Origin & 1st app. Ghost Rider; Kid Colt-reprints begin 4.50 13.50 45.00
2 2.60 7.80 26.00
3-7: 6-Last Kid Colt-r; All Ayers-c/a(p) 2.50 7.50 20.00

GHOST RIDER (See The Champions, Marvel Spotlight #5, Marvel Team-Up #15, 58, Marvel Treasury Edition #18, Marvel Two-In-One #8, The Original Ghost Rider & The Original Ghost Rider Rides Again)
Sept, 1973 - No. 81, June, 1983 (Super-hero)
Marvel Comics Group

1-Johnny Blaze, the Ghost Rider begins; 1st app. Daimon Hellstrom (Son of Satan) in cameo 6.50 19.50 65.00
2-1st full app. Daimon Hellstrom; gives glimpse of costume (1 panel); story continues in Marvel Spotlight #12 2.50 7.50 25.00
3-5: 3-Ghost Rider gets new cycle; Son of Satan app. 1.85 5.50 15.00
6-10: 10-Reprints origin/1st app. from Marvel Spotlight #5; Ploog-a 1.25 3.75 10.00
11-18: 18-Spider-Man-c & app. 1.00 2.80 7.00
19-(Regular 25¢ edition)(8/76) 1.00 2.80 7.00
19-(30¢-c, limited distribution) 2.80 8.40 28.00
20-Daredevil x-over; ties into D.D. #138; Byrne-a 1.10 3.30 9.00
21-30: 22-1st app. Enforcer. 29,30-Vs. Dr. Strange 1.80 4.50
31-34,36-49 1.60 4.00
35-Death Race classic; Starlin-c/a/sty 1.00 2.80 7.00
50-Double size 2.20 5.50
51-67,69-76,78-80: 80-Brief origin recap 1.40 3.50
68,77-Origin retold 2.00 5.00
81-Death of Ghost Rider (Demon leaves Blaze) 2.40 6.50
NOTE: ***Anderson** c-64p. **Infantino** a(p)-43, 44, 51. **G. Kane** a-21p; c(p)-1, 2, 4, 5, 8, 9, 11-13, 19, 20, 24, 25. **Kirby** c-21-23. **Mooney** a-2-9p, 30i. **Nebres** c-26i. **Newton** a-23i. **Perez** c-26p. **Shores** a-2i. J. **Sparling** a-62p, 64p, 65p. **Starlin** a(p)-35. **Sutton** a-1p, 44i, 64i, 65i, 66, 67i. **Tuska** a-13p, 14p, 16p.*

GHOST RIDER (Also see Doctor Strange/Ghost Rider Special, Marvel Comics Presents & Midnight Sons Unlimited)
V2#1, May, 1990 - No. 94, Mar, 1998 ($1.50/$1.75/$1.95/$1.50)
Marvel Comics (Midnight Sons imprint #44 on)

V2#1-($1.95, 52 pgs.)-Origin/1st app. new Ghost Rider; Kingpin app. 2.40 6.00
1-2nd printing (not gold) .80 2.00
2,3,5: 3-Kingpin app. 5-Punisher app.; Jim Lee-c 1.20 3.00
4-Scarcer 1.60 4.00
5-Gold background 2nd printing .80 2.00
6-Punisher app. .80 2.00
7-10: 9-X-Factor app. 10-Reintro Johnny Blaze on the last pg. 1.50
11-14: 11-Stroman-c/a(p). 12,13-Dr. Strange x-over cont'd in D.S. #28. 13-Painted-c. 14-Johnny Blaze vs. Ghost Rider; origin recap 1st Ghost Rider (Blaze) 1.50
15-Glow in the dark-c; begin $1.75-c .80 2.00
15-Gold background 2nd printing 1.50
16,17-Spider-Man/Hobgoblin-c/story 1.50
18-24,29,30,32-39: 18-Painted-c by Nelson. 29-Wolverine-c/story. 32-Dr. Strange x-over; Johnny Blaze app. 34-Williamson-a(i). 36-Daredevil app. 37-Archangel app. 1.50
25-27: 25-($2.75)-Contains pop-up scene insert. 26,27-X-Men x-over; Lee/Williams-c on both 1.10 2.75
28-($2.50, 52 pgs.)-Polybagged w/poster; part 1 of Rise of the Midnight Sons storyline (see Ghost Rider/Blaze #1) 1.00 2.50
31-($2.50, 52 pgs.)-Polybagged w/poster; part 6 of Rise of the Midnight Sons 1.00 2.50
40-Outer-c is Darkhold envelope made of black parchment w/gold ink; Midnight Massacre; Demogoblin app. .90 2.25
41-48: 41-Lilith & Centurious app.; begin $1.75-c. 41-43-Neon ink-c. 43-Has free extra 16 pg. insert on Siege of Darkness. 44,45-Siege of Darkness parts 2 & 10. 44-Spot varnish-c. 46-Intro new Ghost Rider. 48-Spider-Man app. .70 1.75
49,51-60,62-78: 49-Begin $1.95-c; bound-in trading card sheet; Hulk app. 55-Werewolf by Night app. 65-Punisher app. 67,68-Gambit app. 68-Wolverine app. 73,74-Blaze, Vengeance app. 78-New costume. .80 2.00
50-($2.50, 52 pgs.)-Regular edition 1.00 2.50
50-($2.95, 52 pgs.)-Collectors ed. die cut foil-c 1.20 3.00
61-($2.50) 1.00 2.50
75-83: 75-Begin $1.50-c. 76-Vs. Vengeance. 77-Dr. Strange-c/app. 78-Dr. Strange app. 1.50
84-86, -1(7/97): 84-Begin $1.95-c 1.95
87-92,94: 87-Begin $1.99-c. 94-Final issue 1.99
93-($2.99)-Salteres & Texeira-a 2.99
Annual 1 (1993, $2.95, 68 pgs.)-Bagged w/card 1.20 3.00
Annual 2 (1994, $2.95, 68 pgs.) 1.20 3.00
...And Cable 1 (9/92, $3.95, stiff-c, 68 pgs.)-Reprints Marvel Comics Presents #90-98 w/new Kieth-c 1.60 4.00
NOTE: ***Andy & Joe Kubert** c/a-28-31. **Quesada** c-21. **Williamson** a(i)-33-35; c-33i.*

GHOST RIDER/BALLISTIC
Feb, 1997 ($2.95, one-shot)
Marvel Comics

1-Devil's Reign pt. 3 2.95

GHOST RIDER/BLAZE: SPIRITS OF VENGEANCE (Also see Blaze)
Aug, 1992 - No. 23, June, 1994 ($1.75)
Marvel Comics (Midnight Sons imprint #17 on)

1-($2.75, 52 pgs.)-Polybagged w/poster; part 2 of Rise of the Midnight Sons storyline; Adam Kubert-c/a begins 1.10 2.75
2-11,14-21: 4-Art Adams & Joe Kubert-p. 5,6-Spirits of Venom parts 2 & 4 cont'd from Web of Spider-Man #95,96 w/Demogoblin. 14-17-Neon ink-c. 15-Intro Blaze's new costume & power. 17,18-Siege of Darkness parts 8 & 13. 17-Spot varnish-c .70 1.75
12-($2.95)-Glow-in-the-dark-c 1.20 3.00
13-($2.25)-Outer-c is Darkhold envelope made of black parchment w/gold ink; Midnight Massacre x-over .90 2.25
22,23: 22-Begin $1.95-c; bound-in trading card sheet .80 2.00
NOTE: ***Adam & Joe Kubert** c-7, 8. **Adam Kubert/Steacy** c-6. **J. Kubert** a-13p(6 pgs.)*

GHOST RIDER/CAPTAIN AMERICA: FEAR
Oct, 1992 ($5.95, 52 pgs.)
Marvel Comics

nn-Wraparound gatefold-c; Williamson inks 1.00 2.50 6.00

GHOST RIDER 2099

Ghost Rider 2099 #4 © MEG

Ghosts #7 © DC

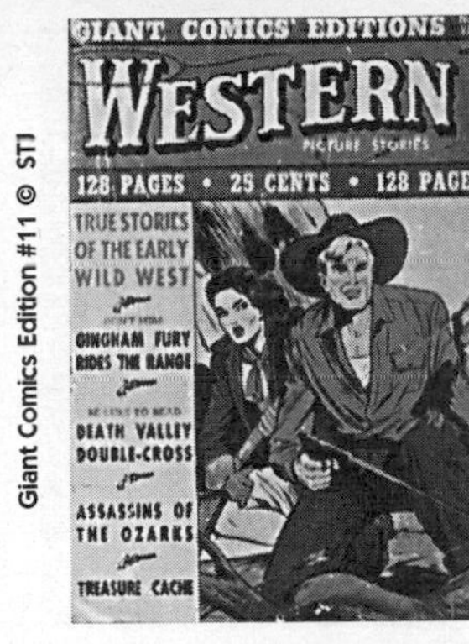

Giant Comics Edition #11 © STI

GD25 FN65 NM94

May, 1994 - No. 25, May, 1996 ($1.50/$1.95)
Marvel Comics

1 ($2.25)-Collector's Edition w/prismatic foil-c .80 2.00
1 ($1.50)-Regular Edition; bound-in trading card sheet 1.50
2-12: 7-Spider-Man 2099 app. 1.50
13-24 ($1.95) .80 2.00
25 ($2.95) 1.20 3.00

GHOST RIDER, WOLVERINE, PUNISHER: THE DARK DESIGN
Dec, 1994 ($5.95, one-shot)
Marvel Comics

nn-Gatefold-c 2.40 6.00

GHOST RIDER; WOLVERINE; PUNISHER: HEARTS OF DARKNESS
Dec, 1991 ($4.95, one-shot, 52 pgs.)
Marvel Comics

1-Double gatefold-c; John Romita, Jr.-c/a(p) 2.00 5.00

GHOSTS (Ghost No. 1)
Sept-Oct, 1971 - No. 112, May, 1982 (No. 1-5: 52 pgs.)
National Periodical Publications/DC Comics

1-Aparo-a 7.00 21.00 70.00
2-Wood-a(i) 3.50 10.50 35.00
3-5 2.50 7.50 25.00
6-10 1.85 5.50 15.00
11-20 1.25 3.75 10.00
21-39 1.10 3.30 9.00
40-68 pgs. 1.85 5.50 15.00
41-60 2.40 6.00
61-96 1.60 4.00
97-99-The Spectre vs. Dr. 13 by Aparo. 97,98-Spectre-c by Aparo.
2.40 6.00
100-112: 100-Infinity-c 1.00 2.50

NOTE: ***B. Baily** a-77. **Buckler** c-99, 100. **J. Craig** a-108. **Ditko** a-77, 111. **Giffen** a-104p, 106p, 111p. **Glanzman** a-2. **Golden** a-88. **Infantino** a-8. **Kaluta** c-7, 93, 101. **Kubert** a-8; c-89, 105-108, 111. **Mayer** a-111. **McWilliams** a-99. **Win Mortimer** a-89, 91, 94. **Nasser/Netzer** a-97. **Newton** a-92p, 94p. **Nino** a-35, 37, 57. **Orlando** a-74i; c-80. **Redondo** a-8, 13, 45. **Sparling** a(p)-90, 93, 94. **Spiegle** a-103, 105. **Tuska** a-2i. Dr. 13, the Ghostbreaker back-ups in 95-99, 101.*

GHOSTS SPECIAL (See DC Special Series No. 7)

GHOST STORIES (See Amazing Ghost Stories)

GHOST STORIES
Sept-Nov, 1962; No. 2, Apr-June, 1963 - No. 37, Oct, 1973
Dell Publishing Co.

12-295-211(#1)-Written by John Stanley 3.50 10.50 35.00
2 2.25 6.75 18.00
3-10: Two No. 6's exist with different c/a(12-295-406 & 12-295-503)
#12-295-503 is actually #9 with indicia to #6 1.75 5.25 14.00
11-20 1.25 3.75 10.00
21-37 1.00 3.00 8.00

NOTE: *#21-34, 36, 37 all reprint earlier issues.*

GHOUL TALES (Magazine)
Nov, 1970 - No. 5, July, 1971 (52 pgs.) (B&W)
Stanley Publications

1-Aragon pre-code reprints; Mr. Mystery as host; bondage-c
5.00 15.00 50.00
2,3: 2-(1/71)Reprint/Climax #1. 3-(3/71) 2.50 7.50 24.00
4-(5/71)Reprints story "The Way to a Man's Heart" used in **SOTI**
3.50 10.50 35.00
5-ACG reprints 2.25 6.75 18.00

NOTE: *No. 1-4 contain pre-code Aragon reprints.*

GIANT BOY BOOK OF COMICS (Also see Boy Comics)
1945 (240 pgs., hard-c)
Newsbook Publications (Gleason)

1-Crimebuster & Young Robin Hood; Biro-c 75.00 225.00 675.00

GIANT COMIC ALBUM
1972 (59¢, 11x14", 52 pgs., B&W, cardboard-c)
King Features Syndicate

Newspaper reprints: Little Iodine, Katzenjammer Kids, Henry, Mandrake the Magician ('59 Falk), Popeye, Beetle Bailey, Barney Google, Blondie, Flash Gordon ('68-69 Dan Barry), & Snuffy Smith
each... 2.50 7.50 24.00

GIANT COMICS
Summer, 1957 - No. 3, Winter, 1957 (25¢, 100 pgs.)
Charlton Comics

1-Atomic Mouse, Hoppy app. 17.50 53.00 140.00
2,3: 2-Romance. 3-Christmas Book; Atomic Mouse, Atomic Rabbit, Li'l Genius, Li'l Tomboy & Atom the Cat stories 12.00 38.00 100.00

NOTE: *The above may be rebound comics; contents could vary.*

GIANT COMICS (See Wham-O Giant Comics)

GIANT COMICS EDITION (See Terry-Toons)
1947 - No. 17, 1950 (25¢, 100-164 pgs.)
St. John Publishing Co.

1-Mighty Mouse 41.00 123.00 410.00
2-Abbie & Slats 19.00 57.00 190.00
3-Terry-Toons Album; 100 pgs. 31.00 93.00 310.00
4-Crime comics; contains Red Seal No. 16, used & illo. in **SOTI**
48.00 145.00 485.00
5-Police Case Book (4/49, 132 pgs.)-Contents varies; contains remaindered St. John books - some volumes contain 5 copies rather than 4, with 160 pages; Matt Baker-c 46.00 138.00 460.00
5A-Terry-Toons Album (132 pgs.)-Mighty Mouse, Heckle & Jeckle, Gandy Goose & Dinky stories 29.00 87.00 290.00
6-Western Picture Stories; Baker-c/a(3); Tuska-a; The Sky Chief, Blue Monk, Ventrilo app., 132 pgs. 43.00 130.00 435.00
7-Contains a teen-age romance plus 3 Mopsy comics
26.00 78.00 260.00
8-The Adventures of Mighty Mouse (10/49) 29.00 87.00 290.00
9-Romance and Confession Stories; Kubert-a(4); Baker-a; photo-c (132 pgs.)
45.00 135.00 450.00
10-Terry-Toons Album (132 pgs.)-Mighty Mouse, Heckle & Jeckle, Gandy Goose stories 29.00 87.00 290.00
11-Western Picture Stories-Baker-c/a(4); The Sky Chief, Desperado, & Blue Monk app.; another version with Son of Sinbad by Kubert (132 pgs.)
41.00 123.00 410.00
12-Diary Secrets; Baker prostitute-c; 4 St. John romance comics; Baker-a
72.00 217.00 725.00
13-Romances; Baker, Kubert-a 38.00 115.00 385.00
14-Mighty Mouse Album (132 pgs.) 29.00 87.00 290.00
15-Romances (4 love comics)-Baker-c 42.00 126.00 420.00
16-Little Audrey; Abbott & Costello, Casper 29.00 87.00 290.00
17(nn)-Mighty Mouse Album (nn, no date, but did follow No. 16); 100 pgs. on cover but has 148 pgs. 29.00 87.00 290.00

NOTE: *The above books contain remaindered comics and contents could vary with each issue. No. 11, 12 have part photo magazine insides.*

GIANT COMICS EDITIONS
1940's (132 pgs.)
United Features Syndicate

1-Abbie & Slats, Abbott & Costello, Jim Hardy, Ella Cinders, Iron Vic, Gordo, & Bill Bumlin 31.00 94.00 250.00
2-Jim Hardy, Ella Cinders, Elmo & Gordo 24.00 71.00 190.00

NOTE: *Above books contain rebound copies; contents can vary.*

GIANT GRAB BAG OF COMICS (See Archie All-Star Specials under Archie Comics)

GIANTS (See Thrilling True Story of the Baseball...)

GIANT-SIZE...

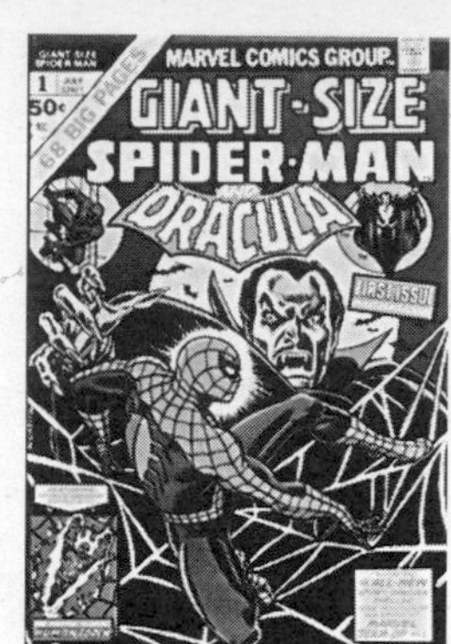

Giant Size Spider-Man #1 © MEG

Giant Size X-Men #1 © MEG

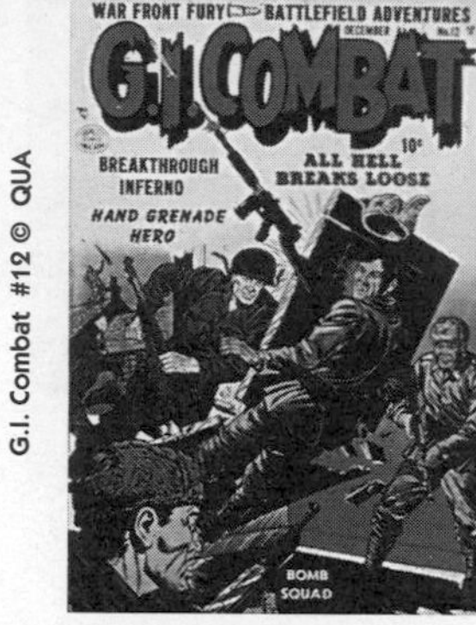

G.I. Combat #12 © QUA

GD25 FN65 NM94

May, 1974 - Dec, 1975 (35/50¢, 52/68 pgs.)(Some titles quarterly)
Marvel Comics Group

Avengers 1(8/74)-New-a plus G.A. H. Torch-r; 1st modern app. The Whizzer; 1st & only modern app. Miss America 1.25 3.75 10.00
Avengers 2,3: 2(11/74)-Death of the Swordsman. 3(2/75) 2.40 6.00
Avengers 4,5: 4(6/75)-Vision marries Scarlet Witch. 5(12/75)-Reprints Avengers Special #1 2.40 6.00
Captain America 1(12/75)-r/stories T.O.S. 59-63 by Kirby (#63 reprints origin) 1.40 4.15 11.00
Captain Marvel 1(12/75)-r/Capt. Marvel #17, 20 by Gil Kane (p) 1.10 3.30 9.00
Chillers 1(6/74, 52 pgs)-Curse of Dracula; origin/1st app. Lilith, Dracula's daughter; Heath-r, Colan-c/a(p); becomes Giant-Size Dracula #2 on 1.85 5.50 15.00
Chillers 1(2/75, 50¢, 68 pgs.)-Alacala-a 1.10 3.30 9.00
Chillers 2(5/75)-All-r; Everett-r from Advs. into Weird Worlds 2.40 6.00
Chillers 3(8/75)-Wrightson-c(new)/a(r); Colan, Kirby, Smith-r 1.00 3.00 8.00
Conan 1(9/74)-B. Smith-r/#3; start adaptation of Howard's "Hour of the Dragon" (ends #4); 1st app. Belit; new-a begins 1.25 3.75 10.00
Conan 2(12/74)-B. Smith-r/#5; Sutton-a(i)(#1 also); Buscema-c 1.00 3.00 8.00
Conan 3-5: 3(4/75)-B. Smith-r/#6; Sutton-a(i). 4(6/75)-B. Smith-r/#7. 5(1975)-B. Smith-r/#14,15; Kirby-c 2.40 6.00
Creatures 1(5/74, 52 pgs.)-Werewolf app; 1st app. Tigra (formerly Cat); Crandall-r; becomes Giant-Size Werewolf w/#2 1.50 4.50 12.00
Daredevil 1(1975) 1.00 3.00 8.00
Defenders 1(7/74)-Silver Surfer app.; Starlin-a; Ditko, Everett & Kirby reprints 1.85 5.50 15.00
Defenders 2(10/74, 68 pgs.)-New G. Kane-c/a(p); Son of Satan app.; Sub-Mariner-r by Everett; Ditko-r/Strange Tales #119 (Dr. Strange); Maneely-r. 1.10 3.30 9.00
Defenders 3-5: 3(1/75)-1st app. Korvac.; Newton, Starlin-a; Ditko, Everett-r. 4(4/75)-Ditko, Everett-r; G. Kane-c. 5-(7/75)-Guardians app. 1.00 2.80 7.00
Doc Savage 1(1975, 68 pgs.)-r/#1,2; Mooney-r 2.40 6.00
Doctor Strange 1(11/75)-Reprints stories from Strange Tales #164-168; Lawrence, Tuska-r 1.00 2.80 7.00
Dracula 2(9/74, 50¢)-Formerly Giant-Size Chillers 1.10 3.30 9.00
Dracula 3(12/74)-Fox-r/Uncanny Tales #6 2.40 6.00
Dracula 4(3/75)-Ditko-r(2) 2.40 6.00
Dracula 5(6/75)-1st Byrne art at Marvel 1.85 5.50 15.00
Fantastic Four 2-4: 2(8/74)-Formerly Giant-Size Super-Stars; Ditko-r. 3(11/74). 4(2/75)-1st Madrox; 2-4-All have Buscema-a 1.25 3.75 10.00
Fantastic Four 5,6: 5(5/75)-All-r; Kirby, G. Kane-r. 6(10/75)-All-r; Kirby-r 1.00 3.00 8.00
Hulk 1(1975) 1.85 5.50 15.00
Invaders 1(6/75, 50¢, 68 pgs.)-Origin; G.A. Sub-Mariner-r/Sub-Mariner #1; intro Master Man 1.00 3.00 8.00
Iron Man 1(1975)-Ditko reprint 1.50 4.50 12.00
Kid Colt 1-3: 1(1/75). 2(4/75). 3(7/75) 1.50 4.50 12.00
Man-Thing 1(8/74)-New Ploog-c/a (25 pgs.); Ditko-r/Amazing Adv. #11; Kirby-r/Strange Tales Ann. #2 & T.O.S. #15; (#1-5 all have new Man-Thing stories, pre-hero-r & are 68 pgs.) 1.10 3.30 9.00
Man-Thing 2,3: 2(11/74)-Buscema-c/a(p); Kirby, Powell-r. 3(2/75)-Alcala-a; Ditko, Kirby, Sutton-r; Gil Kane-c 2.40 6.00
Man-Thing 4,5: 4(5/75)-Howard the Duck by Brunner-c/a; Ditko-r. 5(8/75)-Howard the Duck by Brunner (p); Dracaula cameo in Howard the Duck; Buscema-a(p); Sutton-a(i); G. Kane-c 1.25 3.75 10.00
Marvel Triple Action 1,2: 1(5/75). 2(7/75) 1.00 3.00 8.00
Master of Kung Fu 1(9/74)-Russell-a; Yellow Claw-r in #1-4; Gulacy-a in #1,2 1.10 3.30 9.00

GD25 FN65 NM94

Master of Kung Fu 2(12/74)-r/Yellow Claw #1 2.40 6.00
Master of Kung Fu 3(3/75)-Gulacy-a 2.40 6.00
Master of Kung Fu 4(6/75) 2.40 6.00
Power Man 1(1975) 2.40 6.00
Spider-Man 1(7/74)-Kirby/Ditko, Byrne-r plus new-a (Dracula-c/story) 3.00 9.00 30.00
Spider-Man 2,3: 2(10/74). 3(1/75)-Byrne-r 1.85 5.50 15.00
Spider-Man 4(4/75)-3rd Punisher app.; Byrne, Ditko-r 6.00 18.00 60.00
Spider-Man 5,6: 5(7/75)-Byrne-r. 6(9/75) 1.10 3.30 9.00
Super-Heroes Featuring Spider-Man 1(6/74, 35¢, 52 pgs.)-Spider-Man vs. Man-Wolf; Morbius, the Living Vampire app.; Ditko-r; G. Kane-a(p); Spidey villains app. 4.00 12.00 40.00
Super-Stars 1(5/74, 35¢, 52 pgs.)-Fantastic Four; Thing vs. Hulk; Kirbyish-c/a by Buckler/Sinnott; F.F. villains profiled; becomes Giant-Size Fantastic Four #2 on 1.85 5.50 15.00
Super-Villain Team-Up 1(3/75, 68 pgs.)-Craig-r(i) (Also see Fantastic Four #6 for 1st super-villain team-up) 1.00 2.80 7.00
Super-Villain Team-Up 2(6/75, 68 pgs.)-Dr. Doom, Sub-Mariner app.; Spider-Man-r/Amazing Spider-Man #8 by Ditko; Sekowsky-a(p) 2.00 5.00
Thor 1(7/75) 1.00 2.80 7.00
Werewolf 2(10/74, 68 pgs.)-Formerly Giant-Size Creatures; Ditko-r; Frankenstein app. 1.00 2.80 7.00
Werewolf 3,5: 3(1/75, 68 pgs.). 5(7/75, 68 pgs.) 1.00 2.80 7.00
Werewolf 4(4/75, 68 pgs.)-Morbius the Living Vampire app. 1.25 3.75 10.00
X-Men 1(Summer, 1975, 50¢, 68 pgs.)-1st app. new X-Men; intro Nightcrawler, Storm, Colossus & Thunderbird; 2nd full app. Wolverine after Incredible Hulk #181 40.00 120.00 440.00
X-Men 2(11/75)-N. Adams-r (51 pgs) 4.50 13.50 45.00

GIANT SPECTACULAR COMICS (See Archie All-Star Special under Archie Comics)

GIANT SUMMER FUN BOOK (See Terry-Toons...)

G. I. COMBAT
Oct, 1952 - No. 43, Dec, 1956
Quality Comics Group

1-Crandall-c; Cuidera a-1-43i 47.00 141.00 425.00
2 23.00 68.00 180.00
3-5,10-Crandall-c/a 21.00 64.00 170.00
6-Crandall-a 19.00 56.00 150.00
7-9 15.00 45.00 120.00
11-20 11.30 34.00 90.00
21-31,33,35-43: 41-1st S.A. issue 9.50 28.00 75.00
32-Nuclear attack-c/story "Atomic Rocket Assault" 11.30 34.00 90.00
34-Crandall-a 10.00 30.00 80.00

G. I. COMBAT (See DC Special Series #22)
No. 44, Jan, 1957 - No. 288, Mar, 1987
National Periodical Publications/DC Comics

44-Grey tone-c 42.00 126.00 420.00
45 23.00 69.00 230.00
46-50 17.00 51.00 170.00
51-Grey tone-c 16.00 48.00 160.00
52-60 13.50 41.00 135.00
61-66,68-74: 68-Introduces "The Rock" (Sgt. Rock prototype?) 9.00 27.00 90.00
67-1st Tank Killer 12.50 38.00 125.00
75-80: 75-Greytone-c begin, end #109 9.50 28.50 95.00
81,82,84-86,88-90: 90-Last 10¢ issue 7.50 22.50 75.00
83-1st Big Al, Little Al, & Charlie Cigar 9.50 28.50 95.00
87-1st Haunted Tank 36.00 108.00 400.00
91-100: 91-1st Haunted Tank-c 6.50 19.50 65.00
101-108: 108-1st Sgt. Rock x-over. 5.50 16.50 55.00

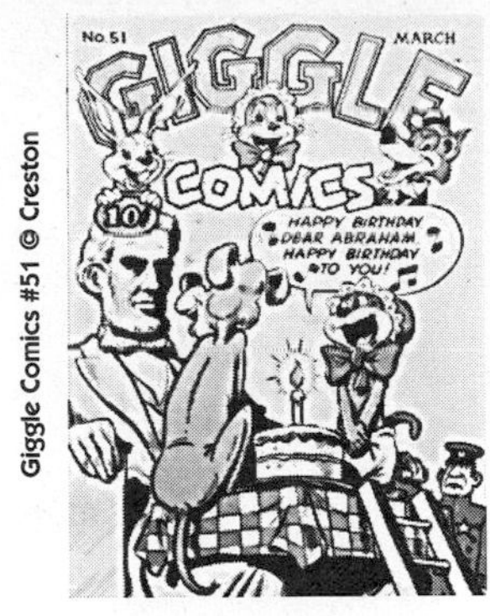

Giggle Comics #51 © Creston

G. I. Joe V2 #6 © Z-D

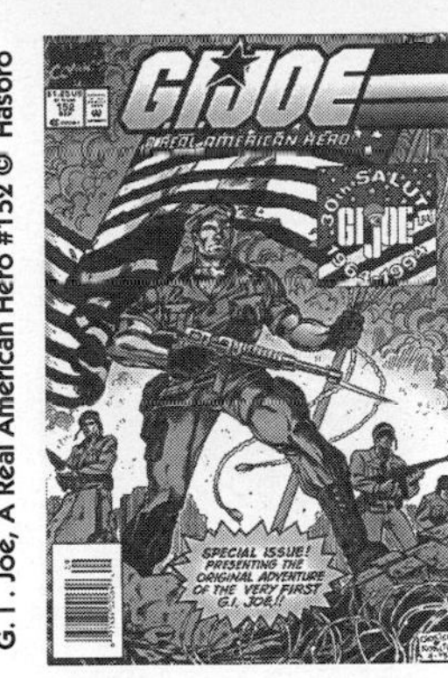

G. I. Joe, A Real American Hero #152 © Hasbro

	GD25	FN65	NM94
109-Grey tone-c	5.50	16.50	55.00
110-113,115-120: 113-Grey tone-c	4.20	12.60	42.00
114-Origin Haunted Tank	10.00	30.00	100.00
121-137,139,140: 121-1st app. Sgt. Rock's father. 136-Last 12¢ issue	2.60	7.80	26.00
138-Intro. The Losers (Capt. Storm, Gunner/Sarge, Johnny Cloud) in Haunted Tank (10-11/69)	6.00	18.00	60.00
141-145, 155-200:		2.40	6.00
146-148 (68pgs.)	1.50	4.50	12.00
149-154 (52 pgs.)-150-Ice Cream Soldier story (tells how he got his name). 151-Capt. Storm story. 151,153-Medal of Honor series by Maurer	1.10	3.30	9.00
201-210 ($1.00 size)	1.00	3.00	8.00
211-230 ($1.00 size)		2.00	5.00
231-259 ($1.00 size).232-Origin Kana the Ninja. 244-Death of Slim Stryker; 1st app. The Mercenaries. 246-(76 pgs., $1.50)-30th Anniversary issue. 257-Intro. Stuart's Raiders		1.60	4.00
281: 201-245,247-259 are $1.00 size. 260-Begin $1.25, 52 pg. issues, end #281. 264-Intro Sgt. Bullet; origin Kana. 269-Intro. The Bravos of Vietnam		1.20	3.00
282-288 (75¢): 282-New advs. begin		1.60	4.00

NOTE: **N. Adams** *c-168, 201, 202.* **Check** *a-168, 173.* **Drucker** *a-48, 61, 63, 66, 71, 72, 76, 134, 140, 141, 144, 147, 148, 153.* **Evans** *a-135, 138, 158, 164, 166, 201, 202, 204, 205, 215, 256. Giffen a-267.* **Glanzman** *a-most issues.* **Kubert/Heath** *a-most issues;* **Kubert** *covers most issues.* **Morrow** *a-159-161(2 pgs.).* **Redondo** *a-189, 240i, 243i.* **Sekowsky** *a-162p.* **Severin** *a-147, 152, 154.* **Simonson** *c-169.* **Thorne** *a-152, 156.* **Wildey** *a-153. Johnny Cloud app.-112, 115, 120. Mlle. Marie app.-123, 132, 200. Sgt. Rock app.-111-113, 115, 120, 125, 141, 146, 147, 149, 200. USS Stevens by* **Glanzman***-145, 150-153, 157.* **Grandenetti** *c-44-48.*

G. I. COMICS (Also see Jeep & Overseas Comics)
1945 - No. 73?, 1946 (Distributed to U. S. armed forces)
Giveaways

	GD25	FN65	NM94
1-73-Contains Prince Valiant by Foster, Blondie, Smilin' Jack, Mickey Finn, Terry & the Pirates, Donald Duck, Alley Oop, Moon Mullins & Capt. Easy strip reprints (at least 73 issues known to exist)	4.25	13.00	28.00

GIDGET (TV)
Apr, 1966 - No. 2, Dec, 1966
Dell Publishing Co.

	GD25	FN65	NM94
1-Sally Field photo-c	9.00	27.00	90.00
2	5.50	16.50	55.00

GIFT (See The Crusaders)

GIFT COMICS
1942 - No. 4, 1949 (50¢/25¢, 324 pgs./152 pgs.)
Fawcett Publications

	GD25	FN65	NM94
1-Captain Marvel, Bulletman, Golden Arrow, Ibis the Invincible, Mr. Scarlet, & Spy Smasher begin; not rebound, remaindered comics, printed at same time as originals; 50¢-c & 324 pgs. begin, end #3.	220.00	660.00	2200.00
2-Commando Yank, Phantom Eagle, others app.	140.00	420.00	1400.00
3	95.00	285.00	950.00
4-(25¢, 152 pgs.)-The Marvel Family, Captain Marvel, etc.; each issue can vary in contents	60.00	180.00	600.00

GIFTS FROM SANTA (See March of Comics No. 137)

GIGGLE COMICS (Spencer Spook No. 100) (Also see Ha Ha Comics)
Oct, 1943 - No. 99, Jan-Feb, 1955
Creston No.1-63/American Comics Group No. 64 on

	GD25	FN65	NM94
1-Funny animal	25.00	75.00	200.00
2	12.00	36.00	95.00
3-5: Ken Hultgren-a begins?	8.75	26.25	70.00
6-10: 9-1st Superkatt (6/44)	7.85	23.50	55.00
11-20	5.70	17.00	40.00
21-40: 32-Patriotic-c. 37,61-X-Mas-c. 39-St. Valentine's Day-c	5.35	16.00	32.00
41-54,56-59,61-99: 95-Spencer Spook begins?	4.25	13.00	28.00
55,60-Milt Gross-a	5.70	17.00	35.00

G-I IN BATTLE (G-I No. 1 only)
Aug, 1952 - No. 9, July, 1953; Mar, 1957 - No. 6, May, 1958
Ajax-Farrell Publ./Four Star

	GD25	FN65	NM94
1	7.85	23.50	55.00
2	4.25	13.00	28.00
3-9	4.00	12.00	24.00
Annual 1(1952, 25¢, 100 pgs.)	20.00	60.00	160.00
1(1957-Ajax)	5.35	16.00	32.00
2-6	4.00	10.00	20.00

G. I. JANE
May, 1953 - No. 11, Mar, 1955 (Misdated 3/54)
Stanhall/Merit No. 11

	GD25	FN65	NM94
1-PX Pete begins; Bill Williams-c/a	8.75	26.25	70.00
2-7(5/54)	5.70	17.00	35.00
8-10(12/54, Stanhall)	4.25	13.00	28.00
11 (3/55, Merit)	4.00	12.00	24.00

G. I. JOE (Also see Advs. of..., Showcase #53, 54 & The Yardbirds)
No. 10, 1950; No. 11, 4-5/51 - No. 51, 6/57 (52pgs.: 10-14,6-17?)
Ziff-Davis Publ. Co. (Korean War)

	GD25	FN65	NM94
10(#1, 1950)-Saunders painted-c begin	10.00	30.00	80.00
11-14(#2-5, 10/51): 11-New logo. 12-New logo	7.15	21.50	50.00
V2#6(12/51)-17-(11/52; Last 52 pgs.?)	6.50	19.50	45.00
18-(25¢, 100 pg. Giant, 12-1/52-53)	15.00	45.00	120.00
19-30: 20-22,24,28-31-The Yardbirds app.	5.70	17.00	35.00
31-47,49-51	5.35	16.00	32.00
48-Atom bomb story	5.70	17.00	35.00

NOTE: **Powell** *a-V2#7, 8, 11.* **Norman Saunders** *painted c-10-14, V2#6-14, 26, 30, 31, 35, 38, 39.* **Tuska** *a-7. Bondage c-29, 35, 38.*

G. I. JOE (America's Movable Fighting Man)
1967 (5-1/8x8-3/8", 36 pgs.)
Custom Comics

	GD25	FN65	NM94
nn-Schaffenberger-a; based on Hasbro toy	1.25	3.75	10.00

G.I. JOE
Dec, 1995 - No. 4, Apr, 1996 ($1.95, limited series)
Dark Horse Comics

	GD25	FN65	NM94
1-4: Mike W. Barr scripts. 1,2-Miller-c. 3-Simonson-c		.80	2.00

G.I. JOE
V2#1, June, 1996 - V2#4, Sept, 1996 ($2.50)
Dark Horse Comics

	GD25	FN65	NM94
V2#1-4: Mike W. Barr scripts. 4-Painted-c		1.00	2.50

G. I. JOE AND THE TRANSFORMERS
Jan, 1987 - No. 4, Apr, 1987 (Limited series)
Marvel Comics Group

	GD25	FN65	NM94
1-4			1.00

G. I. JOE, A REAL AMERICAN HERO (...Starring Snake-Eyes on-c #135 on)
June, 1982 - No. 155, Dec, 1994
Marvel Comics Group

	GD25	FN65	NM94
1-Printed on Baxter paper; based on Hasbro toy		1.20	3.00
2-Printed on reg. paper		1.00	2.50
3-10		.80	2.00
11-20: 11-Intro Airborne			1.50
21,22,26,27: 26,27-Origin Snake-Eyes parts 1 & 2			1.50
23-25,28-30			1.50
31-134,139-143: 33-New headquarters. 60-Todd McFarlane-a. 110-1st Ron Garney-a. 139-142-New Transformers app.		.70	1.75
135-138-($1.75)-Polybagged w/trading card		.70	1.75
144-149,151-155-($1.25): 144-Origin Snake-Eyes			1.25

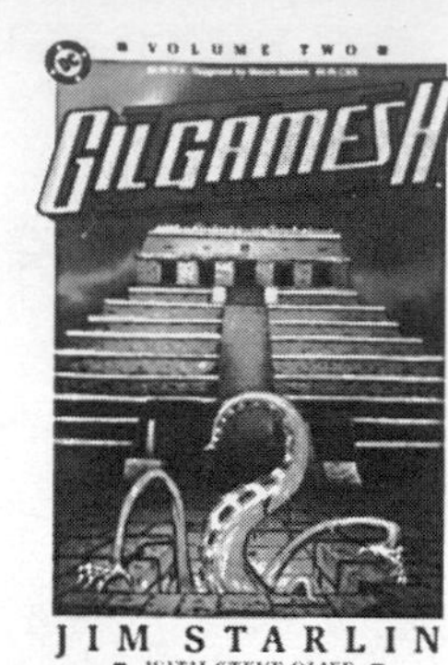

Gilgamesh II #2 © DC

Ginger #5 © AP

Girls' Love Stories #3 © DC

	GD25	FN65	NM94
All 2nd printings			1.00
150-($2.00, 52 pgs.)		.80	2.00
Special Treasury Edition (1982)-r/#1		1.20	3.00
Yearbook 1 (3/85)-r/#1; Golden-c		.80	2.00
Yearbook 2 (3/86)-Golden-c/a , 3(3/87, 68 pgs.)		.80	2.00
Yearbook 4 (2/88)			1.50

NOTE: ***Garney** a(p)-110. **Golden** c-23, 29, 34, 36. **Heath** a-24. **Rogers** a(p)-75, 77-82, 84, 86; c-77.*

G. I. JOE COMICS MAGAZINE
Dec, 1986 - No. 13, 1988 ($1.50, digest-size)
Marvel Comics Group

	GD25	FN65	NM94
1-13: G.I. Joe-r			1.50

G.I. JOE EUROPEAN MISSIONS (Action Force in indicia)
June, 1988 - No. 15, Dec, 1989 ($1.50/$1.75 #12 on)
Marvel Comics Ltd. (British)

	GD25	FN65	NM94
1-15: Reprints Action Force			1.50

G. I. JOE ORDER OF BATTLE, THE
Dec, 1986 - No. 4, Mar, 1987 (limited series)
Marvel Comics Group

	GD25	FN65	NM94
1-4			1.00

G. I. JOE SPECIAL MISSIONS (Indicia title: Special Missions)
Oct, 1986 - No. 28, Dec, 1989 ($1.00)
Marvel Comics Group

	GD25	FN65	NM94
1-28			1.00

G. I. JUNIORS (See Harvey Hits No. 86, 91, 95, 98, 101, 104, 107, 110, 112, 114, 116, 118, 120, 122)

GILGAMESH II
1989 - No. 4, 1989 ($3.95, limited series, prestige format, mature)
DC Comics

	GD25	FN65	NM94
1-4: Starlin-c/a/scripts		1.60	4.00

GIL THORP
May-July, 1963
Dell Publishing Co.

	GD25	FN65	NM94
1-Caniffish-a	2.40	7.20	26.00

GINGER
1951 - No. 10, Summer, 1954
Archie Publications

	GD25	FN65	NM94
1-Teenage humor	9.50	28.50	95.00
2-(1952)	5.00	15.00	50.00
3-6: 6-(Sum/53)	3.50	10.50	35.00
7-10-Katy Keene app.	5.50	16.50	55.00

GINGER FOX (Also see The World of Ginger Fox)
Sept, 1988 - No. 4, Dec, 1988 ($1.75, limited series)
Comico

	GD25	FN65	NM94
1-4: 1-4-part photo-c		.70	1.75

G.I. R.A.M.B.O.T.
Apr, 1987 - No. 2? ($1.95)
Wonder Color Comics/Pied Piper #2

	GD25	FN65	NM94
1,2: 2-Exist?		.80	2.00

GIRL
July, 1996 - No. 3, 1996 ($2.50, limited series, mature)
DC Comics (Vertigo Verite)

	GD25	FN65	NM94
1-3: Peter Milligan scripts; Fegredo-c/a		1.00	2.50

GIRL COMICS (Becomes Girl Confessions No. 13 on)
Oct, 1949 - No. 12, Jan, 1952 (#1-4: 52 pgs.)
Marvel/Atlas Comics(CnPC)

	GD25	FN65	NM94
1-Photo-c	15.00	45.00	120.00
2-Kubert-a; photo-c	8.75	26.25	70.00
3-Everett-a; Liz Taylor photo-c	12.00	36.00	95.00
4-11: 4-Photo-c. 10-12-Sol Brodsky-c	7.15	21.50	50.00
12-Krigstein-a; Al Hartley-c	8.50	26.00	60.00

GIRL CONFESSIONS (Formerly Girl Comics)
No. 13, Mar, 1952 - No. 35, Aug, 1954
Atlas Comics (CnPC/ZPC)

	GD25	FN65	NM94
13-Everett-a	8.75	26.25	70.00
14,15,19,20	5.70	17.00	40.00
16-18-Everett-a	7.15	21.50	50.00
21-35: Robinson-a	4.15	12.50	25.00

GIRL CRAZY
May, 1996 - No. 3, July, 1996 ($2.95, B&W, limited series)
Dark Horse Comics

	GD25	FN65	NM94
1-3: Gilbert Hernandez-a/scripts.		1.20	3.00

GIRL FROM U.N.C.L.E., THE (TV) (Also see The Man From...)
Jan, 1967 - No. 5, Oct, 1967
Gold Key

	GD25	FN65	NM94
1-McWilliams-a; Stephanie Powers photo front/back-c & pin-ups (no ads, 12¢)	8.20	24.60	90.00
2-5-Leonard Swift-Courier No. 5	5.50	16.50	60.00

GIRLS' FUN & FASHION MAGAZINE (Formerly Polly Pigtails)
V5#44, Jan, 1950 - V5#47, July, 1950
Parents' Magazine Institute

	GD25	FN65	NM94
V5#44	4.00	12.00	24.00
45-47	2.80	7.00	14.00

GIRLS IN LOVE
May, 1950 - No. 2, July, 1950
Fawcett Publications

	GD25	FN65	NM94
1,2-Photo-c	7.85	23.50	55.00

GIRLS IN LOVE (Formerly G. I. Sweethearts No. 45)
No. 46, Sept, 1955 - No. 57, Dec, 1956
Quality Comics Group

	GD25	FN65	NM94
46	5.70	17.00	35.00
47-53,55,56	4.00	12.00	24.00
54- 'Commie' story	4.25	13.00	28.00
57-Matt Baker-c/a	5.70	17.00	40.00

GIRLS IN WHITE (See Harvey Comics Hits No. 58)

GIRLS' LIFE (Patsy Walker's Own Magazine For Girls!)
Jan, 1954 - No. 6, Nov, 1954
Atlas Comics (BFP)

	GD25	FN65	NM94
1	7.85	23.50	55.00
2-Al Hartley-c	5.00	15.00	30.00
3-6	4.15	12.50	25.00

GIRLS' LOVE STORIES
Aug-Sept, 1949 - No. 180, Nov-Dec, 1973 (No. 1-13: 52 pgs.)
National Comics(Signal Publ. No. 9-65/Arleigh No. 83-117)

	GD25	FN65	NM94
1-Toth, Kinstler-a, 8 pgs. each; photo-c	43.00	129.00	385.00
2-Kinstler-a?	25.00	75.00	200.00
3-10: 1-9-Photo-c. 7-Infantino-c(p)	16.00	49.00	130.00
11-20	12.00	38.00	100.00
21-33: 21-Kinstler-a. 33-Last pre-code (1-2/55)	7.85	23.50	55.00
34-50	4.60	13.80	46.00
51-99: 83-Last 10¢ issue	3.00	9.00	30.00
100	3.50	10.50	35.00
101-146: 113-117-April O'Day app.	2.50	7.50	22.00
147-151- "Confessions" serial	2.00	6.00	16.00
152-160,171-179	1.50	4.50	12.00
161-170 (52 pgs.)	2.50	7.50	22.00

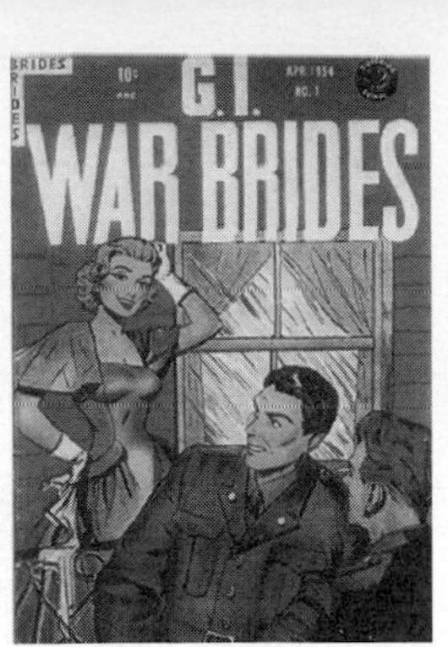

G. I. War Brides #1 © SUPR

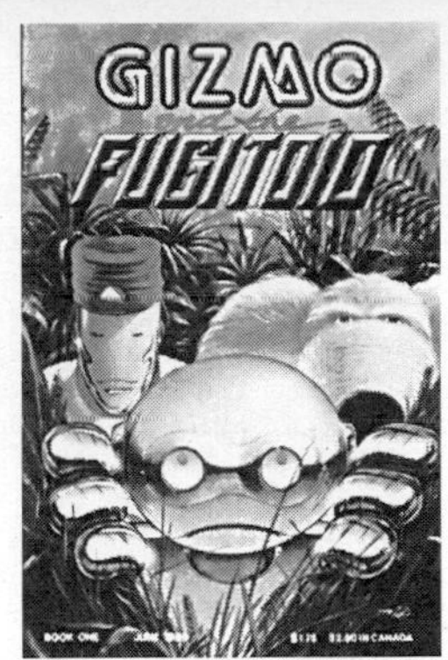

Gizmo #1 © Mirage

Glamorous Romances #60 © ACE

	GD25	FN65	NM94
180 Last issue	2.50	7.50	20.00

GIRLS' ROMANCES
Feb-Mar, 1950 - No. 160, Oct, 1971 (No. 1-11: 52 pgs.)
National Periodical Publ.(Signal Publ. No. 7-79/Arleigh No. 84)

	GD25	FN65	NM94
1-Photo-c	42.00	126.00	375.00
2-Photo-c; Toth-a	24.00	71.00	190.00
3-10: 3-6-Photo-c	16.00	49.00	130.00
11,12,14-20	11.30	34.00	90.00
13-Toth-c	12.00	38.00	100.00
21-31: 31-Last pre-code (2-3/55)	7.15	21.50	50.00
32-50	4.50	13.50	45.00
51-99: 80-Last 10¢ issue	3.00	9.00	30.00
100	3.50	10.50	35.00
101-108,110-120	2.50	7.50	20.00
109-Beatles-c/story	10.00	30.00	100.00
121-133,135-140	2.00	6.00	16.00
134-Neal Adams-c (splash pg. is same as-c)	2.80	8.40	28.00
141-158	1.50	4.50	12.00
159,160-52 pgs.	2.50	7.50	20.00

G. I. SWEETHEARTS (Formerly Diary Loves; Girls In Love #46 on)
No. 32, June, 1953 - No. 45, May, 1955
Quality Comics Group

	GD25	FN65	NM94
32	5.70	17.00	35.00
33-45: 44-Last pre-code (3/55)	4.00	12.00	24.00

G.I. TALES (Formerly Sgt. Barney Barker No. 1-3)
No. 4, Feb, 1957 - No. 6, July, 1957
Atlas Comics (MCI)

	GD25	FN65	NM94
4-Severin-a(4)	5.70	17.00	40.00
5	4.25	13.00	28.00
6-Orlando, Powell, & Woodbridge-a	5.00	15.00	30.00

GIVE ME LIBERTY (Also see Dark Horse Presents Fifth Anniversary Special, Dark Horse Presents #100-4, Happy Birthday Martha Washington, Martha Washington Goes to War, Martha Washington Stranded In Space & San Diego Comicon Comics #2)
June, 1990 - No. 4, 1991 ($4.95, limited series, 52 pgs.)
Dark Horse Comics

	GD25	FN65	NM94
1-4: 1st app. Martha Washington; Frank Miller scripts, Dave Gibbons-c/a in all.		2.00	5.00

G. I. WAR BRIDES
Apr, 1954 - No. 8, June, 1955
Superior Publishers Ltd.

	GD25	FN65	NM94
1	5.70	17.00	40.00
2	4.00	11.00	22.00
3-8: 4-Kamenesque-a; lingerie panels	3.60	9.00	18.00

G. I. WAR TALES
Mar-Apr, 1973 - No. 4, Oct-Nov, 1973
National Periodical Publications

	GD25	FN65	NM94
1-4: Reprints. 2-N. Adams-a(r), 4-Krigstein-a(r)	1.50	4.50	12.00

NOTE: ***Drucker** a-3r, 4r. **Heath** a-4r. **Kubert** a-2, 3; c-4r.*

GIZMO (Also see Domino Chance)
May-June, 1985 (B&W, one-shot)
Chance Ent.

	GD25	FN65	NM94
1		1.20	3.00

GIZMO
1986 - No. 6, July, 1987 ($1.50, B&W)
Mirage Studios

	GD25	FN65	NM94
1-6			1.50

GLADSTONE COMIC ALBUM
1987 - No. 28, 1990 ($5.95/$9.95, 8-1/2x11")(All Mickey Mouse albums are by Gottfredson)
Gladstone

	GD25	FN65	NM94
1-10: 1-Uncle Scrooge; Barks-r; Beck-c. 2-Donald Duck; r/F.C. #108 by Barks. 3-Mickey Mouse-r by Gottfredson. 4-Uncle Scrooge; r/F.C. #456 by Barks w/ unedited story. 5-Donald Duck Advs.; r/F.C. #199. 6-Uncle Scrooge-r by Barks. 7-Donald Duck-r by Barks. 8-Mickey Mouse-r. 9-Bambi; r/F.C. #186? 10-Donald Duck Advs.; r/F.C. #275	1.00	2.80	7.00
11-20: 11-Uncle Scrooge; r/U.S. #4. 12-Donald And Daisy; r/F.C. #1055, WDC&S. 13-Donald Duck Advs.; r/F.C. #408. 14-Uncle Scrooge; Barks-r/ U.S #21. 15-Donald And Gladstone; Barks-r. 16-Donald Duck Advs.; r/F.C. #238. 17-Mickey Mouse strip-r (The World of Tomorrow, The Pirate Ghost Ship). 18-Donald Duck and the Junior Woodchucks; Barks-r. 19-Uncle Scrooge; r/U.S. #12; Rosa-c. 20-Uncle Scrooge; r/F.C. #386; Barks-c/a(r)	1.00	2.80	7.00
21-25: 21-Donald Duck Family; Barks-c/a(r). 22-Mickey Mouse strip-r. 23-Donald Duck; Barks-r/D.D. #26 w/unedited story. 24-Uncle Scrooge; Barks-r; Rosa-c. 25-D. Duck; Barks-c/a-r/F.C. #367	1.00	2.80	7.00
26-28: All have $9.95-c. 26-Mickey and Donald; Gottfredson-c/a(r). 27-Donald Duck; r/WDC&S by Barks; Barks painted-c. 28-Uncle Scrooge & Donald Duck; Rosa-c/a (4 stories)	1.40	4.15	11.00
Special 1 (1989, $9.95)-Donald Duck Finds Pirate Gold; r/F.C. #9	1.40	4.15	11.00
Special 2 (1989, $8.95)-Uncle Scrooge and Donald Duck; Barks-r/Uncle Scrooge #5; Rosa-c	1.25	4.15	10.00
Special 3 (1989, $8.95)-Mickey Mouse strip-r	1.25	4.15	10.00
Special 4 (1989, $11.95)-Uncle Scrooge; Rosa-c/a-r/Son of the Sun from U.S. #219 plus Barks-r/U.S.	1.60	4.85	13.00
Special 5 (1990, $11.95)-Donald Duck Advs.; Barks-r/F.C. #282 & 422 plus Barks painted-c	1.60	4.85	13.00
Special 6 (1990, $12.95)-Uncle Scrooge; Barks-c/a-r/Uncle Scrooge	1.75	5.50	14.00
Special 7 (1990, $13.95)-Mickey Mouse; Gottfredson strip-r	1.85	5.50	15.00

GLADSTONE COMIC ALBUM (2nd Series)(Also see The Original Dick Tracy)
1990 ($5.95, 8-1/2 x 11," stiff-c, 52 pgs.)
Gladstone Publishing

	GD25	FN65	NM94
1,2-The Original Dick Tracy. 2-Origin of the 2-way wrist radio.		2.40	6.00
3-D Tracy Meets the Mole-r by Bould ($6.95).	1.00	2.80	7.00

GLAMOROUS ROMANCES (Formerly Dotty)
No. 41, July, 1949 - No. 90, Oct, 1956 (Photo-c 68-90)
Ace Magazines (A. A. Wyn)

	GD25	FN65	NM94
41-Dotty app.	5.70	17.00	40.00
42-72,74-80: 44-Begin 52 pg. issues. 45,50-61-Painted-c. 80-Last pre-code (2/55)	4.15	12.50	25.00
73-L.B. Cole-r/All Love #27	4.25	13.00	28.00
81-90	4.00	10.00	20.00

GLOBAL FORCE
1987 - No. 2? ($1.95)
Silverline Comics

	GD25	FN65	NM94
1,2		.80	2.00

GLORY
Mar, 1995 - No. 22, Apr, 1997 ($2.50)
Image Comics (Extreme Studios)/Maximum Press

	GD25	FN65	NM94
0-Deodato-c/a		1.00	2.50
1-(3/95)-Deodato-a		1.20	3.00
1A-Variant-c		2.40	6.00
2-11,13-22: 5-Bagged w/Youngblood gaming card. 7,8-Deodato-c/a(p). 8-Babewatch x-over. 9-Cruz-c; Extreme Destroyer Pt. 5; polybagged w/card. 10-Angela-c/app. 11-Deodato-c.		1.00	2.50
4-Variant-c by Quesada & Palmiotti		2.00	5.00

Goddess #5 © Garth Ennis & Phil Winslade

Godwheel #1 © Malibu

Godzilla #17 © RMEG

GD25 FN65 NM94

12-($3.50)-Photo-c 3.50
Trade Paperback (1995, $9.95)-r/#1-4 10.00

GLORY & FRIENDS BIKINI FEST
Sept, 1995 - No. 2, Oct, 1995 ($2.50, limited series)
Image Comics (Extreme Studios)

1,2: 1-Photo-c; centerfold photo; pin-ups 1.00 2.50

GLORY & FRIENDS CHRISTMAS SPECIAL
Dec, 1995 ($2.50, one-shot)
Image Comics (Extreme Studios)

1-Deodato-c 1.00 2.50

GLORY & FRIENDS LINGIRIE SPECIAL
Sept, 1995 ($2.95, one-shot)
Image Comics (Extreme Studios)

1-Pin-ups w/photos; photo-c; varant-c exists 1.20 3.00

GLORY/ANGELA: ANGELS IN HELL (See Angela/Glory: Rage of Angels)
Apr, 1996 ($2.50, one-shot)
Image Comics (Extreme Studios)

1-Flip book w/Darkchylde #1 1.00 2.50

GLORY/AVENGELYNE
Oct, 1995 ($3.95, one-shot)
Image Comics (Extreme Studios)

1-Chromium-c 1.60 4.00
1-Regular-c 1.60 4.00

GLORY/CELESTINE: DARK ANGEL
Sept, 1996 - No. 3, Nov, 1996 ($2.50, limited series)
Image Comics/Maximum Press (Extreme Studios)

1-3 1.00 2.50

GNOME MOBILE, THE (See Movie Comics)

GOBBLEDYGOOK
1984 - No. 2, 1984 (B&W)(1st Mirage comic, published at same time)
Mirage Studios

1,2-(24 pgs.)-1st Teenage Mutant Ninja Turtles 21.00 63.00 210.00

GOBBLEDYGOOK
Dec, 1986 ($3.50, B&W, one-shot, 100 pgs.)
Mirage Studios

1-New 8 pg. TMNT story plus a Donatello/Michaelangelo 7 pg. story & a Gizmo story; Corben-i(r)/TMNT #7 1.60 4.00

GOBLIN, THE
June, 1982 - No. 4, Dec, 1982 (Magazine, $2.25)
Warren Publishing Co.

1-The Gremlin app; Golden-a(p) 1.85 5.50 15.00
2-4: 2-1st Hobgoblin 1.25 3.75 10.00

GODDESS
June, 1995 - No. 8, Jan, 1996 ($2.95, limited series)
DC Comics (Vertigo)

1-8: Garth Ennis scripts; Phil Winslade-c/a 2.00 5.00

GODFATHERS, THE (See The Crusaders)

GOD IS
1973, 1975 (35-49¢)
Spire Christian Comics (Fleming H. Revell Co.)

nn-By Al Hartley 1.00

GOD'S COUNTRY (Also see Marvel Comics Presents)
1994 ($6.95)
Marvel Comics

nn-P. Craig Russell-a; Colossus story; r/Marvel Comics Presents #10-17 1.00 2.80 7.00

GD25 FN65 NM94

GODS FOR HIRE
Dec, 1986 - No. 3? ($1.50)
Hot Comics

1-3: Barry Crain-c/a(p) 1.50

GOD'S HEROES IN AMERICA
1956 (nn) (25¢/35¢, 68 pgs.)
Catechetical Guild Educational Society

307 1.60 4.00 8.00

GOD'S SMUGGLER (Religious)
1972 (39¢/40¢)
Spire Christian Comics/Fleming H. Revell Co.

..1-Two variations exist 1.00

GODWHEEL
No. 0, Jan, 1995 - No. 3, Feb, 1995 ($2.50, limited series)
Malibu Comics (Ultraverse)

0-3: 0-Flip-c. 1-1st app. of Primevil; Thor cameo (1 panel). 3-Perez-a in Chapter 3, Thor app. 1.00 2.50

GODZILLA (Movie)
August, 1977 - No. 24, July, 1979 (Based on movie series)
Marvel Comics Group

1-(Regular 30¢ edition)-Mooney-i 2.40 6.00
1-(35¢-c, limited distribution) 2.50 7.50 24.00
2-(Regular 30¢ edition)-Tuska-i. 1.20 3.00
2-(35¢-c, limited distribution) 1.50 4.50 12.00
3- Champions app.(w/o Ghost Rider) 1.00 2.80 7.00
4-10: 4,5-Sutton-a 1.20 3.00
11-24: 14-Shield app. 20-F.F. app. 21,22-Devil Dinosaur app. 1.00 2.50

GODZILLA (Movie)
May, 1988 - No. 6, 1988 ($1.95, B&W, limited series) (Based on movie series)
Dark Horse Comics

1 2.40 6.00
2-6 1.20 3.00
...Collection (1990, $10.95)-r/1-6 with new-c 1.40 4.15 11.00
...Color Special 1 (Sum, 1992, $3.50, color, 44 pgs.)-Arthur Adams wrap-around-c/a & part scripts 1.60 4.00
...King Of The Monsters Special (8/87, $1.50)-Origin; Bissette-c/a 1.20 3.00
...Vs. Barkley nn (12/93, $2.95, color)-Dorman painted-c 1.20 3.00

GODZILLA (King of the Monsters) (Movie)
May, 1995 - No. 16, Sept, 1996 ($2.50) (Based on movie series)
Dark Horse Comics

0-16: 0-r/Dark Horse Comics #10,11. 1-3-Kevin Maguire scripts. 3-8-Art Adams-c 1.60 4.00
...Vs. Hero Zero ($2.50) 1.00 2.50

GO-GO
June, 1966 - No. 9, Oct, 1967
Charlton Comics

1-Miss Bikini Luv begins; Rolling Stones, Beatles, Elvis, Sonny & Cher, Bob Dylan, Sinatra, parody; Herman's Hermits pin-ups; D'Agostino-c/a in #1-8 4.60 13.80 46.00
2-Ringo Starr, David McCallum & Beatles photos on cover; Beatles story and photos 4.60 13.80 46.00
3,4: 3-Blooperman begins, ends #6; 1 pg. Batman & Robin satire; full pg. photo pin-ups Lovin' Spoonful & The Byrds 2.50 7.50 24.00
5-9: 5 (2/67)-Super Hero & TV satire by Jim Aparo & Grass Green begins; Aparo's 1st published work. 6-8-Aparo-a. 6-Petula Clark photo-c. 7-Photo of Brian Wilson of Beach Boys on-c & Beach Boys photo inside f/b-c. 8-Monkees photo on-c & photo inside f/b-c; 9-Aparo-c/a. 2.50 7.50 24.00

Golden Age #3 © DC

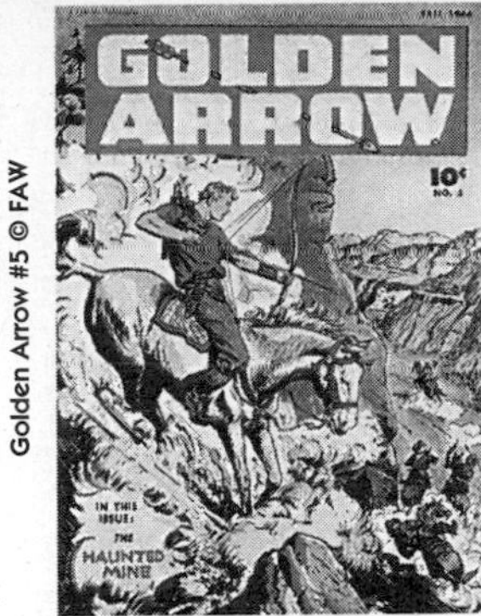

Golden Arrow #5 © FAW

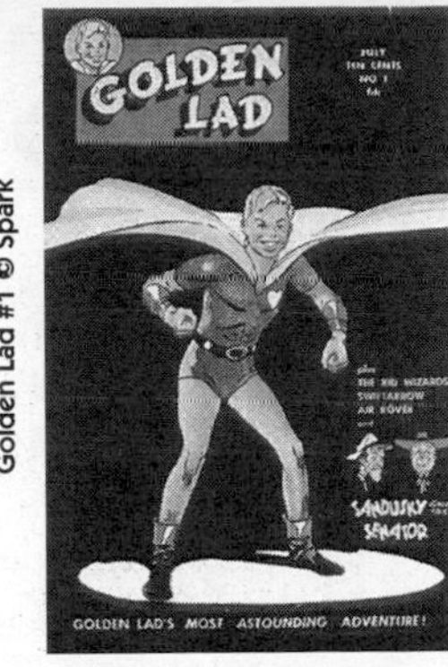

Golden Lad #1 © Spark

	GD25	FN65	NM94

GO-GO AND ANIMAL (See Tippy's Friends...)

GOING STEADY (Formerly Teen-Age Temptations)
No. 10, Dec, 1954 - No. 13, June, 1955; No. 14, Oct, 1955
St. John Publishing Co.

	GD25	FN65	NM94
10(1954)-Matt Baker-c/a	15.00	45.00	120.00
11(2/55, last precode), 12(4/55)-Baker-c	8.50	26.00	60.00
13(6/55)-Baker-c/a	10.00	30.00	80.00
14(10/55)-Matt Baker-c/a, 25 pgs.	12.00	36.00	95.00

GOING STEADY (Formerly Personal Love)
V3#3, Feb, 1960 - V3#6, Aug, 1960; V4#1, Sept-Oct, 1960
Prize Publications/Headline

	GD25	FN65	NM94
V3#3-6, V4#1	2.00	6.00	16.00

GOING STEADY WITH BETTY (Becomes Betty & Her Steady No. 2)
Nov-Dec, 1949
Avon Periodicals

	GD25	FN65	NM94
1	10.50	32.00	85.00

GOLDEN AGE, THE
1993 - No. 4, 1994 ($4.95, limited series)
DC Comics (Elseworlds)

	GD25	FN65	NM94
1-4: James Robinson scripts; Paul Smith-c/a; gold foil embossed-c.		2.40	6.00
Trade Paperback (1995, $19.95)	2.50	7.50	20.00

GOLDEN ARROW (See Fawcett Miniatures, Mighty Midget & Whiz Comics)

GOLDEN ARROW (...Western No. 6)
Spring, 1942 - No. 6, Spring, 1947 (68 pgs.)
Fawcett Publications

	GD25	FN65	NM94
1-Golden Arrow begins	71.00	213.00	640.00
2-(1943)	36.00	108.00	300.00
3-5: 3-(Win/45-46). 4-(Spr/46). 5-(Fall/46)	26.00	80.00	210.00
6-Krigstein-a	29.00	86.00	230.00
...Well Known Comics (1944; 12 pgs.; 8-1/2x10-1/2"; paper-c; glued binding)-Bestmaid/Samuel Lowe giveaway; printed in green	7.15	21.50	50.00

GOLDEN COMICS DIGEST
May, 1969 - No. 48, Jan, 1976
Gold Key
NOTE: *Whitman editions exist of many titles and are generally valued less.*

	GD25	FN65	NM94
1-Tom & Jerry, Woody Woodpecker, Bugs Bunny	2.50	7.50	25.00
2-Hanna-Barbera TV Fun Favorites; Space Ghost, Flintstones, Atom Ant, Jetsons, Yogi Bear, Banana Splits, others app.	3.20	9.60	32.00
3-Tom & Jerry, Woody Woodpecker	1.75	5.25	14.00
4-Tarzan; Manning & Marsh-a	3.20	9.60	32.00
5,8-Tom & Jerry, W. Woodpecker, Bugs Bunny	1.50	4.50	12.00
6-Bugs Bunny	1.50	4.50	12.00
7-Hanna-Barbera TV Fun Favorites	2.50	7.50	20.00
9-Tarzan	3.00	9.00	30.00
10-17: 10-Bugs Bunny. 11-Hanna-Barbera TV Fun Favorites. 12-Tom & Jerry, Bugs Bunny, W. Woodpecker Journey to the Sun. 13-Tom & Jerry. 14-Bugs Bunny Fun Packed Funnies. 15-Tom & Jerry, Woody Woodpecker, Bugs Bunny. 16-Woody Woodpecker Cartoon Special. 17-Bugs Bunny	1.50	4.50	12.00
18-Tom & Jerry; Barney Bear-r by Barks	1.75	5.25	14.00
19-Little Lulu	3.00	9.00	30.00
20-22: 20-Woody Woodpecker Falltime Funtime. 21-Bugs Bunny Showtime. 22-Tom & Jerry Winter Wingding	1.50	4.50	12.00
23-Little Lulu & Tubby Fun Fling	3.00	9.00	30.00
24-26,28: 24-Woody Woodpecker Fun Festival. 25-Tom & Jerry. 26-Bugs Bunny Halloween Hulla-Boo-Loo; Dr. Spektor article, also #25. 28-Tom & Jerry	1.50	4.50	12.00
27-Little Lulu & Tubby in Hawaii	2.50	7.50	24.00
29-Little Lulu & Tubby	2.50	7.50	24.00
30-Bugs Bunny Vacation Funnies	1.50	4.50	12.00
31-Turok, Son of Stone; r/4-Color #596,656; c-r/#9	2.80	8.40	28.00
32-Woody Woodpecker Summer Fun	1.50	4.50	12.00
33,36: 33-Little Lulu & Tubby Halloween Fun; Dr. Spektor app. 36-Little Lulu & Her Friends	3.00	9.00	30.00
34,35,37-39: 34-Bugs Bunny Winter Funnies. 35-Tom & Jerry Snowtime Funtime. 37-Woody Woodpecker County Fair. 38-The Pink Panther. 39-Bugs Bunny Summer Fun	1.50	4.50	12.00
40,43: 40-Little Lulu & Tubby Trick or Treat; all by Stanley. 43-Little Lulu in Paris	3.00	9.00	30.00
41,42,44,45,47: 41-Tom & Jerry Winter Carnival. 42-Bugs Bunny. 44-Woody Woodpecker Family Fun Festival. 45-The Pink Panther. 47-Bugs Bunny	1.25	3.75	10.00
46-Little Lulu & Tubby	1.50	4.50	24.00
48-The Lone Ranger	1.75	5.25	14.00

NOTE: *#1-30, 164 pgs.; #31 on, 132 pgs..*

GOLDEN LAD
July, 1945 - No. 5, June, 1946 (#4, 5: 52 pgs.)
Spark Publications

	GD25	FN65	NM94
1-Origin & 1st app. Golden Lad & Swift Arrow; Sandusky and the Senator begins	56.00	168.00	500.00
2-Mort Meskin-c/a	29.00	86.00	230.00
3,4-Mort Meskin-c/a	25.00	75.00	200.00
5-Origin/1st Golden Girl; Shaman & Flame app.	30.00	90.00	240.00

NOTE: *All have **Robinson,** and **Roussos** art plus **Meskin** covers and art.*

GOLDEN LEGACY
1966 - 1972 (Black History) (25¢)
Fitzgerald Publishing Co.

	GD25	FN65	NM94
1-Toussaint L'Ouverture (1966), 2-Harriet Tubman (1967), 3-Crispus Attucks & the Minutemen (1967), 4-Benjamin Banneker (1968), 5-Matthew Henson (1969), 6-Alexander Dumas & Family (1969), 7-Frederick Douglass, Part 1 (1969), 8-Frederick Douglass, Part 2 (1970), 9-Robert Smalls (1970), 10-J. Cinque & the Amistad Mutiny (1970), 11-Men in Action: White, Marshall J. Wilkins (1970), 12-Black Cowboys (1972), 13-The Life of Martin Luther King, Jr. (1972), 14-The Life of Alexander Pushkin (1971), 15-Ancient African Kingdoms (1972), 16-Black Inventors (1972) each....		2.40	6.00
1-10,12,13,15,16(1976)-Reprints		2.40	6.00

GOLDEN LOVE STORIES (Formerly Golden West Love)
No. 4, April, 1950
Kirby Publishing Co.

	GD25	FN65	NM94
4-Powell-a; Glenn Ford/Janet Leigh photo-c	11.30	34.00	90.00

GOLDEN PICTURE CLASSIC, A
1956-1957 (Text stories w/illustrations in color; 100 pgs. each)
Western Printing Co. (Simon & Shuster)

	GD25	FN65	NM94
CL-401: Treasure Island	7.15	21.50	50.00
CL-402: Tom Sawyer	6.00	18.00	42.00
CL-403: Black Beauty	6.00	18.00	42.00
CL-404: Little Women	6.00	18.00	42.00
CL-405: Heidi	6.00	18.00	42.00
CL-406: Ben Hur	4.25	13.00	28.00
CL-407: Around the World in 80 Days	4.25	13.00	28.00
CL-408: Sherlock Holmes	5.70	17.00	35.00
CL-409: The Three Musketeers	4.25	13.00	28.00
CL-410: The Merry Advs. of Robin Hood	4.25	13.00	28.00
CL-411: Hans Brinker	5.70	17.00	35.00
CL-412: The Count of Monte Cristo	5.70	17.00	35.00

(Both soft & hardcover editions are valued the same)

NOTE: *Recent research has uncovered new information. Apparently #s 1-6 were issued in 1956 and #7-12 in 1957. But they can be found in five different series listings: CL-1 to CL-12 (softbound); CL-401 to CL-412 (also softbound); CL-101 to CL-112 (hardbound); plus two new series discoveries: A Golden Reading Adventure, publ. by Golden Press; edited down to 60 pages and reduced in size to 6x9"; only #s discovered so far are #381 (CL-4), #382 (CL-6) & #387 (CL-3). They have no reorder list and some have covers different from GPC. There have also been found British hardbound editions of GPC with dust jackets. Copies of all five listed series vary from*

Golden Picture Story Book ST-3 © WDC

Good Girl Art Quarterly #2 © AC

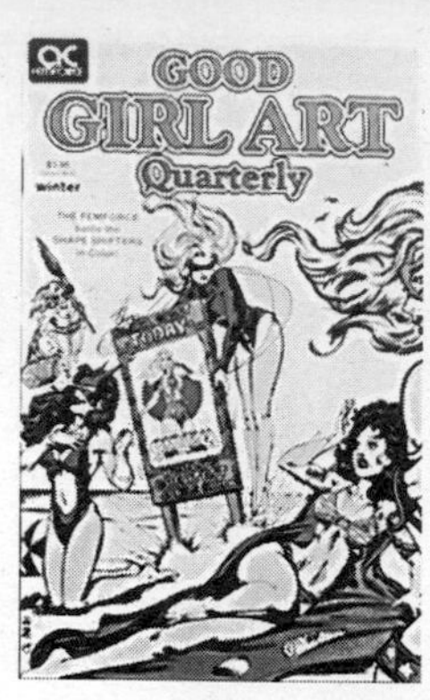

Goofy Comics #26 © Nedor

scarce to very rare. Some editions of some series have not yet been found at all.

GOLDEN PICTURE STORY BOOK
Dec, 1961 (50¢, large size, 52 pgs.)(All are scarce)
Racine Press (Western)

ST-1-Huckleberry Hound (TV) 15.50 47.00 155.00
ST-2-Yogi Bear (TV) 15.50 47.00 155.00
ST-3-Babes in Toyland (Walt Disney's...)-Annette Funicello photo-c 22.00 66.00 220.00
ST-4-(...of Disney Ducks)-Walt Disney's Wonderful World of Ducks (Donald Duck, Uncle Scrooge, Donald's Nephews, Grandma Duck, Ludwig Von Drake, & Gyro Gearloose stories) 22.00 66.00 220.00

GOLDEN RECORD COMIC (See Amazing Spider-Man #1, Avengers #4, Fantastic Four #1, Journey Into Mystery #83)

GOLDEN STORY BOOKS
1949 (Heavy covers, digest size, 128 pgs.) (Illustrated text in color)
Western Printing Co. (Simon & Shuster)
7-Walt Disney's Mystery in Disneyville, a book-length adventure starring Donald and Nephews, Mickey and Nephews, and with Minnie, Daisy and Goofy. Art by Dick Moores & Manuel Gonzales (scarce) 23.00 69.00 185.00
10-Bugs Bunny's Treasure Hunt, a book-length adventure starring Bugs & Porky Pig, with Petunia Pig & Nephew, Cicero. Art by Tom McKimson (scarce) 15.00 45.00 120.00

GOLDEN WEST LOVE (Golden Love Stories No. 4)
Sept-Oct, 1949 - No. 3, Feb, 1950 (All 52 pgs.)
Kirby Publishing Co.

1-Powell-a in all; Roussos-a; painted-c 17.00 49.00 120.00
2,3: Photo-c 11.00 33.00 80.00

GOLDEN WEST RODEO TREASURY (See Dell Giants)

GOLDILOCKS (See March of Comics No. 1)

GOLDILOCKS & THE THREE BEARS
1943 (Giveaway)
K. K. Publications

nn 8.75 26.25 70.00

GOLD KEY CHAMPION
Mar, 1978 - No. 2, May, 1978 (50¢, 52pgs.)
Gold Key

1-Space Family Robinson; half-r 2.00 5.00
2-Mighty Samson; half-r 2.00 5.00

GOLD KEY SPOTLIGHT
May, 1976 - No. 11, Feb, 1978
Gold Key

1-Tom, Dick & Harriet 2.40 6.00
2-5,710,11: 2-Wacky Advs. of Cracky. 3-Wacky Witch. 4-Tom, Dick & Harriet. 5-Wacky Advs. of Cracky. 7-Wacky Witch & Greta Ghost 10-O. G. Whiz. 11-Tom, Dick & Harriet 1.60 4.00
6,8,9: 6-Dagar the Invincible; Santos-a; origin Demonomicon. 8-The Occult Files of Dr. Spektor, Simbar, Lu-sai; Santos-a. 9-Tragg 2.40 6.00

GOLD MEDAL COMICS
1945 (25¢, one-shot, 132 pgs.)
Cambridge House

nn-Captain Truth by Fugitani, Crime Detector, The Witch of Salem, Luckyman, others app. 22.00 66.00 175.00

GOMER PYLE (TV)
July, 1966 - No. 3, Jan, 1967
Gold Key

1-Photo front/back-c 6.00 18.00 65.00
2,3 4.10 12.30 45.00

GON
July, 1996 - No. 4, Oct, 1996 ($5.95, B&W, digest-size, limited series)
DC Comics (Paradox Press)

1-4: Misadventures of baby dinosaur; Tanaka-c/a/scripts in all 2.40 6.00

GON SWIMMIN'
1997 ($6.95, B&W, digest-size)
DC Comics (Paradox Press)

nn-Tanaka-c/a/scripts in all 6.95

GOODBYE, MR. CHIPS (See Movie Comics)

GOOD GIRL ART QUARTERLY
Summer, 1990 - No. 16, 1992? (B&W/color, 52 pgs.)
AC Comics

1,3-16 ($3.50)-All have one new story (often FemForce) & rest reprints by Baker, Ward & other "good girl" artists 1.40 3.50
2 ($3.95) 1.60 4.00

GOOD GUYS, THE
Nov, 1993 - No. 9, July, 1994 ($2.50/$3.25/$3.50)
Defiant

1-($3.50, 52 pgs.)-Glory x-over from Plasm 1.40 3.50
2,3,5-9: 9-Pre-Schism issue 1.00 2.50
4-($3.25, 52 pgs.) 1.30 3.25

GOOFY (Disney)(See Dynabrite Comics, Mickey Mouse Magazine V4#7, Walt Disney Showcase #35 & Wheaties)
No. 468, May, 1953 - Sept-Nov, 1962
Dell Publishing Co.

Four Color 468 (#1) 11.00 34.00 125.00
Four Color 562,627,658,702,747,802,857 6.40 19.00 70.00
Four Color 899,952,987,1053,1094,1149,1201 3.60 11.00 40.00
12-308-211(Dell, 9-11/62) 3.60 11.00 40.00

GOOFY ADVENTURES
June, 1990 - No. 17, 1991 ($1.50)
Disney Comics

1-17: Most new stories. 2-Joshua Quagmire-a w/free poster. 7-WDC&S-r plus new-a. 9-Gottfredson-r. 14-Super Goof story. 15-All Super Goof issue. 17-Gene Colan-a(p) 1.50

GOOFY ADVENTURE STORY (See Goofy No. 857)

GOOFY COMICS (Companion to Happy Comics)(Not Disney)
June, 1943 - No. 48, 1953
Nedor Publ. Co. No. 1-14/Standard No. 14-48 (Animated Cartoons)

1-Funny animal; Oriolo-c 21.00 64.00 170.00
2 10.50 32.00 85.00
3-10 8.75 26.25 65.00
11-19 6.50 19.50 45.00
20-35-Frazetta text illos in all 8.50 26.00 60.00
36-48 5.35 16.00 32.00

GOOFY SUCCESS STORY (See Goofy No. 702)

GOOSE (Humor magazine)
Sept, 1976 - No. 3, 1976 (75¢, 52 pgs.)
Cousins Publ. (Fawcett)

1 1.50 4.50 12.00
2,3 1.00 3.00 8.00

GORDO (See Comics Revue No. 5 & Giant Comics Edition)

GORGO (Based on M.G.M. movie) (See Return of...)
May, 1961 - No. 23, Sept, 1965
Charlton Comics

1-Ditko-a, 22 pgs. 19.00 57.00 190.00
2,3-Ditko-c/a 9.50 28.50 95.00
4-10: 4-Ditko-c 5.50 16.50 55.00
11,13-16-Ditko-a 4.50 13.50 45.00

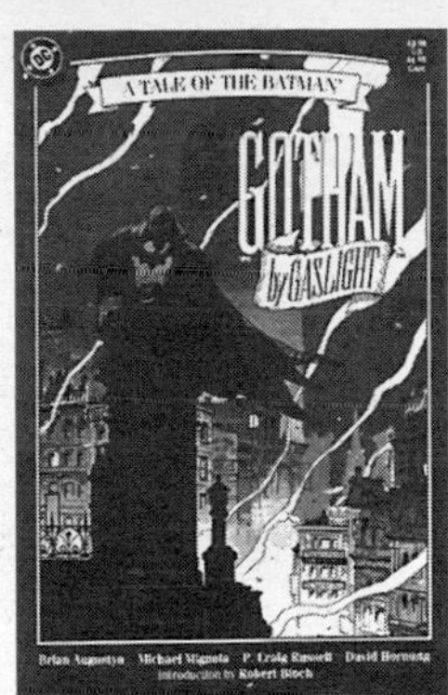

Gotham by Gaslight nn © DC

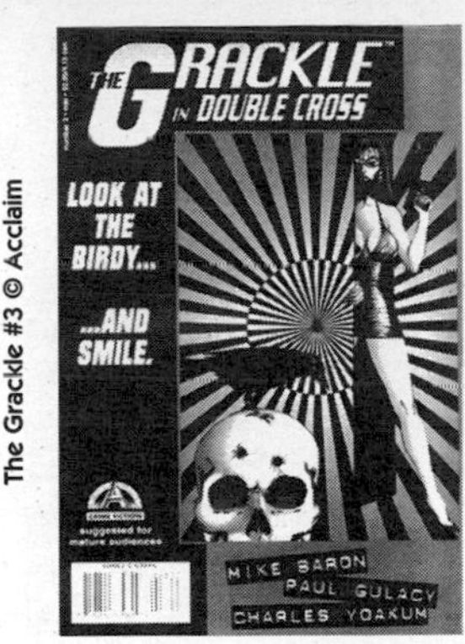

The Grackle #3 © Acclaim

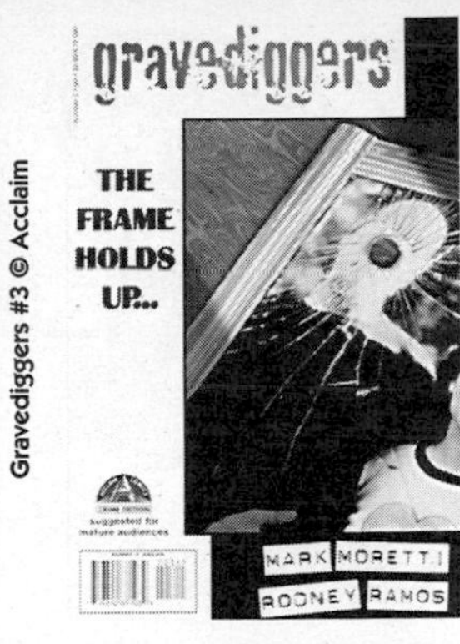

Gravediggers #3 © Acclaim

	GD25	FN65	NM94
12,17-23: 12-Reptisaurus x-over; Montes/Bache-a-No. 17-23. 20-Giordano-c	2.50	7.50	22.00
Gorgo's Revenge('62)-Becomes Return of...	4.00	12.00	40.00

GOSPEL BLIMP, THE
1973, 1974 (35¢/39¢, 36 pgs.)
Spire Christian Comics (Fleming H. Revell Co.)

nn		1.60	4.00

G.O.T.H.
Dec, 1995 - No. 3, June, 1996 ($2.95, limited series, mature)
Verotik

1-3: Danzig scripts; Liam Sharpe-a.		1.20	3.00

GOTHAM BY GASLIGHT (A Tale of the Batman)(See Batman: Master of...)
1989 ($3.95, one-shot, squarebound, 52 pgs.)
DC Comics

nn-Mignola/Russell-a; intro by Robert Bloch		1.60	4.00

GOTHAM NIGHTS (See Batman: Gotham Nights II)
Mar, 1992 - No. 4, June, 1992 ($1.25, limited series)
DC Comics

1-4: Featuring Batman			1.25

GOTHIC ROMANCES
Dec, 1974 (75¢, B&W, magazine)
Atlas/Seaboard Publ.

1-Text w/ illos by N. Adams, Chaykin, Heath (2 pgs. ea.)		.70	1.80

GOVERNOR & J. J., THE (TV)
Feb, 1970 - No. 3, Aug, 1970 (Photo-c)
Gold Key

1	2.75	8.00	30.00
2,3	2.00	6.00	22.00

GRACKLE, THE
Jan, 1997 - No. 4, Apr, 1997 ($2.95, B&W)
Acclaim Comics

1-6: Mike Baron scripts & Paul Gulacy-c/a. 1-4-Doublecross		1.20	3.00

GRAFIK MUZIK
Dec, 1989 - No. 3, May, 1990 ($2.95, 52 pgs.)
Caliber Press

1-3: Mike Allred-c/a/scripts		1.20	3.00

GRANDMA DUCK'S FARM FRIENDS(See Walt Disney's C&S 293 & Wheaties)
No. 763, Jan, 1957 - No. 1279, Feb, 1962 (Disney)
Dell Publishing co.

Four Color 763 (#1)	6.40	19.00	70.00
Four Color 873	4.50	13.50	50.00
Four Color 965,1279	3.60	11.00	40.00
Four Color 1010,1073,1161-Barks-a; 1073,1161-Barks c/a	12.00	37.00	135.00

GRAND PRIX (Formerly Hot Rod Racers)
No. 16, Sept, 1967 - No. 31, May, 1970
Charlton Comics

16-Features Rick Roberts	2.50	7.50	24.00
17-20	2.00	6.00	16.00
21-31	1.50	4.50	12.00

GRAVEDIGGERS
Nov, 1996 - Present ($2.95, B&W)
Acclaim Comics

1-4: Moretti scripts		1.20	3.00

GRAVESTONE
July, 1993 - No. 7, Feb, 1994 ($2.25)
Malibu Comics

1-6: 3-Polybagged w/Skycap		.90	2.25
7-($2.50)		1.00	2.50

GRAVE TALES (Also see Maggots)
Oct, 1991 - No. 3, Feb, 1992 ($3.95, B&W, magazine, 52 pgs.)
Hamilton Comics

1-Staton-c/a	1.00	3.00	8.00
2,3: 2-Staton-a; Morrow-c		2.40	6.00

GRAY GHOST, THE
No. 911, July, 1958 - No. 1000, June-Aug, 1959
Dell Publishing Co.

Four Color 911 (#1)-Photo-c	8.00	25.00	90.00
Four Color 1000-Photo-c	8.00	25.00	90.00

GREAT ACTION COMICS
1958 (Reprints with new covers)
I. W. Enterprises

1-Captain Truth reprinted from Gold Medal #1	2.25	6.75	18.00
8,9-Reprints Phantom Lady #15 & 23	8.00	24.00	80.00

GREAT AMERICAN COMICS PRESENTS - THE SECRET VOICE
1945 (10¢)
Peter George 4-Star Publ./American Features Syndicate

1-Anti-Nazi; "What Really Happened to Hitler"	21.00	62.00	165.00

GREAT AMERICAN WESTERN, THE
1987 - No. 4, 1990? ($1.75/$2.95/$3.50, B&W with some color)
AC Comics

..1($1.75)-Western-r plus Bill Black-a		.90	1.80
..2,3 ($2.95)2-Tribute to ME comics; Durango Kid photo-c 3-Tribute to Tom Mix plus Roy Rogers, Durango Kid; Billy the Kid-r by Severin; photo-c		1.50	3.00
..4 ($3.50, 52 pgs., 16 pgs. color)-Tribute to Lash LaRue; photo-c & interior photos; Fawcett-r		1.75	3.50

GREAT CAT FAMILY, THE (Disney-TV/Movie)
No. 750, Nov, 1956 (one-shot)
Dell Publishing Co.

Four Color 750-Pinocchio & Alice app.	5.50	16.50	60.00

GREAT COMICS
Nov, 1941 - No. 3, Jan, 1942
Great Comics Publications

1-Origin/1st app. The Great Zarro; Madame Strange & Guy Gorham, Wizard of Science & The Great Zarro begin	100.00	300.00	900.00
2-Buck Johnson, Jungle Explorer app.; X-Mas-c	50.00	150.00	450.00
3-Futuro Takes Hitler to Hell-c/s; "The Lost City" movie story (starring William Boyd); continues in Choice Comics #3	100.00	300.00	900.00

GREAT COMICS
1945
Novack Publishing Co./Jubilee Comics/Barrel O' Fun

1-(Novack)-The Defenders, Capt. Power app.; L. B. Cole-c	31.00	94.00	250.00
1-(Jubilee)-Same cover; Boogey Man, Satanas, & The Sorcerer & His Apprentice	22.00	66.00	175.00
1-(Barrel O' Fun)-L. B. Cole-c; Barrel O' Fun overprinted in indicia; Li'l Cactus, Cuckoo Sheriff (humorous)	14.50	43.00	115.00

GREAT DOGPATCH MYSTERY (See Mammy Yokum & the...)

GREATEST BATMAN STORIES EVER TOLD, THE (See Batman)

GREATEST JOKER STORIES EVER TOLD, THE (See Batman)

GREAT EXPLOITS
Oct, 1957
Decker Publ./Red Top

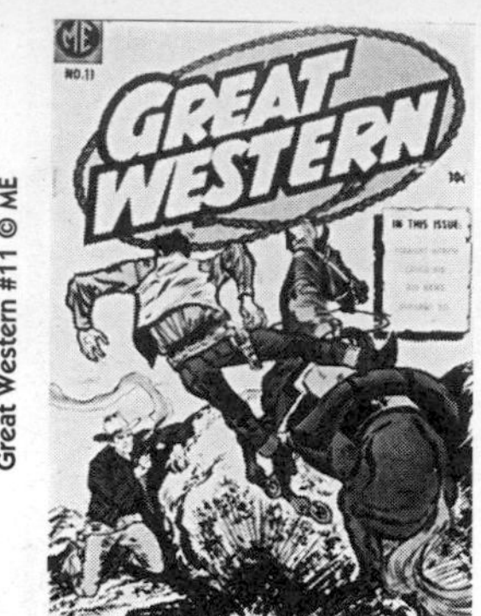

Great Western #11 © ME

Green Arrow #3 (mini series) © DC

Green Arrow #88 © DC

GD25 FN65 NM94

1-Krigstein-a(2) (re-issue on cover); reprints Daring Advs. #6 by Approved Comics 6.50 19.50 45.00

GREAT FOODINI, THE (See Foodini)

GREAT GAZOO, THE (The Flintstones)(TV)
Aug, 1973 - No. 20, Jan, 1977 (Hanna-Barbera)
Charlton Comics

1 2.50 7.50 20.00
2-10 1.25 3.75 10.00
11-20 1.00 3.00 8.00

GREAT GRAPE APE, THE (TV)(See TV Stars #1)
Sept, 1976 - No. 2, Nov, 1976 (Hanna-Barbera)
Charlton Comics

1 1.50 4.50 12.00
2 1.00 3.00 8.00

GREAT LOCOMOTIVE CHASE, THE (Disney)
No. 712, Sept, 1956 (one-shot)
Dell Publishing Co.

Four Color 712-Movie, photo-c 6.40 19.00 70.00

GREAT LOVER ROMANCES (Young Lover Romances #4,5)
3/51; #2, 1951(nd); #3, 1952 (nd); #6, Oct?, 1952 - No. 22, May, 1955
Toby Press (Photo-c #1-5, 10 ,13, 15, 17) (no #4, 5)

1-Jon Juan story-r/Jon Juan #1 by Schomburg; Dr. Anthony King app. 12.00 38.00 100.00
2-Jon Juan, Dr. Anthony King app. 7.15 21.50 50.00
3,7,9-14,16-22: 10-Rita Hayworth photo-c. 17-Rita Hayworth & Aldo Ray photo-c 4.25 13.00 28.00
6-Kurtzman-a (10/52) 7.15 21.50 50.00
8-Five pgs. of "Pin-Up Pete" by Sparling 7.15 21.50 50.00
15-Liz Taylor photo-c 8.50 26.00 60.00

GREAT PEOPLE OF GENESIS, THE
No date (Religious giveaway, 64 pgs.)
David C. Cook Publ. Co.

nn-Reprint/Sunday Pix Weekly 2.40 6.00 12.00

GREAT RACE, THE (See Movie Classics)

GREAT SACRAMENT, THE
1953 (Giveaway, 36 pgs.)
Catechetical Guild

nn 2.00 5.00 10.00

GREAT SCOTT SHOE STORE (See Bulls-Eye)

GREAT WEST (Magazine)
1969 (B&W, 52 pgs.)
M. F. Enterprises

V1#1 1.20 3.00

GREAT WESTERN
No. 8, Jan-Mar, 1954 - No. 11, Oct-Dec, 1954
Magazine Enterprises

8(A-1 93)-Trail Colt by Guardineer; Powell Red Hawk-r/Straight Arrow begins, ends #11; Durango Kid story 17.00 51.00 135.00
9(A-1 105), 11(A-1 127)-Ghost Rider, Durango Kid app. in each. 9-Red Mask-c, but no app. 9.50 28.00 75.00
10(A-1 113)-The Calico Kid by Guardineer-r/Tim Holt #8; Straight Arrow, Durango Kid app. 9.50 28.00 75.00
I.W. Reprint #1,2 9: 1,2-r/Straight Arrow #36,42. 9-r/Straight Arrow #? 2.25 6.75 18.00
I.W. Reprint #8-Origin Ghost Rider(r/Tim Holt #11); Tim Holt app.; Bolle-a 2.50 7.50 22.00

NOTE: ***Guardineer** c-8. **Powell** a(r)-8-11 (from Straight Arrow).*

GREEN ARROW (See Action #440, Adventure, Brave & the Bold, DC Super Stars #17, Detective #521, Flash #217, Green Lantern #76, Justice League of America #4, Leading, More Fun #73 (1st app.), Showcase '95 #9 & World's Finest Comics)

GREEN ARROW
May, 1983 - No. 4, Aug, 1983 (limited series)
DC Comics

1-Origin; Speedy cameo; Mike W. Barr scripts, Trevor Von Eeden-c/a. 1.20 3.00
2-4 .80 2.00

GREEN ARROW
Feb, 1988 - Present ($1.00/$1.50/$1.95/$2.25/$2.50)(Painted-c #1-3)
DC Comics

1-Mike Grell scripts begin, ends #80 1.20 3.00
2 .90 2.25
3-49,51-74,76-86: 27,28-Warlord app. 35-38-Co-stars Black Canary; Bill Wray-i. 40-Grell-a. 47-Begin $1.50-c. 63-No longer has mature readers on-c. 63-66-Shado app. 68-Last $1.50-c. 81-Aparo-a begins, ends #100; Nuklon app. 82-Intro & death of Rival. 83-Huntress-c/story. 84-Deathstroke cameo. 85-Deathstroke-c/app. 86-Catwoman-c/story w/Jim Balent layouts 1.50
50,75-($2.50, 52 pgs.): Anniversary issues. 75-Arsenal (Roy Harper) & Shado app. 1.00 2.50
0,87-96: 87-$1.95-c begins. 88-Guy Gardner, Martian Manhunter, & Wonder Woman-c/app.; Flash-c. 89-Anarky app. 90-(9/94)-Zero Hour tie-in. 0-(10/94)-1st app. Connor Hawke; Aparo-a(p). 91-(11/94). 93-1st app. Camorouge. 95-Hal Jordan cameo. 96-Intro new Force of July; Hal Jordan (Parallax) app; Oliver Queen learns that Connor Hawke is his son .80 2.00
97-99,102-109,112-124: 97-Begin $2.25-c; no Aparo-a. 97-99-Arsenal app. 101-Superman app. 102,103-Underworld Unleashed x-over. 104-GL(Kyle Rainer)-c/app. 105-Robin-c/app. 107-109-Thorn app. 109-Lois Lane cameo; Weeks-c. 110-Intro Hatchet. 114-Final Night. 115-117-Black Canary & Oracle app. .90 2.25
100-($3.95)-Foil-c; Superman app. 1.60 4.00
101-Death of Oliver Queen? 1.00 2.40 6.00
110,111-GL x-over .90 2.25
125-($3.50, 48 pgs)-GL x-over cont. in GL #92 1.40 3.50
126-130-($2.50) 2.50
Annual 1(1988, $2.00)-No Grell scripts .80 2.00
Annual 2(1989, $2.50, 68pgs.)-No Grell scripts; recaps origin Green Arrow, Speedy, Black Canary & others 1.00 2.50
Annual 3(1990, $2.95, 68pgs.)-Bill Wray-a 1.20 3.00
Annual 4(1991, $2.95, 68pgs.)-50th anniversary issue 1.20 3.00
Annual 5(1992, $3.00, 68pgs.)-Batman, Eclipso app. 1.20 3.00
Annual 6(1993, $3.50, 68pgs.)-Bloodlines; Hook app. 1.40 3.50
Annual 7(1995, $3.95)-Year One story 3.95

NOTE: ***Aparo** a-0, 81-85, 86 (partial),87p, 88p, 91-95, 96i, 98-100p, 109p; c-81,98-100p. **Austin** c-96i. **Balent** layouts-86. **Burchett** c-91-95. **Campanella** a-100-108i, 110-113i; c-99i, 101-108i,110-113i. **Denys Cowan** a-39p, 41-43p, 47p, 48p, 60p; c-41-43. **Damaggio** a(p)-97p, 100-108p, 110-112p; c-97-99p, 101-108p, 110-113p. **Mike Grell** c-1-4, 10p, 11, 39, 40, 44, 45, 47-80, Annual 4, 5. **Nasser/Netzer** a-89, 96. **Sienkiewicz** a-109i. **Springer** a-67, 68. **Weeks** c-109.*

GREEN ARROW: THE LONG BOW HUNTERS
Aug, 1987 - No. 3, Oct, 1987 ($2.95, limited series, mature)
DC Comics

1-Grell-c/a in all 1.60 4.00
1,2-2nd printings 1.20 3.00
2,3 1.20 3.00
Trade paperback (1989, $12.95)-r/#1-3 1.60 4.85 13.00

GREEN ARROW: THE WONDER YEAR
Feb, 1993 - No. 4, May, 1993 ($1.75, limited series)
DC Comics

1-4: Mike Grell-a(p)/scripts & Gray Morrow-a(i) .70 1.75

GREEN BERET, THE (See Tales of...)

Green Hornet V2#14 © Now Comics

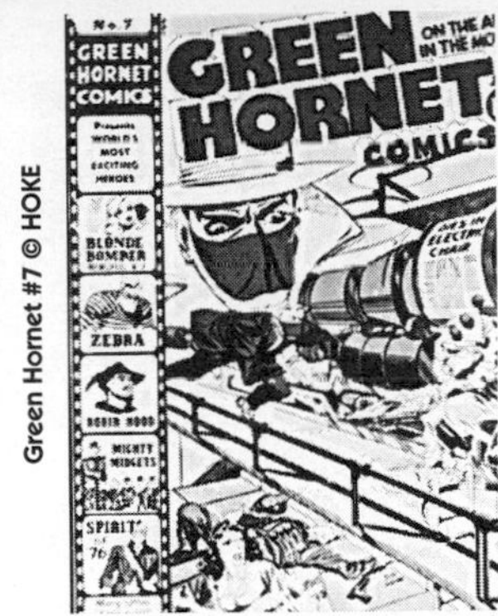

Green Hornet #7 © HOKE

Green Lantern #1 © DC

GREEN CANDLES
Sept, 1995 - No. 3, Dec, 1995 ($5.95, B&W, limited series, digest size)
DC Comics (Paradox Press)
1-3 2.40 6.00

GREEN GIANT COMICS (Also see Colossus Comics)
1940 (No price on cover; distributed in New York City only)
Pelican Publ. (Funnies, Inc.)

	GD25	FN65	VF82	NM94
1-Dr. Nerod, Green Giant, Black Arrow, Mundoo & Master Mystic app.; origin Colossus (Rare)	820.00	2460.00	4920.00	8200.00

(Estimated up to 17 copies exist, 3 in NM/Mint)
NOTE: *The idea for this book came from George Kapitan. Printed by Moreau Publ. of Orange, N.J. as an experiment to see if they could profitably use the idle time of their 40-page Hoe color press. The experiment failed due to the difficulty of obtaining good quality color registration and Mr. Moreau believes the book never reached the stands. The book has no price or date which lends credence to this. Contains five pages reprinted from Motion Picture Funnies Weekly.*

GREEN GOBLIN
Oct, 1995 - No. 13, Oct, 1996 ($2.95/$1.95)
Marvel Comics
1-($2.95)-Scott McDaniel-c/a begins, ends #7; foil-c 1.20 3.00
2-13: 2-Begin $1.95-c. 4-Hobgoblin-c/app; Thing app. 6-Daredevil-c/app. 8-Darrick Robertson-a; McDaniel-c. 10-Arcade app. 12,13-Onslaught x-over. 13-Green Goblin quits; Spider-Man app. .80 2.00

GREENHAVEN
1988 - No. 3, 1988 ($2.00, limited series, 28 pgs.)
Aircel Publishing
..1-3 .80 2.00

GREEN HORNET, THE (TV)
Sept, 1953; Feb, 1967 - No. 3, Aug, 1967
Dell Publishing Co./Gold Key
Four Color 496-Painted-c. 23.00 68.00 250.00
1-All have Bruce Lee photo-c 19.00 57.00 210.00
2,3 13.00 40.00 145.00

GREEN HORNET, THE (Also see Kato of the... & Tales of the...)
Nov, 1989 - No. 14, Feb, 1991 ($1.75)
V2#1, Sept, 1991 - V2#39, Dec, 1994 ($1.95)
Now Comics
1 ($2.95, double-size)-Steranko painted-c; G.A. Green Hornet 1.20 3.00
1-2nd printing ('90, $3.95)-New Butler-c 1.60 4.00
2 .80 2.00
3-8: 5-Death of original (1930s) Green Hornet. 6-Dave Dorman painted-c .80 2.00
9-14: 11-Snyder-c .80 2.00
V2#1-11,13-21,24-26,28-30,32-37,39: 1-Butler painted-c. 9-Mayerik-c .80 2.00
12-($2.50)-Color Green Hornet button polybagged inside 1.00 2.50
22,23-($2.95)-Bagged w/color hologravure card 1.20 3.00
27-($2.95)-Newsstand ed. polybagged w/multi-dimensional card (1993 Anniversary Special on cover) 1.20 3.00
27-($2.95)-Direct Sale ed. polybagged w/multi-dimensional card; cover variations 1.20 3.00
31,38: 31-($2.50)-Polybagged w/trading card 1.00 2.50
1-($2.50)-Polybagged w/button (same as #12) 1.00 2.50
2,3-($1.95)-Same as #13 & 14 .80 2.00
Annual 1 (12/92, $2.50) 1.00 2.50
Annual 1994 (10/94, $2.95) 1.20 3.00

GREEN HORNET: SOLITARY SENTINEL, THE
Dec, 1992 - No. 3, 1993 ($2.50, limited series)
Now Comics
1-3 1.00 2.50

GREEN HORNET COMICS (...Racket Buster #44) (Radio, movies)
Dec, 1940 - No. 47, Sept, 1949 (See All New #13,14)(Early issues: 68 pgs.)
Helnit Publ. Co.(Holyoke) No. 1-6/Family Comics(Harvey) No. 7-on
1-1st app. Green Hornet & Kato; origin of Green Hornet on inside front-c; intro the Black Beauty (Green Hornet's car); painted-c 380.00 1140.00 3800.00
2-Early issues based on radio adventures 133.00 400.00 1200.00
3 108.00 324.00 975.00
4-6: 6-(8/41) 83.00 250.00 750.00
7 (6/42)-Origin The Zebra & begins; Robin Hood, Spirit of '76, Blonde Bomber & Mighty Midgets begin; new logo 71.00 213.00 640.00
8,10 63.00 189.00 565.00
9-Kirby-c 78.00 234.00 700.00
11,12-Mr. Q in both 60.00 180.00 540.00
13-1st Nazi-c; shows Hitler poster on-c 53.00 159.00 475.00
14-20 44.00 132.00 400.00
21-23,25-30 36.00 108.00 325.00
24-Sci-Fi-c 39.00 117.00 350.00
31-The Man in Black Called Fate begins (11-12/45, early app.) 39.00 117.00 350.00
32-36 36.00 108.00 290.00
37-Shock Gibson app. by Powell; S&K Kid Adonis reprinted from Stuntman #3 36.00 108.00 300.00
38-Shock Gibson, Kid Adonis app. 36.00 108.00 285.00
39-Stuntman story by S&K 41.00 123.00 370.00
40,41 26.00 80.00 210.00
42-47-Kerry Drake in all. 45-Boy Explorers on-c only. 46- "Case of the Marijuana Racket" cover/story; Kerry Drake app. 26.00 80.00 210.00
NOTE: *Fuje a-23, 24, 26.* ***Henkle*** *c-7-9.* ***Kubert*** *a-20, 30.* ***Powell*** *a-7-10, 12, 14, 16-21, 30, 31(2), 32(3), 33, 34(3), 35, 36, 37(2), 38.* ***Robinson*** *a-27.* ***Schomburg*** *c-15, 17-23. Kirbyish c-7, 15. Bondage c-8, 14, 18, 26, 36.*

GREEN JET COMICS, THE (See Comic Books, Series 1)

GREEN LAMA (Also see Comic Books, Series 1, Daring Adventures #17 & Prize Comics #7)
Dec, 1944 - No. 8, Mar, 1946
Spark Publications/Prize No. 7 on
1-Intro. Lt. Hercules & The Boy Champions; Mac Raboy-c/a #1-8 106.00 318.00 950.00
2-Lt. Hercules borrows the Human Torch's powers for one panel 64.00 192.00 575.00
3,6,8: 7-X-mas-c; Raboy craft tint-c/a 51.00 153.00 460.00
4-Dick Tracy take-off in Lt. Hercules story by H. L. Gold (sci-fiction writer) 51.00 153.00 460.00
5-Lt. Hercules story; Little Orphan Annie, Smilin' Jack & Snuffy Smith take-off (5/45) 51.00 153.00 460.00
7-X-mas-c; Raboy craft tint-c/a (note: a small quantity of NM copies surfaced) 37.00 110.00 330.00
NOTE: ***Robinson*** *a-3-5, 8. Roussos a-8. Formerly a pulp hero who began in 1940.*

GREEN LANTERN (1st Series) (See All-American, All Flash Quarterly, All Star Comics, The Big All-American & Comic Cavalcade)
Fall, 1941 - No. 38, May-June, 1949 (#1-18 are quarterly)
National Periodical Publications/All-American

	GD25	FN65	VF82	NM94
1-Origin retold	2,300.00	6,900.00	14,950.00	26,000.00

(Estimated up to 200 total copies exist, 8 in NM/Mint)

	GD25	FN65	NM94
2-1st book-length story	570.00	1710.00	5700.00
3-Classic German war-c by Mart Nodell	400.00	1200.00	4000.00
4-Green Lantern & Doiby Dickles join the Army	290.00	870.00	2900.00
5	211.00	633.00	1900.00
6,8: 8-Hop Harrigan begins	167.00	500.00	1500.00
7-Robot-c.	183.00	550.00	1650.00
9,10: 10-Origin/1st app. Vandal Savage	156.00	468.00	1400.00

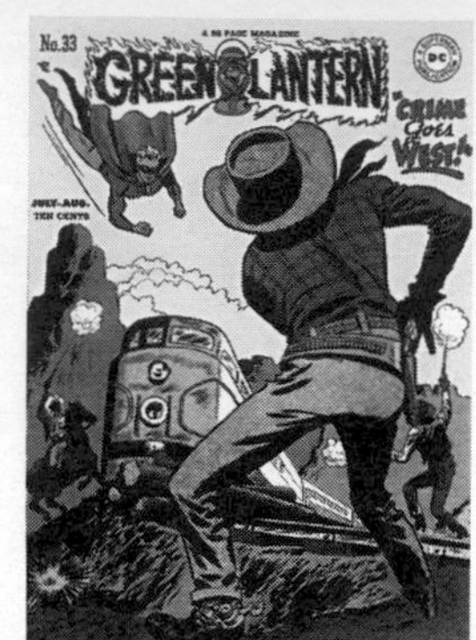

Green Lantern #33 © DC

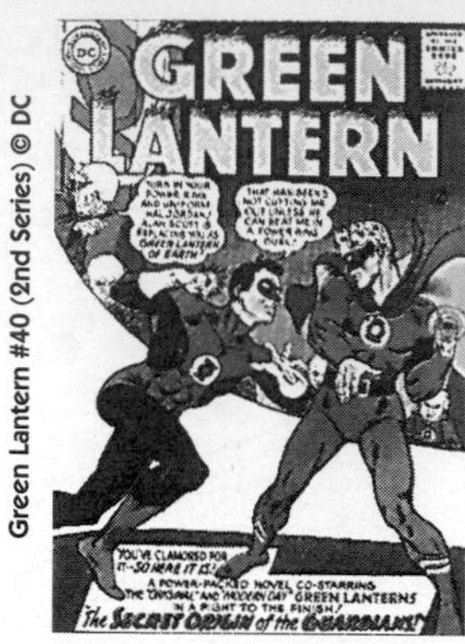

Green Lantern #40 (2nd Series) © DC

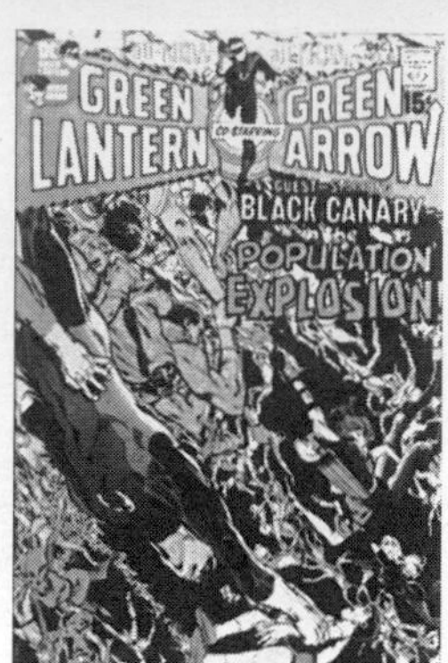

Green Lantern #81 (2nd Series) © DC

	GD25	FN65	NM94
11-17,19,20: 12-Origin/1st app. Gambler	117.00	350.00	1050.00
18-Christmas-c	128.00	384.00	1150.00
21-26,28-30: 30-Origin/1st app. Streak the Wonder Dog by Toth (2-3/48)	106.00	318.00	950.00
27-Origin/1st app. Sky Pirate	108.00	324.00	975.00
31-35: 35-Kubert-c. 35-38-New logo	89.00	267.00	800.00
36-38: 37-Sargon the Sorcerer app.	108.00	324.00	975.00

NOTE: *Book-length stories #2-7.* ***Mayer/Moldoff*** *c-9.* ***Mayer/Purcell*** *c-8.* ***Purcell*** *c-1.* ***Mart Nodell*** *c-2, 3, 7.* ***Paul Reinman*** *c-11, 12, 15-22.* ***Toth*** *a-28, 30, 31, 34-38; c-28, 30, 34p, 36-38p. Cover to #8 says Fall while the indicia says Summer Issue. Streak the Wonder Dog c-30 (w/Green Lantern), 34, 36, 38.*

GREEN LANTERN (See Action Comics Weekly, Adventure Comics, Brave & the Bold, DC Special, DC Special Series, Flash, Guy Gardner, Guy Gardner Reborn, Justice League of America, Parallax: Emerald Night, Showcase, Showcase '93 #12 & Tales of The...Corps)

GREEN LANTERN (2nd Series)(Green Lantern Corps #206 on)
(See Showcase #22-24)
7-8/60 - No. 89, 4-5/72; No. 90, 8-9/76 - No. 205, 10/86
National Periodical Publ./DC Comics

	GD25	FN65	VF82	NM94
1-(7-8/60)-Origin retold; Gil Kane-c/a continues; 1st app. Guardians of the Universe	208.00	624.00	1456.00	2700.00

	GD25	FN65	NM94
2-1st Pieface	64.00	192.00	770.00
3-Contains readers poll	40.00	120.00	440.00
4,5: 5-Origin & 1st app. Hector Hammond	31.00	93.00	350.00
6-Intro Tomar-Re the alien G.L.	31.00	93.00	330.00
7-Origin/1st app. Sinestro (7-8/61)	27.00	82.00	275.00
8-10: 8-1st 5700 A.D. story; grey tone-c. 9-1st Jordan Brothers; last 10¢ issue	25.00	75.00	250.00
11,12	17.00	51.00	170.00
13-Flash x-over	20.00	60.00	200.00
14-20: 14-Origin/1st app. Sonar. 16-Origin & 1st app. Star Sapphire. 20-Flash x-over	15.00	45.00	150.00
21-30: 21-Origin & 1st app. Dr. Polaris. 23-1st Tattooed Man. 24-Origin & 1st app. Shark. 29-JLA cameo; 1st Blackhand	13.50	41.00	135.00
31-39: 37-1st app. Evil Star (villain)	11.00	33.00	110.00
40-1st app. Crisis (10/65); 2nd solo G.A. Green Lantern in Silver Age (see Showcase #55); origin The Guardians; Doiby Dickles app.	41.00	123.00	500.00
41-44,46-50: 42-Zatanna x-over. 43-Flash x-over	7.00	21.00	70.00
45-2nd S.A. app. G.A. Green Lantern in title (6/66)	13.00	39.00	130.00
51,53-58	5.25	15.75	52.00
52-G.A. Green Lantern x-over	7.50	22.50	75.00
59-1st app. Guy Gardner (3/68)	19.00	57.00	210.00
60,62-69: 69-Wood inks; last 12 cent issue	3.05	10.50	35.00
61-G.A. Green Lantern x-over	5.00	15.00	50.00
70-75	2.50	7.50	20.00
76-(4/70)-Begin Green Lantern/Green Arrow series (by Neal Adams #76-89) ends #122 (see Flash #217 for 2nd series)	17.00	51.00	170.00
77	5.00	15.00	50.00
78-80	4.00	12.00	40.00
81-84: 82-Wrightson-i(1 pg.). 83-G.L. reveals i.d. to Carol Ferris. 84-N. Adams/Wrightson-a(22 pgs.); last 15¢-c; partial photo-c	3.50	10.50	35.00
85,86-(52 pgs.)-Anti-drug issues. 86-G.A. Green Lantern-r; Toth-a	5.00	15.00	50.00
87-(52 pgs.): 2nd app. Guy Gardner (cameo); 1st app. John Stewart (12-1/71-72) (becomes 3rd Green Lantern in #182)	3.00	9.00	30.00
88-(2-3/72, 52 pgs.)-Unpubbed G.A. Green Lantern story; Green Lantern-r/Showcase #23. N. Adams-c/a (1 pg.)	1.50	4.50	12.00
89-(4-5/72, 52 pgs.)-G.A. Green Lantern-r; Green Lantern & Green Arrow move to Flash #217 (2nd team-up series)	2.25	6.75	18.00
90 (8-9/76)-Begin 3rd Green Lantern/Green Arrow team-up series; Mike Grell-c/a begins, ends #111	1.10	3.30	9.00
91-99: 90-(8-9/76)-Begin 3rd Green Lantern/Green Arrow team-up series; Mike Grell-c/a begins, ends #111		1.80	4.50
100-(1/78, Giant)-1st app. Air Wave II	1.25	3.75	10.00
101-111,113-115,117-119: 107-1st Tales of the G.L. Corps story. 108-110-(44 pgs)-G.A. Green Lantern back-ups in each. 111-Origin retold; G.A. Green Lantern app.		1.60	4.00
112-G.A. Green Lantern origin retold	1.25	3.75	10.00
116-1st app. Guy Gardner as a G.L. (5/79)	2.50	7.50	25.00
120,121,124-135,138-140,142-149: 130-132-Tales of the G.L. Corps. 132-Adam Strange series begins, ends 147. 142,143-Omega Men app.; Perez-c. 144-Omega Men cameo. 148-Tales of the G.L. Corps begins, ends #173		.80	2.00
122-Last Green Lantern/Green Arrow team-up		.80	2.00
123-Green Lantern back to solo action; 2nd app. Guy Gardner as Green Lantern		1.60	4.00
136,137-1st app. Citadel; Space Ranger app.		.80	2.00
141-1st app. Omega Men (6/81)		.80	2.00
150-Anniversary issue, 52 pgs.; no G.L. Corps		1.20	3.00
151-170: 159-Origin Evil Star. 160,161-Omega Men app. 181-Hal Jordan resigns as G.L. 182-John Stewart becomes new G.L.; origin recap of Hal Jordan as G.L.		.80	2.00
171-193,196-199,201-205: (75¢ cover). 185-Origin new G.L. (John Stewart). 188-I.D. revealed; Alan Moore back-up scripts. 191-Re-intro Star Sapphire (cameo). 192-Re-intro Star Sapphire (1st full app.). 194,198-Crisis x-over. 199-Hal Jordan returns as a member of G.L. Corps (3 G.L.s now). 201-Green Lantern Corps begins (is cover title, says premiere issue)		.80	2.00
194-Hal Jordan/Guy Gardner battle; Guardians choose Guy Gardner to become new Green Lantern		1.20	3.00
195-Guy Gardner becomes Green Lantern; Crisis x-over	1.00	2.80	7.00
200-Double-size		.80	2.00
Annual 1 (See Tales Of The...)			
Annual 3 (See Green Lantern Corps Annual #3)			
Special 1 (1988), 2 (1989)-(Both $1.50, 52 pgs.)		.80	2.00

NOTE: ***N. Adams*** *a-76, 77-87p, 89; c-63, 76-89.* ***M. Anderson*** *a-137i.* ***Austin*** *a-93i, 94i, 171i.* ***Chaykin*** *c-196.* ***Greene*** *a-39-49i, 58-63i; c-54-58i.* ***Grell*** *a-90-106, 108-111; c-90-106, 108-112.* ***Heck*** *a-120-122p.* ***Infantino*** *a-137p, 145-147p, 151, 152p.* ***Gil Kane*** *a-1-49p, 50-57, 58-61p, 68-75p, 85p(r), 87p(r), 88p(r), 156, 177, 184p; c-1-52, 54-61p, 67-75, 123, 154, 156, 165-171, 177, 184.* ***Newton*** *a-148p, 149p, 181.* ***Perez*** *c-132p, 141-144.* ***Sekowsky*** *a-65p, 170p.* ***Simonson*** *c-200.* ***Sparling*** *a-63p.* ***Starlin*** *c-129, 133.* ***Staton*** *a-117p, 123-127p, 128, 129-131p, 132-139, 140p, 141-146, 147p, 148-150, 151-155p; c-107p, 117p, 135(i), 136p, 145p, 146, 147, 148-152p, 155p.* ***Toth*** *a-86r, 171p.* ***Tuska*** *a-166-168p, 170p.*

GREEN LANTERN (3rd Series)
June, 1990 - Present ($1.00/$1.25/$1.50/$1.75)
DC Comics

	GD25	FN65	NM94
1-Hal Jordan, John Stewart & Guy Gardner return; Batman app.		1.20	3.00
2,3		.80	2.00
4-8			1.25
9-12-Guy Gardner solo story		1.00	2.50
13-($1.75, 52 pgs.)		.80	2.00
14-18,20-24,26: 18-Guy Gardner solo story. 26-Last $1.00-c			1.00
19-($1.75, 52 pgs.)-50th anniversary issue; Mart Nodell (original G.A. artist) part-p on G.A. Gr. Lantern; G. Kane-c		.70	1.75
25-($1.75, 52 pgs.)-Hal Jordan/Guy Gardner battle		.80	2.00
27-45,47: 30,31-Gorilla Grodd-c/story(see Flash #69). 38,39-Adam Strange-c/story. 42-Deathstroke-c/s. 47-Green Arrow x-over			1.25
46-Superman app. cont'd in Superman #82		2.00	5.00
48,49: 48-Emerald Twilight part 1; begin $1.50-c		2.00	5.00
50-($2.95, 52 pgs.)-Glow-in-the-dark-c		2.40	6.00
0, 51-62: 51-1st app. New Green Lantern (Kyle Rayner) with new costume. 53-Superman-c/story. 55-(9/94)-Zero Hour. 0-(10/94). 56-(11/94).		.80	2.00
63,64-Kyle Rayner vs. Hal Jordan.		2.00	5.00
65-92: 63-Begin $1.75-c. 65-New Titans app. 66,67-Flash app.			

Green Lantern #86 (3rd Series) © DC

Green Lantern: Emerald Dawn #5 © DC

Grendel #3 © Matt Wagner

GD25 FN65 NM94

71-Batman & Robin app. 72-Shazam!-c/app. 73-Wonder Woman-c/app. 73-75-Adam Strange app. 76,77-Green Arrow x-over. 80-Final Night x-over. 81-(Regular Edition)-Memorial for Hal Jordan (Parallax); most DC heroes app. 87-JLA app. 91-Genesis x-over. 92-Green Arrow x-over. .80 2.00
81-($3.95, Deluxe Edition)-Embossed prism-c 2.00 5.00
93-98: 93-Begin $1.95-c; Deadman app. 94-Superboy app. 95-Starlin-a(p). 98-Legion-c/app. 1.95
Annual 1 (1992, $2.50, 68 pgs.)-Eclipso app. 1.00 2.50
Annual 2 (1993, $2.50, 68 pgs.)-Intro Nightblade 1.00 2.50
Annual 3 (1994, $2.95)-Elseworlds story 1.20 3.00
Annual 4 (1995, $3.50)-Year One story 1.40 3.50
Annual 5 (1996, $2.95)-Legends of the Dead Earth 1.20 3.00
Annual 6 (1997, $3.95)-Pulp Heroes story 3.95
...: Emerald Twilight nn (1994, $5.95)-r/#48-50 2.40 6.00
...: Ganthet's Tale nn (1992, $5.95, 68 pgs.)-Silver foil stamped logo;Larry Niven scripts; Byrne-c/a 2.40 6.00
.../Green Arrow Collection, Vol. 2-r/Gl #84-87,89 & Flash #217-219 & GL/GA #5-7 by O'Neil/Adams/Wrightson 1.60 4.85 13.00
...Plus 1 (12/1996, $2.95)-The Ray & Polaris-c/app. 2.95
...The Road Back nn (1992, $8.95)-r/1-8 w/covers 1.10 3.30 9.00
NOTE: ***Staton*** *a(p)-9-12; c-9-12.*

GREEN LANTERN (See Tangent Comics/ Green Lantern)

GREEN LANTERN CORPS, THE (Formerly Green Lantern; see Tales of...)
No. 206, Nov, 1986 - No. 224, May, 1988
DC Comics

206-223: 220,221-Millennium tie-ins 1.00
224-Double-size last issue 1.50
...Corps Annual 2 (12/86)-Formerly Tales of ...Annual #1; Alan Moore scripts 1.50
...Corps Annual 3 (8/87)-Indicia says Green Lantern Annual #3; Moore scripts; Byrne-a 1.50
NOTE: ***Austin*** *a-Annual 3i.* ***Gil Kane*** *a-223, 224p; c-223, 224, Annual 2.* ***Russell*** *a-Annual 3i.* ***Staton*** *a-207-213p, 217p, 221p, 222p, Annual 3; c-207-213p, 217p, 221p, 222p.* ***Willingham*** *a-213p, 219p, 220p, 218p, 219p, Annual 2, 3p; c-218p, 219p.*

GREEN LANTERN CORPS QUARTERLY
Summer, 1992 - No. 8, Spring, 1994 ($2.50/$2.95, 68 pgs.)
DC Comics

1-5: 1-G.A. Green Lantern story; Staton-a(p). 2-G.A. G.L.-c/story; Austin-c(i); Gulacy-a(p). 3-G.A. G.L. story. 4-Austin-i 1.00 2.50
6-8: 6-Begin $2.95-c. 7-Painted-c; Tim Vigil-a. 8-Lobo-c/s 1.20 3.00

GREEN LANTERN: EMERALD DAWN (Also see Emerald Dawn)
Dec, 1989 - No. 6, May, 1990 ($1.00, limited series)
DC Comics

1-Origin retold; Giffen plots in all .80 2.00
2-6 1.50

GREEN LANTERN: EMERALD DAWN II (Emerald Dawn II #1 & 2)
Apr, 1991 - No. 6, Sept, 1991 ($1.00, limited series)
DC Comics

1 1.25
2-6 1.00

GREEN LANTERN/FLASH: FASTER FRIENDS (See Flash/Green Lantern...)
1997 ($4.95, limited series)
DC Comics

1-Marz-s 4.95

GREEN LANTERN GALLERY
Dec, 1996 ($3.50, one-shot)
DC Comics

1-Wraparound-c; pin-ups by various 1.40 3.50

GREEN LANTERN/GREEN ARROW (Also see The Flash #217)
Oct, 1983 - No. 7, April, 1984 (52-60 pgs.)
DC Comics

1 Reprints Green Lantern #76,77 1.20 3.00
2-7: Reprints Green Lantern #78-89 1.00 2.50
NOTE: ***Neal Adams*** *r-1-7; c-1-4.* ***Wrightson*** *r-4, 5.*

GREEN LANTERN: MOSAIC (Also see Cosmic Odyssey #2)
June, 1992 - No. 18, Nov, 1993 ($1.25)
DC Comics

1-18: Featuring John Stewart. 1-Painted-c by Cully Hamner 1.25

GREEN LANTERN/SILVER SURFER: UNHOLY ALLIANCES
1995 ($4.95, one-shot)(Prelude to DC Versus Marvel)
DC Comics

nn-Hal Jordan app. 2.00 5.00

GREEN MASK, THE (See Mystery Men)
Summer, 1940 - No. 9, 2/42; No. 10, 8/44 - No. 11, 11/44;
V2#1, Spring, 1945 - No. 6, 10-11/46
Fox Features Syndicate

V1#1-Origin The Green Mask & Domino; reprints/Mystery Men #1-3,5-7; Lou Fine-c 270.00 810.00 2700.00
2-Zanzibar The Magician by Tuska 106.00 318.00 950.00
3-Powell-a; Marijuana story 67.00 200.00 600.00
4-Navy Jones begins, ends #6 53.00 159.00 475.00
5 42.00 126.00 375.00
6-The Nightbird begins, ends #9; bondage/torture-c 36.00 108.00 300.00
7-9: 9(2/42)-Becomes The Bouncer #10(nn) on? & Green Mask #10 on 31.00 94.00 250.00
10,11: 10-Origin One Round Hogan & Rocket Kelly 24.00 71.00 190.00
V2#1 18.00 54.00 145.00
2-6 16.00 49.00 130.00

GREEN PLANET, THE
1962 (one-shot) (12¢)
Charlton Comics

nn-Giordano-c 5.00 15.00 50.00

GREEN TEAM (See Cancelled Comic Cavalcade & 1st Issue Special)

GREETINGS FROM SANTA (See March of Comics No. 48)

GRENDEL (Also see Primer #2 and Mage)
Mar, 1983 - No. 3, Feb, 1984 ($1.50, B&W)(#1 has indicia to Skrog #1)
Comico

1-Origin Hunter Rose 10.00 30.00 100.00
2,3: 2-Origin Argent 8.00 24.00 80.00

GRENDEL
Oct, 1986 - No. 40, Feb, 1991 ($1.50/$1.95/$2.50, mature)
Comico

1 1.00 2.80 7.00
1,2: 2nd printings .80 2.00
2 1.60 4.00
3-10: 4-Dave Stevens-c(i) 1.20 3.00
11-15: 13-15-Ken Steacy-c 1.20 3.00
16-Re-intro Mage (series begins, ends #19) 1.60 4.00
17-32: 18-26-$1.75-c; 27-32-$1.95-c. 24-25, 27-28,30-31-Snyder-c/a; 26,29-Snyder-i 1.20 3.00
33-($2.75, 44 pgs.) 1.20 3.00
34-40: 34-Begin $2.50 cover price 1.20 3.00
Devil by the Deed (Graphic Novel, 10/86, $5.95, 52 pgs.)-r/Grendel back-ups/ Mage 6-14; Alan Moore intro. 1.00 2.80 7.00
Devil's Legacy ($14.95, 1988, Graphic Novel) 1.85 5.50 15.00
Devil's Vagary (10/87, B&W & red)-No price; included in Comico Collection 1.50 4.50 12.00

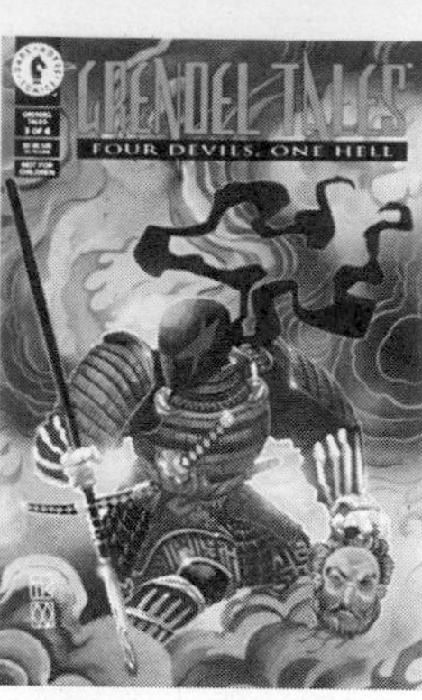

Grendel Tales: Four Devils, One Hell #3 © Matt Wagner

Grendel: War Child #1 © Matt Wagner

Grifter V1 #1 © Aegis Entertainment

	GD25	FN65	NM94
GRENDEL CLASSICS July, 1995 - Aug, 1995 ($3.95, limited series, mature) Dark Horse Comics			
1,2-reprints; new Wagner-c		1.60	4.00
GRENDEL CYCLE Oct, 1995 ($5.95, one shot) Dark Horse Comics			
1-nn-history of Grendel by M. Wagner & others		2.40	6.00
GRENDEL: DEVIL BY THE DEED July, 1993 ($3.95, one shot, spot varnish-c) Dark Horse Comics			
1-nn-M. Wagner-c/a/scripts; r/Grendel back-ups from Mage #6-14.		1.60	4.00
GRENDEL: DEVIL QUEST Nov, 1995 ($4.95, one shot) Dark Horse Comics			
1-nn-Prequel to Batman/Grendel II; M. Wagner story & art; r/back-up story from Grendel Tales series.		2.00	5.00
GRENDEL TALES: DEVILS AND DEATHS Oct, 1994 - Nov, 1994 ($2.95, limited series, mature) Dark Horse Comics			
1,2 (10/94-11/94, $2.95, mature)		1.20	3.00
GRENDEL TALES: DEVIL'S CHOICES Mar, 1995 - Jun, 1995 ($2.95, limited series, mature) Dark Horse Comics			
1-4		1.20	3.00
GRENDEL TALES: FOUR DEVILS, ONE HELL Aug, 1993 - Jan, 1994 ($2.95, limited series, mature) Dark Horse Comics			
1-6-Wagner painted-c		1.20	3.00
TPB (12/94, $17.95) r/#1-6	2.25	6.75	18.00
GRENDEL TALES: HOMECOMING Dec, 1994 - Feb, 1995 ($2.95, limited series, mature) Dark Horse Comics			
1-3		1.20	3.00
GRENDEL TALES: THE DEVIL IN OUR MIDST May, 1994 - Sep, 1995 ($2.95, limited series, mature) Dark Horse Comics			
1-5-Wagner painted-c. in all		1.20	3.00
GRENDEL TALES: THE DEVIL MAY CARE Dec, 1995 - 1996 ($2.95, limited series, mature) Dark Horse Comics			
1-6-Terry LaBan scripts. 5-Batman/Grendel II preview		1.20	3.00
GRENDEL TALES: THE DEVIL'S APPRENTICE Sept, 1997 - No. 3, Nov, 1997 ($2.95, limited series, mature) Dark Horse Comics			
1-3		1.20	3.00
GRENDEL TALES: THE DEVIL'S HAMMER Feb, 1994 - Apr, 1994 ($2.95, limited series, mature) Dark Horse Comics			
1-3		1.20	3.00
GRENDEL: WAR CHILD Aug, 1992 - No. 10, 1993 ($2.50, limited series, mature) Dark Horse Comics			
1-9: Bisley painted-c; Wagner-i & scripts		1.00	2.50
10-($3.50, 52 pgs.)		1.40	3.50

	GD25	FN65	NM94
Limited Edition Hardcover ($99.95)			100.00
GREYFRIARS BOBBY (Disney)(Movie) No. 1189, Nov, 1961 (one-shot) Dell Publishing Co.			
Four Color 1189-Photo-c (scarce)	6.40	19.20	70.00
GREYLORE 12/85 - No. 5, Sept, 1986 ($1.50/$1.75, high quality paper) Sirius			
1-5: Bo Hampton-a in all			1.50
GRIFFIN, THE 1991 - No. 6, 1992 ($4.95, limited series, 52 pgs.) DC Comics			
Book 1-6: Matt Wagner painted-c		2.00	5.00
GRIFTER (Also see Team 7 & WildC.A.T.S) May, 1995 - No. 10, Mar, 1996 ($1.95) Image Comics (Wildstorm Productions)			
1 ($1.95, Newsstand)-WildStorm Rising Pt. 5		1.00	2.50
1 ($2.50, Direct Market)-WildStorm Rising Pt. 5, bound-in trading card		1.20	3.00
2-10		.80	2.00
GRIFTER V2#1, July, 1996 - No. 14, Aug, 1997 ($2.50) Image Comics (Wildstorm Productions)			
V2#1-14: Steven Grant scripts		1.00	2.50
GRIFTER AND THE MASK Sept, 1996 - No. 2, Oct, 1996 ($2.50, limited series) (1st Dark Horse Comics/Image x-over) Dark Horse Comics			
1,2: Steve Seagle scripts		1.00	2.50
GRIFTER/BADROCK (Also see WildC.A.T.S & Youngblood) Oct, 1995 - No.2, Nov, 1995 ($2.50, unfinished limited series) Image Comics (Extreme Studios)			
1,2: 2-Flip book w/Badrock #2		1.00	2.50
GRIFTER: ONE SHOT Jan, 1995 ($4.95, one-shot) Image Comics (Wildstorm Productions)			
1-Flip-c		2.20	5.50
GRIFTER/SHI Apr, 1996 - No. 2, May, 1996 ($2.95, limited series) Image Comics (Wildstorm Productions)			
1,2: 1-Jim Lee-c/a(p); Travis Charest-a(p). 2-Billy Tucci-c/a(p); Travis Charest-a(p)		1.20	3.00
GRIM GHOST, THE Jan, 1975 - No. 3, July, 1975 Atlas/Seaboard Publ.			
1-3: 1-Origin. 3-Heath-c		1.20	3.00
GRIMJACK (Also see Demon Knight & Starslayer) Aug, 1984 - No. 81, Apr, 1991 ($1.00/$1.95/$2.25) First Comics			
1-John Ostrander scripts & Tim Truman-c/a begins.		.80	2.00
2-25: 20-Sutton-c/a begins. 22-Bolland-a.			1.50
26-2nd color Teenage Mutant Ninja Turtles		.80	2.00
27-74,76-81 (Later issues $1.95, $2.25): 30-Dynamo Joe x-over; 31-Mandrake-c/a begins. 73,74-Kelley Jones-a			1.25
75-($5.95, 52 pgs.)-Fold-out map; coated stock		2.40	6.00

NOTE: *Truman c/a-1-17.*

Groo The Wanderer #66 © Sergio Aragones

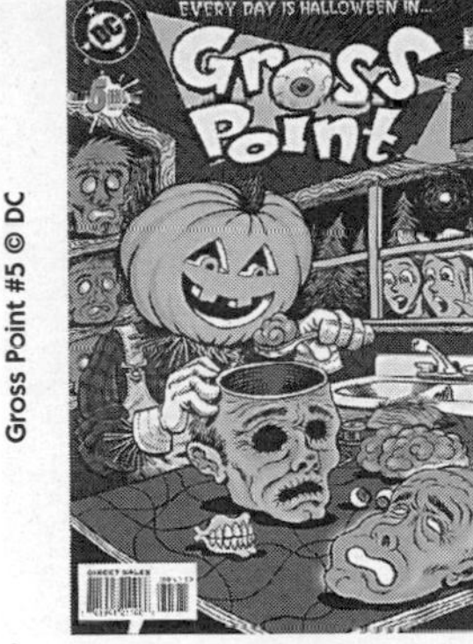

Gross Point #5 © DC

Guardians of the Galaxy #52 © MEG

GD25 FN65 NM94

GRIMJACK CASEFILES
Nov, 1990 - No. 5, Mar, 1991 ($1.95, limited series)
First Comics
1-5 Reprints 1st stories from Starslayer #10 on .80 2.00

GRIMM'S GHOST STORIES (See Dan Curtis)
Jan, 1972 - No. 60, June, 1982 (Painted-c #1-42,44,46-56)
Gold Key/Whitman No. 55 on
1 2.50 7.50 20.00
2-5,8: 5,8-Williamson-a 1.25 3.75 10.00
6,7,9,10 1.00 3.00 8.00
11-20 2.40 6.00
21-42,45-54: 32,34-Reprints. 45-Photo-c 1.60 4.00
43,44,55-60: 43,44-(52 pgs.). 43-Photo-c. 59-Williamson a(r/#8) 2.40 6.00
Mini-Comic No. 1 (3-1/4x6-1/2", 1976) 2.00 5.00
NOTE: *Reprints-#32?, 34?, 39, 43, 44, 47?, 53; 56-60(1/3).* ***Bolle*** *a-8, 17, 22-25, 27, 29(2), 33, 35, 41, 43r, 45(2), 48(2), 50, 52.* ***Celardo*** *a-17, 26, 28p, 30, 31, 43(2), 45.* ***Lopez*** *a-24, 25.* ***McWilliams*** *a-33, 44r, 48, 54(2), 57, 58.* ***Win Mortimer*** *a-31, 33, 49, 51, 55, 56, 58(2), 59, 60.* ***Roussos*** *a-25, 30.* ***Sparling*** *a-23, 24, 28, 30, 31, 33, 43r, 44, 45, 51(2), 52, 56, 58, 59(2), 60.* ***Spiegle*** *a-44.*

GRIN (The American Funny Book) (Satire)
Nov, 1972 - No. 3, April, 1973 (Magazine, 52 pgs.)
APAG House Pubs
1 1.85 5.50 15.00
2,3 1.25 3.75 10.00

GRIN & BEAR IT (See Gags)
No. 28, 1941
Dell Publishing Co.
Large Feature Comic 28 8.00 25.00 90.00

GRIPS (Extreme violence)
Sept, 1986 - No. 4, Dec, 1986 ($1.50, B&W, mature readers)
Silverwolf Comics
1-Tim Vigil-c/a in all .80 2.00
2-4 1.50

GRIT GRADY (See Holyoke One Shot No. 1)

GROO (Sergio Aragones'...)
Dec, 1994 - No. 12, Dec, 1995 ($1.95)
Image Comics
1-12: 2-Indicia reads #1, Jan, 1995; Aragones-c/a in all .80 2.00

GROO CARNIVAL, THE
Dec, 1991 ($8.95, trade paperback)
Marvel Comics (Epic Comics)
nn-Reprints Groo #9-12 by Aragones 1.10 3.30 9.00

GROO CHRONICLES, THE (Sergio Aragones)
June, 1989 - No. 6, Feb, 1990 ($3.50)
Marvel Comics (Epic Comics)
Book 1-6: Reprints early Pacific issues 1.40 3.50

GROO SPECIAL
Oct, 1984 ($2.00, 52 pgs., Baxter paper)
Eclipse Comics
1-Aragones-c/a 1.50 4.50 12.00

GROO THE WANDERER (See Destroyer Duck #1, Marvel Graphic Novel #32 & & Starslayer #5)
Dec, 1982 - No. 8, Apr, 1984
Pacific Comics
1-Aragones-c/a(p) in all; Aragones biog., photo 1.85 5.50 15.00
2 1.25 3.75 10.00
3-8: 5-Deluxe paper (1.00-c) 1.10 3.30 9.00

GD25 FN65 NM94

GROO THE WANDERER (Sergio Aragones'...)
March, 1985 - No. 120, Jan, 1995
Marvel Comics (Epic Comics)
1-Aragones-c/a in all 2.40 6.00
2 1.60 4.00
3-10 1.20 3.00
11-20 1.00 2.50
21-30 .80 2.00
31-86: 50-($1.50, double size) 1.50
87-99,101-120: 87-Begin $2.25, direct sale only, high quality paper issues 1.40 3.50
100-($2.95, 52 pgs.) 2.00 5.00
Marvel Graphic Novel 32: Death of Groo 1.50 4.50 12.00
Death of Groo 2nd printing ($5.95) 2.40 6.00
Groo Garden, The (4/94, $10.95)-r/25-28 1.40 4.15 11.00

GROOVY (Cartoon Comics - not CCA approved)
March, 1968 - No. 3, July, 1968
Marvel Comics Group
1-Monkees, Ringo Starr, Sonny & Cher, Mamas & Papas photos 6.00 18.00 60.00
2,3 4.00 12.00 40.00

GROSS POINT
Aug, 1997 - Present ($2.50)
DC Comics
1-Waid/Augustyn-s 1.20 3.00
2-8: 2.50

GROUP LARUE, THE
1989 - No. 4, 1990 ($1.95, mini-series)
Innovation Publishing
1-4 By Mike Baron; 4-Exist? .80 2.00

GUADALCANAL DIARY (See American Library)

GUARDIANS OF JUSTICE & THE O-FORCE
1990 (no date) ($1.50, 7-1/2 x10-1/4)
Shadow Comics
1-Super-hero group 1.50

GUARDIANS OF METROPOLIS
Nov, 1995 - Feb, 1995 ($1.50, limited series)
DC Comics
1-4: 1-Superman & Granny Goodness app. 1.50

GUARDIANS OF THE GALAXY (Also see The Defenders #26, Marvel Presents #3, Marvel Super-Heroes #18, Marvel Two-In-One #5)
June, 1990 - No. 62, July, 1995 ($1.00/$1.25)
Marvel Comics
1-16: 1-Valentino-c/a(p) begin. 2-Zeck-c(i). 5-McFarlane-c(i). 7-Intro Malevolence (Mephisto's daughter); Perez-c(i). 8-Intro Rancor (descendant of Wolverine) in cameo. 9-1st full app. Rancor; Rob Liefeld-c(i). 10-Jim Lee-c(i). 13,14-1st app. Spirit of Vengeance (futuristic Ghost Rider). 14-Spirit of Vengeance vs. The Guardians. 15-Starlin-c(i). 16-($1.50, 52 pgs.)-Starlin-c(i) .80 2.00
17-23,26-38,40-47: 17-20-31st century Punishers storyline. 20-Last $1.00-c. 21-Rancor app. 22-Reintro Starhawk. 26-Origin retold. 27-28-Infinity War x-over; 27-Inhumans app. 40 Intro Woodon (son of Thor) 1.25
24-Silver Surfer-c/story; Ron Lim-c .80 2.00
25-($2.50)-Prism foil-c; Silver Surfer/Galactus-c/s 1.00 2.50
25-($2.50)-Without foil-c; newsstand edition 1.00 2.50
39-($2.95, 52 pgs.)-Embossed & holo-grafx foil-c; Dr. Doom vs. Rancor 1.20 3.00
48,49,51-62: 48-$1.50-c begins; bound-in trading card sheet 1.50
50-($2.00, 52 pgs.)-Newsstand edition .80 2.00

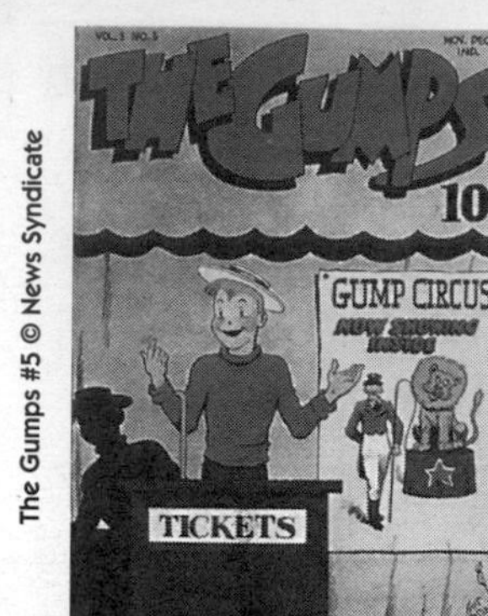

The Gumps #5 © News Syndicate

Gunfire #3 © DC

Gunhawks #11 © MEG

	GD25	FN65	NM94
50-($2.95, 52 pgs.)-Collectors ed. w/foil embossed-c		1.20	3.00
Annual 1 (1991, $2.00, 68 pgs.)-2 pg. origin		.80	2.00
Annual 2 (1992, $2.25, 68 pgs.)-Spirit of Vengeance-c/story		.90	2.25
Annual 3 (1993, $2.95, 68 pgs.)-Bagged w/card		1.20	3.00
Annual 4 (1994, $2.95)		1.20	3.00

GUERRILLA WAR (Formerly Jungle War Stories)
No. 12, July-Sept, 1965 - No. 14, Mar, 1966
Dell Publishing Co.

	GD25	FN65	NM94
12-14	1.50	4.50	12.00

GUILTY (See Justice Traps the Guilty)

GULF FUNNY WEEKLY (Gulf Comic Weekly No. 1-4)
1933 - No. 422, 5/23/41 (in full color; 4 pgs.; tabloid size to 2/3/39; 2/10/39 on, regular comic book size)(early issues undated)
Gulf Oil Company (Giveaway)

	GD25	FN65	NM94
1	53.00	159.00	475.00
2-5	17.00	51.00	135.00
6-30	8.75	26.25	70.00
31-100	7.15	21.50	50.00
101-196	5.35	16.00	32.00
197-Wings Winfair begins(1/29/37); by Fred Meagher beginning in 1938	23.00	69.00	185.00
198-300 (Last tabloid size)	12.00	36.00	95.00
301-350 (Regular size)	6.85	21.00	48.00
351-422	5.35	16.00	32.00

GULLIVER'S TRAVELS (See Dell Jr. Treasury No. 3)
Sept-Nov, 1965 - No. 3, May, 1966
Dell Publishing Co.

	GD25	FN65	NM94
1	4.00	12.00	43.00
2,3	3.00	9.00	32.00

GUMBY'S SUMMER FUN SPECIAL
July, 1987 ($2.50)
Comico

	GD25	FN65	NM94
1-Art Adams-c/a; B. Burden scripts		1.00	2.50

GUMBY'S WINTER FUN SPECIAL
Dec, 1988 ($2.50, 44 pgs.)
Comico

	GD25	FN65	NM94
1-Art Adams-c/a		1.00	2.50

GUMPS, THE (See Merry Christmas..., Popular & Super Comics)
No. 73, 1945; Mar-Apr, 1947 - No. 5, Nov-Dec, 1947
Dell Publ. Co./Bridgeport Herald Corp.

	GD25	FN65	NM94
Four Color 73 (Dell)(1945)	11.00	33.00	120.00
1 (3-4/47)	9.00	27.00	100.00
2-5	5.75	17.00	63.00

GUNFIGHTER (Fat & Slat #1-4) (Becomes Haunt of Fear #15 on)
No. 5, Summer, 1948 - No. 14, Mar-Apr, 1950
E. C. Comics (Fables Publ. Co.)

	GD25	FN65	NM94
5,6-Moon Girl in each	39.00	117.00	350.00
7-14: 14-Bondage-c	30.00	90.00	240.00

NOTE: ***Craig & H. C. Kiefer*** *art in most issues.* ***Craig*** *c-5, 6, 13, 14.* ***Feldstein/Craig*** *a-10.* ***Feldstein*** *a-7-11.* ***Harrison/Wood*** *a-13, 14.* ***Ingels*** *a-5-14; c-7-12.*

GUNFIGHTERS, THE
1963 - 1964
Super Comics (Reprints)

	GD25	FN65	NM94
10-12,15,16,18: 10,11-r/Billy the Kid #s? 12-r/The Rider #5(Swift Arrow). 15-r/Straight Arrow #42; Powell-r. 16-r/Billy the Kid #?(Toby). 18-r/The Rider #3; Severin-c	1.10	3.30	9.00

GUNFIGHTERS, THE (Formerly Kid Montana)
No. 51, 10/66 - No. 52, 10/67; No. 53, 6/79 - No. 85, 7/84
Charlton Comics

	GD25	FN65	NM94
51,52	1.85	5.50	15.00
53,54,56:53,54-Williamson/Torres-r/Six Gun Heroes #47,49. 56-Williamson/Severin-c; Severin-r/Sheriff of Tombstone #1		2.00	5.00
55,57-85: . 85-S&K-r/1955 Bullseye		1.20	3.00

GUNFIRE (See Deathstroke Annual #2 & Showcase 94 #1,2)
May, 1994 - No. 13, June, 1995 ($1.75)
DC Comics

	GD25	FN65	NM94
1-4: 2-Ricochet-c/story. 5-(9/94)		.70	1.75
5,0,6-12: 0-(10/94). 6-(11/94).		.80	2.00
13-$2.25-c begins.		.90	2.25

GUN GLORY (Movie)
No. 846, Oct, 1957 (one-shot)
Dell Publishing Co.

	GD25	FN65	NM94
Four Color 846-Toth-a, photo-c.	9.00	27.00	100.00

GUNHAWK, THE (Formerly Whip Wilson)(See Wild Western)
No. 12, Nov, 1950 - No. 18, Dec, 1951 (Also see Two-Gun Western #5)
Marvel Comics/Atlas (MCI)

	GD25	FN65	NM94
12	14.00	41.00	110.00
13-18: 13-Tuska-a. 16-Colan-a. 18-Maneely-c	10.00	30.00	80.00

GUNHAWKS (Gunhawk No. 7)
Oct, 1972 - No. 7, October, 1973
Marvel Comics Group

	GD25	FN65	NM94
1,6: 1-Reno Jones, Kid Cassidy; Shores-c/a(p). 6-Kid Cassidy dies	1.50	4.50	12.00
2-5,7: 7-Reno Jones solo	1.10-	3.30	9.00

GUNHED
1990 - No. 3, 1991? ($4.95, 7-1/8 x 9-1/8, 52 pgs., bi-monthly)
Vix Comics

	GD25	FN65	NM94
1-3: Japanese sci-fi based on 1991 movie		2.00	5.00

GUNMASTER (Becomes Judo Master #89 on)
9/64 - No. 4, 1965; No. 84, 7/65 - No. 88, 3-4/66; No. 89, 10/67
Charlton Comics

	GD25	FN65	NM94
V1#1	2.50	7.50	24.00
2-4	2.00	6.00	16.00
V5#84-86: 84-Formerly Six-Gun Heroes	2.25	6.75	18.00
V5#87-89	1.50	4.50	12.00

NOTE: *Vol. 5 was originally cancelled with #88 (3-4/66). #89 on, became Judo Master, then later in 1967, Charlton issued #89 as a Gunmaster one-shot.*

GUN RUNNER
Oct, 1993 - No. 6, Mar, 1994 ($1.75, limited series)
Marvel Comics UK

	GD25	FN65	NM94
1-($2.75)-Polybagged w/4 trading cards; Spirits of Vengeance app.		1.10	2.75
2-6: 2-Ghost Rider & Blaze app.		.70	1.75

GUNS AGAINST GANGSTERS (True-To-Life Romances #8 on)
Sept-Oct, 1948 - No. 6, July-Aug, 1949; V2#1, Sept-Oct, 1949 - No. 2, 11-12/49
Curtis Publications/Novelty Press

	GD25	FN65	NM94
1-Toni & Greg Gayle begins by Schomburg; L.B. Cole-c	26.00	80.00	210.00
2-L.B. Cole-c	19.00	56.00	150.00
3-6, V2#1,2: 6-Toni Gayle-c	16.00	49.00	130.00

NOTE: ***L. B. Cole*** *c-1-6, V2#1, 2; a-1, 2, 3(2), 4-6.*

GUNSLINGER
No. 1220, Oct-Dec, 1961 (one-shot)
Dell Publishing Co.

	GD25	FN65	NM94
Four Color 1220--Photo-c	8.00	25.00	90.00

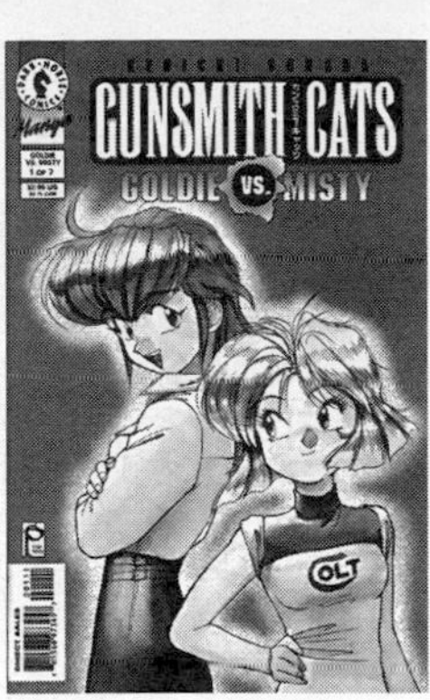

Gunsmith Cats: Goldie vs. Misty #1 © Kodansha, Ltd

Gunsmoke #25 © ATLAS

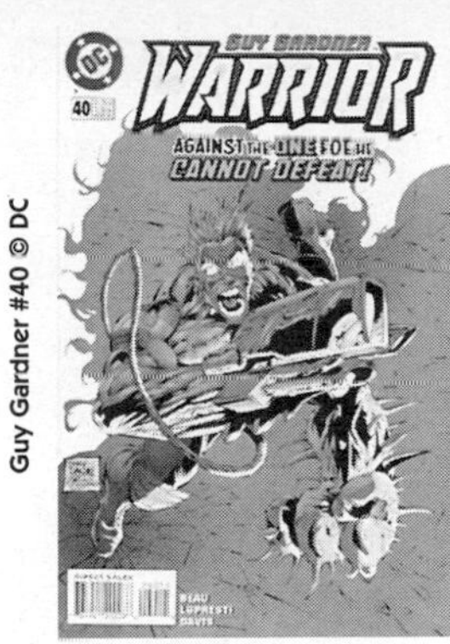

Guy Gardner #40 © DC

GD25 FN65 NM94

GUNSLINGER (Formerly Tex Dawson...)
No. 2, Apr, 1973 - No. 3, June, 1973
Marvel Comics Group

2,3 — 1.10 3.30 9.00

GUNSMITH CATS: GOLDIE VS. MISTY (Manga)
Nov, 1997 - No. 7 ($2.95, B&W, limited series)
Dark Horse Comics

1-7 — 2.95

GUNSMITH CATS: THE RETURN OF GRAY (Manga)
Aug, 1996 - No. 7, Feb, 1997 ($2.95, B&W, limited series)
Dark Horse Comics

1-7 — 1.20 3.00

GUNSMITH CATS: SHADES OF GRAY (Manga)
May, 1997 - No. 5, Sept, 1997 ($2.95, B&W, limited series)
Dark Horse Comics

1-5 — 1.20 3.00

GUNSMOKE (Blazing Stories of the West)
Apr-May, 1949 - No. 16, Jan, 1952
Western Comics (Youthful Magazines)

1-Gunsmoke & Masked Marvel begin by Ingels; Ingels bondage-c — 38.00 114.00 280.00
2-Ingels-c/a(2) — 24.00 71.00 175.00
3-Ingels bondage-c/a — 19.00 56.00 140.00
4-6: Ingels-c — 14.00 43.00 110.00
7-10 — 8.50 26.00 60.00
11-16: 15,16-Western/horror stories — 6.50 19.50 45.00

NOTE: ***Stallman** a-11, 14. **Wildey** a-15, 16.*

GUNSMOKE (TV)
No. 679, Feb, 1956 - No. 27, June-July, 1961; Feb, 1969 - No. 6, Feb, 1970
Dell Publishing Co./Gold Key (All have James Arness photo-c)

Four Color 679(#1) — 14.00 41.00 150.00
Four Color 720,769,797,844 (#2-5) — 6.40 19.00 70.00
6(11-1/57-58), 7 — 6.40 19.00 70.00
8,9,11,12-Williamson-a in all, 4 pgs. each — 7.00 22.00 80.00
10-Williamson/Crandall-a, 4 pgs. — 7.00 22.00 80.00
13-27 — 5.50 16.50 60.00
Gunsmoke Film Story (11/62-G.K. Giant) No. 30008-211 (scarce) — 25.00 75.00 200.00
1 (Gold Key) — 4.00 12.00 45.00
2-6('69-70) — 2.00 6.00 22.00

GUNSMOKE TRAIL
June, 1957 - No. 4, Dec, 1957
Ajax-Farrell Publ./Four Star Comic Corp.

1 — 8.50 26.00 60.00
2-4 — 5.70 17.00 35.00

GUNSMOKE WESTERN (Formerly Western Tales of Black Rider)
No. 32, Dec, 1955 - No. 77, July, 1963
Atlas Comics No. 32-35(CPS/NPI); Marvel No. 36 on

32-Baker & Drucker-a — 12.00 38.00 100.00
33,35,36-Williamson-a in each: 5,6 & 4 pgs. plus Drucker-a #33. 33-Kinstler-a? — 10.00 30.00 80.00
34-Baker-a, 4 pgs.; Kirby-c — 8.50 26.00 60.00
37-Davis-a(2); Williamson text illo — 8.50 26.00 60.00
38,39: 39-Williamson text illo (unsigned) — 6.50 19.50 45.00
40-Williamson/Mayo-a (4 pgs.) — 7.85 23.50 55.00
41,42,45,46,48,49,52-54,57,58,60: 49,52-Kid from Texas story. 57-1st Two Gun Kid by Severin. 60-Sam Hawk app. in Kid Colt — 5.00 15.00 30.00
43,44-Torres-a — 5.35 16.00 32.00
47-Kirby-a — 5.70 17.00 35.00
50-Kirby, Crandall-a — 6.50 19.50 45.00
51,59-Kirby-a — 5.70 17.00 35.00
55,56-Matt Baker-a — 5.70 17.00 40.00
61-Crandall-a — 5.70 17.00 40.00
62-67,69,71,73,77-Kirby-a — 5.00 15.00 30.00
68,70,74-76 — 2.50 7.50 25.00
72-Origin Kid Colt — 3.00 9.00 30.00

NOTE: ***Colan** a-35-37, 39, 72, 76. **Davis** a-37, 52, 54, 55; c-50, 54. **Ditko** a-66; c-56p. **Drucker** a-.32-34. **Heath** c-33. **Jack Keller** a-35, 40, 60, 72; c-72. **Kirby** a-47, 50, 51, 59, 62(3), 63-67, 69, 71, 73, 77; c-56(w/**Ditko**),57, 58, 60, 61(w/**Ayers**), 62, 63, 66, 68, 69, 71-77. **Robinson** a-35. **Severin** a-35, 59-61; c-34, 35, 39, 42, 43. **Tuska** a-34. **Wildey** a-10, 37, 42, 56, 57. Kid Colt in all. Two-Gun Kid in No. 57, 59, 60-63. Wyatt Earp in No. 45, 48, 49, 52, 54, 55, 58.*

GUNS OF FACT & FICTION (Also see A-1 Comics)
No. 13, 1948 (one-shot)
Magazine Enterprises

A-1 13-Used in **SOTI**, pg. 19; Ingels & J. Craig-a — 25.00 75.00 180.00

GUN THAT WON THE WEST, THE
1956 (Giveaway, 24 pgs.)
Winchester-Western Division & Olin Mathieson Chemical Corp.

nn-Painted-c — 5.00 15.00 30.00

GUY GARDNER (Guy Gardner: Warrior #17 on)(Also see Green Lantern #59)
Oct, 1992 - No. 44, July, 1996 ($1.25/$1.50/$1.75)
DC Comics

1-24,0,26-30: 1-Staton-c/a(p) begins. 6-Guy vs. Hal Jordan. 8-Vs. Lobo-c/story. 15-JLA x-over. 16-Begin $1.50-c. 18-Begin 4-part Emerald Fallout story; splash page x-over GL #50. 18-21-Vs. Hal Jordan. 24-(9/94)-Zero Hour. 0-(10/94) — 1.50
25 (11/94, $2.50, 52 pgs.) — 1.00 2.50
29 ($2.95)-Gatefold-c — 1.20 3.00
29-Variant-c (Edward Hopper's Nighthawks) — 1.50
31-44: 31-$1.75-c begins. 40-Gorilla Grodd-c/app. 44-Parallax-c/app. (1 pg.) — .70 1.75
Annual 1 (1995, $3.50)-Year One story — 1.40 3.50
Annual 2 (1996, $2.95)-Legends of the Dead Earth story — 1.20 3.00

GUY GARDNER REBORN
1992 - Book 3, 1992 ($4.95, limited series)
DC Comics

1-3: Staton-c/a(p). 1-Lobo-c/cameo. 2,3-Lobo-c/s — 2.00 5.00

GYPSY COLT
No. 568, June, 1954 (one-shot)
Dell Publishing Co.

Four Color 568--Movie — 3.60 11.00 40.00

GYRO GEARLOOSE (See Dynabrite Comics, Walt Disney's C&S #140 & Walt Disney Showcase #18)
No. 1047, Nov-Jan/1959-60 - May-July, 1962 (Disney)
Dell Publishing Co.

Four Color 1047 (No. 1)-All Barks-c/a — 18.00 55.00 200.00
Four Color 1095,1184-All by Carl Barks — 10.00 30.00 110.00
Four Color 1267-Barks c/a, 4 pgs. — 7.00 20.00 75.00
01329-207 (#1, 5-7/62)-Barks-c only (intended as 4-Color 1329?) — 4.50 13.50 50.00

HACKER FILES, THE
Aug, 1992 - No. 12, July, 1993 ($1.95)
DC Comics

1-12: 1-Sutton-a(p) begins; computer generated-c — .80 2.00

HAGAR THE HORRIBLE (See Comics Reading Libraries)

HA HA COMICS (Teepee Tim No. 100 on; also see Giggle Comics)
Oct, 1943 - No. 99, Jan, 1955
Scope Mag.(Creston Publ.) No. 1-80/American Comics Group

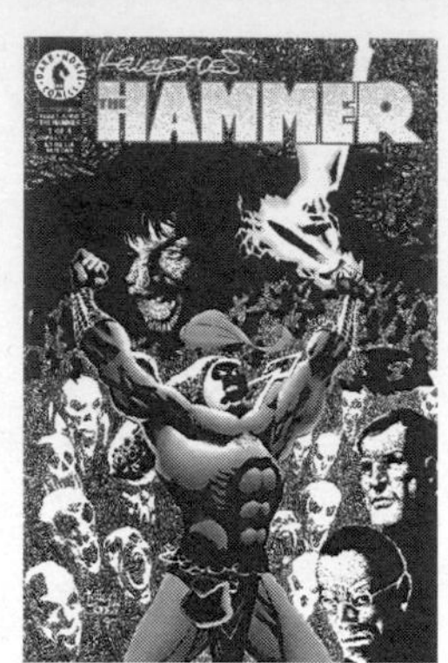

The Hammer #1 © Kelley Jones

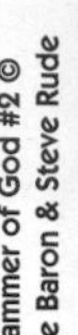
Hammer of God #2 © Mike Baron & Steve Rude

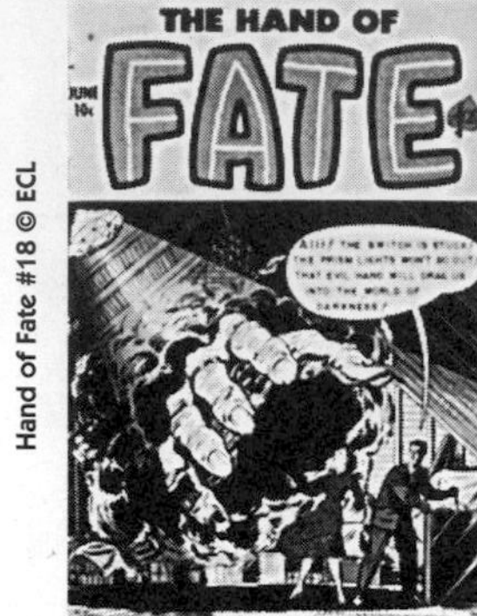

Hand of Fate #18 © ECL

	GD25	FN65	NM94
1-Funny animal	25.00	75.00	200.00
2	12.00	36.00	95.00
3-5: Ken Hultgren-a begins?	8.75	26.25	70.00
6-10	7.85	23.50	55.00
11-20: 14-Infinity-c	5.70	17.00	40.00
21-40	5.35	16.00	32.00
41-94,96-99: 49-X-Mas-c	4.25	13.00	28.00
95-3-D effect-c	11.30	34.00	90.00

HAIR BEAR BUNCH, THE (TV) (See Fun-In No. 13)
Feb, 1972 - No. 9, Feb, 1974 (Hanna-Barbera)
Gold Key

	GD25	FN65	NM94
1	3.00	9.00	30.00
2-9	1.85	5.50	15.00

HALLELUJAH TRAIL, THE (See Movie Classics)

HALL OF FAME FEATURING THE T.H.U.N.D.E.R. AGENTS
May, 1983 - No. 3, Dec, 1983
JC Productions(Archie Comics Group)

	GD25	FN65	NM94
1-3: Thunder Agents-r(Crandall, Tuska, Wood-a)			1.25

HALLOWEEN HORROR
Oct, 1987 (Seduction of the Innocent #7)($1.75)
Eclipse Comics

	GD25	FN65	NM94
1-Pre-code horror-r		.75	1.80

HALLOWEEN MEGAZINE
Dec, 1996 ($3.95, one-shot, 96 pgs.)
Marvel Comics

	GD25	FN65	NM94
1-Reprints Tomb of Dracula		1.60	4.00

HALO, AN ANGEL'S STORY
Apr, 1996 - No. 4, Sept, 1996 ($2.95, limited series)
Sirius Entertainment

	GD25	FN65	NM94
1-4: Knowles-c/a/scripts		1.20	3.00
TPB ($12.95) r/#1-4			12.95

HALO JONES (See The Ballad of...)

HAMMER, THE
Oct, 1997 - No. 4 ($2.95, limited series)
Dark Horse Comics

	GD25	FN65	NM94
1-4-Kelley Jones-s/c/a/		1.20	3.00

HAMMERLOCKE
Sept, 1992 - No. 9, May, 1993 ($1.75, limited series)
DC Comics

	GD25	FN65	NM94
1-($2.50, 52 pgs.)-Chris Sprouse-c/a in all		1.00	2.50
2-9		.70	1.75

HAMMER OF GOD (Also see Nexus)
Feb, 1990 - No. 4, May, 1990 ($1.95, limited series)
First Comics

	GD25	FN65	NM94
1-4		.80	2.00

HAMMER OF GOD: BUTCH
May, 1994 - No. 4, Aug, 1994 ($2.50, limited series)
First Comics

	GD25	FN65	NM94
1-3		1.00	2.50

HAMMER OF GOD: PENTATHLON
Jan, 1994 ($2.50, one shot)
First Comics

	GD25	FN65	NM94
1-character from Nexus		1.00	2.50

HAMMER OF GOD: SWORD OF JUSTICE
Feb 1991 - Mar 1991 ($4.95, limited series, squarebound, 52 pgs.)
First Comics

	GD25	FN65	NM94
V2#1,2		2.00	5.00

HANDBOOK OF THE CONAN UNIVERSE, THE
June, 1985 ($1.25, one-shot)
Marvel Comics

	GD25	FN65	NM94
1-Kaluta-c.			1.25

HAND OF FATE (Formerly Men Against Crime)
No. 8, Dec, 1951 - No. 26, March, 1955 (Weird/horror stories)(Two #25's)
Ace Magazines

	GD25	FN65	NM94
8-Surrealistic text story	30.00	90.00	230.00
9,10	17.00	51.00	125.00
11-18,20,22,23	13.50	41.00	95.00
19-Bondage, hypo needle scenes	15.00	45.00	110.00
21-Necronomicon story; drug belladonna used	17.00	51.00	120.00
24-Electric chair-c	21.00	64.00	160.00
25a(11/54), 25b(12/54)-Both have Cameron-a	10.00	30.00	80.00
26-Nostrand-a; exist?	13.50	41.00	95.00

NOTE: ***Cameron*** *a-9, 10, 19-25a, 25b; c-13.* ***Sekowsky*** *a-8, 9, 13, 14.*

HAND OF FATE
Feb, 1988 - No. 3, Apr, 1988 ($1.75/$2.00, Baxter paper)
Eclipse Comics

	GD25	FN65	NM94
1,2		.90	1.75
3-$2.00-c; B&W		.80	2.00

HANDS OF THE DRAGON
June, 1975
Seaboard Periodicals (Atlas)

	GD25	FN65	NM94
1-Origin; Mooney inks		1.20	3.00

HANGMAN COMICS (Special Comics No. 1; Black Hood No. 9 on)
(Also see Flyman, Mighty Comics, Mighty Crusaders & Pep Comics)
No. 2, Spring, 1942 - No. 8, Fall, 1943
MLJ Magazines

	GD25	FN65	NM94
2-The Hangman, Boy Buddies begin	139.00	417.00	1250.00
3-8: 3-Beheading splash pg.; 1st Nazi war-c. 5-1st Jap war-c. 8-2nd app. Super Duck (ties w/Jolly Jingles #11)	82.00	246.00	730.00

NOTE: ***Fuje*** *a-7(3), 8(3); c-3.* ***Reinman*** *c/a-3. Bondage c-3.* ***Sahle*** *c-6.*

HANK
1946
Pentagon Publishing Co.

	GD25	FN65	NM94
nn-Coulton Waugh's newspaper reprint	6.00	18.00	42.00

HANNA-BARBERA (See Golden Comics Digest No. 2, 7, 11)

HANNA-BARBERA ALL-STARS
Oct, 1995 - No. 6, Sept, 1996 ($1.50, bi-monthly)
Archie Publications

	GD25	FN65	NM94
1-6			1.50

HANNA-BARBERA BAND WAGON (TV)
Oct, 1962 - No. 3, Apr, 1963
Gold Key

	GD25	FN65	NM94
1-Giant, 84 pgs. 1-Augie Doggie & Lippy the Lion app. (pre-#1's)	11.00	33.00	120.00
2-Giant, 84 pgs.	8.00	25.00	90.00
3-Regular size; Mr. & Mrs. J. Evil Scientist app. (pre-#1) & Snagglepuss app.	5.50	16.50	60.00

HANNA-BARBERA GIANT SIZE
Oct, 1992 ($2.25, 68 pgs.)
Harvey Comics

	GD25	FN65	NM94
V2#1-Flintstones, Yogi Bear, Magilla Gorilla, Huckleberry Hound, Quick Draw McGraw, Yakky Doodle & Chopper, Jetsons & others		1.20	3.00

HANNA-BARBERA HI-ADVENTURE HEROES (See Hi-Adventure...)

HANNA-BARBERA PARADE (TV)

Hanna-Barbera Super TV Heroes #1 © H-B

Hap Hazard Comics #1 © ACE

Harbinger #9 © Voyager Comm.

	GD25	FN65	NM94

Sept, 1971 - No. 10, Dec, 1972
Charlton Comics

1	6.00	18.00	60.00
2-6,8-10	3.00	9.00	30.00
7-(52 pgs.)- "Summer Picnic"	4.50	13.50	45.00

NOTE: *No. 4 (1/72) went on sale late in 1972 with the January 1973 issues.*

HANNA-BARBERA PRESENTS
Nov, 1995 - Present ($1.50, bi-monthly
Archie Publications

1-6: 2-Wacky Races. 4-Quick Draw McGraw & Magilla Gorilla. 5-A Pup Named Scooby-Doo 1.50

HANNA-BARBERA SPOTLIGHT (See Spotlight)

HANNA-BARBERA SUPER TV HEROES (TV)
Apr, 1968 - No. 7, Oct, 1969 (Hanna-Barbera)
Gold Key

1-The Birdman, The Herculoids(ends #6; not in #2), Moby Dick, Young Samson & Goliath(ends #2,4), and The Mighty Mightor begin; Spiegle-a in all	14.00	41.00	150.00
2-The Galaxy Trio app.; Shazzan begins; 12 & 15 cent versions exist	9.00	27.00	100.00
3-7: 3,6,7-The Space Ghost app.	8.50	25.50	95.00

HANNA-BARBERA TV FUN FAVORITES (See Golden Comics Digest #2,7,11)

HANNA-BARBERA (TV STARS) (See TV Stars)

HANS BRINKER (Disney)
No. 1273, Feb, 1962 (one-shot)
Dell Publishing Co.

Four Color 1273-Movie, photo-c	5.50	16.50	60.00

HANS CHRISTIAN ANDERSEN
1953 (100 pgs., Special Issue)
Ziff-Davis Publ. Co.

nn-Danny Kaye (movie)-Photo-c; fairy tales	14.00	41.00	110.00

HANSEL & GRETEL
No. 590, Oct, 1954 (one-shot)
Dell Publishing Co.

Four Color 590-Partial photo-c	5.50	16.50	60.00

HANSI, THE GIRL WHO LOVED THE SWASTIKA
1973, 1976 (39¢/49¢)
Spire Christian Comics (Fleming H. Revell Co.)

nn	1.00	3.00	8.00

HAP HAZARD COMICS (Real Love No. 25 on)
Summer, 1944 - No. 24, Feb, 1949 (#1-6 are quarterly issues)
Ace Magazines (Readers' Research)

1	10.00	30.00	80.00
2	5.70	17.00	40.00
3-10	4.25	13.00	28.00
11-13,15-24	4.00	11.00	22.00
14-Feldstein-c (4/47)	6.50	19.50	45.00

HAP HOPPER (See Comics Revue No. 2)

HAPPIEST MILLIONAIRE, THE (See Movie Comics)

HAPPINESS AND HEALING FOR YOU (Also see Oral Roberts'...)
1955 (36 pgs., slick cover) (Oral Roberts Giveaway)
Commercial Comics

nn	7.15	21.50	50.00

NOTE: *The success of this book prompted Oral Roberts to go into the publishing business himself to produce his own material.*

HAPPI TIM (See March of Comics No. 182)

HAPPY BIRTHDAY MARTHA WASHINGTON (Also see Give Me Liberty, Martha Washington Goes To War, & Martha Washington Stranded In Space)
Mar, 1995 ($2.95, one-shot)
Dark Horse Comics

1-Miller script; Gibbons-c/a		1.20	3.00

HAPPY COMICS (Happy Rabbit No. 41 on)
Aug, 1943 - No. 40, Dec, 1950 (Companion to Goofy Comics)
Nedor Publ./Standard Comics (Animated Cartoons)

1-Funny animal	21.00	64.00	170.00
2	10.50	32.00	85.00
3-10	7.85	23.50	55.00
11-19	5.70	17.00	40.00
20-31,34-37-Frazetta text illos in all (2 in #34&35, 3 in #27,28,30). 27-Al Fago-a	7.15	21.50	50.00
32-Frazetta-a, 7 pgs. plus 2 text illos; Roussos-a	15.00	45.00	120.00
33-Frazetta-a(2), 6 pgs. each (Scarce)	21.00	64.00	170.00
38-40	4.15	12.50	25.00

HAPPY DAYS (TV)(See Kite Fun Book)
Mar, 1979 - No. 6, Feb, 1980
Gold Key

1-Photo-c of TV cast	1.00	3.00	8.00
2-6		2.00	5.00

HAPPY HOLIDAY (See March of Comics No. 181)

HAPPY HOULIHANS (Saddle Justice No. 3 on; see Blackstone, The Magician Detective)
Fall, 1947 - No. 2, Winter, 1947-48
E. C. Comics

1-Origin Moon Girl (same date as Moon Girl #1)	36.00	108.00	310.00
2	20.00	60.00	160.00

HAPPY JACK
Aug, 1957 - No. 2, Nov, 1957
Red Top (Decker)

V1#1,2	4.00	10.00	20.00

HAPPY JACK HOWARD
1957
Red Top (Farrell)/Decker

nn-Reprints Handy Andy story from E. C. Dandy Comics #5, renamed "Happy Jack"	4.00	12.00	24.00

HAPPY RABBIT (Formerly Happy Comics)
No. 41, Feb, 1951 - No. 48, April, 1952
Standard Comics (Animated Cartoons)

41-Funny animal	5.00	15.00	30.00
42-48	4.00	10.00	20.00

HARBINGER (Also see Unity)
Jan, 1992 - No. 41, June, 1995 ($1.95/$2.50)
Valiant

0-(Advance)		1.20	3.00
1-1st app.		1.00	2.50
2,3		.80	2.00
4-Low print run		1.00	2.50
5-10: 8,9-Unity x-overs. 8-Miller-c. 9-Simonson-c. 10-1st app. H.A.R.D Corps (10/92)		.80	2.00
11-16: 14-1st app. Stronghold		.80	2.00
17-24,26-41: 18-Intro Screen. 19-1st app. Stunner. 22-Archer & Armstrong app. 24-Cover similar to #1. 26-Intro New Harbingers. 29-Bound-in trading card. 30-H.A.R.D. Corps app. 32-Eternal Warrior app. 33-Dr. Eclipse app.		.80	2.00
25-($3.50, 52 pgs.)-Harada vs. Sting		.80	2.00
...Files 1,2 (8/94,2/95 $2.50)		.80	2.00

Trade paperback nn (11/92, $9.95)-Reprints #1-4 & comes polybagged with a

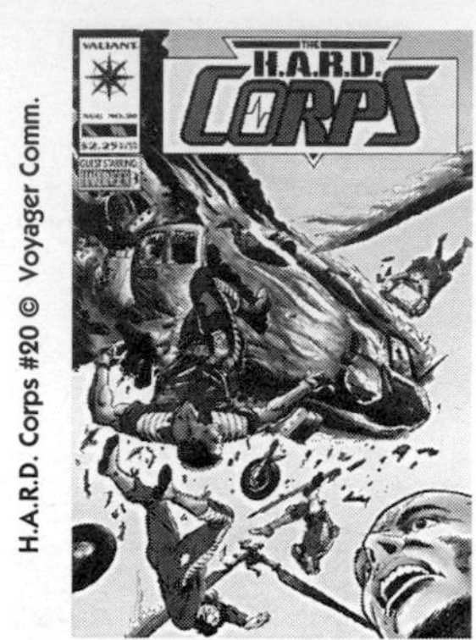

H.A.R.D. Corps #20 © Voyager Comm.

Hardware #21 © Milestone Media

Hari Kari: The Silence of Evil #0 © Blackout

GD25 FN65 NM94

copy of Harbinger #0 w/new-c. 1.25 3.75 10.00
NOTE: *Issues 1-6 have coupons with origin of Harada and are redeemable for Harbinger #0.*

HARD BOILED
9/90 - #3, 1992 ($4.95/$5.95, 8 1/2 x11", limited series, mature)
Dark Horse Comics

1-($4.95)-Miller scripts; Darrow-c/a; sexually explicit & violent 2.40 6.00
2,3-($5.95) 1.00 2.80 7.00

HARDCASE (See Break Thru, Flood Relief & Ultraforce, 1st Series)
June, 1993 - No. 26, Aug, 1995 ($1.95/$2.50)
Malibu Comics (Ultraverse)

1-Intro Hardcase; Dave Gibbons-c; has coupon for Ultraverse Premiere #0; Jim Callahan-a(p) begin, ends #3 .80 2.00
1-With coupon missing 1.00
1-Platinum Edition 1.00 2.50
1-Holographic Cover Edition; 1st full-c holograph tied w/Prime 1 & Strangers 1 1.60 4.00
1-Ultra Limited silver foil-c 1.00 2.50
2,3-Callahan-a 1.00 2.50
2-($2.50)-Newsstand edition bagged w/trading card 1.00 2.50
4,6-15, 17-19: 4-Strangers app. 7-Break-Thru x-over. 8-Solution app. 9-Vs. Turf. 12-Silver foil logo, wraparound-c. 17-Prime app. .80 2.00
5-($2.50, 48 pgs.)-Rune flip-c/story by B. Smith (3 pgs.) 1.00 2.50
16 ($3.50, 68 pgs.)-Rune pin-up 1.40 3.50
20-26: 20-$2.50-c begins. 23-Loki app. 1.00 2.50
NOTE: ***Perez** a-8(2); c-20i.*

H.A.R.D. CORPS, THE (See Harbinger #10)
Dec, 1992 - No. 30, Feb, 1995 ($2.25) (Harbinger spin-off)
Valiant

1-(Advance) 1.20 3.00
1-($2.50)-Gatefold-c by Jim Lee & Bob Layton 1.00 2.50
1-Gold variant 1.20 3.00
2-6: 5-Bloodshot-c/story cont'd from Bloodshot #3 .90 2.25
5-Variant edition; came w/Comic Defense System 1.00 2.50
7-30: 10-Turok app. 17-vs. Armorines. 18-Bound-in trading card. 20-Harbinger app. .90 2.25

HARDWARE
Apr, 1993 - No. 50, Apr, 1997 ($1.50/$1.75/$2.50)
DC Comics (Milestone)

1-($2.95)-Collector's Edition polybagged w/poster & trading card (direct sale only) 1.20 3.00
1-Platinum Edition 2.00 5.00
1-15,17-19: 11-Shadow War x-over. 11,14-Simonson-c. 12-Buckler-a(p). 17-Worlds Collide Pt. 2. 18-Simonson-c; Worlds Collide Pt. 9. 15-1st Humberto Ramos DC work 1.50
16-($3.95, 52 pgs.)-Collector's Edition w/gatefold 2nd cover by Byrne; new armor; Icon app. 1.60 4.00
16-($2.50, 52 pgs.)-Newsstand Edition 1.00 2.50
20-24, 26-28: 20-Begin $1.75-c begins .70 1.75
25-($2.95, 52 pgs.) 1.20 3.00
29-49: 29-Begin $2.50-c. 49-Moebius-c 1.00 2.50
50-($3.95, 52 pgs) 3.95

HARDY BOYS, THE (Disney
No. 760, Dec, 1956 - No. 964, Jan, 1959 (Mickey Mouse Club)
Dell Publishing Co.

Four Color 760 (#1)-Photo-c 10.00 30.00 110.00
Four Color 830(8/57), 887(1/58), 964-Photo-c 9.00 27.00 100.00

HARDY BOYS, THE (TV)
Apr, 1970 - No. 4, Jan, 1971
Gold Key

1 2.75 8.00 30.00

GD25 FN65 NM94

2-4 1.80 5.50 20.00

HARI KARI (See The Death of Hari Kari)
No. 0, 1995 -No. 1, 1995 ($2.95)
Blackout Comics

0,1: Both have pin-ups. 1-Variant-c. 1.20 3.00
1-($9.95)-Commemorative Ed. -New-c; foil stamped; 2,500 copies. 1.25 3.75 10.00

HARI KARI BLOODSHED
1997 ($2.95)
Blackout Comics

1-Virkaitis-s 1.20 3.00
1-($9.95)-Variant-c 1.25 3.75 10.00

HARI KARI LIVE & UNTAMED
No. 0, 1996 ($2.95, one-shot)
Blackout Comics

0-w/photo layout 1.20 3.00
0-($9.95)-Variant-c 1.25 3.75 10.00

HARI KARI POSSESSED BY EVIL
1997($2.95, B&W, one-shot)
Blackout Comics

1 1.20 3.00

HARI KARI PRIVATE GALLERY
No. 0, Feb, 1996 ($2.95, one-shot)
Blackout Comics

0-pin-ups 1.20 3.00
0-($9.95)-Commemorative Ed. 1.25 3.75 10.00

HARI KARI REBIRTH
1996 ($2.95, one-shot)
Blackout Comics

1 Virkaitis-s 1.20 3.00
1-($9.95)-Variant Edition 1.25 3.75 10.00

HARI KARI: RESURRECTION
1997 ($2.95, one-shot)
Blackout Comics

1 Virkaitis-s 1.20 3.00
1-($9.95)-Nude variant Edition 1.25 3.75 10.00

HARI KARI: SEXY SUMMER RAMPAGE
1997 ($2.95, one-shot)
Blackout Comics

1 Pin-ups 1.20 3.00
1-($9.95)-Variant Edition 1.25 3.75 10.00

HARI KARI: THE BEGINNING
1996 ($2.95)
Blackout Comics

1-Origin 1.20 3.00

HARI KARI THE DIARY OF KARI SUN
1997 ($2.95, one-shot)
Blackout Comics

1/2-Text w/art 1.20 3.00
1/2-($9.95) Variant-c 1.25 3.75 10.00

HARI KARI: THE SILENCE OF EVIL
No. 0, 1996 ($2.95, bi-monthly)
Blackout Comics

0 1.20 3.00

HARLAN ELLISON'S DREAM CORRIDOR
Mar, 1995 - No. 5, July, 1995 ($2.95, anthology)
Dark Horse Comics

Harlan Ellison's Dream Corridor #1 © Harlan Ellison

Harvey Comics Hits #48 © HARV

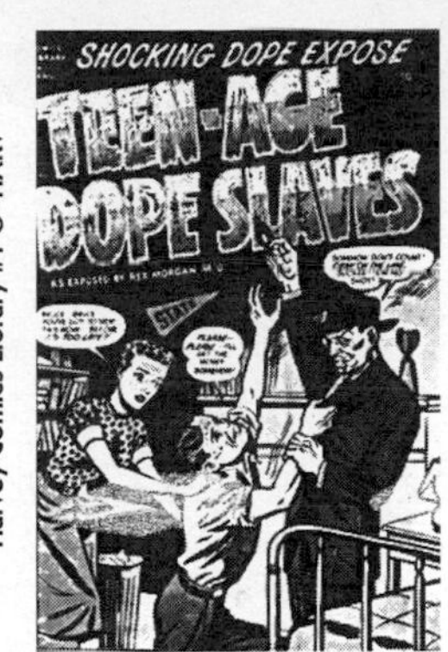

Harvey Comics Library #1 © HARV

GD25 FN65 NM94

1-5: Adaptation of Ellison stories. 1-4-Byrne-a. 1.20 3.00
Special (1/95, $4.95) 2.00 5.00
Trade paperback-(1996, $18.95, 192 pgs)-r/#1-5 & Special #1 19.00

HARLAN ELLISON'S DREAM CORRIDOR QUARTERLY
V2#1, Aug, 1996 ($5.95, anthology, squarebound)
Dark Horse Comics

V2#1-Adaptations of Ellison's stories w/new material; Neal Adams-a
2.40 6.00

HARLEM GLOBETROTTERS (TV) (See Fun-In No. 8, 10)
Apr, 1972 - No. 12, Jan, 1975 (Hanna-Barbera)
Gold Key

1 1.80 5.50 20.00
2-5 1.50 4.50 12.00
6-12 1.10 3.30 9.00
4.00
NOTE: *#4, 8, and 12 contain 16 extra pages of advertising.*

HAROLD TEEN (See Popular Comics, & Super Comics)
No. 2, 1942 - No. 209, Jan, 1949
Dell Publishing Co.

Four Color 2 24.00 71.00 260.00
Four Color 209 3.60 11.00 40.00

HARRIERS
June, 1995 - No. 3, 1995 ($2.50)
Entity Comics

1-Foil-c; polybagged w/PC game 1.20 3.00
1-3 ($2.50) 1.00 2.50

HARROWERS, THE (See Clive Barker's...)

HARSH REALM
1994 ($2.95, one-shot)
Harris Comics

1-4: Painted-c 1.20 3.00

HARVEY
Oct, 1970; No. 2, 12/70; No. 3, 6/72 - No. 6, 12/72
Marvel Comics

1 6.00 18.00 60.00
2-6 3.60 10.80 36.00

HARVEY COLLECTORS COMICS (Richie Rich Collectors Comics #10 on, cover title only)
Sept, 1975 - No. 15, Jan, 1978; No. 16, Oct, 1979 (52 pgs.)
Harvey Publications

1-Reprints Richie Rich #1,2 1.25 3.75 10.00
2-10: 7-Splash pg. shows-c to Friendly Ghost Casper #1 2.40 6.00
11-16: 16-Sad Sack-r 1.60 4.00
NOTE: *All reprints: Casper-#2, 7, Richie Rich-#1, 3, 5, 6, 8-15, Sad Sack-#16. Wendy-#4. #6 titled 'Richie Rich...'on inside.*

HARVEY COMICS HITS (Formerly Joe Palooka #50)
No. 51, Oct, 1951 - No. 62, Apr, 1953
Harvey Publications

51-The Phantom 23.00 68.00 180.00
52-Steve Canyon's Air Power(Air Force sponsored) 10.00 30.00 80.00
53-Mandrake the Magician 17.00 51.00 135.00
54-Tim Tyler's Tales of Jungle Terror 9.50 28.00 75.00
55-Love Stories of Mary Worth 5.35 16.00 32.00
56-The Phantom; bondage-c 19.50 58.00 155.00
57-Rip Kirby Exposes the Kidnap Racket; entire book by Alex Raymond
12.00 36.00 95.00
58-Girls in White (nurses stories) 5.00 15.00 30.00
59-Tales of the Invisible featuring Scarlet O'Neil 8.50 26.00 60.00
60-Paramount Animated Comics #1 (2nd app. Baby Huey); 1st Harvey app. Baby Huey & Casper the Friendly Ghost; 1st app. Herman & Catnip (c/story) & Buzzy the Crow (9/52) 33.00 98.00 260.00
61-Casper the Friendly Ghost #6 (2nd Harvey Casper, 10/52)-Casper-c
33.00 100.00 265.00
62-Paramount Animated Comics #2; Herman & Catnip, Baby Huey & Buzzy the Crow 9.50 28.00 75.00

HARVEY COMICS LIBRARY
Apr, 1952 - No. 2, 1952
Harvey Publications

1-Teen-Age Dope Slaves as exposed by Rex Morgan, M.D.; drug propaganda story; used in **SOTI**, pg. 27 68.00 206.00 575.00
2-Dick Tracy Presents Sparkle Plenty in "Blackmail Terror"
14.00 41.00 110.00

HARVEY COMICS SPOTLIGHT
Sept, 1987 - No. 4, Mar, 1988 (75¢/$1.00)
Harvey Comics

1-New material; begin 75¢, ends #3; Sand Sack 1.20 3.00
2-4: 2,4-All new material. 2-Baby Huey. 3-Little Dot; contains reprints w/5 pg. new story. 4-$1.00-c; Little Audrey .80 2.00
NOTE: No. 5 was advertised but not published.

HARVEY HITS
Sept, 1957 - No. 122, Nov, 1967
Harvey Publications

1-The Phantom 21.00 63.00 210.00
2-Rags Rabbit (10/57) 2.50 7.50 20.00
3-Richie Rich (11/57)-r/Little Dot; 1st book devoted to Richie Rich; see Little Dot for 1st app. 58.00 175.00 700.00
4-Little Dot's Uncles (12/57) 12.00 36.00 120.00
5-Stevie Mazie's Boy Friend (1/58) 1.75 5.25 14.00
6-The Phantom (2/58); Kirby-c; 2pg. Powell-a 15.00 45.00 150.00
7-Wendy the Good Little Witch (3/58, pre-dates Wendy #1; 1st book devoted to Wendy) 14.00 42.00 140.00
8-Sad Sack's Army Life; George Baker-c 4.50 13.50 45.00
9-Richie Rich's Golden Deeds; reprints (2nd book devoted to Richie Rich)
31.00 93.00 340.00
10-Little Lotta's Lunch Box 8.00 24.00 80.00
11-Little Audrey Summer Fun (7/58) 6.00 18.00 60.00
12-The Phantom; Kirby-c; 2pg. Powell-a (8/58) 12.00 36.00 120.00
13-Little Dot's Uncles (9/58); Richie Rich 1pg. 7.50 22.50 75.00
14-Herman & Katnip (10/58, TV/movies) 2.25 6.75 18.00
15-The Phantom (12/58)-1 pg. origin 12.00 36.00 120.00
16-Wendy the Good Little Witch (1/59); Casper app. 7.50 22.50 75.00
17-Sad Sack's Army Life (2/59) 4.00 12.00 40.00
18-Buzzy & the Crow 2.50 7.50 20.00
19-Little Audrey (4/59) 3.50 10.50 35.00
20-Casper & Spooky 4.50 13.50 45.00
21-Wendy the Witch 4.50 13.50 45.00
22-Sad Sack's Army Life 3.20 9.60 32.00
23-Wendy the Witch (8/59) 4.50 13.50 45.00
24-Little Dot's Uncles (9/59); Richie Rich 1pg. 6.00 18.00 60.00
25-Herman & Katnip (10/59) 1.75 5.25 14.00
26-The Phantom (11/59) 9.50 28.50 95.00
27-Wendy the Good Little Witch (12/59) 4.00 12.00 40.00
28-Sad Sack's Army Life (1/60) 2.50 7.50 20.00
29-Harvey-Toon (No.1)('60); Casper, Buzzy 3.00 9.00 30.00
30-Wendy the Witch (3/60) 4.50 13.50 45.00
31-Herman & Katnip (4/60) 1.10 3.30 9.00
32-Sad Sack's Army Life (5/60) 2.00 6.00 16.00
33-Wendy the Witch (6/60) 4.50 13.50 45.00
34-Harvey-Toon (7/60) 2.00 6.00 16.00
35-Funday Funnies (8/60) 1.10 3.30 9.00
36-The Phantom (1960) 8.50 25.50 85.00
37-Casper & Nightmare 3.20 9.60 32.00

Harvey Hits #107 © HARV

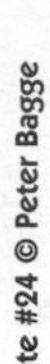

Hate #24 © Peter Bagge

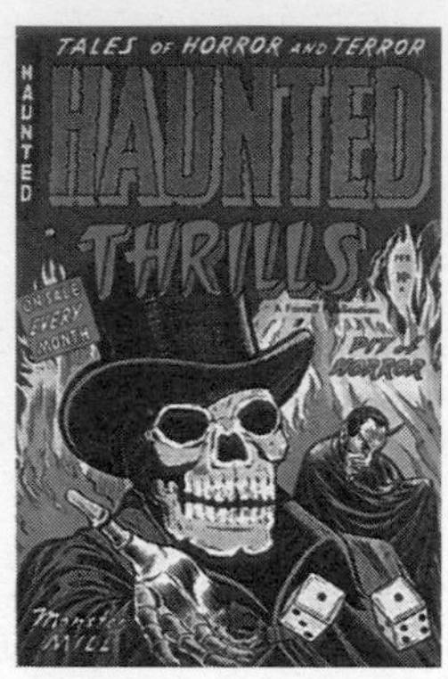

Haunted Thrills #6 © AJAX

	GD25	FN65	NM94
38-Harvey-Toon	2.00	6.00	16.00
39-Sad Sack's Army Life (12/60)	2.00	6.00	16.00
40-Funday Funnies (1/61)		2.40	6.00
41-Herman & Katnip	1.00	3.00	8.00
42-Harvey-Toon (3/61)	1.50	4.50	12.00
43-Sad Sack's Army Life (4/61)	1.75	5.25	14.00
44-The Phantom (5/61)	8.00	24.00	80.00
45-Casper & Nightmare	2.50	7.50	24.00
46-Harvey-Toon (7/61)	1.25	3.75	10.00
47-Sad Sack's Army Life (8/61)	1.75	5.25	14.00
48-The Phantom (9/61)	8.00	24.00	80.00
49-Stumbo the Giant (1st app. in Hot Stuff)	7.00	21.00	70.00
50-Harvey-Toon (11/61)	1.25	3.75	10.00
51-Sad Sack's Army Life (12/61)	1.75	5.25	14.00
52-Casper & Nightmare	2.50	7.50	24.00
53-Harvey-Toons (2/62)	1.00	3.00	8.00
54-Stumbo the Giant	3.20	9.60	32.00
55-Sad Sack's Army Life (4/62)	1.75	5.25	14.00
56-Casper & Nightmare	2.50	7.50	24.00
57-Stumbo the Giant	3.20	9.60	32.00
58-Sad Sack's Army Life	1.75	5.25	14.00
59-Casper & Nightmare (7/62)	2.50	7.50	24.00
60-Stumbo the Giant (9/62)	3.20	9.60	32.00
61-Sad Sack's Army Life	1.50	4.50	12.00
62-Casper & Nightmare	2.50	7.50	20.00
63-Stumbo the Giant	2.80	8.40	28.00
64-Sad Sack's Army Life (1/63)	1.50	4.50	12.00
65-Casper & Nightmare	2.50	7.50	20.00
66-Stumbo The Giant (3/63)	2.80	8.40	28.00
67-Sad Sack's Army Life (4/63)	1.50	4.50	12.00
68-Casper & Nightmare	2.50	7.50	20.00
69-Stumbo the Giant (6/63)	2.80	8.40	28.00
70-Sad Sack's Army Life (7/63)	1.50	4.50	12.00
71-Casper & Nightmare (8/63)	1.75	5.25	14.00
72-Stumbo the Giant	2.80	8.40	28.00
73-Little Sad Sack (10/63)	1.50	4.50	12.00
74-Sad Sack's Muttsy... (11/63)	1.50	4.50	12.00
75-Casper & Nightmare	1.75	5.25	14.00
76-Little Sad Sack	1.50	4.50	12.00
77-Sad Sack's Muttsy...	1.50	4.50	12.00
78-Stumbo the Giant (3/64); JFK caricature	2.80	8.40	28.00
79-87: 79-Little Sad Sack (4/64). 80-Sad Sack's Muttsy... (5/64). 81-Little Sad Sack. 82-Sad Sack's Muttsy... 83-Little Sad Sack(8/64). 84-Sad Sack's Muttsy... 85-Gabby Gob (#1)(10/64). 86-G. I. Juniors (#1)(11/64). 87-Sad Sack's Muttsy... (12/64)	1.50	4.50	12.00
88-Stumbo the Giant (1/65)	2.80	8.40	28.00
89-122: 89-Sad Sack's Muttsy... 90-Gabby Gob. 91-G. I. Juniors. 92-Sad Sack's Muttsy... (5/65). 93-Sadie Sack (6/65). 94-Gabby Gob. 95-G. I. Juniors (8/65). 96-Sad Sack's Muttsy... (9/65). 97-Gabby Gob (10/65). 98-G. I. Juniors (11/65). 99-Sad Sack's Muttsy... (12/65). 100-Gabby Gob(1/66). 101-G. I. Juniors (2/66). 102-Sad Sack's Muttsy... (3/66). 103-Gabby Gob. 104- G. I. Juniors. 105-Sad Sack's Muttsy... 106-Gabby Gob (7/66). 107-G. I. Juniors (8/66). 108-Sad Sack's Muttsy... 109-Gabby Gob. 110-G. I. Juniors (11/66). 111-Sad Sack's Muttsy... (12/66). 112-G. I. Juniors. 113-Sad Sack's Muttsy... 114-G. I. Juniors. 115-Sad Sack's Muttsy... 116-G. I. Juniors (5/67). 117-Sad Sack's Muttsy... 118-G. I. Juniors. 119-Sad Sack's Muttsy... (8/67). 120-G. I. Juniors (9/67). 121-Sad Sack's Muttsy... (10/67). 122-G. I. Juniors (11/67)	1.00	2.80	7.00

HARVEY HITS COMICS
Nov, 1986 - No. 6, Oct, 1987
Harvey Publications

	GD25	FN65	NM94
1-Little Lotta, Little Dot, Wendy & Baby Huey		1.20	3.00
2-6: 3-Xmas-c		.80	2.00

HARVEY POP COMICS (Teen Humor)
Oct, 1968 - No. 2, Nov, 1969 (Both are 68 pg. Giants)
Harvey Publications

	GD25	FN65	NM94
1-The Cowsills	4.00	12.00	40.00
2-Bunny	3.00	9.00	30.00

HARVEY 3-D HITS (See Sad Sack)

HARVEY-TOON (...S) (See Harvey Hits No. 29, 34, 38, 42, 46, 50, 53)

HARVEY WISEGUYS (...Digest #? on)
Nov, 1987; #2, Nov, 1988; #3, Apr, 1989 - No. 4, Nov, 1989 (98 pgs., digest-size, $1.25/$1.75)
Harvey Comics

	GD25	FN65	NM94
1,2: 1-Hot Stuff, Spooky, etc. 2 (68 pgs.)		1.20	3.00
3,4		1.00	2.50

HATARI (See Movie Classics)

HATE
Spr, 1990 - Present ($2.50/$2.95, B&W/color)
Fantagraphics Books

	GD25	FN65	NM94
1	2.50	7.50	20.00
2-3	1.85	5.50	15.00
4-10	1.00	3.00	8.00
11-15		1.60	4.00
16-28: 16-$2.95-c & color begins		1.20	3.00
Buddy Go Home! (1997, $16.95) r/Buddy stories in color			16.95
Hate-Ball Special Edition ($3.95, giveaway)-reprints		1.60	4.00

HATHAWAYS, THE (TV)
No. 1298, Feb-Apr, 1962 (one-shot)
Dell Publishing Co.

	GD25	FN65	NM94
Four Color 1298-Photo-c	3.60	11.00	40.00

HAUNTED (See This Magazine Is Haunted)

HAUNTED (Baron Weirwulf's Haunted Library #21 on)
9/71 - No. 30, 11/76; No. 31, 9/77 - No. 75, 9/84
Charlton Comics

	GD25	FN65	NM94
1	2.00	6.00	16.00
2-5	1.25	3.75	10.00
6-20	1.00	3.00	8.00
21-40		2.40	6.00
41-60: 51-Reprints #1		1.60	4.00
61-75: 64,75-Reprints		1.20	3.00

NOTE: ***Aparo** c-45. **Ditko** a-1-8, 11-16, 18, 23, 24, 28, 30, 34r, 36r, 39-42r, 47r, 49-51r, 57, 60, 74. c-1-7, 11, 13, 14, 16, 30, 41, 47, 49-51, 74. **Howard** a-18, 22, 32. **Morisi** a-13. **Newton** a-17, 21, 59r; c-21, 22(painted). **Staton** a-18, 21, 22, 30, 33; c-18, 33. **Sutton** a-21, 22, 38; c-15, 17, 18, 23(painted), 24(painted), 64r. #49 reprints Tales of the Mysterious Traveler #4.*

HAUNTED LOVE
Apr, 1973 - No. 11, Sept, 1975
Charlton Comics

	GD25	FN65	NM94
1-Tom Sutton-a (16 pgs.)	2.50	7.50	20.00
2,3, 6-11	1.00	3.00	8.00
4,5-Ditko-a	1.25	3.75	10.00
Modern Comics #1(1978)		2.00	5.00

NOTE: ***Howard** a-8i. **Newton** c-8, 9. **Staton** a-5.*

HAUNTED THRILLS (Tales of Horror and Terror)
June, 1952 - No. 18, Nov-Dec, 1954
Ajax/Farrell Publications

	GD25	FN65	NM94
1-r/Ellery Queen #1	34.00	103.00	260.00
2-L. B. Cole-a r-/Ellery Queen #1	21.00	64.00	160.00
3-5: 3-Drug use story	19.00	56.00	140.00
6-10,12: 7-Hitler story.	16.00	47.00	120.00
11-Nazi death camp story	17.00	51.00	130.00
13,16-18: 18-Lingerie panels	13.00	39.00	95.00
14-Jesus Christ apps. in story by Webb	13.00	39.00	95.00

Haunt of Fear #12 © EC

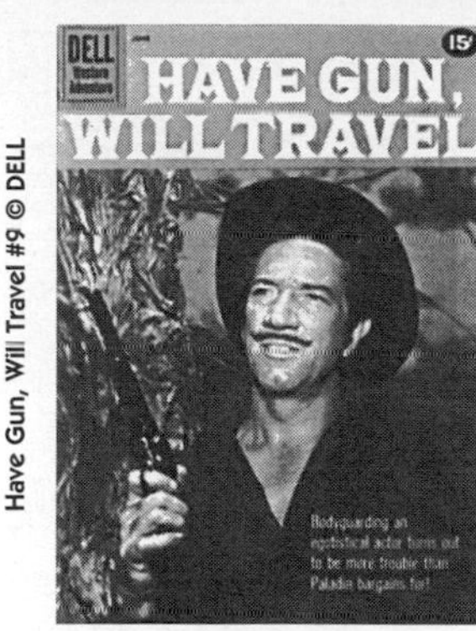

Have Gun, Will Travel #9 © DELL

Hawk and Dove #6 (2nd Series) © DC

	GD25	FN65	NM94
15-Jo-Jo-r	13.00	39.00	95.00

NOTE: ***Kamenish** art in most issues. **Webb** a-12.*

HAUNT OF FEAR (Formerly Gunfighter)
No. 15, May-June, 1950 - No. 28, Nov-Dec, 1954
E. C. Comics

	GD25	FN65	NM94
15(#1, 1950)(Scarce)-1st app. Old Witch	238.00	712.00	2000.00
16	94.00	281.00	775.00
17-Origin of Crypt of Terror, Vault of Horror, & Haunt of Fear; used in **SOTI**, pg. 43; last pg. Ingels-a used by N.Y. Legis. Comm.; story "Monster Maker" based on Frankenstein	94.00	281.00	775.00
4	65.00	197.00	540.00
5-Injury-to-eye panel, pg. 4 of Wood story	49.00	145.00	400.00
6-10: 8-Shrunken head cover. 10-Ingels biog.	36.00	109.00	265.00
11-13,15-18: 11-Kamen biog. 12-Feldstein biog. 16,18-Ray Bradbury adaptations. 18-Ray Bradbury biography	27.00	81.00	200.00
14-Origin Old Witch by Ingels	40.00	120.00	300.00
19-Used in **SOTI**, ill. "A comic book baseball game" & Senate investigation on juvenile delinq. bondage/decapitation-c	37.00	111.00	270.00
20-Feldstein-r/Vault of Horror #12	25.00	75.00	180.00
21,22,25,27: 27-Cannibalism story; Wertham cameo	17.00	49.00	120.00
23-Used in **SOTI**, pg. 241	17.00	51.00	125.00
24-Used in Senate Investigative Report, pg.8	16.00	47.00	115.00
26-Contains anti-censorship editorial, 'Are you a Red Dupe?'	16.00	47.00	115.00
28-Low distribution	17.00	51.00	125.00

NOTE: *(Canadian reprints known; see Table of Contents). **Craig** a-15-17, 5, 7, 10, 12, 13; c-15-17, 5-7. **Crandall** a-20, 21, 26, 27. **Davis** a-4-26, 28. **Evans** a-15-19, 22-25, 27. **Feldstein** a-15-17, 20; c-4, 8-10. **Ingels** a-16, 17, 4-28; c-11-28. **Kamen** a-16, 4, 6, 7, 9-11, 13-19, 21-28. **Krigstein** a-28. **Kurtzman** a-15(#1), 17(#3). **Orlando** a-9, 12. **Wood** a-15, 16, 4-6.*

HAUNT OF FEAR, THE
May, 1991 - No. 2, July, 1991 ($2.00, 68 pgs.)
Gladstone Publishing

	GD25	FN65	NM94
1,2: 1-Ghastly Ingels-c(r); 2-Craig-c(r)		1.00	2.50

HAUNT OF FEAR
Sept, 1991 - No. 5, 1992 ($2.00, 68 pgs.)
Nov, 1992 - Present ($1.50/$2.00/$2.50)
Russ Cochran/Gemstone Publishing

	GD25	FN65	NM94
1-Ingels-c(r)		1.00	2.50
2-5		.80	2.00
1-3: 1-3-r/HOF #15-17 with original-c			1.50
4-15: 4,5-r/HOF #4,5 with original-c		.80	2.00
16-23		1.00	2.50

HAUNT OF HORROR, THE (Magazine)
May, 1974 - No. 5, Jan, 1975 (75¢) (B&W)
Cadence Comics Publ. (Marvel)

	GD25	FN65	NM94
1		2.40	6.00
2,4: 2-Origin & 1st app. Gabriel the Devil Hunter; Satana begins. 4-Neal Adams-a		2.00	5.00
3,5: 5-Evans-a(2)		1.60	4.00

NOTE: ***Alcala** a-2. **Colan** a-2p. **Heath** r-1. **Krigstein** r-3. **Reese** a-1. **Simonson** a-1.*

HAVE GUN, WILL TRAVEL (TV)
No. 931, 8/58 - No. 14, 7-9/62 (All Richard Boone photo-c)
Dell Publishing Co.

	GD25	FN65	NM94
Four Color 931 (#1)	13.00	38.00	140.00
Four Color 983,1044 (#2,3)	8.00	25.00	90.00
4 (1-3/60) - 14	6.40	19.00	70.00

HAVOK & WOLVERINE - MELTDOWN (See Marvel Comics Presents #24)
Mar, 1989 - No. 4, Oct, 1989 ($3.50, mini-series, squarebound, mature)
Marvel Comics (Epic Comics)

	GD25	FN65	NM94
1-4: Violent content		1.40	3.50

HAWAIIAN EYE (TV)
July, 1963 (Troy Donahue, Connie Stevens photo-c)
Gold Key

	GD25	FN65	NM94
1 (10073-307)	3.60	11.00	40.00

HAWAIIAN ILLUSTRATED LEGENDS SERIES
1975 (B&W)(Cover printed w/blue, yellow, and green)
Hogarth Press

	GD25	FN65	NM94
1-Kalelealuaka, the Mysterious Warrior			1.20
2,3(Exist?)			1.00

HAWK, THE (Also see Approved Comics #1, 7 & Tops In Adventure)
Wint/51 - No. 3, 11-12/52; No. 4, 1953 - No. 12, 5/55 (Painted c-1-4)
Ziff-Davis/St. John Publ. Co. No. 4 on

	GD25	FN65	NM94
1-Anderson-a	19.00	56.00	140.00
2 (Sum, '52)-Kubert, Infantino-a	9.50	28.00	75.00
3-7,11: 11-Buckskin Belle & The Texan app.	8.50	26.00	60.00
8-Reprints #3 w/different-c by Baker	8.75	26.25	70.00
9-Baker-c/a; Kubert-a(r)/#2	8.75	26.25	70.00
10-Baker-c/a; r/one story from #2	8.75	26.25	70.00
12-Baker-c/a; Buckskin Belle app.	8.75	26.25	70.00
3-D 1(11/53, 25¢)-Came w/glasses; Baker-c	31.00	94.00	230.00

NOTE: ***Baker** c-8-12. **Larsen** a-10. **Tuska** a-1, 9, 12. Painted c-1, 4, 7.*

HAWK AND THE DOVE, THE (See Showcase #75 & Teen Titans) (1st series)
Aug-Sept, 1968 - No. 6, June-July, 1969
National Periodical Publications

	GD25	FN65	NM94
1-Ditko-c/a	5.00	15.00	50.00
2-6: 5-Teen Titans cameo	3.50	10.50	35.00

NOTE: ***Ditko** c/a-1, 2. **Gil Kane** a-3p, 4p, 5, 6p; c-3-6.*

HAWK AND DOVE (2nd Series)
Oct, 1988 - No. 5, Feb, 1989 ($1.00, limited series)
DC Comics

	GD25	FN65	NM94
1-Rob Liefeld-c/a(p) in all		1.20	3.00
2-5		.80	2.00
Trade paperback ('93, $9.95)-Reprints #1-5	1.25	3.75	10.00

HAWK AND DOVE
June, 1989 - No. 28, Oct, 1991 ($1.00)
DC Comics

	GD25	FN65	NM94
1-28			1.00
Annual 1 (1990, $2.00)-Liefeld pin-up		.80	2.00
Annual 2 (1991)-Armageddon 2001 x-over		.80	2.00

HAWK AND DOVE
Nov, 1997 - No.5, Mar, 1998 ($2.50, limited series)
DC Comics

	GD25	FN65	NM94
1-5-Baron-s/Zachary & Giordano-a			2.50

HAWK AND WINDBLADE (See Elflord)
Aug, 1997 - No.2, Sept, 1997 ($2.95, limited series)
Warp Graphics

	GD25	FN65	NM94
1,2-Blair-s/Chan-c/a			2.95

HAWKEYE (See The Avengers #16 & Tales Of Suspense #57)
Sept, 1983 - No. 4, Dec, 1983 (limited series)
Marvel Comics Group

	GD25	FN65	NM94
1-4: Mark Gruenwald-a/scripts. 1-Origin Hawkeye. 3-Origin Mockingbird. 4-Hawkeye & Mockingbird elope			1.50

HAWKEYE
Jan, 1994 - No. 4, Apr, 1994 ($1.75, limited series)
Marvel Comics

	GD25	FN65	NM94
1-4		.70	1.75

HAWKEYE & THE LAST OF THE MOHICANS (TV)
No. 884, Mar, 1958 (one-shot)

Hawkman #4 (1st Series) © DC

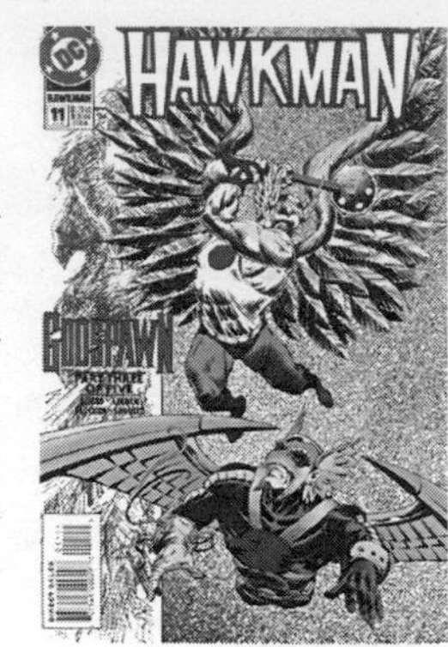

Hawkman #11 (4th Series) © DC

Headline Comics #38 © PRIZE

GD25 FN65 NM94

Dell Publishing Co.
Four Color 884-Photo-c 6.40 19.00 70.00

HAWKMAN (See Atom & Hawkman, The Brave & the Bold, DC Comics Presents, Detective, Flash Comics, Hawkworld, Justice League of America #31, Mystery in Space, Shadow War Of..., Showcase, & World's Finest #256)

HAWKMAN (1st Series) (Also see The Atom #7 & Brave & the Bold #34-36, 42-44, 51)
Apr-May, 1964 - No. 27, Aug-Sept, 1968
National Periodical Publications

1-(4-5/64)-Anderson-c/a begins, ends #21 44.00 132.00 540.00
2 19.00 57.00 190.00
3,5 12.00 36.00 120.00
4-Origin & 1st app. Zatanna (10-11/64) 16.00 48.00 160.00
6 10.00 30.00 100.00
7 9.00 27.00 90.00
8-10: 9-Atom cameo; Hawkman & Atom learn each other's I.D.; 2nd app. Shadow Thief 7.50 22.50 75.00
11-15 5.60 17.00 56.00
16-27: 18-Adam Strange x-over (cameo #19). 25-G.A. Hawkman-r by Moldoff. 27-Kubert-c 4.50 13.50 45.00

HAWKMAN (2nd Series)
Aug, 1986 - No. 17, Dec, 1987
DC Comics

1-17: 10-Byrne-c 1.00
Special #1 (1986, $1.25) 1.50
Trade paperback (1989, $19.95)-r/Brave and the Bold #34-36,42-44 by Kubert; Kubert-c 2.50 7.50 20.00

HAWKMAN (4th Series)(See both Hawkworld limited & ongoing series)
Sept, 1993 - No. 32, July, 1996 ($1.75/$1.95/$2.25)
DC Comics

1-($2.50)-Gold foil embossed-c; storyline cont'd from Hawkworld ongoing series; new costume & powers. 1.00 2.50
2-11: 2-Green Lantern x-over. 3-Airstryke app. 4,6-Wonder Woman app. .70 1.75
12,13,0,14-20: 12-Begin $1.95-c. 13-(9/94)-Zero Hour. 0-(10/94). 14-(11/94). 15-Aquaman-c & app. .80 2.00
21-32: 21-Begin $2.25-c, 23-Wonder Woman app. 25-Kent Williams-c. 29,30-Chaykin-c. 32-Breyfogle-c .90 2.25
Annual 1 (1993, $2.50, 68 pgs.)-Bloodlines Eathplague 1.00 2.50
Annual 2 (1995, $3.95)-Year One story 1.60 4.00

HAWKMOON: THE JEWEL IN THE SKULL
May, 1986 - No. 4, Nov, 1986 ($1.75, limited series, Baxter paper)
First Comics

1-4: Adapts novel by Michael Moorcock .80 2.00

HAWKMOON: THE MAD GOD'S AMULET
Jan, 1987 - No. 4, July, 1987 ($1.75, limited series, Baxter paper)
First Comics

1-4: Adapts novel by Michael Moorcock .80 2.00

HAWKMOON: THE RUNESTAFF
June, 1988 - No. 4, Dec, 1988 ($1.75-$1.95, limited series, Baxter paper)
First Comics

1-4: ($1.75) Adapts novel by Michael Moorcock. 3,4 ($1.95) .80 2.00

HAWKMOON: THE SWORD OF DAWN
Sept, 1987 - No. 4, Mar, 1988 ($1.75, limited series, Baxter paper)
First Comics

1-4: Dorman painted-c; adapts Moorcock novel .80 2.00

HAWKWORLD
1989 - No. 3, 1989 ($3.95, prestige format, limited series)
DC Comics

GD25 FN65 NM94

Book 1-Tim Truman story & art in all; Hawkman dons new costume; reintro Byth. 1.60 4.00
Books 2,3 1.60 4.00

HAWKWORLD (3rd Series)
June, 1990 - No. 32, Mar, 1993 ($1.50/$1.75)
DC Comics

1-Hawkman spin-off; story cont'd from limited series. 1.00 2.50
2-32: 15,16-War of the Gods x-over. 22-J'onn J'onzz app. .70 1.75
Annual 1-3 ('90-'92, $2.95, 68 pgs.) 1.20 3.00
Annual 2-2nd printing with silver ink-c 1.20 3.00
NOTE: ***Truman*** *a-30-32; c-27-32, Annual 1.*

HAWTHORN-MELODY FARMS DAIRY COMICS
No date (1950's) (Giveaway)
Everybody's Publishing Co.

nn-Cheerie Chick, Tuffy Turtle, Robin Koo Koo, Donald & Longhorn Legends 1.60 4.00 8.00

HAYWIRE
Oct, 1988 - No. 13, Sept, 1989 ($1.25, mature)
DC Comics

1-13 1.30

HAZARD
June, 1996 - No. 7, Nov, 1996 ($1.75)
Image Comics (Wildstorm Productions)

1-7: 1-Intro Hazard; Jeff Mariotte scripts begin; Jim Lee-c(p). 1.75

HEADHUNTERS
Apr, 1997 - No. 3, June, 1997 ($2.95, B&W)
Image Comics

1-3: Chris Marrinan-s/a 2.95

HEADLINE COMICS (...For the American Boy) (...Crime No. 32-39)
Feb, 1943 - No. 22, Nov-Dec, 1946; No. 23, 1947 - No. 77, Oct, 1956
Prize Publications

1-Junior Rangers-c/stories begin; Yank & Doodle x-over in Junior Rangers (Junior Rangers are Uncle Sam's nephews) 36.00 108.00 300.00
2 15.50 47.00 125.00
3-Used in **POP**, pg. 84 12.00 38.00 100.00
4-7,9,10: 4,9,10-Hitler stories in each 11.30 34.00 90.00
8-Classic Hitler-c 28.00 83.00 220.00
11,12 8.75 26.25 65.00
13-15-Blue Streak in all 9.50 28.00 75.00
16-Origin & 1st app. Atomic Man (11-12/45) 19.00 56.00 150.00
17,18,20,21: 21-Atomic Man ends (9-10/46) 9.50 28.00 75.00
19-S&K-a 21.00 64.00 170.00
22-Last Junior Rangers; Kiefer-c 7.15 21.50 50.00
23,24: (All S&K-a). 23-Valentine's Day Massacre story; content changes to true crime. 24-Dope-crazy killer story 20.00 60.00 160.00
25-35-S&K-c/a. 25-Powell-a 19.00 56.00 150.00
36-S&K-a; photo-c begin 14.00 41.00 110.00
37-1 pg. S&K, Severin-a; rare Kirby photo-c app. 14.00 41.00 110.00
38,40-Meskin-a 5.70 17.00 35.00
39,41,42,46-48,50,52-55: 41-J. Edgar Hoover 26th Anniversary Issue with photo on-c 4.15 12.50 25.00
43,49-Meskin-a 4.25 13.00 28.00
44-S&K-c; Severin/Elder, Meskin-a 8.75 26.25 65.00
45-Kirby-a 7.15 21.50 50.00
51-Kirby-c 5.00 15.00 30.00
56-S&K-a 8.75 26.25 65.00
57-77: 72-Meskin-c/a(i) 4.00 12.00 20.00
NOTE: ***Hollingsworth*** *a-30. Photo c-36-43.* ***H. C. Kiefer*** *c-12-16, 22. Atomic Man c-17-19.*

HEADMAN

Heartland #1 © DC

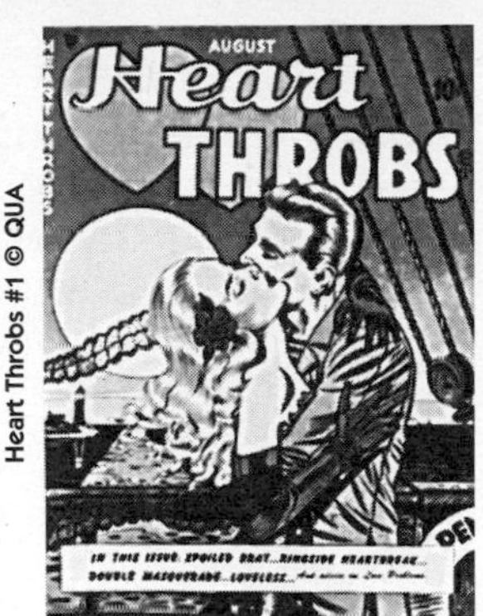

Heart Throbs #1 © QUA

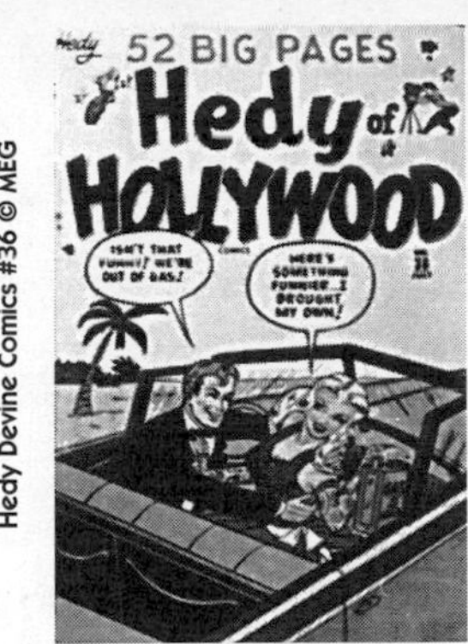

Hedy Devine Comics #36 © MEG

	GD25	FN65	NM94

1990 ($2.50, mature)
Innovation Publishing

1-Sci/fi		1.00	2.50

HEAP, THE
Sept, 1971 (52 pgs.)
Skywald Publications

1-Kinstler-r/Strange Worlds #8	1.25	3.75	10.00

HEART AND SOUL
April-May, 1954 - No. 2, June-July, 1954
Mikeross Publications

1,2	5.70	17.00	35.00

HEARTBREAKERS (Also see Dark Horse Presents)
Apr, 1996 - No. 4, July, 1996 ($2.95, limited series)
Dark Horse Comics

1-4: 1-W/paper doll & pin-up. 2-Hoss pin-up. 3-Evan Dorkin pin upc. 4-Brereton-c; Matt Wagner pin-up		1.20	3.00

HEARTLAND (See Hellblazer)
Mar, 1997 ($4.95, one-shot, mature)
DC Comics (Vertigo)

1-Garth Ennis-s/Steve Dillon-c/a			4.95

HEART OF DARKNESS
1994 ($2.95)
Hardline Studios

1-Brereton-c		1.20	3.00

HEART OF THE BEAST, THE
1994 ($19.95, hardcover, mature)
DC Comics (Vertigo)

1-Dean Motter scripts	2.50	7.50	20.00

HEARTS OF DARKNESS (See Ghost Rider; Wolverine; Punisher: Hearts of…)

HEART THROBS (Love Stories No. 147 on)
8/49 - No. 8, 10/50; No. 9, 3/52 - No. 146, Oct, 1972
Quality Comics/National Periodical #47(4-5/57) on (Arleigh #48-101)

1-Classic Ward-c, Gustavson-a, 9 pgs.	33.00	98.00	260.00
2-Ward-c/a (9 pgs); Gustavson-a	19.00	56.00	150.00
3-Gustavson-a	6.50	19.50	45.00
4,6,8-Ward-a, 8-9 pgs.	9.50	28.00	75.00
5,7	3.60	9.00	28.00
9-Robert Mitchum, Jane Russell photo-c	7.15	21.50	50.00
10,15-Ward-a	8.50	26.00	60.00
11-14,16-20: 12 (7/52)	4.00	12.00	24.00
21-Ward-c	7.15	21.50	50.00
22,23-Ward-a(p)	5.70	17.00	35.00
24-33: 33-Last pre-code (3/55)	4.00	11.00	22.00
34-39,41-46 (12/56; last Quality issue)	3.60	9.00	18.00
40-Ward-a; r-7 pgs./#21	5.35	16.00	32.00
47-(4-5/57; 1st DC issue)	22.00	66.00	220.00
48-60	7.50	22.50	75.00
61-70	5.00	15.00	50.00
71-100: 74-Last 10 cent issue	4.00	12.00	40.00
101-The Beatles app. on-c	12.00	36.00	120.00
102-119: 102-123-(Serial)-Three Girls, Their Lives, Their Loves	2.50	7.50	20.00
120-Neal Adams-c	3.50	10.50	35.00
121-132,143-146	1.50	4.50	12.00
133-142-(52 pgs.)	2.50	7.50	20.00

NOTE: ***Gustavson*** *a-8.* ***Tuska*** *a-128. Photo c-4, 5, 8-10, 15, 17.*

HEART THROBS - THE BEST OF DC ROMANCE COMICS (See Fireside Book Series)

HEATHCLIFF (See Star Comics Magazine)
Apr, 1985 - No. 56, Feb, 1991 (#16-on, $1.00)
Marvel Comics (Star Comics)/Marvel Comics No. 23 on

1-56: Post-a most issues. 43-X-Mas issue. 47-Batman parody (Catman vs. the Soaker)		.80	2.00
Annual 1 ('87)		.80	2.00

HEATHCLIFF'S FUNHOUSE
May, 1987 - No. 10, 1988
Marvel Comics (Star Comics)/Marvel Comics No. 6 on

1-10		.80	2.00

HEAVY HITTERS
1993 ($3.75, 68 pgs.)
Marvel Comics (Epic Comics)

1-Bound w/trading card; Lawdog, Feud, Alien Legion, Trouble With Girls, & Spyke		1.50	3.75

HECKLE AND JECKLE (See Blue Ribbon, Giant Comics Edition #5A & 10, Paul Terry's, Terry-Toons Comics)
10/51 - No. 24, 10/55; No. 25, Fall/56 - No. 34, 6/59
St. John Publ. Co. No. 1-24/Pines No. 25 on

1-Funny animal	22.00	66.00	175.00
2	11.30	34.00	90.00
3-5	8.75	26.25	70.00
6-10	6.50	19.50	45.00
11-20	5.70	17.00	35.00
21-34: 25-Begin CBS Television Presents on-c	4.25	13.00	26.00

HECKLE AND JECKLE (TV) (See New Terrytoons)
11/62 - No. 4, 8/63; 5/66; No. 2, 10/66; No. 3, 8/67
Gold Key/Dell Publishing Co.

1 (11/62; Gold Key)	5.50	16.50	60.00
2-4	2.25	6.75	24.00
1 (5/66; Dell)	2.75	8.00	30.00
2,3	2.00	6.00	22.00

(See March of Comics No. 379, 472, 484)

HECKLE AND JECKLE 3-D
1987 - No. 2?, 1987 ($2.50)
Spotlight Comics

1,2		1.00	2.50

HECTOR COMICS (The Keenest Teen in Town)
Nov, 1953 - No. 3, 1954
Key Publications

1-Teen humor	4.00	11.00	22.00
2,3	2.80	7.00	14.00

HECTOR HEATHCOTE (TV)
Mar, 1964
Gold Key

1 (10111-403)	5.50	16.50	60.00

HECTOR THE INSPECTOR (See Top Flight Comics)

HEDY DEVINE COMICS (Formerly All Winners #21? or Teen #22?(6/47); Hedy of Hollywood #36 on; also see Annie Oakley, Comedy & Venus)
No. 22, Aug, 1947 - No. 50, Sept, 1952
Marvel Comics (RCM)/Atlas #50

22-1st app. Hedy Devine (also see Joker #32)	12.00	38.00	100.00
23,24,27-30: 23-Wolverton-a, 1 pg; Kurtzman's "Hey Look", 2 pgs. 24,27-30-"Hey Look" by Kurtzman, 1-3 pgs.	12.00	36.00	95.00
25-Classic "Hey Look" by Kurtzman, "Optical Illusion"	12.00	38.00	100.00
26- "Giggles 'n' Grins" by Kurtzman	8.75	26.25	65.00
31-34,36-50: 32-Anti-Wertham editorial	6.50	19.50	45.00
35-Four pgs. "Rusty" by Kurtzman	10.00	30.00	80.00

Hellblazer Annual #1 © DC

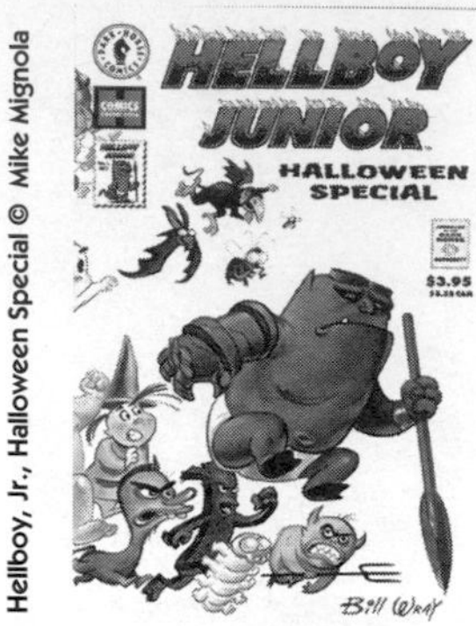

Hellboy, Jr., Halloween Special © Mike Mignola

Hellboy: Wake The Devil #1 © Mike Mignola

GD25 FN65 NM94

HEDY-MILLIE-TESSIE COMEDY (See Comedy Comics)

HEDY WOLFE (Also see Patsy & Hedy & Miss America Magazine V1#2)
Aug, 1957
Atlas Publishing Co. (Emgee)

1-Patsy Walker's rival; Al Hartley-c 8.50 26.00 60.00

HEE HAW (TV)
July, 1970 - No. 7, Aug, 1971
Charlton Press

1 2.50 7.50 24.00
2-7 2.00 6.00 16.00

HEIDI (See Dell Jr. Treasury No. 6)

HELEN OF TROY (Movie)
No. 684, Mar, 1956 (one-shot)
Dell Publishing Co.

Four Color 684-Buscema-a, photo-c 10.00 30.00 110.00

HELLBLAZER (John Constantine) (See Saga of Swamp Thing #37) (Also see Books of Magic limited series)
Jan, 1988 - Present ($1.25/$1.50/$2.25, mature)
DC Comics (Vertigo imprint #63 on)

1-(44 pgs.)-John Constantine 2.00 6.00 20.00
2-5 1.00 3.00 7.50
6-10: 9-X-over w/Swamp Thing #76. 9,10-Swamp Thing cameo 2.00 5.00
11-20: 19-Dave McKean-c 1.60 4.00
21-26,28-30: 24-Contains bound-in Shocker movie poster. 25,26-Grant Morrison scripts. 1.20 3.00
27-Neil Gaiman scripts; Dave McKean-a; fold-out guide to Nightbreed 1.25 3.75 10.00
31-39,41-49: 36-Preview of World Without End. 41-Ennis scripts begins; ends #83. 44-Begin $1.75-c. 44,45-Sutton-a(i) 1.20 3.00
40-($2.25, 52 pgs.)-Dave McKean-a & colors; preview of Kid Eternity 1.40 3.50
50-($3.00, 52 pgs.) 1.60 4.00
51-65: 52-Glenn Fabry painted-c begin. 62-Special Death insert by McKean. 63-Silver metallic ink on-c 1.20 3.00
66-74,76-88: 66-Begin $1.95-c. 77-Totleben-c. 84-Sean Phillips-c/a begins; Delano story. 85-88-Eddie Campbell story. 1.20 3.00
75-($2.95, 52 pgs.) 1.20 3.00
89-99,101-119: 89-Paul Jenkins scripts begin; begin $2.25-c. 108-Adlard-a 1.20 3.00
100 ($3.50, 48 pgs.) 1.40 3.50
120 ($3.50, 48 pgs.) 1.40 3.50
121-123 2.25
Annual 1 (1989, $2.95, 68 pgs.)-Bryan Talbot's 1st work in American comics 2.00 5.00
...Dangerous Habits (1997, $14.95, TPB) r/#41-46 15.00
...Fear and Loathing (1997, $14.95, TPB) r/#62-67 15.00
Special 1 (1993, $3.95, 68 pgs.)-Ennis story; w/pin-ups. 1.25 3.75 10.00

NOTE: ***Alcala*** *a-8i, 9i, 18-22i.* ***Gaiman*** *scripts-27.* ***McKean*** *a-27; c-19.* ***Sutton*** *a-44i, 45i.* ***Talbot*** *a-Annual 1.*

HELLBLAZER/THE BOOKS OF MAGIC
Dec, 1997 - No. 2, Jan, 1998 ($2.50, mini-series)
DC Comics (Vertigo)

1,2-John Constantine and Tim Hunter 1.00 2.50

HELLBOY (Also see Dark Horse Presents, John Byrne's Next Men. San Diego Comic Con #2, Danger Unlimited #4, Gen13 #13B, Ghost/Hellboy, & Savage Dragon)

HELLBOY: ALMOST COLOSSUS
June, 1997 - No. 2, July,1997 ($2.95, limited series)
Dark Horse Comics (Legend)

1,2-Mignola-s/a 1.40 3.50

HELLBOY, JR., HALLOWEEN SPECIAL
Oct, 1997 ($3.95, one-shot)
Dark Horse Comics

nn-"Harvey" style renditions of Hellboy characters; Bill Wray, Mike Mignola & various-s/a; wraparound-c by Wray 3.95

HELLBOY: SEED OF DESTRUCTION
Mar, 1994 - No. 4, June, 1994 ($2.50, limited series)
Dark Horse Comics (Legend)

1-4-Mignola-c/a w/Byrne scripts; Monkeyman & O'Brien back-up story (origin) by Art Adams. 1.60 4.00
Trade paperback (1994, $17.95)-collects all four issues plus r/Hellboy's 1st app. in San Diego Comic Con #2 & pin-ups 2.25 6.75 18.00
Limited edition hardcover (1995, $99.95)-includes everything in trade paperback plus additional material. 10.00 30.00 100.00

HELLBOY: THE CORPSE AND THE IRON SHOES
Jan, 1996 ($2.95, one-shot)
Dark Horse Comics (Legend)

nn-Mignola-c/a/scripts; reprints "The Corpse" serial from Capitol City's Advance Comics catalog w/new story 1.20 3.00

HELLBOY: THE WOLVES OF ST. AUGUST
1995 ($4.95, squarebound, one-shot)
Dark Horse Comics (Legend)

nn-Mignola--c/a/scripts; r/Dark Horse Presents #88-91 with additional story. 2.00 5.00

HELLBOY: WAKE THE DEVIL
June, 1996 - No. 5, Oct, 1996 ($2.95, limited series)(Sequel to Seed of Destruction)
Dark Horse Comics (Legend)

1-5: Mignola-c/a & scripts; The Monstermen back-up story by Gary Gianni 1.20 3.00

HELLHOUNDS (...: Panzer Cops #3-6)
1994 - No. 6, July, 1994 ($2.50, B&W, limited series)
Dark Horse Comics

1,3-5: 1-Hamner-c. 3-(4/94) 1.00 2.50
2,6-($2.95, 52 pgs.): 2-Joe Phillips-c 1.20 3.00

HELLHOUND, THE REDEMPTION QUEST
Dec, 1993 - No. 4, Mar, 1994 ($2.25, limited series, coated stock)
Marvel Comics (Epic Comics)

1-4 .90 2.25

HELLINA
Sept, 1994 ($2.75/$9.95, B&W, one-shot)
Lightning Comics

1-Origin; pin-up gallery 1.20 3.00
1 ($9.95)-Nude Edition 1.25 3.75 10.00

HELLINA/CATFIGHT
Oct, 1995 ($2.75, B&W, one-shot)
Lightning Comics

1 1.10 2.75
1 ($9.95)-Nude Edition 1.25 3.75 10.00
1 (1997, $2.95)-Encore Edition 1.20 3.00

HELLINA: CHRISTMAS IN HELL
Dec, 1996 ($2.95, B&W, one-shot)
Lightning Comics

1, 1b 1.20 3.00
1 ($9.95)-Nude edition; polybagged. 1.25 3.75 10.00
1 ($9.95)-Platinum edition 1.25 3.75 10.00
1 ($29.95)-Platinum Nude edition 3.00 9.00 30.00

Hellina: Hell's Angel #2 © Lightning Comics

Hellshock #4 (1st Series) © Jae Lee

Hellstorm: Prince of Lies #18 © MEG

HELLINA/CYNDER
Sept, 1997 ($2.95, B&W, one-shot)
Lightning Comics

	GD25	FN65	NM94
1,1B-($2.95)-Abrams-c			2.95
1A,1B-($9.95)-Nude Edition; polybagged			9.95

HELLINA/DOUBLE IMPACT
Feb, 1996 ($3.00, one-shot)
Lightning Comics

	GD25	FN65	NM94
1, 1b: 1b-Cleary-c.		1.20	3.00
1 ($9.95)-Nude Edition; polybagged.	1.25	3.75	10.00

HELLINA: GENESIS
Apr, 1996 ($3.50, B&W, one-shot)
Lightning Comics

	GD25	FN65	NM94
1-polybagged w/poster		1.40	3.50
1 ($9.95)-Nude Edition	1.25	3.75	10.00
1 ($20.00)-Platinum Edition	2.50	7.50	20.00

HELLINA: HEART OF THORNS
July, 1996 - No. 2, Sept, 1996 ($2.75/$3.00, limited series)
Lightning Comics

	GD25	FN65	NM94
1-Flip book w/Moxi story		1.20	3.00
1,2A,2B-($9.95): All Nude Editions	1.25	3.75	10.00
2A,2B		1.10	2.75
2-($9.95)-Platinum Edition	1.25	3.75	10.00

HELLINA: HELLBORN
Dec, 1997 ($2.95, B&W)
Lightning Comics

	GD25	FN65	NM94
1-Christina Z. -s		1.20	3.00
1-($9.95)-Nude Edition	1.25	3.75	10.00

HELLINA: HELL'S ANGEL
Nov, 1996 - No. 2, Dec, 1996 ($2.75, B&W, limited series)
Lightning Comics

	GD25	FN65	NM94
1,2-($2.75)		1.10	2.75
1,2-($9.95)-Nude Edition	1.25	3.75	10.00

HELLINA: IN THE FLESH
Aug, 1997 ($2.95, B&W, one-shot)
Lightning Comics

	GD25	FN65	NM94
1a,1b-($2.95)			2.95
1a,1b-($9.95)-Nude Edition			9.95

HELLINA: KISS OF DEATH
July, 1995 ($2.75/$9.95/$20.00, B&W)
Lightning Comics

	GD25	FN65	NM94
1		1.20	3.00
1 ($9.95)-Nude Edition	1.25	3.75	10.00
1 ($20.00)-Gold Edition	2.50	7.50	20.00
1 (Mar, 1997, $2.95) Encore Edition			2.95
1b (Mar, 1997, $2.95)-Encore Edition			2.95

HELLINA:NAKED DESIRE
May, 1997 ($2.95, B&W, one-shot)
Lightning Comics

	GD25	FN65	NM94
1			2.95

HELLINA:NIRA X
Aug, 1996 ($2.95, color, one-shot)
Lightning Comics

	GD25	FN65	NM94
1a,1b-($2.95)		1.20	3.00
1-($9.95)-Commemorative Edition	1.25	3.75	10.00

HELLINA:THE RELIC
June, 1997 ($2.95, B&W, one-shot)
Lightning Comics

	GD25	FN65	NM94
1			2.95

HELLINA:SKYBOLT TOYZ
Aug, 1997 ($1.50, B&W, one-shot)
Lightning Comics

	GD25	FN65	NM94
1,1b-($1.50)-Reprint of Hellina: Wicked Ways			1.50

HELLINA: TAKING BACK THE NIGHT
Apr, 1995 ($2.75, B&W, one-shot)
Lightning Comics

	GD25	FN65	NM94
1		1.20	3.00
1 ($9.95)-Nude Edition	1.25	3.75	10.00

HELLINA: WICKED WAYS
Nov, 1995 ($2.75/$9.95, B&W, one-shot)
Lightning Comics

	GD25	FN65	NM94
1,1b: 1b-Trent Kaniuga-c; polybagged.		1.10	2.75
1-($9.95)-Nude Edition	1.25	3.75	10.00
1a (Apr, 1997, $2.95)-Encore Edition			2.95

HELLO, I'M JOHNNY CASH
1976 (39/49¢)
Spire Christian Comics (Fleming H. Revell Co.)

	GD25	FN65	NM94
nn			1.00

HELL ON EARTH (See DC Science Fiction Graphic Novel)

HELLO PAL COMICS (Short Story Comics)
Jan, 1943 - No. 3, May, 1943 (Photo-c)
Harvey Publications

	GD25	FN65	NM94
1-Rocketman & Rocketgirl begin; Yankee Doodle Jones app.; Mickey Rooney photo-c	52.00	156.00	465.00
2-Charlie McCarthy photo-c (scarce)	43.00	129.00	390.00
3-Bob Hope photo-c	42.00	126.00	380.00

HELLRAISER/NIGHTBREED – JIHAD (Also see Clive Barker's...)
1991 - Book 2, 1991 ($4.50, 52 pgs.)
Epic Comics (Marvel Comics)

	GD25	FN65	NM94
Book 1,2		1.80	4.50

HELL-RIDER (Magazine)
Aug, 1971 - No. 2, Oct, 1971 (B&W)
Skywald Publications

	GD25	FN65	NM94
1-Origin & 1st app.; Butterfly & Wildbunch begins	3.50	10.50	35.00
2	2.50	7.50	24.00

NOTE: *#3 advertised in Psycho #5 but did not come out.* **Buckler** *a-1, 2.* **Morrow** *c-3.*

HELL'S ANGEL (Becomes Dark Angel #6 on)
July, 1992 - No. 5, Nov, 1993 ($1.75)
Marvel Comics UK

	GD25	FN65	NM94
1-5: X-Men (Wolverine, Cyclops)-c/stories. 1-Origin. 3-Jim Lee cover swipe		.70	1.75

HELLSHOCK
July, 1994 - No. 4, Nov, 1994 ($1.95, limited series)
Image Comics

	GD25	FN65	NM94
1-4-Jae Lee-c/a & scripts. 4-variant-c.		.80	2.00

HELLSHOCK
Jan, 1997 - No.2, Feb, 1997 ($2.95/$2.50, limited series)
Image Comics

	GD25	FN65	NM94
1-($2.95)-Jae Lee-c/s/a, Villarrubia-painted-a			2.95
2-($2.50)			2.50

HELLSTORM: PRINCE OF LIES (See Ghost Rider #1 & Marvel Spotlight #12)
Apr, 1993 - No. 21, Dec, 1994 ($2.00)
Marvel Comics

	GD25	FN65	NM94
1-($2.95)-Parchment-c w/red thermographic ink		1.20	3.00
2-21: 14-Bound-in trading card sheet. 18-P. Craig Russell-c		.80	2.00

Herbie #7 © ACG

Hercules #11 © CC

Here Come the Big People #1 © Event Comics

HE-MAN (See Masters Of The Universe)

HE-MAN (Also see Tops In Adventure)
Fall, 1952
Ziff-Davis Publ. Co. (Approved Comics)

	GD25	FN65	NM94
1-Kinstler painted-c; Powell-a	12.00	36.00	90.00

HE-MAN
May, 1954 - No. 2, July, 1954 (Painted-c by B. Safran)
Toby Press

	GD25	FN65	NM94
1	10.50	32.00	85.00
2	8.75	26.25	65.00

HENNESSEY (TV)
No. 1200, Aug-Oct, 1961 - No. 1280, Mar-May, 1962
Dell Publishing Co.

	GD25	FN65	NM94
Four Color 1200-Gil Kane-a, photo-c	5.50	16.50	60.00
Four Color 1280-Photo-c	5.50	16.50	60.00

HENRY (Also see Little Annie Rooney)
1935 (52 pgs.) (Daily B&W strip reprints)(10"x10" cardboard-c)
David McKay Publications

	GD25	FN65	NM94
1-By Carl Anderson	31.00	94.00	250.00

HENRY (See King Comics & Magic Comics)
No. 122, Oct, 1946 - No. 65, Apr-June, 1961
Dell Publishing Co.

	GD25	FN65	NM94
Four Color 122-All new stories begin	12.00	35.00	130.00
Four Color 155 (7/47)	7.00	22.00	80.00
1 (1-3/48)-All new stories	7.00	22.00	80.00
2	3.00	10.00	36.00
3-10	3.00	9.00	32.00
11-20: 20-Infinity-c	1.65	5.00	18.00
21-30	1.50	4.50	14.00
31-40	1.10	3.30	9.00
41-65	1.00	2.80	7.00

HENRY (See Giant Comic Album and March of Comics No. 43, 58, 84, 101, 112, 129, 147, 162, 178, 189)

HENRY ALDRICH COMICS (TV)
Aug-Sept, 1950 - No. 22, Sept-Nov, 1954
Dell Publishing Co.

	GD25	FN65	NM94
1-Part series written by John Stanley; Bill Williams-a	7.00	22.00	80.00
2	3.60	11.00	40.00
3-5	3.00	9.00	35.00
6-10	2.50	7.50	28.00
11-22	1.80	5.50	20.00
Giveaway (16 pgs., soft-c, 1951)-Capehart radio	2.00	6.00	22.00

HENRY BREWSTER
Feb, 1966 - V2#7, Sept, 1967 (All 25¢ Giants)
Country Wide (M.F. Ent.)

	GD25	FN65	NM94
1		2.40	6.00
2-6(12/66)-Powell-a in most		1.60	4.00
V2#7		1.20	3.00

HEPCATS
Nov, 1996 - Present ($2.95, B&W)
Antarctic Press

	GD25	FN65	NM94
0-5-Martin Wagner-c/s/a: 0-color		1.20	3.00
0-($9.95) CD Edition	1.25	3.75	10.00

HERBIE (See Forbidden Worlds & Unknown Worlds)
April-May, 1964 - No. 23, Feb, 1967 (All 12¢)
American Comics Group

	GD25	FN65	NM94
1-Whitney-c/a in most issues	14.00	42.00	140.00
2-4	7.50	22.50	75.00
5-Beatles, Dean Martin, F. Sinatra app.	9.00	27.00	90.00
6,7,9,10	5.50	16.50	55.00
8-Origin & 1st app. The Fat Fury	7.00	21.00	70.00
11-23: 14-Nemesis & Magicman app. 17-r/2nd Herbie from Forbidden Worlds #94. 23-r/1st Herbie from F.W. #73	4.00	12.00	40.00

HERBIE
Oct, 1992 - No. 12, 1993 ($2.50, limited series)
Dark Horse Comics

	GD25	FN65	NM94
1-6: Whitney-r plus new-c/a. 1-Byrne-c/a & scripts. 3-Bob Burden-c/a. 4-Art Adams-c		1.00	2.50

HERBIE GOES TO MONTE CARLO, HERBIE RIDES AGAIN (See Walt Disney Showcase No. 24, 41)

HERCULES (See Hit Comics #1-21, Journey Into Mystery Annual, Marvel Graphic Novel #37, Marvel Premiere #26 & The Mighty...)

HERCULES
Oct, 1967 - No. 13, Sept, 1969; Dec, 1968
Charlton Comics

	GD25	FN65	NM94
1-Thane of Bagarth series begins; Glanzman	1.85	5.50	15.00
2-13: 1-5,7,9,10-Aparo-a	1.25	3.75	10.00
8-(Low distribution)(12/68, 35¢, B&W); magazine format; new Hercules story plus-r story/#1; Thane-r/#1-3	4.00	12.00	40.00
Modern Comics reprint 10('77), 11('78)		2.00	5.00

HERCULES (Prince of Power) (Also see The Champions)
V1#1, 10/82 - V1#4, 12/82; V2#1, 3/84 - V2#4, 6/84 (color, both limited series)
Marvel Comics Group

	GD25	FN65	NM94
1-4: Layton-c/a.			1.60
V2#1-4: Layton-c/a. 4-Death of Zeus.			1.00

NOTE: ***Layton** a-1, 2, 3p, 4p, V2#1-4; c-1-4, V2#1-4.*

HERCULES: HEART OF CHAOS
Aug, 1997 - No. 3, Oct, 1997 ($2.50, limited series)
Marvel Comics

	GD25	FN65	NM94
1-3-DeFalco-s, Frenz-a		1.00	2.50

HERCULES: OFFICIAL COMICS MOVIE ADAPTION
1997 ($4.50, digest size)
Acclaim Books

	GD25	FN65	NM94
nn-Adaption of the Disney animated movie			4.50

HERCULES: THE LEGENDARY JOURNEYS (TV)
June, 1996 - No. 5, Oct, 1996 ($2.95)
Topps Comics

	GD25	FN65	NM94
1-2: 1-Golden-c.			3.00
3-Xena-c/app.	1.00	2.80	7.00
4,5: Xena-c/app.		2.00	5.00

HERCULES UNBOUND
Oct-Nov, 1975 - No. 12, Aug-Sept, 1977
National Periodical Publications

	GD25	FN65	NM94
1-12: 1-Wood-i begin. 7-Adams ad. 10-Atomic Knights x-over		1.60	4.00

NOTE: ***Buckler** c-7p. **Layton** inks-No. 9, 10. **Simonson** a-7-10p, 11, 12; c- 8p, 9-12. **Wood** a-1-8i; c-7i, 8i.*

HERCULES (...Unchained #1121) (Movie)
No. 1006, June-Aug, 1959 - No.1121, Aug, 1960
Dell Publishing Co.

	GD25	FN65	NM94
Four Color 1006-Buscema-a, photo-c	9.00	27.00	100.00
Four Color 1121-Crandall/Evans-a	9.00	27.00	100.00

HERE COMES SANTA (See March of Comics No. 30, 213, 340)

HERE COME THE BIG PEOPLE
Oct, 1997 ($2.95, one-shot)
Event Comics

	GD25	FN65	NM94
1-Trace Beaulieu-s/Conner & Palmiotti-c/a; variant-c by Darrow			2.95

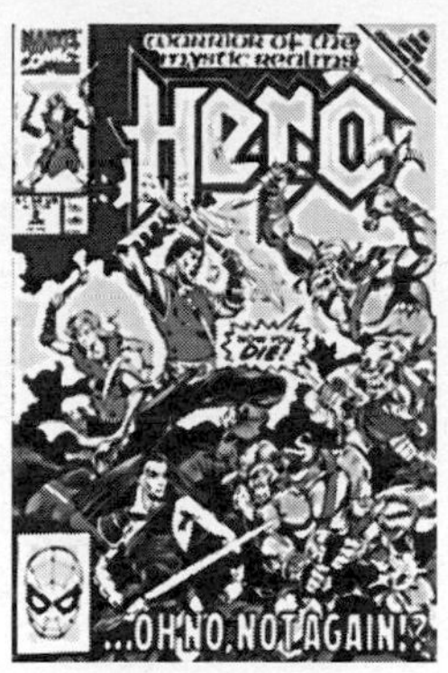

Hero #2 © MEG

Heroes All Catholic Action Illustrated V6 #5 © Heroes All Co.

Heroes Reborn: The Return #1 © MEG

GD25 FN65 NM94

HERE IS SANTA CLAUS
1930s (16 pgs., 8 in color) (stiff paper covers)
Goldsmith Publishing Co. (Kann's in Washington, D.C.)

nn 8.50 26.00 60.00

HERE'S HOW AMERICA'S CARTOONISTS HELP TO SELL U.S. SAVINGS BONDS
1950? (16 pgs., giveaway, paper cover)
Harvey Comics

Contains: Joe Palooka, Donald Duck, Archie, Kerry Drake, Red Ryder, Blondie & Steve Canyon 13.00 39.00 105.00

HERE'S HOWIE COMICS
Jan-Feb, 1952 - No. 18, Nov-Dec, 1954
National Periodical Publications

	GD25	FN65	NM94
1	19.00	56.00	150.00
2	9.50	28.00	75.00
3-5: 5-Howie in the Army issues begin (9-10/52)	7.15	21.50	50.00
6-10	5.70	17.00	40.00
11-18	5.35	16.00	32.00

HERETIC, THE
Nov, 1996 - No. 4, Mar, 1997 ($2.95, limited series)
Dark Horse Comics (Blanc Noir)

1-4:-w/back-up story 1.20 3.00

HERITAGE OF THE DESERT (See Zane Grey, 4-Color 236)

HERMAN & KATNIP (See Harvey Comics Hits #60 & 62, Harvey Hits #14,25,31,41 & Paramount Animated Comics #1)

HERMES VS. THE EYEBALL KID
Dec, 1994 - No. 3,Feb, 1995 ($2.95, B&W, limited series)
Dark Horse Comics

1-3: Eddie Campbell-c/a/scripts 1.20 3.00

HERO (Warrior of the Mystic Realms)
May, 1990 - No. 6, Oct, 1990 ($1.50, limited series)
Marvel Comics

1-6: 1-Portachio-i 1.50

HERO ALLIANCE, THE
Dec, 1985 - No. 2, Sept, 1986 (B&W)
Sirius Comics

1,2: 2-($1.50) 1.50
Special Edition 1 (7/86, color) 1.50

HERO ALLIANCE
May, 1987 ($1.95)
Wonder Color Comics

1-Ron Lim-a .80 2.00

HERO ALLIANCE
V2#1, Sept, 1989 - V2#18?, 1991 ($1.95, 28 pgs.)
Innovation Publishing

V2#1-18: 1,2-Ron Lim-a .80 2.00
Annual 1 (1990, $2.75, 36 pgs.)-Paul Smith-c/a 1.15 2.80
Special 1 (1992, $2.50, 32 pgs.)-Stuart Immonen-a (10 pgs.)

HERO ALLIANCE: END OF THE GOLDEN AGE
July, 1989 - No. 3, Aug, 1989 ($1.75, bi-weekly limited series)
Innovation Publishing

1-3: Bart Sears & Ron Lim-c/a; reprints & new-a .75 1.80

HEROES (Also see Shadow Cabinet & Static)
May, 1996 - No. 6, Nov, 1996 ($2.50, limited series)
DC Comics (Milestone)

1-6: 1-Intro Heroes (Iota, Donner, Blitzen, Starlight, Payback & Static) 1.00 2.50

HEROES AGAINST HUNGER
1986 ($1.50; one-shot for famine relief)
DC Comics

1-Superman, Batman app.; Neal Adams-c(p); includes many artists work; Jeff Jones assist (2 pg.) on B. Smith-a .80 2.00

HEROES ALL CATHOLIC ACTION ILLUSTRATED
1943 - V6#5, Mar 10, 1948 (paper covers)
Heroes All Co.

	GD25	FN65	NM94
V1#1,2-(16 pgs., 8x11")	14.00	41.00	110.00
V2#1(1/44)-3(3/44)-(16 pgs., 8x11")	11.30	34.00	90.00
V3#1(1/45)-10(12/45)-(16 pgs., 8x11")	10.00	30.00	80.00
V4#1-35 (12/20/46)-(16 pgs.)	8.75	26.25	65.00
V5#1(1/10/47)-8(2/28/47)-(16 pgs.)	7.15	21.50	50.00
V5#9(3/7/47)-20(11/25/47)-(32 pgs.)	7.15	21.50	50.00
V6#1(1/10/48)-5(3/10/48)-(32 pgs.)	7.15	21.50	50.00

HEROES FOR HIRE
July, 1997 - Present ($2.99/$1.99)
Marvel Comics

1-($2.99)-Wraparound cover 2.99
2-7: 2-Variant cover. 7-Thunderbolts app. 1.99

HEROES FOR HOPE STARRING THE X-MEN
Dec, 1985 ($1.50, one-shot, 52pgs., proceeds donated to famine relief)
Marvel Comics Group

1-Stephen King scripts; Byrne, Miller, Corben-a; Wrightson/J. Jones-a (3 pgs.); Art Adams-c; Starlin back-c 1.20 3.00

HEROES, INC. PRESENTS CANNON
1969 - No. 2, 1976 (Sold at Army PX's)
Wally Wood/CPL/Gang Publ. No. 2

nn-Ditko, Wood-a; Wood-c; Reese-a(p) 1.50 4.50 12.00
2-Wood-c; Ditko, Byrne, Wood-a; 8-1/2x10-1/2"; B&W; $2.00 1.85 5.50 15.00

NOTE: *First issue not distributed by publisher; 1,800 copies were stored and 900 copies were stolen from warehouse. Many copies have surfaced in recent years.*

HEROES OF THE WILD FRONTIER (Formerly Baffling Mysteries)
No. 27, Jan, 1956 - No. 2, Apr, 1956
Ace Periodicals

27(#1),2-Davy Crockett, Daniel Boone, Buffalo Bill 4.00 12.00 24.00

HEROES REBORN: THE RETURN
Dec, 1997 - No. 4 ($2.50, weekly mini-series)
Marvel Comics

1-4-Avengers, Fantastic Four, Iron Man & Captain America rejoin regular Marvel Universe; Peter David-s/Larocca-c/a 1.00 2.50
..1-4-Variant-c for each 1.00 2.50

HERO FOR HIRE (Power Man No. 17 on; also see Cage)
June, 1972 - No. 16, Dec, 1973
Marvel Comics Group

1-Origin & 1st app. Luke Cage; Tuska-a(p) 3.00 9.00 30.00
2-5: 2,3-Tuska-a(p). 3-1st app. Mace. 4-1st app. Phil Fox of the Bugle 1.00 3.00 7.50
6-10: 8,9-Dr. Doom app. 9-F.F. app. 1.80 4.50
11-16: 14-Origin retold. 15-Everett Subby-r('53). 16-Origin Stilletto; death of Rackham 1.20 3.00

HERO HOTLINE (1st app. in Action Comics Weekly #637)
April, 1989 - No. 6, Sept, 1989 ($1.75, limited series)
DC Comics

1-6: Super-hero humor; Schaffenberger-i .90 1.80

HEROIC ADVENTURES (See Adventures)

HEROIC COMICS (Reg'lar Fellers...#1-15; New Heroic #41 on)

Heroic Comics #18 © EAS

Hero Zero #0 © DH

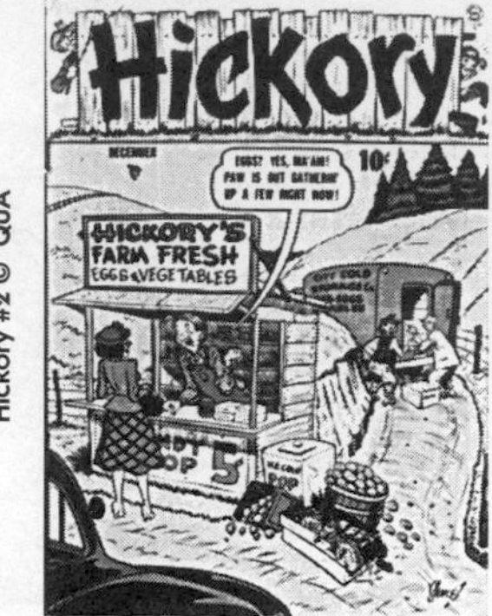

Hickory #2 © QUA

Aug, 1940 - No. 97, June, 1955
Eastern Color Printing Co./Famous Funnies(Funnies, Inc. No. 1)

	GD25	FN65	NM94
1-Hydroman (origin) by Bill Everett, The Purple Zombie (origin) & Mann of India by Tarpe Mills begins (all 1st apps.)	128.00	384.00	1150.00
2	60.00	180.00	540.00
3,4	39.00	117.00	350.00
5,6	35.00	105.00	280.00
7-Origin & 1st app. Man O'Metal (1 pg.)	36.00	108.00	315.00
8-10: 10-Lingerie panels	24.00	71.00	190.00
11,13: 13-Crandall/Fine-a	23.00	68.00	180.00
12-Music Master (origin/1st app.) begins by Everett, ends No. 31; last Purple Zombie & Mann of India	25.00	75.00	200.00
14,15-Hydroman x-over in Rainbow Boy. 14-Origin & 1st app. Rainbow Boy (super hero). 15-1st app. Downbeat	25.00	75.00	200.00
16-20: 16-New logo. 17-Rainbow Boy x-over in Hydroman. 19-Rainbow Boy x-over in Hydroman & vice versa	17.00	51.00	135.00
21-30:25-Rainbow Boy x-over in Hydroman. 28-Last Man O'Metal. 29-Last Hydroman	11.30	34.00	90.00
31,34,38	4.00	12.00	24.00
32,36,37-Toth-a (3-4 pgs. each)	5.70	17.00	38.00
33,35-Toth-a (8 & 9 pgs.)	5.70	17.00	40.00
39-42-Toth, Ingels-a	5.70	17.00	40.00
43,46,47,49-Toth-a (2-4 pgs.). 47-Ingels-a	5.00	15.00	30.00
44,45,50-Toth-a (6-9 pgs.)	5.70	17.00	35.00
48,53,54	4.00	11.00	22.00
51-Williamson-a	5.70	17.00	38.00
52-Williamson-a (3 pg. story)	4.25	13.00	28.00
55-Toth-c/a	5.35	16.00	32.00
56-60-Toth-c. 60-Everett-a	4.25	13.00	28.00
61-Everett-a	4.00	11.00	22.00
62,64-Everett-c/a	4.15	12.50	25.00
63-Everett-c	3.60	9.00	18.00
65-Williamson/Frazetta-a; Evans-a (2 pgs.)	6.50	19.50	45.00
66,75,94-Frazetta-a (2 pgs. each)	4.15	12.50	25.00
67,73-Frazetta-a (4 pgs. each)	5.00	15.00	30.00
68,74,76-80,84,85,88-93,95-97: 95-Last pre-code	3.60	9.00	18.00
69,72-Frazetta-a (6 & 8 pgs. each); 1st (?) app. Frazetta Red Cross ad	6.50	19.50	45.00
70,71,86,87-Frazetta, 3-4 pgs. each; 1 pg. ad by Frazetta in #70	4.15	12.50	25.00
81,82-Frazetta art (1 pg. each): 81-1st (?) app. Frazetta Boy Scout ad (tied w/ Buster Crabbe #9	3.60	9.00	18.00
83-Frazetta-a (1/2 pg.)	3.60	9.00	18.00

NOTE: ***Evans** a-64, 65. **Everett** a-(Hydroman-c/a-No. 1-9), 44, 60-64; c-1-9, 62-64. **Harvey Fuller** c-28-35. **Sid Greene** a-38-43, 46. **Guardineer** a-42(3), 43, 44, 45(2), 49(3), 50, 60, 61(2), 65, 67(2) 70-72. **Ingels** c-41. **Kiefer** a-46, 48; c-19-22, 24, 44, 46, 48, 51-53, 65, 67-69, 71-74, 76, 77, 79, 80, 82, 85, 86, 88, 89, 94, 95. **Mort Lawrence** a-45. **Tarpe Mills** a-2(2), 3(2), 10. **Ed Moore** a-49, 52-54, 56-63, 65-69, 72-74, 76, 77. **H.G. Peter** a-58-74, 76, 77, 87. **Paul Reinman** a-49. **Rico** a-31. Captain Tootsie by **Beck**-31, 32. Painted-c #16 on. Hydroman c-1-11. Music Master c-12, 13, 15. Rainbow Boy c-14.*

HERO ZERO (Also see Comics' Greatest World & Godzilla Versus Hero Zero)
Sept, 1994 ($2.50)
Dark Horse Comics

	GD25	FN65	NM94
0		1.00	2.50

HEX (Replaces Jonah Hex)
Sept, 1985 - No. 18, Feb, 1987 (Story continues from Jonah Hex No. 92)
DC Comics

	GD25	FN65	NM94
1-10,14-18: 1-Hex in post-atomic war world; origin. 6-Origin Stiletta		.80	2.00
11-13: All contain future Batman storyline. 13-Intro The Dogs of War (origin #15)		1.00	2.50

NOTE: ***Giffen** a(p)-15-18; c(p)-15,17,18. **Texeira** a-1, 2p, 3p, 5-7p, 9p, 11-14p; c(p)-1, 2, 4-7, 12.*

HEXBREAKER (See First Comics Graphic Novel #15)

HEY THERE, IT'S YOGI BEAR (See Movie Comics)

HI-ADVENTURE HEROES (TV)
May, 1969 - No. 2, Aug, 1969 (Hanna-Barbera)
Gold Key

	GD25	FN65	NM94
1-Three Musketeers, Gulliver, Arabian Knights	3.60	11.00	40.00
2-Three Musketeers, Micro-Venture, Arabian Knights	2.75	8.00	30.00

HI AND LOIS
No. 683, Mar, 1956 - No. 955, Nov, 1958
Dell Publishing Co.

	GD25	FN65	NM94
Four Color 683 (#1)	2.25	6.75	25.00
Four Color 774(3/57),955	1.80	5.50	20.00

HI AND LOIS
Nov, 1969 - No. 11, July, 1971
Charlton Comics

	GD25	FN65	NM94
1	2.25	6.75	18.00
2-11	1.25	3.75	10.00

HICKORY (See All Humor Comics)
Oct, 1949 - No. 6, Aug, 1950
Quality Comics Group

	GD25	FN65	NM94
1-Sahl-c/a in all; Feldstein?-a	12.00	36.00	95.00
2	6.50	19.50	45.00
3-6	5.70	17.00	40.00

HIDDEN CREW, THE (See The United States Air Force Presents:...)

HIDE-OUT (See Zane Grey, Four Color No. 346)

HIDING PLACE, THE
1973 (39¢/49¢)
Spire Christian Comics (Fleming H. Revell Co.)

	GD25	FN65	NM94
nn		1.60	4.00

HIGH ADVENTURE
Oct, 1957
Red Top(Decker) Comics (Farrell)

	GD25	FN65	NM94
1-Krigstein-r from Explorer Joe (re-issue on-c)	2.50	7.50	24.00

HIGH ADVENTURE (TV)
No. 949, Nov, 1958 - No. 1001, Aug-Oct, 1959 (Lowell Thomas)
Dell Publishing Co.

	GD25	FN65	NM94
Four Color 949 (#1)-Photo-c	4.50	13.50	50.00
Four Color 1001-Lowell Thomas'...(#2)	4.50	13.50	50.00

HIGH CHAPPARAL (TV)
Aug, 1968 (Photo-c)
Gold Key

	GD25	FN65	NM94
1 (10226-808)-Tufts-a	3.60	11.00	40.00

HIGH SCHOOL CONFIDENTIAL DIARY (Confidential Diary #12 on)
June, 1960 - No. 11, Mar, 1962
Charlton Comics

	GD25	FN65	NM94
1	3.00	9.00	30.00
2-11	2.00	6.00	16.00

HIGH VOLTAGE
1996 - Present ($2.95)
Blackout Comics

	GD25	FN65	NM94
0-Mike Baron-s		1.20	3.00

HI-HO COMICS
nd (2/46?) - No. 3, 1946
Four Star Publications

	GD25	FN65	NM94
1-Funny Animal; L. B. Cole-c	28.00	83.00	220.00
2,3: 2-L. B. Cole-c	15.00	45.00	120.00

Hi-School Romance #5 © HARV

Hit Comics #1 © QUA

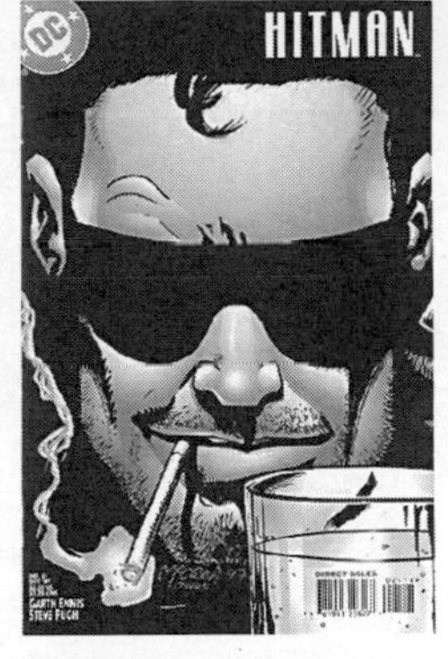

Hitman #21 © DC

HI-JINX (Teen-age Animal Funnies)
1945; July-Aug, 1947 - No. 7, July-Aug, 1948
La Salle Publ. Co./B&I Publ. Co.(American Comics Group)/Creston

	GD25	FN65	NM94
nn-(© 1945, 25 cents, 132 Pgs.)(La Salle)	16.00	49.00	130.00
1-Teen-age, funny animal	12.00	36.00	100.00
2,3	8.50	26.00	60.00
4-7-Milt Gross. 4-X-Mas-c	10.50	32.00	85.00

HI-LITE COMICS
Fall, 1945
E. R. Ross Publishing Co.

	GD25	FN65	NM94
1-Miss Shady	12.00	38.00	100.00

HILLBILLY COMICS
Aug, 1955 - No. 4, July, 1956 (Satire)
Charlton Comics

	GD25	FN65	NM94
1	6.00	18.00	42.00
2-4	4.25	13.00	26.00

HILLY ROSE'S SPACE ADVENTURES
May, 1995 - Present ($2.95, B&W)
Astro Comics

	GD25	FN65	NM94
1	1.85	5.50	15.00
2		2.00	5.00
3-9		1.20	3.00
Trade Paperback (1996, $12.95)-r/#1-5			13.00

HIP-IT-TY HOP (See March of Comics No. 15)

HI-SCHOOL ROMANCE (...Romances No. 41 on)
Oct, 1949 - No. 5, June, 1950; No. 6, Dec, 1950 - No. 73, Mar, 1958; No. 74, Sept, 1958 - No. 75, Nov, 1958
Harvey Publications/True Love(Home Comics)

	GD25	FN65	NM94
1-Photo-c	10.50	32.00	85.00
2-Photo-c	6.50	19.50	45.00
3-9: 3,5-Photo-c	5.00	15.00	30.00
10-Rape story	6.50	19.50	45.00
11-20	3.60	9.00	18.00
21-31	3.00	7.50	15.00
32- "Unholy passion" story	5.00	15.00	30.00
33-36: 36-Last pre-code (2/55)	2.80	7.00	14.00
37-75	2.00	5.00	10.00

NOTE: ***Powell*** *a-1-3, 5, 8, 12-16, 18, 21-23, 25-27, 30-34, 36, 37, 39, 45-48, 50-52, 57, 58, 60, 64, 65, 67, 69.*

HI-SCHOOL ROMANCE DATE BOOK
Nov, 1962 - No. 3, Mar, 1963 (25¢ Giants)
Harvey Publications

	GD25	FN65	NM94
1-Powell, Baker-a	2.50	7.50	25.00
2,3	1.40	4.20	14.00

HIS NAME IS SAVAGE (Magazine format)
June, 1968 (35¢, 52 pgs.)
Adventure House Press

	GD25	FN65	NM94
1-Gil Kane-a	3.50	10.50	35.00

HI-SPOT COMICS (Red Ryder No. 1 & No. 3 on)
No. 2, Nov, 1940
Hawley Publications

	GD25	FN65	NM94
2-David Innes of Pellucidar; art by J. C. Burroughs; written by Edgar Rice Burroughs	94.00	282.00	850.00

HISTORY OF THE DC UNIVERSE (Also see Crisis on Infinite Earths)
Sept, 1986 - No. 2, Nov, 1986 ($2.95, limited series)
DC Comics

	GD25	FN65	NM94
1,2: 1-Perez-c/a		1.20	3.00
Limited Edition hardcover	3.50	10.50	35.00

HITCHHIKERS GUIDE TO THE GALAXY (See Life, the Universe and Everything & Restaraunt at the End of the Universe)
1993 - No. 3, 1993 ($4.95, limited series)
DC Comics

	GD25	FN65	NM94
1-3: Adaptation of Douglas Adams book		2.00	5.00
TPB (1997, $14.95) r/#1-3			15.00

HIT COMICS
July, 1940 - No. 65, July, 1950
Quality Comics Group

	GD25	FN65	NM94
1-Origin/1st app. Neon, the Unknown & Hercules; intro. The Red Bee; Bob & Swab, Blaze Barton, the Strange Twins, X-5 Super Agent, Casey Jones & Jack & Jill (ends #7) begin	500.00	1500.00	5000.00
2-The Old Witch begins, ends #14	211.00	633.00	1900.00
3-Casey Jones ends; transvestism story "Jack & Jill"	189.00	567.00	1700.00
4-Super Agent (ends #17), & Betty Bates (ends #65) begin; X-5 ends	167.00	500.00	1500.00
5-Classic Lou Fine cover	400.00	1200.00	4000.00
6-10: 10-Old Witch by Crandall (4 pgs.); 1st work in comics (4/41)	150.00	450.00	1350.00
11-17: 13-Blaze Barton ends. 17-Last Neon; Crandall Hercules in all; Last Lou Fine-c	93.00	279.00	840.00
18-Origin & 1st app. Stormy Foster, the Great Defender (12/41); The Ghost of Flanders begins; Crandall-c	106.00	318.00	950.00
19,20	86.00	258.00	775.00
21-24: 21-Last Hercules. 24-Last Red Bee & Strange Twins	81.00	243.00	725.00
25-Origin & 1st app. Kid Eternity and begins by Moldoff (12/42); 1st app. The Keeper (Kid Eternity's aide)	122.00	366.00	1100.00
26-Blackhawk x-over in Kid Eternity	81.00	243.00	725.00
27-29	39.00	117.00	350.00
30,31- "Bill the Magnificent" by Kurtzman, 11 pgs. in each	36.00	108.00	315.00
32-40: 32-Plastic Man x-over. 34-Last Stormy Foster	20.00	60.00	160.00
41-50	13.00	39.00	105.00
51-60-Last Kid Eternity	12.00	36.00	95.00
61-63-Crandall-c/a; 61-Jeb Rivers begins	12.00	38.00	100.00
64,65-Crandall-a	12.00	36.00	95.00

NOTE: ***Crandall*** *a-11-17(Hercules), 23, 24(Stormy Foster); c-18-20, 23, 24.* ***Fine*** *c-1-14, 16, 17(most).* ***Ward*** *c-33. Bondage c-7, 64. Hercules c-3, 10-17. Jeb Rivers c-61-65. Kid Eternity c-25-60 (w/Keeper-28-34, 36, 39-43, 45-55). Neon the Unknown c-2, 4, 8, 9. Red Bee c-1, 5-7. Stormy Foster c-18-24.*

HITLER'S ASTROLOGER (See Marvel Graphic Novel #35)

HITMAN (Also see Bloodbath #2, Batman Chronicles #4 & The Demon Annual #2)
May, 1996 - Present ($2.25)
DC Comics

	GD25	FN65	NM94
1-Garth Ennis-s & John McCrea-c/a begin; Batman app.	1.25	3.75	10.00
2-Joker-c; Two Face, Mad Hatter app.; Batman cameo.		2.80	7.00
3-Batman-c/app.; Joker app		1.60	4.00
4-20: 4-1st app. Nightfist. 8-Final Night x-over. 10-GL cameo. 11,12-GL-c/app. 15-20-"Ace of Killers". 16-18-Catwoman app. 17-19-Demon-app		1.20	3.00
21-23			2.25
Annual 1 (1997, $3.95) Pulp Heroes			3.95
TPB-(1997, $9.95) r/Hitman 1-3, Demon Ann. 2, Batman Chronicles 4			9.95

HI-YO SILVER (See Lone Ranger's Famous Horse... and also see The Lone Ranger and March of Comics No. 215)

HOBBIT, THE
1989 - No. 3, 1990 ($4.95, squarebound, 52 pgs.)
Eclipse Comics

Holiday Comics #1 © FAW

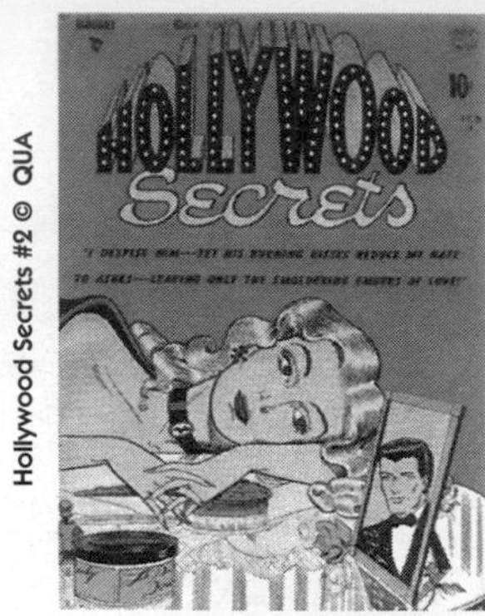

Hollywood Secrets #2 © QUA

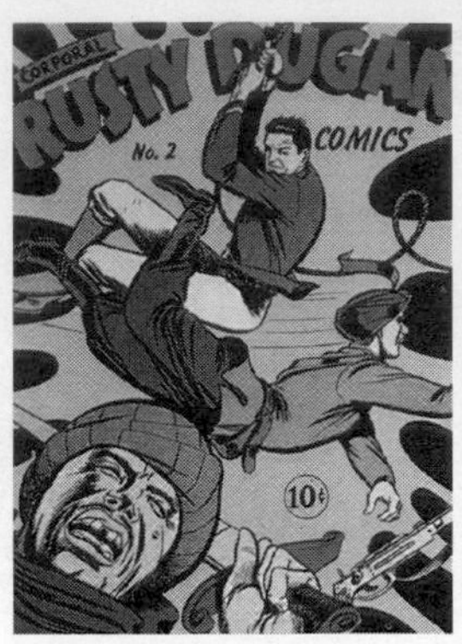

Holyoke One-shot #2 © HOKE

	GD25	FN65	NM94
Book 1-3: Adapts novel (#1has a 2nd printing)		2.00	5.00

HOCUS POCUS (Formerly Funny Book)
No. 9, Aug-Sept, 1946
Parents' Magazine Press

	GD25	FN65	NM94
9	4.25	13.00	28.00

HOGAN'S HEROES (TV)
June, 1966 - No. 8, Sept, 1967; No. 9, Oct, 1969
Dell Publishing Co.

	GD25	FN65	NM94
1: #1-7 photo-c	6.40	19.00	70.00
2,3-Ditko-a(p)	4.00	12.00	45.00
4-9: 9-Reprints #1	2.75	8.00	30.00

HOKUM & HEX (See Razorline)
Sept, 1993 - No. 9, May, 1994 ($1.75/$1.95)
Marvel Comics (Razorline)

	GD25	FN65	NM94
1-($2.50)-Foil embossed-c; by Clive Barker		1.00	2.50
2-8: 5-Hyperkind x-over		.70	1.75
9-($1.95)		.80	2.00

HOLIDAY COMICS
1942 (25¢, 196 pgs.)
Fawcett Publications

	GD25	FN65	NM94
1-Contains three Fawcett comics plus two page portrait of Captain Marvel; Capt. Marvel, Nyoka #1, & Whiz. Not rebound, remaindered comics; printed at the same time as originals	137.00	411.00	1375.00

HOLIDAY COMICS (Becomes Fun Comics #9-12)
Jan, 1951 - No. 8, Oct, 1952
Star Publications

	GD25	FN65	NM94
1-Funny animal contents (Frisky Fables) in all; L. B. Cole X-Mas-c	26.00	80.00	210.00
2-Classic L. B. Cole-c	29.00	88.00	235.00
3-8: 5,8-X-Mas-c; all L.B. Cole-c	18.00	54.00	145.00
Accepted Reprint 4 (nd)-L.B. Cole-c	8.50	26.00	60.00

HOLIDAY DIGEST
1988 ($1.25, digest-size)
Harvey Comics

	GD25	FN65	NM94
1		1.60	4.00

HOLIDAY PARADE (Walt Disney's...)
Winter, 1990-91(no yr. given) - No. 2, Winter, 1990-91 ($2.95, 68 pgs.)
W. D. Publications (Disney)

	GD25	FN65	NM94
1-Reprints 1947 Firestone by Barks plus new-a		1.20	3.00
2-Barks-r plus other stories		1.20	3.00

HOLI-DAY SURPRISE (Formerly Summer Fun)
V2#55, Mar, 1967 (25¢ Giant)
Charlton Comics

	GD25	FN65	NM94
V2#55	1.85	5.50	15.00

HOLLYWOOD COMICS
Winter, 1944 (52 pgs.)
New Age Publishers

	GD25	FN65	NM94
1-Funny animal	14.00	41.00	110.00

HOLLYWOOD CONFESSIONS
Oct, 1949 - No. 2, Dec, 1949
St. John Publishing Co.

	GD25	FN65	NM94
1-Kubert-c/a (entire book)	20.00	60.00	150.00
2-Kubert-c/a (entire book) (Scarce)	29.00	86.00	200.00

HOLLYWOOD DIARY
Dec, 1949 - No. 5, July-Aug, 1950
Quality Comics Group

	GD25	FN65	NM94
1-No photo-c	14.00	43.00	110.00
2-Photo-c	10.00	30.00	70.00
3-5-Photo-c. 5-June Allyson/Peter Lawford photo-c	8.35	25.00	55.00

HOLLYWOOD FILM STORIES
April, 1950 - No. 4, Oct, 1950 (All photo-c; "Fumetti" type movie comic)
Feature Publications/Prize

	GD25	FN65	NM94
1-June Allyson photo-c	14.00	43.00	110.00
2-4: 2-Lizabeth Scott photo-c. 3-Barbara Stanwick photo-c. 4-Betty Hutton photo-c	11.00	33.00	80.00

HOLLYWOOD FUNNY FOLKS (Formerly Funny Folks; Becomes Nutsy Squirrel #61 on)
No. 27, Aug-Sept, 1950 - No. 60, July-Aug, 1954
National Periodical Publications

	GD25	FN65	NM94
27	11.30	34.00	90.00
28-40	8.50	26.00	60.00
41-60	7.15	21.50	50.00

NOTE: ***Sheldon Mayer*** *a-27-35, 37-40, 43-46, 48-51, 53, 56, 57, 60.*

HOLLYWOOD LOVE DOCTOR (See Doctor Anthony King...)

HOLLYWOOD PICTORIAL (...Romances on cover)
No. 3, Jan, 1950
St. John Publishing Co.

	GD25	FN65	NM94
3-Matt Baker-a; photo-c	19.00	58.00	140.00

(Becomes a movie magazine - Hollywood Pictorial Western with No. 4.)

HOLLYWOOD ROMANCES (Formerly Brides In Love; becomes For Lovers Only #60 on)
V2#46, 11/66; #47, 10/67; #48, 11/68; V3#49, 11/69 - V3#59, 6/71
Charlton Comics

	GD25	FN65	NM94
V2#46-Rolling Stones-c/story	6.00	18.00	60.00
V2#47-V3#59: 56- "Born to Heart Break" begins		2.40	6.00

HOLLYWOOD SECRETS
Nov, 1949 - No. 6, Sept, 1950
Quality Comics Group

	GD25	FN65	NM94
1-Ward-c/a (9 pgs.)	26.00	79.00	190.00
2-Crandall-a, Ward-c/a (9 pgs.)	17.00	51.00	125.00
3-6: All photo-c. 5-Lex Barker (Tarzan)-c	9.00	27.00	60.00
...of Romance, I.W. Reprint #9; r/#2 above w/Kinstler-c	2.00	5.00	10.00

HOLLYWOOD SUPERSTARS
Nov, 1990 - No. 5, Apr, 1991 ($2.25)
Marvel Comics (Epic Comics)

	GD25	FN65	NM94
1-($2.95, 52 pgs.)-Spiegle-c/a in all; Aragones-a, inside front-c plus 2-4 pgs.		1.20	3.00
2-5 ($2.25)		.90	2.30

HOLO-MAN (See Power Record Comics)

HOLYOKE ONE-SHOT
1944 - No. 10, 1945 (All reprints)
Holyoke Publishing Co. (Tem Publ.)

	GD25	FN65	NM94
1-Grit Grady (on cover only), Miss Victory, Alias X (origin)-All reprints from Captain Fearless	8.50	26.00	60.00
2-Rusty Dugan (Corporal); Capt. Fearless (origin), Mr. Miracle (origin) app.	8.50	26.00	60.00
3-Miss Victory; r/Crash #4; Cat Man (origin), Solar Legion by Kirby app.; Miss Victory on cover only (1945)	18.00	54.00	145.00
4-Mr. Miracle; The Blue Streak app.	7.15	21.50	50.00
5-U.S. Border Patrol Comics (Sgt. Dick Carter of the...), Miss Victory (story matches cover to #3), Citizen Smith, & Mr. Miracle app.	8.50	26.00	60.00
6-Capt. Fearless, Alias X, Capt. Stone (splash used as-c to #10); Diamond Jim & Rusty Dugan (splash from cover of #2)	7.15	21.50	50.00

7-Secret Agent Z-2, Strong Man, Blue Streak (story matches cover to #8);

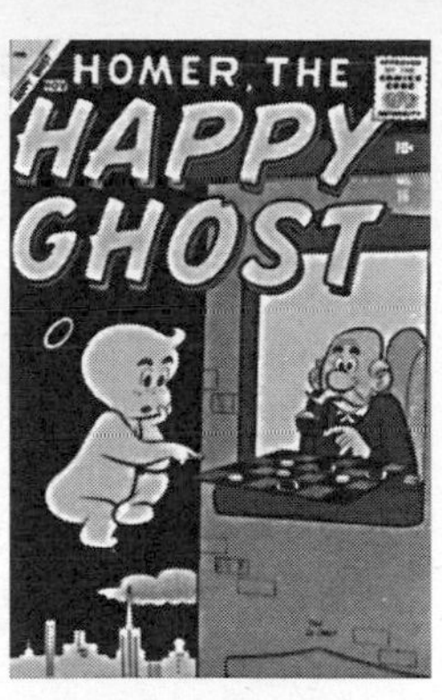

Homer, the Happy Ghost #16 © ACI

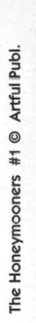

The Honeymooners #1 © Artful Publ.

Hook #1 © MEG

GD25 FN65 NM94

Reprints from Crash #2 8.50 26.00 60.00
8-Blue Streak, Strong Man (story matches cover to #7)-Crash reprints
7.15 21.50 50.00
9-Citizen Smith, The Blue Streak, Solar Legion by Kirby & Strongman, the Perfect Human app.; reprints from Crash #4 & 5; Citizen Smith on cover only-from story in #5 (1944-before #3) 11.30 34.00 90.00
10-Captain Stone; r/Crash; Solar Legion by S&K 11.30 34.00 90.00

HOMER COBB (See Adventures of...)

HOMER HOOPER
July, 1953 - No. 4, Dec, 1953
Atlas Comics
1-Teenage humor 7.50 22.50 52.00
2-4 5.70 17.00 35.00

HOMER, THE HAPPY GHOST (See Adventures of...)
3/55 - No. 22, 11/58; V2#1, 11/69 - V2#5, 7/70
Atlas(ACI/PPI/WPI)/Marvel Comics
V1#1-Dan DeCarlo-c/a begins, ends #22 11.30 34.00 90.00
2-1st code approved issue 6.50 19.50 45.00
3-10 5.70 17.00 35.00
11-22 4.25 12.50 28.00
V2#1 (11/69) 8.00 24.00 80.00
2-4 3.50 10.50 35.00
V2#5 (7/70) 15.00 45.00 150.00

HOME RUN (Also see A-1 Comics)
No. 89, 1953 (one-shot)
Magazine Enterprises
A-1 89 (#3)-Powell-a; Stan Musial photo-c 8.75 26.25 70.00

HOMICIDE (Also see Dark Horse Presents)
Apr, 1990 ($1.95, B&W, one-shot)
Dark Horse Comics
1-Detective story .80 2.00

HOMICIDE: TEARS OF THE DEAD
Apr, 1997 ($2.95, one-shot)
Chaos! Comics
1-Brom-c 2.95
1-Premium Ltd. Ed. w/wraparound-c 2.95

HONEYBEE BIRDWHISTLE AND HER PET PEPI (Introducing...)
1969 (Giveaway, 24 pgs., B&W, slick cover)
Newspaper Enterprise Association
nn-Contains Freckles newspaper strips with a short biography of Henry Fornhals (artist) & Fred Fox (writer) of the strip 3.80 11.40 38.00

HONEYMOON (Formerly Gay Comics)
No. 41, Jan, 1950
A Lover's Magazine(USA) (Marvel)
41-Photo-c; article by Betty Grable 7.15 21.50 50.00

HONEYMOONERS, THE (TV)
Oct, 1986 ($1.50)
Lodestone
1-Photo-c 1.50

HONEYMOONERS, THE (TV)
Sept, 1987 - No. 13? ($2.00)
Triad Publications
1-13 .80 2.00

HONEYMOON ROMANCE
Apr, 1950 - No. 2, July, 1950 (25¢, digest size)
Artful Publications (Canadian)
1,2-(Rare) 31.00 92.00 225.00

GD25 FN65 NM94

HONEY WEST (TV)
Sept, 1966 (Photo-c)
Gold Key
1 (10186-609) 9.00 26.00 95.00

HONG KONG PHOOEY (TV)
June, 1975 - No. 9, Nov, 1976 (Hanna-Barbera)
Charlton Comics
1 3.00 9.00 30.00
2 1.85 5.50 15.00
3-9 1.25 3.75 10.00

HOODED HORSEMAN, THE (Also see Blazing West)
No. 21, 1-2/52 - No. 27, 1-2/53; No. 18, 12-1/54-55 - No. 27, 6-7/56
American Comics Group (Michel Publ.)
21(1-2/52)-Hooded Horseman, Injun Jones continue
12.00 36.00 95.00
22 8.50 26.00 60.00
23-25,27(1-2/53) 6.50 19.50 45.00
26-Origin/1st app. Cowboy Sahib by L. Starr 8.75 26.25 70.00
18(11-12/54)(Formerly Out of the Night) 8.50 26.00 60.00
19-Last precode (1-2/55) 5.70 17.00 40.00
20-Origin Johnny Injun 7.15 21.50 50.00
21-24,26,27(6-7/56) 5.70 17.00 40.00
25-Cowboy Sahib on cover only; Hooded Horseman i.d. revealed
6.50 19.50 45.00
NOTE: ***Whitney*** *c/a-21('52), 20-22.*

HOODED MENACE, THE (Also see Daring Adventures)
1951 (one-shot)
Realistic/Avon Periodicals
nn-Based on a band of hooded outlaws in the Pacific Northwest, 1900-1906; reprinted in Daring Advs. #15 36.00 108.00 325.00

HOODS UP
1953 (15¢, distributed to service station owners, 16 pgs.)
Fram Corp.
1-(Very Rare; only 2 known); Eisner-c/a in all. 42.00 126.00 375.00
2-6-(Very Rare; only 1 known of #3, 4, 2 known of #2)
42.00 126.00 375.00
NOTE: *Convertible Connie gives tips for service stations, selling Fram oil filters.*

HOOK (Movie)
Early Feb, 1992 - No. 4, Late Mar, 1992 ($1.00, limited series)
Marvel Comics
1-4: Adapts movie; Vess-c; 1-Morrow-a(p) 1.00
nn (1991, $5.95, 84 pgs.)-Contains #1-4; Vess-c 2.40 6.00
1 (1991, $2.95, magazine, 84 pgs.)-Contains #1-4; Vess-c (same cover as nn issue) 1.20 3.00

HOOT GIBSON'S WESTERN ROUNDUP (See Western Roundup under Fox Giants)

HOOT GIBSON WESTERN (Formerly My Love Story)
No. 5, May, 1950 - No. 3, Sept, 1950
Fox Features Syndicate
5,6(#1,2): 5-Photo-c. 6-Photo/painted-c 22.00 66.00 175.00
3-Wood-a; painted-c 24.00 71.00 190.00

HOPALONG CASSIDY (Also see Bill Boyd Western, Master Comics, Real Western Hero, Six Gun Heroes & Western Hero; Bill Boyd starred as H. Cassidy in the movies; H. Cassidy in movies, radio & TV)
Feb, 1943; No. 2, Summer, 1946 - No. 85, Nov, 1953
Fawcett Publications
1 (1943, 68 pgs.)-H. Cassidy & his horse Topper begin (on sale 1/8/43)-Captain Marvel app. on-c 420.00 1260.00 4200.00
2-(Sum, '46) 67.00 200.00 600.00
3,4: 3-(Fall, '46, 52 pgs. begin) 31.00 93.00 280.00

Hopalong Cassidy #84 © FAW

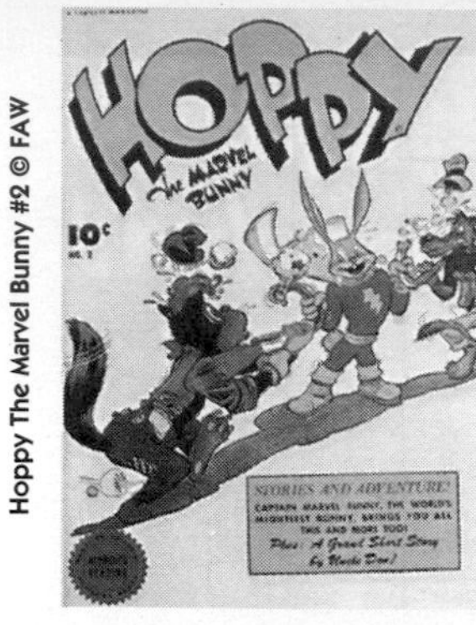

Hoppy The Marvel Bunny #2 © FAW

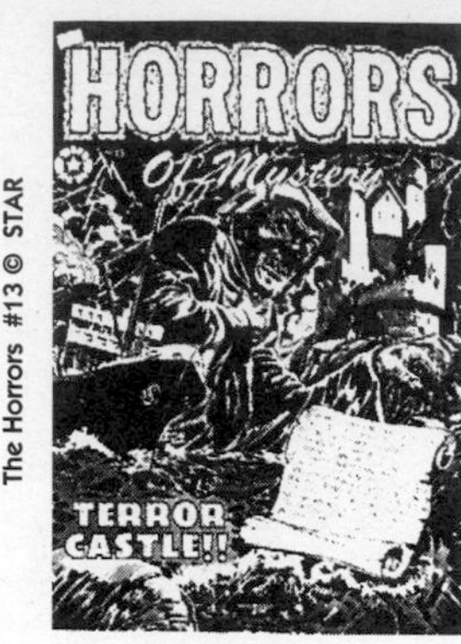

The Horrors #13 © STAR

	GD25	FN65	NM94
5- "Mad Barber" story mentioned in **SOTI**, pgs. 308,309; photo-c	27.00	80.00	240.00
6-10: 8-Photo-c	21.00	63.00	190.00
11-19: 11,13-19-Photo-c	15.50	47.00	140.00
20-29 (52 pgs.)-Painted/photo-c	12.00	36.00	110.00
30,31,33,34,37-39,41 (52 pgs.)-Painted-c	8.75	26.25	70.00
32,40 (36pgs.)-Painted-c	8.50	26.00	60.00
35,42,43,45 (52 pgs.)-Photo-c	8.75	26.25	65.00
36,44,48 (36 pgs.)-Photo-c	7.85	23.50	55.00
46,47,49-51,53,54,56 (52 pgs.)-Photo-c	8.75	26.25	65.00
52,55,57-70 (36 pgs.)-Photo-c	6.50	19.50	45.00
71-84-Photo-c	5.70	17.00	35.00
85-Last Fawcett issue; photo-c	6.50	19.50	45.00

NOTE: *Line-drawn c-1-4, 6, 7, 9, 10, 12.*

	GD25	FN65	NM94
Grape Nuts Flakes giveaway (1950,9x6")	11.30	34.00	90.00
...& the Mad Barber (1951 Bond Bread giveaway)-7x5"; used in **SOTI**, pgs. 308,309	19.00	56.00	150.00
...Meets the Brend Brothers Bandits (1951 Bond Bread giveaway, color, paper-c, 16pgs. 3-1/2x7")-Fawcett Publ.	8.75	26.25	65.00
...Strange Legacy (1951 Bond Bread giveaway)	8.75	26.25	65.00
White Tower Giveaway (1946, 16pgs., paper-c)	8.75	26.25	65.00

HOPALONG CASSIDY (TV)
No. 86, Feb, 1954 - No. 135, May-June, 1959 (All-36 pgs.)
National Periodical Publications

	GD25	FN65	NM94
86-Gene Colan-a begins, ends #117; photo covers continue	31.00	94.00	250.00
87	17.50	53.00	140.00
88-91: 91-1 pg. Superboy-sty (6/54)	12.00	36.00	95.00
92-99 (98 has #93 on-c; last precode issue, 2/55). 95-Reversed photo-c to #52. 98-Reversed photo-c to #61. 99-Reversed photo-c to #60	10.00	30.00	80.00
100-Same cover as #50	11.30	34.00	90.00
101-108: 105-Same photo-c as #54. 107-Same photo-c as #51. 108-Last photo-c	6.00	18.00	60.00
109-135: 118-Gil Kane-a begins. 123-Kubert-a (2 pgs.). 124-Painted-c	5.00	15.00	50.00

HOPE SHIP
June-Aug, 1963
Dell Publishing Co.

	GD25	FN65	NM94
1	1.10	3.30	9.00

HOPPY THE MARVEL BUNNY (See Fawcett's Funny Animals)
Dec, 1945 - No. 15, Sept, 1947
Fawcett Publications

	GD25	FN65	NM94
1	24.00	73.00	195.00
2	12.00	36.00	95.00
3-15: 7-Xmas-c	10.00	30.00	80.00
...Well Known Comics (1944,8-1/2x10-1/2", paper-c) Bestmaid/Samuel Lowe (printed in red or blue)	6.85	21.00	48.00

HORACE & DOTTY DRIPPLE (Dotty Dripple No. 1-24)
No. 25, Aug, 1952 - No. 43, Oct, 1955
Harvey Publications

	GD25	FN65	NM94
25-43	1.60	4.00	8.00

HORIZONTAL LIEUTENANT, THE (See Movie Classics)

HOROBI
1990 - No. 8, 1990 ($3.75, B&W, mature readers, 84 pgs.)
V2#1, 1990 - No. 7, 1991 ($4.25, B&W, 68 pgs.)
Viz Premiere Comics

	GD25	FN65	NM94
1-8: Japanese manga		1.60	4.00
Part Two, #1-7		1.80	4.50

HORRIFIC (Terrific No. 14 on)
Sept, 1952 - No. 13, Sept, 1954
Artful/Comic Media/Harwell/Mystery

	GD25	FN65	NM94
1	29.00	86.00	230.00
2	16.00	47.00	120.00
3-Bullet in head-c	26.00	79.00	200.00
4,5,7,9,10: 4-Shrunken head-c. 7-Guillotine-c	11.00	33.00	85.00
6-Jack The Ripper story	12.00	36.00	95.00
8-Origin & 1st app. The Teller (E.C. parody)	15.00	45.00	120.00
11-13: 11-Swipe/Witches Tales #6,27; Devil-c	10.00	30.00	70.00

NOTE: ***Don Heck** a-8; c-3-13. **Hollingsworth** a-4. **Morisi** a-8. **Palais** a-5, 7-12.*

HORROR FROM THE TOMB (Mysterious Stories No. 2 on)
Sept, 1954
Premier Magazine Co.

	GD25	FN65	NM94
1-Woodbridge/Torres, Check-a; The Keeper of the Graveyard is host	29.00	88.00	225.00

HORRORIST, THE (Also see Hellblazer)
Dec, 1995 - No. 2, Jan, 1996 ($5.95, limited series, mature)
DC Comics (Vertigo)

	GD25	FN65	NM94
1,2: Jamie Delano scripts, David Lloyd-c/a; John Constantine (Hellblazer) app.		2.40	6.00

HORRORS, THE (Formerly Startling Terror Tales #10)
No. 11, Jan, 1953 - No. 15, Apr, 1954
Star Publications

	GD25	FN65	NM94
11-Horrors of War; Disbrow-a(2)	21.00	64.00	160.00
12-Horrors of War; color illo in **POP**	20.00	60.00	150.00
13-Horrors of Mystery; crime stories	19.00	56.00	140.00
14,15-Horrors of the Underworld; crime stories	20.00	60.00	150.00

NOTE: *All have **L. B. Cole** covers; a-12. **Hollingsworth** a-13. **Palais** a-13r.*

HORROR TALES (Magazine)
V1#7, 6/69 - V6#6, 12/74; V7#1, 2/75; V7#2, 5/76 - V8#5, 1977; V9#3, 8/78; (V1-V6: 52 pgs.; V7, V8#2: 112 pgs.; V8#4 on: 68 pgs.) (No V5#3, V8#1,3)
Eerie Publications

	GD25	FN65	NM94
V1#7	3.50	10.50	35.00
V1#8,9	2.50	7.50	24.00
V2#1-6('70), V3#1-6('71)	2.50	7.50	20.00
V4#1-3,5-7('72)	2.50	7.50	20.00
V4#4-LSD story reprint/Weird V3#5	3.00	9.00	30.00
V5#1,2,4,5(6/73),5(10/73),6(12/73),V6#1-6('74),V7#1,2,4('76),V7#3('76)-Giant issue,V8#2,4,5('77),V9#3(8/78, $1.50)	2.50	7.50	24.00

NOTE: *Bondage-c-V6#1, 3, V7#2.*

HORSE FEATHERS COMICS
Nov, 1945 - No. 4, July(Summer on-c), 1948 (52 pgs.)
Lev Gleason Publications

	GD25	FN65	NM94
1-Wolverton's Scoop Scuttle, 2 pgs.	15.50	47.00	125.00
2	8.50	26.00	60.00
3,4: 3-(5/48)	5.70	17.00	40.00

HORSEMAN
Mar, 1996 - No. 2, Jan, 1997 ($2.95)
Crusade Comics/Kevlar Studios

	GD25	FN65	NM94
0-1st Kevlar Studios issue.		1.20	3.00
1-(3/96)-Crusade issue; Shi-c/app.		1.20	3.00
1-(11/96),2-(1/97)-Kevlar Studios		1.20	3.00

HORSEMASTERS, THE (Disney)(TV, Movie)
No. 1260, Dec-Feb, 1961/62
Dell Publishing Co.

	GD25	FN65	NM94
Four Color 1260-Annette Funicello photo-c	11.00	33.00	120.00

HORSE SOLDIERS, THE
No. 1048, Nov-Jan, 1959/60 (Movie-feat. John Wayne)
Dell Publishing Co.

Hot Rods and Racing Cars #1 © CC

Hotspur #2 © ECL

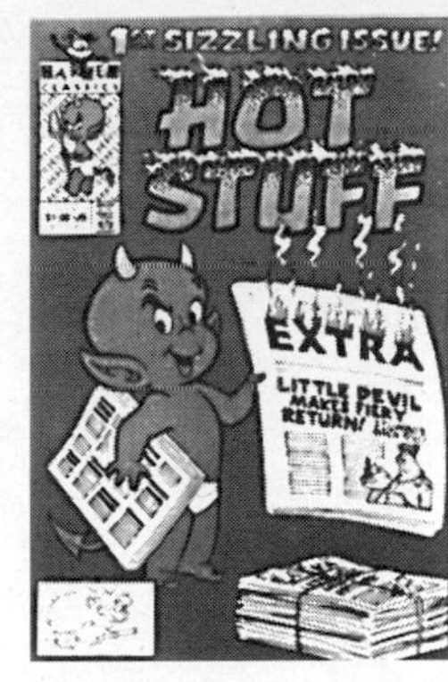

Hot Stuff #1 © HARV

	GD25	FN65	NM94
Four Color 1048-Painted-c, Sekowsky-a	13.00	38.00	140.00

HORSE WITHOUT A HEAD, THE (See Movie Comics)

HOT DOG
June-July, 1954 - No. 4, Dec-Jan, 1954-55
Magazine Enterprises

	GD25	FN65	NM94
1(A-1 #107)	5.70	17.00	40.00
2,3(A-1 #115),4(A-1 #136)	4.25	13.00	28.00

HOT DOG (See Jughead's Pal, Hotdog)

HOTEL DEPAREE - SUNDANCE (TV)
No. 1126, Aug-Oct, 1960 (one-shot)
Dell Publishing Co.

	GD25	FN65	NM94
Four Color 1126-Earl Holliman photo-c	5.50	16.50	60.00

HOT ROD AND SPEEDWAY COMICS
Feb-Mar, 1952 - No. 5, Apr-May, 1953
Hillman Periodicals

	GD25	FN65	NM94
1	20.00	60.00	160.00
2-Krigstein-a	15.00	45.00	120.00
3-5	8.50	26.00	60.00

HOT ROD COMICS (...Featuring Clint Curtis) (See XMas Comics)
Nov, 1951 (no month given) - V2#7, Feb, 1953
Fawcett Publications

	GD25	FN65	NM94
nn (V1#1)-Powell-c/a in all	24.00	71.00	190.00
2 (4/52)	14.00	41.00	110.00
3-6, V2#7	9.50	28.00	75.00

HOT ROD KING (Also see Speed Smith the Hot Rod King)
Fall, 1952
Ziff-Davis Publ. Co.

	GD25	FN65	NM94
1-Giacoia-a; Saunders painted-c	20.00	60.00	160.00

HOT ROD RACERS (Grand Prix No. 16 on)
Dec, 1964 - No. 15, July, 1967
Charlton Comics

	GD25	FN65	NM94
1	6.00	18.00	60.00
2-5	3.50	10.50	35.00
6-15	2.50	7.50	25.00

HOT RODS AND RACING CARS
Nov, 1951 - No. 120, June, 1973
Charlton Comics (Motor Mag. No. 1)

	GD25	FN65	NM94
1-Speed Davis begins; Indianapolis 500 story	21.00	64.00	170.00
2	10.50	32.00	85.00
3-10	7.85	23.50	55.00
11-20	5.70	17.00	40.00
21-34,36-40	5.00	15.00	30.00
35 (6/58, 68 pgs.)	7.15	21.50	50.00
41-60	2.50	7.50	24.00
61-80	2.25	6.75	18.00
81-100	1.50	4.50	12.00
101-120	1.25	3.75	10.00

HOT SHOT CHARLIE
1947 (Lee Elias)
Hillman Periodicals

	GD25	FN65	NM94
1	6.50	19.50	45.00

HOT SHOTS: AVENGERS
Oct, 1995 ($2.95, one-shot)
Marvel Comics

	GD25	FN65	NM94
nn-pin-ups		1.20	3.00

HOTSPUR
June, 1987 - No. 3, Sept, 1987 ($1.75, color, limited series, Baxter paper)
Eclipse Comics

	GD25	FN65	NM94
1-3		.90	1.80

HOT STUFF (See Stumbo Tinytown)
V2#1, Sept, 1991 - No. 12, June, 1994 ($1.00)
Harvey Comics

	GD25	FN65	NM94
V2#1-Stumbo back-up story		1.20	3.00
2-12 ($1.50)		.80	2.00
...Big Book 1 (11/92), 2 (6/93) (Both $1.95, 52 pgs.)		1.20	3.00

HOT STUFF CREEPY CAVES
Nov, 1974 - No. 7, Nov, 1975
Harvey Publications

	GD25	FN65	NM94
1	2.50	7.50	20.00
2-7	1.25	3.75	10.00

HOT STUFF DIGEST
July, 1992 - No. 5, Nov, 1993 ($1.75, digest-size)
Harvey Comics

	GD25	FN65	NM94
V2#1-Hot Stuff, Stumbo, Richie Rich stories		1.20	3.00
2-5		.70	1.75

HOT STUFF GIANT SIZE
Oct, 1992 - No. 3, Oct, 1993 ($2.25, 68 pgs.)
Harvey Comics

	GD25	FN65	NM94
V2#1-Hot Stuff & Stumbo stories		1.20	3.00
2,3		.90	2.25

HOT STUFF SIZZLERS
July, 1960 - No. 59, Mar, 1974; V2#1, Aug, 1992
Harvey Publications

	GD25	FN65	NM94
1: 84 pgs. begin, ends #5; Hot Stuff, Stumbo begin	10.00	30.00	100.00
2-5	4.50	13.50	45.00
6-10: 6-68 pgs. begin, ends #45	2.80	8.40	28.00
11-20	2.00	6.00	20.00
21-45	1.40	4.20	14.00
46-52: 52 pgs. begin	1.00	3.00	10.00
53-59	1.00	3.00	8.00
V2#1-(8/92, $1.25)-Stumbo back-up		1.20	3.00

HOT STUFF, THE LITTLE DEVIL (Also see Devil Kids & Harvey Hits)
10/57 - No. 141, 7/77; No. 142, 2/78 - No. 164, 8/82; No. 165, 10/86 - No. 171, 11/87; No. 172, 11/88; No. 173, Sept, 1990 - No. 177, 1/91
Harvey Publications (Illustrated Humor)

	GD25	FN65	NM94
1	30.00	90.00	300.00
2-1st app. Stumbo the Giant (12/57)	15.00	45.00	150.00
3-5	11.50	35.00	115.00
6-10	6.50	19.50	65.00
11-20	4.50	13.50	45.00
21-40	2.80	8.40	28.00
41-60	1.60	4.80	16.00
61-105	1.00	3.00	10.00
106-112: All 52 pg. Giants	1.40	4.20	14.00
113-125		2.00	5.00
126-177: 172-177-($1.00)		.80	2.00
Shoestore Giveaway('63)	1.20	3.60	12.00

HOT WHEELS (TV)
Mar-Apr, 1970 - No. 6, Jan-Feb, 1971
National Periodical Publications

	GD25	FN65	NM94
1	7.50	22.50	75.00
2,4,5	3.00	9.00	30.00
3-Neal Adams-c	4.00	12.00	40.00
6-Neal Adams-c/a	5.00	15.00	50.00

NOTE: ***Toth*** *a-1p, 2-5; c-1p, 5.*

House of Mystery #64 © DC

House of Mystery #204 © DC

House of Secrets #14 © DC

HOURMAN (See Adventure Comics #48)

HOUSE OF MYSTERY (See Brave and the Bold #93, Elvira's House of Mystery, Limited Collectors' Edition & Super DC Giant)

HOUSE OF MYSTERY, THE
Dec-Jan, 1951-52 - No. 321, Oct, 1983 (No. 199-203: 52 pgs.)
National Periodical Publications/DC Comics

	GD25	FN65	NM94
1	193.00	581.00	1600.00
2	84.00	253.00	700.00
3	62.00	187.00	525.00
4,5	47.00	141.00	400.00
6-10	40.00	120.00	300.00
11-15	34.00	101.00	240.00
16(7/53)-25	25.00	75.00	180.00
26-35(2/55)-Last pre-code issue; 30-Woodish-a	19.00	56.00	140.00
36-50: 50-Text story of Orson Welles' War of the Worlds broadcast	12.00	36.00	120.00
51-60: 55-1st S.A. issue	9.50	28.50	95.00
61,63,65,66,70,72,76,84,85-Kirby-a	9.50	28.50	95.00
62,64,67-69,71,73-75,77-83,86-99	7.50	22.50	75.00
100 (7/60)	8.50	25.50	85.00
101-116: 109-Toth, Kubert-a. 116-Last 10¢ issue	6.50	19.50	65.00
117-130: 117-Swipes-c to HOS #20. 120-Toth-a	6.00	18.00	60.00
131-142	5.00	15.00	50.00
143-J'onn J'onzz, Manhunter begins (6/64), ends #173; story continues from Detective #326	23.50	70.00	235.00
144	12.50	38.00	125.00
145-155,157-159: 149-Toth-a. 155-The Human Hurricane app. (12/65), Red Tornado prototype. 158-Origin/1st app. Diabolu Idol-Head in J'onn J'onzz	8.50	25.50	85.00
156-Robby Reed begins (origin/1st app.), ends #173	11.00	33.00	110.00
160-(7/66)-Robby Reed becomes Plastic Man in this issue only; 1st S.A. app. Plastic Man; intro Marco Xavier (Martian Manhunter) & Vulture Crime Organization; ends #173	13.00	39.00	130.00
161-173: 169-Origin/1st app. Gem Girl	6.00	18.00	60.00
174-Mystery format begins.	4.00	12.00	40.00
175-177,182: 176-1st app. Cain (HOM host). 182-Toth-a.	2.50	7.50	25.00
178-Neal Adams-a (2/68)	2.50	7.50	25.00
179-N. Adams/Orlando, Wrightson-a (1st pro work, 3 pgs.)	6.00	18.00	60.00
180,181,183: Wrightson-a (3,10, & 3 pgs.). 180-Last 12¢ issue; Kane/Wood-a(2). 183-Wood-a	2.25	6.75	18.00
184-Kane/Wood, Toth-a	1.75	5.25	14.00
185-Williamson/Kaluta-a; Howard-a (3 pgs.)	1.85	5.50	15.00
186-N. Adams-c/a; Wrightson-a (10 pgs.)	2.00	6.00	16.00
187,190: Adams-c. 187-Toth-a. 190-Toth-a(r)	1.10	3.30	9.00
188,191-Wrightson-a (8 & 3pgs.); Adams-c	2.00	6.00	16.00
189,192,197: Adams-c; 189-Wood-a(i)	1.50	4.50	12.00
193-Wrightson-c	1.50	4.50	12.00
194-Wrightson-c; 52 pgs begin, end #203; Toth,Kirby-a	1.75	5.25	14.00
195: Wrightson-c. Swamp creature story by Wrightson similar to Swamp Thing (10 pgs.)(10/71)	2.00	6.00	16.00
196,198	1.50	4.50	12.00
199-Adams-c; Wood-a(8pgs.); Kirby-a	1.75	5.50	14.00
200-203-(25¢, 52 pgs.)-One third-r. 200-(3/72)	1.75	5.50	14.00
204-Wrightson-c/a, 9 pgs.	1.25	3.75	10.00
205,206,208,210,212,215,216,218	1.00	2.80	7.00
207-Wrightson c/a; Starlin, Redondo-a	1.25	3.75	10.00
209,211,213,214,217,219-Wrightson-c		2.40	6.00
220,222,223		2.00	5.00
221-Wrightson/Kaluta-a(8 pgs.). 225-Spectre app.	1.25	3.75	10.00
224-Wrightson-r from Spectre #9; Dillin/Adams-r from House of Secrets #82; begin 100 pg. issues; Phantom Stranger-r.	2.60	7.80	26.00
225,227-(100 pgs.)	2.60	7.80	26.00
226-Wrightson/Redondo-a Phantom Stranger-r	2.60	7.80	26.00
228-N. Adams inks; Wrightson-r	2.60	7.80	26.00
229-Wrightson-a(r); Toth-r; last 100 pg. issue.	2.60	7.80	26.00
230-(68 pgs.)	1.00	2.80	7.00
231,236-Wrightson-c	1.00	3.00	8.00
232-235,237-250		1.60	4.00
236-Ditko-a(p); N. Adams-i; Wrightson-c	1.00	3.00	8.00
251-254-(84 pgs.)-Adams-c. 251-Wood-a	1.00	3.00	8.00
255,256-(84 pgs.)-Wrightson-c	1.00	3.00	8.00
257-259-(84 pgs.)	1.00	3.00	8.00
260-321: 282-(68 pgs.)-Has extra story "The Computers That Saved Metropolis" Radio Shack giveaway by Jim Starlin		1.40	3.50

NOTE: ***Neal Adams*** *a-236i; c-175-192, 197, 199, 251-254.* ***Alcala*** *a-209, 217, 219, 224, 227.* ***M. Anderson*** *a-212; c/a-37.* ***Aparo*** *a-209.* ***Aragones*** *a-185, 186, 194, 196, 200, 202, 229, 251.* ***Baily*** *a-279p.* ***Cameron*** *a-76, 79.* ***Colan*** *a-202r.* ***Craig*** *a-263, 275, 295, 300.* ***Dillin/Adams*** *r-224.* ***Ditko*** *a-236p, 247, 254, 258, 276; c-277.* ***Drucker*** *a-37.* ***Evans*** *c-218.* ***Fraden*** *a-251.* ***Giffen*** *a-284.* ***Giunta*** *a-199, 227r.* ***Golden*** *a-257, 259.* ***Heath*** *a-194r; c-203.* ***Howard*** *a-182, 185, 187, 196, 229r, 247i, 254, 279i.* ***Kaluta*** *a-195, 200, 250r; c-200-202, 210, 212, 233, 260, 261, 263, 265, 267, 268, 273, 276, 284, 287, 288, 293-295, 300, 302, 304, 305, 309-319, 321.* ***Bob Kane*** *a-84.* ***Gil Kane*** *a-196p, 253p, 300p.* ***Kirby*** *a-194r, 199r; c-65, 76, 78, 79, 85.* ***Kubert*** *c-282, 283, 285, 286, 289-292, 297-299, 301, 303, 306-308.* ***Maneely*** *a-68, 227r.* ***Mayer*** *a-317p.* ***Meskin*** *a-52-144 (most), 195r, 224r, 229r; c-63, 66, 124, 127.* ***Mooney*** *a-24, 159, 160.* ***Moreira*** *a-3, 4, 20-50, 58, 59, 62, 68, 77, 79, 90, 108, 113, 123, 201r, 228; c-4-28, 44, 47, 50, 54, 59, 62, 64, 68, 70, 73.* ***Morrow*** *a-192, 196, 255, 320i.* ***Mortimer*** *a-204(3 pgs.).* ***Nasser*** *a-276.* ***Newton*** *a-259, 272.* ***Nino*** *a-204, 212, 213, 220, 224, 225, 245, 250, 252-256, 283.* ***Orlando*** *a-175(2 pgs.), 178, 240i; c-240, 258p, 262, 264p, 270p, 271, 272, 274, 275, 278, 296i.* ***Redondo*** *a-194, 195, 197, 202, 203, 207, 211, 214, 217, 219, 226, 227, 229, 235, 241, 287(layout), 302p, 303i, 308; c-229.* ***Reese*** *a-195, 200, 205i.* ***Rogers*** *a-254, 274, 277.* ***Roussos*** *a-65, 84, 224i.* ***Sekowsky*** *a-282p.* ***Sparling*** *a-203.* ***Starlin*** *a-207(2 pgs.), 282p; c-281.* ***Leonard Starr*** *a-9.* ***Staton*** *a-300p.* ***Sutton*** *a-189, 271, 290, 291, 293, 295, 297-299, 302, 303, 306-309, 310-313i, 314.* ***Tuska*** *a-293p, 294p, 316p.* ***Wrightson*** *c-193-195, 204, 207, 209, 211, 213, 214, 217, 219, 221, 231, 236, 255, 256; r-224.*

HOUSE OF SECRETS (Combined with The Unexpected after #154)
11-12/56 - No. 80, 9-10/66; No. 81, 8-9/69 - No. 140, 2-3/76;
No. 141, 8-9/76 - No. 154, 10-11/78
National Periodical Publications/DC Comics

	GD25	FN65	NM94
1-Drucker-a; Moreira-c	96.00	288.00	1150.00
2-Moreira-a	39.00	117.00	440.00
3-Kirby-c/a	32.00	96.00	360.00
4-Kirby-a	27.00	82.00	275.00
5-7	17.50	52.00	175.00
8-Kirby-a	21.00	63.00	215.00
9-11: 11-Lou Cameron-a (unsigned)	15.50	47.00	155.00
12-Kirby-c/a; Lou Cameron-a	16.50	50.00	165.00
13-15: 14-Flying saucer-c	11.50	34.00	115.00
16-20	10.00	30.00	100.00
21,22,24-30	9.50	28.50	95.00
23-1st app. Mark Merlin & begin series (8/59)	10.50	32.00	105.00
31-50: 48-Toth-a. 50-Last 10¢ issue	7.50	22.50	75.00
51-60: 58-Origin Mark Merlin	7.00	21.00	70.00
61-First Eclipso (7-8/63) and begin series	16.50	50.00	165.00
62	8.00	24.00	80.00
63-65,67-Toth-a on Eclipso (see Brave and the Bold #64)	6.50	19.50	65.00
66-1st Eclipso-c (also #67,70,78,79); Toth-a	8.50	25.50	85.00
68-80: 73-Mark Merlin becomes Prince Ra-Man (1st app.). 76-Prince Ra-Man vs. Eclipso. 80-Eclipso, Prince Ra-Man end	6.50	19.50	65.00
81,85,87,90: 81-Mystery format begins; 1st app. Abel (HOS host). 85-N. Adams-a(i). 87-Wrightson & Kaluta-a. 90-Buckler (early work)/N. Adams-a(i)	3.00	9.00	30.00
82-84,86,88,89,91: 82-Neal Adams-c(i).	2.25	6.75	18.00
92-1st app. Swamp Thing-c/story (8 pgs.)(6-7/71) by Berni Wrightson(p) w/JeffJones/Kaluta/Weiss ink assists; classic-c.	51.00	153.00	460.00
93,95-98-(52 pgs.)-Wrightson-c. 94,96-Wrightson-c. 94-Wrightson-a(i); 96-Wood-a	1.85	5.50	15.00

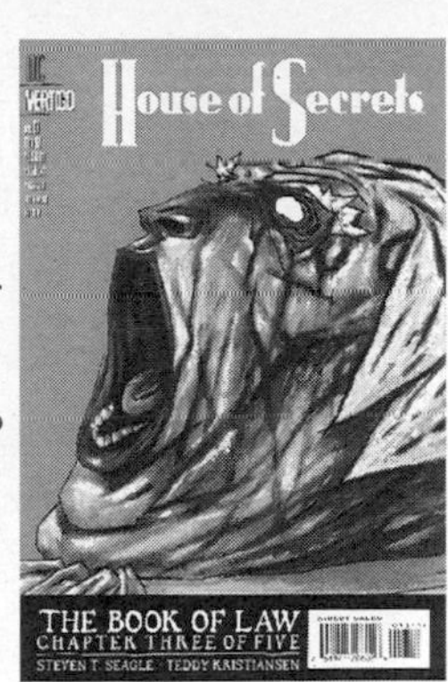

House of Secrets #13 © Steve Seagle & Teddy Kristiansen

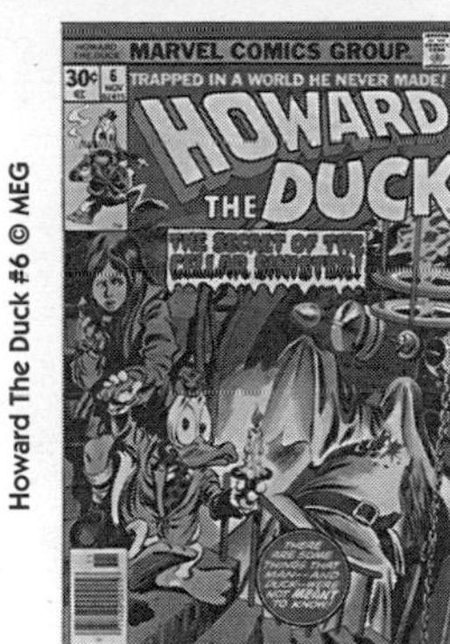

Howard The Duck #6 © MEG

H.P. Lovecraft's Cthulhu #1 © H.P. Lovecraft

	GD25	FN65	NM94
99-Wrightson spash pg.	1.85	5.50	15.00
100-Wrightson-c	2.50	7.50	20.00
101,102,104,105,108-120	1.25	3.75	10.00
103,106,107-Wrightson-c	1.50	4.50	12.00
121-133		2.00	5.00
134-136,139,150,151-Wrightson-a		2.40	6.00
137,138,141-149,152-154		1.60	4.00
140-1st solo origin Patchworkman	1.85	5.50	15.00

NOTE: **Neal Adams** c-81, 82, 84-88, 90, 91. **Alcala** a-104-107. **Anderson** a-91. Aparo a-93, 97, 105. **B. Bailey** a-107. **Cameron** a-13, 15. **Colan** a-63. **Ditko** a-139p, 148. **Elias** a-58. **Evans** a-118. **Finlay** a-7r(Real Fact?). **Glanzman** a-91. **Golden** a-151. **Heath** a-31. **Heck** a-85. **Kaluta** a-87, 98, 99; c-98, 99, 101, 102, 105, 149, 151, 154. **Bob Kane** a-18, 21. **G. Kane** a-85p. **Kirby** c-3, 11, 12. **Kubert** a-39. **Meskin** a-2-68 (most), 94r; c-55-60. **Moreira** a-7, 8, 51, 54, 102-104, 106, 108, 113, 116, 118, 121, 123, 127; c-1, 2, 4-10, 13-20. **Morrow** a-86, 89, 90; c-89, 146-148. **Nino** a-101, 103, 106, 109, 115, 117, 126, 128, 131, 147, 153. **Redondo** a-95, 99, 102, 104p, 113, 116, 134, 136, 139, 140. **Reese** a-85. **Severin** a-91. **Starlin** c-150. **Sutton** a-154. **Toth** a-63-67, 83, 93r, 94r, 96r-98r, 123. **Tuska** a-90, 104. **Wrightson** a-134; c-92-94, 96, 100, 103, 106, 107, 135, 136, 139.

HOUSE OF SECRETS
Oct, 1996 - Present ($2.50) (Creator-owned series)
DC Comics (Vertigo)

	GD25	FN65	NM94
1-Steven Seagle-s/Kristiansen-c/a.		1.60	4.00
2-4		1.20	3.00
5-17: 5,7-Kristiansen-c/a. 6-Fregado-a		1.00	2.50
TPB-(1997, $14.95) r/1-5			14.95

HOUSE OF TERROR (3-D)
Oct, 1953 (25¢, came w/glasses)
St. John Publishing Co.

	GD25	FN65	NM94
1-Kubert, Baker-a	29.00	86.00	210.00

HOUSE OF YANG, THE (See Yang)
July, 1975 - No. 6, June, 1976; 1978
Charlton Comics

	GD25	FN65	NM94
1		2.40	6.00
2-6		1.60	4.00
Modern Comics #1,2(1978)		1.20	3.00

HOUSE II: THE SECOND STORY
Oct, 1987 (One-shot)
Marvel Comics

	GD25	FN65	NM94
1-Adapts movie		.80	2.00

HOWARD CHAYKIN'S AMERICAN FLAGG (See American Flagg!)
V2#1, May, 1988 - V2#12, Apr, 1989 ($1.75/$1.95, Baxter paper)
First Comics

	GD25	FN65	NM94
V2#1-5: ($1.75)-Chaykin-c(p) in all		.70	1.75
6-9,11,12: ($1.95)		.80	2.00
10-Elvis Presley photo-c		1.20	3.00

HOWARD THE DUCK (See Bizarre Adventures #34, Crazy Magazine, Fear, Man-Thing, Marvel Treasury Edition & Sensational She-Hulk #14-17)
Jan, 1976 - No. 31, May, 1979; No. 32, Jan, 1986; No. 33, Sept, 1986
Marvel Comics Group

	GD25	FN65	NM94
1-Brunner-c/a; Spider-Man x-over (low distr.)	1.25	3.75	10.00
2,4-11: 2-Brunner-c/a (low distr.). 8-Howard T.D. for president 9-1st Sgt. Preston Dudley of RCMP. 10-Spider-Man-c/sty		.80	2.00
3-(Regular 25¢ edition)-Buscema-a(p), (7/76)		.80	2.00
3-(30¢-c, limited distribution)	1.00	3.00	8.00
12-1st app. Kiss (cameo, 3/77)		2.40	6.00
13-Kiss app. (1st full story, 6/77); Daimon Hellstrom app. plus cameo of Howard as Son of Satan	1.25	3.75	10.00
14-33: 14-Howard as Son of Satan-c/story; Son of Satan app. 16-Album issue; 3 pgs. comics. 22,23-Man-Thing-c/stories; Star Wars parody. 30,32-P. Smith-a.		.80	2.00
Annual 1(1977, 52 pgs.)-Mayerik-a		.80	2.00

NOTE: **Austin** c-29i. **Bolland** c-33. **Brunner** a-1p, 2p; c-1, 2. **Buckler** c-3p. **Buscema** a-3p. **Colan** a(p)-4-15, 17-20, 24-27, 30, 31; c(p)-4-31, Annual 1p. **Leialoha** a-1-13i; c(i)-3-5, 8-11. **Mayerik** a-22, 23, 33. **Paul Smith** a-30p, 32. Man-Thing app. in #22, 23.

HOWARD THE DUCK (Magazine)
Oct, 1979 - No. 9, Mar, 1981 (B&W, 68 pgs.)
Marvel Comics Group

	GD25	FN65	NM94
1		1.60	4.00
2,3,5-9: 3-Xmas issue. 7-Has poster by Byrne		1.20	3.00
4-Beatles, John Lennon, Elvis, Kiss & Devo cameos; Hitler app.		1.60	4.00

NOTE: **Buscema** a-4p. **Colan** a-1-5p, 7-9p. **Jack Davis** c-3. **Golden** a(p)-1, 5, 6(51pgs.). **Rogers** a-7, 8. **Simonson** a-7.

HOWARD THE DUCK HOLIDAY SPECIAL
Feb, 1997 ($2.50, one-shot)
Marvel Comics

	GD25	FN65	NM94
1-Wraparound-c; Hama-s		1.00	2.50

HOWARD THE DUCK: THE MOVIE
Dec, 1986 - No. 3, Feb, 1987 (Limited series)
Marvel Comics Group

	GD25	FN65	NM94
1-3: Movie adaptation; r/Marvel Super Special			1.00

HOW BOYS AND GIRLS CAN HELP WIN THE WAR
1942 (10¢, one-shot)
The Parents' Magazine Institute

	GD25	FN65	NM94
1-All proceeds used to buy war bonds	20.00	60.00	160.00

HOWDY DOODY (TV)(See Poll Parrot)
1/50 - No. 38, 7-9/56; No. 761, 1/57; No. 811, 7/57
Dell Publishing Co.

	GD25	FN65	NM94
1-(Scarce)-Photo-c; 1st TV comic	73.00	218.00	800.00
2-Photo-c	32.00	95.00	350.00
3-5: All photo-c	18.00	55.00	200.00
6-Used in **SOTI**, pg. 309; painted-c begin	16.00	47.00	170.00
7-10	13.00	38.00	140.00
11-20: 13-X-Mas-c	10.00	30.00	110.00
21-38, Four Color 761,811	9.00	26.00	95.00

HOW IT BEGAN
No. 15, 1939 (one-shot)
United Features Syndicate

	GD25	FN65	NM94
Single Series 15	27.00	81.00	215.00

HOW SANTA GOT HIS RED SUIT (See March of Comics No. 2)

HOW STALIN HOPES WE WILL DESTROY AMERICA
1951 (Giveaway, 16 pgs.)
Joe Lowe Co. (Pictorial News)

	GD25	FN65	NM94
nn	42.00	126.00	375.00

HOW THE WEST WAS WON (See Movie Comics)

HOW TO DRAW FOR THE COMICS
No date (1942?) (10¢, 64 pgs., B&W & color, no ads)
Street and Smith

	GD25	FN65	NM94
nn-Art by Winsor McCay, George Marcoux (Supersnipe artist), Vernon Greene (The Shadow artist), Jack Binder(with biog.), Thorton Fisher, Jon Small, & Jack Farr; has biographies of each artist	21.00	64.00	170.00

H. P. LOVECRAFT'S CTHULHU
Dec, 1991 - No. 3, Feb?, 1992 ($2.50, limited series)
Millennium Publications

	GD25	FN65	NM94
1-3: 1-Contains trading cards on thin stock		1.00	2.50

H. R. PUFNSTUF (TV) (See March of Comics #360)
Oct, 1970 - No. 8, July, 1972
Gold Key

	GD25	FN65	NM94
1-Photo-c (all have photo-c?)	16.00	49.00	180.00
2-8	8.00	25.00	90.00

HUBERT AT CAMP MOONBEAM

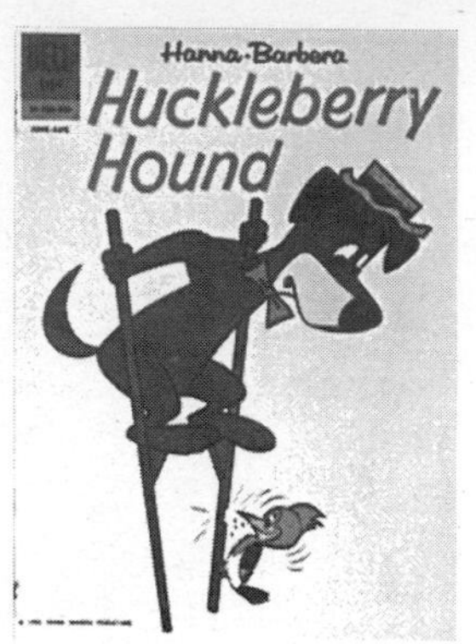

Huckleberry Hound #17 © H-B

Hulk 2099 #7 © MEG

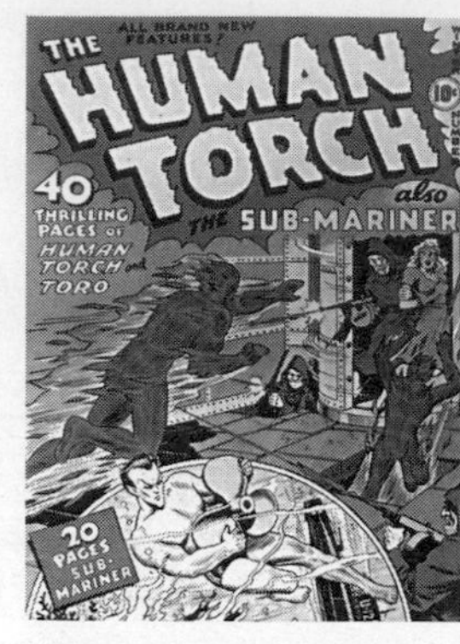

Human Torch #3 (#2) © MEG

GD25 FN65 NM94

No. 251, Oct, 1949 (one shot)
Dell Publishing Co.

Four Color 251 — 3.60 — 11.00 — 40.00

HUCK & YOGI JAMBOREE (TV)
Mar, 1961 ($1.00, 6-1/4x9", 116 pgs., cardboard-c, high quality paper) (B&W original material)
Dell Publishing Co.

nn — 7.00 — 22.00 — 80.00

HUCK & YOGI WINTER SPORTS (TV)
No. 1310, Mar, 1962 (Hanna-Barbara) (one-shot)
Dell Publishing Co.

Four Color 1310 — 7.00 — 22.00 — 80.00

HUCK FINN (See The New Adventures of... & Power Record Comics)

HUCKLEBERRY FINN (Movie)
No. 1114, July, 1960
Dell Publishing Co.

Four Color 1114-Photo-c — 4.50 — 13.50 — 50.00

HUCKLEBERRY HOUND (See Dell Giant #31,44, Golden Picture Story Book, Kite Fun Book, March of Comics #199, 214, 235, Spotlight #1 & Whitman Comic Books)

HUCKLEBERRY HOUND (TV)
No. 990, 5-7/59 - No. 43, 10/70 (Hanna-Barbera)
Dell/Gold Key No. 18 (10/62) on

	GD25	FN65	NM94
Four Color 990(#1)-1st app. Hucklebery Hound, Yogi Bear, & Pixie & Dixie & Mr. Jinx	10.00	30.00	110.00
Four Color 1050,1054 (12/59)	7.30	22.00	80.00
3(1-2/60) - 7 (9-10/60)	7.30	22.00	80.00
Four Color 1141 (10/60)	7.30	22.00	80.00
8-10	5.00	15.00	55.00
11-17 (6-8/62)	3.60	11.00	40.00
18,19 (84pgs.; 18-20 titled ...Chuckleberry Tales)	7.00	20.00	75.00
20-30: 20-Titled Chuckleberry Tales	2.75	8.00	30.00
31-43: 37-Reprints	2.00	6.00	22.00

HUCKLEBERRY HOUND (TV)
Nov, 1970 - No. 8, Jan, 1972 (Hanna-Barbera)
Charlton Comics

	GD25	FN65	NM94
1	3.00	9.00	30.00
2-8	2.25	6.75	18.00

HUEY, DEWEY, & LOUIE (See Donald Duck, 1938 for 1st app. Also see Mickey Mouse Magazine V4#2, V5#7 & Walt Disney's Junior Woodchucks Limited Series)

HUEY, DEWEY, & LOUIE BACK TO SCHOOL (See Dell Giant #22, 35, 49 & Dell Giants)

HUEY, DEWEY AND LOUIE JUNIOR WOODCHUCKS (Disney)
Aug, 1966 - No. 81, 1984 (See Walt Disney's Comics & Stories #125)
Gold Key No. 1-61/Whitman No. 62 on

	GD25	FN65	NM94
1	4.00	12.00	45.00
2,3(12/68)	2.50	7.50	28.00
4,5(4/70)-r/two WDC&S D.Duck stys by Barks	3.00	9.00	35.00
6-17	4.00	12.00	45.00
18,27-30	1.60	4.80	16.00
19-23,25-New storyboarded scripts by Barks, 13-25 pgs. per issue	2.25	6.75	26.00
24,26: 26-r/Barks Donald Duck WDC&S stories	1.60	4.80	16.00
31-57,60-81: 35,41-r/Barks J.W. scripts	.80	2.40	8.00
58,59: 58-r/Barks Donald Duck WDC&S stories	1.00	3.00	10.00

HUGGA BUNCH (TV)
Oct, 1986 - No. 6, Aug, 1987
Marvel Comics (Star Comics)

	GD25	FN65	NM94
1-6		.80	2.00

GD25 FN65 NM94

HULK (Magazine)(Formerly The Rampaging Hulk)(Also see The Incredible Hulk)
No. 10, Aug., 1978 - No. 27, June, 1981 ($1.50)
Marvel Comics

	GD25	FN65	NM94
10-Bill Bixby interview	1.00	3.00	8.00
11-Moon Knight begins, ends 20		2.40	6.00
12-15: Moon Knight stories. 12-Lou Ferrigno interview		1.60	4.00
16,19,21,22,24-27: 24-Part color, Lou Ferrrigno interview. 25-Part color. 26,27-are B&W		1.20	3.00
17,18,20: Moon Knight stories		1.40	3.50
23-Last full color issue; Banner is attacked		1.40	3.50

NOTE: ***Alcala** a(i)-15, 17-20, 22, 24-27. **Buscema** a-23; c-26. **Chaykin** a-21-25. **Colan** a(p)-11, 19, 24-27. **Jusko** painted c-12. **Nebres** a-16. **Severin** a-19i. Moon Knight by **Sienkiewicz** in 13-15, 17, 18, 20. **Simonson** a-27; c-23. Dominic Fortune appears in #21-24.*

HULK: FUTURE IMPERFECT
Jan, 1993 - No. 2, Dec, 1992 (In error) ($5.95, 52 pgs., squarebound, limited series)
Marvel Comics

	GD25	FN65	NM94
1,2: Embossed-c; Peter David story & George Perez-c/a. 1-1st app. Maestro.	1.00	2.80	7.00

HULK/ PITT
1997 ($5.99, one-shot)
Marvel Comics

	GD25	FN65	NM94
1 David-s/Keown-c/a		2.40	5.99

HULK 2099
Dec, 1994 - No. 10, Sept, 1995 ($1.50/$1.95)
Marvel Comics

	GD25	FN65	NM94
1 ($2.50)-Green foil-c		1.00	2.50
2-6: 2-A. Kubert-c			1.50
7-10: 7-begin $1.95-c		.80	2.00

HUMAN FLY
1963 - 1964 (Reprints)
I.W. Enterprises/Super

	GD25	FN65	NM94
I.W. Reprint #1-Reprints Blue Beetle #44('46)	1.25	3.75	10.00
Super Reprint #10-R/Blue Beetle #46('47)	1.25	3.75	10.00

HUMAN FLY, THE
Sept, 1977 - No. 19, Mar, 1979
Marvel Comics Group

	GD25	FN65	NM94
1-Origin; Spider-Man x-over		1.20	3.00
2-Ghost Rider app.		1.60	4.00
3-19: 9-Daredevil x-over; Byrne-c(p)		.75	1.80

NOTE: ***Austin** c-4i, 9i. **Elias** a-1, 3p, 4p, 7p, 10-12p, 15p, 18p, 19p. **Layton** c-19.*

HUMAN TARGET SPECIAL (TV)
Nov, 1991 ($2.00, 52 pgs., one-shot)
DC Comics

	GD25	FN65	NM94
1		.80	2.00

HUMAN TORCH, THE (Red Raven #1)(See All-Select, All Winners, Marvel Mystery, Men's Adventures, Mystic Comics (2nd series), Sub-Mariner, USA & Young Men)
No. 2, Fall, 1940 - No. 15, Spring, 1944;
No. 16, Fall, 1944 - No. 35, Mar, 1949 (Becomes Love Tales #36 on);
No. 36, April, 1954 - No. 38, Aug, 1954
Timely/Marvel Comics (TP 2,3/TCI 4-9/SePI 10/SnPC 11-25/CnPC 26-35/Atlas Comics (CPC 36-38))

	GD25	FN65	VF82	NM94
2(#1)-Intro & Origin Toro; The Falcon, The Fiery Mask, Mantor the Magician, & Microman only app.; Human Torch by Burgos, Sub-Mariner by Everett begin (origin of each in text)	1900.00	5700.00	12,350.00	21,000.00

(Estimated up to 190 total copies exist, 10 in NM/Mint)

	GD25	FN65	NM94
3(#2)-40pg. H.T. story; H.T. & S.M. battle over who is best artist in text-Everett or Burgos	430.00	1290.00	4300.00

Human Torch #36 © MEG

Humbug #1 © Harvey Kurtzman

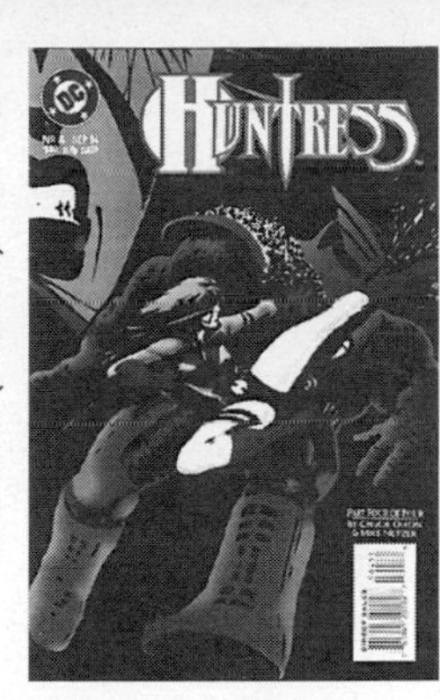

Huntress #4 (2nd Series) © DC

GD25 FN65 NM94

4(#3)-Origin The Patriot in text; last Everett Sub-Mariner; 1st Nazi war-c this title (see Marvel Mystery #4); Sid Greene-a 330.00 990.00 3300.00
5(#4)-The Patriot app; Angel x-over in Sub-Mariner (Summer, 1941) 250.00 750.00 2500.00
5-Human Torch battles Sub-Mariner (Fall, '41); 60 pg. story 370.00 1110.00 3700.00
6,9 167.00 500.00 1500.00
7-1st Japanese war-c 178.00 534.00 1600.00
8-Human Torch battles Sub-Mariner; 52 pg. story; Wolverton-a, 1 pg. 250.00 750.00 2500.00
10-Human Torch battles Sub-Mariner, 45 pg. story; Wolverton-a, 1 pg. 217.00 651.00 1950.00
11,13-15: 14-1st Atlas Globe logo (Winter, 1943-44; see All Winners #11 also) 133.00 400.00 1200.00
12-classic-c 178.00 534.00 1600.00
16-20: 20-Last War issue 94.00 282.00 850.00
21,22,24-30: 89.00 267.00 800.00
23 (Sum/46)-Becomes Junior Miss 24? Classic Schomburg Robot-c 100.00 300.00 900.00
31-Namora x-over in Sub-Mariner (also #30); last Toro 75.00 225.00 675.00
32-Sungirl, Namora app.; Sungirl-c 75.00 225.00 675.00
33-Capt. America x-over 78.00 234.00 700.00
34-Sungirl solo 69.00 207.00 625.00
35-Captain America & Sungirl app. (1949) 78.00 234.00 700.00
36-38(1954)-Sub-Mariner in all 75.00 225.00 675.00

NOTE: *Ayers Human Torch in 36(3). **Brodsky** c-25, 31-33?, 37, 38. **Burgos** c-36. **Everett** a-1-3, 27, 28, 30, 37, 38. **Powell** a-36(Sub-Mariner). **Schomburg** c-1-3, 5-8, 10-23. **Sekowsky** c-28, 34?, 35? **Shores** c-24, 26, 27, 29, 30. **Mickey Spillane** text 4-6. Bondage c-2, 12, 19.*

HUMAN TORCH, THE (Also see Avengers West Coast, Fantastic Four, The Invaders, Saga of the Original... & Strange Tales #101)
Sept, 1974 - No. 8, Nov, 1975
Marvel Comics Group

1: 1-8-r/stories from Strange Tales #101-108 1.25 3.75 10.00
2-8: 1st H.T. title since G.A. 7-vs. Sub-Mariner 2.40 6.00

NOTE: *Golden Age & Silver Age Human Torch-r #1-8. **Ayers** r-6, 7. **Kirby/Ayers** r-1-5, 8.*

HUMBUG (Satire by Harvey Kurtzman)
Aug, 1957 - No. 9, May, 1958; No. 10, June, 1958; No. 11, Oct, 1958
Humbug Publications

1-Wood-a (intro pgs. only) 17.00 51.00 170.00
2 8.00 24.00 80.00
3-9: 8-Elvis in Jailbreak Rock 6.50 19.50 65.00
10,11-Magazine format. 10-Photo-c 9.00 27.00 90.00
Bound Volume(#1-6)-Sold by publisher 26.00 80.00 265.00
Bound Volume(#1-9) 31.00 93.00 315.00

NOTE: ***Davis** a-1-11. **Elder** a-2-4, 6-9, 11. **Heath** a-2, 4-8, 10. **Jaffee** a-2, 4-9. **Kurtzman** a-11.*

HUMDINGER (Becomes White Rider and Super Horse #3 on?)
May-June, 1946 - V2#2, July-Aug, 1947
Novelty Press/Premium Group

1-Jerkwater Line, Mickey Starlight by Don Rico, Dink begin 25.00 75.00 200.00
2 10.50 32.00 85.00
3-6, V2#1,2 7.85 23.50 55.00

HUMONGOUS MAN
Sept, 1997 -Present ($2.25, B&W)
Alternative Press (Ikon Press)

1-3-Stepp & Harrison-c/s/a. 2.25

HUMOR (See All Humor Comics)

HUMPHREY COMICS (Joe Palooka Presents...; also see Joe Palooka)
Oct, 1948 - No. 22, Apr, 1952
Harvey Publications

1-Joe Palooka's pal (r); (52 pgs.)-Powell-a 9.50 28.00 75.00
2,3: Powell-a 5.70 17.00 35.00
4-Boy Heroes app.; Powell-a 5.70 17.00 40.00
5-8,10: 5,6-Powell-a. 7-Little Dot app. 4.25 13.00 26.00
9-Origin Humphrey 5.70 17.00 35.00
11-22 4.00 10.00 20.00

HUNCHBACK OF NOTRE DAME, THE
No. 854, Oct, 1957 (one shot)
Dell Publishing Co.

Four Color 854-Movie, photo-c 12.00 35.00 130.00

HUNK
Aug, 1961 - No. 11, 1963
Charlton Comics

1 2.50 7.50 24.00
2-11 1.50 4.50 12.00

HUNTED (Formerly My Love Memoirs)
No. 13, July, 1950 - No. 2, Sept, 1950
Fox Features Syndicate

13(#1)-Used in **SOTI**, pg. 42 & illo. "Treating police contemptuously" (lower left); Hollingsworth bondage-c 28.00 84.00 200.00
2 11.00 33.00 80.00

HUNTER'S HEART
June, 1995 - No. 3, Aug, 1995 ($5.95, B&W, limited series)
DC Comics

1-3 2.40 6.00

HUNTRESS, THE (See All-Star Comics #69, Batman Family, Brave & the Bold #62, DC Super Stars #17, Detective #652, Infinity, Inc. #1, Sensation Comics #68 & Wonder Woman #271)
Apr, 1989 - No. 19, Oct, 1990 ($1.00, mature)
DC Comics

1-19: Staton-c/a(p) in all. 17-19-Batman-c/stories 1.25

HUNTRESS, THE
June, 1994 - No. 4, Sept, 1994 ($1.50, limited series)
DC Comics

1-4-Netzer-c/a: 2-Batman app. .70 1.75

HURRICANE COMICS
1945 (52 pgs.)
Cambridge House

1-(Humor, funny animal) 17.00 51.00 135.00

HURRICANE KIDS, THE (Also See Magic Morro, The Owl, Popular Comics #45)
1941 (Giveaway, 7-1/2x5-1/4", soft-c)
R.S. Callender

nn-Will Ely-a. 8.50 26.00 60.00

HYBRIDS
Jan, 1994 ($2.50, one-shot)
Continuity Comics

1-Neal Adams-c(p) & part-a(i); embossed-c. 1.00 2.50

HYBRIDS DEATHWATCH 2000
Apr, 1993 - No. 3, Aug, 1993 ($2.50)
Continuity Comics

0-(Giveaway)-Foil-c; Neal Adams-c(i) & plots (also #1,2) 1.00 2.50
1-5: 1-Polybagged w/card; die-cut-c. 2-Thermal-c. 3-Polybagged w/card; indestructible-c; Adams plot. 4,5-Valeria She-Bat; origin Hybrids; Adams-c(p) 1.00 2.50

HYBRIDS ORIGIN
1993 - No. 5, 1994? ($2.50)
Continuity Comics

1-5: 2,3-Neal Adams-c. 4,5-Valeria the She-Bat app. Adams-c(i)

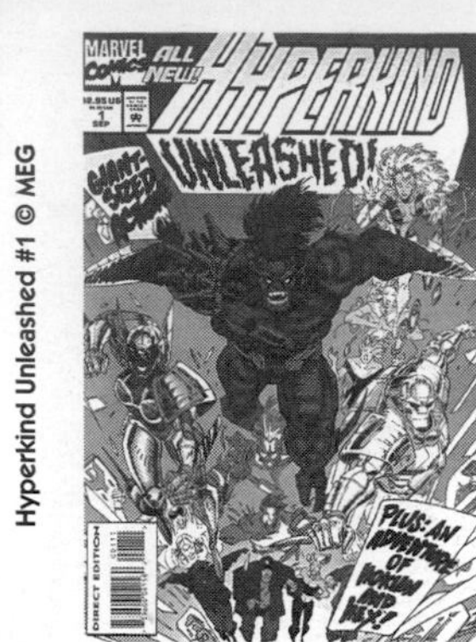

Hyperkind Unleashed #1 © MEG

Ibis, the Invincible #1 © FAW

Icon #15 © Milestone Media

GD25 FN65 NM94

1.00 2.50

HYDE-25
Apr, 1995 ($2.95, one-shot)
Harris Publications

0-coupon for poster; r/Vampirella's 1st app. 1.20 3.00

HYDROMAN (See Heroic Comics)

HYPERKIND (See Razorline)
Sept, 1993 - No. 9, May, 1994 ($1.75/$1.95)
Marvel Comics

1-($2.50)-Foil embossed-c; by Clive Barker 1.00 2.50
2-8 .70 1.75
9-($1.95) .80 2.00

HYPERKIND UNLEASED
Aug, 1994 ($2.95, 52 pgs., one-shot)
Marvel Comics

1 1.20 3.00

HYPER MYSTERY COMICS
May, 1940 - No. 2, June, 1940 (68 pgs.)
Hyper Publications

1-Hyper, the Phenomenal begins; Calkins-a 156.00 468.00 1400.00
2 86.00 258.00 775.00

HYPERSONIC
Nov, 1997 - No. 4 ($2.95, limited series)
Dark Horse Comics

1-Erskine-a 1.20 3.00

I AIM AT THE STARS (Movie)
No. 1148, Nov-Jan/1960-61 (one-shot)
Dell Publishing Co.

Four Color 1148-The Werner Von Braun Sty-photo-c 6.40 19.00 70.00

I AM COYOTE (See Eclipse Graphic Album Series & Eclipse Magazine #2)

I AM LEGEND
1991 - No. 4, 1991 ($5.95, B&W, squarebound, 68 pgs.)
Eclipse Books

1-4: Based on 1954 novel 2.40 6.00

IBIS, THE INVINCIBLE (See Fawcett Miniatures, Mighty Midget & Whiz)
1943 (Feb) - #2, 1943; #3, Wint, 1945 - #5, Fall, 1946; #6, Spring, 1948
Fawcett Publications

1-Origin Ibis; Raboy-c; on sale 1/2/43 139.00 417.00 1250.00
2-Bondage-c 69.00 207.00 625.00
3-Wolverton-a #3-6 (4 pgs. each) 58.00 174.00 520.00
4-6: 5-Bondage-c 40.00 120.00 360.00

NOTE: ***Mac Raboy*** *c(p)-3-5.* ***Shaffenberger*** *c-6.*

I-BOTS (See Isaac Asimov's I-BOTS)

ICE AGE ON THE WORLD OF MAGIC: THE GATHERING (See Magic The Gathering)

ICE KING OF OZ, THE (See First Comics Graphic Novel #13)

ICEMAN (Also see The Champions & X-Men #94)
Dec, 1984 - No. 4, June, 1985 (Limited series)
Marvel Comics Group

1 1.50
2,4 1.50
3-The Defenders, Champions (Ghost Rider) & the original X-Men x-over .80 2.00

NOTE: ***Zeck*** *c-1-4.*

ICON
May, 1993 - No. 42, Feb, 1997($1.50/$1.75/$2.50)
DC Comics (Milestone)

1-($2.95)-Collector's Edition polybagged w/poster & trading card (direct sale only) 1.20 3.00
1-14: 9-Simonson-c 1.50
15-24,26: 15-Begin $1.75-c. 15,16-Worlds Collide Pt. 4 & 11. 15-Superboy app. 16-Superman-c/story .70 1.75
25-($2.95, 52 pgs.) 1.20 3.00
27-30,32-42: Begin $2.50-c. 40-Vs. Blood Syndicate 1.00 2.50
31-(99¢) 1.00

IDAHO
June-Aug, 1963 - No. 8, July-Sept, 1965
Dell Publishing Co.

1 1.75 5.25 14.00
2-8: 5-7-Painted-c 1.00 3.00 8.00

IDEAL (... a Classical Comic) (2nd Series) (Love Romances No. 6 on)
July, 1948 - No. 5, March, 1949 (Feature length stories)
Timely Comics

1-Antony & Cleopatra 29.00 86.00 210.00
2-The Corpses of Dr. Sacotti 26.00 79.00 195.00
3-Joan of Arc; used in **SOTI**, pg. 308 'Boer War' 23.00 69.00 170.00
4-Richard the Lion-hearted; titled "...the World's Greatest Comics"; The Witness app. 40.00 120.00 295.00
5-Ideal Love & Romance; change to love; photo-c 14.00 43.00 105.00

IDEAL COMICS (1st Series) (Willie Comics No. 5 on)
Fall, 1944 - No. 4, Spring, 1946
Timely Comics (MgPC)

1-Funny animal; Super Rabbit in all 15.00 45.00 120.00
2 9.50 28.00 75.00
3,4 8.75 26.25 70.00

IDEAL LOVE & ROMANCE (See Ideal, A Classical Comic)

IDEAL ROMANCE (Formerly Tender Romance)
No. 3, April, 1954 - No. 8, Feb, 1955 (Diary Confessions No. 9 on)
Key Publications

3-Bernard Baily-c 5.70 17.00 40.00
4-8: 4,5-B. Baily-c 4.00 11.00 22.00

IDOL
1992 - No. 3, 1992 ($2.95, mini-series, 52 pgs.)
Marvel Comics (Epic Comics)

Book 1-3 1.20 3.00

I DREAM OF JEANNIE (TV)
Apr, 1965 - No. 2, Dec, 1966 (Photo-c)
Dell Publishing Co.

1-Barbara Eden photo-c, each 14.00 41.00 150.00
2 11.00 32.00 115.00

IF THE DEVIL WOULD TALK
1950; 1958 (32 pgs.; paper cover; in full color)
Roman Catholic Catechetical Guild/Impact Publ.

nn-(Scarce)-About secularism (20-30 copies known to exist); very low distribution 61.00 183.00 550.00
1958 Edition-(Impact Publ.); art & script changed to meet church criticism of earlier edition; 80 plus copies known to exist 22.50 68.00 225.00
Black & White version of nn edition; small size; only 4 known copies exist 25.00 75.00 200.00

NOTE: *The original edition of this book was printed and killed by the Guild's board of directors. It is believed that a very limited number of copies were distributed. The 1958 version was a complete bomb with very limited, if any, circulation. In 1979, 11 original, 4 1958 reprints, and 4 B&W's surfaced from the Guild's old files in St. Paul, Minnesota.*

ILLUMINATOR
1993 - No. 4, 1993 ($4.99/$2.95, 52 pgs.)
Marvel Comics/Nelson Publ.

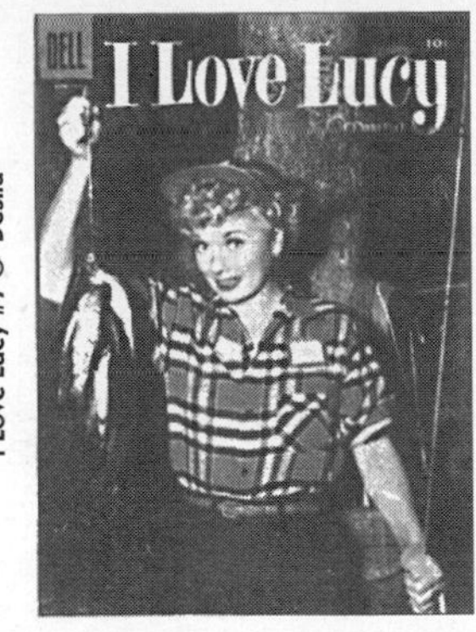

I Love Lucy #7 © Desilu

Images of Shadowhawk #1 © Jim Valentino

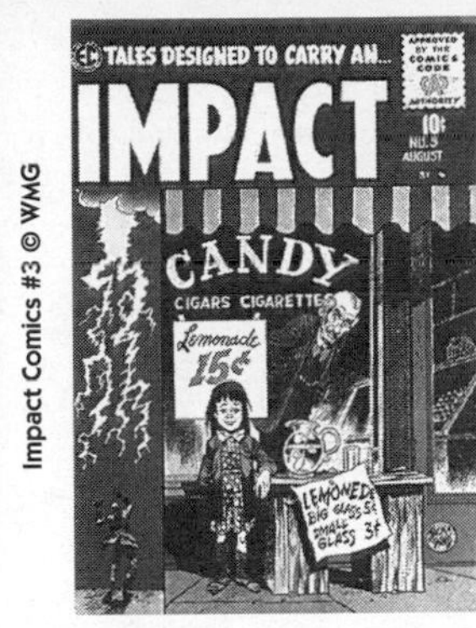

Impact Comics #3 © WMG

	GD25	FN65	NM94
1,2-($4.99)		2.00	5.00
3,4		1.20	3.00

ILLUSTRATED GAGS
No. 16, 1940
United Features Syndicate

	GD25	FN65	NM94
Single Series 16	13.00	39.00	105.00

ILLUSTRATED LIBRARY OF..., AN (See Classics Illustrated Giants)

ILLUSTRATED STORIES OF THE OPERAS
1943 (16 pgs.; B&W) (25 cents) (cover-B&W & red)
Baily (Bernard) Publ. Co.

	GD25	FN65	NM94
nn-(Rare)-Faust (part-r in Cisco Kid #1)	47.00	141.00	420.00
nn-(Rare)-Aida	47.00	141.00	420.00
nn-(Rare)-Carmen; Baily-a	47.00	141.00	420.00
nn-(Rare)-Rigoleito	47.00	141.00	420.00

ILLUSTRATED STORY OF ROBIN HOOD & HIS MERRY MEN, THE
(See Classics Giveaways, 12/44)

ILLUSTRATED TARZAN BOOK, THE (See Tarzan Book)

I LOVED (Formerly Rulah; Colossal Features Magazine No. 33 on)
No. 28, July, 1949 - No. 32, Mar, 1950
Fox Features Syndicate

	GD25	FN65	NM94
28	7.15	21.50	50.00
29-32	5.35	16.00	32.00

I LOVE LUCY
6/90 - No. 6, 1990;V2#1, 11/90 - No. 6, 1991 ($2.95, B&W, mini-series)
Eternity Comics

	GD25	FN65	NM94
..1-6: Reprints 1950s comic strip; photo-c		1.20	3.00
Book II #1-6: Reprints comic strip; photo-c		1.20	3.00
...In Full Color 1 (1991, $5.95, 52 pgs.)-Reprints I Love Lucy Comics #4,5,8,16; photo-c with embossed logo (2 versions exist, one with pgs. 18 & 19 reversed, the other corrected)		2.40	6.00
...In 3-D 1 (1991, $3.95, w/glasses)-Reprints I Love Lucy Comics; photo-c sealed in plastic bag		1.60	4.00

I LOVE LUCY COMICS (TV) (Also see The Lucy Show)
No. 535, Feb, 1954 - No. 35, Apr-June, 1962 (All have Lucille Ball photo-c)
Dell Publishing Co.

	GD25	FN65	NM94
Four Color 535(#1)	48.00	143.00	525.00
Four Color 559(#2, 5/54)	30.00	89.00	325.00
3 (8-10/54) - 5	17.00	52.00	190.00
6-10	14.00	41.00	150.00
11-20	10.00	30.00	110.00
21-35	8.00	23.00	85.00

I LOVE YOU
June, 1950 (one-shot)
Fawcett Publications

	GD25	FN65	NM94
1-Photo-c	10.50	32.00	85.00

I LOVE YOU (Formerly In Love)
No. 7, 9/55 - No. 121, 12/76; No. 122, 3/79 - No. 130, 5/80
Charlton Comics

	GD25	FN65	NM94
7-Kirby-c; Powell-a	7.00	21.00	70.00
8-10	2.50	7.50	24.00
11-16,18-20	1.75	5.50	14.00
17-(68 pg. Giant)	5.00	15.00	50.00
21-25,27-50	2.50	7.50	20.00
26-No Torres-a	1.85	5.50	15.00
51-59	1.50	4.50	12.00
60-(1/66)-Elvis Presley line drawn c/story	11.00	33.00	110.00
61-85	1.00	3.00	8.00
86-110		2.40	6.00
111-130		1.60	4.00

I, LUSIPHER (Becomes Poison Elves, 1st series #8 on)
1991 - No. 7, 1992 (B&W, magazine size)
Mulehide Graphics

	GD25	FN65	NM94
1-Drew Hayes-c/a/scripts	7.50	22.50	75.00
2,4,5	4.50	13.50	45.00
3-Low print run	10.00	30.00	100.00
6,7	4.00	12.00	40.00

I'M A COP
1954 - No. 3, 1954?
Magazine Enterprises

	GD25	FN65	NM94
1(A-1 #111)-Powell-c/a in all	10.00	30.00	80.00
2(A-1 #126), 3(A-1 #128)	6.50	19.50	45.00

IMAGE GRAPHIC NOVEL
1984 ($6.95)(Advertised as Pacific Comics Graphic Novel #1)
Image International

	GD25	FN65	NM94
1-The Seven Samuroid; Brunner-c/a	1.00	2.80	7.00

IMAGES OF A DISTANT SOIL
Feb, 1997 ($2.95, B&W, one-shot)
Image Comics

	GD25	FN65	NM94
1-Sketches by various			2.95

IMAGES OF SHADOWHAWK (Also see Shadowhawk)
Sept, 1993 - No. 3, 1994 ($1.95, limited series)
Image Comics

	GD25	FN65	NM94
1-3: Keith Giffen-c/a; Trencher app.		.80	2.00

IMAGE ZERO
1993 (Received through mail w/coupons from Image books)
Image Comics

	GD25	FN65	NM94
0-Savage Dragon, StormWatch, Shadowhawk, Strykeforce; 1st app. Troll; 1st app. McFarlane's Freak, Blotch, Sweat and Bludd	1.25	3.75	10.00

I'M DICKENS - HE'S FENSTER (TV)
May-July, 1963 - No. 2, Aug-Oct, 1963 (Photo-c)
Dell Publishing Co.

	GD25	FN65	NM94
1,2	3.60	10.80	40.00

I MET A HANDSOME COWBOY
No. 324, Mar, 1951
Dell Publishing Co.

	GD25	FN65	NM94
Four Color 324	8.00	25.00	90.00

IMMORTAL DOCTOR FATE, THE
Jan, 1995 - No. 3, Mar, 1985 ($1.25, limited series)
DC Comics

	GD25	FN65	NM94
1-3: 1-Simonson-c/a. 2-Giffen-c/a(p)			1.30

IMMORTALIS (See Mortigan Goth: Immortalis)

IMMORTAL II
Apr, 1997 -Present ($2.50, B&W& halftones, limited series)
Image Comics

	GD25	FN65	NM94
1-4: 1-B&W w/ color pull-out poster		1.00	2.50

IMPACT
Mar-Apr, 1955 - No. 5, Nov-Dec, 1955
E. C. Comics

	GD25	FN65	NM94
1-Not code approved	14.50	43.00	115.00
2	9.50	28.00	75.00
3-5: 4-Crandall-a	8.50	26.00	60.00

NOTE: ***Crandall** a-1-4. **Davis** a-2-4; c-1-5. **Evans** a-1, 4, 5. **Ingels** a-in all. **Kamen** a-3. **Krigstein** a-1, 5. **Orlando** a-2, 5.*

IMPACT CHRISTMAS SPECIAL
1991 ($2.50, 68 pgs.)

Impulse #21 © DC

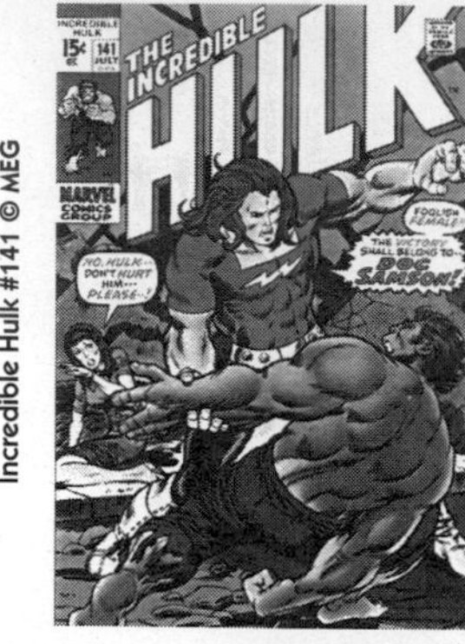

Incredible Hulk #141 © MEG

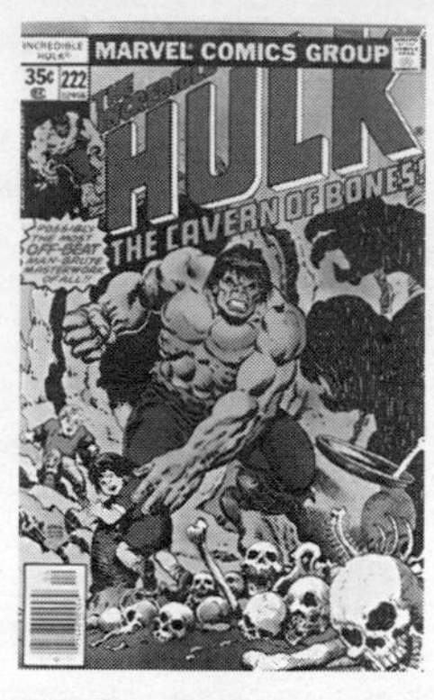

Incredible Hulk #222 © MEG

GD25 FN65 NM94

DC Comics (Impact Comics)
1-Gift of the Magi by Infantino/Rogers; The Black Hood, The Fly, The Jaguar, & The Shield stories 1.00 2.50

IMPOSSIBLE MAN SUMMER VACATION SPECTACULAR, THE
Aug, 1990; No. 2, Sept, 1991 ($2.00, 68 pgs.) (See Fantastic Four#11)
Marvel Comics
..1-Spider Man, Quasar, Dr. Strange, She-Hulk, Punisher & Dr. Doom stories; Barry Crain, Guice-a; Art Adams-c(i) .80 2.00
..2-Ka Zar & Thor app.; Cable Wolverine-c app. .80 2.00

IMPERIAL GUARD
Jan, 1997 - No. 3, Mar, 1997 ($1.95, limited series)
Marvel Comics
1-3: Augustyn-s in all; 1-Wraparound-c 1.95

IMPULSE (See Flash #92, 2nd Series)
Apr, 1995 - Present ($1.50/$1.75/$1.95)
DC Comics
1-Mark Waid scripts & Humberto Ramos-c/a(p) begin; brief retelling of origin 1.00 3.00 8.00
2-4 1.60 4.00
5-9,13-31: 5-Begin $1.75-c. 9-XS from Legion (Impulse's cousin) comes to the 20th Century, returns to the 30th Century in #12. 14-Trickster app. 17-Zatanna-c/app. 21-Legion-c/app. 22-Jesse Quick-c/app. 24-Origin; Flash app. 25-Last Ramos-a. 28-Miss Arrowette (see World's Finest #113) app. 30-Genesis x-over. .70 1.75
10-12:10-Dead Heat Pt. 3 (cont'd in Flash #110). 11-Dead Heat Pt. 4 (cont'd in Flash #111); Johnny Quick dies. 1.00 2.50
32-35: 32-Begin $1.95-c 1.95
Annual 1 (1996, $2.95)-Legends of the Dead Earth; Ramos-c; Mike Parobeck-a 1.20 3.00
Annual 2 (1997, $3.95)-Pulp Heroes stories; Orbik painted-c 3.95
...Plus(9/97, $2.95) w/Gross Out (Scare Tactics)-c/app. 2.95
...Reckless Youth (1997, $14.95, TPB) r/Flash 92-94, Impulse 1-6 14.95

INCAL, THE
Nov, 1988 - No. 3, Jan, 1989 ($10.95/$12.95, mature)
Marvel Comics (Epic Comics)
1,3: Moebius-c/a in all; sexual content 1.40 4.15 11.00
2-($12.95) 1.60 4.85 13.00

INCOMPLETE DEATH'S HEAD (Also see Death's Head)
Jan, 1993 - No. 12, Dec, 1993 ($1.75, limited series)
Marvel Comics UK
1-($2.95, 56 pgs.)-Die-cut cover 1.20 3.00
2-11: 2-Re-intro original Death's Head. 3-Original Death's Head vs. Dragon's Claws .70 1.75
12-($2.50, 52 pgs.)-She Hulk app. 1.00 2.50

INCREDIBLE HULK, THE (See Aurora, The Avengers #1, The Defenders #1, Giant-Size..., Hulk, Marvel Collectors Item Classics, Marvel Comics Presents #26, Marvel Fanfare, Marvel Treasury Edition, Power Record Comics, Rampaging Hulk, She-Hulk & 2099 Unlimited)

INCREDIBLE HULK, THE
May, 1962 - No. 6, Mar, 1963; No. 102, Apr, 1968 - Present
Marvel Comics Group

	GD25	FN65	VF82	NM94
1-Origin & 1st app. (skin is grey colored); Kirby pencils begin, end #5	650.00	1950.00	4875.00	11,000.00
2-1st green skinned Hulk; Kirby/Ditko-a	177.00	530.00	1150.00	2300.00

GD25 FN65 NM94
3-Origin retold; 1st app. Ringmaster & Hercules (9/62) 117.00 350.00 1400.00
4,5: 4-Brief origin retold 108.00 325.00 1300.00
6-Intro. Teen Brigade; all Ditko-a 158.00 475.00 1900.00
102 (Formerly Tales to Astonish)-Origin retold; story continued from Tales to Astonish #101 15.00 45.00 150.00
103 6.80 20.50 68.00
104-Rhino app. 6.20 18.75 62.00
105-108: 105-1st Missing Link. 107-Mandarin app.(9/68). 108-Mandarin & Nick Fury app. (10/68). 5.20 15.75 52.00
109,110: 109-Ka-Zar app. 3.50 10.50 35.00
111-117: 117-Last 12 cent issue 2.90 8.70 29.00
118-Hulk vs. Sub-Mariner 2.60 7.80 26.00
119-121,123-125 2.00 6.00 16.00
122-Hulk battles Thing (12/69) 3.40 10.20 34.00
126-1st Barbara Norriss (Valkyrie) 2.25 6.75 18.00
127-139: 131-Hulk vs. Iron Man; 1st Jim Wilson, Hulk's new sidekick. 136-1st Xeron, The Star-Slayer 1.25 3.75 10.00
140-Written by Harlan Ellison; 1st Jarella, Hulk's love 1.75 5.25 14.00
141-1st app. Doc Samson (7/71) 2.80 8.40 28.00
142-144,146-157-161: 149-1st app. The Inheritor. 155-1st app. Shaper. 158-Warlock cameo(12/72). 161-The Mimic dies; Beast app. 2.00 5.00
145-(52 pgs.)-Origin retold 1.00 2.80 7.00
162-1st app. The Wendigo (4/73); Beast app. 2.40 6.00
163-171,173-175: 163-1st app. The Gremlin. 164-1st Capt. Omen & Colonel John D. Armbruster. 166-1st Zzzax. 168-1st The Harpy; nudity panels of Betty Brant. 169-1st app. Bi-Beast 1.60 4.00
165-Variant w/4 extra pgs. of ads on slick paper(7/73)1.00 2.80 7.00
172-X-Men cameo; origin Juggernaut retold 1.10 3.30 9.00
176-Warlock cameo (2 panels only); same date as Strange Tales #178 (6/74) 2.00 5.00
177-1st actual death of Warlock (last panel only) 1.00 2.80 7.00
178-Rebirth of Warlock 1.00 3.00 8.00
179-No Warlock 1.60 4.00
180-(10/74)-1st app. Wolverine (cameo last pg.) 5.50 16.50 55.00
181-(11/74)-1st full Wolverine story 40.00 120.00 450.00
182-Wolverine cameo; see Giant-Size X-Men #1 for next app.; 1st Crackajack Jackson 5.50 16.50 55.00
183-199: 185-Death of Col. Armbruster 1.60 4.00
200-Silver Surfer app.; anniversary issue 2.50 7.50 25.00
201-240: 201-Conan swipe-c/sty. 212-1st app. The Constrictor. 227-Original Avengers app. 232-Capt. America x-over from C.A. #230. 233-Marvel Man app. 234-(4/79)-1st app. Quasar (formerly Marvel Man & changes name to Quasar) 1.40 3.50
241-249,251-299: 243-Cage app. 271-Rocket Raccoon app. 272-Sasquatch & Wendigo app.; Wolverine & Alpha Flight cameo in flashback. 278,279-Most Marvel characters app. (Wolverine in both). 279-X-Men & Alpha Flight cameos. 282-284-She-Hulk app. 293-F.F. app. 1.00 2.50
250-Giant size; Silver Surfer app. 1.00 3.00 8.00
300-(11/84, 52 pgs.)-Spider-Man app in new black costume on-c & 2 pg. cameo 1.00 2.50
301-313: 312-Origin Hulk retold 1.00 2.50
314-Byrne-c/a begins, ends #319 1.60 4.00
315-319: 319-Bruce Banner & Betty Talbot wed 1.00 2.50
320-323,325,327-329 1.00 2.50
324-1st app. Grey Hulk since #1 (c-swipe of #1) 1.00 3.00 8.00
326-Grey vs. Green Hulk .80 2.00
330-1st McFarlane issue (4/87); death of Thunderbolt Ross 1.75 5.25 14.00
331-Grey Hulk series begins 1.25 3.75 10.00
332-334,336-339: 336,337-X-Factor app. 1.00 2.80 7.00
335-No McFarlane-a 1.00 2.50
340-Hulk battles Wolverine by McFarlane 2.50 7.50 25.00
341-344 1.60 4.00
345-($1.50, 52 pgs.) 1.60 4.00
346-Last McFarlane issue 1.60 4.00
347-349,351-358,360-366: 347-1st app. Marlo 1.50
350-Hulk/Thing battle 1.60 4.00
359-Wolverine app. (illusion only) 1.50

Incredible Hulk #446 © MEG

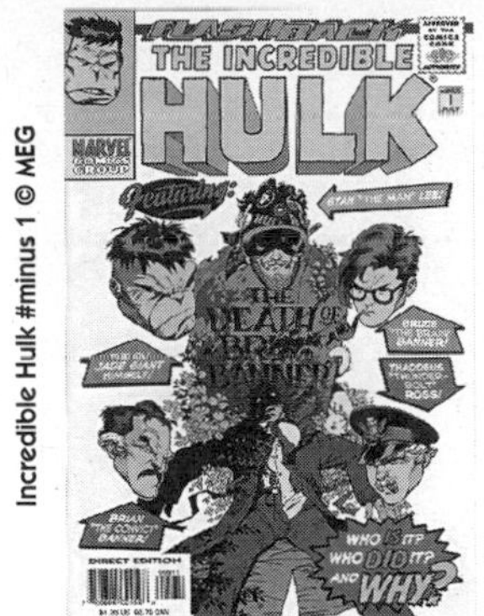

Incredible Hulk #minus 1 © MEG

Indiana Jones and the Golden Fleece #1 © Lucasfilm

GD25 FN65 NM94

367-1st Dale Keown-a on Hulk (3/90) 1.00 2.80 7.00
368-Sam Kieth-c/a, 1st app. Pantheon 1.60 4.00
369,370-Dale Keown-c/a. 370,371-Original Defenders app. 1.40 3.50
371,373-376: Keown-c/a. 376-Green vs. Grey Hulk 1.40 3.50
372-Green Hulk app.; Keown-c/a 1.00 3.00 8.00
377-1st all new Hulk; fluorescent-c; Keown-c/a 1.25 3.75 10.00
377-Fluorescent green logo 2nd printing 1.40 3.50
378,380,389: No Keown-a. 380-Doc Samson app. 1.50
379-Keown-a 1.40 3.50
381-388,390-392-Keown-a. 385-Infinity Gauntlet x-over. 389-Last $1.00-c. 392-X-Factor app. 1.40 3.50
393-($2.50, 72 pgs.)-30th anniversary issue; green foil stamped-c; swipes-c to #1; has pin-ups of classic battles; Keown-c/a 1.40 3.50
393-2nd printing 1.00 2.50
394-397: 394-No Keown-c/a; intro Trauma. 395,396-Punisher-c/stories; Keown-c/a. 397-Begin "Ghost of the Past" 4-part sty; Keown c/a .80 2.00
398,399: 398-Last Keown-c/a .80 2.00
400-($2.50, 68 pgs.)-Holo-grafx foil-c & r/TTA #63 1.00 2.50
401-416: 402-Return of Doc Samson 1.50
417-424: 417-Begin $1.50-c; Rick Jones' bachelor party; Hulk returns from "Future Imperfect"; bound-in trading card sheet. 418-(Regular edition)-Rick Jones marries Marlo; includes cameo apps of various Marvel characters as well as DC's Death & Peter David. 420-Death of Jim Wilson. 1.50
418-($2.50)-Collector's Edition w/gatefold die-cut-c 1.00 2.50
425 ($2.25, 52 pgs.) .90 2.25
425 ($3.50, 52 pgs.)-Holographic-c 1.40 3.50
426-434, 436-442: 426-Begin $1.95-c. 427, 428-Man-Thing app. 431,432-Abomination app. 434-Funeral for Nick Fury. 436-Ghosts of the Future begins, ends #440. 439-Hulk becomes Maestro, Avengers app. 440-Thor-c/app. 441,442-She-Hulk-c/app. 442-Molecule Man app. .80 2.00
435 ($2.50)-Rhino-app; excerpt from "What Savage Beast" 1.00 2.50
443-448: 443-Begin $1.50-c; re-app. of Hulk. 444-Cable-c/app.; "Onslaught". 445-"Onslaught". 446-w/card insert. 447-Begin Deodato-c/a(p). 1.50
447-Variant cover 1.20 3.00
449-Thunderbolts-c/app. 2.40 6.00
450-($2.95)-Thunderbolts app.: two stories: Heroes Reborn-c/app. 1.20 3.00
453,454, -1(7/97):($1.95) 1.95
455-460: 455-Begin $1.99-c, X-Men-c/app. 1.99
Special 1 (10/68, 25¢, 68 pg.)-New 51 pg. story, Hulk battles The Inhumans (early app.); Steranko-c. 7.00 21.00 70.00
Special 2 (10/69, 25¢, 68 pg.)-Origin retold 4.50 13.50 45.00
Special 3 (1/71, 25¢, 68 pg.) 1.85 5.50 15.00
Special 4 (1/72) 1.85 5.50 15.00
Annual 5 (1976) 1.00 3.00 8.00
Annual 6 (1977) 2.00 5.00
Annual 7 (1978)-Byrne/Layton-c/a; Iceman & Angel app. in book-length story 2.00 5.00
Annual 8 ('79)-Book-length Sasquatch-c/sty 1.60 4.00
Annual 9-17: 9('80). 10('81). 11('82)-Doc Samson back-up by Miller(p)(5 pgs.); Spider-Man & Avengers app. Buckler-a(p). 12 ('83). 13('84). 14('85). 15('86). 16('90, $2.00, 68 pgs.)-She-Hulk app. 17(1991, $2.00)-Origin retold 1.20 3.00
Annual 18 (1992, $2.25, 68 pgs.)-Return of the Defenders, Pt. I; no Keown-c/a .90 2.25
Annual 19 (1993, $2.95, 68 pgs.)-Bagged w/card 1.20 3.00
Annual 20 (1994, $2.95, 68 pgs.) 1.20 3.00
...'97 ($2.99) Pollina-c 2.99
...And Wolverine 1 (10/86, $2.50)-r/1st app. #180-181 1.25 3.75 10.00
...Ground Zero ('95, $12.95) r/#340-346 1.60 4.85 13.00

GD25 FN65 NM94

...Hercules Unleashed (10/96, $2.50) David-s/Deodato-c/a 1.00 2.50
...Versus Quasimodo 1 (3/83, one-shot)-Based on Saturday morning cartoon 1.20 3.00
...Versus Venom 1 (4/94, $2.50, one-shot)-Embossed-c; red foil logo 1.10 2.75

NOTE: **Adkins** *a-111-116i.* **Austin** *a(i)-350, 351, 353, 354; c-302i, 350i.* **Ayers** *a-3-5i.* **Buckler** *a-Annual 5; c-252.* **John Buscema** *c-202p.* **Byrne** *a-314-319p; c-314-316, 318, 319, 359, Annual 14i.* **Colan** *c-363.* **Ditko** *a-2i, 6, 249, Annual 2r(5), 3r, 9p; c-2i, 6, 235, 249.* **Everett** *c-133i.* **Golden** *c-248, 251.* **Kane** *c(p)-193, 194, 196, 198.* **Dale Keown** *a(p)-367, 369-377, 379, 381-388, 390-393, 395-398; c-369-377p, 381, 382p, 384, 385, 386, 387p, 388, 390p, 391-393, 395p, 396, 397p, 398.* **Kirby** *a-1-5p, Special 2, 3p, Annual 5p; c-1-5, Annual 5.* **McFarlane** *a-330-334p, 336-339p, 340-343, 344-346p; c-330p, 340p, 341-343, 344p, 345, 346p.* **Mignola** *c-302, 305, 313.* **Miller** *c-258p, 261, 264, 268.* **Mooney** *a-230p, 287i, 288i.* **Powell** *a-Special 3r(2).* **Romita** *a-Annual 17p.* **Severin** *a(i)-108-110, 131-133, 141-151, 153-155; c(i)-109, 110, 132, 142, 144-155.* **Simonson** *c-283, 364-367.* **Starlin** *a-222p; c-217.* **Staton** *a(i)-187-189, 191-209.* **Tuska** *a-102i, 105i, 106i, 218p.* **Williamson** *a-310i; c-310i, 311i.* **Wrightson** *c-197.*

INCREDIBLE MR. LIMPET, THE (See Movie Classics)

INCREDIBLE SCIENCE FICTION (Formerly Weird Science-Fantasy)
No. 30, July-Aug, 1955 - No. 33, Jan-Feb, 1956
E. C. Comics

30,33: 33-Story-r/Weird Fantasy #18 33.00 99.00 240.00
31-Williamson/Krenkel-a, Wood-a(2) 35.00 105.00 250.00
32-Williamson/Krenkel-a 35.00 105.00 250.00

NOTE: **Davis** *a-30, 32, 33; c-30-32.* **Krigstein** *a-in all.* **Orlando** *a-30, 32, 33("Judgement Day" reprint).* **Wood** *a-30, 31, 33; c-33.*

INDEPENDENCE DAY (Movie)
No. 0, June, 1996 - No. 2, Aug, 1996 ($1.95, limited series)
Marvel Comics

0-Special Edition; photo-c 2.00 5.00
0-2 .80 2.00

INDIANA JONES AND THE ARMS OF GOLD
Feb, 1994 - May, 1994 ($2.50, limited series)
Dark Horse Comics

1-4 1.00 2.50

INDIANA JONES AND THE FATE OF ATLANTIS
Mar, 1991 - Sep, 1991 ($2.50, limited series)
Dark Horse Comics

1-4-Dorman painted-c on all; contain trading cards (#1 has a 2nd printing, 10/91) 1.00 2.50

INDIANA JONES AND THE GOLDEN FLEECE
Jun, 1994 - July, 1994 ($2.50, limited series)
Dark Horse Comics

1,2 1.00 2.50

INDIANA JONES AND THE IRON PHOENIX
Dec, 1994 - Mar, 1995 ($2.50, limited series)
Dark Horse Comics

1-4 1.00 2.50

INDIANA JONES AND THE LAST CRUSADE
1989 - No. 4, 1989 ($1.00, limited series, movie adaptation)
Marvel Comics

1-4: Williamson-i assist 1.00
1-(1989, $2.95, B&W mag., 80 pgs.) 1.20 3.00

INDIANA JONES AND THE SHRINE OF THE SEA DEVIL
Sep, 1994 ($2.50, one shot)
Dark Horse Comics

1-Gary Gianni-a 1.00 2.50

INDIANA JONES AND THE SPEAR OF DESTINY
Apr, 1995 - Aug, 1995 ($2.50, limited series)
Dark Horse Comics

1-4 1.00 2.50

Indians #12 © FH

Inferno #1 © DC

The Infinity Gauntlet #3 © MEG

INDIANA JONES: THUNDER IN THE ORIENT
Sep, 1993 - 1994 ($2.50, limited series)
Dark Horse Comics
1-6: Dan Barry story & art in all; 1-Dorman painted-c — 1.00 — 2.50

INDIANA JONES AND THE TEMPLE OF DOOM
Sept, 1984 - No. 3, Nov, 1984 (Movie adaptation)
Marvel Comics Group
1-3-r/Marvel Super Special; Guice-a — 1.00

INDIAN BRAVES (Baffling Mysteries No. 5 on)
March, 1951 - No. 4, Sept, 1951
Ace Magazines

	GD25	FN65	NM94
1-Green Arrowhead begins, ends #3	8.75	26.25	65.00
2	5.35	16.00	32.00
3,4	4.25	13.00	26.00
I.W. Reprint #1 (nd)-r/Indian Braves #4	1.25	3.75	10.00

INDIAN CHIEF (White Eagle...) (Formerly The Chief, Four Color 290)
No. 3, July-Sept, 1951 - No. 33, Jan-Mar, 1959 (All painted-c)
Dell Publishing Co.

	GD25	FN65	NM94
3	3.00	9.00	35.00
4-11: 6-White Eagle app.	2.50	7.50	28.00
12-1st White Eagle(10-12/53)-Not same as earlier character	3.00	9.00	35.00
13-29	1.65	5.00	18.00
30-33-Buscema-a	1.80	5.50	20.00

INDIAN CHIEF (See March of Comics No. 94, 110, 127, 140, 159, 170, 187)

INDIAN FIGHTER, THE (Movie)
No. 687, May, 1956 (one-shot)
Dell Publishing Co.
Four Color 687-Kirk Douglas photo-c — 7.00 — 22.00 — 80.00

INDIAN FIGHTER
May, 1950 - No. 11, Jan, 1952
Youthful Magazines

	GD25	FN65	NM94
1	8.75	26.25	70.00
2-Wildey-a/c(bondage)	5.70	17.00	40.00
3-11: 3,4-Wildey-a	4.25	13.00	28.00

NOTE: ***Walter Johnson** c-1, 3, 4, 6. **Palais** a-10. **Stallman** a-7. **Wildey** a-2-4; c-2, 5.*

INDIAN LEGENDS OF THE NIAGARA (See American Graphics)

INDIANS
Spring, 1950 - No. 17, Spring, 1953 (1-8: 52 pgs.)
Fiction House Magazines (Wings Publ. Co.)

	GD25	FN65	NM94
1-Manzar The White Indian, Long Bow & Orphan of the Storm begin	21.00	64.00	170.00
2-Starlight begins	10.50	32.00	85.00
3-5: 5-17-Most-c by Whitman	8.75	26.25	70.00
6-10	7.85	23.50	55.00
11-17	6.50	19.50	45.00

INDIANS OF THE WILD WEST
Circa 1958? (no date) (Reprints)
I. W. Enterprises
9-Kinstler-c; Whitman-a; r/Indians #? — 1.50 — 4.50 — 12.00

INDIANS ON THE WARPATH
No date (Late 40s, early 50s) (132 pgs.)
St. John Publishing Co.
nn-Matt Baker-c; contains St. John comics rebound. Many combinations possible — 26.00 — 79.00 — 190.00

INDIAN TRIBES (See Famous Indian Tribes)

INDIAN WARRIORS (Formerly White Rider and Super Horse; becomes Western Crime Cases #9)
No. 7, June, 1951 - No. 8, Sept, 1951
Star Publications

	GD25	FN65	NM94
7-White Rider & Superhorse continue; "Last of the Mohicans" serial begins; L.B. Cole-c	13.00	39.00	100.00
8-L. B. Cole-c	11.30	34.00	90.00
3-D 1(12/53, 25¢)-Came w/glasses; L. B. Cole-c	38.00	114.00	280.00
Accepted Reprint(nn)(inside cover shows White Rider & Superhorse #11)-r/cover to #7; origin White Rider &...;. L. B. Cole-c	5.35	16.00	32.00
Accepted Reprint #8 (nd); L.B. Cole-c (r-cover to #8)	5.35	16.00	32.00

INDOORS-OUTDOORS (See Wisco)

INDOOR SPORTS
nd (6x9", 64 pgs., B&W-r, hard-c)
National Specials Co.
nn-By Tad — 5.00 — 15.00 — 30.00

INDUSTRIAL GOTHIC
Dec, 1995 - No. 5, Apr, 1996 ($2.50, limited series)
DC Comics (Vertigo)
1-5: Ted McKeever-c/a/scripts — 1.00 — 2.50

INFERIOR FIVE, THE (Inferior 5 #11, 12) (See Showcase #62, 63, 65)
3-4/67 - No. 10, 9-10/68; No. 11, 8-9/72 - No. 12, 10-11/72
National Periodical Publications (#1-10: 12¢)

	GD25	FN65	NM94
1-(3-4/67)-Sekowsky-a(p); 4th app.	3.50	10.50	35.00
2-Plastic Man, F.F. app.; Sekowsky-a(p)	2.35	7.00	19.00
3-12: 4-Thor app. 6-Stars DC staff. 10-Superman x-over; F.F., Spider-Man & Sub-Mariner app. 11,12-Orlando-c/a; both r/Showcase #62,63	1.75	5.25	14.00

INFERNO
1995 - Present ($2.95, B&W)
Caliber Comics
1-3 — 1.20 — 3.00

INFERNO (See Legion of Super-Heroes)
Oct, 1997 - No. 4, Feb, 1998 ($2.50, limited series)
DC Comics
1-4-Immonen-s/c/a — 2.50

INFINITY CRUSADE
June, 1993 - No. 6, Nov, 1993 ($2.50, limited series, 52 pgs.)
Marvel Comics
1-6: By Jim Starlin & Ron Lim — 1.00 — 2.50

INFINITY GAUNTLET (The... #2 on; see Infinity Crusade, The Infinity War & Warlock & the Infinity Watch)
July, 1991 - No. 6, Dec, 1991 ($2.50, limited series)
Marvel Comics
1-6:Thanos-c/stories in all; Starlin scripts in all; 5,6-Ron Lim-c/a — 1.00 — 2.50

NOTE: ***Lim** a-3p(part), 5p, 6p; c-5i, 6i. **Perez** a-1-3p, 4p(part); c-1(painted), 2-4, 5i, 6i.*

INFINITY, INC. (See All-Star Squadron #25)
Mar, 1984 - No. 53, Aug, 1988 ($1.25, Baxter paper, 36 pgs.)
DC Comics

	GD25	FN65	NM94
1-Brainwave, Jr., Fury, The Huntress, Jade, Northwind, Nuklon, Obsidian, Power Girl, Silver Scarab & Star Spangled Kid begin			1.50
2-5: 2-Dr. Midnite, G.A. Flash, W. Woman, Dr. Fate, Hourman, Green Lantern, Wildcat app. 5-Nudity panels			1.20
6-13,38-49,51-53: 46,47-Millennium tie-ins			1.20
14-Todd McFarlane-a (5/85, 2nd full story)	1.00	3.00	8.00
15-37-McFarlane-a (20,23,24: 5 pgs. only; 33: 2 pgs.); 18-24-Crisis x-over. 21-Intro new Hourman & Dr. Midnight. 26-New Wildcat app. 31-Star Spangled Kid becomes Skyman. 32-Green Fury becomes Green Flame. 33-Origin Obsidian. 35-1st modern app. G.A. Fury		1.20	3.00
50 ($2.50, 52 pgs.)		1.00	2.50

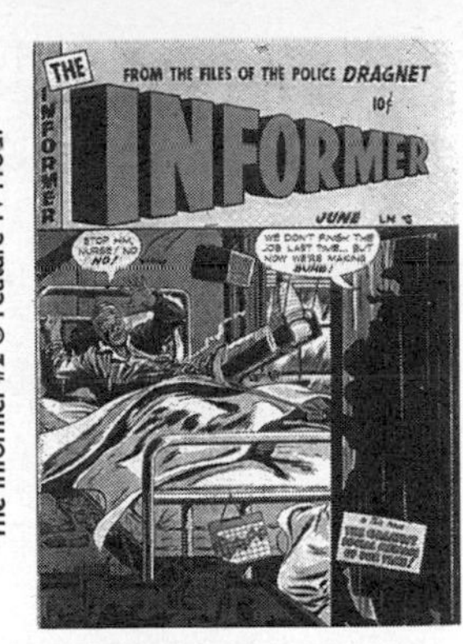

The Informer #2 © Feature TV Prod.

The Inhumans #6 © MEG

The Interface#8 © James D. Hudnall

GD25 FN65 NM94

Annual 1,2: 1(12/85)-Crisis x-over. 2('88, $2.00) .80 2.00
Special 1 (1987, $1.50) 1.50
NOTE: ***Kubert*** *r-4.* ***McFarlane*** *a-14-37p, Annual 1p; c(p)-14-19, 22, 25, 26, 31-33, 37, Annual 1.* ***Newton*** *a-12p, 13p(last work 4/85).* ***Tuska*** *a-11p. JSA app. 3-10.*

INFINITY WAR, THE (Also see Infinity Gauntlet & Warlock and the Infinity...)
June, 1992 - No. 6, Nov, 1992 ($2.50, mini-series)
Marvel Comics
1-Starlin scripts, Lim-c/a(p), Thanos app. in all 1.00 2.50
2-6: All have wraparound gatefold covers 1.00 2.50

INFORMER, THE
April, 1954 - No. 5, Dec, 1954
Feature Television Productions
1-Sekowsky-a begins 8.50 26.00 60.00
2 5.70 17.00 40.00
3-5 5.70 17.00 35.00

IN HIS STEPS
1973, 1977 (39/49¢)
Spire Christian Comics (Fleming H. Revell Co.)
nn 1.60 4.00

INHUMANOIDS, THE (TV)
Jan, 1987 - No. 4, July 1987
Marvel Comics (Star Comics)
1-4: Based on Hasbro toys .80 2.00

INHUMANS, THE (See Amazing Adventures, Fantastic Four #54 & Special #5, Incredible Hulk Special #1, Marvel Graphic Novel & Thor #146)
Oct, 1975 - No. 12, Aug, 1977
Marvel Comics Group
1: #1-4,6 are 25¢ issues 1.00 3.00 8.00
2-12: 9-Reprints Amazing Adventures #1,2('70). 12-Hulk app. 1.60 4.00
Special 1(4/90, $1.50, 52 pgs.)-F.F. cameo .80 2.00
NOTE: ***Buckler*** *c-2-4p, 5.* ***Gil Kane*** *a-5-7p; c-1p, 7p, 8p.* ***Kirby*** *a-9r.* ***Mooney*** *a-11i.* ***Perez*** *a-1-4p, 8p.*

INHUMANS: THE GREAT REFUGE
May, 1995 ($2.95, one-shot)
Marvel Comics
1 1.20 3.00

INKY & DINKY (See Felix's Nephews...)

IN LOVE (...Magazine on-c; I Love You No. 7 on)
Aug-Sept, 1954 - No. 6, July, 1955 ('Adult Reading' on-c)
Mainline/Charlton No. 5 (5/55)-on
1-Simon & Kirby-a; book-length novel in all issues 25.00 75.00 200.00
2-S&K-a 15.00 45.00 120.00
3,4-S&K-a. 3-Last pre-code (12-1/54-55) 12.00 36.00 95.00
5-S&K-c only 7.15 21.50 50.00
6-No S&K-a 4.15 12.50 25.00

IN LOVE WITH JESUS
1952 (Giveaway, 36 pgs.)
Catechetical Educational Society
nn 3.60 9.00 18.00

INNOVATION SPECTACULAR
1991 - No. 2, 1991 ($2.95, squarebound, 100 pgs.)
Innovation Publishing
1,2: Contains rebound comics w/o covers 1.20 3.00

INNOVATION SUMMER FUN SPECIAL
1991 ($3.50, B&W/color, squarebound)
Innovation Publishing
1-Contains rebound comics (Power Factory) 1.40 3.50

INSANE

GD25 FN65 NM94

Feb, 1988 - No. 2? ($1.75, B&W)
Dark Horse Comics
1,2: 1-X-Men, Godzilla parodies. 2-Concrete .70 1.80

IN SEARCH OF THE CASTAWAYS (See Movie Comics)

INSIDE CRIME (Formerly My Intimate Affair)
No. 3, July, 1950 - No. 2, Sept, 1950
Fox Features Syndicate (Hero Books)
3-Wood-a (10 pgs.); L. B. Cole-c 22.00 66.00 170.00
2-Used in **SOTI**, pg. 182,183; r/Spook #24 17.00 49.00 120.00
nn(no publ. listed, nd) 7.15 21.50 50.00

INSPECTOR, THE (TV) (Also see The Pink Panther)
July, 1974 - No. 19, Feb, 1978
Gold Key
1 2.50 7.50 20.00
2-5 1.50 4.50 12.00
6-9 1.10 3.30 9.00
10-19: 11-Reprints 2.40 6.00

INSPECTOR GILL OF THE FISH POLICE (See Fish Police)

INSPECTOR WADE
No. 13, May, 1938
David McKay Publications
Feature Books 13 18.50 56.00 185.00

INSTANT PIANO
Aug, 1994 - No. 4, Feb, 1995 ($3.95, B&W, bimonthly, mature)
Dark Horse Comics
1-4 1.60 4.00

INTERFACE
Dec, 1989 - No. 8, Dec, 1990 ($1.95, mature, coated paper)
Marvel Comics (Epic Comics)
1-5: Based on ESPers; painted-c/a .80 2.00
6-8: 6-Begin $2.25-c .90 2.30

INTERNATIONAL COMICS (...Crime Patrol No. 6)
Spring, 1947 - No. 5, Nov-Dec, 1947
E. C. Comics
1-Schaffenberger-a begins, ends #4 47.00 141.00 420.00
2 36.00 108.00 295.00
3-5 31.00 94.00 250.00

INTERNATIONAL CRIME PATROL (Formerly International Comics #1-5; becomes Crime Patrol No. 7 on)
No. 6, Spring, 1948
E. C. Comics
6-Moon Girl app. 49.00 147.00 440.00

INTERSTATE THEATRES' FUN CLUB COMICS
Mid 1940's (10¢ on cover) (B&W cover) (Premium)
Interstate Theatres
Cover features MLJ characters looking at a copy of Top-Notch Comics, but contains an early Detective Comic on inside; many combinations possible 5.70 17.00 36.00

IN THE DAYS OF THE MOB (Magazine)
Fall, 1971 (B&W)
Hampshire Dist. Ltd. (National)
1-Kirby-a; John Dillinger wanted poster inside 6.50 19.50 65.00

IN THE PRESENCE OF MINE ENEMIES
1973 (35/49¢)
Spire Christian Comics/Fleming H. Revell Co.
nn 1.00

INTIMATE

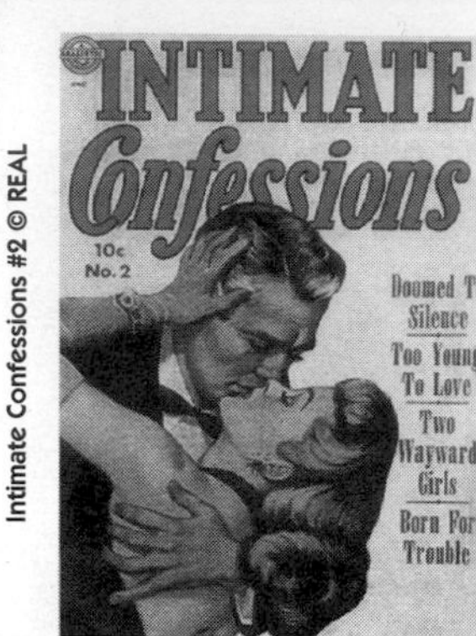

Intimate Confessions #2 © REAL

Invaders #7 © MEG

The Invisibles #8 (1st Series) © Grant Morrison

GD25 FN65 NM94

Dec, 1957 - No. 3, May, 1958
Charlton Comics

1-3 2.40 6.00 12.00

INTIMATE CONFESSIONS (See Fox Giants)

INTIMATE CONFESSIONS
July-Aug, 1951 - No. 7, Aug, 1952; No. 8, Mar, 1953 (All painted-c)
Realistic Comics

1-Kinstler-c/a; c/Avon paperback #222 58.00 174.00 525.00
2 14.00 41.00 110.00
3-c/Avon paperback #250; Kinstler-c/a 16.00 49.00 130.00
4-6,8: 4-c/Avon paperback #304; Kinstler-c. 6-c/Avon paperback #120. 8-c/Avon paperback #375; Kinstler-a 14.00 41.00 110.00
7-Spanking panel 14.00 41.00 110.00

INTIMATE CONFESSIONS
1964
I. W. Enterprises/Super Comics

I.W. Reprint #9,10 1.25 3.75 10.00
Super Reprint #12,18 1.25 3.75 10.00

INTIMATE LOVE
No. 5, 1950 - No. 28, Aug, 1954
Standard Comics

5 5.70 17.00 38.00
6-8-Severin/Elder-a 5.70 17.00 40.00
9 4.00 11.00 22.00
10-Jane Russell, Robert Mitchum photo-c 6.50 19.50 45.00
11-18,20,23,25,27,28 3.00 7.50 15.00
19,21,22,24,26-Toth-a 5.35 16.00 32.00
NOTE: ***Celardo*** *a-8, 10.* ***Colletta*** *a-23.* ***Moreira*** *a-13(2). Photo-c-6, 7, 10, 12, 14, 15, 18-20, 24, 26, 27.*

INTIMATE SECRETS OF ROMANCE
Sept, 1953 - No. 2, Apr, 1954
Star Publications

1,2-L. B. Cole-c 11.30 34.00 90.00

INTRIGUE
Jan, 1955
Quality Comics Group

1-Horror; Jack Cole reprint/Web of Evil 23.00 68.00 180.00

INTRUDER
1990 - No. 10, 1991 ($2.95, 44 pgs.)
TSR, Inc.

1-10 1.20 3.00

INVADERS, THE (TV)
Oct, 1967 - No. 4, Oct, 1968 (All have photo-c)
Gold Key

1-Spiegle-a in all 9.00 26.00 95.00
2-4 6.40 19.00 70.00

INVADERS, THE (Also see The Avengers #71 & Giant-Size Invaders)
August, 1975 - No. 40, May, 1979; No. 41, Sept, 1979
Marvel Comics Group

1-Captain America & Bucky, Human Torch & Toro, & Sub-Mariner begin; cont'd. from Giant Size Invaders #1; #1-7 are 25¢ issues 1.85 5.50 15.00
2-5,7-10: 2-1st app. Mailbag & Brain-Drain. 3-Battle issue; Cap vs. Namor vs. Torch; intro U-Man. 7-Intro Baron Blood & intro/1st app. Union Jack; Human Torch origin retold. 8-Union Jack-c/story. 9-Origin Baron Blood. 10-G.A. Capt. America-r/C.A #22 2.40 6.00
6-(Regular 25¢ edition)(7/76) Liberty Legion app 2.40 6.00
6-(30¢-c, limited distribution) 2.50 7.50 24.00
11-19: 11-Origin Spitfire; intro The Blue Bullet. 14-1st app. The Crusaders. 16-Re-intro The Destroyer. 17-Intro Warrior Woman. 18-Re-intro The Destroyer w/new origin. 19-Hitler-c/story 1.60 4.00
20-Reprints origin/1st app. Sub-Mariner from Motion Picture Funnies Weekly with color added & brief write-up about MPFW; 1st app. new Union Jack II 1.00 3.00 8.00
21-(Regular 30¢ edition)-r/Marvel Mystery #10 (battle issue) 1.60 4.00
21-(35¢-c, limited distribution) 2.00 6.00 16.00
22-30,34-40: 22-New origin Toro. 24-r/Marvel Mystery #17 (team-up issue; all-r). 25-All new-a begins. 28-Intro new Human Top & Golden Girl. 29-Intro Teutonic Knight. 34-Mighty Destroyer joins. 35-The Whizzer app. 1.20 3.00
31-Frankenstein-c/sty 2.40 6.00
32,33-Thor app. 2.00 5.00
41-Double size last issue 2.40 6.00
Annual 1 (9/77)-Schomburg, Rico stories (new); Schomburg-c/a (1st for Marvel in 30 years); Avengers app.; re-intro The Shark & The Hyena 1.00 3.00 8.00
NOTE: ***Buckler*** *a-5.* ***Everett*** *r-20('39), 21(1940), 24, Annual 1.* ***Gil Kane*** *c(p)-13, 17, 18, 20-27.* ***Kirby*** *c(p)-3-12, 14-16, 32, 33.* ***Mooney*** *a-5i, 16, 22.* ***Robbins*** *a-1-4, 6-9, 10(3 pg.), 11-15, 17-21, 23, 25-28; c-28.*

INVADERS (See Namor, the Sub-Mariner #12)
May, 1993 - No. 4, Aug, 1993 ($1.75, limited series)
Marvel Comics Group

1-4 .70 1.75

INVADERS FROM HOME
1990 - No. 6, 1990 ($2.50, mature)
DC Comics (Piranha Press)

1-6 1.00 2.50

INVASION
Holiday, 1988-'89 - No. 3, Jan, 1989 ($2.95, limited series, 84 pgs.)
DC Comics

1-3:1-McFarlane/Russell-a. 2-McFarlane/Russell & Giffen/Gordon-a 1.20 3.00

INVINCIBLE FOUR OF KUNG FU & NINJA
April, 1988 - No. 12?, 1990 ($2.00)
Leung Publications

1-($2.75) 1.10 2.75
2-12: 2-Begin $2.00-c .80 2.00

INVISIBLE BOY (See Approved Comics)

INVISIBLE MAN, THE (See Superior Stories #1 & Supernatural Thrillers #2)

INVISIBLES, THE (1st Series)
Sept, 1994 - No. 25, Oct, 1996 ($1.95/$2.50, mature)
DC Comics (Vertigo)

1-($2.95, 52 pgs.)-Intro King Mob, Ragged Robin, Boy, Lord Fanny & Dane (Jack Frost); Grant Morrison scripts in all 1.40 3.50
2-8: 4-Includes bound-in trading cards. 5-1st app. Orlando; brown paper-c .80 2.00
9-25: 9-Begin $2.50-c. 10-Intro Jim Crow. 13-15-Origin Lord Fanny. 19-Origin King Mob; polybagged. 20-Origin Boy. 21-Mister Six revealed. 25-Intro Division X 1.00 2.50
Say You Want A Revolution (1996, $17.50, TPB)-r/#1-8 17.50
NOTE: ***Buckingham*** *a-25p.* ***Rian Hughes*** *c-1, 5.* ***Phil Jimenez*** *a-17p-19p.* ***Paul Johnson*** *a-16, 21.* ***Sean Phillips*** *c-2-4, 6-25.* ***Weston*** *a-10p.* ***Yeowell*** *a-1p-4p, 22p-24p.*

INVISIBLES, THE (2nd Series)
V2#1, Feb, 1997 - Present ($2.50, mature)
DC Comics (Vertigo)

V2#1-Intro Jolly Roger; Grant Morrison scripts, Phil Jimenez-a, & Brian Bolland-c begins 1.20 3.00
2-11 2.50

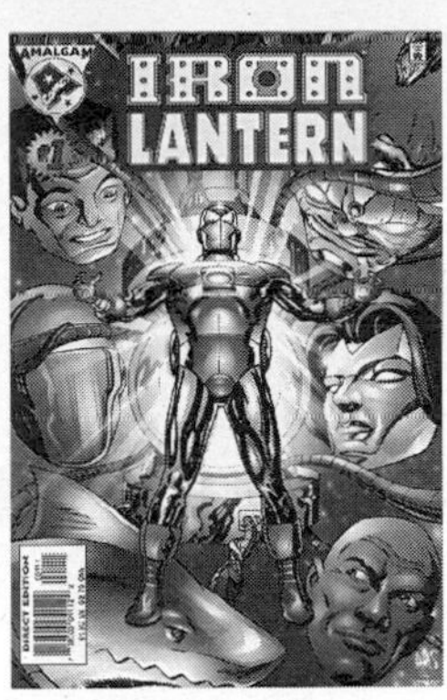

Iron Lantern #1 © MEG

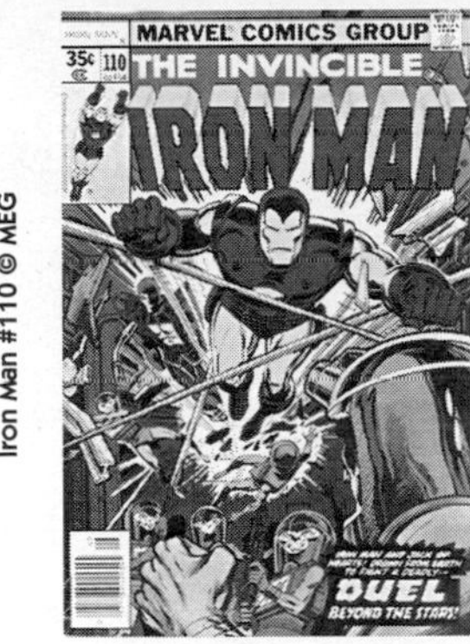

Iron Man #110 © MEG

Iron Man #261 © MEG

GD25 FN65 NM94

INVISIBLE SCARLET O'NEIL (Also see Famous Funnies #81 & Harvey Comics Hits #59)
Dec, 1950 - No. 3, Apr, 1951
Famous Funnies (Harvey)(2-3 pgs. of Powell-a in each issue.)

1- 10.50 32.00 85.00
2,3 8.75 26.25 65.00

IRON CORPORAL, THE (See Army War Heroes #22)
No. 23, Oct, 1985 - No. 25, Feb, 1986
Charlton Comics

23-25: Glanzman-a(r) 1.00

IRON FIST (See Deadly Hands of Kung Fu, Marvel Premiere & Power Man)
Nov, 1975 - No. 15, Sept, 1977
Marvel Comics

1-Iron Fist battles Iron Man (#1-6: 25¢) 2.80 8.40 28.00
2 2.25 6.75 18.00
3-10: 8-Origin retold 1.50 4.50 12.00
4,5-(Regular 25¢ edition)(4,6/76) 1.50 4.50 12.00
4,5-(30¢-c, limited distribution) 4.80 14.40 48.00
11-13: 12-Capt. America app. 1.00 3.00 8.00
14-1st app. Sabretooth (8/77)(see Power Man) 11.00 33.00 110.00
15-(Regular 30¢ ed.) X-Men app., Byrne-a 3.50 10.50 35.00
15-(35¢-c, limited distribution) 10.00 30.00 100.00

NOTE: ***Adkins*** *a-8p, 10i, 13i; c-8i.* ***Byrne*** *a-1-15p; c-8p, 15p.* ***G. Kane*** *c-4-6p.* ***McWilliams*** *a-1i.*

IRON FIST
Sept, 1996 - No. 2, Oct, 1996 ($1.50, limited series)
Marvel Comics

1,2 1.20 3.00

IRONHAND OF ALMURIC (Robert E. Howard's...)
Aug, 1991 - No. 4, 1991 ($2.00, B&W, mini-series)
Dark Horse Comics

1-4: 1-Conrad painted-c .80 2.00

IRON HORSE (TV)
March, 1967 - No. 2, June, 1967
Dell Publishing Co.

1,2-Dale Robertson photo covers 1.50 4.50 12.00

IRONJAW (Also see The Barbarians)
Jan, 1975 - No. 4, July, 1975
Atlas/Seaboard Publ.

1-1st app. Iron Jaw; Neal Adams-c; Sekowsky-a(p) 1.60 4.00
2-4: 2-Neal Adams-c. 4-Origin 1.20 3.00

IRON LANTERN
June, 1997 ($1.95, one-shot)
Marvel Comics (Amalgam)

1-Kurt Busiek-s/Paul Smith & Al Williamson-a 1.95

IRON MAN (Also see The Avengers #1, Giant-Size..., Marvel Collectors Item Classics, Marvel Double Feature, Marvel Fanfare & Tales of Suspense #39)
May, 1968 - No. 332, Sept, 1996
Marvel Comics

1-Origin; Colan-c/a(p); story continued from Iron Man & Sub-Mariner #1
30.00 90.00 300.00
2 9.00 27.00 90.00
3 6.00 18.00 60.00
4,5 5.00 15.00 50.00
6-10: 9-Iron Man battles green Hulk-like android 4.00 12.00 40.00
11-15: 15-Last 12¢ issue 2.50 7.50 24.00
16-20 2.25 6.75 18.00
21-24,26-42: 22-Death of Janice Cord. 27-Intro Fire Brand. 33-1st app. Spymaster. 35-Nick Fury & Daredevil x-over. 42-Last 15¢ issue
1.60 4.85 13.00

GD25 FN65 NM94

25-Iron Man battles Sub-Mariner 1.85 5.50 15.00
43-Intro The Guardsman; 25¢ giant 1.60 4.85 13.00
44-46,48-50: 43-Giant-Man back-up by Ayers. 44-Ant-Man by Tuska. 46-The Guardsman dies. 50-Princess Python app. 1.25 3.75 10.00
47-Origin retold; Barry Smith-a(p) 1.60 4.85 13.00
51-53: 53-Starlin part pencils 1.00 2.80 7.00
54-Iron Man battles Sub-Mariner; 1st app. Moondragon (1/73) as Madame MacEvil; Everett part-c 1.85 5.50 15.00
55-1st app. Thanos (cameo), Drax the Destroyer, Mentor, Starfox & Kronos (2/73); Starlin-c/a 7.50 22.50 75.00
56-Starlin-a 1.85 5.50 15.00
57-67,69,70: 59-Firebrand returns. 65-Origin Dr. Spectrum. 66-Iron Man vs. Thor. 67-Last 20¢ issue 2.40 6.00
68-Sunfire & Unicorn app.; origin retold; Starlin-c 1.00 2.80 7.00
71-99: 72-Cameo portraits of N. Adams. 73-Rename Stark Industries to Stark International; Brunner. 76-r/#9. 86-1st app. Blizzard. 87-Origin Blizzard. 88-Thanos app. 89-Daredevil app.; last 25¢ issue. 96-1st app. new Guardsman
1.60 4.00
100-(7/77)-Starlin-c 1.25 3.75 10.00
101-117: 101-Intro DreadKnight. 109-1st app. new Crimson Dynamo; 1st app. Vanguard. 110-Origin Jack of Hearts retold; death of Count Nefaria. 114-Avengers app. 1.60 4.00
118-Byrne-a(p); 1st app. Jim Rhodes 2.40 6.00
119,120,123-128-Tony Stark recovers from alcohol problem. 120,121-Sub-Mariner x-over. 125-Ant-Man app. 1.40 3.50
121,122,129-149: 122-Origin. 131,132-Hulk x-over 1.20 3.00
150-Double size 1.60 4.00
151-168: 152-New armor. 161-Moon Knight app. 167-Tony Stark alcohol problem starts again 1.00 2.50
169-New Iron Man (Jim Rhodes replaces Tony Stark) 1.80 4.50
170 1.20 3.00
171 1.00 2.50
172-199: 172-Captain America x-over. 186-Intro Vibro. 190-Scarlet Witch app. 191-198-Tony Stark returns as original Iron Man. 192-Both Iron Men battle
.80 2.00
200-(11/85, $1.25, 52 pgs.)-Tony Stark returns as new Iron Man (red & white armor) thru #230 1.20 3.00
201-224: 213-Intro new Dominic Fortune. 214-Spider-Woman apps. in new black costume (1/87) .80 2.00
225-Double size ($1.25) 1.20 3.00
226-243,245-249: 228-vs. Capt. America. 231-Intro new Iron Man. 233-Ant-Man app. 234-Spider-Man x-over. 243-Tony Stark looses use of legs. 247-Hulk x-over .80 2.00
244-($1.50, 52 pgs.)-New Armor makes him walk 1.20 3.00
250-($1.50, 52 pgs.)-Dr. Doom-c/story .80 2.00
251-274,276-281,283,285-287,289,291-299: 258-277-Byrne scripts. 271-Fin Fang Foom app. 276-Black Widow-c/story; last $1.00-c. 281-1st app. ;War Machine (cameo). 283-2nd full app. War Machine .80 2.00
275-($1.50, 52 pgs.) .80 2.00
282-1st full app. War Machine (7/92) 2.00 5.00
284-Death of Iron Man (Tony Stark) 1.20 3.00
288-($2.50, 52pg.)-Silver foil stamped-c; Iron Man's 350th app. in comics
1.00 2.50
290-($2.95, 52pg.)-Gold foil stamped-c; 30th ann. 1.20 3.00
300-($3.95, 68 pgs.)-Collector's Edition w/embossed foil-c; anniversary issue; War Machine-c/story 1.60 4.00
300-($2.50, 68 pgs.)-Newsstand Edition 1.00 2.50
301-303: 302-Venom-c/story (cameo #301) 1.50
304-316,318-324,326-332: 304-Begin $1.50-c; bound-in trading card sheet; Thunderstrike-c/story. 310-Orange logo. 312-w/bound-in Power Ranger Card. 319-Prologue to "The Crossing." 326-New Tony Stark; Pratt-c. 330-War Machine & Stockpile app; return of Morgan Stark. 332-Onsalught x-over 1.50
310 ($2.95)-Polybagged w/ 16 pg. Marvel Action Hour preview & acetate print;

Iron Man Annual #15 © MEG

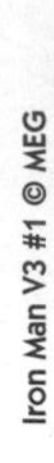
Iron Man V3 #1 © MEG

Isis #3 © DC

	GD25	FN65	NM94
white logo.		1.20	3.00
317 ($2.50)-Flip book		1.00	2.50
325-($2.95)-Wraparound-c		1.20	3.00
Special 1(8/70)-Sub-Mariner x-over; Everett-c	2.50	7.50	20.00
Special 2(11/71)-r/TOS #81,82,91 (all-r)	1.10	3.30	9.00
Annual 3(1976)-Man-Thing app.		1.60	4.00
King Size 4(8/77)-The Champions (w/Ghost Rider) app.; Newton-a(i)		1.20	3.00
Annual 5-9: 5(1982)-New-a. 6(1983)-New Iron Man (J. Rhodes) app. 7(1984). 8(1986)-X-Factor app. 9(1987)		.90	2.25
Annual 10(1989, $2.00, 68 pgs.)-Atlantis Attacks x-over; P. Smith-a; Layton/ Guice-a; Sub-Mariner app.		1.00	2.50
Annual 11,12 ($2.00, 68 pgs.): 11-(1990)-Origin of Mrs. Arbogast by Ditko (p&i). 12-(1991)-1 pg. origin recap; Ant-Man back-up story		.80	2.00
Annual 13 (1992, $2.25, 68 pgs.)-Darkhawk & Avengers West Coast app.; Colan/Williamson-a		.90	2.25
Annual 14 (1993, $2.95, 68 pgs.)-Bagged w/card		1.20	3.00
Annual 15 (1994, $2.95, 68 pgs.)		1.20	3.00
Manual 1 (1993, $1.75)-Operations handbook		.70	1.75
Graphic Novel: Crash (1988, $12.95, Adults, 72 pgs)-Computer generated art & color; violence & nudity	1.60	4.85	13.00
...Collector's Preview 1(11/94, $1.95)-wraparound-c; text & illos-no comics.		.80	2.00
...Vs. Dr. Doom (12/94, $12.95)-r/#149-150, 249,250. J-Bell-c	1.60	4.85	13.00

NOTE: ***Austin** c-105i, 109-111i, 151i. **Byrne** a-118p; c-109p, 197, 253. **Colan** a-1p, 253, Special 1p(3); c-1p. **Craig** a-1i, 2-4, 5-13i, 14, 15-19i, 24p, 25p, 26-28i; c-2-4. **Ditko** a-160p. **Everett** c-29. **Guice** a-233-241p. **G. Kane** c(p)-52-54, 63, 67, 72-75, 77-79, 88, 98. **Kirby** a-Special 1p; c-13, 80p, 90, 92-95. **Mooney** a-40i, 43i, 47i. **Perez** c-103p. **Simonson** c-Annual 8. **B. Smith** a-232p, 243i; c-232. **P. Smith** a-159p, 245p, Annual 10p; c-159. **Starlin** a-53p(part), 55p, 56p; c-55p, 160, 163. **Tuska** a-5-13p, 15-23p, 24i, 32p, 38-46p, 48-54p, 57-61p, 63-69p, 70-72p, 78p, 86-92p, 95-106p, Annual 4p. **Wood** a-Special 1i.*

IRON MAN (The Invincible...) (Volume Two)
Nov, 1996 - No. 13, Nov, 1997 ($2.95/$1.95/$1.99)(Produced by Wildstorm Productions)
Marvel Comics

	GD25	FN65	NM94
V2#1-Heroes Reborn begins; Scott Lobdell scripts & Whilce Portacio-c/a begin; new origin Iron Man & Hulk		1.20	3.00
1-Variant-c		1.60	4.00
2,3: 2-Hulk app. 3-Fantastic Four app.		1.20	3.00
4-10-($1.95): 4-Two covers. 6-Fantastic Four app.; Industrial Revolution; Hulk app. 7-Return of Rebel.		.80	2.00
11-($1.99) Dr. Doom-c/app.			1.99
12-($2.99) "Heroes Reunited"-pt. 3; Hulk-c/app.			2.99
13-($1.99) "World War 3"-pt. 3, x-over w/Image			1.99

IRON MAN (The Invincible...) (Volume Three)
Feb, 1998 - Present ($2.99/$1.99)
Marvel Comics

	GD25	FN65	NM94
V3#1-($2.99)-Follows Heroes Return; Busiek scripts & Chen-c/a begin; Deathsquad app.			2.99
2-4-($1.99)			1.99

IRON MAN & SUB-MARINER
Apr, 1968 (12¢, one-shot) (Pre-dates Iron Man #1 & Sub-Mariner #1)
Marvel Comics Group

	GD25	FN65	NM94
1-Iron Man story by Colan/Craig continued from Tales of Suspense #99 & continued in Iron Man #1; Sub-Mariner story by Colan continued from Tales to Astonish #101 & continued in Sub-Mariner #1; Colan/Everett-c	12.00	36.00	120.00

IRON MAN: THE LEGEND
Sept, 1996 ($3.95, one-shot)
Marvel Comics

	GD25	FN65	NM94
1-Tribute issue		1.60	4.00

IRON MAN 2020 (Also see Machine Man limited series)
June, 1994 ($5.95, one-shot)
Marvel Comics

	GD25	FN65	NM94
nn		2.40	6.00

IRON MAN/X-O MANOWAR: HEAVY METAL (See X-O Manowar/Iron Man: In Heavy Metal)
Sept, 1996 ($2.50, one-shot) (1st Marvel/Valiant x-over)
Marvel Comics

	GD25	FN65	NM94
1-Pt. II of Iron Man/X-O Manowar x-over; Fabian Nicieza scripts; 1st app. Rand Banion		1.00	2.50

IRON MARSHALL
July, 1990 - No. 22, 1992 ($1.75, plastic coated-c)
Jademan Comics

	GD25	FN65	NM94
1-22: Kung Fu stories. 1-Poster centerfold		.75	1.80

IRON VIC (See Comics Revue No. 3 & Giant Comics Editions)
1940; Aug, 1947 - No. 3, 1947
United Features Syndicate/St. John Publ. Co.

	GD25	FN65	NM94
Single Series 22	27.00	81.00	215.00
2,3(St. John)	6.50	19.50	45.00

IRONWOLF
1986 ($2.00, one shot)
DC Comics

	GD25	FN65	NM94
1-r/Weird Worlds 8-10; Chaykin story & art		.80	2.00

IRONWOLF: FIRES OF THE REVOLUTION (See Weird Worlds #8-10)
1992 ($29.95, hardcover)
DC Comics

	GD25	FN65	NM94
nn-Chaykin/Moore story, Mignola-a w/Russell inks.	3.00	9.00	30.00

ISAAC ASIMOV'S I-BOTS
Dec, 1995 - No. 7, May, 1996 ($1.95)
Tekno Comix

	GD25	FN65	NM94
1-7: 1-6-Perez-c/a. 2-Chaykin variant-c exists. 3-Polybagged. 7-Lady Justice-c/app.		.80	2.00

ISAAC ASIMOV'S I-BOTS
V2#1, June, 1996 - Present ($2.25)
BIG Entertainment

	GD25	FN65	NM94
V2#1-9: 1-Lady Justice-c/app. 6-Gil Kane-c		.90	2.25

ISIS (TV) (Also see Shazam)
Oct-Nov, 1976 - No. 8, Dec-Jan, 1977-78
National Periodical Publications/DC Comics

	GD25	FN65	NM94
1-Wood inks	1.00	3.00	8.00
2-8: 5-Isis new look. 7-Origin		1.60	4.00

ISLAND AT THE TOP OF THE WORLD (See Walt Disney Showcase #27)

ISLAND OF DR. MOREAU, THE (Movie)
Oct, 1977 (52 pgs.)
Marvel Comics Group

	GD25	FN65	NM94
1-Gil Kane-c		1.20	3.00

I SPY (TV)
Aug, 1966 - No. 6, Sept, 1968 (All have photo-c)
Gold Key

	GD25	FN65	NM94
1-Bill Cosby, Robert Culp photo covers	22.00	66.00	240.00
2-6: 3,4-McWilliams-a	13.00	39.00	140.00

IS THIS TOMORROW?
1947 (One Shot) (3 editions) (52 pgs.)
Catechetical Guild

	GD25	FN65	NM94
1-Theme of communists taking over the USA; (no price on cover) Used in **POP**, pg. 102	12.00	36.00	95.00
1-(10¢ on cover)	16.00	49.00	130.00

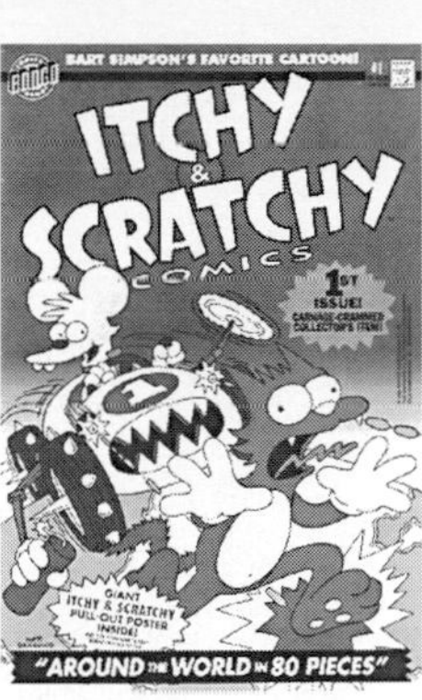

Itchy & Scratchy Comics #1 © Matt Groening

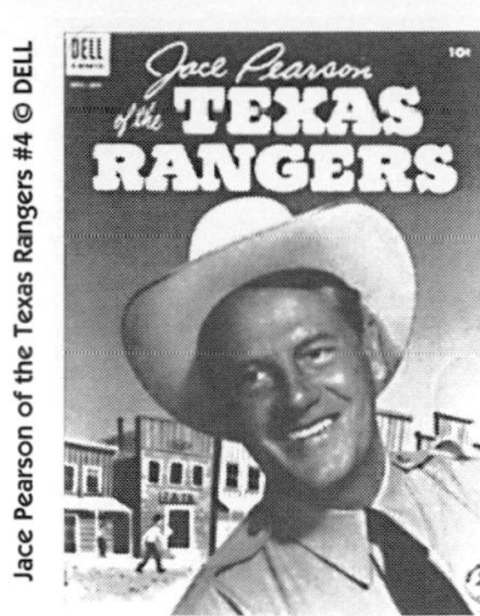

Jace Pearson of the Texas Rangers #4 © DELL

Jackie Chan's Spartan X #1 © Jackie & Willie Productions, Ltd.

GD25 FN65 NM94

1-Has blank circle with no price on cover 16.00 49.00 130.00
Black & White advance copy titled "Confidential" (52 pgs.)-Contains script and art edited out of the color edition, including one page of extreme violence showing mob nailing a Cardinal to a door; (only two known copies) 36.00 108.00 300.00
NOTE: *The original color version first sold for 10 cents. Since sales were good, it was later printed as a giveaway. Approximately four million in total were printed. The two black and white copies listed plus two other versions as well as a full color untrimmed version surfaced in 1979 from the Guild's old files in St. Paul, Minnesota.*

IT! (See Astonishing Tales No. 21-24 & Supernatural Thrillers No. 1)

ITCHY & SCRATCHY COMICS (Simpson's TV show)
1993 - No. 3, 1993 ($1.95)
Bongo Comics
1-($2.25)-Bound-in jumbo poster 1.00 2.50
2 .80 2.00
3-($2.25)-w/decoder screen trading card .90 2.25
Holiday Special ('94, $1.95) .80 2.00

IT REALLY HAPPENED
1944 - No. 11, Oct, 1947
William H. Wise No. 1,2/Standard (Visual Editions)
1-Kit Carson & Ben Franklin stories 14.00 41.00 110.00
2 8.50 26.00 60.00
3,4,6,9,11: 6-Joan of Arc story. 9-Captain Kidd & Frank Buck stories 6.50 19.50 45.00
5-Lou Gehrig & Lewis Carroll stories 10.50 32.00 85.00
7-Teddy Roosevelt story 6.50 19.50 45.00
8-Story of Roy Rogers 12.00 38.00 100.00
10-Honus Wagner & Mark Twain stories 8.75 26.25 70.00
NOTE: ***Guardineer** a-7(2), 8(2), 11. **Schomburg** c-1-7, 9-11.*

IT RHYMES WITH LUST (Also see Bold Stories & Candid Tales)
1950 (Digest size, 128 pgs.)
St. John Publishing Co.
nn (Rare)-Matt Baker & Ray Osrin-a 44.00 132.00 375.00

IT'S ABOUT TIME (TV)
Jan, 1967
Gold Key
1 (10195-701)-Photo-c 3.00 9.00 35.00

IT'S A DUCK'S LIFE
Feb, 1950 - No. 11, Feb, 1952
Marvel Comics/Atlas(MMC)
1-Buck Duck, Super Rabbit begin 10.50 32.00 85.00
2 5.70 17.00 40.00
3-11 5.00 15.00 30.00

IT'S FUN TO STAY ALIVE
1948 (Giveaway, 16 pgs., heavy stock paper)
National Automobile Dealers Association
Featuring: Bugs Bunny, The Berrys, Dixie Dugan, Elmer, Henry, Tim Tyler, Bruce Gentry, Abbie & Slats, Joe Jinks, The Toodles, & Cokey; all art copyright 1946-48 drawn especially for this book. 15.00 45.00 120.00

IT'S GAMETIME
Sept-Oct, 1955 - No. 4, Mar-Apr, 1956
National Periodical Publications
1-(Scarce)-Infinity-c; Davy Crockett app. in puzzle 58.00 174.00 525.00
2-4(Scarce): 2-Dodo & The Frog 47.00 141.00 425.00

IT'S LOVE, LOVE, LOVE
Nov, 1957 - No. 2, Jan, 1958 (10¢)
St. John Publishing Co.
1,2 4.00 12.00 24.00

IVANHOE (See Fawcett Movie Comics No. 20)

GD25 FN65 NM94

IVANHOE
July-Sept, 1963
Dell Publishing Co.
1 (12-373-309) 2.25 6.75 25.00

IWO JIMA (See Spectacular Features Magazine)

JACE PEARSON OF THE TEXAS RANGERS (Radio/TV)(4-Color #396 is titled Tales of the Texas Rangers; ...'s Tales of ... #11-on)(See Western Roundup under Dell Giants)
No. 396, 5/52 - No. 1021, 8-10/59 (No #10) (All-Photo-c)
Dell Publishing Co.
Four Color 396 (#1) 10.00 30.00 110.00
2(5-7/53) - 9(2-4/55) 5.50 16.50 60.00
Four Color 648(#10, 9/55) 4.50 13.50 50.00
11(11-2/55-56) - 14,17-20(6-8/58) 4.00 12.00 45.00
15,16-Toth-a 4.50 13.50 50.00
Four Color 961, 1021: 961--Spiegle-a 4.00 12.00 45.00
NOTE: *Joel McCrea photo c-1-9, F.C. 648 (starred on radio show only); Willard Parker photo c-11-on (starred on TV series).*

JACK & JILL VISIT TOYTOWN WITH ELMER THE ELF
1949 (Giveaway, 16 pgs., paper cover)
Butler Brothers (Toytown Stores)
nn 3.20 8.00 16.00

JACK ARMSTRONG (Radio)(See True Comics)
Nov, 1947 - No. 9, Sept, 1948; No. 10, Mar, 1949 - No. 13, Sept, 1949
Parents' Institute
1-(Scarce) (odd size) 36.00 108.00 300.00
2 15.00 45.00 120.00
3-5 11.30 34.00 90.00
6-13: 7-Vic Hardy's Crime Lab begins? 8.75 26.25 70.00
12-Premium version(distr. in Chicago only); Free printed on upper right-c; no price (Rare) 15.00 45.00 120.00

JACK HUNTER
July, 1987 - No. 4? ($1.25)
Blackthorne Publishing
1-4 1.25

JACKIE CHAN'S SPARTAN X
May, 1997 - No. 6 ($2.95, limited series)
Topps Comics
1-3-Michael Golden-s/a; variant photo-c 2.95

JACKIE GLEASON (TV) (Also see The Honeymooners)
1948 - No. 2, 1948; Sept, 1955 - No. 4, Dec, 1955?
St. John Publishing Co.
1(1948) 61.00 183.00 550.00
2(1948) 47.00 141.00 420.00
1(1955)(TV)-Photo-c 50.00 150.00 450.00
2-4 36.00 108.00 300.00

JACKIE GLEASON AND THE HONEYMOONERS (TV)
June-July, 1956 - No. 12, Apr-May, 1958
National Periodical Publications
1-1st app. Ralph Kramden 72.00 216.00 650.00
2 47.00 141.00 420.00
3-11 35.00 105.00 315.00
12 (Scarce) 52.00 156.00 460.00

JACKIE JOKERS (Became Richie Rich &...)
March, 1973 - No. 4, Sept, 1973 (#5 was advertised, but not published)
Harvey Publications
1-1st app. 1.85 5.50 15.00
2-4: 2-President Nixon app. 1.00 2.80 7.00

Jack Kirby's Fourth World #10 © DC

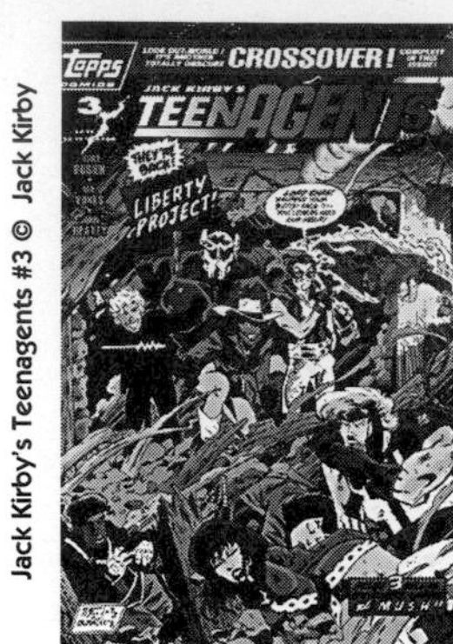

Jack Kirby's Teenagents #3 © Jack Kirby

Jaguar God #0 © Verotik

GD25 FN65 NM94

JACKIE ROBINSON (Famous Plays of...) (Also see Negro Heroes #2 & Picture News #4)
May, 1950 - No. 6, 1952 (Baseball hero) (All photo-c)
Fawcett Publications

nn 71.00 213.00 640.00
2 44.00 132.00 400.00
3-6 36.00 108.00 325.00

JACK IN THE BOX (Formerly Yellowjacket Comics #1-10; becomes Cowboy Western Comics #17 on)
Feb, 1946; No. 11, Oct, 1946 - No. 16, Nov-Dec, 1947
Frank Comunale/Charlton Comics No. 11 on

1-Stitches, Marty Mouse & Nutsy McKrow 10.00 30.00 80.00
11-Yellowjacket (early Charlton comic) 12.00 38.00 100.00
12,14,15 5.70 17.00 35.00
13-Wolverton-a 16.00 49.00 130.00
16-12 pg. adapt. of Silas Marner; Kiefer-a 8.50 26.00 60.00

JACK KIRBY'S FOURTH WORLD (See New Gods, 3rd Series)
Mar, 1997 - Present ($1.95)
DC Comics

1-12: 1-Byrne-a/scripts & Simonson-c begin; story cont'd from New Gods, 3rd Series #15; retells "The Pact" (New Gods, 1st Series #7); 1st DC app. Thor (cameo). 2-Thor vs. Big Barda; "Apokolips Then" back-up begins; Kirby-c/swipe (Thor #126) 8-Genesis x-over. 10-Simonson-s/a .80 2.00

JACK KIRBY'S SECRET CITY SAGA
No. 0, Apr, 1993; No. 1, May, 1993 - No. 4, Aug, 1993 ($2.95, limited series)
Topps Comics (Kirbyverse)

0-(No cover price, 20 pgs.)-Simonson-c/a .80 2.00
1-4-Bagged w/3 trading cards; Ditko-c/a: 1-Ditko/Art Adams-c. 2-Ditko/Byrne-c; has coupon for Pres. Clinton holo-foil trading card. 3-Dorman poster; has coupon for Gore holo-foil trading card. 4-Ditko/Perez-c 1.20 3.00
NOTE: *Issues #1-4 contain coupons redeemable for Kirbychrome version of #1*

JACK KIRBY'S SILVER STAR (Also see Silver Star)
Oct, 1993 ($2.95)(Intended as a 4-issue limited series)
Topps Comics (Kirbyverse)

1-Silver ink-c; Austin-c/a(i); polybagged w/3 cards 1.20 3.00

JACK KIRBY'S TEENAGENTS (See Satan's Six)
Aug, 1993 - No. 3, Oct, 1993 ($2.95)(Intended as a 4-issue limited series)
Topps Comics (Kirbyverse)

1-3: Polybagged with/3 trading cards; 1-3-Austin-c(i): 3-Liberty Project app. 1.20 3.00

JACK OF HEARTS (Also see The Deadly Hands of Kung Fu #22 & Marvel Premiere #44)
Jan, 1984 - No. 4, Apr, 1984 (60¢, limited series)
Marvel Comics Group

1-4 1.00

JACKPOT COMICS (Jolly Jingles #10 on)
Spring, 1941 - No. 9, Spring, 1943
MLJ Magazines

1-The Black Hood, Mr. Justice, Steel Sterling & Sgt. Boyle begin; Biro-c 233.00 700.00 2100.00
2-S. Cooper-c 106.00 318.00 950.00
3-Hubbell-c 78.00 234.00 700.00
4-Archie begins (Win/41; on sale 12/41)-(also see Pep Comics #22); 1st app. Mrs. Grundy, the principal; Novick-c 211.00 633.00 1900.00
5-Hitler-c by Montana; 1st definitive Mr. Weatherbee; 1st app. Reggie in 1 panel cameo 106.00 318.00 950.00
6-9: 6,7-Bondage-c by Novick. 8,9-Sahle-c 83.00 250.00 750.00

JACK Q FROST (See Unearthly Spectaculars)

GD25 FN65 NM94

JACK THE GIANT KILLER (See Movie Classics)

JACK THE GIANT KILLER (New Adventures of...)
Aug-Sept, 1953
Bimfort & Co.

V1#1-H. C. Kiefer-c/a 16.00 49.00 130.00

JACKY'S DIARY
No. 1091, Apr-June, 1960 (one-shot)
Dell Publishing Co.

Four Color 1091 3.60 11.00 40.00

JADEMAN COLLECTION
Dec, 1989 - No. 5?, 1990 ($2.50, plastic coated-c, 68 pgs.)
Jademan Comics

1-5: 1-Wraparound-c w/fold-out poster 1.00 2.50

JADEMAN KUNG FU SPECIAL
1988 ($1.50, 64 pgs.)
Jademan Comics

1 1.50

JAGUAR, THE (Also see The Adventures of...)
Aug, 1991 - No. 14, Oct, 1992 ($1.00)
Impact Comics (DC)

1-14: 4-The Black Hood x-over. 7-Sienkiewicz-c. 9-Contains Crusaders trading card 1.00
Annual 1 (1992, $2.50, 68 pgs.)-With trading card 1.00 2.50

JAGUAR GOD
Mar, 1995 - Present ($2.95, mature)
Verotik

0 (2/96, $3.50)-Embossed Frazetta-c; Bisley-a; w/pin-ups. 1.40 3.50
1-Frazetta-c. 2.40 6.00
2-Frazetta-c 2.00 5.00
3-6: 3-Bisley-c. 4-Emond-c 1.60 4.00
7-($2.95)-Frazetta-c 2.95

JAKE THRASH
1988 - No. 3, 1988 ($2.00)
Aircel Publishing

1-3 .80 2.00

JAM, THE (...Urban Adventure)
Nov, 1989 - Present ($1.95/$2.50/$2.95, B&W)
Slave Labor Nos. 1-5/Dark Horse Comics Nos. 6-8/Caliber Comics No. 9 on

1-5-Bernie Mireault-c/a/scripts .80 2.00
6-7: 6-1st Dark Horse issue; begin $2.50-c. 1.00 2.50
8-13: 8-Begin $2.95-c. 9-1st Caliber issue 1.20 3.00

JAMBOREE
Feb, 1946(no mo. given) - No. 3, Apr, 1946
Round Publishing Co.

1-Funny animal 17.00 51.00 135.00
2,3 10.00 30.00 80.00

JAMES BOND 007: A SILENT ARMAGEDDON
Mar, 1993 - Apr 1993 (limited series)
Dark Horse Comics/Acme Press

1,2 1.40 3.50

JAMES BOND 007: GOLDENEYE (Movie)
Jan, 1996 ($2.95, unfinished limited series of 3)
Topps Comics

1-Movie adaptation; Stelfreeze-c 1.20 3.00

JAMES BOND 007: SERPENT'S TOOTH
July 1992 - Aug 1992 ($4.95, limited series)
Dark Horse Comics/Acme Press

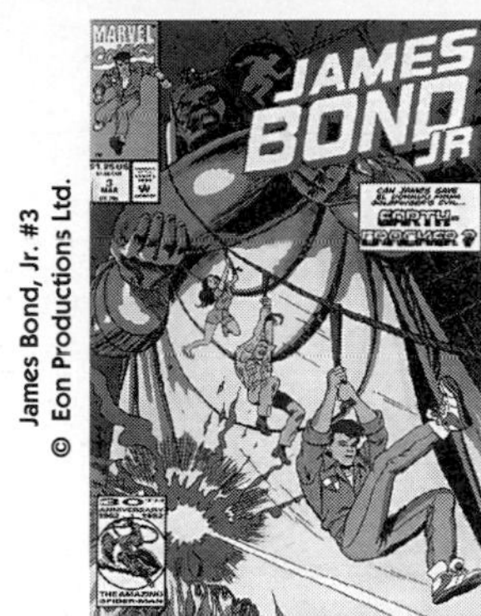

James Bond, Jr. #3 © Eon Productions Ltd.

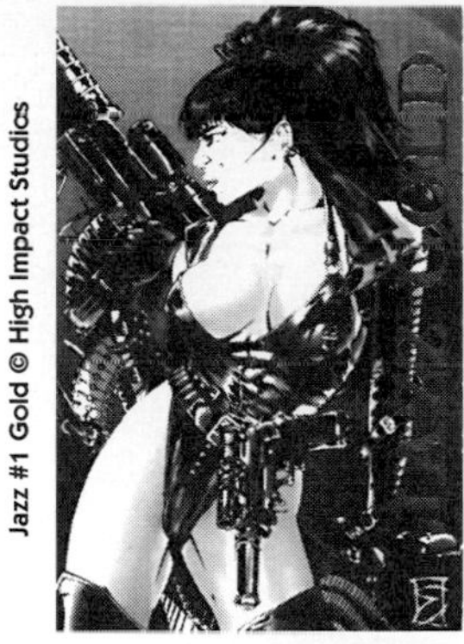
Jazz #1 Gold © High Impact Studios

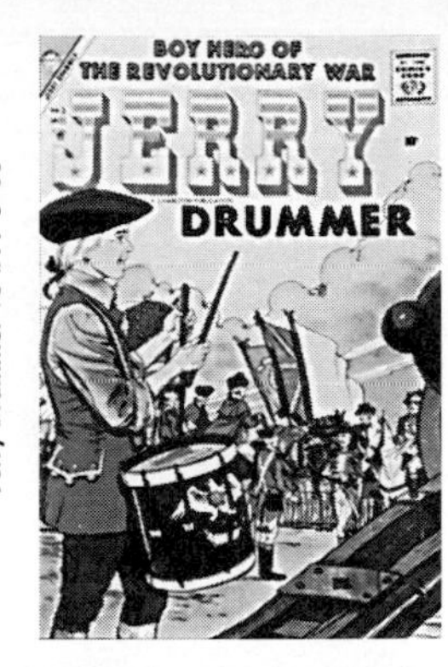

Jerry Drummer V3 #11 © CC

GD25 FN65 NM94

1-3-Paul Gulacy-c/a 2.00 5.00

JAMES BOND 007: SHATTERED HELIX
Jun 1994 - July 1994 ($2.50, limited series)
Dark Horse Comics

1,2 1.20 3.00

JAMES BOND 007: THE QUASIMODO GAMBIT
Jan 1995 - May 1995 ($3.95, limited series)
Dark Horse Comics

1-3 1.80 4.50

JAMES BOND FOR YOUR EYES ONLY
Oct, 1981 - No. 2, Nov, 1981
Marvel Comics Group

1,2-Movie adapt.; r/Marvel Super Special #19 1.50

JAMES BOND JR. (TV)
Jan, 1992 - No. 12, Dec, 1992 (#1: $1.00, #2-on: $1.25)
Marvel Comics

1-12: Based on animated TV show 1.25

JAMES BOND: LICENCE TO KILL (See Licence To Kill)

JAMES BOND: PERMISSION TO DIE
1989 - No. 3, 1991 ($3.95, limited series, squarebound, 52 pgs.)
Eclipse Comics/ACME Press

1-3: Mike Grell-c/a/scripts in all. 3-($4.95) 2.00 5.00

JAM, THE: SUPER COOL COLOR INJECTED TURBO ADVENTURE #1 FROM HELL!
May, 1988 ($2.50, 44 pgs., one-shot)
Comico

1 1.00 2.50

JANE ARDEN (See Feature Funnies & Pageant of Comics)
Mar, 1948 - No. 2, June, 1948
St. John (United Features Syndicate)

1-Newspaper reprints 15.00 45.00 105.00
2 11.00 33.00 75.00

JANN OF THE JUNGLE (Jungle Tales No. 1-7)
No. 8, Nov, 1955 - No. 17, June, 1957
Atlas Comics (CSI)

8(#1) 25.00 75.00 185.00
9,11-15 13.00 39.00 95.00
10-Williamson/Colletta-c 13.50 41.00 100.00
16,17-Williamson/Mayo-a(3), 5 pgs. each 16.00 47.00 110.00
NOTE: ***Everett** c-15-17. **Heck** a-8, 15, 17. **Maneely** c-11. **Shores** a-8.*

JAR OF FOOLS
1994 ($5.95, B&W)
Penny Dreadful Press

1-Jason Lutes-c/a/scripts 2.40 6.00

JAR OF FOOLS
1994 - No. 2, 1994 ($6.95, B&W)
Black Eye Productions

1,2: 1-Reprints of earlier ed. Jason Lutesc/a/scripts 1.00 2.80 7.00

JASON & THE ARGONAUTS (See Movie Classics)

JASON GOES TO HELL: THE FINAL FRIDAY (Movie)
July, 1993 - No. 3, Sept, 1993 ($2.95, limited series)
Topps Comics

1-3: Adaptation of film. 1-Glow-in-the-dark-c 1.20 3.00

JASON'S QUEST (See Showcase #88-90)

JASON VS. LEATHERFACE
Oct, 1995 - No. 3, Jan, 1996 ($2.95, limited series)
Topps Comics

1-3: Collins scripts; Bisley-c 1.20 3.00

JAWS 2 (See Marvel Comics Super Special, A)

JAZZ (Also see Double Impact)
Mar, 1996 - No. 3, June, 1996 ($3.00, B&W, bi-monthly, limited series)
High Impact Studios

1-3 1.20 3.00
1-Gold foil logo (1000 print run) 2.50 7.50 20.00
2-($9.95)-Deluxe Edition; photo-c 1.25 3.75 10.00
3-Variant-c (1000 print run) 1.25 3.75 10.00

JCP FEATURES
Feb, 1982-c; Dec, 1981-indicia ($2.00, one-shot, B&W)
J.C. Productions (Archie)

1-T.H.U.N.D.E.R. Agents; Black Hood by Morrow & Neal Adams .80 2.00

JEANIE COMICS (Formerly All Surprise; Cowgirl Romances #28)
No. 13, April, 1947 - No. 27, Oct, 1949
Marvel Comics/Atlas(CPC)

13-Mitzi, Willie begin 13.00 39.00 95.00
14,15 10.00 30.00 70.00
16-Used in Love and Death by Legman; Kurtzman's "Hey Look" 13.00 39.00 95.00
17-19,22-Kurtzman's "Hey Look", (1-3 pgs. each) 10.00 30.00 60.00
20,21,23-27 7.00 21.00 45.00

JEEP COMICS (Also see G.I. Comics and Overseas Comics)
Winter, 1944 - No. 3, Mar-Apr, 1948
R. B. Leffingwell & Co.

1-Capt. Power, Criss Cross & Jeep & Peep (costumed) begin 34.00 103.00 275.00
2 22.00 66.00 175.00
3-L. B. Cole dinosaur-c 33.00 98.00 260.00
1-46(Giveaways)-Strip reprints in all; Tarzan, Flash Gordon, Blondie, The Nebbs, Little Iodine, Red Ryder, Don Winslow, The Phantom, Johnny Hazard, Katzenjammer Kids; distr. to U.S. Armed Forces from 1945-1946 4.00 10.00 20.00

JEFF JORDAN, U.S. AGENT
Dec, 1947 - Jan, 1948
D. S. Publishing Co.

1 10.00 30.00 75.00

JEMM, SON OF SATURN
Sept, 1984 - No. 12, Aug, 1985 (Maxi-series, mando paper)
DC Comics

1-12: 3-Origin 1.00
NOTE: ***Colan** a-1-12p; c-1-5, 7-12p.*

JERRY DRUMMER (Formerly Soldier & Marine V2#9)
V2#10, Apr, 1957 - V3#12, Oct, 1957
Charlton Comics

V2#10, V3#11,12: 11-Whitman-c/a 2.60 7.80 26.00

JERRY IGER'S... (All titles, Blackthorne/First)(Value: cover or less)

JERRY LEWIS (See The Adventures of...)

JESSE JAMES (The True Story Of..., also seeThe Legend of...)
No. 757, Dec, 1956 (one shot)
Dell Publishing Co.

Four Color 757-Movie, photo-c 9.00 27.00 100.00

JESSE JAMES (See Badmen of the West & Blazing Sixguns)
8/50 - No. 9, 11/52; No. 15, 10/53 - No. 29, 8-9/56
Avon Periodicals

Jesse James #1 © AVON

Jet Aces #4 © FH

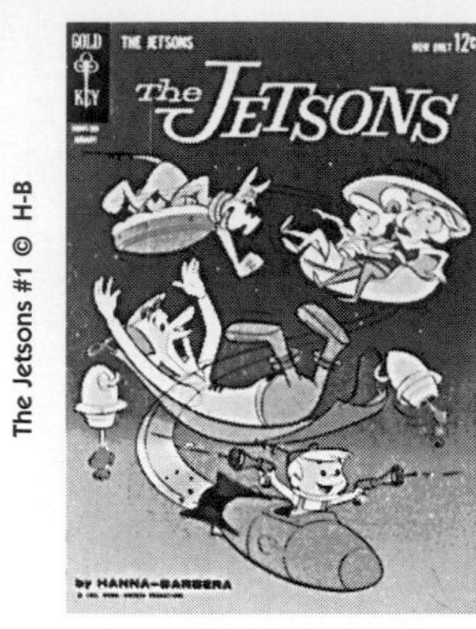

The Jetsons #1 © H-B

	GD25	FN65	NM94
1-Kubert Alabam-r/Cowpuncher #1	14.00	41.00	110.00
2-Kubert-a(3)	11.30	34.00	90.00
3-Kubert Alabam-r/Cowpuncher #2	10.00	30.00	80.00
4,9-No Kubert	5.35	16.00	32.00
5,6-Kubert Jesse James-a(3); 5-Wood-a(1pg.)	10.00	30.00	80.00
7-Kubert Jesse James-a(2)	8.75	26.25	65.00
8-Kinstler-a(3)	6.00	18.00	42.00
15-Kinstler-r/#3	4.25	13.00	28.00
16-Kinstler-r/#3 & story-r/Butch Cassidy #1	5.00	15.00	30.00
17-19,21: 17-Jesse James-r/#4; Kinstler-c idea from Kubert splash in #6. 18-Kubert Jesse James-r/#5. 19-Kubert Jesse James-r/#6. 21-Two Jesse James-r/#4, Kinstler-r/#4	4.00	12.00	24.00
20-Williamson/Frazetta-a; r/Chief Vic. Apache Massacre; Kubert Jesse James-r/#6; Kit West story by Larsen	10.50	32.00	85.00
22,23-No Kubert	4.00	12.00	24.00
24-New McCarty strip by Kinstler; Kinstler-r	4.00	11.00	22.00
25-New McCarty Jesse James strip by Kinstler; Jesse James-r/#7,9	4.00	11.00	22.00
26,27-New McCarty Jesse James strip plus a Kinstler/McCann Jesse James-r	4.00	11.00	22.00
28,29: 28-Reprints most of Red Mountain, Featuring Quantrells Raiders	4.00	11.00	22.00
Annual nn (1952; 25¢, 100 pgs.)- "...Brings Six-Gun Justice to the West"- 3 earlier issues rebound; Kubert, Kinstler-a(3)	23.00	69.00	185.00

NOTE: *Mostly reprints #10 on.* ***Fawcette*** *c-1, 2.* ***Kida*** *a-5.* ***Kinstler*** *a-3, 4, 7-9, 15r, 16r(2), 21-27; c-3, 4, 9, 17-27. Painted c-5-8. 22 has 2 stories r/Sheriff Bob Dixon's Chuck Wagon #1 with name changed to Sheriff Bob Trent.*

JESSE JAMES
July, 1953
Realistic Publications

	GD25	FN65	NM94
nn-Reprints Avon's #1; same-c, colors different	8.50	26.00	60.00

JEST (Formerly Snap; becomes Kayo #12)
No. 10, 1944; No. 11, 1944
Harry 'A' Chesler

	GD25	FN65	NM94
10-Johnny Rebel & Yankee Boy app. in text	11.30	34.00	90.00
11-Little Nemo in Adventure Land	11.30	34.00	90.00

JESTER
No. 10, 1945
Harry 'A' Chesler

	GD25	FN65	NM94
10	9.50	28.00	75.00

JESUS
1979 (49¢)
Spire Christian Comics (Fleming H. Revell Co.)

	GD25	FN65	NM94
nn		1.60	4.00

JET (See Jet Powers)

JET ACES
1952 - No. 4, 1953
Fiction House Magazines

	GD25	FN65	NM94
1	10.00	30.00	80.00
2-4	7.15	21.50	50.00

JET DREAM (...and Her Stunt-Girl Counterspies)(See The Man from Uncle #7)
June, 1968 (12¢)
Gold Key

	GD25	FN65	NM94
1-Painted-c	2.50	7.50	28.00

JET FIGHTERS (Korean War)
No. 5, Nov, 1952 - No. 7, Mar, 1953
Standard Magazines

	GD25	FN65	NM94
5,7-Toth-a. 5-Toth-c	9.50	28.00	75.00
6-Celardo-a	5.00	15.00	30.00

JET POWER
1963
I.W. Enterprises

	GD25	FN65	NM94
I.W. Reprint 1,2-r/Jet Powers #1,2	2.50	7.50	24.00

JET POWERS (American Air Forces No. 5 on)
1950 - No. 4, 1951
Magazine Enterprises

	GD25	FN65	NM94
1(A-1 #30)-Powell-c/a begins	26.00	80.00	210.00
2(A-1 #32)	19.00	56.00	150.00
3(A-1 #35)-Williamson/Evans-a	31.00	94.00	250.00
4(A-1 #38)-Williamson/Wood-a; "The Rain of Sleep" drug story	31.00	94.00	250.00

JET PUP (See 3-D Features)

JETSONS, THE (TV) (See March of Comics #276, 330, 348 & Spotlight #3)
Jan, 1963 - No. 36, Oct, 1970 (Hanna-Barbera)
Gold Key

	GD25	FN65	NM94
1	20.00	60.00	220.00
2	10.50	31.50	115.00
3-10	8.20	24.60	90.00
11-20	5.40	16.20	60.00
21-36	4.50	13.50	50.00

JETSONS, THE (TV) (Also see Golden Comics Digest)
Nov, 1970 - No. 20, Dec, 1973 (Hanna-Barbera)
Charlton Comics

	GD25	FN65	NM94
1	6.00	18.00	60.00
2	3.00	9.00	30.00
3-10	2.50	7.50	24.00
11-20	1.85	5.50	15.00

JETSONS, THE (TV)
V2#1, Sept, 1992 - No. 5, Nov, 1993 ($1.25/$1.50) (Hanna-Barbera)
Harvey Comics

	GD25	FN65	NM94
V2#1-5		.80	2.00
...Big Book V2#1,2,3 ($1.95, 52 pgs.): 1-(11/92). 2-(4/93). 3-(7/93)		1.20	3.00
...Giant Size 1,2,3 ($2.25, 68 pgs): 1-(10/92). 2-(4/93). 3-(10/93)		1.20	3.00

JETSONS, THE (TV)
Sept, 1995 - No. 17, Aug, 1996 ($1.50)
Archie Comics

	GD25	FN65	NM94
1-12			1.50

JETTA OF THE 21ST CENTURY
No. 5, Dec, 1952 - No. 7, Apr, 1953 (Teen-age Archie type)
Standard Comics

	GD25	FN65	NM94
5	17.50	53.00	140.00
6,7	10.00	30.00	80.00

JEZEBEL JADE (Hanna-Barbara)
Oct, 1988 - No. 3, Dec, 1988 ($2.00, mini-series)
Comico

	GD25	FN65	NM94
1-3: Johnny Quest spin-off		.80	2.00

JIGGS & MAGGIE
No. 18, 1941 (one shot)
Dell Publishing Co.

	GD25	FN65	NM94
Four Color 18 (#1)-(1936-38-r)	36.00	109.00	400.00

JIGGS & MAGGIE
No. 11, 1949(June) - No. 21, 2/53; No. 22, 4/53 - No. 27, 2-3/54
Standard Comics/Harvey Publications No. 22 on

	GD25	FN65	NM94
11	8.75	26.25	65.00
12-15,17-21	5.35	16.00	32.00
16-Wood text illos.	6.00	18.00	42.00

Jimmy Wakely #3 © DC

Jingle Jangle Comics #8 © EAS

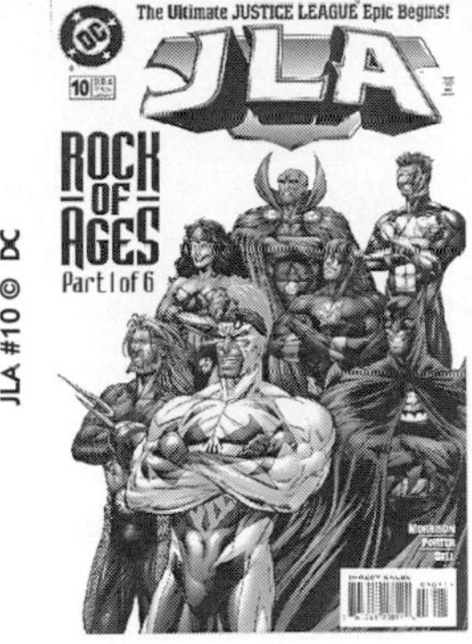

JLA #10 © DC

GD25 FN65 NM94

22-25,27: 22-24-Little Dot app. 4.25 13.00 26.00
26-Four pgs. partially in 3-D 10.50 32.00 85.00
NOTE: *Sunday page reprints by McManus loosely blended into story continuity. Based on Bringing Up Father strip. Advertised on covers as "All New."*

JIGSAW (Big Hero Adventures)
Sept, 1966 - No. 2, Dec, 1966 (36 pgs.)
Harvey Publications (Funday Funnies)
1-Origin & 1st app.; Crandall-a (5 pgs.) 1.25 3.75 10.00
2-Man From S.R.A.M. 1.00 3.00 8.00

JIGSAW OF DOOM (See Complete Mystery No. 2)

JIM BOWIE (Formerly Danger; Black Jack No. 20 on)
No. 15, 1955? - No. 19, Apr, 1957
Charlton Comics
15 5.70 17.00 40.00
16-19 4.25 13.00 26.00

JIM BOWIE (TV, see Western Tales)
No. 893, Mar, 1958 - No. 993, May-July, 1959
Dell Publishing Co.
Four Color 893 (#1), 993-Photo-c 4.50 13.50 50.00

JIM DANDY
May, 1956 - No. 3, Sept, 1956 (Charles Biro)
Dandy Magazine (Lev Gleason)
1-Biro-c 5.70 17.00 40.00
2,3 4.15 12.50 25.00

JIM HARDY (See Giant Comics Eds., Sparkler & Treasury of Comics #2 & 5)
1939; 1942; 1947 - No. 2, 1947
United Features Syndicate/Spotlight Publ.
Single Series 6 ('39) 36.00 108.00 285.00
Single Series 27('42) 28.00 84.00 225.00
1('47)-Spotlight Publ. 10.00 30.00 80.00
2 6.50 19.50 45.00

JIM HARDY
1944 (25¢, 132 pgs.) (Tip Top, Sparkler-r)
Spotlight/United Features Syndicate
nn-Origin Mirror Man; Triple Terror app. 34.00 103.00 275.00

JIMINY CRICKET (Disney,, see Mickey Mouse Mag. V5#3 & Walt Disney Showcase #37)
No. 701, May, 1956 - No. 989, May-July, 1959
Dell Publishing Co.
Four Color 701 8.00 25.00 90.00
Four Color 795, 897, 989 5.50 16.50 60.00

JIMMY DURANTE (Also see A-1 Comics)
No. 18, 1949 - No. 20, 1949
Magazine Enterprises
A-1 18,20-Photo-c 34.00 103.00 275.00

JIMMY OLSEN (See Superman's Pal...)

JIMMY WAKELY (Cowboy movie star)
Sept-Oct, 1949 - No. 18, July-Aug, 1952 (1-13: 52pgs.)
National Periodical Publications
1-Photo-c, 52 pgs. begin; Alex Toth-a; Kit Colby Girl Sheriff begins 89.00 267.00 800.00
2-Toth-a 39.00 117.00 350.00
3,6,7-Frazetta-a in all, 3 pgs. each; Toth-a in all. 7-Last photo-c 40.00 120.00 360.00
4-Frazetta-a (3 pgs.); Kurtzman "Pot-Shot Pete", 1 pg; Toth-a 40.00 120.00 360.00
5,8-15,18-Toth-a; 12,14-Kubert-a (3 & 2 pgs.) 33.00 98.00 260.00
16,17 28.00 83.00 220.00

NOTE: ***Gil Kane** c-10-19p.*

JIM RAY'S AVIATION SKETCH BOOK
Mar-Apr, 1946 - No. 2, May-June, 1946
Vital Publishers
1,2-Picture stories about planes and pilots 21.00 62.00 165.00

JIM SOLAR (See Wisco/Klarer)

JINGLE BELLS (See March of Comics No. 65)

JINGLE BELLS CHRISTMAS BOOK
1971 (20 pgs., B&W inside, slick-c)
Montgomery Ward (Giveaway)
nn .80 2.00

JINGLE DINGLE CHRISTMAS STOCKING COMICS (See Foodini #2)
V2#1, 1951 (no date listed) (25¢, 100 pgs.; giant-size)
Stanhall Publications (Publ. annually)
V2#1-Foodini & Pinhead, Silly Pilly plus games & puzzles 12.00 38.00 100.00

JINGLE JANGLE COMICS (Also see Puzzle Fun Comics)
Feb, 1942 - No. 42, Dec, 1949
Eastern Color Printing Co.
1-Pie-Face Prince of Old Pretzleburg, Jingle Jangle Tales by George Carlson, Hortense, & Benny Bear begin 36.00 108.00 300.00
2,3-No Pie-Face Prince 17.00 51.00 135.00
4-Pie-Face Prince cover 17.00 51.00 135.00
5 15.00 45.00 120.00
6-10: 8-No Pie-Face Prince 12.00 38.00 100.00
11-15 9.50 28.00 75.00
16-30: 17,18-No Pie-Face Prince. 30-XMas-c 8.50 26.00 60.00
31-42: 36,42-Xmas-c 5.70 17.00 40.00
NOTE: ***George Carlson** a-(2) in all except No. 2, 3, 8; c-1-6. **Carlson** 1 pg. puzzles in 9, 10, 12-15, 18, 20. **Carlson** illustrated a series of Uncle Wiggily books in 1930's.*

JING PALS
Feb, 1946 - No. 4, Aug?, 1946 (Funny animal)
Victory Publishing Corporation
1-Wishing Willie, Puggy Panda & Johnny Rabbit begin 10.00 30.00 80.00
2-4 5.70 17.00 40.00

JINKS, PIXIE, AND DIXIE (See Kite Fun Book & Whitman Comic Books)

JINX
1996 - No. 7, 1996 ($2.95, B&W, 32 pgs.)
Caliber Press
1-7: Brian Michael Bendis-c/a/scripts. 2-Photo-c 1.20 3.00

JINX (Volume 2)
1997 - Present ($2.95, B&W, bi-monthly.)
Image Comics
1-3: Brian Michael Bendis-c/a/scripts. 2.95
TPB (1997, $10.95) r/Vol 1,#1-4 10.95

JLA (See Justice League of America)
Jan, 1997 - Present ($1.95)
DC Comics
1-Morrison-s/Porter & Dell-a. The Hyperclan app. 2.50 7.50 20.00
2 2.25 6.75 18.00
3,4 1.25 3.75 10.00
5-9: 5-Membership drive. 8-Green Arrow joins. 2.00 5.00
10-15: 10-Rock of Ages begins. 11-Joker and Luthor-c/app. 1.20 3.00
Annual 1 (1997, $3.95) Pulp Heroes; Augustyn-s/Olivetti & Ha-a 3.95
New World Order (1997, $5.95, TPB) r/1-4 5.95

JLA GALLERY
1997 ($2.95, one-shot)

JLA Paradise Lost #1 © DC

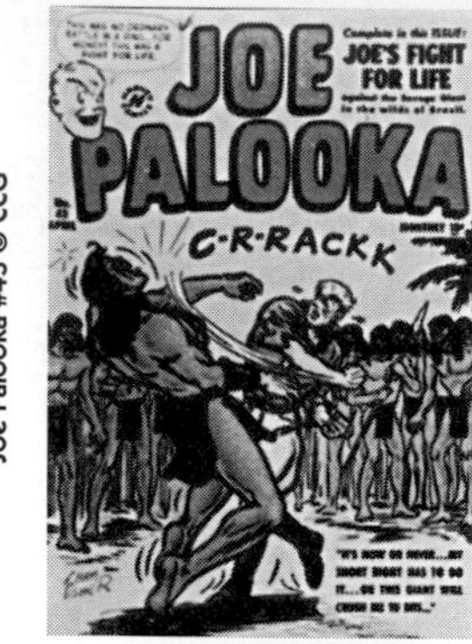

Joe Palooka #43 © CCG

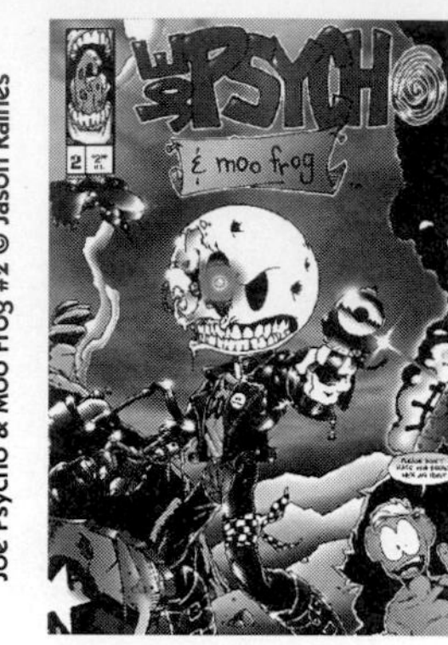

Joe Psycho & Moo Frog #2 © Jason Raines

	GD25	FN65	NM94
DC Comics			
nn-Pin-ups by various, wraparound cover by Frank Quitely			2.95

JLA PARADISE LOST
Jan, 1998 - No. 3, Mar, 1998 ($1.95, limited series)
DC Comics

1-3-Millar-s/Olivetti-a 1.95

JLA SECRET FILES
Sept, 1997 ($4.95, one-shot)
DC Comics

1-Standard Ed. w/origin-s & pin-ups 4.95
1-Collector's Ed. w/origin-s & pin-ups; cardstock-c 4.95

JLA/ WILDC.A.T.S
1997 ($5.95, one-shot, prestige format)
DC Comics

1-Morrison-s/Semeiks & Conrad-a 5.95

JLA: YEAR ONE
Jan, 1998 - Present ($2.95/$1.95, limited series)
DC Comics

1-($2.95)-Waid & Augustyn-s/Kitson-a 2.95
2-4-($1.95) 1.95

JLX
Apr, 1996 ($1.95, one-shot)
DC Comics (Amalgam)

1-Mark Waid scripts 2.00

JLX UNLEASHED
June, 1997 ($1.95, one-shot)
DC Comics (Amalgam)

1-Priest-s/ Jimenez & Rodriquez/a 1.95

JOAN OF ARC (Also see A-1 Comics & Ideal a Classical Comic)
No. 21, 1949 (one shot)
Magazine Enterprises

A-1 21-Movie adaptation; Ingrid Bergman photo-covers & interior photos; Whitney-a 24.00 71.00 170.00

JOAN OF ARC
No date (28 pgs.)
Catechetical Guild (Topix) (Giveaway)

nn 8.50 26.00 60.00
NOTE: *Unpublished version exists which came from the Guild's files.*

JOE COLLEGE
Fall, 1949 - No. 2, Winter, 1950 (Teen-age humor, 52 pgs.)
Hillman Periodicals

1,2: Powell-a; 1-Briefer-a 8.50 26.00 60.00

JOE JINKS
No. 12, 1939
United Features Syndicate

Single Series 12 24.00 71.00 190.00

JOE LOUIS (See Fight Comics #2, Picture News #6 & True Comics #5)
Sept, 1950 - No. 2, Nov, 1950 (Photo-c) (Boxing champ)(See Dick Cole #10)
Fawcett Publications

1-Photo-c; life story 47.00 141.00 420.00
2-Photo-c 34.00 101.00 270.00

JOE PALOOKA (1st Series)(Also see Big Shot Comics, Columbia Comics & Feature Funnies)
1942 - No. 4, 1944
Columbia Comic Corp. (Publication Enterprises)

1-1st to portray American president; gov't permission required 61.00 183.00 550.00
2 (1943)-Hitler-c 36.00 108.00 320.00
3,4: 3-Nazi Sub-c 26.00 80.00 210.00

JOE PALOOKA (2nd Series) (Battle Adv. #68-74; ...Advs. #75, 77-81, 83-85, 87; Champ of the Comics #76, 82, 86, 89-93) (See All-New)
Nov, 1945 - No. 118, Mar, 1961
Harvey Publications

1 37.00 112.00 335.00
2 19.00 56.00 150.00
3,4,6,7-1st Flyin' Fool, ends #25 11.30 34.00 90.00
5-Boy Explorers by S&K (7-8/46) 17.00 51.00 135.00
8-10 8.75 26.25 70.00
11-14,16-20: 19-Freedom Train-c 7.85 23.50 55.00
15-Origin & 1st app. Humphrey (12/47); Super heroine Atoma app. by Powell 11.30 34.00 90.00
21-30: 27-1st app. Little Max? (12/48). 30-Nude female painting 5.70 17.00 40.00
31-61: 35-Little Max-c/story. 36-Humphrey story. 39-Humphrey & Little Max begin (12/49). 41-Bing Crosby photo on-c. 44-Palooka marries Ann Howe. 50-(11/51)-Becomes Harvey Comics Hits #51 5.00 15.00 30.00
62-S&K Boy Explorers-r 5.70 17.00 38.00
63-80: 66,67-'Commie' torture story 4.15 12.50 25.00
81-99,101-115 4.00 11.00 22.00
100 4.35 13.00 26.00
116-S&K Boy Explorers-r (Giant, '60) 5.70 17.00 38.00
117,118-Giants 5.35 16.00 32.00
...Body Building Instruction Book (1958 B&M Sports Toy giveaway, 16pgs., 5-1/4x7")-Origin 8.50 26.00 60.00
...Fights His Way Back (1945 Giveaway, 24 pgs.) Family Comics 15.00 45.00 120.00
...in Hi There! (1949 Red Cross giveaway, 12 pgs., 4-3/4x6") 7.85 23.50 55.00
...in It's All in the Family (1945 Red Cross giveaway, 16 pgs., regular size) 8.75 26.25 70.00
...**Visits the Lost City** nn (1945)(One Shot)(50¢)-164 page continuous story strip reprint. Has biography & photo of Ham Fisher; possibly the single longest comic book story published (159 pgs.?) 130.00 390.00 1300.00
NOTE: ***Nostrand/Powell*** *a-73.* ***Powell*** *a-7, 8, 10, 12, 14, 17, 19, 26-45, 47-53, 70, 73 at least. Black Cat text stories #8, 12, 13, 19.*

JOE PSYCHO & MOO FROG
1996 - Present ($2.50, B&W)
Goblin Studios

1-5: 4-Two covers 1.00 2.50

JOE YANK (Korean War)
No. 5, Mar, 1952 - No. 16, 1954
Standard Comics (Visual Editions)

5-Toth, Celardo, Tuska-a 5.70 17.00 40.00
6-Toth, Severin/Elder-a 7.15 21.50 50.00
7 4.15 12.50 25.00
8-Toth-c 5.70 17.00 38.00
9-16: 9-Andru-c. 12-Andru-a 4.00 11.00 24.00

JOHN BOLTON'S HALLS OF HORROR
June, 1985 - No. 2, June, 1985 ($1.75, limited series)
Eclipse Comics

1,2-British-r; Bolton-c/a .70 1.80

JOHN BYRNE'S NEXT MEN (See Dark Horse Presents #54)
Jan, 1992 - No. 30, Dec, 1994 ($2.50, mature)
Dark Horse Comics (Legend imprint #19 on)

1-Silver foil embossed-c; Byrne-c/a/scripts in all 2.00 5.00
1-4: 1-2nd printing with gold ink logo 1.20 3.00
0-(2/92)-r/chapters 1-4 from DHP w/new Byrne-c .80 2.00

John Byrne's Next Men #21 © John Byrne

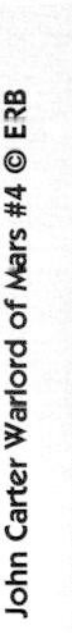

John Carter Warlord of Mars #4 © ERB

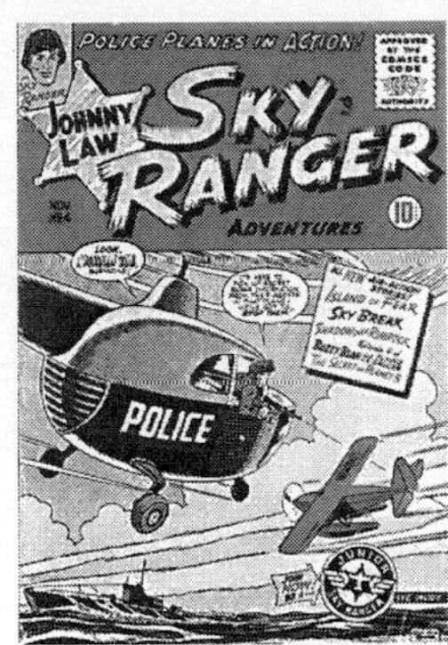

Johnny Law, Sky Ranger #4 © LEV

GD25 FN65 NM94

5-30: 7-10-MA #1-4 mini-series on flip side. 16-Origin of Mark IV. 17-Miller-c. 19-22-Faith storyline. 23-26-Power storyline. 27-30-Lies storyline Pt. 1-4. — 1.00 — 2.50

...Parallel, Book 2 ($16.95)-TPB; r/#7-12 — 17.00
...Fame, Book 3($16.95)-TPB r/#13-18 — 17.00
...Faith, Book 4($14.95)-TPB r/#19-22 — 15.00

NOTE: *Issues 1 through 6 contain certificates redeemable for an exclusive Next Men trading card set by Byrne. Prices are for complete books.* **Cody** *painted c-23-26.* **Mignola** *a-21(part); c-21.*

JOHN CARTER OF MARS (See The Funnies & Tarzan #207)
No. 375, Mar-May, 1952 - No. 488, Aug-Oct, 1953 (Edgar Rice Burroughs)
Dell Publishing Co.

	GD25	FN65	NM94
Four Color 375 (#1)-Origin; Jesse Marsh-a	23.00	68.00	250.00
Four Color 437, 488-Painted-c	14.00	44.00	160.00

JOHN CARTER OF MARS
Apr, 1964 - No. 3, Oct, 1964
Gold Key

	GD25	FN65	NM94
1(10104-404) r/4-Color #375; Jesse Marsh-a	4.00	12.00	45.00
2(407), 3(410)-r/4-Color #437 & 488; Marsh-a	3.00	9.00	32.00

JOHN CARTER OF MARS
1970 (10-1/2x16-1/2", 72 pgs., B&W, paper-c)
House of Greystroke

	GD25	FN65	NM94
1941-42 Sunday strip-r; John Coleman Burroughs-a	2.50	7.50	20.00

JOHN CARTER, WARLORD OF MARS (Also see Weird Worlds)
June, 1977 - No. 28, Oct, 1979
Marvel Comics

	GD25	FN65	NM94
1,18: 18-Frank Miller-a(p)(1st publ. Marvel work)		1.20	3.00
2-17,19-28: 1-Origin. 11-Origin Dejah Thoris		.80	2.00
Annuals 1-3: 1(1977). 2(1978). 3(1979)-All 52 pgs. with new book-length stories		.80	2.00

NOTE: **Austin** *c-24i.* **Gil Kane** *a-1-10p; c-1p, 2p, 3, 4-9p, 10, 15p, Annual 1p.* **Layton** *a-17i.* **Miller** *c-25, 26p.* **Nebres** *a-2-4i, 8-16i; c(i)-6-9, 11-22, 25, Annual 1.* **Perez** *c-24p.* **Simonson** *a-15p.* **Sutton** *a-7i.*

JOHN F. KENNEDY, CHAMPION OF FREEDOM
1964 (no month) (25¢)
Worden & Childs

	GD25	FN65	NM94
nn-Photo-c	4.80	14.40	48.00

JOHN F. KENNEDY LIFE STORY
Aug-Oct, 1964; Nov, 1965; June, 1966 (12¢)
Dell Publishing Co.

	GD25	FN65	NM94
12-378-410-Photo-c	3.00	9.00	32.00
12-378-511 (reprint, 11/65)	2.00	6.00	22.00
12-378-606 (reprint, 6/66)	1.80	5.50	20.00

JOHN FORCE (See Magic Agent)

JOHN HIX SCRAP BOOK, THE
Late 1930's (no date) (10¢, 68 pgs., regular size)
Eastern Color Printing Co. (McNaught Synd.)

	GD25	FN65	NM94
1-Strange As It Seems (resembles Single Series books)	29.00	86.00	230.00
2-Strange As It Seems	21.00	64.00	170.00

JOHN JAKES' MULKON EMPIRE
Sept, 1995 - No. 6, Feb, 1996 ($1.95)
Tekno Comix

	GD25	FN65	NM94
1-6		.80	2.00

JOHN LAW DETECTIVE(See Smash Comics #3)
April, 1983 ($1.50, Baxter paper)
Eclipse Comics

	GD25	FN65	NM94
1-Three Eisner stories originally drawn in 1948 for the never published John Law #1; original cover pencilled in 1948 & inked in 1982 by Eisner		.80	2.00

JOHNNY APPLESEED (See Story Hour Series)

JOHNNY CASH (See Hello, I'm...)

JOHNNY DANGER (See Movie Comics, 1946)
1950 (Based on movie serial)
Toby Press

	GD25	FN65	NM94
1-Photo-c; Sparling-a	13.50	41.00	100.00

JOHNNY DANGER PRIVATE DETECTIVE
Aug, 1954 (Reprinted in Danger #11 by Super)
Toby Press

	GD25	FN65	NM94
1-Photo-c; Opium den story	10.00	30.00	80.00

JOHNNY DYNAMITE (Formerly Dynamite #1-9; Foreign Intrigues #13 on)
No. 10, June, 1955 - No. 12, Oct, 1955
Charlton Comics

	GD25	FN65	NM94
10-12	5.70	17.00	40.00

JOHNNY DYNAMITE
Sept, 1994 - Dec, 1994 ($2.95, B&W & red, limited series)
Dark Horse Comics

	GD25	FN65	NM94
1-4: Max Allan Collins scripts in all.		1.20	3.00

JOHNNY HAZARD
No. 5, Aug, 1948 - No. 8, May, 1949; No. 35, date?
Best Books (Standard Comics) (King Features)

	GD25	FN65	NM94
5-Strip reprints by Frank Robbins (c/a)	11.30	34.00	90.00
6,8-Strip reprints by Frank Robbins	8.75	26.25	70.00
7-New art, not Robbins	7.15	21.50	50.00
35	7.15	21.50	50.00

JOHNNY JASON (...Teen Reporter)
Feb-Apr, 1962 - No. 2, June-Aug, 1962
Dell Publishing Co.

	GD25	FN65	NM94
Four Color 1302, 2(01380-208)	2.75	8.00	30.00

JOHNNY JINGLE'S LUCKY DAY
1956 (16 pgs.; 7-1/4x5-1/8") (Giveaway) (Disney)
American Dairy Association

	GD25	FN65	NM94
nn	4.00	12.00	24.00

JOHNNY LAW, SKY RANGER
Apr, 1955 - No. 3, Aug, 1955; No. 4, Nov, 1955
Good Comics (Lev Gleason)

	GD25	FN65	NM94
1-Edmond Good-c/a	6.50	19.50	45.00
2-4	4.25	13.00	28.00

JOHNNY MACK BROWN (TV western star; see Western Roundup under Dell Giants)
No. 269, Mar, 1950 - No. 963, Feb, 1959 (All Photo-c)
Dell Publishing Co.

	GD25	FN65	NM94
Four Color 269(#1)(3/50, 52pgs.)-Johnny Mack Brown & his horse Rebel begin; photo front/back-c begin; Marsh-a in #1-9	21.00	62.00	225.00
2(10-12/50, 52pgs.)	10.00	30.00	110.00
3(1-3/51, 52pgs.)	9.00	27.00	100.00
4-10 (9-11/52)(36pgs.)	5.50	16.50	60.00
Four Color 455,493,541,584,618	5.50	16.50	60.00
Four Color 645,685,722,776,834,963	5.50	16.50	60.00
Four Color 922-Manning-a	6.40	19.00	70.00

JOHNNY NEMO
Sept, 1985 - No. 3, Feb, 1986 (Mini-series)
Eclipse Comics

	GD25	FN65	NM94
1,2-($1.75)		.70	1.80
3-($2.00)		.80	2.00

JOHNNY PERIL (See Comic Cavalcade #15, Danger Trail #5, Sensation Comics #107 & Sensation Mystery)

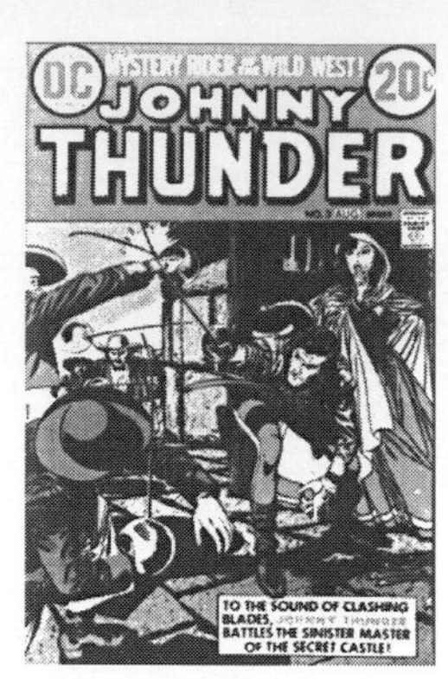

Johnny Thunder #3 © DC

John Wayne Advenmture Comics #28 © TOBY

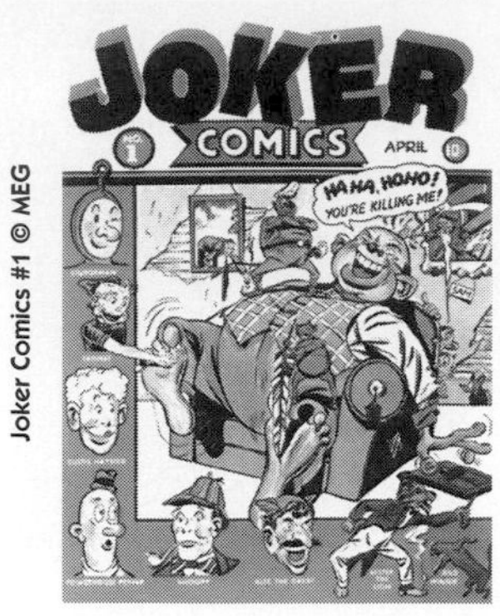

Joker Comics #1 © MEG

GD25 FN65 NM94

JOHNNY RINGO (TV)
No. 1142, Nov-Jan, 1960/61 (one shot)
Dell Publishing Co.

Four Color 1142-Photo-c 6.40 19.00 70.00

JOHNNY STARBOARD (See Wisco)

JOHNNY THE HOMICIDAL MANIAC
Aug, 1995 - No. 7, Jan, 1997 ($2.95, B&W, limited series)
Slave Labor Graphics

1-Jhonen Vasquez-c/s/a 4.00 12.00 40.00
1-Signed & numbered edition 2.50 7.50 25.00
2,3: 2-(11/95). 3-(2/96) 1.50 4.50 12.00
4-7: 4-(5-96). 5-(8/96) 2.00 5.00
Hardcover-($29.95) r/#1-7 29.95
TPB-($19.95) 19.95

JOHNNY THUNDER
Feb-Mar, 1973 - No. 3, July-Aug, 1973
National Periodical Publications

1-Johnny Thunder & Nighthawk-r. in all 1.25 3.75 10.00
2,3: 2-Trigger Twins app. 1.00 2.80 7.00
NOTE: *All contain 1950s DC reprints from All-American Western.* ***Drucker*** *r-2, 3.* ***G. Kane*** *r-2, 3.* ***Moriera*** *r-1.* ***Toth*** *r-1, 3; c-1r, 3r. Also see All-American, All-Star Western, Flash Comics, Western Comics, World's Best & World's Finest.*

JOHN PAUL JONES
No. 1007, July-Sept, 1959 (one-shot)
Dell Publishing Co.

Four Color 1007-Movie, Robert Stack photo-c 4.50 13.50 50.00

JOHN STEED & EMMA PEEL (See The Avengers, Gold Key series)

JOHN STEELE SECRET AGENT (Also see Freedom Agent)
Dec, 1964
Gold Key

1-Freedom Agent 8.00 23.00 85.00

JOHN WAYNE ADVENTURE COMICS (Movie star; See Big Tex, Oxydol-Dreft, Tim McCoy, & With The Marines...#1)
Winter, 1949-50 - No. 31, May, 1955 (Photo-c: 1-12,17,25-on)
Toby Press

1 (36pgs.)-Photo-c begin (1st time in comics on-c) 122.00 366.00 1100.00
2 (4/50, 36pgs.)-Williamson/Frazetta-a(2) 6 & 2 pgs. (one story-r/Billy the Kid #1); photo back-c 51.00 153.00 460.00
3 (36pgs.)-Williamson/Frazetta-a(2), 16 pgs. total; photo back-c 51.00 153.00 460.00
4 (52pgs.)-Williamson/Frazetta-a(2), 16 pgs. total 51.00 153.00 460.00
5 (52pgs.)-Kurtzman-a-(Alfred "L" Newman in Potshot Pete) 38.00 113.00 340.00
6 (52pgs.)-Williamson/Frazetta-a (10 pgs.); Kurtzman-a "Pot-Shot Pete", (5 pgs.); & "Genius Jones", (1 pg.) 48.00 144.00 430.00
7 (52pgs.)-Williamson/Frazetta-a (10 pgs.) 37.00 110.00 330.00
8 (36pgs.)-Williamson/Frazetta-a(2) (12 & 9 pgs.) 48.00 144.00 430.00
9-11: Photo western-c 29.00 88.00 235.00
12,14-Photo war-c. 12-Kurtzman-a(2 pg.) "Genius" 29.00 88.00 235.00
13,15: 13,15-Line-drawn-c begin, end #24 26.00 80.00 210.00
16-Williamson/Frazetta-r/Billy the Kid #1 28.00 83.00 220.00
17-Photo-c 29.00 88.00 235.00
18-Williamson/Frazetta-a (r/#4 & 8, 19 pgs.) 31.00 94.00 250.00
19-24: 23-Evans-a? 23.00 69.00 185.00
25-Photo-c resume; end #31; Williamson/Frazetta-r/Billy the Kid #3 31.00 94.00 250.00
26-28,30-Photo-c 27.00 81.00 215.00
29,31-Williamson/Frazetta-a in each (r/#4, 2) 29.00 86.00 230.00
NOTE: *Williamsonish art in later issues by* ***Gerald McCann.***

JO-JO COMICS (...Congo King #7-29; My Desire #30 on)
(Also see Fantastic Fears and Jungle Jo)
1945 - No. 29, July, 1949 (Two No.7's; no #13)
Fox Feature Syndicate

nn(1945)-Funny animal, humor 11.30 34.00 90.00
2(Sum,'46)-6(4-5/47): Funny animal. 2-Ten pg. Electro story (Fall/46) 6.50 19.50 45.00
7(7/47)-Jo-Jo, Congo King begins (1st app.); Bronze Man & Purlpe Tigress app. 70.00 210.00 600.00
7(#8) (9/47) 51.00 153.00 435.00
8-10(#9-11): 8-Tanee begins 40.00 120.00 335.00
11,12(#12,13),14,16: 11,16-Kamen bondage-c 39.00 116.00 290.00
15-Cited by Dr. Wertham in 5/47 Saturday Review of Literature 40.00 120.00 300.00
17-Kamen bondage-c 40.00 120.00 300.00
18-20 39.00 116.00 290.00
21-29: 21-Hollingsworth-a(4 pgs.; 23-1 pg.) 34.00 103.00 260.00
NOTE: *Many bondage-c/a by* ***Baker/Kamen/Feldstein/Good.*** *No. 7's have Princesses Gwenna, Geesa, Yolda, & Safra before settling down on Tanee.*

JO-JOY (The Adventures of...)
1945 - 1953 (Christmas gift comic, 16 pgs., 7-1/16x10-1/4")
W. T. Grant Dept. Stores

1945-53 issues 4.35 13.00 26.00

JOKEBOOK COMICS DIGEST ANNUAL (...Magazine No. 5 on)
Oct, 1977 - No. 13, Oct, 1983 (Digest Size)
Archie Publications

1(10/77)-Reprints; Neal Adams-a 1.20 3.00
2(4/78)-13 1.20 3.00

JOKER, THE (See Batman #1, Batman: The Killing Joke, Brave & the Bold, Detective, Greatest Joker Stories & Justice League Annual #2)
May, 1975 - No. 9, Sept-Oct, 1976
National Periodical Publications

1-Two-Face app. 2.50 7.50 25.00
2,3: 3-The Creeper app. 1.50 4.50 12.00
4-9: 4-Green Arrow-c/sty. 6-Sherlock Holmes-c/sty. 7-Lex Luthor-c/story. 8-Scarecrow-c/story. 9-Catwoman-c/story 1.25 3.75 10.00

JOKER, THE (See Tangent Comics/ The Joker)

JOKER COMICS (Adventures Into Terror No. 43 on)
Apr, 1942 - No. 42, Aug, 1950
Timely/Marvel Comics No. 36 on (TCI/CDS)

1-(Rare)-Powerhouse Pepper (1st app.) begins by Wolverton; Stuporman app. from Daring Comics 189.00 567.00 1700.00
2-Wolverton-a; 1st app. Tessie the Typist & begin series 69.00 207.00 625.00
3-5-Wolverton-a 44.00 132.00 400.00
6-10-Wolverton-a. 6-Tessie-c begin 34.00 101.00 270.00
11-20-Wolverton-a 26.00 80.00 210.00
21,22,24-27,29,30-Wolverton cont'd. & Kurtzman's "Hey Look" in #23-27 23.00 68.00 180.00
23-1st "Hey Look" by Kurtzman; Wolverton-a 25.00 75.00 200.00
28,32,34,37-41: 28-Millie the Model begins. 32-Hedy begins. 41-Nellie the Nurse app. 6.50 19.50 45.00
31-Last Powerhouse Pepper; not in #28 15.50 47.00 125.00
33,35,36-Kurtzman's "Hey Look" 8.75 26.25 70.00
42-Only app. 'Patty Pinup,' clone of Millie the Model 7.85 23.50 55.00

JOKER: DEVIL'S ADVOCATE
1996 ($24.95/$12.95, one-shot)
DC Comics

nn-(Hardcover)-Dixon scripts/Nolan & Hanna-a 2.50 7.50 25.00
nn-(Softcover) 1.60 4.85 13.00

JOLLY CHRISTMAS, A (See March of Comics No. 269)

Jonah Hex #92 © DC

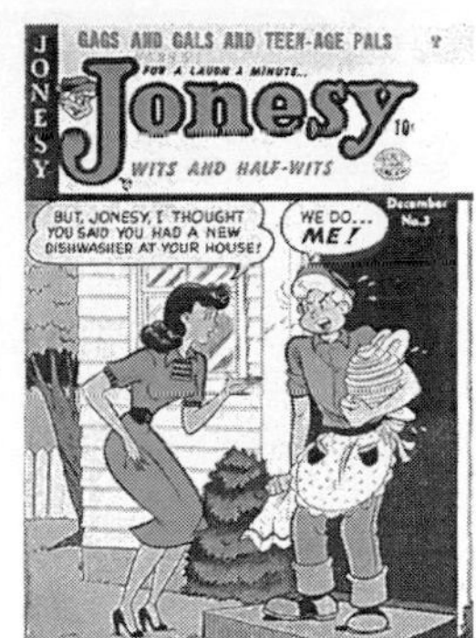

Jonesy #3 © QUA

Jon Sable, Freelance #19 © First Comics

GD25 FN65 NM94

JOLLY CHRISTMAS BOOK (See Christmas Journey Through Space)
1951; 1954; 1955 (36 pgs.; 24 pgs.)
Promotional Publ. Co.

1951-(Woolworth giveaway)-slightly oversized; no slick cover; Marv Levy-c/a 5.70 17.00 40.00
1954-(Hot Shoppes giveaway)-regular size-reprints 1951 issue; slick cover added; 24 pgs.; no ads 5.70 17.00 40.00
1955-(J. M. McDonald Co. giveaway)-reg. size 4.25 13.00 28.00

JOLLY COMICS
1947
Four Star Publishing Co.

1 7.15 21.50 50.00

JOLLY JINGLES (Formerly Jackpot Comics)
No. 10, Sum, 1943 - No. 16, Wint, 1944/45
MLJ Magazines

10-Super Duck begins (origin & 1st app.); Woody The Woodpecker begins (not same as Lantz character) 30.00 90.00 240.00
11 (Fall, '43)-2nd Super Duck(see Hangman #8) 15.00 45.00 120.00
12-Hitler-c 13.00 39.00 105.00
13-16: 13-Sahle-c. 15-Vigoda-c 8.75 26.25 70.00

JONAH HEX (See All-Star Western, Hex and Weird Western Tales)
Mar-Apr, 1977 - No. 92, Aug, 1985
National Periodical Publications/DC Comics

1 4.00 12.00 40.00
2-6,9,10: 9-Wrightson-c. 1.40 4.15 11.00
7,8-Explains Hex's face disfigurement (origin) 1.75 5.25 14.00
11-20: 12-Starlin-c 1.00 2.80 7.00
21-50: 31,32-Origin retold 1.60 4.00
51-91: 89-Mark Texeira-a. 92-Story contd in Hex #1 1.40 3.50
92 1.25 3.75 10.00

NOTE: ***Ayers*** *a(p)-35-37, 40, 41, 44-53, 56, 58-82.* ***Buckler*** *a-11; c-11, 13-16.* ***Kubert*** *c-43-46.* ***Morrow*** *a-90-92; c-10.* ***Spiegle(Tothish)*** *a-34, 38, 40, 49, 52.* ***Texeira*** *a-89p. Batlash back-ups in 49, 52. El Diablo back-ups in 48, 56-60, 73-75. Scalphunter back-ups in 40, 41, 45-47.*

JONAH HEX AND OTHER WESTERN TALES (Blue Ribbon Digest)
Sept-Oct, 1979 - No. 3, Jan-Feb, 1980 (100 pgs.)
DC Comics

1-3: 1-Origin Scalphunter-r, Ayers/Evans, Neal Adams-a.; painted-c. 2-Weird Western Tales-r; Neal Adams, Toth, Aragones-a. 3-Outlaw-r, Scalphunter-r; Gil Kane, Wildey-a 2.40 6.00

JONAH HEX: RIDERS OF THE WORM AND SUCH
Mar, 1995 - No. 5, July, 1995 ($2.95, limited series)
DC Comics (Vertigo)

1-5-Lansdale story, Truman -a 1.20 3.00

JONAH HEX SPECTACULAR (See DC Special Series No. 16)

JONAH HEX: TWO-GUN MOJO
Aug, 1993 - No. 5, Dec, 1993 ($2.95, limited series)
DC Comics (Vertigo)

1-Lansdale scripts in all;Truman/Glanzman-a in all w/Truman-c 1.60 4.00
1-Silver ink edition with no price on cover 1.00 3.00 8.00
2-5 1.20 3.00

JONESY (Formerly Crack Western)
No. 85, Aug, 1953; No. 2, Oct, 1953 - No. 8, Oct, 1954
Comic Favorite/Quality Comics Group

85(#1)-Teen-age humor 5.70 17.00 35.00
2 4.00 12.00 24.00
3-8 3.20 8.00 16.00

JON JUAN (Also see Great Lover Romances)
Spring, 1950
Toby Press

1-All Schomburg-a (signed Al Reid on-c); written by Siegel; used in **SOTI**, pg. 38 (Scarce) 53.00 159.00 435.00

JONNI THUNDER (...A.K.A. Thunderbolt)
Feb, 1985 - No. 4, Aug, 1985 (75¢, limited series)
DC Comics

1-4: 1-Origin & 1st app. 1.00

JONNY DEMON
May, 1994 - No. 3, July, 1994 ($2.50, limited series)
Dark Horse Comics

1-3 1.00 2.50

JONNY QUEST (TV)
Dec, 1964 (Hanna-Barbera)
Gold Key

1 (10139-412) 30.00 89.00 325.00

JONNY QUEST (TV)
June 1986 - No. 31, Dec, 1988 ($1.50/$1.75)(Hanna-Barbera)
Comico

1 2.00 5.00
2,3,5: 3,5-Dave Stevens-c 1.20 3.00
4,6-14 1.50
15-31: 15-Begin $1.75-c. 30-Adapts TV episode .80 2.00
Special 1(9/88, $1.75), 2(10/88, $1.75) .80 2.00

NOTE: ***M. Anderson*** *a-9.* ***Mooney*** *a-Special 1.* ***Pini*** *a-2.* ***Quagmire*** *a-31p.* ***Rude*** *a-1; c-2i.* ***Sienkiewicz*** *c-11.* ***Spiegle*** *a-7, 12, 21; c-21* ***Staton*** *a-2l, 11p.* ***Steacy*** *c-8.* ***Stevens*** *a-4i; c-3,5.* ***Wildey*** *a-1, c-1, 7, 12.* ***Williamson*** *a-4i; c-4i.*

JONNY QUEST CLASSICS (TV)
May, 1987 - No. 3, July, 1987 ($2.00) (Hanna-Barbera)
Comico

1-3: Wildey-c/a; 3-Based on TV episode .80 2.00

JON SABLE, FREELANCE (Also see Mike Grell's Sable & Sable)
6/83 - No. 56, 2/88 (#1-17, $1; #18-33, $1.25, #34-on, $1.75)
First Comics

1-Mike Grell-c/a/scripts 1.40 3.50
2-5: 3-5-Origin, parts 1-3 1.00 2.50
6-10: 6-Origin, part 4 .80 2.00
11-20: 11-1st app. of Maggie the Cat. 14-Mando paper begins. 16-Maggie the Cat. app. .75 1.80
21-33: 25-30-Shatter app. 1.50
34-56: 34-Deluxe format begins ($1.75) .70 1.75

NOTE: ***Aragones*** *a-33; c-33(part).* ***Grell*** *a-1-43;c-1-52, 53p, 54-56.*

JOSEPH & HIS BRETHREN (See The Living Bible)

JOSIE (She's... #1-16) (...& the Pussycats #45 on) (See Archie Giant Series Magazine #528, 540, 551, 562, 571, 584, 597, 610, 622)
Feb, 1963; No. 2, Aug, 1963 - No. 106, Oct, 1982
Archie Publications/Radio Comics

1 14.00 42.00 140.00
2 7.00 21.00 70.00
3-5 4.00 12.00 40.00
6-10 3.00 9.00 30.00
11-20 2.50 7.50 20.00
21-30: 22-Mighty Man & Mighty (Josie Girl) app. 1.75 5.25 14.00
31-54 1.00 3.00 8.00
55-74(52pg. issues) 1.10 3.30 9.00
75-90 1.60 4.00
91-106 1.20 3.00

JOSIE & THE PUSSYCATS (TV)
1993 - No. 2, 1994 ($2.00, 52 pgs.)(Published annually)
Archie Comics

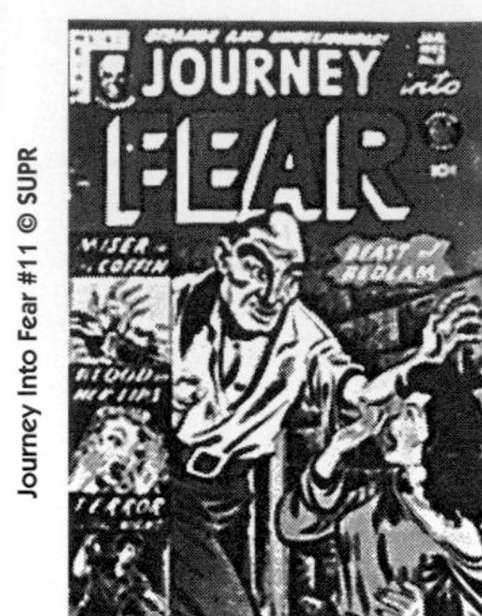

Journey Into Fear #11 © SUPR

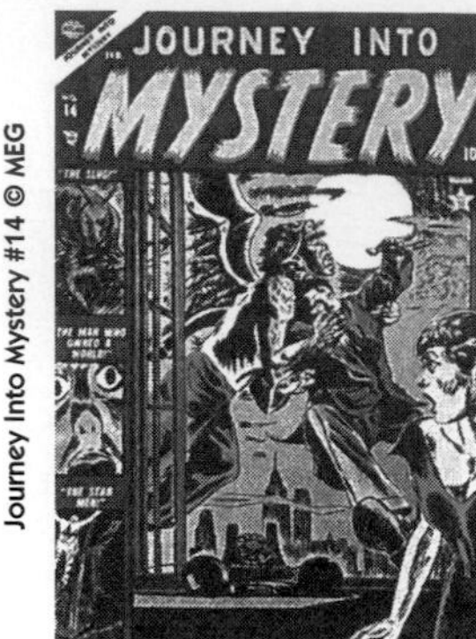

Journey Into Mystery #14 © MEG

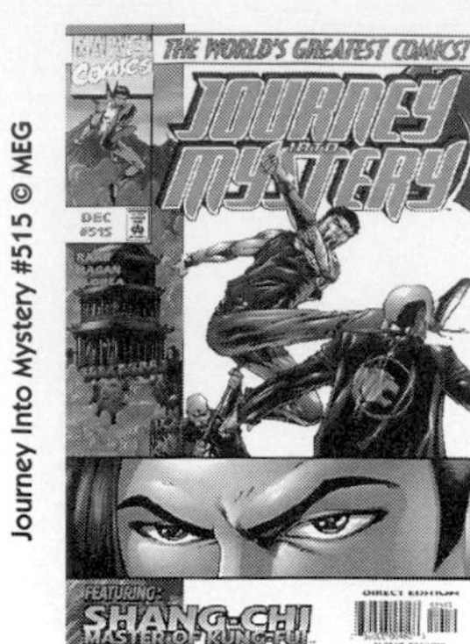

Journey Into Mystery #515 © MEG

GD25 FN65 NM94

1,2-Bound-in pull-out poster in each. 2-(Spr/94) .80 2.00

JOURNAL OF CRIME (See Fox Giants)

JOURNEY (Also see Journey: Wardrums)
1983 - No. 14, 9/84; No. 15, 4/85 - No. 27, 7/86 (B&W)
Aardvark-Vanaheim #1-14/Fantagraphics Books #15-on

1 1.60 4.00
2 .80 2.00
3-27: 20-Sam Kieth-a 1.25

JOURNEY INTO FEAR
May, 1951 - No. 21, Sept, 1954
Superior-Dynamic Publications

1-Baker-r(2) 45.00 136.00 400.00
2 31.00 92.00 235.00
3,4 26.00 77.00 200.00
5-10,15: 15-Used in **SOTI**, pg. 389 18.00 54.00 135.00
11-14,16-21 17.00 49.00 125.00
NOTE: *Kamenish 'headlight'-a most issues.* ***Robinson*** *a-10.*

JOURNEY INTO MYSTERY (1st Series) (Thor Nos. 126-502)
6/52 - No. 48, 8/57; No. 49, 11/58 - No. 125, 2/66; 503, 11/96 - Present
Atlas(CPS No. 1-48/AMI No. 49-68/Marvel No. 69 (6/61) on)

1-Weird/horror stories begin 260.00 780.00 2450.00
2 90.00 270.00 765.00
3,4 68.00 206.00 575.00
5-11 44.00 132.00 370.00
12-20,22: 15-Atomic explosion panel. 22-Davisesque-a; last pre-code issue (2/55) 38.00 116.00 290.00
21-Kubert-a; Tothish-a by Andru 40.00 120.00 295.00
23-32,35-38,40: 24-Torres?-a. 38-Ditko-a 24.00 71.00 175.00
33-Williamson-a; Ditko-a (his 1st for Atlas?) 26.00 77.00 190.00
34,39: 34-Krigstein-a. 39-1st S.A. issue; Wood-a 24.00 73.00 180.00
41-Crandall-a; Frazettaesque-a by Morrow 16.00 48.00 160.00
42,48-Torres-a 16.00 48.00 160.00
43,44-Williamson/Mayo-a in both 17.00 51.00 170.00
45,47,52,53 15.00 45.00 150.00
46-Torres & Krigstein-a 16.00 48.00 160.00
49-Matt Fox, Check-a 16.00 48.00 160.00
50,54: 50-Davis-a. 54-Williamson-a 15.00 45.00 150.00
51-Kirby/Wood-a 17.50 52.00 175.00
55-61,63-65,67-69,71,72,74,75: 73-Story titled "The Spider" but no connection with Spider-Man. 74-Contents change to Fantasy. 75-Last 10¢ issue 15.00 45.00 150.00
62-Prototype ish. (The Hulk); 1st app. Xemnu (Titan) called "The Hulk" 21.00 63.00 210.00
66-Prototype ish. (The Hulk)-Return of Xemnu "The Hulk" 21.00 63.00 210.00
70-Prototype ish. (The Sandman)(7/61); similar to Spidey villain 21.00 63.00 210.00
73-Story titled "The Spider" where a spider is exposed to radiation & gets powers of a human and shoots webbing; a reverse prototype of Spider-Man's origin 30.00 90.00 300.00
76,77,80-82: 80-Anti-communist propaganda story 12.00 36.00 120.00
78-The Sorceror (Dr. Strange prototype) app. (3/62) 21.00 63.00 210.00
79-Prototype issue. (Mr. Hyde) 18.00 54.00 180.00

GD25 FN65 VF82 NM94

83-Origin & 1st app. The Mighty Thor by Kirby (8/62) and begin series; Thor-c also begin 280.00 840.00 1960.00 4000.00

GD25 FN65 NM94

83-Reprint from the Golden Record Comic Set 9.00 27.00 90.00
with the record (1966) 16.00 48.00 160.00
84-2nd app. Thor 77.00 231.00 925.00
85-1st app. Loki & Heimdall; Odin cameo (1 panel) 47.00 141.00 560.00
86-1st full app. Odin 32.00 96.00 350.00
87-89: 89-Origin Thor retold 24.50 74.00 245.00
90-No Kirby-a 14.00 42.00 140.00
91,92,94-96-Sinnott-a 12.00 36.00 120.00
93,97-Kirby-a; Tales of Asgard series begins #97 (origin which concludes in #99) 15.50 47.00 155.00
98-100-Kirby/Heck-a. 98-Origin/1st app. The Human Cobra. 99-1st app. Surtur & Mr. Hyde 11.00 33.00 110.00
101-108,110: 101-(2/64)-2nd Avengers x-over (w/o Capt. America); see Tales Of Suspense #49 for 1st x-over. 102-Intro Sif. 103-1st app. Enchantress. 105-109-Ten extra pgs. Kirby-a in each. 107-1st app. Grey Gargoyle. 108-(9/64)-Early Dr. Strange & Avengers x-over 8.00 24.00 80.00
109-Magneto-c & app. (1st x-over, 10/64) 11.00 33.00 110.00
111,113,114,116-125: 113-Origin Loki. 114-Origin/1st app. Absorbing Man. 118-1st app. Destroyer. 119-Intro Hogun, Fandrall, Volstagg. 124-Hercules-c/story 7.00 21.00 70.00
112-Thor Vs. Hulk (1/65). 112-Origin Loki 18.00 54.00 180.00
115-Origin Loki 9.00 27.00 90.00
503-507: 503-(11/96, $1.50)-The Lost Gods begin; Tom DeFalco scripts & Deodato Studios-c/a. 505-Spider-Man-c/app. 1.50
508-510, -1(7/97)-($1.95): 509-Loki-c/app. 1.95
511-516: 511-Begin $1.99-c. 514-516-Shang-Chi 1.99
Annual 1(1965, 25¢, 72 pgs.)-New Thor vs. Hercules(1st app.)-c/story (see Incredible Hulk #3); Kirby-c/a; r/#85,93,95,97 15.50 47.00 155.00
NOTE: ***Ayers*** *a-14, 39, 64i, 71i, 74i, 80i.* ***Bailey*** *a-43.* ***Briefer*** *a-5, 12.* ***Cameron*** *a-35.* ***Check*** *a-17.* ***Colan*** *a-23, 81; c-14.* ***Ditko*** *a-33, 38, 50-96; c-58, 67, 71, 88i.* ***Kirby/Ditko*** *a-50-83.* ***Everett*** *a-20, 48; c-4-7, 9, 36, 37, 39-42, 44, 45, 47.* ***Forte*** *a-19, 35, 40, 53.* ***Heath*** *a-4-6, 11, 14; c-1, 8, 11, 15, 51.* ***Heck*** *a-53, 73.* ***Kirby*** *a(p)-51, 52, 56, 57, 60, 62, 64, 66, 69, 71-74, 76, 79, 80-89, 93, 97, 98, 100(w/****Heck****), 101-125; c-50-57, 59-66, 68-70, 72-82, 88(w/****Ditko****), 83 & 84(w/****Sinnott****), 85-96(w/****Ayers****), 97-152p.* ***Leiber/Fox*** *a-93, 98-102.* ***Maneely*** *c-20-22.* ***Morisi*** *a-42.* ***Morrow*** *a-41, 42.* ***Orlando*** *a-30, 45, 57.* ***Mac Pakula*** *(Tothish) a-9, 35, 41.* ***Powell*** *a-20, 27, 34.* ***Reinman*** *a-39, 87, 92, 96i.* ***Robinson*** *a-9.* ***Roussos*** *a-39.* ***Robert Sale*** *a-14.* ***Severin*** *a-27; c-30.* ***Sinnott*** *a-41; c-50.* ***Tuska*** *a-11.* ***Wildey*** *a-16.*

JOURNEY INTO MYSTERY (2nd Series)
Oct, 1972 - No. 19, Oct, 1975
Marvel Comics

1-Robert Howard adaptation; Starlin/Ploog-a 1.10 3.30 9.00
2,3,5-Bloch adaptation; 5-Last new story 1.40 3.50
4,6-19: 4-H. P. Lovecraft adaptation .90 2.25
NOTE: ***N. Adams*** *a-2i.* ***Ditko*** *r-7, 10, 12, 14, 15, 19; c-10.* ***Everett*** *r-9, 14.* ***G. Kane*** *a-1p, 2p; c-1-3p.* ***Kirby*** *r-7, 13, 18, 19; c-7.* ***Mort Lawrence*** *r-2.* ***Maneely*** *r-3.* ***Orlando*** *r-16.* ***Reese*** *a-1, 2i.* ***Starlin*** *a-1p, 3p.* ***Torres*** *r-16.* ***Wildey*** *r-9, 14.*

JOURNEY INTO UNKNOWN WORLDS (Formerly Teen)
No. 36, 9/50 - No. 38, 2/51; No. 4, 4/51 - No. 59, 8/57
Atlas Comics (WFP)

36(#1)-Science fiction/weird; "End Of The Earth" c/story 175.00 525.00 1500.00
37(#2)-Science fiction; "When Worlds Collide" c/story; Everett-c/a; Hitler story 84.00 253.00 700.00
38(#3)-Science fiction 68.00 206.00 575.00
4-6,8,10-Science fiction/weird 44.00 132.00 365.00
7-Wolverton-a "Planet of Terror", 6 pgs; electric chair c-inset/story 71.00 215.00 600.00
9-Giant eyeball story 50.00 150.00 420.00
11,12-Krigstein-a 36.00 107.00 265.00
13,16,17,20 26.00 77.00 190.00
14-Wolverton-a "One of Our Graveyards Is Missing", 4 pgs; Tuska-a 53.00 161.00 450.00
15-Wolverton-a "They Crawl by Night", 5 pgs.; 2 pg. Maneely s/f story 53.00 161.00 450.00
18,19-Matt Fox-a 30.00 90.00 220.00
21-33: 21-Decapitation-c. 24-Sci/fic story. 26-Atom bomb panel. 27-Sid Check-a. 33-Last pre-code (2/55) 20.00 60.00 150.00
34-Kubert, Torres-a 15.00 45.00 110.00
35-Torres-a 14.00 43.00 100.00

Journey Into Unknown Worlds #36 © ATLAS

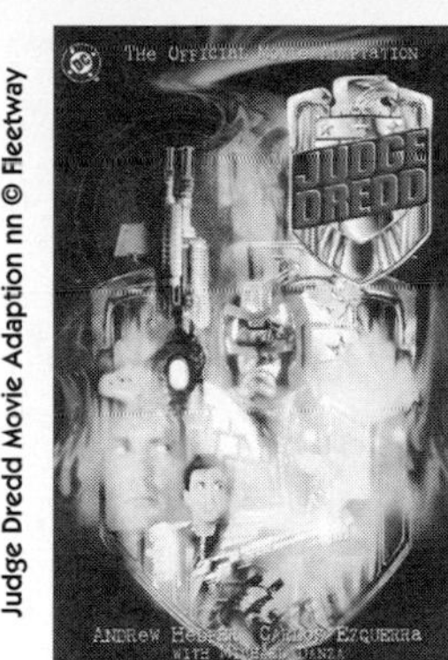

Judge Dredd Movie Adaption nn © Fleetway

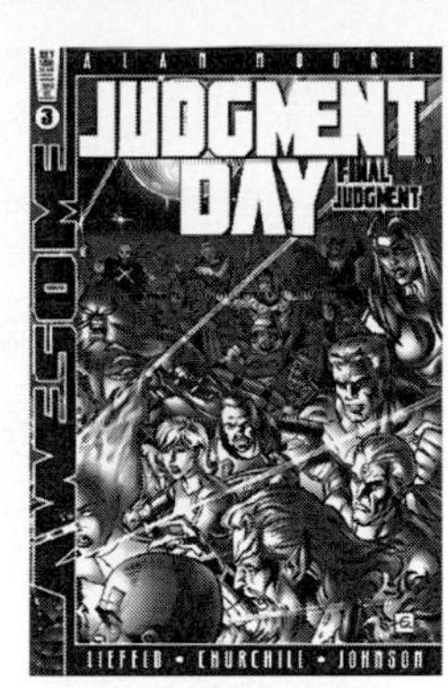

Judgment Day #3 © Awesome Comics

	GD25	FN65	NM94
36-42	13.00	39.00	95.00
43,44: 43-Krigstein-a. 44-Davis-a	13.00	39.00	95.00
45,55,59-Williamson-a in all; with Mayo #55,59. 55-Crandall-a	13.00	39.00	95.00
46,47,49,52,56-58	11.50	34.00	85.00
48,53-Crandall-a (4 pgs. #48). 48-Check-a	13.00	39.00	95.00
50-Davis, Crandall-a	13.00	39.00	95.00
51-Ditko, Wood-a	14.00	43.00	100.00
54-Torres-a	11.50	34.00	85.00

NOTE: ***Ayers** a-24, 43, **Berg** a-38(#3), 43. **Lou Cameron** a-33. **Colan** a-37(#2), 6, 17, 19, 20, 23, 39. **Ditko** a-45, 51. **Drucker** a-35, 58. **Everett** a-37(#2), 11, 14, 41, 55, 56; c-37(#2), 11, 13, 14, 17, 22, 47, 48, 50, 53-55, 59. **Forte** a-49. **Fox** a-21i. **Heath** a-36(#1), 4, 6-8, 17, 20, 22, 36i; c-18. **Keller** a-15. **Mort Lawrence** a-38, 39. **Maneely** a-7, 8, 15, 16, 22, 49, 58; c-19, 25, 52. **Morrow** a-48. **Orlando** a-44, 57. **Pakula** a-36. **Powell** a-42, 53, 54. **Reinman** a-8. **Rico** a-21. **Robert Sale** a-24, 49. **Sekowsky** a-4, 5, 9. **Severin** a-38, 51; c-38, 48i, 56. **Sinnott** a-9, 21, 24. **Tuska** a-38(#3), 14. **Wildey** a-25, 43, 44.*

JOURNEY OF DISCOVERY WITH MARK STEEL (See Mark Steel)

JOURNEY TO THE CENTER OF THE EARTH (Movie)
No. 1060, Nov-Jan, 1959/60 (one-shot)
Doll Publishing Co.

	GD25	FN65	NM94
Four Color 1060-Pat Boone & James Madson photo-c	11.00	33.00	120.00

JUDE, THE FORGOTTEN SAINT
1954 (16 pgs.; 8x11"; full color; paper-c)
Catechetical Guild Education Society

	GD25	FN65	NM94
nn	2.00	5.00	10.00

JUDGE COLT
Oct, 1969 - No. 4, Sept, 1970
Gold Key

	GD25	FN65	NM94
1	1.00	3.00	8.00
2-4		2.00	5.00

JUDGE DREDD (...Classics #62 on; also see Batman - Judge Dredd, Dredd Rules, The Law of Dredd & 2000 A.D. Monthly)
Nov, 1983 - No. 35, 1986; V2#1, Oct, 1986 - No. 77, 1993
Eagle Comics/IPC Magazines Ltd./Quality Comics #34-35, V2#1-37/ Fleetway #38 on

	GD25	FN65	NM94
1-Bolland-c/a		2.40	6.00
2-35		1.00	2.50
V2#1-77: 1-('86)-New look begins. 20-Begin $1.50-c. 21/22, 23/24-Two issue numbers in one. 28-1st app. Megaman (super-hero). 39-Begin $1.75-c. 51-Begin $1.95-c. 53-Bolland-a. 57-Reprints 1st published Judge Dredd story		.80	2.00
Special 1		.80	2.00

NOTE: ***Bolland** a-1-6, 8, 10; c-1-10, 15. **Guice** c-V2#23/24, 26, 27.*

JUDGE DREDD (3rd Series)
Aug, 1994 - No. 18, Jan, 1996 ($1.95)
DC Comics

	GD25	FN65	NM94
1-11		.80	2.00
12-18: 12-Begin $2.25-c		.90	2.25
nn ($5.95)-Movie adaptation, Sienkiewicz-c		2.40	6.00

JUDGE DREDD'S CRIME FILE
Aug, 1989 - No. 6, Feb, 1986 ($1.25, limited series)
Eagle Comics

	GD25	FN65	NM94
1-6: 1-Byrne-a		.80	2.00

JUDGE DREDD: LEGENDS OF THE LAW
Dec, 1994 - No. 13, Dec, 1995 ($1.95)
DC Comics

	GD25	FN65	NM94
1-7: 1-5-Dorman-c		.80	2.00
8-13: 8-Begin $2.25-c		.90	2.25

JUDGE DREDD: THE EARLY CASES
Feb, 1986 - No. 6, July, 1986 ($1.25, Mega-series, Mando paper)
Eagle Comics

	GD25	FN65	NM94
1-6: 2000 A.D.-r			1.50

JUDGE DREDD: THE JUDGE CHILD QUEST (Judge Child in indicia)
Aug, 1984 - No. 5, Oct, 1984 ($1.25, Limited series, Baxter paper)
Eagle Comics

	GD25	FN65	NM94
1-5: 2000A.D.-r; Bolland-c/a			1.50

JUDGE DREDD: THE MEGAZINE
1991 - Present ($4.95, stiff-c, squarebound, 52 pgs.)
Fleetway/Quality

	GD25	FN65	NM94
1-3		2.00	5.00

JUDGEMENT DAY
Sept, 1993 - No. 8, Apr, 1994 ($2.95)
Lightning Comics

	GD25	FN65	NM94
1-($3.50)-Red foil-c		1.40	3.50
1-Gold Prism Edition		1.20	3.00
1-Purple-c Edition		1.20	3.00
2-8: 2-Polybagged with trading card. 7-Origin		1.20	3.00

JUDGE PARKER
Feb, 1956 - No. 2, 1956
Argo

	GD25	FN65	NM94
1-Newspaper strip reprints	5.35	16.00	32.00
2	4.00	11.00	22.00

JUDGMENT DAY
June, 1997 - No. 3, Oct, 1997 ($2.50, limited series)
Awesome Entertainment

	GD25	FN65	NM94
1 Alpha-Moore-s/Liefeld-c/a(p) flashback art by various in all		1.00	2.50
1-Variant cover by Dave Gibbons		1.00	2.50
2 Omega		1.00	2.50
2-Variant cover by Dave Gibbons		1.00	2.50
3 Final Judgment		1.00	2.50
3-Variant cover by Dave Gibbons		1.00	2.50

JUDGMENT PAWNS
Feb, 1997 ($2.95, one-shot)
Antarctic Press

	GD25	FN65	NM94
1			2.95

JUDO JOE
Aug, 1953 - No. 3, Dec, 1953 (Judo lessons in each issue)
Jay-Jay Corp.

	GD25	FN65	NM94
1-Drug ring story	7.50	22.50	45.00
2,3: 3-Hypo needle story	5.00	15.00	30.00

JUDOMASTER (Gun Master #84-89) (Also see Crisis on Infinite Earths, Sarge Steel #6 & Special War Series)
No. 89, May-June, 1966 - No. 98, Dec, 1967 (Two No. 89's)
Charlton Comics

	GD25	FN65	NM94
89-3rd app. Judomaster	2.60	7.80	26.00
90-98: 91-Sarge Steel begins. 93-Intro. Tiger	2.50	7.50	20.00
93,94,96,98 (Modern Comics reprint, 1977)		1.60	4.00

NOTE: ***Morisi** Thunderbolt #90. #91 has 1 pg. biography on writer/artist Frank McLoughlin.*

JUDY CANOVA (Formerly My Experience) (Stage, screen, radio)
No. 23, May, 1950 - No. 3, Sept, 1950
Fox Features Syndicate

	GD25	FN65	NM94
23(#1)-Wood-c,a(p)?	17.00	51.00	120.00
24-Wood-a(p)	17.00	51.00	125.00
3-Wood-c; Wood/Orlando-a	19.00	58.00	140.00

JUDY GARLAND (See Famous Stars)

JUDY JOINS THE WAVES
1951 (For U.S. Navy)
Toby Press

Juggernaut #1 © MEG

Jughead's Pal Hot Dog #2 © AP

Juke Box Comics #1 © FF

	GD25	FN65	NM94
nn	5.35	16.00	32.00

JUGGERNAUT (See X-Men)
Apr, 1997 ($2.95, one-shot)
Marvel Comics

	GD25	FN65	NM94
1-Kelly-s/ Rouleau-a			2.95

JUGHEAD (Formerly Archie's Pal...)
No. 127, Dec, 1965 - No. 352, June, 1987
Archie Publications

	GD25	FN65	NM94
127-130	2.50	7.50	20.00
131,133,135-160	1.85	5.50	15.00
132,134: 132-Shield-c; The Fly & Black Hood app.; Shield cameo. 134-Shield-c	2.50	7.50	20.00
161-200	1.10	3.30	9.00
201-240		2.40	6.00
241-300		1.60	4.00
301-352: 300-Anniversary issue; infinity-c		.80	2.00

JUGHEAD (2nd Series)(Becomes Archie's Pal Jughead Comics #46 on)
Aug, 1987 - No. 45, May, 1993 (.75/$1.00/$1.25)
Archie Enterprises

	GD25	FN65	NM94
1		1.60	4.00
2-10		1.20	3.00
11-45: 4-X-Mas issue. 17-Colan-c/a		.80	2.00

JUGHEAD AS CAPTAIN HERO (See Archie as Purehear the Powerful, Archie Giant Series Magazine #142 & Life With Archie)
Oct, 1966 - No. 7, Nov, 1967
Archie Publications

	GD25	FN65	NM94
1-Super hero parody	4.00	12.00	40.00
2	3.00	9.00	30.00
3-7	2.50	7.50	20.00

JUGHEAD JONES COMICS DIGEST, THE (...Magazine No. 10-64; Jughead Jones Digest Magazine #65)
June, 1977 - Present ($1.35/$1.50/$1.75, digest-size, 128 pgs.)
Archie Publications

	GD25	FN65	NM94
1-Neal Adams-a; Capt. Hero-r	1.85	5.50	15.00
2(9/77)-Neal Adams-a	1.50	4.50	12.00
3-10: 7-Origin Jaguar-r; N. Adams-a.	1.10	3.30	9.00
11-20: 13-r/1957 Jughead's Folly		2.40	6.00
21-50		1.60	4.00
51-70		1.20	3.00
71-94			1.50
95-98		.70	1.75

JUGHEAD'S BABY TALES
Spring, 1994 ($2.00, 52 pgs.)
Archie Comics

	GD25	FN65	NM94
1-Bound-in pull-out poster		1.20	3.00

JUGHEAD'S DINER
Apr, 1990 - No. 7, Apr, 1991 ($1.00)
Archie Comics

	GD25	FN65	NM94
1		1.20	3.00
2-7		.80	2.00

JUGHEAD'S DOUBLE DIGEST (...Magazine #5)
Oct, 1989 - Present ($2.25/$2.50/$2.75/$2.79, 256 pgs.)
Archie Comics

	GD25	FN65	NM94
1	1.00	2.80	7.00
2-10: 2,5-Capt. Hero stories		2.00	5.00
11-25		1.60	4.00
26-53		1.10	2.75

JUGHEAD'S EAT-OUT COMIC BOOK MAGAZINE (See Archie Giant Series Magazine No. 170)

JUGHEAD'S FANTASY
Aug, 1960 - No. 3, Dec, 1960
Archie Publications

	GD25	FN65	NM94
1	15.00	45.00	150.00
2	10.00	30.00	100.00
3	9.00	27.00	90.00

JUGHEAD'S FOLLY
1957 (36 pgs.)(one-shot)
Archie Publications (Close-Up)

	GD25	FN65	NM94
1-Jughead a la Elvis (Rare) (1st reference to Elvis in comics?)	39.00	117.00	350.00

JUGHEAD'S JOKES
Aug, 1967 - No. 78, Sept, 1982
(No. 1-8, 38 on: reg. size; No. 9-23: 68 pgs.; No. 24-37: 52 pgs.)
Archie Publications

	GD25	FN65	NM94
1	5.00	15.00	50.00
2	3.00	9.00	30.00
3-5	2.50	7.50	20.00
6-10: 9,10-68 pgs.	1.50	4.50	12.00
11-30: 11-23, 68 pgs. 24-30, 52 pgs.	1.10	3.30	9.00
31-37: 31-37, 52 pgs.	1.00	2.80	7.00
38-50		1.60	4.00
51-78		.80	2.00

JUGHEAD'S PAL HOT DOG (See Laugh #14 for 1st app.)
Jan, 1990 - No. 5, Oct, 1990 ($1.00)
Archie Comics

	GD25	FN65	NM94
1		1.20	3.00
2-5		.80	2.00

JUGHEAD'S SOUL FOOD
1979 (49 cents)
Spire Christian Comics (Fleming H. Revell Co.)

	GD25	FN65	NM94
nn		2.40	6.00

JUGHEAD'S TIME POLICE
July, 1990 - No. 6, May, 1991 ($1.00, bi-monthly)
Archie Comics

	GD25	FN65	NM94
1		1.20	3.00
2-6: Colan a-3-6p; c-3-6		.80	2.00

JUGHEAD WITH ARCHIE DIGEST (...Plus Betty & Veronica & Reggie Too No. 1,2; ...Magazine #33-?, 101-on; ...Comics Digest Mag.)
March, 1974 - Present (Digest Size; $1.00/$1.25/$1.35/$1.50/$1.75/$1.95)
Archie Publications

	GD25	FN65	NM94
1	3.50	10.50	35.00
2	2.50	7.50	22.00
3-10	1.50	4.50	12.00
11-20: Capt. Hero-r in #14-16; Pureheart the Powerful #18,21,22; Capt. Pureheart #17,19	1.10	3.30	9.00
21-50: 29-The Shield-r. 30-The Fly-r		2.40	6.00
51-100		1.60	4.00
101-121		1.20	3.00
122-137-($1.75)		.70	1.75
138-142-($1.95)			1.95

JUKE BOX COMICS
Mar, 1948 - No. 6, Jan, 1949
Famous Funnies

	GD25	FN65	NM94
1-Toth-c/a; Hollingsworth-a	36.00	108.00	290.00
2-Transvestism story	21.00	64.00	170.00
3-6: 3-Peggy Lee story. 4-Jimmy Durante line drawn-c. 6-Features Desi Arnaz plus Arnaz line drawn-c	15.50	47.00	125.00

JUMBO COMICS (Created by S.M. Iger)

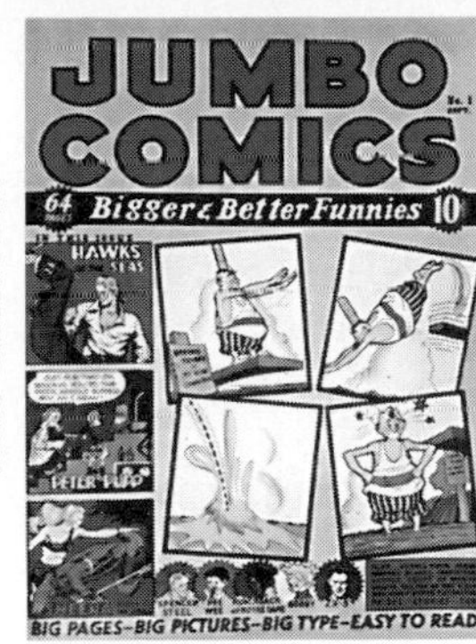

Jumbo Comics #1 © FH

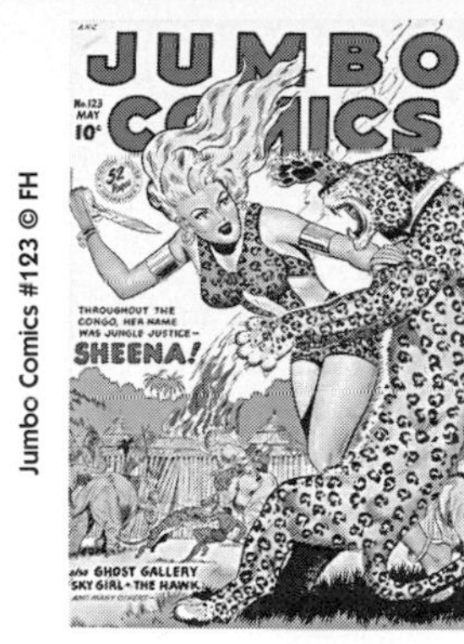

Jumbo Comics #123 © FH

Jungle Comics #30 © FH

GD25 FN65 NM94 | GD25 FN65 NM94

Sept, 1938 - No. 167, Mar, 1953 (No. 1-3: 68 pgs.; No. 4-8: 52 pgs.)
(No. 1-8 oversized-10-1/2x14-1/2"; black & white)
Fiction House Magazines (Real Adv. Publ. Co.) GD25 FN65 VF82

1-(Rare)-Sheena Queen of the Jungle(1st app.) by Meskin, Hawks of the Seas (The Hawk #10 on; see Feature Funnies #3) by Eisner, The Hunchback by Dick Briefer (ends #8), Wilton of the West (ends #24), Inspector Dayton (ends #67) & ZX-5 (ends #140) begin; 1st comic art by Jack Kirby (Count of Monte Cristo & Wilton of the West); Mickey Mouse appears (1 panel) with brief biography of Walt Disney; 1st app. Peter Pupp by Bob Kane. Note: Sheena was created by Iger for publication in England as a newspaper strip. The early issues of Jumbo contain Sheena strip-r; mutiple panel-c 1,2,7 — 1500.00 4500.00 16,500.00
(Estimated up to 45 total copies exist, 1 in NM/Mint)
2-(Rare)-Origin Sheena. Diary of Dr. Hayward by Kirby (also #3) plus 2 other stories; contains strip from Universal Film featuring Edgar Bergen & Charlie McCarthy plus-c (preview of film) — 530.00 1590.00 5300.00
3-Last Kirby issue — 370.00 1110.00 3700.00
4-(Scarce)-Origin The Hawk by Eisner; Wilton of the West by Fine (ends #14)(1st comic work); Count of Monte Cristo by Fine (ends #15); The Diary of Dr. Hayward by Fine (cont'd #8,9) — 350.00 1050.00 3500.00
5-Christmas-c — 290.00 870.00 2900.00
6-8-Last B&W issue. #8 was a 1939 N. Y. World's Fair Special Edition; Frank Buck's Jungleland story — 250.00 750.00 2500.00
9-Stuart Taylor begins by Fine (ends #140); Fine-c; 1st color issue (8-9/39)-1st Sheena (jungle) cover; 8-1/4x10-1/4" (oversized in width only) — 233.00 700.00 2100.00

GD25 FN65 NM94

10-Regular size 68 pg. issues begin; Sheena dons new costume w/ origin costume; Stuart Taylor sci/fi-c; classic Lou Fine-c. — 133.00 400.00 1200.00
11-13: 12-The Hawk-c by Eisner. 13-Eisner-c — 103.00 309.00 925.00
14-Intro. Lightning (super-hero) on-c only — 108.00 324.00 975.00
15,17-20: 15-1st Lightning story and begins, ends #41. 17-Lightning part-c — 64.00 192.00 575.00
16-Lightning-c — 81.00 243.00 725.00
21-30: 22-1st Tom, Dick & Harry; origin The Hawk retold. 25-Midnight the Black Stallion begins, ends #65 — 50.00 150.00 450.00
31-40: 31-(9/41)-1st app. Mars God of War in Stuart Taylor story (see Planet Comics #15. 35-Shows V2#11 (correct number does not appear) — 42.00 126.00 375.00
41-50: 42-Ghost Gallery begins, ends #167 — 36.00 108.00 300.00
51-60: 52-Last Tom, Dick & Harry — 30.00 90.00 240.00
61-70: 68-Sky Girl begins, ends #130; not in #79 — 23.00 69.00 185.00
71-93,95-99: 89-ZX5 becomes a private eye. — 17.50 53.00 140.00
94--Used in Love and Death by Legman — 19.00 56.00 150.00
100 — 18.00 54.00 145.00
101-140,150-158 — 12.00 38.00 100.00
141-149-Two Sheena stories. 141-Long Bow, Indian Boy begins, ends #160 — 12.00 38.00 100.00
155-Used in **POP**, pg. 98 — 12.00 38.00 100.00
159-163: Space Scouts serial in all. 160-Last jungle-c (6/52). 161-Ghost Gallery covers begin, end #167. 163-Suicide Smith app. — 11.30 34.00 90.00
164-The Star Pirate begins, ends #165 — 11.30 34.00 90.00
165-167: 165,167-Space Rangers app. — 11.30 34.00 90.00

NOTE: *Bondage covers, negligee panels, torture, etc. are common in this series. Hawks of the Seas, Inspector Dayton, Spies in Action, Sports Shorts, & Uncle Otto by Eisner, #1-7. Hawk by* ***Eisner****-#10-15.* ***Eisner*** *c-1-8, 12-14. 1pg. Patsy pin-ups in 92-97, 99-101. Sheena by* ***Meskin****-#1, 4; by* ***Powell****-#2, 3, 5-28;* ***Powell*** *c-14, 16, 17, 19.* ***Powell/Eisner*** *c-15. Sky Girl by* ***Matt Baker****-#69-78, 80-130. ZX-5 & Ghost Gallery by* ***Kamen****-#90-130.* ***Bailey*** *a-3-8.* ***Briefer*** *a-1-8, 10.* ***Fine*** *a-14; c-9-11.* ***Kamen*** *a-101, 105, 123, 132; c-105, 121-145.* ***Bob Kane*** *a-1-8.* ***Whitman*** *c-146-167(most). Jungle c-9, 13, 15, 17 on.*

JUMPING JACKS PRESENTS THE WHIZ KIDS
1978 (In 3-D) with glasses (4 pgs.)
Jumping Jacks Stores giveaway

nn — 1.00

JUNGLE ACTION
Oct, 1954 - No. 6, Aug, 1955
Atlas Comics (IPC)

1-Leopard Girl begins by Al Hartley (#1,3); Jungle Boy by Forte; Maneely-a in all — 28.00 83.00 220.00
2-(3-D effect cover) — 30.00 90.00 240.00
3-6: 3-Last precode (2/55) — 17.50 53.00 140.00

NOTE: ***Maneely*** *c-1, 2, 5, 6.* ***Romita*** *a-3, 6.* ***Shores*** *a-3, 6; c-3, 4?.*

JUNGLE ACTION (...& Black Panther #18-21?)
Oct, 1972 - No. 24, Nov, 1976
Marvel Comics Group

1-Lorna, Jann-r (All reprints in 1-4) — 1.50 4.50 12.00
2-4 — 2.40 6.00
5-Black Panther begins (r- Avengers #62)— 2.00 6.00 16.00
6-10: 6-new stories begin; 8-Origin Black Panther. 9-Contains pull-out centerfold ad by Mark Jewelers — 2.40 6.00
11-18: — 1.60 4.00
19-21,23,24: 19-23-KKK x-over. 23-r/#22. 24-1st Wind Eagle; sty contd in Marvel Premiere #51-#53 — 1.20 3.00
22-(Regular 25¢ edition)(7/76) — 1.20 3.00
22-(30¢-c, limited distribution) — 1.50 4.50 12.00

NOTE: ***Buckler*** *a-6-9p, 22; c-8p, 12p.* ***Buscema*** *a-5p; c-22.* ***Byrne*** *c-23.* ***Gil Kane*** *a-8p; c-2, 4, 10p, 11p, 13-17, 19, 24.* ***Kirby*** *c-18.* ***Maneely*** *r-1.* ***Russell*** *a-13i.* ***Starlin*** *c-3p.*

JUNGLE ADVENTURES
1963 - 1964 (Reprints)
Super Comics

10,12,15: 10-r/Terrors of the Jungle #4 & #10(Rulah). 12-r/Zoot #14(Rulah).15-r/Kaanga from Jungle #152 & Tiger Girl — 2.80 8.40 28.00
17-All Jo-Jo reprints — 2.80 8.40 28.00
18-Reprints/White Princess of the Jungle #1; no Kinstler-a; origin of both White Princess & Cap'n Courage — 2.80 8.40 28.00

JUNGLE ADVENTURES
Mar, 1971 - No. 3, June, 1971 (25¢, 52 pgs.)
Skywald Comics

1-Zangar origin; reprints of Jo-Jo, Blue Gorilla(origin)/White Princess #3, Kinstler-r/White Princess #2 — 1.50 4.50 12.00
2-Zangar, Sheena-r/Sheena #17 & Jumbo #162, Jo-Jo, origin Slave Girl Princess-r — 1.10 3.30 9.00
3-Zangar, Jo-Jo, White Princess-r — 1.10 3.30 9.00

JUNGLE BOOK (See King Louie and Mowgli, Movie Comics, Mowgli..., Walt Disney Showcase #45 & Walt Disney's The Jungle Book)

JUNGLE CAT (Disney)
No. 1136, Sept-Nov, 1960 (one shot)
Dell Publishing Co.

Four Color 1136-Movie, photo-c — 5.50 16.50 60.00

JUNGLE COMICS
1/40 - No. 157, 3/53; No. 158, Spr, 1953 - No. 163, Summer, 1954
Fiction House Magazines

1-Origin The White Panther, Kaanga, Lord of the Jungle, Tabu, Wizard of the Jungle; Wambi, the Jungle Boy, Camilla & Capt. Terry Thunder begin (all 1st app.). Lou Fine-c — 340.00 102.00 3400.00
2-Fantomah, Mystery Woman of the Jungle begins, ends #51; The Red Panther begins, ends #26 — 122.00 366.00 1100.00
3,4 — 106.00 318.00 950.00
5-Classic Eisner-c — 111.00 333.00 1000.00
6-10: 7,8-Powell-c — 60.00 180.00 540.00
11-20: 13-Tuska-c — 43.00 129.00 385.00
21-30: 25-Shows V2#1 (correct number does not appear). #27-New origin Fantomah, Daughter of the Pharoahs; Camilla dons new costume — 37.00 110.00 330.00
31-40 — 29.00 86.00 230.00

Jungle Comics #82 © FH

Jungle Tales #5 © ATLAS

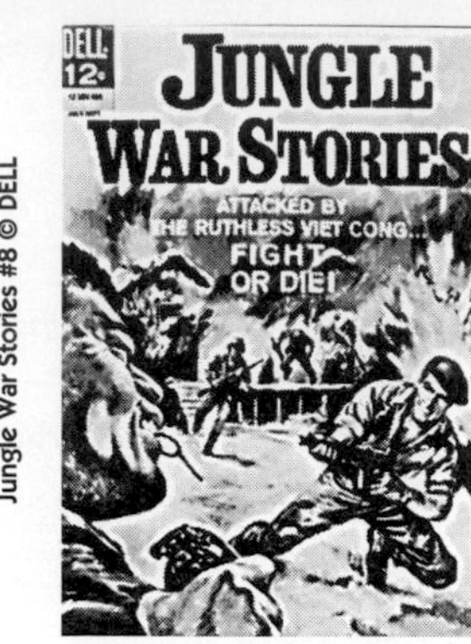

Jungle War Stories #8 © DELL

	GD25	FN65	NM94
41,43-50	25.00	75.00	200.00
42-Kaanga by Crandall, 12 pgs.	28.00	83.00	220.00
51-60	23.00	69.00	185.00
61-70: 67-Cover swipes Crandall splash pg. in #42	19.00	56.00	150.00
71-80: 79-New origin Tabu	17.00	51.00	135.00
81-97,99,101-110	15.00	45.00	120.00
98-Used in **SOTI**, pg. 185 & illo "In ordinary comic books, there are pictures within pictures for children who know how to look;" used by N.Y. Legis. Comm.	27.00	81.00	215.00
100	19.00	56.00	150.00
111-163: 104-In Camilla story villain is Dr. Wertham. 118-Clyde Beatty app. 135-Desert Panther begins in Terry Thunder (origin), not in #137; ends (dies) #138. 139-Last 52 pg. issue. 141-Last Tabu. 143,145-Used in **POP**, pg. 99. 151-Last Camilla & Terry Thunder. 152-Tiger Girl begins. 158-Last Wambi; Sheena app.	12.00	38.00	100.00
I.W. Reprint #1,9: 1-r/? 9-r/#151	2.50	7.50	24.00

NOTE: *Bondage covers, negligee panels, torture, etc. are common to this series. Camilla by* ***Fran Hopper****-#70-92; by* ***Baker****-#69, 100-113, 115, 116; by* ***Lubbers****-#97-99 by* ***Tuska****-#63, 65. Kaanga by* ***John Celardo****-#80-113; by* ***Larsen****-#71, 75-79; by* ***Moreira****-#58, 60, 61, 63-70, 72-74; by* ***Tuska****-#37, 62; by* ***Whitman****-#114-163. Tabu by* ***Larsen****-#59-75, 82-92; by* ***Whitman****-#93-115. Terry Thunder by* ***Hopper****-#71, 72; by* ***Celardo****-#78, 79; by* ***Lubbers****-#80-85. Tiger Girl-r by* ***Baker****-#152, 153, 155-157, 159. Wambi by* ***Baker****-#62-67, 74.* ***Astarita*** *c-45, 46.* ***Celardo*** *a-78; c-98-113.* ***Crandall*** *c-67 from splash pg.* ***Eisner*** *c-2, 5, 6.* ***Fine*** *c-1.* ***Larsen*** *a-65, 66, 71, 72, 74, 75, 79, 83, 84, 87-90.* ***Moriera*** *c-43, 44.* ***Morisi*** *a-51.* ***Powell*** *c-7, 8.* ***Sultan*** *c-3, 4.* ***Tuska*** *c-13.* ***Whitman*** *c-132-163(most).* ***Zolnerowich*** *c-11, 12, 18-41.*

JUNGLE COMICS
May, 1988 - No.4? ($2.00, B&W/color)
Blackthorne Publishing

	GD25	FN65	NM94
1-4: 1-Dave Stevens-c; B. Jones scripts in all. 2-B&W-a begins		.80	2.00

JUNGLE GIRL (See Lorna, the...)

JUNGLE GIRL (Nyoka, Jungle Girl No. 2 on)
Fall, 1942 (one-shot)(No month listed)
Fawcett Publications

	GD25	FN65	NM94
1-Bondage-c; photo of Kay Aldridge who played Nyoka in movie serial app. on-c. Adaptation of the classic Republic movie serial Perils of Nyoka. 1st comic to devote entire contents to a movie serial adaptation	83.00	250.00	750.00

JUNGLE GIRLS
1989 - No. 16, 1993 (B&W)
AC Comics

	GD25	FN65	NM94
1-($1.95)-New story & "good girl" reprints		.80	2.00
2-($2.25)-New story & "good girl" reprints		.90	2.25
3-16: 3,4,10,13-16-New story & g.g. reprints. 5-9,11,12-All g.g. reprints (Baker, Powell, Lubbers, others)		1.00	2.50

JUNGLE JIM (Also see Ace Comics)
No. 11, Jan, 1949 - No. 20, Apr, 1951
Standard Comics (Best Books)

	GD25	FN65	NM94
11	7.15	21.50	50.00
12-20	4.25	13.00	28.00

JUNGLE JIM
No. 490, 8/53 - No. 1020, 8-10/59 (Painted-c)
Dell Publishing Co.

	GD25	FN65	NM94
Four Color 490(#1)	5.50	16.50	60.00
Four Color 565(#2, 6/54)	2.75	8.00	30.00
3(10-12/54)-5	2.50	7.50	28.00
6-19(1-3/59)	2.25	6.75	25.00
Four Color 1020(#20)	2.25	6.75	25.00

JUNGLE JIM
No. 5, Dec, 1967
King Features Syndicate

	GD25	FN65	NM94
5-Reprints Dell #5; Wood-c	1.50	4.50	12.00

JUNGLE JIM (Continued from Dell series)
No. 22, Feb, 1969 - No. 28, Feb, 1970 (#21 was an overseas edition only)
Charlton Comics

	GD25	FN65	NM94
22-Dan Flagg begins; Ditko/Wood-a	2.50	7.50	25.00
23-26: 23-Last Dan Flagg; Howard-c. 24-Jungle People begin	2.00	6.00	16.00
27,28: 27-Ditko/Howard-a. 28-Ditko-a	2.50	7.50	20.00

NOTE: *Ditko cover of #22 reprints story panels*

JUNGLE JO
Mar, 1950 - No. 6, Mar, 1951
Fox Feature Syndicate (Hero Books)

	GD25	FN65	NM94
nn-Jo-Jo blanked out, leaving Congo King; came out after Jo-Jo #29 (intended as Jo-Jo #30?)	34.00	101.00	250.00
1-Tangi begins; part Wood-a	39.00	118.00	290.00
2	29.00	88.00	220.00
3-6	29.00	86.00	210.00

JUNGLE LIL (Dorothy Lamour #2 on; also see Feature Stories Magazine)
April, 1950
Fox Feature Syndicate (Hero Books)

	GD25	FN65	NM94
1	30.00	90.00	220.00

JUNGLE TALES (Jann of the Jungle No. 8 on)
Sept, 1954 - No. 7, Sept, 1955
Atlas Comics (CSI)

	GD25	FN65	NM94
1-Jann of the Jungle	30.00	90.00	220.00
2-7: 3-Last precode (1/55)	21.00	64.00	150.00

NOTE: ***Heath*** *c-5.* ***Heck*** *a-6, 7.* ***Maneely*** *a-2; c-1, 3.* ***Shores*** *a-5-7; c-4, 6.* ***Tuska*** *a-2.*

JUNGLE TALES OF TARZAN
Dec, 1964 - No. 4, July, 1965
Charlton Comics

	GD25	FN65	NM94
1	4.00	12.00	40.00
2-4	3.00	9.00	30.00

NOTE: ***Giordano*** *c-3p.* ***Glanzman*** *a-1-3.* ***Montes/Bache*** *a-4.*

JUNGLE TERROR (See Harvey Comics Hits No. 54)

JUNGLE THRILLS (Formerly Sports Thrills; Terrors of the Jungle #17 on)
No. 16, Feb, 1952; Dec, 1953; No. 7, 1954
Star Publications

	GD25	FN65	NM94
16-Phantom Lady & Rulah story-reprint/All Top No. 15; used in **POP**, pg. 98,99; L. B. Cole-c	40.00	120.00	350.00
3-D 1(12/53, 25¢)-Came w/glasses; Jungle Lil & Jungle Jo appear; L. B. Cole-c	43.00	130.00	375.00
7-Titled 'Picture Scope Jungle Adventures;' (1954, 36 pgs, 15¢)-3-D effect c/stories; story & coloring book; Disbrow-a/script; L.B. Cole-c	40.00	120.00	340.00

JUNGLE TWINS, THE (Tono & Kono)
Apr, 1972 - No. 17, Nov, 1975; No. 18, May, 1982
Gold Key/Whitman No. 18

	GD25	FN65	NM94
1	1.10	3.30	9.00
2-5		2.00	5.00
6-18: 18-Reprints		1.20	3.00

NOTE: *UFO c/story No. 13. Painted-c No. 1-17.* ***Spiegle*** *c-18.*

JUNGLE WAR STORIES (Guerrilla War No. 12 on)
July-Sept, 1962 - No. 11, Apr-June, 1965 (Painted-c)
Dell Publishing Co.

	GD25	FN65	NM94
01-384-209 (#1)	2.50	7.50	20.00
2-11	1.75	5.25	14.00

JUNIE PROM (Also see Dexter Comics)
Winter, 1947-48 - No. 7, Aug, 1949
Dearfield Publishing Co.

	GD25	FN65	NM94
1-Teen-age	9.50	28.00	75.00

Junior Miss #34 © MEG

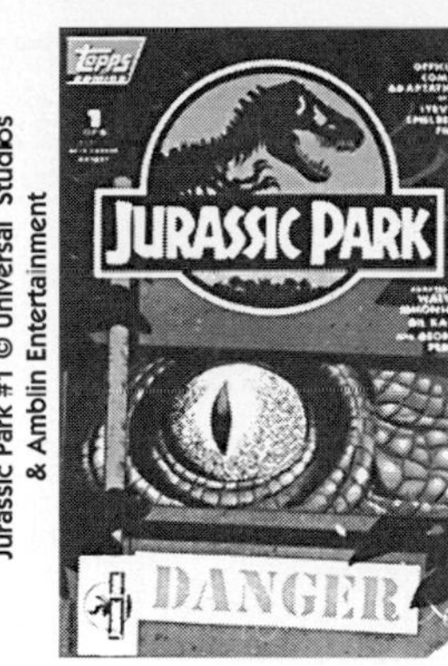

Jurassic Park #1 © Universal Studios & Amblin Entertainment

Justice #1 © MEG

	GD25	FN65	NM94
2	5.70	17.00	40.00
3-7	4.25	13.00	28.00

JUNIOR CARROT PATROL (Jr. Carrot Patrol #2)
May, 1989; No. 2, Nov, 1990 ($2.00, B&W)
Dark Horse Comics

	GD25	FN65	NM94
1,2-Flaming Carrot spin-off. 1-Bob Burden-c(i)		.80	2.00

JUNIOR COMICS (Formerly Li'l Pan; becomes Western Outlaws with #17)
No. 9, Sept, 1947 - No. 16, July, 1948
Fox Feature Syndicate

	GD25	FN65	NM94
9-Feldstein-c/a; headlights-c	62.00	187.00	540.00
10-16-Feldstein-c/a; headlights-c on all	56.00	170.00	475.00

JUNIOR FUNNIES (Formerly Tiny Tot Funnies No. 9)
No. 10, Aug, 1951 - No. 13, Feb, 1952
Harvey Publications (King Features Synd.)

	GD25	FN65	NM94
10-Partial reprints in all; Blondie, Dagwood, Daisy, Henry, Popeye, Felix, Katzenjammer Kids	3.60	9.00	18.00
11-13	3.20	8.00	16.00

JUNIOR HOPP COMICS
Feb, 1952 - No. 3, July, 1952
Stanmor Publ.

	GD25	FN65	NM94
1-Teenage humor	7.15	21.50	50.00
2,3: 3-Dave Berg-a	4.25	13.00	28.00

JUNIOR MEDICS OF AMERICA, THE
No. 1359, 1957 (15¢)
E. R. Squire & Sons

	GD25	FN65	NM94
1359	2.80	7.00	14.00

JUNIOR MISS
Winter, 1944; No. 24, Apr, 1947 - No. 39, Aug, 1950
Timely/Marvel Comics (CnPC)

	GD25	FN65	NM94
1-Frank Sinatra & June Allyson life story	21.00	64.00	160.00
24-Formerly The Human Torch #23?	10.00	30.00	65.00
25-38: 29,31,34-Cindy-c/stories (others?)	5.70	17.00	35.00
39-Kurtzman-a	7.15	21.50	50.00

NOTE: *Painted-c 35-37. 35, 37-all romance. 36, 38-mostly teen humor.*

JUNIOR PARTNERS (Formerly Oral Roberts' True Stories)
No. 120, Aug, 1959 - V3#12, Dec, 1961
Oral Roberts Evangelistic Assn.

	GD25	FN65	NM94
120(#1)	3.20	9.60	32.00
2(9/59)	2.50	7.50	22.00
3-12(7/60)	1.75	5.25	14.00
V2#1(8/60)-5(12/60)	1.10	3.30	9.00
V3#1(1/61)-12	1.00	2.80	7.00

JUNIOR TREASURY (See Dell Junior...)

JUNIOR WOODCHUCKS GUIDE (Walt Disney's...)
1973 (8-3/4"x5-3/4", 214 pgs., hardcover)
Danbury Press

	GD25	FN65	NM94
nn-Illustrated text based on the long-standing J.W. Guide used by Donald Duck's nephews Huey, Dewey & Louie by Carl Barks. The guidebook was a popular plot devise to enable the nephews to solve problems facing their uncle or Scrooge McDuck (scarce)	2.50	7.50	25.00

JUNIOR WOODCHUCKS LIMITED SERIES (Walt Disney's...)
July, 1991 - No. 4, Oct, 1991 ($1.50, limited series; new & reprint-a)
W. D. Publications (Disney)

	GD25	FN65	NM94
1-4: 1-The Beagle Boys app.; Barks-r			1.50

JUNIOR WOODCHUCKS (See Huey, Dewey & Louie...)

JUNK CULTURE
July, 1997 - No. 2, Aug, 1997 ($2.50, limited series)
DC Comics (Vertigo)

	GD25	FN65	NM94
1,2: Ted McKeever-s/a in all		1.00	2.50

JURASSIC JANE
Apr, 1997 - Present ($3.00, B&W)
London Night Studios

	GD25	FN65	NM94
1-8			3.00
1-8-($6.00)-Variant nude-c		2.40	6.00

JURASSIC PARK
6/93 - No. 4, 8/93; #5, 10/94 - #10, 2/95
Topps Comics

	GD25	FN65	NM94
1-($2.50)-Newsstand Edition; Kane/Perez-a in all; 1-4: movie adaptation		1.20	3.00
1-($2.95)-Collector's Ed.; polybagged w/3 cards		1.60	4.00
1-Amberchrome Edition w/no price or ads	1.00	2.80	7.00
2-4-($2.50)-Newsstand Edition		1.00	2.50
2,3-($2.95)-Collector's Ed.; polybagged w/3 cards		1.20	3.00
4-($2.95)-Collector's Ed.; polybagged w/1 of 4 different action hologram trading card; Gil Kane/Perez-a		1.20	3.00
5-10: 5-becomes Advs. of		.80	2.00
Annual 1 ($3.95, 5/95)		1.60	4.00
Trade paperback (1993, $9.95)-r/#1-4; bagged w/#0	1.25	3.75	10.00

JURASSIC PARK: RAPTOR
Nov, 1993 - No. 2, Dec, 1993 ($2.95, limited series)
Topps Comics

	GD25	FN65	NM94
1,2: 1-Bagged w/3 trading cards & Zorro #0; Golden c-1,2		1.20	3.00

JURASSIC PARK: RAPTORS ATTACK
Mar, 1994 - No. 4, June, 1994 ($2.50, limited series)
Topps Comics

	GD25	FN65	NM94
1-4-Michael Golden-c/frontispiece		1.00	2.50

JURASSIC PARK: RAPTORS HIJACK
July, 1994 - No. 4, Oct, 1994 ($2.50, limited series)
Topps Comics

	GD25	FN65	NM94
1-4: Michael Golden-c/front piece		1.00	2.50

JUSTICE
Nov, 1986 - No. 32, June, 1989
Marvel Comics Group (New Universe)

	GD25	FN65	NM94
1-32: 26-32-$1.50-c			1.00

JUSTICE COMICS (Formerly Wacky Duck; Tales of Justice #53 on)
No. 7, Fall/47 - No. 9, 6/48; No. 4, 8/48 - No. 52, 3/55
Marvel/Atlas Comics (NPP 7-9,4-19/CnPC 20-23/MjMC 24-38/Male 39-52

	GD25	FN65	NM94
7(#1, 1947)	21.00	64.00	160.00
8(#2)-Kurtzman-a "Giggles 'n' Grins" (3)	14.00	43.00	100.00
9(#3, 6/48)	13.00	39.00	95.00
4	11.30	34.00	90.00
5-9: 8-Anti-Wertham editorial	10.00	30.00	65.00
10-15-Photo-c	9.00	27.00	60.00
16-30	7.00	21.00	45.00
31-40,42-52: 35-Gene Colan-a. 48-Last precode; Pakula & Tuska-a.	6.35	19.00	40.00
41-Electrocution-c	12.00	36.00	90.00

NOTE: ***Heath** a-24. **Maneely** c-44, 52. **Pakula** a-43, 45, 48. **Louis Ravielli** a-39. **Robinson** a-22, 25, 41. **Shores** c-7(#1), 8(#2)? **Tuska** a-48. **Wildey** a-52.*

JUSTICE: FOUR BALANCE
Sept, 1994 - No. 4, Dec, 1994 ($1.75, limited series)
Marvel Comics

	GD25	FN65	NM94
1-4: 1-Thing & Firestar app.		.70	1.75

JUSTICE, INC. (The Avenger) (Pulp)
May-June, 1975 - No. 4, Nov-Dec, 1975
National Periodical Publications

	GD25	FN65	NM94
1-McWilliams-a, Kubert-c; origin		2.00	5.00

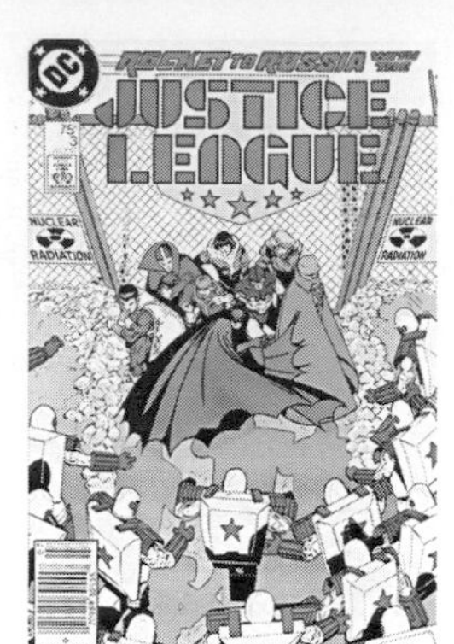

Justice League #3 © DC

Justice League: A Midsummer's Nightmare #3 © DC

Justice League of America #30 © DC

GD25 FN65 NM94

2-4: 2-4-Kirby-a(p), c-2,3p. 4-Kubert-c 1.60 4.00
NOTE: *Adapted from Kenneth Robeson novel, creator of Doc Savage.*

JUSTICE, INC. (Pulp)
1989 - No. 2, 1989 ($3.95, 52 pgs., squarebound, mature)
DC Comics

1,2: Re-intro The Avenger; Andrew Helfer scripts & Kyle Baker-c/a 1.60 4.00

JUSTICE LEAGUE (...International #7-25; ...America #26 on)
May, 1987 - No. 113, Aug, 1996 (Also see Legends #6)
DC Comics

1-Batman, Green Lantern (Guy Gardner), Blue Beetle, Mr. Miracle, Capt. Marvel & Martian Manhunter begin 1.60 4.00
2 1.20 3.00
3-Regular-c (white background) .80 2.00
3-Limited-c (yellow background, Superman logo) 2.50 7.50 20.00
4-6: 4-Booster Gold joins. 5-Origin Gray Man; Batman vs. Guy Gardner; Creeper app. 1.00 2.50
7-($1.25, 52 pgs.)-Capt. Marvel & Dr. Fate resign; Capt. Atom & Rocket Red join 1.20 2.00
8-10: 9,10-Millennium x-over 1.50
11-23: 16-Bruce Wayne-c/story. 18-21-Lobo app. 1.25
24-($1.50)-1st app. Justice League Europe .70 1.75
25-49,51-62: 31,32-Justice League Europe x-over. 58-Lobo app. 61-New team begins; swipes-c to JLA #1(10-11/60). 62-Last $1.00-c 1.25
50-($1.75, 52 pgs.) .70 1.75
63-68,72-82: 80-Intro new Booster Gold. 82,83-Guy Gardner-c/stories 1.25
69-Doomsday tie-in; takes place between Superman: The Man of Steel #18 & Superman #74 2.00 5.00
69,70-2nd printings 1.25
70-Funeral for a Friend part 1; red 3/4 outer-c 1.20 3.00
70-Newsstand version w/o outer-c 1.50
71-Direct sales version w/black outer-c .80 2.00
71-Newsstand version w/o outer-c 1.25
83-92: 83-$1.50-c begins. 92-(9/94)-Zero Hour x-over; Triumph app 1.50
0-(10/94)-New team begins (Hawkman, Wonder Woman, Metamorpho, Flash, Nuklon, Crimson Fox, Obsidian & Fire) 1.50
93-99: 93-(11/94) 1.50
100 ($3.95)-Foil-c; 52 pgs. 1.60 4.00
100 ($2.95)-Newstand 1.20 3.00
101-113: 101-$1.75-c begins. 113-Flash, Green Lantern & Hawkman app .70 1.75
Annual 1-5 (1987-1991): 2-Joker-c/story; Batman cameo. 5-Armageddon 2001 x-over; Silver ink 2nd printing .80 2.00
Annual 6,7 (1992,1993, $2.50, 68 pgs.):7-Bloodlines x-over 1.00 2.50
Annual 8 (1994, $2.95, 68 pgs.)-Elseworlds story 1.20 3.00
Annual 9 (1995, $3.50)-Year One story 1.40 3.50
Special 1 (1990, $1.50, 52 pgs.)-Giffen plots 1.50
Special 2 (1991, $2.95, 52 pgs.)-Staton-a(p) 1.20 3.00
Spectacular 1 (1992, $1.50, 52 pgs.)-Intro new JLI & JLE teams; ties into JLI #61 & JLE #37 1.50
A New Beginning Trade Paperback (1989, $12.95)-r/#1-7 1.60 4.85 13.00
NOTE: ***Anderson*** *c-61i.* ***Austin*** *a-1i, 60i; c-1i.* ***Giffen*** *a-13; c-21p.* ***Guice*** *a-62i.* ***Maguire*** *a-1-12, 16-19, 22, 23.* ***Russell*** *a-Annual 1i; c-54i.* ***Willingham*** *a-30p, Annual 2.*

JUSTICE LEAGUE: A MIDSUMMER'S NIGHTMARE
Sept, 1996 - No. 3, Nov, 1996 ($2.95, limited series, 38 pgs.)
DC Comics

1-3: Re-establishes Superman, Batman, Green Lantern, The Martian Manhunter, Flash, Aquaman & Wonder Woman as the Justice League; Mark Waid & Fabian Nicieza co-scripts; Jeff Johnson & Darick Robertson-a(p); Kevin Maguire-c. 2.00 5.00
TPB-(1997, $8.95) r/1-3 8.95

JUSTICE LEAGUE EUROPE (Justice League International #51 on)
Apr, 1989 - No. 68, Sept., 1994 (75¢/ $1.00/$1.25/$1.50)
DC Comics

1-Giffen plots in all, breakdowns in #1-8,13-30; Justice League #1-c/swipe .80 2.00
2-49,51-57: 5-Begin $1.00-c. 7-9-Batman app. 7,8-JLA x-over. 8,9-Superman app. 12-Metal Men app. 20-22-Rogers-c/a(p). 33,34-Lobo vs. Despero. 37-New team begins; swipes-c to JLA #9; see JLA Spectacular. 1.25
50-($2.50, 68 pgs.)-Battles Sonar 1.00 2.50
58-68: 58-$1.50-c begins. 68-Zero Hour x-over; Triumph joins Justice League Task Force (See JLTF #17) 1.50
Annual 1 (1990, $2.00, 68 pgs.)-Return of the Global Guardians; Giffen plots/ breakdowns .80 2.00
Annual 2 (1991, $2.00, 68pgs.)-Armageddon 2001; Giffen-a(p); Rogers-a(p); Golden-a(i) .80 2.00
Annual 3 (1992, $2.50, 68 pgs.)-Eclipso app. 1.00 2.50
Annual 4 (1993, $2.50, 68 pgs.)-Intro Lionheart 1.00 2.50
Annual 5 (1994, $2.95)-Elseworlds story 1.20 3.00
NOTE: ***Phil Jimenez*** *a-68p.* ***Rogers*** *c/a-20-22.* ***Sears*** *a-1-12, 14-19, 23-29; c-1-10, 12, 14-19, 23-29.*

JUSTICE LEAGUE INTERNATIONAL (See Justice League Europe)

JUSTICE LEAGUE OF AMERICA (See Brave & the Bold #28-30, Mystery In Space #75 & Official... Index)
Oct-Nov, 1960 - No. 261, Apr, 1987 (#91-99,139-157: 52 pgs.)
National Periodical Publ./DC Comics GD25 FN65 VF82 NM94

1-(10-11/60)-Origin & 1st app. Despero; Aquaman, Batman, Flash, Green Lantern, J'onn J'onzz, Superman & Wonder Woman continue from Brave and the Bold 200.00 600.00 1400.00 3000.00

GD25 FN65 NM94

2 62.00 186.00 740.00
3-Origin/1st app. Kanjar Ro (see Mystery in Space #75)(scarce in high grade due to black-c) 52.00 156.00 620.00
4-Green Arrow joins JLA 38.00 114.00 420.00
5-Origin & 1st app. Dr. Destiny 31.00 93.00 320.00
6-8,10: 6-Origin & 1st app. Prof. Amos Fortune. 7-(10-11/61)-Last 10¢ issue. 10-(3/62)-Origin & 1st app. Felix Faust; 1st app. Lord of Time. 27.00 82.00 275.00
9-(2/62)-Origin JLA (1st origin) 38.00 114.00 420.00
11-15: 12-(6/62)-Origin & 1st app. Dr. Light. 13-(8/62)-Speedy app. 14-(9/62)-Atom joins JLA. 19.00 57.00 190.00
16-20: 17-Adam Strange flashback 16.00 48.00 160.00
21-(8/63)-"Crisis on Earth-One"; re-intro. of JSA in this title (see Flash #129) (1st S.A. app. Hourman & Dr. Fate) 31.00 93.00 310.00
22- "Crisis on Earth-Two"; JSA x-over (story continued from #21) 29.00 87.00 290.00
23-28: 24-Adam Strange app. 28-Robin app. 9.50 28.50 95.00
29-JSA x-over; 1st S.A. app. Starman; "Crisis on Earth-Three" 13.00 39.00 130.00
30-JSA x-over 10.50 32.00 105.00
31-Hawkman joins JLA, Hawkgirl cameo (11/64) 8.50 25.50 85.00
32-Intro & Origin Brain Storm 6.00 18.00 60.00
33,35,36,40,41: 40-3rd S.A. Penguin app. 41-Intro & origin The Key 5.00 15.00 50.00
34-Joker-c/story 5.50 16.50 55.00
37,38-JSA x-over (1st S.A. app. Mr. Terrific #37). 37-1st S.A. app. Mr. Terrific; Batman cameo. 38-"Crisis on Earth-A" 8.00 24.00 80.00
39-Giant G-16; r/B&B #28,30 & JLA #5 9.00 27.00 90.00
42-45: 42-Metamorpho app. 43-Intro. Royal Flush Gang 4.00 12.00 40.00
46-JSA x-over; 1st S.A. app. Sandman; 3rd S.A. app. of G.A. Spectre (8/66) 9.00 27.00 90.00
47-JSA x-over; 4th S.A. app of G.A. Spectre. 4.50 13.50 45.00

Justice League of America #94 © DC

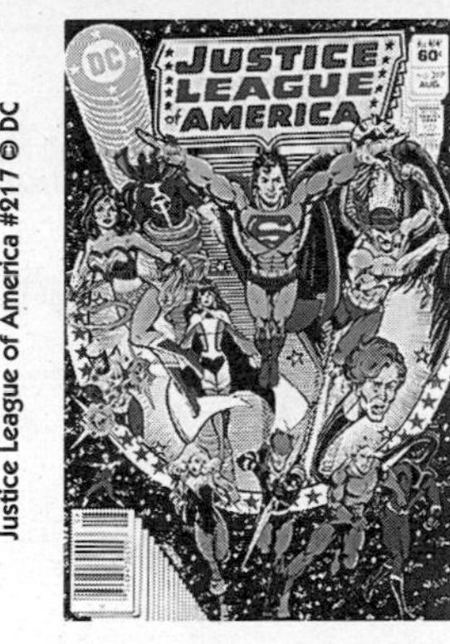

Justice League of America #217 © DC

Justice League Task Force #16 © DC

GD25 FN65 NM94

48-Giant G-29; r/JLA #2,3 & B&B #29 4.50 13.50 45.00
49-54,57,59,60 3.50 10.50 35.00
55-Intro. Earth 2 Robin (1st G.A. Robin in S.A.) 5.00 15.00 50.00
56-JLA vs. JSA (1st G.A. Wonder Woman in S.A.) 3.50 10.50 35.00
58-Giant G-41; r/JLA #6,8,1 4.20 12.60 42.00
61-63,66,68-72: 69-Wonder Woman quits. 71-Manhunter leaves. 72-Last 12¢ issue 2.50 7.50 25.00
64,65-JSA story. 64-(8/68)-Origin/1st app. S.A. Red Tornado 3.00 9.00 30.00
67-Giant G-53; r/JLA #4,14,31 4.00 12.00 40.00
73-1st S.A. app. of G.A. Superman; 1st S.A. app. of Black Canary 3.00 9.00 30.00
74-Black Canary joins; 1st meeting of G.A. & S.A. Superman. 1.85 5.50 15.00
75-2nd app. Green Arrow in new costume (see Brave & the Bold #85) 2.15 6.50 17.00
76-Giant G-65 3.00 9.00 30.00
77-80: 78-Re-intro Vigilante (1st S.A. app?) 1.85 5.50 15.00
81-84,86-90: 82-1st S.A. app. of G.A. Batman (cameo). 83-Death of Spectre. 1.85 5.50 15.00
85,93-(Giant G-77,G-89; 68 pgs.) 2.50 7.50 24.00
91,92: 91-1st meeting of the G.A. & S.A. Robin; begin 25¢, 52 pgs. issues, ends #99. 92-S. A. Robin tries on costume that is similar to that of G.A. Robin in All Star Comics #58. 1.85 5.50 15.00
94-Reprints 1st Sandman story (Adv. #40) & origin/1st app. Starman (Adv. #61); Deadman x-over; N. Adams-a (4 pgs.) 7.50 22.50 75.00
95-Origin Dr. Fate & Dr. Midnight reprint (from More Fun #67, All-American #25) 2.50 7.50 25.00
96-Origin Hourman (Adv. #48); Wildcat-r 2.50 7.50 25.00
97-Origin JLA retold; Sargon, Starman-r 2.50 7.50 20.00
98,99: 98-G.A. Sargon, Starman-r. 99-G.A. Sandman, Starman, Atom-r; last 52 pg. issue 2.50 7.50 20.00
100-(8/72)-1st meeting of G.A. & S.A. W. Woman 3.00 9.00 30.00
101,102: JSA x-overs. 102-Red Tornado dies 1.50 4.50 12.00
103-106,109: 103-Phantom Stranger joins. 105-Elongated Man joins. 106-New Red Tornado joins. 109-Hawkman resigns 1.00 3.00 8.00
107,108-G.A. Uncle Sam, Black Condor, The Ray, Dollman, Phantom Lady & The Human Bomb (JSA) x-over, 1st S.A. app. 1.25 3.75 10.00
110-116: All 100 pgs. 111-JLA vs. Scarecrow & Poison Ivy; Shining Knight, Green Arrow-r. 112-Amazo app; Crimson Avenger, Vigilante-r; origin Starman-r/Adv. #81. 115-Martian Manhunter app. 2.25 6.75 18.00
117-134: 117-Hawkman rejoins. 120,121-Adam Strange app.123-(10/75)-1st named app. Earth-Prime (3rd app. overall) (See Flash; 1st Series #179 & 228); DC editor Julie Schwartz & JLA writers Cary Bates & Elliot S! Maggin appear in story as themselves. 123,124-JLA/JSA app. 125-Two-Face-c/story. 128-Wonder Woman rejoins. 129-Death of Red Tornado 2.00 5.00
135-136: 135-137-G.A. Bulletman, Bulletgirl, Spy Smasher, Mr. Scarlet, Pinky & Ibis x-over, 1st S.A. app. 137-Superman battles G.A. Capt. Marvel. 1.00 3.00 8.00
137-Superman battles G.A. Capt. Marvel 1.25 3.75 10.00
138,158-190: 138-Adam Strange app. w/c by Neal Adams; 1st app. Green Lantern of the 73rd Century. 158-160-(44 pgs.). 161-Zatanna joins & new costume. 171-Mr. Terrific murdered. 178-Cover similar to #1; J'onn J'onzz app. 179-Firestorm joins. 181-Green Arrow leaves JLA 1.60 4.00
139-157-(52 pgs.): 139-Adam Strange app.144-Origin retold; origin J'onn J'onzz. 145-Red Tornado resurrected. 147,148-Legion x-over. 2.40 6.00
191-199: 192,193-Real origin Red Tornado. 193-1st app. All-Star Squadron as free 16 pg. insert .90 2.25
200 ($1.50, Anniversary issue, 76pgs.)-JLA origin retold; Green Arrow rejoins; Bolland, Broderick, Aparo, Giordano, Gil Kane, Infantino, Kubert-a; Perez-c/a. 1.60 4.00
201-250: 203-Intro/origin new Royal Flush Gang. 207,208-JSA, JLA, & All-Star Squadron team-up. 219,220-True origin Black Canary. 228-Re-intro Martian Manhunter. 228-230-War of the Worlds storyline; JLA Satellite destroyed by Martians. 233-Story cont'd from Annual #2. 243-Aquaman leaves. 244,245-Crisis x-over. 250-Batman rejoins .80 2.00
251-259: 253-Origin Despero. 258-Death of Vibe. 258-261-Legends x-over 1.25
260-Death of Steel 1.60 4.00
261-Last issue 2.40 6.00
Annual 1(1983) 1.10 2.75
Annual 2(1984)-Intro new J.L.A. (Aquaman, Martian Manhunter, Steel, Gypsy, Vixen, Vibe, Elongated Man, & Zatanna) .80 2.00
Annual 3(1985)-Crisis x-over .80 2.00

NOTE: ***Neal Adams*** *c-63, 66, 67, 70, 74, 79, 81, 82, 86-89, 91, 92, 94, 96-98, 138, 139.* ***M. Anderson*** *c-1-4, 6, 7, 10, 12-14.* ***Aparo*** *a-200.* ***Austin*** *a-200i.* ***Baily*** *a-96r.* ***Bolland*** *a-200.* ***Buckler*** *c-158, 163, 164.* ***Burnley*** *r-94, 98, 99.* ***Greene*** *a-46-61i, 64-73i, 110i(r).* ***Grell*** *c-117, 122.* ***Kaluta*** *c-154p.* ***Gil Kane*** *a-200.* ***Krigstein*** *a-96(r/Sensation #84).* ***Kubert*** *a-200; c-72, 73.* ***Nino*** *a-228i, 230i.* ***Orlando*** *c-151i.* ***Perez*** *a-184-186p, 192-197p, 200p; c-104p, 186, 192-195, 196p, 197p, 199, 200, 201p, 202, 203-205p, 207-209, 212-215, 217, 219, 220.* ***Reinman*** *r-97.* ***Roussos*** *a-62i.* ***Sekowsky*** *a-37, 38, 44-63p, 110-112p(r); c-46-48p, 51p.* ***Sekowsky/Anderson*** *c-5, 8, 9, 11, 15.* ***B. Smith*** *c-185i.* ***Starlin*** *c-178-180, 183, 185p.* ***Staton*** *a-244p; c-157p, 244p.* ***Toth*** *r-110.* ***Tuska*** *a-153, 228p, 241-243p. JSA x-overs-21, 22, 29, 30, 37, 38, 46, 47, 55, 56, 64, 65, 73, 74, 82, 83, 91, 92, 100, 101, 102, 107, 108, 110, 113, 115, 123, 124, 135-137, 147, 148, 159, 160, 171, 172, 183-185, 195-197, 207-209, 219, 220, 231, 232, 244.*

JUSTICE LEAGUE QUARTERLY (...International Quarterly #6 on)
Winter, 1990-91 - No. 17, Winter, 1994 ($2.95/$3.50, 84 pgs.)
DC Comics

1-6: 1-Intro The Conglomerate (Booster Gold, Praxis, Gypsy, Vapor, Echo, Maxi-Man, & Reverb); Justice League #1-c/swipe. 1,2-Giffen plots/breakdowns. 3-Giffen plot; 72 pg. story. 4-Rogers/Russell-a in back-up. 5,6-Waid scripts 1.20 3.00
7-17: 8,17-Global Guardians app. 12-Waid script 1.40 3.50
NOTE: ***Phil Jimenez*** *a-17p.* ***Sprouse*** *a-1p.*

JUSTICE LEAGUE TASK FORCE
June, 1993 - No. 37, Aug, 1996 ($1.25/$1.50/$1.75)
DC Comics

1-7: Aquaman, Nightwing, Flash, J'onn J'onzz, & Gypsy form team. 5,6-Knightquest tie-ins (new Batman cameo #5, 1 pg.) 1.25
8-16: 8-$1.50-c begins. 15-Triumph cameo. 16-(9/94)-Zero Hour x-over; Triumph app. 1.50
0,17-23: 0-(10/94). 17-(11/94)-Triumph becomes part of Justice League Task Force (See JLE #68) 1.50
24-35: 24-$1.75-c begins, 26-Impulse app. 35-Warlord app. 37-Triumph quits team .70 1.75

JUSTICE MACHINE, THE
June, 1981 - No. 5, Nov, 1983 ($2.00, nos. 1-3 are magazine size)
Noble Comics

1-Byrne-c(p) 2.50 7.50 25.00
2-Austinpc(i) 1.85 5.50 15.00
3 1.25 3.75 10.00
4,5 2.00 5.00
Annual 1 (1/84, 68 pgs.)(published by Texas Comics); 1st app. The Elementals; Golden-c(p) 1.60 4.00

JUSTICE MACHINE (Also see The New Justice Machine)
Jan, 1987 - No. 29, May 1989 ($1.50/$1.75)
Comico/Innovation Publishing

1-29 1.50
Annual 1(6/89, $2.50, 36 pgs.)-Last Comico ish. 1.00 2.50
Summer Spectacular 1 ('89, $2.75)-Innovation Publ.; Byrne/Gustovich cover 1.10 2.75

JUSTICE MACHINE, THE
1990 - No. 4, 1990 ($1.95/$2.25, deluxe format, mature)
Innovation Publishing

1-4: Gustovich-c/a in all .90 2.25

JUSTICE MACHINE FEATURING THE ELEMENTALS

Justice Traps the Guilty #3 © PRIZE

Kaboom #2 © Awesome Comics

Kabuki: Skin Deep #2 © David Mack

May, 1986 - No. 4, Aug, 1986 ($1.50, limited series)
Comico

	GD25	FN65	NM94
1-4			1.50

JUSTICE RIDERS
1997 ($5.95, one-shot, prestige format)
DC Comics

	GD25	FN65	NM94
1-Elseworlds; Dixon-s/Williams & Gray-a		2.40	5.95

JUSTICE SOCIETY OF AMERICA (See Adventure #461 & All-Star #3)
April, 1991 - No. 8, Nov, 1991 ($1.00, limited series)
DC Comics

	GD25	FN65	NM94
1-8: 1-Flash. 2-Black Canary. 3-Green Lantern. 4-Hawkman. 5-Flash/ Hawkman. 6-Green Lantern/Black Canary. 7-JSA			1.00

JUSTICE SOCIETY OF AMERICA (Also see Last Days of the... Special)
Aug, 1992 - No. 10, May, 1993 ($1.25)
DC Comics

	GD25	FN65	NM94
1-10			1.25

JUSTICE TRAPS THE GUILTY (Fargo Kid V11#3 on)
Oct-Nov, 1947 - V11#2(#92), Apr-May, 1958 (True FBI Cases)
Prize/Headline Publications

	GD25	FN65	NM94
V2#1-S&K-c/a; electrocution-c	43.00	128.00	360.00
2-S&K-c/a	27.00	81.00	200.00
3-5-S&K-c/a	25.00	75.00	185.00
6-S&K-c/a; Feldstein-a	27.00	81.00	200.00
7,9-S&K-c/a. 7-9-V2#1-3 in indicia; #7-9 on-c	21.00	64.00	160.00
8,10-Krigstein-a; S&K-c. 10-S&K-a	24.00	73.00	180.00
11,18,19-S&K-c	10.00	30.00	75.00
12,14-17,20-No S&K. 14-Severin/Elder-a (8pg.)	5.70	17.00	35.00
13-Used in **SOTI**, pg. 110-111	8.00	24.00	50.00
21,30-S&K-c/a	8.00	24.00	55.00
22,23,27-S&K-c	5.70	17.00	40.00
24-26,28,29,31-50: 28-Kirby-c. 32-Meskin story	4.15	12.50	25.00
51-55,57,59-70	4.00	11.00	22.00
56-Ben Oda, Joe Simon, Joe Genola, Mort Meskin & Jack Kirby app. in police line-up on-c	5.00	15.00	30.00
58-Illo. in **SOTI**, "Treating police contemptuously" (top left); text on heroin	22.00	66.00	160.00
71-92: 76-Orlando-a	4.00	10.00	20.00

NOTE: ***Bailey*** *a-12, 13.* ***Elder*** *a-8.* ***Kirby*** *a-19p.* ***Meskin*** *a-22, 27, 63, 64; c-45, 46.* ***Robinson/ Meskin*** *a-5, 19.* ***Severin*** *a-8, 11p. Photo c-12, 15-17.*

JUST MARRIED
January, 1958 - No. 114, Dec, 1976
Charlton Comics

	GD25	FN65	NM94
1	5.00	15.00	50.00
2	3.00	9.00	30.00
3-10	2.50	7.50	20.00
11-30	1.50	4.50	12.00
31-50	1.10	3.30	9.00
51-70	1.00	2.80	7.00
71-90		2.00	5.00
91-114		1.60	4.00

JUSTY
Dec 6, 1988 - No. 9, 1989 ($1.75, B&W, bi-weekly mini-series)
Viz Comics

	GD25	FN65	NM94
1-9: Japanese manga		.75	1.80

KA'A'NGA COMICS (...Jungle King)(See Jungle Comics)
Spring, 1949 - No. 20, Summer, 1954
Fiction House Magazines (Glen-Kel Publ. Co.)

	GD25	FN65	NM94
1-Ka'a'nga, Lord of the Jungle begins	42.00	126.00	380.00
2 (Winter, '49-'50)	23.00	68.00	180.00
3,4	16.00	49.00	130.00
5-Camilla app.	12.00	36.00	95.00
6-10: 7-Tuska-a. 9-Tabu, Wizard of the Jungle app. 10-Used in **POP**, pg. 99	10.00	30.00	80.00
11-15: 15-Camilla-r by Baker/Jungle #106	8.75	26.25	65.00
16-Sheena app.	8.75	26.25	70.00
17-20	8.50	26.00	60.00
I.W. Reprint #1,8: 1-r/#18; Kinstler-c. 8-r/#10	2.25	6.75	18.00

NOTE: ***Celardo*** *c-1.* ***Whitman*** *c-8-20(most).*

KABOOM
Sept, 1997 - Present ($2.50)
Awesome Entertainment

	GD25	FN65	NM94
1-4: 1-Matsuda-a/Loeb-s; 4 covers exist (Matsuda, Sale, Polina and McGuiness)			2.50
1-Dynamic Forces Edition			2.50
2-Regular & Gold logo-c exist			2.50
3-Liefeld-c			2.50

KABUKI
Nov, 1994 ($3.50, B&W)
Caliber Press

	GD25	FN65	NM94
1-Intro Kabuki		2.40	6.00
Color Special (1/96, $2.95)-Mack-c/a/scripts; pin-ups by Tucci, Harris & Quesada		1.20	3.00
Gallery (8/95, $2.95)- pinups from Mack, Paul Pope, Tim Bradstreet & others.		1.20	3.00

KABUKI
Oct, 1997 - Present ($2.95, color)
Image Comics

	GD25	FN65	NM94
1-David Mack-c/s/a			2.95
1-($10.00)-Dynamic Forces Edition			10.00

KABUKI: CIRCLE OF BLOOD
Jan, 1995 - No. 6, Nov, 1995 ($2.95, B&W)
Caliber Press

	GD25	FN65	NM94
1-David Mack story/a in all		2.00	5.00
2-6: 3-#1on inside indicia.		1.20	3.00
6-Variant-c		1.20	3.00
TPB ($16.95) r/1-6, intro. by Steranko			16.95
TPB ($24.95) Deluxe Edition			24.95

KABUKI: DANCE OF DEATH
Jan, 1995 ($3.00, B&W, one-shot)
London Night Studios

	GD25	FN65	NM94
1-David Mack-c/a/scripts-		2.40	6.00

KABUKI: DREAMS OF THE DEAD
July, 1996 ($2.95, one-shot)
Caliber

	GD25	FN65	NM94
nn-David Mack-c/a/scripts		1.20	3.00

KABUKI: MASKS OF THE NOH
May, 1996 - No. 4, Feb, 1997 ($2.95, limited series)
Caliber

	GD25	FN65	NM94
1-4: 1-Three-c (1A-Quesada, 1B-Buzz, &1C-Mack). 3-Terry Moore pin-up		1.20	3.00

KABUKI: SKIN DEEP
Oct, 1996 - No. 3, May, 1997 ($2.95)
Caliber Comics

	GD25	FN65	NM94
1-3:David Mack-c/a/scripts. 2-Two-c (1-Mack, 1-Ross)			2.95

KAMANDI: AT EARTH'S END
June, 1993 - No. 6, Nov, 1993 ($1.75, limited series)
DC Comics

	GD25	FN65	NM94
1-6: Elseworlds storyline		.70	1.75

Kamandi, The Last Boy On Earth #45 © DC

Katy Keene #57 © AP

Katzenjammer Kids #16 © DMP

KAMANDI, THE LAST BOY ON EARTH (Also see Alarming Tales #1, Brave and the Bold #120 & 157 & Cancelled Comic Cavalcade)
Oct-Nov, 1972 - V7#59, Sept-Oct, 1978
National Periodical Publications/DC Comics

	GD25	FN65	NM94
1-Origin & 1st app. Kamandi	3.00	12.00	30.00
2	2.25	6.75	18.00
3-5: 4-Intro. Prince Tuftan of the Tigers	1.00	3.00	8.00
6-10		2.40	6.00
11-20		1.60	4.00
21-28,30,31,33-40: 24-Last 20¢ issue. 31-Intro Pyra.		1.20	3.00
29,32: 29-Superman x-over. 32-(68 pgs.)-r/origin from #1 plus one new story; 4 pg. biog. of Jack Kirby with B&W photos		2.40	6.00
41-57,59: 59-(44 pgs.)-Cont'd in B&B #157; The Return of Omac back-up by Starlin c/a(p)		1.60	4.00
58-(44 pgs.)-Karate Kid x-over from LSH		2.40	6.00

NOTE: ***Ayers** a(p)-48-59 (most). **Giffen** a-44p, 45p. **Kirby** a-1-40p; c-1-33. **Kubert** c-34-41. **Nasser** a-45p, 46p. **Starlin** a-59p; c-57, 59p.*

KAMUI (Legend Of...#2 on)
May 12, 1987 - No. 37, Nov. 15, 1988 ($1.50, B&W, bi-weekly)
Eclipse Comics/Viz Comics

	GD25	FN65	NM94
1-37: 1-3 have 2nd printings			1.50

KARATE KID (See Action, Adventure, Legion of Super-Heroes, & Superboy)
Mar-Apr, 1976 - No. 15, July-Aug, 1978 (Legion spin-off)
National Periodical Publications/DC Comics

	GD25	FN65	NM94
1,15: 1-Meets Iris Jacobs; Estrada/Staton-a. 15-Continued into Kamandi #58		1.20	6.00
2-14: 2-Major Disaster app.		1.60	4.00

NOTE: ***Grell** c-1-4, 5p, 6p, 7, 8. **Staton** a-1-9i. Legion x-over-No. 1, 2, 4, 6, 10, 12, 13. Princess Projectra x-over-#8, 9.*

KASCO KOMICS
1945; No. 2, 1949 (Regular size, paper-c)
Kasko Grainfeed (Giveaway)

	GD25	FN65	NM94
1(1945)-Similar to Katy Keene; Bill Woggon-a; 28 pgs.; 6-7/8x9-7/8"	14.00	43.00	100.00
2(1949)-Woggon-c/a	11.50	34.00	80.00

KATHY
Sept, 1949 - No. 17, Sept, 1955
Standard Comics

	GD25	FN65	NM94
1-Teen-age	7.85	23.50	55.00
2-Schomburg-c	5.70	17.00	35.00
3-5	4.00	11.00	22.00
6-17: 17-Code approved	3.00	7.50	15.00

KATHY (The Teenage Tornado)
Oct, 1959 - No. 27, Feb, 1964
Atlas Comics/Marvel (ZPC)

	GD25	FN65	NM94
1-Teen-age	5.00	15.00	50.00
2	2.50	7.50	25.00
3-15	2.00	6.00	16.00
16-27	1.10	3.30	9.00

KAT KARSON
No date (Reprint)
I. W. Enterprises

	GD25	FN65	NM94
1-Funny animals	1.25	3.75	10.00

KATO OF THE GREEN HORNET (Also see The Green Hornet)
Nov, 1991 - No. 4, Feb, 1992 ($2.50, mini-series)
Now Comics

	GD25	FN65	NM94
1-4: Brent Anderson-c/a		1.00	2.50

KATY AND KEN VISIT SANTA WITH MISTER WISH
1948 (Giveaway, 16 pgs., paper-c)
S. S. Kresge Co.

	GD25	FN65	NM94
nn	4.00	12.00	24.00

KATY KEENE (Also see Kasco Komics, Laugh, Pep, Suzie, & Wilbur)
1949 - No. 4, 1951; No. 5, 3/52 - No. 62, Oct, 1961 (50-53-Adventures of...on-c)
Archie Publ./Close-Up/Radio Comics

	GD25	FN65	NM94
1-Bill Woggon-c/a begins; swipes-c to Mopsy #1	83.00	250.00	740.00
2-(1950)	41.00	123.00	370.00
3-5: 3-(1951). 4-(1951)	34.00	103.00	275.00
6-10	29.00	86.00	230.00
11,13-21: 21-Last pre-code issue (3/55)	24.00	73.00	195.00
12-(Scarce)	28.00	83.00	220.00
22-40	14.00	42.00	140.00
41-62: 54-Wedding Album plus wedding pin-up	11.00	33.00	110.00
Annual 1('54, 25¢)-All new stories; last pre-code	39.00	117.00	350.00
Annual 2-6('55-59, 25¢)-All new stories	24.00	73.00	195.00
3-D 1(1953, 25¢, large size)-Came w/glasses	36.00	107.00	285.00
Charm 1(9/58)-Woggon-c/a; new stories, and cut-outs	23.00	69.00	185.00
Glamour 1(1957)-Puzzles, games, cut-outs	23.00	69.00	185.00
Spectacular 1('56)	23.00	69.00	185.00

NOTE: *Debby's Diary in #45, 47-49, 52, 57.*

KATY KEENE COMICS DIGEST MAGAZINE
1987 - No. 10, July, 1990 ($1.25/$1.35/$1.50, digest size)
Close-Up, Inc. (Archie Ent.)

	GD25	FN65	NM94
1		2.40	6.00
2-10		1.20	3.00

KATY KEENE FASHION BOOK MAGAZINE
1955 - No. 13, Sum, '56 - N. 23, Wint, '58-59 (nn 3-10)
Radio Comics/Archie Publications

	GD25	FN65	NM94
1-Bill Woggon-c/a	38.00	113.00	340.00
2	24.00	73.00	195.00
11-18: 18-Photo Bill Woggon	17.50	53.00	140.00
19-23	14.00	41.00	110.00

KATY KEENE HOLIDAY FUN (See Archie Giant Series Magazine No. 7, 12)

KATY KEENE PINUP PARADE
1955 - No. 15, Summer, 1961 (25¢)
Radio Comics/Archie Publications

	GD25	FN65	NM94
1-Cut-outs in all?; last pre-code issue	38.00	113.00	340.00
2-(1956)	22.00	66.00	175.00
3-5: 3-(1957)	19.50	58.00	155.00
6-10,12-14: 8-Mad parody. 10-Bill Woggon photo	13.00	39.00	130.00
11-Story of how comics get CCA approved, narrated by Katy	17.00	51.00	170.00
15(Rare)-Photo artist & family	31.00	93.00	320.00

KATY KEENE SPECIAL (Katy Keene #7 on; see Laugh Comics Digest)
Sept, 1983 - No. 33, 1990 (Later issues published quarterly)
Archie Enterprises

	GD25	FN65	NM94
1-Woggon-r; new Woggon-c		1.20	3.00
2-33: 3-Woggon-r		.80	2.00

KATZENJAMMER KIDS, THE (See Captain & the Kids & Giant Comic Album)
1945-1946; Summer, 1947 - No. 27, Feb-Mar, 1954
David McKay Publ./Standard No. 12-21(Spring/'50 - 53)/Harvey No. 22, 4/53 on

	GD25	FN65	NM94
Feature Books 30	14.50	43.00	115.00
Feature Books 32,35('45),41,44('46)	13.00	39.00	105.00
Feature Book 37-Has photos & biography of Harold Knerr	14.50	43.00	115.00
1(1947)-All new stories begin	14.50	43.00	115.00
2	7.85	23.50	55.00
3-11	5.70	17.00	35.00
12-14(Standard)	4.35	13.00	26.00
15-21(Standard)	4.00	11.00	22.00

Ka-Zar V2 #6 © MEG

Keen Detective Funnies V2 #4 © CEN

Keen Teens nn(#1) © ME

22-25,27(Harvey): 22-24-Henry app. 3.60 9.00 18.00
26-Half in 3-D 15.50 47.00 125.00

KAYO (Formerly Bullseye & Jest; becomes Carnival Comics)
No. 12, Mar, 1945
Harry 'A' Chesler

12-Green Knight, Capt. Glory, Little Nemo (not by McCay) 11.30 34.00 90.00

KA-ZAR (Also see Marvel Comics #1, Savage Tales #6 & X-Men #10)
Aug, 1970 - No. 3, Mar, 1971 (Giant-Size, 68 pgs.)
Marvel Comics Group

1-Reprints earlier Ka-Zar stories; Avengers x-over in Hercules; Daredevil, X-Men app.; hidden profanity-c 2.50 7.50 20.00
2,3-Daredevil-r. 2-r/Daredevil #12 w/Kirby layouts; Ka-Zar origin, Angel-r from X-Men by Tuska. 3-Romita & Heck-a (no Kirby) 1.85 5.50 15.00

NOTE: ***Buscema*** *r-2.* ***Colan*** *a-1p(r).* ***Kirby*** *c/a-1, 2. #1-Reprints X-Men #10? & Daredevil #13?*

KA-ZAR
Jan, 1974 - No. 20, Feb, 1977 (Regular Size)
Marvel Comics Group

1 2.40 6.00
2-Shanna 2.00 5.00
3-10 1.60 4.00
11-16,18-20 1.20 3.00
17-(Regular 25¢ edition)(8/76) 1.20 3.00
17-(30¢-c, limited distribution) 1.50 4.50 12.00

NOTE: ***Alcala*** *a-6i, 8i.* ***Brunner*** *c-4.* ***J. Buscema*** *a-6-10p; c-1, 5, 7.* ***Heath*** *a-12.* ***G. Kane*** *c(p)-3, 5, 8-11, 15, 20.* ***Kirby*** *c-12p.* ***Reinman*** *a-1p.*

KA-ZAR (Volume 2)
May, 1997 - Present ($1.95/$1.99)
Marvel Comics

1-Waid-s/Andy Kubert-c/a. thru #4 1.20 3.00
2,4: 2-Two-c 1.95
3-Alpha Flight #1 preview 1.20 3.00
5-11: 5-Begin $1.99-c. 9-11-Thanos app. 1.99
'97 Annual ($2.99)-Wraparound-c 2.99

KA-ZAR OF THE SAVAGE LAND
Feb, 1997 ($2.50, one-shot)
Marvel Comics

1-Wraparound-c 1.00 2.50

KA-ZAR: SIBLING RIVALRY
July, 1997 ($1.95, one-shot)
Marvel Comics

-1-Flashback story w/Alpha Flight #1 preview 1.95

KA-ZAR THE SAVAGE (See Marvel Fanfare)
Apr, 1981 - No. 34, Oct, 1984 (Regular size) (Mando paper #10 on)
Marvel Comics Group

1-34: 11-Origin Zabu. 12-Two versions: With & without panel missing (1600 printed with panel). 20-Kraven the Hunter-c/story (also apps. in #21). 21-23,25,26-Spider-Man app. 26-Photo-c. 29-Double size; Ka-Zar & Shanna wed 1.00

NOTE: ***B. Anderson*** *a-1-15p, 18, 19; c-1-17, 18p, 20(back).* ***G. Kane*** *a(back-up)-11, 12, 14.*

KEEN DETECTIVE FUNNIES (Formerly Detective Picture Stories?)
No. 8, July, 1938 - No. 24, Sept, 1940
Centaur Publications

V1#8-The Clock continues-r/Funny Picture Stories #1; Roy Crane-a (1st?) 156.00 468.00 1400.00
9-Tex Martin by Eisner; The Gang Buster app. 67.00 200.00 600.00
10,11: 11-Dean Denton story (begins?) 58.00 174.00 525.00
V2#1,2-The Eye Sees by Frank Thomas begins; ends #23(Not in V2#3&5). 2-Jack Cole-a 54.00 162.00 485.00
3-6: 3-TNT Todd begins. 4-Gabby Flynn begins. 5,6-Dean Denton story 51.00 153.00 460.00
7-The Masked Marvel by Ben Thompson begins (7/39, 1st app.)(scarce) 156.00 468.00 1400.00
8-Nudist ranch panel w/four girls 61.00 183.00 550.00
9-11 58.00 174.00 515.00
12(12/39)-Origin The Eye Sees by Frank Thomas; death of Masked Marvel's sidekick ZL 69.00 207.00 615.00
V3#1,2 54.00 162.00 485.00
18,19,21,22: 18-Bondage/torture-c 54.00 162.00 485.00
20-Classic Eye Sees-c by Thomas 72.00 216.00 650.00
23,24: 23-Air Man begins (intro). 23,24-Air Man-c 67.00 200.00 600.00

NOTE: ***Burgos*** *a-V2#2.* ***Jack Cole*** *a-V2#2.* ***Eisner*** *a-10, V2#6r.* ***Ken Ernst*** *a-V2#4-7, 9, 10, 19, 21; c-V2#4.* ***Everett*** *a-V2#6, 7, 9, 11, 12, 20.* ***Guardineer*** *a-V2#5, 66.* ***Gustavson*** *a-V2#4-6.* ***Simon*** *c-V3#1.* ***Thompson*** *c-V2#7, 9, 10, 22.*

KEEN KOMICS
V2#1, May, 1939 - V2#3, Nov, 1939
Centaur Publications

V2#1(Large size)-Dan Hastings (s/f), The Big Top, Bob Phantom the Magician, The Mad Goddess app. 78.00 234.00 700.00
V2#2(Reg. size)-The Forbidden Idol of Machu Picchu; Cut Carson by Burgos begins 50.00 150.00 450.00
V2#3-Saddle Sniffl by Jack Cole, Circus Pays, Kings Revenge app. 50.00 150.00 450.00

NOTE: ***Binder*** *a-V2#2.* ***Burgos*** *a-V2#2, 3.* ***Ken Ernst*** *a-V2#3.* ***Gustavson*** *a-V2#2.* ***Jack Cole*** *a-V2#3.*

KEEN TEENS (Girls magazine)
1945 - No. 6, Aug-Sept, 1947
Life's Romances Publ./Leader/Magazine Enterprises

nn (#1)-14 pgs. Claire Voyant (cont'd. in other nn issue) movie photos, Dotty Dripple, Gertie O'Grady & Sissy; Van Johnson, Frank Sinatra photo-c 21.00 64.00 155.00
nn (#2, 1946)-16 pgs. Claire Voyant & 16 pgs. movie photos 21.00 64.00 155.00
3-6: 4-Glenn Ford photo-c. 5-Perry Como-c 7.00 21.00 45.00

KELLYS, THE (Formerly Rusty Comics; Spy Cases No. 26 on)
No. 23, Jan, 1950 - No. 25, June, 1950 (52 pgs.)
Marvel Comics (HPC)

23-Teenage 10.00 30.00 75.00
24,25: 24-Margie app. 7.50 22.50 45.00

KELVIN MACE
1986 - No. 2, 1986 ($2.00, B&W)
Vortex Publications

1,2: 1-(B&W). 2-(Color) .80 2.00
1-2nd print (1/87, $1.75) .70 1.75

KEN MAYNARD WESTERN (Movie star)(See Wow Comics, 1936)
Sept, 1950 - No. 8, Feb, 1952 (All 36 pgs; photo front/back-c)
Fawcett Publications

1-Ken Maynard & his horse Tarzan begin 50.00 150.00 450.00
2 33.00 98.00 260.00
3-8: 6-Atomic bomb explosion panel 25.00 75.00 200.00

KEN SHANNON (Becomes Gabby #11 on) (Also see Police Comics #103)
Oct, 1951 - No. 10, Apr, 1953 (A private eye)
Quality Comics Group

1-Crandall-a 31.00 94.00 230.00
2-Crandall c/a(2) 25.00 75.00 180.00
3-5-Crandall-a. 3-Horror-c 17.00 51.00 125.00
6-Crandall-c/a; "The Weird Vampire Mob"-c/s 19.00 56.00 135.00
7-Crandall-a 14.00 43.00 105.00
8,9: 8-Opium den drug use story 13.00 39.00 95.00
10-Crandall-c 14.00 43.00 105.00

NOTE: ***Crandall/Cuidera*** *c-1-10.* ***Jack Cole*** *a-1-9. #1-15 published after title change to Gabby.*

Kerry Drake #2 © Life's Romances

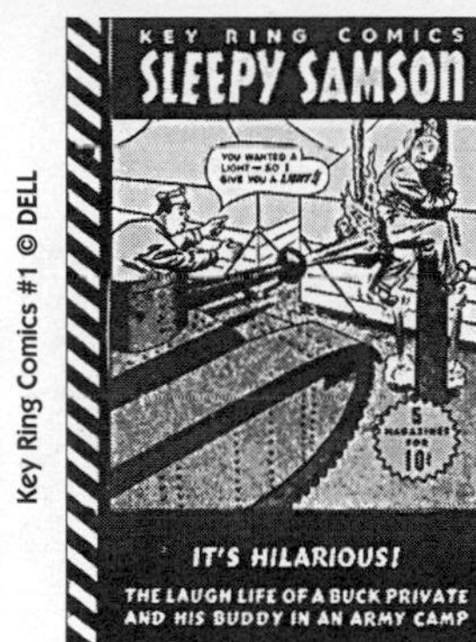

Key Ring Comics #1 © DELL

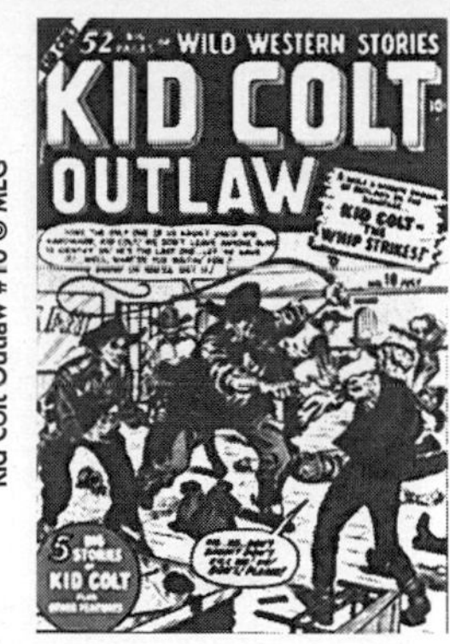

Kid Colt Outlaw #10 © MEG

GD25 FN65 NM94

KEN STUART
Jan, 1949 (Sea Adventures)
Publication Enterprises

1-Frank Borth-c/a 8.00 24.00 50.00

KENT BLAKE OF THE SECRET SERVICE (Spy)
May, 1951 - No. 14, July, 1953
Marvel/Atlas Comics(20CC)

1-Injury to eye, bondage, torture; Brodsky-c 14.00 43.00 110.00
2-Drug use w/hypo scenes; Brodsky-c 10.00 30.00 70.00
3-14: 8-R.Q. Sale-a (2 pgs.) 6.70 20.00 45.00
NOTE: ***Heath** c-5, 7, 8. **Infantino** c-12. **Maneely** c-3. **Sinnott** a-2(3). **Tuska** a-8(3pg.).*

KENTS, THE
Aug, 1997 - No. 12 ($2.50, limited series)
DC Comics

1-12:1-8-Ostrander-s/Truman & Bair-a. 9-12-Ostrander-s/Mandrake-a
1.00 2.50

KERRY DRAKE (Also see A-1 Comics)
1944; Jan, 1956 - No. 2, March, 1956
Life's Romances Publ. nn/Argo

nn- (A-1 Comics on-c)(1944)Kerry Drake, Johnny Devildog, Rocky, Streamer Kelly (Slightly large size) 21.00 62.00 165.00
1,2-Newspaper-r 6.00 18.00 42.00

KERRY DRAKE DETECTIVE CASES (...Racket Buster No. 32,33)
(Also see Chamber of Clues & Green Hornet Comics #42-47)
1944 - No. 5, 1944; No. 6, Jan, 1948 - No. 33, Aug, 1952
Life's Romances/Com/Magazine Ent. No.1-5/Harvey No.6 on

nn(1944)(A-1 Comics)(slightly over-size) 23.00 69.00 165.00
2 14.00 43.00 105.00
3-5(1944) 11.00 33.00 80.00
6,8(1948): Lady Crime by Powell. 8-Bondage-c 7.00 21.00 45.00
7-Kubert-a; biog of Andriola (artist) 9.00 27.00 55.00
9,10-Two-part marijuana story; Kerry smokes marijuana in #10
11.50 34.00 80.00
11-15 6.35 19.00 38.00
16-33 5.00 15.00 30.00
...in the Case of the Sleeping City (1951 Publishers Synd.) 16 pg. giveaway for armed forces; paper cover 4.00 12.00 24.00
NOTE: ***Andiola** c-6-9. **Berg** a-5. **Powell** a-10-23, 28, 29.*

KEWPIES
Spring, 1949
Will Eisner Publications

1-Feiffer-a; Kewpie Doll ad on back cover 36.00 108.00 320.00

KEY COMICS
Jan, 1944 - No. 5, Aug, 1946
Consolidated Magazines

1-The Key, Will-O-The-Wisp begin 30.00 90.00 240.00
2 (3/44) 15.00 45.00 120.00
3,4: 4-(5/46)-Origin John Quincy The Atom (begins); Walter Johnson c-3-5
12.00 38.00 100.00
5-4pg. Faust Opera adaptation; Kiefer-a; back-c advertises "Masterpieces Illustrated" by Lloyd Jacquet after he left Classic Comics (no copies of Masterpieces Illustrated known) 17.50 53.00 140.00

KEY COMICS
1951 - 1956 (32 pgs.) (Giveaway)
Key Clothing Co./Peterson Clothing

Contains a comic from different publishers bound with new cover. Cover changed each year. Many combinations possible. Distributed in Nebraska, Iowa, & Kansas. Contents would determine price, 40-60 percent of original.

KEY RING COMICS
1941 (16 pgs.; two colors) (sold 5 for 10¢)
Dell Publishing Co.

1-Sky Hawk, 1-Viking Carter, 1-Features Sleepy Samson, 1-Origin Greg Gilday-r/War Comics #2, 1-Radior (Super hero) 2.00 6.00 20.00
NOTE: *Each book has two holes in spine to put in binder.*

KICKERS, INC.
Nov, 1986 - No. 12, Oct, 1987
Marvel Comics Goup

1-12 1.00

KID CARROTS
September, 1953
St. John Publishing Co.

1-Funny animal 5.00 15.00 30.00

KID COLT OUTLAW (Kid Colt #1-4; ...Outlaw #5-on)(Also see All Western Winners, Best Western, Black Rider, Giant-Size..., Two-Gun Kid, Two-Gun Western, Western Winners, Wild Western, Wisco)
8/48 - No. 139, 3/68; No. 140, 11/69 - No. 229, 4/79
Marvel Comics(LCC) 1-16; Atlas(LMC) 17-102; Marvel 103-on

1-Kid Colt & his horse Steel begin. 72.00 216.00 650.00
2 36.00 108.00 300.00
3-5: 4-Anti-Wertham editorial; Tex Taylor app. 5-Blaze Carson app.
28.00 84.00 225.00
6-8: 6-Tex Taylor app; 7-Nimo the Lion begins, ends #10
19.00 56.00 150.00
9,10 (52 pgs.) 19.00 56.00 150.00
11-Origin 22.00 66.00 175.00
12-20 14.00 41.00 110.00
21-32 11.30 34.00 90.00
33-45: Black Rider in all 8.75 26.25 70.00
46,47,49,50 7.85 23.50 55.00
48-Kubert-a 8.50 26.00 60.00
51-53,55,56 6.50 19.50 45.00
54-Williamson/Maneely-c 7.15 21.50 50.00
57-60,66: 4-pg. Williamson-a in all. 59-Reprints Rawhide Kid #79; Colan text illo 5.50 16.50 55.00
61-63,67-78,80-86: 70-Severin-c. 73-Maneely-c. 86-Kirby-a(r).
3.20 9.60 32.00
64,65-Crandall-a 3.80 11.40 38.00
79,87: 79-Origin retold. 87-Davis-a(r) 3.80 11.40 38.00
88,89-Williamson-a in both (4 pgs.). 89-Redrawn Matt Slade #2
4.20 12.60 42.00
90-99,101: 91-Kirby/Ayers-c. 95-Kirby/Ayers-c/story. 101-Last 10¢ issue
2.50 7.50 20.00
100 3.00 9.00 30.00
101-120: 110-(5/63)-1st app Iron Mask (Iron Man type villian). 114-(1/64)-2nd app Iron Mask 2.25 6.75 18.00
121-140: 121-Rawhide Kid x-over. 125-Two-Gun Kid x-over. 130-132-68 pg. issues with one new story each. 130-Origin. 140-Reprints begin
1.50 4.50 12.00
141-155,157-160: (later issues all-r) 1.25 3.75 10.00
156-Giant; reprints 1.85 5.50 15.00
161-200: 170-Origin retold. 1.00 3.00 8.00
201-229: 229-Rawhide Kid-r 2.40 6.00
...Album (no date; 1950's; Atlas Comics)-132 pgs.; random binding, cardboard cover, B&W stories; contents can vary (Rare) 63.00 189.00 565.00
NOTE: ***Ayers** a-many. **Colan** a-52, 53; c(p)-223, 228, 229. **Crandall** a-140r, 167r. **Everett** a-90, 137i, 225i(r). **Heath** a-8(2); c-34, 35, 39, 44, 46, 48, 49, 57, 64. **Heck** a-135, 139. **Jack Keller** a-25(2), 26-68(3-4), 78, 94p, 98, 99, 108, 110, 130, 132, 140-150r. **Kirby** a-86r, 93, 96, 119, 176(part); c-87, 92-95, 97, 99-112, 114-117, 121-123, 197r; w/**Ditko** c-89. **Maneely** a-12, 68, 81; c-17, 19, 40-43, 47, 52, 53, 62, 65, 68, 78, 81, 142r, 150r. **Morrow** a-173r, 216r. **Rico** a-13, 18. **Severin** c-58, 59, 143, 148, 149i. **Shores** a-39, 41-43, 143r; c-1-10(most), 24. **Sutton** a-136, 137p, 225p(r). **Wildey** a-47, 54, 82, 144r. **Williamson** r-147, 170, 172, 216. **Woodbridge** a-64, 81. Black Rider in #33-45, 74, 86. Iron Mask in #110, 114, 121, 127. Sam Hawk in #84, 101, 111, 121, 146, 174, 181, 188.*

Kid Eternity #16 © DC

Kid Komics #4 © TCI

Kid Montana V2 #21 © CC

GD25 FN65 NM94

KID COWBOY (Also see Approved Comics #4 & Boy Cowboy)
1950 - No. 14, 1954 (Painted covers #1-10, 14)
Ziff-Davis Publ./St. John (Approved Comics)

1-Lucy Belle & Red Feather begin 10.00 30.00 80.00
2-Maneely-c 7.15 21.50 50.00
3-14: 5-Berg-a. 14-Code approved 5.70 17.00 40.00

KID DEATH & FLUFFY HALLOWEEN SPECIAL
Oct, 1997 ($2.95, B&W, one-shot)
Event Comics

1-Variant-c by Cebollero & Quesada/Palmiotti 2.95

KID DEATH & FLUFFY SPRING BREAK SPECIAL
July, 1996 ($2.50, B&W, one-shot)
Event Comics

1-Quesada & Palmiotti-c/scripts 1.00 2.50

KIDDIE KAPERS
1945?(nd); Oct, 1957; 1963 - 1964
Kiddie Kapers Co., 1945/Decker Publ. (Red Top-Farrell)

1(nd, 1945-46?, 36 pgs.)-Infinity-c; funny animal 5.70 17.00 40.00
1(10/57)(Decker)-Little Bit-r from Kiddie Karnival 4.00 11.00 22.00
Super Reprint #7, 10('63), 12, 14('63), 15,17('64), 18('64): 10, 14-r/Animal Adventures #1. 15-Animal Adventures #? 17-Cowboys 'N' Injuns #? 1.00 3.00 8.00

KIDDIE KARNIVAL
1952 (25¢, 100 pgs.) (One Shot)
Ziff-Davis Publ. Co. (Approved Comics)

nn-Rebound Little Bit #1,2; painted-c 29.00 86.00 230.00

KID ETERNITY (Becomes Buccaneers) (See Hit Comics)
Spring, 1946 - No. 18, Nov, 1949
Quality Comics Group

1 67.00 200.00 600.00
2 33.00 98.00 260.00
3-Mac Raboy-a 36.00 108.00 285.00
4-10 19.00 56.00 150.00
11-18 14.00 43.00 110.00

KID ETERNITY
1991 - No. 3, Nov, 1991 ($4.95, limited series)
DC Comics

1-3: Grant Morrison scripts 2.00 5.00

KID ETERNITY
May, 1993 - No. 16, Sept, 1994 ($1.95, mature)
DC Comics (Vertigo)

1-16: 1-Gold ink-c. 6-Photo-c. All Sean Phillips-c/a except #15 (Phillips-c/i only) .80 2.00

KID FROM DODGE CITY, THE
July, 1957 - No. 2, Sept, 1957
Atlas Comics (MMC)

1-Don Heck-c 7.85 23.50 55.00
2-Everett-c 5.35 16.00 32.00

KID FROM TEXAS, THE (A Texas Ranger)
June, 1957 - No. 2, Aug, 1957
Atlas Comics (CSI)

1-Powell-a; Severin-c 8.50 26.00 60.00
2 5.35 16.00 32.00

KID KOKO
1958
I. W. Enterprises

Reprint #1,2-(r/M.E.'s Koko & Kola #4, 1947) 1.00 3.00 8.00

GD25 FN65 NM94

KID KOMICS (Kid Movie Komics No. 11)
Feb, 1943 - No. 10, Spring, 1946
Timely Comics (USA 1,2/FCI 3-10)

1-Origin Captain Wonder & sidekick Tim Mullrooney, & Subbie; intro the Sea-Going Lad, Pinto Pete, & Trixie Trouble; Knuckles & Whitewash Jones (from Young Allies) app.; Wolverton-a (7 pgs.) 300.00 900.00 3000.00
2-The Young Allies, Red Hawk, & Tommy Tyme begin; last Captain Wonder & Subbie 139.00 417.00 1250.00
3-The Vision, Daredevils & Red Hawk app. 106.00 318.00 950.00
4-The Destroyer begins; Sub-Mariner app.; Red Hawk & Tommy Tyme end 89.00 267.00 800.00
5,6: 5-Tommy Tyme begins, ends #10 69.00 207.00 625.00
7-10: 7,10-The Whizzer app. Destroyer not in #7,8. 10-Last Destroyer, Young Allies & Whizzer 63.00 189.00 565.00

NOTE: ***Brodsky*** *c-5.* ***Schomburg*** *c-2-4, 6-10.* ***Shores*** *c-1. Captain Wonder c-1, 2. The Young Allies c-3-10.*

KID MONTANA (Formerly Davy Crockett Frontier Fighter; The Gunfighters No. 51 on)
V2#9, Nov, 1957 - No. 50, Mar, 1965
Charlton Comics

V2#9 4.00 12.00 40.00
10,13: 13-Williamson-a 3.00 9.00 30.00
11,12,14-20 2.50 7.50 20.00
21-35 1.50 4.50 12.00
36-50 1.00 3.00 8.00

NOTE: *Title change to Montana Kid on cover only #44 & 45; remained Kid Montana on inside.*

KID MOVIE KOMICS (Formerly Kid Komics; Rusty Comics #12 on)
No. 11, Summer, 1946
Timely Comics

11-Silly Seal & Ziggy Pig; 2 pgs. Kurtzman "Hey Look" plus 6 pg. "Pigtales" story 20.00 60.00 160.00

KIDNAPPED (Robert Louis Stevenson's...also see Movie Comics)(Disney)
No. 1101, May, 1960
Dell Publichsing Co.

Four Color 1101-Movie, photo-c 5.50 16.50 60.00

KIDNAP RACKET (See Harvey Comics Hits No. 57)

KID SLADE GUNFIGHTER (Formerly Matt Slade...)
No. 5, Jan, 1957 - No. 8, July, 1957
Atlas Comics (SPI)

5-Maneely, Roth, Severin-a in all; Maneely-c 8.75 26.25 70.00
6,8-Severin-c 5.70 17.00 35.00
7-Williamson/Mayo-a, 4 pgs. 7.85 23.50 55.00

KID SUPREME (See Supreme)
Mar, 1996 - No. 3, July, 1996 ($2.50)
Image Comics (Extreme Studios)

1-3: Fraga-a/scripts. 3-Glory-c/app. 1.00 2.50

KID ZOO COMICS
July, 1948 (52 pgs.)
Street & Smith Publications

1-Funny Animal 21.00 62.00 165.00

KILLER (...Tales By Timothy Truman)
March, 1985 ($1.75, one-shot, Baxter paper)
Eclipse Comics

1-Timothy Truman-c/a .70 1.75

KILLER INSTINCT (Video game)
June, 1996 - Present ($2.50, limited series)
Acclaim Comics

1-6: 1-Bart Sears-a(p). 4-Special #1. 5-Special #2. 6-Special #3 1.00 2.50

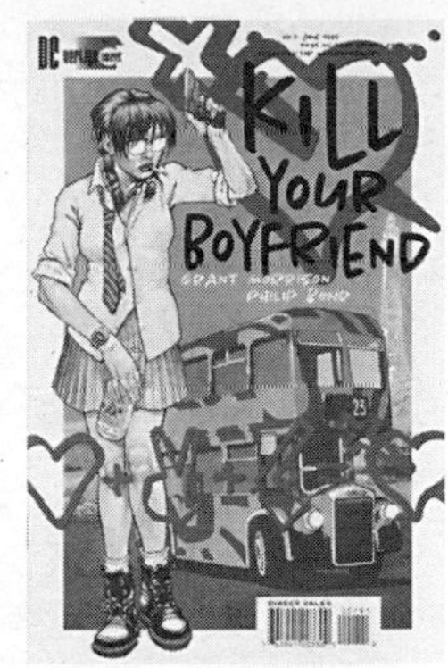

Kill Your Boyfriend #1 © DC

The Kindred #4 © Aegis Entertainment

King Comics #17 © DMP

KILLERS, THE
1947 - No. 2, 1948 (No month)
Magazine Enterprises

1-Mr. Zin, the Hatchet Killer; mentioned in **SOTI**, pgs. 179,180; used by N.Y. Legis. Comm.; L. B. Cole-c 75.00 225.00 650.00
2-(Scarce)-Hashish smoking story; "Dying, Dying, Dead" drug story; Whitney, Ingels-a; Whitney hanging-c 65.00 195.00 550.00

KILLING JOKE, THE (See Batman: The Killing Joke under Batman one-shots)

KILLPOWER: THE EARLY YEARS
Sept, 1993 - No. 4, Dec, 1993 ($1.75, mini-series)
Marvel Comics UK

1-($2.95)-Foil embossed-c 1.20 3.00
2-4: 2-Genetix app. 3-Punisher app. .70 1.75

KILLRAZOR
Aug, 1995 ($2.50, one-shot)
Image Comics (Top Cow Productions)

1 1.00 2.50

KILL YOUR BOYFRIEND
June, 1995 ($4.95, one-shot)
DC Comics (Vertigo)

1-Grant Morrison story 2.00 5.00

KILROY IS HERE
1995 ($2.95, B&W)
Caliber Press

1-4 1.20 3.00

KILROYS, THE
June-July, 1947 - No. 54, June-July, 1955
B&I Publ. Co. No. 1-19/American Comics Group

	GD25	FN65	NM94
1	19.00	56.00	150.00
2	9.50	28.00	75.00
3-5: 5-Gross-a	7.85	23.50	55.00
6-10: 8-Milt Gross's Moronica	5.70	17.00	40.00
11-20: 14-Gross-a	5.70	17.00	35.00
21-30	4.25	13.00	26.00
31-47,50-54	4.00	12.00	24.00
48,49-(3-D effect-c/stories)	14.50	43.00	115.00

KILROY: THE SHORT STORIES
1995 ($2.95, B&W)
Caliber Press

1 1.20 3.00

KINDRED, THE
Mar, 1994 - No. 4, July, 1995 ($1.95, limited series)
Image Comics (Wildstorm Productions)

1-($2.50)-Grifter & Backlash app. in all; bound-in trading card. 2.40 6.00
2,3-($1.95) 1.60 4.00
2-Variant-c 1.00 2.80 7.00
3-Alternate-c by Portacio, see Deathblow #5 2.00 5.00
4-($2.50) 1.00 2.50
Trade paperback (2/95, $9.95) 1.25 3.75 10.00
NOTE: ***Booth** c/a-1-4. The first four issues contain coupons redeemable for a Jim Lee Grifter/Backlash print.*

KING ARTHUR AND THE KNIGHTS OF JUSTICE
Dec, 1993 - No. 3, Feb, 1994 ($1.25, limited series)
Marvel Comics UK

1-3: TV adaptation 1.25

KING CLASSICS
1977 (85¢, 36 pgs., cardboard-c)
King Features (Printed in Spain for U.S. distr.)

1-Connecticut Yankee, 2-Last of the Mohicans, 3-Moby Dick, 4-Robin Hood, 5-Swiss Family Robinson, 6-Robinson Crusoe, 7-Treasure Island, 8-20,000 Leagues, 9-Christmas Carol, 10-Huck Finn, 11-Around the World in 80 Days, 12-Davy Crockett, 13-Don Quixote, 14-Gold Bug, 15-Ivanhoe, 16-Three Musketeers, 17-Baron Munchausen, 18-Alice in Wonderland, 19-Black Arrow, 20-Five Weeks in a Balloon, 21-Great Expectations, 22-Gulliver's Travels, 23-Prince & Pauper, 24-Lawrence of Arabia (Originals, 1977-78)
each.... 1.00 3.00 8.00
Reprints, 1979; HRN-24) 2.40 6.00
NOTE: *The first eight issues were not numbered. Issues No. 25-32 were advertised but not published. The 1977 originals have HRN 32a; the 1978 originals have HRN 32b.*

KING COLT (Luke Short)
No. 651, Sept, 1955
Dell Publishing Co.

Four Color 651-Kinstler-a 3.60 11.00 40.00

KING COMICS (Strip reprints)
4/36 - No. 155, 11-12/49; No. 156, Spr/50 - No. 159, 2/52 (Winter on-c)
David McKay Publications/Standard #156-on

	GD25	FN65	VF82
1-1st app. Flash Gordon by Alex Raymond; Brick Bradford (1st app.), Popeye, Henry (1st app.) & Mandrake the Magician (1st app.) begin; Popeye-c begin	1028.00	3084.00	7200.00

(Estimated up to 25 total copies exist, none in NM/Mint)

	GD25	FN65	NM94
2	314.00	942.00	2200.00
3	200.00	600.00	1400.00
4	157.00	471.00	1100.00
5	114.00	342.00	800.00
6-10: 9-X-Mas-c	82.00	246.00	575.00
11-20	64.00	192.00	450.00
21-30: 21-X-Mas-c	46.00	138.00	325.00
31-40: 33-Last Segar Popeye	37.00	111.00	260.00
41-50: 46-Little Lulu, Alvin & Tubby app. as text illos by Marge Buell. 50-The Lone Ranger begins	29.00	86.00	230.00
51-60: 52-Barney Baxter begins?	20.00	60.00	160.00
61-The Phantom begins	17.50	53.00	140.00
62-80: 76-Flag-c. 79-Blondie begins	15.00	45.00	120.00
81-99	12.00	36.00	95.00
100	14.50	43.00	115.00
101-114: 114-Last Raymond issue (1 pg.); Flash Gordon by Austin Briggs begins, ends #155	10.50	32.00	85.00
115-145: 117-Phantom origin retold	8.75	26.25	65.00
146,147-Prince Valiant in both	7.15	21.50	50.00
148-155: 155-Flash Gordon ends (11-12/49)	7.15	21.50	50.00
156-159: 156-New logo begins (Standard)	6.50	19.50	45.00

NOTE: *Marge Buell text illos in No. 24-46 at least.*

KING CONAN (Conan The King No. 20 on)
Mar, 1980 - No. 19, Nov, 1983 (52 pgs.)
Marvel Comics Group

1 1.00 2.50
2-19: 4-Death of Thoth Amon. 7-1st Paul Smith-a, 1 pg. pin-up (9/81) .70 1.75
NOTE: ***J. Buscema** a-1-9p, 17p; c(p)-1-5, 7-9, 14, 17. **Kaluta** c-19. **Nebres** a-17i, 18, 19i. **Severin** c-18. **Simonson** c-6.*

KINGDOM COME
1996 - No. 4, 1996 ($4.95, painted limited series)
DC Comics (Elseworlds)

1- Mark Waid scripts & Alex Ross-painted c/a in all; tells the last days of the DC Universe; 1st app. Magog. 1.10 3.30 9.00
2-4: 2-Superman forms new Justice League. 3-Return of Capt. Marvel 1.00 2.80 7.00
Deluxe Slipcase Edition-($89.95) w/Revelations companion book, 12 new story pages, foil stamped covers, signed and numbered 11.00 33.00 110.00
Hardcover Edition-($29.95)-Includes 12 new story pages and artwork from

Kingpin nn © MEG

KISS: The Psycho Circus #3 © KISS Catalog Inc

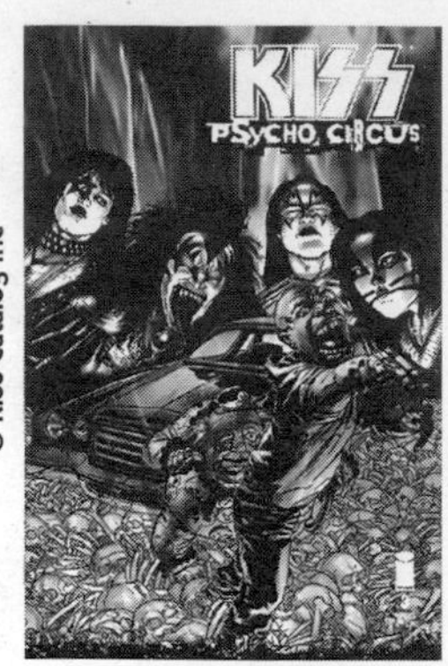

Kit Carson #7 © AVON

	GD25	FN65	NM94
Revelations, new cover artwork with gold foil inlay			29.95
Softcover Edition-($14.95)-Includes 12 new story pages and artwork from Revelations, new cover artwork			14.95

KING KONG (See Movie Comics)

KING LEONARDO & HIS SHORT SUBJECTS (TV)
Nov-Jan, 1961-62 - No. 4, Sept, 1963
Dell Publishing Co./Gold Key

	GD25	FN65	NM94
Four Color 1242,1278	13.00	38.00	140.00
01390-207(5-7/62)(Dell)	10.00	30.00	110.00
1 (10/62)	10.00	30.00	110.00
2-4	8.00	23.00	85.00

KING LOUIE & MOWGLI (See Jungle Book under Movie Comics)
May, 1968 (Disney)
Gold Key

	GD25	FN65	NM94
1 (#10223-805)-Characters from Jungle Book	1.65	5.00	18.00

KING OF DIAMONDS (TV)
July-Sept, 1962
Dell Publishing Co.

	GD25	FN65	NM94
01-391-209-Photo-c	2.75	8.00	30.00

KING OF KINGS (Movie)
No. 1236, Oct-Nov, 1961
Dell Publishing Co.

	GD25	FN65	NM94
Four Color 1236-Photo-c	7.00	22.00	80.00

KING OF THE BAD MEN OF DEADWOOD
1950 (See Wild Bill Hickok #16)
Avon Periodicals

	GD25	FN65	NM94
nn-Kinstler-c; Kamen/Feldstein-r/Cowpuncher #2	13.50	41.00	100.00

KING OF THE ROYAL MOUNTED (See Famous Feature Stories, King Comics, Red Ryder #3 & Super Book #2, 6)

KING OF THE ROYAL MOUNTED (Zane Grey's...)
No. 1, May, 1937; No. 9, 1940; No. 207, Dec, 1948 - No. 935, Sept-Nov, 1958
David McKay/Dell Publishing Co.

	GD25	FN65	NM94
Feature Books 1 (5/37)(McKay)	61.00	184.00	675.00
Large Feature Comic 9 (1940)	33.00	100.00	365.00
Four Color 207(#1, 12/48)	14.00	41.00	150.00
Four Color 265,283	7.00	22.00	80.00
Four Color 310,340	5.50	16.50	60.00
Four Color 363,384, 8(6-8/52)-10	4.50	13.50	50.00
11-20	3.00	9.00	35.00
21-28(3-5/58), Four Color 935(9-11/58)	2.75	8.00	30.00

NOTE: *4-Color No. 207, 265, 283, 310, 340, 363, 384 are all newspaper reprints with* ***Jim Gary*** *art. No. 8 on are all Dell originals. Painted c-No. 9-on.*

KINGPIN
Nov, 1997 ($5.99, squarebound, one-shot)
Marvel Comics

	GD25	FN65	NM94
nn-Spider-Man & Daredevil vs. Kingpin; Stan Lee-s/ John Romita Sr.-a			5.99

KING RICHARD & THE CRUSADERS
No. 588, Oct, 1954
Dell Publishing Co.

	GD25	FN65	NM94
Four Color 588-Movie, Matt Baker-a, photo-c	9.00	27.00	100.00

KINGS OF THE NIGHT
1990 - No. 2, 1990 ($2.25, limited series)
Dark Horse Comics

	GD25	FN65	NM94
1,2-Robert E. Howard adaptation; Bolton-c		.90	2.25

KING SOLOMON'S MINES (Movie)
1951
Avon Periodicals

	GD25	FN65	NM94
nn (#1 on 1st page)	34.00	103.00	250.00

KING TIGER & MOTORHEAD
Aug, 1996 - No. 2, Sept, 1996 ($2.95, limited series)
Dark Horse Comics

	GD25	FN65	NM94
1,2: Chichester scripts		1.20	3.00

KIPLING, RUDYARD (See Mowgli, The Jungle Book)

KISS (See Crazy Magazine, Howard the Duck #12, 13, Marvel Comics Super Special #1, 5, Rock Fantasy Comics #10 & Rock N' Roll Comics #9)

KISS: THE PSYCHO CIRCUS
Aug, 1997 - Present ($1.95)
Image Comics

	GD25	FN65	NM94
1-Holguin-s/Medina-a(p)	1.00	3.00	7.50
2		2.00	5.00
3,4		1.20	3.00

KISSYFUR (TV)
1989 (Sept.) ($2.00, 52 pgs., one-shot)
DC Comics

	GD25	FN65	NM94
1-Based on Saturday morning cartoon		.80	2.00

KIT CARSON (Formerly All True Detective Cases No. 4; Fighting Davy Crockett No. 9; see Blazing Sixguns & Frontier Fighters)
1950; No. 2, 8/51 - No. 3, 12/51; No. 5, 11-12/54 - No. 8, 9/55 (No #4)
Avon Periodicals

	GD25	FN65	NM94
nn(#1) (1950)- "...Indian Scout" ; r-Cowboys 'N' Injuns #?	10.50	32.00	85.00
2(8/51)	7.15	21.50	50.00
3(12/51)- "...Fights the Comanche Raiders"	6.00	18.00	42.00
5-6,8(11-12/54-9/55): 5-Formerly All True Detective Cases (last pre-code); titled "...and the Trail of Doom"	5.70	17.00	40.00
7-McCann-a?	6.00	18.00	42.00
I.W. Reprint #10('63)-r/Kit Carson #1; Severin-c	1.75	5.25	14.00

NOTE: ***Kinstler*** *c-1-3, 5-8.*

KIT CARSON & THE BLACKFEET WARRIORS
1953
Realistic

	GD25	FN65	NM94
nn-Reprint; Kinstler-c	7.85	23.50	55.00

KITE FUN BOOK
1954 - 1981 (16pgs, 5x7-1/4", soft-c)
Pacific, Gas & Electric/Sou. California Edison/Florida Power & Light

	GD25	FN65	NM94
1954-Donald Duck Tells About Kites-Fla. Power, S.C.E. & version with label issues-Barks pencils-8 pgs.; inks-7 pgs. (Rare)	400.00	1200.00	2800.00
1954-Donald Duck Tells About Kites-P.G.&E. issue -7th page redrawn changing middle 3 panels to show P.G.&E. in story line; (All Barks; last page Barks pencils only) Scarce	233.00	700.00	2100.00
1954-Pinocchio Learns About Kites (Disney)	39.00	117.00	350.00
1955-Brer Rabbit in "A Kite Tail" (Disney)	29.00	86.00	230.00
1956-Woody Woodpecker (Lantz)	11.30	34.00	95.00
1957-?			
1958-Tom And Jerry (M.G.M.)	5.50	16.50	55.00
1960-Porky Pig (Warner Bros.)	4.00	12.00	40.00
1960-Bugs Bunny (Warner Bros.)	4.00	12.00	40.00
1961-Huckleberry Hound (Hanna-Barbera)	5.00	15.00	50.00
1962-Yogi Bear (Hanna-Barbera)	3.20	9.60	32.00
1963-Rocky and Bullwinkle (TV)(Jay Ward)	9.50	28.50	95.00
1963-Top Cat (TV)(Hanna-Barbera)	4.00	12.00	40.00
1964-Magilla Gorilla (TV)(Hanna-Barbera)	3.50	10.50	35.00
1965-Jinks, Pixie and Dixie (TV)(Hanna-Barbera)	2.50	7.50	25.00
1965-Tweety and Sylvester (Warner); S.C.E. version with Reddy Kilowatt app.	1.10	3.30	9.00
1966-Secret Squirrel (Hanna-Barbera); S.C.E. version with Reddy Kilowatt app.	6.00	18.00	60.00

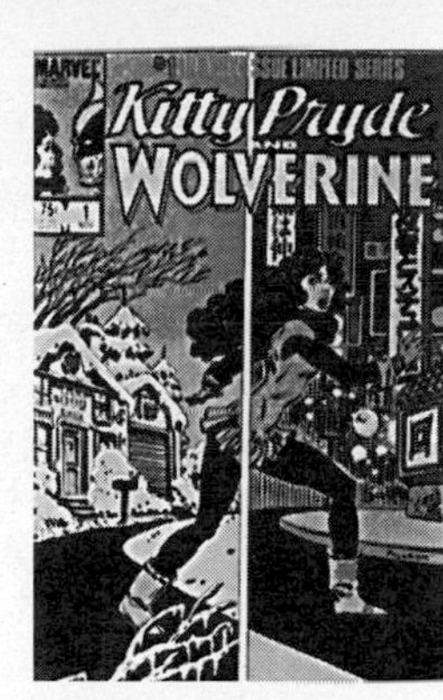

Kitty Pryde and Wolverine #1 © MEG

Knightstrike #1 © Rob Liefeld

Kobra #5 © DC

	GD25	FN65	NM94
1967-Beep! Beep! The Road Runner (TV)(Warner)	2.25	6.75	18.00
1968-Bugs Bunny (Warner Bros.)	2.50	7.50	20.00
1969-Dastardly and Muttley (TV)(Hanna-Barbera)	3.50	10.50	35.00
1970-Rocky and Bullwinkle (TV)(Jay Ward)	6.50	19.50	65.00
1971-Beep! Beep! The Road Runner (TV)(Warner)	1.85	5.50	15.00
1972-The Pink Panther (TV)	1.25	3.75	10.00
1973-Lassie (TV)	2.60	7.80	26.00
1974-Underdog (TV)	2.00	6.00	16.00
1975-Ben Franklin		2.40	6.00
1976-The Brady Bunch (TV)	2.00	6.00	16.00
1977-Ben Franklin		2.40	6.00
1977-Popeye	1.50	4.50	12.00
1978-Happy Days (TV)	1.10	3.30	9.00
1979-Eight is Enough (TV)	1.50	4.50	12.00
1980-The Waltons (TV, released in 1981)	1.50	4.50	12.00

KIT KARTER
May-July, 1962
Dell Publishing Co.

	GD25	FN65	NM94
1	1.80	5.40	18.00

KITTY
Oct, 1948
St. John Publishing Co.

	GD25	FN65	NM94
1-Teenage; Lily Renee-c/a	5.70	17.00	40.00

KITTY PRYDE, AGENT OF S.H.I.E.L.D. (Also see Excalibur)
Dec, 1997 - No. 3, Feb, 1998($2.50, limited series)
Marvel Comics

	GD25	FN65	NM94
1-3-Hama-s		1.00	2.50

KITTY PRYDE AND WOLVERINE (Also see Uncanny X-Men & X-Men)
Nov, 1984 - No. 6, Apr, 1985 (Limited series)
Marvel Comics Group

	GD25	FN65	NM94
1-Characters from X-Men		.80	2.00
2-6			1.50

KLARER GIVEAWAYS (See Wisco)

KNIGHTHAWK
Sept, 1995 - No. 6, Nov, 1995 ($2.50, limited series)
Acclaim Comics (Windjammer)

	GD25	FN65	NM94
1-6: 6-origin		1.00	2.50

KNIGHTMARE
Antarctic Press
July, 1994 ($2.75, B&W, mature readers)

	GD25	FN65	NM94
1		1.10	2.75

KNIGHTMARE
Feb, 1995 - No. 5, June, 1995 ($2.50)
Image Comics (Extreme Studios)

	GD25	FN65	NM94
0 ($3.50)		1.40	3.50
1-5: 5-Flip book w/Warcry		1.00	2.50
4-Quesada & Palmiotti variant-c		1.60	4.00

KNIGHTS OF PENDRAGON, THE (Also see Pendragon)
July, 1990 - No. 18, Dec, 1991 ($1.95)
Marvel Comics Ltd.

	GD25	FN65	NM94
1-18: 1-Capt. Britain app. 2,8-Free poster inside. 9,10-Bolton-c. 11,18-Iron Man app.		.80	2.00

KNIGHTS OF THE ROUND TABLE
No. 540, Mar, 1954
Dell Publishing Co.

	GD25	FN65	NM94
Four Color 540-Movie, photo-c	6.40	19.00	70.00

KNIGHTS OF THE ROUND TABLE
No. 10, April, 1957
Pines Comics

	GD25	FN65	NM94
10	4.00	11.00	22.00

KNIGHTS OF THE ROUND TABLE
Nov-Jan, 1963-64
Dell Publishing Co.

	GD25	FN65	NM94
1 (12-397-401)-Painted-c	2.25	6.75	25.00

KNIGHTSTRIKE (Also see Operation: Knightstrike)
Jan, 1996 ($2.50)
Image Comics (Extreme Studios)

	GD25	FN65	NM94
1-Rob Liefeld & Eric Stephenson story; Extreme Destroyer Part 6.		1.00	2.50

KNIGHT WATCHMAN: GRAVEYARD SHIFT
1994 ($2.95, B&W)
Caliber Press

	GD25	FN65	NM94
1,2-Ben Torres-a		1.20	3.00

KNOCK KNOCK (...Who's There?)
No. 801, 1936 (52 pgs.) (8x9", B&W)
Whitman Publ./Gerona Publications

	GD25	FN65	NM94
801-Joke book; Bob Dunn-a	5.70	17.00	35.00

KNOCKOUT ADVENTURES
Winter, 1953-54
Fiction House Magazines

	GD25	FN65	NM94
1-Reprints Fight Comics #53 w/Rip Carson-c/s	11.30	34.00	90.00

KNOW YOUR MASS
No. 303, 1958 (35¢, 100 Pg. Giant) (Square binding)
Catechetical Guild

	GD25	FN65	NM94
303-In color	2.00	6.00	16.00

KNUCKLES
Apr, 1997 - Present ($1.50/$1.75)
Archie Publications

	GD25	FN65	NM94
1-7			1.50
8-15: 8-Begin $1.75-c			1.75

KNUCKLES' CHAOTIX
Jan, 1996 ($2.00, annual)
Archie Publications

	GD25	FN65	NM94
1		.80	2.00

KOBALT
June, 1994 - No. 15, Sept, 1995 ($1.75/$2.50)
DC Comics (Milestone)

	GD25	FN65	NM94
1-12: 1-Byrne-c. 4-Intro Page		.70	1.75
13-15 ($2.50): 16-Kent Williams-c		1.00	2.50

KOBRA (See DC Special Series No. 1)
Feb-Mar, 1976 - No. 7, Mar-Apr, 1977
National Periodical Publications

	GD25	FN65	NM94
1-1st app.; Kirby-a redrawn by Marcos; only 25¢ issue		2.00	5.00
2-7: (All 30¢ issues) 3-Giffen-a		1.20	3.00

NOTE: ***Austin** a-3i. **Buckler** a-5p; c-5p. **Kubert** c-4. **Nasser** a-6p, 7; c-7.*

KOKEY KOALA (...and the Magic Button)
May, 1952
Toby Press

	GD25	FN65	NM94
1	8.50	25.50	60.00

KOKO AND KOLA (Also see A-1 Comics #16 & Tick Tock Tales)
Fall, 1946 - No. 5, May, 1947; No. 6, 1950
Com/Magazine Enterprises

	GD25	FN65	NM94
1-Funny animal	8.50	25.50	60.00
2-X-Mas-c	5.35	16.00	32.00

Konga #2 © CC

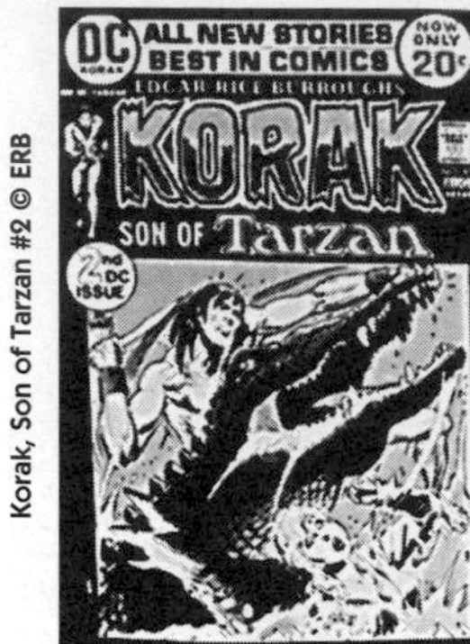

Korak, Son of Tarzan #2 © ERB

Krazy Komics #1 © MEG

	GD25	FN65	NM94
3-6: 6(A-1 28)	4.25	13.00	26.00

KO KOMICS
Oct, 1945
Gerona Publications

	GD25	FN65	NM94
1-The Duke of Darkness & The Menace (hero)	47.00	141.00	420.00

KOMIC KARTOONS
Fall, 1945 - No. 2, Winter, 1945
Timely Comics (EPC)

	GD25	FN65	NM94
1,2-Andy Wolf, Bertie Mouse	15.00	45.00	120.00

KOMIK PAGES (Formerly Snap; becomes Bullseye #11)
Apr, 1945 (All reprints)
Harry 'A' Chesler, Jr. (Our Army, Inc.)

	GD25	FN65	NM94
10(#1 on inside)-Land O' Nod by Rick Yager (2 pgs.), Animal Crackers, Foxy GrandPa, Tom, Dick & Mary, Cheerio Minstrels, Red Starr plus other 1-2 pg. strips; Cole-a	17.50	53.00	140.00

KONA (...Monarch of Monster Isle)
Feb-Apr, 1962 - No. 21, Jan-Mar, 1967 (Painted-c)
Dell Publishing Co.

	GD25	FN65	NM94
Four Color 1256 (#1)	5.50	16.50	60.00
2-10: 4-Anak begins	2.00	6.00	23.00
11-21	1.65	5.50	18.00

NOTE: *Glanzman a-all issues.*

KONGA (Fantastic Giants No. 24) (See Return of...)
1960; No. 2, Aug, 1961 - No. 23, Nov, 1965
Charlton Comics

	GD25	FN65	NM94
1(1960)-Based on movie; Giordano-c	22.00	66.00	220.00
2-Giordano-c	11.00	33.00	110.00
3-5	8.50	25.50	85.00
6-15	6.00	18.00	60.00
16-23	4.00	12.00	40.00

NOTE: ***Ditko** a-1, 3-15; c-4, 6-9. **Glanzman** a-12. **Montes** & **Bache** a-16-23.*

KONGA'S REVENGE (Formerly Return of...)
No. 2, Summer, 1963 - No. 3, Fall, 1964; Dec, 1968
Charlton Comics

	GD25	FN65	NM94
2,3: 2-Ditko-c/a	4.50	13.50	45.00
1(12/68)-Reprints Konga's Revenge #3	2.50	7.50	22.00

KONG THE UNTAMED
June-July, 1975 - V2#5, Feb-Mar, 1976
National Periodical Publications

	GD25	FN65	NM94
1-1st app. Kong; Wrightson-c; Alcala-a		2.00	5.00
2-5: 2-Wrightson-c. 2,3-Alcala-a		1.20	3.00

KOOKIE
Feb-Apr, 1962 - No. 2, May-July, 1962 (15 cents)
Dell Publishing Co.

	GD25	FN65	NM94
1,2: Written by John Stanley; Bill Williams-a	6.00	18.00	65.00

KOOSH KINS
Oct, 1991 - No. 3, Feb, 1992 ($1.00, bi-monthly, limited series)
Archie Comics

	GD25	FN65	NM94
1-3			1.00

NOTE: *No. 4 was planned, but cancelled.*

K. O. PUNCH, THE (Also see Lucky Fights It Through)
1948 (Educational giveaway)
E. C. Comics

	GD25	FN65	NM94
nn-Feldstein-splash; Kamen-a	83.00	250.00	750.00

KORAK, SON OF TARZAN (Edgar Rice Burroughs)(See Tarzan #139)
Jan, 1964 - No. 45, Jan, 1972 (Painted-c No. 1-?)
Gold Key

	GD25	FN65	NM94
1-Russ Manning-a	4.00	12.00	45.00
2-11-Russ Manning-a	2.50	7.50	27.00
12-21: 12,13-Warren Tufts-a. 14-Jon of the Kalahari ends. 15-Mabu, Jungle Boy begins. 21-Manning-a	1.65	5.00	18.00
22-30	1.20	3.60	12.00
31-45	.80	2.40	8.00

KORAK, SON OF TARZAN (Tarzan Family #60 on; see Tarzan #230)
V9#46, May-June, 1972 - V12#56, Feb-Mar, 1974; No. 57, May-June, 1975 - No. 59, Sept-Oct, 1975 (Edgar Rice Burroughs)
National Periodical Publications

	GD25	FN65	NM94
46-(52 pgs.)-Carson of Venus begins (origin), ends #56; Pellucidar feature; Weiss-a	1.25	3.75	10.00
47-59: 49-Origin Korak retold		1.60	4.00

NOTE: ***Kaluta** a-46-56. All have covers by **Joe Kubert**. **Manning** strip reprints-No. 57-59. **Frank Thorn** a-46-51.*

KOREA MY HOME (Also see Yalta to Korea)
nd (1950s)
Johnstone and Cushing

	GD25	FN65	NM94
nn-Anti-communist; Korean War	21.00	62.00	165.00

KORG: 70,000 B. C. (TV)
May, 1975 - No. 9, Nov, 1976 (Hanna-Barbera)
Charlton Publications

	GD25	FN65	NM94
1	1.10	3.30	9.00
2-Painted-c; Byrne text illos	1.25	3.75	10.00
3-9		2.40	6.00

KORNER KID COMICS
1947
Four Star Publications

	GD25	FN65	NM94
1	5.70	17.00	40.00

KRAZY KAT
1946 (Hardcover)
Holt

	GD25	FN65	NM94
Reprints daily & Sunday strips by Herriman	50.00	150.00	450.00
dust jacket only	39.00	117.00	350.00

KRAZY KAT (See Ace Comics & March of Comics No. 72, 87)

KRAZY KAT COMICS (...& Ignatz the Mouse early issues)
May-June, 1951 - F.C. #696, Apr, 1956; Jan, 1964 (None by Herriman)
Dell Publishing Co./Gold Key

	GD25	FN65	NM94
1(1951)	6.40	19.00	70.00
2-5 (#5, 8-10/52)	3.60	11.00	40.00
Four Color 454,504	3.00	9.00	35.00
Four Color 548,619,696 (4/56)	2.75	8.00	30.00
1(10098-401)(1/64-Gold Key)(TV)	2.75	8.00	30.00

KRAZY KOMICS (1st Series) (Cindy Comics No. 27 on)
July, 1942 - No. 26, Spr, 1947 (Also see Ziggy Pig)
Timely Comics (USA No. 1-21/JPC No. 22-26)

	GD25	FN65	NM94
1-Toughy Tomcat, Ziggy Pig (by Jaffee) & Silly Seal begin	42.00	126.00	375.00
2	20.00	60.00	160.00
3-8,10	14.00	41.00	110.00
9-Hitler parody	15.00	45.00	120.00
11,13,14	9.50	28.00	75.00
12-Timely's entire art staff drew themselves into a Creeper story	18.00	54.00	145.00
15-(8-9/44)-Becomes Funny Tunes #16; has "Super Soldier" by Pfc. Stan Lee	9.50	28.00	75.00
16-24,26: 16-(10-11/44). 26-Super Rabbit-c/story	8.50	26.00	60.00
25-Wacky Duck-c/story & begin; Kurtzman-a (6pgs.)	9.50	28.00	75.00

KRAZY KOMICS (2nd Series)

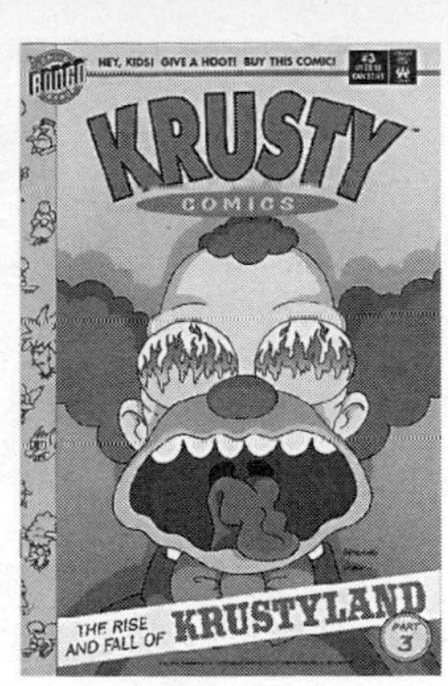

Krusty Comics #3 © Bongo Entertainment

Kull the Conqueror V3 #3 © MEG

Kurt Busiek's Astro City #4 © Juke Box Productions

GD25 FN65 NM94 GD25 FN65 NM94

Aug, 1948 - No. 2, Nov, 1948
Timely/Marvel Comics

1-Wolverton (10 pgs.) & Kurtzman (8 pgs.)-a; Eustice Hayseed begins (Li'l Abner swipe) 34.00 103.00 275.00
2-Wolverton-a (10 pgs.); Powerhouse Pepper cameo 25.00 75.00 200.00

KRAZY KROW (Also see Dopey Duck, Film Funnies, Funny Frolics & Movie Tunes)
Summer, 1945 - No. 3, Wint, 1945/46
Marvel Comics (ZPC)

1 14.00 41.00 110.00
2,3 9.50 28.00 75.00
I.W. Reprint #1('57), 2('58), 7 1.75 5.25 14.00

KRAZYLIFE (Becomes Nutty Life #2)
1945 (no month)
Fox Feature Syndicate

1-Funny animal 10.50 32.00 85.00

KREE/SKRULL WAR STARRING THE AVENGERS, THE
Sept, 1983 - No. 2, Oct, 1983 ($2.50, 68 pgs., Baxter paper)
Marvel Comics Group

1,2 1.00 2.50
NOTE: *Neal Adams p-1r, 2. Buscema a-1r, 2r. Simonson a-1p; c-1p.*

KRIM-KO KOMICS
5/18/35 - No. 6, 6/22/35; 1936 - 1939 (Giveaway, weekly)
Krim-ko Chocolate Drink

1-(16 pgs., soft-c, Dairy giveaways)-Tom, Mary & Sparky Advs. by Russell Keaton, Jim Hawkins by Dick Moores, Mystery Island! by Rick Yager begin 11.30 34.00 90.00
2-6 (6/22/35) 8.75 26.25 65.00
Lola, Secret Agent; 184 issues, 4 pg. giveaways - all original stories each.... 5.70 17.00 40.00

KROFFT SUPERSHOW (TV)
Apr, 1978 - No. 6, Jan, 1979
Gold Key

1-Photo-c 1.20 3.00
2-6: 6-Photo-c 1.50

KRULL
Nov, 1983 - No. 2, Dec, 1983
Marvel Comics Group

1,2-Adaptation of film; r/Marvel Super Special. 1-Photo-c from movie 1.00

KRUSTY COMICS (TV)(See Simpsons Comics)
1995 - No. 3, 1995 ($2.25, limited series)
Bongo Comics

1-3 1.00 2.50

KRYPTON CHRONICLES
Sept, 1981 - No. 3, Nov, 1981
DC Comics

1-3-Buckler-c(p) 1.00

KULL AND THE BARBARIANS
May, 1975 - No. 3, Sept, 1975 ($1.00, B&W, magazine, 84 pgs.)
Marvel Comics Group

1-Andru/Wood-r/Kull #1; 2 pgs. Neal Adams; Gil Kane(p), Marie & John Severin-a(r); Krenkel text illo. 2.40 6.00
2,3: 2-Red Sonja by Chaykin begins; Soloman Kane by Weiss/N. Adams; Gil Kane-a. 3-Origin Red Sonja by Chaykin; N. Adams-a; Solomon Kane app. 1.60 4.00

KULL THE CONQUEROR (...the Destroyer #11 on; see Creatures on the Loose #10, Marvel Preview, & Monsters on the Prowl)
June, 1971 - No. 2, Sept, 1971; No. 3, July, 1972 - No. 15, Aug, 1974; No. 16, Aug, 1976 - No. 29, Oct, 1978
Marvel Comics Group

1-Andru/Wood-a; 2nd app. & origin Kull; 15¢ issue 2.50 7.50 20.00
2-5: 2-Last 15¢ issue. 3-13: 20¢ issues 1.00 3.00 8.00
6-10 2.40 6.00
11-15: 11-15-Ploog-a. 14,15: 25¢ issues 1.60 4.00
16-(Regular 25¢ edition)(8/76) 1.60 4.00
16-(30¢-c, limited distribution) 2.00 6.00 16.00
17-29 1.00 2.50
NOTE: *No. 1, 2, 7-9, 11 are based on Robert E. Howard stories. **Alcala** a-17p, 18-20i; c-24. **Ditko** a-12r, 15r. **Gil Kane** c-15p, 21. **Nebres** a-22i-27i; c-25i, 27i. **Ploog** c-11, 12p, 13. **Severin** a-2-9i; c-2-10i, 19. **Starlin** c-14.*

KULL THE CONQUEROR
Dec, 1982 - No. 2, Mar, 1983 (52 pgs., Baxter paper)
Marvel Comics Group

1,2: 1-Buscema-a(p) .80 2.00

KULL THE CONQUEROR (No. 9,10 titled "Kull")
5/83 - No. 10, 6/85 (52 pgs., Baxter paper)
Marvel Comics Group

V3#1-10: Buscema-a in #1-3,5-10 1.00
NOTE: Bolton a-4. Golden painted c-3-8. Guice a-4p. Sienkiwicz a-4; c-2.

KUNG FU (See Deadly Hands of..., & Master of...)

KUNG FU FIGHTER (See Richard Dragon...)

KURT BUSIEK'S ASTRO CITY
Aug, 1995 - No. 6, Jan, 1996 ($2.25, limited series)
Image Comics (Juke Box Productions)

1-Kurt Busiek scripts, Brent Anderson-a & Alex Ross front & back-c begins; 1st app. Samaritan & Honor Guard (Cleopatra, MHP, Beautie, The Black Rapier, Quarrel & N-Forcer) 1.25 3.75 10.00
2-6: 2-1st app. The Silver Agent, The Old Soldier, & the "original" Honor Guard (Max O'Millions, Starwoman, the "original" Cleopatra, the "original" N-Forcer, the Bouncing Beatnik, Leopardman & Kitkat). 3-1st app. Jack-in-the-Box & The Deacon. 4-1st app. Winged Victory (cameo), The Hanged Man & The First Family. 5-1st app. Crackerjack, The Astro City Irregulars, Nightingale & Sunbird. 6-Origin Samaritan; 1st full app Winged Victory 2.40 6.00

KURT BUSIEK'S ASTRO CITY
V2#1, Sept, 1996 - Present ($2.50) (1st Homage Comics series)
Image Comics (Homage Comics)

V2#1/2-(10/96)-The Hanged Man story; 1st app. The All-American & Slugger, The Lamplighter, The Time-Keeper & Eterneon 2.00 5.00
V2#1- Kurt Busiek scripts, Alex Ross-c, Brent Anderson-p & Will Blyberg-i begin; intro The Gentleman, Thunderhead & Helia. 1.00 2.80 7.00
V2#2,3: 2-Origin The First Family; Astra story 1.60 4.00
V2#4-12: 4-1st app. The Crossbreed, Ironhorse, Glue Gun & The Confessor (cameo) 1.00 2.50
Life In The Big City-(8/96, $19.95, trade paperback)-r/Image Comics limited series w/sketchbook & cover gallery; Ross-c 20.00
Life In The Big City-(8/96, $49.95, hardcover, 1000 print run)-r/Image Comics limited series w/sketchbook & cover gallery; Ross-c 50.00

LABMAN
Nov, 1996 ($3.50, one-shot)
Image Comics

1-Allred-c 1.60 4.00

LABOR IS A PARTNER
1949 (32 pgs., paper-c)
Catechetical Guild Educational Society

nn-Anti-communism 16.00 49.00 130.00
Confidential Preview-(8-1/2x11", B&W, saddle stitched)-only one known copy;

La Cosa Nostroid #4 © Rob Schrab

Lady Death #2 © Chaos!

Lady Luck #88 © QUA

GD25 FN65 NM94

text varies from color version, advertises next book on secularism (If the Devil Would Talk) 31.00 94.00 250.00

LABYRINTH
Nov, 1986 - No. 3, Jan, 1987 (Limited series)
Marvel Comics Group

1-3: Movie adaptation; r/Marvel Super Special #40 1.00

LA COSA NOSTROID
Mar, 1996 - Present ($2.95, B&W)
Fireman Press

1-6-Dan Harmon-s/Rob Schrab-c/a 2.95

LAD: A DOG (Movie)
1961 - No. 2, July-Sept, 1962
Dell Publishing Co.

Four Color 1303, 2 2.75 8.00 30.00

LADY AND THE TRAMP (Disney, See Dell Giants & Movie Comics)
No. 629, May, 1955 - No. 634, June, 1955
Dell Publishing Co.

Four Color 629 (#1)-..with Jock 5.50 16.50 60.00
Four Color 634-...Album 3.65 11.00 40.00

LADY AND THE TRAMP IN "BUTTER LATE THAN NEVER"
1955 (16 pgs., 5x7-1/4", soft-c) (Walt Disney)
American Dairy Association (Premium)

nn 9.50 28.00 75.00

LADY COP (See 1st Issue Special)

LADY DEATH (See Evil Ernie)
Jan, 1994 - No. 3, Mar, 1994 ($2.75, limited series)
Chaos! Comics

1/2: S. Hughes-c/a in all 1.50 4.50 12.00
1/2 Gold 2.50 7.50 20.00
1/2 Velvet 1.50 4.50 12.00
1/2 Signed Limited Edition 2.00 6.00 16.00
1-($3.50)-Chromium-c 4.00 12.00 40.00
1-Commemorative 3.00 9.00 30.00
1-(9/96, $2.95) "Encore Presentation"; r/#1 1.20 3.00
2 2.50 7.50 20.00
3 1.50 4.50 12.00
...And The Women of Chaos! Gallery #1 (11/96, $2.25) pin-ups by various .90 2.25
...Death Becomes Her #0 (11/97, $2.95) Hughes-c/a 2.95
...FAN Edition: All Hallow's Eve #1 (1/97, mail-in) 2.40 6.00
...In Lingerie #1 (8/95, $2.95) pin-ups, wraparound-c 1.20 3.00
...In Lingerie #1-Leather Edition (10,000) 2.50 7.50 20.00
...In Lingerie #1-Micro Premium Edition; Lady Demon-c (2,000) 6.00 18.00 60.00
...Swimsuit Special #1-($2.50)-Wraparound-c 1.60 4.00
...Swimsuit Special #1-Red velvet-c 2.50 7.50 20.00
...: The Reckoning (7/94, $6.95)-r/#1-3 1.00 2.80 7.00
...: The Reckoning (8/95, $12.95)- new printing including Lady Death 1/2 & Swimsuit Special #1 1.30 4.85 13.00

LADY DEATH: THE CRUCIBLE
Nov, 1996 - No. 6, Oct, 1997 ($3.50/$2.95, limited series)
Chaos! Comics

1/2 2.00 5.00
1/2 Cloth Edition 1.25 3.75 10.00
1-Wraparound silver foil embossed-c 2.00 5.00
1-($19.95)-Leather Edition 1.85 5.50 15.00
2-6-($2.95) 1.20 3.00

LADY DEATH: THE ODYSSEY
Apr, 1996 - No. 4, Aug, 1996 ($3.50/$2.95)
Chaos! Comics

1-($1.50)-Sneak Peek Preview 1.50
1-($1.50)-Sneak Peek Preview Micro Premium Edition (2500 print run) 2.50 7.50 20.00
1-($3.50)-Embossed, wraparound goil foil-c 1.00 3.00 8.00
1-Black Onyx Edition (200 print run) 12.50 38.00 125.00
1-($19.95)-Premium Edition (10,000 print run) 2.50 7.50 20.00
2-4-($2.95) 1.60 4.00

LADY DEATH II: BETWEEN HEAVEN & HELL
Mar, 1995 - No. 4, July, 1995 ($3.50, limited series)
Chaos! Comics

1-Chromium wraparound-c; Evil; Ernie cameo 1.25 3.75 10.00
1-Commemorative (4,000) 3.00 9.00 30.00
1-Black Velvet-c 3.00 9.00 30.00
1-Gold 2.50 7.50 20.00
1-"Refractor" edition (5,000) 4.00 12.00 40.00
2-4 1.20 3.00
4-Lady Demon variant-c 1.85 5.50 15.00
Trade paperback-($12.95)-r/#1-4 13.00

LADY FOR A NIGHT (See Cinema Comics Herald)

LADY JUSTICE (See Neil Gaiman's...)

LADY LUCK (Formerly Smash #1-85) (Also see Spirit Sections #1)
No. 86, Dec, 1949 - No. 90, Aug, 1950
Quality Comics Group

86(#1) 73.00 219.00 600.00
87-90 56.00 168.00 450.00

LADY PENDRAGON
Mar, 1996 ($2.50)
Maximum Press

1-Matt Hawkins script 1.00 2.50

LADY RAWHIDE
July, 1995 - No. 5, Mar, 1996 ($2.95, bi-monthly, limited series)
Topps Comics

1-5: Don McGregor scripts & Mayhew-a. in all. 2-Stelfreeze-c. 3-Hughes-c. 4-Golden-c. 5-Julie Bell-c. .80 2.00
Special Edition 1 (6/95, $3.95)-Reprints .80 2.00

LADY RAWHIDE (Volume 2)
Oct, 1996 -No. 5, June, 1997 ($2.95, limited series)
Topps Comics

1-5: 1-Julie Bell-c. .80 2.00

LADY SUPREME (See Asylum)(Also see Supreme & Kid Supreme)
May, 1996 - No. 2, June, 1996 ($2.50, limited series)
Image Comics (Extreme Studios)

1,2-Terry Moore -s: 1-Terry Moore-c. 2-Flip book w/Newmen preview 1.00 2.50

LADY VAMPRE
June, 1995 - No. 1, 1995 ($2.95)
Blackout Comics

0,1 1.20 3.00

LADY VAMPRE: IN THE FLESH
1997 ($2.95, B&W, one-shot)
Blackout Comics

1-Photo-c 1.20 3.00
1-($9.95)-Variant-c 1.25 3.75 10.00

LADY VAMPRE: PLEASURES OF THE FLESH
1996 - Present ($2.95, B&W, limited series)
Blackout Comics

1-Wraparound-c 1.20 3.00

Lana #2 © MEG

Land of Nod #2 © Jay Stephens

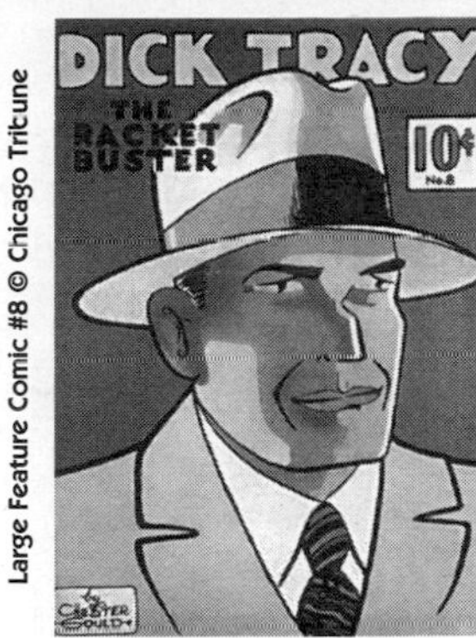

Large Feature Comic #8 © Chicago Tribune

LAFF-A-LYMPICS (TV)(See The Funtastic World of Hanna-Barbera)
Mar, 1978 - No. 13, Mar, 1979 (Hanna-Barbera)
Marvel Comics

	GD25	FN65	NM94
1-Yogi Bear, Scooby Doo, Pixie & Dixie, etc. 11-Jetsons x-over; 1 pg. illustrated bio of Mighty Mightor, Herculoids, Shazzan, Galaxy Trio & Space Ghost	1.25	3.75	10.00
2-13	1.10	3.30	9.00

LAFFY-DAFFY COMICS
Feb, 1945 - No. 2, Mar, 1945
Rural Home Publ. Co.

	GD25	FN65	NM94
1,2-Funny animal	6.50	19.50	45.00

LANA (Little Lana No. 8 on)
Aug, 1948 - No. 7, Aug, 1949 (Also see Annie Oakley)
Marvel Comics (MjMC)

	GD25	FN65	NM94
1-Rusty, Millie begin	14.00	43.00	110.00
2-Kurtzman's "Hey Look" (1); last Rusty	10.00	30.00	70.00
3-7: 3-Nellie begins	7.00	21.00	45.00

LANCELOT & GUINEVERE (See Movie Classics)

LANCELOT LINK, SECRET CHIMP (TV)
Apr, 1971 - No. 8, Feb, 1973
Gold Key

	GD25	FN65	NM94
1-Photo-c	2.75	8.00	30.00
2-8: 2-Photo-c	1.65	5.00	18.00

LANCELOT STRONG (See The Shield)

LANCE O'CASEY (See Mighty Midget & Whiz Comics)
Spring, 1946 - No. 3, Fall, 1946; No. 4, Summer, 1948
Fawcett Publications

	GD25	FN65	NM94
1-Captain Marvel app. on-c	26.00	80.00	210.00
2	17.00	51.00	135.00
3,4	12.00	36.00	95.00

NOTE: *The cover for the 1st issue was done in 1942 but was not published until 1946. The cover shows 68 pages but actually has only 36 pages.*

LANCER (TV)(Western)
Feb, 1969 - No. 3, Sept, 1969 (All photo-c)
Gold Key

	GD25	FN65	NM94
1	2.25	6.75	24.00
2,3	1.65	5.00	18.00

LAND OF NOD, THE
July, 1997 - Present ($2.95, B&W)
Dark Horse Comics

	GD25	FN65	NM94
1,2-Jetcat; Jay Stephens-s/a			2.95

LAND OF THE GIANTS (TV)
Nov, 1968 - No. 5, Sept, 1969 (All have photo-c)
Gold Key

	GD25	FN65	NM94
1	4.00	12.00	45.00
2-5	2.25	6.75	25.00

LAND OF THE LOST COMICS (Radio)
July-Aug, 1946 - No. 9, Spring, 1948
E. C. Comics

	GD25	FN65	NM94
1	25.00	75.00	200.00
2	17.00	51.00	135.00
3-9	14.00	41.00	110.00

LAND UNKNOWN, THE (Movie)
No. 845, Sept, 1957
Dell Publishing Co.

	GD25	FN65	NM94
Four Color 845-Alex Toth-a	11.00	34.00	125.00

LA PACIFICA
1994/1995 ($4.95, B&W, limited series, digest size, mature readers)
DC Comics (Paradox Press)

	GD25	FN65	NM94
1-3		2.00	5.00

LARAMIE (TV)
Aug, 1960 - July, 1962 (All photo-c)
Dell Publishing Co.

	GD25	FN65	NM94
Four Color 1125-Gil Kane/Heath-a	9.00	27.00	100.00
Four Color 1223,1284, 01-418-207 (7/62)	5.50	16.50	60.00

LAREDO (TV)
June, 1966
Gold Key

	GD25	FN65	NM94
1 (10179-606)-Photo-c	2.50	7.50	28.00

LARGE FEATURE COMIC (Formerly called Black & White in previous guides)
1939 - No. 13, 1943
Dell Publishing Co.

Note: See individual alphabetical listings for prices

1 (Series I)-Dick Tracy Meets the Blank
2-Terry and the Pirates (#1)
3-Heigh-Yo Silver! The Lone Ranger (text & ill.)(76 pgs.); also exists as a Whitman #710; based on radio
4-Dick Tracy Gets His Man
5-Tarzan of the Apes (#1) by Harold Foster (origin); reprints 1st Tarzan dailies from 1929
6-Terry & the Pirates & The Dragon Lady; reprints dailies from 1936
7-(Scarce, 52 pgs.)-Hi-Yo Silver the Lone Ranger to the Rescue; also exists as a Whitman #715, based on radio program
8-Dick Tracy the Racket Buster
9-King of the Royal Mounted (Zane Grey's...)
10-(Scarce)-Gang Busters (No. appears on inside front cover); first slick cover (based on radio program)
11-Dick Tracy Foils the Mad Doc Hump
12-Smilin' Jack; no number on-c
13-Dick Tracy and Scottie of Scotland Yard
14-Smilin' Jack Helps G-Men Solve a Case!
15-Dick Tracy and the Kidnapped Princes
16-Donald Duck; 1st app. Daisy Duck on back cover (6/41-Disney)
17-Gang Busters (1941)
18-Phantasmo (see The Funnies #45)
19-Dumbo Comic Paint Book (Disney); partial-r from 4 Color #17
20-Donald Duck Comic Paint Book (rarer than #16) (Disney)
21,22: 21-Private Buck. 22-Nuts & Jolts
23-The Nebbs
24-Popeye in "Thimble Theatre" by Segar
25-Smilin' Jack-1st issue to show title on-c
26-Smitty
27-Terry and the Pirates; Caniff-c/a
28-Grin and Bear It
29-Moon Mullins
30-Tillie the Toiler
1 (Series II)-Peter Rabbit by Harrison Cady; arrival date-3/27/42
2-Winnie Winkle (#1)
3-Dick Tracy
4-Tiny Tim (#1)
5-Toots and Casper
6-Terry and the Pirates; Caniff-a
7-Pluto Saves the Ship (#1) (Disney)-Written by Carl Barks, Jack Hannah, & Nick George (Barks' 1st comic book work)
8-Bugs Bunny (#1)('42)
9-Bringing Up Father
10-Popeye (Thimble Theatre)
11-Barney Google and Snuffy Smith
12-Private Buck
13-(nn)-1001 Hours Of Fun; puzzles & games; by A. W. Nugent. This book was bound as #13 with Large Feature Comics in publisher's files

NOTE: *The Black & White Feature Books are oversized 8-1/2x11-3/8" comics with color covers and black and white interiors. The first nine issues all have rough, heavy stock covers and, except for #7, all have 76 pages, including covers. #7 and #10-on all have 52 pages. Beginning with #10 the covers are slick and thin and, because of their size, are difficult to handle without damaging. For this reason, they are seldom found in fine to mint condition. The paper stock, unlike Wow #1 and Capt. Marvel #1, is itself not unstable ...just thin.*

LARRY DOBY, BASEBALL HERO
1950 (Cleveland Indians)

Lash LaRue Western #46 © FAW

Lassie #1 © DELL

The Last American #1 © Alan Grant

GD25 FN65 NM94

Fawcett Publications
nn-Bill Ward-a; photo-c 61.00 183.00 550.00

LARRY HARMON'S LAUREL AND HARDY (...Comics)
July-Aug, 1972 (Regular & Digest size)
National Periodical Publications
1, Digest 1 5.50 16.50 55.00

LARS OF MARS
No. 10, Apr-May, 1951 - No. 11, July-Aug, 1951 (Painted-c)
Ziff-Davis Publishing Co.
10-Origin; Anderson-a(3) in each 62.00 187.00 550.00
11-Gene Colan-a 50.00 150.00 420.00

LARS OF MARS 3-D
Apr, 1987 ($2.50)
Eclipse Comics
1-r/Lars of Mars #10,11 in 3-D plus new story 1.00 2.50
2-D limited edition (B&W, 100 copies) 1.60 4.00

LASER ERASER & PRESSBUTTON (See Axel Pressbutton & Miracle Man 9)
Nov, 1985 - No. 6, 1987 (95¢/$2.50, limited series)
Eclipse Comics
1-6: 5,6-(95¢) 1.00
...In 3-D 1 (8/86, $2.50) 1.00 2.50
2-D 1 (B&W, limited to 100 copies signed & numbered)
1.00 2.50

LASH LARUE WESTERN (Movie star; king of the bullwhip)(See Fawcett Movie Comic, Motion Picture Comics & Six-Gun Heroes)
Sum, 1949 - No. 46, Jan, 1954 (36pgs., 1-7,9,13,16-on)
Fawcett Publications
1-Lash & his horse Black Diamond begin; photo front/back-c begin
89.00 267.00 800.00
2(11/49) 36.00 108.00 325.00
3-5 34.00 103.00 275.00
6,7,9: 6-Last photo back-c; intro. Frontier Phantom (Lash's twin brother)
26.00 80.00 210.00
8,10 (52pgs.) 28.00 83.00 220.00
11,12,14,15 (52pgs.) 19.00 56.00 150.00
13,16-20 (36pgs.) 15.50 47.00 125.00
21-30: 21-The Frontier Phantom app. 14.00 41.00 110.00
31-45 12.00 36.00 95.00
46-Last Fawcett issue & photo-c 12.00 38.00 100.00

LASH LARUE WESTERN (Continues from Fawcett series)
No. 47, Mar-Apr, 1954 - No. 84, June, 1961
Charlton Comics
47-Photo-c 15.00 45.00 120.00
48 11.30 34.00 90.00
49-60 8.75 26.25 65.00
61-66,69,70: 52-r/#8; 53-r/#22 6.00 18.00 60.00
67,68-(68 pgs.). 68-Check-a 6.00 18.00 60.00
71-83 4.00 12.00 40.00
84-Last issue 5.00 15.00 50.00

LASH LARUE WESTERN
1990 ($3.50, 44 pgs) (24 pgs. of color, 16 pgs. of B&W)
AC Comics
1-Photo covers; r/Lash #6; r/old movie posters 1.40 3.50
Annual 1 (1990, $2.95, B&W, 44 pgs.)-Photo covers 1.20 3.00

LASSIE (TV)(M-G-M's... #1-36; see Kite Fun Book)
June, 1950 - No. 70, July, 1969
Dell Publishing Co./Gold Key No. 59 (10/62) on
1 (52 pgs.)-Photo-c; inside lists One Shot #282 in error
13.00 39.00 140.00
2-Painted-c begin 5.50 16.50 60.00
3-10 3.50 10.50 38.00
11-19: 12-Rocky Langford (Lassie's master) marries Gerry Lawrence. 15-1st app. Timbu 2.50 7.50 28.00
20-22-Matt Baker-a 3.00 9.00 32.00
23-38,40: 33-Robinson-a. 2.00 6.00 22.00
39-1st app. Timmy as Lassie picks up her TV family 3.60 11.00 40.00
2.00 6.00 22.00
41-58,60-70: 63-Last Timmy (10/63). 64-r/#19. 65-Forest Ranger Corey Stuart begins, ends #69. 70-Forest Rangers Bob Ericson & Scott Turner app. (Lassie's new masters) 1.80 5.50 20.00
59 (10/62)-1st Gold Key 3.00 9.00 32.00
11193(1978, $1.95, 224 pgs., Golden Press)-Baker-r (92 pgs.)
1.50 4.50 12.00
The Adventures of... nn-(Red Heart Dog Food giveaway, 1949)-16 pgs, soft-c; 1st app. Lassie in comics 15.00 45.00 160.00
NOTE: *Photo c-57, 63. (See March of Comics #210, 217, 230, 254, 266, 278, 296, 308, 324, 334, 346, 358, 370, 381, 394, 411, 432)*

LAST AMERICAN, THE
Dec, 1990 - No. 4, March, 1991 ($2.25, mini-series)
Marvel Comics (Epic Comics)
1-4: Alan Grant scripts .90 2.25

LAST AVENGERS STORY, THE (Last Avengers #1)
Nov, 1995 - No. 2, Dec, 1995 ($5.95, painted, limited series)
Marvel Comics (Alterniverse)
1,2: Peter David story; acetate-c in all. 1-New team (Hank Pym, Wasp, Human Torch, Cannonball, She-Hulk, Hotshot, Bombshell, Tommy Maximoff, Hawkeye, & Mockingbird) forms to battle Ultron 59, Kang the Conqueror, The Grim Reaper & Oddball 2.40 6.00

LAST DAYS OF THE JUSTICE SOCIETY SPECIAL
1986 ($2.50, one-shot, 68 pgs.)
DC Comics
1-62 pg. JSA story plus unpubbed G.A. pg. 1.00 2.50

LAST GENERATION, THE
1986 - No. 5, 1989 ($1.95, B&W, high quality paper)
Black Tie Studios
1-5 .80 2.00
Book 1 (1989, $6.95)-By Caliber Press 1.00 2.80 7.00

LAST HUNT, THE
No. 678, Feb, 1956
Dell Publishing Co.
Four Color 678-Movie, photo-c 6.40 19.00 70.00

LAST KISS
1988 ($3.95, B&W, squarebound, 52 pgs.)
ACME Press (Eclipse)
1-One story adapts E.A. Poe's The Black Cat 1.60 4.00

LAST OF THE COMANCHES (Movie) (See Wild Bill Hickok #28)
1953
Avon Periodicals
nn-Kinstler-c/a, 21pgs.; Ravielli-a 13.00 39.00 95.00

LAST OF THE ERIES, THE (See American Graphics)

LAST OF THE FAST GUNS, THE
No. 925, Aug, 1958
Dell Publishing Co.
Four Color 925-Movie, photo-c 6.40 19.00 70.00

LAST OF THE MOHICANS (See King Classics & White Rider and...)

LAST OF THE VIKING HEROES, THE (Also see Silver Star #1)

The Last One #2 © J.M DeMatteis & Dan Sweetman

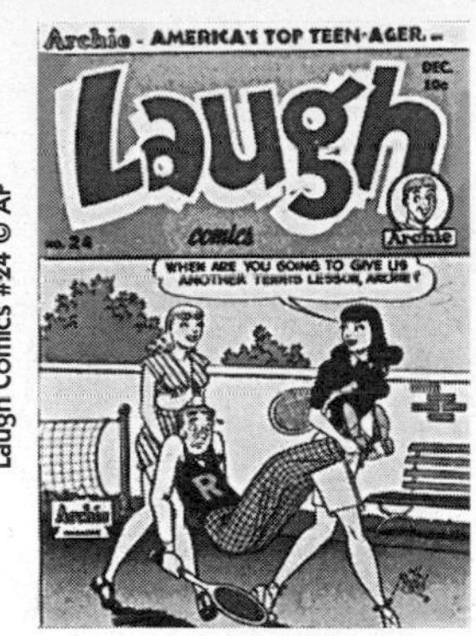

Laugh Comics #24 © AP

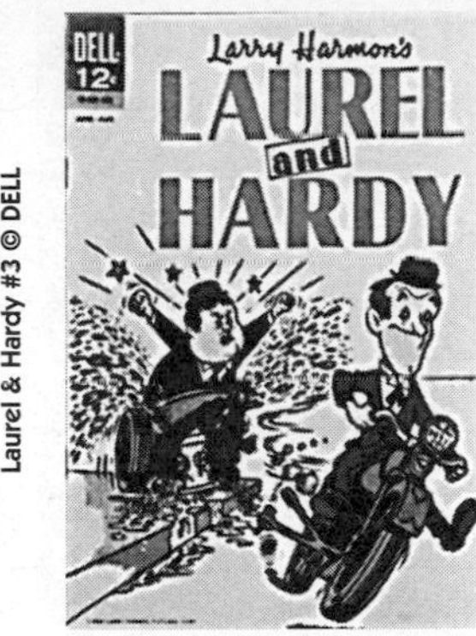

Laurel & Hardy #3 © DELL

GD25 FN65 NM94

Mar, 1987 - No. 12 ($1.50/$1.95)
Genesis West Comics

1-4: 4-Intro The Phantom Force 1.50
1-Signed edition ($1.50) 1.50
5A,5B,6-12: 5A-Kirby/Stevens-c. 5B,6 ($1.95). 7-Art Adams-c. 8-Kirby back-c. 9,10,12-($2.50) .80 2.00
Summer Special 1-3: 1-(1988)-Frazetta-c & illos. 2(1990, $2.50)-A TMNT app. 3 (1991, $2.50)-Teenage Mutant Ninja Turtles 1.00 2.50
Summer Special 1-Signed edition (sold for $1.95) .80 2.00
NOTE: ***Art Adams** c-7. **Byrne** c-3. **Kirby** c-1p, 5p. **Perez** c-2i. **Stevens** c-5Ai.*

LAST ONE, THE
July, 1993 - No. 6, Dec, 1993 ($2.50, limited series, mature readers)
DC Comics (Vertigo)

1-6 1.00 2.50

LAST STARFIGHTER, THE
Oct, 1984 - No. 3, Dec, 1984 (75¢, movie adaptation)
Marvel Comics Group

1-3: r/Marvel Super Special; Guice-c 1.00

LAST TEMPTATION, THE
1994 - No. 3, 1994 ($4.95, limited series)
Marvel Comics

1-3: Alice Cooper story; Neil Gaiman scripts; McKean-c; Zulli-a 2.00 5.00

LAST TRAIN FROM GUN HILL
No. 1012, July, 1959
Dell Publishing Co.

Four Color 1012-Movie, photo-c 8.00 25.00 90.00

LATEST ADVENTURES OF FOXY GRANDPA (See Foxy Grandpa)

LATEST COMICS (Super Duper No. 3?)
Mar, 1945 - No. 2, 1945?
Spotlight Publ./Palace Promotions (Jubilee)

1-Super Duper 11.30 34.00 90.00
2-Bee-29 (nd); Jubilee in indicia blacked out 8.75 26.25 70.00

LAUGH
June, 1987 - No. 29, Aug, 1991 (75¢/$1.00)
Archie Enterprises

V2#1-29: 5,19-X-Mas issues. 14-1st app. Hot Dog. 24-Re-intro Super Duck 1.00

LAUGH COMICS (Teenage) (Formerly Black Hood #9-19) (Laugh #226 on)
No. 20, Fall, 1946 - No. 400, Apr, 1987
Archie Publications (Close-Up)

20-Archie begins; Katy Keene & Taffy begin by Woggon; Suzie & Wilbur also begin; Archie covers begin 47.00 141.00 465.00
21-23,25 28.00 83.00 220.00
24- "Pipsy" by Kirby (6 pgs.) 29.00 86.00 230.00
26-30 14.00 41.00 110.00
31-40 10.00 30.00 80.00
41-60: 41,54-Debbi by Woggon 6.85 21.00 48.00
61-80: 67-Debbi by Woggon 5.70 17.00 35.00
81-99 2.80 8.40 28.00
100 3.20 9.60 32.00
101-126: 125-Debbi app 2.25 6.75 [illegible]
127-144: Super-hero app. in all (see note) 2.50 7.50 24.00
145-160: 157-Josie app. 1.75 5.25 14.00
161-165,167-200 1.25 3.75 10.00
166-Beatles-c 3.00 9.00 30.00
201-240 2.40 6.00
241-280 1.60 4.00
281-350 1.20 3.00
351-400: 381-384-Katy Keene app.; by Woggon-381,382 .80 2.00
NOTE: *The Fly app. in 128, 129, 132, 134, 138, 139. Flygirl app. in 136, 137, 143. Flyman app. in 137. The Jaguar app. in 127, 130, 131, 133, 135, 140-142, 144. Josie app. in 145, 160, 164. Katy Keene app. in 20-125, 129, 130, 133. Many issues contain paper dolls. **Al Fagaly** c-20-29. **Montana** c-33, 36, 37, 42. **BillVigoda** c-30, 50.*

LAUGH COMICS DIGEST (...Magazine #23-89; Laugh Digest Mag. #90 on)
8/74; No. 2, 9/75; No. 3, 3/76 - Present (Digest-size)
Archie Publications (Close-Up No. 1, 3 on)

1-Neal Adams-a 2.50 7.50 24.00
2,7,8,19-Neal Adams-a 1.75 5.25 14.00
3-6,9,10 1.25 3.75 10.00
11-18,20 1.00 3.00 8.00
21-40 2.40 6.00
41-80 1.60 4.00
81-100 1.20 3.00
101-130 .80 2.00
131-139-145: 139-Begin $1.89-c 1.89
NOTE: *Katy Keene in 23, 25, 27, 32-38, 40, 45-48, 50. The Fly-r in 19, 20. The Jaguar-r in 25, 27. Mr. Justice-r in 21. The Web-r in 23.*

LAUGH COMIX (Formerly Top Notch Laugh; Suzie Comics No. 49 on)
No. 46, Summer, 1944 - No. 48, Winter, 1944-45
MLJ Magazines

46-Wilbur & Suzie in all; Harry Sahle-c 17.00 51.00 135.00
47,48: 47-Sahle-c. 48-Bill Vigoda-c 12.00 38.00 100.00

LAUGH-IN MAGAZINE (TV)(Magazine)
Oct, 1968 - No. 12, Oct, 1969 (50¢) (Satire)
Laufer Publ. Co.

V1#1 3.00 9.00 30.00
2-12 2.50 7.50 20.00

LAUREL & HARDY (See Larry Harmon's... & March of Comics No. 302, 314)

LAUREL AND HARDY (...Comics)
3/49 - No. 3, 9/49; No. 26, 11/55 - No. 28, 3/56 (No #4-25)
St. John Publishing Co.

1 54.00 162.00 490.00
2 35.00 105.00 280.00
3 24.00 71.00 190.00
26-28 (Reprints) 13.00 39.00 105.00

LAUREL AND HARDY (TV)
Oct, 1962 - No. 4, Sept-Nov, 1963
Dell Publishing Co.

12-423-210 (8-10/62) 3.60 11.00 42.00
2-4 (Dell) 2.75 8.00 30.00

LAUREL AND HARDY (Larry Harmon's...)
Jan, 1967 - No. 2, Oct, 1967
Gold Key

1-Photo back-c 4.00 12.00 40.00
2 2.75 8.00 30.00

LAW AGAINST CRIME (Law-Crime on cover)
April, 1948 - No. 3, Aug, 1948 (Real Stories from Police Files)
Essenkay Publishing Co.

1-(#1-3 are half funny animal, half crime stories)-L. B. Cole-c/a in all; electrocution-c 53.00 159.00 450.00
2-L. B. Cole-c/a 40.00 120.00 325.00
3-Used in **SOTI**, pg. 180,181 & illo "The wish to hurt or kill couples in lovers' lanes;" reprinted in All-Famous Crime #9 50.00 150.00 425.00

LAW AND ORDER
Sept, 1995 - No. 2, 1995 ($2.50, unfinished limited series)
Maximum Press

1,2 1.00 2.50

Lawbreakers Suspense Stories #15 © CC

Leading Comics #5 © DC

Leave it to Chance #3 © James Robinson & Paul Smith

LAWBREAKERS (...Suspense Stories No. 10 on)
Mar, 1951 - No. 9, Oct-Nov, 1952
Law and Order Magazines (Charlton Comics)

	GD25	FN65	NM94
1	24.00	73.00	180.00
2	12.00	36.00	90.00
3,5,6,8,9	10.00	30.00	65.00
4- "White Death" junkie story	11.50	34.00	85.00
7- "The Deadly Dopesters" drug story	11.50	34.00	85.00

LAWBREAKERS ALWAYS LOSE!
Spring, 1948 - No. 10, Oct, 1949
Marvel Comics (CBS)

	GD25	FN65	NM94
1-2pg. Kurtzman-a, "Giggles 'n' Grins"	26.00	77.00	190.00
2	13.00	39.00	95.00
3-5: 4-Vampire story	10.00	30.00	70.00
6(2/49)-Has editorial defense against charges of Dr. Wertham	10.00	30.00	75.00
7-Used in **SOTI**, illo "Comic-book philosophy"	24.00	71.00	170.00
8-10: 9,10-Photo-c	9.00	27.00	60.00

NOTE: ***Brodsky** c-4, 5. **Shores** c-1-3, 6-8.*

LAWBREAKERS SUSPENSE STORIES (Formerly Lawbreakers; Strange Suspense Stories No. 16 on)
No. 10, Jan, 1953 - No. 15, Nov, 1953
Capitol Stories/Charlton Comics

	GD25	FN65	NM94
10	21.00	64.00	160.00
11 (3/53)-Severed tongues-c/story & woman negligee scene	59.00	178.00	525.00
12-14: 13-Giordana-c begin, end #15	10.00	30.00	65.00
15-Acid-in-face-c/story; hands dissolved in acid sty	31.00	94.00	240.00

LAW-CRIME (See Law Against Crime)

LAWDOG/GRIMROD: TERROR AT THE CROSSROADS
Sept, 1993 ($3.50)
Marvel Comics (Epic Comics)

	GD25	FN65	NM94
1		1.40	3.50

LAWMAN (TV)
No. 970, Feb, 1959 - No. 11, Apr-June, 1962 (All photo-c)
Dell Publishing Co.

	GD25	FN65	NM94
Four Color 970(#1)	12.00	36.00	130.00
Four Color 1035('60), 3(2-4/60)-Toth-a	6.40	19.00	70.00
4-11	4.50	13.50	50.00

LAW OF DREDD, THE (Also see Judge Dredd)
1989 - No. 33, 1992 ($1.50/$1.75)
Quality Comics/Fleetway #8 on

	GD25	FN65	NM94
1-8 ($1.50)-Bolland a-1-6,8,10-12,14(2 pg),15,19			1.50
9-20,24-28: 9-Begin $1.75-c		.70	1.75
21-23,29-33)$1.95-c)		.80	2.00

LAWRENCE (See Movie Classics)

LAZARUS CHURCHYARD
June, 1992 - No. 3, 1992 ($3.95, 44 pgs., coated stock)
Tundra Publishing

	GD25	FN65	NM94
1-3		1.60	4.00

LEADING COMICS (...Screen Comics No. 42 on)
Winter, 1941-42 - No. 41, Feb-Mar, 1950
National Periodical Publications

	GD25	FN65	NM94
1-Origin The Seven Soldiers of Victory; Crimson Avenger, Green Arrow & Speedy, Shining Knight, The Vigilante, Star Spangled Kid & Stripesy begin; The Dummy (Vigilante villain) app.	310.00	930.00	3100.00
2-Meskin-a;Fred Ray-c	122.00	366.00	1100.00
3	103.00	309.00	925.00
4,5	72.00	216.00	650.00
6-10	64.00	192.00	575.00
11-14(Spring, 1945)	44.00	132.00	400.00
15-(Sum,'45)-Contents change to funny animal	23.00	68.00	180.00
16-22,24-30: 16-Nero Fox-c begin, end #22	9.50	28.00	75.00
23-1st app. Peter Porkchops by Otto Feur & begins	22.00	66.00	175.00
31,32,34-41: 34-41-Leading Screen... on-c only	8.75	26.25	65.00
33-(Scarce)	17.00	51.00	135.00

NOTE: ***Rube Grossman**-a(Peter Porkchops)-most #15-on; c-15-41. **Post** a-23-37, 39, 41.*

LEADING SCREEN COMICS (Formerly Leading Comics)
No. 42, Apr-May, 1950 - No. 77, Aug-Sept, 1955
National Periodical Publications

	GD25	FN65	NM94
42-Peter Porkchops-c/stories continue	8.75	26.25	65.00
43-77	7.85	23.50	55.00

NOTE: ***Grossman** a-most. **Mayer** a-45-48, 50, 54-57, 60, 62-74, 75(3), 76, 77.*

LEAGUE OF CHAMPIONS, THE (Also see The Champions)
Dec, 1990 - No. 3?, 1991 ($2.95, 52 pgs.)
Hero Graphics

	GD25	FN65	NM94
1-3: 1-Flare app. 2-Origin Malice		1.20	3.00

LEAGUE OF JUSTICE
1996 - No. 2, 1996 ($5.95, 48 pgs., limited series, squarebound)
DC Comics (Elseworlds)

	GD25	FN65	NM94
1,2: Magic-based alternate DC Universe story; Giordano-i		2.40	6.00

LEATHERFACE
May (April on-c), 1991 ($2.75, painted-c)
Arpad Publishing

	GD25	FN65	NM94
1-Based on Texas Chainsaw movie; Dorman-c		1.10	2.75

LEATHERNECK THE MARINE (See Mighty Midget Comics)

LEAVE IT TO BEAVER (TV)
No. 912, June, 1958; May-July, 1962 (All photo-c)
Dell Publishing Co.

	GD25	FN65	NM94
Four Color 912	17.00	52.00	190.00
Four Color 999,1103,1191,1285, 01-428-207	14.00	44.00	160.00

LEAVE IT TO BINKY (Binky No. 72 on) (Super DC Giant) (No. 1-22: 52 pgs.)
2-3/48 - #60, 10/58; #61, 6-7/68 - #71, 2-3/70 (Teen-age humor)
National Periodical Publications

	GD25	FN65	NM94
1-Lucy wears Superman costume	29.00	86.00	230.00
2	14.50	43.00	115.00
3,4	8.75	26.25	65.00
5-Superman cameo	14.00	41.00	110.00
6-10	7.85	23.50	55.00
11-14,16-22: Last 52pg. issue	6.50	19.50	45.00
15-Scribbly story by Mayer	8.75	26.25	65.00
23-28,30-45: 45-Last pre-code (2/55)	4.25	13.00	26.00
29-Used in **POP**, pg. 78	4.25	13.00	28.00
46-60: 60-(10/58)	2.50	7.50	20.00
61 (6-7/68)	4.00	12.00	40.00
62-69	2.50	7.50	20.00
70-7pg. app. Bus Driver who looks like Ralph from Honey Mooners	3.00	9.00	30.00
71-Last issue	2.50	7.50	24.00

NOTE: ***Aragones**-a-61, 62, 67. **Drucker** a-28. **Mayer** a-1, 2, 15. Created by **Mayer**.*

LEAVE IT TO CHANCE
Sept, 1996 - Present ($2.50)
Homage Comics

	GD25	FN65	NM94
1-Intro Chance Falconer & St. George; James Robinson scripts & Paul Smith-c/a begins		2.40	6.00
2		1.60	4.00
3		1.20	3.00
4-7			2.50
Shaman's Rain(1997, $9.95, TPB) r/#1-4			10.00

Legend of Mother Sarah #5 © DH

Legend of the Shield #3 © DC

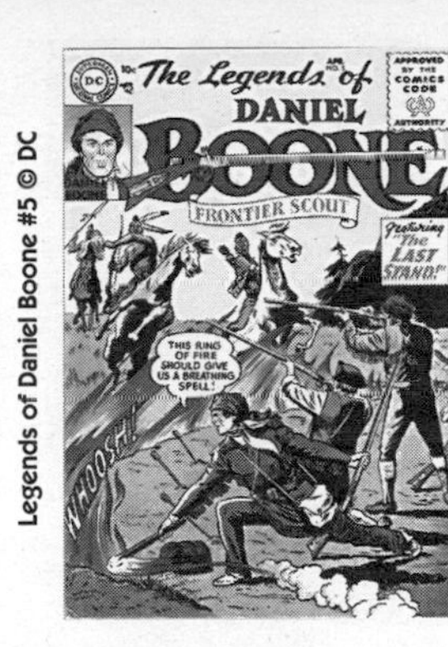

Legends of Daniel Boone #5 © DC

GD25 FN65 NM94

LEE HUNTER, INDIAN FIGHTER
No. 779, Mar, 1957; No. 904, May, 1958
Dell Publishing Co.

	GD25	FN65	NM94
Four Color 779 (#1)	3.60	11.00	40.00
Four Color 904	2.75	8.00	30.00

LEFT-HANDED GUN, THE (Movie)
No. 913, July, 1958
Dell Publishing Co.

	GD25	FN65	NM94
Four Color 913-Paul Newman photo-c	10.00	30.00	110.00

LEGACY
Oct, 1993 - No. 2, Nov, 1993; No. 0, 1994 ($2.25)
Majestic Entertainment

	GD25	FN65	NM94
1-2: 1-Glow-in-the-dark-c		.90	2.25
0-Platinum		1.20	3.00

LEGEND OF CUSTER, THE (TV)
Jan, 1968
Dell Publishing Co.

	GD25	FN65	NM94
1-Wayne Maunder photo-c	1.50	4.50	12.00

LEGEND OF JESSE JAMES, THE (TV)
Feb, 1966
Gold Key

	GD25	FN65	NM94
10172-602-Photo-c	1.80	5.40	18.00

LEGEND OF KAMUI, THE (See Kamui)

LEGEND OF LOBO, THE (See Movie Comics)

LEGEND OF MOTHER SARAH (Manga)
Apr, 1995 - No. 8, Nov, 1995 ($2.50, limited series)
Dark Horse Comics

	GD25	FN65	NM94
1-8: Katsuhiro Otomo scripts		1.00	2.50

LEGEND OF MOTHER SARAH: CITY OF THE ANGELS (Manga)
Oct, 1996 - No. 9, June, 1997 ($3.95, B&W, limited series)
Dark Horse Comics

	GD25	FN65	NM94
1-9: Otomo scripts		1.60	4.00

LEGEND OF MOTHER SARAH: CITY OF THE CHILDREN (Manga)
Jan, 1996 - No. 7, July, 1996 ($3.95, B&W, limited series)
Dark Horse Comics

	GD25	FN65	NM94
1-7: Otomo scripts		1.60	4.00

LEGEND OF SUPREME
Dec, 1994 - No. 3, Feb, 1995 ($2.50, limited series)
Image Comics (Extreme Studios)

	GD25	FN65	NM94
1-3		1.00	2.50

LEGEND OF THE SHIELD, THE
July, 1991 - No. 16, Oct, 1992 ($1.00)
DC Comics (Impact Comics)

	GD25	FN65	NM94
1-16: 6,7-The Fly x-over. 12-Contains trading card			1.00
Annual 1 (1992, $2.50, 68 pgs.)-Snyder-a; w/trading card		1.00	2.50

LEGEND OF WONDER WOMAN, THE
May, 1986 - No. 4, Aug, 1986 (75¢, limited series)
DC Comics

	GD25	FN65	NM94
1-4			1.00

LEGEND OF YOUNG DICK TURPIN, THE (Disney)(TV)
May, 1966
Gold Key

	GD25	FN65	NM94
1 (10176-605)-Photo/painted-c	1.25	3.75	10.00

LEGEND OF ZELDA, THE (Link: The Legend... in indicia)
1990 - No. 4, 1990 ($1.95, coated stiff-c)

V2#1, 1991 - No. 5, 1991 ($1.50)
Valiant Comics

	GD25	FN65	NM94
1-4: 4-Layton-c(i)		.80	2.00
V2#1-5			1.50

LEGENDS
Nov, 1986 - No. 6, Apr, 1987 (75¢, limited series)
DC Comics

	GD25	FN65	NM94
1-6: 1-Byrne-c/a(p) in all; 1st app. new Capt. Marvel. 3-1st app. new Suicide Squad; death of Blockbuster. 6-1st app. new Justice League			1.00

LEGENDS OF DANIEL BOONE, THE (...Frontier Scout)
Oct-Nov, 1955 - No. 8, Dec-Jan, 1956-57
National Periodical Publications

	GD25	FN65	NM94
1 (Scarce)-Nick Cardy c-1-8	50.00	150.00	450.00
2 (Scarce)	36.00	108.00	325.00
3-8 (Scarce)	36.00	108.00	285.00

LEGENDS OF KID DEATH AND FLUFFY
1996 ($2.95, B&W)
Brainstorm Comics

	GD25	FN65	NM94
1-3:1-Lindo-c. 3-Regular -c & nude-c		1.20	3.00

LEGENDS OF LUXURA
Feb, 1997 ($2.95, B&W, one-shot)
Event Comics

	GD25	FN65	NM94
1-Five covers		1.20	3.00

LEGENDS OF NASCAR, THE
Nov, 1990 - No. 14, 1992? (#1 3rd printing (1/91) says 2nd printing inside)
Vortex Comics

	GD25	FN65	NM94
1-Bill Elliott biog.; Trimpe-a ($1.50)		1.20	3.00
1-2nd printing (11/90, $2.00)		.80	2.00
1-3rd print; contains Maxx racecards ($3.00)		1.20	3.00
2-Richard Petty ($2.00)		.80	2.00
3-14: 3-Ken Schrader (7/91). 4-Bobby Allison; Spiegle-a(p); Adkins part-i. 5-Sterling Marlin. 6-Bill Elliott. 7-Junior Johnson; Spiegle-c/a. 8-Benny Parsons; Heck-a		.70	1.80
1-13-Hologram cover versions. 2-Hologram shows Bill Elliott's car by mistake (all are numbered & limited)		1.60	4.00
2-Hologram corrected version		1.60	4.00
Christmas Special ($5.95)		2.40	6.00

LEGENDS OF THE DARK CLAW
Apr, 1996 ($1.95)
DC Comics (Amalgam)

	GD25	FN65	NM94
1-Jim Balent-c/a		2.00	5.00

LEGENDS OF THE DARK KNIGHT (See Batman: ...)

LEGENDS OF THE DC UNIVERSE
Feb, 1998 - Present ($1.95)
DC Comics

	GD25	FN65	NM94
1-Superman; Robinson-s/Orbik-painted-c			1.95

LEGENDS OF THE STARGRAZERS (See Vanguard Illustrated #2)
Aug, 1989 - No. 6, 1990 ($1.95, limited series, mature)
Innovation Publishing

	GD25	FN65	NM94
1-6: 1-Redondo part inks		.80	2.00

LEGENDS OF THE WORLD'S FINEST (See World's Finest)
1994 - No. 3, 1994 ($4.95, squarebound, limited series)
DC Comics

	GD25	FN65	NM94
1-3: Simonson scripts; Brereton-c/a; embossed foil logos		2.00	5.00
TPB-(1995, $14.95) r/#1-3	1.85	5.50	15.00

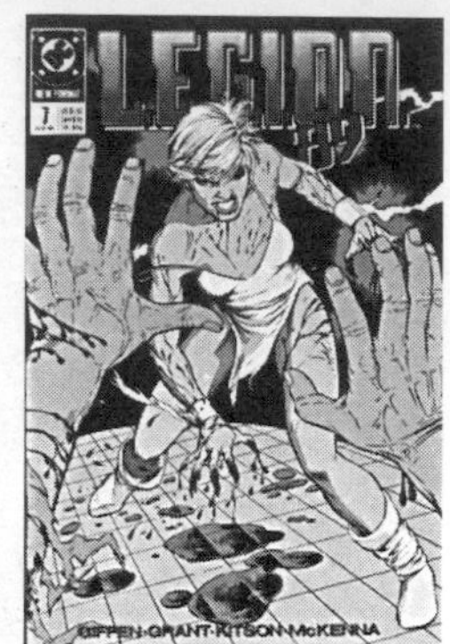

L.E.G.I.O.N. '89 #7 © DC

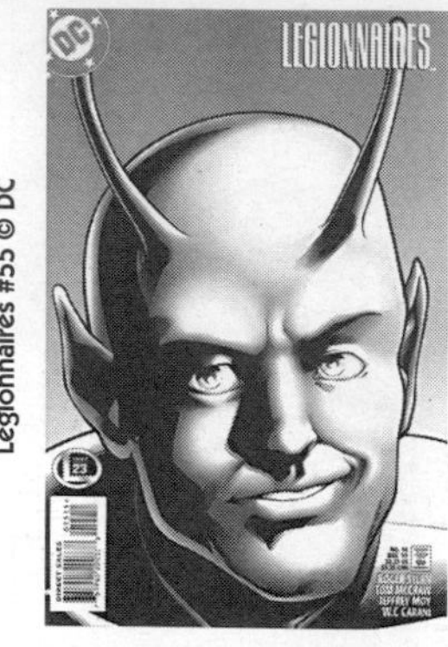

Legionnaires #55 © DC

Legion of Super-Heroes #55 (2nd Series) © DC

GD25 FN65 NM94

L.E.G.I.O.N. (The # to right of title represents year of print)(Also see Lobo & R.E.B.E.L.S.)
Feb, 1989 - No. 70, Sept, 1994 ($1.50/$1.75)
DC Comics

1-Giffen plots/breakdowns in #1-12 .70 1.75
2-22,24-47: 3-Lobo app. #3 on. 4-1st Lobo-c this title. 5-Lobo joins L.E.G.I.O.N. 13-Lar Gand app. 16-Lar Gand joins L.E.G.I.O.N., leaves #19. 28-Giffen-c(p). 31-Capt. Marvel app. 35-L.E.G.I.O.N. '92 begins 1.50
23-($2.50, 52 pgs.)-L.E.G.I.O.N. '91 begins 1.00 2.50
48,49,51-69: 48-Begin $1.75-c. 63-L.E.G.I.O.N. '94 begins; Superman x-over .70 1.75
50-($3.50, 68 pgs.) 1.40 3.50
70-($2.50, 52 pgs.)-Zero Hour 1.00 2.50
Annual 1-3 (1990-1992, $2.95, 68 pgs.): 1-Lobo, Superman app. 2-Alan Grant scripts 1.20 3.00
Annual 4 (1993, $3.50, 68 pgs.) 1.40 3.50
Annual 5 (1994, $3.50, 68 pgs.)-Elseworlds story; Lobo app. 1.40 3.50
NOTE: ***Alan Grant*** *scripts in #1-39, 51, Annual 1, 2.*

LEGIONNAIRES (See Legion of Super-Heroes #40, 41 & Showcase 95 #6)
Apr, 1992 - Present ($1.25/$1.50/$2.25)
DC comics

1-8: 1-Chris Sprouse-c/a; polybagged w/SkyBox trading card 1.50
0,9-25: 9-Begin $1.50-c. 11-Kid Quantum joins. 18-(9/94)-Zero Hour. 0-(10/94). 19-(11/94) 1.50
26-28: 26-Begin $1.75-c 1.75
29-49: 29-Begin $2.25-c. 37-Valor (Lar Gand) becomes M'onel (5/96). 43-Legion tryouts; reintro Princess Projectra, Shadow Lass & others 47-Forms one cover image with LSH #91 .90 2.25
50-($3.95) Pullout poster by Davis/Farmer 3.95
51-58: 52-Shrinking Violet becomes LeViathan. 2.25
Annual 1 (1994, $2.95)-Elseworlds story 1.20 3.00
Annual 2 (1995, $3.95)-Year One story 1.60 4.00
Annual 3 (1996, $2.95)-Legends of the Dead Earth story 1.20 3.00

LEGIONNAIRES THREE
Jan, 1986 - No. 4, May, 1986 (75¢, limited series)
DC comics

1-4 1.00

LEGION OF MONSTERS (Also see Marvel Premiere #28 & Marvel Preview #8)
Sept, 1975 ($1.00, B&W, magazine, 76 pgs.)
Marvel Comics Group

1-Origin & 1st app. Legion of Monsters; Neal Adams-c; Morrow-a; origin & only app. The Manphibian; Frankenstein by Mayerik; Bram Stoker's Dracula adaptation; Reese-a; painted-c (#2 was advertised with Morbius & Satana, but was never published) 2.00 6.00 16.00

LEGION OF NIGHT, THE
Oct, 1991 - No. 2, Oct, 1991 ($4.95, 52 pgs.)
Marvel Comics

1,2-Whilce Portacio-c/a(p) 2.00 5.00

LEGION OF SUBSTITUTE HEROES SPECIAL (See Adventure Comics #306)
July, 1985 ($1.25, one-shot, 52 pgs.)
DC Comics

1-Giffen-c/a(p) 1.25

LEGION OF SUPER-HEROES (See Action, Adventure, All New Collectors Edition, Limited Collectors Edition, Secrets of the..., Superboy & Superman)
Feb, 1973 - No. 4, July-Aug, 1973
National Periodical Publications

1-Legion & Tommy Tomorrow reprints begin 1.75 5.25 14.00
2-4: 2-Forte-r. 3-r/Adv. #340. Action #240. 4-r/Adv. #341, Action #233; Mooney-r 1.00 2.80 7.00

LEGION OF SUPER-HEROES, THE (Formerly Superboy and...; Tales of The Legion No. 314 on)
No. 259, Jan, 1980 - No. 313, July, 1984
DC Comics

259(#1)-Superboy leaves Legion 2.00 5.00
260-270: 265-Contains 28 pg. insert "Superman & the TRS-80 Computer"; origin Tyroc; Tyroc leaves Legion 1.20 3.00
271-284,291-293: 272-Blok joins; origin; 20pg. insert-Dial 'H' For Hero. 277-Intro Reflecto. 280-Superboy re-joins legion. 282-Origin Reflecto. 283-Origin Wildfire 1.50
285-290:285,286-Giffen back up sty. 287-Giffen-a on Legion begins. 290-294-Great Darkness saga 1.20 3.00
294-Double size (52 pgs.) .70 1.75
295-299,301-305: 297-Origin retold. 298-Free 16pg. Amethyst preview 1.50
300-(68 pgs., Mando paper)-Anniversary issue; has c/a by almost everyone at DC 1.20 3.00
306-313 (75¢): 306-Brief origin Star Boy 1.00
Annual 1(1982, 52 pgs.)-Giffen-c/a; 1st app./origin new Invisible Kid who joins Legion .80 2.00
Annual 2,3: 2(1983, 52 pgs.)-Giffen-c; Karate Kid & Princess Projectra wed & resign. 3(1984, 52 pgs.) 1.50
...The Great Darkness Saga (1989, $17.95, 196 pgs.)-r/LSH #287,290-294 & Annual #3; Giffen-c/a 2.25 6.75 18.00
NOTE: ***Aparo*** *c-282, 283, 300(part).* ***Austin*** *c-268i.* ***Buckler*** *c-273p, 274p, 276p.* ***Colan*** *a-311p.* ***Ditko*** *a(p)-267, 268, 272, 274, 276, 281.* ***Giffen*** *a-285-313p, Annual 1p; c-287p, 288p, 289, 290p, 291p, 292, 293, 294-299p, 300, 301-313p, Annual 1p, 2p.* ***Perez*** *c-268p, 277-280, 281p.* ***Starlin*** *a-265.* ***Staton*** *a-259p, 260p, 280.* ***Tuska*** *a-308p.*

LEGION OF SUPER-HEROES (Reprinted in Tales of the Legion)
Aug, 1984 - No. 63, Aug, 1989 ($1.25/$1.75, deluxe format)
DC Comics

1-Silver ink logo 1.50
2-10: 4-Death of Karate Kid. 5-Death of Nemesis Kid 1.50
11-14: 12-Cosmic Boy, Lightning Lad, & Saturn Girl resign. 14-Intro new members: Tellus, Sensor Girl, Quislet 1.25
15-18: 15-17-Crisis tie-ins. 18-Crisis x-over 1.50
19-25: 25-Sensor Girl i.d. revealed as Princess Projectra 1.25
26-36,39-44: 35-Saturn Girl rejoins. 40-$1.75-c. price begins. 42,43-Millennium tie-ins. 44-Origin Quislet 1.25
37,38-Death of Superboy 1.25 3.75 10.00
45 ($2.95, 68 pgs.)-Anniversary issue 1.20 3.00
46-49,51-62 1.25
50-Double size, $2.50 1.00 2.50
63-Final issue 1.50
Annual 1 (10/85, 52 pgs.)-Crisis tie-in .70 1.75
Annual 2,3: 2 (1986, 52 pgs.). 3 (1987, $2.25, 52 pgs.) .90 2.25
Annual 4 (1988, $2.50, 52 pgs.) 1.00 2.50
NOTE: ***Byrne*** *c-36p.* ***Giffen*** *a(p)-1, 2, 50-55, 57-63, Annual 1p, 2; c-1-5p, 54p, Annual 1.* ***Orlando*** *a-6p.* ***Steacy*** *c-45-50, Annual 3.*

LEGION OF SUPER-HEROES
Nov, 1989 - Present ($1.75/$1.95/$2.25)
DC Comics

1-Giffen-c/a(p)/scripts begin (4 pg.-a only #18) .70 1.75
2-49,51-53,55-58: 4-Mon-El (Lar Gand) destroys Time Trapper, changes reality. 5-Alt. reality story where Mordru rules all; Ferro Lad app. 6-1st app. of Laurel Gand (Lar Gand's cousin). 8-Origin. 15-(2/91)-1st reference of Lar Gand as Valor. 13-Free poster by Giffen showing new costumes. 21-24-Lobo & Darkseid storyline. 26-New map of headquarters. 34-Six pg. preview of Timber Wolf mini-series. 40-Minor Legionnaires app. 41-(3/93)-Intro Legionnaires .70 1.75
50-($3.50, 68 pgs.) 1.40 3.50
54-($2.95)-Die-cut & foil stamped-c 1.20 3.00

Legion of Super-Heroes #96 (3rd series) © DC

Leonard Nimoy's Primortals #3 (1st series) © Leonard Nimoy

Liberty Comics #12 © Green Publ. Co.

GD25 FN65 NM94 | GD25 FN65 NM94

59-61: 59-Begin $1.95-c. 61-(9/94)-Zero Hour .80 2.00
0,62-68: 0-(10/94). 62-(11/94) .80 2.00
69-99,101: 69-Begin $2.25-c. 75-XS travels back to the 20th Century (cont'd in Impulse #9). 77-Origin of Brainiac 5. 81-Reintro Sun Boy. 85-Half of the Legion sent to the 20th century, Superman-c/app. 86-Final Night. 87-Deadman-c/app. 88-Impulse-c/app. Adventure Comics #247 cover swipe. 91-Forms one cover image with Legionnaires #47. 96-Wedding of Ultra Boy and Apparition. 99-Robin, Impulse, Superboy app. .90 2.25
100-($5.95, 96 pgs.)-Legionnaires return to the 30th Century; gatefold-c; 5 stories-art by Simonson, Davis and others 5.95
Annual 1-5 (1990-1994, $3.50, 68 pgs.): 4-Bloodlines. 5-Elseworlds story 1.40 3.50
Annual 6 (1995,$3.95)-Year One story 1.60 4.00
Annual 7 (1996, $3.50, 48 pgs.)-Legends of the Dead Earth story; intro 75th Century Legion of Super-Heroes; Wildfire app. 1.40 3.50
Legion: Secret Files 1 (1/98, $4.95) Retold origin & pin-ups by various 4.95
NOTE: ***Giffen** a-1-24; breakdowns-26-32, 34-36; c-1-7, 8(part), 9-24.* ***Brandon Peterson** a(p)-15(1st for DC), 16, 18, Annual 2(54 pgs.); c-Annual 2p.* ***Swan/Anderson** c-8(part).*

LEMONADE KID, THE (See Bobby Benson's B-Bar-B Riders)
1990 ($2.50, 28 pgs.)
AC Comics

1-Powell-c(r); Red Hawk-r by Powell; Lemonade Kid-r/Bobby Benson by Powell (2 stories) 1.00 2.50

LENNON SISTERS LIFE STORY, THE
No. 951, Nov, 1958 - No. 1014, Aug, 1959
Dell Publishing Co.

Four Color 951 (#1)-Toth-a, 32pgs, photo-c 13.00 40.00 145.00
Four Color 1014-Toth-a, photo-c 13.00 40.00 145.00

LEONARD NIMOY'S PRIMORTALS
Mar, 1995 - No. 15, May, 1996 ($1.95)
Tekno Comix

1-15: Concept by Leonard Nimoy & Isaac Asimov 1-3-w/bound-in game piece & trading card. 4-w/Teknophage Steel Edition coupon. 13,14-Art Adams-c. 15-Simonson-c .80 2.00

LEONARD NIMOY'S PRIMORTALS
V2#0, June, 1996 - No. 8, Feb, 1997 ($2.25)
BIG Entertainment

V2#0-8: 0-Includes Pt. 9 of "The Big Bang" x-over. 0,1-Simonson-c. 3-Kelley Jones-c .90 2.25

LEONARD NIMOY'S PRIMORTALS ORIGINS
Nov, 1995 - No. 2, Dec, 1995 ($2.95, limited series)
Tekno Comix

1,2: Nimoy scripts; Art Adams-c; polybagged 1.20 3.00

LEONARDO (Also see Teenage Mutant Ninja Turtles)
Dec, 1986 ($1.50, B&W, one-shot)
Mirage Studios

1 .80 2.00

LEO THE LION
No date(1960s) (10¢)
I. W. Enterprises

1-Reprint 1.10 3.30 9.00

LEROY (Teen-age)
Nov, 1949 - No. 6, Nov, 1950
Standard Comics

1 5.70 17.00 40.00
2-Frazetta text illo. 5.00 15.00 30.00
3-6: 3-Lubbers-a 4.00 12.00 24.00

LETHAL (Also see Brigade)
Feb, 1996 ($2.50, unfinished limited series)
Image Comics (Extreme Studios)

1-Marat Mychaels-c/a. 1.00 2.50

LETHAL FOES OF SPIDER-MAN (Sequel to Deadly Foes of Spider-Man)
Sept, 1993 - No. 4, Dec, 1993 ($1.75, limited series)
Marvel Comics

1-4 .70 1.75

LETHAL STRYKE
June, 1995 - No. 3, 1995 ($3.00)
London Night Studios

0-(8/95, $5.95)-Collector's ed. 2.40 6.00
1/2, 1-3: 1-polybagged w/card 1.20 3.00
Annual 1-(1996, $3.00) 1.20 3.00
Annual 1-Platinum Edition 1.25 3.75 10.00
Trade paperback-(1996, $12.95)-r/#(1/2)-3 12.95

LETHAL STRYKE/DOUBLE IMPACT: LETHAL IMPACT
May, 1996 ($3.00, one-shot)
London Night Studios

1-Hartsoe/Lyon-a(p) 1.20 3.00
1-Natural Born Killers Edition 2.40 6.00

LETHARGIC LAD
June, 1996 - No. 3, Sept, 1996 ($2.95, B&W, limited series)
Crusade Entertainment

1-3: 3-Alex Ross-c/swipe (Kingdom Come) 1.20 3.00

LETHARGIC LAD ADVENTURES
Oct, 1997 - Present ($2.95, B&W)
Crusade Entertainment

1,2-Hyland-s/a 2.95

LET'S PRETEND (CBS radio)
May-June, 1950 - No. 3, Sept-Oct, 1950
D. S. Publishing Co.

1 11.30 34.00 90.00
2,3 8.75 26.25 70.00

LET'S READ THE NEWSPAPER
1974
Charlton Press

nn-Features Quincy by Ted Sheares 1.00

LET'S TAKE A TRIP (TV) (CBS Television Presents)
Spring, 1958
Pines Comics

1-Marv Levy-c/a 2.50 7.50 20.00

LETTERS TO SANTA (See March of Comics No. 228)

LEX LUTHOR: THE UNAUTHORIZED BIOGRAPHY
1989 ($3.95, 52 pgs., one-shot, squarebound)
DC Comics

1-Painted-c; Clark Kent app. 1.60 4.00

LIBERTY COMICS (Miss Liberty No. 1)
No. 4, 1945 - No. 15, July, 1946 (MLJ & other reprints)
Green Publishing Co.

4 12.00 36.00 95.00
5 (5/46)-The Prankster app; Starr-a 10.00 30.00 80.00
10-Hangman & Boy Buddies app.; Suzie & Wilbur begin; reprints Hangman story from Hangman #8 14.00 41.00 110.00
11(V2#2, 1/46)-Wilbur in women's clothes 12.00 36.00 95.00
12-Black Hood & Suzie app. 12.00 36.00 95.00
14,15-Patty of Airliner; Starr-a in both 7.85 23.50 55.00

LIBERTY GUARDS
No date (1946?)

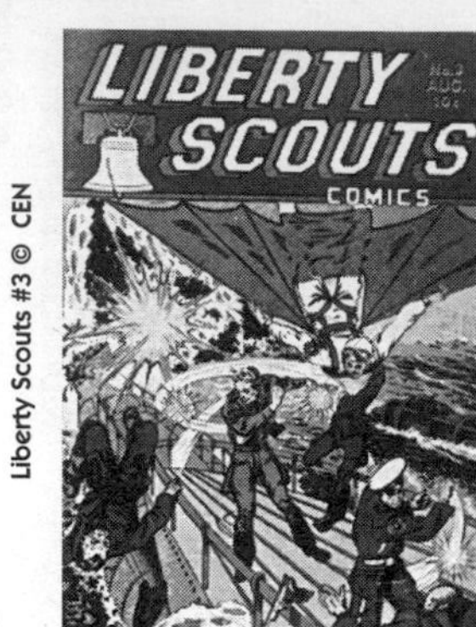

Liberty Scouts #3 © CEN

Life of Captain Marvel #4 © MEG

Life Story #45 © FAW

	GD25	FN65	NM94
Chicago Mail Order			
nn-Reprints Man of War #1 with cover of Liberty Scouts #1; Gustavson-c	26.00	80.00	210.00

LIBERTY PROJECT, THE
June, 1987 - No. 8, May, 1988 ($1.75, color, Baxter paper)
Eclipse Comics

	GD25	FN65	NM94
1-8: 6-Valkyrie app.		.90	1.80

LIBERTY SCOUTS (See Liberty Guards & Man of War)
No. 2, June, 1941 - No. 3, Aug, 1941
Centaur Publications

	GD25	FN65	NM94
2(#1)-Origin The Fire-Man, Man of War; Vapo-Man & Liberty Scouts begin; intro Liberty Scouts; Gustavson-c/a in both	106.00	318.00	950.00
3(#2)-Origin & 1st app. The Sentinel	81.00	243.00	725.00

LICENCE TO KILL (James Bond 007) (Movie)
1989 ($7.95, slick paper, 52 pgs.)
Eclipse Comics

	GD25	FN65	NM94
nn-Movie adaptation; Timothy Dalton photo-c	1.00	3.00	8.00
Limited Hardcover ($24.95)	2.50	7.50	25.00

LIDSVILLE (TV)
Oct, 1972 - No. 5, Oct, 1973
Gold Key

	GD25	FN65	NM94
1-Photo-c	2.75	8.00	30.00
2-5	1.85	5.50	15.00

LIEUTENANT, THE (TV)
April-June, 1964
Dell Publishing Co.

	GD25	FN65	NM94
1-Photo-c	1.40	4.20	14.00

LIEUTENANT BLUEBERRY (Also see Blueberry)
1991 - No. 3, 1991 (Graphic novel)
Marvel Comics (Epic Comics)

	GD25	FN65	NM94
1,2 ($8.95)-Moebius-a in all	1.10	3.30	9.00
3 ($14.95)	1.85	5.50	15.00

LT. ROBIN CRUSOE, U.S.N. (See Movie Comics & Walt Disney Showcase #26)

LIFE OF CAPTAIN MARVEL, THE
Aug, 1985 - No. 5, Dec, 1985 ($2.00, Baxter paper)
Marvel Comics Group

	GD25	FN65	NM94
1-5: 1-All reprint Starlin issues of Iron Man #55, Capt. Marvel #25-34 plus Marvel Feature #12 (all with Thanos). 4-New Thanos back-c by Starlin		.80	2.00

LIFE OF CHRIST, THE
No. 301, 1949 (35¢, 100 pgs.)
Catechetical Guild Educational Society

	GD25	FN65	NM94
301-Reprints from Topix(1949)-V5#11,12	4.00	10.00	20.00

LIFE OF CHRIST: THE EASTER STORY, THE
1993 ($2.99, slick stock)
Marvel Comics/Nelson

	GD25	FN65	NM94
nn		1.20	3.00

LIFE OF CHRIST VISUALIZED
1942 - No. 3, 1943
Standard Publishers

	GD25	FN65	NM94
1-3: All came in cardboard case	4.00	10.00	20.00
With case.....	7.15	21.50	50.00

LIFE OF CHRIST VISUALIZED
1946? (48 pgs. in color)
The Standard Publ. Co.

	GD25	FN65	NM94
nn	2.00	5.00	10.00

LIFE OF ESTHER VISUALIZED
No. 2062, 1947 (48 pgs. in color)
The Standard Publ. Co.

	GD25	FN65	NM94
2062	2.00	5.00	10.00

LIFE OF JOSEPH VISUALIZED
No. 1054, 1946 (48 pgs. in color)
The Standard Publ. Co.

	GD25	FN65	NM94
1054	2.00	5.00	10.00

LIFE OF PAUL (See The Living Bible)

LIFE OF POPE JOHN PAUL II, THE
Jan, 1983
Marvel Comics Group

	GD25	FN65	NM94
1			1.50

LIFE OF RILEY, THE (TV)
No. 917, July, 1958
Dell Publishing Co.

	GD25	FN65	NM94
Four Color 917-Photo-c	11.00	33.00	120.00

LIFE OF THE BLESSED VIRGIN
1950 (68pgs.) (square binding)
Catechetical Guild (Giveaway)

	GD25	FN65	NM94
nn-Contains "The Woman of the Promise" & "Mother of Us All" rebound	4.00	10.00	20.00

LIFE'S LIKE THAT
1945 (25¢, B&W, 68 pgs.)
Croyden Publ. Co.

	GD25	FN65	NM94
nn-Newspaper Sunday strip-r by Neher	5.35	16.00	32.00

LIFE STORIES OF AMERICAN PRESIDENTS (See Dell Giants)

LIFE STORY
Apr, 1949 - V8#46, Jan, 1953; V8#47, Apr, 1953 (All have photo-c?)
Fawcett Publications

	GD25	FN65	NM94
V1#1	10.00	30.00	70.00
2	5.00	15.00	30.00
3-6	4.25	13.00	26.00
V2#7-12	4.25	13.00	26.00
V3#13-Wood-a	11.00	33.00	75.00
V3#14-18, V4#19-24, V5#25-30, V6#31-35	4.00	11.00	22.00
V6#36- "I sold drugs" on-c	4.25	13.00	28.00
V7#37,40-42, V8#44,45	2.80	7.00	14.00
V7#38, V8#43-Evans-a	4.25	13.00	26.00
V7#39-Drug Smuggling & Junkie story	4.00	12.00	24.00
V8#46,47 (Scarce)	4.00	12.00	24.00

NOTE: ***Powell** a-13, 23, 24, 26, 28, 30, 32, 39. **Marcus Swayze** a-1-3, 10-12, 15, 16, 20, 21, 23-25, 31, 35, 37, 40, 44, 46.*

LIFE, THE UNIVERSE AND EVERYTHING (See Hitchhikers Guide to the Galaxy & Restaurant at the End of the Universe)
1996 - No. 3, 1996 ($6.95, squarebound, limited series)
DC Comics

	GD25	FN65	NM94
1-3: Adaptation of novel by Douglas Adams.	1.00	2.80	7.00

LIFE WITH ARCHIE
Sept, 1958 - No. 285, 1991
Archie Publications

	GD25	FN65	NM94
1	26.00	78.00	260.00
2-(9/59)	13.00	39.00	130.00
3-5: 3-(7/60)	9.00	27.00	90.00
6-10	5.50	16.50	55.00
11-20	3.50	10.50	35.00
21-30	2.80	8.40	28.00
31-41	2.50	7.50	20.00

Life With Archie #50 © AP

Lightning Comics Presents #1 © Lightning Comics

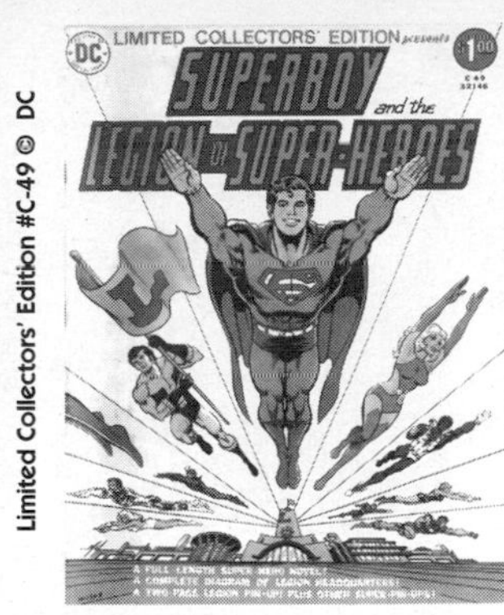

Limited Collectors' Edition #C-49 © DC

	GD25	FN65	NM94
42-Pureheart begins (1st app., 1965?)	3.00	9.00	30.00
43-45	1.85	5.50	15.00
46-Origin Pureheart	2.50	7.50	24.00
47-59: 50-United Three begin: Pureheart (Archie), Superteen (Betty), Captain Hero (Jughead). 59-Pureheart ends	1.50	4.50	12.00
60-100: 60-Archie band begins	1.00	3.00	8.00
101-150		2.40	6.00
151-200		1.60	4.00
201-240		1.20	3.00
241-285: 208-Reintro Veronica. 238-(9/83)-25th anniversary issue; Ol' Betsy (jalopy) replaced. 279-Intro Mustang Sally ($1.00)		.80	2.00

NOTE: ***Gene Colan*** *a-272-279, 285, 286.*

LIFE WITH MILLIE (Formerly A Date With Millie) (Modeling With Millie #21 on)
No. 8, Dec, 1960 - No. 20, Dec, 1962
Atlas/Marvel Comics Group

	GD25	FN65	NM94
8-Teenage	5.50	16.50	55.00
9-11	3.80	11.40	38.00
12-20	2.80	8.40	28.00

LIFE WITH SNARKY PARKER (TV)
Aug, 1950
Fox Feature Syndicate

	GD25	FN65	NM94
1-Early TV comic; photo-c from TV puppet show	21.00	64.00	170.00

LIGHT AND DARKNESS WAR, THE
Oct, 1988 - No. 6, Dec, 1989 ($1.95, limited series)
Marvel Comics (Epic Comics)

	GD25	FN65	NM94
1-6		.80	2.00

LIGHT FANTASTIC, THE (Terry Pratchett's)
June, 1992 - No. 4, Sept, 1992 ($2.50, mini-series)
Innovation Publishing

	GD25	FN65	NM94
1-4: Adapts 2nd novel in Discworld series		1.00	2.50

LIGHT IN THE FOREST (Disney)
No. 891, Mar, 1958
Dell Publishing Co.

	GD25	FN65	NM94
Four Color 891-Movie, Fess Parker photo-c	7.30	22.00	80.00

LIGHTNING COMICS (Formerly Sure-Fire No. 1-3)
No. 4, Dec, 1940 - No. 13(V3#1), June, 1942
Ace Magazines

	GD25	FN65	NM94
4-Characters continue from Sure-Fire	81.00	243.00	725.00
5,6: 6-Dr. Nemesis begins	53.00	159.00	475.00
V2#1-6: 2- "Flash Lightning" becomes "Lash…"	42.00	126.00	375.00
V3#1-Intro. Lightning Girl & The Sword	42.00	126.00	375.00

NOTE: ***Anderson*** *a-V2#6.* ***Mooney*** *c-V1#5, 6, V2#1-6, V3#1. Bondage c-V2#6. Lightning-c on all.*

LIGHTNING COMICS PRESENTS
May, 1994 ($3.50)
Lightning Comics

	GD25	FN65	NM94
1-Red foil-c distributed by Diamond Distributors		1.40	3.50
1-Black/yellow/blue-c distrib. by Capital Distributors		1.40	3.50
1-Red/yellow-c distributed by H. World		1.40	3.50
1-Platinum		1.40	3.50

LI'L (See Little)

LILITH (See Warrior Nun...)
Sept, 1996 - No. 3, Feb, 1997 ($2.95, limited series)
Antarctic Press

	GD25	FN65	NM94
1-3: 1-Variant-c			2.95

LIMITED COLLECTORS' EDITION (See Famous First Edition & Rudolph the Red Nosed Reindeer; becomes All-New Collectors' Edition)
(#21-34,51-59: 84 pgs.; #35-41: 68 pgs.; #42-50: 60 pgs.)
nn, 12/72: C-21, Summer, 1973 - No. C-59, 1978 ($1.00) (10x13-1/2")
National Periodical Publications/DC Comics

	GD25	FN65	NM94
nn(C-20)-Rudolph (12/72)	20.00	60.00	200.00
C-21: Shazam (TV); r/Captain Marvel Jr. #11 by Raboy; C.C. Beck-c, biog. & photo	2.50	7.50	22.00
C-22: Tarzan; complete origin reprinted from #207-210; all Kubert-c/a; Joe Kubert biography & photo inside	2.25	6.75	18.00
C-23: House of Mystery; Wrightson, N. Adams/Orlando, G. Kane/Wood, Toth, Aragones, Sparling reprints	2.50	7.50	24.00
C-24: Rudolph The Red-nosed Reindeer	6.00	18.00	60.00
C-25: Batman; Neal Adams-c/a(r); G.A. Joker-r; Batman/Enemy Ace-r; has photos from TV show	3.00	9.00	30.00
C-26: See Famous First Edition C-26 (same contents)			
C-27: Shazam (TV); G.A. Capt. Marvel & Mary Marvel-r; Beck-r	2.25	6.75	18.00
C-29: Tarzan; reprints "Return of Tarzan" from #219-223 by Kubert; Kubert-c	2.25	6.75	18.00
C-31: Superman; origin-r; N. Adams-a; photos of George Reeves from 1950s TV show on inside b/c; Burnley, Boring-r	2.25	6.75	18.00
C-32: Ghosts (new-a)	2.50	7.50	24.00
C-33: Rudolph The Red-nosed Reindeer(new-a)	5.00	15.00	50.00
C-34: Christmas with the Super-Heroes; unpublished Angel & Ape story by Oksner & Wood; Batman & Teen Titans-r	1.75	5.25	14.00
C-35: Shazam (TV); photo cover features TV's Captain Marvel, Jackson Bostwick; Beck-r; TV photos inside b/c	1.25	3.75	10.00
C-36: The Bible; all new adaptation beginning with Genesis by Kubert, Redondo & Mayer; Kubert-c	1.25	3.75	10.00
C-37: Batman; r-1946 Sundays; inside b/c photos of Batman TV show villains (all villain issue; r/G.A. Joker, Catwoman, Penguin, Two-Face, & Scarecrow stories plus 1946 Sundays-r)	2.50	7.50	20.00
C-38: Superman; 1 pg. N. Adams; part photo-c; photos from TV show on inside back-c	1.25	3.75	10.00
C-39: Secret Origins of Super-Villains; N. Adams-i(r); collection reprints 1950's Joker origin, Luthor origin from Adv. Comics #271, Capt. Cold origin from Showcase #8 among others; G.A. Batman-r; Beck-r.	1.25	3.75	10.00
C-40: Dick Tracy by Gould featuring Flattop; newspaper-r from 12/21/43 - 5/17/44; biog. of Chester Gould	1.25	3.75	10.00
C-41: Super Friends (TV); JLA-r(1965); Toth-c/a	1.50	4.50	12.00
C-42: Rudolph	4.00	12.00	40.00
C-43: Christmas with the Super-Heroes; Wrightson, S&K, Neal Adams-a	1.50	4.50	12.00
C-44: Batman; N. Adams-p(r) & G.A.-r; painted-c	1.50	4.50	12.00
C-45: More Secret Origins of Super-Villains; Flash-r/#105; G.A. Wonder Woman & Batman/Catwoman-r	1.25	3.75	10.00
C-46: Justice League of America(1963-r); 3 pgs. Toth-a	1.25	3.75	10.00
C-47: Superman Salutes the Bicentennial (Tomahawk interior); 2 pgs. new-a	1.25	3.75	10.00
C-48: Superman Vs. The Flash (Superman/Flash race); swipes-c to Superman #199; r/Superman #199 & Flash #175; 6 pgs. Neal Adams-a	1.50	4.50	12.00
C-49: Superboy & the Legion of Super-Heroes	1.25	3.75	10.00
C-50: Rudolph The Red-nosed Reindeer	4.00	12.00	40.00
C-51: Batman; Neal Adams-c/a	1.50	4.50	12.00
C-52: The Best of DC; Neal Adams-c/a; Toth, Kubert-a	1.50	4.50	12.00
C-57: Welcome Back, Kotter-r(TV)(5/78)	1.85	5.50	15.00
C-59: Batman's Strangest Cases; N. Adams-r; Wrightson-r/Swamp Thing #7; N. Adams/Wrightson-c	1.50	4.50	12.00

NOTE: *All-r with exception of some special features and covers.* ***Aparo*** *a-52r; c-37.* ***Grell*** *c-49.* ***Infantino*** *a-25, 39, 44, 45, 52.* ***Bob Kane*** *r-25.* ***Robinson*** *r-25, 44.* ***Sprang*** *r-44. Issues #21-31, 35-39, 45, 48 have back cover cut-outs.*

LINDA (Everybody Loves...) (Phantom Lady No. 5 on)
Apr-May, 1954 - No. 4, Oct-Nov, 1954

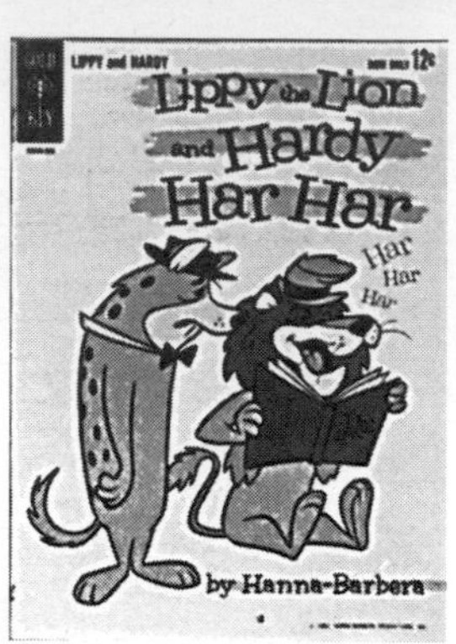

Lippy the Lion & Hardy Har Har #1 © H-B

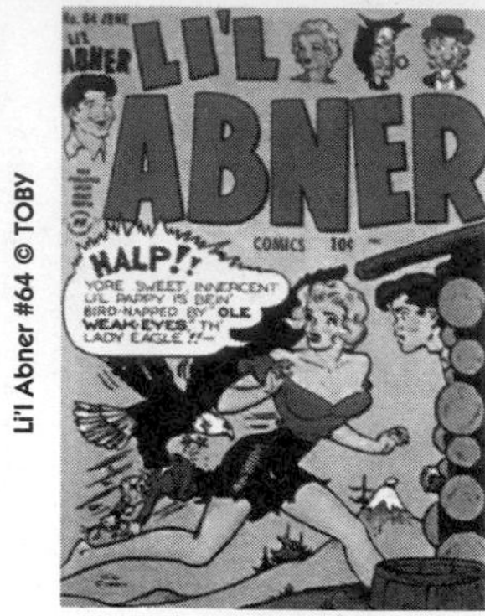

Li'l Abner #64 © TOBY

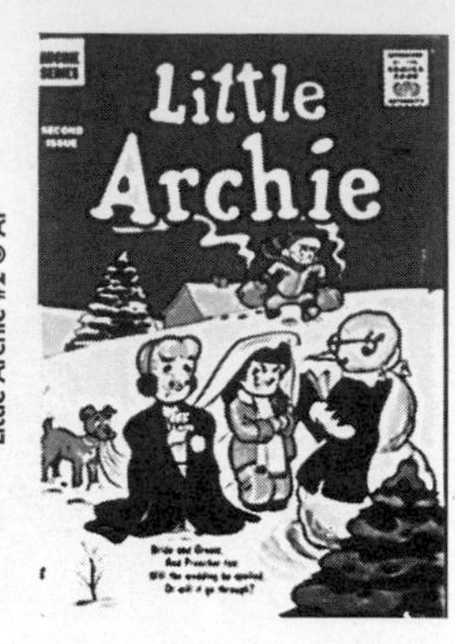

Little Archie #2 © AP

	GD25	FN65	NM94

Ajax-Farrell Publ. Co.

1-Kamenish-a	12.00	36.00	85.00
2-Lingerie panel	10.00	30.00	60.00
3,4	8.35	25.00	50.00

LINDA CARTER, STUDENT NURSE
Sept, 1961 - No. 9, Jan, 1963
Atlas Comics (AMI)

1-Al Hartley-c	3.50	10.50	35.00
2-9	2.50	7.50	25.00

LINDA LARK
Oct-Dec, 1961 - No. 8, Aug-Oct, 1963
Dell Publishing Co.

1	2.25	6.75	18.00
2-8	1.10	3.30	9.00

LINUS, THE LIONHEARTED (TV)
Sept, 1965
Gold Key

1 (10155-509)	7.00	20.00	75.00

LION, THE (See Movie Comics)

LION OF SPARTA (See Movie Classics)

LIPPY THE LION AND HARDY HAR HAR (TV)
Mar, 1963 (Hanna-Barbera) (12¢) (See Hanna-Barbera Band Wagon #1)
Gold Key

1 (10049-303)	7.00	20.00	75.00

LI'L ABNER (See Comics on Parade, Sparkle, Sparkler Comics, Tip Top Comics & Tip Topper)
1939 - 1940
United Features Syndicate

Single Series 4 ('39)	58.00	174.00	525.00
Single Series 18 ('40) (#18 on inside, #2 on-c)	49.00	147.00	440.00

LI'L ABNER (Al Capp's; continued from Comics on Parade #58)
No. 61, Dec, 1947 - No. 97, Jan, 1955 (See Oxydol-Dreft)
Harvey Publ. No. 61-69 (2/49)/Toby Press No. 70 on

61(#1)-Wolverton & Powell-a	28.00	83.00	220.00
62-65: 63-The Wolf Girl app. 65-Powell-a	16.00	49.00	130.00
66,67,69,70	14.00	41.00	110.00
68-Full length Fearless Fosdick-c/story	15.00	45.00	120.00
71-74,76,80	10.50	32.00	85.00
75,77-79,86,91-All with Kurtzman art; 91-r/#77	14.00	41.00	110.00
81-85,87-90,92-94,96,97: 93-reprints #71	9.50	28.00	75.00
95-Full length Fearless Fosdick story	12.00	36.00	95.00
...& the Creatures from Drop-Outer Space-nn (Job Corps giveaway; 36 pgs., in color)(entire book by Frank Frazetta)	25.00	75.00	200.00
...Joins the Navy (1950) (Toby Press Premium)	8.75	26.25	70.00
...by Al Capp Giveaway (Circa 1955, nd)	8.75	26.25	70.00

LI'L ABNER
1951
Toby Press

1	14.50	43.00	115.00

LI'L ABNER'S DOGPATCH (See Al Capp's...)

LISA COMICS (TV)(See Simpsons Comics)
1995 ($2.25)
Bongo Comics

1-Lisa in Wonderland		.90	2.25

LITTLE AL OF THE F.B.I.
No. 10, 1950 (no month) - No. 11, Apr-May, 1951 (Saunders painted-c)
Ziff-Davis Publications

	GD25	FN65	NM94
10(1950)	12.00	36.00	90.00
11(1951)	10.00	30.00	70.00

LITTLE AL OF THE SECRET SERVICE
No. 10, 7-8/51; No, 2, 9-10/51; No. 3, Winter, 1951 (Saunders painted-c)
Ziff-Davis Publications

10(#1)-Spanking panels (2)	14.00	43.00	100.00
2,3	10.00	30.00	70.00

LITTLE ALONZO
1938 (B&W, 5-1/2x8-1/2")(Christmas giveaway)
Macy's Dept. Store

nn-By Ferdinand the Bull's Munro Leaf	6.50	19.50	45.00

LITTLE AMBROSE
September, 1958
Archie Publications

1-Bob Bolling-c	11.30	34.00	90.00

LITTLE ANGEL
No. 5, Sept, 1954; No. 6, Sept, 1955 - No. 16, Sept, 1959
Standard (Visual Editions)/Pines

5-Last pre-code issue	5.70	17.00	35.00
6-16	4.00	10.00	22.00

LITTLE ANNIE ROONEY (Also see Henry)
1935 (25¢, B&W dailies, 48 pgs.)(10"x10", cardboard-c)
David McKay Publications

Book 1-Daily strip-r by Darrell McClure	31.00	94.00	250.00

LITTLE ANNIE ROONEY (See King Comics & Treasury of Comics)
1938; Aug, 1948 - No. 3, Oct, 1948
David McKay/St. John/Standard

Feature Books 11 (McKay, 1938)	31.00	94.00	250.00
1 (St. John)	10.00	30.00	80.00
2,3	6.50	19.50	45.00

LITTLE ARCHIE (The Adventures of... #13-on) (See Archie Giant Series Mag. #527, 534, 538, 545, 549, 556, 560, 566, 570, 583, 594, 596, 607, 609, 619)
1956 - No. 180, Feb, 1983 (Giants No. 3-84)
Archie Publications

1-(Scarce)	45.00	135.00	550.00
2 (1957)	22.50	68.00	225.00
3-5: 3-(1958)-Bob Bolling-c & giant issues begin	12.00	36.00	120.00
6-10	9.00	27.00	90.00
11-20	5.00	15.00	50.00
21-30	3.00	9.00	30.00
31-40: Little Pureheart apps. #40-42,44	2.25	6.75	18.00
41-60: 42-Intro The Little Archies. 59-Little Sabrina begins	1.50	4.50	12.00
61-84: 84-Last Giant-Size	1.00	2.80	7.00
85-100		2.00	5.00
101-140		1.20	3.00
141-180		.80	2.00
...In Animal Land 1 (1957)	10.00	30.00	100.00
...In Animal Land 17 (Winter, 1957-58)-19 (Summer,1958)-Formerly Li'l Jinx	5.00	15.00	50.00

LITTLE ARCHIE CHRISTMAS SPECIAL (See Archie Giant Series #581)

LITTLE ARCHIE COMICS DIGEST ANNUAL (...Magazine #5 on)
10/77 - No. 48, 5/91 (Digest-size, 128 pgs., later issues $1.35-$1.50)
Archie Publications

1(10/77)-Reprints	1.50	4.50	12.00
2(4/78)-Neal Adams-a	1.25	3.75	10.00
3(11/78)-The Fly-r by S&K; Neal Adams-a	1.25	3.75	10.00
4(4/79) - 10	1.00	3.00	8.00
11-20		2.40	6.00

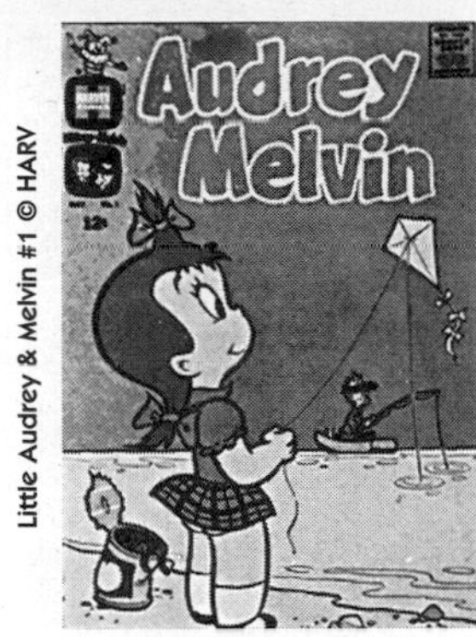
Little Audrey & Melvin #1 © HARV

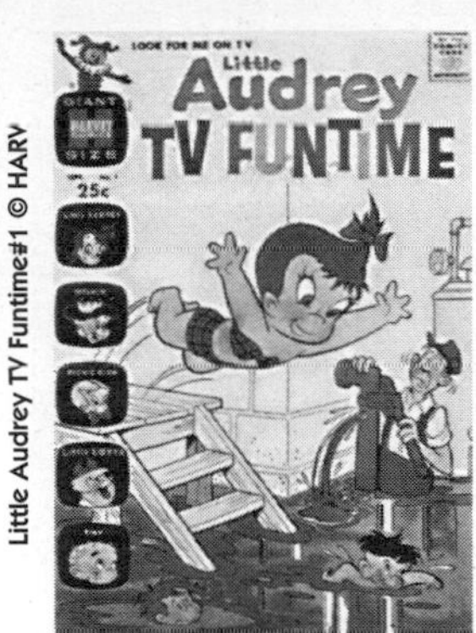
Little Audrey TV Funtime#1 © HARV

Little Dot #11 © HARV

	GD25	FN65	NM94
21-48: 28,40,46-Christmas-c		1.60	4.00

NOTE: *Little Archie, Little Jinx, Little Jughead & Little Sabrina in most issues.*

LITTLE ARCHIE DIGEST MAGAZINE
July, 1991 - Present ($1.50/$1.79/$1.89, digest size, bi-annually)
Archie Comics

	GD25	FN65	NM94
V2#1		1.60	4.00
2-10		1.20	3.00
11-20		.70	1.75
21-25: 21-Begin $1.89-c			1.89

LITTLE ARCHIE MYSTERY
Aug, 1963 - No. 2, Oct, 1963 (12¢ issues)
Archie Publications

	GD25	FN65	NM94
1	0.00	27.00	00.00
2	4.50	13.50	45.00

LITTLE ASPIRIN (See Little Lenny & Wisco)
July, 1949 - No. 3, Dec, 1949 (52 pgs.)
Marvel Comics (CnPC)

	GD25	FN65	NM94
1-Oscar app.; Kurtzman-a (4 pgs.)	12.00	36.00	95.00
2-Kurtzman-a (4 pgs.)	7.85	23.50	55.00
3-No Kurtzman-a	4.25	13.00	26.00

LITTLE AUDREY (Also see Playful...)
Apr, 1948 - No. 24, May, 1952
St. John Publ.

	GD25	FN65	NM94
1-1st app. Little Audrey	34.00	103.00	275.00
2	16.00	49.00	130.00
3-5	10.50	32.00	85.00
6-10	7.85	23.50	55.00
11-20: 16-X-Mas-c	5.35	16.00	32.00
21-24	4.00	12.00	24.00

LITTLE AUDREY (See Harvey Hits #11, 19)
No. 25, Aug, 1952 - No. 53, April, 1957
Harvey Publications

	GD25	FN65	NM94
25-(Paramount Pictures Famous Star... on-c)	7.50	22.50	75.00
26-30: 26-28-Casper app.	4.00	12.00	40.00
31-40: 32-35-Casper app.	3.50	10.50	35.00
41-53	2.00	6.00	20.00
...Clubhouse 1 (9/61, 68 pg. Giant)-New stories & reprints	6.00	18.00	60.00

LITTLE AUDREY
Aug, 1992 - No. 8, July, 1993 ($1.25/$1.50)
Harvey Comics

	GD25	FN65	NM94
V2#1		1.20	3.00
2-8		.80	2.00

LITTLE AUDREY (...Yearbook)
1950 (50¢, 260 pgs.)
St. John Publishing Co.

	GD25	FN65	NM94
Contains 8 complete 1949 comics rebound; Casper, Alice in Wonderland, Little Audrey, Abbott & Costello, Pinocchio, Moon Mullins, Three Stooges (from Jubilee), Little Annie Rooney app. (Rare)	55.00	165.00	550.00

(Also see All Good & Treasury of Comics)

NOTE: *This book contains remaindered St. John comics; many variations possible.*

LITTLE AUDREY & MELVIN (Audrey & Melvin No. 62)
May, 1962 - No. 61, Dec, 1973
Harvey Publications

	GD25	FN65	NM94
1	6.50	19.50	65.00
2-5	3.20	9.60	32.00
6-10	2.20	6.60	22.00
11-20	1.50	4.50	15.00
21-40: 22-Richie Rich app.	1.10	3.30	9.00
41-50,55-61		2.40	6.00
51-54: All 52 pg. Giants	1.00	2.80	7.00

LITTLE AUDREY TV FUNTIME
Sept, 1962 - No. 33, Oct, 1971 (#1-31: 68 pgs.; #32,33: 52 pgs.)
Harvey Publications

	GD25	FN65	NM94
1-Richie Rich app.	5.50	16.50	55.00
2,3: Richie Rich app.	4.00	12.00	40.00
4,5: 5-25¢ & 35¢ issues exist	3.20	9.60	32.00
6-10	1.40	4.20	14.00
11-20	1.10	3.30	9.00
21-33	1.00	2.80	7.00

LITTLE BAD WOLF (Disney; seeWalt Disney's C&S #52, Walt Disney Showcase #21 & Wheaties)
No. 403, June, 1952 - No. 564, June, 1954
Dell Publishing Co.

	GD25	FN65	NM94
Four Color 403 (#1)	6.40	19.00	70.00
Four Color 473 (6/53), 564	3.60	11.00	40.00

LITTLE BEAVER
No. 211, Jan, 1949 - No. 870, Jan, 1958 (All painted-c)
Dell Publishing Co.

	GD25	FN65	NM94
Four Color 211('49)-All Harman-a	7.00	20.00	75.00
Four Color 267,294,332(5/51)	3.50	11.00	38.00
3(10-12/51)-8(1-3/53)	3.00	9.00	35.00
Four Color 483(8-10/53),529	2.75	8.00	30.00
Four Color 612,660,695,744,817,870	2.75	8.00	30.00

LITTLE BIT
Mar, 1949 - No. 2, June, 1949
Jubilee/St. John Publishing Co.

	GD25	FN65	NM94
1,2	4.25	13.00	28.00

LITTLE DOT (See Humphrey, Li'l Max, Sad Sack, and Tastee-Freez Comics)
Sept, 1953 - No. 164, Apr, 1976
Harvey Publications

	GD25	FN65	NM94
1-Intro./1st app. Richie Rich & Little Lotta	78.00	234.00	775.00
2-1st app. Freckles & Pee Wee (Richie Rich's poor friends)	32.50	98.00	325.00
3	20.00	60.00	200.00
4	15.00	45.00	150.00
5-Origin dots on Little Dot's dress	22.00	66.00	220.00
6-Richie Rich, Little Lotta, & Little Dot all on cover; 1st Richie Rich cover featured	18.00	54.00	180.00
7-10: 9-Last pre-code issue (1/55)	11.00	33.00	110.00
11-20	7.50	22.50	75.00
21-40	4.00	12.00	40.00
41-60	2.00	6.00	20.00
61-80	1.40	4.20	14.00
81-100	1.25	3.75	10.00
101-141		2.40	6.00
142-145: All 52 pg. Giants	1.10	3.30	9.00
146-164		1.60	4.00
Shoe store giveaway 2	3.50	10.50	35.00

NOTE: *Richie Rich & Little Lotta in all.*

LITTLE DOT
Sept, 1992 - No. 7, June, 1994 ($1.25/$1.50)
Harvey Comics

	GD25	FN65	NM94
V2#1-Little Dot, Little Lotta, Richie Rich in all		1.20	3.00
2-7 ($1.50)		.80	2.00

LITTLE DOT DOTLAND (Dot Dotland No. 62, 63)
July, 1962 - No. 61, Dec, 1973
Harvey Publications

	GD25	FN65	NM94
1-Richie Rich begins	7.50	22.50	75.00
2,3	3.80	11.40	38.00

Little Eva #2 © STJ

Li'l Ghost #1 © STJ

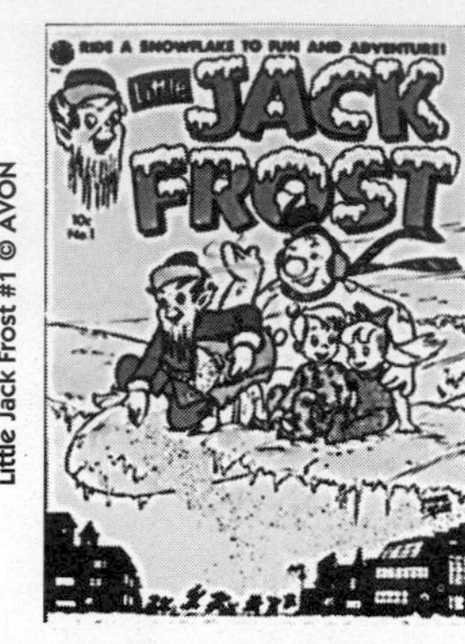

Little Jack Frost #1 © AVON

	GD25	FN65	NM94
4,5	3.20	9.60	32.00
6-10	2.00	6.00	20.00
11-20	1.50	4.50	15.00
21-30	1.00	3.00	8.00
31-50,55-61		2.40	6.00
51-54: All 52 pg. Giants	1.10	3.30	9.00

LITTLE DOT'S UNCLES & AUNTS (See Harvey Hits No. 4, 13, 24)
Oct, 1961; No. 2, Aug, 1962 - No. 52, Apr, 1974
Harvey Enterprises

	GD25	FN65	NM94
1-Richie Rich begins; 68 pgs. begin	9.00	27.00	90.00
2,3	4.50	13.50	45.00
4,5	3.20	9.60	32.00
6-10	2.20	6.60	22.00
11-20	1.60	4.80	16.00
21-37: Last 68 pg. issue	1.50	4.50	12.00
38-52: All 52 pg. Giants	1.25	3.75	10.00

LITTLE DRACULA
Jan, 1992 - No. 3, May, 1992 ($1.25, quarterly, mini-series)
Harvey Comics

	GD25	FN65	NM94
1-3		.80	2.00

LITTLE EVA
May, 1952 - No. 31, Nov, 1956
St. John Publishing Co.

	GD25	FN65	NM94
1	10.00	30.00	80.00
2	5.70	17.00	40.00
3-5	4.15	12.50	25.00
6-10	3.60	9.00	18.00
11-31	3.20	8.00	16.00
3-D 1,2(10/53, 11/53, 25¢)-Both came w/glasses. 1-Infinity-c	15.00	45.00	120.00
I.W. Reprint #1-3,6-8: 1-r/Little Eva #28. 2-r/Little Eva #29. 3-r/Little Eva #24		2.40	6.00
Super Reprint #10,12('63),14,16,18('64): 18-r/Little Eva #25.		2.40	6.00

LITTLE FIR TREE, THE
nd (1942) (8-1/2x11") (12 pgs. with cover, color & B&W, heavy paper)
W. T. Grant Co. (Christmas giveaway)

nn-Story by Hans Christian Anderson; 8 pg. Kelly-r/Santa Claus Funnies (not signed); X-Mas-c
(One copy in Mint sold for $1750.00 in 1986 & another copy in VF sold for $1000.00 in 1991)

LI'L GENIUS (Summer Fun No. 54) (See Blue Bird & Giant Comics #3)
1954 - No. 52, 1/65; No. 53, 10/65; No. 54, 10/85 - No. 55, 1/86
Charlton Comics

	GD25	FN65	NM94
1	8.50	26.00	60.00
2	5.00	15.00	30.00
3-15,19,20	4.00	10.00	20.00
16,17-(68 pgs.)	5.00	15.00	30.00
18-(100 pgs., 10/58)	7.15	21.50	50.00
21-35	2.25	6.75	18.00
36-53	1.50	4.50	12.00
54,55		1.20	3.00

LI'L GHOST
Feb, 1958; Nov?, 1958 - No. 3, Mar, 1959
St. John Publishing Co./Fago No. 1 on

	GD25	FN65	NM94
1(St. John)	6.50	19.50	45.00
1(Fago)-Al Fago-c/a begins	5.00	15.00	30.00
2,3: 2-(1/59)	4.00	11.00	22.00

LITTLE GIANT COMICS
7/38 - No. 3, 10/38; No. 4, 2/39 (132 pgs.) (6-3/4x4-1/2")
Centaur Publications

	GD25	FN65	NM94
1-B&W with color-c; stories, puzzles, magic	49.00	147.00	440.00
2,3-B&W with color-c	42.00	126.00	375.00
4 (6-5/8x9-3/8")(68 pgs., B&W inside)	43.00	129.00	390.00

NOTE: ***Filchock** c-2, 4. **Gustavson** a-1. **Pinajian** a-4. **Bob Wood** a-1.*

LITTLE GIANT DETECTIVE FUNNIES
Oct, 1938 - No. 4, Jan, 1939 (6-3/4x4-1/2", 132 pgs., B&W)
Centaur Publications

	GD25	FN65	NM94
1-B&W with color-c	56.00	168.00	500.00
2,3	42.00	126.00	375.00
4(1/39, B&W; color-c; 68 pgs., 6-1/2x9-1/2")-Eisner-r	44.00	132.00	400.00

LITTLE GIANT MOVIE FUNNIES
Aug, 1938 - No. 2, Oct, 1938 (6-3/4x4-1/2", 132 pgs., B&W)
Centaur Publications

	GD25	FN65	NM94
1-Ed Wheelan's "Minute Movies" reprints	56.00	168.00	500.00
2-Ed Wheelan's "Minute Movies" reprints	42.00	126.00	375.00

LITTLE GROUCHO (...the Red-Headed Tornado; ...Grouchy No. 2)
No. 16; Feb-Mar, 1955 - No. 2, June-July, 1955 (See Tippy Terry)
Reston Publ. Co.

	GD25	FN65	NM94
16, 1 (2-3/55)	6.00	18.00	42.00
2(6-7/55)	4.25	13.00	28.00

LITTLE HIAWATHA (Disney; see Walt Disney's C&S #143)
No. 439, Dec, 1952 - No. 988, May-July, 1959
Dell Publishing Co.

	GD25	FN65	NM94
Four Color 439 (#1)	4.50	13.50	50.00
Four Color 787 (4/57), 901 (5/58), 988	3.60	11.00	40.00

LITTLE IKE
April, 1953 - No. 4, Oct, 1953
St. John Publishing Co.

	GD25	FN65	NM94
1	7.85	23.50	55.00
2	5.00	15.00	30.00
3,4	4.00	12.00	24.00

LITTLE IODINE (See Giant Comic Album)
No. 224, 4/49 - No. 257, 1949: 3-5/50 - No. 56, 4-6/62 (1-4: 52pgs.)
Dell Publishing Co.

	GD25	FN65	NM94
Four Color 224-By Jimmy Hatlo	8.00	25.00	90.00
Four Color 257	6.40	19.00	70.00
1(3-5/50)	8.00	25.00	90.00
2-5	3.00	10.00	36.00
6-10	2.50	7.50	27.00
11-20	1.65	5.00	18.00
21-30: 27-Xmas-c	1.50	4.50	16.00
31-40	1.40	4.20	12.00
41-56	1.10	3.30	9.00

LITTLE JACK FROST
1951
Avon Periodicals

	GD25	FN65	NM94
1	6.50	19.50	45.00

LI'L JINX (Little Archie in Animal Land #17) (Also see Pep Comics #62)
Nov, 1956 - No. 6, Sept, 1957
Archie Publications

	GD25	FN65	NM94
1-By Joe Edwards	8.75	26.25	65.00
2-6	6.50	19.50	45.00

LI'L JINX (See Archie Giant Series Magazine No. 223)

LI'L JINX CHRISTMAS BAG (See Archie Giant Series Mag. No. 195, 206, 219)

LI'L JINX GIANT LAUGH-OUT (See Archie Giant Series Mag. No. 176, 185)
No. 33, Sept, 1971 - No. 43, Nov, 1973 (52 pgs.)

Little Lizzie #2 © MEG

Li'l Menace #1 © Fago

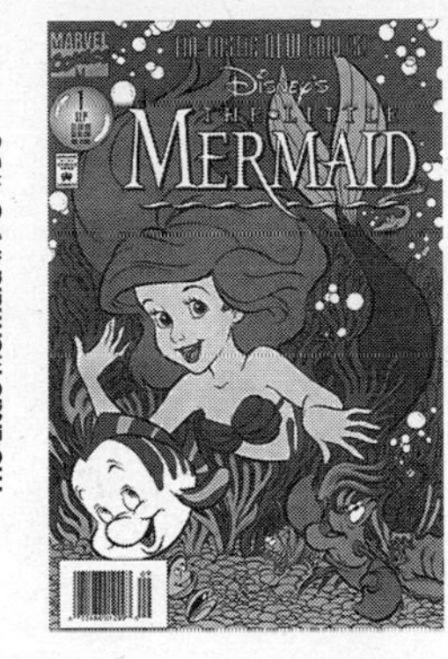

The Little Mermaid #1 © WDC

	GD25	FN65	NM94
Archie Publications			
33-43	1.10	3.30	9.00

LITTLE JOE (See Popular Comics & Super Comics)
No. 1, 1942
Dell Publishing Co.

	GD25	FN65	NM94
Four Color 1	42.00	125.00	460.00

LITTLE JOE
Apr, 1953
St. John Publishing Co.

	GD25	FN65	NM94
1	4.00	10.00	20.00

LI'L KIDS (Also see Li'l Pals)
8/70 - No. 2, 10/70; No. 3, 11/71 - No. 12, 6/73
Marvel Comics Group

	GD25	FN65	NM94
1	3.50	10.50	35.00
2-12: 10-12-Calvin app.	2.25	6.75	18.00

LITTLE KING
No. 494, Aug, 1953 - No. 677, Feb, 1956
Dell Publishing Co.

	GD25	FN65	NM94
Four Color 494 (#1)	9.00	27.00	100.00
Four Color 597, 677	4.50	13.50	70.00

LITTLE KLINKER
Nov, 1960 (20 pgs.) (slick cover)
Little Klinker Ventures (Montgomery Ward Giveaway)

	GD25	FN65	NM94
nn	1.50	4.50	12.00

LITTLE LANA (Formerly Lana)
No. 8, Nov, 1949; No. 9, Mar, 1950
Marvel Comics (MjMC)

	GD25	FN65	NM94
8,9	5.70	17.00	40.00

LITTLE LENNY
June, 1949 - No. 3, Nov, 1949
Marvel Comics (CDS)

	GD25	FN65	NM94
1-Little Aspirin app.	8.50	26.00	60.00
2,3	5.00	15.00	30.00

LITTLE LIZZIE
6/49 - No. 5, 4/50; 9/53 - No. 3, Jan, 1954
Marvel Comics (PrPI)/Atlas (OMC)

	GD25	FN65	NM94
1	8.75	26.25	70.00
2-5	5.70	17.00	40.00
1 (9/53, 2nd series by Atlas)-Howie Post-c	6.50	19.50	45.00
2,3	5.00	15.00	30.00

LITTLE LOTTA (See Harvey Hits No. 10)
11/55 - No. 110, 11/73; No. 111, 9/74 - No. 120, 5/76
V2#1, Oct, 1992 - No. 4, July, 1993 ($1.25)
Harvey Publications

	GD25	FN65	NM94
1-Richie Rich (r) & Little Dot begin	29.00	87.00	290.00
2,3	13.00	39.00	125.00
4,5	6.50	19.50	65.00
6-10	5.50	16.50	55.00
11-20	3.50	10.50	35.00
21-40	2.20	6.60	22.00
41-60	1.80	5.40	18.00
61-80	1.40	4.20	14.00
81-99	1.00	3.00	8.00
100-103: All 52 pg. Giants	1.10	3.30	9.00
104-120		2.00	5.00
V2#1-4 (1992-93)		.80	2.00

NOTE: *No. 121 was advertised, but never released.*

LITTLE LOTTA FOODLAND
9/63 - No. 14, 10/67; No. 15, 10/68 - No. 29, Oct, 1972
Harvey Publications

	GD25	FN65	NM94
1-Little Lotta, Little Dot, Richie Rich, 68 pgs. begin	10.00	30.00	100.00
2,3	6.00	18.00	60.00
4,5	4.00	12.00	40.00
6-10	3.00	9.00	30.00
11-20	2.00	6.00	20.00
21-26: 26-Last 68 pg. issue	1.40	4.20	14.00
27,28: Both 52 pgs.	1.40	4.20	14.00
29-(36 pgs.)	1.00	2.80	7.00

LITTLE LULU (Formerly Marge's...)
No. 207, Sept, 1972 - No. 268, April, 1984
Gold Key 207-257/Whitman 258 on

	GD25	FN65	NM94
207,209,220-Stanley-r. 207-1st app. Henrietta	1.00	3.00	8.00
208,210-219: 208-1st app. Snobbly, Wilbur's brother		2.40	6.00
221-240,242-249, 250(r/#166), 251-254(r/#206)		1.60	4.00
241,263,268-Stanley-r		1.60	4.00
255-262,264-267: 256-r/#212		.80	2.00

LITTLE MARY MIXUP (See Comics On Parade)
No. 10, 1939, - No. 26, 1940
United Features Syndicate

	GD25	FN65	NM94
Single Series 10, 26	28.00	84.00	220.00

LITTLE MAX COMICS (Joe Palooka's Pal; see Joe Palooka)
Oct, 1949 - No. 73, Nov, 1961
Harvey Publications

	GD25	FN65	NM94
1-Infinity-c; Little Dot begins; Joe Palooka on-c	13.00	39.00	105.00
2-Little Dot app.; Joe Palooka on-c	7.50	22.50	52.00
3-Little Dot app.; Joe Palooka on-c	5.70	17.00	36.00
4-10: 5-Little Dot app., 1pg.	4.00	12.00	24.00
11-20	3.60	9.00	18.00
21-73: 23-Little Dot app. 38-r/#20. 63,65,67,69-Include new five pg. Richie Rich stories 70-73-Little Lotta, Richie Rich app.	1.20	3.60	12.00

LI'L MENACE
Dec, 1958 - No. 3, May, 1959
Fago Magazine Co.

	GD25	FN65	NM94
1-Peter Rabbit app.	5.70	17.00	40.00
2-Peter Rabbit (Vincent Fago's)	5.00	15.00	30.00
3	4.15	12.50	25.00

LITTLE MERMAID, THE (Walt Disney's...; also see Disney's...)
1990 (no date given)($5.95, no ads, 52 pgs.)
W. D. Publications (Disney)

	GD25	FN65	NM94
nn-Adapts animated movie		2.40	6.00
nn-Comic version ($2.50)		1.00	2.50

LITTLE MERMAID, THE
1992 - No. 4, 1992 ($1.50, mini-series)
Disney Comics

	GD25	FN65	NM94
1-4: Based on movie			1.50
1-4: 2nd printings sold at Wal-Mart w/different-c			1.50

LITTLE MISS MUFFET
No. 11, Dec, 1948 - No. 13, March, 1949
Best Books (Standard Comics)/King Features Synd.

	GD25	FN65	NM94
11-Strip reprints; Fanny Cory-c/a	6.50	19.50	45.00
12,13-Strip reprints; Fanny Cory-c/a	5.00	15.00	30.00

LITTLE MISS SUNBEAM COMICS
June-July, 1950 - No. 4, Dec-Jan, 1950-51
Magazine Enterprises/Quality Bakers of America

	GD25	FN65	NM94
1	11.30	34.00	90.00
2-4	6.50	19.50	45.00
...Advs. In Space ('55)	4.25	13.00	28.00

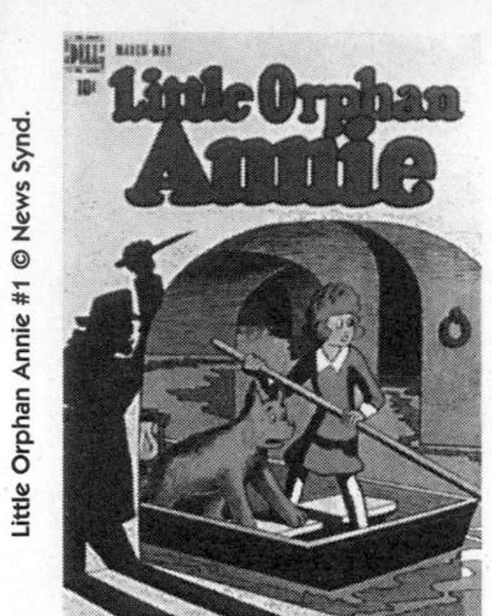

Little Orphan Annie #1 © News Synd.

Li'l Pan #6 © FOX

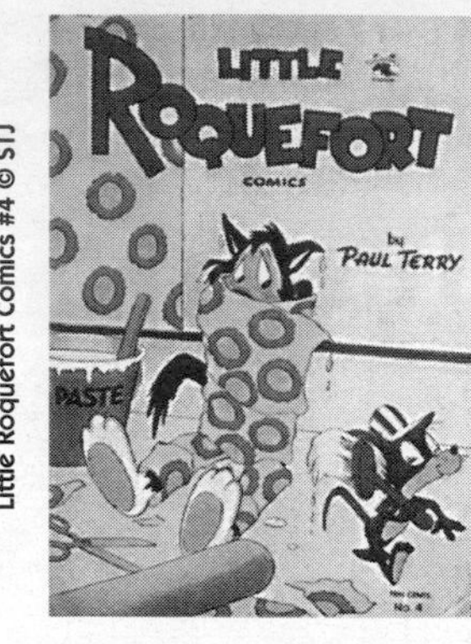

Little Roquefort Comics #4 © STJ

	GD25	FN65	NM94
Bread Giveaway 1-4(Quality Bakers, 1949-50)-14 pgs. each	4.00	12.00	24.00
Bread Giveaway (1957,61; 16pgs, reg. size)	4.00	11.00	22.00

LITTLE MONSTERS, THE (See March of Comics #423, Three Stooges #17)
Nov, 1964 - No. 44, Feb, 1978
Gold Key

	GD25	FN65	NM94
1	3.60	11.00	40.00
2	1.80	5.50	20.00
3-10	1.60	4.80	15.00
11-20	1.50	4.50	12.00
21-30	1.10	3.30	9.00
31-44: 20,34-39,43-Reprints		2.40	6.00

LITTLE MONSTERS (Movie)
1989 - No. 6, June, 1990 ($1.75)
Now Comics

	GD25	FN65	NM94
..1-6: Photo-c from movie		.75	1.80

LITTLE NEMO (See Cocomalt, Future Comics, Help, Jest, Kayo, Punch, Red Seal, & Superworld; most by Winsor McCay Jr., son of famous artist) (Other McCay books: see Little Sammy Sneeze & Dreams of the Rarebit Fiend)

LITTLE NEMO (...in Slumberland)
1945 (11x7-1/4", 28 pgs., B&W)
McCay Features/Nostalgia Press('69)

	GD25	FN65	NM94
1905 & 1911 reprints by Winsor McCay	7.85	23.50	55.00
1969-70 (Exact reprint)	2.00	5.00	10.00

LITTLE ORPHAN ANNIE (See Annie, Famous Feature Stories, Marvel Super Special, Merry Christmas..., Popular Comics, Super Book #7, 11, 23 & Super Comics)

LITTLE ORPHAN ANNIE
No. 7, 1937 - No. 3, Sept-Nov, 1948; No. 206, Dec, 1948
David McKay Publ./Dell Publishing Co.

	GD25	FN65	NM94
Feature Books(McKay) 7-(1937) (Rare)	77.00	231.00	850.00
Four Color 12(1941)	45.00	135.00	495.00
Four Color 18(1943)-Flag-c	36.00	107.00	390.00
Four Color 52(1944)	28.00	85.00	310.00
Four Color 76(1945)	23.00	70.00	255.00
Four Color 107(1946)	19.00	58.00	215.00
Four Color 152(1947)	13.00	38.00	140.00
1(3-5/48)-r/strips from 5/7/44 to 7/30/44	13.00	38.00	140.00
2-r/strips from 7/21/40 to 9/9/40	9.00	26.00	95.00
3-r/strips from 9/10/40 to 11/9/40	9.00	26.00	95.00
Four Color 206(12/48)	7.00	20.00	75.00
Junior Commandos Giveaway (same-c as 4-Color #18, K.K. Publ.)(Big Shoe Store); same back cover as '47 Popped Wheat giveaway; 16 pgs; flag-c; r/strips 9/7/42-10/10/42	27.00	81.00	215.00
Popped Wheat Giveaway ('47)-16 pgs. full color; reprints strips from 5/3/40 to 6/20/40	1.60	4.00	8.00
Quaker Sparkies Giveaway (1940)	15.50	47.00	125.00
Quaker Sparkies Giveaway (1941, full color, 20 pgs.); "LOA and the Rescue"; r/strips 4/13/39-6/21/39 & 7/6/39-7/17/39. "LOA and the Kidnappers"; r/strips 11/28/38-1/28/39	13.00	39.00	105.00
Quaker Sparkies Giveaway (1942, full color, 20 pgs.); "LOA and Mr. Gudge"; r/strips 2/13/38-3/21/38 & 4/18/37-5/30/37. "LOA and the Great Am"	11.30	34.00	90.00

LI'L PALS (Also see Li'l Kids)
Sept, 1972 - No. 5, May, 1973
Marvel Comics Group

	GD25	FN65	NM94
1	2.50	7.50	25.00
2-5	1.85	5.50	15.00

LI'L PAN (Formerly Rocket Kelly; becomes Junior Comics with #9)
No. 6, Dec-Jan, 1946-47 - No. 8, Apr-May, 1947 (Also see Wotalife Comics)
Fox Features Syndicate

	GD25	FN65	NM94
6	7.15	21.50	50.00
7,8: 7-Atomic bomb story	5.70	17.00	35.00

LITTLE PEOPLE
No. 485, Aug-Oct, 1953 - No. 1062, Dec, 1959 (Walt Scott's)
Dell Publishing Co.

	GD25	FN65	NM94
Four Color 485 (#1)	5.50	16.50	60.00
Four Color 573(7/54), 633(6/55)	3.00	9.00	35.00
Four Color 692(3/56),753(11/56),809(7/57),868(12/57),908(5/58), 959(12/58), 1062	3.00	9.00	35.00
Four Color 1024-Darby O'Gill &...-Movie, Toth-a, photo-c	9.00	27.00	100.00

LITTLE RASCALS
No. 674, Jan, 1956 - No. 1297, Mar-May, 1962
Dell Publishing Co.

	GD25	FN65	NM94
Four Color 674 (#1)	6.40	19.00	70.00
Four Color 778(3/57),825(8/57)	3.60	11.00	40.00
Four Color 883(3/58),936(9/58),974(3/59),1030(9/59),1079(2-4/60),1137 (9-11/60)	3.60	11.00	40.00
Four Color 1174(3-5/61),1224(10-12/61),1297	2.75	8.00	30.00

LI'L RASCAL TWINS (Formerly Nature Boy)
No. 6, 1957 - No. 18, Jan, 1960
Charlton Comics

	GD25	FN65	NM94
6-Li'l Genius & Tomboy in all	3.00	9.00	30.00
7-18	2.00	6.00	16.00

LITTLE ROQUEFORT COMICS (See Paul Terry's Comics #105)
June, 1952 - No. 9, Oct, 1953; No. 10, Summer, 1958
St. John Publishing Co.(all pre-code)/Pines No. 10

	GD25	FN65	NM94
1-By Paul Terry	8.50	26.00	60.00
2	4.25	13.00	28.00
3-10: 10-CBS Television Presents on-c	4.00	11.00	22.00

LITTLE SAD SACK (See Harvey Hits No. 73, 76, 79, 81, 83)
Oct, 1964 - No. 19, Nov, 1967
Harvey Publications

	GD25	FN65	NM94
1-Richie Rich app. on cover only	3.00	9.00	30.00
2-19	1.85	5.50	15.00

LITTLE SCOUTS
No. 321, Mar, 1951 - No. 587, Oct, 1954
Dell Publishing Co.

	GD25	FN65	NM94
Four Color #321 (#1, 3/51)	2.75	8.00	30.00
2(10-12/51) - 6(10-12/52)	1.35	4.00	15.00
Four Color #462,506,550,587	1.35	4.00	15.00

LITTLE SHOP OF HORRORS SPECIAL (Movie)
Feb, 1987 ($2.00, 68 pgs.)
DC Comics

	GD25	FN65	NM94
1-Colan-c/a		.80	2.00

LITTLE SPUNKY
No date (1963?) (10¢)
I. W. Enterprises

	GD25	FN65	NM94
1-r/Frisky Fables #1	1.00	2.80	7.00

LITTLE STOOGES, THE (The Three Stooges' Sons)
Sept, 1972 - No. 7, Mar, 1974
Gold Key

	GD25	FN65	NM94
1-Norman Maurer cover/stories in all	1.80	5.50	20.00
2-7	1.25	3.75	10.00

LITTLEST OUTLAW (Disney)
No. 609, Jan, 1955
Dell Publishing Co.

	GD25	FN65	NM94
Four Color 609-Movie, photo-c	5.50	16.50	60.00

Lobo #7 © DC

Lobo Gallery #1 © DC

Lobo: I Quit #1 © DC

GD25 FN65 NM94

LITTLEST SNOWMAN, THE
No. 755, 12/56; No. 864, 12/57; 12-2/1963-64
Dell Publishing Co.
Four Color #755,864, 1(1964) 3.00 10.00 36.00

LI'L TOMBOY (Formerly Fawcett's Funny Animals; see Giant Comics #3)
V14#92, Oct, 1956; No. 93, Mar, 1957 - No. 107, Feb, 1960
Charlton Comics
V14#92 4.25 13.00 26.00
93-107: 97-Atomic Bunny app. 4.00 10.00 20.00

LITTLE TREE THAT WASN'T WANTED, THE
1960, (Color, 28 pgs.)
W. T. Grant Co. (Giveaway)
nn-Christmas giveaway 1.50 4.50 12.00

LI'L WILLIE COMICS (Formerly & becomes Willie Comics #22 on)
No. 20, July, 1949 - No. 21, Sept, 1949
Marvel Comics (MgPC)
20,21: 20-Little Aspirin app. 5.70 17.00 40.00

LITTLE WOMEN (See Power Record Comics)

LIVE IT UP
1973, 1976 (39-49 cents)
Spire Christian Comics (Fleming H. Revell Co.)
nn 1.20 3.00

LIVING BIBLE, THE
Fall, 1945 - No. 3, Spring, 1946
Living Bible Corp.
1-The Life of Paul; all have L. B. Cole-c 31.00 94.00 250.00
2-Joseph & His Brethren; Jonah & the Whale 19.00 56.00 150.00
3-Chaplains At War (classic-c) 31.00 94.00 250.00

LOBO
Dec, 1965; No. 2, Oct, 1966
Dell Publishing Co.
1,2-1st black character to have his own title. 1.85 5.50 15.00

LOBO (Also see Action #650, Adventures of Superman, Demon (2nd series), Justice League, L.E.G.I.O.N., Mister Miracle, Omega Men #3 & Superman #41)
Nov, 1990 - No. 4, Feb, 1991 ($1.50, color, limited series)
DC Comics
1-(99¢)-Giffen plots/Breakdowns in all .80 2.00
2-Legion '89 spin-off .80 2.00
3,4: 1-4 have Bisley painted covers & art .80 2.00
...: Blazing Chain of Love 1 (9/92, $1.50)-Denys Cowan-c/a; Alan Grant scripts 1.50
...Convention Special 1 (1993, $1.75) .70 1.75
...Paramilitary Christmas Special 1 (1991, $2.39, 52 pgs.)-Bisley-c/a 1.50
...: Portrait of a Victim 1 (1993, $1.75) .70 1.75

LOBO (Also see Showcase '95 #9)
Dec, 1993 - Present ($1.75/$1.95, mature)
DC Comics
1 ($2.95)-Foil enhanced-c; Alan Grant scripts begin 1.40 3.50
2-7-Alan Grant scripts .70 1.75
0,8,-15: 8-Begin $1.95-c. 9-(9/94). 0-(10/94)-Origin retold .80 2.00
16-49: 16-Begin $2.25-c .90 2.25
Annual 1 (1993, $3.50, 68 pgs.)-Bloodlines x-over 1.40 3.50
Annual 2 (1994, $3.50)-21 artists (20 listed on-c); Alan Grant script; Elseworlds story .80 2.00
Annual 3 (1995, $3.95)-Year One story 1.60 4.00
...Big Babe Spring Break Special (Spr, '95, $1.95)-Balent-a .80 2.00
...Bounty Hunting for Fun and Profit ('95)-Bisley-c 2.00 5.00
...Chained (5/97, $2.50)-Alan Grant story 1.00 2.50
.../Deadman: The Brave And The Bald (2/95, $3.50) 1.40 3.50
.../Demon: Helloween (12/96, $2.25)-Giarrano-a .90 2.25
...Fragtastic Voyage 1 ('97, $5.95)-Mejia painted-c/a 5.95
...Gallery (9/95, $3.50)-pin-ups. 1.40 3.50
...In the Chair 1 (8/94, $1.95, 36 pgs.) .80 2.00
...I Quit-(12/95, $2.25) .90 2.25
.../Judge Dredd ('95, $4.95). 2.00 5.00
...Lobocop 1 (2/94, $1.95)-Alan Grant scripts; painted-c .80 2.00

LOBO: A CONTRACT ON GAWD
Apr, 1994 - July, 1994 ($1.75, mini-series, mature)
DC Comics
1-4: Alan Grant scripts. 3-Groo cameo .70 1.75

LOBO: DEATH AND TAXES
Oct, 1996 - No. 4, Jan, 1997 ($2.25, mini-series)
DC Comics
1-4-Giffen/Grant scripts .90 2.25

LOBO GOES TO HOLLYWOOD
Aug, 1996 ($2.25, one shot)
DC Comics
1-Grant scripts .90 2.25

LOBO: INFANTICIDE
Oct, 1992 - Jan, 1993 ($1.50, mini-series, mature)
DC Comics
1-4-Giffen-c/a; Alan Grant scripts 1.50

LOBO/ MASK
Feb, 1997 - No.2, Mar, 1997 ($5.95, limited series)
DC Comics
1,2 5.95

LOBO'S BACK
May, 1992 - No. 4, Nov, 1992 ($1.50, mini-series, mature)
DC Comics
1-4: 1-Has 3 outer covers. Bisley painted-c 1,2; a-1-3. 3-Sam Kieth-c; all have Giffen plots/breakdown & Grant scripts 1.50
Trade paperback (1993, $9.95)-r/1-4 1.25 3.75 10.00

LOBO THE DUCK
June, 1997 ($1.95, one-shot)
DC Comics (Amalgam)
1-Alan Grant-s/Val Semeiks & Ray Kryssing-a 1.95

LOBO: UNAMERICAN GLADIATORS
Jun, 1993 - Sep, 1993 ($1.75, mini-series, mature)
DC Comics
1-4-Mignola-c; Grant/Wagner scripts .70 1.75

LOCKE!
1987 - No. 3, ($1.25, limited series)
Blackthorne Publishing
1-3 1.25

LOCO (Magazine) (Satire)
Aug, 1958 - V1#3, Jan, 1959
Satire Publications
V1#1-Chic Stone-a 5.70 17.00 40.00
V1#2,3-Severin-a, 2 pgs. Davis; 3-Heath-a 5.00 15.00 30.00

LOGAN: PATH OF THE WARLORD
Feb, 1996 ($5.95, one-shot)
Marvel Comics
1-John Paul Leon-a 2.40 6.00

LOGAN: SHADOW SOCIETY

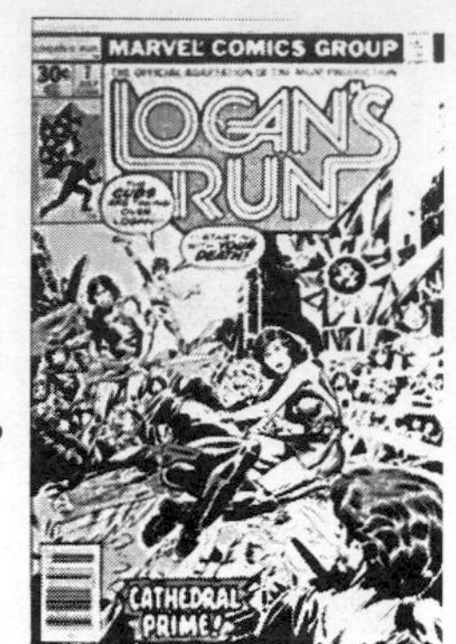

Logan's Run #7 © MEG

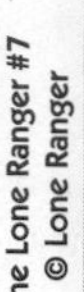
The Lone Ranger #7 © Lone Ranger

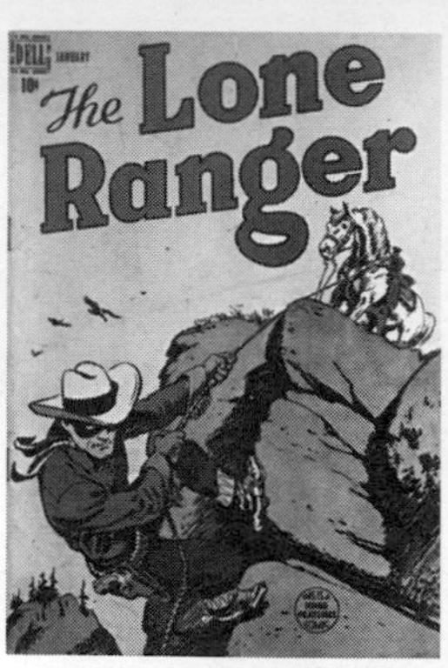

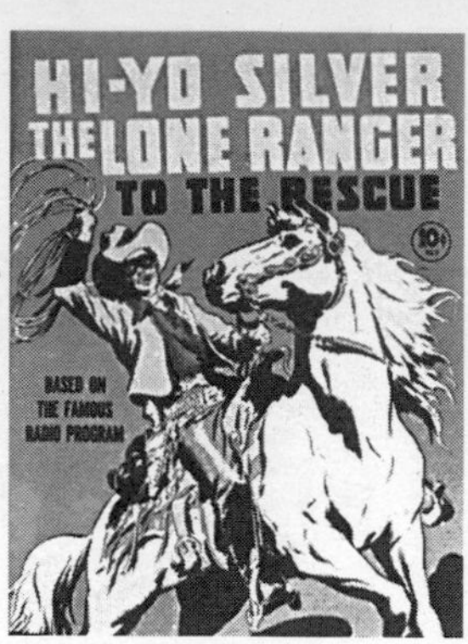

The Lone Ranger Large Feature Comic #7 © Lone Ranger

GD25 FN65 NM94

1996 ($5.95, one-shot)
Marvel Comics

1 2.40 6.00

LOGAN'S RUN
Jan, 1977 - No. 7, July, 1977
Marvel Comics Group

1: 1-5-Based on novel & movie 1.60 4.00
2-5,7: 6,7-New stories adapted from novel 1.20 3.00
6-1st Thanos (also see Iron Man #55) solo story (back-up) by Zeck (6/77) 1.00 3.00 8.00

NOTE: ***Austin*** *a-6i.* ***Gulacy*** *c-6.* ***Kane*** *c-7p.* ***Perez*** *a-1-5p; c-1-5p.* ***Sutton*** *a-6p, 7p.*

LOIS & CLARK, THE NEW ADVENTURES OF SUPERMAN
1994 ($9.95, one-shot)
DC Comics

1-r/Man of Steel #2, Superman Annual 1, Superman #9 & 11, Action #600 & 655, Adventures of Superman #445, 462 & 466 1.25 3.75 10.00

LOIS LANE (Also see Daring New Adventures of Supergirl, Showcase #9,10 & Superman's Girlfriend...)
Aug, 1986 - No. 2, Sept, 1986 ($1.50, 52 pgs.)
DC Comics

1,2-Morrow-c/a in each 1.50

LOLLY AND PEPPER
No. 832, Sept, 1957 - July, 1962
Dell Publishing Co.

Four Color 832(#1) 2.75 8.00 30.00
Four Color 940,978,1086,1206 1.80 5.50 20.00
01-459-207 (7/62) 1.80 5.50 20.00

LOMAX (See Police Action)

LONDON NIGHT LINGERIE SPECIAL
1996 ($3.00/$10.00, one-shot)
London Night Studios

1-($3.00)-"Nice" Edition; JJ North photo-c 1.20 3.00
1-($10.00)-"Naughty" Edition; JJ North naughty photo-c 3.75 10.00

LONDON'S DARK
1989 ($8.95, B&W, graphic novel)
Escape/Titan

nn-James Robinson script; Paul Johnson-c/a 1.10 3.30 9.00

LONE EAGLE (The Flame No. 5 on)
Apr-May, 1954 - No. 4, Oct-Nov, 1954
Ajax/Farrell Publications

1 9.50 28.00 75.00
2-4: 3-Bondage-c 6.50 19.50 45.00

LONELY HEART (Formerly Dear Lonely Hearts; Dear Heart #15 on)
No. 9, Mar, 1955 - No. 14, Feb, 1956
Ajax/Farrell Publ. (Excellent Publ.)

9-Kamenesque-a; (Last precode) 7.00 21.00 45.00
10-14 4.25 13.00 28.00

LONE RANGER, THE (See Ace Comics, Aurora, Dell Giants, Future Comics, Golden Comics Digest #48, King Comics, Magic Comics & March of Comics #165, 174, 193, 208, 225, 238, 310, 322, 338, 350)

LONE RANGER, THE
No. 3, 1939 - No. 167, Feb, 1947
Dell Publishing Co.

Large Feature Comic 3(1939)-Heigh-Yo Silver; text with illus. by Robert Weisman; also exists as a Whitman #710 80.00 240.00 875.00
Large Feature Comic 7(1939)-Illustr. by Henry Vallely; Hi-Yo Silver the Lone Ranger to the Rescue; also exists as a Whitman #715 77.00 231.00 850.00

GD25 FN65 NM94

Feature Book 21(1940), 24(1941) 57.00 171.00 625.00
Four Color 82(1945) 39.00 116.00 425.00
Four Color 98(1945),118(1946) 28.00 85.00 310.00
Four Color 125(1946),136(1947) 19.00 57.00 210.00
Four Color 151,167(1947) 16.00 47.00 170.00

LONE RANGER, THE (Movie, radio & TV; Clayton Moore starred as Lone Ranger in the movies; No. 1-37: strip reprints)(See Dell Giants)
Jan-Feb, 1948 - No. 145, May-July, 1962
Dell Publishing Co.

1 (36 pgs.)-The Lone Ranger, his horse Silver, companion Tonto & his horse Scout begin 54.00 162.00 600.00
2 (52 pgs. begin, end #41) 25.00 75.00 280.00
3-5 19.00 57.00 210.00
6,7,9,10 16.00 48.00 175.00
8-Origin retold; Indian back-c begin, end #35 20.00 60.00 215.00
11-20: 11- "Young Hawk" Indian boy serial begins, ends #145 9.00 29.00 105.00
21,22,24-31: 51-Reprint. 31-1st Mask logo 8.00 25.00 90.00
23-Origin retold 10.50 32.00 115.00
32-37: 32-Painted-c begin. 36-Animal photo back-c begin, end #49. 37-Last newspaper-r issue; new outfit 6.40 19.00 70.00
38-41 (All 52 pgs.) 5.75 17.00 63.00
42-50 (36 pgs.) 5.00 15.00 54.00
51-74 (52 pgs.): 56-One pg. origin story of Lone Ranger & Tonto. 71-Blank inside-c 5.00 15.00 54.00
75,77-99: 79-X-mas-c 4.00 12.00 45.00
76-Flag-c 5.00 15.00 55.00
100 5.75 17.00 63.00
101-111: Last painted-c 4.00 12.00 45.00
112-Clayton Moore photo-c begin, end #145 15.00 45.00 165.00
113-117 8.00 25.00 90.00
118-Origin Lone Ranger, Tonto, & Silver retold; Special anniversary issue 22.00 66.00 240.00
119-145: 139-Last issue by Fran Striker 7.00 20.00 75.00
Cheerios Giveaways (1954, 16 pgs., 2-1/2x7", soft-c) #1- "The Lone Ranger, His Mask & How He Met Tonto". #2- "The Lone Ranger & the Story of Silver" each.... 13.00 39.00 105.00
Doll Giveaways (Gabriel Ind.)(1973, 3-1/4x5")- "The Story of The Lone Ranger" & "The Carson City Bank Robbery" 1.25 3.75 10.00
How the Lone Ranger Captured Silver Book(1936)-Silvercup Bread giveaway 42.00 126.00 375.00
...In Milk for Big Mike (1955, Dairy Association giveaway), soft-c; 5x7-1/4", 16 pgs. 11.30 34.00 90.00
Merita Bread giveaway (1954, 16 pgs., 5x7-1/4")- "How to Be a Lone Ranger Health & Safety Scout" 12.00 38.00 100.00

NOTE: ***Hank Hartman*** *painted c(signed)-65, 66, 70, 75, 82; unsigned-64?, 67-69?, 71, 72, 73?, 74?, 76-78, 80, 81, 83-91, 92?, 93-111.* ***Ernest Nordli*** *painted c(signed)-42, 50, 52, 53, 56, 59, 60; unsigned-39-41, 44-49, 51, 54, 55, 57, 58, 61-63?*

LONE RANGER, THE
9/64 - No. 16, 12/69; No. 17, 11/72; No. 18, 9/74 - No. 28, 3/77
Gold Key (Reprints in #13-20)

1-Retells origin 3.60 11.00 40.00
2 1.80 5.50 20.00
3-10: Small Bear-r in #6-12 1.40 4.20 15.00
11-17 1.25 3.75 10.00
18-28 2.40 6.00
Golden West 1(30029-610, 10/66)-Giant; r/most Golden West #3 including Clayton Moore photo front/back-c 5.50 16.50 60.00
Legend of The Lone Ranger (1969, 16 pgs., giveaway)-Origin The Lone Ranger 1.50 4.50 12.00

LONE RANGER AND TONTO, THE
Aug, 1994 - No. 4, Nov, 1994 ($2.50, limited series)
Topps Comics

Lone Ranger Book #1 1939 © Lone Ranger

Looney Tunes #35 (3rd Series) © Warner Bros.

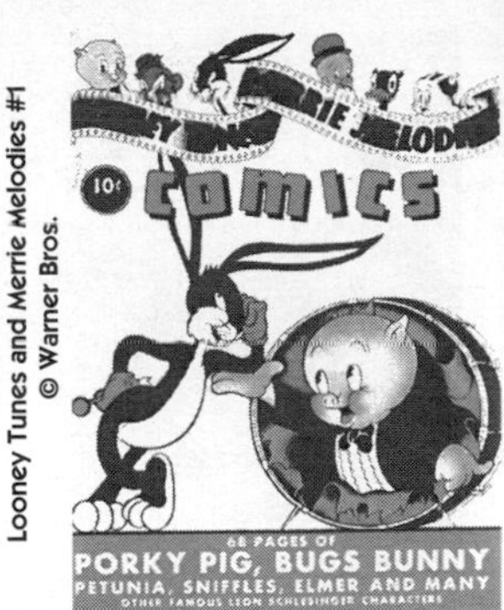

Looney Tunes and Merrie Melodies #1 © Warner Bros.

GD25 FN65 NM94

1-4: 3-Origin of Lone Ranger; Tonto leaves; Lansdale story, Truman-c/a in all. 1.00 2.50
1-4: Silver logo 1.25 3.75 10.00
Trade paperback (1/95, $9.95) 10.00

LONE RANGER COMICS, THE
Book 1, 1939(inside) (shows 1938 on-c) (52 pgs. in color; regular size)
Lone Ranger, Inc. (Ice cream mail order) GD25 FN65 VF82
Book 1-(Scarce)-The first western comic devoted to a single character; not by Vallely 800.00 2400.00 4000.00
(Estimated up to 20 total copies exist, none in NM/Mint)

LONE RANGER'S COMPANION TONTO, THE (TV)
No. 312, Jan, 1951 - No. 33, Nov-Jan/58-59 (All painted-c)
Dell Publishing Co. GD25 FN65 NM94
Four Color 312(#1, 1/51) 9.00 27.00 100.00
2(8-10/51),3: (#2 titled "Tonto") 4.50 13.50 50.00
4-10 0.00 11.00 40.00
11-20 2.75 8.00 30.00
21-33 1.80 5.50 20.00
NOTE: ***Ernest Nordli*** *painted c(signed)-2, 7; unsigned-3-6, 8-11, 12?, 13, 14, 18?, 22-24? See Aurora Comic Booklets.*

LONE RANGER'S FAMOUS HORSE HI-YO SILVER, THE (TV)
No. 369, Jan, 1952 - No. 36, Oct-Dec, 1960 (All painted-c, most by Sam Savitt)
Dell Publishing Co.
Four Color 369(#1)-Silver's origin as told by The Lone Ranger 8.00 25.00 90.00
Four Color 392(#2, 4/52) 4.00 12.00 45.00
3(7-9/52)-10(4-6/52) 3.00 10.00 36.00
11-36 2.50 7.50 27.00

LONE RIDER (Also see The Rider)
April, 1951 - No. 26, July, 1955 (#3-on: 36 pgs.)
Superior Comics(Farrell Publications)
1 (52 pgs.)-The Lone Rider & his horse Lightnin' begin; Kamenish-a begins 15.00 45.00 120.00
2 (52 pgs.)-The Golden Arrow begins (origin) 8.50 26.00 60.00
3-6: 6-Last Golden Arrow 7.15 21.50 50.00
7-Golden Arrow becomes Swift Arrow; origin of his shield 8.50 26.00 60.00
8-Origin Swift Arrow 8.75 26.25 70.00
9,10 6.50 19.50 45.00
11-14 5.35 16.00 32.00
15-Golden Arrow origin-r from #2, changing name to Swift Arrow 6.00 18.00 42.00
16-20,22-26: 23-Apache Kid app. 5.35 16.00 32.00
21-3-D effect-c 10.50 32.00 85.00

LONE WOLF AND CUB
May, 1987 - Jan, 1991 ($1.95-$3.25, B&W, deluxe size)
First Comics
1 .80 2.00
1-2nd print, 3rd print 1.50
2 .80 2.00
2-2nd print 1.50
3-25: 6-72 pgs. origin ish. 8-$2.50-c begins 1.00 2.50
26-30,33 ($2.95) 1.00 2.50
31,32,34-38,40,42 ($3.25): 40,42-Ploog-c 1.30 3.25
39-($5.95, 120 pgs.)-Ploog-c 2.40 6.00
41-($3.95, 84 pgs.)-Ploog-c 1.60 4.00
Deluxe Edition ($19.95, B&W) 2.50 7.50 20.00
NOTE: ***Miller*** *c-1-12p; intro 1-12.* ***Sienkiewicz*** *c-13-24.* ***Matt Wagner*** *c-25-30.*

LONG BOW (...Indian Boy)(See Indians & Jumbo Comics #141)
1951 - No. 9, Wint, 1952/53
Fiction House Magazines (Real Adventures Publ.)

GD25 FN65 NM94

1-Most covers by Maurice Whitman 12.00 36.00 95.00
2 8.50 26.00 60.00
3-9 6.50 19.50 45.00

LONG HOT SUMMER, THE
July, 1995 - No. 3, Sept, 1995 ($2.95/$2.50, limited series)
DC Comics (Milestone)
1 ($2.95) 1.20 3.00
2,3 ($2.50) 1.00 2.50

LONG JOHN SILVER & THE PIRATES (Formerly Terry & the Pirates)
No. 30, Aug, 1956 - No. 32, March, 1957 (TV)
Charlton Comics
30-32: Whitman-c 6.85 21.00 48.00

LONGSHOT (Also see X-Men, 2nd Series #10)
Sept, 1985 - No. 6, Feb, 1986 (60¢, limited series)
Marvel Comics
1-Arthur Adams/Whilce Portacio-c/a in all 1.00 2.50
2-5: 4-Spider-Man app. 1.50
6-Double size .80 2.00
Trade Paperback (1989, $16.95)-r/#1-6 17.00

LOOKERS
Feb, 1997 - Present ($3.00, B&W)
Avatar Press
1 1.20 3.00

LOONEY TUNES (2nd Series)
April, 1975 - No. 47, July, 1984
Gold Key/Whitman
1 -Reprints 1.65 5.00 18.00
2-10: 2,4-reprints 1.25 3.75 10.00
11-20: 16-reprints 1.00 2.80 7.00
21-30 2.00 5.00
31-47: Reprints: #1-4,16; 38-46(1/3-r) 1.20 3.00

LOONEY TUNES (3rd Series)
Apr, 1994 - Present ($1.50/$1.75)
DC Comics
1-22: 1-Marvin Martian-c/sty; Bugs Bunny, Roadrunner, Daffy, Tweety begin 1.50
23-34: 23-Begin $1.75-c 1.75
35-37: 35-Begin $1.95-c 1.95

LOONEY TUNES AND MERRIE MELODIES COMICS ("Looney Tunes" #166 (8/55) on)(Also see Porky's Duck Hunt)
1941 - No. 246, July-Sept, 1962
Dell Publishing Co. GD25 FN65 VF82 NM94
1-Porky Pig, Bugs Bunny, Daffy Duck, Elmer Fudd, Mary Jane & Sniffles, Pat Patsy and Pete begin (1st comic book app. of each). Bugs Bunny story by Win Smith (early Mickey Mouse artist) 864.00 2592.00 5184.00 9500.00
(Estimated up to 171 total copies exist, 8 in NM/Mint)
GD25 FN65 NM94
2 (11/41) 118.00 354.00 1300.00
3-Kandi the Cave Kid begins by Walt Kelly; also in #4-6,8,11,15 100.00 300.00 1100.00
4-Kelly-a 86.00 258.00 950.00
5-Bugs Bunny The Super-Duper Rabbit story (1st funny animal super hero, 3/42; also see Coo Coo); Kelly-a 77.00 231.00 850.00
6,8-Kelly-a 57.00 171.00 625.00
7,9,10: 9-Painted-c. 10-Flag-c 43.00 129.00 465.00
11,15-Kelly-a; 15-X-Mas-c 43.00 129.00 465.00
12-14,16-19 30.00 90.00 330.00
20-25: Pat, Patsy & Pete by Walt Kelly in all 26.00 78.00 290.00
26-30 19.00 57.00 210.00

Lords of Misrue #4 © DH

Lost in Space #1 © Innovation

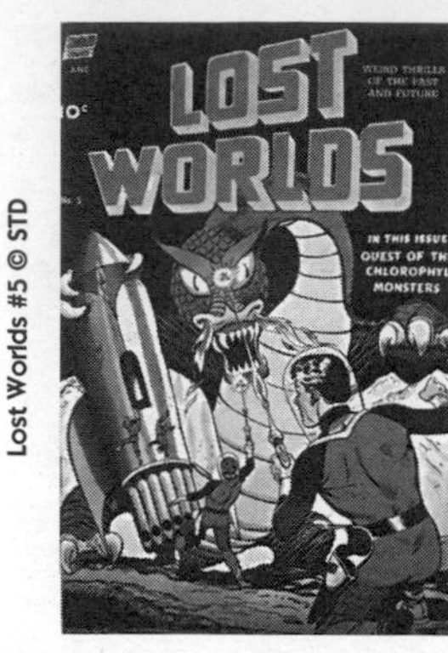

Lost Worlds #5 © STD

	GD25	FN65	NM94
31-40: 33-War bond-c. 39-X-Mas-c	15.00	45.00	170.00
41-50	13.00	39.00	140.00
51-60	8.75	26.50	95.00
61-80	5.90	17.70	65.00
81-99: 87-X-Mas-c	4.10	12.30	45.00
100	4.50	13.50	50.00
101-120	2.70	8.10	30.00
121-150	2.50	7.50	27.00
151-200: 159-X-Mas-c	1.60	4.80	16.00
201-246	1.20	3.60	12.00

LOONY SPORTS (Magazine)
Spring, 1975 (68 pgs.)
3-Strikes Publishing Co.

	GD25	FN65	NM94
1-Sports satire		.80	2.00

LOOSE CANNON (Also see Action Comics Annual #5 & Showcase '94 #5)
June, 1995 - No. 4, Sept, 1995 ($1.75, limited series)
DC Comics

	GD25	FN65	NM94
1-4: Adam Pollina-a. 1-Superman app.		.70	1.75

LOOY DOT DOPE
No. 13, 1939
United Features Syndicate

	GD25	FN65	NM94
Single Series 13	23.00	69.00	185.00

LORD JIM (See Movie Comics)

LORD PUMPKIN
Oct, 1994 ($2.50, one-shot)
Malibu Comics (Ultraverse)

	GD25	FN65	NM94
0		1.00	2.50

LORD PUMPKIN/NECROMANTRA
Apr, 1995 - No. 4, July, 1995 ($2.95, limited series, flip book)
Malibu Comics (Ultraverse)

	GD25	FN65	NM94
1-4		1.20	3.00

LORDS OF MISRULE
Jan, 1997 - No. 6, Jun, 1997 ($2.95, B&W, limited series)
Dark Horse Comics

	GD25	FN65	NM94
1-6: 1-Wraparound-c			2.95

LORDS OF THE ULTRA-REALM
June, 1986 - No. 6, Nov, 1986 (Mini-series)
DC Comics

	GD25	FN65	NM94
1		.80	2.00
2-6		.70	1.75
Special 1(12/87, $2.25)		.90	2.25

LORNA THE JUNGLE GIRL (...Jungle Queen #1-5)
July, 1953 - No. 26, Aug, 1957
Atlas Comics (NPI 1/OMC 2-11/NPI 12-26)

	GD25	FN65	NM94
1-Origin & 1st app.	30.00	90.00	220.00
2-Intro. & 1st app. Greg Knight	14.00	43.00	110.00
3-5	11.50	34.00	85.00
6-11: 11-Last pre-code (1/55)	10.00	30.00	70.00
12-17,19-26: 14-Colletta & Maneely-c	8.35	25.00	55.00
18-Williamson/Colletta-c	9.00	27.00	60.00

NOTE: ***Brodsky** c-1-3, 5, 9. **Everett** c-21, 23-26. **Heath** c-6, 7. **Maneely** c-12, 15. **Romita** a-20, 22, 24, 26. **Shores** a-14-16, 24, 26; c-11, 13, 16. **Tuska** a-6.*

LOSERS SPECIAL (See Our Fighting Forces #123)(Also see G.I. Combat & Our Fighting Forces)
Sept, 1985 ($1.25, one-shot)
DC Comics

	GD25	FN65	NM94
1-Capt. Storm, Gunner & Sarge; Crisis x-over			1.30

LOST, THE
Dec, 1997 - No. 4 ($2.95, B&W, limited series)
Chaos! Comics

	GD25	FN65	NM94
1,2-Andreyko-script: 1-Russell back-c			2.95

LOST CONTINENT
Sept, 1990 - No. 6, 1991 ($3.50, B&W, squarebound, 60 pgs.)
Eclipse International

	GD25	FN65	NM94
1-6: Japanese story translated to English		1.40	3.50

LOST IN SPACE (TV)(Also see Space Family Robinson)
Aug, 1991 - No. 12, Jan, 1993 ($2.50, limited series)
Innovation Publishing

	GD25	FN65	NM94
1-12: Bill Mumy (Will Robinson) scripts in #1-9. 9-Perez-c		1.00	2.50
1,2-Special Ed.; r/#1,2 plus new art & new-c		1.00	2.50
Annual 1,2 (1991, 1992, $2.95, 52 pgs.)		1.20	3.00

LOST IN SPACE: PROJECT ROBINSON (TV)
Nov, 1993 ($2.50, limited series intended)
Innovation Publishing

	GD25	FN65	NM94
1-Takes place after #12		1.00	2.50

LOST IN SPACE: VOYAGE TO THE BOTTOM OF THE SOUL
No. 13, Aug, 1993 - No. 18, 1994 ($2.50, limited series)
Innovation Publishing

	GD25	FN65	NM94
13(V1#1, $2.95)-Embossed silver logo edition; Bill Mumy scripts begin; painted-c		1.00	2.50
13(V1#1, $4.95)-Embossed gold logo edition bagged w/poster		2.00	5.00
14-18: Painted-c		1.00	2.50

NOTE: *Originally intended to be a 12 issue limited series.*

LOST PLANET
5/87 - No. 5, 2/88; No. 6, 3/89 ($1.75/$2.00, mini-series, Baxter paper)
Eclipse Comics

	GD25	FN65	NM94
1,2 ($1.75)-Bo Hampton-c/a in all		.75	1.80
3-6 ($2.00)		.80	2.00

LOST WAGON TRAIN, THE (See Zane Grey Fou r Color 583)

LOST WORLD, THE
No. 1145, Nov-Jan, 1960-61
Dell Publishing Co.

	GD25	FN65	NM94
Four Color 1145-Movie, Gil Kane-a, photo-c; 1pg. Conan Doyle biography by Torres	10.00	30.00	110.00

LOST WORLD, THE (See Jurassic Park)
May, 1997 - No. 4, Aug, 1997 ($2.95, limited series)
Topps Comics

	GD25	FN65	NM94
1-4-Movie adaption			2.95

LOST WORLDS (Weird Tales of the Past and Future)
No. 5, Oct, 1952 - No. 6, Dec, 1952
Standard Comics

	GD25	FN65	NM94
5- "Alice in Terrorland" by Alex Toth; J. Katz-a	36.00	107.00	260.00
6-Toth-a	30.00	90.00	220.00

LOTS 'O' FUN COMICS
1940's? (5¢, heavy stock, blue covers)
Robert Allen Co.

nn-Contents can vary; Felix, Planet Comics known; contents would determine value. Similar to Up-To-Date Comics. Remainders - re-packaged.

LOU GEHRIG (See The Pride of the Yankees)

LOVE ADVENTURES (Actual Confessions #13)
Oct, 1949; No. 2, Jan, 1950; No. 3, Feb, 1951 - No. 12, Aug, 1952
Marvel (IPS)/Atlas Comics (MPI)

	GD25	FN65	NM94
1-Photo-c	11.00	33.00	80.00
2-Powell-a; Tyrone Power, Gene Tierney photo-c	11.00	33.00	80.00

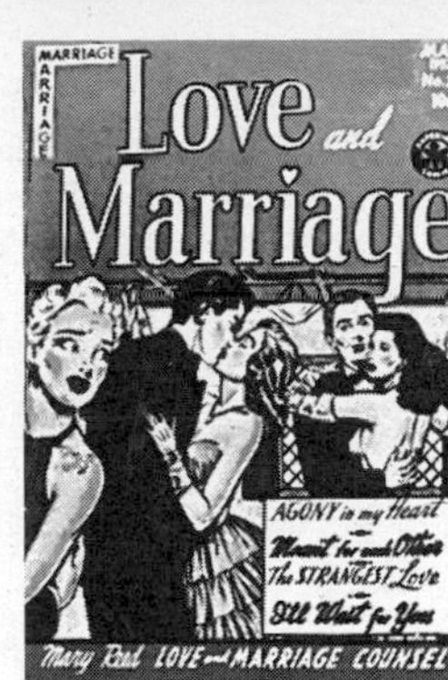

Love and Marriage #7 © SUPR

Love Confession #47 © QUA

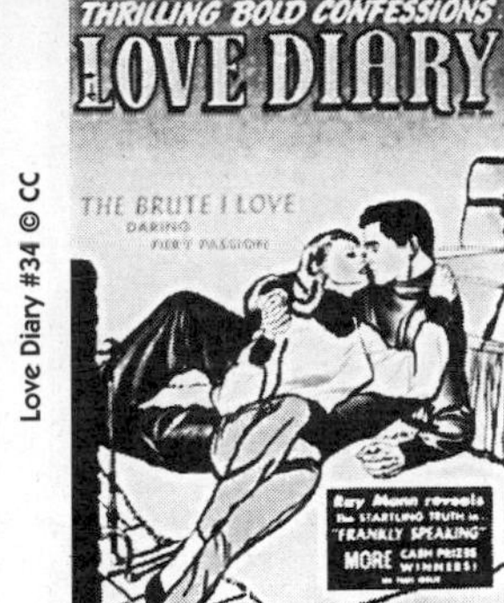

Love Diary #34 © CC

	GD25	FN65	NM94
3-8,10-12: 8-Robinson-a	5.70	17.00	40.00
9-Everett-a	7.00	21.00	45.00

LOVE AND MARRIAGE
Mar, 1952 - No. 16, Sept, 1954
Superior Comics Ltd.

	GD25	FN65	NM94
1	8.75	26.25	70.00
2	5.70	17.00	35.00
3-10	4.15	12.50	25.00
11-16	4.00	11.00	22.00
I.W. Reprint #1,2,8,11,14: 8-r/Love and Marriage #3. 11-r/Love and Marriage #11.	1.00	2.80	7.00
Super Reprint #10('63),15,17('64):15-Love and Marriage #?	1.00	2.80	7.00

NOTE: *All issues have **Kamenish** art.*

LOVE AND ROCKETS
July, 1982 - No. 50, May, 1996 ($2.95/$2.50/$4.95, B&W, mature)
Fantagraphics Books

	GD25	FN65	NM94
1-B&W-c (6/82, $2.95; small size, publ. by Hernandez Bros.)(800 printed)	3.00	9.00	30.00
1 (Fall, '82; color-c)	2.50	7.50	20.00
1-2nd & 3rd printing		1.20	3.00
2	1.00	3.00	8.00
2-11, 29-31: 2nd printings ($2.50)		1.00	2.50
3-5		2.40	6.00
6-10		1.60	4.00
11-49: 30 ($2.95, 52 pgs.). 31-on: $2.50-c		1.20	3.00
50-($4.95)		1.60	4.00

LOVE AND ROMANCE
Sept, 1971 - No. 24, Sept, 1975
Charlton Comics

	GD25	FN65	NM94
1	1.85	5.50	15.00
2-10	1.00	3.00	8.00
11-24		2.00	5.00

LOVE AT FIRST SIGHT
Oct, 1949 - No. 43, Nov, 1956 (Photo-c: 21-42)
Ace Magazines (RAR Publ. Co./Periodical House)

	GD25	FN65	NM94
1-Painted-c	9.50	28.00	75.00
2-Painted-c	5.70	17.00	38.00
3-10: 4-Painted-c	4.15	12.50	25.00
11-20	4.00	11.00	22.00
21-33: 33-Last pre-code	3.20	8.00	16.00
34-43	1.50	4.50	12.00

LOVE BUG, THE (See Movie Comics)

LOVE CLASSICS
Nov, 1949 - No. 2, Feb, 1950 (Photo-c, 52 pgs.)
A Lover's Magazine/Marvel Comics

	GD25	FN65	NM94
1,2: 2-Virginia Mayo photo-c; 30 pg. story "I Was a Small Town Flirt"	10.00	30.00	75.00

LOVE CONFESSIONS
Oct, 1949 - No. 54, Dec, 1956 (Photo-c: 3,4,6,7,9,11-18,21)
Quality Comics Group

	GD25	FN65	NM94
1-Ward-c/a, 9 pgs; Gustavson-a	24.00	73.00	180.00
2-Gustavson-a; Ward-c	10.00	30.00	70.00
3	5.70	17.00	38.00
4-Crandall-a	6.85	21.00	48.00
5-Ward-a, 7 pgs.	10.00	30.00	60.00
6,7,9,11-13,15,16,18: 7-Van Johnson photo-c. 8-Robert Mitchum & Jane Russell photo-c	4.00	11.00	24.00
8,10-Ward-a(2 stories in #10)	10.00	30.00	65.00
14,17,19,22-Ward-a; 17-Faith Domerque photo-c	8.35	25.00	55.00
20-Ward-a(2)	10.00	30.00	65.00
21,23-28,30-38,40-42: Last precode, 4/55	3.20	8.00	16.00
29-Ward-a	8.00	24.00	50.00
39-Matt Baker-a	5.00	15.00	30.00
43,44,46-48,50-54: 47-Ward-c?	1.75	5.25	14.00
45-Ward-a	4.25	13.00	26.00
49-Baker-c/a	5.70	17.00	35.00

LOVE DIARY
July, 1949 - No. 48, Oct, 1955 (Photo-c: 1-24,27-29) (52 pgs. #1-11?)
Our Publishing Co./Toytown/Patches

	GD25	FN65	NM94
1-Krigstein-a	13.00	39.00	95.00
2,3-Krigstein & Mort Leav-a in each	10.00	30.00	65.00
4-8	4.00	13.00	26.00
9,10-Everett-a	5.35	16.00	32.00
11-20: 16- Mort Leav-a, 3 pg. Baker-sty. Leav-a	4.00	11.00	22.00
21-30,32-48: 45-Leav-a. 47-Last precode(12/54)	3.60	9.00	18.00
31-John Buscema headlights-c	4.00	12.00	24.00

LOVE DIARY (Diary Loves #2 on; title changed due to previously published title above?)
Sept, 1949
Quality Comics Group

	GD25	FN65	NM94
1-Ward-c/a, 9 pgs.	24.00	73.00	175.00

LOVE DIARY
July, 1958 - No. 102, Dec, 1976
Charlton Comics

	GD25	FN65	NM94
1	6.50	19.50	45.00
2	5.00	15.00	30.00
3-5,7-10: 10-Photo-c	4.00	10.00	20.00
6-Torres-a	5.00	15.00	30.00
11-20: 20-Photo-c	1.85	5.50	15.00
21-40	1.50	4.50	12.00
41-60	1.00	3.00	8.00
61-102		2.00	5.00

LOVE DOCTOR (See Dr. Anthony King...)

LOVE DRAMAS (True Secrets No. 3 on?)
Oct, 1949 - No. 2, Jan, 1950
Marvel Comics (IPS)

	GD25	FN65	NM94
1-Jack Kamen-a; photo-c	13.00	39.00	95.00
2	10.00	30.00	70.00

LOVE EXPERIENCES (Challenge of the Unknown No. 6)
Oct, 1949 - No. 5, June, 1950; No. 6, Apr, 1951 - No. 38, June, 1956
Ace Periodicals (A.A. Wyn/Periodical House)

	GD25	FN65	NM94
1-Painted-c	8.75	26.25	65.00
2	4.25	13.00	28.00
3-5: 5-Painted-c	2.50	7.50	20.00
6-10	3.20	8.00	16.00
11-30: 30-Last pre-code (2/55)	2.40	6.00	12.00
31-38: 38-Indicia date-6/56; c-date-8/56	2.00	5.00	10.00

NOTE: ***Anne Brewster** a-15. Photo c-4, 15-35, 38.*

LOVE JOURNAL
No. 10, Oct, 1951 - No. 25, July, 1954
Our Publishing Co.

	GD25	FN65	NM94
10	8.35	25.00	55.00
11-25: 19-Mort Leav-a	4.25	13.00	28.00

LOVELAND
Nov, 1949 - No. 2, Feb, 1950 (52 pgs.)
Mutual Mag./Eye Publ. (Marvel)

	GD25	FN65	NM94
1,2-Photo-c	8.00	24.00	50.00

LOVE LESSONS

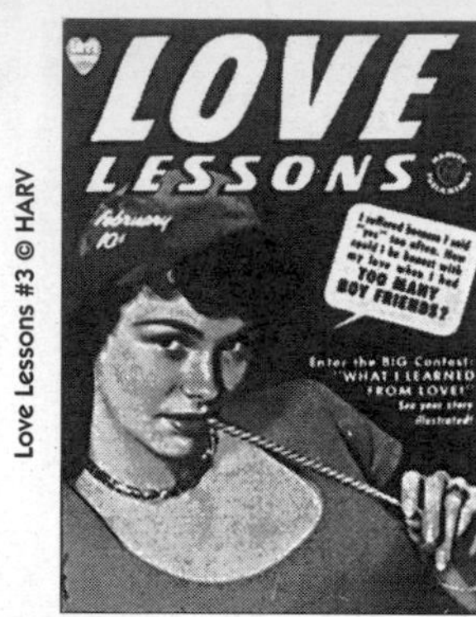

Love Lessons #3 © HARV

Lovers #52 © MEG

Lovers Lane #37 © LEV

Oct, 1949 - No. 5, June, 1950
Harvey Comics/Key Publ. No. 5

	GD25	FN65	NM94
1-Metallic silver-c printed over the cancelled covers of Love Letters #1; indicia title is "Love Letters"	10.00	30.00	70.00
2-Powell-a; photo-c	5.00	15.00	30.00
3-5: 3-Photo-c	4.15	12.50	25.00

LOVE LETTERS (10/49, Harvey; advertised but never published; covers were printed before cancellation and were used as the cover to Love Lessons #1)

LOVE LETTERS (Love Secrets No. 32 on)
11/49 - #6, 9/50; #7, 3/51 - #31, 6/53; #32, 2/54 - #51, 12/56
Quality Comics Group

	GD25	FN65	NM94
1-Ward-c, Gustavson-a	19.00	58.00	140.00
2-Ward-c, Gustavson-a	15.00	45.00	110.00
3-Gustavson-a	10.00	30.00	70.00
4-Ward-a, 9 pgs.	13.50	41.00	100.00
5-8,10	4.25	13.00	26.00
9-One pg. Ward "Be Popular with the Opposite Sex"; Robert Mitchum photo-c	5.70	17.00	38.00
11-Ward-r/Broadway Romances #2 & retitled	6.35	19.00	40.00
12-15,18-20	4.00	11.00	22.00
16,17-Ward-a; 16-Anthony Quinn photo-c. 17-Jane Russell photo-c	9.00	29.00	60.00
21-29	4.00	10.00	20.00
30,31(6/53)-Ward-a	5.70	17.00	35.00
32(2/54)-39: 38-Crandall-a. 39-Last precode (4/55)	3.00	7.50	15.00
40-48	2.40	6.00	12.00
49,50-Baker-a	5.70	17.00	35.00
51-Baker-c	4.25	13.00	28.00

NOTE: *Photo-c on most 3-28.*

LOVE LIFE
Nov, 1951
P. L. Publishing Co.

	GD25	FN65	NM94
1	6.70	20.00	45.00

LOVELORN (Confessions of the Lovelorn #52 on)
Aug-Sept, 1949 - No. 51, July, 1954 (No. 1-26: 52 pgs.)
American Comics Group (Michel Publ./Regis Publ.)

	GD25	FN65	NM94
1	11.00	33.00	75.00
2	6.35	19.00	38.00
3-10	4.25	13.00	28.00
11-20,22-48: 18-Drucker-a(2 pgs.). 46-Lazarus-a	4.00	11.00	22.00
21-Prostitution story	5.35	16.00	32.00
49-51-Has 3-D effect-c/stories	13.00	39.00	90.00

LOVE MEMORIES
1949 (no month) - No. 4, July, 1950 (All photo-c)
Fawcett Publications

	GD25	FN65	NM94
1	10.00	30.00	65.00
2-4: 2-(Win/49-50)	5.70	17.00	38.00

LOVE MYSTERY
June, 1950 - No. 3, Oct, 1950 (All photo-c)
Fawcett Publications

	GD25	FN65	NM94
1-George Evans-a	17.00	51.00	130.00
2,3-Evans-a. 3-Powell-a	13.50	41.00	100.00

LOVE PROBLEMS (See Fox Giants)

LOVE PROBLEMS AND ADVICE ILLUSTRATED (see True Love...)

LOVE ROMANCES (Formerly Ideal #5)
No. 6, May, 1949 - No. 106, July, 1963
Timely/Marvel/Atlas(TCI No. 7-71/Male No. 72-106)

	GD25	FN65	NM94
6-Photo-c	10.00	30.00	70.00
7-Photo-c; Kamen-a	6.50	19.50	45.00
8-Kubert-a; photo-c	6.85	21.00	48.00
9-20: 9-12-Photo-c	5.00	15.00	30.00
21,24-Krigstein-a	6.50	19.50	45.00
22,23,25-35,37,39,40	4.25	13.00	26.00
36,38-Krigstein-a	5.70	17.00	40.00
41-44,46,47: Last precode (2/55)	4.25	13.00	26.00
45,57-Matt Baker-a	5.70	17.00	35.00
48,50-52,54-56,58-74	2.50	7.50	20.00
49,53-Toth-a, 6 & ? pgs.	4.00	12.00	40.00
75,77,82-Matt Baker-a	3.20	9.60	32.00
76,78-81,84,86-95: Last 10¢ issue? 80-Heath-c	2.50	7.50	20.00
83-Kirby-c, Severin-a	3.50	10.50	35.00
85,96-Kirby-c/a	4.00	12.00	40.00
97,100-104	2.25	6.75	18.00
98-Kirby-a(4)	5.50	16.50	55.00
99,105,106-Kirby-a	3.50	10.50	35.00

NOTE: ***Anne Brewster** a-67, 72. **Colletta** a-37, 40, 42, 44, 67(2); c-42, 44, 49, 54, 80. **Everett** c-70. **Heath** a-87. **Kirby** c-80, 85, 88. **Robinson** a-29.*

LOVERS (Formerly Blonde Phantom)
No. 23, May, 1949 - No. 86, Aug?, 1957
Marvel Comics No. 23,24/Atlas No. 25 on (ANC)

	GD25	FN65	NM94
23-Photo-c begin, end #28	10.00	30.00	70.00
24-Tothish plus Robinson-a	5.70	17.00	35.00
25,30-Kubert-a; 7, 10 pgs.	5.70	17.00	40.00
26-29,31-36,39,40	4.25	13.00	26.00
37,38-Krigstein-a	7.00	21.00	45.00
41-Everett-a(2)	5.70	17.00	35.00
42,44-65: 65-Last pre-code (1/55)	4.00	12.00	24.00
43-Frazetta 1 pg. ad	4.00	12.00	24.00
66,68-86	4.00	10.00	20.00
67-Toth-a	5.00	15.00	30.00

NOTE: ***Anne Brewster** a-86. **Colletta** a-54, 59, 62, 64, 65, 69, 85; c-61, 64, 65, 75. **Heath** a-61. **Maneely** a-57. **Powell** a-27, 30. **Robinson** a-54, 56.*

LOVERS' LANE
Oct, 1949 - No. 41, June, 1954 (No. 1-18: 52 pgs.)
Lev Gleason Publications

	GD25	FN65	NM94
1-Biro-c	7.85	23.50	55.00
2-Biro-c	4.25	13.00	28.00
3-20: 3,4-Painted-c. 20-Frazetta 1 pg. ad	4.00	10.00	20.00
21-38,40,41	2.80	7.00	14.00
39-Story narrated by Frank Sinatra	4.25	13.00	26.00

NOTE: ***Briefer** a-6, 21. **Fuje** a-4, 16; c-many. **Guardineer** a-1. **Kinstler** c-41. **Tuska** a-6. Painted c-3-18. Photo c-19-22, 26-28.*

LOVE SCANDALS
Feb, 1950 - No. 5, Oct, 1950 (Photo-c #2-5) (All 52 pgs.)
Quality Comics Group

	GD25	FN65	NM94
1-Ward-c/a, 9 pgs.	21.00	64.00	160.00
2,3: 2-Gustavson-a	8.00	24.00	50.00
4-Ward-a, 18 pgs; Gil Fox-a	17.00	49.00	120.00
5-C. Cuidera-a; tomboy story "I Hated Being a Woman"	8.00	24.00	50.00

LOVE SECRETS
Oct, 1949 - No. 2, Jan, 1950 (52 pgs., photo-c)
Marvel Comics(IPC)

	GD25	FN65	NM94
1	10.00	30.00	70.00
2	7.00	21.00	45.00

LOVE SECRETS (Formerly Love Letters #31)
No. 32, Aug, 1953 - No. 56, Dec, 1956
Quality Comics Group

	GD25	FN65	NM94
32	7.00	21.00	45.00
33,35-39	4.00	12.00	24.00
34-Ward-a	8.00	24.00	50.00

Love Stories of Mary Worth #3 © HARV

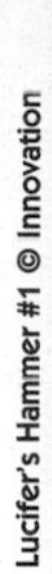
Lucifer's Hammer #1 © Innovation

INNOVATION 1
FROM THE BEST-SELLING NOVEL BY
LARRY NIVEN and JERRY POURNELLE

Luftwaffe: 1946 V2 #5 © Ted Nomura

	GD25	FN65	NM94
40-Matt Baker-c	5.35	16.00	32.00
41-43: 43-Last precode (3/55)	4.00	11.00	22.00
44,47-50,53,54	3.00	7.50	15.00
45,46-Ward-a. 46-Baker-a	5.70	17.00	38.00
51,52-Ward(r). 52-r/Love Confessions #17	4.25	13.00	26.00
55,56: 55-Baker-a. 56-Baker-c	4.25	13.00	28.00

LOVE STORIES (Formerly My Love Affair #5)
No. 6, 1950 - No. 12, 1951
Fox Feature Syndicate

	GD25	FN65	NM94
6,8-Wood-a	14.00	43.00	110.00
7,9-12	6.50	19.50	45.00

LOVE STORIES (Formerly Heart Throbs)
No. 147, Nov, 1972 - No. 152, Oct-Nov, 1973
National Periodical Publications

	GD25	FN65	NM94
147-152	1.10	3.30	9.00

LOVE STORIES OF MARY WORTH (See Harvey Comics Hits #55 & Mary Worth)
Sept, 1949 - No. 5, May, 1950
Harvey Publications

	GD25	FN65	NM94
1-1940's newspaper reprints-#1-4	5.70	17.00	35.00
2	4.25	13.00	28.00
3-5: 3-Kamen/Baker-a?	4.25	13.00	26.00

LOVE TALES (Formerly The Human Torch #35)
No. 36, 5/49 - No. 58, 8/52; No. 59, date? - No. 75, Sept, 1957
Marvel/Atlas Comics (ZPC No. 36-50/MMC No. 67-75)

	GD25	FN65	NM94
36-Photo-c	10.00	30.00	70.00
37	6.35	19.00	40.00
38-44,46-50: 39-41-Photo-c	4.25	13.00	28.00
45-Powell-a	5.00	15.00	30.00
51,69-Everett-a	5.35	16.00	32.00
52-Krigstein-a	5.35	16.00	32.00
53-60: 60-Last pre-code (2/55)	4.00	11.00	22.00
61-68,70-75: 75-Brewster, Cameron, Colletta-a	2.80	7.00	14.00

LOVE THRILLS (See Fox Giants)

LOVE TRAILS (Western romance)
Dec, 1949 - No. 2, Mar, 1950 (52 pgs.)
A Lover's Magazine (CDS)(Marvel)

	GD25	FN65	NM94
1,2: 1-Photo-c	10.00	30.00	65.00

LOWELL THOMAS' HIGH ADVENTURE (See High Adventure)

LT. (See Lieutenant)

LUCIFER'S HAMMER (Larry Niven & Jerry Pournelle's...)
Nov, 1993 - No. 6, 1994 ($2.50, painted, limited series)
Innovation Publishing

	GD25	FN65	NM94
1-6: Adaptatin of novel, painted-c & art		1.00	2.50

LUCKY COMICS
Jan, 1944; No. 2, Summer, 1945 - No. 5, Summer, 1946
Consolidated Magazines

	GD25	FN65	NM94
1-Lucky Starr & Bobbie begin	15.00	45.00	120.00
2-5: 5-Devil-c by Walter Johnson	8.75	26.25	65.00

LUCKY DUCK
No. 5, Jan, 1953 - No. 8, Sept, 1953
Standard Comics (Literary Ent.)

	GD25	FN65	NM94
5-Funny animal; Irving Spector-a	8.75	26.25	70.00
6-8-Irving Spector-a	7.85	23.50	55.00

NOTE: Harvey Kurtzman tried to hire Spector for Mad #1.

LUCKY FIGHTS IT THROUGH (Also see The K. O. Punch)
1949 (Giveaway, 16 pgs. in color, paper-c)
Educational Comics

	GD25	FN65	NM94
nn-(Very Rare)-1st Kurtzman work for E. C.; V.D. prevention	111.00	333.00	1000.00
nn-Reprint in color (1977)		.80	2.00

NOTE: *Subtitled "The Story of That Ignorant, Ignorant Cowboy". Prepared for Communications Materials Center, Columbia University.*

LUCKY "7" COMICS
1944 (No date listed)
Howard Publishers Ltd.

	GD25	FN65	NM94
1-Pioneer, Sir Gallagher, Dick Royce, Congo Raider, Punch Powers; bondage-c	26.00	80.00	210.00

LUCKY STAR (Western)
1950 - No. 7, 1951; No. 8, 1953 - No. 14, 1955 (5x7-1/4"; full color, 5¢)
Nation Wide Publ. Co.

	GD25	FN65	NM94
nn (#1)-(5¢, 52 pgs.)-Davis-a	8.50	26.00	60.00
2,3-(5¢, 52 pgs.)-Davis-a	5.70	17.00	40.00
4-7-(5¢, 52 pgs.)-Davis-a	5.70	17.00	35.00
8-14-(36 pgs.)	4.15	12.50	25.00
Given away with Lucky Star Western Wear by the Juvenile Mfg. Co.	4.00	10.00	20.00

LUCY SHOW, THE (TV) (Also see I Love Lucy)
June, 1963 - No. 5, June, 1964 (Photo-c: 1,2)
Gold Key

	GD25	FN65	NM94
1	11.00	34.00	125.00
2	6.00	18.00	65.00
3-5: Photo back c-1,2,4,5	5.00	15.00	55.00

LUCY, THE REAL GONE GAL (Meet Miss Pepper #5 on)
June, 1953 - No. 4, Dec, 1953
St. John Publishing Co.

	GD25	FN65	NM94
1-Negligee panels	8.75	26.25	65.00
2	5.70	17.00	35.00
3,4: 3-Drucker-a	4.25	13.00	28.00

LUDWIG BEMELMAN'S MADELEINE & GENEVIEVE
No. 796, May, 1957
Dell Publishing Co.

	GD25	FN65	NM94
Four Color 796	2.75	8.00	30.00

LUDWIG VON DRAKE (TV)(Disney)(See Walt Disney's C&S #256)
Nov-Dec, 1961 - No. 4, June-Aug, 1962
Dell Publishing Co.

	GD25	FN65	NM94
1	5.50	16.50	60.00
2-4	3.60	11.00	40.00
...Fish Stampede (1962, Fritos giveaway)-16 pgs., 3-1/4x7", soft-c; also see Donald Duck & Mickey Mouse	3.00	9.00	32.00

LUFTWAFFE: 1946 (Volume 1)
July, 1996 - No.4, Jan, 1997 ($2.95, B&W, limited series)
Antarctic Press

	GD25	FN65	NM94
1-4-Ben Dunn & Ted Nomura-s/a		1.20	3.00
...Special		1.20	3.00

LUFTWAFFE: 1946 (Volume 2)
Mar, 1997 - No.4, Sept, 1997 ($2.95, B&W, limited series)
Antarctic Press

	GD25	FN65	NM94
1-6		1.20	3.00

LUGER
Oct, 1986 - No. 3, Feb, 1987 ($1.75, mini-series, Baxter paper)
Eclipse Comics

	GD25	FN65	NM94
1-3: Bruce Jones scripts; Yeates-c/a		.70	1.80

LUKE CAGE (See Cage & Hero for Hire)

LUKE SHORT'S WESTERN STORIES
No. 580, Aug, 1954 - No. 927, Aug, 1958

Lynch #1 © Aegis Entertainment

Lynch Mob #2 © Chaos!

Mad #7 © WMG

Dell Publishing Co.

	GD25	FN65	NM94
Four Color 580(8/54), 651(9/55)-Kinstler-a	2.75	8.00	30.00
Four Color 739,771,807,875,927	2.75	8.00	30.00
Four Color 848	3.60	11.00	40.00

LUNATIC FRINGE, THE
July, 1989 - No. 2, 1989 ($1.75, deluxe format)
Innovation Publishing

	GD25	FN65	NM94
1,2			1.80

LUNATICKLE (Magazine) (Satire)
Feb, 1956 - No. 2, Apr, 1956
Whitstone Publ.

	GD25	FN65	NM94
1,2-Kubert-a	1.85	5.50	15.00

LUNATIK
Dec, 1995 - No. 3, Feb, 1996 ($1.95, limited series)
Marvel Comics

	GD25	FN65	NM94
1-3		.80	2.00

LUST FOR LIFE
Feb, 1997 - Present ($2.95, B&W)
Slave Labor Graphics

	GD25	FN65	NM94
1-3: 1-Jeff Levin-s/a		1.20	3.00

LYCANTHROPE LEO
1994 - No. 7($2.95, B&W, limited series, 44 pgs.)
Viz Communications

	GD25	FN65	NM94
1-7		1.20	3.00

LYNCH (See Gen 13)
May, 1997 ($2.50, one-shot)
Image Comics (Wildstorm Productions)

	GD25	FN65	NM94
1-Helmut-c/app.		1.00	2.50

LYNCH MOB
June, 1994 - No. 4, Sept, 1994 ($2.50, limited series)
Chaos! Comics

	GD25	FN65	NM94
1-4		1.00	2.50
1-Special edition full foil-c		2.00	5.00

LYNDON B. JOHNSON
Mar, 1965
Dell Publishing Co.

	GD25	FN65	NM94
12-445-503-Photo-c	1.60	4.80	16.00

M
1990 - No. 4, 1991 ($4.95, painted, 52 pgs.)
Eclipse Books

	GD25	FN65	NM94
1-Adapts movie; contains flexi-disc ($5.95)		2.40	6.00
2-4		2.00	5.00

MACHINE, THE
Nov, 1994 - Feb, 1995 ($2.50, color)
Dark Horse Comics

	GD25	FN65	NM94
1-4		1.00	2.50

MACHINE MAN (Also see 2001, A Space Odyssey)
Apr, 1978 - No. 9, Dec, 1978; No. 10, Aug, 1979 - No. 19, Feb, 1981
Marvel Comics Group

	GD25	FN65	NM94
1-Jack Kirby-c/a/scripts begin; end #9		1.60	4.00
2-17: 10-Marv Wolfman scripts & Ditko-a begins		.80	2.00
18-Wendigo, Alpha Flight-ties into X-Men #140			1.25
19-Intro/1st app. Jack O'Lantern (Macendale), later becomes 2nd Hobgoblin	1.10	3.30	9.00

NOTE: ***Austin** c-7i, 19i. **Buckler** c-17p, 18p. **Byrne** c-14p. **Ditko** a-10-19; c-10-13, 14i, 15, 16. **Kirby** a-1-9p; c-1-5, 7-9p. **Layton** c-7i. **Miller** c-19p. **Simonson** c-6.*

MACHINE MAN
Oct, 1984 - No. 4, Jan, 1985 (Limited-series)
Marvel Comics Group

	GD25	FN65	NM94
1-Barry Smith-c/a(i) & colors in all			1.50
2-4			1.25

MACHINE MAN 2020
Aug, 1994 - Nov, 1994 ($2.00, 52 pgs., limited series)
Marvel Comics

	GD25	FN65	NM94
1-4: Reprints Machine Man limited series; Barry Windsor-Smith-c/i(r)		.80	2.00

MACK BOLAN: THE EXECUTIONER (Don Pendleton's...)
July, 1993 ($2.50)
Innovation Publishing

	GD25	FN65	NM94
1-($3.95)-Indestructible Cover Edition		1.60	4.00
1-($2.95)-Collector's Gold Edition; foil stamped		1.20	3.00
1-($3.50)-Double Cover Edition; red foil outer-c		1.40	3.50

MACKENZIE'S RAIDERS (Movie, TV)
No. 1093, Apr-June, 1960
Dell Publishing Co.

	GD25	FN65	NM94
Four Color 1093-Richard Carlson photo-c from TV show	5.50	16.50	60.00

MACO TOYS COMIC
1959 (Giveaway, 36 pgs.)
Maco Toys/Charlton Comics

	GD25	FN65	NM94
1-All military stories featuring Maco Toys		2.40	6.00

MACROSS (Becomes Robotech: The Macross Saga #2 on)
Dec, 1984 ($1.50)
Comico

	GD25	FN65	NM94
1	2.50	7.50	20.00

MACROSS II
1992 - No. 10, 1993 ($2.75, B&W, limited series)
Viz Select Comics

	GD25	FN65	NM94
1-10: Based on video series		1.10	2.75

MAD (Tales Calculated to Drive You...)
Oct-Nov, 1952 - Present (No. 24 on are magazine format)
(Kurtzman editor No. 1-28, Feldstein No. 29 - No. ?)
E. C. Comics (Educational Comics)

	GD25	FN65	NM94
1-Wood, Davis, Elder start as regulars	500.00	1500.00	5000.00
2-Dick Tracy cameo	125.00	375.00	1050.00
3,4: 3-Stan Lee mentioned. 4-Reefer mention story "Flob Was a Slob" by Davis; Superman parody	78.00	234.00	650.00
5-Low distr.; W.M. Gaines biog.	128.00	384.00	1050.00
6-11: 6-Popeye cameo. 7,8- "Hey Look" reprints by Kurtzman. 11-Wolverton-a; Davis story was-r/Crime Suspenstories #12 w/new Kurtzman dialogue	59.00	178.00	490.00
12-15: 15,18-Pot Shot Pete-r by Kurtzman	47.00	141.00	390.00
16-23(5/55): 18-Alice in Wonderland by Jack Davis. 21-1st app. Alfred E. Neuman on-c in fake ad. 22-All by Elder plus photo-montages by Kurtzman. 23-Special cancel announcement	40.00	120.00	300.00
24(7/55)-1st magazine issue (25¢); Kurtzman logo & border on-c; 1st "What? Me Worry?" on-c; 2nd printing exists	92.00	276.00	750.00
25-Jaffee starts as regular writer	40.00	120.00	320.00
26,27: 27-Jaffee starts as story artist; new logo	36.00	107.00	260.00
28-Last issue edited by Kurtzman; (three cover variations exist with different wording on contents banner on lower right of cover; value of each the same)	33.00	99.00	240.00
29-Kamen-a; Don Martin starts as regular; Feldstein editing begins	33.00	99.00	240.00
30-1st A. E. Neuman cover by Mingo; last Elder-a; Bob Clarke starts as regular; Disneyland & Elvis Presley spoof	45.00	135.00	375.00

Mad #41 © WMG

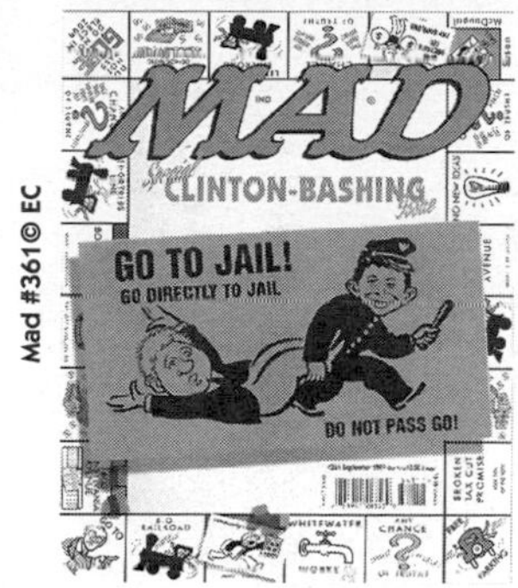

Mad #361© EC

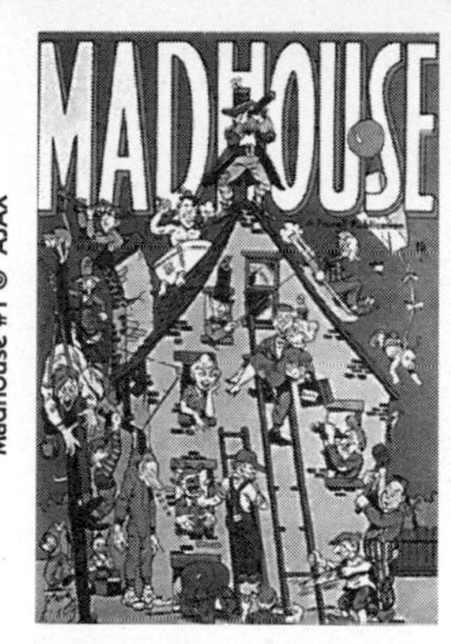

Madhouse #1 © AJAX

	GD25	FN65	NM94
31-Freas starts as regular; last Davis-a until #99	26.00	79.00	190.00
32,33: 32-Orlando, Drucker, Woodbridge start as regulars; Wood back-c. 33-Orlando back-c	24.00	71.00	170.00
34-Berg starts as regular	19.00	56.00	140.00
35-Mingo wraparound-c; Crandall-a	19.00	56.00	140.00
36-40	12.00	36.00	90.00
41-50	10.00	30.00	75.00
51-60: 60-Two Clarke-c; Prohias starts as regular	8.00	24.00	65.00
61-70: 64-Rickard starts as regular. 68-Martin-c	6.00	18.00	50.00
71-80: 76-Aragones starts as regular	4.00	12.00	40.00
81-90: 86-1st Fold-in. 89-One strip by Walt Kelly. 90-Frazetta back-c; Beatles app.	3.50	10.50	35.00
91-100: 91-Jaffee starts as story artist. 99-Davis-a resumes	3.00	9.00	30.00
101-104,106-120: 101-Infinity-c. 106-Frazetta back-c	2.50	7.50	25.00
105-Batman TV show take-off	3.20	9.60	32.00
121-140: 121-Beatles app. 122-Ronald Reagan photo inside; Drucker & Mingo-c. 128-Last Orlando. 130-Torres begins as reg. 131-Reagan photo back-c. 135,139-Davis-c	2.00	6.00	16.00
141-170: 165-Martin-c. 169-Drucker-c	1.75	5.25	14.00
171-200: 182-Bob Jones starts as regular. 186-Star Trek take-off. 187-Harry North starts as regular. 196-Star Wars take-off	1.40	4.15	11.00
201-250: 203-Star Wars take-off. 204-Hulk TV show take-off. 208-Superman movie take-off. 245- Last Rikard-a.		2.40	6.00
251-300: 256-Last issue edited by Feldstein. 274-Last Martin-a. 284-Roger Rabbit-c/story. 289-Batman movie parody. 291-TMNT-c only. 299-Simpson's-c/story		1.60	4.00
301-370: 306-TMNT III movie parody. 308-Terminator parody. 311-Addams Family-c/story. 314-Batman Returns-c/story. 315-Tribute to William Gaines. 316-Photo-c. 322-Batman animated series parody. 347-Broken Arrow & Mission Impossible parody. 350-Polybagged w/CD Rom disc. 358-X-Files.		1.00	2.50
300-303 (1/91-6/91)-Special Hussein Asylum Editions; only distributed to the troops in the Middle East (see Mad Super Spec.)		2.00	5.00

NOTE: ***Aragones*** *c-210, 293.* ***Davis*** *c-2, 27, 135, 139, 173, 178, 212, 213, 219, 246, 260, 296, 308.* ***Drucker*** *c-122, 169, 176, 225, 234, 264, 266, 274, 280, 285, 297, 299, 303, 314, 315, 321.* ***Elder*** *c-5, 259, 261, 268.* ***Elder/Kurtzman*** *a-258-274.* ***Jules Feiffer*** *a(r)-42.* ***Freas*** *c-30-50, 62-67, 69-70, 72, 74.* ***Heath*** *a-14, 27.* ***Jaffee*** *c-199, 217, 224, 258.* ***Kamen*** *a-29.* ***Krigstein*** *a-12, 17, 24, 26.* ***Kurtzman*** *c-1, 3, 4, 6-10, 13, 16, 18.* ***Martin*** *c-68, 165, 229.* ***Mingo*** *c-30-37, 61, 71, 75-80, 82-114, 117-124, 126, 129, 131, 133, 134, 136, 140, 143-148, 150-162, 164, 166-168, 171, 172, 174, 175, 177, 179, 181, 183, 185, 198, 206, 209, 211, 214, 218, 221, 222, 300.* ***John Severin*** *a-1-6, 9, 10.* ***Wolverton*** *c-11; a-11, 17, 29, 31, 36, 40, 82, 137.* ***Wood*** *a-24-45, 59; c-26, 28, 29.* ***Woodbridge*** *a-43. Issues 1-23 are 36 pgs.; 24-28 are 58 pgs.; 29 on are 52 pgs.*

MAD (See Mad Follies, ...Special, More Trash from..., and The Worst from...)

MAD ABOUT MILLIE (Also see Millie the Model)
April, 1969 - No. 17, Dec, 1970
Marvel Comics Group

1-Giant issue	4.00	12.00	40.00
2-17: 16,17-r	2.25	6.75	18.00
Annual 1(11/71)	1.75	5.25	14.00

MADAME XANADU
July, 1981 ($1.00, no ads, 36 pgs.)
DC Comics

1-Marshall Rogers-a(25 pgs.); Kaluta-c/a(2pgs.); pin-up of Madame Xanadu		1.20	3.00

MADBALLS
Sept, 1986 - No. 3, Nov, 1986; No. 4, June, 1987 - No. 10, June, 1988
Star Comics/Marvel Comics #9 on

1-10: Based on toys. 9-Post-a		1.20	3.00

MAD DISCO
1980 (one-shot, 36 pgs.)
E.C. Comics

	GD25	FN65	NM94
1-Includes 30 minute flexi-disc of Mad disco music	1.50	4.50	12.00

MAD DOGS
Feb, 1992 - No. 3, July, 1992 ($2.50, B&W, limited series)
Eclipse Comics

1-3		1.00	2.50

MAD 84 (Mad Extra)
1984 (84 pgs.)
E.C. Comics

1		.80	2.00

MAD FOLLIES (Special)
1963 - No. 7, 1969
E. C. Comics

nn(1963)-Paperback book covers	24.00	72.00	240.00
2(1964)-Calendar	18.00	54.00	180.00
3(1965)-Mischief Stickers	12.00	36.00	120.00
4(1966)-Mobile; Frazetta-r/back-c Mad #90	10.50	32.00	105.00
5(1967)-Stencils	7.00	21.00	70.00
6(1968)-Mischief Stickers	5.50	16.50	55.00
7(1969)-Nasty Cards	5.50	16.50	55.00

NOTE: ***Clarke*** *c-4.* ***Frazetta*** *r-4, 6 (1 pg. ea.).* ***Mingo*** *c-1-3.* ***Orlando*** *a-5.*

MAD HATTER, THE (Costumed Hero)
Jan-Feb, 1946; No. 2, Sept-Oct, 1946
O. W. Comics Corp.

1-Freddy the Firefly begins; Glunta-c/a	64.00	192.00	575.00
2-Has ad for E.C.'s Animal Fables #1	34.00	101.00	270.00

MADHOUSE
3-4/54 - No. 4, 9-10/54; 6/57 - No. 4, Dec?, 1957
Ajax/Farrell Publ. (Excellent Publ./4-Star)

1(1954)	24.00	71.00	170.00
2,3	13.00	39.00	95.00
4-Surrealistic-c	21.00	64.00	155.00
1(1957, 2nd series)	10.00	30.00	70.00
2-4	7.50	22.50	48.00

MAD HOUSE (Formerly Madhouse Glads; ...Comics #104? on)
No. 95, 9/74 - No. 97, 1/75; No. 98, 8/75 - No. 130, 10/82
Red Circle Productions/Archie Publications

95,96-Horror stories through #97	1.00	3.00	8.00
97-Intro. Henry Hobson; Morrow, Thorne-a		1.60	4.00
98-130-Satire/humor stories		1.60	4.00
Annual 8(1970-71)- 12(1974-75)-Formerly Madhouse Ma-ad Annual. 11-Wood-a(r)	1.25	3.75	10.00
...Comics Digest 1('75-76)	1.50	4.50	12.00
2- 8(8/82)(...Mag. #5 on)	1.00	3.00	8.00

NOTE: ***B. Jones*** *a-96.* ***McWilliams*** *a-97.* ***Morrow*** *a-96, 97; c-95-97.* ***Wildey*** *a-95, 96. See Archie Comics Digest #1, 13.*

MADHOUSE GLADS (Formerly ...Ma-ad; Madhouse #95 on)
No. 73, May, 1970 - No. 94, Aug, 1974 (No. 78-92: 52 pgs.)
Archie Publications

73-94	1.00	3.00	8.00

MADHOUSE MA-AD (...Jokes #67-70; ...Freak-Out #71-74)
(Formerly Archie's Madhouse) (Becomes Madhouse Glads #75 on)
No. 67, April, 1969 - No. 72, Jan, 1970
Archie Publications

67-72	1.25	3.75	10.00
...Annual 7(1969-70)-Formerly Archie's Madhouse Annual; becomes Madhouse Annual	1.75	5.25	14.00

MADMAN (See Creatures of the Id #1)
Mar, 1992 - No. 3, 1992 ($3.95, duotone, high quality, limited series, 52 pgs.)

Madman Comics #6 © Mike Allred

Mage #15 © Matt Wagner

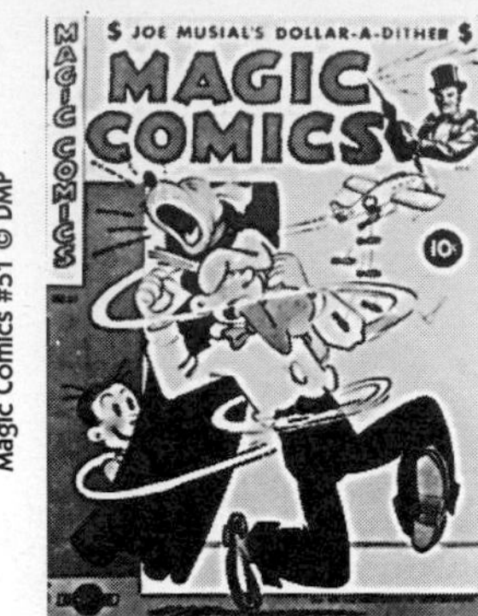

Magic Comics #51 © DMP

GD25 FN65 NM94

Tundra Publishing

1-Mike Allred-c/a in all 1.75 5.25 14.00
1-2nd printing 2.00 5.00
2,3 1.25 4.50 10.00

MADMAN ADVENTURES
1992 - No. 3, 1993 ($2.95, limited series)
Tundra Publishing

1-Mike Allred-c/a in all 1.25 3.75 10.00
2,3 1.00 2.80 7.00

MADMAN COMICS
Apr, 1994 - Present ($2.95, bi-monthly)
Dark Horse Comics (Legend No. 2 on)

1-Allred-c/a; F. Miller back-c. 2.40 6.00
2-3: 3-Alex Toth back-c. 1.60 4.00
4-12: 4-Dave Stevens back-c. 6,7-Miller/Darrow's Big Guy app. 6-Bruce Timm back-c. 7-Darrow back-c. 8-Origin?; Bagge back-c. 10-Allred/Ross-c; Ross back-c. 11-Frazetta back-c 1.40 3.50
Ltd. Ed. Slipcover (1997, $99.95, signed and numbered) w/Vol.1 & Vol. 2. Vol.1- reprints #1-5; Vol. 2- reprints #6-10 100.00
Yearbook '95 (1996, $17.95, TPB)-r/#1-5, intro by Teller 18.00

MAD MONSTER PARTY (See Movie Classics)

MADNESS IN MURDERWORLD
1989 (Came with computer game from Paragon Software)
Marvel Comics

V1#1-Starring The X-Men 1.00

MADRAVEN HALLOWEEN SPECIAL
Oct, 1995 ($2.95, one-shot)
Hamilton Comics

nn-Morrow-a 1.20 3.00

MAD SPECIAL (...Super Special)
Fall, 1970 - Present (84 - 116 pgs.)
E. C. Publications, Inc.

Fall 1970(#1)-Bonus-Voodoo Doll; contains 17 pgs. new material 7.00 21.00 70.00
Spring 1971(#2)-Wall Nuts; 17 pgs. new material 4.00 12.00 40.00
3-Protest Stickers 4.00 12.00 40.00
4-8: 4-Mini Posters. 5-Mad Flag. 6-Mad Mischief Stickers. 7-Presidential candidate posters, Wild Shocking Message posters. 8-TV Guise 3.50 10.50 35.00
9(1972)-Contains Nostalgic Mad #1 (28 pgs.) 2.50 7.50 25.00
10,11,13: 10-Nonsense Stickers (Don Martin). 11-33-1/3 RPM record. 13-Sickie Stickers; 3 pgs. Wolverton-r/Mad #137 2.50 7.50 25.00
12-Contains Nostalgic Mad #2 (36 pgs.); Davis, Wolverton-a 2.50 7.50 25.00
14-Vital Message posters & Art Depreciation paintings 1.75 5.25 14.00
15-Contains Nostalgic Mad #3 (28 pgs.) 2.15 6.50 17.00
16,17,19,20: 16-Mad-hesive Stickers. 17-Don Martin posters. 20-Martin Stickers 1.75 5.25 14.00
18-Contains Nostalgic Mad #4 (36 pgs.) 1.75 5.25 14.00
21,24-Contains Nostalgic Mad #5 (28 pgs.) & #6 (28 pgs.) 1.75 5.25 14.00
22,23,25,27,29,30: 22-Diplomas. 23-Martin Stickers. 25-Martin Posters.27-Mad Shock-Sticks. 29-Mad Collectable-Correctables Posters. 30-The Movies 2.40 6.00
26-Has 33-1/3 RPM record 1.50 4.50 12.00
28-Contains Nostalgic Mad #7 (36 pgs.) 1.00 3.00 8.00
31,33-60: 36-Has 96 pgs. of comic book & comic strip spoofs: titles "The Comics" on-c 2.40 6.00
32-Contains Nostalgic Mad #8 1.00 3.00 8.00

GD25 FN65 NM94

61-88,90-100: 71-Batman parodies-r by Wood, Drucker. 72-Wolverton-c r-from 1st panel in Mad #11; Wolverton-s r/new dialogue. 83-All Star Trek spoof issue 1.40 3.50
76-(Fall, 1991)-Special Hussein Asylum Edition; distributed only to the troops in the Middle East (see Mad #300-303) 2.00 5.00
89-($3.95)-Polybaged w/1st of 3 Spy vs. Spy hologram trading cards (direct sale only issue)(other cards came w/card set) 1.60 4.00
100-126: 100?- ($3.99). 117-Sci-Fi parodies-r. 1.60 4.00
NOTE: *#28-30 have no number on cover.* ***Freas*** *c-76.* ***Mingo*** *c-9, 11, 15, 19, 23.*

MAGE (The Hero Discovered...; also see Grendel #16)
Feb, 1984 (no month) - No. 15, Dec, 1986 ($1.50, Mando paper)
Comico

1-Comico's 1st color comic 1.25 3.75 10.00
2 2.40 6.00
3-5: 3-Intro Edsel 1.60 4.00
6-Grendel begins (1st in color) 2.50 7.50 25.00
7-1st new Grendel story 1.50 4.50 12.00
8-14: 13-Grendel dies. 14-Grendel story ends 2.40 6.00
15-$2.95, Double size w/pullout poster 2.40 6.00

MAGE (The Hero Defined)
July, 1997 - Present ($2.50)
Image Comics

1-Matt Wagner-c/s/a in all 1.20 3.00
2-4 1.00 2.50

MAGGIE AND HOPEY COLOR SPECIAL (See Love and Rockets)
May, 1997 ($3.50, one-shot)
Fantagraphics Books

1 1.40 3.50

MAGGIE THE CAT (Also see Jon Sable, Freelance #11 & Shaman's Tears #12)
Jan, 1996 - No. 2, Feb, 1996 ($2.50, unfinished limited series)
Image Comics (Creative Fire Studio)

1,2: Mike Grell-c/a/scripts 1.00 2.50

MAGIC AGENT (See Forbidden Worlds & Unknown Worlds)
Jan-Feb, 1962 - No. 3, May-June, 1962
American Comics Group

1-Origin & 1st app. John Force 2.00 6.00 18.00
2,3 1.50 4.50 12.00

MAGIC COMICS
Aug, 1939 - No. 123, Nov-Dec, 1949
David McKay Publications

1-Mandrake the Magician, Henry, Popeye , Blondie, Barney Baxter, Secret Agent X-9 (not by Raymond), Bunky by Billy DeBeck & Thornton Burgess text stories illustrated by Harrison Cady begin; Henry covers begin 283.00 850.00 2000.00
2 100.00 300.00 650.00
3 77.00 232.00 500.00
4 66.00 200.00 440.00
5 50.00 150.00 330.00
6-10: 8-11,21-Mandrake/Henry-c 41.00 125.00 270.00
11-16,18,20: 12-Mandrake-c begin. 35.00 107.00 240.00
17-The Lone Ranger begins 38.00 114.00 250.00
19-Robot-c 41.00 125.00 275.00
21-30: 25-Only Blondie-c. 26-Dagwood-c begin 20.00 60.00 150.00
31-40: 36-Flag-c 14.00 41.00 110.00
41-50 10.50 32.00 85.00
51-60 9.50 28.00 75.00
61-70 7.15 21.50 50.00
71-99 5.70 17.00 40.00
100 7.15 21.50 50.00
101-106,109-123: 123-Last Dagwood-c 5.70 17.00 35.00
107,108-Flash Gordon app; not by Raymond 5.70 17.00 40.00

Magneto #4 © MEG

Magnus, Robot Fighter #23 © GK

Magnus Robot Fighter #10 © WEST

GD25 FN65 NM94

MAGICA DE SPELL (See Walt Disney Showcase #30)
MAGIC FLUTE, THE (See Night Music #9-11)
MAGIC MORRO (Also see Super Comics #21, The Owl, & The Hurricane Kids)
1941 (7-1/2x5-1/4, giveaway, soft-c)
K. K. Publications
nn-Ken Ernst-a. 10.00 30.00 80.00

MAGIC OF CHRISTMAS AT NEWBERRYS, THE
1967 (Giveaway) (B&W, slick-c, 20 pgs.)
E. S. London
nn 1.20 3.00

MAGIC SWORD, THE (See Movie Classics)
MAGIC THE GATHERING
Acclaim Comics (Armada)
...**ANTIQUITIES WAR**, Nov, 1995 - Feb, 1996 ($2.50, limited series)
1-4-Paul Smith-a(p). 1-Pratt-c. 1.00 2.50
...**ARABIAN NIGHTS**, Dec, 1995 - Jan, 1996 ($2.50, limited series)
1,2 1.00 2.50
...**COLLECTION** ,1995 ($4.95, limited series)
1,2-polybagged 2.00 5.00
...**CONVOCATIONS**, 1995 ($2.50, one shot)
1-nn-pin-ups 1.00 2.50
...**ELDER DRAGONS** ,1995 ($2.50, limited series)
1,2-Doug Wheatley-a 1.00 2.50
...**FALLEN ANGEL** ,1995 ($5.95, one shot)
nn 2.40 6.00
...**FALLEN EMPIRES** ,Sep, 1995 - Oct, 1995 ($2.75, limited series)
1,2 1.10 2.75
...Collection ($4.95)-polybagged 2.00 5.00
...**HOMELANDS** ,1995 ($5.95, one shot)
nn-polybagged w/card; Hildebrandts-c 2.40 6.00
... **ICE AGE** (On The World of...) ,July, 1995 - Nov, 1995 ($2.50, limited series)
1-4: 1,2-bound-in Magic Card. 3,4-bound-in insert 1.00 2.50
...**LEGEND OF JEDIT OJANEN**, 1996 ($2.50, limited series)
1,2 1.00 2.50
...**NIGHTMARE**, 1995 ($2.50, one shot)
1 1.00 2.50
...**THE SHADOW MAGE**, July, 1995 - Oct, 1995 ($2.50, limited series)
1-4--polybagged w/Magic The Gathering card 1.00 2.50
...Collection 1,2 (1995, $4.95)-Trade paperback; polybagged 2.00 5.00
...**SHANDALAR** ,1996 ($2.50, limited series)
1,2 1.00 2.50
...**WAYFARER** ,Nov, 1995 - Feb, 1996 ($2.50, limited series)
1-5 1.00 2.50

MAGIK (Illyana and Storm Limited Series)
Dec, 1983 - No. 4, Mar, 1984 (60¢, limited series)
Marvel Comics Group
1-4: 1-Characters from X-Men; Inferno begins; X-Men cameo (Buscema pencils in #1,2; c-1p. 2-4: 2-Nightcrawler app. & X-Men cameo
.80 2.00

MAGILLA GORILLA (TV) (See Kite Fun Book)
May, 1964 - No. 10, Dec, 1968 (Hanna-Barbera)
Gold Key
1 7.50 22.50 75.00
2-10: 3-Vs. Yogi Bear for President 4.50 13.50 45.00

MAGILLA GORILLA (TV)(See Spotlight #4)
Nov, 1970 - No. 5, July, 1971 (Hanna-Barbera)
Charlton Comics
1 3.20 9.60 32.00
2-5 2.50 7.50 20.00

MAGNETIC MEN FEATURING MAGNETO
June, 1997 ($1.95, one-shot)
Marvel Comics (Amalgam)
1-Tom Peyer-s/Barry Kitson & Dan Panosian-a .80 2.00

MAGNETO (See X-Men #1)
nd (Sept, 1993) (Giveaway) (one-shot)
Marvel Comics
0-Embossed foil-c by Sienkiewicz; r/Classic X-Men #19 & 12 by John Bolton
2.00 5.00

MAGNETO
Nov, 1996 - No. 4, Feb, 1997 ($1.95, limited series)
Marvel Comics
1-4: Peter Milligan scripts & Kelley Jones-a(p) .80 2.00

MAGNETO AND THE MAGNETIC MEN
Apr, 1996 ($1.95, one-shot)
Marvel Comics (Amalgam)
1-Jeff Matsuda-a(p) .80 2.00

MAGNUS, ROBOT FIGHTER (...4000 A.D.)(See Doctor Solar)
Feb, 1963 - No. 46, Jan, 1977 (All painted covers except #5)
Gold Key
1-Origin & 1st app. Magnus; Aliens (1st app.) series begins
18.00 55.00 200.00
2,3 8.00 25.00 90.00
4-10: 10-Simonson fan club illo (5/65, 1st-a?) 4.50 13.50 50.00
11-20 2.75 8.00 30.00
21,24-28: 28-Aliens ends 1.65 5.00 18.00
22,23-12¢ and 15¢ editions exist: 22-Origin-r/#1 1.80 5.50 20.00
29-46-Reprints 1.00 3.00 10.00
NOTE: ***Manning** a-1-22, 28-43(r). **Spiegle** a-23, 44r.*

MAGNUS ROBOT FIGHTER (Also see Vintage Magnus)
May, 1991 - No. 64, Feb, 1996 ($1.75/$1.95/$2.25/$2.50)
Valiant/Acclaim Comics
1-Nichols/Layton-c/a; 1-8 have trading cards 2.00 5.00
2-5: 4-Rai cameo. 5-Origin & 1st full app. Rai (10/91); 5-8 are in flip book format and back-c & half of book are Rai #1-4 mini-series
1.60 4.00
6-8: 6-1st Solar x-over. 7-Magnus vs. Rai-c/story; 1st X-O Armor. 8-Begin $1.95-c 1.00 2.50
0-Origin issue; Layton-a; ordered through mail w/coupons from 1st 8 issues plus 50¢; B. Smith trading card 1.00 3.00 8.00
0-Sold thru comic shops without trading card 1.20 3.00
9-11: 11-Last $1.95-c .80 2.00
12-(3.25, 44 pgs.)-Turok-c/story (1st app. in Valiant universe, 5/92); has 8 pg. Magnus story insert 1.00 2.80 7.00
13-20,22-24,26-48, 50-63: 14-1st app. Isak. 15,16-Unity x-overs. 15-Miller-c. 16-Birth of Magnus. 24-Story cont'd in Rai & the Future Force #9. 33-Timewalker app.36-Bound-in trading cards. 37-Rai & Starwatchers app. 44-Bound-in sneak peek card .90 2.25
21-New direction & new logo; Reese inks .90 2.25
21-Gold ink variant 1.60 4.00
25-($2.95)-Embossed silver foil-c; new costume 1.20 3.00
49, 64 ($2.50): 64-Magnus dies? 1.00 2.50
...Invasion (1994, $9.95)-r/Rai #1-4 & Magnus #5-8 1.25 3.75 10.00
Yearbook (1994, $3.95, 52 pgs.) 1.60 4.00
NOTE: ***Ditko/Reese** a-18. **Layton** a(i)-5; c-6-9i, 25; back(i)-5-8. **Reese** a(i)-22, 25, 28; c(i)-22, 24, 28. **Simonson** c-16. Prices for issues 1-8 are for trading cards and coupons intact.*

MAGNUS ROBOT FIGHTER

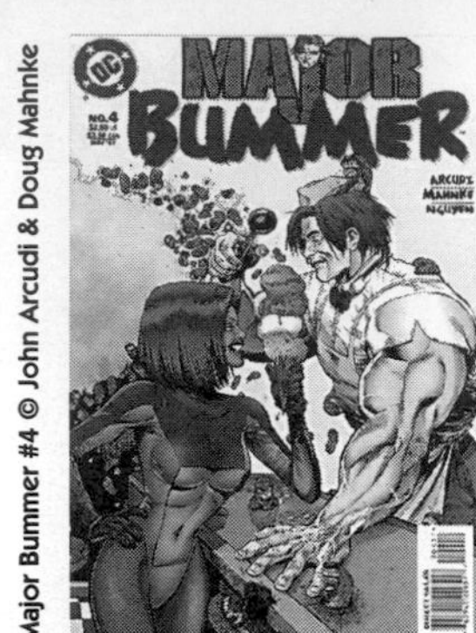

Major Bummer #4 © John Arcudi & Doug Mahnke

Man Called A-X #4 (#5) © Marv Wolfman & Shawn McManus

Man Comics #4 © MEG

GD25 FN65 NM94

V2#1, May, 1997 - Present ($2.50, limited series)
Acclaim Comics (Valiant Heroes)

1-11: 1-Reintro Magnus; Donavon Wylie (X-O Manowar) cameo; Tom Peyer scripts & Mike McKone-c/a begin; painted variant-c exists 1.00 2.50

MAGNUS ROBOT FIGHTER 4000 A.D.
1990 - No. 2?, 1991 ($7.95, high quality paper, card stock-c, 96 pgs.)
Valiant

1,2: Russ Manning-r in all. 1-Origin 1.00 3.00 8.00

MAGNUS ROBOT FIGHTER/NEXUS
Dec, 1993 - No. 2, Apr, 1994 ($2.95, limited series)
Valiant/Dark Horse Comics

1,2: Steve Rude painted-c & pencils in all 1.20 3.00

MAID OF THE MIST (See American Graphics)

MAI, THE PSYCHIC GIRL
May 19, 1987 - No. 28, July, 1989 ($1.50, B&W, bi-weekly, 44pgs.)
Eclipse Comics

1-28 1.30
1,2-2nd print 1.20

MAJOR BUMMER
Aug, 1997 - Present ($2.50)
DC Comics

1-9: 1-Origin and 1st app. Major Bummer 1.20 3.00

MAJOR HOOPLE COMICS (See Crackajack Funnies)
nd (Jan, 1943)
Nedor Publications

1-Mary Worth, Phantom Soldier app. by Moldoff 33.00 98.00 260.00

MAJOR INAPAK THE SPACE ACE
1951 (20 pgs.) (Giveaway)
Magazine Enterprises (Inapac Foods)

1-Bob Powell-c/a 1.00
NOTE: *Many warehouse copies surfaced in 1973.*

MAJOR VICTORY COMICS (Also see Dynamic Comics)
1944 - No. 3, Summer, 1945
H. Clay Glover/Service Publ./Harry 'A' Chesler

1-Origin Major Victory (patriotic hero) by C. Sultan (reprint from Dynamic #1); 1st app. Spider Woman 44.00 132.00 400.00
2-Dynamic Boy app. 33.00 98.00 260.00
3-Rocket Boy app. 28.00 83.00 220.00

MALIBU ASHCAN: RAFFERTY (See Firearm #12)
Nov, 1994 (99¢, B&W w/color-c; one-shot)
Malibu Comics (Ultraverse)

1-Previews "The Rafferty Saga" storyline in Firearm; Chaykin-c. 1.00

MALTESE FALCON
No. 48, 1946
David McKay Publications

Feature Books 48-by Dashiell Hammett 58.00 174.00 520.00

MALU IN THE LAND OF ADVENTURE
1964 (See White Princess of Jungle #2)
I. W. Enterprises

1-r/Avon's Slave Girl Comics #1; Severin-c 3.50 10.50 35.00

MAMMOTH COMICS
1938 (84 pgs.) (B&W, 8-1/2x11-1/2")
Whitman Publishing Co.(K. K. Publications)

1-Alley Oop, Terry & the Pirates, Dick Tracy, Little Orphan Annie, Wash Tubbs, Moon Mullins, Smilin' Jack, Tailspin Tommy, Don Winslow, Dan Dunn, Smokey Stover & other reprints 133.00 400.00 1200.00

GD25 FN65 NM94

MAMMY YOKUM & THE GREAT DOGPATCH MYSTERY
1951 (Giveaway)
Toby Press

nn-Li'l Abner 15.50 47.00 125.00
nn-Reprint (1956) 4.25 13.00 26.00

MAN AGAINST TIME
May, 1996 - No. 3, June, 1996 ($2.25, limited series)
Image Comics (Motown Machineworks)

1-3: 1-Simonson-c. 2,3,-Leon-c. .90 2.25

MAN-BAT (See Batman Family, Brave & the Bold, & Detective #400)
Dec-Jan, 1975-76 - No. 2, Feb-Mar, 1976; Dec, 1984
National Periodical Publications/DC Comics

1-Ditko-a(p); Aparo-c; Batman app.; 1st app. She-Bat? 1.00 3.00 8.00
2-Aparo-c 2.40 6.00
1 (12/84)-N. Adams-r(3)/Det.(Vs. Batman on-c) 1.60 4.00

MAN-BAT
Feb, 1996 - No. 3, Apr, 1996 ($2.25, limited series)
DC Comics

1-3: Dixon scripts in all. 2-Killer Croc-c/app. 2.25

MAN CALLED A-X, THE
Nov, 1994 - No. 4, Jun, 1995 ($2.95, limited series)
Malibu Comics (Bravura)

0-4: Marv Wolfman scripts & Shawn McManus-c/a. 0-(2/95). 1-"1A" on cover 1.20 3.00

MAN CALLED A-X, THE
Oct, 1997 - Present ($2.50)
DC Comics

1-5: Marv Wolfman scripts & Shawn McManus-c/a. 1.00 2.50

MAN COMICS
Dec, 1949 - No. 28, Sept, 1953 (#1-6: 52 pgs.)
Marvel/Atlas Comics (NPI)

1-Tuska-a 17.00 51.00 130.00
2-Tuska-a 10.00 30.00 65.00
3-6 8.35 25.00 55.00
7,8 7.15 21.50 50.00
9-13,15: 9-Format changes to war 5.35 16.00 32.00
14-Henkel (3 pgs.); Pakula-a 6.00 18.00 42.00
16-21,23-28: 28-Crime issue (Bob Brant) 4.25 13.00 28.00
22-Krigstein-a, 5 pgs. 6.50 19.50 45.00
NOTE: ***Berg** a-14, 15, 19. **Colan** a-9, 21. **Everett** a-8, 22; c-22, 25. **Heath** a-11, 17, 21. Kubertish a-by **Bob Brown**-3. **Maneely** a-11; c-10, 11. **Reinman** a-11. **Robinson** a-7, 10, 14. **Robert Sale** a-9, 11. **Sinnott** a-22, 23. **Tuska** a-14, 23.*

MANDRAKE THE MAGICIAN (See Defenders Of The Earth, 123, 46, 52, 55, Giant Comic Album, King Comics, Magic Comics, The Phantom #21, Tiny Tot Funnies & Wow Comics, '36)

MANDRAKE THE MAGICIAN (See Harvey Comics Hits #53)
1938 - 1948; Sept, 1966 - No. 10, Nov, 1967 (Also see Four Color #752)
David McKay Publ./Dell/King Comics (All 12¢)

Feature Books 18,19 (1938) 40.00 120.00 400.00
Feature Books 46 35.00 105.00 280.00
Feature Books 52,55 28.00 84.00 225.00
Four Color 752 (11/56) 9.00 27.00 100.00
1-Begin S.O.S. Phantom, ends #3 2.80 8.40 28.00
2-7,9: 4-Girl Phantom app. 5-Flying Saucer-c/story. 5,6-Brick Bradford app. 7-Origin Lothar. 9-Brick Bradford app. 2.00 6.00 16.00
8-Jeff Jones-a (4 pgs.) 2.50 7.50 22.00
10-Rip Kirby app.; Raymond-a (14 pgs.) 2.70 8.00 27.00

MANDRAKE THE MAGICIAN
Apr, 1995 - No. 2, May, 1995 ($2.95, unfinished limited series)

Man from Atlantis #2 © MEG

Manga Shi 2000 #3 © William Tucci

Man of Steel #3 © DC

GD25 FN65 NM94

Marvel Comics
1,2: Mike Barr scripts 1.20 3.00

MAN-EATING COW (See Tick #7,8)
July, 1992 - No. 10, 1994? ($2.75, B&W, limited series)
New England Comics
1-10 1.20 3.00
Man-Eating Cow Bonanza (6/96, $4.95, 128 pgs.)-r/#1-4. 2.00 5.00

MAN FROM ATLANTIS (TV)
Feb, 1978 - No. 7, Aug, 1978
Marvel Comics
1-($1.00, 84 pgs.)-Sutton-a(p), Buscema-c; origin 1.20 3.00
2-7 (#1: cast photos & origin Mark Harris inside) .80 2.00

MAN FROM PLANET X, THE
1987 (no price;probably unlicensed)
Planet X Productions
1-Reprints Fawcett Movie Comic 1.00

MAN FROM U.N.C.L.E., THE (TV) (Also see The Girl From Uncle)
Feb, 1965 - No. 22, Apr, 1969 (All photo-c)
Gold Key
1 14.00 41.00 150.00
2-Photo back c-2-8 8.00 23.00 85.00
3-10: 7-Jet Dream begins (1st app., also see Jet Dream) (all new stories)
5.00 15.00 55.00
11-22: 21,22-Reprint #10 & 7 4.00 12.00 45.00

MAN FROM U.N.C.L.E., THE (TV)
1987 - No. 11 ($1.50/$1.75, B&W)
Entertainment Publishing
1-7 ($1.50), 8-11 ($1.75) .80 2.00

MAN FROM WELLS FARGO (TV)
No. 1287, Feb-Apr, 1962 - May-July, 1962 (Photo-c)
Dell Publishing Co.
Four Color 1287, #01-495-207 4.50 13.50 50.00

MANGA SHI (See Tomoe)
Aug, 1996 ($2.95)
Crusade Entertainment
1-Printed backwards (manga-style) 1.20 3.00

MANGA SHI 2000
Feb, 1997 - Present ($2.95, mini-series)
Crusade Entertainment
1-3: 1-Two covers 2.95

MANGA ZEN (Also see Zen Intergalactic Ninja)
1996 - No. 3, 1996 ($2.50, B&W)
Zen Comics (Fusion Studios)
1-3 1.00 2.50

MANGLE TANGLE TALES
1990 ($2.95, deluxe format)
Innovation Publishing
1-Intro by Harlan Ellison 1.20 3.00

MANHUNT! (Becomes Red Fox #15 on)
Oct, 1947 - No. 14, 1953
Magazine Enterprises
1-Red Fox by L. B. Cole, Undercover Girl by Whitney, Space Ace begin (1st app.); negligee panels 40.00 120.00 310.00
2-Electrocution-c 33.00 99.00 240.00
3-6 28.00 84.00 200.00
7-10: 7-Space Ace ends. 8-Trail Colt begins (intro/1st app., 5/48) by Guardineer; Trail Colt-c. 10-G. Ingels-a 25.00 75.00 185.00
11(8/48)-Frazetta-a, 7 pgs.; The Duke, Scotland Yard begin
34.00 101.00 250.00
12 18.00 54.00 135.00
13(A-1 #63)-Frazetta, r-/Trail Colt #1, 7 pgs. 31.00 94.00 235.00
14(A-1 #77)-Bondage/hypo-c; last L. B. Cole Red Fox; Ingels-a
25.00 75.00 195.00
NOTE: *Guardineer a-1-5; c-8. Whitney a-2-14; c-1-6, 10. Red Fox by L. B. Cole-#1-14. #15 was advertised but came out as Red Fox #15. Bondage c-6.*

MANHUNTER (See Adventure #58, 73, Brave & the Bold, Detective Comics, 1st Issue Special, House of Mystery #143 and Justice League of America)
1984 ($2.50, 76 pgs; high quality paper)
DC Comics
1-Simonson-c/a(r)/Detective; Batman app. 1.00 2.50

MANHUNTER
July, 1988 - No. 24, Apr, 1990 ($1.00)
DC Comics
1-24: 8,9-Flash app. 9-Invasion. 17-Batman-c/sty 1.00

MANHUNTER
No. 0, Nov, 1994 - No. 12, Nov, 1995 ($1.95/$2.25)
DC Comics
0-7 .80 2.00
8-12: 8-Begin $2.25-c .90 2.25

MAN IN BLACK (See Thrill-O-Rama) (Also see All New Comics, Front Page, Green Hornet #31, Strange Story & Tally-Ho Comics)
Sept, 1957 - No. 4, Mar, 1958
Harvey Publications
1-Bob Powell-c/a 11.50 34.00 85.00
2-4: Powell-c/a 10.00 30.00 65.00

MAN IN BLACK
1990 - No. 2, July, 1991 (B&W)
Lorne-Harvey Publications (Recollections)
1,2 .80 2.00

MAN IN FLIGHT (Disney, TV)
No. 836, Sept, 1957
Dell Publishing Co.
Four Color 836 6.40 19.00 70.00

MAN IN SPACE (Disney, TV, see Dell Giant #27)
No. 716, Aug, 1956 - No. 954, Nov, 1958
Dell Publishing Co.
Four Color 716-A science feat. from Tomorrowland 8.00 25.00 90.00
Four Color 954-Satellites 6.40 19.00 70.00

MAN OF PEACE, POPE PIUS XII
1950 (See Pope Pius XII... & To V2#8)
Catechetical Guild
nn-All Powell-a 4.00 12.00 24.00

MAN OF STEEL, THE (Also see Superman: The Man of Steel)
1986 (June release) - No. 6, 1986 (75¢, limited series)
DC Comics
1-Silver logo; Byrne-c/a/scripts in all; origin 1.20 3.00
1-Alternate-c for newsstand sales 1.20 3.00
1-Distr. to toy stores by So Much Fun 1.20 3.00
2-6: 2-Intro. Lois Lane, Jimmy Olsen. 3-Intro/origin Magpie; Batman-c/story. 4-Intro. new Lex Luthor 1.20 3.00
1-6-Silver Editions (1993, $1.95)-r/1-6 1.20 3.00
...The Complete Saga nn-Contains #1-6, given away in contest 1.20 3.00
Limited Edition, softcover 3.00 9.00 30.00
NOTE: *Issues 1-6 were released between Action #583 (9/86) & Action #584 (1/87) plus Superman #423 (9/86) & Advs. of Superman #424 (1/87).*

MAN OF THE ATOM (See Solar, Man of the Atom Vol. 2)

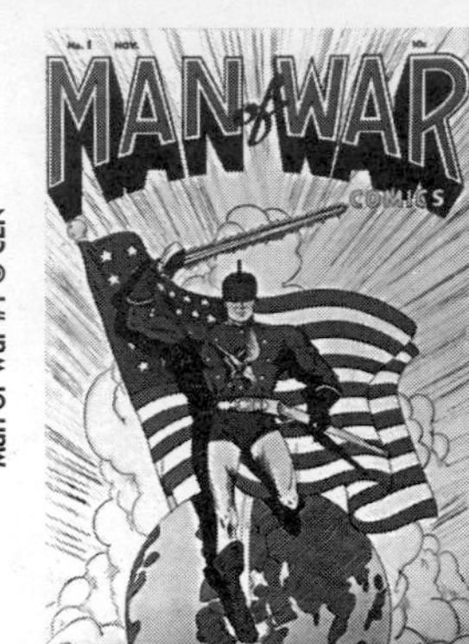

Man of War #1 © CEN

Mantra #13 © Malibu

March of Comics nn (#4) © WDC

MAN OF WAR (See Liberty Guards & Liberty Scouts)
Nov, 1941 - No. 2, Jan, 1942
Centaur Publications

	GD25	FN65	NM94
1-The Fire-Man, Man of War, The Sentinel, Liberty Guards, & Vapo-Man begin; Gustavson-c/a; Flag-c	128.00	384.00	1150.00
2-Intro The Ferret; Gustavson-c/a	103.00	309.00	925.00

MAN OF WAR
Aug, 1987 - No. 3, Feb, 1988 ($1.75, Baxter paper)
Eclipse Comics

	GD25	FN65	NM94
1-3: Bruce Jones scripts			1.80

MAN OF WAR (See The Protectors)
1993 - No, 8, Feb, 1994 ($1.95/$2.50/$2.25)
Malibu Comics

	GD25	FN65	NM94
1-5 ($1.95)-Newsstand Editions w/different-c		.80	2.00
1-5 ($2.50)-Collector's Editions w/poster		1.00	2.50
6-8 ($2.25): 6-Polybagged w/Skycap. 8-Vs. Rocket Rangers		.90	2.25

MAN O' MARS
1953; 1964
Fiction House Magazines

	GD25	FN65	NM94
1-Space Rangers; Whitman-c	36.00	107.00	265.00
I.W. Reprint #1-r/Man O'Mars #1 & Star Pirate; Murphy Anderson-a	4.20	12.60	42.00

MANTECH ROBOT WARRIORS
Sept, 1984 - No. 4, Apr, 1985 (75¢)
Archie Enterprises, Inc.

	GD25	FN65	NM94
1-4: Ayers-c/a(p). 1-Buckler-c(i)			.80

MAN-THING (See Fear, Giant-Size..., Marvel Comics Presents, Marvel Fanfare, Monsters Unleashed, Power Record Comics & Savage Tales)
Jan, 1974 - No. 22, Oct, 1975; V2#1, Nov, 1979 - V2#11, July, 1981
Marvel Comics Group

	GD25	FN65	NM94
1-Howard the Duck(2nd app.) cont'd/Fear #19	1.60	4.85	13.00
2	1.00	2.80	7.00
3-1st app. original Foolkiller		2.40	6.00
4-Origin Foolkiller; last app. 1st Foolkiller		1.20	3.00
5-11-Ploog-a. 11-Foolkiller cameo (flashback)		1.00	2.50
12-22: 19-1st app. Scavenger. 20-Spidey cameo. 21-Origin Scavenger, Man-Thing. 22-Howard the Duck cameo		.80	2.00
V2#1(1979) - 11			1.50

NOTE: ***Alcala*** *a-14.* ***Brunner*** *c-1.* ***J. Buscema*** *a-12p, 13p, 16p.* ***Gil Kane*** *c-4p, 10p, 12-20p, 21.* ***Mooney*** *a-17, 18, 19p, 20-22, V2#1-3p.* ***Ploog*** *Man-Thing-5p, 6p, 7, 8, 9-11p; c-5, 6, 8, 9, 11.* ***Sutton*** *a-13i. No. 19 says #10 in indicia.*

MAN-THING (Volume Three)
Dec, 1997 - Present ($2.99)
Marvel Comics

	GD25	FN65	NM94
1-5-DeMatteis-s/Sharp-a. 2-Two covers			2.99

MANTRA
July, 1993 - No. 24, Aug, 1995 ($1.95/$2.50)
Malibu Comics (Ultraverse)

	GD25	FN65	NM94
1-Polybagged w/trading card & coupon		.80	2.00
1-Newsstand edition w/o trading card or coupon		.80	2.00
1-Full cover holographic edition	1.85	5.50	15.00
1-Ultra-limited silver foil-c		2.40	6.00
2,3,5,6: 3-Intro Warstrike & Kismet. 6-Break-Thru x-over		.90	2.25
2-($2.50- Newsstand edition bagged w/card		1.00	2.50
4-($2.50, 48 pgs.)-Rune flip-c/story by B. Smith (3 pgs.)		1.00	2.50
7-9,11-17: 7-Prime app.; origin Prototype by Jurgens/Austin (2 pgs.). 11-New costume. 17-Intro NecroMantra & Pinnacle; prelude to Godwheel.		.80	2.00
10-($3.50, 68 pgs.)-Flip-c w/Ultraverse Premiere #2		1.40	3.50
18-24: 18-Begin $2.50-c		1.00	2.50
Giant Size 1 (7/94, $2.50, 44 pgs.)		1.00	2.50
...Spear of Destiny 1,2 (4/95, $2.50, 36pgs.)		1.00	2.50

MANTRA (2nd Series) (Also See Black September)
Infinity, Sept, 1995 - No. 7, Apr, 1996 ($1.50)
Malibu Comics (Ultraverse)

	GD25	FN65	NM94
Infinity (9/95, $1.50)-Black September x-over, Intro new Mantra.			1.50
1-7: 1-(10/95). 5-Return of Eden (original Mantra). 6,7-Rush app.			1.50

MAN WITH THE X-RAY EYES, THE (See X,... under Movie Comics)

MANY GHOSTS OF DR. GRAVES, THE (Doctor Graves #73 on)
5/67 - No. 60, 12/76; No. 61, 9/77 - No. 62, 10/77; No. 63, 2/78 - No. 65, 4/78; No. 66, 6/81 - No. 72, 5/82
Charlton Comics

	GD25	FN65	NM94
1-Palais-a; early issues 12¢-c	2.50	7.50	24.00
2-10	1.50	4.50	12.00
11-20	1.10	3.30	9.00
21-44		2.40	6.00
46-72: 47,49-Newton-a		1.60	4.00
45-1st Newton comic work (8 pgs.); new logo	1.00	3.00	8.00
Modern Comics Reprint 12,25 (1978)		1.60	4.00

NOTE: ***Aparo*** *a-4, 5, 7, 8, 66r, 69r; c-8, 14, 19, 66r, 67r.* ***Byrne*** *c-54.* ***Ditko*** *a-1, 7, 9, 11-13, 15-18, 20-22, 24, 26, 27, 35, 37, 38, 40-44, 47, 48, 51-54, 58, 60r-65r, 70, 72; c-11-13, 16-18, 22, 24, 26-35, 38, 40, 55, 58, 62-65.* ***Howard*** *a-45i; c-48.* ***Morisi*** *a-13, 14, 23, 26.* ***Newton*** *a-45, 47p, 49p; c-49, 52.* ***Sutton*** *a-42, 49; c-42, 44, 45; painted c-53.*

MANY LOVES OF DOBIE GILLIS (TV)
May-June, 1960 - No. 26, Oct, 1964
National Periodical Publications

	GD25	FN65	NM94
1-Most covers by Bob Oskner	22.00	66.00	220.00
2-5	12.00	36.00	120.00
6-10	8.50	25.50	85.00
11-26: 20-Drucker-a	7.50	22.50	75.00

MARAUDER'S MOON (See Luke Short, Four Color #848)

MARCH OF COMICS (Boys' and Girls'...#3-353)
1946 - No. 488, April, 1982 (#1-4 are not numbered)
(K.K. Giveaway) (Founded by Sig Feuchtwanger)
K. K. Publications/Western Publishing Co.

Early issues were full size, 32 pages, and were printed with and without an extra cover of slick stock, just for the advertiser. The binding was stapled if the slick cover was added; otherwise, the pages were glued together at the spine. Most 1948 - 1951 issues were full size,24 pages, pulp covers. Starting in 1952 they were half-size and 32 pages with slick covers.1959 and later issues had only 16 pages plus covers. 1952 -1959 issues read oblong; 1960 and later issues read upright. All have new stories except where noted.

	GD25	FN65	NM94
nn (#1, 1946)-Goldilocks; Kelly back-c (16 pgs., stapled)	36.00	107.00	250.00
nn (#2, 1946)-How Santa Got His Red Suit; Kelly-a (11 pgs., r/4-Color #61 from 1944) (16pgs., stapled)	36.00	107.00	250.00
nn (#3, 1947)-Our Gang (Walt Kelly)	46.00	137.00	340.00
nn (#4)-Donald Duck by Carl Barks, "Maharajah Donald", 28 pgs.; Kelly-c? (Disney)	857.00	2571.00	7000.00
5-Andy Panda (Walter Lantz)	20.00	60.00	140.00
6-Popular Fairy Tales; Kelly-c; Noonan-a(2)	24.00	71.00	165.00
7-Oswald the Rabbit	24.00	71.00	165.00
8-Mickey Mouse, 32 pgs. (Disney)	71.00	215.00	500.00
9(nn)-The Story of the Gloomy Bunny	11.00	33.00	75.00
10-Out of Santa's Bag	10.00	30.00	65.00
11-Fun With Santa Claus	8.35	25.00	50.00
12-Santa's Toys	8.35	25.00	50.00
13-Santa's Surprise	8.35	25.00	50.00
14-Santa's Candy Kitchen	8.35	25.00	50.00
15-Hip-It-Ty Hop & the Big Bass Viol	8.35	25.00	50.00

March of Comics #38 © Walter Lantz

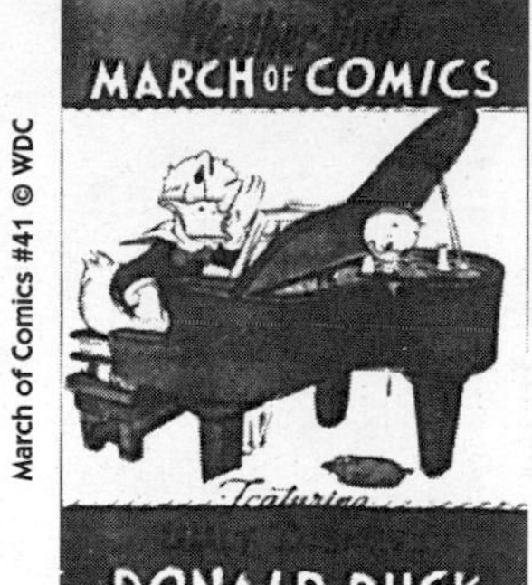

March of Comics #41 © WDC

March of Comics #72 © King Features

	GD25	FN65	NM94
16-Woody Woodpecker (1947)(Walter Lantz)	15.00	45.00	105.00
17-Roy Rogers (1948)	26.00	79.00	185.00
18-Popular Fairy Tales	13.00	39.00	90.00
19-Uncle Wiggily	11.00	33.00	75.00
20-Donald Duck by Carl Barks, "Darkest Africa", 22 pgs.; Kelly-c (Disney)	500.00	1500.00	4000.00
21-Tom and Jerry	12.00	36.00	85.00
22-Andy Panda (Lantz)	11.00	33.00	75.00
23-Raggedy Ann & Andy; Kerr-a	17.00	49.00	115.00
24-Felix the Cat, 1932 daily strip reprints by Otto Messmer	27.00	81.00	190.00
25-Gene Autry	25.00	75.00	175.00
26-Our Gang; Walt Kelly	26.00	77.00	180.00
27-Mickey Mouse; r/in M. M. #240 (Disney)	50.00	150.00	350.00
28-Gene Autry	25.00	75.00	175.00
29-Easter Bonnet Shop	5.85	17.50	35.00
30-Here Comes Santa	4.25	13.00	28.00
31-Santa's Busy Corner	4.25	13.00	28.00
32-No book produced			
33-A Christmas Carol (12/48)	4.25	13.00	28.00
34-Woody Woodpecker	11.00	33.00	75.00
35-Roy Rogers (1948)	26.00	77.00	180.00
36-Felix the Cat(1949); by Messmer; 1934 daily strip-r	24.00	71.00	165.00
37-Popeye	18.00	54.00	125.00
38-Oswald the Rabbit	10.00	30.00	58.00
39-Gene Autry	25.00	75.00	175.00
40-Andy and Woody	10.00	30.00	58.00
41-Donald Duck by Carl Barks, "Race to the South Seas", 22 pgs.; Kelly-c	500.00	1500.00	3500.00
42-Porky Pig	10.00	30.00	58.00
43-Henry	8.00	24.00	48.00
44-Bugs Bunny	11.00	33.00	75.00
45-Mickey Mouse (Disney)	39.00	116.00	270.00
46-Tom and Jerry	11.00	33.00	75.00
47-Roy Rogers	22.00	66.00	155.00
48-Greetings from Santa	4.00	12.00	24.00
49-Santa Is Here	4.00	12.00	24.00
50-Santa Claus' Workshop (1949)	4.00	12.00	24.00
51-Felix the Cat (1950) by Messmer	19.00	58.00	135.00
52-Popeye	15.00	45.00	105.00
53-Oswald the Rabbit	10.00	30.00	58.00
54-Gene Autry	21.00	62.00	145.00
55-Andy and Woody	8.70	26.00	52.00
56-Donald Duck; not by Barks; Barks art on back-c (Disney)	36.00	109.00	255.00
57-Porky Pig	8.70	26.00	52.00
58-Henry	6.35	19.00	38.00
59-Bugs Bunny	10.00	30.00	65.00
60-Mickey Mouse (Disney)	35.00	105.00	245.00
61-Tom and Jerry	8.70	26.00	52.00
62-Roy Rogers	21.00	62.00	145.00
63-Welcome Santa (1/2-size, oblong)	4.00	12.00	24.00
64(nn)-Santa's Helpers (1/2-size, oblong)	4.00	12.00	24.00
65(nn)-Jingle Bells (1950) (1/2-size, oblong)	4.00	12.00	24.00
66-Popeye (1951)	13.00	39.00	90.00
67-Oswald the Rabbit	8.00	24.00	48.00
68-Roy Rogers	19.00	58.00	135.00
69-Donald Duck; Barks-a on back-c (Disney)	31.00	94.00	220.00
70-Tom and Jerry	8.00	24.00	48.00
71-Porky Pig	8.00	24.00	48.00
72-Krazy Kat	10.00	30.00	65.00
73-Roy Rogers	17.00	49.00	115.00
74-Mickey Mouse (1951)(Disney)	29.00	86.00	200.00
75-Bugs Bunny	8.70	26.00	52.00
76-Andy and Woody	8.00	24.00	48.00
77-Roy Rogers	16.00	47.00	110.00
78-Gene Autry (1951); last regular size issue	14.00	43.00	100.00
79-Andy Panda (1952, 5x7" size)	4.25	13.00	28.00
80-Popeye	11.50	34.00	80.00
81-Oswald the Rabbit	5.00	15.00	30.00
82-Tarzan; Lex Barker photo-c	19.00	58.00	135.00
83-Bugs Bunny	6.70	20.00	40.00
84-Henry	4.00	12.00	24.00
85-Woody Woodpecker	4.00	12.00	24.00
86-Roy Rogers	13.50	41.00	95.00
87-Krazy Kat	8.70	26.00	52.00
88-Tom and Jerry	5.70	17.00	34.00
89-Porky Pig	4.00	12.00	24.00
90-Gene Autry	13.00	39.00	90.00
91-Roy Rogers & Santa	13.00	39.00	90.00
92-Christmas with Santa	4.00	10.00	20.00
93-Woody Woodpecker (1953)	4.00	12.00	24.00
94-Indian Chief	10.00	30.00	65.00
95-Oswald the Rabbit	4.00	12.00	24.00
96-Popeye	10.00	30.00	68.00
97-Bugs Bunny	5.70	17.00	34.00
98-Tarzan; Lex Barker photo-c	21.00	62.00	145.00
99-Porky Pig	4.00	12.00	24.00
100-Roy Rogers	10.00	30.00	68.00
101-Henry	4.00	11.00	22.00
102-Tom Corbett (TV)('53, early app).; painted-c	17.00	49.00	115.00
103-Tom and Jerry	4.00	12.00	24.00
104-Gene Autry	11.00	33.00	75.00
105-Roy Rogers	11.00	33.00	75.00
106-Santa's Helpers	4.00	10.00	20.00
107-Santa's Christmas Book - not published			
108-Fun with Santa (1953)	4.00	10.00	20.00
109-Woody Woodpecker (1954)	4.00	11.00	22.00
110-Indian Chief	5.70	17.00	34.00
111-Oswald the Rabbit	4.00	11.00	22.00
112-Henry	4.00	10.00	20.00
113-Porky Pig	4.00	11.00	22.00
114-Tarzan; Russ Manning-a	21.00	62.00	145.00
115-Bugs Bunny	4.25	13.00	28.00
116-Roy Rogers	11.00	33.00	75.00
117-Popeye	10.00	30.00	68.00
118-Flash Gordon; painted-c	13.50	41.00	95.00
119-Tom and Jerry	4.00	11.00	22.00
120-Gene Autry	11.00	33.00	75.00
121-Roy Rogers	11.00	33.00	75.00
122-Santa's Surprise (1954)	3.00	7.50	15.00
123-Santa's Christmas Book	3.00	7.50	15.00
124-Woody Woodpecker (1955)	4.00	10.00	20.00
125-Tarzan; Lex Barker photo-c	19.00	58.00	135.00
126-Oswald the Rabbit	4.00	10.00	20.00
127-Indian Chief	5.00	15.00	30.00
128-Tom and Jerry	4.00	10.00	20.00
129-Henry	3.40	8.50	17.00
130-Porky Pig	4.00	10.00	20.00
131-Roy Rogers	11.00	33.00	75.00
132-Bugs Bunny	4.00	12.00	24.00
133-Flash Gordon; painted-c	12.00	36.00	85.00
134-Popeye	8.00	24.00	48.00
135-Gene Autry	10.00	30.00	68.00
136-Roy Rogers	10.00	30.00	68.00
137-Gifts from Santa	2.40	6.00	12.00
138-Fun at Christmas (1955)	2.40	6.00	12.00

March of Comics #144 © ERB

March of Comics #233 © Jay Ward

March of Comics #240 © ERB

	GD25	FN65	NM94
139-Woody Woodpecker (1956)	4.00	10.00	20.00
140-Indian Chief	5.00	15.00	30.00
141-Oswald the Rabbit	4.00	10.00	20.00
142-Flash Gordon	12.00	36.00	85.00
143-Porky Pig	4.00	10.00	20.00
144-Tarzan; Russ Manning-a; painted-c	18.00	54.00	125.00
145-Tom and Jerry	4.00	10.00	20.00
146-Roy Rogers; photo-c	11.00	33.00	75.00
147-Henry	3.00	7.50	15.00
148-Popeye	8.00	24.00	48.00
149-Bugs Bunny	4.00	11.00	22.00
150-Gene Autry	10.00	30.00	68.00
151-Roy Rogers	10.00	30.00	68.00
152-The Night Before Christmas	2.40	6.00	12.00
153-Merry Christmas (1956)	2.40	6.00	12.00
154-Tom and Jerry (1957)	4.00	10.00	20.00
155-Tarzan; photo-c	18.00	54.00	125.00
156-Oswald the Rabbit	4.00	10.00	20.00
157-Popeye	6.70	20.00	40.00
158-Woody Woodpecker	4.00	10.00	20.00
159-Indian Chief	5.00	15.00	30.00
160-Bugs Bunny	4.00	11.00	22.00
161-Roy Rogers	10.00	30.00	58.00
162-Henry	3.00	7.50	15.00
163-Rin Tin Tin (TV)	7.50	22.50	45.00
164-Porky Pig	4.00	10.00	20.00
165-The Lone Ranger	10.00	30.00	65.00
166-Santa and His Reindeer	2.40	6.00	12.00
167-Roy Rogers and Santa	10.00	30.00	58.00
168-Santa Claus' Workshop (1957)	2.40	6.00	12.00
169-Popeye (1958)	6.70	20.00	40.00
170-Indian Chief	5.00	15.00	30.00
171-Oswald the Rabbit	3.60	9.00	18.00
172-Tarzan	13.50	41.00	95.00
173-Tom and Jerry	3.60	9.00	18.00
174-The Lone Ranger	10.00	30.00	65.00
175-Porky Pig	3.60	9.00	18.00
176-Roy Rogers	9.15	27.00	55.00
177-Woody Woodpecker	3.60	9.00	18.00
178-Henry	3.00	7.50	15.00
179-Bugs Bunny	3.60	9.00	18.00
180-Rin Tin Tin (TV)	6.35	19.00	38.00
181-Happy Holiday	2.00	5.00	10.00
182-Happi Tim	3.20	8.00	16.00
183-Welcome Santa (1958)	2.00	5.00	10.00
184-Woody Woodpecker (1959)	3.20	8.00	16.00
185-Tarzan; photo-c	13.00	39.00	90.00
186-Oswald the Rabbit	3.20	8.00	16.00
187-Indian Chief	4.70	14.00	28.00
188-Bugs Bunny	3.20	8.00	16.00
189-Henry	2.80	7.00	14.00
190-Tom and Jerry	3.20	8.00	16.00
191-Roy Rogers	8.35	25.00	50.00
192-Porky Pig	3.20	8.00	16.00
193-The Lone Ranger	10.00	30.00	60.00
194-Popeye	5.85	17.50	35.00
195-Rin Tin Tin (TV)	5.85	17.50	35.00
196-Sears Special - not published			
197-Santa Is Coming	2.00	5.00	10.00
198-Santa's Helpers (1959)	2.00	5.00	10.00
199-Huckleberry Hound (TV)(1960, early app.)	6.70	20.00	40.00
200-Fury (TV)	5.35	16.00	32.00
201-Bugs Bunny	3.20	8.00	16.00
202-Space Explorer	9.15	27.50	55.00

	GD25	FN65	NM94
203-Woody Woodpecker	2.80	7.00	14.00
204-Tarzan	10.00	30.00	70.00
205-Mighty Mouse	6.35	19.00	38.00
206-Roy Rogers; photo-c	8.35	25.00	50.00
207-Tom and Jerry	2.80	7.00	14.00
208-The Lone Ranger; Clayton Moore photo-c	12.00	36.00	85.00
209-Porky Pig	2.80	7.00	14.00
210-Lassie (TV)	6.35	19.00	38.00
211-Sears Special - not published			
212-Christmas Eve	2.00	5.00	10.00
213-Here Comes Santa (1960)	2.00	5.00	10.00
214-Huckleberry Hound (TV)(1961)	5.85	17.50	35.00
215-Hi Yo Silver	6.35	19.00	38.00
216-Rocky & His Friends (TV)(1961); predates Rocky and His Fiendish Friends #1 (see Four Color #1128)	10.00	30.00	70.00
217-Lassie (TV)	5.00	15.00	30.00
218-Porky Pig	2.80	7.00	14.00
219-Journey to the Sun	5.35	16.00	32.00
220-Bugs Bunny	3.20	8.00	16.00
221-Roy and Dale; photo-c	7.50	22.50	45.00
222-Woody Woodpecker	2.80	7.00	14.00
223-Tarzan	10.00	30.00	70.00
224-Tom and Jerry	2.80	7.00	14.00
225-The Lone Ranger	7.50	22.50	45.00
226-Christmas Treasury (1961)	2.00	5.00	10.00
227-Sears Special - not published?			
228-Letters to Santa (1961)	2.00	5.00	10.00
229-The Flintstones (TV)(1962); early app.; predates 1st Flintstones Gold Key issue (#7)	10.00	30.00	60.00
230-Lassie (TV)	5.00	15.00	30.00
231-Bugs Bunny	3.20	8.00	16.00
232-The Three Stooges	10.00	30.00	65.00
233-Bullwinkle (TV) (1962, very early app.)	11.00	32.00	75.00
234-Smokey the Bear	4.00	10.00	20.00
235-Huckleberry Hound (TV)	5.85	17.50	35.00
236-Roy and Dale	5.85	17.50	35.00
237-Mighty Mouse	4.70	14.00	28.00
238-The Lone Ranger	7.50	22.50	45.00
239-Woody Woodpecker	2.80	7.00	14.00
240-Tarzan	9.15	27.50	55.00
241-Santa Claus Around the World	2.00	5.00	10.00
242-Santa's Toyland (1962)	2.00	5.00	10.00
243-The Flintstones (TV)(1963)	9.15	27.50	55.00
244-Mister Ed (TV); early app.; photo-c	5.85	17.50	35.00
245-Bugs Bunny	3.20	8.00	16.00
246-Popeye	4.35	13.00	26.00
247-Mighty Mouse	4.70	14.00	28.00
248-The Three Stooges	10.00	30.00	65.00
249-Woody Woodpecker	2.80	7.00	14.00
250-Roy and Dale	5.85	17.50	35.00
251-Little Lulu & Witch Hazel	14.00	43.00	100.00
252-Tarzan; painted-c	9.15	27.50	55.00
253-Yogi Bear (TV)	6.35	19.00	38.00
254-Lassie (TV)	5.35	16.00	32.00
255-Santa's Christmas List	2.00	5.00	10.00
256-Christmas Party (1963)	2.00	5.00	10.00
257-Mighty Mouse	4.70	14.00	28.00
258-The Sword in the Stone (Disney)	9.15	27.50	55.00
259-Bugs Bunny	3.20	8.00	16.00
260-Mister Ed (TV)	4.70	14.00	28.00
261-Woody Woodpecker	2.80	7.00	14.00
262-Tarzan	8.35	25.00	50.00
263-Donald Duck; not by Barks (Disney)	10.00	30.00	65.00
264-Popeye	4.35	13.00	26.00

March of Comics #323 © WEST

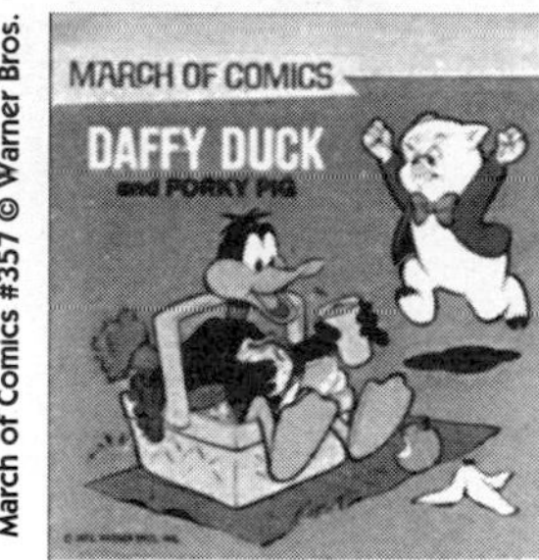

March of Comics #357 © Warner Bros.

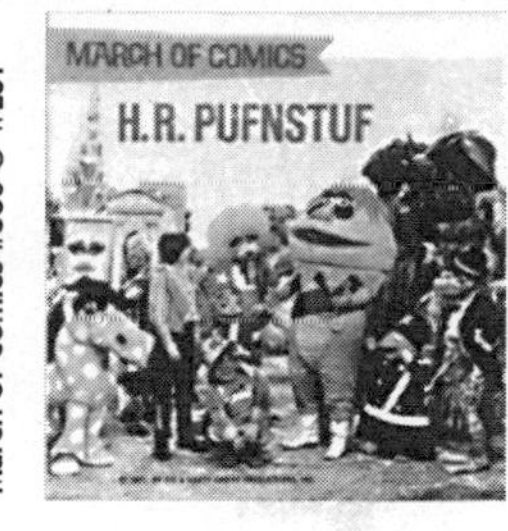

March of Comics #360 © WEST

	GD25	FN65	NM94
265-Yogi Bear (TV)	4.70	14.00	28.00
266-Lassie (TV)	4.15	12.50	25.00
267-Little Lulu; Irving Tripp-a	11.50	34.00	80.00
268-The Three Stooges	10.00	30.00	60.00
269-A Jolly Christmas	2.00	5.00	10.00
270-Santa's Little Helpers	2.00	5.00	10.00
271-The Flintstones (TV)(1965)	9.15	27.50	55.00
272-Tarzan	8.35	25.00	50.00
273-Bugs Bunny	3.20	8.00	16.00
274-Popeye	4.35	13.00	26.00
275-Little Lulu; Irving Tripp-a	10.00	30.00	65.00
276-The Jetsons (TV)	14.00	43.00	100.00
277-Daffy Duck	3.20	8.00	16.00
278-Lassie (TV)	4.15	12.50	25.00
279-Yogi Bear (TV)	4.70	14.00	28.00
280-The Three Stooges; photo-c	10.00	30.00	60.00
281-Tom and Jerry	2.40	6.00	12.00
282-Mister Ed (TV)	4.70	14.00	28.00
283-Santa's Visit	2.00	5.00	10.00
284-Christmas Parade (1965)	2.00	5.00	10.00
285-Astro Boy (TV); 2nd app. Astro Boy	36.00	107.00	250.00
286-Tarzan	7.50	22.50	45.00
287-Bugs Bunny	3.20	8.00	16.00
288-Daffy Duck	2.80	7.00	14.00
289-The Flintstones (TV)	8.35	25.00	50.00
290-Mister Ed (TV); photo-c	4.00	12.00	24.00
291-Yogi Bear (TV)	4.00	12.00	24.00
292-The Three Stooges; photo-c	10.00	30.00	60.00
293-Little Lulu; Irving Tripp-a	9.15	27.50	55.00
294-Popeye	4.35	13.00	26.00
295-Tom and Jerry	2.40	6.00	12.00
296-Lassie (TV); photo-c	4.00	11.00	22.00
297-Christmas Bells	2.00	5.00	10.00
298-Santa's Sleigh (1966)	2.00	5.00	10.00
299-The Flintstones (TV)(1967)	8.35	25.00	50.00
300-Tarzan	7.50	22.50	45.00
301-Bugs Bunny	2.80	7.00	14.00
302-Laurel and Hardy (TV); photo-c	5.00	15.00	30.00
303-Daffy Duck	2.00	5.00	10.00
304-The Three Stooges; photo-c	9.15	27.50	55.00
305-Tom and Jerry	2.00	5.00	10.00
306-Daniel Boone (TV); Fess Parker photo-c	5.85	17.50	35.00
307-Little Lulu; Irving Tripp-a	7.50	22.50	45.00
308-Lassie (TV); photo-c	4.00	11.00	22.00
309-Yogi Bear (TV)	4.00	11.00	22.00
310-The Lone Ranger; Clayton Moore photo-c	12.00	36.00	85.00
311-Santa's Show	2.00	5.00	10.00
312-Christmas Album (1967)	2.00	5.00	10.00
313-Daffy Duck (1968)	2.00	5.00	10.00
314-Laurel and Hardy (TV)	4.70	14.00	28.00
315-Bugs Bunny	2.80	7.00	14.00
316-The Three Stooges	7.50	22.50	45.00
317-The Flintstones (TV)	6.70	20.00	40.00
318-Tarzan	6.70	20.00	40.00
319-Yogi Bear (TV)	4.00	11.00	22.00
320-Space Family Robinson (TV); Spiegle-a	13.00	40.00	90.00
321-Tom and Jerry	2.00	5.00	10.00
322-The Lone Ranger	6.70	20.00	40.00
323-Little Lulu; not by Stanley	4.35	13.00	26.00
324-Lassie (TV); photo-c	4.00	11.00	22.00
325-Fun with Santa	2.00	5.00	10.00
326-Christmas Story (1968)	2.00	5.00	10.00
327-The Flintstones (TV)(1969)	6.70	20.00	40.00
328-Space Family Robinson (TV); Spiegle-a	13.00	40.00	90.00

	GD25	FN65	NM94
329-Bugs Bunny	2.80	7.00	14.00
330-The Jetsons (TV)	10.00	30.00	70.00
331-Daffy Duck	2.00	5.00	10.00
332-Tarzan	5.35	16.00	32.00
333-Tom and Jerry	2.00	5.00	10.00
334-Lassie (TV)	4.00	10.00	20.00
335-Little Lulu	4.35	13.00	26.00
336-The Three Stooges	7.50	22.50	45.00
337-Yogi Bear (TV)	4.00	11.00	22.00
338-The Lone Ranger	6.70	20.00	40.00
339-(Was not published)			
340-Here Comes Santa (1969)	2.00	5.00	10.00
341-The Flintstones (TV)	6.70	20.00	40.00
342-Tarzan	5.35	16.00	32.00
343-Bugs Bunny	2.40	6.00	12.00
344-Yogi Bear (TV)	4.00	10.00	20.00
345-Tom and Jerry	2.00	5.00	10.00
346-Lassie (TV)	4.00	10.00	20.00
347-Daffy Duck	2.00	5.00	10.00
348-The Jetsons (TV)	10.00	30.00	60.00
349-Little Lulu; not by Stanley	4.00	11.00	22.00
350-The Lone Ranger	5.00	15.00	30.00
351-Beep-Beep, the Road Runner (TV)	2.80	7.00	14.00
352-Space Family Robinson (TV); Spiegle-a	13.00	40.00	90.00
353-Beep-Beep, the Road Runner (1971) (TV)	2.80	7.00	14.00
354-Tarzan (1971)	4.70	14.00	28.00
355-Little Lulu; not by Stanley	4.00	11.00	22.00
356-Scooby Doo, Where Are You? (TV)	4.00	11.00	22.00
357-Daffy Duck & Porky Pig	2.00	5.00	10.00
358-Lassie (TV)	4.00	10.00	20.00
359-Baby Snoots	2.80	7.00	14.00
360-H. R. Pufnstuf (TV); photo-c	4.00	10.00	20.00
361-Tom and Jerry	2.00	5.00	10.00
362-Smokey the Bear (TV)	2.00	5.00	10.00
363-Bugs Bunny & Yosemite Sam	2.40	6.00	12.00
364-The Banana Splits (TV); photo-c	2.40	6.00	12.00
365-Tom and Jerry (1972)	2.00	5.00	10.00
366-Tarzan	4.35	13.00	26.00
367-Bugs Bunny & Porky Pig	2.40	6.00	12.00
368-Scooby Doo (TV)(4/72)	4.00	10.00	20.00
369-Little Lulu; not by Stanley	3.60	9.00	18.00
370-Lassie (TV); photo-c	4.00	10.00	20.00
371-Baby Snoots	2.40	6.00	12.00
372-Smokey the Bear (TV)	2.00	5.00	10.00
373-The Three Stooges	6.70	20.00	40.00
374-Wacky Witch	2.00	5.00	10.00
375-Beep-Beep & Daffy Duck (TV)	2.00	5.00	10.00
376-The Pink Panther (1972) (TV)	2.80	7.00	14.00
377-Baby Snoots (1973)	2.40	6.00	12.00
378-Turok, Son of Stone; new-a	14.00	43.00	100.00
379-Heckle & Jeckle New Terrytoons (TV)	2.00	5.00	10.00
380-Bugs Bunny & Yosemite Sam	2.00	5.00	10.00
381-Lassie (TV)	3.20	8.00	16.00
382-Scooby Doo, Where Are You? (TV)	3.60	9.00	18.00
383-Smokey the Bear (TV)	1.60	4.00	8.00
384-Pink Panther (TV)	2.00	5.00	10.00
385-Little Lulu	3.00	7.50	15.00
386-Wacky Witch	1.60	4.00	8.00
387-Beep-Beep & Daffy Duck (TV)	1.60	4.00	8.00
388-Tom and Jerry (1973)	1.60	4.00	8.00
389-Little Lulu; not by Stanley	3.00	7.50	15.00
390-Pink Panther (TV)	1.60	4.00	8.00
391-Scooby Doo (TV)	3.20	8.00	16.00
392-Bugs Bunny & Yosemite Sam	1.20	3.00	6.00

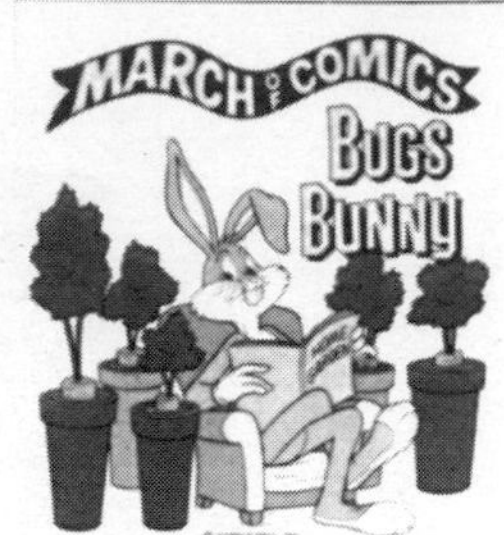

March of Comics #452 © Warner Bros.

March of Comics #453 © WEST

Marc Spector: Moon Knight #34 © MEG

	GD25	FN65	NM94
393-New Terrytoons (Heckle & Jeckle) (TV)	1.20	3.00	6.00
394-Lassie (TV)	2.40	6.00	12.00
395-Woodsy Owl	1.20	3.00	6.00
396-Baby Snoots	1.60	4.00	8.00
397-Beep-Beep & Daffy Duck (TV)	1.20	3.00	6.00
398-Wacky Witch	1.20	3.00	6.00
399-Turok, Son of Stone; new-a	11.00	32.00	75.00
400-Tom and Jerry	1.20	3.00	6.00
401-Baby Snoots (1975) (r/#371)	1.60	4.00	8.00
402-Daffy Duck (r/#313)	1.00	2.50	5.00
403-Bugs Bunny (r/#343)	1.20	3.00	6.00
404-Space Family Robinson (TV)(r/#328)	10.00	30.00	65.00
405-Cracky	1.00	2.50	5.00
406-Little Lulu (r/#355)	2.40	6.00	12.00
407-Smokey the Bear (TV)(r/#362)	1.20	3.00	6.00
408-Turok, Son of Stone; c-r/Turok #20 w/changes; new-a	8.35	25.00	55.00
409-Pink Panther (TV)	1.00	2.50	5.00
410-Wacky Witch	.80	2.00	4.00
411-Lassie (TV)(r/#324)	2.40	6.00	12.00
412-New Terrytoons (1975) (TV)	.80	2.00	4.00
413-Daffy Duck (1976)(r/#331)	.80	2.00	4.00
414-Space Family Robinson (r/#328)	8.35	25.00	55.00
415-Bugs Bunny (r/#329)	.80	2.00	4.00
416-Beep-Beep, the Road Runner (r/#353)(TV)	.80	2.00	4.00
417-Little Lulu (r/#323)	2.40	6.00	12.00
418-Pink Panther (r/#384) (TV)	.80	2.00	4.00
419-Baby Snoots (r/#377)	1.00	2.50	5.00
420-Woody Woodpecker	.80	2.00	4.00
421-Tweety & Sylvester	.80	2.00	4.00
422-Wacky Witch (r/#386)	.80	2.00	4.00
423-Little Monsters	1.00	2.50	5.00
424-Cracky (12/76)	.80	2.00	4.00
425-Daffy Duck	.80	2.00	4.00
426-Underdog (TV)	3.00	7.50	15.00
427-Little Lulu (r/#335)	1.60	4.00	8.00
428-Bugs Bunny	.60	1.50	3.00
429-The Pink Panther (TV)	.60	1.50	3.00
430-Beep-Beep, the Road Runner (TV)	.60	1.50	3.00
431-Baby Snoots	.80	2.00	4.00
432-Lassie (TV)	1.20	3.00	6.00
433-437: 433-Tweety & Sylvester. 434-Wacky Witch. 435-New Terrytoons (TV). 436-Wacky Advs. of Cracky. 437-Daffy Duck	.60	1.50	3.00
438-Underdog (TV)	3.00	7.50	15.00
439-Little Lulu (r/#349)	1.60	4.00	8.00
440-442,444-446: 440-Bugs Bunny. 441-The Pink Panther (TV). 442-Beep-Beep, the Road Runner (TV). 444-Tom and Jerry. 445-Tweety and Sylvester. 446-Wacky Witch	.60	1.50	3.00
443-Baby Snoots	.80	2.00	4.00
447-Mighty Mouse	1.20	3.00	6.00
448-455,457,458: 448-Cracky. 449-Pink Panther (TV). 450-Baby Snoots 451-Tom and Jerry. 452-Bugs Bunny. 453-Popeye. 454-Woody Woodpecker. 455-Beep-Beep, the Road Runner (TV). 457-Tweety & Sylvester. 458-Wacky Witch	.60	1.50	3.00
456-Little Lulu (r/#369)	1.20	3.00	6.00
459-Mighty Mouse	1.20	3.00	6.00
460-466: 460-Daffy Duck. 461-The Pink Panther (TV). 462-Baby Snoots. 463-Tom and Jerry. 464-Bugs Bunny. 465-Popeye. 466-Woody Woodpecker	.60	1.50	3.00
467-Underdog (TV)	2.40	6.00	12.00
468-Little Lulu (r/#385)	.80	2.00	4.00
469-Tweety & Sylvester	.60	1.50	3.00
470-Wacky Witch	.60	1.50	3.00
471-Mighty Mouse	.80	2.50	5.00
472-474,476-478: 472-Heckle & Jeckle(12/80). 473-Pink Panther(1/81)(TV). 474-Baby Snoots. 476-Bugs Bunny. 477-Popeye. 478-Woody Woodpecker	.60	1.50	3.00
475-Little Lulu (r/#323)	.80	2.00	4.00
479-Underdog (TV)	2.00	5.00	10.00
480-482: 480-Tom and Jerry. 481-Tweety and Sylvester. 482-Wacky Witch	.60	1.50	3.00
483-Mighty Mouse	.80	2.00	5.00
484-487: 484-Heckle & Jeckle. 485-Baby Snoots. 486-The Pink Panther (TV). 487-Bugs Bunny	.60	1.50	3.00
488-Little Lulu (4/82) (r/#335)	.80	2.00	4.00

MARCH OF CRIME (Formerly My Love Affair #1-6) (See Fox Giants)
No. 7, July, 1950 - No. 2, Sept, 1950; No. 3, Sept, 1951
Fox Features Syndicate

	GD25	FN65	NM94
7(#1)(7/50)-True crime stories; Wood-a	30.00	94.00	240.00
2(9/50)-Wood-a (exceptional)	29.00	86.00	230.00
3(9/51)	12.00	38.00	100.00

MARCO POLO
1962 (Movie classic)
Charlton Comics Group

	GD25	FN65	NM94
nn (Scarce)-Glanzman-c/a (25 pgs.)	9.50	28.50	95.00

MARC SPECTOR: MOON KNIGHT (Also see Moon Knight)
June, 1989 - No. 60, Mar, 1994 ($1.50/$1.75, direct sales)
Marvel Comics

	GD25	FN65	NM94
1-21: 4-Intro new Midnight. 8,9-Punisher app. 15-Silver Sable app. 20-Guice-c. 21-23-Cowan-c(p). 19-21-Spider-Man & Punisher app.		.80	2.00
22-24,26-31,34: 34-Last $1.50-c		.70	1.75
25-($2.50, 52 pgs.)-Ghost Rider app.		1.00	2.50
32,33,35-38: 32,33-Hobgoblin II (Macendale) & Spider-Man (in black costume) app. 35-38-Punisher story		.80	2.00
39-49,51-54: 42-44-Infinity War x-over. 46-Demogoblin app. 51,53-Gambit app.		.70	1.75
50-($2.95, 56 pgs.)-Special die-cut cover		1.20	3.00
55-New look & Stephen Platt-c/a begin		1.00	2.50
56,57-Platt-c/a. 57-Spider-Man-c/story		1.00	2.50
58-60: 58,59-S. Platt-c only. 60-S.Platt-c/a; Moon Knight dies.		.80	2.00
...: Divided We Fall ($4.95, 52 pgs.)		2.00	5.00
Special 1 (1992, $2.50)		1.00	2.50

NOTE: *Heath c/a-4. Platt c-a*

MARGARET O'BRIEN (See The Adventures of...)

MARGE'S LITTLE LULU (Little Lulu #207 on)
No. 74, 6/45 - No. 164, 7-9/62; No. 165, 10/62 - No. 206, 8/72
Dell Publishing Co./Gold Key #165-206

Marjorie Henderson Buell, born in Philadelphia, Pa., in 1904, created Little Lulu, a cartoon character that appeared weekly in the Saturday Evening Post from Feb. 23, 1935 through Dec. 30, 1944. She was not responsible for any of the comic books. **John Stanley** did pencils only on all Little Lulu comics through at least #135 (1959). He did pencils and inks on Four Color #74 & 97. **Irving Tripp** began inking stories from #1 on, and remained the comic's illustrator throughout its entire run. **Stanley** did storyboards (layouts), pencils, and scripts in all cases and inking only on covers. His word balloons were written in cursive. **Tripp** and occasionally other artists at Western Publ. in Poughkeepsie, N.Y. blew up the pencilled pages, inked the blowups, and lettered them. **Arnold Drake** did storyboards, pencils and scripts starting with #197 (1970) on, amidst reprinted issues. **Buell** sold her rights exclusively to Western Publ. in Dec., 1971. The earlier issues had to be approved by **Buell** prior to publication.

	GD25	FN65	NM94
Four Color 74('45)-Intro Lulu, Tubby & Alvin	91.00	273.00	1000.00
Four Color 97(2/46)	43.00	128.00	470.00
(Above two books are all John Stanley - cover, pencils, and inks.)			
Four Color 110('46)-1st Alvin Story Telling Time; 1st app. Willy	31.00	92.00	335.00
Four Color 115-1st app. Boys' Clubhouse	31.00	92.00	335.00
Four Color 120, 131: 120-1st app. Eddie	26.00	79.00	290.00
Four Color 139('47),146,158	25.00	74.00	270.00

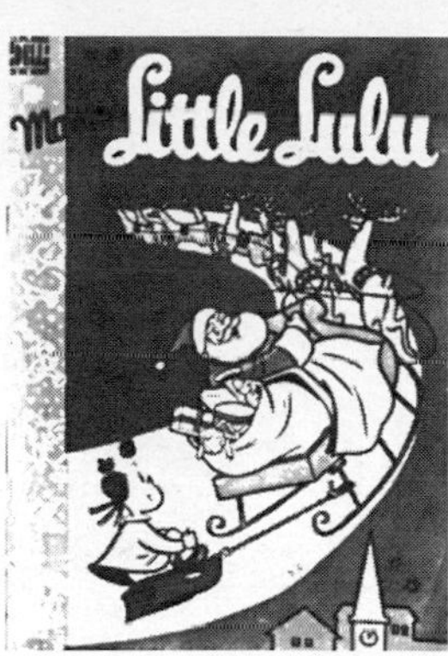

Marge's Little Lulu #7 © WEST

Marines In Battle #1 © ATLAS

The Mark #3 © DH

	GD25	FN65	NM94
Four Color 165 (10/47)-Smokes doll hair & has wild hallucinations. 1st Tubby detective story	25.00	74.00	270.00
1(1-2/48)-Lulu's Diary feature begins	52.00	155.00	565.00
2-1st app. Gloria; 1st Tubby story in a L.L. comic; 1st app. Miss Feeny	26.00	79.00	290.00
3-5	24.00	71.00	260.00
6-10: 7-1st app. Annie; Xmas-c	17.00	52.00	190.00
11-20: 18-X-Mas-c. 19-1st app. Wilbur. 20-1st app. Mr. McNabbem	15.00	45.00	165.00
21-30: 26-r/F.C. 110. 30-Xmas-c	12.00	35.00	130.00
31-38,40: 35-1st Mumday story	11.00	32.00	115.00
39-Intro. Witch Hazel in "That Awful Witch Hazel"	11.00	34.00	125.00
41-60: 42-Xmas-c. 45-2nd Witch Hazel app. 49-Gives Stanley & others credit	10.00	30.00	110.00
61-80: 63-1st app. Chubby (Tubby's cousin). 68-1st app. Prof. Cleff. 78-Xmas-c. 80-Intro. Little Itch (2/55)	7.00	20.00	75.00
81-99: 90-Xmas-c	5.00	15.00	55.00
100	5.50	16.50	60.00
101-130: 123-1st app. Fifi	4.50	13.50	50.00
131-164: 135-Last Stanley-p	3.60	11.00	40.00
165-Giant; ...in Paris ('62)	11.00	33.00	120.00
166-Giant; ...Christmas Diary (1962 - '63)	11.00	33.00	120.00
167-169	2.75	8.00	30.00
170,172,175,176,178-196,198-200-Stanley-r. 182-1st app. Little Scarecrow Boy	1.40	4.20	14.00
171,173,174,177,197	1.00	3.00	8.00
201,203,206-Last issue to carry Marge's name		2.40	6.00
202,204,205-Stanley-r	1.00	3.00	9.00
...& Tubby in Japan (12¢)(5-7/62) 01476-207	5.50	16.50	60.00
...Summer Camp 1(8/67-G.K.-Giant) '57-58-r	3.60	11.00	42.00
...Trick 'N' Treat 1(12¢)(12/62-Gold Key)	4.50	13.50	50.00

NOTE: *See Dell Giant Comics #23, 29, 36, 42, 50, & Dell Giants for annuals. All Giants not by Stanley from L.L. on Vacation (7/54) on. Irving Tripp a-#1-on. Christmas c-7, 18, 30, 42, 78, 90, 126, 166, 250. Summer Camp issues #173, 177, 181, 189, 197, 201, 206.*

MARGE'S LITTLE LULU (See Golden Comics Digest #19, 23, 27, 29, 33, 36, 40, 43, 46, & March of Comics #251, 267, 275, 293, 307, 323, 335, 349, 355, 369, 385, 406, 417, 427, 439, 456, 468, 475, 488)

MARGE'S TUBBY (Little Lulu)(See Dell Giants)
No. 381, Aug, 1952 - No. 49, Dec-Feb, 1961-62
Dell Publishing Co./Gold Key

	GD25	FN65	NM94
Four Color 381(#1)-Stanley script; Irving Tripp-a	17.00	52.00	190.00
Four Color 430,444-Stanley-a	10.00	30.00	110.00
Four Color 461 (4/53)-1st Tubby & Men From Mars story; Stanley-a	9.00	26.00	95.00
5 (7-9/53)-Stanley-a	7.00	20.00	75.00
6-10	5.00	15.00	55.00
11-20	3.60	11.00	42.00
21-30	3.00	9.00	32.00
31-49	2.50	7.50	27.00
...& the Little Men From Mars No. 30020-410(10/64-G.K.)-25¢, 68 pgs.	6.40	19.00	70.00

NOTE: ***John Stanley** did all storyboards & scripts through at least #35 (1959). **Lloyd White** did all art except F.C. 381, 430, 444, 461 & #5.*

MARGIE (See My Little...)

MARGIE (TV)
No. 1307, Mar-May, 1962 - No. 2, July-Sept, 1962 (Photo-c)
Dell Publishing Co.

	GD25	FN65	NM94
Four Color 1307(#1), 2	3.60	11.00	40.00

MARGIE COMICS (Formerly Comedy Comics; Reno Browne #50 on)
(Also see Cindy Comics & Teen Comics)
No. 35, Winter, 1946-47 - No. 49, Dec, 1949
Marvel Comics (ACI)

	GD25	FN65	NM94
35	10.00	30.00	75.00
36-38,42,45,47-49	6.35	19.00	40.00
39,41,43(2),44,46-Kurtzman's "Hey Look"	9.00	27.00	55.00
40-Three "Hey Looks", three "Giggles 'n' Grins" by Kurtzman	10.00	30.00	65.00

MARINES (See Tell It to the...)

MARINES ATTACK
Aug, 1964 - No. 9, Feb-Mar, 1966
Charlton Comics

	GD25	FN65	NM94
1	2.50	7.50	20.00
2-9	1.50	4.50	12.00

MARINES AT WAR (Formerly Tales of the Marines #4)
No. 5, Apr, 1957 - No. 7, Aug, 1957
Atlas Comics (OPI)

	GD25	FN65	NM94
5-7	5.70	17.00	35.00

NOTE: ***Colan** a-5. **Drucker** a-5. **Everett** a-5. **Maneely** a-5. **Orlando** a-7. **Severin** c-5.*

MARINES IN ACTION
June, 1955 - No. 14, Sept, 1957
Atlas News Co.

	GD25	FN65	NM94
1-Rock Murdock, Boot Camp Brady begin	7.85	23.50	55.00
2-14	5.70	17.00	35.00

NOTE: ***Berg** a-2, 8, 9, 11, 14. **Heath** c-2, 9. **Maneely** c-1. **Severin** a-4; c-7-11, 14.*

MARINES IN BATTLE
Aug, 1954 - No. 25, Sept, 1958
Atlas Comics (ACI No. 1-12/WPI No. 13-25)

	GD25	FN65	NM94
1-Heath-c; Iron Mike McGraw by Heath; history of U.S. Marine Corps. begins	13.00	39.00	100.00
2-Heath-c	8.35	25.00	55.00
3-6,8-10: 4-Last precode (2/55)	5.70	17.00	40.00
7-Kubert/Moskowitz-a (6 pgs.)	7.00	21.00	45.00
11-16,18-21,24	5.70	17.00	35.00
17-Williamson-a (3 pgs.)	8.00	24.00	50.00
22,25-Torres-a	5.70	17.00	40.00
23-Crandall-a; Mark Murdock app.	7.00	21.00	45.00

NOTE: ***Berg** a-22. **G. Colan** a-22, 23. **Drucker** a-6. **Everett** a-4, 15; c-21. **Heath** c-1, 2, 4. **Maneely** c-23, 24. **Orlando** a-14. **Pakula** a-6, 23. **Powell** a-16. **Severin** a-22; c-12. **Sinnott** a-23. **Tuska** a-15.*

MARINE WAR HEROES (Charlton Premiere #19 on)
Jan, 1964 - No. 18, Mar, 1967
Charlton Comics

	GD25	FN65	NM94
1-Montes/Bache-c/a	2.50	7.50	20.00
2-18: 14,18-Montes/Bache-a	1.50	4.50	12.00

MARK, THE (Also see Mayhem)
Dec, 1993 - No. 4, Mar, 1994 ($2.50, limited series)
Dark Horse Comics

	GD25	FN65	NM94
1-4		1.00	2.50

MARK HAZZARD: MERC
Nov, 1986 - No. 12, Oct, 1987 (75¢)
Marvel Comics Group

	GD25	FN65	NM94
1-12: Morrow-a			.80
Annual 1 (11/87, $1.25)			1.25

MARK OF ZORRO (See Zorro, Four Color #228)

MARKSMAN, THE (Also see Champions)
Jan, 1988 - No. 5, 1988 ($1.95)
Hero Comics

	GD25	FN65	NM94
1-5: 1-Rose begins. 1-3-Origin The Marksman		.80	2.00
Annual 1 ('88, $2.75, 52pgs)-Champions app.		1.10	2.80

MARK STEEL
1967, 1968, 1972 (Giveaway) (24 pgs.)
American Iron & Steel Institute

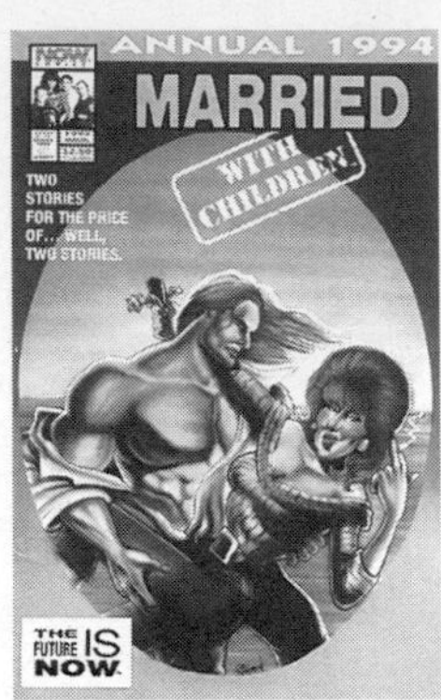

Married... With Children 1994 Annual © FOX

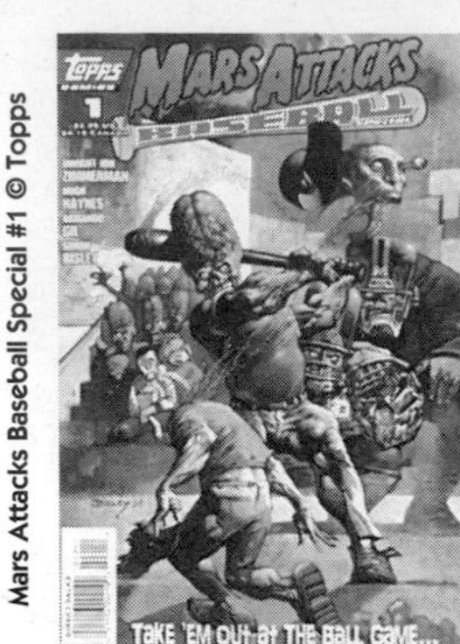

Mars Attacks Baseball Special #1 © Topps

Martha Washington Goes to War #4 © Frank Miller & Dave Gibbons

GD25 FN65 NM94

1967,1968- “Journey of Discovery with...”; Neal Adams art 2.25 6.75 18.00
1972- “...Fights Pollution”; N. Adams-a 1.10 3.30 9.00

MARK TRAIL
Oct, 1955; No. 5, Summer, 1959
Standard Magazines (Hall Syndicate)/Fawcett Publ. No. 5

1(1955)-Sunday strip-r 5.70 17.00 35.00
5(1959) 4.00 10.00 20.00
...Adventure Book of Nature 1 (Summer, 1958, 25¢, Pines)-100 pg. Giant; Special Camp Issue; contains 78 Sunday strip-r 7.15 21.50 50.00

MARMADUKE MONK
No date; 1963 (10¢)
I. W. Enterprises/Super Comics

I.W. Reprint 1 (nd) 2.40 6.00
Super Reprint 14 (1963)-r/Monkeyshines Comics #? 2.40 6.00

MARMADUKE MOUSE
Spring, 1946 - No. 65, Dec, 1956 (Early issues: 52 pgs.)
Quality Comics Group (Arnold Publ.)

1-Funny animal 14.00 41.00 110.00
2 7.85 23.50 55.00
3-10 5.70 17.00 40.00
11-30 5.00 15.00 30.00
31-65: Later issues are 36 pgs. 4.00 12.00 24.00
Super Reprint #14(1963) 1.50 4.50 12.00

MARRIED ... WITH CHILDREN (TV)
June, 1990 - No. 7, Feb, 1991(12/90 inside) ($1.75)
V2#1, Sept, 1991 - No. 12, 1992 ($1.95)
Now Comics

1-7: Based on Fox TV show. 2-Photo-c .70 1.75
1,2-2nd printing ($1.75) .70 1.75
V2#1-12: 1,4,5,9-Photo-c .70 1.75
...Buck's Tale (6/94, $1.95) .80 2.00
...1994 Annual nn (2/94, $2.50, 52 pgs.)-Flip book format 1.00 2.50
Special 1 (7/92, $1.95)-Kelly Bundy photo-c/poster .80 2.00

MARRIED ... WITH CHILDREN: KELLY BUNDY
Aug, 1992 - No. 3, Oct, 1992 ($1.95, limited series)
Now Comics

1-3: Kelly Bundy photo-c & poster in each .80 2.00

MARRIED ... WITH CHILDREN: QUANTUM QUARTET
Oct, 1993 - No. 4, 1994, ($1.95, limited series)
Now Comics

1-4: Fantastic Four parody .80 2.00

MARRIED ... WITH CHILDREN: 2099
June, 1993 - No. 3, Aug, 1993 ($1.95, limited series)
Now Comics

1-3 .80 2.00

MARS
Jan, 1984 - No. 12, Jan, 1985 ($1.00, Mando paper)
First Comics

nn: 1-12: Marc Hempel & Mark Wheatley story & art. 2-The Black Flame begins. 10-Dynamo Joe begins 1.00

MARS & BEYOND (Disney, TV)
No. 866, Dec, 1957
Dell Publishing Co.

Four Color 866-A Science feat. from Tomorrowland 8.00 25.00 90.00

MARS ATTACKS
May, 1994 - No. 5, Sept, 1994 ($2.95, limited series)
Topps Comics

1-5-Giffen story; flip books 1.60 4.00
Special Edition 1.50 4.50 12.00
Trade paperback (12/94, $12.95)-r/limited series plus new 8 pg. story 13.00

MARS ATTACKS
V2#1, 8/95 - V2#3, 10/95; V2#4, 1/96 - Present ($2.95, bi-monthly #6 on)
Topps Comics

V2#1-7: 1-Counterstrike storyline begins. 4-(1/96). 5-(1/96). 5,7-Brereton-c. 6-(3/96)-Simonson-c. 7-Story leads into Baseball Special #1. 1.20 3.00
Baseball Special 1 (6/96, $2.95)-Bisley-c. 1.20 3.00

MARS ATTACKS HIGH SCHOOL
May, 1997 - No. 2, Sept, 1997 ($2.95, B&W, limited series)
Topps Comics

1,2-Stelfreeze-c 1.20 3.00

MARS ATTACKS IMAGE
Dec, 1996 - No. 4, Mar, 1997 ($2.50, limited series)
Topps Comics

1-4-Giffen-s/Smith/Sienkiewicz-a 1.00 2.50

MARS ATTACKS THE SAVAGE DRAGON
Dec, 1996 - No. 4, Mar, 1997 ($2.95, limited series)
Topps Comics

1-4: 1--w/bound-in card 1.20 3.00

MARSHAL BLUEBERRY (See Blueberry)
1991 (14.95, graphic novel)
Marvel Comics (Epic Comics)

1-Moebius-a 1.85 5.50 15.00

MARSHAL LAW (Also see Crime And Punishment: Marshall Law...)
Oct, 1987 - No. 6, May, 1989 ($1.95, mature readers) (See Pinhead Vs....)
Marvel Comics (Epic Comics)

1-6 .80 2.00

M.A.R.S. PATROL TOTAL WAR (Formerly Total War #1,2)
No. 3, Sept, 1966 - No. 10, Aug, 1969 (All-Painted-c except #7)
Gold Key

3-Wood-a 4.00 12.00 45.00
4-10 2.00 6.00 22.00

MARTHA WASHINGTON (Also see Dark Horse Presents Fifth Anniversary Special, Dark Horse Presents #100-4, Give Me Liberty, Happy Birthday Martha Washington & San Diego Comicon Comics #2)

MARTHA WASHINGTON GOES TO WAR
May, 1994 - No. 5, Sept, 1994 ($2.95, limited series)
Dark Horse Comics (Legend)

1-5-Miller scripts; Gibbons-c/a 1.20 3.00
TPB ($17.95) r/#1-5 17.95

MARTHA WASHINGTON STRANDED IN SPACE
Nov, 1995 ($2.95, one-shot)
Dark Horse Comics (Legend)

nn-Miller-s/Gibbons-a; Big Guy app. 1.20 3.00

MARTHA WAYNE (See The Story of...)

MARTIAN MANHUNTER (See Detective Comics & Showcase '95 #9)
May, 1988 - No. 4, Aug,. 1988 ($1.25, limited series)
DC Comics

1-4: 1,4-Batman app. 2-Batman cameo 1.25
Special 1-(1996, $3.50) 3.50

MARTIN KANE (William Gargan as... Private Eye)(Stage/Screen/Radio/TV)
No. 4, June, 1950 - No. 2, Aug, 1950 (Formerly My Secret Affair)
Fox Features Syndicate (Hero Books)

Marvel Adventure #3 © MEG

Marvel Collector's Item Classics #8 © MEG

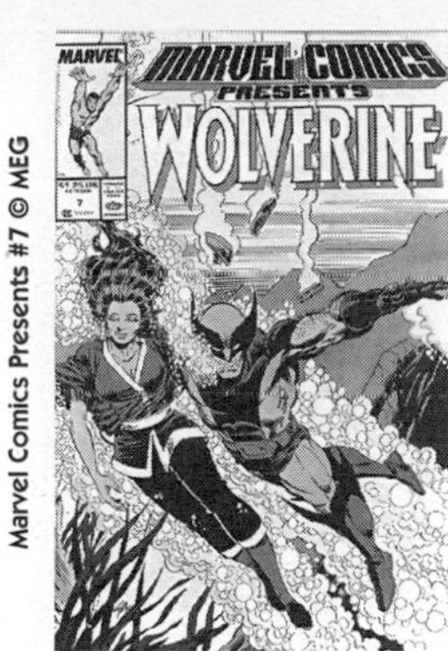

Marvel Comics Presents #7 © MEG

GD25 FN65 NM94

4(#1)-True crime stories; Wood-c/a(2); used in **SOTI**, pg. 160; photo back-c 25.00 75.00 180.00
2-Wood/Orlando story, 5 pgs; Wood-a(2) 19.00 58.00 140.00

MARTY MOUSE
No date (1958?) (10¢)
I. W. Enterprises

1-Reprint 1.00 3.00 8.00

MARVEL ACTION HOUR FEATURING IRON MAN (TV cartoon)
Nov, 1994 - No. 8, June, 1995 ($1.50/$2.95)
Marvel Comics

1-8: Based on cartoon series 1.50
1 ($2.95)-Polybagged w/16 pg Marvel Action Hour Preview & acetate print 1.20 3.00

MARVEL ACTION HOUR FEATURING THE FANTASTIC FOUR (TV cartoon)
Nov, 1994 - No. 8, June, 1995 ($1.50/$2.95)
Marvel Comics

1-8: Based on cartoon series 1.50
1-($2.95)-Polybagged w/ 16 pg. Marvel Action Hour Preview & acetate print 1.20 3.00

MARVEL ACTION UNIVERSE (TV cartoon)
Jan, 1989 ($1.00, one-shot)
Marvel Comics

1-r/Spider-Man And His Amazing Friends 1.00

MARVEL ADVENTURES
Apr, 1997 - Present ($1.50)
Marvel Comics

1-13-"Animated style": 1-Hulk-c/app. 2-Spider-Man. 3-X-Men. 4-Hulk. 5-Spider-Man & X-Men. 6-Spider-Man & Human Torch. 7-Hulk 8-X-Men. 9-Fantastic Four. 10-Silver Surfer 1.50

MARVEL ADVENTURES STARRING DAREDEVIL (...Adventure #3 on)
Dec, 1975 - No. 6, Oct, 1976
Marvel Comics Group

1 2.40 6.00
2-6-r/Daredevil #22-27 by Colan 1.20 3.00

MARVEL AND DC PRESENT FEATURING THE UNCANNY X-MEN AND THE NEW TEEN TITANS
1982 ($2.00, 68 pgs., one-shot, Baxter paper)
Marvel Comics Group/DC Comics

1-3rd app. Deathstroke the Terminator; Darkseid app.; Simonson/Austin-c/a 2.25 6.75 18.00

MARVEL BOY (Astonishing #3 on; see Marvel Super Action #4)
Dec, 1950 - No. 2, Feb, 1951
Marvel Comics (MPC)

1-Origin Marvel Boy by Russ Heath 74.00 225.00 670.00
2-Everett-a 58.00 175.00 525.00

MARVEL CHILLERS (Also see Giant-Size Chillers)
Oct, 1975 - No. 7, Oct, 1976 (All 25¢ issues)
Marvel Comics Group

1,2-Intro. Modred the Mystic, ends #2; Kane-c(p) 1.60 4.00
3-Tigra, the Were-Woman begins (origin), ends #7 (see Giant-Size Creatures #1). Chaykin/Wrightson-c. 1.00 3.00 8.00
4,5,7: 4-Kraven app. 5,6-Red Wolf app. 7-Kirby-c; Tuska-p 1.20 3.00
6-Byrne-a(p); Buckler-c(p) 1.60 4.00
NOTE: ***Bolle** a-1. **Buckler** c-2.*

MARVEL CLASSICS COMICS SERIES FEATURING... (Also see Pendulum Illustrated Classics)
1976 - No. 36, Dec, 1978 (52 pgs., no ads)
Marvel Comics Group

GD25 FN65 NM94

1-Dr. Jekyll and Mr. Hyde 1.50 4.50 12.00
2-27,29-36 2.40 6.00
28-1st Golden-c/a; The Pit and the Pendulum 1.10 3.30 9.00
NOTE: ***Adkins** c-1i, 4i, 12i. **Alcala** a-34i; c-34. **Bolle** a-35. **Buscema** c-17p, 19p, 26p. **Golden** c/a-28. **Gil Kane** c-1-16p, 21p, 22p, 24p, 32p. **Nebres** a-5; c-24i. **Nino** a-2, 8, 12. **Redondo** a-1, 9. No. 1-12 were reprinted from Pendulum Illustrated Classics.*

MARVEL COLLECTOR'S EDITION
1992 (Ordered thru mail with Charleston Chew candy wrapper)
Marvel Comics

1-Flip-book format; Spider-Man, Silver Surfer, Wolverine (by Sam Kieth), & Ghost Rider stories; Wolverine back-c by Kieth .90 2.25

MARVEL COLLECTOR'S EDITION: X-MEN
1993 (3-3/4x6-1/2")
Marvel Comics

1-4-Pizza Hut giveaways .80 2.00

MARVEL COLLECTORS' ITEM CLASSICS (Marvel's Greatest #23 on)
Feb, 1965 - No. 22, Aug, 1969 (25¢, 68 pgs.)
Marvel Comics Group(ATF)

1-Fantastic Four, Spider-Man, Thor, Hulk, Iron Man-r begin 6.00 18.00 60.00
2 (4/66) 3.00 9.00 30.00
3,4 2.50 7.50 24.00
5-10 2.25 6.75 18.00
11-22: 22-r/The Man in the Ant Hill/TTA #27 1.50 4.50 12.00
NOTE: *All reprints; **Ditko, Kirby** art in all.*

MARVEL COMICS (Marvel Mystery Comics #2 on)
Oct, Nov, 1939
Timely Comics (Funnies, Inc.)

NOTE: The first issue was originally dated October 1939. Most copies have a black circle stamped over the date (on cover and inside) with "November" printed over it. However, some copies do not have the November overprint and could have a higher value. Most No. 1's have printing defects, i.e., tilted pages which caused trimming into the panels usually on right side and bottom. Covers exist with and without gloss finish.

GD25 FN65 VF82 NM94

1-Origin Sub-Mariner by Bill Everett(1st newsstand app.); 1st 8 pgs. were produced for Motion Picture Funnies Weekly #1 which was probably not distributed outside of advance copies; intro Human Torch by Carl Burgos, Kazar the Great (1st Tarzan clone), & Jungle Terror(only app.); intro. The Angel by Gustavson, The Masked Raider & his horse Lightning (ends #12); cover by sci/fi pulp illustrator Frank R. Paul 12,000.00 30,700.00 61,400.00 108,000.00
(Estimated up to 50 total copies exist, 4 in NM/Mint)

MARVEL COMICS PRESENTS
Early Sept, 1988 - No. 175, Feb, 1995 ($1.25/$1.50/$1.75, bi-weekly)
Marvel Comics (Midnight Sons imprint #143 on)

GD25 FN65 NM94

1-Wolverine by Buscema in #1-10 2.40 6.00
2-5 1.20 3.00
6-10: 6-Sub-Mariner app. 10-Colossus begins 1.00 2.50
11-32,34-37: 17-Cyclops begins. 19-1st app. Damage Control. 24-Havok begins. 25-Origin/1st app. Nth Man. 26-Hulk begins by Rogers. 29-Quasar app. 31-Excalibur begins by Austin (i). 32-McFarlane-a(p). 37-Devil-Slayer app. 1.50
33-Capt. America; Jim Lee-a 1.10 2.75
38-Wolverine begins by Buscema; Hulk app. 1.20 3.00
39-47,51-53: 39-Spider-Man app. 46-Liefeld Wolverine-c. 51-53-Wolverine by Rob Liefeld 1.00 2.50
48-50-Wolverine & Spider-Man team-up by Erik Larsen-c/a. 48-Wasp app. 49,50-Savage Dragon prototype app. by Larsen. 50-Silver Surfer. 50-53-Comet Man; Bill Mumy scripts 1.20 3.00
54-61-Wolverine/Hulk story: 54-Werewolf by Night begins; The Shroud by Ditko. 58-Iron Man by Ditko. 59-Punisher 1.20 3.00
62-Deathlok & Wolverine stories 1.20 3.00
63-Wolverine 1.00 2.50

Marvel Comics Presents #72 © MEG

Marvel Double Feature #19 © MEG

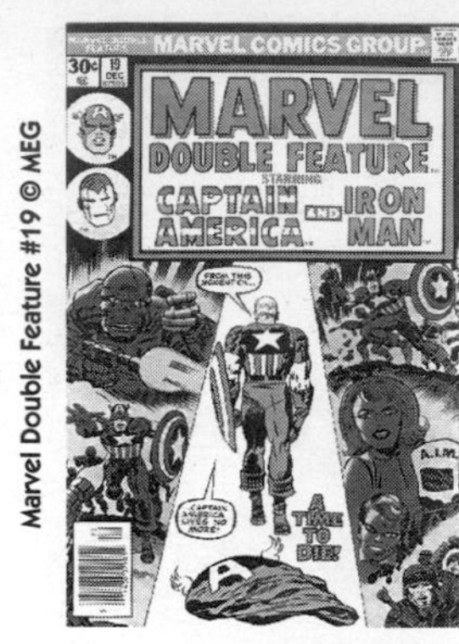

Marvel Family #29 © FAW

64-71-Wolverine/Ghost Rider 8-part story. 70-Liefeld Ghost Rider/ Wolverine-c 1.00 2.50

72-Begin 13-part Weapon-X story (Wolverine origin) by B. Windsor-Smith (prologue) 1.60 4.00

73-Weapon-X part 1; Black Knight, Sub-Mariner 1.20 3.00

74-Weapon-X part 2; Black Knight, Sub-Mariner 1.00 2.50

75-80: 76-Death's Head story. 77-Mr. Fantastic story. 78-Iron Man by Steacy 80,81-Capt. America by Ditko/Austin 1.00 2.50

81-84: 81-Daredevil by Rogers/Williamson. 82-Power Man. 83-Human Torch by Ditko(a&scripts); $1.00-c direct, $1.25 newsstand. 84-Last Weapon-X (24 pg. conclusion) .90 2.25

85-Begin 8-part Wolverine story by Sam Keith (c/a); 1st Kieth-a on Wolverine; begin 8-part Beast story by Jae Lee(p) with Liefeld part pencils #85,86; 1st Jae Lee-a (assisted w/Liefeld, 1991) 1.80 4.50

86-89-Wolverine, Beast stories continue 1.00 2.50

90-Begin 8-part Ghost Rider & Cable story, ends #97; begin flip book format with two covers 1.20 3.00

91-94: 93-Begin 6-part Wolverine story, ends #98 .80 2.00

95-98: 95-Begin $1.50-c. 98-Begin 2-part Ghost Rider story 1.50

99,101-107,112-116: 99-Spider-Man story. 101-Begin 6-part Ghost Rider/Dr. Strange story & begin 8-part Wolverine/Nightcrawler story by Colan/ Williamson; Punisher story. 107-Begin 6-part Ghost Rider/Werewolf by Night story. 112-Demogoblin story by Colan/Williamson; Pip the Troll story w/Starlin scripts & Gamora cameo. 113-Begin 6-part Giant-Man & begin 6-part Ghost Rider/Iron Fist stories 1.50

100-Full-length Ghost Rider/Wolverine story by Sam Keith w/Tim Vigil assists; anniversary issue, non flip-book 1.50

108-111: 108-Begin 4 part Thanos story; Starlin scripts. 109-Begin 8 part Wolverine/Typhoid Mary story. 111-Iron Fist 1.50

117-Preview of Ravage 2099 (1st app.); begin 6 part Wolverine/Venom story w/Kieth-a 1.50

118-Preview of Doom 2099 (1st app.) 1.50

119-142,147-152: 119-Begin Ghost Rider/Cloak & Dagger story by Colan. 120,136,138-Spider-Man. 123-Begin 8-part Ghost Rider/Typhoid Mary story; begin 4-part She Hulk story; begin 8-partWolverine/Lynx story. 125-Begin 6-part Iron Fist story. 129-Jae Lee back-c. 130-Begin 6-part Ghost Rider/ Cage story. 131-Begin 6-part Ghost Rider/Cage story. 132-Begin 5-part Wolverine story. 133-136-Iron Fist vs. Sabretooth. 136-Daredevil. 137-Begin 6-part Wolverine story & 6-part Ghost Rider story. 147-Begin 2-part Vengeance-c/story w/new Ghost Rider. 149-Vengeance-c/story w/new Ghost Rider. 150-Silver ink-c; begin 2-part Bloody Mary story w/Typhoid Mary, Wolverine, Daredevil, new Ghost Rider; intro Steel Raven. 152-Begin 4-part Wolverine, 4-part War Machine, 4-part Vengeance, 3-part Moon Knight stories; same date as War Machine #1 .70 1.75

143-146: ($1.75)-Siege of Darkness parts 3,6,11,14; all have spot-varnished covers. 143-Ghost Rider/Scarlet Witch; intro new Werewolf. 144-Begin 2-part Morbius story. 145-Begin 2-part Nightstalkers story. .70 1.75

153-175: 153-$1.75-c begins. 153-155-Bound-in Spider-Man trading card sheet .70 1.75

NOTE: ***Austin*** *a-31-37i; c(i)-48, 50, 99, 122.* ***Buscema*** *a-1-10, 38-47; c-6.* ***Byrne*** *a-79; c-71.* ***Colan*** *a(p)-36, 37.* ***Colan/Williamson*** *a-101-108.* ***Ditko*** *a-7p, 10, 56p, 58, 80, 81, 83.* ***Guice*** *a-62.* ***Sam Kieth*** *a-85-92, 117-122; c-85-98, 99p, 100-108, 117, 118, 120-122; back c-109-113, 117.* ***Jae Lee*** *c-129(back).* ***Liefeld*** *a-51, 52, 53p(2), 85p; c-46, 70.* ***McFarlane*** *c-32.* ***Mooney*** *a-73.* ***Rogers*** *a-26, 38, 46i, 81p.* ***Russell*** *a-10i; c-4i.* ***Saltares*** *a-8p(early), 38-45p.* ***Simonson*** *c-1.* ***B. Smith*** *a-72-84; c-72-84.* ***P. Smith*** *c-34.* ***Sparling*** *a-33.* ***Starlin*** *a-89i.* ***Staton*** *a-74.* ***Steacy*** *a-78.* ***Sutton*** *a-101-105.* ***Williamson*** *c-62i. Two Gun Kid by* ***Gil Kane*** *in #116, 122.*

MARVEL COMICS SUPER SPECIAL, A (Marvel Super Special #5 on)
Sept, 1977 - No. 41(?), Nov, 1986 (nn 7) ($1.50, magazine)
Marvel Comics Group

1-Kiss, 40 pgs. comics plus photos & features; Simonson-a(p); also see Howard the Duck #12 7.50 22.50 75.00

2-Conan (1978) 2.40 6.00

3-Close Encounters of the Third Kind (1978); Simonson-a 2.40 6.00

4-The Beatles Story (1978)-Perez/Janson-a; has photos & articles 2.50 7.50 24.00

5-Kiss (1978)-Includes poster 6.00 18.00 60.00

6-Jaws II (1978) 2.40 6.00

7-Sgt. Pepper; Beatles movie adaptation; withdrawn from U.S. distribution

8-Battlestar Galactica; tabloid size ($1.50, 1978); adapts TV show 1.25 3.75 10.00

8-Modern-r of tabloid size; scarce 2.50 7.50 25.00

8-Battlestar Galactica; publ. in regular magazine format; low distribution ($1.50, 8-1/2x11") 1.25 3.75 10.00

9,10: 9-Conan. 10-Star-Lord 1.60 4.00

11-13-Weirdworld begins #11; 25 copy special press run of each with gold seal and signed by artists (Proof quality), Spring-June, 1979 8.00 24.00 80.00

11-13-Weirdworld (regular issues): 11-Fold-out centerfold 1.60 4.00

14-Miller-c(p); adapts movie "Meteor." 1.60 4.00

15-Star Trek with photos & pin-ups($1.50) 1.60 4.00

15-With $2.00 price (scarce); the price was changed at tail end of a 200,000 press run 1.60 4.00

16-20 (Movie adaptations): 16-Empire Strikes Back; Williamson-a. 17-Xanadu. 18-Raiders of the Lost Ark. 19-For Your Eyes Only (James Bond). 20-Dragonslayer 1.60 4.00

21-30 (Movie adaptations): 21-Conan. 22-Bladerunner; Williamson-a; Steranko-c. 23-Annie. 24-The Dark Crystal. 25-Rock and Rule-w/photos; artwork is from movie. 26-Octopussy (James Bond). 27-Return of the Jedi. 28-Krull; photo-c. 29-Tarzan of the Apes (Greystoke movie). 30-Indiana Jones and the Temple of Doom 2.00 5.00

31-41: 31-The Last Star Fighter. 32-The Muppets Take Manhattan. 33-Buckaroo Banzai. 34-Sheena. 35-Conan The Destroyer. 36-Dune. 37-2010. 38-Red Sonja. 39-Santa Claus:The Movie. 40-Labyrinth. 41-Howard The Duck 2.40 6.00

NOTE: ***J. Buscema*** *a-1, 2, 9, 11-13, 18p, 21, 35, 40; c-11(part), 12.* ***Chaykin*** *a-9, 19p; c-18, 19.* ***Colan*** *a(p)-6, 10, 14.* ***Morrow*** *a-34; c-1i, 34.* ***Nebres*** *a-11.* ***Spiegle*** *a-29.* ***Stevens*** *a-27.* ***Williamson*** *a-27. #22-28 contain photos from movies.*

MARVEL DOUBLE FEATURE
Dec, 1973 - No. 21, Mar, 1977
Marvel Comics Group

1-Capt. America, Iron Man-r/T.O.S. begin 1.25 3.75 10.00

2-10: 3-Last 20¢ issue 2.40 6.00

11-16,20,21 1.60 4.00

17-Story-r/Iron Man & Sub-Mariner #1; last 25ç issue 1.60 4.00

18,19-Colan/Craig-r from Iron Man #1 in both 2.00 5.00

NOTE: ***Colan*** *r-1-19p.* ***Craig*** *r-17-19i.* ***G. Kane*** *r-15p; c-15p.* ***Kirby*** *r-1-16p, 20, 21; c-17-20.*

MARVEL FAMILY (Also see Captain Marvel Adventures No. 18)
Dec, 1945 - No. 89, Jan, 1954
Fawcett Publications

1-Origin Captain Marvel, Captain Marvel Jr., Mary Marvel, & Uncle Marvel retold; origin/1st app. Black Adam 122.00 366.00 1100.00

2-The 3 Lt. Marvels & Uncle Marvel app. 58.00 174.00 515.00

3 40.00 120.00 360.00

4,5 36.00 108.00 300.00

6-10: 7-Shazam app. 30.00 90.00 240.00

11-20 23.00 68.00 180.00

21-30 17.50 53.00 140.00

31-40 15.00 45.00 120.00

41-46,48-50 12.00 36.00 95.00

47-Flying Saucer-c/story (5/50) 16.00 48.00 130.00

51-76,79,80,82-89: 79-Horror satire-c 11.30 34.00 90.00

77-Communist Threat-c 17.50 53.00 140.00

78,81-Used in **POP**, pg. 92,93. 12.00 38.00 100.00

MARVEL FANFARE (1st Series)
March, 1982 - No. 60, Jan, 1992 ($1.25/$2.25, slick paper, direct sales)
Marvel Comics Group

1-Spider-Man/Angel team-up; 1st Paul Smith-a (1st full story; see King Conan #7); Daredevil app. 2.00 5.00

Marvel Fanfare #55 (1st Series) © MEG

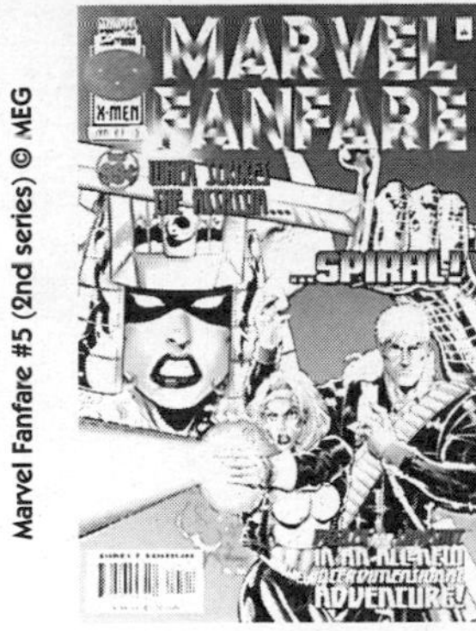

Marvel Fanfare #5 (2nd series) © MEG

Marvel Heroes & Legends 1997 © MEG

GD25 FN65 NM94

2-Spider-Man, Ka-Zar, The Angel. F.F. origin retold 1.60 4.00
3,4-X-Men & Ka-Zar. 4-Deathlok, Spidey app. 1.20 3.00
5-Dr. Strange, Capt. America 1.00 2.50
6-15: 6-Spider-Man, Scarlet Witch. 7-Incredible Hulk; D.D. back-up(also 15). 8-Dr. Strange; Wolf Boy begins. 9-Man-Thing. 10-13-Black Widow. 14-The Vision. 15-The Thing by Barry Smith, c/a .90 2.25
16-32,34-50: 16,17-Skywolf. 16-Sub-Mariner back-up. 17-Hulk back-up. 18-Capt. America by Miller. 19-Cloak and Dagger. 20-Thing/Dr. Strange. 21-Thing/Dr. Strange/Hulk. 22,23-Iron Man vs. Dr. Octopus. 24-26-Weird-world. 24-Wolverine back-up. 27-Daredevil/Spider-Man. 28-Alpha Flight. 29-Hulk. 30-Moon Knight. 31,32-Captain America. 34-37-Warriors Three. 38-Moon Knight/Dazzler. 39-Moon Knight/Hawkeye. 40-Angel/Rogue & Storm. 41-Dr. Strange. 42-Spider-Man. 43-Sub-Mariner/Human Torch. 44-Iron Man vs. Dr. Doom by Ken Steacy. 45-All pin-up issue by Steacy, Art Adams & others. 46-Fantastic Four. 47-Hulk. 48-She-Hulk/Vision. 49-Dr Strange/Nick Fury. 50-X-Factor; begin $2.25-c .90 2.25
33-X-Men, Wolverine app.; Punisher pin-up 1.00 2.50
51-($2.95, 52 pgs.)-Silver Surfer; Fantastic Four & Capt. Marvel app.; 51,52-Colan/Williamson back up (Dr. Strange) 1.20 3.00
52,53: 52-54-Black Knight; 53-Iron Man back up .90 2.25
54,55-Wolverine back-ups. 55-Power Pack 1.00 2.50
56-60: 56-59-Shanna the She-Devil. 58-Vision & Scarlet Witch back-up. 60-Black Panther/Rogue/Daredevil stories .90 2.25

NOTE: ***Art Adams*** *c-13.* ***Austin*** *a-1i, 4i, 33i, 38i; c-8i, 33i.* ***Buscema*** *a-51p.* ***Byrne*** *a-1p, 29, 48; c-29.* ***Chiodo*** *painted c-56-59.* ***Colan*** *a-51p.* ***Cowan/Simonson*** *c/a-60.* ***Golden*** *a-1, 2, 4p, 47; c-1, 2, 47.* ***Infantino*** *c/a(p)-8.* ***Gil Kane*** *a-8-11p.* ***Miller*** *a-18; c-1(Back-c), 18.* ***Perez*** *a-10, 11p, 12, 13p; c-10-13p.* ***Rogers*** *a-5p; c-5p.* ***Russell*** *a-5i, 6i, 8-11i, 43i; c-5i, 6.* ***Paul Smith*** *a-1p, 4p, 32, 60; c-4p. Staton c/a-50(p).* ***Williamson*** *a-30i, 51i.*

MARVEL FANFARE (2nd Series)
Sept, 1996 - No. 6(99¢)
Marvel Comics

1-6: 1-Capt. America & The Falcon-c/story; Deathlok app. 2-Wolverine & Hulk-c/app. 3-Ghost Rider & Spider-Man-c/app. 5-Longshot-c/app. 6-Sabretooth, Power Man, & Iron Fist-c/app 1.00

MARVEL FEATURE (See Marvel Two-In-One)
Dec, 1971 - No. 12, Nov, 1973 (1,2: 25¢ giants)(#1-3: quarterly)
Marvel Comics Group

1-Origin/1st app. The Defenders (Sub-Mariner, Hulk & Dr. Strange); see Sub-Mariner #34,35 for prequel; Dr. Strange solo story (predates D.S. #1) plus 1950s Sub-Mariner-r; Neal Adams-c 10.00 30.00 80.00
2-2nd app. Defenders; 1950s Sub-Mariner-r 3.50 10.50 35.00
3-Defenders ends 3.50 10.50 35.00
4-Re-intro Antman (1st app. since 1960s), begin series; brief origin; Spider-Man app. 1.75 5.25 14.00
5-10: 6-Wasp app. & begins team-ups. 8-Origin Antman & Wasp-r/TTA #44. 9-Iron Man app. 10-Last Antman 2.20 5.50
10-(7/73)-Variant w/4 extra pgs. ads on slick paper 2.40 6.00
11-Thing vs. Hulk; 1st Thing solo book (9/73); origin Fantastic Four retold 1.40 4.15 11.00
12-Thing/Iron Man; early Thanos app.; occurs after Capt. Marvel #33; Starlin-a(p) 1.25 3.75 10.00

NOTE: ***Bolle*** *a-9i.* ***Everett*** *a-1i, 3i.* ***Hartley*** *r-10.* ***Kane*** *c-3p, 7p.* ***Russell*** *a-7-10p.* ***Starlin*** *a-8, 11, 12; c-8.*

MARVEL FEATURE (Also see Red Sonja)
Nov, 1975 - No. 7, Nov, 1976 (Story continues in Conan #68)
Marvel Comics Group

1-Red Sonja begins (pre-dates Red Sonja #1); adapts Howard short story; Adams-r/Savage Sword of Conan #1 2.00 5.00
2,3,6: Thorne-c/a in #2-7 1.20 3.00
4,5-(Regular 25¢ edition)(5,7/76) 1.20 3.00
4,5-(30¢-c, limited distribution) 1.50 4.50 12.00
7-Battles Conan 2.40 6.00

MARVEL FRONTIER COMICS UNLIMITED
Jan, 1994 ($2.95, 68 pgs.)
Marvel Frontier Comics

1-Dances with Demons, Immortalis, Children of the Voyager, Evil Eye, The Fallen stories 1.20 3.00

MARVEL FUMETTI BOOK
Apr, 1984 ($1.00, one-shot)
Marvel Comics Group

1-All photos; Stan Lee photo-c; Art Adams touch-ups 1.20 3.00

MARVEL FUN & GAMES
1979/80 (color comic for kids)
Marvel Comics Group

1-Games, puzzles, etc. 2.40 6.00
2-10,12,13 1.60 4.00
11-X-Men-c 2.40 6.00

MARVEL GRAPHIC NOVEL
1982 - No. 38, 1990? ($5.95/$6.95)
Marvel Comics Group (Epic Comics)

1-Death of Captain Marvel (1st Marvel graphic novel); Capt. Marvel battles Thanos by Jim Starlin (c/a/scripts) 2.50 7.50 20.00
1 (2nd & 3rd printings) 2.00 5.00
2-Elric: The Dreaming City 1.50 4.50 12.00
3-Dreadstar; Starlin-c/a, 52 pgs. 1.50 4.50 12.00
4-Origin/1st app. The New Mutants (1982) 1.75 5.25 14.00
4,5-2nd printings 2.20 5.50
5-X-Men; book-length story (1982) 2.00 6.00 16.00
6-18: 6-The Star Slammers. 7-Killraven. 8-Super Boxers; Byrne scripts. 9-The Futurians. 10-Heartburst. 11-Void Indigo. 12-The Dazzler. 13-Starstruck. 14-The Swords Of The Swashbucklers. 15-The Raven Banner (Asgard). 16-The Aladdin Effect. 17-Revenge Of The Living Monolith. 18-She Hulk 1.00 3.00 8.00
19-21,23-31: 19-The Witch Queen of Acheron (Conan). 20-Greenberg the Vampire. 21-Marada the She-Wolf. 23-Dr. Strange. 24-Love and War (Daredevil); Miller scripts. 25-Alien Legion. 26-Dracula. 27-Avengers (Emperor Doom). 28-Conan the Reaver. 29-The Big Chance (Thing vs. Hulk). 30-A Sailor's Story. 31-Wolfpack. 1.10 3.30 9.00
22-Amaz. Spider-Man in Hooky by Wrightson 1.50 4.50 12.00
32-Death of Groo 1.50 4.50 12.00
32-2nd printing ($5.95) 2.40 6.00
33,34,36,37: 33-Thor. 34-Predator & Prey (Cloak & Dagger). 36-Willow (movie adapt.). 37-Hercules 1.00 3.00 7.50
35-Hitler's Astrologer (The Shadow, $12.95, hard-c) 1.60 4.85 13.00
35-Soft-c reprint (1990, $10.95) 1.40 4.15 11.00
38-Silver Surfer (Judgement Day)($14.95) 1.85 5.50 15.00
nn-Inhumans (1988, $7.95)-Williamson-i 1.00 3.00 8.00
nn-Last of the Dragons (1988, $6.95) 1.00 2.80 7.00
nn-Who Framed Roger Rabbit (1989, $6.95) 1.00 2.80 7.00
nn-Roger Rabbit In The Resurrection Of Doom (1989, $8.95) 1.10 3.30 9.00
nn-Arena by Bruce Jones ($5.95) 2.40 6.00

NOTE: ***Aragones*** *a-27, 32.* ***Buscema*** *a-38.* ***Byrne*** *c/a-18.* ***Heath*** *a-35i.* ***Kaluta*** *a-13, 35p; c-13.* ***Miller*** *a-24p.* ***Simonson*** *a-6; c-6.* ***Starlin*** *c/a-1,3.* ***Williamson*** *a-34.* ***Wrightson*** *c-29i.*

MARVEL-HEROES & LEGENDS
Oct, 1996 ($2.95, one-shot)
Marvel Comics

nn-Wraparound-c 1.20 3.00
...1997 ($2.99) -Original Avengers story 2.99

MARVEL HOLIDAY SPECIAL
No. 1, 1991 ($2.25, 84 pgs.); nn, Jan, 1993 ($2.95, 68 pgs.)
Marvel Comics

1-X-Men, Fantastic Four, Punisher, Thor, Capt. America, Ghost Rider, Capt. Ultra, Spidey stories; Art Adams-c/a .90 2.25

Marvel Masterpieces 2 #2 © MEG

Marvel Mystery Comics #3 © MEG

Marvel Mystery Comics #47 © MEG

GD25 FN65 NM94

nn (1/93)-Wolverine, Thanos (by Starlin/Lim/Austin) 1.20 3.00
NOTE: ***Art Adams*** *c-nn.* ***Golden*** *a-nn.*

MARVEL ILLUSTRATED: SWIMSUIT ISSUE (See Marvel Swimsuit Spec.)
1991 ($3.95, magazine, 52 pgs.)
Marvel Comics

V1#1-Parody of Sports Illustrated swimsuit issue; Mary Jane Parker centerfold pin-up by Jusko; 2nd print exists 1.60 4.00

MARVEL MASTERPIECES COLLECTION, THE
May, 1993 - No. 4, Aug, 1993 ($2.95, coated paper, limited series)
Marvel Comics

1-4-Reprints Marvel Masterpieces trading cards w/ new Jusko paintings in in each; Jusko painted-c/a 1.20 3.00

MARVEL MASTERPIECES 2 COLLECTION, THE
July, 1994 - No. 3, Sept, 1994 ($2.95, limited series)
Marvel Comics

1-3: 1-Kaluta-c; r/trading cards; new Steranko centerfold 1.20 3.00

MARVEL MILESTONE EDITION
1991 - 1995 ($2.95, coated stock)(r/originals with original ads w/silver ink-c)
Marvel Comics

	GD25	NM94
...: X-Men #1-Reprints X-Men #1 (1991)	1.20	3.00
...: Giant Size X-Men #1-(1991, $3.95, 68 pgs.)	1.60	4.00
...: Fantastic Four #1 (11/91)	1.20	3.00
...: Incredible Hulk #1 (3/92, says 3/91 by error)	1.20	3.00
...: Amazing Fantasy #15 (3/92)	1.20	3.00
...: Fantastic Four #5 (11/92)	1.20	3.00
...: Amazing Spider-Man #129 (11/92)	1.20	3.00
...: Iron Man #55 (11/92)	1.20	3.00
...: Iron Fist #14 (11/92)	1.20	3.00
...: Amazing Spider-Man #1 (1/93)	1.20	3.00
...: Tales of Suspense #39 (3/93)	1.20	3.00
...: Avengers #1 (9/93)	1.20	3.00
...: X-Men #9 (10/93)	1.20	3.00
...: Avengers #16 (10/93)	1.20	3.00
...:Amazing Spider-Man #149 (11/94, $2.95)	1.20	3.00
...:X-Men #28 (11/94, $2.95)	1.20	3.00
...:Captain America #1 (3/95, $3.95)	1.60	4.00
...:Amazing Spider-Man #3 (3/95, $2.95)	1.20	3.00
...:Avengers #4 (3/95, $2.95)	1.20	3.00
...:Strange Tales-r/Dr. Strange stories from #110, 111, 114, & 115.	1.20	3.00

MARVEL MINI-BOOKS
1966 (50 pgs., B&W; 5/8x7/8") (6 different issues)
Marvel Comics Group (Smallest comics ever published)

Captain America, Millie the Model, Spider-Man, Sgt. Fury, Hulk, Thor 5.00 15.00 50.00
NOTE: *Each came in six different color covers, usually one color: Pink, yellow, green, etc.*

MARVEL MOVIE PREMIERE (Magazine)
Sept, 1975 (B&W, one-shot)
Marvel Comics Group

1-Burroughs' "The Land That Time Forgot" adapt. 1.00 3.00 8.00

MARVEL MOVIE SHOWCASE FEATURING STAR WARS
Nov, 1982 - No. 2, Dec, 1982 ($1.25, 68 pgs.)
Marvel Comics Group

1,2-Star Wars movie adaptation; reprints Star Wars #1-6 by Chaykin; 1-Reprints-c to Star Wars #1. 2-Stevens-r 1.20 3.00

MARVEL MOVIE SPOTLIGHT FEATURING RAIDERS OF THE LOST ARK
Nov, 1982 ($1.25, 68 pgs.)
Marvel Comics Group

1-Edited-r/Raiders of the Lost Ark #1-3; Buscema-c/a(p); movie adaptation 1.25

GD25 FN65 NM94

MARVEL MYSTERY COMICS (Formerly Marvel Comics) (Becomes Marvel Tales No. 93 on)
No. 2, Dec, 1939 - No. 92, June, 1949
Timely /Marvel Comics (TP #2-17/TCI #18-54/MCI #55-92)

	GD25	FN65	VF82	NM94
2-American Ace begins, ends #3; Human Torch (blue costume) by Burgos, Sub-Mariner by Everett continue; 2 pg. origin recap of Human Torch	1818.00	5455.00	11,817.00	20,000.00

(Estimated up to 50 total copies exist, 5 in NM/Mint)

	GD25	FN65	NM94
3-New logo from Marvel pulp begins	860.00	2580.00	8600.00
4-Intro. Electro, the Marvel of the Age (ends #19), The Ferret, Mystery Detective (ends #9); 1st Nazi war-c on a comic book & 1st German flag (Swastika) on-c of a comic (2/40)	700.00	2100.00	7000.00

	GD25	FN65	VF82	NM94
5 (Scarce)	136500	4100.00	8200.00	15,000.00

(Estimated up to 75 total copies exist, 3 in NM/Mint)

	GD25	FN65	NM94
6,7: 6-Gustavson Angel story	480.00	1440.00	4800.00
8-1st Human Torch & Sub-Mariner battle(6/40)	700.00	2100.00	7000.00

	GD25	FN65	VF82	NM94
9-(Scarce)-Human Torch & Sub-Mariner battle (cover/story); 1st Television in comics?; classic-c	1545.00	4640.00	9600.00	17,000.00

(Estimated up to 75 total copies exist, 6 in NM/Mint)

	GD25	FN65	NM94
10-Human Torch & Sub-Mariner battle, conclusion; Terry Vance, the Schoolboy Sleuth begins, ends #57	490.00	1470.00	4900.00
11	260.00	780.00	2600.00
12-Classic Kirby-c	290.00	870.00	2900.00
13-Intro. & 1st app. The Vision by S&K (11/40); Sub-Mariner dons new costume, ends #15	340.00	1020.00	3400.00
14-16: 14-Shows-c to Human Torch #1 on-c (12/40). 15-S&K Vision, Gustavson Angel story	189.00	567.00	1700.00
17-Human Torch/Sub-Mariner team-up by Burgos/Everett; pin-up on back-c; shows-c to Human Torch #2 on-c	211.00	633.00	1900.00
18	167.00	500.00	1500.00
19-Origin Toro in text; shows-c to Sub-Mariner #1 on-c	183.00	550.00	1650.00
20-Origin The Angel in text	183.00	550.00	1650.00
21-Intro. & 1st app. The Patriot (7/41); not in #46-48; pin-up on back-c	167.00	500.00	1500.00
22-25: 23-Last Gustavson Angel; origin The Vision in text. 24-Injury-to-eye story	144.00	432.00	1300.00
26-30: 27-Ka-Zar ends; last S&K Vision who battles Satan. 28-Jimmy Jupiter in the Land of Nowhere begins, ends #48; Sub-Mariner vs. The Flying Dutchman. 30-1st Japanese war-c	133.00	400.00	1200.00
31-Sub-Mariner by Everett ends, begins again #84	117.00	350.00	1050.00
32-1st app. The Boboes	117.00	350.00	1050.00
33,35-40: 40-Zeppelin-c	117.00	350.00	1050.00
34-Everett, Burgos, Martin Goodman, Funnies, Inc. office appear in story & battles Hitler; last Burgos Human Torch	133.00	400.00	1200.00
41-43,45-48: 46-Hitler-c. 48-Last Vision; flag-c	100.00	300.00	900.00
44-Classic Super Plane-c	100.00	300.00	900.00
49-Origin Miss America	133.00	400.00	1200.00
50-Mary becomes Miss Patriot (origin)	106.00	318.00	950.00
51-60: 53-Bondage-c. 60-Last Japanese war-c	94.00	282.00	840.00
61,62,64-Last German war-c	89.00	267.00	800.00
63-Classic Hitler War-c; The Villainess Cat-Woman only app.	94.00	282.00	850.00
65,66-Last Japanese War-c	89.00	267.00	800.00
67-75: 74-Last Patriot. 75-Young Allies begin	81.00	243.00	725.00
76-78: 76-Ten Chapter Miss America serial begins, ends #85	81.00	243.00	725.00

Marvel No-Prize Book #1 © MEG

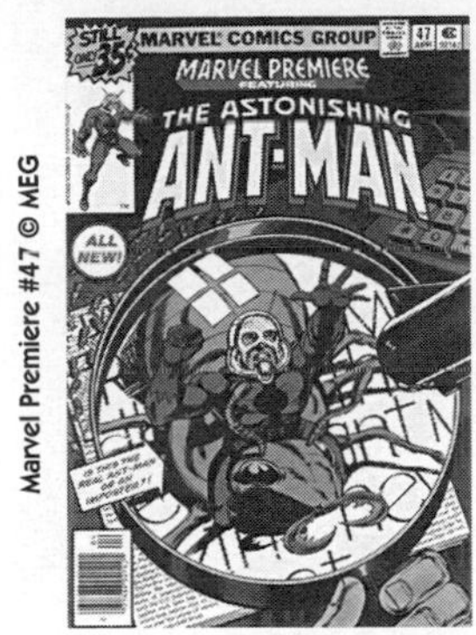

Marvel Premiere #47 © MEG

Marvel Preview #20 © MEG

79-New cover format; Super Villains begin on cover; last Angel 83.00 250.00 750.00
80-1st app. Capt. America in Marvel Comics 106.00 318.00 950.00
81-Captain America app. 81.00 243.00 725.00
82-Origin & 1st app. Namora (5/47); 1st Sub-Mariner/Namora team-up; Captain America app. 189.00 567.00 1700.00
83,85: 83-Last Young Allies. 85-Last Miss America; Blonde Phantom app. 75.00 225.00 675.00
84-Blonde Phantom begins (on-c of #84,88,89); Sub-Mariner by Everett begins; Captain America app. 106.00 318.00 950.00
86-Blonde Phantom i.d. revealed; Captain America app.; last Bucky app. 85.00 255.00 765.00
87-1st Capt. America/Golden Girl team-up 91.00 273.00 815.00
88-Golden Girl, Namora, & Sun Girl (1st in Marvel Comics) x-over; Captain America, Blonde Phantom app.; last Toro 86.00 258.00 775.00
89-1st Human Torch/Sun Girl team-up; 1st Captain America solo; Blonde Phantom app. 85.00 255.00 765.00
90-Blonde Phantom un-masked; Captain America app. 91.00 273.00 815.00
91-Capt. America app.; Blonde Phantom & Sub-Mariner end; early Venus app. (4/49) 91.00 273.00 815.00
92-Feature story on the birth of the Human Torch and the death of Professor Horton (his creator); 1st app. The Witness in Marvel Comics; Captain America app. 211.00 633.00 1900.00
132 Pg. issue, B&W, 25¢ (1943-44)-printed in N. Y.; square binding, blank inside covers; has Marvel No. 33-c in color; contains Capt. America #18 & Marvel Mystery Comics #33; same contents as Captain America Annual

GD25 FN65 VF82

(Less than 5 copies known to exist) 2667.00 8000.00 16,000.00

NOTE: ***Brodsky*** *c-49, 72, 86, 88-92.* ***Crandall*** *a-26i.* ***Everett*** *c-7-9, 27, 84.* ***Gabrielle*** *c-30-32.* ***Schomburg*** *c-3-11, 13-29, 33-36, 39-48, 50-59, 63-69, 74, 76, 132 pg. issue.* ***Shores*** *c-37, 38, 75p, 77, 78p, 79p, 80, 81p, 82-84, 85p, 87p.* ***Sekowsky*** *c-73. Bondage covers-3, 4, 7, 12, 28, 29, 49, 50, 52, 56, 57, 58, 59, 65. Angel c-2, 3, 8, 12. Remember Pearl Harbor issues-#30-32.*

MARVEL NO-PRIZE BOOK, THE (The Official... on-c)
Jan, 1983 (one-shot, direct sales only)
Marvel Comics Group

GD25 FN65 NM94

1-Golden-c .80 2.00

MARVEL PREMIERE
April, 1972 - No. 61, Aug, 1981 (A tryout book for new characters)
Marvel Comics Group

1-Origin Warlock (pre-#1) by Gil Kane/Adkins; origin Counter-Earth; Hulk & Thor cameo (#1-14 are 20¢-c) 3.00 9.00 30.00
2-Warlock ends; Kirby Yellow Claw-r 1.85 5.50 15.00
3-Dr. Strange series begins (pre #1, 7/72), B. Smith-a(p); Smith-c? 2.50 7.50 24.00
4-Smith/Brunner-a 1.10 3.30 9.00
5-9: 8-Starlin-c/a(p) 2.20 5.50
10-Death of the Ancient One 1.00 3.00 8.00
11-14: 11-Dr. Strange origin-r by Ditko. 14-Last Dr. Strange (3/74), gets own title 3 months later 1.80 4.50
15-Origin/1st app. Iron Fist (5/74), ends #25 5.00 15.00 50.00
16-2nd app. Iron Fist; origin cont'd from #15; Hama's 1st Marvel-a 1.85 5.50 15.00
17-24: Iron Fist in all 1.25 3.75 10.00
25-1st Byrne Iron Fist (moves to own title next) 1.85 5.50 15.00
26-Hercules. 1.20 3.00
27-Satana 2.40 6.00
28-Legion of Monsters (Ghost Rider, Man-Thing, Morbius, Werewolf) 1.50 4.50 12.00
29-49,51-56,61: 29,30-The Liberty Legion. 29-1st modern app. Patriot. 31-1st app. Woodgod; last 25¢ issue. 32-1st app. Monark Starstalker. 33,34-1st color app. Solomon Kane (Robert E. Howard adaptation "Red Shadows". 35-Origin/1st app. 3-D Man. 36,37-3-D Man. 38-1st Weirdworld. 39,40-Torpedo. 41-1st Seeker 3001! 42-Tigra. 43-Paladin. 44-Jack of Hearts (1st solo book, 10/78). 45,46-Man-Wolf. 47-Origin/1st app. new Ant-Man. 48-Ant-Man. 49-The Falcon (1st solo book, 8/79). 51-53-Black Panther. 54-1st Caleb Hammer. 55-Wonder Man. 56-1st color app. Dominic Fortune. 61-Star Lord .80 2.00
50-1st app. Alice Cooper; co-plotted by Alice 1.10 3.30 9.00
57-Dr. Who (2nd U.S. app.-see Movie Classics) 1.20 3.00
58-60-Dr. Who .90 2.25

NOTE: ***N. Adams*** *(Crusty Bunkers) part inks-10, 12, 13.* ***Austin*** *a-50i, 56i; c-46i, 50i, 56i, 58.* ***Brunner*** *a-4i, 6p, 9-14p; c-9-14.* ***Byrne*** *a-47p, 48p.* ***Chaykin*** *a-32-34; c-32, 33, 56.* ***Giffen*** *a-31p, 44p; c-44.* ***Gil Kane*** *a(p)-1, 2, 15; c(p)-1, 2, 15, 16, 22-24, 27, 36, 37.* ***Kirby*** *c-26, 29-31, 35.* ***Layton*** *a-47i, 48i; c-47.* ***McWilliams*** *a-25i.* ***Miller*** *c-49p, 53p, 58p.* ***Nebres*** *a-44i; c-38i.* ***Nino*** *a-38i.* ***Perez*** *c/a-38p, 45p, 46p.* ***Ploog*** *a-38; c-5-7.* ***Russell*** *a-7p.* ***Simonson*** *a-60(2pgs.); c-57.* ***Starlin*** *a-8p; c-8.* ***Sutton*** *a-41, 43, 50p, 61; c-50p, 61. #57-60 published w/two different prices on-c.*

MARVEL PRESENTS
October, 1975 - No. 12, Aug, 1977 (#1-5 are 25¢ issues)
Marvel Comics Group

1,2: 1-Origin & 1st app. Bloodstone. 2-Origin Bloodstone continued; Kirby-c 1.60 4.00
3-Guardians of the Galaxy (1st solo book, 2/76) begins, ends #12 1.00 3.00 7.50
4-7,9-12: 9,10-Origin Starhawk 2.00 5.00
8-r/story from Silver Surfer #2 plus 4 pgs. new-a 2.40 6.00

NOTE: ***Austin*** *a-6i.* ***Buscema*** *r-8p.* ***Chaykin*** *a-5p.* ***Kane*** *c-1p.* ***Starlin*** *layouts-10.*

MARVEL PREVIEW (Magazine) (Bizarre Adventures #25 on)
Feb (no month), 1975 - No. 24, Winter, 1980 (B&W) ($1.00)
Marvel Comics Group

1-Man-Gods From Beyond the Stars; Crusty Bunkers (Neal Adams)-a(i) & cover; Nino-a 2.00 5.00
2-1st origin The Punisher (see Amaz. Spider-Man #129 & Classic Punisher); 1st app. Dominic Fortune; Morrow-c 6.00 18.00 60.00
3,8,10: 3-Blade the Vampire Slayer. 8-Legion of Monsters; Morbius app. 10-Thor the Mighty; Starlin frontispiece 1.25 3.75 10.00
4,5: 4-Star-Lord & Sword in the Star (origins & 1st app.). 5,6-Sherlock Holmes. 1.00 3.00 8.00
6,9: 6-Sherlock Holmes; N. Adams frontispiece. 9-Man-God; origin Star Hawk, ends #20 2.00 5.00
7-Satana, Sword in the Star app. 1.00 2.80 7.00
11,16,19: 11-Star-Lord; Byrne-a; Starlin frontispiece. 16-Masters of Terror. 19-Kull. 1.60 4.00
12-15,17,18,20-24: 12-Haunt of Horror. 14,15-Star-Lord. 14-Starlin painted-c. 16-Masters of Terror. 17-Blackmark by G. Kane (see SSOC #1-3). 18-Star-Lord. 20-Bizarre Advs. 21-Moon Knight (Spr/80)-Predates Moon Knight #1; The Shroud by Ditko. 22-King Arthur. 23-Bizarre Advs.; Miller-a. 24-Debut Paradox 1.20 3.00

NOTE: ***N. Adams*** *(C. Bunkers) r-20i.* ***Buscema*** *a-22, 23.* ***Byrne*** *a-11.* ***Chaykin*** *a-20r; c-20 (new).* ***Colan*** *a-8, 16p(3), 18p, 23p; c-16p.* ***Elias*** *a-18.* ***Giffen*** *a-7.* ***Infantino*** *a-14p.* ***Kaluta*** *a-12; c-15.* ***Miller*** *a-23.* ***Morrow*** *a-8i; c-2-4.* ***Perez*** *a-20p.* ***Ploog*** *a-8.* ***Starlin*** *c-13, 14. Nudity in some issues*

MARVEL RIOT
Dec, 1995 ($1.95, one-shot)
Marvel Comics

1-"Age of Apocalypse" spoof; Lobdell script .80 2.00

MARVELS
Jan, 1994 - No. 4, Apr, 1994 ($5.95, painted limited series, 52 pgs.)
No. 1 (2nd Printing), Apr, 1996 - No. 4 (2nd Printing), July, 1996 ($2.95, painted limited series)
Marvel Comics

1-4: Kurt Busiek scripts & Alex Ross painted-c/a in all; double-c w/acetate overlay 1.00 3.00 8.00
Marvel Classic Collectors Pack ($11.90)-Issues #1 & 2 boxed (1st printings). 1.70 5.00 12.00
0-(8/94, $2.95)-no acetate overlay. 1.20 3.00
1-4-(2nd printing): r/original limited series w/o acetate overlay

Marvel Special Edition Featuring The Spectacular Spider-Man #1 © MEG

Marvel Spotlight #9 © MEG

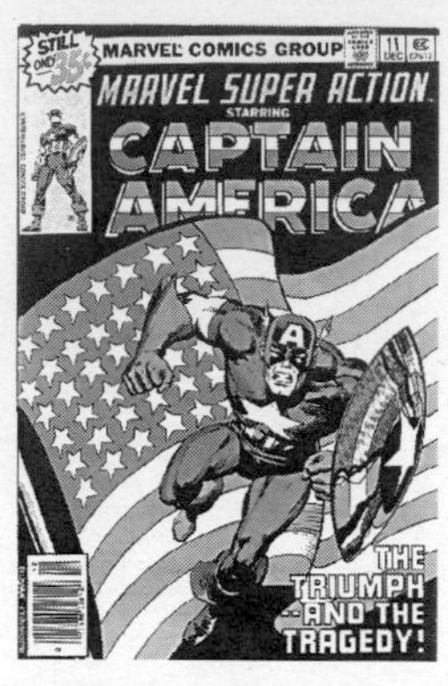

Marvel Super Action #11 © MEG

GD25 FN65 NM94

1.20 3.00
Hardcover (1994, $69.95)-r/#0-4; w/intros by Stan Lee, John Romita, Sr., Kurt Busiek & Scott McCloud. 70.00
Trade paperback ($19.95) 20.00

MARVEL SAGA, THE
Dec, 1985 - No. 25, Dec, 1987
Marvel Comics Group

1 1.50
2-25 1.00
NOTE: ***Williamson*** *a(i)-9, 10; c(i)-7, 10-12, 14, 16.*

MARVEL'S GREATEST COMICS (Marvel Collectors' Item Classics #1-22)
No. 23, Oct, 1969 - No. 96, Jan, 1981
Marvel Comics Group

23-34 (Giants). Begin Fantastic Four-r/#30s?-116 1.50 4.50 12.00
35-37-Silver Surfer-r/Fantastic Four #48-50 2.00 5.00
38-50: 42-Silver Surfer-r/F.F.(others?) 1.60 4.00
51-96 .80 2.00
NOTE: *Dr. Strange, Fantastic Four, Iron Man, Watcher-#23, 24. Capt. America, Dr. Strange, Iron Man, Fantastic Four-#25-28. Fantastic Four-#38-96.* ***Buscema*** *r-85-92; c-87-92r.* ***Ditko*** *r-23-28.* ***Kirby*** *r-23-82; c-75, 77p, 80p. #81 reprints Fantastic Four #100.*

MARVEL'S GREATEST SUPERHERO BATTLES (See Fireside Book Series)

MARVEL: SHADOWS AND LIGHT
Feb, 1997 ($2.95, B&W, one-shot)
Marvel Comics

1-Tony Daniel-c 1.20 3.00

MARVELS OF SCIENCE
March, 1946 - No. 4, June, 1946
Charlton Comics

1-A-Bomb story 16.00 48.00 130.00
2-4 10.00 30.00 80.00

MARVEL SPECIAL EDITION FEATURING... (Also see Special Collectors' Ed.)
1975 - 1978 (84 pgs.) (Oversized)
Marvel Comics Group

1-The Spectacular Spider-Man ($1.50); r/Amazing Spider-Man #6,35, Annual 1; Ditko-a(r) 1.50 4.50 12.00
1-Star Wars (1977, $1.00); r/Star Wars #1-3 1.25 3.75 10.00
2-Star Wars (1978, $1.00); r/Star Wars #4-6 1.25 3.75 10.00
3-Star Wars ('78, $2.50, 116pgs.); r/S. Wars #1-6 1.25 3.75 10.00
3-Close Encounters of the Third Kind (1978, $1.50, 56 pgs.)-Movie adaptation; Simonson-a(p) 1.25 3.75 10.00
V2#2(Spring, 1980, $2.00, oversized)- "Star Wars: The Empire Strikes Back"; r/Marvel Comics Super Special #16 2.50 7.50 20.00
NOTE: ***Chaykin*** *c/a(r)-1(1977), 2, 3.* ***Stevens*** *a(r)-2i, 3i.* ***Williamson*** *a(r)-V2#2.*

MARVEL SPECTACULAR
Aug, 1973 - No. 19, Nov, 1975
Marvel Comics Group

1-Thor-r from mid-sixties begin by Kirby 1.10 3.30 9.00
2-10 2.40 6.00
11-19 1.60 4.00

MARVELS: PORTRAITS
Mar, 1995 - No. 4, June, 1995 ($2.95, limited series)
Marvel Comics

1-4:Different artists renditions of Marvel characters. 1.20 3.00

MARVEL SPOTLIGHT (...& Son of Satan #19, 20, 23, 24)
Nov, 1971 - No. 33, Apr, 1977; V2#1, July, 1979 - V2#11, Mar, 1981
Marvel Comics Group (A try-out book for new characters)

1-Origin Red Wolf (western hero)(1st solo book, pre-#1); Wood inks, Neal Adams-c; only 15¢ issue 2.50 7.50 20.00
2-(25¢, 52 pgs.)-Venus-r by Everett; origin/1st app. Werewolf By Night (begins) by Ploog; N. Adams-c 9.00 27.00 90.00
3,4: 4-Werewolf By Night ends (6/72); gets own title 9/72 2.50 7.50 25.00
5-Origin/1st app. Ghost Rider (8/72) & begins 6.50 19.50 65.00
6-8: 6-Origin G.R. retold. 8-Last Ploog issue 3.00 9.00 30.00
9-11-Last Ghost Rider (gets own title next mo.) 2.50 7.50 20.00
12-Origin & 2nd full app. The Son of Satan (10/73); story cont'd from Ghost Rider #2 & into #3; series begins, ends #24 2.50 7.50 20.00
12-Variant w/4 extra pgs. of ads on slick paper plus a Mark Jeweler pull-out centerfold ad 2.50 7.50 24.00
13-21,23,24: 13-Partial origin Son of Satan. 14-Last 20¢ issue. 24-Last Son of Satan (10/75); gets own title 12/75 2.40 6.00
22-Ghost Rider-c & cameo (5 panels) 2.40 6.00
25,27,30,31: 25-Sinbad; contains pull-out Mark Jewelers ad. 27-Sub-Mariner. 30-The Warriors Three. 31-Nick Fury 1.20 3.00
26-Scarecrow 2.00 5.00
28-1st solo Moon Knight app., (6/76) 1.50 4.50 12.00
29-(Regular 25¢ edition)(8/76) Moon Knight app.; last 25¢ issue 1.50 4.50 12.00
29-(30¢-c, limited distribution) 4.80 14.40 48.00
32-1st app./partial origin Spider-Woman (2/77); Nick Fury app. 1.50 4.50 12.00
33-Deathlok; 1st app. Devil-Slayer 2.00 5.00
V2#1-11: 1-4-Capt. Marvel. 5-Dragon Lord. 6,7-StarLord; origin #6. 9-11-Capt. Universe (see Micronauts #8) .80 2.00
8-Capt. Marvel; Miller-c/a(p) 1.20 3.00
NOTE: ***Austin*** *c-V2#2i, 8.* ***J. Buscema*** *c/a-30p.* ***Chaykin*** *a-31; c-26, 31.* ***Colan*** *a-18p, 19p.* ***Ditko*** *a-V2#4, 5, 9-11; c-V2#4, 9-11.* ***Kane*** *c-21p, 32p.* ***Kirby*** *c-29p.* ***McWilliams*** *a-20i.* ***Miller*** *a-V2#8p; c(p)-V2#2, 5, 7, 8.* ***Mooney*** *a-8i, 10i, 14p, 15, 16p, 17p, 24p, 27, 32i.* ***Nasser*** *a-33p.* ***Ploog*** *a-2-5, 6-8p; c-3-9.* ***Romita*** *c-13.* ***Sutton*** *a-9-11p, V2#6, 7. #29-25¢ & 30¢ issues exist.*

MARVEL SUPER ACTION (Magazine)
Jan, 1976 (B&W, 76 pgs.)
Marvel Comics Group

1-Origin/2nd app. Dominic Fortune(see Marv. Preview); early Punisher app.; Weird World & The Huntress; Evans, Ploog-a 3.50 10.50 35.00

MARVEL SUPER ACTION
May, 1977 - No. 37, Nov, 1981
Marvel Comics Group

1-Reprints Capt. America #100 by Kirby 1.00 2.80 7.00
2,3,5-13: r/Capt. America #101,102,103-111. 11-Origin-r. 12,13-Classic Steranko-c/a(r) 1.60 4.00
4-Marvel Boy-r(origin)/M. Boy #1 1.60 4.00
14-20s: r/Avengers #55,56, Annual 2, others 1.20 3.00
21-37: 30-r/Hulk #6 from U.K. .80 2.00
NOTE: ***Buscema*** *a(r)-14p, 15p; c-18-20, 22, 35r-37.* ***Everett*** *a-4.* ***Heath*** *a-4r.* ***Kirby*** *r-1-3, 5-11.* ***B. Smith*** *a-27r, 28r.* ***Steranko*** *a(r)-12p, 13p; c-12r, 13r.*

MARVEL SUPER HERO CONTEST OF CHAMPIONS
June, 1982 - No. 3, Aug, 1982 (Limited series)
Marvel Comics Group

1-3: Features nearly all Marvel characters currently appearing in their comics; 1st Marvel limited series 1.60 4.00

MARVEL SUPER HEROES
October, 1966 (25¢, 68 pgs.) (1st Marvel one-shot)
Marvel Comics Group

1-r/origin Daredevil from D.D. #1; r/Avengers #2; G.A. Sub-Mariner-r/Marvel Mystery #8 (Human Torch app.). 6.00 18.00 60.00

MARVEL SUPER-HEROES (Formerly Fantasy Masterpieces #1-11)
(Also see Giant-Size Super Heroes) (#12-20: 25¢, 68 pgs.)
No. 12, 12/67 - No. 31, 11/71; No. 32, 9/72 - No. 105, 1/82
Marvel Comics Group

12-Origin & 1st app. Capt. Marvel of the Kree; G.A. Human Torch, Destroyer, Capt. America, Black Knight, Sub-Mariner-r (#12-20 all contain new stories

Marvel Super-Heroes #105 © MEG

Marvel Tales #93 © MEG

Marvel Tales #123 © MEG

GD25 FN65 NM94

and reprints) 8.00 24.00 80.00
13-2nd app. Capt. Marvel; G.A. Black Knight, Torch, Vision, Capt. America, Sub-Mariner-r 4.00 12.00 40.00
14-Amazing Spider-Man (5/68, new-a by Andru/Everett); G.A. Sub-Mariner, Torch, Mercury (1st Kirby-a at Marvel), Black Knight, Capt. America reprints 7.00 21.00 70.00
15-Black Bolt cameo in Medusa (new-a); Black Knight, Sub-Mariner, Black Marvel, Capt. America-r 2.50 7.50 25.00
16-Origin & 1st app. S. A. Phantom Eagle; G.A. Torch, Capt. America, Black Knight, Patriot, Sub-Mariner-r 2.50 7.50 25.00
17-Origin Black Knight (new-a); G.A. Torch, Sub-Mariner-r; reprint from All-Winners Squad #21 (cover & story) 2.50 7.50 25.00
18-Origin/1st app. Guardians of the Galaxy (1/69); G.A. Sub-Mariner, All-Winners Squad-r 4.00 12.00 40.00
19-Ka-Zar (new-a); G.A. Torch, Marvel Boy, Black Knight, Sub-Mariner reprints, Smith-c(p); Tuska-a(r) 1.25 3.75 10.00
20-Doctor Doom (5/69); r/Young Men #24 w/-c 2.50 7.50 20.00
21-31: All-r issues. 21-X-Men, Daredevil, Iron Man-r begin, end #31. 31-Last Giant issue 1.25 3.75 10.00
32-50: 32-Hulk/Sub-Mariner-r begin from TTA. 1.60 4.00
51-105: 56-r/origin Hulk/Inc. Hulk #102; Hulk-r begin .80 2.00
NOTE: **Austin** *a-104.* **Colan** *a(p)-12, 13, 15, 18; c-12, 13, 15, 18.* **Everett** *a-14i(new); r-14, 15i, 18, 19, 33; c-85(r). New* **Kirby** *c-22, 27, 54.* **Maneely** *r-14, 15, 19.* **Severin** *r-83-85i, 100-102; c-100-102r.* **Starlin** *c-47.* **Tuska** *a-19p. Black Knight-r by* **Maneely** *in 12-16, 19. Sub-Mariner-r by* **Everett** *in 12-20.*

MARVEL SUPER-HEROES
May, 1990 - V2#15, Oct, 1993 ($2.95/$2.25/$2.50, quarterly, 68-84 pgs.)
Marvel Comics

1-Moon Knight, Hercules, Black Panther, Magik, Brother Voodoo, Speedball (by Ditko) & Hellcat; Hembeck-a 1.20 3.00
2,4,5: 2-Summer Special(7/90); Rogue, Speedball (by Ditko), Iron Man, Falcon, Tigra & Daredevil. 4-Spider-Man/Nick Fury, Daredevil, Speedball, Wonder Man, Spitfire & Black Knight; Byrne-c. 5-Thor, Dr. Strange, Thing & She-Hulk; Speedball by Ditko(p) .90 2.25
V2#3-Retells origin Capt. America w/new facts; Blue Shield, Capt. Marvel, Speedball, Wasp; Hulk by Ditko/Rogers .90 2.25
V2#6-9: 6-8-$2.25-c. 6,7-X-Men, Cloak & Dagger, The Shroud (by Ditko) & Marvel Boy in each. 8-X-Men, Namor & Iron Man (by Ditko); Larsen-c. 9-W.C Avengers, Iron Man app.; Kieth-c(p); begin $2.50-c .90 2.25
V2#10-Ms. Marvel/Sabretooth-c/story (intended for Ms. Marvel #24; shows-c to #24); Namor, Vision, Scarlet Witch stories 1.00 2.50
V2#11,12 ($2.50): 11-Original Ghost Rider-c/story; Giant-Man, Ms. Marvel stories. 12-Dr. Strange, Falcon, Iron Man 1.00 2.50
V2#13-15 ($2.75, 84 pgs.): 13-All Iron Man issue; 30th anniversary. 15-Iron Man/Thor/Volstagg/Dr. Druid 1.10 2.75

MARVEL SUPER-HEROES MEGAZINE
Oct, 1994 - No. 6, Mar, 1995 ($2.95, 100 pgs.)
Marvel Comics

1-6: 1-r/FF #232, DD #159, Iron Man #115, Incred. Hulk #314 1.20 3.00

MARVEL SUPER-HEROES SECRET WARS (See Secret Wars II)
May, 1984 - No. 12, Apr, 1985 (limited series)
Marvel Comics Group

1 1.20 3.00
1-3-2nd printings (sold in multi-packs) 1.00
2-7,9-12: 6-The Wasp dies. 7-Intro. new Spider-Woman. 12-($1.00, 52 pgs.) .80 2.00
8-Spider-Man's new black costume explained as alien costume (1st app. Venom as alien costume) 2.50 7.50 10.00
NOTE: **Zeck** *a-1-12; c-13, 8-12.*

MARVEL SUPER SPECIAL A (See Marvel Comics Super...)

MARVEL SWIMSUIT SPECIAL (Also see Marvel Illustrated...)
1992 ($3.95/$4.50, magazine, 52 pgs.)
Marvel Comics

1-Silvestri-c; pin-ups by many good artists 1.60 4.00
2-Jusko painted-c; all pin-ups 1.80 4.50

MARVEL TAILS STARRING PETER PORKER THE SPECTACULAR SPIDER-HAM (Also see Peter Porker...)
Nov, 1983 (one-shot)
Marvel Comics Group

1-Peter Porker, the Spectacular Spider-Ham, Captain Americat, Goose Rider, Hulk Bunny app. 1.50

MARVEL TALES (Formerly Marvel Mystery Comics #1-92)
No. 93, Aug, 1949 - No. 159, Aug, 1957
Marvel/Atlas Comics (MCI)

93-Horror/weird stories begin 112.00 338.00 950.00
94-Everett-a 78.00 234.00 650.00
95,96,99,101,103,105: 95-New logo 58.00 174.00 425.00
97-Sun Girl, 2 pgs; Kirbyish-a; one story used in N.Y. State Legislative document 65.00 195.00 525.00
98-Krigstein-a 55.00 165.00 450.00
100 55.00 165.00 450.00
102-Wolverton-a "The End of the World", (6 pgs.) 75.00 225.00 625.00
104-Wolverton-a "Gateway to Horror", (6 pgs.) 71.00 215.00 600.00
106,107-Krigstein-a. 106-Decapitation story 44.00 130.00 350.00
108-120: 118-Hypo-c/panels in End of World story. 120-Jack Katz-a 33.00 99.00 240.00
121,123-131: 128-Flying Saucer-c. 131-Last precode (2/55) 26.00 79.00 190.00
122-Kubert-a 29.00 84.00 195.00
132,133,135-141,143,145 16.00 47.00 120.00
134-Krigstein, Kubert-a; flying saucer-c 18.00 54.00 130.00
142-Krigstein-a 16.00 47.00 120.00
144-Williamson/Krenkel-a, 3 pgs. 16.00 47.00 120.00
146,148-151,154-156,158: 150-1st S.A. issue. 156-Torres-a 12.00 36.00 90.00
147-Ditko-a 16.00 47.00 110.00
152-Wood, Morrow-a 16.00 47.00 110.00
153-Everett End of World c/story 17.00 49.00 120.00
157,159-Krigstein-a 13.50 41.00 95.00
NOTE: **Andru** *a-103.* **Briefer** *a-118.* **Check** *a-147.* **Colan** *a-105, 107, 118, 120, 121, 127, 131* **Drucker** *a-127, 135, 141, 146, 150.* **Everett** *a-98, 104, 106(2), 108(2), 131, 148, 151, 153, 155; c-107, 109, 111, 112, 114, 117, 127, 143, 147-151, 153, 155, 156.* **Forte** *a-119, 125, 130.* **Heath** *a-110, 113, 118, 119; c-104-106, 110, 130.* **Gil Kane** *a-117.* **Lawrence** *a-130.* **Maneely** *a-111, 126, 129; c-108, 116, 120, 129, 152.* **Mooney** *a-114.* **Morisi** *a-153.* **Morrow** *a-150, 152, 156.* **Orlando** *a-149, 151, 157.* **Pakula** *a-119, 121, 135, 144, 150, 152, 156.* **Powell** *a-136, 137, 150, 154.* **Ravielli** *a-117.* **Rico** *a-97, 99.* **Romita** *a-108.* **Sekowsky** *a-96-98.* **Shores** *a-110; c-96.* **Sinnott** *a-105, 116.* **Tuska** *a-114.* **Whitney** *a-107.* **Wildey** *a-126, 138.*

MARVEL TALES (...Annual #1,2; ...Starring Spider-Man #123 on)
1964 - No. 291, Nov, 1994 (No. 1-32: 72 pgs.)
Marvel Comics Group (NPP earlier issues)

1-Reprints origins of Spider-Man/Amazing Fantasy #15, Hulk/Inc. Hulk#1, Ant-Man/T.T.A. #35, Giant Man/T.T.A. #49, Iron Man/T.O.S. #39,48, Thor/J.I.M. #83 & r/Sgt. Fury #1 25.00 76.00 255.00
2 ('65)-r/X-Men #1(origin), Avengers #1(origin), origin Dr. Strange-r/Strange Tales #115 & origin Hulk(Hulk #3) 8.00 24.00 80.00
3 (7/66)-Spider-Man, Strange Tales (H. Torch), Journey into Mystery (Thor), Tales to Astonish (Ant-Man)-r begin (r/Strange Tales #101) 3.70 11.10 37.00
4,5 2.50 7.50 24.00
6-8,10: 10-Reprints 1st Kraven/Amaz. S-M #15 2.00 6.00 16.00
9-r/Amazing Spider-Man #14 w/cover 2.50 7.50 20.00
11-32: 11-Spider-Man battles Daredevil-r/Amaz. Spider-Man #16. 13-Origin Marvel Boy-r/M. Boy #1. 22-Green Goblin-c/story-r/Amaz. Spider-Man #27. 30-New Angel story. 32-Last 72 pg. issue 1.50 4.50 12.00
33-50: 33-(52 pgs.,)-Kraven-r. 34-Begin regular size issues 2.00 5.00
51-67,69,71-105: 75-Origin Spider-Man-r. 77-79-Drug issues-r/A. Spider-Man

Marvel Tales #155 © MEG

Marvel Tales #289 © MEG

Marvel Team-Up #131 © MEG

GD25 FN65 NM94

#96-98. 98-Death of Gwen Stacy-r/A. Spider-Man #121 (Green Goblin). 99-Death Green Goblin-r/A. Spider-Man #122. 100-(52 pgs.)-New Hawkeye/Two Gun Kid story. 101-105-All Spider-Man-r 1.20 3.00
68,70-(Regular 25¢ edition)(6,8/76) 1.20 3.00
68,70-(30¢-c, limited distribution) 1.50 4.50 12.00
106-1st Punisher-r/Amazing Spider-Man #129 1.60 4.00
107-133-All Spider-Man-r. 111,112-r/Spider-Man #134,135 (Punisher). 113, 114-r/Spider-Man #136,137(Green Goblin). 126-128-r/clone story from Amazing Spider-Man #149-151 .80 2.00
134-136-Dr. Strange-r begin; SpM stories continue. 134-Dr. Strange-r/ Strange Tales #110 .80 2.00
137-Origin-r Dr. Strange; shows original unprinted-c & origin Spider-Man/ Amazing Fantasy #15 1.20 3.00
137-Nabisco giveaway 2.40 6.00
138-Reprints all Amazing Spider-Man #1; begin reprints of Spider-Man with covers similar to originals 1.20 3.00
139-144: r/Amazing Spider-Man #2-7 .80 2.00
145-191,193-199: Spider-Man-r continue w/#8 on. 149-Contains skin "Tattooz" decals. 150-($1.00, 52pgs.)-r/Spider-Man Annual 1(Kraven app.). 153-r/1st Kraven/Spider-Man #15. 155-r/2nd Green Goblin/Spider-Man #17. 161,164,165-Gr. Goblin-c/stories-r/Spider-Man #23,26,27. 178,179-Green Goblin-c/story-r/Spider-Man #39,40. 187,189-Kraven-r. 191-($1.50, 68 pgs.)-r/Spider-Man #96-98. 193-Byrne-r/Marvel Team-Up begin w/scripts .80 2.00
192-($1.25, 52 pgs.)-r/Spider-Man #121,122 .80 2.00
200-Double size ($1.25)-Miller-c & r/Annual #14 1.50
201-208,210-222: 208-Last Byrne-r. 210,211-r/Spidey #134,135. 212,213-r/ Giant-Size Spidey #4. 213-r/1st solo Silver Surfer story/F.F. Annual #5. 214, 215-r/Spidey #161,162. 222-Reprints origin Punisher/Spectacular Spider-Man #83; last Punisher reprint 1.00
209-Reprints 1st app. The Punisher/Amazing Spider-Man #129; Punisher reprints begin, end #222 .70 1.75
223-McFarlane-c begins, end #239 1.50
224-249,251,252,254-257: 233-Spider-Man/X-Men team-ups begin; r/X-Men #35. 234-r/Marvel Team-Up #4. 235,236-r/M. Team-Up Annual #1. 237, 238-r/M. Team-Up #150. 239,240-r/M. Team-Up #38,90(Beast). 242-r/M. Team-Up #89. 243-r/M. Team-Up #117(Wolverine). 251-r/Spider-Man #100 (Green Goblin-c/story). 252-r/1st app. Morbius/Amaz. Spider-Man #101. 254-r/M. Team-Up #15(Ghost Rider); new painted-c. 255,256-Spider-Man & Ghost Rider-r/Marvel Team-Up #58,91. 257-Hobgoblin-r begin(r/Amazing Spider-Man #238); last $1.00-c 1.00
250-($1.50, 52pgs.)-r/1st Karma/M. Team-Up #100 1.50
253-($1.50, 52 pgs.)-r/Amaz. S-M #102 1.50
258-289: 258-261-r/A. Spider-Man #239,249-251(Hobgoblin). 262,263-r/Marv. Team-Up #53,54. 262-New X-Men vs. Sunstroke story. 263-New Woodgod origin story. 264,265-r/A. Spider-Man Annual 5. 266-273-Reprints alien costume stories/A. S-M 252-259. 277-r/1st Silver Sable/A. S-M 265. 283-r/ A. S-M 275 (Hobgoblin). 284-r/A. S-M 276 (Hobgoblin) 1.25
285-variant w/Wonder-Con logo on c-no price-giveaway 1.00
286-($2.95)-p/bagged w/16 page insert & animation print 1.20 3.00
290, 291: 290-Begin $1.50-c 1.50

NOTE: *All contain reprints; some have new art. #89-97-r/Amazing Spider-Man #110-118; #98-136-r/#121-159; #137-150-r/Amazing Fantasy #15, #1-12 & Annual 1; #151-167-r/#13-28 & Annual 2; #168-186-r/#29-46.* **Austin** *a-100i; c-272i, 273i.* **Byrne** *a(r)-193-198p, 201-208p.* **Ditko** *a-1-30, 83, 100, 137-155.* **G. Kane** *a-71, 81, 98-101p, 249r; c-125-127p, 130p, 137-155.* **Sam Kieth** *c-255, 262, 263.* **Ron Lim** *c-266p-281p, 283p-285p.* **McFarlane** *c-223-239.* **Mooney** *a-63, 95-97i, 103(i).* **Nasser** *a-100p.* **Nebres** *a-242i.* **Perez** *c-259-261.* **Rogers** *c-240, 241, 243-252.*

MARVEL TEAM-UP (See Marvel Treasury Edition #18 & Official Marvel Index To...) (Replaced by Web of Spider-Man)
March, 1972 - No. 150, Feb, 1985
Marvel Comics Group
NOTE: *Spider-Man team-ups in all but Nos. 18, 23, 26, 29, 32, 35, 97, 104, 105, 137.*

1-Human Torch 10.00 30.00 100.00
2-Human Torch 3.20 9.60 32.00

GD25 FN65 NM94

3-Spider-Man/Human Torch vs. Morbius (part 1); 3rd app. of Morbius (7/72) 3.50 10.50 35.00
4-Spider-Man/X-Men vs. Morbius (part 2 of story); 4th app. of Morbius 4.00 12.00 40.00
5-10: 5-Vision. 6-Thing. 7-Thor. 8-The Cat (4/73, came out between The Cat #3 & 4). 9-Iron Man. 10-H-T 1.85 5.50 15.00
11,13,14,16-20: 11-Inhumans. 13-Capt. America. 14-Sub-Mariner. 16-Capt. Marvel. 17-Mr. Fantastic. 18-H-T/Hulk. 19-Ka-Zar. 20-Black Panther; last 20¢ issue 1.00 3.00 7.50
12-Werewolf (8/73, 1 month before Werewolf #1). 2.25 6.75 18.00
15-1st Spider-Man/Ghost Rider team-up (11/73) 2.50 7.50 20.00
21-30: 21-Dr. Strange. 22-Hawkeye. 23-H-T/Iceman (X-Men cameo). 24-Brother Voodoo. 25-Daredevil. 26-H-T/Thor. 27-Hulk. 28-Hercules. 29-H-T/Iron Man. 30-Falcon 1.60 4.00
31-45,47-50: 31-Iron Fist. 32-H-T/Son of Satan. 33-Nighthawk. 34-Valkyrie. 35-H-T/Dr. Strange. 36-Frankenstein. 37-Man-Wolf. 38-Beast. 39-H-T. 40-Sons of the Tiger/H-T. 41-Scarlet Witch. 42-The Vision. 43-Dr. Doom; retells origin. 44-Moondragon. 45-Killraven. 47-Thing. 48-Iron Man; last 25¢ issue. 49-Dr. Strange; Iron Man app. 50-Iron Man; Dr. Strange app. 1.20 3.00
46-Spider-Man/Deathlok team-up 2.40 6.00
51,52,56,57: 51-Iron Man; Dr. Strange app. 52-Capt. America. 56-Daredevil. 57-Black Widow 2.00 2.50
53-Hulk; Woodgod & X-Men app., 1st Byrne-a on X-Men (1/77) 2.50 7.50 20.00
54,59,60: 54-Hulk; Woodgod app. 59-Yellowjacket/The Wasp. 60-The Wasp (Byrne-a in all) 1.60 4.00
55-Warlock-c/story; Byrne-a 2.00 5.00
58-Ghost Rider 1.60 4.00
61-70: All Byrne-a; 61-H-T. 62-Ms. Marvel; last 30¢ issue. 63-Iron Fist. 64-Daughters of the Dragon. 65-Capt. Britain (1st U.S. app.). 66-Capt. Britain; 1st app. Arcade. 67-Tigra; Kraven the Hunter app. 68-Man-Thing. 69-Havok (from X-Men). 70-Thor 1.20 3.00
71-74,76-78,80: 71-Falcon. 72-Iron Man. 73-Daredevil. 74-Not Ready for Prime Time Players (Belushi). 76-Dr. Strange. 77-Ms. Marvel. 78-Wonder Man. 80-Dr. Strange/Clea; last 35¢ issue .80 2.00
75,79: Byrne-a(p). 75-Power Man; Cage app. 79-Mary Jane Watson as Red Sonja; Clark Kent cameo (1 panel, 3/79) 1.20 3.00
81-85,87,88,90,92-99: 81-Satana. 82-Black Widow. 83-Nick Fury. 84-Shang-Chi. 92-Hawkeye. 93-Werewolf by Night. 94-SpM vs. The Shroud. 95-Mockingbird (intro.); Nick Fury app. 96-Howard the Duck; last 40¢ issue. 97-Spider-Woman/Hulk. 98-Black Widow. 99-Machine Man. 85-Shang-Chi/ Black Widow/Nick Fury. 87-Black Panther. 88-Invisible Girl. 90-Beast .80 2.00
86-Guardians of the Galaxy 1.20 3.00
89-Nightcrawler (from X-Men) 1.20 3.00
91-Ghost Rider 1.20 3.00
100-(Double-size)-Fantastic Four/Storm/Black Panther; origin/1st app. Karma, one of the New Mutants; origin Storm; X-Men x-over; Miller-c/a(p); Byrne-a (on X-Men app. only) 1.60 4.00
101-116: 101-Nighthawk(Ditko-a). 102-Doc Samson. 103-Ant-Man. 104-Hulk/ Ka-Zar. 105-Hulk/Powerman/Iron Fist. 106-Capt. America. 107-She-Hulk. 108-Paladin; Dazzler cameo. 109-Dazzler; Paladin app. 110-Iron Man. 111-Devil-Slayer. 112-King Kull; last 50¢ issue. 113-Quasar. 114-Falcon. 115-Thor. 116-Valkyrie 1.50
117-Wolverine-c/story 1.00 2.80 7.00
118-140,142-149: 118-Professor X; Wolverine app. (4 pgs.); X-Men cameo. 119-Gargoyle. 120-Dominic Fortune. 121-Human Torch. 122-Man-Thing. 123-Daredevil. 124-The Beast. 125-Tigra. 126-Hulk & Powerman/Son of Satan. 127-The Watcher. 128-Capt. America; Spider-Man/Capt. America photo-c. 129-The Vision. 130-Scarlet Witch. 131-Frogman. 132-Mr. Fantastic. 133-Fantastic Four. 134-Jack of Hearts. 135-Kitty Pryde; X-Men cameo. 136-Wonder Man. 137-Aunt May/Franklin Richards. 138-Sandman. 139-Nick Fury. 140-Black Widow. 142-Capt. Marvel. 143-Starfox. 144-Moon Knight. 145-Iron Man. 146-Nomad. 147-Human Torch; SpM

Marvel Team-Up #5 (2nd Sereis) © MEG

Marvel Triple Action #45 © MEG

Marvel Two-in-One #29 © MEG

back to old costume. 148-Thor. 149-Cannonball 1.50
141-Daredevil; SpM/Black Widow app. (Spidey in new black costume; ties w/ Amaz. S-M #252 for 1st black costume) 1.20 3.00
150-X-Men ($1.00, double-size); B. Smith-c 1.60 4.00
Annual 1(1976)-SpM/X-Men (early app.) 1.85 5.50 15.00
Annuals 2-7: 2(1979)-SpM/Hulk. 3(1980)-Hulk/Power Man/Machine Man/Iron Fist; Miller-c(p). 4(1981)-SpM/Daredevil/Moon Knight/Power Man/Iron Fist; brief origins of each; Miller-c; Miller scripts on Daredevil. 5(1982)-SpM/The Thing/Scarlet Witch/Dr. Strange/Quasar. 6(1983)-SpM/New Mutants (early app.), Cloak & Dagger. 7(1984)-Alpha Flight; Byrne-c(i) .80 2.00

NOTE: ***Art Adams** c-141p. **Austin** a-79i; c-76i, 79i, 96i, 101i, 112i, 130i. **Bolle** a-9i. **Byrne** a(p)-53-55, 59-70, 75, 79, 100; c-68p, 70p, 72p, 75, 76p, 79p, 129i, 133i. **Colan** a-87p. **Ditko** a-101. **Kane** a(p)-4-6, 13, 14, 16-19, 23; c(p)-4, 13, 14, 17-19, 23, 25, 26, 32-35, 37, 41, 44, 45, 47, 53, 54. **Miller** a-100p; c-95p, 99p, 100p, 102p, 106. **Mooney** a-2i, 7i, 8, 10p, 11p, 16i, 24-31p, 72, 93i, Annual 5i. **Nasser** a-89p; c-101p. **Simonson** c-99i, 148. **Paul Smith** c-131, 132. **Starlin** c-27. **Sutton** a-93p. "H-T" means Human Torch; "SpM" means Spider-Man; "S-M" means Sub-Mariner.*

MARVEL TEAM-UP
Sept, 1997 - Present ($1.99)
Marvel Comics

1-5: 1-Spider-Man team-ups begin, Generation x-app. 2-Hercules-c/app.; two covers. 3-Sandman. 4-Man-Thing .80 2.00

MARVEL TREASURY EDITION
1974; #2, Dec, 1974 - #28, 1981 ($1.50/$2.50, 100 pgs., oversized, new-a &-r)
Marvel Comics Group

1-Spectacular Spider-Man; story-r/Marvel Super-Heroes #14; Romita-c/a(r); G. Kane, Ditko-r; Green Goblin/Hulk-r 2.50 7.50 24.00
1-1,000 numbered copies signed by Stan Lee & John Romita on front-c & sold thru mail for $5.00; 1st 1,000 copies off the press10.00 30.00 100.00
2-25,27: 2-Fantastic Four-r/F.F. 6,11,48-50(Silver Surfer). 3-The Mighty Thor-r/ Thor #125-130. 4-Conan the Barbarian; Barry Smith-c/a(r)/Conan #11. 5-The Hulk (origin-r/Hulk #3). 6-Dr. Strange. 7-Mighty Avengers. 8-Giant Superhero Holiday Grab-Bag; Spider-Man, Hulk, Nick Fury. 9-Giant; Super-hero Team-up. 10-Thor; r/Thor #154-157. 11-Fantastic Four. 12-Howard the Duck (r/#H. the Duck #1 & G.S. Man-Thing #4,5) plus new Defenders story. 13-Giant Super-Hero Holiday Grab-Bag. 14-The Sensational Spider-Man; r/1st Morbius from Amazing S-M #101,102 plus #100 & r/Not Brand Echh #6. 15-Conan; B. Smith, Neal Adams-i; r/Conan #24. 16-The Defenders (origin) & Valkyrie; r/Defenders #1,4,13,14. 17-The Hulk. 18-The Astonishing Spider-Man; r/Spider-Man's 1st team-ups with Iron Fist, The X-Men, Ghost Rider & Werewolf by Night; inside back-c has photos from 1978 Spider-Man TV show. 19-Conan the Barbarian. 20-Hulk. 21-Fantastic Four. 22-Spider-Man. 23-Conan. 24-Rampaging Hulk. 25-Spider-Man vs. The Hulk. 27-Spider-Man 1.00 3.00 8.00
26-The Hulk; Wolverine app. 1.25 3.75 10.00
28-Spider-Man/Superman; (origin of each) 1.85 5.50 15.00

NOTE: *Reprints-2, 3, 5, 7-9, 13, 14, 16, 17. **Neal Adams** a(i)-6, 15. **Brunner** a-6, 12; c-6. **Buscema** a-15, 19, 28; c-28. **Colan** a-6r; c-12p. **Ditko** a-1, 6. **Gil Kane** c-16p. **Kirby** a-2, 10, 11; c-7. **Romita** c-1, 5. **B. Smith** a-4, 15, 19; c-4, 19.*

MARVEL TREASURY OF OZ FEATURING THE MARVELOUS LAND OF OZ
1975 ($1.50, oversized) (See MGM's Marvelous...)
Marvel Comics Group

1-Buscema-a; Romita-c 1.25 3.75 10.00

MARVEL TREASURY SPECIAL (Also see 2001: A Space Odyssey)
1974; 1976 ($1.50, oversized, 84 pgs.)
Marvel Comics Group

Vol. 1-Spider-Man, Torch, Sub-Mariner, Avengers "Giant Superhero Holiday Grab-Bag"; Wood, Colan/Everett, plus 2 Kirby-r; reprints Hulk vs. Thing from Fantastic Four #25,26 1.25 3.75 10.00
Vol. 1-... Featuring Captain America's Bicentennial Battles (6/76)-Kirby-a; B. Smith inks, 11 pgs. 1.80 5.50 15.00

MARVEL TRIPLE ACTION (See Giant-Size...)
Feb, 1972 - No. 24, Mar, 1975; No. 25, Aug, 1975 - No. 47, Apr, 1979
Marvel Comics Group

1-(25¢ giant, 52 pgs.)-Dr. Doom, Silver Surfer, The Thing begin, end #4 ('66 reprints from Fantastic Four) 1.80 5.50 15.00
2-5 1.00 3.00 8.00
6-10 2.00 5.00
11-20 1.20 3.00
21-47: 45-r/X-Men #45. 46-r/Avengers #53(X-Men) .80 2.00

NOTE: *#5-44, 46, 47 reprint Avengers #11 thru ?. #40-r/Avengers #48(1st Black Knight). **Buscema** a(r)-35p, 36p, 38p, 39p, 41, 42, 43p, 44p, 46p, 47p. **Ditko** a-2r; c-47. **Kirby** a(r)-1-4p. **Starlin** c-7. **Tuska** a(r)-40p, 43i, 46i, 47i. #2 through at least #17 are 20¢-c.*

MARVEL TWO-IN-ONE (...Featuring ... #82? on; also see The Thing)
January, 1974 - No. 100, June, 1983
Marvel Comics Group

1-Thing team-ups begin; Man-Thing 3.50 10.50 35.00
2-4: 2-Sub-Mariner; last 20¢ issue. 3-Daredevil. 4-Capt. America 1.25 3.75 10.00
5-Guardians of the Galaxy (9/74, 2nd app.?) 1.50 4.50 12.00
6-Dr. Strange (11/74) 1.50 4.50 12.00
7,9,10 2.00 5.00
8-Early Ghost Rider app. (3/75) 1.00 2.80 7.00
11-14,17-20: 13-Power Man. 14-Son of Satan (early app.). 17-Spider-Man. 18-Last 25¢ issue 1.40 3.50
15,16-(Regular 25¢ edition)(5-6/76) 1.40 3.50
15,16-(30¢-c, limited distribution) 1.75 5.25 14.00
21-26,29,31-40: 29-Master of Kung Fu; Spider-Woman cameo. 31-33-Spider-Woman. 39-Vision 1.20 3.00
27-Deathlok 1.60 4.00
28-(Regular 30¢ edition)(6/77) 1.20 3.00
28-(35¢-c, limited distribution) 1.50 4.50 12.00
30-2nd full app. Spider-Woman (see Marvel Spotlight #32 for 1st app.) 2.00 5.00
41,42,44-49: 42-Capt. America. 45-Capt. Marvel. 46-Thing battles Hulk-c/story 1.20 3.00
43,50,53,55-Byrne-a(p). 53-Quasar(7/79, 2nd app.) 1.00 2.50
51-The Beast, Nick Fury, Ms. Marvel; Miller-p 1.20 3.00
52-Moon Knight app. 1.20 3.00
54-Death of Deathlok; Byrne-a 1.00 3.00 7.50
56-60,64-68,70-79,81,82: 60-Intro. Impossible Woman. 68-Angel. 71-1st app. Maelstrom. 75-Avengers (52 pgs.). 76-Iceman 1.20 2.00
61-63: 61-Starhawk (from Guardians); "The Coming of Her" storyline begins, ends #63; cover similar to F.F. #67 (Him-c). 62-Moondragon; Thanos & Warlock cameo in flashback; Starhawk app. 63-Warlock?; Warlock revived shortly; Starhawk & Moondragon app. .80 2.00
69-Guardians of the Galaxy 1.20 3.00
80-Ghost Rider 1.20 3.00
83,84: 83-Sasquatch. 84-Alpha Flight app. .80 2.00
85-99: 90-Spider-Man. 93-Jocasta dies. 96-X-Men-c & cameo .80 2.00
100-Double size, Byrne scripts .80 2.00
Annual 1 (1976, 52 pgs.)-Thing/Liberty Legion .80 2.00
Annual 2(1977, 52 pgs.)-Thing/Spider-Man; 2nd death of Thanos; end of Thanos saga; Warlock app.; Starlin-c/a 1.00 3.00 8.00
Annual 3,4 (1978-79, 52 pgs.): 3-Nova. 4-Black Bolt .80 2.00
Annual 5-7 (1980-82, 52 pgs.): 5-Hulk. 6-1st app. American Eagle. 7-The Thing/ Champion; Sasquatch, Colossus app.; X-Men cameo (1 pg.) .80 2.00

NOTE: ***Austin** c(i)-42, 54, 56, 58, 61, 63, 66. **John Buscema** a-30p, 45; c-30p. **Byrne** (p)-43, 50, 53-55; c-43, 53p, 56p, 98i, 99i. **Gil Kane** a-1p, 2p; c(p)-1-3, 9, 11, 14, 28. **Kirby** c-10, 12, 19p, 20, 25, 27. **Mooney** a-18i, 38i, 90i. **Nasser** a-70p. **Perez** a(p)-56-58, 60, 64, 65; c(p)-32, 33, 42, 50-52, 54, 55, 57, 58, 61-66, 70. **Roussos** a-Annual 1i. **Simonson** c-43i, 97p, Annual 6i. **Starlin** c-6, Annual 1. **Tuska** a-6p.*

MARVEL UNIVERSE (See Official Handbook Of The...)

MARVEL VERSUS DC (See DC Versus Marvel) (Also see Amazon, Assassins, Bruce Wayne: Agent of S.H.I.E.L.D., Bullets & Bracelets, Doctor Strangefate, JLX, Legend of the Dark Claw, Magneto & The Magnetic Men, Speed Demon, Spider-Boy, Super Soldier, & X-Patrol)

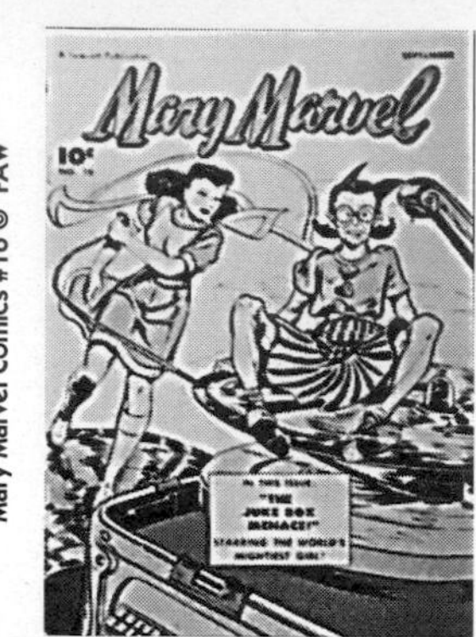

Mary Marvel Comics #16 © FAW

Mary Shelley's Frankenstein #1 © Topps

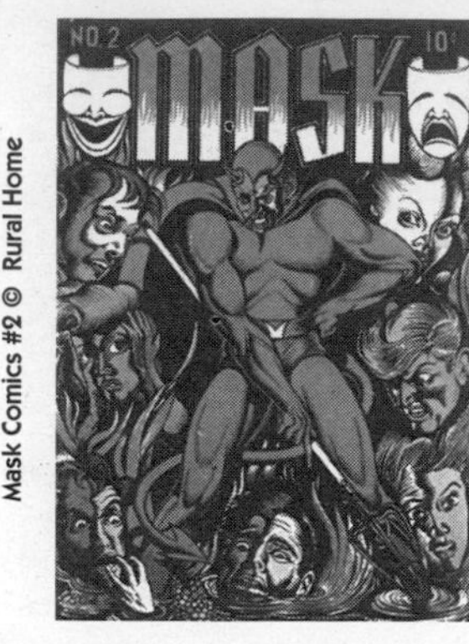

Mask Comics #2 © Rural Home

GD25 FN65 NM94

No. 2, 1996 - No. 3, 1996 ($3.95, limited series)
Marvel Comics
2,3: 2-Peter David script. 3-Ron Marz script; Dan Jurgens-a(p). 1st app. of Super Soldier, Spider-Boy, Dr. Doomsday, Doctor Strangefate, The Dark Claw, Nightcreeper, Amazon, Wraith & others. Storyline continues in Amalgam books. 1.60 4.00

MARVEL X-MEN COLLECTION, THE
Jan, 1994 - No. 3, Mar, 1994 ($2.95, limited series)
Marvel Comics
1-3-r/X-Men trading cards by Jim Lee 1.20 3.00

MARVIN MOUSE
September, 1957
Atlas Comics (BPC)
1-Everett-c/a; Maneely-a 8.75 26.25 70.00

MARY JANE & SNIFFLES (See Looney Tunes)
No. 402, June, 1952 - No. 474, June, 1953
Dell Publishing Co.
Four Color 402 (#1) 7.00 22.00 80.00
Four Color 474 6.40 19.00 70.00

MARY MARVEL COMICS (Monte Hale #29 on) (Also see Captain Marvel #18, Marvel Family, Shazam, & Wow Comics)
Dec, 1945 - No. 28, Sept, 1948
Fawcett Publications
1-Captain Marvel introduces Mary on-c; intro/origin Georgia Sivana 144.00 432.00 1300.00
2 60.00 180.00 540.00
3,4: 3-New logo 39.00 117.00 350.00
5-8: 8-Bulletgirl x-over in Mary Marvel; X-Mas-c 30.00 90.00 240.00
9,10 26.00 80.00 210.00
11-20 17.50 53.00 140.00
21-28: 28-Western-c 15.00 45.00 120.00

MARY POPPINS (See Movie Comics & Walt Disney Showcase No. 17)

MARY'S GREATEST APOSTLE (St. Louis Grignion de Montfort)
No date (16 pgs.; paper cover)
Catechetical Guild (Topix) (Giveaway)
nn 2.40 6.00 12.00

MARY SHELLEY'S FRANKENSTEIN
Oct, 1994 - Jan, 1995 ($2.95, limited series)
Topps Comics
1-4-polybagged w/3 trading cards 1.20 3.00
1-4 ($2.50)-Newstand ed. 1.00 2.50

MARY WORTH (See Harvey Comics Hits #55 & Love Stories of...)
March, 1956 (Also see Romantic Picture Novelettes)
Argo
1 5.70 17.00 40.00

MASK (TV)
Dec, 1985 - No. 4, Mar, 1986; Feb, 1987 - No. 9, Oct, 1987 (limited series)
DC Comics
1-Sat. morning TV show. .80 2.00
2-4 1.40
1-(2nd series) 1.20
2-9 .90

MASK, THE
Aug, 1991 - No. 4, Oct, 1991; No. 0, Dec, 1991 ($2.50, 36 pgs., limited series)
Dark Horse Comics
1-4: 1-1st app. Lt. Kellaway as The Mask 1.00 2.80 7.00
0-(12/91, B&W, 56 pgs.)-r/Mayhem #1-4 2.00 5.00

MASK: HUNT FOR GREEN OCTOBER
July, 1995 - Oct, 1995 ($2.50, limited series)
Dark Horse Comics
1-4-Evan Dorkin scripts 1.00 2.50

MASK: OFFICIAL MOVIE ADAPTATION
July, 1994 - Aug, 1994 ($2.50, limited series)
Dark Horse Comics
1,2 1.00 2.50

MASK RETURNS
Oct, 1992 - Mar, 1993 ($2.50, limited series)
Dark Horse Comics
1-4 1.60 4.00

MASK SOUTHERN DISCOMFORT
Mar, 1996 - July, 1996 ($2.50, limited series)
Dark Horse Comics
1-4 1.00 2.50

MASK STRIKES BACK
Feb, 1995 - Jun, 1995 ($2.50, limited series)
Dark Horse Comics
1-5 1.00 2.50

MASK SUMMER VACATION
July, 1995 ($10.95, one shot, hard-c)
Dark Horse Comics
1-nn-Rick Geary-c/a 1.40 4.15 11.00

MASK VIRTUAL SURREALITY
July, 1997 ($2.95, one shot)
Dark Horse Comics
nn-Mignola, Aragonés, and others-s/a 1.20 3.00

MASK WORLD TOUR
Dec, 1995 - Mar, 1996 ($2.50, limited series)
Dark Horse Comics
1-4-3-X & Ghost-c/app. 1.00 2.50

MASK COMICS
Feb-Mar, 1945 - No. 2, Apr-May, 1945; No. 2, Fall, 1945
Rural Home Publications
1-Classic L. B. Cole Satan-c/a; Palais-a 200.00 600.00 1800.00
2-(Scarce)-Classic L. B. Cole Satan-c; Black Rider, The Boy Magician, & The Collector app. 133.00 400.00 1200.00
2-(Fall, 1945)-No publ.-same as regular #2; L. B. Cole-c 100.00 300.00 900.00

MASKED BANDIT, THE
1952
Avon Periodicals
nn-Kinstler-a 13.00 39.00 95.00

MASKED MAN, THE
12/84 - #10, 4/86; #11, 10/87; #12, 4/88 ($1.75/$2.00, color/B&W #9 on, Baxter paper)
Eclipse Comics
1-Origin retold .80 2.00
2-12: 3-Origin Aphid-Man; begin $2.00-c .75 1.80

MASKED MARVEL (See Keen Detective Funnies)
Sept, 1940 - No. 3, Dec, 1940
Centaur Publications
1-The Masked Marvel begins 139.00 417.00 1250.00
2,3: 2-Gustavson, Tarpe Mills-a 94.00 282.00 850.00

MASKED PILOT, THE (See Popular Comics #43)
1939 (7-1/2x5-1/4", 16 pgs., premium, non-slick-c)
R.S. Callender

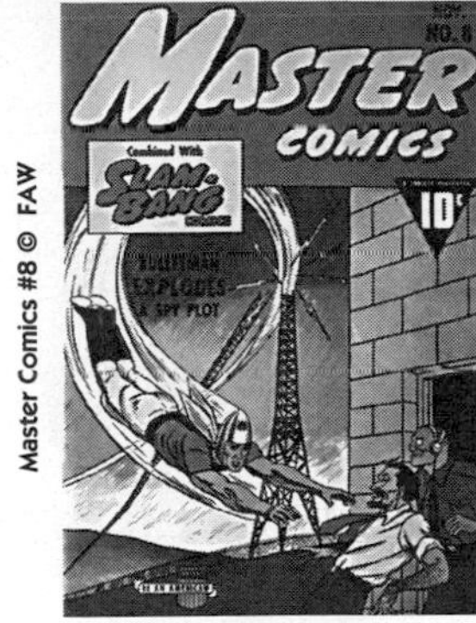

Master Comics #8 © FAW

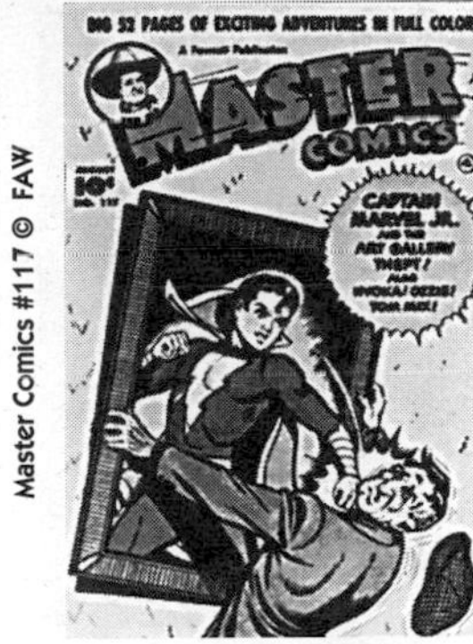

Master Comics #117 © FAW

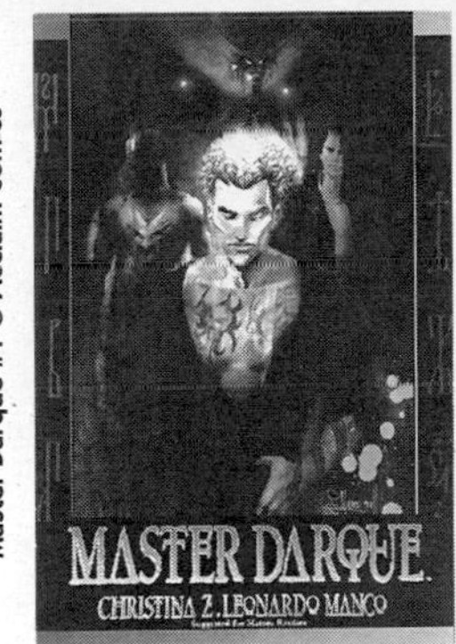

Master Darque #1 © Acclaim Comics

GD25 FN65 NM94

nn-Bob Jenney-a 8.50 26.00 60.00

MASKED RAIDER, THE (Billy The Kid #9 on; Frontier Scout, Daniel Boone #10-13) (Also see Blue Bird)
June, 1955 - No. 8, July, 1957; No. 14, Aug, 1958 - No. 30, June, 1961
Charlton Comics

1-Masked Raider & Talon the Golden Eagle begin; painted-c 8.75 26.25 70.00
2 5.70 17.00 40.00
3-8: 8-Billy The Kid app. 4.25 13.00 28.00
14,16-30: 22-Rocky Lane app. 4.00 11.00 22.00
15-Williamson-a, 7 pgs. 4.25 13.00 28.00

MASKED RANGER
Apr, 1954 - No. 9, Aug, 1955
Premier Magazines

1-The Masked Ranger, his horse Streak, & The Crimson Avenger (origin) begin, end #9; Woodbridge/Frazetta-a 34.00 101.00 250.00
2,3 10.00 30.00 75.00
4-8-All Woodbridge-a. 5-Jesse James by Woodbridge. 6-Billy The Kid by Woodbridge. 7-Wild Bill Hickok by Woodbridge. 8-Jim Bowie's Life Story 11.50 34.00 85.00
9-Torres-a; Wyatt Earp by Woodbridge; Says Death of Masked Ranger on-c 12.00 36.00 90.00

NOTE: *Check a-1.* ***Woodbridge*** *c/a-1, 4-9.*

MASK OF DR. FU MANCHU, THE (See Dr. Fu Manchu)
1951
Avon Periodicals

1-Sax Rohmer adapt.; Wood-c/a (26 pgs.); Hollingsworth-a 78.00 234.00 650.00

MASQUE OF THE RED DEATH (See Movie Classics)

MASTER COMICS (Combined with Slam Bang Comics #7 on)
Mar, 1940 - No. 133, Apr, 1953 (No. 1-6: oversized issues)
(#1-3: 15¢, 52 pgs.; #4-6: 10¢, 36 pgs.; #7-Begin 68 pg. issues)
Fawcett Publications

GD25 FN65 VF82 NM94

1-Origin & 1st app. Master Man; The Devil's Dagger, El Carim, Master of Magic, Rick O'Say, Morton Murch, White Rajah, Shipwreck Roberts, Frontier Marshal, Streak Sloan, Mr. Clue begin (all features end #6) 680.00 2040.00 4080.00 6800.00
(Estimated up to 100 total copies exist, 4 in NM/Mint)

GD25 FN65 NM94

2 178.00 534.00 1600.00
3-5 139.00 417.00 1250.00
6-Last Master Man 139.00 417.00 1250.00

NOTE: *#1-6 rarely found in near mint to mint condition due to large-size format.*

7-(10/40)-Bulletman, Zoro, the Mystery Man (ends #22), Lee Granger, Jungle King, & Buck Jones begin; only app. The War Bird & Mark Swift & the Time Retarder; Zoro, Lee Granger, Jungle King & Mark Swift all continue from Slam Bang; Bulletman moves from Nickel 222.00 667.00 2000.00
8-The Red Gaucho (ends #13), Captain Venture (ends #22) & The Planet Princess begin 117.00 350.00 1050.00
9,10: 10-Lee Granger ends 94.00 282.00 850.00
11-Origin & 1st app. Minute-Man (2/41) 211.00 633.00 1900.00
12 106.00 318.00 950.00
13-Origin & 1st app. Bulletgirl; Hitler-c 161.00 483.00 1450.00
14-16: 14-Companions Three begins, ends #31 86.00 258.00 775.00
17-20: 17-Raboy-a on Bulletman begins. 20-Captain Marvel cameo app. in Bulletman 82.00 246.00 735.00

GD25 FN65 VF82 NM94

21-(12/41; Scarce)-Captain Marvel & Bulletman team up against Capt. Nazi; origin & 1st app. Capt. Marvel Jr's most famous nemesis Captain Nazi who will cause creation of Capt. Marvel Jr. in Whiz #25. Part I of trilogy origin of Capt. Marvel Jr.; 1st Mac Raboy-c for Fawcett; Capt. Nazi-c 430.00 1290.00 2580.00 4300.00
(Estimated up to 110 total copies exist, 6 in NM/Mint)
22-(1/42)-Captain Marvel Jr. moves over from Whiz #25 & teams up with Bulletman against Captain Nazi; part III of trilogy origin of Capt. Marvel Jr. & his 1st cover and adventure 390.00 1170.00 2340.00 3900.00
(Estimated up to 135 total copies exist, 7 in NM/Mint)

GD25 FN65 NM94

23-Capt. Marvel Jr. c/stories begin (1st solo story); fights Capt. Nazi by himself. 233.00 700.00 2100.00
24,25 81.00 243.00 725.00
26-28,30-Captain Marvel Jr. vs. Capt. Nazi. 30-Flag-c 73.00 219.00 660.00
29-Hitler & Hirohito-c 78.00 234.00 700.00
31,32: 32-Last El Carim & Buck Jones; intro Balbo, the Boy Magician in El Carim story 52.00 156.00 470.00
33-Balbo, the Boy Magician (ends #47), Hopalong Cassidy (ends #49) begins 52.00 156.00 470.00
34-Capt. Marvel Jr. vs. Capt. Nazi-c/story 58.00 174.00 525.00
35 52.00 156.00 470.00
36-40: 40-Flag-c 47.00 141.00 425.00
41-Bulletman, Capt. Marvel Jr. & Bulletgirl x-over in Minute-Man; only app. Crime Crusaders Club (Capt. Marvel Jr., Minute-Man, Bulletman & Bulletgirl); only team in Fawcett Comics 52.00 156.00 470.00
42-47,49: 47-Hitler becomes Corpl. Hitler Jr. 49-Last Minute-Man 33.00 100.00 265.00
48-Intro. Bulletboy; Capt. Marvel cameo in Minute-Man 36.00 108.00 310.00
50-Intro Radar & Nyoka the Jungle Girl & begin series (5/44); Radar also intro in Captain Marvel #35 (same date); Capt. Marvel x-over in Radar; origin Radar; Capt. Marvel & Capt. Marvel, Jr. introduce Radar on-c 25.00 75.00 200.00
51-58 17.00 51.00 135.00
59-62: Nyoka serial "Terrible Tiara" in all; 61-Capt. Marvel Jr. 1st meets Uncle Marvel 19.50 58.00 155.00
63-80 13.00 39.00 105.00
81,83-87,89-91,95-99: 88-Hopalong Cassidy begins (ends #94). 95-Tom Mix begins (ends #133) 12.00 36.00 95.00
82,88,92-94-Krigstein-a 13.00 39.00 105.00
100 12.00 36.00 95.00
101-106-Last Bulletman 10.50 32.00 85.00
107-131 9.50 28.00 75.00
132-B&W and color illos in **POP** 10.00 30.00 80.00
133-Bill Battle app. 12.00 36.00 95.00

NOTE: ***Mac Raboy*** *a-15-39, 40(part), 42, 58. c-21-49, 51, 52, 54, 56, 58, 68(part), 69(part). Bulletman c-7-11, 13(half), 15, 18(part), 19, 20, 21(w/Capt. Marvel & Capt. Nazi), 22(w/Capt. Marvel, Jr.). Capt. Marvel, Jr. c-23-133.* ***Master Man*** *c-1-6. Minute Man c-12, 13(half), 14, 16, 17, 18(part).*

MASTER DARQUE
Feb, 1998 - Present ($3.95, limited series)
Acclaim Comics (Valiant)

1-Manco-a/Christina Z.-s 3.95

MASTER DETECTIVE
1964 (Reprints)
Super Comics

17-r/Criminals on the Loose V4 #2; r/Young King Cole #?; McWilliams-r 1.10 3.30 9.00

MASTER OF KUNG FU (Formerly Special Marvel Edition; see Deadly Hands of Kung Fu & Giant-Size...)
No. 17, April, 1974 - No. 125, June, 1983
Marvel Comics Group

17-Starlin-a; intro Black Jack Tarr; 3rd Shang-Chi (ties w/Deadly Hands #1) 2.15 6.50 17.00
18-20: 19-Man-Thing-c/story 1.10 3.30 9.00
21-23,25-30 2.20 5.50

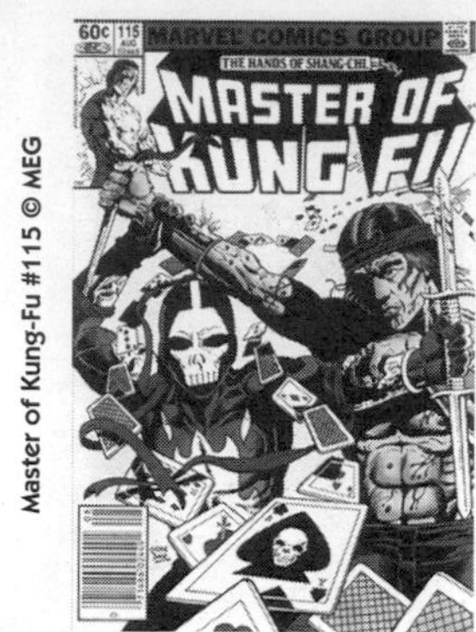

Master of Kung-Fu #115 © MEG

Maximage #6 © Rob Liefeld

Maxx #2 © I Before E

	GD25	FN65	NM94
24-Starlin, Simonson-a	1.00	2.80	7.00
31-99: 33-1st Leiko Wu. 43-Last 25¢ issue		1.40	3.50
100-Double size		1.80	4.50
101-117,119-124		1.20	3.00
118,125-Double size issues		1.60	4.00
Annual 1(4/76)-Iron Fist app.	1.00	2.80	7.00

NOTE: ***Austin** c-63i, 74i. **Buscema** c-44p. **Gulacy** a(p)-18-20, 22, 25, 29-31, 33-35, 38, 39, 40(p&i), 42-50, 53r(#20); c-51, 55, 64, 67. **Gil Kane** c(p)-20, 38, 39, 42, 45, 59, 63. **Nebres** c-73i. **Starlin** a-17p, 24; c-54. **Sutton** a-42i. #53 reprints #20.*

MASTER OF KUNG-FU: BLEEDING BLACK
Feb, 1991 ($2.95, 84 pgs., one-shot)
Marvel Comics

1-The Return of Shang-Chi — 1.20 3.00

MASTER OF THE WORLD
No. 1157, July, 1961
Dell Publishing Co.

Four Color 1157-Movie — 4.50 13.50 50.00

MASTERS OF TERROR (Magazine)
July, 1975 - No. 2, Sept, 1975 (B&W) (All reprints)
Marvel Comics Group

1-Brunner, Barry Smith-a; Morrow/Steranko-c; Starlin-a(p); Gil Kane-a — 1.00 3.00 8.00
2-Reese, Kane, Mayerik-a; Adkins/Steranko-c — 1.00 3.00 8.00

MASTERS OF THE UNIVERSE
Dec, 1982 - No. 3, Feb, 1983 (Mini-series)
DC Comics

1-3: 2-Origin He-Man & Ceril — 1.00

NOTE: ***Alcala** a-1i,, 2i. **Tuska** a-1-3p; c-1-3p. #2 has 75 & 95 cent cover price.*

MASTERS OF THE UNIVERSE (Comic Album)
1984 (8-1/2x11", $2.95, 64 pgs.)
Western Publishing Co.

11362-Based on Mattel toy & cartoon — 1.20 3.00

MASTERS OF THE UNIVERSE
May 1986 - No. 12, March, 1988 (75¢/$1.00)
Star Comics/Marvel #7 on

1-12: 8-Begin $1.00-c — 1.00
The Motion Picture (11/87, $2.00)-Tuska-p — .80 2.00

MASTERWORKS SERIES OF GREAT COMIC BOOK ARTISTS, THE
May, 1983 - No. 3, Dec, 1983 (Baxter paper)
Sea Gate Distributors/DC Comics

1-3: 1,2-Shining Knight by Frazetta r-/Adventure. 2-Tomahawk by Frazetta-r. 3-Wrightson-c/a(r) — .80 2.00

MATT SLADE GUNFIGHTER (Kid Slade Gunfighter #5 on; See Western Gunfighters)
May, 1956 - No. 4, Nov, 1956
Atlas Comics (SPI)

	GD25	FN65	NM94
1-Intro Matt & horse Eagle; Williamson/Torres-a	15.00	45.00	120.00
2-Williamson-a	8.75	26.25	65.00
3,4	7.15	21.50	50.00

NOTE: ***Maneely** a-1, 3, 4; c-1, 2, 4. **Roth** a-2-4. **Severin** a-1, 3, 4. **Maneely** c/a-1.*

MAVERICK (TV)
No. 892, 4/58 - No. 19, 4-6/62 (All have photo-c)
Dell Publishing Co.

	GD25	FN65	NM94
Four Color 892 (#1)-James Garner photo-c begin	25.00	75.00	275.00
Four Color 930,945,962,980,1005 (6-8/59): 945-James Garner/Jack Kelly photo-c begin	10.00	30.00	110.00
7 (10-12/59) - 14: Last Garner/Kelly-c	8.00	23.00	85.00
15-18: Jack Kelly/Roger Moore photo-c	6.50	19.50	72.00
19-Jack Kelly photo-c	6.50	19.50	72.00

MAVERICK (See X-Men)
Jan, 1997 ($2.95, one-shot)
Marvel Comics

1-Hama-s — 1.20 3.00

MAVERICK (See X-Men)
Sept, 1997 - Present ($2.99/$1.99)
Marvel Comics

1-($2.99)-Wraparound-c. — 3.00
2-6: 2-Two covers. 4-Wolverine-c — 1.99

MAVERICK MARSHAL
Nov, 1958 - No. 7, May, 1960
Charlton Comics

	GD25	FN65	NM94
1	5.00	15.00	30.00
2-7	4.00	10.00	20.00

MAVERICKS
Jan, 1994 - No. 5, 1994 (#1-$2.75, #2-5-$2.50)
Daggar Comics Group

1-5: 1-Bronze. 1-Gold. 1-Silver — 1.00 2.50

MAX BRAND (See Silvertip)

MAXIMAGE
Dec, 1995 - No. 7, June 1996 ($2.50)
Image Comics (Extreme Studios)

1-7: 1-Liefeld-c. 2-Extreme Destroyer Pt. 2; polybagged w/card. 4-Angela & Glory-c/app. — 1.00 2.50

MAXIMUM MANGA
Nov, 1997 ($4.95, B&W, bi-monthy)
London Knight Studios

1-Anthology w/Jurassic Jane, Demonique, CYJAX and others — 4.95

MAXX (Also see Darker Image, Primer #5, & Friends of Maxx)
Mar, 1993 - Present ($1.95)
Image Comics (I Before E)

	GD25	FN65	NM94
1/2	1.25	3.75	10.00
1/2 (Gold)	2.50	7.50	25.00
1-Sam Kieth-c/a/scripts		2.40	6.00
1-Glow-in-the-dark variant	1.85	5.50	15.00
2-10: 6-Savage Dragon cameo(1 pg.). 7,8-Pitt-c & story		1.20	3.00
11-20		1.00	2.50
21-33: 21-Alan Moore-s		.80	2.00

MAYA (See Movie Classics)
Mar, 1968
Gold Key

1 (10218-803)(TV) — 1.50 4.50 12.00

MAYHEM
May, 1989 - No. 4, Sept, 1989 ($2.50, B&W, 52 pgs.)
Dark Horse Comics

	GD25	FN65	NM94
1- 4-part Stanley Ipkiss/Mask story begins; Mask-c	1.25	3.75	10.00
2-4: 2-Mask 1/2 back-c. 4-Mask-c	1.00	3.00	8.00

MAZE AGENCY, THE
Dec, 1988 - No. 20, 1991 ($1.95-$2.50, color)
Comico/Innovation Publishing #8 on

	GD25	FN65	NM94
1-6,8-15 ($1.95): 9-Ellery Queen app.		.80	2.00
7,16-20: 7 ($2.50)-Last Comico issue		1.00	2.50
Annual 1 (1990, $2.75)-Ploog-c; Spirit tribute ish		1.10	2.80
Special 1 (1989, $2.75)-Staton-p (Innovation)		1.10	2.80

MAZE AGENCY, THE (Vol. 2)
July, 1997 - Present ($2.95, B&W)
Caliber Comics

'Mazing Man #6 © DC

Medieval Spawn/Witchblade #3 © Top Cow

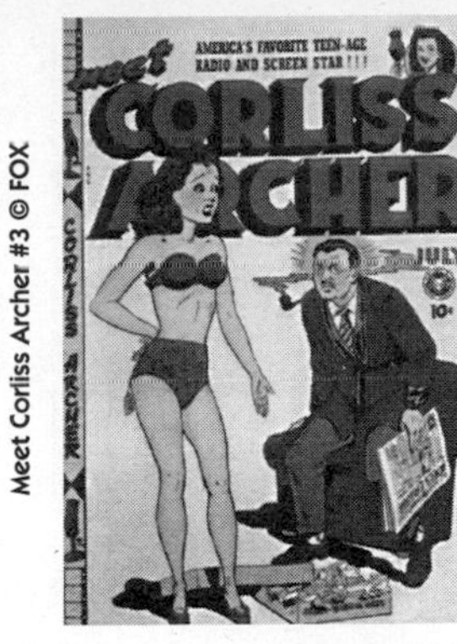

Meet Corliss Archer #3 © FOX

	GD25	FN65	NM94
1-Barr-s/Gonzales-a(p)			2.95

MAZIE (...& Her Friends) (See Flat-Top, Mortie, Stevie & Tastee-Freez)
1953 - #12, 1954; #13, 12/54 - #22, 9/56; #23, 9/57 - #28, 8/58
Mazie Comics(Magazine Publ.)/Harvey Publ. No. 13-on

	GD25	FN65	NM94
1-(Teen-age)-Stevie's girl friend	5.70	17.00	38.00
2	3.60	9.00	18.00
3-10	2.80	7.00	14.00
11-28	1.80	4.50	9.00

MAZIE
1950 - No. 7, 1951 (5¢) (5x7-1/4"-miniature)(52 pgs.)
Nation Wide Publishers

	GD25	FN65	NM94
1-Teen-age	10.00	30.00	80.00
2-7	5.70	17.00	40.00

MAZINGER (See First Comics Graphic Novel #17)

'MAZING MAN
Jan, 1986 - No. 12, Dec, 1986
DC Comics

	GD25	FN65	NM94
1-12: 7,8-Hembeck-a. 12-Dark Knight part-c by Miller			.80
Special 1 ('87), 2 (4/88), 3 ('90)-All $2.00, 52pgs.		.80	2.00

McCRORY'S CHRISTMAS BOOK
1955 (36 pgs., slick-c)
Western Printing Co. (McCrory Stores Corp. giveaway)

	GD25	FN65	NM94
nn-Painted-c	3.20	8.00	16.00

McCRORY'S TOYLAND BRINGS YOU SANTA'S PRIVATE EYES
1956 (16 pgs.)
Promotional Publ. Co. (Giveaway)

	GD25	FN65	NM94
nn-Has 9 pg. story plus 7 pgs. toy ads	2.40	6.00	12.00

McCRORY'S WONDERFUL CHRISTMAS
1954 (20 pgs., slick-c)
Promotional Publ. Co. (Giveaway)

	GD25	FN65	NM94
nn	3.20	8.00	16.00

McHALE'S NAVY (TV) (See Movie Classics)
May-July, 1963 - No. 3, Nov-Jan, 1963-64 (All have photo-c)
Dell Publishing Co.

	GD25	FN65	NM94
1	4.50	13.50	50.00
2,3	3.60	11.00	40.00

McKEEVER & THE COLONEL (TV)
Feb-Apr, 1963 - No. 3, Aug-Oct, 1963
Dell Publishing Co.

	GD25	FN65	NM94
1-Photo-c	4.50	13.50	50.00
2,3	3.60	11.00	40.00

McLINTOCK (See Movie Comics)

MD
Apr-May, 1955 - No. 5, Dec-Jan, 1955-56
E. C. Comics

	GD25	FN65	NM94
1-Not approved by code	11.30	34.00	90.00
2-5	8.75	26.25	70.00

NOTE: ***Crandall, Evans, Ingels, Orlando*** *art in all issues;* ***Craig*** *c-1-5.*

M.D. GEIST
1995 - No. 3, 1995 (Limited series)
CPM Comics

	GD25	FN65	NM94
1-3		1.20	3.00

M.D. GEIST DATA ALBUM
June, 1996 ($9.95, trade paperback)
CPM Comics

	GD25	FN65	NM94
1			10.00

M.D. GEIST: GROUND ZERO
Mar, 1996 - No. 3, May, 1996 ($2.95, limited series)
CPM Comics

	GD25	FN65	NM94
1-3		1.20	3.00

MEAT CAKE
1992 (B&W)
Iconographix

	GD25	FN65	NM94
1			1.00

MEAT CAKE
No. 1, Oct, 1993 - No. 5 (B&W)
Fantagraphics Books

	GD25	FN65	NM94
0-5: 3-Sal Buscema-a. 0 (1996)-reprints Meat Cake #1 from Iconographix.		1.00	2.50

MECHA (Also see Mayhem)
June, 1987 - No. 6, 1988 ($1.50/$1.95, color/B&W)
Dark Horse Comics

	GD25	FN65	NM94
1-6: 1,2 ($1.95, color), 3,4-($1.75, B&W), 5,6-($1.50, B&W)		.80	2.00

MECHA SPECIAL
May, 1995 ($2.95, one-shot)
Dark Horse Comics

	GD25	FN65	NM94
1		1.20	3.00

MEDAL FOR BOWZER, A
1966 (8 pgs.)
American Visuals

	GD25	FN65	NM94
nn-Eisner-c/script	20.00	60.00	200.00

MEDAL OF HONOR COMICS
Spring, 1946
A. S. Curtis

	GD25	FN65	NM94
1-War stories	8.75	26.25	65.00

MEDAL OF HONOR SPECIAL
1994 ($2.50, one-shot)
Dark Horse Comics

	GD25	FN65	NM94
1-Kubert-c/a (first story)		1.00	2.50

MEDIA STARR
July, 1989 - No. 3, Sept, 1989 ($1.95, color, mini-series, 28pgs.)
Innovation Publishing

	GD25	FN65	NM94
1-3: Deluxe format		.80	2.00

MEDIEVAL SPAWN/WITCHBLADE
May, 1996 - No. 3, June, 1996 ($2.95, limited series)
Image Comics (Top Cow Productions)

	GD25	FN65	NM94
1-Garth Ennis scripts in all	1.00	3.00	8.00
1-Platinum (500 copies) foil-c	4.0o0	12.00	40.00
1-Gold	1.85	5.50	15.00
1-ETM Exclusive Edition; gold foil logo	1.25	3.75	10.00
2,3		2.00	5.00
TPB ($9.95) r/#1-3	1.25	3.75	10.00

MEET ANGEL (Formerly Angel & the Ape)
No. 7, Nov-Dec, 1969
National Periodical Publications

	GD25	FN65	NM94
7-Wood-a(i)	1.25	3.75	10.00

MEET CORLISS ARCHER (Radio/Movie)(My Life #4 on)
Mar, 1948 - No. 3, July, 1948
Fox Features Syndicate

	GD25	FN65	NM94
1-(Teen-age)-Feldstein-c/a; headlight-c	58.00	174.00	475.00
2-Feldstein-c only	45.00	136.00	370.00
3-Part Feldstein-c only	40.00	120.00	290.00

NOTE: *No. 1-3 used in Seduction of the Innocent, pg. 39.*

Meet Hiya A Friend of Santa Claus nn © Julian J. Proskauer

Megaton #3 © Megaton

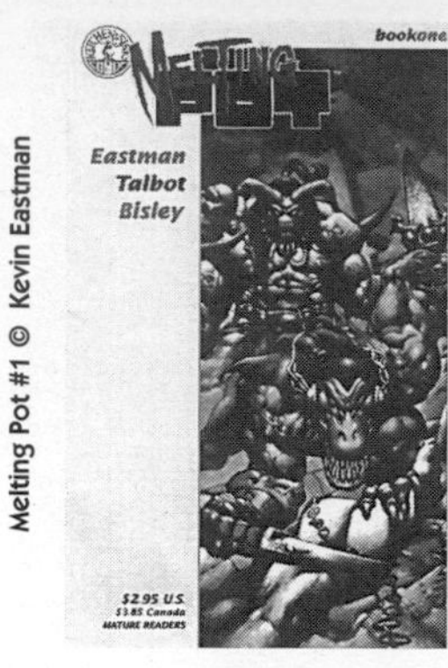

Melting Pot #1 © Kevin Eastman

MEET HERCULES (See Three Stooges)

MEET HIYA A FRIEND OF SANTA CLAUS
1949 (18 pgs.?, paper-c)
Julian J. Proskauer/Sundial Shoe Stores, etc. (Giveaway)

	GD25	FN65	NM94
nn	5.70	17.00	35.00

MEET MERTON
Dec, 1953 - No. 4, June, 1954
Toby Press

	GD25	FN65	NM94
1-(Teen-age)-Dave Berg-c/a	6.00	18.00	42.00
2-Dave Berg-c/a	4.25	13.00	26.00
3,4-Dave Berg-c/a	4.00	12.00	24.00
I.W. Reprint #9		2.40	6.00
Super Reprint #11('63), 18		2.40	6.00

MEET MISS BLISS (Becomes Stories Of Romance #5 on)
May, 1955 - No. 4, Nov, 1955
Atlas Comics (LMC)

	GD25	FN65	NM94
1-Al Hartley-c/a	10.00	30.00	70.00
2-4	6.50	19.50	45.00

MEET MISS PEPPER (Formerly Lucy, The Real Gone Gal)
No. 5, April, 1954 - No. 6, June, 1954
St. John Publishing Co.

	GD25	FN65	NM94
5-Kubert/Maurer-a	16.00	47.00	120.00
6-Kubert/Maurer-a; Kubert-c	13.00	39.00	90.00

MEET THE NEW POST GAZETTE SUNDAY FUNNIES
3/12/49 (7-1/4x10-1/4", 16 pgs., paper-c)
Commercial Comics (insert in newspaper)
Pittsburgh Post Gazette

Dick Tracy by Gould, Gasoline Alley, Terry & the Pirates, Brenda Starr, Buck Rogers by Yager, The Gumps, Peter Rabbit by Fago, Superman, Funnyman by Siegel & Shuster, The Saint, Archie, & others done especially for this book. A fine copy sold at auction in 1985 for $276.00.
Estimated value.... $300 – $800

MEGAHURTZ
Aug, 1997 - Present ($2.95, B&W)
Image Comics

	GD25	FN65	NM94
1-3-St. Pierre-s		1.20	3.00

MEGALITH DEATHWATCH 2000 (Megalith #3 on)
Apr, 1993 - No. 7, Jan, 1994 ($2.50)
Continuity

	GD25	FN65	NM94
0-Foil-c; no c-price, giveaway; Adams plot		1.00	2.50
1-3-Bagged w/card: 1-Gatefold-c by Nebres; Adams plot. 2-Fold-out-c; Adams plot. 3-Indestructible-c		1.00	2.50
4-7-Embossed-c: 4-Adams/Nebres-c; Adams part-i. 5-Sienkiewicz-i. 6-Adams part-i. 7-Adams-c(p); Adams plot		1.00	2.50

MEGATON (A super hero)
Nov, 1983; No. 2, Oct, 1985 - No. 8, Aug, 1987 (B&W)
Megaton Publ. (#3: 44 pgs.; #4: 52 pgs.)

	GD25	FN65	NM94
1-($2.00, 68 pgs.)-Erik Larsen's 1st pro work; Vanguard by Larsen begins (1st app.), ends #4; 1st app. Megaton, Berzerker, & Ethrian; Guice-c/a(p); Gustovich-a(p) in #1,2	1.00	3.00	8.00
2-($2.00, 68 pgs.)-The Dragon cameo (1 pg.) by Larsen (later The Savage Dragon in Image Comics); Guice-c/a(p)		1.60	4.00
3-1st full app. Savage Dragon-c/story by Larsen; 1st comic book work by Angel Medina (pin-up)	1.50	4.50	12.00
4-2nd full app. Savage Dragon by Larsen; 4,5-Wildman by Grass Green	1.10	3.30	9.00
5-1st Liefeld published-a (inside f/c, 6/86)		1.20	3.00
6,7: 6-Larsen-c		1.20	3.00
8-1st Liefeld story-a (7 pg. super hero story) plus 1 pg. Youngblood ad		1.20	3.00
...Explosion (6/87, 16 pg. color giveaway)-1st app. Youngblood by Rob Liefeld (2 pg. spread); shows Megaton heroes	1.85	5.50	15.00
...Holiday Special 1 (1994, $2.95, color, 40 pgs., publ. by Entity Comics)-Gold foil logo; bagged w/Kelley Jones card; Vanguard, Megaton plus shows unpublished-c to 1987 Youngblood #1 by Liefeld/Ordway		1.20	3.00

NOTE: *Copies of Megaton Explosion were also released in early 1992 all signed by Rob Liefeld and were made available to retailers.*

MEGATON MAN (See Don Simpson's Bizarre Heroes)
Nov, 1984 - No. 10, 1986
Kitchen Sink Enterprises

	GD25	FN65	NM94
1-10		.80	2.00
1-2nd printing (1989)		.80	2.00
...Meets The Uncategorizable X-Thems 1 (4/89, $2.00)		.80	2.00

MEGATON MAN VS. FORBIDDEN FRANKENSTEIN
Apr, 1996 ($2.95, B&W, one-shot)
Fiasco Comics

	GD25	FN65	NM94
1-Intro The Tomb Team (Forbidden Frankenstein, Drekula, Bride of the Monster, & Moon Wolf).		1.20	3.00

MEL ALLEN SPORTS COMICS (The Voice of the Yankees)
No. 5, Nov, 1949; No. 6, June, 1950
Standard Comics

	GD25	FN65	NM94
5(#1 on inside)-Tuska-a	16.00	49.00	130.00
6(#2)-Lou Gehrig story	11.30	34.00	90.00

MELTING POT
Dec, 1993 - No. 4, Sept, 1994 ($2.95)
Kitchen Sink Press

	GD25	FN65	NM94
1-4: Bisley-painted-c		1.20	3.00

MELVIN MONSTER (See Peter, the Little Pest)
Apr-June, 1965 - No. 10, Oct, 1969
Dell Publishing Co.

	GD25	FN65	NM94
1-By John Stanley	10.00	30.00	110.00
2-10-All by Stanley. #10-r/#1	7.00	20.00	75.00

MELVIN THE MONSTER (Dexter The Demon #7)
July, 1956 - No. 6, July, 1957
Atlas Comics (HPC)

	GD25	FN65	NM94
1-Maneely-c/a	7.00	22.00	80.00
2-6: 4-Maneely-c/a	4.50	13.50	50.00

MENACE
Mar, 1953 - No. 11, May, 1954
Atlas Comics (HPC)

	GD25	FN65	NM94
1-Horror & sci/fi stories begin; Everett-c/a	50.00	150.00	425.00
2-Post-atom bomb disaster by Everett; anti-Communist propaganda/torture scenes; Sinnott sci/fi story "Rocket to the Moon"	38.00	114.00	275.00
3,4,6-Everett-a. 4-Sci/fi story "Escape to the Moon". 6-Romita sci/fi story "Science Fiction"	29.00	86.00	215.00
5-Origin & 1st app. The Zombie by Everett (reprinted in Tales of the Zombie #1)(7/53); 5-Sci/fi story "Rocket Ship"	40.00	120.00	315.00
7,8,10,11: 7-Frankenstein story. 8-End of world story; Heath 3-D art(3 pgs.). 10-H-Bomb panels	21.00	62.00	155.00
9-Everett-a r-in Vampire Tales #1	25.00	75.00	185.00

NOTE: ***Brodsky** c-7, 8, 11. **Colan** a-6; c-9. **Everett** a-1-6, 9; c-1-6. **Heath** a-1-8; c-10. **Katz** a-11. **Maneely** a-3, 5, 7-9. **Powell** a-11. **Romita** a-3, 6, 8, 11. **Shelly** a-10. **Shores** a-7. **Sinnott** a-2, 7. **Tuska** a-1, 2, 5.*

MEN AGAINST CRIME (Formerly Mr. Risk; Hand of Fate #8 on)
No. 3, Feb, 1951 - No. 7, Oct, 1951
Ace Magazines

	GD25	FN65	NM94
3-Mr. Risk app.	8.35	25.00	55.00
4-7: 4-Colan-a; entire book-r as Trapped! #4. 5-Meskin-a	5.00	15.00	30.00

MEN, GUNS, & CATTLE (See Classics Illustrated Special Issue)

Men in Black Book 2 #1 © Lowell Cunningham

Men of War #20 © DC

Menz Insana © Christopher Fowler & John Bolton

GD25 FN65 NM94

MEN IN ACTION (Battle Brady #10 on)
April, 1952 - No. 9, Dec, 1952 (War stories)
Atlas Comics (IPS)

1-Berg, Reinman-a 11.30 34.00 90.00
2 7.15 21.50 50.00
3-6,8,9: 3-Heath-c/a 5.70 17.00 38.00
7-Krigstein-a; Heath-c 8.50 26.00 60.00
NOTE: *__Brodsky__ c-1, 4-6. __Maneely__ c-5. __Pakula__ a-1, 6. __Robinson__ c-8. __Shores__ c-9.*

MEN IN ACTION
April, 1957 - No. 9, 1958
Ajax/Farrell Publications

1 6.50 19.50 45.00
2 4.25 13.00 26.00
3-9 4.00 11.00 22.00

MEN IN BLACK (1st series)
Jan, 1990 - No. 3 ($2.25, B&W, limited series)
Aircel Comics (Malibu Graphics)

1-Cunningham-s/a in all 9.00 27.00 90.00
2 7.50 22.50 75.00
3 5.00 15.00 50.00
Graphic Novel (Jan, 1991) r/#1-3 2.50 7.50 25.00

MEN IN BLACK (2nd series)
May, 1991 - No. 3 ($2.50, B&W, limited series)
Aircel Comics (Malibu Graphics)

1-Cunningham-s/a in all 4.00 12.00 40.00
2 2.50 7.50 25.00
3 1.85 5.50 15.00

MEN IN BLACK: RETRIBUTION
Dec, 1997 ($3.99, color, one-shot)
Marvel Comics

1-Cunningham-s; continuation of the movie 3.99

MEN IN BLACK: THE MOVIE
Oct, 1997 ($3.99, one-shot, movie adaption)
Marvel Comics

1-Cunningham-s 3.99

MEN INTO SPACE
No. 1083, Feb-Apr, 1960
Dell Publishing Co.

Four Color 1083-Anderson-a, photo-c 4.50 13.50 50.00

MEN OF BATTLE (Also see New Men of Battle)
V1#5, March, 1943 (Hardcover)
Catechetical Guild

V1#5-Topix reprints 3.60 9.00 18.00

MEN OF COURAGE
1949
Catechetical Guild

Bound Topix comics-V7#2,4,6,8,10,16,18,20 3.60 9.00 18.00

MEN OF WAR
August, 1977 - No. 26, March, 1980 (#9,10: 44 pgs.)
DC Comics, Inc.

1-Enemy Ace, Gravedigger (origin #1,2) begin 2.00 5.00
2-26: 9-Unknown Soldier app. 1.20 3.00
NOTE: *__Chaykin__ a-9, 10, 12-14, 19, 20. __Evans__ c-25. __Kubert__ c-2-23, 24p, 26.*

MEN'S ADVENTURES (Formerly True Adventures)
No. 4, Aug, 1950 - No. 28, July, 1954
Marvel/Atlas Comics (CCC)

4(#1)(52 pgs.) 23.00 69.00 170.00
5-Flying Saucer story 13.00 39.00 95.00
6-8: 7-Buried alive story. 8-Sci/fic story 10.00 30.00 75.00
9-20: All war format 8.35 25.00 55.00
21,22,24-26: All horror format. 25-Shrunken head-c 10.00 30.00 70.00
23-Crandall-a; Fox-a(i); horror format 11.00 33.00 80.00
27,28-Human Torch & Toro-c/stories; Captain America & Sub-Mariner stories in each (also see Young Men #24-28) 90.00 271.00 750.00
NOTE: *__Ayers__ a-27(H. Torch). __Berg__ a-15, 16. __Brodsky__ c-4-9, 11, 12, 16-18, 24. __Burgos__ c-27, 28(Human Torch). __Colan__ a-14, 19. __Everett__ a-10, 14, 22, 25, 28; c-14, 21-23. __Heath__ a-8, 11, 24; c-13, 20, 26. __Lawrence__ a-23; 27(Captain America). __Maneely__ a-24; c-10, 15. __Mac Pakula__ a-15, 25. __Post__ a-23. __Powell__ a-27(Sub-Mariner). __Reinman__ a-11, 12. __Robinson__ c-19. __Romita__ a-22. __Shores__ c-25. __Sinnott__ a-21. __Tuska__ a-24. Adventure-#4-8; War-#9-20; Weird/Horror-#21-26.*

MEN WHO MOVE THE NATION
(Giveaway) (B&W)
Publisher unknown

nn-Neal Adams-a 4.25 13.00 26.00

MENZ INSANA
1997 ($7.95, one-shot)
DC Comics (Vertigo)

nn-Fowler-s/Bolton painted art 1.00 3.00 8.00

MEPHISTO VS... (See Silver Surfer #3)
Apr, 1987 - No. 4, July, 1987 ($1.50, mini-series)
Marvel Comics Group

1-4: 1-Fantastic Four; Austin-i. 2-X-Factor. 3-X-Men. 4-Avengers .70 1.75

MERC (See Mark Hazzard: Merc)

MERCHANTS OF DEATH
July, 1988 - No. 4, Nov, 1988 ($3.50, B&W/16 pgs. color, 44pg. mag.)
Acme Press (Eclipse)

1-4: 4-Toth-c 1.40 3.50

MERCY
1993 ($5.95, 68 pgs., mature)
DC Comics (Vertigo)

nn 2.40 6.00

MERLIN JONES AS THE MONKEY'S UNCLE (See Movie Comics and The Misadventures of... under Movie Comics)

MERRILL'S MARAUDERS (See Movie Classics)

MERRY CHRISTMAS (See A Christmas Adventure, Donald Duck..., Dell Giant #39, & March of Comics #153)

MERRY CHRISTMAS, A
1948 (Giveaway)
K. K. Publications (Child Life Shoes)

nn 4.25 13.00 26.00

MERRY CHRISTMAS
1956 (7-1/4x5-1/4")
K. K. Publications (Blue Bird Shoes Giveaway)

nn 1.80 4.50 9.00

MERRY CHRISTMAS FROM MICKEY MOUSE
1939 (16 pgs.) (Color & B&W)
K. K. Publications (Shoe store giveaway)

nn-Donald Duck & Pluto app.; text with art (Rare); c-reprint/Mickey Mouse Mag. V3#3 (12/37)(Rare) 178.00 534.00 1600.00

MERRY CHRISTMAS FROM SEARS TOYLAND
1939 (16 pgs.) (Color)
Sears Roebuck Giveaway

nn-Dick Tracy, Little Orphan Annie, The Gumps, Terry & the Pirates 89.00 267.00 800.00

MERRY COMICS
Dec, 1945 (No cover price)

Metal Men #3 (mini-series) © DC

Metamorpho #10 © DC

Meteor Man #1 © MGM

Carlton Publishing Co.

	GD25	FN65	NM94
nn-Boogeyman app.	15.00	45.00	120.00

MERRY COMICS
1947
Four Star Publications

	GD25	FN65	NM94
1	10.00	30.00	80.00

MERRY-GO-ROUND COMICS
1944 (25¢, 132 pgs.); 1946; 9-10/47 - No. 2, 1948
LaSalle Publ. Co./Croyden Publ./Rotary Litho.

	GD25	FN65	NM94
nn(1944)(LaSalle)-Funny animal; 29 new features	14.00	41.00	110.00
21	5.70	17.00	35.00
1(1946)(Croyden)-Al Fago-c; funny animal	7.85	23.50	55.00
V1#1,2(1947-48; 52 pgs.)(Rotary Litho. Co. Ltd., Canada); Ken Hultgren-a	5.70	17.00	40.00

MERRY MAILMAN (See Fawcett's Funny Animals #87-89)

MERRY MOUSE (Also see Funny Tunes & Space Comics)
June, 1953 - No. 4, Jan-Feb, 1954
Avon Periodicals

	GD25	FN65	NM94
1-1st app.; funny animal; Frank Carin-c/a	6.50	19.50	45.00
2-4	4.25	13.00	28.00

META-4
Feb, 1991 - No. 4, 1991 ($2.25)
First Comics

	GD25	FN65	NM94
1-($3.95, 52pgs.)		1.60	4.00
2-4		.90	2.25

METAL MEN (See Brave & the Bold, DC Comics Presents, and Showcase #37-40)
4-5/63 - No. 41, 12-1/69-70; No. 42, 2-3/73 - No. 44, 7-8/73; No. 45, 4-5/76 - No. 56, 2-3/78
National Periodical Publications/DC Comics

	GD25	FN65	NM94
1-(4-5/63)-5th app. Metal Men	40.00	120.00	450.00
2	13.00	40.00	150.00
3-5	9.00	27.00	100.00
6-10	6.00	18.00	65.00
11-20: 12-Beatles cameo (12/65)	5.00	15.00	50.00
21-26,28-30: 21-Batman, Robin & Flash x-over	3.50	10.50	35.00
27-Origin Metal Men retold	5.50	16.50	55.00
31-41(1968-70): 38-Last 12¢ issue. 41-Last 15¢	2.50	7.50	25.00
42-44(1973)-Reprints	1.25	3.75	10.00
45('76)-49-Simonson-a in all: 48,49-Re-intro Eclipso		2.40	6.00
50-56: 50-Part-r. 54,55-Green Lantern x-over		2.40	6.00

NOTE: ***Andru/Esposito*** *c-1-29.* ***Aparo*** *c-53-56.* ***Giordano*** *c-45, 46.* ***Kane*** *a-30, 31p; c-31.* ***Simonson*** *a-45-49; c-47-52.* ***Staton*** *a-50-56.*

METAL MEN
Oct, 1993 - No. 4, Jan, 1994 ($1.25, mini-series)
DC Comics

	GD25	FN65	NM94
1-($2.50)-Multi-colored foil-c		1.00	2.50
2-4: 2-Origin			1.25

METAL MEN (See Tangent Comics/ Metal Men)

METAMORPHO (See Action Comics #413, Brave & the Bold #57,58, 1st Issue Special,& World's Finest #217)
July-Aug, 1965 - No. 17, Mar-Apr, 1968 (All 12¢ issues)
National Periodical Publications

	GD25	FN65	NM94
1-(7-8/65)-3rd app. Metamorpho	9.50	28.50	95.00
2,3	5.50	16.50	55.00
4-6	3.50	10.50	35.00
7-9	3.00	9.00	30.00
10-Origin & 1st app. Element Girl (1-2/67)	3.50	10.50	35.00
11-17	2.50	7.50	20.00

NOTE: ***Ramona Fraden*** *a-B&B 57, 58, 1-4.* ***Orlando*** *a-5, 6; c-5-9, 11.* ***Sal Trapani*** *a-7-16.*

METAMORPHO
Aug, 1993 - No. 4, Nov, 1993 ($1.50, mini-series)
DC Comics

	GD25	FN65	NM94
1-4			1.50

METAPHYSIQUE
Apr, 1995 - No. 6, Oct, 1995 ($2.95, limited series)
Malibu Comics (Bravura)

	GD25	FN65	NM94
1-6: Norm Breyfogle-c/a/scripts		1.20	3.00

METEOR COMICS
Nov, 1945
L. L. Baird (Croyden)

	GD25	FN65	NM94
1-Captain Wizard, Impossible Man, Race Wilkins app.; origin Baldy Bean, Capt. Wizard's sidekick; bare-breasted mermaids story	31.00	94.00	250.00

METEOR MAN
Aug, 1993 - No. 6, Jan, 1994 ($1.25, limited series)
Marvel Comics

	GD25	FN65	NM94
1-6: 1-Polybagged w/button & rap newspaper. 4-Night Thrasher-c/story. 6-Terry Austin-c(i)			1.25

METROPOL (See Ted McKeever's...)

METROPOL A.D. (See Ted McKeever's...)

METROPOLIS S.C.U. (Also see Showcase '96 #1)
Nov, 1995 - No. 4, Feb, 1996 ($1.50, limited series)
DC Comics

	GD25	FN65	NM94
1-4:1-Superman-c & app.			1.50

MEZZ: GALACTIC TOUR 2494 (Also See Nexus)
May, 1994 ($2.50, one-shot)
Dark Horse Comics

	GD25	FN65	NM94
1		1.00	2.50

MGM'S MARVELOUS WIZARD OF OZ (See Marvel Treasury of Oz)
1975 ($1.50, 84 pgs.; oversize)
Marvel Comics Group/National Periodical Publications

	GD25	FN65	NM94
1-Adaptation of MGM's movie; J. Buscema-a		1.60	4.00

M.G.M'S MOUSE MUSKETEERS (Formerly M.G.M.'s The Two Mouseketeers)
No. 670, Jan, 1956 - No. 1290, Mar-May, 1962
Dell Publishing Co.

	GD25	FN65	NM94
Four Color 670 (#4)	2.75	8.00	30.00
Four Color 711,728,764	1.80	5.50	20.00
8 (4-6/57) - 21 (3-5/60)	1.65	5.00	18.00
Four Color 1135,1175,1290	1.80	5.50	20.00

M.G.M.'S SPIKE AND TYKE (also see Tom & Jerry #79)
No. 499, Sept, 1953 - No. 1266, Dec-Feb, 1961-62
Dell Publishing Co.

	GD25	FN65	NM94
Four Color 499 (#1)	2.75	8.00	30.00
Four Color 577,638	1.80	5.50	20.00
4(12-2/55-56)-10	1.65	5.00	18.00
11-24(12-2/60-61)	1.50	4.50	15.00
Four Color 1266	1.65	5.00	18.00

M.G.M.'S THE TWO MOUSKETEERS
No. 475, June, 1953 - No. 642, July, 1955
Dell Publishing Co.

	GD25	FN65	NM94
Four Color 475 (#1)	6.40	19.00	70.00
Four Color 603 (11/54), 642	3.60	11.00	40.00

MICHAELANGELO CHRISTMAS SPECIAL (See Teenage Mutant Ninja Turtles Christmas Special)

MICHAELANGELO, TEENAGE MUTANT NINJA TURTLE

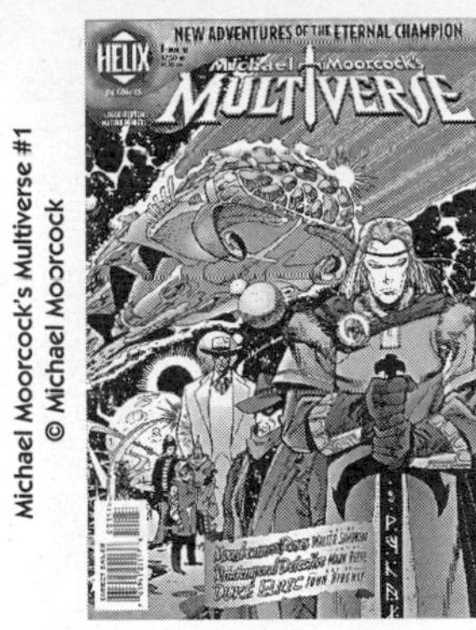

Michael Moorcock's Multiverse #1 © Michael Moorcock

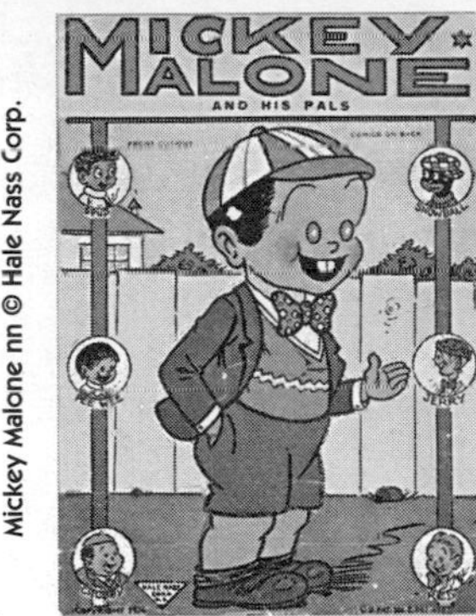

Mickey Malone nn © Hale Nass Corp.

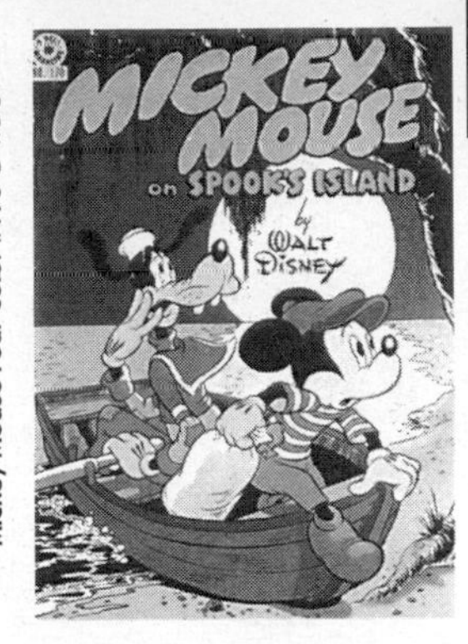

Mickey Mouse Four Color #170 © WDC

GD25 FN65 NM94

1986 (One shot) ($1.50, B&W)
Mirage Studios
1 1.20 3.00
1-2nd printing ('89, $1.75)-Reprint plus new-a .80 2.00

MICHAEL MOORCOCK'S MULTIVERSE
Nov, 1997 - No. 12 ($2.50, limited series)
DC Comics (Helix)
1-6: Simonson, Reeve & Ridgway-a 1.00 2.50

MICKEY AND DONALD (See Walt Disney's...)

MICKEY AND DONALD IN VACATIONLAND (See Dell Giant No. 47)

MICKEY & THE BEANSTALK (See Story Hour Series)

MICKEY & THE SLEUTH (See Walt Disney Showcase #38, 39, 42)

MICKEY FINN (Also see Big Shot Comics #74 & Feature Funnies)
Nov?, 1942 - V3#2, May, 1952
Eastern Color 1-4/McNaught Synd. #5 on (Columbia)/Headline V3#2
1 25.00 75.00 200.00
2 12.00 38.00 100.00
3-Charlie Chan story 8.75 26.25 70.00
4 7.15 21.50 50.00
5-10 5.70 17.00 38.00
11-15(1949): 12-Sparky Watts app. 4.25 13.00 28.00
V3#1,2(1952) 4.00 11.00 22.00

MICKEY MALONE
1936 (Color, punchout-c) (B&W-a on back)
Hale Nass Corp. GD FN VF
nn-1pg. of comics 125.00 250.00 400.00

MICKEY MANTLE (See Baseball's Greatest Heroes #1)

MICKEY MOUSE (See Adventures of Mickey Mouse, The Best of Walt Disney Comics, Cheerios giveaways, Donald Donald and ..., Dynabrite Comics, 40 Big Pages..., Gladstone Comic Album, Merry Christmas From..., Walt Disney's Mickey and Donald, Walt Disney's Comics & Stories, Walt Disney's..., & Wheaties)

MICKEY MOUSE (...Secret Agent #107-109; Walt Disney's... #148-205?)
(See Dell Giants for annuals)
#16, 1941 - #84, 7-9/62; #85, 11/62 - #218, 7/84; #219, 10/86 - #256, 4/90
Dell Publ. Co./Gold Key #85-204/Whitman #205-218/Gladstone #219 on
GD25 FN65 VF82
Four Color 16(1941)-1st Mickey Mouse comic book; "...vs. the Phantom Blot" by Gottfredson 654.00 1961.00 8500.00
(Estimated up to 200 total copies exist, 5 in VF-NM)
GD25 FN65 NM94
Four Color 27(1943)- "7 Colored Terror" 77.00 232.00 850.00
Four Color 79(1945)-By Carl Barks (1 story) 95.00 286.00 1050.00
Four Color 116(1946) 21.00 64.00 235.00
Four Color 141,157(1947) 18.00 55.00 200.00
Four Color 170,181,194('48) 14.00 44.00 160.00
Four Color 214('49),231,248,261 13.00 38.00 140.00
Four Color 268-Reprints/WDC&S #22-24 by Gottfredson ("Surprise Visitor") 12.00 35.00 130.00
Four Color 279,286,296 9.00 27.00 100.00
Four Color 304,313(#1),325(#2),334 7.00 22.00 80.00
Four Color 343,352,362,371,387 5.50 16.50 60.00
Four Color 401,411,427(10-11/52) 3.60 11.00 40.00
Four Color 819-Mickey Mouse in Magicland 3.00 9.00 35.00
Four Color 1057,1151,1246(1959-61)-Album 2.75 8.00 30.00
28(12-1/52-53)-32,34 2.25 6.75 26.00
33-(Exists with 2 dates, 10-11/53 & 12-1/54) 2.25 6.75 26.00
35-50 1.65 5.00 18.00
51-73,75-80 1.20 3.60 12.00
74-Story swipe "The Rare Stamp Search" from 4-Color #422- "The Gilded Man" 1.40 4.20 14.00

GD25 FN65 NM94

81-99: 93,95-titled "Mickey Mouse Club Album" 1.20 3.60 12.00
100-105: Reprint 4-Color #427,194,279,170,343,214 in that order 1.20 3.60 12.00
106-120 1.00 3.00 10.00
121-130 .90 2.70 9.00
131-146 .70 2.10 7.00
147,148: 147-Reprints "The Phantom Fires" from WDC&S #200-202.148-Reprints "The Mystery of Lonely Valley" from WDC&S #208-210 .70 2.10 7.00
149-158 2.00 5.00
159-Reprints "The Sunken City" from WDC&S #205-207 2.00 6.00
160-170: 162-170-r 1.60 4.00
171-178,180-207,209-218: 200-r/Four Color #371 .80 2.00
179-(52 pgs.) .80 2.00
208-(8-12/80)-Only distr. in Whitman 3-pack 2.25 6.75 25.00
219-1st Gladstone issue; The Seven Ghosts serial-r begins by Gottfredson 1.85 5.50 15.00
220,221 1.00 3.00 8.00
222-225: 222-Editor-in Grief strip-r 1.20 3.00
226-230 1.20 3.00
231-243,245-254: 240-r/March of Comics #27. 245-r/F.C. #279. 250-r/F.C. #248 1.20 3.00
244 (1/89, $2.95, 100 pgs.)-Squarebound 60th anniversary issue; gives history of Mickey 1.60 4.00
245, 256: 245-r/F.C. #279. 256-$1.95, 68 pgs. 1.60- 4.00
255 ($1.95, 68 pgs.) .80 2.00
NOTE: *Reprints #195-197, 198(2/3), 199(1/3), 200-208, 211(1/2), 212, 213, 215(1/3), 216-on.* ***Gottfredson*** *Mickey Mouse serials in #219-239, 241-244, 246-249, 251-253, 255.*
Album 01-518-210(Dell), 1(10082-309)(9/63-Gold Key) 1.20 3.60 12.00
...& Goofy "Bicep Bungle"(1952, 16 pgs., 3-1/4x7") Fritos giveaway, soft-c (also see Donald Duck & Ludwig Von Drake) 5.35 16.00 32.00
...& Goofy Explore Business(1978) .80 2.00
...& Goofy Explore Energy(1976-1978, 36 pgs.); Exxon giveaway in color; regular size .80 2.00
...& Goofy Explore Energy Conservation(1976-1978)-Exxon .80 2.00
...& Goofy Explore The Universe of Energy(1985, 20 pgs.); Exxon giveaway in color; regular size .80 2.00
...Club 1(1/64-Gold Key)(TV) 2.50 7.50 20.00
Mini Comic 1(1976)(3-1/4x6-1/2")-Reprints 158 2.00 5.00
New Mickey Mouse Club Fun Book 11190 (Golden Press, 1977, $1.95, 224 pgs.) 1.20 3.00
The Perils of Mickey nn (1993, 5-1/4x7-1/4", 16 pgs.)-Nabisco giveaway w/ games, Nabisco coupons & 6 pgs. of stories; Phantom Blot app. 1.00
Surprise Party 1(30037-901, G.K.)(1/69)-40th Anniversary (see Walt Disney Showcase #47) 2.50 7.50 20.00
Surprise Party 1(1979)-r/1969 issue 1.00 2.50

MICKEY MOUSE ADVENTURES
June, 1990 - No. 18, Nov, 1991 ($1.50)
Disney Comics
1-18: 1-Bradbury, Murry-r/M.M. #45,73 plus new-a. 2-Begin all new stories. 8-Byrne-c. 9-Fantasia 50th ann. issue w/new adapt. of movie. 10-r/F.C. #214 1.50

MICKEY MOUSE
ca. 1933-1934 (10"x8-3/4", 34 pgs., cardboard-c)
Whitman Publishing Co.
948-1932 & 1933 Sunday strips in color, printed from the same plates as Mickey Mouse Book #3 by David McKay, but only pages 5-17 & 32-48 (including all of the "Wolf Barker" continuity) 131.00 395.00 1050.00
NOTE: Some copies bound with back cover upside down. Variance doesn't affect value. Same art appears on front and back covers of all copies. Height of Whitman reissue of McKay book

Mickey Mouse Magazine #1 © WDC

Mickey Mouse Magazine V3#6 © WDC

Mickey Mouse Magazine V4#7 © WDC

GD25 FN65 NM94

trimmed 1/2 inch.

MICKEY MOUSE CLUB MAGAZINE (See Walt Disney...)

MICKEY MOUSE CLUB SPECIAL (See The New Mickey Mouse...)

MICKEY MOUSE COMICS DIGEST
1986 - No. 5, 1987 (96 pgs.)
Gladstone

1,2 ($1.25) 2.00 5.00
3-5 ($1.50) 1.20 3.00

MICKEY MOUSE IN COLOR
1988 (Deluxe, 13"x17", hard-c, $250.00)(Trade, 9-7/8"x11-1/2", hard-c, $39.95)
Another Rainbow/Pantheon

Deluxe limited edition of 3,000 copies signed by Floyd Gottfredson and Carl Barks, designated as the "Official Mickey Mouse 60th Anniversary" book. Mickey Sunday and daily reprints, plus Barks "Riddle of the Red Hat" from Four Color #79. Comes with 45 r.p.m. record interview with Gottfredson and Barks. 240 pgs. 25.00 75.00 250.00
Deluxe, limited to 100 copies, as above, but with a unique colored pencil original drawing of Mickey Mouse by Carl Barks. Add value of art to book price. 750.00
Pantheon trade edition, edited down & without Barks, 192 pgs. 4.00 12.00 40.00

MICKEY MOUSE MAGAZINE
V1#1, Jan, 1933 - V1#9, Sept, 1933 (5-1/4x7-1/4")
No. 1-3 published by Kamen-Blair (Kay Kamen, Inc.)
Walt Disney Productions GD25 FN65 VF82
(Scarce)-Distributed by dairies and leading stores through their local theatres. First few issues had 5¢ listed on cover, later ones had no price.
V1#1 357.00 1071.00 3000.00
2-9 117.00 350.00 900.00

MICKEY MOUSE MAGAZINE
V1#1, 11/33 - V2#12, 10/35 (Mills giveaways issued by different dairies)
Walt Disney Productions GD25 FN65 NM94
V1#1 125.00 375.00 1000.00
2-12: 2-X-Mas issue 44.00 132.00 350.00
V2#1-12: 2-X-Mas issue. 4-St. Valentine-c 34.00 101.00 235.00

MICKEY MOUSE MAGAZINE (Becomes Walt Disney's Comics & Stories)
(No V3#1, V4#6)
Summer, 1935 (June-Aug, indicia) - V5#12, Sept, 1940
V1#1-5, V3#11,12, V4#1-3 are 44 pgs; V2#3-100 pgs; V5#12-68 pgs; rest are 36 pgs.
K. K. Publ./Western Publishing Co. GD25 FN65 VF82 NM94
V1#1 (Large size, 13-1/4x10-1/4"; 25¢)-Contains puzzles, games, cels, stories & comics of Disney characters. Promotional magazine for Disney cartoon movies and paraphernalia 1100.00 3300.00 7150.00 11000.00
(Estimated up to 100 total copies exist, 3 in NM/Mint)
Note: *Some copies were autographed by the editors & given away with all early one year subscriptions.* GD25 FN65 VF82
2 (Size change, 11-1/2x8-1/2"; 10/35; 10¢)-High quality paper begins; Messmer-a 131.00 395.00 1050.00
3,4: 3-Messmer-a 72.00 216.00 575.00
5-1st Donald Duck solo-c; last 44 pg. & high quality paper issue 81.00 244.00 650.00
6-9: 6-36 pg. issues begin; Donald becomes editor. 8-2nd Donald solo-c. 9-1st Mickey/Minnie-c 64.00 193.00 525.00
10-12, V2#1,2: 11-1st Pluto/Mickey-c; Donald fires himself and appoints Mickey as editor 61.00 182.00 475.00
V2#3-Special 100 pg. Christmas issue (25¢); Messmer-a; Donald becomes editor of Wise Quacks 287.00 862.00 2300.00
4-Mickey Mouse Comics & Roy Ranger (adventure strip) begin; both end V2#9; Messmer-a 54.00 160.00 420.00
GD25 FN65 NM94
5-Ted True (adventure strip, ends V2#9) & Silly Symphony Comics (ends V3#3) begin 43.00 130.00 330.00
6-9: 6-1st solo Minnie-c. 6-9-Mickey Mouse Movies cut-out in each 43.00 130.00 330.00
10-1st full color issue; Mickey Mouse (by Gottfredson; ends V3#12) & Silly Symphony (ends V3#3) full color Sunday-r, Peter The Farm Detective (ends V5#8) & Ole Of The North (ends V3#3) begins 67.00 200.00 525.00
11-13: 12-Hiawatha-c & feature story 43.00 130.00 330.00
V3#2-Big Bad Wolf Halloween-c 52.00 155.00 410.00
3 (12/37)-1st app. Snow White & The Seven Dwarfs (before release of movie)(possibly 1st in print); Mickey X-Mas-c 90.00 270.00 675.00
4 (1/38)-Snow White & The Seven Dwarfs serial begins (on stands before release of movie); Ducky Symphony (ends V3#11) begins 72.00 215.00 550.00
5-1st Snow White & Seven Dwarfs-c (St. Valentine's Day) 93.00 280.00 700.00
6-Snow White serial ends; Lonesome Ghosts app. (2 pp.) 50.00 150.00 390.00
7-Seven Dwarfs Easter-c 49.00 145.00 375.00
8-10: 9-Dopey-c. 10-1st solo Goofy-c 40.00 120.00 310.00
11,12 (44 pgs; 8 more pgs. color added). 11-Mickey the Sheriff serial (ends V4#3) & Donald Duck strip-r (ends V3#12) begin. Color feature on Snow White's Forest Friends 43.00 130.00 330.00
V4#1 (10/38; 44 pgs.)-Brave Little Tailor-c/feature story, nominated for Academy Award; Bobby & Chip by Otto Messmer (ends V4#2) & The Practical Pig (ends V4#2) begin 43.00 130.00 330.00
2 (44 pgs.)-1st Huey, Dewey & Louie-c 43.00 130.00 330.00
3 (12/38, 44 pgs.)-Ferdinand The Bull-c/feature story, Academy Award winner; Mickey Mouse & The Whalers serial begins, ends V4#12 43.00 130.00 330.00
4-Spotty, Mother Pluto strip-r begin, end V4#8 40.00 120.00 310.00
5-St. Valentine's day-c. 1st Pluto solo-c 47.00 141.00 360.00
7 (3/39)-The Ugly Duckling-c/feature story, Academy Award winner 43.00 130.00 330.00
7 (4/39)-Goofy & Wilbur The Grasshopper classic-c/feature story from 1st Goofy solo cartoon movie; Timid Elmer begins, ends V5#5 43.00 130.00 330.00
8-Big Bad Wolf-c from Practical Pig movie poster; Practical Pig feature story 43.00 130.00 330.00
9-Donald Duck & Mickey Mouse Sunday-r begin; The Pointer feature story, nominated for Academy Award 43.00 130.00 330.00
10-Classic July 4th drum & fife-c; last Donald Sunday-r 54.00 160.00 425.00
11-1st slick-c; last over-sized issue 40.00 120.00 310.00
12 (9/39; format change, 10-1/4x8-1/4")-1st full color, cover to cover issue; Donald's Penguin-c/feature story 48.00 145.00 375.00
V5#1-Black Pete-c; Officer Duck-c/feature story; Autograph Hound feature story; Robinson Crusoe serial begins 48.00 145.00 375.00
2-Goofy-c; 1st app. Pinocchio (cameo) 64.00 195.00 500.00
3 (12/39)-Pinocchio Christmas-c (Before movie release). 1st app. Jiminy Cricket; Pinocchio serial begins 72.00 215.00 550.00
4,5: 5-Jiminy Cricket-c; Pinocchio serial ends; Donald's Dog Laundry feature story 48.00 145.00 375.00
6-Tugboat Mickey feature story; Rip Van Winkle feature begins, ends V5#8 47.00 140.00 360.00
7-2nd Huey, Dewey & Louie-c 47.00 140.00 360.00
8-Last magazine size issue; 2nd solo Pluto-c; Figaro & Cleo feature story 47.00 140.00 360.00
9 (6/40; change to comic book size)-Jiminy Cricket feature story; Donald-c & Sunday-r begin 52.00 155.00 400.00
10-Special Independence Day issue 52.00 155.00 400.00
11-Hawaiian Holiday & Mickey's Trailer feature stories; last 36 pg. issue 52.00 155.00 400.00

Micronauts #7 © MEG

Midnight Sons Unlimited #6 © MEG

Midnight Tales #3 © CC

GD25 FN65 NM94 | GD25 FN65 NM94

12 (Format change)-The transition issue (68 pgs.) becoming a comic book. With only a title change to follow, becomes Walt Disney's Comics & Stories #1 with the next issue 411.00 1233.00 3700.00
V4#1 (Giveaway) 38.00 114.00 265.00
NOTE: ***Otto Messmer**-a is in many issues of the first two-three years. The following story titles and issues have gags created by **Carl Barks:** V4#3(12/38)-'Donald's Better Self' & 'Donald's Golf Game;' V4#4(1/39)-'Donald's Lucky Day;' V4#7(3/39)-'Hockey Champ;' V4#7(4/39)-'Donald's Cousin Gus;' V4#9(6/39)-'Sea Scouts;' V4#12(9/39)-'Donald's Penguin;' V5#9 (6/40)-'Donald's Vacation;' V5#10(7/40)-'Bone Trouble;' V5#12(9/40)-'Window Cleaners.'*

MICKEY MOUSE MARCH OF COMICS (See March of Comics #8,27,45,60,74)

MICKEY MOUSE SUMMER FUN (See Dell Giants)

MICKEY MOUSE'S SUMMER VACATION (See Story Hour Series)

MICKEY SPILLANE'S MIKE DANGER
Sept, 1995 - No. 11, May, 1996 ($1.95)
Tekno Comix

1-11: 1-Frank Miller-c. 7-polybagged; Simonson-c. 8,9-Simonson-c. .80 2.00

MICKEY SPILLANE'S MIKE DANGER
V2#1, June, 1996 - No. 10, Apr, 1997 ($2.25)
Big Entertainment

V2#1-10: Max Allan Collins scripts 2.25

MICROBOTS, THE
Dec, 1971 (one-shot)
Gold Key

1 (10271-112) 1.00 2.80 7.00

MICRONAUTS (Toys)
Jan, 1979 - No. 59, Aug, 1984 (Mando paper #53 on)
Marvel Comics Group

1-Intro/1st app. Baron Karza .90 2.20
2-5 1.20
6-36,39-59: 7-Man-Thing app. 8-1st app. Capt. Universe (8/79). 9-1st app. Cilicia. 13-1st app. Jasmine. 15-Death of Microtron. 15-17-Fantastic Four app. 17-Death of Jasmine. 20-Ant-Man app. 21-Microverse series begins. 25-Origin Baron Karza. 25-29-Nick Fury app. 27-Death of Biotron. 34,35-Dr. Strange app. 35-Double size; origin Microverse; intro Death Squad. 40-Fantastic Four app. 57-(52 pgs.). 59-Golden painted-c 1.00
37-Nightcrawler app.; X-Men cameo (2 pgs.) .80 2.00
38-First direct sale 1.60
nn-Reprints #1-3; blank UPC; diamond on top 1.20 3.00
Annual 1(12/79)-Ditko-c/a 1.00 2.50
Annual 2(10/80)-Ditko-c/a .80 2.00
NOTE: *#38 on distributed only through comic shops. **N. Adams** c-7i. **Chaykin** a-13-18p. **Ditko** a-39p. **Giffen** a-36p, 37p(part). **Golden** a-1-12p; c-2-7p, 8-23, 24p, 38, 39, 59. **Guice** a-48-58p; c-49-58. **Gil Kane** a-38, 40-45p; c-40-45. **Layton** c-33-37. **Miller** c-31.*

MICRONAUTS (Toys)
Oct, 1984 - No. 20, May, 1986
Marvel Comics Group

V2#1-20 .75
NOTE: ***Kelley Jones** a-1; c-1, 6. **Guice** a-4p; c-2p.*

MICRONAUTS SPECIAL EDITION
Dec, 1983 - No. 5, Apr, 1984 ($2.00, limited series, Baxter paper)
Marvel Comics Group

1-5: r-/original series 1-12; Guice-c(p)-all .80 2.00

MIDGET COMICS (Fighting Indian Stories)
Feb, 1950 - No. 2, Apr, 1950 (5-3/8x7-3/8", 68 pgs.)
St. John Publishng Co.

1-Fighting Indian Stories; Matt Baker-c 14.00 43.00 110.00
2-Tex West, Cowboy Marshal (also in #1) 7.15 21.50 50.00

MIDNIGHT (See Smash Comics #18)

MIDNIGHT
Apr, 1957 - No. 6, June, 1958
Ajax/Farrell Publ. (Four Star Comic Corp.)

1-Reprints from Voodoo & Strange Fantasy with some changes 10.00 30.00 75.00
2-6 6.35 19.00 40.00

MIDNIGHT EYE
1991 - No. 6, 1992 ($4.95, 44 pgs., mature)
Viz Premiere Comics

1-6: Japanese stories translated into English 2.00 5.00

MIDNIGHT MEN
June, 1993 - No. 4, Sept, 1993 ($2.50/$1.95, limited series)
Marvel Comics (Epic Comics/Heavy Hitters)

1-($2.50)-Embossed-c; Chaykin-c/a & scripts in all. 1.00 2.50
2-4 .80 2.00

MIDNIGHT MYSTERY
Jan-Feb, 1961 - No. 7, Oct, 1961
American Comics Group

1-Sci/Fi story 7.50 22.50 75.00
2-7: 7-Gustavson-a 3.80 11.40 38.00
NOTE: ***Reinman** a-1, 3. **Whitney** a-1, 4-6; c-1-3, 5, 7.*

MIDNIGHT SONS UNLIMITED
Apr, 1993 - No. 9, May, 1995 ($3.95, 68 pgs.)
Marvel Comics (Midnight Sons imprint #4 on)

1-9: Blaze, Darkhold (by Quesada #1), Ghost Rider, Morbius & Nightstalkers in all. 1-Painted-c. 3-Spider-Man app. 4-Siege of Darkness part 17; new Dr. Strange & new Ghost Rider app.; spot varnish-c 1.60 4.00
NOTE: ***Sears** a-2.*

MIDNIGHT TALES
Dec, 1972 - No. 18, May, 1976
Charlton Press

V1#1 1.85 5.50 15.00
2-10 1.00 3.00 8.00
11-18: 11-14-Newton-a(p) 2.40 6.00
12,17(Modern Comics reprint, 1977) 1.60 4.00
NOTE: ***Adkins** a-12i, 13i. **Ditko** a-12. **Howard** (Wood imitator) a-1-15, 17, 18; c-1-18. **Don Newton** a-11-14p. **Staton** a-1, 3-11, 13. **Sutton** a-3-10.*

MIGHTY ATOM, THE (...& the Pixies #6) (Formerly The Pixies #1-5)
No. 6, 1949; Nov, 1957 - No. 6, Aug-Sept, 1958
Magazine Enterprises

6(1949-M.E.)-no month (1st Series) 4.25 13.00 28.00
1-6(2nd Series)-Pixies-r 3.20 8.00 16.00
I.W. Reprint #1(nd) 1.20 3.00
Giveaway(1959, '63, Whitman)-Evans-a 1.00 3.00 8.00
Giveaway ('64r, '65r, '66r, '67r, '68r, '73r, '76r)-Evans-r? 1.00

MIGHTY BEAR (Formerly Fun Comics; becomes Unsane #15)
No. 13, Jan, 1954 - No. 14, Mar, 1954; 9/57 - No. 3, 2/58
Star Publ. No. 13,14/Ajax-Farrell (Four Star)

13,14-L. B. Cole-c 12.00 36.00 95.00
1-3('57-58)Four Star; becomes Mighty Ghost #4 4.00 12.00 24.00

MIGHTY COMICS (...Presents) (Formerly Flyman)
No. 40, Nov, 1966 - No. 50, Oct, 1967 (All 12¢ issues)
Radio Comics (Archie)

40-Web 2.50 7.50 20.00
41-50: 41-Shield, Black Hood. 42-Black Hood. 43-Shield, Web & Black Hood. 44-Black Hood, Steel Sterling & The Shield. 45-Shield & Hangman; origin Web retold. 46-Steel Sterling, Web & Black Hood. 47-Black Hood & Mr. Justice. 48-Shield & Hangman; Wizard x-over in Shield. 49-Steel Sterling & Fox; Black Hood x-over in Steel Sterling. 50-Black Hood & Web; Inferno x-over in Web 2.25 6.75 18.00
NOTE: ***Paul Reinman** a-40-50.*

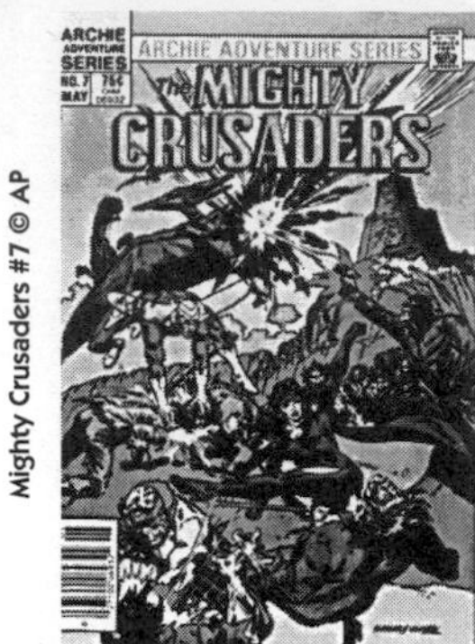

Mighty Crusaders #7 © AP

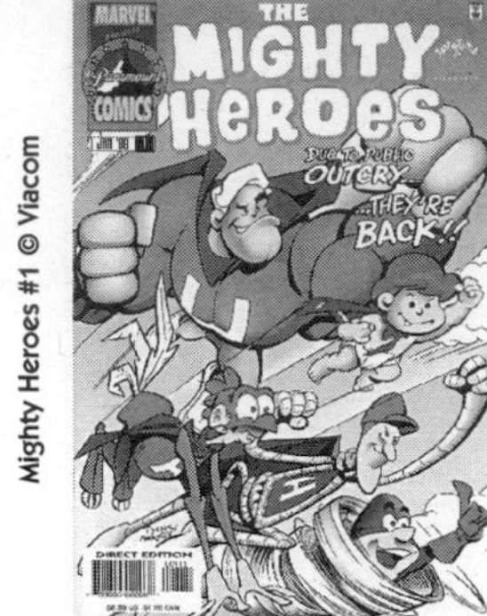

Mighty Heroes #1 © Viacom

Mighty Mouse #8 © Terry Toons

GD25 FN65 NM94

MIGHTY CRUSADERS, THE (Also see Adventures of the Fly, The Crusaders & Fly Man)
Nov, 1965 - No. 7, Oct, 1966 (All 12¢ issues)
Mighty Comics Group (Radio Comics)

1-Origin The Shield 4.00 12.00 40.00
2-Origin Comet 2.50 7.50 24.00
3-Origin Fly-Man 2.50 7.50 20.00
4-1st S.A. app. Fireball, Inferno & Fox; Firefly, Web, Bob Phantom, Blackjack, Hangman, Zambini, Kardak, Steel Sterling, Mr. Justice, Wizard, Capt. Flag, Jaguar x-over 2.50 7.50 22.00
5-Intro. Ultra-Men (Fox, Web, Capt. Flag) & Terrific Three (Jaguar, Mr. Justice, Steel Sterling) 2.50 7.50 20.00
6,7: 7-Steel Sterling feature; origin Fly-Girl 2.50 7.50 20.00
NOTE: ***Reinman** a-6.*

MIGHTY CRUSADERS, THE (All New Advs. of...#2)
Mar, 1983 - No. 13, Sept, 1985 ($1.00, 36 pgs, Mando paper)
Red Circle Prod./Archie Ent. No. 6 on

1-Origin Black Hood, The Fly, Fly Girl, The Shield, The Wizard, The Jaguar, Pvt. Strong & The Web. .80 2.00
2-15: 2-Mister Midnight begins. 4-Darkling replaces Shield. 5-Origin Jaguar, Shield begins. 7-Untold origin Jaguar 1.50
NOTE: ***Buckler** a-1-3, 4i, 5p, 7p, 8i, 9i; c-1-10p.*

MIGHTY GHOST (Formerly Mighty Bear #1-3)
No. 4, June, 1958
Ajax/Farrell Publ.

4 4.00 11.00 22.00

MIGHTY HERCULES, THE (TV)
July, 1963 - No. 2, Nov, 1963
Gold Key

1,2(10072-307, 10072-311) 13.00 38.00 140.00

MIGHTY HEROES, THE (TV) (Funny)
Mar, 1967 - No. 4, July, 1967
Dell Publishing Co.

1-Also has a 1957 Heckle & Jeckle-r 12.00 37.00 135.00
2-4: 4-Has two 1958 Mighty Mouse-r 9.00 27.00 100.00

MIGHTY HEROES
1987 (B&W, one-shot)
Spotlight Comics

1-Heckle & Jeckle backup 1.00

MIGHTY HEROES
Jan, 1998 ($2.99, one-shot)
Marvel Comics

1-Origin of the Mighty Heroes 2.99

MIGHTY MARVEL WESTERN, THE
Oct, 1968 - No. 46, Sept, 1976 (#1-14: 68 pgs.; #15,16: 52 pgs.)
Marvel Comics Group (LMC earlier issues)

1-Begin Kid Colt, Rawhide Kid, Two-Gun Kid-r 2.50 7.50 24.00
2-16: (2-14-68 pgs./ 15,16-52 pgs.) 2.00 6.00 16.00
17-20 1.10 3.30 9.00
21-46: 24-Kid Colt-r end. 25-Matt Slade-r begin. 31-Baker-r. 32-Origin-r/Rawhide Kid #23; Williamson-r/Kid Slade #7. 37-Williamson, Kirby-r/Two-Gun Kid 51 1.00 2.80 7.00
NOTE: ***Jack Davis** a(r)-21-24. **Keller** r-1-13, 22. **Kirby** a(r)-1-3, 6, 9, 12-14, 16, 26, 29, 32, 36, 41, 43, 44; c-29. **Maneely** a(r)-22. **Severin** c-3i, 9. No Matt Slade-#43.*

MIGHTY MIDGET COMICS, THE (Miniature)
No date; circa 1942-1943 (Sold 2 for 5¢, B&W and red, 36 pgs, approx. 5x4")
Samuel E. Lowe & Co.

Bulletman #11(1943)-r/cover/Bulletman #3 14.00 41.00 110.00
Captain Marvel Adventures #11 14.00 41.00 110.00
Captain Marvel #11 (Same as above except for full color ad on back cover; this issue was glued to cover of Captain Marvel #20 and is not found in fine-mint condition) 233.00 700.00 –
Captain Marvel Jr. #11 (Same-c as Master #27 14.00 41.00 110.00
Captain Marvel Jr. #11 (Same as above except for full color ad on back-c; this issue was glued to cover of Captain Marvel #21 and is not found in fine-mint condition) 233.00 700.00 –
Golden Arrow #11 12.00 38.00 100.00
Ibis the Invincible #11(1942)-Origin; reprints cover to Ibis #1 (Predates Fawcett's Ibis the Invincible #1). 14.00 41.00 110.00
Spy Smasher #11(1942) 14.00 41.00 110.00
NOTE: *The above books came in a box called "box full of books" and was distributed with other Samuel Lowe puzzles, paper dolls, coloring books, etc. They are not titled Mighty Midget Comics. All have a war bond seal on back cover which is otherwise blank. These books came in a "Mighty Midget" flat cardboard counter display rack.*
Balbo, the Boy Magician #12 (1943)-1st book devoted entirely to character. 5.70 17.00 35.00
Bulletman #12 9.50 28.00 75.00
Commando Yank #12 (1943)-Only comic devoted entirely to character. 7.15 21.50 50.00
Dr. Voltz the Human Generator (1943)-Only comic devoted entirely to character. 5.70 17.00 35.00
Lance O'Casey #12 (1943)-1st comic devoted entirely to character (Predates Fawcett's Lance O'Casey #1). 5.70 17.00 35.00
Leatherneck the Marine (1943)-Only comic devoted entirely to character. 5.70 17.00 35.00
Minute Man #12 9.50 28.00 75.00
Mister "Q" (1943)-Only comic devoted entirely to character. 5.70 17.00 35.00
Mr. Scarlet and Pinky #12 (1943)-Only comic devoted entirely to character. 8.50 26.00 60.00
Pat Wilton and His Flying Fortress (1943)-1st comic devoted entirely to character. 5.70 17.00 35.00
The Phantom Eagle #12 (1943)-Only comic devoted entirely to character. 5.70 17.00 40.00
State Trooper Stops Crime (1943)-Only comic devoted entirely to character. 5.70 17.00 35.00
Tornado Tom (1943)-Origin, r/from Cyclone #1-3; only comic devoted entirely to character. 5.70 17.00 35.00

MIGHTY MORPHIN' POWER RANGERS: THE MOVIE (Also see Saban's Mighty Morphin' Power Rangers)
Sept, 1995 ($3.95, one-shot)
Marvel Comics

nn-adaptation of movie 1.60 4.00

MIGHTY MOUSE (See Adventures of..., Dell Giant #43, Giant Comics Edition, March of Comics #205, 237, 247, 257, 447, 459, 471, 483, Oxydol-Dreft, Paul Terry's, & Terry-Toons Comics)

MIGHTY MOUSE (1st Series)
Fall, 1946 - No. 4, Summer, 1947
Timely/Marvel Comics (20th Century Fox)

1 94.00 282.00 850.00
2 44.00 132.00 400.00
3,4 34.00 103.00 275.00

MIGHTY MOUSE (2nd Series) (Paul Terry's... #62-71)
Aug, 1947 - No. 67, 11/55; No. 68, 3/56 - No. 83, 6/59
St. John Publishing Co./Pines No. 68 (3/56) on (TV issues #72 on)

5(#1) 33.00 98.00 260.00
6-10 16.00 49.00 130.00
11-19 10.00 30.00 80.00
20 (11/50) - 25-(52 pg. editions) 8.50 26.00 60.00
20-25-(36 pg. editions) 7.15 21.50 50.00
26-37: 35-Flying saucer-c 5.70 17.00 40.00
38-45-(100 pgs.) 15.00 45.00 120.00

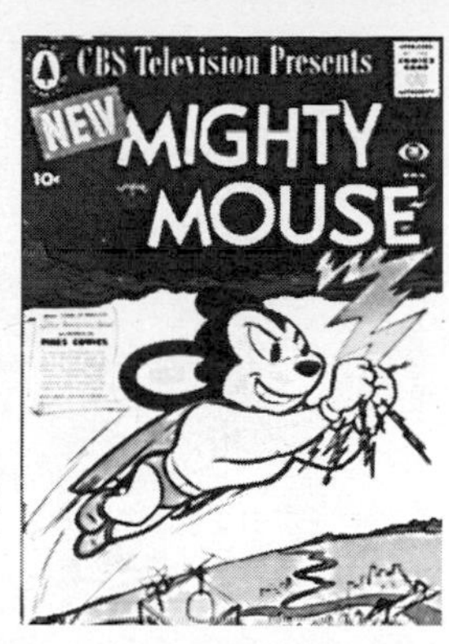

Mighty Mouse #72 © Terry Toons

Mike Grell's Sable #2 © Mike Grell

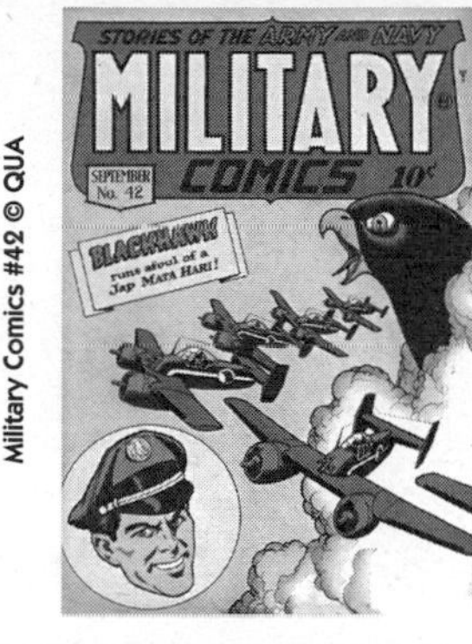

Military Comics #42 © QUA

	GD25	FN65	NM94
46-83: 62-64,67-Painted-c. 82-Infinity-c	5.70	17.00	38.00
Album 1(10/52, 25¢, 100 pgs., St. John)-Gandy Goose app.	24.00	71.00	190.00
Album 2,3(11/52 & 12/52, St. John) (100 pgs.)	19.00	56.00	150.00
Fun Club Magazine 1(Fall, 1957-Pines, 25¢, 100 pgs.) (CBS TV)-Tom Terrific, Heckle & Jeckle, Dinky Duck, Gandy Goose	13.00	39.00	105.00
Fun Club Magazine 2-6(Winter, 1958-Pines)	8.75	26.25	65.00
3-D 1-(1st printing-9/53, 25¢)(St. John)-Came w/glasses; stiff covers; says World's First! on-c; 1st 3-D comic	25.00	75.00	200.00
3-D 1-(2nd printing-10/53, 25¢)-Came w/glasses; slick, glossy covers, slightly smaller	23.00	68.00	180.00
3-D 2,3(11/53, 12/53, 25¢)-(St. John)-With glasses	21.00	64.00	170.00

MIGHTY MOUSE (TV)(3rd Series)(Formerly Adventures of Mighty Mouse)
No. 161, Oct, 1964 - No. 172, Oct, 1968
Gold Key/Dell Publishing Co. No. 166-on

	GD25	FN65	NM94
161(10/64)-165(9/65)-(Becomes Adventures of... No. 166 on)	3.50	10.50	35.00
166(3/66), 167(6/66)-172	2.50	7.50	24.00

MIGHTY MOUSE (TV)
1987 - No. 2, 1987 ($1.50, color)
Spotlight Comics

	GD25	FN65	NM94
1,2-New stories			1.50
...And Friends Holiday Special (11/87, $1.75)		.70	1.75

MIGHTY MOUSE (TV)
Oct, 1990 - No. 10, July, 1991 ($1.00)(Based on Sat. cartoon)
Marvel Comics

	GD25	FN65	NM94
1-10: 1-Dark Knight-c parody. 2-10: 3-Intro Bat-Bat; Byrne-c. 4,5-Crisis-c/story parodies w/Perez-c. 6-Spider-Man-c parody. 7-Origin Bat-Bat			1.00

MIGHTY MOUSE ADVENTURE MAGAZINE
1987 ($2.00, B&W, 52 pgs., magazine size, one-shot)
Spotlight Comics

	GD25	FN65	NM94
1-Deputy Dawg, Heckle & Jeckle backup stories		.80	2.00

MIGHTY MOUSE ADVENTURES (Adventures of... #2 on)
November, 1951
St. John Publishing Co.

	GD25	FN65	NM94
1	29.00	86.00	230.00

MIGHTY MOUSE ADVENTURE STORIES (Paul Terry's... on-c only)
1953 (50¢, 384 pgs.)
St. John Publishing Co.

	GD25	FN65	NM94
nn-Rebound issues	36.00	108.00	325.00

MIGHTY MUTANIMALS (See Teenage Mutant Ninja Turtles Adventures #19)
May, 1991 - No. 3, July, 1991 ($1.00, limited series)
Apr, 1992 - Present ($1.25)
Archie Comics

	GD25	FN65	NM94
1-3: 1-Story cont'd from TMNT Advs. #19			1.00
1-8 (1992): 7-1st app. Merdude			1.25

MIGHTY SAMSON (Also see Gold Key Champion)
7/64 - #20, 11/69; #21, 8/72; #22, 12/73 - #31, 3/76; #32, 8/82
Gold Key (Painted c-1-31)

	GD25	FN65	NM94
1-Origin/1st app.; Thorne-a begins	5.50	16.50	60.00
2-5	2.75	8.00	30.00
6-10: 7-Tom Morrow begins, ends #20	2.50	7.50	20.00
11-20	1.85	5.50	15.00
21-32: 21,22,32-r	1.00	2.80	7.00

MIGHTY THOR (See Thor)

MIKE BARNETT, MAN AGAINST CRIME (TV)
Dec, 1951 - No. 6, Oct, 1952
Fawcett Publications

	GD25	FN65	NM94
1	14.00	43.00	110.00
2	9.15	27.00	60.00
3,4,6	7.50	22.50	50.00
5- "Market for Morphine" cover/story	10.00	30.00	65.00

MIKE DANGER (See Mickey Spillane's...)

MIKE DEODATO'S...
Caliber Comics

...FALLOUT 3000, 1996 ($2.95, B&W, one-shot)

	GD25	FN65	NM94
1		1.20	3.00

...PRIME CUTS, 1996 ($2.95, B&W, magazine size)

	GD25	FN65	NM94
1		1.20	3.00

...PROTHEUS, 1996 - No. 2, 1996 ($2.95, B&W, limited series)

	GD25	FN65	NM94
1,2		1.20	3.00

...RAMTHAR, 1996 ($2.95, B&W, one-shot)

	GD25	FN65	NM94
1		1.20	3.00

...RAZOR NIGHTS, 1996 ($2.95, B&W, one-shot)

	GD25	FN65	NM94
1		1.20	3.00

MIKE GRELL'S SABLE (Also see Jon Sable & Sable)
Mar, 1990 - No. 10, Dec, 1990 ($1.75)
First Comics

	GD25	FN65	NM94
1-10: r/Jon Sable Freelance #1-10 by Grell		.75	1.80

MIKE MIST MINUTE MIST-ERIES (See Ms. Tree/Mike Mist in 3-D)
April, 1981 ($1.25, B&W, one-shot)
Eclipse Comics

	GD25	FN65	NM94
1			1.25

MIKE SHAYNE PRIVATE EYE
Nov-Jan, 1962 - No. 3, Sept-Nov, 1962
Dell Publishing Co.

	GD25	FN65	NM94
1	1.65	5.00	18.00
2,3	1.20	3.60	12.00

MILITARY COMICS (Becomes Modern Comics #44 on)
Aug, 1941 - No. 43, Oct, 1945
Quality Comics Group

	GD25	FN65	VF82	NM94
1-Origin/1st app. Blackhawk by C. Cuidera (Eisner scripts); Miss America, The Death Patrol by Jack Cole (also #2-7,27-30), & The Blue Tracer by Guardineer; X of the Underground, The Yankee Eagle, Q-Boat & Shot & Shell, Archie Atkins, Loops & Banks by Bud Ernest (Bob Powell)(ends #13) begin	780.00	2340.00	4680.00	7800.00

(Estimated up to 160 total copies exist, 9 in NM/Mint)

	GD25	FN65	NM94
2-Secret War News begins (by McWilliams #2-16); Cole-a; new uniform with yellow circle & hawk's head for Blackhawk	217.00	650.00	1950.00
3-Origin/1st app. Chop Chop	183.00	550.00	1650.00
4	144.00	432.00	1300.00
5-The Sniper begins; Miss America in costume #4-7	122.00	366.00	1100.00
6-9: 8-X of the Underground begins (ends #13). 9-The Phantom Clipper begins (ends #16)	92.00	276.00	825.00
10-Classic Eisner-c	94.00	282.00	850.00
11-Flag-c	72.00	216.00	650.00
12-Blackhawk by Crandall begins, ends #22	94.00	282.00	850.00
13-15: 14-Private Dogtag begins (ends #83)	69.00	207.00	625.00
16-20: 16-Blue Tracer ends. 17-P.T. Boat begins	61.00	183.00	550.00
21-31: 22-Last Crandall Blackhawk. 23-Shrunken head-c. 27-Death Patrol revived	53.00	159.00	475.00
32-43	47.00	141.00	420.00

NOTE: ***Berg*** *a-6.* ***Al Bryant*** *c-31-34, 38, 40-43.* ***J. Cole*** *a-1-3, 27-32.* ***Crandall*** *a-12-22; c-13-20.* ***Cuidera*** *c-2-9.* ***Eisner*** *c-1, 2(part), 9, 10.* ***Kotsky*** *c-21-29, 35, 37, 39.* ***McWilliams*** *a-2-16.* ***Powell*** *a-1-13.* ***Ward*** *Blackhawk-30, 31(15 pgs. each); c-30.*

MILK AND CHEESE (Also see Cerebus Bi-Weekly #20)

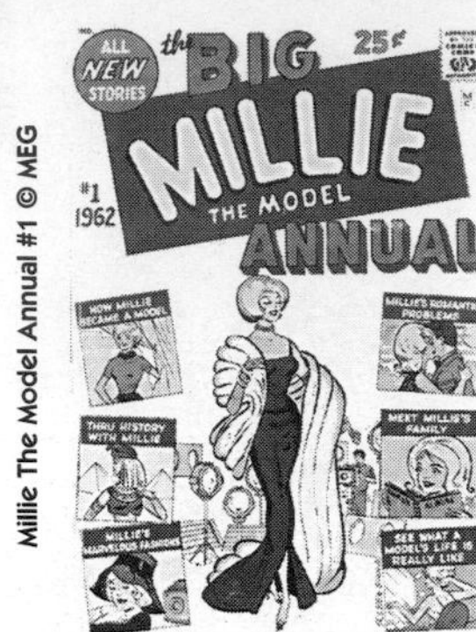

Millie The Model Annual #1 © MEG

Minimum Wage V2#5 © Fantagraphics Books

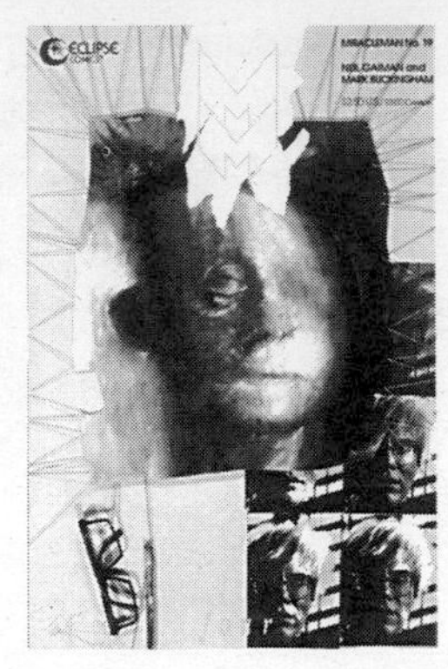
Miracleman #19 © ECL

GD25 FN65 NM94

1991 - Present ($2.50, B&W)
Slave Labor

1-Evan Dorkin story & art in all. 7.50 22.50 75.00
1-2nd-6th printings 1.60 4.00
2-"Other #1" 4.50 13.50 45.00
2-reprint 1.20 3.00
3-"Third #1" 3.50 10.50 35.00
4-"Fourth #1", 5-"First Second Issue" 2.25 6.75 18.00
6-"#666",7 1.10 3.30 9.00
NOTE: *Multiple printings of all issues exist and are worth cover price unless listed here.*

MILLENNIUM
Jan, 1988 - No. 6, Feb, 1988 (Weekly limited series)
DC Comics

1-Staton c/a(p) begins 1.00 2.50
2-8 1.60

MILLENNIUM FEVER
Oct, 1995 - No.4, Jan, 1996 ($2.50, limited series)
DC Comics (Vertigo)

1-4: Duncan Fegredo-c/a 1.00 2.50

MILLENNIUM INDEX
Mar, 1988 - No. 2, Mar, 1988 ($2.00)
Independent Comics Group

1,2 .80 2.00

MILLIE, THE LOVABLE MONSTER
Sept-Nov, 1962 - No. 6, Jan, 1973
Dell Publishing Co.

12-523-211, 2(8-10/63)-Bill Woggon c/a 3.00 9.00 35.00
3(8-10/64) 2.25 6.75 26.00
4(7/72), 5(10/72), 6(1/73) 1.40 4.20 14.00
NOTE: ***Woggon** a-3-6; c-3-6. 4 reprints 1; 5 reprints 2; 6 reprints 3.*

MILLIE THE MODEL (See Comedy Comics, A Date With..., Joker Comics #28, Life With..., Mad About..., Marvel Mini-Books & Modeling With...)
1945 - No. 207, December, 1973
Marvel/Atlas/Marvel Comics (CnPC #1)(SPI/Male/VPI)

1-Origin 56.00 168.00 500.00
2 (10/46)-Millie becomes The Blonde Phantom to sell Blonde Phantom perfume; a pre-Blonde Phantom app. (see All-Select #11, Fall, 1946) 33.00 98.00 260.00
3-7: 4-7- Willie app. 7-Willie smokes extra strong tobacco 20.00 60.00 160.00
8,10-Kurtzman's "Hey Look". 8-Willie & Rusty app. 20.00 60.00 160.00
9-Powerhouse Pepper by Wolverton, 4 pgs. 24.00 71.00 190.00
11-Kurtzman-a, "Giggles 'n' Grins" 14.00 41.00 110.00
12,15,17-20: 12-Rusty & Hedy Devine app. 9.50 28.00 75.00
13,14,16-Kurtzman's "Hey Look". 13-Hedy Devine app. 10.50 32.00 85.00
21-30 7.15 21.50 50.00
31-60 3.50 10.50 35.00
61-99 2.50 7.50 25.00
100 3.20 9.60 32.00
101-153,155-190: 107-Jack Kirby app. in story 2.00 6.00 16.00
154-New Millie begins (10/67) 2.50 7.50 20.00
191-207: 192-(52 pgs.) 1.50 4.50 12.00
Annual 1(1962)-Early Marvel annual (2nd?) 13.50 41.00 135.00
Annual 2(1963) 11.00 33.00 110.00
Annual 3-5 (1964-1966) 5.50 16.50 55.00
Annual 6-10(1967-11/71) 4.50 13.50 45.00
Queen-Size 11(9/74), 12(1975) 3.50 10.50 35.00
NOTE: ***Dan DeCarlo** a-18-93.*

MILLION DOLLAR DIGEST (Richie Rich... #23 on; also see Richie Rich...)
11/86 - No. 7, 11/87; No. 8, 4/88 - No. 34, Nov, 1994 ($1.25/$1.75, digest size)
Harvey Publications

1-8: 8-(68 pgs.) 1.25
9-34: 9-Begin $1.75-c. 14-May not exist .70 1.75

GD25 FN65 NM94

MILT GROSS FUNNIES (Also see Picture News #1)
Aug, 1947 - No. 2, Sept, 1947
Milt Gross, Inc. (ACG?)

1,2 9.50 28.00 75.00

MILTON THE MONSTER & FEARLESS FLY (TV)
May, 1966
Gold Key

1 (10175-605) 8.00 25.00 90.00

MINIMUM WAGE
V1#1, July, 1995 ($9.95, B&W, graphic novel, mature)
V2#1, 1995 - Present ($2.95, B&W, mature)
Fantagraphics Books

V1#1-Bob Fingerman story & art 1.25 3.75 10.00
V2#1-7($2.95): Bob Fingerman story & art. 2-Kevin Nowlan back-c. 4-w/pin-ups 1.20 3.00

MINUTE MAN (See Master Comics & Mighty Midget Comics)
Summer, 1941 - No. 3, Spring, 1942 (68 pgs.)
Fawcett Publications

1 133.00 400.00 1200.00
2,3 89.00 267.00 800.00

MINUTE MAN
No date (16 pgs., B&W, paper-c blue & red)
Sovereign Service Station giveaway

nn-American history 2.40 6.00

MINUTE MAN ANSWERS THE CALL, THE
1942 (4 pgs.)
By M. C. Gaines (Giveaway inserted in Jr. JSA Membership Kit)

nn-Sheldon Moldoff-a 8.75 26.25 65.00

MIRACLE COMICS
Feb, 1940 - No. 4, Mar, 1941
Hillman Periodicals

1-Sky Wizard Master of Space, Dash Dixon, Man of Might, Pinkie Parker, Dusty Doyle, The Kid Cop, K-7, Secret Agent, The Scorpion, & Blandu, Jungle Queen begin; Masked Angel only app. (all 1st app.) 139.00 417.00 1250.00
2 69.00 207.00 625.00
3,4: 3-Bill Colt, the Ghost Rider begins. 4-The Veiled Prophet & Bullet Bob (by Burnley) app. 64.00 192.00 575.00

MIRACLEMAN
Aug, 1985 - No. 15, Nov, 1988; No. 16, Dec, 1989 - No. 24, 1994
Eclipse Comics

1-r/British Marvelman series; Alan Moore scripts in #1-16 2.00 5.00
1-Gold & Silver editions 1.60 4.00
2-12: 8-Airboy preview. 9,10-Origin Miracleman. 9-Shows graphic scenes of childbirth. 10-Snyder-c 1.60 4.00
13-15-($1.75) 1.60 4.00
16-18-($1.95): 17-"The Golden Age" begins, ends #22. Dave McKean-c begins, end #22; Neil Gaiman scripts in #17-24 1.60 4.00
19-24-($2.50); 23-"The Silver Age" begins. 23,24-B. Smith-c. 1.60 4.00
3-D 1 (12/85) 1.20 3.00
The Golden Age (1997, $12.99, TPB) r/#17-22 13.00
NOTE: ***Chaykin** c-3. **Gulacy** c-7. **McKean** c-17-22. **B. Smith** c-23, 24. **Starlin** c-4. **Totleben** a-11-13; c-9, 11-13. **Truman** c-6.*

MIRACLEMAN: APOCRYPHA
Nov, 1991 - No. 3, Feb, 1992 ($2.50, limited series)
Eclipse Comics

Miss America Comics #1 © MEG

Miss America Magazine V7 #24 © MEG

Miss Fury Comics #3 © MEG

GD25 FN65 NM94

1-3: 1-Stories by Neil Gaiman, Mark Buckingham, Alex Ross & others. 3-Stories by James Robinson, Kelley Jones, Matt Wagner, Neil Gaiman, Mark Buckingham & others 1.00 2.50

MIRACLEMAN FAMILY
May, 1988 - No. 2, Sept, 1988 ($1.95, limited series, Baxter paper)
Eclipse Comics

1,2: 2-Gulacy-c .80 2.00

MIRACLE OF THE WHITE STALLIONS, THE (See Movie Comics)

MIRACLE ON BROADWAY
Dec, 1995 (Giveaway)
Broadway Comics

1-Ernie Colon-c/a; Jim Shooter &Co. story; 1st known digitally printed comic book; 1st app. Spiro & Knights on Broadway (1150 print run) 20.00

NOTE: *Miracle on Broadway was a limited edition comic given to 1100 VIPs in the entertainment industry for the 1995 Holiday Season.*

MIRACLE SQUAD, THE
Aug, 1986 - No. 4, 1987 ($2.00, limited series)
Upshot Graphics (Fantagraphics Books)

1-4 .80 2.00

MIRACLE SQUAD: BLOOD AND DUST, THE
Jan, 1989 - No. 4, July, 1989 ($1.95, B&W, limited series)
Apple Comics

1-4 .80 2.00

MIRRORWORLD: RAIN
Feb, 1997 - No. 0, Apr, 1997 ($3.25, limited series)
NetCo Partners (Big Entertainment)

0,1-Tad Williams-s 3.25

MISADVENTURES OF MERLIN JONES, THE (See Movie Comics & Merlin Jones as the Monkey's Uncle under Movie Comics)

MISS AMERICA COMICS (Miss America Magazine #2 on; also see Blonde Phantom & Marvel Mystery Comics)
1944 (one-shot)
Marvel Comics (20CC)

1-2 pgs. pin-ups 128.00 384.00 1150.00

MISS AMERICA MAGAZINE (Formerly Miss America; Miss America #51 on)
V1#2, Nov, 1944 - No. 93, Nov, 1958
Miss America Publ. Corp./Marvel/Atlas (MAP)

V1#2-Photo-c of teenage girl in Miss America costume; Miss America, Patsy Walker (intro.) comic stories plus movie reviews & stories; intro. Buzz Baxter & Hedy Wolfe; 1 pg. origin Miss America 106.00 318.00 950.00
3-5-Miss America & Patsy Walker stories 39.00 117.00 350.00
6-Patsy Walker only 8.50 26.00 60.00
V2#1(4/45)-6(9/45)-Patsy Walker continues 5.00 15.00 30.00
V3#1(10/45)-6(4/46) 5.00 15.00 30.00
V4#1(5/46),2,5(9/46) 4.25 13.00 28.00
V4#3(7/46)-Liz Taylor photo-c 7.15 21.50 50.00
V4#4 (8/46; 68 pgs.) 4.25 13.00 26.00
V4#6 (10/46; 92 pgs.) 4.25 13.00 26.00
V5#1(11/46)-6(4/47), V6#1(5/47)-3(7/47) 4.25 13.00 26.00
V7#1(8/47)-14,16-23(#56, 6/49) 4.00 11.00 22.00
V7#15-All comics 4.25 13.00 26.00
V7#24(#57, 7/49)-Kamen-a (becomes Best Western #58 on?) 4.00 12.00 24.00
V7#25(8/49), 27-44(3/52), VII,nn(5/52) 4.00 10.00 20.00
V7#26(9/49)-All comics 4.25 13.00 26.00
V1,nn(7/52)-V1,nn(1/53)(#46-49) 4.00 10.00 20.00
V7#50(Spring '53), V1#51-V7?#54(7/53) 4.00 10.00 20.00
55-93 4.00 10.00 20.00

NOTE: *Photo-c #1, 4, V2#1, 4, 5, V3#5, V4#3, 4, 6, V7#15, 16, 24, 26, 34, 37, 38. Painted c-3.* ***Powell** a-V7#31.*

MISS BEVERLY HILLS OF HOLLYWOOD (See Adventures of Bob Hope)
Mar-Apr, 1949 - No. 9, July-Aug, 1950 (52 pgs.)
National Periodical Publications

1 (Meets Alan Ladd) 48.00 144.00 430.00
2-William Holden photo on-c 36.00 108.00 310.00
3-5: 2-9-Part photo-c. 5-Bob Hope photo on-c 31.00 92.00 245.00
6,7,9: 6-Lucille Ball photo on-c 29.00 86.00 230.00
8-Reagan photo on-c 35.00 105.00 285.00

NOTE: *Beverly meets Alan Ladd in #1, Eve Arden #2, Betty Hutton #4, Bob Hope #5.*

MISS CAIRO JONES
1945
Croyden Publishers

1-Bob Oksner daily newspaper-r (1st strip story); lingerie panels 17.00 51.00 135.00

MISS FURY COMICS (Newspaper strip reprints)
Winter, 1942-43 - No. 8, Winter, 1946 (Published quarterly)
Timely Comics (NPI 1/CmPI 2/MPC 3-8)

1-Origin Miss Fury by Tarpe' Mills (68 pgs.) in costume w/pin-ups 250.00 750.00 2500.00
2-(60 pgs.)-In costume w/pin-ups 128.00 384.00 1150.00
3-(60 pgs.)-In costume w/pin-ups; Hitler-c 105.00 315.00 940.00
4-(52 pgs.)-In costume, 2 pgs. w/pin-ups 81.00 243.00 725.00
5-(52 pgs.)-In costume w/pin-ups 75.00 225.00 675.00
6-(52 pgs.)-Not in costume in inside stories, w/pin-ups 69.00 207.00 625.00
7,8-(36 pgs.)-In costume 1 pg. each; no pin-ups 64.00 192.00 575.00

NOTE: ***Schomburg** c-1, 5, 6.*

MISS FURY
1991 - No. 4, 1991 ($2.50, limited series)
Adventure Comics

1-4: 1-Origin; granddaughter of original Miss Fury 1.00 2.50
1-Limited ed. ($4.95) 2.00 5.00

MISSION IMPOSSIBLE (TV)
May, 1967 - No. 4, Oct, 1968; No. 5, Oct, 1969 (All have photo-c)
Dell Publishing Co.

1 8.00 25.00 90.00
2-5: 5-Reprints #1 5.50 16.50 60.00

MISSION IMPOSSIBLE (Movie)
May, 1996 ($2.95, one-shot) (1st Paramount Comics book)
Marvel Comics (Paramount Comics)

1-Liefeld-c & back-up story 1.20 3.00

MISS LIBERTY (Becomes Liberty Comics)
1945 (MLJ reprints)
Burten Publishing Co.

1-The Shield & Dusty, The Wizard, & Roy, the Super Boy app.; r/Shield-Wizard #13 24.00 71.00 190.00

MISS MELODY LANE OF BROADWAY (See The Adventures of Bob Hope)
Feb-Mar, 1950 - No. 3, June-July, 1950 (52 pgs.)
National Periodical Publications

1-Movie stars photos app. on all-c. 50.00 150.00 420.00
2,3: 3-Ed Sullivan photo on-c. 36.00 107.00 260.00

MISS PEACH
Oct-Dec, 1963; 1969
Dell Publishing Co.

1-Jack Mendelsohn-a/script 6.40 19.00 70.00
...Tells You How to Grow (1969; 25¢)-Mel Lazarus-a; also given away (36 pgs.) 3.60 11.00 40.00

Mr. & Mrs. J. Evil Scientist #1 © H-B

Mr. District Attorney © #2 DC

Mister Miracle #2 © DC

GD25 FN65 NM94

MISS PEPPER (See Meet Miss Pepper)

MISS SUNBEAM (See Little Miss...)

MISS VICTORY (See Captain Fearless #1,2, Holyoke One-Shot #3, Veri Best Sure Fire & Veri Best Sure Shot Comics)

MISTER AMERICA
Apr, 1994 - No. 2, May, 1994 ($2.95, limited series)
Endeavor Comics

1,2 1.20 3.00

MR. & MRS. BEANS
No. 11, 1939
United Features Syndicate

Single Series 11 28.00 83.00 220.00

MR. & MRS. J. EVIL SCIENTIST (TV)(See The Flintstones & Hanna-Barbera Band Wagon #3)
Nov, 1963 - No. 4, Sept, 1966 (Hanna-Barbera, all 12¢)
Gold Key

1-From The Flintstones 6.40 19.00 70.00
2-4 3.60 11.00 40.00

MR. ANTHONY'S LOVE CLINIC (Based on radio show)
Nov, 1949 - No. 5, Apr-May, 1950 (52 pgs.)
Hillman Periodicals

1-Photo-c 10.00 30.00 70.00
2 6.70 20.00 40.00
3-5: 5-Photo-c 5.70 17.00 35.00

MR. BUG GOES TO TOWN (See Cinema Comics Herald)
1941 (Giveaway, 52 pgs.)
K.K. Publications

nn-Cartoon movie (scarce) 50.00 150.00 450.00

MR. DISTRICT ATTORNEY (Radio/TV)
Jan-Feb, 1948 - No. 67, Jan-Feb, 1959 (1-23: 52 pgs.)
National Periodical Publications

1-Howard Purcell c-5-23 (most) 90.00 270.00 750.00
2 40.00 120.00 325.00
3-5 30.00 90.00 220.00
6-10 23.00 69.00 170.00
11-20 18.00 54.00 130.00
21-43: 43-Last pre-code (1-2/55) 13.50 41.00 95.00
44-67 11.00 33.00 75.00

MR. DISTRICT ATTORNEY (SeeThe Funnies #35)
No. 13, 1942
Dell Publishing Co.

Four Color 13-See The Funnies #35 for 1st app. 27.00 82.00 300.00

MISTER E (Also see Books of Magic limited series)
Jun, 1991- No. 4, Sept, 1991($1.75, limited series)
DC Comics

1-4-Snyder III-c/a; follow-up to Books of Magic limited series. .80 2.00

MISTER ED, THE TALKING HORSE (TV)
Mar-May, 1962 - No. 6, Feb, 1964 (All photo-c; photo back-c: 1-6)
Dell Publishing Co./Gold Key

Four Color 1295 12.00 35.00 130.00
1(11/62) (Gold Key)-Photo-c 9.00 27.00 100.00
2-6: Photo-c 4.50 13.50 50.00

(See March of Comics #244, 260, 282, 290)

MR. HERO, THE NEWMATIC MAN (See Neil Gaiman's...)

MR. MAGOO (TV) (The Nearsighted..., ...& Gerald McBoing Boing 1954 issues; formerly Gerald McBoing-Boing And ...)
No. 6, Nov-Jan, 1953-54; 5/54 - 3-5/62; 9-11/63 - 3-5/65
Dell Publishing Co.

6 11.00 33.00 120.00
Four Color 561(5/54),602(11/54) 11.00 33.00 120.00
Four Color 1235(#1, 12-2/62),1305(#2, 3-5/62) 9.00 27.00 100.00
3(9-11/63) - 5 8.00 23.00 85.00
Four Color 1235(12-536-505)(3-5/65)-2nd Printing 5.50 16.50 60.00

MISTER MIRACLE (1st series) (See Cancelled Comic Cavalcade)
3-4/71 - V4#18, 2-3/74; V5#19, 9/77 - V6#25, 8-9/78; 1987 (Fourth World)
National Periodical Publications/DC Comics

1-1st app. Mr. Miracle (#1-3 are 15¢) 2.80 8.40 28.00
2,3 1.75 5.25 14.00
4-8: 4-Boy Commandos-r begin; all 52 pgs. 1.50 4.50 12.00
9,10: 9-Origin Mr. Miracle; Darkseid cameo 1.10 3.30 9.00
11-18: 15-Intro/1st app. Shilo Norman. 18-Barda & Scott Free wed; New Gods app. & Darkseid cameo; Last Kirby issue. 1.10 3.30 9.00
19-25 (1977-78) 2.40 6.00
Special 1(1987, $1.25, 52 pgs.) 1.20 3.00

NOTE: ***Austin*** *a-19i.* ***Ditko*** *a-6r.* ***Golden*** *a-23-25p; c-25p.* ***Heath*** *a-24i, 25i; c-25i.* ***Kirby*** *a(p)/c-1-18.* ***Nasser*** *a-19i.* ***Rogers*** *a-19-22p; c-19, 20p, 21p, 22-24. 4-8 contain* ***Simon & Kirby*** *Boy Commandos reprints from Detective 82,76, Boy.Commandos 1, 3 & Detective 64 in that order.*

MISTER MIRACLE (2nd Series) (See Justice League)
Jan, 1989 - No. 28, June, 1991 ($1.00)
DC Comics

1-28: 13,14-Lobo app. 22-1st new Mr. Miracle w/new costume 1.00

MISTER MIRACLE (3rd Series)
Apr, 1996 - No. 7, Oct, 1996 ($1.95)
DC Comics

1-7: 2-Vs. JLA. .80 2.00

MR. MIRACLE (See Capt. Fearless #1 & Holyoke One-Shot #4)

MR. MONSTER (1st Series)(Doc Stearn... #7 on; See Airboy-Mr. Monster Special, Dark Horse Presents, Super Duper Comics & Vanguard Illustrated #7)
Jan, 1985 - No. 10, June, 1987 ($1.75, Baxter paper)
Eclipse Comics

1-1st story-r from Vanguard Ill. #7(1st app.) 1.00 2.50
2-Dave Stevens-c .70 1.75
3-10: 3-Alan Moore scripts; Wolverton-r/Weird Mysteries #5. 6-Ditko-r/Fantastic Fears #5 plus new Giffen-a 10 6-D issue .70 1.75

MR. MONSTER
Feb, 1988 - No. 8, July, 1991 ($1.75, B&W)
Dark Horse Comics

1-7 .70 1.75
8-($4.95, 60 pgs.)-Origins conclusion 2.00 5.00

MR. MONSTER ATTACKS! (Doc Stearn...)
Aug, 1992 - No. 3, Oct, 1992 ($3.95, limited series, 32 pgs.)
Tundra Publishing

1-3: Michael T. Gilbert-a/scripts; Gilbert/Dorman painted-c 1.60 4.00

MR. MONSTER PRESENTS (CRACK-A-BOOM!)
1997 ($2.95, B&W&Red, limited series)
Caliber Comics

1-2: Michael T. Gilbert-a/scripts: 1-Wraparound-c 1.20 3.00

MR. MONSTER'S SUPER-DUPER SPECIAL
May, 1986 - No. 8, July, 1987
Eclipse Comics

1-(5/86)...3-D High Octane Horror #1 .80 2.00
1-(5/86)...2-D version, 100 copies .80 3.00
2-(8/86)...High Octane Horror #1, 3-(9/86)...True Crime #1, 4-(11/86)...True Crime #2, 5-(1/87)...Hi-Voltage Super Science #1, 6-(3/87)...High Shock Schlock #1, 7-(5/87)...High Shock Schlock #2, 8-(7/87)...Weird Tales Of The Future #1 .80 2.00

Mr. T and the T-Force #1 © NOW

Mister X V2 #10 © Mr. Publ.

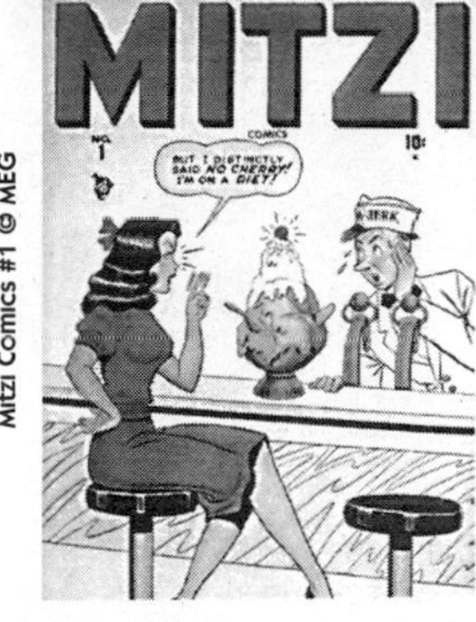

Mitzi Comics #1 © MEG

	GD25	FN65	NM94

NOTE: ***Jack Cole*** *r-3, 4.* ***Evans*** *a-2r.* ***Kubert*** *a-1r.* ***Powell*** *a-5r.* ***Wolverton*** *a-2r, 7r, 8r.*

MR. MUSCLES (Formerly Blue Beetle #18-21)
No. 22, Mar, 1956; No. 23, Aug, 1956
Charlton Comics

	GD25	FN65	NM94
22,23	5.35	16.00	32.00

MISTER MYSTERY (Tales of Horror and Suspense)
Sept, 1951 - No. 19, Oct, 1954
Mr. Publ. (Media Publ.) No. 1-3/SPM Publ./Stanmore (Aragon)

	GD25	FN65	NM94
1-Kurtzmanesque horror story	62.00	187.00	525.00
2,3-Kurtzmanesque story. 3-Anti-Wertham edit.	41.00	124.00	340.00
4,6: Bondage-c; 6-Torture	41.00	124.00	340.00
5,8,10	39.00	116.00	280.00
7 "The Brain Bats of Venus" by Wolverton; partially re-used in Weird Tales of the Future #7	87.00	262.00	725.00
9-Nostrand-a	39.00	116.00	280.00
11-Wolverton "Robot Woman" story/Weird Mysteries #2, cut up, rewritten & partially redrawn	59.00	178.00	500.00
12-Classic injury to eye-c	87.00	262.00	725.00
13,14,17,19: 17-Severed heads-c. 19-Reprints	26.00	77.00	190.00
15- "Living Dead" junkie story	26.00	77.00	190.00
16-Bondage-c	26.00	77.00	190.00
18- "Robot Woman" by Wolverton reprinted from Weird Mysteries #2; decapitation, bondage-c	44.00	135.00	375.00

NOTE: ***Andru*** *a-1, 2p, 3p.* ***Andru/Esposito*** *c-1-3.* ***Baily*** *c-10-18(most).* ***Mortellaro*** *c-5-7. Bondage c-7. Some issues have graphic dismemberment scenes.*

MR. MYSTIC (See Will Eisner Presents)

MR. PUNCH
1994 ($24.95, one-shot)
DC Comics (Vertigo)

	GD25	FN65	NM94
nn (Hard-c)-Gaiman scripts; McKean-c/a	2.50	7.50	25.00
nn (Soft-c)	1.85	5.50	15.00

MISTER Q (See Mighty Midget Comics & Our Flag Comics #5)

MR. RISK (Formerly All Romances; Men Against Crime #3 on)(Also see Our Flag Comics & Super-Mystery Comics)
No. 7, Oct, 1950 - No. 2, Dec, 1950
Ace Magazines

	GD25	FN65	NM94
7,2	6.35	19.00	40.00

MR. SCARLET & PINKY (See Mighty Midget Comics)

MR. T AND THE T-FORCE
June, 1993 - No. 10, May, 1994 ($1.95, color)
Now Comics

	GD25	FN65	NM94
1-10-Newsstand editions: 1-7-polybagged with photo trading card in each. 1,2-Neal Adams-c/a(p). 3-Dave Dorman painted-c		.80	2.00
1-10-Direct Sale editions polybagged w/line drawn trading cards. 1-Contains gold foil trading card by Neal Adams		.80	2.00

MISTER UNIVERSE (Professional wrestler)
July, 1951; No. 2, Oct, 1951 - No. 5, April, 1952
Mr. Publications Media Publ. (Stanmor, Aragon)

	GD25	FN65	NM94
1	17.00	49.00	125.00
2- "Jungle That Time Forgot", (24 pg. story); Andru/Esposito-c	11.00	33.00	80.00
3-Marijuana story	11.00	33.00	80.00
4,5- "Goes to War" cover/stories	8.35	25.00	55.00

MISTER X (See Vortex)
6/84 - No. 14, 8/88 ($1.50/$2.25, direct sales, coated paper)
V2#1, Apr, 1989 - V2#12, Mar, 1990 ($2.00/$2.50, B&W, newsprint)
V3#1, 1996 - Present ($2.95, B&W)
Mr. Publications/Vortex Comics/Caliber V3#1 on

	GD25	FN65	NM94
1		1.20	3.00
2		1.00	2.50
3-14: 11-Dave McKean story & art (6 pgs.)		.80	2.00
V2#1-11 (Second Coming, $2.00, B&W): 1-Four different covers. 10-Photo-c		.80	2.00
V2#12 ($2.50)		1.00	2.50
V3#1-3(2.95, B&W): 1-1st Caliber issue		1.20	3.00
Return of... ($11.95, graphic novel)-r/1-4	1.50	4.50	12.00
Return of... ($34.95, hardcover limited edition)-r/1-4	3.50	10.50	35.00
Special (no date, 1990?)		.80	2.00

MISTY
Dec, 1985 - No. 6, May, 1986 (Limited series)
Marvel Comics (Star Comics)

	GD25	FN65	NM94
1-6: Millie The Model's niece			.80

MITZI COMICS (Becomes Mitzi's Boy Friend #2 on)(See All Teen)
Spring, 1948 (one-shot)
Timely Comics

	GD25	FN65	NM94
1-Kurtzman's "Hey Look" plus 3 pgs. "Giggles 'n' Grins"	17.00	49.00	120.00

MITZI'S BOY FRIEND (Formerly Mitzi Comics; becomes Mitzi's Romances)
No. 2, June, 1948 - No. 7, April, 1949
Marvel Comics (TCI)

	GD25	FN65	NM94
2	8.50	26.00	60.00
3-7	6.50	19.50	45.00

MITZI'S ROMANCES (Formerly Mitzi's Boy Friend)
No. 8, June, 1949 - No. 10, Dec, 1949
Timely/Marvel Comics (TCI)

	GD25	FN65	NM94
8-Becomes True Life Tales #8 (10/49) on?	8.50	26.00	60.00
9,10: 10-Painted-c	6.50	19.50	45.00

MOBFIRE
Dec, 1994 - No. 6, May, 1995 ($2.50, limited series)
DC Comics (Vertigo)

	GD25	FN65	NM94
1-6		1.00	2.50

MOBY DICK (See Feature Presentations #6, and King Classics)
No. 717, Aug, 1956
Dell Publishing Co.

	GD25	FN65	NM94
Four Color 717-Movie, Gregory Peck photo-c	8.00	25.00	90.00

MOBY DUCK (See Donald Duck #112 & Walt Disney Showcase #2,11)
Oct, 1967 - No. 11, Oct, 1970; No. 12, Jan, 1974 - No. 30, Feb, 1978
Gold Key (Disney)

	GD25	FN65	NM94
1	1.50	4.50	12.00
2-5	1.00	2.80	7.00
6-11		1.60	4.00
12-30: 21,30-r		.80	2.00

MODEL FUN (With Bobby Benson)
No. 3, Winter, 1954-55 - No. 5, July, 1955
Harle Publications

	GD25	FN65	NM94
3-Bobby Benson	5.70	17.00	38.00
4,5-Bobby Benson	4.00	12.00	24.00

MODELING WITH MILLIE (Formerly Life With Millie)
No. 21, Feb, 1963 - No. 54, June, 1967
Atlas/Marvel Comics Group (Male Publ.)

	GD25	FN65	NM94
21	6.50	19.50	65.00
22-30	3.80	11.40	38.00
31-54	2.50	7.50	25.00

MODERN COMICS (Formerly Military Comics #1-43)
No. 44, Nov, 1945 - No. 102, Oct, 1950
Quality Comics Group

	GD25	FN65	NM94
44-Blackhawk continues	44.00	132.00	400.00

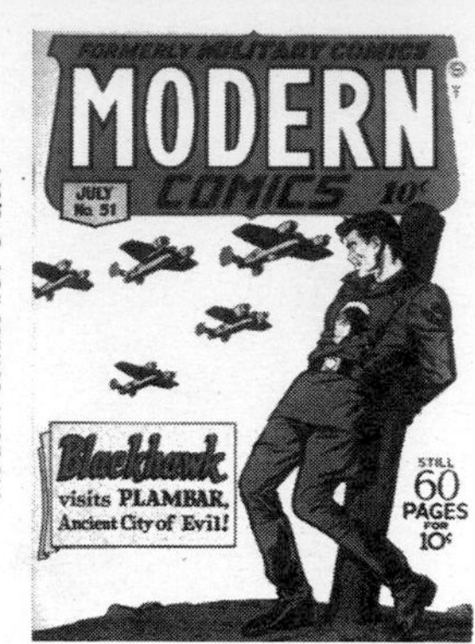

Modern Comics #51 © QUA

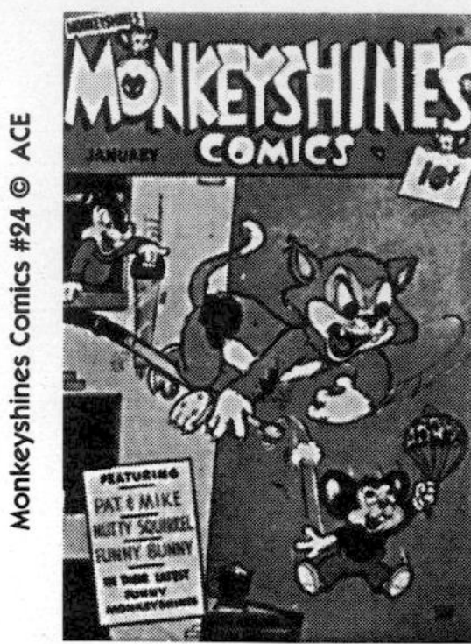

Monkeyshines Comics #24 © ACE

The Monroes #1 © DELL

	GD25	FN65	NM94
45-52: 49-1st app. Fear, Lady Adventuress	36.00	108.00	285.00
53-Torchy by Ward begins (9/46)	36.00	108.00	315.00
54-60: 55-J. Cole-a	29.00	88.00	235.00
61-77,79,80: 73-J. Cole-a	26.00	80.00	210.00
78-1st app. Madame Butterfly	29.00	88.00	235.00
81-99,101: 82,83-One pg. J. Cole-a. 83-The Spirit app.; last 52 pg. issue? 99-Blackhawks on the moon-c/story	26.00	80.00	210.00
100	26.00	80.00	210.00
102-(Scarce)-J. Cole-a; Spirit by Eisner app.	31.00	92.00	245.00

NOTE: ***Al Bryant** c-44-51, 54, 55, 66, 69. **Jack Cole** a-55, 73. **Crandall** Blackhawk-#46, 47, 50, 51, 54, 56, 58-60, 64, 67-70, 73, 74, 76-78, 80-83; c-60-65, 67, 68, 70-95. **Crandall/Cuidera** c-56-59, 96-102. **Gustavson** a-47. **Ward** Blackhawk-#52, 53, 55 (15 pgs. each). Torchy in #53-102; by **Ward** only in #53-89(9/49); by **Gil Fox** #93, 102.*

MODERN LOVE
June-July, 1949 - No. 8, Aug-Sept, 1950
E. C. Comics

	GD25	FN65	NM94
1	50.00	150.00	420.00
2-Craig/Feldstein-c	40.00	120.00	310.00
3-Spanking panel	36.00	107.00	260.00
4-6 (Scarce): 4-Bra/panties panels	47.00	141.00	385.00
7,8	39.00	118.00	280.00

NOTE: ***Craig** a-3. **Feldstein** a-in most issues; c-1, 2i, 3-8. **Harrison** a-4. **Iger** a-6-8. **Ingels** a-1, 2, 4-7. **Palais** a-5. **Wood** a-7. **Wood/Harrison** a-5-7. (Canadian reprints known; see Table of Contents.)*

MOD LOVE
1967 (50¢, 36 pgs.)
Western Publishing Co.

	GD25	FN65	NM94
1	2.50	7.50	24.00

MODNIKS, THE
Aug, 1967 - No. 2, Aug, 1970
Gold Key

	GD25	FN65	NM94
10206-708(#1)	2.50	7.50	20.00
2	1.50	4.50	12.00

MOD SQUAD (TV)
Jan, 1969 - No. 3, Oct, 1969 - No. 8, April, 1971
Dell Publishing Co.

	GD25	FN65	NM94
1-Photo-c	4.00	12.00	45.00
2-8: 2-4-Photo-c. 8-Photo-c; Reprints #2	2.00	6.00	23.00

MOD WHEELS
Mar, 1971 - No. 19, Jan, 1976
Gold Key

	GD25	FN65	NM94
1	2.50	7.50	20.00
2-9	1.75	5.25	14.00
10-19: 11,15-Extra 16 pgs. ads	1.25	3.75	10.00

MOE & SHMOE COMICS
Spring, 1948 - No. 2, Summer, 1948
O. S. Publ. Co.

	GD25	FN65	NM94
1	6.50	19.50	45.00
2	5.35	16.00	32.00

MOEBIUS (Graphic novel)
Oct, 1987 - No. 6, 1988; No. 7, 1990; No. 8, 1991 ($9.95, 8x11", mature)
Marvel Comics (Epic Comics)

	GD25	FN65	NM94
1,2,4-6,8: (#2, 2nd printing, $9.95)	1.25	3.75	10.00
3,7: 3-(1st & 2nd printings, $12.95)	1.60	4.85	13.00
0 (1990, $12.95)	1.60	4.85	13.00
Moebius I-Signed & numbered hard-c ($45.95, Graphitti Designs, 1,500 copies printed)-r/#1-3	4.60	13.80	46.00

MOEBIUS COMICS
May, 1996 - No. 2 ($2.95, B&W)
Caliber

	GD25	FN65	NM94
1,2: Moebius-c/a. 1-William Stout-a		1.20	3.00

MOEBIUS: THE MAN FROM CIGURI
1996 ($7.95, digest-size)
Dark Horse Comics

	GD25	FN65	NM94
nn-Moebius-c/a	1.00	3.00	8.00

MOLLY MANTON'S ROMANCES (Romantic Affairs #3)
Sept, 1949 - No. 2, Dec, 1949 (52 pgs.)
Marvel Comics (SePI)

	GD25	FN65	NM94
1-Photo-c (becomes Blaze the Wonder Collie #2 (10/49) on? & Molly Manton's Romances #2	10.00	30.00	75.00
2-Titled "Romances of…"; photo-c	8.00	24.00	50.00

MOLLY O'DAY (Super Sleuth)
February, 1945 (1st Avon comic)
Avon Periodicals

	GD25	FN65	NM94
1-Molly O'Day, The Enchanted Dagger by Tuska (r/Yankee #1), Capt'n Courage, Corporal Grant app.	40.00	120.00	320.00

MONKEES, THE (TV)(Also see Circus Boy, Groovy, Not Brand Echh #3, Teen-Age Talk, Teen Beam & Teen Beat)
March, 1967 - No. 17, Oct, 1969 (#1-4,6,7,9,10,12,15,16 have photo-c)
Dell Publishing Co.

	GD25	FN65	NM94
1-Photo-c	8.00	25.00	90.00
2-4,6,7,9,10,12,15,16: All photo-c	5.00	15.00	55.00
5,8,11,13,14,17-No photo-c: 17-Reprints #1	3.50	11.00	38.00

MONKEY AND THE BEAR, THE
Sept, 1953 - No. 3, Jan, 1954
Atlas Comics (ZPC)

	GD25	FN65	NM94
1-Howie Post-c/a in all; funny animal	5.70	17.00	40.00
2,3	4.00	12.00	24.00

MONKEYMAN AND O'BRIEN (Also see Dark Horse Presents #80, 100-5, Hellboy: Seed of Destruction, & San Diego Comic Con #2)
July, 1996 - No. 3, Sept, 1996 ($2.95, limited series)
Dark Horse Comics (Legend)

	GD25	FN65	NM94
1-3: New stories; Art Adams-c/a/scripts		1.40	3.50
nn-(2/96, $2.95)-r/back-up stories from Hellboy: Seed of Destruction; Adams-c/a/scripts		1.40	3.50

MONKEYSHINES COMICS
Summer, 1944 - No. 27, July, 1949
Ace Periodicals/Publishers Specialists/Current Books/Unity Publ.

	GD25	FN65	NM94
1-Funny animal	8.75	26.25	70.00
2-(Aut/44)	5.70	17.00	35.00
3-10: 3-(Win/44)	4.25	13.00	28.00
11-27: 23,24-Fago-c/a	4.00	12.00	24.00

MONKEY'S UNCLE, THE (See Merlin Jones As... under Movie Comics)

MONROES, THE (TV)
Apr, 1967
Dell Publishing Co.

	GD25	FN65	NM94
1-Photo-c	1.80	5.50	20.00

MONSTER
1953 - No. 2, 1953
Fiction House Magazines

	GD25	FN65	NM94
1-Dr. Drew by Grandenetti; reprint from Rangers Comics #48; Whitman-c	36.00	108.00	320.00
2-Whitman-c	30.00	90.00	240.00

MONSTER CRIME COMICS (Also see Crime Must Stop)
Oct, 1952 (15¢, 52 pgs.)
Hillman Periodicals

	GD25	FN65	NM94
1 (Scarce)	75.00	225.00	650.00

Monster Matinee #1 © Chaos!

Monte Hale Western #46 © FAW

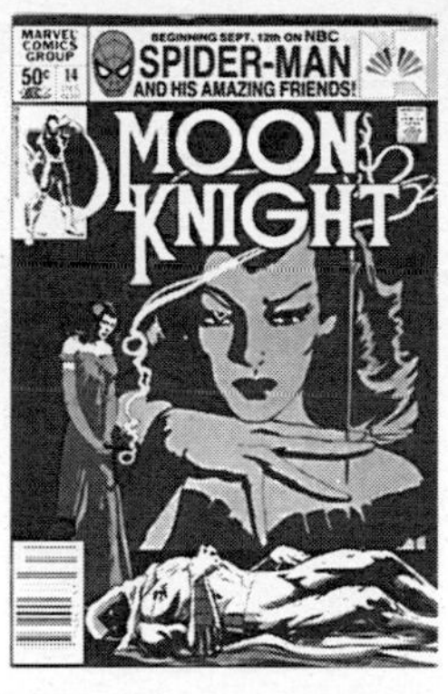

Moon Knight #14 © MEG

MONSTER HOWLS (Magazine)
December, 1966 (Satire) (35¢, 68 pgs.)
Humor-Vision

	GD25	FN65	NM94
1	3.50	10.50	35.00

MONSTER HUNTERS
Aug, 1975 - No. 9, Jan, 1977; No. 10, Oct, 1977 - No. 18, Feb, 1979
Charlton Comics

	GD25	FN65	NM94
1-Howard-a; Newton-c.	1.50	4.50	12.00
2-10: 2-Ditko-a	1.00	3.00	8.00
11-13,15-18		2.00	5.00
14-Special all-Ditko issue	1.25	3.75	10.00
1,2 (Modern Comics reprints, 1977)		1.20	3.00

NOTE: ***Ditko*** *a-2, 6, 8, 10, 13-15r, 18r; c-13-15, 18.* ***Howard*** *r-13.* ***Morisi*** *a-1.* ***Staton*** *a-1, 13.* ***Sutton*** *a-2, 4; c-2, 4. Reprints in #12-18.*

MONSTER MADNESS (Magazine)
1972 - #3, 1973 (60¢, B&W)
Marvel Comics

	GD25	FN65	NM94
1-3: Stories by "Sinister" Stan Lee	2.50	7.50	20.00

MONSTER MAN
Sept, 1997 - Present ($2.95, B&W)
Image Comics (Action Planet)

	GD25	FN65	NM94
1-Mike Manley-c/s/a			2.95

MONSTER MATINEE
Oct, 1997 - No. 3, Oct, 1997 ($2.50, limited series)
Chaos! Comics

	GD25	FN65	NM94
1-3: pin-ups			2.50

MONSTER MENACE
Dec, 1993 - No. 4, Mar, 1994 ($1.25, limited series)
Marvel Comics

	GD25	FN65	NM94
1-4: Pre-code Atlas horror reprints.		.80	2.00

NOTE: ***Ditko-r*** *&* ***Kirby-r*** *in all.*

MONSTER OF FRANKENSTEIN (See Frankenstein)

MONSTERS ON THE PROWL (Chamber of Darkness #1-8)
No. 9, 2/71 - No. 27, 11/73; No. 28, 6/74 No. 30, 10/74
Marvel Comics Group (No. 13,14: 52 pgs.)

	GD25	FN65	NM94
9-Barry Smith inks	2.50	7.50	20.00
10-12,15-30	1.00	2.80	7.00
13,14-52 pgs.	1.50	4.50	12.00
16-(4/72)-King Kull app.; Severin-c	1.50	4.50	12.00

NOTE: ***Ditko*** *r-5, 9, 14, 16.* ***Gil Kane*** *c-7.* ***Kirby*** *r-10-17, 21, 23, 25, 27, 28, 30; c-9, 25.* ***Kirby/Ditko*** *r-14, 17-20, 22, 24, 26, 29.* ***Reinman*** *r-5.* ***Marie/John Severin*** *a-16(Kull). 9-13, 15 contain one new story. Woodish art by* ***Reese****-11. King Kull created by Robert E. Howard.*

MONSTERS UNLEASHED (Magazine)
July, 1973 - No. 11, Apr, 1975; Summer, 1975 (B&W)
Marvel Comics Group

	GD25	FN65	NM94
1-Soloman Kane sty; Werewolf app.	2.50	7.50	24.00
2-4: 2-The Frankenstein Monster begins, ends #10. 3-Neal Adams-c/a; The Man-Thing begins (origin-r); Son of Satan preview. 4-Intro. Satana, the Devil's daughter; Werewolf app.	2.50	7.50	20.00
5-7: Werewolf in all. 5-Man-Thing. 7-Williamson-a(r)	1.25	3.75	10.00
8-11: 8-Man-Thing; N. Adams-r. 9-Man-Thing; Wendigo app. 10-Origin Tigra	1.60	4.85	13.00
Annual 1 (Summer,1975, 92 pgs.)-Kane-a	1.50	4.50	12.00

NOTE: ***Boris*** *c-2, 6.* ***Brunner*** *a-2; c-11.* ***J. Buscema*** *a-2p, 4p, 5p.* ***Colan*** *a-1, 4r.* ***Davis*** *a-3r.* ***Everett*** *a-2r.* ***G. Kane*** *a-3.* ***Krigstein*** *r-4.* ***Morrow*** *a-3; c-1.* ***Perez*** *a-8.* ***Ploog*** *a-6.* ***Reese*** *a-1, 2.* ***Tuska*** *a-3p.* ***Wildey*** *a-1r.*

MONTANA KID, THE (See Kid Montana)

MONTE HALE WESTERN (Movie star; Formerly Mary Marvel #1-28; also see Fawcett Movie Comic, Motion Picture Comics, Picture News #8, Real Western Hero, Six-Gun Heroes, Western Hero & XMas Comics)
No. 29, Oct, 1948 - No. 88, Jan, 1956
Fawcett Publications/Charlton No. 83 on

	GD25	FN65	NM94
29-(#1, 52 pgs.)-Photo-c begin, end #82; Monte Hale & his horse Pardner begin	41.00	123.00	370.00
30-(52 pgs.)-Big Bow and Little Arrow begin, end #34; Captain Tootsie by Beck	21.00	64.00	170.00
31-36,38-40-(52 pgs.): 34-Gabby Hayes begins, ends #80. 39-Captain Tootsie by Beck	15.50	47.00	125.00
37,41,45,49-(36 pgs.)	10.50	32.00	85.00
42-44,46-48,50-(52 pgs.): 47-Big Bow & Little Arrow app.	11.30	34.00	90.00
51,52,54-56,58,59-(52 pgs.)	8.75	26.25	70.00
53,57-(36 pgs.): 53-Slim Pickens app.	7.85	23.50	55.00
60-81: 36 pgs. #60-on. 80-Gabby Hayes ends	7.85	23.50	55.00
82-Last Fawcett issue (6/53)	8.75	26.25	70.00
83-1st Charlton issue (2/55); B&W photo back-c begin. Gabby Hayes returns, ends #86	8.75	26.25	70.00
84 (4/55)	7.85	23.50	55.00
85-86	7.15	21.50	50.00
87-Wolverton-r, 1/2 pg.	7.85	23.50	55.00
88-Last issue	7.85	23.50	55.00

NOTE: ***Gil Kane*** *a-33?, 34? Rocky Lane -1 pg. (Carnation ad)-38, 40, 41, 43, 44, 46, 55.*

MONTY HALL OF THE U.S. MARINES (See With the Marines…)
Aug, 1951 - No. 11, Apr, 1953
Toby Press

	GD25	FN65	NM94
1	9.00	27.00	55.00
2	5.70	17.00	35.00
3-5	5.00	15.00	30.00
6-11	4.25	13.00	26.00

NOTE: *Full page pin-ups (Pin-Up Pete) by* ***Jack Sparling*** *in #1-9.*

MOON, A GIRL...ROMANCE, A (Becomes Weird Fantasy #13 on; formerly Moon Girl #1-8)
No. 9, Sept-Oct, 1949 - No. 12, Mar-Apr, 1950
E. C. Comics

	GD25	FN65	NM94
9-Moon Girl cameo; spanking panel	60.00	180.00	475.00
10,11	45.00	135.00	360.00
12-(Scarce)	63.00	190.00	485.00

NOTE: ***Feldstein, Ingels*** *art in all.* ***Feldstein*** *c-9-12.* ***Wood/Harrison*** *a-10-12. Canadian reprints known; see Table of Contents.*

MOON GIRL AND THE PRINCE (#1) (Moon Girl #2-6; Moon Girl Fights Crime #7, 8; becomes A Moon, A Girl, Romance #9 on)(Also see Animal Fables #7 and Happy Houlihans)
Fall, 1947 - No. 8, Summer, 1949
E. C. Comics

	GD25	FN65	NM94
1-Origin Moon Girl (see Happy Houlihans #1)	71.00	213.00	640.00
2	37.00	110.00	330.00
3,4: 4-Moon Girl vs. a vampire	36.00	108.00	285.00
5-E.C.'s 1st horror story, "Zombie Terror"	84.00	252.00	760.00
6-8 (Scarce): 7-Origin Star (Moongirl's sidekick)	41.00	123.00	365.00

NOTE: ***Craig*** *a-2, 5.* ***Moldoff*** *a-1-8; c-2-6.* ***Wheelan's*** *Fat and Slat app. in #3, 4, 6. #2 & #3 are 52 pgs., #4 on, 36 pgs. Canadian reprints known; (see Table of Contents.)*

MOON KNIGHT (Also see The Hulk, Marc Spector…, Marvel Preview #21, Marvel Spotlight & Werewolf by Night #32)
November, 1980 - No. 38, July, 1984 (Mando paper No. 33 on)
Marvel Comics Group

	GD25	FN65	NM94
1-Origin resumed in #4; begin Sienkiewicz-c/a		1.20	3.00
2-34,36-38: 4-Intro Midnight Man. 16-The Thing app. 25-Double size			1.50
35-($1.00, 52 pgs.)-X-men app.; F.F. cameo			1.50

NOTE: ***Austin*** *c-27i, 31i.* ***Cowan*** *a-16; c-16, 17.* ***Kaluta*** *c-36-38; back c-35.* ***Miller*** *c-9, 12p, 13p, 15p, 27p.* ***Ploog*** *back c-35.* ***Sienkiewicz*** *a-1-15, 17-20, 22-26, 28-30, 33i, 36(4), 37; c-1-5, 7, 8, 10, 11, 14-16, 18-26, 28-30, 31p, 33, 34.*

MOON KNIGHT

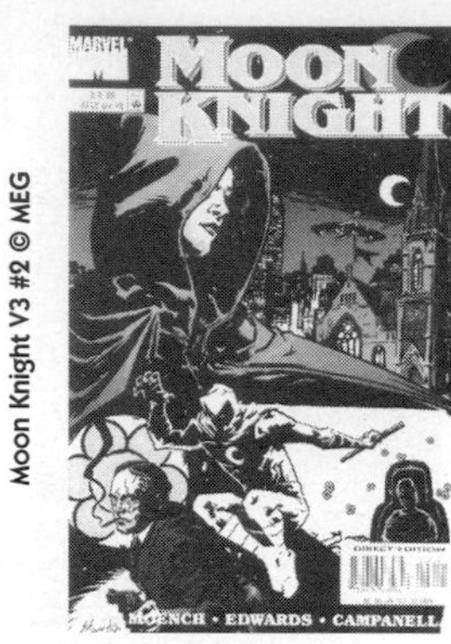

Moon Knight V3 #2 © MEG

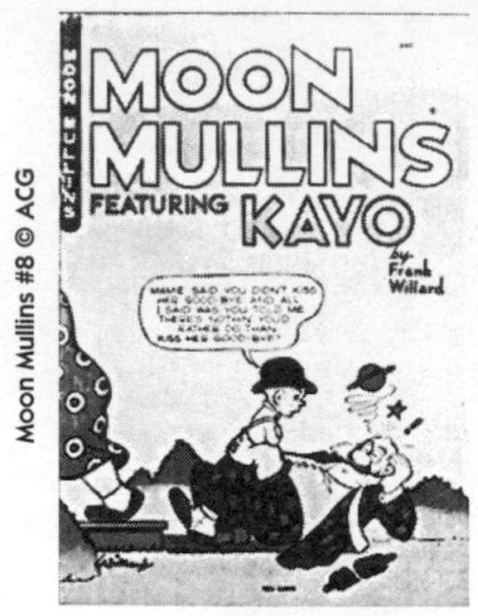

Moon Mullins #8 © ACG

Moonshadow #1 © J.M. DeMatteis & Jon J. Muth

GD25 FN65 NM94

June, 1985 - V2#6, Dec, 1985
Marvel Comics Group

V2#1-6: 1-Double size; new costume. 6-Sienkiewicz painted-c. 1.00

MOON KNIGHT (Volume 3)
Jan, 1998 - No. 4, Apr, 1998 ($2.50, limited series)
Marvel Comics

1-Moench-s/Edwards-c/a 2.50

MOON KNIGHT: DIVIDED WE FALL
1992 ($4.95, 52 pgs.)
Marvel Comics

nn-Denys Cowan-c/a(p) 2.00 5.00

MOON KNIGHT SPECIAL
Oct, 1992 ($2.50, 52 pgs.)
Marvel Comics

1-Shang Chi, Master of Kung Fu-c/story 1.00 2.50

MOON KNIGHT SPECIAL EDITION
Nov, 1983 - No. 3, Jan, 1984 ($2.00, limited series, Baxter paper)
Marvel Comics Group

1-3: Reprints from Hulk mag. by Sienkiewicz .80 2.00

MOON MULLINS (See Popular Comics, Super Book #3 & Super Comics)
1941 - 1945
Dell Publishing Co.

	GD25	FN65	NM94
Four Color 14(1941)	33.00	98.00	360.00
Large Feature Comic 29(1941)	24.00	71.00	260.00
Four Color 31(1943)	17.00	50.00	185.00
Four Color 81(1945)	9.00	27.00	100.00

MOON MULLINS
Dec-Jan, 1947-48 - No. 8, 1949 (52 pgs.)
Michel Publ. (American Comics Group)

	GD25	FN65	NM94
1-Alternating Sunday & daily strip-r	17.50	53.00	140.00
2	8.75	26.25	70.00
3-8: 8-...Featuring Kayo on-c	7.85	23.50	55.00

NOTE: *Milt Gross a-2-6, 8. Frank Willard r-all.*

MOON PILOT
No. 1313, Mar-May, 1962
Dell Publishing Co.

Four Color 1313-Movie, photo-c 6.40 19.00 70.00

MOONSHADOW (Also see Farewell, Moonshadow)
5/85 - #12, 2/87 ($1.50/$1.75, mature)(1st fully painted comic book)
Marvel Comics (Epic Comics)

1-Origin; J. M. DeMatteis scripts & Jon J. Muth painted-c/a. 2.00 5.00
2-12: 11-Origin 1.20 3.00
Trade paperback (1987?)-r/#1-12 14.00
Signed & numbered hard-c ($39.95, 1,200 copies)-r/#1-12 7.50 22.50 75.00

MOONSHADOW
Oct, 1994 - No. 12, Aug, 1995 ($2.25/$2.95, painted limited series, mature)
DC Comics (Vertigo)

1-11: Reprints Epic series. 1.00 2.50
12 ($2.95)-w/expanded ending 1.20 3.00

MOON-SPINNERS, THE (See Movie Comics)

MOPSY (See Pageant of Comics & TV Teens)
Feb, 1948 - No. 19, Sept, 1953
St. John Publ. Co.

	GD25	FN65	NM94
1-Part-r; reprints "Some Punkins" by Neher	16.00	47.00	110.00
2	10.00	30.00	60.00
3-10(1953): 8-Lingerie panels	7.50	22.50	45.0
11-19: 19-Lingerie-c	6.35	19.00	38.0

NOTE: *#1, 3-6, 13, 18, 19 have paper dolls.*

MORBID ANGEL
Oct, 1995 ($3.00, B&W)
London Night Studios

1-Hartsoe-c 1.20 3.0

MORBID ANGEL
July, 1996 - No. 3, Jan, 1997 ($3.00, limited series)
London Night Studios

1/2-($9.95)-Angel Tear Edition; foil logo 10.0
1-3 1.20 3.0
1-Penance-c 1.60 4.0

MORBID ANGEL-TO HELL AND BACK
Oct, 1996 - Present ($3.00, B&W)
London Night Studios

1 1.20 3.0

MORBIUS REVISITED
Aug, 1993 - No. 5, Dec, 1993 ($1.95, mini-series)
Marvel Comic

1-5-Reprints Fear #27-31 .80 2.0

MORBIUS: THE LIVING VAMPIRE (Also see Amazing Spider-Man #101, 102, Fear #20, Marvel Team-Up #3, 4, Midnight Sons Unl. & Vampire Tales)
Sept, 1992 - No. 32, Apr, 1995 ($1.75/$1.95)
Marvel Comics (Midnight Sons imprint #16 on)

1-($2.75, 52 pgs.)-Polybagged w/poster; Ghost Rider & Johnny Blaze x-over (part 3 of Rise of the Midnight Sons) 1.20 3.0
2-5: 3,4-Vs. Spider-Man-c/story .80 2.0
6-11,13-20: 15-Ghost Rider app. 16-Spot varnish-c. 16,17-Siege of Darkness parts 5 &13. 18-Deathlok app. .70 1.7
12-($2.25)-Outer-c is a Darkhold envelope made of black parchment w/gold ink; Midnight Massacre x-over .90 2.2
21-24,26-32: 21-Begin $1.95-c; bound-in Spider-Man trading card sheet; S-M app. .80 2.0
25-($2.50, 52 pgs.)-Gold foil logo 1.00 2.5

MORE FUN COMICS (Formerly New Fun Comics #1-6)
No. 7, Jan, 1936 - No. 127, Nov-Dec, 1947 (No. 7,9-11: paper-c)
National Periodical Publications

	GD25	FN65	VF82
7(1/36)-Oversized, paper-c; 1 pg. Kelly-a	766.00	2300.00	4700.0
(Estimated up to 15 total copies exist, none in NM/Mint)			
8(2/36)-Oversized (10x12"), slick-c; 1 pg. Kelly-a	766.00	2300.00	4700.0
9(3-4/36)(Very rare, 1st comic-sized issue)-Last multiple panel-c	950.00	2850.00	5800.0
10,11(7/36): 10-Last Henri Duval by Siegel & Shuster. 11-1st "Calling All Cars" by Siegel & Shuster; new classic logo begins	533.00	1600.00	3300.0
12(8/36)-Slick-c begin	416.00	1250.00	2600.0
V2#1(9/36, #13)	383.00	1150.00	2400.0
2(10/36, #14)-Dr. Occult in costume (1st in color)(Superman proto-type; 1st DC appearance) continues from The Comics Magazine, ends #17	1915.00	5750.00	11,500.0
(Estimated up to 10 total copies exist, none in NM/Mint)			
V2#3(11/36, #15), 16(V2#4), 17(V2#5): 16-Cover numbering begins; Xmas-c; last Superman tryout issue	750.00	2250.00	4600.0
18-20(V2#8, 5/37)	283.00	850.00	1800.0

	GD25	FN65	NM94
21(V2#9)-24(V2#12, 9/37)	283.00	850.00	1800.0
25(V3#1, 10/37)-27(V3#3, 12/37): 27-Xmas-c	283.00	850.00	1800.0
28-30: 30-1st non-funny cover	250.00	750.00	1600.0
31-Has ad for Action #1	266.00	800.00	1700.0
32-35: 32-Last Dr. Occult	250.00	750.00	1600.0

36-40: 36-(10/38)-The Masked Ranger & sidekick Pedro begins; Ginger Snap

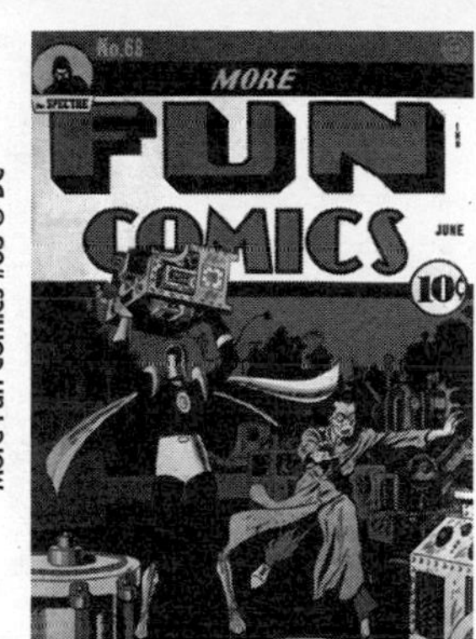

More Fun Comics #68 © DC

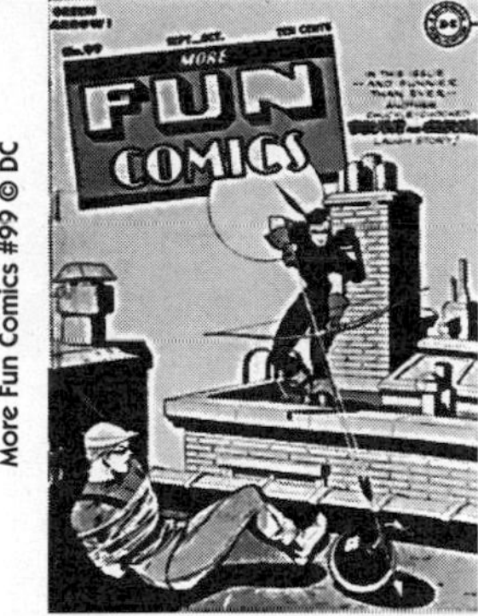

More Fun Comics #99 © DC

More Than Mortal #1 © Liar

GD25 FN65 NM94

by Bob Kane (2 pgs.; 1st-a?). 39-Xmas-c 250.00 750.00 1600.00
41-50: 41-Last Masked Ranger 191.00 575.00 1200.00
51-The Spectre app. (in costume) in one panel ad at end of Buccaneer story
733.00 2200.00 4500.00

GD25 FN65 VF82 NM94

52-(2/40)-Origin/1st app. The Spectre (in costume splash panel only), part 1 by Bernard Baily (parts 1 & 2 written by Jerry Siegel; Spectre's costume changes color from purple & blue to green & grey; last Wing Brady
4270.00 12,820.00 27,755.00 47,000.00
(Estimated up to 60 total copies exist, 3 in NM/Mint)
53-Origin The Spectre (in costume at end of story), part 2; Capt. Desmo begins
2900.00 8700.00 18,850.00 32,000.00
(Estimated up to 60 total copies exist, 3 in NM/Mint)
54-The Spectre in costume; last King Carter; classic-c
820.00 2460.00 4920.00 8200.00
55-(Scarce, 5/40)-Dr. Fate begins (Intro & 1st app.); last Bulldog Martin
1046.00 3138.00 6800.00 11,500.00
(Estimated up to 100 total copies exist, 6 in NM/Mint)

GD25 FN65 NM94

56-Congo Bill begins (6/40), 1st app.; 1st Dr. Fate-c (classic), origin continues.
430.00 1290.00 4300.00
57,59,60 280.00 840.00 2800.00
58-Classic Spectre-c 300.00 900.00 3000.00
62-64,66: 63-Last St. Bob Neal. 64-Lance Larkin begins.
256.00 768.00 2300.00
61,65: 61-Classic Dr. Fate-c. 65-Classic Spectre-c
250.00 750.00 2500.00

GD25 FN65 VF82 NM94

67-(5/41)-Origin (1st) Dr. Fate; last Congo Bill & Biff Bronson (C.B. continues in Action Comics #37 (6/41) 630.00 1890.00 3780.00 6300.00
(Estimated up to 105 total copies exist, 6 in NM/Mint)

GD25 FN65 NM94

68-70: 68-Clip Carson begins. 70-Last Lance Larkin
200.00 600.00 1800.00

GD25 FN65 VF82 NM94

71-Origin & 1st app. Johnny Quick by Mort Weisinger (9/41); sci/fi-c
490.00 1470.00 2940.00 4900.00
(Estimated up to 90 total copies exist, 6 in NM/Mint)

GD25 FN65 NM94

72-Dr. Fate's new helmet; last Sgt. Carey, Sgt. O'Malley & Captain Desmo; German submarine-c (only German war-c) 167.00 500.00 1500.00

GD25 FN65 VF82 NM94

73-Origin & 1st app. Aquaman (11/41) & begins; intro. Green Arrow & Speedy
955.00 2865.00 5730.00 10,500.00
(Estimated up to 85 total copies exist, 5 in NM/Mint)

GD25 FN65 NM94

74-2nd Aquaman 211.00 633.00 1900.00
75-80: 76-Last Clip Carson; Johnny Quick (by Meskin #76-97) begins, ends #107. 80-Last large logo 189.00 567.00 1700.00
81-88: 82-1st small logo. 84-Only Japanese war-c. 87-Last Radio Squad
106.00 318.00 950.00
89-Origin Green Arrow & Speedy Team-up 122.00 366.00 1100.00
90-99: 91-1st bi-monthly issue. 93-Dover & Clover begin (1st app., 9-10/43). 97-Kubert-a. 98-Last Dr. Fate 75.00 225.00 675.00
100 106.00 318.00 950.00

GD25 FN65 VF82 NM94

101-Origin & 1st app. Superboy (1-2/45)(not by Siegel & Shuster); last Spectre issue 700.00 2100.00 4200.00 7000.00
(Estimated up to 200 total copies exist, 9 in NM/Mint)

GD25 FN65 NM94

102-2nd Superboy 106.00 318.00 950.00
103-3rd Superboy 81.00 243.00 725.00
104-107: 107-Last Johnny Quick & Superboy 67.00 200.00 600.00
108-120: 108-Genius Jones begins (3-4/46; cont'd from Adventure Comics #102) 17.50 53.00 140.00
121-124,126: 121-123,126-Post-c (Jimminy-c) 12.00 38.00 100.00
125-Superman on cover 61.00 183.00 550.00
127-(Scarce)-Post-c/a 28.00 83.00 220.00

NOTE: *All issues are scarce to rare. Cover features: The Spectre-#52-55, 57-60, 62-67. Dr. Fate-#56, 61, 68-76. The Green Arrow & Speedy-#77-85, 88-97, 99, 101 (w/Dover & Clover-#98, 103). Johnny Quick-#86, 87, 100. Dover & Clover-#102, (104, 106 w/Superboy), 107, 108(w/Genius Jones), 110, 112, 114, 117, 119. Genius Jones-#109, 111, 113, 115, 118, 120.* ***Baily*** *a-45, 50-on; c-52-55, 57-60, 62-67.* ***Al Capp*** *a-45(signed Koppy).* ***Ellsworth*** *c-7.* ***Craig Flessel*** *c-30, 31, 35-48(most).* ***Guardineer*** *c-47, 49, 50.* ***Kiefer*** *a-20.* ***Meskin*** *c-86, 87, 100?* ***Moldoff*** *c-51.* ***George Papp*** *c-77-85.* ***Post*** *c-121-127.* ***Vincent Sullivan*** *c-8-28, 32-34.*

MORE SEYMOUR (See Seymour My Son)
Oct, 1963
Archie Publications

1 1.50 4.50 12.00

MORE THAN MORTAL
June, 1997 - Present ($2.95)
Liar Comics

1 1.60 4.00
1-Variant-c 2.00 5.00
1-White-c 1.25 3.75 10.00
2 2.95

MORE TRASH FROM MAD (Annual)
1958 - No. 12, 1969
E. C. Comics

nn(1958)-8 pgs. color Mad reprint from #20 17.50 52.00 175.00
2(1959)-Market Product Labels 12.00 36.00 120.00
3(1960)-Text book covers 11.00 33.00 110.00
4(1961)-Sing Along with Mad booklet 11.00 33.00 110.00
5(1962)-Window Stickers; r/from Mad #39 7.50 22.50 75.00
6(1963)-TV Guise booklet 8.50 25.50 85.00
7(1964)-Alfred E. Neuman commemorative stamps 6.00 18.00 60.00
8(1965)-Life size poster-Alfred E. Neuman 4.00 12.00 40.00
9,10(1966-67)-Mischief Sticker 3.50 10.50 35.00
11(1968)-Campaign poster & bumper sticker 3.50 10.50 35.00
12(1969)-Pocket medals 3.50 10.50 35.00

NOTE: ***Kelly Freas*** *c-1, 2, 4.* ***Mingo*** *c-3, 5-9, 12.*

MORGAN THE PIRATE (Movie)
No. 1227, Sept-Nov, 1961
Dell Publishing Co.

Four Color 1227-Photo-c 7.00 22.00 80.00

MORLOCK 2001
Feb, 1975 - No. 3, July, 1975
Atlas/Seaboard Publ.

1,2: 1-(Super-hero)-Origin & 1st app. 1.20 3.00
3-Ditko/Wrightson-a; origin The Midnight Man & The Midnight Men
2.00 5.00

MORNINGSTAR SPECIAL
Apr, 1990 ($2.50)
Comico

1-From the Elementals; Willingham-c/a/scripts 1.00 2.50

MORRIGAN
Aug, 1993 ($2.75, B&W)
Dimension X

1-Foil stamped-c 1.10 2.75

MORRIGAN
1997 ($2.95, limited series)
Sirius Entertainment

1-Tenuta-c/a 2.95

MORTAL KOMBAT

Mortal Kombat #2 © Midway

Mortigan Goth: Immortalis #4 © MEG

Motormouth #9 © MEG

July, 1994 - No. 6, Dec, 1994 ($2.95)
Malibu Comics

	GD25	FN65	NM94
1-6: 1-Two variant covers exist		1.20	3.00
1-Limited edition gold foil embossed-c		1.60	4.00
0 (12/94), Special Edition 1 (11/94)		1.20	3.00
Tournament Edition (12/94, $3.95)		1.60	4.00
Tournament Edition II (1995, $3.95)		1.60	4.00
...: **BARAKA** ,June, 1995 ($2.95, one-shot)			
1		1.20	3.00
...: **BATTLEWAVE** ,Feb, 1995 - No. 6, July, 1995 ($2.95)			
1-6		1.20	3.00
...: **GORO, PRINCE OF PAIN** ,Sept, 1994 - No. 3, Nov, 1994 ($2.95)			
1-3		1.20	3.00
...: **KITANA AND MILEENA** ,Aug, 1995 ($2.95, one-shot)			
1		1.20	3.00
...: **KUNG LAO** ,July, 1995 ($2.95, one shot)			
1		1.20	3.00
...: **RAYDON & KANO** ,Mar, 1995 - No. 3, May, 1995 ($2.95)			
1-3		1.20	3.00
...: **U.S. SPECIAL FORCES** ,Jan, 1995 - No. 2, Feb, 1995 ($3.50)			
1,2		1.20	3.50

MORTIE (Mazie's Friend; also see Flat-Top)
Dec, 1952 - No. 4, June, 1953?
Magazine Publishers

	GD25	FN65	NM94
1	5.85	17.50	38.00
2-4	4.00	10.00	22.00

MORTIGAN GOTH: IMMORTALIS (See Marvel Frontier Comics Unlimited)
Sept, 1993 - No. 4, Mar, 1994 ($1.95, mini-series)
Marvel Comics

	GD25	FN65	NM94
1-($2.95)-Foil-c		1.20	3.00
2-4		.80	2.00

MORT THE DEAD TEENAGER
Nov, 1993 - No. 4, Mar, 1994 ($1.75, mini-series)
Marvel Comics

	GD25	FN65	NM94
1-4		.70	1.75

MORTY MEEKLE
No. 793, May, 1957
Dell Publishing Co.

	GD25	FN65	NM94
Four Color 793	1.80	5.50	20.00

MOSES & THE TEN COMMANDMENTS (See Dell Giants)

MOTHER GOOSE AND NURSERY RHYME COMICS (See Christmas With Mother Goose)
No. 41, 1944 - No. 862, Nov, 1957
Dell Publishing Co.

	GD25	FN65	NM94
Four Color 41-Walt Kelly-c/a	21.00	63.00	230.00
Four Color 59, 68-Kelly c/a	18.00	53.00	195.00
Four Color 862-The Truth About..., Movie (Disney)	6.40	19.00	70.00

MOTHER OF US ALL
1950? (32 pgs.)
Catechetical Guild Giveaway

	GD25	FN65	NM94
nn	1.60	4.00	8.00

MOTHER TERESA OF CALCUTTA
1984
Marvel Comics Group

	GD25	FN65	NM94
1			1.25

MOTION PICTURE COMICS (See Fawcett Movie Comics)
No. 101, 1950 - No. 114, Jan, 1953 (All-photo-c)
Fawcett Publications

	GD25	FN65	NM94
101- "Vanishing Westerner"; Monte Hale (1950)	26.00	77.00	205.00
102- "Code of the Silver Sage"; Rocky Lane (1/51)	24.00	71.00	190.00
103- "Covered Wagon Raid"; Rocky Lane (3/51)	24.00	71.00	190.00
104- "Vigilante Hideout"; Rocky Lane (5/51)-Book length Powell-a	24.00	71.00	190.00
105- "Red Badge of Courage"; Audie Murphy; Bob Powell-a (7/51)	29.00	86.00	230.00
106- "The Texas Rangers"; George Montgomery (9/51)	24.00	73.00	195.00
107- "Frisco Tornado"; Rocky Lane (11/51)	21.00	64.00	170.00
108- "Mask of the Avenger"; John Derek	15.00	45.00	120.00
109- "Rough Rider of Durango"; Rocky Lane	22.00	66.00	175.00
110- "When Worlds Collide"; George Evans-a (5/52); Williamson & Evans drew themselves in story; (also see Famous Funnies No. 72-88)	84.00	253.00	675.00
111- "The Vanishing Outpost"; Lash LaRue	26.00	80.00	210.00
112- "Brave Warrior"; Jon Hall & Jay Silverheels	14.50	53.00	115.00
113- "Walk East on Beacon"; George Murphy; Schaffenberger-a	10.00	30.00	80.00
114- "Cripple Creek"; George Montgomery (1/53)	11.30	34.00	90.00

MOTION PICTURE FUNNIES WEEKLY (Amazing Man #5 on?)
1939 (Giveaway)(B&W, 36 pgs.)
No month given; last panel in Sub-Mariner story dated 4/39
(Also see Colossus, Green Giant & Invaders No. 20)
First Funnies, Inc.

	GD25	FN65	NM94
1-Origin & 1st printed app. Sub-Mariner by Bill Everett (8 pgs.); Fred Schwab-c; reprinted in Marvel Mystery #1 with color added over the craft tint which was used to shade the black & white version; Spy Ring, American Ace (reprinted in Marvel Mystery #3) app. (Rare)-only eight (8) known copies,one near mint with white pages, the rest with brown pages.	2600.00	5500.00	15,000.00
Covers only to #2-4 (set)			500.00

NOTE: The only eight known copies (with a ninth suspected) were discovered in 1974 in the estate of the deceased publisher. Covers only to issues No. 2-4 were also found which evident were printed in advance along with #1. #1 was to be distributed only through motion picture movie houses. However, it is believed that only advanced copies were sent out and the motion picture houses not going for the idea. Possible distribution at local theaters in Boston suspected The last panel of Sub-Mariner contains a rectangular box with "Continued Next Week" printed in it. When reprinted in Marvel Mystery, the box was left in with lettering omitted.

MOTORHEAD (See Comic's Greatest World)
Aug, 1995 - No. 6, Jan, 1996 ($2.50)
Dark Horse Comics

	GD25	FN65	NM94
1-6: Bisley-c on all. 1-Predator app.		1.00	2.50
Special 1 (3/94, $3.95, 52pgs.)-Jae Lee-c; Barb Wire, The Machine & Wolf Gang app.		1.60	4.00

MOTORMOUTH (... & Killpower #7? on)
June, 1992 - No. 13, June, 1993 ($1.75)
Marvel Comics UK

	GD25	FN65	NM94
1-13: 1,2-Nick Fury app. 3-Punisher-c/story. 5,6-Nick Fury & Punisher app. 6-Cable cameo. 7-9-Cable app.		.70	1.80

MOUNTAIN MEN (See Ben Bowie)

MOUSE MUSKETEERS (See M.G.M.'s...)

MOUSE ON THE MOON, THE (See Movie Classics)

MOVIE CLASSICS
Jan, 1963 - Dec, 1969
Dell Publishing Co.

(Before 1963, most movie adaptations were part of the 4-Color series)
(Disney movie adaptations after 1970 are in Walt Disney Showcase)

	GD25	FN65	NM94
Around the World Under the Sea 12-030-612 (12/66)	2.50	7.50	25.00
Bambi 3(4/56)-Disney; r/4-Color #186	2.80	8.40	28.00
Battle of the Bulge 12-056-606 (6/66)	2.60	7.80	26.00
Beach Blanket Bingo 12-058-509	5.50	16.50	55.00

Movie Classics - Operation Bikini © DELL

Movie Comics #6 © DC

Movie Comics #2 © FH

	GD25	FN65	NM94
Bon Voyage 01-068-212 (12/62)-Disney; photo-c	2.80	8.40	28.00
Castilian, The 12-110-401	2.80	8.40	28.00
Cat, The 12-109-612 (12/66)	2.20	6.60	22.00
Cheyenne Autumn 12-112-506 (4-6/65)	4.50	13.50	45.00
Circus World, Samuel Bronston's 12-115-411; John Wayne app.; John Wayne photo-c	8.50	25.50	85.00
Countdown 12-150-710 (10/67)-James Caan photo-c	2.80	8.40	28.00
Creature, The 1 (12-142-302) (12-2/62-63)	4.00	12.00	40.00
Creature, The 12-142-410 (10/64)	2.40	7.20	24.00
David Ladd's Life Story 12-173-212 (10-12/62)-Photo-c	6.50	19.50	65.00
Die, Monster, Die 12-175-603 (3/66)-Photo-c	3.50	10.50	35.00
Dirty Dozen 12-180-710 (10/67)	3.20	9.60	32.00
Dr. Who & the Daleks 12-190-612 (12/66)-Peter Cushing photo-c; 1st U.S. app. of Dr. Who	8.50	25.50	85.00
Dracula 12-231-212 (10-12/62)	3.50	10.50	35.00
El Dorado 12-240-710 (10/67)-John Wayne; photo-c	11.50	34.00	115.00
Ensign Pulver 12-257-410 (8-10/64)	2.40	7.20	24.00
Frankenstein 12-283-305 (3-5/63)	3.30	9.90	33.00
Great Race, The 12-299-603 (3/66)-Natallie Wood, Tony Curtis photo-c	3.50	10.50	35.00
Hallelujah Trail, The 12-307-602 (2/66) (Shows 1/66 inside); Burt Lancaster, Lee Remick photo-c	4.00	12.00	40.00
Hatari 12-340-301 (1/63)-John Wayne	7.00	21.00	70.00
Horizontal Lieutenant, The 01-348-210 (10/62)	2.40	7.20	24.00
Incredible Mr. Limpet, The 12-370-408; Don Knotts photo-c	3.00	9.00	30.00
Jack the Giant Killer 12-374-301 (1/63)	6.50	19.50	65.00
Jason & the Argonauts 12-376-310 (8-10/63)-Photo-c	8.00	24.00	80.00
Lancelot & Guinevere 12-416-310 (10/63)	4.50	13.50	45.00
Lawrence 12-426-308 (8/63)-Story of Lawrence of Arabia; movie ad on back-c; not exactly like movie	4.50	13.50	45.00
Lion of Sparta 12-439-301 (1/63)	2.40	7.20	24.00
Mad Monster Party 12-460-801 (9/67)-Based on Kurtzman's screenplay	4.80	14.40	48.00
Magic Sword, The 01-496-209 (9/62)	4.50	13.50	45.00
Masque of the Red Death 12-490-410 (8-10/64)-Vincent Price photo-c	4.00	12.00	40.00
Maya 12-495-612 (12/66)-Clint Walker & Jay North part photo-c	3.50	10.50	35.00
McHale's Navy 12-500-412 (10-12/64)	2.60	7.80	26.00
Merrill's Marauders 12-510-301 (1/63)-Photo-c	2.40	7.20	24.00
Mouse on the Moon, The 12-530-312 (10/12/63)-Photo-c	2.60	7.80	26.00
Mummy, The 12-537-211 (9-11/62) 2 versions with different back-c	3.70	11.10	37.00
Music Man, The 12-538-301 (1/63)	2.40	7.20	24.00
Naked Prey, The 12-545-612 (12/66)-Photo-c	5.00	15.00	50.00
Night of the Grizzly, The 12-558-612 (12/66)-Photo-c	3.00	9.00	30.00
None But the Brave 12-565-506 (4-6/65)	5.00	15.00	50.00
Operation Bikini 12-597-310 (10/63)-Photo-c	2.80	8.40	28.00
Operation Crossbow 12-590-512 (10-12/65)	2.80	8.40	28.00
Prince & the Pauper, The 01-654-207 (5-7/62)-Disney	3.00	9.00	30.00
Raven, The 12-680-309 (9/63)-Vincent Price photo-c	3.50	10.50	35.00
Ring of Bright Water 01-701-910 (10/69) (inside shows #12-701-909)	3.00	9.00	30.00
Runaway, The 12-707-412 (10-12/64)	2.50	7.50	25.00
Santa Claus Conquers the Martians #? (1964)-Photo-c	6.00	18.00	60.00
Santa Claus Conquers the Martians 12-725-603 (3/66, 12¢)-Reprints 1964 issue; photo-c	5.00	15.00	50.00
Another version given away with a Golden Record, SLP 170, nn, no price (3/66)-Complete with record	13.00	39.00	130.00
Six Black Horses 12-750-301 (1/63)-Photo-c	2.80	8.40	28.00
Ski Party 12-743-511 (9-11/65)-Frankie Avalon photo-c	3.50	10.50	35.00
Smoky 12-746-702 (2/67)	2.50	7.50	25.00
Sons of Katie Elder 12-748-511 (9-11/65); John Wayne app.; photo-c	12.00	36.00	120.00
Tales of Terror 12-793-302 (2/63)-Evans-a	2.40	7.20	24.00
Three Stooges Meet Hercules 01-828-208 (8/62)-Photo-c	7.00	21.00	70.00
Tomb of Ligeia 12-830-506 (4-6/65)	2.40	7.20	24.00
Treasure Island 01-845-211 (7-9/62)-Disney; r/4-Color #624	2.80	8.40	28.00
Twice Told Tales (Nathaniel Hawthorne) 12-840-401 (11-1/63-64); Vincent Price photo-c	3.30	10.00	33.00
Two on a Guillotine 12-850-506 (4-6/65)	2.40	7.20	24.00
Valley of Gwangi 01-880-912 (12/69)	7.50	22.50	75.00
War Gods of the Deep 12-900-509 (7-9/65)	2.60	7.80	26.00
War Wagon, The 12-533-709 (9/67); John Wayne app.	7.50	22.50	75.00
Who's Minding the Mint? 12-924-708 (8/67)	2.40	7.20	24.00
Wolfman, The 12-922-308 (6-8/63)	2.60	7.80	26.00
Wolfman, The 1(12-922-410)(8-10/64)-2nd printing; r/#12-922-308	2.60	7.80	26.00
Zulu 12-950-410 (8-10/64)-Photo-c	7.00	21.00	70.00

MOVIE COMICS (See Cinema Comics Herald & Fawcett Movie Comics)

MOVIE COMICS
April, 1939 - No. 6, Sept-Oct, 1939 (Most all photo-c)
National Periodical Publications/Picture Comics

	GD25	FN65	NM94
1- "Gunga Din", "Son of Frankenstein", "The Great Man Votes", "Fisherman's Wharf", & "Scouts to the Rescue" part 1; Wheelan "Minute Movies" begin	260.00	780.00	2600.00
2- "Stagecoach", "The Saint Strikes Back", "King of the Turf","Scouts to the Rescue" part 2, "Arizona Legion", Andy Devine photo-c	189.00	567.00	1700.00
3- "East Side of Heaven", "Mystery in the White Room", "Four Feathers", "Mexican Rose" with Gene Autry, "Spirit of Culver", "Many Secrets", "The Mikado"	139.00	417.00	1250.00
4- "Captain Fury", Gene Autry in "Blue Montana Skies", "Streets of N.Y." with Jackie Cooper, "Oregon Trail" part 1 with Johnny Mack Brown, "Big Town Czar" with Barton MacLane, & "Star Reporter" with Warren Hull	108.00	324.00	975.00
5- "The Man in the Iron Mask", "Five Came Back", "Wolf Call", "The Girl & the Gambler", "The House of Fear", "The Family Next Door", "Oregon Trail" part 2	122.00	366.00	1100.00
6- "The Phantom Creeps", "Chumps at Oxford", & "The Oregon Trail" part 3; 2nd Robot-c	150.00	450.00	1350.00

NOTE: *Above books contain many original movie stills with dialogue from movie scripts. All issues are scarce. 2-Andy Devine photo-c.*

MOVIE COMICS
Dec, 1946 - No. 4, 1947
Fiction House Magazines

	GD25	FN65	NM94
1-Big Town (by Lubbers), Johnny Danger begin; Celardo-a; Mitzi of the Movies by Fran Hopper	44.00	132.00	400.00
2-(2/47)- "White Tie & Tails" with William Bendix; Mitzi of the Movies begins by Matt Baker, ends #4	36.00	108.00	300.00
3-(6/47)-Andy Hardy starring Mickey Rooney	36.00	108.00	300.00
4-Mitzi In Hollywood by Matt Baker; Merton of the Movies with Red Skelton; Yvonne DeCarlo & George Brent in "Slave Girl"	41.00	123.00	365.00

MOVIE COMICS
Oct, 1962 - Mar, 1972
Gold Key/Whitman

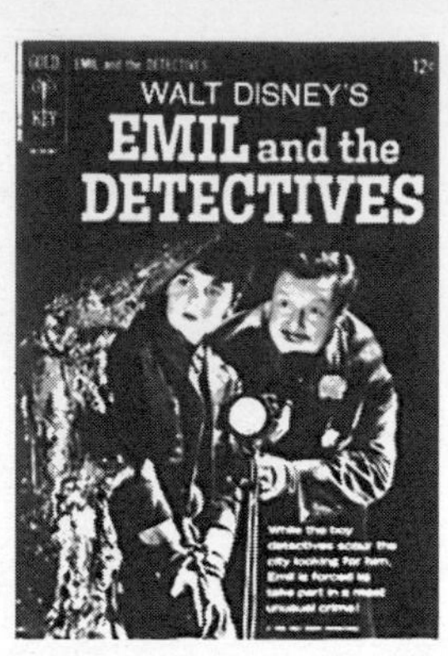

Movie Comics - Emil & the Detectives © WDC

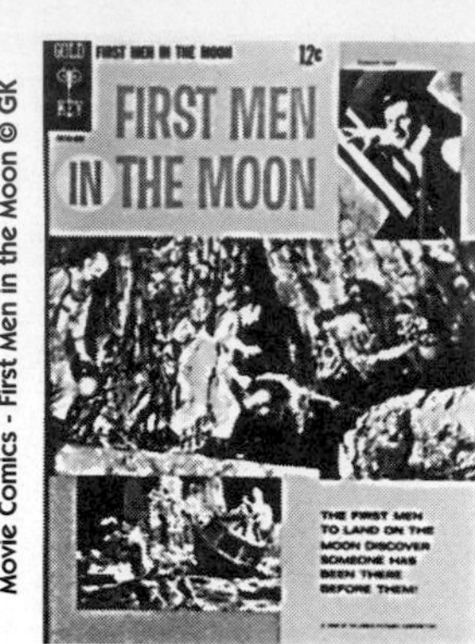

Movie Comics - First Men in the Moon © GK

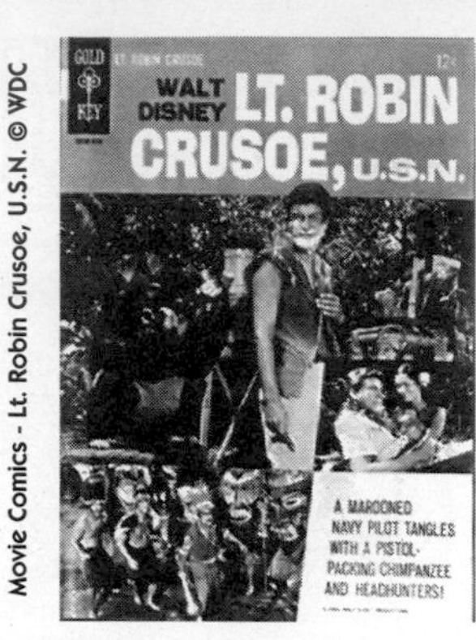

Movie Comics - Lt. Robin Crusoe, U.S.N. © WDC

GD25 FN65 NM94

Alice in Wonderland 10144-503 (3/65)-Disney; partial reprint of 4-Color #331
2.80 8.40 28.00
Aristocats, The 1 (30045-103)(3/71)-Disney; with pull-out poster (25¢)
5.50 16.50 55.00
Bambi 1 (10087-309)(9/63)-Disney; r/4-C #186 2.60 7.80 26.00
Bambi 2 (10087-607)(7/66)-Disney; r/4-C #186 2.20 6.60 22.00
Beneath the Planet of the Apes 30044-012 (12/70)-with pull-out poster; photo-c 6.00 18.00 60.00
Big Red 10026-211 (11/62)-Disney; photo-c 2.20 6.60 22.00
Big Red 10026-503 (3/65)-Disney; reprints 10026-211; photo-c
2.20 6.60 22.00
Blackbeard's Ghost 10222-806 (6/68)-Disney 2.00 6.00 20.00
Bullwhip Griffin 10181-706 (6/67)-Disney; Manning-a; photo-c
2.80 8.40 28.00
Captain Sindbad 10077-309 (9/63)-Manning-a; photo-c
4.50 13.50 45.00
Chitty Chitty Bang Bang 1 (30038-902)(2/69)-with pull-out poster; Disney; photo-c 5.50 16.50 55.00
Cinderella 10152-508 (8/65)-Disney; r/4-C #786 2.40 7.20 24.00
Darby O'Gill & the Little People 10251-001(1/70)-Disney; reprints 4-Color #1024 (Toth-a); photo-c 4.00 12.00 40.00
Dumbo 1 (10090-310)(10/63)-Disney; r/4-C #668 2.40 7.20 24.00
Emil & the Detectives 10120-502 (2/65)-Disney; photo-c
2.60 7.80 26.00
Escapade in Florence 1 (10043-301)(1/63)-Disney; starring Annette Funicello
7.00 21.00 70.00
Fall of the Roman Empire 10118-407 (7/64); Sophia Loren photo-c
2.80 8.40 28.00
Fantastic Voyage 10178-702 (2/67)-Wood/Adkins-a; photo-c
4.00 12.00 40.00
55 Days at Peking 10081-309 (9/63)-Photo-c 2.80 8.40 28.00
Fighting Prince of Donegal, The 10193-701 (1/67)-Disney
2.40 7.20 24.00
First Men in the Moon 10132-503 (3/65)-Fred Fredericks-a; photo-c
2.60 7.80 26.00
Gay Purr-ee 30017-301(1/63, 84 pgs.) 3.50 10.50 35.00
Gnome Mobile, The 10207-710 (10/67)-Disney 2.60 7.80 26.00
Goodbye, Mr. Chips 10246-006 (6/70)-Peter O'Toole photo-c
2.80 8.40 28.00
Happiest Millionaire, The 10221-804 (4/68)-Disney 2.50 7.50 25.00
Hey There, It's Yogi Bear 10122-409 (9/64)-Hanna-Barbera
5.00 15.00 50.00
Horse Without a Head, The 10109-401 (1/64)-Disney 2.40 7.20 24.00
How the West Was Won 10074-307 (7/63)-Tufts-a 3.00 9.00 30.00
In Search of the Castaways 10048-303 (3/63)-Disney; Hayley Mills photo-c
5.80 17.40 58.00
Jungle Book, The 1 (6022-801)(1/68-Whitman)-Disney; large size (10x13-1/2"); 59¢ 4.50 13.50 45.00
Jungle Book, The 1 (30033-803)(3/68, 68 pgs.)-Disney; same contents as Whitman #1 3.00 9.00 30.00
Jungle Book, The 1 (6/78, $1.00 tabloid) 1.50 4.50 15.00
Jungle Book (1984)-r/Giant 2.00 5.00
Kidnapped 10080-306 (6/63)-Disney; reprints 4-Color #1101; photo-c
2.50 7.50 25.00
King Kong 30036-809(9/68-68 pgs.)-painted-c 2.00 6.00 20.00
King Kong nn-Whitman Treasury($1.00, 68 pgs.,1968), same cover as Gold Key issue 3.50 10.50 35.00
King Kong 11299(#1-786, 10x13-1/4", 68 pgs., $1.00, 1978)
1.20 3.60 12.00
Lady and the Tramp 10042-301 (1/63)-Disney; r/4-Color #629
2.60 7.80 26.00
Lady and the Tramp 1 (1967-Giant; 25¢)-Disney; reprints part of Dell #1
4.20 12.60 42.00
Lady and the Tramp 2 (10042-203)(3/72)-Disney; r/4-Color #629
1.90 5.70 19.00
Legend of Lobo, The 1 (10059-303)(3/63)-Disney; photo-c
3.60 11.00 20.00
Lt. Robin Crusoe, U.S.N. 10191-610 (10/66)-Disney; Dick Van Dyke photo-c
1.80 5.40 18.00
Lion, The 10035-301 (1/63)-Photo-c 1.60 4.80 16.00
Lord Jim 10156-509 (9/65)-Photo-c 2.00 6.00 20.00
Love Bug, The 10237-906 (6/69)-Disney; Buddy Hackett photo-c
2.00 6.00 20.00
Mary Poppins 10136-501 (1/65)-Disney; photo-c 3.50 10.50 35.00
Mary Poppins 30023-501 (1/65-68 pgs.)-Disney; photo-c
5.50 16.50 55.00
McLintock 10110-403 (3/64); John Wayne app.; John Wayne & Maureen O'Hara photo-c 11.00 33.00 110.00
Merlin Jones as the Monkey's Uncle 10115-510 (10/65)-Disney; Annette Funicello front/back photo-c 4.20 12.60 42.00
Miracle of the White Stallions, The 10065-306 (6/63)-Disney
2.40 7.20 24.00
Misadventures of Merlin Jones, The 10115-405 (5/64)-Disney; Annette Funicello photo front/back-c 4.20 12.60 42.00
Moon-Spinners, The 10124-410 (10/64)-Disney; Haley Mills photo-c
5.80 17.40 58.00
Mutiny on the Bounty 1 (10040-302)(2/63)-Marlon Brando photo-c
2.80 8.40 28.00
Nikki, Wild Dog of the North 10141-412 (12/64)-Disney; reprints 4-Color #1226
2.00 6.00 20.00
Old Yeller 10168-601 (1/66)-Disney; reprints 4-Color #869; photo-c
2.00 6.00 20.00
One Hundred & One Dalmations 1 (10247-002) (2/70)-Disney; reprints Four Color #1183 2.20 6.60 22.00
Peter Pan 1 (10086-309)(9/63)-Disney; reprints Four Color #442
2.60 7.80 26.00
Peter Pan 2 (10086-909)(9/69)-Disney; reprints Four Color #442
2.00 6.00 20.00
Peter Pan 1 ('83)-r/4-Color #442 1.00
P.T. 109 10123-409 (9/64)-John F. Kennedy 3.50 10.50 35.00
Rio Conchos 10143-503(3/65) 3.00 9.00 30.00
Robin Hood 10163-506 (6/65)-Disney; reprints Four Color #413
2.20 6.60 22.00
Shaggy Dog & the Absent-Minded Professor 30032-708 (8/67-Giant, 68 pgs.) Disney; reprints 4-Color #985,1199 4.20 12.60 42.00
Sleeping Beauty 1 (30042-009)(9/70)-Disney; reprints Four Color #973; with pull-out poster 5.00 15.00 50.00
Snow White & the Seven Dwarfs 1 (10091-310)(10/63)-Disney; reprints Four Color #382 2.00 6.00 20.00
Snow White & the Seven Dwarfs 10091-709 (9/67)-Disney; reprints Four Color #382 1.80 5.40 18.00
Snow White & the Seven Dwarfs 90091-204 (2/84)-Reprints Four Color #382
1.00
Son of Flubber 1 (10057-304)(4/63)-Disney; sequel to "The Absent-Minded Professor" 2.20 6.60 22.00
Summer Magic 10076-309 (9/63)-Disney; Hayley Mills photo-c; Manning-a
5.80 17.40 58.00
Swiss Family Robinson 10236-904 (4/69)-Disney; reprints Four Color #1156; photo-c 2.20 6.60 22.00
Sword in the Stone, The 30019-402 (2/64-Giant, 68 pgs.)-Disney (see March of Comics #258 & Wart and the Wizard 4.70 14.10 47.00
That Darn Cat 10171-602 (2/66)-Disney; Hayley Mills photo-c
5.20 15.60 52.00
Those Magnificent Men in Their Flying Machines 10162-510 (10/65); photo-c
2.40 7.20 24.00
Three Stooges in Orbit 30016-211 (11/62-Giant, 32 pgs.)-All photos from movie; stiff-photo-c 8.00 24.00 80.00
Tiger Walks, A 10117-406 (6/64)-Disney; Torres?, Tufts-a; photo-c

Movie Love #8 © FF

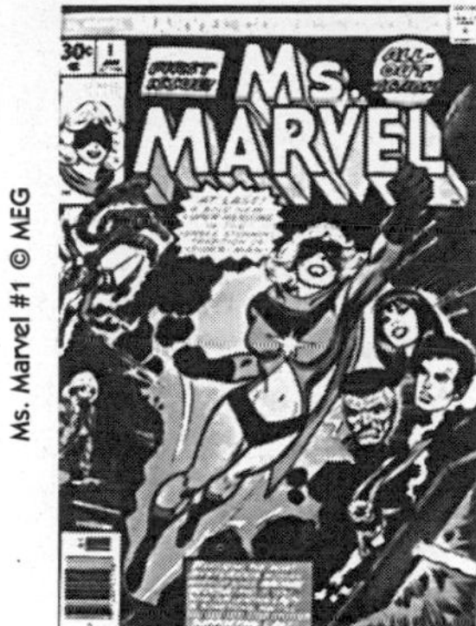

Ms. Marvel #1 © MEG

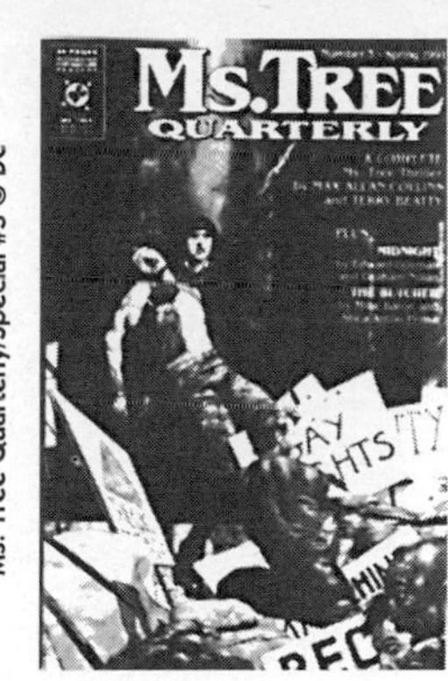

Ms. Tree Quarterly/Special #3 © DC

GD25 FN65 NM94

3.60 10.80 36.00
Toby Tyler 10142-502 (2/65)-Disney; reprints Four Color #1092; photo-c
2.20 6.60 22.00
Treasure Island 1 (10200-703)(3/67)-Disney; reprints Four Color #624; photo-c
2.00 6.00 20.00
20,000 Leagues Under the Sea 1 (10095-312)(12/63)-Disney; reprints
Four Color #614 2.00 6.00 20.00
Wonderful Adventures of Pinocchio, The 1 (10089-310)(10/63)-Disney; reprints
Four Color #545 (see Wonderful Advs. of...) 2.20 6.60 22.00
Wonderful Adventures of Pinocchio, The 10089-109 (9/71)-Disney; reprints
Four Color #545 2.20 6.60 22.00
Wonderful World of the Brothers Grimm 1 (10008-210)(10/62)
3.50 10.50 35.00
X, the Man with the X-Ray Eyes 10083-309 (9/63)-Ray Milland photo on-c
6.20 18.60 62.00
Yellow Submarine 35000-902 (2/69-Giant, 68 pgs.)-With pull-out poster;
The Beatles cartoon movie 20.00 60.00 200.00
Without poster 5.00 15.00 50.00

MOVIE LOVE (Also see Personal Love)
Feb, 1950 - No. 22, Aug, 1953
Famous Funnies

1-Dick Powell, Evelyn Keyes, & Mickey Rooney photo-c
10.00 30.00 80.00
2-Myrna Loy photo-c 5.70 17.00 40.00
3-7,9: 6-Ricardo Montalban photo-c. 9-Gene Tierney, John Lund, Glenn Ford,
& Rhonda Fleming photo-c. 5.35 16.00 32.00
8-Williamson/Frazetta-a, 6 pgs. 28.00 83.00 220.00
10-Frazetta-a, 6 pgs. 33.00 98.00 260.00
11,14-16: 14-Janet Leigh photo-c 4.25 13.00 28.00
12-Dean Martin & Jerry Lewis photo-c (12/51, pre-dates Advs. of Dean
Martin & Jerry Lewis comic) 5.70 17.00 40.00
13-Ronald Reagan photo-c with 1 pg. biog. 16.00 49.00 130.00
17-Leslie Caron & Ralph Meeker photo-c; 1 pg. Frazetta ad
4.25 13.00 28.00
18-22: 19-John Derek photo-c. 21-Paul Henreid & Patricia Medina photo-c.
22-John Payne & Coleen Gray photo-c 4.15 12.50 25.00
NOTE: *Each issue has a full-length movie adaptation with photo covers.*

MOVIE THRILLERS (Movie)
1949
Magazine Enterprises

1-Adaptation of "Rope of Sand" w/Burt Lancaster; Burt Lancaster photo-c
27.00 81.00 190.00

MOVIE TOWN ANIMAL ANTICS (Formerly Animal Antics; becomes Raccoon Kids #52 on)
No. 24, Jan-Feb, 1950 - No. 51, July-Aug, 1954
National Periodical Publications

24-Raccoon Kids continue 9.50 28.00 75.00
25-51 8.75 26.25 65.00
NOTE: ***Sheldon Mayer** a-28-33, 35, 37-41, 43, 44, 47, 49-51.*

MOVIE TUNES COMICS (Formerly Animated...; Frankie No. 4 on)
No. 3, Fall, 1946
Marvel Comics (MgPC)

3-Super Rabbit, Krazy Krow, Silly Seal & Ziggy Pig 8.75 26.25 70.00

MOWGLI JUNGLE BOOK
No. 487, Aug-Oct, 1953 - No. 620, Apr, 1955 (Rudyard Kipling's..)
Dell Publishing Co.

Four Color 487 (#1) 4.50 13.50 50.00
Four Color 582 (8/54), 620 3.60 11.00 40.00

MOXI
July, 1996 ($3.00)
Lightning Comics

1-Flip book w/Hellina; two covers 1.20 3.00
1-($9.95)-Commemorative Edition; polybagged 1.25 3.75 10.00

MOXI'S FRIENDS...BOBBY JOE & NITRO
Sept, 1996 ($2.75, B&W, one-shot)
Lightning Comics

1-Regular Edition 1.10 2.75
1($9.95)-Commemorative Edition 1.25 3.75 10.00

MOXI: STRANGE DAZE
Nov, 1996 ($2.75, B&W, one-shot)
Lightning Comics

1, 1b-Regular Edition 1.10 2.75
1($9.95)-Platinum Edition 1.25 3.75 10.00

MR. (See Mister)

MS. CYANIDE & ICE
June, 1995 - No. 1, 1995 ($2.95, B&W)
Blackout Comics

0,1 1.20 3.00

MS. MARVEL (Also see The Avengers #183)
Jan, 1977 - No. 23, Apr, 1979
Marvel Comics Group

1-1st app. Ms. Marvel; Scorpion app. in #1,2 1.60 4.00
2-Origin 1.00 2.50
3-10: 5-Vision app. 10-Last 30¢ issue .80 2.00
11-15,19-23: 19-Capt. Marvel app. 20-New costume. 23-Vance Astro (leader of
the Guardians) app. 1.50
16,17-Mystique cameo 1.00 3.00 8.00
18-1st full Mystique; Avengers x-over 1.50 4.50 12.00
NOTE: ***Austin** c-14i, 16i, 17i, 22i. **Buscema** a-1-3p; c(p)-2, 4, 6, 7, 15. **Infantino** a-14p, 19p. **Gil Kane** c-8. **Mooney** a-4-8p, 13p, 15-18p. **Starlin** c-12.*

MS. MYSTIC
Oct, 1982 - No. 2, Feb, 1984 ($1.00/$1.50)
Pacific Comics

1-Origin; intro Erth, Ayre, Fyre & Watr; Neal Adams-c/a/script 1.50
2 ($1.50)-N. Adams-c/a/script 1.50

MS. MYSTIC
V2#1, Oct, 1993 - V2#4, Jan?, 1994 ($2.50)
Continunity Comics

V2#1-4: 1-Adams-c(i)/part-i. 2-4-Embossed-c. 2-Nebres part-i.
3-Adams-c(i)/plot. 4-Adams-c(p)/plot 1.00 2.50

MS. MYSTIC DEATHWATCH 2000 (Ms. Mystic #3)
May, 1993 - No. 3, Aug, 1993 ($2.50)
Continuity

1-Bagged w/card; Adams-c & plot 1.00 2.50
2-Bagged w/card; Adams plot 1.00 2.50
3-Bagged w/card; wraparound indestructible-c by Golden/Cory; Adams plot
1.00 2.50

MS. TREE QUARTERLY/SPECIAL
Summer, 1990 -No. 10, 1992 ($3.95/$3.50, 84 pgs, mature)
DC Comics

1-Midnight story; Batman text story, Grell-a. 1.60 4.00
2-9: 2,3-Midnight stories; The Butcher text stories. 1.60 4.00
10 ($3.50) 3.50
NOTE: ***Cowan** c-2. **Grell** c-1, 6. **Infantino** a-8.*

MS. TREE'S THRILLING DETECTIVE ADVS (Ms. Tree #4 on; also see The Best of Ms. Tree)(Baxter paper #4-9)
2/83 - #9, 7/84; #10, 8/84 - #18, 5/85; #19, 6/85 - #50, 6/89
Eclipse Comics/Aardvark-Vanaheim 10-18/Renegade Press 19 on

1 .80 2.00
2-8: 2-Schythe begins .75 1.80

Munsters #2 © TV Comics

Murder Incorporated #14 © FOX

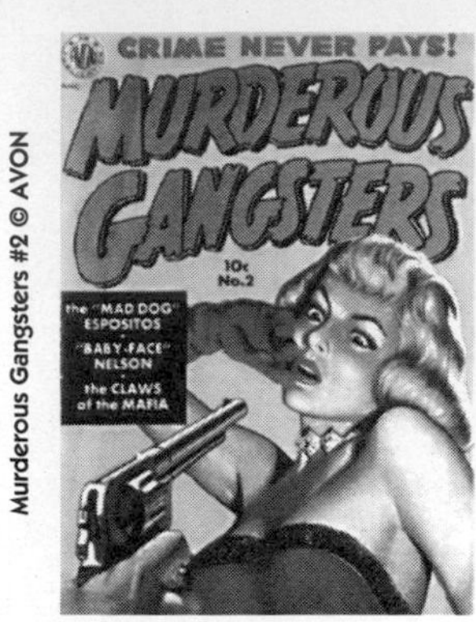

Murderous Gangsters #2 © AVON

	GD25	FN65	NM94
9-Last Eclipse & last color issue		.75	1.80
10-49: 10,11-2-tone; ($1.70; $2.00 #34 on)		.75	1.80
50-Contains flexi-disc ($3.95, 52pgs.)		1.60	4.00
Summer Special 1 (8/86)		1.20	3.00
1950s 3-D Crime (7/87, no glasses)-Johnny Dynamite in 3-D		1.00	2.50
Mike Mist in 3-D (8/85)-With glasses		1.20	3.00

NOTE; ***Miller** pin-up 1-4. Johnny Dynamite-r begin #36 by **Morisi**.*

MS. VICTORY SPECIAL(Also see Capt. Paragon & Femforce)
Jan, 1985 (nd)
Americomics

	GD25	FN65	NM94
1			1.70

MUGGSY MOUSE (Also see Tick Tock Tales)
1951 - No. 3, 1951; No. 4, 1954 - No. 5, 1954; 1963
Magazine Enterprises

	GD25	FN65	NM94
1(A-1 #33)	5.70	17.00	35.00
2(A-1 #36)-Racist-c	7.15	21.50	50.00
3(A-1 #39), 4(A-1 #95), 5(A-1 #99)	4.00	10.00	20.00
Super Reprint #14(1963)	1.00	2.80	7.00
I.W. Reprint #1,2 (nd)	1.00	2.80	7.00

MUGGY-DOO, BOY CAT
July, 1953 - No. 4, Jan, 1954
Stanhall Publ.

	GD25	FN65	NM94
1-Funny animal; Irving Spector-a	5.70	17.00	40.00
2-4	4.25	13.00	28.00
Super Reprint #12('63), 16('64)	1.00	2.80	7.00

MULLKON EMPIRE (See John Jake's...)

MUMMY, THE (See Universal Presents... under Dell Giants & Movie Classics)

MUNDEN'S BAR ANNUAL
Apr, 1988 ($2.95, 52 pgs.)
First Comics

	GD25	FN65	NM94
1-r/from Grimjack; Fish Police story		1.20	3.00

MUNSTERS, THE (TV)
Jan, 1965 - No. 16, Jan, 1968 (All photo-c)
Gold Key

	GD25	FN65	NM94
1 (10134-501)	17.00	52.00	190.00
2	8.00	25.00	90.00
3-5	6.40	19.00	70.00
6-16	5.50	16.50	60.00

MUNSTERS, THE (TV)
Aug, 1997 - Present ($2.95, B&W)
TV Comics!

	GD25	FN65	NM94
1,2-All have photo-c			2.95
1-($7.95)-Variant-c			7.95
2-Variant-c w/Beverly Owens as Marilyn			2.95

MUPPET BABIES, THE (TV)(See Star Comics Magazine)
Aug, 1985 - No. 26, July, 1989 (Children's book)
Marvel Comics (Star Comics)/Marvel #18 on

	GD25	FN65	NM94
1-13 (75¢)			.75
14-26 ($1.00)			1.00

MUPPETS TAKE MANHATTAN, THE
Nov, 1984 - No. 3, Jan, 1985
Marvel Comics (Star Comics)

	GD25	FN65	NM94
1-3-Movie adapt. r-/Marvel Super Special			.60

MURCIELAGA, SHE-BAT
Jan, 1993 - No. 2, 1993 (B&W)
Heroic Publishing

	GD25	FN65	NM94
1-($1.50, 28 pgs.)			1.50
2-($2.95, 36 pgs.)-Coated-c		1.20	3.00

MURDER INCORPORATED (My Private Life #16 on)
1/48 - No. 15, 12/49; (2 No.9's); 6/50 - No. 3, 8/51
Fox Feature Syndicate

	GD25	FN65	NM94
1 (1st Series); 1,2 have 'For Adults Only' on-c	40.00	120.00	320.00
2-Electrocution story	32.00	96.00	240.00
3-7,9(4/49),10(5/49),11-15	17.00	51.00	130.00
8-Used in **SOTI**, pg. 160	19.00	58.00	140.00
9(3/49)-Possible use in **SOTI**, pg. 145; r/Blue Beetle #56('48)	18.00	56.00	130.00
5(#1, 6/50)(2nd Series)-Formerly My Desire #4; bondage-c.	11.50	34.00	90.00
2(8/50)-Morisi-a	11.00	33.00	80.00
3(8/51)-Used in **POP**, pg. 81; Rico-a; lingerie-c/panels	13.00	39.00	90.00

MURDEROUS GANGSTERS
July, 1951; No. 2, Dec, 1951 - No. 4, June, 1952
Avon Periodicals/Realistic No. 3 on

	GD25	FN65	NM94
1-Pretty Boy Floyd, Leggs Diamond; 1 pg. Wood-a	35.00	105.00	280.00
2-Baby-Face Nelson; 1 pg. Wood-a; painted-c	21.00	64.00	170.00
3-Painted-c	16.00	49.00	130.00
4- "Murder by Needle" drug story; Mort Lawrence-a; Kinstler-c	21.00	64.00	170.00

MURDER TALES (Magazine)
V1#10, Nov, 1970 - V1#11, Jan, 1971 (52 pgs.)
World Famous Publications

	GD25	FN65	NM94
V1#10-One pg. Frazetta ad	2.50	7.50	22.00
11-Guardineer-r; bondage-c	1.75	5.25	14.00

MUSHMOUSE AND PUNKIN PUSS (TV)
September, 1965 (Hanna-Barbera)
Gold Key

	GD25	FN65	NM94
1 (10153-509)	7.00	22.00	80.00

MUSIC MAN, THE (See Movie Classics)

MUTANT CHRONICLES (Video game)
May, 1996 - No. 4, Aug, 1996 ($2.95, limited series)
Acclaim Comics (Armada)

	GD25	FN65	NM94
1-4: Simon Bisley-c on all		1.20	3.00
Sourcebook (#5)		1.20	3.00

MUTANT MISADVENTURES OF CLOAK AND DAGGER, THE (Becomes Cloak and Dagger #14 on)
Oct, 1988 - No. 19, Aug, 1991 ($1.25/$1.50)
Marvel Comics

	GD25	FN65	NM94
1-8,10-18: 1-$.25-c. X-Factor app. 2-Begin $1.50-c. 9,10-Painted-c. 12-Dr. Doom app. 14-Begin new direction. 16-18-Spider-Man x-over. 18-Infinity Gauntlet x-over; Thanos cameo; Ghost Rider app.			1.50
9-($2.50, 52 pgs.)-The Avengers x-over		1.00	2.50
19-($2.50, 52 pgs.)-Origin Cloak & Dagger		1.00	2.50

NOTE: ***Austin** a-12i; c(i)-4, 12, 13; scripts-all. **Russell** a-2i. **Williamson** a-14i-16i; c-15i.*

MUTANTS & MISFITS
1987 - No. 3, 1987 ($1.95)
Silverline Comics (Solson)

	GD25	FN65	NM94
1-3		.80	2.00

MUTANTS VS. ULTRAS
Nov, 1995 ($6.95, one-shot)
Malibu Comics (Ultraverse)

	GD25	FN65	NM94
1-r/Exiles vs. X-Men, NIght Man vs. Wolverine, Prime vs. Hulk	1.00	2.80	7.00

MUTATIS
1992 - No. 3, 1992 ($2.25, mini-series)

Mutt and Jeff #14 © DC

My Desire #3 © FOX

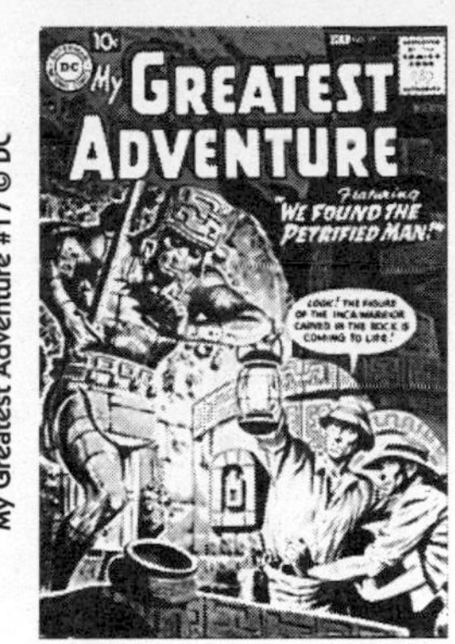

My Greatest Adventure #17 © DC

	GD25	FN65	NM94

Marvel Comics (Epic Comics)

	GD25	FN65	NM94
1-3: Painted-c		.90	2.25

MUTINY (Stormy Tales of the Seven Seas)
Oct, 1954 - No. 3, Feb, 1955
Aragon Magazines

	GD25	FN65	NM94
1	13.00	39.00	90.00
2,3: 2-Capt. Mutiny. 3-Bondage-c	10.00	30.00	65.00

MUTINY ON THE BOUNTY (See Classics Illustrated #100 & Movie Comics)

MUTT AND JEFF (See All-American, All-Flash #18, Cicero's Cat, Comic Cavalcade, Famous Feature Stories, The Funnies, Popular & Xmas Comics)
Summer, 1939 (nd) - No. 148, Nov, 1965
All American/National 1-103(6/58)/Dell 104(10/58)-115 (10-12/59)/ Harvey 116(2/60)-148

	GD25	FN65	NM94
1(nn)-Lost Wheels	128.00	384.00	1150.00
2(nn)-Charging Bull (Summer, 1940, nd; on sale 6/20/40)	69.00	207.00	625.00
3(nn)-Bucking Broncos (Summer, 1941, nd)	50.00	150.00	450.00
4(Winter, '41), 5(Summer, '42)	44.00	132.00	400.00
6-10	23.00	69.00	185.00
11-20: 20-X-Mas-c	14.50	43.00	115.00
21-30	10.50	32.00	85.00
31-50: 32-X-Mas-c	8.50	26.00	60.00
51-75-Last Fisher issue. 53-Last 52 pgs.	6.50	19.50	45.00
76-99,101-103: 76-Last precode issue(1/55)	5.35	16.00	32.00
100	5.70	17.00	38.00
104-148: 116-131-Richie Rich app.	2.20	6.60	22.00
...Jokes 1-3(8/60-61, Harvey)-84 pgs.; Richie Rich in all; Little Dot in #2,3	2.60	7.80	26.00
...New Jokes 1-4(10/63-11/65, Harvey)-68 pgs.; Richie Rich in #1-3; Stumbo in #1	2.00	6.00	16.00

NOTE: *Most all issues by* ***Al Smith****. Issues from 1963 on have* ***Fisher*** *reprints. Clarification: early issues signed by Fisher are mostly drawn by Smith.*

MY BROTHERS' KEEPER
1973 (35/49¢, 36 pgs.)
Spire Christian Comics (Fleming H. Revell Co.)

	GD25	FN65	NM94
nn		1.20	3.00

MY CONFESSIONS (My Confession #7&8; formerly Western True Crime; A Spectacular Feature Magazine #11)
No. 7, Aug, 1949 - No. 10, Jan-Feb, 1950
Fox Feature Syndicate

	GD25	FN65	NM94
7-Wood-a (10 pgs.)	16.00	47.00	115.00
8,9: 8-Harrison/Wood-a (19 pgs.). 9-Wood-a	14.00	43.00	105.00
10	7.50	22.50	48.00

MY DATE COMICS (Teen-age)
July, 1947 - V1#4, Jan, 1948 (2nd Romance comic; see Young Romance)
Hillman Periodicals

	GD25	FN65	NM94
1-S&K-c/a	26.00	79.00	200.00
2-4-S&K-c/a; Dan Barry-a	17.00	51.00	130.00

MY DESIRE (Formerly Jo-Jo Comics; becomes Murder, Inc. #5 on)
No. 30, Aug, 1949 - No. 4, April, 1950
Fox Feature Syndicate

	GD25	FN65	NM94
30(#1)	10.00	30.00	75.00
31 (#2, 10/49),3(2/50),4	7.50	22.50	48.00
31 (Canadian edition)	5.35	16.00	32.00
32(12/49)-Wood-a	14.00	43.00	105.00

MY DIARY (Becomes My Friend Irma #3 on?)
Dec, 1949 - No. 2, Mar, 1950
Marvel Comics (A Lovers Mag.)

	GD25	FN65	NM94
1,2-Photo-c	10.00	30.00	75.00

MY DOG TIGE (Buster Brown's Dog)
1957 (Giveaway)
Buster Brown Shoes

	GD25	FN65	NM94
nn	4.00	11.00	22.00

MY EXPERIENCE (Formerly All Top; becomes Judy Canova #23 on)
No. 19, Sept, 1949 - No. 22, Mar, 1950
Fox Feature Syndicate

	GD25	FN65	NM94
19-Wood-a	17.00	49.00	120.00
20	7.50	22.50	48.00
21-Wood-a(2)	17.00	51.00	125.00
22-Wood-a (9 pgs.)	14.00	43.00	105.00

MY FAVORITE MARTIAN (TV)
1/64; No.2, 7/64 - No. 9, 10/66 (No. 1,3-9 have photo-c)
Gold Key

	GD25	FN65	NM94
1-Russ Manning-a	12.00	35.00	130.00
2	6.00	18.00	65.00
3-9	5.00	15.00	55.00

MY FRIEND IRMA (Radio/TV) (Formerly My Diary? and/or Western Life Romances?)
No. 3, June, 1950 - No. 47, Dec, 1954; No. 48, Feb, 1955
Marvel/Atlas Comics (BFP)

	GD25	FN65	NM94
3-Dan DeCarlo-a in all; 52 pgs. begin, end ?	11.00	33.00	80.00
4-Kurtzman-a (10 pgs.)	13.50	41.00	95.00
5- "Egghead Doodle" by Kurtzman (4 pgs.)	10.00	30.00	70.00
6,8-10: 9-paper dolls, 1 pg; Millie app. (5 pgs.)	6.70	20.00	45.00
7-One pg. Kurtzman-a	6.70	20.00	45.00
11-23: 23-One pg. Frazetta-a	4.25	13.00	28.00
24-48	4.00	11.00	22.00

MY GIRL PEARL
4/55 - #4, 10/55; #5, 7/57 - #6, 9/57; #7, 8/60 - #11, ?/61
Atlas Comics

	GD25	FN65	NM94
1-Dan DeCarlo-c/a in #1-6	9.50	28.00	75.00
2	5.70	17.00	38.00
3-6	4.00	11.00	22.00
7-11	2.25	6.75	18.00

MY GREATEST ADVENTURE (Doom Patrol #86 on)
Jan-Feb, 1955 - No. 85, Feb, 1964
National Periodical Publications

	GD25	FN65	NM94
1-Before CCA	120.00	360.00	1200.00
2	45.00	135.00	550.00
3-5	32.00	96.00	355.00
6-10: 6-Science fiction format begins	31.00	93.00	310.00
11-15: 12-1st S.A. issue	21.00	63.00	210.00
16-18: Kirby-a in all. 18-Kirby-c	23.00	69.00	230.00
19,22-25	18.00	54.00	180.00
20,21,28-Kirby-a	21.00	63.00	210.00
26,27,29,30	13.00	39.00	130.00
31-40	10.50	32.00	105.00
41-61: 58,60,61-Toth-a; Last 10¢ issue	8.00	24.00	80.00
62-79: 77-Toth-a	4.50	13.50	45.00
80-(6/63)-Intro/origin Doom Patrol and begin series; origin & 1st app. Negative Man, Elasti-Girl & S.A. Robotman	33.00	100.00	370.00
81-85: 81,85-Toth-a	15.00	45.00	150.00

NOTE: ***Anderson*** *a-42.* ***Cameron*** *a-24.* ***Colan*** *a-77.* ***Meskin*** *a-25, 26, 32, 39, 45, 50, 56, 57, 61, 64, 70, 73, 74, 76, 79; c-76.* ***Moreira*** *a-11, 12, 15, 17, 20, 23, 25, 27, 37, 40-43, 46, 48, 55-57, 59, 60, 62-65, 67, 69, 70; c-1-4, 7-10.* ***Roussos*** *c/a-71-73.* ***Wildey*** *a-32.*

MY GREATEST THRILLS IN BASEBALL
Date? (16 pg. Giveaway)
Mission of California

	GD25	FN65	NM94
nn-By Mickey Mantle	44.00	142.00	400.00

My Intimate Affair #1 © FOX

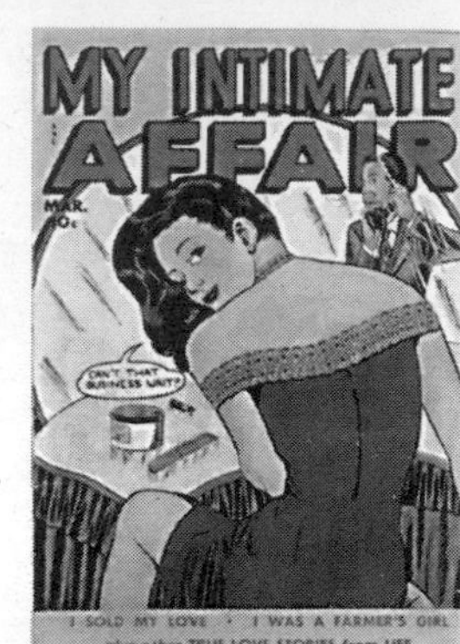

My Love Memoirs #11 © FOX

My Love Story #4 © FOX

MY GREAT LOVE (Becomes Will Rogers Western #5)
Oct, 1949 - No. 4, Apr, 1950
Fox Feature Syndicate

	GD25	FN65	NM94
1	10.00	30.00	75.00
2-4	6.35	19.00	40.00

MY INTIMATE AFFAIR (Inside Crime #3)
Mar, 1950 - No. 2, May, 1950
Fox Feature Syndicate

	GD25	FN65	NM94
1	10.00	30.00	75.00
2	6.35	19.00	40.00

MY LIFE (Formerly Meet Corliss Archer)
No. 4, Sept, 1948 - No. 15, July, 1950
Fox Feature Syndicate

	GD25	FN65	NM94
4-Used in **SOTI**, pg. 39; Kamen/Feldstein-a	31.00	94.00	220.00
5-Kamen-a	15.00	45.00	110.00
6-Kamen/Feldstein-a	16.00	47.00	120.00
7-Wood-a; wash cover	14.00	43.00	100.00
8,9,11-15	6.35	19.00	40.00
10-Wood-a	13.00	39.00	90.00

MY LITTLE MARGIE (TV)
July, 1954 - No. 54, Nov, 1964
Charlton Comics

	GD25	FN65	NM94
1-Photo front/back-c	25.00	75.00	190.00
2-Photo front/back-c	11.50	34.00	85.00
3-7,10	7.00	21.00	45.00
8,9-Infinity-c	7.50	22.50	50.00
11-14: Part-photo-c (#13, 8/56)	6.35	19.00	40.00
15-19	3.00	9.00	30.00
20-(25¢, 100 pg. issue)	7.00	21.00	70.00
21-38-Last 10¢ issue?	2.50	7.50	25.00
39-53	2.00	6.00	20.00
54-Beatles on cover; lead story spoofs the Beatle haircut craze of the 1960's	12.00	36.00	120.00

NOTE: *Doll cut-outs in 32, 33, 40, 45, 50.*

MY LITTLE MARGIE'S BOY FRIENDS (TV) (Freddy V2#12 on)
Aug, 1955 - No. 11, Apr?, 1958
Charlton Comics

	GD25	FN65	NM94
1-Has several Archie swipes	9.50	28.00	75.00
2	6.50	19.50	45.00
3-11	5.00	15.00	30.00

MY LITTLE MARGIE'S FASHIONS (TV)
Feb, 1959 - No. 5, Nov, 1959
Charlton Comics

	GD25	FN65	NM94
1	8.75	26.25	70.00
2-5	5.70	17.00	40.00

MY LOVE (Becomes Two Gun Western #5 (11/50) on?)
July, 1949 - No. 4, Apr, 1950 (All photo-c)
Marvel Comics (CLDS)

	GD25	FN65	NM94
1	10.00	30.00	70.00
2,3	6.70	20.00	42.00
4-Betty Page photo-c (see Cupid #2)	24.00	73.00	180.00

MY LOVE
Sept, 1969 - No. 39, Mar, 1976
Marvel Comics Group

	GD25	FN65	NM94
1	2.50	7.50	24.00
2-9: 4-6-Colan-a	1.50	4.50	12.00
10-Williamson-r/My Own Romance #71; Kirby-a	2.00	6.00	16.00
11-13,15-20	1.25	3.75	10.00
14-(52 pgs.)-Woodstock-c/sty; Morrow-c/a; Kirby/Colletta-r	2.50	7.50	20.00
21,22,24-38: 38-Reprints	1.00	2.80	7.00
23-Steranko-r/Our Love Story #5	1.50	4.50	12.00
39-Last issue; reprints	1.50	4.50	12.00
Special(12/71)(52 pgs.)	2.50	7.50	20.00

NOTE: ***John Buscema** a-1-7, 10, 22r(2), 24r, 25r, 29r, 34r, 36r, 37r, Spec. (r)(4); c-13, 15, 25, 27, Spec. **Colan** a-16,22,24r,35r,39r. **Colan/Everett** a-13, 15, 16, 27(r/#13). **Kirby** a-(r)-14,28.*

MY LOVE AFFAIR (March of Crime #7 on)
July, 1949 - No. 6, May, 1950
Fox Feature Syndicate

	GD25	FN65	NM94
1	10.00	30.00	75.00
2	6.70	20.00	40.00
3-6-Wood-a. 5-(3/50)-Becomes Love Stories #6	13.00	39.00	90.00

MY LOVE LIFE (Formerly Zegra)
No. 6, June, 1949 - No. 13, Aug, 1950; No. 13, Sept, 1951
Fox Feature Syndicate

	GD25	FN65	NM94
6-Kamenish-a	11.50	34.00	80.00
7-13	6.70	20.00	42.00
13 (9/51)	5.70	17.00	38.00

MY LOVE MEMOIRS (Formerly Women Outlaws; Hunted #13 on)
No. 9, Nov, 1949 - No. 12, May, 1950
Fox Feature Syndicate

	GD25	FN65	NM94
9,11,12-Wood-a	12.00	36.00	90.00
10	6.70	20.00	40.00

MY LOVE SECRET (Formerly Phantom Lady; Animal Crackers #31)
No. 24, June, 1949 - No. 30, June, 1950; No. 53, 1954
Fox Feature Syndicate/M. S. Distr.

	GD25	FN65	NM94
24-Kamen/Feldstein-a	11.30	34.00	90.00
25-Possible caricature of Wood on-c?	7.50	22.50	45.00
26,28-Wood-a	11.30	34.00	90.00
27,29,30: 30-Photo-c	5.70	17.00	40.00
53-(Reprint, M.S. Distr.) 1954? nd given; formerly Western Thrillers; becomes Crimes by Women #54; photo-c	4.25	13.00	26.00

MY LOVE STORY (Hoot Gibson Western #5 on)
Sept, 1949 - No. 4, Mar, 1950
Fox Feature Syndicate

	GD25	FN65	NM94
1	10.00	30.00	75.00
2	6.35	19.00	40.00
3,4-Wood-a	13.00	39.00	90.00

MY LOVE STORY
April, 1956 - No. 9, Aug, 1957
Atlas Comics (GPS)

	GD25	FN65	NM94
1	8.50	26.00	60.00
2	4.25	13.00	28.00
3-Matt Baker-a	6.35	19.00	40.00
4-6,8,9	4.15	12.50	25.00
7-Matt Baker, Toth-a	6.35	19.00	40.00

NOTE: ***Brewster** a-3. **Colletta** a-1(2), 3, 4(2), 5; c-3.*

MY NAME IS CHAOS
1992 - No. 4, 1992 ($4.95, limited series, 52 pgs.)
DC Comics

	GD25	FN65	NM94
Book 1-4: Tom Veitch scripts; painted-c		2.00	5.00

MY NAME IS HOLOCAUST
May, 1995 - No. 5, Sept, 1995 ($2.50, limited series)
DC Comics

	GD25	FN65	NM94
1-5		1.00	2.50

MY ONLY LOVE
July, 1975 - No. 9, Nov, 1976
Charlton Comics

	GD25	FN65	NM94
1	1.25	3.75	10.00

My Personal Problem #1 © AJAX

My Secret Confession #1 © Sterling

My Secret Story #29 © FOX

	GD25	FN65	NM94
2,4-9		2.40	6.00
3-Toth-a	1.25	3.75	10.00

MY OWN ROMANCE (Formerly My Romance; Teen-Age Romance #77 on)
No. 4, Mar, 1949 - No. 76, July, 1960
Marvel/Atlas (MjPC/RCM No. 4-59/ZPC No. 60-76)

	GD25	FN65	NM94
4-Photo-c	10.00	30.00	75.00
5-10: 5,6,8-10-Photo-c	5.70	17.00	35.00
11-20: 14-Powell-a	5.00	15.00	30.00
21-42: 42-Last precode (2/55)	4.25	13.00	28.00
43-54,56-60	2.50	7.50	22.00
55-Toth-a	3.00	9.00	30.00
61-70,72-76	2.25	6.75	18.00
71-Williamson-a	3.20	9.60	32.00

NOTE: ***Brewster** a-59. **Colletta** a-45(2), 48, 50, 55, 57(2), 59; c-58i, 59, 61. **Everett** a-25; c-58p. **Morisi** a-18. **Orlando** a-61. **Romita** a-36. **Tuska** a-10.*

MY PAL DIZZY (See Comic Books, Series I)

MY PAST (...Confessions) (Formerly Western Thrillers)
No. 7, Aug, 1949 - No. 11, April, 1950 (Crimes Inc. #12)
Fox Feature Syndicate

	GD25	FN65	NM94
7	10.00	30.00	70.00
8-10	6.30	19.00	40.00
11-Wood-a	12.00	36.00	90.00

MY PERSONAL PROBLEM
11/55; No. 2, 2/56; No. 3, 9/56 - No. 4, 11/56; 10/57 - No. 3, 5/58
Ajax/Farrell/Steinway Comic

	GD25	FN65	NM94
1	6.50	19.50	45.00
2-4	4.25	13.00	28.00
1-3('57-'58)-Steinway	4.00	12.00	24.00

MY PRIVATE LIFE (Formerly Murder, Inc.; becomes Pedro #18)
No. 16, Feb, 1950 - No. 17, April, 1950
Fox Feature Syndicate

	GD25	FN65	NM94
16,17	8.50	26.00	60.00

MYRA NORTH (See The Comics, Crackajack Funnies & Red Ryder)
No. 3, Jan, 1940
Dell Publishing Co.

	GD25	FN65	NM94
Four Color 3	68.00	205.00	750.00

MY REAL LOVE
No. 5, June, 1952 (Photo-c)
Standard Comics

	GD25	FN65	NM94
5-Toth-a, 3 pgs.; Tuska, Cardy, Vern Greene-a	10.00	30.00	65.00

MY ROMANCE (Becomes My Own Romance #4 on)
Sept, 1948 - No. 3, Jan, 1949
Marvel Comics (RCM)

	GD25	FN65	NM94
1	10.00	30.00	75.00
2,3: 2-Anti Wertham editorial (11/48)	6.35	19.00	40.00

MY ROMANTIC ADVENTURES (Formerly Romantic Adventures)
No. 68, 8/56 - No. 115, 12/60; No. 116, 7/61 - No. 138, 3/64
American Comics Group

	GD25	FN65	NM94
68	6.50	19.50	45.00
69-85	4.00	12.00	24.00
86-Three pg. Williamson-a (2/58)	5.70	17.00	38.00
87-100	2.00	6.00	16.00
101-138	1.25	3.75	10.00

NOTE: ***Whitney** art in most issues.*

MY SECRET (Becomes Our Secret #4 on)
Aug, 1949 - No. 3, Oct, 1949
Superior Comics, Ltd.

	GD25	FN65	NM94
1	10.00	30.00	75.00
2,3	6.85	21.00	48.00

MY SECRET AFFAIR (Becomes Martin Kane #4)
Dec, 1949 - No. 3, April, 1950
Hero Book (Fox Feature Syndicate)

	GD25	FN65	NM94
1-Harrison/Wood-a (10 pgs.)	14.00	43.00	110.00
2-Wood-a (poor)	10.00	30.00	65.00
3-Wood-a	12.00	36.00	90.00

MY SECRET CONFESSION
September, 1955
Sterling Comics

	GD25	FN65	NM94
1-Sekowsky-a	6.70	20.00	40.00

MY SECRET LIFE (Formerly Western Outlaws; Romeo Tubbs #26 on)
No. 22, July, 1949 - No. 27, May, 1950
Fox Feature Syndicate

	GD25	FN65	NM94
22	8.35	25.00	55.00
23,26-Wood-a, 6 pgs.	12.00	36.00	90.00
24,25,27	5.70	17.00	38.00

NOTE: *The title was changed to Romeo Tubbs after #25 even though #26 & 27 did come out.*

MY SECRET LIFE (Formerly Young Lovers; Sue & Sally Smith #48)
No. 19, Aug, 1957 - No. 47, Sept, 1962
Charlton Comics

	GD25	FN65	NM94
19	2.25	6.75	18.00
20-35	1.10	3.30	9.00
36-47: 44-Last 10¢ issue		2.00	5.00

MY SECRET MARRIAGE
May, 1953 - No. 24, July, 1956
Superior Comics, Ltd.

	GD25	FN65	NM94
1	8.50	26.00	60.00
2	4.25	13.00	28.00
3-24	4.00	10.00	20.00
I.W. Reprint #9		2.40	6.00

NOTE: *Many issues contain **Kamenish** art.*

MY SECRET ROMANCE (Becomes A Star Presentation #3)
Jan, 1950 - No. 2, March, 1950
Hero Book (Fox Feature Syndicate)

	GD25	FN65	NM94
1	9.00	29.00	60.00
2-Wood-a	12.00	36.00	90.00

MY SECRET STORY (Formerly Captain Kidd #25; Sabu #30 on)
No. 26, Oct, 1949 - No. 29, April, 1950
Fox Feature Syndicate

	GD25	FN65	NM94
26	10.00	30.00	65.00
27-29	6.70	20.00	40.00

MYS-TECH WARS
Mar, 1993 - No. 4, June, 1993 ($1.75, mini-series)
Marvel Comics UK

	GD25	FN65	NM94
1-4: 1-Gatefold-c		.70	1.75

MYSTERIES (...Weird & Strange)
May, 1953 - No. 11, Jan, 1955
Superior/Dynamic Publ. (Randall Publ. Ltd.)

	GD25	FN65	NM94
1	26.00	79.00	200.00
2-A-Bomb blast story	14.00	43.00	110.00
3-9,11	11.30	34.00	90.00
10-Kamenish-c/a reprinted from Strange Mysteries #2; cover is from a panel in Strange Mysteries #2	12.00	36.00	90.00

MYSTERIES OF SCOTLAND YARD (Also see A-1 Comics)
No. 121, 1954 (one shot)
Magazine Enterprises

	GD25	FN65	NM94
A-1 121-Reprinted from Manhunt (5 stories)	13.00	39.00	100.00

MYSTERIES OF UNEXPLORED WORLDS (See Blue Bird) (Becomes Son of

Mysterious Adventures #2 © Story

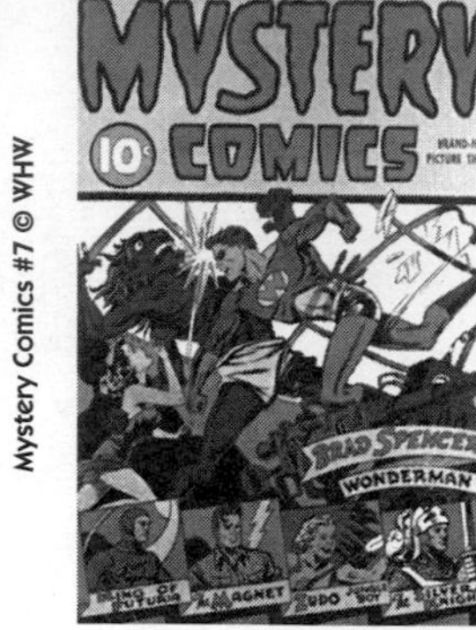

Mystery Comics #7 © WHW

Mystery in Space #24 © DC

Vulcan V2#49 on)
Aug, 1956; No. 2, Jan, 1957 - No. 48, Sept, 1965
Charlton Comics

1 28.00 83.00 220.00
2-No Ditko 10.00 30.00 80.00
3,4,8,9 Ditko-a. 3-Diko c/a (4). 4-Ditko c/a (2). 19.00 58.00 155.00
5-7,10,11: 5,6-Ditko-c/a (all). 7-(2/58, 68 pgs.); Ditko-a(4). 10-Ditko-c/a(4). 11-Ditko-c/a(3); signed J. Kotdi 21.00 64.00 170.00
12,19,21-24,26-Ditko-a. 12-Ditko sty (3); Baker story "The Charm Bracelet." 14.00 41.00 110.00
13-18,20 5.00 15.00 30.00
25,27-30 2.50 7.50 20.00
31-45 1.75 5.25 14.00
46(5/65)-Son of Vulcan begins (origin/1st app.) 3.00 9.00 30.00
47,48 1.75 5.25 14.00

NOTE: ***Ditko*** *c-3-6, 10, 11, 19, 21-24. Covers to #19, 21-24 reprint story panels.*

MYSTERIOUS ADVENTURES
Mar, 1951 - No. 24, Mar, 1955; No. 25, Aug, 1955
Story Comics

1-All horror stories 40.00 120.00 300.00
2 21.00 64.00 160.00
3,4,6,10 18.00 54.00 140.00
5-Bondage-c 21.00 64.00 160.00
7-Daggar in eye panel 30.00 90.00 225.00
8-Eyeball story 31.00 94.00 240.00
9-Extreme violence 24.00 73.00 180.00
11(12/52)-Used in **SOTI**, pg. 84 24.00 73.00 180.00
12,13 21.00 64.00 160.00
14-E.C. Old Witch swipe 20.00 60.00 150.00
15-21: 18-Used in Senate Investigative report, pgs. 5,6; E.C. swipe/TFTC #35; The Coffin-Keeper & Corpse (hosts). 20-Used by Wertham in the Senate hearings. 21-Bondage/beheading-c 30.00 90.00 230.00
22- "Cinderella" parody 20.00 60.00 150.00
23-Disbrow-a (6 pgs.); E.C. swipe "The Mystery Keeper's Tale" (host) and "Mother Ghoul's Nursery Tale" 20.00 60.00 150.00
24,25 15.00 45.00 120.00

NOTE: ***Tothish*** *art by* ***Ross Andru****-#22, 23.* ***Bache*** *a-8.* ***Cameron*** *a-5-7.* ***Harrison*** *a-12.* ***Hollingsworth*** *a-3-8, 12.* ***Schaffenberger*** *a-24, 25.* ***Wildey*** *a-15, 17.*

MYSTERIOUS ISLAND
No. 1213, July-Sept, 1961
Dell Publishing Co.

Four Color 1213-Movie, photo-c 8.00 25.00 90.00

MYSTERIOUS ISLE
Nov-Jan, 1963/64 (Jules Verne)
Dell Publishing Co.

1 1.50 4.50 12.00

MYSTERIOUS RIDER, THE (See Zane Grey, 4-Color 301)

MYSTERIOUS STORIES (Formerly Horror From the Tomb #1)
No. 2, Dec-Jan, 1954-1955 - No. 7, Dec, 1955
Premier Magazines

2-Woodbridge-c; last pre-code issue 29.00 86.00 220.00
3-Woodbridge-c/a 19.00 58.00 150.00
4-7: 5-Cinderella parody. 6-Woodbridge-c 18.00 54.00 140.00

NOTE: ***Hollingsworth*** *a-2, 4.*

MYSTERIOUS SUSPENSE
Oct, 1968 (12¢)
Charlton Comics

1-Return of the Question by Ditko (c/a) 4.20 12.60 42.00

MYSTERIOUS TRAVELER (See Tales of the...)

MYSTERIOUS TRAVELER COMICS (Radio)
Nov, 1948
Trans-World Publications

1-Powell-c/a(2); Poe adaptation, "Tell Tale Heart" 47.00 141.00 390.00

MYSTERY COMICS
1944 - No. 4, 1944 (No months given)
William H. Wise & Co.

1-The Magnet, The Silver Knight, Brad Spencer, Wonderman, Dick Devins, King of Futuria, & Zudo the Jungle Boy begin (all 1st app.); Schomburg-c on all 83.00 250.00 750.00
2-Bondage-c 56.00 168.00 500.00
3-Lance Lewis, Space Detective begins (1st app.); Robot-c 49.00 147.00 440.00
4(V2#1 inside) 49.00 147.00 440.00

MYSTERY COMICS DIGEST
Mar, 1972 - No. 26, Oct, 1975
Gold Key

1-Ripley's Believe It or Not; reprint of Ripley's #1 origin Ra-Ka-Tep the Mummy; Wood-a 2.25 6.75 24.00
2-9: 2-Boris Karloff Tales of Mystery; Wood-a; 1st app. Werewolf Count Wulfstein 3-Twilight Zone (TV); Crandall, Toth & George Evans-a; 1st app. Tragg & Simbar the Lion Lord; (2) Crandall/Frazetta-r/Twilight Zone #1 4-Ripley's Believe It or Not; 1st app. Baron Tibor, the Vampire. 5-Boris Karloff Tales of Mystery; 1st app. Dr. Spektor. 6-Twilight Zone (TV); 1st app. U.S. Marshal Reid & Sir Duane; Evans-r. 7-Ripley's Believe It or Not; origin The Lurker in the Swamp; 1st app. Duroc. 8-Boris Karloff Tales of Mystery; McWilliams-r; Orlando-r. 9-Twilight Zone (TV); Williamson, Crandall, McWilliams-a; 2nd Tragg app.;Torres, Evans, Heck/Tuska-r 1.60 4.80 16.00
10-26: 10,13-Ripley's Believe It or Not: 13-Orlando-r. 11,14-Boris Karloff Tales of Mystery. 14-1st app. Xorkon. 12,15-Twilight Zone (TV). 16,19,22,25-Ripley's Believe It or Not. 17-Boris Karloff Tales of Mystery; Williamson-r; Orlando-r. 18,21,24-Twilight Zone (TV). 20,23,26-Boris Karloff Tales of Mystery 1.20 3.60 12.00

NOTE: *Dr. Spektor app.-#5, 10-12, 21. Durak app.-#15. Duroc app.-#14 (later called Durak). King George 1st app.-#8.*

MYSTERY IN SPACE
4-5/51 - No. 110, 9/66; No. 111, 9/80 - No. 117, 3/81 (#1-3: 52 pgs.)
National Periodical Publications

1-Frazetta-a, 8 pgs.; Knights of the Galaxy begins, ends #8 200.00 600.00 2600.00
2 83.00 250.00 1000.00
3 67.00 200.00 800.00
4,5 54.00 162.00 650.00
6-10: 7-Toth-a 45.00 135.00 540.00
11-15: 13-Toth-a 34.00 102.00 380.00
16-18,20-25: Interplanetary Insurance feature by Infantino in all. 21-1st app. Space Cabbie. 24-Last pre-code issue 31.00 93.00 340.00
19-Virgil Finlay-a 33.00 100.00 370.00
26-40: 26-Space Cabbie feature begins. 34-1st S.A. issue 28.00 84.00 280.00
41-52: 47-Space Cabbie feature ends 21.00 63.00 210.00

GD25 FN65 VF82 NM94

53-Adam Strange begins (8/59, 10pg. sty) 133.00 400.00 800.00 1600.00

GD25 FN65 NM94

54 37.00 111.00 410.00
55-Grey tone-c 28.00 84.00 280.00
56-60: 59-Kane/Anderson-a 20.00 60.00 200.00
61-71: 61-1st app. Adam Strange foe Ulthoon. 62-1st app. A.S. foe Mortan. 63-Origin Vandor. 66-Star Rovers begin (1st app.). 68-1st app. Dust Devils (6/61). 69-1st Mailbag. 70-2nd app. Dust Devils. 71-Last 10¢ issue 15.50 47.00 155.00

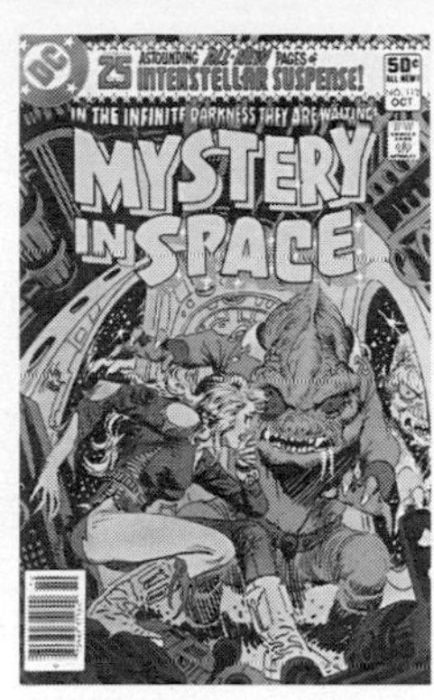

Mystery in Space #112 © DC

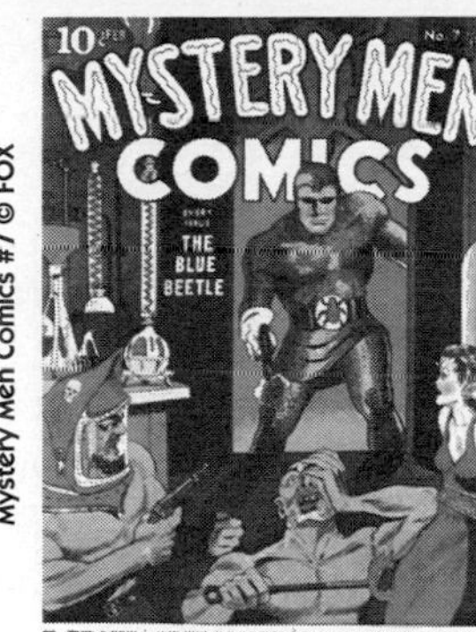

Mystery Men Comics #7 © FOX

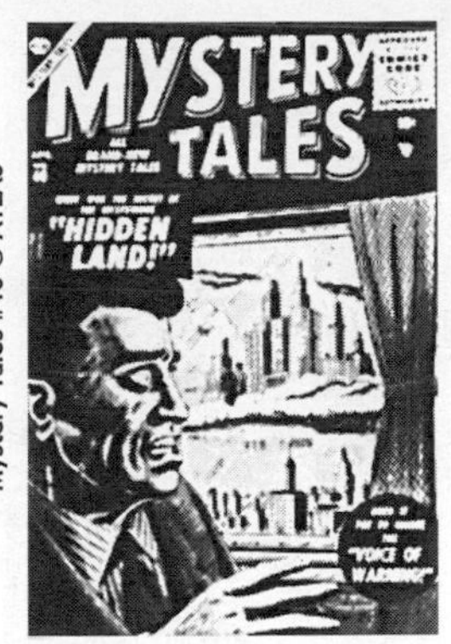

Mystery Tales #40 © ATLAS

	GD25	FN65	NM94
72-74,76-80	11.00	33.00	110.00
75-JLA x-over in Adam Strange (5/62)(sequel to JLA #3)	23.50	70.00	235.00
81-86	7.50	22.50	75.00
87-(11/63)-Adam Strange/Hawkman double feat begins; 3rd Hawkman tryout series	18.50	55.00	185.00
88-Adam Strange & Hawkman stories	16.50	50.00	165.00
89-Adam Strange & Hawkman stories	15.50	47.00	155.00
90-Adam Strange & Hawkman team-up for 1st time (3/64); Hawkman moves to own title next month	17.50	52.00	175.00
91-103: 91-End Infantino art on Adam Strange; double-length Adam Strange story. 92-Space Ranger begins (6/64), ends #103. 92-94,96,98-Space Ranger-c. 94,98-Adam Strange/Space Ranger team-up. 102-Adam Strange ends (no Space Ranger). 103-Origin Ultra, the Multi-Alien; last Space Ranger	3.50	10.50	35.00
104-110: 110-(9/66)-Last 12¢ issue	2.15	6.50	17.00
V17#111(9/80)-117: 117-Newton-a(3 pgs.)		2.00	5.00

NOTE: ***Anderson*** *a-2, 4, 8-10, 12-17, 19, 45-48, 51, 57, 59i, 61-64, 70, 76, 87-91; c-9, 10, 15-25, 87, 89, 105-108, 110.* ***Aparo*** *a-111.* ***Austin*** *a-112i.* ***Bolland*** *a-115.* ***Craig*** *a-114, 116.* ***Ditko*** *a-111, 114-116.* ***Drucker*** *a-13, 14.* ***Elias*** *a-98, 102, 103.* ***Golden*** *a-113p.* ***Sid Greene*** *a-78, 91.* ***Infantino*** *a-1-8, 11, 14-25, 27-46, 48, 49, 51, 53-91, 103, 117; c-60-86, 88, 90, 91, 105, 107.* ***Gil Kane*** *a-14p, 15p, 18p, 19p, 26p, 29-59p(most), 100-102; c-52, 101.* ***Kubert*** *a-113; c-111-115.* ***Moriera*** *c-27, 28.* ***Rogers*** *a-111.* ***Sekowsky*** *a-52.* ***Simon*** *&* ***Kirby*** *a-4(2 pgs.).* ***Spiegle*** *a-111, 114.* ***Starlin*** *c-116.* ***Sutton*** *a-112.* ***Tuska*** *a-115p, 117p.*

MYSTERY MEN COMICS
Aug, 1939 - No. 31, Feb, 1942
Fox Features Syndicate

	GD25	FN65	NM94
1-Intro. & 1st app. The Blue Beetle, The Green Mask, Rex Dexter of Mars by Briefer, Zanzibar by Tuska, Lt. Drake, D-13-Secret Agent by Powell, Chen Chang, Wing Turner, & Captain Denny Scott	940.00	2820.00	9400.00
2-Robot & sci/fi-c (2nd Robot-c w/Movie #6)	250.00	750.00	2500.00
3 (10/39)-Classic Lou Fine-c	320.00	960.00	3200.00
4,5: 4-Capt. Savage begins (11/39)	200.00	600.00	1800.00
6-Tuska-c	167.00	500.00	1500.00
7-1st Blue Beetle-c app.	200.00	600.00	1800.00
8-Lou Fine-c	178.00	534.00	1600.00
9-The Moth begins; Lou Fine-c	89.00	267.00	800.00
10-12: All Joe Simon-c. 10-Wing Turner by Kirby. 11-Intro. Domino	78.00	234.00	700.00
13-Intro. Lynx & sidekick Blackie (8/40)	52.00	156.00	465.00
14-18	49.00	147.00	440.00
19-Intro. & 1st app. Miss X (ends #21)	51.00	153.00	460.00
20-31: 26-The Wraith begins	44.00	132.00	400.00

NOTE: ***Briefer*** *a-1-15, 20, 24; c-9.* ***Cuidera*** *a-22.* ***Lou Fine*** *c-1-5,8,9.* ***Powell*** *a-1-15, 24.* ***Simon*** *c-10-12.* ***Tuska*** *a-1-16, 22, 24, 27; c-6. Bondage-c 1, 3, 7, 8, 25, 27-29, 31. Blue Beetle c-7, 8, 10-31. D-13 Secret Agent c-6. Green Mask c-1, 3-5. Rex Dexter of Mars c-2, 9.*

MYSTERY TALES
Mar, 1952 - No. 54, Aug, 1957
Atlas Comics (20CC)

	GD25	FN65	NM94
1 Horror/weird stories in all	65.00	195.00	550.00
2-Krigstein-a	40.00	120.00	290.00
3-10: 6-A-Bomb panel. 10-Story similar to "The Assassin" from Shock SuspenStories	29.00	88.00	220.00
11,13-21: 14-Maneely s/f story. 20-Electric chair issue. 21-Matt Fox-a; decapitation story	21.00	64.00	160.00
12,22: 12-Matt Fox-a. 22-Forte/Matt Fox-c; a(i)	23.00	69.00	170.00
23-26 (2/55)-Last precode issue	17.00	51.00	125.00
27,29-35,37,38,41-43,48,49: 43-Morisi story contains Frazetta art swipes from Untamed Love	13.50	41.00	95.00
28,36,39,40,45: 28-Jack Katz-a. 36,39-Krigstein-a. 40,45-Ditko-a (#45 is 3 pgs. only)	14.00	43.00	100.00
44,46,47,51: 44,51-Williamson/Krenkel-a	15.00	45.00	110.00
46-Williamson/Krenkel-a; Crandall text illos	15.00	45.00	110.00
47-Crandall, Ditko, Powell-a	15.00	45.00	110.00
50-Torres, Morrow-a	14.00	43.00	100.00
52,53	12.00	36.00	90.00
54-Crandall, Check-a	13.50	41.00	95.00

NOTE: ***Ayers*** *a-18, 49, 52.* ***Berg*** *a-17, 51.* ***Colan*** *a-1, 3, 18, 35, 43.* ***Colletta*** *a-18.* ***Drucker*** *a-41.* ***Everett*** *a-2, 29, 33, 35, 41; c-8-11, 14, 38, 39, 41, 43, 44, 46, 48-51, 53.* ***Fass*** *a-16.* ***Forte*** *a-21, 22, 45, 46.* ***Matt Fox*** *a-12?, 21, 22; c-22.* ***Heath*** *a-3; c-3, 15, 17, 26.* ***Heck*** *a-25.* ***Kinstler*** *a-15.* ***Mort Lawrence*** *a-26, 32, 34.* ***Maneely*** *a-1, 9, 14, 22; c-12, 23, 24, 27.* ***Mooney*** *a-3, 40.* ***Morisi*** *a-43, 49, 52.* ***Morrow*** *a-50.* ***Orlando*** *a-51.* ***Pakula*** *a-16.* ***Powell*** *a-21, 29, 37, 38, 47.* ***Reinman*** *a-1, 14, 17.* ***Robinson*** *a-7p, 42.* ***Romita*** *a-37.* ***Roussos*** *a-4, 44.* ***R.Q. Sale*** *a-45, 46, 49.* ***Severin*** *c-52.* ***Shores*** *a-17, 45.* ***Tuska*** *a-10, 12, 14.* ***Whitney*** *a-2.* ***Wildey*** *a-37.*

MYSTERY TALES
1964
Super Comics

	GD25	FN65	NM94
Super Reprint #16,17('64): 16-r/Tales of Horror #2. 17-r/Eerie #14(Avon), 18-Kubert-r/Strange Terrors #4	1.50	4.50	12.00

MYSTIC (3rd Series)
March, 1951 - No. 61, Aug, 1957
Marvel/Atlas Comics (CLDS 1/CSI 2-21/OMC 22-35/CSI 35-61)

	GD25	FN65	NM94
1-Atom bomb panels; horror/weird stories in all	68.00	206.00	600.00
2	40.00	120.00	325.00
3-Eyes torn out	34.00	103.00	250.00
4- "The Devil Birds" by Wolverton (6 pgs.)	60.00	180.00	500.00
5,7-10	25.00	75.00	185.00
6- "The Eye of Doom" by Wolverton (7 pgs.)	60.00	180.00	500.00
11-20: 16-Bondage/torture c/story	22.00	66.00	165.00
21-25,27-36-Last precode (3/55). 25-E.C. swipe	17.00	49.00	125.00
26-Atomic War, severed head stories	17.00	51.00	130.00
37-51,53-57,61: 57-Story "Trapped in the Ant-Hill" (1957) is very similar to "The Man in the Ant Hill" in TTA #27	13.50	41.00	100.00
52-Wood-a; Crandall-a?	16.00	47.00	115.00
58,59-Krigstein-a	14.00	43.00	105.00
60-Williamson/Mayo-a (4 pgs.)	14.00	43.00	105.00

NOTE: ***Andru*** *a-23, 25.* ***Ayers*** *a-35, 53; c-8.* ***Berg*** *a-49.* ***Cameron*** *a-49, 51.* ***Check*** *a-31, 60.* ***Colan*** *a-3, 7, 12, 21, 37, 60.* ***Colletta*** *a-29.* ***Drucker*** *a-46, 52, 56.* ***Everett*** *a-8, 9, 17, 40, 44, 57; c-13, 18, 21, 42, 47, 49, 51-55, 57-59, 61.* ***Forte*** *a-35, 52, 58.* ***Fox*** *a-24i.* ***Al Hartley*** *a-35.* ***Heath*** *a-10; c-10, 20, 22, 23, 25, 30.* ***Infantino*** *a-12.* ***Kane*** *a-8, 24p.* ***Jack Katz*** *a-31, 33.* ***Mort Lawrence*** *a-19, 37.* ***Maneely*** *a-22, 24, 58; c-7, 15, 28, 29, 31.* ***Moldoff*** *a-29.* ***Morisi*** *a-48, 49, 52.* ***Morrow*** *a-51.* ***Orlando*** *a-57, 61.* ***Pakula*** *a-52, 57, 59.* ***Powell*** *a-52, 54-56.* ***Robinson*** *a-5.* ***Romita*** *a-11, 15.* ***R.Q. Sale*** *a-35, 53, 58.* ***Sekowsky*** *a-1, 2, 4, 5.* ***Severin*** *c-56, 60.* ***Tuska*** *a-15.* ***Whitney*** *a-33.* ***Wildey*** *a-28, 30.* ***Ed Win*** *a-17, 20. Canadian reprints known-title 'Startling.'*

MYSTICAL TALES
June, 1956 - No. 8, Aug, 1957
Atlas Comics (CCC 1/EPI 2-8)

	GD25	FN65	NM94
1-Everett-c/a	37.00	111.00	275.00
2,4: 2-Berg-a	20.00	60.00	150.00
3,5: 3,4-Crandall-a. 5-Williamson-a (4 pgs.)	21.00	62.00	155.00
6-Torres, Krigstein-a	19.00	58.00	145.00
7-Bolle, Forte, Torres, Orlando-a	19.00	56.00	140.00
8-Krigstein, Check-a	17.00	49.00	125.00

NOTE: ***Everett*** *a-1; c-1-4, 6, 7.* ***Orlando*** *a-1, 2, 7.* ***Pakula*** *a-3.* ***Powell*** *a-1, 4.*

MYSTIC COMICS (1st Series)
March, 1940 - No. 10, Aug, 1942
Timely Comics (TPI 1-5/TCI 8-10)

	GD25	FN65	VF82	NM94
1-Origin The Blue Blaze, The Dynamic Man, & Flexo the Rubber Robot; Zephyr Jones, 3X's & Deep Sea Demon app.; The Magician begins (all 1st app.); c-from Spider pulp V18#1, 6/39	1090.00	3272.00	6540.00	12,000.00

(Estimated up to 110 total copies exist, 4 in NM/Mint)

	GD25	FN65	NM94
2-The Invisible Man & Master Mind Excello begin; Space Rangers, Zara of the Jungle, Taxi Taylor app.	300.00	900.00	3000.00
3-Origin Hercules, who last appears in #4	240.00	720.00	2400.00
4-Origin The Thin Man & The Black Widow; Merzak the Mystic app.; last Flexo, Dynamic Man, Invisible Man & Blue Blaze (some issues have date sticker on cover; others have July w/August overprint in silver color); Roosevelt assassination-c	260.00	780.00	2600.00

Mythos: The Final Tour #1 © DC

The 'Nam #79 © MEG

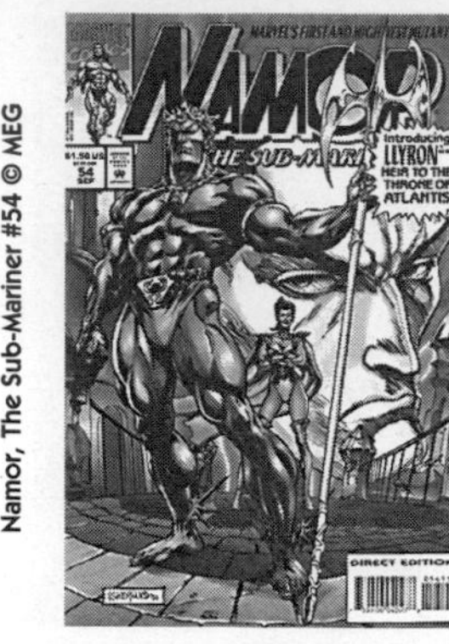

Namor, The Sub-Mariner #54 © MEG

GD25 FN65 NM94

5-(3/41)-Origin The Black Marvel, The Blazing Skull, The Sub-Earth Man, Super Slave & The Terror; The Moon Man & Black Widow app.; 5-German war-c begin, end #10 240.00 720.00 2400.00
6-(10/41)-Origin The Challenger & The Destroyer (1st app.?; also see All-Winners #2, Fall, 1941) 260.00 780.00 2600.00
7-The Witness begins (12/41, origin & 1st app.); origin Davey & the Demon; last Black Widow; Hitler opens his trunk of terror-c by Simon & Kirby (classic-c) 270.00 810.00 2700.00
8,9: 9-Gary Gaunt app.; last Black Marvel, Mystic & Blazing Skull; Hitler-c 156.00 468.00 1400.00
10-Father Time, World of Wonder, & Red Skeleton app.; last Challenger & Terror 156.00 468.00 1400.00

NOTE: ***Gabrielle*** *c-8-10.* ***Kirby/Schomburg*** *c-6.* ***Rico*** *a-9(2).* ***Schomburg*** *a-1-4; c-1-5.* ***Sekowsky*** *a-9.* ***Sekowsky/Klein*** *a-8(Challenger). Bondage c-1, 2, 9.*

MYSTIC COMICS (2nd Series)
Oct, 1944 - No. 3, Win, 1944-45; No. 4, Mar, 1945
Timely Comics (ANC)

1-The Angel, The Destroyer, The Human Torch, Terry Vance the Schoolboy Sleuth, & Tommy Tyme begin 178.00 534.00 1600.00
2-(Fall/44)-Last Human Torch & Terry Vance; bondage/hypo-c 94.00 282.00 850.00
3-Last Angel (two stories) & Tommy Tyme 92.00 276.00 825.00
4-The Young Allies-c & app.; Schomburg-c 86.00 258.00 775.00

MYSTIQUE & SABRETOOTH (Sabretooth and Mystique on-c)
Dec, 1996 - No. 4, Mar, 1997 ($1.95, limited series)
Marvel Comics

1-4: Characters from X-Men .80 2.00

MY STORY (...True Romances in Pictures #5,6) (Formerly Zago)
No. 5, May, 1949 - No. 12, Aug, 1950
Hero Books (Fox Features Syndicate)

5-Kamen/Feldstein-a 14.00 43.00 100.00
6-8,11,12: 12-Photo-c 7.50 22.50 45.00
9,10-Wood-a 13.00 39.00 90.00

MYTHOGRAPHY
Sept, 1996 - Present ($3.95, B&W, anthology)
Bardic Press

1-3: 1-Drew Hayes-s/a 1.00 2.80 7.00
4,5-($4.25) 4.25

MYTHOS: THE FINAL TOUR
Dec, 1996 - No. 3, Feb, 1997 ($5.95, limited series)
DC Comics/Vertigo

1-3: 1-Ney Rieber-s/Amaro-a. 2-Snejbjerg-a; Constantine-app. 3-Kristiansen-a; Black Orchid-app. 2.40 6.00

MY TRUE LOVE (Formerly Western Killers #64; Frank Buck #70 on)
No. 65, July, 1949 - No. 69, March, 1950
Fox Features Syndicate

65 10.00 30.0 65.00
66,68,69: 69-Morisi-a 7.50 22.50 45.00
67-Wood-a 13.50 41.00 95.00

NAKED PREY, THE (See Movie Classics)

'NAM, THE (See Savage Tales #1, 2nd series)
Dec, 1986 - No. 84, Sept, 1993
Marvel Comics Group

1-Golden a(p)/c begins, ends #13 1.50
1 (2nd printing) 1.00
2-7: 7 Golden-a (2 pgs.) 1.50
8-64: 32-Death R. Kennedy. 52,53-Frank Castle (The Punisher) app. 52,53-Gold 2nd printings. 58-Silver logo 1.25
65-74,76-84: 65-Heath-c/a; begin $1.75-c. 67-69-Punisher 3 part story. 70-Lomax scripts begin 1.50
75-($2.25, 52 pgs.) .90 2.25
Trade Paperback 1,2: 1-r/#1-4. 2-r/#5-8 1.80 4.50

'NAM MAGAZINE, THE
Aug, 1988 - No. 10, May, 1989 ($2.00, B&W, 52pgs.)
Marvel Comics

1-10: Each issue reprints 2 of the comic .80 2.00

NAMELESS, THE
May, 1997 - Present ($2.95, B&W)
Image Comics

1-5: Pruett/Hester-s/a 3.00

NAMORA (See Marvel Mystery Comics #82 & Sub-Mariner Comics)
Fall, 1948 - No. 3, Dec, 1948
Marvel Comics (PrPl)

1-Sub-Mariner x-over in Namora; Namora by Everett(2), Sub-Mariner by Rico (10 pgs.) 178.00 534.00 1600.00
2-The Blonde Phantom & Sub-Mariner story; Everett-a 106.00 318.00 950.00
3-(Scarce)-Sub-Mariner app.; Everett-a 106.00 318.00 950.00

NAMOR, THE SUB-MARINER (See Prince Namor & Sub-Mariner)
Apr, 1990 - No. 62, May, 1995 ($1.00/$1.25/$1.50)
Marvel Comics

1-Byrne-c/a/scripts in 1-25 (scripts only #26-32) 1.20 3.00
2-5: 5-Iron Man app. 1.50
6-11: 8,10,16-Re-intro Iron Fist (8-cameo only) 1.25
12-($1.50, 52 pgs.)-Re-intro. The Invaders .70 1.75
13-22: 18-Punisher cameo (1 panel); 21-23,25-Wolverine cameos. 22-Last $1.00-c. 22,23-Iron Fist app. 1.00
23-25: 24-Namor vs. Wolverine 1.25
26-New look for Namor w/new costume; 1st Jae Lee-c/a this title (5/92) & begins 1.20 3.00
27-30: 28-Iron Fist-c/story .80 2.00
31-36,38-49: 31-Dr. Doom-c/story. 33,34-Iron Fist cameo. 35-New Tiger Shark-c/story. 48-The Thing app. 1.25
37-($2.00)-Aqua holo-grafx foil-c .90 2.25
50-($1.75, 52 pgs.)-Newsstand edition; w/bound-in S-M trading card sheet (both versions) .70 1.75
50-($2.95, 52 pgs.)-Collector edition w/foil-c 1.20 3.00
51-62: 51-Begin $1.50-c 1.50
Annual 1 (1991, $2.00, 68 pgs.)-3 pg. origin recap .80 2.00
Annual 2 (1992, $2.25, 68 pgs.)-Return/Defenders .90 2.25
Annual 3 (1993, $2.95, 68 pgs.)-Bagged w/card 1.20 3.00
Annual 4 (1994, $2.95, 68 pgs.)-Painted-c 1.20 3.00

NOTE: ***Jae Lee*** *a-26-30p, 31-37, 38p, 39, 40; c-26-40.*

NANCY AND SLUGGO (See Comics On Parade & Sparkle Comics)
No. 16, 1949 - No. 23, 1954
United Features Syndicate

16(#1) 6.50 19.50 45.00
17-23 4.25 13.00 28.00

NANCY & SLUGGO (Nancy #146-173; formerly Sparkler Comics)
No. 121, Apr, 1955 - No. 192, Oct, 1963
St. John/Dell #146-187/Gold Key #188 on

121(4/55)(St. John) 5.70 17.00 35.00
122-145(7/57)(St. John) 4.25 13.00 26.00
146(9/57)-Peanuts begins, ends #192 (Dell) 3.50 11.00 38.00
147-161 (Dell) 2.75 8.00 30.00
162-165,177-180-John Stanley-a 6.40 19.00 70.00
166-176-Oona & Her Haunted House series; Stanley-a 7.00 22.00 80.00
181-187(3-5/62)(Dell) 2.75 8.00 30.00
188(10/62)-192 (Gold Key) 2.75 8.00 30.00

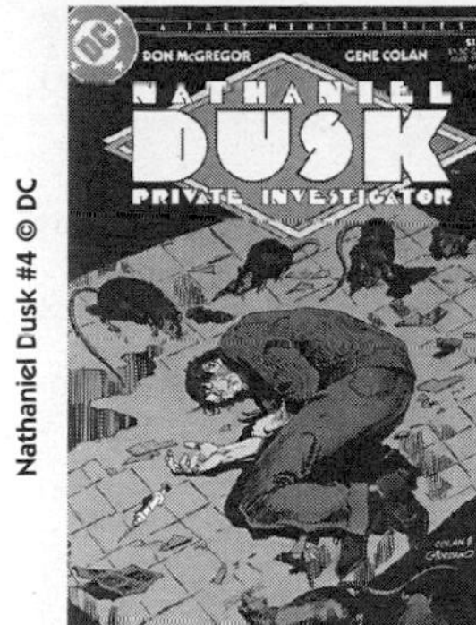

Nathaniel Dusk #4 © DC

National Comics #16 © QUA

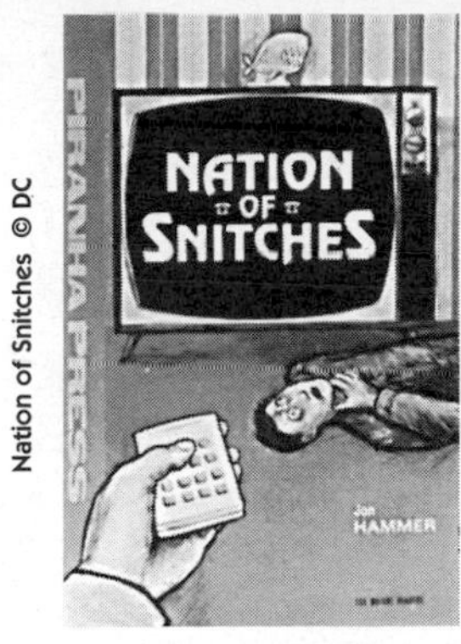

Nation of Snitches © DC

GD25 FN65 NM94

Four Color 1034(9-11/59)-Summer Camp 2.75 8.00 30.00
(See Dell Giant #34, 45 & Dell Giants)

NANNY AND THE PROFESSOR (TV)
Aug, 1970 - No. 2, Oct, 1970 (Photo-c)
Dell Publishing Co.

1(01-546-008), 2 2.75 8.00 30.00

NAPOLEON
No. 526, Dec, 1953
Dell Publishing Co.

Four Color 526 1.80 5.50 20.00

NAPOLEON & SAMANTHA (See Walt Disney Showcase No. 10)

NAPOLEON & UNCLE ELBY (See Clifford McBride's…)
July, 1942 (68 pgs.) (One Shot)
Eastern Color Printing Co.

1 33.00 98.00 260.00
1945-American Book-Strafford Press (128 pgs.) (8x10-1/2"; B&W reprints; hardcover) 11.30 34.00 90.00

NARRATIVE ILLUSTRATION, THE STORY OF THE COMICS
Summer, 1942 (32 pgs., 7-1/4"x10", B&W w/color inserts)
M.C. Gaines

nn-16pgs. text with illustrations of ancient art, strips and comic covers; 4 pg. WWII War Bond promo, "The Minute Man Answers the Call" color comic drawn by Shelly and a special 8-page color comic insert of "The Story of Saul" from Picture Stories from the Bible #1 or soon to appear in PS #1. Insert has special title page indicating it was No. 10 of a Sunday newspaper supplement insert series that had already run in a New England "Sunday Herald." (very rare; only one known copy.) Estimated value... 1,100.00

NATHANIEL DUSK
Feb, 1984 - No. 4, May, 1984 ($1.25, mini-series, direct sales, Baxter paper)
DC Comics

1-4: 1-Intro/origin; Gene Colan-c/a in all 1.25

NATHANIEL DUSK II
Oct, 1985 - No. 4, Jan, 1986 ($2.00, mini-series, Baxter paper)
DC Comics

1-4: Gene Colan-c/a in all .80 2.00

NATIONAL COMICS
July, 1940 - No. 75, Nov, 1949
Quality Comics Group

1-Uncle Sam begins (1st app.); origin sidekick Buddy by Eisner; origin Wonder Boy & Kid Dixon; Merlin the Magician (ends #45); Cyclone, Kid Patrol, Sally O'Neil Policewoman, Pen Miller (by Klaus Nordling; ends #22), Prop Powers (ends #26), & Paul Bunyan (ends #22) begin 430.00 1290.00 4300.00
2 183.00 550.00 1650.00
3-Last Eisner Uncle Sam 128.00 384.00 1150.00
4-Last Cyclone 103.00 309.00 925.00
5-(11/40)-Quicksilver begins (1st app.)(3rd w/lightning speed?); origin Uncle Sam; bondage-c 117.00 350.00 1050.00
6,8-11: 8-Jack & Jill begins (ends #22). 9-Flag-c 103.00 309.00 925.00
7-Classic Lou Fine-c 133.00 400.00 1200.00
12 78.00 234.00 700.00
13-16-Lou Fine-a 69.00 207.00 625.00
17,19-22: 22-Last Pen Miller (moves to Crack #23) 51.00 153.00 460.00
18-(12/41)-Shows orientals attacking Pearl Harbor; on stands one month before actual event 92.00 276.00 825.00
23-The Unknown & Destroyer 171 begin 52.00 156.00 470.00
24-Japanese War-c 50.00 150.00 450.00
25,26,28,30: 26-Wonder Boy ends 36.00 108.00 320.00
27-G-2 the Unknown begins (ends #46) 36.00 108.00 320.00
29-Origin The Unknown 36.00 108.00 320.00
31-33: 33-Chic Carter begins (ends #47) 36.00 108.00 290.00
34-40: 35-Last Kid Patrol. 39-Hitler-c 28.00 83.00 220.00
41-50: 42-The Barker begins (1st app?, 5/44); The Barker covers begin. 48-Origin The Whistler 17.00 51.00 135.00
51-Sally O'Neil by Ward, 8 pgs. (12/45) 23.00 68.00 180.00
52-60 14.00 41.00 110.00
61-67: 67-Format change; Quicksilver app. 10.00 30.00 80.00
68-75: The Barker ends 8.50 26.00 60.00

NOTE: ***Cole*** *Quicksilver-13;* ***Barker****-43; c-43, 46, 47, 49-51.* ***Crandall*** *Uncle Sam-11-13 (with* ***Fine****), 25, 26; c-24-26, 30-33, 43.* ***Crandall*** *Paul Bunyan-10-13.* ***Fine*** *Uncle Sam-13 (w/****Crandall****), 17, 18; c-1-14, 16, 18, 21.* ***Gill Fox*** *c-69-74.* ***Guardineer*** *Quicksilver-27, 35.* ***Gustavson*** *Quicksilver-14-26.* ***McWilliams*** *a-23-28, 55, 57. Uncle Sam c-1-41. Barker c-42-75.*

NATIONAL CRUMB, THE (Magazine-Size)
August, 1975 (52 pgs.) (Satire)
Mayfair Publications

1 1.00 3.00 8.00

NATIONAL VELVET (TV)
May-July, 1961 - No. 2, March, 1963 (All photo-c)
Dell Publishing Co./Gold Key

Four Color 1195 (#1) 5.50 16.50 60.00
Four Color 1312 2.75 8.00 30.00
01-556-207, 12-556-210 (Dell) 2.75 8.00 30.00
1(12/62), 2(3/63) (Gold Key) 2.75 8.00 30.00

NATION OF SNITCHES
1990 ($4.95, color, 52 pgs.)
Piranha Press (DC)

nn 2.00 5.00

NATURE BOY (Formerly Danny Blaze; Li'l Rascal Twins #6 on)
No. 3, March, 1956 - No. 5, Feb, 1957
Charlton Comics

3-Origin; Blue Beetle story; Buscema-c/a 19.00 56.00 150.00
4,5 14.00 41.00 110.00

NOTE: ***John Buscema*** *a-3, 4p, 5; c-3.* ***Powell*** *a-4.*

NATURE OF THINGS (Disney, TV/Movie)
No. 727, Sept, 1956 - No. 842, Sept, 1957
Dell Publishing Co.

Four Color 727 (#1), 842-Jesse Marsh-a 4.50 13.50 50.00

NAUSICAA OF THE VALLEY OF WIND
1988 - No. 7, 1989; 1989 - No. 4, 1990 ($2.50-$2.95, B&W, 68pgs.)
Viz Comics

Book 1-7: ($2.50) 1-Contains Moebius poster 1.00 2.50
Part II, Book 1-3 ($2.95) 1.20 3.00
Part II, Book 4 ($3.25) 1.30 3.25

NAVY ACTION (Sailor Sweeney #12-14)
Aug, 1954 - No. 11, Apr, 1956; No. 15, 1/57 - No. 18, 8/57
Atlas Comics (CDS)

1-Powell-a 13.00 39.00 95.00
2-Lawrence-a 8.00 24.00 50.00
3-11: 4-Last precode (2/55) 5.35 16.00 32.00
15-18 4.25 13.00 28.00

NOTE: ***Berg*** *a-7, 9.* ***Colan*** *a-8.* ***Drucker*** *a-7, 17.* ***Everett*** *a-3, 7, 16; c-16, 17.* ***Heath*** *c-1, 2, 6.* ***Maneely*** *a-7, 8, 18; c-9, 11.* ***Pakula*** *a-2, 3, 9.* ***Reinman*** *a-17.*

NAVY COMBAT
June, 1955 - No. 20, Oct, 1958
Atlas Comics (MPI)

1-Torpedo Taylor begins by Don Heck 13.00 39.00 95.00
2 8.00 24.00 50.00
3-10 5.35 16.00 32.00
11,13,15,16,18-20 5.00 15.00 30.00
12-Crandall-a 7.15 21.50 50.00

Navy Heroes #1 © Almanac Pub.

Negative Burn #48 © Caliber

Neil Gaiman and Charles Vess' Stardust #1 © Neil Gaiman and Charles Vess

	GD25	FN65	NM94
14-Torres-a	5.70	17.00	38.00
17-Williamson-a, 4 pgs.; Torres-a	5.70	17.00	40.00

NOTE: ***Berg*** *a-10, 11.* ***Colan*** *a-11.* ***Drucker*** *a-7.* ***Everett*** *a-3, 20; c-8 & 9 w/****Tuska****, 10, 13-16.* ***Heck*** *a-11(2).* ***Maneely*** *c-1, 6, 11, 17.* ***Morisi*** *a-8.* ***Pakula*** *a-7.* ***Powell*** *a-20.*

NAVY HEROES
1945
Almanac Publishing Co.

1-Heavy in propaganda 8.75 26.25 65.00

NAVY: HISTORY & TRADITION
1958 - 1961 (nn) (Giveaway)
Stokes Walesby Co./Dept. of Navy

1772-1778, 1778-1782, 1782-1817, 1817-1865, 1865-1936, 1940-1945:
1772-1778-16 pg. in color 4.25 13.00 28.00
1861: Naval Actions of the Civil War: 1865-36 pg. in color; flag-c 4.25 13.00 28.00

NAVY PATROL
May, 1955 - No. 4, Nov, 1955
Key Publications

1 5.70 17.00 35.00
2-4 4.00 10.00 20.00

NAVY TALES
Jan, 1957 - No. 4, July, 1957
Atlas Comics (CDS)

1-Everett-c; Berg, Powell-a 11.00 33.00 80.00
2-Williamson/Mayo-a(5 pgs); Crandall-a 10.00 30.00 70.00
3,4-Reinman-a; Severin-c. 4-Crandall-a 9.00 27.00 60.00

NOTE: ***Colan*** *a-4.* ***Maneely*** *c-2.* ***Sinnott*** *a-4.*

NAVY TASK FORCE
Feb, 1954 - No. 8, April, 1956
Stanmor Publications/Aragon Mag. No. 4-8

1 6.35 19.00 38.00
2 4.00 10.00 20.00
3-8: #8-r/Navy Patrol #1 3.20 8.00 16.00

NAVY WAR HEROES
Jan, 1964 - No. 7, Mar-Apr, 1965
Charlton Comics

1 2.50 7.50 20.00
2-7 1.50 4.50 12.00

NAZA (Stone Age Warrior)
Nov-Jan, 1963-64 - No. 9, March, 1966
Dell Publishing Co.

12-555-401 (#1)-Painted-c 3.00 9.00 30.00
2-9: 2-4-Painted-c 2.50 7.50 20.00

NAZZ, THE
1990 - No. 4, 1991 ($4.95, 52 pgs., mature)
DC Comics

1-4 2.00 5.00

NEBBS, THE (Also see Crackajack Funnies)
1941; 1945
Dell Publishing Co./Croydon Publishing Co.

Large Feature Comic 23(1941) 13.00 40.00 145.00
1(1945, 36 pgs.)-Reprints 7.00 21.00 75.00

NECROMANCER: THE GRAPHIC NOVEL
1989 ($8.95)
Marvel Comics (Epic Comics)

nn 1.10 3.30 9.00

NEGATIVE BURN
1993 - No. 50, 1997 ($2.95, B&W, anthology)
Caliber

1,2,4-12,26-30,32-35: Anthology by various including Bolland, Burden, Doran, Gaiman, Moebius, Moore, & Pope 1.60 4.00
3-Bone story 2.50 7.50 20.00
13-Strangers in Paradise story 2.50 7.50 20.00
25,31,36-47-($3.95): 25-Gaiman, Moore & Pope 1.60 4.00
48,49-($4.95) 4.95
50-($6.95, 96 pgs.)-Gaiman, Robinson, Bolland 6.95

NEGRO (See All-Negro)

NEGRO HEROES (Calling All Girls, Real Heroes, & True Comics reprints)
Spring, 1947 - No. 2, Summer, 1948
Parents' Magazine Institute

1 68.00 206.00 600.00
2-Jackie Robinson-c/story 75.00 225.00 650.00

NEGRO ROMANCE (Negro Romances #4)
June, 1950 - No. 3, Oct, 1950 (All photo-c)
Fawcett Publications

1-Evans-a 96.00 290.00 800.00
2,3 75.00 225.00 600.00

NEGRO ROMANCES (Formerly Negro Romance; Romantic Secrets #5 on)
No. 4, May, 1955
Charlton Comics

4-Reprints Fawcett #2 59.00 178.00 475.00

NEIL GAIMAN AND CHARLES VESS' STARDUST
1997 - No. 4, 1998 ($5.95/$6.95, square-bound, limited series)
DC Comics (Vertigo)

1-3: Gaiman text with Vess paintings in all 5.95
4-($6.95) 6.95

NEIL GAIMAN'S LADY JUSTICE
Sept, 1995 - No. 11, May, 1996 ($1.95/$2.25)
Tekno Comix

1-($2.25)-Sienkiewicz-c; pin-ups .90 2.25
1-5-($1.95): Brereton-c in all. .80 2.00
6-11: 6-Begin $2.25-c. 7-polybagged. 11-Includes The Big Bang Pt. 7 .90 2.25

NEIL GAIMAN'S LADY JUSTICE
V2#1, June, 1996 - No. 9, Feb, 1997 ($2.25)
BIG Entertainment

V2#1-9: Dan Brereton-c on all. 6-8-Dan Brereton script .90 2.25

NEIL GAIMAN'S MR. HERO-THE NEWMATIC MAN
Mar, 1995 - No. 17, May, 1996 ($1.95/$2.25)
Tekno Comix

1-Intro Mr. Hero & Teknophage; bound-in game piece and trading card 1.00 2.50
2-11: 4-w/Steel edition Neil Gaiman's Teknophage #1 coupon .80 2.00
12-17: 12-Begin $2.25-c. 13-polybagged. .90 2.25

NEIL GAIMAN'S MR. HERO-THE NEWMATIC MAN
V2#1, June, 1996 ($2.25)
BIG Entertainment

V2#1-Teknophage destroys Mr. Hero; includes The Big Bang Pt. 10 .90 2.25

NEIL GAIMAN'S PHAGE-SHADOWDEATH
June, 1996 - No. 6, Nov, 1996 ($2.25, limited series)
BIG Entertainment

1-6: Bryan Talbot-c & scripts in all. 1-1st app. Orlando Holmes .90 2.25

NEIL GAIMAN'S TEKNOPHAGE

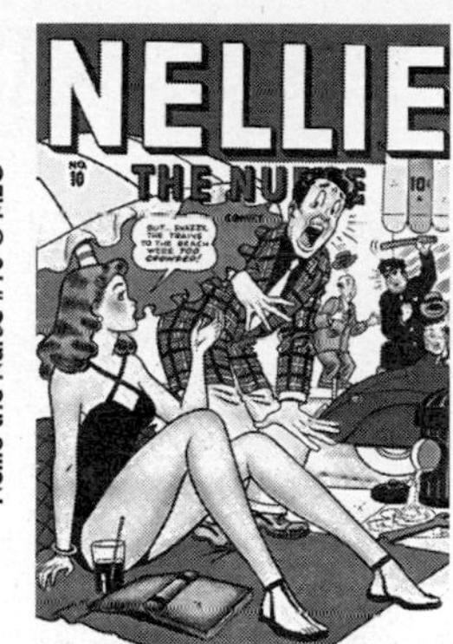

Nellie the Nurse #10 © MEG

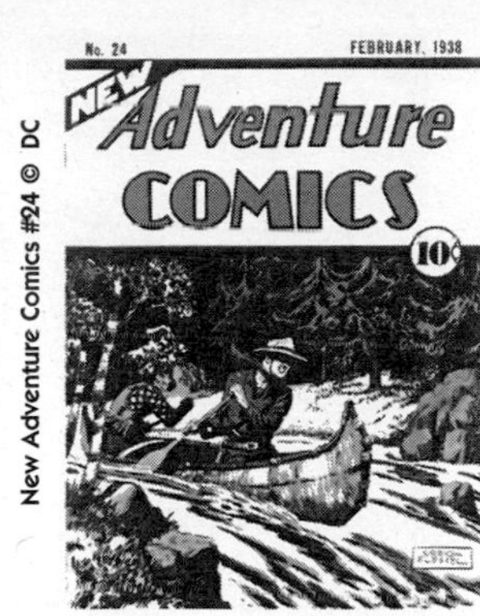

New Adventure Comics #24 © DC

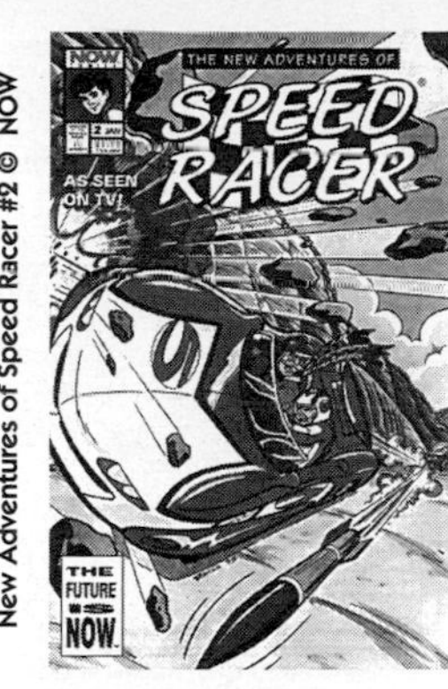

New Adventures of Speed Racer #2 © NOW

GD25 FN65 NM94

Aug, 1995 - No. 10, Mar, 1996 ($1.95/$2.25)
Tekno Comix

1-6-Rick Veitch scripts & Bryan Talbot-c/a. .80 2.00
1-Steel Edition 2.00 5.00
7-10: Paul Jenkins scripts in all. 7-$2.25-c begins. 8-polybagged. .90 2.25

NEIL GAIMAN'S WHEEL OF WORLDS
Apr, 1995 - No. 1, May, 1996 ($2.95/$3.25)
Tekno Comix

0-1st app. Lady Justice; 48 pgs.; bound-in poster 1.20 3.00
0-Regular edition .80 2.00
1 ($3.25, 5/96)-Bruce Jones scripts; Lady Justice & Teknophage app.; computer-generated photo-c. 1.30 3.25

NEIL THE HORSE (See Charlton Bullseye #2)
2/83 - No. 10, 12/84; No. 11, 4/85 - #15, 1985 (B&W)
Aardvark-Vanaheim #1-10/Renegade Press #11 on

1($1.40) .80 2.00
1-2nd print 1.50
2-13: 13-Double size; 11,13-w/paperdolls .80 2.00
14,15: Double size ($3.00). 15 is a flip book(2-c) 1.20 3.00

NELLIE THE NURSE (Also see Gay Comics & Joker Comics)
1945 - No. 36, Oct, 1952; 1957
Marvel/Atlas Comics (SPI/LMC)

	GD25	FN65	NM94
1-(1945)	31.00	94.00	240.00
2-(Spring/46)	14.00	43.00	110.00
3,4: 3-New logo (9/46)	11.00	33.00	80.00
5-Kurtzman's "Hey Look" (3); Georgie app.	13.00	39.00	95.00
6-8,10: 7,8-Georgie app. 10-Millie app.	10.00	30.00	70.00
9-Wolverton-a (1 pg.); Mille the Model app.	10.00	30.00	75.00
11,14-16,18-Kurtzman's "Hey Look"	11.00	33.00	80.00
12- "Giggles 'n' Grins" by Kurtzman	10.00	30.00	70.00
13,17,19,20: 17-Annie Oakley app.	8.00	24.00	50.00
21-27,29,30	6.35	19.00	40.00
28-Mr. Nexdoor-r (3 pgs.) by Kurtzman/Rusty #22	7.00	21.00	45.00
31-36: 36-Post-c	5.70	17.00	35.00
1('57)-Leading Mag. (Atlas)-Everett-a, 20 pgs	7.00	21.00	45.00

NELLIE THE NURSE
No. 1304, Mar-May, 1962
Dell Publishing Co.

Four Color 1304-Stanley-a 6.40 19.00 70.00

NEMESIS THE WARLOCK (Also see Spellbinders)
Sept, 1984 - No. 7, Mar, 1985 (36 pgs, limited series)
Eagle Comics (Baxter paper)

1-7: 2000 A.D. reprints 1.50

NEMESIS THE WARLOCK
1989 - No. 10, 1990 ($1.95, B&W)
Quality Comics/Fleetway Quality #2 on

1-10 .80 2.00

NEURO JACK
Aug, 1996 ($2.25)
BIG Entertainment Interactive

1-Digital art .90 2.25

NEUTRO
Jan, 1967
Dell Publishing Co.

1-Jack Sparling-c/a (super hero) 2.50 7.50 24.00

NEVADA (See Zane Grey's Four Color 412, 996 & Zane Grey's Stories of the West #1)

NEVER AGAIN (War stories; becomes Soldier & Marine V2#9)
Aug, 1955 - No. 2, Oct?, 1955; No. 8, July, 1956 (No #3-7)
Charlton Comics

1 5.70 17.00 40.00
2-(Becomes Fightin' Air Force #3), 8-(Formerly Foxhole?) 4.00 12.00 24.00

NEW ADVENTURE COMICS (Formerly New Comics; becomes Adventure Comics #32 on; V1#12 indicia says NEW COMICS #12)
V1#12, Jan, 1937 - No. 31, Oct, 1938
National Periodical Publications

	GD25	FN65	VF82	NM94
V1#12-Federal Men by Siegel & Shuster continues; Jor-L mentioned; Whitney Ellsworth-c begin, end #14	483.00	1450.00	3000.00	–
V2#1(2/37, #13)-(Rare)	450.00	1350.00	2800.00	–
V2#2 (#14)	400.00	1200.00	2500.00	–

	GD25	FN65	NM94
15(V2#3)-20(V2#8): 15-1st Adventure logo; Creig Flessel-c begin, end #31. 16-1st Shuster-c; 1st non-funny cover. 17-Nadir, Master of Magic begins, ends #30	400.00	1200.00	2400.00
21(V2#9),22(V2#10, 2/37): 22-X-Mas-c	366.00	1100.00	2200.00
23-31	308.00	924.00	1850.00

NEW ADVENTURE OF WALT DISNEY'S SNOW WHITE AND THE SEVEN DWARFS, A (See Snow White Bendix Giveaway)

NEW ADVENTURES OF CHARLIE CHAN, THE (TV)
May-June, 1958 - No. 6, Mar-Apr, 1959
National Periodical Publications

1 (Scarce)-Gil Kane/Sid Greene-a in all 53.00 160.00 480.00
2 (Scarce) 36.00 108.00 325.00
3-6 (Scarce)-Greene/Giella-a 34.00 101.00 270.00

NEW ADVENTURES OF HUCK FINN, THE (TV)
December, 1968 (Hanna-Barbera)
Gold Key

1- "The Curse of Thut"; part photo-c 2.75 8.00 30.00

NEW ADVENTURES OF PETER PAN (Disney)
1953 (5x7-1/4", 36 pgs.) (Admiral giveaway)
Western Publishing Co.

nn 8.75 26.25 70.00

NEW ADVENTURES OF PINOCCHIO (TV)
Oct-Dec, 1962 - No. 3, Sept-Nov, 1963
Dell Publishing Co.

12-562-212(#1) 8.00 23.00 85.00
2,3 5.00 15.00 55.00

NEW ADVENTURES OF ROBIN HOOD (See Robin Hood)

NEW ADVENTURES OF SHERLOCK HOLMES (Also see Sherlock Holmes)
No. 1169, Mar-May, 1961 - No. 1245, Nov-Jan, 1961/62
Dell Publishing Co.

Four Color 1169(#1), 1245 14.00 44.00 160.00

NEW ADVENTURES OF SPEED RACER
Dec, 1993 - No. 7, 1994? ($1.95)
Now Comics

1-7 .80 2.00
0-(Premiere)-3-D cover 1.20 3.00

NEW ADVENTURES OF SUPERBOY, THE (Also see Superboy)
Jan, 1980 - No. 54, June, 1984
DC Comics

1-54: 7-Has extra story "The Computers That Saved Metropolis" by Starlin (Radio Shack giveaway w/indicia). 11-Superboy gets new power. 14-Lex Luthor app. 15-Superboy gets new parents. 28-Dial "H" For Hero begins, ends #49. 45-47-1st app. Sunburst. 48-Begin 75¢-c. 50-Legion app. 1.00

New Force #4 © Rob Liefeld

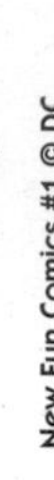

New Fun Comics #1 © DC

The New Gods #4 © DC

NOTE: *Buckler a-9p; c-36p.* ***Giffen*** *a-50; c-50. 40i.* ***Gil Kane*** *c-32p, 33p, 35, 39, 41-49.* ***Miller*** *c-51.* ***Starlin*** *a-7. Krypto back-ups in 17, 22. Superbaby in 11, 14, 19, 24.*

NEW ADVENTURES OF THE PHANTOM BLOT, THE (See The Phantom Blot)

NEW AMERICA
Nov, 1987 - No. 4, Feb, 1988 ($1.75, Baxter paper)
Eclipse Comics

	GD25	NM94
1-4: Scout limited series	.75	1.80

NEW ARCHIES, THE (TV)
Oct, 1987 - No. 22, May, 1990 (75¢)
Archie Comic Publications

	GD25	NM94
1	1.20	3.00
2-22: 3-Xmas issue; 17-22 (.95-$1.00): 21-Xmas issue	.80	2.00

NEW ARCHIES DIGEST (TV)(...Comics Digest Magazine #4?-10; ...Digest Magazine #11 on)
May, 1988 - No. 14, July, 1991 ($1.35/$1.50, digest-size, quarterly)
Archie Comics

	GD25	NM94
1	2.00	5.00
2-14: 6-Begin $1.50-c	1.20	3.00

NEW BOOK OF COMICS (Also see Big Book Of Fun)
1937; No. 2, Spring, 1938 (100 pgs. each) (Reprints)
National Periodical Publ.

	GD25	FN65	VF82	NM94
1(Rare)-1st regular size comic annual; 2nd DC annual; contains r/New Comics #1-4 & More Fun #9; r/Federal Men (8 pgs.), Henri Duval (1 pg.), & Dr. Occult in costume (1 pg.) by Siegel & Shuster; Moldoff, Sheldon Mayer (15 pgs.)-a	1833.00	5500.00	11,500.00	-
(Estimated up to 50 total copies exist, none in NM/Mint)				
2-Contains-r/More Fun #15 & 16; r/Dr. Occult in costume (a Superman prototype), & Calling All Cars (4 pgs.) by Siegel & Shuster	916.00	2750.00	5800.00	-

NEW COMICS (New Adventure #12 on)
12/35 - No. 11, 12/36 (No. 1-6: paper cover) (No. 1-5: 84 pgs.)
National Periodical Publ.

	GD25	FN65	VF82	NM94
V1#1-Billy the Kid, Sagebrush 'n' Cactus, Jibby Jones, Needles, The Vikings, Sir Loin of Beef, Now-When I Was a Boy, & other 1-2 pg. strips; 2 pgs. Kelly art(1st)-(Gulliver's Travels); Sheldon Mayer-a(1st)(2 2pg. strips); Vincent Sullivan-c(1st)	2417.00	7250.00	15,000.00	-
(Estimated up to 50 total copies exist, none in NM/Mint)				
2-1st app. Federal Men by Siegel & Shuster & begins (also see The Comics Magazine #2); Mayer, Kelly-a (Rare)(1/36)	916.00	2750.00	5800.00	-
3-6: 3,4-Sheldon Mayer-a which continues in The Comics Magazine #1. 3-Vincent Sullivan-c. 4-Dickens' "A Tale of Two Cities" adaptation begins. 5-Junior Federal Men Club; Kiefer-a. 6- "She" adaptation begins	550.00	1650.00	3400.00	-
7-11: 11-Christmas-c	433.00	1300.00	2700.00	-

NOTE: *#1-6 rarely occur in mint condition.* ***Whitney Ellsworth*** *c-4-11.*

NEW DEFENDERS (See Defenders)

NEW DNAGENTS, THE (Formerly DNAgents)
V2#1, Oct, 1985 - V2#17, Mar, 1987 (Whole #s 25-40; Mando paper)
Eclipse Comics

	GD25	NM94
V2#1-12: 1-Origin recap. 7-Begin 95 cent-c. 9,10-Airboy preview		1.00
13-17 ($1.25)		1.25
3-D 1 (1/86, $2.25)	.90	2.25
2-D 1 (1/86)-Limited ed. (100 copies)	1.60	4.00

NEWFORCE (Also see Newmen)
Jan, 1996 - No. 4, Apr, 1996 ($2.50, limited series)
Image Comics (Extreme Studios)

	GD25	NM94
1-4: 1-"Extreme Destroyer" Pt. 8; polybagged w/gaming card. 4-Newforce disbands.	1.00	2.50

NEW FUN COMICS (More Fun #7 on; see Big Book of Fun Comics)
Feb, 1935 - No. 6, Oct, 1935 (10x15", No. 1-4,: slick-c)
(No. 1-5: 36 pgs; 40 pgs. No. 6)
National Periodical Publications

	GD25	FN65	VF82	NM94
V1#1 (1st DC comic); 1st app. Oswald The Rabbit; Jack Woods (cowboy) begins	6170.00	18,500.00	37,500.00	-
(Estimated up to 10 total copies exist, 1 in VF/NM)				
2(3/35)-(Very Rare)	2590.00	7750.00	16,000.00	-
(Estimated up to 5 total copies exist)				
3-5(8/35): 3-Don Drake on the Planet Soro-c/story (sci/fi, 4/35). 5-Soft-c	1300.00	3900.00	8000.00	-
6(10/35)-1st Dr. Occult by Siegel & Shuster (Leger & Reuths); last "New Fun" title. "New Comics" #1 begins in Dec. which is reason for title change to More Fun; Henri Duval (ends #10) by Siegel & Shuster begins; paper-c	2917.00	8750.00	18,000.00	-
(Estimated up to 10 total copies exist of #3-6)				

NEW FUNNIES (The Funnies #1-64; Walter Lantz...#109 on; New TV... #259, 260, 272, 273; TV Funnies #261-271)
No. 65, July, 1942 - No. 288, Mar-Apr, 1962
Dell Publishing Co.

	GD25	FN65	NM94
65(#1)-Andy Panda in a world of real people, Raggedy Ann & Andy, Oswald the Rabbit (with Woody Woodpecker x-overs), Li'l Eight Ball & Peter Rabbit begin	58.00	175.00	640.00
66-70: 66-Felix the Cat begins. 67-Billy & Bonnie Bee by Frank Thomas begins. 69-Kelly-a (2 pgs.); The Brownies begin (not by Kelly)	27.00	82.00	300.00
71-75: 72-Kelly illos. 75-Brownies by Kelly?	16.00	49.00	180.00
76-Andy Panda (Carl Barks & Pabian-a); Woody Woodpecker x-over in Oswald ends	91.00	273.00	1000.00
77,78: 77-Kelly-c. 78-Andy Panda in a world with real people ends	16.00	49.00	180.00
79-81	12.00	35.00	130.00
82-Brownies by Kelly begins; Homer Pigeon begins	13.00	38.00	140.00
83-85-Brownies by Kelly in ea. 83-X-mas-c. 85-Woody Woodpecker, 1 pg. strip begins	13.00	38.00	140.00
86-90: 87-Woody Woodpecker stories begin	9.00	27.00	100.00
91-99	5.50	16.50	60.00
100 (6/45)	6.40	19.00	70.00
101-110	3.60	11.00	40.00
111-120: 119-X-Mas-c	3.00	9.00	35.00
121-150: 131,143-X-Mas-c	2.75	8.00	30.00
151-200: 155-X-Mas-c. 168-X-Mas-c. 182-Origin & 1st app. Knothead & Splinter. 191-X-Mas-c	1.65	5.00	18.00
201-240	1.25	3.75	10.00
241-288: 270,271-Walter Lantz c-app. 281-1st story swipes/WDC&S #100	1.00	2.80	7.00

NOTE: *Early issues written by* ***John Stanley.***

NEW GODS, THE (1st Series)(New Gods #12 on)(See Adventure #459, DC Graphic Novel #4, 1st Issue Special #13 & Super-Team Family)
2-3/71 - V2#11, 10-11/72; V3#12, 7/77 - V3#19, 7-8/78 (Fourth World)
National Periodical Publications/DC Comics

	GD25	FN65	NM94
1-Intro/1st app. Orion; 4th app. Darkseid (cameo; 3 weeks after Forever People #1) (#1-3 are 15¢ issues)	5.00	15.00	50.00
2-Darkseid-c/story (2nd full app., 4-5/71)	2.50	7.50	25.00
3-1st app. Black Racer	2.25	6.75	18.00
4-9: (25¢, 52 pg. giants): 4-Darkseid cameo; origin Manhunter-r. 5,7,8-Young Gods feature. 7-Darkseid app. (2-3/72); origin Orion; 1st origin of all New Gods as a group. 9-1st app. Bug	1.50	4.50	12.00
10,11: 11-Last Kirby issue.	1.10	3.30	9.00
12-19: Darkseid storyline w/minor apps. 12-New costume Orion (see 1st Issue Special #13 for 1st new costume). 19-Story continued in Adventure Comics #459,460		2.00	5.00

NOTE: *#4-9(25¢, 52 pgs.) contain Manhunter-r by* ***Simon*** *&* ***Kirby*** *from Adventure #73, 74, 75,*

New Gods #2 © DC

New Love #6 © Gilbert Hernandez

New Mutants #95 © MEG

GD25 FN65 NM94

76, 77, 78 with covers in that order. ***Adkins*** *i-12-14, 17-19.* ***Buckler*** *a(p)-15.* ***Kirby*** *c/a-1-11p.* ***Newton*** *a(p)-12-14, 16-19.* ***Starlin*** *c-17.* ***Staton*** *c-19p.*

NEW GODS (Also see DC Graphic Novel #4)
May, 1984 - No. 6, Nov, 1984 ($2.00, Baxter paper)
DC Comics

1-6: 1-5: New Kirby-c; r/New Gods #1-10. 6-Reprints New Gods #11 w/48 pgs of new Kirby story & art; leads into DC Graphic Novel #4 .90 2.25

NEW GODS (2nd Series)
Feb, 1989 - No. 28, Aug, 1991 ($1.50)
DC Comics

1-28 1.50

NEW GODS (3rd Series) (Becomes Jack Kirby's Fourth World) (Also see Showcase '94 #1 & Showcase '95 #7)
Oct, 1995 - No. 15, Feb, 1997 ($1.95)
DC Comics

1-11,13-15: 9-Giffen-a(p). 10,11-Superman app. 13-Takion, Mr. Miracle & Big Barda app. 13-15-Byrne-a(p)/scripts & Simonson-c. 15-Apokolips merged w/ New Genesis; story cont'd in Jack Kirby's Fourth World .80 2.00
12-(11/96, 99¢)-Byrne-a(p)/scripts & Simonson-c begin; Takion cameo; indicia reads October 1996 1.00

NEW GUARDIANS, THE
Sept, 1988 - No. 12, Sept, 1989 ($1.25)
DC Comics

1-($2.00, 52pgs)-Staton-c/a in #1-9 .80 2.00
2-12 1.25

NEW HEROIC (See Heroic)

NEW JUSTICE MACHINE, THE (Also see The Justice Machine)
1989 - No. 3, 1989 ($1.95, limited series)
Innovation Publishing

1-3 .80 2.00

NEW KIDS ON THE BLOCK, THE (Also see Richie Rich and...)
Dec, 1990 -1991 ($1.25)
Harvey Comics

1-5 1.25
...**Backstage Pass** 1(12/90) - 5 **Chillin'** 1(12/90) - 5: 1-Photo-c...**Comics Tour** '90/91 1 (12/90) - 5 **Hanging Tough** 1 (2/91) - 3 **Live** 1 (2/91) - 3 **Magic Summer Tour** 1 (Fall/90, one-shot) **Step By Step** 1 (Fall/90, one-shot) **Valentine Girl** 1 (Fall/90, one-shot)-Photo-c 1.25

NEW LOVE (See Love & Rockets)
Aug, 1996 - No. 6, Dec, 1997($2.95, B&W, limited series)
Fantagraphics Books

1-6: Gilbert Hernandez-s/a 1.20 3.00

NEWMAN
Jan, 1996 - No. 4, Apr, 1996 ($2.50, limited series)
Image Comics (Extreme Studios)

1-4: 1-Extreme Destroyer Pt. 3; polybagged w/card. 4-Shadowhunt tie-in; Eddie Collins becomes new Shadowhawk 1.00 2.50

NEWMEN (becomes The Adventures Of The...#22)
Apr, 1994 - No. 20, Nov, 1995; No. 21, Nov, 1996 ($1.95/$2.50)
Image Comics (Extreme Studios)

1-5: Matsuda-c/a. 1-Liefeld/Matsuda plot .80 2.00
6-21: 6-(9/94)-Begin $2.50-c. 10-Polybagged w/trading card. 11-Polybagged. 20-Variant-c; Babewatch! x-over. 21-(11/96)-Series relaunch; Chris Sprouse-a begins; pin-up 1.00 2.50
16-Quesada & Palmiotti variant-c 1.20 3.00
TPB-(1996, $12.95) r/#1-4 w/pin-ups 13.00

NEW MEN OF BATTLE, THE
1949 (nn) (Carboard-c)
Catechetical Guild

nn(V8#1-3,5,6)-192 pgs.; contains 5 issues of Topix rebound 4.25 13.00 28.00
nn(V8#7-V8#11)-160 pgs.; contains 5 iss. of Topix 4.25 13.00 28.00

NEW MUTANTS, THE (See Marvel Graphic Novel #4 for 1st app.)(Also see X-Force & Uncanny X-Men #167)
Mar, 1983 - No. 100, Apr, 1991
Marvel Comics Group

1 2.40 6.00
2,3: 3,4-Ties into X-Men #167 1.20 3.00
4-10: 10-1st app. Magma 1.20 3.00
11-17,19,20: 13-Kitty Pryde app. 16-1st app. Warpath (w/out costume); see X-Men #193 1.00 2.50
18-Intro. new Warlock 1.60 4.00
21-Double size; origin new Warlock; newsstand version has cover price written in by Sienkiewicz 1.60 4.00
22-24,29,30: 23-25-Cloak & Dagger app. 1.00 2.50
25-Legion app. (cameo) 1.60 4.00
26-1st full Legion app. 1.60 4.00
27,28 1.20 3.00
31-58: 35-Magneto intro'd as new headmaster. 43-Portacio-i. 50-Double size. 58-Contains pull-out mutant registration form .80 2.00
59-Fall of The Mutants begins, ends #61 1.40 3.50
60-($1.25, 52 pgs.) 1.00 2.50
61-Fall of The Mutants ends .80 2.00
62,64-72,74-85: 68-Intro Spyder. 76-X-Factor & X-Terminator app. 85-Liefeld-c begin 1.25
63-X-Men & Wolverine clones app.; begin $1.00-c 1.40 3.50
73-($1.50, 52 pgs.) .80 2.00
86-Rob Liefeld-a begins; McFarlane-c(i) swiped from Ditko splash pg.; Cable cameo (last page teaser) 1.00 2.80 7.00
87-1st full app. Cable (3/90) 1.85 5.50 15.00
87-2nd printing; gold metallic ink-c ($1.00) .80 2.00
88-2nd app. Cable 1.00 3.00 8.00
89-3rd app. Cable 2.00 5.00
90,91: 90-New costumes. 90,91-Sabretooth app. 2.00 5.00
92-No Liefeld-a; Liefeld-c 1.00 2.50
93,94-Cable vs. Wolverine 2.00 5.00
95-97-X-Tinction Agenda x-over. 95-Death of new Warlock. 97-Wolverine & Cable-c, but no app. 2.00 5.00
95-Gold 2nd printing 1.00 2.50
98-1st app. Deadpool, Gideon & Domino (2/91); 2nd Shatterstar (cameo) 2.40 6.00
99-1st app. of Feral (of X-Force); Byrne-c/swipe (X-Men, 1st Series #138) 2.40 6.00
100-($1.50, 52 pgs.)-1st app. X-Force (cameo) 1.20 3.00
100-Gold 2nd printing 1.20 2.00
100-Silver ink 3rd printing 1.50
Annual 1 (1984) 1.20 3.00
Annual 2 (1986, $1.25)-1st Psylocke 1.00 3.00 7.50
Annual 3 (1987, $1.25) .80 2.00
Annual 4 (1988, $1.75)-Evolutionary War x-over .80 2.00
Annual 5 (1989, $2.00, 68 pgs.)-Atlantis Attacks; 1st Liefeld-a on New Mutants 2.00 5.00
Annual 6 (1990, $2.00, 68 pgs.)-1st new costumes by Liefeld (3 pgs.); 1st app. (cameo) Shatterstar (of X-Force) .80 2.00
Annual 7 (1991, $2.00, 68 pgs.)-Liefeld pin-up only; X-Terminators back-up story; 2nd app. X-Force (continued in New Warriors Annual #1) .80 2.00
Special 1-Special Edition ('85, 68 pgs.)-Ties in w/X-Men Alpha Flight limited series; cont'd in X-Men Annual #9; Art Adams/Austin-a 2.00 5.00

New Statesmen #1 © QUA

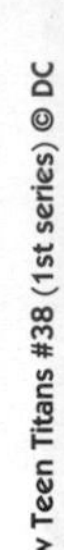

New Teen Titans #38 (1st series) © DC

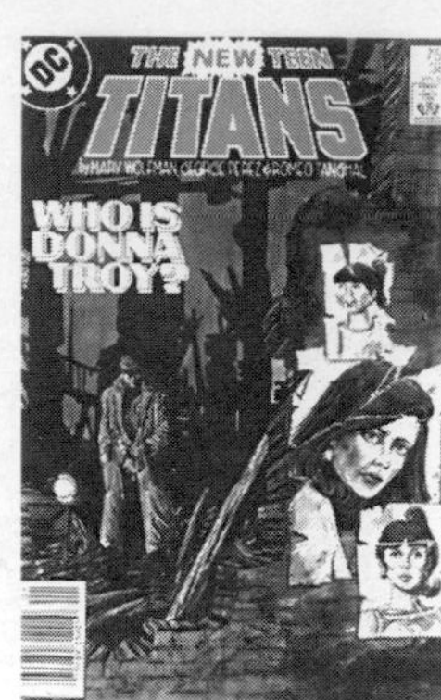

New Teen Titans #9 (2nd series) © DC

GD25 FN65 NM94

Summer Special 1(Sum/90, $2.95, 84 pgs.) 1.20 3.00

NOTE: ***Art Adams*** *c-38, 39.* ***Austin*** *c-57i.* ***Byrne*** *c/a-75p.* ***Liefeld*** *a-86-91p, 93-96p, 98-100, Annual 5p, 6(3 pgs.); c-85-91p, 92, 93p, 94, 95, 96p, 97-100, Annual 5, 6p.* ***McFarlane*** *c-85-89i, 93i.* ***Portacio*** *a(i)-43.* ***Russell*** *a-48i.* ***Sienkiewicz*** *a-18-31, 35-38i; c-17-31, 35i, 37i, Annual 1.* ***Simonson*** *c-11p.* ***B. Smith*** *c-36, 40-48.* ***Williamson*** *a(i)-69, 71-73, 78-80, 82, 83; c(i)-69, 72, 73, 78i.*

NEW MUTANTS, THE: TRUTH OR DEATH
Nov, 1997 - No. 3, Jan, 1998 ($2.50, limited series)
Marvel Comics

1-3-Raab-s/Chang-a(p) 2.50

NEW ORDER, THE
Nov, 1994 ($2.95)
CFD Publishing

1 1.20 3.00

NEW PEOPLE, THE (TV)
Jan, 1970 - No. 2, May, 1970
Dell Publishing Co.

1,2 1.50 4.50 12.00

NEW ROMANCES
No. 5, May, 1951 - No. 21, May, 1954
Standard Comics

5-Photo-c 8.75 26.25 65.00
6-9: 6-Barbara Bel Geddes, Richard Basehart "Fourteen Hours" photo-c. 7-Ray Milland & Joan Fontaine photo-c. 9-Photo-c from '50s movie 5.70 17.00 35.00
10,14,16,17-Toth-a 6.00 18.00 42.00
11-Toth-a; Liz Taylor, Montgomery Cliff photo-c 10.50 32.00 85.00
12,13,15,18-21 4.15 12.50 25.00

NOTE: ***Celardo*** *a-9.* ***Moreira*** *a-6.* ***Tuska*** *a-7, 20. Photo c-5-16.*

NEW SHADOWHAWK, THE (Also see Shadowhawk & Shadowhunt)
June, 1995 - No. 7, Mar, 1996 ($2.50)
Image Comics (Shadowline Ink)

1-7: Kurt Busiek scripts in all 1.00 2.50

NEW STATESMEN, THE
1989 - No. 5, 1990 ($3.95, limited series, mature readers, 52pgs.)
Fleetway Publications (Quality Comics)

1-5: Futuristic; squarebound; 3-Photo-c 1.60 4.00

NEWSTRALIA
July, 1989 - No. 5, 1989 ($1.75, color)(#2 on, $2.25,, B&W)
Innovation Publishing

1,2: Timothy Truman-c/a; Gustovich-i .70 1.75
3-5 ($2.25, B&W) .90 2.25

NEW TALENT SHOWCASE (Talent Showcase #16 on)
Jan, 1984 - No. 19, Oct, 1985 (Direct sales only)
DC Comics

1-10: Features new strips & artists .70
11-19 ($1.25): 18-Williamson-c(i) 1.25

NEW TEEN TITANS, THE (See DC Comics Presents 26, Marvel and DC Present & Teen Titans; Tales of the Teen Titans #41 on)
Nov, 1980 - No. 40, Mar, 1984
DC Comics

1-Robin, Kid Flash, Wonder Girl, The Changeling (1st app.), Starfire, The Raven, Cyborg begin; partial origin 1.00 3.00 8.00
2-1st app. Deathstroke the Terminator 1.00 3.00 8.00
3-9: 3-Origin Starfire; Intro The Fearsome Five. 4-Origin continues; J.L.A. app. 6-Origin Raven. 7-Cyborg origin. 8-Origin Kid Flash retold. 9-Minor cameo Deathstroke on last pg. 1.20 3.00
10-2nd app. Deathstroke the Terminator (see Marvel & DC Present for 3rd app.); origin Changeling retold 2.00 5.00

GD25 FN65 NM94

11-20: 13-Return of Madame Rouge & Capt. Zahl; Robotman revived. 14-Return of Mento; origin Doom Patrol. 15-Death of Madame Rouge & Capt. Zahl; intro. new Brotherhood of Evil. 16-1st app. Captain Carrot (free 16 pg. preview). 18-Return of Starfire. 19-Hawkman teams-up 1.50
21-30: 21-Intro Night Force in free 16 pg. insert; intro Brother Blood. 23-1st app. Vigilante (not in costume), & Blackfire. 24-Omega Men app. 25-Omega Men cameo; free 16 pg. preview Masters of the Universe. 26-1st app. Terra. 27-Free 16 pg. preview Atari Force. 29-The New Brotherhood of Evil & Speedy app. 30-Terra joins the Titans .80 2.00
31-33,35-38,40: 37-Batman & The Outsiders x-over. 38-Origin Wonder Girl .80 2.00
34-4th app. Deathstroke the Terminator 1.20 3.00
39-Last Dick Grayson as Robin; Kid Flash quits .80 2.00
Annual 1(11/82)-Omega Men app. .80 2.00
Annual V2#2(9/83)-1st app. Vigilante in costume .80 2.00
Annual 3 (See Tales of the Teen Titans Annual #3)
nn(11/83-Keebler Co. Giveaway)-In cooperation with "The President's Drug Awareness Campaign"; came in Presidential envelope w/letter from White House (Nancy Reagan) 1.00
nn-(re-issue of above on Mando paper for direct sales market); American Soft Drink Ind. version; I.B.M. Corp. version 1.00

NOTE: ***Perez*** *a-1-4p, 6-34p, 37-40p, Annual 1p, 2p; c-1-12, 13-17p, 18-21, 22p, 23p, 24-37, 38, 39(painted), 40, Annual 1, 2.*

NEW TEEN TITANS, THE (Becomes The New Titans #50 on)
Aug, 1984 - No. 49, Nov, 1988 ($1.25/$1.75; deluxe format)
DC Comics

1-New storyline; Perez-c/a begins 1.20 3.00
2,3: 2-Re-intro Lilith 1.00 2.50
4-10: 5-Death of Trigon. 7-9-Origin Lilith. 8-Intro Kole. 10-Kole joins .80 2.00
11-19: 13,14-Crisis x-over 1.25
20-Robin (Jason Todd) joins; original Teen Titans return .80 2.00
21-49: 37-Begin $1.75-c. 38-Infinity, Inc. x-over. 47-Origin of all Titans; Titans (East & West) pin-up by George Perez. .80 2.00
Annual 1 (9/85)-Intro. Vanguard .80 2.00
Annual 2 (8/86; $2.50): Byrne c/a(p); origin Brother Blood; intro new Dr. Light 1.00 2.50
Annual 3 (11/87)-Intro. Danny Chase .90 2.25
Annual 4 ('88, $2.50)-Perez-c 1.00 2.50

NOTE: ***Buckler*** *c-10.* ***Kelley Jones*** *a-47, Annual 4.* ***Erik Larsen*** *a-33.* ***Orlando*** *c-33p.* ***Perez*** *a-1-5; c-1-7, 19-23, 43.* ***Steacy*** *c-47.*

NEW TERRYTOONS (TV)
6-8/60 - No. 8, 3-5/62; 10/62 - No. 54, 1/79
Dell Publishing Co./Gold Key

1(1960-Dell)-Deputy Dawg, Dinky Duck & Hashimoto San begin (1st app. of each) 4.00 12.00 45.00
2-8(1962) 2.25 6.75 26.00
1(30010-210)(10/62-Gold Key, 84 pgs.)-Heckle & Jeckle begins 5.50 16.50 60.00
2(30010-301)-84 pgs. 4.50 13.50 50.00
3-10 1.75 5.25 14.00
11-20 1.25 3.75 10.00
21-30 1.00 3.00 8.00
31-54 2.00 5.00

NOTE: *Reprints: #4-12, 38, 40, 47. (See March of Comics #379, 393, 412, 435)*

NEW TESTAMENT STORIES VISUALIZED
1946 - 1947
Standard Publishing Co.

"New Testament Heroes–Acts of Apostles Visualized, Book I"
"New Testament Heroes–Acts of Apostles Visualized, Book II"
"Parables Jesus Told" Set.... 8.75 26.25 70.00

NOTE: *All three are contained in a cardboard case, illustrated on front and info about the set.*

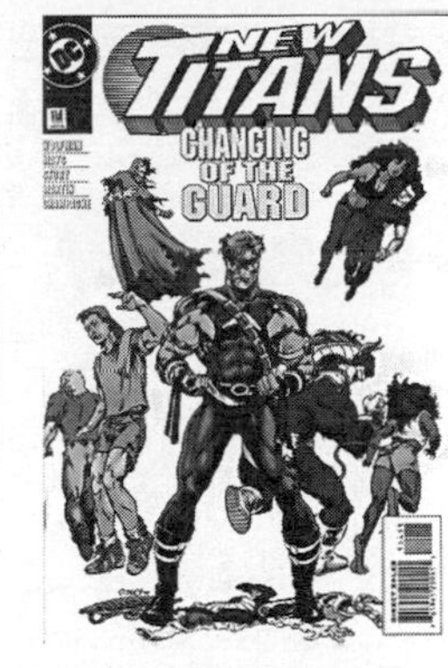
New Titans #114 © DC

New Warriors #51 © MEG

Next Nexus #3 © Mike Baron & Steve Rude

GD25 FN65 NM94

NEW TITANS, THE (Formerly The New Teen Titans)
No. 50, Dec, 1988 - No. 130, Feb, 1996 ($1.75/$2.25)
DC Comics

50-Perez-c/a begins; new origin Wonder Girl 1.20 3.00
51-59: 50-55-Painted-c. 55-Nightwing (Dick Grayson) forces Danny Chase to resign; Batman app. in flashback, Wonder Girl becomes Troia .90 2.25
60-A Lonely Place of Dying Part 2 continues from Batman #440; new Robin tie-in; Timothy Drake app. 1.60 4.00
61-A Lonely Place of Dying Part 4 1.20 3.00
62-65: Deathstroke the Terminator app. 65-Timothy Drake (Robin) app. 1.20 3.00
66-69,71: 71-(44 pgs.)-10th anniversary issue; Deathstroke cameo 1.00 2.50
70-1st Deathstroke solo cover/story 1.00 2.50
72-79-Deathstroke in all: 74-Intro. Pantha. 79-Terra brought back to life; 1 panel cameo Team Titans (1st app.) 1.00 2.50
80-99,101-111: Deathstroke in #80-84,86. 80-2nd full app. Team Titans. 83, 84-Deathstroke kills his son, Jericho. 85-Team Titans app. 86-Deathstroke vs. Nightwing-c/story; last Deathstroke app. 87-New costume Nightwing. 90-92-Parts 2,5,8 Total Chaos (Team Titans) .70 1.75
100-($3.50, 52 pgs.)-Holo-grafx foil-c 1.40 3.50
112-114: 112-Begin $1.95-c. 114-(9/94) .80 2.00
0,115-121: 0-(10/94). 115-(11/94) .80 2.00
122-130: 122-begin $2.25-c. 130-Perez-c .90 2.25
125 (3.50)-wraparound-c 1.40 3.50
Annual 5,6 (1989, 1990, $3.50, 68 pgs.) 1.40 3.50
Annual 7 (1991, $3.50, 68 pgs.)-Armaggedon 2001 x-over; 1st full app. Teen (Team) Titans (new group) 1.40 3.50
Annual 8,9 (1992, '93, $3.50, 68 pgs.): 8-Deathstroke app.; Eclipso app. (minor) 1.40 3.50
Annual 10 (1994, $3.50, 68 pgs.)-Elseworlds story 1.40 3.50
NOTE: ***Perez*** *a-50-55p, 57-60p, 61(layouts); c-50-61, 62-67i, Annual 5i; co-plots-66.*

NEW TV FUNNIES (See New Funnies)

NEW TWO-FISTED TALES, THE
1993 ($4.95, limited series, 52 pgs.)
Dark Horse Comics/Byron Preiss

1-Kurtzman-r & new-a 2.00 5.00
NOTE: ***Eisner*** *c-1i.* ***Kurtzman*** *c-1p, 2.*

NEW WARRIORS, THE (See Thor #411,412)
July, 1990 - No. 75, 1996 ($1.00/$1.25/$1.50)
Marvel Comics

1-Williamson-i; Bagley-c/a(p) in 1-13, Annual 1 1.20 3.00
1-Gold 2nd printing (7/91) 1.00
2-5: 1,3-Guice-c(i). 2-Williamson-c/a(i). .80 2.00
6-10: 7-Punisher cameo (last pg.). 8,9-Punisher app. .80 2.00
11-14: 14-Darkhawk & Namor x-over .80 2.00
15-19: 17-Fantastic Four & Silver Surfer x-over. 19-Gideon (of X-Force) app.; last $1.00-c 1.25
20-24,26-46: 28-Intro Turbo & Cardinal. 31-Cannonball & Warpath app. 42-Nova vs. Firelord. 46-Photo-c 1.25
25-($2.50, 52 pgs.)-Die-cut cover 1.00 2.50
40-($2.25)-Gold foil collector's edition .90 2.25
47-49,51-59, 61-75: 47-Begin $1.50-c; bound-in S-M trading card sheet. 52-12 pg. ad insert. 62-Scarlet Spider-c/app. 70-Spider-Man-c/app. 72-Avengers-c/app. 1.50
50-($2.95, 52 pgs.)-Glow in the dark-c 1.20 3.00
60 ($2.50) 1.00 2.50
Annual 1 (1991, $2.00, 68 pgs.)-Origins all members; 3rd app. X-Force (cont'd from New Mutants Ann. #7 & cont'd in X-Men Ann. #15); x-over before X-Force #1 1.00 2.50
Annual 2 (1992, $2.25, 68 pgs.) .90 2.25
Annual 3 (1993, $2.95, 68 pgs.)-Bagged w/card 1.20 3.00

GD25 FN65 NM94

Annual 4 (1994, $2.95, 68 pgs.) 1.20 3.00

NEW WAVE, THE
6/10/86 - No. 13, 3/87 (#1-8: bi-weekly, 20pgs; #9-13: monthly)
Eclipse Comics

1-8 (50 cents): 1-Origin, concludes #5. 6-Origin Megabyte. 8,9-The Heap returns .50
9-13 ($1.50): 13-Synder-c 1.50
Versus the Volunteers 3-D #1,2(4/87): 1-Snyder-c 1.00 2.50

NEW WORLD (See Comic Books, series I)

NEW WORLDS
1996 - Present ($2.95, 80 pgs., B&W, anthology)
Caliber

1-Mister X & other stories 1.20 3.00

NEW YORK GIANTS (See Thrilling True Story of the Baseball Giants)

NEW YORK STATE JOINT LEGISLATIVE COMMITTEE TO STUDY THE PUBLICATION OF COMICS, THE
1951, 1955
N.Y. State Legislative Document

This document was referenced by Wertham for **Seduction of the Innocent.** Contains numerous repros from comics showing violence, sadism, torture, and sex. 1955 version (196p, No. 37, 2/23/55)-Sold for $180 in 1986.

NEW YORK WORLD'S FAIR (Also see Big Book of Fun & New Book of Fun)
1939, 1940 (100 pgs.; cardboard covers) (DC's 4th & 5th annuals)
National Periodical Publ. GD25 FN65 VF82 NM94

1939-Scoop Scanlon, Superman (blond haired Superman on-c), Sandman, Zatara, Slam Bradley, Ginger Snap by Bob Kane begin; 1st published app. The Sandman (see Adventure #40 for his 1st drawn story); Vincent Sullivan-c; cover background by Guardineer 2200.00 6600.00 14,300.00 24,000.00
(Estimated up to 110 total copies exist, 4 in NM/Mint)
1940-Batman, Hourman, Johnny Thunderbolt, Red, White & Blue & Hanko (by Creig Flessel) app.; Superman, Batman & Robin-c (1st time they all appear together); early Robin app.; 1st Burnley-c/a (per Burnley) 1180.00 3545.00 7670.00 13,000.00
NOTE: *The 1939 edition was published 4/29/39 and released 4/30/39, the day the fair opened, at 25¢, and was first sold only at the fair. Since all other comics were 10¢, it didn't sell. Remaining copies were advertised beginning in the August issues of most DC comics for 25¢, but soon the price was dropped to 15¢. Everyone that sent a quarter through the mail for it received a free Superman #1 or a #2 to make up the dime difference. 15¢ stickers were placed over the 25¢ price. Four variations on the 15¢ stickers are known. The 1940 edition was published 5/11/40 and was priced at 15¢. It was a precursor to World's Best #1.*

NEW YORK: YEAR ZERO
July, 1988 - No. 4, Oct, 1988 ($2.00, B&W, limited series)
Eclipse Comics

1-4 .80 2.00

NEXT MAN
Mar, 1985 - No. 5, Oct, 1985 ($1.50, color, Baxter paper)
Comico

1-5 1.50

NEXT MEN (See John Byrne's...)

NEXT NEXUS, THE
Jan, 1989 - No. 4, April, 1989 ($1.95, limited series, Baxter paper)
First Comics

1-4: Mike Baron scripts & Steve Rude-c/a. .80 2.00

NEXUS (See First Comics Graphic Novel #4, 19 & The Next Nexus)
June, 1981 - No. 6, Mar, 1984; No. 7, Apr, 1985 - No. 80?, May, 1991
(Direct sales only, 36 pgs.; V2#1('83)-printed on Baxter paper
Capital Comics/First Comics No. 7 on

1-B&W version; mag. size; w/double size poster 1.25 3.75 10.00
1-B&W 1981 limited edition; 500 copies printed and signed; same as above

Nexus #16 © Mike Baron & Steve Rude

Nick Fury, Agent of S.H.I.E.L.D. V2 #6 © MEG

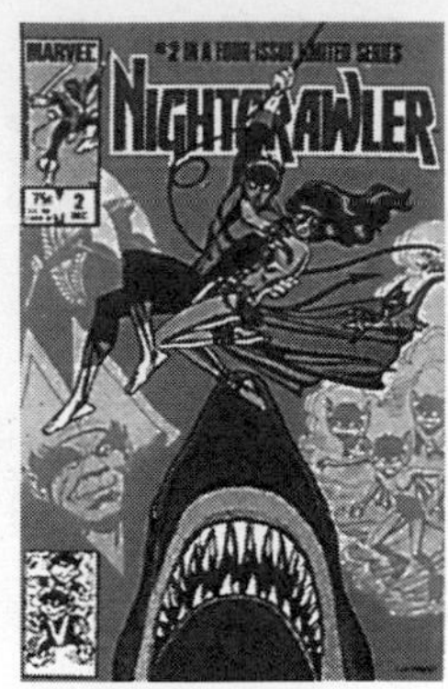

Nightcrawler #2 © MEG

GD25 FN65 NM94

except this version has a 2-pg. poster & a pencil sketch on paperboard by Rude 1.85 5.50 15.00
2-B&W, magazine size 1.00 3.00 8.00
3-B&W, magazine size; contains 33-1/3 rpm record ($2.95 price) 2.00 5.00
V2#1-Color version 1.60 4.00
2-80: 2-Nexus' origin begins. 50-($3.50, 52 pgs.). 67-Snyder-c/a. 73-Begin $2.25-c 1.00 2.50

NOTE: ***Bissette*** *c-V2#29.* ***Giffen*** *c/a-V2#23.* ***Gulacy*** *c-1 (B&W), 2(B&W).* ***Mignola*** *c/a-V2#28.* ***Rude*** *c-3(B&W), V2#1-22, 24-27, 33-36, 39-42, 45-48, 50, 58-60, 75; a-1-3, V2#1-7, 8-16p, 18-22p, 24-27p, 33-36p, 39-42p, 45-48p, 50, 58, 59p, 60.* ***Paul Smith*** *a-V2#37, 38, 43, 44, 51-55p; c-V2#37, 38, 43, 44, 51-55.*

NEXUS: ALIEN JUSTICE
Dec, 1992 - No. 3, Feb, 1993 ($3.95, limited series)
Dark Horse Comics

1-3: Mike Baron scripts & Steve Rude-c/a 1.60 4.00

NEXUS: EXECUTIONER'S SONG
June, 1996 - No. 4, Sept, 1996 ($2.95, limited series)
Dark Horse Comics

1-4: Mike Baron scripts & Steve Rude-c/a 1.20 3.00

NEXUS FILES
1989 ($4.50, color/16pgs. B&W, one-shot, squarebound, 52pgs.)
First Comics

1-New Rude-a; info on Nexus 1.80 4.50

NEXUS: GOD CON
Apr, 1997 - No. 2, May, 1997 ($2.95, limited series)
Dark Horse Comics

1,2-Baron-s/Rude-c/a 1.20 3.00

NEXUS LEGENDS
May, 1989 - No. 23, Mar, 1991 ($1.50, Baxter paper)\
First Comics

1-23: R/1-3(Capital) & early First Comics issues w/new Rude covers #1-6,9,10 1.50

NEXUS MEETS MADMAN (...Special)
May, 1996 ($2.95, one-shot)
Dark Horse Comics

nn-Mike Baron & Mike Allred scripts, Steve Rude-c/a. 1.20 3.00

NEXUS: NIGHTMARE IN BLUE
July, 1997 - No. 4, Oct, 1997 ($2.95, B&W, limited series)
Dark Horse Comics

1-4-Baron-s/Rude-c/a 1.20 3.00

NEXUS: THE WAGES OF SIN
Mar, 1995 - No. 4, June, 1995 ($2.95, limited series)
Dark Horse Comics

1-4 1.20 3.00

NICKEL COMICS
1938 (Pocket size - 7-1/2x5-1/2")(132 pgs.)
Dell Publishing Co.

1- "Bobby & Chip" by Otto Messmer, Felix the Cat artist. Contains some English reprints 53.00 159.00 480.00

NICKEL COMICS
May, 1940 - No. 8, Aug, 1940 (36 pgs.; Bi-Weekly; 5¢)
Fawcett Publications

1-Origin/1st app. Bulletman 300.00 900.00 3000.00
2 103.00 309.00 925.00
3 75.00 225.00 675.00
4-The Red Gaucho begins 67.00 200.00 600.00
5-8: 8-World's Fair-c; Bulletman moved to Master Comics #7 in October 61.00 183.00 550.00

NOTE: ***Beck*** *c-5-8.* ***Jack Binder*** *c-1-4. Bondage c-5. Bulletman c-1-8.*

NICK FURY, AGENT OF SHIELD (See Fury, Marvel Spotlight #31 & Shield)
6/68 - No. 15, 11/69; No. 16, 11/70 - No. 18, 3/71
Marvel Comics Group

1 6.00 18.00 60.00
2-4: 4-Origin retold 3.50 10.50 35.00
5-Classic-c 4.00 12.00 40.00
6,7: 7-Salvador Dali painting swipe 2.50 7.50 22.00
8-11,13: 9-Hate Monger begins, ends #11. 10-Smith layouts/pencil. 11-Smith-c. 13-1st app. Super-Patriot; last 12¢ issue 1.25 3.75 10.00
12-Smith-c/a 1.40 4.15 11.00
14-Begin 15¢ issues 2.40 6.00
15-1st app. & death of Bullseye-c/story(11/69); Nick Fury shot & killed 4.50 13.50 45.00
16-18-(25¢, 52 pgs.)-r/Str. Tales #135-143 1.00 2.50

NOTE: ***Adkins*** *a-3i.* ***Craig*** *a-10i.* ***Sid Greene*** *a-12i.* ***Kirby*** *a-16-18r.* ***Springer*** *a-4, 6, 7, 8p, 9, 10p, 11; c-8, 9.* ***Steranko*** *a(p)-1-3, 5; c-1-7.*

NICK FURY AGENT OF SHIELD (Also see Strange Tales #135)
Dec, 1983 - No. 2, Jan, 1984 (2.00, 52 pgs., Baxter paper)
Marvel Comics

1,2-r/Nick Fury #1-4; new Steranko-c .80 2.00

NICK FURY, AGENT OF S.H.I.E.L.D.
Sept, 1989 - No. 47, May, 1993 ($1.50/$1.75)
Marvel Comics

V2#1-26: 10-Capt. America app. 13-Return of The Yellow Claw. 15-Fantastic Four app. 1.50
27-29-Wolverine-c/stories .80 2.00
30-47: 30,31-Deathlok app. 32-Begin $1.75-c. 36-Cage app. 37-Woodgod c/story. 38-41-Flashes back to pre-Shield days after WWII. 44-Capt. America-c/s. 45-Viper-c/s. 46-Gideon x-over .70 1.75

NOTE: ***Alan Grant*** *scripts-11.* ***Guice*** *a(p)-20-23, 25, 26; c-20-28.*

NICK FURY VS. S.H.I.E.L.D.
June, 1988 - No. 6, Nov, 1988 ($3.50, 52 pgs, deluxe format)
Marvel Comics

1-Steranko-c 1.60 4.00
2-(Low print run) Sienkiewicz-c 1.60 4.00
3-6 1.20 3.00

NICK HALIDAY (Thrill of the Sea)
May, 1956
Argo

1-Daily & Sunday strip-r by Petree 6.50 19.50 45.00

NIGHT AND THE ENEMY (Graphic Novel)
1988 (8-1/2x11") ($11.95, color, 80 pgs.)
Comico

1-Harlan Ellison scripts/Ken Steacy-c/a; r/Epic Illustrated & new-a (1st and 2nd printings) 1.50 4.50 12.00
1-Limited edition ($39.95) 4.00 12.00 40.00

NIGHT BEFORE CHRISTMAS, THE (See March of Comics No. 152)

NIGHT BEFORE CHRISTMASK, THE
Nov, 1994 ($9.95, one-shot)
Dark Horse Comics

nn-Hardcover book; Rick Geary -c/a 1.25 3.75 10.00

NIGHTBREED (See Clive Barker's Nightbreed)

NIGHTCRAWLER
Nov, 1985 - No. 4, Feb, 1986 (Mini-series from X-Men)
Marvel Comics Group

1-4: 1-Cockrum-c/a .80 2.00

NIGHT FORCE

Night Force #12 © DC

Nightmare Infinity © MAL

Nightmare & Casper #3 © Paramount

GD25 FN65 NM94

Dec, 1996 - No. 12, Nov, 1997 ($2.25)
DC Comics

1-12: 1-3-Wolfman-s/Anderson-a(p)
8-"Convergence" part 2 .90 2.25

NIGHT FORCE, THE (See New Teen Titans #21)
Aug, 1982, No. 14, Sept, 1983 (60¢)
DC Comics

1 1.20 3.00
2-14: 13-Origin Baron Winter. 14-Nudity panels .80 2.00
NOTE: ***Colan*** *c/a-1-14p.* ***Giordano*** *c-1i, 2i, 4i, 5i, 7i, 12i.*

NIGHT GLIDER
April, 1993 ($2.95, one-shot)
Topps Comics (Kirbyverse)

1-Kirby c-1, Heck-a; polybagged w/Kirbychrome trading card. 1.20 3.00

NIGHTINGALE, THE
1948 (10¢, 7-1/4x10-1/4", 14 pgs., 1/2 B&W)
Henry H. Stansbury Once-Upon-A-Time Press, Inc.

(Very Rare)-Low distribution; distributed to Westchester County & Bronx, N.Y. only; used in **Seduction of the Innocent**, pg. 312,313 as the 1st and only "good" comic book ever published. Ill. by Dong Kingman; 1,500 words of text, printed on high quality paper & no word balloons. Copyright registered 10/22/48, distributed week of 12/5/48. (By Hans Christian Andersen)
Estimated value........ $200

NIGHT MAN, THE (See Sludge #1)
Oct, 1993 - No. 23, Aug, 1995 ($1.95/$2.50)
Malibu Comics (Ultraverse)

1-($2.50, 48 pgs.)-Rune flip-c/story by B. Smith (3 pgs.) 1.00 2.50
1-Ultra-Limited silver foil-c 1.25 3.75 10.00
2-15, 17: 3-Break-Thru x-over; Freex app. 4-Origin Firearm (2 pgs.) by Chaykin. 6-TNTNT app. 8-1st app. Teknight .80 2.00
16 ($3.50)-flip book (Ultraverse Premiere #11) 1.40 3.50
...:The Pilgrim Conundrum Saga (1/95, $3.95, 68 pgs.)-Strangers app. 1.60 4.00
18-23: 22-Loki-c/a 1.00 2.50
Infinity ($1.50) 1.50
...Vs. Wolverine #0-Kelley Jones-c; mail in offer 1.25 3.75 10.00
NOTE: ***Zeck*** *a-16.*

NIGHT MAN, THE
Sept, 1995 - No.4, Dec, 1995 ($1.50, limited series)
Malibu Comics (Ultraverse)

1-4: Post Black September storyline 1.50

NIGHT MAN, THE /GAMBIT
Mar, 1996 - No. 3, May, 1996 ($1.95, limited series)
Malibu Comics (Ultraverse)

0-Limited Premium Edition 2.00 5.00
1-3: David Quinn scripts in all. 3-Rhiannon discovered to be The Night Man's mother .80 2.00

NIGHTMARE
Summer, 1952 - No. 3, Winter, 1952, 53 (Painted-c)
Ziff-Davis (Approved Comics)/St. John No. 3,4

1-1 pg. Kinstler-a; Tuska-a(2) 43.00 128.00 360.00
2-Kinstler-a-Poe's "Pit & the Pendulum" 34.00 101.00 250.00
3-Kinstler-a 27.00 81.00 200.00

NIGHTMARE (Weird Horrors #1-9) (Amazing Ghost Stories #14 on)
No. 10, Dec, 1953 - No. 13, Aug, 1954
St. John Publishing Co.

10-Reprints Ziff-Davis Weird Thrillers #2 w/new Kubert-c plus 2 pgs. Kinstler-a; Anderson, Colan & Toth-a 44.00 132.00 360.00
11-Krigstein-a; painted-c; Poe adapt., "Hop Frog" 36.00 107.00 250.00
12-Kubert bondage-c; adaptation of Poe's "The Black Cat"; Cannibalism story 29.00 86.00 210.00
13-Reprints Z-D Weird Thrillers #3 with new cover; Powell-a(2), Tuska-a; Baker-c 22.00 66.00 160.00

NIGHTMARE (Magazine)
Dec, 1970 - No. 23, Feb, 1975 (B&W, 68 pgs.)
Skywald Publishing Corp.

1-Everett-a 5.00 15.00 50.00
2-5: 4-Decapitation story 2.50 7.50 24.00
6-Kaluta-a; Jeff Jones photo & interview 2.50 7.50 24.00
7,10 2.25 6.75 18.00
8,9: 8-Features E. C. movie "Tales From the Crypt"; reprints some E.C. comics panels. 9-Wrightson-a 2.50 7.50 24.00
11-20: 12-Excessive gore, severed heads. 20-Byrne's 1st artwork (8/74); severed head-c 2.00 6.00 16.00
21-23: 21-(1974 Summer Special)-Kaluta-a. 22-Tomb of Horror issue. 23-(1975 Winter Special) 2.50 7.50 20.00
Annual 1(1972)-B. Jones-a 2.50 7.50 24.00
Winter Special 1(1973) 2.50 7.50 20.00
Yearbook nn(1974) 2.25 6.75 18.00
NOTE: ***Adkins*** *a-5.* ***Boris*** *c-2, 3, 5 (#4 is not by Boris).* ***Byrne*** *a-20p.* ***Everett*** *a-4, 5.* ***Jeff Jones*** *a-6, 21r(Psycho #6); c-6.* ***Katz*** *a-5.* ***Reese*** *a-4, 5.* ***Wildey*** *a-5, 6, 21, '74 Yearbook.*

NIGHTMARE (Alex Nino's)
1989 ($1.95)
Innovation Publishing

1-Alex Nino-a .80 2.00

NIGHTMARE
Dec, 1994 - No. 4, Mar, 1995 ($1.95, limited series)
Marvel Comics

1-4 .80 2.00

NIGHTMARE & CASPER (See Harvey Hits #71) (Casper & Nightmare #6 on) (See Casper The Friendly Ghost #19)
Aug, 1963 - No. 5, Aug, 1964 (25¢)
Harvey Publications

1-All reprints? 4.80 14.40 48.00
2-5: All reprints? 3.00 9.00 30.00

NIGHTMARE ON ELM STREET, A (See Freddy Krueger's...)

NIGHTMARES (See Do You Believe in Nightmares)

NIGHTMARES
May, 1985 - No. 2, May, 1985 ($1.75, Baxter paper)
Eclipse Comics

1,2 .70 1.75

NIGHTMARE THEATER
Nov, 1997 - No. 4, Nov, 1997 ($2.50, mini-series)
Chaos! Comics

1-4-Horror stories by various; Wrightson-a 1.00 2.50

NIGHTMARK: BLOOD & HONOR
1994 - No. 3, 1994 ($2.50, B&W, mini-series)
Alpha Productions

1,2 1.00 2.50

NIGHTMARK MYSTERY SPECIAL
Jan, 1994 ($2.50, B&W)
Alpha Productions

1 1.00 2.50

NIGHTMASK
Nov, 1986 - No. 12, Oct, 1987
Marvel Comics Group

1-12 .75

NIGHT MASTER

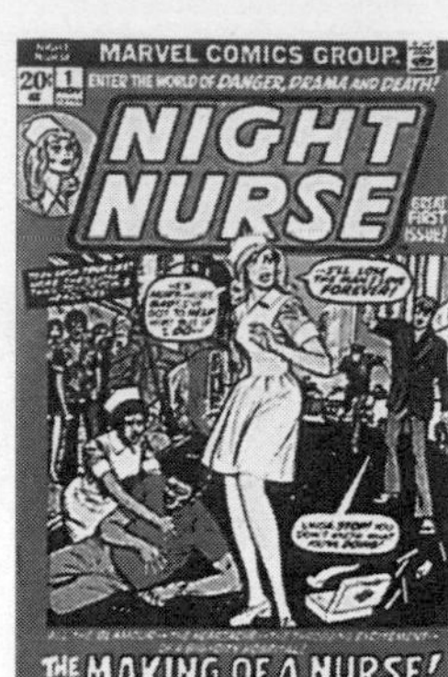

Night Nurse #1 © MEG

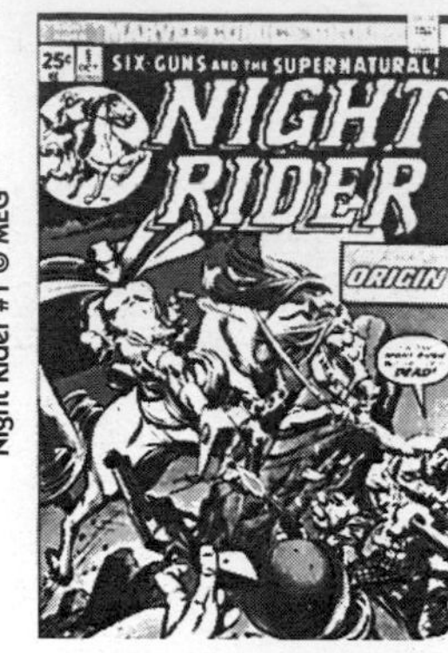

Night Rider #1 © MEG

Nightwing #10 © DC

Feb, 1987 ($1.50, B&W)
Silverwolf

1-Tim Vigil-c/a 1.50

NIGHT MUSIC (See Exlispe Graphic Album Series, The Magic Flute)
Dec, 1984 - No. 7, Feb, 1988 ($1.75, Baxter paper)
Eclipse Comics

1-7: 3-Russell's Jungle Book adapt. 4,5-Pelleas And Melisande (double titled) 6-Salome' (double titled). 7-Red Dog #1 .70 1.75

NIGHT NURSE
Nov, 1972 - No. 4, May, 1973
Marvel Comics Group

1 8.00 24.00 80.00
2-4 4.50 13.50 45.00

NIGHT OF MYSTERY
1953 (no month) (one-shot)
Avon Periodicals

nn-1 pg. Kinstler-a, Hollingsworth-c 36.00 107.00 260.00

NIGHT OF THE GRIZZLY, THE (See Movie Classics)

NIGHTRAVEN: THE COLLECTED STORIES
1991 ($9.95, graphic novel)
Marvel Comics UK, Ltd.

nn-Bolton-r/British Hulk mag.; David Lloyd-c/a 1.25 3.75 10.00

NIGHT RIDER (Western)
Oct, 1974 - No. 6, Aug, 1975
Marvel Comics Group

1: 1-6 reprint Ghost Rider #1-6 (#1-origin) 1.10 3.30 9.00
2-6 2.40 6.00

NIGHT'S CHILDREN: THE VAMPIRE
July, 1995 - No. 2, Aug, 1995 ($2.95, B&W)
Millenium

1,2: Wendy Snow-Lang story & art 1.20 3.00

NIGHTSHADE
Aug, 1997 - Present ($2.50)
No Mercy Comics

1-Mark Williams-s/a 1.00 2.50

NIGHTSTALKERS (Also see Midnight Sons Unlimited)
Nov, 1992 - No. 21, Apr, 1994 ($1.75)
Marvel Comics (Midnight Sons imprint #14 on)

1-($2.75, 52 pgs.)-Polybagged w/poster; part 5 of Rise of the Midnight Sons storyline; Garney/Palmer-c/a begins; Hannibal King, Blade & Frank Drake begin (see Tomb of Dracula for & Dr. Strange) 1.10 2.75
2-9,11-21: 5-Punisher app. 7-Ghost Rider app. 8,9-Morbius app. 14-Spot varnish-c. 14,15-Siege of Darkness Pts 1 & 9 .70 1.75
10-($2.25)-Outer-c is a Darkhold envelope made of black parchment w/gold ink; Midnight Massacre part 1 .90 2.25

NIGHT THRASHER (Also see The New Warriors)
Aug, 1993 - No. 21, Apr, 1995 ($1.75/$1.95)
Marvel Comics

1-($2.95, 52 pgs.)-Red holo-grafx foil-c; origin 1.20 3.00
2-9: 2-Intro Tantrum. 3-Gideon (of X-Force) app. .70 1.75
10-21: 10-Begin $1.95-c; bound-in trading card sheet; Iron Man app. 15-Hulk app. .80 2.00

NIGHT THRASHER: FOUR CONTROL
Oct, 1992 - No. 4, Jan, 1993 ($2.00, limited series)
Marvel Comics

1-4: 1-Hero from New Warriors. 2-Intro Tantrum. 3-Gideon (of X-Force) app. .80 2.00

NIGHTVEIL (Also see Femforce)
Nov, 1984 - No. 7, 1985 ($1.75)
Americomics/AC Comics

1-7 .80 2.00
...'s Cauldron Of Horror 1 (1989, B&W)-Kubert, Powell, Wood-r plus new Nightveil story 1.00 2.50
...'s Cauldron Of Horror 2 (1990, $2.95, B&W, 44pgs)-Pre-code horror-r by Kubert & Powell 1.20 3.00
Special 1 ('88, $1.95)-Kaluta-c .80 2.00
One Shot ('96, $5.95)-Flip book w/ Colt 2.40 6.00

NIGHTWATCH
Apr, 1994 - No. 12, Mar, 1995 ($1.50)
Marvel Comics

1-($2.95)-Collectors edition; foil-c; Ron Lim-c/a begins; Spider-Man app. 1.20 3.00
1-($1.50)-Regular edition 1.50
2-12: 2-Bound-in S-M trading card sheet; 5,6-Venom-c & app. 7,11-Cardiac app. 1.50

NIGHTWING (Also see New Teen Titans, New Titans, Showcase '93 #11,12, Tales of the New Teen Titans & Teen Titans Spotlight)
Sept, 1995 - No. 4, Dec, 1995 ($2.25, limited series)
DC Comics

1-4-Dennis O'Neil story 1.00 2.50

NIGHTWING
Oct, 1996 - Present ($1.95)
DC Comics

1-Chuck Dixon scripts & Scott McDaniel-c/a 2.40 6.00
2 2.00 5.00
3 1.60 4.00
4-19: 6-Robin-c/app. 13-15-Batman app .80 2.00
Annual 1(1997, $3.95) Pulp Heroes 3.95
...Ties That Bind (1997, $12.95, TPB) r/mini-series & Alfred's Return 12.95

NIGHTWING (See Tangent Comics/ Nightwing)

NIGHTWING: ALFRED'S RETURN
July, 1995 ($3.50, one-shot)
DC Comics

1 1.80 4.50

NIGHTWINGS (See DC Science Fiction Graphic Novel)

NIKKI, WILD DOG OF THE NORTH (Disney, see Movie Comics)
No. 1226, Sept, 1961
Dell Publishing Co.

Four Color 1226-Movie, photo-c 4.50 13.50 50.00

1963
Apr, 1993 - No. 6, Oct, 1993 ($1.95, limited series)
Image Comics (Shadowline Ink)

1-6: Alan Moore scripts; Veitch, Bissette & Gibbons-a(p) .80 2.00
1-Gold 1.60 4.00
NOTE: ***Bissette*** *a-2-4;* ***Gibbons*** *a-1i, 2i, 6i; c-2.*

1984 (Magazine) (1994 #11 on)
June, 1978 - No. 10, Jan, 1980 ($1.50)
Warren Publishing Co.

1-Nino-a in all 1.85 5.50 15.00
2-10 1.25 3.75 10.00
NOTE: ***Alacla*** *a-1-3, 5i.* ***Corben*** *a-1-8; c-1, 2.* ***Thorne*** *a-7-10.* ***Wood*** *a-1, 2, 5i.*

1994 (Formerly 1984) (Magazine)
No. 11, Feb, 1980 - No. 29, Feb, 1983
Warren Publishing Co.

11-29: 27-The Warhawks return 1.00 3.00 8.00
NOTE: ***Corben*** *c-26.* ***Nino*** *a-11-19, 20(2), 21, 25, 26, 28; c-21.* ***Redondo*** *c-20.* ***Thorne*** *a-11-14,*

Ninjak #2 © VAL

Nocturnals #2 © Daniel Brereton

Nomad #18 © MEG

GD25 FN65 NM94

17-21, 25, 26, 28, 29.

NINE VOLT
July, 1997 - Present ($2.50)
Image Comics (Top Cow Productions)

1-4 1.00 2.50

NINJAK (See Bloodshot #6, 7 & Deathmate)
Feb, 1994 - No. 26, Nov. 1995 ($2.25/$2.50)
Valiant/Acclaim Comics (Valiant) No. 16 on

1 ($3.50)-Chromium-c; Quesada-c/a(p) in #1-3 1.40 3.50
1-Gold 1.60 4.00
2-13: 3-Batman, Spawn & Random (from X-Factor) app. as costumes at party (cameo). 4-w/bound-in trading card. 5,6-X-O app. .90 2.25
0,00,14-26: 14-(4/95)-Begin $2.50-c. 0-(6/95, $2.50). 00-(6/95, $2.50) 1.00 2.50
Yearbook 1 (1994, $3.95) 1.20 3.00

NINJAK
V2#1, Mar, 1997 -No. 12, Feb, 1998 ($2.50)
Acclaim Comics (Valiant Heroes)

V2#1-12: 1-Intro new Ninjak; 1st app. Brutakon; Kurt Busiek scripts begin; painted variant-c exists. 2-1st app. Karnivor & Zeer. 3-1st app. Gigantik, Shurikai, & Nixie. 4-Origin; 1st app. Yasuiti Motomiya; intro The Dark Dozen; Colin King (original Ninjak) cameo. 9-Copycat-c 1.00 2.50

NINTENDO COMICS SYSTEM
1990 - No. 3, 1990 ($4.95, card stock-c, 68pgs.)
Valiant Comics

1-3: 3-Layton-c (features 8 stories each) 2.00 5.00

NIRA X: ANIME
No. 0, Mar, 1997 ($2.75,one-shot)
Entity Comics

0a,0b-Manga Swimsuit Edition 1.10 2.75

NIRA X: CYBERANGEL
Dec, 1994 - No. 4, 1995 ($2.95, limited series)
Entity Comics

1-Foil logo 1.20 3.00
2-4 ($2.50) 1.00 2.50
4-($6.95)-bagged w/PC Game 1.00 2.80 7.00

NIRA X: CYBERANGEL SERIES II
1995 - No. 4, 1995 ($2.50, limited series)
Entity Comics

1-4 1.00 2.50

NIRA X: CYBERANGEL SERIES III
1995 - No. 3, 1995 ($2.50/$2.95, limited series)
Entity Comics

1,2-($2.50) 1.00 2.50
3-($2.95) 1.20 3.00
1-($6.95)-Bagged w/PC Game 1.00 2.80 7.00

NIRA X-CYNDER: ENDANGERED SPECIES
Feb, 1996 ($2.95, one-shot)
Entity Comics

1-Maus-a(p)/scripts 1.20 3.00
1-($12.95)-Commemorative 13.00

NIRA X: EXODUS
1997 - No. 2, 1997 ($3.00, limited series)
Entity Comics

0-2-Wraparound-c 3.00
0-2-($4.95) Nude-c 4.95

NIRA X: HEATWAVE
July, 1997 ($3.75, one-shot)
Entity Comics

1-Wraparound chromium-c 1.50 3.75

NIRA X: HELLINA
Aug, 1996 ($2.95, one-shot)
Entity Comics

1-Two covers (1 gold foil & 1 red foil) 1.20 3.00
1-($12.95)-Platinum Edition; polybagged w/certificate 13.00

NIRA X: SOUL SKURGE
Nov, 1996 - No. 2, Dec, 1996 ($2.75, B&W, limited series)
Entity Comics

1,2 1.10 2.75

NIRA X UNLIMITED SERIES
No. 0, Mar, 1996 - No. 4, Aug, 1996 ($2.75, B&W)
Entity Comics

0-4 1.10 2.75
Annual 1-($2.75) 1.10 2.75

NOAH'S ARK
1973 (35/49¢)
Spire Christian Comics/Fleming H. Revell Co.

nn-By Al Hartley 1.00

NOCTURNALS, THE
Jan, 1995 - No. 6, Aug, 1995 ($2.95, painted limited series)
Malibu Comics (Bravura)

1-6: Dan Brereton painted-c/a & scripts 1.20 3.00
1-Glow-in-the-Dark premium edition 2.00 5.00

NOCTURNE
June, 1995 - No. 4, Sept. 1995 ($1.50, limited series)
Marvel Comics

1-4 1.50

NO ESCAPE (Movie)
June, 1994 - No. 3, Aug, 1994 ($1.50)
Marvel Comics

1-3: Based on movie 1.50

NOMAD (See Captain America #180)
Nov, 1990 - No. 4, Feb, 1991 ($1.50, limited series)
Marvel Comics

1-4: 1,4-Captain America app. 1.50

NOMAD
V2#1, May, 1992 - No. 25, May, 1994 ($1.75)
Marvel Comics

V2#1-($2.00)-Has gatefold-c w/map/wanted poster 1.00 2.50
2-5: 4-Deadpool x-over. 5-Punisher vs. Nomad-c/story .75 1.80
6-25: 6-Punisher & Daredevil-c/story cont'd in Punisher War Journal #48. 7-Gambit-c/story. 10-Red Wolf app. 21-Man-Thing-c/story. 25-Bound-in trading card sheet .70 1.75

NOMAN (See Thunder Agents)
Nov, 1966 - No. 2, March, 1967 (25¢, 68 pgs.)
Tower Comics

1-Wood/Williamson-c; Lightning begins; Dynamo cameo; Kane-a(p) & Whitney-a 5.00 15.00 50.00
2-Wood-c only; Dynamo x-over; Whitney-a 3.50 10.50 35.00

NONE BUT THE BRAVE (See Movie Classics)

NOODNIK COMICS (See Pinky the Egghead)
Dec, 1953; No. 2, Feb, 1954 - No. 5, Aug, 1954
Comic Media/Mystery/Biltmore

3-D(1953, 25¢; Comic Media)(#1)-Came w/glasses 28.00 84.00 225.00

Not Brand Ecch #1 © MEG

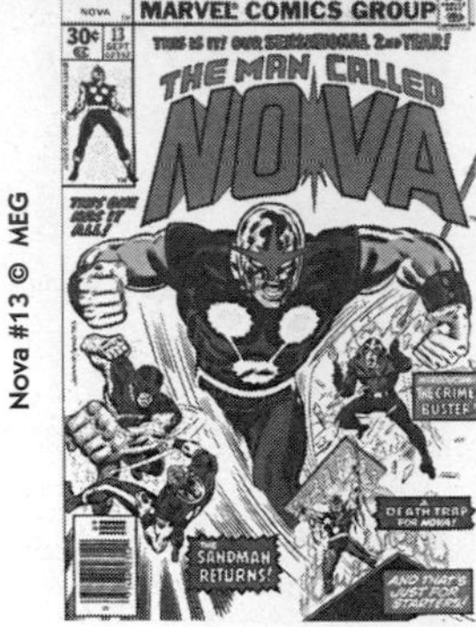

Nova #13 © MEG

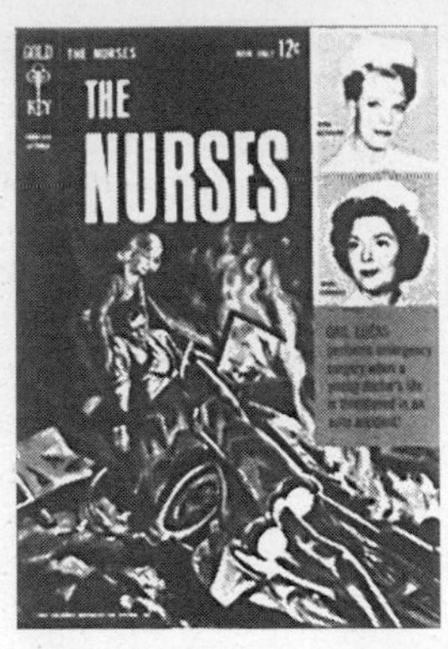

Nurses #3 © GK

GD25 FN65 NM94

2-5 5.70 17.00 35.00

NORMALMAN (See Cerebus the Aardvark #55, 56)
Jan, 1984 - No. 12, Dec, 1985 ($1.70/$2.00)
Aardvark-Vanaheim/Renegade Press #6 on

1-5 ($1.70, color)-Jim Valentino-c/a in all .70 1.70
6-12 ($2.00, B&W): 10-Cerebus cameo; Sim-a (2 pgs.) .80 2.00
...3-D 1 (Annual, 1986, $2.25) .90 2.25

NORMALMAN-MEGATON MAN SPECIAL
Aug, 1994 ($2.50, color)
Image Comics

1 1.00 2.50

NORTH AVENUE IRREGULARS (See Walt Disney Showcase #49)

NORTHSTAR
Apr, 1994 - No. 4, July, 1994 ($1.75, mini-series)
Marvel Comics

1-4: Character from Alpha Flight .70 1.75

NORTH TO ALASKA
No. 1155, Dec, 1960
Dell Publishing Co.

Four Color 1155-Movie, John Wayne photo-c 16.00 47.00 170.00

NORTHWEST MOUNTIES (Also see Approved Comics #12)
Oct, 1948 - No. 4, July, 1949
Jubilee Publications/St. John

1-Rose of the Yukon by Matt Baker; Walter Johnson-a; Lubbers-c
40.00 120.00 325.00
2-Baker-a; Lubbers-c. Ventrilo app. 33.00 99.00 240.00
3-Bondage-c, Baker-a; Sky Chief, K-9 app. 34.00 103.00 250.00
4-Baker-c/a(2 pgs.); Blue Monk & The Desperado app.
34.00 103.00 250.00

NO SLEEP 'TIL DAWN
No. 831, Aug, 1957
Dell Publishing Co.

Four Color 831-Movie, Karl Malden photo-c 5.50 16.50 60.00

NOT BRAND ECHH (Brand Echh #1-4; See Crazy, 1973)
Aug, 1967 - No. 13, May, 1969 (1st Marvel parody book)
Marvel Comics Group (LMC)

1: 1-8 are 12¢ issues 3.00 9.00 30.00
2-4: 3-Origin Thor, Hulk & Capt. America; Monkees, Alfred E. Neuman cameo. 4-X-Men app. 2.25 6.75 18.00
5-8: 5-Origin/intro. Forbush Man. 7-Origin Fantastical-4 & Stuporman. 8-Beatles cameo; X-Men satire 2.25 6.75 18.00
9-13 (25¢, 68 pgs., all Giants) 9-Beatles cameo. 10-All-r; The Old Witch, Crypt Keeper & Vault Keeper cameos. 12,13-Beatles cameo
2.50 7.50 24.00

NOTE: ***Colan** a(p)-4, 5, 8, 9, 13. **Everett** a-1i. **Kirby** a(p)-1, 3, 5-7, 10r; c-1p. **J. Severin** a-1; c-3, 6-8, 11. **M. Severin** a-1-13; c-2, 9, 10, 12, 13. **Sutton** a-3, 4, 5i, 6i, 8, 9, 10r, 11-13; c-5. Archie satire in #9. Avengers satire in #8, 12.*

NOTHING CAN STOP THE JUGGERNAUT
1989 ($3.95)
Marvel Comics

1-r/Amazing Spider-Man #229 & 230 1.60 4.00

NO TIME FOR SERGEANTS (TV)
No. 914, July, 1958; Feb-Apr, 1965 - No. 3, Aug-Oct, 1965
Dell Publishing Co.

Four Color 914 (Movie)-Toth-a; Andy Griffith photo-c 9.00 27.00 100.00
1(2-4/65)-3 (TV): Photo-c 3.60 11.00 40.00

NOVA (The Man Called... No. 22-25)(See New Warriors)
Sept, 1976 - No. 25, May, 1979
Marvel Comics Group

1-Origin/1st app. Nova 1.20 3.00
2-11: 4-Thor x-over 1.20 3.00
12-Spider-Man x-over 1.00 2.50
13-(Regular 30¢ edition)(9/77) Intro Crime-Buster. 1.20 3.00
13-(35¢-c, limited distribution) 1.50 4.50 12.00
14-24: 14-Last 30¢ issue. 18-Yellow Claw app. 19-Wally West (Kid Flash) cameo 1.20 3.00
25-Last issue 1.60 4.00

NOTE: ***Austin** c-21i, 23i. **John Buscema** a(p)-1-3, 8, 21; c-1p, 2, 15. **Infantino** a(p)-15-20, 22-25; c-17-20, 21p, 23p, 24p. **Kirby** c-4p, 5, 7. **Nebres** c-25i. **Simonson** a-23i.*

NOVA
Jan, 1994 - June, 1995 ($1.75/$1.95)(Started as 4-part mini-series)
Marvel Comics

1-($2.95, 52 pgs.)-Collector's Edition w/gold foil-c; new costume for Nova
1.20 3.00
1-($2.25, 52 pgs.)-Newsstand Edition w/o foil-c .90 2.25
2-4: 3-Spider-Man-c/story. 5-Stan Lee app. .70 1.75
5-18: 5-Begin $1.95-c; bound-in card sheet. 13-Firestar & Night Thrasher app.14-Darkhawk .80 2.00

NOW AGE ILLUSTRATED (See Pendulum Illustrated Classics)

NTH MAN THE ULTIMATE NINJA (See Marvel Comics Presents 25)
Aug, 1989 - No. 16, Sept, 1990 ($1.00)
Marvel Comics

1-7,9-16-Ninja mercenary 1.00
8-Dale Keown's 1st Marvel work (1/90, pencils) .80 2.00

NUCLEUS (Also see Cerebus)
May, 1979 ($1.50, B&W, adult fanzine)
Heiro-Graphic Publications

1-Contains "Demonhorn" by Dave Sim; early app. of Cerebus The Aardvark (4 pg. story) 2.80 8.40 28.00

NUKLA
Oct-Dec, 1965 - No. 4, Sept, 1966
Dell Publishing Co.

1-Origin & 1st app. Nukla (super hero) 2.80 8.40 28.00
2,3 1.85 5.50 15.00
4-Ditko-a, c(p) 2.60 7.80 26.00

NURSE BETSY CRANE (Formerly Teen Secret Diary)
V2#12, Aug, 1961 - V2#27, Mar, 1964 (See Soap Opera Romances)
Charlton Comics

V2#12-27 1.25 3.75 10.00

NURSE HELEN GRANT (See The Romances of...)

NURSE LINDA LARK (See Linda Lark)

NURSERY RHYMES
No. 10, July-Aug, 1951 - No. 2, Winter, 1951 (Painted-c)
Ziff-Davis Publ. Co. (Approved Comics)

10 (#1), 2: 10-Howie Post-a 11.30 34.00 90.00

NURSES, THE (TV)
April, 1963 - No. 3, Oct, 1963 (Photo-c: #1,2)
Gold Key

1 2.50 7.50 24.00
2,3 2.00 6.00 16.00

NUTS! (Satire)
March, 1954 - No. 5, Nov, 1954
Premiere Comics Group

1-Hollingsworth-a 22.00 66.00 175.00
2,4,5: 5-Capt. Marvel parody 15.50 47.00 125.00
3-Drug "reefers" mentioned 16.00 49.00 130.00

NUTS (Magazine) (Satire)

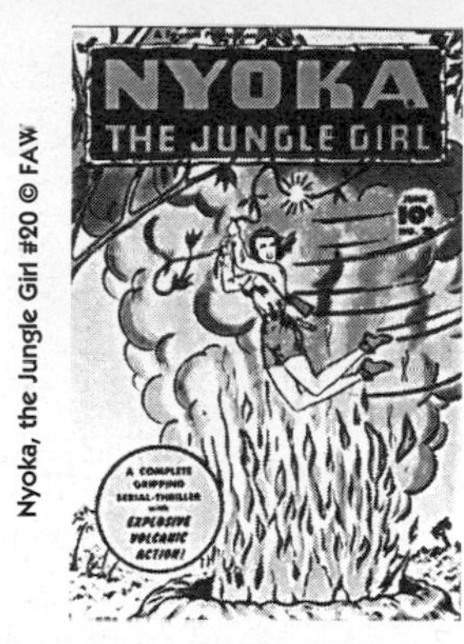

Nyoka, the Jungle Girl #20 © FAW

Oblivion #2 © Comico

Offcastes #2 © MEG

Feb, 1958 - No. 2, April, 1958
Health Knowledge

	GD25	FN65	NM94
1	4.50	13.50	45.00
2	3.50	10.50	35.00

NUTS & JOLTS
No. 22, 1941
Dell Publishing Co.

	GD25	FN65	NM94
Large Feature Comic 22	9.00	26.00	95.00

NUTSY SQUIRREL (Formerly Hollywood Funny Folks)(See Comic Cavalcade)
#61, 9-10/54 - #69, 1-2/56; #70, 8-9/56 - #71, 10-11/56; #72, 11/57
National Periodical Publications

	GD25	FN65	NM94
61-Mayer-a; Grossman-a in all	11.30	34.00	90.00
62-72: Mayer a-62,65,67-72	8.50	26.00	60.00

NUTTY COMICS
Winter, 1946 (Funny animal)
Fawcett Publications

	GD25	FN65	NM94
1-Capt. Kidd story; 1 pg. Wolverton-a	10.00	30.00	80.00

NUTTY COMICS
1945 - No. 8, June-July, 1947
Home Comics (Harvey Publications)

	GD25	FN65	NM94
nn-Helpful Hank, Bozo Bear & others (funny animal)	6.50	19.50	45.00
2-4	4.25	13.00	28.00
5-8: 5-Rags Rabbit begins(1st app.); infinity-c	4.00	11.00	22.00

NUTTY LIFE (Formerly Krazy Life #1; becomes Wotalife Comics #3 on)
No. 2, Summer, 1946
Fox Features Syndicate

	GD25	FN65	NM94
2	7.85	23.50	55.00

NYOKA, THE JUNGLE GIRL (Formerly Jungle Girl; see The Further Adventures of..., Master Comics #50 & XMas Comics)
No. 2, Winter, 1945 - No. 77, June, 1953 (Movie serial)
Fawcett Publications

	GD25	FN65	NM94
2	44.00	132.00	400.00
3	25.00	75.00	200.00
4,5	21.00	64.00	170.00
6-10	15.50	47.00	125.00
11,13,14,16-18-Krigstein-a: 17-Sam Spade ad by Lou Fine	15.50	47.00	125.00
12,15,19,20	14.00	41.00	110.00
21-30: 25-Clayton Moore photo-c?	8.75	26.25	65.00
31-40	7.15	21.50	50.00
41-50	5.70	17.00	40.00
51-60	5.00	15.00	30.00
61-77	4.15	12.50	25.00

NOTE: *Photo-c from movies 25, 30-70, 72, 75-77. Bondage c-4, 5, 7, 8, 14, 24.*

NYOKA, THE JUNGLE GIRL (Formerly Zoo Funnies; Space Adventures #23 on)
No. 14, Nov, 1955 - No. 22, Nov, 1957
Charlton Comics

	GD25	FN65	NM94
14	7.85	23.50	55.00
15-22	5.70	17.00	40.00

OAKLAND PRESS FUNNYBOOK, THE
9/17/78 - 4/13/80 (16 pgs.) (Weekly)
Full color in comic book form; changes to tabloid size 4/20/80-on
The Oakland Press

	GD25	FN65	NM94
Contains Tarzan by Manning, Marmaduke, Bugs Bunny, etc. (low distribution); 9/23/79 - 4/13/80 contain Buck Rogers by Gray Morrow & Jim Lawrence		.80	2.00

OAKY DOAKS (See Famous Funnies #190)
July, 1942 (One Shot)
Eastern Color Printing Co.

	GD25	FN65	NM94
1	28.00	83.00	220.00

OBIE
1953 (6¢)
Store Comics

	GD25	FN65	NM94
1		1.60	4.00

OBLIVION
Aug, 1995 - Present ($2.50)
Comico

	GD25	FN65	NM94
1-3: 1-Art Adams-c. 2-(1/96)-Polybagged w/gaming card. 3-(5/96)-Darrow-c		1.00	2.50

OBNOXIO THE CLOWN
April, 1983 (one-shot) (Character from Crazy Magazine)
Marvel Comics Group

	GD25	FN65	NM94
1-Vs. the X-Men			1.00

OCCULT FILES OF DR. SPEKTOR, THE
Apr, 1973 - No. 24, Feb, 1977; No. 25, May, 1982 (Painted-c #1-24)
Gold Key/Whitman No. 25

	GD25	FN65	NM94
1-1st app. Lakota; Baron Tibor begins	1.80	5.50	20.00
2-5	1.00	3.00	8.00
6-10: 8-Dracula app.		2.40	6.00
11-13,15-25: 11-1st app. Spektor as Werewolf. 25-Reprints		1.60	4.00
14-Dr. Solar app.	1.50	4.50	15.00
9(Modern Comics reprint, 1977)(exist?)	1.80	5.50	20.00

NOTE: *Also see Dan Curtis, Golden Comics Digest 33, Gold Key Spotlight, Mystery Comics Digest 5, & Spine Tingling Tales.*

ODELL'S ADVENTURES IN 3-D (See Adventures in 3-D)

OFFCASTES
July, 1993 - No. 3, Sept, 1993 ($1.95, limited series)
Marvel Comics (Epic Comics/Heavy Hitters)

	GD25	FN65	NM94
1-3: Mike Vosburg-c/a/scripts in all		.80	2.00

OFFICIAL CRISIS ON INFINITE EARTHS INDEX, THE
Mar, 1986 ($1.75)
Independent Comics Group (Eclipse)

	GD25	FN65	NM94
1		.70	1.75

OFFICIAL CRISIS ON INFINITE EARTHS CROSSOVER INDEX, THE
July, 1986 ($1.75)
Independent Comics Group (Eclipse)

	GD25	FN65	NM94
1-Perez-c.		.70	1.75

OFFICIAL DOOM PATROL INDEX, THE
Feb, 1986 - No. 2, Mar, 1986 ($1.50, limited series)
Independent Comics Group (Eclipse)

	GD25	FN65	NM94
1,2: Byrne-c.			1.50

OFFICIAL HANDBOOK OF THE CONAN UNIVERSE (See Handbook of...)

OFFICIAL HANDBOOK OF THE MARVEL UNIVERSE, THE
Jan, 1983 - No. 15, May, 1984 (Limited series)
Marvel Comics Group

	GD25	FN65	NM94
1-Lists Marvel heroes & villains (letter A)		1.20	3.00
2 (B-C)		1.00	2.50
3-5: 3-(C-D). 4-(D-G). 5-(H-J)		.80	2.00
6-9: 6-(K-L). 7-(M). 8-(N-P); Punisher-c. 9-(Q-S)			1.50
10-15: 10-(S). 11-(S-U). 12-(V-Z); Wolverine-c. 13,14-Book of the Dead. 15-Weaponry catalogue			1.25

NOTE: ***Bolland** a-8. **Byrne** c/a(p)-1-14; c-15p. **Grell** a-6, 9. **Kirby** a-1, 3. **Layton** a-2, 5, 7. **Mignola** a-3, 4, 5, 6, 8, 12. **Miller** a-4-6, 8, 10. **Nebres** a-3, 4, 8. **Redondo** a-3, 4, 8, 13, 14. **Simonson** a-1, 4, 6-13. **Paul Smith** a-1-12. **Starlin** a-5, 7, 8, 10, 13, 14. **Steranko** a-8p. **Zeck**-2-14.*

Official Hawkman Index #2 © DC

Oh My Goddess #1 © DH

O.K. Comics #2 © UFS

OFFICIAL HANDBOOK OF THE MARVEL UNIVERSE, THE
Dec, 1985 - No. 20, Feb, 1988 ($1.50, maxi-series)
Marvel Comics Group

	GD25	FN65	NM94
V2#1-Byrne-c		1.20	3.00
2-5: 2,3-Byrne-c		.80	2.00
6-10			1.50
11-20			1.50
Trade paperback Vol. 1-10 ($6.95)	1.00	2.80	7.00

NOTE: ***Art Adams*** *a-7, 8, 11, 12, 14.* ***Bolland*** *a-8, 10, 13.* ***Buckler*** *a-1, 3, 5, 10.* ***Buscema*** *a-1, 5, 8, 9, 10, 13, 14.* ***Byrne*** *a-1-14; c-1-11.* ***Ditko*** *a-1, 2, 4, 6, 7, 11, 13. a-7, 11.* ***Mignola*** *a-2, 4, 9, 11, 13.* ***Miller*** *a-2, 4, 12.* ***Simonson*** *a-1, 2, 4-13, 15.* ***Paul Smith*** *a-1-5, 7-12, 14.* ***Starlin*** *a-6, 8, 9, 12, 16.* ***Zeck*** *a-1-4, 6, 7, 9-14, 16.*

OFFICIAL HANDBOOK OF THE MARVEL UNIVERSE, THE
July, 1989 - No. 8, Mid-Dec, 1990 ($1.50, limited series, 52 pgs.)
Marvel Comics

	GD25	FN65	NM94
V3#1-8: 1-McFarlane-a(2 pgs.)			1.50

OFFICIAL HAWKMAN INDEX, THE
Nov, 1986 - No. 2, Dec, 1986 ($2.00)
Independent Comics Group

	GD25	FN65	NM94
1,2		.80	2.00

OFFICIAL JUSTICE LEAGUE OF AMERICA INDEX, THE
April, 1986 - No. 8, Mar, 1987 ($2.00, Baxter)
Independent Comics Group (Eclipse)

	GD25	FN65	NM94
1-8: 1,2-Perez-c.		.80	2.00

OFFICIAL LEGION OF SUPER-HEROES INDEX, THE
Dec, 1986 - No. 5, 1987 ($2.00, limited series)(No Official in Title #2 on)
Independent Comics Group (Eclipse)

	GD25	FN65	NM94
1-5: 4-Mooney-c		.80	2.00

OFFICIAL MARVEL INDEX TO MARVEL TEAM-UP
Jan, 1986 - No. 6, 1986 ($1.25, limited series)
Marvel Comics Group

	GD25	FN65	NM94
1-6			1.30

OFFICIAL MARVEL INDEX TO THE AMAZING SPIDER-MAN
Apr, 1985 - No. 9, Dec, 1985 ($1.25, limited series)
Marvel Comics Group

	GD25	FN65	NM94
1 ($1.00)-Byrne-c.		1.00	2.50
2-9: 5,6,8,9-Punisher-c.		.80	2.00

OFFICIAL MARVEL INDEX TO THE AVENGERS, THE
V2#1, Oct, 1994 - V2#6, 1995 ($1.95, limited series)
Marvel Comics

	GD25	FN65	NM94
V2#1-#6		.80	2.00

OFFICIAL MARVEL INDEX TO THE FANTASTIC FOUR
Dec, 1985 - No. 5, 1986 ($1.25, limited series)
Marvel Comics Group

	GD25	FN65	NM94
1-5: 1-Byrne-c			1.50

OFFICIAL MARVEL INDEX TO THE X-MEN, THE
V2#1, Apr, 1994 - V2#5, 1994 ($1.95, limited series)
Marvel Comics

	GD25	FN65	NM94
V2#1-5: 1-Covers X-Men #1-51. 2-Covers #52-122,Special #1,2,Giant-Size #1,2. 3-Byrne-c; covers #123-177, Annuals 3-7, Spec. Ed. #1. 4-Covers Uncanny X-Men #178-234, Annuals 8-12. 5-Covers #235-287, Annuals 13-15		.80	2.00

OFFICIAL SOUPY SALES COMIC (See Soupy Sales)

OFFICIAL TEEN TITANS INDEX, THE
Aug, 1985 - No. 5, 1986 ($1.50, limited series)
Independent Comics Group (Eclipse)

	GD25	FN65	NM94
1-5			1.50

OFFICIAL TRUE CRIME CASES (Formerly Sub-Mariner #23; All-True Crime Cases #26 on)
No. 24, Fall, 1947 - No. 25, Winter, 1947-48
Marvel Comics (OCI)

	GD25	FN65	NM94
24(#1)-Burgos-a; Syd Shores-c	19.00	58.00	140.00
25-Syd Shores-c; Kurtzman's "Hey Look"	16.00	47.00	110.00

OF SUCH IS THE KINGDOM
1955 (15¢, 36 pgs.)
George A. Pflaum

	GD25	FN65	NM94
nn-Reprints from 1951 Treasure Chest	2.00	5.00	10.00

O.G. WHIZ (See Gold Key Spotlight #10)
2/71 - No. 6, 5/72; No. 7, 5/78 - No. 11, 1/79 (No. 7: 52 pgs.)
Gold Key

	GD25	FN65	NM94
1,2-John Stanley scripts	5.00	15.00	55.00
3-6(1972)	2.50	7.50	28.00
7-11(1978-79)-Part-r: 9-Tubby app.	1.50	4.50	12.00

OH, BROTHER! (Teen Comedy)
Jan, 1953 - No. 5, Oct, 1953
Stanhall Publ.

	GD25	FN65	NM94
1-By Bill Williams	5.70	17.00	35.00
2-5	4.00	11.00	22.00

OH MY GODDESS! (Manga)
Aug, 1994 - No. 6, Jan, 1995($2.50, B&W, limited series)
Dark Horse Comics

	GD25	FN65	NM94
1-6		1.60	4.00

OH MY GODDESS! PART II (Manga)
Feb, 1995 - No. 9, Sept, 1995 ($2.50, B&W, limited series)
Dark Horse Comics

	GD25	FN65	NM94
1-9		1.20	3.00

OH MY GODDESS! PART III (Manga)
Nov, 1995 - No. 11, Sept, 1996 ($2.95, B&W, limited series)
Dark Horse Comics

	GD25	FN65	NM94
1-11		1.20	3.00

OH MY GODDESS! PART IV (Manga)
Dec, 1996 - No. 8, July, 1997 ($2.95, B&W, limited series)
Dark Horse Comics

	GD25	FN65	NM94
1-11		1.20	3.00

OH MY GODDESS! PART V (Manga)
Sept, 1997 - Present ($2.95, B&W, limited series)
Dark Horse Comics

	GD25	FN65	NM94
1,2,4			2.95
3-($3.95, 48 pgs.)			3.95

OH SUSANNA (TV)
No. 1105, June-Aug, 1960 (Gale Storm)
Dell Publishing Co.

	GD25	FN65	NM94
Four Color 1105-Toth-a, photo-c	12.00	35.00	130.00

OKAY COMICS
July, 1940
United Features Syndicate

	GD25	FN65	NM94
1-Captain & the Kids & Hawkshaw the Detective reprints	36.00	108.00	300.00

O.K. COMICS
July, 1940 - No. 2, Oct, 1940
United Features Syndicate/Hit Publications

	GD25	FN65	NM94
1-Little Giant (w/super powers), Phantom Knight, Sunset Smith, & The Teller Twins begin	61.00	183.00	550.00
2 (Rare)-Origin Mister Mist by Chas. Quinlan	61.00	183.00	550.00

Omac #3 © DC

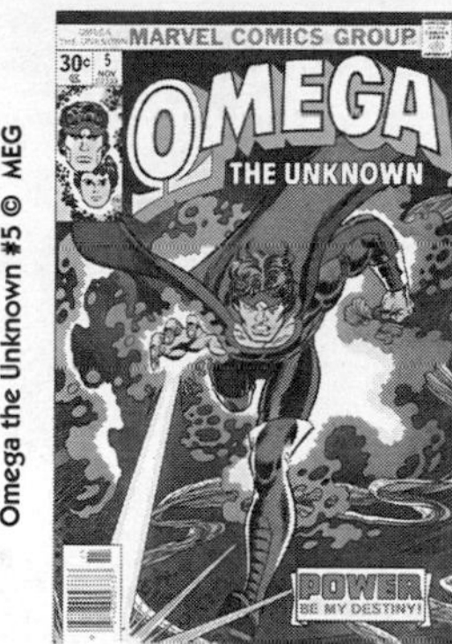

Omega the Unknown #5 © MEG

101 Ways to End the Clone Saga #1 © MEG

OKLAHOMA KID
June, 1957 - No. 4, 1958
Ajax/Farrell Publ.

	GD25	FN65	NM94
1	8.50	26.00	60.00
2-4	5.70	17.00	35.00

OKLAHOMAN, THE
No. 820, July, 1957
Dell Publishing Co.

	GD25	FN65	NM94
Four Color 820-Movie, photo-c	9.00	27.00	100.00

OKTANE
Aug, 1995 - Nov, 1995($2.50, color, limited series)
Dark Horse Comics

	GD25	FN65	NM94
1-4-Gene Ha-a		1.00	2.50

OLD GLORY COMICS
1944 (Giveaway)
Chesapeake & Ohio Railway

	GD25	FN65	NM94
nn-Capt. Fearless reprint	5.70	17.00	35.00

OLD IRONSIDES (Disney)
No. 874, Jan, 1958
Dell Publishing Co.

	GD25	FN65	NM94
Four Color 874-Movie w/Johnny Tremain	5.50	16.50	60.00

OLD YELLER (Disney, see Movie Comics, and Walt Disney Showcase #25)
No. 869, Jan, 1958
Dell Publishing Co.

	GD25	FN65	NM94
Four Color 869-Movie, photo-c	4.50	13.50	50.00

OMAC (One Man Army; ...Corps. #4 on; also see Kamandi #59 & Warlord)
Sept-Oct, 1974 - No. 8, Nov-Dec, 1975
National Periodical Publications

	GD25	FN65	NM94
1-Origin	1.25	3.75	10.00
2-8: 8-2 pg. Neal Adams ad		2.40	6.00

NOTE: ***Kirby** a-1-8p; c-1-7p. **Kubert** c-8. See Cancelled Comic Cavalcade.*

OMAC: ONE MAN ARMY CORPS
1991 - No. 4, 1991 ($3.95, B&W, mini-series, mature readers, 52 pgs.)
DC Comics

	GD25	FN65	NM94
Book One - Four: John Byrne-c/a & scripts		1.60	4.00

O'MALLEY AND THE ALLEY CATS
April, 1971 - No. 9, Jan, 1974 (Disney)
Gold Key

	GD25	FN65	NM94
1	1.75	5.25	14.00
2-9	1.10	3.30	9.00

OMEGA ELITE
1987 ($1.25)
Blackthorne Publishing

	GD25	FN65	NM94
1-Starlin-c			1.25

OMEGA MEN, THE (See Green Lantern #141)
Dec, 1982 - No. 38, May, 1986 ($1.00/$1.50; Baxter paper)
DC Comics

	GD25	FN65	NM94
1			1.50
2,4,6-8,11-18,21-36,38: 2-Origin Broot. 7-Origin The Citadel. 26,27-Alan Moore scripts. 30-Intro new Primus. 31-Crisis x-over. 34,35-Teen Titans x-over			1.00
3-1st app. Lobo (5 pgs.)(6/83); Lobo-c		1.20	3.00
5,9-2nd & 3rd app. Lobo (cameo, 2 pgs. each)		.80	2.00
10-1st full Lobo story		1.20	3.00
19-Lobo cameo			1.50
20-2nd full Lobo story		1.20	3.00
37-1st solo Lobo story (8 pg. back-up by Giffen)		.80	2.00
Annual 1(11/84, 52 pgs.), 2(11/85)			1.50

NOTE: ***Giffen** c/a-1-6p. **Morrow** a-24r. **Nino** c/a-16, 21; a-Annual 1i.*

OMEGA THE UNKNOWN
March, 1976 - No. 10, Oct, 1977
Marvel Comics Group

	GD25	FN65	NM94
1-1st app. Omega		1.60	4.00
2-(Regular 25¢ edition)-Hulk-c/story.		1.60	4.00
2-(30¢-c, limited distribution)	2.00	6.00	16.00
3,8: 3-Electro-c/story. 8-1st app. 2nd Foolkiller (Greg Salinger), 1 panel only (cameo)		1.60	4.00
4-7,10		1.20	3.00
9-(Regular 30¢ edition)(7/77)-1st full app. 2nd Foolkiller		1.60	4.00
9-(35¢-c, limited distribution)	2.00	6.00	16.00

NOTE: ***Kane** c(p)-3, 5, 8, 9. **Mooney** a-1-3, 4p, 5, 6p, 7, 8i, 9, 10.*

OMEN
1989 - No. 3?, 1989 ($2.00, B&W, mature)
Northstar Publishing

	GD25	FN65	NM94
1-Tim Vigil-c/a in all		.80	2.00
1, (2nd printing), 2,3		.80	2.00

OMNI MEN
1987 - No. 3, 1987 ($1.25)
Blackthorne Publishing

	GD25	FN65	NM94
1-3			1.25

ONE, THE
July, 1985 - No. 6, Feb, 1986 (Limited series, mature)
Marvel Comics (Epic Comics)

	GD25	FN65	NM94
1-6: Post nuclear holocaust super-hero. 2-Intro The Other			1.50

ONE-ARM SWORDSMAN, THE
1987 - No. 12, 1990 ($2.75/$1.80, 52pgs.)
Victory Prod./Lueng's Publications #4 on

	GD25	FN65	NM94
1-3 ($2.75)		1.10	2.75
4-12: 4-6-$1.80-c. 7-12-$2.00-c			1.80

ONE HUNDRED AND ONE DALMATIANS (Disney, see Cartoon Tales, Movie Comics, and Walt Disney Showcase #9, 51)
No. 1183, Mar, 1961
Dell Publishing Co.

	GD25	FN65	NM94
Four Color 1183-Movie	9.00	27.00	100.00

101 DALMATIONS (Movie)
1991 (52 pgs., graphic novel)
Disney Comics

	GD25	FN65	NM94
nn-($4.95, direct sales)-r/movie adaptation & more		2.00	5.00
1-($2.95, newsstand edition)		1.20	3.00

101 WAYS TO END THE CLONE SAGA (See Spider-Man)
Jan, 1997 ($2.50, one-shot)
Marvel Comics

	GD25	FN65	NM94
1		1.00	2.50

100 PAGES OF COMICS
1937 (Stiff covers, square binding)
Dell Publishing Co.

	GD25	FN65	NM94
101(Found on back cover)-Alley Oop, Wash Tubbs, Capt. Easy, Og Son of Fire, Apple Mary, Tom Mix, Dan Dunn, Tailspin Tommy, Doctor Doom	128.00	384.00	1150.00

100 PAGE SUPER SPECTACULAR (See DC 100 Page...)

100% TRUE?
Summer 1996 - Present ($4.95, B&W)
DC Comics (Paradox Press)

	GD25	FN65	NM94
1,2-Reprints stories from various Paradox Press books.		2.00	5.00

$1,000,000 DUCK (See Walt Disney Showcase #5)

On the Spot © FAW

Open Space #1 © MEG

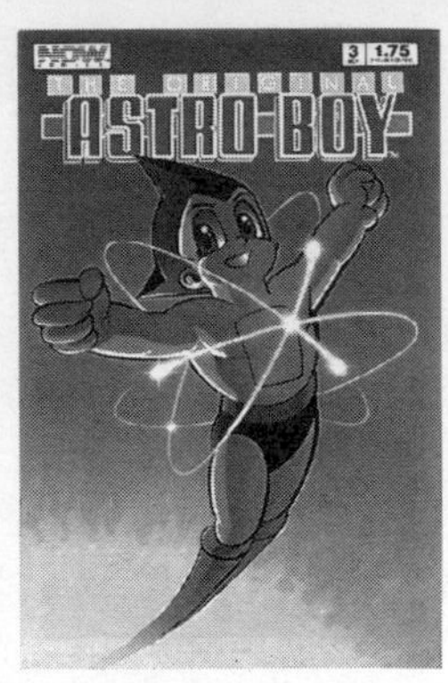

The Original Astro Boy #3 © Suzuki Assoc. Int.

GD25 FN65 NM94

ONE MILLION YEARS AGO (Tor #2 on)
Sept, 1953
St. John Publishing Co.

1-Origin & 1st app. Tor; Kubert-c/a; Kubert photo inside front cover — 15.50 47.00 125.00

ONE SHOT (See Four Color...)

1001 HOURS OF FUN
No. 13, 1943
Dell Publishing Co.

Large Feature Comic 13 (nn)-Puzzles & games; by A.W. Nugent. This book was bound as #13 w/Large Feature Comics in publisher's files — 16.00 49.00 180.00

ONE TRICK RIP OFF, THE (See Dark Horse Presents)

ONSLAUGHT: EPILOGUE
Feb, 1997 ($2.95, one-shot)
Marvel Comics

1-Hama-s/Green-a; Xavier-c; Bastion-app. — 1.20 3.00

ONSLAUGHT: MARVEL
Oct, 1996 ($3.95, one-shot)
Marvel Comics

1-Conclusion to Onslaught x-over; wraparound-c — 1.00 2.80 7.00

ONSLAUGHT: X-MEN
Aug, 1996 ($3.95, one-shot)
Marvel Comics

1-Mark Waid & Scott Lobdell script; Fantastic Four & Avengers app.; Xavier as Onslaught — 2.00 5.00
1-Variant-c — 1.50 4.50 12.00

ON STAGE
No. 1336, Apr-June, 1962
Dell Publishing Co.

Four Color 1336-Not by Leonard Starr — 3.60 11.00 40.00

ON THE AIR
1947 (Giveaway, paper-c)
NBC Network Comic

nn-(Rare) — 21.00 64.00 170.00

ON THE DOUBLE (Movie)
No. 1232, Sept-Nov, 1961
Dell Publishing Co.

Four Color 1232 — 3.60 11.00 40.00

ON THE ROAD WITH ANDRAE CROUCH
1973, 1977 (39¢)
Spire Christian Comics (Fleming H. Revell)

nn — 1.00

ON THE SPOT (Pretty Boy Floyd...)
Fall, 1948
Fawcett Publications

nn-Pretty Boy Floyd photo on-c; bondage-c — 27.00 81.00 200.00

ONYX OVERLORD
Oct, 1992 - No. 4, Jan, 1993 ($2.75, mini-series)
Marvel Comics (Epic Comics)

1-4: Moebius scripts — 1.10 2.75

OPEN SPACE
Mid-Dec, 1989 - No. 4, Aug, 1990 ($4.95, bi-monthly, 68 pgs.)
Marvel Comics

1-4: 1-Bill Wray-a; Freas-c — 2.00 5.00

OPERATION BIKINI (See Movie Classics)

GD25 FN65 NM94

OPERATION BUCHAREST (See The Crusaders)

OPERATION CROSSBOW (See Movie Classics)

OPERATION: KNIGHTSTRIKE (See Knightstrike)
May, 1995 - No.3, July, 1995 ($2.50)
Image Comics (Extreme Studios)

1-3 — 1.00 2.50

OPERATION PERIL
Oct-Nov, 1950 - No. 16, Apr-May, 1953 (#1-5: 52 pgs.)
American Comics Group (Michel Publ.)

1-Time Travelers, Danny Danger (by Leonard Starr) & Typhoon Tyler (by Ogden Whitney) begin — 33.00 99.00 235.00
2 — 20.00 60.00 145.00
3-5: 3-Horror story. 5-Sci/fi-c/story — 17.00 51.00 125.00
6-12-Last Time Travelers. 6,8,9-Sci/fi-c — 14.00 43.00 105.00
13-16: All war format — 7.50 22.50 48.00

NOTE: ***Starr** a-2, 5. **Whitney** a-1, 2, 5-10, 12; c-1, 3, 5, 8, 9.*

OPERATION: STORMBREAKER
Aug, 1997 ($3.95, one-shot)
Acclaim Comics (Valiant Heroes)

1-Waid/Augustyn-s, Braithwaite-a — 3.95

OPTIC NERVE
Apr, 1995 - Present ($2.95, bi-annual)
Drawn and Quarterly

1,2: Adrian Tomine-c/a/scripts in all — 2.00 5.00
3,4 — 1.20 3.00
32 Stories-($9.95, trade paperback)-r/Optic Nerve mini-comics — 10.00
32 Stories-($29.95, hardcover)-r/Optic Nerve mini-comics; signed & numbered — 30.00

ORAL ROBERTS' TRUE STORIES (Junior Partners #120 on)
1956 (no month) - No. 119, 7/59 (15¢)(No #102: 25¢)
TelePix Publ. (Oral Roberts' Evangelistic Assoc./Healing Waters)

V1#1(1956)-(Not code approved)- "The Miracle Touch" — 15.50 47.00 125.00
102-(Only issue approved by code, 10/56) — 9.50 28.00 75.00
103-119: 115-(114 on inside) — 6.50 19.50 45.00

NOTE: *Also see Happiness & Healing For You.*

ORANGE BIRD, THE
No date (1980) (36 pgs.; in color; slick cover)
Walt Disney Educational Media Co.

nn-Included with educational kit on foods — 1.00
...in Nutrition Adventures nn (1980) — .60
...and the Nutrition Know-How Revue nn (1983) — .60

ORBIT
1990 - No. 3, 1990 ($4.95, 52 pgs., squarebound)
Eclipse Books

1-3: Reprints from Isaac Asimov's Science Fiction Magazine; 1-Dave Stevens-c, Bolton-a. 3-Bolton-c/a, Yeates-a — 2.00 5.00

ORIENTAL HEROES
Aug, 1988 - No. 26, 1991 ($1.50/$1.95, 68pgs.)
Jademan Comics

1-9 ($1.50) — 1.50
10-26 ($1.95) — .80 2.00

ORIGINAL ASTRO BOY, THE
Sept, 1987 - No. 19, 1989 ($1.50/$1.75)
Now Comics

1-All have Ken Steacy painted-c/a — .80 2.00
2,3: 3-Begin $1.75-c — .70 1.75
4-19 — 1.50

Original Ghost Rider Rides Again #4 © MEG

Oscar Comics #3 © MEG

Others #0 © Aegis Entertainment

GD25 FN65 NM94

ORIGINAL BLACK CAT, THE
Oct. 6, 1988 - No. 3, 1989 ($2.00, limited series)
Recollections

1-3: Elias-r; 1-Bondage-c. 2-M. Anderson-c .80 2.00

ORIGINAL DICK TRACY, THE
Sept, 1990 - No. 5, 1991 ($1.95, bi-monthly, 68pgs.)
Gladstone Publishing

1-5: 1-Vs. Pruneface. 2-& the Evil influence; begin $2.00-c .80 2.00

NOTE: *#1 reprints strips 7/16/43 - 9/30/43. #2 reprints strips 12/1/46 - 2/2/47. #3 reprints 8/31/46 - 11/14/46. #4 reprints 9/17/45 - 12/23/45. #5 reprints 6/10/46 - 8/28/46.*

ORIGINAL DOCTOR SOLAR, MAN OF THE ATOM, THE
Apr, 1995 ($2.95, one-shot)
Valiant

1-Reprints Doctor Solar, Man of the Atom #1,5; Bob Fugitani-r; Paul Smith-c; afterword by Seaborn Adamson 1.20 3.00

ORIGINAL E-MAN AND MICHAEL MAUSER, THE
Oct, 1985 - No. 7, April, 1986 ($1.75, Baxter paper)
First Comics

1-Has r-/Charlton's E-Man, Vengeance Squad .80 2.00
2-6: 2-Shows #4 in indicia by mistake .75 1.80
7 ($2.00, 44pgs.)-Staton-a .80 2.00

ORIGINAL GHOST RIDER, THE
July, 1992 - No. 20, Feb, 1994 ($1.75)
Marvel Comics

1-20: 1-7-r/Marvel Spotlight #5-11 by Ploog w/new-c. 3-New Phantom Rider (former Night Rider) back-ups begin by Ayers. 4-Quesada-c(p). 8-Ploog-c. 8,9-r/Ghost Rider #1,2. 10-r/Marvel Spotlight #12. 11-18,20-r/Ghost Rider #3-12. 19-r/Marvel Two-in-One #8 .70 1.75

ORIGINAL GHOST RIDER RIDES AGAIN, THE
July, 1991 - No. 7, Jan, 1992, ($1.50, limited series, 52 pgs.)
Marvel Comics

1-Reprints Ghost Rider #68(origin),69 w/covers 1.50
2-7: Reprints G.R. #70-81 w/covers 1.50

ORIGINAL MAGNUS ROBOT FIGHTER, THE
Apr, 1995 ($2.95, one-shot)
Valiant

1-Reprints Magnus, Robot Fighter 4000 #2; Russ Manning-r; Rick Leonardi-c; afterword by Seaborn Adamson 1.20 3.00

ORIGINAL NEXUS GRAPHIC NOVEL (See First Comics Graphic Novel #19)

ORIGINAL SHIELD, THE
Apr, 1984 - No. 4, Oct, 1984
Archie Enterprises, Inc.

1-4: 1,2-Origin Shield; Ayers p-1-4, Nebres c-1,2 1.00

ORIGINAL SWAMP THING SAGA, THE (See DC Special Series #2, 14, 17, 20)

ORIGINAL TUROK, SON OF STONE, THE
Apr, 1995 - No. 2, May, 1995 ($2.95, limited series)
Valiant

1,2: 1-Reprints Turok, Son of Stone #24,25,42; Alberto Gioletti-r; Rags Morales-c; afterword by Seaborn Adamson. 2-Reprints Turok, Son of Stone #24,33; Gioletti-r; Mike McKone-c 1.20 3.00

ORIGIN OF GALACTUS (See Fantastic Four #48-50)
Feb, 1996 ($2.50, one-shot)
Marvel Comics

1-Lee & Kirby reprints w/pin-ups 1.00 2.50

ORIGIN OF THE DEFIANT UNIVERSE, THE
Feb, 1994 ($1.50, 20 pgs., one-shot)
Defiant Comics

1-David Lapham, Adam Pollina & Alan Weiss-a; Weiss-c 1.50

NOTE: *The comic was originally published as Defiant Genesis and was distributed at the 1994 Philadelphia ComicCon.*

ORIGINS OF MARVEL COMICS (See Fireside Book Series)

ORION (Manga)
Sept, 1992 - No. 6, July, 1993 ($2.95/$3.95, B&W, bimonthly, limited series)
Dark Horse Comics

1,2,6-($3.95, squarebound): 1-Masamune Shirow-c/a/s in all 1.60 4.00
4,5-($2.95) 1.20 3.00

OSBORNE JOURNALS (See Spider-Man titles)
Feb, 1997 ($2.95, one-shot)
Marvel Comics

1-Hotz-c/a 2.95

OSCAR COMICS (Formerly Funny Tunes; Awful...#11 & 12)
(Also see Cindy Comics)
No. 24, Spring, 1947 - No. 10, Apr, 1949; No. 13, Oct, 1949
Marvel Comics

24(#1, Spring, 1947) 11.50 34.00 85.00
25(#2, Sum, 1947)-Wolverton-a plus Kurtzman's "Hey Look" 14.00 43.00 110.00
26(#3)-Same as regular #3 except #26 was printed over in black ink with #3 appearing on-c below the over print 8.50 26.00 60.00
3-9,13: 8-Margie app. 8.50 26.00 60.00
10-Kurtzman's "Hey Look" 10.00 30.00 70.00

OSWALD THE RABBIT (Also see New Fun Comics #1)
No. 21, 1943 - No. 1268, 12-2/61-62 (Walter Lantz)
Dell Publishing Co.

	GD25	FN65	NM94
Four Color 21(1943)	46.00	139.00	510.00
Four Color 39(1943)	33.00	98.00	360.00
Four Color 67(1944)	16.00	48.00	175.00
Four Color 102(1946)-Kelly-a, 1 pg.	14.00	41.00	150.00
Four Color 143,183	8.00	25.00	90.00
Four Color 225,273	4.50	13.50	50.00
Four Color 315,388	3.60	11.00	40.00
Four Color 458,507,549,593	2.75	8.00	30.00
Four Color 623,697,792,894,979,1268	1.80	5.50	20.00

OSWALD THE RABBIT (See The Funnies, March of Comics #7, 38, 53, 67, 81, 95, 111, 126, 141, 156, 171, 186, New Funnies & Super Book #8, 20)

OTHERS, THE
1995 - No. 3, 1995 ($2.50)
Image Comics (Shadowline Ink)

0 ($1.00)-16 pg. preview 1.00
1-3 1.00 2.50

OTIS GOES TO HOLLYWOOD
Apr, 1997 - No.2, May, 1997 ($2.95, B&W, mini-series)
Dark Horse Comics

1,2-Fingerman-c/s/a 1.20 3.00

OUTCAST, THE
Dec, 1995 ($2.50, one-shot)
Valiant

1-Breyfogle-a. 1.00 2.50

OUR ARMY AT WAR (Becomes Sgt. Rock #302 on; also see Army At War)
Aug, 1952 - No. 301, Feb, 1977
National Periodical Publications

	GD25	FN65	NM94
1	139.00	417.00	1250.00
2	64.00	192.00	575.00
3,4: 4-Krigstein-a	47.00	141.00	425.00
5-7	39.00	117.00	350.00

Our Army at War #9 © DC

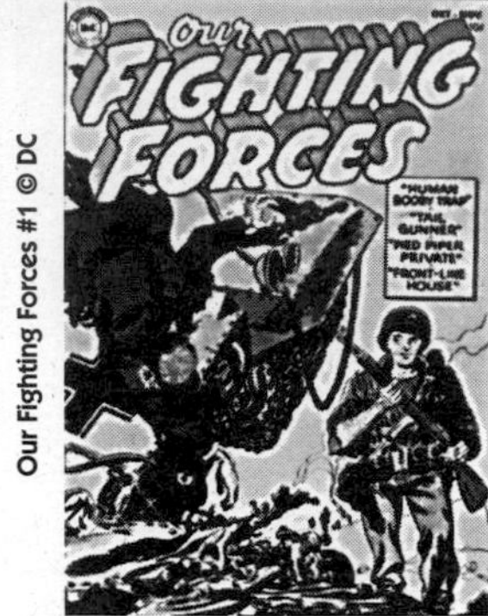

Our Fighting Forces #1 © DC

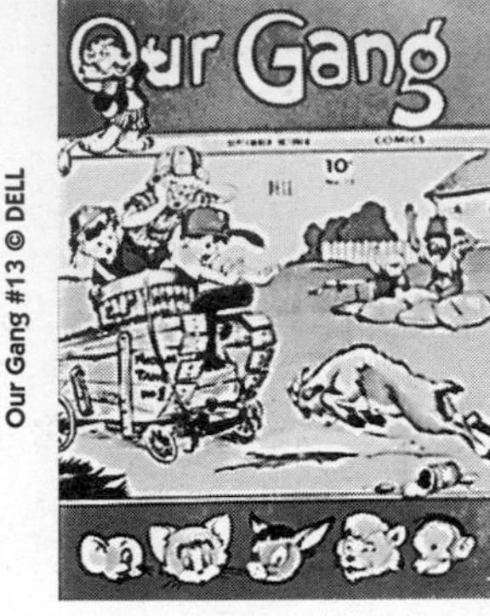

Our Gang #13 © DELL

	GD25	FN65	NM94
8-11,14-Krigstein-a	36.00	108.00	310.00
12,15-20	33.00	98.00	260.00
13-Krigstein-c/a; flag-c	36.00	108.00	320.00
21-31: Last precode (2/55)	22.00	66.00	175.00
32-40	19.00	56.00	150.00
41-60: 51-1st S.A. issue	15.50	47.00	125.00
61-70	13.00	39.00	105.00
71-80	11.30	34.00	90.00
81-1st Sgt. Rock app. (4/59) by Andru & Esposito in Easy Co. story	177.00	531.00	2300.00
82-Sgt. Rock cameo in Easy Co. story (6 panels)	45.00	135.00	550.00
83-1st Kubert Sgt. Rock (6/59)	69.00	217.00	825.00
84,86-90	20.00	60.00	200.00
85-Origin & 1st app. Ice Cream Soldier	28.00	84.00	280.00
91-All Sgt. Rock issue	43.00	130.00	525.00
92-100: 95-1st app. Bulldozer; 1st app. Zack. 99-Sgt. Rock-c by Kubert	12.50	38.00	125.00
101-120: 101-1st app. Buster. 111-1st app. Wee Willie & Sunny. 113-1st app. Wildman & Jackie Johnson. 115-Rock revealed as orphan; 1st x-over Mlle Marie. 118-Sunny dies	8.00	24.00	80.00
121-127,129-150: 126-1st app. Canary; grey tone-c. 127-1st app. Little Sure Shot. 140-All Sgt. Rock issue	5.00	15.00	50.00
128-Training & origin Sgt. Rock	18.00	54.00	180.00
151-Intro. Enemy Ace by Kubert (2/65)	30.00	90.00	300.00
152,154,156,157,159-163,165-170: 157-2 pg. pin-up. 162,163-Viking Prince x-over in Sgt. Rock	4.20	12.60	42.00
153-2nd app. Enemy Ace (4/65)	12.50	38.00	125.00
155-3rd app. Enemy Ace (6/65)(see Showcase)	8.00	24.00	80.00
158-Origin & 1st app. Iron Major(9/65), formerly Iron Captain	5.00	15.00	50.00
164-Giant G-19	7.00	21.00	70.00
171-176,178-181	3.20	9.60	32.00
177-(80 pg. Giant G-32)	4.50	13.50	45.00
182,183,186-Neal Adams-a. 186-Origin retold	3.40	10.20	34.00
184,185,187-189,191-199: 184-Wee Willie dies. 189-Intro. The Teen-age Underground Fighters of Unit 3	2.60	7.80	26.00
190-(80 pg. Giant G-44)	4.00	12.00	40.00
200-12 pg. Rock story told in verse; Evans-a	3.00	9.00	30.00
201-Krigstein-r/#14	2.00	6.00	16.00
202,204-215: 204,205-All reprints; no Sgt. Rock	2.00	6.00	16.00
203-(80 pg. Giant G-56)-All-r, Sgt. Rock story	3.50	10.50	35.00
216,229-(80 pg. Giants G-68, G-80): 216-Has G-58 on-c by mistake	3.50	10.50	35.00
217-228,230-239,241	1.60	4.85	13.00
240-Neal Adams-a	2.50	7.50	20.00
242-(50¢ issue DC-9)-Kubert-c (see DC 100 pg. Super Spect. #9 for price)			
243,245-269,271-274,276-279,281-301	1.25	3.75	10.00
244-N.Adams-a?	1.85	5.50	15.00
270,275-(100 pgs.)	2.50	7.50	24.00
280-(68 pgs.)-200th app. Sgt. Rock; reprints Our Army at War #81,83	2.25	6.75	18.00

NOTE *Alcala a-251. Drucker a-27, 67, 68, 79, 82, 83, 96, 164, 177, 203, 212, 243r, 244, 269r, 275r, 280r. Evans a-165-175, 200, 266, 269, 270, 274, 276, 278, 280. Glanzman a-218, 220, 222, 223, 225, 227, 230-232, 238-241, 244, 247, 248, 256-259, 261, 265-267, 271, 282, 283, 298. Grandenetti c-91. Grell a-287. Heath a-50, 164, & most 176-281. Kubert a-38, 59, 67, 68 & most issues from 83-165, 233, 236, 267, 275, 300; c-84, 280. Maurer a-233, 237, 239, 240, 45, 280, 284, 288, 290, 291, 295. Severin a-236, 252, 265, 267, 269r, 272. Toth a-235, 241, 254. Wildey a-283-285, 287p. Wood a-249.*

OUR FIGHTING FORCES
Oct-Nov, 1954 - No. 181, Sept-Oct, 1978
National Periodical Publications/DC Comics

	GD25	FN65	NM94
1-Grandenetti-c/a	80.00	240.00	720.00
2	38.00	113.00	340.00
3-Kubert-c; last precode issue (3/55)	36.00	108.00	290.00
4,5	28.00	83.00	220.00
6-9: 7-1st S.A. issue	23.00	68.00	180.00
10-Wood-a	24.00	71.00	190.00
11-20: 20-Grey tone-c (4/57)	15.00	45.00	150.00
21-30	10.00	30.00	100.00
31-40	9.50	28.50	95.00
41-Unknown Soldier tryout	11.50	34.00	115.00
42-44	8.50	25.50	85.00
45-Gunner & Sarge begins, end #94	28.00	85.00	285.00
46	11.50	34.00	115.00
47	8.50	25.50	85.00
48,50	6.50	19.50	65.00
49-1st Pooch	9.50	28.50	95.00
51-64: 51-Grey tone-c. 64-Last 10¢ issue	6.00	18.00	60.00
65-70	4.20	12.60	42.00
71-80: 71-Grey tone-c	2.50	7.50	24.00
81-90	2.50	7.50	22.00
91-98,100: 95-Devil-Dog begins, ends 98.	1.85	5.50	15.00
99-Capt. Hunter begins, ends #106	2.50	7.50	20.00
101-122: 106-Hunters Hellcats begin. 116-Mlle. Marie app. 121-Intro. Heller	1.85	5.50	15.00
123-Losers (Capt. Storm, Gunner & Sarge, Johnny Cloud) begin	3.50	10.50	35.00
124-132	1.50	4.50	12.00
133-137 (Giants). 134-Toth-a	1.85	5.50	15.00
138-150: 146-Toth-a	1.25	3.75	10.00
151-162-Kirby a(p)	1.50	4.50	12.00
163-180	1.00	3.00	8.00
181-Last issue	1.25	3.75	10.00

NOTE: *N. Adams c-147. Drucker a-28, 37, 39, 42-44, 49, 53, 133r. Evans a-149, 164-174, 177 181. Glanzman a-125-128, 132, 134, 138-141, 143, 144. Heath a-2, 16, 18, 28, 41, 44, 49, 114, 135-138r; c-51. Kirby a-151-162p; c-152-159. Kubert c/a in many issues. Maurer a-135. Redondo a-166. Severin a-123-130, 131i, 132-150.*

OUR FIGHTING MEN IN ACTION (See Men In Action)

OUR FLAG COMICS
Aug, 1941 - No. 5, April, 1942
Ace Magazines

	GD25	FN65	NM94
1-Captain Victory, The Unknown Soldier (intro.) & The Three Cheers begin	178.00	534.00	1600.00
2-Origin The Flag (patriotic hero); 1st app?	92.00	276.00	825.00
3-5: 5-Intro & 1st app. Mr. Risk	74.00	222.00	665.00

NOTE: *Anderson a-1, 4. Mooney a-1, 2; c-2.*

OUR GANG COMICS (With Tom & Jerry #39-59; becomes Tom & Jerry #60 on; based on film characters)
Sept-Oct, 1942 - No. 59, June, 1949
Dell Publishing Co.

	GD25	FN65	NM94
1-Our Gang & Barney Bear by Kelly, Tom & Jerry, Pete Smith, Flip & Dip, The Milky Way begin (all 1st app.)	77.00	232.00	850.00
2-Benny Burro begins (#2 by Kelly)	41.00	123.00	450.00
3-5	27.00	82.00	300.00
6-Bumbazine & Albert only app. by Kelly	41.00	123.00	450.00
7-No Kelly story	21.00	63.00	230.00
8-Benny Burro begins by Barks	52.00	157.00	575.00
9-Barks-a(2): Benny Burro & Happy Hound; no Kelly story	47.00	142.00	520.00
10-Benny Burro by Barks	34.00	101.00	370.00
11-1st Barney Bear & Benny Burro by Barks (5-6/44); Happy Hound by Barks	47.00	142.00	520.00
12-20	21.00	63.00	230.00
21-30: 30-X-Mas-c	14.00	41.00	150.00
31-36-Last Barks issue	9.00	29.00	105.00
37-40	5.00	15.00	55.00
41-50	3.60	11.00	42.00
51-57	3.00	9.00	32.00
58,59-No Kelly art or Our Gang stories	2.50	7.50	28.00

Our Love #2 © MEG

Outcasts #11 © DC

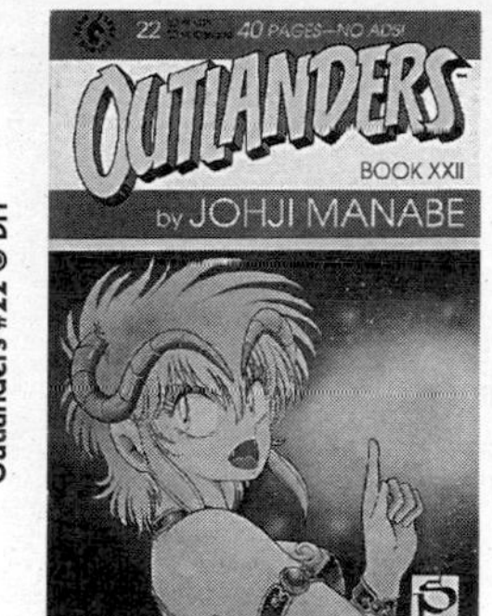

Outlanders #22 © DH

GD25 FN65 NM94

NOTE: ***Barks** art in part only. **Barks** did not write Barney Bear stories #30-34. (See March of Comics #3, 26). Early issues have photo back-c.*

OUR LADY OF FATIMA
3/11/55 (15¢) (36 pgs.)
Catechetical Guild Educational Society

	GD25	FN65	NM94
395	3.00	7.50	15.00

OUR LOVE (True Secrets #3 on? or Romantic Affairs #3 on?)
Sept, 1949 - No. 2, Jan, 1950
Marvel Comics (SPC)

	GD25	FN65	NM94
1-Photo-c	10.00	30.00	75.00
2-Photo-c	6.70	20.00	45.00

OUR LOVE STORY
Oct, 1969 - No. 38, Feb, 1976
Marvel Comics Group

	GD25	FN65	NM94
1	2.50	7.50	24.00
2-4,6-13	1.50	4.50	12.00
5-Steranko-a	3.50	10.50	35.00
14-New story by Gary Fredrich & Tarpe' Mills	2.00	6.00	16.00
15-37: 27-Colan/Everett-a(r?); Kirby/Colletta-r	1.00	3.00	8.00
38-Last issue	1.50	4.50	12.00

NOTE: ***J. Buscema** a-1-3, 5-7, 9, 13r, 16r, 19r(2), 21r, 22r(2), 23r, 34r, 35r; c-11, 13, 16, 22, 23, 24, 27, 35. **Colan** a-3-6, 21r(#6), 22r, 23r(#3), 24r(#4), 27; c-19. **Katz** a-17. **Weiss** a-16, 17, 29r(#17).*

OUR MISS BROOKS
No. 751, Nov, 1956
Dell Publishing Co.

	GD25	FN65	NM94
Four Color 751-Photo-c	7.00	22.00	80.00

OUR SECRET (Exciting Love Stories)(Formerly My Secret)
No. 4, Nov, 1949 - No. 8, Jun, 1950
Superior Comics Ltd.

	GD25	FN65	NM94
4-Kamen-a; spanking scene	13.00	39.00	100.00
5,6,8	8.00	24.00	50.00
7-Contains 9 pg. story intended for unpublished Ellery Queen #5; lingerie panels	10.00	30.00	60.00

OUTBREED 999
May, 1994 - No. 6, 1994 ($2.95)
Blackout Comics

	GD25	FN65	NM94
1-6: 4-1st app. of Extreme Violet in 7 pg. backup story		1.20	3.00

OUTCASTS
Oct, 1987 - No. 12, Sept, 1988 ($1.75, limited series)
DC Comics

	GD25	FN65	NM94
1-12: John Wagner & Alan Grant scripts in all		.75	1.80

OUTER LIMITS, THE (TV)
Jan-Mar, 1964 - No. 18, Oct, 1969 (All painted-c)
Dell Publishing Co.

	GD25	FN65	NM94
1	8.00	25.00	90.00
2	4.50	13.50	50.00
3-10	3.60	11.00	40.00
11-18: 17-Reprints #1. 18-r/#2	2.75	8.00	30.00

OUTER SPACE (Formerly This Magazine Is Haunted, 2nd Series)
No. 17, May, 1958 - No. 25, Dec, 1959; Nov, 1968
Charlton Comics

	GD25	FN65	NM94
17-Williamson/Wood style art; not by them (Sid Check?)	10.00	30.00	80.00
18-20-Ditko-a	15.00	45.00	120.00
21-25: 21-Ditko-c	8.75	26.25	70.00
V2#1(11/68)-Ditko-a, Boyette-c	3.50	10.50	35.00

OUTER SPACE BABES, THE
Feb, 1994 ($2.95)
Silhouette Studios

	GD25	FN65	NM94
V3#1		1.20	3.00

OUTLANDERS (Manga)
Dec, 1988 - No. 33, Sept,1991 ($2.00-$2.50, B&W, 44pgs.)
Dark Horse Comics

	GD25	FN65	NM94
1-7: Japanese Sci-fi manga		.80	2.00
8-21 ($2.25)		.90	2.25
22-33 ($2.50)		1.00	2.50

OUTLAW (See Return of the...)

OUTLAW FIGHTERS
Aug, 1954 - No. 5, Apr, 1955
Atlas Comics (IPC)

	GD25	FN65	NM94
1-Tuska-a	9.50	28.00	75.00
2-5: 5-Heath-c/a, 7 pgs.	6.50	19.50	45.00

NOTE: ***Heath** c/a-5. **Maneely** c-2. **Pakula** a-2. **Reinman** a-2. **Tuska** a-1, 2.*

OUTLAW KID, THE (1st Series; see Wild Western)
Sept, 1954 - No. 19, Sept, 1957
Atlas Comics (CCC No. 1-11/EPI No. 12-29)

	GD25	FN65	NM94
1-Origin; The Outlaw Kid & his horse Thunder begin; Black Rider app.	19.00	56.00	150.00
2-Black Rider app.	9.50	28.00	75.00
3-7,9: 3-Wildey-a(3)	8.75	26.25	65.00
8-Williamson/Woodbridge-a, 4 pgs.	8.75	26.25	70.00
10-Williamson-a	8.75	26.25	65.00
11-17,19: 13-Baker text illo. 15-Williamson text illo (unsigned)	5.70	17.00	40.00
18-Williamson/Mayo-a	7.15	21.50	50.00

NOTE: ***Berg** a-4, 7, 13. **Maneely** c-1-3, 5-8, 11-13, 15, 16, 18. **Pakula** a-3. **Severin** c-10, 17, 19. **Shores** a-1. **Wildey** a-1(3), 2-8, 10, 11, 12(4), 13(4), 15-19(4 each); c-4.*

OUTLAW KID, THE (2nd Series)
Aug, 1970 - No. 30, Oct, 1975
Marvel Comics Group

	GD25	FN65	NM94
1-Reprints; 1-Orlando-r, Wildey-r(3)	2.00	6.00	16.00
2,3,8-10: 2-Reprints. 3,9-Williamson-a(r). 8-Double size; Crandall-r. 10-Origin	1.50	4.50	12.00
4-7	1.25	3.75	10.00
11-20: new-a in #10-16	1.00	3.00	8.00
21-30: 27-Origin-r/#10		2.40	6.00

NOTE: ***Ayers** a-10, 27r. **Berg** a-7, 25r. **Everett** a-2(2 pgs.). **Gil Kane** c-10, 11, 15, 27r, 28. **Roussos** a-10i, 27i(r). **Severin** c-1, 9, 20, 25. **Wildey** r-1-4, 6-9, 19-22, 25, 26. **Williamson** a-28r. **Woodbridge/Williamson** a-9r.*

OUTLAWS
Feb-Mar, 1948 - No. 9, June-July, 1949
D. S. Publishing Co.

	GD25	FN65	NM94
1-Violent & suggestive stories	25.00	75.00	190.00
2-Ingels-a; Baker-a	25.00	75.00	190.00
3,5,6: 3-Not Frazetta. 5-Sky Sheriff by Good app. 6-McWilliams-a	11.00	33.00	80.00
4-Orlando-a	13.00	39.00	95.00
7,8-Ingels-a in each	19.00	58.00	140.00
9-(Scarce)-Frazetta-a (7 pgs.)	40.00	120.00	320.00

NOTE: *Another #3 was printed in Canada with **Frazetta** art "Prairie Jinx," 7 pgs.*

OUTLAWS, THE (Formerly Western Crime Cases)
No. 10, May, 1952 - No. 13, Sept, 1953; No. 14, April, 1954
Star Publishing Co.

	GD25	FN65	NM94
10-L. B. Cole-c	14.00	41.00	110.00
11-14-L. B. Cole-c. 14-Reprints Western Thrillers #4 (Fox) w/new L.B. Cole-c; Kamen, Feldstein-r	10.00	30.00	80.00

OUTLAWS
Sept, 1991 - No. 8, Apr, 1992 ($1.95, limited series)

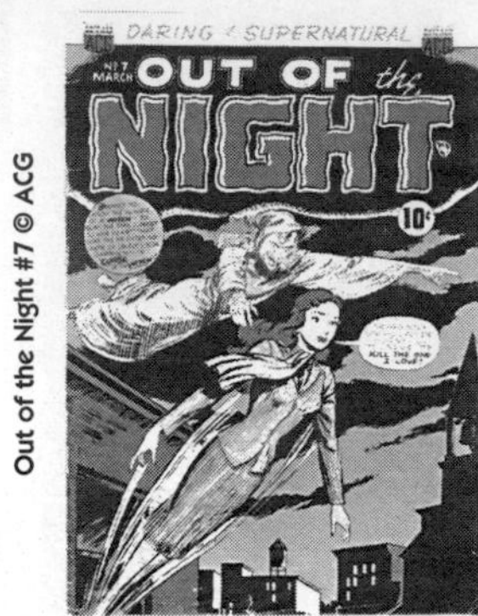

Out of the Night #7 © ACG

Out of the Vortex #10 © DH

Over the Edge #1 © MEG

	GD25	FN65	NM94

DC Comics

	GD25	FN65	NM94
1-8: Post-apocalyptic Robin Hood.		.80	2.00

OUTLAWS OF THE WEST (Formerly Cody of the Pony Express #10)
No. 11, 7/57 - No. 81, 5/70; No. 82, 7/79 - No. 88, 4/80
Charlton Comics

	GD25	FN65	NM94
11	6.50	19.50	45.00
12,13,15-17,19,20	4.00	11.00	22.00
14-(68 pgs., 2/58)	5.70	17.00	40.00
18-Ditko-a	7.85	23.50	55.00
21-30	2.00	6.00	16.00
31-50	1.50	4.50	12.00
51-70: 54-Kid Montana app. 64-Captain Doom begins (1st app.)	1.25	3.75	10.00
71-81: 73-Origin & 1st app. The Sharp Shooter, last app. #74. 75-Last Capt. Doom. 80,81-Ditko-a	1.00	3.00	8.00
82-88		1.20	3.00
64,79(Modern Comics-r, 1977, '78)		1.20	3.00

OUTLAWS OF THE WILD WEST
1952 (25¢, 132 pgs.) (4 rebound comics)
Avon Periodicals

	GD25	FN65	NM94
1-Wood back-c; Kubert-a (3 Jesse James-r)	25.00	75.00	200.00

OUTLAW TRAIL (See Zane Grey 4-Color 511)

OUT OF SANTA'S BAG (See March of Comics #10)

OUT OF THE NIGHT (The Hooded Horseman #18 on)
Feb-Mar, 1952 - No. 17, Oct-Nov, 1954
American Comics Group (Creston/Scope)

	GD25	FN65	NM94
1-Williamson/LeDoux-a (9 pgs.)	53.00	159.00	450.00
2-Williamson-a (5 pgs.)	44.00	132.00	365.00
3,5-10: 9-Sci/Fic story	21.00	64.00	160.00
4-Williamson-a (7 pgs.)	40.00	120.00	300.00
11-17: 13-Nostrand-a? 17-E.C. Wood swipe	17.00	49.00	120.00

NOTE: ***Landau** a-14, 16, 17. **Shelly** a-12.*

OUT OF THE PAST A CLUE TO THE FUTURE
1946? (16 pgs.) (paper cover)
E. C. Comics (Public Affairs Comm.)

	GD25	FN65	NM94
nn-Based on public affairs pamphlet "What Foreign Trade Means to You"	21.00	62.00	165.00

OUT OF THE SHADOWS
No. 5, July, 1952 - No. 14, Aug, 1954
Standard Comics/Visual Editions

	GD25	FN65	NM94
5-Toth-p; Moreira, Tuska-a; Roussos-c	40.00	120.00	300.00
6-Toth/Celardo-a; Katz-a(2)	29.00	86.00	210.00
7-Jack Katz-c/a(2)	19.00	56.00	140.00
8,10: 8-Katz shrunken head-c. 10-Sekowsky-a	15.00	45.00	110.00
9-Crandall-a(2)	19.00	56.00	140.00
11-Toth-a, 2 pgs.; Katz-a; Andru-c	19.00	56.00	140.00
12-Toth/Peppe-a(2); Katz-a	29.00	86.00	210.00
13-Cannabalism story; Sekowsky-a; Roussos-c	21.00	62.00	150.00
14-Toth-a	21.00	62.00	150.00

OUT OF THE VORTEX (Comics' Greatest World:... #1-4)
Oct., 1993 - No. 12, Oct, 1994 ($2.00, limited series)
Dark Horse Comics

	GD25	FN65	NM94
1-11: 1-Foil logo. 4-Dorman-c(p). 6-Hero Zero x-over		.80	2.00
12 ($2.50)		1.00	2.50

NOTE: ***Art Adams** c-7. **Golden** c-8. **Mignola** c-2. **Simonson** c-3. **Zeck** c-10.*

OUT OF THIS WORLD
Aug, 1956 - No. 16, Dec, 1959
Charlton Comics

	GD25	FN65	NM94
1	19.00	58.00	140.00
2	11.00	33.00	75.00
3-6-Ditko-c/a (3) each	24.00	73.00	180.00
7-(2/58, 15¢, 68 pgs.)-Ditko-c/a(4)	24.00	73.00	180.00
8-(5/58, 15¢, 68 pgs.)-Ditko-a(2)	20.00	60.00	150.00
9,10,12,16-Ditko-a.	17.00	49.00	120.00
11-Ditko c/a (3)	18.00	54.00	130.00
13-15	8.00	24.00	50.00

NOTE: ***Ditko** c-3-12, 16. **Reinman** a-10.*

OUT OF THIS WORLD (...Adventures #2)
June, 1950; No. 2, Dec, 1950 (25¢ pulp)
Avon Periodicals

	GD25	FN65	NM94
1-Kubert-a(2) (one reprinted/Eerie #1, 1947) plus Crom the Barbarian by Gardner Fox & John Giunta (origin); Fawcette-c.; pulp magazine w/comic insert	53.00	159.00	440.00
2-Kubert-a plus The Spider God of Akka by Gardner Fox & John Giunta.	4000	120.00	320.00

NOTE: *Out of This World Adventures is a sci-fi pulp magazine w/32 pgs. of color comics.*

OUT OUR WAY WITH WORRY WART
No. 680, Feb, 1956
Dell Publishing Co.

	GD25	FN65	NM94
Four Color 680	1.80	5.50	20.00

OUTPOSTS
June, 1987 - No. 4, 1987 ($1.25)
Blackthorne Publishing

	GD25	FN65	NM94
1-4: 1-Kaluta-c(p)			1.25

OUTSIDERS, THE
Nov, 1987 - No. 28, Feb, 1988
DC Comics

	GD25	FN65	NM94
1			1.50
2-28: 18-26-Batman returns. 21-Intro. Strike Force Kobra. 22-E.C. parody; Orlando-a. 21-1st app. Clayface IV. 25-Atomic Knight app. 27,28-Millennium tie-ins.			1.00
Annual 1 (12/86, $2.50)		.80	2.00
Special 1 (7/87, $1.50)			1.50

NOTE: ***Aparo** a-1-7, 9-14, 17-22, 25, 26; c-1-7, 9-14, 17, 19-26. **Byrne** a-11. **Bolland** a-6, 18; c-16. **Ditko** a-13p. **Erik Larsen** a-24, 27 28; c-27, 28. **Morrow** a-12.*

OUTSIDERS
Nov, 1993 - No. 24, Nov, 1995 ($1.75/$1.95/$2.25)
DC Comics

	GD25	FN65	NM94
1-Alpha; Travis Charest-c		.70	1.75
1-Omega; Travis Charest-c		.70	1.75
2-9: 5-Atomic Knight app. 8-New Batman-c/story		.70	1.75
10,11: 10-Begin $1.95-c. 11-(9/94)-Zero Hour		.80	2.00
0,12-18: 0-(10/94).12-(11/94).		.80	2.00
19-24: 19-Begin $2.25-c. 21-Darkseid cameo. 22-New Gods app.		.90	2.25

OUTSTANDING AMERICAN WAR HEROES
1944 (16 pgs., paper-c)
The Parents' Institute

	GD25	FN65	NM94
nn-Reprints from True Comics	4.00	10.00	20.00

OVERSEAS COMICS (Also see G.I. Comics & Jeep Comics)
1944 - No. 105?, 1946 (7-1/4x10-1/4"; 16 pgs. in color)
Giveaway (Distributed to U.S. armed forces)

	GD25	FN65	NM94
23-105-Bringing Up Father (by McManus), Popeye, Joe Palooka, Dick Tracy, Superman, Gasoline Alley, Buz Sawyer, Li'l Abner, Blondie, Terry & the Pirates, Out Our Way	5.00	15.00	30.00

OVER THE EDGE
Nov, 1995 - No. 10, Aug, 1996 (99¢)
Marvel Comics

1-10: 1,6,10-Daredevil-c/story. 2,7-Dr. Strange-c/story. 3-Hulk-c/story.

Oz #1 © Caliber

Ozark Ike # B11 © STD

Painkiller Jane #5 © Event

GD25 FN65 NM94

4,9-Ghost Rider-c/story. 5-Punisher-c/story. 8-Elektra-c/story 1.00

OWL, THE (See Crackajack Funnies #25 & Popular Comics #72)(Also see The Hurricane Kids & Magic Morro
1940 (Giveaway)(7-1/2x5-1/4")(Soft-c, color)
Western Publ. Co./R.S. Callender

nn-Frank Thomas-a 16.00 49.00 130.00

OWL, THE (See Crackajack Funnies #25 & Popular Comics #72)
April, 1967; No. 2, April, 1968
Gold Key

1,2-Written by Jerry Siegel; '40s super hero 2.75 8.00 30.00

OXYDOL-DREFT
1950 (Set of 6 pocket-size giveaways; distributed through the mail as a set)
Oxydol-Dreft (Scarce)

1-3: 1-Li'l Abner. 2-Daisy Mae. 3-Shmoo 8.75 26.25 70.00
4-John Wayne; Williamson/Frazetta-c from John Wayne #3
14.00 41.00 105.00
5-Archie 9.50 28.00 75.00
6-Terrytoons Mighty Mouse 8.75 26.25 70.00
NOTE: *Set is worth more with original envelope.*

OZ (See First Comics Graphic Novel, Marvel Treaury Of Oz & MGM's Marvelous...)

OZ
1994 - Present ($2.95, B&W)
Caliber Press

0-22 1.60 4.00
1 ($5.95)-Limited Edition; double-c 2.40 6.00

OZARK IKE
Feb, 1948; Nov, 1948 - No. 24, Dec, 1951; No. 25, Sept, 1952
Dell Publishing Co./Standard Comics B11 on

Four Color 180(1948-Dell) 9.00 27.00 100.00
B11, B12, 13-15 7.15 21.50 50.00
16-25 5.70 17.00 38.00

OZ: ROMANCE IN RAGS
1996 ($2.95, B&W, limited series)
Caliber Press

1-3 1.20 3.00
...Special 1.20 3.00
...Specials: Freedom Fighters. Lion. Scarecrow. Tin Man 1.20 3.00

OZ SQUAD
1992 - No. 4, 1994 ($2.50/$2.75, B&W)
Brave New Worlds/Patchwork Press (No. 4)

1-3 1.00 2.50
4 1.10 2.75

OZ SQUAD
Dec, 1995 - No. 10, 1996 ($2.95, B&W)
Patchwork Press

1 ($3.95) 1.60 4.00
2-10 1.20 3.00

OZ-WONDERLAND WARS, THE
Jan, 1986 - No. 3, March, 1986 (Mini-series)
DC Comics

1-3 .80 2.00

OZZIE & BABS (TV Teens #14 on)
Dec, 1947 - No. 13, Fall, 1949
Fawcett Publications

1-Teen-age 7.15 21.50 50.00
2 4.25 13.00 26.00
3-13 4.00 10.00 20.00

OZZIE & HARRIET (See The Adventures of...)

PACIFIC COMICS GRAPHIC NOVEL (See Image Graphic Novel)

PACIFIC PRESENTS (Also see Starslayer #2, 3)
Oct, 1982 - No. 2, Apr, 1983; No. 3, Mar, 1984 - No. 4, June, 1984
Pacific Comics

1-Chapter 3 of The Rocketeer; Stevens-c/a 2.40 6.00
2-Chapter 4 of The Rocketeer (4th app.); nudity; Stevens-c/a 2.00 5.00
3,4: 3-1st app. Vanity .80 2.00
NOTE: ***Conrad** a-3, 4; c-3. **Ditko** a-1-3; c-1(1/2). **Dave Stevens** a-1, 2; c-1(1/2), 2.*

PACT, THE
Feb, 1994 - No. 3, June, 1994 ($1.95, limited series)
Image Comics

1-3: Valentino co-scripts & layouts .80 2.00

PADRE OF THE POOR
nd (Giveaway) (16 pgs., paper-c)
Catechetical Guild

nn 1.25 3.75 10.00

PAGEANT OF COMICS (See Jane Arden & Mopsy)
Sept, 1947 - No. 2, Oct, 1947
Archer St. John

1-Mopsy strip-r 7.85 23.50 55.00
2-Jane Arden strip-r 7.85 23.50 55.00

PAINKILLER JANE
June, 1997 - Present ($3.95/$2.95)
Event Comics

1-Augustyn/Waid-s/Leonardi/Palmiotti-a, variant-c 1.60 3.95
2-5: Two covers (Quesada, Leonardi) 1.20 2.95

PAINKILLER JANE VS. THE DARKNESS
Apr, 1997 ($2.95, one-shot)
Event Comics

1-Ennis-s; four variant-c 1.40 3.50

PAKKIN'S LAND
1996 - No. 6 ($2.95, B&W)
Caliber Comics (Tapestry)

1-6-Gary and Rhoda Shipman-s/a 1.20 3.00

PAKKIN'S LAND: QUEST FOR KINGS
Aug, 1997 - Present ($2.95, B&W)
Caliber Comics

1-4-Gary and Rhoda Shipman-s/a 1.20 3.00

PANCHO VILLA
1950
Avon Periodicals

nn-Kinstler-c 20.00 60.00 150.00

PANDORA
Jan, 1997 - No. 2, Feb, 1997 ($3.00, B&W, limited series)
Avatar Press

0,1,2: 1-Lindo-c 1.20 3.00
...Demonography (5/97, $3.00) 1.20 3.00

PANDORA PIN-UP
July, 1997 ($3.00, B&W, one-shot)
Avatar Press

1-($3.00)-Regular ed. 1.20 3.00
1-($4.95)-Nude ed. 2.00 5.00

PANDORA/WIDOW
Sept, 1997 ($3.95, B&W, one-shot)
Avatar Press

Panic #10 © WMG

Paradox #1 © Dark Visions

Pat Boone #5 © DC

GD25 FN65 NM94

1-($3.95)-Regular ed. 1.60 3.95
1-($4.95)-Nude ed. 2.00 4.95
1-($25.00)-Leather ed. 25.00

PANHANDLE PETE AND JENNIFER (TV) (See Gene Autry #20)
July, 1951 - No. 3, Nov, 1951
J. Charles Laue Publishing Co.

1 8.50 26.00 60.00
2,3 5.70 17.00 40.00

PANIC (Companion to Mad)
Feb-Mar, 1954 - No. 12, Dec-Jan, 1955-56
E. C. Comics (Tiny Tot Comics)

1-Used in Senate Investigation hearings; Elder draws entire E. C. staff; Santa Claus & Mickey Spillane parody 22.00 66.00 175.00
2 10.00 30.00 80.00
3,4: 3-Senate Subcommittee parody; Davis draws Gaines, Feldstein & Kelly, 1 pg.; Old King Cole smokes marijuana. 4-Infinity-c; John Wayne parody 8.75 26.25 70.00
5-11: 8-Last pre-code issue (5/55). 9-Superman, Smilin' Jack & Dick Tracy app. on-c; has photo of Walter Winchell on-c 8.50 26.00 60.00
12 (Low distribution; thousands were destroyed) 10.00 30.00 80.00

NOTE: ***Davis** a-1-12; c-12. **Elder** a-1-12. **Feldstein** c-1-3, 5. **Kamen** a-1. **Orlando** a-1-9. **Wolverton** c-4, panel-3. **Wood** a-2-9, 11, 12.*

PANIC (Magazine) (Satire)
July, 1958 - No. 6, July, 1959; V2#10, Dec, 1965 - V2#12, 1966
Panic Publications

1 8.50 26.00 60.00
2-6 5.00 15.00 30.00
V2#10-12: Reprints earlier issues 2.50 7.50 22.00

NOTE: ***Davis** a-3(2 pgs.), 4, 5, 10; c-10. **Elder** a-5. **Powell** a-V2#10, 11. **Torres** a-1-5. **Tuska** a-V2#11.*

PANTHA: HAUNTED PASSION
May, 1997 ($2.95, B&W, one-shot)
Harris Comics

1-r/Vampirella #30,31 1.20 3.00

PARADAX (Also see Strange Days)
1986 (one-shot)
Eclipse Comics

1 .80 2.00

PARADAX
April, 1987 - No. 2, Aug, 1987 ($1.75, mature)
Vortex Comics

1,2-Nudity, adult language .75 1.80

PARADE (See Hanna-Barbera...)

PARADE COMICS (Frisky Animals on Parade #2 on)
Sept, 1957
Ajax/Farrell Publ. (World Famous Publ.)

1 5.70 17.00 35.00

NOTE: *Cover title: Frisky Animals on Parade.*

PARADE OF PLEASURE
1954 (192 pgs.) (Hardback book)
Derric Verschoyle Ltd., London, England

By Geoffrey Wagner. Contains section devoted to the censorship of American comic books with illustrations in color and black and white. (Also see **Seduction of the Innocent**). Distributed in USA by Library Publishers, N. Y. 34.00 103.00 275.00
with dust jacket.... 61.00 183.00 550.00

PARADOX
June, 1994 - No. 2, July?, 1994 ($2.95, B&W, mature)
Dark Visions Publishing

GD25 FN65 NM94

1,2: 1-Linsner-c. 2-Boris-c. 1.20 3.00

PARALLAX: EMERALD NIGHT (See Final Night)
Nov, 1996 ($2.95, one-shot, 48 pgs.)
DC Comics

1-Final Night tie-in; Green Lantern (Kyle Rayner) app. 1.60 4.00

PARAMOUNT ANIMATED COMICS (See Harvey Comics Hits #60, 62)
Feb, 1953 - No. 22, July, 1956
Harvey Publications

1-Baby Huey, Herman & Katnip, Buzzy the Crow begin 16.00 49.00 130.00
2 8.75 26.25 70.00
3-6 7.15 21.50 50.00
7-Baby Huey becomes permanent cover feature; cover title becomes Baby Huey with #9 15.50 47.00 125.00
8-10: 9-Infinity-c 6.85 21.00 48.00
11-22 5.35 16.00 32.00

PARENT TRAP, THE (Disney)
No. 1210, Oct-Dec, 1961
Dell Publishing Co.

Four Color 1210-Movie, Haley Mills photo-c 8.00 25.00 90.00

PARODY
Mar, 1977 - No. 3, Aug, 1977 (B&W humor magazine)
Armour Publishing

1 1.50 4.50 12.00
2,3 1.10 3.30 9.00

PAROLE BREAKERS
Dec, 1951 - No. 3, July, 1952
Avon Periodicals/Realistic #2 on

1(#2 on inside)-r-c/Avon paperback #283 (painted) 38.00 114.00 265.00
2-Kubert-a; r-c/Avon paperback #114 (photo-c) 26.00 77.00 180.00
3-Kinstler-c 24.00 71.00 165.00

PARTRIDGE FAMILY, THE (TV)(Also see David Cassidy)
Mar, 1971 - No. 21, Dec, 1973
Charlton Comics

1 3.50 10.50 35.00
2-4,6-10 2.00 6.00 16.00
5-Partridge Family Summer Special (52 pgs.); The Shadow, Lone Ranger, Charlie McCarthy, Flash Gordon, Hopalong Cassidy, Gene Autry & others app. 4.50 13.50 45.00
11-21 1.75 5.25 14.00

PARTS UNKNOWN
July, 1992 - No. 4, Oct, 1992 ($2.50, B&W, mini-series, mature)
Eclipse Comics/FX

1-4: All contain FX gaming cards 1.00 2.50

PASSION, THE
No. 394, 1955
Catechetical Guild

394 2.80 7.00 14.00

PASSOVER (See Avengelyne)
Dec, 1996 ($2.99, one-shot)
Maximum Press

1 1.20 3.00

PAT BOONE (TV)(Also see Superman's Girlfriend Lois Lane #9)
Sept-Oct, 1959 - No. 5, May-Jun, 1960 (All have photo-c)
National Periodical Publications

1 36.00 107.00 320.00
2-5: 3-Fabian, Connie Francis & Paul Anka photos on-c. 4-Previews "Journey To The Center Of The Earth". 4-Johnny Mathis & Bobbie Darin photos on-c.

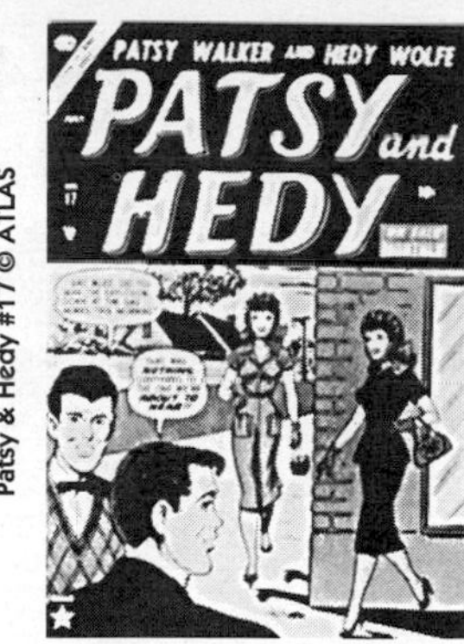

Patsy & Hedy #17 © ATLAS

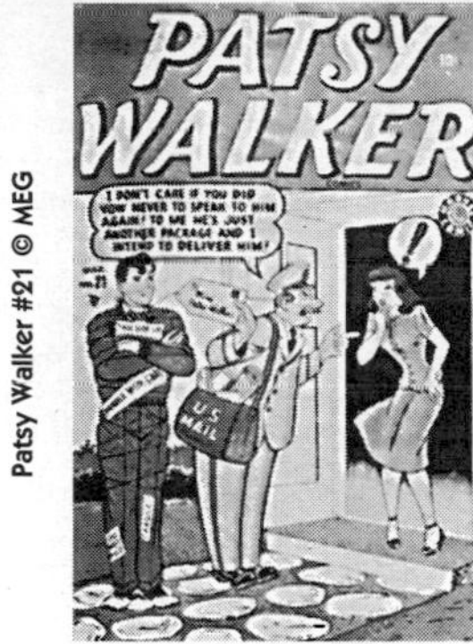

Patsy Walker #21 © MEG

Paul the Samurai #4 © New England

	GD25	FN65	NM94
5-Dick Clark & Frankie Avalon photos on-c	31.00	94.00	250.00

PATCHES
Mar-Apr, 1945 - No. 11, Nov, 1947
Rural Home/Patches Publ. (Orbit)

	GD25	FN65	NM94
1-L. B. Cole-c	26.00	80.00	210.00
2	10.00	30.00	80.00
3,4,6,8-11: 6-Henry Aldrich story. 8-Smiley Burnette-c/s (6/47); pre-dates Smiley Burnette #1. 9-Mr. District Attorney story (radio). Leav/Keigstein-a (16 pgs.). 9-11-Leav-c. 10-Jack Carson (radio) c/story; Leav-c. 11-Red Skelton story	9.50	28.00	75.00
5-Danny Kaye-c/story; L.B. Cole-c.	14.00	41.00	110.00
7-Hopalong Cassidy-c/story	11.30	34.00	90.00

PATHWAYS TO FANTASY
July, 1984
Pacific Comics

	GD25	FN65	NM94
1-Barry Smith-c/a; Jeff Jones-a (4 pgs.)			1.50

PATORUZU (See Adventures of...)

PATSY & HEDY (Teenage)(Also see Hedy Wolfe)
Feb, 1952 - No. 110, Feb, 1967
Atlas Comics/Marvel (GPI/Male)

	GD25	FN65	NM94
1-Patsy Walker & Hedy Wolfe; Al Jaffee-c	15.00	45.00	120.00
2	8.50	26.00	60.00
3-10: 3,8-Al Jaffee-c	6.50	19.50	45.00
11-20	5.35	16.00	32.00
21-40	4.15	12.50	25.00
41-60	2.50	7.50	20.00
61-110: 88-Lingerie panel	1.50	4.50	12.00
Annual 1(1963)-Early Marvel annual	7.00	21.00	70.00

PATSY & HER PALS (Teenage)
May, 1953 - No. 29, Aug, 1957
Atlas Comics (PPI)

	GD25	FN65	NM94
1-Patsy Walker	12.00	36.00	100.00
2	7.15	21.50	50.00
3-10	5.70	17.00	40.00
11-29: 24-Everett-c	5.00	15.00	30.00

PATSY WALKER (See All Teen, A Date With Patsy, Girls' Life, Miss America Magazine, Patsy & Hedy, Patsy & Her Pals & Teen Comics)
1945 (no month) - No. 124, Dec, 1965
Marvel/Atlas Comics (BPC)

	GD25	FN65	NM94
1-Teenage	36.00	108.00	320.00
2	19.00	56.00	150.00
3,4,6-10	14.00	41.00	110.00
5-Injury-to-eye-c; spanking panel	16.00	49.00	130.00
11,12,15,16,18	8.75	26.25	70.00
13,14,17,19-22-Kurtzman's "Hey Look"	9.50	28.00	75.00
23,24	7.15	21.50	50.00
25-Rusty by Kurtzman; painted-c	9.50	28.00	75.00
26-29,31: 26-31: 52 pgs.	5.70	17.00	40.00
30(52 pgs.)-Egghead Doodle by Kurtzman (1 pg.)	7.15	21.50	50.00
32-57: Last precode (3/55)	4.00	12.00	24.00
58-80	2.25	6.75	18.00
81-99: 92,98-Millie x-over	1.75	5.25	14.00
100	2.00	6.00	16.00
101-124	1.50	4.50	12.00
Fashion Parade 1(1966, 68 pgs.)	5.50	16.50	55.00

NOTE: *Painted c-25-28. Anti-Wertham editorial in #21. Georgie app. in #8, 11. Millie app. in #10, 92, 98. Mitzi app. in #11. Rusty app. in #12, 25. Willie app. in #12.* ***Al Jaffee*** *c-57, 58.*

PAT THE BRAT (Adventures of Pipsqueak #34 on)
June, 1953; Summer, 1955 - No. 4, 5/56; No. 15, 7/56 - No. 33, 7/59
Archie Publications (Radio)

	GD25	FN65	NM94
nn(6/53)	10.00	30.00	80.00
1(Summer, 1955)	7.15	21.50	50.00
2-4-(5/56) (#5-14 not published)	5.00	15.00	30.00
15-(7/56)-33	2.25	6.75	18.00

PAT THE BRAT COMICS DIGEST MAGAZINE
October, 1980
Archie Publications

	GD25	FN65	NM94
1	1.25	3.75	10.00

PATTY POWERS (Formerly Della Vision #3)
No. 4, Oct, 1955 - No. 7, Oct, 1956
Atlas Comics

	GD25	FN65	NM94
4	7.15	21.50	50.00
5-7	4.15	12.50	25.00

PAT WILTON (See Mighty Midget Comics)

PAUL
1978 (49¢)
Spire Christian Comics (Fleming H. Revell Co.)

	GD25	FN65	NM94
nn			1.00

PAULINE PERIL (See The Close Shaves of...)

PAUL REVERE'S RIDE (TV, Disney, see Walt Disney Showcase #34)
No. 822, July, 1957
Dell Publishing Co.

	GD25	FN65	NM94
Four Color 822-w/Johnny Tremain, Toth-a	9.00	27.00	100.00

PAUL TERRY'S ADVENTURES OF MIGHTY MOUSE (See Adventures of...)

PAUL TERRY'S COMICS (Formerly Terry-Toons Comics; becomes Adventures of Mighty Mouse No. 126 on)
No. 85, Mar, 1951 - No. 125, May, 1955
St. John Publishing Co.

	GD25	FN65	NM94
85,86-Same as Terry-Toons #85, & 86 with only a title change; published at same time?; Mighty Mouse, Heckle & Jeckle & Gandy Goose continue from Terry-Toons	8.75	26.25	70.00
87-99	6.00	18.00	42.00
100	7.15	21.50	50.00
101-104,107-125: 121,122,125-Painted-c	5.70	17.00	40.00
105,106-Giant Comics Edition (25¢, 100 pgs.) (9/53 & ?). 105-Little Roquefort-c/story	15.00	45.00	120.00

PAUL TERRY'S HOW TO DRAW FUNNY CARTOONS
1940's (14 pgs.) (Black & White)
Terrytoons, Inc. (Giveaway)

	GD25	FN65	NM94
nn-Heckle & Jeckle, Mighty Mouse, etc.	10.50	32.00	85.00

PAUL TERRY'S MIGHTY MOUSE (See Mighty Mouse)

PAUL TERRY'S MIGHTY MOUSE ADVENTURE STORIES (See Mighty Mouse Adventure Stories)

PAUL THE SAMURAI (See The Tick #4)
July, 1992 - No. 6, July, 1993 ($2.75, B&W)
New England Comics

	GD25	FN65	NM94
1-6		1.10	2.75

PAWNEE BILL
Feb, 1951 - No. 3, July, 1951
Story Comics (Youthful Magazines?)

	GD25	FN65	NM94
1-Bat Masterson, Wyatt Earp app.	8.75	26.25	70.00
2,3: 3-Origin Golden Warrior; Cameron-a	5.70	17.00	40.00

PAY-OFF (This Is the..., ...Crime, ...Detective Stories)
July-Aug, 1948 - No. 5, Mar-Apr, 1949 (52 pgs.)
D. S. Publishing Co.

	GD25	FN65	NM94
1-True Crime Cases #1,2	19.00	56.00	140.00
2	11.50	34.00	85.00

Pebbles & Bamm Bamm Giant Size #1 © H-B

Pendragon #1 © MEG

Penthouse Comix #3 © General Media

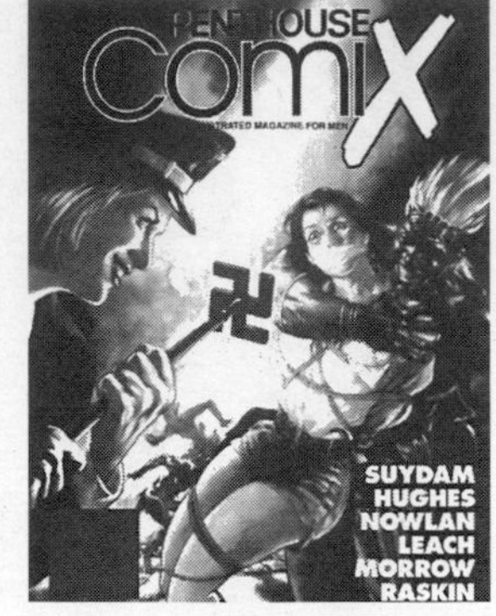

GD25 FN65 NM94

3-5-Thrilling Detective Stories 10.00 30.00 75.00

PEACEMAKER, THE (Also see Fightin' Five)
V3#1, Mar, 1967 - No. 5, Nov, 1967 (All 12¢ cover price)
Charlton Comics

1-Fightin' Five begins 2.80 8.40 28.00
2,3,5 1.85 5.50 15.00
4-Origin The Peacemaker 2.50 7.50 25.00
1,2(Modern Comics reprint, 1978) .80 2.00

PEACEMAKER (Also see Crisis On Infinite Earths & Showcase '93 #7,9,10)
Jan, 1988 - No. 4, Apr, 1988 ($1.25, limited series)
DC Comics

1-4 1.25

PEANUTS (Charlie Brown) (See Fritzi Ritz, Nancy & Sluggo, Tip Top, Tip Topper & United Comics)
1953-54; No. 878, 2/58 - No. 13, 5-7/62; 5/63 - No. 4, 2/64
Dell Publishing Co./Gold Key

1(1953-54)-Reprints United Features' Strange As It Seems, Willie, Ferdnand
11.00 33.00 120.00
Four Color 878(#1) 14.00 41.00 150.00
Four Color 969,1015('59) 10.00 30.00 110.00
4(2-4/60) 7.00 22.00 80.00
5-13 5.00 15.00 55.00
1(Gold Key, 5/63) 9.00 29.00 105.00
2-4 6.00 18.00 65.00

PEBBLES & BAMM BAMM (TV) (See Cave Kids #7, 12)
Jan, 1972 - No. 36, Dec, 1976 (Hanna-Barbera)
Charlton Comics

1-From the Flintstones 3.60 11.00 40.00
2-10 1.80 5.50 20.00
11-20 1.70 5.00 15.00
21-36 1.50 4.50 12.00

PEBBLES & BAMM BAMM (TV)
Nov, 1993 - No. 3, Mar, 1994 ($1.50) (Hanna-Barbera)
Harvey Comics

V2#1-3 1.20 3.00
...Giant Size 1 (10/93, $2.25, 68 pgs.)("Summer Special" on-c) 1.20 3.00

PEBBLES FLINTSTONE (TV) (See The Flintstones #11)
Sept, 1963 (Hanna-Barbera)
Gold Key

1 (10088-309)-Early Pebbles app. 8.00 25.00 90.00

PEDRO (Formerly My Private Life #17; also see Romeo Tubbs)
No. 18, June, 1950 - No. 2, Aug, 1950?
Fox Features Syndicate

18(#1)-Wood-c/a(p) 17.50 53.00 140.00
2-Wood-a? 14.00 41.00 110.00

PEE-WEE PIXIES (See The Pixies)

PELLEAS AND MELISANDE (See Night Music #4, 5)

PENALTY (See Crime Must Pay the...)

PENDRAGON (Knights of... #5 on; also see Knights of...)
July, 1992 - No. 15, Sept, 1993 ($1.75)
Marvel Comics UK, Ltd.

1-15: 1-4-Iron Man app. 6-8-Spider-Man app. .70 1.75

PENDULUM ILLUSTRATED BIOGRAPHIES
1979 (B&W)
Pendulum Press

19-355x-George Washington/Thomas Jefferson, 19-3495-Charles Lindbergh/Amelia Earhart, 19-3509-Harry Houdini/Walt Disney, 19-3517-Davy Crockett/Daniel Boone-Redondo-a, 19-3525-Elvis Presley/Beatles, 19-3533-Benjamin Franklin/Martin Luther King Jr, 19-3541-Abraham Lincoln/Franklin D. Roosevelt, 19-3568-Marie Curie/Albert Einstein-Redondo-a, 19-3576-Thomas Edison/Alexander Graham Bell-Redondo-a, 19-3584-Vince Lombardi/Pele, 19-3592-Babe Ruth/Jackie Robinson, 19-3606-Jim Thorpe/Althea Gibson

Softback 1.50
Hardback 4.50

NOTE: *Above books still available from publisher.*

PENDULUM ILLUSTRATED CLASSICS (Now Age Illustrated)
1973 - 1978 (75¢, 62pp, B&W, 5-3/8x8") (Also see Marvel Classics)
Pendulum Press

64-100x(1973)-Dracula-Redondo art, 64-131x-The Invisible Man-Nino art, 64-0968-Dr. Jekyll and Mr. Hyde-Redondo art, 64-1005-Black Beauty, 64-1010-Call of the Wild, 64-1020-Frankenstein, 64-1025-Hucklebury Finn, 64-1030-Moby Dick-Nino-a, 64-1040-Red Badge of Courage, 64-1045-The Time Machine-Nino-a, 64-1050-Tom Sawyer, 64-1055-Twenty Thousand Leagues Under the Sea, 64-1069-Treasure Island, 64-1328(1974)-Kidnapped, 64-1336-Three Musketeers-Nino art, 64-1344-A Tale of Two Cities, 64-1352-Journey to the Center of the Earth, 64-1360-The War of the Worlds-Nino-a, 64-1379-The Greatest Advs. of Sherlock Holmes-Redondo art, 64-1387-Mysterious Island, 64-1395-Hunchback of Notre Dame, 64-1409-Helen Keller-story of my life, 64-1417-Scarlet Letter, 64-1425-Gulliver's Travels, 64-2618(1977)-Around the World in Eighty Days, 64-2626-Captains Courageous, 64-2634-Connecticut Yankee, 64-2642-The Hound of the Baskervilles, 64-2650-The House of Seven Gables, 64-2669-Jane Eyre, 64-2677-The Last of the Mohicans, 64-2685-The Best of O'Henry, 64-2693-The Best of Poe-Redondo-a, 64-2707-Two Years Before the Mast, 64-2715-White Fang, 64-2723-Wuthering Heights, 64-3126(1978)-Ben Hur-Redondo art, 64-3134-A Christmas Carol, 64-3142-The Food of the Gods, 64-3150-Ivanhoe, 64-3169-The Man in the Iron Mask, 64-3177-The Prince and the Pauper, 64-3185-The Prisoner of Zenda, 64-3193-The Return of the Native, 64-3207-Robinson Crusoe, 64-3215-The Scarlet Pimpernel, 64-3223-The Sea Wolf, 64-3231-The Swiss Family Robinson, 64-3851-Billy Budd, 64-386x-Crime and Punishment, 64-3878-Don Quixote, 64-3886-Great Expectations, 64-3894-Heidi, 64-3908-The Iliad, 64-3916-Lord Jim, 64-3924-The Mutiny on Board H.M.S. Bounty, 64-3932-The Odyssey, 64-3940-Oliver Twist, 64-3959-Pride and Prejudice, 64-3967-The Turn of the Screw

Softback 1.45
Hardback 4.50

NOTE: *All of the above books can be ordered from the publisher; some were reprinted as Marvel Classic Comics #1-12. In 1972 there was another brief series of 12 titles which contained Classics Ill. artwork. They were entitled* ***Now Age Books*** *Illustrated, but can be easily distinguished from later series by the small Classics Illustrated logo at the top of the front cover. The format is the same as the later series. The 48 pg. C.I. art was stretched out to make 62 pgs. After Twin Circle Publ. terminated the Classics Ill. series in 1971, they made a one year contract with Pendulum Press to print these twelve titles of C.I. art. Pendulum was unhappy with the contract, and at the end of 1972 began their own art series, utilizing the talents of the Filipino artist group. One detail which makes this rather confusing is that when they redid the art in 1973, they gave it the same identifying no. as the 1972 series. All 12 of the 1972 C.I. editions have new covers, taken from internal art panels. In spite of their recent age, all of the 1972 C.I. series are very rare. Mint copies would fetch at least $50. Here is a list of the 1972 series, with C.I. title no. counterpart:*

64-1005 (CI#60-A2) 64-1010 (CI#91) 64-1015 (CI-Jr #503) 64-1020 (CI#26)
64-1025 (CI#19-A2) 64-1030 (CI#5-A2) 64-1035 (CI#169) 64-1040 (CI#98)
64-1045 (CI#133) 64-1050 (CI#50-A2) 64-1055 (CI#47) 64-1060 (CI-Jr#535)

PENDULUM ILLUSTRATED ORIGINALS
1979 (In color)
Pendulum Press

94-4254-Solarman: The Beginning .65 1.60

PENDULUM'S ILLUSTRATED STORIES
1990 - No. 72, 1990? (No cover price ($4.95), squarebound, 68 pgs.)
Pendulum Press

1-72: Reprints Pendulum Ill. Classics series 2.00 5.00

PENNY
1947 - No. 6, Sept-Oct, 1949 (Newspaper reprints)
Avon Comics

1-Photo & biography of creator 10.00 30.00 68.00
2-5 6.35 19.00 38.00
6-Perry Como photo on-c 7.00 21.00 42.00

PENTHOUSE COMIX
1994 - Present ($4.95, bimonthly, magazine, mature)
General Media International

1 1.25 3.75 10.00
2,3 1.00 2.80 7.00

Pep Comics #16 © AP

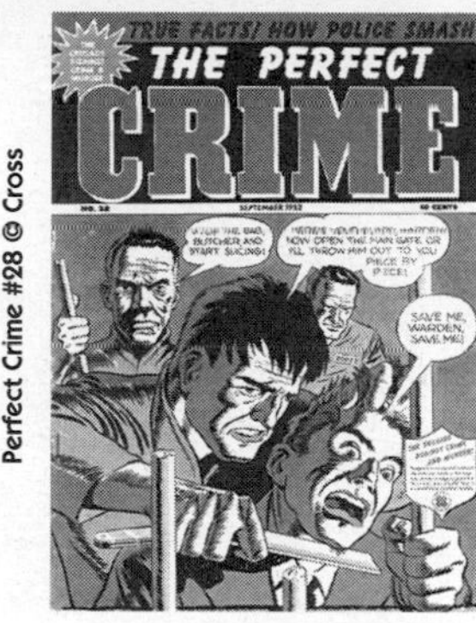

Perfect Crime #28 © Cross

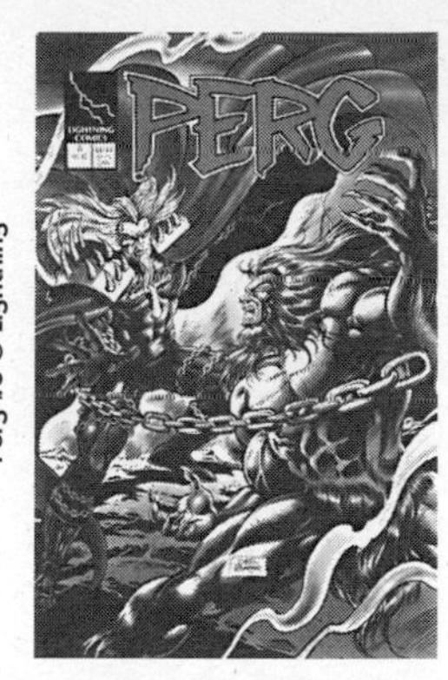

Perg #3 © Lightning

GD25 FN65 NM94

4-28: 15-Corben-c. 16-Dorman-c. 17-Manara-c. 20-Chiodo-c. 21,23-Boris-c
24-Scott Hampton-c 2.00 5.00

PENTHOUSE MAX
July, 1996 - No. 3 ($4.95, magazine, mature)
General Media International

1-3: 1-Giffen, Sears, Maguire-a. 2-Political satire. 3-Mr. Monster-c/app.;
Dorman-c 2.00 5.00

PENTHOUSE MEN'S ADVENTURE COMIX
1995 - No. 7, 1996 ($4.95, magazine, mature)
General Media International

1-7 (Magazine Size): 1-Boris-c 2.00 5.00
1-5 (Comic Size): 1-Boris-c 2.00 5.00

PEP COMICS (See Archie Giant Series #576, 589, 601, 614, 624)
Jan, 1940 - No. 411, Mar, 1989
MLJ Magazines/Archie Publications No. 56 (3/46) on

GD25 FN65 VF82 NM94
1-Intro. The Shield by Irving Novick (1st patriotic hero); origin & 1st app. The Comet by Jack Cole, The Queen of Diamonds & Kayo Ward; The Rocket, The Press Guardian (The Falcon #1 only), Sergeant Boyle, Fu Chang, & Bentley of of Scotland Yard; Robot-c; Shield-c begin
660.00 1980.00 3960.00 6600.00
(Estimated up to 150 total copies exist, 7 in NM/Mint)

GD25 FN65 NM94
2-Origin The Rocket 172.00 516.00 1550.00
3 122.00 366.00 1100.00
4-Wizard cameo 100.00 300.00 900.00
5-Wizard cameo in Shield story 100.00 300.00 900.00
6-10: 8-Last Cole Comet; no Cole-a in #6,7 78.00 234.00 700.00
11-Dusty, Shield's sidekick begins (1st app.); last Press Guardian, Fu Chang
83.00 250.00 750.00
12-Origin & 1st app. Fireball (2/41); last Rocket & Queen of Diamonds; Danny in Wonderland begins 100.00 300.00 900.00
13-15 64.00 192.00 575.00
16-Origin Madam Satan; blood drainage-c 100.00 300.00 900.00
17-Origin/1st app. The Hangman (7/41); death of The Comet; Comet is revealed as Hangman's brother 250.00 750.00 2500.00
18-21: 20-Last Fireball. 21-Last Madam Satan 64.00 192.00 575.00

GD25 FN65 VF82 NM94
22-Intro. & 1st app. Archie, Betty, & Jughead(12/41); (also see Jackpot)
900.00 2700.00 5400.00 9000.00
(Estimated up to 150 total copies exist, 7 in NM/Mint)

GD25 FN65 NM94
23 106.00 318.00 950.00
24,25: 24-Coach Kleets app. (unnamed until Archie #94); bondage/torture-c. 25-1st app. Archie's jalopy; 1st skinny Mr. Weatherbee prototype
89.00 267.00 800.00
26-1st app. Veronica Lodge (4/42) 122.00 366.00 1100.00
27-30: 29-Origin Shield retold; 30-Capt. Commando begins; bondage/torture-c; 1st Miss Grundy (definitive version); see Jackpot #4
72.00 216.00 650.00
31-35: 31-MLJ offices & artists are visited in Sgt. Boyle story; 1st app. Mr. Lodge. 32-Shield dons new costume. 34-Bondage/Hypo-c. 33-Pre-Moose tryout (see Jughead #1) 56.00 168.00 500.00
36-1st Archie-c (2/43) w/Shield & Hangman 122.00 366.00 1100.00
37-40 42.00 126.00 375.00
41-50: 41-Archie-c begin. 47-Last Hangman issue; infinity-c. 48-Black Hood begins (5/44); ends #51,59,60 30.00 90.00 240.00
51-60: 52-Suzie begins. 56-Last Capt. Commando. 59-Black Hood not in costume; spanking & lingerie panels; Archie dresses as his aunt; Suzie ends. 60-Katy Keene begins(3/47), ends #154 21.00 64.00 170.00
61-65-Last Shield. 62-1st app. Li'l Jinx (7/47) 17.50 53.00 140.00
66-80: 66-G-Man Club becomes Archie Club (2/48); Nevada Jones by Bill Woggon. 78-1st app. Dilton 10.50 32.00 85.00

GD25 FN65 NM94

81-99 8.75 26.25 65.00
100 10.00 30.00 80.00
101-130 5.00 15.00 30.00
131-149 2.25 6.75 18.00
150-160-Super-heroes app. in each (see note). 150 (10/61?)-2nd or 3rd app. The Jaguar? 152-157-Sci/Fi-c. 157-Li'l Jinx story 2.50 7.50 24.00
161-167,169-200 1.25 3.75 10.00
168-Jaguar app. 1.50 4.50 12.00
201-260 2.40 6.00
261-300 1.60 4.00
301-360 1.20 3.00
361-411: 383-Marvelous Maureen begins (Sci/fi). 393-Thunderbunny begins. 400-Story featuring Archie staff (DeCarlo-a) .80 2.00

NOTE: ***Biro** a-2, 4, 5. **Jack Cole** a-1-5, 8. **Al Fagaly** c-55-72. **Fuje** a-39, 45, 47; c-34. **Meskin** a-2, 4, 5, 11(2). **Montana** c-30, 32, 33, 36, 73-87(most). **Novick** c-1-28, 29(w/**Schomburg**), 31i. **Harry Sahle** c-35, 39-50. **Schomburg** c-38. **Bob Wood** a-2, 4-6, 11. The Fly app. in 151, 154, 160. Flygirl app. in 153, 155, 156, 158. Jaguar app. in 150, 152, 157, 159, 168. Katy Keene by **Bill Woggon** in many later issues. Bondage c-7, 12, 13, 15, 18, 21, 31, 32. Cover features: Shield #1-16; Shield/Hangman #17-27, 29-41; Hangman #28, Archie #36, 41-on.*

PEPE
No. 1194, Apr, 1961
Dell Publishing Co.

Four Color 1194-Movie, photo-c 1.80 5.50 20.00

PERFECT CRIME, THE
Oct, 1949 - No. 33, May, 1953 (#2-12, 52 pgs.)
Cross Publications

1-Powell-a(2) 24.00 71.00 175.00
2 (4/50) 13.00 39.00 95.00
3-10: 7-Steve Duncan begins, ends #30. 10-Flag-c 11.00 33.00 80.00
11-Used in **SOTI**, pg. 159 13.00 39.00 95.00
12-14 10.00 30.00 65.00
15- "The Most Terrible Menace" 2 pg. drug editorial 10.00 30.00 75.00
16,17,19-25,27-29,31-33 7.50 22.50 50.00
18-Drug cover, heroin drug propaganda story, plus 2 pg. anti-drug editorial
17.00 49.00 120.00
26-Drug-c with hypodermic; drug propaganda story 17.00 51.00 125.00
30-Strangulation cover 18.00 54.00 130.00

NOTE: ***Powell** a-No. 1, 2, 4. **Wildey** a-1, 5. Bondage c-11*

PERFECT LOVE
#10, 8-9/51 (cover date; 5-6/51 indicia date); #2, 10-11/51 - #10, 12/53
Ziff-Davis(Approved Comics)/St. John No. 9 on

10(#1)(8-9/51)-Painted-c 14.00 43.00 110.00
2(10-11/51) 10.00 30.00 70.00
3,5-7: 3-Painted-c. 5-Photo-c 7.50 22.50 50.00
4,8 (Fall, 1952)-Kinstler-a; last Z-D issue 8.35 25.00 55.00
9,10 (10/53, 12/53, St. John): 9-Painted-c. 10-Photo-c
6.50 19.50 45.00

PERG (Also see Hellina)
Oct, 1993 - No. 8, May, 1994 ($2.95)
Lightning Comics

1-($3.50)-Flip-c is glow-in-the-dark by Saltares 1.40 3.50
1-4: Platinum Editions 1.20 3.00
2-8: 4-Origin Perg. 7-Blue & Pink cover versions 1.20 3.00

PERRI (Disney)
No. 847, Jan, 1958
Dell Publishing Co.

Four Color 847-Movie, w/2 diff-c publ. 4.50 13.50 50.00

PERRY MASON
No. 49, 1946 - No. 50, 1946
David McKay Publications

Feature Books 49, 59-Based on Gardner novels 20.00 60.00 160.00

Personal Love #28 © FF

Peter Panda #9 © DC

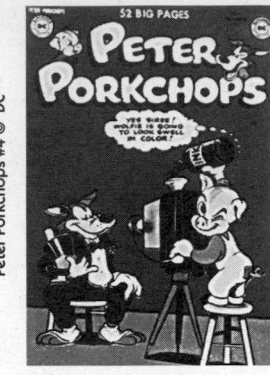

Peter Porkchops #4 © DC

GD25 FN65 NM94

PERRY MASON MYSTERY MAGAZINE (TV)
June-Aug, 1964 - No. 2, Oct-Dec, 1964
Dell Publishing Co.

	GD25	FN65	NM94
1,2: 2-Raymond Burr photo-c	2.00	6.00	22.00

PERSONAL LOVE (Also see Movie Love)
Jan, 1950 - No. 33, June, 1955
Famous Funnies

	GD25	FN65	NM94
1-Photo-c	12.00	36.00	95.00
2-Kathryn Grayson & Mario Lanza photo-c	7.15	21.50	50.00
3-7,10: 7-Robert Walker & Joanne Dru photo-c. 10-Loretta Young & Joseph Cotton photo-c	5.70	17.00	38.00
8,9: 8-Esther Williams & Howard Keel photo-c. 9-Debra Paget & Louis Jourdan photo-c	5.70	17.00	40.00
11-Toth-a; Glenn Ford & Gene Tierney photo-c	8.75	26.25	65.00
12,16,17-One pg. Frazetta each. 17-Rock Hudson & Yvonne DeCarlo photo-c	5.70	17.00	38.00
13-15,18-23: 12-Jane Greer & William Lundigan photo-c. 14-Kirk Douglas photo-c. 15-Dale Robertson & Joanne Dru photo-c. 18-Gregory Peck & Susan Hayworth photo-c. 19-Anthony Quinn & Suzan Ball photo-c. 20-Robert Wagner & Kathleen Crowley photo-c. 21-Roberta Peters & Byron Palmer photo-c. 22-Dale Robertson photo-c. 23-Rhonda Fleming-c	5.35	16.00	32.00
24,27,28-Frazetta-a in each (8,8&6 pgs.). 27-Rhonda Fleming & Fernando Lamas photo-c. 28,30-Mitzi Gaynor photo-c	28.00	83.00	220.00
25-Frazetta-a (tribute to Betty Page, 7 pg. story); Tyrone Power/Terry Moore photo-c from "King of the Khyber Rifles"	28.00	83.00	220.00
26,29,30,33: 26-Constance Smith & Byron Palmer photo-c. 29-Charlton Heston & Nicol Morey photo-c. 30-Johnny Ray & Mitzi Gaynor photo-c. 33-Dana Andrews & Piper Laurie photo-c	5.00	15.00	30.00
31-Marlon Brando & Jean Simmons photo-c; last pre-code (2/55)	7.15	21.50	50.00
32-Classic Frazetta-a (8 pgs.); Kirk Douglas & Bella Darvi photo-c	38.00	113.00	340.00

NOTE: *All have photo-c. Many feature movie stars.* ***Everett*** *a-5, 9, 10, 24.*

PERSONAL LOVE (Going Steady V3#3 on)
V1#1, Sept, 1957 - V3#2, Nov-Dec, 1959
Prize Publ. (Headline)

	GD25	FN65	NM94
V1#1	5.70	17.00	40.00
2	4.00	12.00	24.00
3-6(7-8/58)	4.00	12.00	22.00
V2#1(9-10/58)-V2#6(7-8/59)	3.60	9.00	18.00
V3#1-Wood?/Orlando-a	4.25	13.00	26.00
2	3.20	8.00	16.00

PETER CANNON - THUNDERBOLT (See Crisis on Infinite Earths)(Also see Thunderbolt)
Sept, 1992 - No. 12, Aug, 1993 ($1.25)
DC Comics

	GD25	FN65	NM94
1-12			1.25

PETER COTTONTAIL
Jan, 1954; Feb, 1954 - No. 2, Mar, 1954 (Says 3/53 in error)
Key Publications

	GD25	FN65	NM94
1(1/54)-Not 3-D	5.70	17.00	40.00
1(2/54)-(3-D, 25¢)-Came w/glasses; written by Bruce Hamilton	18.00	54.00	145.00
2-Reprints 3-D #1 but not in 3-D	5.00	15.00	30.00

PETER GUNN (TV)
No. 1087, Apr-June, 1960
Dell Publishing Co.

	GD25	FN65	NM94
Four Color 1087-Photo-c	9.00	27.00	100.00

PETER PAN (Disney) (See Hook, Movie Classics & Comics, New Adventures of... & Walt Disney Showcase #36)
No. 442, Dec, 1952 - No. 926, Aug, 1958
Dell Publishing Co.

	GD25	FN65	NM94
Four Color 442 (#1)-Movie	8.00	25.00	90.00
Four Color 926-Reprint of 442	3.60	11.00	40.00

PETER PAN
1991 ($5.95, graphic novel, 68 pgs.)(Celebrates release of video)
Disney Comics

	GD25	FN65	NM94
nn-r/Peter Pan Treasure Chest from 1953		2.40	6.00

PETER PANDA
Aug-Sept, 1953 - No. 31, Aug-Sept, 1958
National Periodical Publications

	GD25	FN65	NM94
1-Grossman-c/a in all	34.00	101.00	270.00
2	15.00	45.00	120.00
3-10	12.00	36.00	90.00
11-31	8.50	26.00	60.00

PETER PAN TREASURE CHEST (See Dell Giants)

PETER PARKER (See The Spectacular Spider-Man)

PETER PAT
No. 8, 1939
United Features Syndicate

	GD25	FN65	NM94
Single Series 8	27.00	81.00	215.00

PETER PAUL'S 4 IN 1 JUMBO COMIC BOOK
No date (1953)
Capitol Stories (Charlton)

	GD25	FN65	NM94
1-Contains 4 comics bound; Space Adventures, Space Western, Crime & Justice, Racket Squad in Action	34.00	101.00	270.00

PETER PENNY AND HIS MAGIC DOLLAR
1947 (16 pgs.; paper cover; regular size)
American Bankers Association, N. Y. (Giveaway)

	GD25	FN65	NM94
nn-(Scarce)-Used in **SOTI**, pg. 310, 311	14.00	41.00	110.00
Diff. version (7-1/4x11")-redrawn, 16 pgs., paper-c	8.50	26.00	60.00

PETER PIG
No. 5, May, 1953 - No. 6, Aug, 1953
Standard Comics

	GD25	FN65	NM94
5,6	4.25	13.00	28.00

PETER PORKCHOPS (See Leading Comics #23)
11-12/49 - No. 61, 9-11/59; No. 62, 10-12/60 (1-11: 52 pgs.)
National Periodical Publications

	GD25	FN65	NM94
1	28.00	84.00	225.00
2	14.00	41.00	110.00
3-10: 6- "Peter Rockets to Mars!" c/story	10.00	30.00	80.00
11-30	8.50	26.00	60.00
31-62	7.15	21.50	50.00

NOTE: ***Otto Feur*** *a-all.* ***Sheldon Mayer*** *a-30-38, 40-44, 46-52, 61.*

PETER PORKER, THE SPECTACULAR SPIDER-HAM
May, 1985 - No. 17, Sept, 1987 (Also see Marvel Tails)
Star Comics (Marvel)

	GD25	FN65	NM94
1-Michael Golden-c		.80	2.00
2-17: 12-Origin/1st app. Bizarro Phil. 13-Halloween issue			1.00

NOTE: *Back-up features: 2-X-Bugs. 3-Iron Mouse. 4-Croctor Strange. 5-Thrr, Dog of Thunder.*

PETER POTAMUS (TV)
Jan, 1965 (Hanna-Barbera)
Gold Key

	GD25	FN65	NM94
1	7.00	20.00	75.00

PETER RABBIT (See New Funnies #65 & Space Comics)
No. 1, 1942
Dell Publishing Co.

Peter Rabbit #4 © AVON

Peter Wheat #40 © Bakers Ass

The Phantom #7 © KFS

	GD25	FN65	NM94
Large Feature Comic 1	36.00	107.00	385.00

PETER RABBIT (Adventures of...; New Advs. of... #9 on)(Also see Funny Tunes & Space Comics)
1947 - No. 34, Aug-Sept, 1956
Avon Periodicals

	GD25	FN65	NM94
1(1947)-Reprints 1943-44 Sunday strips; contains a biography & drawing of Cady	29.00	86.00	230.00
2 (4/48)	21.00	64.00	170.00
3 ('48) - 6(7/49)-Last Cady issue	19.00	56.00	150.00
7-10(1950-8/51): 9-New logo	5.35	16.00	32.00
11(11/51)-34('56)-Avon's character	4.00	11.00	22.00
...Easter Parade (1952, 25¢, 132 pgs.)	13.00	39.00	105.00
...Jumbo Book (1954-Giant Size, 25¢)-Jesse James by Kinstler (6 pgs.); space ship-c	18.00	54.00	145.00

PETER RABBIT
1958
Fago Magazine Co.

	GD25	FN65	NM94
1	6.70	20.00	40.00

PETER RABBIT 3-D
April, 1990 ($2.95, with glasses; sealed in plastic bag)
Eternity Comics

	GD25	FN65	NM94
1-By Harrison Cady (reprints)		1.20	3.00

PETER, THE LITTLE PEST (#4 titled Petey)
Nov, 1969 - No. 4, May, 1970
Marvel Comics Group

	GD25	FN65	NM94
1	3.00	9.00	30.00
2-4-r-Dexter the Demon & Melvin the Monster	2.50	7.50	20.00

PETER WHEAT (The Adventures of...)
1948 - 1956? (16 pgs. in color) (paper covers)
Bakers Associates Giveaway

	GD25	FN65	NM94
nn(No.1)-States on last page, end of 1st Adventure of...; Kelly-a	25.00	75.00	200.00
nn(4 issues)-Kelly-a	16.00	49.00	130.00
6-10-All Kelly-a	11.30	34.00	90.00
11-20-All Kelly-a	9.50	28.00	75.00
21-35-All Kelly-a	8.50	26.00	60.00
36-66	5.70	17.00	40.00
...Artist's Workbook ('54, digest size)	5.70	17.00	40.00
...Four-In-One Fun Pack (Vol. 2, '54), oblong, comics w/puzzles	7.15	21.50	50.00
...Fun Book ('52, 32 pgs., paper-c, B&W & color, 8-1/2x10-3/4")-Contains cut-outs, puzzles, games, magic & pages to color	8.75	26.25	70.00

NOTE: ***Al Hubbard** art #36 on; written by Del Connell.*

PETER WHEAT NEWS
1948 - No. 30, 1950 (4 pgs. in color)
Bakers Associates

	GD25	FN65	NM94
Vol. 1-All have 2 pgs. Peter Wheat by Kelly	21.00	62.00	165.00
2-10	12.00	38.00	100.00
11-20	7.15	21.50	50.00
21-30	5.35	16.00	32.00

NOTE: *Early issues have no date & **Kelly** art.*

PETE'S DRAGON (See Walt Disney Showcase #43)

PETE THE PANIC
November, 1955
Stanmor Publications

	GD25	FN65	NM94
nn-Code approved	4.00	11.00	22.00

PETEY (See Peter, the Little Pest)

PETTICOAT JUNCTION (TV)
Oct-Dec, 1964 - No. 5, Oct-Dec, 1965 (#1-3, 5 have photo-c)
Dell Publishing Co.

	GD25	FN65	NM94
1	5.00	15.00	55.00
2-5	3.60	11.00	40.00

PETUNIA (Also see Looney Tunes and Porky Pig)
No. 463, Apr, 1953
Dell Publishing Co.

	GD25	FN65	NM94
Four Color 463	3.00	9.00	35.00

PHAGE (See Neil Gaiman's Teknophage & Neil Gaiman's Phage-Shadowdeath)

PHANTASMO (See The Funnies #45)
No. 18, 1941
Dell Publishing Co.

	GD25	FN65	NM94
Large Feature Comic 18	24.00	71.00	260.00

PHANTOM, THE
1939 - 1949
David McKay Publishing Co.

	GD25	FN65	NM94
Feature Books 20	59.00	177.00	650.00
Feature Books 22	50.00	150.00	550.00
Feature Books 39	40.00	120.00	365.00
Feature Books 53,56,57	34.00	103.00	275.00

PHANTOM, THE (See Ace Comics, Defenders Of The Earth, Eat Right to Work and Win, Future Comics, Harvey Comics Hits #51,56, Harvey Hits #1, 6, 12, 15, 26, 36, 44, 48, & King Comics)

PHANTOM, THE (nn 29-Published overseas only) (Also see Comics Reading Library)
Nov, 1962 - No. 17, July, 1966; No. 18, Sept, 1966 - No. 28, Dec, 1967; No. 30, Feb, 1969 - No. 74, Jan, 1977
Gold Key (#1-17)/King (#18-28)/Charlton (#30 on)

	GD25	FN65	NM94
1-Manning-a; origin revealed on inside-c. & back-c.	12.00	36.00	120.00
2-King, Queen & Jack begins, ends #11	5.50	16.50	60.00
3-10	4.00	12.00	45.00
11-17: 12-Track Hunter begins	3.50	11.00	38.00
18-Flash Gordon begins; Wood-a	3.00	9.00	34.00
19,20-Flash Gordon ends (both by Gil Kane)	2.25	6.75	24.00
21-24,26,27: 21-Mandrake begins. 20,24-Girl Phantom app. 26-Brick Bradford app.	2.25	6.75	24.00
25-Jeff Jones-a(4 pgs.); 1 pg. Williamson ad	2.25	6.75	24.00
28(nn)-Brick Bradford app.	1.80	5.50	20.00
30-40: 36,39-Ditko-a	1.50	4.50	15.00
41-66: 46-Intro. The Piranha. 62-Bolle-c	1.20	3.60	12.00
67-Origin retold	1.20	3.60	12.00
68-73-Newton-c/a	1.00	3.00	8.00
74-Newton flag-c; Newton-a; classic flag-c	1.25	3.75	10.00

NOTE: ***Aparo** a-31-34, 36-38; c-31-38, 60, 61. Painted c-1-17.*

PHANTOM, THE
May, 1988 - No. 4, Aug, 1988 ($1.25, mini-series)
DC Comics

	GD25	FN65	NM94
1-4: Orlando-c/a in all			1.25

PHANTOM, THE
Mar, 1989 - No. 13, Mar, 1990 ($1.50)
DC Comics

	GD25	FN65	NM94
1-13: 1-Brief origin			1.50

PHANTOM, THE
1992 - No. 8, 1993? ($2.25)
Wolf Publishing

	GD25	FN65	NM94
1-8		.90	2.25

PHANTOM BLOT, THE (#1 titled New Adventures of...)
Oct, 1964 - No. 7, Nov, 1966 (Disney)
Gold Key

	GD25	FN65	NM94
1 (Meets The Beagle Boys)	3.60	11.00	40.00

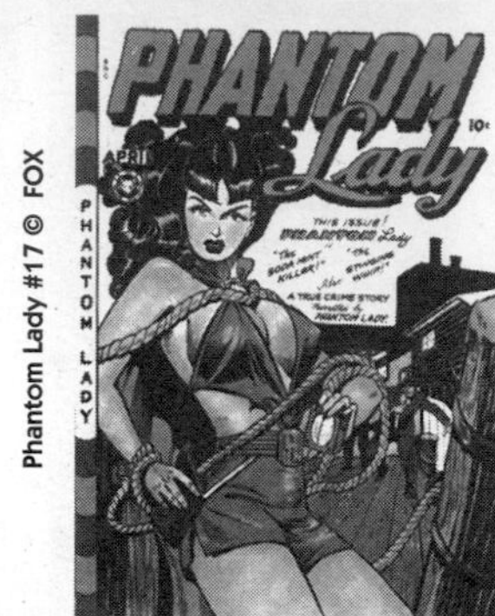

Phantom Lady #17 © FOX

Phantom Stranger #1 © DC

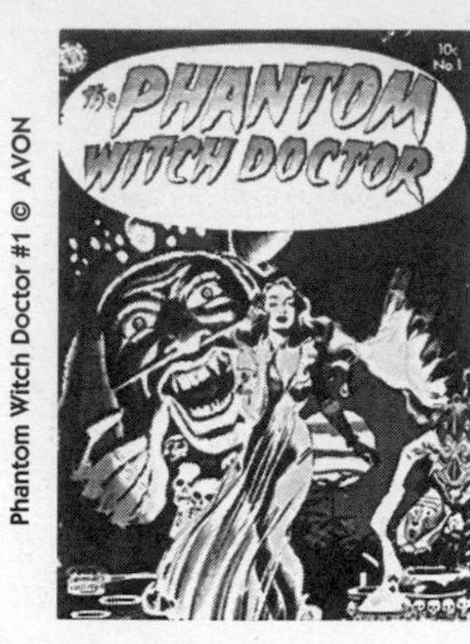

Phantom Witch Doctor #1 © AVON

	GD25	FN65	NM94
2-1st Super Goof	3.00	9.00	35.00
3-7	1.80	5.50	20.00

PHANTOM EAGLE (See Mighty Midget, Marvel Super Heroes #16 & Wow #6)

PHANTOM FORCE
12/93 - #2, 1994; #0, 3/94; #3, 5/94 - #7, 10/94 ($2.50/$3.50, limited series)
Image Comics/Genesis West #0, 3-7

0 (3/94, $2.50)-Kirby/Jim Lee-c; Kirby-p pgs. 1,5,24-29. 1.00 2.50
1 (12/93, $2.50)-Polybagged w/trading card; Kirby Liefeld-c; Kirby plots/pencils w/inks by Liefeld, McFarlane, Jim Lee, Silvestri, Larsen, Williams, Ordway & Miki. 1.00 2.50
2 ($3.50)-Kirby-a(p); Kirby/Larson-c 1.40 3.50
3-7: 3-(5/94, $2.50)-Kirby/McFarlane-c 4-(5/94)-Kirby-c(p). 5-(6/94). 1.00 2.50

PHANTOM GUARD
Oct, 1997 - Present ($2.50)
Image Comics (WildStorm Productions)

1,2: 1-Two covers 2.50
1-($3.50)-Voyager Pack w/Wildcore preview 3.50

PHANTOM LADY (1st Series) (My Love Secret #24 on) (Also see All Top, Daring Adventures, Freedom Fighters, Jungle Thrills, & Wonder Boy)
No. 13, Aug, 1947 - No. 23 Apr, 1949
Fox Features Syndicate

	GD25	FN65	NM94
13(#1)-Phantom Lady by Matt Baker begins (1st app.); The Blue Beetle story	300.00	900.00	2900.00
14(#2)-Not Baker-c	200.00	600.00	1700.00
15-P.L. injected with experimental drug	200.00	600.00	1700.00
16-Negligee-c, panels; true crime stories begin	200.00	600.00	1700.00
17-Classic bondage cover; used in **SOTI**, illo "Sexual stimulation by combining 'headlights' with the sadist's dream of tying up a woman"	422.00	1266.00	4000.00
18,19	143.00	431.00	1200.00
20-23: 23-Bondage-c	112.00	338.00	900.00

NOTE: ***Matt Baker*** *a-in all; c-13, 15-21.* ***Kamen*** *a-22, 23.*

PHANTOM LADY (2nd Series) (See Terrific Comics) (Formerly Linda)
V1#5, Dec-Jan, 1954/1955 - No. 4, June, 1955
Ajax/Farrell Publ.

	GD25	FN65	NM94
V1#5(#1)-By Matt Baker	87.00	262.00	750.00
V1#2-Last pre-code	73.00	219.00	600.00
3,4-Red Rocket. 3-Heroin story	58.00	174.00	475.00

PHANTOM PLANET, THE
No. 1234, 1961
Dell Publishing Co.

	GD25	FN65	NM94
Four Color 1234-Movie	6.40	19.00	70.00

PHANTOM STRANGER, THE (1st Series)(See Saga of Swamp Thing)
Aug-Sept, 1952 - No. 6, June-July, 1953
National Periodical Publications

	GD25	FN65	NM94
1(Scarce)-1st app.	156.00	468.00	1400.00
2 (Scarce)	100.00	300.00	800.00
3-6 (Scarce)	87.00	262.00	700.00

PHANTOM STRANGER, THE (2nd Series) (See Showcase #80)
May-June, 1969 - No. 41, Feb-Mar, 1976
National Periodical Publications

	GD25	FN65	NM94
1-2nd S.A. app. P. Stranger; only 12¢ issue	7.00	21.00	70.00
2,3	2.80	8.40	28.00
4-1st new look Phantom Stranger; N. Adams-a	3.20	9.60	32.00
5-7	2.50	7.50	20.00
8-14: 14-Last 15¢ issue	2.00	6.00	16.00
15-19: All 25¢ giants (52 pgs.)	1.75	5.25	14.00
20-Dark Circle begins, ends #24.	1.50	4.50	12.00
21,22:	1.00	2.80	7.00
23-Spawn of Frankenstein begins by Kaluta	1.85	5.50	15.00
24,25,27-30-Last Spawn of Frankenstein	1.25	3.75	10.00
26- Book-length story featuring Phantom Stranger, Dr.13 & Spawn of Frankenstein	1.50	4.50	12.00
31-The Black Orchid begins (6-7/74).	1.85	5.50	15.00
32-38: 33-Deadman-c/story. 34-Last 20¢ issue (#35 on are 25¢).	1.00	3.00	8.00
39-41-Deadman app.	1.50	4.50	12.00

NOTE: ***N. Adams*** *a-4; c-3-19.* ***Anderson*** *a-4, 5i.* ***Aparo*** *a-7-17, 19-26; c-20-24, 33-41.* ***B. Bailey*** *a-27-30.* ***DeZuniga*** *a-12-16, 18, 19, 21, 22, 31, 34.* ***Grell*** *a-33.* ***Kaluta*** *a-23-25; c-26.* ***Meskin*** *r-15, 16, 18, 19.* ***Redondo*** *a-32, 35, 36.* ***Sparling*** *a-20.* ***Starr*** *a-17r.* ***Toth*** *a-15r. Black Orchid by* ***Carrilo****-38-41. Dr. 13 solo in-13, 18, 19, 20, 21, 34. Frankenstein by* ***Kaluta****-23-25; by* ***Baily****-27-30. No Black Orchid-33, 34, 37.*

PHANTOM STRANGER (See Justice League of America #103)
Oct, 1987 - No. 4, Jan, 1988 (75¢, limited series)
DC Comics

	GD25	FN65	NM94
1-Mignola/Russell-c/a & Eclipso app. in all		.80	2.00
2-4: 3,4-Eclipso-c			1.25

PHANTOM: THE GHOST WHO WALKS
Feb, 1995 - No. 3, Apr, 1995 ($2.95, limited series)
Marvel Comics

	GD25	FN65	NM94
1-3		1.20	3.00

PHANTOM 2040 (TV cartoon)
May, 1995 - No. 4, Aug, 1995 ($1.50)
Marvel Comics

	GD25	FN65	NM94
1-4-Based on animated series			1.50

PHANTOM WITCH DOCTOR (Also see Durango Kid #8 & Eerie #8)
1952
Avon Periodicals

	GD25	FN65	NM94
1-Kinstler-c/a (7 pgs.)	40.00	120.00	300.00

PHANTOM ZONE, THE (See Adventure #283 & Superboy #100, 104)
January, 1982 - No. 4, April, 1982
DC Comics

	GD25	FN65	NM94
1-Superman app. in all			1.10
2-4: Batman, Green Lantern app.			1.35

NOTE: ***Colan*** *a-1-4p; c-1-4p.* ***Giordano*** *c-1-4i.*

PHAZE
Apr, 1988 - No. 2, Oct, 1988 ($2.25)
Eclipse Comics

	GD25	FN65	NM94
1,2: 2-Gulacy painted-c		.90	2.25

PHIL RIZZUTO (Baseball Hero)(See Sport Thrills, Accepted reprint)
1951 (New York Yankees)
Fawcett Publications

	GD25	FN65	NM94
nn-Photo-c	53.00	159.00	480.00

PHOENIX
Jan, 1975 - No. 4, Oct, 1975
Atlas/Seaboard Publ.

	GD25	FN65	NM94
1-Origin		1.60	4.00
2-4: 3-Origin & only app. The Dark Avenger. 4-New origin/costume The Protector (formerly Phoenix)		1.20	3.00

NOTE: ***Infantino*** *appears in #1, 2.* ***Austin*** *a-3i.* ***Thorne*** *c-3.*

PHOENIX (...The Untold Story)
April, 1984 ($2.00, one-shot)
Marvel Comics Group

	GD25	FN65	NM94
1-Byrne/Austin-r/X-Men #137 with original unpublished ending	1.25	3.75	10.00

PHOENIX RESURRECTION, THE
1995 - 1996 ($3.95)
Malibu Comics (Ultraverse)

Pictorial Romances #10 © STJ

Picture Parade #2 © GIL

Pinhead #2 © Clive Barker

GD25 FN65 NM94

Genesis #1 (12/95)-X-Men app; wraparound-c 1.60 4.00
Revelations #1 (12/95)-X-Men app; wraparound-c 1.60 4.00
Aftermath #1 (1/96)-X-Men app. 1.60 4.00
0-($1.95)-r/series .80 2.00
0-American Entertainment Ed. 2.00 5.00

PICNIC PARTY (See Dell Giants)

PICTORIAL CONFESSIONS (Pictorial Romances #4 on)
Sept, 1949 - No. 3, Dec, 1949
St. John Publishing Co.

1-Baker-c/a(3) 22.00 66.00 175.00
2-Baker-a; photo-c 14.00 41.00 110.00
3-Kubert, Baker-a; part Kubert-c 14.00 41.00 110.00

PICTORIAL LOVE STORIES (Formerly Tim McCoy)
No. 22, Oct, 1949 - No. 26, July, 1950 (all photo-c)
Charlton Comics

22-26: All have "Me-Dan Cupid". 25-Fred Astaire-c 15.00 45.00 110.00

PICTORIAL LOVE STORIES
October, 1952
St. John Publishing Co.

1-Baker-c 21.00 64.00 160.00

PICTORIAL ROMANCES (Formerly Pictorial Confessions)
No. 4, Jan, 1950; No. 5, Jan, 1951 - No. 24, Mar, 1954
St. John Publishing Co.

4-Baker-a; photo-c 21.00 64.00 170.00
5,10-All Matt Baker issues. 5-Reprints all stories from #4 w/new Baker-c
15.50 47.00 125.00
6-9,12,13,15,16-Baker-c, 2-3 stories 11.30 34.00 90.00
11-Baker-c/a(3); Kubert-r/Hollywood Confessions #1
12.00 36.00 95.00
14,21-24: Baker-c/a each. 21,24-Each has signed story by Estrada
10.00 30.00 75.00
17-20(7/53, 25¢, 100 pgs.): Baker-c/a; each has two signed stories by Estrada
21.00 64.00 160.00

NOTE: ***Matt Baker** art in most issues. **Estrada** a-17-20(2), 21, 24.*

PICTURE NEWS
Jan, 1946 - No. 10, Jan-Feb, 1947
Lafayette Street Corp.

1-Milt Gross begins, ends No. 6; 4 pg. Kirby-a; A-Bomb-c/story
31.00 94.00 250.00
2-Atomic explosion panels; Frank Sinatra/Perry Como story
15.00 45.00 120.00
3-Atomic explosion panels; Frank Sinatra, June Allyson, Benny Goodman stories 12.00 36.00 95.00
4-Atomic explosion panels; "Caesar and Cleopatra" movie adapt. w/Claude Raines & Vivian Leigh; Jackie Robinson story 15.00 45.00 120.00
5-7: 5-Hank Greenberg story. 6-Joe Louis-c/story 9.50 28.00 75.00
8-Monte Hale story (9-10/46; 1st?) 10.50 32.00 85.00
9-A-Bomb story; "Crooked Mile" movie adaptation; Joe DiMaggio story
10.50 32.00 85.00
10-Dick Quick; A-Bomb story; Krigstein, Gross-a 10.50 32.00 85.00

PICTURE PARADE (Picture Progress #5 on)
Sept, 1953 - V1#4, Dec, 1953 (28 pgs.)
Gilberton Company (Also see A Christmas Adventure)

V1#1-Andy's Atomic Adventures; A-bomb blast-c; (Teachers version distributed to schools exists) 14.00 41.00 110.00
2-Around the World with the United Nations 8.75 26.25 65.00
3-Adventures of the Lost One(The American Indian), 4-A Christmas Adventure (r-under same title in 1969) 8.75 26.25 65.00

PICTURE PROGRESS (Formerly Picture Parade)
V1#5, Jan, 1954 - V3#2, Oct, 1955 (28-36 pgs.)
Gilberton Corp.

V1#5-9,V2#1-9: 5-News in Review 1953. 6-The Birth of America. 7-The Four Seasons. 8-Paul Revere's Ride. 9-The Hawaiian Islands(5/54). V2#1-The Story of Flight(9/54). 2-Vote for Crazy River(The Meaning of Elections). 3-Louis Pasteur. 4-The Star Spangled Banner. 5-News in Review 1954. 6-Alaska: The Great Land. 7-Life in the Circus. 8-The Time of the Cave Man. 9-Summer Fun(5/55) 4.25 13.00 28.00
V3#1,2: 1-The Man Who Discovered America. 2-The Lewis & Clark Expedition
4.25 13.00 28.00

PICTURE SCOPE JUNGLE ADVENTURES (See Jungle Thrills)

PICTURE STORIES FROM AMERICAN HISTORY
1945 - No. 4, Sum, 1947 (#1,2: 10¢, 56 pgs.; #3,4: 15¢, 52 pgs.)
National/All-American/E. C. Comics

1 22.00 66.00 175.00
2-4 17.50 53.00 140.00

PICTURE STORIES FROM SCIENCE
Spring, 1947 - No. 2, Fall, 1947
E.C. Comics

1,2: 1-(15¢). 2-(10¢) 22.00 66.00 175.00

PICTURE STORIES FROM THE BIBLE (See Narrative Illustration, the Story of the Comics by M.C. Gaines)
1942 - No. 4, Fall, 1943; 1944-46
National/All-American/E.C. Comics

1-4('42-Fall, '43)-Old Testament (DC) 19.00 56.00 150.00
Complete Old Testament Edition, (12/43-DC, 50¢, 232 pgs.);-1st printing; contains #1-4; 2nd - 8th (1/47) printings exist; later printings by E.C.
23.00 68.00 180.00
Complete Old Testament Edition (1945-publ. by Bible Pictures Ltd.)-232 pgs., hardbound, in color with dust jacket 23.00 68.00 180.00

NOTE: *Both Old and New Testaments published in England by Bible Pictures Ltd. in hardback, 1943, in color, 376 pgs. (2 vols.: O.T. 232 pgs. & N.T. 144 pgs.), and were also published by Scarf Press in 1979 (Old Test., $9.95) and in 1980 (New Test., $7.95)*

1-3(New Test.; 1944-46, DC)-52 pgs. ea. 14.00 41.00 110.00
The Complete Life of Christ Edition (1945, 25¢, 96 pgs.)-Contains #1&2 of the New Testament Edition 19.00 56.00 150.00
1,2(Old Testament-r in comic book form)(E.C., 1946; 52 pgs.)
14.00 41.00 110.00
1(DC),2(AA),3(EC)(New Testament-r in comic book form)(E.C., 1946; 52 pgs.)
14.00 41.00 110.00
Complete New Testament Edition (1946-E.C., 50¢, 144 pgs.)-Contains #1-3
19.00 56.00 150.00

NOTE: *Another British series entitled **The Bible Illustrated** from 1947 has recently been discovered, with the same internal artwork. This eight edition series (5-OT, 3-NT) is of particular interest to Classics Ill. collectors because it exactly copied the C.I. logo format. The British publisher was Thorpe & Porter, who in 1951 began publishing the British Classics Ill. series. All editions of The Bible Ill. have new British painted covers. While this market is still new, and not all editions have as yet been found, current market value is about the same as the first U.S. editions of Picture Stories From The Bible.*

PICTURE STORIES FROM WORLD HISTORY
Spring, 1947 - No. 2, Summer, 1947 (52, 48 pgs.)
E.C. Comics

1,2: 1-(15¢). 2-(10¢) 22.00 66.00 175.00

PINHEAD
Dec, 1993 - No. 9, 1994 ($2.50)
Marvel Comics (Epic Comics)

1-($2.95)-Embossed foil-c by Kelley Jones; Intro Pinhead & Disciples (Snakeoil, Hangman, Fan Dancer & Dixie) 1.20 3.00
2-9 1.00 2.50

PINHEAD & FOODINI (TV)(Also see Foodini & Jingle Dingle Christmas…)
July, 1951 - No. 4, Jan, 1952 (Early TV comic)
Fawcett Publications

Pinky & The Brain #5 © Warner Bros.

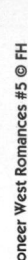

Pioneer West Romances #5 © FH

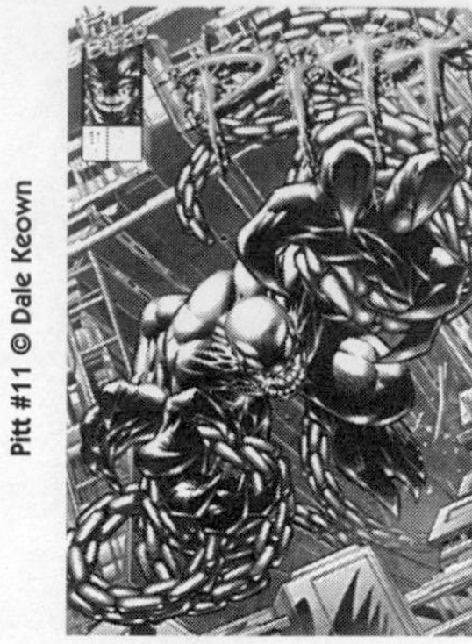
Pitt #11 © Dale Keown

	GD25	FN65	NM94
1-(52 pgs.)-Photo-c; based on TV puppet show	26.00	80.00	210.00
2-Photo-c	12.00	36.00	95.00
3,4: 3-Photo-c	9.50	28.00	75.00

PINHEAD VS. MARSHALL LAW (Law in Hell)
Nov, 1993 - No. 2, Dec, 1993 ($2.95, limited series)
Marvel Comics (Epic Comics)

	GD25	FN65	NM94
1,2: 1-Embossed red foil-c. 2-Embossed silver foil-c		1.20	3.00

PINK PANTHER, THE (TV)(See The Inspector & Kite Fun Book)
April, 1971 - No. 87, 1984
Gold Key

	GD25	FN65	NM94
1-The Inspector begins	3.60	11.00	40.00
2-5	1.65	5.00	18.00
6-10	1.40	4.20	14.00
11-30: Warren Tufts-a #16-on	1.00	3.00	10.00
31-60	.80	2.40	8.00
61-87		2.00	5.00
Mini-comic No. 1(1976)(3-1/4x6-1/2")		2.40	6.00

NOTE: *Pink Panther began as a movie cartoon. (See Golden Comics Digest #38, 45 and March of Comics #376, 384, 390, 409, 418, 429, 441, 449, 461, 473, 486); #37, 72, 80-85 contain reprints.*

PINK PANTHER SUPER SPECIAL (TV)
Oct, 1993 ($2.25, 68 pgs.)
Harvey Comics

	GD25	FN65	NM94
V2#1-The Inspector & Wendy Witch stories also		1.20	3.00

PINK PANTHER, THE
Nov, 1993 - No. 9, July, 1994 ($1.50)
Harvey Comics

	GD25	FN65	NM94
V2#1-9		.80	2.00

PINKY & THE BRAIN (See Animaniacs)
July, 1996 - Present ($1.75/$1.95)
DC Comics

	GD25	FN65	NM94
1-17			1.75
18-20-($1.95)			1.95
Christmas Special (1/96, $1.50)			1.50

PINKY LEE (See Adventures of...)

PINKY THE EGGHEAD
1963 (Reprints from Noodnik)
I.W./Super Comics

	GD25	FN65	NM94
I.W. Reprint #1,2(nd)		2.40	6.00
Super Reprint #14-r/Noodnik Comics #4		2.40	6.00

PINOCCHIO (See 4-Color #92, 252, 545, 1203, Mickey Mouse Mag. V5#3, Movie Comics under Wonderful Advs. of..., New Advs. of..., Thrilling Comics #2, Walt Disney Showcase, Walt Disney's..., Wonderful Advs. of..., & World's Greatest Stories #2)
No. 92, 1945 - No. 1203, Mar, 1962 (Disney)
Dell Publishing Co.

	GD25	FN65	NM94
Four Color 92-The Wonderful Adventures of...; 16 pg. Donald Duck story ; entire book by Kelly	55.00	164.00	600.00
Four Color 252 (10/49)-Origin, not by Kelly	9.00	27.00	100.00
Four Color 545 (3/54)-The Wonderful Advs. of...; part-r of 4-Color #92; Disney-movie	6.40	19.00	70.00
Four Color 1203 (3/62)	4.50	13.50	50.00

PINOCCHIO
1940 (10 pgs.; linen-like paper)
Cocomalt/Montgomery Ward Co. (Giveaway)

	GD25	FN65	NM94
nn-Cocomalt edition	14.50	43.00	115.00
nn-store edition	11.30	34.00	90.00

PINOCCHIO AND THE EMPEROR OF THE NIGHT
Mar, 1988 ($1.25, 52 pgs.)
Marvel Comics

	GD25	FN65	NM94
1-Adapts film			1.25

PINOCCHIO LEARNS ABOUT KITES (See Kite Fun Book)

PIN-UP PETE (Also see Great Lover Romances & Monty Hall...)
1952
Toby Press

	GD25	FN65	NM94
1-Jack Sparling pin-ups	14.00	41.00	110.00

PIONEER MARSHAL (See Fawcett Movie Comics)

PIONEER PICTURE STORIES
Dec, 1941 - No. 9, Dec, 1943
Street & Smith Publications

	GD25	FN65	NM94
1-The Legless Air Ace begins	23.00	68.00	180.00
2 -True life story of Errol Flynn	11.30	34.00	90.00
3-9	9.50	28.00	75.00

PIONEER WEST ROMANCES (Firehair #1,2,7-11)
No. 3, Spring, 1950 - No. 6, Winter, 1950-51
Fiction House Magazines

	GD25	FN65	NM94
3-(52 pgs.)-Firehair continues	17.00	49.00	120.00
4-6	17.00	49.00	120.00

PIPSQUEAK (See The Adventures of...)

PIRACY
Oct-Nov, 1954 - No. 7, Oct-Nov, 1955
E. C. Comics

	GD25	FN65	NM94
1-Williamson/Torres-a	24.00	71.00	190.00
2-Williamson/Torres-a	15.00	45.00	120.00
3-7	12.00	38.00	100.00

NOTE: ***Crandall*** *a-in all; c-2-4.* ***Davis*** *a-1, 2, 6.* ***Evans*** *a-3-7; c-7.* ***Ingels*** *a-3-7.* ***Krigstein*** *a-3-5, 7; c-5, 6.* ***Wood*** *a-1, 2; c-1.*

PIRANA (See The Phantom #46 & Thrill-O-Rama #2, 3)

PIRATE CORPS, THE
1987 - No. 5, 1988 ($1.95)
Eternity Comics/Slave Labor Graphics

	GD25	FN65	NM94
1-5: 3-Color begins		.80	2.00
Special 1 ('89, $1.95, B&W)-Slave Labor Publ.		.80	2.00

PIRATE OF THE GULF, THE (See Superior Stories #2)

PIRATES COMICS
Feb-Mar, 1950 - No. 4, Aug-Sept, 1950 (All 52 pgs.)
Hillman Periodicals

	GD25	FN65	NM94
1	20.00	60.00	150.00
2-Dave Berg-a	14.00	43.00	100.00
3,4-Berg-a	13.00	39.00	90.00

P.I.'S: MICHAEL MAUSER AND MS. TREE, THE
Jan, 1985 - No. 3, May, 1985 ($1.25, limited series)
First Comics

	GD25	FN65	NM94
1-3: Staton-c/a(p)			1.25

PITT, THE (Also see The Draft & The War)
Mar, 1988 ($3.25, 52 pgs., one-shot)
Marvel Comics

	GD25	FN65	NM94
1-Ties into Starbrand, D.P.7		1.40	3.50

PITT (See Youngblood #4 & Gen 13 #3,#4)
Jan, 1993 - Present ($1.95, intended as a four part limited series)
Image Comics #1-9/Full Bleed #1/2,10-on

	GD25	FN65	NM94
1/2-(12/95)-1st Full Bleed issue			1.50
1-Dale Keown-c/a. 1-1st app. The Pitt		1.40	3.50
2,4: Dale Keown-c/a		.80	2.00
3 (Low distribution)		1.20	3.00
5-13: All Dale Keown-c/a. 10 (1/96)-Indicia reads "January 1995"			

The Pixies #3 © ME

Planet Comics #1 © FH

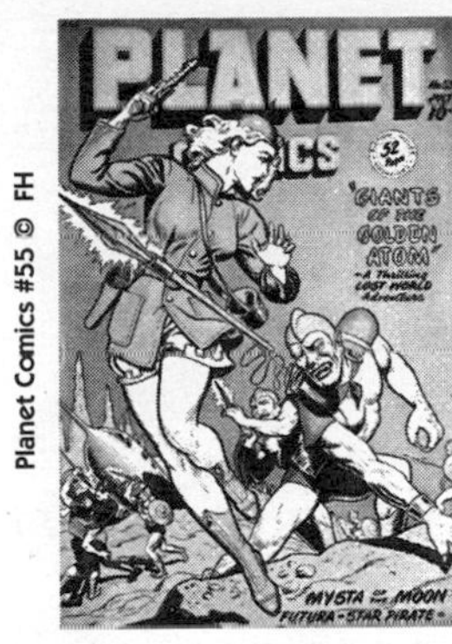

Planet Comics #55 © FH

GD25 FN65 NM94

.80 2.00
14-16: 14-Begin $2.50-c, pullout poster 1.00 2.50
TPB-(1997, $9.95) r/#1/2, 1-4 1.25 3.75 10.00

PITT IN THE BLOOD
Aug, 1996 ($2.50, one-shot)
Full Bleed Studios
nn-Richard Pace-a/script 1.00 2.50

PIUS XII MAN OF PEACE
No date (12 pgs.; 5-1/2x8-1/2") (B&W)
nn-Catechetical Guild Giveaway 4.00 10.50 21.00

PIXIE & DIXIE & MR. JINKS (TV)(See Jinks, Pixie, and Dixie & Whitman Comic Books)
July-Sept, 1960 - Feb, 1963 (Hanna-Barbera)
Dell Publishing Co./Gold Key
Four Color 1112 6.40 19.00 70.00
Four Color 1196,1264 4.50 13.50 50.00
01-631-207 (Dell, 7/62), 1(2/63-Gold Key) 4.50 13.50 50.00

PIXIE PUZZLE ROCKET TO ADVENTURELAND
Nov, 1952
Avon Periodicals
1 9.50 28.00 75.00

PIXIES, THE (Advs. of...)(The Mighty Atom and ...#6 on)(See A-1 Comics #16)
Winter, 1946 - No. 4, Fall?, 1947; No. 5, 1948
Magazine Enterprises
1-Mighty Atom 5.70 17.00 40.00
2-5-Mighty Atom 4.00 11.00 22.00
I.W. Reprint #1(1958), 8-(Pee-Wee Pixies), 10-I.W. on cover, Super on inside 1.10 3.30 9.00

PIZZAZZ
1977 - 1979 (slick-color kids mag. w/puzzles, games, comics)
Marvel Comics Group
1-Star Wars photo-c/article; origin Tarzan 2.50 7.50 20.00
2-Spider-Man-c 1.50 4.50 12.00
3-8: 3-Close Encounters-c. 4-Alice Cooper. 7-James Bond. 8-TV Spider-Man photo-c/article 1.25 3.75 10.00
9-16: 10-Sgt. Pepper-c. 12-Battlestar Galactica-c; Spider-Man app. 13-TV Hulk-c/sty. 15-Battlestar Galactica-c/sty. 16-Movie Superman photo-c/sty. 2.40 6.00
NOTE: **Star Wars** comics in all. **Tarzan** comics, 1pg.-#1-8. 1pg. "Hey Look" by Kurtzman #12-16.

PLANET COMICS
1/40 - No. 62, 9/49; No. 63, Wint, 1949-50; No. 64, Spring, 1950; No. 65, 1951(nd); No. 66-68, 1952(nd); No. 69, Wint, 1952-53; No. 70-72, 1953(nd); No. 73, Winter, 1953-54
Fiction House Magazines

	GD25	FN65	VF82	NM94
1-Origin Auro, Lord of Jupiter by Briefer (ends #61); Flint Baker & The Red Comet begin; Eisner/Fine-c	900.00	2700.00	5400.00	9000.00

(Estimated up to 160 total copies exist, 10 in NM/Mint)

	GD25	FN65	NM94
2-Lou Fine-c (Scarce)	340.00	1020.00	3400.00
3-Eisner-c	240.00	720.00	2400.00
4-Gale Allen and the Girl Squadron begins	211.00	633.00	1900.00
5,6-(Scarce): 5-Eisner/Fine-c	200.00	600.00	1800.00
7-12: 8-Robot-c. 12-The Star Pirate begins	167.00	500.00	1500.00
13-14: 13-Reff Ryan begins	122.00	366.00	1100.00
15-(Scarce)-Mars, God of War begins (11/41); see Jumbo Comics #31 for 1st app.	240.00	720.00	2200.00
16-20,22	111.00	333.00	1000.00
21-The Lost World & Hunt Bowman begin	114.00	342.00	1025.00
23-26: 26-Space Rangers begin (9/43), end #71	106.00	318.00	950.00
27-30	86.00	258.00	775.00
31-35: 33-Origin Star Pirates Wonder Boots, reprinted in #52. 35-Mysta of the Moon begins, ends #62	72.00	216.00	650.00
36-45: 38-1st Mysta of the Moon-c. 41-New origin of "Auro, Lord of Jupiter". 42-Last Gale Allen. 43-Futura begins	64.00	192.00	575.00
46-60: 48-Robot-c. 53-Used in **SOTI**, pg. 32	50.00	150.00	450.00
61-68,70: 61-Last 68 pg. issue. 64,70-Robot-c. 65-70-All partial-r of earlier issues. 70-r/stories from #41	36.00	108.00	325.00
69-Used in **POP**, pgs. 101,102	36.00	108.00	325.00
71-73-No series stories. 71-Space Rangers strip	30.00	90.00	240.00
I.W. Reprint #1(nd)-r/#70; cover-r from Attack on Planet Mars	6.00	18.00	60.00
I.W. Reprint #8 (r/#72), 9-r/#73	6.00	18.00	60.00

NOTE: ***Anderson*** *a-33-38, 40-51 (Star Pirate).* ***Matt Baker*** *a-53-59 (Mysta of the Moon).* ***Celardo*** *c-12.* ***Bill Discount*** *a-71 (Space Rangers).* ***Elias*** *c-70.* ***Evans*** *a-46-49 (Auro, Lord of Jupiter), 50-64 (Lost World).* ***Fine*** *c-2, 5.* ***Hopper*** *a-31, 35 (Gale Allen), 41, 42, 48, 49 (Mysta of the Moon).* ***Ingels*** *a-24-31 (Lost World), 56-61 (Auro, Lord of Jupiter).* ***Lubbers*** *a-44-47 (Space Rangers); c-40, 41.* ***Moriera*** *a-43, 44 (Mysta of the Moon.* ***Renee*** *a-40-49 (Lost World); c-33, 35, 39.* ***Tuska*** *a-30 (Star Pirate).* ***M. Whitman*** *a-50-52 (Mysta of the Moon), 53-58 (Star Pirate); c-71-73.* ***Starr*** *a-59.* ***Zolnerwich*** *c-10. 13-25. Bondage c-53.*

PLANET COMICS
Apr, 1988 - No. 3 (2.00, color/B&W #3)
Blackthorne Publishing
1-3: New stories. 1-Dave Stevens-c .80 2.00

PLANET OF THE APES (Magazine) (Also see Adventures on the... & Power Record Comics)
Aug, 1974 - No. 29, Feb, 1977 (B&W) (Based on movies)
Marvel Comics Group
1-Ploog-a 2.50 7.50 24.00
2-Ploog-a 1.50 4.50 12.00
3-20 1.10 3.30 9.00
21-29 1.50 4.50 12.00
NOTE: ***Alcala*** *a-7-11, 17-22, 24.* ***Ploog*** *a-1-4, 6, 8, 11, 13, 14, 19.* ***Sutton*** *a-11, 12, 15, 17, 19, 20, 23, 24, 29.* ***Tuska*** *a-1-6.*

PLANET OF THE APES
Apr, 1990 - No. 24, 1992 ($2.50, B&W)
Adventure Comics
1-New movie tie-in; comes w/outer-c (3 colors) 2.00 5.00
1-Limited serial numbered edition ($5.00) 2.00 5.00
1-2nd printing (no outer-c, $2.50) 1.00 2.50
2-24 1.00 2.50
Annual 1 ($3.50) 1.40 3.50
...Urchak's Folly 1-4 ($2.50, mini-series) 1.00 2.50

PLANET OF VAMPIRES
Feb, 1975 - No. 3, July, 1975
Seaboard Publications (Atlas)
1-Neal Adams-c(i); 1st Broderick c/a(p) 1.60 4.00
2,3: 2-Neal Adams-c. 3-Heath-c/a 1.20 3.00

PLANET TERRY
April, 1985 - No. 12, March, 1986 (Children's comic)
Marvel Comics (Star Comics)/Marvel
1-12 .80 2.00

PLASM (See Warriors of Plasm)
June, 1993
Defiant Comics
0-Came bound into Diamond Previews V3#6 (6/93); price is for complete Previews with comic still attached 1.20 3.00
0-Comic only removed from Previews .80 2.00

PLASMER
Nov, 1993 - No. 4, Feb, 1994 ($1.95, limited series)
Marvel Comics UK

Plastic Man #61 © QUA

Plop #7 © DC

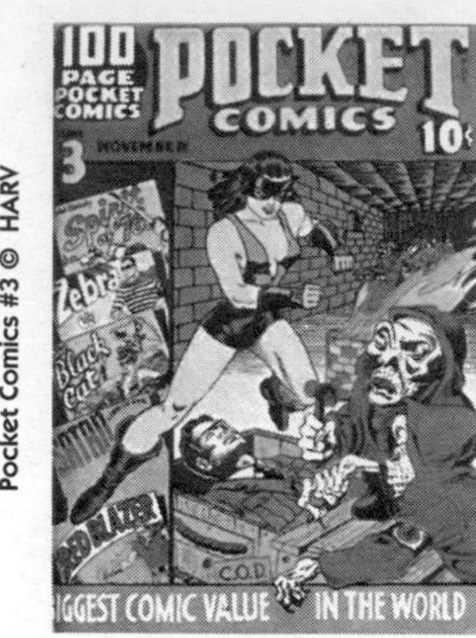

Pocket Comics #3 © HARV

	GD25	FN65	NM94
1-($2.50)-Polybagged w/4 trading cards		1.00	2.50
2-4: Capt. America & Silver Surfer app.		.80	2.00

PLASTIC FORKS
1990 - No. 5, 1990 ($4.95, 68 pgs., limited series, mature)
Marvel Comis (Epic Comics)

	GD25	FN65	NM94
Book 1-5: Squarebound		2.00	5.00

PLASTIC MAN (Also see Police Comics & Smash Comics #17)
Sum, 1943 - No. 64, Nov, 1956
Vital Publ. No. 1,2/Quality Comics No. 3 on

	GD25	FN65	NM94
nn(#1)- "In The Game of Death"; Skull-c; Jack Cole-c/a begins; ends-#64?	290.00	870.00	2900.00
nn(#2, 2/44)- "The Gay Nineties Nightmare"	133.00	400.00	1200.00
3 (Spr, '46)	86.00	258.00	775.00
4 (Sum, '46)	69.00	207.00	625.00
5 (Aut, '46)	58.00	174.00	525.00
6-10	47.00	141.00	425.00
11-20	42.00	126.00	375.00
21-30: 26-Last non-r issue?	36.00	108.00	300.00
31-40: 40-Used in POP, pg. 91	28.00	84.00	225.00
41-64: 53-Last precode issue. 54-Robot-c	24.00	71.00	190.00
Super Reprint 11,16,18: 11('63)-r/#16. 16-r/#18 & #21; Cole-a. 18('64)-Spirit-r by Eisner from Police #95	4.00	12.00	40.00

NOTE: ***Cole** r-44, 49, 56, 58, 59 at least. **Cuidera** c-32-64i.*

PLASTIC MAN (See DC Special #15 & House of Mystery #160)
11-12/66 - No. 10, 5-6/68; V4#11, 2-3/76 - No. 20, 10-11/77
National Periodical Publications/DC Comics

	GD25	FN65	NM94
1-Real 1st app. Silver Age Plastic Man (House of Mystery #160 is actually tryout); Gil Kane-c/a; 12¢ issues begin	6.50	19.50	65.00
2-5: 4-Infantino-c; Mortimer-a	3.00	9.00	30.00
6-10('68): 7-G.A. Plastic Man & Woozy Winks (1st S.A. app.) app.; origin retold. 10-Sparling-a; last 12¢ issue	2.25	6.75	18.00
V4#11('76)-20: 11-20-Fraden-p. 17-Origin retold		2.00	5.00

PLASTIC MAN
Nov, 1988 - No. 4, Feb, 1989 ($1.00, mini-series)
DC Comics

	GD25	FN65	NM94
1-4: 1-Origin; Woozy Winks app.			1.00

PLASTRON CAFE
Dec, 1992 - 1993 ($2.25, B&W)
Mirage Studios

	GD25	FN65	NM94
1-4: 1-Teenage Mutant Ninja Turtles app.; Kelly Freas-c. 2-Hildebrandt painted-c. 4-Spaced & Alien Fire stories		.90	2.25

PLAYFUL LITTLE AUDREY (TV)(Also see Little Audrey #25)
6/57 - No. 110, 11/73; No. 111, 8/74 - No. 121, 4/76
Harvey Publications

	GD25	FN65	NM94
1	17.00	51.00	170.00
2	9.00	27.00	90.00
3-5	6.00	18.00	60.00
6-10	3.80	11.40	38.00
11-20	2.60	7.80	26.00
21-40	2.25	6.75	18.00
41-60	1.75	5.25	14.00
61-80	1.25	3.75	10.00
81-99	1.00	2.80	7.00
100-52 pg. Giant	1.25	3.75	10.00
101-103: 52 pg. Giants	1.10	3.30	9.00
104-121		1.60	4.00
...In 3-D (Spring, 1988, $2.25, Blackthorne #66)		.90	2.25

PLOP! (Also see The Best of DC #60)
Sept-Oct, 1973 - No. 24, Nov-Dec, 1976
National Periodical Publications

	GD25	FN65	NM94
1,5: 1-Sergio Aragonés-a; 1,5-Wrightson-a	1.85	5.50	15.00
2-20	1.00	3.00	8.00
21-24 (52 pgs.). 23-No Aragonés-a (52 pgs.)	1.50	4.50	12.00

NOTE: ***Alcala** a-1-3. **Anderson** a-5. **Aragonés** a-1-22, 24. **Ditko** a-16p. **Evans** a-1. **Mayer** a-1. **Orlando** a-21, 22; c-21. **Sekowsky** a-5, 6p. **Toth** a-11. **Wolverton** r-4, 22-24(1 pg.ea.); c-1-12, 14, 17, 18. **Wood** a-14, 16i, 18-24; c-13, 15, 16, 19.*

PLUTO (See Cheerios Premiums, Four Color #537, Mickey Mouse Magazine, Walt Disney Showcase #4, 7, 13, 20, 23, 33 & Wheaties)
No. 7, 1942; No. 429, 10/52 - No. 1248, 11-1/61-62 (Walt Disney)
Dell Publishing Co.

	GD25	FN65	NM94
Large Feature Comic 7(1942)-Written by Carl Barks, Jack Hannah, & Nick George (Barks' 1st comic book work)	105.00	315.00	1150.00
Four Color 429 (#1)	8.00	23.00	85.00
Four Color 509	4.50	13.50	50.00
Four Color 595,654,736,853	2.75	8.00	30.00
Four Color 941,1039,1143,1248	2.75	8.00	30.00

POCAHONTAS
1941 - No. 2, 1942
Pocahontas Fuel Company (Coal)

	GD25	FN65	NM94
nn(#1), 2	9.50	28.00	75.00

POCKET COMICS (Becomes Super Duper #5?; also see Double Up)
Aug, 1941 - No. 4, Jan, 1942 (Pocket size; 100 pgs.)
Harvey Publications (1st Harvey comic)

	GD25	FN65	NM94
1-Origin & 1st app. The Black Cat, Cadet Blakey the Spirit of '76, The Red Blazer, The Phantom, Sphinx, & The Zebra; Phantom Ranger, British Agent #99, Spin Hawkins, Satan, Lord of Evil begin (1st app. of each); Simon-c/a in #1-3	78.00	234.00	700.00
2-Black Cat on-c #2-4	53.00	159.00	475.00
3,4	40.00	120.00	360.00

POGO PARADE (See Dell Giants)

POGO POSSUM (Also see Animal Comics & Special Delivery)
No. 105, 4/46 - No. 148, 5/47; 10-12/49 - No. 16, 4-6/54
Dell Publishing Co.

	GD25	FN65	NM94
Four Color 105(1946)-Kelly-c/a	61.00	184.00	675.00
Four Color 148-Kelly-c/a	55.00	164.00	600.00
1-(10-12/49)-Kelly-c/a in all	46.00	137.00	500.00
2	36.00	109.00	400.00
3-5	25.00	74.00	270.00
6-10: 10-Infinity-c	21.00	63.00	230.00
11-16: 11-X-Mas-c	16.00	49.00	180.00

NOTE: *#1-4, 9-13: 52 pgs.; #5-8, 14-16: 36 pgs.*

POINT BLANK
May, 1989 - No. 2, 1989 ($2.95, B&W, magazine)
Acme Press (Eclipse)

	GD25	FN65	NM94
1,2-European-r		1.20	3.00

POISON ELVES (Formerly I, Lusipher)
No. 8, 1993- No. 20, 1995 (B&W, magazine/comic size, mature readers)
Mulehide Graphics

	GD25	FN65	NM94
8-Drew Hayes-c/a/scripts.	4.00	12.00	40.00
9-11: 11-1st comic size issue	4.00	12.00	40.00
12,14,16,20	2.80	8.40	28.00
13,15-scarce	5.00	15.00	50.00
15-2nd print		2.00	5.00
17-19	3.00	9.00	30.00

POISON ELVES (See I, Lusiphur)
June, 1995 - Present ($2.50, B&W, mature readers)
Sirius Entertainment

	GD25	FN65	NM94
1-Linsner-c; Drew Hayes-a/scripts in all.	1.50	4.50	12.00
1-2nd print		1.20	3.00
2-24: 12-Purple Marauder-c/app.		1.60	4.00

Police Against Crime #2 © FG

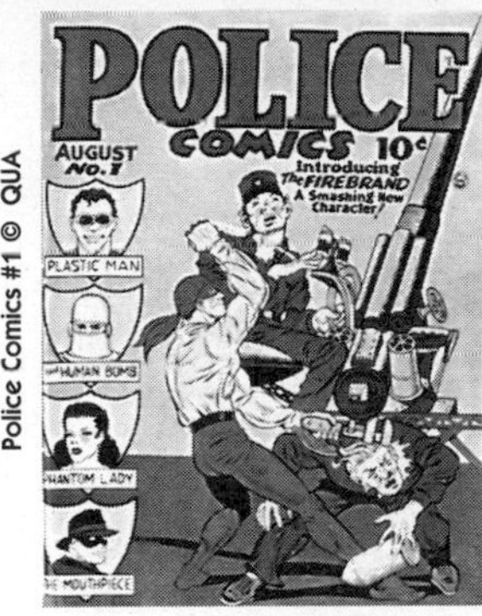

Police Comics #1 © QUA

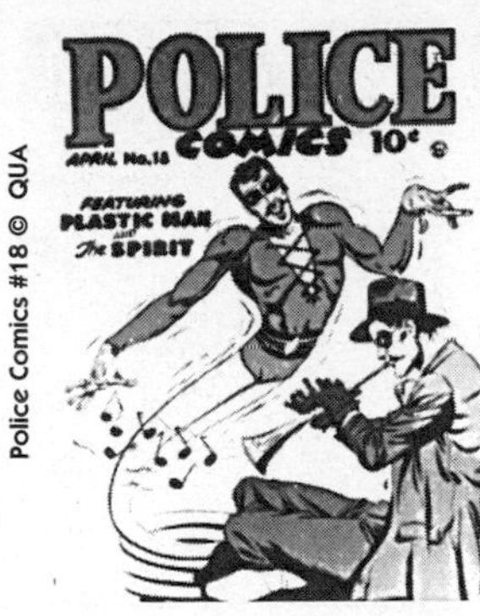

Police Comics #18 © QUA

GD25 FN65 NM94

25-($2.95) 1.20 3.00
26-30 1.00 2.50
... FAN Edition #1 mail-in offer; Drew Hayes-c/s/a 1.50 4.50 12.00
...Requiem For An Elf (6/96, $14.95, trade paperback)-Reprints I, Lusiphur #1-6 15.00
TPB-(1996, $14.95)-Reprints I, Lusiphur #7-12 15.00
TPB-(1997, $14.95)-Reprints I, Lusiphur #13-18 15.00

POIZON
Oct, 1995 - Present ($3.00)
London NIght Studios

0,1/2-3: 1/2-Razor-c/app. 1-Razor & Stryke app.; wraparound-c. 2-Razor & Stryke app. 3-Razor-c/app. 1.20 3.00
0-($5.00) Nude photo-c 2.00 5.00
0-Gothchik Edition 2.00 5.00
1-($5.95)-Necro-Nude Edition 2.40 6.00
1-Purple Reign Edition 2.00 5.00
1-($15.00)-Green Death Edition; in green envelope w/certificate 15.00

POIZON: CADILLACS AND GREEN TOMATOES
1997 - Present ($3.00)
London NIght Studios

1-3 1.20 3.00
1-3-($6.00) Nude photo-c 2.40 6.00

POLICE ACADEMY (TV)
Nov, 1989 - No. 6, Feb, 1990 ($1.00)
Marvel Comics

1-6: Based on TV cartoon; Post-c/a(p) in all 1.00

POLICE ACTION
Jan, 1954 - No. 7, Nov, 1954
Atlas News Co.

1-Violent-a by Robert Q. Sale 16.00 47.00 120.00
2 9.00 27.00 60.00
3-7: 7-Powell-a 7.50 22.50 50.00
NOTE: ***Ayers** a-4, 5. **Colan** a-1. **Forte** a-1, 2. **Mort Lawrence** a-5. **Maneely** a-3; c-1, 5. **Reinman** a-6, 7.*

POLICE ACTION
Feb, 1975 - No. 3, June, 1975
Atlas/Seaboard Publ.

1-3: 1-Lomax, N.Y.P.D., Luke Malone begin; McWilliams-a. 2-Origin Luke Malone, Manhunter 1.20 3.00
NOTE: ***Ploog** art in all. **Sekowsky/McWilliams** a-1-3. **Thorne** c-3.*

POLICE AGAINST CRIME
April, 1954 - No. 9, Aug, 1955
Premiere Magazines

1-Disbrow-a; extreme violence (man's face slashed with knife); Hollingsworth-a 19.00 58.00 140.00
2-Hollingsworth-a 10.00 30.00 70.00
3-9 9.00 27.00 60.00

POLICE BADGE #479 (Formerly Spy Thrillers #1-4)
No. 5, Sept, 1955
Atlas Comics (PrPI)

5-Maneely-c/a (6 pgs.) 9.00 27.00 60.00

POLICE CASE BOOK (See Giant Comics Editions)

POLICE CASES (See Authentic... & Record Book of...)

POLICE COMICS
Aug, 1941 - No. 127, Oct, 1953
Quality Comics Group (Comic Magazines)

1-Origin/1st app. Plastic Man by Jack Cole (r-in DC Special #15), The Human Bomb by Gustavson, & No. 711; intro. Chic Carter by Eisner, The Firebrand by Reed Crandall, The Mouthpiece by Guardineer, Phantom Lady, & The Sword; Firebrand-c 1-4 600.00 1800.00 6000.00
2-Plastic Man smuggles opium 240.00 720.00 2200.00
3 167.00 500.00 1500.00
4 156.00 468.00 1400.00
5-Plastic Man-c begin; Plastic Man forced to smoke marijuana; Plastic Man covers begin, end #102 139.00 417.00 1250.00
6,7 128.00 384.00 1150.00
8-Manhunter begins (origin/1st app.) (3/42) 156.00 468.00 1400.00
9,10 108.00 324.00 975.00
11-The Spirit strip reprints begin by Eisner (origin-strip #1); 1st comic book app. The Spirit & 1st cover app. (9/42) 178.00 534.00 1600.00
12-Intro. Ebony 108.00 324.00 975.00
13-Intro. Woozy Winks; last Firebrand 108.00 324.00 975.00
14-19: 15-Last No. 711; Destiny begins 78.00 234.00 700.00
20-The Raven x-over in Phantom Lady; features Jack Cole himself 78.00 234.00 700.00
21,22: 21-Raven & Spider Widow x-over in Phantom Lady (cameo in #22) 63.00 189.00 565.00
23-30: 23-Last Phantom Lady. 24-26-Flatfoot Burns by Kurtzman in all 58.00 174.00 525.00
31-41: 37-1st app. Candy by Sahle & begins (12/44). 41-Last Spirit-r by Eisner 39.00 117.00 350.00
42,43-Spirit-r by Eisner/Fine 36.00 108.00 285.00
44-Fine Spirit-r begin, end #88,90,92 31.00 94.00 250.00
45-50: 50-(#50 on-c, #49 on inside, 1/46) 31.00 94.00 250.00
51-60: 58-Last Human Bomb 26.00 80.00 210.00
61-88: 63-(Some issues have #65 printed on cover, but #63 on inside) Kurtzman a, 6 pgs. 20.00 60.00 160.00
89,91,93-No Spirit stories 17.50 53.00 140.00
90,92-Spirit by Fine 22.00 66.00 175.00
94-99,101,102: Spirit by Eisner in all; 101-Last Manhunter. 102-Last Spirit & Plastic Man by Jack Cole 28.00 83.00 220.00
100 34.00 101.00 270.00
103-Content change to crime; Ken Shannon & T-Man begin (1st app. of each, 12/50) 20.00 60.00 160.00
104-111,114-127: Crandall-a most issues (not in 104,105,122,125-127). 109-Atomic bomb story 15.50 47.00 125.00
112-Crandall-a 15.50 47.00 125.00
113-Crandall-c/a(2), 9 pgs. each 16.00 49.00 130.00
NOTE: *Most Spirit stories signed by Eisner are not by him; all are reprints. **Cole** c-17, 19-21, 24-26, 28-31, 36-38, 40-42, 45-48, 65-68, 69, 73, 75. **Crandall** Firebrand-1-8. Spirit by **Eisner** 1-41, 94-102; by **Eisner/Fine**-42, 43; by **Fine**-44-88, 90, 92. 103, 109. **Al Bryant** c-33, 34. **Cole** c-17-32, 35-102(most). **Crandall** c-13, 14. **Crandall/Cuidera** c-105-127. **Eisner** c-4i. **Gill Fox** c-1-3, 4p, 5-12, 15. Bondage c-103, 109, 125.*

POLICE LINE-UP
Aug, 1951 - No. 4, July, 1952 (Painted-c #1-3)
Avon Periodicals/Realistic Comics #3,4

1-Wood-a, 1 pg. plus part-c; spanking panel-r/Saint #5 33.00 99.00 240.00
2-Classic story "The Religious Murder Cult", drugs, perversion; r/Saint #5; c-r/Avon paperback #329 23.00 69.00 170.00
3-Kubert-a(r?)/part-c; Kinstler-a (inside-c only) 17.00 49.00 120.00
4 17.00 49.00 120.00

POLICE TRAP (Public Defender In Action #7 on)
8-9/54 - No. 4, 2-3/55; No. 5, 7/55 - No. 6, 9/55
Mainline No. 1-4/Charlton No. 5,6

1-S&K covers-all issues; Meskin-a; Kirby scripts 21.00 64.00 170.00
2-4 13.00 39.00 100.00
5,6-S&K-c/a 19.00 56.00 140.00

POLICE TRAP
No. 11, 1963; No. 16-18, 1964
Super Comics

Reprint #11,16-18: 11-r/Police Trap #3. 16-r/Justice Traps the Guilty #?

Poly Pigtails #2 © PMI

Popeye #48 © KFS

Popeye Summer Special V2 #1 © KFS

GD25 FN65 NM94

17-r/Inside Crime #3 & r/Justice Traps The Guilty #83; 18-r/Inside Crime #3 1.10 3.30 9.00

POLL PARROT
Poll Parrot Shoe Store/International Shoe
1950 - No. 4, 1951; No. 2, 1959 - No. 16, 1962
K. K. Publications (Giveaway)

1 ('50)-Howdy Doody; small size 11.30 34.00 90.00
2-4('51)-Howdy Doody 8.75 26.25 70.00
2('59)-16('62): 2-The Secret of Crumbley Castle. 5-Bandit Busters. 7-The Make-Believe Mummy. 8-Mixed Up Mission('60). 10-The Frightful Flight. 11-Showdown at Sunup. 12-Maniac at Mubu Island. 13-...and the Runaway Genie. 14-Bully for You. 15-Trapped In Tall Timber. 16-...& the Rajah's Ruby('62) 2.25 6.75 18.00

POLLY & HER PALS (See Comic Monthly #1)

POLLYANNA (Disney)
No. 1129, Aug-Oct, 1960
Dell Publishing Co.

Four Color 1129-Movie, Haley Mills photo-c 7.00 22.00 80.00

POLLY PIGTAILS (Girls' Fun & Fashion Magazine #44 on)
Jan, 1946 - V4#43, Oct-Nov, 1949
Parents' Magazine Institute/Polly Pigtails

1-Infinity-c; photo-c 8.75 26.25 65.00
2-Photo-c 5.35 16.00 32.00
3-5: 3,4-Photo-c 4.00 12.00 24.00
6-10: 7-Photo-c 4.00 10.00 20.00
11-30: 22-Photo-c 2.80 7.00 14.00
31-43 2.40 6.00 12.00

PONY EXPRESS (See Tales of the...)

PONYTAIL
7-9/62 - No. 12, 10-12/65; No. 13, 11/69 - No. 20, 1/71
Dell Publishing Co./Charlton No. 13 on

12-641-209(#1) 1.80 5.50 20.00
2-12 1.50 4.50 12.00
13-20 1.00 3.00 8.00

POP COMICS
1955 (36 pgs.; 5x7"; in color) (7¢)
Modern Store Publ.

1-Funny animal 2.00 5.00

POPEYE (See Comic Album #7, 11, 15, Comics Reading Libraries, Eat Right to Work and Win, Giant Comic Album, King Comics, Kite Fun Book, Magic Comics, March of Comics #37, 52, 66, 80, 96, 117, 134, 148, 157, 169, 194, 246, 264, 274, 294, 453, 465, 477 & Wow Comics, 1st series)

POPEYE (See Thimble Theatre)
1935 (25¢; 52 pgs.; B&W) (By Segar)
David McKay Publications

1-Daily strip serial reprints- "The Gold Mine Thieves" 59.00 177.00 590.00
2-Daily strip-r 46.00 138.00 460.00
NOTE: *Popeye first entered Thimble Theatre in 1929.*

POPEYE
1937 - 1939 (All by Segar)
David McKay Publications

Feature Books nn (100 pgs.) (Very Rare) 545.00 1635.00 6000.00
Feature Books 2 (52 pgs.) 61.00 184.00 675.00
Feature Books 3 (100 pgs.)-r/nn issue with a new-c 57.00 170.00 625.00
Feature Books 5,10 (76 pgs.) 52.00 157.00 575.00
Feature Books 14 (76 pgs.) (Scarce) 61.00 184.00 675.00

POPEYE (Strip reprints through 4-Color #70)
1941 - 1947; #1, 2-4/48 - #65, 7-9/62; #66, 10/62 - #80, 5/66; #81, 8/66 - #92, 12/67; #94, 2/69 - #138, 1/77; #139, 5/78 - #171, 7/84 (no #93,160,161)
Dell #1-65/Gold Key #66-80/King #81-92/Charlton #94-138/Gold Key #139-155/ Whitman #156 on

GD25 FN65 NM94

Large Feature Comic 24('41)-Half by Segar 50.00 150.00 550.00
Four Color 25('41)-by Segar 66.00 197.00 720.00
Large Feature Comic 10('43) 42.00 125.00 460.00
Four Color 17('43),26('43)-by Segar 48.00 143.00 535.00
Four Color 43('44) 30.00 89.00 325.00
Four Color 70('45)-Title: ...& Wimpy 24.00 72.00 265.00
Four Color 113('46-original strips begin),127,145('47),168 12.00 35.00 130.00
1(2-4/48)(Dell)-All new stories continue 26.00 77.00 280.00
2 13.00 38.00 140.00
3-10: 5-Popeye on moon w/rocket-c 11.00 32.00 115.00
11-20 9.00 27.00 100.00
21-40 7.00 22.00 80.00
41-45,47-50 5.00 15.00 55.00
46-Origin Swee' Pee 7.00 22.00 80.00
51-60 4.50 13.50 50.00
61-65 (Last Dell issue) 3.60 11.00 40.00
66,67-Both 84 pgs. (Gold Key) 5.00 15.00 55.00
68-80 1.80 5.50 20.00
81-92,94-100 1.40 4.20 14.00
101-130 1.00 3.00 8.00
131-159,162-171: 144-50th Anniversary issue 2.00 5.00
Bold Detergent giveaway (Same as regular issue #94) 1.20 3.00
NOTE: *Reprints-#145, 147, 149, 151, 153, 155, 157, 163-68(1/3), 170.*

POPEYE
1972 - 1974 (36 pgs. in color)
Charlton (King Features) (Giveaway)

E-1 to E-15 (Educational comics) .80 2.00
nn-Popeye Gettin' Better Grades-4 pgs. used as intro. to above giveaways (in color) .80 2.00

POPEYE
Nov, 1993 - No. 7, Aug, 1994 ($1.50)
Harvey Comics

V2#1-7 1.50
...Summer Special V2#1-(10/93, $2.25, 68 pgs.)-Sagendorf-r & others .90 2.25

POPEYE CARTOON BOOK
1934 (8-1/2x13", 40 pgs., cardboard-c)
The Saalfield Publ. Co.

2095-(Rare)-1933 strip reprints in color by Segar; each page contains a vertical half of a Sunday strip, so the continuity reads row by row completely across each double page spread. If each page is read by itself, the continuity makes no sense. Each double page spread reprints one complete Sunday page (from 1933) 118.00 354.00 1300.00
12 Page Version 57.00 170.00 625.00

POPEYE SPECIAL
Summer, 1987 - No. 2, Sept, 1988 ($1.75/$2.00)
Ocean Comics

1-Origin ($1.75) 1.75
2 ($2.00) .80 2.00

POPPLES (TV, movie)
Dec, 1986 - No. 5, Aug, 1987
Star Comics (Marvel)

1-3-Based on toys .70
4,5 ($1.00) 1.00

POPPO OF THE POPCORN THEATRE
10/29/55 - No. 13, 1956 (weekly)
Fuller Publishing Co. (Publishers Weekly)

Popular Comics #3 © DELL

Popular Teen-Agers #10 © STAR

Porky Pig Four Color #260 © Warner Bros.

	GD25	FN65	NM94
1	6.85	21.00	48.00
2-5	5.00	15.00	30.00
6-13	4.00	12.00	24.00

NOTE: *By **Charles Biro**. 10¢ cover, given away by supermarkets such as IGA.*

POP-POP COMICS
No date (Circa 1945) (52 pgs.)
R. B. Leffingwell Co.

	GD25	FN65	NM94
1-Funny animal	8.50	26.00	60.00

POPSICLE PETE FUN BOOK (See All-American Comics #6)
1947, 1948
Joe Lowe Corp.

	GD25	FN65	NM94
nn-36 pgs. in color; Sammy 'n' Claras, The King Who Couldn't Sleep & Popsicle Pete stories, games, cut-outs	7.85	23.50	55.00
Adventure Book ('48)-Has Classics ad with checklist to HRN #343 (Great Expectations #43)	6.50	19.50	45.00

POPULAR COMICS
Feb, 1936 - No. 145, July-Sept, 1948
Dell Publishing Co.

	GD25	FN65	VF82
1-Dick Tracy (1st comic book app.), Little Orphan Annie, Terry & the Pirates, Gasoline Alley, Don Winslow (1st app.), Harold Teen, Little Joe, Skippy, Moon Mullins, Mutt & Jeff, Tailspin Tommy, Smitty, Smokey Stover, Winnie Winkle & The Gumps begin (all strip-r)	566.00	1700.00	3600.00
(Estimated up to 90 total copies exist, 4 in NM/Mint)			
2	183.00	550.00	1200.00
3	145.00	437.00	900.00
4,5: 5-Tom Mix begins	119.00	357.00	750.00
6-10: 8,9-Scribbly, Reglar Fellers app.	91.00	275.00	570.00

	GD25	FN65	NM94
11-20: 12-X-Mas-c	78.00	234.00	475.00
21-27: 27-Last Terry & the Pirates, Little Orphan Annie, & Dick Tracy	54.00	162.00	340.00
28-37: 28-Gene Autry app. 31,32-Tim McCoy app. 35-Christmas-c; Tex Ritter app.	45.00	137.00	290.00
38-43: Tarzan in text only. 38-(4/39)-Gang Busters (Radio, 2nd app.) & Zane Grey's Tex Thorne begins? 43-The Masked Pilot app.; 1st non-funny-c?	36.00	108.00	315.00
44,45: 45-Hurricane Kid-c	26.00	80.00	210.00
46-Origin/1st app. Martan, the Marvel Man(12/39)	36.00	108.00	300.00
47-50	25.00	75.00	200.00
51-Origin The Voice (The Invisible Detective) strip begins (5/40)	26.00	80.00	210.00
52-59: 55-End of World story	20.00	60.00	160.00
60-Origin/1st app. Professor Supermind and Son (2/41)	21.00	64.00	170.00
61-71: 63-Smilin' Jack begins	16.00	49.00	130.00
72-The Owl & Terry & the Pirates begin (2/42); Smokey Stover reprints begin	36.00	108.00	290.00
73-75	21.00	64.00	170.00
76-78-Capt. Midnight in all	29.00	86.00	230.00
79-85-Last Owl	19.00	56.00	150.00
86-99: 98-Felix the Cat, Smokey Stover-r begin	14.00	41.00	110.00
100	15.00	45.00	120.00
101-130	8.75	26.25	65.00
131-145: 142-Last Terry & the Pirates	8.50	26.00	60.00

NOTE: *Martan, the Marvel Man c-47-49, 52, 57-59. Professor Supermind c-60-63, 64(1/2), 65, 66. The Voice c-53.*

POPULAR FAIRY TALES (See March of Comics #6, 18)

POPULAR ROMANCE
No. 5, Dec, 1949 - No. 29, July, 1954
Better-Standard Publications

	GD25	FN65	NM94
5	7.15	21.50	50.00
6-9: 7-Palais-a; lingerie panels	5.00	15.00	30.00
10-Wood-a (2 pgs.)	6.50	19.50	45.00
11,12,14-16,18-21,28,29	4.15	12.50	25.00
13,17-Severin/Elder-a (3&8 pgs.)	5.00	15.00	30.00
22-27-Toth-a	6.85	21.00	48.00

NOTE: *All have photo-c. **Tuska** art in most issues.*

POPULAR TEEN-AGERS (Secrets of Love) (School Day Romances #1-4)
No. 5, Sept, 1950 - No. 23, Nov, 1954
Star Publications

	GD25	FN65	NM94
5-Toni Gay, Midge Martin & Eve Adams continue from School Day Romances; Ginger Bunn (formerly Ginger Snapp & becomes Honey Bunn #6 on) begins; all features end #8	24.00	73.00	190.00
6-8 (7/51)-Honey Bunn begins; all have L. B. Cole-c; 6-Negligee panels	21.00	64.00	170.00
9-(...Romances; 1st romance issue, 10/51)	12.00	36.00	95.00
10-(...Secrets of Love thru #23)	12.00	36.00	95.00
11,16,18,19,22,23	9.50	28.00	75.00
12,13,17,20,21-Disbrow-a	10.50	32.00	85.00
14-Harrison/Wood-a; 2 spanking scenes	18.00	54.00	125.00
15-Wood?, Disbrow-a	13.50	41.00	105.00
Accepted Reprint 5,6 (nd); L.B. Cole-c	5.70	17.00	38.00

NOTE: *All have **L. B. Cole** covers.*

PORKY PIG (See Bugs Bunny &..., Kite Fun Book, Looney Tunes, March of Comics #42, 57, 71, 89, 99, 113, 130, 143, 164, 175, 192, 209, 218, 367, and Super Book #6, 18, 30)

PORKY PIG (...& Bugs Bunny #40-69)
No. 16, 1942 - No. 81, Mar-Apr, 1962; Jan, 1965 - No. 109, July, 1984
Dell Publishing Co./Gold Key No. 1-93/Whitman No. 94 on

	GD25	FN65	NM94
Four Color 16(#1, 1942)	72.00	215.00	790.00
Four Color 48(1944)-Carl Barks-a	91.00	273.00	1000.00
Four Color 78(1945)	22.00	65.00	240.00
Four Color 112(7/46)	13.00	38.00	140.00
Four Color 156,182,191('49)	9.00	27.00	100.00
Four Color 226,241('49),260,271,277,284,295	7.00	22.00	80.00
Four Color 303,311,322,330: 322-Sci/fi-c/story	4.50	13.50	50.00
Four Color 342,351,360,370,385,399,410,426	3.60	11.00	40.00
25 (11-12/52)-30	2.75	8.00	30.00
31-40	1.40	4.20	14.00
41-60	1.20	3.60	12.00
61-81(3-4/62)	1.20	3.60	12.00
1(1/65-Gold Key)(2nd Series)	2.75	8.00	30.00
2,4,5-r/4-Color 226,284 & 271 in that order	1.80	5.50	20.00
3,6-10: 3-r/Four Color #342	1.20	3.60	12.00
11-30	1.10	3.30	9.00
31-54	1.00	2.80	7.00
55-70		2.00	5.00
71-109		1.20	3.00

NOTE: *Reprints-#1-8, 9-35(2/3); 36-46, 58, 67, 69-74, 76, 78, 102-109(1/3-1/2).*

PORKY PIG'S DUCK HUNT
1938 (12pgs.)(large size)(heavy linen-like paper)
Saalfield Publishing Co.

	GD25	FN65	NM94
2178-1st app. Porky Pig & Daffy Duck by Leon Schlesinger. Illustrated text story book written in verse. 1st book ever devoted to these characters. (see Looney Tunes #1 for their 1st comic book app.)	56.00	168.00	500.00

PORKY'S BOOK OF TRICKS
1942 (8-1/2x5-1/2", 48 pgs.)
K. K. Publications (Giveaway)

	GD25	FN65	NM94
nn-7 pg. comic story, text stories, plus games & puzzles	36.00	108.00	300.00

PORTIA PRINZ OF THE GLAMAZONS
Dec, 1986 - No. 6, Oct, 1987 ($2.00, B&W, Baxter paper)
Eclipse Comics

	GD25	FN65	NM94
1-6		.80	2.00

Power Comics #1 © HOKE

Power Man & Iron Fist #75 © MEG

The Power of Shazam! #1 © DC

POST GAZETTE (See Meet the New...)

POWDER RIVER RUSTLERS (See Fawcett Movie Comics)

POWER & GLORY (Also See American Flagg! & Howard Chaykin's American Flagg!
Feb, 1994 - No. 4, May, 1994 ($2.50, limited series, mature)
Malibu Comics (Bravura)

1A, 1B-By Howard Chaykin; w/Bravura stamp 1.00 2.50
1-Newsstand ed. (polybagged w/children's warning on bag), Gold ed., Silver-foil ed., Blue-foil ed.(print run of 10,000), Serigraph ed. (print run of 3,000)-($2.95)-Howard Chaykin-c/a begin 1.20 3.00
2-4-Contains Bravura stamp 1.00 2.50
Holiday Special (Win '94, $2.95) 1.20 3.00

POWER COMICS
1944 - No. 4, 1945
Holyoke Publ. Co./Narrative Publ.

1-L. B. Cole-c 111.00 333.00 1000.00
2-Hitler, Hirohito-c (scarce) 111.00 333.00 1000.00
3-Classic L.B. Cole-c; Dr. Mephisto begins? 122.00 366.00 1100.00
4-L.B. Cole-c; Miss Espionage app. #3,4; Leav-a 111.00 333.00 1000.00

POWER COMICS
1977 - No. 5, Dec, 1977 (B&W)
Power Comics Co.

1- "A Boy And His Aardvark" by Dave Sim; first Dave Sim aardvark (not Cerebus) 2.40 6.00
1-Reprint (3/77, black-c) 1.60 4.00
2-Cobalt Blue by Gustovich 1.00 2.50
3-5: 3-Nightwitch. 4-Northern Light. 5-Bluebird 1.00 2.50

POWER COMICS
Mar, 1988 - No. 4, Sept, 1988 ($2.00, B&W, mini-series)
Eclipse Comics (Acme Press)

1-4: Bolland, Gibbons-r in all .80 2.00

POWER FACTOR
May, 1987 - No. 3, 1987 ($1.95)
Wonder Color Comics

1-3: Super team. 2-Infantino-c .80 2.00

POWER FACTOR
Oct, 1990 - No. 3, 1991 ($1.95/$2.25)
Innovation Publishing

1-Reprints 1st story plus new-a .80 2.00
2,3: 2-Begin $2.25-c; r/2nd story plus new-a. 3-Infantino-a .90 2.25

POWER GIRL (See All-Star 58, Infinity; Inc., Showcase #97-99)
June, 1988 - No. 4, Sept, 1988 ($1.00, color, limited series)
DC Comics

1-4 1.00

POWERHOUSE PEPPER COMICS (See Gay Comics, Joker Comics & Tessie the Typist)
No. 1, 1943; No. 2, May, 1948 - No. 5, Nov, 1948
Marvel Comics (20CC)

1-(60 pgs.)-Wolverton-a in all; c-2,3 122.00 366.00 1100.00
2 67.00 200.00 600.00
3,4 61.00 183.00 550.00
5-(Scarce) 75.00 225.00 675.00

POWER LINE
May, 1988 - No. 8, Sept, 1989 ($1.25/$1.50)
Marvel Comics (Epic Comics)

1-3: 2-Williamson-i. 3-Austin-i, Dr. Zero app. 1.25
4-8: 4-Begin $1.50-c. 4-7-Morrow-a. 8-Williamson-i 1.50

POWER LORDS
Dec, 1983 - No. 3, Feb, 1984 (Limited series, Mando paper)
DC Comics

1-3: Based on Revell toys .80

POWER MAN (Formerly Hero for Hire; ...& Iron Fist #68 on; see Cage & Giant-Size...)
No. 17, Feb, 1974 - No. 125, Sept, 1986
Marvel Comics Group

17-Luke Cage continues; Iron Man app. 2.40 6.00
18-20: 18-Last 20¢ issue 2.00 5.00
21-30 1.60 4.00
31-Part Neal Adams-i 2.40 6.00
32-46: 34-Last 25¢ issue. 36-r/Hero For Hire #12. 41-1st app. Thunderbolt. 45-Starlin-c. 1.20 3.00
47-Barry Smith-a 1.00 2.80 7.00
48-50-Byrne-a(p); 48-Power Man/Iron Fist 1st meet. 50-Iron Fist joins Cage 1.00 2.80 7.00
51-56,58-60: 58-Intro El Aguila .80 2.00
57-New X-Men app. (6/79) 1.10 3.30 9.00
61-65,67-77,79-83,85-124: 75-Double size. 77-Daredevil app. 87-Moon Knight app. 90-Unus app. 109-The Reaper app. 100-Double size; origin K'un L'un 1.00
66-2nd app. Sabretooth (see Iron Fist #14) 2.50 7.50 25.00
78-3rd app. Sabretooth (cameo under cloak) 1.25 3.75 10.00
84-4th app. Sabretooth 1.25 3.75 10.00
125-Double size; death of Iron Fist .80 2.00
Annual 1(1976)-Punisher cameo in flashback 2.40 6.00

NOTE: ***Austin*** *c-102i.* ***Byrne*** *a-48-50; c-102, 104, 106, 107, 112-116.* ***Kane*** *c(p)-24, 25, 28, 48.* ***Miller*** *a-68, 76(2 pgs.); c-66-68, 70-74, 80i.* ***Mooney*** *a-38i, 53i, 55i.* ***Nebres*** *a-76p.* ***Nino*** *a-42i, 43i.* ***Perez*** *a-27.* ***B. Smith*** *a-47i.* ***Tuska*** *a(p)-17, 20, 24, 26, 28, 29, 36, 47. Painted c-75, 100.*

POWER OF PRIME
July, 1995 - No. 4, Nov, 1995 ($2.50, limited series)
Malibu Comics (Ultraverse)

1-4 1.00 2.50

POWER OF SHAZAM!, THE (See SHAZAM!)
1994 (Painted graphic novel) (Prequel to new series)
DC Comics

Hardcover-($19.95)-New origin of Shazam!; Ordway painted-c/a & script 20.00
Softcover-($9.95)-New-c. 10.00

POWER OF SHAZAM!, THE
Mar, 1995 - Present ($1.50/$1.75/$1.95)
DC Comics

1-Jerry Ordway scripts begin .80 2.00
2,3 1.50
4-31: 4-Begin $1.75-c. 6:Re-intro of Capt. Nazi. 8-Re-intro of Spy Smasher, Bulletman & Minuteman; Swan-a (7 pgs.). 11-Re-intro of Ibis, Swan-a (2 pgs.). 14-Gil Kane-a(p). 20-Superman-c/app.; "Final Night." 21-Plastic Man-c/app. 22-Batman-c/app. .70 1.75
32-38: 32-Begin $1.95-c. 35,36-Crossover w/Starman #39,40 1.95
Annual 1 (1996, $2.95)-Legends of the Dead Earth story; Jerry Ordway-c; Mike Manley-a 1.20 3.00

POWER OF STRONGMAN, THE (Also see Strongman)
1989 ($2.95)
AC Comics

1-Powell G.A.-r 1.20 3.00

POWER OF THE ATOM (See Secret Origins #29)
Aug, 1988 - No. 18, Nov, 1989 ($1.00)
DC Comics

1-18: 6-Chronos returns; Byrne-p. 9-JLI app. 1.00

POWER PACHYDERMS

Power Record Comics PR-15 © MEG

Preacher #4 © Garth Ennis & Steve Dillon

Predator: Big Game #4 © 20th Cent. Fox

Sept, 1989 ($1.25, one-shot)
Marvel Comics

	GD25	FN65	NM94
1-Elephant super-heroes			1.30

POWER PACK
Aug, 1984 - No. 62, Feb, 1991
Marvel Comics Group

	GD25	FN65	NM94
1-($1.00, 52 pgs.)-Origin & 1st app. Power Pack			1.00
2-18,20-26,28,30-45,47-62			1.00
19-(52 pgs.)-Cloak & Dagger, Wolverine app.		.80	2.00
27-Mutant massacre; Wolverine & Sabretooth app.		.80	2.00
29-Spider-Man & Hobgoblin app.		.80	2.00
46-Punisher app.		.80	2.00
...Holiday Special 1 (2/92, $2.25, 68 pgs.)		.90	2.25

NOTE: ***Austin*** *scripts-53.* ***Mignola*** *c-20.* ***Morrow*** *a-51.* ***Spiegle*** *a-55i.* ***Williamson*** *a(i)-43, 50, 52.*

POWER RANGERS ZEO (TV)(Saban's...)(Also see Saban's Mighty Morphin Power Rangers)
Aug, 1996 ($2.50)
Image Comics (Extreme Studios)

	GD25	FN65	NM94
1-Based on TV show		1.00	2.50

POWER RECORD COMICS
1974 - 1978 ($1.49, 7x10" comics, 20 pgs. with 45 R.P.M. record)
Marvel Comics/Power Records

PR10-Spider-Man-r/from #124,125; Man-Wolf app. PR11-Hulk-r. PR12-Captain America-r/#168. PR13-Fantastic Four-r/#126. PR14-Frankenstein-Ploog-r/#1. PR15-Tomb of Dracula-Colan-r/#2. PR16-Man-Thing-Ploog-r/#5. PR17-Werewolf By Night-Ploog r/Marvel Spotlight #2. PR18-Planet of the Apes-r. PR19-Escape From the Planet of the Apes-r. PR20-Beneath the Planet of the Apes-r. PR21-Battle for the Planet of the Apes-r. PR24-Spider-Man II-New-a begins. PR25-Star Trek "Passage to Moauv". PR26-Star Trek "Crier in Emptiness." PR27-Batman "Stacked Cards"; N. Adams-a(p). PR28-Superman "Alien Creatures". PR29-Space: 1999 "Breakaway". PR30-Batman; N. Adams-r/Det.(7 pgs.). PR31-Conan-N. Adams-a; reprinted in Conan #116. PR32-Space: 1999 "Return to the Beginning". PR33-Superman-G.A. origin, Buckler-a(p). PR34-Superman. PR35-Wonder Woman-Buckler-a(p). PR36-Holo-Man. PR37-Robin Hood. PR39-Huckleberry Finn. PR40-Davy Crockett. PR41-Robinson Crusoe. PR42-20,000 Leagues Under the Sea. PR46-Star Trek "The Robot Masters". PR47-Little Women

	GD25	FN65	NM94
With record; each...	1.50	4.50	12.00

POWERS THAT BE (Becomes Star Seed No.7 on)
Nov, 1995 - No. 6, June, 1996 ($2.50)
Broadway Comics

	GD25	FN65	NM94
1-5: 1-Intro of Fatale & Star Seed.		1.00	2.50
6-Begin $2.95-c.		1.20	3.00
Preview Editions 1-3 (9/95 - 11/95, B&W)		1.00	2.50

POW MAGAZINE (Bob Sproul's) (Satire Magazine)
Aug, 1966 - No. 3, Feb, 1967 (30¢)
Humor-Vision

	GD25	FN65	NM94
1-3: 2-Jones-a. 3-Wrightson-a	4.00	11.00	22.00

PREACHER
Apr, 1995 - Present ($2.50, mature)
DC Comics (Vertigo)

	GD25	FN65	NM94
nn-Preview	7.00	21.00	70.00
1 ($2.95)-Ennis scripts, Dillon-a & Fabry-c in all; 1st app. Jesse, Tulip, & Cassidy	4.20	12.60	42.00
2,3: 2-1st app. Saint of Killers.	3.00	9.00	30.00
4,5,12: 12-Polybagged w/videogame w/Ennis text	2.50	7.50	20.00
6-11,13-15: 13-Hunters storyline begins; ends #17	1.25	3.75	10.00
16-20: 19-Saint of Killers app.; begin "Crusaders", ends #24.		2.40	6.00
21-25: 21-24Saint of Killers app. 25-Origin of Cassidy.		1.60	4.00
26-37		1.00	2.50
Gone To Texas ($14.95, 1996, TPB)-r/#1-7; Fabry-c			15.00
Proud Americans ($20.95, 1997, TPB)-r/#18-26; Fabry-c			21.00
Until the End of the World ($14.95, 1996, TPB)-r/#8-17; Fabry-c			15.00

PREACHER SPECIAL: SAINT OF KILLERS
Aug, 1996 - No. 4, Nov, 1996 ($2.50, limited series, mature)
DC Comics (Vertigo)

	GD25	FN65	NM94
1,2: Ennis-scripts/Fabry-c/Pugh-a in all.		2.40	6.00
1-Signed & numbered			25.00
3,4-		1.60	4.00

PREACHER SPECIAL: THE GOOD OLD BOYS
Aug, 1997 ($4.95, one-shot, mature)
DC Comics (Vertigo)

	GD25	FN65	NM94
1-Ennis-scripts/Fabry-c /Esquerra-a		2.00	5.00

PREACHER SPECIAL: THE STORY OF YOU-KNOW-WHO
Dec, 1996 ($4.95, one-shot, mature)
DC Comics (Vertigo)

	GD25	FN65	NM94
1-Ennis-scripts/Fabry-c/Case-a		2.00	5.00

PREDATOR (Also see Aliens Vs. ..., Batman vs. ..., Dark Horse Comics, & Dark Horse Presents)
June, 1989 - No. 4, Mar, 1990 ($2.25, limited series)
Dark Horse Comics

	GD25	FN65	NM94
1-Based on movie; 1st app. Predator		2.40	6.00
1-2nd printing		1.60	4.00
2		2.00	5.00
3,4		1.20	3.00
Trade paperback (1990, $12.95)-r/#1-4	1.60	4.85	13.00

PREDATOR: BAD BLOOD
Dec, 1993 - No. 4, 1994 ($2.50, limited series)
Dark Horse Comics

	GD25	FN65	NM94
1-4		1.00	2.50

PREDATOR: BIG GAME
Mar, 1991 - No. 4, June, 1991 ($2.50, limited series)
Dark Horse Comics

	GD25	FN65	NM94
1: 1-3-Contain 2 Dark Horse trading cards		1.20	3.00
2-4		1.10	2.75

PREDATOR BLOODY SANDS OF TIME
Feb, 1992 - No. 2, Feb, 1992 ($2.50, limited series)
Dark Horse Comics

	GD25	FN65	NM94
1,2-Dan Barry-c/a(p)/scripts		1.00	2.50

PREDATOR COLD WAR
Sept, 1991 - No. 4, Dec, 1991 ($2.50, limited series)
Dark Horse Comics

	GD25	FN65	NM94
1-4: All have painted-c		1.00	2.50

PREDATOR: DARK RIVER
July, 1996 - No.4, Oct, 1996 ($2.95, limited series)
Dark Horse Comics

	GD25	FN65	NM94
1-4: Miran Kim-c			3.00

PREDATOR: HELL & HOT WATER
Apr, 1997 - No. 3, June, 1997 ($2.95, limited series)
Dark Horse Comics

	GD25	FN65	NM94
1-3			2.95

PREDATOR: INVADERS FROM THE FOURTH DIMENSION
July, 1994 ($3.95, one-shot, 52 pgs.)
Dark Horse Comics

	GD25	FN65	NM94
1		1.60	4.00

PREDATOR: JUNGLE TALES
Mar, 1995 ($2.95, one-shot)
Dark Horse Comics

	GD25	FN65	NM94
1-r/Dark Horse Comics		1.20	3.00

PREDATOR: KINDRED

Predator vs. Judge Dredd #2 © 20th Cent. Fox/ Fleetway

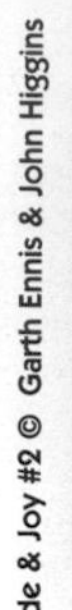

Pride & Joy #2 © Garth Ennis & John Higgins

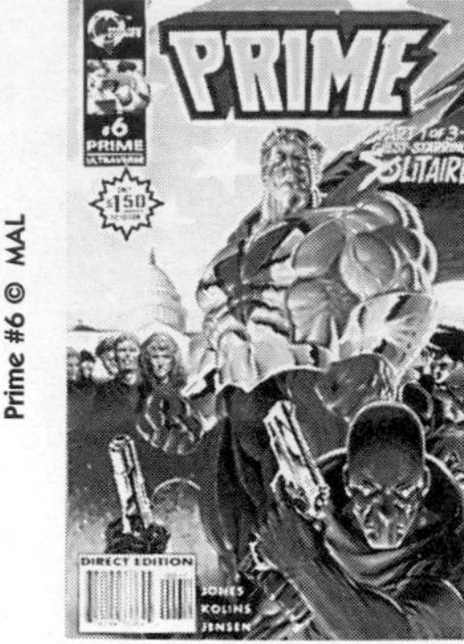

Prime #6 © MAL

GD25 FN65 NM94

Dec, 1996 - No. 4, Mar, 1997 ($2.50, limited series)
Dark Horse Comics
1-4 — 1.00 2.50

PREDATOR: PRIMAL
July, 1997 - No. 2, Aug, 1997 ($2.95, limited series)
Dark Horse Comics
1,2 — 2.95

PREDATOR: RACE WAR (See Dark Horse Presents #67)
Feb, 1993 - No. 4, Oct, 1993 ($2.50, color, limited series)
Dark Horse Comics
1-4-Dorman painted-c #1-4 — 1.00 2.50
0-(4/93) — 1.00 2.50

PREDATOR: STRANGE ROUX
Nov, 1996 ($2.95, one-shot)
Dark Horse Comics
1 — 1.20 3.00

PREDATOR 2
Feb, 1991 - No. 2, June, 1991 ($2.50, limited series)
Dark Horse Comics
1-Adapts movie; 2 trading cards inside; photo-c — 1.00 2.50
2-Photo-c; w/2 trading cards inside — 1.00 2.50

PREDATOR VS. JUDGE DREDD
Oct, 1997 - No. 3 ($2.50, limited series)
Dark Horse Comics
1-3-Wagner-s/Alcatena-a/Bolland-c — 2.50

PREDATOR VS. MAGNUS ROBOT FIGHTER
Oct, 1992 - No. 2, 1993 ($2.95, limited series)(1st Dark Horse/Valiant x-over)
Dark Horse/Valiant
1 (Regular)-Barry Smith-c; Lee Weeks-a in both — 1.20 3.00
1 (Platinum edition, 11/92)-Barry Smith-c — 2.00 5.00
2-Contains 2 bound-in trading cards; Barry Smith-c. — 1.20 3.00

PREHISTORIC WORLD (See Classics Illustrated Special Issue)

PREMIERE (See Charlton Premiere)

PRESTO KID, THE (See Red Mask)

PRETTY BOY FLOYD (See On the Spot)

PREZ (See Cancelled Comic Cavalcade & Supergirl #10)
Aug-Sept, 1973 - No. 4, Feb-Mar, 1974
National Periodical Publications
1-Origin; Joe Simon scripts — 1.85 5.50 15.00
2-4 — 1.10 3.30 9.00

PRICE, THE (See Eclipse Graphic Album Series)

PRIDE & JOY
July, 1997 - No. 4, Oct, 1997 (2.50, limited series)
DC Comics (Vertigo)
1-4-Ennis-s — 1.00 2.50

PRIDE AND THE PASSION, THE
No. 824, Aug, 1957
Dell Publishing Co.
Four Color 824-Movie, Frank Sinatra & Cary Grant photo-c — 8.00 25.00 90.00

PRIDE OF THE YANKEES, THE (See Real Heroes & Sport Comics)
1949 (The Life of Lou Gehrig)
Magazine Enterprises
nn-Photo-c; Ogden Whitney-a — 66.00 198.00 590.00

PRIEST (Also see Asylum)
Aug, 1996 - No. 3 ($2.99)
Maximum Press
1-3 — 1.20 3.00

PRIMAL FORCE
No. 0, Oct, 1994 - No. 14, Dec, 1995 ($1.95/$2.25)
DC Comics
0-8: Red Tornado, Golem, Jack O'Lantern, Meridian & Silver Dragon — .80 2.00
9-14: 9-begin $2.25-c — .80 2.25

PRIMAL MAN (See The Crusaders)

PRIMAL RAGE
1996 ($2.95)
Sirius Entertainment
1-Dark One-c; based of video game — 1.20 3.00

PRIME (See Break-Thru, Flood Relief & Ultraforce)
June, 1993 - No. 26, Aug, 1995 ($1.95/$2.50)
Malibu Comics (Ultraverse)
1-1st app. Prime; has coupon for Ultraverse Premiere #0 — 1.20 3.00
1-With coupon missing — 1.50
1-Full cover holographic edition; 1st of kind w/Hardcase #1 & Strangers #1 — 1.20 3.00
1-Ultra 5,000 edition w/silver ink-c — 1.20 3.00
2-Polybagged w/card & coupon for U. Premiere #0 — 1.20 3.00
3,4-Prototype app. 4-Direct sale w/o card — 1.10 2.75
4-($2.50)-Newsstand ed. polybagged w/card — 1.00 2.50
5-($2.50, 48 pgs.)-Rune flip-c/story part B by Barry Smith; see Sludge #1 for 1st app. Rune; 3-pg. Night Man preview — 1.00 2.50
6-11,14-19: 6-Bill & Chelsea Clinton app. 7-Break-Thru x-over. 8-Mantra app.; 2-pg. origin Freex by Simonson. 10-Firearm app.15-Intro Papa Verite; Perez-c/a. 16-Intro Turbo Charge — .80 2.00
12-($3.50, 68 pgs.)-Flip book w/Ultraverse Premiere #3; silver foil logo — 1.40 3.50
13-($2.95, 52 pgs.)-Variant covers — 1.20 3.00
20-26: 20-$2.50-c begins.) — 1.00 2.50
...: Gross and Disgusting 1 (10/94, $3.95)-Boris-c; "Annual" on cover, published monthly in indicia — 1.80 4.50
...Month "Ashcan" (8/94, 75¢)-Boris-c — .75
... Time: A Prime Collection (1994, $9.95)-r/1-4 — 1.25 3.75 10.00
...Vs. The Incredible Hulk (1995)-mail away limited edition — 1.25 3.75 10.00
...Vs. The Incredible Hulk Premium edition — 1.25 3.75 10.00
...Vs. The Incredible Hulk Super Premium edition — 2.50 7.50 25.00
NOTE: ***Perez*** *a-15; c-15, 16.*

PRIME (Also see Black September)
Infinity, Sept, 1995 - V2#15, Dec, 1996 ($1.50)
Malibu Comics (Ultraverse)
Infinity, V2#1-8: Post Black September storyline. 6-8-Solitaire app. 9-Breyfogle-c/a. 10-12-Ramos-c. 15-Lord Pumpkin app. — 1.50
Infinity Signed Edition (2,000 printed) — 2.00 5.00

PRIME/CAPTAIN AMERICA
Mar, 1996 ($3.95, one-shot)
Marvel Comics
1-Norm Breyfogle-a — 1.60 4.00

PRIMER (Comico...)
Oct (no month), 1982 - No. 6, Feb, 1984 (B&W)
Comico
1 (52 pgs.) — 2.00 5.00
2-1st app. Grendel & Argent by Wagner — 12.00 36.00 120.00
3,4 — 2.00 5.00
5-1st Sam Kieth art in comics ('83) & 1st The Maxx — 4.00 12.00 40.00

Prince Valiant #3 © KFS

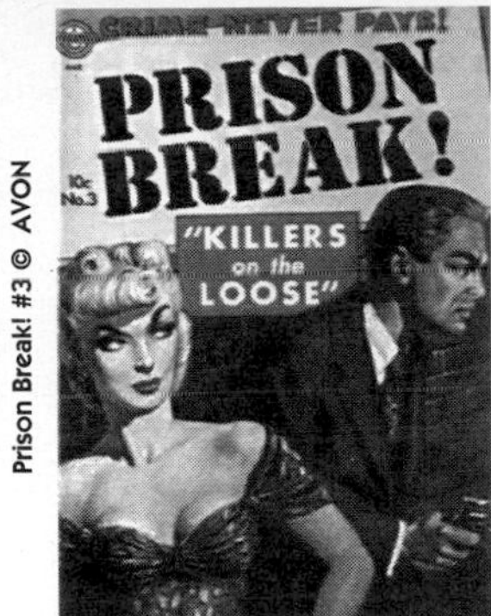

Prison Break! #3 © AVON

Prize Comics #25 © PRIZE

GD25 FN65 NM94

6-Intro & 1st app. Evangeline 1.60 4.00

PRIMORTALS (Leonard Nimoy's...)

PRIMUS (TV)
Feb, 1972 - No. 7, Oct, 1972
Charlton Comics

1-Staton-a in all 1.50 4.50 12.00
2-7: 6-Drug propaganda story 1.00 3.00 8.00

PRINCE NAMOR, THE SUB-MARINER (Also see Namor ...)
Sept, 1984 - No. 4, Dec, 1984 (Limited-series)
Marvel Comics Group

1 .75 1.80
2-4 1.20

PRINCE NIGHTMARE
1987 ($2.95, 68pgs.)
Aaaargh! Associated Artists

Book 1 1.20 3.00

PRINCE VALIANT (See Ace Comics, Comics Reading Libraries, & King Comics #146, 147)
No. 26, 1941; No. 67, June, 1954 - No. 900, May, 1958
Feature Books 26 ('41)-Harold Foster-c/a; newspaper strips reprinted, pgs. 1-28,30-63; color & 68 pgs; Foster cover is only original comic book artwork by him 66.00 198.00 725.00
Four Color 567 ((6/54)(#1)-By Bob Fuje-Movie, photo-c 10.00 30.00 110.00
Four Color 650 (9;55), 699 (4/56), 719 (8/56),-Fuje-a 5.50 16.50 60.00
Four Color 788 (4/57), 849 (1/58), 900-Fuje-a 5.50 16.50 60.00

PRINCE VALIANT
Dec, 1994 - No. 4, Mar, 1995 ($3.95, limited series)
Marvel Comics

1-4 1.60 4.00

PRINCE VANDAL
Nov, 1993 - Apr?, 1994 ($2.50)
Triumphant Comics

1-6: 1,2-Triumphant Unleashed x-over 1.00 2.50

PRINCESS SALLY (Video game)
Apr, 1995 - No. 3, June, 1995 ($1.50, limited series)
Archie Publications

1-3: Spin-off from Sonic the Hedgehog 1.50

PRIORITY: WHITE HEAT
1986 - No. 2, 1986 ($1.75, mini-series)
AC Comics

1,2-Bill Black-a .75 1.75

PRISCILLA'S POP
No. 569, June, 1954 - No. 799, May, 1957
Dell Publishing Co.

Four Color 569 (#1) 2.75 8.00 30.00
Four Color 630 (5/55), 704 (5/56), 799 2.75 8.00 30.00

PRISON BARS (See Behind...)

PRISON BREAK!
Sept, 1951 - No. 5, Sept, 1952 (Painted c-3)
Avon Periodicals/Realistic No. 3 on

1-Wood-c & 1 pg.; has-r/Saint #7 retitled Michael Strong Private Eye 38.00 114.00 275.00
2-Wood-c; Kubert-a; Kinstler inside front-c 24.00 73.00 180.00
3-Orlando, Check-a; c-/Avon paperback 179 21.00 62.00 150.00
4,5: 4-Kinstler-c & inside f/c; Lawrence, Lazarus-a. 5-Kinstler-c; Infantino-a 18.00 54.00 130.00

PRISONER, THE (TV)
1988 - No. 4, 1989 ($3.50, squarebound, mini-series)
DC Comics

1-4 (Books a-d) 1.40 3.50

PRISON RIOT
1952
Avon Periodicals

1-Marijuana Murders-1 pg. text; Kinstler-c; 2 Kubert illos on text pages 24.00 71.00 170.00

PRISON TO PRAISE
1974 (35¢)
Logos International

nn-True Story of Merlin R. Carothers 1.60 4.00

PRIVATE BUCK
No. 21, 1941 - No. 12, 1942
Dell Publishing Co.

Large Feature Comic 21 (#1)(1941)(Series I) 9.00 26.00 95.00
Large Feature Comic 22 (1941)(Series I), 12 (1942)(Series II) 9.00 26.00 95.00

PRIVATEERS
Aug, 1987 - No. 2, 1987 ($1.50)
Vanguard Graphics

1,2 1.50

PRIVATE EYE (Cover title: Rocky Jorden...#6-8)
Jan, 1951 - No. 8, March, 1952
Atlas Comics (MCI)

1-Cover title: Crime Cases... #1-5 17.00 51.00 125.00
2,3-Tuska c/a(3) 10.00 30.00 70.00
4-8 9.00 27.00 60.00
NOTE: ***Henkel** a-6(3), 7; c-7. **Sinnott** a-6.*

PRIVATE EYE (See Mike Shayne...)

PRIVATE SECRETARY
Dec-Feb, 1962-63 - No. 2, Mar-May, 1963
Dell Publishing Co.

1,2 2.50 7.50 20.00

PRIVATE STRONG (See The Double Life of...)

PRIZE COMICS (...Western #69 on) (Also see Treasure Comics)
March, 1940 - No. 68, Feb-Mar, 1948
Prize Publications

1-Origin Power Nelson, The Futureman & Jupiter, Master Magician; Ted O'Neil, Secret Agent M-11, Jaxon of the Jungle, Bucky Brady & Storm Curtis begin (1st app. of each) 178.00 534.00 1600.00
2-The Black Owl begins (1st app.) 83.00 250.00 750.00
3,4: 4-Robot-c 72.00 216.00 650.00
5,6: Dr. Dekkar, Master of Monsters app. in each 67.00 200.00 600.00
7-(Scarce)-Black Owl by S&K; origin/1st app. Dr. Frost & Frankenstein; The Green Lama, Capt. Gallant, The Great Voodini & Twist Turner begin; 1st app. The Green Lama (12/40) 139.00 417.00 1250.00
8,9-Black Owl & Ted O'Neil by S&K 75.00 225.00 675.00
10-12,14-20: 11-Origin Bulldog Denny. 16-Spike Mason begins 53.00 159.00 480.00
13-Yank & Doodle begin (8/41, origin/1st app.) 58.00 174.00 525.00
21-24 36.00 108.00 325.00
25-30 23.00 68.00 180.00
31-33 19.00 56.00 150.00
34-Origin Airmale, Yank & Doodle; The Black Owl joins army, Yank & Doodle's father assumes Black Owl's role 23.00 68.00 180.00
35-36,38-40: 35-Flying Fist & Bingo begin 15.00 45.00 120.00
37-Intro. Stampy, Airmale's sidekick; Hitler-c 23.00 68.00 180.00
41-50: 45-Yank & Doodle learn Black Owl's I.D. (their father). 48-Prince Ra

Prize Comics Western #74 © PRIZE

Propeller Man #5 © DH

Prophet #2 © Rob Liefeld

GD25 FN65 NM94

begins 11.30 34.00 90.00
51-62,64,67,68: 53-Transvestism story. 55-No Frankenstein. 57-X-Mas-c.
64-Black Owl retires 10.00 30.00 80.00
63-Simon & Kirby c/a 12.00 36.00 95.00
65,66-Frankenstein-c by Briefer 10.50 32.00 85.00
NOTE: ***Briefer*** *a 7-on; c-65, 66.* ***J. Binder*** *a-16; c-21-29.* ***Guardineer*** *a-62.* ***Kiefer*** *c-62.* ***Palais*** *c-68.* ***Simon & Kirby*** *c-63, 75, 83.*

PRIZE COMICS WESTERN (Formerly Prize Comics #1-68)
No. 69(V7#2), Apr-May, 1948 - No. 119, Nov-Dec, 1956
Prize Publications (Feature) (No. 69-84: 52 pgs.)

69(V7#2) 12.00 36.00 95.00
70-75: 74-Kurtzman-a (8 pgs.) 10.00 30.00 80.00
76-Randolph Scott photo-c; "Canadian Pacific" movie adaptation
11.30 34.00 90.00
77-Photo-c; Severin/Elder, Mart Bailey-a; "Streets of Laredo" movie adaptation
10.00 30.00 80.00
78-Photo-c; S&K-a, 10 pgs.; Severin, Mart Bailey-a; "Bullet Code", & "Roughshod" movie adaptations 15.00 45.00 120.00
79-Photo-c; Kurtzman-a, 8 pgs.; Severin/Elder, Severin, Mart Bailey-a; "Stage To Chino" movie adaptation w/George O'Brien 15.00 45.00 120.00
80,81-Photo-c; Severin/Elder-a(2) 10.50 32.00 85.00
82-Photo-c; 1st app. The Preacher by Mart Bailey; Severin/Elder-a(3)
10.50 32.00 85.00
83,84 8.75 26.25 70.00
85-1st app. American Eagle by John Severin & begins (V9#6, 1-2/51)
21.00 64.00 170.00
86,101-105 10.00 30.00 80.00
87-99,110,111-Severin/Elder-a(2-3) each 10.50 32.00 85.00
100 12.00 36.00 95.00
106-108,112 8.50 26.00 60.00
109-Severin/Williamson-a 10.00 30.00 80.00
113-Williamson/Severin-a(2)/Frazetta? 10.50 32.00 85.00
114-119: Drifter series in all; by Mort Meskin #114-118
6.50 19.50 45.00
NOTE: ***Fass*** *a-81.* ***Severin & Elder*** *c-84-99.* ***Severin*** *a-72, 75, 77-79, 83-86, 96, 97, 100-105; c-92,100-109(most), 110-119.* ***Simon & Kirby*** *c-75, 83.*

PRIZE MYSTERY
May, 1955 - No. 3, Sept, 1955
Key Publications

1 7.50 22.50 45.00
2,3 5.70 17.00 35.00

PROFESSIONAL FOOTBALL (See Charlton Sport Library)

PROFESSOR COFFIN
No. 19, Oct, 1985 - No. 21, Feb, 1986
Charlton Comics

19-21: Wayne Howard-a(r) 1.20 3.00

PROFESSOR OM
May, 1990 - No. 2, 1990 ($2.50, limited series)
Innovation Publishing

1,2-East Meets West spin-off 1.00 2.50

PROFESSOR XAVIER AND THE X-MEN (Also see X-Men, 1st series)
Nov, 1995 - No. 18 (99¢)
Marvel Comics

1-18: Stories featuring the Original X-Men. 2-vs. The Blob. 5-Vs. the Original Brotherhood of Evil Mutants. 10-Vs The Avengers 1.00

PROJECT A-KO (Manga)
Mar, 1994 - No. 4, June, 1994 ($2.95)
Malibu Comics

1-4-Based on anime film 1.20 3.00

PROJECT A-KO 2 (Manga)
May, 1995 - No. 3, Aug, 1995 ($2.95, limited series)
CPM Comics

1-3 1.20 3.00

PROJECT A-KO VERSUS THE UNIVERSE (Manga)
Oct, 1995 - No. 5, June, 1996 ($2.95, limited series, bi-monthly)
CPM Comics

1-5 1.20 3.00

PROJECT: HERO
Aug, 1987 ($1.50)
Vanguard Graphics (Canadian)

1 1.50

PROPELLERMAN
Jan, 1993 - No. 8, Mar, 1994 ($2.95, limited series)
Dark Horse Comics

1-8: 2,4,8-Contain 2 trading cards 1.20 3.00

PROPHET (See Youngblood #2)
Oct, 1993 - No. 10, 1995 ($1.95)
Image Comics (Extreme Studios)

1-($2.50)-Liefeld/Panosian-c/a; 1st app. Mary McCormick; Liefeld scripts in 1-4; #1-3 contain coupons for Prophet #0 1.20 3.00
1-Gold foil embossed-c edition rationed to dealers 2.00 5.00
2-4: 2-Liefeld-c(p). 3-1st app. Judas. 4-1st app. Omen; Black and White Pt. 3 by Thibert .80 2.00
4-Alternate-c by Stephen Platt 1.20 3.00
5,6-Platt-c/a .80 2.00
0-(7/94, $2.50)-San Diego Comic Con ed. (2200 copies) 2.00 5.00
7-10: 7-(9/94, $2.50)-Platt-c/a. 8-Bloodstrike app. 10-Polybagged w/trading card; Platt-c. 1.00 2.50

PROPHET
V2#1, Aug, 1995 - No. 8 ($3.50)
Image Comics (Extreme Studios)

V2#1-8: Dixon scripts in all. 1-4-Platt-a. 1-Boris-c; F. Miller variant-c. 4-Newmen app. 5,6-Wraparound-c 1.00 2.50
Annual 1 (9/95, $2.50)-Bagged w/Youngblood gaming card; Quesada-c
1.00 2.50
Babewatch Special 1 (12/95, $2.50)-Babewatch tie-in 1.00 2.50
1995 San Diego Edition-B&W preview of V2#1. 2.00 5.00
TPB-(1996, $12.95) r/#1-7 13.00

PROPHET/CABLE
Jan, 1997 - No. 2, Mar, 1997 ($3.50, limited series)
Image Comics (Extreme Studios)

1,2-Liefeld-c/a: 2-#1 listed on cover 1.40 3.50

PROPHET/CHAPEL: SUPER SOLDIERS
May, 1996 - No. 2, June, 1996 ($2.50, limited series)
Image Comics (Extreme Studios)

1,2: 1-Two covers exist 1.00 2.50
1-San Diego Edition; B&W-c 2.00 5.00

PROTECTORS (Also see The Ferret)
Sept, 1992 - No. 20, May, 1994 ($1.95-$2.50/$2.25/$2.50)
Malibu Comics

1-12 ($2.50, direct sale)-With poster & diff-c: 1-Origin; has 3/4 outer-c
1.00 2.50
1-12 ($1.95, newsstand)-Without poster .80 2.00
13-16 ($2.25): 13-Polybagged w/Skycap .90 2.25
17-20: 17-Begin $2.50-c 1.00 2.50

PROTOTYPE (Also see Flood Relief & Ultraforce)
Aug, 1993 - No. 18, Feb, 1995 ($1.95/$2.50)
Malibu Comics (Ultraverse)

Prototype #15 © MAL

Prudence & Caution #1 © DEF

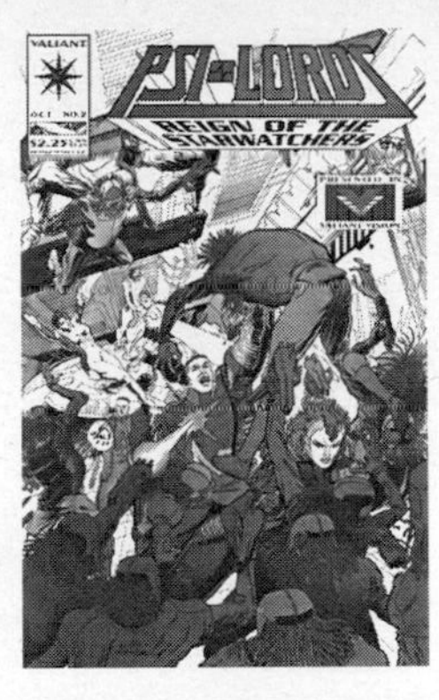

Psi-Lords #2 © VAL

GD25 FN65 NM94

1,2 .80 2.00
1-Holo-c 2.00 5.00
1-Ultra Limited silver foil-c 1.60 4.00
3-($2.50, 48 pgs.)-Rune flip-c/story by B. Smith (3 pgs.) 1.00 2.50
4-12: 4-Intro Wrath. 5-Break-Thru & Strangers x-over. 6-Arena cameo. 7,8-Arena-c/story. 12-(7/94) .80 2.00
0-(8/94,$ 2.50, 44 pgs.) 1.00 2.50
13 (8/94, $3.50)-Flip book(Ultraverse Premiere #6) 1.40 3.50
14-17: 14-(10/94) .80 2.00
18 ($2.50) 1.00 2.50
Giant Size 1 (10/94, $2.50, 44 pgs.) 1.00 2.50

PROWLER (Also see Revenge of the…)
July, 1987 - No. 4, Oct, 1987 ($1.75)
Eclipse Comics

1-4: Snyder-c/a. 3,4-Origin .75 1.80

PROWLER, THE
Nov, 1994 ($1.75)
Marvel Comics

1-4: 1-Spider-Man app. .70 1.75

PROWLER IN "WHITE ZOMBIE", THE
Oct, 1988 ($2.00, B&W, Baxter paper)
Eclipse Comics

1-Adapts Bela Lugosi movie White Zombie .80 2.00

PRUDENCE & CAUTION (Also see Dogs of War & Warriors of Plasm)
May, 1994 - No. 2, June, 1994 ($3.50/$2.50)(Spanish versions exist)
Defiant

1-($3.50, 52 pgs.)-Chris Claremont scripts in all 1.40 3.50
2-($2.50) 1.00 2.50

PRYDE AND WISDOM (Also see Excalibur)
Sept, 1996 - No. 3, Nov, 1996 ($1.95, limited series)
Marvel Comics

1-3: Warren Ellis scripts; Terry Dodson & Karl Story-c/a 2.00

PSI-FORCE
Nov, 1986 - No. 32, June, 1989 (75¢/$1.50)
Marvel Comics Group

1-32: 11-13-Williamson-i 1.25
Annual 1 (10/87) 1.25

PSI-JUDGE ANDERSON
1989 No. 10, 1990 ($1.95, B&W)
Fleetway Publications (Quality)

1-10 1.00 2.50

PSI-LORDS
Sept, 1994 - No. 10, June, 1995 ($2.25)
Valiant

1-($3.50)-Chromium wraparound-c 1.40 3.50
1-Gold 1.60 4.00
2-10: 3-Chaos Effect Epsilon Pt. 2 .90 2.25

PSYBA-RATS (Also see Showcase '94 #3,4)
Apr, 1995-No. 3, June, 1995 ($2.50, limited series)
DC Comics

1-3 1.00 2.50

PSYCHO (Magazine)
Jan, 1971 - No. 24, Mar, 1975 (68 pgs.; B&W) (No #22?)
Skywald Publishing Corp.

1-All reprints 4.50 13.50 45.00
2-Origin & 1st app. The Heap, & Frankenstein series by Adkins 3.00 9.00 30.00
3-10 2.50 7.50 20.00
11-24: 13-Cannabalism; 3 pgs of Christopher Lee as Dracula photos. 18-Injury to eye-c. 20-Severed Head-c. 24-1975 Winter Special 2.00 6.00 16.00
Annual 1(1972) 2.50 7.50 24.00
Fall Special (1974)-Reese, Wildey-a(r) 2.25 6.75 18.00
Winter Special 1 (1975)-Dave Sim scripts 2.25 6.75 18.00
Yearbook(1974-nn) 2.50 7.50 20.00
NOTE: ***Boris*** *c-3, 5.* ***Buckler*** *a-4, 5.* ***Everett*** *a-3-6.* ***Jeff Jones*** *a-6, 7, 9; c-12.* ***Kaluta*** *a-13.* ***Katz/Buckler*** *a-3.* ***Morrow*** *a-1.* ***Reese*** *a-5.* ***Sutton*** *a-3.* ***Wildey*** *a-5.*

PSYCHOANALYSIS
Mar-Apr, 1955 - No. 4, Sept-Oct, 1955
E. C. Comics

1-All Kamen-c/a; not approved by code 17.00 49.00 120.00
2-4-Kamen-c/a in all 13.00 39.00 95.00

PSYCHOBLAST
Nov, 1987 - No. 9, July, 19898 ($1.75)
First Comics

1-9 .75 1.80

PSYCHONAUTS
Oct, 1993 - No. 4, Jan, 1994 ($4.95, limited series)
Marvel Comics (Epic Comics)

1-4: American/Japanese co-produced comic 2.00 5.00

PSYLOCKE & ARCHANGEL CRIMSON DAWN
Aug, 1997 - No. 4, Nov, 1997 ($2.50, limited series)
Marvel Comics

1-4-Raab-s/Larroca-a(p) 1.00 2.50

P.T. 109 (See Movie Comics)

PUBLIC DEFENDER IN ACTION (Formerly Police Trap)
No. 7, Mar, 1956 - No. 12, Oct, 1957
Charlton Comics

7 7.15 21.50 50.00
8-12 5.35 16.00 32.00

PUBLIC ENEMIES
1948 - No. 9, June-July, 1949
D. S. Publishing Co.

1-True Crime Stories 17.50 53.00 140.00
2-Used in **SOTI**, pg. 95 19.00 56.00 130.00
3-5: 5-Arrival date of 10/1/48 10.00 30.00 75.00
6,8,9 10.00 30.00 65.00
7-McWilliams-a; injury to eye panel 10.00 30.00 75.00

PUDGY PIG
Sept, 1958 - No. 2, Nov, 1958
Charlton Comics

1,2 2.50 7.50 20.00

PUMA BLUES
1986 - No. 26, 1990 ($1.70-$1.75, B&W)
Aardvark One International/Mirage Studios #21 on

1-19, 21-26: 1-1st & 2nd printings. 25,26-$1.75-c .80 2.00
20 ($2.25)-By Alan Moore, Miller, Grell, others 1.00 2.50
Trade Paperback (12/88, $14.95) 14.95

PUMPKINHEAD: THE RITES OF EXORCISM (Movie)
1993 - No. 2, 1993 ($2.50, limited series)
Dark Horse Comics

1,2: Based on movie; painted-c by McManus 1.00 2.50

PUNCH & JUDY COMICS
1944; No. 2, Fall, 1944 - V3#2, 12/47; V3#3, 6/51 - V3#9, 12/51
Hillman Periodicals

V1#1-(60 pgs.) 15.50 47.00 125.00

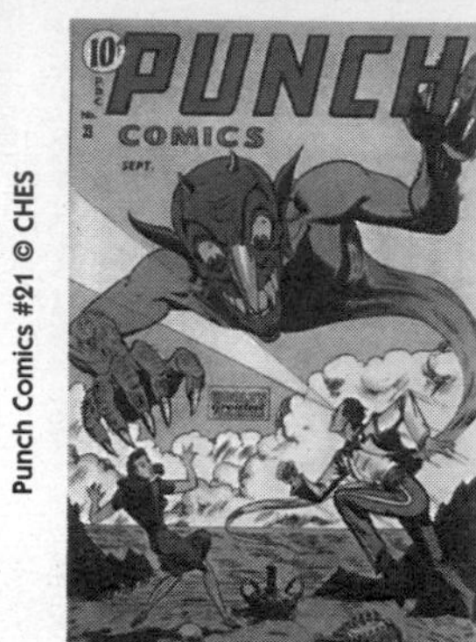

Punch Comics #21 © CHES

Punisher #92 © MEG

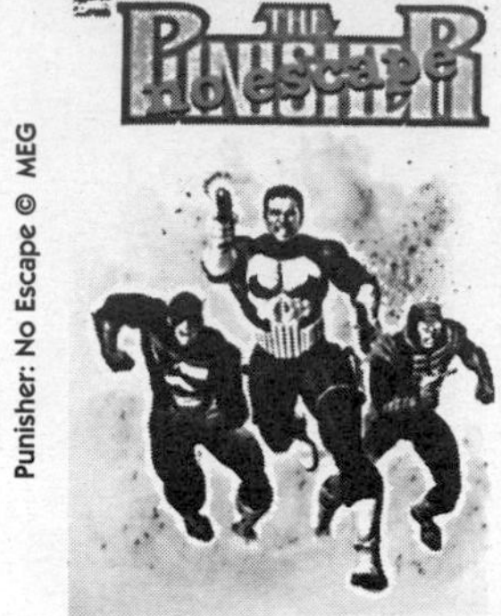

Punisher: No Escape © MEG

	GD25	FN65	NM94
2	8.75	26.25	70.00
3-12(7/46)	7.15	21.50	50.00
V2#1(8/49),3-9	4.35	13.00	28.00
V2#2,10-12, V3#1-Kirby-a(2) each	16.00	49.00	130.00
V3#2-Kirby-a	15.00	45.00	120.00
3-9	4.25	13.00	28.00

PUNCH COMICS
12/41; #2, 2/42; #9, 7/44 - #19, 10/46; #20, 7/47 - #23, 1/48
Harry 'A' Chesler

	GD25	FN65	NM94
1-Mr. E, The Sky Chief, Hale the Magician, Kitty Kelly begin	100.00	300.00	900.00
2-Captain Glory app.	67.00	200.00	600.00
9-Rocketman & Rocket Girl & The Master Key begin	56.00	168.00	500.00
10-Sky Chief app.; J. Cole-a; Master Key-r/Scoop #3	47.00	141.00	420.00
11-Origin Master Key-r/Scoop #1; Sky Chief, Little Nemo app.; Jack Cole-a; Fineish art by Sultan	44.00	132.00	400.00
12-Rocket Boy & Capt. Glory app; classic Skull-c	83.00	250.00	750.00
13-Cover has list of 4 Chesler artists' names on tombstone	47.00	141.00	425.00
14-17,19:	42.00	126.00	375.00
18-Bondage-c; hypodermic panels	50.00	150.00	450.00
20-Unique cover with bare-breasted women	67.00	200.00	600.00
21-Hypo needle story	42.00	126.00	375.00
22,23-Little Nemo-not by McCay. 22-Intro Baxter (teenage)	23.00	68.00	180.00

PUNCHY AND THE BLACK CROW
No. 10, Oct, 1985 - No. 12, Feb, 1986
Charlton Comics

	GD25	FN65	NM94
10-12: Al Fago funny animal-r			1.00

PUNISHER (See Amazing Spider-Man #129, Blood and Glory, Captain America #241, Classic Punisher, Daredevil #182-184, 257, Daredevil and the..., Ghost Rider V2#5, 6, Marc Spector #8 & 9, Marvel Preview #2, Marvel Super Action, Marvel Tales, Power Pack #46, Spectacular Spider-Man #81-83, 140, 141, 143 & new Strange Tales #13 & 14)

PUNISHER (The...)
Jan, 1986 - No. 5, May, 1986 (Limited series)
Marvel Comics Group

	GD25	FN65	NM94
1-Double size		2.00	5.00
2		1.20	3.00
3-5: 3-Has 2 diff. cover prices, 75¢ & 95¢(w/UPC)			1.50
Trade Paperback (1988)-r/#1-5	1.40	4.15	11.00

NOTE: ***Zeck*** *a-1-4; c-1-5.*

PUNISHER (The...)
July, 1987 - No. 104, July, 1995
Marvel Comics

	GD25	FN65	NM94
V2#1		1.60	4.00
2-9: 7-Last 75¢ issue. 8-Portacio/Williams-c/a begins, ends #18. 9-Scarcer, low distribution		.80	2.00
10-Daredevil app.; ties in w/Daredevil #257		1.20	3.00
11-15: 13-18-Kingpin app.		.80	2.00
16-20: 19-Stroman-c/a. 20-Portacio-c(p)		.80	2.00
21-24,26-40: 24-1st app. Shadowmasters			1.50
25,50:($1.50, 52 pgs.). 25-Shadowmasters app.			1.50
41-49 ($1.25)			1.25
51-59: 57-Photo-c; came w/outer-c (newsstand ed. w/o outer-c). 59-Punisher is severely cut & has skin grafts (has black skin); last $1.00-c			1.00
60-74,76-85,87-89: 60-Begin $1.25-c. 60-62-Luke Cage app. 62-Punisher back to white skin. 68-Tarantula-c/story. 85-Prequel to Suicide Run Pt. 0. 87,88-Suicide Run Pt. 6 & 9			1.00
75-($2.75, 52 pgs.)-Embossed silver foil-c		1.10	2.75
86-($2.95, 52 pgs.)-Embossed & foil stamped-c; Suicide Run part 3		1.20	3.00
90-99, 101-104: 90-Begin $1.50-c; bound-in card sheet. 99-Cringe app. 102-Bullseye.			1.50
100-($2.95, 68 pgs.)		1.20	3.00
100-($3.95, 68 pgs.)-Foil cover		1.60	4.00
"Ashcan" edition (75¢)-Joe Kubert-c			.75
Annual 1 (1988)-Evolutionary War x-over		.80	2.00
Annual 2 (1989, $2.00, 68 pgs.)-Atlantis Attacks x-over; Jim Lee-a(p) (back-up story, 6 pgs.); Moon Knight app.		.80	2.00
Annual 3,4 ('90, '91, $2.00, 68 pgs.): 4-Golden-c(p)		.80	2.00
Annual 5 (1992, $2.25, 68 pgs.)		.90	2.25
Annual 6 (1993, $2.95, 68 pgs.)-Bagged w/card		1.20	3.00
Annual 7 (1994, $2.95)-Rapido app.		1.20	3.00
...: A Man Named Frank (1994, $6.95, TPB)	1.00	2.80	7.00
...and Wolverine in African Saga nn (1989, $5.95, 52 pgs.)-Reprints Punisher War Journal #6 & 7; Jim Lee-c/a(r)		1.60	4.00
Back to School Special 1 (11/92, $2.95, 68 pgs.)		1.20	3.00
Back to School Special 2 (10/93, $2.95, 68 pgs.)		1.20	3.00
Back to School Special 3 (10/94, $2.95)		1.20	3.00
.../Batman: Deadly Knights (10/94, $4.95)		2.00	5.00
...Bloodlines nn (1991, $5.95, 68 pgs.)		2.40	6.00
...: Die Hard in the Big Easy nn ('92, $4.95, 52 pgs.)		2.00	5.00
...: Empty Quarter nn ('94, $6.95)	1.00	2.80	7.00
...G-Force nn (1992, $4.95, 52 pgs.)-Painted-c		2.00	5.00
...Holiday Special 1 (1/93, $2.95, 52 pgs.)-Foil-c		1.20	3.00
...Holiday Special 2 (1/94, $2.95, 68 pgs.)		1.20	3.00
...Holiday Special 3 (1/95, $2.95, 68 pgs.)		1.20	3.00
...Invades the 'Nam: Final Invasion nn (2/94, $6.95)-J. Kubert-c & chapter break art; reprints The 'Nam #52,53,67-69	1.00	2.80	7.00
...Meets Archie (8/94, $3.95, 52 pgs.)-Die cut-c; no ads; same contents as Archie Meets The Punisher		1.60	4.00
...Movie Special 1 (6/90, $5.95, 68 pgs.)		2.40	6.00
...: No Escape nn (1990, $4.95, 52 pgs.)-New-a		2.00	5.00
...The Prize nn (1990, $4.95, 68 pgs.)-New-a		2.00	5.00
Summer Special 1 (8/91, $2.95, 52 pgs.)-No ads		1.20	3.00
Summer Special 2 (8/92, $2.50, 52 pgs.)-Bisley painted-c; Austin-a(i)		1.00	2.50
Summer Special 3 (8/93, $2.50, 52 pgs.)-No ads		1.00	2.50
Summer Special 4 (7/94, $2.95, 52 pgs.)		1.20	3.00

NOTE: ***Austin*** *c(i)-47, 48.* ***Cowan*** *c-39.* ***Golden*** *c-50, 85, 86, 100.* ***Heath*** *a-26, 27, 89, 90; c-26, 27.* ***Quesada*** *c-56p, 62p.* ***Sienkiewicz*** *c-Back to School 1.* ***Stroman*** *a-76p(9 pgs.).* ***Williamson*** *a(i)-25, 60-62i, 64-70, 74, Annual 5; c(i)-62, 65-68.*

PUNISHER (Also see Double Edge)
Nov, 1995 - No. 18, Apr, 1997 ($2.95/$1.95/$1.50)
Marvel Comics

	GD25	FN65	NM94
1 ($2.95)-Ostrander scripts begin; foil-c.		1.20	3.00
2-8: 7-Vs. S.H.I.E.L.D.			
9-18: 9-Begin $1.50-c. 11-"Onslaught." 12-17-X-Cutioner-c/app. 17-Daredevil, Spider-Man-c/app.		.80	2.00

PUNISHER AND WOLVERINE: DAMAGING EVIDENCE (See Wolverine and...)

PUNISHER ARMORY, THE
7/90 ($1.50); No. 2, 6/91; No. 3, 4/92 - 10/94($1.75/$2.00)
Marvel Comics

	GD25	FN65	NM94
1($1.50)-r/weapons pgs. from War Journal; Jim Lee-c			1.50
2 ($1.75)-Jim Lee-c		.80	2.00
3-10 ($2.00): All new material. 3-Jusko painted-c		.80	2.00

PUNISHER KILLS THE MARVEL UNIVERSE
Nov, 1995 ($5.95, one-shot)
Marvel Comics

	GD25	FN65	NM94
1-Garth Ennis script			6.00

PUNISHER MAGAZINE, THE
Oct, 1989 - No. 16, Nov, 1990 ($2.25, B&W, Magazine, 52 pgs.)

Punisher 2099 #20 © MEG

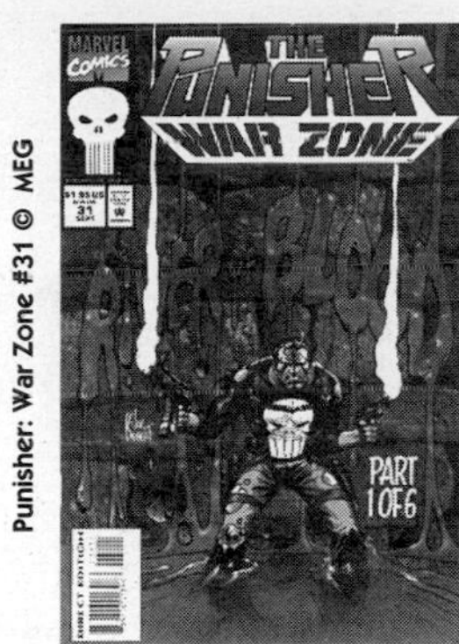

Punisher: War Zone #31 © MEG

Punx #3 © Acclaim

GD25 FN65 NM94

Marvel Comics
1-3: 1-r/Punisher #1('86). 2,3-r/Punisher 2-5 .90 2.25
4-16: 4-7-r/Punisher V2#1-8. 4-Chiodo-c. 8-r/Punisher #10 & Daredevil #257; Portacio & Lee-r. 14-r/Punisher War Journal #1,2 w/new Lee-c. 16-r/Punisher W. J. #3,8 .90 2.25

NOTE: ***Chiodo** painted c-4, 7, 16. **Jusko** painted c-6, 8. **Jim Lee** r-8, 14-16; c-14. **Portacio/Williams** r-7-12.*

PUNISHER MOVIE COMIC
Nov, 1989 - No. 3, Dec, 1989 ($1.00, limited series)
Marvel Comics
1-3: Movie adaptation 1.25
1 (1989, $4.95, squarebound)-contains #1-3 2.00 5.00

PUNISHER: ORIGIN OF MICRO CHIP, THE
July, 1993 - No. 2, Aug, 1993 ($1.75, limited series)
Marvel Comics
1,2 .70 1.75

PUNISHER: P.O.V.
1991 - No. 4, 1991 ($4.95, painted, limited series, 52 pgs.)
Marvel Comics
1-4: Starlin scripts & Wrightson painted-c/a in all. 2-Nick Fury app. 2.00 5.00

PUNISHER: THE GHOSTS OF INNOCENTS
Jan, 1993 - No. 2, Jan, 1993 ($5.95, 52 pgs.)
Marvel Comics
1,2-Starlin scripts 2.40 6.00

PUNISHER 2099 (See Punisher War Journal #50)
Feb, 1993 - No. 34, Nov, 1995 ($1.25/$1.50/$1.95)
Marvel Comics
1-($1.75)-Foil stamped-c .80 2.00
1-($1.75)-Second printing .70 1.75
2-15: 13-Spider-Man 2099 x-over; Ron Lim-c(p) 1.25
16-24, 26,27: 16-Begin $1.50-c; bound-in card sheet 1.50
25 ($2.95, 52 pgs.)-Deluxe edition; embossed foil-cover 1.20 3.00
25 ($2.25, 52 pgs.) .90 2.25
28-34: 28-Begin $1.95-c .80 2.00

PUNISHER WAR JOURNAL, THE
Nov, 1988 - No. 80, July, 1995 ($1.50/$1.75/$1.95)
Marvel Comics
1-Origin The Punisher; Matt Murdock cameo; Jim Lee inks begin. 1.20 3.00
2-5: 2,3-Daredevil x-over; Jim Lee-c(i). 4-Jim Lee c/a begins. .80 2.00
6-Two part Wolverine story begins .80 2.00
7-Wolverine-c, story ends 1.50
8-12,17-19: 19-Last Jim Lee-c/a 1.50
13-16,20-22: No Jim Lee-a. 13-Lee-c only. 13-15-Heath-i. 14,15-Spider-Man x-over 1.50
23-28,31-49,51-60,62,63,65: 23-Begin $1.75-c. 31-Andy & Joe Kubert art. 36-Photo-c. 47,48-Nomad/Daredevil-c/stories; see Nomad. 57,58-Daredevil & Ghost Rider-c/stories. 62,63-Suicide Run Pt. 4 & 7 1.00
29,30-Ghost Rider app. 1.50
50-($2.95, 52 pgs.)-Preview of Punisher 2099 (1st app.); embossed-c. 1.20 3.00
61-($2.95, 52 pgs.)-Embossed foil cover; Suicide Run Pt. 1 1.20 3.00
64-($2.95, 52 pgs.)-Die-cut-c; Suicide Run Pt. 10 1.20 3.00
64-($2.25, 52 pgs.)-Regular cover edition .90 2.25
66-74. 76-80: 66-Begin $1.95-c; bound-in card sheet .80 2.00
75 ($2.50, 52 pgs.) 1.00 2.50

NOTE: ***Golden** c-25-30, 40, 61, 62. **Jusko** painted c-31, 32. **Jim Lee** a-1i-3i, 4p-13p, 17p-19p; c-2i, 3i, 4p-15p, 17p, 18p, 19p. Painted c-40.*

GD25 FN65 NM94

PUNISHER: WAR ZONE, THE
Mar, 1992 - No. 40, July, 1995 ($1.75/$1.95)
Marvel Comics
1-($2.25, 40 pgs.)-Die cut-c; Romita, Jr.-c/a begins .90 2.25
2 .80 2.00
3-22,24,26: 8-Last Romita, Jr.-c/a. 19-Wolverine app. 24-Suicide Run Pt. 5 .70 1.75
23-($2.95, 52 pgs.)-Enbossed foil-c; Suicide Run part 2; Buscema-a(part) 1.20 3.00
25-($2.25, 52 pgs.)-Suicide Run part 8; painted-c .90 2.25
27-40: 27-Begin 1.95-c; bound-in card sheet .80 2.00
Annual 1 (1993, $2.95, 68 pgs.)-Bagged w/card; John Buscema-a 1.20 3.00
Annual 2 (1994, $2.95, 68 pgs.) 1.20 3.00

NOTE: ***Golden** c-23. **Romita, Jr.** c/a-1-8.*

PUNISHER: YEAR ONE
Dec, 1994 - No. 4, Apr, 1995 ($2.50, limited series)
Marvel Comics
1-4 1.00 2.50

PUNX
Nov, 1995 - No. 3, Jan, 1996 ($2.50, unfinished limited series)
Acclaim (Valiant)
1-3: Giffen story & art in all. 2-Satirizes Scott McCloud's Understanding Comics 1.00 2.50
(Manga) Special 1 (3/96, $2.50)-Giffen scripts 1.00 2.50

PUPPET COMICS
Spring, 1946 - No. 2, Summer, 1946
George W. Dougherty Co.
1,2-Funny animal 8.50 26.00 60.00

PUPPETOONS (See George Pal's...)

PURE OIL COMICS (Also see Salerno Carnival of Comics, 24 Pages of Comics, & Vicks Comics)
Late 1930's (24 pgs., regular size, paper-c)
Pure Oil Giveaway
nn-Contains 1-2 pg. strips; i.e., Hairbreadth Harry, Skyroads, Buck Rogers by Calkins & Yager, Olly of the Movies, Napoleon, S'Matter Pop, etc. 34.00 103.00 275.00
Also a 16 pg. 1938 giveaway w/Buck Rogers 33.00 98.00 260.00

PURGATORI
Prelude #-1, 5/96 ($1.50, 16 pgs.); 1996 - No. 3 Dec, 1996 ($3.50/$2.95, limited series)
Chaos! Comics
Prelude #-1-Brian Pulido story; Jim Balent-c/a; contains sketches & interviews. 1.50
1-($3.50)-Wraparound cover; red foil embossed-c; Jim Balent-a 1.00 2.80 7.00
1-($19.95)-Premium Edition (1000 print run) 2.50 7.50 20.00
2-($3.00)-Wraparound-c 1.20 3.00
2-Variant-c 2.00 5.00
...The Dracula Gambit-($2.95) 1.20 3.00
...The Dracula Gambit Sketchbook-($2.95) 1.20 3.00
...The Vampire's Myth 1-($19.95) Premium ed. (10,000) 2.50 7.50 20.00

PURGE
Aug, 1993 ($1.95, unfinished limited series)
ANIA/U.P. Comics
1 .80 2.00

PURPLE CLAW, THE (Also see Tales of Horror)
Jan, 1953 - No. 3, May, 1953
Minoan Publishing Co./Toby Press

Purple Claw #2 © TOBY

Pussycat #1 MEG

The Question Quarterly #1 © DC

	GD25	FN65	NM94
1-Origin; horror/weird stories in all	24.00	73.00	180.00
2,3: 1-3 r-in Tales of Horror #9-11	18.00	54.00	130.00
I.W. Reprint #8-Reprints #1	2.50	7.50	20.00

PUSSYCAT (Magazine)
Oct, 1968 (B&W reprints from Men's magazines)
Marvel Comics Group

	GD25	FN65	NM94
1-(Scarce)-Ward, Everett, Wood-a; Everett-c	17.00	51.00	135.00

PUZZLE FUN COMICS (Also see Jingle Jangle)
Spring, 1946 - No. 2, Summer, 1946 (52 pgs.)
George W. Dougherty Co.

	GD25	FN65	NM94
1-Gustavson-a	17.50	53.00	140.00
2	12.00	38.00	100.00

NOTE: *#1 & 2('46) each contain a* ***George Carlson*** *cover plus a 6 pg. story "Alec in Fumbleland"; also many puzzles in each.*

QUACK!
July, 1976 - No. 6, 1977? ($1.25, B&W)
Star Reach Productions

	GD25	FN65	NM94
1-Brunner-c/a on Duckaneer (Howard the Duck clone); Dave Stevens, Gilbert, Shaw-a	1.85	5.50	15.00
1-2nd printing (10/76)			1.50
2,4-6: 2-Newton the Rabbit Wonder by Aragones/Leialoha; Gilbert, Shaw-a; Leialoha-c. 6-Brunner-a (Duckeneer); Gilbert-a		2.40	6.00
3-The Beavers by Dave Sim begin, end #5; Gilbert, Shaw-a; Sim/Leialoha-c	1.00	3.00	8.00

QUADRANT
1983 - No. 8, 1986 (B&W, nudity, adults)
Quadrant Publications

	GD25	FN65	NM94
1-Peter Hsu-c/a in all		1.20	3.00
2		.80	2.00
3-8		.75	1.90

QUAKER OATS (Also see Cap'n Crunch)
1965 (Giveaway) (2-1/2x5-1/2") (16 pgs.)
Quaker Oats Co.

	GD25	FN65	NM94
"Plenty of Glutton", starring Quake & Quisp;	2.50	7.50	20.00
"Lava Come-Back", "Kite Tale", "A Witch in Time"		1.60	4.00

QUANTUM & WOODY
June, 1997 - Present ($2.50)
Acclaim Comics

	GD25	FN65	NM94
1-10: 1-1st app.; two covers. 6-Copycat-c. 9-Troublemakers app.		1.00	2.50
The Director's Cut TPB ('97, $7.95) r/#1-4 plus extra pages			7.95

QUANTUM LEAP (TV) (See A Nightmare on Elm Street)
Sept, 1991 - No. 12, June?, 1993 ($2.50, color, painted-c)
Innovation Publishing

	GD25	FN65	NM94
1-12: Based on TV show; all have painted-c. 8-Has photo gallery		1.00	2.50
Special Edition 1 (10/92)-r/#1 w/8 extra pgs. of photos & articles		1.00	2.50
Time and Space Special 1 (#13) ($2.95)-Foil logo		1.20	3.00

QUASAR (See Avengers #302, Captain America #217, Incredible Hulk #234, Marvel Team-Up #113 & Marvel Two-in-One #53)
Oct, 1989 - July, 1994 ($1.00/$1.25) (Direct sales #17 on)
Marvel Comics

	GD25	FN65	NM94
1-Origin; formerly Marvel Boy/Marvel Man		.80	2.00
2-5: 3-Human Torch app.			1.50
6-Venom cameo (2 pgs.)		.80	2.00
7-Cosmic Spidey app.		1.00	2.50
8-15,18-24: 11-Excalibur x-over. 14-McFarlane-c. 20-Fantastic Four app. 23-Ghost Rider x-over			1.20
16-($1.50, 52 pgs.)			1.50
17-Flash parody (Buried Alien)		.80	2.00
25-($1.50, 52 pgs.)-New costume Quasar			1.50
26-Infinity Gauntlet x-over; Thanos-c/story		.80	2.00
27-Infinity Gauntlet x-over			1.50
28-30: 30-Thanos cameo in flashback; last $1.00-c			1.00
31-49,51-60: 31-Begin $1.25-c; D.P. 7 guest stars. 38-40-Infinity War x-overs. 38-Battles Warlock. 39-Thanos-c & cameo. 40-Thanos app. 42-Punisher-c/story. 53-Warlock & Moondragon app. 58-w/bound-in card sheet			1.25
50-($2.95, 52 pgs.)-Holo-grafx foil-c; Silver Surfer, Man-Thing, Ren & Stimpy app.		1.20	3.00
Special #1-3 ($1.25, newsstand)-Same as #32-34			1.25

QUEEN OF THE WEST, DALE EVANS (TV)(See Dale Evans Comics & Western Roundup under Dell Giants)
No. 479, 7/53 - No. 22, 1-3/59 (All photo-c; photo back c-4-8, 15)
Dell Publishing Co.

	GD25	FN65	NM94
Four Color 479(#1, '53)	20.00	60.00	220.00
Four Color 528(#2, '54)	9.00	27.00	100.00
3,4: 3(4-6/54)-Toth-a. 4-Toth, Manning-a	8.00	23.00	85.00
5-10-Manning-a. 5-Marsh-a	6.00	18.00	65.00
11,19,21-No Manning 21-Tufts-a	4.00	12.00	45.00
12-18,20,22-Manning-a	5.00	15.00	54.00

QUENTIN DURWARD
No. 672, Jan, 1956
Dell Publishing Co.

	GD25	FN65	NM94
Four Color 672-Movie, photo-c	5.50	16.50	60.00

QUESTAR ILLUSTRATED SCIENCE FICTION CLASSICS
1977 (224 pgs.) ($1.95)
Golden Press

	GD25	FN65	NM94
11197-Stories by Asimov, Sturgeon, Silverberg & Niven; Starstream-r	2.50	7.50	20.00

QUEST FOR DREAMS LOST (Also see Word Warriors)
July 4, 1987 ($2.00, B&W, 52 pgs.)(Proceeds donated to help illiteracy)
Literacy Volunteers of Chicago

	GD25	FN65	NM94
1-Teenage Mutant Ninja Turtles by Eastman/Laird, Trollords, Silent Invasion, The Realm, Wordsmith, Reacto Man, Eb'nn, Aniverse		.80	2.00

QUESTION, THE (See Americomics, Blue Beetle (1967), Charlton Bullseye & Mysterious Suspense)

QUESTION, THE (Also see Showcase '95 #3)
Feb, 1987 - No. 36, Mar, 1990 ($1.50)
DC Comics

	GD25	FN65	NM94
1-36: Denny O'Neil scripts in all			1.50
Annual 1 (1988, $2.50)		1.00	2.50
Annual 2 (1989, $3.50)		1.40	3.50

QUESTION QUARTERLY, THE
Summer, 1990 - No. 5, Spring, 1992 ($2.50, 52pgs.)
DC Comics

	GD25	FN65	NM94
1-5		1.00	2.50

NOTE: ***Cowan*** *a-1, 2, 4, 5; c-1-3, 5.* ***Mignola*** *a-5i.* ***Quesada*** *a-3-5.*

QUESTION RETURNS, THE
Feb, 1997 ($3.50, one-shot)
DC Comics

	GD25	FN65	NM94
1-Brereton-c		1.40	3.50

QUESTPROBE
8/84; No. 2, 1/85; No. 3, 11/85 - No. 4, 12/85 (limited series)
Marvel Comics Group

	GD25	FN65	NM94
1-4: 1-The Hulk app. by Romita. 2-Spider-Man; Mooney-a(i). 3-Human Torch & Thing			1.00

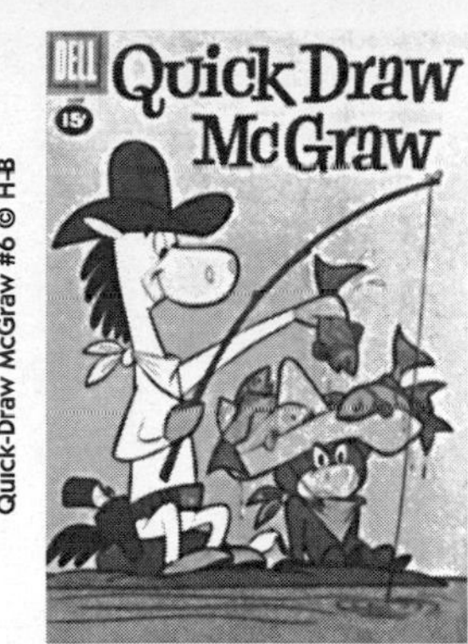

Quick-Draw McGraw #6 © H-B

Rack & Pain #2 © Brian Pulido

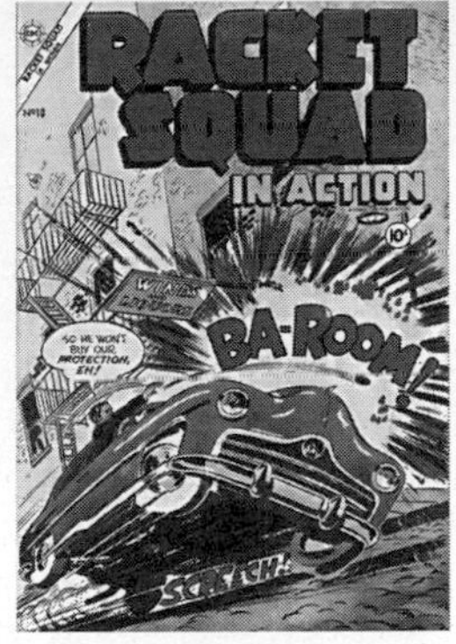

Racket Squad in Action #10 © CC

QUICK-DRAW McGRAW (TV) (Hanna-Barbera)(See Whitman Comic Books)
No. 1040, 12-2/59-60 - No. 11, 7-9/62; No. 12, 11/62; No. 13, 2/63; No. 14, 4/63; No. 15, 6/69 (1st show aired 9/29/59)
Dell Publishing Co./Gold Key No. 12 on

Four Color 1040(#1) 11.00 34.00 125.00
2(4-6/60)-6: 2-Augie Doggie & Snooper & Blabber stories (8 pgs. each); pre-dates both of their #1 issues. 4-Augie Doggie & Snooper & Blabber stories.
5-Early Snagglepuss app.; last 10¢ issue 6.40 19.00 70.00
7-11 4.50 13.50 50.00
12,13-Title change to ...Fun-Type Roundup (84pgs.) 7.00 22.00 80.00
14,15 3.60 11.00 40.00

QUICK-DRAW McGRAW (TV)(See Spotlight #2)
Nov, 1970 - No. 8, Jan, 1972 (Hanna-Barbera)
Charlton Comics

1 4.00 12.00 40.00
2-8 2.50 7.50 24.00

QUICKSILVER (See Avengers)
Nov, 1997 - Present ($2.99/$1.99)
Marvel Comics

1-($2.99)-Peyer-s/Casey Jones-a; wraparound-c 2.99
2-4: 2-Two covers-variant by Golden 1.99

QUICK-TRIGGER WESTERN (...Action #12; Cowboy Action #5-11)
No. 12, May, 1956 - No. 19, Sept, 1957
Atlas Comics (ACI No. 12/WPI No. 13-19)

12-Baker-a 11.30 34.00 90.00
13-Williamson-a, 5 pgs. 10.50 32.00 85.00
14-Everett, Crandall, Torres-a; Heath-c 9.50 28.00 75.00
15-Torres, Crandall-a 8.50 26.00 60.00
16-Orlando, Kirby-a 7.85 23.50 55.00
17,18: 18-Baker-a 7.85 23.50 55.00
19 5.70 17.00 40.00

NOTE: ***Ayers** a-17. **Colan** a-16. **Maneely** a-15, 17; c-15, 18. **Morrow** a-18. **Powell** a-14. **Severin** a-19; c-12, 13, 16, 17, 19. **Shores** a-16. **Tuska** a-17.*

QUINCY (See Comics Reading Libraries)

Q-UNIT
Dec, 1993 ($2.95)
Harris Comics

1-($2.95)-Polybagged w/trading card version 1.2 1.20 3.00

RABID
1994 ($5.95, B&W)
FantaCo Enterprises

1 2.40 6.00

RACCOON KIDS, THE (Formerly Movietown Animal Antics)
No. 52, Sept-Oct, 1954 - No. 64, Nov, 1957
National Periodical Publications (Arleigh No. 63,64)

52-Doodles Duck by Mayer 12.00 38.00 100.00
53-64: 53-62-Doodles Duck by Mayer 8.75 26.25 70.00

RACE FOR THE MOON
Mar, 1958 - No. 3, Nov, 1958
Harvey Publications

1-Powell-a(5); 1/2-pg. S&K-a; cover redrawn from Galaxy Science Fiction pulp (5/53) 11.50 34.00 80.00
2-Kirby/Williamson-c(r)/a(3); Kirby-p 7 more stys 24.00 71.00 165.00
3-Kirby/Williamson-c/a(4); Kirby-p 6 more stys 25.00 75.00 175.00

RACE OF SCORPIONS
1990 - No. 2, 1990 ($4.50/$4.95, 52pgs.)
Dark Horse Comics

1-r/stories from Dark Horse Presents #23-27 1.80 4.50
2-($4.95-c); r/Dark Horse Presents 2.00 5.00

RACER-X
8/88 - No. 11, 8/89; V2#1, 9/89 - V2#10, 1990 ($1.75)
Now Comics

0-Deluxe ($3.50) 1.40 3.50
1 (9/88) - 11, V2#1-10 .75 1.80

RACK & PAIN
Mar, 1994 - No. 4, June, 1994 ($2.50, limited series)
Dark Horse Comics

1-4: Brian Pulido scripts in all. 1-Greg Capullo-c 1.20 3.00

RACK & PAIN: KILLERS
Sept, 1996 - No. 4, Jan, 1997 ($2.95, limited series)
Chaos! Comics

1-4: Brian Pulido scripts; Jae Lee-c 1.20 3.00

RACKET SQUAD IN ACTION
May-June, 1952 - No. 29, Mar, 1958
Capitol Stories/Charlton Comics

1 23.00 69.00 170.00
2-4,6: 3,4,6-Dr. Neff, Ghost Breaker app. 11.00 33.00 80.00
5-Dr. Neff, Ghost Breaker app; headlights-c 19.00 47.00 120.00
7-10: 10-Explosion-c 10.00 30.00 70.00
11-Ditko-c/a 22.00 66.00 170.00
12-Ditko explosion-c (classic); Shuster-a(2) 40.00 120.00 300.00
13-Shuster-c(p)/a. 9.00 27.00 60.00
14-Marijuana story "Shakedown" 10.00 30.00 75.00
15-28 8.35 25.00 55.00
29-(15¢, 68 pgs.) 9.00 27.00 60.00

RADIANT LOVE (Formerly Daring Love #1)
No. 2, Dec, 1953 - No. 6, Aug, 1954
Gilmor Magazines

2 5.70 17.00 38.00
3-6 4.00 12.00 24.00

RADICAL DREAMER
No. 0, May, 1994 - No. 4, Nov, 1994 ($1.99, bi-monthly)(1st poster format comic)
Blackball Comics

0-2-($1.99, poster format); 0-1st app. Max Wrighter .80 2.00
3,4-($2.50) 1.00 2.50

RADICAL DREAMER
V2#1, June, 1995 - V2#6, Feb, 1996 ($2.95, B&W, limited series)
Mark's Giant Economy Size Comics

V2#1-6 1.20 3.00
Prime (5/96, $2.95) 1.20 3.00
Dreams Cannot Die!-(1996, $20.00, softcover)-Collects V1#0-4 & V2#1-6; intro by Kurt Busiek; afterward by Mark Waid 20.00
Dreams Cannot Die!-(1996, $60.00, hardcover)-Signed & limited edition; collects V1#0-4 & V2#1-6; intro by Kurt Busiek; afterward by Mark Waid 60.00

RADIOACTIVE MAN (Simpsons TV show)
1993 - No. 6, 1994 ($1.95/$2.25, limited series)
Bongo Comics

1-($2.95)-Glow-in-the-dark-c; bound-in jumbo poster; origin Radioactive Man; (cover dated Nov. 1952) 1.30 3.25
2-Says #88 on-c & inside & dated May 1962; cover parody of Atlas Kirby monster-c; Superior Squad app.; origin Fallout Boy .80 2.00
3-($1.95)-Cover "dated" Aug 1972 #216 .80 2.00
4-($2.25)-Cover "dated" Oct 1980 #412; w/trading card .90 2.25
5-($2.25)-Cover "dated" Jan 1986 #679; w/trading card .90 2.25
6-($2.25)-Cover "dated" Jan 1995 #1000 .90 2.25
Colossal #1-($4.95) 4.95

RAGAMUFFINS
Jan, 1985 ($1.75, one shot)

Raggedy Ann and Andy #20 © DELL

Rai #26 © VAL

Ralph Kiner, Home Run King © FAW

GD25 FN65 NM94

Eclipse Comics

1-Eclipse Magazine-r, w/color .75 1.80

RAGGEDY ANN AND ANDY (See Dell Giants, March of Comics #23 & New Funnies)
No. 5, 1942 - No. 533, 2/54; 10-12/64 - No. 4, 3/66
Dell Publishing Co.

Four Color 5(1942) 46.00 139.00 510.00
Four Color 23(1943) 35.00 104.00 380.00
Four Color 45(1943) 28.00 85.00 310.00
Four Color 72(1945) 24.00 71.00 260.00
1(6/46)-Billy & Bonnie Bee by Frank Thomas 23.00 68.00 250.00
2,3: 3-Egbert Elephant by Dan Noonan begins 12.00 35.00 130.00
4-Kelly-a, 16 pgs. 13.00 38.00 140.00
5-10: 7-Little Black Sambo, Black Mumbo & Black Jumbo only app; Christmas-c 9.00 27.00 100.00
11-21: 21-Alice In Wonderland cover/story 8.00 25.00 90.00
22-27,29-39(8/49), Four Color 262(1/50): 34-"...In Candyland" 6.40 19.00 70.00
28-Kelly-c 7.00 22.00 80.00
Four Color 306,354,380,452,533 4.50 13.50 50.00
1(10-12/64-Dell) 2.50 7.50 27.00
2,3(10-12/65), 4(3/66) 2.00 6.00 16.00

NOTE: ***Kelly** art ("Animal Mother Goose")-#1-34, 36, 37; c-28. Peterkin Pottle by **John Stanley** in 32-38.*

RAGGEDY ANN AND ANDY
Dec, 1971 - No. 6, Sept, 1973
Gold Key

1 2.50 7.50 20.00
2-6 1.25 3.75 10.00

RAGGEDY ANN & THE CAMEL WITH THE WRINKLED KNEES (See Dell Jr. Treasury #8)

RAGMAN (See Batman Family #20, The Brave & The Bold #196 & Cancelled Comic Cavalcade)
Aug-Sept, 1976 - No. 5, June-July, 1977
National Periodical Publications/DC Comics No. 5

1-Origin & 1st app. 2.40 6.00
2-5: 2-Origin ends; Kubert-c. 4-Drug use story 1.20 3.00

NOTE: ***Kubert** a-4, 5; c-1-5. **Redondo** studios a-1-4.*

RAGMAN (2nd Series)
Oct, 1991 - No. 8, May, 1992 ($1.50, limited series)
DC Comics

1-Giffen plots/breakdowns .80 2.00
2-8: 3-Origin. 8-Batman-c/story 1.50

RAGMAN: CRY OF THE DEAD
Aug, 1993 - No. 6, Jan, 1994 ($1.75, limited series)
DC Comics

1-6: Joe Kubert-c .70 1.75

RAGMOP
Sept, 1997 - Present ($2.95, B&W)
Image Comics

1,2-Rob Walton-c/s/a 2.95

RAGS RABBIT (Formerly Babe Ruth Sports #10 or Little Max #10?; also see Harvey Hits #2, Harvey Wiseguys & Tastee Freez)
No. 11, June, 1951 - No. 18, March, 1954 (Written & drawn for little folks)
Harvey Publications

11-(See Nutty Comics #5 for 1st app.) 3.60 9.00 18.00
12-18 3.20 8.00 16.00

RAI (Rai and the Future Force #9-23) (See Magnus #5-8)
Mar, 1992 - No. 0, Oct, 1992; No. 9, May, 1993 - No. 33, Jun, 1995 ($1.95/$2.25)

GD25 FN65 NM94

Valiant

1,2-Valiant's 1st original character 2.40 6.00
3,4: 4-Low print run; last $1.95-c 1.00 3.00 8.00
5-8: 6,7-Unity x-overs. 7-Death of Rai 1.20 3.00
0-(11/92)-Origin/1st app. new Rai (Rising Spirit) & 1st full app. & partial origin Bloodshot; also see Eternal Warrior #4; tells future of all characters 1.60 4.00
9-($2.50)-Gatefold-c; story cont'd from Magnus #24; Magnus, Eternal Warrior & X-O app. 1.00 2.50
10-33: 15-Manowar Armor app. 17-19-Magnus x-over. 21-1st app. The Starwatchers (cameo); bound-in trading card. 22-Death of Rai. 26-Chaos Effect Epsilon Pt. 3 .90 2.25

NOTE: ***Layton** c-2i, 9i. **Miller** c-6. **Simonson** c-7.*

RAIDERS OF THE LOST ARK (Movie)
Sept, 1981 - No. 3, Nov, 1981 (Movie adaptation)
Marvel Comics Group

1-r/Marvel Comics Super Special #18 1.50
2,3 1.00

NOTE: ***Buscema** a(p)-1-3; c(p)-1. **Simonson** a-3i; scripts-1-3.*

RAINBOW BRITE AND THE STAR STEALER
1985
DC Comics

nn-Movie adaptation .80

RALPH KINER, HOME RUN KING
1950 (Pittsburgh Pirates)
Fawcett Publications

nn-Photo-c; life story 47.00 141.00 425.00

RALPH SNART ADVENTURES
June, 1986 - V2#9, 1987; V3#1 - #26, Feb, 1991; V4#1, 1992 - #4, 1992
Now Comics

1-($1.00, B&W) 1.00
2,3 1.25
V2#1 (11/86, B&W) - 9 1.50
V3#1-23,25,26: 1 (9/88, $1.75)-Color series begins .70 1.75
24-($2.50)-3-D issue 1.00 2.50
V4#1-4-Direct sale versions w/cards 1.00 2.50
V4#1-4-Newsstand versions w/random cards .80 2.00
Book 1 1.00 3.00 8.00
3-D Special (11/92, $3.50)-Complete 12-card set w/3-D glasses 1.40 3.50

RAMAR OF THE JUNGLE (TV)
1954 (no month); No. 2, Sept, 1955 - No. 5, Sept, 1956
Toby Press No. 1/Charlton No. 2 on

1-Jon Hall photo-c; last pre-code issue 16.00 47.00 120.00
2-5: 2-Jon Hall photo-c 11.00 33.00 80.00

RAMM
May, 1987 - No. 2, Sept, 1987 ($1.50, B&W)
Megaton Comics

1,2-Both have 1 pg. Youngblood ad by Liefeld 1.50

RAMPAGING HULK (The Hulk #10 on; see Marvel Treasury Edition)
Jan, 1977 - No. 9, June, 1978 ($1.00, B&W magazine)
Marvel Comics Group

1-6,8: Bloodstone story 1.00 3.00 8.00
2-Old X-Men app; origin old & new X-Men in text w/Cockrum illos 1.00 3.00 8.00
3,7,9: 7-Man-Thing story. 9-Thor vs. Hulk battle; Shanna the She-Devil story.
10-Color issue 1.60 4.00

NOTE: ***Alcala** a-1-3i, 5i, 8i. **Buscema** a-1. **Giffen** a-4. **Nino** a-4i. **Simonson** a-1-3p. **Starlin** a-4(w/Nino), 7; c-4, 5, 7.*

RANDOLPH SCOTT (Movie star)(See Crack Western #67, Prize Comics Western #76,

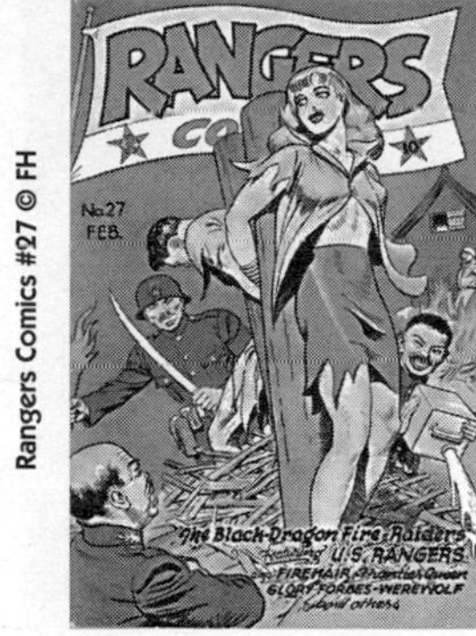

Rangers Comics #27 © FH

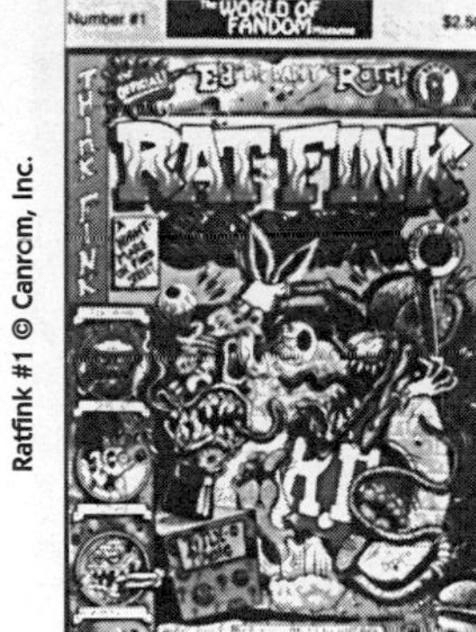

Ratfink #1 © Canrom, Inc.

Ravage 2099 #22 © MEG

	GD25	FN65	NM94

Western Hearts #8, Western Love #1 & Western Winners #7)

RANGE BUSTERS
Sept, 1950 - No. 8, 1951
Fox Features Syndicate

1	14.00	43.00	110.00
2	10.00	30.00	65.00
3-8	8.35	25.00	55.00

RANGE BUSTERS (Formerly Cowboy Love?; Wyatt Earp, Frontier Marshall #11 on)
No. 8, May, 1955 - No. 10, Sept, 1955
Charlton Comics

8	5.70	17.00	40.00
9,10	4.15	12.50	25.00

RANGELAND LOVE
Dec, 1949 - No. 2, Mar, 1950 (52 pgs.)
Atlas Comics (CDS)

1-Robert Taylor & Arlene Dahl photo-c	12.00	36.00	90.00
2-Photo-c	11.00	33.00	75.00

RANGER, THE (See Zane Grey, Four Color #255)

RANGE RIDER, THE (TV)(See Flying A's...)

RANGE ROMANCES
Dec, 1949 - No. 5, Aug, 1950 (#5: 52 pgs.)
Comic Magazines (Quality Comics)

1-Gustavson-c/a	20.00	60.00	150.00
2-Crandall-c/a; "spanking" scene	26.00	77.00	180.00
3-Crandall, Gustavson-a; photo-c	17.00	51.00	130.00
4-Crandall-a; photo-c	14.00	43.00	110.00
5-Gustavson-a; Crandall-a(p); photo-c	14.00	43.00	110.00

RANGERS COMICS (...of Freedom #1-7)
10/41 - No. 67, 10/52; No. 68, Fall, 1952; No. 69, Winter, 1952-53
Fiction House Magazines (Flying stories)

1-Intro. Ranger Girl & The Rangers of Freedom; ends #7, cover app. only #5	178.00	534.00	1600.00
2	67.00	200.00	600.00
3	56.00	168.00	500.00
4,5	50.00	150.00	450.00
6-10: 8-U.S. Rangers begin	39.00	117.00	350.00
11,12-Commando Rangers app.	36.00	108.00	325.00
13-Commando Ranger begins-not same as Commando Rangers	36.00	108.00	300.00
14-20	31.00	94.00	250.00
21-Intro/origin Firehair (begins, 2/45)	34.00	103.00	275.00
22-30: 23-Kazanda begins, ends #28. 28-Tiger Man begins (origin/1st app., 4/46), ends #46. 30-Crusoe Island begins, ends #40	24.00	71.00	190.00
31-40: 33-Hypodermic panels	20.00	60.00	160.00
41-46: 41-Last Werewolf Hunter	15.50	47.00	125.00
47-56- "Eisnerish" Dr. Drew by Grandenetti. 48-Last Glory Forbes. 53-Last 52 pg. issue. 55-Last Sky Rangers	15.50	47.00	125.00
57-60-Straight Dr. Drew by Grandenetti	12.00	36.00	95.00
61,62,64-66: 64-Suicide Smith begins	10.50	32.00	85.00
63-Used in **POP**, pgs. 85, 99	10.50	32.00	85.00
67-69: 67-Space Rangers begin, end #69	10.50	32.00	85.00

NOTE: *Bondage, discipline covers, lingerie panels are common. Crusoe Island by* ***Larsen****-#30-36. Firehair by* ***Lubbers****-#30-49. Glory Forbes by* ***Baker****-#36-45, 47; by* ***Whitman****-#34, 35. I Confess in #41-53. Jan of the Jungle in #42-58. King of the Congo in #49-53. Tiger Man by* ***Celardo****-#30-39.* ***M. Anderson*** *a-30?* ***Baker*** *a-36-38, 42, 44.* ***John Celardo*** *a-34, 36-39.* ***Lee Elias*** *a-21-28.* ***Evans*** *a-19, 38-46, 48-52.* ***Hopper*** *a-25, 26.* ***Ingels*** *a-13-16.* ***Larsen*** *a-34.* ***Bob Lubbers*** *a-30-38, 40-44; c-40-45.* ***Moreira*** *a-41-47.* ***Tuska*** *a-16, 17, 19, 22.* ***M. Whitman*** *c-61-66.* ***Zolnerwich*** *c-1-17.*

RANGO (TV)
Aug, 1967
Dell Publishing Co.

1-Tim Conway photo-c	1.65	5.00	18.00

RAPHAEL (See Teenage Mutant Ninja Turtles)
1985 ($1.50, 7-1/2x11", B&W w/2 color cover, one-shot)
Mirage Studios

1-1st Turtles one-shot spin-off; contains 1st drawing of the Turtles as a group from 1983		1.20	3.00
1-2nd printing (11/87); new-c & 8 pgs. art		.80	2.00

RASCALS IN PARADISE
Aug, 1994 - No. 3, Dec, 1994 ($3.95, limited series, magazine size)
Dark Horse Comics

1-3-Jim Silke-a/story		1.60	4.00
Trade paperback-($16.95)-r/#1-3			17.00

RATFINK (See Frantic & Zany)
Oct, 1964
Canrom, Inc.

1-Woodbridge-a	2.50	7.50	24.00

RAT PATROL, THE (TV)
Mar, 1967 - No. 5, Nov, 1967; No. 6, Oct, 1969
Dell Publishing Co.

1-Christopher George photo-c	5.00	15.00	55.00
2	3.00	9.00	35.00
3-6: 3-6-Photo-c	2.50	7.50	28.00

RAVAGE 2099 (See Marvel Comics Presents #117)
Dec, 1992 - No. 33, Aug, 1995($1.25/$1.50)
Marvel Comics

1-($1.75)-Gold foil stamped-c; Stan Lee scripts		.70	1.75
1-($1.75)-2nd printing		.70	1.75
2,3		.70	1.75
4-17: 5-Last Ryan-c. 6-Last Ryan-a. 14-Punisher 2099 x-over. 15-Ron Lim-c(p)			1.25
18-24, 26-30: 18-Begin $1.50-c; bound-in card sheet			1.50
25 ($2.25, 52 pgs.)		.90	2.25
25 ($2.95, 52 pgs.)-Silver foil embossed-c		1.20	3.00
31-33: 31-Begin $1.95-c		.80	2.00

RAVEN, THE (See Movie Classics)

RAVEN CHRONICLES
1995 - Present ($2.95, B&W)
Caliber (New Worlds)

1-15: 10-Flip book w/Wordsmith #6. 15-Flip book w/High Caliber #4		1.20	3.00

RAVENING, THE
June, 1997 - No. 2 ($3.00, B&W, limited series)
Avatar Press

1,2		1.20	3.00

RAVENS AND RAINBOWS
Dec, 1983 (Baxter paper)(Reprints fanzine work in color)
Pacific Comics

1-Jeff Jones-c/a(r); nudity scenes			1.50

RAWHIDE (TV)
Sept-Nov, 1959 - June-Aug, 1962; July, 1963 - No. 2, Jan, 1964
Dell Publishing Co./Gold Key

Four Color 1028 (#1)	22.00	65.00	240.00
Four Color 1097,1160,1202,1261,1269	14.00	41.00	150.00
01-684-208(8/62-Dell)	12.00	35.00	130.00
1(10071-307, G.K.), 2-(12¢)	11.00	32.00	115.00

NOTE: *All have Clint Eastwood photo-c.* ***Tufts*** *a-1028.*

Rawhide Kid #33 © MEG

The Ray #3 © DC

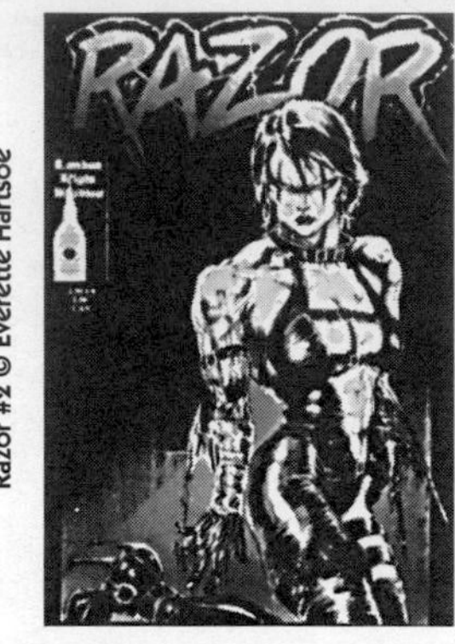

Razor #2 © Everette Hartsoe

RAWHIDE KID
3/55 - No. 16, 9/57; No. 17, 8/60 - No. 151, 5/79
Atlas/Marvel Comics (CnPC No. 1-16/AMI No. 17-30)

	GD25	FN65	NM94
1-Rawhide Kid, his horse Apache & sidekick Randy begin; Wyatt Earp app.; #1 was not code approved; Maneely splash pg.	67.00	200.00	600.00
2	30.00	90.00	240.00
3-5	20.00	60.00	160.00
6-10: 7-Williamson-a (4 pgs.)	15.50	47.00	125.00
11-16: 16-Torres-a	12.00	38.00	100.00
17-Origin by Jack Kirby; Kirby-a begins	19.00	57.00	190.00
18-20,24-30	9.00	27.00	90.00
22-Monster-c/story by Kirby/Ayers	11.00	33.00	110.00
23-Origin retold by Jack Kirby	14.00	42.00	140.00
31-37,39-41: 31,32-Kirby-a. 33-35-Davis-a. 34-Kirby-a. 35-Intro & death of The Raven. 40-Two-Gun Kid x-over.	7.00	21.00	70.00
38-Red Raven-c/story; Kirby-c (2/64).	8.00	24.00	80.00
42,43-Kirby-a; 42-1st Larry Lieber issue	7.00	21.00	70.00
44,46: 46-Toth-a	5.50	16.50	55.00
45-Origin retold	7.00	21.00	70.00
47-60: 50-Kid Colt x-over.	3.00	9.00	30.00
61-70: 64-Kid Colt story. 66-Two-Gun Kid story. 67-Kid Colt story	2.50	7.50	24.00
71-83,85: 79-Williamson-a(r).	1.75	5.25	14.00
84,86: Kirby-a. 86-Origin-r; Williamson-r/Ringo Kid #13 (4 pgs.)	2.00	6.00	16.00
87-91,94-99	1.50	4.50	12.00
92,93 (Giants). 92-Kirby-a	2.50	7.50	20.00
100-Origin retold & expanded	1.85	5.50	15.00
101-120: 115-Last new story	1.25	3.75	10.00
121-151	1.00	3.00	8.00
Special 1(9/71, 25¢, 68 pgs.)-All Kirby/Ayers-r	2.25	6.75	18.00

NOTE: ***Ayers** a-13, 14, 16. **Colan** a-5, 35, 37; c-145p, 148p, 149p. **Davis** a-125r. **Everett** a-54i, 65, 66, 88, 96i, 148i(r). **Gulacy** c-147. **Heath** c-4. **G. Kane** c-101, 144. **Keller** a-5, 144r. **Kirby** a-17-32, 34, 42, 43, 84, 86, 92, 109r, 112r, 137r, Spec. 1; c-17-35, 37, 38, 40, 41, 43-47, 137r. **Maneely** c-1, 2, 5, 6, 14. **Morisi** a-13. **Morrow/Williamson** r-111. **Roussos** r-146i, 147i, 149-151i. **Severin** a-16; c-8, 13. **Torres** a-99r. **Tuska** a-14. **Wildey** r-146-151(Outlaw Kid). **Williamson** r-79, 86, 95.*

RAWHIDE KID
Aug, 1985 - No. 4, Nov, 1985 (Mini-series)
Marvel Comics Group

	GD25	FN65	NM94
1-4		.80	2.00

RAY, THE (See Freedom Fighters & Smash Comics #14)
Feb, 1992 - No. 6, July, 1992 ($1.00, mini-series)
DC Comics

	GD25	FN65	NM94
1-Sienkiewicz-c; Joe Quesada-a(p) in 1-5		2.40	6.00
2		1.40	3.50
3: 3-6-Quesada-c(p)		1.20	3.00
4-6: 6-Quesada layouts only		1.00	2.50
...In a Blaze of Power (1994, $12.95)-r/#1-6 w/new Quesada-c	1.60	4.85	13.00

RAY, THE
May, 1994 - No. 28, Oct, 1996 ($1.75/$1.95/$2.25)
DC Comics

	GD25	FN65	NM94
1-3: 1,2-Quesada-c(p); Superboy app.		.70	1.75
1-($2.95)-Collectors Edition w/different Quesada-c; embossed foil-c		1.20	3.00
4,5: 4-Begin $1.95-c. 5-(9/94)		.80	2.00
0,6-12: 0-(10/94)		.80	2.00
13-24, 26-28: 13-Begin $2.25-c		.90	2.25
25-($3.50)-Future Flash (Bart Allen)-c/app; double size		1.40	3.50
Annual 1 ($3.95, 68 pgs.)-Superman app.		1.60	4.00

RAY BRADBURY COMICS
Feb, 1993 - V4#1, June, 1994 ($2.95)
Topps Comics

	GD25	FN65	NM94
1-5-Polybagged w/3 trading cards each. 1-All dinosaur issue; Corben-a; Williamson/Torres/Krenkel-r/Weird Science-Fantasy #25. 3-All dinosaur issue; Steacy painted-c; Stout-a		1.20	3.00
Special Edition 1 (1994, $2.95)-The Illustrated Man		1.20	3.00
...Trilogy of Terror V3#1 (5/94, $2.50)		1.00	2.50
...Martian Chronicles V4#1 (6/94, $2.50)-Steranko-c		1.00	2.50

NOTE: ***Kelley Jones** a-Trilogy of Terror V3#1. **Kaluta** a-Martian Chronicles V4#1. **Kurtzman/Matt Wagner** c-2. **McKean** c-4. **Mignola** a-4. **Wood** a-Trilogy of Terror V3#1r.*

RAZOR
May, 1992 - Present ($3.95, B&W, mature)
London Night Studios

	GD25	FN65	NM94
0 (5/92, $3.95)-Direct market	2.25	6.75	18.00
0 (4/95, $3.00)-London Night edition		1.60	4.00
1/2 (4/95, mail-in offer)-1st Poizon; Linsner-c	1.00	2.80	7.00
1 (8/92, $2.50)-Fathom Press	2.25	6.75	18.00
1-2nd printing		1.60	4.00
2 ($2.95)-J. O'Barr-c	1.75	5.25	14.00
2-Limited editions in red & blue	2.00	6.00	16.00
2-Platinum; no price on cover	2.00	6.00	16.00
3-($3.95)-Jim Balent-c	1.00	3.00	8.00
3-w/poster insert	1.10	3.30	9.00
4-Vigil-c		2.40	6.00
4-w/poster insert	1.00	2.80	7.00
5-Linsner-c	1.10	3.30	9.00
5-Platinum	1.75	5.25	14.00
6,7		1.60	4.00
8-10: 10-1st app. Stryke		1.20	3.00
11-31, 33, 34:11,12 -Rituals Pt. 1 & 2. 21-Rose & Gunn app. 25-Photo-c		1.20	3.00
25-Uncut ($10.00)-Nude Edition; double-c	1.10	3.30	9.00
32-($3.50)		1.40	3.50
32-($5.00)-Nude Edition; Nude-c		2.00	5.00
.35-41		1.20	3.00
40-Uncut ($6.00)-Nude Edition		2.40	6.00
Annual 1 (1993, $2.95)-1st app. Shi	3.50	10.50	35.00
Annual 1-Gold (1200 printed)	3.50	10.50	35.00
Annual 2 (Late 1994, $3.00)		1.60	4.00
.../Cry No More 1-($3.95)-Origin Razor; variant-c exists		1.60	4.00
.../Shi Special 1 (7/94, $3.00)	1.00	2.80	7.00
...: Swimsuit Special-painted-c		1.20	3.00
.../Warrior Nun Areala-Faith-(5/96, $3.95)		1.60	4.00
.../Warrior Nun Areala-Faith-(5/96, $3.95)-Virgin-c		2.40	6.00

RAZOR AND THE LADIES OF LONDON NIGHT
March, 1997 ($3.95, one-shot, mature)
London Night Studios

	GD25	FN65	NM94
1-Photo-c & insides			3.95

RAZOR: ARCHIVES
May, 1997 - Present ($3.95/$5.00, mature)
London Night Studios

	GD25	FN65	NM94
1-($3.95)			3.95
2-4-($5.00)			5.00

RAZOR: BURN
1994 - No. 5, 1994 ($3.00, limited series, mature)
London Night Studios

	GD25	FN65	NM94
1-5		1.20	3.00
TPB-($14.95) r/ #1-5			10.00

RAZOR/DARK ANGEL: THE FINAL NAIL
June, 1994 -No. 2, June, 1994 ($2.95, B&W, limited series, mature)
Boneyard Press #1/London Night Studios #2

	GD25	FN65	NM94
1,2		1.20	3.00

Real Clue Crime Stories V2 #5 © HILL

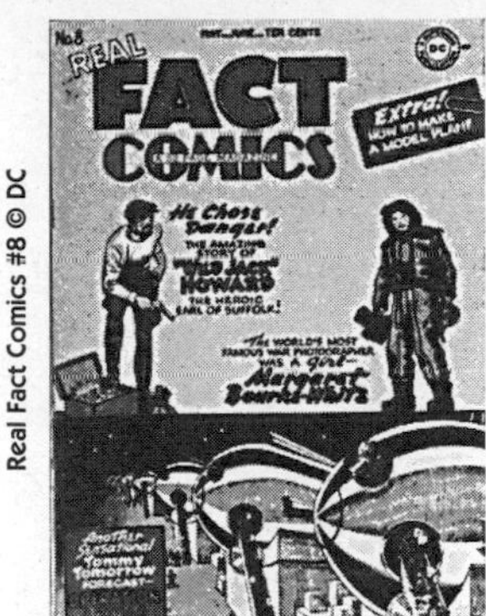

Real Fact Comics #8 © DC

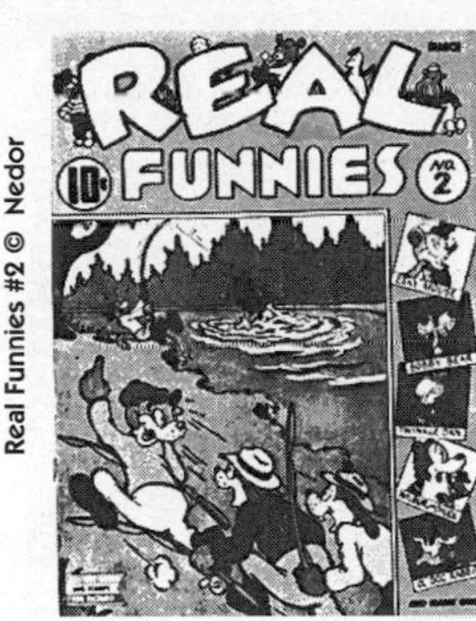

Real Funnies #2 © Nedor

GD25 FN65 NM94

RAZOR• DEEP CUTS
Sept, 1997 ($5.00, one-shot, mature)
London Night Studios

	GD25	FN65	NM94
1-Photo-c & insides		2.00	5.00
1-($10.00)-Nude Edition; Photo-c & insides	1.25	3.75	10.00

RAZOR/MORBID ANGEL: SOUL SEARCH
Sept, 1996 - No. 3, 1997 ($3.00, limited series, mature)
London Night Studios

	GD25	FN65	NM94
1-3		1.20	3.00

RAZOR: THE SUFFERING
1994 - No. 3, 1995 ($2.95, limited series, mature)
London Night Studios

	GD25	FN65	NM94
1-3 ($2.95): 2-(9/94)		1.20	3.00
1-($3.00)-Director's Cut		1.20	3.00
1-Platinum	1.00	2.80	7.00
Trade paperback-($12.95)	1.60	4.85	13.00

RAZOR: TORTURE
1995 - No. 6, 1995 ($3.00, limited series, mature)
London Night Studios

	GD25	FN65	NM94
0-($3.95)-Wraparound, chromium-c; polybagged w/card; alternate-c exists?		1.60	4.00
1-6 ($3.00): 3-Error & corrected issues exist		1.20	3.00

RAZOR: VOLUME TWO
Oct, 1996 - Present ($3.95/$3.00, mature)
London Night Studios

	GD25	FN65	NM94
1-Wraparound foil-c; Quinn-s			3.95
2-7-($3.00):3-Error & corrected issues exist			3.00

RAZORLINE
Sept, 1993 (75¢, one-shot)
Marvel Comics

	GD25	FN65	NM94
1-Clive Barker super-heroes: Ectokid, Hokum & Hex, Hyperkind & Saint Sinner (all 1st app.)			1.00

REAL ADVENTURE COMICS (Action Adventure #2 on)
Apr, 1955
Gillmor Magazines

	GD25	FN65	NM94
1	4.25	13.00	26.00

REAL ADVENTURES OF JONNY QUEST, THE
Sept, 1996 - No. 12, Sept, 1997 ($2.95)
Dark Horse Comics

	GD25	FN65	NM94
1-12		1.20	3.00

REAL CLUE CRIME STORIES (Formerly Clue Comics)
V2#4, June, 1947 - V8#3, May, 1953
Hillman Periodicals

	GD25	FN65	NM94
V2#4(#1)-S&K c/a(3); Dan Barry-a	39.00	118.00	300.00
5-7-S&K c/a(3-4). 7-Iron Lady app.	29.00	86.00	220.00
8-12	8.35	25.00	55.00
V3#1-8,10-12, V4#1-3,5-8,11,12	6.70	20.00	45.00
V3#9-Used in **SOTI**, pg. 102	10.00	30.00	65.00
V4#4-S&K-a	10.00	30.00	75.00
V4#9,10-Krigstein-a	9.00	27.00	55.00
V5#1-5,7,8,10,12	5.70	17.00	35.00
6,9,11-Krigstein-a	9.00	27.00	55.00
V6#1-5,8,9,11	5.00	15.00	30.00
6,7,10,12-Krigstein-a. 10-Bondage-c	8.35	25.00	50.00
V7#1-3,5-11, V8#1-3: V7#6-1 pg. Frazetta ad "Prayer" - 1st app.?	5.00	15.00	30.00
4,12-Krigstein-a	8.35	25.00	50.00

NOTE: ***Barry*** *a-9, 10; c-V2#8.* ***Briefer*** *a-V6#6.* ***Fuje*** *a- V2#7(2), 8, 11.* ***Infantino*** *a-V2#8; c-V2#11.* ***Lawrence*** *a-V3#8, V5#7.* ***Powell*** *a-V4#11, 12. V5#4, 5, 7 are 68 pgs.*

REAL EXPERIENCES (Formerly Tiny Tessie)
No. 25, Jan, 1950
Atlas Comics (20CC)

	GD25	FN65	NM94
25-Virginia Mayo photo-c from movie "Red Light"	5.70	17.00	35.00

REAL FACT COMICS
Mar-Apr, 1946 - No. 21, July-Aug, 1949
National Periodical Publications

	GD25	FN65	NM94
1-S&K-c/a; Harry Houdini story; Just Imagine begins (not by Finlay); Fred Ray-a	50.00	150.00	450.00
2-S&K-a; Rin-Tin-Tin & P. T. Barnum stories	36.00	108.00	300.00
3-H.G. Wells, Lon Chaney stories; 1st DC letter column	31.00	94.00	250.00
4-Virgil Finlay-a on 'Just Imagine' begins, ends #12 (2 pgs. each); Jimmy Stewart & Jack London stories; Joe DiMaggio 1 pg. biography	36.00	108.00	300.00
5-Batman/Robin-c taken from cover of Batman #9; 5 pg. story about creation of Batman & Robin; Tom Mix story	156.00	468.00	1400.00
6-Origin & 1st app. Tommy Tomorrow by Finlay (1-2/47); Flag-c; 1st writing by Harlan Ellison (letter column, non-professional); "First Man to Reach Mars" epic-c/story	97.00	291.00	875.00
7-(No. 6 on inside)-Roussos-a; D. Fairbanks sty.	15.50	47.00	125.00
8-2nd app. Tommy Tomorrow by Finlay (5-6/47)	50.00	150.00	450.00
9-S&K-a; Glenn Miller, Indianapolis 500 stories	25.00	75.00	200.00
10-Vigilante by Meskin (based on movie serial); 4 pg. Finlay s/f story	23.00	69.00	185.00
11,12: 11-Annie Oakley, G-Men stories; Kinstler-a	13.00	39.00	105.00
13-Dale Evans and Tommy Tomorrow-c/stories	44.00	132.00	400.00
14,17,18: 14-Will Rogers story	12.00	36.00	95.00
15-Nuclear explosion part-c ("Last War on Earth" story); Clyde Beatty story	15.50	47.00	125.00
16-Tommy Tomorrow app.; 1st Planeteers?	39.00	117.00	350.00
19-Sir Arthur Conan Doyle story	14.00	41.00	110.00
20-Kubert-a, 4 pgs; Daniel Boone story	15.00	45.00	120.00
21-Kubert-a, 2 pgs; Kit Carson story	12.00	36.00	95.00

NOTE: ***Barry*** *c-16.* ***Virgil Finlay*** *c-6, 8.* ***Meskin*** *c-10.* ***Roussos*** *a-1-4, 6.*

REAL FUN OF DRIVING!!, THE
1965, 1967 (Regular size)
Chrysler Corp.

	GD25	FN65	NM94
nn-Schaffenberger-a (12 pgs.)		1.20	3.00

REAL FUNNIES
Jan, 1943 - No. 3, June, 1943
Nedor Publishing Co.

	GD25	FN65	NM94
1-Funny animal, humor; Black Terrier app. (clone of The Black Terror)	25.00	75.00	200.00
2,3	12.00	38.00	95.00

REAL GHOSTBUSTERS, THE (Also see Slimer)
Aug, 1988 - No. 32, 1991 ($1.75/$1.95)
Now Comics

	GD25	FN65	NM94
1-32: 1-Based on Ghostbusters movie. 30-Begin $1.95-c		.80	1.95

REAL HEROES COMICS
Sept, 1941 - No. 16, Oct, 1946
Parents' Magazine Institute

	GD25	FN65	NM94
1-Roosevelt-c/story	26.00	80.00	210.00
2-J. Edgar Hoover-c/story	11.30	34.00	90.00
3-5,7-10: 4-Churchill, Roosevelt stories	9.50	28.00	75.00
6-Lou Gehrig-c/story	15.50	47.00	125.00
11-16: 13-Kiefer-a	6.50	19.50	45.00

REAL HIT
1944 (Savings Bond premium)
Fox Features Publications

Real Life Comics #26 © Pictorial Magazine

Real Screen Comics #43 © DC

Real Secrets #2 © ACE

	GD25	FN65	NM94
1-Blue Beetle-r	14.50	43.00	115.00

NOTE: *Two versions exist, with and without covers. The coverless version has the title, No. 1 and price printed at top of splash page.*

REALISTIC ROMANCES
July-Aug, 1951 - No. 17, Aug-Sept, 1954 (No #9-14)
Realistic Comics/Avon Periodicals

	GD25	FN65	NM94
1-Kinstler-a; c-/Avon paperback #211	16.00	47.00	120.00
2	8.35	25.00	55.00
3,4	6.70	20.00	42.00
5,8-Kinstler-a	7.00	21.00	45.00
6-c-/Diversey Prize Novels #6; Kinstler-a	8.00	24.00	50.00
7-Evans-a?; c-/Avon paperback #360	8.00	24.00	50.00
15,17: 17-Kinstler-c	6.35	19.00	40.00
16-Kinstler marijuana story-r/Romantic Love #6	8.00	24.00	50.00
I.W. Reprint #1,8,9: #1-r/Realistic Romances #4; Astarita-a. 9-r/Women To Love #1	1.00	2.80	7.00

NOTE: ***Astarita** a-2-4, 7, 8, 17. Photo c-1, 2. Painted c-3, 4.*

REAL LIFE COMICS
Sept, 1941 - No. 59, Sept, 1952
Nedor/Better/Standard Publ./Pictorial Magazine No. 13

	GD25	FN65	NM94
1-Uncle Sam-c/story; Daniel Boone story	39.00	117.00	350.00
2	17.50	53.00	140.00
3-Hitler cover	36.00	108.00	300.00
4,5: 4-Story of American flag "Old Glory"	11.30	34.00	90.00
6-10: 6-Wild Bill Hickok story	10.50	32.00	85.00
11-20: 17-Albert Einstein story	8.75	26.25	70.00
21-23,25,26,28-30: 29-A-Bomb story	7.85	23.50	55.00
24-Story of Baseball (Babe Ruth)	12.00	36.00	95.00
27-Schomburg A-Bomb-c; story of A-Bomb	12.00	36.00	95.00
31-33,35,36,42-44,48,49: 49-Baseball issue	5.70	17.00	40.00
34,37-41,45-47: 34-Jimmy Stewart story. 37-Story of motion pictures; Bing Crosby story. 38-Jane Froman story. 39- "1,000,000 A.D." story. 40-Bob Feller story. 41-Jimmie Foxx story; "Home Run" Baker story. 45-Story of Olympic games; Burl Ives & Kit Carson story. 46-Douglas Fairbanks Jr. & Sr. story. 47-George Gershwin story	7.85	23.50	55.00
50-Frazetta-a (5 pgs.)	20.00	60.00	160.00
51-Jules Verne "Journey to the Moon" by Evans	14.00	41.00	110.00
52-Frazetta-a (4 pgs.); Severin/Elder-a(2); Evans-a	20.00	60.00	160.00
53-57-Severin/Elder-a. 54-Bat Masterson-c/story	8.75	26.25	70.00
58-Severin/Elder-a(2)	9.50	28.00	75.00
59-1 pg. Frazetta; Severin/Elder-a	8.75	26.25	65.00

NOTE: *Some issues had two titles.* ***Guardineer** a-40(2), 44.* ***Meskin** a-52.* ***Roussos** a-50.* ***Schomburg** c-1, 2, 4, 5, 7, 11, 13-21, 23, 24, 26, 28, 30-32, 34-40, 42, 44-47, 55.* ***Tuska** a-53. Photo-c 5, 6.*

REAL LIFE SECRETS (Real Secrets #2 on)
Sept, 1949 (one-shot)
Ace Periodicals

	GD25	FN65	NM94
1-Painted-c	7.15	21.50	50.00

REAL LIFE STORY OF FESS PARKER (Magazine)
1955
Dell Publishing Co.

	GD25	FN65	NM94
1	9.00	27.00	90.00

REAL LIFE TALES OF SUSPENSE (See Suspense)

REAL LOVE (Formerly Hap Hazard)
No. 25, April, 1949 - No. 76, Nov, 1956
Ace Periodicals (A. A. Wyn)

	GD25	FN65	NM94
25	8.75	26.25	65.00
26	5.70	17.00	35.00
27-L. B. Cole-a	8.50	26.00	60.00
28-35	4.15	12.50	25.00
36-66: 66-Last pre-code (2/55)	4.00	11.00	22.00
67-76	1.75	5.25	14.00

NOTE: *Photo c-50-76. Painted c-46.*

REALM, THE
Feb, 1986 - No. 20? ($1.50/$1.95/$2.50, B&W)
Arrow Comics/WeeBee Comics #13/Caliber Press #14 on

	GD25	FN65	NM94
1-16: 4-1st app. Deadworld (9/86). 13-Begin $1.95-c			1.50
17-20: 17-Begin $2.50-c		1.00	2.50
Book 1 ($4.95, B&W)		2.00	5.00

REAL McCOYS, THE (TV)
No. 1071, 1-3/60 - 5-7/1962 (All have Walter Brennan photo-c)
Dell Publishing Co.

	GD25	FN65	NM94
Four Color 1071,1134-Toth-a in both	9.00	27.00	100.00
Four Color 1193,1265	8.00	25.00	90.00
01-689-207 (5-7/62)	7.00	22.00	80.00

REAL SCREEN COMICS (#1 titled Real Screen Funnies; TV Screen Cartoons #129-138)
Spring, 1945 - No. 128, May-June, 1959 (#1-40: 52 pgs.)
National Periodical Publications

	GD25	FN65	NM94
1-The Fox & the Crow, Flippity & Flop, Tito & His Burrito begin	89.00	267.00	800.00
2	42.00	126.00	375.00
3-5	28.00	83.00	220.00
6-10 (2-3/47)	18.00	54.00	145.00
11-20 (10-11/48): 13-The Crow x-over in Flippity & Flop	14.00	41.00	110.00
21-30 (6-7/50)	10.00	30.00	80.00
31-50	8.75	26.25	70.00
51-99	7.15	21.50	50.00
100	7.85	23.50	55.00
101-128	5.70	17.00	38.00

REAL SECRETS (Formerly Real Life Secrets)
No. 2, Nov, 1950 - No. 5, May, 1950
Ace Periodicals

	GD25	FN65	NM94
2-Painted-c	7.15	21.50	50.00
3-5: 3-Photo-c	5.00	15.00	30.00

REAL SPORTS COMICS (All Sports Comics #2 on)
Oct-Nov, 1948 (52 pgs.)
Hillman Periodicals

	GD25	FN65	NM94
1-Powell-a (12 pgs.)	31.00	94.00	250.00

REAL WAR STORIES
July, 1987; No. 2, Jan, 1991 ($2.00, 52 pgs.)
Eclipse Comics

	GD25	FN65	NM94
1-Bolland-a(p), Bissette-a, Totleben-a(i); Alan Moore scripts (2nd printing exists, 2/88)		.80	2.00
2-($4.95)		2.00	5.00

REAL WESTERN HERO (Formerly Wow #1-69; Western Hero #76 on)
No. 70, Sept, 1948 - No. 75, Feb, 1949 (All 52 pgs.)
Fawcett Publications

	GD25	FN65	NM94
70(#1)-Tom Mix, Monte Hale, Hopalong Cassidy, Young Falcon begin	30.00	90.00	240.00
71-75: 71-Gabby Hayes begins. 71,72-Captain Tootsie by Beck. 75-Big Bow and Little Arrow app.	19.00	56.00	150.00

NOTE: *Painted/photo c-70-73; painted c-74, 75.*

REAL WEST ROMANCES
4-5/49 - V1#6, 3/50; V2#1, Apr-May, 1950 (All 52 pgs. & photo-c)
Crestwood Publishing Co./Prize Publ.

	GD25	FN65	NM94
V1#1-S&K-a(p)	17.00	51.00	130.00
2-Spanking panel	13.50	41.00	95.00
3-Kirby-a(p) only	10.00	30.00	70.00
4-S&K-a; Whip Wilson, Reno Browne photo-c	15.00	45.00	110.00

R.E.B.E.L.S. '94 #1 © DC

Rebel Sword #6 © DH

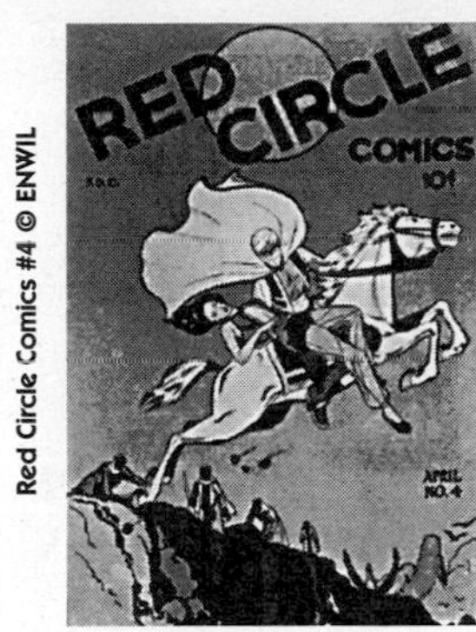

Red Circle Comics #4 © ENWIL

GD25 FN65 NM94

5-Audie Murphy, Gale Storm photo-c; S&K-a 13.50 41.00 100.00
6-Produced by S&K, no S&K-a; Robert Preston & Cathy Downs photo-c
10.00 30.00 75.00
V2#1-Kirby-a(p) 8.50 26.00 60.00
NOTE: ***Meskin** a-V1#5, 6. **Severin/Elder** a-V1#3-6, V2#1. **Meskin** a-V1#6. **Leonard Starr** a-1-3. Photo-c V1#1-6, V2#1.*

RE-ANIMATOR IN FULL COLOR
Oct, 1991 - No. 3, 1992 ($2.95, mini-series)
Adventure Comics
1-3: Adapts horror movie. 1-Dorman painted-c 1.20 3.00

REAP THE WILD WIND (See Cinema Comics Herald)

REBEL, THE (TV)
No. 1076, Feb-Apr, 1960 - No. 1262, Dec-Feb, 1961-62
Dell Publishing Co.
Four Color 1076 (#1)-Sekowsky-a, photo-c 10.00 30.00 110.00
Four Color 1138 (9-11/60), 1207 (9-11/61), 1262-Photo-c
8.00 25.00 90.00

R.E.B.E.L.S. '94 (Becomes R.E.B.E.L.S. '95 & R.E.B.E.L.S. '96)
No. 0, Oct, 1994 - No. 17, Mar, 1996 ($1.95/$2.25)
DC Comics
0-7 .80 2.00
8-17: 8-$2.25-c begins. 15-R.E.B.E.L.S '96 begins. .90 2.25

REBEL SWORD (Manga)
Oct, 1994 - No. 6, Feb, 1995 ($2.50, B&W)
Dark Horse Comics
1-6 1.00 2.50

RECORD BOOK OF FAMOUS POLICE CASES
1949 (25¢, 132 pgs.)
St. John Publishing Co.
nn-Kubert-a(3); r/Son of Sinbad; Baker-c 30.00 90.00 240.00

RED ARROW
May-June, 1951 - No. 3, Oct, 1951
P. L. Publishing Co.
1 8.50 26.00 60.00
2,3 6.50 19.50 45.00

RED BALL COMIC BOOK
1947 (Red Ball Shoes giveaway)
Parents' Magazine Institute
nn-Reprints from True Comics 2.40 6.00 12.00

RED BAND COMICS
Feb, 1945 - No. 4, May, 1945
Enwil Associates
1 28.00 83.00 220.00
2-Origin Bogeyman & Santanas; c-reprint/#1 22.00 66.00 175.00
3,4-Captain Wizard app. in both (1st app.); each has identical contents/cover
20.00 60.00 160.00

REDBLADE
Apr, 1993 - No. 3, July, 1993 ($2.50, mini-series)
Dark Horse Comics
1-3; 1-Double gatefold-c 1.00 2.50

RED CIRCLE COMICS
Jan, 1945 - No. 4, April, 1945
Rural Home Publications (Enwil)
1-The Prankster & Red Riot begin 26.00 80.00 210.00
2-Starr-a; The Judge (costumed hero) app. 21.00 64.00 170.00
3,4-Starr-c/a. 3-The Prankster not in costume 16.00 49.00 130.00
4-(Dated 4/45)-Leftover covers to #4 were later restapled over early 1950s coverless comics; variations in the coverless comics used are endless; Woman Outlaws, Dorothy Lamour, Crime Does Not Pay, Sabu, Diary Loves, Love Confessions & Young Love V3#3 known 10.50 32.00 75.00

RED CIRCLE SORCERY (Chilling Adventures in Sorcery #1-5)
No. 6, Apr, 1974 - No. 11, Feb, 1975 (All 25¢ issues)
Red Circle Productions (Archie)
6-11: 8-Only app. The Cobra. 10-Wood-a(i) 1.60 4.00
NOTE: ***Chaykin** a-6, 10. **B. Jones** a-7(w/**Wrightson**, **Kaluta**, **J. Jones**). **McWilliams** a-10(2 & 3 pgs.). **Mooney** a-11p. **Morrow** a-6-8, 9(text illos), 10, 11i; c-6-11. **Thorne** a-8, 10. **Toth** a-8, 9.*

RED DOG (See Night Music #7)

RED DRAGON
June, 1996 ($2.95)
Comico
1-Bisley-c 1.20 3.00

RED DRAGON COMICS (1st Series) (Formerly Trail Blazers; see Super Magician V5#7, 8)
No. 5, Jan, 1943 - No. 9, Jan, 1944
Street & Smith Publications
5-Origin Red Rover, the Crimson Crimebuster; Rex King, Man of Adventure, Captain Jack Commando, & The Minute Man begin; text origin Red Dragon; Binder-c 78.00 234.00 700.00
6-Origin The Black Crusader & Red Dragon (3/43); 1st story app. Red Dragon & 1st cover (classic-c) 144.00 432.00 1300.00
7-Classic-c 94.00 282.00 850.00
8-The Red Knight app. 53.00 159.00 475.00
9-Origin Chuck Magnon, Immortal Man 53.00 159.00 475.00

RED DRAGON COMICS (2nd Series)(See Super Magician V2#8)
Nov, 1947 - No. 6, Jan, 1949; No. 7, July, 1949
Street & Smith Publications
1-Red Dragon begins; Elliman, Nigel app.; Edd Cartier-c/a
75.00 225.00 650.00
2-Cartier-c 56.00 168.00 475.00
3-1st app. Dr. Neff Ghost Breaker by Powell; Elliman, Nigel app.
48.00 144.00 400.00
4-Cartier c/a 62.00 187.00 525.00
5-7 38.00 114.00 275.00
NOTE: ***Maneely** a-5, 7. **Powell** a-2-7; c-3, 5, 7.*

REDDY GOOSE
No #, 1958?; No. 2, Jan, 1959 - No. 16, July, 1962 (Giveaway)
International Shoe Co. (Western Printing)
nn (#1) 4.00 12.00 40.00
2-16 2.50 7.50 21.00

REDDY KILOWATT (5¢) (Also see Story of Edison)
1946 - No. 2, 1947; 1956 - 1960 (no month) (16 pgs., paper-c)
Educational Comics (E. C.)
nn-Reddy Made Magic (1946, 5¢) 8.75 26.25 70.00
nn-Reddy Made Magic (1958) 5.35 16.00 32.00
2-Edison, the Man Who Changed the World (3/4" smaller than #1) (1947, 5¢)
8.75 26.25 70.00
...Comic Book 2 (1954)- "Light's Diamond Jubilee" 6.50 19.50 40.00
...Comic Book 2 (1958, 16 pgs.)- "Wizard of Light" 5.35 16.00 32.00
...Comic Book 3 (1956, 8 pgs.)- "The Space Kite"; Orlando story; regular size
5.35 16.00 32.00
...Comic Book 3 (1960, 8 pgs.)- "The Space Kite"; Orlando story; regular size
4.25 13.00 28.00
NOTE: *Several copies surfaced in 1979.*

REDDY MADE MAGIC
1956, 1958 (16 pgs., paper-c)
Educational Comics (E. C.)
1-Reddy Kilowatt-r (splash panel changed) 6.85 21.00 48.00
1 (1958 edition) 5.00 15.00 30.00

Red Mask #49 © ME

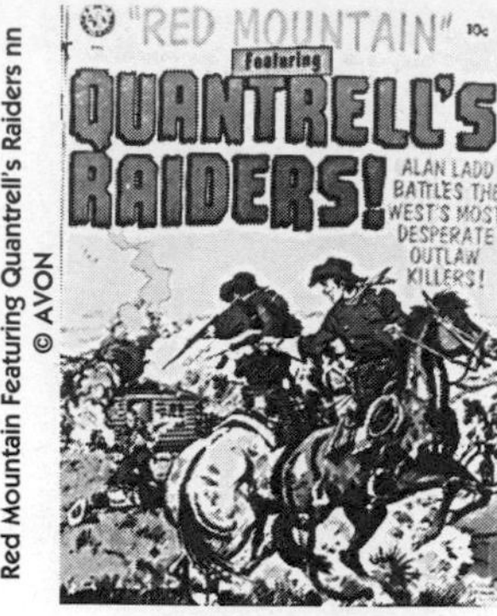

Red Mountain Featuring Quantrell's Raiders nn © AVON

Red Ryder Comics #11 © DELL

GD25 FN65 NM94

RED EAGLE
No. 16, Aug, 1938
David McKay Publications

Feature Books 16 — 14.00 44.00 160.00

REDEYE (See Comics Reading Libraries)

RED FOX (Formerly Manhunt! #1-14; also see Extra Comics)
No. 15, 1954
Magazine Enterprises

15(A-1 #108)-Undercover Girl story; L.B. Cole-c/a (Red Fox); r-from Manhunt; Powell-a — 14.50 43.00 115.00

RED FURY
1997 ($2.95, B&W)
High Impact Entertainment

1 — 2.95

RED GOOSE COMIC SELECTIONS (See Comic Selections)

RED HAWK (See A-1 Comics, Bobby Benson's ..#14-16 & Straight Arrow #2)
No. 90, 1953
Magazine Enterprises

A-1 90-Powell-c/a — 9.50 28.00 75.00

RED ICEBERG, THE
1960 (10¢, 16 pgs.) (Communist propaganda)
Impact Publ. (Catechetical Guild)

nn-(Rare)- 'We The People' back-c — 27.00 81.00 270.00
2nd version- 'Impact Press' back-c — 30.00 90.00 300.00
3rd version-"Explains comic" back-c — 30.00 90.00 300.00
NOTE: *This book was the Guild's last anti-communist propaganda book and had very limited circulation. 3 - 4 copies surfaced in 1979 from the defunct publisher's files. Other copies do turn up.*

RED MASK (Formerly Tim Holt; see Best Comics, Blazing Six-Guns)
No. 42, June-July, 1954 - No. 53, May, 1956; No. 54, Sept, 1957
Magazine Enterprises No. 42-53/Sussex No. 54 (M.E. on-c)

42-Ghost Rider by Ayers continues, ends #50; Black Phantom continues; 3-D effect c/stories begin — 17.50 53.00 140.00
43-3-D effect-c/stories — 15.50 47.00 125.00
44-50: 3-D effect stories only. 47-Last pre-code issue. 50-Last Ghost Rider — 14.50 43.00 115.00
51-The Presto Kid begins by Ayers (1st app.); Presto Kid-c begins, ends #54; last 3-D effect story — 14.50 43.00 115.00
52-Origin The Presto Kid — 14.50 43.00 115.00
53,54-Last Black Phantom — 10.50 32.00 85.00
I.W. Reprint #1 (r-/#52). 2 (nd, r/#51 w/diff.-c). 3, 8 (nd; Kinstler-c); 8-r/Red Mask #52 — 2.50 7.50 20.00
NOTE: ***Ayers** art on Ghost Rider & Presto Kid. **Bolle** art in all (Red Mask); c-43, 44, 49. **Guardineer** a-52. Black Phantom in #42-44, 47-50, 53, 54.*

REDMASK OF THE RIO GRANDE
1990 ($2.50, 28pgs.)(Has photos of movie posters)
AC Comics

1-Bolle-c/a(r); photo inside-c — 1.00 2.50

RED MOUNTAIN FEATURING QUANTRELL'S RAIDERS (Movie)(Also see Jesse James #28)
1952
Avon Periodicals

nn-Alan Ladd; Kinstler-c — 23.00 69.00 170.00

"RED" RABBIT COMICS
Jan, 1947 - No. 22, Aug-Sept, 1951
Dearfield Comic/J. Charles Laue Publ. Co.

1 — 8.75 26.25 70.00
2 — 5.70 17.00 38.00
3-10 — 4.25 13.00 28.00
11-17,19-22 — 4.00 12.00 24.00
18-Flying Saucer-c (1/51) — 5.70 17.00 35.00

RED RAVEN COMICS (Human Torch #2 on)(Also see X-Men #44 & Sub-Mariner #26, 2nd series)
August, 1940
Timely Comics

GD25 FN65 VF82 NM94

1-Origin & 1st app. Red Raven; Comet Pierce & Mercury by Kirby, The Human Top & The Eternal Brain; intro. Magar, the Mystic & only app.; Kirby-c (his 1st signed work) — 960.00 2880.00 5760.00 9600.00
(Estimated up to 50 total copies exist, 6 in NM/Mint)

RED ROCKET 7
Aug, 1997 - No. 7 ($2.95, square format, limited series)
Dark Horse Comics

1-7-Mike Allred-c/s/a — 2.95

RED RYDER COMICS (Hi Spot #2)(Movies, radio)(See Crackajack Funnies)
9/40; No. 3, 8/41 - No. 5, 12/41; No. 6, 4/42 - No. 151, 4-6/57
Hawley Publ. No. 1/Dell Publishing Co.(K.K.) No. 3 on

GD25 FN65 NM94

1-Red Ryder, his horse Thunder, Little Beaver & his horse Papoose strip reprints begin by Fred Harman; 1st meeting of Red & Little Beaver; Harman line-drawn-c #1-85 — 240.00 720.00 2400.00
3-(Scarce)-Alley Oop, King of the Royal Mtd., Capt. Easy, Freckles & His Friends, Myra North, Dan Dunn strip-r begin — 82.00 245.00 900.00
4-6: 6-1st Dell issue (4/42) — 39.00 116.00 425.00
7-10 — 32.00 95.00 350.00
11-20 — 23.00 68.00 250.00
21-32-Last Alley Oop, Dan Dunn, Capt. Easy, Freckles — 14.00 44.00 160.00
33-40 (52 pgs.) — 9.00 27.00 100.00
41 (52 pgs.)-Rocky Lane photo back-c; photo back-c begin, end #57 — 9.00 29.00 105.00
42-46 (52 pgs.): 46-Last Red Ryder strip-r — 8.00 23.00 85.00
47-53 (52 pgs.): 47-New stories on Red Ryder begin. 49,52-Harmon photo back-c — 6.40 19.00 70.00
54-57 (36 pgs.) — 5.00 15.00 54.00
58-73 (36 pgs.): 59-Harmon photo back-c. 73-Last King of the Royal Mtd; strip-r by Jim Gary — 5.00 15.00 54.00
74-85,93 (52 pgs.)-Harman line-drawn-c — 5.00 15.00 54.00
86-92 (52 pgs.)-Harman painted-c — 5.00 15.00 54.00
94-96 (36 pgs.)-Harman painted-c — 3.60 11.00 40.00
97,98,107,108 (36 pgs.)-Harman line-drawn-c — 3.60 11.00 40.00
99,101-106 (36 pgs.)-Jim Bannon Photo-c — 3.60 11.00 40.00
100 (36 pgs.)-Bannon photo-c — 4.00 12.00 45.00
109-118 (52 pgs.)-Harman line-drawn-c — 3.00 9.00 32.00
119-129 (52 pgs.): 119-Painted-c begin, not by Harman, end #151 — 2.75 8.00 30.00
130-144 (#130 on have 36 pgs.) — 2.50 7.50 27.00
145-148: 145-Title change to Red Ryder Ranch Magazine with photos — 2.00 6.00 22.00
149-151: 149-Title changed to Red Ryder Ranch Comics — 2.00 6.00 22.00
Four Color 916 (7/58) — 2.75 8.00 30.00
Buster Brown Shoes Giveaway (1941, color, soft-c, 32 pgs.) — 23.00 69.00 185.00
Red Ryder Super Book Of Comics 10 (1944; paper-c; 32 pgs.; blank back-c)-Magic Morro app. — 23.00 69.00 185.00
Red Ryder Victory Patrol-nn(1944, 32 pgs.)-r-/#43,44; comic has a paper-c & is stapled inside a triple cardboard fold-out-c; contains membership card, decoder, map of R.R. home range, etc. Herky app. (Langendorf Bread give-away; sub-titled 'Super Book of Comics')(Rare) — 378.00 1133.00 3400.00
Wells Lamont Corp. giveaway (1950)-16 pgs. in color; regular size; paper-c; 1941-r — 21.00 64.00 170.00
NOTE: ***Fred Harman** a-1-99; c-1-98, 107-118. Don Red Barry, Allan Rocky Lane, Wild Bill Elliott*

Red Seal Comics #19 © SUPR

Red Sonja V3 #3 © MEG

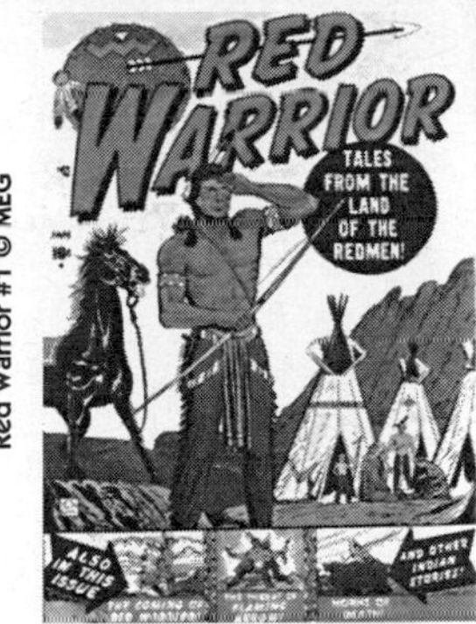

Red Warrior #1 © MEG

GD25 FN65 NM94

& Jim Bannon starred as Red Ryder in the movies. Robert Blake starred as Little Beaver.

RED RYDER PAINT BOOK
1941 (8-1/2x11-1/2", 148 pgs.)
Whitman Publishing Co.

	GD25	FN65	NM94
nn-Reprints 1940 daily strips	56.00	168.00	500.00

RED SEAL COMICS (Formerly Carnival Comics, and/or Spotlight Comics?)
No. 14, 10/45 - No. 18, 10/46; No. 19, 6/47 - No. 22, 12/47
Harry 'A' Chesler/Superior Publ. No. 19 on

	GD25	FN65	NM94
14-The Black Dwarf begins (continued from Spotlight?); Little Nemo app; bondage/hypo-c; Tuska-a	53.00	159.00	460.00
15-Torture story; funny-c	40.00	120.00	310.00
16-Used in **SOTI**, pg. 181, illo "Outside the forbidden pages of de Sade, you find draining a girl's blood only in children's comics;" drug club story r-later in Crime Reporter #1; Veiled Avenger & Barry Kuda app; Tuska-a; funny-c	50.00	150.00	430.00
17-Lady Satan, Yankee Girl & Sky Chief app; Tuska-a	40.00	120.00	310.00
18,20-Lady Satan & Sky Chief app.	40.00	120.00	310.00
19-No Black Dwarf (on-c only); Zor, El Tigre app.	32.00	96.00	250.00
21-Lady Satan & Black Dwarf app.	27.00	81.00	200.00
22-Zor, Rocketman app. (68 pgs.)	27.00	81.00	200.00

REDSKIN (Thrilling Indian Stories)(Famous Western Badmen #13 on)
Sept, 1950 - No. 12, Oct, 1952
Youthful Magazines

	GD25	FN65	NM94
1-Walter Johnson-a (7 pgs.)	11.00	33.00	80.00
2	9.00	27.00	60.00
3-12: 3-Daniel Boone story. 6-Geronimo story	7.50	22.50	50.00

NOTE: ***Walter Johnson** c-3, 4. **Palais** a-11. **Wildey** a-5, 11. Bondage c-6, 12.*

RED SONJA (Also see Conan #23, Kull & The Barbarians, Marvel Feature & Savage Sword Of Conan #1)
1/77 - No. 15, 5/79; V1#1, 2/83 - V2#2, 3/83; V3#1, 8/83 - V3#4, 2/84; V3#5, 1/85 - V3#13, 1986
Marvel Comics Group

	GD25	FN65	NM94
1-Created by Robert E. Howard		2.40	6.00
2-10: 5-Last 30¢ issue		1.60	4.00
11-15, V1#1,V2#2: 14-Last 35¢ issue		1.20	3.00
V3#1-4 ($1.00, 52 pgs.)		.80	2.00
5-13 (65-75¢)			1.50

NOTE: ***Brunner** c-12-14. **J. Buscema** a(p)-12, 13, 15; c-V#1. **Nebres** a-V3#3i(part). **N. Redondo** a-8i, V3#2i, 3i. **Simonson** a-V3#1. **Thorne** c/a-1-11.*

RED SONJA: SCAVENGER HUNT
Dec, 1995 ($2.95, one-shot)
Marvel Comics

	GD25	FN65	NM94
1		1.20	3.00

RED SONJA: THE MOVIE
Nov, 1985 - No. 2, Dec, 1985 (Limited series)
Marvel Comics Group

	GD25	FN65	NM94
1,2-Movie adapt-r/Marvel Super Spec. #38			.80

RED TORNADO (See All-American #20 & Justice League of America #64)
July, 1985 - No. 4, Oct, 1985 (Limited series)
DC Comics

	GD25	FN65	NM94
1-4: Kurt Busiek scripts in all. 1-3-Superman cameos. 1,3-Batman cameos			1.00

RED WARRIOR
Jan, 1951 - No. 6, Dec, 1951
Marvel/Atlas Comics (TCI)

	GD25	FN65	NM94
1-Red Warrior & his horse White Wing; Tuska-a	12.00	38.00	100.00
2-Tuska-c	8.50	26.00	60.00
3-6: 4-Origin White Wing. 6-Maneely-c	7.15	21.50	50.00

GD25 FN65 NM94

RED WOLF (See Avengers #80 & Marvel Spotlight #1)
May, 1972 - No. 9, Sept, 1973
Marvel Comics Group

	GD25	FN65	NM94
1-(Western hero); Gil Kane/Severin-c; Shores-a	1.50	4.50	12.00
2-9: 2-Kane-c; Shores-a. 6-Tuska-r in back-up. 7-Red Wolf as super hero begins. 9-Origin sidekick, Lobo (wolf)		2.40	6.00

REESE'S PIECES
Oct, 1985 - No.2, Oct, 1985 ($1.75, Baxter paper)
Eclipse Comics

	GD25	FN65	NM94
1,2-B&W-r in color		.75	1.80

REFORM SCHOOL GIRL!
1951
Realistic Comics

	GD25	FN65	NM94
nn-Used in **SOTI**, pg. 358, & cover ill. with caption "Comic books are supposed to be like fairy tales"	106.00	318.00	900.00

(Prices vary widely on this book)

NOTE: *The cover and title originated from a digest-sized book published by Diversey Publishing Co. of Chicago in 1948. The original book "House of Fury", Doubleday, came out in 1941. The girl's real name which appears on the cover of the digest and comic is Marty Collins, Canadian model and ice skating star who posed for this special color photograph for the Diversey novel.*

REGENTS ILLUSTRATED CLASSICS
1981 (Plus more recent reprintings)
(48 pgs., B&W-a with 14 pgs. of teaching helps)
Prentice Hall Regents, Englewood Cliffs, NJ 07632

NOTE: *This series contains Classics Ill. art, and was produced from the same illegal source as **Cassette Books.** But when Twin Circle sued to stop the sale of the Cassette Books, they decided to permit this series to continue. This series was produced as a teaching aid. The 20 title series is divided into four levels based upon number of basic words used therein. There is also a teacher's manual for each level. All of the titles are still available from the publisher for about $5 each retail. The number to call for mail order purchases is (201)767-5937. Almost all of the issues have new covers taken from some interior art panel. Here is a list of the series by Regents ident. no. and the Classics Ill. counterpart.*

16770(Cl#24-A2)18333(Cl#3-A2)21668(Cl#13-A2)32224(Cl#21)33051(Cl#26)
35788(Cl#84)37153(Cl#16)44460(Cl#19-A2)44808(Cl#18-A2)52395(Cl#4-A2)
58627(Cl#5-A2)60067(Cl#30)68405(Cl#23-A1)70302(Cl#29)78192(Cl#7-A2)
78193(Cl#10-A2)79679(Cl#85)92046(Cl#1-A2)93062(Cl#64)93512(Cl#25)

REGGIE (Formerly Archie's Rival...; Reggie & Me #19 on)
No. 15, Sept, 1963 - No. 18, Nov, 1965
Archie Publications

	GD25	FN65	NM94
15(9/63), 16(10/64), 17(8/65), 18(11/65)	4.00	12.00	40.00

NOTE: *Cover title No. 15 & 16 is Archie's Rival Reggie.*

REGGIE AND ME (Formerly Reggie)
No. 19, Aug, 1966 - No. 126, Sept, 1980 (No. 50-68: 52 pgs.)
Archie Publications

	GD25	FN65	NM94
19-Evilheart app.	2.50	7.50	20.00
20-23-Evilheart app.; with Pureheart #22	1.75	5.25	14.00
24-40	1.00	2.80	7.00
41-49		2.00	5.00
50-68 (52 pgs.)		2.40	6.00
69-126		1.20	3.00

REGGIE'S JOKES (See Reggie's Wise Guy Jokes)

REGGIE'S REVENGE!
Spring, 1994 - No. 3 ($2.00, 52 pgs.)(Published semi-annually)
Archie Comic Publications, Inc.

	GD25	FN65	NM94
1-Bound-in pull-out poster		1.20	3.00
2,3		.80	2.00

REGGIE'S WISE GUY JOKES
Aug, 1968 - No. 60, Jan, 1982 (#5-28 are Giants)
Archie Publications

	GD25	FN65	NM94
1	3.00	9.00	30.00
2-4	1.25	3.75	10.00
5-10 (Giants)	1.50	4.50	12.00

The Ren & Stimpy Show #23 © Nickelodeon

Renfield #1 © Caliber

Replacement God #1 (2nd Series) © Zander Cannon

	GD25	FN65	NM94
11-28 (Giants)	1.10	3.30	9.00
29-40		1.60	4.00
41-60		1.20	3.00

REGISTERED NURSE
Summer, 1963
Charlton Comics

	GD25	FN65	NM94
1-r/Nurse Betsy Crane & Cynthia Doyle	1.85	5.50	15.00

REG'LAR FELLERS
No. 5, Nov, 1947 - No. 6, Mar, 1948
Visual Editions (Standard)

	GD25	FN65	NM94
5,6	6.85	21.00	48.00

REG'LAR FELLERS HEROIC (See Heroic Comics)

REGULATORS
June, 1995 - No. 3, Aug, 1995 ($2.50)
Image Comics

	GD25	FN65	NM94
1-3: Kurt Busiek scripts		1.00	2.50

REID FLEMING, WORLD'S TOUGHEST MILKMAN
8/86; V2#1, 12/86 - V2#3, 12/88; V2#4, 11/89; V2#5, 11/90 (B&W)
Eclipse Comics/ Deep Sea Comics

	GD25	FN65	NM94
1 (3rd print, large size, 8/86, $2.50)		1.00	2.50
1-4th & 5th printings ($2.50)		1.00	2.50
V2#1 (10/86, regular size, $2.00)		.80	2.00
1-2nd print, 3rd print ($2.00, 2/89)		.80	2.00
2-8 , V2#2-2nd & 3rd printings, V2#4-2nd printing, V2#5 ($2.00)		.80	2.00

RELUCTANT DRAGON, THE (Walt Disney's...)
No. 13, 1940
Dell Publishing Co.

	GD25	FN65	NM94
Four Color 13-Contains 2 pgs. of photos from film; 2 pg. foreword to Fantasia by Leopold Stokowski; Donald Duck, Goofy, Baby Weems & Mickey Mouse (as the Sorcerer's Apprentice) app.	147.00	443.00	1625.00

REMEMBER PEARL HARBOR
1942 (68 pgs.) (Illustrated story of the battle)
Street & Smith Publications

	GD25	FN65	NM94
nn-Uncle Sam-c; Jack Binder-a	36.00	108.00	320.00

REN & STIMPY SHOW, THE (TV) (Nicklodeon cartoon characters)
Dec, 1992 - No. 44, July, 1996 ($1.75/$1.95)
Marvel Comics

	GD25	FN65	NM94
1-($2.25)-Polybagged w/scratch & sniff Ren or Stimpy air fowler (equal amounts of each were made)		1.20	3.00
1-2nd printing; different dialogue on-c		.80	2.00
1-3rd printing; yet different dialogue on-c		.80	2.00
2,3		.80	2.00
4-6: 4-Muddy Mudskipper back-up. 5-Bill Wray painted-c. 6-Spider-Man vs. Powered Toast Man		.80	2.00
7-17: 12-1st solo back-up story w/Tank & Brenner		.70	1.75
18-44: 18-Begin $1.95-c; Powered Toast Man app.		.80	2.00
25($2.95) Deluxe edition w/die cut cover		1.20	3.00
...Don't Try This at Home (3/94, $12.95, TPB)-r/#9-12	1.60	4.85	13.00
...Eenteractive Special ('95, $2.95)		1.20	3.00
...Holiday Special 1994 (2/95, $2.95, 52 pgs.)		1.20	3.00
...Pick of the Litter nn (1993, $12.95, TPB)-r/#1-4	1.60	4.85	13.00
...Radio Daze (11/95, $1.95)		.80	2.00
...Running Joke nn (1993, $12.95, TPB)-r/#1-4 plus new-a	1.60	4.85	13.00
...Seeck Little Monkeys (1/95, $12.95)-r/#17-20	1.60	4.85	13.00
...Special 2 (7/94, $2.95, 52 pgs.)		1.20	3.00
...Special 3 (10/94, $2.95, 52 pgs.)-Choose adventure		1.20	3.00
...Special: Around the World in a Daze ($2.95)		1.20	3.00
...Special: Four Swerks (1/95, $2.95, 52 pgs.)-FF #1 cover swipe; cover reads "Four Swerks w/5 pg. coloring book."		1.20	3.00
...Special: Powered Toast Man 1 (4/94, $2.95, 52 pgs.)		1.20	3.00
...Special: Powdered Toast Man's Cereal Serial (4/95, $2.95)		1.20	3.00
...Special: Sports (10/95, $2.95)		1.20	3.00
...Tastes Like Chicken nn (11/93,$12.95,TPB)-r/#5-8	1.60	4.85	13.00
...Your Pals (1994, $12.95, TPB)-r/#13-16	1.60	4.85	13.00

RENFIELD
1994 - No. 3, 1995 ($2.95, B&W, limited series)
Caliber Press

	GD25	FN65	NM94
1-3		1.20	3.00

RENO BROWNE, HOLLYWOOD'S GREATEST COWGIRL (Formerly Margie Comics; Apache Kid #53 on; also see Western Hearts, Western Life Romances & Western Love)
No. 50, April, 1950 - No. 52, Sept, 1950 (52 pgs.)
Marvel Comics (MPC)

	GD25	FN65	NM94
50-Reno Browne photo-c on all	27.00	81.00	200.00
51,52	24.00	73.00	170.00

REPLACEMENT GOD
June, 1995 - Present ($2.95, B&W)
Amaze Ink

	GD25	FN65	NM94
1-8-Zander Cannon-s/a		1.20	3.00

REPLACEMENT GOD
May, 1997 - Present ($2.95, B&W)
Image Comics

	GD25	FN65	NM94
1-Flip book w/"Knute's Escapes", r/original series			2.95
2-Flip book w/"Harris Thermidor"			2.95
3-Flip book w/"Myth and Legend"			2.95

REPTILICUS (Becomes Reptisaurus #3 on)
Aug, 1961 - No. 2, Oct, 1961
Charlton Comics

	GD25	FN65	NM94
1 (Movie)	10.50	32.00	105.00
2	6.50	19.50	65.00

REPTISAURUS (Reptilicus #1,2)
V2#3, Jan, 1962 - No. 8, Dec, 1962; Summer, 1963
Charlton Comics

	GD25	FN65	NM94
V2#3-8: 8-Montes/Bache-c/a	4.00	12.00	40.00
Special Edition 1 (Summer, 1963)	3.50	10.50	35.00

REQUIEM FOR DRACULA
Feb, 1993 ($2.00, 52 pgs.)
Marvel Comics

	GD25	FN65	NM94
nn-r/Tomb of Dracula #69,70 by Gene Colan		.80	2.00

RESCUERS, THE (See Walt Disney Showcase #40)

RESTAURANT AT THE END OF THE UNIVERSE, THE (See Hitchhiker's Guide to the Galaxy & Life, the Universe & Everything)
1994 - No. 3, 1994 ($6.95, limited series)
DC Comics

	GD25	FN65	NM94
1-3	1.00	2.80	7.00

RESTLESS GUN (TV)
No. 934, Sept, 1958 - No. 1146, Nov-Jan, 1960-61
Dell Publishing Co.

	GD25	FN65	NM94
Four Color 934 (#1)-Photo-c	10.00	30.00	110.00
Four Color 986 (5/59), 1045 (11-1/60), 1089 (3/60), 1146-Wildey-a; all photo-c	7.00	22.00	80.00

RESURRECTION MAN
May, 1997 - Present ($2.50)
DC Comics

Resurrection Man #8 © DC

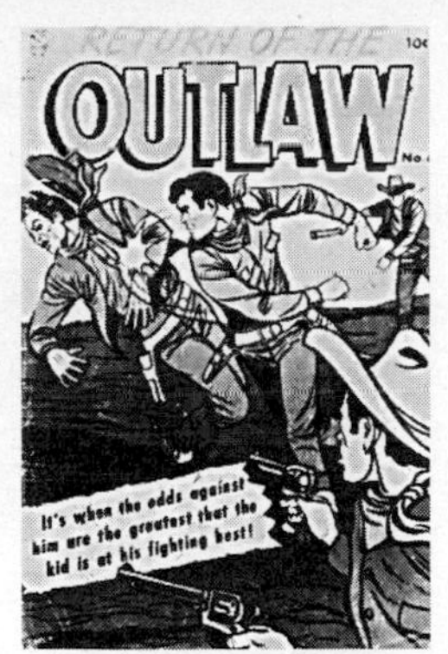

Return of the Outlaw #6 © TOBY

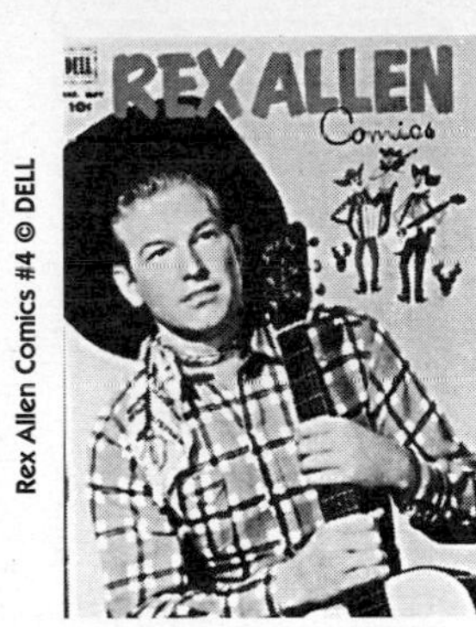

Rex Allen Comics #4 © DELL

	GD25	FN65	NM94
1-Lenticular disc on cover		2.40	6.00
2-JLA app.		2.00	5.00
3-13: 6-Genesis-x-over. 7-Batman app.			2.50

RETIEF (Keith Laumer's)
Dec, 1989 - No.2?, Jan, 1990 ($2.25, B&W)
Adventure Comics (Malibu)

	GD25	FN65	NM94
1,2: 2-exist?		.90	2.25
...and The Warlords #1 (1/91)		1.00	2.50
...: Diplomatic Immunity #1 (4/91)		1.00	2.50
...: Giant Killer #1 (9/91)		1.00	2.50
...: Crime & Punishment #1 (11/91)		1.00	2.50

RETURN FROM WITCH MOUNTAIN (See Walt Disney Showcase #44)

RETURN OF GORGO, THE (Formerly Gorgo's Revenge)
No. 2, Aug, 1963; No. 3, Fall, 1964 (12¢)
Charlton Comics

	GD25	FN65	NM94
2,3-Ditko-c/a; based on M.G.M. movie	5.50	16.50	55.00

RETURN OF KONGA, THE (Konga's Revenge #2 on)
1962
Charlton Comics

	GD25	FN65	NM94
nn	5.50	16.50	55.00

RETURN OF MEGATON MAN
July, 1988 - No. 3, 1988 ($2.00, limited series)
Kitchen Sink Press

	GD25	FN65	NM94
1-3: Simpson-c/a		.80	2.00

RETURN OF THE OUTLAW
Feb, 1953 - No. 11, 1955
Toby Press (Minoan)

	GD25	FN65	NM94
1-Billy the Kid	7.85	23.50	55.00
2	5.00	15.00	30.00
3-11	4.00	12.00	24.00

RETURN TO JURASSIC PARK
Apr, 1995 - No. 9, Feb, 1996 ($2.50/$2.95)
Topps Comics

	GD25	FN65	NM94
1,2		1.00	2.50
3-9: 3-Begin $2.95-c. 9-Artist's Jam issue		1.20	3.00

RETURN TO THE AMALGAM AGE OF COMICS: THE MARVEL COMICS COLLECTION
1997 ($12.95, TPB)
Marvel Comics

nn-Reprints Amalgam one-shots: Challengers of the Fantastic #1, The Exciting X-Patrol #1, Iron Lantern# 1, The Magnetic Men Featuring Magneto #1, Spider-Boy Team-Up #1 & Thorion of the New Asgods #1 — 12.95

REVEALING LOVE STORIES (See Fox Giants)

REVEALING ROMANCES
Sept, 1949 - No. 6, Aug, 1950
Ace Magazines

	GD25	FN65	NM94
1	7.15	21.50	50.00
2	4.15	12.50	25.00
3-6	4.00	10.00	20.00

REVENGE OF THE PROWLER (Also see The Prowler)
Feb, 1988 - No. 4, June, 1988 ($1.75/$1.95)
Eclipse Comics

	GD25	FN65	NM94
1,3,4: 1-$1.75. 3,4-$1.95-c; Snyder III-a(p)		.80	2.00
2 ($2.50)-Contains flexi-disc		1.00	2.50

REVENGERS FEATURING MEGALITH
Sept, 1985; 1987 - No. 5, 1988 ($2.00, Baxter paper)
Continuity Comics

	GD25	FN65	NM94
1 (1985)-Origin; Neal Adams-c/a, scripts		.80	2.00
1 (1987, newsstand)- 5		.80	2.00

REX ALLEN COMICS (Movie star)(Also see Four Color #877 & Western Roundup under Dell Giants)
No. 316, Feb, 1951 - No. 31, Dec-Feb, 1958-59 (All-photo-c)
Dell Publishing Co.

	GD25	FN65	NM94
Four Color 316(#1)(52 pgs.)-Rex Allen & his horse Koko begin; Marsh-a	13.00	38.00	140.00
2 (9-11/51, 36 pgs.)	8.00	23.00	85.00
3-10	5.50	16.50	60.00
11-20	4.50	13.50	50.00
21-23,25-31	4.00	12.00	45.00
24-Toth-a	5.00	15.00	55.00

NOTE: ***Manning*** *a-20, 27-30. Photo back-c F.C. #316, 2-12, 20, 21.*

REX DEXTER OF MARS (See Mystery Men Comics)
Fall, 1940 (68 pgs.)
Fox Features Syndicate

	GD25	FN65	NM94
1-Rex Dexter, Patty O'Day, & Zanzibar (Tuska-a) app.; Briefer-c/a	156.00	468.00	1400.00

REX HART (Formerly Blaze Carson; Whip Wilson #9 on)
No. 6, Aug, 1949 - No. 8, Feb, 1950 (All photo-c)
Timely/Marvel Comics (USA)

	GD25	FN65	NM94
6-Rex Hart & his horse Warrior begin; Black Rider app; Captain Tootsie by Beck	22.00	66.00	175.00
7,8: 18 pg. Thriller in each. 8-Blaze the Wonder Collie app. in text	15.00	45.00	120.00

REX MORGAN, M.D. (Also see Harvey Comics Library)
Dec, 1955 - No. 3, Apr?, 1956
Argo Publ.

	GD25	FN65	NM94
1-r/Rex Morgan daily newspaper strips & daily panel-r of "These Women" by D'Alessio & "Timeout" by Jeff Keate	9.50	28.00	75.00
2,3	7.15	21.50	50.00

REX THE WONDER DOG (See The Adventures of...)

RHUBARB, THE MILLIONAIRE CAT
No. 423, Sept-Oct, 1952 - No. 563, June, 1954
Dell Publishing Co.

	GD25	FN65	NM94
Four Color 423 (#1)	4.50	13.50	50.00
Four Color 466(5/53),563	3.60	11.00	40.00

RIB
Oct, 1995 - April, 1996 ($1.95, B&W)
Dilemma Productions

	GD25	FN65	NM94
Ashcan, 1		.80	2.00

RIB
1996 ($2.95, B&W)
Bookmark Productions

	GD25	FN65	NM94
1-Sakai-c; Andrew Ford-s/a		1.20	3.00

RIB
May, 1997 ($2.95, B&W)
Caliber Comics

	GD25	FN65	NM94
1-"Beginnings" pts. 1 & 2		1.20	3.00

RIBIT!
Jan, 1989 - No. 4, April?, 1989 ($1.95, limited series)
Comico

	GD25	FN65	NM94
1-4: Frank Thorne-c/a/scripts		.80	2.00

RIBTICKLER (Also see Fox Giants)
1945 - No. 9, Aug, 1947; 1957; 1959
Fox Feature Synd./Green Publ. (1957)/Norlen (1959)

	GD25	FN65	NM94
1-Funny animal	11.30	34.00	90.00

Richard Dragon, Kung-Fu Fighter #1 © DC

Richie Rich #4 © HARV

Richie Rich and Cadbury #24 © HARV

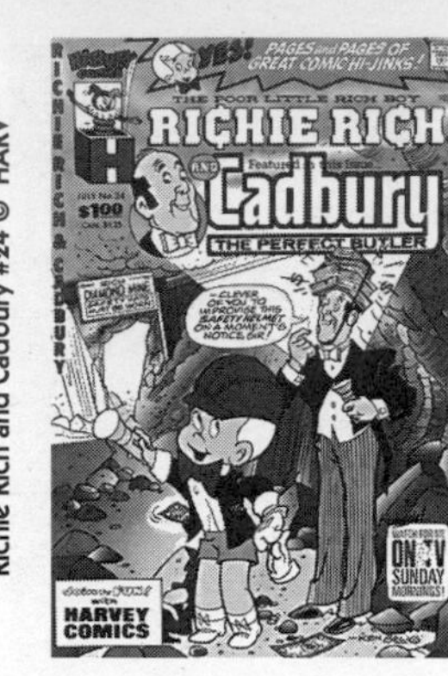

	GD25	FN65	NM94
2-(1946)	6.50	19.50	45.00
3-9: 3,7-Cosmo Cat app.	5.70	17.00	35.00
3,7,8 (Green Publ.-1957)	2.00	6.00	16.00
3,7,8 (Norlen Mag.-1959)	2.00	6.00	16.00

RICHARD DRAGON, KUNG-FU FIGHTER (See The Batman Chronicles, Brave & the Bold, & The Question)
Apr-May, 1975 - No. 18, Nov-Dec, 1977
National Periodical Publications/DC Comics

	GD25	FN65	NM94
1-3: 1-Intro Richard Dragon, Ben Stanley & O-Sensei; 1st app. Barney Ling; adaptation of Jim Dennis novel "Dragon's Fists" begins, ends #4. 2-Intro Carolyn Woosan; Starlin/Weiss-c/a; bondage-c. 3-Kirby-a(p); Giordano bondage-c		2.40	6.00
4-8-Wood inks. 4-Carolyn Woosan dies. 5-1st app. Lady Shiva		1.60	4.00
9-13,15-18: 9-Ben Stanley becomes Ben Turner; intro Preying Mantis. 16-1st app. Prof Ojo. 18-1st app. Ben Turner as The Bronze Tiger		1.20	3.00
14-"Spirit of Bruce Lee"		2.40	6.00

NOTE: ***Buckler*** *a-14. c-15, 18.* ***Chua*** *c-13.* ***Estrada*** *a-9, 13-18.* ***Estrada/Abel*** *a-10-12.* ***Estrada/Wood*** *a-4-8.* ***Giordano*** *c-1, 3-11.* ***Weiss*** *a-2(partial) c-2i.*

RICHARD THE LION-HEARTED (See Ideal a Classical Comic)

RICHIE RICH (See Harvey Collectors Comics, Harvey Hits, Little Dot, Little Lotta, Little Sad Sack, Million Dollar Digest, Mutt & Jeff, Super Richie, and 3-D Dolly)

RICHIE RICH (...the Poor Little Rich Boy) (See Harvey Hits #3, 9)
Nov, 1960 - #218, Oct, 1982; #219, Oct, 1986 - #254, Jan, 1991
Harvey Publications

	GD25	FN65	NM94
1-(See Little Dot for 1st app.)	140.00	420.00	1400.00
2	47.50	142.00	475.00
3-5	27.00	81.00	270.00
6-10: 8-Christmas-c	16.50	50.00	165.00
11-20	10.00	30.00	100.00
21-30	8.00	24.00	80.00
31-40	6.00	18.00	60.00
41-50	4.00	12.00	40.00
51-60: 56-1st app. Super Richie. 59-Buck, prototype of Dollar the Dog	3.00	10.00	30.00
61-80: 65-1st app. Dollar the Dog. 71-Nixon & Robert Kennedy caricatures	2.00	6.00	16.00
81-99	1.25	3.75	10.00
100(12/70)-1st app. Irona the robot maid	1.85	5.50	15.00
101-111,117-120	1.00	3.00	8.00
112-116: All 52 pg. Giants	1.50	4.50	12.00
121-140: 137-1st app. Mr. Cheepers		2.40	6.00
141-160: 145-Infinity-c. 155-3rd app. The Money Monster		1.60	4.00
161-180		1.20	3.00
181-254: 210-Stone-Age Riches app. 237-Last original material		.80	2.00

RICHIE RICH
Mar, 1991 - No. 28, Nov, 1994 ($1.00, bi-monthly)
Harvey Comics

	GD25	FN65	NM94
1		1.20	3.00
2-28: Reprints best of Richie Rich		.80	2.00
Giant Size 1-4 (10/91-10/93, $2.25, 68 pgs.)		1.20	3.00

RICHIE RICH ADVENTURE DIGEST MAGAZINE
1992 ($1.25, quarterly, digest-size)
Harvey Comics

	GD25	FN65	NM94
1		1.60	4.00

RICHIE RICH AND...
Oct, 1987 - No. 11, May, 1990 ($1.00)
Harvey Comics

	GD25	FN65	NM94
1-Professore Keenbean		1.60	4.00
2-11: 2-Casper. 3-Dollar the Dog. 4-Cadbury. 5 Mayda Munny. 6-Irona. 7-Little Dot. 8-Professor Keenbean. 9-Little Audrey. 10-Mayda Munny. 11-Cadbury.		.80	2.00

RICHIE RICH AND BILLY BELLHOPS
Oct, 1977 (52 pgs., one-shot)
Harvey Publications

	GD25	FN65	NM94
1	1.00	3.00	8.00

RICHIE RICH AND CADBURY
10/77; #2, 9/78 - #23, 7/82; #24, 7/90 - #29, 1/91 (1-10: 52pgs.)
Harvey Publications

	GD25	FN65	NM94
1	1.25	3.75	10.00
2-5		2.40	6.00
6-23		1.60	4.00
24-29: 24-Begin $1.00-c		.80	2.00

RICHIE RICH AND CASPER
Aug, 1974 - No. 45, Sept, 1982
Harvey Publications

	GD25	FN65	NM94
1	2.50	7.50	20.00
2-5	1.25	3.75	10.00
6-10: 10-Xmas-c		2.40	6.00
11-20		1.60	4.00
21-45: 22-Xmas-c		1.20	3.00

RICHIE RICH AND DOLLAR THE DOG (See Richie Rich #65)
Sept, 1977 - No. 24, Aug, 1982 (#1-10: 52 pgs.)
Harvey Publications

	GD25	FN65	NM94
1	1.00	3.00	8.00
2-10		2.00	5.00
11-24		1.20	3.00

RICHIE RICH AND DOT
Oct, 1974 (one-shot)
Harvey Publications

	GD25	FN65	NM94
1	1.50	4.50	12.00

RICHIE RICH AND GLORIA
Sept, 1977 - No. 25, Sept, 1982 (#1-11: 52 pgs.)
Harvey Publications

	GD25	FN65	NM94
1	1.00	3.00	8.00
2-11		2.00	5.00
12-25		1.20	3.00

RICHIE RICH AND HIS GIRLFRIENDS
April, 1979 - No. 16, Dec, 1982
Harvey Publications

	GD25	FN65	NM94
1-(52 pg. Giant)	1.00	3.00	8.00
2-(52 pg. Giant)		2.00	5.00
3-10		1.60	4.00
11-16		1.20	3.00

RICHIE RICH AND HIS MEAN COUSIN REGGIE
April, 1979 - No. 3, 1980 (50¢) (#1,2: 52 pgs.)
Harvey Publications

	GD25	FN65	NM94
1	1.00	3.00	8.00
2-3:		2.00	5.00

NOTE: *No. 4 was advertised, but never released.*

RICHIE RICH AND JACKIE JOKERS (Also see Jackie Jokers)
Nov, 1973 - No. 48, Dec, 1982
Harvey Publications

	GD25	FN65	NM94
1: 52 pg. Giant; contains material from unpublished Jackie Jokers #5	3.00	9.00	30.00
2,3-(52 pg. Giants). 2-R.R. & Jackie 1st meet	2.25	6.75	18.00
4,5	1.25	3.75	10.00
6-10	1.00	2.80	7.00
11-20: 11-1st app. Kool Katz		2.00	5.00
21-40: 26-Star Wars parody		1.60	4.00

Richie Rich and Jackie Jokers #42 © HARV

Richie Rich and Jackie Jokers #48 © HARV

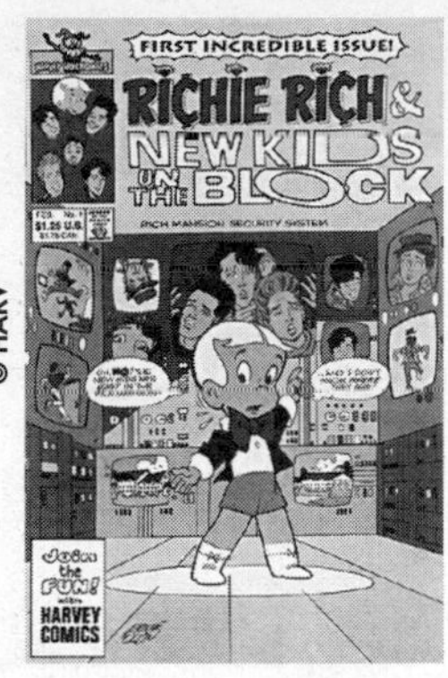

Richie Rich & The New Kids On The Block #1 © HARV

	GD25	FN65	NM94
41-48		1.20	3.00

RICHIE RICH AND PROFESSOR KEENBEAN
Sept, 1990 - No. 2, Nov, 1990 ($1.00)
Harvey Comics

	GD25	FN65	NM94
1,2		.80	2.00

RICHIE RICH AND THE NEW KIDS ON THE BLOCK
Feb, 1991 - No. 3, June, 1991 ($1.25)
Harvey Publications

	GD25	FN65	NM94
1-3		.80	2.00

RICHIE RICH AND TIMMY TIME
Sept, 1977 (50¢, 52 pgs, one-shot)
Harvey Publications

	GD25	FN65	NM94
1	1.00	3.00	8.00

RICHIE RICH BANK BOOKS
Oct, 1972 - No. 59, Sept, 1982
Harvey Publications

	GD25	FN65	NM94
1	3.50	10.50	35.00
2-5: 2-2nd app. The Money Monster	2.50	7.50	20.00
6-10	1.50	4.50	12.00
11-20: 18-Super Richie app.	1.00	3.00	8.00
21-30		2.00	5.00
31-40		1.60	4.00
41-59		1.20	3.00

RICHIE RICH BEST OF THE YEARS
Oct, 1977 - No. 6, June, 1980 (128 pgs., digest-size)
Harvey Publications

	GD25	FN65	NM94
1(10/77)-Reprints	1.00	3.00	8.00
2-6(11/79-6/80, 95¢). #2(10/78)-Reprints. #3(6/79, 75¢)		2.00	5.00

RICHIE RICH BIG BUCKS
Apr, 1991 - No. 8, July, 1992 ($1.00, bi-monthly)
Harvey Publications

	GD25	FN65	NM94
1-8		.80	2.00

RICHIE RICH BILLIONS
Oct, 1974 - No. 48, Oct, 1982 (#1-33: 52 pgs.)
Harvey Publications

	GD25	FN65	NM94
1	2.50	7.50	24.00
2-5	1.50	4.50	12.00
6-10	1.00	3.00	8.00
11-20		2.40	6.00
21-33		1.60	4.00
34-48: 35-Onion app.		1.20	3.00

RICHIE RICH CASH
Sept, 1974 - No. 47, Aug, 1982
Harvey Publications

	GD25	FN65	NM94
1-1st app. Dr. N-R-Gee	2.50	7.50	24.00
2-5	1.50	4.50	12.00
6-10	1.10	3.30	9.00
11-20		2.40	6.00
21-30		1.60	4.00
31-47: 33-Dr. Blemish app.		1.20	3.00

RICHIE RICH CASH MONEY
May, 1992 - No. 2, Aug, 1992 ($1.25)
Harvey Comics

	GD25	FN65	NM94
1,2		.80	2.00

RICHIE RICH, CASPER & WENDY NATIONAL LEAGUE
June, 1976 (52 pgs.)
Harvey Publications

	GD25	FN65	NM94
1 (Released-3/76 with 6/76 date)	1.25	3.75	10.00
1 (6/76)-2nd version w/San Francisco Giants & KTVU 2 logos; has "Compliments of Giants and Straw Hat Pizza" on-c	1.25	3.75	10.00

RICHIE RICH COLLECTORS COMICS (See Harvey Collectors Comics)

RICHIE RICH DIAMONDS
Aug, 1972 - No. 59, Aug, 1982 (#1, 23-45: 52 pgs.)
Harvey Publications

	GD25	FN65	NM94
1-(52 pg. Giant)	4.00	12.00	40.00
2-5	2.50	7.50	20.00
6-10	1.50	4.50	12.00
11-22	1.00	3.00	8.00
23-30		2.00	5.00
31-45: 39-Origin Little Dot		1.60	4.00
46-50		1.20	3.00
51-59		.80	2.00

RICHIE RICH DIGEST
Oct, 1986 - No. 42, Oct, 1994 ($1.25/$1.75, digest-size)
Harvey Publications

	GD25	FN65	NM94
1		2.40	6.00
2-20		1.60	4.00
21-42		1.20	3.00

RICHIE RICH DIGEST STORIES (...Magazine #?-on)
Oct, 1977 - No., 17, Oct, 1982 (75¢/95¢, digest-size)
Harvey Publications

	GD25	FN65	NM94
1-Reprints	1.00	3.00	8.00
2-10: Reprints		2.00	5.00
11-17: Reprints		1.60	4.00

RICHIE RICH DIGEST WINNERS
Dec, 1977 - No. 16, Sept, 1982 (75¢/95¢, 132 pgs., digest-size)
Harvey Publications

	GD25	FN65	NM94
1	1.00	3.00	8.00
2-5		2.00	5.00
6-16		1.60	4.00

RICHIE RICH DOLLARS & CENTS
Aug, 1963 - No. 109, Aug, 1982 (#1-43: 68 pgs.; 44-60, 71-94: 52 pgs.)
Harvey Publications

	GD25	FN65	NM94
1: (#1-64 are all reprint issues)	14.00	42.00	140.00
2	6.50	19.50	65.00
3-5: 5-r/1st app. of R.R. from Little Dot #1	4.00	12.00	40.00
6-10	2.60	7.80	26.00
11-20	2.50	7.50	22.00
21-30: 25-1st app. Nurse Jenny	2.00	6.00	16.00
31-43: 43-Last 68 pg. issue	1.50	4.50	12.00
44-60: All 52 pgs.	1.10	3.30	9.00
61-71		2.00	5.00
72-94: All 52 pgs.	1.00	2.80	7.00
95-109: 100-Anniversary issue		1.20	3.00

RICHIE RICH FORTUNES
Sept, 1971 - No. 63, July, 1982 (#1-15: 52 pgs.)
Harvey Publications

	GD25	FN65	NM94
1	4.00	12.00	40.00
2-5	2.50	7.50	20.00
6-10	1.50	4.50	12.00
11-15: 11-1st app. The Onion	1.00	3.00	8.00
16-30		1.60	4.00
31-40		1.20	3.00
41-63: 62-Onion app.		.80	2.00

RICHIE RICH GEMS
Sept, 1974 - No. 43, Sept, 1982
Harvey Publications

	GD25	FN65	NM94
1	2.50	7.50	24.00
2-5	1.50	4.50	12.00

Richie Rich Millions #1 © HARV

Richie Rich Summer Bonanza #1 © HARV

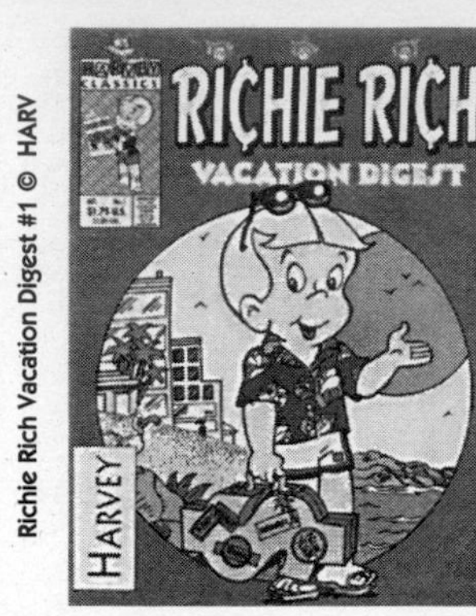

Richie Rich Vacation Digest #1 © HARV

	GD25	FN65	NM94
6-10	1.00	3.00	8.00
11-20		2.00	5.00
21-30		1.60	4.00
31-43: 36-Dr. Blemish, Onion app. 38-1st app. Stone-Age Riches		1.20	3.00

RICHIE RICH GOLD AND SILVER
Sept, 1975 - No. 42, Oct, 1982 (#1-27: 52 pgs.)
Harvey Publications

	GD25	FN65	NM94
1	2.50	7.50	20.00
2-5	1.25	3.75	10.00
6-10	1.00	2.80	7.00
11-27		2.00	5.00
28-42: 34-Stone-Age Riches app.		1.20	3.00

RICHIE RICH GOLD NUGGETS DIGEST
Feb., 1991 - No.5, June, 1991 ($1.75, digest-size)
Harvey Publications

	GD25	FN65	NM94
1		1.20	3.00
2-5		.70	1.75

RICHIE RICH HOLIDAY DIGEST MAGAZINE (...Digest #4)
Jan, 1980 - #3, Jan, 1982; #4, 3/88; #5, 2/89 (Published annually)
Harvey Publications

	GD25	FN65	NM94
1-X-Mas-c		2.40	6.00
2-5: 2,3: All X-Mas-c. 4-(3/88, $1.25), 5-(2/89, $1.75)		1.60	4.00

RICHIE RICH INVENTIONS
Oct, 1977 - No. 26, Oct, 1982 (#1-11: 52 pgs.)
Harvey Publications

	GD25	FN65	NM94
1	1.00	3.00	8.00
2-5		2.00	5.00
6-11		1.60	4.00
12-26		1.20	3.00

RICHIE RICH JACKPOTS
Oct, 1972 - No. 58, Aug, 1982 (#41-43: 52 pgs.)
Harvey Publications

	GD25	FN65	NM94
1	4.00	12.00	40.00
2-5	2.50	7.50	20.00
6-10	1.50	4.50	12.00
11-20: 16-Super Richie app.	1.00	3.00	8.00
21-30		2.00	5.00
31-40,44-50: 37-Caricatures of Frank Sinatra, Dean Martin, Sammy Davis, Jr. 45-Dr. Blemish app.		1.60	4.00
41-43 (52 pgs.)		2.00	5.00
51-58		1.20	3.00

RICHIE RICH MILLION DOLLAR DIGEST (...Magazine #?-on)(See Million Dollar Digest)
Oct, 1980 - No. 10, Oct, 1982 ($1.50)
Harvey Publications

	GD25	FN65	NM94
1		2.40	6.00
2-10		1.60	4.00

RICHIE RICH MILLIONS
9/61; #2, 9/62 - #113, 10/82 (#1-48: 68 pgs.; 49-64, 85-97: 52 pgs.)
Harvey Publications

	GD25	FN65	NM94
1: (#1-3 are all reprint issues)	17.00	51.00	170.00
2	9.00	27.00	90.00
3-10: All other giants are new & reprints. 5-1st 15 pg. Richie Rich story	7.00	21.00	70.00
11-20	3.20	9.60	32.00
21-30	2.50	7.50	24.00
31-48: 48-Last 68 pg. Giant	1.85	5.50	15.00
49-64: 52 pg. Giants	1.25	3.75	10.00
65-67,69-84: 74-1st app. Mr. Woody; Super Richie app.	2.40	6.00	
68- 1st Super Richie-c (11/74)	1.50	4.50	12.00
85-97: 52 pg. Giants	1.00	3.00	8.00
98-100		1.60	4.00
101-113		1.20	3.00

RICHIE RICH MONEY WORLD
Sept, 1972 - No. 59, Sept, 1982
Harvey Publications

	GD25	FN65	NM94
1-(52 pg. Giant)-1st app. Mayda Munny	4.00	12.00	40.00
2-5: 2-Super Richie app.	2.00	6.00	16.00
6-10: 9,10-Richie Rich mistakenly named Little Lotta on covers	1.10	3.30	9.00
11-20: 16,20-Dr. N-R-Gee		2.00	5.00
21-30		1.60	4.00
31-50		1.20	3.00
51-59		.80	2.00
Digest 1 (2/91, $1.75)		1.60	4.00
2 - 8 (12/93, $1.75)		.70	1.75

RICHIE RICH PROFITS
Oct, 1974 - No. 47, Sept, 1982
Harvey Publications

	GD25	FN65	NM94
1	3.00	9.00	30.00
2-5	1.50	4.50	12.00
6-10: 10-Origin of Dr. N-R-Gee	1.00	3.00	8.00
11-20: 15-Christmas-c		2.00	5.00
21-30		1.60	4.00
31-47		1.20	3.00

RICHIE RICH RELICS
Jan, 1988 - No.4, Feb, 1989 (75¢/$1.00, reprints)
Harvey Comics

	GD25	FN65	NM94
1-4		1.20	3.00

RICHIE RICH RICHES
July, 1972 - No. 59, Aug, 1982 (#1, 2, 41-45: 52 pgs.)
Harvey Publications

	GD25	FN65	NM94
1-(52 pg. Giant)-1st app. The Money Monster	4.20	12.60	42.00
2-(52 pg. Giant)	2.50	7.50	20.00
3-5	1.50	4.50	12.00
6-10	1.10	3.30	9.00
11-20: 17-Super Richie app. (3/75)		2.40	6.00
21-40		1.60	4.00
41-45: 52 pg. Giants		2.00	5.00
46-59: 56-Dr. Blemish app.		1.20	3.00

RICHIE RICH SUCCESS STORIES
Nov, 1964 - No. 105, Sept, 1982 (#1-38: 68 pgs., 39-55, 67-90: 52 pgs.)
Harvey Publications

	GD25	FN65	NM94
1	15.00	45.00	150.00
2-5	7.00	21.00	70.00
6-10	3.50	10.50	35.00
11-30: 27-1st Penny Van Dough (8/69)	2.50	7.50	20.00
31-38: 38-Last 68 pg. Giant	1.85	5.50	15.00
39-55-(52 pgs.): 44-Super Richie app.	1.50	4.50	12.00
56-66	1.00	2.80	7.00
67-90: 52 pgs. (Majority of early issues are reprints)		2.00	5.00
91-105: 91-Onion app. 101-Dr. Blemish app.		1.20	3.00

RICHIE RICH SUMMER BONANZA
Oct, 1991 ($1.95, one-shot, 68 pgs.)
Harvey Comics

	GD25	FN65	NM94
1-Richie Rich, Little Dot, Little Lotta		1.20	3.00

RICHIE RICH TREASURE CHEST DIGEST (...Magazine #3)
Apr, 1982 - No. 3, Aug, 1982 (95¢, Digest Mag.)(#4 advertised but not publ.)
Harvey Publications

	GD25	FN65	NM94
1		2.40	6.00

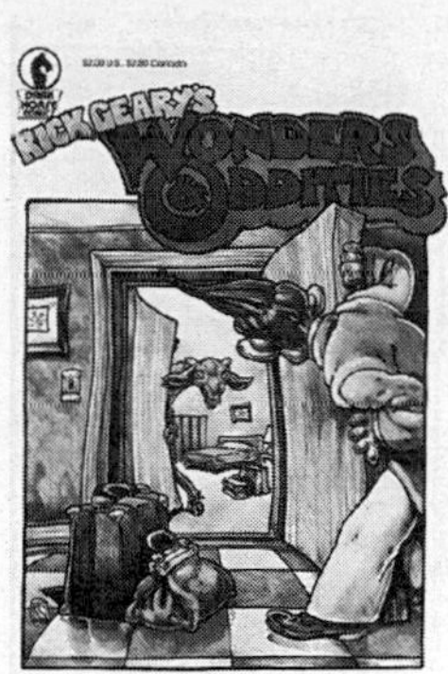

Rick Geary's Wonders and Oddities #1 © DH

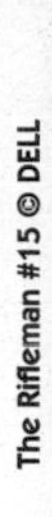

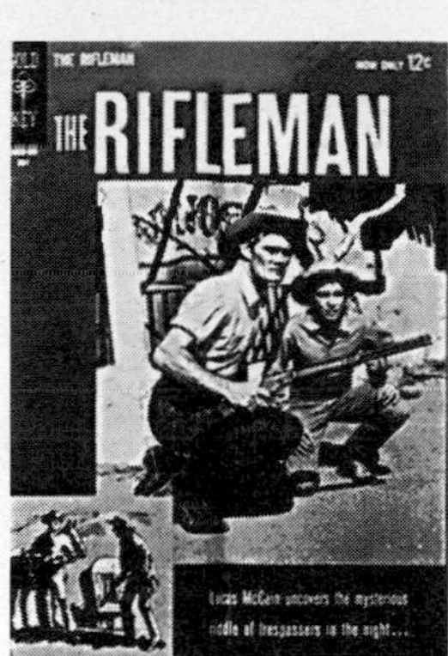

The Rifleman #15 © DELL

Rin Tin Tin #28 © DELL

	GD25	FN65	NM94
2,3		1.60	4.00

RICHIE RICH VACATION DIGEST
Oct, 1991 ($1.75, digest-size)
Harvey Comics

1		1.20	3.00

RICHIE RICH VACATION DIGEST
Oct, 1992 ($1.75, digest size)
Harvey Comics

1		1.20	3.00

RICHIE RICH VACATION DIGEST
Oct, 1993 ($1.75, digest-size)
Harvey Comics

1		1.20	3.00

RICHIE RICH VACATIONS DIGEST
11/77; No. 2, 10/78 - No. 7, 10/81; No. 8, 8/82; No. 9, 10/82 (Digest, 132 pgs.)
Harvey Publications

1-Reprints	1.00	3.00	8.00
2-9		2.00	5.00

RICHIE RICH VAULT OF MYSTERY
Nov, 1974 - No. 47, Sept, 1982
Harvey Publications

1	2.50	7.50	20.00
2-10	1.25	3.75	10.00
11-20		2.40	6.00
21-30		1.60	4.00
31-47		1.20	3.00

RICHIE RICH ZILLIONZ
Oct, 1976 - No. 33, Sept, 1982 (#1-4: 68 pgs.; #5-18: 52 pgs.)
Harvey Publications

1	2.50	7.50	20.00
2-4: 4-Last 68 pg. Giant	1.10	3.30	9.00
5-10		2.40	6.00
11-18: 18-Last 52 pg. Giant		1.60	4.00
19-33		1.00	2.50

RICK GEARY'S WONDERS AND ODDITIES
Dec, 1988 ($2.00, B&W, one-shot)
Dark Horse Comics

1		.80	2.00

RICKY
No. 5, Sept, 1953
Standard Comics (Visual Editions)

5-Teenage humor	4.00	12.00	24.00

RICKY NELSON (TV)(See Sweethearts V2#42)
No. 956, Dec, 1958 - No. 1192, June, 1961 (All photo-c)
Dell Publishing Co.

Four Color 956,998	18.00	55.00	200.00
Four Color 1115	14.00	41.00	150.00
Four Color 1192-Manning-a	14.00	41.00	150.00

RIDER, THE (Frontier Trail #6; also see Blazing Sixguns I.W. Reprint #10, 11)
Mar, 1957 - No. 5, 1958
Ajax/Farrell Publ. (Four Star Comic Corp.)

1-Swift Arrow, Lone Rider begin	8.75	26.25	65.00
2-5	5.70	17.00	35.00

RIDERS OF THE PURPLE SAGE (See Zane Grey & Four Color #372)

RIFLEMAN, THE (TV)
No. 1009, 7-9/59 - No. 12, 7-9/62; No. 13, 11/62 - No. 20, 10/64
Dell Publ. Co./Gold Key No. 13 on

Four Color 1009 (#1)	22.00	65.00	240.00
2 (1-3/60)	11.00	33.00	120.00
3-Toth-a (4 pgs.)	12.00	35.00	130.00
4,5,7-10	9.00	27.00	100.00
6-Toth-a (4 pgs.)	9.00	27.00	100.00
11-20	7.00	20.00	75.00

NOTE: ***Warren Tufts** a-2-9. All have Chuck Connors photo-c. Photo back c-13-15.*

RIMA, THE JUNGLE GIRL
Apr-May, 1974 - No. 7, Apr-May, 1975
National Periodical Publications

1-Origin, part 1 (#1-5: 20¢; 6,7: 25¢)	1.00	2.80	7.00
2-4-Origin, parts 2-4		1.60	4.00
5-6		1.60	4.00
7-Origin & only app. Space Marshal	1.00	3.00	8.00

NOTE: ***Kubert** c-1-7. **Nino** a-1-7. **Redondo** a-1-7.*

RING OF BRIGHT WATER (See Movie Classics)

RING OF THE NIBELUNG, THE
1989 - No. 4, 1990 ($4.95, squarebound, 52 pgs., mature readers)
DC Comics

1-4: Adapts novel, Gil Kane-c/a		2.00	5.00

RINGO KID, THE (2nd Series)
Jan, 1970 - No. 23, Nov, 1973; No. 24, Nov, 1975 - No. 30, Nov, 1976
Marvel Comics Group

1-Williamson-a r-from #10, 1956.	2.25	6.75	18.00
2-11: 2-Severin-c	1.25	3.75	10.00
12 (Giant)	1.85	5.50	15.00
13-20: 13-Wildey-r. 20-Williamson-r/#1	1.00	3.00	8.00
21-30		2.40	6.00

RINGO KID WESTERN, THE (1st Series) (See Wild Western & Western Trails)
Aug, 1954 - No. 21, Sept, 1957
Atlas Comics (HPC)/Marvel Comics

1-Origin; The Ringo Kid begins	23.00	68.00	180.00
2-Black Rider app.; origin/1st app. Ringo's Horse Arab	11.30	34.00	90.00
3-5	8.50	26.00	60.00
6-8-Severin-a(3) each	8.75	26.25	70.00
9,11,12,14-21: 12-Orlando-a (4 pgs.)	6.50	19.50	45.00
10,13-Williamson-a (4 pgs.)	7.15	21.50	50.00

NOTE: ***Berg** a-8. **Maneely** a-1-5, 15, 16(text illos only), 17(4), 18, 20, 21; c-1-6, 8, 13, 15-18, 20. **J. Severin** c-10, 11. **Sinnott** a-1. **Wildey** a-16-18.*

RIN TIN TIN (See March of Comics #163,180,195)

RIN TIN TIN (TV) (...& Rusty #21 on; see Western Roundup under Dell Giants)
Nov, 1952 - No. 38, May-July, 1961; Nov, 1963 (All Photo-c)
Dell Publishing Co./Gold Key

Four Color 434 (#1)	14.00	41.00	150.00
Four Color 476,523	7.00	22.00	80.00
4(3-5/54)-10	5.50	16.50	60.00
11-20	5.00	15.00	55.00
21-38: 36-Toth-a (4 pgs.)	3.60	11.00	40.00
... & Rusty 1 (11/63-Gold Key)	4.50	13.50	50.00

RIO (Also see Eclipse Monthly)
June, 1987 ($8.95, 64 pgs.)
Comico

1-Wildey-c/a	1.10	3.30	9.00

RIO AT BAY
July, 1992 - No. 2, Aug, 1992 ($2.95, limited series)
Dark Horse Comics

1,2-Wildey-c/a		1.20	3.00

RIO BRAVO (Movie) (See 4-Color #1018)

Riot #4 © ATLAS

Ripclaw #1 © Top Cow Productions

Rip Hunter Time Master #10 © DC

	GD25	FN65	NM94

June, 1959
Dell Publishing Co.

	GD25	FN65	NM94
Four Color #1018-Toth-a; John Wayne, Dean Martin, & Ricky Nelson photo-c.	18.00	55.00	200.00

RIO CONCHOS (See Movie Comics)

RIOT (Satire)
Apr, 1954 - No. 3, Aug, 1954; No. 4, Feb, 1956 - No. 6, June, 1956
Atlas Comics (ACI No. 1-5/WPI No. 6)

	GD25	FN65	NM94
1-Russ Heath-a	23.00	68.00	180.00
2-Li'l Abner satire by Post	17.50	53.00	140.00
3-Last precode (8/54)	15.00	45.00	120.00
4-Infinity-c; Marilyn Monroe "7 Year Itch" movie satire; Mad Rip-off ads	19.50	58.00	155.00
5-Marilyn Monroe, John Wayne parody; part photo-c	20.00	60.00	160.00
6-Lorna of the Jungle satire by Everett; Dennis the Menace satire-c/story; part photo-c	15.00	45.00	120.00

NOTE: ***Berg** a-3. **Burgos** c-1, 2. **Colan** a-1. **Everett** a-1, 4, 6. **Heath** a-1. **Maneely** a-1, 2, 4-6; c-3, 4, 6. **Post** a-1-4. **Reinman** a-2. **Severin** a-4-6.*

RIOT GEAR
Sept, 1993 - No. 11, July, 1994 ($2.50, serially numbered comics)
Triumphant Comics

	GD25	FN65	NM94
1-11: 1-2nd app. Riot Gear. 2-1st app. Rabin. 3,4-Triumphant Unleashed x-over. 3-1st app. Surzar. 4-Death of Captain Tich		1.00	2.50
Violent Past 1,2: 1-(2/94, $2.50)		1.00	2.50

R.I.P.
1990 - No. 8, 1991 ($2.95, 44 pgs.)
TSR, Inc.

	GD25	FN65	NM94
1-8-Based on TSR game		1.20	3.00

RIPCLAW (See Cyberforce)
Apr, 1995 - No. 3, June, 1995 (Limited series)
Image Comics (Top Cow Productions)

	GD25	FN65	NM94
1/2-Gold	1.75	5.25	14.00
1/2-San Diego ed.	1.40	4.15	11.00
1/2-Chicago ed.	1.40	4.15	11.00
1-3: Brandon Peterson-a(p)		1.00	2.50

RIPCLAW
V2#1, Dec, 1995 - No. 6, June, 1996 ($2.50)
Image Comics (Top Cow Productions)

	GD25	FN65	NM94
V2#1-6: 5-Medieval Spawn/Witchblade Preview		1.00	2.50
Special (10/95, $2.50)		1.00	2.50

RIPCORD (TV)
Mar-May, 1962
Dell Publishing Co.

	GD25	FN65	NM94
Four Color 1294	6.40	19.00	70.00

RIPFIRE
No. 0, Apr, 1995 ($2.50, one-shot)
Malibu Comics (Ultraverse)

	GD25	FN65	NM94
0		1.00	2.50

RIP HUNTER TIME MASTER (See Showcase #20, 21, 25, 26 & Time Masters)
Mar-Apr, 1961 - No. 29, Nov-Dec, 1965
National Periodical Publications

	GD25	FN65	NM94
1-(3-4/61)	41.00	123.00	470.00
2	22.50	68.00	225.00
3-5: 5-Last 10¢ issue	13.00	39.00	130.00
6,7-Toth-a in each	10.00	30.00	100.00
8-15	7.00	21.00	70.00
16-20: 20-Hitler c/s	6.00	18.00	60.00
21-29: 29-Gil Kane-c	5.00	15.00	50.00

RIP IN TIME (Also see Teenage Mutant Ninja Turtles #5-7)
Aug, 1986 - No.5, 1987 ($1.50, B&W)
Fantagor Press

	GD25	FN65	NM94
1-5: Corben-c/a in all			1.50

RIP KIRBY (Also see Harvey Comics Hits #57, & Street Comix)
1948 David McKay Publications

	GD25	FN65	NM94
Feature Books 51,54: Raymond-c; 51-Origin	28.00	84.00	225.00

RIPLEY'S BELIEVE IT OR NOT! (See Ace Comics, All-American Comics, Mystery Comics Digest #1, 4, 7, 10, 13, 16, 19, 22, 25)

RIPLEY'S BELIEVE IT OR NOT!
Sept, 1953 - No. 4, March, 1954
Harvey Publications

	GD25	FN65	NM94
1-Powell-a	10.00	30.00	70.00
2-4	7.50	22.50	45.00
J. C. Penney giveaway (1948)	7.50	22.50	45.00

RIPLEY'S BELIEVE IT OR NOT! (Formerly ...True War Stories)
No. 4, April, 1967 - No. 94, Feb, 1980
Gold Key

	GD25	FN65	NM94
4-Photo-c; McWilliams-a	2.00	6.00	22.00
5-Subtitled "True War Stories"; Evans-a; 1st Jeff Jones-a in comics? (2 pgs.)	1.80	5.50	20.00
6-10: 6-McWilliams-a. 10-Evans-a(2)	1.80	5.50	20.00
11-20: 15-Evans-a	1.25	3.75	14.00
21-30	1.00	2.80	10.00
31-38,40-60	1.00	3.00	8.00
39-Crandall-a	1.10	3.30	9.00
61-73		2.40	6.00
74,77-83-(52 pgs.)	1.00	3.00	8.00
75,76,84-94		1.60	4.00
Story Digest Mag. 1(6/70)-4-3/4x6-1/2"	3.00	9.00	30.00

NOTE: ***Evanish** art by **Luiz Dominguez** #22-25, 27, 30, 31, 40. **Jeff Jones** a-5(2 pgs.). **McWilliams** a-65, 66, 70, 89. **Orlando** a-8. **Sparling** c-68. Reprints-74, 77-84, 87 (part); 91, 93 (all). **Williamson, Wood** a-80r/#1.*

RIPLEY'S BELIEVE IT OR NOT! TRUE GHOST STORIES (Becomes ...True War Stories) (See Dan Curtis)
June, 1965 - No. 2, Oct, 1966
Gold Key

	GD25	FN65	NM94
1-Williamson, Wood & Evans-a; photo-c	3.60	11.00	40.00
2-Orlando, McWilliams-a; photo-c	2.50	7.50	28.00
Mini-Comic 1(1976-3-1/4x6-1/2")		2.00	5.00
11186(1977)-Golden Press; ($1.95, 224 pgs.)-All-r	2.50	7.50	20.00
11401(3/79)-Golden Press; ($1.00, 96 pgs.)-All-r	1.50	4.50	12.00

RIPLEY'S BELIEVE IT OR NOT! TRUE WAR STORIES (Formerly ...True Ghost Stories; becomes Ripley's Believe It or Not! #4 on)
Nov, 1966
Gold Key

	GD25	FN65	NM94
1(#3)-No Williamson-a	2.20	6.60	22.00

RIPLEY'S BELIEVE IT OR NOT! TRUE WEIRD
June, 1966 - No. 2, Aug, 1966 (B&W Magazine)
Ripley Enterprises

	GD25	FN65	NM94
1,2-Comic stories & text		2.40	6.00

RIPTIDE
Sep, 1995 - No. 2, Oct, 1995 ($2.50, limited series)
Image Comics

	GD25	FN65	NM94
1,2: Rob Liefeld-c		1.00	2.50

RISE OF APOCALYPSE
Oct, 1996 - No. 4, Jan, 1997 ($1.95, limited series)
Marvel Comics

Riverdale High #1 © AP

Roarin' Rick's Rare Bit Fiends #1 © Rick Veitch

Robin #34 © DC

GD25 FN65 NM94

1-4: Adam Pollina-c/a .80 2.00

RIVERDALE HIGH (Archie's... #7,8)
Aug, 1990 - No. 8, Oct, 1991 ($1.00, bi-monthly)
Archie Comics

1-8 1.00

RIVER FEUD (See Zane Grey & Four Color #484)

RIVETS
No. 518, Nov, 1953
Dell Publishing Co.

Four Color 518 2.25 6.75 25.00

RIVETS (A dog)
Jan, 1956 - No. 3, May, 1956
Argo Publ.

1-Reprints Sunday & daily newspaper strips 4.25 13.00 26.00
2,3 3.60 9.00 18.00

ROACHMILL
Dec, 1986 - No. 6, Oct, 1987 ($1.75, B&W)
Blackthorne Publ.

1-6 .70 1.75

ROACHMILL
May, 1988 - No. 10, Dec, 1990 ($1.75, B&W)
Dark Horse Comics

1-10: 10-Contains trading cards .70 1.75

ROAD RUNNER (See Beep Beep, the...)

ROADWAYS
May, 1994 ($2.75, B&W, limited series)
Cult Press

1 1.10 2.75

ROARIN' RICK'S RARE BIT FIENDS
July, 1994 - Present ($2.95, B&W, mature)
King Hell Press

1-21: Rick Veitch-c/a/scripts in all. 20-(5/96). 21-(8/96)-Reads Subtleman #1 on cover 1.20 3.00
RABID EYE: THE DREAM ART OF RICK VEITCH ($14.95, B&W, TPB)-r/#1-8 & the appendix from #12 15.00
POCKET UNIVERSE (6/96, $14.95, B&W, TPB)-Reprints 15.00

ROBERT E. HOWARD'S CONAN THE BARBARIAN
1983 ($2.50, 68 pgs., Baxter paper)
Marvel Comics

1-r/Savage Tales #2,3 by Smith, c-r/Conan #21 by Smith. 1.00 2.50

ROBERT LOUIS STEVENSON'S KIDNAPPED (See Kidnapped)

ROBIN (See Aurora, Detective Comics #38, New Teen Titans, Robin II, Robin III, Robin 3000, Star Spangled Comics #65 & Teen Titans)

ROBIN (See Batman #457)
Jan, 1991 - No. 5, May, 1991 ($1.00, limited series)
DC Comics

1-Free poster by N. Adams; Bolland-c on all 1.60 4.00
1-2nd & 3rd printings (without poster) 1.50
2 .70 1.75
2-2nd printing 1.00
3-5 1.50
Annual 1,2 (1992-93, $2.50, 68 pgs.): 1-Grant/Wagner scripts; Sam Kieth-c. 2-Intro Razorsharp; Jim Balent-c(p) 1.00 2.50

ROBIN (See Detective #668)
Nov, 1993 - Present ($1.50/$1.95)
DC Comics

1-($2.95)-Collector's edition w/foil embossed-c; 1st app. Robin's car, The Redbird; Azrael as Batman app. 1.20 3.00
1-Newsstand ed. .70 1.75
0,2-13,15,16-Regular editions: 3-5-The Spoiler app. 6-The Huntress-c/story cont'd from Showcase '94 #5. 7-Knightquest: The Conclusion w/new Batman (Azrael) vs. Bruce Wayne. 8-KnightsEnd Pt. 5. 9-KnightsEnd Aftermath; Batman-c & app. 10-(9/94)-Zero Hour. 0-(10/94). 11-(11/94) 1.50
14 ($2.50)-Embossed-c; Troika Pt. 4 1.00 2.50
14 ($1.50)-Regular edition 1.50
17-49: 17-Begin $1.95-c. 25-Green Arrow-c/app. 26-Batman app. 27-Contagion Pt. 3; Catwoman-c/app; Penguin & Azrael app. 28-Contagion Pt. 11. 29-Penguin app. 31-Wildcat-c/app. 32-Legacy Pt. 3. 33-Legacy Pt. 7 35-Final Night. 46-Genesis .80 2.00
50-($2.95)-Lady Shiva & King Snake app. 2.95
51-53 1.95
Annual 3-5: 3-(1994, $2.95)-Elseworlds story. 4-(1995, $2.95)-Year One story. 5-(1996, $2.95)-Legends of the Dead Earth story 1.20 3.00
Annual 6 (1997, $3.95)-Pulp Heroes story. 3.95
.../Argent 1 (2/98, $1.95) Argent (Teen Titans) app. 1.95
...Plus 1 (12/96, $2.95) Impulse-c/app.; Waid-s 1.20 3.00
...Plus 2 (12/97, $2.95) Fang (Scare Tactics) app. 2.95

ROBIN: A HERO REBORN
1991 ($4.95, squarebound, trade paperback)
DC Comics

nn-r/Batman #455-457 & Robin #1-5; Bolland-c 2.00 5.00

ROBIN HOOD (See The Advs. of..., Brave and the Bold, Four Color #413, 669, King Classics, Movie Comics & Power Record Comics)

ROBIN HOOD (...& His Merry Men, The Illustrated Story of...) (See Classic Comics #7 & Classics Giveaways, 12/44)

ROBIN HOOD (New Adventures of...)
1952 (Flour giveaways, 5x7-1/4", 36 pgs.)
Walt Disney Productions

"New Adventures of Robin Hood", "Ghosts of Waylea Castle", & "The Miller's Ransom" each.... 4.25 13.00 26.00

ROBIN HOOD (Adventures of... #7, 8)
No. 52, Nov, 1955 - No. 6, June, 1957
Magazine Enterprises (Sussex Publ. Co.)

52 (#1)-Origin Robin Hood & Sir Gallant of the Round Table 13.00 39.00 105.00
53 (#2), 3-6: 6-Richard Greene photo-c (TV) 9.50 28.00 75.00
I.W. Reprint #1,2,9: 1-r/#3. 2-r/#4. 9-r/#52 (1963) 1.85 5.50 15.00
Super Reprint #10,15: 10-r/#53. 15-r/#5 1.85 5.50 15.00
NOTE: ***Bolle*** *a-in all; c-52.* ***Powell*** *a-6.*

ROBIN HOOD (Not Disney)
May-July, 1963 (one-shot)
Dell Publishing Co.

1 1.65 5.00 18.00

ROBIN HOOD (Disney)
1973 ($1.50, 8-1/2x11", 52 pgs., cardboard-c)
Western Publishing Co.

96151- "Robin Hood", based on movie, 96152- "The Mystery of Sherwood Forest", 96153- "In King Richard's Service", 96154- "The Wizard's Ring" each.... 1.60 4.00

ROBIN HOOD
July, 1991 - No. 3, 1991 ($2.50, limited series)
Eclipse Comics

1-3: Timothy Truman layouts 1.00 2.50

ROBIN HOOD AND HIS MERRY MEN (Formerly Danger & Adventure)
No. 28, Apr, 1956 - No. 38, Aug, 1958
Charlton Comics

28 7.15 21.50 50.00

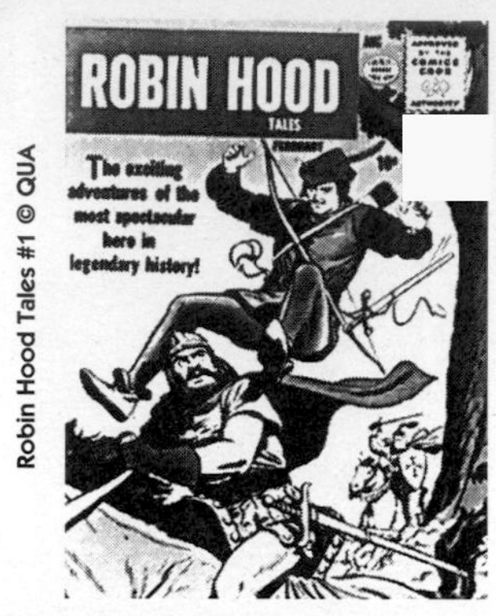

Robin Hood Tales #1 © QUA

Robin III #3 © DC

Robocop 2 #1 © Orion Pictures

	GD25	FN65	NM94
29-37	5.70	17.00	40.00
38-Ditko-a (5 pgs.); Rocke-c	10.50	32.00	85.00

ROBIN HOOD'S FRONTIER DAYS (...Western Tales, Adventures of... #1)
No date (Circa 1955) 20 pgs., slick-c (Seven issues?)
Shoe Store Giveaway (Robin Hood Stores)

	GD25	FN65	NM94
nn	4.25	13.00	28.00
nn-Issues with Crandall-a	6.85	21.00	48.00

ROBIN HOOD TALES (Published by National Periodical #7 on)
Feb, 1956 - No. 6, Nov-Dec, 1956
Quality Comics Group (Comic Magazines)

	GD25	FN65	NM94
1-All have Baker/Cuidera-c	26.00	80.00	210.00
2-6-Matt Baker-a	25.00	75.00	200.00

ROBIN HOOD TALES (Cont'd from Quality series)(See Brave & the Bold #5)
No. 7, Jan-Feb, 1957 - No. 14, Mar-Apr, 1958
National Periodical Publications

	GD25	FN65	NM94
7-All have Andru/Esposito-c	25.00	75.00	250.00
8-14	20.00	60.00	200.00

ROBINSON CRUSOE (See King Classics & Power Record Comics)
Nov-Jan, 1963-64
Dell Publishing Co.

	GD25	FN65	NM94
1	1.00	3.00	8.00

ROBIN II (The Joker's Wild)
Oct, 1991 - No. 4, Dec, 1991 ($1.50, mini-series)
DC Comics

	GD25	FN65	NM94
1-(Direct sales, $1.50)-With 4 different-c; same hologram on each			1.50
1-(Newsstand, $1.00)-No hologram; 1 version			1.00
1-Collector's set ($10.00)-Contains all 5 versions bagged with hologram trading card inside	1.25	3.75	10.00
2-(Direct sales, $1.50)-With 3 different-c			1.50
2-4-(Newsstand, $1.00)-1 version of each			1.00
2-Collector's set ($8.00)-Contains all 4 versions bagged with hologram trading card inside	1.00	3.00	8.00
3-(Direct sale, $1.50)-With 2 different-c			1.50
3-Collector's set ($6.00)-Contains all 3 versions bagged with hologram trading card inside		2.40	6.00
4-(Direct sales, $1.50)-Only one version			1.50
4-Collector's set ($4.00)-Contains both versions bagged with Bat-Signal hologram trading card		1.60	4.00
Multi-pack (All four issues w/hologram sticker)		1.60	4.00
Deluxe Complete Set ($30.00)-Contains all 14 versions of #1-4 plus a new hologram trading card; numbered & limited to 25,000; comes with slipcase & 2 acid free backing boards	3.00	9.00	30.00

ROBIN III: CRY OF THE HUNTRESS
Dec, 1992 - No. 6, Mar, 1993 (Limited series)
DC Comics

	GD25	FN65	NM94
1-6 ($2.50, collector's ed.)-Polybagged w/movement enhanced-c plus mini-poster of newsstand-c by Zeck		1.00	2.50
1-6 ($1.25, newsstand ed.): All have Zeck-c			1.25

ROBIN 3000
1992 - No. 2, 1992 ($4.95, mini-series, 52 pgs.)
DC Comics (Elseworlds)

	GD25	FN65	NM94
1,2-Foil logo; Russell-c/a		2.00	5.00

ROBOCOP
Oct, 1987 ($2.00, B&W, magazine, one-shot)
Marvel Comics

	GD25	FN65	NM94
1-Movie adaptation		.80	2.00

ROBOCOP (Also see Dark Horse Comics)
Mar, 1990 - No. 23, Jan, 1992 ($1.50)
Marvel Comics

	GD25	FN65	NM94
1-Based on movie		1.20	3.00
2-6		.80	2.00
7-23			1.50
nn (7/90, $4.95, 52 pgs.)-r/B&W magazine in color; adapts 1st movie		2.00	5.00

ROBOCOP: MORTAL COILS
Sept, 1993 - No. 4, Dec, 1993 ($2.50, limited series)
Dark Horse Comics

	GD25	FN65	NM94
1-4: 1,2-Cago painted-c		1.00	2.50

ROBOCOP: PRIME SUSPECT
Oct, 1992 - No. 4, Jan, 1993 ($2.50, limited series)
Dark Horse Comics

	GD25	FN65	NM94
1-4: 1,3-Nelson painted-c. 2,4-Bolton painted-c		1.00	2.50

ROBOCOP: ROULETTE
Dec, 1993 - No. 4, 1994 ($2.50, limited series)
Dark Horse Comics

	GD25	FN65	NM94
1-4: 1,3-Nelson painted-c. 2,4-Bolton painted-c		1.00	2.50

ROBOCOP 2
Aug, 1990 ($2.25, B&W, magazine, 68 pgs.)
Marvel Comics

	GD25	FN65	NM94
1-Adapts movie sequel		.90	2.25

ROBOCOP 2
Aug, 1990; Late Aug, 1990 - #3, Late Sept, 1990 ($1.00, limited series)
Marvel Comics

	GD25	FN65	NM94
nn-(8/90, $4.95, 68 pgs., color)-Same contents as B&W magazine		2.00	5.00
1: #1-3 reprint no number issue		1.20	3.00
2,3: 2-Guice-c(i)			1.50

ROBOCOP 3
July, 1993 - No. 3, Nov, 1993 ($2.50, limited series)
Dark Horse Comics

	GD25	FN65	NM94
1-3: Nelson painted-c; Nguyen-a(p)		1.00	2.50

ROBOCOP VERSUS THE TERMINATOR
Sept, 1992 - No. 4, 1992 (Dec.) ($2.50, limited series)
Dark Horse Comics

	GD25	FN65	NM94
1-4: Miller scripts & Simonson-c/a in all		1.00	2.50
1-Platinum Edition	1.25	3.75	10.00

NOTE: *All contain a different Robocop cardboard cut-out stand-up.*

ROBO-HUNTER (Also see Sam Slade...)
Apr, 1984 - No. 6, 1984 ($1.00)
Eagle Comics

	GD25	FN65	NM94
1-6-2000 A.D.			1.00

R.O.B.O.T. BATTALION 2050
Mar, 1988 ($2.00, B&W, one-shot)
Eclipse Comics

	GD25	FN65	NM94
1		.80	2.00

ROBOT COMICS
No. 0, June, 1987 ($2.00, B&W, one-shot)
Renegade Press

	GD25	FN65	NM94
0-Bob Burden story & art		.80	2.00

ROBOTECH
Mar, 1997 - Present ($2.95)
Antarctic Press

	GD25	FN65	NM94
1-4			2.95

ROBOTECH DEFENDERS
Mar, 1985 - No. 2, Apr, 1985 (Mini-series)

Robotech: The Macross Saga #4 © Comico

Rocketeer Adventure Magazine #3 © Dave Stevens

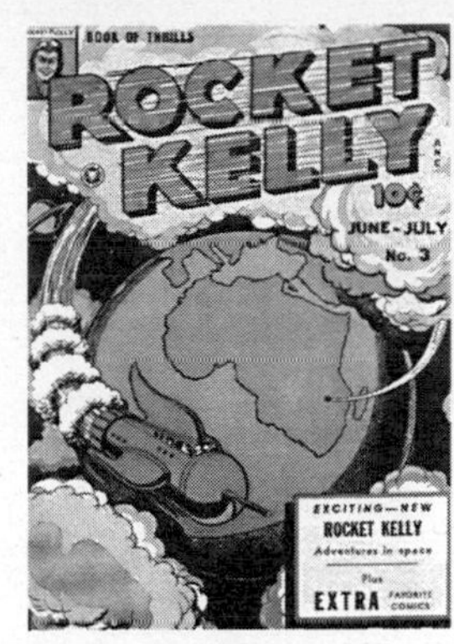

Rocket Kelly #3 © FOX

GD25 FN65 NM94

DC Comics
1,2 — 1.00

ROBOTECH IN 3-D (TV)
Aug, 1987 ($2.50)
Comico
1-Steacy painted-c — 1.00 2.50

ROBOTECH MASTERS (TV)
July, 1985 - No. 23, Apr, 1988 ($1.50)
Comico
1 — 1.00 2.50
2-23 — .80 2.00

ROBOTECH SPECIAL
May, 1988 ($2.50, one-shot, 44 pgs.)
Comico
1-Steacy wraparound-c; partial photo-c — 1.00 2.50

ROBOTECH THE GRAPHIC NOVEL
Aug, 1986 ($5.95, 8-1/2x11", 52pgs.)
Comico
1-Origin SDF-1; intro T.R. Edwards, Steacy-c/a; 2nd printing also exists (12/86). — 2.40 6.00

ROBOTECH: THE MACROSS SAGA (TV)(Formerly Macross)
No. 2, Feb, 1985 - No. 36, Feb, 1989 ($1.50)
Comico
2-10 — 1.00 2.50
11-36: 12,17-Ken Steacy painted-c. 26-Begin $1.75-c. 35,36-($1.95) — .80 2.00

ROBOTECH: THE NEW GENERATION
July, 1985 - No. 25, July, 1988
Comico
1-25 — .80 2.00

ROBOTECH: VERMILION
Mar, 1997 - No. 4, ($2.95, B&W, limited series)
Antarctic Press
1-3 — 2.95

ROBOTIX
Feb, 1986 (75¢, one-shot)
Marvel Comics
1-Based on toy — 1.00

ROBOTMEN OF THE LOST PLANET (Also see Space Thrillers)
1952 (Also see Strange Worlds #19)
Avon Periodicals
1-McCann-a (3 pgs.); Fawcette-a — 81.00 243.00 700.00

ROB ROY
1954 (Disney-Movie)
Dell Publishing Co.
Four Color 544-Manning-a, photo-c — 7.00 22.00 80.00

ROCK & ROLL HIGH SCHOOL
Oct, 1995 ($2.50)
Roger Corman's Cosmic Comics
1-Bob Fingerman scripts — 1.00 2.50

ROCK AND ROLLO (Formerly TV Teens)
V2#14, Oct, 1957 - No. 19, Sept, 1958
Charlton Comics
V2#14-19 — 4.00 12.00 24.00

ROCKET COMICS
Mar, 1940 - No. 3, May, 1940
Hillman Periodicals
1-Rocket Riley, Red Roberts the Electro Man (origin), The Phantom Ranger, The Steel Shark, The Defender, Buzzard Barnes and his Sky Devils, Lefty Larson, & The Defender, the Man with a Thousand Faces begin (1st app. of each); all have Rocket Riley-c — 189.00 567.00 1700.00
2,3 — 100.00 300.00 900.00

ROCKETEER, THE (See Eclipse Graphic Album Series, Pacific Presents & Starslayer)

ROCKETEER ADVENTURE MAGAZINE, THE
July, 1988 ($2.00); No. 2, July, 1989 ($2.75); No. 3, Jan, 1995 ($2.95)
Comico/Dark Horse Comics No. 3
1-(7/88, $2.00)-Dave Stevens-c/a in all; Kaluta back-up-a; 1st app. Jonas (character based on The Shadow) — 1.25 3.75 10.00
2-(6/88, $2.75)-Stevens/Dorman painted-c — 1.00 2.80 7.00
3-(1/95, $2.95)-Includes pinups by Stevens, Gulacy, Plunkett, & Mignola — 3.00
Volume 2-(9/96, $9.95, magazine size TPB)-Reprints #1-3 — 10.00

ROCKETEER SPECIAL EDITION, THE
Nov, 1984 ($1.50, Baxter paper)(Chapter 5 of Rocketeer serial)
Eclipse Comics
1-Stevens-c/a; Kaluta back-c; pin-ups inside — 1.50 4.50 12.00
NOTE: *Originally intended to be published in Pacific Presents.*

ROCKETEER: THE OFFICIAL MOVIE ADAPTATION, THE
1991
W. D. Publications (Disney)
nn-($5.95, 68 pgs.)-Squarebound deluxe edition — 2.40 6.00
nn-($2.95, 68 pgs.)-Stapled regular edition — 1.20 3.00
3-D Comic Book (1991, $7.98, 52 pgs.) — 1.00 3.00 8.00

ROCKET KELLY (See The Bouncer, Green Mask #10); becomes Li'l Pan #6)
1944; Fall, 1945 - No. 5, Oct-Nov, 1946
Fox Feature Syndicate
nn (1944) — 22.00 66.00 175.00
1 — 22.00 66.00 175.00
2-The Puppeteer app. (costumed hero) — 17.50 53.00 140.00
3-5: 5-(#5 on cover, #4 inside) — 15.50 47.00 125.00

ROCKETMAN (Strange Fantasy #2 on) (See Hello Pal & Scoop Comics)
June, 1952 (Strange Stories of the Future)
Ajax/Farrell Publications
1-Rocketman & Cosmo — 37.00 111.00 280.00

ROCKET RACCOON
May, 1995 - No. 4, Aug, 1985 (color, limited series)
Marvel Comics
1-4: Mignola-a — 1.50

ROCKETS AND RANGE RIDERS
May, 1957 (Giveaway, 16 pgs., soft-c)
Richfield Oil Corp.
nn-Toth-a — 15.00 45.00 120.00

ROCKET SHIP X
September, 1951; 1952
Fox Features Syndicate
1 — 51.00 155.00 435.00
1952 (nn, nd, no publ.)-Edited 1951-c — 38.00 114.00 280.00

ROCKET TO ADVENTURE LAND (See Pixie Puzzle...)

ROCKET TO THE MOON
1951
Avon Periodicals
nn-Orlando-c/a; adapts Otis Aldebert Kline's "Maza of the Moon" — 85.00 256.00 725.00

ROCK FANTASY COMICS

Rock N Roll Comics #18 © Revolutionary

Rocko's Modern Life #4 © Nickelodeon

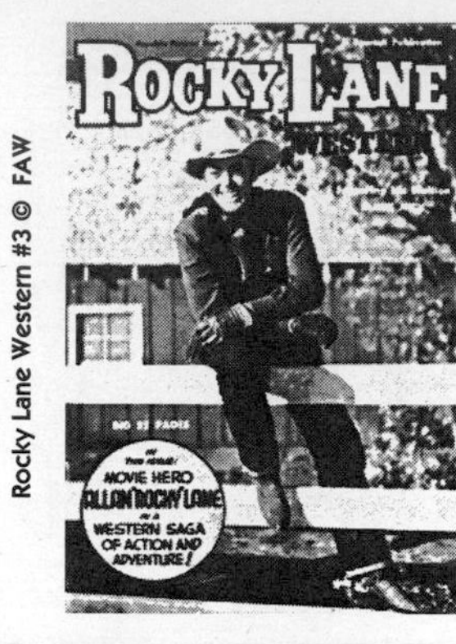

Rocky Lane Western #3 © FAW

GD25 FN65 NM94

Dec, 1989 - No. 16?, 1991 ($2.25/$3.00, B&W)(No cover price)
Rock Fantasy Comics

1-Pink Floyd part 1 1.00 2.50
1-2nd printing ($3.00-c) 1.20 3.00
2,3: 2-Rolling Stones #1. 3-Led Zeppelin #1 1.20 3.00
2,3: 2nd printings ($3.00-c, 1/90 & 2/90) 1.20 3.00
4-Stevie Nicks Not published
5-Monstrosities of Rock #1; photo back-c 1.00 2.50
5-2nd printing ($3.00, 3/90 indicia, 2/90-c) 1.20 3.00
6-15,17,18: 6-Guns n' Roses #1 (1st & 2nd printings, 3/90)-Begin $3.00-c. 7-Sex Pistols #1. 8-Alice Cooper; not published. 9-Van Halen #1; photo back-c. 10-Kiss #1; photo back-c. 11-Jimi Hendrix #1; wraparound-c 1.20 3.00
16-($5.00, 68 pgs.)-The Great Gig in the Sky(Floyd) 2.00 5.00

ROCK HAPPENING (Harvey Pop Comics:...)(See Bunny)
Sept, 1969 - No. 2, Nov, 1969
Harvey Publications

1,2: Featuring Bunny 2.00 6.00 20.00

ROCK N' ROLL COMICS
June, 1989 - No. 24?, 1992 ($1.50/$1.95, B&W/color #15 on)
Revolutionary Comics

1-Guns N' Roses .80 2.00
1-2nd thru 6th printings 1.50
1-7th printing (full color w/new-c/a; $1.95) .80 2.00
2-Metallica .80 2.00
2-2nd thru 6th printings (6th in color) 1.50
3-Bon Jovi (no reprints) .80 2.00
4-8,10-24: 4-Motley Crue(2nd printing only, 1st destroyed). 5-Def Leppard (2 printings). 6-Rolling Stones(4 printings). 7-The Who(3 printings). 8-Skid Row; not published. 10-Warrant/Whitesnake(2 printings; 1st has 2 diff.-c). 11-Aerosmith (2 printings?). 12-New Kids on the Block(2 printings). 12-3rd printing; rewritten & titled NKOTB Hate Book. 13-Led Zeppelin. 14-Sex Pistols. 15-Poison; 1st color issue. 16-Van Halen. 17-Madonna. 18-Alice Cooper. 19-Public Enemy/2 Live Crew. 20-Queensryche/Tesla. 21-Prince? 22-AC/DC; begin $2.50-c. 23-Living Colour. 24-Anthrax 1.00 2.50
9-Kiss 1.60 4.00
9-2nd & 3rd printings .80 2.00

NOTE: *Most issues were reprinted except #3. Later reprints are in color. #8 was not released.*

ROCKO'S MODERN LIFE (TV)
June, 1994 - No. 7, Dec, 1994 ($1.95) (Nickelodeon cartoon)
Marvel Comics

1-7 .80 2.00

ROCKY AND HIS FIENDISH FRIENDS (TV)(Bullwinkle)
Oct, 1962 - No. 5, Sept, 1963 (Jay Ward)
Gold Key

1 (25¢, 80 pgs.) 20.00 60.00 220.00
2,3 (25¢, 80 pgs.) 14.00 42.00 155.00
4,5 (Regular size, 12¢) 9.00 29.00 105.00

ROCKY AND HIS FRIENDS (See Kite Fun Book & March of Comics #216)

ROCKY AND HIS FRIENDS (TV)
No. 1128, 8-10/60 - No.1311,1962 (Jay Ward)
Dell Publishing Co.

Four Color #1128 (#1) (8-10/60) 36.00 109.00 400.00
Four Color #1152 (12-2/61), 1166, 1208, 1275, 1311('62) 23.00 68.00 250.00

ROCKY HORROR PICTURE SHOW THE COMIC BOOK, THE
July, 1990 - No. 3, 1990 ($2.95, mini-series, 52 pgs.)(Photo-c #1)
Caliber Press

1-Adapts cult film plus photos, etc. 1.20 3.00
1-2nd printing 1.20 3.00
2,3 1.20 3.00

GD25 FN65 NM94

...Collection ($4.95) 2.00 5.00

ROCKY JONES SPACE RANGER (See Space Adventures #15-18)

ROCKY JORDEN PRIVATE EYE (See Private Eye)

ROCKY LANE WESTERN (Allan Rocky Lane starred in Republic movies & TV (for a short time as Allan Lane, Red Ryder & Rocky Lane) (See Black Jack Fawcett Movie Comics, Motion Picture Comics & Six-Gun Heroes)
May, 1949 - No. 87, Nov, 1959
Fawcett Publications/Charlton No. 56 on

1 (36 pgs.)-Rocky, his stallion Black Jack, & Slim Pickens begin; photo-c begin, end #57; photo back-c 83.00 250.00 750.00
2 (36 pgs.)-Last photo back-c 36.00 108.00 300.00
3-5 (52 pgs.): 4-Captain Tootsie by Beck 24.00 71.00 190.00
6,10 (36 pgs.): 10-Complete western novelette "Badman's Reward" 17.50 53.00 140.00
7-9 (52 pgs.) 19.00 56.00 150.00
11-13,15-17 (52 pgs.): 15-Black Jack's Hitching Post begins, ends #25 14.00 41.00 110.00
14,18 (36 pgs.) 11.30 34.00 90.00
19-21,23,24 (52 pgs.): 20-Last Slim Pickens. 21-Dee Dickens begins, ends #55,57,65-68 11.30 34.00 90.00
22,25-28,30 (36 pgs. begin) 10.50 32.00 85.00
29-Classic complete novel "The Land of Missing Men" with hidden land of ancient temple ruins (r-in #65) 15.00 45.00 120.00
31-40 9.50 28.00 75.00
41-54 8.75 26.25 65.00
55-Last Fawcett issue (1/54) 8.75 26.25 70.00
56-1st Charlton issue (2/54)-Photo-c 15.00 45.00 120.00
57,60-Photo-c 8.75 26.25 70.00
58,59,61-64: 59-61-Young Falcon app. 64-Slim Pickens app. 7.15 21.50 50.00
65-r/#29, "The Land of Missing Men" 8.50 26.00 60.00
66-68: Reprints #30,31,32 7.15 21.50 50.00
69-78,80-86 7.15 21.50 50.00
79-Giant Edition (68 pgs.) 8.50 26.00 60.00
87-Last issue 8.50 26.00 60.00

NOTE: *Complete novels in #10, 14, 18, 22, 25, 30-32, 36, 38, 39, 49. Captain Tootsie in #4, 12, 20. Big Bow and Little Arrow in #11, 28, 63. Black Jack's Hitching Post in #15-25, 64, 73.*

ROCKY LANE WESTERN
1989 ($2.50, B&W, one-shot?)
AC Comics

1-Photo-c; Giordano reprints 1.00 2.50
Annual 1 (1991, $2.95, B&W, 44 pgs.)-photo front/back & inside-c; reprints. 1.20 3.00

ROD CAMERON WESTERN (Movie star)
Feb, 1950 - No. 20, Apr, 1953
Fawcett Publications

1-Rod Cameron, his horse War Paint, & Sam The Sheriff begin; photo front/back-c begin 44.00 132.00 400.00
2 23.00 68.00 180.00
3-Novel length story "The Mystery of the Seven Cities of Cibola" 19.00 56.00 150.00
4-10: 9-Last photo back-c 15.00 45.00 120.00
11-19 12.00 36.00 95.00
20-Last issue & photo-c 12.00 38.00 100.00

NOTE: *Novel length stories in No. 1-8, 12-14.*

RODEO RYAN (See A-1 Comics #8)

ROEL
Feb, 1997 ($2.95, B&W, one-shot)
Sirius

1 2.95

ROGAN GOSH

Roly Poly Comic Book #10 © Green Publ.

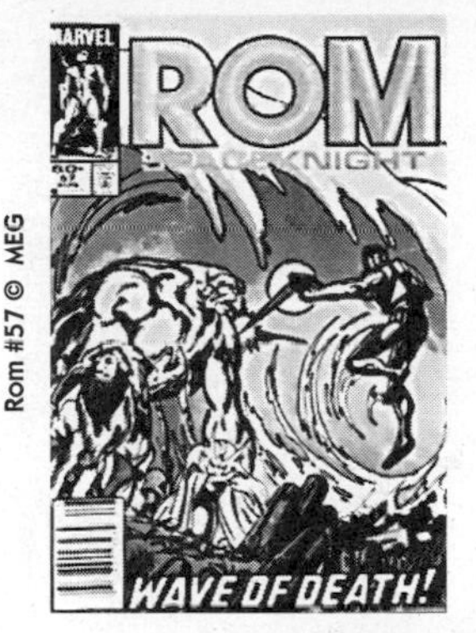

Rom #57 © MEG

Romance and Confession Stories #1 © STJ

1994 ($6.95, one-shot)
DC Comics (Vertigo)

	GD25	FN65	NM94
nn-Peter Milligan scripts	1.00	2.80	7.00

ROGER DODGER (Also in Exciting Comics #57 on)
No. 5, Aug, 1952
Standard Comics

	GD25	FN65	NM94
5-Teen-age	4.00	12.00	24.00

ROGER RABBIT (Also see Marvel Graphic Novel)
June, 1990 - No. 18, Nov, 1991 ($1.50)
Disney Comics

	GD25	FN65	NM94
1-18-All new stories			1.50
In 3-D 1 (1992, $2.50)-Sold at Wal-Mart?; w/glasses		1.00	2.50

ROGER RABBIT'S TOONTOWN
Aug, 1991 - No. 5, Dec, 1991 ($1.50)
Disney Comics

	GD25	FN65	NM94
1-5			1.50

ROGER ZELANY'S AMBER: THE GUNS OF AVALON
1996 - No. 3, 1996 ($6.95, limited series)
DC Comics

	GD25	FN65	NM94
1-3: Based on novel	1.00	2.80	7.00

ROG 2000
June, 1982 ($2.95, one-shot)
Pacific Comics

	GD25	FN65	NM94
nn-Byrne-c/a (r); 2nd printing (7/82) exists		1.20	3.00

ROG 2000
1987 - No. 2, 1987 ($2.00, limited series)
Fantagraphics Books

	GD25	FN65	NM94
1,2-Byrne-r		.80	2.00

ROGUE
Jan, 1995 - No. 4, Apr, 1995 ($2.95, limited series)
Marvel Comics

	GD25	FN65	NM94
1-4: 1-Gold foil logo		1.40	3.50
TPB-($12.95) r/#1-4	1.60	4.85	13.00

ROGUES GALLERY
1996 ($3.50, one-shot)
DC Comics

	GD25	FN65	NM94
1-Pinups of DC villains by various artists		1.40	3.50

ROGUE TROOPER
Oct, 1986 - No. 49, 1991 ($1.25/$1.50/$1.75)
Quality Comics/Fleetway Quality #38-on

	GD25	FN65	NM94
1-19:($1.25). 6-Double size			1.25
20-38- ($1.50): 21,22,25-27-Guice-c			1.50
39-49 ($1.75): 47,48-Alan Moore scripts		.70	1.75

ROLY POLY COMIC BOOK
1945 - No. 15, 1946 (MLJ reprints)
Green Publishing Co.

	GD25	FN65	NM94
1-Red Rube & Steel Sterling begin; Sahle-c	22.00	66.00	175.00
6-The Blue Circle & The Steel Fist app.	12.00	36.00	95.00
10-Origin Red Rube retold; Steel Sterling story (Zip #41)	11.30	34.00	90.00
11,12,14: The Black Hood app. in each. 14-Decapitation-c	13.00	39.00	105.00
15-The Blue Circle & The Steel Fist app.; cover exact swipe from Fox Blue Beetle #1	26.00	80.00	210.00

ROM (Based on toy)
Dec, 1979 - No. 75, Feb, 1986
Marvel Comics Group

	GD25	FN65	NM94
1-16,19-24,26-30: Based on a Parker Bros. toy; 1-Origin/1st app. 13-Saga of the Space Knights begins. 19-X-Men cameo. 24-F.F. cameo; Skrulls, Nova & The New Champions app. 26,27-Galactus app.			1.00
17,18-X-Men app.			1.50
25-Double size			1.20
31-60: 31,32-Brotherhood of Evil Mutants app. 32-X-Men cameo. 34,35-Sub-Mariner app. 41,42-Dr. Strange app. 50-Skrulls app. (52 pgs.). 56,57-Alpha Flight app. 58,59-Ant-Man app.			1.00
61-75: 65-West Coast Avengers & Beta Ray Bill app. 65,66-X-Men app.		.80	2.00
Annual 1,4: 1(1982, 52 pgs.). 4(1985, 52 pgs.)			1.20
Annual 2,3: 2(1983, 52 pgs.). 3(1984, 52 pgs.)			1.00

NOTE: ***Austin*** *c-3i, 18i, 61i.* ***Byrne*** *a-74i; c-56, 57, 74.* ***Ditko*** *a-59-75p, Annual 4.* ***Golden*** *c-7-12, 19.* ***Guice*** *a-61i; c-55, 58, 60p, 70p.* ***Layton*** *a-59i, 72i; c-15, 59i, 69.* ***Miller*** *c-2p?, 3p, 17p, 18p.* ***Russell*** *a(i)-64, 65, 67, 69, 71, 75; c-64, 65i, 66, 71i, 75.* ***Severin*** *c-41p.* ***Sienkiewicz*** *a-53i; c-46, 47, 52-54, 68, 71p, Annual 2.* ***Simonson*** *c-18.* ***P. Smith*** *c-59p.* ***Starlin*** *c-67.* ***Zeck*** *c-50.*

ROMANCE (See True Stories of...)

ROMANCE AND CONFESSION STORIES (See Giant Comics Edition)
No date (1949) (25¢, 100 pgs.)
St. John Publishing Co.

	GD25	FN65	NM94
1-Baker-c/a; remaindered St. John love comics	34.00	101.00	250.00

ROMANCE DIARY
Dec, 1949 - No. 2, Mar, 1950
Marvel Comics (CDS)(CLDS)

	GD25	FN65	NM94
1,2	10.00	30.00	70.00

ROMANCE OF FLYING, THE
1942
David McKay Publications

	GD25	FN65	NM94
Feature Books 33 (nn)-WW II photos	11.30	34.00	90.00

ROMANCES OF MOLLY MANTON (See Molly Manton)

ROMANCES OF NURSE HELEN GRANT, THE
Aug, 1957
Atlas Comics (VPI)

	GD25	FN65	NM94
1	5.35	16.00	32.00

ROMANCES OF THE WEST (Becomes Romantic Affairs #3?)
Nov, 1949 - No. 2, Mar, 1950 (52 pgs.)
Marvel Comics (SPC)

	GD25	FN65	NM94
1-Movie photo-c of Yvonne DeCarlo & Howard Duff (Calamity Jane & Sam Bass)	18.00	54.00	130.00
2-Photo-c	12.00	35.00	90.00

ROMANCE STORIES OF TRUE LOVE (Formerly True Love Problems & Advice Illustrated)
No. 45, 5/57 - No. 50, 3/58; No. 51, 9/58 - No. 52, 11/58
Harvey Publications

	GD25	FN65	NM94
45-51: 45,46,48-50-Powell-a	4.00	10.00	20.00
52-Matt Baker-a	5.70	17.00	38.00

ROMANCE TALES (Formerly Western Winners #6?)
No. 7, Oct, 1949 - No. 9, Mar, 1950 (7,8: photo-c)
Marvel Comics (CDS)

	GD25	FN65	NM94
7	10.00	30.00	70.00
8,9: 8-Everett-a	7.50	22.50	50.00

ROMANCE TRAIL
July-Aug, 1949 - No. 6, May-June, 1950 (All photo-c & 52 pgs.)
National Periodical Publications

	GD25	FN65	NM94
1-Kinstler, Toth-a; Jimmy Wakely photo-c	50.00	150.00	420.00
2-Kinstler-a; Jim Bannon photo-c	26.00	79.00	190.00
3-Photo-c; Kinstler, Toth-a	29.00	86.00	210.00
4-Photo-c; Toth-a	22.00	66.00	160.00
5,6: Photo-c on both. 5-Kinstler-a	19.00	56.00	140.00

Romantic Adventures #32 © ACG

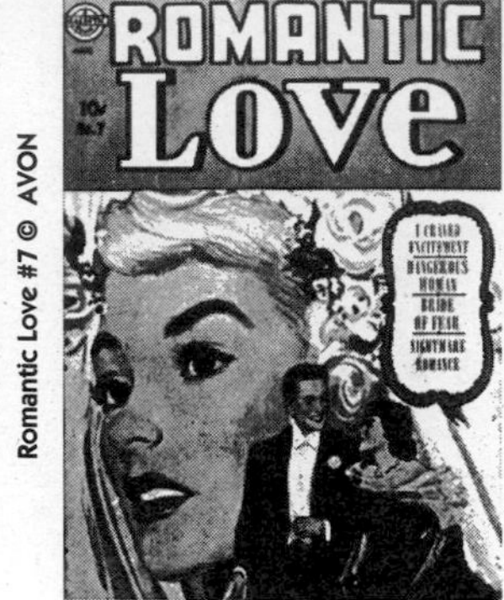

Romantic Love #7 © AVON

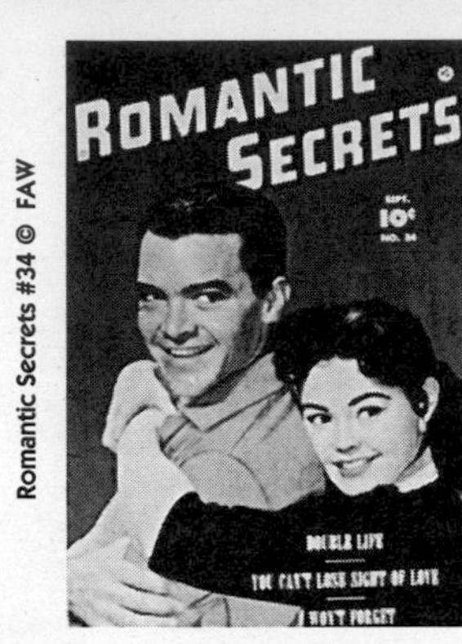

Romantic Secrets #34 © FAW

ROMAN HOLIDAYS, THE (TV)
Feb, 1973 - No. 4, Nov, 1973 (Hanna-Barbera)
Gold Key

	GD25	FN65	NM94
1	2.75	8.00	30.00
2-4	1.65	5.00	18.00

ROMANTIC ADVENTURES (My... #49-67, covers only)
Mar-Apr, 1949 - No. 67, July, 1956 (Becomes My... #68 on)
American Comics Group (B&I Publ. Co.)

	GD25	FN65	NM94
1	12.00	36.00	95.00
2	6.85	21.00	48.00
3-10	5.00	15.00	30.00
11-20 (4/52)	4.15	12.50	25.00
21-45,49,51,52: 52-Last Pre-code (2/55)	4.00	10.00	20.00
46-48-3-D effect-c/stories (TrueVision)	8.50	26.00	60.00
50-Classic cover/story "Love of A Lunatic"	6.50	19.50	45.00
53-67	2.60	6.50	13.00

NOTE: *#1-23, 52 pgs.* ***Shelly*** *a-40. Whitney c/art in many issues.*

ROMANTIC AFFAIRS (Formerly Molly Manton's Romances #2 and/or Romances of the West #2 and/or Our Love #2?)
No. 3, Mar, 1950
Marvel Comics (SPC)

	GD25	FN65	NM94
3-Photo-c from Molly Manton's Romances #2	6.50	19.50	45.00

ROMANTIC CONFESSIONS
Oct, 1949 - V3#1, Apr-May, 1953
Hillman Periodicals

	GD25	FN65	NM94
V1#1-McWilliams-a	11.00	33.00	80.00
2-Briefer-a; negligee panels	7.00	21.00	45.00
3-12	5.00	15.00	30.00
V2#1,2,4-8,10-12: 2-McWilliams-a	4.15	12.50	25.00
3-Krigstein-a	7.00	21.00	45.00
9-One pg. Frazetta ad	4.00	12.00	24.00
V3#1	4.00	12.00	24.00

ROMANTIC HEARTS
Mar, 1951 - No. 10, Oct, 1952; July, 1953 - No. 12, July, 1955
Story Comics/Master/Merit Pubs.

	GD25	FN65	NM94
1(3/51) (1st Series)	10.00	30.00	70.00
2	5.70	17.00	35.00
3-10: Cameron-a	4.25	13.00	28.00
1(7/53) (2nd Series)-Some say #11 on-c	6.70	20.00	40.00
2	4.00	12.00	24.00
3-12	4.00	10.00	20.00

ROMANTIC LOVE
9-10/49 - #3, 1-2/50; #4, 2-3/51 - #13, 10/52; #20, 3-4/54 - #23, 9-10/54
Avon Periodicals/Realistic (No #14-19)

	GD25	FN65	NM94
1-c-/Avon paperback #252	18.00	54.00	130.00
2-5: 3-c-/paperback Novel Library #12. 4-c-/paperback Diversey Prize Novel #5. 5-c-/paperback Novel Library #34	11.00	33.00	80.00
6- "Thrill Crazy" marijuana story; c-/Avon paperback #207; Kinstler-a	14.00	41.00	110.00
7,8: 8-Astarita-a(2)	10.00	30.00	70.00
9-12: 9-c-/paperback Novel Library #41; Kinstler-a. 10-c-/Avon paperback #212. 11-c-/paperback Novel Library #17; Kinstler-a. 12-c-/paperback Novel Library #13	11.00	33.00	80.00
13,21,22: 22-Kinstler-c	10.00	30.00	70.00
20-Kinstler-c/a	10.00	30.00	70.00
23-Kinstler-c	8.35	25.00	55.00
nn(1-3/53)(Realistic-r)	7.50	22.50	50.00

NOTE: ***Astarita*** *a-7, 10, 11, 21. Painted c-1-3, 5, 7-11, 13. Photo c-4, 6.*

ROMANTIC LOVE
No. 4, June, 1950
Quality Comics Group

	GD25	FN65	NM94
4 (6/50)(Exist?)	5.70	17.00	35.00
I.W. Reprint #2,3,8: 2-r/Romantic Love #2		2.40	6.00

ROMANTIC MARRIAGE (Cinderella Love #25 on)
#1-3 (1950, no months); #4, 5-6/51 - #17, 9/52; #18, 9/53 - #24, 9/54
Ziff-Davis/St. John No. 18 on (#1-8: 52 pgs.)

	GD25	FN65	NM94
1-Photo-c; Cary Grant/Betsy Drake photo back-c.	14.00	43.00	110.00
2-Painted-c; Anderson-a (also #15)	9.00	27.00	60.00
3-9: 3,4,8,9-Painted-c; 5-7-Photo-c	7.50	22.50	50.00
10-Unusual format; front-c is a painted-c; back-c is a photo-c complete with logo, price, etc.	13.00	39.00	100.00
11-17 13-Photo-c. 15-Signed story by Anderson. 17-(9/52)-Last Z-D issue	6.50	19.50	45.00
18-22,24: 20-Photo-c	6.50	19.50	45.00
23-Baker-c; all stories are reprinted from #15	7.15	21.50	50.00

ROMANTIC PICTURE NOVELETTES
1946
Magazine Enterprises

	GD25	FN65	NM94
1-Mary Worth-r; Creig Flessel-c	13.00	39.00	90.00

ROMANTIC SECRETS (Becomes Time For Love)
Sept, 1949 - No. 39, 4/53; No. 5, 10/55 - No. 52, 11/64 (#1-5: photo-c)
Fawcett/Charlton Comics No. 5 (10/55) on

	GD25	FN65	NM94
1-(52 pg. issues begin, end #?)	10.50	32.00	85.00
2,3	6.50	19.50	45.00
4,9-Evans-a	7.15	21.50	50.00
5-8,10	5.00	15.00	30.00
11-23	4.25	13.00	28.00
24-Evans-a	5.70	17.00	38.00
25-39('53)	4.00	11.00	22.00
5 (Charlton, 2nd Series)(10/55, formerly Negro Romances #4)	6.50	19.50	45.00
6-10	4.15	12.50	30.00
11-20	2.50	7.50	20.00
21-35: Last 10¢ issue?	1.85	5.50	15.00
36-52('64)	1.25	3.75	10.00

NOTE: ***Bailey*** *a-20.* ***Powell*** *a(1st series)-5, 7, 10, 12, 16, 17, 20, 26, 29, 33, 34, 36, 37.* ***Sekowsky*** *a-26. Photo c(1st series)-1-5, 16, 25, 27, 33.* ***Swayze*** *a(1st series)-16, 18, 19, 23, 26-28, 31, 32, 39.*

ROMANTIC STORY (Cowboy Love #28 on)
11/49 - #22, Sum, 1953; #23, 5/54 - #27, 12/54; #28, 8/55 - #130, 11/73
Fawcett/Charlton Comics No. 23 on

	GD25	FN65	NM94
1-Photo-c begin, end #24; 52 pgs. begins	11.30	34.00	90.00
2	6.50	19.50	45.00
3-5	5.70	17.00	40.00
6-14	5.00	15.00	30.00
15-Evans-a	5.70	17.00	40.00
16-22(Sum, '53; last Fawcett issue). 21-Toth-a?	4.00	11.00	22.00
23-39: 26,29-Wood swipes	4.00	11.00	22.00
40-(100 pgs.)	7.15	21.50	50.00
41-50	1.85	5.50	15.00
51-80: 57-Hypo needle story	1.25	3.75	10.00
81-100	1.00	3.00	8.00
101-130		2.40	6.00

NOTE: ***Jim Aparo*** *a-94.* ***Powell*** *a-7, 8, 16, 20, 30.* ***Marcus Swayze*** *a-2, 12, 20, 32.*

ROMANTIC THRILLS (See Fox Giants)

ROMANTIC WESTERN
Winter, 1949 - No. 3, June, 1950 (All Photo-c)
Fawcett Publications

	GD25	FN65	NM94
1	16.00	47.00	120.00
2-(Spr/50)-Williamson, McWilliams-a	16.00	47.00	120.00
3	11.50	34.00	80.00

ROMEO TUBBS (...That Lovable Teenager; formerly My Secret Life)

Ronin #4 © Frank Miller

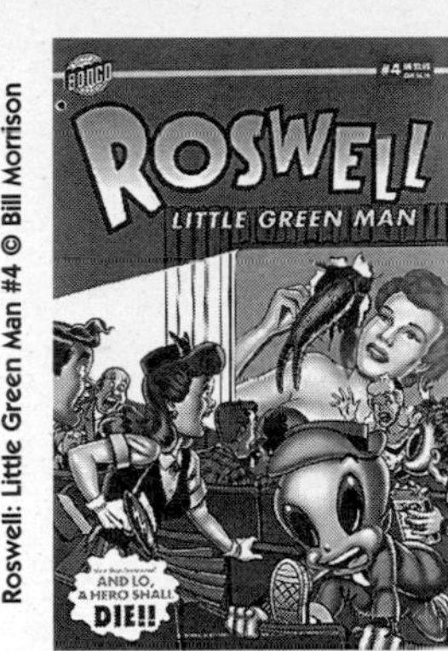

Roswell: Little Green Man #4 © Bill Morrison

Roy Rogers Comics #1 © DELL

No. 26, 5/50 - No. 28, 7/50; No. 1, 1950; No. 27, 12/52
Fox Feature Syndicate/Green Publ. Co. No. 27

	GD25	FN65	NM94
26-Teen-age	8.75	26.25	65.00
27-Contains Pedro on inside; Wood-a	12.00	36.00	95.00
28, 1	7.85	23.50	55.00

RONALD McDONALD (TV)
Sept, 1970 - No. 4, March, 1971
Charlton Press (King Features Synd.)

	GD25	FN65	NM94
1	4.00	12.00	40.00
2-4 (#4 exist?)	2.50	7.50	24.00

RONIN
July, 1983 - No. 6, Aug, 1984 ($2.50, limited series, 52 pgs.)
DC Comics

	GD25	FN65	NM94
1-Frank Miller-c/a/scripts in all		2.00	5.00
2-5		1.20	3.00
6-Scarcer; has fold out poster.	1.00	3.00	8.00
Trade paperback (1987, $12.95)-Reprints #1-6	1.60	4.85	13.00

RONNA
Apr, 1997 ($2.95, B&W, one-shot)
Knight Press

	GD25	FN65	NM94
1-Beau Smith-s			2.95

ROOK (See Eerie Magazine & Warren Presents: The Rook)
Nov, 1979 - No. 14, April, 1982
Warren Publications

	GD25	FN65	NM94
1-Nino-a	1.50	4.50j	12.00
2-14: 3,4-Toth-a	1.00	3.00	8.00

ROOK
No. 0, Jun, 1995 - No. 4, 1995 ($2.95)
Harris Comics

	GD25	FN65	NM94
0-4: 0-short stories (3) w/preview. 4-Brereton-c.		1.20	3.00

ROOKIE COP (Formerly Crime and Justice?)
No. 27, Nov, 1955 - No. 33, Aug, 1957
Charlton Comics

	GD25	FN65	NM94
27	6.85	21.00	48.00
28-33	5.35	16.00	32.00

ROOM 222 (TV)
Jan, 1970; No. 2, May, 1970 - No. 4, Jan, 1971
Dell Publishing Co.

	GD25	FN65	NM94
1	3.60	11.00	40.00
2-4: 2,4-Photo-c. 3-Marijuana story. 4 r/#1	2.00	6.00	23.00

ROOTIE KAZOOTIE (TV)(See 3-D-ell)
No. 415, Aug, 1952 - No. 6, Oct-Dec, 1954
Dell Publishing Co.

	GD25	FN65	NM94
Four Color 415 (#1)	10.00	30.00	110.00
Four Color 459,502(#2,3)	6.40	19.00	70.00
4(4-6/54)-6	6.40	19.00	70.00

ROOTS OF THE SWAMP THING
July, 1986 - No.5, Nov, 1986 ($2.00, Baxter paper, 52 pgs.)
DC Comics

	GD25	FN65	NM94
1-5: r/Swamp Thing #1-10 by Wrightson & House of Mystery-r. 1-new Wrightson-c (2-5 reprinted covers).		.80	2.00

ROSE N'GUNN
Jan, 1995 - No. 6, May, 1996 ($2.95, B&W, mature)
Bishop Press

	GD25	FN65	NM94
1-6		1.20	3.00
Creator's Choice ($2.95)-reprints w/pin-ups		1.20	3.00

ROSE N'GUNN
June, 1996 ($3.00, B&W, mature)
London Night Studios

	GD25	FN65	NM94
1		1.20	3.00
1-($6.00)-Blood & Glory Edition		2.40	6.00

ROSWELL: LITTLE GREEN MAN
1996 - Present ($2.95, quarterly)
Bongo Comics

	GD25	FN65	NM94
1-4		1.40	3.50
...Walks Among Us ('97, $12.95, TPB) r/ #1-3			12.95

ROUND THE WORLD GIFT
No date (mid 1940's) (4 pgs.)
National War Fund (Giveaway)

	GD25	FN65	NM94
nn	10.50	32.00	85.00

ROUNDUP (...Western Crime Stories)
July-Aug, 1948 - No. 5, Mar-Apr, 1949 (All 52 pgs.)
D. S. Publishing Co.

	GD25	FN65	NM94
1-Kiefer-a	17.00	49.00	120.00
2-5: 2-Marijuana drug mention story	11.00	33.00	80.00

ROYAL ROY
May, 1985 - No.6, Mar, 1986 (Children's book)
Marvel Comics (Star Comics)

	GD25	FN65	NM94
1-6			1.00

ROY CAMPANELLA, BASEBALL HERO
1950 (Brooklyn Dodgers)
Fawcett Publications

	GD25	FN65	NM94
nn-Photo-c; life story	47.00	141.00	425.00

ROY ROGERS (See March of Comics #17, 35, 47, 62, 68, 73, 77, 86, 91, 100, 105, 116, 121, 131, 136, 146, 151, 161, 167, 176, 191, 206, 221, 236, 250)

ROY ROGERS AND TRIGGER
Apr, 1967
Gold Key

	GD25	FN65	NM94
1-Photo-c; reprints	3.00	9.00	35.00

ROY ROGERS COMICS (See Western Roundup under Dell Giants)
No. 38, 4/44 - No. 177, 12/47 (#38-166: 52 pgs.)
Dell Publishing Co.

	GD25	FN65	NM94
Four Color 38 (1944)-49 pg. story; photo front/back-c on all 4-Color issues (1st western comic with photo-c)	164.00	490.00	1800.00
Four Color 63 (1945)-Color photos on all four-c	43.00	130.00	475.00
Four Color 86,95 (1945)	32.00	95.00	350.00
Four Color 109 (1946)	23.00	70.00	255.00
Four Color 117,124,137,144	16.00	49.00	180.00
Four Color 153,160,166: 166-48 pg. story	14.00	42.00	155.00
Four Color 177 (36 pgs.)-32 pg. story	14.00	42.00	155.00

ROY ROGERS COMICS (...& Trigger #92(8/55)-on)(Roy starred in Republic movies, radio & TV) (Singing cowboy) (Also see Dale Evans, It Really Happened #8, Queen of the West Dale Evans, & Roy Rogers' Trigger)
Jan, 1948 - No. 145, Sept-Oct, 1961 (#1-19: 36 pgs.)
Dell Publishing Co.

	GD25	FN65	NM94
1-Roy, his horse Trigger, & Chuck Wagon Charley's Tales begin; photo-c begin, end #145	64.00	191.00	700.00
2	23.00	68.00	250.00
3-5	16.00	49.00	180.00
6-10	12.00	37.00	135.00
11-19: 19-Chuck Wagon Charley's Tales ends	9.00	27.00	100.00
20 (52 pgs.)-Trigger feature begins, ends #46	9.00	27.00	100.00
21-30 (52 pgs.)	8.00	22.00	85.00
31-46 (52 pgs.): 37-X-Mas-c	6.00	18.00	65.00
47-56 (36 pgs.): 47-Chuck Wagon Charley's Tales returns, ends #133. 49-X-mas-c. 55-Last photo back-c	4.25	13.00	48.00

Rudolph, the Red-Nosed Reindeer 1952 © DC

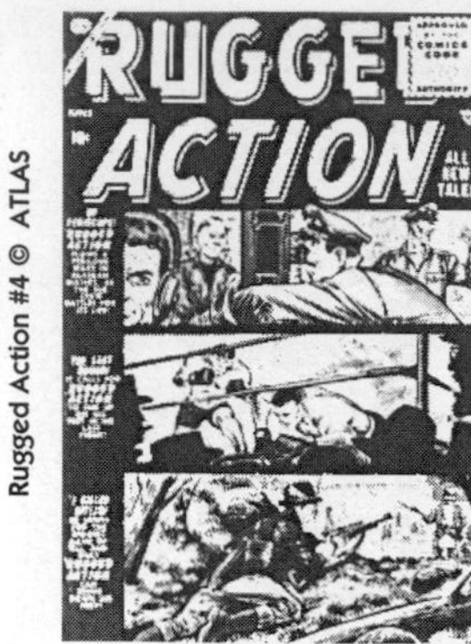

Rugged Action #4 © ATLAS

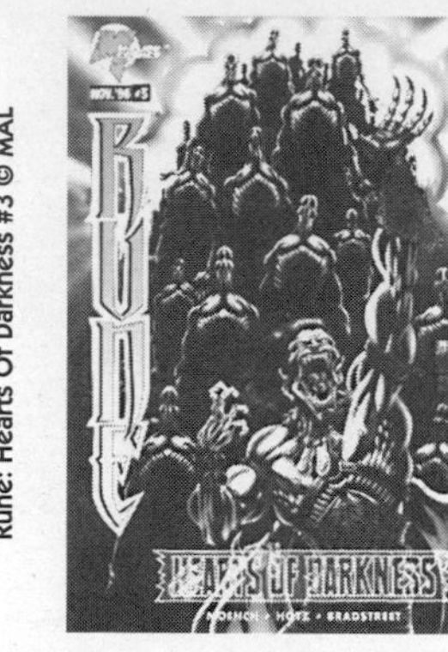

Rune: Hearts Of Darkness #3 © MAL

GD25 FN65 NM94

57 (52 pgs.)-Heroin drug propaganda story 5.00 15.00 56.00
58-70 (52 pgs.): 58-Heroin drug use/dealing story. 61-X-Mas-c 4.25 13.00 48.00
71-80 (52 pgs.): 73-X-Mas-c 3.50 11.00 38.00
81-91 (36 pgs. #81-on): 85-X-Mas-c 3.00 9.00 34.00
92-99,101-110,112-118: 92-Title changed to Roy Rogers and Trigger (8/55) 3.00 9.00 34.00
100-Trigger feature returns, ends #131 4.25 13.00 48.00
111,119-124-Toth-a 4.50 13.50 50.00
125-131: 125-Toth-a (1 pg.) 3.50 11.00 38.00
132-144-Manning-a. 132-1st Dale Evans-sty by Russ Manning138,144-Dale Evans featured 3.60 11.00 42.00
145-Last issue 5.00 15.00 55.00
...& the Man From Dodge City (Dodge giveaway, 16 pgs., 1954)-Frontier, Inc. (5x7-1/4") 7.00 22.00 80.00
Official Roy Rogers Riders Club Comics (1952; 16 pgs., reg. size, paper-c) 16.00 49.00 180.00
NOTE: ***Buscema*** *a-74-108(2 stories each).* ***Manning*** *a-123, 124, 132-144.* ***Marsh*** *a-110. Photo back-c No. 1-9, 11-35, 38-55.*

ROY ROGERS' TRIGGER (TV)
No. 329, May, 1951 - No. 17, June-Aug, 1955
Dell Publishing Co.

Four Color 329 (#1)-Painted-c 10.00 30.00 110.00
2 (9-11/51)-Photo-c 9.00 26.00 95.00
3-5: 3-Painted-c begin, end #17, most by S. Savitt 3.50 11.00 38.00
6-17: Title merges with Roy Rogers after #17 2.50 7.50 28.00

ROY ROGERS WESTERN CLASSICS
1989 -Present? ($2.95/$3.95, 44pgs.) (24 pgs in color, 16 pgs. in B&W)
AC Comics

1-Dale Evans-r by Manning, Trigger-r by Buscema; photo covers & interior photos by Roy & Dale 1.20 3.00
2-Buscema-r (3); photo-c & B&W photos inside 1.20 3.00
3,4 ($3.95): 3-Dale Evans-r by Manning; Trigger-r by Buscemaplus other Buscema-r; photo-c. 1.60 4.00

RUDOLPH, THE RED NOSED REINDEER (See Limited Collectors' Edition #20, 24, 33, 42, 50)

RUDOLPH, THE RED-NOSED REINDEER
1939 (2,400,000 copies printed); Dec, 1951
Montgomery Ward (Giveaway)

Paper cover-1st app. in print; written by Robert May; ill. by Denver Gillen 10.00 30.00 80.00
Hardcover version 14.00 41.00 110.00
1951 Edition (Has 1939 date)-36 pgs., slick-c printed in red & brown; pulp interior printed in four mixed-ink colors: red, green, blue & brown 6.50 19.50 45.00
1951 Edition with red-spiral promotional booklet printed on high quality stock, 8-1/2"x11", in red & brown, 25 pages composed of 4 fold outs, single sheets and the Rudolph comic book inserted (rare) 43.00 129.00 385.00

RUDOLPH, THE RED-NOSED REINDEER
1950 - No. 9?, Winter, 1962-63 (Issues are not numbered)
National Periodical Publications

1950 issue (#1); Grossman-c/a begins 14.00 41.00 110.00
1951-53 issues (3? total) 8.75 26.25 65.00
1954-55, 56-57, 58-59, 60-61, 62-63 issues (5 total) 6.50 19.50 45.00
NOTE: *The 1962-63 issue is 84 pages. 9? total issues published. Has games & puzzles also.*

RUFF AND REDDY (TV)
No. 937, 9/58 - No. 12, 1-3/62 (Hanna-Barbera)(#9 on: 15¢)
Dell Publishing Co.

Four Color 937(#1)(1st Hanna-Barbera comic book) 11.00 33.00 120.00
Four Color 981,1038 7.00 22.00 80.00
4(1-3/60)-12: 8-Last 10¢ issue 5.50 16.50 60.00

GD25 FN65 NM94

RUGGED ACTION (Strange Stories of Suspense #5 on)
Dec, 1954 - No. 4, June, 1955
Atlas Comics (CSI)

1-Brodsky-c 10.00 30.00 75.00
2-4: 2-Last precode (2/55) 6.50 19.50 45.00
NOTE: ***Ayers*** *a-2, 3.* ***Maneely*** *c-2, 3.* ***Severin*** *a-2.*

RUINS
July, 1995 - No. 2, Sept, 1995 ($5.00, painted, limited series)
Marvel Comics (Alterniverse)

1,2: Phil Sheldon from Marvels; Warren Ellis scripts; acetate-c 2.00 5.00

RULAH JUNGLE GODDESS (Formerly Zoot; I Loved #28 on) (Also see All Top Comics & Terrors of the Jungle)
No. 17, Aug, 1948 - No. 27, June, 1949
Fox Features Syndicate

17 71.00 215.00 625.00
18-Classic girl-fight interior splash 54.00 163.00 465.00
19,20 50.00 150.00 430.00
21-Used in **SOTI**, pg. 388,389 54.00 163.00 465.00
22-Used in **SOTI**, pg. 22,23 50.00 150.00 430.00
23-27 40.00 120.00 335.00
NOTE: ***Kamen*** *c-17-19, 21, 22.*

RUNAWAY, THE (See Movie Classics)

RUN BABY RUN
1974 (39¢)
Logos International

nn-By Tony Tallarico from Nicky Cruz's book 1.00

RUN, BUDDY, RUN (TV)
June, 1967 (Photo-c)
Gold Key

1 (10204-706) 1.65 5.00 18.00

RUNE (See Curse of Rune, Sludge & all other Ultraverse titles for previews)
1994 - No. 9, Apr, 1995 ($1.95)
Malibu Comics (Ultraverse)

1,2,4-9: 1-Barry Windsor-Smith-c/a/stories begin, ends #6. 5-1st app. of Gemini. 6-Prime & Mantra app. .80 2.00
1-(1/94)-"Ashcan" edition flip book w/Wrath #1 1.00
1-Ultra 5000 Limited silver foil edition 1.00 2.80 7.00
0-Obtained by sending coupons from 11 comics; came w/Solution #0, poster, temporary tattoo, card 1.10 3.30 9.00
3-(3/94, $3.50, 68 pgs.)-Flip book w/Ultraverse Premiere #1 1.40 3.50
Giant Size 1 ($2.50, 44 pgs.)-B.Smith story & art. 1.00 2.50

RUNE (2nd Series)(Formerly Curse of Rune)(See Ultraverse Unlimited #1)
Infinity, Sept, 1995 - V2#7, Apr, 1996 ($1.50)
Malibu Comics (Ultraverse)

Infinity, V2#1-7: Infinity-Black September tie-in; black-c & painted-c exist. 1,3-7-Marvel's Adam Warlock app; regular & painted-c exist. 2-Flip book w/"Phoenix Resurrection" Pt. 6. 1.50
...Vs. Venom 1 (12/95, $3.95) 1.60 4.00

RUNE: HEARTS OF DARKNESS
Sept, 1996 - No. 3, Nov, 1996 ($1.50, limited series)
Malibu Comics (Ultraverse)

1-3: Doug Moench scripts & Kyle Hotz-c/a; flip books w/6 pg. Rune story by the Pander Bros. 1.50

RUNE/SILVER SURFER
Apr, 1995 ($5.95/$2.95, one-shot)
Marvel Comics/Malibu Comics (Ultraverse)

1 ($5.95, direct market)-BWS-c 2.40 6.00
1 ($2.95, newstand)-BWS-c 1.20 3.00

Saari #1 © P.L. Publ.

Sable #24 © Mike Grell

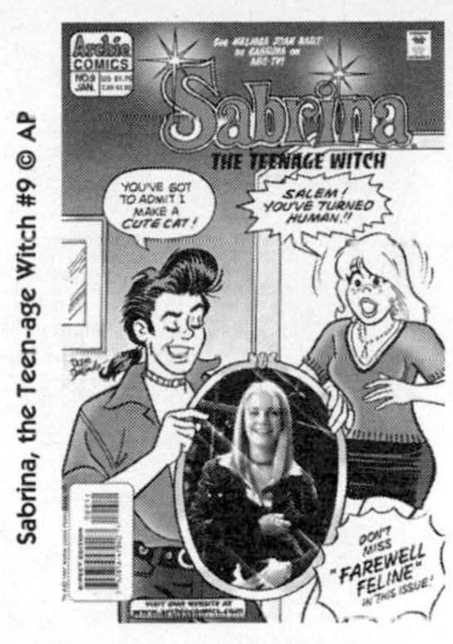

Sabrina, the Teen-age Witch #9 © AP

	GD25	FN65	NM94
1-Collector's limited edition		2.00	5.00

RUST
7/87 - No. 15, 11/88; V2#1, 2/89 - No. 7, 1989 ($1.50/$1.75)
Now Comics

	GD25	FN65	NM94
1-3 ($1.50)			1.50
4-11,13-15, V2#1-7 ($1.75)		.70	1.75
12-(8/88, $1.75)-5 pg. preview of The Terminator (1st app.)		.70	1.75

RUST
1996/1997 ($2.95, B&W)
Caliber Comics

	GD25	FN65	NM94
1,2			2.95

RUSTLERS, THE (See Zane Grey Four Color 532)

RUSTY, BOY DETECTIVE
Mar-April, 1955 - No. 5, Nov, 1955
Good Comics/Lev Gleason

	GD25	FN65	NM94
1-Bob Wood, Carl Hubbell-a begins	7.15	19.50	50.00
2-5	5.00	15.00	30.00

RUSTY COMICS (Formerly Kid Movie Comics; Rusty and Her Family #21, 22; The Kelleys #23 on; see Millie The Model)
No. 12, Apr, 1947 - No. 22, Sept, 1949
Marvel Comics (HPC)

	GD25	FN65	NM94
12-Mitzi app.	14.00	41.00	110.00
13	7.85	23.50	55.00
14-Wolverton's Powerhouse Pepper (4 pgs.) plus Kurtzman's "Hey Look"	17.00	51.00	120.00
15-17-Kurtzman's "Hey Look"	13.50	41.00	95.00
18,19	7.00	21.00	45.00
20-Kurtzman-a (5 pgs.)	13.50	41.00	95.00
21,22-Kurtzman-a (17 & 22 pgs.)	18.00	54.00	125.00

RUSTY DUGAN (See Holyoke One-Shot #2)

RUSTY RILEY
No. 418, Aug, 1952 - No. 554, April, 1954 (Frank Godwin strip reprints)
Dell Publishing Co.

	GD25	FN65	NM94
Four Color 418 (...a Boy, a Horse, and a Dog #1	3.60	11.00	40.00
Four Color #451(2/53), 486 ('53), 554	2.75	8.00	30.00

SAARI ("The Jungle Goddess")
November, 1951
P. L. Publishing Co.

	GD25	FN65	NM94
1	39.00	116.00	280.00

SABAN POWERHOUSE (TV)
1997 - Present ($4.50, digest size)
Acclaim Books

	GD25	FN65	NM94
1,2-Power Rangers, BeetleBorgs, and others			4.50

SABAN PRESENTS POWER RANGERS TURBO VS. BEETLEBORGS METALLIX (TV)
1997 ($4.50, digest size, one-shot)
Acclaim Books

	GD25	FN65	NM94
nn			4.50

SABAN'S MIGHTY MORPHIN POWER RANGERS
Dec, 1994 - No. 6, May, 1995 ($1.95, limited series)
Hamilton Comics

	GD25	FN65	NM94
1-6: 1-w/bound-in Power Ranger Barcode Card		.80	2.00

SABAN'S MIGHTY MORPHIN POWER RANGERS (TV)
1995 - No. 8, 1996 ($1.75)
Marvel Comics

	GD25	FN65	NM94
1-8		.70	1.75

SABAN'S NINJA RANGERS
Dec, 1995 - No. 4, Mar, 1995 ($1.95, limited series)
Hamilton Comics

	GD25	FN65	NM94
1-4: Flip book w/Saban's V.R. Troopers		.80	2.00

SABAN'S V.R. TROOPERS (See Saban's Ninja Rangers)

SABLE (Formerly Jon Sable, Freelance; also see Mike Grell's...)
Mar, 1988 - No. 27, May, 1990 ($1.75/$1.95)
First Comics

	GD25	FN65	NM94
1-27: 10-Begin $1.95-c		.70	1.75

SABRE (See Eclipse Graphic Album Series)
Aug, 1982 - No. 14, Aug, 1985 (Baxter paper #4 on)
Eclipse Comics

	GD25	FN65	NM94
1 ($1.00)-Sabre & Morrigan Tales begin			1.00
2-14: 4-6-Incredible Seven origin			1.00

SABRETOOTH (See Iron Fist, Power Man, X-Factor #10 & X-Men)
Aug, 1993 - No. 4, Nov, 1993 ($2.95, limited series, coated paper)
Marvel Comics

	GD25	FN65	NM94
1-4: 1-Die-cut-c. 3-Wolverine app.		1.20	3.00
...Special 1 "In the Red Zone"(1995, $4.95) Chromium wraparound-c		2.40	6.00
Trade paperback (12/94, $12.95) r/#1-4			13.00

SABRETOOTH AND MYSTIQUE (See Mystique and Sabretooth)

SABRETOOTH CLASSIC
May, 1994 - No. 15, July, 1995 ($1.50)
Marvel Comics

	GD25	FN65	NM94
1-15: 1-3-r/Power Man & Iron Fist #66,78,84. 4-r/Spec. S-M #116. 9-Uncanny X-Men #212, 10-r/Uncanny X-Men #213. 11-0r/ Daredevil #238. 12-r/Classic X-Men #10			1.50

SABRINA'S CHRISTMAS MAGIC (See Archie Giant Series Magazine #196, 207, 220, 231, 243, 455, 467, 479, 491, 503, 515)

SABRINA'S HALLOWEEN SPOOOKTACULAR
1993 ($2.00, 52 pgs.)
Archie Publications

	GD25	FN65	NM94
1-Neon orange ink-c; bound-in poster		.80	2.00

SABRINA, THE TEEN-AGE WITCH (TV)(See Archie Giant Series 544, Archie's Madhouse 22, Archie's TV..., Chilling Advs. In Sorcery)
April, 1971 - No. 77, Jan, 1983 (Giants No. 1-17)
Archie Publications

	GD25	FN65	NM94
1	6.50	19.50	65.00
2	3.00	9.00	30.00
3-5: 3,4-Archie's Group x-over	2.50	7.50	20.00
6-10	1.85	5.50	15.00
11-17	1.50	4.50	12.00
18-40		2.40	6.00
41-60		1.60	4.00
61-77		.80	2.00

SABRINA, THE TEEN-AGE WITCH
1996 ($1.50, 32 pgs., one-shot)
Archie Publications

	GD25	FN65	NM94
1-Updated origin			1.50

SABRINA, THE TEEN-AGE WITCH
May, 1997 - Present ($1.50, 32 pgs)
Archie Publications

	GD25	FN65	NM94
1-8-Photo-c with Melissa Joan Hart			1.50
9-16: 9-Begin $1.75-c			1.75

SABU, "ELEPHANT BOY" (Movie; formerly My Secret Story)
No. 30, June, 1950 - No. 2, Aug, 1950
Fox Features Syndicate

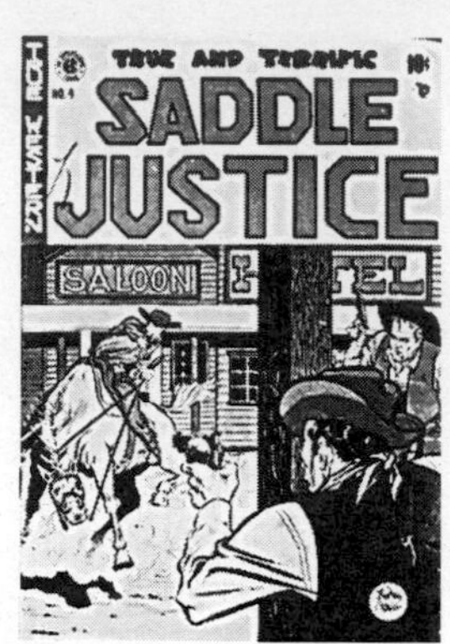

Saddle Justice #4 © EC

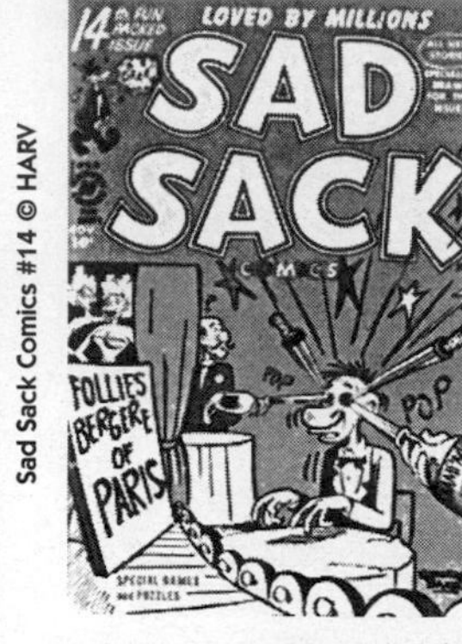

Sad Sack Comics #14 © HARV

Sad Sack Laugh Special #6 © HARV

	GD25	FN65	NM94
30(#1)-Wood-a; photo-c from movie	21.00	64.00	160.00
2-Photo-c from movie; Kamen-a	15.00	45.00	110.00

SACHS & VIOLENS
Nov, 1993 - No. 4, July, 1994 ($2.25, limited series, mature)
Marvel Comics (Epic Comics)

	GD25	FN65	NM94
1-($2.75)-Embossed-c w/bound-in trading card		1.10	2.75
1-($3.50)-Platinum edition (1 for each 10 ordered)		1.60	4.00
2-4: Perez-c/a; bound-in trading card: 2-(5/94)		.90	2.25

SACRAMENTS, THE
Oct, 1955 (25¢)
Catechetical Guild Educational Society

	GD25	FN65	NM94
304	2.40	6.00	12.00

SACRED AND THE PROFANE, THE (See Eclipse Graphic Album Series #9 & Epic Illustrated #20)

SAD CASE OF WAITING ROOM WILLIE, THE
1950? (nd) (14 pgs. in color; paper covers; regular size)
American Visuals Corp. (For Baltimore Medical Society)

	GD25	FN65	NM94
nn-By Will Eisner (Rare)	39.00	117.00	350.00

SADDLE JUSTICE (Happy Houlihans #1,2) (Saddle Romances #9 on)
No. 3, Spring, 1948 - No. 8, Sept-Oct, 1949
E. C. Comics

	GD25	FN65	NM94
3-The 1st E.C. by Bill Gaines to break away from M. C. Gaines' old Educational Comics format. Craig, Feldstein, H. C. Kiefer, & Stan Asch-a; mentioned in Love and Death	39.00	118.00	285.00
4-1st Graham Ingels-a for E.C.	39.00	118.00	285.00
5-8-Ingels-a in all	36.00	109.00	265.00

NOTE: ***Craig** and **Feldstein** art in most issues. Canadian reprints known; see Table of Contents. **Craig** c-3, 4. **Ingels** c-5-8. #4 contains a biography of **Craig**.*

SADDLE ROMANCES (Saddle Justice #3-8; Weird Science #12 on)
No. 9, Nov-Dec, 1949 - No. 11, Mar-Apr, 1950
E. C. Comics

	GD25	FN65	NM94
9-Ingels-c/a	39.00	118.00	285.00
10-Wood's 1st work at E. C.; Ingels-a; Feldstein-c	40.00	120.00	300.00
11-Ingels-a; Feldstein-c	39.00	118.00	285.00

NOTE: *Canadian reprints known; see Table of Contents. **Wood/Harrison** a-10, 11.*

SADE
No. 0, May, 1995 - No. 2, 1996 ($2.95, B&W, mature)
Bishop Press/London Night Studios

	GD25	FN65	NM94
0-2: All Bishop Press issues. 1-Razor app; w/pin-ups		1.20	3.00
1($3.00)-London Night Studio's Encore Edition.		1.20	3.00
Special 1-Razor app.		1.20	3.00
Special 1 ($4.95, limited edition)-Razor app.		2.00	5.00

SADE
June, 1996 - No. 4 ($3.00, B&W, mature)
London Night Studios

	GD25	FN65	NM94
1-4		1.20	3.00
1-Balance of Pain Edition		1.20	3.00

SADE AND ROSE & GUNN CONFEDERATE MISTS
Mar, 1996 ($3.00, B&W, one-shot, mature)
Bishop Press

	GD25	FN65	NM94
1-w/pin-ups.		1.20	3.00

SADIE SACK (See Harvey Hits #93)

SAD SACK AND THE SARGE
Sept, 1957 - No. 155, June, 1982
Harvey Publications

	GD25	FN65	NM94
1	11.00	33.00	110.00
2	5.00	15.00	50.00
3-10	3.50	10.50	35.00
11-20	3.00	9.00	30.00
21-30	2.25	6.75	18.00
31-50	1.50	4.50	12.00
51-70	1.10	3.30	9.00
71-90,97-100		2.40	6.00
91-96: All 52 pg. Giants	1.00	3.00	8.00
101-155		1.60	4.00

SAD SACK COMICS (See Harvey Collector's Comics #16, Little Sad Sack, Tastee Freez Comics #4 & True Comics #55)
Sept, 1949 - No. 287, Oct, 1982; No. 288, 1992 - No. 293?, 1993
Harvey Publications/Lorne-Harvey Publications (Recollections) #288 0n

	GD25	FN65	NM94
1-Infinity-c; Little Dot begins (1st app.); civilian issues begin, end #21; based on comic strip	34.00	102.00	375.00
2-Flying Fool by Powell	18.50	55.00	185.00
3	10.00	30.00	100.00
4-10	7.50	22.50	75.00
11-21	5.00	15.00	50.00
22-("Back In The Army Again" on covers #22-36); "The Specialist" story about Sad Sack's return to Army	3.00	9.00	30.00
23-50	2.50	7.50	20.00
51-100: 62-"The Specialist" reprinted	1.75	5.25	14.00
101-150	1.25	3.75	10.00
151-222		2.40	6.00
223-228 (25¢ Giants, 52 pgs.)	1.00	3.00	8.00
229-285		1.60	4.00
286,287 had limited distribution		2.40	6.00
288,289 ($2.75, 1992): 289-50th anniversary issue		2.00	5.00
290-293 ($1.00, 1993, B&W)		1.20	3.00
3-D 1 (1/54, 25¢)-Came with 2 pairs of glasses; titled "Harvey 3-D Hits"	15.50	47.00	155.00
Armed Forces Complimentary copies, HD #1-40 (1957-1962)		2.40	6.00
...At Home for the Holidays 1 (1993, no-c price)-Publ. by Lorne-Harvey' X-Mas issue		.80	2.00

NOTE: *The Sad Sack Comics comic book was a spin-off from a Sunday Newspaper strip launched through John Wheeler's Bell Syndicate. The previous Sunday page and the first 21 comics depicted the Sad Sack in civvies. Unpopularity caused the Sunday page to be discontinued in the early '50s. Meanwhile Sad Sack returned to the Army, by popular demand, in issue No. 22, remaining there ever since. Incidentally, relatively few of the first 21 issues were ever collected and remain scarce due to this.*

SAD SACK FUN AROUND THE WORLD
1974 (no month)
Harvey Publications

	GD25	FN65	NM94
1-About Great Britain	1.50	4.50	12.00

SAD SACK GOES HOME
1951 (16 pgs. in color, no cover price)
Harvey Publications

	GD25	FN65	NM94
nn-By George Baker	4.20	12.60	42.00

SAD SACK LAUGH SPECIAL
Winter, 1958-59 - No. 93, Feb, 1977 (#1-9: 84 pgs.; #10-60: 68 pgs.; #61-76: 52 pgs.)
Harvey Publications

	GD25	FN65	NM94
1-Giant 25¢ issues begin	8.50	25.50	85.00
2	4.20	12.60	42.00
3-10	3.00	9.00	30.00
11-30	2.50	7.50	24.00
31-60: 31-1st app. Hi-Fi Tweeter. 60-Last 68 pg. Giant	1.75	5.25	14.00
61-76-(All 52 pg. issues)	1.10	3.30	9.00
77-93		2.00	5.00

SAD SACK NAVY, GOBS 'N' GALS
Aug, 1972 - No. 8, Oct, 1973

The Saga of Ra's Al Ghul #2 © DC

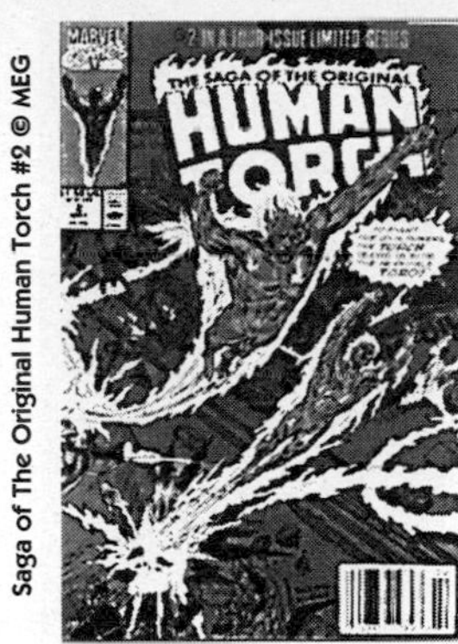

Saga of The Original Human Torch #2 © MEG

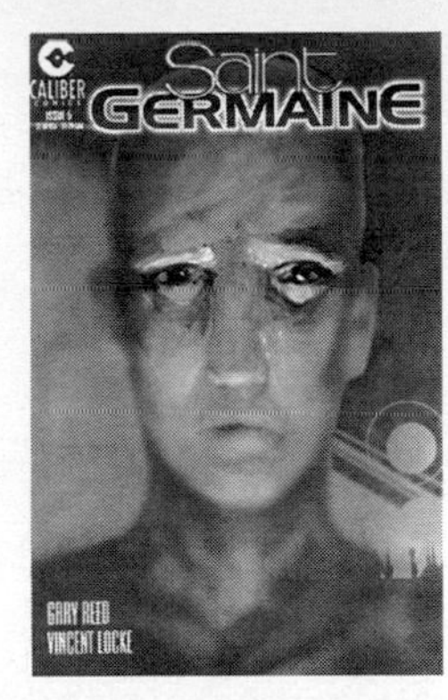

Saint Germaine #5 © Caliber

	GD25	FN65	NM94
Harvey Publications			
1: 52 pg. Giant	1.85	5.50	15.00
2-8	1.00	2.80	7.00

SAD SACK'S ARMY LIFE (See Harvey Hits #8, 17, 22, 28, 32, 39, 43, 47, 51, 55, 58, 61, 64, 67, 70)

SAD SACK'S ARMY LIFE (...Parade #1-57, ...Today #58 on)
Oct, 1963 - No. 60, Nov, 1975; No. 61, May, 1976
Harvey Publications

	GD25	FN65	NM94
1-(68 pg. issues begin)	4.50	13.50	45.00
2-10	2.50	7.50	22.00
11-20	1.50	4.50	12.00
21-34: Last 68 pg. issue	1.25	3.75	10.00
35-51: All 52 pgs.	1.00	3.00	8.00
52-61		1.60	4.00

SAD SACK'S FUNNY FRIENDS (See Harvey Hits #75)
Dec, 1955 - No. 75, Oct, 1969
Harvey Publications

	GD25	FN65	NM94
1	7.50	22.50	75.00
2-10	3.80	11.40	38.00
11-20	2.00	6.00	16.00
21-30	1.50	4.50	12.00
31-75	1.00	3.00	8.00

SAD SACK'S MUTTSY (See Harvey Hits #74, 77, 80, 82, 84, 87, 89, 92, 96, 99, 102, 105, 108, 111, 113, 115, 117, 119, 121)

SAD SACK USA (...Vacation #8)
Nov, 1972 - No. 7, Nov, 1973; No. 8, Oct, 1974
Harvey Publications

	GD25	FN65	NM94
1	1.50	4.50	12.00
2-8		2.40	6.00

SAD SACK WITH SARGE & SADIE
Sept, 1972 - No. 8, Nov, 1973
Harvey Publications

	GD25	FN65	NM94
1-(52 pg. Giant)	1.85	5.50	15.00
2-8		2.40	6.00

SAD SAD SACK WORLD
Oct, 1964 - No. 46, Dec, 1973 (#1-31: 68 pgs.; #32-38: 52 pgs.)
Harvey Publications

	GD25	FN65	NM94
1	4.00	12.00	40.00
2-10	2.50	7.50	20.00
11-31: 31-Last 68 pg. issue	1.85	5.50	15.00
32-39-(All 52 pgs)	1.25	3.75	10.00
40-46		2.00	5.00

SAFEST PLACE IN THE WORLD, THE
1993 ($2.50, one-shot)
Dark Horse Comics

	GD25	FN65	NM94
1-Steve Ditko-c/a/scripts		1.00	2.50

SAFETY-BELT MAN ALL HELL
June, 1996 - Present ($2.95)
Sirius Entertainment

	GD25	FN65	NM94
1-3,5-Horan-s/Fillbach Bros.-a			2.95
4-Linsner back-c			5.00

SAGA OF BIG RED, THE
Sept, 1976 ($1.25) (In color)
Omaha World-Herald

	GD25	FN65	NM94
nn-by Win Mumma; story of the Nebraska Cornhuskers (sports)		.80	2.00

SAGA OF CRYSTAR, CRYSTAL WARRIOR, THE
May, 1983 - No. 11, Feb, 1985 (Remco toy tie-in)
Marvel Comics

	GD25	FN65	NM94
1 ($2.00, baxter paper)		.80	2.00
2-5,7-11: 3-Dr. Strange app. 3-11-Golden-c (painted-4,5). 11-Alpha Flight app.			1.00
6-Nightcrawler app; Golden-c.			1.50

SAGA OF RA'S AL GHUL, THE
Jan, 1988 - No. 4, Apr, 1988 ($2.50, limited series)
DC Comics

	GD25	FN65	NM94
1-4-r/N. Adams Batman		1.00	2.50

SAGA OF SABAN'S MIGHTY MORPHIN POWER RANGERS (Also see Saban's Mighty Morphin Power Rangers)
1995 - No. 4, 1995 ($1.95, limited series)
Hamilton Comics

	GD25	FN65	NM94
1-4		.80	2.00

SAGA OF THE SWAMP THING, THE (See Swamp Thing)

SAGA OF THE ORIGINAL HUMAN TORCH
Apr, 1990 - No. 4, July, 1990 ($1.50, limited series)
Marvel Comics

	GD25	FN65	NM94
1-4: 1-Origin; Buckler-c/a(p). 3-Hitler-c			1.50

SAGA OF THE SUB-MARINER, THE
Nov, 1988 - No. 12, Oct, 1989 ($1.25/$1.50 #5 on)
Marvel Comics

	GD25	FN65	NM94
1-12: 9-Original X-Men app.			1.50

SAILOR ON THE SEA OF FATE (See First Comics Graphic Novel #11)

SAILOR SWEENEY (Navy Action #1-11, 15 on)
No. 12, July, 1956 - No. 14, Nov, 1956
Atlas Comics (CDS)

	GD25	FN65	NM94
12-14: 12-Shores-a. 13-Severin-c	6.50	19.50	45.00

SAINT, THE (Also see Movie Comics(DC) #2 & Silver Streak #18)
Aug, 1947 - No. 12, Mar, 1952
Avon Periodicals

	GD25	FN65	NM94
1-Kamen bondage-c/a	60.00	181.00	500.00
2	38.00	114.00	275.00
3,4: 4-Lingerie panels	28.00	84.00	200.00
5-Spanking panel	35.00	105.00	250.00
6-Miss Fury app. by Tarpe Mills (14 pgs.)	40.00	120.00	300.00
7-c-/Avon paperback #118	23.00	69.00	160.00
8,9(12/50): Saint strip-r in #8-12; 9-Kinstler-c	20.00	60.00	140.00
10-Wood-a, 1 pg; c-/Avon paperback #289	20.00	60.00	140.00
11	13.50	41.00	95.00
12-c-/Avon paperback #123	17.00	49.00	115.00

NOTE: *Lucky Dale, Girl Detective in #1,2,4,6.* **Hollingsworth** *a-4, 6. Painted-c 7, 8, 10-12.*

ST. GEORGE
June, 1988 - No.8, Oct, 1989 ($1.25,/$1.50)
Marvel Comics (Epic Comics)

	GD25	FN65	NM94
1-8: Sienkiewicz-c 3-begin $1.50-c			1.50

SAINT GERMAINE
1997 - Present ($2.95)
Caliber Comics

	GD25	FN65	NM94
1-5: 1,5-Alternate covers			2.95

SAINT SINNER (See Razorline)
Oct, 1993 - No. 7, Apr, 1994 ($1.75)
Marvel Comics (Razorline)

	GD25	FN65	NM94
1-($2.50)-Foil embossed-c; created by Clive Barker		1.00	2.50
2-7: 5-Ectokid x-over		.70	1.75

ST. SWITHIN'S DAY
Apr, 1990 ($2.50, one-shot)

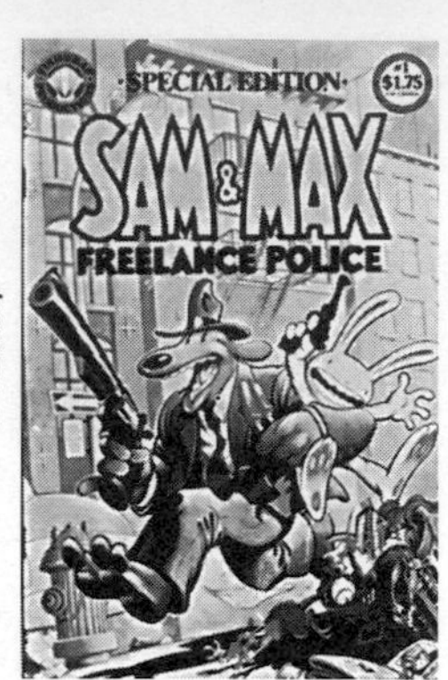

Sam and Max, Freelance Police Special #1 © Fishwrap

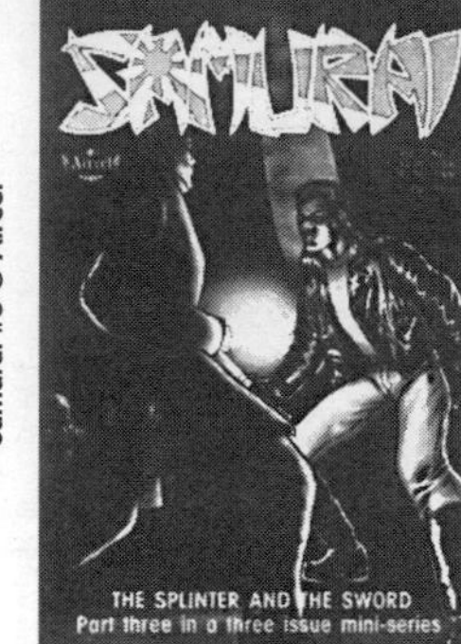

Samurai #3 © Aircel

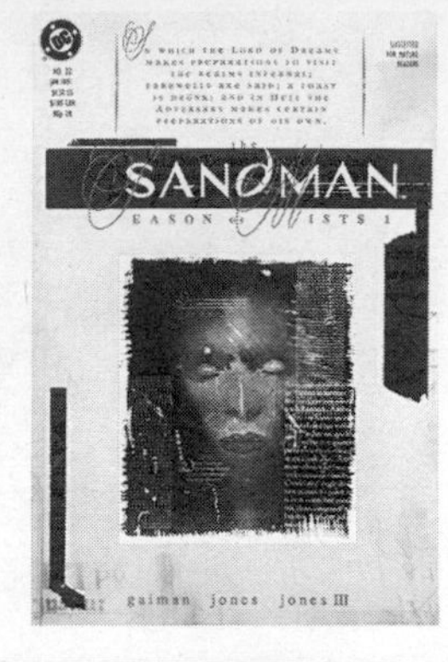

Sandman #22 © DC

GD25 FN65 NM94

Trident Comics
1-Grant Morrison scripts 1.00 2.50

SALERNO CARNIVAL OF COMICS (Also see Pure Oil Comics, 24 Pages of Comics, & Vicks Comics)
Late 1930s (Giveaway, 16 pgs, paper-c)
Salerno Cookie Co.
nn-Color reprints of Calkins' Buck Rogers & Skyroads, plus other strips from Famous Funnies 43.00 129.00 385.00

SALOME' (See Night Music #6)

SAM AND MAX, FREELANCE POLICE SPECIAL
1987 ($1.75, B&W); Jan, 1989 ($2.75, 44 pgs.)
Fishwrap Productions/Comico
1 ($1.75, B&W, Fishwrap) .70 1.75
2 ($2.75, color, Comico) 1.10 2.75

SAM HILL PRIVATE EYE
1950 - No. 7, 1951
Close-Up (Archie)
1 13.00 39.00 95.00
2 8.35 25.00 50.00
3-7 7.50 22.50 45.00

SAM SLADE ROBOHUNTER
Oct, 1986 - No. 31, 1989 ($1.25/$1.50)
Quality Comics
1-19 ($1.25) 1.25
20-31 ($1.50) 1.50

SAMSON (1st Series) (Captain Aero #7 on; see Big 3 Comics)
Fall, 1940 - No. 6, Sept, 1941 (See Fantastic Comics)
Fox Features Syndicate
1-Samson begins, ends #6; Powell-a, signed 'Rensie;' Wing Turner by Tuska app; Fine-c? 167.00 500.00 1500.00
2-Dr. Fung by Powell; Fine-c? 67.00 200.00 600.00
3-Navy Jones app.; Joe Simon-c 53.00 159.00 475.00
4-Yarko the Great, Master Magician begins 44.00 132.00 400.00
5,6: 6-Origin The Topper 36.00 108.00 320.00

SAMSON (2nd Series) (Formerly Fantastic Comics #10, 11)
No. 12, April, 1955 - No. 14, Aug, 1955
Ajax/Farrell Publications (Four Star)
12-Wonder Boy 23.00 68.00 180.00
13,14: 13-Wonder Boy, Rocket Man 20.00 60.00 160.00

SAMSON (See Mighty Samson)

SAMSON & DELILAH (See A Spectacular Feature Magazine)

SAMUEL BRONSTON'S CIRCUS WORLD (See Circus World under Movie Comics)

SAMURAI (Also see Eclipse Graphic Album Series #14)
1985 - No. 22, 1988? ($1.70, B&W)
Aircel Publications
1 1.20 3.00
1-2nd & 3rd printings .70 1.70
2-12,17-22 .70 1.70
2-2nd printing .70 1.70
13-Dale Keown's 1st published artwork (1987) 2.00 5.00
14-16-Dale Keown-a 1.20 3.00

SAMURAI
May, 1997 - Present ($2.95, B&W)
Warp Graphics
1 2.95

SAMURAI CAT
June, 1991 - No. 3, Sept, 1991 ($2.25, limited series)
Marvel Comics (Epic Comics)
1-3: 3-Darth Vader-c/story parody .90 2.25

GD25 FN65 NM94

SAMUREE
May, 1987 - No. 12, 1988?
Continuity Comics
1-12 .80 2.00

SAMUREE
V2#1, May, 1993 - V2#4, Jan,1994 ($2.50)
Continuity Comics
V2#1-4-Embossed-c: 2,4-Adams plot, Nebres-i. 3-Nino-c(i) 1.00 2.50

SAMUREE
Oct, 1995 - No. 3, Dec,1995 ($2.50, limited series)
Acclaim Comics (Windjammer)
1-3 1.00 2.50

SAN DIEGO COMIC CON COMICS
1992 - No.4, 1995 (B&W, promo comic for the San Diego Comic Con)
Dark Horse Comics
1 (1992)-Includes various characters published from Dark Horse including Concrete, The Mask, RoboCop and others; 1st app. of Sprint from John Byrne's Next Men; art by Quesada, Byrne, Rude, Burden, Moebius & others; pin-ups by Rude, Dorkin, Allred & others; Chadwick-c. 1.60 4.00
2 (1993)-Intro of Legend imprint; 1st app. of John Byrne's Danger Unlimited, Mike Mignola's Hellboy, Art Adams' Monkeyman & O'Brien; contains stories featuring Concrete, Sin City, Martha Washington & others; Grendel, Madman, & Big Guy pin-ups; Don Martin-c. 2.00 5.00
3 (1994)-Contains stories featuring Barb Wire, The Mask, The Dirty Pair, & Grendel by Matt Wagner; contains pin-ups of Ghost, Predator & Rascals In Paradise; The Mask-c. 1.60 4.00
4 (1995)-Contains Sin City story by Miller (3pg.) 1.60 4.00

SANDMAN, THE (1st Series) (Also see Adventure Comics #40, New York World's Fair & World's Finest #3)
Winter, 1974; No. 2, Apr-May, 1975 - No. 6, Dec-Jan, 1975-76
National Periodical Publications
1-1st app. Bronze Age Sandman by Simon & Kirby (last S&K collaboration) 1.75 5.25 14.00
2-6: 6-Kirby/Wood-c/a 2.40 6.00
NOTE: ***Kirby*** *a-1p, 4-6p; c-1-5, 6p.*

SANDMAN (2nd Series) (See Books of Magic, Vertigo Jam & Vertigo Preview)
Jan, 1989 - No. 75, Mar, 1996 ($1.50/$1.75/$2.50, mature)
DC Comics (Vertigo imprint #47 on)
1 ($2.00, 52 pgs.)-1st app. Modern Age Sandman (Morpheus); Neil Gaiman scripts begin; Sam Kieth-a(p) in #1-5; Wesley Dodds (G.A. Sandman) cameo. 5.00 15.00 50.00
2-Cain & Abel app. (from HOM & HOS) 2.25 6.75 18.00
3-5: 3-John Constantine app. 1.85 5.50 15.00
6,7 1.25 3.75 10.00
8-Regular ed. has Jeanette Kahn publishorial & American Cancer Society ad w/no indicia on inside front-c; Death-c/story (1st app.) 3.00 9.00 30.00
8-Limited ed. (600+ copies?); has Karen Berger editorial and next issue teaser on inside covers (has indicia) 7.50 22.50 75.00
9-13: 10-Has explaination about #8 mixup; has bound-in Shocker movie poster 1.00 3.00 8.00
14-($2.50, 52 pgs.)-Bound-in Nightbreed fold-out 1.00 3.00 8.00
15-20: 16-Photo-c. 17,18-Kelley Jones-a. 19-Vess-a. 2.00 5.00
18-Error version w/1st 3 panels on pg. 1 in blue ink 2.50 7.50 20.00
19-Error version w/switched pgs. (no 2 pg. spread) 2.50 7.50 20.00
21,23-27: Seasons of Mist storyline. 22-World Without End preview. 24-Kelley Jones/Russell-a 2.00 5.00
22-1st Daniel (Later becomes new Sandman) 1.85 5.50 15.00

Sandman #62 © DC

Sandman Mystery Theatre #45 © DC

Santa Claus Funnies © DELL

GD25 FN65 NM94

28-30 1.20 3.00
31-35,37-48: 41,44-48-Metallic ink on-c. 48-Cerebus appears as a doll 1.00 2.50
36-($2.50, 52 pgs.) 1.00 2.50
49,51-53,55: 49-Begin $1.95-c 1.20 3.00
50-($2.95, 52 pgs.)-Black-c w/metallic ink by McKean; Russell-a; McFarlane pin-up 1.60 4.00
50-($2.95)-Signed & limited (5,000) Treasury Edition with sketch of Neil Gaiman 1.25 3.75 10.00
50-Platinum 3.50 10.50 35.00
54-Re-intro Prez; Death app.; Belushi, Nixon & Wildcat cameos. 1.00 2.50
56-68: 57-Metallic ink on c. 65-w/bound-in trading card .80 2.00
69-Death of Sandman 1.20 3.00
70-75: 70-73-Zulli-a. 74-Jon J. Muth-a. 75-Vess-a. 1.00 2.50
Annual 1 (10/94, $3.95) 1.60 4.00
Special 1 (1991, $3.50, 68 pgs.)-Glow-in-the-dark-c 1.40 3.50
...: A Gallery of Dreams ($2.95)-Intro by N. Gaiman 1.20 3.00
...: Preludes & Nocturnes ($29.95, HC)-r/#1-8. 30.00
...: The Doll's House (1990, $29.95, HC)-r/#8-16. 30.00
...: Dream Country ($29.95, HC)-r/#17-20. 30.00
...: Season of Mists ($29.95, Leatherbound HC)-r/21-28. 30.00
...: A Game of You ($29.95, HC)-r/32-37. 30.00
...: Fables and Reflections ($29.95, HC)-r/Vertigo Preview #1, Sandman Special #1, #29-31, #38-40 & #50. 30.00
...: Brief Lives ($29.95, HC)-r/#41-49. 30.00
...: World's End ($29.95, HC)-r/#51-56. 30.00
...: The Kindly Ones (1996, $34.95, HC)-r/#57-69 & Vertigo Jam#1 35.00
...: The Wake ($29.95, HC)-r/#70-75. 30.00
NOTE: *Multiple printings exist of softcover collections.* **Bachalo** *a-12;* **Kelley Jones** *a-17, 18, 22, 23, 26, 27.* **Vess** *a-19, 75.*

SANDMAN MIDNIGHT THEATRE
Sept, 1995 ($6.95, squarebound, one-shot)
DC Comics (Vertigo)
nn-Modern Age Sandman (Morpheus) meets G.A. Sandman; Gaiman & Wagner story; McKean-c; Kristiansen-a 1.00 2.80 7.00

SANDMAN MYSTERY THEATRE (Also see Sandman (2nd Series) #1)
Apr, 1993 - Present ($1.95/$2.25, mature)
DC Comics (Vertigo)
1-G.A. Sandman advs. begin; Matt Wagner scripts begin. 1.60 4.00
2-27: 5-Neon ink logo. 1.20 3.00
28-49: 28-Begin $2.25-c. 29-32-Hourman app. 38-Ted Knight (G.A. Starman) app. 42-Jim Corrigan (Spectre) app. 45-48-Blackhawk app. 1.20 3.00
50-($3.50, 48 pgs.) w/bonus story of S.A. Sandman, Torres-a 3.50
51-62 2.25
Annual 1 (10/94, $3.95, 68 pgs.)-Bolton, Ross & others-a. 1.60 4.00

SANDS OF THE SOUTH PACIFIC
Jan, 1953
Toby Press
1 18.00 54.00 125.00

SANTA AND HIS REINDEER (See March of Comics #166)

SANTA AND POLLYANNA PLAY THE GLAD GAME
Aug, 1960 (16 pgs.) (Disney giveaway)
Sales Promotion
nn 2.40 6.00 12.00

SANTA AND THE ANGEL (See Dell Junior Treasury #7)
Dec, 1949 (Combined w/Santa at the Zoo) (Gollub-a condensed from FC#128)
Dell Publishing Co.
Four Color 259 3.60 11.00 50.00

SANTA & THE BUCCANEERS
1959 (Giveaway)
Promotional Publ. Co.
nn-Reprints 1952 Santa & the Pirates 1.10 3.30 9.00

SANTA & THE CHRISTMAS CHICKADEE
1974 (Giveaway, 20 pgs.)
Murphy's
nn 2.00 5.00

SANTA & THE PIRATES
1952 (Giveaway)
Promotional Publ. Co.
nn-Marv Levy-c/a 2.40 6.00 12.00

SANTA AT THE ZOO (See Santa And The Angel)

SANTA CLAUS AROUND THE WORLD (See March of Comics #241)

SANTA CLAUS CONQUERS THE MARTIANS (See Movie Classics)

SANTA CLAUS FUNNIES (Also see The Little Fir Tree)
nd; 1940 (Giveaway, 8x10"; 12 pgs., color & B&W, heavy paper)
W. T. Grant Co./Whitman Publishing
nn-(2 versions) 10.50 32.00 85.00

SANTA CLAUS FUNNIES (Also see Dell Giants)
Dec?, 1942 - No. 1274, Dec, 1961
Dell Publishing Co.
nn(#1)(1942)-Kelly-a 36.00 107.00 390.00
2(12/43)-Kelly-a 23.00 70.00 255.00
Four Color 61(1944)-Kelly-a 22.00 67.00 245.00
Four Color 91(1945)-Kelly-a 16.00 49.00 180.00
Four Color 128('46),175('47)-Kelly-a 13.00 38.00 140.00
Four Color 205,254-Kelly-a 12.00 35.00 130.00
Four Color 302,361 3.60 11.00 40.00
Four Color 525,607,666,756,867 3.60 11.00 40.00
Four Color 958,1063,1154,1274 3.00 9.00 35.00
NOTE: *Most issues contain only one Kelly story.*

SANTA CLAUS PARADE
1951; No. 2, Dec, 1952; No. 3, Jan, 1955 (25¢)
Ziff-Davis (Approved Comics)/St. John Publishing Co.
nn(1951-Ziff-Davis)-116 pgs. (Xmas Special 1,2) 23.00 68.00 180.00
2(12/52-Ziff-Davis)-100 pgs.; Dave Berg-a 17.50 53.00 140.00
V1#3(1/55-St. John)-100 pgs.; reprints-c/#1 15.00 45.00 120.00

SANTA CLAUS' WORKSHOP (See March of Comics #50, 168)

SANTA IS COMING (See March of Comics #197)

SANTA IS HERE (See March of Comics #49)

SANTA ON THE JOLLY ROGER
1965
Promotional Publ. Co. (Giveaway)
nn-Marv Levy-c/a 1.60 4.00

SANTA! SANTA!
1974 (20 pgs.)
R. Jackson (Montgomery Ward giveaway)
nn 1.20 3.00

SANTA'S BUSY CORNER (See March of Comics #31)

SANTA'S CANDY KITCHEN (See March of Comics #14)

SANTA'S CHRISTMAS BOOK (See March of Comics #123)

SANTA'S CHRISTMAS COMICS
Dec, 1952 (100 pgs.)
Standard Comics (Best Books)
nn-Supermouse, Dizzy Duck, Happy Rabbit, etc. 14.00 41.00 110.00

SANTA'S CHRISTMAS COMIC VARIETY SHOW

Santa's Gift Book nn

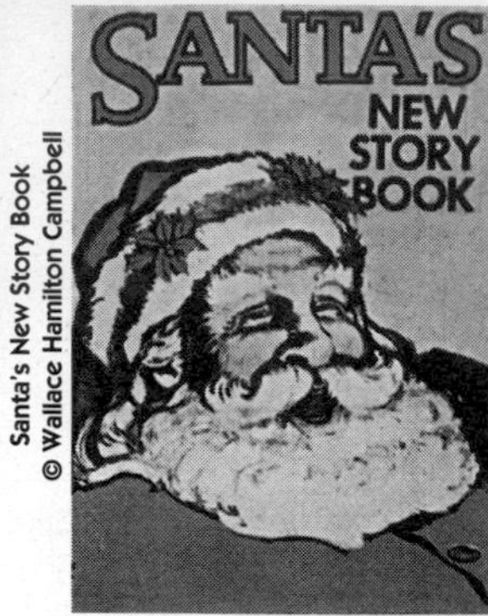

Santa's New Story Book
© Wallace Hamilton Campbell

Satan's Six Hellspawn #3 © Topps

GD25 FN65 NM94

1943 (24 pgs.)
Sears Roebuck & Co.

Contains puzzles & new comics of Dick Tracy, Little Orphan Annie, Moon Mullins, Terry & the Pirates, etc. 25.00 75.00 200.00

SANTA'S CHRISTMAS LIST (See March of Comics #255)

SANTA'S CHRISTMAS TIME STORIES
nd (Late 1940s) (16 pgs., paper-c)
Premium Sales, Inc. (Giveaway)

nn 5.35 16.00 32.00

SANTA'S CIRCUS
1964 (Giveaway, half-size)
Promotional Publ. Co.

nn-Marv Levy-c/a 2.40 6.00

SANTA'S FUN BOOK
1951, 1952 (Regular size, 16 pgs., paper-c)
Promotional Publ. Co. (Murphy's giveaway)

nn 3.00 7.50 15.00

SANTA'S GIFT BOOK
No date (16 pgs.)
No Publisher

nn-Puzzles, games only 2.40 6.00 12.00

SANTA'S HELPERS (See March of Comics #64, 106, 198)

SANTA'S LITTLE HELPERS (See March of Comics #270)

SANTA'S NEW STORY BOOK
1949 (16 pgs., paper-c)
Wallace Hamilton Campbell (Giveaway)

nn 5.00 15.00 30.00

SANTA'S REAL STORY BOOK
1948, 1952 (Giveaway, 16 pgs.)
Wallace Hamilton Campbell/W. W. Orris

nn 4.25 13.00 28.00

SANTA'S RIDE
1959 (Giveaway)
W. T. Grant Co.

nn 1.75 5.25 14.00

SANTA'S RODEO
1964 (Giveaway, half-size)
Promotional Publ. Co.

nn-Marv Levy-a 2.00 5.00

SANTA'S SECRETS
1951, 1952? (16 pgs., paper-c)
Sam B. Anson Christmas giveaway

nn-Has games, stories & pictures to color 3.20 8.00 16.00

SANTA'S SHOW (See March of Comics #311)

SANTA'S SLEIGH (See March of Comics #298)

SANTA'S STORIES
1953 (Regular size, paper-c)
K. K. Publications (Klines Dept. Store)

nn-Kelly-a 14.50 43.00 115.00
nn-Another version (1953, glossy-c, half-size, 7-1/4x5-1/4")-Kelly-a 9.50 28.00 75.00

SANTA'S SURPRISE (See March of Comics #13)

SANTA'S SURPRISE
1947 (Giveaway, 36 pgs., slick-c)
K. K. Publications

nn 5.35 16.00 32.00

SANTA'S TINKER TOTS
1958
Charlton Comics

1-Based on "The Tinker Tots Keep Christmas" 1.75 5.25 14.00

SANTA'S TOYLAND (See March of Comics #242)

SANTA'S TOYS (See March of Comics #12)

SANTA'S TOYTOWN FUN BOOK
1953 (Giveaway)
Promotional Publ. Co.

nn-Marv Levy-c 1.40 3.50 7.00

SANTA'S VISIT (See March of Comics #283)

SANTA THE BARBARIAN
Dec, 1996 ($2.99, one-shot)
Maximum Press

1-Fraga/Mhan-s/a 1.20 3.00

SANTIAGO (Movie)
Sept, 1956 (Alan Ladd photo-c)
Dell Publishing Co.

Four Color 723-Kinstler-a 10.00 30.00 110.00

SARGE SNORKEL (Beetle Bailey)
Oct, 1973 - No. 17, Dec, 1976
Charlton Comics

1 1.25 3.75 10.00
2-17 2.00 5.00

SARGE STEEL (Becomes Secret Agent #9 on; also see Judomaster)
Dec, 1964 - No. 8, Mar-Apr, 1966 (All 12¢ issues)
Charlton Comics

1-Origin & 1st app. 2.50 7.50 20.00
2-5,7,8 1.50 4.50 12.00
6-2nd app. Judomaster 2.00 6.00 16.00

SATANIKA
Jan, 1995 - No. 2, 1995 ($2.95, limited series, mature)
Verotik

0-2: Danzig story in all. 0-(7/95)-Frazetta-c; 1-Bisley-c. 2.40 6.00
The Brimstone Trail (1996, $9.95, TPB)-r/#0-2. 10.00

SATANIKA
Feb, 1996 - Present ($2.95, mature)
Verotik

1-8: Danzig story in all. 2-Igrat cameo; indicia reads "Satanika #1." 4,5-nudity-c 1.20 3.00

SATANIKA X
Feb, 1996 ($4.95, one-shot, mature)
Verotik

1-Embossed-c. 2.00 5.00

SATAN'S SIX
Apr, 1993 - No. 4, July, 1993 ($2.95, limited series)
Topps Comics (Kirbyverse)

1-Polybagged w/Kirbychrome trading card; Kirby/McFarlane-c plus 8 pgs. Kirby-a(p); has coupon for Kirbychrome ed. of Secret City Saga #0 1.20 3.00
2-4-Polybagged w/3 cards. 4-Teenagents preview 1.20 3.00
NOTE: *Ditko a-1.* ***Miller*** *a-1.*

SATAN'S SIX: HELLSPAWN
June, 1994 - No. 3, July, 1994 ($2.50, limited series)
Topps Comics (Kirbyverse)

1-3: 1-(6/94)-Indicia incorrectly shows "Vol 1 #2". 2-(6/94) 1.00 2.50

Savage Dragon #15 © Erik Larsen

The Savage She-Hulk #2 © MEG

Savage Sword of Conan #89 © MEG

GD25 FN65 NM94

SAVAGE COMBAT TALES
Feb, 1975 - No. 3, July, 1975
Atlas/Seaboard Publ.

1-3: 1-Sgt. Stryker's Death Squad begins (origin). 2-Only app. Warhawk 1.20 3.00

NOTE: ***Buckler*** *c-3.* ***McWilliams*** *a-1-3; c-1.* ***Sparling*** *a-1, 3.* ***Toth*** *a-2.*

SAVAGE DRAGON, THE (See Megaton #3 & 4)
July, 1992 - No. 3, Dec, 1992 ($1.95, limited series)
Image Comics (Highbrow Entertainment)

1-Erik Larsen-c/a/scripts & bound-in poster in all; 4 cover color variations w/4 different posters; 1st Highbrow Entertainment title. 1.20 3.00
2-Intro SuperPatriot-c/story (10/92) 1.20 3.00
3-Contains coupon for Image Comics #0 .80 2.00
3-With coupon missing 1.00
...Vs. Savage Megaton Man 1 (3/93, $1.95)-Larsen & Simpson-c/a. .80 2.00

SAVAGE DRAGON, THE
June, 1993 - Present ($1.95/$2.50)
Image Comics (Highbrow Entertainment)

1-Erik Larsen-c/a/scripts .80 2.00
3-7: Erik Larsen-c/a/scripts. 3-Mighty Man back-up story w/Austin-a(i). 4-Flip book w/Ricochet. 5-Mighty Man flip-c & back-up plus poster. 6-Jae Lee poster. 7-Vanguard poster .90 2.25
2,27-(Wondercon Exclusive): 2-($2.95, 52 pgs.)-Teenage Mutant Ninja Turtles-c/story; flip book features Vanguard #0 (See Megaton for 1st app.). 27 (Wondercon Exclusive)-new-c. .80 2.00
8-12,13B,14-15: 8-Deadly Duo poster by Larsen. 13B (6/95)-Larsen story. 15-Dragon poster by Larsen. .80 2.00
13A,16-24,26-44: 13A (10/94)-Jim Lee-c/a; 1st app. Max Cash (Condition Red). 16-$2.50-c begins. 22-TMNT-c/a; Bisley pin-up. 28-Maxx-c/app. 29-Wildstar-c/app. 30-Spawn app. 31-God vs. The Devil; alternate version exists w/o expletives (has "God Is Good" inside Image logo) 33-Birth of Dragon/Rapture's baby. 34,35-Hellboy-c/app. 1.00 2.50
25 ($3.95)-variant-c exists. 1.60 4.00
27-"Wondercon Exclusive" new-c 1.20 3.00

SAVAGE DRAGON/DESTROYER DUCK, THE
Nov, 1996 ($3.95, one-shot)
Image Comics/ Highbrow Entertainment

1 1.60 4.00

SAVAGE DRAGON/MARSHALL LAW
July, 1997 - No. 2, Aug, 1997 ($2.95, B&W, limited series)
Image Comics

1,2-Pat Mills-s, Kevin O'Neill-a 2.95

SAVAGE DRAGON: SEX & VIOLENCE
Aug, 1997 - No. 2, Sept, 1997 ($2.50, limited series)
Image Comics

1,2-T&M Bierbaum-s, Mays, Lupka, Adam Hughes-a 2.50

SAVAGE DRAGON/TEENAGE MUTANT NINJA TURTLES CROSSOVER
Sept, 1993 ($2.75, one-shot)
Mirage Studios

1-Erik Larsen-c(i) only 1.10 2.75

SAVAGE DRAGON: THE RED HORIZON
Feb, 1997 - No. 3 ($2.50, limited series)
Image Comics/ Highbrow Entertainment

1-3 2.50

SAVAGE FISTS OF KUNG FU
1975 (Treasury)
Marvel Comics Group

1-Iron Fist, Shang Chi, Sons of Tiger; Adams, Starlin-a 1.25 3.75 10.00

SAVAGE HENRY
Jan, 1987 - No. 16?, 1990 ($1.75/$2.00, B&W, mature)
Vortex Comics

1-9 ($1.75) .70 1.75
10-15 ($2.00) .80 2.00
16-Begin $2.50-c 1.00 2.50

SAVAGE HULK, THE (Also see Incredible Hulk)
Jan, 1996 ($6.95, one-shot)
Marvel Comics

1-Bisley-c; David, Lobdell, Wagner, Loeb, Gibbons, Messner-Loebs scripts; McKone, Kieth, Ramos & Sale-a. 1.00 2.80 7.00

SAVAGE RAIDS OF GERONIMO (See Geronimo #4)

SAVAGE RANGE (See Luke Short, Four Color 807)

SAVAGE RETURN OF DRACULA
1992 ($2.00, 52 pgs.)
Marvel Comics

1-r/Tomb of Dracula #1,2 by Gene Colan .80 2.00

SAVAGE SHE-HULK, THE (See The Avengers, Marvel Graphic Novel #18 & The Sensational She-Hulk)
Feb, 1980 - No. 25, Feb, 1982
Marvel Comics Group

1-Origin & 1st app. She-Hulk 1.00 2.80 7.00
2-10 1.20 3.00
11-25: 25-(52 pgs.) .90 2.25

NOTE: ***Austin*** *a-25i; c-23i-25i.* ***J. Buscema*** *a-1p; c-1, 2p.* ***Golden*** *c-8-11.*

SAVAGE SWORD OF CONAN (The... #41 on; ...The Barbarian #175 on)
Aug, 1974 - No. 235, July, 1995 ($1.00/$1.25/$2.25, B&W magazine, mature)
Marvel Comics Group

1-Smith-r; J. Buscema/N. Adams/Krenkel-a; origin Blackmark by Gil Kane (part 1, ends #3); Blackmark's 1st app. in magazine form-r/from paperback) & Red Sonja (3rd app.) 7.50 22.50 75.00
2-Neal Adams-c; Chaykin/N. Adams-a 3.00 9.00 30.00
3-Severin/B. Smith-a; N. Adams-a 2.25 6.75 18.00
4-Neal Adams/Kane-a(r) 1.85 5.50 15.00
5-10: 5-Jeff Jones frontispiece (r) 1.75 5.25 14.00
11-20 1.50 4.50 12.00
21-50: 34-3 pg. preview of Conan newspaper strip. 35-Cover similar to Savage Tales #1. 45-Red Sonja returns; begin $1.25-c 1.25 3.75 10.00
51-100: 63-Toth frontispiece. 65-Kane-a w/Chaykin/Miller/Simonson/Sherman finishes. 70-Article on movie. 83-Red Sonja-r by Neal Adams from #1 2.00 5.00
101-176: 163-Begin $2.25-c. 169-King Kull story. 171-Soloman Kane by Williamson (i). 172-Red Sonja story 1.40 3.50
177-235: 179,187,192-Red Sonja app. 190-193-4 part King Kull story. 196, 202-King Kull story. 200-New Buscema-a; Robert E. Howard app. with Conan in story. 204-60th anniversary (1932-92). 211-Rafael Kayanan's 1st Conan-a. 214-Sequel to Red Nails by Robert E. Howard .90 2.25
Special 1(1975, B&W)-B. Smith-r/Conan #10,13 1.50 4.50 12.00

NOTE: ***N. Adams*** *a-14p, 60, 83p(r).* ***Alcala*** *a-2 ,4, 7, 12, 15-20, 23, 24, 28, 59, 67, 69, 75, 76i, 80i, 82i, 83i, 89, 180i, 184i, 187i, 189i, 216p.* ***Austin*** *a-78i.* ***Boris*** *painted c-1, 4, 5, 7, 9, 10, 12, 15.* ***Brunner*** *a-30; c-8, 30.* ***Buscema*** *a-1-5, 7, 10-12, 15-24, 26-28, 31, 32, 36-43, 45, 47-58p, 60-67p, 70, 71-74p, 76-81p, 87-96p, 98, 99-101p, 190-204p; painted c-40.* ***Chaykin*** *c-31.* ***Chiodo*** *painted c-71, 76, 79, 81, 84, 85, 178.* ***Conrad*** *c-215, 217.* ***Corben*** *a-4, 16, 29.* ***Finlay*** *a-16.* ***Golden*** *a-98, 101; c-98, 101, 105, 106, 117, 124, 150.* ***Kaluta*** *a-11, 18; c-3, 91, 93.* ***Gil Kane*** *a-2, 3, 8, 13r, 29, 47, 64, 65, 67, 85p, 86p.* ***Rafael Kayanan*** *a-211-213, 215, 217.* ***Krenkel*** *a-9, 11, 14, 16, 24.* ***Morrow*** *a-7.* ***Nebres*** *a-93i, 101i, 107, 114.* ***Newton*** *a-6.* ***Nino*** *c/a-6.* ***Redondo*** *painted c-48-50, 52, 56, 57, 85i, 90, 96i.* ***Marie & John Severin*** *a-Special 1.* ***Simonson*** *a-7, 8, 12, 15-17.* ***Barry Smith*** *a-7, 16, 24, 82r, Special 1r.* ***Starlin*** *c-26.* ***Toth*** *a-64.* ***Williamson*** *a(i)-162, 171, 186. No. 8 , 10 & 16 contain a Robert E. Howard Conan adaptation.*

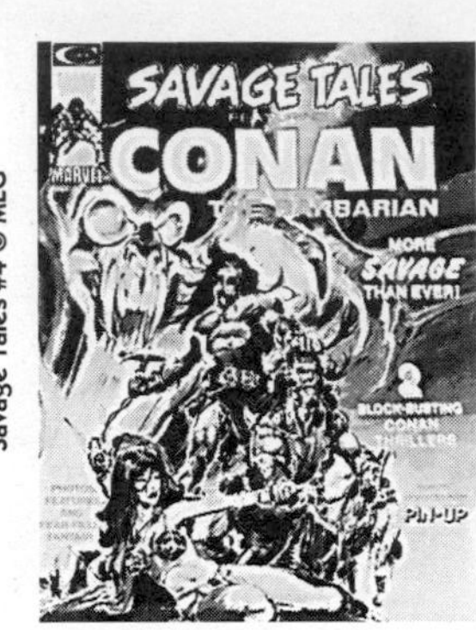

Savage Tales #4 © MEG

Scarab #5 © John Smith & Scot Eaton

Scarlett #13 © DC

GD25 FN65 NM94

SAVAGE TALES (...Featuring Conan #4 on)(Magazine)
May, 1971; No. 2, 10/73; No. 3, 2/74 - No. 12, Summer, 1975 (B&W)
Marvel Comics Group

1-Origin/1st app. The Man-Thing by Morrow; Conan the Barbarian by Barry Smith (1st Conan x-over outside his own title); Femizons by Romita-r/in #3; Ka-Zar story by Buscema 12.00 36.00 120.00
2-B. Smith, Brunner, Morrow, Williamson-a; Wrightson King Kull reprint/ Creatures on the Loose #10 3.50 10.50 35.00
3-B. Smith, Brunner, Steranko, Williamson-a 2.50 7.50 22.00
4,5-N. Adams-c; last Conan (Smith-r/#4) plus Kane/N. Adams-a. 5-Brak the Barbarian begins, ends #8 2.25 6.75 18.00
6-Ka-Zar begins; Williamson-r; N. Adams-c 1.25 3.75 10.00
7-N. Adams-i 1.00 3.00 8.00
8-Shanna, the She-Devil app. thru #10; Williamson-r1.00 2.80 7.00
9,11 2.40 6.00
10-Neal Adams-a(i), Williamson-r 2.40 6.00
...Featuring Ka-Zar Annual 1 (Summer, '75, B&W)(#12 on inside)-Ka-Zar origin by G. Kane; B. Smith-r/Astonishing Tales 1.50 4.50 12.00
NOTE: *Boris c-7, 10. Buscema a-5r, 6p, 8p; c-2. Colan a-1p. Fabian c-8. Golden a-1, 4; c-1. Heath a-10p, 11p. Kaluta c-9. Maneely r-2, 4(The Crusader in both). Morrow a-1, 2, Annual 1. Reese a-2. Severin a-1-7. Starlin a-5. Robert E. Howard adaptations-1-4.*

SAVAGE TALES
Nov, 1985 - No. 9, Mar, 1987 ($1.50, B&W, magazine, mature)
Marvel Comics Group

1-1st app. The Nam; Golden, Morrow-a 1.20 3.00
2-9: 2,7-Morrow-a. 4-2nd Nam story; Golden-a 1.50

SAVANT GARDE (See WildC.A.T.S)
Mar, 1997 - No. 7, Sept, 1997 ($2.50)
Image Comics/WildStorm Productions

1-7 2.50

SAVED BY THE BELL (TV)
Mar, 1992 - No. 4, Aug, 1992? ($1.25, limited series)
Harvey Comics

1-4 1.25
Special 1 (9/92, $1.50)-photo-c 1.50

SCAMP (Walt Disney)(See Walt Disney's Comics & Stories #204)
No. 703, 5/56 - No. 1204, 8-10/61; 11/67 - No. 45, 1/79
Dell Publishing Co./Gold Key

Four Color 703(#1) 8.00 25.00 90.00
Four Color 777,806('57),833 5.50 16.50 60.00
5(3-5/58)-10(6-8/59) 4.50 13.50 50.00
11-16(12-2/60-61), Four Color 1204(1961) 3.00 9.00 35.00
1(12/67-Gold Key)-Reprints begin 2.75 8.00 30.00
2(3/69)-10 1.50 4.50 12.00
11-20 1.00 3.00 8.00
21-45 2.40 6.00
NOTE: *New stories-#20(in part), 22-25, 27, 29-31, 34, 36-40, 42-45. New covers-#11, 12, 14, 15, 17-25, 27, 29-31, 34, 36-38.*

SCARAB
Nov, 1993 - No. 8, June, 1994 ($1.95, limited series)
DC Comics (Vertigo)

1-8-Glenn Fabry painted-c: 1-Silver ink-c. 2-Phantom Stranger app. .80 2.00

SCAR FACE (See The Crusaders)

SCARECROW OF ROMNEY MARSH, THE (See W. Disney Showcase #53)
April, 1964 - No. 3, Oct, 1965 (Disney TV Show)
Gold Key

10112-404 (#1) 2.25 6.75 24.00
2,3 1.65 5.00 18.00

SCARE TACTICS
Dec, 1996 - No. 12, Mar, 1998 ($2.25)
DC Comics

1-12: 1-1st app. 2.25

SCARLET O'NEIL (See Harvey Comics Hits #59 & Invisible...)

SCARLET SPIDER
Nov, 1995 - No. 4, Feb, 1996 ($1.95)
Marvel Comics

1-4: Replaces Spider-Man .80 2.00

SCARLET SPIDER UNLIMITED
Nov, 1995 ($3.95, one-shot)
Marvel Comics

1-Replaces Spider-Man Unlimited 1.60 4.00

SCARLETT
Jan, 1993 - No. 14, Feb, 1994 (1.75)
DC Comics

1-($2.95) 1.20 3.00
2-14 .70 1.75

SCARLET THUNDER
Nov, 1995, - Present ($1.50, B&W)
Amaze Ink

1-3: 3-(5/96) 1.50

SCARLET WITCH (See Avengers #16, Vision &... & X-Men #4)
Jan, 1994 - No. 4, Apr, 1994 ($1.75, limited series)
Marvel Comics

1-4 .70 1.75

SCARY TALES
8/75 - #9, 1/77; #10, 9/77 - #20, 6/79; #21, 8/80 - #46, 10/84
Charlton Comics

1-Origin/1st app. Countess Von Bludd, not in #2 1.25 3.75 10.00
2-11: 3-Sutton painted-c 2.40 6.00
12-20 1.60 4.00
21-46: 39,46-All reprints. 37,38,40-45-New-a. 38-Mr. Jigsaw app. 1.20 3.00
1(Modern Comics reprint, 1977) 1.60 4.00
NOTE: *Adkins a-31i; c-31i. Ditko a-3, 5, 7, 8(2), 11, 12, 14-16r, 18(3)r, 19r, 21r, 30r, 32, 39r; c-5, 11, 14, 18, 30, 32. Newton a-31p; c-31p. Powell a-18r. Staton a-1(2 pgs.), 4, 20r; c-1, 20. Sutton a-9; c-4, 9.*

SCAVENGERS
Feb, 1988 - No. 14, 1989 ($1.25/$1.50)
Quality Comics

1-7 ($1.25) 1.25
8-14 ($1.50): 9-13-Guice-c 1.50

SCAVENGERS
1993(nd, July) - No. 11, May, 1994 ($2.50, serially numbered)
Triumphant Comics

1-9: 5,6-Triumphant Unleashed x-over. 9-(3/94) 1.00 2.50
0-Retail edition (3/94, $2.50, 36 pgs.) 1.00 2.50
0-Giveaway edition (3/94, 20 pgs.) 1.00 2.50
0-Coupon redemption edition 1.00 2.50
10,11: 10-(4/94) 1.00 2.50

SCHOOL DAY ROMANCES (...of Teen-Agers #4; Popular Teen-Agers #5 on)
Nov-Dec, 1949 - No. 4, May-June, 1950 (Teenage)
Star Publications

1-Toni Gayle (later Toni Gay), Ginger Snapp, Midge Martin & Eve Adams begin 20.00 60.00 160.00
2,3: 3-Jane Powell photo on-c & true life story 14.00 41.00 110.00
4-Ronald Reagan photo on-c; L.B. Cole-c 22.00 66.00 175.00
NOTE: *All have L. B. Cole covers.*

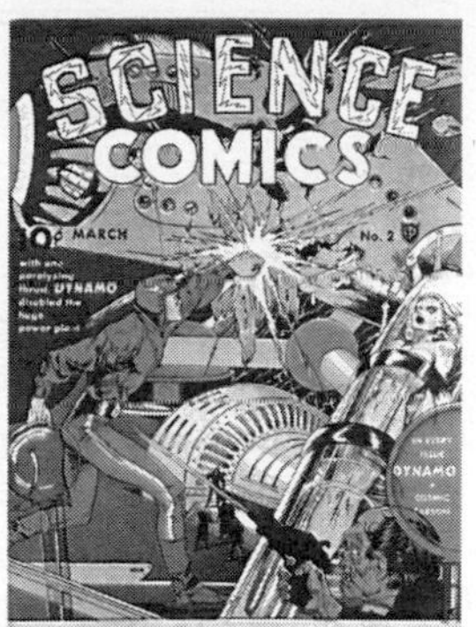

Science Comics #2 © FOX

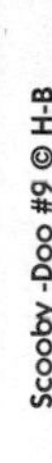

Scooby -Doo #9 © H-B

Scorpion Corps #7 © Dagger

GD25 FN65 NM94

SCHWINN BICYCLE BOOK (...Bike Thrills, 1959)
1949; 1952; 1959 (10¢)
Schwinn Bicycle Co.

1949 5.00 15.00 30.00
1952-Believe It or Not facts; comic format; 36 pgs. 4.00 10.00 20.00
1959 2.00 5.00 10.00

SCIENCE COMICS (1st Series)
Feb, 1940 - No. 8, Sept, 1940
Fox Features Syndicate

1-Origin Dynamo (1st app., called Electro in #1), The Eagle (1st app.), & Navy Jones; Marga, The Panther Woman (1st app.), Cosmic Carson & Perisphere Payne, Dr. Doom begin; bondage/hypo-c; Electro-c 320.00 960.00 3200.00
2-Lou Fine Dynamo-c 167.00 500.00 1500.00
3-Classic Lou Fine Dynamo-c 139.00 417.00 1250.00
4-Kirby-a; Cosmic Carson-c by Joe Simon 122.00 366.00 1100.00
5-8: 5,8-Eagle-c. 6,7-Dynamo-c 72.00 216.00 650.00
NOTE: *Cosmic Carson by* ***Tuska****-#1-3; by* ***Kirby****-#4.* **Lou Fine** *c-1-3 only.*

SCIENCE COMICS (2nd Series)
Jan, 1946 - No. 5, 1946
Humor Publications (Ace Magazines?)

1-Palais-c/a in #1-3; A-Bomb-c 12.00 36.00 95.00
2 6.50 19.50 45.00
3-Feldstein-a (6 pgs.) 11.30 34.00 90.00
4,5: 4-Palais-c 5.70 17.00 35.00

SCIENCE COMICS
May, 1947 (8 pgs. in color)
Ziff-Davis Publ. Co.

nn-Could be ordered by mail for 10¢; like the nn Amazing Adventures (1950) & Boy Cowboy (1950); used to test the market 31.00 94.00 250.00

SCIENCE COMICS (True Science Illustrated)
Mar, 1951
Export Publication Ent., Toronto, Canada
Distr. in U.S. by Kable News Co.

1-Science Adventure stories plus some true science features; man on moon story 7.15 21.50 50.00

SCIENCE FICTION SPACE ADVENTURES (See Space Adventures)

SCOOBY DOO (TV)(...Where are you? #1-16,26; ...Mystery Comics #17-25, 27 on)(See March Of Comics #356, 368, 382, 391)
Mar, 1970 - No. 30, Feb, 1975 (Hanna-Barbera)
Gold Key

1 6.00 18.00 60.00
2-5 4.00 12.00 40.00
6-10 3.00 9.00 30.00
11-20: 11-Tufts-a 2.50 7.50 20.00
21-30 1.85 5.50 15.00

SCOOBY DOO (TV)
Apr, 1975 - No. 11, Dec, 1976 (Hanna-Barbera)
Charlton Comics

1 3.00 9.00 30.00
2-5 2.25 6.75 18.00
6-11 1.50 4.50 12.00

SCOOBY-DOO (TV)
Oct, 1977 - No. 9, Feb, 1979 (Hanna-Barbera)
Marvel Comics Group

1-Dyno-Mutt begins 1.25 3.75 10.00
2-9 1.10 3.30 9.00

SCOOBY-DOO (TV)
Sept, 1992 - No. 3, May, 1993 ($1.25)
Harvey Comics

V2#1,2 1.25
Big Book 1,2 (11/92, 4/93, $1.95, 52 pgs.) .80 2.00
Giant Size 1,2 (10/92, 3/93, $2.25, 68 pgs.) .90 2.25

SCOOBY DOO (TV)
Oct, 1995 -No. 21, June, 1997 ($1.50)
Archie Comics

1-21: 12-Cover by Scooby Doo creative designer Iwao Takamoto 1.50

SCOOBY DOO (TV)
Aug, 1997 - Present ($1.75/$1.95)
DC Comics

1-4 1.75
5-10: 5-Begin-$1.95-c 1.95

SCOOP COMICS (Becomes Yankee Comics #4-7, a digest sized cartoon book not listed in this guide; becomes Snap #9)
November, 1941 - No. 3, Mar, 1943; No. 8, 1944
Harry 'A' Chesler (Holyoke)

1-Intro. Rocketman & Rocketgirl & begins; origin The Master Key & begins; Dan Hastings begins; Charles Sultan-c/a 106.00 318.00 950.00
2-Rocket Boy begins; injury to eye story (reprinted in Spotlight #3); classic-c 100.00 300.00 900.00
3-Injury to eye story-r from #2; Rocket Boy 52.00 156.00 470.00
8-Formerly Yankee Comics; becomes Snap 33.00 100.00 265.00

SCOOTER (See Swing With...)

SCOOTER COMICS
Apr, 1946
Rucker Publ. Ltd. (Canadian)

1-Teen-age/funny animal 7.85 23.50 55.00

SCORCHED EARTH
Apr, 1991 - No. 6, 1991 ($2.95, stiff-c)
Tundra Publishing

1-6 1.20 3.00

SCORE, THE
1989 - No. 4, 1990 ($4.95, 52 pgs, squarebound, mature)
DC Comics (Piranha Press)

Books One - Four 1.20 3.00

SCORPION
Feb, 1975 - No. 3, July, 1975
Atlas/Seaboard Publ.

1-Intro.; bondage-c by Chaykin 1.60 4.00
2-Chaykin-a w/Wrightson, Kaluta, Simonson assists(p) 1.60 4.00
3 1.20 3.00
NOTE: ***Chaykin*** *a-1, 2; c-1.* ***Colon*** *c-2.* ***Craig*** *c/a-3.*

SCORPION CORPS
Nov, 1993 - No. 7, May, 1994? ($2.75/$2.50)
Dagger Comics Group

1,2-($2.75): 1-Intro Angel Dust, Shellcase, Tork, Feedback & Magnon 1.10 2.75
2-Bronze, 2-Gold, 2-Silver 1.10 2.75
3-7-($2.50) 1.00 2.50

SCORPIO ROSE
Jan, 1983 - No. 2, Oct, 1983 ($1.25, Baxter paper)
Eclipse Comics

1,2: Dr. Orient back-up story begins. 2-origin. 1.25

SCOTLAND YARD (Inspector Farnsworth of)(Texas Rangers in Action #5 on?)
June, 1955 - No. 4, Mar, 1956
Charlton Comics Group

Scout: War Shaman #7 © ECL

Sea Devils #10 © DC

Seaquest #1 © Nemesis

	GD25	FN65	NM94
1-Tothish-a	12.00	36.00	90.00
2-4: 2-Tothish-a	10.00	30.00	60.00

SCOUT (See Eclipse Graphic Album #16, New America & Swords of Texas)(Becomes Scout: War Shaman)
Dec, 1985 - No. 27, Oct, 1987($1.75/$1.25, Baxter paper)
Eclipse Comics

	GD25	FN65	NM94
1-8,11,12: 11-Monday, the Eliminator begins		.75	1.80
9,10 ($1.25): 9-Airboy preview. 10-Bissette-a			1.25
13-15,17,18,20-24 ($1.75): 15-Swords of Texas		.75	1.80
16-Scout 3-D Special ($2.50)		1.00	2.50
16-Scout 2-D Limited Edition		1.00	2.50
19-contains flexi-disk ($2.50)		1.00	2.50
...Handbook 1 (8/87, $1.75, B&W)		.70	1.75

SCOUT: WAR SHAMAN (Formerly Scout)
Mar, 1988 - No. 16, Dec, 1989 ($1.95)
Eclipse Comics

	GD25	FN65	NM94
1-16		.80	2.00

SCREAM (...Comics) (Andy Comics #20 on)
Autumn, 1944 - No. 19, Apr, 1948
Humor Publications/Current Books(Ace Magazines)

	GD25	FN65	NM94
1-Teenage humor	12.00	38.00	100.00
2	7.15	21.50	50.00
3-16: 11-Racist humor (Indians). 16-Intro. Lily-Belle	5.70	17.00	40.00
17,19	5.00	15.00	30.00
18-Hypo needle story	5.70	17.00	40.00

SCREAM
Aug, 1973 - No. 11, Feb, 1975 (68 pgs., B&W, magazine)
Skywald Publishing Corp.

	GD25	FN65	NM94
1	2.80	8.40	28.00
2-5: 2-Origin Lady Satan. 3 (12/73)-#3 found on pg. 22	2.00	6.00	16.00
6-11: 6-Origin The Victims. 9-Severed head-c. 11- "Mr. Poe and the Raven" story	1.50	4.50	12.00

SCREWBALL SQIRREL
July, 1995 - No. 3, Sept, 1995 ($2.50, limited series)
Dark Horse Comics

	GD25	FN65	NM94
1-3: Characters created by Tex Avery		1.00	2.50

SCRIBBLY (See All-American Comics, Buzzy, The Funnies, Leave It To Binky & Popular Comics)
8-9/48 - No. 13, 8-9/50; No. 14, 10-11/51 - No. 15, 12-1/51-52
National Periodical Publications

	GD25	FN65	NM94
1-Sheldon Mayer-c/a in all; 52 pgs. begin	83.00	250.00	750.00
2	54.00	162.00	490.00
3-5	43.00	129.00	390.00
6-10	33.00	98.00	260.00
11-15: 13-Last 52 pgs.	29.00	86.00	230.00

SCUD: THE DISPOSABLE ASSASSIN
Feb, 1994 - Present ($2.95, B&W)
Fireman Press

	GD25	FN65	NM94
1	1.50	4.50	12.00
1-2nd printing in color		1.20	3.00
2,3	1.00	3.00	8.00
4-9		2.00	5.00
10-17		1.20	3.00

SEA DEVILS (See Limited Collectors' Edition #39,45, & Showcase #27-29)
Sept-Oct, 1961 - No. 35, May-June, 1967
National Periodical Publications

	GD25	FN65	NM94
1-(9-10/61)	41.00	123.00	500.00
2-Last 10¢ issue	25.00	75.00	250.00
3-Begin 12¢ issues thru #35	16.00	48.00	160.00
4,5	14.50	44.00	145.00
6-10	8.50	25.50	85.00
11,12,14-20	6.00	18.00	60.00
13-Kubert, Colan-a; Joe Kubert app. in story	6.50	19.50	65.00
21-35: 22-Intro. International Sea Devils; origin & 1st app. Capt. X & Man Fish	4.00	12.00	40.00

NOTE: ***Heath*** *a-B&B 27-29, 1-10; c-B&B 27-29, 1-10, 14-16.* ***Moldoff*** *a-16i.*

SEA DEVILS (See Tangent Comics/ Sea Devils)

SEADRAGON (Also see the Epsilion Wave)
May, 1986 - No. 8, 1987 ($1.75)
Elite Comics

	GD25	FN65	NM94
1-8: 1-1st & 2nd printings exist		.70	1.75

SEA HOUND, THE (Captain Silver's Log Of The...)
1945 (no month) - No. 2, Sept-Oct, 1945
Avon Periodicals

	GD25	FN65	NM94
nn (#1)-29 pg. novel length sty-"The Esmeralda's Treasure"	12.00	36.00	95.00
2	8.75	26.25	70.00

SEA HOUND, THE (Radio)
No. 3, July, 1949 - No. 4, Sept, 1949
Capt. Silver Syndicate

	GD25	FN65	NM94
3,4	7.15	21.50	50.00

SEA HUNT (TV)
No. 928, 8/58 - No. 1041, 10-12/59; No. 4, 1-3/60 - No. 13, 4-6/62
Dell Publishing Co. (All have Lloyd Bridges photo-c)

	GD25	FN65	NM94
Four Color 928(#1)	11.00	33.00	120.00
Four Color 994(#2), 4-13: Manning-a #4-6,8-11,13	8.00	23.00	85.00
Four Color 1041(#3)-Toth-a	8.00	25.00	90.00

SEAQUEST (TV)
Mar, 1994 ($2.25)
Nemesis Comics

	GD25	FN65	NM94
1-Has 2 diff-c stocks (slick & cardboard); Alcala-i		.90	2.25

SEARCH FOR LOVE
Feb-Mar, 1950 - No. 2, Apr-May, 1950 (52 pgs.)
American Comics Group

	GD25	FN65	NM94
1	8.75	26.25	65.00
2,3(6-7/50): 3-Exist?	6.00	18.00	42.00

SEARCHERS, THE (Movie)
No. 709, 1956
Dell Publishing Co.

	GD25	FN65	NM94
Four Color 709-John Wayne photo-c	24.00	71.00	260.00

SEARS (See Merry Christmas From...)

SEASON'S GREETINGS
1935 (6-1/4x5-1/4", 32 pgs. in color)
Hallmark (King Features)

	GD25	FN65	NM94
nn-Cover features Mickey Mouse, Popeye, Jiggs & Skippy. "The Night Before Christmas" told one panel per page, each panel by a famous artist featuring their character. Art by Alex Raymond, Gottfredson, Swinnerton, Segar, Chic Young, Milt Gross, Sullivan (Messmer), Herriman, McManus, Percy Crosby & others (22 artists in all) Estimated value...		500.00	

SEBASTION O
May, 1993 - No. 3, July, 1993 ($1.95, limited series)
DC Comics (Vertigo)

	GD25	FN65	NM94
1-3-Grant Morrison scripts		.80	2.00

SECOND LIFE OF DOCTOR MIRAGE, THE (See Shadowman #16)
Nov, 1993 - No. 18, May, 1995 ($2.50)

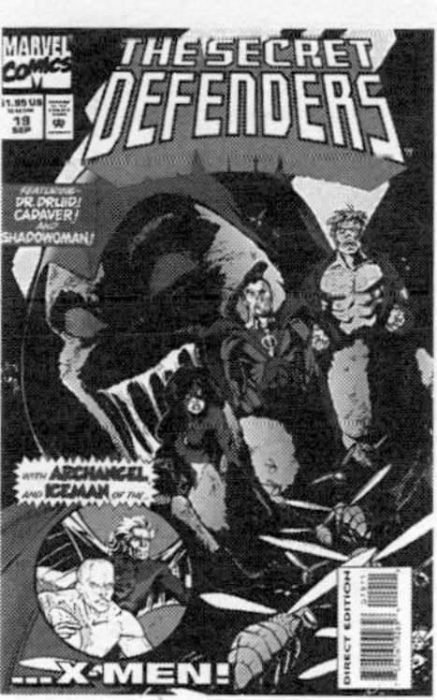

Secret Defenders #19 © MEG

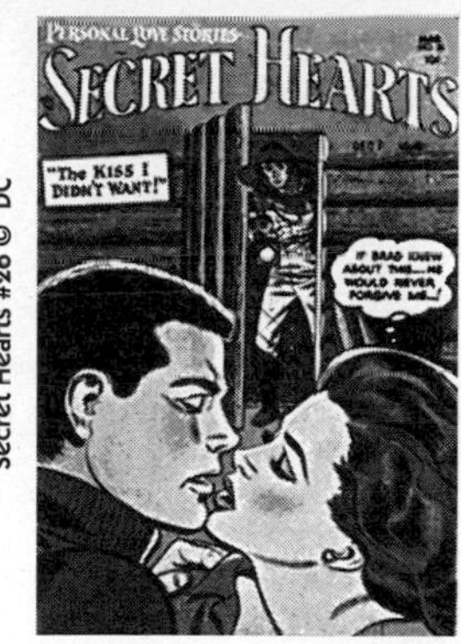

Secret Hearts #26 © DC

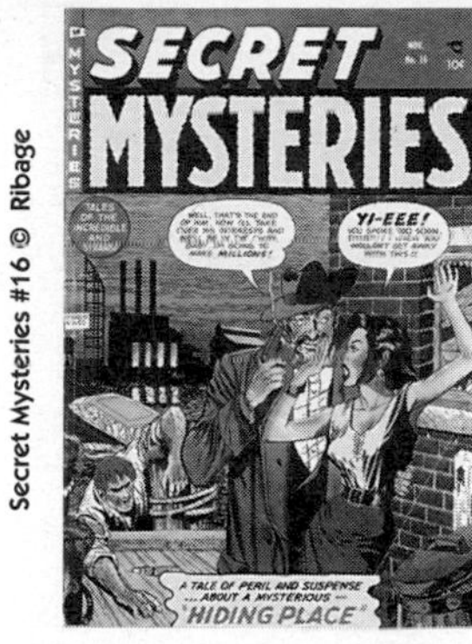

Secret Mysteries #16 © Ribage

GD25 FN65 NM94

Valiant

1-18: 1-With bound-in poster. 5-Shadowman x-over. 7-Bound-in trading card 1.00 2.50
1-Gold ink logo edition; no price on-c 1.20 3.00

SECRET AGENT (Formerly Sarge Steel)
V2#9, Oct, 1966; V2#10, Oct, 1967
Charlton Comics

V2#9-Sarge Steel part-r begins 1.85 5.50 15.00
10-Tiffany Sinn, CIA app. (from Career Girl Romances #39); Aparo-a 1.25 3.75 10.00

SECRET AGENT (TV) (See Four Color #1231)
Nov, 1966; No. 2, Jan, 1968
Gold Key

1-Photo-c 11.00 34.00 125.00
2-Photo-c 7.00 20.00 75.00

SECRET AGENT X-9 (See Flash Gordon #4 by King)
1934 (Book 1: 84 pgs., Book 2: 124 pgs.) (8x7-1/2")
David McKay Publications

Book 1-Contains reprints of the first 13 weeks of the strip by Alex Raymond; complete except for 2 dailies 36.00 108.00 315.00
Book 2-Contains reprints immediately following contents of Book 1, for 20 weeks by Alex Raymond; complete except for two dailies. Note: Raymond mis-dated the last five strips from 6/34, and while the dating sequence is confusing, the continuity is correct 34.00 101.00 270.00

SECRET AGENT X-9 (See Magic Comics)
Dec, 1937 (Not by Raymond)
Dell Publishing Co.

Feature Books 8 35.00 104.00 380.00

SECRET AGENT Z-2 (See Holyoke One-Shot No. 7)

SECRET CITY SAGA (See Jack Kirby's Secret City Saga)

SECRET DEFENDERS (Also see The Defenders & Fantastic Four #374)
Mar, 1993 - No. 25, Mar, 1995 ($1.75/$1.95)
Marvel Comics

1-($2.50)-Red foil stamped-c; Dr. Strange, Nomad, Wolverine, Spider Woman & Darkhawk begin 1.00 2.50
2-11,13,14: 9-New team w/Silver Surfer, Thunderstrike, Dr. Strange & War Machine. 13-Thanos replaces Dr. Strange as leader; leads into Cosmic Powers limited series; 14-Dr. Druid .70 1.75
12-($2.50)-Prismatic foil-c 1.00 2.50
15-24: 15-Begin $1.95-c.; bound-in card sheet. 18-Giant Man & Iron Fist app. .80 2.00
25 ($2.50, 52 pgs.) 1.00 2.50

SECRET DIARY OF EERIE ADVENTURES
1953 (25¢ giant, 100 pgs., one-shot)
Avon Periodicals

nn-(Rare)-Kubert-a; Hollingsworth-c; Sid Check back-c 125.00 375.00 1100.00

SECRET FILES
Spring 1997 ($2.95, B&W, limited series)
Angel Entertainment

1 2.95

SECRET HEARTS
9-10/49 - No. 6, 7-8/50; No. 7, 12-1/51-52 - No. 153, 7/71 (All 52 pgs.)
National Periodical Publications (Beverly)(Arleigh No. 50-113)

1-Kinstler-a; photo-c begin, end #6 41.00 123.00 370.00
2-Toth-a (1 pg.); Kinstler-a 22.00 66.00 175.00
3,6 (1950) 19.00 56.00 150.00
4,5-Toth-a 19.50 58.00 155.00
7(12-1/51-52) (Rare) 31.00 94.00 250.00
8-10 (1952) 12.00 38.00 100.00
11-20 10.50 32.00 85.00
21-26: 26-Last precode (2-3/55) 8.75 26.25 70.00
27-40 5.00 15.00 50.00
41-50 3.50 10.50 35.00
51-60 2.80 8.40 28.00
61-75: 75-Last 10¢ issue 2.50 7.50 22.00
76-109 2.00 6.00 16.00
110- "Reach for Happiness" serial begins, ends #138 1.50 4.50 12.00
111-119,121-126,128-133,135-138-140 1.00 3.00 8.00
120,134-Neal Adams-c 1.25 3.75 10.00
127 (4/68)-Beatles cameo 1.75 5.25 14.00
141,142- "20 Miles to Heartbreak", Chapter 2 & 3 (see Young Love for Chapters 1 & 4); Toth, Colletta-a 1.25 3.75 10.00
143-148,150-153: 144-Morrow-a. 153-Kirby-i 1.00 2.80 7.00
149-Toth-a 1.00 3.00 8.00

SECRET ISLAND OF OZ, THE (See First Comics Graphic Novel)

SECRET LOVE (See Fox Giants & Sinister House of...)

SECRET LOVE
12/55 - No. 3, 8/56; 4/57 - No. 5, 2/58; No. 6, 6/58
Ajax-Farrell/Four Star Comic Corp. No. 2 on

1(12/55-Ajax, 1st series) 7.15 21.50 50.00
2,3 5.00 15.00 30.00
1(4/57-Ajax, 2nd series) 5.70 17.00 40.00
2-6: 5-Bakerish-a 4.15 12.50 25.00

SECRET LOVES
Nov, 1949 - No. 6, Sept, 1950 (#5: photo-c)
Comic Magazines/Quality Comics Group

1-Ward-c 18.00 54.00 140.00
2-Ward-c 16.00 47.00 110.00
3-Crandall-a 10.00 30.00 75.00
4,6 7.00 21.00 45.00
5-Suggestive art "Boom Town Babe" 10.00 30.00 65.00

SECRET LOVE STORIES (See Fox Giants)

SECRET MISSIONS (Admiral Zacharia's...)
February, 1950
St. John Publishing Co.

1-Joe Kubert-c; stories of U.S. foreign agents 17.00 49.00 120.00

SECRET MYSTERIES (Formerly Crime Mysteries & Crime Smashers)
No. 16, Nov, 1954 - No. 19, July, 1955
Ribage/Merit Publications No. 17 on

16-Horror, Palais-a; Myron Fass-c 19.00 56.00 140.00
17-19-Horror. 17-Fass-c; mis-dated 3/54? 12.00 36.00 90.00

SECRET ORIGINS (1st Series) (See 80 Page Giant #8)
Aug-Oct, 1961 (Annual) (Reprints)
National Periodical Publications

1-Origin Adam Strange (Showcase #17), Green Lantern (Green Lantern #1), Challengers (partial-r/Showcase #6, 6 pgs. Kirby-a), J'onn J'onzz (Det. #225), The Flash (Showcase #4), Green Arrow (1 pg. text), Superman-Batman team (W. Finest #94), Wonder Woman (Wonder Woman #105) 58.00 174.00 520.00

SECRET ORIGINS (2nd Series)
Feb-Mar, 1973 - No. 6, Jan-Feb, 1974; No. 7, Oct-Nov, 1974 (All 20¢ issues)
National Periodical Publications (All origin reprints)

1-Superman(r/1 pg. origin/Action #1, 1st time since G.A.), Batman(Det. #33), Ghost(Flash #88), The Flash(Showcase #4) 2.50 7.50 24.00
2-4: 2-Green Lantern & The Atom(Showcase #22 & 34), Supergirl(Action #252). 3-Wonder Woman(W.W. #1), Wildcat(Sensation #1). 4-Vigilante

Secret Origins #1 (3rd series) © DC

The Secret Society of Super-Villains #9 © DC

Secrets of Haunted House #30 © DC

	GD25	FN65	NM94
(Action #42) by Meskin, Kid Eternity(Hit #25)	1.25	3.75	10.00
5-7: 5-The Spectre by Baily (More Fun #52,53). 6-Blackhawk(Military #1) & Legion of Super-Heroes(Superboy #147). 7-Robin(Detective #38), Aquaman (More Fun #73)	1.25	3.75	10.00

NOTE: *Infantino a-1. Kane a-2. Kubert a-1.*

SECRET ORIGINS (3rd Series)
4/86 - No. 50, 8/90 (All origins)(52 pgs. #6 on)(#27 on: $1.50)
DC Comics

	GD25	FN65	NM94
1-Origin Superman		.80	2.00
2-Blue Beetle			1.50
3-5: 3-Shazam. 4-Firestorm. 5-Crimson Avenger			1.50
6-Halo/G.A. Batman			1.50
7-12,14-26: 7-Green Lantern(Guy Gardner)/G.A. Sandman. 8-Shadow Lass/ Doll Man. 9-G.A. Flash/Skyman. 10-Phantom Stranger w/Alan Moore scripts; Legends spin-off. 11-G.A. Hawkman/Power Girl. 12-Challengers of Unknown/ G.A. Fury (2nd modern app.). 14-Suicide Squad; Legends spin-off. 15-Spectre/Deadman. 16-G.A. Hourman/Warlord. 17-Adam Strange story by Carmine infantino; Dr. Occult. 18-G.A. Gr. Lantern/The Creeper. 19-Uncle Sam/The Guardian. 20-Batgirl/G.A. Dr. Mid-Nite. 21-Jonah Hex/Black Condor. 22-Manhunters. 23-Floronic Man/Guardians of the Universe. 24-Blue Devil/Dr. Fate. 25-LSH/Atom. 26-Black Lightning/Miss America			1.50
13-Origin Nightwing; Johnny Thunder app.			1.50
27-38,40-44: 27-Zatara/Zatanna. 28-Midnight/Nightshade. 29-Power of the Atom/Mr. America; new 3 pg. Red Tornado story by Mayer (last app. of Scribbly, 8/88). 30-Plastic Man/Elongated Man. 31-JSA. 32-JLA. 33-35-JLI. 36-Poison Ivy by Neil Gaiman & Mark Buckingham/Green Lantern. 37-Legion Of Substitute Heroes/Doctor Light. 38-Green Arrow/Speedy; Grell scripts. 40-All Ape issue. 41-Rogues Gallery of Flash. 42-Phantom Girl/Grim Ghost. 43-Original Hawk & Dove/Cave Carson/Chris KL-99. 44-Batman app.; story based on Det. #40			1.50
39-Animal Man-c/story continued in Animal Man #10; Grant Morrison scripts; Batman app.			1.50
45-49: 45-Blackhawk/El Diablo. 46-JLA/LSH/New Titans. 47-LSH. 48-Ambush Bug/Stanley & His Monster/Rex the Wonder Dog/Trigger Twins. 49-Newsboy Legion/Silent Knight/brief origin Bouncing Boy			1.50
50-($3.95, 100 pgs.)-Batman & Robin in text, Flash of Two Worlds, Johnny Thunder, Dolphin, Black Canary & Space Museum		1.60	4.00
Annual 1 (8/87)-Capt. Comet/Doom Patrol		.80	2.00
Annual 2 ('88, $2.00)-Origin Flash II & Flash III		.80	2.00
Annual 3 ('89, $2.95, 84 pgs.)-Teen Titans; 1st app. new Flamebird who replaces original Bat-Girl		1.20	3.00
Special 1 (10/89, $2.00)-Batman villains: Penguin, Riddler, & Two-Face; Bolland-c; Sam Kieth-a; Neil Gaiman scripts(2)		.80	2.00

NOTE: ***Art Adams** a-33i(part). **M. Anderson** 8, 19, 21, 25i; c-19(part). **Aparo** c/a-10. **Bissette** c-23. **Bolland** c-7. **Byrne** c/a-Annual 1. **Colan** c/a-5p. **Forte** a-37. **Giffen** a-18p, 44p, 48. **Infantino** a-17, 50p. **Kaluta** c-39. **Gil Kane** a-2, 28; c-2p. **Kirby** c-19(part). **Erik Larsen** a-13. **Mayer** a-29. **Morrow** a-21. **Orlando** a-10. **Perez** a-50i, Annual 3i; c- Annual 3. **Rogers** a-6p. **Russell** a-27i. **Simonson** c-22. **Staton** a-36, 50p. **Steacy** a-35. **Tuska** a-4p, 9p.*

SECRET ORIGINS OF SUPER-HEROES (See DC Special Series #10, 19)

SECRET ORIGINS OF THE WORLD'S GREATEST SUPER-HEROES
1989 ($4.95, 148 pgs.)
DC Comics

	GD25	FN65	NM94
nn-Reprints Batman, Superman, JLA.origins; Bolland-c.		2.20	5.50

SECRET ROMANCE
Oct, 1968 - No. 41, Nov, 1976; No. 42, Mar, 1979 - No. 48, Feb, 1980
Charlton Comics

	GD25	FN65	NM94
1-Begin 12¢ issues, ends #?	1.00	3.00	8.00
2-10: 9-Reese-a		2.60	4.00
11-48		.80	2.00

NOTE: *Beyond the Stars app.-No. 9, 11, 12, 14.*

SECRET ROMANCES (Exciting Love Stories)
Apr, 1951 - No. 27, July, 1955
Superior Publications Ltd.

	GD25	FN65	NM94
1	9.50	28.00	75.00
2	6.50	19.50	45.00
3-10	5.35	16.00	32.00
11-13,15-18,20-27	4.00	12.00	24.00
14,19-Lingerie panels	5.00	15.00	30.00

SECRET SERVICE (See Kent Blake of the...)

SECRET SIX (See Action Comics Weekly)
Apr-May, 1968 - No. 7, Apr-May, 1969 (12¢)
National Periodical Publications

	GD25	FN65	NM94
1-Origin/1st app.	4.50	13.50	45.00
2-7	2.50	7.50	25.00

SECRET SIX (See Tangent Comics/ Secret Six)

SECRET SOCIETY OF SUPER-VILLAINS
May-June, 1976 - No. 15, June-July, 1978
National Periodical Publications/DC Comics

	GD25	FN65	NM94
1-Origin; JLA cameo & Capt. Cold app.	1.00	2.80	7.00
2,4,15: 2-Re-intro/origin Capt. Comet; Green Lantern x-over.15-G.A. Atom, Dr. Midnite, & JSA app.		2.00	5.00
3,5: 5-Green Lantern, Hawkman x-over; Darkseid app.		2.40	6.00
6-9: 9-Creeper x-over		1.60	4.00
10-14: 10-Creeper x-over. 11-Capt. Comet; Orlando-i.		1.20	3.00

SECRET SOCIETY OF SUPER-VILLAINS SPECIAL (See DC Special Series #6)

SECRETS OF HAUNTED HOUSE
4-5/75 - #5, 12-1/75-76; #6, 6-7/77 - #14, 10-11/78; #15, 8/79 - #46, 3/82
National Periodical Publications/DC Comics

	GD25	FN65	NM94
1	2.50	7.50	20.00
2-4	1.00	3.00	8.00
5-Wrightson-c	1.25	3.75	10.00
6-14		2.40	6.00
15-30		1.60	4.00
31-Mr. E series begins, ends #41		2.00	5.00
32-43,45,46		1.20	3.00
44-Wrightson-c		2.40	6.00

NOTE: ***Aparo** c-7. **Aragones** a-1. **B. Bailey** a-8. **Bissette** a-46. **Buckler** c-32-40p. **Ditko** a-9, 12, 41, 45. **Golden** a-10. **Howard** a-13i. **Kaluta** c-8, 10, 11, 14, 16, 29. **Kubert** c-41, 42. **Sheldon Mayer** a-43p. **McWilliams** a-35. **Nasser** a-24. **Newton** a-30p. **Nino** a-1, 13, 19. **Orlando** c-13, 30, 43, 45i. **N. Redondo** a-4, 5, 29. **Rogers** c-26. **Spiegle** a-31-41. **Wrightson** c-5, 44.*

SECRETS OF HAUNTED HOUSE SPECIAL (See DC Special Series #12)

SECRETS OF LIFE (Movie)
1956 (Disney)
Dell Publishing Co.

	GD25	FN65	NM94
Four Color 749-Photo-c	3.60	11.00	40.00

SECRETS OF LOVE (See Popular Teen-Agers...)

SECRETS OF LOVE AND MARRIAGE
V2#1, Aug, 1956 - V2#25, June, 1961
Charlton Comics

	GD25	FN65	NM94
V2#1	3.00	9.00	30.00
V2#2-6	2.50	7.50	20.00
V2#7-9-(All 68 pgs.)	3.00	9.00	30.00
10-25	1.50	4.50	12.00

SECRETS OF MAGIC (See Wisco)

SECRETS OF SINISTER HOUSE (Sinister House of Secret Love #1-4)
No. 5, June-July, 1972 - No. 18, June-July, 1974
National Periodical Publications

	GD25	FN65	NM94
5-(52 pgs.).	2.50	7.50	20.00
6-9: 7-Redondo-a	1.50	4.50	12.00
10-Neal Adams-a(i)	2.50	7.50	20.00

Secrets of the Legion of Super-Heroes #2 ©DC

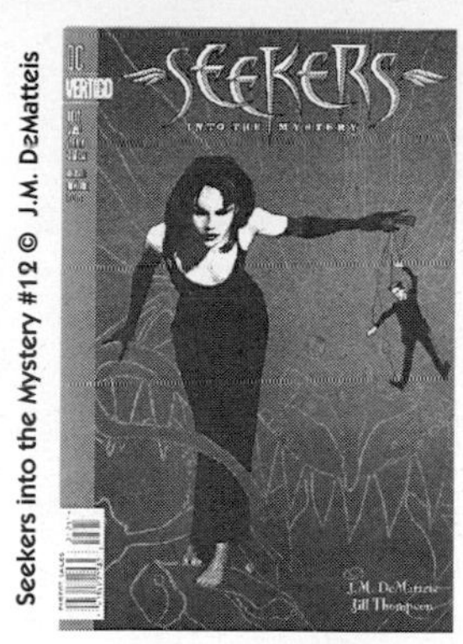

Seekers into the Mystery #12 © J.M. DeMatteis

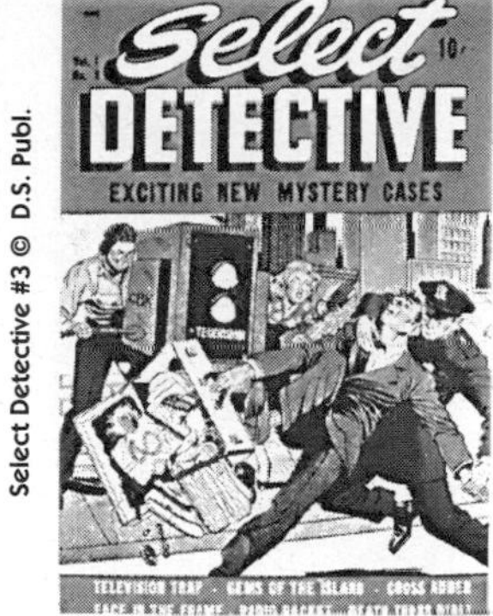

Select Detective #3 © D.S. Publ.

GD25 FN65 NM94

11-18: 15-Redondo-a. 17-Barry-a; early Chaykin 1 pg. strip 1.00 3.00 8.00

NOTE: ***Alcala*** *a-6, 13, 14.* ***Glanzman*** *a-7.* ***Kaluta*** *c-6, 7.* ***Nino*** *a-8, 11-13. Ambrose Bierce adapt.-#14.*

SECRETS OF THE LEGION OF SUPER-HEROES
Jan, 1981 - No. 3, Mar, 1981 (Limited series)
DC Comics

1-3: 1-Origin of the Legion. 2-Retells origins of Brainiac 5, Shrinking Violet, Sun-Boy, Bouncing Boy, Ultra-Boy, Matter-Eater Lad, Mon-El, Karate Kid, & Dream Girl .80 2.00

SECRETS OF TRUE LOVE
Feb, 1958
St. John Publishing Co.

1 4.00 12.00 24.00

SECRETS OF YOUNG BRIDES
No. 5, Sept, 1957 - No. 44, Oct, 1964; July, 1975 - No. 9, Nov, 1976
Charlton Comics

5 3.00 9.00 30.00
6-10: 8-Negligee panel 2.50 7.50 20.00
11-20 1.85 5.50 15.00
21-30: Last 10¢ issue? 1.25 3.75 10.00
31-44 2.40 6.00
1-9 (2nd series) 1.50

SECRET SQUIRREL (TV)(See Kite Fun Book)
Oct, 1966 (12¢) (Hanna-Barbera)
Gold Key

1 11.00 32.00 115.00

SECRET STORY ROMANCES (Becomes True Tales of Love)
Nov, 1953 - No. 21, Mar, 1956
Atlas Comics (TCI)

1-Everett-a; Jay Scott Pike-c 9.50 28.00 75.00
2 5.70 17.00 38.00
3-11: 11-Last pre-code (2/55) 5.00 15.00 30.00
12-21 4.15 12.50 25.00

NOTE: ***Colletta*** *a-10, 14, 15, 17, 21; c-10, 14, 17.*

SECRET VOICE, THE (See Great American Comics Presents...)

SECRET WARS II (Also see Marvel Super Heroes...)
July, 1985 - No. 9, Mar, 1986 (Maxi-series)
Marvel Comics Group

1-9: 2-1st app. Boom Boom. 2,8,9-X-Men app. 5,8,9-Spider-Man app. 9-(75¢, 52 pgs.) 1.00

SECRET WEAPONS
Sept, 1993 - No. 21, May, 1995 ($2.25)
Valiant

1-10,12-21: 3-Reese-a(i). 5-Ninjak app. 9-Bound-in trading card. 12-Bloodshot app. .90 2.25
11-(Sept. on envelope, Aug on-c, $2.50)-Enclosed in manilla envelope; Blootshot app; intro new team. 1.00 2.50

SECTAURS
June, 1985 - No. 10?, 1986 (75¢) (Based on Coleco Toys)
Marvel Comics

1-10 1.00
1-Coleco giveaway; different-c 1.00

SEDUCTION OF THE INNOCENT (Also see New York State Joint Legislative Committee to Study...)
1953, 1954 (400 pgs.) (Hardback, $4.00)(Written by Fredric Wertham, M.D.)
Rinehart & Co., Inc., N. Y. (Also printed in Canada by Clarke, Irwin & Co. Ltd., Toronto)

(1st Version)-with bibliographical note intact (pages 399 & 400)(several copies got out before the comic publishers forced the removal of this page) 42.00 126.00 375.00
Dust jacket only 31.00 94.00 250.00
(1st Version)-without bibliographical note 25.00 75.00 200.00
Dust jacket only 14.00 41.00 110.00
(2nd Version)-Published in England by Kennikat Press, 1954, 399 pgs. has bibliographical page 8.75 26.25 65.00
1972 r-/of 2nd version; 400 pgs. w/bibliography page; Kennikat Press 2.50 7.50 24.00

NOTE: *Material from this book appeared in the November, 1953(Vol.70, pp50-53,214) issue of the* ***Ladies' Home Journal*** *under the title "What Parents Don't Know About Comic Books". With the release of this book, Dr. Wertham reveals seven years of research attempting to link juvenile delinquency to comic books. Many illustrations showing excessive violence, sex, sadism, and torture are shown. This book was used at the Kefauver Senate hearings which led to the Comics Code Authority. Because of the influence this book had on the comic industry and the collector's interest in it, we feel this listing is justified. Also see* ***Parade of Pleasure.***

SEDUCTION OF THE INNOCENT! (Also see Halloween Horror)
Nov, 1985 - 3-D#2, Apr, 1986 ($1.75)
Eclipse Comics

1-6: Double listed under cover title from #7 on .75 1.80
3-D 1 (10/85, $2.25, 36 pgs.)-contains unpublished Advs. Into Darkness #15 (pre-code);Dave Stevens-c .90 2.25
2D 1 (100 copy limited signed & numbered edition)(B&W) 2.00 5.00
3-D 2 (4/86)-Baker, Toth, Wrightson-c 1.00 2.50
2-D 2 (100 copy limited signed & numbered edition)(B&W) 2.00 5.00

NOTE: ***Anderson*** *r-2, 3.* ***Crandall*** *c/a(r)-1.* ***Meskin*** *c/a(r)-3, 3-D 1.* ***Moreira*** *r-2.* ***Toth*** *a-1-6r; c-4r.* ***Tuska*** *r-6.*

SEEKER
Apr, 1994 ($2.50, one-shot)
Sky Comics

1 1.00 2.50

SEEKERS INTO THE MYSTERY
Jan, 1996 - No. 15, Apr, 1997 ($2.50)
DC Comics (Vertigo)

1-14: J.M. DeMatteis scripts in all. 1-4-Glenn Barr-a. 5,10-Muth-c/a. 6-9-Zulli-c/a. 11-14-Bolton-c; Jill Thompson-a 1.00 2.50
15-($2.95)-Muth-c/a 2.95

SELECT DETECTIVE (Exciting New Mystery Cases)
Aug-Sept, 1948 - No. 3, Dec-Jan, 1948-49
D. S. Publishing Co.

1-Matt Baker-a 21.00 62.00 160.00
2-Baker, McWilliams-a 13.00 39.00 100.00
3 11.00 33.00 80.00

SELF-LOATHING COMICS
Feb, 1995 ($2.95, B&W)
Fantagraphics Books

1,2-Crumb 1.20 3.00

SEMPER FI (Tales of the Marine Corp)
Dec, 1988- No.9, Aug, 1989 (75¢)
Marvel Comics

1-9: Severin-c/a 1.00

SENSATIONAL POLICE CASES (Becomes Captain Steve Savage, 2nd Series)
1952; 1954 - No. 4, July-Aug, 1954
Avon Periodicals

nn-(1952, 25¢, 100 pgs.)-Kubert-a?; Check, Larsen, Lawrence & McCann-a; Kinstler-c 36.00 107.00 250.00
1 (1954)-Exists? 12.00 36.00 90.00
2-4: 2-Kirbyish-a (3-4/54). 4-Reprint/Saint #5; spanking panel 10.00 30.00 70.00
I.W. Reprint #5-(1963?, nd)-Reprints Prison Break #5(1952-Realistic); Infantino-a 2.50 7.50 20.00

Sensational She-Hulk #12 © MEG

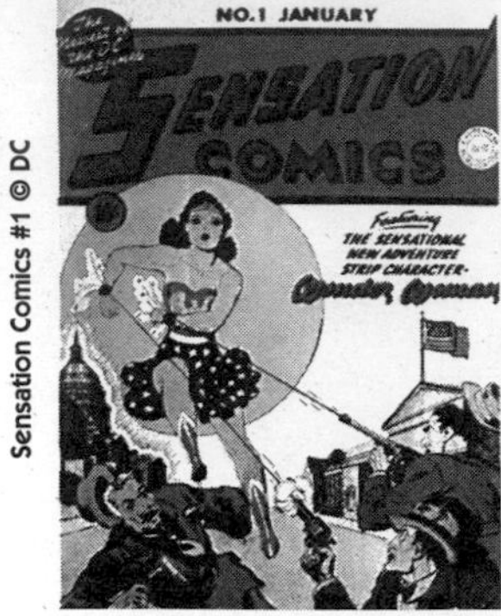

Sensation Comics #1 © DC

Sgt. Bilko's Pvt. Doberman #5 © DC

GD25 FN65 NM94

SENSATIONAL SHE-HULK, THE (She-Hulk #21-23) (See Savage She-Hulk)
V2#1, 5/89 - No. 60, Feb, 1994 ($1.50/$1.75, deluxe format)
Marvel Comics

V2#1-Byrne-c/a(p)/scripts begin, end #8 1.20 3.00
2-8: 3-Spidey. 4-Reintro G.A. Blonde Phantom .90 2.25
9-49,51-60: 14-17-Howard the Duck app. 21-23-Return of the Blonde Phantom. 22-All Winners Squad app. 25-Thor app. 26-Excalibur app.; Guice-c. 29-Wolverine app. (3 pgs.). 30-Hobgoblin-c & cameo. 31-Byrne-c/a/scripts begin again. 35-Last $1.50-c. 37-Wolverine/Punisher/Spidey-c, but no app. 39-Thing app. 56-War Zone app.; Hulk cameo. 57-Vs. Hulk-c/story. 58-Electro-c/story. 59-Jack O'Lantern app. .80 2.00
50-($2.95, 52 pgs.)-Embossed green foil-c; Byrne app.; last Byrne-c/a; Austin, Chaykin, Simonson-a; Miller-a(2 pgs.) 1.30 3.25
NOTE: ***Dale Keown*** *a(p)-13, 15-22.*

SENSATIONAL SHE-HULK IN CEREMONY, THE
1989 - No. 2, 1989 ($3.95, squarebound, 52 pgs.)
Marvel Comics

nn-Part 1, nn-Part 2 1.60 4.00

SENSATIONAL SPIDER-MAN
Apr, 1989 ($5.95, squarebound, 80 pgs.)
Marvel Comics

1-r/Amazing Spider-Man Annual #14,15 by Miller & Annual #8 by Kirby & Ditko. 2.40 6.00

SENSATIONAL SPIDER-MAN, THE
Jan, 1996 - Present ($1.95)
Marvel Comics

0 ($4.95)-Lenticular-c; Jurgens-a/scripts 1.00 2.00 5.00
1-17, -1(7/97), 18: 2-Kaine & Rhino app. 3-Giant-Man app. 9-Onslaught tie-in; revealed that Peter & Mary Jane's unborn baby is a girl. 11-Revelations. 13-15-Ka-Zar app. 14,15-Hulk app. .80 2.00
1-($2.95) variant-c; polybagged w/cassette 1.20 3.00
19-24: 19 Begin-$1.99-c; Living Pharoah app. 22,23-Dr. Strange app. 1.99
'96 Annual ($2.95) 2.95

SENSATION COMICS (Sensation Mystery #110 on)
Jan, 1942 - No. 109, May-June, 1952
National Per. Publ./All-American

	GD25	FN65	VF82	NM94
1-Origin Mr. Terrific(1st app.), Wildcat(1st app.), The Gay Ghost, & Little Boy Blue; Wonder Woman(cont'd from All Star #8), The Black Pirate begin; intro. Justice & Fair Play Club	1909.00	5727.00	12,408.00	21,000.00

(Estimated up to 150 total copies exist, 7 in NM/Mint)

1-Reprint, Oversize 13-1/2x10". WARNING: This comic is an exact duplicate reprint of the original except for its size. DC published it in 1974 with a second cover titling it as a Famous First Edition. There have been many reported cases of the outer cover being removed and the interior sold as the original edition. The reprint with the new outer cover removed is practically worthless. See Famous First Edition for value.

	GD25	FN65	NM94
2-Etta Candy begins	340.00	1020.00	3400.00
3-W. Woman gets secretary's job	200.00	600.00	1800.00
4-1st app. Stretch Skinner in Wildcat	144.00	432.00	1300.00
5-Intro. Justin, Black Pirate's son	117.00	350.00	1050.00
6-Origin/1st app. Wonder Woman's magic lasso	117.00	350.00	1050.00
7-10	83.00	250.00	750.00
11,12,14-20	75.00	225.00	675.00
13-Hitler, Tojo, Mussolini-c (as bowling pins)	93.00	279.00	840.00
21-30	58.00	174.00	525.00
31-33	44.00	132.00	400.00
34-Sargon, the Sorcerer begins (10/44), ends #36; begins again #52	47.00	141.00	420.00
35-40: 38-X-Mas-c	39.00	117.00	350.00
41-50: 43-The Whip app.	36.00	108.00	300.00
51-60: 51-Last Black Pirate. 56,57-Sargon by Kubert	31.00	94.00	250.00
61-67,69-80: 63-Last Mr. Terrific. 66-Wildcat by Kubert	31.00	94.00	250.00
68-Origin & 1st app.Huntress (8/47)	33.00	98.00	260.00
81-Used in **SOTI**, pg. 33,34; Krigstein-a	33.00	98.00	260.00
82-90: 83-Last Sargon. 86-The Atom app. 90-Last Wildcat	24.00	71.00	190.00
91-Streak begins by Alex Toth	24.00	73.00	195.00
92,93: 92-Toth-a (2 pgs.)	24.00	73.00	195.00
94-1st all girl issue	36.00	108.00	300.00
95-99,101-106: 95-Unmasking of Wonder Woman-c/story. 99-1st app. Astra, Girl of the Future, ends #106. 103-Robot-c. 105-Last 52 pgs. 106-Wonder Woman ends	35.00	105.00	280.00
100-(11-12/50)	44.00	132.00	400.00
107-(Scarce, 1-2/52)-1st mystery issue; Johnny Peril by Toth(p), 8 pgs. & begins; continues from Danger Trail #5 (3-4/51)(see Comic Cavalcade #15 for 1st app.)	52.00	156.00	465.00
108-(Scarce)-Johnny Peril by Toth(p)	42.00	126.00	380.00
109-(Scarce)-Johnny Peril by Toth(p)	52.00	156.00	465.00

NOTE: ***Krigstein*** *a-(Wildcat)-81, 83, 84.* ***Moldoff*** *Black Pirate-1-25; Black Pirate not in 34-36, 43-48.* ***Oskner*** *c(i)-89-91, 94-106. Wonder Woman by* ***H. G. Peter****, all issues except #8, 17-19, 21; c-4-7, 9-18, 20-88, 92, 93.* ***Toth*** *a-91, 98; c-107. Wonder Woman c-1-106.*

SENSATION MYSTERY (Formerly Sensation Comics #1-109)
No. 110, July-Aug, 1952 - No. 116, July-Aug, 1953
National Periodical Publications

110-Johnny Peril continues 34.00 103.00 270.00
111-116-Johnny Peril in all. 116-M. Anderson-a 34.00 103.00 270.00
NOTE: ***M. Anderson*** *c-110.* ***Colan*** *a-114p.* ***Giunta*** *a-112.* ***G. Kane*** *c(p)-108, 109, 111-115.*

SENTINELS OF JUSTICE, THE (See Americomics & Captain Paragon &...)

SENTRY SPECIAL
1991 ($2.75, one-shot)(Hero Alliance spin-off)
Innovation Publishing

1-Lost in Space preview (3 pgs.) 1.10 2.75

SERAPHIM
May, 1990 ($2.50, mature readers)
Innovation Publishing

1 1.00 2.50

SERGEANT BARNEY BARKER (Becomes G. I. Tales #4 on)
Aug, 1956 - No. 3, Dec, 1956
Atlas Comics (MCI)

1-Severin-c/a(4) 15.00 45.00 120.00
2,3: 2-Severin-c/a(4). 3-Severin-c/a(5) 10.00 30.00 80.00

SERGEANT BILKO (Phil Silvers Starring as...) (TV)
May-June, 1957 - No. 18, Mar-Apr, 1960
National Periodical Publications

1-All have Bob Oskner-c 60.00 180.00 540.00
2 34.00 103.00 275.00
3-5 28.00 83.00 220.00
6-18: 11,12,15,17-Photo-c 23.00 68.00 180.00

SGT. BILKO'S PVT. DOBERMAN (TV)
June-July, 1958 - No. 11, Feb-Mar, 1960
National Periodical Publications

1-Bob Oskner c-1-4,7,11 36.00 108.00 300.00
2 23.00 68.00 180.00
3-5: 5-Photo-c 16.00 49.00 130.00
6-11: 6,9-Photo-c 12.00 36.00 95.00

SGT. DICK CARTER OF THE U.S. BORDER PATROL (See Holyoke One-Shot)

SGT. FURY (& His Howling Commandos)(See Fury & Special Marvel Edition)
May, 1963 - No. 167, Dec, 1981
Marvel Comics Group (BPC earlier issues)

1-1st app. Sgt. Nick Fury (becomes agent of Shield in Strange Tales #135);

Sgt. Fury #149 © MEG

Sergeant Preston of the Yukon #6 © DELL

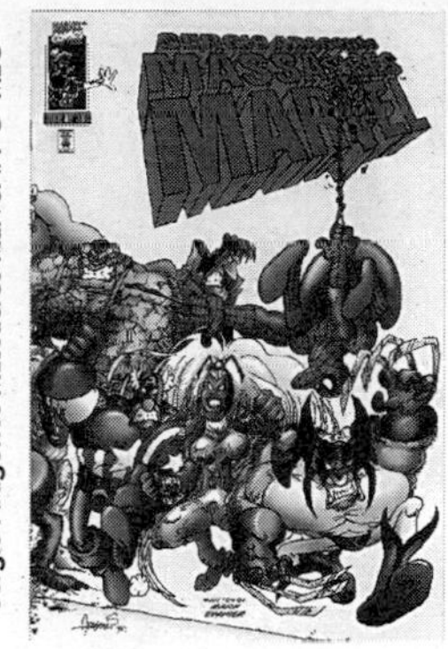
Sergio Aragonés Massacres Marvel #1 © MEG

GD25 FN65 NM94

Kirby/Ayers-c/a; 1st Dum-Dum Dugan & the Howlers
83.00 250.00 1000.00
2-Kirby-a 29.00 88.00 295.00
3-5: 3-Reed Richards x-over. 4-Death of Junior Juniper. 5-1st Baron Strucker app.; Kirby-a 17.00 51.00 170.00
6-10: 8-Baron Zemo, 1st Percival Pinkerton app. 9-Hitler-c & app. 10-1st app. Capt. Savage (the Skipper)(9/64) 11.00 33.00 110.00
11,12,14-20: 14-1st Blitz Squad. 18-Death of Pamela Hawley
5.50 16.50 55.00
13-Captain America & Bucky app.(12/64); 2nd solo Capt. America x-over outside The Avengers; Kirby-a 28.00 84.00 280.00
21-30: 25-Red Skull app. 27-1st app. Eric Koenig; origin Fury's eye patch
4.00 12.00 40.00
31-50: 34-Origin Howling Commandos. 35-Eric Koenig joins Howlers. 43-Bob Hope, Glen Miller app. 44-Flashback on Howlers 1st mission
2.50 7.50 20.00
51-60 2.25 6.75 18.00
61-80: 64-Capt. Savage & Raiders x-over. 76-Fury's Father app. in WWI story
1.85 5.50 15.00
81-100: 98-Deadly Dozen x-over. 100-Capt. America, Fantastic 4 cameos; Stan Lee, Martin Goodman & others app. 1.50 4.50 12.00
101-120: 101-Origin retold 1.25 3.75 10.00
121-130: 121-123-r/#19-21 1.00 3.00 8.00
131-167: 167-Reprints (from 1963) 1.00 2.80 7.00
Annual 1(1965, 25¢, 72 pgs.)-r/#4,5 & new-a 12.00 36.00 120.00
Special 2(1966) 4.00 12.00 40.00
Special 3(1967) 2.50 7.50 25.00
Special 4(1968) 2.25 6.75 18.00
Special 5-7(1969-11/71) 1.50 4.50 12.00

NOTE: *Ayers a-8, Annual 1. Ditko a-15i. Gil Kane c-37, 96. Kirby a-1-7, 13p, 167p(r). Special 5; c-1-20, 25, 167p. Severin a-44-46, 48, 162, 164; inks-49-79, Special 4, 6; c-4i, 5, 6, 44, 46, 110, 149i, 155i, 162-166. Sutton a-57p. Reprints in #80, 82, 85, 87, 89, 91, 93, 95, 99, 101, 103, 105, 107, 109, 111, 121-123, 145-155, 167.*

SGT. FURY AND HIS HOWLING DEFENDERS (See The Defenders #147)

SERGEANT PRESTON OF THE YUKON (TV)
No. 344, Aug, 1951 - No. 29, Nov-Jan, 1958-59
Dell Publishing Co.

Four Color 344(#1)-Sergeant Preston & his dog Yukon King begin; painted-c begin, end #18 11.00 33.00 120.00
Four Color 373,397,419('52) 6.40 19.00 70.00
5(11-1/52-53)-10(2-4/54): 6-Bondage-c. 4.50 13.50 50.00
11,12,14-17 3.60 11.00 40.00
13-Origin Sgt. Preston 4.50 13.50 50.00
18-Origin Yukon King; last painted-c 4.50 13.50 50.00
19-29: All photo-c 5.50 16.50 60.00

SERGEANT PRESTON OF THE YUKON
1956 (4 comic booklets) (Soft-c, 16 pgs., 7x2-1/2" & 5x2-1/2")
Giveaways with Quaker Cereals

"How He Found Yukon King", "The Case That Made Him A Sergeant", "How Yukon King Saved Him From The Wolves", "How He Became A Mountie" each... 7.15 21.50 50.00

SGT. ROCK (Formerly Our Army at War; see Brave & the Bold #52 & Showcase #45)
No. 302, Mar, 1977 - No. 422, July, 1988 (See G.I. Combat #108)
National Periodical Publications/DC Comics

302 3.00 9.00 30.00
303-310 1.85 5.50 15.00
311-320: 318-Reprints 1.25 3.75 10.00
321-350 1.00 3.00 8.00
351-399,401-421 2.00 5.00
400,422: 422-1st Joe, Adam, Andy Kubert-a team 1.00 2.80 7.00
Annual 2-4: 2(1982)-Formerly Sgt. Rock's Prize Battle Tales #1. 3(1983). 4(1984) 2.00 5.00

GD25 FN65 NM94

NOTE: *Estrada a-322, 327, 331, 336, 337, 341, 342i. Glanzman a-384, 421. Kubert a-302, 303, 305r, 306, 328, 351, 356, 368, 373, 422; c-317, 318r, 319-323, 325-333-on, Annual 2, 3. Severin a-347. Spiegle a-382, Annual 2, 3. Thorne a-384. Toth a-385r. Wildey a-307, 311, 313, 314.*

SGT. ROCK SPECIAL (Sgt. Rock #14 on; see DC Special Series #3)
Oct, 1988 - No. 21, Feb, 1992; No. 1, 1992 ($2.00, quarterly, 52 pgs.)
DC Comics

1 1.10 2.75
2-8,10-21: All-r; 5-r/1st Sgt. Rock/Our Army at War #81. 7-Tomahawk-r by Thorne. 10-All Rock issue. 11-r/1st Haunted Tank story. 12-All Kubert issue; begins monthly. 13-Dinosaur story by Heath(r). 14-Enemy Ace-r (22 pgs.) by Adams/Kubert. 15-Enemy Ace (22 pgs.) by Kubert. 16-Iron Major-c/story. 16,17-Enemy Ace-r. 19-r/Batman/Sgt. Rock team-up/B&B #108 by Aparo
.90 2.25
9-Enemy Ace-r by Kubert 1.20 3.00
1,2: 1 (1992, $2.95, 68 pgs.)-Simonson-c; unpubbed Kubert-a; Glanzman, Russell, Pratt, & Wagner-a 1.40 3.50

NOTE: *Neal Adams r-1, 8, 14p. Chaykin a-2; r-3, 9(2pgs.); c-3. Drucker r-6. Glanzman r-20. Golden a-1. Heath a-2; r-5, 9-13, 16, 19, 21. Krigstein r-4, 8. Kubert r-1-17, 20, 21; c-1p, 2, 8, 14-21. Miller r-6p. Severin r-3, 6, 10. Simonson r-2, 4; c-4. Thorne r-7. Toth r-2, 8, 11. Wood r-4.*

SGT. ROCK SPECTACULAR (See DC Special Series #13)

SGT. ROCK'S PRIZE BATTLE TALES (Becomes Sgt. Rock Annual #2 on; see DC Special Series #18 & 80 Page Giant #7)
Winter, 1964 (Giant - 80 pgs., one-shot)
National Periodical Publications

1-Kubert, Heath-r; new Kubert-c 27.00 81.00 270.00

SGT. STRYKER'S DEATH SQUAD (See Savage Combat Tales)

SERGIO ARAGONES DESTROYS DC
June, 1996 ($3.50, one-shot)
DC Comics

1-DC Superhero parody book; Aragonés-c/a; Evanier scripts.
1.40 3.50

SERGIO ARAGONES' LOUDER THAN WORDS
July, 1997 - No. 6, Dec, 1997 ($2.95, B&W, limited series)
Dark Horse Comics

1-6-Aragonés-c/a 2.95

SERGIO ARAGONES MASSACRES MARVEL
June, 1996 ($3.50, one-shot)
Marvel Comics

1-Marvel Superhero parody book; Aragonés-c/a; Evanier scripts.
1.40 3.50

SERGIO ARAGONES' GROO THE WANDERER (See Groo...)

SERRA ANGEL ON THE WORLDS OF MAGIC THE GATHERING
Aug, 1996 ($5.95, one-shot)
Acclaim Comics (Armada)

1 2.40 6.00

SERINA
Mar, 1996 - No. 2 ($2.95)
Antarctic Press

1,2: Warrior Nun app. 1.20 3.00

SEVEN BLOCK
1990 ($4.50, one-shot, 52 pgs.)
Marvel Comics (Epic Comics)

1 1.80 4.50

SEVEN DEAD MEN (See Complete Mystery #1)

SEVEN DWARFS (Also see Snow White)
No. 227, 1949 (Disney-Movie)
Dell Publishing Co.

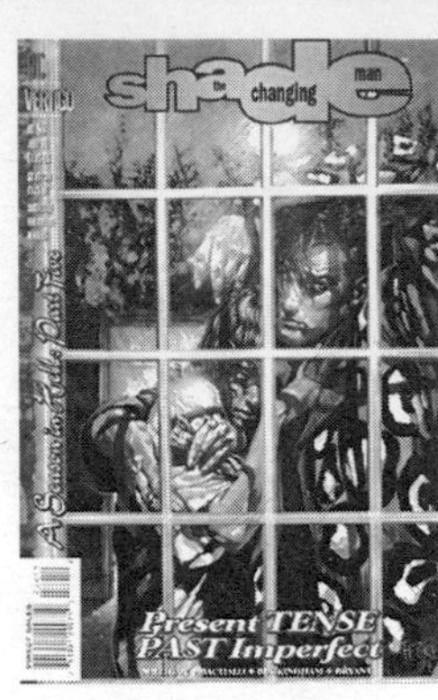

Shade, The Changing Man #49 © DC

The Shadow #1 © Conde Nast

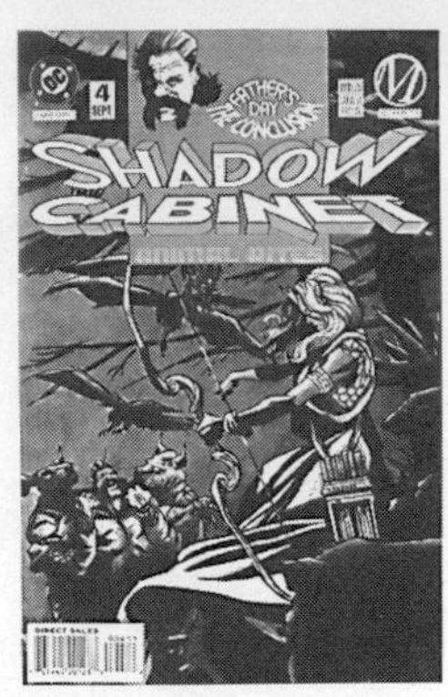

Shadow Cabinet #4 © DC

	GD25	FN65	NM94
Four Color #227	10.00	30.00	110.00

SEVEN MILES A SECOND
1996 ($7.95, one-shot)
DC Comics (Vertigo Verité)

nn-Wojnarowicz-s/Romberg-a	1.00	3.00	8.00

SEVEN SAMUROID, THE (See Image Graphic Novel)

SEVEN SEAS COMICS
Apr, 1946 - No. 6, 1947 (no month)
Universal Phoenix Features/Leader No. 6

1-South Sea Girl by Matt Baker, Capt. Cutlass begin; Tugboat Tessie by Baker app.	66.00	200.00	575.00
2	58.00	174.00	480.00
3-6: 3-Six pg. Feldstein-a	51.00	153.00	425.00

NOTE: ***Baker*** *a-1-6; c-3-6.*

1776 (See Charlton Classic Library)

7TH VOYAGE OF SINBAD, THE (Movie)
Sept, 1958 (photo-c)
Dell Publishing Co.

Four Color 944-Buscema-a	12.00	35.00	130.00

77 SUNSET STRIP (TV)
No. 1066, Jan-Mar, 1960 - No. 2, Feb, 1963 (All photo-c)
Dell Publ. Co./Gold Key

Four Color 1066-Toth-a	11.00	33.00	120.00
Four Color 1106,1159-Toth-a	9.00	27.00	100.00
Four Color 1211,1263,1291, 01-742-209(7-9/62)-Manning-a in all	8.00	25.00	90.00
1(11/62-G.K.), 2-Manning-a in each	8.00	25.00	90.00

77TH BENGAL LANCERS, THE (TV)
May, 1957
Dell Publishing Co.

Four Color 791-Photo-c	6.40	19.00	70.00

SEYMOUR, MY SON (See More Seymour)
Sept, 1963
Archie Publications (Radio Comics)

1	2.50	7.50	22.00

SHADE, THE (See Starman)
Apr, 1997 - No. 4, July, 1997 ($2.25, limited series)
DC Comics

1-4-Robinson-s/Harris-c: 1-Gene Ha-a. 2-Williams/Gray-a 3-Blevins-a. 4-Zulli-a		1.60	4.00

SHADE, THE CHANGING MAN (See Cancelled Comic Cavalcade)
June-July, 1977 - No. 8, Aug-Sept, 1978
National Periodical Publications/DC Comics

1-1st app. Shade; Ditko-c/a in all		2.40	6.00
2-8		1.60	4.00

SHADE, THE CHANGING MAN (2nd series) (Also see Suicide Squad #16)
July, 1990 - No.70, 1996 ($1.50/$1.75/$1.95/$2.25, mature)
DC Comics (Vertigo imprint #33 on)

1-($2.50, 52 pgs.)-Peter Milligan scripts in all		1.60	4.00
2-49,51-59: 6-Preview of World Without End. 17-Begin $1.75-c. 33-Metallic ink on-c. 41-Begin $1.95-c. 42-44-John Constantine app.		.80	2.00
50-($2.95, 52 pgs.)		1.40	3.50
60-70: 60-begin $2.25-c		.90	2.25

NOTE: ***Bachalo*** *a-1-9, 11-13, 15-21, 23-26, 33-39, 42-45, 47-50; c-30, 33-39.*

SHADO: SONG OF THE DRAGON (See Green Arrow #63-66)
1992 - No. 4, 1992 ($4.95, limited series, 52 pgs.)
DC Comics

Book One - Four: Grell scripts; Morrow-a(i)		2.00	5.00

SHADOW, THE (See Batman #253, 259 & Marvel Graphic Novel #35)

SHADOW, THE (Pulp, radio)
Aug, 1964 - No. 8, Sept, 1965 (All 12¢)
Archie Comics (Radio Comics)

	GD25	FN65	NM94
1-Jerrry Siegel scripts in all; Shadow-c.	4.50	13.50	45.00
2-8: 2-App. in super-hero costume on-c only; Reinman-a(backup). 3-Superhero begins; Reinman-a (book-length novel). 3,4,6,7-The Fly 1 pg. strips. 4-8-Reinman-a. 5-8-Jerry Siegel scripts. 7-Shield app.	2.50	7.50	25.00

SHADOW, THE
Oct-Nov, 1973 - No. 12, Aug-Sept, 1975
National Periodical Publications

1-Kaluta-a begins	2.50	7.50	20.00
2	1.25	3.75	10.00
3-Kaluta/Wrightson-a	1.60	4.85	13.00
4,6-Kaluta-a ends. 4-Chaykin, Wrightson part-i	1.00	3.00	8.00
5,7-12: 11-The Avenger (pulp character) x-over		2.00	5.00

NOTE: ***Craig*** *a-10.* ***Cruz*** *a-10-12.* ***Kaluta*** *a-1, 2, 3p, 4, 6; c-1-4, 6, 10-12.* ***Kubert*** *c-9.* ***Robbins*** *a-5, 7-9; c-5, 7, 8.*

SHADOW, THE
May, 1986 - No. 4, Aug, 1986 (limited series)
DC Comics

1-4: Howard Chaykin art in all		1.00	2.50
Blood & Judgement ($12.95)-r/1-4	1.60	4.85	13.00

SHADOW, THE
Aug, 1987 - No. 19, Jan, 1989 ($1.50)
DC Comics

1-19: Andrew Helfer scripts in all.		.70	1.75
Annual 1 (12/87, $2.25)		1.00	2.50
Annual 2 (1988, $2.50)-The Shadow dies; origin retold (story inspired by the movie "Citizen Kane").		1.10	2.75

NOTE: ***Kyle Baker*** *a-7i, 8-19, Annual 2.* ***Chaykin*** *c-Annual 1.* ***Helfer*** *scripts in all.* ***Orlando*** *a-Annual 1.* ***Rogers*** *c/a-7.* ***Sienkiewicz*** *c/a-1-6.*

SHADOW, THE (Movie)
June, 1994 - No. 2, July, 1994 ($2.50, limited series)
Dark Horse Comics

1,2-Adaptation from Universal Pictures film		1.20	3.00

NOTE: ***Kaluta*** *c/a-1, 2.*

SHADOW AND DOC SAVAGE, THE
July, 1995 - No. 2, Aug, 1995 ($2.95, limited series)
Dark Horse Comics

1,2		1.40	3.50

SHADOW AND THE MYSTERIOUS 3, THE
Sept, 1994 ($2.95, one-shot)
Dark Horse Comics

1-Kaluta co-scripts.		1.20	3.00

NOTE: ***Stevens*** *c-1.*

SHADOW CABINET (See Heroes)
Jan, 1994 - No. 17, Oct, 1995 ($1.75/$2.50)
DC Comics (Milestone)

0-($2.50, 52 pgs.)-Silver ink-c; Simonson-c		1.00	2.50
1-13: 1-Byrne-c		.70	1.75
14-17: 14-begin $2.50-c		1.00	2.50

SHADOW COMICS (Pulp, radio)
Mar, 1940 - V9#5, Aug-Sept, 1949
Street & Smith Publications

NOTE: *The Shadow first appeared on radio in 1929 and was featured in pulps beginning in April, 1931, written by Walter Gibson. The early covers of this series were reprinted from the pulp covers.*

V1#1-Shadow, Doc Savage, Bill Barnes, Nick Carter (radio), Frank Merriwell, Iron Munro, the Astonishing Man begin	390.00	1170.00	3900.00

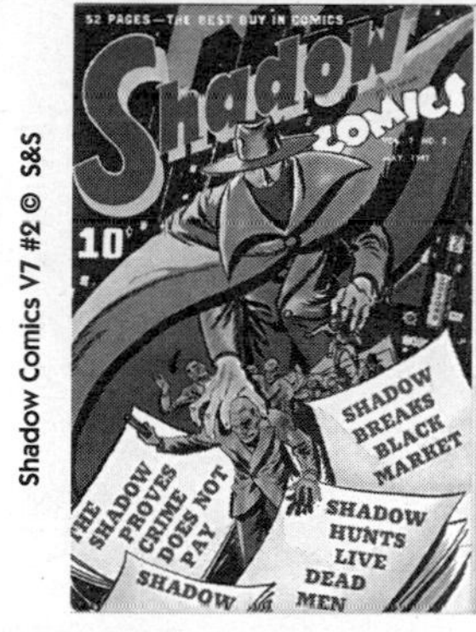

Shadow Comics V7 #2 © S&S

Shadowhawk/Vampirella nn © Shadowline Ink

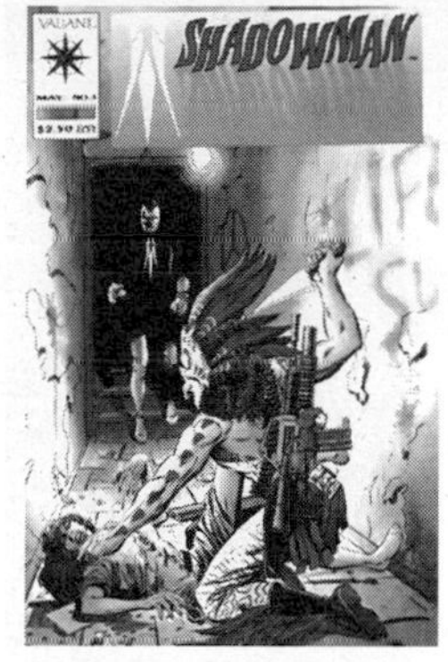

Shadowman #1 © VAL

GD25 FN65 NM94

2-The Avenger begins, ends #6; Capt. Fury only app. 150.00 450.00 1350.00
3(nn-5/40)-Norgil the Magician app.; cover is exact swipe of Shadow pulp from 1/33 106.00 318.00 950.00
4,5: 4-The Three Musketeers begins, ends #8. 5-Doc Savage ends 86.00 258.00 775.00
6,8,9: 9-Norgil the Magician app. 75.00 225.00 675.00
7-Origin/1st app. The Hooded Wasp & Wasplet (11/40); series ends V3#8; Hooded Wasp/Wasplet app. on-c thru #9 83.00 250.00 740.00
10-Origin The Iron Ghost, ends #11; The Dead End Kids begins, ends #14 75.00 225.00 675.00
11-Origin Hooded Wasp & Wasplet retold 75.00 225.00 675.00
12-Dead End Kids app. 58.00 174.00 525.00
V2#1,2(11/41): 2-Dead End Kids story 52.00 156.00 470.00
3-Origin & 1st app. Supersnipe (3/42); series begins; Little Nemo story 75.00 225.00 675.00
4,5: 4,8-Little Nemo story 47.00 141.00 425.00
6-9: 6-Blackstone the Magician story 41.00 123.00 370.00
10-12: 10-Supersnipe app. 41.00 123.00 370.00
V3#1-12: 10-Doc Savage begins, not in V5#5, V6#10-12, V8#4 39.00 117.00 350.00
V4#1-12 36.00 108.00 320.00
V5#1-12 36.00 107.00 285.00
V6#1-11: 9-Intro. Shadow, Jr. (12/46) 31.00 94.00 250.00
12-Powell-c/a; atom bomb panels 36.00 107.00 285.00
V7#1,2,5,7-9,12: 2,5-Shadow, Jr. app.; Powell-a 36.00 108.00 315.00
3,6,11-Powell-c/a 39.00 117.00 345.00
4-Powell-c/a; Atom bomb panels 41.00 123.00 370.00
10(1/48)-Flying Saucer-c/story (2nd of this theme; see The Spirit 9/28/47); Powell-c/a 47.00 141.00 420.00
V8#1-12-Powell-a. 8-Powell Spider-c/a 39.00 117.00 345.00
V9#1,5-Powell-a 36.00 108.00 310.00
2-4-Powell-c/a 39.00 117.00 345.00

NOTE: ***Binder** c-V3#1. **Powell** art in most issues beginning V6#12. Painted c-1-6.*

SHADOWDRAGON
1995 ($3.50, annual)
DC Comics

Annual 1-Year One story 1.40 3.50

SHADOW EMPIRES: FAITH CONQUERS
Aug, 1994 - No. 4, Nov, 1994 ($2.95, limited series)
Dark Horse Comics

1-4 1.20 3.00

SHADOWHAWK (See Images of Shadowhawk, New Shadowhawk, Shadowhawk II, Shadowhawk III & Youngblood #2)
Aug, 1992 - No. 4, Mar, 1993; No. 12, Aug, 1994 - No. 18, May, 1995 ($1.95/$2.50)
Image Comics (Shadowline Ink)

1-($2.50)-Embossed silver foil stamped-c; Valentino/Liefeld-c; Valentino-c/a/scripts in all; has coupon for Image #0; 1st Shadowline Ink title. .80 2.00
1-With coupon missing .80 2.00
1-($1.95)-Newsstand version w/o foil stamp .80 2.00
2-Shadowhawk poster w/McFarlane-i; brief Spawn app.; wraparound-c w/silver ink highlights .80 2.00
3-($2.50)-Glow-in-the-dark-c 1.00 2.50
4-($1.95)-Savage Dragon-c/story; Valentino/Larsen-c .80 2.00
12,13:12-Cont'd from Shadowhawk III; pull-out poster by Texeira. 13-w/ShadowBone poster; WildC.A.T.s app. .80 2.00
0 (10/94)-Liefeld c/a/story; ShadowBart poster. .80 2.00
14-18: 14-(10/94, $2.50)-The Others app. 16-Supreme app. 17-Spawn app.; story cont'd from Badrock & Co. #6. 18-Shadowhawk dies; Savage Dragon & Brigade app. 1.00 2.50
Special 1(12/94, $3.50, 52 pgs.)-Silver Age Shadowhawk flip book 1.40 3.50
Gallery (4/94, $1.95) .80 2.00
Out of the Shadows ($19.95)-r/Youngblood #2, Shadowhawk #1-4, Image Zero #0, Operation :Urban Storm (Never published) 2.50 7.50 20.00
.../Vampirella (2/95, $4.95)-Pt.2 of x-over (See Vampirella/Shadowhawk for Pt. 1) 2.00 5.00

NOTE: *Shadowhawk was originally a four issue limited series. The story continued in Shadowhawk II, Shadowhawk III & then became Shadowhawk again with issue #12.*

SHADOWHAWK II
V2#1, May, 1993 - V2#3, Aug, 1993 ($3.50/$1.95/$2.95, limited series)
Image Comics (Shadowline Ink)

V2#1 ($3.50)-Cont'd from Shadowhawk #4; die-cut mirricard-c. 1.40 3.50
2 ($1.95)-Foil embossed logo; reveals identity; gold-c variant exists .80 2.00
3 ($2.95)-Pop-up-c w/Pact ashcan insert 1.20 3.00

SHADOWHAWK III
V3#1, Nov, 1993 - V3#4, Mar, 1994 ($1.95, limited series);
Image Comics (Shadowline Ink)

V3#1-4: 1-Cont'd from Shadowhawk II; intro Valentine; gold foil & red foil stamped-c variations. 2-(52 pgs.)-Shadowhawk contracts HIV virus; U.S. Male by M. Anderson (p) in free 16 pg.insert. 4-Continues in Shadowhawk #12. .80 2.00

SHADOWHAWKS OF LEGEND
Nov, 1995 ($4.95, one-shot)
Image Comics (Shadowline Ink)

nn-Stories of past Shadowhawks by Kurt Busiek, Beau Smith & Alan Moore. 2.00 5.00

SHADOW, THE: HELL'S HEAT WAVE (Movie, pulp, radio)
Apr, 1995 - No. 3, June, 1995 ($2.95, limited series)
Dark Horse Comics

1-3: Kaluta story 1.40 3.50

SHADOWHUNT SPECIAL
Apr, 1996 ($2.50)
Image Comics (Extreme Studios)

1-Retells origin of past Shadowhawks; Jim Valentino script; Chapel app. 1.00 2.50

SHADOW, THE: IN THE COILS OF THE LEVIATHAN (Movie, pulp, radio)
Oct, 1993 - No. 4, Apr, 1994 ($2.95, limited series)
Dark Horse Comics

1-4-Kaluta-c & co-scripter 1.40 3.50
Trade paperback (10/94, $13.95)-r/1-4 1.75 5.25 14.00

SHADOWLINE SAGA: CRITICAL MASS, A
Jan, 1990 - No. 7, July, 1990 ($4.95, limited series, 68 pgs.)
Marvel Comics (Epic)

1-6: Dr. Zero, Powerline, St. George 2.00 5.00
7 ($5.95, 84 pgs.)-Morrow-a, Williamson-c(i) 2.40 6.00

SHADOWMAN (See X-O Manowar #4)
May, 1992 - No. 43, Dec, 1995 ($2.50)
Valiant/Acclaim Comics (Valiant)

1-Partial origin 1.60 4.00
2-5: 3-1st app. Sousa the Soul Eater 1.20 3.00
6-15,17: 8-1st app. Master Darque .80 2.00
16-1st app. Dr. Mirage (8/93) 1.50
18-43: 15-Minor Turok app. 17,18-Archer & Armstrong x-over. 19-Aerosmith-c/story. 23-Dr. Mirage x-over. 24-(4/94). 25-Bound-in trading card. 29-Chaos Effect. 43-Shadowman jumps to his death 1.00 2.50
0-($2.50, 4/94)-Regular edition 1.00 2.50
0-($3.50)-Wraparound chromium-c edition 1.40 3.50

Shadowman V2 #13 © Acclaim

Shaman's Tears #2 © Mike Grell

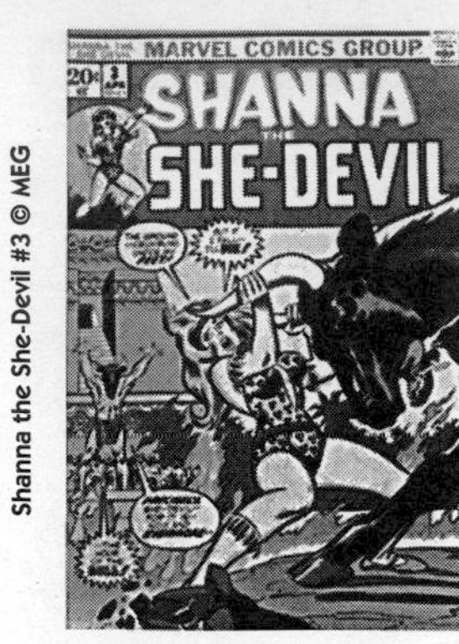

Shanna the She-Devil #3 © MEG

GD25 FN65 NM94

0-Gold 2.40 6.00
Yearbook 1 (12/94, $3.95) 1.60 4.00

SHADOWMAN
V2#1, Mar, 1997 - Present ($2.50, mature)
Acclaim Comics (Valiant Heroes)

V2#1-13: 1-1st app. Zero; Garth Ennis scripts begin, end #4. 2-Zero becomes new Shadowman. 4-Origin; Jack Boniface (original Shadowman) rises from the grave. 5-Jamie Delano scripts begin. 9-Copycat-c 1.00 2.50
V2#1-Variant painted cover 1.00 2.50

SHADOWMASTERS
10/89 - No.4, 1/90 ($3.95, squarebound, limited series, 52 pgs.)
Marvel Comics

1-Jim Lee-c; Heath-a(i); story cont'd from Punisher 1.60 4.00
2-4: Heath-a(i) 1.60 4.00

SHADOW OF THE BATMAN
Dec, 1985 - No. 5, Apr, 1986 ($1.75, limited series)
DC Comics

1-Detective-r (all have wraparound-c) 2.20 5.50
2,3,5: 3-Penguin-c & cameo. 5-Clayface app. 1.40 3.50
4-Joker-c/story 1.90 4.75

NOTE: ***Austin*** *a(new)-2i, 3i; r-2-4i.* ***Rogers*** *a(new)-1, 2p, 3p, 4, 5; r-1-5p; c-1-5.* ***Simonson*** *a-1r.*

SHADOW OF THE TORTURER, THE
July, 1991 - No. 6, 1992 ($2.50, limited series)
Innovation

1-6: Based on Pocket Books novel 1.00 2.50

SHADOW ON THE TRAIL (See Zane Grey & Four Color #604)

SHADOW PLAY (Tales of the Supernatural)
June, 1982
Whitman Publications

1-Painted-c 1.60 4.00

SHADOW RIDERS
June, 1993 - No. 4, Sept, 1993 ($1.75, limited series)
Marvel Comics UK, Ltd.

1-($2.50)-Embossed-c; Cable-c/story 1.00 2.50
2-4-Cable app. 2-Ghost Rider app. .70 1.75

SHADOWS FROM BEYOND (Formerly Unusual Tales)
V2#50, October, 1966
Charlton Comics

V2#50-Ditko-c 2.00 6.00 16.00

SHADOW SLASHER
No. 0, 1994 - No. 6, 1995? ($2.50, B&W)
Pocket Change Comics

0-6 1.00 2.50

SHADOW'S FALL
Nov, 1994 - No. 6, Apr, 1995 ($2.95, limited series)
DC Comics (Vertigo)

1-6: Van Fleet-c/a in all. 1.20 3.00

SHADOW STATE
Dec, 1995 - No. 5, Apr, 1996 ($2.50)
Broadway Comics

1-5: 1,2-Fatale back-up story; Cockrum-a(p) 1.00 2.50
Preview Edition 1,2 (10-11/95, $2.50, B&W) 1.00 2.50

SHADOW STRIKES!, THE (Pulp, radio)
Sept, 1989 - No.31, May, 1992 ($1.75)
DC Comics

1-18: 5,6-Doc Savage x-over .75 1.80
19-31: 19-begin $2.00-c. 31-Mignola-c. .80 2.00

GD25 FN65 NM94

Annual 1 (1989, $3.50, 68 pgs.)-Spiegle a; Kaluta-c 1.40 3.50

SHADOW WAR OF HAWKMAN
May, 1985 - No. 4, Aug, 1985 (limited series)
DC Comics

1-4 1.00

SHAGGY DOG & THE ABSENT-MINDED PROFESSOR (See Movie Comics & Walt Disney Showcase #46)(Disney-Movie)
No. 985, May, 1959 (photo-all four covers; Annette on back-c)
Dell Publishing Co.

Four Color 985 6.40 19.00 70.00

SHALOMAN
Aug, 1988 - V2#5, 1994? (B&W)
Al Wiesner

V1#1-9 .70 1.75
V2#1 .80 2.00
2-4, 6-10 1.00 2.50
5 (Color)-Shows Vol 2, No. 4 in indicia 1.20 3.00

SHAMAN'S TEARS (Also see Maggie the Cat)
5/93 - No. 2, 8/93; No. 3, 11/94 - No. 0, 1/96 ($2.50/$1.95)
Image Comics (Creative Fire Studio)

0-2: 0-(DEC-c, 1/96)-Last Issue. 1-(5/93)-Embossed red foil stamped-c; Mike Grell-c/a & scripts in all. 2-Cover unfolds into poster (8/93-c, 7/93 inside). 1.00 2.50
3-12: 3-Begin $1.95-c. 5-Re-intro Jon Sable. 12-Re-intro Maggie the Cat (1 pg.) .80 2.00

SHANNA, THE SHE-DEVIL (See Savage Tales #8)
Dec, 1972 - No. 5, Aug, 1973 (All are 20¢ issues)
Marvel Comics Group

1-1st app. Shanna; Steranko-c; Tuska-a(p) 1.25 3.75 10.00
2-Steranko-c; heroin drug story 1.00 3.00 8.00
3-5 2.40 6.00

SHARDS
Apr, 1994 ($2.50, B&W, unfinished limited series)
Ascension Comics

1-Flip-c. 1.00 2.50

SHARK FIGHTERS, THE (Movie)
Jan, 1957
Dell Publishing Co.

Four Color 762-Buscema-a; photo-c 7.00 22.00 80.00

SHARP COMICS (Slightly large size)
Winter, 1945-46 - V1#2, Spring, 1946 (52 pgs.)
H. C. Blackerby

V1#1-Origin Dick Royce Planetarian 34.00 101.00 270.00
2-Origin The Pioneer; Michael Morgan, Dick Royce, Sir Gallagher, Planetarian, Steve Hagen, Weeny and Pop app. 30.00 90.00 240.00

SHARPY FOX (See Comic Capers & Funny Frolics)
1958; 1963
I. W. Enterprises/Super Comics

1,2-I.W. Reprint (1958): 2-r/Kiddie Kapers #1 1.00 3.00 8.00
14-Super Reprint (1963) 1.00 3.00 8.00

SHATTER (See Jon Sable #25-30)
June, 1985; Dec, 1985 - No. 14, Apr, 1988. ($1.75, Baxter paper/deluxe paper)
First Comics

1 (6/85)-1st computer gernerated-a in a comic book (1st & 2nd printings) .70 1.75
1-14: computer-generated-a & lettering in all. 1-(12/85) .70 1.75

SHATTERED IMAGE
Aug, 1996 - No. 4, Dec, 1996 ($2.50, limited series)

Shazam! #19 © DC

Sheena, Queen of the Jungle #15 © FH

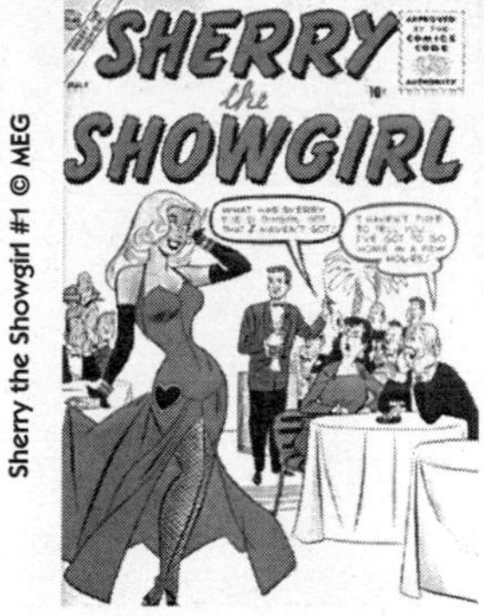

Sherry the Showgirl #1 © MEG

GD25 FN65 NM94

Image Comics (Wildstorm Productions)
1-4: 1st Image company-wide x-over; Kurt Busiek scripts in all. 1-Tony Daniel-c/a(p). 2-Alex Ross-c/swipe (Kingdom Come) by Ryan Benjamin & Travis Charest 1.00 2.50

SHAZAM (See Giant Comics to Color, Limited Collectors' Edition & The Power Of Shazam!)

SHAZAM! (TV)(See World's Finest #253)
Feb, 1973 - No. 35, May-June, 1978
National Periodical Publications/DC Comics
1-1st revival of original Captain Marvel since G.A. (origin retold), by Beck; Captain Marvel Jr. & Mary Marvel x-over; Superman-c. 1.00 3.00 8.00
2-7,9-11,18-35: 2,6-Infinity photo-c. 2-Re-intro Mr. Mind & Tawny. 3-Capt. Marvel-r. (10/46, 8 pgs.). 4-Origin retold; Capt. Marvel-r. (1949, 6 pgs.). 5-Capt. Marvel Jr. origin retold; Capt. Marvel-r. (1948, 7 pgs.). 6-photo-c; Capt. Marvel-r (1950, 6 pgs.). 9-Mr. Mind app. 10-Last C.C. Beck issue. 11-Schaffenberger-a begins. 21-24-All reprints. 25-1st app. Isis. 26-Sivana app. (10/76). 27-Kid Eternity teams up w/Capt. Marvel. 28-1st S.A. app. of Black Adam. 30-1st DC app. 3 Lt. Marvels. 31-1st DC app. Minuteman. 34-Origin Capt. Nazi & Capt. Marvel Jr. retold. 1.60 4.00
8 (100 pgs.) 8-r/Capt. Marvel Jr. by Raboy; origin/C.M. #80; origin Mary Marvel/C.M. #18; origin Mr. Tawny/C.M. #79 2.50 7.50 24.00
12-17-(All 100 pgs.). 15-vs. Lex Luthor & Mr. Mind. 2.00 6.00 16.00
NOTE: *Reprints in #1-8, 10, 12-17, 21-24.* ***Beck*** *a-1-10, 12-17r, 21-24r; c-1, 3-9.* ***Nasser*** *c-35p.* ***Newton*** *a-35p.* ***Raboy*** *a-5r, 8r, 17r.* ***Schaffenberger*** *a-11, 14-20, 25, 26, 27p, 28, 29-31p, 33i, 35i; c-20, 22, 23, 25, 26i, 27i, 28-33.*

SHAZAM: THE NEW BEGINNING
Apr, 1987 - No. 4, July, 1987 (Legends spin-off) (Limited series)
DC Comics
1-4: 1-New origin & 1st modern app. Captain Marvel; Marvel Family cameo. 2-4-Sivana & Black Adam app. 1.00

SHEA THEATRE COMICS (Also see Theatre Comics)
No date (1940's) (32 pgs.)
Shea Theatre
nn-Contains Rocket Comics; MLJ cover in one color 8.50 26.00 60.00

SHE-BAT (See Murcielaga, She-Bat & Valeria the She-Bat)

SHEENA (Movie)
Dec, 1984 - No. 2, Feb, 1985 (limited series)
Marvel Comics
1,2-r/Marvel Comics Super Special #34 1.00

SHEENA, QUEEN OF THE JUNGLE (See Jerry Iger's Classic..., Jumbo Comics, & 3-D Sheena)
Spring, 1942; No. 2, Wint, 1942-43; No. 3, Spring, 1943; No. 4, Fall, 1948; No. 5, Sum, 1949; No. 6, Spring, 1950; No. 7-10, 1950(nd); No. 11, Spring, 1951 - No. 18, Winter, 1952-53 (#1-3: 68 pgs.; #4-7: 52 pgs.)
Fiction House Magazines
1-Sheena begins 189.00 567.00 1700.00
2 (Winter, 1942-43) 86.00 258.00 775.00
3 (Spring, 1943) 64.00 192.00 575.00
4,5 (Fall, 1948, Sum, 1949): 4-New logo; cover swipe from Jumbo #20 39.00 117.00 350.00
6,7 (Spring, 1950, 1950) 36.00 108.00 290.00
8-10(1950 - Win/50, 36 pgs.) 34.00 101.00 270.00
11-18: 15-Cover swipe from Jumbo #43. 18-Used in **POP**, pg. 98 27.00 81.00 215.00
I.W. Reprint #9-r/#18; c-r/White Princess #3 4.00 12.00 40.00
NOTE: ***Baker*** *c-5-10?* ***Whitman*** *c-11-18(most).*

SHEENA 3-D SPECIAL (Also see Blackthorne 3-D Series #1)
Jan, 1985 ($2.00)
Eclipse Comics
1-Dave Stevens-c .80 2.00

SHE-HULK (See The Savage She-Hulk & The Sensational She-Hulk)

SHERIFF BOB DIXON'S CHUCK WAGON (TV) (See Wild Bill Hickok #22)
Nov, 1950
Avon Periodicals
1-Kinstler-c/a(3) 10.00 30.00 80.00

SHERIFF OF COCHISE, THE (TV)
1957 (16 pgs.)
Mobil Giveaway
nn-Shaffenberger-a 2.40 6.00 12.00

SHERIFF OF TOMBSTONE
Nov, 1958 - No. 17, Sept, 1961
Charlton Comics
V1#1-Giordano-c; Severin-a 6.00 18.00 60.00
2 3.50 10.50 35.00
3-17 2.50 7.50 22.00

SHERLOCK HOLMES (See Marvel Preview, New Adventures of..., & Spectacular Stories)

SHERLOCK HOLMES (All New Baffling Adventures of...)(Young Eagle #3 on?)
Oct, 1955 - No. 2, Mar, 1956
Charlton Comics
1-Dr. Neff, Ghost Breaker app. 36.00 108.00 300.00
2 31.00 94.00 250.00

SHERLOCK HOLMES (Also see The Joker)
Sept-Oct, 1975
National Periodical Publications
1-Cruz-a; Simonson-c 1.85 5.50 15.00

SHERRY THE SHOWGIRL (Showgirls #4)
July, 1956 - No. 3, Dec, 1956; No. 5, Apr, 1957 - No. 7, Aug, 1957
Atlas Comics
1-Dan DeCarlo-c/a in all 9.50 28.00 75.00
2 7.15 21.50 50.00
3,5-7 5.70 17.00 40.00

SHE'S JOSIE (See Josie)

SHI/CYBLADE: THE BATTLE FOR THE INDEPENDENTS
Sept, 1995 ($2.95)
Crusade Comics
1-Tucci c; features Cerebus, Bone, Hellboy, as well as others. 1.60 4.00
1-Silvestri variant-c 1.25 3.75 10.00

SHI/DAREDEVIL: HONOR THY MOTHER (See Daredevil/Shi..)
Jan, 1997 ($2.95, one-shot)
Crusade Comics
1-Flip book 2.95

SHI: EAST WIND RAIN
Nov, 1997 - No. 2 ($3.50, limited series)
Crusade Comics
1-Shi at WW2 Pearl Harbor 3.50

S.H.I.E.L.D. (Nick Fury & His Agents of...) (Also see Nick Fury)
Feb, 1973 - No. 5, Oct, 1973 (All 20¢ issues)
Marvel Comics Group
1-Steranko-c 1.00 3.00 8.00
2-5: 2-Steranko flag-c. 1-5 all contain-r from Str. Tales #146-155. 3-5-are cover-r; 3-Kirby/Steranko-c(r). 4-Steranko-c(r) 2.00 5.00
NOTE: ***Buscema*** *a-3p(r).* ***Kirby*** *layouts 1-5; c-3 (w/****Steranko****).* ***Steranko*** *a-3r, 4r(2).*

SHIELD, THE (Becomes Shield-Steel Sterling #3; #1 titled Lancelot Strong; also see Advs. of the Fly, Double Life of Private Strong, Fly Man, Mighty

Shield Wizard Comics #2 © MLJ

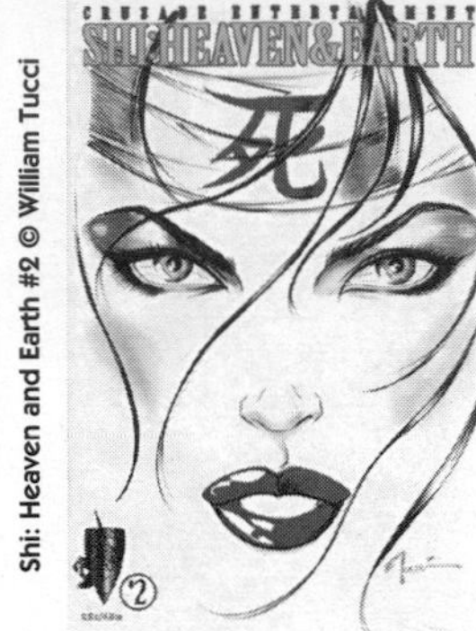

Shi: Heaven and Earth #2 © William Tucci

Shi: The Way of the Warrior #2 © William Tucci

GD25 FN65 NM94

Comics, The Mighty Crusaders, The Original... & Pep Comics #1)
June, 1983 - No. 2, Aug, 1983
Archie Enterprises, Inc.

1,2: Steel Sterling app. 1.00

SHIELD-STEEL STERLING (Formerly The Shield)
No. 3, Dec, 1983 (Becomes Steel Sterling No. 4)
Archie Enterprises, Inc.

3-Nino-a 1.00

SHIELD WIZARD COMICS (Also see Pep Comics & Top-Notch Comics)
Summer, 1940 - No. 13, Spring, 1944
MLJ Magazines

1-(V1#5 on inside)-Origin The Shield by Irving Novick & The Wizard by Ed Ashe, Jr; Flag-c 320.00 960.00 3200.00
2-(Winter/40)-Origin The Shield retold; Wizard's sidekick, Roy the Super Boy begins (see Top-Notch #8 for 1st app.) 156.00 468.00 1400.00
3,4 97.00 291.00 875.00
5-Dusty, the Boy Detective begins 86.00 258.00 775.00
6-8: 6-Roy the Super Boy begins. 7-Shield dons new costume (Summer, 1942); S & K-c? 80.00 240.00 715.00
9-13: 13-Bondage-c 67.00 200.00 600.00
NOTE: ***Bob Montana** c-13. **Novick** c-1-6,8-11. **Harry Sahle** c-12.*

SHI: FAN EDITIONS
1997
Crusade Comics

1-3-Two covers polybagged in FAN #19-21 2.00 5.00
1-3-Gold editions 1.25 3.75 10.00

SHI: HEAVEN AND EARTH
June, 1997 - Present ($2.95)
Crusade Comics

1,2 2.95
Rising Sun Edition-signed by Tucci in FanClub Starter Pack 2.95
"Tora No Shi" variant-c 2.95

SHI: KAIDAN
Oct, 1996 ($2.95)
Crusade Comics

1-Two covers; Tucci-c; Jae Lee wraparound-c 2.95

SHI: NIGHTSTALKERS
Sept, 1997 ($3.50, one-shot)
Crusade Comics

1-Painted art by Val Mayerik 3.50

SHINING KNIGHT (See Adventure Comics #66)

SHIP AHOY
Nov, 1944 (52 pgs.)
Spotlight Publishers

1-L. B. Cole-c 12.00 38.00 100.00

SHIP OF FOOLS
Aug, 1997 - Present ($2.95, B&W)
Image Comics

0,1-Glass-s/Oeming-a 2.95

SHIPWRECKED! (Disney-Movie)
1990 ($5.95, graphic novel, 68 pgs.)
Disney Comics

nn-adaptation; Spiegle-a 2.40 6.00

SHI: REKISHI
Jan, 1997 ($2.95)
Crusade Comics

1-Character bios and story summaries of Shi: The Way of the Warrior told in Detective Joe Labianca's point of view; Christopher Golden script; Tucci-c; J.G. Jones-a; flip book w/Shi: East Wind Rain preview 1.20 3.00

SHI: SENRYAKU
Aug, 1995 - No. 3, Nov, 1995 ($2.95, limited series)
Crusade Comics

1-3: 1-Tucci-c; Quesada, Darrow, Sim, Lee, Smith-a. 2-Tucci-c; Silvestri, Balent, Perez, Mack-a. 3-Jusko-c; Hughes, Ramos, Bell, Moore-a. 2.00 5.00
1-variant-c (no logo) 1.25 3.75 10.00
Hardcover ($24.95)-r/#1-3; Frazetta-c. 25.00
Trade Paperback ($13.95)-r/#1-3; Frazetta-c. 14.00

SHI: THE SERIES
Aug, 1997 - Present ($2.95)
Crusade Comics

1-4 2.95

SHI: THE WAY OF THE WARRIOR (See Razor Annual #1 for 1st app.)
Mar, 1994 - No. 12, Apr, 1997 ($2.50/$2.95)
Crusade Comics

1 3.00 9.00 30.00
1-Commemorative ed., B&W, new-c; given out at 1994 San Diego Comic Con 5.00 15.00 50.00
1-Fan appreciation edition -r/#1 1.20 3.00
1-Fan appreciation edition (variant) 2.25 6.75 18.00
2 2.50 7.50 20.00
2-Commemorative edition (3,000) 4.00 12.00 40.00
2-Fan appreciation edition -r/#2 1.60 4.00
3 1.25 3.75 10.00
4-6: 4-Silvestri poster 1.60 4.00
5-Silvestri variant-c 2.00 6.00 16.00
5-Gold edition 5.00 15.00 50.00
6-Tomoe #1 variant-c 1.85 5.50 15.00
6-Fan appreciation edition 1.20 3.00
7-Tomoe app. 1.60 4.00
8-12: 8-Begin $2.95-c 1.20 3.00
8-Signed Edition-(5000) 2.00 5.00
Trade paperback (1995, $12.95)-r/#1-4 13.00
Trade paperback (1995, $14.95)-r/#1-4 revised; Julie Bell-c 15.00

SHI/ VAMPIRELLA
Oct, 1997 ($2.95, one-shot)
Crusade Comics

1-Ellis-s/Lau-a 2.00 5.00

SHI VS. TOMOE
Aug, 1996 ($3.95, one-shot)
Crusade Comics

1-Tucci-a/scripts; wraparound foil-c 1.60 4.00
1-(6/96, $5.00. B&W)-Preview Edition; sold at San Diego Comic Con 2.00 5.00

SHMOO (See Al Capp's... & Washable Jones &...)

SHOCK (Magazine)
May, 1969 - V3#4, Sept, 1971 (B&W)(Reprints from horror comics)
Stanley Publications

V1#1-Cover-r/Weird Tales of the Future #7 by Bernard Baily; r/Weird Chills #1 3.00 9.00 30.00
2-Wolverton-r/Weird Mysteries 5; r-Weird Mysteries #7 used in **SOTI**; cover reprints cover to Weird Chills #1 2.60 7.80 26.00
3,5,6 2.25 6.75 18.00
4-Harrison/Williamson-r/Forbid. Worlds #6 2.50 7.50 20.00
V2#2, V1#8, V2#4-6, V3#1-4: V2#4-Cover swipe from Weird Mysteries #6 2.00 6.00 16.00
NOTE: ***Disbrow** r-V2#4; Bondage c-V1#4, V2#6, V3#1.*

Shock SuspenStories #6 © EC

Showcase #9 © DC

Showcase #14 © DC

GD25 FN65 NM94

SHOCK DETECTIVE CASES (Formerly Crime Fighting Detective)
(Becomes Spook Detective Cases No. 22)
No. 20, Sept, 1952 - No. 21, Nov, 1952
Star Publications

20,21-L.B. Cole-c; based on true crime cases 16.00 47.00 120.00
NOTE: ***Palais** a-20. No. 21-Fox-r.*

SHOCK ILLUSTRATED (...Adult Crime Stories; Magazine format)
Sept-Oct, 1955 - No. 3, Spring, 1956 (Adult Entertainment on-c #1,2)(All 25¢)
E. C. Comics

1-All by Kamen; drugs, prostitution, wife swapping 5.70 17.00 40.00
2-Williamson-a redrawn from Crime SuspenStories #13 plus Ingels, Crandall, Evans & part Torres-i; painted-c 6.50 19.50 45.00
3 Only 100 known copies bound & given away at E.C. office; Crandall, Evans-a; painted-c; shows May, 1956 on-c 78.00 234.00 700.00

SHOCKING MYSTERY CASES (Formerly Thrilling Crime Cases)
No. 50, Sept, 1952 - No. 60, Oct, 1954 (All crime reprints?)
Star Publications

50-Disbrow "Frankenstein" story 31.00 94.00 250.00
51-Disbrow-a 17.50 53.00 140.00
52-60: 56-Drug use story 16.00 49.00 130.00
NOTE: ***L. B. Cole** covers on all; a-60(2 pgs.). **Hollingsworth** a-52. **Morisi** a-55.*

SHOCKING TALES DIGEST MAGAZINE
Oct, 1981 (95¢)
Harvey Publications

1-1957-58-r; Powell, Kirby, Nostrand-a .80 2.00

SHOCK SUSPENSTORIES
Feb-Mar, 1952 - No. 18, Dec-Jan, 1954-55
E. C. Comics

1-Classic Feldstein electrocution-c 68.00 206.00 575.00
2 40.00 120.00 325.00
3,4: 4-Used in **SOTI**, pg. 387,388 29.00 86.00 210.00
5-Hanging-c 29.00 86.00 210.00
6,7: 6-Classic bondage-c. 7-Classic face melting-c 34.00 103.00 250.00
8-Williamson-a 29.00 86.00 210.00
9-11: 9-Injury to eye panel. 10-Junkie story 24.00 71.00 175.00
12- "The Monkey" classic junkie cover/story; anti-drug propaganda issue 27.00 81.00 210.00
13-Frazetta's only solo story for E.C., 7 pgs. 34.00 103.00 260.00
14-Used in Senate Investigation hearings 18.00 54.00 130.00
15-Used in 1954 Reader's Digest article, "For the Kiddies to Read"; Bill Gaines stars in prose story "The EC Caper" 18.00 54.00 130.00
16- "Red Dupe" editorial; rape story 17.00 49.00 120.00
17,18 17.00 49.00 120.00
NOTE: ***Ray Bradbury** adaptations-1, 7, 9. **Craig** a-11; c-11. **Crandall** a-9-13, 15-18. **Davis** a-1-5. **Evans** a-7, 8, 14-18; c-16-18. **Feldstein** c-1, 7-9, 12. **Ingels** a-1, 2, 6. **Kamen** a-in all; c-10, 13, 15. **Krigstein** a-14, 18. **Orlando** a-1, 3-7, 9, 10, 12, 16, 17. **Wood** a-2-15; c-2-6, 14.*

SHOCK SUSPENSTORIES
Sept, 1992 - Present ($1.50/$2.00/$2.50, quarterly)
Russ Cochran/Gemstone Publishing

1,2-r/#1,2 above with original-c 1.50
3-16: 3-r/#3-7 above with original-c .80 2.00
17-20: 17-r/HOF #17 1.00 2.50

SHOGUN WARRIORS
Feb, 1979 - No. 20, Sept, 1980 (Based on Mattel toys)
Marvel Comics Group (1-3: 35¢; 4-19: 40¢; 20: 50¢)

1-3: Reprints. 1-Raydeen, Combatra, & Dangard Ace begin 1.20 3.00
4-20: 11-Austin-c. 12-Simonson-c. 19,20-FF x-over 1.50

SHOOK UP (Magazine) (Satire)
Nov, 1958
Dodsworth Publ. Co.

GD25 FN65 NM94

V1#1 2.50 7.50 20.00

SHORT RIBS
No. 1333, Apr - June, 1962
Dell Publishing Co.

Four Color 1333 4.50 13.50 50.00

SHORT STORY COMICS (See Hello Pal,...)

SHORTY SHINER (The Five-Foot Fighter in the Ten Gallon Hat)
June, 1956 - No. 3, Oct, 1956
Dandy Magazine (Charles Biro)

1 5.35 16.00 32.00
2,3 4.00 11.00 22.00

SHOTGUN MARY
Sept, 1995 - No. 2 ($2.95)
Antarctic Press

1,2-w/pin-ups 1.20 3.00
1-($8.95)-Bagged w/CD 1.10 3.30 9.00
...Deviltown-(7/96, $2.95) 1.20 3.00
...Shooting Gallery-(6/96, $2.95) 1.20 3.00
...Son Of The Beast-(10/97, $2.95) Painted-a by Esad Ribic 2.95

SHOTGUN MARY: BLOOD LORE
Feb, 1997 - No.4, Aug, 1997 (2.95, mini-series)
Antarctic Press

1-4 2.95

SHOTGUN SLADE (TV)
No. 1111, July-Sept, 1960
Dell Publishing Co.

Four Color 1111-Photo-c 5.50 16.50 60.00

SHOWCASE (See Cancelled Comic Cavalcade & New Talent...)
3-4/56 - No. 93, 9/70; No. 94, 8-9/77 - No. 104, 9/78
National Per. Publ./DC Comics

GD25 FN65 VF82 NM94
1-Fire Fighters; w/Fireman Farrell 214.00 642.00 1491.00 3000.00

GD25 FN65 NM94
2-King of the Wild; Kubert-a (animal stories) 67.00 200.00 800.00
3-The Frogmen by Russ Heath, Heath greytone-c (early DC example, 7-8/56) 66.00 198.00 785.00

GD25 FN65 VF82 NM94
4-Origin/1st app. The Flash (1st DC S.A. hero, Sept-Oct, 1956) & The Turtle; Kubert-a; r/in Secret Origins #1 ('61 & '73); Flash shown reading G.A. Flash #13; Infantino/Kubert-c 1100.00 3300.00 11,000.00 25,000.00

GD25 FN65 NM94
5-Manhunters 75.00 225.00 900.00

GD25 FN65 VF82 NM94
6-Origin/1st app. Challengers of the Unknown by Kirby, partly r/in Secret Origins #1 & Challengers #64,65 (1st S.A. super-hero team & 1st original concept S.A. series)(1-2/56) 243.00 729.00 1700.00 3400.00

GD25 FN65 NM94
7-Challengers of the Unknown by Kirby (2nd app.) reprinted in Challengers of the Unknown #75 123.00 369.00 1600.00

GD25 FN65 VF82 NM94
8-The Flash (5-6/57, 2nd app.); origin & 1st app. Capt. Cold 800.00 2400.00 6000.00 12,500.00
9-Lois Lane (Pre-#1, 7-8/57) (1st Showcase character to win own series) Superman app. on-c 533.00 1600.00 3500.00 6000.00

GD25 FN65 NM94
10-Lois Lane; Jor-el cameo; Superman app. on-c 171.00 515.00 2400.00
11-Challengers of the Unknown by Kirby (3rd) 115.00 345.00 1500.00
12-Challengers of the Unknown by Kirby (4th) 115.00 345.00 1500.00
13-The Flash (3rd app.); origin Mr. Element 286.00 857.00 4000.00
14-The Flash (4th app.); origin Dr. Alchemy, former Mr. Element (rare in NM) 333.00 1000.00 5000.00

Showcase #48 © DC

Showcase #97 © DC

Showcase '95 #2 © DC

	GD25	FN65	VF82	NM94
15-Space Ranger (7-8/58, 1st app.)	119.00	357.00	714.00	1650.00

	GD25	FN65	NM94
16-Space Ranger (9-10/58, 2nd app.)	75.00	225.00	900.00

	GD25	FN65	VF82	NM94
17-(11-12/58)-Adventures on Other Worlds; origin/1st app. Adam Strange by Gardner Fox & Mike Sekowsky.	150.00	450.00	1050.00	2100.00
18-Adventures on Other Worlds (2nd A. Strange)	85.00	255.00		1100.00
19-Adam Strange; 1st Adam Strange logo	92.00	276.00		1200.00
20-Rip Hunter; origin & 1st app. (5-6/59); Moriera-a	67.00	201.00		800.00
21-Rip Hunter (7-8/59, 2nd app.); Sekowsky-c/a	42.00	126.00		460.00

	GD25	FN65	VF82	NM94
22-Origin & 1st app. Silver Age Green Lantern by Gil Kane (9-10/59); reprinted in Secret Origins #2	280.00	840.00	1960.00	4200.00
23-Green Lantern (3-4.60, 2nd app.); nuclear explosion-c	113.00	339.00	680.00	1475.00
24-Green Lantern (1-2/60, 3rd app.)	113.00	339.00	680.00	1475.00

	GD25	FN65	NM94
25,26-Rip Hunter by Kubert. 25-Grey tone-c	29.00	87.00	290.00
27-Sea Devils (7-8/60, 1st app.); Heath-c/a	60.00	180.00	715.00
28-Sea Devils (9-10/60, 2nd app.); Heath-c/a	34.00	102.00	375.00
29-Sea Devils; Heath-c/a; grey tone c-27-29	33.00	100.00	370.00
30-Origin Silver Age Aquaman (1-2/61) (see Adventure #260 for 1st S.A. origin)	58.00	174.00	690.00
31,32-Aquaman	34.00	102.00	375.00
33-Aquaman	38.00	114.00	420.00

	GD25	FN65	VF82	NM94
34-Origin & 1st app. Silver Age Atom by Kane & Anderson (9-10/61); reprinted in Secret Origins #2	92.00	276.00	552.00	1200.00

	GD25	FN65	NM94
35-The Atom by Gil Kane (2nd); last 10¢ issue	60.00	180.00	725.00
36-The Atom by Gil Kane (1-2/62, 3rd app.)	43.00	129.00	545.00
37-Metal Men (3-4/62, 1st app.)	45.00	135.00	550.00
38-Metal Men (5-6/62, 2nd app.)	38.00	114.00	420.00
39-Metal Men (7-8/62, 3rd app.)	31.00	93.00	320.00
40-Metal Men (9-10/62, 4th app.)	29.00	87.00	290.00
41,42-Tommy Tomorrow (parts 1 & 2). 42-Origin	16.00	48.00	160.00
43-Dr. No (James Bond); Nodel-a; originally published as British Classics Illustrated #158A & as #6 in a European Detective series, all with diff. painted-c. This Showcase #43 version is actually censored, deleting all racial skin color and dialogue thought to be racially demeaning (1st DC S.A. movie adaptation)(based on Ian Fleming novel & movie)	36.00	108.00	400.00
44-Tommy Tomorrow	11.00	33.00	110.00
45-Sgt. Rock (7-8/63); pre-dates B&B #52; origin retold; Heath-c	23.00	69.00	230.00
46,47-Tommy Tomorrow	9.00	27.00	90.00
48,49-Cave Carson (3rd tryout series; see B&B)	7.00	21.00	70.00
50,51-I Spy (Danger Trail-r by Infantino), King Farady story (#50 has new 4 pg. story)	7.00	21.00	70.00
52-Cave Carson	5.50	16.50	55.00
53,54-G.I. Joe (11-12/64, 1-2/65); Heath-a	9.00	27.00	90.00
55-Dr. Fate & Hourman (3-4/65); origin of each in text; 1st solo app. G.A. Green Lantern in Silver Age (pre-dates Gr. Lantern #40); 1st S.A. app. Solomon Grundy	22.50	68.00	225.00
56-Dr. Fate & Hourman	9.00	27.00	90.00
57-Enemy Ace by Kubert (7-8/65, 4th app. after Our Army at War #155)	17.00	51.00	170.00
58-Enemy Ace by Kubert (5th app.)	15.00	45.00	150.00
59-Teen Titans (11-12/65, 3rd app.)	9.50	28.50	95.00
60-1st S. A. app. The Spectre; Anderson-a (1-2/66); origin in text	24.00	72.00	240.00
61-The Spectre by Anderson (2nd app.)	13.00	39.00	130.00
62-Origin & 1st app. Inferior Five (5-6/66)	8.50	25.50	85.00
63,65-Inferior Five. 65-X-Men parody (11-12/66)	4.50	13.50	45.00
64-The Spectre by Anderson (5th app.)	12.50	38.00	125.00
66,67-B'wana Beast	2.80	8.40	28.00
68,69,71-Maniaks	2.80	8.40	28.00
70-Binky (9-10/67)-Tryout issue	2.80	8.40	28.00
72-Top Gun (Johnny Thunder-r)-Toth-a	2.80	8.40	28.00
73-Origin/1st app. Creeper; Ditko-c/a (3-4/68)	10.50	32.00	105.00
74-Intro/1st app. Anthro; Post-c/a (5/68)	7.00	21.00	70.00
75-Origin/1st app. Hawk & the Dove; Ditko-c/a	9.00	27.00	90.00
76-1st app. Bat Lash (8/68)	5.00	15.00	50.00
77-1st app. Angel & The Ape (9/68)	5.00	15.00	50.00
78-1st app. Jonny Double (11/68)	2.80	8.40	28.00
79-1st app. Dolphin (12/68); Aqualad origin-r	4.50	13.50	45.00
80-1st S.A. app. Phantom Stranger (1/69); Neal Adams-c	3.00	9.00	30.00
81-Windy & Willy	2.50	7.50	25.00
82-1st app. Nightmaster (5/69) by Grandenetti & Giordano; Kubert-c	5.50	16.50	55.00
83,84-Nightmaster by Wrightson w/Jones/Kaluta ink assist in each; Kubert-c. 83-Last 12¢ issue 84-Origin retold; begin 15¢	5.00	15.00	50.00
85-87-Firehair; Kubert-a	1.85	5.50	15.00
88-90-Jason's Quest: 90-Manhunter 2070 app.	1.00	3.00	8.00
91-93-Manhunter 2070: 92-Origin	1.25	3.75	10.00
94-Intro/origin new Doom Patrol & Robotman	1.10	3.30	9.00
95,96-The Doom Patrol. 95-Origin Celsius	1.00	3.00	8.00
97-99-Power Girl; origin-97,98; JSA cameos	1.00	3.00	8.00
100-(52 pgs.)-Most Showcase characters featured	1.00	3.00	8.00
101-103-Hawkman; Adam Strange x-over	1.00	3.00	8.00
104-(52 pgs.)-O.S.S. Spies at War	1.00	3.00	8.00

NOTE: ***Anderson** a-22-24i, 34-36i, 55, 56, 60, 61, 64, 101-103i; c-50i, 51i, 55, 56, 60, 61, 64. **Aparo** c-94-96. **Boring** c-10. **Estrada** a-104. **Fraden** c(p)-30, 31, 33. **Heath** c-3, 27-29. **Infantino** c/a(p)-4, 8, 13, 14; c-50p, 51p. **Gil Kane** a-22-24p, 34-36p; c-17-19, 22-24p(w/ Giella), 31. **Kane/Anderson** c-34-36. **Kirby** c-11, 12. **Kirby/Stein** c-6, 7. **Kubert** a-2, 4i, 25, 26, 45, 53, 54, 72; c-25, 26, 53, 54, 57, 58, 82-87, 101-104; c-2, 4i. **Moriera** c-5. **Orlando** a-62p, 63p, 97i; c-62, 63, 97i. **Sekowsky** a-65p. **Sparling** a-78. **Staton** a-94, 95-99p, 100; c-97-100p.*

SHOWCASE '93
Jan, 1993 - No. 12, Dec, 1993 ($1.95, limited series, 52 pgs.)
DC Comics

1-12: 1-Begin 4 part Catwoman story & 6 part Blue Devil story; begin Cyborg story; Art Adams/Austin-c. 2-Flash by Travis Charest (p) 6-Azrael in Bat-costume (2 pgs.). 7,8-Knightfall parts 13 & 14. 6-10-Deathstroke app. (6,10-cameo). 9,10-Austin-i. 10-Azrael as Batman in new costume app.; Gulacy-c. 11-Perez-c. 12-Creeper app.; Alan Grant scripts. .80 2.00

NOTE: ***Chaykin** c-9. **Fabry** c-8. **Giffen** a-12. **Golden** c-3. **Zeck** c-6.*

SHOWCASE '94
Jan, 1994 - No. 12, Dec, 1994 ($1.95, limited series, 52 pgs.)
DC Comics

1-12: 1,2-Joker & Gunfire stories. 1-New Gods. 4-Riddler story. 5-Huntress-c/story w/app. new Batman. 6-Huntress-c/story w/app. Robin; Atom story. 7-Penguin story.by Peter David, P. Craig Russell, & Michael T. Gilbert; Penguin-c by Jae Lee. 8,9-Scarface origin story by Alan Grant, John Wagner,& Teddy Kristiansen; Prelude to Zero Hour. 10-Zero Hour tie-in story. 11-Man-Bat. .80 2.00

NOTE: ***Alan Grant** scripts-3, 4. **Kelley Jones** c-12. **Mignola** c-3. **Nebres** a(i)-2. **Quesada** c-10. **Russell** a-7p. **Simonson** c-5.*

SHOWCASE '95
Jan, 1995 - No. 12, Dec, 1995 ($2.50/$2.95, limited series)
DC Comics

1-4-Supergirl story. 3-Eradicator-c.; The Question story. 4-Thorn c/story 1.00 2.50

5-12: 5-Thorn-c/story; begin $2.95-c. 8-Spectre story. 12-The Shade story by James Robinson & Wade Von Grawbadger; Maitresse story by Chris Claremont & Alan Davis. 1.20 3.00

SHOWCASE '96

Showcase '96 #12 © DC

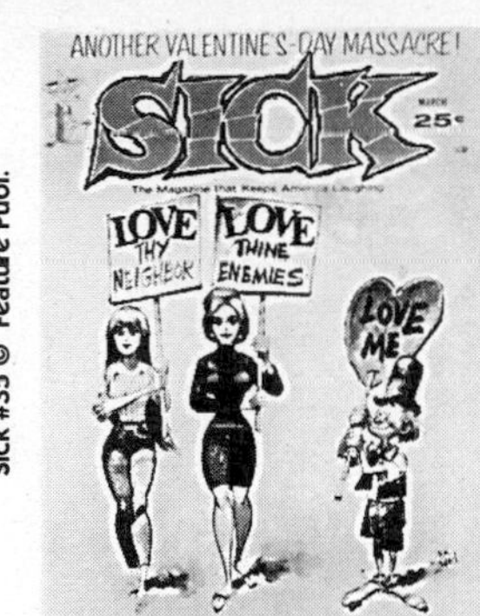

Sick #35 © Feature Publ.

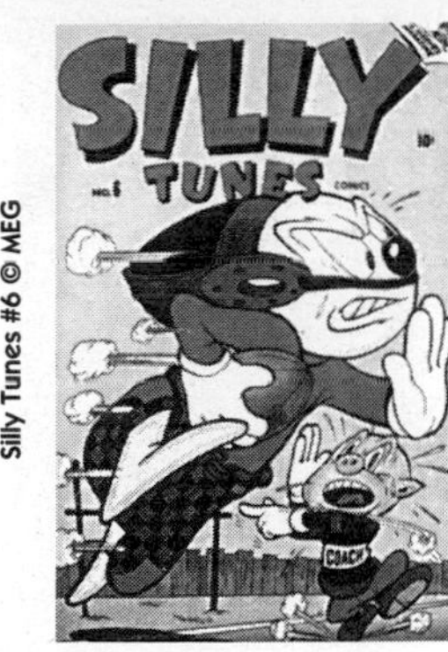

Silly Tunes #6 © MEG

GD25 FN65 NM94

Jan, 1996 - No. 12, Dec, 1996 ($2.95, limited series)
DC Comics

1-12: 1-Steve Geppi cameo. 3-Black Canary & Lois Lane-c/story; Deadman story by Jamie Delano & Wade Von Grawbadger, Gary Frank-c. 4-Firebrand & Guardian-c/story; The Shade & Dr. Fate "Times Past" story by James Robinson & Matt Smith begins, ends #5. 6-Superboy-c/app.; Atom app.; Capt. Marvel (Mary Marvel)-c/app. 8-Supergirl by David & Dodson. 11-Scare Tactics app. 11,12-Legion of Super-Heroes vs. Brainiac. 12-Jesse Quick app. 1.20 3.00

SHOWGIRLS (Formerly Sherry the Showgirl #3)
No. 4, 2/57; June, 1957 - No. 2, Aug, 1957
Atlas Comics (MPC No. 2)

4-Dan DeCarlo-c/a begins 5.70 17.00 40.00
1-Millie, Sherry, Chili, Pearl & Hazel begin 8.50 26.00 60.00
2 5.70 17.00 40.00

SHROUD, THE (See Super-Villain Team-Up #5)
Mar, 1994 - No. 4, June, 1994 ($1.75, mini-series)
Marvel Comics

1-4: 1,2,4-Spider-Man & Scorpion app. .70 1.75

SHROUD OF MYSTERY
June, 1982
Whitman Publications

1 1.60 4.00

SICK (Sick Special #131) (Magazine) (Satire)
Aug, 1960 - No. 131, Feb, 1980
Feature Publ./Headline Publ./Crestwood Publ. Co./Hewfred Publ./Pyramid Comm./Charlton Publ. No. 109 (4/76) on

V1#1-Jack Paar photo on-c; Torres-a 12.00 36.00 120.00
2-5-Torres-a in all 6.00 18.00 60.00
6 3.80 11.40 38.00
V2#1-8(#7-14) 3.00 9.00 30.00
V3#1-8(#15-22) 2.50 7.50 24.00
V4#1-5(#23-27) 2.25 6.75 18.00
28-32,34-40: 29-Beatles-c by Jack Davis 1.50 4.50 12.00
33-Ringo Starr photo-c & spoof on "A Hard Day's Night"; inside-c has Beatles photos 2.80 8.40 28.00
41-70: 45 has #44 on-c & #45 on inside. 70-John & Yoko-c 1.25 3.75 10.00
71-100 1.00 3.00 8.00
101-131: 128-Superman-c/movie parody. 131-Superman parody 2.40 6.00
Annual 1969, 1970, 1971 1.85 5.50 15.00
Annual 2-4(1980) 1.00 2.80 7.00
Big Sick Laff-in (1968)-w/psychedelic posters 2.25 6.75 18.00
Birthday Annual (1967)-3 pg. Huckleberry Fink fold out 2.25 6.75 18.00
7th Annual Yearbook (1967)-Davis-c, 2 pg. glossy poster insert 2.25 6.75 18.00
Special 2 (1978) 2.00 5.00
Yearbook 14(1974), 15(1975, 84 pgs.) 2.40 6.00

*NOTE: **Davis** a-42, 87; c-22, 23, 25, 29, 31, 32. **Powell** a-7, 31, 57. **Simon** a-1-3, 10, 41, 42, 87, 99; c-1, 47, 57, 59, 69, 91, 95-97, 99, 100, 102, 107, 112. **Torres** a-1-3, 29, 31, 47, 49. **Tuska** a-14, 41-43. Civil War Blackouts-23, 24. #42 has biography of Bob Powell.*

SIDESHOW
1949 (one-shot)
Avon Periodicals

1-(Rare)-Similar to Bachelor's Diary 26.00 79.00 195.00

SIEGE
Jan, 1997 - No. 4, Apr, 1997 ($2.50)
Image Comics (WildStorm Productions)

1-4 1.00 2.50

GD25 FN65 NM94

SIEGEL AND SHUSTER: DATELINE 1930s
Nov, 1984 - No. 2, Sept, 1985 ($1.50/$1.75, Baxter paper #1)
Eclipse Comics

1-Unpublished samples of strips from the '30s; includes 'Interplanetary Police'; Shuster-c 1.50
2 ($1.75, B&W)-unpublished strips; Shuster-c .70 1.75

SIGMA
March, 1996 - No. 3, June, 1996 ($2.50, limited series)
Image Comics (WildStorm Productions)

1-3: 1-"Fire From Heaven" prelude #2; Coker-a 2-"Fire From Heaven" pt. 6. 3-"Fire From Heaven" pt. 14. 1.00 2.50

SILENT INVASION, THE
Apr, 1986 - No.12, Mar, 1988 ($1.70/$2.00, B&W)
Rengade Press

1-12-UFO sightings of the '50's .80 2.00
Book 1- reprints ($7.95) 1.00 3.00 8.00

SILENT MOBIUS
1991 - No. 5, 1992 ($4.95, color, squarebound, 44 pgs.)
Viz Select Comics

1-5: Japanese stories translated to English 2.00 5.00

SILENT RAPTURE
Jan, 1997 - No.2 ($3.00, B&W, limited series)
Avatar Press

1,2 1.20 3.00

SILLY PILLY (See Frank Luther's...)

SILLY SYMPHONIES (See Dell Giants)

SILLY TUNES
Fall, 1945 - No. 7, June, 1947
Timely Comics

1-Silly Seal, Ziggy Pig begin 15.00 45.00 120.00
2-(2/46) 8.75 26.25 65.00
3-7: 6-New logo 7.15 21.50 50.00

SILVER (See Lone Ranger's Famous Horse...)

SILVERBACK
1989 - No. 3, 1990 ($2.50, color, limited series, mature readers)
Comico

1-3: Character from Grendel: Matt Wagner-a 1.20 3.00

SILVERBLADE
Sept, 1987 - No. 12, Sept, 1988
DC Comics

1-12: Colan -c/a in all 1.50

SILVER CROSS (See Warrior Nun series)
Nov, 1997 - Present ($2.95)
Antarctic Press

1-Ben Dunn-s/a 2.95

SILVERHAWKS
Aug, 1987 - No. 6, June, 1988 ($1.00)
Star Comics/Marvel Comics #6

1-6 1.00

SILVERHEELS
Dec, 1983 - No. 3, May, 1984 ($1.50)
Pacific Comics

1-3 1.50

SILVER KID WESTERN
Oct, 1954 - No. 5, July?, 1955
Key/Stanmor Publications

Silver Sable and the Wild Pack #28 © MEG

Silver Streak Comics #17 © New Friday Publ.

Silver Surfer #50 © MEG

GD25 FN65 NM94

1 8.50 26.00 60.00
2 5.00 15.00 30.00
3-5 4.25 13.00 28.00
I.W. Reprint #1,2-Severin-c: 1-r/#? 2-r/#1 1.10 3.30 9.00

SILVER SABLE AND THE WILD PACK (See Amazing Spider-Man #265)
June, 1992 - No. 35, Apr, 1995 ($1.25/$1.50
Marvel Comics

1-($2.00)-Embossed & foil stamped-c; Spider-Man app. 1.00 2.50
2-4: 4,5-Dr. Doom-c/story .70 1.75
5-23: 6,7-Deathlok-c/story. 9-Origin Silver Sable. 10-Punisher-c/s. 15-Capt. America-c/s. 16,17-Intruders app. 18,19-Venom-c/s. 19-Siege of Darkness x-over. 23-Daredevil (in new costume) & Deadpool app. 1.25
24,26-35: 24-Begin $1.50-c; bound-in card sheet. Li'l Sylvie backup story 1.50
25-($2.00, 52 pgs.)-Li'l Sylvie backup story .80 2.00

SILVER STAR (Also see Jack Kirby's...)
Feb, 1983 - No. Jan, 1984 ($1.00)
Pacific Comics

1-6: 1-1st app. Last of the Viking Heroes. 1-5-Kirby-c/a. 2-Ditko-a 1.00

SILVER STREAK COMICS (Crime Does Not Pay #22 on)
Dec, 1939 - No. 21, May, 1942; No. 22-24, 1946 (Silver logo-#1-5)
Your Guide Publs. No. 1-7/New Friday Publs. No. 8-17/Comic House Publ./Newsbook Publ.

GD25 FN65 VF82 NM94

1-(Scarce)-Intro The Claw by Cole (r-/in Daredevil #21), Red Reeves, Boy Magician, & Captain Fearless; The Wasp, Mister Midnight begin; Spirit Man app. Silver metallic-c begin, end #5; Claw c-1,2,6-8 910.00 2730.00 5460.00 10,000.00
(Estimated up to 100 total copies exist, 6 in NM/Mint)

GD25 FN65 NM94

2-The Claw by Cole; Simon-c/a 320.00 960.00 3200.00
3-1st app. & origin Silver Streak (2nd with lightning speed); Dickie Dean the Boy Inventor, Lance Hale, Ace Powers, Bill Wayne, & The Planet Patrol begin 270.00 810.00 2700.00
4-Sky Wolf begins; Silver Streak by Jack Cole (new costume); 1st app. Jackie, Lance Hale's sidekick 133.00 400.00 1200.00
5-Jack Cole c/a(2) 156.00 468.00 1400.00

GD25 FN65 VF82 NM94

6-(Scarce, 9/40)-Origin & 1st app. Daredevil (blue & yellow costume) by Jack Binder; The Claw returns; classic Cole Claw-c 1000.00 3000.00 6000.00 11,000.00
7-Claw vs. Daredevil (new costume-blue & red) by Jack Cole & 3 other Cole stories (38 pgs.) 700.00 2100.00 4200.00 7000.00
(#6, 7-Estimated up to 120 total copies of each exist, 7-10 in NM/Mint)

GD25 FN65 NM94

8-Claw vs. Daredevil by Cole; last Cole Silver Streak 240.00 720.00 2200.00
9-Claw vs. Daredevil by Cole 156.00 468.00 1400.00
10-Origin & 1st app. Captain Battle (5/41); Claw vs. Daredevil by Cole; Robot-c 133.00 400.00 1200.00
11-Intro. Mercury by Bob Wood, Silver Streak's sidekick; conclusion Claw vs. Daredevil by Rico; in 'Presto Martin,' 2nd pg., newspaper says 'Roussos does it again' 92.00 276.00 825.00
12-14: 13-Origin Thun-Dohr 71.00 213.00 640.00
15, 17-Last Daredevil issue. 64.00 192.00 575.00
16-Hitler-c 71.00 213.00 640.00
18-The Saint begins (2/42, 1st app.) by Leslie Charteris (see Movie Comics #2 by DC); The Saint-c 54.00 162.00 485.00
19-21(1942): 20,21 have Wolverton's Scoop Scuttle. 21-Hitler app. in strip on cover 42.00 126.00 375.00
22,24(1946)-Reprints 25.00 75.00 200.00
23-Reprints?; bondage-c 25.00 75.00 200.00

GD25 FN65 NM94

nn(11/46)(Newsbook Publ.)-R-/S.S. story from #4-7 plus 2 Captain Fearless stories, all in color; bondage/torture-c 36.00 108.00 325.00

NOTE: ***Binder** c-3, 4, 13-15, 17. **Jack Cole** a-(Daredevil)-#6-10, (Dickie Dean)-#3-10, (Pirate Prince)-#7, (Silver Streak)-#4-8, nn; c-5 (Silver Streak), 6 (Claw), 7, 8 (Daredevil). **Everett** Red Reed begins #20. **Guardineer** a-#8-13. **Don Rico** a-11-17 (Daredevil); c-11, 12, 16. **Simon** a-3 (Silver Streak). **Bob Wood** a-9 (Silver Streak); c-9, 10. Captain Battle c-11, 13-15, 17. Claw c-#1, 2, 6-8. Daredevil c-7, 8, 12. Dickie Dean c-19. Ned of the Navy c-20 (war). The Saint c-18. Silver Streak c-5, 9, 10, 16, 23.*

SILVER SURFER (See Fantastic Four, Fantasy Masterpieces V2#1, Fireside Book Series, Marvel Graphic Novel, Marvel Presents #8, Marvel's Greatest Comics & Tales To Astonish #92)

SILVER SURFER, THE
Aug, 1968 - No. 18, Sept, 1970; June, 1982 (No. 1-7: 25¢, 68 pgs.)
Marvel Comics Group

1-More detailed origin by John Buscema (p); The Watcher back-up stories begin (origin), end #7 39.00 117.00 435.00
2 17.50 52.00 175.00
3-1st app. Mephisto 13.50 41.00 135.00
4-Low distribution; Thor & Loki app. 36.00 108.00 400.00
5-7-Last giant size. 5-The Stranger app.; Fantastic Four app. 6-Brunner inks. 7-(8/69)-1st app. Frankenstein's monster (cameo) 8.50 25.50 85.00
8-10: 8-18-(15¢ issues) 6.50 19.50 65.00
11-13,15-18: 15-Silver Surfer vs. Human Torch; Fantastic Four app. 17-Nick Fury app. 18-Vs. The Inhumans; Kirby-c/a 5.00 15.00 50.00
14-Spider-Man x-over 7.00 21.00 70.00
V2#1 (6/82, 52 pgs.)-Byrne-c/a 1.10 3.30 9.00

NOTE: ***Adkins** a-8-15i. **Brunner** a-6i. **J. Buscema** a-1-17p. **Colan** a-1-3p. **Reinman** a-1-4i. #1-14 were reprinted in Fantasy Masterpieces V2#1-14.*

SILVER SURFER (See Marvel Graphic Novel #38)
V3#1, July, 1987 - Present
Marvel Comics Group

V3#1-Double size ($1.25) 1.00 3.00 8.00
2 1.60 4.00
3-17: 15-Ron Lim-c/a begins (9/88) 1.60 4.00
18-20 1.20 3.00
21-33,39-43: 25,31 ($1.50, 52 pgs.). 25-Skrulls app. 32,39-No Ron Lim-c/a.
39-Alan Grant scripts .80 2.00
34-Thanos returns (cameo); Starlin scripts begin 1.60 4.00
35-1st full Thanos app. in Silver Surfer (3/90); reintro Drax the Destroyer on last pg. (cameo) 2.40 6.00
36-38: 36-Recaps history of Thanos; Capt. Marvel & Warlock app. in recap 37-1st full app. Drax the Destroyer; Drax-c. 38-Silver Surfer battles Thanos 2.00 5.00
44,45,49-Thanos stories (c-44,45) 1.00 2.50
46,47: 46-Return of Adam Warlock (2/91); re-intro Gamora & Pip the Troll. 47-Warlock battles Drax 1.60 4.00
48-Last Starlin scripts (also #50) .80 2.00
50-($1.50, 52 pgs.)-Embossed & silver foil-c; Silver Surfer has brief battle w/Thanos; story cont'd in Infinity Gauntlet #1 1.00 2.80 7.00
50-2nd & 3rd printings .80 2.00
51-53: Infinity Gauntlet x-over 1.00 2.50
54-57: Infinity Gauntlet x-overs. 54-Rhino app. 55,56-Thanos-c & app. 57-Thanos-c & cameo .80 2.00
58,59-Infinity Guantlet x-overs; 58-Ron Lim-c only. 59-Thanos battles Silver Surfer-c/story; Thanos joins 1.20 3.00
60-66: 61-Last $1.00-c. 63-Capt. Marvel app. 1.50
67-69-Infinity War x-overs .80 2.00
70-74,76-81,83-91: 76-78-Jack of Hearts-c/s. 83-85-Infinity Crusade x-over; 83,84-Thanos cameo. 85-Storm, Wonder Man x-over. 86-Thor-c/s. 87-Dr. Strange & Warlock app. 88-Thanos-c/s 1.25
75-($2.50, 52 pgs.)-Embossed foil-c; Lim-c/a 1.40 3.50
82-($1.75, 52 pgs.) .70 1.75
92-99; 101-109: 92-Begin $1.50-c; bound-in card sheet. 95-FF app. 96-Hulk & FF app. 97-Terrax & Nova app. 106-Doc Doom app. 1.50
100 ($2.25, 52 pgs.)-Wraparound-c .90 2.25

Silver Surfer/ Superman #1 © MEG/ DC

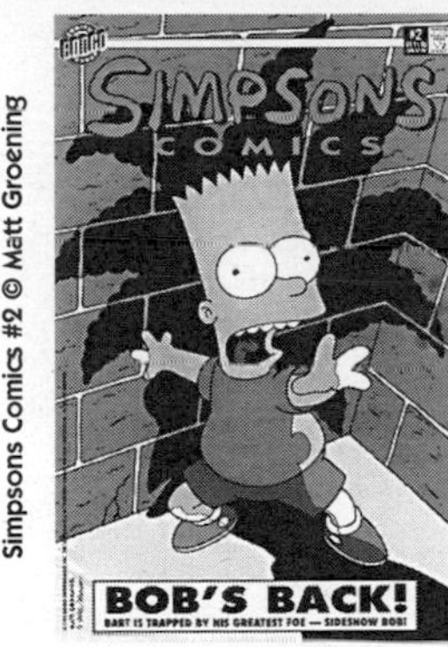

Simpsons Comics #2 © Matt Groening

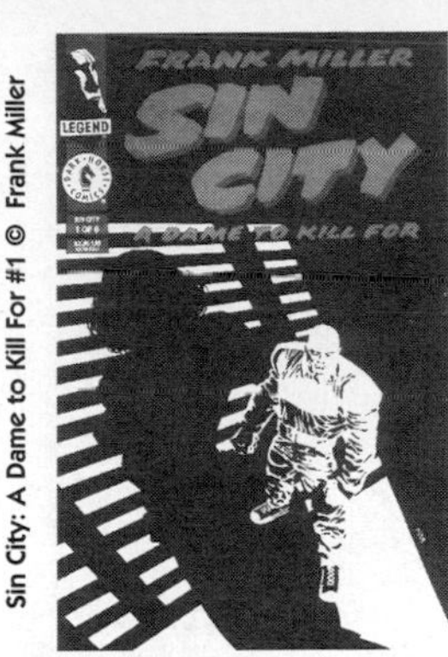

Sin City: A Dame to Kill For #1 © Frank Miller

GD25 FN65 NM94

100 ($3.95, 52 pgs.)-Enhanced-c 1.60 4.00
110-117: 110-Begin $1.95-c .80 2.00
118-124,126: 118-Begin $1.50-c. 121-Quasar & Beta Ray Bill app. 123-w/card insert; begin Garney-a. 126-Dr. Strange-c/app. 1.50
125 ($2.95)-Wraparound-c; Vs. Hulk-c/app. 2.95
127-129, -1(7/97)-($1.95): 128-Spider-Man & Daredevil-c/app. 1.95
130-139-($1.99) 1.99
Annual 1 (1988, $1.75)-Evolutionary War app.; 1st Ron Lim-a on Silver Surfer (20 pg. back-up story & pin-ups) 1.00 2.00 5.00
Annual 2-4 (1989-91, $2.00, 68 pgs.): 2-Atlantis Attacks. 4-3 pg. origin story; Silver Surfer battles Guardians of the Galaxy 1.00 2.50
Annual 5 (1992, $2.25, 68 pgs.)-Return of the Defenders, part 3; Lim-c/a (3 pgs. of pin-ups only) 1.00 2.50
Annual 6 (1993, $2.95, 68 pgs.)-Polybagged w/trading card; 1st app. Legacy; card is by Lim/Austin 1.20 3.00
Annual 7 (1994, $2.95) 1.20 3.00
Annual '97 (1997, $2.99) 3.00
Graphic Novel (Hardcover, $14.95) 1.85 5.50 15.00
Graphic Novel (The Enslavers, $16.95) 2.15 6.50 17.00
...Dangerous Artifacts-(1996, $3.95)-Ron Marz scripts; Galactus-c/app. 1.60 4.00
...: The First Coming of Galactus nn (11/92, $5.95, 68 pgs.)-Reprints Fantastic Four #48-50 with new Lim-c 2.40 6.00

NOTE: ***Austin** c(i)-71, 73, 74, 76, 79. **Cully Hamner** a-83p. **Ron Lim** a(p)-15-31, 33-38, 40-55, (56, 57-part-p), 60-65, 73-82; c(p)-15-31, 32-38, 40-84, 86-92, Annual 5, 6. **M. Rogers** a-1-10, 12, 19, 21; c-1-12, 21.*

SILVER SURFER, THE
Dec, 1988 - No. 2, Jan, 1989 ($1.00, limited series)
Marvel Comics (Epic Comics)

1,2: By Stan Lee scripts & Moebius-c/a 1.60 4.00

SILVER SURFER/SUPERMAN
1996 ($5.95,one-shot)
Marvel Comics

1-Perez-s/Lim-c/a(p) 2.40 6.00

SILVER SURFER VS. DRACULA
Feb, 1994 ($1.75, one-shot)
Marvel Comics

1-r/Tomb of Dracula #50; Everett Vampire-r/Venus #19; Howard the Duck back-up by Brunner; Lim-c(p) .70 1.75

SILVER SURFER/WARLOCK: RESURRECTION
Mar, 1993 - No. 4, June, 1993 ($2.50, limited series)
Marvel Comics

1-4: Starlin-c/a & scripts 1.00 2.50

SILVER SURFER/WEAPON ZERO
Apr, 1997 ($2.95,one-shot)
Marvel Comics

1-"Devil's Reign" pt. 8 2.95

SILVERTIP (Max Brand)
No. 491, Aug, 1953 - No. 898, May, 1958
Dell Publishing Co.

Four Color 491 (#1); all painted-c 7.00 22.00 80.00
Four Color 572,608,637,667,731,789,898-Kinstler-a 3.60 11.00 40.00
Four Color 835 3.60 11.00 40.00

SIMPSONS COMICS (See Bartman, Itchy & Scratchy & Radioactive Man)
1993 - Present ($1.95, color)
Bongo Comics Group

1-($2.25)-FF#1-c swipe; pull-out poster; flip book 1.20 3.00
2,3-($1.95): 2-Patty & Selma on flip side. 3-Krusty, Agent of K.L.O.W.N. flip-c/story 1.00 2.50
4-($2.25)-Infinity-c; flip-c of Busman #1; w/trading card .90 2.25
5-Wraparound-c w/trading card .90 2.25
6-35: All Flip books. 6-w/Chief Wiggum's "Crime Comics". 7-w/"McBain Comics". 8-w/"Edna, Queen of the Congo". 9-w/"Barney Gumble". 10-w/"Apu". 11-w/"Homer". 12-w/"White Knuckled War Stories". 13-w/"Jimbo Jones' Wedgie Comics". 14-w/"Grampa". 15-w/"Itchy & Scratchy". 16-w/"Bongo Grab Bag". 17-w/"Headlight Comics". 18-w/"Milhouse". 19-22-w/"Roswell". 23-w/"Hellfire Comics". 24-w/"Lil' Homey" .90 2.25
...Extravaganza (1994, $10.00)-r/#1-4; infinity-c 10.00
...Simpsorama (1996, $10.95)-r/#11-14 11.00

SIMPSONS COMICS AND STORIES
1993 ($2.95, one-shot)
Welsh Publishing Group

1-(Direct Sale)-Polybagged w/Bartman poster 1.20 3.00
1-(Newsstand Edition)-Without poster 1.20 3.00

SIMULATORS, THE
1991 ($2.50, stiff-c)
Neatly Chiseled Features

1-Super hero group 1.00 2.50

SINBAD, JR (TV Cartoon)
Sept-Nov, 1965 - No. 3, May, 1966
Dell Publishing Co.

1 2.00 6.00 16.00
2,3 1.50 4.50 12.00

SINDBAD (See Capt. Sindbad under Movie Comics, and Fantastic Voyages of Sindbad)

SIN CITY (See Dark Horse Presents, Decade of Dark Horse, A & San Diego Comic Con Comics #2,4)

SIN CITY: A DAME TO KILL FOR
Nov, 1993 - No. 6, May, 1994 ($2.95, B&W, limited series)
Dark Horse Comics (Legend)

1-6: Frank Miller-c/a & story in all. 1-1st app. Dwight. 1.20 3.00
Limited Edition Hardcover 100.00
Hardcover 25.00

SIN CITY: FAMILY VALUES
Oct, 1997 ($10.00, B&W, square bound, one-shot)
Dark Horse Comics (Legend)

nn-Miller-c/a & story 10.00

SIN CITY: JUST ANOTHER SATURDAY NIGHT
Aug, 1997 (Wizard 1/2 offer, B&W, one-shot)
Dark Horse Comics (Legend)

1/2-Miller-c/a & story 2.50

SIN CITY: LOST, LONELY & LETHAL
Dec, 1996 ($2.95, B&W and blue, one-shot)
Dark Horse Comics (Legend)

nn-Miller-c/s/a; w/pin-ups 1.20 3.00

SIN CITY: SEX AND VIOLENCE
Mar, 1997 ($2.95, B&W and blue, one-shot)
Dark Horse Comics (Legend)

nn-Miller-c/a & story 1.20 3.00

SIN CITY: SILENT NIGHT
Dec, 1995 ($2.95, B&W, one-shot)
Dark Horse Comics (Legend)

1-Miller-c/a & story; Marv app. 1.20 3.00

SIN CITY: THAT YELLOW BASTARD
Feb, 1996 - No. 6, July, 1996 ($2.95/$3.50, B&W and yellow, limited series)
Dark Horse Comics (Legend)

1-5: Miller-c/a & story in all. 1-1st app. Hartigan. 1.60 4.00
6-($3.50) Error & corrected 3.50

Sin City: The Big Fat Kill #4 © Frank Miller

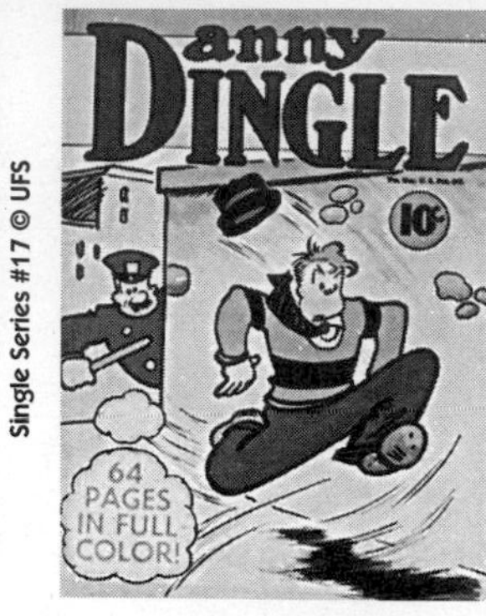

Single Series #17 © UFS

Sisterhood of Steel #4 © MEG

	GD25	FN65	NM94
Limited Edition Hardcover			25.00

SIN CITY: THE BABE WORE RED AND OTHER STORIES
Nov, 1994 ($2.95, B&W and red, one-shot)
Dark Horse Comics (Legend)

1-r/serial run in Previews as well as other stories; Miller-c/a & scripts; Dwight app.		1.20	3.00

SIN CITY: THE BIG FAT KILL
Nov, 1994 - No. 5, Mar, 1995 ($2.95, B&W, limited series)
Dark Horse Comics (Legend)

1-4-Miller story & art in all; Dwight app.		1.60	4.00
5 ($3.50)-Dwight app.		1.60	4.00
Hardcover			25.00

SINGING GUNS (See Fawcett Movie Comics)

SINGLE SERIES (Comics on Parade #30 on)(Also see John Hix...)
1938 - No. 28, 1942 (All 68 pgs.)
United Features Syndicate

Note: See Individual Alphabetical Listings for prices

1-Captain and the Kids (#1)
2-Broncho Bill (1939) (#1)
3-Ella Cinders (1939)
4-Li'l Abner (1939) (#1)
5-Fritzi Ritz (#1)
6-Jim Hardy by Dick Moores (#1)
7-Frankie Doodle
8-Peter Pat (On sale 7/14/39)
9-Strange As It Seems
10-Little Mary Mixup
11-Mr. and Mrs. Beans
12-Joe Jinks
13-Looy Dot Dope
14-Billy Make Believe
15-How It Began (1939)
16-Illustrated Gags (1940)-Has ad for Captain and the Kids #1 reprint listed below
17-Danny Dingle
18-Li'l Abner (#2 on-c)
19-Broncho Bill (#2 on-c)
20-Tarzan by Hal Foster
21-Ella Cinders (#2 on-c; on sale 3/19/40)
22-Iron Vic
23-Tailspin Tommy by Hal Forrest (#1)
24-Alice in Wonderland (#1)
25-Abbie and Slats
26-Little Mary Mixup (#2 on-c, 1940)
27-Jim Hardy by Dick Moores (1942)
28-Ella Cinders & Abbie and Slats (1942)
1-Captain and the Kids (1939 reprint)-2nd Edition
1-Fritzi Ritz (1939 reprint)-2nd ed.

NOTE: *Some issues given away at the 1939-40 New York World's Fair (#6).*

SINISTER HOUSE OF SECRET LOVE, THE (Becomes Secrets of Sinister House No. 5 on)
Oct-Nov, 1971 - No. 4, Apr-May, 1972 (52 pgs.)
National Periodical Publications

1	2.80	8.40	28.00
2-4: 2-Jeff Jones-c. 3-Toth-a (36 pgs.)	1.75	5.25	14.00

SINJA
June, 1996 ($3.00, one-shot)
Lightning Comics

1,1b-Cleary-c			3.00
1-($9.95) "Nude" Edition; polybagged			10.00
1-($5.95)Commemorative Edition; polybagged			6.00
1-American Entertainment Exclusive Ed.; polybagged w/certificate			5.00

SINJA: RESURRECTION
Aug, 1996 ($3.00, one-shot)
Lightning Comics

1-Flip book w/Kunichi #1			3.00
1-($5.95) Platinum Edition			6.00
1-($9.95) "Nude" Edition			10.00

SIR CHARLES BARKLEY AND THE REFEREE MURDERS
1993 ($9.95, 8-1/2" x 11", 52 pgs.)
Hamilton Comics

	GD25	FN65	NM94
nn-Photo-c; Sports fantasy comic book fiction (uses real names of NBA super stars). Script by Alan Dean Foster, art by Joe Staton. Comes with bound-in sheet of 35 gummed "Moods of Charles Barkley" stamps. Photo/story on Barkley	1.25	3.75	10.00
Special Edition of 100 copies for charity signed on an affixed book plate by Barkley, Foster & Staton			150.00
Ashcan edition given away to dealers, distributors & promoters (low distribution). Four pages in color, balance of story in b&w	1.25	3.75	10.00

SIREN (Also see Eliminator & Ultraforce)
Sept, 1995 - No. 3, Dec, 1995 ($1.50)
Malibu Comics (Ultraverse)

Infinity, 1-3: Infinity-Black-c & painted-c exists. 1-Regular-c & painted-c; War Machine app. 2-Flip book w/Phoenix Resurrection Pt. 3			1.50
Special 1-(2/96, $1.95, 28 pgs.)-Origin Siren; Marvel Comic's Juggernaut-c/app.		.80	2.00

SIR LANCELOT (TV)
No. 606, Dec, 1954 - No. 775, Mar, 1957
Dell Publishing Co.

Four Color 606 (not TV)	6.40	19.00	70.00
Four Color 775(...and Brian)-Buscema-a; photo-c	7.00	22.00	80.00

SIR WALTER RALEIGH (Movie)
May, 1955 (Based on movie "The Virgin Queen")
Dell Publishing Co.

Four Color 644-Photo-c	5.50	16.50	60.00

SISTERHOOD OF STEEL (See Eclipse Graphic Novel #13)
Dec, 1984 -No. 8, Feb, 1986 ($1.50, Baxter paper, mature)
Marvel Comics (Epic Comics)

1-8			1.50

SISTERS OF MERCY
Dec, 1995 - No. 5, Oct, 1996 ($2.50)
Maximum Press/No Mercy Comics No. 3 on

1-5: 1-Liefeld variant-c exists		1.00	2.50
V2#0-(3/97, $1.50) Liefeld-c			1.50

SISTERS OF MERCY: PARADISE LOST
Apr, 1997 - Present ($2.50)
London Night Studios

1-3		1.00	2.50

SISTERS OF MERCY: WHEN RAZORS CRY CRIMSON TEARS
Oct, 1996 ($2.50, one-shot)
No Mercy Comics

1		1.00	2.50

6, THE
Oct, 1996 - No. 3, Dec, 1996 ($2.50, limited series)
Virtual Comics (Byron Preiss Multimedia)

1-3: L. Simonson-s		1.00	2.50

6 BLACK HORSES (See Movie Classics)

SIX FROM SIRIUS
July, 1984 - No. 4, Oct, 1984 ($1.50, limited series, mature)
Marvel Comics (Epic Comics)

1-4: Moench scripts; Gulacy-c/a in all			1.50

SIX FROM SIRIUS II
Feb, 1986 - No. 4, May, 1986 ($1.50, limited series, mature)
Marvel Comics (Epic Comics)

1-4: Moench scripts; Gulacy-c/a in all			1.50

SIX-GUN HEROES
March, 1950 - No. 23, Nov, 1953 (Photo-c #1-23)
Fawcett Publications

1-Rocky Lane, Hopalong Cassidy, Smiley Burnette begin (same date as Smiley Burnette #1)	38.00	113.00	340.00

Six-Gun Heroes #20 © FAW

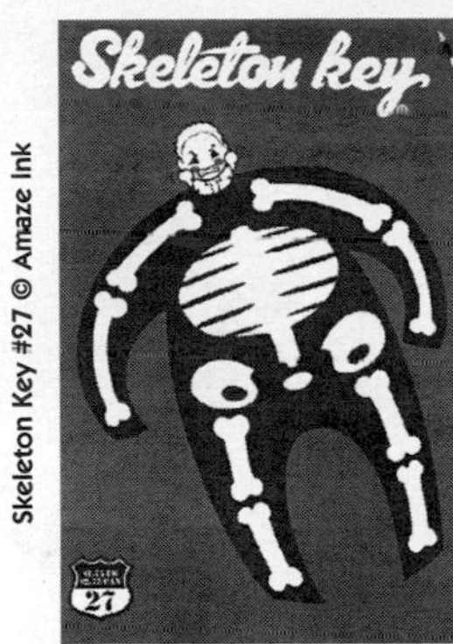

Skeleton Key #27 © Amaze Ink

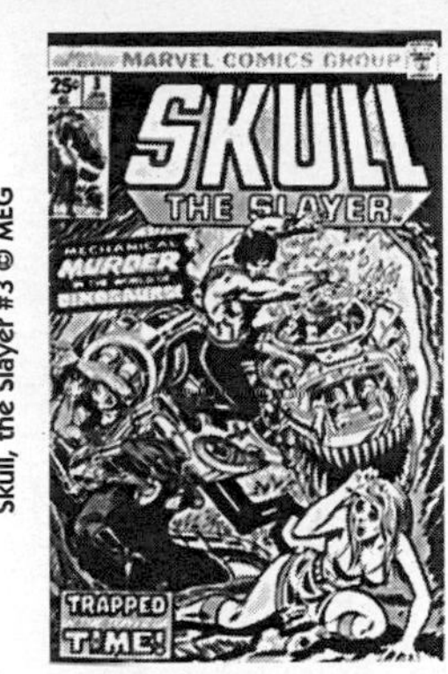

Skull, the Slayer #3 © MEG

	GD25	FN65	NM94
2	23.00	68.00	180.00
3-5: 5-Lash LaRue begins	15.00	45.00	120.00
6-15	12.00	36.00	95.00
16-22: 17-Last Smiley Burnette. 18-Monte Hale begins	10.00	30.00	80.00
23-Last Fawcett issue	11.30	34.00	90.00

NOTE: *Hopalong Cassidy photo c-1-3. Monte Hale photo c-18. Rocky Lane photo c-4, 5, 7, 9, 11, 13, 15, 17, 20, 21, 23. Lash LaRue photo c-6, 8, 10, 12, 14, 16, 19, 22.*

SIX-GUN HEROES (Continued from Fawcett; Gunmasters #84 on)
No. 24, Jan, 1954 - No. 83, Mar-Apr, 1965 (All Vol. 4)(See Blue Bird)
Charlton Comics

	GD25	FN65	NM94
24-Lash LaRue, Hopalong Cassidy, Rocky Lane & Tex Ritter begin; photo-c	15.50	47.00	125.00
25	8.50	26.00	60.00
26-30: 26-Rod Cameron story. 28-Tom Mix begins?	7.15	21.50	50.00
31-40: 38-Jingles & Wild Bill Hickok (TV)	6.00	18.00	42.00
41-46,48,50	5.70	17.00	40.00
47-Williamson-a, 2 pgs; Torres-a	6.50	19.50	45.00
49-Williamson-a (5 pgs.)	6.50	19.50	45.00
51-56,58-60: 58-Gunmaster app.	2.50	7.50	25.00
57-Origin & 1st app. Gunmaster	3.20	9.60	32.00
61-70: 62-Origin Gunmaster	2.50	7.50	20.00
71-83: 76-Gunmaster begins. 79-1st app. & origin of Bullet, the Gun-Boy	1.75	5.25	14.00

SIXGUN RANCH (See Luke Short & Four Color #580)

SIX-GUN WESTERN
Jan, 1957 - No. 4, July, 1957
Atlas Comics (CDS)

	GD25	FN65	NM94
1-Crandall-a; two Williamson text illos	15.00	45.00	120.00
2,3-Williamson-a in both	11.30	34.00	90.00
4-Woodbridge-a	7.15	21.50	50.00

NOTE: ***Ayers** a-2, 3. **Maneely** a-1; c-2, 3. **Orlando** a-2. **Pakula** a-2. **Powell** a-3. **Romita** a-1, 4. **Severin** c-1, 4. **Shores** a-2.*

SIX MILLION DOLLAR MAN, THE (TV)
6/76 - No. 4, 12/76; No. 5, 10/77; No. 6, 2/78 - No. 9, 6/78
Charlton Comics

	GD25	FN65	NM94
1-Staton-c/a; Lee Majors photo on-c		2.40	6.00
2-9: 2-Neal Adams-c; Staton-a		1.60	4.00

SIX MILLION DOLLAR MAN, THE (TV)(Magazine)
July, 1976 - No. 7, Nov, 1977 (B&W)
Charlton Comics

	GD25	FN65	NM94
1-Neal Adams-c/a	1.25	3.75	10.00
2-Neal Adams-c		2.40	6.00
3-7: 3-N. Adams part inks; Chaykin-a		1.60	4.00

67 SECONDS
1992 ($15.95, 54 pgs., graphic novel)
Marvel Comics (Epic Comics)

	GD25	FN65	NM94
nn-James Robinson scripts; Steve Yeowell-c/a	2.00	6.00	16.00

SKATEMAN
Nov, 1983 (Baxter paper, one-shot)
Pacific Comics

	GD25	FN65	NM94
1-Adams-c/a			1.50

SKATING SKILLS
1957 (36 & 12 pgs.; 5x7", two versions) (10¢)
Custom Comics, Inc./Chicago Roller Skates

	GD25	FN65	NM94
nn-Resembles old ACG cover plus interior art	3.20	8.00	16.00

SKELETON HAND (...In Secrets of the Supernatural)
Sept-Oct, 1952 - No. 6, July-Aug, 1953
American Comics Group (B&M Dist. Co.)

	GD25	FN65	NM94
1	37.00	111.00	280.00
2	25.00	75.00	180.00
3-6	21.00	62.00	150.00

SKELETON KEY
July, 1995 - Present ($1.25/$1.50/$1.75)
Amaze Ink

	GD25	FN65	NM94
1			1.25
2-9: 2-Begin $1.50			1.50
10-29: 10-Begin $1.75			1.75
Beyond The Threshold (6/96. $11.95, trade paperback)-r/#1-6			12.00

SKELETON WARRIORS
Apr, 1995 - No. 4, July, 1995 ($1.50)
Marvel Comics

	GD25	FN65	NM94
1-4: Based on animated series.			1.50

SKIN GRAFT: THE ADVENTURES OF A TATTOOED MAN
July, 1993 - No. 4, Oct, 1993 ($2.50, limited series, mature)
DC Comics (Vertigo)

	GD25	FN65	NM94
1-4		1.00	2.50

SKI PARTY (See Movie Classics)

SKIPPY'S OWN BOOK OF COMICS (See Popular Comics)
1934 (Giveaway, 52 pgs., strip reprints)
No publisher listed

	GD25	FN65	NM94
nn-(Scarce)-By Percy Crosby	450.00	1350.00	4500.00

(Estimated up to 40 total copies exist, 2 in NM/Mint)

Published by Max C. Gaines for Phillip's Dental Magnesia to be advertised on the Skippy Radio Show and given away with the purchase of a tube of Phillip's Tooth Paste. This is the first four-color comic book of reprints about one character.

SKREEMER
May, 1989 - No. 6, Oct, 1989 ($2.00, limited series, mature)
DC Comics

	GD25	FN65	NM94
1-6: Contains graphic violence		.80	2.00

SKRULL KILL KREW
Sept, 1995 - No. 5, Dec, 1995 ($2.95, limited series)
Marvel Comics

	GD25	FN65	NM94
1-5: Grant Morrison scripts. 2,3-Cap America app.		1.20	3.00

SKUL, THE
Oct, 1996 - No. 3, Dec, 1996 ($2.50, limited series)
Virtual Comics (Byron Preiss Multimedia)

	GD25	FN65	NM94
1-3: Ron Lim & Jimmy Palmiotti-a		1.00	2.50

SKULL & BONES
1992 - No. 3, 1992 ($4.95, limited series, 52 pgs.)
DC Comics

	GD25	FN65	NM94
Book 1-3: 1-1st app.		2.00	5.00

SKULL, THE SLAYER
Aug, 1975 - No. 8, Nov, 1976 (20¢/25¢)
Marvel Comics Group

	GD25	FN65	NM94
1-Origin & 1st app.; Gil Kane-c		2.00	5.00
2-8: 2-Gil Kane-c. 8-Kirby-c		1.20	3.00

SKY BLAZERS (CBS Radio)
Sept, 1940 - No. 2, Nov, 1940
Hawley Publications

	GD25	FN65	NM94
1-Sky Pirates, Ace Archer, Flying Aces begin	49.00	157.00	440.00
2	34.00	101.00	270.00

SKY KING "RUNAWAY TRAIN" (TV)
1964 (Regular size, 16 pgs.)
National Biscuit Co.

	GD25	FN65	NM94
nn	2.25	6.75	18.00

SKYMAN (See Big Shot Comics & Sparky Watts)

Slaine, the Berserker #21 © QUA

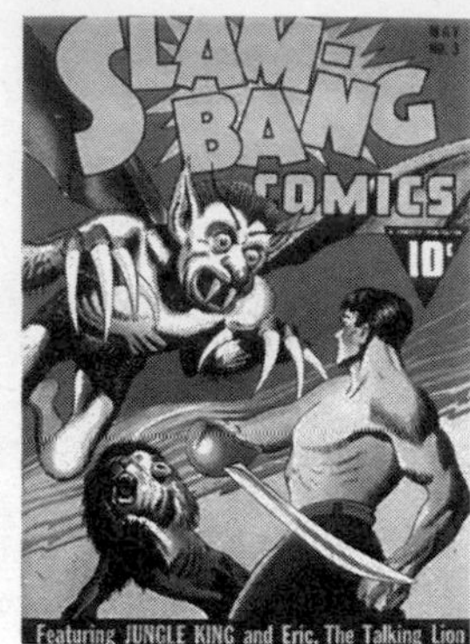

Slam-Bang Comics
10¢
Featuring JUNGLE KING and Eric, The Talking Lion

Slam Bang Comics #3 © FAW

Sleepwalker #2 © MEG

GD25 FN65 NM94

Fall?, 1941 - No. 2, Fall?, 1942; No. 3, 1948 - No. 4, 1948
Columbia Comics Group

1-Origin Skyman, The Face, Sparky Watts app.; Whitney-c/a; 3rd story-r from Big Shot #1; Whitney c-1-4 83.00 250.00 750.00
2 (1942)-Yankee Doodle 44.00 132.00 400.00
3,4 (1948) 31.00 94.00 250.00

SKYPILOT
No. 10, 1950(nd) - No. 11, Apr-May, 1951 (Saunders painted-c)
Ziff-Davis Publ. Co.

10,11-Frank Borth-a 10.00 30.00 80.00

SKY RANGER (See Johnny Law...)

SKYROCKET
1944
Harry 'A' Chesler

nn-Alias the Dragon, Dr. Vampire, Skyrocket & The Desperado app. 21.00 64.00 170.00

SKY SHERIFF (Breeze Lawson...) (Also see Exposed & Outlaws)
Summer, 1948
D. S. Publishing Co.

1-Edmond Good-c/a 10.00 30.00 70.00

SKY WOLF (Also see Airboy)
Mar, 1988 - No. 3, Oct, 1988 ($1.25/$1.50/$1.95, limited series)
Eclipse Comics

1,2-($1.75) .70 1.75
3-($1.95) .80 1.95

SLACKER COMICS
Aug, 1994 - Present ($2.95, B&W, quarterly)
Slave Labor Graphics

1-15 1.20 3.00
1 (2nd printing)-Reads "2nd print" in indicia 1.20 3.00

SLAINE, THE BERSERKER (Slaine the King #21 on)
July, 1987 - No. 28, 1989 ($1.25/$1.50)
Quality

1-12 1.25
13-28: 13-Begin $1.50-c 1.50

SLAM BANG COMICS (Western Desperado #8)
Mar, 1940 - No. 7, Sept, 1940 (Combined with Master Comics #7)
Fawcett Publications

1-Diamond Jack, Mark Swift & The Time Retarder, Lee Granger, Jungle King begin & continue in Master 156.00 468.00 1400.00
2 67.00 200.00 600.00
3-Classic-c 89.00 267.00 800.00
4-7: 6-Intro Zoro, the Mystery Man (also in #7). 56.00 168.00 500.00

SLAM BANG COMICS
No. 9, No date
Post Cereal Giveaway

9-Dynamic Man, Echo, Mr. E, Yankee Boy app. 4.00 12.00 24.00

SLAPSTICK
Nov, 1992 - No. 4, Feb, 1993 ($1.25, limited series)
Marvel Comics

1-4: Fry/Austin-c/a. 4-Ghost Rider, D.D., F.F. app. 1.25

SLAPSTICK COMICS
nd (1946?) (36 pgs.)
Comic Magazines Distributors

nn-Firetop feature; Post-a(2) 17.50 53.00 140.00

SLASH-D DOUBLECROSS
1950 (Pocket-size, 132 pgs.)

GD25 FN65 NM94

St. John Publishing Co.

nn-Western comics 16.00 49.00 130.00

SLASH MARAUD
Nov, 1987 - No. 6, Apr, 1988 ($1.75, limited series)
DC Comics

1-6 .70 1.75

SLAUGHTERMAN
Feb, 1983 - No. 2, 1983 ($1.50, B&W)
Comico

1,2 1.50

SLAVE GIRL COMICS (See Malu... & White Princess of the Jungle #2)
Feb, 1949 - No. 2, Apr, 1949 (52 pgs.); Mar, 1989 (B&W, 44 pgs)
Avon Periodicals/Eternity Comics (1989)

1-Larsen-c/a 73.00 221.00 600.00
2-Larsen-a 55.00 165.00 450.00
1-(3/89, $2.25, B&W, 44 pgs.)-r/#1 .90 2.25

SLEDGE HAMMER (TV)
Feb, 1988 - No. 2, Mar,1988 ($1.00, limited series)
Marvel Comics

1,2 1.00

SLEEPING BEAUTY (See Dell Giants & Movie Comics)
No. 973, May, 1959 - No. 984, June, 1959 (Disney)
Dell Publishing Co.

Four Color 973 (...and the Prince) 11.00 33.00 120.00
Four Color 984 (...Fairy Godmother's) 8.00 25.00 90.00

SLEEPWALKER
June, 1991 - No. 33, Feb, 1994 ($1.00/$1.25)
Marvel Comics

1-1st app. Sleepwalker 1.50
2-5: 4-Williamson-i. 5-Spider-Man-c/story 1.50
6-10: 7-Infinity Gauntlet x-over. 8-Vs. Deathlok-c/story 1.50
11-18,20-24,26-33: 11-Ghost Rider-c/story. 12-Quesada-c/a(p) 14-Intro Spectra. 15-F.F.-c/story. 17-Darkhawk & Spider-Man x-over. 18-Infinity War x-over; Quesada/Williamson-c. 21,22-Hobgoblin app. 1.25
19-($2.00)-Die-cut Sleepwalker mask cover .80 2.00
25-($2.95, 52 pgs.)-Holo-grafx foil-c; origin 1.20 3.00
Holiday Special 1 (1/93, $2.00, 52 pgs.)-Quesada-c(p) .80 2.00

SLEEPWALKING
Jan, 1996 ($2.50, B&W)
Hall of Heroes

1-Kelley Jones-c 1.00 2.50

SLEEZE BROTHERS, THE
Aug, 1989 - No. 6, Jan, 1990 ($1.75, mature)
Marvel Comics (Epic Comics)

1-6: 4-6 (9/89 - 11/89 indicia dates) 1.80
nn-(1991, $3.95, 52 pgs.) 1.60 4.00

SLICK CHICK COMICS
1947(nd) - No. 3, 1947(nd)
Leader Enterprises

1-Teenage humor 8.75 26.25 70.00
2,3 7.15 21.50 50.00

SLIDERS (TV)
June, 1996 - No. 2, July, 1996 ($2.50, limited series)
Acclaim Comics (Armada)

1,2: D.G. Chichester scripts; Dick Giordano-a. 1.00 2.50

SLIDERS: DARKEST HOUR (TV)
Oct, 1996 - No. 3, Dec, 1996 ($2.50, limited series)

Sludge #7 © MAL

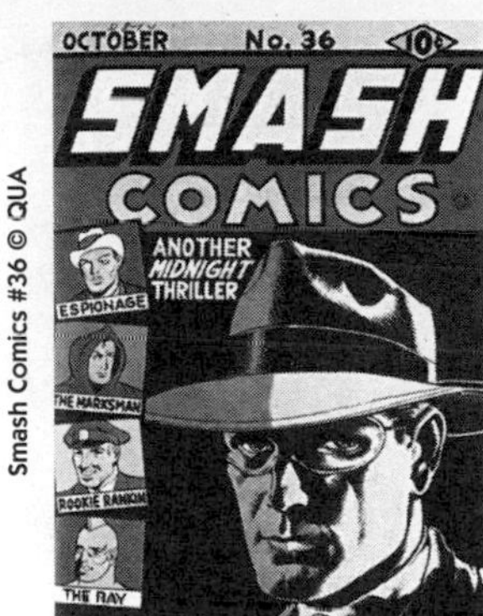

Smash Comics #36 © QUA

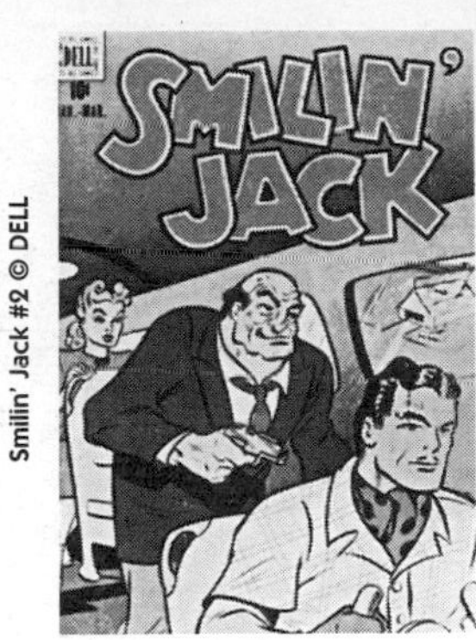

Smilin' Jack #2 © DELL

	GD25	FN65	NM94

Acclaim Comics (Armada)

1-3 — 1.00 — 2.50

SLIDERS SPECIAL
Nov, 1996 - No 3, Mar, 1997 ($3.95, limited series)
Acclaim Comics (Armada)

1-Narcotica-Jerry O'Connell-s — 1.60 — 4.00
2-Blood and Splendor — 1.60 — 4.00
3-Deadly Secrets — 1.60 — 4.00

SLIDERS: ULTIMATUM (TV)
Sept, 1996 - No. 2, Sept, 1996 ($2.50, limited series)
Acclaim Comics (Armada)

1,2 — 1.00 — 2.50

SLIMER! (TV cartoon) (Also see the Real Ghostbusters)
1989 - No. 19, Feb?, 1991 ($1.75)
Now Comics

1-19: Based on animated cartoon — .70 — 1.75

SLIM MORGAN (See Wisco)

SLUDGE
Oct, 1993 - No. 12, Dec, 1994 ($2.50/$1.95)
Malibu Comics (Ultraverse)

1-($2.50, 48 pgs.)-Intro/1st app. Sludge; Rune flip-c/story Pt. 1 (1st app., 3 pgs.) by Barry Smith; The Night Man app. (3 pg. preview); The Mighty Magnor 1 pg strip begins by Aragones (cont. in other titles) — 1.00 — 2.50
1-Ultra 5000 Limited silver foil — 2.00 — 5.00
2-11: 3-Break-Thru x-over. 4-2 pg. Mantra origin. 8-Bloodstorm app. — .80 — 2.00
12 ($3.50)-Ultraverse Premiere #8 flip book; Alex Ross poster. — 1.40 — 3.50
...:Red Xmas (12/94, $2.50, 44 pgs.) — 1.00 — 2.50

SLUGGER (Little Wise Guys Starring...)(Also see Daredevil Comics)
April, 1956
Lev Gleason Publications

1-Biro-c — 5.35 — 16.00 — 32.00

SMASH COMICS (Becomes Lady Luck #86 on)
Aug, 1939 - No. 85, Oct, 1949
Quality Comics Group

1-Origin Hugh Hazard & His Iron Man, Bozo the Robot, Espionage, Starring Black X by Eisner, & Hooded Justice (Invisible Justice #2 on); Chic Carter & Wings Wendall begin; 1st Robot on the cover of a comic book (Bozo) — 200.00 — 600.00 — 1800.00
2-The Lone Star Rider app; Invisible Hood gains power of invisibility — 78.00 — 234.00 — 700.00
3-Captain Cook & Eisner's John Law begin — 50.00 — 150.00 — 450.00
4,5: 4-Flash Fulton begins — 44.00 — 132.00 — 400.00
6-12: 12-One pg. Fine-a — 39.00 — 117.00 — 350.00
13-Magno begins (8/40); last Eisner issue; The Ray app. in full page ad; The Purple Trio begins — 40.00 — 120.00 — 360.00
14-Intro. The Ray (9/40) by Lou Fine & others — 222.00 — 667.00 — 2000.00
15,16: 16-The Scarlet Seal begins — 100.00 — 300.00 — 900.00
17-Wun Cloo becomes plastic super-hero by Jack Cole (9-months before Plastic Man) — 106.00 — 318.00 — 950.00
18-Midnight by Jack Cole begins (origin & 1st app., 1/41) — 122.00 — 366.00 — 1100.00
19-22: Last Ray by Fine; The Jester begins-#22 — 67.00 — 200.00 — 600.00
23,24: 24-The Sword app.; last Chic Carter; Wings Wendall dons new costume #24,25 — 53.00 — 159.00 — 475.00
25-Origin/1st app. Wildfire; Rookie Rankin begins — 63.00 — 189.00 — 570.00
26-30: 28-Midnight-c begin, end #85 — 50.00 — 150.00 — 450.00
31,32,34: Ray by Rudy Palais; also #33 — 39.00 — 117.00 — 350.00
33-Origin The Marksman — 50.00 — 150.00 — 450.00
35-37 — 39.00 — 117.00 — 350.00
38-The Yankee Eagle begins; last Midnight by Jack Cole — 44.00 — 132.00 — 400.00
39,40-Last Ray issue — 37.00 — 110.00 — 330.00
41,43-50 — 25.00 — 75.00 — 200.00
42-Lady Luck begins by Klaus Nordling — 53.00 — 159.00 — 475.00
51-60 — 19.00 — 56.00 — 150.00
61-70 — 15.50 — 47.00 — 125.00
71-85: 79-Midnight battles the Men from Mars-c/s — 15.00 — 45.00 — 120.00

NOTE: ***Al Bryant*** *c-54, 63-68.* ***Cole*** *a-17-38, 68, 69, 72, 73, 78, 80, 83, 85; c-38, 60-62, 69-84.* ***Crandall*** *a-(Ray)-23-29, 35-38; c-36, 39, 40, 42-44, 46.* ***Fine*** *a(Ray)-14, 15, 16(w/****Tuska****), 17-22.* ***Fox*** *c-24-35.* ***Fuje*** *Ray-30.* ***Gil Fox*** *a-6-7, 9, 11-13.* ***Guardineer*** *a-(The Marksman)-39-?, 49, 52.* ***Gustavson*** *a-4-7, 9, 11-13 (The Jester)-22-46; (Magno)-13-21; (Midnight)-39(Cole inks), 49, 52, 63-65.* ***Kotzky*** *a-(Espionage)-33-38; c-45, 47-53.* ***Nordling*** *a-49, 52, 63-65.* ***Powell*** *a-11, 12, (Abdul the Arab)-13-24.Black X c-2, 6, 9, 11, 13, 16. Bozo the Robot c-1, 3, 5, 8, 10, 12, 14, 18, 20, 22, 24, 26. Midnight c-28-85. The Ray c-15, 17, 19, 21, 23, 25, 27. Wings Wendall c-4, 7.*

SMASH HIT SPORTS COMICS
V2#1, Jan, 1949
Essankay Publications

V2#1-L.B. Cole-c/a — 24.00 — 71.00 — 180.00

SMILE COMICS (Also see Gay Comics, Tickle, & Whee)
1955 (52 pgs.; 5x7-1/4") (7¢)
Modern Store Publ.

1 — 1.20 — 3.00

SMILEY BURNETTE WESTERN (Also see Patches #8 & Six-Gun Heroes)
March, 1950 - No. 4, Oct, 1950 (All photo front & back-c)
Fawcett Publications

1-Red Eagle begins — 38.00 — 113.00 — 340.00
2-4 — 28.00 — 84.00 — 225.00

SMILIN' JACK (See Famous Feature Stories, Popular Comics, Super Book #1, 2, 7, 19 & Super Comics)
No. 5, 1940 - No. 8, Oct-Dec, 1949
Dell Publishing Co.

Four Color 5 — 54.00 — 162.00 — 595.00
Four Color 10 (1940) — 49.00 — 146.00 — 535.00
Large Feature Comic 12,14,25 (1941) — 47.00 — 140.00 — 515.00
Four Color 4 (1942) — 40.00 — 121.00 — 445.00
Four Color 14 (1943) — 32.00 — 97.00 — 355.00
Four Color 36,58 (1943-44) — 21.00 — 64.00 — 235.00
Four Color 80 (1945) — 14.00 — 42.00 — 155.00
Four Color 149 (1947) — 9.00 — 27.00 — 100.00
1 (1-3/48) — 9.00 — 27.00 — 100.00
2 — 5.00 — 15.00 — 54.00
3-8 (10-12/49) — 3.00 — 10.00 — 36.00
Popped Wheat Giveaway (1947)-1938 strip reprints; 16 pgs. in full color — 1.00 — 2.00 — 5.00
Shoe Store Giveaway-1938 strip reprints; 16 pgs. — 4.25 — 13.00 — 28.00
Sparked Wheat Giveaway (1942)-16 pgs. in full color — 4.25 — 13.00 — 28.00

SMILING SPOOK SPUNKY (See Spunky)

SMITTY (See Popular Comics, Super Book #2, 4 & Super Comics)
No. 11, 1940 - No. 7, Aug-Oct, 1949; No. 909, Apr, 1958
Dell Publishing Co.

Four Color 11 (1940) — 34.00 — 101.00 — 370.00
Large Feature Comic 26 (1941) — 24.00 — 71.00 — 260.00
Four Color 6 (1942) — 20.00 — 60.00 — 220.00
Four Color 32 (1943) — 14.00 — 44.00 — 160.00
Four Color 65 (1945) — 11.00 — 34.00 — 125.00
Four Color 99 (1946) — 9.00 — 29.00 — 105.00
Four Color 138 (1947) — 8.00 — 25.00 — 90.00
1 (2-4/48) — 8.00 — 25.00 — 90.00
2-(5-7/48) — 4.00 — 12.00 — 45.00

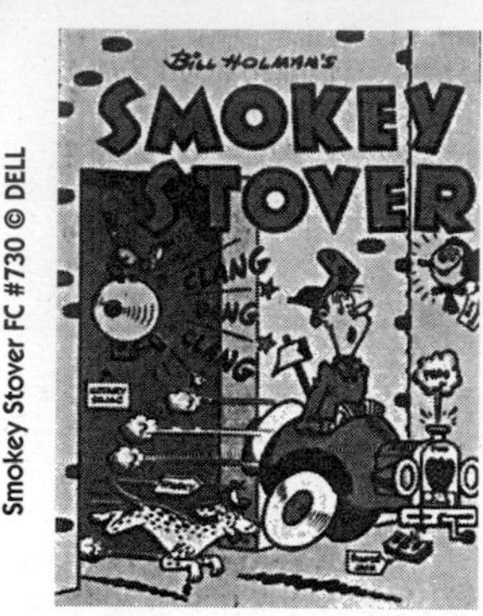

Smokey Stover FC #730 © DELL

Snagglepuss #4 © H-B

Snowman Dead and Dying #1 © Avatar

	GD25	FN65	NM94
3,4: 3-(8-10/48), 4-(11-1/48-49)	3.00	10.00	36.00
5-7, Four Color 909 (4/58)	1.80	5.50	20.00

SMOKEY BEAR (TV) (See March Of Comics #234, 362, 372, 383, 407)
Feb, 1970 - No. 13, Mar, 1973
Gold Key

	GD25	FN65	NM94
1	1.80	5.50	20.00
2-5		2.40	6.00
6-13		1.60	4.00

SMOKEY STOVER (See Popular Comics, Super Book #5, 17, 29 & Super Comics)
No. 7, 1942 - No. 827, Aug, 1957
Dell Publishing Co.

	GD25	FN65	NM94
Four Color 7 (1942)-Reprints	30.00	90.00	330.00
Four Color 35 (1943)	16.00	47.00	170.00
Four Color 64 (1944)	11.00	34.00	125.00
Four Color 229 (1949)	4.50	13.50	50.00
Four Color 730,827	3.50	11.00	38.00
General Motors giveaway (1953)	2.75	8.00	30.00
National Fire Protection giveaway(1953 & 1954)-16 pgs., paper-c	2.75	8.00	30.00

SMOKEY THE BEAR (See Forest Fire for 1st app.)
No. 653, 10/55 - No. 1214, 8/61 (See March of Comics #234)
Dell Publishing Co.

	GD25	FN65	NM94
Four Color 653 (#1)	9.00	27.00	100.00
Four Color 708,754,818,932	4.50	13.50	50.00
Four Color 1016,1119,1214	2.75	8.00	30.00
True Story of..., The('59)-U.S. Forest Service giveaway-Publ. by Western Printing Co. (reprinted in 1964 & 1969)-Reprints 1st 16 pgs. of Four Color 932	3.20	8.00	16.00

SMOKY (See Movie Classics)

SMURFS (TV)
1982 (Dec) - No. 3, 1983
Marvel Comics

	GD25	FN65	NM94
1-3		1.20	3.00
...Treasury Edition 1 (64 pgs.)-r/#1-3	2.25	6.75	18.00

SNAFU (Magazine)
Nov, 1955 - V2#2, Mar, 1956 (B&W)
Atlas Comics (RCM)

	GD25	FN65	NM94
V1#1-Heath/Severin-a; Everett, Maneely-a	9.50	28.00	75.00
V2#1,2-Severin-a	7.85	23.50	55.00

SNAGGLEPUSS (TV)(See Hanna-Barbera Band Wagon #3, Quick-Draw McGraw & Spotlight #4)
Oct, 1962 - No. 4, Sept, 1963 (Hanna-Barbera)
Gold Key

	GD25	FN65	NM94
1	6.40	19.00	70.00
2-4	4.50	13.50	50.00

SNAP (Formerly Scoop #8; becomes Jest #10,11 & Komik Pages #10)
No. 9, 1944
Harry 'A' Chesler

	GD25	FN65	NM94
9-Manhunter, The Voice	14.50	43.00	115.00

SNAPPY COMICS
1945
Cima Publ. Co. (Prize Publ.)

	GD25	FN65	NM94
1-Airmale app.; 9 pg. Sorcerer's Apprentice adapt; Kiefer-a	23.00	69.00	185.00

SNARKY PARKER (See Life With...)

SNIFFY THE PUP
No. 5, Nov, 1949 - No. 18, Sept, 1953
Standard Publications (Animated Cartoons)

	GD25	FN65	NM94
5-Two Frazetta text illos	8.75	26.25	65.00
6-10	4.00	12.00	24.00
11-18	3.60	9.00	18.00

SNOOPER AND BLABBER DETECTIVES (TV) (See Whitman Comic Books)
Nov, 1962 - No. 3, May, 1963 (Hanna-Barbera)
Gold Key

	GD25	FN65	NM94
1	6.40	19.00	70.00
2,3	5.00	15.00	55.00

SNOW FOR CHRISTMAS
1957 (16 pgs.) (Giveaway)
W. T. Grant Co.

	GD25	FN65	NM94
nn	3.20	8.00	16.00

SNOWMAN
1996 ($2.50, B&W)
Hall of Heroes

	GD25	FN65	NM94
1	2.25	6.75	18.00
1-Ltd. Ed.	3.20	9.60	32.00
2		2.40	6.00
2,3-Ltd. Ed.	1.50	4.50	12.00
3		2.00	5.00

SNOWMAN DEAD AND DYING
Nov,1997 - No. 3 ($3.00, B&W, limited series)
Avatar Press

	GD25	FN65	NM94
1		1.20	3.00
1-($4.95) Ltd. Edition			4.95

SNOWMAN 1944
1997 ($2.75, B&W)
Hall of Heroes

	GD25	FN65	NM94
1		1.60	4.00
1-Ltd. Ed.	1.00	3.00	8.00
2		1.60	4.00
3,4			2.75
3-Ltd. Ed.		1.20	3.00
...Special 1 (10/97, $3.95)			3.95

SNOW WHITE (See Christmas With..., Mickey Mouse Mag., Movie Comics & Seven Dwarfs)
No. 49, July, 1944 - No. 382, Mar, 1952 (Disney-Movie)
Dell Publishing Co.

	GD25	FN65	NM94
Four Color 49 (...& the Seven Dearfs)	56.00	169.00	620.00
Four Color 382 (1952)-origin; partial reprint of Four Color 49	10.00	30.00	110.00

SNOW WHITE
Jan, 1995 ($1.95, one-shot)
Marvel Comics

	GD25	FN65	NM94
1-r/1937 Sunday newspaper pages		.80	2.00

SNOW WHITE AND THE SEVEN DWARFS
1952 (32 pgs., 5x7-1/4", soft-c) (Disney)
Bendix Washing Machines

	GD25	FN65	NM94
nn	9.50	28.00	75.00

SNOW WHITE AND THE SEVEN DWARFS
1957 (Small size)
Promotional Publ. Co.

	GD25	FN65	NM94
nn	4.00	10.50	21.00

SNOW WHITE AND THE SEVEN DWARFS
1958 (16 pgs, 5x7-1/4", soft-c) (Disney premium)
Western Printing Co.

	GD25	FN65	NM94
nn- "Mystery of the Missing Magic"	5.70	17.00	40.00

Solar #12 © WEST

Solar, Man of the Atom: Hell on Earth #3 © VAL

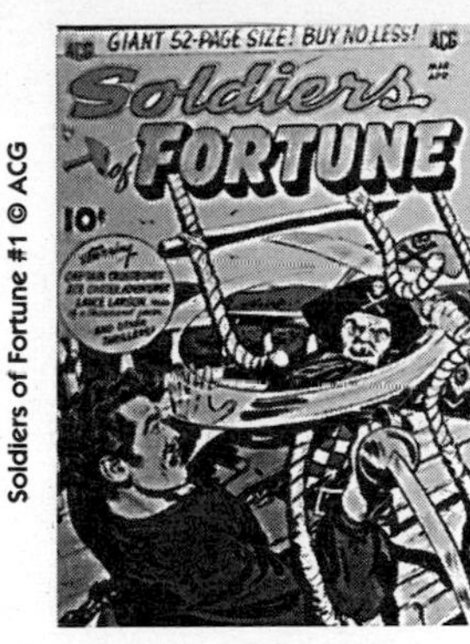

Soldiers of Fortune #1 © ACG

GD25 FN65 NM94

SNOW WHITE AND THE SEVEN DWARFS
April, 1982 (60¢)
Whitman Publications

nn-r/Four Color 49 — 1.20 3.00

SNOW WHITE AND THE SEVEN DWARFS GOLDEN ANNIVERSARY
Fall, 1987 ($2.95, magazine size, 52 pgs.)
Gladstone

1-Contains poster — 1.00 3.00 8.00

SNOW WHITE AND THE 7 DWARFS IN "MILKY WAY"
1955 (16 pgs., soft-c, 5x7-1/4") (Disney premium)
American Dairy Association

nn — 9.50 28.00 75.00

SOAP OPERA LOVE
Feb, 1983 - No. 3, June, 1983
Charlton Comics

1-3 — 1.00

SOAP OPERA ROMANCES
July, 1982 - No. 5, March, 1983
Charlton Comics

1-5-Nurse Betsy Crane-r — 1.00

SO DARK THE ROSE
Oct, 1995 ($2.95)
CFD Productions

1-Wrightson-c — 1.20 3.00

SOJOURN
Sept, 1977 - No. 2, 1978 ($1.50, B&W & color, full tabloid size)
White Cliffs Publ. Co.

1,2: 1-Tor by Kubert, Eagle by Severin, E. V. Race, Private Investigator by Doug Wildey, T. C. Mars by Aragones begin plus other strips — .70 1.75

SOLAR (...Man of the Atom) (Also see Doctor Solar)
Sept, 1991 - No. 60, Apr, 1996 ($1.75/$1.95/$2.50, 44 pgs.)
Valiant/Acclaim Comics (Valiant)

1-Layton-a(i) on Solar; Barry Windsor-Smith-c/a — 2.00 5.00
2,3: 2-Layton-a(i) on Solar, B. Smith-a. 3-1st app. Harada (11/91) — 1.20 3.00
4-9: 7-vs. X-O Armor; last $1.95-c. 8-$2.25-c begins — .80 2.00
10-(6/92, $3.95)-1st app. Eternal Warrior (6 pgs.); black embossed-c; origin & 1st app. Geoff McHenry (Geomancer) — 1.60 4.00
10-($3.95)-2nd printing — 1.60 4.00
11-15: 11-1st full app. Eternal Warrior. 12,13-Unity x-overs. 14-1st app. Fred Bender (becomes Dr. Eclipse). 15-2nd Dr. Eclipse — 1.20 3.00
16-45: 17-X-O Manowar app. 23-Solar splits. 29-1st Valiant Vision book. 33-Valiant Vision; bound-in trading card. 38-Chaos Effect Epsilon Pt.1 — .90 2.25
46-60: 46-$2.50-c begins. 46-52-Dan Jurgens-a(p)/scripts w/Giordano-i 53,54-Jurgens scripts only. 60-Keith Giffen scripts; Jeff Johnson-a(p) — 1.00 2.50
0-($9.95, trade paperback)-r/Alpha and Omega origin story; polybagged w/poster — 1.25 3.75 10.00
...:Second Death (1994, $9.95)-r/issues #1-4. — 1.25 3.75 10.00

NOTE: *#1-10 all have free 8 pg. insert "Alpha and Omega" which is a 10 chapter Solar origin story. All 10 centerfolds can pieced together to show climax of story.* ***Ditko*** *a-11p, 14p.* ***Giordano*** *a-46, 47, 48, 49, 50, 51, 52i.* ***Johnson*** *a-60p.* ***Jurgens*** *a-46, 47, 48, 49, 50 , 51, 52p.* ***Layton*** *a-1-3i; c-2i, 11i, 17i, 25i.* ***Miller*** *c-12.* ***Quesada*** *c-17p, 20-23p, 29p.* ***Simonson*** *c-13.* ***B. Smith*** *a-1-10; c-1, 3, 5, 7, 19i.* ***Thibert*** *c-22i, 23i.*

SOLARMAN
Jan, 1989 - No. 2, May, 1990 ($1.00, limited series)
Marvel Comics

1,2 — 1.00

SOLAR, MAN OF THE ATOM (Man of the Atom on cover)
Vol. 2, May, 1997 ($3.95, one-shot, 46 pgs.) (1st Valiant Heroes Special Event)
Acclaim Comics (Valiant Heroes)

Vol. 2-Reintro Solar; Ninjak cameo; Warren Ellis scripts; Darick Robertson-a — 1.60 4.00

SOLAR, MAN OF THE ATOM: HELL ON EARTH
Jan, 1998 - No. 4 ($2.50, limited series)
Acclaim Comics (Valiant Heroes)

1,3-Priest-s/ Zircher-a(p) — 2.50

SOLAR, MAN OF THE ATOM: REVELATIONS
Nov, 1997 ($3.95, one-shot, 46 pgs.)
Acclaim Comics (Valiant Heroes)

1-Krueger-s/ Zircher-a(p) — 1.60 4.00

SOLDIER & MARINE COMICS (Fightin' Army #16 on)
No. 11, Dec, 1954 - No. 15, Aug, 1955; V2#9, Dec, 1956
Charlton Comics (Toby Press of Conn. V1#11)

V1#11 (12/54)-Bob Powell-a — 5.35 16.00 32.00
V1#12(2/55)-15: 12-Photo-c — 4.00 10.00 20.00
V2#9(Formerly Never Again; Jerry Drummer V2#10 on) — 4.00 10.00 20.00

SOLDIER COMICS
Jan, 1952 - No. 11, Sept, 1953
Fawcett Publications

1 — 8.75 26.25 70.00
2 — 5.70 17.00 35.00
3-5 — 4.25 13.00 28.00
6-11: 8-Illo. in **POP** — 4.00 12.00 24.00

SOLDIERS OF FORTUNE
Mar-Apr, 1951 - No. 13, Feb-Mar, 1953
American Comics Group (Creston Publ. Corp.)

1-Capt. Crossbones by Shelly, Ace Carter, Lance Larson begin — 20.00 60.00 140.00
2 — 11.50 34.00 80.00
3-10: 6-Bondage-c — 10.00 30.00 70.00
11-13 (War format) — 5.00 15.00 30.00

NOTE: ***Shelly*** *a-1-3, 5.* ***Whitney*** *a-6, 8-11, 13; c-1-3, 5, 6.*

SOLDIERS OF FREEDOM
1987 - No. 2? ($1.75)
Americomics

1,2 — .75 1.80

SOLITAIRE (Also See Prime V2#6-8)
Nov, 1993 - No. 12, Dec, 1994 ($1.95)
Malibu Comics (Ultraverse)

1-($2.50)-Collector's edition bagged w/playing card — 1.00 2.50
1-12: 1-Regular edition w/o playing card. 2,4-Break-Thru x-over. 3-2 pg. origin The Night Man. 4-Gatefold-c. 5-Two pg. origin the Strangers — .80 2.00

SOLO
Sept, 1994 - No. 4, Dec, 1994 ($1.75, limited series)
Marvel Comics

1-4: Spider-Man app. — .70 1.75

SOLO (Movie)
July, 1996 - No. 2, Aug, 1996 ($2.50, limited series)
Dark Horse Comics

1,2: Adaptation of film; photo-c — 1.00 2.50

SOLO AVENGERS (Becomes Avenger Spotlight #21 on)
Dec, 1987 - No. 20, July, 1989 (75¢/$1.00)
Marvel Comics

1-Jim Lee-a on back-up story — 1.00 2.50

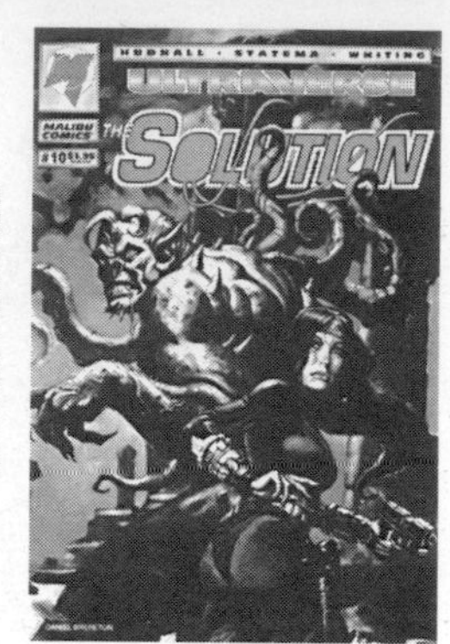

The Solution #10 © MAL

Son of Satan #2 © MEG

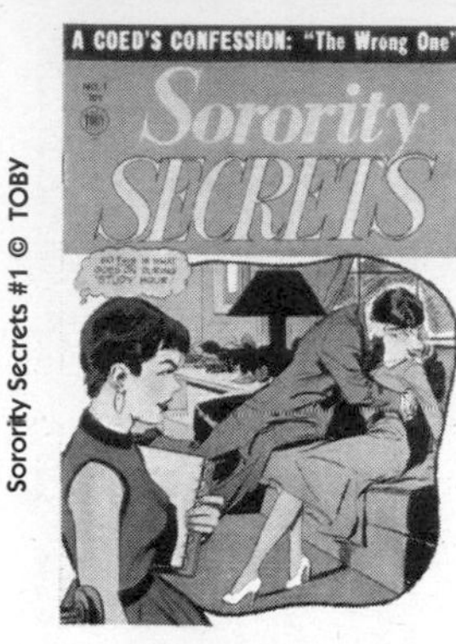

Sorority Secrets #1 © TOBY

	GD25	FN65	NM94
2-5			1.50
6-20: 11-Intro Bobcat			1.00

SOLOMON AND SHEBA (Movie)
No. 1070, Jan-Mar, 1960
Dell Publishing Co.

	GD25	FN65	NM94
Four Color 1070-Sekowsky-a; photo-c	9.00	27.00	100.00

SOLOMON KANE (Also see Blackthorne 3-D Series #60 & Marvel Premiere)
Sept, 1985 - No. 6, July, 1986 (Limited series)
Marvel Comics

	GD25	FN65	NM94
1-6: 1-Double size. 3-6-Williamson-a(i)			1.00

SOLUTION, THE
Sept, 1993 - No. 17, Feb, 1995 ($1.95)
Malibu Comics (Ultraverse)

	GD25	FN65	NM94
1,3-13: 1-Intro Meathook, Deathdance, Black Tiger, Tech. 4-Break-Thru x-over; gatefold-c. 5-2 pg. origin The Strangers. 11-Brereton-c		.80	2.00
1-($2.50)-Newsstand ed. polybagged w/trading card		1.00	2.50
1-Ultra 5000 Limited silver foil		2.00	5.00
0-Obtained w/Rune #0 by sending coupons from 11 comics		1.20	3.00
2-($2.50, 48 pgs.)-Rune flip-c/story by B. Smith; The Mighty Magnor 1 pg. strip by Aragones		1.00	2.50
11-15: 11-Brereton-c		.80	2.00
16 ($3.50)-Flip-c Ultraverse Premiere #10		1.40	3.50
17 ($2.50)		1.00	2.50

SOMERSET HOLMES (See Eclipse Graphic Novel Series)
Sept, 1983 - No. 6, Dec, 1984 ($1.50, Baxter paper)
Pacific Comics/ Eclipse Comics No. 5, 6

	GD25	FN65	NM94
1-Brent Anderson-c/a. Cliff Hanger by Williamson begins, ends #6.			1.50
2-6			1.50

SONG OF THE SOUTH (See Brer Rabbit)
No. 693, Mar, 1956 (Disney)
Dell Publishing Co.

	GD25	FN65	NM94
Four Color 693-Partial-r/Four Color 129	8.00	25.00	90.00

SONIC & KNUCKLES
Aug, 1995 ($2.00)
Archie Comics

	GD25	FN65	NM94
1		.80	2.00

SONIC DISRUPTORS
Dec, 1987 - No. 7, July, 1988 ($1.75, limited series, mature)
DC Comics

	GD25	FN65	NM94
1-7		.70	1.75

SONIC THE HEDGEHOG (TV, video game)
Feb, 1993 - No. 3, May, 1993 ($1.25, mini-series)
July, 1993 - Present ($1.25/$1.50)
Archie Comics

	GD25	FN65	NM94
0(2/93),1-3: Shaw-a(p) & covers			1.25
1-20: 8-Neon ink-c.			1.25
20-53 ($1.50): 25-Silver ink-c			1.50
54-60: 54-Begin $1.75-c			1.75
Triple Trouble Special (10/95, $2.00, 48 pgs.)		.80	2.00

SONIC'S FRIENDLY NEMESIS KNUCKLES
July, 1996 - No. 3, Sept, 1996 ($1.50, limited series)
Archie Publications

	GD25	FN65	NM94
1-3			1.50

SONIC SUPER SPECIAL (BRAVE NEW WORLD)
1997 ($2.00, 48 pgs)
Archie Publications

	GD25	FN65	NM94
1,2		.80	2.00

SONIC VS. KNUCKLES "BATTLE ROYAL" SPECIAL
1997 ($2.00, one-shot)
Archie Publications

	GD25	FN65	NM94
1		.80	2.00

SON OF AMBUSH BUG (See Ambush Bug)
July, 1986 - No. 6, Dec, 1986 (75¢)
DC Comics

	GD25	FN65	NM94
1-6: Giffen-c/a in all. 5-Bissette-a.			.75

SON OF BLACK BEAUTY (Also see Black Beauty)
No. 510, Oct, 1953 - No. 566, June, 1954
Dell Publishing Co.

	GD25	FN65	NM94
Four Color 510, 566	2.75	8.00	30.00

SON OF FLUBBER (See Movie Comics)

SON OF MUTANT WORLD
1990 - No. 5, 1990? ($2.00, bi-monthly)
Fantagor Press

	GD25	FN65	NM94
1-3: Corben-c/a		.80	2.00
4,5 ($1.75, B&W)		.70	1.75

SON OF ORIGINS OF MARVEL COMICS (See Fireside Book Series)

SON OF SATAN (Also see Ghost Rider #1 & Marvel Spotlight #12)
Dec, 1975 - No. 8, Feb, 1977 (25¢)
Marvel Comics Group

	GD25	FN65	NM94
1-Mooney-a; Kane-c(p), Starlin splash(p)	1.85	5.50	15.00
2,4,6-8: 2-Origin The Possessor. 8-Heath-a	1.10	3.30	9.00
3,5-(Regular 25¢ edition)(4,8/76): 5-Russell-p	1.10	3.30	9.00
3,5-(30¢-c, limited distribution)	3.60	10.80	36.00

SON OF SINBAD (Also see Abbott & Costello & Daring Adventures)
Feb, 1950
St. John Publishing Co.

	GD25	FN65	NM94
1-Kubert-c/a	37.00	111.00	270.00

SON OF TOMAHAWK (See Tomahawk)

SON OF VULCAN (Formerly Mysteries of Unexplored Worlds #1-48; Thunderbolt V3#51 on)
V2#49, Nov, 1965 - V2#50, Jan, 1966
Charlton Comics

	GD25	FN65	NM94
V2#49,50: 50-Roy Thomas scripts (1st pro work)	1.85	5.50	15.00

SON OF YUPPIES FROM HELL (See Yuppies From Hell)
1990 ($3.50, B&W, squarebound, 52 pgs.)
Marvel Comics

	GD25	FN65	NM94
nn		1.40	3.50

SONS OF KATIE ELDER (See Movie Classics)

SORCERY (See Chilling Adventures in... & Red Circle...)

SORORITY SECRETS
July, 1954
Toby Press

	GD25	FN65	NM94
1	6.35	19.00	40.00

SOULSEARCHERS AND COMPANY
June, 1995 - Present ($2.50, B&W)
Claypool Comics

	GD25	FN65	NM94
1-26: Peter David scripts		1.00	2.50

SOULQUEST
Apr, 1989 ($3.95, squarebound, 52 pgs.)
Innovation

	GD25	FN65	NM94
1-Blackshard app.		1.60	4.00

Sovereign Seven #28 © Chris Claremont

Space Adventures #15 © CC

Spaced #12 © ECL

GD25 FN65 NM94

SOULWIND
Mar, 1997 - Present ($2.95, B&W, limited series)
Image Comics
1-5 3.00
...The Kid From Planet Earth (1997, $9.95, TPB) 9.95

SOUPY SALES COMIC BOOK (TV)(The Official...)
1965
Archie Publications
1 8.00 24.00 80.00

SOUTHERN KNIGHTS, THE (See Crusaders #1)
1983 - No. 34? (B&W)
Guild Publ/Fictioneer Books
2-Magazine size 1.50
3-34 1.50
Dread Halloween Special 1 .90 2.25
Special 1 (Spring, 1989, $2.25) .90 2.25
Graphic Novels #1-4 1.60 4.00

SOVEREIGN SEVEN (Also see Showcase '95 #12)
July, 1995 - Present ($1.95) (1st creator-owned mainstream DC comic)
DC Comics
1-Gold 1.00 3.00 8.00
1-25: 1-1st app. Sovereign Seven (Reflex, Indigo, Cascade, Finale, Cruiser, Network & Rampart); 1st app. Maitresse; Darkseid app.; Chris Claremont scripts & Dwayne Turner-c/a begins. 2-Wolverine cameo. 4-Neil Gaiman cameo. 5,8-Batman app. 7-Ramirez cameo (from the movie Highlander). 9-Humphrey Bogart cameo from Casablanca. 10-Impulse app; Manoli Wetherell & Neal Conan cameo from Uncanny X-Men #226. 11-Robin app. 16-Final Night. 24-Superman app. 25-Power Girl app. .80 2.00
26-34: 26-Begin $2.25-c. 28-Impulse-c/app. 2.25
Annual 1 (1995, $3.95)-Year One story; Big Barda & Lobo app.; Jeff Johnson-c/a. 1.60 4.00
Annual 2 (1996, $2.95)-Legends of the Dead Earth; Leonardi-c/a 1.20 3.00
...Plus 1(2/97, $2.95)-Legion-c/app. 1.20 3.00
TPB-($12.95) r/#1-5, Annual #1 & Showcase '95 #12 13.00

SPACE: ABOVE AND BEYOND (TV)
Jan, 1996 - No. 3, Mar, 1996 ($2.95, limited series)
Topps Comics
1-3: Adaptation of pilot episode; Steacy-c. 1.20 3.00

SPACE: ABOVE AND BEYOND--THE GAUNTLET (TV)
May, 1996 -No. 2, June, 1996 ($2.95, limited series)
Topps Comics
1,2 1.20 3.00

SPACE ACE (Also see Manhunt!)
No. 5, 1952
Magazine Enterprises
5(A-1 #61)-Guardineer-a 38.00 113.00 340.00

SPACE ACTION
June, 1952 - No. 3, Oct, 1952
Ace Magazines (Junior Books)
1-Cameron-a in all (1 story) 56.00 168.00 500.00
2,3 44.00 132.00 400.00

SPACE ADVENTURES (War At Sea #22 on)
7/52 - No. 21, 8/56; No. 23, 5/58 - No. 59, 11/64; V3#60, 10/67; V1#2, 7/68 - V1#8, 7/69; No. 9, 5/78 - No. 13, 3/79
Capitol Stories/Charlton Comics
1 40.00 120.00 300.00
2 21.00 62.00 145.00
3-5: 4,6-Flying saucer-c/stories 17.00 49.00 115.00
6-9: 7-Sex change story "Transformation". 9-A-Bomb panel 14.00 43.00 100.00
10,11-Ditko-c/a; 11-Two Ditko stories 39.00 118.00 290.00
12-Ditko-c (classic) 40.00 120.00 350.00
13-(Fox-r, 10-11/54); Blue Beetle-c/story 17.00 49.00 115.00
14-Blue Beetle-c/story; Fox-r (12-1/54-55, last pre-code) 15.00 45.00 105.00
15,17,18-Rocky Jones-c/s.(TV); 15-Part photo-c 16.00 47.00 110.00
16-Krigstein-a; Rocky Jones-c/story (TV) 18.00 54.00 125.00
19 11.00 33.00 75.00
20-Reprints Fawcett's "Destination Moon" 24.00 71.00 165.00
21-(8/56) (no #22)(Becomes War At Sea) 11.00 33.00 75.00
23-(5/58; formerly Nyoka, The Jungle Girl)-Reprints Fawcett's "Destination Moon" 19.00 56.00 130.00
24,25,31,32-Ditko-a. 24-Severin-a(signed "LePoer") 16.00 47.00 115.00
26,27-Ditko-a(4) each. 26,28-Flying saucer-c 17.00 51.00 125.00
28-30 6.35 19.00 38.00
33-Origin/1st app. Capt. Atom by Ditko (3/60) 31.00 93.00 350.00
34-40,42-All Captain Atom by Ditko 13.00 39.00 130.00
41,43-59: 44-1st app. Mercury Man; also in #45 2.50 7.50 22.00
V3#60(#1, 10/67)-Origin & 1st app. Paul Mann & The Saucers From the Future 2.80 8.40 28.00
2-8(1968-69)-2,5,6,8-Ditko-a; 2,4-Aparo-c/a 1.85 5.50 15.00
9-13(1978-79)-Capt. Atom-r/Space Adventures by Ditko; 9-Reprints origin/1st app. Capt. Atom from #33 1.60 4.00
NOTE: ***Aparo** a-V3#60. c-V3#8. **Ditko** c-12, 31-42. **Giordano** c-3, 4, 7-9, 18p. **Krigstein** c-15. **Shuster** a-11. Issues 13 & 14 have Blue Beetle logos; #15-18 have Rocky Jones logos.*

SPACE ARK
June, 1985 - No. 5, Sept, 1987 ($1.75)
Americomics (AC Comics)/ Apple Comics #3 on
1-5: Funny animal (#1,2-color; #3-5-B&W) .75 1.80

SPACE BUSTERS
Spring, 1952 - No. 2, Fall, 1952 (Painted-c by Norman Saunders)
Ziff-Davis Publ. Co.
1-Krigstein-a(3) 68.00 206.00 575.00
2-Kinstler-a(2 pgs.) 55.00 165.00 450.00
NOTE: ***Anderson** a-2. Bondage c-2.*

SPACE CADET (See Tom Corbett,...)

SPACE COMICS (Formerly Funny Tunes)
No. 4, Mar-Apr, 1954 - No. 5, May-June, 1954
Avon Periodicals
4,5-Space Mouse, Peter Rabbit, Super Pup (formerly Spotty the Pup), & Merry Mouse continue from Funny Tunes 5.35 16.00 32.00
I.W. Reprint #8 (nd)-Space Mouse-r 1.00 3.00 8.00

SPACED
1982 - No. 13, 1988 ($1.25/$1.50, B&W, quarterly)
Anthony Smith Publ. #1,2/Unbridled Ambition/Eclipse Comics #10 on
1-($1.25-c) 1.60 4.00
2-($1.25-c) 1.20 3.00
3-13: 3-Begin $1.50-c 1.50
Special Edition (1983, Mimeo) 1.20 3.00

SPACE DETECTIVE
July, 1951 - No. 4, July, 1952
Avon Periodicals
1-Rod Hathway, Space Detective begins, ends #4; Wood-c/a(3)-23 pgs.; "Opium Smugglers of Venus" drug story; Lucky Dale-r/Saint #4 86.00 260.00 740.00
2-Tales from the Shadow Squad story; Wood/Orlando-c; Wood inside layouts; "Slave Ship of Saturn" story 56.00 168.00 490.00
3,4: 3-Kinstler-c. 4-Kinstlerish-a by McCann 34.00 103.00 250.00
I.W. Reprint #1(Reprints #2), 8(Reprints cover #1 & part Famous Funnies #191) 2.80 8.40 28.00

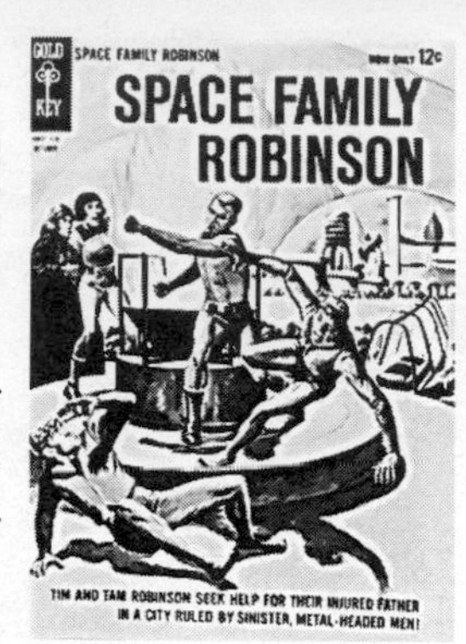

Space Family Robinson #10 © GK

Space Patrol #2 © Z-D

Space Squadron #2 © MEG

	GD25	FN65	NM94
I.W. Reprint #9-Exist?	2.80	8.40	28.00

SPACE EXPLORER (See March of Comics #202)

SPACE FAMILY ROBINSON (TV)(...Lost in Space #15-37, ...Lost in Space On Space Station One #38 on)(See Gold Key Champion)
Dec, 1962 - No. 36, Oct, 1969; No. 37, 10/73 - No. 54, 11/78;
No. 55, 3/81 - No. 59, 5/82 (All painted covers)
Gold Key

	GD25	FN65	NM94
1-(Low distribution); Spiegle-a in all	22.00	65.00	240.00
2(3/63)-Family becomes lost in space	10.00	30.00	110.00
3-10: 6-Captain Venture back-up stories begin	5.00	15.00	55.00
11-20: 14-(10/65). 15-Title change (1/66)	3.00	9.00	35.00
21-36: 28-Last 12¢ issue. 36-Captain Venture ends	1.80	5.50	20.00
37-48: 37-Origin retold	1.00	2.80	7.00
49-59: Reprints #49,50,55-59		1.60	4.00

NOTE: *The TV show first aired on 9/15/65. Title changed after TV show debuted.*

SPACE FAMILY ROBINSON (See March of Comics #320, 328, 352, 404, 414)

SPACE GHOST (TV) (Also see Golden Comics Digest #2 & Hanna-Barbera Super TV Heroes #3-7)
March, 1967 (Hanna-Barbera) (TV debut was 9/10/66)
Gold Key

	GD25	FN65	NM94
1 (10199-703)-Spiegle-a	29.00	87.00	320.00

SPACE GHOST (TV cartoon)
Mar, 1987 ($3.50, deluxe format, one-shot) (Hanna-Barbera)
Comico

	GD25	FN65	NM94
1-Steve Rude-c/a		2.40	6.00

SPACE GIANTS, THE (TV cartoon)
1979 ($1.00, B&W, one-shots)
FBN Publications

	GD25	FN65	NM94
1-Based on Japanese TV series		.80	2.00

SPACEHAWK
1989 - No. 3, 1990 ($2.00, B&W)
Dark Horse Comics

	GD25	FN65	NM94
1-3-Wolverton-c/a(r) plus new stories by others.		.80	2.00

SPACE JAM
1996 ($5.95, one-shot)
DC Comics

	GD25	FN65	NM94
1-Wraparound photo cover of Michael Jordan; movie adaption			5.95

SPACE KAT-ETS (...in 3-D)
Dec, 1953 (25¢, came w/glasses)
Power Publishing Co.

	GD25	FN65	NM94
1	31.00	92.00	220.00

SPACEMAN (Speed Carter...)
Sept, 1953 - No. 6, July, 1954
Atlas Comics (CnPC)

	GD25	FN65	NM94
1-Grey tone-c	52.00	157.00	450.00
2	37.00	111.00	275.00
3-6: 4-A-Bomb explosion-c	33.00	99.00	240.00

NOTE: ***Everett** c-1, 3. **Heath** a-1. **Maneely** a-1(3), 2(4), 3(3), 4-6; c-5, 6. **Romita** a-1. **Sekowsky** c-4. **Sekowsky/Abel** a-4(3). **Tuska** a-5(3).*

SPACE MAN
No. 1253, 1-3/62 - No. 8, 3-5/64; No. 9, 7/72 - No. 10, 10/72
Dell Publishing Co.

	GD25	FN65	NM94
Four Color 1253 (#1)(1-3/62)	6.40	19.00	70.00
2,3	3.00	10.00	36.00
4-8	2.50	7.50	27.00
9,10: 9-Reprints #1253. 10-Reprints #2		2.40	6.00

SPACE MOUSE (Also see Funny Tunes & Space Comics)
April, 1953 - No. 5, Apr-May, 1954
Avon Periodicals

	GD25	FN65	NM94
1	7.15	21.50	50.00
2	5.35	16.00	32.00
3-5	4.00	11.00	22.00

SPACE MOUSE (Walter Lantz...#1; see Comic Album #17)
No. 1132, Aug-Oct, 1960 - No. 5, Nov, 1963 (Walter Lantz)
Dell Publishing Co./Gold Key

	GD25	FN65	NM94
Four Color 1132,1244	3.60	11.00	40.00
1(11/62)(G.K.)	3.60	11.00	40.00
2-5	2.75	8.00	30.00

SPACE MYSTERIES
1964 (Reprints)
I.W. Enterprises

	GD25	FN65	NM94
1-r/Journey Into Unknown Worlds #4 w/new-c	1.50	4.50	12.00
8,9: 9-r/Planet Comics #73	1.75	5.25	14.00

SPACE: 1999 (TV) (Also see Power Record Comics)
Nov, 1975 - No. 7, Nov, 1976
Charlton Comics

	GD25	FN65	NM94
1-Origin Moonbase Alpha; Staton-c/a		2.00	5.00
2,7: 2-Staton-a		1.60	4.00
3-6: All Byrne-a; c-3,5,6		2.40	6.00

SPACE: 1999 (TV)(Magazine)
Nov, 1975 - No. 8, Nov, 1976 (B&W) (#7 shows #6 on inside)
Charlton Comics

	GD25	FN65	NM94
1-Origin Moonbase Alpha; Morrow-c/a	1.00	3.00	8.00
2-8: 2,3-Morrow-c/a. 4-6-Morrow-c. 5,8-Morrow-a		2.00	5.00

SPACE PATROL (TV)
Summer, 1952 - No. 2, Oct-Nov, 1952 (Painted-c by Norman Saunders)
Ziff-Davis Publishing Co. (Approved Comics)

	GD25	FN65	NM94
1-Krigstein-a	72.00	217.00	650.00
2-Krigstein-a(3)	53.00	159.00	465.00
...'s Special Mission (8 pgs., B&W, Giveaway)	59.00	178.00	475.00

SPACE PIRATES (See Archie Giant Series #533)

SPACE RANGER (See Mystery in Space #92, Showcase #15 & Tales of the Unexpected)

SPACE SQUADRON (In the Days of the Rockets)(Becomes Space Worlds #6)
June, 1951 - No. 5, Feb, 1952
Marvel/Atlas Comics (ACI)

	GD25	FN65	NM94
1-Space team; Brodsky c-1,5	52.00	157.00	450.00
2: Tuska c-2-4	45.00	136.00	375.00
3-5: 3-Capt. Jet Dixon by Tuska(3). 4-Weird advs. begin	40.00	120.00	300.00

SPACE THRILLERS
1954 (25¢ Giant)
Avon Periodicals

	GD25	FN65	NM94
nn-(Scarce)-Robotmen of the Lost Planet; contains 3 rebound comics of The Saint & Strange Worlds. Contents could vary	93.00	281.00	790.00

SPACE TRIP TO THE MOON (See Space Adventures #23)

SPACE USAGI
June, 1992 - No. 3, 1992 ($2.00, B&W, mini-series)
V2#1, Nov, 1993 - V2#3, Jan, 1994 ($2.75)
Mirage Studios

	GD25	FN65	NM94
1-3: Stan Sakai-c/a/scripts		.80	2.00
V2#1-3		1.10	2.75

SPACE USAGI
Jan, 1996 - No. 3, Mar, 1996 ($2.00, B&W, limited series)
Dark Horse Comics

	GD25	FN65	NM94
1-3: Stan Sakai-c/a/scripts		.80	2.00

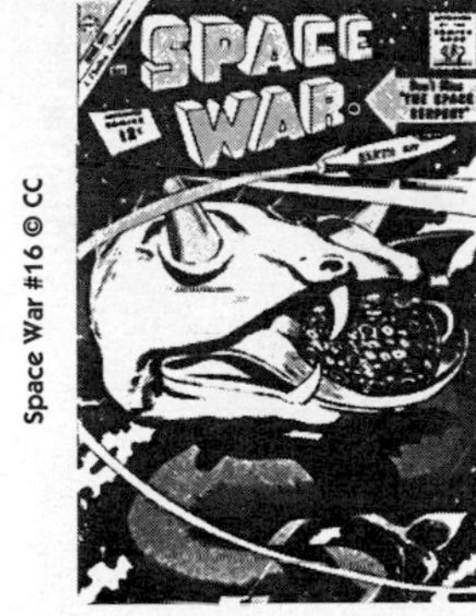

Space War #16 © CC

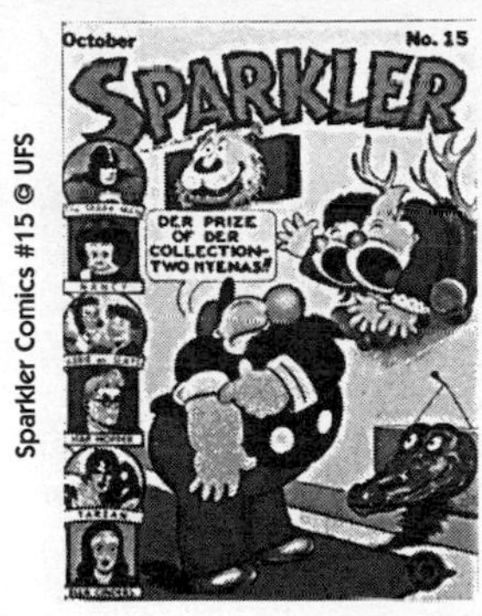

Sparkler Comics #15 © UFS

Sparkling Stars #5 © HOKE

GD25 FN65 NM94

SPACE WAR (Fightin' Five #28 on)
Oct, 1959 - No. 27, Mar, 1964; No. 28, Mar, 1978 - No. 34, 3/79
Charlton Comics

V1#1-Giordano-c begin, end #3 12.00 36.00 120.00
2,3 5.50 16.50 55.00
4-6,8,10-Ditko-c/a 12.00 36.00 120.00
7,9,11-15: Last 10¢ issue? 2.80 8.40 28.00
16-27 (3/64) 2.50 7.50 25.00
28(3/78),29,33,34-Ditko-c/a(r) 2.00 5.00
30-Ditko-c/a(r); Staton, Sutton/Wood-a 2.00 5.00
31-Ditko-c/a(3); same-c as Strange Suspense Stories #2 (1968); atom blast-c 2.00 5.00
32-r/Charlton Premiere V2#2; Sutton-a 1.20 3.00

SPACE WESTERN (Formerly Cowboy Western Comics; becomes Cowboy Western Comics #46 on)
No. 40, Oct, 1952 - No. 45, Aug, 1953
Charlton Comics (Capitol Stories)

40-Intro Spurs Jackson & His Space Vigilantes; flying saucer story 47.00 141.00 400.00
41,43-45: 41-Flying saucer-c. 45-Hitler app. 39.00 116.00 280.00
42-Atom bomb explosion-c 40.00 120.00 310.00

SPACE WORLDS (Formerly Space Squadron #1-5)
No. 6, April, 1952
Atlas Comics (Male)

6-Sol Brodsky-c 39.00 116.00 280.00

SPANKY & ALFALFA & THE LITTLE RASCALS (See The Little Rascals)

SPANNER'S GALAXY
Dec, 1984 - No. 6, May, 1985 (limited series)
DC Comics

1-6: Mandrake-c/a in all. 1.00

SPARKIE, RADIO PIXIE (Radio)(Becomes Big Jon & Sparkie #4)
Winter, 1951 - No. 3, July-Aug, 1952 (Painted-c)(Sparkie #2,3; #1?)
Ziff-Davis Publ. Co.

1-Based on children's radio program 17.50 53.00 140.00
2,3: 3-Big Jon and Sparkie on-c only 12.00 38.00 100.00

SPARKLE COMICS
Oct-Nov, 1948 - No. 33, Dec-Jan, 1953-54 (#1-3: 52 pgs.)
United Features Syndicate

1-Li'l Abner, Nancy, Captain & the Kids, Ella Cinders 11.30 34.00 90.00
2 6.50 19.50 45.00
3-10 5.70 17.00 35.00
11-20 5.00 15.00 30.00
21-33 4.00 12.00 24.00

SPARKLE PLENTY (See Harvey Comics Library #2)
No. 215, 1949 (Dick Tracy reprint by Gould)
Dell Publishing Co.

Four Color 215 9.00 27.00 100.00

SPARKLER COMICS (1st series)
July, 1940 - No. 2, 1940
United Feature Comic Group

1-Jim Hardy 33.00 98.00 260.00
2-Frankie Doodle 25.00 75.00 200.00

SPARKLER COMICS (2nd series)(Nancy & Sluggo #121 on)(Cover title becomes Nancy and Sluggo #101? on)
July, 1941 - No. 120, Jan, 1955
United Features Syndicate

1-Origin 1st app. Sparkman; Tarzan (by Hogarth in all issues), Captain & the Kids, Ella Cinders, Danny Dingle, Dynamite Dunn, Nancy, Abbie & Slats, Broncho Bill, Frankie Doodle, begin; Sparkman c-1-9,11,12; Hap Hopper c-10,13 178.00 534.00 1600.00
2 64.00 192.00 575.00
3,4 50.00 150.00 450.00
5-10: 9-Sparkman's new costume 44.00 132.00 400.00
11-13,15-20: 12-Sparkman's new costume (color change). 19-1st Race Riley and the Commandos plus-c 36.00 108.00 310.00
14-Tarzan-c by Hogarth 41.00 123.00 370.00
21,25,28,31,34,37,39-Tarzan-c by Hogarth 36.00 108.00 300.00
22-24,26,27,29,30: 22-Race Riley & the Commandos strips begin, ends #44 29.00 86.00 230.00
32,33,35,36,38,40 15.50 47.00 125.00
41,43,45,46,48,49 11.30 34.00 90.00
42,44,47,50-Tarzan-c (42,47,50 by Hogarth) 21.00 64.00 170.00
51,52,54-70: 57-Li'l Abner begins (not in #58); Fearless Fosdick app. in #58 9.50 28.00 75.00
53-Tarzan-c by Hogarth 17.50 53.00 140.00
71-80 6.50 19.50 45.00
81,82,84-90: 85-Li'l Abner ends. 86-Lingerie panels 5.70 17.00 40.00
83-Tarzan-c 8.75 26.25 70.00
91-96,98-99 5.70 17.00 40.00
97-Origin Casey Ruggles by Warren Tufts 10.00 30.00 80.00
100 7.15 21.50 50.00
101-107,109-112,114-120 4.25 13.00 28.00
108,113-Toth-a 7.15 21.50 50.00

SPARKLING LOVE
June, 1950; 1953
Avon Periodicals/Realistic (1953)

1(Avon)-Kubert-a; photo-c 17.00 51.00 130.00
nn(1953)-Reprint; Kubert-a 7.50 22.50 45.00

SPARKLING STARS
June, 1944 - No. 33, March, 1948
Holyoke Publishing Co.

1-Hell's Angels, FBI, Boxie Weaver, Petey & Pop, & Ali Baba begin 12.00 38.00 100.00
2-Speed Spaulding story 8.50 26.00 60.00
3-Actual FBI case photos & war photos 6.50 19.50 45.00
4-10: 7-X-Mas-c 5.70 17.00 38.00
11-19: 13-Origin/1st app. Jungo the Man-Beast-c/s 5.35 16.00 32.00
20-Intro Fangs the Wolf Boy 5.70 17.00 38.00
21-29,32,33: 29-Bondage-c 5.35 16.00 32.00
31-Sid Greene-a 5.70 17.00 38.00

SPARK MAN (See Sparkler Comics)
1945 (36 pgs., one-shot)
Frances M. McQueeny

1-Origin Spark Man r/Sparkler #1-3; female torture story; cover redrawn from Sparkler #1 25.00 75.00 200.00

SPARKY WATTS (Also see Big Shot Comics & Columbia Comics)
Nov?, 1942 - No. 10, 1949
Columbia Comic Corp.

1(1942)-Skyman & The Face app; Hitler-c 36.00 108.00 310.00
2(1943) 20.00 60.00 160.00
3(1944) 14.00 41.00 110.00
4(1944)-Origin 12.00 38.00 100.00
5(1947)-Skyman app.; Boody Rogers-c/a 10.00 30.00 80.00
6,7,9,10: 6(1947),10(1949) 7.15 21.50 50.00
8(1948)-Surrealistic-c 10.00 30.00 80.00

NOTE: *Boody Rogers c-1-8.*

SPARTACUS (Movie)
No. 1139, Nov, 1960 (Kirk Douglas photo-c)
Dell Publishing Co.

Spawn #19 © Todd McFarlane

Spawn #67 © Todd McFarlane

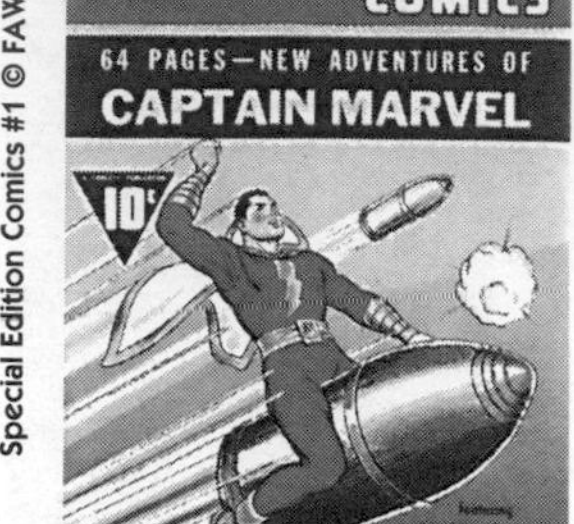

SPECIAL EDITION
NUMBER ONE
COMICS
64 PAGES—NEW ADVENTURES OF
CAPTAIN MARVEL
10¢

Special Edition Comics #1 © FAW

GD25 FN65 NM94

Four Color 1139-Buscema-a 12.00 35.00 130.00

SPARTAN: WARRIOR SPIRIT (Also see WildC.A.T.S: Covert Action Teams)
July, 1995 - No. 4, Nov, 1995 ($2.50, limited series)
Image Comics (Wildstorm Productions)

1-4: Kurt Busiek scripts; Mike McKone-c/a 1.00 2.50

SPAWN (Also see Curse of the Spawn)
May, 1992 - Present ($1.95)
Image Comics (Todd McFarlane Productions)

1-1st app. Spawn; McFarlane-c/a begins; McFarlane/Steacy-c; 1st Todd McFarlane Productions title. 2.50 7.50 20.00
2,3: 2-1st app. Violator; McFarlane/Steacy-c 1.75 5.25 14.00
4-Contains coupon for Image Comics #0 1.75 5.25 14.00
4-With coupon missing 1.60 4.00
4-Newstand edition w/o poster or coupon 2.40 6.00
5-Cerebus cameo (1 pg.) as stuffed animal; Spawn mobile poster #1 1.00 3.00 8.00
6-8,10: 7-Spawn Mobile poster #2. 8-Alan Moore scripts; Miller poster. 10-Cerebus app.; Dave Sim scripts; 1 pg. cameo app. by Superman. 1.00 2.80 7.00
9-Neil Gaiman scripts; Jim Lee poster; 1st Angela. 1.10 3.30 9.00
11-17,19,20,22-30: 11-Miller script; Darrow poster. 12-Bloodwulf poster by Liefeld. 14,15-Violator app. 16,17-Grant Morrison scripts; Capullo-c/a(p). 23,24-McFarlane-a/stories. 25-(10/94). 19-(10/94). 20-(11/94) 2.40 6.00
18,21: 18-Grant Morrison script, Capullo-c/a(p); low distribution. 2.00 6.00 16.00
31-49, 51-60: 31-1st app. The Redeemer; new costume cameo. 32-1st full app new costume. 38-40,42,44,46,48-Tony Daniel-c/a(p). 38-1st app. Cy-Gor. 40,41-Cy-Gor & Curse app. 52-Savage Dragon app. 56-w/ Darkchylde preview. 57-Cy-Gor-c/app. 1.60 4.00
50-($3.95, 48 pgs.) 1.80 4.50
61-67: 64-Polybagged w/McFarlane Toys catalog. 65-Photo-c of movie Spawn and McFarlane .80 1.95
...Bible-(8/96, $1.95)-Character bios .80 1.95

NOTE: ***Capullo** a-16p-18p; c-16p-18p. **Daniel** a-38-40, 42, 44, 46. **McFarlane** a-1-15; c-1-15p. **Thibert** a-16i(part). Posters come with issues 1, 4, 7-9, 11, 12. #25 was released before #19 & 20.*

SPAWN-BATMAN (Also see Batman/Spawn: War Devil under Batman: One-Shots)
1994 ($3.95, one-shot)
Image Comics (Todd McFarlane Productions)

1-Miller scripts; McFarlane-c/a 1.60 4.00

SPAWN: BLOOD FEUD
June, 1995 - No. 3, Sept, 1995 ($2.25, limited series)
Image Comics (Todd McFarlane Productions)

1-3-Alan Moore scripts, Tony Daniel-a .90 2.25

SPAWN FAN EDITION
Aug, 1996 - No. 3, Oct, 1996 (Giveaway, 12 pgs.)
(Polybagged w/Overstreet's FAN)
Image Comics (Todd McFarlane Productions)

1-3: Beau Smith scripts; Brad Gorby-a(p). 1-1st app. Nordik, the Norse Hellspawn. 2-1st app. McFallon, the Dragon Master. 3-1st app. Mercy 1.00 3.00 7.50
1-3-(Gold): All retailer incentives 2.00 6.00 16.00
1-3-Variant-c 2.40 6.00
2-(Platinum)-Retailer incentive 2.50 7.50 25.00

SPAWN THE IMPALER
Oct, 1996 - No. 3, Dec, 1996 ($2.95, limited series)
Image Comics (Todd McFarlane Productions)

1-3-Mike Grell scripts, painted-a 2.95

SPAWN/WILDC.A.T.S

GD25 FN65 NM94

Jan, 1996 - No. 4, Apr, 1996 ($2.50, limited series)
Image Comics (Wildstorm Productions)

1-4: Alan Moore scripts in all. 1.00 2.50

SPECIAL AGENT (Steve Saunders...)(Also see True Comics #68)
Dec, 1947 - No. 8, Sept, 1949 (Based on true FBI cases)
Parents' Magazine Institute (Commended Comics No. 2)

1-J. Edgar Hoover photo on-c 8.75 26.25 65.00
2 5.70 17.00 35.00
3-8 4.25 13.00 28.00

SPECIAL COLLECTORS' EDITION
Dec, 1975 (No month given) (10-1/4x13-1/2")
Marvel Comics Group

1-Kung Fu, Iron Fist (early), Sons of the Tiger 1.25 3.75 10.00

SPECIAL COMICS (Becomes Hangman #2 on)
Winter, 1941-42
MLJ Magazines

1-Origin The Boy Buddies (Shield & Wizard x-over); death of The Comet; origin The Hangman retold; Hangman-c 211.00 633.00 1900.00

SPECIAL DELIVERY
1951 (32 pgs.; B&W)
Post Hall Synd. (Giveaway)

nn-Origin of Pogo, Swamp, etc.; 2 pg. biog. on Walt Kelly
(One copy sold in 1980 for $150.00)

SPECIAL EDITION (See Gorgo and Reptisaurus)

SPECIAL EDITION (U. S. Navy Giveaways)
1944 - 1945 (Regular comic format with wording simplified, 52 pgs.)
National Periodical Publications

1-Action (1944)-Reprints Action #80 56.00 168.00 500.00
2-Action (1944)-Reprints Action #81 56.00 168.00 500.00
3-Superman (1944)-Reprints Superman #33 56.00 168.00 500.00
4-Detective (1944)-Reprints Detective #97 58.00 174.00 525.00
5-Superman (1945)-Reprints Superman #34 56.00 168.00 500.00
6-Action (1945)-Reprints Action #84 56.00 168.00 500.00

NOTE: ***Wayne Boring** c-1, 2, 6. **Dick Sprang** c-4.*

SPECIAL EDITION COMICS
1940 (August) (68 pgs., one-shot)
Fawcett Publications

GD25 FN65 VF82 NM94

1-1st book devoted entirely to Captain Marvel; C.C. Beck-c/a; only app. of Capt. Marvel with belt buckle; Capt. Marvel appears with button-down flap; 1st story (came out before Captain Marvel #1) 800.00 2400.00 4800.00 8000.00
(Estimated up to 150 total copies exist, 7 in NM/Mint)

NOTE: *Prices vary widely on this book. Since this book is all Captain Marvel stories, it is actually a pre-Captain Marvel #1. There is speculation that this book almost became **Captain Marvel** #1. After **Special Edition** was published, there was an editor change at Fawcett. The new editor commissioned Kirby to do a nn **Captain Marvel** book early in 1941. This book was followed by a 2nd book several months later. This 2nd book was advertised as a #3 (making Special Edition the #1, & the nn issue the #2). However, the 2nd book did come out as a #2.*

SPECIAL EDITION: SPIDER-MAN VS. THE HULK (See listing under The Amazing Spider-Man)

SPECIAL EDITION X-MEN
Feb, 1983 ($2.00, one-shot, Baxter paper)
Marvel Comics Group

GD25 FN65 NM94

1-r/Giant-Size X-Men #1 plus one new story 1.25 3.75 10.00

SPECIAL MARVEL EDITION (Master of Kung Fu #17 on)
Jan, 1971 - No. 16, Feb, 1974 (#1-4: 25¢, 68 pgs.; #5-16: 20¢, regular ed.)
Marvel Comics Group

1-Thor-r by Kirby; 68 pgs. 2.00 6.00 16.00
2-4: Thor-r by Kirby; 68 pg. Giant 1.25 3.75 10.00

Spectacular Feature #11 © FOX

Spectacular Spider-Man #18 © MEG

Spectacular Spider-Man #238 © MEG

GD25 FN65 NM94

5-14: Sgt. Fury-r; 11-r/Sgt. Fury #13 (Capt. America) 2.40 6.00
15-Master of Kung Fu (Shang-Chi) begins (1st app., 12/73); Starlin-a; origin/ 1st app. Nayland Smith & Dr. Petric 4.00 12.00 40.00
16-1st app. Midnight; Starlin-a (2nd Shang-Chi) 1.85 5.50 15.00

SPECIAL MISSIONS (See G.I. Joe...)

SPECIAL WAR SERIES (Attack V4#3 on?)
Aug, 1965 - No. 4, Nov, 1965
Charlton Comics

V4#1-D-Day (also see D-Day listing) 2.50 7.50 20.00
2-Attack! 1.50 4.50 12.00
3-War & Attack (also see War & Attack) 1.50 4.50 12.00
4-Judomaster (intro/1st app.; see Sarge Steel) 4.00 12.00 40.00

SPECIES (Movie)
June, 1995 - No. 4, Sept, 1995 ($2.50, limited series)
Dark Horse Comics

1-4: Adaptation of film 1.00 2.50

SPECIES: HUMAN RACE (Movie)
Nov, 1996 - No. 4, Feb, 1997 ($2.95, limited series)
Dark Horse Comics

1-4 2.95

SPECTACULAR ADVENTURES (See Adventures)

SPECTACULAR FEATURE MAGAZINE, A (Formerly My Confessions) (Spectacular Features Magazine #12)
No. 11, April, 1950
Fox Feature Syndicate

11 (#1)-Samson and Delilah 26.00 77.00 190.00

SPECTACULAR FEATURES MAGAZINE (Formerly A Spectacular Feature Magazine)
No. 12, June, 1950 - No. 3, Aug, 1950
Fox Feature Syndicate

12 (#2)-Iwo Jima; photo flag-c 26.00 77.00 190.00
3-True Crime Cases From Police Files 19.00 56.00 140.00

SPECTACULAR SCARLET SPIDER
Nov, 1995 - No. 2, Dec, 1995 ($1.95, limited series)
Marvel Comics

1,2: Replaces Spectacular Spider-Man .80 2.00

SPECTACULAR SPIDER-MAN, THE (See Marvel Special Edition and Marvel Treasury Edition)

SPECTACULAR SPIDER-MAN, THE (Magazine)
July, 1968 - No. 2, Nov, 1968 (35¢)
Marvel Comics Group

1-(B&W)-Romita/Mooney 52 pg. story plus updated origin story with Everett-a(i) 6.50 19.50 65.00
1-Variation w/single c-price of 40¢ 8.00 24.00 80.00
2-(Color) Green Goblin-c & 58 pg. story; Romita painted-c (story reprinted in King Size Spider-Man #9); Romita/Mooney-a 8.50 25.50 85.00

SPECTACULAR SPIDER-MAN, THE (Peter Parker...#54-132, 134)
Dec, 1976 - Present
Marvel Comics Group

1-Origin recap in text; return of Tarantula 2.50 7.50 25.00
2-Kraven the Hunter app. 1.50 4.50 12.00
3-5: 3-Intro Lightmaster. 4-Vulture app. 1.00 3.00 8.00
6-8-Morbius app.; 6-r/Marvel Team-Up #3 w/Morbius 1.50 4.50 12.00
9-20: 9,10-White Tiger app. 11-Last 30¢-c. 17,18-Angel & Iceman app. (from Champions); Ghost Rider cameo in flashback 2.40 6.00
21,24-26: 21-Scorpion app. 26-Daredevil app. 2.00 5.00
22,23-Moon Knight app. 1.00 2.80 7.00
27-Miller's 1st art on Daredevil (2/79); also see Captain America #235 2.25 6.75 18.00
28-Miller Daredevil (p) 1.75 5.25 14.00
29-55,57,59: 33-Origin Iguana. 38-Morbius app. 2.00 5.00
56-2nd app. Jack O'Lantern (Macendale) & 1st Spidey/Jack O'Lantern battle (7/81) 2.40 6.00
58-Byrne-a(p) 2.00 5.00
60-Double size; origin retold with new facts revealed 2.40 6.00
61-63,65-68,71-74: 65-Kraven the Hunter app. 1.60 4.00
64-1st app. Cloak & Dagger (3/82) 2.00 5.00
69,70-Cloak & Dagger app. 1.00 3.00 8.00
75-Double size 2.00 5.00
76-80: 78,79-Punisher cameo 1.60 4.00
81,82-Punisher, Cloak & Dagger app. 1.60 4.00
83-Origin Punisher retold (10/83) 1.25 3.75 10.00
84,86-99: 90-Spider-man's new black costume, last panel(ties w/Amazing Spider-Man #252 & Marvel Team-Up #141 for 1st app.). 94-96-Cloak & Dagger app. 98-Intro The Spot 1.20 3.00
85-Hobgoblin (Ned Leeds) app. (12/83); gains powers of original Green Goblin (see Amazing Spider-Man #238) 1.25 3.75 10.00
100-(3/85)-Double size 2.00 5.00
101-115,117,118,120-129: 107-110-Death of Jean DeWolff. 111-Secret Wars II tie-in. 128-Black Cat new costume 1.00 2.50
116,119-Sabretooth-c/story 1.80 4.50
130-Hobgoblin app. 2.00 5.00
131-Six part Kraven tie-in 1.00 2.80 7.00
132-Kraven tie-in 2.40 6.00
133-139: 138-1st full app. Tombstone (origin #139) .80 2.00
140-Punisher cameo app. .80 2.00
141-Punisher app. 1.20 3.00
142,143-Punisher app. 1.20 3.00
144-146,148-157: 151-Tombstone returns .90 2.25
147-1st app. new Hobgoblin (Macendale) in 1 pg. cameo; continued in Web of Spider-Man #48 1.25 3.75 10.00
158-Spider-Man gets new powers (1st Cosmic Spidey, cont'd in Web of Spider-Man #59) 2.00 5.00
159-Cosmic Spider-Man app. 2.40 6.00
160-170: 161-163-Hobgoblin app. 168-170-Avengers x-over. 169-1st app. The Outlaws .80 2.00
171-184: 180,181,183,184-Green Goblin app. 1.50
185-188,190-199: 197-199-Original X-Men-c/story 1.50
189-($2.95, 52 pgs.)-Silver hologram on-c; battles Green Goblin; origin Spidey retold; Vess poster w/Spidey & Hobgoblin 1.60 4.00
189-(2nd printing)-Gold hologram on-c 1.20 3.00
195-(Deluxe ed.)-Polybagged w/audio cassette 1.20 3.00
200-($2.95)-Holo-grafx foil-c; Green Goblin-c/story 1.20 3.00
201-211: 203-Maximum Carnage x-over. 204-Begin 4 part death of Tombstone story. 207,208-The Shroud-c/story. 208-Siege of Darkness x-over (#207 is a tie-in). 209-Black Cat back-up 1.50
212-219,221,222,224,226-228,230-247,-1(7/97): 212-Begin $1.50-c; w/card sheet. 215,216-Scorpion app. 217-Power & Responsibility Pt. 4. 231-Return of Kaine; Spider-Man corpse discovered. 232-New Doc Octopus app. 233-Carnage-c/app. 235-Dragon Man cameo. 236-Dragon Man-c/app; Lizard app.; Peter Parker regains powers. 238,239-Lizard app. 239-w/card insert. 240-Revelations storyline begins. -1-Flashback 1.50
213-Collectors ed. polybagged w/16 pg. preview & animation cel; foil-c; 1st meeting Spidey & Typhoid Mary 1.20 3.00
213-Version polybagged w/Gamepro #7; no-c date, price 1.50
217 ($2.95)-Deluxe edition foil-c; flip book 1.20 3.00
219-($2.95)-Deluxe edition foil-c; flip book 1.20 3.00
220 ($2.25, 52 pgs.)-Flip book, Mary Jane reveals pregnancy 1.20 3.00
223 ($2.50) 1.00 2.50
223 ($2.95)-Die Cut-c 1.20 3.00

Spectacular Spider-Man Annual #14 © MEG

The Spectre #43 (3rd Series) © DC

Speed Comics #43 © HARV

GD25 FN65 NM94

225 ($3.95)-Direct Market Holodisk-c (Green Goblin) 1.60 4.00
225 ($2.95)-Newsstand-Green Goblin 1.20 3.00
229 ($3.95)-Acetate-c, Spidey quits 1.60 4.00
229 ($2.50)-Spidey quits 1.00 2.50
240-Variant-c 1.20 3.00
248,249,251-257: 248-Begin $1.99-c. 249-Return of Norman Osborne 1.99
250-($3.25) Double gatefold-c 3.25
Annual 1 (1979)-Doc Octopus-c & 46 pg. story 1.00 2.80 7.00
Annual 2 (1980)-Origin/1st app. Rapier 2.00 5.00
Annual 3-7: 3(1981)-Last Man-Wolf. 4(1984). 5(1985). 6(10/86). 7(1987) 1.20 3.00
Annual 8 (1988,$ 1.75)-Evolutionary War x-over; Daydreamer returns Gwen Stacy "clone" back to real self (not Gwen Stacy) 1.60 4.00
Annual 9 (1989, $2.00, 68 pgs.)-Atlantis Attacks 1.20 3.00
Annual 10 (1990, $2.00, 68 pgs.)-McFarlane-a 1.00 2.50
Annual 11 (1991, $2.00, 68 pgs.)-Iron Man app. .80 2.00
Annual 12 (1992, $2.25, 68 pgs.)-Venom solo story cont'd from Amazing Spider-Man Annual #26 .90 2.25
Annual 13 (1993, $2.95, 68 pgs.)-Polybagged w/trading card; John Romita, Sr. back-up-a 1.20 3.00
Annual 14 (1994, $2.95) 1.20 3.00
Special 1 (1995, $3.95)-Flip book 1.60 4.00

NOTE: ***Austin*** *c-21i, Annual 11i.* ***Buckler*** *a-103, 107-111, 116, 117, 119, 122, Annual 1, Annual 10; c-103, 107-111, 113, 116-119, 122, Annual 1.* ***Buscema*** *a-121.* ***Byrne*** *c(p)-17, 43, 58, 101, 102.* ***Giffen*** *a-120p.* ***Hembeck*** *c/a-86p.* ***Larsen*** *c-Annual 11p.* ***Miller*** *c-46p, 48p, 50, 51p, 52p, 54p, 55, 56p, 57, 60.* ***Mooney*** *a-7i, 11i, 21p, 23p, 25p, 26p, 29-34p, 36p, 37p, 39i, 41, 42i, 49p, 50i, 51i, 53p, 54-57i, 59-66i, 68i, 71i, 73-79i, 81-83i, 85i, 87-99i, 102i, 125p, Annual 1i, 2p.* ***Nasser*** *c-37p.* ***Perez*** *c-10.* ***Simonson*** *c-54i.* ***Zeck*** *a-118, 131, 132; c-131, 132.*

SPECTACULAR STORIES MAGAZINE (Formerly A Star Presentation)
No. 4, July, 1950 - No. 3, Sept, 1950
Fox Feature Sydicate (Hero Books)

4-Sherlock Holmes (true crime stories) 34.00 101.00 250.00
3-The St. Valentine's Day Massacre (true crime) 22.00 66.00 165.00

SPECTRE, THE (1st Series) (See Adventure Comics #431, More Fun & Showcase)
Nov-Dec, 1967 - No. 10, May-June, 1969 (All 12¢)
National Periodical Publications

1-(11-12/67)-Anderson-c/a 10.00 30.00 100.00
2-5-Neal Adams-c/a; 3-Wildcat x-over 7.00 21.00 70.00
6-8,10: 6-8-Anderson inks. 7-Hourman app. 4.50 13.50 45.00
9-Wrightson-a 5.00 15.00 50.00

SPECTRE, THE (2nd Series) (See Saga of the Swamp Thing #58, Showcase '95 #8 & Wrath of the...)
Apr, 1987 - Oct, 1989 ($1.00, new format)
DC Comics

1-31: 1-Colan-a begins. 9-Nudity panels. 10-Batman cameo. 10,11-Millenium tie-ins 1.50
Annual 1 (1988, $2.00)-Deadman app. .90 2.25

NOTE: ***Art Adams*** *c-Annual 1.* ***Colan*** *a-1-6.* ***Kaluta*** *c-1-3.* ***Mignola*** *c-7-9.* ***Morrow*** *a-9-15.* ***Sears*** *c/a-22.* ***Vess*** *c-13-15.*

SPECTRE, THE (3rd Series) (Also see Brave and the Bold #72, 75, 116, 180, 199 & Showcase '95 #8)
Dec, 1992 - No. 62, Feb, 1998 ($1.75/$1.95/$2.25)
DC Comics

1-($1.95)-Glow-in-the-dark-c; Mandrake-a begins 1.00 3.00 8.00
2,3 1.80 4.50
4-7,9-12,14-20: 10-Kaluta-c. 11-Hildebrandt painted-c. 16-Aparo/K. Jones-a. 20-Sienkiewicz-c 1.40 3.50
8,13-($2.50)-Glow-in-the-dark-c 1.60 4.00
21,22: 21-Begin $1.95-c. 22-(9/94)-Superman-c & app. .90 2.25
0,23-29: 0-(10/94). 23-(11/94) .90 2.25
30-49: 30-Begin-$2.25-c. 42-Kent Williams-c. 44-Kaluta-c. 47-Final Night x-over 1.10 2.75
50-62: 50-Begin-$2.50-c.; Bolton-c. 51-Batman-c/app. 52-Gianni-c. 54-Corben-c. 60-Harris-c 1.10 2.75
Annual 1 (1995, $3.95)-Year One story 1.70 4.25

NOTE: ***Bisley*** *c-27.* ***Fabry*** *c-2.* ***Kelley Jones*** *c-31.* ***Vess*** *c-5.*

SPEEDBALL (See Amazing Spider-Man Annual #12, Marvel Super-Heroes & The New Warriors)
Sept, 1988(10/88-inside) - No. 11, July, 1989 (75¢)
Marvel Comics

1-11: Ditko/Guice a-1-4, c-1; Ditko a-1-10; c-1-11p 1.00

SPEED BUGGY (TV)(Also see Fun-In #12, 15)
July, 1975 - No. 9, Nov, 1976 (Hanna-Barbera)
Charlton Comics

1 1.85 5.50 15.00
2-9 1.10 3.30 9.00

SPEED CARTER SPACEMAN (See Spaceman)

SPEED COMICS (New Speed)(Also see Double Up)
10/39 - #11, 8/40; #12, 3/41 - #44, 1-2/47 (#14-16: pocket size, 100 pgs.)
Brookwood Publ./Speed Publ./Harvey Publications No. 14 on

1-Origin & 1st app. Shock Gibson; Ted Parrish, the Man with 1000 Faces begins; Powell-a; becomes Champion #2 on? 240.00 720.00 2300.00
2-Powell-a 83.00 250.00 740.00
3 47.00 141.00 425.00
4,5: 4-Powell-a?5-Dinosaur-c 40.00 120.00 360.00
6-11: 7-Mars Mason begins, ends #11 36.00 108.00 310.00
12 (3/41; shows #11 in indicia)-The Wasp begins; Major Colt app. (Capt. Colt #12) 40.00 120.00 360.00
13-Intro. Captain Freedom & Young Defenders; Girl Commandos, Pat Parker (costumed heroine), War Nurse begins; Major Colt app. 47.00 141.00 425.00
14-16 (100 pg. pocket size, 1941): 14-2nd Harvey comic (See Pocket); Shock Gibson dons new costume. 15-Pat Parker dons costume, last in costume #23; no Girl Commandos 49.00 147.00 440.00
17-Black Cat begins (4/42, early app.; see Pocket #1); origin Black Cat-r/ Pocket #1; not in #40,41; S&K-c 57.00 171.00 510.00
18-20-S&K-c 41.00 123.00 370.00
21,22-Kirby-c 41.00 123.00 370.00
23-Origin Girl Commandos; Kirby-c 44.00 132.00 400.00
24-Pat Parker team-up with Girl Commandos 33.00 98.00 260.00
25-30: 26-Flag-c 34.00 101.00 270.00
31-Schomburg Hitler & Hirohito-c 38.00 113.00 340.00
32-36-Schomburg-c 36.00 108.00 320.00
37,39-42, 44 33.00 100.00 265.00
38-Iwo-Jima Flag-c 35.00 105.00 285.00
43-Robot-c 36.00 108.00 300.00

NOTE: ***Al Avison*** *c-14-16, 30, 43.* ***Briefer*** *a-6, 7.* ***Jon Henri*** *(Kirbyesque) c-17-20.* ***Kubert*** *a-7-11(Mars Mason), 37, 38, 42-44.* ***Kirby/Caseneuve*** *c-21-23.* ***Palais*** *c-37, 39-42.* ***Powell*** *a-1, 2, 4-7, 28, 31, 44.* ***Schomburg*** *c-31-36.* ***Tuska*** *a-3, 6, 7. Bondage c-18, 35. Captain Freedom c-16-24, 25(part), 26-44(w/Black Cat #27, 29, 31, 32-40). Shock Gibson c-1-15.*

SPEED DEMON (Also see Marvel Versus DC #3 & DC Versus Marvel #4)
Apr, 1996 ($1.95, one-shot)
Marvel Comics (Amalgam)

1 .80 2.00

SPEED DEMONS (Formerly Frank Merriwell at Yale #1-4?; Submarine Attack #11 on)
No. 5, Feb, 1957 - No. 10, 1958
Charlton Comics

5-10 4.00 12.00 24.00

SPEED FORCE (See The Flash)
Nov, 1997 ($3.95, one-shot)
DC Comics

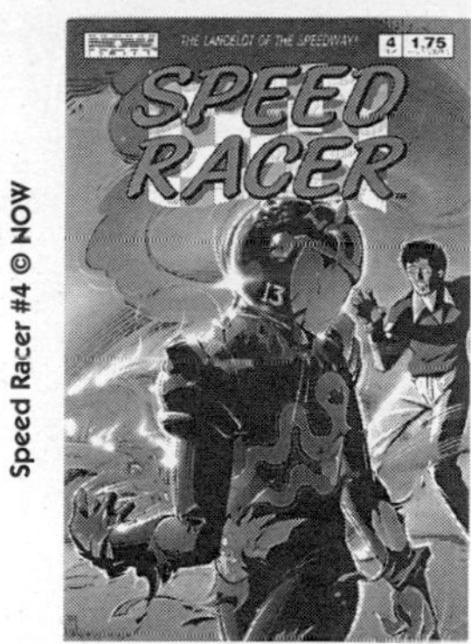

Speed Racer #4 © NOW

Spellbound #17 © ATLAS

Spider-Man #4 © MEG

	GD25	FN65	NM94
1-Flash & Kid Flash vs. Cobalt Blue; Waid-s/Aparo & Sienkiewicz-a; Flash family stories and pin-ups by various		1.60	4.00

SPEED RACER (Also see The New Adventures of...)
July, 1987 - No. 38, Nov, 1990 ($1.75)
Now Comics

	GD25	FN65	NM94
1-38, 1-2nd printing		.80	2.00
Special 1 (1988, $2.00)		.80	2.00
Special 2 (1988, $3.50)		1.40	3.50

SPEED RACER FEATURING NINJA HIGH SCHOOL
Aug, 1993 - No. 2, 1993 ($2.50, mini-series)
Now Comics

	GD25	FN65	NM94
1,2: 1-Polybagged w/card. 2-Exists?		1.00	2.50

SPEED RACER: RETURN OF THE GRX
Mar, 1994 - No. 2, Apr, 1994 ($1.95, limited series)
Now Comics

	GD25	FN65	NM94
1,2		.90	2.25

SPEED SMITH-THE HOT ROD KING (Also see Hot Rod King)
Spring, 1952
Ziff-Davis Publishing Co.

	GD25	FN65	NM94
1-Saunders painted-c	17.50	53.00	140.00

SPEEDY GONZALES
No. 1084, Mar, 1960
Dell Publishing Co.

	GD25	FN65	NM94
Four Color 1084	2.75	8.00	30.00

SPEEDY RABBIT (See Television Puppet Show)
nd (1953); 1963
Realistic/I. W. Enterprises/Super Comics

	GD25	FN65	NM94
nn (1953)-Realistic Reprint?	2.40	6.00	12.00
I.W. Reprint #1 (2 versions w/diff. c/stories exist)-Peter Cottontail #?		2.40	6.00
Super Reprint #14(1963)		2.40	6.00

SPELLBINDERS
Dec, 1986 - No. 12, Jan, 1988 ($1.25)
Quality

	GD25	FN65	NM94
1-12: Nemesis the Warlock, Amadeus Wolf			1.25

SPELLBOUND (See The Crusaders)

SPELLBOUND (Tales to Hold You... #1, Stories to Hold You...)
Mar, 1952 - #23, June, 1954; #24, Oct, 1955 - #34, June, 1957
Atlas Comics (ACI 1-15/Male 16-23/BPC 24-34)

	GD25	FN65	NM94
1-Horror/weird stories in all	50.00	150.00	425.00
2-Edgar A. Poe app.	31.00	92.00	225.00
3-5: 3 Whitney-a; cannibalism story	26.00	77.00	190.00
6-Krigstein-a	26.00	77.00	190.00
7-10: 8-Ayers-a	21.00	62.00	155.00
11-16,18-20. 14-Ed Win-a	17.00	49.00	120.00
17-Krigstein-a	18.00	54.00	130.00
21-23: 23-Last precode (6/54)	15.00	45.00	110.00
24-28,30,31,34: 25-Orlando-a	13.50	41.00	95.00
29-Ditko-a (4 pgs.)	15.00	45.00	110.00
32,33-Torres-a	13.50	41.00	95.00

NOTE: ***Brodsky*** *a-5; c-1, 5-7, 10, 11, 13, 15, 25-27, 32.* ***Colan*** *a-17.* ***Everett*** *a-2, 5, 7, 10, 16, 28, 31; c-2, 8, 9, 14, 17-19, 28, 30.* ***Forgione/Abel*** *a-29.* ***Forte/Fox*** *a-16.* ***Al Hartley*** *a-2.* ***Heath*** *a-2, 4, 8, 9, 12, 14, 16; c-3, 4, 12, 16, 20, 21.* ***Infantino*** *a-15.* ***Keller*** *a-5.* ***Kida*** *a-2, 14.* ***Maneely*** *a-7, 14, 27; c-24, 29, 31.* ***Mooney*** *a-5, 13, 18.* ***Mac Pakula*** *a-22, 32.* ***Post*** *a-8.* ***Powell*** *a-19, 20, 32.* ***Robinson*** *a-1.* ***Romita*** *a-24, 26, 27.* ***R.Q. Sale*** *a-29.* ***Sekowsky*** *a-5.* ***Severin*** *c-29.* ***Sinnott*** *a-8, 16, 17.*

SPELLBOUND
Jan, 1988 - Apr, 1988 ($1.50, bi-weekly, Baxter paper)
Marvel Comics

	GD25	FN65	NM94
1-5			1.50
6 ($2.25, 52 pgs.)		.90	2.25

SPELLJAMMER (Also see TSR Worlds Comics Annual)
Sept, 1990 - Feb, 1992 ($1.75)
DC Comics

	GD25	FN65	NM94
1-18: Based on TSR game. 11-Heck-a.		.75	1.80

SPENCER SPOOK (Formerly Giggle Comics; see Adventures of...)
No. 100, Mar-Apr, 1955 - No. 101, May-June, 1955
American Comics Group

	GD25	FN65	NM94
100,101	5.70	17.00	34.00

SPIDER, THE
1991 - Book 3, 1991 ($4.95, 52 pgs., limited series)
Eclipse Books

	GD25	FN65	NM94
Book 1-3-Truman-c/a		2.00	5.00

SPIDER-BOY (Also see Marvel Versus DC #3)
Apr, 1996 ($1.95)
Marvel Comics (Amalgam)

	GD25	FN65	NM94
1-Mike Wieringo-c/a; Karl Kesel story; 1st app. of Bizarnage, Insect Queen, Challengers of the Fantastic, Sue Storm: Agent of S.H.I.E.L.D., & King Lizard.		.80	2.00

SPIDER-BOY TEAM-UP
June, 1997 ($1.95, one-shot)
Marvel Comics (Amalgam)

	GD25	FN65	NM94
1-Karl Kesel & Roger Stern-s/Jo Ladronn-a(p)			1.95

SPIDER-MAN (See Amazing..., Giant-Size..., Marvel Tales, Marvel Team-Up, Spectacular..., Spidey Super Stories, Venom, & Web Of...)

SPIDER-MAN
Aug, 1990 - Present ($1.75)
Marvel Comics

	GD25	FN65	NM94
1-Silver edition, direct sale only (unbagged)		.80	2.00
1-Silver bagged edition; direct sale, no price on comic, but $2.00 on plastic bag (125,000 print run)		2.00	5.00
1-Regular edition w/Spidey face in UPC area (unbagged); green-c		.80	2.00
1-Regular bagged edition w/Spidey face in UPC area; green cover (125,000)		1.60	4.00
1-Newsstand bagged w/UPC code		1.20	3.00
1-Gold edition, 2nd printing (unbagged) with Spider-Man in box (400,000-450,000)		.80	2.00
1-Gold 2nd printing w/UPC code; sold in Wal-Mart; not scarce		1.00	2.50
1-Platinum ed. mailed to retailers only (10,000 print run); has new McFarlane-a & editorial material instead of ads; stiff-c, no cover price			100.00
2-McFarlane-c/a/scripts continue		1.20	3.00
3-5		.80	2.00
6,7-Ghost Rider & Hobgoblin app.		1.00	2.50
8-12: 8-Wolverine cameo; Wolverine storyline begins. 12-Wolverine storyline ends		.80	2.00
13-Spidey's black costume returns; Morbius app.		1.00	2.50
14,15: 14-Morbius app. 15-Erik Larsen-c/a; Beast c/s		.90	2.25
16,17: 16-X-Force-c/story w/Liefeld assists; continues in X-Force #4; reads sideways; last McFarlane issue. 17-Thanos-c/story; Leonardi/Williamson-c/a		1.00	2.50
18-23,25: 13,14-Spidey in black costume. 18-Ghost Rider-c/story. 18-23-Sinister Six storyline w/Erik Larsen-c/a/scripts. 19-Hulk & Hobgoblin-c & app. 20-22-Deathlok app. 22,23-Ghost Rider, Hulk, Hobgoblin app. 23-Wrap-around gatefold-c. 24-Infinity War x-over w/Demogoblin & Hobgoblin-c/story		.80	2.00
24-Demogoblin dons new costume & battles Hobgoblin-c/story		.80	2.00

Spider-Man #44 © MEG

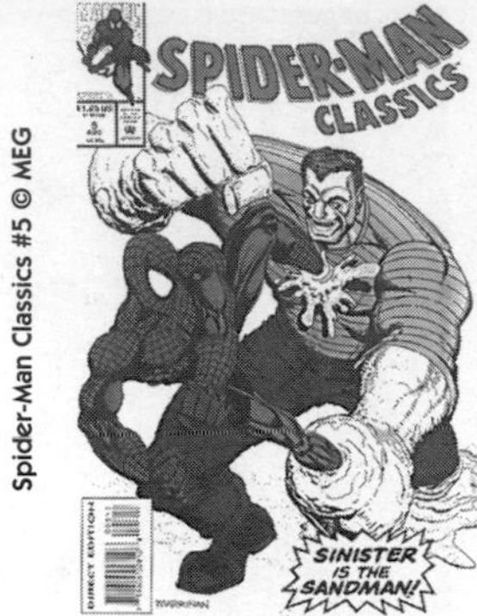

Spider-Man Classics #5 © MEG

Spider-Man/ Gen 13 © MEG/ Aegis Entertainment

GD25 FN65 NM94

26-($3.50, 52 pgs.)-Silver hologram on-c w/gatefold poster by Ron Lim; Spidey retells his origin 1.60 4.00
26-2nd printing; gold hologram on-c 1.60 4.00
27-45: 32-34-Punisher-c/story. 37-Maximum Carnage x-over. 39,40-Electro-c/s (cameo #38). 41-43-Iron Fist-c/stories w/Jae Lee-c/a. 42-Intro Platoon. 44-Hobgoblin app .70 1.75
46-49,51-53, 55, 56,58-74,76-81 -1(7/97): 46-Begin $1.95-c; bound-in card sheet. 51-Power & Responsibility Pt. 3. 52,53-Venom app. 60-Kaine revealed. 61-Origin Kaine. 65-Mysterio app. 66-Kaine-c/app.; Peter Parker app. 67-Carnage-c/app. 68,69-Hobgoblin-c/app. 72-Onslaught x-over; Spidey vs. Sentinels. 74-Daredevil-c/app. 77-80-Morbius-c/app. .90 2.25
46-($2.95)-Polybagged; silver ink-c w/16 pg. preview of cartoon series & animation style print; bound-in trading card sheet 1.20 3.00
50-($2.50)-Newsstand edition 1.00 2.50
50-($3.95)-Collectors edition w/holographic-c 1.60 4.00
51-($2.95)-Deluxe edition foil-c; flip book 1.20 3.00
54 ($2.75, 52 pgs.)-Flip book 1.10 2.75
57 ($2.50) 1.00 2.50
57 ($2.95)-Die cut-c 1.20 3.00
65-($2.95)-Variant-c; polybagged w/cassette 1.20 3.00
75-($2.95)-Wraparound-c; return of the Green Goblin; death of Ben Reilly (who was the clone) 1.20 3.00
82-91: 82-Begin $1.99-c. 84-Juggernaut app. .80 2.00
Annual '97 ($2.99) 1.20 3.00
Super Special (7/95, $3.95)-Planet of the Symbiotes 1.60 4.00
...: Carnage nn (6/93, $6.95, TPB)-r/Amazing S-M #344,345,359-363; spot varnish-c 1.00 2.80 7.00
.../Dr. Strange: "The Way to Dusty Death" nn (1992, $6.95, 68 pgs.) 1.00 2.80 7.00
...Revelations ('97, $14.99, TPB) r/end of Clone Saga plus 14 new pages by Romita Jr. 14.99
Special Edition 1 (12/92-c, 11/92 inside)-The Trial of Venom; ordered thru mail with $5.00 donation or more to UNICEF; embossed metallic ink; came bagged w/bound-in poster; Daredevil app. 1.25 3.75 10.00
...Vs. Venom nn (1990, $8.95, TPB)-r/Amaz. S-M #300,315-317 w/new McFarlane-c 1.10 3.30 9.00

NOTE: *Erik Larsen c/a-15, 18-23. M. Rogers/Keith Williams c/a-27, 28.*

SPIDER-MAN ADVENTURES
Dec, 1994 - No. 15, Mar, 1996 ($1.50)
Marvel Comics

1-15 ($1.50)-Based on animated series 1.50
1-($2.95)-Foil embossed-c 1.20 3.00

SPIDER-MAN AND BATMAN
1995 ($5.95, one-shot)
Marvel Comics

nn-DeMatteis-s; Joker, Carnage app. 2.40 6.00

SPIDER-MAN AND DAREDEVIL
Mar, 1984 ($2.00, one-shot, deluxe paper)
Marvel Comics Group

1-r/Spectacular Spider-Man #26-28 by Miller 1.20 3.00

SPIDER-MAN AND HIS AMAZING FRIENDS (See Marvel Action Universe)
Dec, 1981 (one-shot)
Marvel Comics Group

1-Adapted from NBC TV cartoon show; Green Goblin-c/story; 1st Spidey, Firestar, Iceman team-up; Spiegle-p 1.20 3.00

SPIDER-MAN AND THE INCREDIBLE HULK (See listing under Amazing...)

SPIDER-MAN AND THE UNCANNY X-MEN
Mar, 1996 ($16.95, trade paperback)
Marvel Comics

nn-r/Uncanny X-Men #27, Uncanny X-men #35, Amazing Spider-Man #92, Marvel Team-Up Annual #1, Marvel Team-Up #150, & Spectacular Spider-Man #197-199 17.00

SPIDER-MAN AND X-FACTOR
May, 1994 - No. 3, July, 1994 ($1.95, limited series)
Marvel Comics

1-3 .80 2.00

SPIDER-MAN /BADROCK
Mar, 1997 ($2.99, one-shot)
Maximum Press

1A, 1B-Jurgens-s 1.50

SPIDER-MAN CLASSICS
Apr, 1993 - No. 16, July, 1994 ($1.25)
Marvel Comics

1-14,16: 1-r/Amaz. Fantasy #15 & Strange Tales #115. 2-16-r/Amaz. Spider-Man #1-15. 6-Austin-c(i) 1.25
15-($2.95)-Polybagged w/16 pg. insert & animation style print; r/Amazing S-M #14 (1st Green Goblin) 1.20 3.00

SPIDER-MAN COLLECTOR'S PREVIEW
Dec, 1994 ($1.50, 100 pgs., one-shot)
Marvel Comics

1-wraparound-c; no comics 1.50

SPIDER-MAN COMICS MAGAZINE
Jan, 1987 - No. 13, 1988 ($1.50, digest-size)
Marvel Comics Group

1-13-Reprints 1.50

SPIDER-MAN: DEAD MAN'S HAND
Apr, 1997 ($2.99, one-shot)
Marvel Comics

1 1.20 3.00

SPIDER-MAN: FRIENDS AND ENEMIES
Jan, 1995 - No. 4, Apr, 1995 ($1.95, limited series)
Marvel Comics

1-4-Darkhawk, Nova & Speedball app. .80 2.00

SPIDER-MAN: FUNERAL FOR AN OCTOPUS
Mar, 1995 - No. 3, May, 1995 ($1.50, limited series)
Marvel Comics

1-3 1.50

SPIDER-MAN/GEN 13
Nov, 1996 ($4.95, one-shot)
Marvel Comics

nn-Peter David-s/Stuart Immonen-a 4.95

SPIDER-MAN: HOBGOBLIN LIVES
Jan, 1997 - No. 3, Mar, 1997 ($2.50, limited series)
Marvel Comics

1-3-Wraparound-c 1.00 2.50

SPIDER-MAN: HOT SHOTS
Jan, 1996 ($2.95, one-shot)
Marvel Comics

nn-fold out posters by various, inc. Vess and Ross 1.20 3.00

SPIDER-MAN: LEGACY OF EVIL
June, 1996 ($3.95, one-shot)
Marvel Comics

1-Kurt Busiek script & Mark Texiera-c/a 1.60 4.00

SPIDER-MAN MAGAZINE
1994 - No. 3, 1994 ($1.95, magazine)
Marvel Comics

Spider-Man Megazine #1 © MEG

Spider-Man 2099 #23 © DC

Spider-Man: Venom Agenda #1 © MEG

GD25 FN65 NM94

1-Contains 4 S-M promo cards & 4 X-Men Ultra Fleer cards; Spider-Man story by Romita, Sr.; X-Men story; puzzles & games .80 2.00
2,3: 2-Doc Octopus & X-Men stories .80 2.00

SPIDER-MAN: MAXIMUM CLONAGE
1995 ($4.95)
Marvel Comics

Alpha #1-Acetate-c. 2.00 5.00
Omega #1-Chromium-c. 2.00 5.00

SPIDER-MAN MEGAZINE
Oct, 1994 - No. 6, Mar, 1995 ($2.95, 100 pgs.)
Marvel Comics

1-6: 1-r/ASM #16,224,225, Marvel Team-Up #1 1.20 3.00

SPIDER-MAN: POWER OF TERROR
Jan, 1995 - No. 4, Apr, 1995 ($1.95, limited series)
Marvel Comics

1-4-Silvermane & Deathlok app. .80 2.00

SPIDER-MAN: REDEMPTION
Sept, 1996 - No. 4, Dec, 1996 ($1.50, limited series)
Marvel Comics

1-4: DeMatteis scripts; Zeck-a 1.50

SPIDER-MAN SAGA
Nov, 1991 - No. 4, Feb, 1992 ($2.95, limited series)
Marvel Comics

1-4: Gives history of Spider-Man: text & illustrations 1.20 3.00

SPIDER-MAN TEAM-UP
Dec, 1995 - No. 7, June, 1996 ($2.95)
Marvel Comics

1-7: 1-w/ X-Men. 2-w/ Silver Surfer. 3-w/Fantastic Four. 4-w/Avengers. 5-Gambit & Howard the Duck-c/app. 7-Thunderbolts-c/app. 1.20 3.00

SPIDER-MAN: THE ARACHNIS PROJECT
Aug, 1994 - No. 6, Jan, 1995 ($1.75, limited series)
Marvel Comics

1-6-Venom, Styx, Stone & Jury app. .70 1.75

SPIDER-MAN: THE CLONE JOURNAL
Mar, 1995 ($2.95, one-shot)
Marvel Comics

1 1.20 3.00

SPIDER-MAN: THE FINAL ADVENTURE
Nov, 1995 - No. 4, Feb, 1996 ($2.95, limited series)
Marvel Comics

1-4: 1-Nicieza scripts; foil-c 1.20 3.00

SPIDER-MAN: THE JACKAL FILES
Aug, 1995 ($1.95, one-shot)
Marvel Comics

1 .80 2.00

SPIDER-MAN: THE LOST YEARS
Aug, 1995 - No. 3, Oct, 1995; No. 0, 1996 ($2.95/$3.95, limited series)
Marvel Comics

0-(1/96, $3.95)-Reprints.
1-3-DeMatteis scripts, Romita, Jr.-c/a 1.20 3.00
NOTE: ***Romita*** *c-0i.* ***Romita, Jr.*** *a-0r, 1-3p. c-0-3p.* ***Sharp*** *a-0r.*

SPIDER-MAN: THE MANGA
Dec, 1997 - Present ($3.99/$2.99, B&W, bi-weekly)
Marvel Comics

1-($3.99)-English translation of Japanese Spider-Man 3.99
2-10-($2.99) 2.99

SPIDER-MAN: THE MUTANT AGENDA
No. 0, Feb, 1994; No. 1, Mar, 1994 - No. 3, May, 1994 ($1.75, limited series)
Marvel Comics

0-(2/94, $1.25, 52 pgs.)-Crosses over w/newspaper strip; has empty pages to paste in newspaper strips; gives origin of Spidey 1.25
1-3: Beast & Hobgoblin app. 1-X-Men app. .70 1.75

SPIDER-MAN: THE PARKER YEARS
Nov, 1995 ($2.50, one-shot)
Marvel Comics

1 1.00 2.50

SPIDER-MAN 2099 (See Amazing Spider-Man #365)
Nov, 1992 - No. 46, Aug, 1996 ($1.25/$1.50/$1.95)
Marvel Comics

1-($1.75, stiff-c)-Red foil stamped-c; begins origin of Miguel O'Hara (Spider-Man 2099); Leonardi/Williamson-c/a begins 1.00 2.50
1-2nd printing ($1.75) 1.50
2-Origin continued, ends #3 1.50
3,4: 4-Doom 2099 app. 1.50
5-18: 13-Extra 16 pg. insert on Midnight Sons 1.25
19-24,26-31: 19-Begin$ 1.50-c; bound-in trading card sheet 1.50
25-($2.25, 52 pgs.)-Newsstand edition .90 2.25
25-($2.95, 52 pgs.)-Deluxe edition w/embossed foil-c 1.20 3.00
32-46: 32-Begin $1.95-c. 35-variant-c. 36-two-c; Jae Lee-a. 37,38-two-c. 46-The Vulture app; Mike McKone-a(p). .80 2.00
Annual 1 (1994, $2.95, 68 pgs.) 1.20 3.00
Special 1 (1995, $3.95) 1.60 4.00
NOTE: ***Chaykin*** *c-37.* ***Ron Lim*** *a(p)-18; c(p)-13, 16, 18.* ***Kelley Jones*** *c/a-9.* ***Leonardi/Williamson*** *a-1-8, 10-13, 15-17, 19, 20, 22-25; c-1-13, 15, 17-19, 20, 22-25, 35.*

SPIDER-MAN 2099 MEETS SPIDER-MAN
1995 ($5.95, one-shot)
Marvel Comics

nn-Peter David script; Leonardi/Williamson-c/a. 2.40 6.00

SPIDER-MAN UNLIMITED
May, 1993 - Present ($3.95, quarterly, 68 pgs.)
Marvel Comics

1-Begin Maximum Carnage storyline, ends; Carnage-c/story. 2.00 5.00
2-19: 2-Venom & Carnage-c/story; Ron Lim-c/a(p) in #2-6. 10-Vulture app., McManus-a 1.60 4.00

SPIDER-MAN UNMASKED
Nov, 1996 ($5.95, one-shot)
Marvel Comics

nn-Art w/text 2.40 6.00

SPIDER-MAN: VENOM AGENDA
Jan, 1998 ($2.99, one-shot)
Marvel Comics

1-Hama-s/Lyle-c/a 2.99

SPIDER-MAN VS. DRACULA
Jan, 1994 ($1.75, 52 pgs., one-shot)
Marvel Comics

1-r/Giant-Size Spider-Man #1 plus new Matt Fox-a .70 1.75

SPIDER-MAN VS. WOLVERINE
Feb, 1987; V2#1, 1990 (68 pgs.)
Marvel Comics Group

1-Williamson-c/a(i); intro Charlemagne; death of Ned Leeds (old Hobgoblin) 2.50 7.50 20.00
V2#1 (1990, $4.95)-Reprints #1 (2/87) 2.00 5.00

SPIDER-MAN: WEB OF DOOM
Aug, 1994 - No. 3, Oct, 1994 ($1.75, limited series)
Marvel Comics

Spider-Woman #4 © MEG

Spinworld #3 © Eric Vinicott & Brent Anderson

The Spirit 6/16/40 © Will Eisner

GD25 FN65 NM94

1-3 .70 1.75

SPIDER REIGN OF THE VAMPIRE KING, THE (Also see The Spider)
1992 - No. 3, 1992 ($4.95, limited series, coated stock, 52 pgs.)
Eclipse Books

Book One - Three: Truman scripts & painted-c 2.00 5.00

SPIDER'S WEB, THE (See G-8 and His Battle Aces)

SPIDER-WOMAN (Also see The Avengers #240, Marvel Spotlight #32, Marvel Super Heroes Secret Wars #7 & Marvel Two-In-One #29)
April, 1978 - No. 50, June, 1983 (New logo #47 on)
Marvel Comics Group

1-New complete origin & mask added 2.00 5.00
2-5,7-18,21-27,30-36,39-49: 13,15-The Shroud-c/s. 46-Kingpin app. 49-Tigra-c/story .80 2.00
6,19,20,28,29: 6,19-Werewolf by Night-c/stories. 20,28,29-Spider-Man app. 1.20 3.00
37,38-X-Men x-over; 37-1st app. Siryn of X-Force; origin retold 1.60 4.00
50-(52 pgs.)-Death of Spider-Woman; photo-c 2.00 5.00
NOTE: ***Austin** a-37i. **Byrne** c-26p. **Layton** c-19. **Miller** c-32p.*

SPIDER-WOMAN
Nov, 1993 - No. 4, Feb, 1994 ($1.75, mini-series)
Marvel Comics

V2#1-4: 1,2-Origin; U.S. Agent app. .70 1.75

SPIDEY SUPER STORIES (Spider-Man)
Oct, 1974 - No. 57, Mar, 1982 (35¢, no ads)
Marvel/Children's TV Workshop

1-Origin (stories simplified) 1.85 5.50 15.00
2-12,15: 2-Kraven. 6-Iceman. 15-Storm-c/sty 1.25 3.75 10.00
11-14,16-20 1.00 3.00 8.00
21-30 2.40 6.00
31-38,40-44,46-55,57: 31-Moondragon-c/story; Dr. Doom app. 33-Hulk. 34-Sub-Mariner. 38-F.F. 44-Vision. 1.60 4.00
39-Thanos-c/story 1.00 3.00 8.00
45-Silver Surfer & Dr. Doom app. 2.40 6.00
56-Battles Jack O'Lantern-c/sty (exactly one year after 1st app. in Machine Man #19) 2.40 6.00

SPIKE AND TYKE (See M.G.M.'s...)

SPIN & MARTY (TV) (Walt Disney's)(See Walt Disney Showcase #32)
No. 714, June, 1956 - No. 1082, Mar-May, 1960 (All photo-c)
Dell Publishing Co. (Mickey Mouse Club)

Four Color 714 (#1) 10.00 30.00 110.00
Four Color 767,808 (#2,3) 9.00 27.00 100.00
Four Color 826 (#4)-Annette Funicello photo-c 23.00 68.00 250.00
5(3-5/58) - 9(6-8/59) 7.00 20.00 75.00
Four Color 1026,1082 7.00 20.00 75.00

SPINE-TINGLING TALES (Doctor Spektor Presents...)
May, 1975 - No. 4, Jan, 1976 (All 25¢ issues)
Gold Key

1-1st Tragg-r/Mystery Comics Digest #3 2.40 6.00
2-4: 2-Origin Ra-Ka-Tep-r/Mystery Comics Digest #1; Dr. Spektor #12. 3-All Durak-r issue; 4-Baron Tibor's 1st app.-r/Mystery Comics Digest #4; painted-c 1.60 4.00

SPINWORLD
July, 1997 - No. 4 ($2.95, B&W, mini-series)
Amaze Ink (Slave Labor Graphics)

1-3-Brent Anderson-a(p) 2.95

SPIRAL PATH, THE
July, 1986 - No. 2 ($1.75, Baxter paper, limited series)
Eclipse Comics

1,2 .75 1.80

GD25 FN65 NM94

SPIRAL ZONE
Feb, 1988 - No. 4, May, 1988 ($1.00, mini-series)
DC Comics

1-4-Based on Tonka toys 1.00

SPIRIT, THE (Weekly Comic Book)
6/2/40 - 10/5/52 (16 pgs.; 8 pgs.) (no cover) (in color)
(Distributed through various newspapers and other sources)
Will Eisner
NOTE: **Eisner** script, pencils/inks for the most part from 6/2/40-4/26/42; a few stories assisted by Jack Cole, Fine, Powell and Kotsky.

6/2/40(#1)-Origin/1st app. The Spirit; reprinted in Police #11; Lady Luck (Brenda Banks)(1st app.) by Chuck Mazoujian & Mr. Mystic (1st. app.) by S. R. (Bob) Powell begin 65.00 195.00 525.00
6/9/40(#2) 31.00 92.00 215.00
6/16/40(#3)-Black Queen app. in Spirit 18.00 54.00 125.00
6/23/40(#4)-Mr. Mystic receives magical necklace 15.00 45.00 105.00
6/30/40(#5) 15.00 45.00 105.00
7/7/40(#6)-1st app.: Spirit carplane; Black Queen app. in Spirit 15.00 45.00 105.00
7/14/40(#7)-8/4/40(#10): 7/21/40-Spirit becomes fugitive wanted for murder 12.00 36.00 85.00
8/11/40-9/22/40 11.00 33.00 75.00
9/29/40-Ellen drops engagement with Homer Creep 10.00 30.00 65.00
10/6/40-11/3/40 10.00 30.00 65.00
11/10/40-The Black Queen app. 10.00 30.00 65.00
11/17/40, 11/24/40 10.00 30.00 65.00
12/1/40-Ellen spanking by Spirit on cover & inside; Eisner-1st 3 pgs., J. Cole rest 14.00 43.00 100.00
12/8/40-3/9/41 8.35 25.00 50.00
3/16/41-Intro. & 1st app. Silk Satin 13.00 39.00 90.00
3/23/41-6/1/41: 5/11/41-Last Lady Luck by Mazoujian; 5/18/41-Lady Luck by Nick Viscardi begins, ends 2/22/42 8.35 25.00 50.00
6/8/41-2nd app. Satin; Spirit learns Satin is also a British agent 10.00 30.00 70.00
6/15/41-1st app. Twilight 10.00 30.00 60.00
6/22/41-Hitler app. in Spirit 8.35 25.00 50.00
6/29/41-1/25/42,2/8/42 6.70 20.00 40.00
2/1/42-1st app. Duchess 10.00 30.00 60.00
2/15/42-4/26/42-Lady Luck by Klaus Nordling begins 3/1/42 7.50 22.50 45.00
5/3/42-8/16/42-Eisner/Fine/Quality staff assists on Spirit 5.00 15.00 30.00
8/23/42-Satin cover splash; Spirit by Eisner/Fine although signed by Fine 9.30 28.00 65.00
8/30/42,9/27/42-10/11/42,10/25/42-11/8/42-Eisner/Fine/Quality staff assists on Spirit 5.00 15.00 30.00
9/6/42-9/20/42,10/18/42-Fine/Belfi art on Spirit; scripts by Manly Wade Wellman 3.00 9.00 21.00
11/15/42-12/6/42,12/20/42,12/27/42,1/17/43-4/18/43,5/9/43-8/8/43-Wellman/Woolfolk scripts, Fine pencils, Quality staff inks 3.00 9.00 21.00
12/13/42,1/3/43,1/10/43,4/25/43,5/2/43-Eisner scripts/layouts; Fine pencils, Quality staff inks 3.75 11.25 26.00
8/15/43-Eisner script/layout; pencils/inks by Quality staff; Jack Cole-a 2.30 6.75 16.00
8/22/43-12/12/43-Wellman/Woolfolk scripts, Fine pencils, Quality staff inks; Mr. Mystic by Guardineer-10/10/43-10/24/43 2.30 6.75 16.00
12/19/43-8/13/44-Wellman/Woolfolk/Jack Cole scripts; Cole, Fine & Robin King-a; Last Mr. Mystic-5/14/44 2.00 6.00 14.00
8/20/44-12/16/45-Wellman/Woolfolk scripts; Fine art with unknown staff assists 2.00 6.00 14.00
NOTE: *Scripts/layouts by Eisner, or Eisner/Nordling, Eisner/Mercer or Spranger/Eisner; inks by Eisner or Eisner/Spranger in issues 12/23/45-2/2/47.*
12/23/45-1/6/46: 12/23/45-Christmas-c 3.75 11.25 28.00
1/13/46-Origin Spirit retold 6.00 18.00 45.00

The Spirit 3/12/50 © Will Eisner

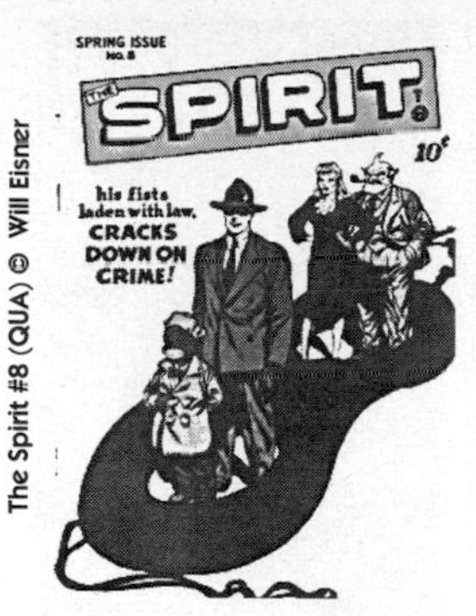

The Spirit #8 (QUA) © Will Eisner

The Spirit #1 (FH) © Will Eisner

	GD25	FN65	NM94
1/20/46-1st postwar Satin app.	5.00	15.00	38.00
1/27/46-3/10/46: 3/3/46-Last Lady Luck by Nordling	3.70	11.00	28.00
3/17/46-Intro. & 1st app. Nylon	5.00	15.00	38.00
3/24/46,3/31/46,4/14/46	3.70	11.00	28.00
4/7/46-2nd app. Nylon	4.30	13.00	32.00
4/21/46-Intro. & 1st app. Mr. Carrion & His Pet Buzzard Julia	5.70	17.00	45.00
4/28/46-5/12/46,5/26/46-6/30/46: Lady Luck by Fred Schwab in issues 5/5/46-11/3/46	3.70	11.00	28.00
5/19/46-2nd app. Mr. Carrion	4.30	13.00	32.00
7/7/46-Intro. & 1st app. Dulcet Tone & Skinny	5.50	16.50	40.00
7/14/46-9/29/46	3.70	11.00	28.00
10/6/46-Intro. & 1st app. P'Gell	6.00	18.00	45.00
10/13/46-11/3/46,11/16/46-11/24/46	3.70	11.00	28.00
11/10/46-2nd app. P'Gell	4.50	14.00	35.00
12/1/46-3rd app. P'Gell	4.30	13.00	32.00
12/8/46-2/2/47	3.40	10.00	24.00

NOTE: *Scripts, pencils/inks by Eisner except where noted in issues 2/9/47-12/19/48.*

	GD25	FN65	NM94
2/9/47-7/6/47: 6/8/47-Eisner self satire	3.40	10.00	24.00
7/13/47- "Hansel & Gretel" fairy tales	5.00	15.00	38.00
7/20/47-Li'L Abner, Daddy Warbucks, Dick Tracy, Fearless Fosdick parody; A-Bomb blast-c	5.50	16.50	40.00
7/27/47-9/14/47	3.40	10.00	24.00
9/21/47-Pearl Harbor flashback	4.00	12.00	30.00
9/28/47-1st mention of Flying Saucers in comics-3 months after 1st sighting in Idaho on 6/25/47	9.30	28.00	65.00
10/5/47- "Cinderella" fairy tales	5.00	15.00	38.00
10/12/47-11/30/47	3.40	10.00	24.00
12/7/47-Intro. & 1st app. Powder Pouf	5.70	17.00	45.00
12/14/47-12/28/47	3.40	10.00	24.00
1/4/48-2nd app. Powder Pouf	4.30	13.00	32.00
1/11/48-1st app. Sparrow Fallon; Powder Pouf app.	4.30	13.00	32.00
1/18/48-He-Man ad cover; satire issue	4.30	13.00	32.00
1/25/48-Intro. & 1st app. Castanet	5.50	16.50	40.00
2/1/48-2nd app. Castanet	3.70	11.00	28.00
2/8/48-3/7/48	3.40	10.00	24.00
3/14/48-Only app. Kretchma	3.70	11.00	28.00
3/21/48,3/28/48,4/11/48-4/25/48	3.40	10.00	24.00
4/4/48-Only app. Wild Rice	3.70	11.00	28.00
5/2/48-2nd app. Sparrow	3.40	10.00	24.00
5/9/48-6/27/48,7/11/48,7/18/48: 6/13/48-Television issue	3.40	10.00	24.00
7/4/48-Spirit by Andre Le Blanc	2.60	7.50	18.00
7/25/48-Ambrose Bierce's "The Thing" adaptation classic by Eisner/ Grandenetti	9.30	28.00	65.00
8/1/48-8/15/48,8/29/48-9/12/48	3.40	10.00	24.00
8/22/48-Poe's "Fall of the House of Usher" classic by Eisner/Grandenetti	9.30	28.00	65.00
9/19/48-Only app. Lorelei	4.50	14.00	35.00
9/26/48-10/31/48	3.40	10.00	24.00
11/7/48-Only app. Plaster of Paris	4.50	14.00	35.00
11/14/48-12/19/48	3.40	10.00	24.00

NOTE: *Scripts by Eisner or Feiffer or Eisner/Feiffer or Nordling. Art by Eisner with backgrounds by Eisner, Grandenetti, Le Blanc, Stallman, Nordling, Dixon and/or others in issues 12/26/48-4/1/51 except where noted.*

	GD25	FN65	NM94
12/26/48-Reprints some covers of 1948 with flashbacks	3.40	10.00	24.00
1/2/49-1/16/49	3.40	10.00	24.00
1/23/49,1/30/49-1st & 2nd app. Thorne	4.50	14.00	35.00
2/6/49-8/14/49	3.40	10.00	24.00
8/21/49,8/28/49-1st & 2nd app. Monica Veto	4.50	14.00	35.00
9/4/49,9/11/49	3.40	10.00	24.00
9/18/49-Love comic cover; has gag love comic ads on inside	4.50	14.00	35.00
9/25/49-Only app. Ice	4.00	12.00	30.00
10/2/49,10/9/49-Autumn News appears & dies in 10/9 issue	4.00	12.00	30.00
10/16/49-11/27/49,12/18/49,12/25/49	3.40	10.00	24.00
12/4/49,12/11/49-1st & 2nd app. Flaxen	3.70	11.00	28.00
1/1/50-Flashbacks to all of the Spirit girls-Thorne, Ellen, Satin, & Monica	6.00	18.00	45.00
1/8/50-Intro. & 1st app. Sand Saref	8.50	26.00	65.00
1/15/50-2nd app. Saref	5.70	17.00	45.00
1/22/50-2/5/50	3.40	10.00	24.00
2/12/50-Roller Derby issue	4.30	13.00	32.00
2/19/50-Half Dead Mr. Lox - Classic horror	4.30	13.00	32.00
2/26/50-4/23/50,5/14/50,5/28/50,7/23/50-9/3/50	3.40	10.00	24.00
4/30/50-Script/art by Le Blanc with Eisner framing	1.70	5.00	12.00
5/7/50,6/4/50-7/16/50-Abe Kanegson-a	1.70	5.00	12.00
5/21/50-Script by Feiffer/Eisner, art by Blaisdell, Eisner framing	1.70	5.00	12.00
9/10/50-P'Gell returns	4.50	14.00	35.00
9/17/50-1/7/51	3.40	10.00	24.00
1/14/51-Life Magazine cover; brief biography of Comm. Dolan, Sand Saref, Silk Satin, P'Gell, Sammy & Willum, Darling O'Shea, & Mr. Carrion & His Pet Buzzard Julia, with pin-ups by Eisner	4.50	14.00	35.00
1/21/51,2/4/51-4/1/51	3.40	10.00	24.00
1/28/51- "The Meanest Man in the World" classic by Eisner	4.50	14.00	35.00
4/8/51-7/29/51,8/12/51-Last Eisner issue	3.40	10.00	24.00
8/5/51,8/19/51-7/20/52-Not Eisner	1.70	5.00	12.00
7/27/52-(Rare)-Denny Colt in Outer Space by Wally Wood; 7 pg. S/F story of E.C. vintage	32.00	95.00	225.00
8/3/52-(Rare)- "Mission…The Moon" by Wood	32.00	95.00	225.00
8/10/52-(Rare)- "A DP On The Moon" by Wood	32.00	95.00	225.00
8/17/52-(Rare)- "Heart" by Wood/Eisner	27.00	81.00	190.00
8/24/52-(Rare)- "Rescue" by Wood	32.00	95.00	225.00
8/31/52-(Rare)- "The Last Man" by Wood	32.00	95.00	225.00
9/7/52-(Rare)- "The Man in The Moon" by Wood	32.00	95.00	225.00
9/14/52-(Rare)-Eisner/Wenzel-a	8.50	26.00	60.00
9/21/52-(Rare)- "Denny Colt, Alias The Spirit/Space Report" by Eisner/Wenzel	11.50	34.00	80.00
9/28/52-(Rare)- "Return From The Moon" by Wood	32.00	95.00	225.00
10/5/52-(Rare)- "The Last Story" by Eisner	11.50	34.00	80.00

Large Tabloid pages from 1946 on (Eisner) - Price 200 percent over listed prices.
NOTE: *Spirit sections came out in both large and small format. Some newspapers went to the 8-pg. format months before others. Some printed the pages so they cannot be folded into a small comic book section; these are worth less. (Also see Three Comics & Spiritman).*

SPIRIT, THE (1st Series)(Also see Police Comics #11)
1944 - No. 22, Aug, 1950
Quality Comics Group (Vital)

	GD25	FN65	NM94
nn(#1)- "Wanted Dead or Alive"	56.00	168.00	495.00
nn(#2)- "Crime Doesn't Pay"	36.00	108.00	285.00
nn(#3)- "Murder Runs Wild"	27.00	81.00	215.00
4,5: 4-Flatfoot Burns begins, ends #22. 5-Wertham app.	22.00	66.00	175.00
6-10	19.00	56.00	150.00
11	16.00	49.00	130.00
12-17-Eisner-c. 19-Honeybun app.	26.00	80.00	210.00
18-21-Strip-r by Eisner; Eisner-c	35.00	105.00	280.00
22-Used by N.Y. Legis. Comm; classic Eisner-c	43.00	129.00	390.00
Super Reprint #11-r/Quality Spirit #19 by Eisner	2.50	7.50	22.00
Super Reprint #12-r/Spirit #17 by Fine; Sol Brodsky-c	2.50	7.50	20.00

SPIRIT, THE (2nd Series)
Spring, 1952 - No. 5, 1954
Fiction House Magazines

	GD25	FN65	NM94
1-Not Eisner	30.00	90.00	240.00

The Spirit #1 (HARV) © Will Eisner

Spitfire #132 © Malverne Herald

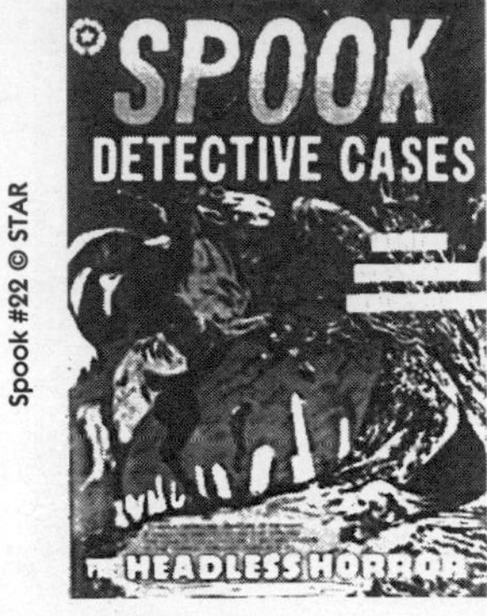

Spook #22 © STAR

GD25 FN65 NM94

2-Eisner-c/a(2) 28.00 84.00 225.00
3-Eisner/Grandenetti-c 19.50 58.00 155.00
4-Eisner/Grandenetti-c; Eisner-a 22.00 66.00 175.00
5-Eisner-c/a(4) 27.00 81.00 215.00

SPIRIT, THE
Oct, 1966 - No. 2, Mar, 1967 (Giant Size, 25¢, 68 pgs.)
Harvey Publications

1-Eisner-r plus 9 new pgs.(origin Denny Colt, Take 3, plus 2 filler pgs.) (#3 was advertised, but never published) 4.80 14.40 48.00
2-Eisner-r plus 9 new pgs.(origin of the Octopus) 4.80 14.40 48.00

SPIRIT, THE (Underground)
Jan, 1973 - No. 2, Sept, 1973 (Black & White)
Kitchen Sink Enterprises (Krupp Comics)

1-New Eisner-c & 4 pgs. new Eisner-a plus-r (titled Crime Convention) 1.25 3.75 10.00
2-New Eisner-c & 4 pgs. new Eisner-a plus-r (titled Meets P'Gell) 1.50 4.50 12.00

SPIRIT, THE (Magazine)
4/74 - No. 16, 10/76; No. 17, Winter, 1977 - No. 41, 6/83 (B&W w/color)
Warren Publ. Co./Krupp Comic Works No. 17 on

1-Eisner-r begin 2.50 7.50 25.00
2-5 1.85 5.50 15.00
6-9,11-15: 7-All Ebony issue. 8-Female Foes issue. 12-X-Mas issue 1.25 3.75 10.00
10-Giant Summer Special ($1.50)-Origin 5.00 15.00 50.00
16-Giant Summer Special ($1.50) 4.00 12.00 40.00
17,18(8/78): 17-Lady Luck-r 1.00 3.00 8.00
19-21-New Eisner-a. 20,21-Wood-r (#21-r/A DP on the Moon by Wood). 20-Outer Space-r 2.40 6.00
22-41: 22,23-Wood-r (#22-r/Mission the Moon by Wood). 28-r/last story (10/5/52). 30-(7/81)-Special Spirit Jam issue w/Caniff, Corben, Bolland, Byrne, Miller, Kurtzman, Rogers, Sienkiewicz-a & 40 others. 36-Begin Spirit Section-r; r/1st story (6/2/40) in color; new Eisner-c/a(18 pgs.)($2.95). 37-r/2nd story in color plus 18 pgs. new Eisner-a. 38-41: r/3rd - 6th stories in color. 41-Lady Luck Mr. Mystic in color 2.40 6.00
Special 1(1975)-All Eisner-a 2.40 6.00

NOTE: *Covers pencilled/inked by* **Eisner** *only #1-9,12-16; painted by Eisner & Ken Kelly #10 & 11; painted by Eisner #17-up; one color story reprinted in #1-10.* **Austin** *a-30i.* **Byrne** *a-30p.* **Miller** *a-30p.*

SPIRIT, THE (See Will Eisner's 3-D Classics Featuring…)
Oct, 1983 - No. 87, Jan, 1992 (Baxter paper) ($2.00)
Kitchen Sink Enterprises

1-4: 1-Origin-r/12/23/45 Spirit Section. 2-r/sections 1/20/46-2/10/46. 3-r/2/17/46-3/10/46. 4-r/3/17/46-4/7/46 1.00 2.50
5-11 ($2.95 cover): 11-Last color issue 1.00 2.50
12-87 ($1.95/$2.00, B&W): 54-r/section 2/19/50. 85-87-Reprint the Outer Space Spirit stories by Wood. 86-r/A DP on the Moon by Wood from 1952 1.00 2.50

SPIRIT: THE ORIGIN YEARS
May, 1992 - No. 4, Aug, 1992 ($2.95, B&W, high quality paper)
Kitchen Sink Press

1-4: 1-r/sections 6/2/40(origin)-6/23/40 (all 1940s) 1.20 3.00

SPIRITMAN (Also see Three Comics)
No date (1944) (10¢)
(Triangle Sales Co. ad on back cover)
No publisher listed

1-Three 16pg. Spirit sections bound together, (1944, 10¢, 52 pgs.) 17.00 51.00 135.00
2-Two Spirit sections (3/26/44, 4/2/44) bound together; by Lou Fine 14.50 43.00 115.00

SPIRIT OF THE BORDER (See Zane Grey & Four Color #197)

SPIRIT OF WONDER (Manga)
Apr, 1996 - No. 5, Aug, 1996 ($2.95, B&W, limited series)
Dark Horse Comics

1-5 1.20 3.00

SPIRIT WORLD (Magazine)
Fall, 1971 (B&W)
National Periodical Publications

1-New Kirby-a; Neal Adams-c; poster inside 5.00 15.00 50.00

SPITFIRE
No. 132, 1944 (Aug) - No. 133, 1945 (Female undercover agent)
Malverne Herald (Elliot)(J. R. Mahon)

132,133: Both have Classics Gift Box ads on b/c with checklist to #20 19.00 56.00 150.00

SPITFIRE AND THE TROUBLESHOOTERS
Oct, 1986 - No. 9, June, 1987 (Codename: Spitfire #10 on)
Marvel Comics

1-9: 4-McFarlane-a 1.00

SPITFIRE COMICS (Also see Double Up)
Aug, 1941 - No. 2, Oct, 1941 (Pocket size; 100 pgs.)
Harvey Publications

1-Origin The Clown, The Fly-Man, The Spitfire & The Magician From Bagdad 47.00 141.00 475.00
2 44.00 132.00 400.00

SPLITTING IMAGE
Mar, 1993 - No. 2, 1993 ($1.95)
Image Comics

1,2-Simpson-c/a; parody comic .80 2.00

SPOOF
Oct, 1970; No. 2, Nov, 1972 - No. 5, May, 1973
Marvel Comics Group

1-Infinity-c; Dark Shadows-c & parody 1.25 3.75 10.00
2-5: 3-Beatles, Osmond's, Jackson 5, David Cassidy, Nixon & Agnew-c. 5-Rod Serling, Woody Allen, Ted Kennedy-c 1.00 3.00 8.00

SPOOK (Formerly Shock Detective Cases)
No. 22, Jan, 1953 - No. 30, Oct, 1954
Star Publications

22-Sgt. Spook-r; acid in face story; hanging-c 27.00 81.00 210.00
23,25,27: 25-Jungle Lil-r. 27-Two Sgt. Spook-r 17.50 53.00 140.00
24-Used in **SOTI**, pgs. 182,183-r/Inside Crime #2; Transvestism story 20.00 60.00 160.00
26-Disbrow-a 17.50 53.00 140.00
28,29-Rulah app. 29-Jo-Jo app. 17.50 53.00 140.00
30-Disbrow-c/a(2); only Star-c 17.50 53.00 140.00

NOTE: **L. B. Cole** *covers-all issues; a-28(1 pg.).* **Disbrow** *a-26(2), 28, 29(2), 30(2); No. 30 r/Blue Bolt Weird Tales #114.*

SPOOK COMICS
1946
Baily Publications/Star

1-Mr. Lucifer story 24.00 71.00 175.00

SPOOKY (The Tuff Little Ghost; see Casper The Friendly Ghost)
11/55 - 139, 11/73; No. 140, 7/74 - No. 155, 3/77; No. 156, 12/77 - No. 158, 4/78; No. 159, 9/78; No. 160, 10/79; No. 161, 9/80
Harvey Publications

1-Nightmare begins (see Casper #19) 27.00 81.00 270.00
2 13.50 41.00 135.00
3-10(1956-57) 8.00 24.00 80.00
11-20(1957-58) 4.00 12.00 40.00
21-40(1958-59) 2.50 7.50 25.00
41-60 2.00 6.00 16.00

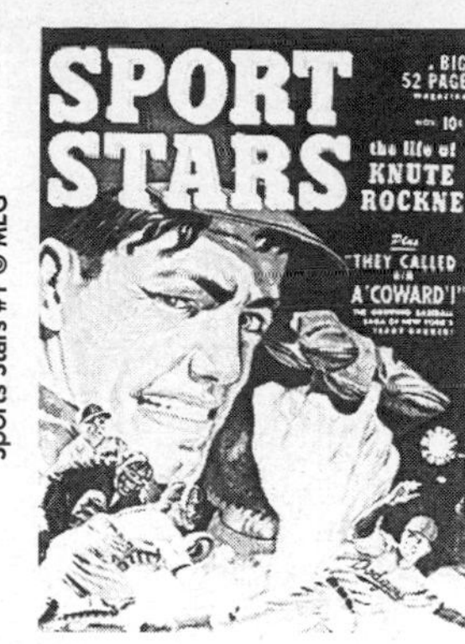

Sports Stars #1 © MEG

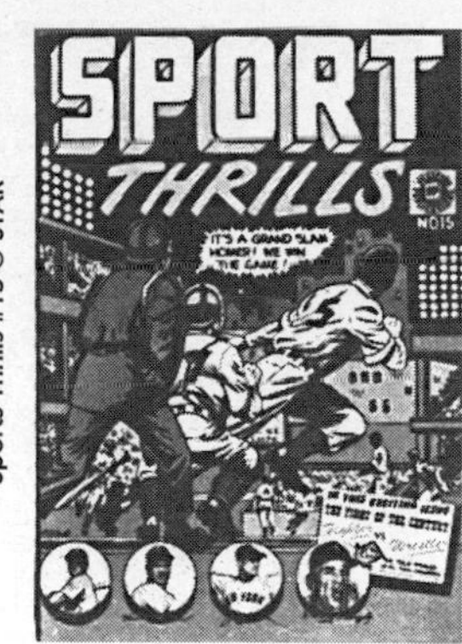

Sports Thrills #15 © STAR

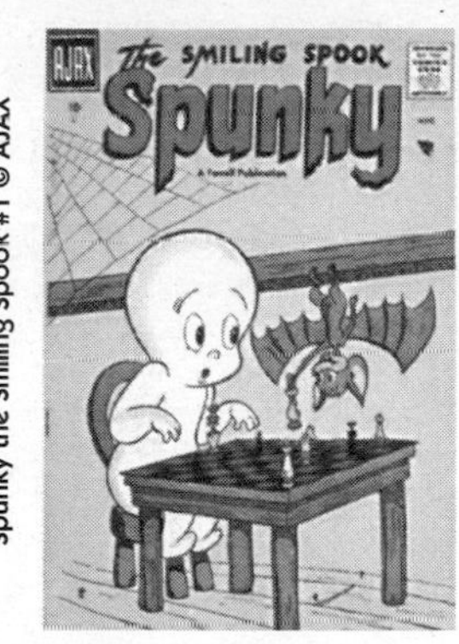

Spunky the Smiling Spook #1 © AJAX

	GD25	FN65	NM94
61-80	1.50	4.50	12.00
81-120	1.00	3.00	8.00
121-126,133-140		2.40	6.00
127-132: All 52 pg. Giants	1.00	3.00	8.00
141-161		1.60	4.00

SPOOKY
Nov, 1991 - No. 4, Sept, 1992 ($1.00/$1.25)
Harvey Comics

	GD25	FN65	NM94
1		1.20	3.00
2-4: 3-Begin $1.25-c		.80	2.00
...Digest 1-3 (10/92, 6/93, 10/93, $1.75, 100 pgs.)-Casper, Wendy, etc.		1.20	3.00

SPOOKY HAUNTED HOUSE
Oct, 1972 - No. 15, Feb, 1975
Harvey Publications

	GD25	FN65	NM94
1	2.50	7.50	24.00
2-5	1.25	3.75	10.00
6-10	1.00	2.80	7.00
11-15		2.00	5.00

SPOOKY MYSTERIES
No date (1946) (10¢)
Your Guide Publ. Co.

	GD25	FN65	NM94
1-Mr. Spooky, Super Snooper, Pinky, Girl Detective app.	13.50	41.00	110.00

SPOOKY SPOOKTOWN
9/61; No. 2, 9/62 - No. 52, 12/73; No. 53, 10/74 - No. 66, Dec, 1976
Harvey Publications

	GD25	FN65	NM94
1-Casper, Spooky; 68 pgs. begin	12.00	36.00	120.00
2	6.50	19.50	65.00
3-5	4.00	12.00	40.00
6-10	2.60	7.80	26.00
11-20	2.25	6.75	18.00
21-39: 39-Last 68 pg. issue	1.75	5.25	14.00
40-45: All 52 pgs.	1.25	3.75	10.00
46-66: 61-Hot Stuff/Spooky team-up story		2.00	5.00

SPORT COMICS (Becomes True Sport Picture Stories #5 on)
Oct, 1940 (No mo.) - No. 4, Nov, 1941
Street & Smith Publications

	GD25	FN65	NM94
1-Life story of Lou Gehrig	42.00	126.00	375.00
2	24.00	71.00	190.00
3,4	20.00	60.00	160.00

SPORT LIBRARY (See Charlton Sport Library)

SPORTS ACTION (Formerly Sport Stars)
No. 2, Feb, 1950 - No. 14, Sept, 1952
Marvel/Atlas Comics (ACI No. 2,3/SAI No. 4-14)

	GD25	FN65	NM94
2-Powell painted-c; George Gipp life story	28.00	83.00	220.00
3-Everett-a	17.50	53.00	140.00
4-11,14: Weiss-a	15.50	47.00	125.00
12,13: 12-Everett-c. 13-Krigstein-a	17.50	53.00	140.00

NOTE: *Title may have changed after No. 3, to Crime Must Lose No. 4 on, due to publisher change.* ***Sol Brodsky*** *c-4-7, 13, 14.* ***Maneely*** *c-3, 8-11.*

SPORT STARS
Feb-Mar, 1946 - No. 4, Aug-Sept, 1946 (Half comic, half photo magazine)
Parents' Magazine Institute (Sport Stars)

	GD25	FN65	NM94
1- "How Tarzan Got That Way" story of Johnny Weissmuller	31.00	94.00	250.00
2-Baseball greats	20.00	60.00	160.00
3,4	17.50	53.00	140.00

SPORT STARS (Becomes Sports Action #2 on)
Nov, 1949 (52 pgs.)
Marvel Comics (ACI)

	GD25	FN65	NM94
1-Knute Rockne; painted-c	28.00	84.00	225.00

SPORT THRILLS (Formerly Dick Cole; becomes Jungle Thrills #16)
No. 11, Nov, 1950 - No. 15, Nov, 1951
Star Publications

	GD25	FN65	NM94
11-Dick Cole begins, ends #13?; Ted Williams & Ty Cobb life stories	23.00	68.00	180.00
12-Joe DiMaggio, Phil Rizzuto stories & photos on-c; L.B. Cole-c/a	17.50	53.00	140.00
13-15-All L. B. Cole-c. 13-Jackie Robinson, Pee Wee Reese stories & photo on-c. 14-Johnny Weissmuler life story	17.50	53.00	140.00
Accepted Reprint #11 (#15 on-c, nd); L.B. Cole-c	5.70	17.00	35.00
Accepted Reprint #12 (nd); L.B. Cole-c; Joe DiMaggio & Phil Rizzuto life stories-r/#12	5.70	17.00	35.00

SPOTLIGHT (TV)
Sept, 1978 - No. 4, Mar, 1979 (Hanna-Barbera)
Marvel Comics Group

	GD25	FN65	NM94
1-Huckleberry Hound, Yogi Bear; Shaw-a	1.85	5.50	15.00
2,4: 2-Quick Draw McGraw, Augie Doggie, Snooper & Blabber. 4-Magilla Gorilla, Snagglepuss	1.25	3.75	10.00
3-The Jetsons; Yakky Doodle	1.85	5.50	15.00

SPOTLIGHT COMICS (Becomes Red Seal Comics #14 on?)
Nov, 1944 - No. 3, 1945
Harry 'A' Chesler (Our Army, Inc.)

	GD25	FN65	NM94
1-The Black Dwarf (cont'd in Red Seal?), The Veiled Avenger, & Barry Kuda begin; Tuska-c	47.00	141.00	425.00
2	40.00	120.00	360.00
3-Injury to eye story (reprinted from Scoop #3)	41.00	123.00	370.00

SPOTTY THE PUP (Becomes Super Pup #4, see Television Puppet Show)
No. 2, Oct-Nov, 1953 - No. 3, Dec-Jan, 1953-54 (Also see Funny Tunes)
Avon Periodicals/Realistic Comics

	GD25	FN65	NM94
2,3	4.00	12.00	24.00
nn (1953, Realistic-r)	2.80	7.00	14.00

SPUNKY (...Junior Cowboy)(...Comics #2 on)
April, 1949 - No. 7, Nov, 1951
Standard Comics

	GD25	FN65	NM94
1,2-Text illos by Frazetta	6.85	21.00	48.00
3-7	4.00	11.00	22.00

SPUNKY THE SMILING SPOOK
Aug, 1957 - No. 4, May, 1958
Ajax/Farrell (World Famous Comics/Four Star Comic Corp.)

	GD25	FN65	NM94
1-Reprints from Frisky Fables	6.50	19.50	45.00
2-4	4.25	13.00	28.00

SPY AND COUNTERSPY (Becomes Spy Hunters #3 on)
Aug-Sept, 1949 - No. 2, Oct-Nov, 1949 (52 pgs.)
American Comics Group

	GD25	FN65	NM94
1-Origin, 1st app. Jonathan Kent, Counterspy	18.00	56.00	140.00
2	12.00	36.00	90.00

SPY CASES (Formerly The Kellys)
No. 26, Sept, 1950 - No. 19, Oct, 1953
Marvel/Atlas Comics (Hercules Publ.)

	GD25	FN65	NM94
26 (#1)	17.00	51.00	130.00
27(#2),28(#3, 2/51): 27-Everett-a; bondage-c	10.00	30.00	75.00
4(4/51) - 7,9,10	9.00	27.00	60.00
8-A-Bomb-c/story	10.00	30.00	70.00
11-19: 10-14-War format	7.50	22.50	50.00

NOTE: ***Sol Brodsky*** *c-1-5, 8, 9, 11-14, 17, 18.* ***Maneely*** *a-8; c-7, 10.* ***Tuska*** *a-7.*

Spy-Hunters #5 © ACG

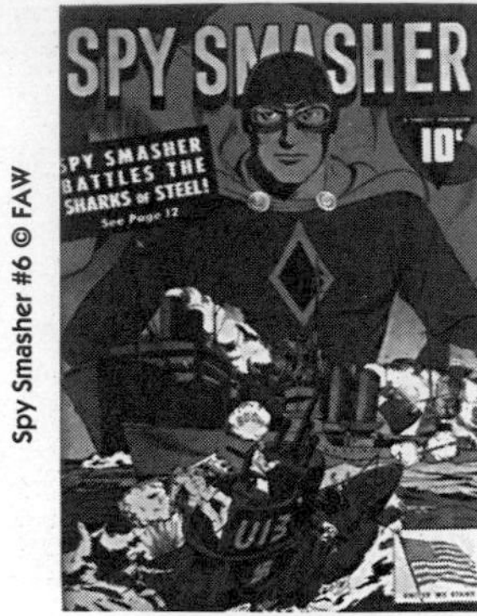

Spy Smasher #6 © FAW

Squee #3 © Jhonen Vasquez

SPY FIGHTERS
March, 1951 - No. 15, July, 1953 (Cases from official records)
Marvel/Atlas Comics (CSI)

	GD25	FN65	NM94
1-Clark Mason begins; Tuska-a; Brodsky-c	19.00	56.00	140.00
2-Tuska-a	10.00	30.00	70.00
3-13: 3-5-Brodsky-c. 7-Heath-c	9.00	27.00	60.00
14,15-Pakula-a(3), Ed Win-a. 15-Brodsky-c	10.00	30.00	65.00

SPY-HUNTERS (Formerly Spy & Counterspy)
No. 3, Dec-Jan, 1949-50 - No. 24, June-July, 1953 (#3-14: 52 pgs.)
American Comics Group

	GD25	FN65	NM94
3-Jonathan Kent continues, ends #10	19.00	56.00	140.00
4-10: 4,8,10-Starr-a	11.00	33.00	80.00
11-15,17-22,24: 18-War-c begin. 21-War-c/stories begin	9.00	27.00	60.00
16-Williamson-a (9 pgs.)	13.00	39.00	95.00
23-Graphic torture, injury to eye panel	17.00	51.00	125.00

NOTE: ***Drucker** a-12. **Whitney** a-many issues; c-7, 8, 10-12, 15, 16.*

SPYMAN (Top Secret Adventures on cover)
Sept, 1966 - No. 3, Feb, 1967 (12¢ issues)
Harvey Publications (Illustrated Humor)

	GD25	FN65	NM94
1-Origin and 1st app. of Spyman. Steranko-a(p)-1st pro work; 1 pg. Neal Adams ad; Tuska-c/a, Crandall-a(i)	4.00	12.00	40.00
2,3: Simon-c. 2-Steranko-a(p)	2.80	8.40	28.00

SPY SMASHER (See Mighty Midget, Whiz & Xmas Comics) (Also see Crime Smasher)
Fall, 1941 - No. 11, Feb, 1943
Fawcett Publications

	GD25	FN65	NM94
1-Spy Smasher begins; silver metallic-c	270.00	810.00	2700.00
2-Raboy-c	133.00	400.00	1200.00
3,4: 3-Bondage-c	89.00	267.00	800.00
5-7: Raboy-a; 6-Raboy-c/a. 7-Part photo-c (movie).	81.00	243.00	725.00
8,11	64.00	192.00	575.00
9-Hitler, Tojo, Mussolini-c.	72.00	216.00	650.00
10-Hitler-c	69.00	207.00	625.00
Well Known Comics (1944, 12 pgs., 8-1/2x10-1/2"), paper-c, glued binding, printed in green; Bestmaid/Samuel Lowe giveaway	13.00	39.00	105.00

SPY THRILLERS (Police Badge No. 479 #5)
Nov, 1954 - No. 4, May, 1955
Atlas Comics (PrPI)

	GD25	FN65	NM94
1-Brodsky c-1,2	16.00	47.00	120.00
2-Last precode (1/55)	10.00	30.00	65.00
3,4	8.35	25.00	55.00

SQUADRON SUPREME
Aug, 1985 - No. 12, Aug, 1986 (Maxi-series)
Marvel Comics Group

	GD25	FN65	NM94
1-Double size			1.50
2-12			1.00
TPB ($24.99) r/#1-12; Alex Ross painted-c; printing inks contain some of the cremated remains of late writer Mark Gruenwald			24.99

SQUALOR
Dec, 1989 - Aug, 1990 ($2.75, limited series)
First Comics

	GD25	FN65	NM94
1-4: Sutton-a		1.10	2.75

SQUEE
Apr, 1997 - Present ($2.95, B&W)
Slave Labor Graphics

	GD25	FN65	NM94
1-3-Jhonen Vasquez-s/a		1.20	3.00

SQUEEKS (Also see Boy Comics)
Oct, 1953 - No. 5, June, 1954
Lev Gleason Publications

	GD25	FN65	NM94
1-Funny animal; Biro-c; Crimebuster's pet monkey "Squeeks" begins	5.70	17.00	40.00
2-Biro-c	4.00	11.00	22.00
3-5: 3-Biro-c	3.60	9.00	18.00

S.R. BISSETTE'S SPIDERBABY COMIX
Aug, 1996 - Present ($3.95, B&W, magazine size)
SpiderBaby Grafix

	GD25	FN65	NM94
Preview-(8/96, $3.95)-Graphic violence & nudity; Laurel & Hardy app.		1.60	4.00
1,2			3.95

S.R. BISSETTE'S TYRANT
Sept, 1994 - Present ($2.95, B&W)
SpiderBaby Grafix

	GD25	FN65	NM94
1-4		2.00	5.00

STAINLESS STEEL RAT
Oct, 1985 - No. 6, Mar, 1986 (Limited series)
Eagle Comics

	GD25	FN65	NM94
1 (52 pgs.; $2.25-c)		.90	2.25
2-6 ($1.50)			1.50

STALKER
June-July, 1975 - No. 4, Dec-Jan, 1975-76
National Periodical Publications

	GD25	FN65	NM94
1-Origin & 1st app; Ditko/Wood-c/a		2.00	5.00
2-4-Ditko/Wood-c/a		1.20	3.00

STALKERS
Apr, 1990 - No. 12, Mar, 1991 ($1.50)
Marvel Comics (Epic Comics)

	GD25	FN65	NM94
1-12: 1-Chadwick-c			1.50

STAMP COMICS (Stamps... on-c; Thrilling Adventures In...#8)
Oct, 1951 - No. 7, Oct, 1952 (No. 1: 15¢)
Youthful Magazines/Stamp Comics, Inc.

	GD25	FN65	NM94
1-('Stamps' on indicia No. 1-3,5,7)	25.00	75.00	200.00
2	14.00	41.00	110.00
3-6: 3,4-Kiefer, Wildey-a	12.00	38.00	100.00
7-Roy Krenkel (4 pgs.)	15.00	45.00	120.00

NOTE: *Promotes stamp collecting; gives stories behind various commemorative stamps. No. 2, 10¢ printed over 15¢ c-price. **Kiefer** a-1-7. **Kirkel** a-1-6. **Napoli** a-2-7. **Palais** a-2-4, 7.*

STANLEY & HIS MONSTER (Formerly The Fox & the Crow)
No. 109, Apr-May, 1968 - No. 112, Oct-Nov, 1968
National Periodical Publications

	GD25	FN65	NM94
109-112	1.85	5.50	15.00

STANLEY & HIS MONSTER
Feb, 1993 - No. 4, May, 1993 ($1.50, limited series)
DC Comics

	GD25	FN65	NM94
1-4			1.50

STAN SHAW'S BEAUTY & THE BEAST
Nov, 1993 ($4.95, one-shot)
Dark Horse Comics

	GD25	FN65	NM94
1		2.00	5.00

STAR
June, 1995 - No. 4, Oct, 1995 ($2.50, limited series)
Image Comics (Highbrow Entertainment)

	GD25	FN65	NM94
1-4		1.00	2.50

STARBLAST
Jan, 1994 - No. 4, Apr, 1994 ($1.75, limited series)

Star Comics V2 #1 © CHES

Star Crossed #3 © Matt Howarth

Stargate: Doomsday World #2 © Le Studio Canal

GD25 FN65 NM94

Marvel Comics

1-($2.00, 52 pgs.)-Nova, Quasar, Black Bolt; painted-c .80 2.00
2-4 .70 1.75

STAR BLAZERS
Apr, 1987 - No. 4, July, 1987 ($1.75, limited series)
Comico

1-4 .70 1.75

STAR BLAZERS
1989 ($1.95/$2.50, limited series)
Comico

1 ($1.95)- Steacy wraparound painted-c on all .80 2.00
2-5 ($2.50) 1.00 2.50

STAR BLAZERS (The Magazine of Space Battleship Yamato)
No. 0, Aug, 1995 - No. 3, Dec, 1995 ($2.95)
Argo Press

0-3 1.20 3.00

STAR BRAND
Oct, 1986 - No. 19, May, 1989 (75¢/$1.25)
Marvel Comics (New Universe)

1-19: 14-begin $1.25-c. 16-19-Byrne story & art. 1.00
Annual 1 (10/87) 1.25

STARCHILD
1992 - No. 12($2.25/$2.50, B&W)
Tailspin Press

1,2-(1992) 1.60 4.00
0-(4/93)-Illos by Chadwick, Eisner, Sim, M. Wagner; $2.50-c begins
1.60 4.00
3-12: 3-(7/93). 4-(11/93). 6-(2/94) 1.60 4.00

STARCHILD: MYTHOPOLIS
July, 1997 - Present ($2.95, B&W, limited series)
Image Comics

0-2-James Owen-s/a 2.95

STAR COMICS
Feb, 1937 - V2#7 (No. 23), Aug, 1939 (#1-6: large size)
Ultem Publ. (Harry 'A' Chesler)/Centaur Publications

V1#1-Dan Hastings (s/f) begins 117.00 350.00 1050.00
2 56.00 168.00 500.00
3-6 (#6, 9/37): 4,5-Little Nemo-c/stories 52.00 156.00 470.00
7-9: 8-Severed head centerspread; Impy & Little Nemo by Winsor McCay Jr, Popeye app. by Bob Wood; Mickey Mouse & Popeye app. as toys in Santa's bag on-c; X-Mas-c 46.00 138.00 410.00
10 (1st Centaur; 3/38)-Impy by Winsor McCay Jr; Don Marlow by Guardineer begins 64.00 192.00 580.00
11-1st Jack Cole comic-a, 1 pg. (4/38) 46.00 138.00 410.00
12-15: 12-Riders of the Golden West begins; Little Nemo app. 15-Speed Silvers by Gustavson & The Last Pirate by Burgos begins
40.00 120.00 360.00
16 (12/38)-The Phantom Rider & his horse Thunder begins, ends V2#6
40.00 120.00 360.00
V2#1(#17, 2/39)-Phantom Rider-c (only non-funny-c)
40.00 120.00 360.00
2-7(#18-23): 2-Diana Deane by Tarpe Mills app. 3-Drama of Hollywood by Mills begins. 7-Jungle Queen app. 36.00 108.00 320.00

NOTE: *Biro c-6, 9, 10.* ***Burgos*** *a-15, 16, V2#1-7.* ***Ken Ernst*** *a-10, 12, 14.* ***Filchock*** *c-15, 18, 22.* ***Gill Fox*** *c-14, 19.* ***Guardineer*** *a-6, 8-14.* ***Gustavson*** *a-13-16, V2#1-7.* ***Winsor McCay*** *c-4, 5.* ***Tarpe Mills*** *a-15, V2#1-7.* ***Schwab*** *c-20, 23.* ***Bob Wood*** *a-10, 12, 13; c-7, 8.*

STAR COMICS MAGAZINE
Dec, 1986 - No. 13, 1988 ($1.50, digest-size)
Marvel Comics (Star Comics)

1-13 2.00 5.00

S.T.A.R. CORPS
Nov, 1993 - No. 6, Apr, 1994 ($1.50, limited series)
DC Comics

1-6: 1,2-Austin-c(i). 1-Superman app. 1.50

STAR CROSSED
June, 1997 - No. 3, Aug, 1997 ($2.50, limited series)
DC Comics (Helix)

1-3-Matt Howarth-s/a 1.00 2.50

STARDUST (See Neil Gaiman and Charles Vess' Stardust)

STAR FEATURE COMICS
1963
I. W. Enterprises

Reprint #9-Stunt-Man Stetson-r/Feat. Comics #141 2.00 5.00

STARFIRE (See New Teen Titans & Teen Titans #18)
Aug-Sept, 1976 - No. 8, Oct-Nov, 1977
National Periodical Publications/DC Comics

1-Origin (CCA stamp fell off cover art; so it was approved by code)
2.40 6.00
2-8 1.60 4.00

STARGATE (Movie)
July, 1996 - No. 4, Oct, 1996 ($2.95, limited series)
Entity Comics

1-4: Based on film 1.20 3.00
1-4-($3.50): Special Edition foil-c 1.40 3.50

STARGATE: DOOMSDAY WORLD (Movie)
Nov, 1996 - No. 3, Jan, 1997 ($2.95, limited series)
Entity Comics

1-3 1.20 3.00
1-3-($3.50)-Foil-c 1.40 3.50

STARGATE: ONE NATION UNDER RA (Movie)
Apr, 1997 ($2.75, B&W, one-shot)
Entity Comics

1-($2.75) 1.10 2.75
1-($3.50)-Foil-c 1.40 3.50

STARGATE: REBELLION (Movie)
May/June, 1997 - No. 3, Nov, 1997 ($2.75, B&W, limited series)
Entity Comics

1-3 1.10 2.75
1-3-($3.50)-Gold foil-c 1.40 3.50

STARGATE: THE NEW ADVENTURES COLLECTION (Movie)
Dec, 1997 ($5.95, B&W)
Entity Comics

1-Regular and photo-c 5.95

STARGATE: UNDERWORLD (Movie)
May, 1997 ($2.75, B&W, one-shot)
Entity Comics

1 1.10 2.75

STAR HUNTERS (See DC Super Stars #16)
Oct-Nov, 1977 - No. 7, Oct-Nov, 1978
National Periodical Publications/DC Comics

1,7: 1-Newton-a(p). 7-Giant 1.60 4.00
2-6 1.20 3.00

NOTE: ***Buckler*** *a-4-7p; c-1-7p.* ***Layton*** *a-1-5i; c-1-6i.* ***Nasser*** *a-3p.* ***Sutton*** *a-6i.*

STARJAMMERS (See X-Men Spotlight on Starjammers)

STARJAMMERS (Also see Uncanny X-Men)

Starlord #2 © MEG

Starmam #29 (2nd Series) © DC

Star Ranger V2 #51 © CEN

Oct, 1995 - No. 4, Jan, 1996 ($2.95, limited series)
Marvel Comics

1-4: Foil-c; Ellis scripts 1.20 3.00

STARK TERROR
Dec, 1970 - No. 5, Aug, 1971 (B&W, magazine, 52 pgs.)
Stanley Publications

1-Bondage, torture-c 3.50 10.50 35.00
2-4 (Gillmor/Aragon-r) 2.50 7.50 20.00
5 (ACG-r) 2.00 6.00 16.00

STARLET O'HARA IN HOLLYWOOD (Teen-age) (Also see Cookie)
Dec, 1948 - No. 4, Sept, 1949
Standard Comics

1-Owen Fitzgerald-a in all 15.00 45.00 120.00
2 10.00 30.00 80.00
3,4 8.75 26.25 70.00

STAR-LORD THE SPECIAL EDITION (Also see Marvel Comics Super Special #10, Marvel Premiere & Preview & Marvel Spotlight V2#6,7)
Feb, 1982 (one-shot, direct sales) (1st Baxter paper comic)
Marvel Comics Group

1-Byrne/Austin-a; Austin-c; 8 pgs. of new-a by Golden (p); Dr. Who story by Dave Gibbons; 1st deluxe format comic 1.20 3.00

STARLORD
Dec, 1996 - No. 3, Feb, 1997 ($2.50, limited series)
Marvel Comics

1-3-Timothy Zahn-s 1.00 2.50

STARLORD MEGAZINE
Nov, 1996 ($2.95, one-shot)
Marvel Comics

1-Reprints w/preview of new series 1.20 3.00

STARMAN (1st Series) (Also see Justice League & War of the Gods)
Oct, 1988 - No. 45, Apr, 1992 ($1.00)
DC Comics

1-25,27-45: 1-Origin. 4-Intro The Power Elite. 9,10,34-Batman app. 14-Superman app. 17-Power Girl app. 27-Starman (David Knight) app. 28-Starman disguised as Superman; leads into Superman #50. 38-War of the Gods x-over. 42-Lobo cameo.42-45-Eclipso-c/stories (#43,44 with Lobo) .80 2.00
26-Ist app. David Knight (G.A.Starman's son). 1.20 3.00

STARMAN (2nd Series) (Also see The Golden Age, Showcase 95 #12, Showcase 96 #4,5)
No. 0, Oct, 1994 - Present ($1.95/$2.25)
DC Comics

0,1: 0-James Robinson scripts, Tony Harris-c/a(p) & Wade Von Grawbadger-a(i) begins; Sins of the Father storyline begins, ends #3; 1st app. new Starman (Jack Knight); reintro of the G.A. Mist & G.A. Shade; 1st app. Nash; David Knight dies 1.25 3.75 10.00
2-8: 2-Reintro Charity from Forbidden Tales of Dark Mansion. 3-Reintro/2nd app "Blue" Starman (1st app. in 1st Issue Special #12); Will Payton app. (both cameos). 5-David Knight app. 6-The Shade "Times Past" story; Teddy Kristiansen-a. 7-The Black Pirate cameo 2.00 5.00
9-32: 9-Begin $2.25-c. 10-1st app. new Mist.(Nash) 11-JSA "Times Past" story; Matt Smith-a. 12-Sins of the Child storyline begins, ends #16. 17-The Black Pirate app. 18-G.A. Starman "Times Past" story; John Watkiss-a. 19-David Knight app. 20-23-G.A. Sandman app. 24-26-Demon Quest; all 3 covers make-up triptych. 1.20 3.00
33-38: 33-36-Batman-c/app. 37-David Knight and deceased JSA members app. 38-Nash vs. Justice League Europe. 39,40-Crossover w/ Power of Shazam! #35,36; Bulletman app 2.25
Annual 1 (1996, $3.50)-Legends of the Dead Earth story; Prince Gavyn & G.A. Starman stories; J.H. Williams III, Bret Blevins, Craig Hamilton-c/a(p) 1.60 4.00
Annual 2 (1997, $3.95)-Pulp Heroes story; 3.95
Night and Day-($14.95, trade paperback)-r/#7-10,12-16 15.00
Sins of the Father-($12.95, trade paperback)-r/#0-5 13.00

STARMASTERS
Mar, 1984 ($1.50, one-shot)
Americomics

1-Origin The Women of W.O.S.P. & Breed 1.50

STAR PRESENTATION, A (Formerly My Secret Romance #1,2; Spectacular Stories #4 on) (Also see This Is Suspense)
No. 3, May, 1950
Fox Features Syndicate (Hero Books)

3-Dr. Jekyll & Mr. Hyde by Wood & Harrison (reprinted in Startling Terror Tales #10); "The Repulsing Dwarf" by Wood; Wood-c 42.00 126.00 375.00

STAR QUEST COMIX (Warren Presents... on cover)
Oct, 1978
Warren Publications

1-Corben, Maroto, Neary-a 1.00 3.00 8.00

STAR RAIDERS (See DC Graphic Novel #1)

STAR RANGER (Cowboy Comics #13 on)
Feb, 1937 - No. 12, May, 1938 (Large size: No. 1-6)
Ultem Publ./Centaur Publications

1-(1st Western comic)-Ace & Deuce, Air Plunder; Creig Flessel-a 122.00 366.00 1100.00
2 54.00 162.00 490.00
3-6 47.00 141.00 425.00
7-9: 8-Christmas-c 38.00 113.00 340.00
V2#10 (1st Centaur; 3/38) 66.00 198.00 590.00
11,12 50.00 150.00 450.00

NOTE: ***J. Cole*** *a-10, 12; c-12.* ***Ken Ernst*** *a-11.* ***Gill Fox*** *a-8(illo), 9, 10.* ***Guardineer*** *a-1, 3, 6, 7, 8(illos), 9, 10, 12.* ***Gustavson*** *a-8-10, 12.* ***Fred Schwab*** *c-2-11.* ***Bob Wood*** *a-8-10.*

STAR RANGER FUNNIES (Formerly Cowboy Comics)
V1#15, Oct, 1938 - V2#5, Oct, 1939
Centaur Publications

V1#15-Eisner, Gustavson-a 78.00 234.00 700.00
V2#1 (1/39) 54.00 162.00 490.00
2-5: 2-Night Hawk by Gustavson. 4-Kit Carson app. 48.00 144.00 430.00

NOTE: ***Jack Cole*** *a-V2#1, 3; c-V2#1.* ***Filchock*** *c-V2#2, 3.* ***Guardineer*** *a-V2#3.* ***Gustavson*** *a-V2#2.* ***Pinajian*** *c/a-V2#5.*

STAR REACH CLASSICS
Mar, 1984 - No. 6, Aug, 1984 ($1.50, Baxter paper)
Eclipse Comics

1-6: Neal Adams-r/Star Reach #1 1.50

NOTE: ***Dave Sim*** *a-1.* ***Starlin*** *a-1.*

STARR FLAGG, UNDERCOVER GIRL (See Undercover...)

STARRIORS
Aug, 1984 - Feb, 1985 (Limited series) (Based on Tomy toys)
Marvel Comics

1-4 1.00

STARS AND STRIPES COMICS
No. 2, May, 1941 - No. 6, Dec, 1941
Centaur Publications

2(#1)-The Shark, The Iron Skull, A-Man, The Amazing Man, Mighty Man, Minimidget begin; The Voice & Dash Dartwell, the Human Meteor, Reef Kinkaid app.; Gustavson Flag-c 178.00 534.00 1600.00
3-Origin Dr. Synthe; The Black Panther app. 103.00 309.00 925.00
4-Origin/1st app. The Stars and Stripes; injury to eye-c

Star Slammers #1 © Walt Simonson

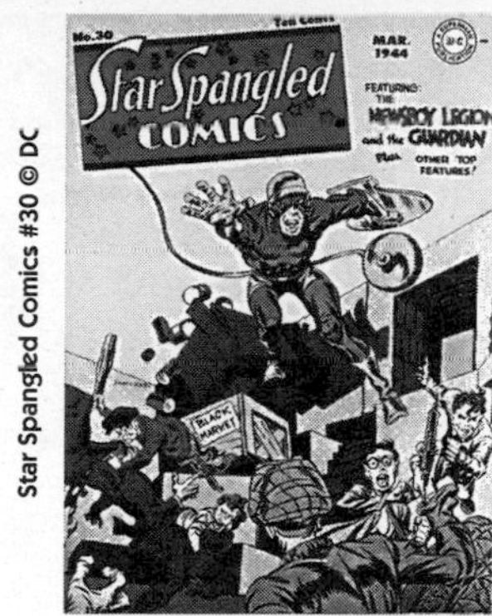

Star Spangled Comics #30 © DC

Star Spangled War Stories #4 © DC

GD25 FN65 NM94

92.00 276.00 825.00
5(#5 on cover & inside) 64.00 192.00 575.00
5(#6)-(#5 on cover, #6 on inside) 64.00 192.00 575.00
NOTE: ***Gustavson** c/a-3. **Myron Strauss** c-4, 5(#5), 5(#6).*

STAR SEED (Formerly Powers That Be)
No. 7, 1996 - Present ($2.95)
Broadway Comics

7-9 1.20 3.00

STARSHIP TROOPERS
1997 - No. 2, 1997 ($2.95, limited series)
Dark Horse Comics

1,2-Movie adaption 2.95

STARSHIP TROOPERS: BRUTE CREATIONS
1997 ($2.95, one-shot)
Dark Horse Comics

1 2.95

STARSHIP TROOPERS: INSECT TOUCH
1997 - No. 3, 1997 ($2.95, limited series)
Dark Horse Comics

1-3 2.95

STAR SLAMMERS (See Marvel Graphic Novel #6)
May, 1994 - No. 4, Aug, 1994 ($2.50, unfinished limited series)
Malibu Comics (Bravura)

1-4: W. Simonson-a/stories; contain Bravura stamps 1.00 2.50

STAR SLAMMERS SPECIAL
June, 1996 ($2.95, one-shot)
Dark Horse Comics (Legend)

nn-Simonson-c/a/scripts; concludes Bravura limited series. 1.20 3.00

STARSLAYER
Feb, 1982 - No. 6, Apr, 1983; No. 7, Aug, 1983 - No. 34, Nov, 1985
Pacific Comics/First Comics No. 7 on

1-Origin & 1st app.; excessive blood & gore; 1 pg. Rocketeer cameo which continues in #2 1.20 3.00
2-Origin/1st full app. the Rocketeer (4/82) by Dave Stevens (Chapter 1 of Rocketeer saga; see Pacific Presents #1,2) 1.00 3.00 8.00
3-Chapter 2 of Rocketeer saga by Stevens 2.00 5.00
4,6,7: 7-Grell-a ends .80 2.00
5-2nd app. Groo the Wanderer by Aragones 2.40 6.00
8-34: 10-1st app. Grimjack (11/83, ends #17). 18-Starslayer meets Grimjack. 20-The Black Flame begins (9/84, 1st app.), ends #33. 27-Book length Black Flame story 1.00
NOTE: ***Grell** a-1-7; c-1-8. **Stevens** back c-2, 3. **Sutton** a-17p, 20-22p, 24-27p, 29-33p.*

STARSLAYER (The Director's Cut)
June, 1994 - No. 8, Dec, 1995 ($2.50)
Acclaim Comics (Windjammer)

1-8: Mike Grell-c/a/scripts 1.00 2.50

STAR SPANGLED COMICS (Star Spangled War Stories #131 on)
Oct, 1941 - No. 130, July, 1952
National Periodical Publications

1-Origin/1st app. Tarantula; Captain X of the R.A.F., Star Spangled Kid (see Action #40), Armstrong of the Army begin; Robot-c 350.00 1050.00 3500.00
2 133.00 400.00 1200.00
3-5 83.00 250.00 750.00
6-Last Armstrong/Army; Penniless Palmer begins 53.00 159.00 475.00

GD25 FN65 VF82 NM94

7-(4/42)-Origin/1st app. The Guardian by S&K, & Robotman (by Paul Cassidy & created by Siegel);The Newsboy Legion (1st app.), Robotman & TNT begin; last Captain X 600.00 1800.00 3600.00 6000.00

GD25 FN65 NM94

(Estimated up to 100 total copies exist, 5 in NM/Mint)

GD25 FN65 NM94

8-Origin TNT & Dan the Dyna-Mite 178.00 534.00 1600.00
9,10 144.00 432.00 1300.00
11-17 106.00 318.00 950.00
18-Origin Star Spangled Kid 133.00 400.00 1200.00
19-Last Tarantula 104.00 312.00 935.00
20-Liberty Belle begins (5/43) 104.00 312.00 935.00
21-29-Last S&K issue; 23-Last TNT. 25-Robotman by Jimmy Thompson begins. 29-Intro Robbie the Robotdog 86.00 258.00 775.00
30-40: 31-S&K-c 44.00 132.00 400.00
41-50: 41,49,-Kirby-c. 50-1st S.A. issue 40.00 120.00 360.00
51-64: Last Newsboy Legion & The Guardian; last Liberty Belle? 51-Kirby-c. 53 by S&K 40.00 120.00 360.00
65-Robin begins with c/app. (2/47); Batman cameo in 1 panel; Robin-c begins, end #95 122.00 366.00 1100.00
66-Batman cameo in Robin story 72.00 216.00 650.00
67,68,70-80: 72-Burnley Robin-c 58.00 174.00 525.00
69-Origin/1st app. Tomahawk by F. Ray (6/47) 89.00 267.00 800.00
81-Origin Merry, Girl of 1000 Gimmicks in Star Spangled Kid story 44.00 132.00 400.00
82,85: 82-Last Robotman? 44.00 132.00 400.00
83-Tomahawk enters the lost valley, a land of dinosaurs; Capt. Compass begins, ends #130 44.00 132.00 400.00
84,87 (Rare): 87-Batman cameo in Robin 69.00 207.00 625.00
86-Batman cameo in Robin story; last Star Spangled Kid 50.00 150.00 450.00
88(1/49)-94: Batman-c/stories in all. 91-Federal Men begin, end #93. 94-Manhunters Around the World begin, end #121 53.00 159.00 475.00
95-Batman story; last Robin-c 49.00 147.00 440.00
96,98-Batman cameo in Robin stories. 96-1st Tomahawk-c (also #97-121) 35.00 105.00 280.00
97,99 29.00 88.00 235.00
100 (1/50)-Pre-Bat-Hound tryout in Robin story (pre-dates Batman #92). 36.00 108.00 290.00
101-109,118,119,121: 121-Last Tomahawk-c 27.00 81.00 215.00
110,111,120-Batman cameo in Robin stories. 120-Last 52 pg. issue 28.00 84.00 225.00
112-Batman & Robin story 30.00 90.00 240.00
113-Frazetta-a (10 pgs.) 36.00 108.00 310.00
114-Retells Robin's origin (3/51); Batman & Robin story 37.00 112.00 335.00
115,117-Batman app. in Robin stories 29.00 88.00 235.00
116-Flag-c 29.00 86.00 230.00
122-(11/51)-Ghost Breaker-c/stories begin (origin/1st app.), ends #130 (Ghost Breaker covers #122-130) 33.00 98.00 260.00
123-126,128,129 22.00 66.00 175.00
127-Batman cameo 23.00 69.00 185.00
130-Batman cameo in Robin story 24.00 73.00 195.00
NOTE: *Most all issues after #29 signed by Simon & Kirby are not by them. **Bill Ely** c-122-130. **Mortimer** c-65-74(most), 76-95(most). **Fred Ray** c-96-106, 109, 110, 112, 113, 115-120. **S&K** c-7-31, 33, 34, 36, 37, 39, 40, 48, 49, 50-54, 56-58. **Hal Sherman** c-1-6. **Dick Sprang** c-75.*

STAR SPANGLED KID (See Action #40, Leading Comics & Star Spangled Comics)

STAR SPANGLED WAR STORIES (Formerly Star Spangled Comics #1-130; Becomes The Unknown Soldier #205 on) (See Showcase)
No. 131, 8/52 - No. 133, 10/52; No. 3, 11/52 - No. 204, 2-3/77
National Periodical Publications

131(#1) 86.00 258.00 775.00
132 63.00 189.00 565.00
133-Used in **POP**, pg. 94 52.00 156.00 470.00
3-6: 4-Devil Dog Dugan app. 6-Evans-a 31.00 94.00 250.00
7-10 25.00 75.00 200.00
11-20 22.00 66.00 175.00
21-30: 30-Last precode (2/55) 19.00 56.00 150.00

Star Spangled War Stories #38 © DC

Startling Comics #8 © NEDOR

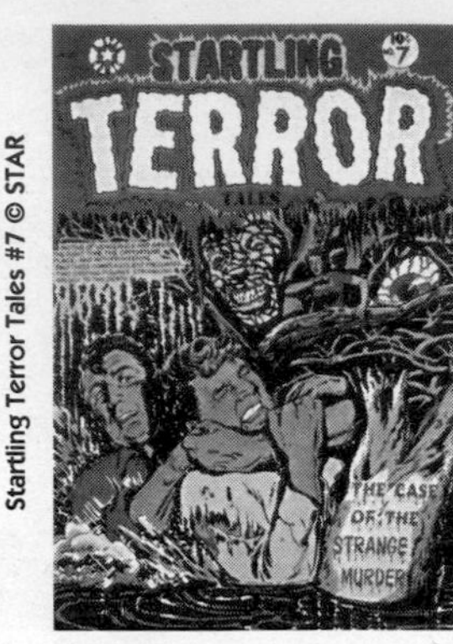

Startling Terror Tales #7 © STAR

	GD25	FN65	NM94
31-33,35-40	10.50	32.00	105.00
34-Krigstein-a	11.00	33.00	110.00
41-50: 45-1st DC grey tone-c (5/56)	10.00	30.00	100.00
51-83: 67-Easy Co. story without Sgt. Rock	7.00	21.00	70.00
84-Origin Mlle. Marie	15.00	45.00	150.00
85-89-Mlle. Marie in all	8.50	25.50	85.00
90-1st dinosaur issue-c/story (4-5/60)	35.00	105.00	380.00
91,93-No dinosaur stories	6.00	18.00	60.00
92,95-99: All dinosaur-c/s.	12.00	36.00	120.00
94 (12/60)- "Ghost Ace" story; Baron Von Richter as The Enemy Ace (pre-dates Our Army... #151)	14.50	44.00	145.00
100-Dinosaur-c/story.	14.00	42.00	140.00
101-115: All dinosaur issues	8.50	25.50	85.00
116-125,127-133,135-137-Last dinosaur story; Heath Birdman-#129,131	7.50	22.50	75.00
126-No dinosaur story	5.00	15.00	50.00
134-Dinosaur story; Neal Adams-a	8.50	25.50	85.00
138-New Enemy Ace-c/stories begin by Joe Kubert (4-5/68), end #150 (also see Our Army at War #151 and Showcase #57)	9.00	27.00	90.00
139-Origin Enemy Ace (7/68)	8.00	24.00	80.00
140-143,145: 145-Last 12¢ issue (6-7/69)	5.00	15.00	50.00
144-Neal Adams/Kubert-a	5.50	16.50	55.00
146-Enemy Ace-c only	3.30	9.90	33.00
147,148-New Enemy Ace stories	4.00	12.00	40.00
149,150-Last new Enemy Ace by Kubert. Viking Prince by Kubert	3.50	10.50	35.00
151-1st Unknown Soldier (6-7/70); Enemy Ace-r begin (from Our Army at War, Showcase & SSWS); end #161	12.00	36.00	120.00
152,153,155-Enemy Ace reprints	2.50	7.50	20.00
154-Origin Unknown Soldier	9.00	27.00	90.00
156-1st Battle Album; Unknown Soldier story; Kubert-c/a	2.50	7.50	20.00
157-Sgt. Rock x-over in Unknown Soldier story.	1.50	4.50	12.00
158-163-(52 pgs.): 160-Unknown Soldier story; Kubert-c/a. 161-Last Enemy Ace-r	1.50	4.50	12.00
164-199,201-204: 181-183-Enemy Ace vs. Balloon Buster serial app; Frank Thorne-a.	1.00	2.80	7.00
200-Enemy Ace back-up	1.00	3.00	8.00

NOTE: ***Chaykin*** *a-167.* ***Drucker*** *a-59, 61, 64, 66, 67, 73-84.* ***Estrada*** *a-149.* ***John Giunta*** *a-72.* ***Glanzman*** *a-167, 171, 172, 174.* ***Heath*** *a-122, 132, 133; c-67, 122, 132-134.* ***Kaluta*** *a-197i; c-167.* ***G. Kane*** *a-169.* ***Kubert*** *a-6-163(most later issues), 200.* ***Maurer*** *a-160, 165.* ***Severin*** *a-65, 162.* ***S&K*** *c-7-31, 33, 34, 37, 40.* ***Simonson*** *a-170, 172, 174, 180.* ***Sutton*** *a-168.* ***Thorne*** *a-183.* ***Toth*** *a-164.* ***Wildey*** *a-161. Suicide Squad in 110, 116-118, 120, 121, 127.*

STARSTREAM (Adventures in Science Fiction)(See Questar illustrated)
1976 (79¢, 68 pgs, cardboard-c)
Whitman/Western Publishing Co.

	GD25	FN65	NM94
1-4: 1-Bolle-a. 2-4-McWilliams & Bolle-a	1.00	3.00	8.00

STARSTRUCK
Feb, 1985 - No. 6, Feb, 1986 ($1.50, mature)
Marvel Comics (Epic Comics)

	GD25	FN65	NM94
1-6: Kaluta-a.		1.20	3.00

STARSTRUCK
Aug, 1990 - No. 4, Nov?, 1990 ($2.95, B&W, limited series, 52pgs.)
Dark Horse Comics

	GD25	FN65	NM94
1-3:Kaluta-r/Epic series plus new-c/a in all		1.20	3.00
4 (68, pgs.)-contains 2 trading cards		1.20	3.00

STAR STUDDED
1945 (25¢, 132 pgs.); 1945 (196 pgs.)
Cambridge House/Superior Publishers

	GD25	FN65	NM94
nn-Captain Combat by Giunta, Ghost Woman, Commandette, & Red Rogue app.; Infantino-a	23.00	69.00	185.00
nn-The Cadet, Edison Bell, Hoot Gibson, Jungle Lil (196 pgs.); copies vary; Blue Beetle in some	19.00	56.00	150.00

STAR TEAM
1977 (6-1/2x5", 20 pgs.)
Marvel Comics Group (Ideal Toy Giveaway)

	GD25	FN65	NM94
nn	1.00	3.00	8.00

STARTLING COMICS
June, 1940 - No. 53, May, 1948
Better Publications (Nedor)

	GD25	FN65	NM94
1-Origin Captain Future-Man Of Tomorrow, Mystico (By Eisner/Fine), The Wonder Man; The Masked Rider & his horse Pinto begins; Masked Rider formerly in pulps; drug use story	178.00	534.00	1600.00
2 -Don Davis, Espionage Ace begins	71.00	213.00	640.00
3	58.00	174.00	515.00
4	43.00	129.00	390.00
5-9	36.00	108.00	315.00
10-The Fighting Yank begins (9/41, origin/1st app.)	240.00	720.00	2400.00
11-2nd app. Fighting Yank	83.00	240.00	740.00
12-Hitler, Hirohito, Mussolini-c	58.00	174.00	520.00
13-15	43.00	129.00	390.00
16-Origin The Four Comrades; not in #32,35	49.00	147.00	440.00
17-Last Masked Rider & Mystico	36.00	108.00	300.00
18-Pyroman begins (12/42, origin)(also see America's Best Comics #3 for 1st app., 11/42)	75.00	225.00	675.00
19	36.00	108.00	310.00
20-The Oracle begins (3/43); not in issues 26,28,33,34	36.00	108.00	310.00
21-Origin The Ape, Oracle's enemy	36.00	108.00	325.00
22-33	36.00	108.00	300.00
34-Origin The Scarab & only app.	36.00	108.00	300.00
35-Hypodermic syringe attacks Fighting Yank in drug story	36.00	108.00	300.00
36-43: 36-Last Four Comrades. 38-Bondage/torture-c. 40-Last Capt. Future & Oracle. 41-Front Page Peggy begins; A-Bomb-c. 43-Last Pyroman	33.00	98.00	260.00
44-Lance Lewis, Space Detective begins; Ingels-c; sci/fi-c begin	44.00	132.00	400.00
45-Tygra begins (intro/origin, 5/47); Ingels-c/a (splash pg. & inside f/c B&W ad	44.00	132.00	400.00
46-Ingels-c/a	44.00	132.00	400.00
47,48,50-53: 50,51-Sea-Eagle app.	42.00	126.00	375.00
49-Classic Schomburg Robot-c; last Fighting Yank	240.00	720.00	2300.00

NOTE: ***Ingels*** *a-44, 45; c-44, 45, 46(wash).* ***Schomburg*** *(**Xela**) c-21-43; 47-53 (airbrush).* ***Tuska*** *c-45? Bondage c-16, 21, 37, 46-49. Captain Future c-1-9, 13, 14. Fighting Yank c-10-12, 15-17, 21, 22, 24, 26, 28, 30, 32, 34, 36, 38, 40, 42. Pyroman c-18-20, 23, 25, 27, 29, 31, 33, 35, 37, 39, 41, 43.*

STARTLING TERROR TALES
No. 10, May, 1952 - No. 14, Feb, 1953; No. 4, Apr, 1953 - No. 11, 1954
Star Publications

	GD25	FN65	NM94
10-(1st Series)-Wood/Harrison-a (r/A Star Presentation #3) Disbrow/Cole-c; becomes 4 different titles after #10; becomes Confessions of Love #11 on, The Horrors #11 on, Terrifying Tales #11 on, Terrors of the Jungle #11 on & continues w/Startling Terror #11	51.00	155.00	450.00
11-(8/52)-L. B. Cole Spider-c; r-Fox's "A Feature Presentation" #5 (blue-c)	42.00	126.00	375.00
11-Black-c (variant; believed to be a pressrun change) (Unique)			600.00
12,14	17.50	53.00	140.00
13-Jo-Jo-r; Disbrow-a	19.00	56.00	150.00
4-7,9,11(1953-54) (2nd Series): 11-New logo	15.50	47.00	125.00
8-Spanking scene-r from inside front-c of All Famous Crime Stories (Fox Giant) (1949)	15.50	47.00	125.00
10-Disbrow-a	17.50	53.00	140.00

NOTE: ***L. B. Cole*** *covers-all issues.* ***Palais*** *a-V2#8r, V2#11r.*

Star Trek #3 © Paramount

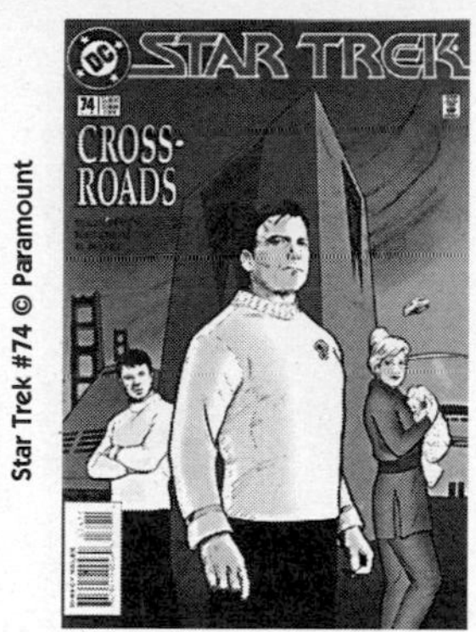

Star Trek #74 © Paramount

MARVEL
STAR TREK
Paramount COMICS
DEEP SPACE NINE
PLAGUE!
A FATHER IN GRIEF... A STATION IN PANIC!

Star Trek: Deep Space Nine #4 © Paramount

STAR TREK (TV) (See Dan Curtis Giveaways, Dynabrite Comics & Power Record Comics)
7/67; No. 2, 6/68; No. 3, 12/68; No. 4, 6/69 - No. 61, 3/79
Gold Key

	GD25	FN65	NM94
1-Photo-c begin, end #9	42.00	125.00	460.00
2	26.00	78.00	285.00
2 (rare variation w/photo back-c)	18.00	55.00	400.00
3-5	17.00	52.00	190.00
3 (rare variation w/photo back-c)	26.00	77.00	280.00
6-9	14.00	42.00	155.00
10-20	7.00	22.00	80.00
21-30	5.50	16.50	60.00
31-40	3.60	11.00	40.00
41-61: 52-Drug propaganda story	2.25	6.75	25.00
...the Enterprise Logs nn (8/76)-Golden Press, ($1.95, 224 pgs.)-r/#1-8 plus 7 pgs. by McWilliams (#11185)-Photo-c	2.50	7.50	24.00
...the Enterprise Logs Vol. 2 ('76)-r/#9-17 (#11187)-Photo-c	2.50	7.50	24.00
...the Enterprise Logs Vol. 3 ('77)-r/#18-26 (#11188); McWilliams-a (4 pgs.)-Photo-c	2.50	7.50	24.00
Star Trek Vol. 4 (Winter '77)-Reprints #27,28,30-34,36,38 (#11189) plus 3 pgs. new art	2.50	7.50	24.00

NOTE: ***McWilliams*** *a-38, 40-44, 46-61. #29 reprints #1; #35 reprints #4; #37 reprints #5; #45 reprints #7. The tabloids all have photo covers and blank inside covers. Painted covers #10-44, 46-59.*

STAR TREK
April, 1980 - No. 18, Feb, 1982
Marvel Comics Group

	GD25	FN65	NM94
1: 1-3-r/Marvel Super Special; movie adapt.		2.40	6.00
2-16: 5-Miller-c		2.00	5.00
17 (scarce)	1.25	3.75	10.00
18-Last issue	2.50	7.50	20.00

NOTE: ***Austin*** *c-18i.* ***Buscema*** *a-13.* ***Gil Kane*** *a-15.* ***Nasser*** *c/a-7.* ***Simonson*** *c-17.*

STAR TREK (Also see Who's Who In Star Trek)
Feb, 1984 - No. 56, Nov, 1988 (75¢, Mando paper)
DC Comics

	GD25	FN65	NM94
1-Sutton-a(p) begins	1.10	3.30	9.00
2-5		2.00	5.00
6-10: 7-Origin Saavik		1.60	4.00
11-20: 19-Walter Koenig story		1.20	3.00
21-32		1.00	2.50
33-($1.25, 52 pgs.)-20th anniversary issue		1.20	3.00
34-49: 37-Painted-c. 49-Begin $1.00-c		.80	2.00
50-($1.50, 52 pgs.)		.80	2.00
51-56		.70	1.75
Annual 1-3: 1(1985). 2(1986). 3(1988, $1.50)		1.00	2.50

NOTE: ***Morrow*** *a-28, 35, 36, 56.* ***Orlando*** *c-8i.* ***Perez*** *c-1-3.* ***Spiegle*** *a-19.* ***Starlin*** *c-24, 25.* ***Sutton*** *a-1-6p, 8-18p, 20-27p, 29p, 31-34p, 39-52p, 55p; c-4-6p, 8-22p, 46p.*

STAR TREK
Oct, 1989 - No. 80, Jan, 1996 ($1.50/$1.75/$1.95/$2.50)
DC Comics

	GD25	FN65	NM94
1-Capt. Kirk and crew		2.00	5.00
2,3		1.20	3.00
4-23,25-30: 10-12-The Trial of James T. Kirk. 21-Begin $1.75-c		.80	2.00
24-($2.95, 68 pgs.)-40 pg. epic w/pin-ups		1.40	3.50
31-49,51-60		.80	2.00
50-($3.50, 68 pgs.)-Painted-c		1.40	3.50
61-70: 61-Begin $1.95-c		.90	2.25
71-74, 76-80: 71-begin $2.50-c		1.00	2.50
75 ($3.95)		1.60	4.00
Annual 1,2('90, '91, $2.95, 68 pgs.): 1-Morrow-a		1.40	3.50
Annual 3,4 ('92,93, $3.50, 68 pgs.): 3-Painted-c		1.60	4.00
Annual 5 (1994, $3.95)		1.60	4.00
Annual 6 (1995, $3.95)		1.60	4.00
Special 1 (1994, $3.50, 68 pgs.)-Sutton-a.		1.40	3.50
Special 2 (1995, $3.50, 68 pgs.)		1.40	3.50
Special 3 (1995, $3.95)		1.60	4.00
...: The Ashes of Eden (1995, $14.95, 100 pgs.)-Shatner story	1.85	5.50	15.00
...Generations (1994, $3.95, 68 pgs.)-Movie adaptation		1.60	4.00
...Generations (1994, $5.95, 68 pgs.)-Squarebound		2.40	6.00

STAR TREK: DEEP SPACE NINE (TV)
Aug, 1993 - No. 32, Jan, 1996 ($2.50)
Malibu Comics

	GD25	FN65	NM94
1-Direct Sale Edition w/line drawn-c		1.00	2.50
1-Newsstand Edition with photo-c		1.00	2.50
0 (1/95, $2.95)-Terok Nor		1.00	2.50
2-32: 2-Polybagged w/trading card. 9-4 pg. prelude to Hearts & Minds		1.00	2.50
Annual 1 (1/95, $3.95, 68 pgs.)		1.60	4.00
Special 1 (1995, $3.50)		1.40	3.50
Ultimate Annual 1 (12/95, $5.95)		2.40	6.00
...:Lightstorm (12/94, $3.50)		1.40	3.50

STAR TREK: DEEP SPACE NINE (TV)
Nov, 1996 - No. 15, Mar, 1998 ($1.95/$1.99)
Marvel Comics (Paramount Comics)

	GD25	FN65	NM94
1-3		.80	2.00
4-15: 4-Begin $1.99-c. 12,13-"Telepathy War" pt. 2,3		.80	2.00

STAR TREK DEEP SPACE NINE-THE CELEBRITY SERIES; BLOOD AND HONOR
May, 1995 ($2.95)
Malibu Comics

	GD25	FN65	NM94
1-Mark Lenard script		1.20	3.00
1-Aron Eisenberg script		1.20	3.00

STAR TREK: DEEP SPACE NINE HEARTS AND MINDS
June, 1994 - No. 4, Sept, 1994 ($2.50, limited series)
Mailbu Comics

	GD25	FN65	NM94
1-4		1.00	2.50
1-Holographic-c		1.60	4.00

STAR TREK: DEEP SPACE NINE, THE MAQUIS
Feb, 1995 - No. 3, Apr, 1995 ($2.50, limited series)
Malibu Comics

	GD25	FN65	NM94
1-3-Newstand-c, 1-Photo-c		1.00	2.50

STAR TREK: DEEP SPACE NINE/THE NEXT GENERATION
Oct, 1994 - No. 2, Nov, 1994 ($2.50, limited series)
Malibu Comics

	GD25	FN65	NM94
1,2: Parts 2 & 4 of "Prophet & Losses."		1.00	2.50

STAR TREK: DEEP SPACE NINE WORF SPECIAL
Dec, 1995 ($3.95, one-shot)
Marvel Comics

	GD25	FN65	NM94
1-Includes pinups		1.60	4.00

STAR TREK EARLY VOYAGES(TV)
Feb, 1997 - Present ($2.95/$1.95/$1.99)
Marvel Comics (Paramount Comics)

	GD25	FN65	NM94
1-($2.95)		1.20	3.00
2-6-($1.95)		.80	2.00
7-12: 7-Begin- $1.99-c		.80	2.00

STAR TREK: FIRST CONTACT (Movie)
Nov, 1996 ($5.95, one-shot)
Marvel Comics (Paramount Comics)

Star Trek: The Next Generation #61 © Paramount

Star Trek Unlimited #5 © Paramount

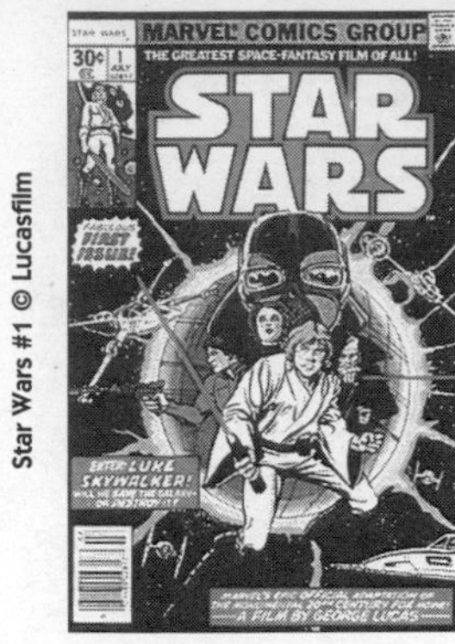

Star Wars #1 © Lucasfilm

GD25 FN65 NM94

nn-Movie adaption 2.40 6.00

STAR TREK: MIRROR MIRROR
Feb, 1997 ($3.95, one-shot)
Marvel Comics (Paramount Comics)

1-DeFalco-s 1.60 4.00

STAR TREK MOVIE SPECIAL
1984 (June) - No. 2, 1987 ($1.50, 68 pgs); No. 1, 1989 ($2.00, 52 pgs.)
DC Comics

nn-(#1)-Adapts Star Trek III; Sutton-p (68 pgs.) .70 1.75
2-Adapts Star Trek IV; Sutton-a; Chaykin-c. (68 pgs.) .70 1.75
1 (1989)-Adapts Star Trek V; painted-c .90 2.25

STAR TREK: OPERATION ASSIMILATION
Dec, 1996 ($2.95, one-shot)
Marvel Comics (Paramount Comics)

1 1.20 3.00

STAR TREK VI: THE UNDISCOVERED COUNTRY (Movie)
1992
DC Comics

1-($2.95, regular edition, 68 pgs.)-Adaptation of film 1.20 3.00
nn-($5.95, prestige edition)-Has photos of movie not included in regular edition; painted-c by Palmer; photo back-c 2.40 6.00

STAR TREK: STARFLEET ACADEMY
Dec, 1996 - Present ($1.95/$1.99)
Marvel Comics (Paramount Comics)

1-8-Begin new series .80 2.00
9-15: 9-Begin $1.99-c. 12-"Telepathy War" pt. 1 .80 2.00

STAR TREK: TELEPATHY WAR
Nov, 1997 ($2.99, 48 pgs., one-shot)
Marvel Comics (Paramount Comics)

1-"Telepathy War" x-over pt. 6 1.20 3.00

STAR TREK - THE ASHES OF EDEN
1995 ($14.95, 100 pgs., one-shot)
DC Comics

nn-Shatner scripts 1.85 5.50 15.00

STAR TREK - THE MODALA IMPERATIVE
Late July, 1991 - No. 4, Late Sept, 1991 ($1.75, limited series)
DC Comics

1 1.00 2.50
2-4 .80 2.00

STAR TREK: THE NEXT GENERATION (TV)
Feb, 1988 - No. 6, July, 1988 (limited series)
DC Comics

1 ($1.50, 52 pgs.)-Sienkiewicz painted-c 2.00 5.00
2-6 ($1.00) 1.20 3.00

STAR TREK: THE NEXT GENERATION (TV)
Oct, 1989 -No. 80, 1995 ($1.50/$1.75/$1.95)
DC Comics

1-Capt. Picard and crew from TV show 2.00 5.00
2,3 1.20 3.00
4,5 1.00 2.50
6-10 1.00 2.50
11-23,25-30: 21-Begin $1.75-c .80 2.00
24-($2.50, 52 pgs.) 1.20 3.00
31-49,51-60 .80 2.00
50-($3.50, 68 pgs.)-Painted-c 1.60 4.00
61-70: 61-Begins $1.95-c .90 2.25
71-74,76-80: 71-begin $2.50-c 1.00 2.50
75-($3.95, 50 pgs.) 1.60 4.00

GD25 FN65 NM94

Annual 1 (1990, $2.95, 68 pgs.) 1.60 4.00
Annual 2-4 (1991-93, $3.50, 68 pgs.) 1.80 4.50
Annual 5 (1994, $3.95, 68 pgs.) 1.60 4.00
Annual 6 (1995, $3.95) 1.60 4.00
Special 1 (1993, $3.50, 68 pgs.)-Contains 3 stories 1.60 4.00
Special 2 (Sum/94, $3.95, 68 pgs.) 1.60 4.00
Special 3 ('95, $3.95) 1.60 4.00
...-The Series Finale (1994, $3.95, 68 pgs.) 1.60 4.00

STAR TREK: THE NEXT GENERATION/DEEP SPACE NINE (TV)
Dec, 1994 - No. 2, Jan, 1995 ($2.50, limited series)
DC Comics

1,2-Parts 1 & 3 of "Prophets & Losses" 1.00 2.50

STAR TREK: THE NEXT GENERATION - ILL WIND
Nov, 1995 - No. 3, Feb, 1996 ($2.50, limited series)
DC Comics

1-3 1.00 2.50

STAR TREK: THE NEXT GENERATION - THE MODALA IMPERATIVE
Early Sept, 1991 - No. 4, Late Oct, 1991 ($1.75, limited series)
DC Comics

1 1.00 2.50
2-4 .80 2.00

STAR TREK: THE NEXT GENERATION-SHADOWHEART
Dec, 1994 - No. 4, Mar, 1995 ($1.95, limited series)
DC Comics

1-4 .80 2.00

STAR TREK UNLIMITED
Nov, 1996 - Present ($2.95/$2.99)
Marvel Comics (Paramount Comics)

1,2-Stories from all series .80 2.00
3-6: 3-Begin $2.99-c. 6-"Telepathy War" pt. 3 1.20 3.00

STAR TREK: VOYAGER
Nov, 1996 - No. 15, Mar, 1998 ($1.95/$1.99)
Marvel Comics (Paramount Comics)

1-4 .80 2.00
5-15: 5-Begin $1.99-c. 13-"Telepathy War" pt. 5. 14-Seven of Nine joins crew .80 2.00

STAR WARS (Movie) (See Classic..., Contemporary Motivators, Dark Horse Comics, The Droids, The Ewoks, Marvel Movie Showcase, Marvel Special Ed.)
July, 1977 - No. 107, Sept, 1986
Marvel Comics Group

1-(Regular 30¢ edition)-Price in square w/UPC code; #1-6 adapt first movie 3.50 10.50 35.00
1-(35¢-c; limited distribution - 1500 copies?)- Price in square w/UPC code (see note below) 41.00 123.00 490.00
2-6: 2-4-30¢ issues. 4-Battle with Darth Vader. 6-Dave Stevens-a(i). 2.25 6.75 18.00
2-4-35¢ with UPC code; not reprints 7.20 21.60 72.00
7-20 1.25 3.75 10.00
21-91, 93-99: 39-44-The Empire Strikes Back-r by Al Williamson in all. 81-Reintro Boba Fett. 98-Williamson-a. 1.00 3.00 8.00
92,100-106: 92,100-($1.00, 52 pgs.). 1.25 3.75 10.00
107 (scarce); Portacio-a(i) 5.00 15.00 50.00
1-9: Reprints; has "reprint" in upper lefthand corner of cover or on inside or price and number inside a diamond with no date or UPC on cover; 30¢ and 35¢ issues published .80 2.00
Annual 1 (12/79, 52 pgs.)-Simonson-c 2.40 6.00
Annual 2 (11/82, 52 pgs.), 3(12/83, 52 pgs.) 2.00 5.00

NOTE: *The rare 35¢ edition has the cover price in a square box, and the UPC box in the lower left hand corner has the UPC code lines running through it.* **Austin** *c-11-15i, 21i, 38; c-12-15i, 21i.* **Byrne** *c-13p.* **Chaykin** *a-1-10p; c-1.* **Golden** *c/a-38.* **Miller** *c-47p; pin-up-43.* **Nebres** *c/a-Annual 2i.* **Portacio** *a-107i.* **Sienkiewicz** *c-92i, 98.* **Simonson** *a-16p, 49p, 51-63p, 65p, 66p; c-*

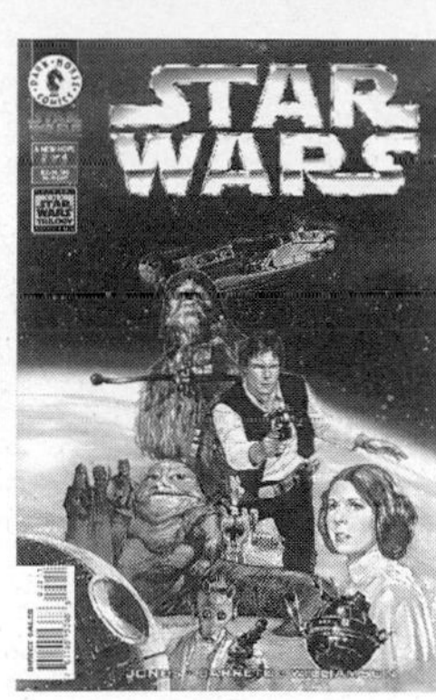

Star Wars: A New Hope- The Special Edition #2 © Lucasfilm

Star Wars: Dark Empire #4 © Lucasfilm

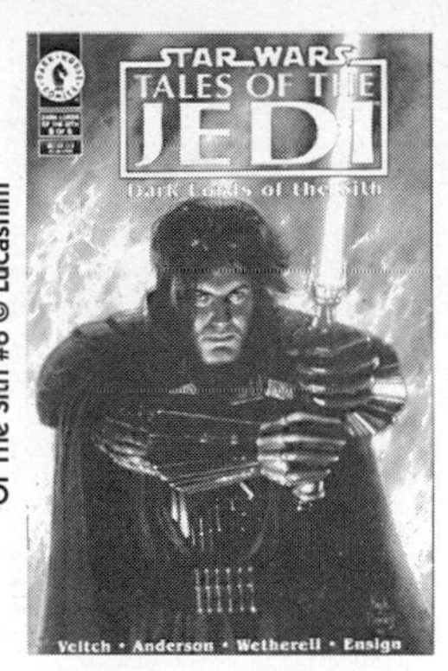

Star Wars: Tales Of The Jedi -Dark Lords Of The Sith #6 © Lucasfilm

GD25 FN65 NM94

16, 49-51, 52p, 53-62, Annual 1. ***Steacy*** *painted a-105i, 106i; c-105.* ***Williamson*** *a-39-44p, 50p, 98; c-39, 40, 41-44p. Painted c-81, 87, 92, 95, 98, 100, 105.*

STAR WARS: A NEW HOPE- THE SPECIAL EDITION
Jan, 1997 - No. 4, Apr, 1997 ($2.95, limited series)
Dark Horse Comics

1-4-Dorman-c 1.20 3.00

STAR WARS: BOBA FETT
Dec, 1995 - No. 3 ($3.95) (Originally intended as a one-shot)
Dark Horse Comics

1-Kennedy-c/a 2.00 5.00
2,3 1.60 4.00
Twin Engines of Destruction (1/97, $2.95) r/#1-3 1.20 3.00

STAR WARS: DARK EMPIRE
Dec, 1991 - No. 6, Oct, 1992 ($2.95, limited series)
Dark Horse Comics

1-All have Dorman painted-c 1.85 5.50 15.00
1-2nd printing 2.00 5.00
2-Low print run 2.50 7.50 20.00
2,3-2nd printings 2.00 5.00
3 1.00 3.00 8.00
4-6 1.60 4.00
Gold Embossed Set (#1-6)-With gold embossed foil logo (price is for set) 80.00
Platinum Embossed Set (#1-6) 150.00
... (4/93, $16.95, TPB) 17.00
Trade paperback (4/93, 16.95) 17.00
Ltd. Ed. Hardcover ($99.95) Signed & numbered 125.00

STAR WARS: DARK EMPIRE II
Dec, 1994 - No. 6, May, 1995 ($2.95, limited series)
Dark Horse Comics

1-Dave Dorman painted-c 2.00 5.00
2-6: Dorman-c in all. 1.60 4.00
Platinum Embossed Set (#1-6) 35.00
Trade paperback ($17.95) 18.00

STAR WARS: DARK FORCE RISING
May, 1997 - No. 6, Oct, 1997 ($2.95, limited series)
Dark Horse Comics

1-6 1.20 3.00

STAR WARS: DROIDS (See Dark Horse Comics #17-19)
Apr, 1994 - #6, Sept, 1994; V2#1, Apr, 1995 - V2#8, Dec, 1995 ($2.50, limited series)
Dark Horse Comics

1-($2.95)-Embossed-c 1.20 3.00
2-6 ($2.25) 1.00 2.50
Special 1 (1/95, $2.50) 1.00 2.50
V2#1-8 1.00 2.50

STAR WARS: EMPIRE'S END
Oct, 1995 - No. 2, Nov, 1995 ($2.95, limited series)
Dark Horse Comics

1,2-Dorman-c 1.20 3.00

STAR WARS : HEIR TO THE EMPIRE
Oct, 1995 - No.6, Apr, 1996 ($2.95, limited series)
Dark Horse Comics

1-6: Adaptation of Zahn novel 1.20 3.00

STAR WARS: JABBA THE HUTT
Apr, 1995 ($2.50, one-shots)
Dark Horse Comics

nn 1.00 2.50
...The Betrayal 1.00 2.50
...The Dynasty Trap 1.00 2.50
...The Hunger of Princess Nampi 1.00 2.50

STAR WARS: RETURN OF THE JEDI (Movie)
Oct, 1983 - No. 4, Jan, 1984 (limited series)
Marvel Comics Group

1-4-Williamson-p in all; r/Marvel Super Special #27 2.00 5.00
Oversized issue (1983, $2.95, 10-3/4x8-1/4", 68 pgs., cardboard-c)-r/#1-4 1.20 3.00

STAR WARS: RIVER OF CHAOS
June, 1995 - No. 4, Sept, 1995 ($2.95, limited series)
Dark Horse Comics

1-4: Louise Simonson scripts 1.00 2.50

STAR WARS: SHADOWS OF THE EMPIRE
May, 1996 - No. 6, Oct, 1996 ($2.95, limited series)
Dark Horse Comics

1-6: Story details events between The Empire Strikes Back & Return of the Jedi; Russell-a(i). 1.20 3.00

STAR WARS: SHADOW STALKER
Sept, 1997 ($2.95, one-shot)
Dark Horse Comics

nn-Windham-a. 1.20 3.00

STAR WARS: TALES FROM MOS EISLY
Mar, 1996 ($2.95, one-shot)
Dark Horse Comics

nn-Bret Blevins-a. 1.20 3.00

STAR WARS: TALES OF THE JEDI (See Dark Horse Comics #7)
Oct, 1993 - No. 5, Feb, 1994 ($2.50, limited series)
Dark Horse Comics

1-5: All have Dave Dorman painted-c. 3-r/Dark Horse Comics #7-9 w/new coloring & some panels redrawn 1.20 3.00
1-5-Gold foil embossed logo; limited # printed-7500 5.00 15.00 50.00

STAR WARS: TALES OF THE JEDI-DARK LORDS OF THE SITH
Oct, 1994 - No. 6, Mar, 1995 ($2.50, limited series)
Dark Horse Comics

1-6: 1-Polybagged w/trading card 1.20 3.00

STAR WARS: TALES OF THE JEDI-THE FALL OF THE SITH
June, 1997 - No. 5, Oct, 1997 ($2.95, limited series)
Dark Horse Comics

1-5 1.20 3.00

STAR WARS: TALES OF THE JEDI-THE FREEDOM NADD UPRISING
Aug, 1994 - No. 2, Nov, 1994 ($2.50, limited series)
Dark Horse Comics

1,2 1.00 2.50

STAR WARS: TALES OF THE JEDI-THE GOLDEN AGE OF THE SITH
July, 1996 - No. 5, Feb, 1997 (99¢/$2.95, limited series)
Dark Horse Comics

0-(99¢)-Anderson-s 1.00
1-5-Anderson-s 1.20 3.00

STAR WARS: TALES OF THE JEDI-THE SITH WAR
Aug, 1995 - No. 6, Jan, 1996 ($2.50, limited series)
Dark Horse Comics

1-6: Anderson scripts 1.00 2.50

STAR WARS: THE LAST COMMAND
Nov, 1997 - No. 6 ($2.95, limited series)
Dark Horse Comics

1-6:Based on the Timothy Zaun novel 2.95

Steel #7 © DC

Steve Canyon Comics #5 © HARV

Steve Roper #1 © FF

STAR WARS: THE PROTOCOL OFFENSIVE
Sept, 1997 ($4.95, one-shot)
Dark Horse Comics

	GD25	FN65	NM94
nn-Anthony Daniels & Ryder Windham-s		2.00	5.00

STAR WARS: X-WING ROGUE SQUADRON (Star Wars: X-Wing Rogue Squadron-The Phantom Affair #5-8 appears on cover only))
July, 1995 - Present ($2.95)
Dark Horse Comics

	GD25	FN65	NM94
1/2		2.00	5.00
1-24: 1-4-Baron scripts. 5-20-Stackpole scripts		1.20	3.00

S.T.A.T.
Dec, 1993 ($2.25)
Majestic Entertainment

	GD25	FN65	NM94
1		.90	2.25

STATIC (Also see Eclipse Monthly)
No, 11, Oct, 1985 - No. 12, Dec, 1985
Charlton Comics

	GD25	FN65	NM94
11,12-Ditko-c/a			1.00

STATIC (See Heroes)
June, 1993 - No. 45, Mar, 1997 ($1.50/$1.75/$2.50)
DC Comics (Milestone)

	GD25	FN65	NM94
1-($2.95)-Collector's Edition; polybagged w/poster & trading card & backing board (direct sales only)		1.20	3.00
1-13: 2-Origin. 8-Shadow War; Simonson silver ink-c			1.50
14-($2.50, 52 pgs.)-Worlds Collide Pt. 14		1.00	2.50
15-24: 15-Begin $1.75-c		.70	1.75
25 ($3.95)		1.60	4.00
26-30,32-45: 26-Begin $2.50-c. 27-Kent Williams-c		1.00	2.50
31-(99¢)			1.00

STEALTH SQUAD
Sept, 1993 ($2.50, unfinished limited series)
Petra Comics

	GD25	FN65	NM94
1-Super hero team		1.00	2.50

STEED AND MRS. PEEL (TV)(Also see The Avengers)
1990 - No. 3, 1991 ($4.95, limited series)
Eclipse Books/ ACME Press

	GD25	FN65	NM94
Books One - Three: Grant Morrison scripts		2.00	5.00

STEEL
Feb, 1994 - Present ($1.50/$1.95)
DC Comics

	GD25	FN65	NM94
1-8: 1-From Reign of the Supermen storyline. 6,7-Worlds Collide Pt. 5 & 12. 8-(9/94)			1.50
0,9-15: 0-(10/94). 9-(11/94)			1.50
16-49: 16-Begin $1.95-c. 46-Superboy-c/app.		.80	2.00
Annual 1 (1994, $2.95)-Elseworlds story		1.20	3.00
Annual 2 (1995, $3.95)-Year One story		1.60	4.00
...Forging of a Hero (1997, $19.95, TPB) r/ early app.			20.00

STEEL: THE OFFICIAL COMIC ADAPTION OF THE WARNER BROS. MOTION PICTURE
1997 ($4.95, Prestige format, one-shot)
DC Comics

	GD25	FN65	NM94
nn-Movie adaption; Bogdanove & Giordano-a		2.00	5.00

STEELGRIP STARKEY
June, 1986 - No. 6, July, 1987 ($1.50, limited series, Baxter paper)
Marvel Comics (Epic Comics)

	GD25	FN65	NM94
1-6			1.50

STEEL STERLING (Formerly Shield-Steel Sterling; see Blue Ribbon, Jackpot, Mighty Comics, Mighty Crusaders, Roly Poly & Zip Comics)
No. 4, Jan, 1984 - No. 7, July, 1984
Archie Enterprises, Inc.

	GD25	FN65	NM94
4-7: 6-McWilliams-a			1.00

STEEL, THE INDESTRUCTIBLE MAN (See All-Star Squadron #8)
Mar, 1978 - No. 5, Oct-Nov, 1978
DC Comics

	GD25	FN65	NM94
1,5: 5-Giant		1.40	4.00
2-4		1.20	3.00

STEELTOWN ROCKERS
Apr, 1987 - No. 6, Sept, 1990 ($1.00, limited series)
Marvel Comics

	GD25	FN65	NM94
1-6: Small town teens form rock band			1.00

STEVE CANYON (See Harvey Comics Hits #52)
No. 519, 11/53 - No. No. 1033, 9/59 (All Milton Caniff-a except #519, 939, 1033)
Dell Publishing Co.

	GD25	FN65	NM94
Four Color 519 (1, '53)	8.00	25.00	90.00
Four Color 578 (8/54), 641 (7/55), 737 (10/56), 804 (5/57), 939 (10/58), 1033 (9/59) (photo-c)	4.50	13.50	50.00

STEVE CANYON
1959 (6-3/4x9", 96 pgs., B&W, no text, hardcover)
Grosset & Dunlap

	GD25	FN65	NM94
100100-Reprints 2 stories from strip (1953, 1957)	4.15	12.50	25.00
100100 (softcover edition)	4.00	10.00	20.00

STEVE CANYON COMICS
Feb, 1948 - No. 6, Dec, 1948 (Strip reprints, No. 4,5: 52pgs.)
Harvey Publications

	GD25	FN65	NM94
1-Origin; has biography of Milton Caniff; Powell-a, 2 pgs.; Caniff-a	17.50	53.00	140.00
2-Caniff, Powell-a in #2-6	11.30	34.00	90.00
3-6: 6-Intro Madame Lynx-c/story	10.00	30.00	80.00
Dept. Store giveaway #3(6/48, 36pp)	8.75	26.25	70.00
...'s Secret Mission (1951, 16 pgs., Armed Forces giveaway); Caniff-a	8.75	26.25	65.00
Strictly for the Smart Birds (1951, 16 pgs.)-Information Comics Div. (Harvey) Premium	8.00	24.00	56.00

STEVE CANYON IN 3-D
June, 1986 ($2.25, one-shot)
Kitchen Sink Press

	GD25	FN65	NM94
1-Contains unpublished story from 1954		.90	2.25

STEVE DITKO'S STRANGE AVENGING TALES
Feb, 1997 - Present ($2.95, B&W)
Fantagraphics Books

	GD25	FN65	NM94
1-Ditko-c/s/a		1.20	3.00

STEVE DONOVAN, WESTERN MARSHAL (TV)
No. 675, Feb, 1956 - No. 880, Feb, 1958 (All photo-c)
Dell Publishing Co.

	GD25	FN65	NM94
Four Color 675-Kinstler-a	7.00	22.00	80.00
Four Color 768-Kinstler-a	5.50	16.50	60.00
Four Color 880	3.60	11.00	40.00

STEVE ROPER
Apr, 1948 - No. 5, Dec, 1948
Famous Funnies

	GD25	FN65	NM94
1-Contains 1944 daily newspaper-r	9.50	28.00	75.00
2	5.70	17.00	40.00
3-5	5.35	16.00	32.00

STEVE SAUNDERS SPECIAL AGENT (See Special Agent)

STEVE SAVAGE (See Captain...)

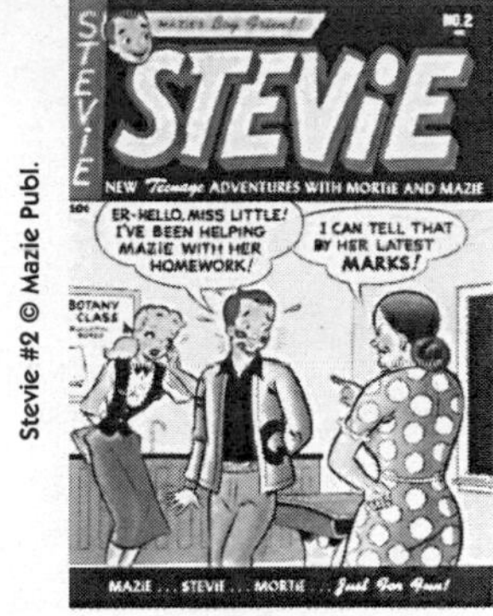

Stevie #2 © Mazie Publ.

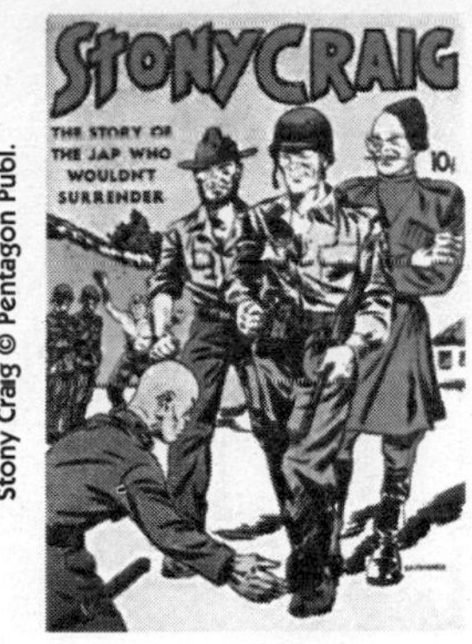

Stony Craig © Pentagon Publ.

StormWatch #20 © Aegis Entertainment

	GD25	FN65	NM94

STEVE ZODIAC & THE FIRE BALL XL-5 (TV)
Jan, 1964
Gold Key

10108-401 (#1)	6.40	19.00	70.00

STEVIE (Mazie's boy friend)(Also see Flat-Top, Mazie & Mortie)
Nov, 1952 - No. 6, Apr, 1954
Mazie (Magazine Publ.)

1-Teenage humor; Stevie, Mortie & Mazie begin	5.70	17.00	40.00
2-6	4.15	12.50	25.00

STEVIE MAZIE'S BOY FRIEND (See Harvey Hits #5)

STEWART THE RAT (See Eclipse Graphic Album Series)

ST. GEORGE (See listing under Saint...)

STIGG'S INFERNO
1985 - No. 7, Mar, 1987 ($1.95, B&W)
Vortex/Eclipse

1-7 ($1.95)		.80	2.00
Graphic Album (1988, $6.95, B&W, 100 pgs.)	1.00	2.80	7.00

STING OF THE GREEN HORNET (See The Green Hornet)
June, 1992 - No. 4, 1992 ($2.50, limited series)
Now Comics

1-4: Butler-c/a		1.00	2.50
1-4 ($2.75)-Collectors Ed.; polybagged w/poster		1.10	2.75

STONEY BURKE (TV)
June-Aug, 1963 - No. 2, Sept-Nov, 1963
Dell Publishing Co.

1,2: Jack Lord photo-c	1.50	4.50	12.00

STONY CRAIG
1946 (No #)
Pentagon Publishing Co.

nn-Reprints Bell Syndicate's "Sgt. Stony Craig" newspaper strips	5.70	17.00	40.00

STORIES BY FAMOUS AUTHORS ILLUSTRATED (Fast Fiction #1-5)
No. 6, Aug, 1950 - No. 13, Mar, 1951
Seaboard Publ./Famous Authors Ill.

1-Scarlet Pimpernel-Baroness Orczy	28.00	84.00	225.00
2-Capt. Blood-Raphael Sabatini	28.00	84.00	225.00
3-She, by Haggard	35.00	105.00	280.00
4-The 39 Steps-John Buchan	19.00	56.00	150.00
5-Beau Geste-P. C. Wren	19.00	56.00	150.00

NOTE: *The above five issues are exact reprints of Fast Fiction #1-5 except for the title change and new Kiefer covers on #1 and 2. Kiefer c(r)-3-5. The above 5 issues were released before Famous Authors #6.*

6-Macbeth, by Shakespeare; Kiefer art (8/50); used in **SOTI**, pg. 22,143; Kiefer-c; 36 pgs.	24.00	71.00	190.00
7-The Window; Kiefer-c/a; 52 pgs.	17.50	53.00	140.00
8-Hamlet, by Shakespeare; Kiefer-c/a; 36 pgs.	22.00	66.00	175.00
9-Nicholas Nickleby, by Dickens; G. Schrotter-a; 52 pgs.	19.00	56.00	150.00
10-Romeo & Juliet, by Shakespeare; Kiefer-c/a; 36 pgs.	19.00	56.00	150.00
11-Ben-Hur; Schrotter-a; 52 pgs.	19.00	56.00	150.00
12-La Svengali; Schrotter-a; 36 pgs.	19.00	56.00	150.00
13-Scaramouche; Kiefer-c/a; 36 pgs.	19.00	56.00	150.00

NOTE: *Artwork was prepared/advertised for #14, The Red Badge Of Courage. Gilberton bought out Famous Authors, Ltd. and used that story as C.I. #98. Famous Authors, Ltd. then published the Classics Junior series. The Famous Authors titles were published as part of the regular Classics Ill. Series in Brazil starting in 1952.*

STORIES OF CHRISTMAS
1942 (Giveaway, 32 pgs., paper cover)
K. K. Publications

nn-Adaptation of "A Christmas Carol"; Kelly story "The Fir Tree"; Infinity-c	31.00	94.00	250.00

STORIES OF ROMANCE (Formerly Meet Miss Bliss)
No. 5, Mar, 1956 - No. 13, Aug, 1957
Atlas Comics (LMC)

5-Baker-a?	7.15	21.50	50.00
6-10,12,13	5.00	15.00	30.00
11-Baker, Romita-a; Colletta-c/a	5.70	17.00	35.00

NOTE: ***Ann Brewster** a-13. **Colletta** a-9(2), 11; c-5, 11.*

STORM
Feb, 1996 - No. 4, May, 1996 ($2.95, limited series)
Marvel Comics

1-4-Foil-c; Dodson-a(p); Ellis-s: 2-4-Callisto;		1.20	3.00

STORMQUEST
Nov, 1994 - No. 6, Apr, 1995 ($1.95)
Caliber Press (Sky Universe)

1-6		.80	2.00

STORMWATCH
May, 1993 - No. 50, July, 1997 ($1.95/$2.50)
Image Comics (WildStorm Productions)

1-8: 1-Intro StormWatch (Battalion, Diva, Winter, Fuji, & Hellstrike); 1st app. Weatherman; Jim Lee-c & part scripts; Lee plots in all. 1-Gold edition. 1-3-Includes coupon for limited edition StormWatch trading card #00 by Lee. 3-1st app. Backlash (cameo).		.80	2.00
0-($2.50)-Polybagged w/card; 1st full app. Backlash		1.00	2.50
9-(4/94, $2.50)-Intro Defile		1.00	2.50
10-17: 10-(6/94), 11,12-Both (8/94). 13,14-(9/94). 15-(10/94)		.80	2.00
10-Alternate Portacio-c, see Deathblow #5		2.40	6.00
18-21: 18-$2.50-c begins. 21-Reads #1 on-c.		1.00	2.50
22-36: 22-Direct Market; Wildstorm Rising Pt. 9, bound-in card. 23-Spartan joins team. 25-(6/94, June 1995 on-c, $2.50). 35-Fire From Heaven Pt. 5. 36-Fire From Heaven Pt. 12		1.00	2.50
22-($1.95)-Newsstand, Wildstorm Rising Pt. 9		.80	2.00
37-(7/96, $3.50, 38 pgs.)-Weatherman forms new team; 1st app. Jenny Sparks, Jack Hawksmoor & Rose Tattoo; Warren Ellis scripts begin; Justice League #1-c/swipe		1.40	3.50
38-49: 38-Begin $2.50-c. 44-Three covers.		1.00	2.50
50-($4.50)		1.80	4.50
Special 1 (1/94, $3.50, 52 pgs.)		1.40	3.50
Special 2 (5/95, $3.50, 52 pgs.)		1.40	3.50
Sourcebook 1 (1/94, $2.50)		1.00	2.50

STORMWATCH
Oct, 1997 - Present ($2.50)
Image Comics (WildStorm Productions)

1-Ellis-s/Jimenez-a(p); two covers by Bennett			2.50
1-($3.50)-Voyager Pack bagged w/Gen 13 preview			3.50
2,3			2.50

STORMWATCHER
Apr, 1989 - No. 4, Dec, 1989 ($2.00, B&W, limited series)
Eclipse Comics (Acme Press)

1-4		.80	2.00

STORMY (Disney) (Movie)
No. 537, Feb, 1954
Dell Publishing Co.

Four Color 537 (...the Thoroughbred)-on top 2/3 of each page; Pluto story on bottom 1/3	2.75	8.00	30.00

STORY HOUR SERIES (Disney)
1948, 1949; 1951-1953 (36 pgs., paper-c) (4-3/4x6-1/2")
Given away with subscription to Walt Disney's Comics & Stories
Whitman Publishing Co.

Straight Arrow #13 © ME

Strange Adventures #1 © DC

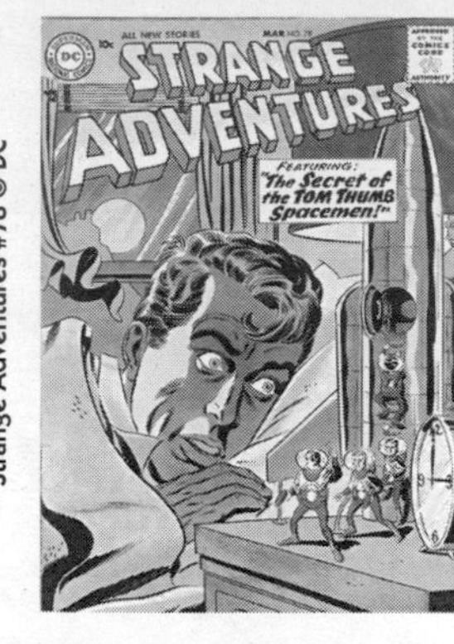

Strange Adventures #78 © DC

	GD25	FN65	NM94
nn(1948)-Mickey Mouse and the Boy Thursday	10.50	32.00	85.00
nn(1948)-Mickey Mouse the Miracle Master	10.50	32.00	85.00
nn(1948)-Minnie Mouse and Antique Chair	10.50	32.00	85.00
nn(1949)-The Three Orphan Kittens(B&W & color)	6.50	19.50	45.00
nn(1949)-Danny-The Little Black Lamb	6.50	19.50	45.00
800(1948)-Donald Duck in "Bringing Up the Boys"	12.00	38.00	100.00
1953 edition	7.85	23.50	55.00
801(1948)-Mickey Mouse's Summer Vacation	8.75	26.25	65.00
1951, 1952 editions	4.25	13.00	28.00
802(1948)-Bugs Bunny's Adventures	7.15	21.50	50.00
803(1948)-Bongo	5.70	17.00	35.00
804(1948)-Mickey and the Beanstalk	7.15	21.50	50.00
805-15(1949)-Andy Panda and His Friends	5.70	17.00	40.00
806-15(1949)-Tom and Jerry	6.50	19.50	45.00
808-15(1949)-Johnny Appleseed	5.70	17.00	35.00
1948, 1949 Hard Cover Edition of each....	$3.00 - $5.00 more.		

STORY OF EDISON, THE
1956 (16 pgs.) (Reddy Killowatt)
Educational Comics

nn-Reprint of Reddy Kilowatt #2(1947)	5.00	15.00	30.00

STORY OF HARRY S. TRUMAN, THE
1948 (Giveaway, regular size, soft-c, 16 pgs.)
Democratic National Committee

nn-Gives biography on career of Truman; used in **SOTI**, pg. 311	8.75	26.25	70.00

STORY OF JESUS (See Classics Illustrated Special Issue)

STORY OF MANKIND, THE (Movie)
No. 851, Jan, 1958
Dell Publishing Co.

Four Color 851-Vincent Price/Hedy Lamarr photo-c	6.40	19.00	70.00

STORY OF MARTHA WAYNE, THE
April, 1956
Argo Publ.

1-Newspaper strip-r	4.25	13.00	28.00

STORY OF RUTH, THE
No. 1144, Nov-Jan, 1961 (Movie)
Dell Publishing Co.

Four Color #1144-Photo-c	9.00	27.00	100.00

STORY OF THE COMMANDOS, THE (Combined Operations)
1943 (15¢, B&W, 68 pgs.)
Long Island Independent (Distr. by Gilberton)

nn-All text (no comics); photos & illustrations; ad for Classic Comics on back cover (Rare)	24.00	71.00	190.00

STORY OF THE GLOOMY BUNNY, THE (See March of Comics #9)

STRAIGHT ARROW (Radio)(See Best of the West & Great Western)
Feb-Mar, 1950 - No. 55, Mar, 1956 (All 36 pgs.)
Magazine Enterprises

1-Straight Arrow (alias Steve Adams) & his palomino Fury begin; 1st mention of Sundown Valley & the Secret Cave	35.00	105.00	280.00
2-Red Hawk begins (1st app?) by Powell (origin), ends #55	17.00	51.00	135.00
3-Frazetta-c	24.00	71.00	190.00
4,5: 4-Secret Cave-c	15.50	47.00	125.00
6-10	14.50	43.00	115.00
11-Classic story "The Valley of Time", with an ancient civilization made of gold	15.50	47.00	125.00
12-19	12.00	36.00	95.00
20-Origin Straight Arrow's Shield	13.00	39.00	105.00
21-Origin Fury	15.50	47.00	125.00
22-Frazetta-c	16.00	49.00	130.00
23,25-30: 25-Secret Cave-c. 28-Red Hawk meets The Vikings	7.85	23.50	55.00
24-Classic story "The Dragons of Doom!" with prehistoric pteradactyls	8.75	26.25	65.00
31-38: 36-Red Hawk drug story by Powell	5.70	17.00	40.00
39-Classic story "The Canyon Beast", with a dinosaur egg hatching a Tyranosaurus Rex	8.50	26.00	60.00
40-Classic story "Secret of The Spanish Specters", with Conquistadors' lost treasure	8.50	26.00	60.00
41,42,44-54: 45-Secret Cave-c	5.70	17.00	35.00
43-Intro & 1st app. Blaze, S. Arrow's Warrior dog	7.15	21.50	50.00
55-Last issue	8.50	26.00	60.00

NOTE: ***Fred Meagher** a 1-55; c-1, 2, 4-21, 23-55. **Powell** a 2-55. **Whitney** a-1. Many issues advertise the radio premiums associated with Straight Arrow.*

STRAIGHT ARROW'S FURY (Also see A-1 Comics)
No. 119, 1954 (one-shot)
Magazine Enterprises

A-1 119-Origin; Fred Meagher-c/a	10.50	32.00	85.00

STRANGE (Tales You'll Never Forget)
March, 1957 - No. 6, May, 1958
Ajax-Farrell Publ. (Four Star Comic Corp.)

1	14.00	41.00	110.00
2-Censored r/Haunted Thrills	8.35	25.00	55.00
3-6	6.50	19.50	45.00

STRANGE ADVENTURES
Aug-Sept, 1950 - No. 244, Oct-Nov, 1973 (No. 1-12: 52 pgs.)
National Periodical Publications

1-Adaptation of "Destination Moon"; preview of movie w/photo-c from movie (also see Fawcett Movie Comic #2); adapt. of Edmond Hamilton's "Chris KL-99" in #1-3; Darwin Jones begins	256.00	768.00	2300.00
2	117.00	350.00	1050.00
3,4	75.00	225.00	675.00
5-8,10: 7-Origin Kris KL-99	67.00	200.00	600.00
9-(6/51)-Origin/1st app. Captain Comet (c/story).	156.00	468.00	1400.00
11-20: 12,13,17,18-Toth-a	47.00	141.00	425.00
21-30: 28-Atomic explosion panel. 30-Robot-c	38.00	114.00	340.00
31,34-38	36.00	108.00	300.00
32,33-Krigstein-a	36.00	108.00	310.00
39-Ill. in **SOTI** "Treating police contemptuously" (top right)	40.00	120.00	360.00
40-49-Last Capt. Comet; not in 45,47,48	34.00	103.00	275.00
50-53-Last precode issue (2/55)	26.00	80.00	210.00
54-70	15.50	47.00	155.00
71-99	11.00	33.00	110.00
100	12.50	38.00	125.00
101-110: 104-Space Museum begins by Sekowsky.	8.50	25.50	85.00
111-116,118,119: 114-Star Hawkins begins, ends #185; Heath-a in Wood E.C. style	7.50	22.50	75.00
117-(6/60)-Origin/1st app. Atomic Knights.	46.00	138.00	560.00
120-2nd app. Atomic Knights	22.00	66.00	220.00
121,122,125,127,128,130,131,133,134: 134-Last 10¢ issue	6.50	19.50	65.00
123,126-3rd & 4th app. Atomic Knights	13.00	39.00	130.00
124-Intro/origin Faceless Creature	7.00	21.00	70.00
129,132,135,138,141,147-Atomic Knights app.	8.00	24.00	80.00
136,137,139,140,143,145,146,148,149,151,152,154,155,157-159	4.50	13.50	45.00
142-2nd app. Faceless Creature	5.00	15.00	50.00
144-Only Atomic Knights-c (by M. Anderson)	9.00	27.00	90.00

150,153,156,160: Atomic Knights in each. 153-(6/63)-3rd app. Faceless Creature; atomic explosion-c. 159-Star Rovers app.; Gil Kane/Anderson-a.

Strange Adventures #206 © DC

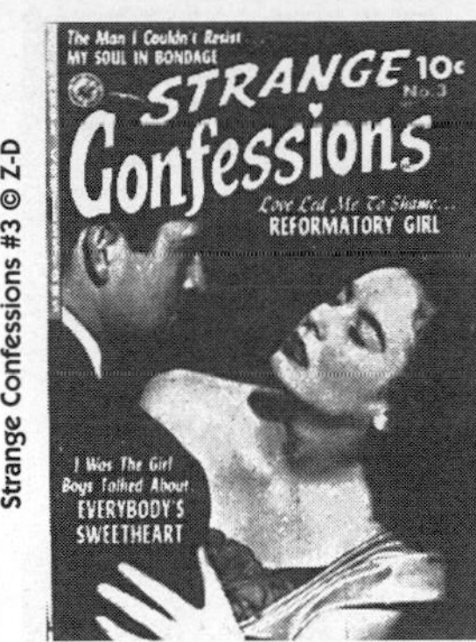

Strange Confessions #3 © Z-D

Strange Fantasy #3 © AJAX

GD25 FN65 NM94

160-Last Atomic Knights 6.00 18.00 60.00
161-179: 161-Last Space Museum. 163-Star Rovers app. 170-Infinity-c. 177-Intro/origin Immortal Man 3.50 10.50 35.00
180-Origin/1st app. Animal Man 19.00 51.00 190.00
181-183,185-189: 187-Intro/origin The Enchantress 1.85 5.50 15.00
184-2nd app. Animal Man by Gil Kane 12.50 38.00 125.00
190-1st app. Animal Man in costume 15.00 45.00 150.00
191-194,196-200,202-204 1.60 4.85 13.00
195-1st full app. Animal Man 8.50 25.50 85.00
201-Last Animal Man; 2nd full app. 4.50 13.50 45.00
205-(10/67)-Intro/origin Deadman by Infantino & begin series, ends #216 9.00 27.00 90.00
206-Neal Adams-a begins 6.00 18.00 60.00
207-210 4.80 14.40 48.00
211-216: 211-Space Museum-r. 216-(1-2/69)-Deadman story finally concludes in Brave & the Bold #86 (10-11/69); secret message panel by Neal Adams (pg. 13); tribute to Steranko 3.60 10.80 36.00
217-221,223-225: 217-r/origin & 1st app. Adam Strange from Showcase #17, begin-r; Atomic Knights-r begin. 218-Last 12¢ issue. 225-Last 15¢ issue 1.10 3.30 9.00
222-New Adam Strange story; Kane/Anderson-a 2.50 7.50 24.00
226,227,230-236-(68-52 pgs.): 226, 227-New Adam Strange text story w/illos by Anderson (8,6 pgs.) 231-Last Atomic Knights-r. 235-JLA-c 1.50 4.50 12.00
228,229 (68 pgs.) 1.85 5.50 15.00
237-243 1.00 3.00 8.00
244-Last issue 1.25 3.75 10.00

NOTE: ***Neal Adams*** *a-206-216; c-207-216, 228, 235.* ***Anderson*** *a-8-52, 94, 96, 99, 115, 117, 119-163, 217r, 218r, 222, 223-225r, 226, 229r, 242i(r); c-18, 19, 21, 23, 24, 27, 30, 32-44(most); c/r-157i, 190i, 217-224, 228-231, 233, 235-239, 241-243.* ***Ditko*** *a-188, 189.* ***Drucker*** *a-42, 43, 45.* ***Elias*** *a-212.* ***Finlay*** *a-2, 3, 6, 7, 210r, 229r.* ***Giunta*** *a-237r.* ***Heath*** *a-116.* ***Infantino*** *a-10-101, 106-151, 154, 157-163, 180, 190, 218-221r, 223-244p(r); c-50; c(r)-190p, 197, 199-211, 218-221, 223-244.* ***Kaluta*** *c-238, 240.* ***Gil Kane*** *a-8-116, 124, 125, 130, 138, 146-157, 173-186, 204r, 222r, 227-231r; c(p)-11-17, 25, 154, 157.* ***Kubert*** *a-55(2 pgs.), 226; c-219, 220, 225-227, 232, 234.* ***Moriera*** *c-26, 28, 29, 71.* ***Morrow*** *c-230.* ***Mortimer*** *c-8.* ***Powell*** *a-4.* ***Sekowsky*** *a-71p, 97-162p, 217p(r), 218p(r); c-206, 217-219r.* ***Simon & Kirby*** *a-2r (2 pgs)* ***Sparling*** *a-201.* ***Toth*** *a-8, 12, 13, 17-19.* ***Wood*** *a-154i. Atomic Knights in #117, 120, 123, 126, 129, 132, 135, 138, 141, 144, 147, 150, 153, 156, 160. Atomic Knights reprints by* ***Anderson*** *in 217-221, 223-231. Chris KL99 in 1-3, 5, 7, 9, 11, 15. Capt. Comet covers-9-14, 17-19, 24, 26, 27, 32-44.*

STRANGE AS IT SEEMS (See Famous Funnies-A Carnival of Comics, Feature Funnies #1, The John Hix Scrap Book & Peanuts)

STRANGE AS IT SEEMS
1936 (B&W, 5x7", 24 pgs.)
McNaught Syndicate

nn-Ex-Lax giveaway 3.60 9.00 18.00

STRANGE AS IT SEEMS
1939
United Features Syndicate

Single Series 9, 1, 2 28.00 83.00 220.00

STRANGE ATTRACTORS
1993 - Present ($2.50, B&W)
RetroGraphix

1-15: 1-(5/93), 2-(8/93), 3-(11/93), 4-(2/94) 1.00 2.50
Volume One-($14.95, trade paperback)-r/#1-7 15.00

STRANGE ATTRACTORS: MOON FEVER
Feb, 1997 - Present ($2.95, B&W, mini-series)
Caliber Comics

1,2 1.20 3.00

STRANGE COMBAT TALES
Oct, 1993 - No. 4, Jan, 1994 ($2.50, limited series)
Marvel Comics (Epic Comics)

1-4 1.00 2.50

STRANGE CONFESSIONS
Jan-Mar (Spring on-c), 1952 - No. 4, Fall, 1952 (All have photo-c)
Ziff-Davis Publ. Co. (Approved)

1(Scarce)-Kinstler-a 38.00 114.00 280.00
2(Scarce, 7-8/52) 26.00 79.00 190.00
3(Scarce, 9-10/52)-#3 on-c, #2 on inside; Reformatory girl story; photo-c 26.00 79.00 190.00
4(Scarce) 26.00 79.00 190.00

STRANGE DAYS
Oct, 1984 - No. 3, Apr, 1985 ($1.75, Baxter paper)
Eclipse Comics

1-3: Freakwave, Johnny Nemo, & Paradax from Vanguard Illustrated; nudity, violence & strong language .75 1.80

STRANGE DAYS (Movie)
Dec, 1995 ($5.95, squarebound, one-shot)
Marvel Comics

1-Adaptation of film 2.40 6.00

STRANGE FANTASY (Eerie Tales of Suspense!)(Formerly Rocketman #1)
Aug, 1952 - No. 14, Oct-Nov, 1954
Ajax-Farrell

2(#1, 8/52)-Jungle Princess story; Kamenish-a; reprinted from Ellery Queen #1 34.00 101.00 250.00
2(10/52)-No Black Cat or Rulah; Bakerish, Kamenish-a; hypo/meathook-c 26.00 77.00 200.00
3-Rulah story, called Pulah 24.00 73.00 190.00
4-Rocket Man app. (2/53) 21.00 64.00 170.00
5,6,8,10,12,14 17.00 49.00 125.00
7-Madam Satan/Slave story 21.00 64.00 170.00
9(w/Black Cat), 9(w/Boy's Ranch; S&K-a)(A rebinding of Harvey interiors; not publ. by Ajax) 20.00 60.00 160.00
9-Regular issue; Steve Ditko's 3rd published work (tied with Captain 3D) 31.00 92.00 245.00
11-Jungle story 22.00 66.00 170.00
13-Bondage-c; Rulah (Kolah) story 21.00 64.00 170.00

STRANGE GALAXY
V1#8, Feb, 1971 - No. 11, Aug, 1971 (B&W, magazine)
Eerie Publications

V1#8-Reprints-c/Fantastic V19#3 (2/70) (a pulp) 2.50 7.50 24.00
9-11 2.00 6.00 16.00

STRANGEHAVEN
June, 1995 - Present ($2.95, B&W)
Abiogenesis Press

1-8 1.20 3.00

STRANGE JOURNEY
Sept, 1957 - No. 4, June, 1958 (Farrell reprints)
America's Best (Steinway Publ.) (Ajax/Farrell)

1 14.00 43.00 110.00
2-4: 2-Flying saucer-c 10.00 30.00 70.00

STRANGE LOVE (See Fox Giants)

STRANGELOVE
1995 ($2.50)
Entity Comics

1 1.00 2.50

STRANGE MYSTERIES
Sept, 1951 - No. 21, Jan, 1955
Superior/Dynamic Publications

1-Kamenish-a & horror stories begin 44.00 132.00 370.00
2 24.00 73.00 180.00
3-5 21.00 64.00 160.00

The Strangers #8 © MAL

Sttrangers In Paradise V3 #1 © Terry Moore

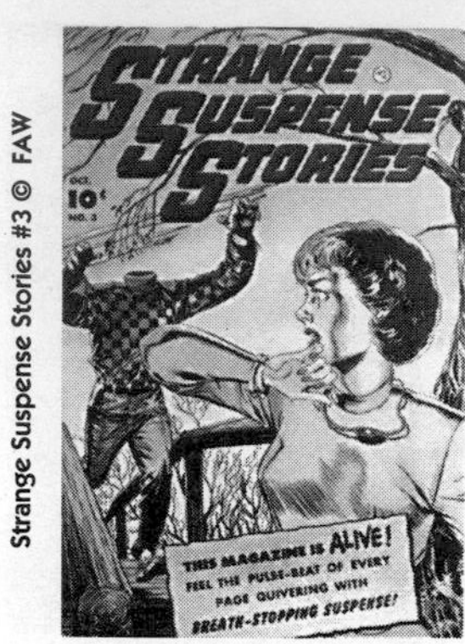

Strange Suspense Stories #3 © FAW

GD25 FN65 NM94

6-8 17.00 51.00 130.00
9-Bondage 3-D effect-c 24.00 71.00 175.00
10-Used in **SOTI**, pg. 181 17.00 49.00 125.00
11-18 13.50 41.00 105.00
19-r/Journey Into Fear #1; cover is a splash from one story; Baker-r(2) 17.00 49.00 120.00
20,21-Reprints; 20-r/#1 with new-c 10.00 30.00 75.00

STRANGE MYSTERIES
1963 - 1964
I. W. Enterprises/Super Comics

I.W. Reprint #9; Rulah-r/Spook #28; Disbrow-a 2.50 7.50 20.00
Super Reprint #10-12,15-17(1963-64): 10,11-r/Strange #2,1. 12-r/Tales of Horror #5 (3/53) less-c. 15-r/Dark Mysteries #23. 16-r/The Dead Who Walk. 17-r/Dark Mysteries #22 2.50 7.50 20.00
Super Reprint #18-r/Witchcraft #1; Kubert-a 2.50 7.50 20.00

STRANGE PLANETS
1958; 1963-64
I. W. Enterprises/Super Comics

I.W. Reprint #1(nd)-Reprints E. C. Incredible S/F #30 plus-c/Strange Worlds #3 5.50 16.50 55.00
I.W. Reprint #9-Orlando/Wood-r/Strange Worlds #4; cover-r from Flying Saucers #1 7.50 22.50 75.00
Super Reprint #10-Wood-r (22 pg.) from Space Detective #1; cover-r/Attack on Planet Mars 7.00 21.00 70.00
Super Reprint #11-Wood-r (25 pg.) from An Earthman on Venus 8.50 25.50 85.00
Super Reprint #12-Orlando-r/Rocket to the Moon 7.00 21.00 70.00
Super Reprint #15-Reprints Journey Into Unknown Worlds #8; Heath, Colan-r 3.00 9.00 30.00
Super Reprint #16-Reprints Avon's Strange Worlds #6; Kinstler, Check-a 3.50 10.50 35.00
Super Reprint #18-r/Great Exploits #1 (Daring Adventures #6); Space Busters, Explorer Joe, The Son of Robin Hood; Krigstein-a 2.50 7.50 25.00

STRANGERS, THE
June, 1993 - No. 24, May, 1995 ($1.95/$2.50)
Malibu Comics (Ultraverse)

1-4,6-12,14-20: 1-1st app. The Strangers; has coupon for Ultraverse Premiere #0; 1st app. the Night Man (not in costume). 2-Polybagged w/trading card. 7-Break-Thru x-over. 8-2 pg. origin Solution. 12-Silver foil logo; wraparound-c. 17-Rafferty app. .80 2.00
1-With coupon missing 1.50
1-Full cover holographic edition, 1st of kind w/Hardcase #1 & Prime #1 2.00 5.00
1-Ultra 5000 limited silver foil 1.60 4.00
4-($2.50)-Newsstand edition bagged w/card 1.00 2.50
5-($2.50, 52 pgs.)-Rune flip-c/story by B. Smith (3 pgs.); The Mighty Magnor 1 pg. strip by Aragones; 3-pg. Night Man preview 1.00 2.50
13-($3.50, 68 pgs.)-Mantra app.; flip book w/Ultraverse Premiere #4 1.40 3.50
21-24 ($2.50) 1.00 2.50
...:The Pilgrim Conundrum Saga (1/95, $3.95, 68pgs.) 1.60 4.00

STRANGERS IN PARADISE
Nov, 1994 - No. 3, Feb, 1994 ($2.75, B&W, limited series)
Antarctic Press

1 6.50 19.50 65.00
1-2nd/3rd prints 1.00 2.80 7.00
2 (2300 printed) 5.00 15.00 50.00
3 3.00 9.00 30.00
Trade paperback (Antarctic Press, $6.95)-Red -c (5000 print run) 15.00
Trade paperback (Abstract Studios, $6.95)-Red-c (2000 print run) 20.00
Trade paperback (Abstract Studios, $6.95, 1st-4th printing)-Blue- 7.00

STRANGERS IN PARADISE
Sept, 1994 - No. 14, July, 1996 ($2.75, B&W)
Abstract Studios

1 2.50 7.50 20.00
1,3- 2nd printings 2.00 5.00
2,3: 2-Color dream sequence. 2.00 10.00
4-10 1.10 5.00
4-6-2nd printings 2.75
11-14: 14-The Letters of Molly & Poo 1.20 3.00
I Dream Of You ($16.95, TPB) r/#1-9 17.00
It's a Good Life ($8.95, TPB) r/#10-13 9.00

STRANGERS IN PARADISE (Volume Three)
Oct, 1996 - Present ($2.75, color #1-5, B&W #6-on)
Homage Comics #1-8/Abstract Studios #9-on

1-Terry Moore-c/s/a in all; dream seq. by Jim Lee-a 2.00 5.00
1-Jim Lee variant-c 1.00 2.80 7.00
2-5 1.20 3.00
6-12: 6-Return to B&W 2.75
Love Me Tender ($12.95, TPB) r/#1-5 in B&W w/ color Lee seq. 12.95

STRANGE SPORTS STORIES (See Brave & the Bold #45-49, DC Special, and DC Super Stars #10)
Sept-Oct, 1973 - No. 6, July-Aug, 1974
National Periodical Publications

1 2.50 7.50 20.00
2-6: 3-Swan/Anderson-a 1.50 4.50 12.00

STRANGE STORIES FROM ANOTHER WORLD (Unknown World #1)
No. 2, Aug, 1952 - No. 5, Feb, 1953
Fawcett Publications

2-Saunders painted-c 40.00 120.00 310.00
3-5-Saunders painted-c 31.00 92.00 225.00

STRANGE STORIES OF SUSPENSE (Rugged Action #1-4)
No. 5, Oct, 1955 - No. 16, Aug, 1957
Atlas Comics (CSI)

5(#1) 29.00 86.00 215.00
6,9 17.00 51.00 130.00
7-E. C. swipe cover/Vault of Horror #32 18.00 54.00 135.00
8-Morrow/Williamson-a; Pakula-a 18.00 54.00 135.00
10-Crandall, Torres, Meskin-a 18.00 54.00 135.00
11-13: 12-Torres, Pakula-a. 13-E.C. art swipes 13.50 41.00 105.00
14-16: 14-Williamson/Mayo-a. 15-Krigstein-a. 16-Fox, Powell-a 14.00 43.00 110.00

NOTE: ***Everett** a-6, 7, 13; c-8, 9, 11-14. **Heath** a-5. **Maneely** c-5. **Morisi** a-11. **Morrow** a-13. **Powell** a-8. **Severin** c-7. **Wildey** a-14.*

STRANGE STORY (Also see Front Page)
June-July, 1946 (52 pgs.)
Harvey Publications

1-The Man in Black Called Fate by Powell 22.00 66.00 175.00

STRANGE SUSPENSE STORIES (Lawbreakers Suspense Stories #10-15; This Is Suspense #23-26; Captain Atom V1#78 on)
6/52 - No. 5, 2/53; No. 16, 1/54 - No. 22, 11/54; No. 27, 10/55 - No. 77, 10/65; V3#1, 10/67 - V1#9, 9/69
Fawcett Publications/Charlton Comics No. 16 on

1-(Fawcett)-Powell, Sekowsky-a 58.00 174.00 485.00
2-George Evans horror story 40.00 120.00 290.00
3-5 (2/53)-George Evans horror stories 36.00 107.00 260.00
16(1-2/54)-Formerly Lawbreakers S.S. 21.00 64.00 160.00
17,21: 21-Shuster-a 17.00 49.00 125.00
18-E.C. swipe/HOF 7; Ditko-c/a(2) 30.00 90.00 215.00
19-Ditko electric chair-c; Ditko-a 38.00 114.00 275.00
20-Ditko-c/a(2) 29.00 84.00 205.00

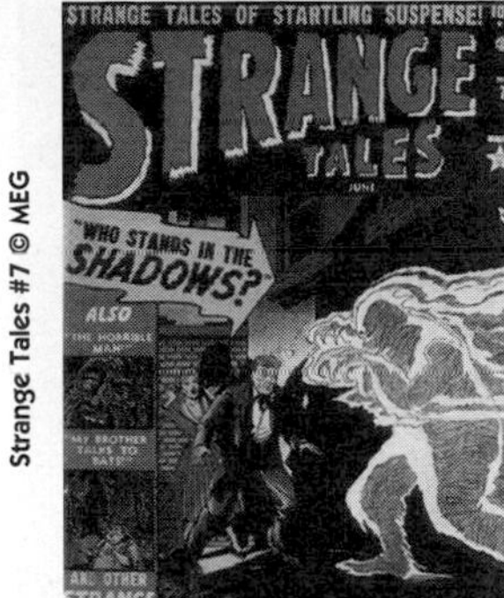

Strange Tales #7 © MEG

Strange Tales #15 © MEG

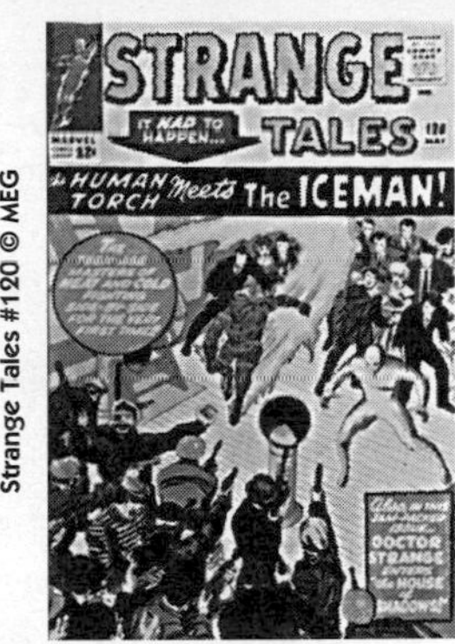

Strange Tales #120 © MEG

GD25 FN65 NM94

22(11/54)-Ditko-c, Shuster-a; last pre-code issue; becomes This Is Suspense 25.00 75.00 185.00
27(10/55)-(Formerly This Is Suspense #26) 10.00 30.00 75.00
28-30,38 6.85 21.00 48.00
31-33,35,37,40-Ditko-c/a(2-3 each) 16.00 47.00 120.00
34-Story of ruthless business man, Wm. B. Gaines; Ditko-c/a 31.00 94.00 250.00
36-(15¢, 68 pgs.); Ditko-a(4) 16.00 49.00 130.00
39,41,52,53-Ditko-a 12.00 38.00 100.00
42-44,46,49,54-60 3.00 9.00 30.00
45,47,48,50,51-Ditko-c/a 8.00 24.00 80.00
61-74 1.50 4.50 14.00
75(6/65)-Reprints origin/1st app. Captain Atom by Ditko from Space Advs. #33; r/Severin-a/Space Advs. #24 (75-77: 12¢ issues) 10.00 30.00 100.00
76,77-Captain Atom-r by Ditko/Space Advs. 4.50 13.50 45.00
V3#1(10/67): 12¢ issues begin 2.50 7.50 20.00
V1#2-Ditko-c/a; atom bomb-c 1.85 5.50 15.00
V1#3-9: All 12¢ issues 1.25 3.75 10.00

NOTE: ***Alascia** a-19. **Aparo** a-60, V3#1, 2, 4; c-V1#4, 8. **Baily** a-1-3; c-2, 5. **Evans** c-3, 4. **Giordana** c-16, 17p, 24p, 25p. **Montes/Bache** c-66. **Powell** a-4. **Shuster** a-19, 21. **Marcus Swayze** a-27.*

STRANGE TALES (...Featuring Warlock #178-181; Doctor Strange #169 on)
June, 1951 - #168, May, 1968; #169, Sept, 1973 - #188, Nov, 1976
Atlas (CCPC #1-67/ZPC #68-79/VPI #80-85)/Marvel #86(7/61) on

1-Horror/weird stories begin 255.00 766.00 2400.00
2 95.00 286.00 785.00
3,5: 3-Atom bomb panels 70.00 211.00 580.00
4-Cosmic eyeball story "The Evil Eye" 76.00 230.00 630.00
6-9: 6-Heath-c/a 53.00 159.00 440.00
10-Krigstein-a 58.00 172.00 475.00
11-14,16-20 38.00 114.00 280.00
15-Krigstein-a 39.00 116.00 285.00
21,23-27,29-34: 27-Atom bomb panels. 33-Davis-a. 34-Last pre-code issue (2/55) 30.00 90.00 215.00
22-Krigstein, Forte/Fox-a 31.00 92.00 220.00
28-Jack Katz story used in Senate Investigation report, pgs. 7 & 169 31.00 94.00 225.00
35-41,43,44: 37-Vampire story by Colan 18.00 54.00 180.00
42,45,59,61-Krigstein-a; #61 (2/58) 18.50 55.00 185.00
46-57,60: 51-1st S.A. issue. 53,56-Crandall-a. 60-(8/57) 16.00 48.00 160.00
58,64-Williamson-a in each, with Mayo-#58 16.00 48.00 160.00
62,63,65,66: 62-Torres-a. 66-Crandall-a 15.00 45.00 150.00
67-Prototype ish. (Quicksilver) 18.00 54.00 180.00
68,71,72,74,77,80: Ditko/Kirby-a in #67-80 16.00 48.00 160.00
69-Prototype ish. (Prof. X) 22.00 66.00 220.00
70-Prototype ish. (Giant Man) 22.00 66.00 220.00
73-Prototype ish. (Ant-Man) 22.00 66.00 220.00
75-Prototype ish. (Iron Man) 22.00 66.00 220.00
76-Prototype ish. (Human Torch) 22.00 66.00 220.00
78-Prototype ish. (Ant-Man) 22.00 66.00 220.00
79-Prototype ish. (Dr. Strange) (12/60) 22.00 66.00 220.00
81-83,85-88,90,91-Ditko/Kirby-a in all: 90-(11/61)-Atom bomb blast panel 14.00 42.00 140.00
84-Prototype ish. (Magneto)(5/61); has powers like Magneto of X-Men over two years later; Ditko/Kirby-a 18.00 54.00 180.00
89-1st app. Fin Fang Foom (10/61) by Kirby 36.00 108.00 395.00
92-Prototype ish. (Ancient One); last 10¢ issue 15.00 45.00 150.00
93,95,96,98-100: Kirby-a 13.00 39.00 130.00
94-Prototype ish. (The Thing); Kirby-a 15.00 45.00 150.00
97-1st app. Aunt May & Uncle Ben by Ditko (6/62), before Amazing Fantasy #15; (see Tales Of Suspense #7); Kirby-a 31.00 93.00 325.00

GD25 FN65 VF82 NM94

101-Human Torch begins by Kirby (10/62); origin recap Fantastic Four & Human Torch; H. Torch-c begin 73.00 219.00 438.00 875.00

GD25 FN65 NM94

102-1st app. Wizard 29.00 87.00 290.00
103-105: 104-1st app. Trapster. 105-2nd Wizard 24.00 72.00 240.00
106,108,109: 106-Fantastic Four guests (3/63) 15.50 47.00 155.00
107-(4/63)-Human Torch/Sub-Mariner battle; 4th S.A. Sub-Mariner app. & 1st x-over outside of Fantastic Four 18.50 55.00 185.00

GD25 FN65 VF82 NM94

110-(7/63)-Intro Doctor Strange, Ancient One & Wong by Ditko 81.00 243.00 486.00 975.00

GD25 FN65 NM94

111-2nd Dr. Strange 31.00 93.00 310.00
112,113 10.50 32.00 105.00
114-Acrobat disguised as Captain America, 1st app. since the G.A.; intro. & 1st app. Victoria Bentley; 3rd Dr. Strange app. & begin series (11/63) 32.00 96.00 360.00
115-Origin Dr. Strange; Human Torch vs. Sandman (Spidey villain; 2nd app. & brief origin); early Spider-Man x-over, 12/63 40.00 120.00 460.00
116-(1/64)-Human Torch battles The Thing; 1st Thing x-over 10.00 30.00 100.00
117,118,120: 120-1st Iceman x-over (from X-Men) 6.50 19.50 65.00
119-Spider-Man x-over (2 panel cameo) 11.50 34.00 115.00
121,122,124,126-134: Thing/Torch team-up in 121-134. 126-Intro Clea. 128-Quicksilver & Scarlet Witch app. (1/65). 130-The Beatles cameo. 134-Last Human Torch; The Watcher-c/story; Wood-a(i) 4.50 13.50 45.00
123-1st app. The Beetle (see Amazing Spider-Man #21 for next app.); 1st Thor x-over (8/64); Loki app. 5.00 15.00 50.00
125-Torch & Thing battle Sub-Mariner (10/64) 4.50 13.50 45.00
135-Col. (formerly Sgt.) Nick Fury becomes Nick Fury Agent of Shield (origin/1st app.) by Kirby (8/65); series begins 10.00 30.00 100.00
136-147,149: 138-Intro Eternity. 145-Begins alternating-c features w/Nick Fury (odd #'s) & Dr. Strange (even #'s). 146-Last Ditko Dr. Strange who is in consecutive stories since #113. 146-Only Ditko Dr. Strange-c this title. 147-Dr. Strange (by Everett #147-152) continues thru #168, then Dr. Strange #169 3.00 9.00 30.00
148-Origin Ancient One 5.50 16.50 55.00
150(11/66)-John Buscema's 1st work at Marvel 3.00 9.00 30.00
151-Kirby/Steranko-c/a; 1st Marvel work by Steranko 3.80 11.40 38.00
152,153-Kirby/Steranko-a 2.80 8.40 28.00
154-158-Steranko-a/script 2.80 8.40 28.00
159-Origin Nick Fury retold; Intro Val; Captain America-c/story; Steranko-a 3.00 9.00 30.00
160-162-Steranko-a/scripts; Capt. America app. 2.50 7.50 25.00
163-166,168-Steranko-a(p). 168-Last Nick Fury (gets own book next month) & last Dr. Strange who also gets own book 2.50 7.50 25.00
167-Steranko pen/script; classic flag-c 3.80 11.40 38.00
169-1st app. Brother Voodoo(origin in 169,170) & begin series, ends #173. 1.25 3.75 10.00
170-173 1.00 3.00 8.00
174-Origin Golem 2.40 6.00
175-177: 177-Brunner-c 1.60 4.00
178-(2/75)-Warlock by Starlin begins; origin Warlock & Him retold; 1st app. Magus; Starlin-c/a/scripts in 178-181 (all before Warlock #9) 1.85 5.50 15.00
179-181-All Warlock. 179-Intro/1st app. Pip the Troll. 180-Intro Gamora. 181-(8/75)-Warlock story continued in Warlock #9 1.10 3.30 9.00
182-188 1.40 3.50
Annual 1(1962)-Reprints from Strange Tales #73,76,78, Tales of Suspense #7,9, Tales to Astonish #1,6,7, & Journey Into Mystery #53,55,59; (1st Marvel annual?) 39.00 117.00 440.00
Annual 2(7/63)-Reprints from Strange Tales #67, Strange Worlds (Atlas) #1-3, World of Fantasy #16; new Human Torch vs. Spider-Man story by Kirby/Ditko (1st Spidey x-over; 4th app.); Kirby-c 40.00 120.00 470.00

NOTE: ***Briefer** a-17. **Burgos** a-123p. **J. Buscema** a-174p. **Colan** a-11, 20, 37, 53, 169-173p,*

Strange Terrors #3 © STJ

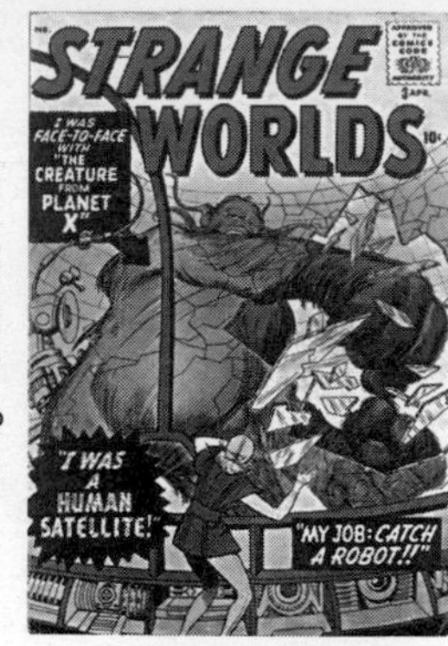

Strange Worlds #3 © AVON

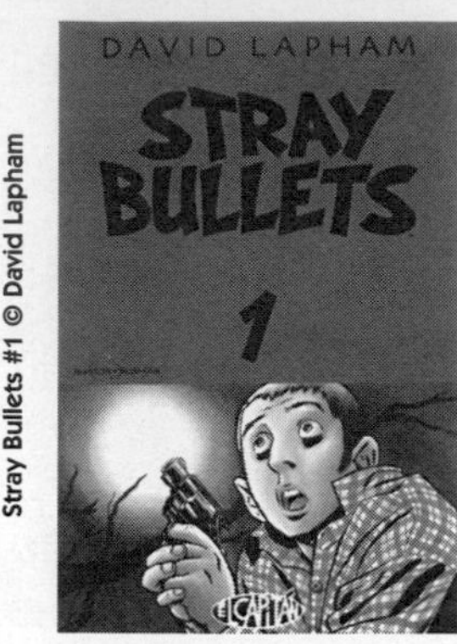

Stray Bullets #1 © David Lapham

GD25 FN65 NM94

188p. ***Davis*** *c-71.* ***Ditko*** *a-46, 50, 67-122, 123-125p, 126-146, 175r, 182-188r; c-51, 93, 115, 121, 146.* ***Everett*** *a-4, 21, 40-42, 73, 147-152, 164i; c-8, 10, 11, 13, 15, 24, 45, 49-54, 56, 58, 60, 61, 63, 148, 150, 152, 158i.* ***Forte*** *a-27, 43, 50, 53, 54, 60.* ***Heath*** *a-6; c-6, 18-20.* ***Kamen*** *a-45.* ***G. Kane*** *c-170-173, 182p.* ***Kirby*** *Human Torch-101-105, 108, 109, 114, 120; Nick Fury-135p, 141-143p; (Layouts)-135-153; other* ***Kirby*** *a-67-100p; c-68-70, 72-74, 76-92, 94, 95, 101-114, 116-123, 125-130, 132-135, 136p, 138-145, 147, 149, 151p.* ***Kirby/Ayers*** *c-101-106, 108-110.* ***Kirby/Ditko*** *a-80, 88, 121; c-75, 93, 97, 100. .* ***Lawrence*** *a-29.* ***Leiber/ Fox*** *a-110, 111, 113.* ***Maneely*** *a-3, 37, 42; c-33, 40.* ***Moldoff*** *a-20.* ***Mooney*** *a-174i.* ***Morisi*** *a-53, 56.* ***Morrow*** *a-54.* ***Orlando*** *a-41, 44, 46, 49, 52.* ***Powell*** *a-42, 44, 49, 54, 130-134p; c-131p.* ***Reinman*** *a-11, 50, 74, 88, 91, 95, 104, 106, 112i, 124-127i.* ***Robinson*** *a-17.* ***Romita*** *c-169.* ***Roussos*** *c-201i.* ***R.Q. Sale*** *a-56; c-16.* ***Sekowski*** *a-3, 11.* ***Severin*** *a(i)-136-138; c-137.* ***Starlin*** *a-178, 179, 180p, 181p; c-178-180, 181p.* ***Steranko*** *a-151-161, 162-168p; c-151i, 153, 155, 157, 159, 161, 163, 165, 167.* ***Torres*** *a-53, 62.* ***Tuska*** *a-14, 166p.* ***Whitney*** *a-149.* ***Wildey*** *a-42, 56.* ***Woodbridge*** *a-59. Fantastic Four cameos #101-134. Jack Katz app.-26.*

STRANGE TALES
Apr, 1987 - No. 19, Oct, 1988
Marvel Comics Group

V2#1-19 1.00

STRANGE TALES
Nov, 1994 ($6.95, one-shots)
Marvel Comics

V3#1-acetate-c 1.00 2.80 7.00

STRANGE TALES OF THE UNUSUAL
Dec, 1955 - No. 11, Aug, 1957
Atlas Comics (ACI No. 1-4/WPI No. 5-11)

1-Powell-a 38.00 114.00 285.00
2 21.00 62.00 155.00
3-Williamson-a (4 pgs.) 21.00 64.00 160.00
4,6,8,11 13.50 41.00 105.00
5-Crandall, Ditko-a 18.00 54.00 135.00
7,9: 7-Kirby, Orlando-a. 9-Krigstein-a 15.00 45.00 115.00
10-Torres, Morrow-a 13.50 41.00 105.00

NOTE: ***Baily*** *a-6.* ***Brodsky*** *c-2-4.* ***Everett*** *a-2, 6; c-6, 9, 11.* ***Heck*** *a-1.* ***Maneely*** *c-1.* ***Orlando*** *a-7.* ***Pakula*** *a-10.* ***Romita*** *a-1.* ***R.Q. Sale*** *a-3.* ***Wildey*** *a-3.*

STRANGE TERRORS
June, 1952 - No. 7, Mar, 1953
St. John Publishing Co.

1-Bondage-c; Zombies spelled Zoombies on-c; Fine-*esque* -a 39.00 118.00 300.00
2 21.00 64.00 160.00
3-Kubert-a; painted-c 28.00 84.00 210.00
4-Kubert-a (reprinted in Mystery Tales #18); Ekgren painted-c; Fine-*esque* -a; Jerry Iger caricature 38.00 114.00 275.00
5-Kubert-a; painted-c 28.00 84.00 210.00
6-Giant (25¢, 100 pgs.)(1/53); bondage-c 38.00 114.00 275.00
7-Giant (25¢, 100 pgs.); Kubert-c/a 40.00 120.00 310.00

NOTE: ***Cameron*** *a-6, 7.* ***Morisi*** *a-6.*

STRANGE WORLD OF YOUR DREAMS
Aug, 1952 - No. 4, Jan-Feb, 1953
Prize Publications

1-Simon & Kirby-a 50.00 150.00 425.00
2,3-Simon & Kirby-a. 2-Meskin-a 40.00 120.00 330.00
4-S&K-c; Meskin-a 38.00 114.00 270.00

STRANGE WORLDS (#18 continued from Avon's Eerie #1-17)
11/50 - No. 9, 11/52; No. 18, 10-11/54 - No. 22, 9-10/55 (No #11-17)
Avon Periodicals

1-Kenton of the Star Patrol by Kubert (r/Eerie #1 from 1947); Crom the Barbarian by John Giunta 68.00 206.00 600.00
2-Wood-a; Crom the Barbarian by Giunta; Dara of the Vikings app.; used in **SOTI**, pg. 112; injury to eye panel 65.00 195.00 575.00
3-Wood/Orlando-a (Kenton), Wood/Williamson/Frazetta/Krenkel/Orlando-a (7 pgs.); Malu Slave Girl Princess app.; Kinstler-c 131.00 393.00 1150.00

GD25 FN65 NM94

4-Wood-c/a (Kenton); Orlando-a; origin The Enchanted Daggar; Sultan-a 62.00 187.00 560.00
5-Orlando/Wood-a (Kenton); Wood-c 44.00 130.00 375.00
6-Kinstler-a(2); Orlando/Wood-c; Check-a 34.00 101.00 250.00
7-Fawcette & Becker/Alascia-a 26.00 79.00 200.00
8-Kubert, Kinstler, Hollingsworth & Lazarus-a; Lazarus Robot-c 26.00 79.00 200.00
9-Kinstler, Fawcette, Alascia-a 25.00 75.00 190.00
18-(Formerly Eerie #17)-Reprints "Attack on Planet Mars" by Kubert 25.00 75.00 180.00
19-r/Avon's "Robotmen of the Lost Planet"; last pre-code issue; Robot-c 25.00 75.00 180.00
20-War-c/story; Wood-c(r)/U.S. Paratroops #1 7.50 22.50 45.00
21,22-War-c/stories. 22-New logo 5.70 17.00 35.00
I.W. Reprint #5-Kinstler-a(r)/Avon's #9 2.00 6.00 16.00

STRANGE WORLDS
Dec, 1958 - No. 5, Aug, 1959
Marvel Comics (MPI No. 1,2/Male No. 3,5)

1-Kirby & Ditko-a; flying saucer issue 68.00 206.00 575.00
2-Ditko-c/a 40.00 120.00 320.00
3-Kirby-a(2) 33.00 99.00 250.00
4-Williamson-a 31.00 94.00 235.00
5-Ditko-a 26.00 77.00 195.00

NOTE: ***Buscema*** *a-3, 4.* ***Ditko*** *a-1-5; c-2..* ***Heck*** *a-2.* ***Kirby*** *a-1, 3.* ***Kirby/Brodsky*** *c-1, 3-5.*

STRAWBERRY SHORTCAKE
June, 1985 - No. 7, Apr, 1986 (Children's comic)
Marvel Comics (Star Comics)

1-7: Howie Post-a 1.00

STRAY BULLETS
1995 - Present ($2.95, B&W, mature readers)
El Capitan Books

1-David Lapham-c/a/scripts 1.85 5.50 15.00
2,3 1.25 3.75 10.00
4,6-8 1.10 3.30 9.00
5 ($3.50) 2.40 6.00
9-13: Begin $2.95-c 2.00 5.00
14-($3.50) 3.50
Volume 1 ($29.95, hardcover) 30.00

NOTE: *Multiple issues of all issues exist & are worth cover price.*

STRAY TOASTERS
Jan, 1988 - No. 4, April, 1989 ($3.50, squarebound, limited series)
Marvel Comics (Epic Comics)

1-4: Sienkiewicz-c/a/scripts 1.40 3.50

STREET COMIX
1973 (50¢, B&W, 36 pgs.) (20,000 print run)
Street Enterprises/King Features

1,2: 1-Rip Kirby. 2-Flash Gordon 1.50

STREETFIGHTER
Aug, 1986 - No. 4, Spr, 1987 ($1.75, limited series)
Ocean Comics

1-4: 2-Origin begins .75 1.80

STREET FIGHTER
Sept, 1993 - No. 3, Nov, 1993 ($2.95)
Malibu Comics

1-3: 3-Includes poster; Ferret x-over 1.20 3.00

STREET FIGHTER: THE BATTLE FOR SHADALOO
1995 ($3.95, one-shot)
DC Comics/CAP Co. Ltd.

1-polybagged w/trading card & Tattoo 1.60 4.00

Strike! #3 © ECL

Strikeback! #4 © Jonathan Peterson & Kevin Maguire

Stygmata #2 © Entity

	GD25	FN65	NM94

STREET FIGHTER II
Apr, 1994 - No. 8, Nov, 1994 ($2.95, limited series)
Tokuma Comics (Viz)

	GD25	FN65	NM94
1-8		1.20	3.00

STREET POET RAY
Spring, 1989; 1990 - No. 4, 1990 ($2.95, B&W, squarebound)
Blackthorne Publ./Marvel Comics

	GD25	FN65	NM94
1 (Blackthorne, $2.00)		1.00	2.00
1-4 (Marvel, $2.95, thick-c & paper)		1.20	3.00

STREETS
1993 - No. 3, 1993 ($4.95, limited series, 52 pgs.)
DC Comics

	GD25	FN65	NM94
Book 1-3-Estes painted-c		2.00	5.00

STREET SHARKS
Jan, 1996 - No. 3, Mar, 1996 ($1.50, limited series)
Archie Publications

	GD25	FN65	NM94
1-3			1.50

STREET SHARKS
May, 1996 - Present ($1.50, published 8 times a year)
Archie Publications

	GD25	FN65	NM94
1-6			1.50

STRICTLY PRIVATE (You're in the Army Now)
July, 1942 (#1 on sale 6/15/42)
Eastern Color Printing Co.

	GD25	FN65	NM94
1,2: Private Peter Plink. 2-Says 128 pgs. on-c	18.00	54.00	145.00

STRIKE!
Aug, 1987 - No. 6, Jan, 1988 ($1.75)
Eclipse Comics

	GD25	FN65	NM94
1-6		.75	1.80
...Vs. Sgt. Strike Special 1 (5/88, $1.95)		.80	2.00

STRIKEBACK! (The Hunt For Nikita)
Oct, 1994 - No. 3, Jan, 1995 ($2.95, unfinished limited series)
Malibu Comics (Bravura)

	GD25	FN65	NM94
1-3: Jonathon Peterson script, Kevin Maguire-c/a		1.20	3.00
1-Gold foil embossed-c	1.00	3.00	8.00

STRIKEBACK!
Jan, 1996 - No. 5, May, 1996 ($2.50, limited series)
Image Comics (Wildstorm Productions)

	GD25	FN65	NM94
1-6: Reprints original Bravura series w/additional story & art by Kevin Maguire & Jonathon Peterson; new Maguire-c in all. 4,5-New story & art.		1.00	2.50

STRIKEFORCE: AMERICA
Dec, 1995 ($2.95)
Comico

	GD25	FN65	NM94
V2#1-Polybagged w/gaming card; S. Clark-a(p)		1.20	3.00

STRIKEFORCE: MORITURI
Dec, 1986 - No. 31, July, 1989
Marvel Comics Group

	GD25	FN65	NM94
1-12, 14: 14-Williamson-i			1.00
13-Double size			1.50
15-23 ($1.00-$1.25)			1.25
24-31 ($1.50): 25-Heath-c			1.50

STRIKEFORCE MORITURI: ELECTRIC UNDERTOW
Dec, 1989 - No. 5, Mar, 1990 ($3.95, 52 pgs., limited series)
Marvel Comics

	GD25	FN65	NM94
1-5 Squarebound		1.60	4.00

STRONG GUY REBORN (See X-Factor)
Sept, 1997 ($2.99, one-shot)
Marvel Comics

	GD25	FN65	NM94
1-Dezago-s/Andy Smith, Art Thibert-a		1.20	3.00

STRONG MAN (Also see Complimentary Comics & Power of...)
Mar-Apr, 1955 - No. 4, Sept-Oct, 1955
Magazine Enterprises

	GD25	FN65	NM94
1(A-1 #130)-Powell-c/a	17.50	53.00	140.00
2-4: (A-1 #132,134,139)-Powell-a. 2-Powell-c	14.50	43.00	115.00

STRONTIUM DOG
Dec, 1985 - No. 4, Mar, 1986 ($1.25, limited series)
Eagle Comics

	GD25	FN65	NM94
1-4: 4-Moore scripts.			1.30
Special 1 (1986)-Moore scripts			1.50

STRYFE'S STRIKE FILE
Jan, 1993 ($1.75, one-shot, no ads)
Marvel Comics

	GD25	FN65	NM94
1-Stroman, Capullo, Andy Kubert, Brandon Peterson-a; silver metallic ink-c; X-Men tie-in to X-Cutioner's Song		.70	1.75
1-Gold metallic ink 2nd printing		.70	1.75

STRYKE
1995 ($3.00)
London Night Studios

	GD25	FN65	NM94
0		1.20	3.00
0-Alternate-c		2.00	5.00

STUMBO THE GIANT (See Harvey Hits #49, 54, 57, 60, 63, 66, 69, 72, 78, 88 & Hot Stuff #2)

STUMBO TINYTOWN
Oct, 1963 - No. 13, Nov, 1966 (All 25¢ giants)
Harvey Publications

	GD25	FN65	NM94
1-Stumbo, Hot Stuff & others begin	12.00	36.00	125.00
2	7.00	21.00	70.00
3-5	4.50	13.50	45.00
6-13	3.60	10.80	36.00

STUNT DAWGS
Mar, 1993 ($1.25, one-shot)
Harvey Comics

	GD25	FN65	NM94
1			1.25

STUNTMAN COMICS (Also see Thrills Of Tomorrow)
Apr-May, 1946 - No. 2, June-July, 1946; No. 3, Oct-Nov, 1946
Harvey Publications

	GD25	FN65	NM94
1-Origin Stuntman by S&K reprinted in Black Cat #9; S&K-c	83.00	250.00	750.00
2-S&K-c/a; The Duke of Broadway story	56.00	168.00	500.00

3-Small size (5-1/2x8-1/2"; B&W; 32 pgs.); distributed to mail subscribers only; S&K-a; Kid Adonis by S&K reprinted in Green Hornet #37
Estimated value... $250.00-$400.00
(Also see All-New #15, Boy Explorers #2, Flash Gordon #5 & Thrills of Tomorrow)

STUPID HEROES
Sept, 1993 ($2.75, unfinished limited series)
Mirage Studios

	GD25	FN65	NM94
1-Laird-c/a & scripts; 2 trading cards bound in		1.10	2.75

STYGMATA
No. 0, July, 1994 - No. 3, Oct, 1994 ($2.95, B&W, limited series)
Entity Comics

	GD25	FN65	NM94
0, 1-3: 0,1-Foil-c. 3-Silver foil logo		1.20	3.00
Yearbook 1 (1995, $2.95)		1.20	3.00

SUBMARINE ATTACK (Formerly Speed Demons)

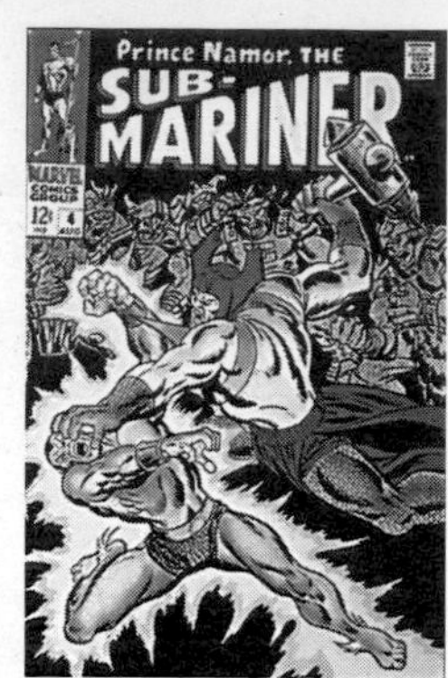

The Sub-Mariner #4 © MEG

Sub-Mariner Comics #1 © MEG

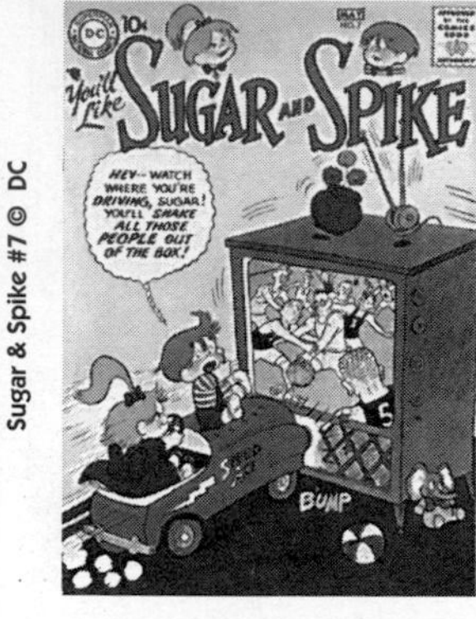

Sugar & Spike #7 © DC

GD25 FN65 NM94

No. 11, May, 1958 - No. 54, Feb-Mar, 1966
Charlton Comics

11 2.50 7.50 24.00
12-20 2.50 7.50 20.00
21-54 1.85 5.50 15.00
NOTE: *Glanzman c/a-25.* ***Montes/Bache*** *a-38, 40, 41.*

SUB-MARINER (See All-Select, All-Winners, Blonde Phantom, Daring, The Defenders, Fantastic Four #4, Human Torch, The Invaders, Iron Man &..., Marvel Mystery, Marvel Spotlight #27, Men's Adventures, Motion Picture Funnies Weekly, Namora, Namor, The..., Prince Namor, The Sub-Mariner, Saga Of The..., Tales to Astonish #70 & 2nd series, USA & Young Men)

SUB-MARINER, THE (2nd Series)(Sub-Mariner #31 on)
May, 1968 - No. 72, Sept, 1974 (No. 43: 52 pgs.)
Marvel Comics Group

1-Origin Sub-Mariner; story continued from Iron Man & Sub-Mariner #1
10.00 30.00 100.00
2-Triton app. 4.50 13.50 45.00
3-10: 5-1st Tiger Shark (9/68). 6-Tiger Shark-c & 2nd app., cont'd from #5. 7-Photo-c. (1968). 8-Sub-Mariner vs. Thing. 9-1st app. Serpent Crown (origin in #10 & 12) 3.00 9.00 30.00
11-13,15: 15-Last 12¢ issue 2.50 7.50 20.00
14-Sub-Mariner vs. G.A. Human Torch; death of Toro (1st modern app. & only app. Toro, 6/69) 3.00 9.00 30.00
16-20: 19-1st Sting Ray (11/69); Stan Lee, Romita, Heck, Thomas, Everett & Kirby cameos. 20-Dr. Doom app. 1.25 3.75 10.00
21-33,36-40: 22-Dr. Strange x-over. 25-Origin Atlantis. 30-Capt. Marvel x-over. 37-Death of Lady Dorma. 38-Origin retold. 40-Spider-Man x-over
1.00 2.80 7.00
34,35-Prelude to 1st Defenders story. 34-Hulk & Silver Surfer x-over. 35-Namor/Hulk/Silver Surfer team-up to battle The Avengers-c/story (3/71); hints at teaming up again 1.50 4.50 12.00
41-49,56,62,64-72: 42-Last 15¢ issue. 43-King Size Special (52 pgs.). 44,45-Sub-Mariner vs. H. Torch. 47,48-Dr. Doom app. 49-Cosmic Cube story. 62-1st Tales of Atlantis, ends #66. 64-Hitler cameo. 67-New costume; F.F. x-over. 69-Spider-Man x-over (6 panels) 1.60 4.00
50-1st app. Nita, Namor's niece (later Namorita in New Warriors)
1.00 2.60 6.50
51-55,57-61,63-Everett issues: 59-1st battle with Thor. 61-Last artwork by Everett; 1st 4 pgs. completed by Mortimer; pgs. 5-20 by Mooney.
1.60 4.00
Special 1 (1/71)-r/Tales to Astonish #70-73 1.00 3.00 7.50
Special 2 (1/72)-r/T.T.A. #74-76; Everett-a 1.00 2.60 6.50
NOTE: ***Bolle*** *a-67i.* ***Buscema*** *a(p)-1-8, 20, 24.* ***Colan*** *a(p)-10, 11, 40, 43, 46-49, Special 1, 2; c(p)-10, 11, 40.* ***Craig*** *a-17i, 19-23i.* ***Everett*** *a-45r, 50-55, 57, 58, 59-61(plot), 63(plot); c-47, 48i, 55, 57-59i, 61, Spec. 2.* ***G. Kane*** *c(p)-42-52, 58, 66, 70, 71.* ***Mooney*** *a-24i, 25i, 32-35i, 39i, 42i, 44i, 45i, 60i, 61i, 65p, 66p, 68i. Severin c/a-38i.* ***Starlin*** *c-59p.* ***Tuska*** *a-41p, 42p, 69-71p.* ***Wrightson*** *a-36i. #53, 54-r/stories Sub-Mariner Comics #41 & 39.*

SUB-MARINER COMICS (1st Series) (The Sub-Mariner #1, 2, 33-42)(Official True Crime Cases #24 on; Amazing Mysteries #32 on; Best Love #33 on)
Spring, 1941 - No. 23, Sum, 1947; No. 24, Wint, 1947 - No. 31, 4/49; No. 32, 7/49; No. 33, 4/54 - No. 42, 10/55
Timely/Marvel Comics (TCI 1-7/SePI 8/MPI 9-32/Atlas Comics (CCC 33-42))

GD25 FN65 VF82 NM94
1-The Sub-Mariner by Everett & The Angel begin
1818.00 5455.00 11,817.00 20,000.00
(Estimated up to 190 total copies exist, 8 in NM/Mint)

GD25 FN65 NM94
2-Everett-a 430.00 1290.00 4300.00
3-Churchill assassination-c; 40 pg. Sub-Mariner story
300.00 900.00 3000.00
4-Everett-a, 40 pgs.; 1 pg. Wolverton-a 250.00 750.00 2500.00
5: 5,8-Gabrielle/Klein-c 189.00 567.00 1700.00
6-10: 9-Wolverton-a, 3 pgs.; flag-c 156.00 468.00 1400.00
11-15 111.00 333.00 1000.00
16-20 100.00 300.00 900.00
21-Last Angel; Everett-a 83.00 250.00 750.00
22-Young Allies app. 83.00 250.00 750.00
23-The Human Torch, Namora x-over (Sum/47); 2nd app. Namora after Marvel Mystery #82 83.00 250.00 750.00
24-Namora x-over (3rd app.) 83.00 250.00 750.00
25-The Blonde Phantom begins (Spr/48), ends No. 31; Kurtzman-a; Namora x-over; last quarterly issue 100.00 300.00 900.00
26-28: 28-Namora cover; Everett-a 83.00 250.00 750.00
29-31 (4/49): 29-The Human Torch app. 31-Capt. America app.
83.00 250.00 750.00
32 (7/49, Scarce)-Origin Sub-Mariner 133.00 400.00 1200.00
33 (4/54)-Origin Sub-Mariner; The Human Torch app.; Namora x-over in Sub-Mariner #33-42 77.00 231.00 695.00
34,35-Human Torch in each 62.00 187.00 560.00
36,37,39-41: 36,39-41-Namora app. 62.00 187.00 560.00
38-Origin Sub-Mariner's wings; Namora app.; last pre-code (2/55)
71.00 212.00 635.00
42-Last issue 73.00 220.00 660.00
NOTE: *Angel by* ***Gustavson****-#1, 8.* ***Brodsky*** *c-34-36, 42.* ***Everett*** *a-1-4, 22-24, 26-42; c-32, 33, 40.* ***Maneely*** *a-38; c-37, 39-41.* ***Rico*** *c-27-31.* ***Schomburg*** *c-1-4, 6, 8-18, 20.* ***Sekowsky*** *c-24. 25, 26(w/****Rico****).* ***Shores*** *c-21-23, 38. Bondage c-13, 22, 24, 25, 34.*

SUBSPECIES
May, 1991 - No. 4, Aug, 1991 ($2.50, limited series)
Eternity Comics

1-4: New stories based on horror movie 1.00 2.50

SUBTLE VIOLENTS
1991 ($2.50, B&W, mature)
CFD Productions

1-Linsner-c & story 2.50 7.50 20.00
San Diego Limited Edition 9.50 28.50 95.00

SUE & SALLY SMITH (Formerly My Secret Life)
V2#48, Nov, 1962 - No. 54, Nov, 1963 (Flying Nurses)
Charlton Comics

V2#48 1.85 5.50 15.00
49-54 1.25 3.75 10.00

SUGAR & SPIKE (Also see The Best of DC & DC Silver Age Classics)
Apr-May, 1956 - No. 98, Oct-Nov, 1971
National Periodical Publications

1 (Scarce) 122.00 366.00 1100.00
2 53.00 159.00 475.00
3-5: 3-Letter column begins 46.00 138.00 410.00
6-10 31.00 94.00 250.00
11-20 28.00 83.00 220.00
21-29,31-40: 26-Christmas-c 13.00 39.00 130.00
30-Scribbly & Scribbly, Jr. x-over 14.00 42.00 140.00
41-60 7.50 22.50 75.00
61-80: 69-1st app. Tornado-Tot-c/story. 72-Origin & 1st app. Bernie the Brain
5.00 15.00 50.00
81-95: 84-Bernie the Brain apps. as Superman in 1 panel (9/69). 85-(68 pgs.); r-#72 3.50 10.50 35.00
96 (68 pgs.) 6.00 18.00 60.00
97,98 (52 pgs.) 4.50 13.50 45.00
NOTE: *All written and drawn by* ***Sheldon Mayer.***

SUGAR BEAR
No date, circa 1975? (2-1/2x4-1/2", 16 pgs.)
Post Cereal Giveaway

"The Almost Take Over of the Post Office", "The Race Across the Atlantic", "The Zoo Goes Wild" each... 1.00

SUGAR BOWL COMICS (Teen-age)
May, 1948 - No. 5, Jan, 1949

Suicide Squad #13 © DC

Sun Girl #1 © MEG

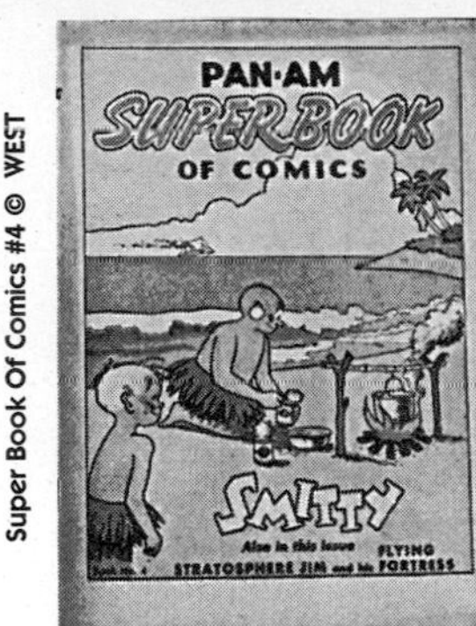

Super Book Of Comics #4 © WEST

	GD25	FN65	NM94
Famous Funnies			
1-Toth-c/a	12.00	36.00	95.00
2,4,5	5.70	17.00	40.00
3-Toth-a	8.75	26.25	65.00

SUGARFOOT (TV)
No. 907, May, 1958 - No. 1209, Oct-Dec, 1961
Dell Publishing Co.

	GD25	FN65	NM94
Four Color 907 (#1)-Toth-a, photo-c	12.00	37.00	135.00
Four Color 992 (5-7/59), Toth-a, photo-c	11.00	34.00	125.00
Four Color 1059 (11-1/60), 1098 (5-7/60), 1147 (11-1/61), 1209-all photo-c	8.00	25.00	90.00

SUICIDE SQUAD (See Brave & the Bold and Doom Patrol & Suicide Squad Spec., Legends #3 & note under Star Spangled War stories)
May, 1987 - No. 66, June, 1992 (Direct sales only #32 on)
DC Comics

	GD25	FN65	NM94
1-66: 9-Millennium x-over. 10-Batman-c/story. 13-JLI app. (Batman). 16-Re-intro Shade The Changing Man. 27-34-Snyder-a. 36,37-Snyder-a. 40-43-"The Phoenix Gambit" Batman storyline. 40-Free Batman/Suicide Squad poster			1.00
Annual 1 (1988, $1.50)-Manhunter x-over			1.50

NOTE: ***Chaykin** c-1.*

SUIT, THE
Oct, 1996 - No. 3, Dec, 1996 ($2.50, limited series)
Virtual Comics (Byron Preiss Multimedia)

	GD25	FN65	NM94
1-3		1.00	2.50

SUMMER FUN (See Dell Giants)

SUMMER FUN (Formerly Li'l Genius; Holiday Surprise #55)
No. 54, Oct, 1966 (Giant)
Charlton Comics

	GD25	FN65	NM94
54	2.50	7.50	25.00

SUMMER FUN (Walt Disney's...)
Summer, 1991 ($2.95, annual, 68 pgs.)
Disney Comics

	GD25	FN65	NM94
1 D. Duck, M. Mouse, Brer Rabbit, Chip 'n' Dale & Pluto, Li'l Bad Wolf, Super Goof, Scamp stories		1.20	3.00

SUMMER LOVE (Formerly Brides in Love?)
V2#46, Oct, 1965; V2#47, Oct, 1966; V2#48, Nov, 1968
Charlton Comics

	GD25	FN65	NM94
V2#46-Beatles-c/story	9.00	27.00	90.00
47-Beatles story	9.00	27.00	90.00
48	1.25	3.75	10.00

SUMMER MAGIC (See Movie Comics)

SUNDANCE (See Hotel Deparee...)

SUNDANCE KID (Also see Blazing Six-Guns)
June, 1971 - No. 3, Sept, 1971 (52 pgs.)
Skywald Publications

	GD25	FN65	NM94
1-Durango Kid; Two Kirby Bullseye-r	1.00	3.00	8.00
2,3: 2-Swift Arrow, Durango Kid, Bullseye by S&K; Meskin plus 1 pg. origin. 3-Durango Kid, Billy the Kid, Red Hawk-r		2.00	5.00

SUNDAY FUNNIES
1950
Harvey Publications

	GD25	FN65	NM94
1	4.00	11.00	22.00

SUN DEVILS
July, 1984 - No. 12, June, 1985 ($1.25, maxi series)
DC Comics

	GD25	FN65	NM94
1-12: 6-Death of Sun Devil			1.25

SUN FUN KOMIKS
1939 (15¢, B&W & red)
Sun Publications

	GD25	FN65	NM94
1-Satire on comics	23.00	69.00	185.00

SUN GIRL (See The Human Torch & Marvel Mystery Comics #88)
Aug, 1948 - No. 3, Dec, 1948
Marvel Comics (CCC)

	GD25	FN65	NM94
1-Sun Girl begins; Miss America app.	122.00	366.00	1100.00
2,3: 2-The Blonde Phantom begins	92.00	276.00	825.00

SUNGLASSES
Nov, 1995 - No. 6, Nov, 1996 ($2.95, limited series, mature)
Verotik

	GD25	FN65	NM94
1-5: Nancy Collins scripts, adapt. of "Sunglasses after Dark"		1.20	3.00
6-($3.95)		1.60	4.00

SUNNY, AMERICA'S SWEETHEART (Formerly Cosmo Cat #1-10)
No. 11, Dec, 1947 - No. 14, June, 1948
Fox Features Syndicate

	GD25	FN65	NM94
11-Feldstein-c/a	56.00	168.00	500.00
12-14-Feldstein-c/a; 14-Lingerie panels	47.00	141.00	400.00
I.W. Reprint #8-Feldstein-a; r/Fox issue	9.50	28.50	95.00

SUN-RUNNERS (Also see Tales of the...)
2/84 - No. 3, 5/84; No. 4, 11/84 - No. 7, 1986 (Baxter paper)
Pacific Comics/Eclipse Comics/Amazing Comics

	GD25	FN65	NM94
1-7: P. Smith-a in some			1.60
Christmas Special 1 (1987, $1.95)-By Amazing		.80	2.00

SUNSET CARSON (Also see Cowboy Western)
Feb, 1951 - No. 4, 1951 (No month) (Sunset Carson photo on-c of each)
Charlton Comics

	GD25	FN65	NM94
1-Photo/retouched-c (Scarce, all issues)	71.00	213.00	640.00
2-Kit Carson story; adapts "Kansas Raiders" w/Brian Donlevy, Audie Murphy & Margaret Chapman	53.00	159.00	475.00
3,4	40.00	120.00	360.00

SUNSET PASS (See Zane Grey & 4-Color #230)

SUPER ANIMALS PRESENTS PIDGY & THE MAGIC GLASSES
Dec, 1953 (25¢, came w/glasses)
Star Publications

	GD25	FN65	NM94
1-(3-D Comics)-L. B. Cole-c	36.00	108.00	320.00

SUPER BOOK OF COMICS
nd (1943?) (Soft-c, 32 pgs.) (Pan-Am/Gilmore Oil/Kelloggs premiums)
Western Publishing Co.

	GD25	FN65	NM94
nn-Dick Tracy (Gilmore)-Magic Morro app.	36.00	108.00	295.00
1-Dick Tracy & The Smuggling Ring; Stratosphere Jim app. (Rare) (Pan-Am)	31.00	92.00	245.00
1-Smilin' Jack, Magic Morro (Pan-Am)	9.50	28.00	75.00
2-Smilin' Jack, Stratosphere Jim (Pan-Am)	9.50	28.00	75.00
2-Smitty, Magic Morro (Pan-Am)	9.50	28.00	75.00
3-Captain Midnight, Magic Morro (Pan-Am)	15.00	45.00	120.00
3-Moon Mullins?	8.75	26.25	65.00
4-Red Ryder, Magic Morro (Pan-Am)	8.75	26.25	65.00
4-Smitty, Stratosphere Jim (Pan-Am)	8.75	26.25	65.00
5-Don Winslow, Magic Morro (Gilmore)	8.75	26.25	70.00
5-Don Winslow, Stratosphere Jim (Pan-Am)	8.75	26.25	70.00
5-Terry & the Pirates	14.00	41.00	110.00
6-Don Winslow, Stratosphere Jim (Pan-Am)-McWilliams-a	10.00	30.00	80.00
6-King of the Royal Mounted, Magic Morro (Pan-Am)	9.50	28.00	75.00
7-Dick Tracy, Magic Morro (Pan-Am)	15.00	45.00	120.00
7-Little Orphan Annie	9.50	28.00	75.00

Super-Book Of Comics #1 © WEST

Superboy #53 © DC

Superboy #100 © DC

	GD25	FN65	NM94
8-Dick Tracy, Stratosphere Jim (Pan-Am)	15.00	45.00	120.00
8-Dan Dunn, Magic Morro (Pan-Am)	9.50	28.00	75.00
9-Terry & the Pirates, Magic Morro (Pan-Am)	12.00	38.00	100.00
10-Red Ryder, Magic Morro (Pan-Am)	8.75	26.25	65.00

SUPER-BOOK OF COMICS
(Omar Bread & Hancock Oil Co. giveaways)
1944 - No. 30, 1947 (Omar); 1947 - 1948 (Hancock) (16 pgs.)
Western Publishing Co.

Note: The Hancock issues are all exact reprints of the earlier Omar issues. The issue numbers were removed in some of the reprints.

	GD25	FN65	NM94
1-Dick Tracy (Omar, 1944)	19.00	56.00	150.00
1-Dick Tracy (Hancock, 1947)	14.00	41.00	110.00
2-Bugs Bunny (Omar, 1944)	6.50	19.50	45.00
2-Bugs Bunny (Hancock, 1947)	5.70	17.00	35.00
3-Terry & the Pirates (Omar, 1944)	10.50	32.00	85.00
3-Terry & the Pirates (Hancock, 1947)	9.50	28.00	75.00
4-Andy Panda (Omar, 1944)	6.50	19.50	45.00
4-Andy Panda (Hancock, 1947)	5.70	17.00	35.00
5-Smokey Stover (Omar, 1945)	5.70	17.00	35.00
5-Smokey Stover (Hancock, 1947)	4.15	12.50	25.00
6-Porky Pig (Omar, 1945)	6.50	19.50	45.00
6-Porky Pig (Hancock, 1947)	5.70	17.00	35.00
7-Smilin' Jack (Omar, 1945)	6.50	19.50	45.00
7-Smilin' Jack (Hancock, 1947)	5.70	17.00	35.00
8-Oswald the Rabbit (Omar, 1945)	5.70	17.00	35.00
8-Oswald the Rabbit (Hancock, 1947)	4.15	12.50	25.00
9-Alley Oop (Omar, 1945)	11.30	34.00	90.00
9-Alley Oop (Hancock, 1947)	10.00	30.00	80.00
10-Elmer Fudd (Omar, 1945)	5.70	17.00	35.00
10-Elmer Fudd (Hancock, 1947)	4.15	12.50	25.00
11-Little Orphan Annie (Omar, 1945)	7.15	21.50	50.00
11-Little Orphan Annie (Hancock, 1947)	5.70	17.00	38.00
12-Woody Woodpecker (Omar, 1945)	5.70	17.00	35.00
12-Woody Woodpecker (Hancock, 1947)	4.15	12.50	25.00
13-Dick Tracy (Omar, 1945)	11.30	34.00	90.00
13-Dick Tracy (Hancock, 1947)	10.00	30.00	80.00
14-Bugs Bunny (Omar, 1945)	5.70	17.00	35.00
14-Bugs Bunny (Hancock, 1947)	4.15	12.50	25.00
15-Andy Panda (Omar, 1945)	5.00	15.00	30.00
15-Andy Panda (Hancock, 1947)	4.15	12.50	25.00
16-Terry & the Pirates (Omar, 1945)	10.00	30.00	80.00
16-Terry & the Pirates (Hancock, 1947)	8.75	26.25	65.00
17-Smokey Stover (Omar, 1946)	5.70	17.00	35.00
17-Smokey Stover (Hancock, 1948?)	4.15	12.50	25.00
18-Porky Pig (Omar, 1946)	5.00	15.00	30.00
18-Porky Pig (Hancock, 1948?)	4.15	12.50	25.00
19-Smilin' Jack (Omar, 1946)	5.70	17.00	35.00
nn-Smilin' Jack (Hancock, 1948)	4.15	12.50	25.00
20-Oswald the Rabbit (Omar, 1946)	5.00	15.00	30.00
nn-Oswald the Rabbit (Hancock, 1948)	4.00	12.00	24.00
21-Gasoline Alley (Omar, 1946)	7.15	21.50	50.00
nn-Gasoline Alley (Hancock, 1948)	5.70	17.00	38.00
22-Elmer Fudd (Omar, 1946)	5.00	15.00	30.00
nn-Elmer Fudd (Hancock, 1948)	4.00	12.00	24.00
23-Little Orphan Annie (Omar, 1946)	6.50	19.50	45.00
nn-Little Orphan Annie (Hancock, 1948)	5.70	17.00	35.00
24-Woody Woodpecker (Omar, 1946)	5.00	15.00	30.00
nn-Woody Woodpecker (Hancock, 1948)	4.00	12.00	24.00
25-Dick Tracy (Omar, 1946)	10.00	30.00	80.00
nn-Dick Tracy (Hancock, 1948)	8.50	26.00	60.00
26-Bugs Bunny (Omar, 1946))	5.00	15.00	30.00
nn-Bugs Bunny (Hancock, 1948)	4.00	12.00	24.00
27-Andy Panda (Omar, 1946)	5.00	15.00	30.00
27-Andy Panda (Hancock, 1948)	4.00	12.00	24.00
28-Terry & the Pirates (Omar, 1946)	10.00	30.00	80.00
28-Terry & the Pirates (Hancock, 1948)	8.50	26.00	60.00
29-Smokey Stover (Omar, 1947)	5.00	15.00	30.00
29-Smokey Stover (Hancock, 1948)	4.00	12.00	24.00
30-Porky Pig (Omar, 1947)	5.00	15.00	30.00
30-Porky Pig (Hancock, 1948)	4.00	12.00	24.00
nn-Bugs Bunny (Hancock, 1948)-Does not match any Omar book	4.00	12.00	24.00

SUPERBOY (See Adventure, Aurora, DC Comics Presents, DC 100 Page Super Spectacular #15, DC Super Stars, 80 Page Giant #10, More Fun Comics, The New Advs. of... & Superman Family #191)

SUPERBOY (1st Series)(...& the Legion of Super-Heroes with #231)(Becomes The Legion of Super-Heroes No. 259 on)
Mar-Apr, 1949 - No. 258, Dec, 1979 (#1-16: 52 pgs.)
National Periodical Publications/DC Comics

	GD25	FN65	VF82	NM94
1-Superman cover	650.00	1950.00	3900.00	6500.00

(Estimated up to 275 total copies exist, 15 in NM/Mint)

	GD25	FN65	NM94
2-Used in **SOTI**, pg. 35-36,226	161.00	483.00	1450.00
3	122.00	366.00	1100.00
4,5: 5-1st pre-Supergirl tryout (c/story, 11-12/49)	83.00	250.00	750.00
6-10: 8-1st Superbaby. 10-1st app. Lana Lang	72.00	216.00	650.00
11-15	56.00	168.00	500.00
16-20	36.00	108.00	325.00
21-26,28-30: 21-Lana Lang app.	33.00	98.00	260.00
27-Low distribution	34.00	101.00	270.00
31-38: 38-Last pre-code issue (1/55)	24.00	71.00	190.00
39-48,50 (7/56)	17.00	51.00	170.00
49 (6/56)-1st app. Metallo (Jor-El's robot)	20.00	60.00	200.00
51-60: 52-1st S.A. issue	13.50	41.00	135.00
61-67	11.00	33.00	110.00
68-Origin/1st app. original Bizarro (10-11/58)	42.00	125.00	460.00
69-77,79: 75-Spanking-c. 76-1st Supermonkey. 77-Pre-Pete Ross tryout	8.50	25.50	85.00
78-Origin Mr. Mxyzptlk & Superboy's costume	15.00	45.00	150.00
80-1st meeting Superboy/Supergirl (4/60)	12.50	38.00	125.00
81,83-85,87,88: 83-Origin/1st app. Kryptonite Kid	7.00	21.00	70.00
82-1st Bizarro Krypto	7.50	22.50	75.00
86-(1/61)-4th Legion app; Intro Pete Ross	12.50	38.00	125.00
89-(6/61)-1st app. Mon-el; 2nd Phantom Zone	23.00	69.00	230.00
90-92: 90-Pete Ross learns Superboy's I.D. 92-Last 10¢ issue	7.00	21.00	70.00
93-10th Legion app.(12/61); Chameleon Boy app.	8.00	24.00	80.00
94-97,99	4.50	13.50	45.00
98-(7/62)-18th Legion app; origin & 1st app. Ultra Boy; Pete Ross joins Legion	9.00	27.00	90.00
100-(10/62)-Ultra Boy app; 1st app. Phantom Zone villains, Dr. Xadu & Erndine. 2 pg. map of Krypton; origin Superboy retold; r-cover of Superman #1	17.00	51.00	170.00
101-120: 104-Origin Phantom Zone. 115-Atomic bomb-c. 117-Legion app.	3.50	10.50	35.00
121-128: 124-(10/65)-1st app. Insect Queen (Lana Lang). 125-Legion cameo. 126-Origin Krypto the Super Dog retold with new facts	3.20	9.60	32.00
129-(80-pg. Giant G-22)-Reprints origin Mon-el	3.60	10.80	36.00
130-137,139,140: 131-Legion statues cameo in Dog Legionnaires story. 132-1st app. Supremo. 133-Superboy meets Robin	2.50	7.50	20.00
138 (80-pg. Giant G-35)	3.60	10.80	36.00
141-146,148-155,157-164,166-173,175,176: 145-Superboy's parents regain their youth. 171-1st app. Aquaboy? 172,173,176-Legion app.; 172-Origin Yango (Super Ape). 176-Partial photo-c	1.50	4.50	12.00

147(6/68)-Giant G-47; 1st origin of L.S.H. (Saturn Girl, Lightning Lad, Cosmic

Superboy #205 © DC

Superboy #32 (3rd Series) © DC

Super Brat #7 © TOBY

GD25 FN65 NM94

Boy); origin Legion of Super-Pets-r/Adv. #293? 2.50 7.50 22.00
156,165,174 (Giants G-59,71,83): 165-r/1st app. Krypto the Superdog from Adventure Comics #210 1.75 5.25 14.00
177-184,186,187 (All 52 pgs.): 182-All new origin of the classic World's Finest team (Superman & Batman) as teenagers (2/72, 22pgs). 184-Origin Dial H for Hero-r. 1.00 3.00 7.50
185-DC 100 Pg. Super Spectacular #12; Legion-c/story; Teen Titans, Kid Eternity(r/Hit #46), Star Spangled Kid-r(S.S. 55)(see DC 100 pg. Super Spec. #12 for price)
188-196: 188-Origin Karkan. 191-Origin Sunboy retold; Legion app. 193-Chameleon Boy & Shrinking Violet get new costumes. 195-1st app. Erg/Wildfire; Phantom Girl gets new costume. 196-Last Superboy solo story 2.40 6.00
197-Legion series begins; Lightning Lad's new costume 1.25 3.75 10.00
198,199: 198-Element Lad & Princess Projectra get new costumes 2.40 6.00
200-Bouncing Boy & Duo Damsel marry; J'onn J'onzz cameo 1.25 3.75 10.00
201,204,206,207,209: 201-Re-intro Erg as Wildfire. 204-Supergirl resigns from Legion. 206-Ferro Lad & Invisible Kid app. 209-Karate Kid gets new costume 2.00 5.00
202,205-(100 pgs.): 202-Light Lass gets new costume; Mike Grell's 1st comic work-i (5-6/74) 2.50 7.50 20.00
203-Invisible Kid dies 1.00 3.00 8.00
208,210: 208-(68 pgs.). 210-Origin Karate Kid 1.00 3.00 8.00
211-220: 212-Matter-Eater Lad resigns. 216-1st app. Tyroc who joins the Legion in #218 1.60 4.00
221-230,246-249: 226-Intro. Dawnstar. 228-Death of Chemical King. 1.20 3.00
231-245: (Giants). 240-Origin Dawnstar. 242-(52 pgs.). 243-Legion of Substitute Heroes app. 243-245-(44 pgs.). 1.60 4.00
250-258: 253-Intro Blok. 257-Return of Bouncing Boy & Duo Damsel by Ditko .80 2.00
Annual 1 (Sum/64, 84 pgs.)-Origin Krypto-r 16.50 50.00 165.00
Spectacular 1 (1980, Giant)-Distr. through comic stores; mostly-r .80 2.00

NOTE: ***Neal Adams*** *c-143, 145, 146, 148-155, 157-161, 163, 164, 166-168, 172, 173, 175, 176, 178.* ***M. Anderson*** *a-245i.* ***Ditko*** *a-257p.* ***Grell*** *a-202i, 203-219, 220-224p, 235p; c-207-232, 235, 236p, 237, 239p, 240p, 243p, 246, 258.* ***Nasser*** *a(p)-222, 225, 226, 230, 231, 233, 236.* ***Simonson*** *a-237p.* ***Starlin*** *a(p)-239, 250, 251; c-238.* ***Staton*** *a-227p, 243-249p, 252-258p; c-247-251p.* ***Swan/Moldoff*** *c-109.* ***Tuska*** *a-172, 173, 176, 183, 235p.* ***Wood*** *inks-153-155, 157-161. Legion app.-172, 173, 176, 177, 183, 184, 188, 190, 191, 193, 195.*

SUPERBOY (TV)(2nd Series)(The Adventures of...#19 on)
Feb, 1990 - No. 22, Dec, 1991 ($1.00/$1.25)
DC Comics

1-15: Mooney-a(p) in 1-8,18-20; 1-Photo-c from TV show. 8-Bizarro-c/story; Arthur Adams-a(i). 9-12,14-17-Swan-p 1.00
16-22: 16-Begin $1.25-c 1.30

SUPERBOY (3rd Series)
Feb, 1994 - Present ($1.50/$1.95)
DC Comics

1-5-Metropolis Kid from Reign of the Supermen 1.50
6-8: 6,7-Worlds Collide Pts. 3 & 8. 8-(9/94)-Zero Hour x-over 1.50
0, 9-15: 0-(10/94). 9-(11/94)-King Shark app. 1.50
16-24,26-41: 16-$1.95-c begins. 21-Legion app. 28-Supergirl-c/app. 33-Final Night. 38-41-"Meltdown" .80 2.00
25-($2.95)-New Gods & Female Furies app.; w/pin-ups 1.20 2.95
42-49: 45-Legion-c/app. 47-Green Lantern-c/app 1.95
Annual 1 (1994, $2.95, 68 pgs.)-Elseworlds story, Pt. 2 of The Super Seven (see Adventures Of Superman Annual #6) 1.20 2.95
Annual 2 (1995, $3.95)-Year One story 1.60 3.95
Annual 3 (1996, $2.95)-Legends of the Dead Earth 1.20 2.95
Annual 4 (1997, $3.95)-Pulp Heroes story 1.60 3.95

GD25 FN65 NM94

...Plus 1 (Jan, 1997, $2.95) w/Capt. Marvel Jr. 1.20 2.95
...Plus 2 (Fall, 1997, $2.95) w/Slither (Scare Tactics) 1.20 2.95
.../Risk Double-Shot 1 (Feb, 1998, $1.95) w/Risk (Teen Titans) 1.95

SUPERBOY & THE RAVERS
Sept, 1996 - No. 19, March, 1998 ($1.95)
DC Comics

1-19: 4-Adam Strange app. 7-Impulse-c/app. 9-Superman-c/app. .80 2.00

SUPERBOY/ROBIN: WORLD'S FINEST THREE
1996 - No. 2, 1996 ($4.95, squarebound, limited series)
DC Comics

1,2: Superboy & Robin vs. Metallo & Poison Ivy; Karl Kesel & Chuck Dixon scripts; Tom Grummett-c(p)/a(p) 2.00 5.00

SUPER BRAT
Jan, 1954 - No. 4, July, 1954
Toby Press

1 5.70 17.00 35.00
2-4: 4-Li'l Teevy by Mel Lazarus 4.00 11.00 22.00
I.W. Reprint #1,2,3,7,8('58): 1-r/#1 2.00 5.00
I.W. (Super) Reprint #10('63) 2.00 5.00

SUPERCAR (TV)
Nov, 1962 - No. 4, Aug, 1963 (All painted-c)
Gold Key

1 22.00 65.00 235.00
2,3 10.00 30.00 110.00
4 14.00 44.00 160.00

SUPER CAT (Formerly Frisky Animals; also see Animal Crackers)
No. 56, Nov, 1953 - No. 58, May, 1954; Aug, 1957 - No. 4, May, 1958
Star Publications #56-58/Ajax/Farrell Publ. (Four Star Comic Corp.)

56-58-L.B. Cole-c on all 15.00 45.00 120.00
1(1957-Ajax)- "The Adventures of..." c-only 7.15 21.50 50.00
2-4 5.00 15.00 30.00

SUPER CIRCUS (TV)
Jan, 1951 - No. 5, Sept, 1951 (Mary Hartline)
Cross Publishing Co.

1-(52 pgs.)-Cast photos on-c 8.75 26.25 70.00
2-Cast photos on-c 7.15 21.50 50.00
3-5 5.70 17.00 40.00

SUPER CIRCUS (TV)
No. 542, Mar, 1954 - No. 694, Mar, 1956 (Featuring Mary Hartline)
Dell Publishing Co.

Four Color 542: Mary Hartline photo-c 6.40 19.00 70.00
Four Color 592,694: Mary Hartline photo-c 5.50 16.50 60.00

SUPER COMICS
May, 1938 - No. 121, Feb-Mar, 1949
Dell Publishing Co.

1-Terry & The Pirates, The Gumps, Dick Tracy, Little Orphan Annie, Little Joe, Gasoline Alley, Smilin' Jack, Smokey Stover, Smitty, Tiny Tim, Moon Mullins, Harold Teen, Winnie Winkle begin 266.00 800.00 1800.00
2 100.00 300.00 650.00
3 91.00 275.00 600.00
4,5: 4-Dick Tracy-c; also #8-10,17,26(part),31 73.00 219.00 475.00
6-10 58.00 174.00 375.00
11-20: 20-Smilin' Jack-c (also #29,32) 45.00 137.00 300.00
21-29: 21-Magic Morro begins (origin & 1st app., 2/40). 22,27-Ken Ernst-c (also #25?); Magic Morro c-22,25,27,34 34.00 101.00 270.00
30- "Sea Hawk" movie adaptation-c/story with Errol Flynn 34.00 101.00 270.00
31-40: 31-1st Dick Tracy-c. 34-Ken Ernst-c 26.00 80.00 210.00

Super Comics #79 © DELL

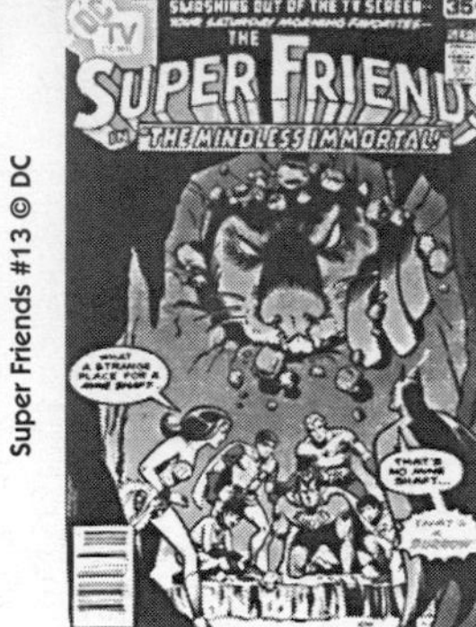

Super Friends #13 © DC

Supergirl #6 (1st Series) © DC

GD25 FN65 NM94

41-50: 41-Intro Lightning Jim. 43-Terry & The Pirates ends 21.00 64.00 170.00
51-60 15.50 47.00 125.00
61-70: 62-Flag-c. 65-Brenda Starr-r begin? 67-X-Mas-c 14.00 41.00 110.00
71-80 10.50 32.00 85.00
81-99 8.75 26.25 70.00
100 10.00 30.00 80.00
101-115-Last Dick Tracy (moves to own title) 6.50 19.50 45.00
116-121: 116,118-All Smokey Stover. 117-All Gasoline AlleY. 119-121-Terry & The Pirates app. in all 5.70 17.00 38.00

SUPER COPS, THE
July, 1974 (one-shot)
Red Circle Productions (Archie)

1-Morrow-c/a 1.00

SUPER COPS
Sept, 1990 - No. 4, Dec?, 1990 ($1.75)
Now Comics

1-($2.75, 52 pgs.)-Dave Dorman painted-c 1.10 2.80
1-2nd printing ($2.75) 1.10 2.80
2-4 .75 1.80

SUPER CRACKED (See Cracked)

SUPER DC GIANT (25-50¢, all 68-52 pg. Giants)
No. 13, 9-10/70 - No. 26, 7-8/71; V3#27, Summer, 1976 (No #1-12)
National Periodical Publications

S-13-Binky 7.50 22.50 75.00
S-14-Top Guns of the West; Kubert-c; Trigger Twins, Johnny Thunder, Wyoming Kid-r; Moreira-r (9-10/70) 2.50 7.50 20.00
S-15-Western Comics; Kubert-c; Pow Wow Smith, Vigilante, Buffalo Bill-r; new Gil Kane-a (9-10/70) 2.50 7.50 20.00
S-16-Best of the Brave & the Bold; Batman-r & Metamorpho origin-r from Brave & the Bold; Spectre pin-up. 2.50 7.50 20.00
S-17-Love 1970 (scarce) 15.00 45.00 150.00
S-18-Three Mouseketeers; Dizzy Dog, Doodles Duck, Bo Bunny-r; Sheldon Mayer-a 6.00 18.00 60.00
S-19-Jerry Lewis; no Neal Adams-a 6.00 18.00 60.00
S-20-House of Mystery; N. Adams-c; Kirby-r(3) 4.00 12.00 40.00
S-21-Love 1971 (scarce) 17.50 52.00 175.00
S-22-Top Guns of the West; Kubert-c 1.85 5.50 15.00
S-23-The Unexpected 2.50 7.50 20.00
S-24-Supergirl 2.50 7.50 20.00
S-25-Challengers of the Unknown; all Kirby/Wood-r 1.85 5.50 15.00
S-26-Aquaman (1971)-r/S.A. Aquaman origin story from Showcase #30 1.85 5.50 15.00
27-Strange Flying Saucers Adventures (Sum, 1976) 1.00 2.80 7.00
NOTE: ***Sid Greene*** *r-27p(2),* ***Heath*** *r-27.* ***G. Kane*** *a-14r(2), 15, 27r(p).* ***Kubert*** *r-16.*

SUPER-DOOPER COMICS
1946 - No. 8, 1946 (10¢, 32 pgs., paper-c)(#1-4 exist?)
Able Manufacturing Co.

1-The Clock, Gangbuster app. 13.00 39.00 105.00
2 8.75 26.25 65.00
3,4,6 7.85 23.50 55.00
5,7-Capt. Freedom & Shock Gibson 8.75 26.25 70.00
8-Shock Gibson, Sam Hill 8.75 26.25 70.00

SUPER DUCK COMICS (The Cockeyed Wonder) (See Jolly Jingles)
Fall, 1944 - No. 94, Dec, 1960 (Also see Laugh #24)(#1-5 are quarterly)
MLJ Mag. No. 1-4(9/45)/Close-Up No. 5 on (Archie)

1-Origin; Hitler & Hirohito-c 36.00 108.00 320.00
2-Bill Vigoda-c 17.50 53.00 140.00
3-5: 4-20-Al Fagaly-c (most) 12.00 38.00 100.00
6-10 10.00 30.00 80.00

GD25 FN65 NM94

11-20 8.50 26.00 60.00
21,23-40 (10/51) 5.70 17.00 50.00
22-Used in **SOTI**, pg. 35,307,308 7.85 23.50 55.00
41-60 (2/55) 5.70 17.00 35.00
61-94 4.00 12.00 24.00

SUPER DUPER (Formerly Pocket Comics #1-4?)
No. 5, 1941 - No. 11, 1941
Harvey Publications

5-Captain Freedom & Shock Gibson app. 23.00 69.00 185.00
8,11 14.00 41.00 110.00

SUPER DUPER COMICS (Formerly Latest Comics?)
No. 3, May-June, 1947
F. E. Howard Publ.

3-1st app. Mr. Monster 8.50 26.00 60.00

SUPER FRIENDS (TV) (Also see Best of DC & Limited Collectors' Edition)
Nov, 1976 - No. 47, Aug, 1981 (#14 is 44 pgs.)
National Periodical Publications/DC Comics

1-Superman, Batman, Robin, Wonder Woman, Aquaman, Atom, Wendy, Marvin & Wonder Dog begin (1st Super Friends) 1.85 5.50 15.00
2-Penquin-c/sty 1.00 3.00 8.00
3-5 2.40 6.00
6-10,14:7-1st app. Wonder Twins & The Seraph. 8-1st app. Jack O'Lantern. 9-1st app. Icemaiden. 14-Origin Wonder Twins 2.00 5.00
11-13,15-20: 13-1st app. Dr. Mist. 1.60 4.00
21-30,32-46: 25-1st app. Fire & Green Fury. 28-Bizarro app. 36,43-Plastic Man app. 1.20 3.00
31,47: 31-Black Orchid app. 47-Origin Fire & Green Fury 1.60 4.00
...Special 1 (1981, giveaway, no ads, no code or price)-r/Super Friends #19 & 36 .80 2.00
NOTE: ***Estrada*** *a-1p, 2p.* ***Orlando*** *a-1p.* ***Staton*** *a-43, 45.*

SUPER FUN
Jan, 1956 (By A.W. Nugent)
Gillmor Magazines

1-Comics, puzzles, cut-outs by A.W. Nugent 3.20 8.00 16.00

SUPER FUNNIES (...Western Funnies #3,4)
Dec, 1953 - No. 4, Sept, 1954
Superior Comics Publishers Ltd. (Canada)

1-(3-D, 10¢)-...Presents Dopey Duck; make your own 3-D glasses cut-out inside front-c; did not come w/glasses 33.00 98.00 260.00
2-Horror & crime satire 8.75 26.25 70.00
3-Phantom Ranger-c/s; Geronimo, Billy the Kid app. 5.35 16.00 32.00
4-Phantom Ranger-c/story 5.35 16.00 32.00

SUPERGEAR COMICS
1976 (Giveaway, 4 pgs. in color, slick paper)
Jacobs Corp.

nn-(Rare)-Superman, Lois Lane; Steve Lombard app. (500 copies printed, over half destroyed?) 2.40 6.00

SUPERGIRL (See Action, Adventure #281, Brave & the Bold, Crisis on Infinite Earths #7, Daring New Advs. of..., Super DC Giant, Superman Family, & Super-Team Family)

SUPERGIRL
Nov, 1972 - No. 9, Dec-Jan, 1973-74; No. 10, Sept-Oct, 1974 (1st solo title)(20¢)
National Periodical Publications

1-Zatanna back-up stories begin, end #5 2.50 7.50 24.00
2-4,6,7,9 1.10 3.30 9.00
5,8,10: 5-Zatanna origin-r. 8-JLA x-over; Batman cameo. 10-Prez 1.50 4.50 12.00
NOTE: *Zatanna in #1-5, 7(Guest); Prez app. in #10. #1-10 are 20¢ issues.*

SUPERGIRL (Formerly Daring New Adventures of...)
No. 14, Dec, 1983 - No. 23, Sept, 1984
DC Comics

Supergirl #9 (4th Series) © DC

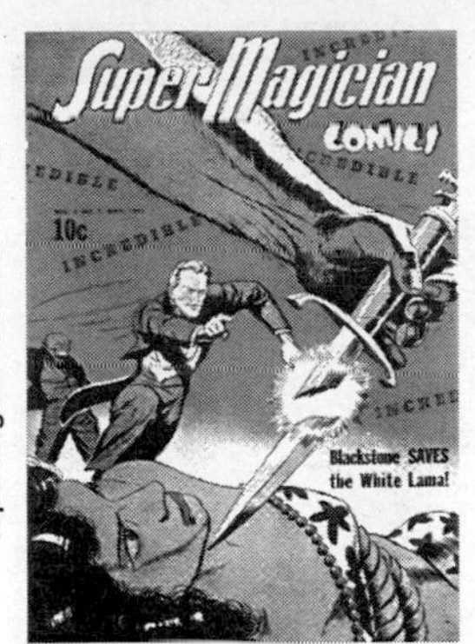

Super Magician Comics #10 © S&S

Superman #1 © DC

GD25 FN65 NM94

14-23: 16-Ambush Bug app. 20-JLA & New Teen Titans app. 1.00
...Movie Special (1985)-Adapts movie; Morrow-a; photo back-c 1.25
Giveaway ('84, '86 Baxter, nn)(American Honda/U.S. Dept. Transportation)-Torres-c/a 1.25

SUPERGIRL
Feb, 1994 - No. 4, May, 1994 ($1.50, limited series)
DC Comics
1-4: Guice-a(i) 1.50

SUPERGIRL (See Showcase '96 #8)
Sept, 1996 - Present ($1.95)
DC Comics
1: Peter David scripts & Gary Frank-c/a; DC cover logo in upper left is blue 1.25 3.75 10.00
1-2nd printing-DC cover logo in upper left is red 1.60 4.00
2 2.40 6.00
3-Final Night, Gorilla Grodd app. 1.20 3.00
4-13: 4-Gorilla Grodd-c/app. 6-Superman-c/app. 1.20 3.00
14-19:14-Genesis x-over. 16-Power Girl app. 1.95
Annual 1 (1996, $2.95)-Legends of the Dead Earth; Dixon & Lansdale scripts 1.20 3.00
Annual 2 (1997, $3.95)-Pulp Heroes; LSH app. 1.60 4.00
...Plus (2/97, $2.95) Capt.(Mary) Marvel-c/app.; David-s/Frank-a 1.20 3.00
.../Prysm Double-Shot 1 (Feb, 1998, $1.95) w/Prysm (Teen Titans) 1.95

SUPERGIRL/LEX LUTHOR SPECIAL (Supergirl and Team Luthor on-c)
1993 ($2.50, 68 pgs., one-shot)
DC Comics
1-Pin-ups by Byrne & Thibert 1.00 2.50

SUPER GOOF (Walt Disney) (See Dynabrite & The Phantom Blot)
Oct, 1965 - No. 74, 1982
Gold Key No. 1-57/Whitman No. 58 on
1 2.50 7.50 20.00
2-5 1.25 3.75 10.00
6-10 1.00 3.00 8.00
11-20 2.40 6.00
21-30 1.20 3.00
31-50 .80 2.00
51-74 1.00
NOTE: *Reprints in #16, 24, 28, 29, 37, 38, 43, 45, 46, 54(1/2), 56-58, 65(1/2), 72(r-#2).*

SUPER GREEN BERET (Tod Holton...)
April, 1967 - No. 2, June, 1967 (25¢, 68 pgs.)
Lightning Comics (Milson Publ. Co.)
1,2 3.00 9.00 30.00

SUPER HEROES (See Giant-Size... & Marvel...)

SUPER HEROES
Jan, 1967 - No. 4, June, 1967
Dell Publishing Co.
1-Origin & 1st app. Fab 4 2.50 7.50 25.00
2-4 2.00 6.00 16.00

SUPER-HEROES BATTLE SUPER-GORILLAS (See DC Special #16)
Winter, 1976 (52 pgs., all reprints, one-shot)
National Periodical Publications
1-Superman, Batman, Flash stories; Infantino-a(p) 2.00 5.00

SUPER HEROES PUZZLES AND GAMES
1979 (32 pgs., regular size)
General Mills Giveaway (Marvel Comics Group)
nn-Four 2-pg. origin stories of Spider-Man, Captain America, The Hulk, & Spider-Woman 1.25 3.75 10.00

SUPER HEROES VERSUS SUPER VILLAINS
July, 1966 (no month given)(68 pgs.)
Archie Publications (Radio Comics)
1-Flyman, Black Hood, Web, Shield-r; Reinman-a 4.00 12.00 40.00

SUPERHERO WOMEN, THE - FEATURING THE FABULOUS FEMALES OF MARVEL COMICS (See Fireside Book Series)

SUPERICHIE (Formerly Super Richie)
No. 5, Oct, 1976 - No. 18, Jan, 1979 (52 pgs. giants)
Harvey Publications
5-18: 5-Origin/1st app. new costumes for Rippy & Crashman 2.00 5.00

SUPERIOR STORIES
May-June, 1955 - No. 4, Nov-Dec, 1955
Nesbit Publishers, Inc.
1-The Invisible Man by H.G. Wells 15.00 45.00 120.00
2-The Pirate of the Gulf by J.H. Ingrahams 8.50 26.00 60.00
3-Wreck of the Grosvenor by William Clark Russell 8.50 26.00 60.00
4-The Texas Rangers by O'Henry 8.50 26.00 60.00
NOTE: ***Morisi** c/a in all. Kiwanis stories in #3 & 4. #4 has photo of Gene Autry on-c.*

SUPER MAGIC (Super Magician Comics #2 on)
May, 1941
Street & Smith Publications
V1#1-Blackstone the Magician-c/story; origin/1st app. Rex King (Black Fury); Charles Sultan-c; Blackstone-c begin 100.00 300.00 900.00

SUPER MAGICIAN COMICS (Super Magic #1)
No. 2, Sept, 1941 - V5#8, Feb-Mar, 1947
Street & Smith Publications
V1#2-Blackstone the Magician continues; Rex King, Man of Adventure app. 42.00 126.00 375.00
3-Tao-Anwar, Boy Magician begins 29.00 86.00 230.00
4-Origin Transo 26.00 80.00 210.00
5-7,9-12: 11-Supersnipe app. 26.00 80.00 210.00
8-Abbott & Costello story (1st app?, 11/42) 29.00 86.00 230.00
V2#1-The Shadow app. 31.00 94.00 250.00
2-12: 5-Origin Tigerman. 8-Red Dragon begins 12.00 38.00 100.00
V3#1-12: 5-Origin Mr. Twilight 12.00 38.00 100.00
V4#1-12: 11-Nigel Elliman Ace of Magic begins (3/46) 10.50 32.00 85.00
V5#1-6 10.50 32.00 85.00
7,8-Red Dragon by Edd Cartier-c/a 28.00 83.00 220.00
NOTE: ***Jack Binder** c-1-14(most). Red Dragon c-V5#7, 8.*

SUPERMAN (See Action Comics, Advs. of..., All-New Coll. Ed., All-Star Comics, Best of DC, Brave & the Bold, Cosmic Odyssey, DC Comics Presents, Heroes Against Hunger, The Kents, Krypton Chronicles, Limited Coll. Ed., Man of Steel, Phantom Zone, Power Record Comics, Special Edition, Steel, Super Friends, Superman: The Man of Steel, Superman: The Man of Tomorrow, Taylor's Christmas Tabloid, Three-Dimension Advs., World Of Krypton, World Of Metropolis, World Of Smallville & World's Finest)

SUPERMAN (Becomes Adventures of...#424 on)
Summer, 1939 - No. 423, Sept, 1986 (#1-5 are quarterly)
National Periodical Publications/DC Comics
GD25 FN65 VF82 NM94
1(nn)-1st four Action stories reprinted; origin Superman by Siegel & Shuster; has a new 2 pg. origin plus 4 pgs. omitted in Action story; see The Comics Magazine #1 & More Fun #14-17 for Superman proto-type app.; cover r/splash page from Action #10; 1st pin-up Superman on back-c - 1st pin-up in comics 12,500.00 37,500.00 75,000.00 125,000.00
(Estimated up to 190 total copies exist, 3 in NM/Mint)
1-Reprint, Oversize 13-1/2x10". **WARNING**: This comic is an exact duplicate reprint of the original except for its size. DC published it in 1978 with a second cover titling it as a Famous First Edition. There have been many reported cases of the outer cover being removed and the interior sold as the original edition. The reprint with the new outer cover removed is practically worthless. See Famous First Edition for value.
GD25 FN65 NM94
2-All daily strip-r; full pg. ad for N.Y. World's Fair 950.00 2850.00 9500.00
3-2nd story-r from Action #5; 3rd story-r from Action #6

Superman #16 © DC

Superman #70 © DC

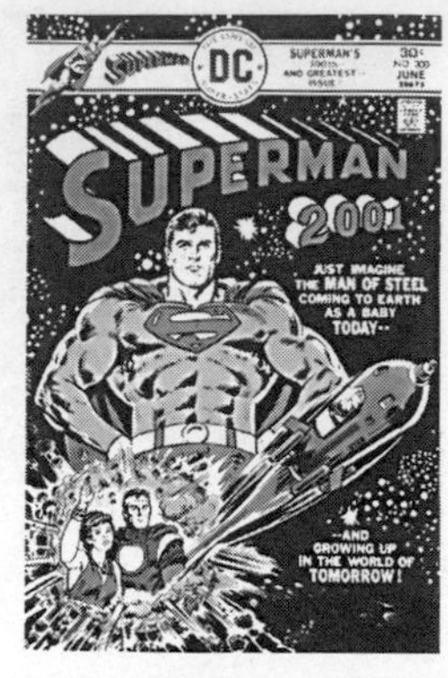

Superman #300 © DC

GD25 FN65 NM94

630.00 1890.00 6300.00
4-2nd mention of Daily Planet (Spr/40); also see Action #23; 2nd & 3rd app. Luthor (red-headed; also see Action #23) 470.00 1410.00 4700.00
5-4th Luthor app. (red hair) 330.00 990.00 3300.00
6,7: 6-1st splash pg. in a Superman comic. 7-1st Perry White? (11-12/40) 240.00 720.00 2400.00
8-10: 10-5th app. Luthor (1st bald Luthor, 5-6/41) 233.00 700.00 2100.00
11-13,15: 13-Jimmy Olsen & Luthor app. 167.00 500.00 1500.00
14-Patriotic Shield-c classic by Fred Ray 240.00 720.00 2400.00
16,18-20: 16-1st Lois Lane-c this title (5-6/42); 2nd Lois-c after Action #29 139.00 417.00 1250.00
17-Hitler, Hirohito-c 150.00 450.00 1350.00
21-23,25: 25-Clark Kent's only military service; Fred Ray's only super-hero story 105.00 315.00 940.00
24-Jack Burnley flag-c 133.00 400.00 1200.00
26-29: 27,29-31-Lois Lane-c. 28-Lois Lane Girl Reporter series begins, ends #40,42 94.00 282.00 850.00
28-Overseas edition for Armed Forces; same as reg. #28 94.00 282.00 850.00
30-Origin & 1st app. Mr. Mxyztplk (9-10/44)(pronounced "Mix-it-plk") in comic books; name later became Mxyzptlk ("Mix-yez-pit-l-ick"); the character was inspired by a combination of the name of Al Capp's Joe Blyfstyk (the little man with the black cloud over his head) & the devilish antics of Bugs Bunny; he 1st app. in newspapers 3/7/44 150.00 450.00 1350.00
31-40: 33-(3-4/45)-3rd app. Mxyztplk. 35,36-Lois Lane-c. 38-Atomic bomb story (1-2/46); delayed because of gov't censorship; Superman shown reading Batman #32 on cover 83.00 250.00 750.00
41-50: 42-Lois Lane-c. 45-Lois Lane as Superwoman (see Action #60 for 1st app.). 46-(5-6/47)-1st app. Superboy this title? 48-1st time Superman travels thru time 63.00 189.00 570.00
51,52: 51-Lois Lane-c 52.00 156.00 470.00
53-Origin Superman retold; 10th anniversary ('48) 222.00 667.00 2000.00
54,56-60: 58-Intro Tiny Trix 52.00 156.00 470.00
55-Used in **SOTI**, pg. 33 56.00 168.00 500.00
61-Origin Superman retold; origin Green Kryptonite (1st Kryptonite story); Superman returns to Krypton for 1st time & sees his parents for 1st time since infancy, discovers he's not an Earth man 105.00 315.00 940.00
62-65,67-70: 62-Orson Welles-c/story. 65-1st Krypton Foes: Mala, K120, & U-Ban. 67-Perry Como-c/story. 68-1st Luthor-c this title (see Action Comics) 50.00 150.00 450.00
66-2nd Superbaby story 50.00 150.00 450.00
71-75: 74-2nd Luthor-c this title. 75-Some have #74 on-c 47.00 141.00 425.00
72-Giveaway(9-10/51)-(Rare)-Price blackened out; came with banner wrapped around book; without banner 58.00 174.00 525.00
72-Giveaway with banner 83.00 250.00 750.00
76-Batman x-over; Superman & Batman learn each other's I.D. for the 1st time (5-6/52)(also see World's Finest #71) 139.00 417.00 1250.00
77-81: 78-Last 52 pg. issue. 81-Used in **POP**, pg. 88 44.00 132.00 400.00
82-87,89,90 42.00 126.00 375.00
88-Prankster, Toyman & Luthor team-up 44.00 132.00 400.00
91-95: 95-Last precode issue (2/55) 36.00 108.00 325.00
96-99: 96-Mr. Mxyztplk-c/story 29.00 87.00 290.00

GD25 FN65 VF82 NM94
100 (9-10/55)-Shows cover to #1 on-c 150.00 450.00 900.00 1600.00

GD25 FN65 NM94
101-105,107-110: 109-1st S.A. issue 27.00 82.00 275.00
106 (7/56)-Retells origin 30.00 90.00 300.00
111-120 23.00 69.00 230.00
121,122,124-127,129: 127-Origin/1st app. Titano. 129-Intro/origin Lori Lemaris, The Mermaid 19.00 57.00 190.00
123-Pre-Supergirl tryout-c/story (8/58). 20.00 60.00 200.00
128-(4/59)-Red Kryptonite used. Bruce Wayne x-over who protects Superman's i.d. (3rd story) 20.00 60.00 200.00
130-(7/59)-1st app, Krypto, the Superdog with Superman (all previous app. w/Superboy 19.00 57.00 190.00
131-139: 139-Lori Lemaris app.; "Untold Story of Red Kryptonite" back-up story 15.00 45.00 150.00
140-1st Blue Kryptonite & Bizarro Supergirl; origin Bizarro Jr. #1 16.50 50.00 165.00
141-145,148: 142-2nd Batman x-over 12.00 36.00 120.00
146-(7/61)-Superman's life story; back-up hints at Earth II. Classic-c 15.00 45.00 150.00
147(8/61)-7th Legion app; 1st app. Legion of Super-Villains; 1st app. Adult Legion; swipes-c to Adv. #247 14.00 42.00 140.00
149(11/61)-9th Legion app. (cameo); "The Death of Superman" imaginary story; last 10¢ issue 12.50 38.00 125.00
150-162: 152(4/62)-15th Legion app. 155-(8/62)-19th Legion app; Lightning Man & Cosmic Man, & Adult Legion app. 156,162-Legion app. 157-Gold Kryptonite used (see Adv. 299); Mon-el app.; Lightning Lad cameo (11/62). 158-1st app. Flamebird & Nightwing & Nor-Kan of Kandor (12/62). 161-1st told death of Ma and Pa Kent 7.00 21.00 70.00
161-2nd printing (1987, $1.25)-New DC logo; sold thru So Much Fun Toy Stores (cover title: Superman Classic) .90 2.25
163-166,168-180: 166-XMas-c. 168-All Luthor issue; JFK tribute/memorial. 169-Bizarro Invasion of Earth-c/story; last Sally Selwyn. 170-Pres. Kennedy story is finally published after delay from #169 due to assassination. 172,173-Legion cameos. 174-Super-Mxyzptlk; Bizarro app. 5.50 16.50 55.00
167-New origin Brainiac & Brainiac 5; intro Tixarla (later Luthor's wife) 8.50 25.50 85.00
181,182,184-186,188-192,194-196,198,200: 181-1st 2965 story/series. 182-1st S.A. app. of The Toyman (1/66). 189-Origin/destruction of Krypton II. 4.50 13.50 45.00
183,187,193,197 (Giants G-18,G-23,G-31,G-36) 5.00 15.00 50.00
199-1st Superman/Flash race (8/67): also see Flash #175 & World's Finest #198,199 (r-in Limited Coll. Ed. #48) 21.00 63.00 210.00
201,203-206,208-211,213-216: 213-Brainiac-5 app. 2.80 8.40 28.00
202 (80-pg. Giant G-42)-All Bizarro issue 3.50 10.50 35.00
207,212,217,222,239 (Giants G-48,G-54,G-60,G-66,G-84): 207-Legion app.; 30th anniversary Superman (6/68) 3.50 10.50 35.00
218-221,223-226,228-231 2.50 7.50 22.00
227,232(Giants, G-72,G-78)-All Krypton issues 3.30 9.90 33.00
233-2nd app. Morgan Edge; Clark Kent switches from newspaper reporter to TV newscaster; all Kryptonite on earth destroyed 3.50 10.50 35.00
234-238 2.00 6.00 16.00
240-Kaluta-a 1.00 2.80 7.00
241-244 (All 52 pgs.): 243-G.A.-r/#38 1.25 3.75 10.00
245-DC 100 Pg. Super Spectacular #7; Air Wave, Kid Eternity, Hawkman-r; Atom-r/Atom #3 (see DC 100 Pg. Super Spect. #7 for price)
246-248,250,251,253 (All 52 pgs.): 246-G.A.-r/#40. 248-World of Krypton story. 251-G.A.-r/#45. 253-Finlay-a, 2 pgs., G.A.-r/#1 1.25 3.75 10.00
249,254-Neal Adams-a. 249-(52 pgs.); origin & 1st app. Terra-Man by Neal Adams (inks) 1.85 5.50 15.00
252-DC 100 Pg. Super Spectacular #13; Ray(r/Smash #17), Black Condor, (r/Crack #18), Hawkman(r/Flash #24); Starman-r/Adv. #67; Dr. Fate & Spectre-r/More Fun #57; N. Adams-c (see DC 100 Pg. Super Spect. #13 for price)
255-271,273-277,279-283: 263-Photo-c. 264-1st app. Steve Lombard. 276-Intro Capt. Thunder. 279-Batman, Batgirl app. 2.00 5.00
272,278,284-All 100 pgs. G.A.-r in all. 272-r/2nd app. Mr. Mxyztplk from Action #80 2.50 7.50 20.00
285-299: 289-Partial photo-c. 292-Origin Lex Luthor retold 1.60 4.00
300-Retells origin (6/76) 1.85 5.50 15.00
301-399: 301,320-Solomon Grundy app. 323-Intro. Atomic Skull. 327-329-(44 pgs.). 330-More facts revealed about I. D. 338-The bottled city of Kandor enlarged. 344-Frankenstein & Dracula app. 353-Brief origin. 354,355,357-Superman 2020 stories (354-Debut of Superman III). 356-World of Krypton

Superman #416 © DC

Superman #93 (2nd Series) © DC

Superman #130 (2nd Series) © DC

GD25 FN65 NM94

story (also #360,367,375). 366-Fan letter by Todd McFarlane. 372-Superman 2021 story. 376-Free 16 pg. preview Daring New Advs. of Supergirl. 377-Free 16 pg. preview Masters of the Universe 1.00 2.50
400 (10/84, $1.50, 68 pgs.)-Many top artists featured; Chaykin painted cover, Miller back-c 2.00 5.00
401-422: 405-Super-Batman story. 408-Nuclear Holocaust-c/story. 411-Special Julius Schwartz tribute issue. 414,415-Crisis x-over. 422-Horror-c 1.00 2.50
423-Alan Moore scripts; Perez-a(i); last Earth I Superman story, cont'd in Action #583 1.00 2.80 7.00
Annual 1(10/60, 84 pgs.)-Reprints 1st Supergirl story/Action #252; r/Lois Lane #1; Krypto-r (1st Silver Age DC annual) 71.00 213.00 850.00
Annual 2(Win, 1960-61)-Super-villain issue; Brainiac, Titano, Metallo, Bizarro origin-r 35.00 105.00 390.00
Annual 3(Sum, 1961)-Strange Lives of Superman 27.00 82.00 275.00
Annual 4(Win, 1961-62)-11th Legion app; 1st Legion origins (text & pictures); advs. in time, space & on alien worlds 22.50 68.00 225.00
Annual 5(Sum, 1962)-All Krypton issue 18.00 54.00 180.00
Annual 6(Win, 1962-63)-Legion-r/Adv. #247 16.50 50.00 165.00
Annual 7(Sum, 1963)-Origin-r/Superman-Batman team/Adv. 275; r/1955 Superman dailies 12.00 36.00 120.00
Annual 8(Win, 1963-64)-All origins issue 10.50 32.00 105.00
Annual 9(8/64)-Was advertised but came out as 80 Page Giant #1 instead
Annual 9(1983)-Toth/Austin-a 2.00 5.00
Annuals 10-12: 10(1984, $1.25)-M. Anderson inks. 11(1985)-Moore scripts. 12(1986)-Bolland-c 1.60 4.00
Special 1(1983)-G. Kane-c/a; contains German-r 1.60 4.00
Special 2,3(1984, 1985, $1.25, 52 pgs.) 1.60 4.00
The Amazing World of Superman "Official Metropolis Edition" (1973, $2.00, 14x10-1/2")-Origin retold; Wood-r(i) from Superboy #153,161 2.50 7.50 20.00
Kelloggs Giveaway-(2/3 normal size, 1954)-r-two stories/Superman #55 29.00 86.00 230.00
...Meets the Quik Bunny (1987, Nestles Quik premium, 36 pgs.) 1.50
Pizza Hut Premiums (12/77)-Exact reprints of 1950s comics except for paid ads (set of 6 exist?); Vol. 1-r#97 (#113-r also known) .80 2.00
Radio Shack Giveaway-36 pgs. (7/80) "The Computers That Saved Metropolis", Starlin/Giordano a; advertising insert in Action #509, New Advs. of Superboy #7, Legion of Super-Heroes #265, & House of Mystery #282. (All comics were 68 pgs.) Cover of inserts printed on newsprint. Giveaway contains 4 extra pgs. of Radio Shack advertising that inserts do not .80 2.00
Radio Shack Giveaway-(7/81) "Victory by Computer" .80 2.00
Radio Shack Giveaway-(7/82) "Computer Masters of Metropolis" .80 2.00
11195 (2/79, $1.95, 224 pgs.)-Golden Press 1.00 2.50

NOTE: **N. Adams** *a-249i, 254p; c-204-208, 210, 212-215, 219, 231, 233-237, 240-243, 249-252, 254, 263, 307, 308, 313, 314, 317.* **Adkins** *a-323i.* **Austin** *c-368i.* **Wayne Boring** *art-late 1940's to early 1960's.* **Buckler** *a(p)-352, 363, 364, 369; c(p)-324-327, 356, 363, 368, 369, 373, 376, 378.* **Burnley** *a-252r; c-19-25, 30, 33, 34, 35p, 38p, 39p, 45p.* **Fine** *a-252r.* **Kaluta** *a-400.* **Gil Kane** *a-272r, 367, 372, 375, Special 2; c-374p, 375p, 377, 381, 382, 384-390, 392, Annual 9, Special 2.* **Joe Kubert** *c-216.* **Miller**-*pin-up.* **Morrow** *a-238.* **Mortimer** *a-250r.* **Perez** *c-364p.* **Fred Ray** *a-25; c-6, 8-18.* **Starlin** *c-355.* **Staton** *a-354i, 355i.* **Swan/Moldoff** *c-149.* **Williamson** *a(i)-408-410, 412-416; c-408i, 409i.* **Wrightson** *a-400, 416.*

SUPERMAN (2nd Series)
Jan, 1987 - Present (75¢/$1.00/$1.25/$1.50/$1.95)
DC Comics

1-Byrne-c/a begins; intro new Metallo 1.60 4.00
2-8,10: 3-Legends x-over; Darkseid-c & app. 7-Origin/1st app. Rampage. 8-Legion app. .80 2.00
9-Joker-c 1.60 4.00
11-49,51,52,54-56,58-67: 11-1st new Mr. Mxyzptlk. 12-Lori Lemaris revived. 13-1st app. new Toyman. 13,14-Millennium x-over. 16-1st app. new Supergirl (4/88). 20-Doom Patrol app.; Supergirl cameo. 21-Supergirl-c/story; 1st app. Matrix who becomes new Supergirl. 31-Mr. Mxyzptlk app. 37-Newsboy Legion app. 41-Lobo app. 44-Batman storyline, part 1. 45-Free extra 8 pgs. 54-Newsboy Legion story. 63-Aquaman x-over. 67-Last $1.00-c .80 2.00
50-($1.50, 52 pgs.)-Clark Kent proposes to Lois 1.80 4.50
50-2nd printing .70 1.75
53-Clark reveals i.d. to Lois (Cont'd from Action #662) 1.20 3.00
53-2nd printing 1.50
57-($1.75, 52 pgs.) .70 1.75
68-72: 65,66,68-Deathstroke-c/stories. 70-Superman & Robin team-up 1.50
73-Doomsday cameo 1.20 3.00
74-Doomsday Pt. 2 (Cont'd from Justice League #69); Superman battles Doomsday 1.60 4.00
73,74-2nd printings .80 2.00
75-($2.50)-Collector's Ed.; Doomsday Pt. 6; Superman dies; polybagged w/poster of funeral, obituary from Daily Planet, postage stamp & armband premiums (direct sales only) 1.25 3.75 10.00
75-Direct sales copy (no upc code, 1st print) 1.20 3.00
75-Direct sales copy (no upc code, 2nd print) 1.25
75-Direct sales copy (no upc code, 3rd, 4th prints) 1.25
75-Newsstand copy w/upc code 1.40 3.50
75-Platinum Edition; given away to retailers 3.00 9.00 30.00
76,77-Funeral For a Friend parts 4 & 8 .90 2.25
78-($1.95)-Collector's Edition with die-cut outer-c & bound-in mini poster; Doomsday cameo .90 2.25
78-($1.50)-Newsstand Edition w/poster and different-c; Doomsday-c & cameo .80 2.00
79-81,83-89: 83-Funeral for a Friend epilogue; new Batman (Azrael) cameo. 87,88-Bizarro-c/story .80 2.00
82-($3.50)-Collector's Edition w/all chromium c; real Superman revealed; Green Lantern x-over from G.L. #46; no ads 1.40 3.50
82-($2.00, 44 pgs.)-Regular Edition w/different-c .80 2.00
90-93: 93-(9/94)-Zero Hour 1.50
0, 94-99: 0-(10/94). 94-(11/94). 95-Atom app. 96-Return of Brainiac. 1.50
100-Death of Clark Kent foil-c 1.60 4.00
100-Newsstand 1.20 3.00
101-122: 101-Begin $1.95-c; Black Adam app. 105-Green Lantern app. 110-Plastic Man-c/app. 114-Brainiac app; Dwyer-c. 115-Lois leaves Metropolis. 116-(10/96)-1st app. Teen Titans by Dan Jurgens & George Perez in 8 pg. preview. 117-Final Night. 118-Wonder Woman app. 119-Legion app. 122-New powers .80 2.00
123-Collector's Edition w/glow in the dark-c, new costume 1.60 4.00
123-Standard ed., new costume 1.20 3.00
124-134: 128-Cyborg-c/app. 131-Birth of Lena Luthor. 132-Superman Red/Superman Blue 1.95
Annual 1,2: 1 (1987)-No Byrne-a. 2 (1988)-Byrne-a; Newsboy Legion; return of the Guardian .80 4.00
Annual 3 (1991, $2.00, 68 pgs.)-Armageddon 2001 x-over; Batman app.; Austin-c(i) & part inks .90 2.25
Annual 3-2nd & 3rd printings; 3rd has silver ink .80 2.00
Annual 4 (1992, $2.50, 68 pgs.)-Eclipso app. 1.00 2.50
Annual 5 (1993, $2.50, 68 pgs.) 1.00 2.50
Annual 6 (1994, $2.95, 68 pgs.)-Elseworlds story 1.20 3.00
Annual 7 (1995, $3.95, 69 pgs.)-Year One story 1.60 4.00
Annual 8 (1996, $2.95)-Legends of the Dead Earth story 1.20 3.00
Annual 9 (1997, $3.95)-Pulp Heroes story 1.60 4.00
...Plus 1(2/97, $2.95)-Legion of Super-Heroes-c/app. 1.20 3.00
Special 1 (1992, $3.50, 68 pgs.)-Simonson-c/a 1.40 3.50
...: TIME AND TIME AGAIN (1994, $7.50)-Reprints 1.00 3.00 7.50
THE DEATH OF CLARK KENT TPB nn (1997, $19.95)-Reprints Man of Steel #43 (1 page), Superman #99 (1 page),#100-102, Action #709 (1 page), #710,711, Advs. of Superman #523-525, Superman:The Man of Tomorrow #1 2.50 7.50 20.00
THE DEATH OF SUPERMAN TPB nn (1993, $4.95)-Reprints Man of Steel #17-19, Superman #73-75, Advs. of Superman #496,497, Action

The Superman Adventures #16 © DC

Superman Family #222 © DC

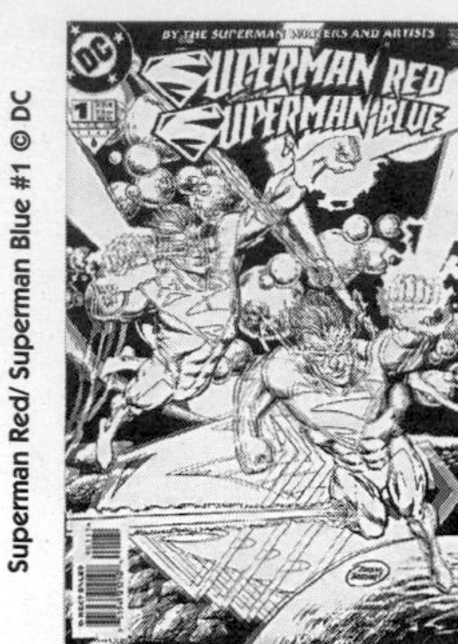

Superman Red/ Superman Blue #1 © DC

GD25 FN65 NM94

#683,684 & Justice League #69 6.00
THE DEATH OF SUPERMAN, 2nd & 3rd printings 2.00 5.00
THE DEATH OF SUPERMAN Platinum Edition 2.85 6.50 15.00
NOTE: **Austin** *a(i)-1-3.* **Byrne** *a-1-16p, 17, 19-21p, 22; c-1-17, 20-22; scripts-1-22.* **Guice** *c/a-64.* **Kirby** *c-37p.* **Joe Quesada** *c-Annual 4.* **Russell** *c/a-23i.* **Simonson** *c-69i. #19-21 2nd printings sold in multi-packs.*

SUPERMAN (one-shots)
DAILY NEWS MAGAZINE PRESENTS DC COMICS' SUPERMAN
nn-(1987, 8 pgs.)-Supplement to New York Daily News; Perez-c/a 1.50
...: AT EARTH'S END (1995, $4.95)-Elseworlds story 2.00 5.00
...FOR EARTH (1991, $4.95, 52 pgs, printed on recycled paper)-Ordway wraparound-c. 2.00 5.00
...IV MOVIE SPECIAL (1987, $2.00)-Movie adaptation; Heck-a .80 2.00
...GALLERY, THE 1 (1993, $2.95)-Poster-a 1.20 3.00
...: KAL (1995, $5.95)-Elseworlds story 2.40 6.00
...MOVIE SPECIAL-(9/83)-Adaptation of Superman III; other versions exist with store logos on bottom 1/3 of-c 1.00
...'S METROPOLIS-(1996, $5.95, prestige format)-Elseworlds Ted McKeever-c/a 2.40 6.00
...: SPEEDING BULLETS-(1993, $4.95, 52 pgs.)-Elseworlds 2.00 5.00
.../SPIDER-MAN-(1995, $3.95)-r/DC and Marvel Presents...
...: THE EARTH STEALERS 1-(1988, $2.95, 52 pgs, prestige format) 1-Byrne script; painted-c 1.40 3.50
...: THE EARTH STEALERS 1-2nd printing 1.20 3.00
...: THE LEGACY OF SUPERMAN #1 (3/93, $2.50, 68 pgs.)-Art Adams-c; Simonson-a 1.00 2.50
.../TOYMAN-(1996, $1.95) 2.00
...: UNDER A YELLOW SUN nn (1994, $5.95, 68 pgs.)-A Novel by Clark Kent; embossed-c 2.40 6.00

SUPERMAN ADVENTURES, THE (TV)
Oct, 1996 - Present ($1.75) (Based on animated series)
DC Comics
1-Rick Burchett-c/a begins; Paul Dini script; Lex Luthor app.; silver ink, wraparound-c. .80 2.00
2-13: 2-Scott McCloud scripts begin; Metallo-c/app. 3-Brainiac-c/app. 6-Mxyzptlk-c/app. 1.75
14-19: 14-Begin $1.95-c 1.95
Annual 1 (1997, $3.95)-Zatanna and Bruce Wayne app. 1.60 4.00

SUPERMAN AND THE GREAT CLEVELAND FIRE
1948 (Giveaway, 4 pgs., no cover) (Hospital Fund)
National Periodical Publications
nn-In full color 53.00 159.00 475.00

SUPERMAN/BATMAN: ALTERNATE HISTORIES
1996 ($14.95, trade paperback)
DC Comics
nn-Reprints Detective Comics Annual #7, Action Comics Annual #6, Steel Annual #1, Legends of the Dark Knight Annual #4 15.00

SUPERMAN/DOOMSDAY: HUNTER/PREY
1994 - No. 3, 1994 ($4.95, limited series, 52 pgs.)
DC Comics
1-3 2.00 5.00

SUPERMAN FAMILY, THE (Formerly Superman's Pal Jimmy Olsen)
No. 164, Apr-May, 1974 - No. 222, Sept, 1982
National Periodical Publications/DC Comics
164-Jimmy Olsen, Supergirl, Lois Lane begin 2.50 7.50 24.00
165-169 (100 pgs.) 2.00 6.00 16.00
170-176 (68 pgs.) 1.25 3.75 10.00
177-181 (52 pgs.) 2.00 5.00
182-Marshall Rogers-a; $1.00 issues begin; Krypto begins, ends #192 2.40 6.00
183-193,195-199: 183-Nightwing-Flamebird begins, ends #194. 189-Brainiac 5, Mon-el app. 191-Superboy begins, ends #198 1.60 4.00
194,200: 194-Marshall Rogers-a. 200-Book length sty 2.40 6.00
201-222: 211-Earth II Batman & Catwoman marry 1.20 3.00
NOTE: **N. Adams** *c-182-185.* **Anderson** *a-186i.* **Buckler** *c(p)-190, 191, 209, 210, 215, 217, 220.* **Jones** *a-191-193.* **Gil Kane** *c(p)-221, 222.* **Mortimer** *a(p)-191-193, 199, 201-222.* **Orlando** *a(i)-186, 187.* **Rogers** *a-182, 194.* **Staton** *a-191-194, 196p.* **Tuska** *a(p)-203, 207-209.*

SUPERMAN FOR EARTH (See Superman one-shots)

SUPERMAN/MADMAN HULLABALOO!
June, 1997 - No. 3, Aug, 1997 ($2.95, limited series)
Dark Horse Comics
1-3-Mike Allred-c/s/a 2.95

SUPERMAN (Miniature)
1942; 1955 - 1956 (3 issues, no #'s, 32 pgs.)
The pages are numbered in the 1st issue: 1-32; 2nd: 1A-32A, and 3rd: 1B-32B
National Periodical Publications
No date-Py-Co-Pay Tooth Powder giveaway (8 pgs.; circa 1942) 69.00 207.00 625.00
1-The Superman Time Capsule (Kellogg's Sugar Smacks)(1955) 47.00 142.00 425.00
1A-Duel in Space (1955) 42.00 125.00 375.00
1B-The Super Show of Metropolis (also #1-32, no B)(1955) 42.00 125.00 375.00
NOTE: *Numbering variations exist. Each title could have any combination-#1, 1A, or 1B.*

SUPERMAN RECORD COMIC
1966 (Golden Records)
National Periodical Publications
(With record)-Record reads origin of Superman from comic; came with iron-on patch, decoder, membership card & button; comic-r/Superman #125,146 18.00 54.00 125.00
Comic only 11.50 34.00 80.00

SUPERMAN RED/ SUPERMAN BLUE
Feb, 1998 ($4.95, one shot)
DC Comics
1-Polybagged w/3-D glasses and reprint of Superman 3-D (1955); Jurgens-plot/3-D cover; script and art by various 4.95
1-($3.95)-Standard Ed.; comic only, non 3-D cover 3.95

SUPERMAN'S BUDDY (Costume Comic)
1954 (4 pgs., slick paper-c; one-shot) (Came in box w/costume)
National Periodical Publications
1-w/box & costume 111.00 333.00 1000.00
Comic only 50.00 150.00 450.00
1-(1958 edition)-Printed in 2 colors 14.00 41.00 110.00

SUPERMAN'S CHRISTMAS ADVENTURE
1940, 1944 (Giveaway, 16 pgs.)
Distributed by Nehi drinks, Bailey Store, Ivey-Keith Co., Kennedy's Boys Shop, Macy's Store, Boston Store
National Periodical Publications
1(1940)-Burnley-a; F. Ray-c/r from Superman #6 (Scarce)-Superman saves Santa Claus. Santa makes real Superman Toys offered in 1940. 1st merchandising story 500.00 1500.00 4000.00
nn(1944) w/Santa Claus & X-mas tree-c 94.00 282.00 850.00
nn(1944) w/Candy cane & Superman-c 83.00 250.00 750.00

SUPERMAN SCRAPBOOK (Has blank pages; contains no comics)

SUPERMAN: SECRET FILES
Jan, 1998 ($4.95, one shot)
DC Comics
1-Retold origin story, "lost" pages & pin-ups 4.95

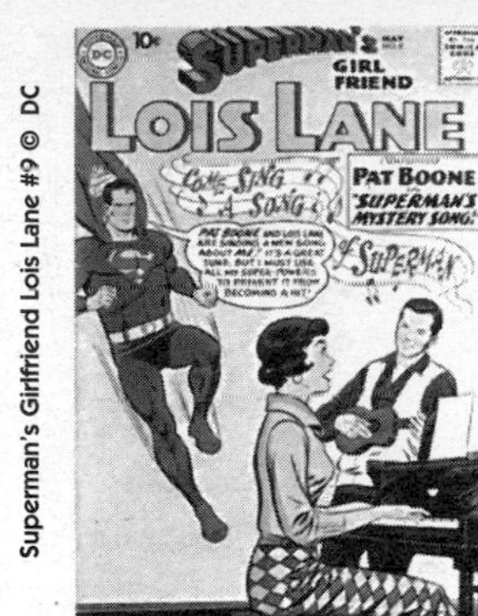

Superman's Girlfriend Lois Lane #9 © DC

Superman's Pal Jimmy Olsen #115 © DC

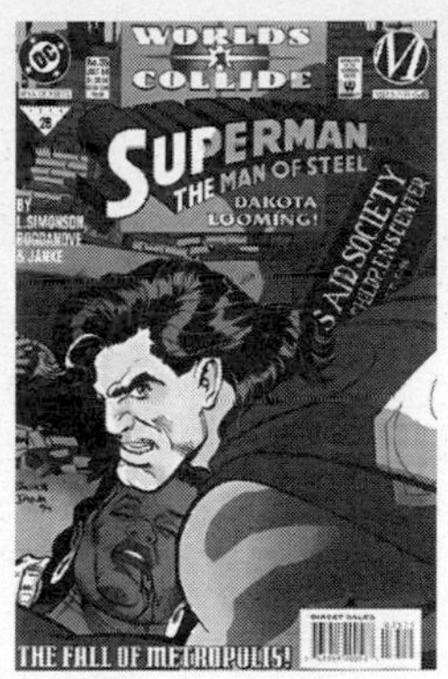

Superman: The Man of Steel #28 © DC

GD25 FN65 NM94 GD25 FN65 NM94

SUPERMAN'S GIRLFRIEND LOIS LANE (See Action Comics #1, 80 Page Giant #3, 14, Lois Lane, Showcase #9, 10, Superman #28 & Superman Family)

SUPERMAN'S GIRLFRIEND LOIS LANE (See Showcase #9,10)
Mar-Apr, 1958 - No. 136, Jan-Feb, 1974; No. 137, Sept-Oct, 1974
National Periodical Publ.

	GD25	FN65	VF82	NM94
1-(3-4/58)	192.00	576.00	1344.00	2500.00

	GD25	FN65	NM94
2	60.00	180.00	725.00
3	40.00	120.00	470.00
4,5	34.00	102.00	375.00
6,7	29.00	88.00	295.00
8-10: 9-Pat Boone-c/story	25.00	75.00	250.00
11-20: 12-(10/59)-Aquaman app. 14-Supergirl x-over; Batman app? 20-Supergirl-c/sty	15.00	45.00	150.00
21-28: 23-1st app. Lena Thorul, Lex Luthor's sister. 27-Bizarro-c/story	11.50	34.00	115.00
29-Aquaman, Batman, Green Arrow cover app. and cameo; last 10¢ issue	12.50	38.00	125.00
30-32,34-46,48,49	6.00	18.00	60.00
33(5/62)-Mon-el app.	6.50	19.50	65.00
47-Legion app.	6.50	19.50	65.00
50(7/64)-Triplicate Girl, Phantom Girl & Shrinking Violet app.	5.00	15.00	50.00
51-55,57-67,69: 59-Jor-el app.; Batman back-up sty	4.20	12.60	42.00
56-Saturn Girl app.	4.20	12.60	42.00
68-(Giant G-26)	5.00	15.00	50.00
70-Penguin & Catwoman app. (1st S.A. Catwoman, 11/66; also see Detective #369 for 3rd app.); Batman & Robin cameo	21.50	65.00	215.00
71-Batman & Robin cameos (3 panels); Catwoman story cont'd from #70 (2nd app.); see Detective #369 for 3rd app	12.50	38.00	125.00
72,73,75,76,78	2.50	7.50	22.00
74-1st Bizarro Flash (5/67); JLA cameo	3.20	9.60	32.00
77-(Giant G-39)	4.00	12.00	40.00
79-Neal Adams-c begin, end #95,108	1.50	4.50	12.00
80-85,87-94: 89-Batman x-over; all N. Adams-c. 93-Wonder Woman-c/story	1.50	4.50	12.00
86,95: (Giants G-51,G-63)-Both have Neal Adams-c. 95-Wonder Woman x-over	3.00	9.00	30.00
96-103,106-111: 108-Neal Adams-c. 111-Morrow-a	1.25	3.75	10.00
104,113-(Giants G-75,87): 113-Kubert-a (previously unpublished G.A. story)	3.00	9.00	30.00
105-Origin/1st app. The Rose & the Thorn.	3.00	9.00	30.00
112,114-123 (52 pgs.): 122-G.A. Lois Lane-r/Superman #30. 123-G.A. Batman-r/Batman #35 (w/Catwoman)	1.50	4.50	12.00
124-135: 130-Last Rose & the Thorn. 132-New Zatanna story		2.00	5.00
136,137: 136-Wonder Woman x-over	1.00	3.00	8.00
Annual 1(Sum, 1962)-r/L. Lane #12; Aquaman app.	17.00	51.00	170.00
Annual 2(Sum, 1963)	11.00	33.00	110.00

NOTE: *Buckler a-117-121p.* ***Curt Swan (or Kurt Schaffenberger)*** *a-1-50(most); c(p)-1-15.*

SUPERMAN'S PAL JIMMY OLSEN (Superman Family #164 on)
(See Action Comics #6 for 1st app. & 80 Page Giant)
Sept-Oct, 1954 - No. 163, Feb-Mar, 1974 (Fourth World #133-148)
National Periodical Publ.

	GD25	FN65	VF82	NM94
1	257.00	771.00	1800.00	3600.00

	GD25	FN65	NM94
2	96.00	288.00	1150.00
3-Last pre-code issue	53.00	159.00	640.00
4,5	40.00	120.00	450.00
6-10	30.00	90.00	300.00
11-20: 15-1st S.A. issue	20.00	60.00	200.00
21-30: 29-1st app. Krypto in Jimmy Olsen	13.50	41.00	135.00
31-40: 31-Origin & 1st app.Elastic Lad (Jimmy Olsen). 33-One pg. biography of Jack Larson (TV Jimmy Olsen). 36-Intro Lucy Lane. 37-2nd app. Elastic Lad & 1st cover app.	9.50	28.50	95.00
41-50: 41-1st J.O. Robot. 48-Intro/origin Superman Emergency Squad	7.50	22.50	75.00
51-56: 56-Last 10¢ issue	6.00	18.00	60.00
57-62,64-70: 57-Olsen marries Supergirl. 62-Mon-el & Elastic Lad app. but not as Legionnaires. 70-Element Lad app.	3.20	9.60	32.00
63(9/62)-Legion of Super-Villains app.	3.80	11.40	38.00
71,74,75,78,80-84,86,89,90: 86-Jimmy Olsen Robot becomes Congorilla	2.80	8.40	28.00
72(10/63)-Legion app; Elastic Lad (Olsen) joins	3.00	9.00	30.00
73-Ultra Boy app.	3.00	9.00	30.00
76,85-Legion app.	3.00	9.00	30.00
77,79: 77-Olsen with Colossal Boy's powers & costume; origin Titano retold. 79-(9/64)-Titled The Red-headed Beatle of 1000 B.C.	3.00	9.00	30.00
87-Legion of Super-Villains app.	3.00	9.00	30.00
88-Star Boy app.	3.00	9.00	30.00
91-94,96-99: 99-Olsen w/powers & costumes of Lightning Lad, Sun Boy & Star Boy	2.50	7.50	22.00
95,104 (Giants G-25,G-38)	3.50	10.50	35.00
100-Legion cameo	3.20	9.60	32.00
101-103,105-112,114-121,123-130,132: 106-Legion app. 110-Infinity-c. 117-Batman & Legion cameo	1.50	4.50	12.00
113,122,131,140 (Giants G-50,G-62,G-74,G-86): 113-Unpublished G.A. Kubert-a (2 pgs.)	3.00	9.00	30.00
133-(10/70)-Re-intro Newsboy Legion; Kirby story & art begins; 1st app. Morgan Edge.	4.00	12.00	40.00
134-1st app. Darkseid (1 panel, 12/70)	6.00	18.00	60.00
135-2nd app. Darkseid (1 pg. cameo; see New Gods & Forever People); G.A. Guardian app.	2.50	7.50	20.00
136-139: 136-Origin new Guardian. 138-Partial photo-c. 139-Last 15¢ issue	1.85	5.50	15.00
141-150: (25¢,52 pgs.). 141-Photo-c; Newsboy Legion-r by S&K begin; full pg. self-portrait Kirby; Don Rickles cameo. 149,150-G.A. Plastic Man-r in both; 150-Newsboy Legion app.	1.85	5.50	15.00
151-163:	1.10	3.30	9.00

NOTE: *Issues #141-148 contain* ***Simon & Kirby*** *Newsboy Legion reprints from Star Spangled #7, 8, 9, 10, 11, 12, 13, 14 in that order.* ***N. Adams*** *c-109-112, 115, 117, 118, 120, 121, 132, 134-136, 147, 148.* ***Kirby*** *a-133-139p, 141-148p; c-133, 137, 139, 142, 145p.* ***Kirby/N. Adams*** *c-137, 138, 141-144, 146.* ***Curt Swan*** *c-1-14(most)., 140.*

SUPERMAN SPECTACULAR (Also see DC Special Series #5)
1982 (Magazine size, square binding)
DC Comics

	GD25	FN65	NM94
1		.80	2.00

SUPERMAN: THE MAN OF STEEL (Also see Man of Steel, The)
July, 1991 - Present ($1.00/$1.25/$1.50/$1.95)
DC Comics

	GD25	FN65	NM94
1-($1.75, 52 pgs.)-Painted-c		1.20	3.00
2-16: 3-War of the Gods x-over. 5-Reads sideways. 10-Last $1.00-c. 14-Superman & Robin team-up			1.25
17-1st app. Doomsday (cameo)		2.00	5.00
17-2nd printing			1.25
18-1st full app. Doomsday	1.00	2.80	7.00
18-2nd & 3rd printings			1.25
19-Doomsday battle issue (c/story)		1.20	3.00
20,21-Funeral for a Friend		.80	2.00
22-($1.95)-Collector's Edition w/die-cut outer-c & bound-in poster; Steel-c/story		.80	2.00
22-($1.50)-Newsstand Ed. w/poster & different-c			1.50
23-37: 23-$1.50-c begins. 30-Regular edition. 32-Bizarro-c/story. 35,36-Worlds Collide Pt. 1 & 10. 37-(9/94)-Zero Hour x-over			1.50
30-($2.50)-Collector's Edition; polybagged with Superman & Lobo vinyl clings that stick to wraparound-c; Lobo-c/story		1.00	2.50

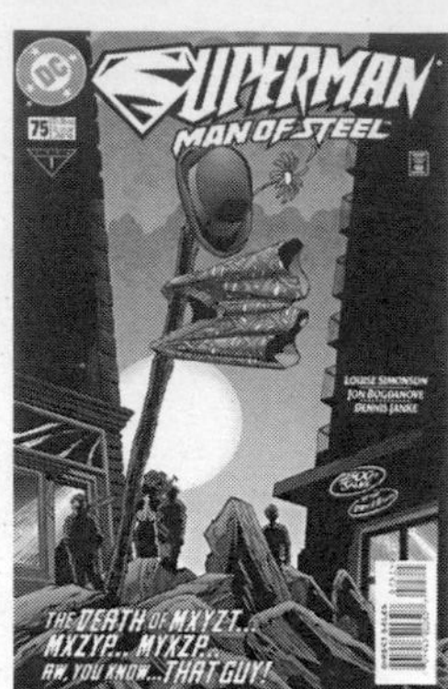

Superman: The Man of Steel #75 © DC

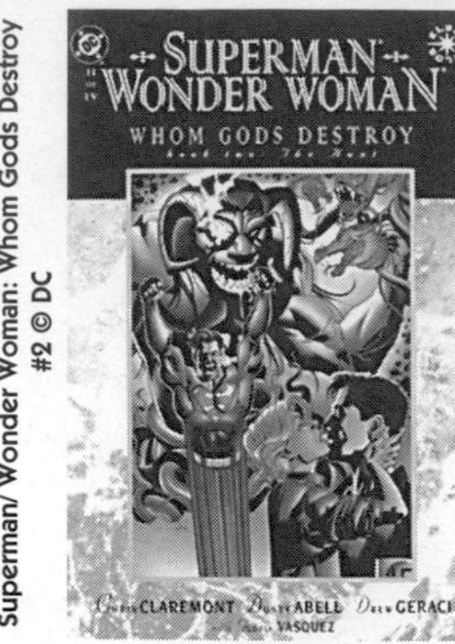

Superman/ Wonder Woman: Whom Gods Destroy #2 © DC

Super-Mystery Comics V4 #3 © ACE

GD25 FN65 NM94

0, 38-44-(10/94). 38-(11/94) 1.50
45-49,51-79: 45-$1.95-c begins. 48-Aquaman app. 54-Spectre-c/app; Lex Luthor app. 56-Mxyzptlk-c/app. 57-G.A. Flash app. 58-Supergirl app. 59-Parasite-c/app.; Steel app. 60-Reintro Bottled City of Kandor 62-Final Night. 64-New Gods app. 67-New powers. 75-"Death" of Mxyzptlk 1.95
50 ($2.95)-The Trial of Superman 1.20 3.00
Annual 1,2 (1992-93, $2.50, 68 pgs.): 1-Eclipso app.; Joe Quesada-c(p). 2-Intro Edge 1.00 2.50
Annual 3 (1994, $2.95, 68 pgs.)-Elseworlds story; Mignola-c; Batman app. 1.20 3.00
Annual 4 (1995, $2.95)-Year One story 1.20 3.00
Annual 5 (1996, $2.95)-Legends of the Dead Earth story 1.20 3.00
Annual 6 (1997, $3.95)-Pulp Heroes story 1.60 4.00
...Gallery (1995, $3.50) Pin-ups by various 1.40 3.50

SUPERMAN: THE MAN OF TOMORROW
1995 - Present ($1.95, quarterly)
DC Comics

1-9: 1-Lex Luthor app. 3-Lex Luthor-c/app; Joker app. 4-Shazam! app. 5-Wedding of Lex Luthor. .80 2.00

SUPERMAN: THE SECRET YEARS
Feb, 1985 - No. 4, May, 1985 (limited series)
DC Comics

1-Miller-c on all 1.50
2-4 1.00

SUPERMAN: THE WEDDING ALBUM
Dec, 1996 ($4.95, 96 pgs, one-shot)
DC Comics

1-Standard Edition-Story & art by past and present Superman creators; gatefold back-c. Byrne-c 2.00 5.00
1-Collector's Edition-Embossed cardstock variant-c w/ metallic silver ink and matte and gloss varnishes 2.00 5.00

SUPERMAN 3-D (See Three-Dimension Adventures)

SUPERMAN-TIM (Becomes Tim)
Aug, 1942 - May, 1950 (Half size) (B&W Giveaway w/2 color covers)
Superman-Tim Stores/National Periodical Publications

8/42(#1) 72.00 216.00 650.00
2/43(#2)-Two pg. Superman illo 34.00 103.00 275.00
3/43, 5/43, 6/43, 8/43, 9/43(#6)-Two pg. Superman illo 25.00 75.00 200.00
3/44, 2/45, 11/49 issues-Two pg. Superman illos 19.00 56.00 150.00
10/43, 12/43, 2/44-no Superman 17.50 53.00 140.00
4/44-1/45, 3/45, 4/45, 5/45, 11/45, 4/46, 5/46, 6/46, 7/46, 8/46 issues-no Superman 16.00 49.00 130.00
9/46-1st stamp album issue (worth more if complete with Superman stamps) 34.00 103.00 275.00
10/46-1st Superman story 25.00 75.00 200.00
11/46, 12/46, 1/47, 2/47, 3/47, 4/47, 5/47-8/47 issues-Superman story in each; 2/47-Infinity-c 25.00 75.00 200.00
9/47-Stamp album issue & Superman story 33.00 98.00 260.00
10/47, 11/47, 12/47-Superman stories 25.00 75.00 200.00
1/48, 2/48, 6/48, 8/48, 10/48, 11/48, 2/49-10/49 issues-no Superman 19.00 56.00 150.00
9/48-Stamp album issue 20.00 60.00 160.00
12/49-5/50 Superman stories 23.00 68.00 180.00

NOTE: *16 pgs. through 9/47; 8 pgs. 10/47 on? The stamp album issues (3) may contain Superman stamps that were made to glue in these books. Books with the stamps in cluded would be worth more, and the value would depend upon completeness of the album. There is no stamp album in the 9/49 issue.*

SUPERMAN VS. ALIENS
July, 1995 - No. 3, Sept, 1995 ($4.95, limited series)
DC Comics/Dark Horse Comics

GD25 FN65 NM94

1-3: Jurgens/Nowlan-a 2.00 5.00

SUPERMAN VS. THE AMAZING SPIDER-MAN (Also see Marvel Treasury Edition No. 28)
1976 ($2.00, over-sized, 100 pgs.)
National Periodical Publications/Marvel Comics Group

1-Andru/Giordano-a; 1st Marvel/DC x-over. 6.00 18.00 60.00
1-2nd printing; 5000 numbered copies signed by Stan Lee & Carmine Infantino on front cover & sold through mail 12.00 36.00 120.00
nn-(1995, $5.95)-r/#1 2.40 6.00

SUPERMAN/WONDER WOMAN: WHOM GODS DESTROY
1997 ($4.95, prestige format, limited series)
DC Comics

1-4-Elseworlds; Claremont-s 2.00 5.00

SUPERMAN WORKBOOK
1945 (B&W, one-shot, reprints, 68 pgs)
National Periodical Publ./Juvenile Group Foundation

nn-Cover-r/Superman #14 117.00 350.00 1050.00

SUPER MARIO BROS. (Also see Adventures of the…)
1990 - No. 5?, 1991 ($1.95, slick-c)
V2#1, 1991 - No. 5, 1991 ($1.50)
Valiant Comics

1-5: 1-Wildman-a .80 2.00
V2#1-5 1.50
Special Edition 1 (1990, $1.95)-Wildman-a .80 2.00

SUPERMOUSE (…the Big Cheese; see Coo Coo Comics)
Dec, 1948 - No. 34, Sept, 1955; No. 35, Apr, 1956 - No. 45, Fall, 1958
Standard Comics/Pines No. 35 on (Literary Ent.)

1-Frazetta text illos (3) 25.00 75.00 200.00
2-Frazetta text illos 10.00 30.00 100.00
3,5,6-Text illos by Frazetta in all 10.00 30.00 80.00
4-Two pg. text illos by Frazetta 10.50 32.00 85.00
7-10 5.00 15.00 30.00
11-20: 13-Racist humor (Indians) 4.00 12.00 24.00
21-45 3.60 9.00 18.00
1-Summer Holiday issue (Summer, 1957, 25¢, 100 pgs.)-Pines 10.00 30.00 80.00
2-Giant Summer issue (Summer, 1958, 25¢, 100 pgs.)-Pines; has games, puzzles & stories 8.50 26.00 60.00

SUPER-MYSTERY COMICS
July, 1940 - V8#6, July, 1949
Ace Magazines (Periodical House)

V1#1-Magno, the Magnetic Man & Vulcan begins (1st app.); Q-13, Corp. Flint, & Sky Smith begin 139.00 417.00 1250.00
2 67.00 200.00 600.00
3-The Black Spider begins (1st app.) 58.00 174.00 520.00
4-Origin Davy 44.00 132.00 400.00
5-Intro. The Clown & begin series (12/40) 44.00 132.00 400.00
6(2/41) 36.00 108.00 325.00
V2#1(4/41)-Origin Buckskin 36.00 108.00 325.00
2-6(2/42): 6-Vulcan begins again 36.00 108.00 300.00
V3#1(4/42),2: 1-Black Ace begins 33.00 98.00 260.00
3-Intro. The Lancer; Dr. Nemesis & The Sword begin; Kurtzman-c/a(2) (Mr. Risk & Paul Revere Jr.); Robot-c 39.00 117.00 350.00
4-Kurtzman-c/a 36.00 108.00 300.00
5-Kurtzman-a(2); L.B. Cole-a; Mr. Risk app. 39.00 117.00 350.00
6(10/43)-Mr. Risk app.; Kurtzman's Paul Revere Jr.; L.B. Cole-a 39.00 117.00 350.00
V4#1(1/44)-L.B. Cole-a 36.00 108.00 290.00
2-6(4/45): 2,5,6-Mr. Risk app. 23.00 68.00 180.00
V5#1(7/45)-6 24.00 71.00 190.00

Supernatural Thrillers #7 © MEG

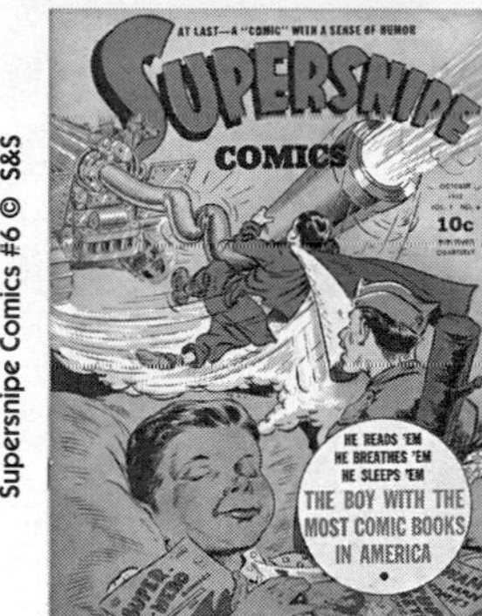

Supersnipe Comics #6 © S&S

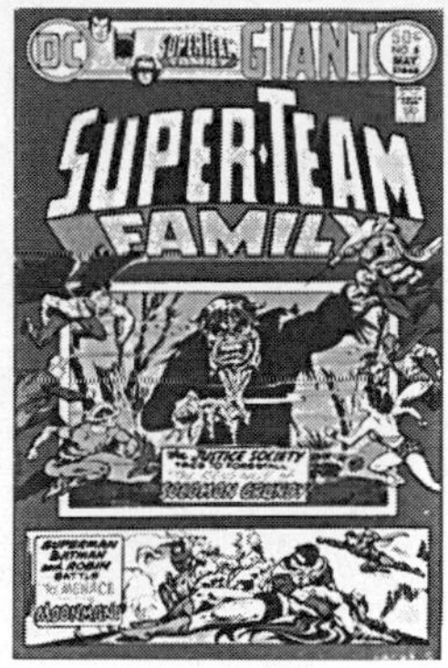

Super-Team Family #4 © DC

GD25 FN65 NM94

V6#1-6: 3-Torture story. 4-Last Magno. Mr. Risk app. in #2,4-6. 6-New logo 19.00 56.00 150.00
V7#1-6, V8#1-4,6 19.00 56.00 150.00
V8#5-Meskin, Tuska, Sid Greene-a 19.00 56.00 150.00
NOTE: ***Sid Greene*** *a-V7#4.* ***Mooney*** *c-V1#5, 6, V2#1-6.* ***Palais*** *a-V5#3, 4; c-V4#6-V5#4, V6#2, V8#4. Bondage c-V2#5, 6, V3#2, 5. Magno c-V1#1-V3#6, V4#2-V5#5, V6#2. The Sword c-V4#1, 6(w/Magno).*

SUPERNATURAL THRILLERS
Dec, 1972 - No. 6, Nov, 1973; No. 7, July, 1974 - No. 15, Oct, 1975
Marvel Comics Group
1-It!; Sturgeon adap. (see Astonishing Tales #21). 1.85 5.50 15.00
2-4: 2-The Invisible Man; H.G. Wells adapt. 3-The Valley of the Worm; R.E. Howard adapt. 4-Dr. Jekyll & Mr. Hyde; R.L. Stevenson adapt. 1.25 3.75 10.00
5-1st app. The Living Mummy 3.00 9.00 30.00
6-15: 6-The Headless Horseman; last 20¢ issue. 7-The Living Mummy begins 2.40 6.00
NOTE: ***Brunner*** *c-11.* ***Buckler*** *a-5p.* ***Ditko*** *a-8r, 9r.* ***G. Kane*** *a-3p; c-3, 9p, 15p.* ***Mayerik*** *a-2p, 7, 8, 9p, 10p, 11.* ***McWilliams*** *a-14i.* ***Mortimer*** *a-4.* ***Steranko*** *c-1, 2.* ***Sutton*** *a-15.* ***Tuska*** *a-6p.*

SUPERPATRIOT (Also see Freak Force & Savage Dragon #2)
July, 1993 - No. 4, Dec, 1993 ($1.95, limited series)
Image Comics (Highbrow Entertainment)
1-4: Dave Johnson-c/a; Larsen scripts; Giffen plots .80 2.00

SUPERPATRIOT: LIBERTY & JUSTICE
July, 1995 - No. 4, Oct, 1995 ($2.50, limited series)
Image Comics (Highbrow Entertainment)
1-4: Dave Johnson-c/a. 1-1st app. Liberty & Justice 1.00 2.50

SUPER POWERS (1st Series)
July, 1984 - No. 5, Nov, 1984
DC Comics
1-Joker/Penguin-c/story; Batman app. .80 2.00
2-5: 1-5-Kirby-c; 5-Kirby-c/a .80 2.00

SUPER POWERS (2nd Series)
Sept, 1985 - No. 6, Feb, 1986
DC Comics
1-Kirby-c/a in all; Capt. Marvel & Firestorm join; Batman cameo; Darkseid storyline in #1-6 .80 2.00
2-6: 4-Batman cameo. 5,6-Batman app. .80 2.00

SUPER POWERS (3rd Series)
Sept, 1986 - No. 4, Dec, 1986
DC Comics
1-4: 1-Cyborg joins; 1st app. Samurai from Super Friends TV show. 1-4-Batman cameos; Darkseid storyline in #1-4 .80 2.00

SUPER PUP (Formerly Spotty The Pup) (See Space Comics)
No. 4, Mar-Apr, 1954 - No. 5, 1954
Avon Periodicals
4,5: 5-Robot-c 4.25 13.00 28.00

SUPER RABBIT (See All Surprise, Animated Movie Tunes, Comedy Comics, Comic Capers, Ideal Comics, It's A Duck's Life, Movie Tunes & Wisco)
Fall, 1944 - No. 14, Nov, 1948
Timely Comics (CmPl)
1-Hitler & Hirohito-c; war effort paper recycling PSA by S&K; Ziggy Pig & Silly begin? 53.00 159.00 480.00
2 29.00 86.00 230.00
3-5 19.00 56.00 150.00
6-Origin 20.00 60.00 160.00
7-10: 9-Infinity-c 11.30 34.00 90.00
11-Kurtzman's "Hey Look" 12.00 36.00 95.00
12-14 10.50 32.00 85.00
I.W. Reprint #1,2('58),7,10('63): 1-r/#13. 2-r/#10. 1.75 5.25 14.00

SUPER RICHIE (Superichie #5 on) (See Richie Rich Millions #68)
Sept, 1975 - No. 4, Mar, 1976 (All 52 pg. Giants)
Harvey Publications
1 1.50 4.50 12.00
2-4 1.00 2.80 7.00

SUPERSNIPE COMICS (Formerly Army & Navy #1-5)
V1#6, Oct, 1942 - V5#1, Aug-Sept, 1949 (See Shadow Comics V2#3)
Street & Smith Publications
V1#6-Rex King - Man of Adventure (costumed hero, see Super Magic/Magician) by Jack Binder begins; Supersnipe by George Marcoux continues from Army & Navy #5; Bill Ward-a 64.00 192.00 575.00
7,10-12: 10,11-Little Nemo app. 39.00 117.00 350.00
8-Hitler, Tojo, Mussolini in Hell with Devil-c 42.00 126.00 380.00
9-Doc Savage x-over in Supersnipe; Hitler-c 53.00 159.00 475.00
V2#1-12: Both V2#1(2/44) & V2#2(4/44) has V2#1 on outside-c. 1-Huck Finn by Clare Dwiggins begins, ends V3#5; V2#2 shows V2#1 on cover 30.00 90.00 240.00
V3#1-12: 8-Bobby Crusoe by Dwiggins begins, ends V3#12. 9-X-Mas-c 26.00 80.00 210.00
V4#1-12, V5#1: V4#10-X-Mas-c 19.00 56.00 150.00
NOTE: ***George Marcoux*** *c-V1#6-V3#4. Doc Savage app. in some issues.*

SUPER SOLDIER (See Marvel Versus DC #3)
Apr, 1996 ($1.95, one-shot)
DC Comics (Amalgam)
1-Mark Waid script & Dave Gibbons-c/a. .80 2.00

SUPER SOLDIER: MAN OF WAR
June, 1997 ($1.95, one-shot)
DC Comics (Amalgam)
1-Waid & Gibbons-s/Gibbons & Palmiotti-c/a. .80 2.00

SUPER SOLDIERS
Apr, 1993 - No. 8, Nov, 1993 ($1.75)
Marvel Comics UK
1-($2.50)-Embossed silver foil logo 1.00 2.50
2-8: 5-Capt. America app. 6-Origin; Nick Fury app.; neon ink-c .70 1.75

SUPERSPOOK (Formerly Frisky Animals on Parade)
No. 4, June, 1958
Ajax/Farrell Publications
4 5.70 17.00 40.00

SUPER SPY (See Wham Comics)
Oct, 1940 - No. 2, Nov, 1940 (Reprints)
Centaur Publications
1-Origin The Sparkler 94.00 282.00 850.00
2-The Inner Circle, Dean Denton, Tim Blain, The Drew Ghost, The Night Hawk by Gustavson, & S.S. Swanson by Glanz app. 58.00 174.00 525.00

SUPER STAR HOLIDAY SPECIAL (See DC Special Series #21)

SUPER-TEAM FAMILY
Oct-Nov, 1975 - No. 15, Mar-Apr, 1978
National Periodical Publications/DC Comics
1-Reprints by Neal Adams & Kane/Wood; 68 pgs. begin, ends #4. New Gods app. 1.00 2.80 7.00
2,3: New stories 2.00 5.00
4-7: Reprints. 4-G.A. JSA-r & Superman/Batman/Robin-r from World's Finest. 5-52 pgs. begin 2.00 5.00
8-10: New Challengers of the Unknown stories 2.40 6.00
11-14: New stories 2.40 6.00
15-New Gods app. New stories 1.00 2.80 7.00
NOTE: ***Neal Adams*** *r-1-3.* ***Brunner*** *c-3.* ***Buckler*** *c-8p.* ***Tuska*** *a-7r.* ***Wood*** *a-1i(r), 3.*

SUPER TV HEROES (See Hanna-Barbera...)

Superworld Comics #1 © Hugo Gernsback

Supreme #53 © Awesome Entertainment

Suspense #6 © MEG

GD25 FN65 NM94 GD25 FN65 NM94

SUPER-VILLAIN CLASSICS
May, 1983
Marvel Comics Group
1-Galactus - The Origin 1.20 3.00

SUPER-VILLAIN TEAM-UP (See Fantastic Four #6 & Giant-Size...)
8/75 - No. 14, 10/77; No. 15, 11/78; No. 16, 5/79; No. 17, 6/80
Marvel Comics Group
1-Giant-Size Super-Villian Team-Up #2; Sub-Mariner & Dr. Doom begin, end #10 1.10 3.30 9.00
2 2.40 6.00
3-5,7-17: 5-1st app. The Shroud. 7-Origin Shroud. 9-Avengers app. 11-15-Dr. Doom & Red Skull app. 1.20 3.00
6-(Regular 25¢ edition)(6/76)-F.F., Shroud app. 1.20 3.00
6-(30¢-c, limited distribution) 1.50 4.50 12.00
NOTE: ***Buckler** c-4p, 5p, 7p. **Buscema** c-1. **Byrne/Austin** c-14. **Evans** a-1p, 3p. **Everett** a-1p. **Giffen** a-8p, 13p; c-13p. **Kane** c-2p, 9p. **Mooney** a-4i. **Starlin** c-6. **Tuska** r-1p, 15p. **Wood** r-15p.*

SUPER WESTERN COMICS (Also see Buffalo Bill)
Aug, 1950 - No. 4, Mar, 1951
Youthful Magazines
1-Buffalo Bill begins; Wyatt Earp, Calamity Jane & Sam Slade app; Powell-c/a 10.00 30.00 80.00
2-4 6.50 19.50 45.00

SUPER WESTERN FUNNIES (See Super Funnies)

SUPERWORLD COMICS
Apr, 1940 - No. 3, Aug, 1940 (All have 68 pgs.)
Hugo Gernsback (Komos Publ.)
1-Origin & 1st app. Hip Knox, Super Hypnotist; Mitey Powers & Buzz Allen, the Invisible Avenger, Little Nemo begin; cover by Frank R. Paul (all have sci/fi-c)(Scarce) 420.00 1260.00 4200.00
2-Marvo 1-2 Go+, the Super Boy of the Year 2680 (1st app.); Paul-c (Scarce) 260.00 780.00 2600.00
3 (Scarce) 200.00 600.00 1800.00

SUPREME (Becomes ...The New Adventures #43-48)(See Youngblood #3) (Also see Bloodwulf Special, Legend of Supreme, & Trencher #3)
V2#1, Nov, 1992 - V2#42, Sept, 1996; V3#49 - Present ($1.95/$2.50/$2.99)
Image Comics (Extreme Studios)/ Awesome Entertainment #49 on
V2#1-Liefeld-a(i) & scripts; embossed foil logo 1.40 3.50
1-Gold Edition 1.00 3.00 8.00
2-(3/93)-Liefeld co-plots & inks; 1st app. Grizlock .80 2.00
3-12,25: 3-Intro Bloodstrike; 1st app. Khrome. 5-1st app. Thor. 6-The Starguard cameo. 7-1st full app. The Starguard. 10-Black and White Pt 1 (1st app.) by Art Thibert (2 pgs. ea. installment). 25-(5/94)-Platt-c .80 2.00
13-24, 26-40: 11-Coupon #4 for Extreme Prejudice #0; Black and White Pt. 7 by Thibert. 12-(4/94)-Platt-c. 13,14-(6/94). 15 (7/94). 16 (7/94)-Stormwatch app. 18-Kid Supreme Sneak Preview; Pitt app. 19,20-Polybagged w/trading card. 20-1st app. Woden & Loki (as a dog); Overtkill app. 21-1st app. Loki (in true form). 21-23-Polybagged trading card. 32-Lady Supreme cameo. 33-Origin & 1st full app. of Lady Supreme (Probe from the Starguard); Babewatch! tie-in. 37-Intro Loki; Fraga-c. 40-Retells Supreme's past advs. 1.00 2.50
41-Alan Moore scripts begin; Supreme revised; intro The Supremacy; Jerry Ordway-c (Joe Bennett variant-c exists). 1.00 3.00 8.00
42-New origin w/Rick Veitch-a; intro Radar, The Hound Supreme & The League of Infinity 2.40 6.00
V3#49,51: 49-Begin $2.99-c 2.99
50-($3.95)-Double sized, 2 covers, pin-up gallery 3.95
52a,52b-($3.50) 3.50
53-($2.50)-Sprouse-a begins 2.50
54-($2.99) 2.99
Annual 1-(1995, $2.95) 1.20 3.00
NOTE: ***Rob Liefeld** a(i)-1, 2; co-plots-2-4; scripts-1, 5, 6. **Ordway** c-41. **Platt** c-12, 25. **Thibert** c(i)-7-9.*

SUPREME: GLORY DAYS
Oct, 1994 - No. 2, Dec, 1994 ($2.95/$2.50, limited series)
Image Comics (Extreme Studios)
1 1.20 3.00
2-Diehard, Roman, Superpatriot, & Glory app. 1.00 2.50

SUPREME: THE NEW ADVENTURES (Formerly Supreme)
V3#43, Oct, 1996 - V3#48, May, 1997 ($2.50)
Maximum Press
V3#43-48: 43-Alan Moore scripts begin; Joe Bennett-a; Rick Veitch-a (8 pgs.); Dan Jurgens-a (1 pg.); intro Citadel Supreme & Suprematons; 1st app. Allied Supermen of America 1.20 3.00

SURE-FIRE COMICS (Lightning Comics #4 on)
June, 1940 - No. 4, Oct, 1940 (Two No. 3's)
Ace Magazines
V1#1-Origin Flash Lightning & begins; X-The Phantom Fed, Ace McCoy, Buck Steele, Marvo the Magician, The Raven, Whiz Wilson (Time Traveler) begin (all 1st app.); Flash Lightning c-1-4 122.00 366.00 1100.00
2 64.00 192.00 575.00
3(9/40), 3(#4)(10/40)-nn on-c, #3 on inside 50.00 150.00 450.00

SURF 'N' WHEELS
Nov, 1969 - No. 6, Sept, 1970
Charlton Comics
1 2.50 7.50 20.00
2-6 1.85 5.50 15.00

SURGE
July, 1984 - No. 4, Jan, 1985 ($1.50, limited series, Baxter paper)
Eclipse Comics
1-4 Ties into DNAgents series 1.50

SURPRISE ADVENTURES (Formerly Tormented)
No. 3, Mar, 1955 - No. 5, July, 1955
Sterling Comic Group
3-5: 3,5-Sekowsky-a 5.35 16.00 32.00

SUSIE Q. SMITH
No. 323, Mar, 1951 - No. 553, Apr, 1954
Dell Publishing Co.
Four Color 323 (#1) 3.00 9.00 35.00
Four Color 377, 453 (2/53), 553 2.75 8.00 30.00

SUSPENSE (Radio/TV issues #1-11; Real Life Tales of... #1-4) (Amazing Detective Cases #3 on?)
Dec, 1949 - No. 29, Apr, 1953 (#1-8,17-23: 52 pgs.)
Marvel/Atlas Comics (CnPC No. 1-10/BFP No. 11-29)
1-Powell-a; Peter Lorre, Sidney Greenstreet photo-c from Hammett's "The Verdict" 47.00 141.00 400.00
2-Crime stories; Dennis O'Keefe & Gale Storm photo-c from Universal movie "Abandoned" 26.00 77.00 200.00
3-Change to horror 27.00 81.00 210.00
4,7-10: 7-Dracula-sty 21.00 62.00 160.00
5-Krigstein, Tuska, Everett-a 22.00 66.00 170.00
6-Tuska, Everett, Morisi-a 21.00 62.00 160.00
11-17,19,20: 14-Hypo-c; A-Bomb panels 15.00 45.00 120.00
18,22-Krigstein-a 18.00 54.00 140.00
21,23,24,26-29: 24-Tuska-a 14.00 43.00 110.00
25-Electric chair-c/story 20.00 60.00 150.00
NOTE: ***Ayers** a-20. **Briefer** a-5, 7, 27. **Brodsky** c-4, 6-9, 11, 16, 17, 25. **Colan** a-8(2), 9. **Everett** a-5, 6(2), 19, 23, 28; c-21-23, 26. **Fuje** a-29. **Heath** a-5, 6, 8, 10, 12, 14; c-14, 19, 24. **Maneely** a-12, 23, 24, 28, 29; c-5, 6p, 10, 13, 15, 18. **Mooney** a-24, 28. **Morisi** a-6, 12. **Palais** a-10. **Rico** a-7-9. **Robinson** a-29. **Romita** a-20(2), 25. **Sekowsky** a-11, 13, 14. **Sinnott** a-23, 25. **Tuska** a-*

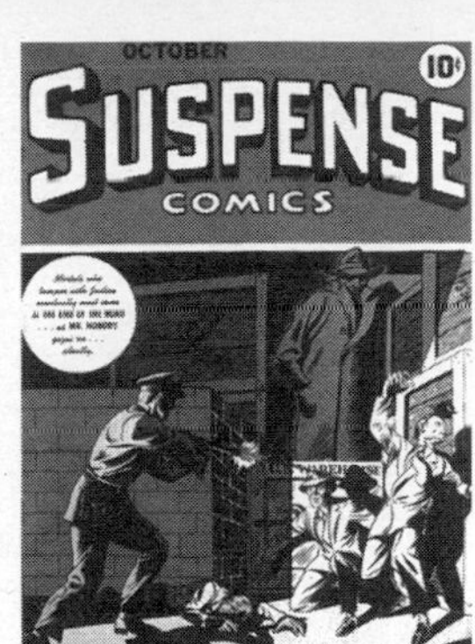

Suspense Comics #6 © Continental Magazines

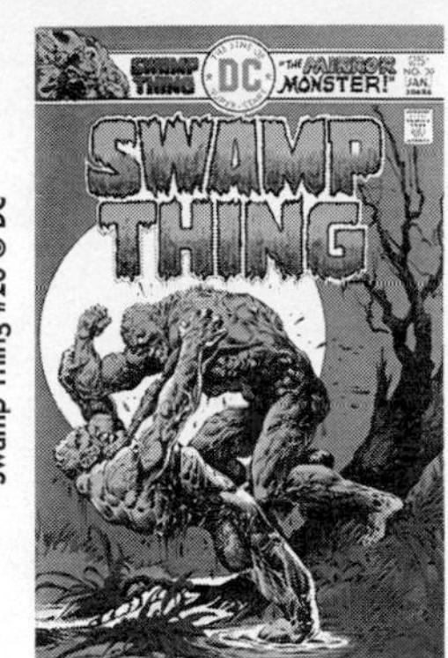

Swamp Thing #20 © DC

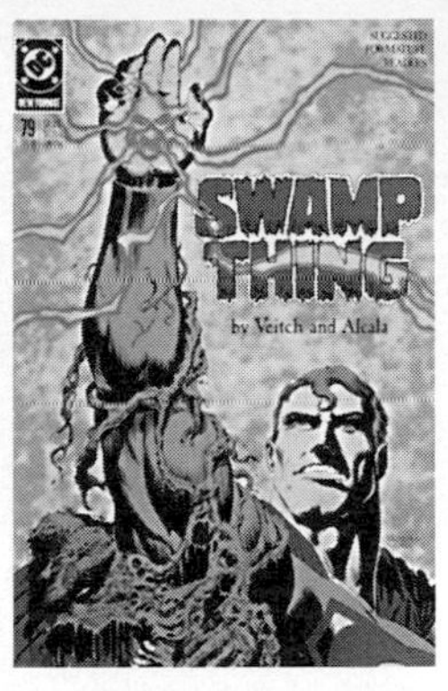

Swamp Thing #79 © DC

GD25 FN65 NM94

*5, 6(2), 12; c-12. **Whitney** a-15, 16, 22. **Ed Win** a-27.*

SUSPENSE COMICS
Dec, 1943 - No. 12, Sept, 1946
Continental Magazines

	GD25	FN65	NM94
1-The Grey Mask begins; bondage/torture-c; L. B. Cole-a (7 pgs.)	280.00	840.00	2800.00
2-Intro. The Mask; Rico, Giunta, L. B. Cole-a (7 pgs.)	233.00	700.00	2100.00
3-L.B. Cole-a; classic Schomburg-c (Scarce)	900.00	2700.00	9500.00
4-6: 5-L. B. Cole-c begin	167.00	500.00	1500.00
7,9,10,12: 9-L.B. Cole eyeball-c	133.00	400.00	1200.00
8-Classic L. B. Cole spider-c	300.00	900.00	3000.00
11-Classic Devil-c	250.00	750.00	2500.00

*NOTE: **L. B. Cole** c-5-12. **Fuje** a-8. **Larsen** a-11. **Palais** a-10, 11. Bondage c-1, 3, 4.*

SUSPENSE DETECTIVE
June, 1952 - No. 5, Mar, 1953
Fawcett Publications

	GD25	FN65	NM94
1-Evans-a (11 pgs); Baily-c/a	36.00	107.00	270.00
2-Evans-a (10 pgs.)	21.00	64.00	160.00
3-5	17.00	51.00	130.00

*NOTE: **Baily** a-4, 5; c-1-3. **Sekowsky** a-2, 4, 5; c-5.*

SUSPENSE STORIES (See Strange Suspense Stories)

SUSPIRA: THE GREAT WORKING
Apr, 1997 - No. 4, Aug, 1997 ($2.95, limited series)
Chaos! Comics

	GD25	FN65	NM94
1-4		1.20	3.00

SUSSEX VAMPIRE, THE (Sherlock Holmes)
1996 ($2.95, 32 pgs., B&W, one-shot)
Caliber Comics

	GD25	FN65	NM94
nn-Adapts Sir Arthur Conan Doyle's story; Warren Ellis scripts		1.20	3.00

SUZIE COMICS (Formerly Laugh Comix; see Laugh Comics, Liberty Comics #10, Pep Comics & Top-Notch Comics #28)
No. 49, Spring, 1945 - No. 100, Aug, 1954
Close-Up No. 49,50/MLJ Mag./Archie No. 51 on

	GD25	FN65	NM94
49-Ginger begins	20.00	60.00	160.00
50-55: 54-Transvestism story	12.00	38.00	100.00
56-Katy Keene begins by Woggon	11.30	34.00	90.00
57-65	8.75	26.25	65.00
66-80	8.50	26.00	60.00
81-87,89-100: 100-Last Katy Keene	7.85	23.50	55.00
88-Used in **POP**, pgs. 76,77; Bill Woggon draws himself in story	8.50	26.00	60.00

*NOTE: **Al Fagaly** c-49-67. Katy Keene app. in 53-82, 85-100.*

SWAMP FOX, THE (TV, Disney)(See Walt Disney Presents #2)
No. 1179, Dec, 1960
Dell Publishing Co.

	GD25	FN65	NM94
Four Color 1179-Leslie Nielson photo-c	8.00	25.00	90.00

SWAMP FOX, THE
1960 (14 pgs, small size) (Canada Dry Premiums)
Walt Disney Productions

Titles: (A)-Tory Masquerade, (B)-Rindau Rampage, (C)-Turnabout Tactics; each came in paper sleeve, books 1,2 & 3;

	GD25	FN65	NM94
Set with sleeves	3.00	9.00	30.00
Comic only	1.10	3.30	9.00

SWAMP THING (See Brave & the Bold, Challengers of the Unknown #82, DC Comics Presents #8 & 85, DC Special Series #2, 14, 17, 20, House of Secrets #92, Limited Collectors' Edition C-59, & Roots of the...)

SWAMP THING
Oct-Nov, 1972 - No. 24, Aug-Sept, 1976
National Periodical Publications/DC Comics

	GD25	FN65	NM94
1-Wrightson-c/a begins; origin	7.50	22.50	75.00
2-1st app. Patchwork Man (1 panel cameo)	4.00	12.00	40.00
3-1st full app. Patchwork Man	2.50	7.50	25.00
4-6,8-10: 10-Last Wrightson issue	2.50	7.50	20.00
7-Batman-c/story	2.50	7.50	25.00
11-19-Redondo-a. 13-Origin retold (1 pg.).		2.40	6.00
20-24: 23,24-Swamp Thing reverts back to Dr. Holland. 23-New logo	1.00	2.80	7.00

*NOTE: **J. Jones** a-9i(assist). **Kaluta** a-9i. **Redondo** c-12-19, 21. **Wrightson** issues (#1-10) reprinted in DC Special Series #2, 14, 17, 20 & Roots of the Swampthing.*

SWAMP THING (Saga Of The... #1-38,42-45)
May, 1982 - No. 171, Oct, 1996 (Direct sales #65 on)
DC Comics (Vertigo imprint #129 on)

	GD25	FN65	NM94
1-Origin retold; Phantom Stranger series begins; ends #13; Yeates-c/a begins		.80	2.00
2-15: 2-Photo-c from movie			1.50
16-19: Bissette-a. 13-Last Yeates-a		1.00	2.50
20-1st Alan Moore issue	1.85	5.50	15.00
21-New origin	1.50	4.50	12.00
22-25: 24-JLA x-over; Last Yeates-c		2.40	6.00
26-30		1.60	4.00
31-33,35,36: 33-r/1st app. from House of Secrets #92		1.20	3.00
34	1.00	2.80	7.00
37-1st app. John Constantine (Hellblazer) (6/85)	1.50	4.50	12.00
38-40: John Constantine app.		2.40	6.00
41-51: 44-Batman cameo. 44-51-John Constantine app. 46-Crisis x-over; Batman cameo. 49-Spectre app. 50-($1.25, 52 pgs.)-Deadman, Dr. Fate, Demon		.80	2.00
52-Arkham Asylum-c/story; Joker-c/cameo		1.20	3.00
53-($1.25, 52 pgs.)-Arkham Asylum; Batman-c/story		1.60	4.00
54-64: 58-Spectre preview. 64-Last Moore issue		.80	2.00
65-83,85-99,101-124,126-130: 65-Direct sales only begins. 66-Batman & Arkham Asylum story. 70,76-John Constantine x-over; 76-X-over w/Hellblazer #9. 79-Superman-c/story. 85-Jonah Hex app. 102-Preview of World Without End. 116-Photo-c. 129-Metallic ink on-c		.80	2.00
84-Sandman (Morpheus) cameo.		2.00	5.00
100 ($2.50, 52 pgs.)		1.00	2.50
125-($2.95, 52 pgs.)-20th anniversary issue		1.40	3.50
131-149, 151-154: 131-$1.95-c begins. 140-Millar scripts begin, end #171.		1.20	3.00
150 ($2.95, 52 pgs.)-Anniversary issue		1.20	3.00
155-171: 155-$2.25-c begins. 165-Curt Swan-a(p). 166,169,171-John Constantine & Phantom Stranger app. 168-Arcane returns		.90	2.25
Annual 1(1982, $1.00)-Movie Adaptation; painted-c			1.50
Annual 2(1985)-Alan Moore scripts; Bissette-a(p); Spectre app.		1.20	3.00
Annual 3(1987, $2.00)-New format; Bolland-c		.80	2.00
Annual 4(1988, $2.00)-Batman-c/story		1.20	3.00
Annual 5(1989, $2.95, 68 pgs.)-Batman cameo; re-intro Brother Power (Geek), 1st app. since 1968		1.20	3.00
Annual 6(1991, $2.95, 68 pgs.)		1.20	3.00
Annual 7(1993, $3.95)-Children's Crusade		1.60	4.00
Saga of the Swamp Thing (1987, $10.95)-r/#21-27	1.40	4.15	11.00
Saga of the Swamp Thing (1989, $12.95, 2nd Printing)	1.60	4.85	13.00
...Love and Death (1990, $17.95)-r/#28-34 & Annual #2; Totleben painted-c	2.25	6.75	18.00

*NOTE: **Bissette** a(p)-16-19, 21-27, 29, 30, 34-36, 39-42, 44, 46, 50, 64; c-17i, 24-32p, 35-37p, 40p, 44p, 46-50p, 51-58, 61, 62, 63p. **Kaluta** c/a-74. **Spiegle** a-1-3, 6. **Sutton** a-98p. **Totleben** a(i)-10, 16-27, 29, 31, 34-40, 42, 44, 46, 48, 50, 53, 55i; c-25-32i, 33, 35-40i, 42i, 44i, 46-50i, 53, 55i, 59p, 64, 65, 68, 73, 76, 80, 82, 84, 89, 91-100, Annual 4, 5. **Vess** painted c-121, 129-139, Annual 7. **Williamson** 86i. **Wrightson** a-18i(r), 33r. John Constantine appears in #37-40, 44-51, 65-67, 70-77, 80-90, 99, 114, 115, 130, 134-138.*

Sweetheart Diary V2 #8 © FAW

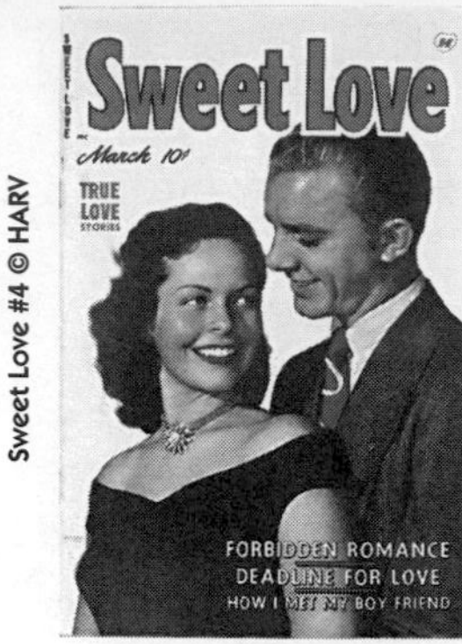

Sweet Love #4 © HARV

Swift Arrow #1 © AJAX

SWARM (See Futuretech)
Jan, 1996 - Present ($2.50, limited series)
Mushroom Comics

	GD25	FN65	NM94
1-Flip book w/Futuretech #1		1.00	2.50

SWAT MALONE (America's Home Run King)
Sept, 1955
Swat Malone Enterprises

	GD25	FN65	NM94
V1#1-Hy Fleishman-a	8.50	26.00	60.00

SWEENEY (Formerly Buz Sawyer)
No. 4, June, 1949 - No. 5, Sept, 1949
Standard Comics

	GD25	FN65	NM94
4,5: 5-Crane-a	7.15	21.50	50.00

SWEE'PEA (Also see Popeye #46)
No. 219, Mar, 1949
Dell Publishing Co.

	GD25	FN65	NM94
Four Color 219	8.00	25.00	90.00

SWEET CHILDE
1995 - No. 2, 1995 ($2.95, B&W, limited series, mature)
Advantage Graphics Press

	GD25	FN65	NM94
1,2		1.20	3.00

SWEETHEART DIARY (Cynthia Doyle #66-on)
Wint, 1949; #2, Spr, 1950; #3, 6/50 - #5, 10/50; #6, 1951(nd); #7, 9/51 - #14, 1/53; #32, 10/55; #33, 4/56 - #65, 8/62 (#1-14: photo-c)
Fawcett Publications/Charlton Comics No. 32 on

	GD25	FN65	NM94
1	12.00	36.00	90.00
2	7.50	22.50	45.00
3,4-Wood-a	13.00	39.00	90.00
5-10: 8-Bailey-a	6.35	19.00	38.00
11-14: 13-Swayze-a. 14-Last Fawcett issue	4.00	12.00	24.00
32 (10/55; 1st Charlton issue)(Formerly Cowboy Love #31)	5.00	15.00	30.00
33-40: 34-Swayze-a	3.00	7.50	15.00
41-60	1.50	4.50	12.00
61-65	1.10	3.30	9.00

SWEETHEARTS (Formerly Captain Midnight)
#68, 10/48 - #121, 5/53; #122, 3/54; V2#23, 5/54 - #137, 12/73
Fawcett Publications/Charlton No. 122 on

	GD25	FN65	NM94
68-Photo-c begin	11.30	34.00	90.00
69-80	5.00	15.00	30.00
81-84,86-93,95-99,105	4.00	12.00	24.00
85,94,103,110,117-George Evans-a	5.70	17.00	38.00
100	4.25	13.00	28.00
101,107-Powell-a	4.25	13.00	26.00
102,104,106,108,109,112-116,118	3.60	9.00	18.00
111-1 pg. Ronald Reagan biography	5.70	17.00	38.00
119-Marilyn Monroe & Richard Widmark photo-c (1/54?); also appears in story; part Wood-a	29.00	86.00	230.00
120-Atom Bomb story	7.15	21.50	50.00
121-Liz Taylor/Fernanado Lamas photo-c	5.70	17.00	38.00
122-(1st Charlton? 3/54)-Marijuana story	6.50	19.50	45.00
V2#23 (5/54)-28: 28-Last precode issue (2/55)	3.60	9.00	18.00
29-39,41,43-45,47-50	1.25	3.75	10.00
40-Photo-c; Tommy Sands story	2.50	7.50	20.00
42-Ricky Nelson photo-c/story	5.50	16.50	55.00
46-Jimmy Rodgers photo-c/story	2.50	7.50	20.00
51-60	1.85	5.50	15.00
61-80	1.50	4.50	12.00
81-100	1.25	3.75	10.00
101-110	1.00	3.00	8.00
111-137		2.40	6.00

NOTE: *Photo c-68-121(Fawcett), 40, 42, 46(Charlton).* **Swayze** *a(Fawcett)-70-118(most).*

SWEETHEART SCANDALS (See Fox Giants)

SWEETIE PIE
No. 1185, May-July, 1961 - No. 1241, Nov-Jan, 1961/62
Dell Publishing Co.

	GD25	FN65	NM94
Four Color 1185 (#1), 1241	2.75	8.00	30.00

SWEETIE PIE
Dec, 1955 - No. 15, Fall, 1957
Ajax-Farrell/Pines (Literary Ent.)

	GD25	FN65	NM94
1-By Nadine Seltzer	5.70	17.00	35.00
2 (5/56; last Ajax?)	4.00	11.00	22.00
3-15 (#3-10, exist?)	2.60	6.50	13.00

SWEET LOVE
Sept, 1949 - No. 5, May, 1950 (All photo-c)
Home Comics (Harvey)

	GD25	FN65	NM94
1	7.15	21.50	50.00
2	4.25	13.00	28.00
3,4: 3-Powell-a	4.00	11.00	22.00
5-Kamen, Powell-a	5.70	17.00	38.00

SWEET ROMANCE
Oct, 1968
Charlton Comics

	GD25	FN65	NM94
1		1.60	4.00

SWEET SIXTEEN (...Comics and Stories for Girls)
Aug-Sept, 1946 - No. 13, Jan, 1948 (All have movie stars photos on covers)
Parents' Magazine Institute

	GD25	FN65	NM94
1-Van Johnson's life story; Dorothy Dare, Queen of Hollywood Stunt Artists begins (in all issues); part photo-c	14.00	41.00	110.00
2-Jane Powell, Roddy McDowall "Holiday in Mexico" photo on-c; Alan Ladd story	9.50	28.00	75.00
3-6,8-11: 4-Elizabeth Taylor photo on-c. 5-Ann Francis photo on-c; Gregory Peck story. 6-Dick Haymes story. 8-Shirley Jones photo on-c. 10-Jean Simmons photo on-c; James Stewart story	7.85	23.50	55.00
7-Ronald Reagan's life story	14.50	43.00	115.00
12-Bob Cummings, Vic Damone story	7.85	23.50	55.00
13-Robert Mitchum's life story	8.50	26.00	60.00

SWEET XVI
May, 1991 - No. 5, Sept, 1991($1.00, color)
Marvel Comics

	GD25	FN65	NM94
..1-5: Barbara Slate story & art			1.00

SWIFT ARROW (Also see Lone Rider & The Rider)
Feb-Mar, 1954 - No. 5, Oct-Nov, 1954; Apr, 1957 - No. 3, Sept, 1957
Ajax/Farrell Publications

	GD25	FN65	NM94
1(1954) (1st Series)	10.50	32.00	85.00
2	6.50	19.50	45.00
3-5: 5-Lone Rider story	5.70	17.00	35.00
1 (2nd Series) (Swift Arrow's Gunfighters #4)	5.70	17.00	40.00
2,3: 2-Lone Rider begins	4.25	13.00	28.00

SWIFT ARROW'S GUNFIGHTERS (Formerly Swift Arrow)
No. 4, Nov, 1957
Ajax/Farrell Publ. (Four Star Comic Corp.)

	GD25	FN65	NM94
4	5.00	15.00	30.00

SWING WITH SCOOTER
June-July, 1966 - No. 35, Aug-Sept, 1971; No. 36, Oct-Nov, 1972
National Periodical Publications

	GD25	FN65	NM94
1	5.00	15.00	50.00
2,6-10: 9-Alfred E. Newman swipe in last panel	2.25	6.75	18.00
3-5: 3-Batman cameo on-c. 4-Batman cameo inside. 5-JLA cameo			

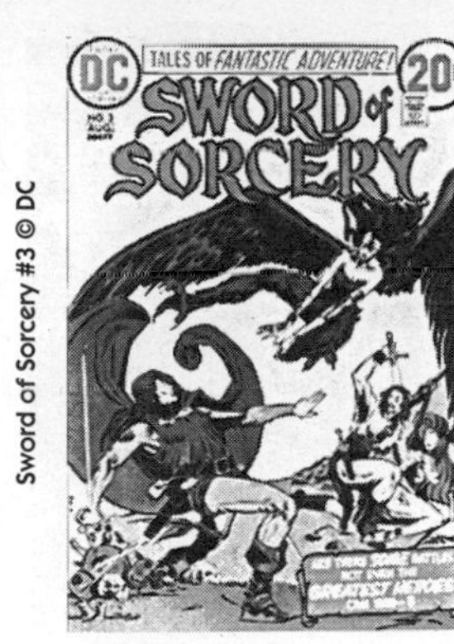

Sword of Sorcery #3 © DC

Syphons #2 © NOW

Taffy Comics #2 © Orbit Publ.

GD25 FN65 NM94

2.50 7.50 25.00
11-13,15-19: 18-Wildcat of JSA 1pg. text 1.75 5.25 14.00
14-Alfred E. Neuman cameo 2.25 6.75 18.00
20 (68 pgs.) 3.00 9.00 30.00
21-31: 24-Frankenstein-c. 1.50 4.50 12.00
32-34 (68 pgs.). 33-Interview with David Cassidy. 34-Interview with Ron Ely (Doc Savage) 2.50 7.50 24.00
35-(52 pgs.). 1 pg. app. Clark Kent and 4 full pgs. of Superman 6.00 18.00 60.00
36-Bat-signal refererence to Batman 1.85 5.50 15.00
NOTE: *Aragones* a-13 (1pg.), 18(1pg.), 30(2pgs.) *Orlando* a-1-11; c-1-11, 13. #20, 33, 34: 68 pgs.; #35: 52 pgs.

SWISS FAMILY ROBINSON (Walt Disney's..; see King Classics & Movie Comics)
No. 1156, Dec, 1960
Dell Publishing Co.
Four Color 1156-Movie-photo-c 6.40 19.00 70.00

SWORD & THE DRAGON, THE
No. 1118, June, 1960
Dell Publishing Co.
Four Color 1118-Movie, photo-c 7.00 22.00 80.00

SWORD & THE ROSE, THE (Disney)
No. 505, Oct, 1953 - No. 682, Feb, 1956
Dell Publishing Co.
Four Color 505-Movie, photo-c 8.00 25.00 90.00
Four Color 682-When Knighthood Was in Flower-Movie, reprint of #505; Renamed the Sword & the Rose for the novel; photo-c 6.40 19.00 70.00

SWORD IN THE STONE, THE (See March of Comics #258 & Movie Comics & Wart and the Wizard)

SWORD OF DAMOCLES
Mar, 1996 - No. 2, Apr, 1996 ($2.50, limited series)
Image Comics (Wildstorm Productions)
1,2: Warren Ellis scripts. 1-Prelude to "Fire From Heaven" x-over; 1st app. Sword 1.00 2.50

SWORD OF SORCERY
Feb-Mar, 1973 - No. 5, Nov-Dec, 1973 (20¢)
National Periodical Publications
1-Leiber Fafhrd & The Grey Mouser; Chaykin/Neal Adams (Crusty Bunkers) art; Kaluta-c 1.10 3.30 9.00
2,3: 2-Wrightson-c(i); Neal Adams-a(i). 3-Wrightson-i(5 pgs.) 2.40 6.00
4,5: . 5-Starlin-a(p); Conan cameo 1.60 4.00
NOTE: *Chaykin* a-1-4p; c-2p, 3-5. *Kaluta* a-3i. *Simonson* a-3i, 4i, 5p; c-5.

SWORD OF THE ATOM
Sept, 1983 - No. 4, Dec, 1983 (Limited series)
DC Comics
1-4: Kane-c/a in all 1.50
Special 1(1984), 2(1985): Kane-c/a each 1.50
Special 3(1988, $1.50) 1.50

SWORDS OF TEXAS (See Scout #15)
Oct, 1987 - No. 4, Jan, 1988 ($1.75, color, Baxter paper)
Eclipse Comics
1-4: Scout app. .75 1.80

SWORDS OF THE SWASHBUCKLERS (See Marvel Graphic Novel)
May, 1985 - No. 12, June, 1987 ($1.50; Mature readers)
Marvel Comics (Epic Comics)
1-12-Butch Guice-c/a (Cont'd from Marvel G.N.) 1.60

SWORN TO PROTECT
Sept, 1995 ($1.95) (Based on card game)
Marvel Comics
nn-Overpower Game Guide; Jubilee story .80 2.00

SYNDICATE FEATURES (Sci/fi)
V1#3, 11/15/37 (Tabloid size, 3 colors, 4 pgs.) (Editors premium)
Harry A. Chesler Syndicate
V1#3-Dan Hastings daily strips-Guardineer-a 240.00 720.00 2200.00

SYPHONS
V2#1, May, 1994 - V2#3, 1994 ($2.50, limited series)
Now Comics
V2#1-3: 1-Stardancer, Knightfire, Raze & Brigade begin 1.00 2.50

SYSTEM, THE
May, 1996 - No. 3, July, 1996 ($2.95, limited series)
DC Comics (Vertigo Verite)
1-3: Kuper-c/a 1.20 3.00
TPB (1997, $12.95) r/#1-3 12.95

TAFFY COMICS
Mar-Apr, 1945 - No. 12, 1948
Rural Home/Orbit Publ.
1-L.B. Cole-c; origin & 1st app. of Wiggles The Wonderworm plus 7 chapter WWII funny animal adventures 36.00 108.00 300.00
2-L.B. Cole-c; Wiggles-c/stories in #1-4 17.50 53.00 140.00
3,4,6-12: 6-Perry Como-c/story. 7-Duke Ellington, 2 pgs. 8-Glenn Ford-c/story. 9-Lon McCallister part photo-c & story. 10-Mort Leav-c. 11-Mickey Rooney-c/story 8.50 26.00 60.00
5-L.B. Cole-c; Van Johnson-c/story 14.00 41.00 110.00

TAILGUNNER JO
Sept, 1988 - No. 6, Jan, 1989 ($1.25)
DC Comics
1-6 1.25

TAILS
Dec, 1995 - No. 3, Feb, 1996 ($1.50, limited series)
Archie Publications
1-3: Based on Sonic, the Hedgehog video game 1.50

TAILSPIN
November, 1944
Spotlight Publishers
nn-Firebird app.; L.B. Cole-c 20.00 60.00 160.00

TAILSPIN TOMMY (Also see Popular Comics)
1940; 1946
United Features Syndicate/Service Publ. Co.
Single Series 23(1940) 33.00 98.00 260.00
Best Seller (nd, 1946)-Service Publ. Co. 11.30 34.00 90.00

TAINTED
Jan, 1995 ($4.95, one-shot)
DC Comics (Vertigo)
1-Jamie Delano scripts; Al Davison-c/a; reads February '95 on-c 2.00 5.00

TAKION
June, 1996 - No. 7, Dec, 1996 ($1.75)
DC Comics
1-7: Aaron Lopresti-c/a(p). 1-Origin; Green Lantern app. 6-Final Night x-over 1.75

TALENT SHOWCASE (See New Talent Showcase)

TALE OF ONE BAD RAT, THE
Oct, 1994 - No. 4, Jan, 1995 ($2.95, limited series)
Dark Horse Comics

Tales From The Crypt #45 © WMG

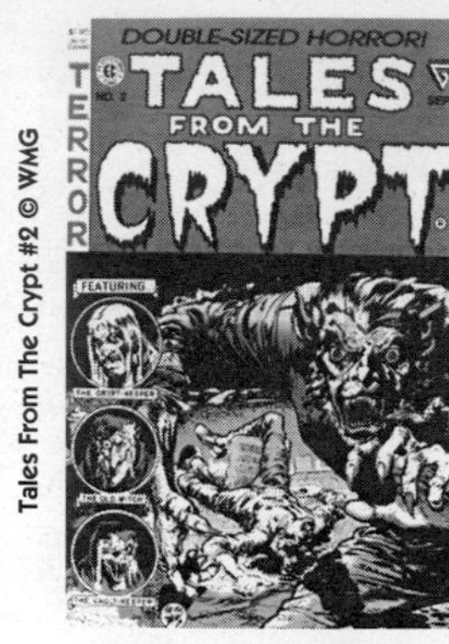

Tales From The Crypt #2 © WMG

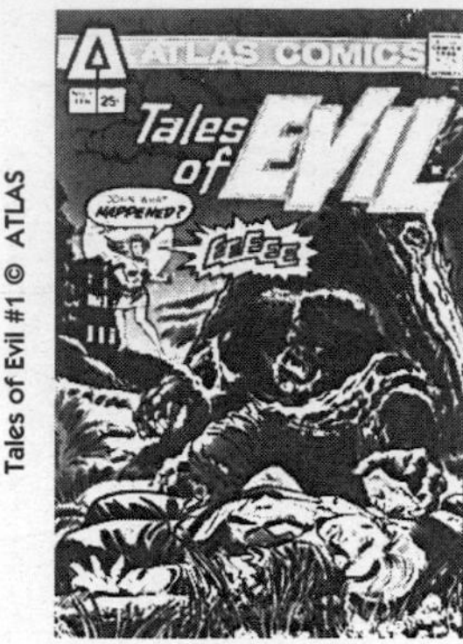

Tales of Evil #1 © ATLAS

	GD25	FN65	NM94
1-4: Bryan Talbot-c/a/scripts		1.20	3.00

TALES CALCULATED TO DRIVE YOU BATS
Nov, 1961 - No. 7, Nov, 1962; 1966 (Satire)
Archie Publications

	GD25	FN65	NM94
1-Only 10¢ issue; has cut-out Werewolf mask (price includes mask)	8.50	25.50	85.00
2-Begin 12¢ issues	4.50	13.50	45.00
3-6	3.50	10.50	35.00
7-Storyline change	3.00	9.00	30.00
1(1966, 25¢, 44 pgs.)-r/#1	3.20	9.60	32.00

TALES CALCULATED TO DRIVE YOU MAD
Summer, 1997 - Present ($3.99, satire)
E.C. Publications

	GD25	FN65	NM94
1-Full color reprints of Mad#1-3		1.60	4.00
2-Full color reprints of Mad#4-6		1.60	4.00

TALES FROM THE AGE OF APOCALYPSE
1996 ($5.95, prestige format, one-shot)
Marvel Comics

	GD25	FN65	NM94
1		2.40	6.00

TALES FROM THE BOG
Nov, 1995 - Present ($2.95/$3.95, B&W)
Aberration Press

	GD25	FN65	NM94
1-4		1.20	3.00
5-7-($3.95)			3.95

TALES FROM THE CRYPT (Formerly The Crypt Of Terror; see Three Dimensional...)
No. 20, Oct-Nov, 1950 - No. 46, Feb-Mar, 1955
E.C. Comics

	GD25	FN65	NM94
20-See Crime Patrol #15 for 1st Crypt Keeper	106.00	320.00	900.00
21-Kurtzman-r/Haunt of Fear #15(#1)	88.00	262.00	725.00
22-Moon Girl costume at costume party, one panel	69.00	206.00	575.00
23-25: 24-E. A. Poe adaptation	52.00	156.00	425.00
26-30	40.00	120.00	325.00
31-Williamson-a(1st at E.C.); B&W and color illos. in **POP**; Kamen draws himself, Gaines & Feldstein; Ingels, Craig & Davis draw themselves in his story	42.00	128.00	350.00
32,35-39: 38-Censored-c	36.00	109.00	265.00
33-Origin The Crypt Keeper	59.00	178.00	475.00
34-Used in **POP**, pg. 83; lingerie panels	36.00	109.00	265.00
40-Used in Senate hearings & in Hartford Cournat anti-comics editorials-1954	36.00	109.00	265.00
41-45: 45-2 pgs. showing E.C. staff	36.00	109.00	265.00
46-Low distribution; pre-advertised cover for unpublished 4th horror title "Crypt of Terror" used on this book	40.00	120.00	310.00

NOTE: ***Ray Bradbury** adaptations-34, 36. **Craig** a-20, 22-24; c-20. **Crandall** a-38, 44. **Davis** a-24-46; c-29-46. **Elder** a-37, 38. **Evans** a-32-34, 36, 40, 41, 43, 46. **Feldstein** a-20-23; c-21-25, 28. Ingels a-in all. **Kamen** a-20, 22, 25, 27-31, 33-36, 39, 41-45. **Krigstein** a-40, 42, 45. **Kurtzman** a-21. **Orlando** a-27-30, 35, 37, 39, 41-45. **Wood** a-21, 24, 25; c-26, 27. Canadian reprints known; see Table of Contents.*

TALES FROM THE CRYPT (Magazine)
No. 10, July, 1968 (35¢, B&W)
Eerie Publications

	GD25	FN65	NM94
10-Contains Farrell reprints from 1950s	2.50	7.50	24.00

TALES FROM THE CRYPT
July, 1990 - No. 6, May, 1991 ($1.95/$2.00, 68 pgs.)
Gladstone Publishing

	GD25	FN65	NM94
1-r/TFTC #33 & Crime S.S. #17; Davis-c(r)		.80	2.00
2-6: 2,3,5,6-Davis-c(r). 4-Begin $2.00-c; Craig-c(r)		.80	2.00

TALES FROM THE CRYPT
July, 1991 - Present ($3.95, 10 1/4 x13 1/4", 68 pgs.)
Extra-Large Comics (Russ Cochran)/Gemstone Publishing

	GD25	FN65	NM94
1-Davis-c(r); Craig back-c(r); E.C. reprints		1.60	4.00
2-6 ($2.00, comic sized)		.80	2.00

TALES FROM THE CRYPT
Sept, 1992 - Present ($1.50, quarterly)
Russ Cochran/Gemstone Publishing

	GD25	FN65	NM94
1-4-r/Crypt of Terror #17-19, TFTC #20 w/original-c			1.50
5-15 ($2.00)-r/TFTC #21-23 w/original-c		.80	2.00
16-23($2.50)		1.00	2.50

TALES FROM THE GREAT BOOK
Feb, 1955 - No. 4, Jan, 1956
Famous Funnies

	GD25	FN65	NM94
1-Story of Samson; John Lehti-a in all	6.50	19.50	45.00
2-4: 2-Joshua. 3-Joash the Boy King. 4-David	4.15	12.50	25.00

TALES FROM THE HEART OF AFRICA (The Temporary Natives)
Aug, 1990 ($3.95, 52 pgs.)
Marvel Comics (Epic Comics)

	GD25	FN65	NM94
1		1.60	4.00

TALES FROM THE TOMB (Also see Dell Giants)
Oct, 1962 (25¢ giant)
Dell Publishing Co.

	GD25	FN65	VF82	NM94
1(02-810-210)-All stories written by John Stanley	9.50	28.00	67.00	170.00

TALES FROM THE TOMB (Magazine)
V1#6, July, 1969 - V7#1, Feb, 1975 (52 pgs.)
Eerie Publications

	GD25	FN65	NM94
V1#6-8	5.00	15.00	50.00
V2#1-6: 4-LSD story-r/Weird V3#5. 6-Rulah-r	3.50	10.50	35.00
V3#1-Rulah-r	3.50	10.50	35.00
2-6('70),V4#1-5('72),V5#1-6('73),V6#1-6('74),V7#1('75)	3.00	9.00	30.00

TALES OF ASGARD
Oct, 1968 (25¢, 68 pgs.); Feb, 1984 ($1.25, 52 pgs.)
Marvel Comics Group

	GD25	FN65	NM94
1-Reprints Tales of Asgard (Thor) back-up stories from Journey into Mystery #97-106; new Kirby-c	2.50	7.50	25.00
V2#1 (2/84)-Thor-r; Simonson-c			1.00

TALES OF DEMON DICK & BUNKER BILL
1934 (B&W, 5x10-1/2", hardcover, 78 pgs.)
Whitman Publishing Co.

	GD25	FN65	NM94
793-By Dick Spencer	21.00	64.00	170.00

TALES OF EVIL
Feb, 1975 - No. 3, July, 1975 (All 25¢ issues)
Atlas/Seaboard Publ.

	GD25	FN65	NM94
1-3: 2-Intro. The Bog Beast; Sparling-a. 3-Origin The Man-Monster; Buckler-a(p)		1.20	3.00

NOTE: ***Grandenetti** a-1, 2. **Lieber** c-1. **Sekowsky** a-1. **Sutton** a-2. **Thorne** c-2.*

TALES OF GHOST CASTLE
May-June, 1975 - No. 3, Sept-Oct, 1975 (All 25¢ issues)
National Periodical Publications

	GD25	FN65	NM94
1-3: 1,3-Redondo-a. 2-Nino-a	1.25	3.75	10.00

TALES OF G.I. JOE
Jan, 1988 - No. 15, Mar, 1989
Marvel Comics

	GD25	FN65	NM94
1 ($2.25, 52 pgs.)		.90	2.25
2-15 ($1.50): 1-15-r/G.I. Joe #1-15			1.50

TALES OF HORROR

Tales Of Suspense #20 © MEG

Tales Of Suspense #29 © MEG

Tales Of Suspense V2 #1 © MEG

June, 1952 - No. 13, Oct, 1954
Toby Press/Minoan Publ. Corp.

	GD25	FN65	NM94
1	30.00	90.00	225.00
2-Torture scenes	24.00	73.00	180.00
3-8,13	15.00	45.00	110.00
9-11-Reprints Purple Claw #1-3	15.00	45.00	110.00
12-Myron Fass-c/a; torture scenes	17.00	49.00	120.00

NOTE: ***Andru** a-5. **Baily** a-5. **Myron Fass** a-2, 3, 12; c-1-3, 12. **Hollingsworth** a-2. **Sparling** a-6, 9; c-9.*

TALES OF JUSTICE
No. 53, May, 1955 - No. 67, Aug, 1957
Atlas Comics(MjMC No. 53-66/Male No. 67)

	GD25	FN65	NM94
53	12.00	36.00	90.00
54-57: 54-Powell-a	9.00	27.00	60.00
58,59-Krigstein-a	10.00	30.00	70.00
60-63,65: 60-Powell-a	7.50	22.50	50.00
64,67-Crandall-a	9.15	27.50	60.00
66-Torres, Orlando-a	9.15	27.50	60.00

NOTE: ***Everett** a-53, 60. **Orlando** a-65, 66. **Severin** a-64; c-58, 60, 65. **Wildey** a-64, 67.*

TALES OF SUSPENSE (Becomes Captain America #100 on)
Jan, 1959 - No. 99, Mar, 1968
Atlas (WPI No. 1,2/Male No. 3-12/VPI No. 13-18)/Marvel No. 19 on

	GD25	FN65	NM94
1-Williamson-a (5 pgs.); Heck-c; #1-4 have sci/fi-c	116.00	348.00	1400.00
2,3: 3-Flying saucer-c/story	44.00	132.00	540.00
4-Williamson-a (4 pgs.); Kirby/Everett-c/a	39.00	118.00	470.00
5,6,8,10: 5-Kirby monster-c begin	31.00	93.00	310.00
7-Prototype ish. (Lava Man); 1 panel app. Aunt May (see Str. Tales #97)	31.00	93.00	350.00
9-Prototype ish. (Iron Man)	35.00	104.00	380.00
11,12,15,17-19: 12-Crandall-a.	24.00	72.00	240.00
13,14: 13-Elektro-c/story. 14-Intro/1st app. Colossus-c/sty.	24.00	72.00	240.00
16-1st Metallo-c/story (4/61, Iron Man prototype)	30.00	90.00	300.00
20-Colossus-c/story (2nd app.)	24.00	72.00	240.00
21-25: 25-Last 10¢ issue	18.00	54.00	180.00
26,27,29,30,33,34,36-38: 33-(9/62)-Hulk 1st x-over cameo (picture on wall)	16.00	48.00	160.00
28-Prototype ish. (Stone Men)	17.00	51.00	170.00
31-Prototype ish. (Dr. Doom)	21.00	63.00	210.00
32-Prototype ish. (Dr. Strange)(8/62)-Sazzik The Sorcerer app.; "The Man and the Beehive" story, 1 month before TTA #35 (2nd Antman), came out after "The Man in the Ant Hill" in TTA #27 (1/62) (1st Antman)-Characters from both stories were tested to see which got best fan response	31.00	93.00	310.00
35-Prototype issue (The Watcher)	21.00	63.00	210.00

	GD25	FN65	VF82	NM94
39 (3/63)-Origin/1st app. Iron Man & begin series; 1st Iron Man story has Kirby layouts	250.00	750.00	1750.00	3700.00

	GD25	FN65	NM94
40-2nd app. Iron Man (in new armor)	100.00	300.00	1200.00
41-3rd app. Iron Man; Dr. Strange (villain) app.	54.00	162.00	650.00
42-45: 45-Intro. & 1st app. Happy & Pepper	31.00	93.00	320.00
46,47: 46-1st app. Crimson Dynamo	19.50	58.00	195.00
48-New Iron Man armor by Ditko	24.00	72.00	240.00
49-1st X-Men x-over (same date as X-Men #3, 1/64); also 1st Avengers x-over (w/o Captain America); 1st Tales of the Watcher back-up story & begins (2nd app. Watcher; see F.F. #13)	17.00	51.00	170.00
50-1st app. Mandarin	12.50	38.00	125.00
51-1st Scarecrow	10.00	30.00	100.00
52-1st app. The Black Widow (4/64)	13.50	41.00	135.00
53-Origin The Watcher; 2nd Black Widow app.	12.00	36.00	120.00
54-56: 56-1st app. Unicorn; 4th Avengers x-over	7.00	21.00	70.00
57-Origin/1st app. Hawkeye (9/64)	15.50	47.00	155.00
58-Captain America battles Iron Man (10/64)-Classic-c; 2nd Kraven app. (Cap's 1st app. in this title)	26.00	80.00	265.00
59-Iron Man plus Captain America double feature begins (11/64); 1st S.A. Captain America solo story; intro Jarvis, Avenger's butler; classic-c	26.00	80.00	265.00
60-2nd app. Hawkeye (#64 is 3rd app.)	12.00	36.00	120.00
61,62,64: 62-Origin Mandarin (2/65)	7.00	21.00	70.00
63-1st Silver Age origin Captain America (3/65)	20.00	60.00	200.00
65,66-G.A. Red Skull in WWII stories: 65-1st Silver-Age Red Skull (5/65). 66-Origin Red Skull	13.50	41.00	135.00
67-78,81-98: 69-1st app. Titanium Man. 70-Begin alternating-c features w/Capt. America (even #'s) & Iron Man (odd #'s). 75-1st app. Agent 13 later named Sharon Carter. 76-Intro Batroc & Sharon Carter, Agent 13 of Shield. 78-Col. Nick Fury app. 81-Intro the Adaptoid by Kirby (also in #82-84). 88-Mole Man app. in Iron Man story. 92-1st Nick Fury x-over (cameo, as Agent of Shield, 8/67). 94-Intro Modok. 95-Capt. America's i.d. revealed. 98-1st app. new Zemo (son?) in cameo (#99 is 1st full app.)	4.00	12.00	40.00
79-Begin 3 part Iron Man Sub-Mariner battle story; Sub-Mariner-c & cameo; 1st app. Cosmic Cube; 1st modern Red Skull	5.50	16.50	55.00
80-Iron Man battles Sub-Mariner story cont'd in Tales to Astonish #82	5.00	15.00	50.00
99-Captain America story cont'd in Captain America #100; Iron Man story cont'd in Iron Man & Sub-Mariner #1	5.50	16.50	55.00

NOTE: ***Abel** a-73-81i(as Gary Michaels), **J. Buscema** a-1; c-3. **Colan** a-39, 73-99p; c(p)-73, 75, 77, 79, 81, 83, 85-87, 89, 91, 93, 95, 97, 99. **Crandall** a-12. **Davis** a-38. **Ditko** a-1-15, 17-44, 46, 47-49p; c-2, 10i, 13i, 23i. **Kirby/Ditko** a-7; c-10, 13, 22, 28, 34. **Everett** a-8. **Forte** a-5, 9. **Giacoia** a-82. **Heath** a-2, 10. **Gil Kane** a-88p, 89-91; c-88, 89-91p. **Kirby** a(p)-2-4, 6-35, 40, 41, 43, 59-75, 77-86, 92-99; layouts-69-75, 77; c(p)4-28(most), 29-56, 58-72, 74, 76, 78, 80, 82, 84, 86, 92, 94, 96, 98. **Leiber/Fox** a-42, 43, 45, 51. **Reinman** a-26, 44i, 49i, 52i, 53i. **Tuska** a-58, 70-74. **Wood** c/a-71i.*

TALES OF SUSPENSE
V2#1, Jan, 1995 ($6.95, one-shot)
Marvel Comics

	GD25	FN65	NM94
V2#1-James Robinson script; acetate-c.	1.00	2.80	7.00

TALES OF SWORD & SORCERY (See Dagar)

TALES OF TERROR
1952 (no month)
Toby Press Publications

	GD25	FN65	NM94
1-Fawcette-c; Ravielli-a	18.00	54.00	140.00

NOTE: *This title was cancelled due to similarity to the E.C. title.*

TALES OF TERROR (See Movie Classics)

TALES OF TERROR (Magazine)
Summer, 1964
Eerie Publications

	GD25	FN65	NM94
1	2.50	7.50	24.00

TALES OF TERROR
July, 1985 - No. 13, July, 1987 ($2.00, Baxter paper, mature)
Eclipse Comics

	GD25	FN65	NM94
1-8 ($1.75-c): 5-1st Lee Weeks-a. 7-Sam Kieth-a.		.75	1.80
9-13 ($2.00-c): 10-Snyder-a. 12-Vampire story		.80	2.00

TALES OF TERROR ANNUAL
1951 - No. 3, 1953 (25¢, 132 pgs., 16 stories each)
E.C. Comics

	GD25	FN65	VF82
nn(1951)(Scarce)-Feldstein infinity-c	371.00	1115.00	3200.00
(Estimated up to 35 total copies exist, 3 in NM/Mint)			

	GD25	FN65	NM94
2(1952)-Feldstein-c	156.00	468.00	1400.00
3(1953)-Feldstein bondage/torture-c	122.00	366.00	1100.00

NOTE: *No. 1 contains three horror and one science fiction comic which came out in 1950. No. 2 contains a horror, crime, and science fiction book which generally had cover dates in 1951, and No. 3 had horror, crime, and shock books that generally appeared in 1952. All E.C. annuals contain four complete books that did not sell on the stands which were rebound in the annual format, minus the covers, and sold from the E.C. office and on the stands in key cities. The contents of*

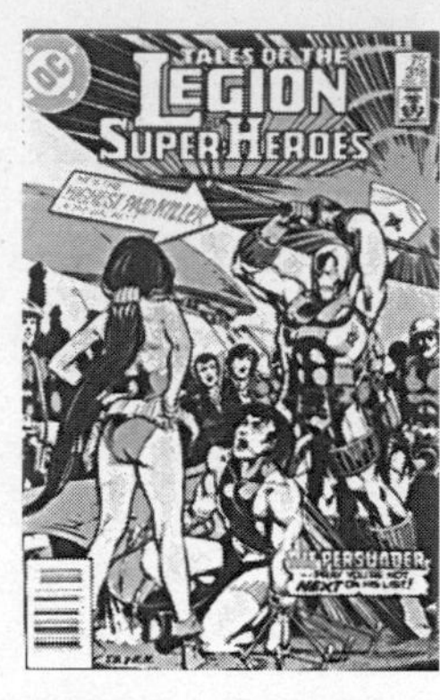

Tales of the Legion #318 © DC

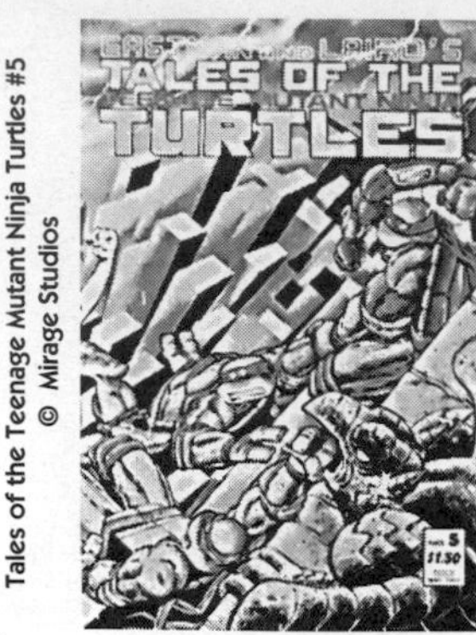

Tales of the Teenage Mutant Ninja Turtles #5 © Mirage Studios

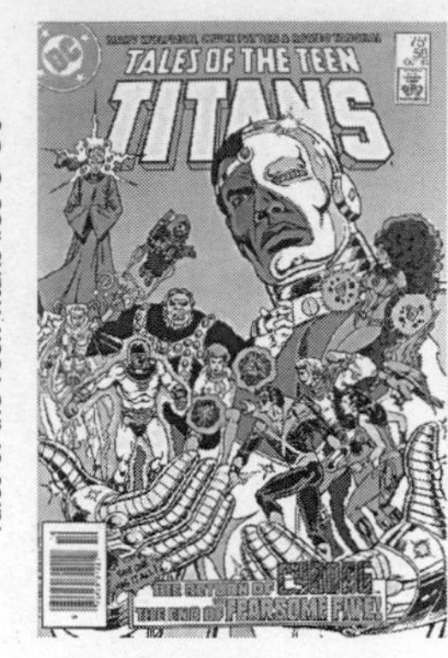

Tales of the Teen Titans #58 © DC

each annual may vary in the same year. Crypt Keeper, Vault Keeper, Old Witch app. on all-c.

TALES OF TERROR ILLUSTRATED (See Terror Illustrated)

TALES OF TEXAS JOHN SLAUGHTER (See Walt Disney Presents, 4-Color #997)

TALES OF THE BEANWORLD
Feb, 1985 - No. 19, 1991; No. 20, 1993 - No. 21, 1993 ($1.50/$2.00, B&W)
Beanworld Press/Eclipse Comics

	GD25	FN65	NM94
1		1.20	3.00
2-19		.80	2.00
20 ($2.50)		1.00	2.50
21 ($2.95)		1.20	3.00

TALES OF THE GREEN BERET
Jan, 1967 - No. 5, Oct, 1969
Dell Publishing Co.

	GD25	FN65	NM94
1-Glanzman-a in 1-4 & 5r	1.80	5.50	20.00
2-5: 5-Reprints #1	1.40	4.20	14.00

TALES OF THE GREEN HORNET
Sept, 1990 - No. 2, 1990 ($1.75); V3#1, Sept, 1992 - No. 3, Nov, 1992
Now Comics

	GD25	FN65	NM94
1,2			1.75
V3#1 ($2.75)-Polybagged w/hologram trading card		1.10	2.75
V3#2,3 ($2.50)		1.00	2.50

TALES OF THE GREEN LANTERN CORPS (See Green Lantern #107)
May, 1981 - No. 3, July, 1981 (Limited series)
DC Comics

	GD25	FN65	NM94
1-3: 1-Origin of G.L. & the Guardians			1.50
Annual 1 (1/85)-Gil Kane-c/a		.70	1.75
Annual 2 (1986)-Alan Moore script			1.75

TALES OF THE INVISIBLE SCARLET O'NEIL (See Harvey Comics Hits #59)

TALES OF THE KILLERS (Magazine)
V1#10, Dec, 1970 - V1#11, Feb, 1971 (B&W, 52 pgs.)
World Famous Periodicals

	GD25	FN65	NM94
V1#10-One pg. Frazetta; contains r/Crime Does Not Pay	2.50	7.50	24.00
11-similar cover to Crime Does Not Pay #47; contains r/Crime Does Not Pay	2.25	6.75	18.00

TALES OF THE LEGION (Formerly Legion of Super-Heroes)
No. 314, Aug, 1984 - No. 354, Dec, 1987
DC Comics

	GD25	FN65	NM94
314-354: 321-Reprints begin			1.25
Annual 4,5 (1986, 1987)-Formerly LSH Annual			1.40

TALES OF THE MARINES (Formerly Devil-Dog Dugan #1-3)
No. 4, Feb, 1957 (Marines At War #5 on)
Atlas Comics (OPI)

	GD25	FN65	NM94
4-Powell-a; Severin-c	5.35	16.00	32.00

TALES OF THE MARVELS
1995/1996 (all acetate, painted-c)
Marvel Comics

	GD25	FN65	NM94
....BLOCKBUSTER 1 (1995, $5.95, one-shot		2.40	6.00
INNER DEMONS 1 (1996, $5.95, one shot)		2.40	6.00
....WONDER YEARS 1,2 (1995, $4.95, limited series		2.00	5.00

TALES OF THE MARVEL UNIVERSE
Feb, 1997 ($2.95, one-shot)
Marvel Comics

	GD25	FN65	NM94
1-Anthology; wraparound-c; Thunderbolts, Ka-Zar app.		1.20	3.00

TALES OF THE MYSTERIOUS TRAVELER (See Mysterious...)
Aug, 1956 - No. 13, June, 1959; V2#14, Oct, 1985 - No. 15, Dec, 1985
Charlton Comics

	GD25	FN65	NM94
1-No Ditko-a; Giordano/Alascia-c	39.00	116.00	290.00
2-Ditko-a(1)	33.00	99.00	245.00
3-Ditko-c/a(1)	33.00	99.00	245.00
4-6-Ditko-c/a(3-4 stories each)	38.00	114.00	280.00
7-9-Ditko-a(1-2 each). 8-Rocke-c	31.00	94.00	230.00
10,11-Ditko-c/a(3-4 each)	34.00	103.00	250.00
12	11.30	34.00	90.00
13-Baker-a (r?)	14.00	43.00	110.00
V2#14,15 (1985)-Ditko-c/a			1.00

TALES OF THE NEW TEEN TITANS
June, 1982 - No. 4, Sept, 1982 (Limited series)
DC Comics

	GD25	FN65	NM94
1-4			1.00

TALES OF THE PONY EXPRESS (TV)
No. 829, Aug, 1957 - No. 942, Oct, 1958
Dell Publishing Co.

	GD25	FN65	NM94
Four Color 829 (#1)--Painted-c	3.60	11.00	40.00
Four Color 942-Title -Pony Express	3.60	11.00	40.00

TALES OF THE SUN RUNNERS
V2#1, July, 1986 - V2#3, 1986? ($1.50)
Sirius Comics/Amazing Comics No. 3

	GD25	FN65	NM94
V2#1			1.50
V2#2,3 ($1.95)		.80	2.00
Christmas Special 1(12/86)			1.50

TALES OF THE TEENAGE MUTANT NINJA TURTLES
May, 1987 - No. 7, Aug (Apr-c), 1989 (B&W, $1.50)(See Teenage Mutant...)
Mirage Studios

	GD25	FN65	NM94
1		.80	2.00
2-7: Title merges w/Teenage Mutant Ninja...			1.50

TALES OF THE TEEN TITANS (Formerly The New Teen Titans)
No. 41, Apr, 1984 - No. 91, July, 1988 (75¢)
DC Comics

	GD25	FN65	NM94
41,45-59: 46-Aqualad & Aquagirl join. 50-Double size; app. Betty Kane (Bat-Girl) out of costume. 52-1st app. Azrael in cameo (not same as newer character). 53-1st full app. Azrael; Deathstroke cameo (1 panel). 54,55-Deathstroke-c/stories. 56-Intro Jinx. 57-Neutron app. 59-r/DC Comics Presents #26			1.00
42-44: The Judas Contract part 1-3 with Deathstroke the Terminator in all; concludes in Annual #3. 44-Dick Grayson becomes Nightwing (3rd to be Nightwing) & joins Titans; Jericho (Deathstroke's son) joins; origin Deathstroke		1.20	3.00
60-91-r/New Teen Titans Baxter series. 68-B. Smith-c. 70-Origin Kole. 83-91 are $1.00 cover			1.00
Annual 3(1984, $1.25)-Part 4 of The Judas Contract; Deathstroke-c/story; Death of Terra; indicia says Teen Titans Annual; formerly New Teen Titans Annual #1,2		1.20	3.00
Annual 4,5: 4-(1986, $1.25)-Reprints. 5-(1987)			1.25

TALES OF THE TEXAS RANGERS (See Jace Pearson...)

TALES OF THE UNEXPECTED (Becomes The Unexpected #105 on)(See Adventure #75, Super DC Giant)
Feb-Mar, 1956 - No. 104, Dec-Jan, 1967-68
National Periodical Publications

	GD25	FN65	NM94
1	83.00	250.00	1000.00
2	40.00	120.00	485.00
3-5	31.00	93.00	330.00
6-10: 6-1st Silver Age issue	25.00	75.00	250.00
11,14,19,20	15.50	47.00	155.00
12,13,15-18,21-24: All have Kirby-a. 15,17-Grey tone-c. 16-Character named 'Thor' with a magic hammer by Kirby (8/57, not like later Thor)	19.00	57.00	190.00

Tales of the Unexpected #43 © DC

Tales of the Witchblade #1 © Top Cow

Tales to Astonish #6 © MEG

GD25 FN65 NM94

25-30 15.00 45.00 150.00
31-39 12.00 36.00 120.00
40-Space Ranger begins (8/59, 3rd ap.), ends #82 73.00 219.00 875.00
41,42-Space Ranger stories 28.00 85.00 285.00
43-1st Space Ranger-c this title; grey tone-c 56.00 168.00 670.00
44-46 21.00 63.00 210.00
47-50 15.00 45.00 150.00
51-60: 54-Dinosaur-c/story 13.00 39.00 130.00
61-67: 67-Last 10¢ issue 10.50 32.00 105.00
68-82: 82-Last Space Ranger 6.00 18.00 60.00
83-100: 91-1st Automan (also in #94,97) 4.00 12.00 40.00
101-104 3.20 9.60 32.00

NOTE: ***Neal Adams*** *c-104.* ***Anderson*** *a-50.* ***Brown*** *a-50-82(Space Ranger); c-19, 40, & many Space Ranger-c.* ***Cameron*** *a-24, 27, 29; c-24.* ***Heath*** *a-49.* ***Bob Kane*** *a-24, 48.* ***Kirby*** *a-12, 13, 15-18, 21-24; c-13, 18, 22.* ***Meskin*** *a-15, 18, 26, 27, 35, 66.* ***Moreira*** *a-16, 20, 29, 38, 44, 62, 71; c-38.* ***Roussos*** *c-10.* ***Wildey*** *a-31.*

TALES OF THE WEST (See 3-D...)

TALES OF THE WITCHBLADE
Nov, 1996 - Present ($2.95)
Image Comics (Top Cow Productions)

1-Daniel-c/a(p) 2.00 5.00
1-Variant-c by Turner 1.00 3.00 8.00
1-Platinum Edition 2.50 7.50 20.00
2,3 2.95

TALES OF THE WIZARD OF OZ (See Wizard of OZ, 4-Color #1308)

TALES OF THE ZOMBIE (Magazine)
Aug, 1973 - No. 10, Mar, 1975 (75¢, B&W)
Marvel Comics Group

V1#1-Reprint/Menace #5; origin 2.25 6.75 18.00
2,3: 2-Everett biog. & memorial 1.50 4.50 12.00
V2#1(#4)-Photos & text of James Bond movie "Live & Let Die"
1.50 4.50 12.00
5-10: 8-Kaluta-a 1.50 4.50 12.00
Annual 1(Summer,'75)(#11)-B&W; Everett, Buscema-a
1.50 4.50 12.00

NOTE: Brother Voodoo app. 2, 5, 6, 10. ***Alcala*** *a-7-9.* ***Boris*** *c-1-4.* ***Colan*** *a-2r, 6.* ***Heath*** *a-5r.* ***Reese*** *a-2.* ***Tuska*** *a-2r.*

TALES OF THUNDER
Mar, 1985
Deluxe Comics

1-Dynamo, Iron Maiden, Menthor app.; Giffen-a.35 .80 2.00

TALES OF VOODOO
V1#11, Nov, 1968 - V7#6, Nov, 1974 (Magazine)
Eerie Publications

V1#11 4.00 12.00 40.00
V2#1(3/69)-V2#4(9/69) 3.00 9.00 30.00
V3#1-6('70): 4- "Claws of the Cat" redrawn from Climax #1
2.50 7.50 24.00
V4#1-6('71), V5#1-7('72), V6#1-6('73), V7#1-6('74) 2.50 7.50 24.00
Annual 1 2.50 7.50 24.00

NOTE: *Bondage-c-V1#10, V2#4, V3#4.*

TALES OF WELLS FARGO (TV)(See Western Roundup under Dell Giants)
No. 876, Feb, 1958 - No. 1215, Oct-Dec, 1961
Dell Publishing Co.

Four Color 876 (#1)-Photo-c 9.00 27.00 100.00
Four Color 968 (2/59), 1023, 1075 (3/60), 1113 (7-9/60)-All photo-c
8.00 25.00 90.00
Four Color 1167 (3-5/61), 1215-Photo-c 7.00 22.00 80.00

TALESPIN (Also see Cartoon Tales & Disney's Talespin Limited Series)
June, 1991 - No. 7, Dec, 1991 ($1.50)
Disney Comics

GD25 FN65 NM94

1-7 1.50

TALES TO ASTONISH (Becomes The Incredible Hulk #102 on)
Jan, 1959 - No. 101, Mar, 1968
Atlas (MAP No. 1/ZPC No. 2-14/VPI No. 15-21/Marvel No. 22 on

1-Jack Davis-a; monster-c. 120.00 360.00 1450.00
2-Ditko flying saucer-c (Martians); #2-4 have sci/fi-c.
50.00 150.00 600.00
3,4 36.00 108.00 400.00
5-Prototype issue (Stone Men); Williamson-a (4 pgs.); Kirby monster-c begin
38.00 114.00 420.00
6-Prototype issue (Stone Men) 31.00 93.00 350.00
7-Prototype issue (Toad Men) 31.00 93.00 340.00
8-10 31.00 93.00 310.00
11-14,17-20: 13-Swipes story from Monaco #8 23.00 69.00 230.00
15-Prototype issue (Electro) 32.00 96.00 360.00
16-Prototype issue (Stone Men) 26.00 78.00 260.00
21-(7/61)-Hulk prototype 26.00 78.00 260.00
22-26,28-34 17.00 51.00 170.00

GD25 FN65 VF82 NM94

27-1st Ant-Man app. (1/62); last 10¢ issue (see Strange Tales #73,78 & Tales of Suspense #32) 242.00 726.00 1694.00 3100.00
35-(9/62)-2nd app. Ant-Man, 1st in costume; begin series & Ant-Man-c
100.00 300.00 650.00 1400.00

GD25 FN65 NM94

36-3rd app. Ant-Man 47.00 141.00 570.00
37-40: 38-1st app. Egghead 32.00 96.00 360.00
41-43 22.00 66.00 220.00
44-Origin & 1st app. The Wasp (6/63) 25.00 75.00 250.00
45-48: Origin & 1st app. The Porcupine. 14.00 42.00 140.00
49-Ant-Man becomes Giant Man (11/63) 17.00 51.00 170.00
50-56,58: 50-Origin/1st app. Human Top (alias Whirlwind). 52-Origin/1st app. Black Knight (2/64). 53-Origin Colossus 9.50 28.50 95.00
57-Early Spider-Man app. (7/64) 13.00 39.00 130.00
59-Giant Man vs. Hulk feature story (9/64); Hulk's 1st app. this title
15.00 45.00 150.00
60-Giant Man & Hulk double feature begins 17.00 51.00 170.00
61-69: 61-All Ditko issue; 1st mailbag. 62-1st app./origin The Leader; new Wasp costume. 63-Origin Leader; 65-New Giant Man costume. 68-New Human Top costume. 69-Last Giant Man. 5.00 15.00 50.00
70-Sub-Mariner & Incredible Hulk begins (8/65) 6.00 18.00 60.00
71-81,83-91,94-99: 72-Begin alternating-c features w/Sub-Mariner (even #'s) & Hulk (odd #'s). 79-Hulk vs. Hercules-c/story. 81-1st app. Boomerang. 90-1st app. The Abomination. 97-X-Men cameo (brief) 4.00 12.00 40.00
82-Iron Man battles Sub-Mariner (1st Iron Man x-over outside The Avengers & TOS); story cont'd from Tales of Suspense #80 4.50 13.50 45.00
92-1st Silver Surfer x-over (outside of Fantastic Four, 6/67); 1 panel cameo only 5.00 15.00 50.00
93-Hulk battles Silver Surfer-c/story (1st full x-over) 5.00 15.00 50.00
100-Hulk battles Sub-Mariner full-length story 5.00 15.00 50.00
101-Hulk story cont'd in Incredible Hulk #102; Sub-Mariner story continued in Iron Man & Sub-Mariner #1 6.00 18.00 60.00

NOTE: ***Ayers*** *c(i)-9-12, 16, 18, 19.* ***Berg*** *a-1.* ***Burgos*** *a-62-64p.* ***Buscema*** *a-85-87p.* ***Colan*** *a(p)-70-76, 78-82, 84, 85, 101; c(p)-71-76, 78, 80, 82, 84, 86, 88, 90.* ***Ditko*** *a-1, 3-48, 50i, 60-67p; c-2, 7i, 8i, 14i, 17i.* ***Everett*** *a-78, 79i, 80-84, 85-90i, 94i, 95, 96; c(i)-79-81, 83, 86, 88.* ***Forte*** *a-6.* ***Kane*** *a-76, 88-91; c-89, 91.* ***Kirby*** *a(p)-1, 5-34-40, 44, 49-51, 68-70, 82, 83; layouts-71-84; c(p)-1, 3-48, 50-70, 72, 73, 75, 77, 78, 79, 81, 85, 90.* ***Kirby/Ditko*** *a-7, 8, 12, 13, 50; c-7, 8, 10, 13.* ***Leiber/Fox*** *a-47, 48, 50, 51.* ***Powell*** *a-65-69p, 73, 74.* ***Reinman*** *a-6, 36, 45, 46, 54i, 56-60i.*

TALES TO ASTONISH (2nd Series)
Dec, 1979 - No. 14, Jan, 1981
Marvel Comics Group

V1#1-Reprints Sub-Mariner #1 by Buscema .80 2.00
2-14: Reprints Sub-Mariner #2-14 1.50

TALES TO ASTONISH
V3#1, Oct, 1994 ($6.95, one-shot)

Tangent Comics/ The Joker #1 © DC

Tank Girl: The Odyssey #3 © Deadline Publ.

Target Comics V3 #2 © NOVP

GD25 FN65 NM94

Marvel Comics
V3#1-Peter David scripts; acetate, painted-c 1.00 2.80 7.00

TALES TO HOLD YOU SPELLBOUND (See Spellbound)

TALES TO OFFEND
July, 1997 ($2.95, one-shot)
Dark Horse Comics
1-Frank Miller-s/a, EC-style cover 1.40 3.50

TALKING KOMICS
1947 (20 pgs, slick-c)
Belda Record & Publ. Co.
Each comic contained a record that followed the story - much like the Golden Record sets. Known titles: Chirpy Cricket, Lonesome Octopus, Sleepy Santa, Grumpy Shark, Flying Turtle, Happy Grasshopper
with records... 2.00 5.00 10.00

TALLY-HO COMICS
Dec, 1944
Swappers Quarterly (Baily Publ. Co.)
nn-Frazetta's 1st work as Giunta's assistant; Man in Black horror story; violence; Giunta-c 30.00 90.00 240.00

TALOS OF THE WILDERNESS SEA
Aug, 1987 ($2.00, one-shot)
DC Comics
1 .80 2.00

TALULLAH (See Comic Books Series I)

TAMMY, TELL ME TRUE
No. 1233, 1961
Dell Publishing Co.
Four Color 1233-Movie 5.50 16.50 60.00

TANGENT COMICS/ THE ATOM, Dec, 1997 ($2.95, one-shot), DC Comics
1-Dan Jurgens-s/Jurgens & Paul Ryan-a 2.95

TANGENT COMICS/ DOOM PATROL, Dec, 1997 ($2.95, one-shot), DC
1- Dan Jurgens-s/Sean Chen & Kevin Conrad-a 2.95

TANGENT COMICS/ THE FLASH, Dec, 1997 ($2.95, one-shot), DC Comics
1-Todd Dezago-s/Gary Frank & Cam Smith-a 2.95

TANGENT COMICS/ GREEN LANTERN, Dec, 1997 ($2.95, one-shot), DC
1-James Robinson-s/J.H. Williams III & Mick Gray-a 2.95

TANGENT COMICS/ THE JOKER, Dec, 1997 ($2.95, one-shot), DC Comics
1-Karl Kesel-s/Matt Haley & Tom Simmons-a 2.95

TANGENT COMICS/ METAL MEN, Dec, 1997 ($2.95, one-shot), DC Comics
1-Ron Marz-s/Mike McKone & Mark McKenna-a 2.95

TANGENT COMICS/ NIGHTWING, Dec, 1997 ($2.95, one-shot), DC Comics
1-John Ostrander-s/Jan Duursema-a 2.95

TANGENT COMICS/ SEA DEVILS, Dec, 1997 ($2.95, one-shot), DC Comics
1-Kurt Busiek-s/Vince Giarrano & Tom Palmer-a 2.95

TANGENT COMICS/ SECRET SIX, Dec, 1997 ($2.95, one-shot), DC Comics
1-Chuck Dixon-s/Tom Grummett & Lary Stucker-a 2.95

TANK GIRL
May, 1991 - No. 4, Aug, 1991 ($2.25, B&W, mini-series)
Dark Horse Comics
1-4: 1-Contains Dark Horse trading cards .90 2.25

TANK GIRL: APOCALYPSE
Nov, 1995 - No. 4, Feb, 1996 ($2.25, limited series)
DC Comics
1-4 .90 2.25

TANK GIRL: MOVIE ADAPTATION
1995 ($5.95, 68 pgs., one-shot)
DC Comics
nn-Peter Milligan scripts 2.40 6.00

TANK GIRL: THE ODYSSEY
May, 1995 - No.4, Oct, 1995 ($2.25, limited series)
DC Comics
1-4: Peter Milligan scripts; Hewlett-a .90 2.25

TANK GIRL 2
Feb, 1995 ($17.95, one-shot, mature)
Dark Horse Comics
1 2.25 6.75 18.00

TAPPAN'S BURRO (See Zane Grey & 4-Color #449)

TAPPING THE VEIN (Clive Barker's...)
1989 - No. 4, 1990 ($6.95, squarebound, mature readers, 68 pgs.)
Eclipse Comics
Book 1-4: 1-Russell-a, Bolton-c. 2-Bolton-a. 4-Die-cut-c 1.00 2.80 7.00

TARANTULA (See Weird Suspense)

TARGET: AIRBOY
Mar, 1988 ($1.95)
Eclipse Comics
1 .80 2.00

TARGET COMICS (...Western Romances #106 on)
Feb, 1940 - V10#3 (#105), Aug-Sept, 1949
Funnies, Inc./Novelty Publications/Star Publications

V1#1-Origin & 1st app. Manowar, The White Streak by Burgos, & Bulls-Eye Bill by Everett; City Editor (ends #5), High Grass Twins by Jack Cole (ends #4), T-Men by Joe Simon(ends #9), Rip Rory (ends #4), Fantastic Feature Films by Tarpe Mills (ends #39), & Calling 2-R (ends #14) begin; marijuana use story 350.00 1050.00 3500.00
2 194.00 582.00 1750.00
3,4 106.00 318.00 950.00
5-Origin The White Streak in text; Space Hawk by Wolverton begins (6/40) (see Blue Bolt & Circus) 300.00 900.00 3000.00
6-The Chameleon by Everett begins (7/40, 1st app.); White Streak origin cont'd. in text; early mention of comic collecting in letter column; 1st letter column in comics? (7/40) 133.00 400.00 1200.00
7-Wolverton Spacehawk-c/story (Scarce) 360.00 1080.00 3600.00
8,9,12: 12-(1/41) 106.00 318.00 950.00
10-Intro/1st app. The Target (11/40); Simon-c 133.00 400.00 1200.00
11-Origin The Target & The Targeteers 122.00 366.00 1100.00
V2#1-Target by Bob Wood; Uncle Sam flag-c 64.00 192.00 580.00
2-Ten part Treasure Island serial begins; Harold Delay-a; reprinted in Catholic Comics V3#1-10 (see Key Comics #5) 58.00 174.00 520.00
3-5: 4-Kit Carter, The Cadet begins 43.00 129.00 390.00
6-9: Red Seal with White Streak in #6-10 43.00 129.00 390.00
10-Classic-c 75.00 225.00 675.00
11,12: 12-10-part Last of the Mohicans serial begins; Delay-a 42.00 126.00 375.00
V3#1-10: 8-Flag-c; 6-part Gulliver Travels serial begins; Delay-a. 10-Last Wolverton issue 42.00 126.00 375.00
11,12 10.00 30.00 80.00
V4#1-12: 6-Targetoons by Wolverton (1 pg.). 8-X-Mas-c 8.50 26.00 60.00
V5#1-8 7.85 23.50 55.00
V6#1-10, V7#1-12 7.15 21.50 50.00
V8#1,3-5,8,9,11,12 6.50 19.50 45.00
2,6,7-Krigstein-a 7.15 21.50 50.00
10-L.B. Cole-c 24.00 71.00 190.00
V9#1,4,6,8,10,12, V10#2,3-L.B. Cole-c 24.00 71.00 190.00

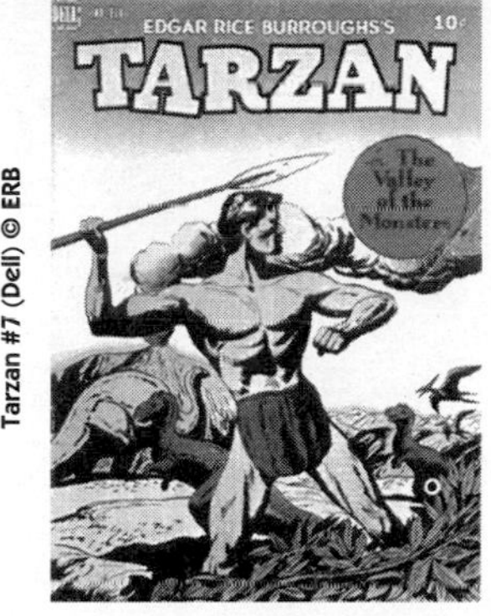

Tarzan #7 (Dell) © ERB

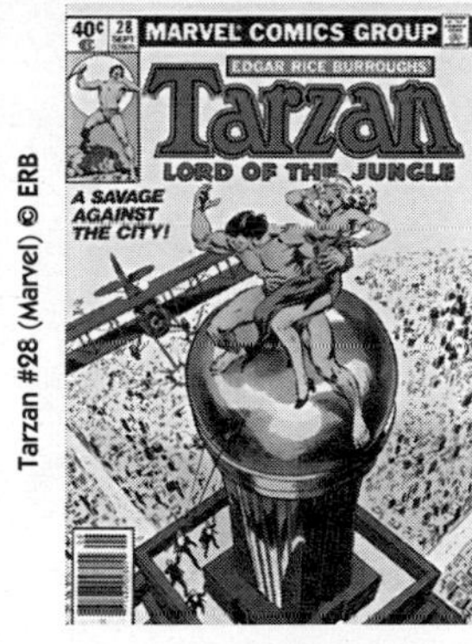

Tarzan #28 (Marvel) © ERB

Tarzan Family #62 © ERB

	GD25	FN65	NM94
V9#2,3,5,7,9,11, V10#1	6.00	18.00	42.00

NOTE: ***Certa*** *c-V8#9, 11, 12, V9#5, 9, 11, V10#1.* ***Jack Cole*** *a-1-8.* ***Everett*** *a-1-9; c(signed Blake)-1, 2.* ***Al Fago*** *c-V6#8.* ***Sid Greene*** *c-V2#9, 12, V3#3.* ***Walter Johnson*** *c-V5#6, V6#4.* ***Tarpe Mills*** *a-1-4, 6, 8, 11, V3#1.* ***Rico*** *a-V7#4, 10, V8#5, 6, V9#3; c-V7#6, 8, 10, V8#2, 4, 6, 7.* ***Simon*** *a-1, 2.* ***Bob Wood*** *c-V2#2, 3, 5, 6.*

TARGET: THE CORRUPTORS (TV)
No. 1306, Mar-May, 1962 - No. 3, Oct-Dec, 1962 (All have photo-c)
Dell Publishing Co.

	GD25	FN65	NM94
Four Color 1306(#1), #2,3	4.50	13.50	50.00

TARGET WESTERN ROMANCES (Formerly Target Comics; becomes Flaming Western Romances #3)
No. 106, Oct-Nov, 1949 - No. 107, Dec-Jan, 1949-50
Star Publications

	GD25	FN65	NM94
106(#1)-Silhouette nudity panel; L.B. Cole-c	30.00	90.00	230.00
107(#2)-L.B. Cole-c; lingerie panels	25.00	75.00	190.00

TARGITT
March, 1975 - No. 3, July, 1975
Atlas/Seaboard Publ.

	GD25	FN65	NM94
1-3: 1-Origin; Nostrand-a in all. 2-1st in costume		1.20	3.00

TARZAN (See Aurora, Comics on Parade, Crackajack, DC 100-Page Super Spec., Famous Feature Stories #1, Golden Comics Digest #4, 9, Jeep Comics #1-29, Jungle Tales of..., Limited Collectors' Edition, Popular, Sparkler, Sport Stars #1, Tip Top & Top Comics)

TARZAN
No. 5, 1939 - No. 161, Aug, 1947
Dell Publishing Co./United Features Syndicate

	GD25	FN65	NM94
Large Feature Comic 5('39)-(Scarce)-By Hal Foster; reprints 1st dailies from 1929	118.00	355.00	1300.00
Single Series 20(:40)-By Hal Foster	91.00	273.00	1000.00
Four Color 134(2/47)-Marsh-c/a	59.00	177.00	650.00
Four Color 161(8/47)-Marsh-c/a	50.00	150.00	550.00

TARZAN (...of the Apes #138 on)
1-2/48 - No. 131, 7-8/62; No. 132, 11/62 - No. 206, 2/72
Dell Publishing Co./Gold Key No. 132 on

	GD25	FN65	NM94
1-Jesse Marsh-a begins	82.00	245.00	900.00
2	46.00	137.00	500.00
3-5	32.00	95.00	350.00
6-10: 6-1st Tantor the Elephant. 7-1st Valley of the Monsters	26.00	77.00	280.00
11-15: 11-Two Against the Jungle begins, ends #24. 13-Lex Barker photo-c begin	21.00	63.00	230.00
16-20	16.00	49.00	180.00
21-24,26-30	13.00	38.00	140.00
25-1st "Brothers of the Spear" episode; series ends #156,160,161,196-206	15.00	45.00	165.00
31-40	8.00	25.00	90.00
41-54: Last Barker photo-c	5.50	16.50	60.00
55-60: 56 Eight pg. Boy story	3.60	11.00	40.00
61,62,64-70	3.00	9.00	32.00
63-Two Tarzan stories, 1 by Manning	3.00	9.00	35.00
71-79	2.25	6.75	24.00
80-99: 80-Gordon Scott photo-c begin	2.25	6.75	26.00
100	3.00	9.00	32.00
101-109	2.00	6.00	22.00
110 (Scarce)-Last photo-c	2.50	7.50	28.00
111-120	1.65	5.00	18.00
121-131: Last Dell issue	1.40	4.20	14.00
132-1st Gold Key issue	2.75	8.00	30.00
133-154: 139-(12/63)-1st app. Korak (Boy); leaves Tarzan & gets own book 1/64	2.25	6.75	24.00
155-Origin Tarzan	2.50	7.50	28.00
156-161: 157-Banlu, Dog of the Arande begins, ends #159, 195. 169-Leopard Girl app.	1.65	5.00	18.00
162,165,168,171 (TV)-Ron Ely photo covers	2.25	6.75	24.00
163,164,166,167,169,170: 169-Leopard Girl app.	1.45	4.35	16.00
172-199,201-206: 178-Tarzan origin-r/#155; Leopard Girl app., also in #179, 190-193	1.45	4.35	15.00
200 (Scarce)	1.80	5.50	20.00
Story Digest 1-(6/70, G.K.)(scarce)	6.00	18.00	60.00

NOTE: *#162, 165, 168, 171 are TV issues. #1-153 all have* ***Marsh*** *art on Tarzan. #154-161, 163, 164, 166, 167, 172-177 all have* ***Manning*** *art on Tarzan. #178, 202 have* ***Manning*** *Tarzan reprints. No "Brothers of the Spear" in #1-24, 157-159, 162-195. #39-126, 128-156 all have* ***Russ Manning*** *art on "Brothers of the Spear". #196-201, 203-205 all have* ***Manning*** *B.O.T.S. reprints; #25-38, 127 all have Jesse* ***Marsh*** *art on B.O.T.S. #206 has a Marsh B.O.T.S. reprint.* ***Gollub*** *c-8-12.* ***Marsh*** *c-1-7.* ***Doug Wildey*** *a-162, 179-187. Many issues have front and back photo covers.*

TARZAN (Continuation of Gold Key series)
No. 207, Apr, 1972 - No. 258, Feb, 1977
National Periodical Publications

	GD25	FN65	NM94
207-Origin Tarzan by Joe Kubert, part 1; John Carter begins (origin); 52 pg. issues thru #209	2.25	6.75	18.00
208,209: 208-210-Parts 2-4 of origin. 209-Last John Carter	1.25	3.75	10.00
210-229,236,237,239-258: 210-Kubert-a. 211-Hogarth, Kubert-a. 212-214: Adaptations from "Jungle Tales of Tarzan". 213-Beyond the Farthest Star begins, ends #218. 215-218,224,225-All by Kubert. 215-part Foster-r. 219-223: Adapts "The Return of Tarzan" by Kubert. 226-Manning-a. 240-243 adapts "Tarzan & the Castaways". 250-256 adapts "Tarzan the Untamed." 252,253-r/#213	1.00	3.00	8.00
230-DC 100 Page Super Spectacular; Kubert, Kaluta-a(p); Korak begins, ends #234; Carson of Venus app.	2.25	6.75	18.00
231-235-New Kubert-a.: 231-234-(All 100 pgs.)-Adapts "Tarzan and the Lion Man"; Rex, the Wonder Dog r-#232, 233. 235-(100 pgs.)-Last Kubert issue.	2.00	6.00	16.00
238-(68 pgs.)	1.50	4.50	12.00
Comic Digest 1-(Fall, 1972, 50¢, 164 pgs.)(DC)-Digest size; Kubert-c; Manning-a	4.00	12.00	40.00

NOTE: ***Anderson*** *a-207, 209, 217, 218.* ***Chaykin*** *a-216.* ***Finlay*** *a(r)-212.* ***Foster*** *strip-r #207-209, 211, 212, 221.* ***Heath*** *a-230i.* ***G. Kane*** *a(r)-232p, 233p.* ***Kubert*** *a-207-225, 227-235, 257r, 258r; c-207-249, 253.* ***Lopez*** *a-250-255p; c-250p, 251, 252, 254.* ***Manning*** *strip-r 230-235, 238.* ***Morrow*** *a-208.* ***Nino*** *a-231-234.* ***Sparling*** *a-230, 231.* ***Starr*** *a-233r.*

TARZAN
June, 1977 - No. 29, Oct, 1979
Marvel Comics Group

	GD25	FN65	NM94
1		1.20	3.00
2-29: 2-Origin by John Buscema		.80	2.00
Annual 1-3: 1-(1977). 2-(1978). 3-(1979)		.80	2.00

NOTE: ***N. Adams*** *c-11i, 12i.* ***Alcala*** *a-9i, 10i; c-8i, 9i.* ***Buckler*** *c-25-27p, Annual 3p.* ***John Buscema*** *a-1-3, 4-18p, Annual 1; c-1-7, 8p, 9p, 10, 11p, 12p, 13, 14-19p, 21p, 22, 23p, 24p, 28p, Annual 1.* ***Mooney*** *a-22i.* ***Nebres*** *a-22i.* ***Russell*** *a-29i.*

TARZAN
July, 1996 - Present ($2.95)
Dark Horse Comics

	GD25	FN65	NM94
1-16: All Suydam-c		1.20	3.00

TARZAN FAMILY, THE (Formerly Korak, Son of Tarzan)
No. 60, Nov-Dec, 1975 - No. 66, Nov-Dec, 1976
(#60-62: 68 pgs.; #63 on: 52 pgs.)
National Periodical Publications

	GD25	FN65	NM94
60-66: 60-Korak begins; Kaluta-r		2.40	6.00

NOTE: *Carson of Venus-r 60-65. New John Carter-62-64, 65r, 66r. New Korak-60-66. Pellucidar feature-66. Foster strip r-60(9/4/32-10/16/32), 62(6/29/32-7/31/32), 63(10/11/31-12/13/31).* ***Kaluta*** *Carson of Venus-60-65.* ***Kubert*** *a-61, 64; c-60-64.* ***Manning*** *strip-r 60-62, 64.* ***Morrow*** *a-66r.*

TARZAN/JOHN CARTER: WARLORDS OF MARS
Jan, 1996 - No. 4, June, 1996 ($2.50, limited series)
Dark Horse Comics

1-4: Bruce Jones scripts in all. 1,2,4-Bret Blevins-c/a. 2-(4/96)-Indicia reads #3

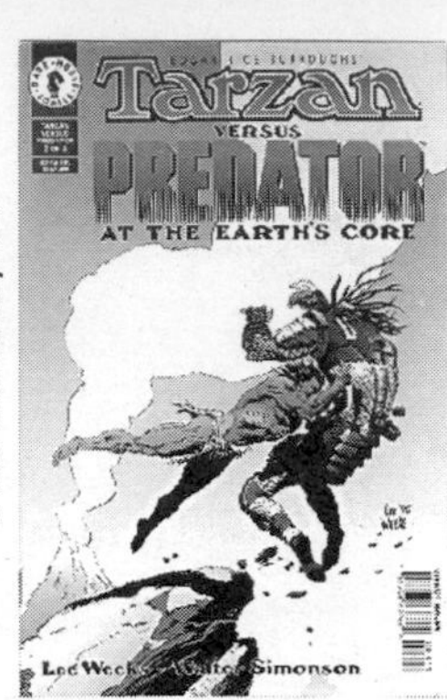

Tarzan vs. Predator at the Earth's Core #3 © ERB/ 20th Century FOX

Team America #9 © MEG

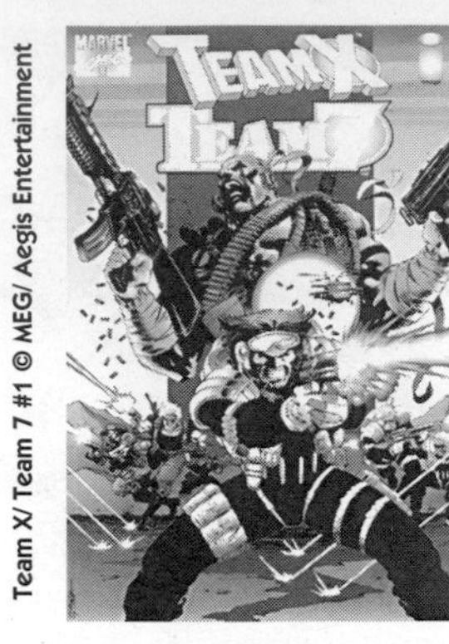

Team X/ Team 7 #1 © MEG/ Aegis Entertainment

	GD25	FN65	NM94
		1.00	2.50

TARZAN KING OF THE JUNGLE (See Dell Giant #37, 51)

TARZAN, LORD OF THE JUNGLE
Sept, 1965 (Giant) (25¢, soft paper-c)
Gold Key

	GD25	FN65	NM94
1-Marsh-r	6.40	19.00	70.00

TARZAN: LOVE, LIES AND THE LOST CITY (See Tarzan the Warrior)
Aug. 10, 1992 - No. 3, Sept, 1992 ($2.50, limited series)
Malibu Comics

	GD25	FN65	NM94
1-($3.95, 68 pgs.)-Flip book format; Simonson & Wagner scripts		1.60	4.00
2,3-No Simonson or Wagner scripts		1.00	2.50

TARZAN MARCH OF COMICS (See March of Comics #82, 98, 114, 125, 144, 155, 172, 185, 204, 223, 240, 252, 262, 272, 286, 300, 332, 342, 354, 366)

TARZAN OF THE APES
1934? (Hardcover, 4x12", 68 pgs.)
Metropolitan Newspaper Service

	GD25	FN65	NM94
1-Strip reprints	17.50	53.00	140.00

TARZAN OF THE APES
July, 1984 - No. 2, Aug, 1984 (Movie adaptation)
Marvel Comics Group

	GD25	FN65	NM94
1,2: Origin-r/Marvel Super Spec.			1.50

TARZAN'S JUNGLE ANNUAL (See Dell Giants)

TARZAN'S JUNGLE WORLD (See Dell Giant #25)

TARZAN: THE LOST ADVENTURE (See Edgar Rice Burroughs' ...)

TARZAN THE WARRIOR (Also see Tarzan: Love, Lies and the Lost City)
Mar, 19, 1992 - No. 5, 1992 ($2.50, limited series)
Malibu Comics

	GD25	FN65	NM94
1-5: 1-Bisley painted pack-c (flip book format-c)		1.20	3.00
1-2nd printing w/o flip-c by Bisley		1.00	2.50

TARZAN VS. PREDATOR AT THE EARTH'S CORE
Jan, 1996 - No. 4, June, 1996 ($2.50, limited series)
Dark Horse Comics

	GD25	FN65	NM94
1-4: Lee Weeks-c/a; Walt Simonson scripts		1.00	2.50

TASMANIAN DEVIL & HIS TASTY FRIENDS
Nov, 1962 (12¢)
Gold Key

	GD25	FN65	NM94
1-Bugs Bunny & Elmer Fudd x-over	11.00	32.00	115.00

TASTEE-FREEZ COMICS
1957 (10¢, 36 pgs.)(6 different issues given away)
Harvey Comics

	GD25	FN65	NM94
1,3: 1-Little Dot. 3-Casper	3.80	11.40	38.00
2,4,5: 2-Rags Rabbit. 4-Sad Sack. 5-Mazie	2.40	7.20	24.00
6-Dick Tracy	3.50	10.50	35.00

TAYLOR'S CHRISTMAS TABLOID
Mid 1930s, Cleveland, Ohio
Dept. Store Giveaway (Tabloid size; in color)

	GD25	FN65	NM94
nn-(Very Rare)-Among the earliest pro work of Siegel & Shuster; one full color page called "The Battle in the Stratosphere", with a pre-Superman look; Shuster art thoughout. (Only 1 known copy) Estimated value...			3000.00

TEAM AMERICA (See Captain America #269)
June, 1982 - No. 12, May, 1983
Marvel Comics Group

	GD25	FN65	NM94
1-Origin; Ideal Toy motorcycle characters			1.00
2-10: 9-Iron man app.			1.00
11-Ghost Rider app.		1.20	3.00
12-Double size		.80	2.00

TEAM ANARCHY
Oct, 1993 - No.8, 1994? ($2.50)
Dagger Comics

	GD25	FN65	NM94
1-($2.75)-Red foil logo; intro Team Anarchy		1.10	2.75
1-Platinum		1.10	2.75
2,3,3-Bronze,3-Gold,3-Silver,4-8		1.10	2.75

TEAM HELIX
Jan, 1993 - No. 4, Apr, 1993 ($1.75, limited series)
Marvel Comics

	GD25	FN65	NM94
1-4: Teen Super Group. 1,2-Wolverine app.		.70	1.75

TEAM ONE: STORMWATCH (Also see StormWatch)
June, 1995 - No. 2, Aug, 1995 ($2.50, limited series)
Image Comics (Wildstorm Productions)

	GD25	FN65	NM94
1,2: Steven T. Seagle scripts		1.00	2.50

TEAM ONE: WILDC.A.T.S (Also see WildC.A.T.S)
July, 1995 - No. 2, Aug, 1995 ($2.50, limited series)
Image Comics (Wildstorm Productions)

	GD25	FN65	NM94
1,2: James Robinson scripts		1.00	2.50

TEAM 7
Oct, 1994 - No.4, Feb, 1995 ($2.50, limited series)
Image Comics (Wildstorm Productions)

	GD25	FN65	NM94
1-Dixon scripts in all		1.60	4.00
1-Portacio variant-c		2.40	6.00
2-4		1.00	2.50

TEAM 7-DEAD RECKONING
Jan, 1996 - No. 4, Apr, 1996 ($2.50, limited series)
Image Comics (Wildstorm Productions)

	GD25	FN65	NM94
1-4: Dixon scripts in all		1.00	2.50

TEAM 7-OBJECTIVE HELL
May, 1995 - No. 3, July, 1995 ($1.95/$2.50, limited series)
Image Comics (Wildstorm Productions)

	GD25	FN65	NM94
1-($1.95)-Newstand; Dixon scripts in all; Barry Smith-c		.80	2.00
1-($2.50)-Direct Market; Barry Smith-c, bound-in card		1.00	2.50
2,3-($2.50)		1.00	2.50

TEAM TITANS (See Deathstroke & New Titans Annual #7)
Sept, 1992 - No. 24, Sept, 1994 ($1.75/$1.95)
DC Comics

	GD25	FN65	NM94
1-Five different #1s exist w/origins in 1st half & the same 2nd story in each: Kilowat, Mirage, Nightrider w/Netzer/Perez-a, Redwing, & Terra w/part Perez-p; Total Chaos Pt. 3		.90	2.25
2-Total Chaos Pt 6		.80	2.00
3-21: 11-Metallik app.		.70	1.75
22-24: 22-$1.95-c begins. 24-Zero Hour x-over		.80	2.00
Annual 1 (1993, $3.50, 68 pgs.)		1.40	3.50
Annual 2 (1994, $3.50, 68 pgs.)-Elseworlds story		1.40	3.50

TEAM X/TEAM 7
Nov, 1996 ($4.95, one-shot)
Marvel Comics

	GD25	FN65	NM94
1		2.00	5.00

TEAM YANKEE
Jan, 1989 - No. 6, Feb, 1989 ($1.95, weekly limited series)
First Comics

	GD25	FN65	NM94
1-6		.80	2.00

TEAM YOUNGBLOOD (Also see Youngblood)
Sept, 1993 - No. 22, Sept, 1995 ($1.95/$2.50)

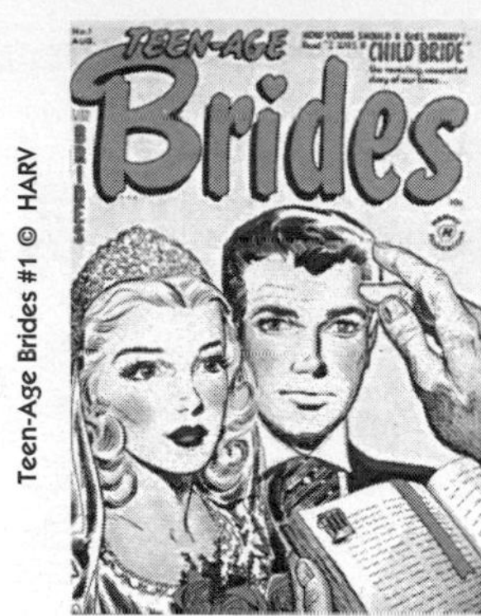

Teen-Age Brides #1 © HARV

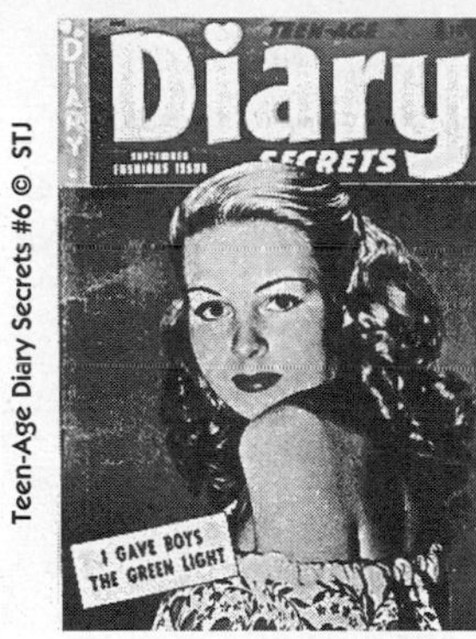

Teen-Age Diary Secrets #6 © STJ

Teenage Mutant Ninja Turtles #25 © Mirage Studios

GD25 FN65 NM94

Image Comics (Extreme Studios)

1-9-Liefeld scripts in all: 1,2,4-6,8-Thibert-c(i). 1-1st app. Dutch & Masada. 3-Spawn cameo. 5-1st app. Lynx. 7,8-Coupons 1 & 4 for Extreme Prejudice #0; Black and White Pt. 4 & 8 by Thibert. 8-Coupon #4 for E. P. #0. 9-Liefeld wraparound-c(p)/a(p) on Pt. I .80 2.00
10-22: 10-$2.50-c begin; Liefeld-c(p). 16-Polybagged w/trading card 17-Polybagged w/trading card. 18-Extreme 3000 Prelude. 19-Cruz-a. 21-Angela & Glory-app. 22-Shadowhawk-c/app 1.00 2.50

TEDDY ROOSEVELT & HIS ROUGH RIDERS (See Real Heroes #1)
1950
Avon Periodicals

1-Kinstler-c; Palais-a; Flag-c 15.00 45.00 110.00

TEDDY ROOSEVELT ROUGH RIDER (See Battlefield #22 & Classics Illustrated Special Issue)

TED MCKEEVER'S METROPOL
Mar, 1991 - No. 12, Mar, 1992 ($2.95, limited series)
Marvel Comics (Epic Comics)

V1#1-12: Ted McKeever-c/a/scripts 1.20 3.00

TED MCKEEVER'S METROPOL A.D.
Oct, 1992 - No. 3, Dec, 1992 ($3.50, limited series)
Marvel Comics (Epic Comics)

V2#1-3: Ted McKeever-c/a/scripts 1.40 3.50

TEE AND VEE CROSLEY IN TELEVISION LAND COMICS
(Also see Crosley's House of Fun)
1951 (52 pgs.; 8x11"; paper cover; in color)
Crosley Division, Avco Mfg. Corp. (Giveaway)

Many stories, puzzles, cut-outs, games, etc. 4.25 13.00 28.00

TEENA
No. 11, 1948 - No. 15, 1948; No. 20, Aug, 1949 - No. 22, Oct, 1950
Magazine Enterprises/Standard Comics No. 20 on

A-1 #11-Teen-age; Ogden Whitney-c 6.50 19.50 45.00
A-1 #12, 15 5.70 17.00 40.00
20-22 (Standard) 4.00 12.00 24.00

TEEN-AGE BRIDES (True Bride's Experiences #8 on)
Aug, 1953 - No. 7, Aug, 1954
Harvey/Home Comics

1-Powell-a 8.50 26.00 60.00
2-Powell-a 5.70 17.00 40.00
3-7: 3,6-Powell-a 5.00 15.00 30.00

TEEN-AGE CONFESSIONS (See Teen Confessions)

TEEN-AGE CONFIDENTIAL CONFESSIONS
July, 1960 - No. 22, 1964
Charlton Comics

1 2.50 7.50 24.00
2-10 1.85 5.50 15.00
11-22 1.25 3.75 10.00

TEEN-AGE DIARY SECRETS (Formerly Blue Ribbon Comics; becomes Diary Secrets #10 on)
No. 4, 9/49; nn (#5), 9/49 - No. 7, 11/49; No. 8, 2/50; No. 9, 8/50
St. John Publishing Co.

4(9/49)-Oversized; part mag., part comic 21.00 62.00 150.00
nn(#5),6,8: 6,8-Photo-c; Baker-a(2-3) in each 16.00 47.00 120.00
7,9-Digest size 19.00 58.00 140.00

TEEN-AGE DOPE SLAVES (See Harvey Comics Library #1)

TEENAGE HOTRODDERS (Top Eliminator #25 on; see Blue Bird)
Apr, 1963 - No. 24, July, 1967
Charlton Comics

1 3.50 10.50 35.00
2-10 2.50 7.50 20.00
11-24 2.00 6.00 16.00

TEEN-AGE LOVE (See Fox Giants)

TEEN-AGE LOVE (Formerly Intimate)
V2#4, July, 1958 - No. 96, Dec, 1973
Charlton Comics

V2#4 3.00 9.00 30.00
5-9 2.50 7.50 20.00
10(9/59)-20 1.85 5.50 15.00
21-35 1.50 4.50 12.00
36-70 1.10 3.30 9.00
71-96: 61&62-Jonnie Love begins (origin) 2.40 6.00

TEENAGE MUTANT NINJA TURTLES (Also see Anything Goes, Donatello, First Comics Graphic Novel, Gobbledygook, Grimjack #26, Leonardo, Michaelangelo, Raphael & Tales Of The...)
1984 - No. 62, Aug, 1993 ($1.50/$1.75, B&W; all 44-52 pgs.)
Mirage Studios

1-1st printing (3000 copies)-Only printing to have ad for Gobbledygook #1 & 2; Shredder app. (#1-4: 7-1/2x11") 12.50 38.00 125.00
1-2nd printing (6/84)(15,000 copies) 1.25 3.75 10.00
1-3rd printing (2/85)(36,000 copies) 2.00 5.00
1-4th printing, new-c (50,000 copies) 1.60 4.00
1-5th printing, new-c (8/88-c, 11/88 inside) .80 2.00
1-Counterfeit. **Note**: Most counterfeit copies have a half inch wide white streak or scratch marks across the center of back cover. Black part of cover is a bluish black instead of a deep black. Inside paper is very white & inside cover is bright white. These counterfeit the 1st printings (no value).
2-1st printing (1984; 15,000 copies) 3.50 10.50 35.00
2-2nd printing 2.40 6.00
2-3rd printing; new Corben-c/a (2/85) 1.10 2.75
2-Counterfeit with glossy cover stock (no value).
3-1st printing (1985, 44 pgs.) 2.25 6.75 18.00
3-Variant, 500 copies, given away in NYC. Has 'Laird's Photo' in white rather than light blue 5.00 15.00 50.00
3-2nd printing; contains new back-up story 1.10 2.75
4-1st printing (1985, 44 pgs.) 1.25 3.75 10.00
4-2nd printing (5/87) .70 1.75
5-Fugitoid begins, ends #7; 1st full color-c (1985) 1.00 3.00 7.50
5-2nd printing (11/87) .70 1.75
6-1st printing (1986) 2.00 5.00
6-2nd printing (4/88-c, 5/88 inside) .70 1.75
7-4 pg. Eastman/Corben color insert; 1st color TMNT (1986, $1.75-c); Bade Biker back-up story 2.00 5.00
7-2nd printing (1/89) w/o color insert .70 1.75
8-Cerebus-c/story with Dave Sim-a (1986) 1.80 4.50
9,10: 9 (9/86)-Rip In Time by Corben 1.60 4.00
11-15 1.20 3.00
16-18: 18-Mark Bode'-a 1.00 2.50
18-2nd printing ($2.25, color, 44 pgs.)-New-c .90 2.25
19-51: 19-Begin $1.75-c. 24-26-Veitch-c/a. 35-Begin $2.00-c. 50-Features pin-ups by Larsen, McFarlane, Simonson, etc. .70 1.80
32-2nd printing ($2.75, 52 pgs., full color) 1.10 2.75
52-62: 52-Begin $2.25-c .90 2.25
Book 1,2($1.50, B&W): 2-Corben-c 1.50
...Christmas Special 1 (12/90, $1.75, B&W, 52 pgs.)-Cover title: Michaelangelo Christmas Special; r/Michaelangelo one-shot plus new Raphael story .70 1.75
...Special (The Maltese Turtle) nn (1/93, $2.95, color, 44 pgs.) 1.20 3.00
...Special: "Times" Pipeline nn (9/92, $2.95, color, 44 pgs.)-Mark Bode-c/a 1.20 3.00
Hardcover ($100)-r/#1-10 plus one-shots w/dust jackets - limited to 1000 w/letter of authenticity 10.00 30.00 100.00

Teenage Mutant Ninja Turtles V2 #9 © Mirage Studios

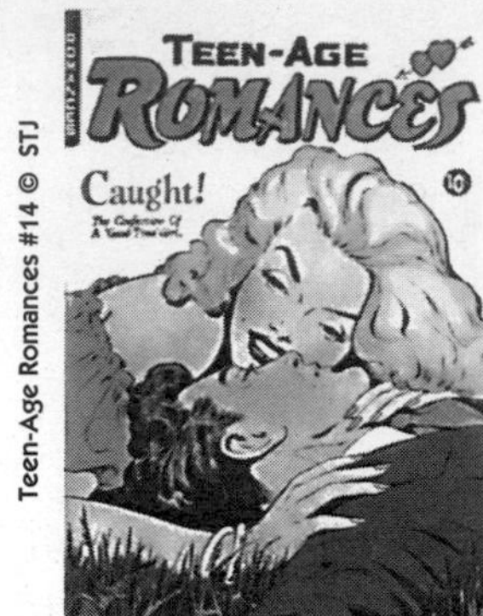

Teen-Age Romances #14 © STJ

Teen-Age Temptations #1 © STJ

GD25 FN65 NM94

Softcover ($40)-r/#1-10 4.00 12.00 40.00

TEENAGE MUTANT NINJA TURTLES
V2#1, Oct, 1993 - V2#10, July, 1994? ($2.75)
Mirage Studios

V2#1-10: 1-Wraparound-c 1.10 2.75

TEENAGE MUTANT NINJA TURTLES ADVENTURES (TV)
8/88 - No. 3, 12/88; 3/89 - No. 62, 1995? ($1.00/$1.25/$1.50/$1.75)
Archie Comics

1-Adapts TV cartoon; not by Eastman/Laird .80 2.00
2,3 (Mini-series) 1.50
1 (2nd on going series) .80 2.00
2-5: 5-Begins original stories not based on TV 1.50
1-11: 2nd printings 1.00
6-49,51-58: 14-Simpson-a(p). 19-1st Mighty Mutanimals (also in #20, 51-54). 20-Begin $1.25-c. 22-Gene Colan-c/a 1.25
50-($1.50)-Poster by Eastman/Laird 1.50
59-61,63-73: 59-Begin $1.50-c 1.50
62-($1.75)-w/poster .70 1.75
nn (1990, $5.95)-Movie adaptation 2.40 6.00
nn (Spring, 1991, $2.50, 68 pgs.)-(Meet Archie) 1.00 2.50
nn (Sum, 1991, $2.50, 68 pgs.)-(Movie II)-Adapts movie sequel 1.00 2.50
...Meet the Conservation Corps 1 (1992, $2.50, 68 pgs.) 1.00 2.50
...III The Movie: The Turtles are Back...In Time (1993, $2.50, 68 pgs.) 1.00 2.50
Special 1 (Sum/92, $2.50, 68 pgs.)-Bill Wray-c 1.00 2.50
Special 4 (Spr/93, $2.50, 68 pgs.) 1.00 2.50
Special 5 (Sum/93, $2.50, 68 pgs.) 1.00 2.50
Giant Size Special 6 (Fall/93, $1.95, 52 pgs.) .80 2.00
Special 7,8 (Win/93, Spr/94, $1.95, 52 pgs.) .80 2.00
Special 9 (Sum/94, $1.95, 52 pgs.)-Jeff Smith-c .80 2.00
Special 10 (Fall/94, $2.00, 52 pgs.) .80 2.00
NOTE: *There are 2nd printings of #1-11 w/B&W inside covers. Originals are color.*

TEENAGE MUTANT NINJA TURTLES (Adventures)
Jan, 1996 - No. 3, Mar, 1996 ($1.50, limited series)
Archie Publications

1-3 1.50

TEENAGE MUTANT NINJA TURTLES
June, 1996 - Present ($1.95)
Image Comics (Highbrow Entertainment)

1-8: Eric Larsen-c(i) on all .80 2.00
9-11-($2.95) 10-Savage Dragon-c/app. 1.20 3.00

TEENAGE MUTANT NINJA TURTLES CLASSICS DIGEST (TV)
Aug, 1993 - No. 8, Mar, 1995? ($1.75)
Archie Comics

1-8: Reprints TMNT Advs. .70 1.75

TEENAGE MUTANT NINJA TURTLES/FLAMING CARROT CROSSOVER
Nov, 1993 - No. 4, Feb, 1994 ($2.75, limited series)
Mirage Publishing

1-4: Bob Burden story 1.10 2.75

TEENAGE MUTANT NINJA TURTLES PRESENTS: APRIL O'NEIL
Mar, 1993 - No. 3, June, 1993 ($1.25, limited series)
Archie Comics

1-3 1.25

TEENAGE MUTANT NINJA TURTLES PRESENTS: DONATELLO AND LEATHERHEAD
July, 1993 - No. 3, Sept, 1993 ($1.25, limited series)
Archie Comics

1-3 1.25

GD25 FN65 NM94

TEENAGE MUTANT NINJA TURTLES PRESENTS: MERDUDE
Oct, 1993 - No. 3, Dec, 1993 ($1.25, limited series)
Archie Comics

1-3-See Mighty Mutanimals #7 for 1st app. Merdude 1.25

TEENAGE MUTANT NINJA TURTLES/SAVAGE DRAGON CROSSOVER
Aug, 1995 ($2.75, one-shot)
Mirage Studios

1 1.10 2.75

TEEN-AGE ROMANCE (Formerly My Own Romance)
No. 77, Sept, 1960 - No. 86, Mar, 1962
Marvel Comics (ZPC)

77-86 2.00 6.00 16.00

TEEN-AGE ROMANCES
Jan, 1949 - No. 45, Dec, 1955
St. John Publ. co. (Approved Comics)

1-Baker-c/a(1) 31.00 94.00 240.00
2-Baker-c/a 17.00 51.00 130.00
3-Baker-c/a(3); spanking panel 19.00 56.00 140.00
4,5,7,8-Photo-c; Baker-a(2-3) each 14.00 41.00 110.00
6-Slightly large size; photo-c; part magazine; Baker-a (10/49) 15.00 45.00 120.00
9-Baker-c/a; Kubert-a 18.00 54.00 140.00
10-12,20-Baker-c/a(2-3) each 13.00 39.00 100.00
13-19,21,22-Complete issues by Baker 18.00 54.00 140.00
23-25-Baker-c/a(2-3) each 11.30 34.00 90.00
26,27,33,34,36-40,42: Baker-a. 33-Signed story by Estrada. 38-Suggestive-c. 42-r/Cinderella Love #9; Last pre-code (3/55) 8.50 26.00 60.00
28-30-No Baker-a 4.15 12.50 25.00
31,32-Baker-c 5.70 17.00 40.00
35-Baker-c/a (16 pgs.) 8.50 26.00 60.00
41-Baker-c; Infantino-a(r); all stories are Ziff-Davis-r 6.50 19.50 45.00
43-45-Baker-a 6.50 19.50 45.00

TEEN-AGE TALK
1964
I.W. Enterprises

Reprint #1 1.75 5.25 14.00
Reprint #5,8,9: 5-r/Hector #? 9-Punch Comics #?; L.B. Cole-c reprint from School Day Romances #1 1.00 3.00 8.00

TEEN-AGE TEMPTATIONS (Going Steady #10 on)(See True Love Pictorial)
Oct, 1952 - No. 9, Aug, 1954
St. John Publishing co.

1-Baker-c/a; has story "Reform School Girl" by Estrada 38.00 114.00 280.00
2,4-Baker-c 11.30 34.00 90.00
3,5-7,9-Baker-c/a 17.00 51.00 130.00
8-Teenagers smoke reefers; Baker-c/a 17.00 51.00 130.00
NOTE: ***Estrada** a-1, 3-5.*

TEEN BEAM (Formerly Teen Beat #1)
No. 2, Jan-Feb, 1968
National Periodical Publications

2-Orlando, Drucker-a(r); Monkees photo-c 5.00 15.00 50.00

TEEN BEAT (Becomes Teen Beam #2)
Nov-Dec, 1967
National Periodical Publications

1-Photos & text only; Monkees photo-c 6.00 18.00 60.00

TEEN COMICS (Formerly All Teen; Journey Into Unknown Worlds #36 on)
No. 21, Apr, 1947 - No. 35, May, 1950
Marvel comics (WFP)

21-Kurtzman's "Hey Look"; Patsy Walker, Cindy (1st app.?), Georgie, Margie

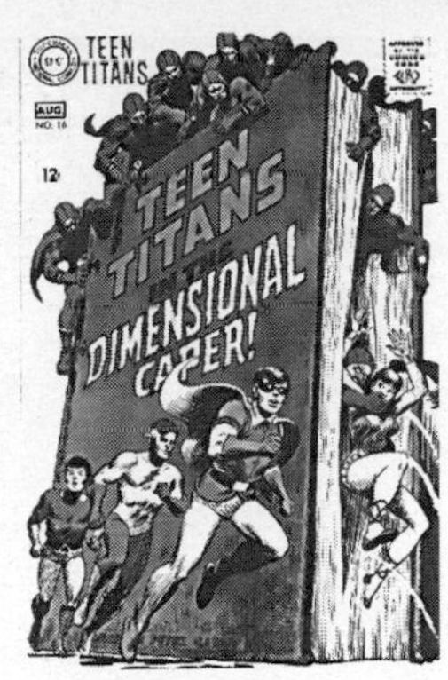

Teen Titans #16 (1st Series) © DC

Teen Titans #12 (2nd Series) © DC

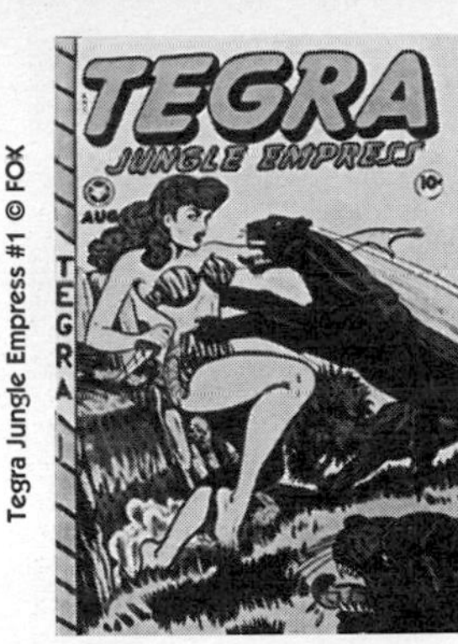

Tegra Jungle Empress #1 © FOX

app.; Syd Shores-a begins, end #23 10.00 30.00 80.00
22,23,25,27,29,31-35: 22-(6/47)-Becomes Hedy Devine #22 (8/47) on? 7.50 22.50 50.00
24,26,28,30-Kurtzman's "Hey Look" 10.00 30.00 70.00

TEEN CONFESSIONS
Aug, 1959 - No. 97, Nov, 1976
Charlton Comics

1 6.00 18.00 60.00
2 3.00 9.00 30.00
3-10 2.25 6.75 18.00
11-30 1.50 4.50 12.00
31-Beatles-c 9.00 27.00 90.00
32-36,38-55 1.25 3.75 10.00
37 (1/66)-Beatles Fan Club story; Beatles-c 9.00 27.00 90.00
56-58,60-97: 89,90-Newton-c 2.00 5.00
59-Kaluta's 1st pro work? (12/69) 1.50 4.50 12.00

TEENIE WEENIES, THE (America's Favorite Kiddie Comic)
No. 10, 1950 - No. 11, Apr-May, 1951 (Newspaper reprints)
Ziff-Davis Publishing Co.

10,11-Painted-c 15.00 45.00 120.00

TEEN-IN (Tippy Teen)
Summer, 1968 - No. 4, Fall, 1969
Tower Comics

nn(#1, Summer, 1968) 4.00 12.00 40.00
nn(#2, Spring, 1969),3,4 2.80 8.40 28.00

TEEN LIFE (Formerly Young Life)
No. 3, Winter, 1945 - No. 5, Fall, 1945 (Teenage magazine)
New Age/Quality Comics Group

3-June Allyson photo on-c & story 8.75 26.25 70.00
4-Duke Ellington photo on-c & story 7.15 21.50 50.00
5-Van Johnson, Woody Herman & Jackie Robinson articles; Van Johnson & Woody Herman photos on-c 10.00 30.00 75.00

TEEN ROMANCES
1964
Super Comics

10,11,15-17 Reprints 2.00 5.00

TEEN SECRET DIARY (Nurse Betsy Crane #12 on)
Oct, 1959 - No. 11, June, 1961; No. 1, 1972
Charlton Comics

1 2.50 7.50 24.00
2 1.85 5.50 15.00
3-11 1.50 4.50 12.00
1 (1972) 1.25 3.75 10.00

TEEN TALK (See Teen)

TEEN TITANS(See Brave & the Bold #54,60, DC Super-Stars #1, Marvel & DC Present, New Teen Titans, New Titans, Official...Index and Showcase #59)
1-2/66 - No. 43, 1-2/73; No. 44, 11/76 - No. 53, 2/78
National Periodical Publications/DC Comics

1-(1-2/66)-Titans join Peace Corps; Batman, Flash, Aquaman, Wonder Woman cameos 23.00 69.00 185.00
2 9.00 27.00 90.00
3-5: 4-Speedy app. 5.50 16.50 55.00
6-10: 6-Doom Patrol app.; Beast Boy x-over; readers polled on him joining Titans 4.20 12.60 42.00
11-19: 11-Speedy app. 13-X-Mas-c. 18-1st app. Starfire (11-12/68). 19-Wood-i; Speedy begins as regular 3.50 10.50 35.00
20-22: All Neal Adams-a. 21-Hawk & Dove app.; last 12¢ issue. 22-Origin Wonder Girl 3.80 11.40 38.00
23-30: 23-Wonder Girl dons new costume. 25-Flash, Aquaman, Batman, Green Arrow, Green Lantern, Superman, & Hawk & Dove guests; 1st app. Lilith who joins T.T. West in #50. 29-Hawk & Dove & Ocean Master app. 30-Aquagirl app. 1.85 5.50 15.00
31-35,40-43: 31-Hawk & Dove app. 1.25 3.75 10.00
36-39-52 pgs.: 36,37-Superboy-r. 38-Green Arrow/Speedy-r; Aquaman/Aqualad story. 39-Hawk & Dove-r. 1.50 4.50 12.00
44,45,47,49,51,52: 44-Mal becomes the Guardian 2.00 5.00
46-Joker's daughter begins (see Batman Family) 1.40 4.15 11.00
48-Intro Bumblebee; Joker's daughter becomes Harlequin 1.40 4.15 11.00
50-1st revival original Bat-Girl; intro. Teen Titans West 2.60 7.80 26.00
53-Origin retold 2.20 5.50

NOTE: *Aparo a-36.* ***Buckler*** *c-46-53.* ***Cardy*** *c-1-16.* ***Kane*** *a(p)-19, 22-24, 39r.* ***Tuska*** *a(p)-31, 36, 38, 39. DC Super-Stars #1 (3/76) was released before #44.*

TEEN TITANS
Oct, 1995 - Present ($1.95)
DC Comics

1-Dan Jurgens-c/a(p)/scripts & George Perez-c/a(i) begin; Atom forms new team (Risk, Argent, Prysm, & Joto); 1st app.Loren Jupiter & Omen; no indicia. 1-3-Origin. .80 2.00
2-11: 4,5-Robin, Nightwing, Supergirl, Capt. Marvel Jr. app. .80 2.00
12-($2.95)"Then and Now" begins w/original Teen Titans-c/app. 2.95
13-17: 15-Death of Joto 1.95
Annual 1 (1997, $3.95)-Pulp Heroes story 1.60 4.00

TEEN TITANS SPOTLIGHT
Aug, 1986 - No. 21, Apr, 1988
DC Comics

1-21: 7-Guice's 1st work at DC. 14-Nightwing; Batman app. 15-Austin-c(i). 18,19-Millenium x-over. 21-($1.00-c)-Original Teen Titans; Spiegle-a 1.00

Note: ***Guice*** *a-7p, 8p; c-7,8.* ***Orlando*** *c/a-11p.* ***Perez*** *c-1, 17i, 19.* ***Sienkiewicz*** *c-10*

TEEPEE TIM (...Heap Funny Indian Boy)(Formerly Ha Ha Comics)
No. 100, Feb-Mar, 1955 - No. 102, June-July, 1955
American Comics Group

100-102 4.00 10.00 20.00

TEGRA JUNGLE EMPRESS (Zegra Jungle Empress #2 on)
August, 1948
Fox Features Syndicate

1-Blue Beetle, Rocket Kelly app.; used in **SOTI**, pg. 31 43.00 128.00 360.00

TEKNO COMIX HANDBOOK
May, 1996 ($3.95, one-shot)
Tekno Comix

1-Guide to the Tekno Universe 1.60 4.00

TEKNOPHAGE (See Neil Gaiman's...)

TEKNOPHAGE VERSUS ZEERUS
July, 1996 ($3.25, one-shot)
BIG Entertainment

1-Paul Jenkins script 1.30 3.25

TEKWORLD (William Shatner's... on-c only)
Sept, 1992 - Aug, 1994 ($1.75)
Epic Comics (Marvel)

1-Based on Shatner's novel, TekWar, set in L.A. in the year 2120 1.00 2.50
2-24 .70 1.75

TELEVISION (See TV)

TELEVISION COMICS
No. 5, Feb, 1950 - No. 8, Nov, 1950

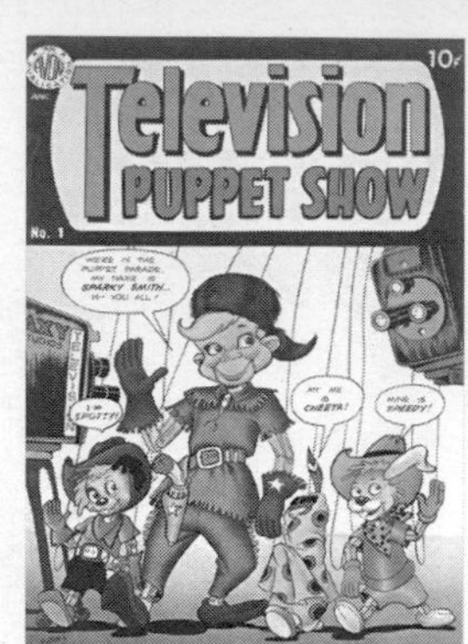

Television Puppet Show #1 © AVON

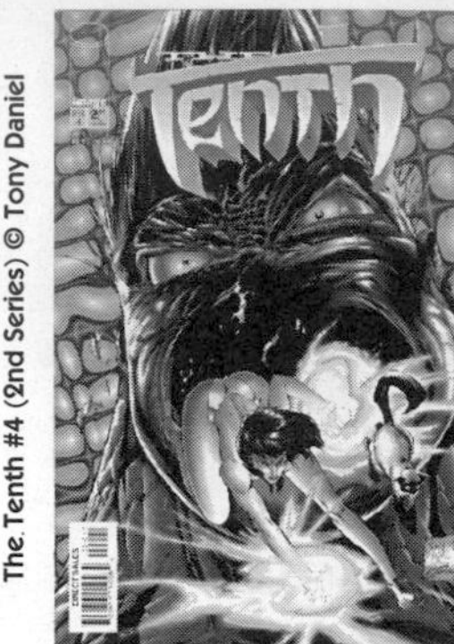

The Tenth #4 (2nd Series) © Tony Daniel

Terminal City #3 © Dean Motter

GD25 FN65 NM94

Standard Comics (Animated Cartoons)
5-1st app. Willy Nilly 7.85 23.50 55.00
6-8: 6 has #2 on inside 6.00 18.00 42.00

TELEVISION PUPPET SHOW (See Spotty the Pup)
1950 - No. 2, Nov, 1950
Avon Periodicals
1-1st app. Speedy Rabbit, Spotty The Pup 13.00 39.00 110.00
2 11.30 34.00 90.00

TELEVISION TEENS MOPSY (See TV Teens)

TELL IT TO THE MARINES
Mar, 1952 - No. 15, July, 1955
Toby Press Publications
1-Lover O'Leary and His Liberty Belles (with pin-ups), ends #6; Spike & Bat begin, end #6 16.00 47.00 120.00
2-Madame Cobra-c/story 9.15 27.00 60.00
3-5 6.35 19.00 40.00
6-12,14,15: 7-9,14,15-Photo-c 5.00 15.00 30.00
13-John Wayne photo-c 10.00 30.00 70.00
I.W. Reprint #9-r/#1 above 1.00 2.80 7.00
Super Reprint #16(1964)-r/#4 above 1.00 2.80 7.00

TEMPEST (See Aquaman, 3rd Series)
Nov, 1996 - No. 4, Feb, 1997 ($1.75, limited series)
DC Comics
1-4: Formerly Aqualad; Phil Jimenez-c/a/scripts in all 1.75

TEMPUS FUGITIVE
1990 - No. 4, 1991 ($4.95, squarebound, 52 pgs.)
DC Comics
Book 1,2: Ken Steacy painted-c/a & scripts 2.00 5.00
Book 3,4-($5.95-c) 2.40 6.00
TPB (Dark Horse Comics, 1/97, $17.95) 18.00

TEN COMMANDMENTS (See Moses & the... and Classics Illustrated Special)

TENDER LOVE STORIES
Feb, 1971 - No. 4, July, 1971 (All 25¢, 52 pgs.)
Skywald Publ. Corp.
1-4 1.20 3.00

TENDER ROMANCE (Ideal Romance #3 on)
Dec, 1953 - No. 2, Feb, 1954
Key Publications (Gilmour Magazines)
1-Headlight & lingerie panels; B. Baily-c 12.00 36.00 90.00
2-Bernard Baily-c 7.50 22.50 50.00

TENNESSEE JED (Radio)
nd (1945) (16 pgs.; paper cover; regular size; giveaway)
Fox Syndicate? (Wm. C. Popper & Co.)
nn 14.50 43.00 115.00

TENNIS (...For Speed, Stamina, Strength, Skill)
1956 (16 pgs.; soft cover; 10¢)
Tennis Educational Foundation
Book 1-Endorsed by Gene Tunney, Ralph Kiner, etc. showing how tennis has helped them 4.00 12.00 24.00

TENSE SUSPENSE
Dec, 1958 - No. 2, Feb, 1959
Fago Publications
1,2 6.70 20.00 45.00

TEN STORY LOVE (Formerly a pulp magazine with same title)
V29#3, June-July, 1951 - V36#5(#209), Sept, 1956 (#3-6: 52 pgs.)
Ace Periodicals
V29#3(#177)-Part comic, part text; painted-c 8.50 26.00 60.00
4-6(1/52) 4.25 13.00 28.00
V30#1(3/52)-6(1/53) 4.00 12.00 24.00
V31#1(2/53),V32#2(4/53)-6(12/53) 3.60 9.00 18.00
V33#1(1/54)-3(5#54, #195), V34#4(7/54, #196)-6(10/54, #198) 3.60 9.00 18.00
V35#1(12/54, #199)-3(4/55, #201)-Last precode 2.80 7.00 14.00
V35#4-6(9/55, #201-204), V36#1(11/55, #205)-3, 5(9/56, #209) 2.40 6.00 12.00
V36#4-L.B. Cole-a 5.70 17.00 40.00

TENTH, THE
Jan, 1997 - No. 4 ($2.50)
Image Comics
1-4-Tony Daniel-c/a, Beau Smith-s 1.00 2.80 7.00
Abuse of Humanity TPB ($10.95) r/#1-4 10.95

TENTH, THE
Sept, 1997 - Present ($2.50)
Image Comics
1-5-Tony Daniel-c/a, Beau Smith-s 1.00 2.50

TEN WHO DARED (Disney)
No. 1178, Dec, 1960
Dell Publishing Co.
Four Color 1178-Movie, painted-c; cast member photo on back-c 6.40 19.00 70.00

TERMINAL CITY
July, 1996 - No. 9, Mar, 1997 ($2.50, limited series)
DC Comics (Vertigo)
1-9: Dean Motter scripts, 7,8-Matt Wagner-c 1.00 2.50
TPB ('97, $19.95) r/series 19.95

TERMINAL CITY: AERIAL GRAFFITI
Nov, 1997 - No. 5, ($2.50, limited series)
DC Comics (Vertigo)
1-5: Dean Motter-s/Lark-a/Chiarello-c 1.00 2.50

TERMINATOR, THE (See Robocop vs. ... & Rust #12 for 1st app.)
Sept, 1988 - No. 17, 1989 ($1.75, Baxter paper)
Now Comics
1-Based on movie 2.40 6.00
2-10,12: 12-($2.95, 52 pgs.)-Intro. John Connor 1.20 3.00
11,13-17 .80 2.00
Trade paperback (1989, $9.95) 1.25 3.75 10.00

TERMINATOR, THE
Aug, 1990 - No. 4, Nov, 1990 ($2.50, limited series)
Dark Horse Comics
1-Set 39 years later than the movie 1.60 4.00
2-4 1.00 2.50

TERMINATOR, THE: ALL MY FUTURES PAST
V3#1, Aug, 1990 - V3#2, Sept, 1990 ($1.75, limited series)
Now Comics
V3#1,2 .70 1.75

TERMINATOR, THE: ENDGAME
Sept, 1992 - No. 3, Nov, 1992 ($2.50, limited series)
Dark Horse Comics
1-3: Guice-a(p); painted-c 1.00 2.50

TERMINATOR, THE: HUNTERS AND KILLERS
Mar, 1992 - No. 3, May, 1992 ($2.50, limited series)
Dark Horse Comics
1-3 1.00 2.50

TERMINATOR, THE: ONE SHOT

The Terminator: The Enemy Within #3 © Cinema 84

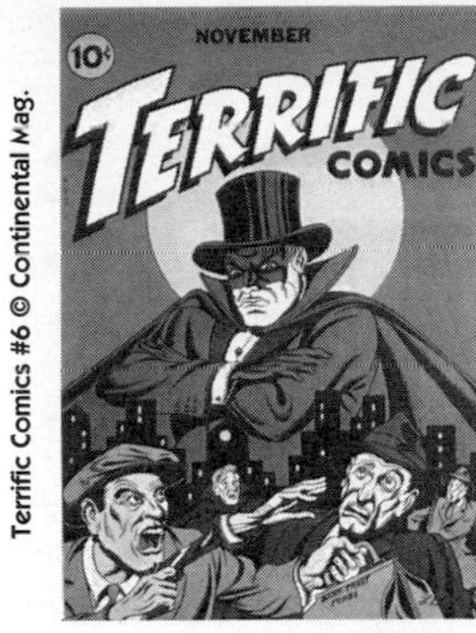

Terrific Comics #6 © Continental Mag.

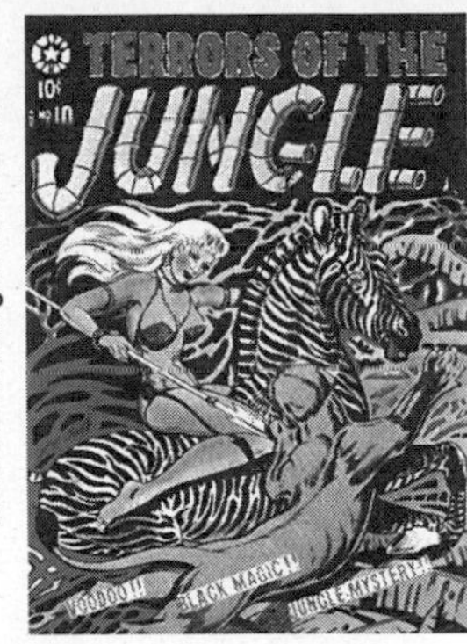

Terrors of the Jungle #10 © STAR

GD25 FN65 NM94

July, 1991 ($5.95, 56 pgs.)
Dark Horse Comics

nn-Matt Wagner-a; contains stiff pop-up inside 2.40 6.00

TERMINATOR, THE: SECONDARY OBJECTIVES
July, 1991 - No. 4, Oct, 1991 ($2.50, limited series)
Dark Horse Comics

1-Gulacy-c/a(p) in all 1.00 2.50
2-4 1.00 2.50

TERMINATOR, THE: THE BURNING EARTH
V2#1, Mar, 1990 - V2#5, July, 1990 ($1.75, limited series)
Now Comics

V2#1-5 .70 1.75
Trade paperback (1990, $9.95)-Reprints V2#1-5 1.25 3.75 10.00

TERMINATOR: THE ENEMY WITHIN, THE
Nov, 1991 - No. 4, Feb, 1992 ($2.50, limited series)
Dark Horse Comics

1-4: All have Simon Bisley painted-c 1.00 2.50

TERMINATOR 2: CYBERNETIC DAWN
Nov, 1995 - No.4, Feb, 1996; No. 0. Apr, 1996 ($2.50, limited series)
Malibu Comics

0-4: Continuation of film. 0 (4/96)-flip book w/Terminator 2: Nuclear Twilight. 1.00 2.50

TERMINATOR 2: JUDGEMENT DAY
Early Sept, 1991 - No. 3, Early Oct, 1991 ($1.00, limited series)
Marvel Comics

1-3: Based on movie sequel; 1-3-Same as nn issues 1.00
nn (1991, $4.95, squarebound, 68 pgs.)-Photo-c 2.00 5.00
nn (1991, $2.25, B&W, magazine, 68 pgs.) .90 2.25

TERMINATOR 2: NUCLEAR TWILIGHT
Nov, 1995 - No.4, Feb, 1996; No. 0, Apr, 1996 ($2.50, limited series)
Malibu Comics

0-4:Continuation of film. 0 (4/96)-Gary Erskine-c/a; flip book w/Terminator 2: Cybernetic Dawn. 1.00 2.50

TERRAFORMERS
April, 1987 - No. 2, 1987 ($1.95, limited series)
Wonder Color Comics

1,2-Kelley Jones-a .80 2.00

TERRANAUTS
Aug, 1986 - No. 2, 1986 ($1.75, limited series)
Fantasy General Comics

1,2 .75 1.80

TERRARISTS
Nov, 1993 - No. 4, Feb, 1994 ($2.50, limited series)
Marvel Comics (Epic Comics)

1-4-Bound-in trading cards in all 1.00 2.50

TERRIFIC COMICS (Also see Suspense Comics)
Jan, 1944 - No. 6, Nov, 1944
Continental Magazines

1-Kid Terrific; opium story 240.00 720.00 2400.00
2-1st app. The Boomerang by L.B. Cole & Ed Wheelan's "Comics" McCormick, called the world's #1 comic book fan begins 200.00 600.00 1800.00
3-Diana becomes Boomerang's costumed aide; L.B. Cole-c 200.00 600.00 1800.00
4-Classic war-c (Scarce) 300.00 900.00 3000.00
5-The Reckoner begins; Boomerang & Diana by L.B. Cole; Schomburg bondage-c (Scarce) 420.00 1260.00 4200.00
6-L.B. Cole-c/a 178.00 534.00 1600.00

NOTE: ***L.B. Cole*** *a-1, 2(2), 3-6.* ***Fuje*** *a-5, 6.* ***Rico*** *a-2; c-1.* ***Schomburg*** *c-2, 5.*

GD25 FN65 NM94

TERRIFIC COMICS (Formerly Horrific; Wonder Boy #17 on)
No. 14, Dec, 1954; No. 16, Mar, 1955 (No #15)
Mystery Publ.(Comic Media)/(Ajax/Farrell)

14-Art swipe/Advs. into the Unknown #37; injury-to-eye-c; pg. 2, panel 5 swiped from Phantom Stranger #4; surrealistic Palais-a; Human Cross story 21.00 64.00 160.00
16-Wonder Boy-c/story (last pre-code) 14.00 43.00 110.00

TERRIFYING TALES (Formerly Startling Terror Tales #10)
No. 11, Jan, 1953 - No. 15, Apr, 1954
Star Publications

11-Used in **POP**, pgs. 99,100; all Jo-Jo-r 40.00 120.00 300.00
12-Reprints Jo-Jo #19 entirely; L.B. Cole splash 37.00 111.00 275.00
13-All Rulah-r; classic devil-c 40.00 120.00 325.00
14-All Rulah reprints 37.00 111.00 275.00
15-Rulah, Zago-r; used in **SOTI**-r/Rulah #22 37.00 111.00 275.00

NOTE: *All issues have* ***L.B. Cole*** *covers; bondage covers-No. 12-14.*

TERROR ILLUSTRATED (Adult Tales of...)
Nov-Dec, 1955 - No. 2, Spring (April on-c), 1956 (Magazine, 25¢)
E.C. Comics

1-Adult Entertainment on-c 10.50 32.00 85.00
2-Charles Sultan-a 8.75 26.25 70.00

NOTE: ***Craig, Evans, Ingels, Orlando*** *art in each.* ***Crandall*** *c-1, 2.*

TERROR INC. (See A Shadowline Saga #3)
July, 1992 - No. 13, July, 1993 ($1.75)
Marvel Comics

1-13: 6,7-Punisher-c/story. 9,10-Wolverine-c/story. 13-Ghost Rider app. .70 1.75

TERRORS OF THE JUNGLE (Formerly Jungle Thrills)
No. 17, 5/52 - No. 21, 2/53; No. 4, 4/53 - No. 10, 9/54
Star Publications

17-Reprints Rulah #21, used in **SOTI**; L.B. Cole bondage-c 40.00 120.00 310.00
18-Jo-Jo-r 26.00 77.00 200.00
19,20(1952)-Jo-Jo-r; Disbrow-a 24.00 73.00 190.00
21-Jungle Jo, Tangi-r; used in **POP**, pg. 100 & color illos.; shrunken heads on-c 27.00 81.00 210.00
4-10: All Disbrow-a. 5-Jo-Jo-r. 8-Rulah, Jo-Jo-r. 9-Jo-Jo-r; Disbrow-a; Tangi by Orlando10-Rulah-r 24.00 73.00 190.00

NOTE: ***L.B. Cole*** *c-all; bondage c-17, 19, 21, 5, 7.*

TERROR TALES (See Beware Terror Tales)

TERROR TALES (Magazine)
V1#7, 1969 - V6#6, Dec, 1974; V7#1, Apr, 1976 - V10, 1979?
(V1-V6: 52 pgs.; V7 on: 68 pgs.)
Eerie Publications

V1#7 4.00 12.00 40.00
V1#8-11('69): 9-Bondage-c 3.00 9.00 30.00
V2#1-6('70), V3#1-6('71), V4#1-7('72), V5#1-6('73), V6#1-6('74) 2.50 7.50 24.00
V7#1,4(no V7#2), V8#1-3('77), V9, V10 2.50 7.50 24.00
V7#3-LSD story-r/Weird V3#5 2.50 7.50 24.00

TERRY AND THE PIRATES (See Famous Feature Stories, Merry Christmas From Sears Toyland, Popular Comics, Super Book #3,5,9,16,28, & Super Comics)

TERRY AND THE PIRATES
1939 - 1953 (By Milton Caniff)
Dell Publishing Co.

Large Feature Comic 2(1939) 57.00 172.00 630.00
Large Feature Comic 6(1938)-r/1936 dailies 57.00 172.00 630.00
Four Color 9(1940) 54.00 161.00 590.00
Large Feature Comic 27('41), 6('42) 47.00 142.00 520.00
Four Color 44('43) 37.00 112.00 410.00

Terry and the Pirates #3 © NY News Synd.

Terry-Toons Comics #10 © MEG

Tessie the Typist #5 © MEG

GD25 FN65 NM94

Four Color 101('45) 25.00 74.00 270.00
Buster Brown Shoes giveaway(1938)-32 pgs.; in color
25.00 75.00 200.00
Canada Dry Premiums-Books #1-3(1953, 36 pgs.; 2x5")-Harvey
12.00 36.00 95.00
Family Album(1942) 16.00 49.00 130.00
Gambles Giveaway (1938, 16 pgs.) 7.85 23.50 55.00
Gillmore Giveaway (1938, 24 pgs.) 8.50 26.00 60.00
Popped Wheat Giveaway(1938)-Strip reprints in full color; Caniff-a
1.00 2.00 5.00
Shoe Store giveaway (Weatherbird)(1938, 16 pgs., soft-c)(2-diff.)
7.85 23.50 55.00
Sparked Wheat Giveaway(1942, 16 pgs.)-In color 7.85 23.50 55.00

TERRY AND THE PIRATES
1941 (16 pgs.; regular size)(shipped folded in the mail)
Libby's Radio Premium GD25 FN65 VF82
"Adventure of the Ruby of Genghis Khan" - Each pg. is a puzzle that must be completed to read the story 189.00 567.00 1700.00

TERRY AND THE PIRATES (Formerly Boy Explorers; Long John Silver & the Pirates #30 on) (Daily strip-r) (Two #26's)
No. 3, 4/47 - No. 26, 4/51; No. 26, 6/55 - No. 28, 10/55
Harvey Publications/Charlton No. 26-28 GD25 FN65 NM94
3(#1)-Boy Explorers by S&K; Terry & the Pirates begin by Caniff; 1st app. The Dragon Lady 33.00 98.00 260.00
4-S&K Boy Explorers 17.50 53.00 140.00
5-11: 11-Man in Black app. by Powell 8.75 26.25 65.00
12-20: 16-Girl threatened with red hot poker 7.15 21.50 50.00
21-26(4/51)-Last Caniff issue & last pre-code issue 6.50 19.50 45.00
26-28('55)(Formerly This Is Suspense)-No Caniff-a 5.70 17.00 35.00
NOTE: ***Powell*** *a (Tommy Tween)-5-10, 12, 14; 15-17(1/2 to 2 pgs. each).*

TERRY BEARS COMICS (TerryToons, The... #4)
June, 1952 - No. 3, Mar, 1953
St. John Publishing Co.
1-By Paul Terry 5.70 17.50 40.00
2,3 5.00 15.00 30.00

TERRY-TOONS ALBUM (See Giant Comics Edition)

TERRY-TOONS COMICS (1st Series) (Becomes Paul Terry's Comics #85 on; later issues titled "Paul Terry's...")
Oct, 1942 - No. 86, May, 1951
Timely/Marvel No. 1-59 (8/47)(Becomes Best Western No. 58 on?, Marvel)/ St. John No. 60 (9/47) on
1 (Scarce)-Features characters that 1st app. on movie screen; Gandy Goose & Sourpuss begin; war-c; Gandy Goose c-1-37 122.00 366.00 1100.00
2 50.00 150.00 450.00
3-5 36.00 108.00 300.00
6,8-10 26.00 80.00 210.00
7-Hitler, Hirohito, Mussolini-c 33.00 98.00 260.00
11-20 16.00 49.00 130.00
21-37 11.30 34.00 90.00
38-Mighty Mouse begins (1st app., 11/45); Mighty Mouse-c begin, end #86; Gandy, Sourpuss welcome Mighty Mouse on-c 89.00 267.00 800.00
39-2nd app. Mighty Mouse 28.00 83.00 220.00
40-49: 43-Infinity-c 13.00 39.00 105.00
50-1st app. Heckle & Jeckle (11/46) 29.00 88.00 235.00
51-60: 55-Infinity-c. 60-(9/47)-Atomic explosion panel; 1st St. John issue
8.75 26.25 70.00
61-84 7.85 23.50 55.00
85,86-Same book as Paul Terry's Comics #85,86 with only a title change; published at same time? 7.85 23.50 55.00

TERRY-TOONS COMICS (2nd Series)
June, 1952 - No. 9, Nov, 1953; 1957; 1958
St. John Publishing Co./Pines
1-Gandy Goose & Sourpuss begin by Paul Terry 14.00 41.00 110.00
2 7.15 21.50 50.00
3-9 6.50 19.50 45.00
Giant Summer Fun Book 101,102-(Sum, 1957, Sum, 1958, 25¢, Pines)(TV) CBS Television Presents...; Tom Terrific, Mighty Mouse, Heckle & Jeckle Gandy Goose app. 10.00 30.00 80.00

TERRYTOONS, THE TERRY BEARS (Formerly Terry Bears Comics)
No. 4, Summer, 1958 (CBS Television Presents...)
Pines Comics
4 4.25 13.00 28.00

TESSIE THE TYPIST (Tiny Tessie #24; see Comedy Comics, Gay Comics & Joker Comics)
Summer, 1944 - No. 23, Aug, 1949
Timely/Marvel Comics (20CC)
1-Doc Rockblock & others by Wolverton 47.00 141.00 420.00
2-Wolverton's Powerhouse Pepper 29.00 86.00 230.00
3-(3/45)-No Wolverton 8.75 26.25 70.00
4,5,7,8-Wolverton-a. 4-(Fall/45) 19.00 56.00 150.00
6-Kurtzman's "Hey Look", 2 pgs. Wolverton-a 19.00 56.00 150.00
9-Wolverton's Powerhouse Pepper (8 pgs.) & 1 pg. Kurtzman's "Hey Look"
22.00 66.00 175.00
10-Wolverton's Powerhouse Pepper (4 pgs.) 20.00 60.00 160.00
11-Wolverton's Powerhouse Pepper (8 pgs.) 22.00 66.00 175.00
12-Wolverton's Powerhouse Pepper (4 pgs.) & 1 pg. Kurtzman's "Hey Look"
20.00 60.00 160.00
13-Wolverton's Powerhouse Pepper (4 pgs.) 20.00 60.00 160.00
14-Wolverton's Dr. Whackyhack (1 pg.); 1-1/2 pgs. Kurtzman's "Hey Look"
15.00 45.00 120.00
15-Kurtzman's "Hey Look" (3 pgs.) & 3 pgs. Giggles 'n' Grins
15.00 45.00 120.00
16-18-Kurtzman's "Hey Look" (?, 2 & 1 pg.) 10.50 32.00 85.00
19-Annie Oakley story (8 pgs.) 8.50 26.00 60.00
20-23: 20-Anti-Wertham editorial (2/49) 7.15 21.50 50.00
NOTE: *Lana app.-21. Millie The Model app.-13, 15, 17, 21. Rusty app.-10, 11, 13, 15, 17.*

TEXAN, THE (Fightin' Marines #15 on; Fightin' Texan #16 on)
Aug, 1948 - No. 15, Oct, 1951
St. John Publishing Co.
1-Buckskin Belle 13.00 39.00 95.00
2 7.50 22.50 50.00
3,10: 10-Oversized issue 7.00 21.00 45.00
4,5,7,15-Baker-c/a 11.30 34.00 90.00
6,9-Baker-c 8.50 26.00 60.00
8,11,13,14-Baker-c/a(2-3) each 11.30 34.00 90.00
12-All Matt Baker-c/a; Peyote story 16.00 47.00 120.00
NOTE: ***Matt Baker*** *c-4-9, 11-15.* ***Larsen*** *a-4-6, 8-10, 15.* ***Tuska*** *a-1, 2, 7-9.*

TEXAN, THE (TV)
No. 1027, Sept-Nov, 1959 - No. 1096, May-July, 1960
Dell Publishing Co.
Four Color 1027 (#1)-Photo-c 8.00 25.00 90.00
Four Color 1096-Rory Calhoun photo-c 7.00 22.00 80.00

TEXAS JOHN SLAUGHTER (See Walt Disney Presents, 4-Color #997, 1181 & #2)

TEXAS KID (See Two-Gun Western, Wild Western)
Jan, 1951 - No. 10, July, 1952
Marvel/Atlas Comics (LMC)
1-Origin; Texas Kid (alias Lance Temple) & his horse Thunder begin; Tuska-a 17.50 53.00 140.00
2 8.75 26.25 70.00
3-10 7.85 23.50 55.00
NOTE: ***Maneely*** *a-1-4; c-1, 3, 5-10.*

TEXAS RANGERS, THE (See Jace Pearson of... and Superior Stories #4)

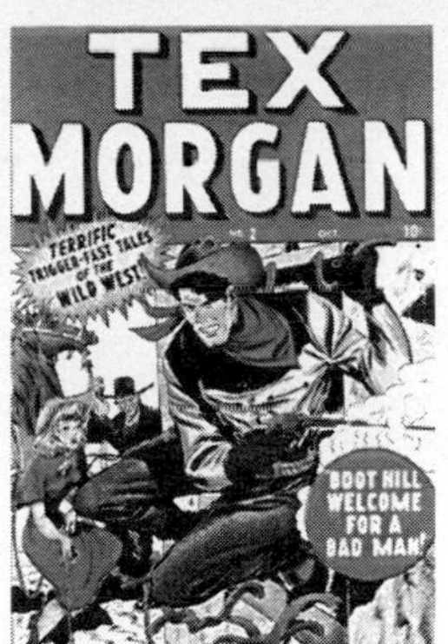

Tex Morgan #2 © MEG

Tex Ritter Western #11 © FAW

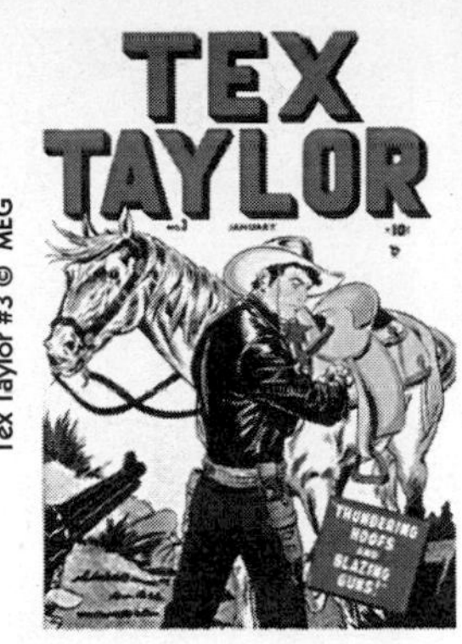

Tex Taylor #3 © MEG

TEXAS RANGERS IN ACTION (Formerly Captain Gallant or Scotland Yard?)
No. 5, July, 1956 - No. 79, Aug, 1970 (See Blue Bird Comics)
Charlton Comics

	GD25	FN65	NM94
5	6.50	19.50	45.00
6,7,9,10	4.25	13.00	26.00
8-Ditko-a (signed)	6.50	19.50	45.00
11-Williamson-a(5&8 pgs.); Torres/Williamson-a (5 pgs.)	7.15	21.50	50.00
12,14-20	4.00	10.00	20.00
13-Williamson-a (5 pgs); Torres, Morisi-a	5.70	17.00	40.00
21-30: 31-Last 10¢ issue?	2.00	6.00	16.00
31-59	1.75	5.25	14.00
60-Riley's Rangers begin	1.25	3.75	10.00
61-70: 65-1st app. 67-The Man Called Loco, origin	1.00	3.00	8.00
71-79		2.40	6.00
76(Modern Comics-r, 1977)		1.60	4.00

TEXAS SLIM (Also see A-1 Comics)
No. 2, 1947 - No.10, 1948
Magazine Enterprises

	GD25	FN65	NM94
A-1 2-8,10: Texas Slim & Dirty Dalton, The corsair, Teddy Rich, Dotty Dripple, Inca Iinca, Tommy Tinker, Little Mexico & Tugboat Tim, The Masqu´rader & others. 7-Corsair-c/s. 8-Intro Rodeo Ryan	4.25	13.00	28.00
A-1 9-All Texas Slim	5.00	15.00	30.00

TEX DAWSON, GUN-SLINGER (Gunslinger #2 on)
January, 1973 (20¢)(Also see Western Kid, 1st series)
Marvel Comics Group

	GD25	FN65	NM94
1-Steranko-c; Williamson-r (4 pgs.); Tex Dawson-r by Romita(3) from 1955; Tuska-r	1.50	4.50	12.00

TEX FARNUM (See Wisco)

TEX FARRELL (...Pride of the Wild West)
Mar-Apr, 1948
D. S. Publishing Co.

	GD25	FN65	NM94
1-Tex Farrell & his horse Lightning; Shelly-c	10.00	30.00	80.00

TEX GRANGER (Formerly Calling All Boys; see True Comics)
No. 18, June, 1948 - No. 24, Sept, 1949
Parents' Magazine Institute/Commondod

	GD25	FN65	NM94
18-Tex Granger & his horse Bullet begin	8.75	26.25	70.00
19	7.15	21.50	50.00
20-24: 22-Wild Bill Hickok story. 23-Vs. Billy the Kid; Tim Holt app.	5.70	17.00	40.00

TEX MORGAN (See Blaze Carson and Wild Western)
Aug, 1948 - No. 9, Feb, 1950
Marvel Comics (CCC)

	GD25	FN65	NM94
1-Tex Morgan, his horse Lightning & sidekick Lobo begin	21.00	64.00	170.00
2	15.00	45.00	120.00
3-6: 3,4-Arizona Annie app.	9.50	28.00	75.00
7-9: All photo-c. 7-Captain Tootsie by Beck. 8-18 pg. story "The Terror of Rimrock Valley"; Diablo app.	15.00	45.00	120.00

NOTE: *Tex Taylor app.-6, 7, 9.* ***Brodsky*** *c-6.* ***Syd Shores*** *c-2, 5.*

TEX RITTER WESTERN (Movie star; singing cowboy; see Six-Gun Heroes and Western Hero)
Oct, 1950 - No. 46, May, 1959 (Photo-c: 1-21)
Fawcett No. 1-20 (1/54)/Charlton No. 21 on

	GD25	FN65	NM94
1-Tex Ritter, his stallion White Flash & dog Fury begin; photo front/back-c begin	58.00	174.00	520.00
2	26.00	80.00	210.00
3-5: 5-Last photo back-c	20.00	60.00	160.00
6-10	15.50	47.00	125.00
11-19	10.50	32.00	85.00
20-Last Fawcett issue (1/54)	12.00	36.00	95.00
21-1st Charlton issue; photo-c (3/54)	13.00	39.00	105.00
22-B&W photo back-c begin, end #32	8.75	26.25	65.00
23-30: 23-25-Young Falcon app.	7.85	23.50	55.00
31-38,40-45	6.50	19.50	45.00
39-Williamson-a; Whitman-c (1/58)	8.50	26.00	60.00
46-Last issue	7.85	23.50	55.00

TEX TAYLOR (...The Fighting Cowboy on-c #1, 2)(See Blaze Carson, Kid Colt, Tex Morgan, Wild West, Wild Western, & Wisco)
Sept, 1948 - No. 9, March, 1950
Marvel Comics (HPC)

	GD25	FN65	NM94
1-Tex Taylor & his horse Fury begin	23.00	68.00	180.00
2	12.00	38.00	100.00
3	11.30	34.00	90.00
4-6: All photo-c. 4-Anti-Wertham editorial. 5,6-Blaze Carson app.	13.00	39.00	105.00
7-Photo-c; 18 pg. Movie-Length Thriller "Trapped in Time's Lost Land!" with sabre toothed tigers, dinosaurs; Diablo app.	15.00	45.00	120.00
8-Photo-c; 18 pg. Movie-Length Thriller "The Mystery of Devil-Tree Plateau!" with dwarf horses, dwarf people & a lost miniature Inca type village; Diablo app.	15.00	45.00	120.00
9-Photo-c; 18 pg. Movie-Length Thriller "Guns Along the Border!" Captain Tootsie by Schreiber; Nimo the Mountain Lion app.	15.00	45.00	120.00

NOTE: ***Syd Shores*** *c-1-3.*

THANE OF BAGARTH (Also see Hercules, 1967 series)
No. 24, Oct, 1985 - No. 25, Dec, 1985
Charlton Comics

	GD25	FN65	NM94
24,25			1.00

THANOS QUEST, THE (See Capt. Marvel #25, Infinity Gauntlet, Iron Man #55, Logan's Run, Marvel Feature #12, Silver Surfer #34 & Warlock #9)
1990 - No. 2, 1990 ($4.95, squarebound, 52 pgs.)
Marvel Comics

	GD25	FN65	NM94
1,2-Both have Starlin scripts & covers		2.00	5.00
1,2-($4.95, 2nd printings)		2.00	5.00

THAT CHEMICAL REFLEX
1994 ($2.50, B&W, one-shot, mature)
CFD Productions

	GD25	FN65	NM94
1-Dan Brereton-c/a		1.00	2.50

THAT DARN CAT (See Movie Comics & Walt Disney Showcase #19)

THAT'S MY POP! GOES NUTS FOR FAIR
1939 (76 pgs., B&W)
Bystander Press

	GD25	FN65	NM94
nn-by Milt Gross	21.00	64.00	170.00

THAT THE WORLD MAY BELIEVE
No date (16 pgs.) (Graymoor Friars distr.)
Catechetical Guild Giveaway

	GD25	FN65	NM94
nn	1.60	4.00	8.00

THAT WILKIN BOY (Meet Bingo...)
Jan, 1969 - No. 52, Oct, 1982
Archie Publications

	GD25	FN65	NM94
1	2.50	7.50	20.00
2-26: 12-26-Giants	1.10	3.30	9.00
27-40		1.60	4.00
41-52		.80	2.00

THB
Oct, 1994 - Present ($5.50/$2.50/$2.95, B&W)
Horse Press

	GD25	FN65	NM94
1 ($5.50)	1.50	4.50	12.00

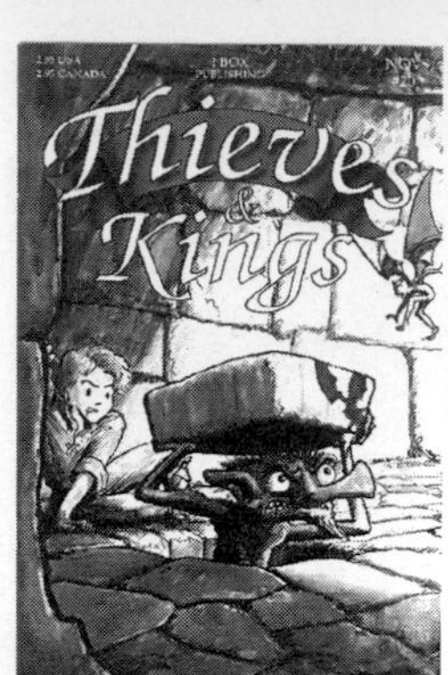

Thieves & Kings #20 © Mark Oakley

The Thing! #9 © CC

This is War #7 © STD

GD25 FN65 NM94

1 (2nd Printing)-r/#1 w/new material 1.00 2.50
2 ($2.50) 1.25 3.75 10.00
3-5 1.60 4.00
69 (1995, no price, low distribution, 12 pgs.)-story reprinted in #1 (2nd Printing). 1.20 3.00
Giant THB-($4.95) 2.00 5.00

T.H.E. CAT (TV)
Mar, 1967 - No. 4, Oct, 1967 (All have photo-c)
Dell Publishing Co.
1 2.50 7.50 22.00
2-4 2.00 6.00 16.00

THERE'S A NEW WORLD COMING
1973 (35/49¢)
Spire Christian Comics/Fleming H. Revell Co.
nn 1.00

THEY ALL KISSED THE BRIDE (See Cinema Comics Herald)

THEY RING THE BELL
1946
Fox Feature Syndicate
1 9.50 28.00 75.00

THIEF OF BAGHDAD
No. 1229, Oct-Dec, 1961 (one-shot)
Dell Publishing Co.
Four Color 1229-Movie, Crandall/Evans-a, photo-c 5.50 16.50 60.00

THIEVES & KINGS
1994 - Present ($2.35, B&W, bi-monthly)
I Box
1 2.40 6.00
1-(2nd printing), 2-16 1.20 3.00
17,18 .90 2.35

THIMK (Magazine) (Satire)
May, 1958 - No. 6, May, 1959
Counterpoint
1 5.70 17.00 38.00
2-6 4.00 12.00 24.00

THING!, THE (Blue Beetle #18 on)
Feb, 1952 - No. 17, Nov, 1954
Song Hits No. 1,2/Capitol Stories/Charlton
1-Weird/horror stories in all; shrunken head-c 61.00 183.00 525.00
2,3 43.00 129.00 360.00
4-6,8,10: 5-Severed head-c; headlights 40.00 120.00 300.00
7-Injury to eye-c & inside panel; E.C. swipes from Vault of Horror #28 53.00 159.00 450.00
9-Used in **SOTI**, pg. 388 & illo "Stomping on the face is a form of brutality which modern children learn early" 60.00 181.00 500.00
11-Necronomicon story; Hansel & Gretel parody; Injury-to-eye panel; Check-a 47.00 141.00 400.00
12-1st published Ditko-c; "Cinderella" parody; lingerie panels. Ditko-a 62.00 187.00 525.00
13,15-Ditko-c/a(3 & 5); 13-Ditko E.C. swipe/Haunt of Fear #15(#1) "House of Horror" 62.00 187.00 525.00
14-Extreme violence/torture; Rumpelstiltskin story; Ditko-c/a(4) 62.00 187.00 525.00
16-Injury to eye panel 40.00 120.00 320.00
17-Ditko-c; classic parody "Through the Looking Glass"; Powell-r/Beware Terror Tales #1 & recolored 58.00 174.00 480.00
NOTE: *Excessive violence, severed heads, injury to eye are common No. 5 on.* ***Al Fago*** *c-4.* ***Forgione*** *c-1i, 2, 6, 8, 9.* ***Palais*** *c-16. All* ***Ditko*** *issues #14, 15.*

THING, THE (See Fantastic Four, Marvel Fanfare, Marvel Feature #11, 12 & Marvel Two-In-One)
July, 1983 - No. 36, June, 1986
Marvel Comics Group
1-Life story of Ben Grimm; Byrne scripts begin .90 2.25
2-36: 5-Spider-Man, She-Hulk app. 1.30
NOTE: ***Byrne*** *a-2i, 7; c-1, 7, 36i; scripts-1-13, 19-22.* ***Sienkiewicz*** *c-13i.*

THING, THE (From Another World)
1991 - No. 2, 1992 ($2.95, mini-series, stiff-c)
Dark Horse Comics
1,2-Based on Universal movie; painted-c/a 1.20 3.00

THING FROM ANOTHER WORLD: CLIMATE OF FEAR, THE
July, 1992 - No. 4, Dec, 1992 ($2.50, mini-series)
Dark Horse Comics
1-4: Painted-c 1.00 2.50

THING FROM ANOTHER WORLD: ETERNAL VOWS
Dec, 1993 - No. 4, 1994 ($2.50, mini-series)
Dark Horse Comics
1-4-Gulacy-c/a 1.00 2.50

THIRD WORLD WAR
1990 - No. 6, 1991 ($2.50, high quality, thick-c, mature)
Fleetway Publications (Quality)
1-6 1.25 2.50

THIRTEEN (...Going on 18)
11-1/61-62 - No. 25, 12/67; No. 26, 7/69 - No. 29, 1/71
Dell Publishing Co.
1 5.00 15.00 50.00
2-10 4.00 12.00 40.00
11-29: 26-29-r 3.00 9.00 30.00
NOTE: ***John Stanley*** *script-No. 3-29; art?*

13: ASSASSIN
1990 - No. 8, 1991 ($2.95, 44 pgs.)
TSR, Inc.
1-8: Agent 13; Alcala-a(i); Springer back-up-a 1.20 3.00

THIRTY SECONDS OVER TOKYO (See American Library)

THIS IS SUSPENSE! (Formerly Strange Suspense Stories; Strange Suspense Stories #27 on)
No. 23, Feb, 1955 - No. 26, Aug, 1955
Charlton Comics
23-Wood-a(r)/A Star Presentation #3 "Dr. Jekyll & Mr. Hyde"; last pre-code issue 22.00 66.00 155.00
24-Censored Fawcett-r; Evans-a (r/Suspense Detective #1) 12.00 36.00 85.00
25,26: 26-Marcus Swayze-a 8.35 25.00 50.00

THIS IS THE PAYOFF (See Pay-Off)

THIS IS WAR
No. 5, July, 1952 - No. 9, May, 1953
Standard Comics
5-Toth-a 11.50 34.00 80.00
6,9-Toth-a 10.00 30.00 65.00
7,8: 8-Ross Andru-c 5.00 15.00 30.00

THIS IS YOUR LIFE, DONALD DUCK (See Donald Duck..., Four Color #1109)

THIS MAGAZINE IS CRAZY (Crazy #? on)
V3#2, July, 1957 - V4#8, Feb, 1959 (25¢, magazine, 68 pgs.)
Charlton Publ. (Humor Magazines)
V3#2-V4#7: V4#5-Russian Sputnik-c parody 5.00 15.00 30.00
V4#8-Davis-a (8 pgs.) 5.70 17.00 38.00

THIS MAGAZINE IS HAUNTED (Danger and Adventure #22 on)

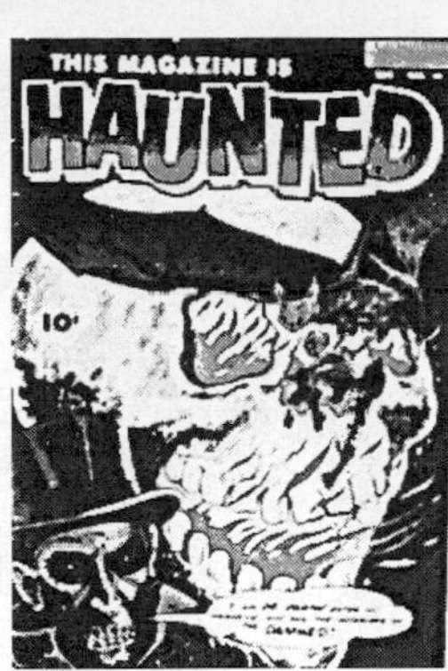

This Magazine is Haunted #14 © FAW

Thor #366 © MEG

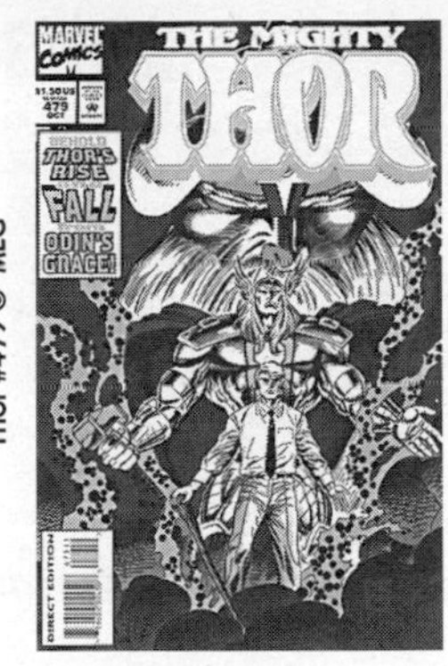

Thor #479 © MEG

GD25 FN65 NM94 — GD25 FN65 NM94

Oct, 1951 - No. 14, 12/53; No. 15, 2/54 - V3#21, Nov, 1954
Fawcett Publications/Charlton No. 15(2/54) on

1-Evans-a; Dr. Death as host begins 46.00 138.00 400.00
2,5-Evans-a 35.00 105.00 275.00
3,4: 3-Vampire-c/story 21.00 64.00 170.00
6-9,11,12,14 17.00 49.00 120.00
10-Severed head-c 24.00 73.00 190.00
13-Severed head-c/story 24.00 71.00 180.00
15,20: 15-Dick Giordano-c. 20-Cover is swiped from panel in The Thing #16 13.50 41.00 100.00
16,19-Ditko-c. 19-Injury-to-eye panel; story-r/#1 29.00 86.00 220.00
17-Ditko-c/a(4); blood drainage story 36.00 107.00 270.00
18-Ditko-c/a(1 story); E.C. swipe/Haunt of Fear #5; injury-to-eye panel; reprints "Caretaker of the Dead" from Beware Terror Tales & recolored 30.00 90.00 230.00
21-Ditko-c, Evans-r/This Magazine Is Haunted #1 27.00 81.00 210.00

NOTE: ***Baily*** *a-1, 3, 4, 21r/#1.* ***Moldoff*** *c/a-1-13.* ***Powell*** *a-3-5, 11, 12, 17.* ***Shuster*** *a-18-20. Issues 19-21 have reprints which have been recolored from This Magazine is Haunted #1.*

THIS MAGAZINE IS HAUNTED (2nd Series) (Formerly Zaza the Mystic; Outer Space #17 on)
V2#12, July, 1957 - V2#16, May, 1958
Charlton Comics

V2#12-14-Ditko-c/a in all 30.00 90.00 230.00
15-No Ditko-c/a 5.70 17.00 35.00
16-Ditko-a 19.00 58.00 140.00

THIS MAGAZINE IS WILD (See Wild)

THIS WAS YOUR LIFE (Religious)
1964 (3 1/2 x 5 1/2", 40 pgs., B&W and red)
Jack T. Chick Publ.

nn 1.00
Another version (5x2 3/4", 26 pgs.) 1.20

THOR (See Avengers #1, Giant-Size..., Marvel Collectors Item Classics, Marvel Graphic Novel #33, Marvel Preview, Marvel Spectacular, Marvel Treasury Edition, Special Marvel Edition & Tales of Asgard)

THOR (Journey Into Mystery #1-125, 503-on)(The Mighty Thor #413-490)
No. 126, Mar, 1966 - No. 502, Sept, 1996
Marvel Comics Group

126-Thor continues (#125-130 Thor vs. Hercules) 12.50 38.00 125.00
127-133,135-140: 127-1st app. Pluto 4.50 13.50 45.00
134-Intro High Evolutionary 5.65 17.00 56.00
141-157,159,160: 146-Inhumans begin (early app.), end #151 (see Fantastic Four #45 for 1st app.). 146,147-Origin The Inhumans. 148,149-Origin Black Bolt in each. 149-Origin Medusa, Crystal, Maximus, Gorgon, Kornak 3.00 9.00 30.00
158-Origin-r/#83; 158,159-Origin Dr. Blake (Thor) 6.25 18.75 62.00
161,167,170-179: 179-Last Kirby issue 2.50 7.50 20.00
162,168,169-Origin Galactus; Kirby-a 3.20 9.60 32.00
163,164-2nd & 3th brief cameo Warlock (Him) 2.50 7.50 20.00
165-1st full app. Warlock (Him) (6/69, see Fantastic Four #67); last 12¢ issue; Kirby-a 5.50 16.50 55.00
166-2nd full app. Warlock (Him); battles Thor 4.20 12.60 42.00
180,181-Neal Adams-a 1.75 5.25 14.00
182-192,194-200 1.00 2.80 7.00
193-(25¢, 52 pgs.); Silver Surfer x-over 4.00 12.00 40.00
201-247,249: 225-Intro. Firelord 2.00 5.00
248,250-(Regular 25¢ edition)(6,8/76) 2.00 5.00
248,250-(30¢-c, limited distribution) 2.50 7.50 20.00
251-280: 271-Iron Man x-over. 274-Death of Balder the Brave 1.30 3.25
281-299: 294-Origin Asgard & Odin 1.10 2.75
300-(12/80)-End of Asgard; origin of Odin & The Destroyer 2.40 6.00
301-336: 316-Iron Man x-over .80 2.00
337-Simonson-c/a begins, ends #382; Beta Ray Bill becomes new Thor 2.40 6.00
338-Two variants exist, 60¢ & 75¢ cover price .80 2.00
339,340: 340-Donald Blake returns as Thor .80 2.00
341-373,375-381,383: 341-Clark Kent & Lois Lane cameo. 373-X-Factor tie-in 1.50
374-Mutant Massacre; X-Factor app. 1.20 3.00
382-($1.25)-Anniversary issue; last Simonson-a 1.00 2.50
384-Intro. new Thor .80 2.00
385-399,401-410,413-428: 385-Hulk x-over. 391-Spider-Man x-over; 1st Eric Masterson. 395-Intro Earth Force. 408-Eric Masterson becomes Thor. 427, 428-Excalibur x-over 1.25
400-($1.75, 68 pgs.)-Origin Loki 1.00 2.50
411-Intro New Warriors (appears in costume in last panel); Juggernaut-c/story 1.20 3.00
412-1st full app. New Warriors (Marvel Boy, Kid Nova, Namorita, Night Thrasher, Firestar & Speedball) 1.60 4.00
429,430-Ghost Rider x-over .80 2.00
431,434-443: 434-Capt. America x-over. 437-Thor vs. Quasar; Hercules app.; Tales of Asgard back-up stories begin. 443-Dr. Strange & Silver Surfer x-over; last $1.00-c 1.50
432-($1.50, 52 pgs.)-Thor's 300th app. (vs. Loki); reprints origin & 1st app. from Journey into Mystery #83 1.30 3.25
433-Intro new Thor 1.60 4.00
444-449,451-473: 448-Spider-Man-c/story. 455,456-Dr. Strange back-up. 457-Old Thor returns (3 pgs.). 459-Intro Thunderstrike. 460-Starlin scripts begin. 465-Super Skrull app. 466-Drax app. 469,470-Infinity Watch x-over. 472-Intro the Godlings 1.50
450-($2.50, 68 pgs.)-Flip-book format; r/story JIM #87 (1st Loki) plus-c plus a gallery of past-c; gatefold-c 1.20 3.00
474,476-481,483-499,501,502: 474-Begin $1.50-c; bound-in trading card sheet. 459-Intro Thunderstrike, 460-Starlin scripts begin. 472-Intro the Godlings. 49The Absorbing Man app. 491-Warren Ellis scripts begins, ends #494; Deodato-c/a begins. 492-Reintro The Enchantress; Beta Ray Bill dies. 495-Wm. Messner-Loebs scripts begin; Isherwood-c/a. 501-Reintro Red Norvell. 502-Onslaught tie-in; Red Norvell, Jane Foster & Hela app. 1.50
475 ($2.00, 52 pgs.)-Regular edition .80 2.00
475 ($2.50, 52 pgs.)-Collectors edition w/foil embossed-c 1.00 2.50
482 ($2.95, 84 pgs.)-400th issue 1.20 3.00
500 ($2.50)-Double-size; wraparound-c; Deodato-c/a; Dr. Strange app. 2.00 5.00
Special 2(9/66)-See Journey Into Mystery for 1st annual 5.00 15.00 50.00
King Size Special 3(1/71) 1.25 3.75 10.00
Special 4(12/71)-r/Thor #131,132 & JIM #113 1.25 3.75 10.00
Annual 5-8: 5(11/76). 6(10/77)-Guardians of the Galaxy app. 7(1978). 8(1979)-Thor vs. Zeus-c/story 1.00 2.80 7.00
Annual 9-12: 9('81). 10('82). 11('83). 12('84) 1.40 3.50
Annual 13-16: 13(1985). 14('89, $2.00, 68 pgs.)-Atlantis Attacks. 15('90, $2.00, 68 pgs.). 16('91, $2.00, 68 pgs.)-3 pg. origin; Guardians of the Galaxy x-over .80 2.00
Annual 17 (1992, $2.25, 68 pgs.) .90 2.25
Annual 18 (1993, $2.95, 68 pgs.)-Polybagged w/card 1.20 3.00
Annual 19 (1994, $2.95, 68 pgs.) 1.20 3.00
...Alone Against the Celestials nn (6/92, $5.95)-r/Thor #387-389 2.40 6.00
...: Worldengine (8/96, $9.95)-r/#491-494; Deodato-c/a; story & new intermission by Warren Ellis.

NOTE: ***Neal Adams*** *a-180,181; c-179-181.* ***Austin*** *a-342i, 346i; c-312i.* ***Buscema*** *a(p)-178, 182-213, 215-226, 231-238, 241-253, 254r, 256-259, 272-278, 283-285, 370, Annual 6, 8, 11i; c(p)-175, 182-196, 198-200, 202-204, 206, 211, 212, 215, 219, 221, 226, 256, 259, 261, 262, 272-278, 283, 289, 370, Annual 6.* ***Everett*** *a(i)-143, 170-175; c(i)-171, 172, 174, 176, 241.* ***Gil Kane*** *a-318p; c(p)-201, 205, 207-210, 216, 220, 222, 223, 231, 233-240, 242, 243, 318.* ***Kirby*** *a(p)-126-177, 179, 194r, 254r; c(p)-126-169, 171-174, 176-178, 249-253, 255, 257, 258, Annual*

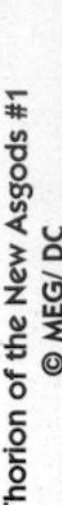
Thorion of the New Asgods #1 © MEG/ DC

3-D Batman 1953 © DC

Three Dimensional Tales From The Crypt #2 © EC

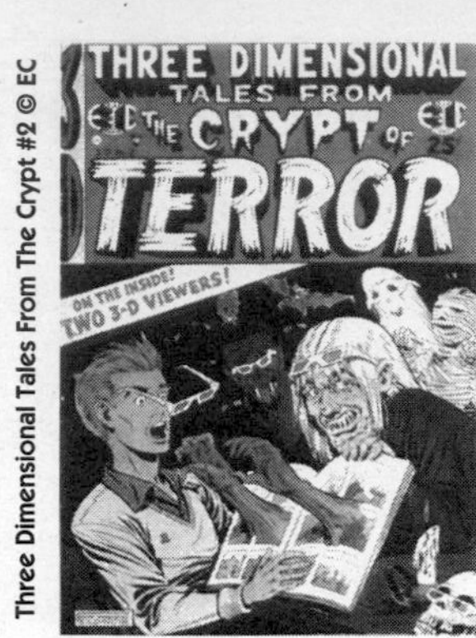

GD25 FN65 NM94

5, Special 1-4. ***Mooney*** *a(i)-201, 204, 214-216, 218, 322i, 324i, 325i, 327i.* ***Sienkiewicz*** *c-332, 333, 335.* ***Simonson*** *a-260-271p, 337-354, 357-367, 380, Annual 7p; c-260, 263-271, 337-355, 357-369, 371, 373-382, Annual 7.* ***Starlin*** *c-213.*

THOR CORPS
Sept, 1993 - No. 4, Jan, 1994 ($1.75, limited series)
Marvel Comics

1-4: 1-Invaders cameo. 2-Invaders app. 3-Spider-Man 2099, Rawhide Kid, Two-Gun Kid & Kid Colt app. 4-Painted-c .70 1.75

THORION OF THE NEW ASGODS
June, 1997 ($1.95, one-shot)
Marvel Comics (Amalgam)

1-Keith Giffen-s/John Romita Jr.-c/a .80 2.00

THOR: THE LEGEND
Sept, 1996 ($3.95, one-shot)
Marvel Comics

nn-Tribute issue 1.60 4.00

THOSE MAGNIFICENT MEN IN THEIR FLYING MACHINES (See Movie Comics)

THRAX
Nov, 1996 ($2.95, one-shot)
Event Comics

1 1.20 3.00

THREE CABALLEROS (Walt Disney's...)
No. 71, 1945
Dell Publishing Co.

Four Color 71-by Walt Kelly, c/a 75.00 225.00 825.00

THREE CHIPMUNKS, THE (TV)
No. 1042, Oct-Dec, 1959
Dell Publishing Co.

Four Color 1042 (#1)-(Alvin, Simon & Theodore) 4.50 13.50 50.00

THREE COMICS (Also see Spiritman)
1944 (10¢, 52 pgs.) (2 different covers exist)
The Penny King Co.

1,3,4-Lady Luck, Mr. Mystic, The Spirit app. (3 Spirit sections bound together); Lou Fine-a 19.00 56.00 150.00

NOTE: *No. 1 contains Spirit Sections 4/9/44 - 4/23/44, and No. 4 is also from 4/44.*

3-D (NOTE: The prices of all the 3-D comics listed include glasses. Deduct 40-50 percent if glasses are missing, and reduce slightly if glasses are loose.)

3-D ACTION
Jan, 1954 (Oversized, 15¢)(2 pairs of glasses included)
Atlas Comics (ACI)

1-Battle Brady; Sol Brodsky-c 33.00 98.00 260.00

3-D ADVENTURE COMICS
Aug, 1986 (one shot)
Stats, Etc.

1-Promo material 1.50

3-D ALIEN TERROR
June, 1986 ($2.50)
Eclipse Comics

1-Old Witch, Crypt-Keeper, Vault Keeper cameo; Morrow, John Pound-a, Yeates-c 1.00 2.50
...in 2-D: 100 copies signed, numbered(B&W) 2.00 5.00

3-D ANIMAL FUN (See Animal Fun)

3-D BATMAN (Also see Batman 3-D)
1953 (Reprinted in 1966)
National Periodical Publications

1953-(25¢)-Reprints Batman #42 & 48 (Penguin-c/story); Tommy Tomorrow app.; came with pair of 3-D Bat glasses 92.00 276.00 825.00
1966-Tommy Tomorrow app.; Penguin-c/story(r); has inside-c photos of Batman & Robin from TV show (50¢) 31.00 94.00 250.00

3-D CIRCUS
1953 (25¢, came w/glasses)
Fiction House Magazines (Real Adventures Publ.)

1 34.00 101.00 270.00

3-D COMICS (See Mighty Mouse, Tor and Western Fighters)

3-D DOLLY
December, 1953 (25¢, came with 2 pairs of glasses)
Harvey Publications

1-Richie Rich story redrawn from his 1st app. in Little Dot #1; shows cover in 3-D on inside 20.00 60.00 160.00

3-D-ELL
1953 - No. 3, 1953 (3-D comics) (25¢, came w/glasses)
Dell Publishing Co.

1,2-Rootie Kazootie (#2 exist?) 36.00 108.00 290.00
3-Flukey Luke 33.00 98.00 260.00

3-D EXOTIC BEAUTIES
Nov, 1990 ($2.95, 28 pgs.)
The 3-D Zone

1-L.B. Cole-c 1.20 3.00

3-D FEATURES PRESENTS JET PUP
Oct-Dec (Winter on-c), 1953 (25¢, came w/glasses)
Dimensions Publications

1-Irving Spector-a(2) 34.00 101.00 270.00

3-D FUNNY MOVIES
1953 (25¢, came w/glasses)
Comic Media

1-Bugsey Bear & Paddy Pelican 34.00 101.00 270.00

THREE-DIMENSION ADVENTURES (Superman)
1953 (25¢, large size, came w/glasses)
National Periodical Publications

nn-Origin Superman (new art) 92.00 276.00 825.00

THREE DIMENSIONAL ALIEN WORLDS (See Alien Worlds)
July, 1984 (1st Ray Zone 3-D book)(one-shot)
Pacific Comics

1-Bolton-p(a); Stevens-p(i); Art Adams 1st published-p(a) 1.20 3.00

THREE DIMENSIONAL DNAGENTS (See New DNAgents)

THREE DIMENSIONAL E. C. CLASSICS (Three Dimensional Tales From the Crypt No. 2)
Spring, 1954 (Prices include glasses; came with 2 pair)
E. C. Comics

1-Stories by Wood (Mad #3), Krigstein (W.S. #7), Evans (F.C. #13), & Ingels (CSS #5); Kurtzman-c (rare in high grade due to unstable paper) 70.00 210.00 630.00

NOTE: *Stories redrawn to 3-D format. Original stories not necessarily by artists listed. CSS: Crime SuspenStories; F.C.: Frontline Combat; W.S.: Weird Science.*

THREE DIMENSIONAL TALES FROM THE CRYPT (Formerly Three Dimensional E. C. Classics)(Cover title: ...From the Crypt of Terror)
No. 2, Spring, 1954 (Prices include glasses; came with 2 pair)
E. C. Comics

2-Davis (TFTC #25), Elder (VOH #14), Craig (TFTC #24), & Orlando (TFTC #22) stories; Feldstein-c (rare in high grade due to unstable paper) 72.00 216.00 650.00

NOTE: *Stories redrawn to 3-D format. Original stories not necessarily by artists listed. TFTC: Tales From the Crypt; VOH: Vault of Horror.*

3-D Tales of the West #1 © ATLAS

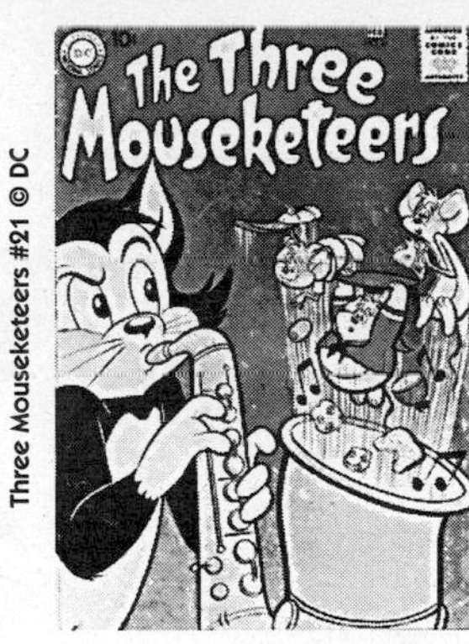

Three Mouseketeers #21 © DC

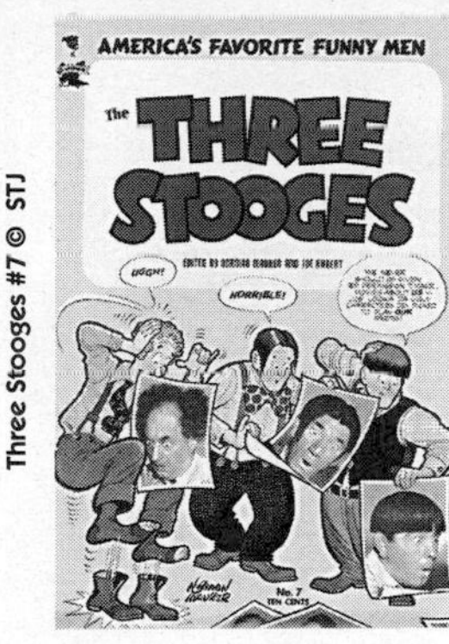

Three Stooges #7 © STJ

GD25 FN65 NM94

3-D LOVE
Dec, 1953 (25¢, came w/glasses)
Steriographic Publ. (Mikeross Publ.)

1 34.00 101.00 270.00

3-D NOODNICK (See Noodnick)

3-D ROMANCE
Jan, 1954 (25¢, came w/glasses)
Steriographic Publ. (Mikeross Publ.)

1 34.00 101.00 270.00

3-D SHEENA, JUNGLE QUEEN (Also see Sheena 3-D)
1953 (25¢, came w/glasses)
Fiction House Magazines

1-Maurice Whitman-c 58.00 174.00 525.00

3-D SUBSTANCE
July, 1990 ($2.95, 28 pgs.)
The 3-D Zone

1-Ditko-c/a(r) 1.20 3.00

3-D TALES OF THE WEST
Jan, 1954 (Oversized) (15¢, came with 2 pair of glasses)
Atlas Comics (CPS)

1 (3-D)-Sol Brodsky-c 35.00 105.00 280.00

3-D THREE STOOGES (Also see Three Stooges)
Sept, 1986 - No. 2, Nov, 1986; No. 3, Oct, 1987; No. 4, 1989 ($2.50)
Eclipse Comics

1-3 (10/87)-Maurer-r 1.00 2.50
4 (1989, $3.50)-Reprints "Three Missing Links" 1.40 3.50
1-3 (2-D) 1.20 3.00

3-D WHACK (See Whack)

3-D ZONE, THE
Feb, 1987 - No. 20, 1989 ($2.50)
The 3-D Zone (Renegade Press)/Ray Zone

1-10: 1-r/A Star Presentation, 2-Wolverton-r, 3-Picture Scope Jungle Advs., 4-Electric Fear, 5-Krazy Kat-r, 6-Ratfink, 7-Hollywood 3-D Jayne Mansfield photo-c, 8-High Seas 3-D, 9-Redmask-r, 10-Jet 3-D; Powell & Williamson-r 1.00 2.50
11-20: 11-Danse MAcabre; Matt Fox c/a(r). 12-3-D Presidents. 13-Flash Gordon. 14-Tyranostar. 15-3-Dementia Comics; Kurtzman-c, Kubert, Maurer-a. 16-Space Vixens; Dave Stevens-c/a. 17-Thrilling Love. 18-Spacehawk; Wolverton-r. 19-Cracked Classics. 20-Commander Battle and His Atomic Submarine 1.00 2.50

NOTE: ***Davis** r-19. **Ditko** r-19. **Elder** r-19. **Everett** r-19. **Feldstein** r-17. **Frazetta** r-17. **Heath** r-19. **Kamen** r-17. **Severin** r-19. **Ward** r-17,19. **Wolverton** r-2,18,19. **Wood** r-1,17. Photo c-12*

3 LITTLE PIGS (Disney)(...and the Wonderful Magic Lamp)
No. 218, Mar, 1949
Dell Publishing Co.

Four Color 218 (#1) 11.00 33.00 120.00

3 LITTLE PIGS, THE (See Walt Disney Showcase #15 & 21)
May, 1964; No. 2, Sept, 1968 (Walt Disney)
Gold Key

1-Reprints Four Color #218 2.50 7.50 20.00
2 1.50 4.50 12.00

THREE MOUSEKETEERS, THE (1st Series)(See Funny Stuff #1)
3-4/56 - No. 24, 9-10/59; No. 25, 8-9/60 - No. 26, 10-12/60
National Periodical Publications

1 17.50 52.00 175.00
2 9.00 27.00 90.00
3-10: 6,8-Grey tone-c 7.00 21.00 70.00
11-26: 24-Cover says 11/59, inside says 9-10/59 5.50 16.50 55.00

GD25 FN65 NM94

NOTE: ***Rube Grossman** a-1-26. **Sheldon Mayer** a-1-8; c-1-7.*

THREE MOUSEKETEERS, THE (2nd Series) (See Super DC Giant)
May-June, 1970 - No. 7, May-June, 1971 (#5-7: 68 pgs.)
National Periodical Publications

1-Mayer-r in all 3.00 9.00 30.00
2-4 2.25 6.75 18.00
5-7: (68 pgs.). 5-Dodo & the Frog, Bo Bunny & Doodles Duck begin 3.00 9.00 30.00

THREE MUSKETEERS, THE (See Disney's The Three Musketeers)

THREE NURSES (Confidential Diary #12-17; Career Girl Romances #24 on)
V3#18, May, 1963 - V3#23, Mar, 1964
Charlton Comics

V3#18-23 1.50 4.50 12.00

THREE RASCALS
1958; 1963
I. W. Enterprises

I.W. Reprint #1,2,10: 1-(Says Super Comics on inside)-(M.E.'s Clubhouse Rascals). #2-(1958). 10-(1963)-r/#1 2.40 6.00

THREE RING COMICS
March, 1945
Spotlight Publishers

1-Funny animal 10.50 32.00 85.00

THREE RING COMICS (Also see Captain Wizard & Meteor Comics)
April, 1946
Century Publications

1-Prankster-c; Captain Wizard, Impossible Man, Race Wilkins, King O'Leary, & Dr. Mercy app. 26.00 80.00 210.00

THREE ROCKETEERS (See Blast-Off)

THREE STOOGES (See Comic Album #18, Top Comics, The Little Stooges, March of Comics #232, 248, 268, 280, 292, 304, 316, 336, 373, Movie Classics & Comics & 3-D Three Stooges)

THREE STOOGES
Feb, 1949 - No. 2, May, 1949; Sept, 1953 - No. 7, Oct, 1954
Jubilee No. 1/St. John No. 1 (9/53) on

1-(Scarce, 1949)-Kubert-a; infinity-c 83.00 250.00 750.00
2-(Scarce)-Kubert, Maurer-a 64.00 192.00 575.00
1(9/53)-Hollywood Stunt Girl by Kubert (7 pgs.) 56.00 168.00 500.00
2(3-D, 10/53, 25¢)-Came w/glasses; Stunt Girl story by Kubert 36.00 108.00 325.00
3(3-D, 10/53, 25¢)-Came w/glasses; has 3-D-c 36.00 108.00 325.00
4(3/54)-7(10/54): 4-1st app. Li'l Stooge? 31.00 94.00 250.00

NOTE: *All issues have **Kubert-Maurer** art & **Maurer** covers. 6, 7-Partial photo-c.*

THREE STOOGES
No. 1043, Oct-Dec, 1959 - No. 55, June, 1972
Dell Publishing Co./Gold Key No. 10 (10/62) on

Four Color 1043 (#1) 18.00 55.00 200.00
Four Color 1078,1127,1170,1187 10.00 30.00 110.00
6(9-11/61) - 10: 6-Professor Putter begins; ends #16 8.00 25.00 90.00
11-14,16-20: 17-The Little Monsters begin (5/64)(1st app.?) 6.40 19.00 70.00
15-Go Around the World in a Daze (movie scenes) 7.00 22.00 80.00
21,23-30 5.50 16.50 60.00
22-Movie scenes from "The Outlaws Is Coming" 6.40 19.00 70.00
31-55 4.50 13.50 50.00

NOTE: *All Four Colors, 6-50, 52-55 have photo-c.*

THREE STOOGES IN 3-D, THE
1991 ($3.95, high quality paper, w/glasses)
Eternity Comics

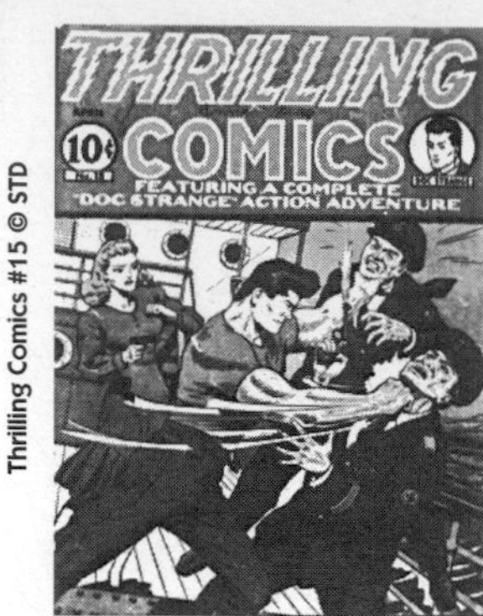

Thrilling Comics #15 © STD

Thrilling Romances #8 © STD

Thrillkiller #2 © DC

GD25 FN65 NM94

1-Reprints Three Stooges by Gold Key; photo-c 1.60 4.00

3 WORLDS OF GULLIVER
No. 1158, July, 1961 (2 issues exist with diff. covers)
Dell Publishing Co.

Four Color 1158-Movie, photo-c 5.50 16.50 60.00

THRILL COMICS (See Flash Comics, Fawcett)

THRILLER
Nov, 1983 - No. 12, Nov, 1984 ($1.25, Baxter paper)
DC Comics

1-9,11,12: 1-Intro Seven Seconds; Von Eeden-c/a begins. 2-Origin. 5,6-Elvis satire. 1.30
10-($2.00) .80 2.00

THRILLING ADVENTURES IN STAMPS COMICS (Formerly Stamp Comics)
V1#8, Jan, 1953 (25¢, 100 pgs.)
Stamp Comics, Inc. (Very Rare)

V1#8-Harrison, Wildey, Kiefer, Napoli-a 61.00 183.00 550.00

THRILLING ADVENTURE STORIES (See Tigerman)
Feb, 1975 - No. 2, Aug, 1975 (B&W, 68 pgs.)
Atlas/Seaboard Publ.

1-Tigerman, Kromag the Killer begin; Heath, Thorne-a. 1.10 3.30 9.00
2-Heath, Toth, Severin, Simonson-a; Neal Adams-c 1.85 5.50 15.00

THRILLING COMICS
Feb, 1940 - No. 80, April, 1951
Better Publ./Nedor/Standard Comics

1-Origin & 1st app. Dr. Strange (37 pgs.), ends #?; Nickie Norton of the Secret Service begins 200.00 600.00 1800.00
2-The Rio Kid, The Woman in Red, Pinocchio begins 94.00 282.00 850.00
3-The Ghost & Lone Eagle begin 58.00 174.00 525.00
4-10: 5-Dr. Strange changed to Doc Strange 49.00 147.00 440.00
11-18,20 41.00 123.00 370.00
19-Origin & 1st app. The American Crusader (8/41), ends #39,41 49.00 147.00 440.00
21-30: 24-Intro. Mike, Doc Strange's sidekick (1/42). 29-Last Rio Kid 36.00 108.00 300.00
31-41: 36-Commando Cubs begin (7/43, 1st app.) 30.00 90.00 240.00
42,43,45-52: 52-The Ghost ends. 45-Hitler pict. on-c 23.00 69.00 185.00
44-Hitler-c 34.00 103.00 275.00
53-The Phantom Detective begins; The Cavalier app.; no Commando Cubs 22.00 66.00 175.00
54-The Cavalier app.; no Commando Cubs 22.00 66.00 175.00
55-Lone Eagle ends 22.00 66.00 175.00
56-Princess Pantha begins (10/46, 1st app.) 36.00 108.00 300.00
57-66: 61-Ingels-a; The Lone Eagle app. 65-Last Phantom Detective & Commando Cubs. 66-Frazetta text illo 30.00 90.00 240.00
67,70-73: Frazetta-a(5-7 pgs.) in each. 72-Sea Eagle app.; Buck Ranger, Cowboy Detective begins 36.00 108.00 300.00
68,69-Frazetta-a(2), 8 & 6 pgs.; 9 & 7 pgs. 36.00 108.00 325.00
74-Last Princess Pantha; Tara app. 23.00 69.00 185.00
75-78: 75-All western format begins 10.50 32.00 85.00
79-Krigstein-a 11.30 34.00 90.00
80-Severin & Elder, Celardo, Moreira-a 11.30 34.00 90.00

NOTE: *Bondage c-5, 9, 13, 20, 22, 27-30, 38, 41, 52, 54, 70.* ***Kinstler*** *a-45.* ***Leo Morey*** *a-7.* ***Schomburg (Xela)*** *c-7, 9-19, 36-80 (airbrush 62-71).* ***Tuska*** *a-62, 63. Woman in Red not in #19, 23, 31-33, 39-45. No. 45 exists as a Canadian reprint but numbered #48. No. 72 exists as a Canadian reprint with no* ***Frazetta*** *story. American Crusader c-20-24. Buck Ranger c-72-80. Commando Cubs c-37, 39, 41, 43, 45, 47, 49, 51. Doc Strange c-1-19, 25-36, 38, 40, 42, 44, 46, 48, 50, 52-57, 59. Princess Pantha c-58, 60-71.*

THRILLING CRIME CASES (Formerly 4Most; becomes Shocking Mystery Cases #50 on)
No. 41, June-July, 1950 - No. 49, July, 1952
Star Publications

41 20.00 60.00 160.00
42-45: 42-L. B. Cole-c/a (1); Chameleon story (Fox-r) 17.50 53.00 140.00
46-48: 47-Used in **POP**, pg. 84 16.00 49.00 130.00
49-(7/52)-Classic L. B. Cole-c 33.00 98.00 260.00

NOTE: ***L. B. Cole*** *c-all; a-43p, 45p, 46p, 49(2 pgs.).* ***Disbrow*** *a-48.* ***Hollingsworth*** *a-48.*

THRILLING ROMANCES
No. 5, Dec, 1949 - No. 26, June, 1954
Standard Comics

5 8.75 26.25 65.00
6,8 5.00 15.00 30.00
7-Severin/Elder-a (7 pgs.) 7.15 21.50 50.00
9,10-Severin/Elder-a; photo-c 5.70 17.00 40.00
11,14-21,26: 12-Tyrone Power/ Susan Hayward photo-c.14-Gene Tierney & Danny Kaye photo-c from movie "On the Riviera". 15-Tony Martin/Janet Leigh photo-c 4.15 12.50 25.00
12-Wood-a (2 pgs.) 8.50 26.00 60.00
13-Severin-a 5.70 17.00 35.00
22-25-Toth-a 6.50 19.50 45.00

NOTE: *All photo-c.* ***Celardo*** *a-9, 16.* ***Colletta*** *a-23, 24(2).* ***Toth*** *text illos-19.* ***Tuska*** *a-9.*

THRILLING SCIENCE TALES
1989 - No. 2? ($3.50, 2/3 color, 52 pgs.)
AC Comics

1-r/Bob Colt #6(saucer); Frazetta, Guardineer (Space Ace), Wood, Krenkel, Orlando, WIlliamson-r; Kaluta-c 1.40 3.50
2-Capt. Video-r by Evans, Capt. Science-r by Wood, Star Pirate-r by Whitman & Mysta of the Moon-r by Moreira 1.40 3.50

THRILLING TRUE STORY OF THE BASEBALL...
1952 (Photo-c, each)
Fawcett Publications

...Giants-photo-c; has Willie Mays rookie photo-biography; Willie Mays, Eddie Stanky & others photos on-c 54.00 162.00 490.00
...Yankees-photo-c; Yogi Berra, Joe DiMaggio, Mickey Mantle & others photos on-c 50.00 150.00 450.00

THRILLKILLER
Jan, 1997 - No. 3, Mar, 1997($2.50, limited series)
DC Comics

1-3-Elseworlds Robin & Batgirl; Chaykin-s/Brereton-c/a 1.20 3.00

THRILLOGY
Jan, 1984 (One-shot, color)
Pacific Comics

1-Conrad-c/a 1.00

THRILL-O-RAMA
Oct, 1965 - No. 3, Dec, 1966
Harvey Publications (Fun Films)

1-Fate (Man in Black) by Powell app.; Doug Wildey-a(2); Simon-c 3.00 9.00 30.00
2-Pirana begins (see Phantom #46); Williamson 2 pgs.; Fate (Man in Black) app.; Tuska/Simon-c 2.50 7.50 20.00
3-Fate (Man in Black) app.; Sparling-c 2.00 6.00 16.00

THRILLS OF TOMORROW (Formerly Tomb of Terror)
No. 17, Oct, 1954 - No. 20, April, 1955
Harvey Publications

17-Powell-a (horror); r/Witches Tales #7 8.75 26.25 70.00
18-Powell-a (horror); r/Tomb of Terror #1 7.85 23.50 55.00
19,20-Stuntman-c/stories by S&K (r/from Stuntman #1 & 2); 19 has origin & is last pre-code (2/55) 24.00 71.00 190.00

Thun'da #1 © ME

Thunderbolts #11 © MEG

Thunderstrike #11 © MEG

GD25 FN65 NM94

NOTE: ***Kirby** c-19, 20. **Palais** a-17. **Simon** c-18?*

THROBBING LOVE (See Fox Giants)

THROUGH GATES OF SPLENDOR
1973, 1974 (36 pages) (39-49 cents)
Spire Christian Comics (Flemming H. Revell Co.)

nn 1.00

THUMPER (Disney)
No, 19, 1942 - No. 243, Sept, 1949
Dell Publishing Co.

Four Color 19-Walt Disney's...Meets the Seven Dwarfs; reprinted in Silly Symphonies 51.00 153.00 560.00
Four Color 243-...Follows His Nose 9.00 27.00 100.00

THUMPER (Disney)
1942 (50 cents, 32pgs., hardcover book, 7"x8-1/2" w/dust jacket)
Grosset & Dunlap
nn-Given away (along with a copy of Bambi) for a $2.00, 2-year subscription to WDC&S in 1942. (Xmas offer). Book only 14.00 41.00 110.00
Dust jacket only 7.85 23.50 55.00

THUN'DA (...King of the Congo)
1952 - No. 6, 1953
Magazine Enterprises

1(A-1 #47)-Origin; Frazetta c/a; only comic done entirely by Frazetta; all Thun'da stories, no Cave Girl 86.00 258.00 775.00
2(A-1 #56)-Powell-c/a begins, ends #6; Intro/1st app. Cave Girl in filler strip (also app. in 3-6) 16.00 49.00 130.00
3(A-1 #73), 4(A-1 #78) 11.30 34.00 90.00
5(A-1 #83), 6(A-1 #86) 10.00 30.00 80.00

THUN'DA TALES (See Frank Frazetta's...)

THUNDER AGENTS (See Dynamo, Noman & Tales Of Thunder)
11/65 - No. 17, 12/67; No. 18, 9/68, No. 19, 11/68, No. 20, 11/69
(No. 1-16: 68 pgs.; No. 17 on: 52 pgs.)(All are 25¢)
Tower Comics

1-Origin & 1st app. Dynamo, Noman, Menthor, & The Thunder Squad; 1st app. The Iron Maiden 12.00 36.00 120.00
2-Death of Egghead; A-bomb blast panel 7.00 21.00 70.00
3-5: 4-Guy Gilbert becomes Lightning who joins Thunder Squad; Iron Maiden app. 4.50 13.50 45.00
6-10: 7-Death of Menthor. 8-Origin & 1st app. The Raven 3.20 9.60 32.00
11-15: 13-Undersea Agent app.; no Raven story 2.50 7.50 22.00
16-19 2.50 7.50 20.00
20-Special Collectors Edition; all reprints 1.25 3.75 10.00
NOTE: ***Crandall** a-1, 4p, 5p, 18, 20r; c-18. **Ditko** a-6, 7p, 12p, 13?, 14p, 16, 18. **Giunta** a-6. **Kane** a-1, 5p, 6p?, 14, 16p; c-14, 15. **Reinman** a-13. **Sekowsky** a-6. **Tuska** a-1p, 7, 8, 10, 13-17, 19. **Whitney** a-9p, 10, 13, 15, 17, 18; c-17. **Wood** a-1-11, 15(w/**Ditko**-12, 18), (inks-#9, 13, 14, 16, 17), 19i, 20r; c-1-8, 9i, 10-13(#10 w/**Williamson**(p)), 16.*

T.H.U.N.D.E.R. AGENTS (See Blue Ribbon Comics, Hall of Fame Featuring the..., JCP Features & Wally Wood's...)
May, 1983 - No. 2, Jan, 1984
JC Comics (Archie Publications)

1,2-New material 1.20 3.00

THUNDER BIRDS (See Cinema Comics Herald)

THUNDERBOLT (See The Atomic...)

THUNDERBOLT (Peter Cannon...; see Crisis on Infinite Earths & Peter...)
Jan, 1966; No. 51, Mar-Apr, 1966 - No. 60, Nov, 1967
Charlton Comics

1-Origin & 1st app. Thunderbolt 2.00 6.00 16.00
51-(Formerly Son of Vulcan #50) 1.50 4.50 12.00
52-59: 54-Sentinels begin. 59-Last Thunderbolt & Sentinels (back-up story) 1.10 3.30 9.00
60-Prankster app. 1.50 4.50- 12.00
57,58 ('77)-Modern Comics-r 1.60 4.00
NOTE: ***Aparo** a-60. **Morisi** a-1, 51-56, 58; c-1, 51-56, 58, 59.*

THUNDERBOLTS
Apr, 1997 - Present ($1.95/$1.99)
Marvel Comics

1-($2.99)-Busiek-s/Bagley-c/a 2.00 5.00
2-4: 2-Two covers. 4-Intro. Jolt 1.00 2.50
5-14: 5-Begin $1.99-c 1.99
Annual '97 ($2.99)-Wraparound-c 2.99
First Strikes (1997, $4.99,TPB) r/#1,2 4.99

THUNDERBOLTS: DISTANT RUMBLINGS
July, 1997 ($1.95, one-shot)
Marvel Comics

minus 1-Flashback; Busiek-s .80 2.00

THUNDERBUNNY (Also see Blue Ribbon Comics #13,Charlton Bullseye & Pep Comics #393)
Jan, 1984 (Direct sale only)
Red Circle Comics

1-Origin 1.20

THUNDERCATS (TV)
Dec, 1985 - No. 24, June, 1988 (75¢)
Marvel Comics (Star Comics)/Marvel #22 on

1-Mooney-c/a begins 1.20 3.00
2-24: 2-(65 & 75 cent cover exists). 12-Begin $1.00-c. 18-20-Williamson-i. 23-Williamson-c(i) 1.20 3.00

THUNDERGOD
July, 1996 - No. 3 ($2.95, B&W)
Crusade Entertainment

1-3: Christopher Golden scripts; painted-c 1.20 3.00

THUNDERGOD
1997 ($2.95, B&W, one-shot)
Caliber Comics

1 1.20 3.00

THUNDER MOUNTAIN (See Zane Grey, Four Color #246)

THUNDERSTRIKE (See Thor #459)
June, 1993 - No. 24, July, 1995 ($1.25)
Marvel Comics

1-($2.95, 52 pgs.)-Holo-grafx lightning patterned foil-c; Bloodaxe returns 1.20 3.00
2-7: 2-Juggernaut-c/s. 4-Capt. America app. 4-6-Spider-Man app. 1.25
8-24: 8-Begin $1.50-c; bound-in trading card sheet. 18-Bloodaxe app. 24-Death of Thunderstrike. 1.50
Marvel Double Feature...Thunderstrike/Code Blue #13 ($2.50)-Same as Thunderstrike #13 w/Code Blue flip book 1.00 2.50

TICK, THE (Also see The Chroma-Tick)
June, 1988 - No. 12, May, 1993 ($1.75/$1.95/$2.25; B&W, over-sized)
New England Comics Press

Special Edition 1-1st comic book app. serially numbered & limited to 5,000 copies 4.00 12.00 40.00
Special Edition 1-(5/96, $5.95)-Double-c; foil-c; serially numbered (5,001 thru 14,000) & limited to 9,000 copies 2.40 6.00
Special Edition 2-Serially numbered and limited to 3000 copies 4.00 12.00 40.00
Special Edition 2-(8/96, $5.95)-Double-c; foil-c; serially numbered (5,001 thru 14,000) & limited to 9,000 copies 2.40 6.00
1-Reprints Special Ed. 1 w/minor changes 3.00 9.00 30.00
1-2nd printing 2.00 5.00
1-3rd printing ($1.95, 6/89) 1.20 3.00

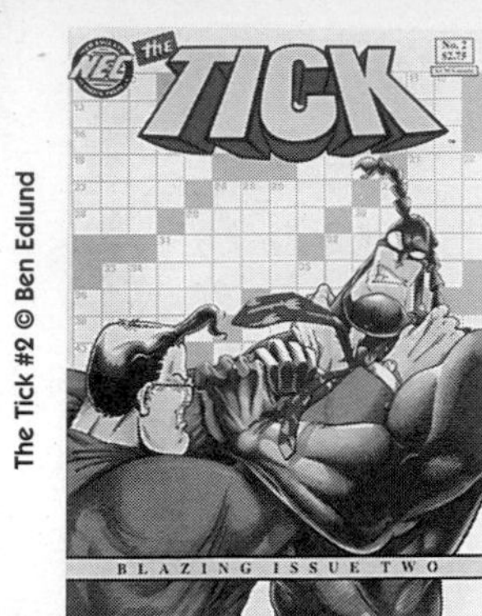

The Tick #2 © Ben Edlund

The Tick Big Blue Yule Log Special #1 © Ben Edlund

Timecop #2 © Mark Verhaiden

	GD25	FN65	NM94
1-4th printing ($2.25)		1.00	2.50
1-5th printing ($2.75)		1.20	3.00
2-Reprints Special Ed. 2 w/minor changes	2.50	7.50	20.00
2-2nd printing ($1.95)		2.00	5.00
2-3rd & 4th printings ($2.25)		1.00	2.50
2-5th printing ($2.75)		1.20	3.00
3-5 ($1.95): 4-1st app. Paul the Samurai		2.00	5.00
3-2nd & 3rd printings ($2.25)		1.00	2.50
3-4th printing ($2.75)		1.20	3.00
4-2nd printing ($2.25)		1.00	2.50
4-3rd - 5th printings ($2.75)		1.20	3.00
6-8 ($2.25): 7-1st app. Man-Eating Cow.		1.60	4.00
5-8-2nd printings ($2.75)		1.20	3.00
6-3rd printing ($2.75)		1.20	3.00
8-Variant with no logo, price, issue number or company logos.	1.85	5.50	15.00
9-12 ($2.75)		1.20	3.00
12-Special Edition; card-stock, virgin foil-c; numbered edition	2.50	7.50	20.00
Promo Sampler-(1990)-Tick-c/story	1.25	3.75	10.00

TICK BIG BLUE DESTINY, THE
Oct, 1997 - Present ($2.95)
New England Comics

	GD25	FN65	NM94
1-"Keen" Ed			2.95
1-($4.95) "Wicked Keen" Ed. w/die cut-c			4.95

TICK BIG BLUE YULE LOG SPECIAL, THE
Dec, 1997 ($2.95, B&W)
New England Comics

	GD25	FN65	NM94
1-"Jolly" and "Traditional" covers; flip book w/"Arthur Teaches the Tick About Hanukkah"			2.95

TICK'S BACK, THE
Aug, 1997 ($2.95, B&W, one-shot)
New England Comics

	GD25	FN65	NM94
0		1.20	3.00

TICK'S GIANT CIRCUS OF THE MIGHTY, THE
Summer, 1992 - No. 3, Fall, 1993 ($2.75, B&W, magazine size)
New England Comics

	GD25	FN65	NM94
1-(A-O). 2-(P-Z). 3-1993 Update		1.40	3.50

TICK KARMA TORNADO (The...)
Oct, 1993 - No. 9, Mar, 1995 ($2.75, B&W)
New England Comics Press

	GD25	FN65	NM94
1-($3.25)		1.40	3.50
2-9: 2-$2.75-c begins		1.20	3.00

TICKLE COMICS (Also see Gay, Smile, & Whee Comics)
1955 (7¢, 5x7-1/4", 52 pgs)
Modern Store Publ.

	GD25	FN65	NM94
1		1.00	2.50

TICK TOCK TALES
Jan, 1946 - V3#33, Jan-Feb, 1951
Magazine Enterprises

	GD25	FN65	NM94
1-Koko & Kola begin	9.50	28.00	75.00
2	5.70	17.00	38.00
3-10	5.00	15.00	30.00
11-33: 19-Flag-c. 23-Muggsy Mouse, The Pixies & Tom-Tom the Jungle Boy app. 25-The Pixies & Tom-Tom app.	4.00	11.00	22.00

TIGER (Also see Comics Reading Libraries)
Mar, 1970 - No. 6, Jan, 1971 (15¢)
Charlton Press (King Features)

	GD25	FN65	NM94
1	1.25	3.75	10.00
2-6		2.40	6.00

TIGER BOY (See Unearthly Spectaculars)

TIGER GIRL
Sept, 1968 (15¢)
Gold Key

	GD25	FN65	NM94
1(10227-809)-Sparling-c/a; Jerry Siegel scripts	2.50	7.50	25.00

TIGERMAN (Also see Thrilling Adventure Stories)
Apr, 1975 - No. 3, Sept, 1975 (All 25¢ issues)
Seaboard Periodicals (Atlas)

	GD25	FN65	NM94
1-3: 2,3-Ditko-p in each		1.20	3.00

TIGER WALKS, A (See Movie Comics)

TIGRESS, THE
Aug, 1992 - No. 6?, July, 1993 ($3.95/$2.95/$3.95, B&W)
Hero Graphics

	GD25	FN65	NM94
1-Tigress vs. Flare		1.40	3.50
2-5: 2-$2.95-c begins		1.20	3.00
6-(6/93, $3.95, 44 pgs.)		1.60	4.00

TILLIE THE TOILER (See Comic Monthly)
No. 15, 1941 - No. 237, July, 1949
Dell Publishing Co.

	GD25	FN65	NM94
Four Color 15(1941)	32.00	95.00	360.00
Large Feature Comic 30(1941)	21.00	63.00	230.00
Four Color 8(1942)	21.00	63.00	230.00
Four Color 22(1943)	16.00	49.00	180.00
Four Color 55(1944), 89(1945)	12.00	37.00	135.00
Four Color 106('45),132('46): 132-New stories begin	9.00	27.00	100.00
Four Color 150,176,184	8.00	25.00	90.00
Four Color 195,213,237	5.50	16.50	60.00

TILLY AND TED-TINKERTOTLAND
1945 (Giveaway, 20 pgs.)
W. T. Grant Co.

	GD25	FN65	NM94
nn-Christmas comic	5.70	17.00	38.00

TIM (Formerly Superman-Tim; becomes Gene Autry-Tim)
June, 1950 - Oct, 1950 (B&W, half-size)
Tim Stores

	GD25	FN65	NM94
4 issues; 6/50, 9/50, 10/50 known	6.00	18.00	42.00

TIMBER WOLF (See Action Comics #372, & Legion of Super-Heroes)
Nov, 1992 - No. 5, Mar, 1993 ($1.25, limited series)
DC Comics

	GD25	FN65	NM94
1-5			1.25

TIME BANDITS
Feb, 1982 (one-shot)
Marvel Comics Group

	GD25	FN65	NM94
1-Movie adaptation			1.00

TIME BEAVERS (See First Comics Graphic Novel #2)

TIME BREAKERS
Jan, 1997 - No. 5, May, 1997 ($2.25, limited series)
DC Comics (Helix)

	GD25	FN65	NM94
1-5-Pollack-s		.90	2.25

TIMECOP (Movie)
Sept, 1994 - No. 2, Nov, 1994 ($2.50, limited series)
Dark Horse Comics

	GD25	FN65	NM94
1,2-Adaptation of film		1.00	2.50

TIME FOR LOVE (Formerly Romantic Secrets)
V2#53, Oct, 1966; Oct, 1967 - No. 47, May, 1976
Charlton Comics

Timewalker #14 © VAL

Tim Holt #17 © ME

Tim Holt #26 © ME

GD25 FN65 NM94

V2#53(10/66), 2(12/67)-20 1.25 3.75 10.00
1(10/67) 2.50 7.50 20.00
21-47 2.40 6.00
30-(10/72)-Full-length portrait of David Cassidy 1.25 3.75 10.00

TIMELESS TOPIX (See Topix)

TIME MACHINE, THE
No. 1085, Mar, 1960 (H.G. Wells)
Dell Publishing Co.

Four Color 1085-Movie, Alex Toth-a; Rod Taylor photo-c 14.00 44.00 160.00

TIME MASTERS
Feb, 1990 - No. 8, Sept, 1990 ($1.75, mini-series)
DC Comics

1-8: New Rip Hunter series. 5-Cave Carson, Viking Prince app. 6-Dr. Fate app. .75 1.80

TIMESPIRITS
Oct, 1984 - No. 8, Mar, 1986 ($1.50, Baxter paper, direct sales)
Marvel Comics (Epic Comics)

1-8: 4-Williamson-a 1.50

TIME TUNNEL, THE (TV)
Feb, 1967 - No. 2, July, 1967 (12¢)
Gold Key

1,2-Photo back-c 3.60 11.00 40.00

TIME TWISTERS
Sept, 1987 - No. 21, 1989 ($1.25/$1.50)
Quality Comics

1-10: Alan Moore scripts in 1-4, 6-9, 14 (2 pg.) 1.25
11-21 ($1.50): 14-Bolland-a (2 pg.). 15,16 Guice-c 1.50

TIME 2: THE EPIPHANY (See First Comics Graphic Novel #9)

TIMEWALKER (Also see Archer & Armstrong)
Jan, 1994 - No. 15, Oct, 1995 ($2.50)
Valiant

1-15: 2-"JAN" on-c, February, 1995 in indicia. 1.00 2.50
Yearbook 1 (5/95, $2.95) 1.20 3.00

TIME WARP (See The Unexpected #210)
Oct-Nov, 1979 - No. 5, June-July, 1980 ($1.00, 68 pgs.)
DC Comics, Inc.

1-5 2.00 5.00

NOTE: ***Aparo*** *a-1.* ***Buckler*** *a-1p.* ***Chaykin*** *a-2.* ***Ditko*** *a-1-4.* ***Kaluta*** *c-1-5.* ***G. Kane*** *a-2.* ***Nasser*** *a-4.* ***Newton*** *a-1-5p.* ***Orlando*** *a-2.* ***Sutton*** *a-1-3.*

TIME WARRIORS THE BEGINNING
1986 (Aug) - No. 2, 1986? ($1.50)
Fantasy General Comics

1,2-Alpha Track/Skellon Empire 1.50

TIM HOLT (Movie star) (Becomes Red Mask #42 on; also see Crack Western #72, & Great Western)
1948 - No. 41, April-May, 1954 (All 36 pgs.)
Magazine Enterprises

1-(A-1 #14)-Line drawn-c w/Tim Holt photo on-c; Tim Holt, His horse Lightning & sidekick Chito begin 53.00 159.00 475.00
2-(A-1 #17)(9-10/48)-Photo-c begin, end #18 30.00 90.00 240.00
3-(A-1 #19)-Photo back-c 23.00 68.00 180.00
4(1-2/49),5: 5-Photo front/back-c 17.00 51.00 135.00
6-(5/49)-1st app. The Calico Kid (alias Rex Fury), his horse Ebony & Sidekick Sing-Song (begin series); photo back-c 29.00 86.00 230.00
7-10: 7-Calico Kid by Ayers. 8-Calico Kid by Guardineer (r-in/Great Western #10). 9-Map of Tim's Home Range 14.00 41.00 110.00
11-The Calico Kid becomes The Ghost Rider (origin & 1st app.) by Dick Ayers (r-in/Great Western I.W. #8); his horse Spectre & sidekick Sing-Song begin series 36.00 108.00 310.00
12-16,18-Last photo-c 10.50 32.00 85.00
17-Frazetta Ghost Rider-c 28.00 84.00 225.00
19,22,24: 19-Last Tim Holt-c; Bolle line-drawn-c begin; Tim Holt photo on covers #19-28,30-41. 22-interior photo-c 8.75 26.25 70.00
20-Tim Holt becomes Redmask (origin); begin series; Redmask-c #20-on 14.00 41.00 110.00
21-Frazetta Ghost Rider/Redmask-c 25.00 75.00 200.00
23-Frazetta Redmask-c 21.00 64.00 170.00
25-1st app. Black Phantom 16.00 49.00 130.00
26-30: 28-Wild Bill Hickok, Bat Masterson team up with Redmask. 29-B&W photo-c 8.50 26.00 60.00
31-33-Ghost Rider ends 7.85 23.50 55.00
34-Tales of the Ghost Rider begins (horror)-Classic "The Flower Women" & "Hard Boiled Harry!" 9.50 28.00 75.00
35-Last Tales of the Ghost Rider 8.50 26.00 60.00
36-The Ghost Rider returns, ends #41; liquid hallucinogenic drug story 8.75 26.25 70.00
37-Ghost Rider classic "To Touch Is to Die!", about Inca treasure 8.75 26.25 70.00
38-The Black Phantom begins (not in #39); classic Ghost Rider "The Phantom Guns of Feather Gap!" 8.75 26.25 70.00
39-41: All 3-D effect c/stories 12.00 36.00 95.00

NOTE: ***Dick Ayers*** *a-7, 9-41.* ***Bolle*** *a-1-41; c-19, 20, 22, 24-28, 30-41.*

TIM IN SPACE (Formerly Gene Autry Tim; becomes Tim Tomorrow)
1950 (1/2 size giveaway) (B&W)
Tim Stores

nn 4.00 11.00 22.00

TIM McCOY (Formerly Zoo Funnies; Pictorial Love Stories #22 on)
No. 16, Oct, 1948 - No. 21, Aug, 1949 (Western Movie Stories)
Charlton Comics

16-John Wayne, Montgomery Clift app. in "Red River"; photo back-c 36.00 108.00 320.00
17-21: 17-Allan "Rocky" Lane guest stars. 18-Rod Cameron guest stars. 19-Whip Wilson, Andy Clyde guest star; Jesse James story. 20-Jimmy Wakely guest stars. 21-Johnny Mack Brown guest stars 35.00 105.00 200.00

TIM McCOY, POLICE CAR 17
No. 674, 1934 (32 pgs.) (11x14-3/4") (B&W) (Like Feature Books)
Whitman Publishing Co.

674-1933 movie ill. 23.00 69.00 185.00

TIMMY
No. 715, Aug, 1956 - No. 1022, Aug-Oct, 1959
Dell Publishing Co.

Four Color 715 (#1) 2.75 8.00 30.00
Four Color 823 (8/57), 923 (8/58), 1022 1.80 5.50 20.00

TIMMY THE TIMID GHOST (Formerly Win-A-Prize?; see Blue Bird)
No. 3, 2/56 - No. 44, 10/64; No. 45, 9/66; 10/67 - No. 23, 7/71; V4#24, 9/85 - No. 26, 1/86
Charlton Comics

3(1956) (1st Series) 7.15 21.50 50.00
4,5 4.15 12.50 25.00
6-10 2.00 6.00 16.00
11,12(4/58,10/58)(100 pgs.) 5.00 15.00 50.00
13-20 1.50 4.50 12.00
21-45(1966) 1.10 3.30 9.00
1(10/67, 2nd series) 1.50 4.50 12.00
2-23 2.40 6.00
24-26 (1985-86): Fago-r 1.20 3.00

TIM TOMORROW (Formerly Tim In Space)
8/51, 9/51, 10/51, Christmas, 1951 (5x7-3/4")

Tim Tyler Cowboy #11 © STD

Tiny Tots Comics #2 © EC

Tip Top Comics #39 © UFS

	GD25	FN65	NM94
Tim Stores			
nn-Prof. Fumble & Captain Kit Comet in all	4.25	13.00	26.00

TIM TYLER (See Harvey Comics Hits #54)

TIM TYLER (Also see Comics Reading Libraries)
1942
Better Publications

	GD25	FN65	NM94
1	10.00	30.00	80.00

TIM TYLER COWBOY
No. 11, Nov, 1948 - No. 18, 1950
Standard Comics (King Features Synd.)

	GD25	FN65	NM94
11-By Lyman Young	7.15	21.50	50.00
12-18: 13-15-Full length western adventures	5.70	17.00	35.00

TINKER BELL (Disney, TV)(See Walt Disney Showcase #37)
No. 896, Mar, 1958 - No. 982, Apr-June, 1959
Dell Publishing Co.

	GD25	FN65	NM94
Four Color 896 (#1)-The Adventures of...	7.00	22.00	80.00
Four Color 982-The New Advs. of...	7.00	22.00	80.00

TINY FOLKS FUNNIES
No. 60, 1944
Dell Publishing Co.

	GD25	FN65	NM94
Four Color 60	13.00	40.00	145.00

TINY TESSIE (Tessie #1-23; Real Experiences #25)
No. 24, Oct, 1949 (52 pgs.)
Marvel Comics (20CC)

	GD25	FN65	NM94
24	6.50	19.50	45.00

TINY TIM (Also see Super Comics)
No. 4, 1941 - No. 235, July, 1949
Dell Publishing Co.

	GD25	FN65	NM94
Large Feature Comic 4('41)	29.00	87.00	320.00
Four Color 20(1941)	27.00	80.00	295.00
Four Color 42(1943)	16.00	47.00	170.00
Four Color 235	3.60	11.00	40.00

TINY TOT COMICS
Mar, 1946 - No. 10, Nov-Dec, 1947 (For younger readers)
E. C. Comics

	GD25	FN65	NM94
1(nn)-52 pg. issues begin, end #4	26.00	80.00	210.00
2 (5/46)	15.50	47.00	125.00
3-10: 10-Christmas-c	14.00	41.00	110.00

TINY TOT FUNNIES (Formerly Family Funnies; becomes Junior Funnies)
No. 9, June, 1951
Harvey Publ. (King Features Synd.)

	GD25	FN65	NM94
9-Flash Gordon, Mandrake, Dagwood, Daisy, etc.	5.00	15.00	30.00

TINY TOTS COMICS
1943 (Not reprints)
Dell Publishing Co.

	GD25	FN65	NM94
1-Kelly-a(2); fairy tales	36.00	108.00	290.00

TIPPY & CAP STUBBS (See Popular Comics)
No. 210, Jan, 1949 - No. 242, Aug, 1949
Dell Publishing Co.

	GD25	FN65	NM94
Four Color 210 (#1)	3.60	11.00	40.00
Four Color 242	2.75	8.00	30.00

TIPPY'S FRIENDS GO-GO & ANIMAL
July, 1966 - No. 15, Oct, 1969 (25¢)
Tower Comics

	GD25	FN65	NM94
1	4.00	12.00	40.00
2-5,7,9-15: 12-15 titled "Tippy's Friend Go-Go"	2.50	7.50	20.00
6-The Monkees photo-c	4.50	13.50	45.00
8-Beatles app. on front/back-c	7.50	22.50	75.00

TIPPY TEEN (See Vicki)
Nov, 1965 - No. 27, Feb, 1970 (25¢)
Tower Comics

	GD25	FN65	NM94
1	4.00	12.00	40.00
2-4,6-10	2.50	7.50	25.00
5-1 pg. Beatles pin-up	3.00	9.00	30.00
11-20: 16-Twiggy photo-c	2.50	7.50	20.00
21-27	1.85	5.50	15.00
Special Collectors' Editions nn-(1969, 25¢)	2.50	7.50	24.00

TIPPY TERRY
1963
Super/I. W. Enterprises

	GD25	FN65	NM94
Super Reprint #14('63)-r/Little Groucho #1	1.00	2.80	7.00
I.W. Reprint #1 (nd)-r/Little Groucho #1	1.00	2.80	7.00

TIP TOP COMICS
4/36 - No. 210, 1957; No. 211, 11-1/57-58 - No. 225, 5-7/61
United Features #1-187/St. John #188-210/Dell Publishing Co. #211 on

	GD25	FN65	VF82	NM94
1-Tarzan by Hal Foster, Li'l Abner, Broncho Bill, Fritzi Ritz, Ella Cinders, Capt. & The Kids begin; strip-r (1st comic book app. of each)	916.00	2750.00	4122.00	6000.00

(Estimated up to 80 total copies exist, 4 in NM/Mint)

	GD25	FN65	VF82
2	200.00	600.00	1300.00
3-Tarzan-c	183.00	549.00	1200.00
4	108.00	324.00	725.00
5-8,10: 7-Photo & biography of Edgar Rice Burroughs. 8-Christmas-c	79.00	237.00	550.00
9-Tarzan-c	100.00	300.00	650.00

	GD25	FN65	NM94
11,13,16,18-Tarzan-c: 11-Has Tarzan pin-up	79.00	237.00	525.00
12,14,15,17,19,20: 20-Christmas-c	64.00	192.00	400.00
21,24,27,30-(10/38)-Tarzan-c	64.00	192.00	400.00
22,23,25,26,28,29	36.00	108.00	310.00
31,35,38,40	36.00	108.00	290.00
32,36-Tarzan-c: 32-1st published Jack Davis-a (cartoon). 36-Kurtzman panel (1st published comic work)	44.00	132.00	400.00
33,34,37,39-Tarzan-c	42.00	126.00	375.00
41-Reprints 1st Tarzan Sunday; Tarzan-c	44.00	132.00	400.00
42-50: 43-Mort Walker panel	34.00	101.00	270.00
51,53	29.00	86.00	230.00
52-Tarzan-c	36.00	108.00	290.00
54-Origin Mirror Man & Triple Terror, also featured on cover	35.00	105.00	280.00
55,56,58,60: Last Tarzan by Foster	23.00	68.00	180.00
57,59,61,62-Tarzan by Hogarth	28.00	84.00	225.00
63-80: 65,67-70,72-74,77,78-No Tarzan	14.00	41.00	110.00
81-90	12.00	36.00	95.00
91-99	10.00	30.00	80.00
100	11.30	34.00	90.00
101-140: 110-Gordo story. 111-Li'l Abner app. 118, 132-No Tarzan. 137-Sadie Hawkins Day story	7.15	21.50	50.00
141-170: 145,151-Gordo stories. 157-Last Li'l Abner; lingerie panels	5.70	17.00	35.00
171-188-Tarzan reprints by B. Lubbers in all. 177-Peanuts by Schulz begins?; no Peanuts in #178,179,181-183	5.70	17.00	38.00
189-225	4.15	12.50	25.00
Bound Volumes (Very Rare) sold at 1939 World's Fair; bound by publisher in pictorial comic boards (also see Comics on Parade)			
Bound issues 1-12	183.00	550.00	1650.00
Bound issues 13-24	122.00	366.00	1100.00

Titans: Scissors, Paper, Stone #1 © DC

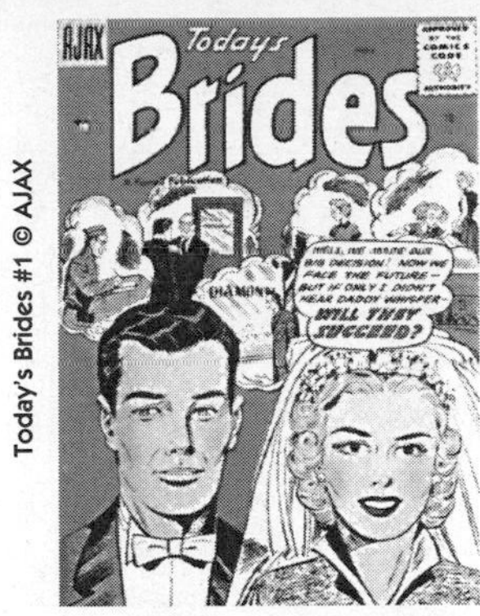

Today's Brides #1 © AJAX

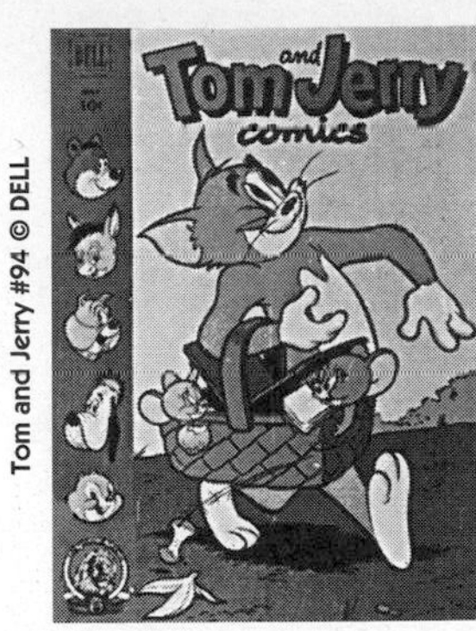

Tom and Jerry #94 © DELL

	GD25	FN65	NM94
Bound issues 25-36	106.00	318.00	950.00

NOTE: *Tarzan covers-#1(part), 2(part), 3, 9, 11, 13, 16, 18, 21, 24, 27, 30, 32-34, 36, 37, 39, 41, 43, 45, 47, 50, 52 (all worth 10-20 percent more). Tarzan by* ***Foster****-#1-40, 44-50; by* ***Rex Maxon****-#41-43; by* ***Burne Hogarth****-#57, 59, 62.*

TIP TOPPER COMICS
Oct-Nov, 1949 - No. 28, 1954
United Features Syndicate

	GD25	FN65	NM94
1-Li'l Abner, Abbie & Slats	8.50	26.00	60.00
2	5.70	17.00	35.00
3-5: 5-Fearless Fosdick app.	5.00	15.00	30.00
6-10: 6-Fearless Fosdick app.	4.15	12.50	25.00
11-25: 17-22,24,26-Peanuts app. (2 pgs.)	4.00	10.00	20.00
26-28-Twin Earths	5.00	15.00	30.00

NOTE: *Many lingerie panels in Fritzi Ritz stories.*

TITAN SPECIAL
June, 1994 ($3.95, one-shot)
Dark Horse Comics

	GD25	FN65	NM94
1-($3.95, 52 pgs.)		1.60	4.00

TITANS: SCISSORS, PAPER, STONE
1997 ($4.95, one-shot)
DC Comics

	GD25	FN65	NM94
1-Manga style Elseworlds; Adam Warren-s/a(p)		2.00	5.00

TITANS SELL-OUT SPECIAL
Nov, 1992 ($3.50, 52 pgs., one-shot)
DC Comics

	GD25	FN65	NM94
1-Fold-out Nightwing poster; 1st Teeny Titans		1.40	3.50

T-MAN (Also see Police Comics #103)
Sept, 1951 - No. 38, Dec, 1956
Quality Comics Group

	GD25	FN65	NM94
1-Pete Trask, T-Man begins; Jack Cole-a	34.00	103.00	250.00
2-Crandall-c	18.00	54.00	130.00
3,7,8: All Crandall-c	15.00	45.00	110.00
4,5-Crandall-c/a each	16.00	47.00	120.00
6-"The Man Who Could Be Hitler" c/story; Crandall-c.	17.00	51.00	130.00
9,10-Crandall-c	13.00	39.00	95.00
11-Used in **POP**, pg. 95 & color illo.	10.00	30.00	70.00
12,13,15-19,21,22-26: 21- "The Return of Mussolini" c/story. 23-H-Bomb panel. 24-Last pre-code issue (4/55). 25-Not Crandall-a	8.35	25.00	55.00
14-Hitler-c	9.00	27.00	60.00
20-H-Bomb explosion-c/story	11.00	33.00	80.00
27-38	7.50	22.50	50.00

NOTE: *Anti-communist stories common.* ***Crandall*** *c-2-10p.* ***Cuidera*** *c(i)-1-38. Bondage c-15.*

TMNT MUTANT UNIVERSE SOURCEBOOK
1992 - No. 3, 1992? ($1.95, 52 pgs.)(Lists characters from A-Z)
Archie Comics

	GD25	FN65	NM94
1-3: 3-New characters; fold-out poster		.80	2.00

TNT COMICS
Feb, 1946 (36 pgs.)
Charles Publishing Co.

	GD25	FN65	NM94
1-Yellowjacket app.	21.00	62.00	165.00

TOBY TYLER (Disney, see Movie Comics)
No. 1092, Apr-June, 1960
Dell Publishing Co.

	GD25	FN65	NM94
Four Color 1092-Movie, photo-c	5.50	16.50	60.00

TODAY'S BRIDES
Nov, 1955; No. 2, Feb, 1956; No. 3, Sept, 1956; No. 4, Nov, 1956
Ajax/Farrell Publishing Co.

	GD25	FN65	NM94
1	5.70	17.00	40.00
2-4	4.15	12.50	25.00

TODAY'S ROMANCE
No. 5, March, 1952 - No. 8, Sept, 1952 (All photo-c?)
Standard Comics

	GD25	FN65	NM94
5-Photo-c	5.70	17.00	40.00
6-Photo-c; Toth-a	6.50	19.50	45.00
7,8	4.15	12.50	25.00

TOKA (Jungle King)
Aug-Oct, 1964 - No. 10, Jan, 1967 (Painted-c #1,2)
Dell Publishing Co.

	GD25	FN65	NM94
1	2.50	7.50	24.00
2	2.00	6.00	16.00
3-10	1.50	4.50	12.00

TOMAHAWK (Son of... on-c of #131-140; see Star Spangled Comics #69 & World's Finest Comics #65)
Sept-Oct, 1950 - No. 140, May-June, 1972
National Periodical Publications

	GD25	FN65	NM94
1-Tomahawk & boy sidekick Dan Hunter begin by Fred Ray	133.00	400.00	1200.00
2-Frazetta/Williamson-a (4 pgs.)	53.00	159.00	475.00
3-5	36.00	108.00	300.00
6-10: 7-Last 52 pg. issue	26.00	80.00	210.00
11-20	19.00	56.00	150.00
21-27,30: 30-Last precode (2/55)	15.00	45.00	120.00
28-1st app. Lord Shilling (arch-foe)	16.00	49.00	130.00
29-Frazetta-r/Jimmy Wakely #3 (3 pgs.)	20.00	60.00	160.00
31-40	9.50	28.50	95.00
41-50	7.50	22.50	75.00
51-56,58-60	5.25	15.75	52.00
57-Frazetta-r/Jimmy Wakely #6 (3 pgs.)	8.50	25.50	85.00
61-77: 77-Last 10¢ issue	4.20	12.60	42.00
78-85: 81-1st app. Miss Liberty. 83-Origin Tomahawk's Rangers	2.80	8.40	28.00
86-100: 96-Origin/1st app. The Hood, alias Lady Shilling	2.00	6.00	16.00
101-110: 107-Origin/1st app. Thunder-Man	1.75	5.25	14.00
111-130	1.50	4.50	12.00
131-Frazetta-r/Jimmy Wakely #7 (3 pgs.); origin Firehair retold	1.85	5.50	15.00
132-135,140	1.10	3.30	9.00
136-138,140 (52 pg. Giants)	1.50	4.50	12.00
139-Frazetta-r/Star Spangled #113	1.85	5.50	15.00

NOTE: ***Neal Adams*** *c-116-119, 121, 123-130.* ***Fred Ray*** *c-1, 2, 8, 11, 30, 34, 35, 40-43, 45, 46, 82. Firehair by* ***Kubert****-131-134, 136.* ***Maurer*** *a-138.* ***Severin*** *a-135.* ***Starr*** *a-5.* ***Thorne*** *a-137, 140.*

TOM AND JERRY (See Comic Album #4, 8, 12, Dell Giant #21, Dell Giants, Golden Comics Digest #1, 5, 8, 13, 15, 18, 22, 25, 28, 35, Kite fun Book & March of Comics #21, 46, 61, 70, 88, 103, 119, 128, 145, 154, 173, 190, 207, 224, 281, 295, 305, 321,333, 345, 361, 365, 388, 400, 444, 451, 463, 480)

TOM AND JERRY (...Comics, early issues) (M.G.M.)
(Formerly Our Gang No. 1-59) (See Dell Giants for annuals)
No. 193, 6/48; No. 60, 7/49 - No. 212, 7-9/62; No. 213, 11/62 - No. 291, 2/75; No. 292, 3/77 - No. 342, 5/82 - No. 344, 1982?
Dell Publishing Co./Gold Key No. 213-327/Whitman No. 328 on

	GD25	FN65	NM94
Four Color 193 (#1)-Titled "M.G.M. Presents..."	13.00	38.00	140.00
60-Barney Bear, Benny Burro cont. from Our Gang; Droopy begins	7.00	22.00	80.00
61	6.40	19.00	70.00
62-70: 66-X-Mas-c	4.50	13.50	50.00
71-80: 77,90-X-Mas-c. 79-Spike & Tyke begin	3.60	11.00	40.00
81-99	2.75	8.00	30.00
100	3.00	9.00	32.00

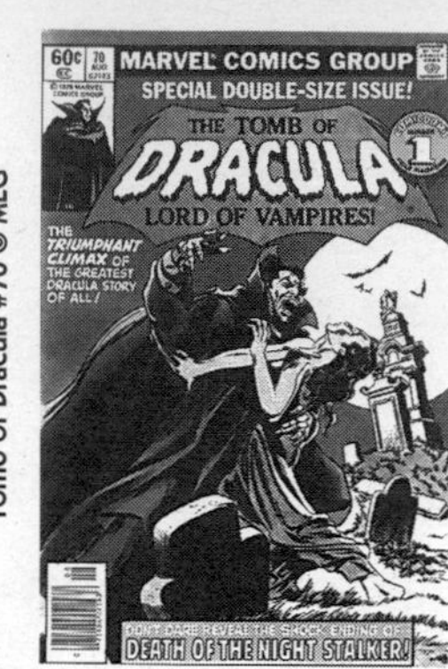

Tomb of Dracula #70 © MEG

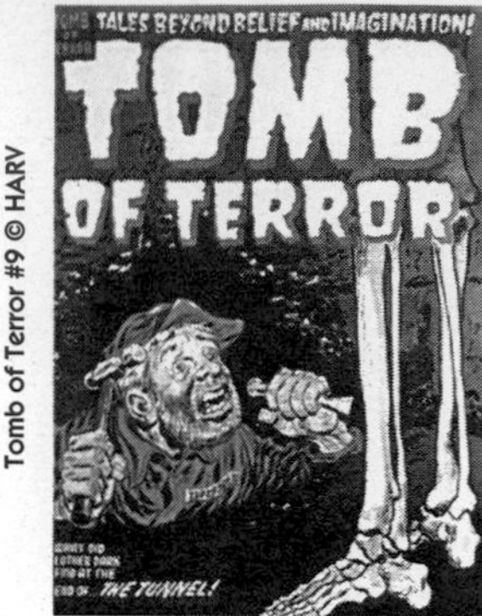

Tomb of Terror #9 © HARV

Tommi Gunn: Killer's Lust #1 © Everette Hartsoe

	GD25	FN65	NM94
101-120	2.25	6.75	24.00
121-140: 126-X-Mas-c	2.00	6.00	22.00
141-160	1.60	4.80	16.00
161-200	1.40	4.20	14.00
201-212(7-9/62)(Last Dell issue)	1.10	3.30	9.00
213,214-(84 pgs.)-Titled "...Funhouse"	3.50	10.50	35.00
215-240: 215-Titled "...Funhouse"	1.85	5.50	15.00
241-270	1.25	3.75	10.00
271-300: 286- "Tom & Jerry"		2.40	6.00
301-344		1.20	3.00
Mouse From T.R.A.P. 1(7/66)-Giant, G. K.	2.60	7.80	26.00
Summer Fun 1(7/67, 68 pgs.)(Gold Key)-Reprints Barks' Droopy from Summer Fun #1	2.60	7.80	26.00

NOTE: *#60-87, 98-121, 268, 277, 289, 302 are 52 pgs.. Reprints-#225, 241, 245, 247, 252, 254, 266, 268, 270, 292-327, 329-342, 344.*

TOM & JERRY
Sept, 1991 - No. 4, 1992 ($1.25)
Harvey Comics

	GD25	FN65	NM94
1-4: 1-Tom & Jerry, Barney Bear-r by Barks			1.30
50th Anniversary Special 1 (10/91, $2.50, 68 pgs.)-Benny the Lonesome Burro-r by Barks (story/a)/Our Gang #9		1.00	2.50

TOMB OF DARKNESS (Formerly Beware)
No. 9, July, 1974 - No. 23, Nov, 1976
Marvel Comics Group

	GD25	FN65	NM94
9	1.50	4.50	12.00
10-23: 15,19-Ditko-r. 17-Woodbridge-r/Astonishing #62; Powell-r. 20-Everett Venus-r/Venus #19. 22-r/Venus #19. 23-Everett-r	1.00	3.00	8.00

TOMB OF DRACULA (See Giant-Size Dracula, Dracula Lives, Nightstalkers, Power Record Comics & Requiem for Dracula)
Apr, 1972 - No. 70, Aug, 1979
Marvel Comics Group

	GD25	FN65	NM94
1-1st app. Dracula & Frank Drake; Colan-p in all	9.00	27.00	90.00
2	4.50	13.50	45.00
3-5: 3-Intro. Dr. Rachel Van Helsing & Inspector Chelm	3.00	9.00	30.00
6-9	2.50	7.50	25.00
10-1st app. Blade the Vampire Slayer	3.00	9.00	30.00
11-20: 12-Brunner-c(p). 13-Origin Blade	1.85	5.50	15.00
21-40: 25-1st app. & origin Hannibal King	1.50	4.50	12.00
41-45,48,49,51-60		2.40	6.00
46,47-(Regular 25¢ edition)(7-8/76)		2.40	6.00
46,47-(30¢-c, limited distribution)	2.50	7.50	24.00
50-Silver Surfer app.	1.60	4.85	13.00
61-69		2.40	6.00
70-Double size	1.00	3.00	7.00

NOTE: ***N. Adams** c-1, 6. **Colan** a-1-70p; c(p)-8, 38-42, 44-56, 58-70. **Wrightson** c-43.*

TOMB OF DRACULA, THE (Magazine)
Oct, 1979 - No. 6, Aug, 1980 (B&W)
Marvel Comics Group

	GD25	FN65	NM94
1,4-6		2.00	5.00
2,3: 2-Ditko-a (36 pgs.). 3-Miller-a(2 pg. sketch)		2.00	5.00

NOTE: ***Buscema** a-4p, 5p. **Chaykin** c-5, 6. **Colan** a(p)-1, 3-6. **Miller** a-3. **Romita** a-2p.*

TOMB OF DRACULA
1991 - No. 4, 1992 ($4.95, 52 pgs., squarebound, mini-series)
Marvel Comics (Epic Comics)

	GD25	FN65	NM94
Book 1-4: Colan/Williamson-a; Colan painted-c		1.20	3.00

TOMB OF LEGEIA (See Movie Classics)

TOMB OF TERROR (Thrills of Tomorrow #17 on)
June, 1952 - No. 16, July, 1954
Harvey Publications

	GD25	FN65	NM94
1	31.00	94.00	240.00
2	17.00	49.00	125.00
3-Bondage-c; atomic disaster story	18.00	54.00	135.00
4-12: 4-Heart ripped out. 8-12-Nostrand-a	17.00	49.00	125.00
13,14-Special S/F issues. 14-Check-a	20.00	60.00	150.00
15-S/F issue; c-shows head exploding	24.00	73.00	180.00
16-Special S/F issue; Nostrand-a	20.00	60.00	150.00

NOTE: ***Edd Cartier** a-13? **Elias** c-2, 5-16. **Kremer** a-1, 7; c-1. **Nostrand** a-8-12, 15r 16. **Palais** a-2, 3, 5-7. **Powell** a-1, 3, 5, 9-16. **Sparling** a-12, 13, 15.*

TOMBSTONE TERRITORY (See Four Color #1123)

TOM CAT (Formerly Bo; Atom The Cat #9 on)
No. 4, Apr, 1956 - No. 8, July, 1957
Charlton Comics

	GD25	FN65	NM94
4-Al Fago-c/a	5.70	17.00	40.00
5-8	4.25	13.00	28.00

TOM CORBETT, SPACE CADET (TV)
No. 378, Jan-Feb, 1952 - No. 11, Sept-Nov, 1954 (All painted covers)
Dell Publishing Co.

	GD25	FN65	NM94
Four Color 378 (#1)-McWilliams-a	16.00	48.00	175.00
Four Color 400,421-McWilliams-a	9.00	27.00	100.00
4(11-1/53) - 11	6.40	19.00	70.00

TOM CORBETT SPACE CADET (See March of Comics #102)

TOM CORBETT SPACE CADET (TV)
V2#1, May-June, 1955 - V2#3, Sept-Oct, 1955
Prize Publications

	GD25	FN65	NM94
V2#1	24.00	73.00	180.00
2,3-Meskin-c	21.00	64.00	160.00

TOM, DICK & HARRIET (See Gold Key Spotlight)

TOM LANDRY AND THE DALLAS COWBOYS
1973 (35/49¢)
Spire Christian Comics/Fleming H. Revell Co.

	GD25	FN65	NM94
nn			1.00

TOMMI GUNN
May, 1996 - No. 3, Aug, 1996 ($3.00, limited series, mature)
London Night Studios

	GD25	FN65	NM94
1/2,1-3: W/J.J. North centerfold		1.20	3.00
1/2-($10.00)-Naughty Edition; photo-c	1.25	3.75	10.00
1-Naughty Platinum; embossed nude-c w/nude J.J. North centerfold inside	1.25	3.75	10.00
2-Variant nude-c		2.00	5.00
Annual 1(1997, $3.00)		1.20	3.00
Annual 1(1997, $6.00)"Naughty Ed."; photo-c		2.40	6.00

TOMMI GUNN: KILLER'S LUST
Feb, 1997 - Present ($3.00, mature)
London Night Studios

	GD25	FN65	NM94
0,1,2,3		1.20	3.00
0,1,2,3-($6.00)-"Naughty Ed."; photo-c (Elizabeth Parkhurst)		2.40	6.00

TOM MIX (...Commandos Comics #10-12)
Sept, 1940 - No. 12, Nov, 1942 (36 pgs.); 1983 (one-shot)
Given away for two Ralston box-tops; 1983 came in cereal box
Ralston-Purina Co.

	GD25	FN65	NM94
1-Origin (life) Tom Mix; Fred Meagher-a	270.00	810.00	2700.00
2	89.00	267.00	800.00
3-9	56.00	168.00	500.00
10-12: 10-Origin Tom Mix Commando Unit; Speed O'Dare begins; Japanese sub-c. 12-Sci/fi-c	44.00	132.00	400.00
1983- "Taking of Grizzly Grebb", Toth-a; 16 pg. miniature		2.40	6.00

TOM MIX WESTERN (Movie, radio star) (Also see The Comics, Crackajack Funnies, Master Comics, 100 Pages Of Comics, Popular Comics, Real Western Hero, Six Gun Heroes, Western Hero & XMas Comics)

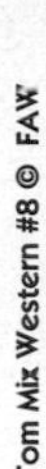
Tom Mix Western #8 © FAW

Tomoe-Witchblade/ Fire Sermon #1 © Crusade/ Top Cow

Too Much Coffee Man Full Color Special #1 © Shannon Wheeler

GD25 FN65 NM94

Jan, 1948 - No. 61, May, 1953 (1-17: 52 pgs.)
Fawcett Publications

1 (Photo-c, 52 pgs.)-Tom Mix & his horse Tony begin; Tumbleweed Jr. begins, ends #52,54,55 83.00 250.00 750.00
2 (Photo-c) 36.00 108.00 320.00
3-5 (Painted/photo-c): 5-Billy the Kid & Oscar app. 29.00 86.00 230.00
6,7 (Painted/photo-c) 24.00 71.00 190.00
8-Kinstler tempera-c 24.00 71.00 190.00
9,10 (Painted/photo-c)-Used in **SOTI**, pgs. 323-25 22.00 66.00 175.00
11-Kinstler oil-c 20.00 60.00 160.00
12 (Painted/photo-c) 17.50 53.00 140.00
13-17 (Painted-c, 52 pgs.) 17.50 53.00 140.00
18,22 (Painted-c, 36 pgs.) 15.00 45.00 120.00
19 (Photo-c, 52 pgs.) 15.50 47.00 125.00
20,21,23 (Painted-c, 52 pgs.) 12.00 38.00 100.00
24,25,27-29 (52 pgs.): 24-Photo-c begin, end #61. 29-Slim Pickens app. 12.00 38.00 100.00
26,30 (36 pgs.) 11.30 34.00 90.00
31-33,35-37,39,40,42 (52 pgs.): 39-Red Eagle app. 10.50 32.00 85.00
34,38 (36 pgs. begin) 9.50 28.00 75.00
41,43-60: 57-(9/52)-Dope smuggling story 7.85 23.50 55.00
61-Last issue 8.75 26.25 70.00

NOTE: *Photo-c from 1930s Tom Mix movies (he died in 1940). Many issues contain ads for Tom Mix, Rocky Lane, Space Patrol and other premiums. Captain Tootsie by* ***C.C. Beck*** *in #6-11, 20.*

TOM MIX WESTERN
1988 - No. 2, 1989? ($2.95, B&W w/16 pgs. color, 44 pgs.)
AC Comics

1-Tom Mix-r/Master #124,128,131,102 plus Billy the Kid-r by Severin; photo front/back/inside-c 1.20 3.00
2-($2.50, B&W)-Gabby Hayes-r; photo covers 1.00 2.50
...Holiday Album 1 (1990, $3.50, B&W, one-shot, 44 pgs.)-Contains photos & 1950s Tom Mix-r; photo inside-c 1.40 3.50

TOMMY OF THE BIG TOP (Thrilling Circus Adventures)
No. 10, Sept, 1948 - No. 12, Mar, 1949
King Features Syndicate/Standard Comics

10-By John Lehti 5.70 17.00 35.00
11,12 4.00 11.00 22.00

TOMMY TOMORROW (See Action Comics #127, Real Fact #6, Showcase #41,42,44,46,47 & World's Finest #102)

TOMOE (Also see Shi: The Way Of the Warrior #6)
July, 1995 - Present ($2.95)
Crusade Comics

0-3: 2-B&W Dogs o' War preview. 3-B&W Demon Gun preview. 1.20 3.00
0 (3/96, $2.95)-variant-c. 1.20 3.00
0-Commemorative edition (5,000) 2.15 6.50 17.00
1-Commemorative edition (5,000) 2.50 7.50 20.00
1-($2.95)-FAN Appreciation edition 1.20 3.00
TPB (1997, $14.95) r/#0-3 1.85 5.50 15.00

TOMOE: UNFORGETTABLE FIRE
June, 1997 - Present ($2.95, limited series)
Crusade Comics

1 1.20 3.00

TOMOE-WITCHBLADE/FIRE SERMON
Sept, 1996 ($3.95, one-shot)
Crusade Comics

1-Tucci-c 1.60 4.00
1-($9.95)-Avalon Ed. w/gold foil-c 1.25 3.75 10.00

TOMOE-WITCHBLADE/MANGA SHI PREVIEW EDITION
July, 1996 ($5.00, B&W)
Crusade Comics

nn-San Diego Preview Edition 2.00 5.00

TOMORROW KNIGHTS
June, 1990 - No. 6, Mar, 1991 ($1.50)
Marvel Comics (Epic Comics)

1-($1.95, 52 pgs.) .80 2.00
2-6 1.50

TOM SAWYER (See Adventures of... & Famous Stories)

TOM SAWYER COMICS
1951? (Paper cover)
Giveaway

nn-Contains a coverless Hopalong Cassidy from 1951; other combinations known 2.00 5.00 10.00

TOM SKINNER-UP FROM HARLEM (See Up From Harlem)

TOM TERRIFIC! (TV)(See Mighty Mouse Fun Club Magazine #1)
Summer, 1957 - No. 6, Fall, 1958 (See Terry Toons Giant Summer Fun Book)
Pines Comics (Paul Terry)

1-1st app.?; CBS Television Presents... 17.50 53.00 140.00
2-6 12.00 38.00 100.00

TOM THUMB
No. 972, Jan, 1959
Dell Publishing Co.

Four Color 972-Movie, George Pal 9.00 27.00 100.00

TOM-TOM, THE JUNGLE BOY (See A-1 Comics & Tick Tock Tales)
1947 - No. 3, 1947; Nov, 1957 - No. 3, Mar, 1958
Magazine Enterprises

1-Funny animal 7.15 21.50 50.00
2,3(1947): 3-Christmas issue 5.70 17.00 35.00
Tom-Tom & Itchi the Monk 1(11/57) - 3(3/58) 1.75 5.25 14.00
I.W. Reprint No. 1,2,8,10: 1,2,8-r/Koko & Kola #? 2.40 6.00

TONGUE LASH
Aug, 1996 - No. 2, Sept, 1996 ($2.95, limited series, mature)
Dark Horse Comics

1,2: Taylor-c/a 1.20 3.00

TONKA (Disney)
No. 966, Jan, 1959
Dell Publishing Co.

Four Color 966-Movie (Starring Sal Mineo)-photo-c 7.00 22.00 80.00

TONTO (See The Lone Ranger's Companion...)

TONY TRENT (The Face #1,2)
No. 3, 1948 - No. 4, 1949
Big Shot/Columbia Comics Group

3,4: 3-The Face app. by Mart Bailey 12.00 38.00 100.00

TOODLES, THE (The Toodle Twins with #1)
No. 10, July-Aug, 1951; Mar, 1956 (Newspaper-r)
Ziff-Davis (Approved Comics)/Argo

10-Painted-c, some newspaper-r by The Baers 7.15 21.50 50.00
...Twins 1(Argo, 3/56)-Reprints by The Baers 5.70 17.00 35.00

TOO MUCH COFFEE MAN
July, 1993 - Present ($2.50, B&W)
Adhesive Comics

1-Shannon Wheeler story & art 2.00 6.00 16.00
2,3 1.40 4.15 11.00
4,5 1.00 3.00 8.00
Full Color Special-($2.95) 1.30 3.25
Full Color Special 2-(7/97, $3.95) 1.60 4.00

TOO MUCH COFFEE MAN SPECIAL

Top Cat #2 © H-B

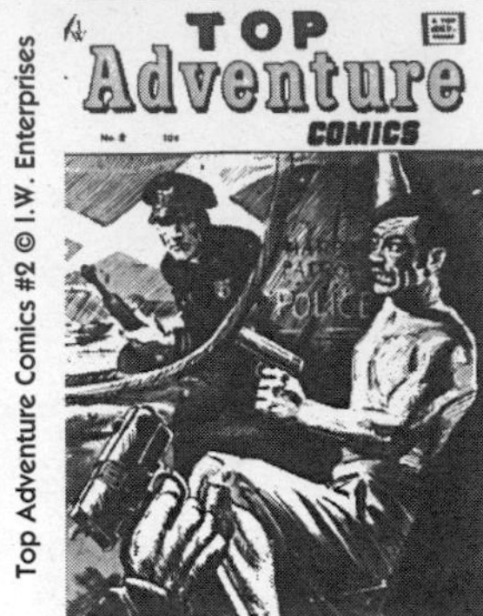

Top Adventure Comics #2 © I.W. Enterprises

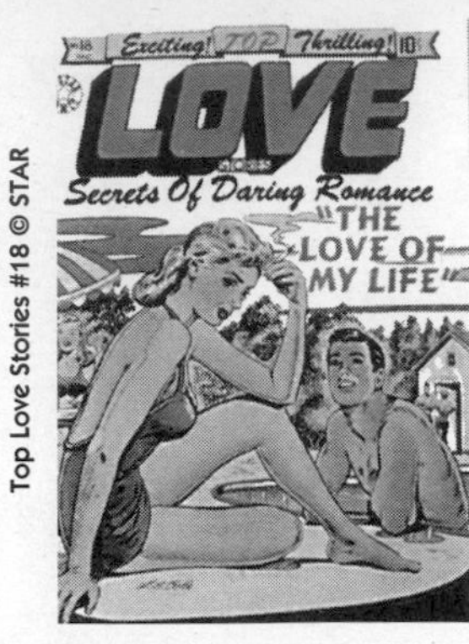

Top Love Stories #18 © STAR

	GD25	FN65	NM94
July, 1997 ($2.95, B&W)			
Dark Horse Comics			
nn-Reprints Dark Horse Presents #92-95		1.20	3.00

TOOTS & CASPER
No. 5, 1942
Dell Publishing Co.

	GD25	FN65	NM94
Large Feature Comic 5	10.00	30.00	110.00

TOP ADVENTURE COMICS
1964 (Reprints)
I. W. Enterprises

	GD25	FN65	NM94
1-r/High Adv. (Explorer Joe #2); Krigstein-r	2.00	6.00	16.00
2-Black Dwarf-r/Red Seal #22; Kinstler-c	2.00	6.00	16.00

TOP CAT (TV) (Hanna-Barbera)(See Kite Fun Book)
12-2/61-62 - No. 3, 6-8/62; No. 4, 10/62 - No. 31, 9/70
Dell Publishing Co./Gold Key No. 4 on

	GD25	FN65	NM94
1 (TV show debuted 9/27/61)	13.00	40.00	145.00
2-Augie Doggie back-ups in #1-4	7.00	22.00	80.00
3-5: 3-Last 15¢ issue. 4-Begin 12¢ issues; 1st app. Yakky Doodle in 1 pg. strip. 5-1st app. Touche' Turtle	5.50	16.50	60.00
6-10	3.60	11.00	40.00
11-20	2.75	8.00	30.00
21-31: 21,24,25,29-Reprints	1.80	5.50	20.00

TOP CAT (TV) (Hanna-Barbera)(See TV Stars #4)
Nov, 1970 - No. 20, Nov, 1973
Charlton Comics

	GD25	FN65	NM94
1	4.00	12.00	40.00
2-10	2.50	7.50	22.00
11-20	2.00	6.00	16.00

NOTE: *#8 (1/72) went on sale late in 1972 between #14 and #15 with the 1/73 issues.*

TOP COMICS
July, 1967 (All reprints)
K. K. Publications/Gold Key

	GD25	FN65	NM94
nn-The Gnome-Mobile (Disney-movie)	1.00	3.00	8.00
1-Beagle Boys (#7), Beep Beep the Road Runner (#5), Bugs Bunny, Chip 'n' Dale, Daffy Duck (#50), Flipper, Huckleberry Hound, Huey, Dewey & Louie, Junior Woodchucks, Lassie, The Little Monsters (#71), Moby Duck, Porky Pig (has Gold Key label - says Top Comics on inside), Scamp, Super Goof, Tarzan of the Apes (#169), Three Stooges (#35), Tom & Jerry Top Cat (#21), Tweety & Sylvester (#7), Walt Disney C&S (#322), Woody Woodpecker, Yogi Bear, Zorro (r/G.K. Zorro #7 w/Toth-a; says 2nd printing) known; each character given own book	1.00	3.00	8.00
1-Uncle Scrooge (#70)	1.50	4.50	12.00
1-Donald Duck (not Barks), Mickey Mouse	1.25	4.50	10.00
1-Flintstones	2.50	7.50	25.00
1-The Jetsons	3.50	10.50	35.00
2-Bugs Bunny, Daffy Duck, Donald Duck (not Barks), Mickey Mouse (#114), Porky Pig, Super Goof, Three Stooges, Tom & Jerry, Tweety & Sylvester, Uncle Scrooge (#71)-Barks-c, Walt Disney's C&S (r/#325), Woody Woodpecker, Yogi Bear (#30), Zorro (r/#8; Toth-a)	1.00	3.00	8.00
2-Snow White & 7 Dwarfs(6/67)(1944-r)	1.25	3.75	10.00
3-Donald Duck	1.10	3.30	9.00
3-Uncle Scrooge (#72)	1.50	4.50	12.00
3,4-The Flintstones	2.50	7.50	25.00
3-Mickey Mouse (r/#115), Tom & Jerry, Woody Woodpecker, Yogi Bear	1.00	3.00	8.00
4-Mickey Mouse, Woody Woodpecker	1.00	3.00	8.00

NOTE: *Each book in this series is identical to its counterpart except for cover, and came out at same time. The number in parentheses is the original issue it contains.*

TOP COW PRODUCTIONS, INC./BALLISTIC STUDIOS SWIMSUIT SPECIAL
May, 1995 ($2.95, one-shot)
Image Comics (Top Cow Productions)

	GD25	FN65	NM94
1		2.00	5.00

TOP COW SECRETS:SPECIAL WINTER LINGERIE EDITION
Jan, 1996 ($2.95, one-shot)
Image Comics (Top Cow Productions)

	GD25	FN65	NM94
1-Pin-ups		1.20	3.00

TOP DETECTIVE COMICS
1964 (Reprints)
I. W. Enterprises

	GD25	FN65	NM94
9-r/Young King Cole #14; Dr. Drew (not Grandenetti)	1.50	4.50	12.00

TOP DOG (See Star Comics Magazine, 75¢)
Apr, 1985 - No. 14, June, 1987 (Children's book)
Star Comics (Marvel)

	GD25	FN65	NM94
1-14: 10-Peter Parker & J. Jonah Jameson cameo			1.00

TOP ELIMINATOR (Teenage Hotrodders #1-24; Drag 'n' Wheels #30 on)
No. 25, Sept, 1967 - No. 29, July, 1968
Charlton Comics

	GD25	FN65	NM94
25-29	1.50	4.50	12.00

TOP FLIGHT COMICS
1947; July, 1949
Four Star Publications/St. John Publishing Co.

	GD25	FN65	NM94
1(1947)	10.00	30.00	70.00
1(7/49, St. John)-Hector the Inspector; funny animal	7.00	21.00	45.00

TOP GUN (See Luke Short, 4-Color #927 & Showcase #72)

TOP GUNS OF THE WEST (See Super DC Giant)

TOPIX (...Comics) (Timeless Topix-early issues) (Also see Men of Battle, Men of Courage & Treasure Chest)(V1-V5#1,V7#1-20-paper-c)
11/42 - V10#15, 1/28/52 (Weekly - later issues)
Catechetical Guild Educational Society

	GD25	FN65	NM94
V1#1(8 pgs.,8x11")	17.50	53.00	140.00
2,3(8 pgs.,8x11")	10.00	30.00	80.00
4-8(16 pgs.,8x11")	8.50	26.00	60.00
V2#1-10(16 pgs.,8x11"): V2#8-Pope Pius XII	7.15	21.50	50.00
V3#1-10(16 pgs.,8x11")	7.15	21.50	50.00
V4#1-10	5.70	17.00	35.00
V5#1(10/46,52 pgs.)-9,12-15(12/47): 13-Lists V5#4	4.25	13.00	28.00
10,11-Life of Christ editions	6.50	19.50	45.00
V6#1-14	4.00	10.00	20.00
V7#1(9/1/48)-20(6/15/49), 32 pgs.	4.00	10.00	20.00
V8#1(9/19/49)-3,5-11,13-30(5/15/50)	4.00	10.00	20.00
4-Dagwood Splits the Atom(10/10/49)-Magazine format	4.15	12.50	25.00
12-Ingels-a	6.50	19.50	45.00
V9#1(9/25/50)-11,13-30(5/14/51)	3.60	9.00	18.00
12-Special 36 pg. Xmas issue, text illos format	4.00	10.00	20.00
V10#1(10/1/51)-15: 14-Hollingsworth-a	3.60	9.00	18.00

TOP JUNGLE COMICS
1964 (Reprint)
I. W. Enterprises

	GD25	FN65	NM94
1(nd)-Reprints White Princess of the Jungle #3, minus cover; Kintsler-a	2.50	7.50	20.00

TOP LOVE STORIES (Formerly Gasoline Alley #2)
No. 3, 5/51 - No. 19, 3/54
Star Publications

	GD25	FN65	NM94
3(#1)	16.00	47.00	120.00
4,5,7-9: 8-Wood story	12.00	36.00	95.00
6-Wood-a	19.00	56.00	140.00
10-16,18,19-Disbrow-a	12.00	36.00	95.00
17-Wood art (Fox-r)	14.00	43.00	110.00

NOTE: *All have **L. B. Cole** covers.*

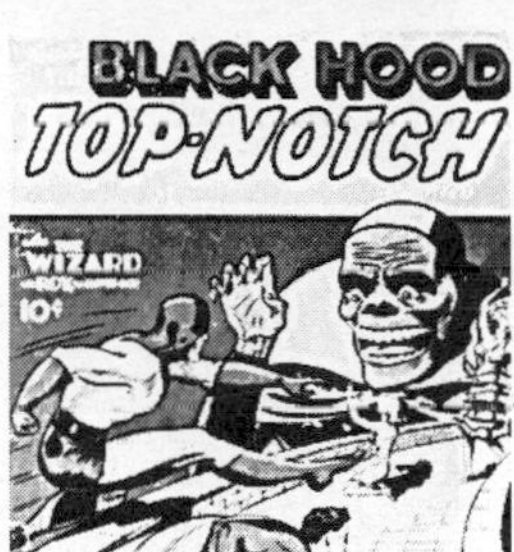

Top Notch Comics #21 © MLJ

Top Spot Comics #1 © Top Spot Publ. Co.

Tor #2 © DC

GD25 FN65 NM94

TOP-NOTCH COMICS (...Laugh #28-45; Laugh Comix #46 on)
Dec, 1939 - No. 45, June, 1944
MLJ Magazines

1-Origin/1st app. The Wizard; Kardak the Mystic Magician, Swift of the Secret Service (ends #3), Air Patrol, The Westpointer, Manhunters (by J. Cole), Mystic (ends #2) & Scott Rand (ends #3) begin; Wizard covers begin, end #8 — 450.00 1350.00 4500.00
2-Dick Storm (ends #8), Stacy Knight M.D. (ends #4) begin; Jack Cole-a — 178.00 534.00 1600.00
3-Bob Phantom, Scott Rand on Mars begin; J. Cole-a — 122.00 366.00 1100.00
4-Origin/1st app. Streak Chandler on Mars; Moore of the Mounted only app.; J. Cole-a — 100.00 300.00 900.00
5-Flag-c; origin/1st app. Galahad; Shanghai Sheridan begins (ends #8); Shield cameo; Novick-a; classic-c — 108.00 324.00 975.00
6-Meskin-a — 81.00 243.00 725.00
7-The Shield x-over in Wizard; The Wizard dons new costume — 97.00 291.00 875.00
8-Origin/1st app. The Firefly & Roy, the Super Boy (9/40, 2nd costumed boy hero after Robin?; also see Toro in Human Torch #1 (Fall/40) — 108.00 324.00 975.00
9-Origin & 1st app. The Black Hood; 1st Black Hood-c & logo (10/40); Fran Frazier begins (Scarce) — 420.00 1260.00 4200.00
10-2nd app. Black Hood — 122.00 366.00 1100.00
11-15 — 75.00 225.00 675.00
16-20 — 67.00 200.00 600.00
21-30: 23-26-Roy app. 24-No Wizard. 25-Last Bob Phantom. 27-Last Firefly. 28-Suzie, Pokey Oakey begin. 29-Last Kardak — 53.00 159.00 475.00
31-44: 33-Dotty & Ditto by Woggon begins (2/43, 1st app.). 44-Black Hood series ends — 34.00 101.00 270.00
45-Last issue — 36.00 108.00 295.00

NOTE: *J. Binder a-1-3. Meskin a-2, 3, 6, 15. Bob Montana a-30; c-28-31. Harry Sahle c-42-45. Woggon a-33-40, 42. Bondage c-17, 19. Black Hood also appeared on radio in 1944. Black Hood app. on c-9-34, 41-44. Roy the Super Boy app. on c-8, 9, 11-27. The Wizard app. on c-1-8, 11-13, 15-22, 24, 25, 27. Pokey Oakey app. on c-28-43. Suzie app. on c-44-on.*

TOPPER & NEIL (TV)
No. 859, Nov, 1957
Dell Publishing Co.

Four Color 859 — 3.60 11.00 40.00

TOPPS COMICS
1947
Four Star Publications

1-L. B. Cole-c — 17.50 53.00 140.00

TOPPS COMICS PRESENTS
No. 0, 1993 (Giveaway, B&W, 36 pgs.)
Topps Comics

0-Dracula vs. Zorro, Teenagents, Silver Star, & Bill the Galactic Hero stories — 1.00

TOPS
July, 1949 - No. 2, Sept, 1949 (25¢, 10-1/4x13-1/4", 68 pgs.)
(Large size-magazine format; for the adult reader)
Tops Magazine, Inc. (Lev Gleason)

1 (Rare)-Story by Dashiell Hammett; Crandall/Lubbers, Tuska, Dan Barry, Fuje-a; Biro painted-c — 83.00 250.00 750.00
2 (Rare)-Crandall/Lubbers, Biro, Kida, Fuje, Guardineer-a — 78.00 234.00 700.00

TOPS COMICS
1944 (10¢, 132 pgs.)
Consolidated Book Publishers

2000-(Color-c, inside in red shade & some in full color)-Ace Kelly by Rick Yager, Black Orchid, Don on the Farm, Dinky Dinkerton (Rare) — 23.00 68.00 180.00

NOTE: *This book is printed in such a way that when the staple is removed, the strips on the left side of the book correspond with the same strips on the right side. Therefore, if strips are removed from the book, each strip can be folded into a complete comic section of its own.*

TOPS COMICS (See Tops in Humor)
1944 (7-1/4x5", 32 pgs.)
Consolidated Book (Lev Gleason)

2001-The Jack of Spades (costumed hero) — 12.00 36.00 95.00
2002-Rip Raider — 7.50 22.50 52.00
2003-Red Birch (gag cartoons) — 2.00 5.00 10.00

TOP SECRET
Jan, 1952
Hillman Publ.

1 — 17.00 49.00 125.00

TOP SECRET ADVENTURES (See Spyman)

TOP SECRETS (...of the F.B.I.)
Nov, 1947 - No. 10, July-Aug, 1949
Street & Smith Publications

1-Powell-c/a — 29.00 86.00 210.00
2-Powell-c/a — 21.00 62.00 150.00
3-6,8,10-Powell-a — 18.00 54.00 130.00
9-Powell-c/a — 19.00 56.00 140.00
7-Used in **SOTI**, pg. 90 & illo. "How to hurt people"; used by N.Y. Legis. Comm.; Powell-c/a — 29.00 86.00 200.00

NOTE: ***Powell** c-1-3, 5-10.*

TOPS IN ADVENTURE
Fall, 1952 (25¢, 132 pgs.)
Ziff-Davis Publishing Co.

1-Crusader from Mars, The Hawk, Football Thrills, He-Man; Powell-a; painted-c — 40.00 120.00 300.00

TOPS IN HUMOR (See Tops Comics?)
1944 (7-1/4x5")
Consolidated Book Publ. (Lev Gleason)

2001(#1)-Origin The Jack of Spades, Ace Kelly by Rick Yager, Black Orchid (female crime fighter) app. — 13.00 39.00 105.00
2 — 8.75 26.25 65.00

TOP SPOT COMICS
1945
Top Spot Publ. Co.

1-The Menace, Duke of Darkness app. — 24.00 71.00 190.00

TOPSY-TURVY
Apr, 1945
R. B. Leffingwell Publ.

1-1st app. Cookie — 8.50 26.00 60.00

TOR (Prehistoric Life on Earth) (Formerly One Million Years Ago)
No. 2, Oct, 1953; No. 3, May, 1954 - No. 5, Oct, 1954
St. John Publishing Co.

3-D 2(10/53)-Kubert-c/a — 10.50 32.00 85.00
3-D 2(10/53)-Oversized, otherwise same contents — 9.50 28.00 75.00
3-D 2(11/53)-Kubert-c/a; has 3-D cover — 9.50 28.00 75.00
3-5-Kubert-c/a: 3-Danny Dreams by Toth; Kubert 1 pg. story (w/self portrait) — 10.50 32.00 85.00

NOTE: *The two October 3-D's have same contents and **Powell** art; the October & November issues are titled 3-D Comics. All 3-D issues are 25¢ and came with 3-D glasses.*

TOR (See Sojourn)
May-June, 1975 - No. 6, Mar-Apr, 1976
National Periodical Publications

1-6: 1-New origin by Kubert. 2-Origin-r/St. John #1 — 1.20 3.00

NOTE: ***Kubert** a-1, 2-6r; c-1-6. **Toth** a(p)-3r.*

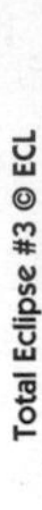
Total Eclipse #3 © ECL

Total Justice #3 © DC

Toyland Comics #3 © FH

GD25 FN65 NM94

TOR (3-D)
July, 1986 - No. 2, Aug, 1987 ($2.50)
Eclipse Comics
1,2: 1-r/One Million Years Ago. 2-r/Tor 3-D #2 1.00 2.50
...2-D: 1,2-Limited signed & numbered editions 1.00 2.50

TOR
June, 1993 - No. 4, 1993 ($5.95, limited series)
Marvel Comics (Epic Comics/Heavy Hitters)
1-4: Joe Kubert-c/a/scripts 2.40 6.00

TORCH OF LIBERTY SPECIAL
Jan, 1995 ($2.50, one-shot)
Dark Horse Comics (Legend)
1-Byrne scripts 1.00 2.50

TORCHY (...Blonde Bombshell) (See Dollman, Military, & Modern)
Nov, 1949 - No. 6, Sept, 1950
Quality Comics Group
1-Bill Ward-c, Gil Fox-a 110.00 331.00 925.00
2,3-Fox-c/a 53.00 159.00 450.00
4-Fox-c/a(3), Ward-a (9 pgs.) 67.00 202.00 575.00
5,6-Ward-c/a, 9 pgs; Fox-a(3) each 90.00 271.00 750.00
Super Reprint #16(1964)-r/#4 with new-c 7.50 22.50 75.00

TO RIVERDALE AND BACK AGAIN (Archie Comics Presents...)
1990 ($2.50, 68 pgs.)
Archie Comics
nn-Byrne-c, Colan-a(p); adapts NBC TV movie 1.00 2.50

TORMENTED, THE (Becomes Surprise Adventures #3 on)
July, 1954 - No. 2, Sept, 1954
Sterling Comics
1,2: Weird/horror stories 17.00 51.00 125.00

TORNADO TOM (See Mighty Midget Comics)

TOTAL ECLIPSE
May, 1988 - No. 5, Apr, 1989 ($3.95, 52 pgs., deluxe size)
Eclipse Comics
Book 1-5: 3-Intro/1st app. new Black Terror 1.60 4.00

TOTAL ECLIPSE: THE SERAPHIM OBJECTIVE
Nov, 1988 ($1.95, one-shot, Baxter paper)
Eclipse Comics
1-Airboy, Valkyrie, The Heap app. .80 2.00

TOTAL JUSTICE
Oct, 1996 - No. 3, Nov, 1996 ($2.25, bi-weekly limited series)(Based on toyline)
DC Comics
1-3 .90 2.25

TOTAL RECALL (Movie)
1990 ($2.95, 68 pgs., movie adaptation, one-shot)
DC Comics
1-Arnold Schwarzenegger photo-c 1.20 3.00

TOTAL WAR (M.A.R.S. Patrol #3 on)
July, 1965 - No. 2, Oct, 1965 (Painted-c)
Gold Key
1,2: Wood-a in each 3.60 11.00 40.00

TO THE LAST MAN (See Zane Grey Four Color #616)

TOUCH OF SILVER, A
Jan, 1997 - Present ($2.95, B&W, bi-monthly)
Image Comics
1-5-Valentino-s/a; photo-c: 5-color pgs. w/Round Table 1.20 3.00

TOUGH KID SQUAD COMICS
Mar, 1942
Timely Comics (TCI)
GD25 FN65 VF82 NM94
1-(Scarce)-Origin & 1st app.The Human Top & The Tough Kid Squad; The Flying Flame app. 790.00 2370.00 4740.00 7900.00
(Estimated up to 100 total copies exist, 6 in NM/Mint)

TOUR OF TORTURE
June, 1996 ($10.00, one-shot)
London Night Studios
nn-Photo-c 1.25 3.75 10.00

TOWER OF SHADOWS (Creatures on the Loose #10 on)
Sept, 1969 - No. 9, Jan, 1971
Marvel Comics Group
GD25 FN65 NM94
1-Steranko, Craig-a(p) 3.50 10.50 35.00
2,3: 2-Neal Adams-a. 3-Barry Smith, Tuska-a 2.50 7.50 20.00
4-Marie Severin-c 1.50 4.50 12.00
5,7-B. Smith-a(p), Wood-a. 5-Wood draws himself (1st pg., 1st panel) 2.50 7.50 20.00
6-9: 6,8-Wood-a; 8-Wrightson-c. 9-Wrightson-c; Roy Thomas app. 1.50 4.50 12.00
Special 1(12/71)-Neal Adams-a 1.50 4.50 12.00
NOTE: ***J. Buscema*** *a-1p, 2p, Special 1r.* ***Colan*** *a-3p, 6p, Special 1.* ***J. Craig*** *a(r)-1p.* ***Ditko*** *a-6, 8, 9r, Special 1.* ***Everett*** *a-9(i)r; c-5i.* ***Kirby*** *a-9(p)r.* ***Severin*** *c-5p, 6.* ***Steranko*** *a-1p.* ***Tuska*** *a-3.* ***Wood*** *a-5-8. Issues 1-9 contain new stories with some pre-Marvel age reprints in 6-9.* ***H. P. Lovecraft*** *adaptation-9.*

TOWN & COUNTRY
May, 1940
Publisher?
nn-Origin The Falcon 38.00 113.00 340.00

TOWN THAT FORGOT SANTA, THE
1961 (Giveaway, 24 pgs.)
W. T. Grant Co.
nn 2.00 6.00 16.00

TOXIC AVENGER (Movie)
Apr, 1991 - No. 11, Feb, 1992 ($1.50)
Marvel Comics
1-10: Based on movie character. 3,10-Photo-c 1.50
11-($1.75) .75 1.80

TOXIC CRUSADERS (TV)
May, 1992 - No. 8, Dec, 1992 ($1.25)
Marvel Comics
1-3-Sam Kieth-c; based on USA network cartoon 1.50
4-8: 8-Kieth-c(i) 1.25

TOYBOY
Oct, 1986 - No. 7?, 1991 ($2.00, Baxter paper)
Continuity Comics
1-7 .80 2.00
NOTE: ***N. Adams*** *a-1; c-1, 2,5.* ***Golden*** *a-7p; c-6,7.* ***Nebres*** *a(i)-1,2.*

TOYLAND COMICS
Jan, 1947 - No. 2, Mar, 1947; No. 3, July, 1947 - No. 4, 1947
Fiction House Magazines
1-Wizard of the Moon begins 20.00 60.00 160.00
2-4: 2,3-Bob Lubbers-c. 3-Tuska-a 12.00 38.00 100.00
148 pg. issue 22.00 66.00 175.00
NOTE: *All above contain strips by* ***Al Walker.***

TOY TOWN COMICS
1945 - No. 7, May, 1947
Toytown/Orbit Publ./B. Antin/Swapper Quarterly
1-Mertie Mouse; L. B. Cole-c/a; funny animal 26.00 80.00 210.00
2-L. B. Cole-a 17.00 51.00 135.00

Transformers #60 © Hasbro

Transmetropolitan #1 © Warren Ellis & Darick Robertson

Trapped! #1 © HARV

	GD25	FN65	NM94
3-7-L. B. Cole-a. 5-Wiggles the Wonderworm-c	14.50	43.00	115.00

TRAGG AND THE SKY GODS (See Gold Key Spotlight, Mystery Comics Digest #3,9 & Spine Tingling Tales)
June, 1975 - No. 8, Feb, 1977; No. 9, May, 1982 (Painted-c #3-8)
Gold Key/Whitman No. 9

	GD25	FN65	NM94
1-Origin		2.00	5.00
2-9: 4-Sabre-Fang app. 8-Ostellon app.; 9-r/#1		1.20	3.00

NOTE: ***Santos*** *a-1, 2, 9r; c-3-7.* ***Spiegel*** *a-3-8.*

TRAIL BLAZERS (Red Dragon #5 on)
1941; No. 2, Apr, 1942 - No. 4, Oct, 1942 (True stories of American heroes)
Street & Smith Publications

	GD25	FN65	NM94
1-Life story of Jack Dempsey & Wright Brothers	29.00	86.00	230.00
2-Brooklyn Dodgers-c/story; Ben Franklin story	17.50	53.00	140.00
3,4: 3-Fred Allen, Red Barber, Yankees stories	16.00	49.00	130.00

TRAIL COLT (Also see Extra Comics & Manhunt!)
1949 - No. 2, 1949
Magazine Enterprises

	GD25	FN65	NM94
nn(A-1 #24)-7 pg. Frazetta-a r-in Manhunt #13; Undercover Girl app.; The Red Fox by L. B. Cole; Ingels-c; Whitney-a (Scarce)	33.00	98.00	260.00
2(A-1 #26)-Undercover Girl; Ingels-c; L. B. Cole-a (6 pgs.)	28.00	83.00	220.00

TRANSFORMERS, THE (TV)(See G.I. Joe and...)
Sept, 1984 - No. 80, July, 1991 (75¢/$1.00)
Marvel Comics Group

	GD25	FN65	NM94
1-Based on Hasbro Toys		1.00	2.50
2,3		.75	1.80
4-10,75: 75-($1.50, 52 pgs.)			1.50
11-74,76-80: 21-Intro Aerialbots. 54-Intro Micromasters			1.00

NOTE: *Second and third printings of all issues exist and are worth less than originals. Was originally planned as a four issue mini-series.* ***Wrightson*** *a-64i(4 pgs.).*

TRANSFORMERS: GENERATION 2
Nov, 1993 - No. 12, Oct, 1994 ($1.75)
Marvel Comics

	GD25	FN65	NM94
1-($2.95, 68 pgs.)-Collector's ed. w/bi-fold metallic-c		1.20	3.00
1-11: 1-Newsstand edition (68 pgs.)		.70	1.75
12-($2.25, 52 pgs.)		.90	2.25

TRANSMETROPOLITAN
Sept, 1997 - Present ($2.50)
DC Comics (Vertigo)

	GD25	FN65	NM94
1,3-9-Warren Ellis-s/Darick Robertson-a(p)			2.50
2			4.00

TRANSMUTATION OF IKE GARUDA, THE
July, 1991 - No. 2, 1991 ($3.95, 52 pgs.)
Marvel Comics (Epic Comics)

	GD25	FN65	NM94
1,2		1.60	4.00

TRAPMAN
June, 1994 - No. 2, 1994? ($2.95, quarterly, unfinished limited series)
Phantom Comics

	GD25	FN65	NM94
1,2		1.20	3.00

TRAPPED
1951 (Giveaway, soft-c, 16 pgs.)
Harvey Publications (Columbia University Press)

	GD25	FN65	NM94
nn-Drug education comic (30,000 printed?) distributed to schools.; mentioned in **SOTI**, pgs. 256,350	1.60	4.00	8.00

NOTE: *Many copies surfaced in 1979 causing a setback in price; beware of trimmed edges, because many copies have a brittle edge.*

TRAPPED!
Oct, 1954 - No. 5, June?, 1955
Periodical House Magazines (Ace)

	GD25	FN65	NM94
1 (All reprints)	8.70	26.00	55.00
2-5: 4-r/Men Against Crime #4 in its entirety	5.70	17.00	35.00

NOTE: ***Colan*** *a-1, 4.* ***Sekowsky*** *a-1.*

TRASH
Mar, 1978 - No. 2, June, 1978 (B&W, magazine)
Trash Publ. Co.

	GD25	FN65	NM94
1,2	1.50	4.50	10.00

TRAVELS OF JAIMIE McPHEETERS, THE (TV)
Dec, 1963
Gold Key

	GD25	FN65	NM94
1-Kurt Russell photo on-c plus photo back-c	2.00	6.00	22.00

TREASURE CHEST (Catholic Guild; also see Topix)
3/12/46 - V27#8, July, 1972 (Educational comics)
George A. Pflaum (not publ. during Summer)

	GD25	FN65	NM94
V1#1	19.00	56.00	150.00
2-6 (5/21/46): 5-Dr. Styx app. by Baily	8.75	26.25	70.00
V2#1-20 (9/3/46-5/27/47)	7.15	21.50	50.00
V3#1-5,7-20 (1st slick cover)	5.70	17.00	40.00
V3#6-Jules Verne's "Voyage to the Moon"	8.50	26.00	60.00
V4#1-20 (9/9/48-5/31/49)	5.00	15.00	30.00
V5#1-20 (9/6/49-5/31/50)	4.15	12.50	25.00
V6#1-20 (9/14/50-5/31/51)	4.15	12.50	25.00
V7#1-20 (9/13/51-6/5/52)	4.00	10.00	20.00
V8#1-20 (9/11/52-6/4/53)	3.60	9.00	18.00
V9#1-20 ('53-'54)	3.20	8.00	16.00
V10#1-20 ('54-'55)	3.20	8.00	16.00
V11('55-'56), V12('56-'57)	2.80	7.00	14.00
V13#1,3-5,7,9-V17#1 ('57-'63)	2.40	6.00	12.00
V13#2,6,8-Ingels-a	4.50	13.50	45.00
V17#2- "This Godless Communism" series begins(not in odd #'d issues); cover shows hammer & sickle over Statue of Liberty; 8 pg. Crandall-a of family life under communism	14.00	42.00	140.00
V17#3,5,7,9,11,13,15,17,19	1.00	2.80	7.00
V17#4,6,14- "This Godless Communism" stories	9.00	27.00	90.00
V17#8-Shows red octopus encompassing Earth, firing squad; 8 pgs. Crandall-a	11.00	33.00	110.00
V17#10- "This Godless Communism" - how Stalin came to power, part I; Crandall-a	9.50	28.50	95.00
V17#12-Stalin in WWII, forced labor, death by exhaustion; Crandall-a	9.50	28.50	95.00
V17#16-Kruschev takes over; de-Stalinization	9.50	28.50	95.00
V17#18-Kruschev's control; murder of revolters, brainwash, space race by Crandall	9.50	28.50	95.00
V17#20-End of series; Kruschev-people are puppets, firing squads hammer & sickle over Statue of Liberty, snake around communist manifesto by Crandall	11.00	33.00	110.00
V18#1-20, V19#11-20, V20#1-20(1964-65): V18#11-Crandall draws himself & 13 other artists on cover	1.25	3.75	10.00
V18#5- "What About Red China?" - describes how communists took over China	4.00	12.00	40.00
V19#1-10- "Red Victim" anti-communist series in all	4.00	12.00	40.00
V21-V25(1965-70)-(two V24#5's 11/7/68 & 11/21/68) (no V24#6)	1.00	3.00	8.00
V26, V27#1-8 (V26,27-68 pgs.)	1.25	3.75	10.00
Summer Edition V1#1-6('66), V2#1-6('67)	1.85	5.50	15.00

NOTE: ***Anderson*** *a-V18#13.* ***Borth*** *a-V7#10-19 (serial), V8#8-17 (serial), V9#1-10 (serial), V13#2, 6, 11, V14-V25 (except V22#1-3, 11-13), Summer Ed. V1#3-6.* ***Crandall*** *a-V16#7, 9, 12, 14, 16-18, 20; V17#1, 2, 4-6, 10, 12, 14, 16-18, 20; V18#1, 2, 3(2 pg.), 7, 9-20; V19#4, 11, 13, 16, 19, 20; V20#1, 2, 4, 6, 8-10, 12, 14-16, 18, 20; V21#1-5, 8-11, 13, 16-18; V22#3, 7, 9-11, 14; V23#3, 6, 9, 16, 18; V24#7, 8, 10, 13, 16; V25#8, 16; V27#1-7r, 8r(2 pg.), Summer Ed. V1#3-5, V2#3; c-V16#7, V18#2(part), 7, 11, V19#4, 19, 20, V20#15, V21#5, 9, V22#3, 7, 9, 11, V23#9, 16, V24#13, 16, V25#8, Summer Ed. V1#2 (back c-V1#2-5).* ***Powell*** *a-V10#11. V19#11, 15, V10#13, V13#6, 8 all have wraparound covers. All the above Crandall issues should be priced by condition from $4-8.00 in mint unless already priced.*

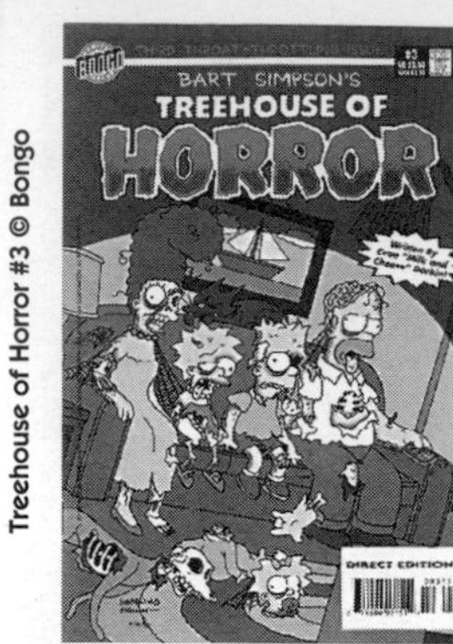

Treehouse of Horror #3 © Bongo

Tribe #3 © Axis

Trinity Angels #9 © Acclaim

GD25 FN65 NM94

TREASURE CHEST OF THE WORLD'S BEST COMICS
1945 (500 pgs., hard-c)
Superior, Toronto, Canada

Contains Blue Beetle, Captain Combat, John Wayne, Dynamic Man, Nemo, Li'l Abner; contents can vary - represents random binding of extra books; Capt. America on-c 72.00 216.00 650.00

TREASURE COMICS
No date (1943) (50¢, 324 pgs., cardboard-c)
Prize Publications? (no publisher listed)

1-(Rare)-Contains rebound Prize Comics #7-11 from 1942 (blank inside-c) 167.00 500.00 1500.00

TREASURE COMICS
June-July, 1945 - No. 12, Fall, 1947
Prize Publications (American Boys' Comics)

1-Paul Bunyan & Marco Polo begin; Highwayman & Carrot Topp only app.; Kiefer-a 24.00 71.00 190.00
2-Arabian Knight, Gorilla King, Dr. Styx begin 12.00 36.00 95.00
3,4,9,12: 9-Kiefer-a 8.75 26.25 70.00
5-Marco Polo-c; Krigstein-a 15.00 45.00 120.00
6,11-Krigstein-a; 11-Krigstein-c 14.00 41.00 110.00
7,8-Frazetta-a (5 pgs. each). 7-Capt. Kidd Jr. app. 28.00 83.00 220.00
10-Simon & Kirby-c/a 23.00 68.00 180.00
NOTE: ***Barry*** *a-9-11; c-12.* ***Kiefer*** *a-3, 5, 7; c-2, 6, 7.* ***Roussos*** *a-11.*

TREASURE ISLAND (See Classics Illustrated #64, Doc Savage Comics #1, King Classics, Movie Classics & Movie Comics)
No. 624, Apr, 1955 (Disney)
Dell Publishing Co.

Four Color 624-Movie, photo-c 8.00 25.00 90.00

TREASURY OF COMICS
1947; No. 2, July, 1947 - No. 4, Sept, 1947; No. 5, Jan, 1948
St. John Publishing Co.

nn(#1)-Abbie an' Slats (nn on-c, #1 on inside) 12.00 38.00 100.00
2-Jim Hardy Comics; featuring Windy & Paddles 8.75 26.25 70.00
3-Bill Bumlin 7.15 21.50 50.00
4-Abbie an' Slats 8.75 26.25 70.00
5-Jim Hardy Comics #1 8.75 26.25 70.00

TREASURY OF COMICS
Mar, 1948 - No. 5, 1948 (Reg. size); 1948-1950 (Over 500 pgs., $1.00)
St. John Publishing Co.

1 15.50 47.00 125.00
2(#2 on-c, #1 on inside) 8.75 26.25 70.00
3-5 8.50 26.00 60.00
1-(1948, 500 pgs., hard-c)-Abbie & Slats, Abbott & Costello, Casper, Little Annie Rooney, Little Audrey, Jim Hardy, Ella Cinders (16 books bound together) (Rare) 89.00 267.00 800.00
1(1949, 500 pgs.)-Same format as above 89.00 267.00 800.00
1(1950, 500 pgs.)-Same format as above; different-c; (also see Little Audrey Yearbook) (Rare) 89.00 267.00 800.00

TREASURY OF DOGS, A (See Dell Giants)

TREASURY OF HORSES, A (See Dell Giants)

TREEHOUSE OF HORROR (Bart Simpson's...)
1995 -Present ($2.95/$2.50, annual)
Bongo Comics

1-(1995, $2.95)-Groening-c; Allred, Robinson & Smith stories. 1.60 4.00
2-(1996, $2.50)-Stories by Dini & Bagge; infinity-c by Groening 1.20 3.00
3-(1997, $2.50)-Dorkin-s/Groening-c 2.50

TREKKER (See Dark Horse Presents #6)
May, 1987 - No. 9?, 1988 ($1.50, B&W)
Dark Horse Comics

GD25 FN65 NM94

1-9: Sci/Fi stories 1.50
Color Special 1 (1989, $2.95, 52 pgs.) 1.20 3.00
Collection ($5.95, B&W) 2.40 6.00

TRENCHER (See Blackball Comics)
May, 1993 - No. 4, Oct, 1993 ($1.95, unfinished limited series)
Image Comics

1-4: Keith Giffen-c/a/scripts. 3-Supreme-c/story .80 2.00

TRIBAL FORCE
Aug, 1996 ($2.50)
Mystic Comics

1-Reads "Special Edition" on-c 1.00 2.50

TRIB COMIC BOOK, THE
Sept. 24, 1977 - Vol.4, #36, 1980 (8-1/2"x11", 24 pgs., weekly)
Winnipeg Tribune (155 total issues)

V1# 1-Color pages (Sunday strips)-Spiderman, Asterix, Disney's Scamp, Wizard of Id, Doonesbury, Inside Woody Allen, Mary Worth, & others (similar to Spirit sections) 1.85 5.50 14.00
V2#2-15, V3#1-53, V4#1-33 1.25 3.75 10.00
V4#34-36 (not distributed) 2.50 7.50 20.00
Note: All issues have Spider-Man. Later issues contain Star Trek and Star Wars. 20 strips in ea. The first newspaper to put Sunday pages into a comic book format.

TRIBE (See WildC.A.T.S #4)
Apr, 1993; No. 2, Sept, 1993 - No. 3, 1994 ($2.50/$1.95)
Image Comics/Axis Comics No. 2 on

1-By Johnson & Stroman; gold foil & embossed on black-c 1.00 2.50
1-($2.50)-Ivory Edition; gold foil & embossed on white-c; available only through the creators 1.00 2.50
2,3: 2-1st Axis Comics issue. 3-Savage Dragon app. .80 2.00

TRIGGER (See Roy Rogers'...)

TRIGGER TWINS
Mar-Apr, 1973 (20¢, one-shot)
National Periodical Publications

1-Trigger Twins & Pow Wow Smith-r/All-Star Western #94,103 & Western Comics #81; Infantino-r(p) 1.85 5.50 15.00

TRINITY (See DC Universe: Trinity)

TRINITY ANGELS
July, 1997 - Present ($2.50)
Acclaim Comics (Valiant Heroes)

1-10-Maguire-s/a(p):4-Copycat-c 1.00 2.50

TRIPLE GIANT COMICS (See Archie All-Star Specials under Archie Comics)

TRIPLE THREAT
Winter, 1945
Special Action/Holyoke/Gerona Publ.

1-Duke of Darkness, King O'Leary 16.00 49.00 130.00

TRIPLE-X
Dec, 1994 - No. 7, June, 1995 ($3.95, B&W, limited series)
Dark Horse Comics

1-7 1.60 4.00

TRIP TO OUTER SPACE WITH SANTA
1950s (self-c)
Sales Promotions, Inc/Peoria Dry Goods

nn-Comics, games & puzzles 3.60 9.00 18.00

TRIP WITH SANTA ON CHRISTMAS EVE, A
No date (Early 1950s) (Giveaway, 16 pgs., paper-c)
Rockford Dry Goods Co.

nn 3.60 9.00 18.00

TRIUMPH (Also see Justice League Task Force & Zero Hour)

Troll II #1 © Rob Liefeld

Troublemakers #8 © Acclaim

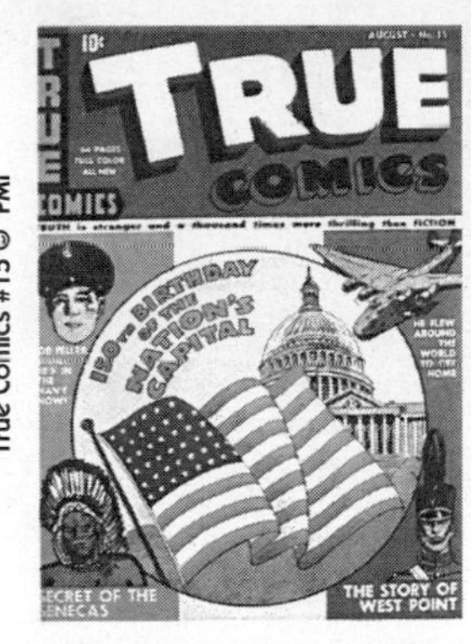

True Comics #15 © PMI

GD25 FN65 NM94

June, 1995 - No. 4, Sept, 1995 ($1.75, limited series)
DC Comics

1-4: 3-Hourman, JLA app. .70 1.75

TRIUMPHANT UNLEASHED
No. 0, Nov, 1993 - No. 1, Nov, 1993 ($2.50, limited series)
Triumphant Comics

0-Serially numbered, 0-Red logo 1.00 2.50
0-White logo (no cover price; giveaway) 1.00 2.50
1-Cover is negative & reverse of #0-c 1.00 2.50

TROLL (Also see Brigade)
Dec, 1993 ($2.50, one-shot, 44 pgs.)
Image Comics (Extreme Studios)

1-1st app. Troll; Liefeld scripts; Matsuda-c/a(p) 1.00 2.50
Halloween Special (1994, $2.95)-Maxx app. 1.20 3.00
...Once A Hero (8/94, $2.50) 1.00 2.50

TROLLORDS
2/86 - No. 15, 1988; V2#1, 11/88 - V2#4, 1989 (1-15: $1.50, B&W)
Tru Studios/Comico V2#1 on

1-1st & 2nd printings 1.50
2-15: 6-Christmas issue; silver logo 1.50
V2#1 ($1.75, color, Comico) .75 1.80
V2#2,3 ($1.95, color) .80 2.00
4 ($2.50, color) 1.00 2.50
Special 1 ($1.75, 2/87, color)-Jerry's Big Fun Bk. .75 1.80

TROLLORDS
July, 1989 - No. 6, 1990 ($2.25, B&W, limited series)
Apple Comics

1-6: 1-"The Big Batman Movie Parody" .90 2.30

TROLL PATROL
Jan, 1993 ($1.95, 52 pgs.)
Harvey Comics

1 .80 2.00

TROLL II (Also see Brigade)
July, 1994 ($3.95, one-shot)
Image Comics (Extreme Studios)

1 1.60 4.00

TROUBLED SOULS
1990 ($9.95, trade paperback)
Fleetway

nn-Garth Ennis scripts & John McCrea painted-c/a. 1.25 3.75 10.00

TROUBLEMAKERS
Apr, 1997 - Present ($2.50)
Acclaim Comics (Valiant Heroes)

1-13: Fabian Nicieza scripts in all. 1-1st app. XL, Rebound & Blur. 8-Copycat-c. 12-Shooting of Parker 1.00 2.50

TROUBLEMAN
June, 1996 - No. 3, Aug, 1996 ($2.25, limited series)
Image Comics (Motown Machineworks)

1-3 .90 2.25

TROUBLE SHOOTERS, THE (TV)
No. 1108, Jun-Aug, 1960
Dell Publishing Co.

Four Color 1108-Keenan Wynn photo-c 4.50 13.50 50.00

TROUBLE WITH GIRLS, THE
8/87 - #14, 1988; V2#1, 2/89 - V2#10, 1990? ($1.95, B&W/color)
Malibu Comics (Eternity Comics) #7-14/Comico V2#1-4/Eternity V2#5 on

1-14 ($1.95, B&W, Eternity)-Gerard Jones scripts & Tim Hamilton-c/a in all. .80 2.00
V2#1-10-Jones scripts, Hamilton-c/a. .80 2.00
Annual 1 (1988, $2.95) 1.20 3.00
Christmas Special 1 (12/91, $2.95, B&W, Eternity)-Jones scripts, Hamilton-c/a. 1.20 3.00
Graphic Novel 1 (7/88, $6.95, B&W)-r/#1-3 1.00 2.80 7.00
Graphic Novel 2 (1989, $7.95, B&W)-r/#4-6 1.00 3.00 8.00

TROUBLE WITH GIRLS, THE: NIGHT OF THE LIZARD
1993 - No. 4, 1993 ($2.50/$1.95, limited series)
Marvel Comics (Epic Comics/Heavy Hitters)

1-Embossed-c; Gerard Jones scripts & Bret Blevins-c/a in all. 1.00 2.50
2-4: 2-Begin $1.95-c. .80 2.00

TRUE ADVENTURES (Formerly True Western)(Men's Adventures #4 on)
No. 3, May, 1950 (52 pgs.)
Marvel Comics (CCC)

3-Powell, Sekowsky-a; Brodsky-c 13.00 39.00 95.00

TRUE ANIMAL PICTURE STORIES
Winter, 1947 - No. 2, Spring-Summer, 1947
True Comics Press

1,2 7.85 23.50 55.00

TRUE AVIATION PICTURE STORIES (Becomes Aviation Adventures & Model Building #16 on)
1942; No. 2, Jan-Feb, 1943 - No. 15, Sept-Oct, 1946
Parents' Magazine Institute

1-(#1 & 2 titled ...Aviation Comics Digest)(not digest size) 11.30 34.00 90.00
2 7.15 21.50 50.00
3-14: 3-10-Plane photos on-c. 11,13-Photo-c 6.50 19.50 45.00
15-(Titled "True Aviation Adventures & Model Building") 5.70 17.00 40.00

TRUE BRIDE'S EXPERIENCES (Formerly Teen-Age Brides)
(True Bride-To-Be Romances No. 17 on)
No. 8, Oct, 1954 - No. 16, Feb, 1956
True Love (Harvey Publications)

8 6.35 19.00 38.00
9,10: 10-Last pre-code (2/55) 4.00 12.00 24.00
11-15 4.00 10.00 20.00
16-Spanking panels (3) 5.85 17.50 35.00
NOTE: ***Powell*** *a-8-10, 12, 13.*

TRUE BRIDE-TO-BE ROMANCES (Formerly True Bride's Experiences)
No. 17, Apr, 1956 - No. 30, Nov, 1958
Home Comics/True Love (Harvey)

17-S&K-c, Powell-a 7.85 23.50 55.00
18-20,22,25-28,30 4.00 10.00 20.00
21,23,24,29-Powell-a. 29-Baker-a (1 pg.) 4.00 12.00 24.00

TRUE COMICS (Also see Outstanding American War Heroes)
April, 1941 - No. 84, Aug, 1950
True Comics/Parents' Magazine Press

1-Marathon run story; life story Winston Churchill 25.00 75.00 200.00
2-Red Cross story; Everett-a 12.00 38.00 100.00
3-Baseball Hall of Fame story 14.50 43.00 115.00
4,5: 4-Story of American flag "Old Glory". 5-Life story of Joe Louis 10.00 30.00 80.00
6-Baseball World Series story 14.00 41.00 110.00
7-10: 7-Buffalo Bill story. 10,11-Teddy Roosevelt 7.85 23.50 55.00
11-16,18-20: 11-Thomas Edison, Douglas MacArthur stories. 13-Harry Houdini story. 14-Charlie McCarthy story. 15-Flag-c; Bob Feller story. 18-Story of America begins, ends #26. 19-Eisenhower-c/s 7.15 21.50 50.00
17-Brooklyn Dodgers story 8.50 26.00 60.00

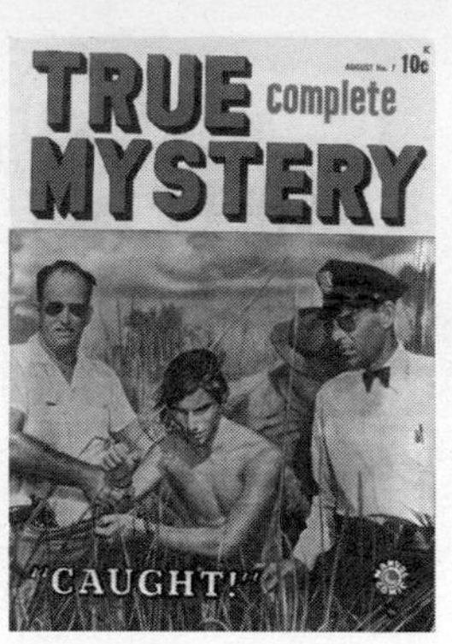

True Complete Mystery #7 © MEG

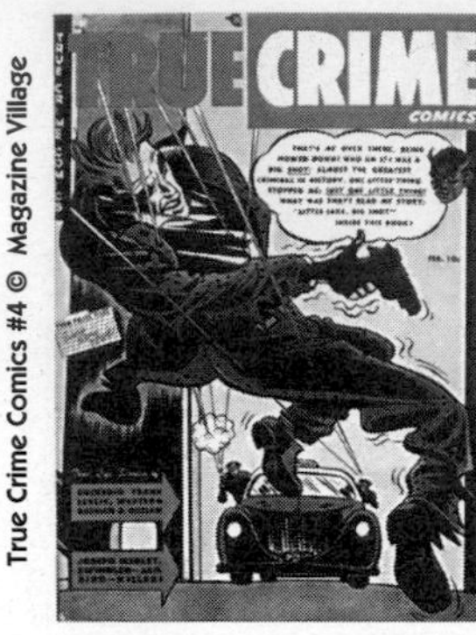

True Crime Comics #4 © Magazine Village

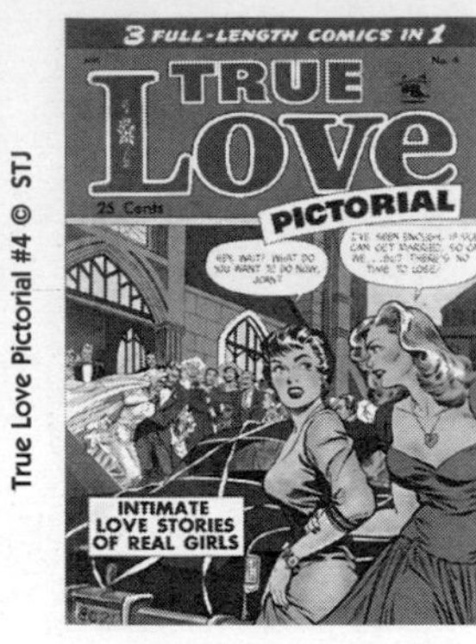

True Love Pictorial #4 © STJ

GD25 FN65 NM94

21-30: 24-Marco Polo story 6.00 18.00 42.00
31-Red Grange "Galloping Ghost" story 5.00 15.00 30.00
32-46: 33-Origin/1st app. Steve Saunders, Special Agent. 39-FDR story. 46-George Gershwin story 4.25 13.00 26.00
47-Atomic bomb issue (c/story, 3/46) 7.85 23.50 55.00
48-66: 55-(12/46)-1st app. Sad Sack by Baker (1/2 pg.). 58-Jim Jeffries (boxer) story; Harry Houdini story. 59-Bob Hope story. 60-Speedway Speed Demon-c/story. 66-Will Rogers-c/story 4.00 12.00 24.00
67-1st oversized issue (12/47); Steve Saunders, Special Agent begins 5.70 17.00 35.00
68-70,72,74-79: 68-70,72,74-78-Features True FBI advs. 69-Jack Benny story. 72-Jackie Robinson story. 74-Amos 'n' Andy story. 78-Stan Musial-c/story. 4.00 12.00 24.00
71-Joe DiMaggio-c/story. 5.00 15.00 30.00
73-Walt Disney's life story 5.70 17.00 35.00
80-84 (Scarce)-All distr. to subscribers through mail only; paper-c. 80-Rocket trip to the moon story. 81-Red Grange story 14.00 41.00 110.00
(Prices vary widely on issues 80-84)

NOTE: ***Bob Kane** a-7. **Palais** a-80. **Powell** c/a-80. #80-84 have soft covers and combined with Tex Granger, Jack Armstrong, and Calling All Kids. #68-78 featured true FBI adventures.*

TRUE COMICS AND ADVENTURE STORIES
1965 (Giant) (25¢)
Parents' Magazine Institute

1,2: 1-Fighting Hero of Viet Nam; LBJ on-c 1.00 2.80 7.00

TRUE COMPLETE MYSTERY (Formerly Complete Mystery)
No. 5, Apr, 1949 - No. 8, Oct, 1949
Marvel Comics (PrPI)

5 20.00 60.00 150.00
6-8: 6-8-Photo-c 16.00 47.00 120.00

TRUE CONFIDENCES
1949 (Fall) - No. 4, June, 1950 (All photo-c)
Fawcett Publications

1-Has ad for Fawcett Love Adventures #1, but publ. as Love Memoirs #1 as Marvel published the title first; Swayze-a 12.00 36.00 95.00
2-4: 3-Swayze-a. 4-Powell-a 8.50 26.00 60.00

TRUE CRIME CASES (...From Official Police Files)
1944 (25¢, 100 pg. Giant)
St. John Publishing Co.

nn-Matt Baker-c 38.00 114.00 285.00

TRUE CRIME COMICS (Also see Complete Book of...)
No. 2, May, 1947; No. 3, July-Aug, 1948 - No. 6, June-July, 1949; V2#1, Aug-Sept, 1949 (52 pgs.)
Magazine Village

2-Jack Cole-c/a; used in **SOTI**, pgs. 81,82 plus illo. "A sample of the injury-to-eye motif" & illo. "Dragging living people to death"; used in **POP**, pg. 105; "Murder, Morphine and Me" classic drug propaganda story used by N.Y. Legis. Comm. 115.00 346.00 975.00
3-Classic Cole-c/a; drug story with hypo, opium den & with drawing addict 84.00 253.00 725.00
4-Jack Cole-c/a; c-taken from a story panel in #3 (r-(2) **SOTI** & **POP** stories/#2?) 76.00 228.00 650.00
5-Jack Cole-c, Marijuana racket story (Canadian ed. w/cover similar to #3 exists w/out drug story) 48.00 146.00 425.00
6-Not a reprint, original story (Canadian ed. reprints #4 w/different coloring on-c) 40.00 120.00 325.00
V2#1-Used in **SOTI**, pgs. 81,82 & illo. "Dragging living people to death"; Toth, Wood (3 pgs.), Roussos-a; Cole-r from #2 68.00 206.00 550.00

NOTE: *V2#1 was reprinted in Canada as V2#9 (12/49); same-c & contents minus Wood-a.*

TRUE FAITH
1990 ($9.95, graphic novel)
Fleetway

nn-Garth Ennis scripts 2.50 7.50 25.00
Reprinted by DC/Vertigo ('97, $12.95) 13.00

TRUE GHOST STORIES (See Ripley's...)

TRUE LIFE ROMANCES (...Romance on cover)
Dec, 1955 - No. 3, Aug, 1956
Ajax/Farrell Publications

1 7.85 23.50 55.00
2 5.00 15.00 30.00
3-Disbrow-a 5.70 17.00 36.00

TRUE LIFE SECRETS
Mar-April, 1951 - No. 28, Sept, 1955; No. 29, Jan, 1956
Romantic Love Stories/Charlton

1-Photo-c begin, end #3? 8.75 26.25 65.00
2 5.35 16.00 32.00
3-19 4.00 12.00 24.00
20-29: 25-Last precode(3/55) 4.00 10.00 20.00

TRUE LIFE TALES (Formerly Mitzi's Romances #8?)
No. 8, Oct, 1949 - No. 2, Jan, 1950 (52 pgs.)
Marvel Comics (CCC)

8(#1, 10/49), 2-Both have photo-c 8.00 24.00 50.00

TRUE LOVE
Jan, 1986 - No. 2, Jan, 1986 ($2.00, Baxter paper)
Eclipse Comics

1,2-Love stories reprinted from pre-code Standard Comics; Toth-a(p) in both; 1-Dave Stevens-c. 2-Mayo-a .80 2.00

TRUE LOVE CONFESSIONS
May, 1954 - No. 11, Jan, 1956
Premier Magazines

1-Marijuana story 7.85 23.50 55.00
2 4.25 13.00 26.00
3-11 4.00 11.00 22.00

TRUE LOVE PICTORIAL
1952 - No. 11, Aug, 1954
St. John Publishing Co.

1-Only photo-c 12.0 36.00 90.00
2-Baker-c/a 12.00 38.00 100.00
3-5(All 25¢, 100 pgs.): 4-Signed story by Estrada. 5-(4/53)-Formerly Teen-Age Temptations; Kubert-a in #3; Baker-a in #3-5 26.00 77.00 190.00
6,7: Baker-c/a. 7-Signed story by Estrada 13.00 39.00 95.00
8,10,11-Baker-c/a 12.00 36.00 90.00
9-Baker-c 10.00 30.00 70.00

TRUE LOVE PROBLEMS AND ADVICE ILLUSTRATED (Becomes Romance Stories of True Love No. 45 on)
June, 1949 - No. 6, Apr, 1950; No. 7, Jan, 1951 - No. 44, Mar, 1957
McCombs/Harvey Publ./Home Comics

V1#1 11.50 34.00 80.00
2 6.70 20.00 40.00
3-10: 7-9-Elias-c 5.00 15.00 30.00
11-13,15-23,25-31: 31-Last pre-code (1/55) 4.00 10.00 20.00
14,24-Rape scene 4.25 13.00 26.00
32-37,39-44 3.20 8.00 16.00
38-S&K-c 5.85 17.50 35.00

NOTE: ***Powell** a-1, 2, 7-14, 17-25, 28, 29, 33, 40, 41. #3 has True Love... on inside.*

TRUE MOVIE AND TELEVISION (Part teenage magazine)
Aug, 1950 - No. 3, Nov, 1950; No. 4, Mar, 1951 (52 pgs.) (1-3: 10¢)
Toby Press

1-Elizabeth Taylor photo-c; Gene Autry, Shirley Temple, Li'l Abner app. 37.00 111.00 270.00
2-(9/50)-Janet Leigh/Liz Taylor/Ava Gardner & others photo-c; Frazetta John

True Sport Picture Stories V3 #11 © S&S

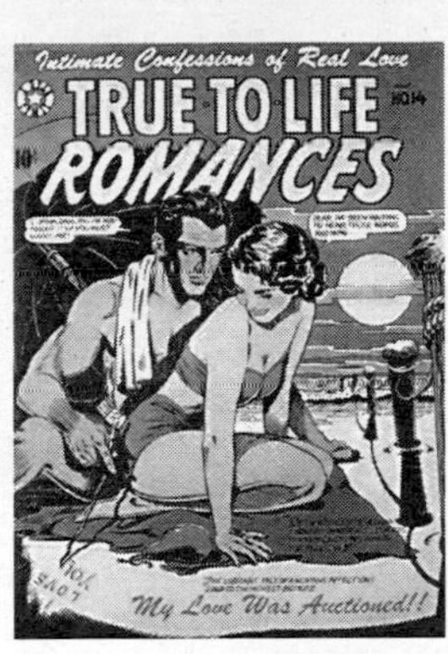

True-To-Life Romances #14 © STAR

Tuff Ghosts Starring Spooky #1 © HARV

	GD25	FN65	NM94
Wayne illo from J.Wayne Adv. Comics #2 (4/50)	27.00	81.00	200.00
3-June Allyson photo-c; Montgomery Cliff, Esther Williams, Andrews Sisters app; Li'l Abner featured; Sadie Hawkins' Day	24.00	73.00	180.00
4-Jane Powell photo-c (15¢)	11.00	33.00	80.00

OTE: *16 pgs. in color, rest movie material in black & white.*

RUE SECRETS (Formerly Our Love?)
lo. 3, Mar, 1950; No. 4, Feb, 1951 - No. 40, Sept, 1956
larvel (IPS)/Atlas Comics (MPI) #4 on

	GD25	FN65	NM94
3 (52 pgs.)(IPS one-shot)`	8.75	26.25	70.00
4,5,7-10	5.70	17.00	35.00
6,22-Everett-a	6.50	19.50	45.00
11-20	5.00	15.00	30.00
21,23-28: 24-Colletta-c. 28-Last pre-code (2/55)	4.00	11.00	22.00
29-40: 34,36-Colletta-a	2.50	7.50	20.00

RUE SPORT PICTURE STORIES (Formerly Sport Comics)
'1#5, Feb, 1942 - V5#2, July-Aug, 1949
treet & Smith Publications

	GD25	FN65	NM94
'1#5-Joe DiMaggio-c/story	28.00	83.00	220.00
6-12 (1942-43): 12-Jack Dempsey story	15.00	45.00	120.00
'2#1-12 (1944-45): 7-Stan Musial-c/story; photo story of the New York Yankees	14.00	41.00	110.00
'3#1-12 (1946-47): 7-Joe DiMaggio, Stan Musial, Bob Feller & others back from the armed service story. 8-Billy Conn vs. Joe Louis-c/story	12.00	36.00	95.00
'4#1-12 (1948-49), V5#1,2	10.50	32.00	85.00

OTE: ***Powell** a-V3#10, V4#1-4, 6-8, 10-12; V5#1, 2; c-V3#11, V4#3-7, 9-12. **Ravielli** c-V5#2.*

'RUE STORIES OF ROMANCE
an, 1950 - No. 3, May, 1950 (All photo-c)
'awcett Publications

	GD25	FN65	NM94
1	8.75	26.25	70.00
2,3: 3-Marcus Swayze-a	7.15	21.50	50.00

'RUE STORY OF JESSE JAMES, THE (See Jesse James, Four Color 757)

'RUE SWEETHEART SECRETS
/50; No. 2, 7/50; No. 3, 1951(nd); No. 4, 9/51 - No. 11, 1/53
awcett Publications (All photo-c)

	GD25	FN65	NM94
1-Photo-c; Debbie Reynolds?	10.00	30.00	75.00
2-Wood-a (11 pgs.)	14.00	43.00	105.00
3-11: 4,5-Powell-a. 8-Marcus Swayze-a. 11-Evans-a	7.50	22.50	50.00

'RUE TALES OF LOVE (Formerly Secret Story Romances)
lo. 22, April, 1956 - No. 31, Sept, 1957
tlas Comics (TCI)

	GD25	FN65	NM94
22	5.70	17.00	40.00
23-24,26-31-Colletta-a in most:	4.00	11.00	22.00
25-Everett-a; Colletta-a	4.25	13.00	28.00

'RUE TALES OF ROMANCE
lo. 4, June, 1950
'awcett Publications

	GD25	FN65	NM94
4-Photo-c	6.00	18.00	42.00

'RUE 3-D
)ec, 1953 - No. 2, Feb, 1954 (25¢)(Both came with 2 pair of glasses)
larvey Publications

	GD25	FN65	NM94
1-Nostrand, Powell-a	5.00	15.00	50.00
2-Powell-a	5.00	15.00	50.00

IOTE: *Many copies of #1 surfaced in 1984.*

'RUE-TO-LIFE ROMANCES (Formerly Guns Against Gangsters)
#8, 11-12/49; #9, 1-2/50; #3, 4/50 - #5, 9/50; #6, 1/51 - #23, 10/54
Star Publications

	GD25	FN65	NM94
8(#1, 1949)	17.00	49.00	125.00
9(#2),4-10	12.00	36.00	95.00
3-Janet Leigh/Glenn Ford photo on-c plus true life story of each	14.00	41.00	110.00
11,22,23	10.00	30.00	80.00
12-14,17-21-Disbrow-a	12.00	36.00	95.00
15,16-Wood & Disbrow-a in each	14.00	43.00	110.00

NOTE: ***Kamen** a-13. **Kamen/Feldstein** a-14. All have **L.B. Cole** covers.*

TRUE WAR EXPERIENCES
Aug, 1952 - No. 4, Dec, 1952
Harvey Publications

	GD25	FN65	NM94
1	7.50	22.50	75.00
2-4	3.50	10.50	35.00

TRUE WAR ROMANCES (Becomes Exotic Romances #22 on)
Sept, 1952 - No. 21, June, 1955
Quality Comics Group

	GD25	FN65	NM94
1-Photo-c	10.00	30.00	70.00
2	5.70	17.00	35.00
3-10: 9-Whitney-a	4.25	13.00	26.00
11-21: 20-Last precode (4/55). 14-Whitney-a	4.00	11.00	22.00

TRUE WAR STORIES (See Ripley's...)

TRUE WESTERN (True Adventures #3)
Dec, 1949 - No. 2, March, 1950
Marvel Comics (MMC)

	GD25	FN65	NM94
1-Photo-c; Billy The Kid story	12.00	38.00	100.00
2: Alan Ladd photo-c	16.00	49.00	130.00

TRUMP
Jan, 1957 - No. 2, Mar, 1957 (50¢, magazine)
HMH Publishing Co.

	GD25	FN65	NM94
1-Harvey Kurtzman satire	18.00	54.00	145.00
2-Harvey Kurtzman satire	15.00	45.00	120.00

NOTE: ***Davis, Elder, Heath, Jaffee** art-#1,2; **Wood** a-1. Article by Mel Brooks in #2.*

TRUMPETS WEST (See Luke Short, Four Color #875)

TRUTH ABOUT CRIME (See Fox Giants)

TRUTH ABOUT MOTHER GOOSE (See Mother Goose, Four Color #862)

TRUTH BEHIND THE TRIAL OF CARDINAL MINDSZENTY, THE (See Cardinal Mindszenty)

TRUTHFUL LOVE (Formerly Youthful Love)
No. 2, July, 1950
Youthful Magazines

	GD25	FN65	NM94
2-Ingrid Bergman's true life story	7.50	22.50	50.00

TRY-OUT WINNER BOOK
Mar, 1988
Marvel Comics

	GD25	FN65	NM94
1-Spider-Man vs. Doc Octopus			1.25

TSR WORLD (...Annual on cover only)
1990 ($3.95, 84 pgs.)
DC Comics

	GD25	FN65	NM94
1-Advanced D&D, ForgottenReals, Dragonlance & 1st app. Spelljammer		1.60	4.00

TUBBY (See Marge's...)

TUFF GHOSTS STARRING SPOOKY
July, 1962 - No. 39, Nov, 1970; No. 40, Sept, 1971 - No. 43, Oct, 1972
Harvey Publications

	GD25	FN65	NM94
1-12¢ issues begin	8.00	24.00	80.00
2-5	4.00	12.00	40.00
6-10	2.50	7.50	22.00
11-20	2.00	6.00	16.00
21-30: 29-Hot Stuff/Spooky team-up story	1.25	3.75	10.00

Tug & Buster #1 © Marc Hempel

Turok, Child of Blood #1 © Acclaim

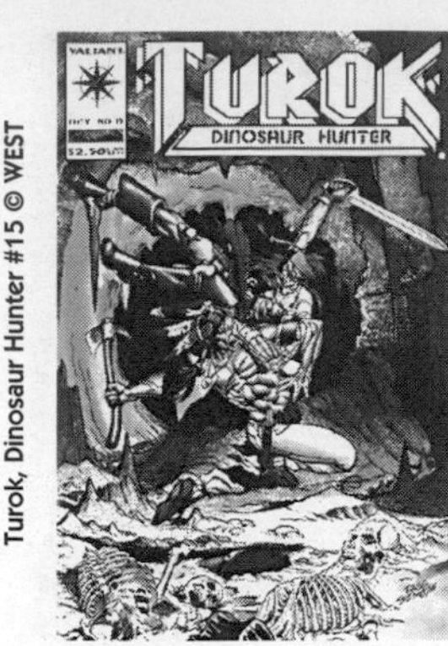

Turok, Dinosaur Hunter #15 © WEST

	GD25	FN65	NM94
31-39,43	1.00	2.80	7.00
40-42: 52 pg. Giants	1.25	3.75	10.00

TUFFY
No. 5, July, 1949 - No. 9, Oct, 1950
Standard Comics

	GD25	FN65	NM94
5-All by Sid Hoff	4.25	13.00	26.00
6-9	3.20	8.00	16.00

TUFFY TURTLE
No date
I. W. Enterprises

	GD25	FN65	NM94
1-Reprint	1.00	2.80	7.00

TUG & BUSTER
Nov, 1995 - Present ($2.95, B&W, bi-monthly)
Art & Soul Comics

	GD25	FN65	NM94
1-6: Marc Hempel--c/a/scripts		1.20	3.00

TUROK, CHILD OF BLOOD
Jan, 1998 ($3.95, one-shot)
Acclaim Comics (Valiant)

	GD25	FN65	NM94
1-Nicieza-s/Kayanan-a			3.95

TUROK, DINOSAUR HUNTER (See Magnus Robot Fighter #12 & Archer & Armstrong #2)
June, 1993 - No. 47, Aug, 1996 ($2.50)
Valiant/Acclaim Comics

	GD25	FN65	NM94
1-($3.50)-Chromium & foil-c		1.40	3.50
1-Gold foil-c variant		2.00	5.00
0, 2-47: 4-Andar app. 5-Death of Andar. 7-9-Truman/Glanzman-a. 11-Bound-in trading card. 16-Chaos Effect		1.00	2.50
Yearbook 1 (1994, $3.95, 52 pgs.)		1.60	4.00

TUROK, REDPATH
Oct, 1997 ($3.95, one-shot)
Acclaim Comics (Valiant)

	GD25	FN65	NM94
1-Nicieza-s/Kayanan-a		1.60	4.00

TUROK, SON OF STONE (See Dan Curtis, Golden Comics Digest #31 & March of Comics #378, 399, 408)
No. 596, 12/54 - No. 29, 9/62; No. 30, 12/62 - No. 91, 7/74; No. 92, 9/74 - No. 125, 1/80; No. 126, 3/81 - No. 130, 4/82
Dell Publ. Co. #1-29(9/62)/Gold Key #30(12/62)-85(7/73)/Gold Key or Whitman #86(9/73)-125(1/80)/Whitman #126(3/81) on

	GD25	FN65	NM94
Four Color 596 (12/54)(#1)-1st app./origin Turok & Andar; dinosaur-c. Created by Matthew H. Murphy; written by Alberto Giolitti	57.00	170.00	625.00
Four Color 656 (10/55)(#2)-1st mention of Lanok	34.00	102.00	375.00
3(3-5/56)-5: 3-Cave men	18.00	55.00	200.00
6-10: 8-Dinosaur of the deep; Turok enters Lost Valley; series begins	12.00	35.00	130.00
11-20: 17-Prehistoric Pygmies	8.00	23.00	85.00
21-30: 30-33-Painted back-c pin-ups	5.50	16.50	60.00
31-Drug use story	5.50	16.50	60.00
32-40	3.60	11.00	40.00
41-50	2.75	8.00	30.00
51-60: 58-Flying Saucer c/story	2.25	6.75	25.00
61-70: 62-12 & 15¢-c. 63-Only line drawn-c	1.65	5.00	18.00
71-84: 84-Origin & 1st app. Hutec	1.50	4.50	12.00
85-99		2.40	6.00
100-129: 93-r-c/#19 w/changes. 94-r-c/#28 w/changes. 97-r-c/#31 w/changes. 98-r/#58 w/o spaceship & spacemen on-c. 99-r-c/#52 w/changes. 114,115-(52 pgs.)	1.50	4.50	12.00
130-Last issue	1.85	5.50	15.00
Giant 1(30031-611) (11/66)-Slick-c; r/#10-12 & 16 plus cover to #11	8.00	25.00	90.00
Giant 1-Same as above but with paper-c	9.00	27.00	100.00

NOTE: *Most painted-c; line-drawn #63 & 130.* ***Alberto Gioletti*** *a-24-27, 30-119, 123; painted-c No. 30-129.* ***Sparling*** *a-117, 120-130. Reprints-#36, 54, 57, 75, 112, 114(1/3), 115(1/3), 118, 121, 125, 127(1/3), 128, 129(1/3), 130(1/3), Giant 1. Cover r-93, 94, 97-99, 126(all different from original covers.*

TUROK: SPRING BREAK IN THE LOST LAND
July, 1997 ($3.95, one-shot)
Acclaim Comics (Valiant)

	GD25	FN65	NM94
1-Nicieza-s/Kayanan-a		1.60	4.0

TUROK: THE EMPTY SOULS
Apr, 1997 ($3.95, one-shot)
Acclaim Comics (Valiant)

	GD25	FN65	NM94
1-Nicieza-s/Kayanan-a; variant-c		1.60	4.0

TUROK THE HUNTED
Mar, 1995 - No. 2, Apr, 1995 ($2.50, limited series)
Valiant/Acclaim Comics

	GD25	FN65	NM94
1,2-Mike Deodato-a(p); price omitted on #1		1.00	2.5

TUROK THE HUNTED
Feb, 1996 - No. 2, Mar, 1996 ($2.50, limited series)
Acclaim Comics (Valiant)

	GD25	FN65	NM94
1,2-Mike Grell story		1.00	2.5

TUROK, TIMEWALKER
Aug, 1997 - No. 2, Sept, 1997 ($2.50, limited series)
Acclaim Comics (Valiant)

	GD25	FN65	NM94
1,2-Nicieza story		1.00	2.50

TURTLE SOUP
Sept, 1987 ($2.00, 76 pgs., B&W, one-shot)
Mirage Studios

	GD25	FN65	NM94
1-Featuring Teenage Mutant Ninja Turtles		.80	2.00

TURTLE SOUP
Nov, 1991 - No. 4, 1992 ($2.50, limited series, coated paper)
Mirage Studios

	GD25	FN65	NM94
1-4: Features the Teenage Mutant Ninja Turtles		1.00	2.50

TV CASPER & COMPANY
Aug, 1963 - No. 46, April, 1974 (25¢ Giants)
Harvey Publications

	GD25	FN65	NM94
1: 68 pg. Giants begin; Casper, Little Audrey, Baby Huey, Herman & Catnip, Buzzy the Crow begin	8.50	25.50	85.00
2-5	4.00	12.00	40.00
6-10	3.00	9.00	30.00
11-20	2.25	6.75	16.00
21-31: 31-Last 68 pg. issue	1.50	4.50	12.00
32-46: All 52 pgs.	1.10	3.30	9.00

NOTE: *Many issues contain reprints.*

TV FUNDAY FUNNIES (See Famous TV...)
TV FUNNIES (See New Funnies)
TV FUNTIME (See Little Audrey)
TV LAUGHOUT (See Archie's...)

TV SCREEN CARTOONS (Formerly Real Screen)
No. 129, July-Aug, 1959 - No. 138, Jan-Feb, 1961
National Periodical Publications

	GD25	FN65	NM94
129-138 (Scarce)	7.00	21.00	70.00

TV STARS (TV)
Aug, 1978 - No. 4, Feb, 1979 (Hanna-Barbera)
Marvel Comics Group

	GD25	FN65	NM94
1-Great Grape Ape app.	1.85	5.50	15.00
2,4: 4-Top Cat app.	1.50	4.50	12.00
3-Toth-c/a; Dave Stevens inks	1.85	5.50	18.00

Tweety and Sylvester #7 © Warner Bros.

2099 Unlimited #6 © MEG

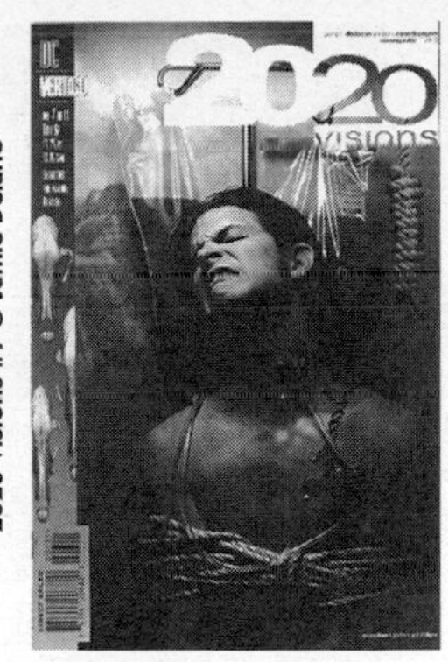

2020 Visions #7 © Jamie Delano

GD25 FN65 NM94

TV TEENS (Formerly Ozzie & Babs; Rock and Rollo #14 on)
V1#14, Feb, 1954 - V2#13, July, 1956
Charlton Comics

V1#14 (#1)-Ozzie & Babs 6.50 19.50 45.00
15 (#2) 4.00 12.00 24.00
V2#3(6/54) - 6-Don Winslow 4.25 13.00 26.00
7-13-Mopsy. 8(7/55) 4.00 12.00 24.00

TWEETY AND SYLVESTER (1st Series)
No. 406, June, 1952 - No. 37, June-Aug, 1962
Dell Publishing Co.

Four Color 406 (#1)-1st app.? 7.00 22.00 80.00
Four Color 489,524 3.00 9.00 35.00
4 (3-5/54) - 20 1.65 5.00 18.00
21-37 1.25 3.75 10.00
(See March of Comics #421, 433, 445, 457, 469, 481)

TWEETY AND SYLVESTER (2nd Series)(See Kite Fun Book)
Nov, 1963; No. 2, Nov, 1965 - No. 121, July, 1984
Gold Key No. 1-102/Whitman No. 103 on

1 1.85 5.50 15.00
2-10 1.00 2.80 7.00
11-30 1.60 4.00
31-70 .80 2.00
71-121: 99,119-r(1/3) 1.00
Mini Comic No. 1(1976, 3-1/4x6-1/2") 1.60 4.00

12 O'CLOCK HIGH (TV)
Jan-Mar, 1965 - No. 2, Apr-June, 1965 (Photo-c)
Dell Publishing Co.

1 4.50 13.50 50.00
2 3.60 11.00 40.00

24 PAGES OF COMICS (No title) (Also see Pure Oil Comics, Salerno Carnival of Comics, & Vicks Comics)
Late 1930s
Giveaway by various outlets including Sears

nn-Contains strip reprints-Buck Rogers, Napoleon, Sky Roads, War on Crime
29.00 88.00 235.00

2099 A.D.
May, 1995 ($3.95, one-shot)
Marvel Comics

1-Acetate-c by Quesada & Palmiotti. 1.60 4.00

2099 APOCALYPSE
Dec, 1995 ($4.95, one-shot)
Marvel Comics

1-Chromium wraparound-c; Ellis script 2.00 5.00

2099 GENESIS
Jan, 1996 ($4.95, one-shot)
Marvel Comics

1-Chromium wraparound-c; Ellis script 2.00 5.00

2099 UNLIMITED
Sept, 1993 - No. 10, 1996 ($3.95, 68 pgs.)
Marvel Comics

1-10: 1-1st app. Hulk 2099 & begins. 1-3-Spider-Man 2099 app. 9-Joe Kubert-c; Len Wein & Nancy Collins scripts 1.60 4.00

2099 WORLD OF DOOM SPECIAL
May, 1995 ($2.25, one-shot)
Marvel Comics

1-Doom's "Contract w/America" .90 2.25

2099 WORLD OF TOMORROW
Sept, 1996 - No. 8, Apr, 1997 ($2.50) (Replaces 2099 titles)
Marvel Comics

1-8: 1-Wraparound-c. 2-w/bound-in card. 4,5-Phalanx 1.00 2.50

21
Feb, 1996 - No. 3, Apr, 1996 ($2.50)
Image Comics (Top Cow Productions)

1-3: Len Wein scripts 1.00 2.50
1-Variant-c 2.00 5.00

2020 VISIONS
May, 1997 - No. 12, Apr, 1998 ($2.25, limited series)
DC Comics (Vertigo)

1-12-Delano-s: 1-3-Quitely-a. 4-"la tormenta"-Pleece-a .90 2.25

20,000 LEAGUES UNDER THE SEA (Movie)(See King Classics, Movie Comics & Power Record Comics)
No. 614, Feb, 1955 (Disney)
Dell Publishing Co.

Four Color 614-Movie, painted-c 9.00 27.00 100.00

22 BRIDES (See Ash/)
Mar, 1996 - No. 4 ($2.95)
Event Comics

1-4: Fabian Nicieza scripts 1.20 3.00
2,3-Variant-c 1.80 4.50

TWICE TOLD TALES (See Movie Classics)

TWILIGHT
1990 - No. 3, 1991 ($4.95, 52 pgs, limited series, squarebound, mature)
DC Comics

1-3: Tommy Tomorrow app; Chaykin scripts, Garcia-Lopez-c/a.
2.00 5.00

TWILIGHT AVENGER, THE
July, 1986 - No. 2, 1987 ($1.75, 28 pgs, limited series)
Elite Comics

1,2 .75 1.80

TWILIGHT MAN
June, 1989 - No. 4, Sept, 1989 ($2.75, limited series)
First Publishing

1-4 1.10 2.80

TWILIGHT ZONE, THE (TV) (See Dan Curtis)
No. 1173, 3-5/61 - No. 91, 4/79; No. 92, 5/82
Dell Publishing Co./Gold Key/Whitman No. 92

Four Color 1173 (#1)-Crandall-c/a 18.00 55.00 200.00
Four Color 1288-Crandall/Evans-c/a 11.00 32.00 115.00
01-860-207 (5-7/62-Dell, 15¢) 7.00 22.00 80.00
12-860-210 on-c; 01-860-210 on inside(8-10/62-Dell)-Evans-c/a (3 stories)
7.00 22.00 80.00
1(11/62-Gold Key)-Crandall/Frazetta-a (10 & 11 pgs.); Evans-a
9.00 26.00 95.00
2 6.00 18.00 65.00
3-11: 3(11 pgs.),4(10 pgs.),9-Toth-a 4.00 12.00 45.00
12-15: 12-Williamson-a. 13,15-Crandall-a. 14-Orlando/Crandall/Torres-a
3.00 9.00 32.00
16-20 1.80 5.50 20.00
21-27: 21-Crandall-a(r). 25-Evans/Crandall-a(r); Toth-r/#4. 26-Flying Saucer-c/story; Crandall, Evans-a(r). 27-Evans-r(2) 1.50 4.50 15.00
28-32: 32-Evans-a(r) 1.25 3.75 10.00
33-51: 43-Celardo-a. 51-Williamson-a 1.00 3.00 8.00
52-70 2.40 6.00
71-82,85-91: 71-Reprint 1.20 3.00
83,84-(52 pgs.). 84-Frank Miller's 1st comic book work. 2.40 6.00
92-Last issue; r/#1. 1.60 4.00

Two Faces of Tomorrow #2 © James P. Hogan

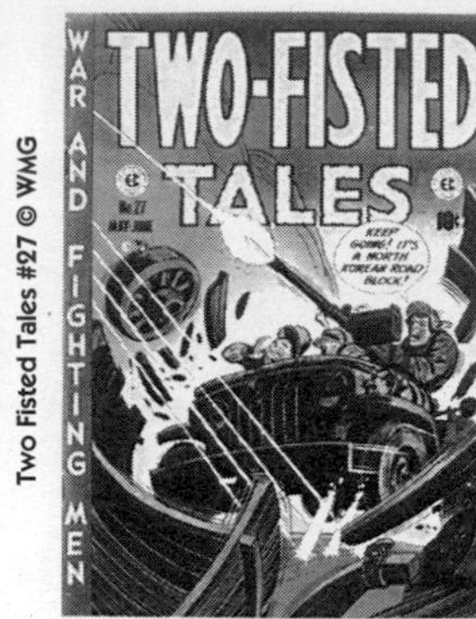

Two Fisted Tales #27 © WMG

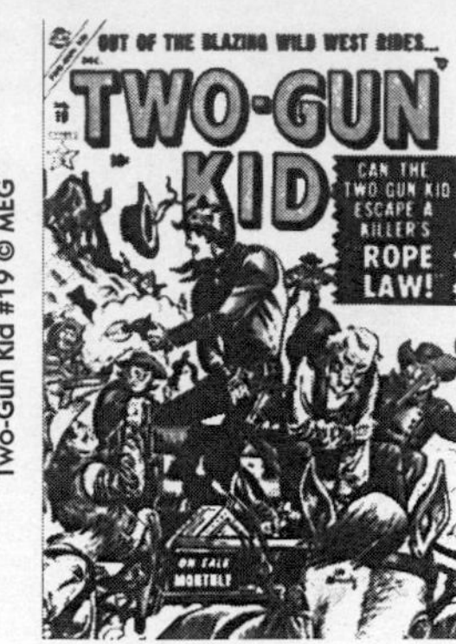

Two-Gun Kid #19 © MEG

GD25 FN65 NM94

Mini Comic #1(1976, 3-1/4x6-1/2") 2.00 5.00

*NOTE: **Bolle** a-13(w/**McWilliams**), 50, 55, 57, 59, 77, 78, 80, 83, 84. **McWilliams** a-59, 78, 80, 82, 84. **Miller** a-84, 85. **Orlando** a-15, 19, 20, 22, 23. **Sekowsky** a-3. **Simonson** a-50, 54, 55, 83r. **Weiss** a-39, 79r(#39). (See Mystery Comics Digest 3, 6, 9, 12, 15, 18, 21, 24). Reprints-26(1/3), 71, 73, 79, 83, 84, 86, 92. Painted c-1-91.*

TWILIGHT ZONE, THE (TV)
Nov, 1990 ($2.95)
Oct, 1991; V2#1, Nov, 1991 - No. 14? 1992 ($1.95)
V3#1, 1993 - No. 4, 1993 ($2.50)
Now Comics

1-(11/90, $2.95, 52 pgs.)-Direct sale edition; Neal Adams-a, Sienkiewicz-c; Harlan Ellison scripts 1.20 3.00
1-(11/90, $1.75)-Newsstand ed. w/N. Adams-c .80 2.00
1-Prestige Format (10/91, $4.95)-Reprints above with extra Harlan Ellison short story 2.00 5.00
1-Collector's Edition (10/91, $2.50)-None-code approved and polybagged; reprints 11/90 issue; gold logo 1.00 2.50
1-Reprint ($2.50)-r/direct sale 11/90 version 1.00 2.50
1-Reprint ($2.50)-r/newsstand 11/90 version 1.00 2.50
V2#1-Direct sale & newsstand ed. w/different-c .80 2.00
V2#2-8,10-14 .80 2.00
V2#9-($2.95)-3-D Special; polybagged w/glasses & hologram on-c 1.20 3.00
V2#9-($4.95)-Prestige Edition; contains 2 extra stories & a different hologram on-c; polybagged w/glasses 2.00 5.00
V3#1-4 1.00 2.50
Anniversary Special 1 (1992, $2.50) 1.00 2.50
Annual 1 (4/93, $2.50)-No ads 1.00 2.50

TWINKLE COMICS
May, 1945
Spotlight Publishers

1 17.50 53.00 140.00

TWIST, THE
July-Sept, 1962
Dell Publishing Co.

01-864-209-Painted-c 2.75 8.00 30.00

TWISTED TALES (See Eclipse Graphic Album Series #15)
11/82 - No. 8, 5/84; No. 9, 11/84; No. 10, 12/84 (Baxter paper)
Pacific Comics/Independent Comics Group (Eclipse) #9,10

1-B. Jones/Corben-c; nudity/violence in all .80 2.00
2-10 1.50

*NOTE: **Alcala** a-1. **Bolton** painted c-4, 6, 7; a-7. **Conrad** a-1, 3, 5; c-1i, 3, 5. **Guice** a-8. **Morrow** a-10. **Ploog** a-2. **Wildey** a-3. **Wrightson** a(Painted)-10; c-2.*

TWO BIT THE WACKY WOODPECKER (See Wacky...)
1951 - No. 3, May, 1953
Toby Press

1 6.50 19.50 45.00
2,3 4.00 12.00 24.00

TWO FACES OF COMMUNISM (Also see Double Talk)
1961 (Giveaway, paper-c, 36 pgs.)
Christian Anti-Communism Crusade, Houston, Texas
nn 10.50 32.00 85.00

TWO FACES OF TOMORROW, THE
Aug, 1997 - Present ($2.95, B&W, limited series)
Dark Horse Comics

1-Manga 1.20 3.00
2-4-($3.95) 1.60 4.00

TWO-FISTED TALES (Formerly Haunt of Fear #15-17)
No. 18, Nov-Dec, 1950 - No. 41, Feb-Mar, 1955
E. C. Comics

GD25 FN65 NM94

18(#1)-Kurtzman-c 79.00 235.00 640.00
19-Kurtzman-c 57.00 171.00 470.00
20-Kurtzman-c 38.00 114.00 275.00
21,22-Kurtzman-c 29.00 86.00 210.00
23-25-Kurtzman-c 22.00 66.00 160.00
26-35: 33- "Atom Bomb" by Wood 16.00 47.00 115.00
36-41 11.50 34.00 85.00
Two-Fisted Annual (1952, 25¢, 132 pgs.) 70.00 210.00 575.00
Two-Fisted Annual (1953, 25¢, 132 pgs.) 52.00 156.00 400.00

*NOTE: **Berg** a-29. **Colan** a-39p. **Craig** a-18, 19, 32. **Crandall** a-35, 36. **Davis** a-20-36, 40; c-30, 34, 35, 41, Annual 2. **Evans** a-34, 40, 41; c-40. **Feldstein** a-18. **Krigstein** a-41. **Kubert** a-32, 33. **Kurtzman** a-18-25; c-18-29, 31, Annual 1. **Severin** a-26, 28, 29, 31, 34-41 (No. 37-39 are all-**Severin** issues); c-36-39. **Severin/Elder** a-19-29, 31, 33, 36. **Wood** a-18-28, 30-35, 41; c-32, 33. Special issues: #26 (ChanJin Reservoir), 31 (Civil War), 35 (Civil War). Canadian reprints known; see Table of Contents. #25-Davis biog. #27-Wood biog. #28-Kurtzman biog.*

TWO-FISTED TALES
Oct, 1992 - Present ($1.50/$2.00/$2.50)
Russ Cochran/Gemstone Publishing

1-15: 1-4r/Two-Fisted Tales #18-21 w/original-c .80 2.00
16-19 1.00 2.50

TWO-GUN KID (Also see All Western Winners, Best Western, Black Rider, Blaze Carson, Kid Colt, Western Winners, Wild West, & Wild Western)
3/48(No mo.) - No. 10, 11/49; No. 11, 12/53 - No. 59, 4/61; No. 60, 11/62 - No. 92, 3/68; No. 93, 7/70 - No. 136, 4/77
Marvel/Atlas (MCI No. 1-10/HPC No. 11-59/Marvel No. 60 on)

1-Two-Gun Kid & his horse Cyclone begin; The Sheriff begins 81.00 243.00 725.00
2 36.00 108.00 290.00
3,4: 3-Annie Oakley app. 27.00 81.00 215.00
5-Pre-Black Rider app. (Wint. 48/49); spanking panel; Anti-Wertham editorial (1st?) 33.00 98.00 260.00
6-10(11/49): 8-Blaze Carson app. 9-Black Rider app. 21.00 64.00 170.00
11(12/53)-Black Rider app.; explains how Kid Colt became an outlaw 16.00 49.00 130.00
12-Black Rider app. 16.00 49.00 130.00
13-20: 13-1st to have Atlas globe on-c. 14-Opium story 11.30 34.00 90.00
21-24,26-29 10.00 30.00 80.00
25,30: 25-Williamson-a (5 pgs.). 30-Williamson/Torres-a (4 pgs.) 10.50 32.00 85.00
31-33,35,37-40 5.50 16.50 55.00
34-Crandall-a 6.00 18.00 60.00
36,41,42,48-Origin in all 6.00 18.00 60.00
43,44,47 4.20 12.60 42.00
45,46-Davis-a 4.80 14.40 48.00
49,50,52,55,57-Severin-a(2) in each 3.80 11.40 38.00
51-Williamson-a (5 pgs.) 4.80 14.40 48.00
53,54-Severin-a(3) in each 4.20 12.60 42.00
56,59: 59-Last 10¢ issue (4/61) 2.50 7.50 20.00
58,60-New origin. 58-Kirby/Ayers-c/a "The Monster of Hidden Valley" cover/story (Kirby monster-c) 2.50 7.50 22.00
61-80: 64-Intro. Boom-Boom 1.85 5.50 15.00
81-92: 92-Last new story; last 12¢ issue 1.50 4.50 12.00
93-101: 101-Origin retold/#58 1.25 3.75 10.00
102-120 1.00 3.00 8.00
121-136 2.40 6.00

*NOTE: **Ayers** a-26, 27. **Davis** c-45-47. **Drucker** a-23. **Everett** a-82, 91. **Fuje** a-13. **Heath** a-3(2), 4(3), 5(2), 7; c-13, 21, 23, 53. **Keller** a-16, 19, 28. **Kirby** a-54, 55, 57-62, 75-77, 90, 95, 101, 119, 120, 129; c-10, 52, 54-65, 67-72, 74-76, 116. **Maneely** a-20; c-11, 12, 16, 19, 20, 25-28, 35, 49. **Powell** a-38, 102, 104. **Severin** a-9, 29, 51, 55, 57, 99r(3); c-9, 51, 99. **Shores** c-1-8, 11. **Tuska** a-11, 12. **Whitney** a-87, 89-91, 98-113, 124, 129; c-87, 89, 91, 113. **Wildey** a-21. **Williamson** a-110r. Kid Colt in #13, 14, 16-21.*

TWO GUN KID:SUNSET RIDERS
Nov, 1995 - No. 2, Dec, 1995 ($6.95, squarebound, limited series)

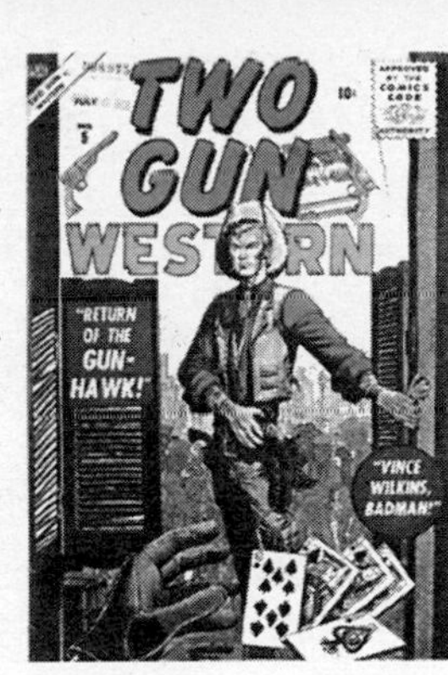

Two-Gun Western #5 (2nd Series) © MEG

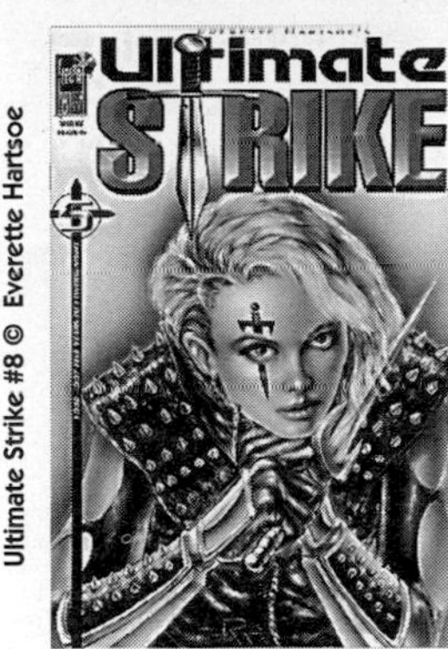

Ultimate Strike #8 © Everette Hartsoe

Ultraforce #1 © MAL

Marvel Comics
1,2: Fabian Nicieza scripts in all. 1-painted-c. 1.00 2.80 7.00

TWO GUN WESTERN (1st Series) (Formerly Casey Crime Photographer #1-4? or My Love #1-4?)
No. 5, Nov, 1950 - No. 14, June, 1952
Marvel/Atlas Comics (MPC)
5-The Apache Kid (Intro & origin) & his horse Nightwind begin by Buscema 20.00 60.00 160.00
6-10: 8-Kid Colt, The Texas Kid & his horse Thunder begin? 14.00 41.00 110.00
11-14: 13-Black Rider app. 9.50 28.00 75.00
NOTE: ***Maneely** a-6, 7, 9; c-6, 11-13. **Morrow** a-9. **Romita** a-8. **Wildey** a-8.*

2-GUN WESTERN (2nd Series) (Formerly Billy Buckskin #1-3; Two-Gun Western #5 on)
No. 4, May, 1956
Atlas Comics (MgPC)
4-Colan, Ditko, Severin, Sinnott-a; Maneely-c 12.00 38.00 100.00

TWO-GUN WESTERN (Formerly 2-Gun Western)
No. 5, July, 1956 - No. 12, Sept, 1957
Atlas Comics (MgPC)
5-Return of the Gun-Hawk-c/story; Black Rider app. 10.00 30.00 80.00
6,7 7.85 23.50 55.00
8,10,12-Crandall-a 8.75 26.25 65.00
9,11-Williamson-a in both (5 pgs. each) 8.75 26.25 65.00
NOTE: ***Ayers** a-9. **Colan** a-5. **Everett** c-12. **Forgione** a-5, 6. **Kirby** a-12. **Maneely** a-6, 8, 12; c-5, 6, 8, 11. **Morrow** a-9, 10. **Powell** a-7, 11. **Severin** c-10. **Sinnott** a-6. **Wildey** a-9.*

TWO MOUSEKETEERS, THE (See 4-Color #475, 603, 642 under M.G.M.'s...;

TWO ON A GUILLOTINE (See Movie Classics)

2000 A.D. MONTHLY/PRESENTS (Showcase #25 on)
4/85 - #6, 9/85; 4/86 - #54, 1991 ($1.25-$1.50, Mando paper)
Eagle Comics/Quality Comics No. 5 on
1-6 ($1.25): 1-4 r/British series featuring Judge Dredd; Alan Moore scripts begin 1.25
1-25 ($1.25)-Reprints from British 2000 AD 1.25
26,27/28, 29/30, 31-44: 27/28, 29/30,31-Guice-c 1.25
45-54: 45-Begin $1.75-c .75 1.75

2001, A SPACE ODYSSEY (Movie)
Dec, 1976 - No. 10, Sept, 1977 (30¢)
Marvel Comics Group
1-Adaptation of film; Kirby-c/a in all 1.20 3.00
2-10: 8-Original/1st app. Machine Man (called Mr. Machine) .80 2.00
Howard Johnson giveaway (1968, 8pp); 6 pg. movie adaptation, 2 pg. games, puzzles; McWilliams-a .80 2.00
...Treastury 1 ('76, 84 pgs.)-All new Kirby-a 1.25 3.75 10.00

2001 NIGHTS
1990 - No. 10, 1991 ($3.75, B&W, limited series, mature readers, 84 pgs.)
Viz Premiere Comics
1-5: Japanese sci-fi. 1-Wraparound-c 1.50 3.75
6-10: 6-Begin $4.25-c 1.70 4.25

2010 (Movie)
Apr, 1985 - No. 2, May, 1985
Marvel Comics Group
1,2-r/Marvel Super Special movie adaptation. 1.00

TYPHOID (Also see Daredevil)
Nov, 1995 - No. 4, Feb, 1996 ($3.95, squarebound, limited series)
Marvel Comics
1-4: Van Fleet-c/a 1.60 4.00

UFO & ALIEN COMIX
Jan, 1978 (one-shot)
Warren Publishing Co.
nn-Toth, Severin-a(r) 1.10 3.30 9.00

UFO & OUTER SPACE (Formerly UFO Flying Saucers)
No. 14, June, 1978 - No. 25, Feb, 1980 (All painted covers)
Gold Key
14-Reprints UFO Flying Saucers #3 2.40 6.00
15,16-Reprints 1.60 4.00
17-20-New material 2.00 5.00
21-25: 23-McWilliams-a. 24-(3 pg.-r). 25-Reprints UFO Flying Saucers #2 w/cover 1.60 4.00

UFO ENCOUNTERS
May, 1978 ($1.95, 228 pgs.)
Western Publishing Co.
11192-Reprints UFO Flying Saucers 2.50 7.50 20.00
11404-Vol.1 (128 pgs.)-See UFO Mysteries for Vol.2 1.85 5.50 15.00

UFO FLYING SAUCERS (UFO & Outer Space #14 on)
Oct, 1968 - No. 13, Jan, 1977 (No. 2 on, 36 pgs.)
Gold Key
1(30035-810) (68 pgs.) 2.25 6.75 25.00
2(11/70), 3(11/72), 4(11/74) 1.50 4.50 12.00
5(2/75)-13: Bolle-a #4 on 1.10 3.30 9.00

UFO MYSTERIES
1978 ($1.00, reprints, 96 pgs.)
Western Publishing Co.
11400, 11404(Vol.2)-Cont'd from UFO Encounters, pgs. 129-224 1.50 4.50 12.00

ULTIMATE STRIKE (See Razor, Stryke)
Dec, 1996 - Present ($3.95/$3.00, B&W)
London Night Studios
1-($3.95)-Wraparound chromium-c 1.60 4.00
1-12-($6.00) Nude Edition 2.40 6.00
2-12-($3.00) 1.20 3.00

ULTRACYBERNETIC DOLPHINDROIDS, THE
Dec, 1993 ($2.50, unfinished limited series)
Polestar Comics
1 1.00 2.50

ULTRAFORCE (1st Series) (Also see Avengers/Ultraforce #1)
Aug, 1994 - No. 10, Aug, 1995 ($1.95/$2.50)
Malibu Comics (Ultraverse)
0 (9/94, $2.50)-Perez-c/a. 1.00 2.50
1-($2.50, 44 pgs.)-Bound-in trading card; team consisting of Prime, Prototype, Hardcase, Pixx, Ghoul, Contrary & Topaz; Gerard Jones scripts begin, ends #6; Perez-c/a begins. 1.00 2.50
1-Ultra 5000 Limited Silver Foil Edition 1.60 4.00
1-Holographic-c, no price 2.00 5.00
2-5: Perez-c/a in all. 2 (10/94, $1.95)-Prime quits, Strangers cameo. 3-Origin of Topaz; Prime rejoins. 5-Pixx dies. .80 2.00
2 ($2.50)-Flourescent logo; limited edition stamp on-c 1.00 2.50
6-10: 6-Begin $2.50-c, Perez-c/a. 7-Ghoul story, Steve Erwin-a. 8-Marvel's Black Knight enters the Ultraverse (last seen in Avengers #375); Perez-c/a. 9,10-Black Knight app.; Perez-c. 10-Leads into Ultraforce/Avengers Prelude. 1.00 2.50
Malibu "Ashcan ": Ultraforce (6/94) .75
.../Avengers Prelude 1 (8/95, $2.50)-Perez-c. 1.00 2.50
.../Avengers 1 (8/95, $3.95)-Warren Ellis script; Perez-c/a; foil-c. 1.60 4.00

ULTRAFORCE (2nd Series)(Also see Black September)
Infinity, Sept, 1995 - V2#15, Dec, 1996 ($1.50)

Ultragirl #3 © MEG

Ultraverse Premiere #2 © MAL

Uncanny Tales #20 © MEG

	GD25	FN65	NM94
Malibu Comics (Ultraverse)			
Infinity, V2#1-15: Infinity-Team consists of Marvel's Black Knight, Ghoul, Topaz, Prime & redesigned Prototype; Warren Ellis scripts begin, ends #3; variant-c exists. 1-1st app.Cromwell, Lament & Wreckage. 2-Contains free encore presentation of Ultraforce #1; flip book "Phoenix Resurrection" Pt. 7. 7-Darick Robertson, Jeff Johnson & others-a. 8,9-Intro. Future Ultraforce (Prime, Hellblade, Angel of Destruction, Painkiller & Whipslash); Gary Erskine-c/a. 9-Foxfire app. 10-Len Wein scripts & Deodato Studios-c/a begin. 10-Lament back-up story. 11-Ghoul back-up story by Pander Bros. 12-Ultraforce vs. Maxis (cont'd in Ultraverse Unlimited #2); Exiles & Iron Clad app. 13-Prime leaves; Hardcase returns			1.50
Infinity (2000 signed)		1.60	4.00
.../Spider-Man ($3.95)-Marv Wolfman script; Green Goblin app; 2 covers exist.		1.60	4.00
Unlimited #2-(9/96, $2.50) Black Knight returns to Marvel Universe		1.00	2.50

ULTRAGIRL
Nov, 1996 - No. 3 Mar, 1997($1.50, limited series)
Marvel Comics

1-3: 1-1st app.			1.50

ULTRA KLUTZ
1981; 6/86 - #27, 1/89, #28, 4/90 - #31, 1990? ($1.50/$1.75/$2.00, B&W)
Onward Comics

1 (1981)-Re-released after 2nd #1			1.50
1-22: 1-(6/86)			1.50
23-30: 23-$2.00-c begins. 27-Photo back-c		.80	2.00
31-($2.95, 52 pgs.)		1.20	3.00

ULTRAMAN
Mar, 1994 - No. 4, 1995? ($1.75/$1.95)
Nemesis Comics

1-($2.25)-Collector's edition; foil-c; special 3/4 wraparound-c		.90	2.25
1-($1.75)-Newsstand edition		.70	1.75
2-4: 3-$1.95-c begins		.80	2.00

ULTRAVERSE DOUBLE FEATURE
Jan, 1995 ($3.95, one-shot, 68 pgs.)
Malibu Comics (Ultraverse)

1-Flip-c featuring Prime & Solitaire.		1.60	4.00

ULTRAVERSE ORIGINS
Jan, 1994 (99¢, one-shot)
Malibu Comics (Ultraverse)

1-Gatefold-c; 2 pg. origins all characters			1.00
1-Newsstand edition; different-c, no gatefold			1.00

ULTRAVERSE PREMIERE
1994 (one-shot)
Malibu Comics (Ultraverse)

0-Ordered thru mail w/coupons		2.00	5.00

ULTRAVERSE UNLIMITED
June, 1996; No. 2, Sept, 1996 ($2.50)
Malibu Comics (Ultraverse)

1,2: 1-Adam Warlock returns to the Marvel Universe; Rune-c/app. 2-Black Knight, Reaper & Sierra Blaze return to the Marvel Universe		1.00	2.50

ULTRAVERSE YEAR ONE
1994 ($4.95, one-shot)
Malibu Comics (Ultraverse)

nn-In-depth synopsis of the first year's titles & stories.		2.00	5.00

ULTRAVERSE YEAR TWO
Aug, 1995 ($4.95, one-shot)
Malibu Comics (Ultraverse)

	GD25	FN65	NM94
nn-In-depth synopsis of second year's titles & stories		2.00	5.00

ULTRAVERSE YEAR ZERO: THE DEATH OF THE SQUAD
Apr, 1995 - No. 4, July, 1995 ($2.95, limited series)
Malibu Comics (Ultraverse)

1-4: 3-Codename: Firearm back-up story.		1.20	3.00

UNBIRTHDAY PARTY WITH ALICE IN WONDERLAND (See Alice In Wonderland, Four Color #341)

UNCANNY ORIGINS
Sept, 1996 - No. 14, Oct, 1997 (99¢)
Marvel Comics

1-14: 1-Cyclops. 2-Quicksilver. 3-Archangel. 4-Firelord. 5-Hulk. 6-Beast 7-Venom. 8-Nightcrawler. 9-Storm. 10-Black Cat. 11-Black Knight. 12-Dr. Strange. 13-Daredevil. 14-Iron Fist			1.00

UNCANNY TALES
June, 1952 - No. 56, Sept, 1957
Atlas Comics (PrPl/PPI)

1-Heath-a; horror/weird stories begin	68.00	206.00	575.00
2	40.00	120.00	310.00
3-5	34.00	103.00	260.00
6-Wolvertonish-a by Matt Fox	34.00	103.00	260.00
7-10: 8-Atom bomb story; Tothish-a (by Sekowsky?). 9-Crandall-a	29.00	88.00	220.00
11-20: 17-Atom bomb panels; anti-communist story; Hitler story. 19-Krenkel-a	23.00	69.00	170.00
21-25,27: 25-Nostrand-a?	19.00	56.00	140.00
26-Spider-Man prototype c/story	27.00	80.00	205.00
28-Last precode issue (1/55); Kubert-a; #1-28 contain 2-3 sci/fi stories each	20.00	60.00	150.00
29-41,43-49,51,52: 52-Oldest? Iron Man prototype (2/57)	11.30	34.00	90.00
42,54,56-Krigstein-a	13.50	41.00	100.00
50,53,55-Torres-a	12.00	36.00	90.00

NOTE: ***Andru** a-15, 27. **Ayers** a-22. **Bailey** a-51. **Briefer** a-19, 20. **Brodsky** c-1, 3, 4, 6, 8, 12-16, 19. **Brodsky/Everett** c-9. **Cameron** a-47. **Colan** a-11, 16, 17, 52. **Drucker** a-37, 42, 45. **Everett** a-2, 9, 12, 32, 36, 39, 48; c-7, 11, 17, 39, 41, 50, 52, 53. **Fass** a-9, 10, 15, 24. Forte a-18, 27, 34, 52, 53. **Heath** a-13, 14; c-5, 10, 18. **Keller** a-3. **Lawrence** a-14, 17, 19, 23, 27, 28, 35. **Maneely** a-4, 8, 10, 16, 29, 35; c-2, 22, 26, 33, 38. **Moldoff** a-23. **Morisi** a-48, 52. **Morrow** a-46, 51. **Orlando** a-49, 50, 53. **Powell** a-12, 18, 34, 36, 38, 43, 50, 56. **Robinson** a-3, 13. **Reinman** a-12. **Romita** a-10. **Roussos** a-8. **Sale** a-47, 53; c-20. **Sekowsky** a-25. **Sinnott** a-15, 52. **Torres** a-53. **Tothish**-a by **Andru**-27. **Wildey** a-22, 48.*

UNCANNY TALES
Dec, 1973 - No. 12, Oct, 1975
Marvel Comics Group

1-Crandall-r/Uncanny Tales #9('50s)	1.50	4.50	12.00
2-12	1.00	3.00	8.00

NOTE: ***Ditko** reprints-#4, 6-8, 10-12.*

UNCANNY X-MEN, THE (Formerly The X-Men))
No. 142, Feb, 1981 - Present
Marvel Comics Group

142-Rachel app.; deaths of alt. future Wolverine, Storm & Colossus	1.50	4.50	12.00
143-Last Byrne issue		2.00	5.00
144-150: 144-Man-Thing app. 145-Old X-Men app. 148-Spider-Woman, Dazzler app. 150-Double size		1.60	4.00
151-157,159-161,163,164: 161-Origin Magneto. 163-Origin Binary. 164-1st app. Binary as Carol Danvers		1.20	3.00
158-1st app. Rogue in X-Men (6/82, see Avengers Annual #10)	1.00	2.80	7.00
162-Wolverine solo story		2.00	5.00
165-Paul Smith-c/a begins, ends #175		1.60	4.00

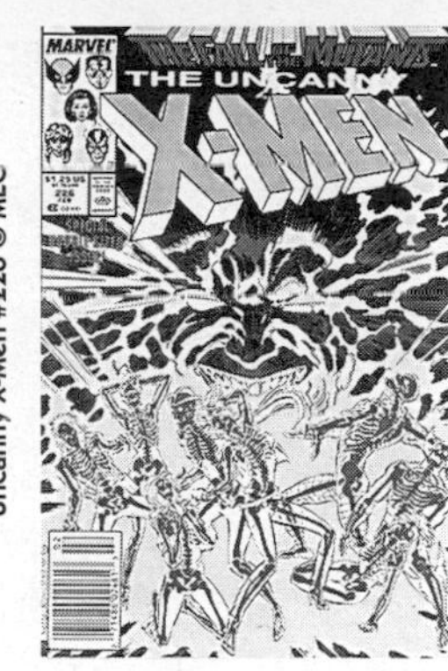

Uncanny X-Men #226 © MEG

Uncanny X-Men #317 © MEG

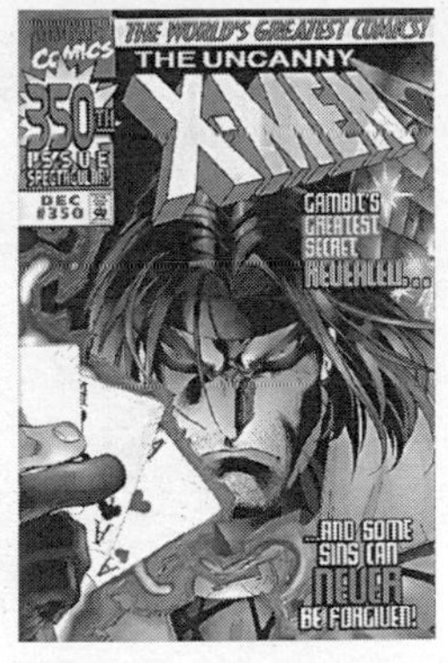

Uncanny X-Men #350 © MEG

GD25 FN65 NM94

166-Double size; Paul Smith-a 1.20 3.00
167-170: 167-New Mutants app. (3/83); same date as New Mutants #1; 1st meeting w/X-Men; ties into N.M. #3,4; Starjammers app.; contains skin "Tattooz" decals. 168-1st app. Madelyne Pryor (last pg. cameo) in X-Men (see Avengers Annual #10) 1.20 3.00
171-Rogue joins X-Men; Simonson-c/a 1.00 2.80 7.00
172-174: 172,173-Two part Wolverine solo story. 173-Two cover variations, blue & black. 174-Phoenix cameo 1.60 4.00
175-(52 pgs.)-Anniversary issue; Phoenix returns 2.00 5.00
176-185: 181-Sunfire app. 182-Rogue solo story. 184-1st app. Forge (8/84) 1.20 3.00
186-Double-size; Barry Smith/Austin-a 1.20 3.00
187-192,194-199: 190,191-Spider-Man & Avengers x-over. 195-Power Pack x-over .80 2.00
193-Double size; 100th app. New X-Men; 1st app. Warpath in costume (see New Mutants #16) 1.60 4.00
200-(12/85, $1.25, 52 pgs.) 2.00 5.00
201-(1/86)-1st app. Cable? (as baby Nathan; see X-Factor #1); 1st Whilce Portacio-c/a(i) on X-Men (guest artist) 1.25 3.75 10.00
202-204,206-209: 204-Nightcrawler solo story; 2nd Portacio-a(i) on X-Men. 207-Wolverine/Phoenix story 1.20 3.00
205-Wolverine solo story by Barry Smith 1.00 2.80 7.00
210,211-Mutant Massacre begins 1.10 3.30 9.00
212,213-Wolverine vs. Sabretooth (Mutant Mass.) 1.50 4.50 12.00
214-221,223,224: 219-Havok joins (7/87); brief app. Sabretooth 1.20 3.00
222-Wolverine battles Sabretooth-c/story 1.00 3.00 8.00
225-227: Fall Of The Mutants. 226-Double size 1.60 4.00
228-239,241: 229-$1.00 begin 1.20 3.00
240-Sabretooth app. 1.40 3.50
242-Double size, X-Factor app., Inferno tie-in 1.20 3.00
243,245-247: 245-Rob Liefeld-a(p) 1.00 2.50
244-1st app. Jubilee 1.50 4.50 12.00
248-1st Jim Lee art on X-Men (1989) 1.50 4.50 12.00
248-2nd printing (1992, $1.25) 1.25
249-252: 252-Lee-c .80 2.00
253-255: 253-All new X-Men begin. 254-Lee-c 1.60 4.00
256,257-Jim Lee-c/a begins 2.00 5.00
258-Wolverine solo story; Lee-c/a 2.40 6.00
259-Silvestri-c/a; no Lee-a 1.20 3.00
260-265-No Lee-a. 260,261,264-Lee-c .80 2.00
266-1st full app. Gambit (see Ann. #14)-No Lee-a 1.85 5.50 15.00
267-Jim Lee-c/a resumes; 2nd full Gambit app. 1.00 2.80 7.00
268-Capt. America, Black Widow & Wolverine team-up; Lee-a 1.25 3.75 10.00
268-2nd printing .80 2.00
269-Lee-a 1.20 3.00
270-X-Tinction Agenda begins 2.40 6.00
270-Gold 2nd printing .80 2.00
271,272-X-Tinction Agenda 1.60 4.00
273-New Mutants (Cable) & X-Factor x-over; Golden, Byrne & Lee part pencils 1.20 3.00
274 1.00 2.50
275-($1.50, 52 pgs.)-Tri-fold-c by Jim Lee (p); Prof. X 1.20 3.00
275-Gold 2nd printing .80 2.00
276-280: 277-Last Lee-c/a. 280-X-Factor x-over 1.50
281 (10/91) New team begins (Storm, Archangel, Colossus, Iceman & Marvel Girl); Whilce Portacio-c/a begins; Byrne scripts begin; wraparound-c (white logo) 1.20 3.00
281-2nd printing with red metallic ink logo w/o UPC box ($1.00-c); does not say 2nd printing inside 1.25
282-1st app. Bishop (cover & 1 pg. cameo) 1.00 2.80 7.00
282-Gold ink 2nd printing ($1.00-c) 1.00
283-1st full app. Bishop (12/91) 1.00 2.80 7.00

GD25 FN65 NM94

284-293,297-299: 284-Last $1.00-c. 286,287-Lee plots. 287-Bishop joins team. 288-Lee/Portacio plots. 290-Last Portacio-c/a. 294-Brandon Peterson-a(p) begins (#292 is 1st Peterson-c) 1.25
294-296 ($1.50)-Polybagged w/trading card in each; X-Cutioner's Song x-overs; all have Peterson/Austin-c/a 1.50
300-($3.95, 68 pgs.)-Holo-grafx foil-c; Magneto app. 1.60 4.00
301-303,305-309,311 1.25
304-($3.95, 68 pgs.)-Wraparound-c with Magneto hologram on-c; 30th anniversary issue; Jae Lee-a (4 pgs.) 1.60 4.00
307-Gold Edition 1.20 3.00
310-($1.95)-Bound-in trading card sheet .80 2.00
312-321: 312-$1.50-c begins; bound-in card sheet 1.50
316,317-($2.95)-Foil enhanced editions 1.20 3.00
318-321-($1.95)-Deluxe editions .80 2.00
322-Onslaught 2.00 5.00
323,324,326-345, -1(7/97), 346: 323-Return from Age of Apocalypse. 328-Sabretooth-c. 329,330-Dr. Strange app. 331-White Queen-c/app. 334-Juggernaut app.; w/Onslaught Update. 335-Onslaught, Avengers, Apocalypse, & X-Man app. 336-Onslaught. 338-Archangel's wings return to normal. 339-Havok vs. Cyclops; Spider-Man app. 341-Gladiator-c/app. 342-Deathbird cameo; two covers. 343,344-Phalanx 1.00 2.50
325-($3.95)-Anniversary issue; gatefold-c 1.60 4.00
342-Variant-c 1.10 3.30 9.00
347-349:347-Begin $1.99-c. 349-"Operation Zero Tolerance" .80 2.00
350-($3.99, 48 pgs.) Prismatic etched foil gatefold wraparound-c; Trial of Gambit; Seagle-s begin 3.99
351-355 1.99
Special 1(12/70)-Kirby-c/a; origin The Stranger 6.00 18.00 60.00
Special 2(11/71) 5.00 15.00 50.00
Annual 3(1979, 52 pgs.)-New story; Miller/Austin-c; Wolverine still in old yellow costume 2.25 6.75 18.00
Annual 4(1980, 52 pgs.)-Dr. Strange guest stars 1.00 3.00 7.50
Annual 5(1981, 52 pgs.) 2.40 6.00
Annual 6(1982, 52 pgs.)-Dracula app. 2.00 5.00
Annual 7,8: 7-(1983, 52 pgs.). 8-(1984, 52 pgs.) 2.00 5.00
Annual 9(1985)-New Mutants x-over cont'd from New Mutants Special Ed. #1; Art Adams-a 1.60 4.85 13.00
Annual 10(1986)-Art Adams-a 1.40 4.15 11.00
Annual 11(1987) 1.20 3.00
Annual 12(1988, $1.75)-Evolutionary War; A.Adams-a(p) 1.60 4.00
Annual 13(1989, $2.00, 68 pgs.)-Atlantis Attacks 1.20 3.00
Annual 14(1990, $2.00, 68 pgs.)-1st app. Gambit (minor app., 5 pgs.); Fantastic Four, New Mutants (Cable) & X-Factor x-over; Arthur Adams-c/a(p) 1.00 3.00 8.00
Annual 15 (1991, $2.00, 68 pgs.)-4 pg. origin; New Mutants x-over; 4 pg. Wolverine solo back-up story; 4th app. X-Force cont'd from New Warriors Annual #1 1.60 4.00
Annual 16 (1992, $2.25, 68 pgs.)-Jae Lee-c/a(p)(2) 1.00 2.50
Annual 17 (1993, $2.95, 68 pgs.)-Bagged w/card 1.60 4.00
Annual 18 (1994, $2.95, 68 pgs.) 1.20 3.00
...'95-(11/95, $3.95)-Wraparound-c 1.60 4.00
...'96-(1996, $2.95)-Wraparound-c 1.20 3.00
...'97-(1997, $2.99)-Wraparound-c 3.00
...: THE DARK PHOENIX SAGA (1990, $12.95, trade paperback) 1.60 4.85 13.00
...IN THE DAYS OF FUTURE PAST (1989, $3.95, trade paperback, 52 pgs.) 1.60 4.00

NOTE: **Art Adams** *a-Annual 9, 10p, 12p, 14p; c-218p.* **Neal Adams** *a-56-63p, 65p; c-56-63.* **Adkins** *a-34, 35p; c-31, 34, 35.* **Austin** *a-108i, 109i, 111-117i, 119-143i, 186i, 204i, 228i, 294-297i, Annual 3i, 7i, 9i, 13; c-109-111i, 114-122i, 123, 124-141i, 142, 143, 196i, 204i, 228i, 294-297i, Annual 3i.* **J. Buscema** *c-42, 43, 45.* **Buscema/Tuska** *a-45.* **Byrne** *a(p)-108, 109, 111-143, 273; c(p)-113-116, 127, 129, 131-141.* **Capullo** *c-14.* **Ditko** *r-86, 89-91, 93.* **Everett** *c-73.* **Golden** *a-273, Annual 7p.* **Guice** *a-216p, 217p.* **G. Kane** *c(p)-33, 74-76, 79, 80, 94, 95.* **Kirby** *a(p)-1-17 (#12-17, 67r-layouts); c(p)-1-17, 25, 30 (18, 26-parts).* **Layton** *a-105i; c-112i, 113i.* **Jim Lee** *a(p)-248, 256-258, 267-277; c(p)-252, 254, 256-261, 264, 267, 270, 275-277, 286.* **Perez** *a-Annual 3p; c(p)-112, 128, Annual 3.* **Peterson** *a(p)-294-300, 304(part); c(p)-294-299.* **Whilce**

Uncle Milty #1 © True Cross Publ.

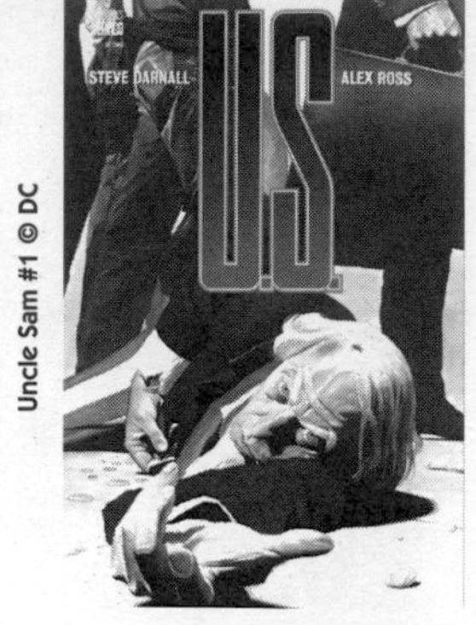

Uncle Sam #1 © DC

Uncle Scrooge #14 © WDC

GD25 FN65 NM94

__Portacio__ a(p)-281-286, 289, 290; a(i)-267; c-281-285p, 289p, 290; c(i)-267. __Romita, Jr.__ a-300; c-300. __Roussos__ a-84i. __Simonson__ a-171p; c-171, 217. __B. Smith__ a-53, 186p, 198p, 205, 214; c-53-55, 186p, 198, 205, 212, 214, 216. __Paul Smith__ a(p)-165-170, 172-175, 278; c-165-170, 172-175, 278. __Sparling__ a-78p. __Steranko__ a-50p, 51p; c-49-51. __Sutton__ a-106i. __Art Thibert__ a(i)-281-286; c(i)-281, 282, 284, 285. __Toth__ a-12p, 67p(r). __Tuska__ a-40-42i, 43-46p, 88i(r); c-39-41, 77p, 78p. __Williamson__ a-202i, 203i, 211i; c-202i, 203i, 206i. __Wood__ c-14i.

UNCANNY X-MEN AND THE NEW TEEN TITANS (See Marvel and DC Present...)

UNCANNY X-MEN AT THE STATE FAIR OF TEXAS, THE
1983 (36 pgs., one-shot)
Marvel Comics Group

nn-Supplement to the Dallas Times Herald 1.00 2.80 7.00

UNCENSORED MOUSE, THE
Apr, 1989 - No. 2, Apr, 1989 ($1.95, B&W)(Came sealed in plastic bag)
Eternity Comics

1-Early Gottfredson strip-r in each .80 2.00
2-Both contain racial stereotyping & violence 1.20 3.00
NOTE: *Both issues contain unauthorized reprints. Series was cancelled.* **Win Smith** *r-1, 2.*

UNCLE CHARLIE'S FABLES
Jan, 1952 - No. 5, Sept, 1952 (All have Biro painted-c)
Lev Gleason Publications

1-Norman Maurer-a; has Biro's picture 10.00 30.00 80.00
2-Fuje-a; Biro photo 7.15 21.50 50.00
3-5 5.70 17.00 40.00

UNCLE DONALD & HIS NEPHEWS DUDE RANCH (See Dell Giant #52)

UNCLE DONALD & HIS NEPHEWS FAMILY FUN (See Dell Giant #38)

UNCLE JOE'S FUNNIES
1938 (B&W)
Centaur Publications

1-Games, puzzles & magic tricks, some interior art; Bill Everett-c
36.00 108.00 320.00

UNCLE MILTY (TV)
Dec, 1950 - No. 4, July, 1951 (52 pgs.)(Early TV comic)
Victoria Publications/True Cross

1-Milton Berle photo on-c of #1,2 40.00 120.00 350.00
2 26.00 77.00 190.00
3,4 21.00 64.00 160.00

UNCLE REMUS & HIS TALES OF BRER RABBIT (See Brer Rabbit, 4-Color #129, 208, 693)

UNCLE SAM
1997 - No. 2, 1997 ($4.95, limited series)
DC Comics (Vertigo)

1,2-Alex Ross painted c/a. Story by Ross and Steve Darnell 4.95

UNCLE SAM QUARTERLY (Blackhawk #9 on)(See Freedom Fighters)
Autumn, 1941 - No. 8, Fall, 1943 (Also see National Comics)
Quality Comics Group

1-Origin Uncle Sam; Fine/Eisner-c, chapter headings, 2 pgs. by Eisner; (2 versions: dark cover, no price; light cover with price sticker); Jack Cole-a
270.00 810.00 2700.00
2-Cameos by The Ray, Black Condor, Quicksilver, The Red Bee, Alias the Spider, Hercules & Neon the Unknown; Eisner, Fine-c/a
106.00 318.00 950.00
3-Tuska-c/a; Eisner-a(2) 78.00 234.00 700.00
4 69.00 207.00 625.00
5,7-Hitler, Mussolini & Tojo-c 72.00 216.00 650.00
6,8 56.00 167.00 500.00
NOTE: ***Kotzky** (or **Tuska**) a-3-8.*

UNCLE SAM'S CHRISTMAS STORY
1958 (Giveaway)
Promotional Publ. Co.

nn-Reprints 1956 Christmas USA 1.50 4.50 12.00

UNCLE SCROOGE (Disney) (Becomes Walt Disney's... #210 on) (See Cartoon Tales, Dell Giants #33, 55, Disney Comic Album, Donald and Scrooge, Dynabrite, Four Color #178, Gladstone Comic Album, Walt Disney's Comics & Stories #98, Walt Disney's ...)
No. 386, 3/52 - No. 39, 8-10/62; No. 40, 12/62 - No. 209, 1984
Dell #1-39/Gold Key #40-173/Whitman #174-209

Four Color 386(#1)-in "Only a Poor Old Man" by Carl Barks; r-in Uncle Scrooge & Donald Duck #1('65) & The Best of Walt Disney Comics (1974). The very 1st cover app. of Uncle Scrooge 86.00 259.00 950.00
1-(1986)-Reprints F.C. #386; given away with lithograph "Dam Disaster at Money Lake" & as a subscription offer giveaway to Gladstone subscribers
2.25 6.75 18.00
Four Color 456(#2)-in "Back to the Klondike" by Carl Barks; r-in Best of U.S. & D.D. #1('66) & Gladstone C.A. #4 57.00 170.00 625.00
Four Color 495(#3)-r-in #105 43.00 130.00 475.00
4(12-2/53-54)-r-in Gladstone Comic Album #11 32.00 95.00 350.00
5-r-in Gladstone Special #2 & W.D. Digest #1 26.00 79.00 290.00
6-r-in U.S. #106,165,233 & Best of U.S. & D.D. #1('66)
20.00 60.00 220.00
7-The Seven Cities of Cibola by Barks; r-in #217 & Best of D.D. & U.S. #2 ('67)
18.00 55.00 200.00
8-10: 8-r-in #111,222. 9-r-in #104,214. 10-r-in #67 15.00 45.00 165.00
11-20: 11-r-in #237. 17-r-in #215. 19-r-in Gladstone C.A. #1. 20-r-in #213
14.00 41.00 150.00
21-30: 24-X-Mas-c. 26-r-in #211 11.00 34.00 125.00
31-35,37-40: 34-r-in #228. 40-X-Mas-c 9.00 29.00 105.00
36-1st app. Magica De Spell; Number one dime 1st identified by name
11.00 32.00 115.00
41-60: 48-Magica De Spell-c/story (3/64). 49-Sci/fi-c. 51-Beagle Boys-c/story (8/64) 8.00 23.00 85.00
61-63,65,66,68-71:71-Last Barks issue w/original story (#71-he only storyboarded the script) 6.40 19.00 70.00
64-Barks Vietnam War story "Treasure of Marco Polo" banned for reprints by Disney since the 1970s because of its third world revolutionary war theme
9.00 27.00 100.00
67,72,73: 67,72,73-Barks-r 6.40 19.00 70.00
74-84: 74-Barks-r(1pg.). 75-81,83-Not by Barks. 82,84-Barks-r begin
4.00 12.00 45.00
85-110 3.00 10.00 36.00
111-141,143-152,154-157 1.65 5.00 18.00
142-Reprints Four Color #456 with-c 2.00 6.00 22.00
153,158,162-164,166,168-170,178,180: No Barks 1.00 2.80 7.00
159-160,165,167,172-176-Barks-a 1.25 3.75 10.00
161(r/#14), 171(r/#11), 177(r/#16),183(r/#6)-Barks-r 1.25 3.75 10.00
179(4/#9) (8-12/80)-Distr. only in Whitman 3-pack 7.00 20.00 75.00
181(r/4-Color #495), 195(r/4-Color #386) 1.25 3.75 10.00
182,186,191-194,197-202,204-206: No Barks 2.40 6.00
184,185,187,188-Barks-a 1.00 3.00 8.00
189(r/#5), 190(r/#4), 196(r/#13), 203(r/#12), 207(r/#93,92), 208(r/U.S. #18), 209(r/U.S. #21)-Barks-r 1.00 3.00 8.00
Uncle Scrooge & Money(G.K.)-Barks-r/from WDC&S #130 (3/67)
3.00 9.00 35.00
Mini Comic #1(1976)(3-1/4x6-1/2")-r/U.S. #115; Barks-c 2.40 6.00
NOTE: ***Barks** c-Four Color 386, 456, 495, #4-37, 39, 40, 43-71.*

UNCLE SCROOGE & DONALD DUCK
June, 1965 (25¢, paper cover)
Gold Key

1-Reprint of Four Color #386(#1) & lead story from Four Color #29
6.40 19.00 70.00

UNCLE SCROOGE COMICS DIGEST
Dec, 1986 - No. 5, Aug, 1987 ($1.25, Digest-size)
Gladstone Publishing

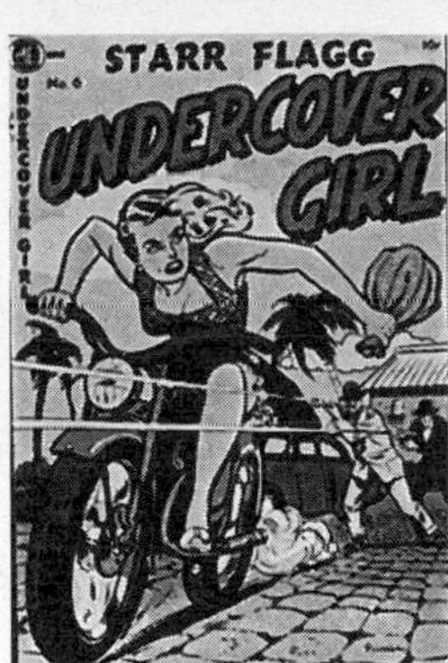

Undercover Girl #6 © ME

Underworld #3 © D. S. Pub.

Underworld Unleashed: Patterns of Fear #1 © DC

GD25 FN65 NM94

1,3 2.00 5.00
2,4 1.20 3.00
5 (scarce) 2.40 6.00

UNCLE SCROOGE GOES TO DISNEYLAND (See Dell Giants)
Aug, 1985 ($2.50)
Gladstone Publishing Ltd.

1-Reprints Dell Giant w/new-c by Mel Crawford, based on old cover 1.25 3.75 10.00
...Comics Digest 1 ($1.50, digest size) 1.50 4.50 12.00

UNCLE SCROOGE IN COLOR
1987 ($29.95, Hardcover, 9-1/4"X12-1/4", 96 Pgs.)
Gladstone Publishing

nn-Reprints "Christmas on Bear Mountain" from Four Color 178 by Barks; Uncle Scrooge's Christmas Carol (published as Donald Duck & the Christmas Carol, A Little Golden Book), reproduced from the original art as adapted by Norman McGary from pencils by Barks; and Uncle Scrooge the Lemonade King, reproduced from the original art, plus Barks' original pencils 5.00 15.00 50.00
nn-Slipcase edition of 750, signed by Barks, issued at $79.95 90.00 300.00

UNCLE SCROOGE THE LEMONADE KING
1960 (A Top Top Tales Book, 6-3/8"x7-5/8", 32 pgs.)
Whitman Publishing Co.

2465-Storybook pencilled by Carl Barks, finished art adapted by Norman McGary 36.00 108.00 400.00

UNCLE WIGGILY (See March of Comics #19)
No. 179, Dec, 1947 - No. 543, Mar, 1954
Dell Publishing Co.

Four Color 179 (#1)-Walt Kelly-c 14.00 44.00 160.00
Four Color 221 (3/49)-Part Kelly-c 9.00 27.00 100.00
Four Color 276 (5/50), 320 (#1, 3/51) 7.00 22.00 80.00
Four Color 349 (9-10/51), 391 (4-5/52) 5.50 16.50 60.00
Four Color 428 (10/52), 503 (10/53), 543 3.60 11.00 40.00

UNDERCOVER GIRL (Starr Flagg) (See Extra Comics & Manhunt!)
No. 5, 1952 - No. 7, 1954
Magazine Enterprises

5(#1)(A-1 #62)-Fallon of the F.B.I. in all 36.00 107.00 260.00
6(A-1 #98), 7(A-1 #118)-All have Starr Flagg 33.00 99.00 240.00
NOTE: ***Powell** c-6, 7. **Whitney** a-5-7.*

UNDERDOG (TV)(See Kite Fun Book, March of Comics #426, 438, 467, 479)
July, 1970 - No. 10, Jan, 1972; Mar, 1975 - No. 23, Feb, 1979
Charlton Comics/Gold Key

1 (1st series, Charlton)-1st app. Underdog 6.00 18.00 60.00
2-10 3.50 10.50 35.00
1 (2nd series, Gold Key) 4.00 12.00 45.00
2-10 2.50 7.50 28.00
11-23: 13-1st app. Shack of Solitude 1.65 5.00 18.00

UNDERDOG
1987 - No. 3?, 1987 ($1.50)
Spotlight Comics

1-3 1.50

UNDERDOG SUMMER SPECIAL (TV)
Oct, 1993 ($2.25, 68 pgs.)
Harvey Comics

1 .90 2.25

UNDERSEA AGENT
Jan, 1966 - No. 6, Mar, 1967 (25¢, 68 pgs.)
Tower Comics

1-Davy Jones, Undersea Agent begins 4.80 14.40 48.00
2-6: 2-Jones gains magnetic powers. 5-Origin & 1st app. of Merman. 6-Kane/Wood-c(r) 3.20 9.60 32.00
NOTE: ***Gil Kane** a-3-6; c-4, 5. **Moldoff** a-2i.*

UNDERSEA FIGHTING COMMANDOS (See Fighting Undersea...)
1964
I.W. Enterprises

I.W. Reprint #1,2('64): 1-r/#? 2-r/#1; Severin-c 1.00 3.00 8.00

UNDERWATER CITY, THE
No. 1328, 1961
Dell Publishing Co.

Four Color 1328-Movie, Evans-a 6.40 19.00 70.00

UNDERWORLD (...True Crime Stories)
Feb-Mar, 1948 - No. 9, June-July, 1949 (52 pgs.)
D. S. Publishing Co.

1-Moldoff (Shelly)-c; excessive violence 38.00 114.00 280.00
2-Moldoff (Shelly)-c; Ma Barker story used in **SOTI**, pg. 95; female electrocution panel; lingerie art 38.00 114.00 280.00
3-McWilliams-c/a; extreme violence, mutilation 32.00 96.00 240.00
4-Used in Love and Death by Legman; Ingels-a 24.00 73.00 180.00
5-Ingels-a 18.00 54.00 140.00
6-9: 8-Ravielli-a 13.50 41.00 100.00

UNDERWORLD
Dec, 1987 - No. 4, Mar, 1988 ($1.00, limited series, mature)
DC Comics

1-4 1.00

UNDERWORLD CRIME
June, 1952 - No. 9, Oct, 1953
Fawcett Publications

1 24.00 73.00 180.00
2 16.00 47.00 115.00
3-6,8,9 (8,9-exist?) 13.50 41.00 100.00
7-(6/53)-Bondage/torture-c 23.00 69.00 160.00

UNDERWORLD STORY, THE (Movie)
1950
Avon Periodicals

nn-(Scarce)-Ravielli-c 24.00 71.00 175.00

UNDERWORLD UNLEASHED
Nov, 1995 - No. 3, Jan, 1996 ($2.95, limited series)
DC Comics

1-3: Mark Waid scripts & Howard Porter-c/a(p) 1.60 4.00
...: Abyss: Hell's Sentinel 1-($2.95)-Alan Scott, Phantom Stranger, Zatanna app. 1.20 3.00
...: Apokolips-Dark Uprising 1 ($1.95) .80 2.00
...: Batman-Devil's Asylum 1-($2.95)-Batman app. 1.20 3.00
...: Patterns of Fear-($2.95) 1.20 3.00

UNEARTHLY SPECTACULARS
Oct, 1965 - No. 3, Mar, 1967
Harvey Publications

1-(12¢)-Tiger Boy; Simon-c 2.50 7.50 22.00
2-(25¢ giants)-Jack Q. Frost, Tiger Boy & Three Rocketeers app.; Williamson, Wood, Kane-a; r-1 story/Thrill-O-Rama #2 2.80 8.40 28.00
3-(25¢ giants)-Jack Q. Frost app.; Williamson/Crandall-a; r-from Alarming Advs. #1,1962 2.80 8.40 28.00
NOTE: ***Crandall** a-3r. **G. Kane** a-2. **Orlando** a-3. **Simon, Sparling, Wood** c-2. **Simon/Kirby** a-3r. **Torres** a-1?. **Wildey** a-1(3). **Williamson** a-2, 3r. **Wood** a-2(2).*

UNEXPECTED, THE (Formerly Tales of the...)
No. 105, Feb-Mar, 1968 - No. 222, May, 1982
National Periodical Publications/DC Comics

105-Begin 12¢ cover price 3.50 10.50 35.00

Union #3 © Aegis Entertainment

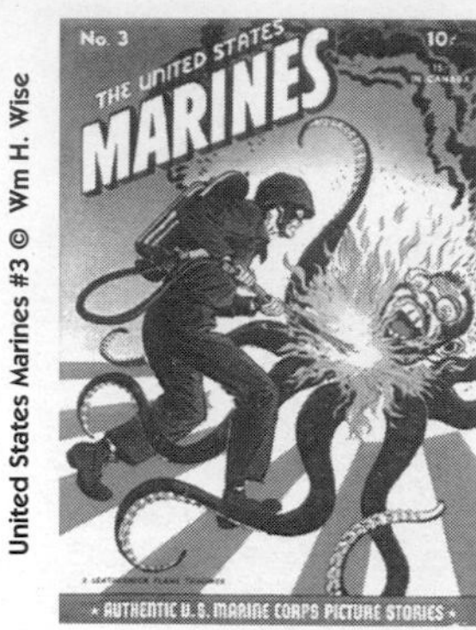

United States Marines #3 © Wm H. Wise

Unknown Soldier #236 © DC

	GD25	FN65	NM94
106-113: 113-Last 12¢ issue (6-7/69)	2.50	7.50	20.00
114,115,117,118,120,122-125	1.50	4.50	12.00
116,119,121 (36 pgs.),128(52 pgs.)-Wrightson-a	2.50	7.50	20.00
126,127,129-136-(52 pgs.)	1.85	5.50	12.00
137-156	1.10	3.30	9.00
157-162-(100 pgs.)	2.00	6.00	18.00
163-188: 187,188-(44 pgs.)		1.20	4.00
189,190,192-195 ($1.00, 68 pgs.): 189 on are combined with House of Secrets & The Witching Hour		2.40	6.00
191-Rogers-a(p) ($1.00, 68 pgs.)		1.60	7.00
196-221: 200-Return of Johhny Peril by Tuska. 205-213-Johnny Peril app. 210-Time Warp story			3.00

NOTE: ***Neal Adams*** *c-110, 112-115, 118, 121, 124.* ***J. Craig*** *a-195.* ***Ditko*** *a-189, 221p, 222p; c-222.* ***Drucker*** *a-107r, 132r.* ***Giffen*** *a-219, 222.* ***Kaluta*** *c-203, 212.* ***Kirby*** *a-127r, 162.* ***Kubert*** *c-204, 214-216, 219-221.* ***Mayer*** *a-217p, 220, 221p.* ***Moldoff*** *a-136r.* ***Moreira*** *a-133.* ***Mortimer*** *a-212p.* ***Newton*** *a-204p.* ***Orlando*** *a-202; c-191.* ***Perez*** *a-217p.* ***Redondo*** *a-155, 166, 195.* ***Reese*** *a-145.* ***Sparling*** *a-107, 205-209p, 212p.* ***Spiegle*** *a-217.* ***Starlin*** *c-198.* ***Toth*** *a-126r, 127r.* ***Tuska*** *a-127, 132, 134, 136, 139, 152, 180, 200p.* ***Wildey*** *a-128r, 193.* ***Wood*** *a-122i, 133i, 137i, 138i.* ***Wrightson*** *a-161r(2 pgs.). Johnny Peril in #106-114, 116, 117, 200, 205-213.*

UNEXPECTED ANNUAL, THE (See DC Special Series #4)

UNIDENTIFIED FLYING ODDBALL (See Walt Disney Showcase #52)

UNION
June, 1993 - No. 0, July, 1994 ($1.95, limited series)
Image Comics (WildStorm Productions)

	GD25	FN65	NM94
0-(7/94, $2.50)		1.00	2.50
0-Alternate Portacio-c (See Deathblow #5)		2.00	5.00
1-($2.50)-Embossed foil-c; Texeira-c/a in all		1.00	2.50
1-($1.95)-Newsstand edition w/o foil-c		.80	2.00
2-4: 4-(7/94)		.80	2.00

UNION
Feb, 1995 - No. 9, Dec, 1995 ($2.50)
Image Comics (WildStorm Productions)

	GD25	FN65	NM94
1-3,5-9: 3-Savage Dragon app. 6-Fairchild from Gen 13 app.		1.00	2.50
4-($1.95, Newsstand)-Wildstorm Rising Pt. 3		.80	2.00
4-($2.50, Direct Market)-Wildstorm Rising Pt. 3, bound-in card		1.00	2.50

UNION: FINAL VENGEANCE
Oct, 1997 - Present ($2.50)
Image Comics (WildStorm Productions)

	GD25	FN65	NM94
1-Golden-c/Heisler-s		1.00	2.50

UNITED COMICS (Formerly Fritzi Ritz #7; has Fritzi Ritz logo)
Aug, 1940; No. 8, 1950 - No. 26, Jan-Feb, 1953
United Features Syndicate

	GD25	FN65	NM94
1(68 pgs.)-Fritzi Ritz & Phil Fumble	19.00	56.00	150.00
8-Fritzi Ritz, Abbie & Slats	4.25	13.00	28.00
9-26: 20-Strange As It Seems; Russell Patterson Cheesecake-a. 22,25-Peanuts app.	4.00	12.00	24.00

NOTE: *Abbie & Slats reprinted from Tip Top.*

UNITED NATIONS, THE (See Classics Illustrated Special Issue)

UNITED STATES AIR FORCE PRESENTS: THE HIDDEN CREW
1964 (36 pgs.)
U.S. Air Force

	GD25	FN65	NM94
nn-Schaffenberger-a		1.60	4.00

UNITED STATES FIGHTING AIR FORCE (Also see U.S. Fighting Air Force)
Sept, 1952 - No. 29, Oct, 1956
Superior Comics Ltd.

	GD25	FN65	NM94
1	7.15	21.50	50.00
2	4.25	13.00	26.00
3-10	2.00	6.00	16.00
11-29	1.75	5.25	14.00

UNITED STATES MARINES
1943 - No. 4, 1944; No. 5, 1952 - No. 8, 1952; No. 7 - No. 11, 1953
William H. Wise/Life's Romances Publ. Co./Magazine Enterprises #5-8/ Toby Press #7-11

	GD25	FN65	NM94
nn-Mart Bailey-a	10.00	30.00	75.00
2-Bailey-a; Tojo classic-c	14.00	41.00	110.00
3-Tojo-c	9.50	28.00	75.00
4	6.50	19.50	45.00
5(A-1 #55)-Bailey-a, 6(A-1 #60), 7(A-1 #68), 8(A-1 #72)	5.35	16.00	32.00
7-11 (Toby)	3.60	9.00	18.00

NOTE: ***Powell*** *a-5-7.*

UNITY
No. 0, Aug, 1992 - No. 1, 1992 (Free comics w/limited distribution, 20 pgs.)
Valiant

	GD25	FN65	NM94
0 (Blue)-Prequel to Unity x-overs in all Valiant titles; B. Smith-c/a. (Free to everyone that bought all 8 titles that month.)		.80	2.00
0 (Red)-Same as above, but w/red logo (5,000).		1.60	4.00
0 (Gold)-Promotional copy.		1.20	3.00
1-Epilogue to Unity x-overs; B. Smith-c/a. (1 copy available for every 8 Valiant books ordered by dealers.)		.80	2.00
1 (Gold)-Promotional copy.		1.20	3.00
1 (Platinum)-Promotional copy.		1.60	4.00
Yearbook 1 (2/95, $3.95)-"1994" in indicia.		1.60	4.00

UNIVERSAL MONSTERS
1993 ($4.95/$5.95, 52 pgs.)(All adapt original movies)
Dark Horse Comics

	GD25	FN65	NM94
Frankenstein nn-($3.95)-Painted-c/a		1.60	4.00
Dracula nn-($4.95)		2.00	5.00
The Mummy nn-($4.95)-Painted-c		2.00	5.00
Creature From the Black Lagoon nn-($4.95)-Art Adams/Austin-c/a		2.00	5.00

UNIVERSAL PRESENTS DRACULA-THE MUMMY& OTHER STORIES
Sept-Nov, 1963 (one-shot, 84 pgs.) (Also see Dell Giants)
Dell Publishing Co.

	GD25	FN65	VF82	NM94
02-530-311-r/Dracula 12-231-212, The Mummy 12-437-211 & part of Ghost Stories No. 1	12.00	36.00	84.00	210.00

UNIVERSAL SOLDIER (Movie)
Sept, 1992 - No. 3, Nov, 1992 (Limited series, polybagged, mature)
Now Comics

	GD25	FN65	NM94
1-3 ($2.50, Direct Sales) 1-Movie adapatation; hologram on-c (all direct sales editions have painted-c)		1.00	2.50
1-3 ($1.95, Newstand)-Rewritten & redrawn code approved version; all newsstand editions have photo-c		.80	2.00

UNKEPT PROMISE
1949 (Giveaway, 24 pgs.)
Legion of Truth

	GD25	FN65	NM94
nn-Anti-alcohol	7.15	21.50	50.00

UNKNOWN MAN, THE (Movie)
1951
Avon Periodicals

	GD25	FN65	NM94
nn-Kinstler-c	24.00	71.00	170.00

UNKNOWN SOLDIER (Formerly Star-Spangled War Stories)
No. 205, Apr-May, 1977 - No. 268, Oct, 1982
National Periodical Publications/DC Comics

	GD25	FN65	NM94
205	1.25	3.75	10.00
206-210,220,221,251: 220,221 (44pgs.). 251-Enemy Ace begins	1.00	2.80	7.00
211-218,222-247,250,252-264		2.00	5.00
219-Miller-a (44 pgs.)	1.25	3.75	10.00
248,249,265-267: 248,249-Origin. .265-267-Enemy Ace vs. Balloon Buster.		2.40	6.00

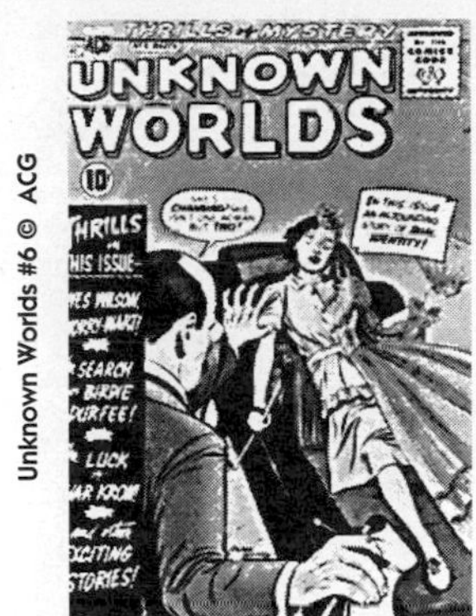

Unknown Worlds #6 © ACG

Unlimited Access #2 © MEG/ DC

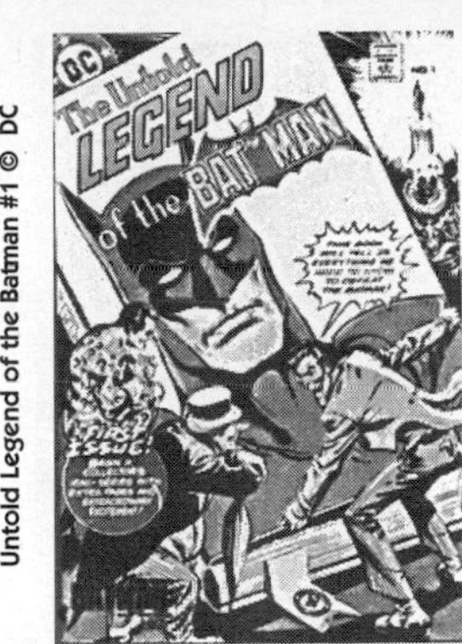

Untold Legend of the Batman #1 © DC

GD25 FN65 NM94

268-Death of Unknown Soldier 1.25 3.75 10.00
NOTE: ***Chaykin** a-234.* ***Evans** a-265-267; c-235.* ***Kubert** c-Most.* ***Miller** a-219p.* ***Severin** a-251-253, 260, 261, 265-267.* ***Simonson** a-254-256.* ***Spiegle** a-258, 259, 262-264.*

UNKNOWN SOLDIER, THE (Also see Brave &the Bold #146)
Winter, 1988-'89 - No. 12, Dec, 1989 ($1.50, maxi-series, mature)
DC Comics
1-12: 8-Begin $1.75-c 1.50

UNKNOWN SOLDIER
Apr, 1997 - No 4, July, 1997 ($2.50, mini-series)
DC Comics (Vertigo)
1-Ennis-s/Plunkett-a/Bradstreet-c in all 1.00 3.00 8.00
2 2.00 5.00
3,4 1.40 3.50

UNKNOWN WORLD (Strange Stories From Another World #2 on)
June, 1952
Fawcett Publications
1-Norman Saunders painted-c 36.00 107.00 260.00

UNKNOWN WORLDS (See Journey Into...)

UNKNOWN WORLDS
Aug, 1960 - No. 57, Aug, 1967
American Comics Group/Best Synd. Features
1-Schaffenberger-c 15.50 47.00 155.00
2-5: 2-Dinosaur-c/story 9.00 27.00 90.00
6-11: 9-Dinosaur-c/story. 11-Last 10¢ issue 6.50 19.50 65.00
12-19: 12-Begin 12¢ issues?; ends #57 5.50 16.50 55.00
20-Herbie cameo (12-1/62-63) 6.00 18.00 60.00
21-35 3.20 9.60 32.00
36- "The People vs. Hendricks" by Craig; most popular ACG story ever
3.50 10.50 35.00
37-46 2.80 8.40 28.00
47-Williamson-a r-from Adventures Into the Unknown #96, 3 pgs.; Craig-a
3.00 9.00 30.00
48-57: 53-Frankenstein app. 2.50 7.50 25.00
NOTE: ***Ditko** a-49, 50p, 54.* ***Forte** a-3, 6, 11.* ***Landau** a-56(2).* ***Reinman** a-3, 9, 13, 20, 22, 23, 36, 38, 54.* ***Whitney** c/a-most issues. John Force, Magic Agent app.-35, 36, 48, 50, 52, 54, 56.*

UNKNOWN WORLDS OF FRANK BRUNNER
Aug, 1985 - No. 2, Aug, 1985 ($1.75)
Eclipse Comics
1,2-B&W-r in color .75 1.80

UNKNOWN WORLDS OF SCIENCE FICTION
Jan, 1975 - No. 6, Nov, 1975; 1976 ($1.00, B&W Magazine)
Marvel Comics Group
1-Williamson/Krenkel/Torres/Frazetta-r/Witzend #1, Neal Adams-r/Phase 1;
Brunner & Kaluta-r; Freas/Romita-c 2.40 6.00
2-6: 5-Kaluta text illos 2.00 5.00
Special 1(1976,100 pgs.)-Newton painted-c 2.40 6.00
NOTE: ***Brunner** a-2; c-4, 6.* ***Buscema** a-Special 1p.* ***Chaykin** a-5.* ***Colan** a(p)-1, 3, 5, 6.* ***Corben** a-4.* ***Kaluta** a-2, Special 1(ext illos); c-2.* ***Morrow** a-3, 5.* ***Nino** a-3, 6, Special 1.* ***Perez** a-2, 3. Ray Bradbury interview in #1.*

UNLIMITED ACCESS (Also see Marvel Vs. DC))
Dec, 1997 - No. 4, Mar, 1998 ($2.99/$1.99, limited series)
Marvel Comics
1-Spider-Man, Wonder Woman, Green Lantern & Hulk app. 2.99
2,3-($1.99): 2-X-Men, Legion of Super-Heroes app. 3-Original Avengers vs.
original Justice League 1.99
4-($2.99) 2.99

UNSANE (Formerly Mighty Bear #13, 14? or The Outlaws #10-14?)
No. 15, June, 1954
Star Publications
15-Disbrow-a(2); L. B. Cole-c 28.00 84.00 225.00

GD25 FN65 NM94

UNSEEN, THE
No. 5, 1952 - No. 15, July, 1954
Visual Editions/Standard Comics
5-Horror stories in all; Toth-a 30.00 90.00 225.00
6,7,9,10-Jack Katz-a 21.00 62.00 155.00
8,11,13,14 13.50 41.00 100.00
12,15-Toth-a. 12-Tuska-a 21.00 62.00 155.00
NOTE: ***Nick Cardy** c-12.* ***Fawcette** a-13, 14.* ***Sekowsky** a-7, 8(2), 10, 13, 15.*

UNTAMED
June, 1993 - No. 3, Aug, 1993 ($1.95, limited series)
Marvel Comics (Epic Comics/Heavy Hitters)
1-($2.50)-Embossed-c 1.00 2.50
2,3 .80 2.00

UNTAMED LOVE (Also see Frank Frazetta's Untamed Love)
Jan, 1950 - No. 5, Sept, 1950
Quality Comics Group (Comic Magazines)
1-Ward-c, Gustavson-a 20.00 60.00 150.00
2,4: 2-5-Photo-c 11.50 34.00 85.00
3,5-Gustavson-a 13.00 39.00 95.00

UNTOLD LEGEND OF CAPTAIN MARVEL, THE
Apr, 1997 - No. 3, June, 1997 ($2.50, limited series)
Marvel Comics
1-3 1.00 2.50

UNTOLD LEGEND OF THE BATMAN, THE
July, 1980 - No. 3, Sept, 1980 (Limited series)
DC Comics
1-Origin; Joker-c; Byrne's 1st work at DC 1.60 4.00
2,3 1.20 3.00
1-3: Batman cereal premiums (1989, 28 pgs., 6X9"); 1st & 2nd printings
known 1.00 2.50
NOTE: ***Aparo** a-1i, 2, 3.* ***Byrne** a-1p.*

UNTOLD ORIGIN OF THE FEMFORCE, THE (Also see Femforce)
1989 ($4.95, 68 pgs.)
AC Comics
1-Origin Femforce, Bill Black-a(i) & scripts 2.00 5.00

UNTOLD TALES OF SPIDER-MAN (Also see Amazing Fantasy #16-18)
Sept, 1995 - No. 25, Sept, 1997(99¢)
Marvel Comics
1-Kurt Busiek scripts begin; Pat Olliffe-c/a in all (except #9). 1.00
2-22, -1(7/97), 23-25: 2-1st app. Batwing. 4-1st app. The Spacemen (Gantry, Orbit, Satellite & Vacuum). 8-1st app. The Headsman; The Enforcers (The Big Man, Montana, The Ox & Fancy Dan) app. 9-Ron Frenz-a. 10-1st app. Commanda. 16-Reintro Mary Jane Watson. 21-X-Men-c/app. 25-Green Goblin 1.00
...'96-(1996, $1.95, 46 pgs.)-Kurt Busiek scripts; Mike Allred-c/a; Kurt Busiek & Pat Olliffe app. in back-up story; contains pin-ups .80 2.00
...'97-(1997, $1.95)-Wraparound-c .80 2.00

UNTOUCHABLES, THE (TV)
No. 1237, 10-12/61 - No. 4, 8-10/62 (All have Robert Stack photo-c)
Dell Publishing Co.
Four Color 1237(#1) 22.00 65.00 240.00
Four Color 1286 16.00 47.00 170.00
01-879-207, 12-879-210(01879-210 on inside) 8.00 25.00 90.00
Topps Bubblegum premiums produced by Leaf Brands, Inc.-2-1/2x4-1/2", 8 pgs. (3 diff. issues) "The Organization, Jamaica Ginger, The Otto Frick Story (drug), 3000 Suspects, The Antidote, Mexican Stakeout, Little Egypt, Purple Gang, Bugs Moran Story, & Lily Dallas Story" 2.00 6.00 16.00

UNTOUCHABLES
Aug, 1997 - Present ($2.95, B&W)
Caliber Comics

Unusual Tales #18 © CC

USA Comics #1 © TCI

Usagi Yojimbo V3 #16 © Stan Sakai

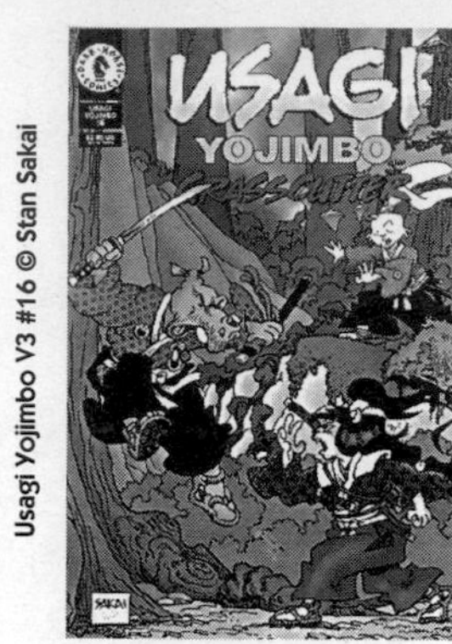

1,2: 1-Pruett-s; variant covers by Kaluta & Showman 2.95

UNUSUAL TALES (Blue Beetle & Shadows From Beyond #50 on)
Nov, 1955 - No. 49, Mar-Apr, 1965
Charlton Comics

	GD25	FN65	NM94
1	20.00	60.00	150.00
2	10.00	30.00	75.00
3-5	7.15	21.50	50.00
6-Ditko-c only	8.50	26.00	60.00
7,8-Ditko-c/a	17.50	53.00	140.00
9-Ditko-c/a (20 pgs.)	19.00	56.00	150.00
10-Ditko-c/a(4)	21.00	64.00	170.00
11-(3/58, 68 pgs.)-Ditko-a(4)	20.00	60.00	160.00
12,14-Ditko-a	12.00	38.00	100.00
13,16-20	3.50	10.50	35.00
15-Ditko-c/a	11.00	33.00	110.00
21,24,28	2.50	7.50	25.00
22,23,25-27,29-Ditko-a	7.00	21.00	70.00
30-49	2.50	7.50	20.00

NOTE: ***Colan** a-11. **Ditko** c-22, 23, 25-27, 31(part).*

UP FROM HARLEM (Tom Skinner...)
1973 (35/49¢)
Spire Christian Comics (Fleming H. Revell Co.)

nn 1.20 3.00

UP-TO-DATE COMICS
No date (1938) (36 pgs.; B&W cover) (10¢)
King Features Syndicate

nn-Popeye & Henry cover; The Phantom, Jungle Jim & Flash Gordon by Raymond, The Katzenjammer Kids, Curley Harper & others. Note: Variations in content exist. 20.00 60.00 160.00

UP YOUR NOSE AND OUT YOUR EAR (Satire)
Apr, 1972 - No. 2, June, 1972 (52 pgs., magazine)
Klevart Enterprises

V1#1,2 1.20 3.00

URBAN
1994 ($1.75, B&W)
Moving Target Entertainment

1 .70 1.75

URTH 4
1990 - No. 4, 1990 ($2.00, deluxe format)
Continuity Comics

1-4: Ms. Mystic characters. 2-Neal Adams-c(i) .80 2.00

URZA-MISHRA WAR ON THE WORLD OF MAGIC THE GATHERING
1996 - No. 2, 1996 ($5.95, limited series)
Acclaim Comics (Armada)

1,2 2.40 6.00

U.S. (See Uncle Sam)

USA COMICS
Aug, 1941 - No. 17, Fall, 1945
Timely Comics (USA)

GD25 FN65 VF82 NM94

1-Origin Major Liberty (called Mr. Liberty #1), Rockman by Wolverton, & The Whizzer by Avison; The Defender with sidekick Rusty & Jack Frost begin; The Young Avenger only app.; S&K-c plus 1 pg. art
930.00 2790.00 5580.00 9300.00
(Estimated up to 145 total copies exist, 7 in NM/Mint)

GD25 FN65 NM94

2-Origin Captain Terror & The Vagabond; last Wolverton Rockman
270.00 810.00 2700.00
3-No Whizzer 222.00 666.00 2000.00
4-Last Rockman, Major Liberty, Defender, Jack Frost, & Capt. Terror; Corporal Dix app. 189.00 567.00 1700.00
5-Origin American Avenger & Roko the Amazing; The Blue Blade, The Black Widow & Victory Boys, Gypo the Gypsy Giant & Hills of Horror only app.; Sergeant Dix begins; no Whizzer; Hitler, Mussolini & Tojo-c
167.00 500.00 1500.00
6-Captain America (ends #17), The Destroyer, Jap Buster Johnson, Jeep Jones begin; Terror Squad only app. 222.00 666.00 2000.00
7-Captain Daring, Disk-Eyes the Detective by Wolverton app.; origin & only app. Marvel Boy (3/43); Secret Stamp begins; no Whizzer, Sergeant Dix
189.00 567.00 1700.00
8-10: 9-Last Secret Stamp. 10-The Thunderbird only app.
150.00 450.00 1350.00
11,12: 11-No Jeep Jones 122.00 366.00 1100.00
13-17: 13-No Whizzer; Jeep Jones ends. 15-No Destroyer; Jap Buster Johnson ends 89.00 267.00 800.00

NOTE: ***Brodsky** c-14. **Gabrielle** c-4, 8. **Schomburg** c-6-8, 10, 12, 13, 15-17. **Shores** a-1, 4; c-9, 11. **Ed Win** a-4. Cover features: 1-The Defender; 2, 3-Captain Terror; 4-Major Liberty; 5-Victory Boys; 6-17-Captain America & Bucky.*

U.S. AGENT (See Jeff Jordan...)

U.S. AGENT (See Captain America #354)
June, 1993 - No. 4, Sept, 1993 ($1.75, limited series)
Marvel Comics

1-4 .70 1.75

USAGI YOJIMBO (See Albedo, Doomsday Squad #3 & Space Usagi)
July, 1987 - No. 38 ($2.00/$2.25, B&W)
Fantagraphics Books

	FN65	NM94
1	1.00	2.50
1,8,10-2nd printings	.80	2.00
2-9,11-28: 11-Aragonés-a	.80	2.00
10-Leonardo app. (TMNT)	1.00	2.50
29-38: 29-Begin $2.25-c	.90	2.25
Color Special 1 (11/89, $2.95, 68 pgs.)-new & r	1.20	3.00
Color Special 2 (10/91, $3.50)	1.40	3.50
Color Special #3 (10/92, $3.50)-Jeff Smith's Bone promo on inside cover	1.40	3.50
Summer Special 1 (1986, B&W, $2.75)-r/early Albedo issues	1.20	3.00

USAGI YOJIMBO
V2#1, Mar, 1993 - No. 16, 1994 ($2.75)
Mirage Studios

V2#1-16: 1-Teenage Mutant Ninja Turtles app. 1.10 2.75

USAGI YOJIMBO
V3#1, Apr, 1996 - Present ($2.95, B&W)
Dark Horse Comics

V3#1-16: Stan Sakai-c/a 1.20 3.00

U.S. AIR FORCE COMICS (Army Attack #38 on)
Oct, 1958 - No. 37, Mar-Apr, 1965
Charlton Comics

	GD25	FN65	NM94
1	3.60	10.80	36.00
2	2.50	7.50	20.00
3-10	1.85	5.50	15.00
11-20	1.50	4.50	12.00
21-37	1.10	3.30	9.00

NOTE: ***Glanzman** c/a-9, 10, 12. **Montes/Bache** a-33.*

USA IS READY
1941 (68 pgs., one-shot)
Dell Publishing Co.

1-War propaganda 34.00 101.00 270.00

U.S. BORDER PATROL COMICS (Sgt. Dick Carter of the...) (See Holyoke One Shot)

U.S. FIGHTING AIR FORCE (Also see United States Fighting Air Force)
No date (1960s?)

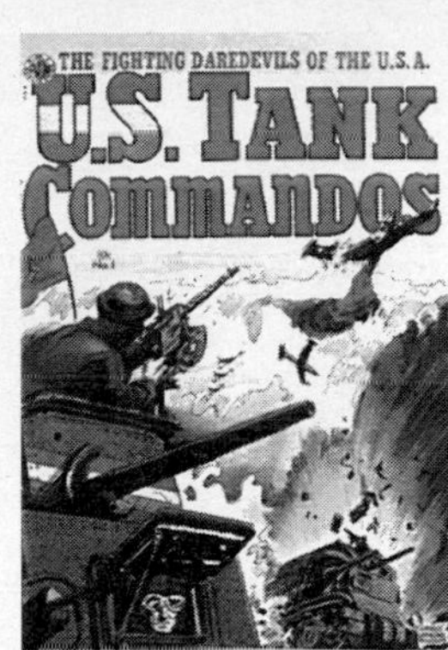

U.S Tank Commandos #1 © AVON

Valeria the She Bat #1 © Neal Adams

Valor #21 © DC

GD25 FN65 NM94

I. W. Enterprises

1,9(nd): 1-r/United States Fighting...#?. 9-r/#1 — 2.00 5.00

U.S. FIGHTING MEN
1963 - 1964 (Reprints)
Super Comics

10-r/With the U.S. Paratroops #4(Avon) 1.00 2.80 7.00
11,12,15-18: 11-r/Monty Hall #10. 12,16,17,18-r/U.S. Fighting Air Force #10,3,?&? 15-r/Man Comics #11 — 2.40 6.00

U.S. JONES (Also see Wonderworld Comics #28)
Nov, 1941 - No. 2, Jan, 1942
Fox Features Syndicate

1-U.S. Jones & The Topper begin; Nazi-c 100.00 300.00 900.00
2-Nazi-c 72.00 216.00 650.00

U.S. MARINES
Fall, 1964 (12¢, one-shot)
Charlton Comics

1 1.85 5.50 15.00

U.S. MARINES IN ACTION
Aug, 1952 - No. 3, Dec, 1952
Avon Periodicals

1-Louis Ravielli-c/a 6.50 19.50 45.00
2,3: 3-Kinstler-c 4.15 12.50 25.00

U.S. 1
May, 1983 - No. 12, Oct, 1984 (7,8: painted-c)
Marvel Comics Group

1-12: 2-Sienkiewicz-c. 3-12-Michael Golden-c 1.00

U.S. PARATROOPS (See With the...)

U.S. PARATROOPS
1964?
I. W. Enterprises

1,8: 1-r/With the U.S. Paratroops #1; Wood-c. 8-r/With the U.S. Paratroops #6; Kinstler-c 1.00 3.00 8.00

U.S. TANK COMMANDOS
June, 1952 - No. 4, Mar, 1953
Avon Periodicals

1-Kinstler-c 7.15 21.50 50.00
2-4: Kinstler-c 5.70 17.00 35.00
I.W. Reprint #1,8: 1-r/#1. 8-r/#3 1.00 3.00 8.00
NOTE: ***Kinstler** a-I.W. #1; c-1-4, I.W. #1, 8.*

"V" (TV)
Feb, 1985 - No. 18, July, 1986
DC Comics

1-Based on TV movie & series (Sci/Fi) 1.50
2-18: 17,18-Denys Cowan-c/a 1.00

VACATION COMICS (Also see A-1 Comics)
No. 16, 1948 (one-shot)
Magazine Enterprises

A-1 16-The Pixies, Tom Tom, Flying Fredd & Koko & Kola 4.00 12.00 24.00

VACATION DIGEST
Sept, 1987 ($1.25, digest size)
Harvey Comics

1 1.25

VACATION IN DISNEYLAND (Also see Dell Giants)
Aug-Oct, 1959; May, 1965 (Walt Disney)
Dell Publishing Co./Gold Key (1965)

Four Color 1025-Barks-a 18.00 55.00 200.00
1(30024-508)(G.K., 5/65, 25¢)-r/Dell Giant #30 & cover to #1 ('58); celebrates Disneyland's 10th anniversary 3.60 11.00 40.00

VACATION PARADE (See Dell Giants)

VALERIA THE SHE BAT
May, 1993 - No. 5, Nov, 1993
Continuity Comics

1-Premium; glow-in-the-dark-c; N. Adams-a/scripts; given as gift to retailers 2.00 5.00
2-5: 5 (11/93)-Embossed-c; N. Adams-a/scripts 1.00 2.50
NOTE: *Due to lack of continuity, #2-4 do not exist.*

VALERIA THE SHE BAT
Sept, 1995 - No.2, Oct, 1995 ($2.50, limited series)
Acclaim Comics (Windjammer)

1,2 1.00 2.50

VALKYRIE (See Airboy)
May,1987 - No. 3, July, 1987 ($1.75, limited series)
Eclipse Comics

1-3: 2-Holly becomes new Black Angel 1.00 2.50

VALKYRIE
Jan, 1997 ($2.95, one-shot)
Marvel Comics

1-w/pin-ups 1.20 3.00

VALKYRIE!
July, 1988 - No. 3, Sept, 1988 ($1.95, limited series)
Eclipse Comics

1-3 .80 2.00

VALLEY OF THE DINOSAURS (TV)
Apr, 1975 - No. 11, Dec, 1976 (Hanna-Barbara)
Charlton Comics

1,3: 3-Byrne text illos (early work, 7/75) 1.00 3.00 8.00
2,4-11 2.00 5.00

VALLEY OF GWANGI (See Movie Classics)

VALOR
Mar-Apr, 1955 - No. 5, Nov-Dec, 1955
E. C. Comics

1-Williamson/Torres-a; Wood-c/a 25.00 75.00 200.00
2-Williamson-c/a; Wood-a 22.00 66.00 175.00
3,4: 3-Williamson, Crandall-a. 4-Wood-c 15.00 45.00 120.00
5-Wood-c/a; Williamson/Evans-a 14.00 41.00 110.00
NOTE: ***Crandall** a-3, 4. **Ingels** a-1, 2, 4, 5. **Krigstein** a-1-5. **Orlando** a-3, 4; c-3. **Wood** a-1, 2, 5; c-1, 4, 5.*

VALOR (Also see Legion of Super-Heroes & Legionnaires)
Nov, 1992 - No. 23, Sept, 1994 ($1.25/$1.50)
DC Comics

1-12: 1-Eclipso The Darkness Within aftermath. 2-Vs. Supergirl. 4-Vs. Lobo. 12-Lobo cameo 1.25
13-22: 13-Begin $1.50-c. 14-Legionnaires, JLA app. 17-Austin-c(i); death of Valor. 18-22-Build-up to Zero Hour 1.50
23-Zero Hour tie-in .70 1.75

VALOR THUNDERSTAR AND HIS FIREFLIES
Dec, 1986 ($1.50)
Now Comics

1-Ordway-c(p) 1.50

VAMPFIRE EROTIC ECHO
1997 ($2.95, B&W)
Brainstorm Comics

1-Regular, nude and photo-c 1.20 3.00

VAMPFIRE TOUR BOOK

Vampire Girls: California 1969 #0 © Angel Entertainment

Vampirella #1(1992) © Harris

Vampirella Classics #3 © Harris

	GD25	FN65	NM94

Apr, 1997 ($2.95, B&W)
Brainstorm Comics

	GD25	FN65	NM94
1-($2.95)		1.20	3.00
1-($3.95) Nude-c		1.60	4.00

VAMPIRE BITES
May, 1995 ($2.95, B&W)
Brainstorm Comics

	GD25	FN65	NM94
1-Color pin-up		1.20	3.00

VAMPIRE GIRLS: CALIFORNIA 1969
No. 0, May, 1996 - No. 1($2.95, B&W)
Angel Entertainment

	GD25	FN65	NM94
0,1		1.20	3.00
0-($10.00)-Nude-c	1.25	3.75	10.00
0-($20.00)-3-D Platinum; embossed-c			20.00
1-($10.00)-Nude Edition	1.25	3.75	10.00

VAMPIRE GIRLS: NEW YORK
No. 0, Spring, 1997 - No. 1($2.95, B&W)
Angel Entertainment

	GD25	FN65	NM94
0,1		1.20	3.00

VAMPIRE GIRLS, POETS OF BLOOD: SAN FRANCISCO 1997
Spring, 1997 - No. 2 ($2.95, B&W)
Angel Entertainment

	GD25	FN65	NM94
1,2		1.20	3.00

VAMPIRE LESTAT, THE
Jan, 1990 - No. 12, 1991 ($2.50, painted limited series)
Innovation Publishing

	GD25	FN65	NM94
1-Adapts novel; Bolton painted-c on all	2.50	7.50	25.00
1-2nd printing (has UPC code, 1st prints don't)		1.60	4.00
1-3rd & 4th printings		1.00	2.50
2-1st printing	1.50	4.50	12.00
2-2nd & 3rd printings		1.00	2.50
3-5	1.00	3.00	8.00
3-6,9-2nd printings		1.00	2.50
6-12		1.60	4.00

VAMPIRELLA (Magazine)(See Warren Presents)
Sept, 1969 - No. 112, Feb, 1983; No. 113, Jan, 1988? (B&W)
Warren Publishing Co./Harris Publications #113

	GD25	FN65	NM94
1-Intro. Vampirella	34.00	102.00	385.00
2-Amazonia series begins, ends #12	12.50	38.00	125.00
3 (Low distribution)	31.00	93.00	330.00
4-7	8.00	24.00	80.00
8-Vampi begins by Tom Sutton as serious strip (early issues-gag line)	9.00	27.00	90.00
9-Barry Smith-a; Boris-c	8.00	24.00	80.00
10-No Vampi story	3.00	9.00	30.00
11-15: 11-Origin & 1st app. Pendragon. 12-Vampi by Gonzales begins	4.50	13.50	45.00
16-18,20-25: 17-Tomb of the Gods begins, ends #22. 25-Begin partial color issues	3.50	10.50	35.00
19 (1973 Annual)	5.00	15.00	50.00
26,28-36,38-40: 30-Intro. Pantha; Corben-a(color). 31-Origin Luana, the Beast Girl. 33-Pantha ends	2.50	7.50	22.00
27 (1974 Annual)	3.00	9.00	30.00
37 (1975 Annual)	2.80	8.40	28.00
41-45,47-50: 49-1st app. The Blood Red Queen of Hearts. 50-Spirit cameo by Eisner	2.00	6.00	16.00
46-Origin retold (10/75)	2.50	7.50	23.00
51-66,68,70,72,73,75-99: 60-62,65,66-The Blood Red Queen of Hearts app. 93-Cassandra St. Knight begins, ends #103; new Pantha series begins, ends #108	1.60	4.85	13.00
67,69,71,74,77-photo-c	2.50	7.50	20.00
100 (96 pg. r-special)-Origin reprinted; Vampirella appears topless	5.00	15.00	50.00
101-110,112: 101,102-The Blood Red Queen of Hearts app. 108-Torpedo series by Toth begins	3.00	9.00	30.00
111-Giant Collector's Edition ($2.50)	4.00	12.00	40.00
113 (1988)-1st Harris Issue	25.00	75.00	250.00
Annual 1(1972)-New origin Vampirella by Gonzales; reprints by Neal Adams (from #1), Wood (from #9)	25.00	75.00	250.00
Special 1 (1977; large-square bound)(soft-c)	6.50	19.50	65.00
Special 1 (color, 1977; large-square bound)-Only available through mail order (scarce)(hard-c)	15.00	45.00	150.00

NOTE: ***Neal Adams** a-1, 10p, 19p(r/#10). **Alcala** a-90, 93i. **Bode'/Todd** c-3. **Bode'/Jones** c-4. **Boris** c-9. **Brunner** a-10, 12(1 pg.). **Corben** a-30, 31, 33, 54. **Crandall** a-1, 19(r/#1). **Frazetta** c-1, 5, 7, 11, 31. **Heath** a-76-78, 83. **Jones** a-5, 9, 12, 27, 32, 33(2 pg.), 34, 50i, 83r. **Nino** a-59i, 61i, 67, 76, 85, 90. **Ploog** a-14. **Barry Smith** a-9. **Starlin** a-78. **Sutton** a-11. **Toth** a-90i, 108, 110. **Wood** a-9, 10, 12, 19(r/#12), 27r; c-9. **Wrightson** a-33(w/**Jones**), 63r. All reprint issues-37, 74, 83, 87, 91, 105, 107, 109, 111. Annuals from 1973 on are included in regular numbering. Later annuals are same format as regular issues.*

VAMPIRELLA (Also see Cain/... & Vengeance of...)
Nov, 1992 - No. 5, Nov, 1993 ($2.95)
Harris Publications

	GD25	FN65	NM94
0		1.60	4.00
0-Gold	3.50	10.50	35.00
1-Jim Balent inks in #1-3; Adam Hughes c-1-3	3.00	9.00	30.00
1-2nd printing	1.00	2.80	7.00
1-(11/97) Commemorative Edition		1.20	3.00
2	2.50	7.50	20.00
3-5: 4-Snyder III-c. 5-Brereton painted-c	1.00	2.80	7.00
Trade paperback nn (10/93, $5.95)-r/#1-4; Jusko-c		2.40	6.00

NOTE: *Issues 1-5 contain certificates for free **Dave Stevens** Vampirella poster.*

VAMPIRELLA & PANTHA SHOWCASE
Jan, 1997 ($1.50, one-shot)
Harris Publications

	GD25	FN65	NM94
1-Millar-s/Texeira-c/a; flip book w/"Blood Lust"; Robinson-s/Jusko-c/a			1.50

VAMPIRELLA & THE BLOOD RED QUEEN OF HEARTS
Sept, 1996 ($9.95, 96 pgs., B&W, squarebound, one-shot)
Harris Publications

	GD25	FN65	NM94
nn-r/Vampirella #49,60-62,65,66,101,102; John Bolton-c; Michael Bair back-c	1.25	3.75	10.00

VAMPIRELLA: BLOODLUST
July, 1997 - No. 2, Aug, 1997 ($4.95, limited series)
Harris Publications

	GD25	FN65	NM94
1,2-Robinson-s/Jusko-painted c/a		2.00	5.00

VAMPIRELLA CLASSICS
Feb, 1995 - No. 5, Nov, 1995 ($2.95, limited series)
Harris Publications

	GD25	FN65	NM94
1-5: Reprints Archie Goodwin stories.		1.20	3.00

VAMPIRELLA: CROSSOVER GALLERY
Sept, 1997 ($2.95, one-shot)
Harris Publications

	GD25	FN65	NM94
1-Wraparound-c by Campbell, pinups by Jae Lee, Mack, Allred, Art Adams, Quesada & Palmiotti and others			2.95

VAMPIRELLA: DEATH & DESTRUCTION
July, 1996 - No. 3, Sept, 1996 ($2.95, limited series)
Harris Publications

	GD25	FN65	NM94
1-3: Amanda Conner-a(p) in all. 1-Tucci-c. 2-Hughes-c. 3-Jusko-c		1.20	3.00

VAMPIRELLA/DRACULA & PANTHA SHOWCASE
Aug, 1997 ($1.50, one-shot)
Harris Publications

Vampirella Lives #2 © Harris

Vampirella: Sad Wings of Destiny #1 © Harris

Vamps #2 © Elaine Lee & William Simpson

GD25 FN65 NM94

1-Ellis, Robinson, and Moore-s; flip book w/"Pantha" 1.50

VAMPIRELLA/DRACULA: THE CENTENNIAL
Oct, 1997 ($5.95, one-shot)
Harris Publications

1-Ellis, Robinson, and Moore-s; Beachum, Frank/Smith, and Mack/Mays-a Bolton-painted-c 5.95

VAMPIRELLA LIVES
Dec, 1996 - No. 3, Feb, 1997 ($3.50/$2.95, limited series)
Harris Publications

1-Die cut-c; Quesada & Palmiotti-c, Ellis-s/Conner-a 1.40 3.50
1-Deluxe Ed.-photo-c 1.40 3.50
2,3-($2.95)-Two editions (1 photo-c): 3-J. Scott Campbell-c 1.20 3.00

VAMPIRELLA: MORNING IN AMERICA
1991 - No. 4, 1992 ($3.95, B&W, limited series, 52 pgs.)
Harris Publications/Dark Horse Comics

1-All have Kaluta painted-c 1.00 2.80 7.00
2-4 2.00 5.00

VAMPIRELLA OF DRAKULON
Jan, 1996 - Present ($2.95)
Harris Publications

0-5: All reprints. 0-Jim Silke-c. 3-Polybagged w/card. 4-Texiera-c 1.20 3.00

VAMPIRELLA PIN-UP SPECIAL
Oct, 1995 ($2.95, one-shot)
Harris Publications

1-Hughes-c, pin-ups by various 1.20 3.00
1-Variant-c 1.20 3.00

VAMPIRELLA: SAD WINGS OF DESTINY
Sept, 1996 ($3.95, one-shot)
Harris Publications

1-Jusko-c 1.60 4.00

VAMPIRELLA/SHADOWHAWK: CREATURES OF THE NIGHT (Also see Shadowhawk)
1995 ($4.95, one-shot)
Harris Publications

1 2.00 5.00

VAMPIRELLA/SHI (SeeShi/Vampirella)
Oct, 1997 ($2.95, one-shot)
Harris Publications

1-Ellis-s 2.95

VAMPIRELLA: SILVER ANNIVERSARY COLLECTION
Jan, 1997 - Present ($2.50, limited series)
Harris Publications

1-4: Two editions: Bad Girl by Beachum, Good Girl by Silke 1.00 2.50

VAMPIRELLA STRIKES
Sept, 1995 - Present ($2.95, limited series)
Harris Publications

1-8: 1-Photo-c. 2-Deodato-c; polybagged w/card. 5-Eudaemon-c/app; wraparound-c; alternate-c exists. 6-(6/96)-Mark Millar script; Texeira-c; alternate-c exists. 7-Flip book 1.20 3.00
1-Newsstand Edition; different photo-c. 1.20 3.00
1-Limited Edition; different photo-c. 1.20 3.00
Annual 1-(12/96, $2.95) Delano-s; two covers 1.20 3.00

VAMPIRELLA: 25TH ANNIVERSARY SPECIAL
Oct, 1996 ($5.95, squarebound, one-shot)
Harris Publications

nn-Reintro The Blood Red Queen of Hearts; James Robinson, Grant Morrison & Warren Ellis scripts; Mark Texeira, Michael Bair & Amanda Connor-a(p); Frank Frazetta-c 2.40 6.00
nn-($6.95)-Silver Edition 1.00 2.80 7.00

VAMPIRELLA VS. HEMORRHAGE
Apr, 1997 - Present ($3.50, mini-series)
Harris Publications

1 1.40 3.50

VAMPIRELLA VS. PANTHA
Mar, 1997 - Present ($3.50, mini-series)
Harris Publications

1-Two covers; Millar-s/Texiera-c/a 1.40 3.50

VAMPIRELLA/WETWORKS (See Wetworks/Vampirella)
June, 1997 ($2.95, one-shot)
Harris Publications

1 2.95

VAMPIRE TALES
Aug, 1973 - No. 11, June, 1975 (75¢, B&W, magazine)
Marvel Comics Group

1-Morbius, the Living Vampire begins by Pablo Marcos (1st solo Morbius series & 5th Morbius app.) 3.50 10.50 35.00
2-Intro. Satana; Steranko-r 3.00 9.00 30.00
3,5,6,8: 3-Satana app. 5-Origin Morbius. 6-1st Lilith app. 8-Blade app. (see Tomb of Dracula) 2.50 7.50 20.00
4,7,9-11: 9-Blade app. 1.85 5.50 15.00
Annual 1(10/75)-Heath-r/#9 1.50 4.50 12.00

NOTE: ***Alcala*** *a-6, 8, 9i.* ***Boris*** *c-4, 6.* ***Chaykin*** *a-7.* ***Everett*** *a-1r.* ***Gulacy*** *a-7p.* ***Heath*** *a-9.* ***Infantino*** *a-3r.* ***Gil Kane*** *a-4, 5r.*

VAMPIRE VERSES, THE
Aug, 1995 - No. 3, 1995 ($2.95, B&W, mature)
CFD Productions

1-3 1.20 3.00

VAMPRESS LUXURA, THE
Feb, 1996 ($2.95)
Brainstorm Comics

1-Lindo c/a/scripts 1.20 3.00
1-($10.00, Gold edition)-Gold foil logo 1.25 3.75 10.00
Leather Special-(3/96, $2.95) 1.20 3.00

VAMPS
Aug, 1994 - No. 6, Jan, 1995 ($1.95, limited series, mature)
DC Comics (Vertigo)

1-Bolland-c 2.00 5.00
2-6: Bolland-c in all 1.20 3.00
Trade paperback ($9.95)-r/#1-6 1.25 3.75 10.00

VAMPS: HOLLYWOOD & VEIN
Feb, 1996 - No. 6, July, 1996 ($2.25, limited series, mature)
DC Comics (Vertigo)

1-6: Winslade-c .90 2.25

VANGUARD (...Outpost: Earth) (See Megaton)
1987 ($1.50)
Megaton Comics

1-Erik Larsen-c(p) 1.20 3.00

VANGUARD (See Savage Dragon #2)
Oct, 1993 - No.6, 1994 ($1.95)
Image Comics (Highbrow Entertainment)

1-6: 1-Wraparound gatefold-c; Erik Larsen back-up-a; Supreme x-over. 3-(12/93)-Indicia says December 1994. 4-Berzerker back-up. 5-Angel Medina-a(p). .80 2.00

VANGUARD (See Savage Dragon #2)

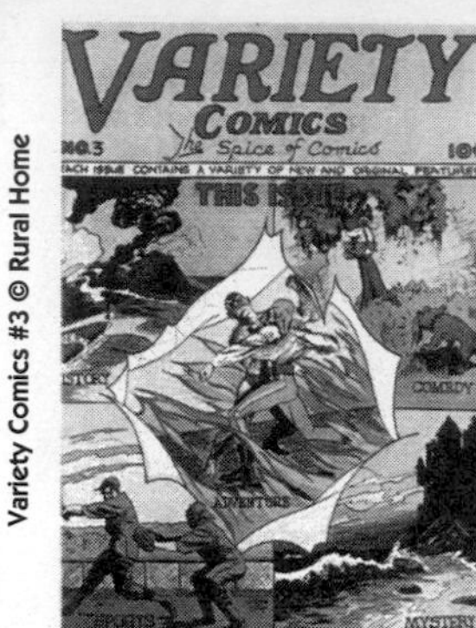

Variety Comics #3 © Rural Home

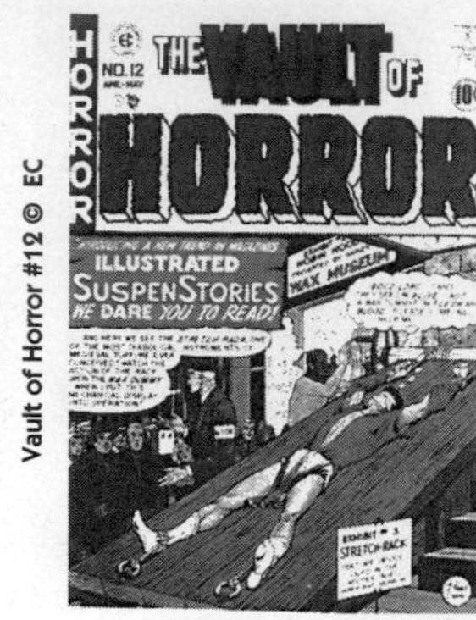

Vault of Horror #12 © EC

Vengeance of Vampirella #4 © Harris

GD25 FN65 NM94

Aug, 1996 - No.4, Feb, 1997 ($2.95, B&W, limited series)
Image Comics

1-4 — 1.20 — 3.00

VANGUARD ILLUSTRATED
Nov, 1983 - No. 11, Oct, 1984 (Baxter paper)(Direct sales only)
Pacific Comics

1-6,8-11: 1,7-Nudity scenes. 2-1st app. Stargrazers (see Legends of the Stargrazers; Dave Stevens-c — 1.50
7-1st app. Mr. Monster (r-in Mr. Monster #1) — 2.00 — 5.00

NOTE: ***Evans*** *a-7.* ***Kaluta*** *c-5, 7p.* ***Perez*** *a-6; c-6.* ***Rude*** *a-1-4; c-4.* ***Williamson*** *c-3.*

VANGUARD: STRANGE VISITORS
Oct, 1996 - No.4, Feb, 1997 ($2.95, B&W, limited series)
Image Comics

1-4: 3-Supreme-c/app. — 1.20 — 3.00

VANITY (See Pacific Presents #3)
Jun, 1984 - No. 2, Aug, 1984 ($1.50, direct sales)
Pacific Comics

1,2: Origin — 1.50

VARIETY COMICS (The Spice of Comics)
1944 - No. 2, 1945; No. 3, 1946
Rural Home Publications/Croyden Publ. Co.

1-Origin Captain Valiant — 15.50 — 47.00 — 125.00
2-Captain Valiant — 8.75 — 26.25 — 70.00
3(1946-Croyden)-Captain Valiant — 8.50 — 26.00 — 60.00

VARIETY COMICS (See Fox Giants)

VARIOGENESIS
June, 1994 ($3.50)
Dagger Comics Group

0 — 1.40 — 3.50

VARSITY
1945
Parents' Magazine Institute

1 — 6.50 — 19.50 — 40.00

VAULT OF EVIL
Feb, 1973 - No. 23, Nov, 1975
Marvel Comics Group

1 (1950s reprints begin) — 1.25 — 3.75 — 10.00
2-23: 3,4-Brunner-c — 1.00 — 3.00 — 8.00

NOTE: ***Ditko*** *a-14r, 15r, 20-22r.* ***Drucker*** *a-10r(Mystic #52), 13r(Uncanny Tales #42).* ***Everett*** *a-11r(Menace #2), 13r(Menace #4); c-10.* ***Heath*** *a-5r.* ***Gil Kane*** *c-1, 6.* ***Krigstein*** *a-20r(Uncanny Tales #54).* ***Reinman*** *r-1.* ***Tuska*** *a-6r.*

VAULT OF HORROR (Formerly War Against Crime #1-11)
No. 12, Apr-May, 1950 - No. 40, Dec-Jan, 1954-55
E. C. Comics

12 (Scarce) — 389.00 — 1167.00 — 3600.00
13-Morphine story — 88.00 — 265.00 — 700.00
14 — 81.00 — 2427.00 — 625.00
15- "Terror in the Swamp" is same story w/minor changes as "The Thing in the Swamp" from Haunt of Fear #15 — 66.00 — 197.00 — 525.00
16 — 48.00 — 145.00 — 400.00
17-19 — 40.00 — 120.00 — 300.00
20-25: 22-Frankenstein-c & adaptation. 23-Used in **POP**, pg. 84; Davis-a(2). 24-Craig biography — 33.00 — 99.00 — 240.00
26-B&W & color illos in **POP** — 33.00 — 99.00 — 240.00
27-35: 30-Dismemberment-c. 31-Ray Bradbury biog. 32-Censored-c. 35-X-Mas-c — 24.00 — 73.00 — 180.00
36- "Pipe Dream" classic opium addict story by Krigstein; "Twin Bill" cited in articles by T.E. Murphy, Wertham — 24.00 — 73.00 — 180.00
37-1st app. Drusilla, a Vampirella look alike; Williamson-a — 24.00 — 73.00 — 180.00
38-39: 39-Bondage-c — 20.00 — 60.00 — 150.00
40-Low distribution — 24.00 — 73.00 — 190.00

NOTE: ***Craig*** *art in all but No. 13 & 33; c-12-40.* ***Crandall*** *a-33, 34, 39.* ***Davis*** *a-17-38.* ***Evans*** *a-27, 28, 30, 32, 33.* ***Feldstein*** *a-12-16.* ***Ingels*** *a-13-20, 22-40.* ***Kamen*** *a-15-22, 25, 29, 35.* ***Krigstein*** *a-36, 38-40.* ***Kurtzman*** *a-12, 13.* ***Orlando*** *a-24, 31, 40.* ***Wood*** *a-12-14. #22, 29 & 31 have Ray Bradbury adaptations. #16 & 17 have H. P. Lovecraft adaptations.*

VAULT OF HORROR, THE
Aug, 1990 - No. 6, June, 1991 ($1.95, 68 pgs.)(#4 on: $2.00)
Gladstone Publishing

1-Craig-c(r); all contain EC reprints — 1.60 — 4.00
2-6: 2,4-6-Craig-c(r). 3-Ingels-c(r) — .80 — 2.00

VAULT OF HORROR
Sept, 1991 - No. 5, May, 1992? ($2.00); Oct, 1992 - Present ($1.50)
Russ Cochran/Gemstone Publishing

1-5: E.C reprints — .80 — 2.00
1-16: 1-4r/VOH #12-15 w/original-c — 1.50

V...–COMICS (Morse code for "V" - 3 dots, 1 dash)
Jan, 1942 - No. 2, Mar-Apr, 1942
Fox Features Syndicate

1-Origin V-Man & the Boys; The Banshee & The Black Fury, The Queen of Evil, & V-Agents begin; Nazi-c — 100.00 — 300.00 — 900.00
2-Nazi bondage/torture-c — 75.00 — 225.00 — 675.00

VECTOR
1986 - No. 4, 1986? ($1.50, 1st color comic by Now Comics)
Now Comics

1-4: Computer-generated art — 1.50

VEGAS KNIGHTS
1989 ($1.95, one-shot)
Pioneer Comics

1 — .80 — 2.00

VELOCITY (Also see Cyberforce)
Nov, 1995 - No. 3, Jan, 1996 ($2.50, limited series)
Image Comics (Top Cow Productions)

1-3: Kurt Busiek scripts in all. 2-Savage Dragon-c/app. — 1.00 — 2.50

VENGEANCE OF VAMPIRELLA (Becomes Vampirella: Death & Destruction)
Apr, 1994 - No. 25, Apr, 1996 ($2.95)
Harris Comics

1-($3.50)-Quesada/Palmiotti "bloodfoil" wraparound-c — 1.50 — 4.50 — 12.00
1-2nd printing; blue foil-c — 1.60 — 4.00
1-Gold — 2.50 — 7.50 — 25.00
2 — 1.00 — 3.00 — 8.00
3,4 — 2.00 — 5.00
5-25: 8-Polybagged w/trading card; 10-w/coupon for Hyde -25 poster. 11, 19-Polybagged w/ trading card. 25-Quesada & Palmiotti red foil-c. — 1.20 — 3.00
...: Bloodshed (1995, $6.95) — 1.00 — 2.80 — 7.00

VENGEANCE OF VAMPIRELLA: THE MYSTERY WALK
Nov, 1995 ($2.95, one-shot)
Harris Comics

0 — 1.20 — 3.00

VENGEANCE SQUAD
July, 1975 - No. 6, May, 1976 (#1-3 are 25¢ issues)
Charlton Comics

1-Mike Mauser, Private Eye begins by Staton — 2.40 — 6.00
2-6: Morisi-a in all — 1.60 — 4.00
5,6(Modern Comics-r, 1977) — 1.20 — 3.00

VENOM: ALONG CAME A SPIDER (See Amazing Spider-Man #298 & Marvel

Venom: Nights of Vengeance #2 © MEG

Venom: Tooth and Claw #2 © MEG

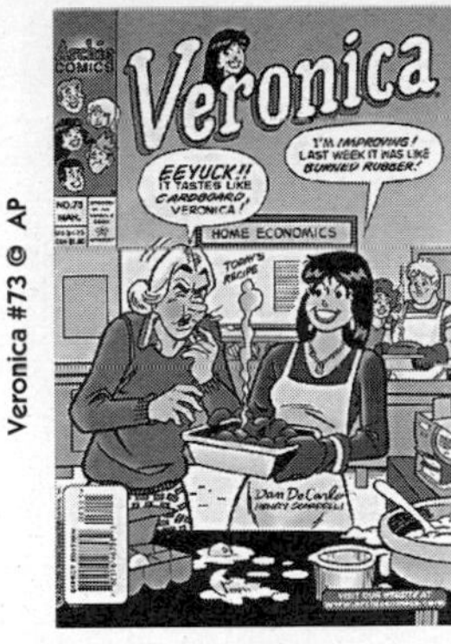

Veronica #73 © AP

GD25 FN65 NM94

Comics Presents)
Jan, 1996 - No. 4, Apr, 1996 ($2.95, limited series)
Marvel Comics

1-4:Spider-Man & Carnage app. 1.20 3.00

VENOM: CARNAGE UNLEASHED, 4/95 - No. 4, 7/95 ($2.95), Marvel Comics
1-4 1.20 3.00

VENOM: FINALE, 11/97 - No. 3, 1/98 ($1.99), Marvel Comics
1-3: Hama-s 1.99

VENOM: FUNERAL PYRE, 8/93- No. 3, 10/93 ($2.95), Marvel Comics
1-3: 1-Holo-grafx foil-c; Punisher app. in all 1.20 3.00

VENOM: LETHAL PROTECTOR
Feb, 1993 - No. 6, July, 1993 ($2.95, limited series)
Marvel Comics

1-Red holo-grafx foil-c; Bagley-c/a in all 2.00 5.00
1-Gold variant sold to retailers 2.50 7.50 20.00
1-Black-c 15.00 45.00 150.00
2-6: Spider-Man app. in all 1.20 3.00

VENOM: LICENSE TO KILL, 6/97 - No. 3, 8/97 ($1.95), Marvel Comics
1-3 .80 2.00

VENOM: NIGHTS OF VENGEANCE, 8/94 - No. 4, 11/94 ($2.95), MarvelComics
1-4: 1-Red foil-c 1.20 3.00

VENOM ON TRIAL, 3/97 - No. 3, 5/97 ($1.95), Marvel Comics
1-3 .80 2.00

VENOM: SEED OF DARKNESS, 7/97 ($1.95, one-shot), Marvel Comics
-1-Flashback story .80 2.00

VENOM: SEPARATION ANXIETY, 12/94- No. 4, 3/95 ($2.95), Marvel Comics
1-4: 1-Embossed-c 1.20 3.00

VENOM: SIGN OF THE BOSS, 3/97 - No. 2, 10/97 ($1.99), Marvel Comics
1,2 .80 2.00

VENOM: SINNER TAKES ALL, 8/95 - No. 5, 10/95 ($2.95), Marvel Comics
1-5 1.20 3.00

VENOM: SUPER SPECIAL, 8/95($3.95, one-shot), Marvel Comics
1-Flip book 1.60 4.00

VENOM: THE ENEMY WITHIN , 2/94 - No. 3, 4/94 ($2.95), Marvel Comics
1-3: Demogoblin & Morbius app. 1-Glow-in-the-dark-c. 1.20 3.00

VENOM: THE HUNGER, 8/96- No. 4, 11/96 ($1.95), Marvel Comics
1-4 .80 2.00

VENOM: THE HUNTED, 5/96-No. 3, 7/96($2.95), Marvel Comics
1-3 1.20 3.00

VENOM: THE MACE, 5/94 - No. 3, 7/94 ($2.95), Marvel Comics
1-3: 1-Embossed-c 1.20 3.00

VENOM: THE MADNESS, 11/93- No. 3, 1/94($2.95), Marvel Comics
1-3: Kelley Jones-c/a(p). 1-Embossed-c; Juggernaut app. 1.20 3.00

VENOM: TOOTH AND CLAW, 12/96 - No. 3, 2/97($1.95), Marvel Comics
1-3: Wolverine-c/app. .80 2.00

VENTURE
Aug, 1986 - No. 3, 1986? ($1.75)
AC Comics (Americomics)

1-3: 1-3-Bolt. 1-Astron. 2-Femforce. 3-Fazers .75 1.80

VENUS (See Marvel Spotlight #2 & Weird Wonder Tales)
Aug, 1948 - No. 19, Apr, 1952 (Also see Marvel Mystery #91)
Marvel/Atlas Comics (CMC 1-9/LCC 10-19)

1-Venus & Hedy Devine begin; 1st app. Venus; Kurtzman's "Hey Look"
106.00 318.00 875.00
2 61.00 185.00 510.00
3,5 52.00 157.00 430.00
4-Kurtzman's "Hey Look" 53.00 161.00 440.00
6-9: 6-Loki app. 7,8-Painted-c. 9-Begin 52 pgs.; book-length feature "Whom the Gods Destroy!" 47.00 142.00 390.00
10-S/F-horror issues begin (7/50) 52.00 157.00 430.00
11-S/F end of the world (11/50) 65.00 195.00 530.00
12-Colan-a 41.00 124.00 340.00
13-19-Venus by Everett, 2-3 stories each; covers-#13,15-19; 14-Everett part cover (Venus). 17-Bondage-c 65.00 195.00 530.00

NOTE: ***Berg*** *s/f story-13.* ***Everett*** *c-13, 14(part; Venus only), 15-19.* ***Heath*** *s/f story-11.* ***Maneely*** *s/f story-10(3pg.), 16.* ***Morisi*** *a-19.* ***Syd Shores*** *c-6.*

VENUS DOMINA
July, 1996 - Present ($2.95/$4.95, mature)
Verotik

1-($4.95)-Embossed-c w/nudity by Dave Stevens 2.00 5.00
1-($2.95, San Diego Edition)-Wing Bird-c/a 1.20 3.00
2,3-($4.95) 2.00 5.00
Candlemass Eve Special Ed.-($4.95) 2.00 5.00

VENUS WARS, THE (Manga)
Apr, 1991 - No.14, May, 1992 ($2.25, B&W)
Dark Horse Comics

1-6,8,9,11-14: 1-3 Contain 2 Dark Horse trading cards .90 2.25
7,10 ($2.50): 1,3,7,10-(44 pgs.) 1.00 2.50

VERI BEST SURE FIRE COMICS
No date (circa 1945) (Reprints Holyoke one-shots)
Holyoke Publishing Co.

1-Captain Aero, Alias X, Miss Victory, Commandos of the Devil Dogs, Red Cross, Hammerhead Hawley, Capt. Aero's Sky Scouts, Flagman app.; same-c as Veri Best Sure Shot #1 30.00 90.00 240.00

VERI BEST SURE SHOT COMICS
No date (circa 1945) (Reprints Holyoke one-shots)
Holyoke Publishing Co.

1-Capt. Aero, Miss Victory by Quinlan, Alias X, The Red Cross, Flagman, Commandos of the Devil Dogs, Hammerhead Hawley, Capt. Aero's Sky Scouts; same-c as Veri Best Sure Fire #1 30.00 90.00 240.00

VERMILLION
Oct, 1996 - No. 12, Sept, 1997 ($2.25/$2.50)
DC Comics (Helix)

1-4: Lucius Shepard scripts. 4-Kaluta-c .90 2.25
5-12: 5-Begin $2.50-c. 12-Kaluta-c 1.00 2.50

VERONICA (Also see Archie's Girls, Betty &...)
Apr, 1989 - Present
Archie Comics

1-21: 1,2-(75¢). 3-30-(95¢-$1.00) 1.00
21-36: 21-Begin $1.25-c. 34-Neon ink-c 1.25
36-70 1.50
71-75: 71-Begin $1.75-c 1.75

VERONICA'S PASSPORT DIGEST MAGAZINE (Becomes Veronica's Digest Magazine #3 on)
Nov, 1992 - Present ($1.50/$1.79, digest size)
Archie Comics

1-5 1.50
6-($1.79) 1.79

VERONICA'S SUMMER SPECIAL (See Archie Giant Series Magazine #615, 625)

VEROTIKA
Mar, 1995 - Present ($2.95, mature) (1st Verotik title)
Verotik

1,2 1.00 3.00 8.00
3-6 1.60 4.00
7-14: 9-Adam Pollina-a. 10,13-Nudity-c 1.20 3.00

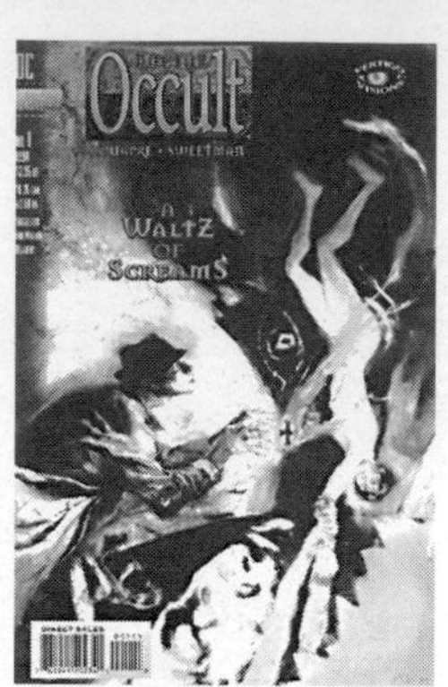

Vertigo Visions: Dr. Occult #1 © DC

Vertigo Winter's Edge #1 © DC

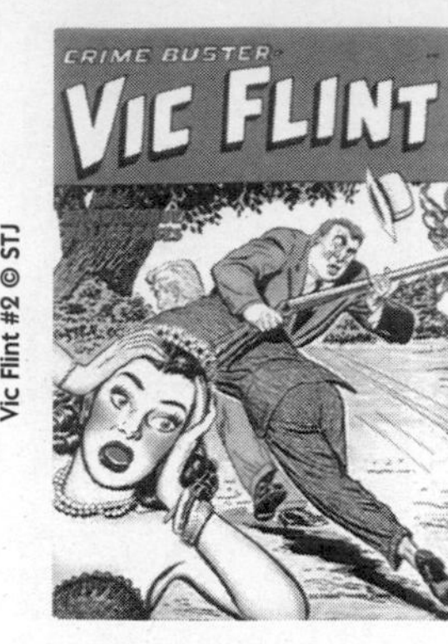

Vic Flint #2 © STJ

GD25 FN65 NM94

15-($3.95) 1.60 4.00

VEROTIK EAST
Jan, 1997 ($11.95, mature, one-shot)
Verotik

nn-Manga style 1.50 4.50 12.00

VEROTIK ILLUSTRATED
Aug, 1997 ($6.95, mature, one-shot)
Verotik

1-Bisley-c 1.00 2.80 7.00

VERTIGO GALLERY, THE: DREAMS AND NIGHTMARES
1995 ($3.50, one-shot)
DC Comics (Vertgo)

1-Pin-ups of Vertigo characters by Sienkiewicz, Toth, Van Fleet & others; Dave McKean-c 1.60 4.00

VERTIGO JAM
Aug, 1993 ($3.95, one-shot, 68 pgs.)(Painted-c by Fabry)
DC Comics (Vertigo)

1-Sandman by Neil Gaiman, Hellblazer, Animal Man, Doom Patrol, Swamp Thing, Kid Eternity & Shade the Changing Man 2.00 5.00

VERTIGO PREVIEW
1992 (75¢, one-shot, 36 pgs.)
DC Comics (Vertigo)

1-Vertigo previews; Sandman story by Neil Gaiman .80 2.00

VERTIGO VERITE: THE UNSEEN HAND
Sept, 1996 - No. 4, Dec, 1996 ($2.50, limited series)
DC Comics (Vertigo)

1-4: Terry LaBan scripts in all 1.00 2.50

VERTIGO VISIONS
June, 1993 - Present (68 pgs.)
DC Comics (Vertigo)

The Geek 1 (6/93, $3.95) 1.60 4.00
The Eaters ($4.95, 1995)-Milligan story. 2.00 5.00
The Phantom Stranger 1 (10/93, $3.50) 1.40 3.50
Dr. Occult 1 (7/94, $3.95) 1.60 4.00
Prez 1 (7/95, $3.95) 1.60 4.00

VERTIGO WINTER'S EDGE
1998 ($7.95, square-bound, one-shot)
DC Comics (Vertigo)

1-Winter stories by Vertigo creators; Desire story by Gaiman/Bolton; Bolland wraparound-c 7.95

VERY BEST OF DENNIS THE MENACE, THE
July, 1979 - No. 2, Apr, 1980 (95¢/$1.00, digest-size, 132 pgs.)
Fawcett Publications

1,2-Reprints .80 2.00

VERY BEST OF DENNIS THE MENACE, THE
Apr, 1982 - No. 3, Aug, 1982 ($1.25, digest-size)
Marvel Comics Group

1-3: Reprints 2.40 6.00
NOTE: ***Hank Ketcham*** *c-all. A few thousand of #1 & 2 were printed with DC emblem.*

VERY VICKY
1993? - No. 8, 1995 ($2.50, B&W)
Meet Danny Ocean

1-8 1.00 2.50
...:Calling All Hillbillies (1995, $2.50) 1.00 2.50

V FOR VENDETTA
Sept, 1988 - No. 10, May, 1989 ($2.00, maxi-series)
DC Comics

1-10: Alan Moore scripts in all .80 2.00
Trade paperback (1990, $14.95) 1.85 5.50 15.00

VIC BRIDGES FAZERS SKETCHBOOK AND FACT FILE
Nov, 1986 ($1.75)
AC Comics

1 .75 1.80

VIC FLINT(Crime Buster...)(See Authentic Police Cases #10-14 & Fugitives From Justice #2)
August, 1948 - No. 5, April, 1949 (Newspaper reprints; NEA Service)
St. John Publishing Co.

1 10.00 30.00 75.00
2 7.50 22.50 50.00
3-5 5.85 17.50 38.00

VIC FLINT (Crime Buster...)
Feb, 1956 - No. 2, May, 1956 (Newspaper reprints)
Argo Publ.

1,2 6.70 20.00 40.00

VIC JORDAN (Also see Big Shot Comics #32)
April, 1945
Civil Service Publ.

1-1944 daily newspaper-r 11.50 34.00 80.00

VICKI (Humor)
Feb, 1975 - No. 4, Aug, 1975 (No. 1,2: 68 pgs.)
Atlas/Seaboard Publ.

1,2 (68 pgs.)-Reprints Tippy Teen 1.85 5.50 15.00
2-4 1.00 3.00 8.00

VICKI VALENTINE (...Summer Special #1)
July, 1985 - No. 4, July, 1986 ($1.70, B&W)
Renegade Press

1-4: Woggon, Rausch-a; all have paper dolls. 2-Christmas issue 1.70

VICKS COMICS (See Pure Oil Comics, Salerno Carnival of Comics & 24 Pages of Comics)
nd (circa 1938) (Giveaway, 68 pgs. in color)
Eastern Color Printing Co. (Vicks Chemical Co.)

nn-Famous Funnies-r (before #40); contains 5 pgs. Buck Rogers (4 pgs. from F.F. #15, & 1 pg. from #16) Joe Palooka, Napoleon, etc. app. 61.00 183.00 550.00
nn-16 loose, untrimmed page giveaway; paper-c; r/Famous Funnies #14; Buck Rogers, Joe Palooka app. 23.00 69.00 185.00

VICKY
Oct, 1948 - No. 5, June, 1949
Ace Magazine

nn(10/48)-Teenage humor 5.35 16.00 32.00
4(12/48), nn(2/49), 4(4/49), 5(6/49): 5-Dotty app. 4.25 13.00 26.00

VIC TORRY & HIS FLYING SAUCER (Also see Mr. Monster's...#5)
1950 (one-shot)
Fawcett Publications

nn-Book-length saucer story by Powell; photo/painted-c 50.00 150.00 400.00

VICTORY
June, 1994 ($2.50, unfinished limited series)
Topps Comics

1-Kurt Busiek script; Giffen-c/a; Rob Liefeld variant-c exists 1.00 2.50

VICTORY COMICS
Aug, 1941 - No. 4, Dec, 1941 (#1 by Funnies, Inc.)
Hillman Periodicals

1-The Conqueror by Bill Everett, The Crusader, & Bomber Burns begin;

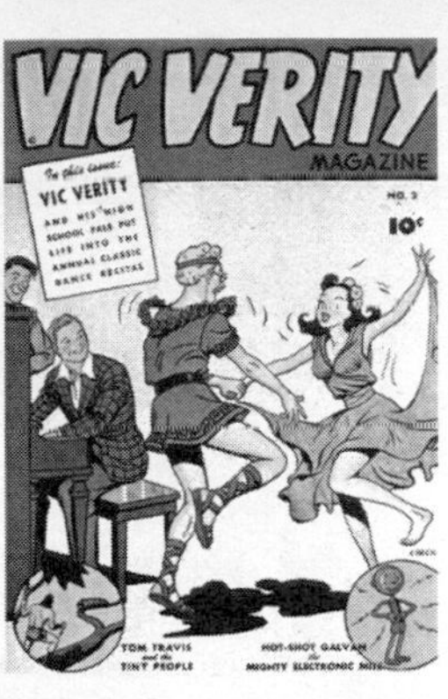

Vic Verity Magazine #2 © Vic Verity Publ.

Vigilante #17 © DC

Viper #2 © Paramount

GD25 FN65 NM94

Conqueror's origin in text; Everett-c 233.00 700.00 2100.00
2-Everett-c/a 100.00 300.00 900.00
3,4 67.00 200.00 600.00

VIC VERITY MAGAZINE
1945; No. 2, Jan?, 1947 - No. 7, Sept, 1946 (A comic book)
Vic Verity Publications
1-C. C. Beck-c/a 14.00 41.00 110.00
2-Beck-c 8.50 26.00 60.00
3-7: 6-Beck-a. 7-Beck-c 7.15 21.50 50.00

VIDEO JACK
Nov, 1987 - No. 6, Nov, 1988 ($1.25)
Marvel Comics (Epic Comics)
1-6: 6-Neal Adams, Keith Giffen, Wrightson, others-a 1.30

VIETNAM JOURNAL
Nov, 1987 - No. 11, July, 1989 ($1.75/$1.95, B&W)
Apple Comics
1-Don Lomax-c/a/scripts in all .80 2.00
1-2nd print .80 2.00
2-11: 10,11-$2.00/$2.25-c .80 2.00
...: Indian Country Vol. 1 (1990, $12.95)-r/#1-4 plus one new story 1.60 4.85 13.00

VIETNAM JOURNAL: VALLEY OF DEATH
June, 1994 - No. 2, Aug, 1994 ($2.75, B&W, limited series)
Apple Comics
1,2: By Don Lomax 1.10 2.75

VIGILANTE, THE (Also see New Teen Titans #23 & Annual V2#2)
Oct, 1983 - No. 50, Feb, 1988 ($1.25, Baxter paper)
DC Comics
1-Origin 1.20 3.00
2-10: 3-Cyborg app. 4-1st app. The Exterminator; Newton-a(p). 6,7-Origin 1.50
11-50: 17,18-Alan Moore scripts. 20,21-Nightwing app. 35-Origin Mad Bomber. 47-Batman-c/story. 50-Ken Steacy painted-c 1.25
Annual (1985) 1.00 2.50
Annual 2 (1986) .80 2.00

VIGILANTE: CITY LIGHTS, PRAIRIE JUSTICE (Also see Action Comics #42, Justice League of America #78, Leading Comics & World's Finest #244)
Nov, 1995 - No. 4, Feb, 1995 ($2.50, limited series)
DC Comics
1-4: James Robinson scripts in all 1.00 2.50

VIGILANTES, THE
No. 839, Sept, 1957
Dell Publishging Col.
Four Color 839-Movie 6.40 19.00 70.00

VIKINGS, THE (Movie)
No. 910, May, 1958
Dell Publishing Co.
Four Color 910-Buscema-a, Kirk Douglas photo-c 8.00 25.00 90.00

VILLAINS AND VIGILANTES
Dec, 1986 - No. 4, May, 1987 ($1.50/$1.75, limited series, Baxter paper)
Eclipse Comics
1-4: Based on role-playing game. 2-4 ($1.75-c) .70 1.75

VINTAGE MAGNUS (...Robot Fighter)
Jan, 1992 - No. 4, Apr, 1992 ($2.25, limited series)
Valiant
1-4: 1-Layton-c; r/origin from Magnus R.F. #22 .90 2.25

VIOLATOR (Also see Spawn #2)
May, 1994 - No. 3, Aug, 1994 ($1.95, limited series)
Image Comics (Todd McFarlane Productions)
1-Alan Moore scripts in all 2.00 5.00
2,3: Bart Sears-c(p)/a(p) 1.60 4.00

VIOLATOR VS. BADROCK
May, 1995 - No. 4, Aug, 1995 ($2.50, limited series)
Image Comics (Extreme Studios)
1-4: Alan Moore scripts in all. 1-1st app Celestine; variant-c (3?) 1.00 2.50

VIPER (TV)
Aug, 1994 - No. 4, Nov, 1994 ($1.95, limited series)
DC Comics
1-4-Adaptation of television show .80 2.00

VIRGINIAN, THE (TV)
June, 1963
Gold Key
1(10060-306)-Part photo-c of James Drury plus photo back-c 2.75 8.00 30.00

VIRTUA FIGHTER (Video Game)
Aug, 1995 (2.95, one-shot)
Marvel Comics
1-Sega Saturn game 1.20 3.00

VIRUS (Manga)
1993 - No. 4, 1993 ($2.50, limited series)
Dark Horse Comics
1-4: Ploog-c 1.00 2.50

VISION, THE
Nov, 1994 - No. 4, Feb, 1995 ($1.75, limited series)
Marvel Comics
1-4 .70 1.75

VISION AND THE SCARLET WITCH, THE (See Marvel Fanfare)
Nov, 1982 - No. 4, Feb, 1983 (Limited series)
Marvel Comics Group
1 .75 1.80
2-4: 2-Nuklo & Future Man app. 1.25

VISION AND THE SCARLET WITCH, THE
Oct, 1985 - No. 12, Sept, 1986 (Maxi-series)
Marvel Comics Group
V2#1-Origin; 1st app. in Avengers #57 .75 1.80
2-5: 2-West Coast Avengers x-over 1.50
6-12 1.30

VISIONARIES
Nov, 1987 - No. 6, Sept, 1988
Marvel Comics (Star Comics)/Marvel Comics #3 on
1-6 1.00

VISIONS
1979 - No. 5, 1983 (B&W, fanzine)
Vision Publications
1-Flaming Carrot begins(1st app?); N. Adams-c 2.50 7.50 25.00
2-N. Adams, Rogers-a; Gulacy back-c; signed & numbered to 2000 2.50 7.50 20.00
3-Williamson-c(p); Steranko back-c 1.25 3.75 10.00
4-Flaming Carrot-c & info. 1.25 3.75 10.00
5-1 pg. Flaming Carrot 2.00 5.00
*NOTE: **Eisner** a-4. **Miller** a-4. **Starlin** a-3. **Williamson** a-5. After #4, Visions became an annual publication of The Atlanta Fantasy Fair.*

VISITOR, THE

Vooda #20 © AJAX

Voodoo #1 © AJAX

Vortex #15 © Vortex

GD25 FN65 NM94

Apr, 1995 - No. 13, Nov, 1995 ($2.50)
Valiant/Acclaim Comics (Valiant)

1-13: 8-Harbinger revealed. 13-Visitor revealed to be Sting from Harbinger. 1.00 2.50

VISITOR, VS. THE VALIANT UNIVERSE, THE
Feb, 1995 - No. 2, Mar, 1995 ($2.95, limited series)
Valiant

1,2 1.20 3.00

VOGUE (Also see Youngblood)
Oct, 1995 - No.3, Jan, 1996 ($2.50, limited series)
Image Comics (Extreme Studios)

1-3: 1-Liefeld-c 1.00 2.50
1-Variant-c 1.20 3.00

VOID INDIGO (Also see Marvel Graphic Novel)
11/84 - No. 2, 3/85 ($1.50, direct sales, unfinished series, mature)
Marvel Comics (Epic Comics)

1,2: Cont'd from Marvel G.N.; graphic sex & violence 1.50

VOLTRON (TV)
1985 - No. 3, 1985 (75¢, limited series)
Modern Publishing

1-3: Ayers-a in all 1.00

VOODA (Jungle Princess) (Formerly Voodoo)
No. 20, April, 1955 - No. 22, Aug, 1955
Ajax-Farrell (Four Star Publications)

20-Baker-c/a (r/Seven Seas #6) 28.00 84.00 210.00
21,22-Baker-a plus Kamen/Baker story, Kimbo Boy of Jungle, & Baker-c (p) in all. 22-Censored Jo-Jo-r (name Powaa) 24.00 73.00 180.00

NOTE: *#20-22 each contain one heavily censored-r of South Sea Girl by **Baker** from Seven Seas Comics with name changed to Vooda. #20-r/Seven Seas #6; #21-r/#4; #22-4/#3.*

VOODOO (Weird Fantastic Tales) (Vooda #20 on)
May, 1952 - No. 19, Jan-Feb, 1955
Ajax-Farrell (Four Star Publ.)

1-South Sea Girl-r by Baker 40.00 120.00 350.00
2-Rulah story-r plus South Sea Girl from Seven Seas #2 by Baker (name changed from Alani to El'nee) 37.00 111.00 280.00
3-Bakerish-a; man stabbed in face 25.00 75.00 190.00
4,8-Baker-r. 8-Severed head panels 25.00 75.00 190.00
5-7,9,10: 5-Nazi death camp story (flaying alive). 6-Severed head panels 20.00 60.00 150.00
11-14,16-18: 14-Zombies take over America. 16-Post nuclear world story. 17-Electric chair panels 17.00 51.00 130.00
15-Opium drug story-r/Ellery Queen #3 19.00 56.00 140.00
19-Bondage-c; Baker-r(2)/Seven Seas #5 w/minor changes & #1, heavily modified; last pre-code; contents & covers chane to jungle theme 23.00 69.00 170.00
Annual 1(1952, 25¢, 100 pgs.)-Baker-a (scarce) 50.00 150.00 450.00

VOODOO
Nov, 1997 - No. 4 ($2.50, limited series)
Image Comics (WildStorm Productions)

1-3:Alan Moore-s in all 1.00 2.50

VOODOO (See Tales of...)

VOODOO-ZEALOT: SKIN TRADE (See WildC.A.T.S: Covert Action Teams)
Aug, 1995 ($4.95, one-shot)
Image Comics (Wildstorm Productions)

1 2.00 5.00

VORTEX
Nov, 1982 - No. 15, 1988 (No month) ($1.50/$1.75, B&W)
Vortex Publs.

GD25 FN65 NM94

1 ($1.95)-Peter Hsu-a; Ken Steacy-c; nudity 2.40 6.00
2-1st app. Mister X (on-c only) 1.20 3.00
3 .80 2.00
4-15: 12-Sam Kieth-a .70 1.75

VORTEX
1991 - No. 2? ($2.50, limited series)
Comico

1,2: Heroes from The Elementals 1.00 2.50

VORTEX
1996 ($2.95)
Entity Comics

1,1b: 1b-Kaniuga-c 1.20 3.00

VOYAGE TO THE BOTTOM OF THE SEA (Movie, TV)
No. 1230, Sept-Nov, 1961; Dec, 1964 - #16, Apr, 1970 (Painted-c)
Dell Publishing Co./Gold Key

Four Color 1230 (1961) 9.00 27.00 100.00
10133-412(#1, 12/64)(Gold Key) 5.50 16.50 60.00
2(7/65) - 5: Photo back-c, 1-5 3.60 11.00 40.00
6-14 2.75 8.00 30.00
15,16-Reprints 2.00 6.00 16.00

VOYAGE TO THE DEEP
Sept-Nov, 1962 - No. 4, Nov-Jan, 1964 (Painted-c)
Dell Publishing Co.

1 3.80 11.40 38.00
2-4 2.80 8.40 28.00

VR VIXEN
July, 1997 ($3.00, B&W)
London Night Studios

0 1.20 3.00
0-($6.00) Nude Edition 3.00 6.00

WACKO
Sept, 1980 - No. 3, Oct, 1981 (84 pgs., B&W, magazine)
Ideal Publ. Corp.

1-3 .80 2.00

WACKY ADVENTURES OF CRACKY (Also see Gold Key Spotlight)
Dec, 1972 - No. 12, Sept, 1975
Gold Key

1 1.25 3.75 10.00
2 2.00 5.00
3-12 1.20 3.00

(See March of Comics #405, 424, 436, 448)

WACKY DUCK (...Comics #3-6; formerly Dopey Duck; Justice Comics #7 on) (See Film Funnies)
No. 3, Fall, 1946 - No. 6, Summer, 1947; Aug, 1948 - No. 2, Oct, 1948
Marvel Comics (NPP)

3 14.00 41.00 110.00
4-Infinity-c 15.00 45.00 120.00
5,6(1947)-Becomes Justice comics 11.30 34.00 90.00
1,2(1948) 8.50 26.00 60.00
I.W. Reprint #1,2,7('58): 1-r/Wacky Duck #6 1.10 3.30 9.00
Super Reprint #10(I.W. on-c, Super-inside) 1.10 3.30 9.00

WACKY QUACKY (See Wisco)

WACKY RACES (TV)
Aug, 1969 - No. 7, Apr, 1972 (Hanna-Barbera)
Gold Key

1 2.75 8.00 30.00
2-7 1.65 5.00 18.00

WACKY SQUIRREL (Also see Dark Horse Presents)

The Waiting Place #1 © SLG

Walt Disney Giant #6 © WDC

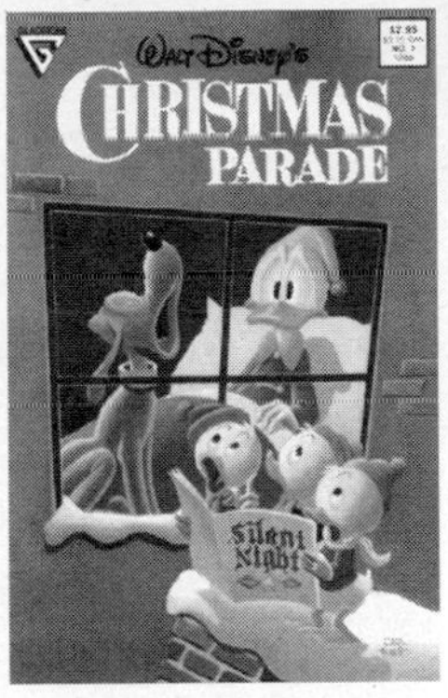

Walt Disney's Christmas Parade #1 © WDC

GD25 FN65 NM94

Oct, 1987 - No. 4, 1988 ($1.75, B&W)
Dark Horse Comics
1-4: 4-Superman parody .70 1.75
Halloween Adventure Special 1 (1987, $2.00) .80 2.00
Summer Fun Special 1 (1988, $2.00) .80 2.00

WACKY WITCH (Also see Gold Key Spotlight)
March, 1971 - No. 21, Dec, 1975
Gold Key
1 1.85 5.50 20.00
2 1.10 3.30 9.00
3-10 1.00 2.80 7.00
11-21 1.20 3.00
(See March of Comics #374, 398, 410, 422, 434, 446, 458, 470, 482)

WACKY WOODPECKER (See Two Bit the...)
1958; 1963
I. W. Enterprises/Super Comics
I.W. Reprint #1,2,7 (nd-reprints Two Bit...): 7-r/Two-Bit, the Wacky Woodpecker #1. 1.00 2.80 7.00
Super Reprint #10('63): 10-r/Two-Bit, The Wacky Woodpecker #? 1.00 2.80 7.00

WAGON TRAIN (1st Series) (TV) (See Western Roundup under Dell Giants)
No. 895, Mar, 1958 - No. 13, Apr-June, 1962 (All photo-c)
Dell Publishing Co.
Four Color 895 (#1) 11.00 33.00 120.00
Four Color 971(#2),1019(#3) 6.00 18.00 65.00
4(1-3/60),6-13 5.00 15.00 55.00
5-Toth-a 5.50 16.50 60.00

WAGON TRAIN (2nd Series)(TV)
Jan, 1964 - No. 4, Oct, 1964 (All front & back photo-c)
Gold Key
1-Tufts-a in all 4.00 12.00 45.00
2-4 2.75 8.00 30.00

WAITING PLACE, THE
Apr, 1997 - Present ($2.95)
Slave Labor Graphics
1-6-Sean McKeever-s 1.20 3.00

WAITING ROOM WILLIE (See Sad Case of...)

WALLY (Teen-age)
Dec, 1962 - No. 4, Sept, 1963
Gold Key
1 2.50 7.50 24.00
2-4 2.00 6.00 16.00

WALLY THE WIZARD
Apr, 1985 - No. 12, Mar, 1986 (Children's comic)
Marvel Comics (Star Comics)
1-12: Bob Bolling a-1,3; c-1,9,11,12 1.00

WALLY WOOD'S T.H.U.N.D.E.R. AGENTS (See Thunder Agents)
Nov, 1984 - No. 5, Oct, 1986 ($2.00, 52 pgs.)
Deluxe Comics
1-5: 5-Jerry Ordway-c/a in Wood style 1.20 3.00
NOTE: *Anderson a-2i, 3i. Buckler a-4. Ditko a-3, 4. Giffen a-1p-4p. Perez a-1p, 2, 4; c-1-4.*

WALT DISNEY CHRISTMAS PARADE (Also see Christmas Parade)
Winter, 1977 ($1.95, cardboard covers, 224 pgs.)
Whitman Publishing Co. (Golden Press)
11191-Barks-r/Christmas in Disneyland #1, Dell Christmas Parade #9 & Dell Giant #53 1.20 3.00

WALT DISNEY COMICS DIGEST
June, 1968 - No. 57, Feb, 1976 (50¢, digest size)
Gold Key
1-Reprints Uncle Scrooge #5; 192 pgs. 6.40 19.00 70.00
2-4-Barks-r 3.60 11.00 40.00
5-Daisy Duck by Barks (8 pgs.); last published story by Barks (art only) plus 21 pg. Scrooge-r by Barks 7.00 22.00 80.00
6-13-All Barks-r 2.75 8.00 30.00
14,15 2.00 6.00 16.00
16-Reprints Donald Duck #26 by Barks 2.75 8.00 30.00
17-20-Barks-r 2.25 6.75 24.00
21-31,33,35-37-Barks-r; 24-Toth Zorro 1.80 5.50 20.00
32,41,45,47-49 1.50 4.50 12.00
34-Reprints 4-Color #318 1.80 5.50 20.00
38-Reprints Christmas in Disneyland #1 1.80 5.50 20.00
39-Two Barks-r/WDC&S #272, 4-Color #1073 plus Toth Zorro-r 1.80 5.50 20.00
40-Mickey Mouse-r by Gottfredson 1.75 5.25 14.00
42,43-Barks-r 1.75 5.25 14.00
44-(Has Gold Key emblem, 50¢)-Reprints 1st story of 4-Color #29,256,275,282 3.60 11.00 40.00
44-Republished in 1976 by Whitman; not identical to original; a bit smaller, blank back-c, 69¢ 2.00 6.00 16.00
46,50,52-Barks-r. 52-Barks-r/WDC&S #161,132 1.50 4.50 12.00
51-Reprints 4-Color #71 1.80 5.50 20.00
53-55: 53-Reprints Dell Giant #30. 54-Reprints Donald Duck Beach Party #2. 55-Reprints Dell Giant #49 1.25 3.75 10.00
56-r/Uncle Scrooge #32 (Barks) 1.75 5.25 14.00
57-r/Mickey Mouse Almanac('57) & two Barks stories 1.50 4.50 12.00
NOTE: *Toth a-52r. #1-10, 196 pgs.; #11-41, 164 pgs.; #42 on, 132 pgs. Old issues were being reprinted & distributed by Whitman in 1976.*

WALT DISNEY GIANT (Disney)
Sept, 1995 - No. 7, Sept, 1996 ($2.25, bi-monthly, 48 pgs.)
Bruce Hamilton Company (Gladstone)
1-7: 1-Scrooge McDuck in the Yukon; Rosa-c/a/scripts plus r/F.C. #218. 2-Uncle Scrooge-r by Barks plus 17 pg. text story. 3-Donald the Mighty Duck; Rosa-c; Barks & Rosa-r. 4-Mickey and Goofy; new-a (story actually stars Goofy. Mickey Mouse by Caesar Ferioli; Donald Duck by Giorgio Cavazzano (1st in U.S.). 6-Uncle Scrooge & the Jr. Woodchucks; new-a and Barks-r. 7-Uncle Scrooge-r by Barks plus new-a .90 2.25
NOTE: *Series was initially solicited as Uncle Walt's Collectory. Issue #8 was advertised, but later cancelled.*

WALT DISNEY PRESENTS (TV)(Disney)
No. 997, 6-8/59 - No. 6, 12-2/1960-61; No. 1181, 4-5/61 (All photo-c)
Dell Publishing Co.
Four Color 997 (#1) 6.40 19.00 70.00
2(12-2/60)-The Swamp Fox(origin), Elfego Baca, Texas John Slaughter (Disney TV show) begin 4.00 12.00 45.00
3-6: 5-Swamp Fox by Warren Tufts 3.60 11.00 40.00
Four Color 1181-Texas John Slaughter 6.40 19.00 70.00

WALT DISNEY'S CHRISTMAS PARADE (Also see Christmas Parade)
Winter, 1988; No. 2, Winter, 1989 ($2.95, 100 pgs.)
Gladstone
1-Barks-r/painted-c 1.25 3.75 10.00
2-Barks-r 1.00 3.00 8.00

WALT DISNEY'S COMICS AND STORIES (Cont. of Mickey Mouse Magazine)
(#1-30 contain Donald Duck newspaper reprints) (Titled "Comics And Stories" #264 to #?; titled "Walt Disney's Comics And Stories" #511 on)
10/40 - #263, 8/62; #264, 10/62 - #510, 1984; #511, 10/86 - Present
Dell Publishing Co./Gold Key #264-394/Whitman #395-510/Gladstone #511-547(4/90)/Disney Comics #548(6/90)-#585/Gladstone #586(8/93) on

NOTE: The whole number can always be found at the bottom of the title page in the lower left-hand or right hand panel.

Walt Disney's Comics & Stories #3 © WDC

Walt Disney's Comics & Stories V3 #1 (#25) © WDC

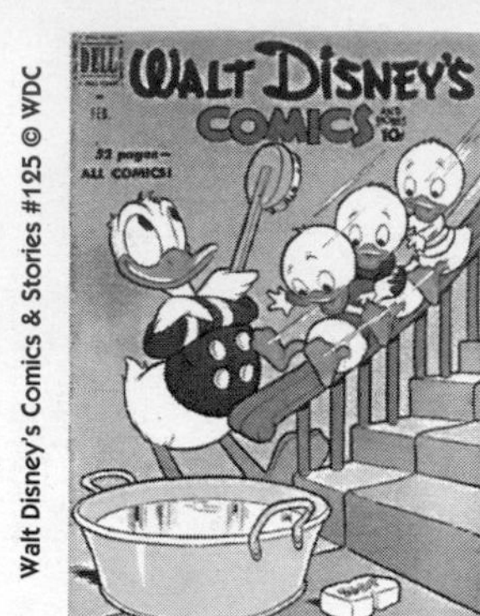

Walt Disney's Comics & Stories #125 © WDC

GD25 FN65 VF82 NM94
1(V1#1-c; V2#1-indicia)-Donald Duck strip-r by Al Taliaferro & Gottfredson's Mickey Mouse begin 1454.00 4360.00 9450.00 16,000.00
(Estimated up to 245 total copies exist, 12 in NM/Mint)

GD25 FN65 NM94
2 550.00 1650.00 6000.00
3 185.00 555.00 1850.00
4-X-Mas-c; 1st Huey, Dewey & Louie-c this title (See Mickey Mouse Magazine V4#2 for 1st-c ever) 130.00 390.00 1300.00
4-Special promotional, complimentary issue; cover same except one corner was blanked out & boxed in to identify the giveaway (not a paste-over). This special pressing was probably sent out to former subscribers to Mickey Mouse Mag. whose subscriptions had expired. (Very rare-5 known copies) 220.00 660.00 2200.00
5-Goofy-c 100.00 300.00 1000.00
6-10: 8-Only Clarabelle Cow-c. 9-Taliaferro-c (1st) 85.00 255.00 850.00
11-14: 11-Huey, Dewey & Louie-c/app. 70.00 210.00 700.00
15-17: 15-The 3 Little Kittens (17 pgs.). 16-The 3 Little Pigs (29 pgs.); X-Mas-c. 17-The Ugly Duckling (4 pgs.) 64.00 192.00 640.00
18-21 52.00 156.00 525.00
22-30: 22-Flag-c. 24-The Flying Gauchito (1st original comic book story done for WDC&S). 27-Jose Carioca by Carl Buettner (2nd original story in WDC&S) 45.00 135.00 450.00
31-New Donald Duck stories by Carl Barks begin (See F.C. #9 for 1st Barks Donald Duck) 290.00 870.00 2900.00
32-Barks-a 125.00 375.00 1250.00
33-Barks-a; infinity-c 90.00 270.00 900.00
34-Gremlins by Walt Kelly begin, end #41; Barks-a 75.00 225.00 750.00
35,36-Barks-a 67.00 202.00 675.00
37-Donald Duck by Jack Hannah 34.00 102.00 340.00
38-40-Barks-a. 39-X-Mas-c. 40,41-Gremlins by Kelly 45.00 135.00 450.00
41-50-Barks-a. 43-Seven Dwarfs-c app. (4/44). 45-50-Nazis in Gottfredson's Mickey Mouse Stories 36.00 108.00 360.00
51-60-Barks-a. 51-X-Mas-c. 52-Li'l Bad Wolf begins, ends #203 (not in #55). 58-Kelly flag-c 25.00 75.00 250.00
61-70: Barks-a. 61-Dumbo story. 63,64-Pinocchio stories. 63-Cover swipe from New Funnies #94. 64-X-Mas-c. 65-Pluto story. 66-Infinity-c. 67,68-Mickey Mouse Sunday-r by Bill Wright 21.00 63.00 210.00
71-80: Barks-a. 75-77-Brer Rabbit stories, no Mickey Mouse. 76-X-Mas-c 16.00 48.00 155.00
81-87,89,90: Barks-a. 82-Goofy-c. 82-84-Bongo stories. 86-90-Goofy & Agnes app. 89-Chip 'n' Dale story 14.00 42.00 140.00
88-1st app. Gladstone Gander by Barks (1/48) 19.00 57.00 185.00
91-97,99: Barks-a. 95-1st WDC&S Barks-c. 96-No Mickey Mouse; Little Toot begins, ends #97. 99-X-Mas-c 12.00 36.00 120.00
98-1st Uncle Scrooge app. in WDC&S (11/48) 24.00 72.00 240.00
100-(1/49)-Barks-a 15.00 45.00 150.00
101-110-Barks-a. 107-Taliaferro-c; Donald acquires super powers 11.00 33.00 110.00
111,114,117-All Barks 8.50 25.50 85.00
112-Drug (ether) issue (Donald Duck) 8.50 25.50 85.00
113,115,116,118-123: No Barks. 116-Dumbo x-over. 121-Grandma Duck begins, ends #168; not in #135,142,146,155 3.80 11.40 38.00
124,126-130-All Barks. 124-X-Mas-c 7.00 21.00 70.00
125-1st app. Junior Woodchucks (2/51); Barks-a 10.50 32.00 105.00
131,133,135-137,139-All Barks 7.00 21.00 70.00
132-Barks-a(2) (D. Duck & Grandma Duck) 7.50 22.50 75.00
134-Intro. & 1st app. The Beagle Boys (11/51) 16.00 48.00 160.00
138-Classic Scrooge money story 12.00 36.00 120.00
140-(5/52)-1st app. Gyro Gearloose by Barks; 2nd Barks Uncle Scrooge-c; 3rd Uncle Scrooge-c app. 16.00 48.00 160.00
141-150-All Barks. 143-Little Hiawatha begins, ends #151,159 5.00 15.00 50.00
151-170-All Barks 4.00 12.00 40.00
171-199-All Barks 3.50 10.50 35.00
200 4.50 13.50 45.00
201-240: All Barks. 204-Chip 'n' Dale & Scamp begin 3.50 10.50 35.00
241-283: Barks-a. 241-Dumbo x-over. 247-Gyro Gearloose begins, ends #274. 256-Ludwig Von Drake begins, ends #274 2.60 7.80 26.00
284,285,287,290,295,296,309-311-Not by Barks 1.50 4.50 12.00
286,288,289,291-294,297,298,308-All Barks stories; 293-Grandma Duck's Farm Friends. 297-Gyro Gearloose. 298-Daisy Duck's Diary-r 2.00 6.00 16.00
299-307-All contain early Barks-r (#43-117). 305-Gyro Gearloose 2.25 6.75 18.00
312-Last Barks issue with original story 2.25 6.75 18.00
313-315,317-327,329-334,336-341 1.50 4.50 12.00
316-Last issue published during life of Walt Disney 1.50 4.50 12.00
328,335,342-350-Barks-r 1.50 4.50 12.00
351-360-With posters inside; Barks reprints (2 versions of each with & without posters)-without posters... 1.50 4.50 12.00
351-360-With posters... 2.25 6.75 18.00
361-400-Barks-r 1.50 4.50 12.00
401-429-Barks-r 1.50 4.50 12.00
430,433,437,438,441,444,445,466,506-No Barks 2.40 6.00
431,432,434-436,439,440,442,443-Barks-r 2.40 6.00
446-465,467-479,481-505,507-510: All Barks-r. 494-r/WDC&S #98 2.00 5.00
480 (8-12/80)-Distr. only in Whitman 3-pack 3.00 9.00 35.00
511-Donald Duck by Daan Jippes (1st in U.S.; in all through #518); Gyro Gearloose Barks-r begins (in most through #547); Wuzzles by Disney studio (1st by Gladstone) 2.50 7.50 20.00
512,513 1.50 4.50 12.00
514-516,520,523: 523-1st Rosa 10 pager 1.00 2.80 7.00
517-519,521,522,524-547: 518-Infinity-c. 522-r/1st app. Huey, Dewey & Louie from D. Duck Sunday. 535-546-Barks-r. 537-1st Donald Duck by William Van Horn in WDC&S. 541-545-52 pgs. 546,547-68 pgs. 546-Kelly-r. 547-Rosa-a 1.20 3.00
548-($1.50, 6/90)-1st Disney issue; new-a; no M. Mouse .70 1.75
549,551-570,572,573,577-579,581,584 ($1.50): 549-Barks-r begin, ends #585, not in #555, 556, & 564. 551-r/1 story from F.C. #29. 556,578-r/Mickey Mouse Cheerios Premium by Dick Moores. 562,563,568-570, 572, 581-Gottfredson strip-r. 570-Valentine issue; has Mickey/Minnie centerfold. 584-Taliaferro strip-r 1.60
550 ($2.25, 52 pgs.)-Donald Duck by Barks; previously only printed in The Netherlands (1st time in U.S.); also r/Chip 'n Dale & Scamp from #204 1.00 2.50
571-($2.95, 68 pgs)-r/Donald Duck's Atomic Bomb by Barks from 1947 Cheerios premium 1.60 4.00
574-576,580,582,583 ($2.95, 68 pgs.): 574-r/1st Pinocchio Sunday strip (1939-40). 575-Gottfredson-r, Pinocchio-r/WDC&S #64. 580-r/Donald Duck's 1st app. from Silly Symphony strip 12/16/34 by Taliaferro; Gottfredson strip-r begin; not in #584 & 600. 582,583-r/Mickey Mouse on Sky Island from WDC&S #1,2 1.30 3.25
585 ($2.50, 52 pgs.)-r/#140; Barks-r/WDC&S #140 1.30 3.25
586,587: 586-Gladstone issues begin again; begin $1.50-c; Gottfredson-r begins (not in #600). 587-Donald Duck by William Van Horn begins .80 2.00
588-597: 588,591-599-Donald Duck by William Van Horn 1.50
598,599 ($1.95, 36 pgs.): 598-r/1st drawings of Mickey Mouse by Ub Iwerks .80 2.00
600 ($2.95, 48 pgs.)-L.B. Cole-c(r)/WDC&S #1; Barks-r/WDC&S #32 plus Rosa, Jippes, Van Horn-r and new Rosa centerspread 1.20 3.00
601-611 ($5.95, 64 pgs., squarebound, bi-monthly): 601-Barks-c, r/Mickey Mouse V1#1, Rosa-a/scripts. 602-Rosa-c. 604-Taliaferro strip-r/1st Silly Symphony Sundays from 1932. 604,605-Jippes-a. 605-Walt Kelly-c; Gottfredson "Mickey Mouse Outwits the Phantom Blot" r/F.C. #16

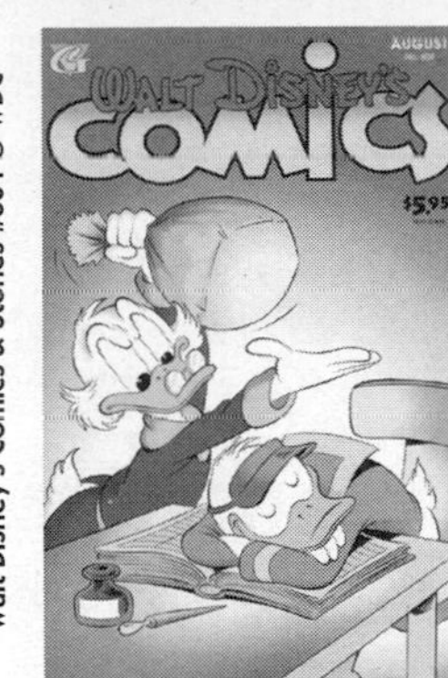

Walt Disney's Comics & Stories #604 © WDC

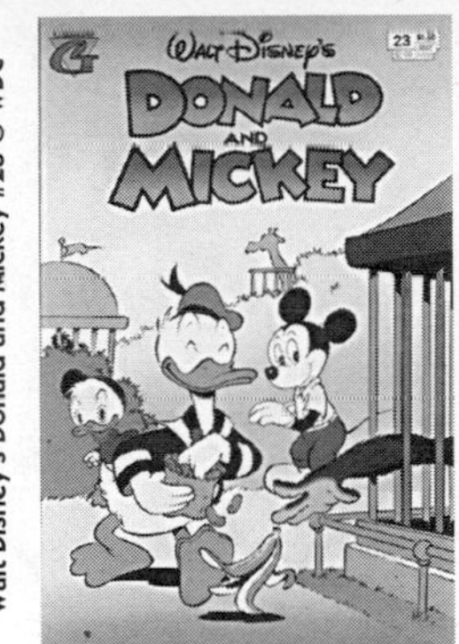

Walt Disney's Donald and Mickey #23 © WDC

Walt Disney's Donald Duck Adventures #28 (2nd Series) © WDC

GD25 FN65 NM94

2.40 6.00
612-615 ($6.95) 1.00 2.80 7.00

NOTE: *(#1-38, 68 pgs.; #39-42, 60 pgs.; #43-57, 61-134, 143-168, 446, 447, 52 pgs.; #58-60, 135-142, 169-540, 36 pgs.)*

NOTE: **Barks** *art in all issues #31 on, except where noted; c-95, 96, 104, 108, 109, 130-172, 174-178, 183, 198-200, 204, 206-209, 212-216, 218, 220, 226, 228-233, 235-238, 240-243, 247, 250, 253, 256, 260, 261, 276-283, 288-292, 295-298, 301, 303, 304, 306, 307, 309, 310, 313-316, 319, 321, 322, 324, 326, 328, 329, 331, 332, 334, 341, 342, 350, 351, 527r, 530r, 540(never before published), 546r, 557-586r(most), 596p, 601p.* **Kelly** *a-24p, 34-41, 43; r-522-524, 546, 547, 582, 583; covers(most)-34-118, 531r, 537r, 541r-543r, 562r, 571r, 605r. Walt Disney's Comics & Stories featured Mickey Mouse serials which were in practically every issue from #1 through #394 and #511 to date. The titles of the serials, along with the issues they are in, are listed in previous editions of this price guide.* **Floyd Gottfredson** *Mickey Mouse serials in issues #1-14, 18-66, 69-74, 78-100, 128, 562, 563, 568-572, 582, 583, 586-599 , 601-603 , 605-present , plus "Service with a Smile" in #13; "Mickey Mouse in a Warplant" (3 pgs.), and "Pluto Catches a Nazi Spy" (4 pgs.) in #62; "Mystery Next Door", #93; "Sunken Treasure", #94; "Aunt Marissa", #95 (r in #575), "Gangland", #98 (r in #582), "Thanksgiving Dinner", #99 (r in #587), and "The Talking Dog", #100 (r in #563); "Morty's Escapade," #128. "The Brave Little Tailor", #580; "Introducing Mickey Mouse Movies ", #581; Circus Roustabout, #585; "Rumplewatt the Giant", #604. Mickey Mouse by* **Paul Murry** *#152-547 except 155-57 (***Dick Moore***), 327-29 (***Tony Strobl***), 348-50 (***Jack Manning***), 533 (***Bill Wright***).* **Don Rosa** *story/a-523, 524, 526, 528, 531, 547, 601-present.* **Al Taliaferro** *Silly Symphonies in #5-"Three Little Pigs"; #13-"Birds of a Feather"; #14-"The Boarding School Mystery"; #15-"Cookieland" and "Three Little Kittens"; #16-"The Practical Pig"; #17-"The Ugly Duckling"; "The Wise Little Hen" in #580; and "Ambrose the Robber Kitten"; #19-"Penguin Isle"; and "Bucky Bug" in #20-23, 25, 26, 28 (one continuous story from 1932-34; first 2 pgs. not Taliaferro).* **Gottfredson** *strip r-562, 563, 568-572, 581, 585, 586, 590.* **Taliaferro** *strip r-584, 580.* **Van Horn** *a-537, 545, 561, 574, 587, 588, 591-present.*

WALT DISNEY'S COMICS & STORIES
1943 (36 pgs.) (Dept. store Xmas giveaway)
Walt Disney Productions

nn-X-Mas-c with Donald & the Boys; Donald Duck by Jack Hannah; Thumper by Ken Hultgren 39.00 117.00 390.00

WALT DISNEY'S COMICS & STORIES
1942-1963 known (7-1/3"x10-1/4", 4 pgs. in color, slick paper)
(folded horizontally once or twice as mailers)
K.K. Publications (Xmas subscription offer)

1942 mailer-r/Kelly cover to WDC&S 25; 2-year subscription + two Grosset & Dunlap hardcover books (32-pages each), of Bambi and of Thumper, offered for $2.00; came in an illustrated C&S envelope with an enclosed postage paid envelope (Rare) Mailer only 16.00 48.00 165.00
with envelopes 23.00 69.00 230.00

1949 mailer-A rare Barks item: Same WDC&S cover as 1942 mailer, but with art changed so that newphew is handing teacher Donald a comic book rather than an apple, as originally drawn by Kelly. The tiny, 7/8"x1-1/4" cover shown was a rejected cover by Barks that was intended for C&S 110, but was redrawn by Kelly for C&S 111. The original art has been lost and this is its only app. (Rare) 32.00 96.00 320.00

1950 mailer-P.1 r/Kelly cover to Dell Xmas Parade 1 (without title); p.2 r/Kelly cover to C&S 101 (w/o title), but with the art altered to show Donald reading C&S 122 (by Kelly); hardcover book, "Donald Duck in Bringing Up the Boys" given with a $1.00 one-year subscription; P.4 r/full Kelly Xmas cover to C&S 99 (Rare) 11.00 33.00 115.00

1953 mailer-P.1 r/cover Dell Xmas Parade 4 (w/o title); insides offer "Donald Duck Full Speed Ahead," a 28-page, color, 5-5/8"x6-5/8" book, not of the Story Hour series; P.4 r/full Barks C&S 148 cover (Rare)
7.00 21.00 70.00

1963 mailer-Pgs. 1,2 & 4 r/GK Xmas art; P.3 r/a 1963 C&S cover (Scarce)
4.00 12.00 40.00

NOTE: *It is assumed a different mailer was printed each Xmas for at least twenty years. A 1952 mailer is known.*

WALT DISNEY'S COMICS DIGEST
Dec, 1986 - No. 7, Sept, 1987
Gladstone

1 2.40 6.00
2-7 1.60 4.00

WALT DISNEY'S COMICS PENNY PINCHER
May, 1997 - No. 3, July, 1997 (99¢, limited series)
Gladstone

1 1.00

WALT DISNEY'S DONALD AND MICKEY (Formerly Walt Disney's Mickey and Donald)
No. 19, Sept, 1993 - No. 30, 1995 ($1.50, 36 & 68 pgs.)
Gladstone (Bruce Hamilton Company)

19,21-24,26-30: New & reprints. 19,21,23,24-Barks-r. 19,26-Murry-r. 22-Barks "Omelet" story r/WDC&S #146. 27-Mickey Mouse story by Caesar Ferioli (1st U.S work). 29-Rosa-c; Mickey Mouse story actually starring Goofy (does not include Mickey except on title page. 1.60 4.00
20,25-($2.95, 68 pgs.): 20-Barks, Gottfredson-r 2.00 5.00

NOTE: *Donald Duck stories were all reprints.*

WALT DISNEY'S DONALD DUCK ADVENTURES (D.D. Adv. #1 3)
11/87-No. 20, 4/90 (1st Series); No. 21, 8/93-Present (3rd Series)
Gladstone

1 1.00 2.80 7.00
2-r/F.C. #308 1.20 3.00
3,4,6,7,9-11,13,15-18: 3-r/F.C. #223. 4-r/F.C. #62. 9-r/F.C. #159, "Ghost of the Grotto". 11-r/F.C. #159, "Adventure Down Under." 16-r/F.C. #291; Rosa-c. 18-r/FC #318; Rosa-c 1.00 2.50
5,8-Don Rosa-c/a 1.60 4.00
12($1.50, 52pgs)-Rosa-c/a w/Barks poster 1.60 4.00
14-r/F.C. #29, "Mummy's Ring" 1.20 3.00
19($1.95, 68 pgs.)-Barks-r/F.C. #199 (1 pg.) 1.20 3.00
20($1.95, 68 pgs.)-Barks-r/F.C. #189 & cover-r; William Van Horn-a
1.20 3.00
21,22: 21-r/D.D. #46. 22-r/F.C. #282 .90 2.25
23-27,29,31,32-($1.50, 36 pgs.): 21,23,29-Rosa-c. 23-Intro/1st app. Andold Wild Duck by Marco Rota. 24-Van Horn-a. 27-1st Pat Block-a, "Mystery of Widow's Gap." 31,32-Block-c. .80 2.00
26,28($2.95, 68 pgs.): 26-Barks-r/F.C. #108, "Terror of the River". 28-Barks-r/F.C. #199, "Sheriff of Bullet Valley" 1.60 4.00
30($2.95, 68 pgs.)-r/F.C. #367, Barks' "Christmas for Shacktown"
1.60 4.00
34-44: 34-Begin $1.50-c. 34,35,37-Block-a/scripts. 38-Van Horn-c/a
1.50

NOTE: **Barks** *a-1-22r, 26r, 28r, 33r, 36r; c-10r, 14r, 20r.* **Block** *a-27, 30, 34, 35, 37; c-27, 30-32, 34, 35, 37; c-27, 30, 31, 32, 34, 35, 37.* **Rosa** *a-5, 8, 12; c-13, 16-18, 21, 23.*

WALT DISNEY'S DONALD DUCK ADVENTURES (2nd Series)
June, 1990 - No. 38, July, 1993 ($1.50)
Disney Comics

1-Rosa-a & scripts 1.20 3.00
2-38: 2-Barks-r/WDC&S #35; William Van Horn-a begins, ends #20. 9-Barks-r/F.C. #178. 9,11,14,17-No Van Horn-a. 11-Mad #1 cover parody. 14-Barks-r. 17-Barks-r. 21-r/FC #203 by Barks. 22-Rosa-a (10 pgs.) & scripts. 24-Rosa-a & scripts. 26-r/March of Comics #41 by Barks. 29-r/MOC #20 by Barks. 34-Rosa-c/a. 37-Rosa-a; Barks-r .80 2.00

NOTE: **Barks** *r-2, 4, 9(F.C. #178), 14(D.D. #45), 17, 21, 26, 27, 29 , 35, 36(D.D #60)-38.* **Taliaferro** *a-34r, 36r.*

WALT DISNEY'S DONALD DUCK AND MICKEY MOUSE (Formerly Walt Disney's Donald and Mickey)
Sept, 1995 - No. 7, Sept, 1996 ($1.50, 32 pgs.)
Gladstone (Bruce Hamilton Company)

1-7: 1-Barks-r and new Mickey Mouse stories in all. 5,6-Mickey Mouse stories by Caesar Ferioli. 7-New Donald Duck and Mickey Mouse x-over story; Barks-r/WDC&S #51 1.50

NOTE: *Issue #8 was advertised, but cancelled.*

WALT DISNEY SHOWCASE
Oct, 1970 - No. 54, Jan, 1980 (No. 44-48: 68pgs., 49-54: 52pgs.)
Gold Key

1-Boatniks (Movie)-Photo-c 2.50 7.50 22.00

Walt Disney's Mickey and Donald #12 © WDC

Walt Disney's The Jungle Book © WDC

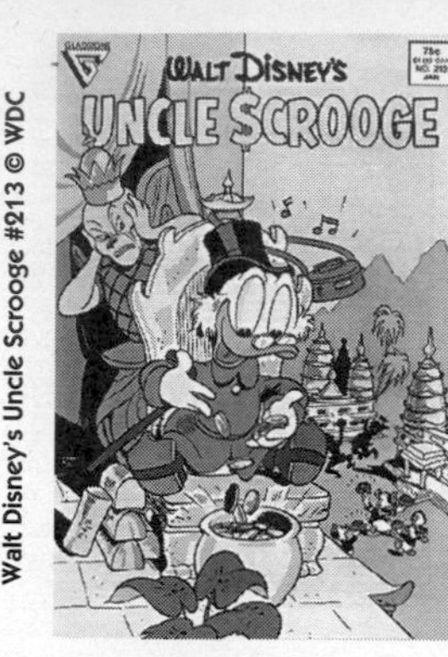

Walt Disney's Uncle Scrooge #213 © WDC

	GD25	FN65	NM94
2-Moby Duck	1.50	4.50	12.00
3,4,7: 3-Bongo & Lumpjaw-r. 4,7-Pluto-r	1.10	3.30	9.00
5-$1,000,000 Duck (Movie)-Photo-c	1.75	5.25	14.00
6-Bedknobs & Broomsticks (Movie)	1.75	5.25	14.00
8-Daisy & Donald	1.10	3.30	9.00
9-101 Dalmatians (cartoon feat.); r/F.C. #1183	1.50	4.50	12.00
10-Napoleon & Samantha (Movie)-Photo-c	1.75	5.25	14.00
11-Moby Duck-r	1.00	3.00	8.00
12-Dumbo-r/Four Color #668	1.10	3.30	9.00
13-Pluto-r	1.00	3.00	8.00
14-World's Greatest Athlete (Movie)-Photo-c	1.75	5.25	14.00
15-3 Little Pigs-r	1.10	3.30	9.00
16-Aristocats (cartoon feature); r/Aristocats #1	1.75	5.25	14.00
17-Mary Poppins; r/M.P. #10136-501-Photo-c	1.75	5.25	14.00
18-Gyro Gearloose; Barks-r/F.C. #1047,1184	2.50	7.50	20.00
19-That Darn Cat; r/That Darn Cat #10171-602-Hayley Mills photo-c	1.50	4.50	14.00
20,23-Pluto-r	1.10	3.30	9.00
21-Li'l Bad Wolf & The Three Little Pigs	1.00	3.00	8.00
22-Unbirthday Party with Alice in Wonderland; r/Four Color #341	1.50	4.50	12.00
24-26: 24-Herbie Rides Again (Movie); sequel to "The Love Bug"; photo-c. 25-Old Yeller (Movie); r/F.C. #869; Photo-c. 26-Lt. Robin Crusoe USN (Movie); r/Lt. Robin Crusoe USN #10191-601; photo-c	1.10	3.30	9.00
27-Island at the Top of the World (Movie)-Photo-c	1.50	4.50	12.00
28-Brer Rabbit, Bucky Bug-r/WDC&S #58	1.10	3.30	9.00
29-Escape to Witch Mountain (Movie)-Photo-c	1.50	4.50	12.00
30-Magica De Spell; Barks-r/Uncle Scrooge #36 & WDC&S #258	2.50	7.50	24.00
31-Bambi (cartoon feature); r/Four Color #186	1.50	4.50	12.00
32-Spin & Marty-r/F.C. #1026; Mickey Mouse Club (TV)-Photo-c	1.75	5.25	14.00
33-39: 33-Pluto-r/F.C. #1143. 34-Paul Revere's Ride with Johnny Tremain (TV); r/F.C. #822. 35-Goofy-r/F.C. #952. 36-Peter Pan-r/F.C. #442. 37-Tinker Bell & Jiminy Cricket-r/F.C. #982,989. 38,39-Mickey & the Sleuth, Parts 1 & 2	1.00	2.80	7.00
40-The Rescuers (cartoon feature)	1.00	3.00	8.00
41-Herbie Goes to Monte Carlo (Movie); sequel to "Herbie Rides Again"; photo-c	1.10	3.30	9.00
42-Mickey & the Sleuth	1.00	2.80	7.00
43-Pete's Dragon (Movie)-Photo-c	1.50	4.50	12.00
44-Return From Witch Mountain (new) & In Search of the Castaways-r (Movies)-Photo-c; 68 pg. giants begin	1.50	4.50	12.00
45-The Jungle Book (Movie); r/#30033-803	1.50	4.50	12.00
46-The Cat From Outer Space (Movie)(new), & The Shaggy Dog (Movie)-r/F.C. #985; photo-c	1.00	3.00	8.00
47-Mickey Mouse Surprise Party-r	1.00	3.00	8.00
48-The Wonderful Advs. of Pinocchio-r/F.C. #1203; last 68 pg. issue	1.00	3.00	8.00
49-54: 49-North Avenue Irregulars (Movie); Zorro-r/Zorro #11; 52 pgs. begin; photo-c. 50-Bedknobs & Broomsticks-r/#6; Mooncussers-r/World of Adv. #1; photo-c. 51-101 Dalmatians-r. 52-Unidentified Flying Oddball (Movie); r/Picnic Party #8; photo-c. 53-The Scarecrow-r (TV). 54-The Black Hole (Movie)-Photo-c (predates Black Hole #1)		2.40	6.00

WALT DISNEY'S MAGAZINE (TV)(Formerly Walt Disney's Mickey Mouse Club Magazine) (50¢, bi-monthly)
V2#4, June, 1957 - V4#6, Oct, 1959
Western Publishing Co.

	GD25	FN65	NM94
V2#4-Stories & articles on the Mouseketeers, Zorro, & Goofy and other Disney characters & people	4.50	13.50	45.00
V2#5, V2#6(10/57)	3.50	10.50	35.00
V3#1(12/57), V3#3-5	2.80	8.40	28.00
V3#2-Annette Funicello photo-c	9.00	27.00	90.00
V3#6(10/58)-TV Zorro photo-c	6.00	18.00	60.00
V4#1(12/58) - V4#2-4,6(10/59)	2.80	8.40	28.00
V4#5-Annette Funicello photo-c, w/ 2-photo articles	9.00	27.00	90.00

NOTE: *V2#4-V3#6 were 11-1/2x8-1/2", 48 pgs.; V4#1 on were 10x8", 52 pgs. (Peak circulation of 400,000).*

WALT DISNEY'S MERRY CHRISTMAS (See Dell Giant #39)

WALT DISNEY'S MICKEY AND DONALD(M & D #1,2)(Becomes Walt Disney's Donald & Mickey #19 on)
Mar, 1988 - No. 18, May, 1990 (95¢)
Gladstone

	GD25	FN65	NM94
1-Don Rosa-a; r/1949 Firestone giveaway		2.40	6.00
2-8: 3-Infinity-c. 4-8-Barks-r		1.20	3.00
9-15: 9-r/1948 Firestone giveaway; X-Mas-c		1.20	3.00
16($1.50, 52 pgs.)-r/FC #157		2.00	5.00
17,18($1.95, 68 pgs.): 17-Barks M.M.-r/FC #79 plus Barks D.D.-r; Rosa-a; X-Mas-c. 18-Gottfredson-r/WDC&S #13,72-74; Kelly-c(r); Barks-r		2.00	5.00

NOTE: ***Barks** reprints in 1-15, 17, 18. **Kelly** c-13r, 14 (r/Walt Disney's C&S #58), 18r.*

WALT DISNEY'S MICKEY MOUSE CLUB MAGAZINE (TV)(Becomes Walt Disney's Magazine)
Winter, 1956 - V2#3, Apr, 1957 (11-1/2x8-1/2", quarterly, 48 pgs.)
Western Publishing Co.

	GD25	FN65	NM94
V1#1	12.00	36.00	120.00
2-4	6.00	18.00	60.00
V2#1,2	4.50	13.50	45.00
3-Annette photo-c	10.00	30. 00	100.00
Annual(1956)-Two different issues; ($1.50-Whitman); 120 pgs., cardboard covers, 11-3/4x8-3/4"; reprints	13.00	39.00	130.00
Annual(1957)-Same as above	11.00	33.00	115.00

WALT DISNEY'S PINOCCHIO SPECIAL
Spring, 1990 ($1.00)
Gladstone

	GD25	FN65	NM94
1-50th anniversary edition; Kelly-r/F.C. #92		1.20	3.00

WALT DISNEY'S SEBASTIAN (See Sebastian)

WALT DISNEY'S THE JUNGLE BOOK
1990 ($5.95, graphic novel, 68 pgs.)
W.D. Publications (Disney Comics)

	GD25	FN65	NM94
nn-Movie adaptation; movie rereleased in 1990		2.40	6.00
nn-($2.95, 68 pgs.)-Comic edition; wraparound-c		1.20	3.00

WALT DISNEY'S UNCLE SCROOGE (Formerly Uncle Scrooge #1-209)
No. 210, 10/86 - No. 242, 4/90; No. 243, 6/90 - Present
Gladstone #210-242/Disney Comics #243-280/Gladstone #281 on

	GD25	FN65	NM94
210-1st Gladstone issue; r/WDC&S #134 (1st Beagle Boys)	1.85	5.50	15.00
211-218: 216-New story ("Go Slowly Sands of Time") plotted and partly scripted by Barks. 217-r/U.S. #7, "Seven Cities of Cibola"	1.85	5.50	15.00
219-"Son Of The Sun" by Rosa	2.50	7.50	25.00
220-Don Rosa-a/scripts		2.00	5.00
221-230: 224-Rosa-c/a. 226,227-Rosa-a		1.20	3.00
231-240: 235-Rosa-a/scripts		1.20	3.00
241-($1.95, 68 pgs.)-Rosa finishes over Barks-r		1.20	3.00
242-($1.95, 68 pgs.)-Barks-r; Rosa-a(1 pg.)		1.20	3.00
243-249,251-280,282-284-($1.50): 243-1st by Disney Comics. 261-263, 276-Don Rosa-c/a. 274-All Barks issue. 275-Contains poster by Rosa. 283-r/WDC&S #98		.90	2.25
250-($2.25, 52 pgs.)-Barks-r; wraparound-c		1.20	3.00
281-Gladstone issues start again; Rosa-c		2.00	5.00
285-The Life and Times of Scrooge McDuck Pt. 1; Rosa-c/a/scripts	1.25	3.75	10.00
286-292: The Life and Times of Scrooge McDuck Pt. 2-8; Rosa-c/a/scripts		2.00	5.00
293-($1.95, 36 pgs.)-The Life and Times of Scrooge McDuck Pt. 9			

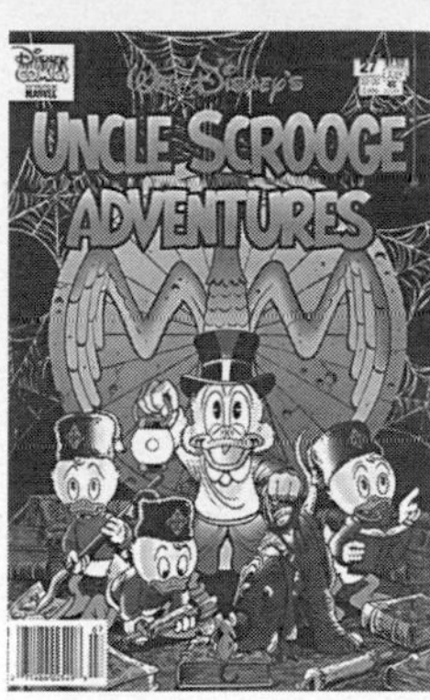

Walt Disney's Uncle Scrooge Adventures #27 © WDC

Wanderers #10 © DC

Wanted Comics #28 © Toytown Publ.

	GD25	FN65	NM94
294-299, 301,304-($1.50, 32 pgs.): 294-296-The Life and Times of Scrooge McDuck Pt. 10-12. 297-The Life and Times of Uncle Scrooge Pt. 0; Rosa-c/a/scripts			1.50
300-($2.25, 48 pgs.)-Rosa-c; Barks-r/WDC&S #104 and U.S. #216; r/U.S. #220; includes new centerfold.		.90	2.25

NOTE: ***Barks** r-210-218, 220-223, 224(2pg.), 225-234, 236-242, 245, 246, 250-253, 255, 256, 258, 261(2 pg.), 265, 267, 268, 270(2), 272-284, 299-present; c(r)-210, 212, 221, 228, 229, 232, 233, 284. scripts-287, 293. **Rosa** a-219, 220, 224, 226, 227, 235, 261-263, 268, 275-277, 285-289; c-219, 224, 231, 261-263, 276, 278-281, 285-289; scripts-219, 220, 224, 235, 261-263, 268, 276, 285-289.*

WALT DISNEY'S UNCLE SCROOGE ADVENTURES (U. Scrooge Advs. #1-3)
Nov, 1987 - No. 21, May, 1990; No. 22, Sept, 1993 - Present
Gladstone Publishing

	GD25	FN65	NM94
1-Barks-r begin, ends #26	1.00	3.00	8.00
2-5: 5-Rosa-c/a; no Barks-r		1.60	4.00
6-19: 9,14-Rosa-a. 10-r/U.S. #18(all Barks)		1.20	3.00
20,21 ($1.95, 68 pgs.) 20-Rosa-c/a. 21-Rosa-a		1.20	3.00
22 ($1.50)-Rosa-c; r/U.S. #26		2.00	5.00
23-($2.95, 68 pgs.)-Vs. The Phantom Blot-r/P.B. #3; Barks-r		1.60	4.00
24-26,29,31,32,34-36: 24,25,29,31,32-Rosa-c. 25-r/U.S. #21		.80	2.00
27-Guardians of the Lost Library - Rosa-c/a/story; origin of Junior Woodchuck Guidebook		1.20	3.00
28-($2.95, 68 pgs.)-r/U.S. #13 w/restored missing panels		1.60	4.00
30-($2.95, 68 pgs.)-r/U.S. #12; Rosa-c		1.60	4.00
33-($2.95, 64 pgs.)-New Barks story		1.20	3.00
37-45: 37-Begin $1.50-c			1.50
46-50: 46-Begin-$1.95-c			1.95

NOTE: ***Barks** r-1-4, 6-8, 10-13, 15-21, 23, 22, 24; c(r)-15, 16, 17, 21. **Rosa** a-5, 9, 14, 20, 21, 27; c-5, 13, 14, 17(finishes), 20, 22, 24, 25, 27, 28; scripts-5, 9, 14, 27.*

WALT DISNEY'S UNCLE SCROOGE ADVENTURES IN COLOR
Dec, 1995 - Present ($8.95, squarebound, 56 issue limited series)(Polybagged w/card)(Series chronologically reprints all the stories written & drawn by Carl Barks)

	GD25	FN65	NM94
1-32: 1-(12/95)-r/FC #386. 15-(12/96)-r/US #15. 16-(12/96)-r/US #16. 18-(1/97)-r/US #18	1.10	3.30	9.00

WALT DISNEY'S WHEATIES PREMIUMS (See Wheaties)

WALTER (Campaign of Terror) (Also see The Mask)
Feb, 1996 - No. 4, May, 1996 ($2.50, limited series)
Dark Horse Comics

	GD25	FN65	NM94
1-4		1.00	2.50

WALTER LANTZ ANDY PANDA (Also see Andy Panda)
Aug, 1973 - No. 23, Jan, 1978 (Walter Lantz)
Gold Key

	GD25	FN65	NM94
1-Reprints	1.10	3.30	9.00
2-10-All reprints		2.00	5.00
11-23: 15,17-19,22-Reprints		1.20	3.00

WALT KELLY'S...
Dec, 1987; Apr, 1988 ($1.75/$2.50, Baxter paper)
Eclipse Comics

	GD25	FN65	NM94
...Christmas Classics 1 (12/87, $1.75)-Kelly-r/Peter Wheat & Santa Claus Funnies		.70	1.75
...Springtime Tales 1 (4/88, $2.50)-Kelly-r		1.00	2.50

WALTONS, THE (See Kite Fun Book)

WALT SCOTT (See Little People)

WALT SCOTT'S CHRISTMAS STORIES (See Christmas Stories, 4-Color #959, 1062)

WAMBI, JUNGLE BOY (See Jungle Comics)
Spr, 1942; No. 2, Win, 1942-43; No. 3, Spr, 1943; No. 4, Fall, 1948; No. 5, Sum, 1949; No. 6, Spr, 1950; No. 7-10, 1950(nd); No. 11, Spr, 1951 - No. 18, Win, 1952-53 (#1-3: 68 pgs.)
Fiction House Magazines

	GD25	FN65	NM94
1-Wambi, the Jungle Boy begins	75.00	225.00	675.00
2 (1942)-Kiefer-c	42.00	126.00	375.00
3 (1943)-Kiefer-c/a	29.00	86.00	230.00
4 (1948)-Origin in text	17.50	53.00	140.00
5 (Fall, 1949, 36 pgs.)-Kiefer-c/a	15.00	45.00	120.00
6-10: 7-(52 pgs.)-New logo	14.00	41.00	110.00
11-18	9.50	28.00	75.00
I.W. Reprint #8('64)-r/#12 with new-c	2.25	6.75	18.00

NOTE: ***Alex Blum** c-8. **Kiefer** c-1-5. **Whitman** c-11-18.*

WANDERERS (See Adventure Comics #375, 376)
June, 1988 - No. 13, Apr, 1989 ($1.25) (Legion of Super-Heroes spin off)
DC Comics

	GD25	FN65	NM94
1-13: 1,2-Steacy-c. 3-Legion app.			1.30

WANDERING STAR
1993 - No. 21, March, 1997 ($2.50/$2.75, B&W)
Pen & Ink Comics/Sirius Entertainment No. 12 on

	GD25	FN65	NM94
1-1st printing; Teri Sue Wood c/a/scripts in all	1.25	3.75	10.00
1-2nd and 3rd printings		1.00	2.50
2-1st printing		2.00	5.00
2-2nd printing		1.00	2.50
3-9: 1st and 2nd printings exist		1.20	3.00
10-11: 10-$2.75-c begins		1.10	2.75
12-21: 12-(1/96)-1st Sirius issue; $2.50-c begins		1.00	2.50
Trade paperback ($11.95)-r/1-7; 1st printing of 1000, signed and numbered			15.00
Trade paperback-2nd printing, 2000 signed			12.00

WANTED COMICS
No. 9, Sept-Oct, 1947 - No. 53, April, 1953 (#9-33: 52 pgs.)
Toytown Publications/Patches/Orbit Publ.

	GD25	FN65	NM94
9-True crime cases; radio's Mr. D. A. app.	14.00	43.00	110.00
10,11: 10-Giunta-a; radio's Mr. D. A. app.	10.00	30.00	65.00
12-Used in **SOTI**, pg. 277	10.00	30.00	75.00
13-Heroin drug propaganda story	9.00	27.00	60.00
14-Marijuana drug mention story (2 pgs.)	7.50	22.50	50.00
15-17,19,20	5.70	17.00	40.00
18-Marijuana story, "Satan's Cigarettes"; r-in #45 & retitled	19.00	47.00	120.00
21,22: 21-Krigstein-a. 22-Extreme violence	7.50	22.50	50.00
23,25-34,36-38,40-44,46-48,53	4.25	13.00	28.00
24-Krigstein-a; "The Dope King", marijuana mention story	7.50	22.50	50.00
35-Used in **SOTI**, pg. 160	7.50	22.50	50.00
39-Drug propaganda story "The Horror Weed"	10.00	30.00	70.00
45-Marijuana story from #18	6.35	19.00	40.00
49-Has unstable pink-c that fades easily; rare in mint condition	5.35	16.00	32.00
50-Has unstable pink-c like #49; surrealist-c by Buscema; horror stories	10.00	30.00	65.00
51- "Holiday of Horror" junkie story; drug-c	7.15	21.50	50.00
52-Classic "Cult of Killers" opium use story	7.15	21.50	50.00

NOTE: ***Buscema** c-50, 51. **Lawrence** and **Leav** c/a most issues. **Syd Shores** c/a-48; c-37. Issues 9-46 have wanted criminals with their descriptions & drawn picture on cover.*

WANTED: DEAD OR ALIVE (TV)
No. 1102, May-July, 1960 - No. 1164, Mar-May, 1961
Dell Publishing Co.

	GD25	FN65	NM94
Four Color 1102 (#1)-Steve McQueen photo-c	12.00	37.00	125.00
Four Color 1164-Steve McQueen photo-c	9.00	27.00	100.00

WANTED, THE WORLD'S MOST DANGEROUS VILLAINS (See DC Special)
July-Aug, 1972 - No. 9, Aug-Sept, 1973 (All reprints & 20¢ issues)
National Periodical Publications

1-Batman, Green Lantern (story r-from G.L. #1), & Green Arrow

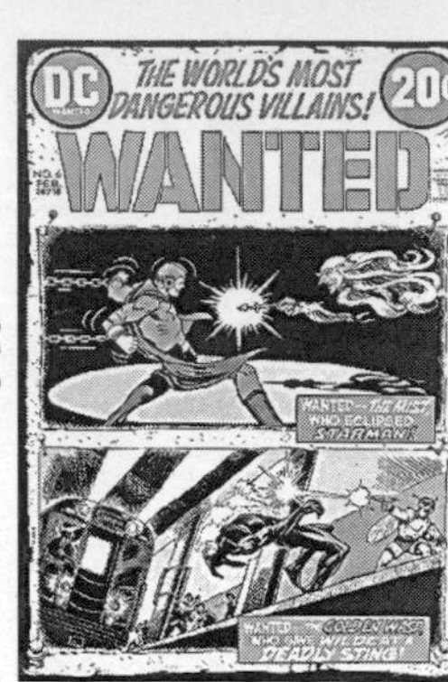

Wanted, The World's Most Dangerous Villains #6 © DC

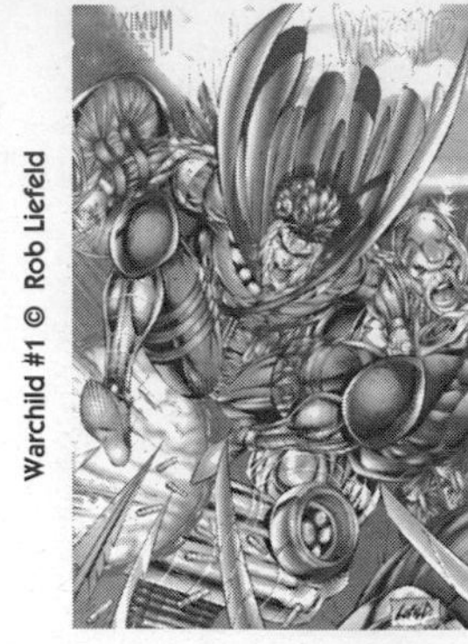
Warchild #1 © Rob Liefeld

War Comics #26 © MEG

	GD25	FN65	NM94
	2.50	7.50	20.00
2-Batman/Joker/Penguin-c/story r-from Batman #25; plus Flash story (r-from Flash #121)	2.50	7.50	20.00
3-9: 3-Dr. Fate(r/More Fun #65), Hawkman(r/Flash #100), & Vigilante(r/Action #69). 4-Gr. Lantern(r/All-American #61) & Kid Eternity(r/Kid Eternity #15). 5-Dollman/Green Lantern. 6-Burnley Starman; Wildcat/Sargon. 7-Johnny Quick(r/More fun #76), Hawkman(r/Flash #90), Hourman by Baily(r/Adv. #72). 8-Dr. Fate/Flash(r/Flash #114). 9-S&K Sandman/Superman	1.25	3.75	10.00

NOTE: ***B. Bailey** a-7r. **Infantino** a-2r. **Kane** r-1, 5. **Kubert** r-3i, 6, 7. **Meskin** r-3, 7. **Reinman** r-4, 6.*

WAR
July, 1975 - No. 9, Nov, 1976; No. 10, Sept, 1978 - No. 49?, 1984
Charlton Comics

	GD25	FN65	NM94
1	1.00	3.00	8.00
2-10		2.00	5.00
11-49: 47-Reprints		1.20	3.00
7,9 (Modern Comics-r, 1977)		1.20	3.00

WAR, THE (See The Draft & The Pitt)
1989 - No. 4, 1990 ($3.50, squarebound, 52 pgs.)
Marvel Comics

	GD25	FN65	NM94
1-4: Characters from New Universe		1.40	3.50

WAR ACTION (Korean War)
April, 1952 - No. 14, June, 1953
Atlas Comics (CPS)

	GD25	FN65	NM94
1	14.00	41.00	110.00
2	10.00	30.00	60.00
3-10,14: 7-Pakula-a	6.70	20.00	45.00
11-13-Krigstein-a	8.35	25.00	55.00

NOTE: ***Brodsky** c-1-4. **Heath** a-1; c-7, 14. **Keller** a-6. **Maneely** a-1. **Tuska** a-2, 8.*

WAR ADVENTURES
Jan, 1952 - No. 13, Feb, 1953
Atlas Comics (HPC)

	GD25	FN65	NM94
1-Tuska-a	12.00	36.00	95.00
2	7.50	22.50	50.00
3-7,9-13: 3-Pakula-a. 7-Maneely-c	5.70	17.00	35.00
8-Krigstein-a	8.35	25.00	55.00

NOTE: ***Brodsky** c-1-3, 6, 8, 11, 12. **Heath** a-5, 7, 10; c-4, 5, 9, 13. **Robinson** a-3; c-10.*

WAR ADVENTURES ON THE BATTLEFIELD (See Battlefield)

WAR AGAINST CRIME! (Becomes Vault of Horror #12 on)
Spring, 1948 - No. 11, Feb-Mar, 1950
E. C. Comics

	GD25	FN65	NM94
1-Real Stories From Police Records on-c #1-9	56.00	170.00	475.00
2,3	33.00	99.00	240.00
4-9	30.00	90.00	220.00
10-1st Vault Keeper app. & 1st Vault of Horror	169.00	506.00	1400.00
11-2nd Vault Keeper app.; 1st horror-c	96.00	290.00	800.00

NOTE: *All have **Johnny Craig** covers. **Feldstein** a-4, 7-9. **Harrison/Wood** a-11. **Ingels** a-1, 2, 8. **Palais** a-8. Changes to horror with #10.*

WAR AND ATTACK (Also see Special War Series #3)
Fall, 1964; V2#54, June, 1966 - V2#63, Dec, 1967
Charlton Comics

	GD25	FN65	NM94
1-Wood-a	2.50	7.50	25.00
V2#54(6/66)-#63 (Formerly Fightin' Air Force)	1.25	3.75	10.00

NOTE: ***Montes/Bache** a-55, 56, 60, 63.*

WAR AT SEA (Formerly Space Adventures)
No. 22, Nov, 1957 - No. 42, June, 1961
Charlton Comics

	GD25	FN65	NM94
22	4.00	11.00	22.00
23-30	1.85	5.50	15.00
31-42	1.50	4.50	12.00

WAR BATTLES
Feb, 1952 - No. 9, Dec, 1953
Harvey Publications

	GD25	FN65	NM94
1-Powell-a; Elias-c	8.50	25.50	85.00
2-Powell-a	4.50	13.50	45.00
3-5,7-9: 3,7-Powell-a	3.80	11.40	38.00
6-Nostrand-a	5.00	15.00	50.00

WAR BIRDS
1952(nd) - No. 3, Winter, 1952-53
Fiction House Magazines

	GD25	FN65	NM94
1	12.00	36.00	90.00
2,3	8.35	25.00	50.00

WARBLADE: ENDANGERED SPECIES (Also see WildC.A.T.S: Covert Action Teams)
Jan, 1995 - No. 4, Apr, 1995 ($2.50, limited series)
Image Comics (Wildstorm Productions)

	GD25	FN65	NM94
1-4: 1-Gatefold wraparound-c		1.00	2.50

WARCHILD
Jan. 1995 - No. 4, Aug, 1995 ($2.50)
Maximum Press

	GD25	FN65	NM94
1-4-Rob Liefeld-c/a/scripts		1.00	2.50
1-4: Variant-c		1.20	3.00
Trade paperback (1/96, $12.95)-r/#1-4.			13.00

WAR COMBAT (Becomes Combat Casey #6 on)
March, 1952 - No. 5, Nov, 1952
Atlas Comics (LBI No. 1/SAI No. 2-5)

	GD25	FN65	NM94
1	10.00	30.00	80.00
2	6.70	20.00	45.00
3-5	5.00	15.00	30.00

NOTE: ***Berg** a-2, 4, 5. **Brodsky** c-1, 2, 4, 5. **Henkel** a-5. **Maneely** a-1, 4; c-3.*

WAR COMICS (War Stories #5 on)(See Key Ring Comics)
May, 1940 (No mo. given) - No. 4, Sept, 1941?
Dell Publishing Co.

	GD25	FN65	NM94
1-Sikandur the Robot Master, Sky Hawk, Scoop Mason, War Correspondent begin; McWilliams-c; 1st war comic	44.00	132.00	400.00
2-Origin Greg Gilday (5/41)	28.00	83.00	220.00
3-Joan becomes Greg Gilday's aide	17.50	53.00	140.00
4-Origin Night Devils	20.00	60.00	160.00

WAR COMICS
Dec, 1950 - No. 49, Sept, 1957
Marvel/Atlas (USA No. 1-41/JPI No. 42-49)

	GD25	FN65	NM94
1	19.00	58.00	150.00
2	10.00	30.00	75.00
3-10	9.00	27.00	60.00
11-Flame thrower w/burning bodies on-c	10.00	30.00	65.00
12-20	7.50	22.50	50.00
21,23-32: 26-Valley Forge story. 32-Last precode issue (2/55)	5.70	17.00	35.00
22-Krigstein-a	9.00	27.50	55.00
33-37,39-42,44,45,47,48	5.70	17.00	35.00
38-Kubert/Moskowitz-a	7.50	22.50	45.00
43,49-Torres-a. 43-Severin/Elder E.C. swipe from Two-Fisted Tales #31	7.50	22.50	45.00
46-Crandall-a	7.50	22.50	45.00

NOTE: ***Colan** a-4, 36, 48, 49. **Drucker** a-37, 43, 48. **Everett** a-17. **Heath** a-7-9, 16, 19, 25, 36; c-11, 16, 19, 25, 26, 29-31, 36. **G. Kane** a-19. **Lawrence** a-36. **Maneely** a-7, 9; c-6, 27, 37. **Orlando** a-42, 48. **Pakula** a-26. **Ravielli** a-27. **Reinman** a-26. **Robinson** a-15; c-13. **Severin** a-26, 27; c-48.*

WAR DANCER (Also see Charlemagne, Doctor Chaos #2 & Warriors of Plasm)
Feb, 1994 - No. 6, July, 1994 ($2.50)
Defiant

Warfront #1 © HARV

War Heroes #7 © DELL

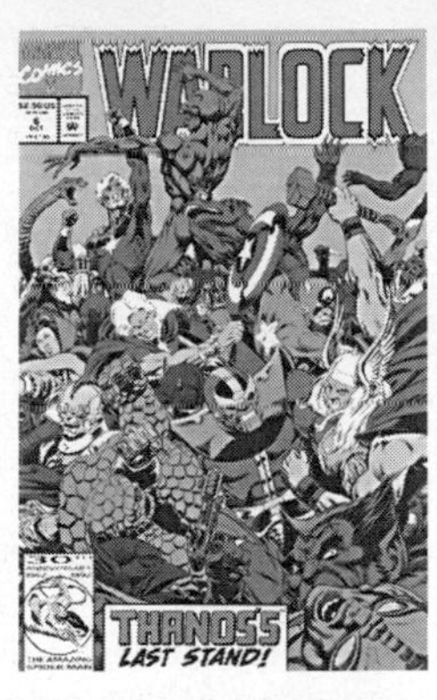

Warlock #6 © MEG

	GD25	FN65	NM94
1-3,5,6: 1-Intro War Dancer; Weiss-c/a begins. 1-3-Weiss-a(p). 6-Pre-Schism issue		1.00	2.50
4-($3.25, 52 pgs.)-Charlemagne app.		1.30	3.25

WAR DOGS OF THE U.S. ARMY
1952
Avon Periodicals

	GD25	FN65	NM94
1-Kinstler-c/a	11.30	34.00	90.00

WARFRONT
9/51 - #35, 11/58; #36, 10/65; #39, 2/67
Harvey Publications

	GD25	FN65	NM94
1-Korean War	8.50	25.50	85.00
2	4.50	13.50	45.00
3-10	3.20	9.60	32.00
11,12,14,16-20	2.20	6.60	22.00
13,15,22-Nostrand-a	5.00	15.00	50.00
21,23-27,29,31-33,35	2.20	6.60	22.00
28,30,34-Kirby-c	4.50	13.50	45.00
36-(12/66)-Dynamite Joe begins, ends #39; Williamson-a	3.00	9.00	30.00
37-Wood-a (17 pgs.)	3.00	9.00	30.00
38,39-Wood-a, 2-3 pgs.; Lone Tiger app.	2.00	6.00	20.00

NOTE: ***Powell*** *a-1-6, 9-11, 14, 17, 20, 23, 25-28, 30, 31, 34, 36.* ***Powell/Nostrand*** *a-12, 13, 15.* ***Simon*** *c-36?, 38.*

WAR FURY
Sept, 1952 - No. 4, Mar, 1953
Comic Media/Harwell (Allen Hardy Associates)

	GD25	FN65	NM94
1-Heck-c/a in all; Palais-a; bullet hole in forehead-c; all issues are very violent	9.00	27.00	70.00
2-4: 4-Morisi-a	5.70	17.00	40.00

WAR GODS OF THE DEEP (See Movie Classics)

WARHAWKS
1990 - No. 10, 1991 ($2.95, 44 pgs.)
TSR, Inc.

	GD25	FN65	NM94
1-10-Based on TSR game, Spiegle a-1-6		1.20	3.00

WARHEADS
June, 1992 - No. 14, Aug, 1993 ($1.75)
Marvel Comics UK

	GD25	FN65	NM94
1-Wolverine-c/story; indicia says #2 by mistake		.80	2.00
2-14: 2-Nick Fury app. 3-Iron Man-c/story. 4,5-X-Force. 5-Liger vs. Cable. 6,7-Death's Head II app. (#6 is cameo)		.70	1.75

WAR HEROES (See Marine War Heroes)

WAR HEROES
7-9/42 (no month); No. 2, 10-12/42 - No. 11, 3/45
Dell Publishing Co. (Published quarterly)

	GD25	FN65	NM94
1-General Douglas MacArthur-c	20.00	60.00	160.00
2	10.50	32.00	85.00
3,5: 3-Pro-Russian back-c	8.75	26.25	65.00
4-Disney's Gremlins app.	14.50	43.00	115.00
6-11: 6-Tothish-a by Discount	7.50	22.50	52.00

NOTE: *No. 1 was to be released in July, but was delayed. Painted c-4, 6-9.*

WAR HEROES
May, 1952 - No. 8, Apr, 1953
Ace Magazines

	GD25	FN65	NM94
1	9.00	27.00	55.00
2-Lou Cameron-a	5.35	16.00	32.00
3-8: 6,7-Cameron-a	4.00	12.00	24.00

WAR HEROES (Also see Blue Bird Comics)
Feb, 1963 - No. 27, Nov, 1967
Charlton Comics

	GD25	FN65	NM94
1,2: 2-John F. Kennedy story	2.50	7.50	20.00
3-10	1.50	4.50	12.00
11-27	1.00	3.00	8.00
27-1st Devils Brigade by Glanzman	1.25	3.75	10.00

NOTE: ***Montes/Bache*** *a-3-7, 21, 25, 27; c-3-7.*

WAR IS HELL
Jan, 1973 - No. 15, Oct, 1975
Marvel Comics Group

	GD25	FN65	NM94
1-Williamson-a(r), 5 pgs.; Ayers-a	1.25	3.75	10.00
2-8-Reprints	1.00	2.80	7.00
9-Intro Death	2.50	7.50	20.00
10-15-Death app.	1.00	3.00	8.00

NOTE: ***Bolle*** *a-3r.* ***Powell*** *a-1.* ***Woodbridge*** *a-1. Sgt. Fury reprints-7, 8.*

WARLOCK (The Power of...)(Also see Fantastic Four #66, 67, Incredible Hulk #178, Infinity Crusade, Infinity Gauntlet, Infinity War, Marvel Premiere #1, Silver Surfer V3#46, Strange Tales #178-181 & Thor #165)
Aug, 1972 - No. 8, Oct, 1973; No. 9, Oct, 1975 - No. 15, Nov, 1976
Marvel Comics Group

	GD25	FN65	NM94
1-Origin by Kane	1.85	5.50	15.00
2,3		2.40	6.00
4-8: 4-Death of Eddie Roberts		2.00	5.00
9-Starlin's 2nd Thanos saga begins, ends #15; new costume Warlock; Thanos cameo only; story cont'd from Strange Tales #178-181; Starlin-c/a in #9-15	1.00	3.00	7.50
10-Origin Thanos & Gamora; recaps events from Capt. Marvel #25-34. Thanos vs.The Magus-c/story	2.25	6.75	18.00
11-Thanos app.; Warlock dies	1.50	4.50	12.00
12,14: 14-Origin Star Thief; last 25¢ issue		2.00	5.00
13-(Regular 25¢ edition)(6/76)		2.40	6.00
13-(30¢-c, limited distribution)	2.50	7.50	24.00
15-Thanos-c/story	1.25	3.75	10.00

NOTE: ***Buscema*** *a-2p; c-8p.* ***G. Kane*** *a-1p, 3-5p; c-1p, 2, 3, 4p, 5p, 7p.* ***Starlin*** *a-9-14p, 15; c-9, 10, 11p, 12p, 13-15.* ***Sutton*** *a-1-8i.*

WARLOCK (...Special Edition on-c)
Dec, 1982 - No. 6, May, 1983 ($2.00, slick paper, 52 pgs.)
Marvel Comics Group

	GD25	FN65	NM94
1-6: 1-Warlock-r/Strange Tales #178-180. 2-r/Str. Tales #180,181 & Warlock #9. 3-r/Warlock #10-12(Thanos origin recap). 4-r/Warlock #12-15. 5-r/Warlock #15, Marvel Team-Up #55 & Avengers Ann. #7. 6-r/2nd half Avengers Annual #7 & Marvel Two-in-One Annual #2		2.00	5.00
Special Edition #1(12/83)		.90	2.25

NOTE: ***Byrne*** *a-5r.* ***Starlin*** *a-1-6r; c-1-6(new). Direct sale only.*

WARLOCK
V2#1, May, 1992 - No. 6, Oct, 1992 ($2.50, limited series)
Marvel Comics

	GD25	FN65	NM94
V2#1-6: 1-Reprints 1982 reprint series w/Thanos		1.00	2.50

WARLOCK AND THE INFINITY WATCH (Also see Infinity Gauntlet)
Feb, 1992 - No. 42, July, 1995 ($1.75) (Sequel to Infinity Gauntlet)
Marvel Comics

	GD25	FN65	NM94
1-Starlin scripts begin; brief origin recap Warlock; sequel to Infinity Gauntlet		1.00	2.50
2,3: 2-Reintro Moondragon		.80	2.00
4-24,26: 7-Reintro The Magus; Moondragon app.; Thanos cameo on last 2 pgs. 8,9-Thanos battles Gamora-c/story. 8-Magus & Moondragon app. 10-Thanos-c/story; Magus app. 13-Hulk x-over. 21-Drax vs. Thor		.70	1.75
25-($2.95, 52 pgs.)-Die-cut & embossed double-c; Thor & Thanos app.		1.20	3.00
28-42: 28-$1.95-c begins; bound-in card sheet		.80	2.00

NOTE: ***Austin*** *c/a-1-4i, 7i.* ***Leonardi*** *a(p)-3, 4.* ***Medina*** *c/a(p)-1, 2, 5; 6, 9, 10, 14, 15, 20.* ***Williams*** *a(i)-8, 12, 13, 16-19.*

WARLOCK CHRONICLES

Warlord #58 © DC

War Machine #6 © MEG

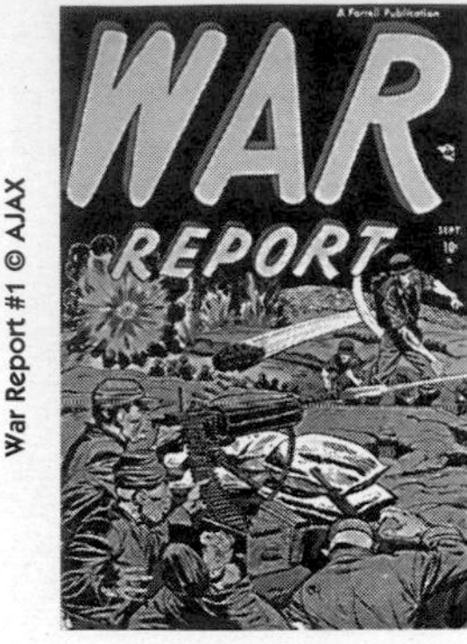

War Report #1 © AJAX

GD25 FN65 NM94

June, 1993 - No. 8, Feb, 1994 ($2.00, limited series)
Marvel Comics

1-($2.95)-Holo-grafx foil & embossed-c; origin retold; Starlin scripts begin; Keith Williams-a(i) in all 1.20 3.00
2-8: 3-Thanos & Mephisto-c/story. 4-Vs. Magus-c/s. 8-Contains free 16 pg. Razorline insert .80 2.00

WARLOCK 5
11/86 - No. 22, 5/89; V2#1, June, 1989 - V2#5?, 1989 ($1.70, B&W)
Aircel Publishing

1-9-All issues by Barry Blair. 5-Green Cyborg on-c. 6-Misnumbered; Blue Girl on-c. 1.70
10-22: 18-$1.95-c begins .80 2.00
V2#1-5 ($2.00, B&W) .80 2.00
Compilation 1-r/#1-5 (1988, $5.95) 2.40 6.00
Compilation 2-r/#6-9 ($5.95) 2.40 6.00

WARLORD (See 1st Issue Special #8)
1-2/76; No.2, 3-4/76; No.3, 10-11/76 - No. 133, Win, 1988-89
National Periodical Publications/DC Comics #123 on

1-Story cont'd. from 1st Issue Special #8 2.40 6.00
2-Intro. Machiste 1.20 3.00
3-5 1.00 2.50
6-10: 6-Intro Mariah. 7-Origin Machiste. 9-Dons new costume .80 2.00
11-20: 11-Origin-r. 12-Intro Aton. 15-Tara returns; Warlord has son 1.20 3.00
21-36,40: 27-New facts about origin. 28-1st app. Wizard World. 32-Intro Shakira. 40-Warlord gets new costume .80 2.00
37-39: 37,38-Origin Omac by Starlin. 38-Intro Jennifer Morgan, Warlord's daughter. 39-Omac ends. 1.20 3.00
41,49-52: 49-Claw The Unconquered app. 50-Death of Aton. 51-Reprints #1 1.50
42-47-Omac back-up series .80 2.00
48-(52 pgs.)-1st app. Arak; contains free 14 pg. Arak Son of Thunder; Claw The Unconquered app. .80 2.00
53-130,132: 55-Arion Lord of Atlantis begins, ends #62. 63-The Barren Earth begins; free 16pg. Masters of the Universe preview. 91-Origin w/new facts. 114,115-Legends x-over. 100-($1.25, 52 pgs.). 125-Death of Tara 1.50
131-1st DC work by Rob Liefeld (9/88) 2.40 6.00
133-($1.50, 52 pgs.) 1.60 4.00
Remco Toy Giveaway (2-3/4x4") 1.00
Annual 1(1982)-Grell-c,/a(p) .80 2.00
Annual 2-6: 2(1983). 3(1984). 4(1985). 5(1986). 6(1987, $1.25)-New Gods app. 1.00

NOTE: ***Grell*** *a-1-15, 16-50p, 51r, 52p, 59p, Annual 1p; c-1-70, 100-104, 112, 116, 117, Annual 1, 5.* ***Wayne Howard*** *a-64i.* ***Starlin*** *a-37-39p.*

WARLORD
Jan, 1992 - No. 6, June, 1992 ($1.75, limited series)
DC Comics

1-6: Grell-c & scripts in all .70 1.75

WARLORDS (See DC Graphic Novel #2)

WAR MAN
Nov, 1993 - No. 2, Dec, 1993 ($2.50, limited series)
Marvel Comics (Epic Comics)

1,2 1.00 2.50

WAR MACHINE (Also see Iron Man #281,282 & Marvel Comics Presents #152)
Apr, 1994 - No. 25, Apr, 1996 ($1.50)
Marvel Comics

"Ashcan" edition (nd, 75¢, B&W, 16 pgs.) .75
1-($2.00, 52 pgs.)-Newsstand edition; Cable app. .80 2.00
1-($2.95, 52 pgs.)-Collectors ed.; embossed foil-c 1.20 3.00
2-14, 16-25: 2-Bound-in trading card sheet; Cable app. 2,3-Deathlok app. 8-red logo 1.50
8-($2.95)-Polybagged w/16 pg. Marvel Action Hour preview & acetate print; yellow logo 1.20 3.00
15 ($2.50)-Flip book 1.00 2.50

WAR OF THE GODS
Sept, 1991 - No. 4, Dec, 1991 ($1.75, limited series)
DC Comics

1-4: Perez layouts, scripts & covers. 1-Contains free mini posters (Robin, Deathstroke). 2-4-Direct sale versions include 4 pin-ups printed on cover stock plus different-c .75 1.80

WAR OF THE WORLDS, THE
1996 - Present ($2.95, B&W, 32 pgs.)(Based on H. G. Wells novel)
Caliber

1-Randy Zimmerman scripts begin 1.20 3.00

WARP
Mar, 1983 - No. 19, Feb, 1985 ($1.00/$1.25, Mando paper)
First Comics

1-Sargon-Mistress of War app. 1.00
2-19: 2-Faceless Ones begin. 10-New Warp advs., & Outrider begin 1.25
Special 1-3: 1(7/83, 36 pgs.)-Origin Chaos-Prince of Madness; origin of Warp Universe begins, ends #3. 2(1/84)-Lord Cumulus vs. Sargon Mistress of War ($1.00). 3(6/84)-Chaos-Prince of Madness 1.00

WAR PARTY
Oct, 1994 (2.95, B&W)
Lightning Comics

1-1st app. Deathmark 1.20 3.00

WARPED
June, 1990 - No. 2, Oct-Nov, 1990 (B&W magazine)
Empire Entertainment (Solson)

1,2 .80 2.00

WARPATH (Indians on the...)
Nov, 1954 - No. 3, Apr, 1955
Key Publications/Stanmor

1 8.50 26.00 60.00
2,3 5.70 17.00 35.00

WARP GRAPHICS ANNUAL
Dec, 1985; 1988 ($2.50)
WaRP Graphics

1-Elfquest, Blood of the Innocent, Thunderbunny & Myth Adventures app. 1.00 2.50
1 (1988) 1.00 2.50

WARREN PRESENTS
Jan, 1979 - No. 14, Nov, 1981
Warren Publications

1-Eerie, Creepy, & Vampirella-r begin 1.85 5.50 15.00
2-14 1.25 3.75 10.00
...The Rook 1 (5/79)-r/Eerie #82-85 1.25 3.75 10.00

WAR REPORT
Sept, 1952 - No. 5, May, 1953
Ajax/Farrell Publications (Excellent Publ.)

1 10.00 30.00 60.00
2 5.70 17.00 35.00
3-5: 4-Used in **POP**, pg. 94 5.00 15.00 30.00

WARRIOR (Wrestling star)
May, 1996 - Present ($2.95)
Ultimate Creations

1-4: Warrior scripts; Callahan-c/a. 3-Wraparound-c. 4-Warrior #3 in indicia; pin-ups 1.20 3.00

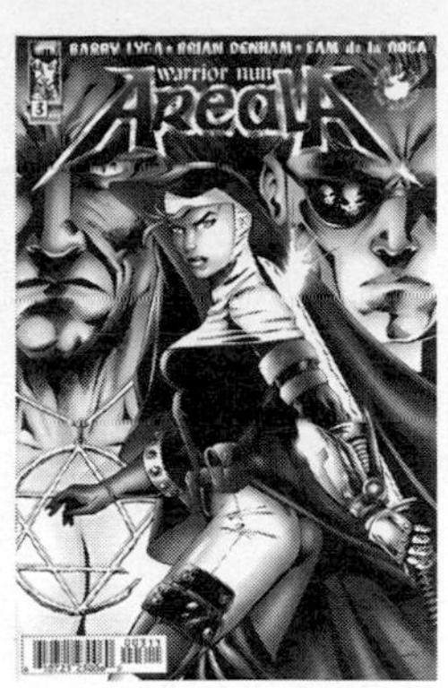

Warrior Nun Areala #3 © Antarctic Press

Warstrike #4 © MAL

War Victory Adventures #2 © HARV

GD25 FN65 NM94

1-Variant-c. 1.00 2.80 7.00

WARRIOR COMICS
1945 (1930s DC reprints)
H.C. Blackerby

1-Wing Brady, The Iron Man, Mark Markon 15.50 47.00 125.00

WARRIOR NUN AREALA
Dec, 1994 - No. 3, Apr, 1995 ($2.95, limited series)
Antarctic Press

1 1.25 3.75 10.00
1-Special Edition (5000) 1.85 5.50 15.00
2-3 1.00 2.80 7.00
3-Bagged w/CD 1.00 2.80 7.00

WARRIOR NUN AREALA, 7/97 - Present ($2.95), Antarctic Press
1-3-Lyga-s 2.95

WARRIOR NUN AREALA AND AVENGELYNE 1996 (See Avengelyne/...)
Dec, 1996 ($2.95), Antarctic Press

1 1.20 3.00

WARRIOR NUN AREALA AND GLORY, 9/97 - '97, Antarctic Press
1-Ben Dunn-s/a ($2.95, color) 2.95
1-($5.95) Ltd. Poster Edition w/pin-ups 5.95

WARRIOR NUN AREALA: BLACK AND WHITE, 2/97 - Present ($2.95, B&W)
Antarctic Press

1-5 1.20 3.00

WARRIOR NUN AREALA: HAMMER AND THE HOLOCAUST
6/97- Present ($2.95), Antarctic Press

1,2 1.20 3.00

WARRIOR NUN AREALA: PORTRAITS, 3/96 ($3.95, one-shot), Antarctic Press
1-Pin-ups 1.60 4.00

WARRIOR NUN AREALA: RITUALS, 7/95 - No. 6, 6/96 ($2.95), Antarctic Press
1-6: 6-($3.50) 1.20 3.00

WARRIOR NUN AREALA: SCORPIO ROSE, 9/96 - #4, '96($2.95, color)
Antarctic Press

1-4 1.20 3.00

WARRIOR NUN AREALA VS. RAZOR (See Razor/...), 5/96 ($3.95, one-shot)
Antarctic Press

1-Dunn-c/a 1.60 4.00
1-($9.95)-Comic polybagged w/CD 1.25 3.75 10.00

WARRIOR NUN DEI: AFTERTIME, 1/97 - No. 3, ($2.95), Antarctic Press
1-3-Patrick Thornton-s/a 1.20 3.00

WARRIOR OF WAVERLY STREET, THE
Nov, 1996 - No. 2, Dec, 1996 ($2.95, mini-series)
Dark Horse Comics

1,2-Darrow-c 1.20 3.00

WARRIORS
1993 (B&W, one-shot)
CFD Productions

1-Linsner, Dark One-a 2.50 7.50 25.00

WARRIORS OF PLASM (Also see Plasm)
Aug, 1993 - No. 13, Aug, 1995 ($2.95/$2.50)
Defiant

1-4: Shooter-scripts; Lapham-c/a: 1-1st app. Glory. 4-Bound-in fold-out poster
1.20 3.00
5-7,10-13: 5-Begin $2.50-c. 13-Schism issue 1.00 2.50
8,9-($2.75, 44 pgs.) 1.10 2.75
The Collected Edition (2/94, $9.95)-r/Plasm #0, WOP #1-4 & Splatterball
1.25 3.75 10.00

GD25 FN65 NM94

WAR ROMANCES (See True...)

WAR SHIPS
1942 (36 pgs.)(Similar to Large Feature Comics)
Dell Publishing Co.

nn-Cover by McWilliams; contains photos & drawings of U.S. war ships
14.00 41.00 100.00

WAR STORIES (Formerly War Comics)
No. 5, 1942(nd); No. 6, Aug-Oct, 1942 - No. 8, Feb-Apr, 1943
Dell Publishing Co.

5-Origin The Whistler 21.00 62.00 165.00
6-8: 6-8-Night Devils app. 8-Painted-c 15.00 45.00 120.00

WAR STORIES (Korea)
Sept, 1952 - No. 5, May, 1953
Ajax/Farrell Publications (Excellent Publ.)

1 9.00 27.00 55.00
2 4.25 13.00 28.00
3-5 4.00 12.00 24.00

WAR STORIES (See Star Spangled...)

WARSTRIKE
May, 1994 - No. 7, Nov, 1995 ($1.95)
Malibu Comics (Ultraverse)

1-7: 1-Simonson-c .80 2.00
1-Ultra 5000 Limited silver foil 1.60 4.00
Giant Size 1 (12/94, 2.50, 44pgs.)-Prelude to Godwheel 1.00 2.50

WART AND THE WIZARD (See The Sword & the Stone under Movie Comics)
Feb, 1964 (Walt Disney)(Characters from Sword in the Stone movie)
Gold Key

1 (10102-402) 2.75 8.00 30.00

WARTIME ROMANCES
July, 1951 - No. 18, Nov, 1953
St. John Publishing Co.

1-All Baker-c/a 24.00 73.00 180.00
2-All Baker-c/a 17.00 49.00 125.00
3,4-All Baker-c/a 15.00 45.00 110.00
5-8-Baker-c/a(2-3) each 12.00 36.00 90.00
9,11,12,16,18: Baker-c/a each. 9-Two signed stories by Estrada
10.00 30.00 70.00
10,13-15,17-Baker-c only 5.70 17.00 40.00

WAR VICTORY ADVENTURES (#1 titled War Victory Comics)
Summer, 1942 - No. 3, Winter, 1943-44 (5¢)
U.S. Treasury Dept./War Victory/Harvey Publ.

1-(Promotion of Savings Bonds)-Featuring America's greatest comic art by top syndicated cartoonists; Blondie, Joe Palooka, Green Hornet, Dick Tracy, Superman, Gumps, etc.; (36 pgs.); all profits were contributed to U.S.O. & Army/Navy relief funds 30.00 90.00 240.00
2-Battle of Stalingrad story; Powell-a (8/43); flag-c 15.00 45.00 120.00
3-Capt. Red Cross-c & text only; Powell-a 14.00 41.00 110.00

WAR WAGON, THE (See Movie Classics)

WAR WINGS
Oct, 1968
Charlton Comics

1 1.50 4.50 12.00

WARWORLD!
Feb, 1989 ($1.75, B&W, one-shot)
Dark Horse Comics

1-Gary Davis sci/fi art in Moebius style .75 1.80

WARZONE

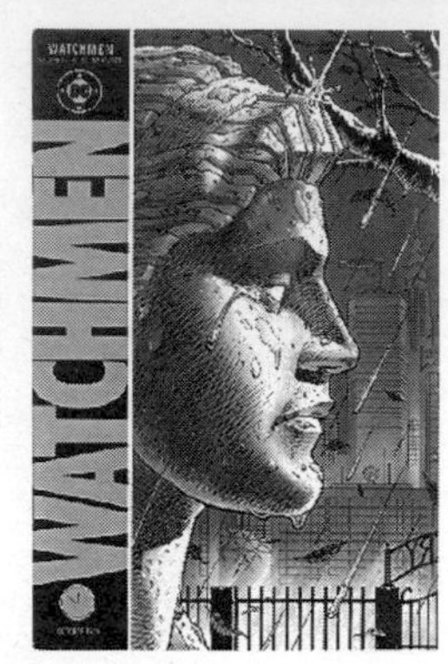

Watchmen #2 © DC

Weapon Zero #9 © Top Cow

Web of Evil #10 © CM

1995 ($2.95, B&W)
Entity Comics

	GD25	FN65	NM94
1-3		1.20	3.00

WASHABLE JONES AND THE SHMOO (Also see Al Capp's Shmoo)
June, 1953
Toby Press

	GD25	FN65	NM94
1- "Super-Shmoo"	16.00	49.00	130.00

WASH TUBBS (See The Comics, Crackajack Funnies)
No. 11, 1942 - No. 53, 1944
Dell Publishing Co.

	GD25	FN65	NM94
Four Color 11 (#1)	27.00	80.00	295.00
Four Color 28 (1943)	20.00	59.00	215.00
Four Color 53	14.00	44.00	160.00

WASTELAND
Dec, 1987 - No. 18, May, 1989 ($1.75-$2.00 #13 on, mature)
DC Comics

	GD25	FN65	NM94
1-5(4/88), 5(5/88), 6(5/88)-18: 13,15-Orlando-a		.80	2.00

NOTE: ***Orlando*** *a-12, 13, 15.* ***Truman*** *a-10; c-13.*

WATCHMEN
Sept, 1986 - No. 12, Oct, 1987 (maxi-series)
DC Comics

	GD25	FN65	NM94
1-Alan Moore scripts & Dave Gibbons-c/a in all		2.00	5.00
2-12		1.20	3.00
Hardcover Collection-Slip-cased-r/#1-12 w/new material; produced by Graphitti Designs	5.00	15.00	50.00
Trade paperback (1987, $14.95)-r/#1-12	1.85	5.50	15.00

WATCH OUT FOR BIG TALK
1950
Giveaway

	GD25	FN65	NM94
nn-Dan Barry-a; about crooked politicians	4.00	12.00	24.00

WATER BIRDS AND THE OLYMPIC ELK (Disney)
No. 700, Apr, 1956
Dell Publishing Co.

	GD25	FN65	NM94
Four Color 700-Movie	4.50	13.50	50.00

WATERWORLD: CHILDREN OF LEVIATHAN
Aug, 1997 - No. 4, Nov, 1997 ($2.50, mini-series)
Acclaim Comics

	GD25	FN65	NM94
1-4		1.00	2.50

WEAPON X
Apr, 1994 ($12.95, one-shot)
Marvel Comics

	GD25	FN65	NM94
nn-r/Marvel Comics Presents #72-84	1.60	4.85	13.00

WEAPON X
Mar, 1995 - No. 4, June, 1995 ($1.95)
Marvel Comics

	GD25	FN65	NM94
1-Age of Apocalypse		1.70	4.20
2-4		.80	2.00

WEAPON ZERO
No. T-4(#1), June, 1995 - No. T-0(#5), Dec, 1995 ($2.50, limited series)
Image Comics (Top Cow Productions)

	GD25	FN65	NM94
T-4(#1): Walt Simonson scripts in all.	1.10	3.30	9.00
T-3(#2) - T-1(#4)		2.40	6.00
T-0(#5)		2.00	5.00

WEAPON ZERO
V2#1, Mar, 1996 - Present ($2.50)
Image Comics (Top Cow Productions)

	GD25	FN65	NM94
V2#1-Walt Simonson scripts.		2.00	5.00
2-10: 8-Begin Top Cow. 10-Devil's Reign		1.60	4.00
11-14		1.00	2.50
15-($3.50) Benitez-a			3.50

WEAPON ZERO/SILVER SURFER
Jan, 1997($2.95, one-shot)
Image Comics/Marvel Comics

	GD25	FN65	NM94
1-Devil's Reign Pt. 1		1.20	3.00

WEASEL PATROL SPECIAL, THE (Also see Fusion #17)
Apr, 1989 ($2.00, B&W, one-shot)
Eclipse Comics

	GD25	FN65	NM94
1-Funny animal		.80	2.00

WEATHER-BIRD (See Comics From..., Dick Tracy, Free Comics to You... & Terry and the Pirates)
1958 - No. 16, July, 1962 (Shoe store giveaway)
International Shoe Co./Western Printing Co.

	GD25	FN65	NM94
1	2.50	7.50	22.00
2-16	1.50	4.50	12.00

NOTE: *The numbers are located in the lower bottom panel, pg. 1. All feature a character called Weather-Bird.*

WEATHER BIRD COMICS (See Comics From Weather Bird)
1957 (Giveaway)
Weather Bird Shoes

nn-Contains a comic bound with new cover. Several combinations possible; contents determines price (40 - 60 percent of contents).

WEAVEWORLD
Dec, 1991 - No. 3, 1992 ($4.95, limited series, 68 pgs.)
Marvel Comics (Epic Comics)

	GD25	FN65	NM94
1-3: Clive Barker adaptation		2.00	5.00

WEB, THE (Also see Mighty Comics & Mighty Crusaders)
Sept, 1991 - No. 14, Oct, 1992 ($1.00)
DC Comics (Impact Comics)

	GD25	FN65	NM94
1-14: 5-The Fly x-over 9-Trading card inside			1.00
Annual 1 (1992, $2.50, 68 pgs.)-With Trading card		1.00	2.50

NOTE: ***Gil Kane*** *c-5, 9, 10, 12-14.* ***Bill Wray*** *a(i)-1-9, 10(part).*

WEB OF EVIL
Nov, 1952 - No. 21, Dec, 1954
Comic Magazines/Quality Comics Group

	GD25	FN65	NM94
1-Used in **SOTI**, pg. 388. Jack Cole-a; morphine use story	43.00	128.00	365.00
2-4,6,7: 2,3-Jack Cole-a. 4,6,7-Jack Cole-c/a	33.00	99.00	240.00
5-Electrocution-c/story; Jack Cole-c/a	37.00	111.00	270.00
8-11-Jack Cole-a	28.00	84.00	210.00
12,13,15,16,19-21	14.00	41.00	110.00
14-Part Crandall-c; Old Witch swipe	15.00	45.00	120.00
17-Opium drug propaganda story	14.00	41.00	110.00
18-Acid-in-face story	17.00	49.00	125.00

NOTE: ***Jack Cole*** *a(2 each)-2, 6, 8, 9.* ***Cuidera*** *c-1-21i.* ***Ravielli*** *a-13.*

WEB OF HORROR
Dec, 1969 - No. 3, Apr, 1970 (Magazine)
Major Magazines

	GD25	FN65	NM94
1-Jeff Jones painted-c; Wrightson-a	7.50	22.50	75.00
2-Jones painted-c; Wrightson-a(2), Kaluta-a	5.00	15.00	50.00
3-Wrightson-c/a (1st published-c); Brunner, Kaluta, Bruce Jones-a	5.00	15.00	50.00

WEB OF MYSTERY
Feb, 1951 - No. 29, Sept, 1955
Ace Magazines (A. A. Wyn)

	GD25	FN65	NM94
1	40.00	120.00	300.00
2-Bakerish-a	21.00	62.00	155.00

Web of Spider-Man #13 © MEG

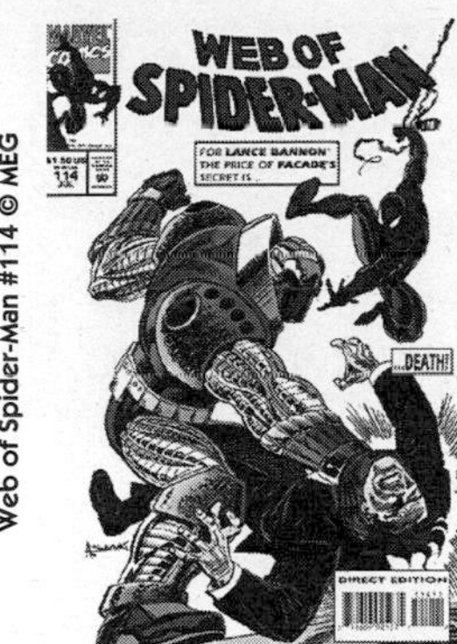

Web of Spider-Man #114 © MEG

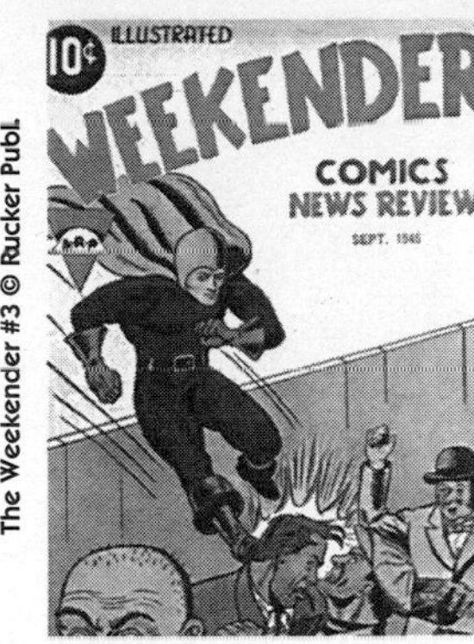

The Weekender #3 © Rucker Publ.

GD25 FN65 NM94

3-10: 4-Colan-a 19.00 58.00 145.00
11-18,20-26: 12-John Chilly's 1st cover art. 13-Surrealistic-c. 20-r/The Beyond #1 17.00 49.00 125.00
19-Reprints Challenge of the Unknown #6 used in N.Y. Legislative Committee 17.00 49.00 125.00
27-Bakerish-a(r/The Beyond #2); last pre-code ish 16.00 47.00 120.00
28,29: 28-All-r 11.50 34.00 85.00

NOTE: *This series was to appear as "Creepy Stories", but title was changed before publication.* ***Cameron*** *a-6, 8, 11-13, 17-20, 22, 24, 25, 27; c-8, 13, 17.* ***Palais*** *a-28r.* ***Sekowsky*** *a-1-3, 7, 8, 11, 14, 21, 29.* ***Tothish*** *a-by* ***Bill Discount*** *#16. 29-all-r, 19-28-partial-r.*

WEB OF SCARLET SPIDER
Oct, 1995 - No. 4, Jan, 1996 ($1.95, limited series)
Marvel Comics

1-4: Replaces "Web of Spider-Man" .80 2.00

WEB OF SPIDER-MAN (Replaces Marvel Team-Up)
Apr, 1985 - No. 129, Sept, 1995
Marvel Comics Group

1-Painted-c (5th app. black costume?) 2.00 6.00 16.00
2,3 2.40 6.00
4-8: 7-Hulk x-over; Wolverine splash 2.00 5.00
9-13: 10-Dominic Fortune guest stars; painted-c 1.60 4.00
14-28: 18-1st app. Venom (behind the scenes, 9/86). 19-Intro Humbug & Solo 1.20 3.00
29-Wolverine, new Hobgoblin (Macendale) app. 1.40 6.00
30-Origin recap The Rose & Hobgoblin I (entire book is flashback story); Punisher & Wolverine cameo 1.40 6.00
31,32-Six part Kraven storyline begins 2.00 5.00
33-37,39-47,49: 36-1st app. Tombstone (cameo) .80 2.00
38-Hobgoblin app.; begin $1.00-c 1.60 4.00
48-Origin Hobgoblin II(Demogoblin) cont'd from Spectacular Spider-Man #147; Kingpin app. 1.60 4.85 13.00
50-($1.50, 52 pgs.) 1.50
51-58 1.50
59-Cosmic Spidey cont'd from Spect. Spider-Man 2.00 5.00
60-65,68-85,87-89,91-94: 69,70-Hulk x-over. 74-76-Austin-c(i). 76-Fantastic Four x-over. 78-Cloak & Dagger app. 81-Origin/1st app. Bloodshed. 84-Begin 6 part Rose & Hobgoblin II storyline; last $1.00-c. 93-Gives brief history of Hobgoblin. 93,94-Hobgoblin (Macendale) Reborn-c/story, parts 1,2; Moon Knight app. 94-Venom cameo 1.50
66,67-Green Goblin (Norman Osborn) app. as a super-hero 1.50
86-Demon leaves Hobgoblin; 1st Demogoblin 1.50
90-($2.95, 52 pgs.)-Polybagged w/silver hologram-c, gatefold poster showing Spider-Man & Spider-Man 2099 (Williamson-i) .80 2.00
90-2nd printing; gold hologram-c 1.50
95-Begin 4 part x-over w/Spirits of Venom w/Ghost Rider/Blaze/Spidey vs. Venom & Demogoblin (cont'd in Ghost Rider/Blaze #5,6) 1.50
96-99,101-106: 96-Spirits of Venom part 3; painted-c. 101,103-Maximum Carnage x-over. 103-Venom & Carnage app. 104-106-Nightwatch back-up stories 1.50
100-($2.95, 52 pgs.)-Holo-grafx foil-c; intro new Spider-Armor 1.30 3.25
107-111: 107-Intro Sandstorm; Sand & Quicksand app. 1.25
112,-116, 118, 119, 121-124, 126-129: 112-Begin $1.50-c; bound-in trading card sheet. 113-Gambit & Black Cat app. 117-Flip book; Power & Responsibility Pt. 1. 110 1st solo clone story; Venom app 1.50
113 ($2.95)-Collector's ed. polybagged w/foil-c; 16 pg. preview of Spider-Man cartoon & animation cel 1.60 4.00
117 ($1.50)-Flip book; Power & Responsibility Pt.1 1.50
117 ($2.95)-Collector's edition; foil-c; flip book 1.20 3.00
119 ($6.45)-Direct market edition; polybagged w/ Marvel Milestone Amazing Spider-Man #150 & coupon for Amazing Spider-Man #396, Spider-Man #53, & Spectacular Spider-Man #219. 1.00 2.60 6.50
120 ($2.25)-Flip book w/ preview of the Ultimate Spider-Man. .90 2.25
125 ($3.95)-Holodisk-c; Gwen Stacy clone 1.60 4.00
125 ($2.95)-Newsstand 1.20 3.00
Annual 1 (1985) 1.20 3.00
Annual 2 (1986)-New Mutants; Art Adams-a 1.00 3.00 8.00
Annual 3 (1987) 1.20 3.00
Annual 4 (1988, $1.75)-Evolutionary War x-over 1.40 3.50
Annual 5 (1989, $2.00, 68 pgs.)-Atlantis Attacks; Captain Universe by Ditko (p) & Silver Sable stories; F.F. app. 1.10 2.75
Annual 6 ('90, $2.00, 68 pgs.)-Punisher back-up plus Capt. Universe by Ditko; G. Kane-a 1.10 2.75
Annual 7 (1991, $2.00, 68 pgs.)-Origins of Hobgoblin I, Hobgoblin II, Green Goblin I & II & Venom; Larsen/Austin-c 1.10 2.75
Annual 8 (1992, $2.25, 68 pgs.)-Part 3 of Venom story; New Warriors x-over; Black Cat back-up story 1.10 2.75
Annual 9 (1993, $2.95, 68 pgs.)-Bagged w/card 1.20 3.00
Annual 10 (1994, $2.95, 68 pgs.) 1.20 3.00
Super Special 1 (1995, $3.95)-flip book 1.60 4.00

NOTE: ***Art Adams*** *a-Annual 2.* ***Byrne*** *c-3-6.* ***Chaykin*** *c-10.* ***Mignola*** *a-Annual 2.* ***Vess*** *c-1, 8, Annual 1, 2.* ***Zeck*** *a-6i, 31, 32; c-31, 32.*

WEBWITCH
May, 1997 - Present ($3.00, B&W)
Avatar Press

1,2 1.20 3.00

WEDDING BELLS
Feb, 1954 - No. 19, Nov, 1956
Quality Comics Group

1-Whitney-a 11.50 34.00 80.00
2 7.00 21.00 42.00
3-9: 8-Last precode (4/55) 4.25 13.00 28.00
10-Ward-a (9 pgs.) 10.00 30.00 68.00
11-14,17 4.00 11.00 22.00
15-Baker-c 4.15 12.50 25.00
16-Baker-c/a 6.50 19.50 45.00
18,19-Baker-a each 5.70 17.00 35.00

WEDDING OF DRACULA
Jan, 1993 ($2.00, 52 pgs.)
Marvel Comics

1-Reprints Tomb of Dracula #30,45,46 .80 2.00

WEEKENDER, THE (Illustrated...)
V1#3, Sept, 1945 - V1#4, Nov, 1945; V2#1, Jan, 1946 (52 pgs.)
Rucker Publ. Co.

V1#3,4: 3-Super hero-c. 4-Same-c as Punch Comics #10 (9/44); r/Hale the Magician (7 pgs.) & r/Mr. E (8 pgs.-Lou Fine? or Gustavson?) plus 3 humor strips & many B&W photos & r/newspaper articles plus cheesecake photos of Hollywood stars 12.00 38.00 100.00
V2#1-36 pgs. comics, 16 in newspaper format with photos; partial Dynamic Comics reprints; 4 pgs. of cels from the Disney film Pinocchio; Little Nemo story by Winsor McCay, Jr.; Jack Cole-a; same-c as Dynamic #11 15.00 45.00 120.00

WEEKLY COMIC MAGAZINE
May 12, 1940 (16 pgs.) (Others exist w/o super-heroes)
Fox Publications

(1st Version)-8 pg. Blue Beetle story, 7 pg. Patty O'Day story, two copies known to exist. Estimated value... 500.00
(2nd Version)-7 two-pg. adventures of Blue Beetle, Patty O'Day, Yarko, Dr. Fung, Green Mask, Spark Stevens, & Rex Dexter; one copy known to exist. Estimated value... 400.00

Discovered with business papers, letters and exploitation material promoting **Weekly Comic Magazine** for use by newspapers in the same manner of **The Spirit** weeklies. Interesting note: these are dated three weeks before the first Spirit comic. Letters indicate that samples may have been sent to a few newspapers. These sections were actually 15-1/2x22" pages which will fold down to an approximate 8x10" comic booklet. Other various comic sections were found with the above, but were more like the Sunday comic sections in format.

The Weird #3 © DC

Weird Comics #4 © FOX

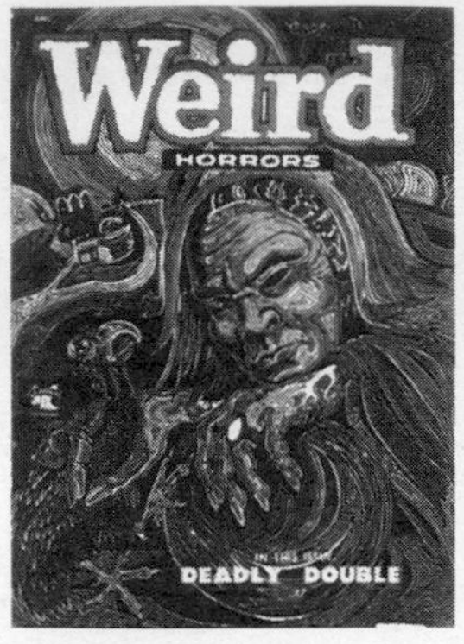

Weird Horrors #7 © STJ

GD25 FN65 NM94

WEEZUL
Aug, 1996 ($2.75/$3.00, B&W)
Lightning Comics
1-($2.75) 1.10 2.75
1b-($3.00) 1.20 3.00
1-($9.95) Commemorative Edition 1.25 3.75 10.00

WEIRD
V1#10, 1/66 - V8#6, 12/74; V9#1, 1/75 - V11#4, Dec, 1978 (Magazine)
(V1-V8: 52 pgs.; V9 on: 68 pgs.)
Eerie Publications
V1#10(#1)-Intro. Morris the Caretaker of Weird (ends V2#10); Burgos-a 5.00 15.00 50.00
11,12 3.00 9.00 30.00
V2#1-4(10/67), V3#1(1/68), V2#6(4/68)-V2#7,9,10(12/68), V3#1(2/69)-V3#4 3.00 9.00 30.00
V2#8-r/Ditko's 1st story/Fantastic Fears #5 4.00 12.00 40.00
5(12/69)-Rulah reprint; "Rulah" changed to "Pulah", LSD story reprinted in Horror Tales V4#4, Tales From the Tomb V2#4, & Terror Tales V7#3 3.00 9.00 30.00
V4#1-6('70), V5#1-6('71), V6#1-7('72), V7#1-7('73), V8#1-6('74), V9#1-4 (1/75-'76)(no V9#1), V10#1-3('77), V11#1-4 3.00 9.00 30.00
NOTE: *V9#4 (12/76) has a cover swipe from Horror Tales V5#1 (2/73).*

WEIRD
Summer, 1997 - Present ($2.99, B&W, magazine size)
DC Comics (Paradox Press)
1 1.20 3.00

WEIRD, THE
Apr, 1988 - No. 4, July, 1988 ($1.50, limited series)
DC Comics
1-4: Wrightson-c/a in all .80 2.00

WEIRD ADVENTURES
May-June, 1951 - No. 3, Sept-Oct, 1951
P. L. Publishing Co. (Canada)
1- "The She-Wolf Killer" by Matt Baker (6 pgs.) 40.00 120.00 315.00
2-Bondage/hypodermic panel 33.00 99.00 250.00
3-Male bondage/torture-c; severed head story 29.00 86.00 220.00

WEIRD ADVENTURES
No. 10, July-Aug, 1951
Ziff-Davis Publishing Co.
10-Painted-c 33.00 99.00 240.00

WEIRD CHILLS
July, 1954 - No. 3, Nov, 1954
Key Publications
1-Wolverton-r/Weird Mysteries No. 4; blood transfusion-c by Baily 50.00 150.00 440.00
2-Extremely violent injury to eye-c by Baily; Hitler story 50.00 150.00 440.00
3-Bondage E.C. swipe-c by Baily 35.00 105.00 265.00

WEIRD COMICS
Apr, 1940 - No. 20, Jan, 1942
Fox Features Syndicate
1-The Birdman, Thor, God of Thunder (ends #5), The Sorceress of Zoom, Blast Bennett, Typhon, Voodoo Man, & Dr. Mortal begin; Lou Fine bondage-c 350.00 1050.00 3500.00
2-Lou Fine-c 167.00 500.00 1500.00
3,4: 3-Simon-c. 4-Torture-c 94.00 282.00 850.00
5-Intro. Dart & sidekick Ace (8/40) (ends #20); bondage/hypo-c 97.00 291.00 875.00
6,7-Dynamite Thor app. in each. 6-Super hero covers begin 78.00 234.00 700.00
8-Dynamo, the Eagle (11/40, early app.; see Science #1) & sidekick Buddy & Marga, the Panther Woman begin 78.00 234.00 700.00
9,10: 10-Navy Jones app. 64.00 192.00 575.00
11-19: 16-Flag-c. 17-Origin The Black Rider. 47.00 141.00 425.00
20-Origin The Rapier; Swoop Curtis app; Churchill & Hitler-c 53.00 159.00 475.00
NOTE *Cover features: Sorceress of Zoom-4; Dr. Mortal-5; Dart & Ace-6-13, 15; Eagle-14, 16-20.*

WEIRD FANTASY (Formerly A Moon, A Girl, Romance; becomes Weird Science-Fantasy #23 on)
No. 13, May-June, 1950 - No. 22, Nov-Dec, 1953
E. C. Comics
13(#1) (1950) 162.00 488.00 1400.00
14-Necronomicon story; cosmic ray bomb explosion-c 62.00 188.00 550.00
15,16: 16-Used in **SOTI**, pg. 144 50.00 150.00 425.00
17 (1951) 44.00 132.00 375.00
6-10: 6-Robot-c 34.00 101.00 270.00
11-13 (1952): 12-E.C. artists cameo. 13-Anti-Wertham "Cosmic Correspondence" 29.00 86.00 210.00
14-Frazetta/Williamson(1st team-up at E.C.)/Krenkel-a (7 pgs.); Orlando draws E.C. staff; "Cosmic Ray Bomb Explosion" by Feldstein stars Gaines & Feldstein 40.00 120.00 320.00
15-Williamson/Evans-a(3), 4,3,&7 pgs. 29.00 86.00 210.00
16-19-Williamson/Krenkel-a in all. 18-Williamson/Feldstein-c 27.00 81.00 200.00
20-Frazetta/Williamson-a (7 pgs.) 29.00 86.00 210.00
21-Frazetta/Williamson-c & Williamson/Krenkel-a 40.00 120.00 320.00
22-Bradbury adaptation 20.00 60.00 150.00
NOTE: ***Ray Bradbury** adaptations-13, 17-20, 22. **Crandall** a-22. **Elder** a-17. **Feldstein** a-13(#1)-8; c-13(#1)-18 (#18 w/**Williamson**), 20. **Harrison/Wood** a-13. **Kamen** a-13(#1)-16, 18-22. **Krigstein** a-22. **Kurtzman** a-13(#1)-17(#5), 6. **Orlando** a-9-22 (2 stories in #16); c-19, 22. **Severin/Elder** a-18-21. **Wood** a-13(#1)-14, 17(2 stories ea. in #10-13). Ray Bradbury adaptations in #17-19, 22. Canadian reprints exist; see Table of Contents.*

WEIRD FANTASY
Oct, 1992 - Present ($1.50)
Russ Cochran/Gemstone Publishing
1,2: 1,2-r/Weird Fantasy #13,14; Feldstein-c .80 2.00
3-17: 3-5-r/Weird Fantasy #15-17 1.00 2.50

WEIRD HORRORS (Nightmare #10 on)
June, 1952 - No. 9, Oct, 1953
St. John Publishing Co.
1-Tuska-a 40.00 120.00 325.00
2,3: 3-Hashish story 23.00 69.00 175.00
4,5 20.00 60.00 150.00
6-Ekgren-c; atomic bomb story 34.00 103.00 260.00
7-Ekgren-c; Kubert, Cameron-a 39.00 116.00 290.00
8,9-Kubert-c/a 31.00 92.00 230.00
NOTE: ***Cameron** a-7, 9. **Finesque** a-1-5. **Forgione** a-6. **Morisi** a-3. Bondage c-8.*

WEIRD MYSTERIES
Oct, 1952 - No. 12, Sept, 1954
Gillmore Publications
1-Partial Wolverton-c swiped from splash page "Flight to the Future" in Weird Tales of the Future #2; "Eternity" has an Ingels swipe 53.00 161.00 460.00
2- "Robot Woman" by Wolverton; Bernard Baily-c reprinted in Mister Mystery #18; acid in face panel 75.00 225.00 630.00
3,6: Both have decapitation-c 40.00 120.00 310.00
4- "The Man Who Never Smiled" (3 pgs.) by Wolverton; B. Baily skull-c 64.00 193.00 580.00
5-Wolverton story "Swamp Monster" (6 pgs.) 62.00 186.00 560.00
7-Used in **SOTI**, illo "Indeed", illo "Sex and blood" 57.00 172.00 475.00
8-Wolverton-c panel-r/#5; used in a '54 Readers Digest anti-comics article by T. E. Murphy entitled "For the Kiddies to Read" 40.00 120.00 310.00

Weird Science #12 © WMG

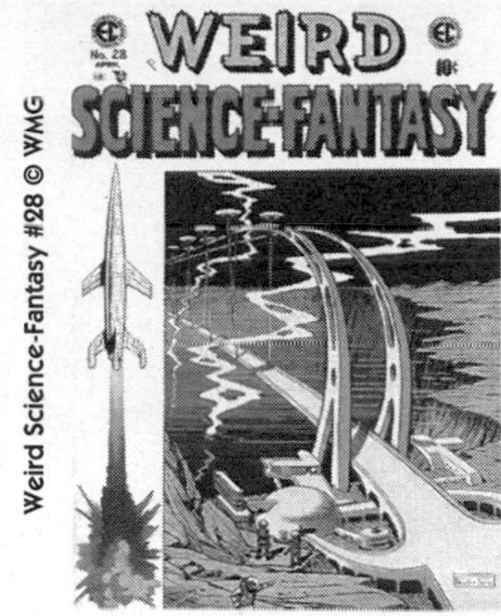

Weird Science-Fantasy #28 © WMG

Weird Tales of the Future #7 © Aragon Publ.

GD25 FN65 NM94

9-Excessive violence, gore & torture 40.00 120.00 300.00
10-Silhouetted nudity panel 34.00 103.00 250.00
11,12: 12-r/Mr. Mystery #8(2), Weird Mysteries #3 & Weird Tales of the Future #6 31.00 92.00 235.00

NOTE: ***Baily** c-2-12. Anti-Wertham column in #5. #1-12 all have 'The Ghoul Teacher' (host).*

WEIRD MYSTERIES (Magazine)
Mar-Apr, 1959 (35¢, B&W, 68 pgs.)
Pastime Publications

1-Torres-a; E. C. swipe from Tales From the Crypt #46 by Tuska "The Ragman" 5.70 17.00 38.00

WEIRD MYSTERY TALES (See DC 100 Page Super Spectacular)

WEIRD MYSTERY TALES (See Cancelled Comic Cavalcade)
July-Aug, 1972 - No. 24, Nov, 1975
National Periodical Publications

1-Kirby-a; Wrightson splash pg. 2.50 7.50 24.00
2,3,21: 21-Wrightson-c 1.50 4.50 12.00
4-10 1.25 3.75 10.00
11-20,22-24 1.00 3.00 8.00

NOTE: ***Alcala** a-5, 10, 13, 14. **Aparo** c-4. **Bailey** a-8. **Bolle** a-8?. **Howard** a-4. **Kaluta** a-4, 24; c-1. **G. Kane** a-10. **Kirby** a-1, 2p, 3p. **Nino** a-5, 6, 9, 13, 16, 21. **Redondo** a-9, 17. **Sparling** c-6. **Starlin** a-3?, 4. **Wood** a-23.*

WEIRD ROMANCE (Seduction of the Innocent #9)
Feb, 1988 ($2.00, B&W)
Eclipse Comics

1-Pre-code horror-r; Lou Cameron-r(2) .80 2.00

WEIRD SCIENCE (Formerly Saddle Romances) (Becomes Weird Science-Fantasy #23 on)
No. 12, May-June, 1950 - No. 22, Nov-Dec, 1953
E. C. Comics

12(#1) (1950)-"Lost in the Microcosm" classic-c/story by Kurtzman 162.00 488.00 1400.00
13-Flying saucers over Washington-c/story, 2 years before the actual event 69.00 206.00 600.00
14-Robot-c/story by Feldstein 69.00 206.00 600.00
15 (1950) 69.00 206.00 600.00
5-10: 5-Atomic explosion-c 40.00 120.00 320.00
11-14 (1952): 12- "Dream of Doom" stars Gaines & E.C. artists 29.00 86.00 210.00
15-18-Williamson/Krenkel-a in each; 15-Williamson-a. 17-Used in **POP**, pgs. 81,82. 18-Bill Gaines doll app. in story 31.00 92.00 225.00
19,20-Williamson/Frazetta-a (7 pgs. each). 19-Used in **SOTI**, illo "A young girl on her wedding night stabs her sleeping husband to death with a hatpin..." 40.00 120.00 300.00
21-Williamson/Frazetta-a (6 pgs.); Wood draws E.C. staff; Gaines & Feldstein app. in story 40.00 120.00 300.00
22-Williamson/Frazetta/Krenkel/Krigstein-a (8 pgs.); Wood draws himself in his story (last pg. & panel) 40.00 120.00 300.00

NOTE: ***Elder** a-14, 19. **Evans** a-22. **Feldstein** a-12(#1)-8; c-12(#1)-8, 11. **Ingels** a-15. **Kamen** a-12(#1)-13, 15-18, 20, 21. **Kurtzman** a-12(#1)-7. **Orlando** a-10-22. **Wood** a-12(#1), 13(#2), 5-22 (#9, 10, 12, 13 all have 2 **Wood** stories); c-9, 10, 12-22. Canadian reprints exist; see Table of Contents. Ray Bradbury adaptations in #17-20.*

WEIRD SCIENCE
Sept, 1990 - No. 4, Mar, 1991 ($1.95/$2.00, 68 pgs.)
Gladstone Publishing

1-4: Wood-c(r); all reprints in each 1.20 3.00

WEIRD SCIENCE
Sept, 1992 - Present ($1.50/$2.00/$2.50)
Russ Cochran/Gemstone Publishing

1,2: r/Weird Science #12,13 w/original-c .80 2.00
3-18: 3,4-r/#14,15. 5-7-w/original-c. 1.00 2.50

WEIRD SCIENCE-FANTASY (Formerly Weird Science & Weird Fantasy) (Becomes Incredible Science Fiction #30)
No. 23 Mar, 1954 - No. 29, May-June, 1955 (#23,24: 15¢)
E. C. Comics

23-Williamson, Wood-a; Bradbury adaptation 29.00 86.00 210.00
24-Williamson & Wood-a; Harlan Ellison's 1st professional story, "Upheaval!", later adapted into a short story as "Mealtime", and then into a TV episode of Voyage to the Bottom of the Sea as "The Price of Doom" 29.00 86.00 210.00
25-Williamson-c; Williamson/Torres/Krenkel-a plus Wood-a; Bradbury adaptation; cover price back to 10¢ 33.00 99.00 240.00
26-Flying Saucer Report; Wood, Crandall-a; A-bomb panels 27.00 81.00 200.00
27-Adam Link/I Robot series begins? 29.00 86.00 210.00
28-Williamson/Krenkel/Torres-a; Wood-a 31.00 94.00 230.00
29-Frazetta-c; Williamson/Krenkel & Wood-a; last pre-code issue; new logo 45.00 135.00 400.00

NOTE: ***Crandall** a-26, 27, 29. **Evans** a-26. **Feldstein** c-24, 26, 28. **Kamen** a-27, 28. **Krigstein** a-23-25. **Orlando** a-in all. **Wood** a-in all; c-23, 27. The cover to #29 was originally intended for Famous Funnies #217 (Buck Rogers), but was rejected for being "too violent."*

WEIRD SCIENCE-FANTASY
Nov, 1992 - Present ($1.50/$2.00/$2.50)
Russ Cochran/Gemstone Publishing

1,2: r/Weird Science-Fantasy #23,24 .80 2.00
3-18: r/#25-27 1.00 2.50

WEIRD SCIENCE-FANTASY ANNUAL
1952, 1953 (Sold thru the E. C. office & on the stands in some major cities) (25¢, 132 pgs.)
E. C. Comics

1952-Feldstein-c 162.00 488.00 1400.00
1953-Feldstein-c 100.00 300.00 900.00

NOTE: *The 1952 annual contains books cover-dated in 1951 & 1952, and the 1953 annual from 1952 & 1953. Contents of each annual may vary in same year.*

WEIRD SUSPENSE
Feb, 1975 - No. 3, July, 1975
Atlas/Seaboard Publ.

1-3: 1-Tarantula begins. 1.20 3.00

NOTE: ***Buckler** c-1, 3.*

WEIRD SUSPENSE STORIES (Canadian reprint of Crime SuspenStories #1-3; see Table of Contents)

WEIRD TALES ILLUSTRATED
1992 - No. 2, 1992 ($2.95, high quality paper)
Millennium Publications

1,2-Bolton painted-c. 1-Adapts E.A. Poe & Harlan Ellison stories. 2-E.A. Poe & H.P. Lovecraft adaptations 1.40 3.50
1-($4.95, 52 pgs.)-Deluxe edition w/Tim Vigil-a not in regular #1; stiff-c; Bolton painted-c 2.00 5.00

WEIRD TALES OF THE FUTURE
Mar, 1952 - No. 8, July-Aug, 1953
S.P.M. Publ. No. 1-4/Aragon Publ. No. 5-8

1-Andru-a(2); Wolverton partial-c 60.00 181.00 525.00
2,3-Wolverton-c/a(3) each. 2- "Jumpin Jupiter" satire by Wolverton begins, ends #5 96.00 290.00 800.00
4- "Jumpin Jupiter" satire & "The Man From the Moon" by Wolverton; partial Wolverton-c 61.00 183.00 550.00
5-Wolverton-c/a(2); "Jumpin Jupiter" satire 96.00 290.00 800.00
6-Bernard Baily-c 40.00 120.00 325.00
7- "The Mind Movers" from the art to Wolverton's "Brain Bats of Venus" from Mr. Mystery #7 which was cut apart, pasted up, partially redrawn, and rewritten by Harry Kantor, the editor; Baily-c 57.00 172.00 500.00
8-Reprints Weird Mysteries #1(10/52) minus cover; gory cover showing heart ripped out by B. Baily 44.00 133.00 400.00

Weird Terror #3 © Comic Media

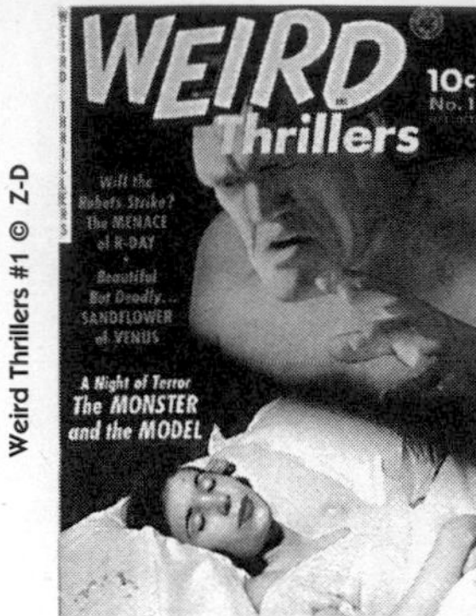

Weird Thrillers #1 © Z-D

Welcome Back Kotter #1 © Wolper Organization

GD25 FN65 NM94

WEIRD TALES OF THE MACABRE (Magazine)
Jan, 1975 - No. 2, Mar, 1975 (75¢, B&W)
Atlas/Seaboard Publ.

1-Jeff Jones painted-c 1.25 3.75 10.00
2-Boris Vallejo painted-c; Severin-a 1.85 5.50 15.00

WEIRD TERROR (Also see Horrific)
Sept, 1952 - No. 13, Sept, 1954
Allen Hardy Associates (Comic Media)

1- "Portrait of Death", adapted from Lovecraft's "Pickman's Model"; lingerie panels, Hitler story 37.00 111.00 285.00
2-Text on Marquis DeSade, Torture, Demonology, & St. Elmo's Fire 25.00 75.00 190.00
3-Extreme violence, whipping, torture; article on sin eating, dowsing 25.00 75.00 190.00
4-Dismemberment, decapitation, article on human flesh for sale, Devil, whipping 29.00 86.00 225.00
5-Article on body snatching, mutilation; cannibalism story 23.00 69.00 180.00
6-Dismemberment, decapitation, man hit by lightning 27.00 81.00 210.00
7,9,10 21.00 62.00 160.00
8-Decapitation story; Ambrose Bierce adapt. 26.00 77.00 200.00
11-End of the world story with atomic blast panels; Tothish-a by Bill Discount 26.00 77.00 200.00
12-Discount-a 19.00 58.00 150.00
13-Severed head panels 21.00 62.00 160.00

NOTE: ***Don Heck*** *a-most issues; c-1-13.* ***Landau*** *a-6.* ***Morisi*** *a-2-5, 7, 9, 12.* ***Palais*** *a-1, 5, 6, 8(2), 10, 12.* ***Powell*** *a-10.* ***Ravielli*** *a-11, 20.*

WEIRD THRILLERS
Sept-Oct, 1951 - No. 5, Oct-Nov, 1952 (#2-5: painted-c)
Ziff-Davis Publ. Co. (Approved Comics)

1-Rondo Hatton photo-c 53.00 159.00 475.00
2-Toth, Anderson, Colan-a 40.00 120.00 350.00
3-Two Powell, Tuska-a; classic-c 50.00 150.00 450.00
4-Kubert, Tuska-a 39.00 118.00 325.00
5-Powell-a 36.00 107.00 280.00

NOTE: ***M. Anderson*** *a-2, 3.* ***Roussos*** *a-4. #2, 3 reprinted in Nightmare #10 & 13; #4, 5 reprinted in Amazing Ghost Stories #16 & #15.*

WEIRD WAR TALES
Sept-Oct, 1971 - No. 124, June, 1983 (#1-5: 52 pgs.)
National Periodical Publications/DC Comics

1-Kubert-a in #1-4,7; c-1-7 15.00 45.00 150.00
2,3-Drucker-a: 2-Crandall-a. 3-Heath-a 5.00 15.00 50.00
4,5: 5-Toth-a; Heath-a 4.00 12.00 40.00
6,7,9,10: 6,10-Toth-a. 7-Heath-a 2.50 7.50 20.00
8-Neal Adams-c/a(i) 3.50 10.50 35.00
11-20 1.50 4.50 12.00
21-35 1.00 3.00 8.00
36-(68 pgs.)-Crandall & Kubert-r/#2; Heath-r/#3; Kubert-c 1.50 4.50 12.00
37-60: 38-Kubert-c 2.40 6.00
61-63,65-67,69-124: 93-Intro/origin Creature Commandos. 101-Intro/origin G.I. Robot 1.20 3.00
64,68-Frank Miller-a in both. 64-Miller's 1st DC work. 1.50 4.50 12.00

WEIRD WAR TALES
June, 1997 - No. 4, Sept, 1997 ($2.50)
DC Comics (Vertigo)

1-4-Anthology by various 1.00 2.50

WEIRD WESTERN TALES (Formerly All-Star Western)
No. 12, June-July, 1972 - No. 70, Aug, 1980
National Periodical Publications/DC Comics

GD25 FN65 NM94

12-(52 pgs.)-3rd app. Jonah Hex; Bat Lash, Pow Wow Smith reprints; El Diablo by Neal Adams/Wrightson 3.50 10.50 50.00
13-Jonah Hex-c (1st?) & 4th app.; Neal Adams-a 2.80 8.40 40.00
14,15: 14-Toth-a. 15-Neal Adams-c/a; no Jonah Hex 1.75 5.25 20.00
16,17,19,20 1.50 4.50 12.00
18,29: 18-1st all Jonah Hex issue (7-8/73) & begins. 29-Origin Jonah Hex 2.25 6.75 20.00
21-28,30-38: Jonah Hex in all. 38-Last Jonah Hex 1.00 2.80 7.00
39-Origin/1st app. Scalphunter & begins 1.00 3.00 8.00
40-47,50-69: 64-Bat Lash-c/story 2.00 5.00
48,49: (44 pgs.)-1st & 2nd app. Cinnamon 2.40 6.00
70-Last issue 2.40 6.00

NOTE: ***Alcala*** *a-16, 17.* ***Evans*** *inks-39-48; c-39i, 40, 47.* ***G. Kane*** *a-15, 20.* ***Kubert*** *c-12, 33.* ***Starlin*** *c-44, 45.* ***Wildey*** *a-26. 48 & 49 are 44 pgs..*

WEIRD WONDER TALES
Dec, 1973 - No. 22, May, 1977
Marvel Comics Group

1-Wolverton-r/Mystic #6 (Eye of Doom) 1.25 3.75 10.00
2-10 1.00 3.00 8.00
11-22: 16-18-Venus-r by Everett from Venus #19,18 & 17. 19-22-Dr. Druid (Droom)-r 2.40 6.00

NOTE: *All 1950s & early 1960s reprints.* ***Check*** *r-1.* ***Colan*** *r-17.* ***Ditko*** *r-4, 5, 10-13, 19-21.* ***Drucker*** *r-12, 20.* ***Everett*** *r-3(Spellbound #16), 6(Astonishing #10), 9(Adv. Into Mystery #5).* ***Heath*** *a-13r.* ***Heck*** *a-10r, 14r.* ***Gil Kane*** *c-1, 2, 10.* ***Kirby*** *r-6, 11, 13, 16-22; c-17, 19, 20.* ***Krigstein*** *r-19.* ***Kubert*** *r-22.* ***Maneely*** *r-8.* ***Mooney*** *r-7p.* ***Powell*** *r-3, 7.* ***Torres*** *r-7.* ***Wildey*** *r-2, 7.*

WEIRD WORLDS (See Adventures Into...)

WEIRD WORLDS (Magazine)
V1#10(12/70), V2#1(2/71) - No. 4, Aug, 1971 (52 pgs.)
Eerie Publications

V1#10 3.00 9.00 30.00
V2#1-4 2.50 7.50 24.00

WEIRD WORLDS (Also see Ironwolf: Fires of the Revolution)
Aug-Sept, 1972 - No. 9, Jan-Feb, 1974; No. 10, Oct-Nov, 1974 (All 20¢ issues)
National Periodical Publications

1-Edgar Rice Burrough's John Carter Warlord of Mars & David Innes begin (1st DC app.); Kubert-c 1.10 3.30 9.00
2-4: 2-Infantino/Orlando-c. 3-Murphy Anderson-c. 4-Kaluta-a 1.00 2.80 7.00
5-7: .5-Kaluta-c. 7-Last John Carter. 2.00 5.00
8-10: 8-Iron Wolf begins by Chaykin (1st app.) 1.60 4.00

NOTE: ***Neal Adams*** *a-2i, 3i. John Carter by* ***Andersonin*** *#1-3.* ***Chaykin*** *c-7, 8.* ***Kaluta*** *a-4; c-4-6, 10.* ***Orlando*** *a-4i; c-2, 3, 4i.* ***Wrightson*** *a-2i, 4i.*

WELCOME BACK, KOTTER (TV) (See Limited Collectors' Edition #57)
Nov, 1976 - No. 10, Mar-Apr, 1978
National Periodical Publications/DC Comics

1-Sparling-a(p) 1.50 4.50 12.00
2-10: 3-Estrada-a 1.00 3.00 8.00

WELCOME SANTA (See March of Comics #63,183)

WELCOME TO THE LITTLE SHOP OF HORRORS
May, 1995 -No. 3, July, 1995 ($2.50, limited series)
Roger Corman's Cosmic Comics

1-3 1.00 2.50

WELLS FARGO (See Tales of...)

WENDY AND THE NEW KIDS ON THE BLOCK
Mar?, 1991 - No. 4, 1991 ($1.25/$1.50)
Harvey Comics

1-4: 4-$1.50-c 1.30

WENDY DIGEST
Oct, 1990 - No. 2, Nov, 1990 ($1.75, digest size)
Harvey Comics

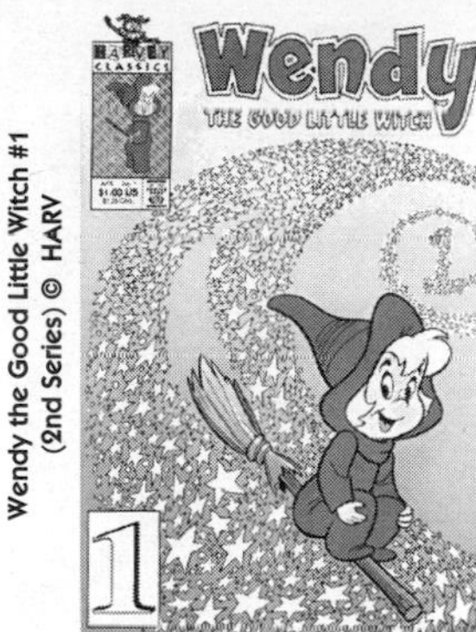

Wendy the Good Little Witch #1 (2nd Series) © HARV

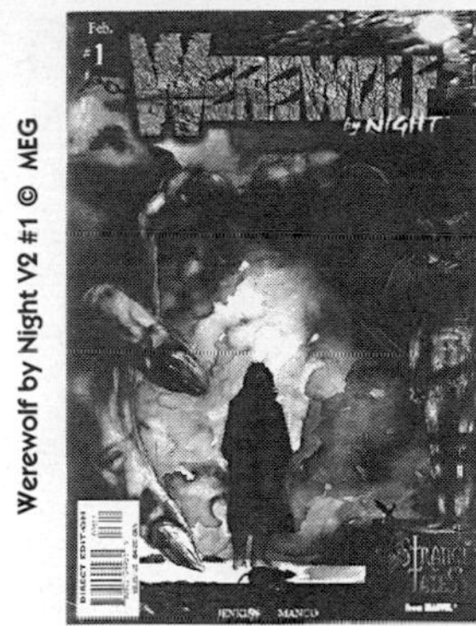

Werewolf by Night V2 #1 © MEG

Western Bandit Trails #1 © STJ

	GD25	FN65	NM94
1,2		.75	1.80

WENDY PARKER COMICS
July, 1953 - No. 8, July, 1954
Atlas Comics (OMC)

	GD25	FN65	NM94
1	8.50	26.00	60.00
2	5.70	17.00	35.00
3-8	5.00	15.00	30.00

WENDY, THE GOOD LITTLE WITCH (TV)
8/60 - #82, 11/73; #83, 8/74 - #93, 4/76; #94, 9/90 - #97, 12/90
Harvey Publications

	GD25	FN65	NM94
1-Wendy & Casper the Friendly Ghost begins	14.00	42.00	140.00
2	6.00	18.00	60.00
3-5	4.50	13.50	45.00
6-10	3.50	10.50	35.00
11-20	2.00	6.00	20.00
21-30	1.75	5.25	14.00
31-50	1.25	3.75	10.00
51-69: 65 (2/71)-Wendy origin.	1.00	3.00	8.00
70-74: All 52 pg. Giants	1.50	4.50	12.00
75-93		2.00	5.00
94-97 (1990, $1.00-c): 94-Has #194 on-c		.80	2.00

(See Casper the Friendly Ghost #20 & Harvey Hits #7, 16, 21, 23, 27, 30, 33)

WENDY THE GOOD LITTLE WITCH (2nd Series)
Apr, 1991 - No. 15, Aug, 1994 ($1.00/$1.25 #7-11/$1.50 #12-15)
Harvey Comics

	GD25	FN65	NM94
1-15-Reprints Wendy & Casper stories. 12-Bunny app.		.80	2.00

WENDY WITCH WORLD
10/61; No. 2, 9/62 - No. 52, 12/73; No. 53, 9/74
Harvey Publications

	GD25	FN65	NM94
1-(25¢, 68 pg. Giants begin)	9.00	27.00	90.00
2-5	4.50	13.50	45.00
6-10	2.50	7.50	24.00
11-20	2.50	7.50	20.00
21-30	1.85	5.50	15.00
31-39: 39-Last 68 pg. issue	1.50	4.50	12.00
40-45: 52 pg. issues	1.10	3.30	9.00
46-53		2.00	5.00

WEREWOLF (Super Hero) (Also see Dracula & Frankenstein)
Dec, 1966 - No. 3, April, 1967
Dell Publishing Co.

	GD25	FN65	NM94
1-1st app.	1.85	5.50	15.00
2,3	1.00	3.00	8.00

WEREWOLF BY NIGHT (See Giant-Size..., Marvel Spotlight #2-4 & Power Record Comics)
Sept, 1972 - No. 43, Mar, 1977
Marvel Comics Group

	GD25	FN65	NM94
1-Ploog-a cont'd. from Marvel Spotlight #4	4.00	12.00	40.00
2	2.00	6.00	16.00
3-5	1.75	5.25	14.00
6-10	1.10	3.30	9.00
11-20: 15-New origin Werewolf; Dracula-c/story cont'd from Tomb of Dracula #18	1.00	2.80	7.00
21-31		2.00	5.00
32-Origin & 1st app. Moon Knight (8/75)	7.50	22.50	75.00
33-2nd app. Moon Knight	3.20	9.60	32.00
34-36,38-43: 35-Starlin/Wrightson-c		2.00	5.00
37-Moon Knight app; part Wrightson-c	1.00	3.00	8.00

NOTE: ***Bolle** a-6i. **G. Kane** a-11p, 12p; c-21, 22, 24-30, 34p. **Mooney** a-7i. **Ploog** 1-4p, 5, 6p, 7p, 13-16p; c-5-8, 13-16. **Reinman** a-8i. **Sutton** a(i)-9, 11, 16, 35.*

WEREWOLF BY NIGHT (Vol. 2)
Feb, 1998 - Present ($2.99)
Marvel Comics Group

	GD25	FN65	NM94
1-Manco-a			2.99

WEREWOLVES & VAMPIRES (Magazine)
1962 (One Shot)
Charlton Comics

	GD25	FN65	NM94
1	6.00	18.00	60.00

WEST COAST AVENGERS
Sept, 1984 - No. 4, Dec, 1984 (limited series, Mando paper)
Marvel Comics Group

	GD25	FN65	NM94
1-Origin & 1st app. W.C. Avengers (Hawkeye, Iron Man, Mockingbird & Tigra)		.80	2.00
2-4			1.50

WEST COAST AVENGERS (Becomes Avengers West Coast #48 on)
Oct, 1985 - No. 47, Aug, 1989
Marvel Comics Group

	GD25	FN65	NM94
V2#1-20			1.50
21-41, 101,102			1.00
42-Byrne-a(p)/scripts begin		.80	2.00
43-74,76-99: 46-Byrne-c; 1st app. Great Lakes Avengers			1.00
75			1.50
100		1.60	4.00
Annual 1-3 (1986-1988): 3-Evolutionary War app.		.80	2.00
Annual V2#4-6 ('89-'91, $2.00, 68 pgs.)-4-Atlantis Attacks; Byrne/Austin-a		.80	2.00
Annual V2#7 (1992, $2.25, 68 pgs.)-Darkhawk app.		.90	2.25
Annual V2#8 (1993, $2.95)-Polybagged w/card		1.20	3.00

WESTERN ACTION
No. 7, 1964
I. W. Enterprises

	GD25	FN65	NM94
7-Reprints Cow Puncher #? by Avon	1.00	2.80	7.00

WESTERN ACTION
Feb, 1975
Atlas/Seaboard Publ.

	GD25	FN65	NM94
1-Kid Cody by Wildey & The Comanche Kid stories; intro. The Renegade		1.20	3.00

WESTERN ACTION THRILLERS
Apr, 1937 (10¢, square binding; 100 pgs.)
Dell Publishers

	GD25	FN65	NM94
1-Buffalo Bill, The Texas Kid, Laramie Joe, Two-Gun Thompson, & Wild West Bill app.	67.00	200.00	600.00

WESTERN ADVENTURES COMICS (Western Love Trails #7 on)
Oct, 1948 - No. 6, Aug, 1949
Ace Magazines

	GD25	FN65	NM94
nn(#1)-Sheriff Sal, The Cross-Draw Kid, Sam Bass begin	17.00	51.00	135.00
nn(#2)(12/48)	8.75	26.25	70.00
nn(#3)(2/49)-Used in **SOTI**, pgs. 30,31	9.50	28.00	75.00
4-6	8.50	26.00	60.00

WESTERN BANDITS
1952 (Painted-c)
Avon Periodicals

	GD25	FN65	NM94
1-Butch Cassidy, The Daltons by Larsen; Kinstler-a; c-part-r/paperback Avon Western Novel #1	13.00	39.00	95.00

WESTERN BANDIT TRAILS (See Approved Comics)
Jan, 1949 - No. 3, July, 1949
St. John Publishing Co.

	GD25	FN65	NM94
1-Tuska-a; Baker-c; Blue Monk, Ventrilo app.	20.00	60.00	155.00
2-Baker-c	15.00	45.00	120.00

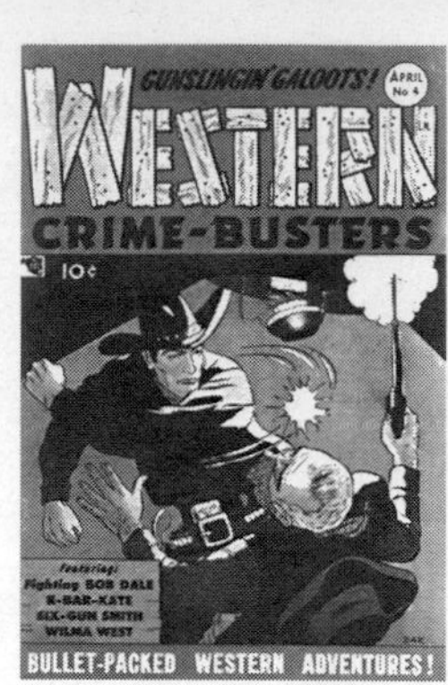

Western Crime Busters #4 © TM

Western Fighters #1 © HILL

Western Hearts #2 © STD

	GD25	FN65	NM94
3-Baker-c/a; Tuska-a	18.00	54.00	140.00

WESTERN COMICS (See Super DC Giant #15)
Jan-Feb, 1948 - No. 85, Jan-Feb, 1961 (1-27: 52pgs.)
National Periodical Publications

	GD25	FN65	NM94
1-Wyoming Kid & his horse Racer, The Vigilante in "Jesse James Rides Again" (Meskin-a), Cowboy Marshal, Rodeo Rick begin	64.00	192.00	575.00
2	36.00	108.00	290.00
3,4-Last Vigilante	29.00	88.00	235.00
5-Nighthawk & his horse Nightwind begin (not in #6); Captain Tootsie by Beck	25.00	75.00	200.00
6,7,9,10	19.00	56.00	150.00
8-Origin Wyoming Kid; 2 pg. pin-ups of rodeo queens	26.00	80.00	210.00
11-20	15.50	47.00	125.00
21-40: 24-Starr-a. 27-Last 52 pgs. 28-Flag-c	11.30	34.00	90.00
41-49: Last precode issue (2/55). 43-Pow Wow Smith begins, ends #85	10.00	30.00	80.00
50-60	8.75	26.25	70.00
61-85-Last Wyoming Kid. 77-Origin Matt Savage Trail Boss. 82-1st app. Fleetfoot, Pow Wow's girlfriend	8.50	26.00	60.00

NOTE: ***G. Kane, Infantino** art in most. **Meskin** a-1-4. **Moreira** a-28-39. **Post** a-3-5.*

WESTERN CRIME BUSTERS
Sept, 1950 - No. 10, Mar-Apr, 1952
Trojan Magazines

	GD25	FN65	NM94
1-Six-Gun Smith, Wilma West, K-Bar-Kate, & Fighting Bob Dale begin; headlight-a	26.00	79.00	190.00
2	13.50	41.00	100.00
3-5: 3-Myron Fass-c	12.00	36.00	90.00
6-Wood-a	26.00	79.00	190.00
7-Six-Gun Smith by Wood	26.00	79.00	190.00
8	12.00	36.00	90.00
9-Tex Gordon & Wilma West by Wood; Lariat Lucy app.	26.00	79.00	190.00
10-Wood-a	25.00	75.00	180.00

WESTERN CRIME CASES (Formerly Indian Warriors #7,8; becomes The Outlaws #10 on)
No. 9, Dec, 1951
Star Publications

	GD25	FN65	NM94
9-White Rider & Super Horse; L. B. Cole-c	13.00	39.00	100.00

WESTERN DESPERADO COMICS (Formerly Slam Bang Comics)
No. 8, 1940 (Oct.?)
Fawcett Publications

	GD25	FN65	NM94
8-(Rare)	58.00	174.00	520.00

WESTERNER, THE (Wild Bill Pecos)
No. 14, June, 1948 - No. 41, Dec, 1951 (#14-31: 52 pgs.)
"Wanted" Comic Group/Toytown/Patches

	GD25	FN65	NM94
14	9.50	28.00	75.00
15-17,19-21: 19-Meskin-a	5.70	17.00	35.00
18,22-25-Krigstein-a	8.50	26.00	60.00
26(4/50)-Origin & 1st app. Calamity Kate, series ends #32; Krigstein-a	9.50	28.00	75.00
27-Krigstein-a(2)	9.50	28.00	75.00
28-41: 33-Quest app. 37-Lobo, the Wolf Boy begins	4.25	13.00	26.00

NOTE: ***Mort Lawrence** a-20-27, 29, 37, 39; c-19, 22-24, 26, 27. **Leav** c-14-18, 20, 31. **Syd Shores** a-39; c-34, 35, 37-41.*

WESTERNER, THE
1964
Super Comics

	GD25	FN65	NM94
Super Reprint 15-17: 15-r/Oklahoma Kid #? 16-r/Crack West. #65; Severin-c; Crandall-r. 17-r/Blazing Western #2; Severin-c		2.40	6.00

WESTERN FIGHTERS
Apr-May, 1948 - V4#7, Mar-Apr, 1953 (#1-V3#2: 52 pgs.)
Hillman Periodicals/Star Publ.

	GD25	FN65	NM94
V1#1-Simon & Kirby-c	28.00	83.00	220.00
2-Not Kirby-a	7.85	23.50	55.00
3-Fuje-c	7.15	21.50	50.00
4-Krigstein, Ingels, Fuje-a	8.50	26.00	60.00
5,6,8,9,12	5.70	17.00	35.00
7,10-Krigstein-a	8.50	26.00	60.00
11-Williamson/Frazetta-a	23.00	69.00	185.00
V2#1-Krigstein-a	8.50	26.00	60.00
2-12: 4-Berg-a	4.00	12.00	24.00
V3#1-11	4.00	11.00	22.00
12-Krigstein-a	7.85	23.50	55.00
V4#1,4-7	4.00	11.00	22.00
2,3-Krigstein-a	7.85	23.50	55.00
3-D 1(12/53, 25¢, Star Publ.)-Came w/glasses; L. B. Cole-c	30.00	90.00	240.00

NOTE: ***Kinstlerish** a-V2#6, 8, 9, 12; V3#2, 5-7, 11, 12; V4#1(plus cover). **McWilliams** a-11. **Powell** a-V2#2. **Reinman** a-1-12, V4#3. **Rowich** c-5, 6i. **Starr** a-5.*

WESTERN FRONTIER
Apr-May, 1951 - No. 7, 1952
P. L. Publishers

	GD25	FN65	NM94
1	8.75	26.25	70.00
2	5.70	17.00	40.00
3-7	4.25	13.00	28.00

WESTERN GUNFIGHTERS (1st Series) (Apache Kid #11-19)
No. 20, June, 1956 - No. 27, Aug, 1957
Atlas Comics (CPS)

	GD25	FN65	NM94
20	8.75	26.25	70.00
21-Crandall-a	8.75	26.25	70.00
22-Wood & Powell-a	14.00	41.00	110.00
23,24: 23-Williamson-a. 24-Toth-a	8.75	26.25	70.00
25-27	7.15	21.50	50.00

NOTE: ***Berg** a-20. **Colan** a-20, 26, 27. **Crandall** a-21. **Heath** a-25. **Maneely** a-24, 25; c-22, 23, 25. **Morisi** a-24. **Morrow** a-26. **Pakula** a-23. **Severin** c-20, 27. **Torres** a-26. **Woodbridge** a-27.*

WESTERN GUNFIGHTERS (2nd Series)
Aug, 1970 - No. 33, Nov, 1975 (#1-6: 25¢, 68 pgs.)
Marvel Comics Group

	GD25	FN65	NM94
1-Ghost Rider begins; Fort Rango, Renegades & Gunhawk app.	1.85	5.50	15.00
2-6: 2-Origin Nightwind (Apache Kid's horse)	1.50	4.50	12.00
7-(52 pgs) Origin Ghost Rider retold	1.25	3.75	10.00
8-14	1.10	3.30	9.00
15-33: 10-Origin Black Rider. 12-Origin Matt Slade		2.40	6.00

NOTE: ***Baker** r-2, 3. **Colan** r-2. **Drucker** r-3. **Everett** a-6i. **G. Kane** c-29, 31. **Kirby** a-1p(r), 10, 11. **Kubert** r-2. **Maneely** r-2, 10. **Morrow** r-29. **Severin** c-10. **Shores** a-3, 4. **Barry Smith** a-4. **Steranko** c-14. **Sutton** a-1, 2i, 5, 4. **Torres** r-26('57). **Wildey** r-8, 9. **Williamson** r-2, 18. **Woodbridge** r-27('57). Renegades in #4, 5; Ghost Rider in #1-7.*

WESTERN HEARTS
Dec, 1949 - No. 10, Mar, 1952 (All photo-c)
Standard Comics

	GD25	FN65	NM94
1-Severin-a; Whip Wilson & Reno Browne photo-c	15.50	47.00	125.00
2-Beverly Tyler & Jerome Courtland photo-c from movie "Palomino"; Williamson/Frazetta-a (2 pgs.)	15.00	45.00	120.00
3-Rex Allen photo-c	8.75	26.25	65.00
4-7,10-Severin & Elder, Al Carreno-a. 5-Ray Milland & Hedy Lamarr photo-c from movie "Copper Canyon". 6-Fred MacMurray & Irene Dunn photo-c from movie "Never a Dull Moment". 7-Jock Mahoney photo-c. 10-Bill Williams & Jane Nigh photo-c	8.75	26.25	65.00
8-Randolph Scott & Janis Carter photo-c from "Santa Fe"; Severin & Elder-a	8.75	26.25	70.00
9-Whip Wilson & Reno Browne photo-c; Severin & Elder-a	10.00	30.00	80.00

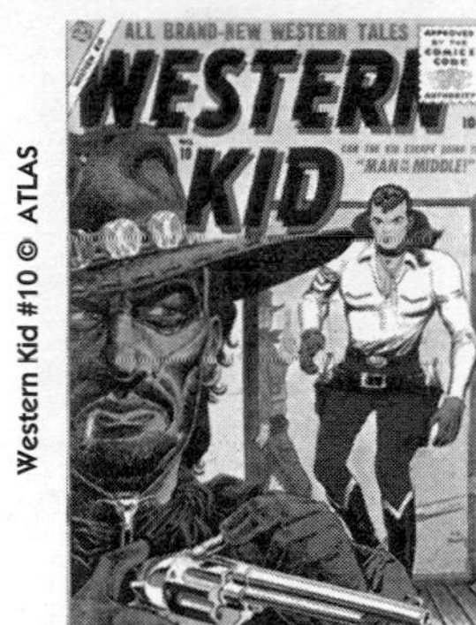

Western Kid #10 © ATLAS

Western Love #2 © PRIZE

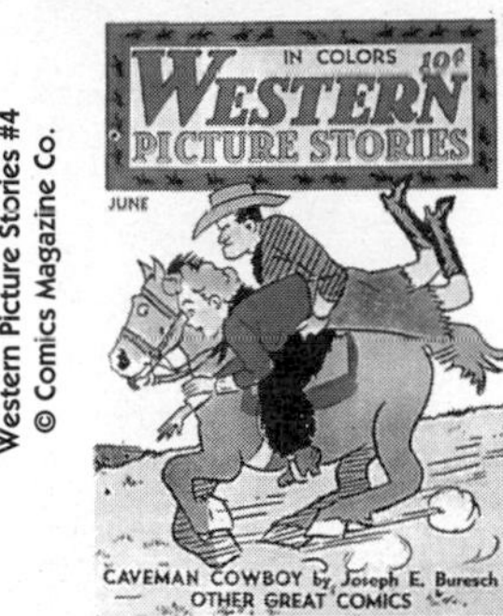

Western Picture Stories #4 © Comics Magazine Co.

WESTERN HERO (Wow Comics #1-69; Real Western Hero #70-75)
No. 76, Mar, 1949 - No. 112, Mar, 1952
Fawcett Publications

	GD25	FN65	NM94
76(#1, 52 pgs.)-Tom Mix, Hopalong Cassidy, Monte Hale, Gabby Hayes, Young Falcon (ends #78,80), & Big Bow and Little Arrow (ends #102,105) begin; painted-c begin	25.00	75.00	200.00
77 (52 pgs.)	14.00	41.00	110.00
78,80-82 (52 pgs.): 81-Capt. Tootsie by Beck	14.00	41.00	110.00
79,83 (36 pgs.): 83-Last painted-c	11.30	34.00	90.00
84-86,88-90 (52 pgs.): 84-Photo-c begin, end #112. 86-Last Hopalong Cassidy	12.00	36.00	95.00
87,91,95,99 (36 pgs.): 87-Bill Boyd begins, ends #95	10.00	30.00	80.00
92-94,96-98,101 (52 pgs.): 96-Tex Ritter begins. 101-Red Eagle app.	11.30	34.00	90.00
100 (52 pgs.)	12.00	36.00	95.00
102-111: 102-Begin 36 pg. issues	10.00	30.00	80.00
112-Last issue	11.30	34.00	90.00

NOTE: *1/2 to 1 pg. Rocky Lane (Carnation) in 80-83, 86, 88, 97. Photo covers feature Hopalong Cassidy #84, 86, 89; Tom Mix #85, 87, 90, 92, 94, 97; Monte Hale #88, 91, 93, 95, 98, 100, 104, 107, 110; Tex Ritter #96, 99, 101, 105, 108, 111; Gabby Hayes #103.*

WESTERN KID (1st Series)
Dec, 1954 - No. 17, Aug, 1957
Atlas Comics (CPC)

	GD25	FN65	NM94
1-Origin; The Western Kid (Tex Dawson), his stallion Whirlwind & dog Lightning begin	15.00	45.00	120.00
2 (2/55)-Last pre-code	8.50	26.00	60.00
3-8	7.85	23.50	55.00
9,10-Williamson-a in both (4 pgs. each)	8.50	26.00	60.00
11-17	5.70	17.00	40.00

NOTE: ***Ayers** a-6, 7. **Maneely** c-2-7, 10, 14. **Romita** a-1-17; c-1, 12. **Severin** c-17.*

WESTERN KID, THE (2nd Series)
Dec, 1971 - No. 5, Aug, 1972 (All 20¢ issues)
Marvel Comics Group

	GD25	FN65	NM94
1-Reprints; Romita-c/a(3)	1.50	4.50	12.00
2,4,5: 2-Romita-a; Severin-c. 4-Everett-r	1.25	3.75	10.00
3-Williamson-4	1.50	4.50	12.00

WESTERN KILLERS
nn, July?, 1948; No. 60, Sept, 1948 - No. 64, May, 1949; No. 6, July, 1949
Fox Features Syndicate

	GD25	FN65	NM94
nn(#59?)(nd, F&J Trading Co.)-Range Busters; formerly Blue Beetle #57?	19.00	56.00	140.00
60 (#1, 9/48)-Extreme violence; lingerie panel	21.00	64.00	160.00
61-Jack Cole, Starr-a	17.00	49.00	120.00
62-64, 6	15.00	45.00	110.00

WESTERN LIFE ROMANCES (My Friend Irma #3 on?)
Dec, 1949 - No. 2, Mar, 1950 (52 pgs.)
Marvel Comics (IPP)

	GD25	FN65	NM94
1-Whip Wilson & Reno Browne photo-c	14.50	43.00	115.00
2-Audie Murphy & Gale Storm photo-c; spanking scene	12.00	36.00	95.00

WESTERN LOVE
July-Aug, 1949 - No. 5, Mar-Apr, 1950 (All photo-c & 52 pgs.)
Prize Publications

	GD25	FN65	NM94
1-S&K-a; Randolph Scott photo-c from movie "Canadian Pacific" (see Prize Comics #76)	23.00	68.00	180.00
2,5-S&K-a: 2-Whip Wilson & Reno Browne photo-c. 5-Dale Robertson photo-c	19.00	56.00	150.00
3,4: 3-Reno Browne? photo-c	11.30	34.00	90.00

NOTE: ***Meskin** & **Severin/Elder** a-2-5.*

WESTERN LOVE TRAILS (Formerly Western Adventures)
No. 7, Nov, 1949 - No. 9, Mar, 1950
Ace Magazines (A. A. Wyn)

	GD25	FN65	NM94
7	8.75	26.25	65.00
8,9	7.15	21.50	50.00

WESTERN MARSHAL (See Steve Donovan...)
No. 534, 2-4/54 - No. 640, 7/55 (Based on Ernest Haycox's "Trailtown")
Dell Publishing Co.

	GD25	FN65	NM94
Four Color 534 (#1)-Kinstler-a	4.50	13.50	50.00
Four Color 591 (10/54), 613 (2/55), 640-All Kinstler-a	4.50	13.50	50.00

WESTERN OUTLAWS (Junior Comics #9-16; My Secret Life #22 on)
No. 17, Sept, 1948 - No. 21, May, 1949
Fox Features Syndicate

	GD25	FN65	NM94
17-Kamen-a; Iger shop-a in all; 1 pg. "Death and the Devil Pills" r-in Ghostly Weird #122	26.00	80.00	210.00
18-21	15.50	47.00	125.00

WESTERN OUTLAWS
Feb, 1954 - No. 21, Aug, 1957
Atlas Comics (ACI No. 1-14/WPI No. 15-21)

	GD25	FN65	NM94
1-Heath, Powell-a; Maneely hanging-c	15.00	45.00	120.00
2	8.75	26.25	65.00
3-10: 7-Violent-a by R.Q. Sale	7.15	21.50	50.00
11,14-Williamson-a in both (6 pgs. each)	8.50	26.00	60.00
12,18,20,21: Severin covers	6.50	19.50	45.00
13,15: 13-Baker-a. 15-Torres-a	7.15	21.50	50.00
16-Williamson text illo	6.50	19.50	45.00
17,19-Crandall-a. 17-Williamson text illo	7.15	21.50	50.00

NOTE: ***Ayers** a-7, 10, 18, 20. **Bolle** a-21. **Colan** a-5, 10, 11, 17. **Drucker** a-11. **Everett** a-9, 10. **Heath** a-1; c-3, 4, 8, 16. **Kubert** a-9p. **Maneely** a-13, 16, 17, 19; c-1, 5, 7, 9, 10, 12, 13. **Morisi** a-18. **Powell** a-3, 16. **Romita** a-7, 13. **Severin** a-8, 16, 19; c-17, 18, 20, 21. **Tuska** a-6, 15.*

WESTERN OUTLAWS & SHERIFFS (Formerly Best Western)
No. 60, Dec, 1949 - No. 73, June, 1952
Marvel/Atlas Comics (IPC)

	GD25	FN65	NM94
60 (52 pgs.)	17.50	53.00	140.00
61-65: 61-Photo-c	15.00	45.00	120.00
66-Story contains 5 hangings	12.00	36.00	95.00
68-72	10.50	32.00	85.00
67-Cannibalism story	14.00	41.00	110.00
73-Black Rider story; Everett-c	11.30	34.00	90.00

NOTE: ***Maneely** a-62, 67; c-62, 69-73. **Robinson** a-68. **Sinnott** a-70. **Tuska** a-69-71.*

WESTERN PICTURE STORIES (1st Western comic)
Feb, 1937 - No. 4, June, 1937
Comics Magazine Company

	GD25	FN65	NM94
1-Will Eisner-a	139.00	417.00	1250.00
2-Will Eisner-a	83.00	250.00	750.00
3,4: 3-Eisner-a. 4-Caveman Cowboy story	67.00	200.00	600.00

WESTERN PICTURE STORIES (See Giant Comics Edition #6, 11)

WESTERN ROMANCES (See Target...)

WESTERN ROUGH RIDERS
Nov, 1954 - No. 4, May, 1955
Gillmor Magazines No. 1,4 (Stanmor Publications)

	GD25	FN65	NM94
1	6.50	19.50	45.00
2-4	5.00	15.00	30.00

WESTERN ROUNDUP (See Dell Giants & Fox Giants)

WESTERN TALES (Formerly Witches...)
No. 31, Oct, 1955 - No. 33, July-Sept, 1956
Harvey Publications

	GD25	FN65	NM94
31,32-All S&K-a; Davy Crockett app. in each	15.00	45.00	120.00
33-S&K-a; Jim Bowie app.	15.00	45.00	120.00

NOTE: *#32 & 33 contain Boy's Ranch reprints. **Kirby** c-31.*

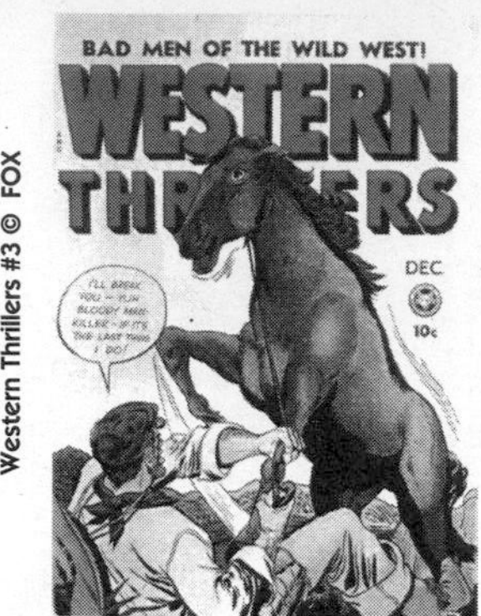

Western Thrillers #3 © FOX

Wetworks #1 © Aegis Entertainment

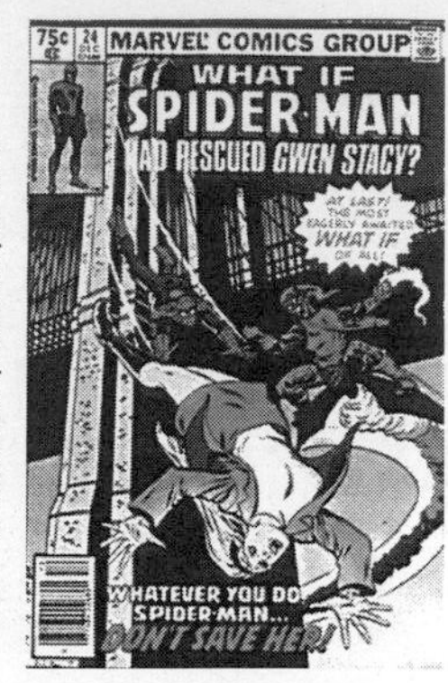

What If? #24 (1st Series) © MEG

WESTERN TALES OF BLACK RIDER (Formerly Black Rider; Gunsmoke Western #32 on)
No. 28, May, 1955 - No. 31, Nov, 1955
Atlas Comics (CPS)

28 (#1): The Spider (a villain) dies 14.00 41.00 110.00
29-31 9.50 28.00 75.00
NOTE: ***Lawrence** a-30. **Maneely** c-28-30. **Severin** a-28. **Shores** c-31.*

WESTERN TEAM-UP
Nov, 1973 (20¢)
Marvel Comics Group

1-Origin & 1st app. The Dakota Kid; Rawhide Kid-r; Gunsmoke Kid-r by Jack Davis 2.25 6.75 18.00

WESTERN THRILLERS (My Past Confessions #7 on)
Aug, 1948 - No. 6, June, 1949; No. 52, 1954?
Fox Features Syndicate/M.S. Distr. No. 52

1- "Velvet Rose" (Kamenish-a); "Two-Gun Sal", "Striker Sisters" (all women outlaws issue); Brodsky-c 40.00 120.00 325.00
2 17.00 49.00 120.00
3,6 14.00 43.00 110.00
4,5-Bakerish-a; 5-Butch Cassidy app. 17.00 49.00 120.00
52-(Reprint, M.S. Dist.)-1954? No date given (becomes My Love Secret #53) 7.00 21.00 42.00

WESTERN THRILLERS (Cowboy Action #5 on)
Nov, 1954 - No. 4, Feb, 1955 (All-r/Western Outlaws & Sheriffs)
Atlas Comics (ACI)

1 11.30 34.00 90.00
2-4 7.15 21.50 50.00
NOTE: ***Heath** c-3. **Maneely** a-1; c-2. **Powell** a-4. **Robinson** a-4. **Romita** c-4. **Tuska** a-2.*

WESTERN TRAILS (Ringo Kid Starring in…)
May, 1957 - No. 2, July, 1957
Atlas Comics (SAI)

1-Ringo Kid app.; Severin-c 8.75 26.25 70.00
2-Severin-c 6.50 19.50 45.00
NOTE: ***Bolle** a-1, 2. **Maneely** a-1, 2. **Severin** c-1, 2.*

WESTERN TRUE CRIME (Becomes My Confessions)
No. 15, Aug, 1948 - No. 6, June, 1949
Fox Features Syndicate

15(#1)-Kamen-a; formerly Zoot #14 (5/48)? 23.00 69.00 170.00
16(#2)-Kamenish-a; headlight panels, violence 21.00 62.00 150.00
3,4: 3-Kamen-a. 4-Johnny Craig-a 17.00 51.00 130.00
5,6 11.00 33.00 80.00

WESTERN WINNERS (Formerly All-Western Winners; becomes Black Rider #8 on & Romance Tales #7 on?)
No. 5, June, 1949 - No. 7, Dec, 1949
Marvel Comics (CDS)

5-Two-Gun Kid, Kid Colt, Black Rider; Shores-c 25.00 75.00 200.00
6-Two-Gun Kid, Black Rider, Heath Kid Colt story; Captain Tootsie by C.C. Beck 21.00 64.00 170.00
7-Randolph Scott Photo-c w/true stories about the West 21.00 64.00 170.00

WEST OF THE PECOS (See Zane Grey, 4-Color #222)

WESTWARD HO, THE WAGONS (Disney)
No. 738, Sept, 1956 (Movie)
Dell Publishing Co.

Four Color 738-Fess Parker photo-c 7.00 22.00 80.00

WETWORKS (See WildC.A.T.S: Covert Action Teams #2)
June, 1994 - Present ($1.95/$2.50)
Image Comics (WildStorm Productions)

1-"July" on-c; gatefold wraparound-c; Portacio/Williams-c/a 1.20 3.00
1-Chicago Comicon edition 2.40 6.00
2-4 .80 2.00
2-Alternate Portacio-c, see Deathblow #5 1.00 3.00 8.00
5-7,9-24,26-35: 5-($2.50). 13-Portacio-c. 16-Fire From Heaven Pt. 4. 17-Fire From Heaven Pt. 11 1.00 2.50
8 ($1.95)-Newstand, Wildstorm Rising Pt. 7 .80 2.00
8 ($2.50)-Direct Market, Wildstorm Rising Pt. 7 1.00 2.50
25-($3.95) 3.95
Sourcebook 1 (10/94, $2.50)-Text & illustrations (no comics) 1.00 2.50
Voyager Pack (8/97, $3.50)- #32 w/Phantom Guard preview 3.50

WETWORKS/VAMPIRELLA (See Vampirella/Wetworks)
July, 1997 ($2.95, one-shot)
Image Comics (WildStorm Productions)

1-Gil Kane-c 1.20 3.00

WHACK (Satire)
Oct, 1953 - No. 3, May, 1954
St. John Publishing Co. (Jubilee Publ.)

1-(3-D, 25¢)-Kubert-a; Maurer-c; came w/glasses 25.00 75.00 200.00
2,3-Kubert-a in each. 2-Bing Crosby on-c; Mighty Mouse & Steve Canyon parodies. 3-Li'l Orphan Annie parody; Maurer-c 14.00 41.00 110.00

WHACKY (See Wacky)

WHAM COMICS (See Super Spy)
Nov, 1940 - No. 2, Dec, 1940
Centaur Publications

1-The Sparkler, The Phantom Rider, Craig Carter and his Magic Ring, Detecto, Copper Slug, Speed Silvers by Gustavson, Speed Centaur & Jon Linton (s/f) begin 122.00 366.00 1100.00
2-Origin Blue Fire & Solarman; The Buzzard app. 86.00 258.00 775.00

WHAM-O GIANT COMICS
April, 1967 (98¢, newspaper size, one-shot)
Wham-O Mfg. Co. (Six issue subscription was advertised)

1-Radian & Goody Bumpkin by Wood; 1 pg. Stanley-a; Fine, Tufts-a; flying saucer reports; wraparound-c 4.50 13.50 45.00

WHAT DO YOU KNOW ABOUT THIS COMICS SEAL OF APPROVAL?
nd (1955) (4 pgs., slick paper-c)
No publisher listed (DC Comics Giveaway)

nn-(Rare) 50.00 150.00 450.00

WHAT IF? (1st Series) (What If? Featuring… #13 & #?-33)
Feb, 1977 - No. 47, Oct, 1984; June, 1988 (All 52 pgs.)
Marvel Comics Group

1-Brief origin Spider-Man, Fantastic Four 1.85 5.50 15.00
2-Origin The Hulk retold 1.00 2.80 7.00
3-5: 3-Avengers. 4-Invaders. 5-Capt. America 1.60 4.00
6-12,14,16: 8-Daredevil; Spidey parody. 9-Origins Venus, Marvel Boy, Human Robot, 3-D Man. 11-Marvel Bullpen as F. F. 1.20 3.00
13-Conan app.; John Buscema-c/a(p) 1.60 4.00
17-Ghost Rider & Son of Satan app. 2.00 5.00
18-26,29: 18-Begin 75¢-c; Dr. Strange. 19-Spider-Man. 22-Origin Dr. Doom retold 1.20 3.00
27-X-Men app.; Miller-c 1.00 3.00 8.00
28-Daredevil by Miller; Ghost Rider app. 1.00 3.00 8.00
30-"What If…Spider-Man's Clone Had Lived?" 1.00 3.00 8.00
31-Begin $1.00-c; featuring Wolverine & the Hulk; X-Men app.; death of Hulk, Wolverine & Magneto 1.50 4.50 12.00
32-34,36-47: 32,36-Byrne-a. 34-Marvel crew each draw themselves. 37-Old X-Men & Silver Surfer app. 39-Thor battles Conan 1.20 3.00
35-What if Elektra had lived?; Miller/Austin-a. 2.00 5.00
Special 1 ($1.50, 6/88)-Iron Man, F.F., Thor app. .80 2.00
NOTE: ***Austin** a-27p, 32i, 34, 35i; c-35i, 36i. **J. Buscema** a-13p, 15p; c-10, 13p, 23p. **Byrne** a-32i, 36; c-36p. **Colan** a-21p; c-17p, 18p, 21p. **Ditko** a-35, Special 1. **Golden** c-29, 40-42. **Guice***

What If? #103 (2nd Series) © MEG

What The--?! #8 © MEG

Where in the World is Carmen Sandiego #4 © Broderbund

GD25 FN65 NM94

a-40p. ***Gil Kane*** *a-3p, 24p; c(p)-2-4, 7, 8.* ***Kirby*** *a-11p; c-9p, 11p.* ***Layton*** *a-32i, 33i; c-30, 32p, 33i, 34.* ***Mignola*** *c-39i.* ***Miller*** *a-28p, 32i, 34(1), 35p; c-27, 28p.* ***Mooney*** *a-8i, 30i.* ***Perez*** *a-15p.* ***Robbins*** *a-4p.* ***Sienkiewicz*** *c-43-46.* ***Simonson*** *a-15p, 32i.* ***Starlin*** *a-32i.* ***Stevens*** *a-8, 16i(part).* ***Sutton*** *a-2i, 18p, 28.* ***Tuska*** *a-5p.* ***Weiss*** *a-37p.*

WHAT IF...? (2nd Series)
V2#1, July, 1989 - Present ($1.25/$1.50)
Marvel Comics

V2#1-...The Avengers Had Lost the Evol. War 1.60 4.00
2-5: 2-Daredevil, Punisher app. 1.00 2.50
6-X-Men app. 1.20 3.00
7-Wolverine app.; Liefeld-c/a(1st on Wolvie?) 1.60 4.00
8,11: 11-Fantastic Four app.; McFarlane-c(i) .80 2.00
9,12-X-Men 1.20 3.00
10-Punisher 1.00 2.50
13-15,17-21,23,27-29: 13-Prof. X; Jim Lee-c. 14-Capt. Marvel; Lim/Austin-c. 15-F.F.; Capullo-c/a(p). 17-Spider-Man/Kraven. 18-F.F. 19-Vision. 20,21-Spider-Man. 23-X-Men. 27-Namor/F.F. 28,29-Capt. America. 29-Swipes cover to Avengers #4 1.50
16-Wolverine battles Conan; Red Sonja app.; X-Men cameo 1.20 3.00
22-Silver Surfer by Lim/Austin-c/a .80 2.00
24-Wolverine; Punisher app. 1.10 2.75
25-($1.50, 52 pgs.)-Wolverine app. 1.20 3.00
26-Punisher app. 1.50
30-($1.75, 52 pgs.)-Sue Richards/F.F. .70 1.75
31-40: 31-Cosmic Spider-Man & Venom app.; Hobgoblin cameo. 32,33-Phoenix; X-Men app. 35-Fantastic Five (w/Spidey). 36-Avengers vs. Guardians of the Galaxy. 37-Wolverine; Thibert-c(i). 38-Thor; Rogers-p (part). 40-Storm; X-Men app. 1.50
41-($1.75, 52 pgs.)-Avengers vs. Galactus .70 1.75
42-49,51-60: 42-Spider-Man. 43-Wolverine. 44-Venom/Punisher. 45-Ghost Rider. 46-Cable. 47-Magneto. 49-Infinity Gauntlet w/Silver Surfer & Thanos. 52-Dr. Doom. 54-Death's Head. 57-Punisher as Shield. 58-"What if Punisher Had Killed Spider-Man" w/cover similar to Amazing S-M #129. 59-...Wolverine led Alpha Flight. 60-X-Men Wedding Album 1.25
50-($2.95, 52 pgs.)-Foil embossed-c; "What If Hulk Had Killed Wolverine" 1.20 3.00
61-99: 61-$1.50-c begins; bound-in card sheet. 61,86,88-Spider-Man. 74,77,81,84,85-X-Men. 76-Last app. Watcher in title. 78-Bisley-c. 80-Hulk. 87-Sabretooth. 89-Fantastic Four. 90-Cyclops & Havok. 91-The Hulk. 93-Wolverine. 94-Juggernaut. 95-Ghost Rider 1.50
96-98,-1(7/97)-($1.95): 97-Black Knight .80 2.00
99,101-108: 99-Begin $1.99-c .80 2.00
100-($2.99, double-sized) Gambit and Rogue, Fantastic Four 1.20 3.00

WHAT'S BEHIND THESE HEADLINES
1948 (16 pgs.)
William C. Popper Co.

nn-Comic insert "The Plot to Steal the World" 4.25 13.00 28.00

'WHAT'S NEW? - THE COLLECTED ADVENTURES OF PHIL & DIXIE'
Oct, 1991 - No. 2, 1991? ($5.95, mostly color, squarebound, 52 pgs.)
Palliard Press

1,2-By Phil Foglio 2.40 6.00

WHAT THE- -?!
Aug, 1988 - No. 26, 1993 ($1.25/$1.50/$2.50, semi-annually #5 on)
Marvel Comics

1-All contain parodies 1.00 2.50
2,4,5: 5-Punisher/Wolverine parody; Jim Lee-a 1.50
3-X-Men parody; Todd McFarlane-a .80 2.00
6-25: 6-($1.00)-Punisher, Wolverine, Alpha Flight. 9-Wolverine. 16-EC back-c parody. 17-Wolverine/Punisher parody. 18-Star Trek parody w/Wolverine. 19-Punisher, Wolverine, Ghost Rider. 21-Weapon X parody. 22-Punisher/Wolverine parody 1.25
26-Fall Special ($2.50, 68 pgs.)-Spider-Ham 2099-c/story; origin Silver Surfer; Hulk & Doomsday parody; indica reads "Winter Special." 1.00 2.50
Summer Special 1 (1993, $2.50)-X-Men parody 1.00 2.50
NOTE: ***Austin*** *a-6i.* ***Byrne*** *a-2, 6, 10; c-2, 6-8, 10, 12, 13.* ***Golden*** *a-22.* ***Dale Keown*** *a-8p(8 pgs.).* ***McFarlane*** *a-3.* ***Rogers*** *c-15i, 16p.* ***Severin*** *a-2.* ***Staton*** *a-21p.* ***Williamson*** *a-2i.*

WHEATIES (Premiums)
1950 & 1951 (32 titles, pocket-size, 32 pgs.)
Walt Disney Productions

(Set A-1 to A-8, 1950)
A-1-Mickey Mouse & the Disappearing Island, A-2-Grandma Duck, Homespun Detective, A-3-Donald Duck & the Haunted Jewels, A-4-Donald Duck & the Giant Ape, A-5-Mickey Mouse, Roving Reporter, A-6-Li'l Bad Wolf, Forest Ranger, A-7-Goofy, Tightrope Acrobat, A-8-Pluto & the Bogus Money
each... 4.15 12.50 25.00

(Set B-1 to B-8, 1950)
B-1-Mickey Mouse & the Pharoah's Curse, B-2-Pluto, Canine Cowpoke, B-3-Donald Duck & the Buccaneers, B-4-Mickey Mouse & the Mystery Sea Monster, B-5-Li'l Bad Wolf in the Hollow Tree Hideout, B-6-Donald Duck, Trail Blazer, B-7-Goofy & the Gangsters, B-8-Donald Duck, Klondike Kid
each... 4.15 12.50 25.00

(Set C-1 to C-8, 1951)
C-1-Donald Duck & the Inca Idol, C-2-Mickey Mouse & the Magic Mountain, C-3-Li'l Bad Wolf, Fire Fighter, C-4-Gus & Jaq Save the Ship, C-5-Donald Duck in the Lost Lakes, C-6-Mickey Mouse & the Stagecoach Bandits, C-7-Goofy, Big Game Hunter, C-8-Donald Duck Deep-Sea Diver
each... 4.15 12.50 25.00

(Set D-1 to D-8, 1951)
D-1-Donald Duck in Indian Country, D-2-Mickey Mouse and the Abandoned Mine, D-3-Pluto & the Mysterious Package, D-4-Bre'r Rabbit's Sunken Treasure, D-5-Donald Duck, Mighty Mystic, D-6-Mickey Mouse & the Medicine Man, D-7-Li'l Bad Wolf and the Secret of the Woods, D-8-Minnie Mouse, Girl Explorer each... 4.15 12.50 25.00
NOTE: *Some copies lack the Wheaties ad.*

WHEE COMICS (Also see Gay, Smile & Tickle Comics)
1955 (7¢, 5x7-1/4", 52 pgs.)
Modern Store Publications

1-Funny animal 1.00 4.00

WHEELIE AND THE CHOPPER BUNCH (TV)
July, 1975 - No. 7, July, 1976 (Hanna-Barbera)
Charlton Comics

1-3: 1-Byrne text illo (see Nightmare for 1st art); Staton-a. 2-Byrne-c/a. 2,3-Mike Zeck text illos. 3-Staton-a; Byrne-c/a 1.85 5.50 15.00
4-7-Staton-a 1.10 3.30 9.00

WHEN KNIGHTHOOD WAS IN FLOWER (See The Sword & the Rose, 4-Color #505, 682)

WHEN SCHOOL IS OUT (See Wisco)

WHERE CREATURES ROAM
July, 1970 - No. 8, Sept, 1971
Marvel Comics Group

1-Kirby/Ayers-r 2.50 7.50 20.00
2-8-Kirby-r 1.50 4.50 12.00
NOTE: ***Ditko*** *r-1-6, 7.* ***Heck*** *r-2, 5.* ***Kirby*** *r-2-5. All contain pre super-hero reprints.*

WHERE IN THE WORLD IS CARMEN SANDIEGO (TV)
June, 1996 - No. 4, Dec, 1996 ($1.75)
DC Comics

1-4: Adaptation of TV show 1.75

WHERE MONSTERS DWELL
Jan, 1970 - No. 38, Oct, 1975
Marvel Comics Group

1-Kirby/Ditko-r; all contain pre super-hero-r 2.50 7.50 20.00

Where Monsters Dwell #12 © MEG

White Princess Of The Jungle #3 © AVON

Whiz Comics #2 (#1) © FAW

	GD25	FN65	NM94
2-10,12: 4-Crandall-a(r). 12-Giant issue	1.50	4.50	12.00
11,13-20: 18,20-Starlin-c	1.25	3.75	10.00
21-37	1.00	3.00	8.00
38-Williamson-r/World of Suspense #3	1.25	3.75	10.00

NOTE: ***Colan** r-12. **Ditko** a(r)-4, 6, 8, 10, 12, 17-19, 23-25, 37. **Kirby** r-1-6; c-12? **Reinman** a-3r, 4r, 12r. **Severin** c-15.*

WHERE'S HUDDLES? (TV) (See Fun-In #9)
Jan, 1971 - No. 3, Dec, 1971 (Hanna-Barbera)
Gold Key

	GD25	FN65	NM94
1	2.25	6.75	24.00
2,3: 3-r/most #1	1.85	5.50	15.00

WHIP WILSON (Movie star) (Formerly Rex Hart; Gunhawk #12 on; see Western Hearts, Western Life Romances, Western Love)
No. 9, April, 1950 - No. 11, Sept, 1950 (#9,10: 52 pgs.)
Marvel Comics

	GD25	FN65	NM94
9-Photo-c; Whip Wilson & his horse Bullet begin; origin Bullet; issue #23 listed on splash page; cover changed to #9	47.00	141.00	415.00
10,11: Both have photo-c. 11-36 pgs.	28.00	84.00	225.00
I.W. Reprint #1(1964)-Kinstler-c; r-Marvel #11	2.50	7.50	22.00

WHIRLWIND COMICS (Also see Cyclone Comics)
June, 1940 - No. 3, Sept, 1940
Nita Publication

	GD25	FN65	NM94
1-Origin & 1st app. Cyclone; Cyclone-c	122.00	366.00	1100.00
2,3: Cyclone-c	83.00	250.00	750.00

WHIRLYBIRDS (TV)
No. 1124, Aug, 1960 - No. 1216, Oct-Dec, 1961
Dell Publishing Co.

	GD25	FN65	NM94
Four Color 1124 (#1)-Photo-c	8.00	25.00	90.00
Four Color 1216-Photo-c	7.00	22.00	80.00

WHISPER (Female Ninja)
Dec, 1983 - No. 2, 1984 ($1.75, Baxter paper)
Capital Comics

	GD25	FN65	NM94
1,2: 1-Origin; Golden-c		.70	1.75

WHITE CHIEF OF THE PAWNEE INDIANS
1951
Avon Periodicals

	GD25	FN65	NM94
nn-Kit West app.; Kinstler-c	12.00	36.00	95.00

WHITE EAGLE INDIAN CHIEF (See Indian Chief)

WHITE FANG
1990 ($5.95, 68 pgs.)
Disney Comics

	GD25	FN65	NM94
nn-Graphic novel adapting new Disney movie		2.40	6.00

WHITE INDIAN
No. 11, July, 1953 - No. 15, 1954
Magazine Enterprises

	GD25	FN65	NM94
11(A-1 94), 12(A-1 101), 13(A-1 104)-Frazetta-r(Dan Brand) in all from Durango Kid. 11-Powell-c	18.00	54.00	145.00
14(A-1 117), 15(A-1 135)-Check-a; Torres-a-#15	8.75	26.25	70.00

NOTE: *#11 contains reprints from Durango Kid #1-4; #12 from #5, 9, 10, 11; #13 from #7, 12, 13, 16. #14 & 15 contain all new stories.*

WHITE PRINCESS OF THE JUNGLE (Also see Jungle Adventures & Top Jungle Comics)
July, 1951 - No. 5, Nov, 1952
Avon Periodicals

	GD25	FN65	NM94
1-Origin of White Princess (Taanda) & Capt'n Courage (r); Kinstler-c	39.00	117.00	350.00
2-Reprints origin of Malu, Slave Girl Princess from Avon's Slave Girl Comics #1 w/Malu changed to Zora; Kinstler-c/a(2)	33.00	98.00	260.00
3-Origin Blue Gorilla; Kinstler-c/a	26.00	80.00	210.00
4-Jack Barnum, White Hunter app.; r/Sheena #9	24.00	71.00	190.00
5-Blue Gorilla by McCann?; Kinstler inside-c; Fawcette/Alascia-a(3)	24.00	71.00	190.00

WHITE RIDER AND SUPER HORSE (Formerly Humdinger V2#2; Indian Warriors #7 on; also see Blue Bolt #1, 4Most & Western Crime Cases)
1950 - No. 6, Mar, 1951
Novelty-Star Publications/Accepted Publ.

	GD25	FN65	NM94
1: 1-3-Exist?	15.00	45.00	120.00
2,3	12.00	38.00	100.00
4-6-Adapts "The Last of the Mohicans". 4-(9/50)-Says #11 on inside	12.00	38.00	100.00
Accepted Reprint #5(r/#5),6 (nd); L.B. Cole-c	6.50	19.50	45.00

NOTE: *All have **L. B. Cole** covers.*

WHITE WILDERNESS (Disney)
No. 943, Oct, 1958
Dell Publishing Co.

	GD25	FN65	NM94
Four Color 943-Movie	5.50	16.50	70.00

WHITMAN COMIC BOOK, A
Sept., 1962 (136 pgs.; 7-3/4x5-3/4; hardcover) (B&W)
Whitman Publishing Co.

	GD25	FN65	NM94
1-7: 1-Yogi Bear. 2-Huckleberry Hound. 3-Mr. Jinks and Pixie & Dixie. 4-The Flintstones. 5-Augie Doggie & Loopy de Loop. 6-Snooper & Blabber Fearless Detectives/Quick DrawMcGraw of the Wild West. 7-Bugs Bunny-r from #47,51,53,54 & 55	1.00	2.80	7.00
8-Donald Duck-reprints most of WDC&S #209-213. Includes 5 Barks stories, 1 complete Mickey Mouse serial by Paul Murry & 1 Mickey Mouse serial missing the 1st episode	7.00	21.00	70.00

NOTE: *Hanna-Barbera #1-4,6,8(TV), original stories. Dell reprints-#5, 7.*

WHIZ COMICS (Formerly Flash Comics & Thrill Comics #1)
No. 2, Feb, 1940 - No. 155, June, 1953
Fawcett Publications

	GD25	FN65	VF82	NM94
1-(nn on cover, #2 inside)-Origin & 1st newsstand app. Captain Marvel (formerly Captain Thunder) by C. C. Beck (created by Bill Parker), Spy Smasher, Golden Arrow, Ibis the Invincible, Dan Dare, Scoop Smith, Sivana, & Lance O'Casey begin	7,000.00	21,000.00	35,000.00	63,000.00

(Estimated up to 100 total copies exist, 3 in NM/Mint)
(The only Mint copy sold in 1995 for $176,000 cash)

1-Reprint, oversize 13-1/2x10". **WARNING**: This comic is an exact duplicate reprint (except for dropping "Gangway for Captain Marvel" from-c) of the original except for its size. DC published it in 1974 with a second cover titling it as a Famous First Edition. There have been many reported cases of the outer cover being removed and the interior sold as the original edition. The reprint with the new outer cover removed is practically worthless. See Famous First Edition for value.

	GD25	FN65	NM94
2-(3/40, nn on cover, #3 inside); cover to Flash #1 redrawn, pg. 12, panel 4; Spy Smasher reveals I.D. to Eve	390.00	1170.00	3900.00
3-(4/40, #3 on-c, #4 inside)-1st app. Beautia	240.00	720.00	2400.00
4-(5/40, #4 on cover, #5 inside)-Brief origin Capt. Marvel retold	222.00	667.00	2000.00
5-Captain Marvel wears button-down flap on splash page only	183.00	550.00	1650.00
6-10: 7-Dr. Voodoo begins (by Raboy-#9-22)	139.00	417.00	1250.00
11-14: 12-Capt. Marvel does not wear cape	98.00	294.00	880.00
15-Origin Sivana; Dr. Voodoo by Raboy	106.00	318.00	950.00
16-18-Spy Smasher battles Captain Marvel	106.00	318.00	950.00
19,20	68.00	204.00	610.00
21-Origin & 1st app. Lt. Marvels	72.00	216.00	650.00
22-24: 23-Only Dr. Voodoo by Tuska	56.00	168.00	500.00
25-(12/41)-Captain Nazi jumps from Master Comics #21 to take on Capt. Marvel solo after being beaten by Capt. Marvel/Bulletman team, causing the creation of Capt. Marvel Jr.; 1st app./origin of Capt. Marvel Jr. (part II of trilogy origin by CC. Beck & Mac Raboy); Captain Marvel sends Jr. back to Master #22 to aid Bulletman against Capt. Nazi; origin Old Shazam in text.	480.00	1440.00	4800.00

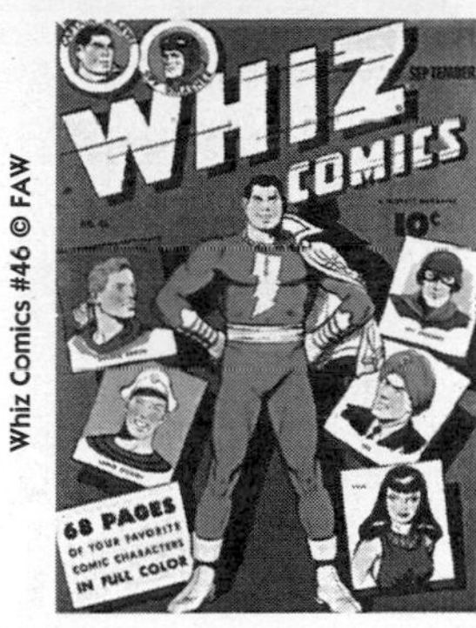

Whiz Comics #46 © FAW

Who's Who: The Definitive Directory of the DC Universe #2 © DC

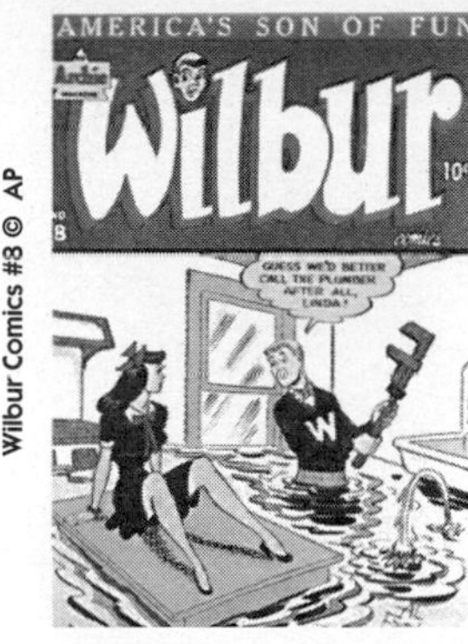

Wilbur Comics #3 © AP

GD25 FN65 NM94

26-30 49.00 147.00 440.00
31,32: 32-1st app. The Trolls; Hitler/Mussolini satire by Beck 42.00 126.00 375.00
33-Spy Smasher, Captain Marvel x-over on cover and inside 49.00 147.00 440.00
34,36-40: 37-The Trolls app. by Swayze 36.00 108.00 300.00
35-Captain Marvel & Spy Smasher-c 39.00 117.00 350.00
41-50: 43-Spy Smasher, Ibis, Golden Arrow x-over in Capt. Marvel. 44-Flag-c. 47-Origin recap (1 pg.) 26.00 80.00 210.00
51-60: 52-Capt. Marvel x-over in Ibis. 57-Spy Smasher, Golden Arrow, Ibis cameo 23.00 68.00 180.00
61-70 20.00 60.00 160.00
71,77-80 18.00 54.00 145.00
72-76-Two Captain Marvel stories in each; 76-Spy Smasher becomes Crime Smasher 19.00 56.00 150.00
81-99: 86-Captain Marvel battles Sivana Family. 91-Infinity-c 18.00 54.00 145.00
100-(8/48)-Anniversary issue 21.00 64.00 170.00
101-106: 102-Commando Yank app. 106-Bulletman app. 17.50 53.00 140.00
107-152: 107-White House photo-c. 108-Brooklyn Bridge photo-c. 112-Photo-c 139-Infinity-c. 140-Flag-c. 142-Used in **POP**, pg. 89 17.50 53.00 140.00
153-155-(Scarce):154,155-1st/2nd Dr. Death stories 22.00 66.00 175.00
Wheaties Giveaway(1946, Miniature, 6-1/2x8-1/4", 32 pgs.); all copies were taped at each corner to a box of Wheaties and are never found in fine or mint condition; "Capt. Marvel & the Water Thieves", plus Golden Arrow, Ibis, Crime Smasher stories 75.00 300.00 –

NOTE: ***C.C. Beck*** *Captain Marvel-No. 25(part).* ***Krigstein*** *Golden Arrow-No. 75, 78, 91, 95, 96, 98-100.* ***Mac Raboy*** *Dr. Voodoo-No. 9-22. Captain Marvel-No. 25(part).* ***M.Swayze*** *a-37, 38, 59; c-38.* ***Schaffenberger*** *c-138-158(most).* ***Wolverton*** *1/2 pg. "Culture Corner"-No. 65-67, 68(2 1/2 pgs), 70-85, 87-96, 98-100, 102-109, 112-121, 123, 125, 126, 128-131, 133, 134, 136, 142, 143, 146.*

WHOA, NELLIE (Also see Love & Rockets)
July, 1996 - No. 3, Sept, 1996 ($2.95, B&W, limited series)
Fantagraphics Books

1-3: Jamie Hernandez-c/a/scripts 1.20 3.00

WHODUNIT
Aug-Sept, 1948 - No. 3, Dec-Jan, 1948-49 (#1,2: 52 pgs.)
D.S. Publishing Co.

1-Baker-a (7 pgs.) 20.00 60.00 150.00
2,3 10.00 30.00 70.00

WHODUNNIT?
June, 1986 - No. 3, Apr, 1987 ($2.00, limited series)
Eclipse Comics

1-3: Spiegle-a. 2-Gulacy-c .80 2.00

WHO FRAMED ROGER RABBIT (See Marvel Graphic Novel)

WHO IS NEXT?
No. 5, Jan, 1953
Standard Comics

5-Toth, Sekowsky, Andru-a 17.00 49.00 120.00

WHO IS THE CROOKED MAN?
Sept, 1996 ($3.50, B&W, 40 pgs.)
Crusade

1-Intro The Martyr, Scarlet 7 & Garrison 1.40 3.50

WHO'S MINDING THE MINT? (See Movie Classics)

WHO'S WHO IN STAR TREK
Mar, 1987 - #2, Apr, 1987 ($1.50, limited series)
DC Comics

1,2 2.00 5.00

NOTE: ***Byrne*** *a-1, 2.* ***Chaykin*** *c-1, 2.* ***Morrow*** *a-1, 2.* ***McFarlane*** *a-2.* ***Perez*** *a-1, 2.* ***Sutton*** *a-1, 2.*

WHO'S WHO IN THE LEGION OF SUPER-HEROES
Apr, 1987 - No. 7, Nov, 1988 ($1.25, limited series)
DC Comics

1-7 1.30

WHO'S WHO: THE DEFINITIVE DIRECTORY OF THE DC UNIVERSE
Mar, 1985 - No. 26, Apr, 1987 (Maxi-series, no ads)
DC Comics

1-DC heroes from A-Z .80 2.00
2-26: All have 1-2 pgs-a by most DC artists 1.50

NOTE: ***Art Adams*** *a-4, 11, 18, 20.* ***Anderson*** *a-1-5, 7-12, 14, 15, 19, 21, 23-25.* ***Aparo*** *a-2, 3, 9, 10, 12, 13, 14, 15, 17, 18, 21, 23.* ***Byrne*** *a-4, 7, 14, 16, 18i, 19, 22i, 24; c-22.* ***Cowan*** *a-3-5, 8, 10-13, 16-18, 22-25.* ***Ditko*** *a-19-22.* ***Evans*** *a-20.* ***Giffen*** *a-1, 3,-6, 8, 13, 15, 17, 18, 23.* ***Grell*** *a-6, 9, 14, 20, 23, 25, 26.* ***Infantino*** *a-1-10, 12, 15, 17-22, 24, 25.* ***Kaluta*** *a-14, 21.* ***Gil Kane*** *a-1-11, 13, 14, 16, 19, 21-23, 25.* ***Kirby*** *a-2-6, 8-18, 20, 22, 25.* ***Kubert*** *a-2, 3, 7-11, 19, 20, 25.* ***Erik Larsen*** *a-24.* ***McFarlane*** *a-10-12, 17, 19, 25, 26.* ***Morrow*** *a-4, 7, 25, 26.* ***Orlando*** *a-1, 4, 10, 11, 21i.* ***Perez*** *a-1-5, 8-19, 22-26; c-1-4, 13-18.* ***Rogers*** *a-1, 2, 5-7, 11, 12, 15, 24.* ***Starlin*** *a-13, 14, 16.* ***Stevens*** *a-4, 7, 18.*

WHO'S WHO UPDATE '87
Aug, 1987 - No. 5, Dec, 1987 ($1.25, limited series)
DC Comics

1-5: Contains art by most DC artists 1.50

NOTE: ***Giffen*** *a-1.* ***McFarlane*** *a-1-4; c-4.* ***Perez*** *a-1-4.*

WHO'S WHO UPDATE '88
Aug, 1988 - No. 4, Nov, 1988 ($1.25, limited series)
DC Comics

1-4: Contains art by most DC artists 1.25

NOTE: ***Giffen*** *a-1.* ***Erik Larsen*** *a-1.*

WIDOW: BOUND BY BLOOD
Aug, 1996 - No. 5, 1996 ($3.50/$3.00, B&W/color, limited series, mature)
Ground Zero Comics

1-(B&W, $3.50) 1.40 3.50
3-5: 2-Begin $3.00-c & color 1.20 3.00
Platinum Ed.-(4/96, B&W)-Complete 1st issue prev. 1.25 3.75 10.00

WIDOW: METAL GYPSIES
Aug, 1995 - No. 2, 1995 ($3.00)
London Night Studios

1,2 1.20 3.00
1-Platinum 1.60 4.00

WILBUR COMICS (Teen-age) (Also see Laugh Comics, Laugh Comix, Liberty Comics #10 & Zip Comics)
Sum', 1944 - No. 87, 11/59; No. 88, 9/63; No. 89, 10/64; No. 90, 10/65 (No. 1-46: 52 pgs.)(#1-11 are quarterly)
MLJ Magazines/Archie Publ. No. 8, Spring, 1946 on

1 40.00 120.00 360.00
2(Fall, 1944) 23.00 68.00 180.00
3,4(Wint, '44-45; Spr, '45) 16.00 49.00 130.00
5-1st app. Katy Keene (Sum, '45) & begin series; Wilbur story same as Archie story in Archie #1 except Wilbur replaces Archie 50.00 150.00 450.00
6-10: 10-(Fall, 1946) 15.00 45.00 120.00
11-20 8.75 26.25 70.00
21-30: 30-(4/50) 6.50 19.50 45.00
31-50 5.00 15.00 30.00
51-70 4.00 11.00 22.00
71-90: 88-Last 10¢ issue (9/63) 1.75 5.25 14.00

NOTE: *Katy Keene in No. 5-56, 58-69.* ***Al Fagaly*** *c-6-9, 12-24 at least.* ***Vigoda*** *c-2.*

WILD
Feb, 1954 - No. 5, Aug, 1954
Atlas Comics (IPC)

1 20.00 60.00 160.00
2 12.00 36.00 95.00

Wild Bill Elliott-Four Color #520 © DELL

Wild Boy of the Congo #8 © Z-D

WildC.A.T.S. #10 © Aegis Entertainment

GD25 FN65 NM94

3-5 9.50 28.50 75.00

NOTE: ***Berg** a-5; c-4. **Burgos** c-3. **Colan** a-4. **Everett** a-1-3. **Heath** a-2, 3, 5. **Maneely** a-1-3, 5; c-1, 5. **Post** a-2, 5. **Ed Win** a-1, 3.*

WILD (This Magazine Is...) (Satire)
Jan, 1968 - No. 3, 1968 (Magazine, 52 pgs.)
Dell Publishing Co.

1-3 2.40 6.00

WILD ANIMALS
Dec, 1982 ($1.00, one-shot, direct sales)
Pacific Comics

1-Funny animal; Sergio Aragones-a; Shaw-c/a 1.00

WILD BILL ELLIOTT (Also see Western Roundup under Dell Giants)
No. 278, 5/50 - No. 643, 7/55 (No #11,12) (All photo-c)
Dell Publishing Co.

Four Color 278(#1, 52pgs.)-Titled "Bill Elliott"; Bill & his horse Stormy begin; photo front/back-c begin 12.00 35.00 130.00
2 (11/50), 3 (52 pgs.) 6.40 19.00 70.00
4-10(10-12/52) 4.50 13.50 50.00
Four Color 472(6/53),520(12/53)-Last photo back-c 3.60 11.00 40.00
13(4-6/54) - 17(4-6/55) 3.00 9.00 35.00
Four Color 643 (7/55) 2.75 8.00 30.00

WILD BILL HICKOK (Also see Blazing Sixguns)
Sept-Oct, 1949 - No. 28, May-June, 1956
Avon Periodicals

1-Ingels-c 17.50 53.00 140.00
2-Painted-c; Kit West app. 8.75 26.25 65.00
3-5-Painted-c (4-Cover by Howard Winfield) 5.70 17.00 35.00
6-10,12: 8-10-Painted-c. 12-Kinsler-c? 5.70 17.00 35.00
11,13,14-Kinstler-c/a (#11-c & inside-f/c art only) 5.70 17.00 40.00
15,17,18,20: 18-Kit West story. 20-Kit West by Larsen 4.25 13.00 28.00
16-Kamen-a; r-3 stories/King of the Badmen of Deadwood 5.70 17.00 35.00
19-Meskin-a 4.25 13.00 28.00
21-Reprints 2 stories/Chief Crazy Horse 4.00 12.00 24.00
22-McCann-a?; r/Sheriff Bob Dixon's... 4.00 12.00 24.00
23-27: 23-Kinstler-c. 24-27-Kinstler-c/a(r) (24,25-r?) 4.25 13.00 28.00
28-Kinstler-c/a (new); r-/Last of the Comanches 4.25 13.00 28.00
I.W. Reprint #1-r/#2; Kinstler-c 1.25 3.75 10.00
Super Reprint #10-12: 10-r/#18. 11-r/#?. 12-r/#8 1.25 3.75 10.00

NOTE: *#23, 25 contain numerous editing deletions in both art and script due to code. **Kinstler** c-6, 7, 11-14, 17, 18, 20-22, 24-28. **Howard Larsen** a-1, 2, 4, 5, 6(3), 7-9, 11, 12, 17, 18, 20-24, 26. **Meskin** a-7. **Reinman** a-6, 17.*

WILD BILL HICKOK AND JINGLES (TV)(Formerly Cowboy Western) (Also see Blue Bird)
No. 68, Aug, 1958 - No. 75, Dec, 1959
Charlton Comics

68,69-Williamson-a (all are 10¢ issues) 8.50 26.00 60.00
70-Two pgs. Williamson-a 5.70 17.00 38.00
71-75 (#76, exist?) 4.00 12.00 24.00

WILD BILL PECOS WESTERN (Also see The Westerner)
1989 ($3.50, 1/2 color/1/2 B&W, 52 pgs.)
AC Comics

1-Syd Shores-c/a(r)/Westerner; photo back-c 1.40 3.50

WILD BOY OF THE CONGO (Also see Approved Comics)
No. 10, 2-3/51 - No. 12, 8-9/51; No. 4, 10-11/51 - No. 15, 6/55
Ziff-Davis No. 10-12,4-8/St. John No. 9 on

10(#1)(2-3/51)-Origin; bondage-c by Saunders (painted); used in **SOTI**, pg. 189; painted-c begin, end #9 17.00 51.00 130.00
11(4-5/51),12(8-9/51)-Norman Saunders painted-c 10.00 30.00 70.00
4(10-11/51)-Saunders painted bondage-c 10.00 30.00 70.00

GD25 FN65 NM94

5(Winter,'51)-Saunders painted-c 9.00 27.00 60.00
6,8,9(10/53),10: 6-Saunders-c. 8,9-Painted-c 9.00 27.00 60.00
7(8-9/52)-Kinstler-a 10.00 30.00 70.00
11-13-Baker-c. 11-r/#7 w/new Baker-c; Kinstler-a (2 pgs.) 10.00 30.00 75.00
14(4/55)-Baker-c; r-#12('51) 10.00 30.00 75.00
15(6/55) 7.50 22.50 50.00

WILD CARDS
Sept, 1990 - No. 4, 1990 ($4.50, limited series, 52 pgs.)
Marvel Comics (Epic Comics)

1-4 1.80 4.50

NOTE: ***Guice** a-1; c-1-4p. **Morrow** a-4. **Rogers** a-1, 4. **Williamson** a-3.*

WILDCAT (See Sensation Comics #1)

WILDC.A.T.S ADVENTURES (TV cartoon)
Sept, 1994 - No. 10, June, 1995 ($1.95/$2.50)
Image Comics (WildStorm Productions)

1-5 .80 2.00
6-10: 6-$2.50-c begins 1.00 2.50
Sourcebook 1 (1/95, $2.95) 1.20 3.00

WILDC.A.T.S: COVERT ACTION TEAMS
Aug, 1992 - No. 4, Mar, 1993; No. 5, Nov, 1993 - Present ($1.95/$2.50)
Image Comics (WildStorm Productions)

1-1st app; Jim Lee/Williams-c/a & Lee scripts begin; contains 2 trading cards (Two diff versions of cards inside); 1st WildStorm Productions title. 2.00 5.00
1-All gold foil signed edition 1.50 4.50 12.00
1-All gold foil unsigned edition 1.00 3.00 8.00
1-Newsstand edition w/o cards 1.20 3.00
1-"3-D Special"(8/97, $4.95) w/3-D glasses; variant-c by Jim Lee 2.00 5.00
2-($2.50)-Prism foil stamped-c; contains coupon for Image Comics #0 & 4 pg. preview to Portacio's Wetworks (back-up) 1.60 4.00
2-With coupon missing .80 2.00
2-Direct sale misprint w/o foil-c 1.20 3.00
2-Newsstand ed., no prism or coupon 1.20 3.00
3-Lee/Liefeld-c (1/93-c, 12/92 inside) 1.60 4.00
4-($2.50)-Polybagged w/Topps trading card; 1st app. Tribe by Johnson & Stroman; Youngblood cameo 1.60 4.00
4-variant w/red card 2.40 6.00
5-7-Jim Lee/Williams-c/a; Lee script 1.20 3.00
8-Begin $2.50-c; X-Men's Jean Grey & Scott Summers cameos. 2.40 6.00
9-12: 10-1st app. Huntsman & Soldier; Claremont scripts begin, ends #13. 11-1st app. Savant, Tapestry & Mr. Majestic. 1.20 3.00
11-Alternate Portacio-c, see Deathblow #5 2.00 5.00
13-19,21-24,26-41: 15-James Robinson scripts begin, ends #20. 15,16-Black Razor story. 21-Alan Moore scripts begin, end #34; intro Tao & Ladytron; new WildC.A.T.S team forms (Mr. Majestic, Savant, Condition Red (Max Cash), Tao & Ladytron). 22-Maguire-a. 29-(5/96)-Fire From Heaven Pt 7; reads Apr on-c. 30-(6/96)-Fire From Heaven Pt. 13; Spartan revealed to have transplanted personality of John Colt (from Team One: WildC.A.T.S). 31-(9/96)-Grifter rejoins team; Ladytron dies 1.00 2.50
20-($2.50)-Direct Market, WildStorm Rising Pt. 2 w/bound-in card 1.00 2.50
20-($1.95)-Newsstand, WildStorm Rising Part 2 .80 2.00
25-($4.95)-Alan Moore script; wraparound foil-c. 2.00 5.00
Compendium (1993, $9.95)-r/#1-4; bagged w/#0 1.25 3.75 10.00
Sourcebook 1 (9/93, $2.50)-Foil embossed-c 1.00 2.50
Sourcebook 1-($1.95)-Newsstand ed. w/o foil embossed-c .80 2.00
Sourcebook 2 (11/94, $2.50)-wraparound-c 1.00 2.50
Special 1 (11/93, $3.50, 52 pgs.)-1st Travis Charest WildC.A.T.S-a. 1.40 3.50

WILDC.A.T.S TRILOGY
June, 1993 - No. 3, Dec, 1993 ($1.95, limited series)

Wildcore #1 © Aegis Entertainment

WildStorm Rising #1 © Aegis Entertainment

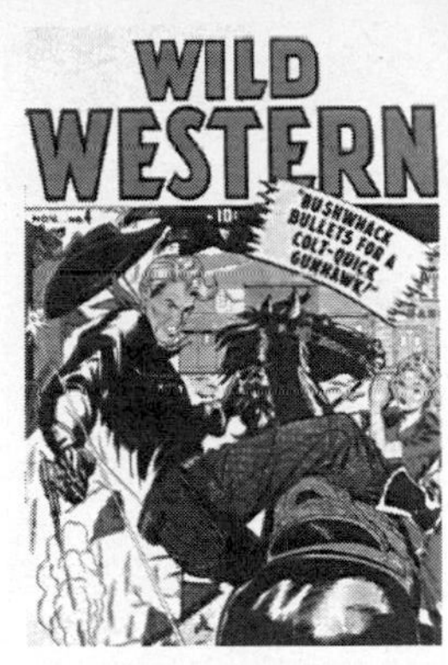

Wild Western #4 © MEG

GD25 FN65 NM94

Image Comics (WildStorm Productions)

1-($2.50)-1st app. Gen 13 (Fairchild, Burnout, Grunge, Freefall) Multi-color foil-c; Jae Lee-c/a in all 2.00 5.00
1-($1.95)-Newsstand ed. w/o foil-c .80 2.00
2,3-($1.95)-Jae Lee-c/a .80 2.00

WILDC.A.T.S/ X-MEN: THE GOLDEN AGE
Feb, 1997 ($4.50, one-shot)
Image Comics (WildStorm Productions)

1-Lobdell-s/Charest-a; Two covers(Charest, Jim Lee) 4.50
1-"3-D" Edition ($6.50) w/glasses 6.50

WILDC.A.T.S/ X-MEN: THE MODERN AGE
Aug, 1997 ($4.50, one-shot)
Image Comics (WildStorm Productions)

1-Robinson-s/Hughes-a; Two covers(Hughes, Paul Smith) 4.50
1-"3-D" Edition ($6.50) w/glasses 6.50

WILDC.A.T.S/ X-MEN: THE SILVER AGE
June, 1997 ($4.50, one-shot)
Image Comics (WildStorm Productions)

1-Lobdell-s/Jim Lee-a; Two covers(Neal Adams, Jim Lee) 4.50
1-"3-D" Edition ($6.50) w/glasses 6.50

WILDCORE
Nov, 1997 - Present ($2.50)
Image Comics (WildStorm Productions)

1-Two covers (Booth/McWeeney, Charest) 2.50
1-($3.50)-Voyager Pack w/DV8 preview 3.50

WILD DOG
Sept, 1987 - No. 4, Dec, 1987 (75¢, limited series)
DC Comics

1-4 1.00
Special 1 (1989, $2.50, 52 pgs.) 1.00 2.50

WILDERNESS TREK (See Zane Grey, Four Color 333)

WILDFIRE (See Zane Grey, FourColor 433)

WILD FRONTIER (Cheyenne Kid #8 on)
Oct, 1955 - No. 7, Apr, 1957
Charlton Comics

1-Davy Crockett 7.15 21.50 50.00
2-6-Davy Crockett in all 5.00 15.00 30.00
7-Origin & 1st app. Cheyenne Kid 5.35 16.00 32.00

WILD KINGDOM (TV)
1965 (Giveaway, regular size, slick-c, 16 pgs.)
Western Printing Co.

nn-Mutual of Omaha's... 1.75 5.25 14.00

WILDSTAR (Also see The Dragon & The Savage Dragon)
Sept, 1995 - No. 3, Jan, 1996 ($2.50, limited series)
Image Comics (Highbrow Entertainment)

1-3: Al Gordon scripts; Jerry Ordway-c/a 1.00 2.50

WILDSTAR: SKY ZERO
Mar, 1993 - No. 4, Nov, 1993 ($1.95, limited series)
Image Comics (Highbrow Entertainment)

1-($2.50)-Embossed-c w/silver ink; Ordway-c/a in all 1.00 2.50
1-($1.95)-Newsstand ed. w/silver ink-c, not embossed .80 2.00
1-Gold variant 1.00 3.00 8.00
2-4 .80 2.00

WILDSTORM
1994/1995 ($2.50/$2.95/$4.95)
Image Comics (WildStorm Publishing)

...Chamber of Horrors (10/95, $3.50)-Bisley-c 1.40 3.50
...Halloween 1 (10/97, $2.50) Warner-c 1.00 2.50
...Rarities 1(12/94, $4.95, 52 pgs.)-r/Gen 13 1/2 & other stories 1.00 3.00 8.00
...Swimsuit Special 1 (12/94, $2.95) 1.60 4.00
...Swimsuit Special 2 (1995, $2.50) 1.20 3.00
...Swimsuit Special '97 #1 (7/97, $2.50) 1.00 2.50
...Ultimate Sports 1 (8/97, $2.50) 1.00 2.50
...Universe Sourcebook (5/95, $2.50) 1.00 2.50

WILDSTORM!
Aug, 1995 - No. 4, Nov, 1995 ($2.50, B&W/color, anthology)
Image Comics (WildStorm Publishing)

1-4: 1-Simonson-a 1.00 2.50

WILDSTORM RISING
May, 1995 - No.2, June, 1995 ($1.95/$2.50)
Image Comics (WildStorm Publishing)

1 ($2.50)-Direct Market, WildStorm Rising Pt. 1 w/bound-in card 1.00 2.50
1 ($1.95)-Newstand, WildStorm Rising Pt. 1 .80 2.00
2 ($2.50)-Direct Market, WildStorm Rising Pt. 10 w/bound-in card; continues in WildC.A.T.S #21. 1.00 2.50
2 ($1.95)-Newstand, WildStorm Rising Pt. 10 .80 2.00
Trade paperback (1996, $19.95)-Collects x-over; B. Smith-c 20.00

WILDSTORM SPOTLIGHT
Feb, 1997 - Present ($2.50)
Image Comics (WildStorm Publishing)

1-4: 1-Alan Moore-s 1.00 2.50

WILDSTORM UNIVERSE '97
Dec, 1996 - No. 3 ($2.50, limited series)
Image Comics (WildStorm Publishing)

1-3: 1-Wraparound-c. 3-Gary Frank-c 1.00 2.50

WILDTHING
Apr, 1993 - No. 7, Oct, 1993 ($1.75)
Marvel Comics UK

1-($2.50)-Embossed-c; Venom & Carnage cameo 1.00 2.50
2-7: 2-Spider-Man & Venom. 6-Mysterio app. .70 1.75

WILD WEST (Wild Western #3 on)
Spring, 1948 - No. 2, July, 1948
Marvel Comics (WFP)

1-Two-Gun Kid, Arizona Annie, & Tex Taylor begin; Shores-c 28.00 83.00 220.00
2-Captain Tootsie by Beck; Shores-c 19.00 56.00 150.00

WILD WEST (Black Fury #1-57)
V2#58, Nov, 1966
Charlton Comics

V2#58 1.25 3.75 10.00

WILD WEST C.O.W.-BOYS OF MOO MESA (TV)
Dec, 1992 - No. 3, Feb, 1993 (limited series)
V2#1, Mar, 1993 - No. 3, July, 1993 ($1.25)
Archie Comics

1-3 1.25
V2#1-3 1.25

WILD WESTERN (Formerly Wild West #1,2)
No. 3, 9/48 - No. 57, 9/57 (3-11: 52 pgs, 12-on: 36 pgs)
Marvel/Atlas Comics (WFP)

3(#1)-Tex Morgan begins; Two-Gun Kid, Tex Taylor, & Arizona Annie continue from Wild West 21.00 64.00 170.00
4-Last Arizona Annie; Captain Tootsie by Beck; Kid Colt app. 16.00 49.00 130.00

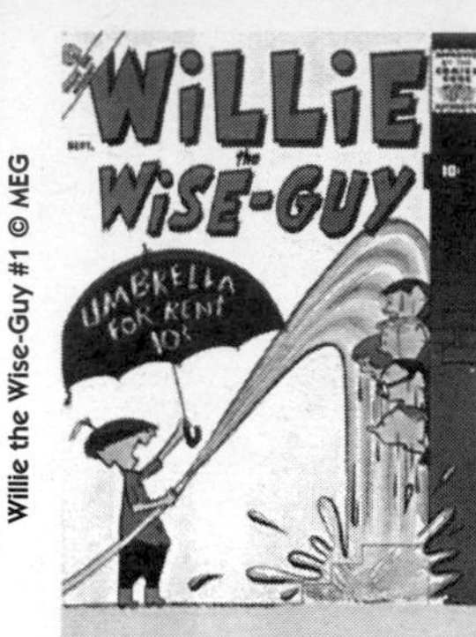

Willie the Wise-Guy #1 © MEG

Will To Power #2 © DH

Win a Prize Comics V1 #1 © CC

GD25 FN65 NM94

5-2nd app. Black Rider (1/49); Blaze Carson, Captain Tootsie (by Beck) app. 19.00 56.00 150.00
6-8: 6-Blaze Carson app; anti-Wertham editorial 11.30 34.00 90.00
9-Photo-c; Black Rider begins, ends #19 15.00 45.00 120.00
10-Charles Starrett photo-c 17.50 53.00 140.00
11-(Last 52 pg. issue) 10.50 32.00 85.00
12-14,16-19: All Black Rider-c/stories. 12-14-The Prairie Kid & his horse Fury app. 9.50 28.00 75.00
15-Red Larabee, Gunhawk (origin), his horse Blaze, & Apache Kid begin, end #22; Black Rider-c/story 10.00 30.00 80.00
20-30: 20-Kid Colt-c begin. 24-Has 2 Kid Colt stories. 26-1st app. The Ringo Kid? (2/53); 4 pg. story. 30-Katz-a 8.75 26.25 65.00
31-40 6.50 19.50 45.00
41-47,49-51,53,57 5.70 17.00 35.00
48-Williamson/Torres-a (4 pgs); Drucker-a 7.85 23.50 55.00
52-Crandall-a 7.85 23.50 55.00
54,55-Williamson-a in both (5 & 4 pgs.), #54 with Mayo plus 2 text illos 7.85 23.50 55.00
56-Baker-a? 5.70 17.00 35.00

NOTE: *Annie Oakley in #46, 47. Apache Kid in #15-22, 39. Arizona Kid in #21, 23. Arrowhead in #34-39. Black Rider in #5, 9-19, 33-44. Fighting Texan in #17. Kid Colt in #4-6, 9-11, 20-47, 52, 54-56. Outlaw Kid in #43. Red Hawkins in #13, 14. Ringo Kid in #26, 39, 41, 43, 44, 46, 47, 50, 52-56. Tex Morgan in #3, 4, 6, 9, 11. Tex Taylor in #3-6, 9, 11. Texas Kid in #23-25. Two-Gun Kid in #3-6, 9, 11, 12, 33-39, 41. Wyatt Earp in #47.* ***Ayers*** *a-41, 42.* ***Berg*** *a-26; c-24.* ***Colan*** *a-49.* ***Forte*** *a-28, 30.* ***Al Hartley*** *a-16.* ***Heath*** *a-4, 5, 8; c-34, 44.* ***Keller*** *a-24, 26(2), 29-40, 44-46, 48, 52.* ***Maneely*** *a-10, 12, 15, 16, 28, 35, 38, 40-45; c-18-22, 33, 35, 36, 38, 39, 41, 42, 45.* ***Morisi*** *a-23, 52.* ***Pakula*** *a-42, 52.* ***Powell*** *a-51.* ***Romita*** *a-24(2).* ***Severin*** *a-46, 47; c-48.* ***Shores*** *a-3, 5, 30, 31, 33, 35, 36, 38, 41; c-3-5.* ***Sinnott*** *a-34-39.* ***Wildey*** *a-43. Bondage c-19.*

WILD WESTERN ACTION (Also see The Bravados)
Mar, 1971 - No. 3, June, 1971 (25¢, reprints, 52 pgs.)
Skywald Publishing Corp.

1-Durango Kid, Straight Arrow-r; with all references to "Straight" in story relettered to "Swift"; Bravados begin; Shores-a (new) 1.00 3.00 8.00
2,3: 2-Billy Nevada, Durango Kid. 3-Red Mask, Durango Kid 2.00 5.00

WILD WESTERN ROUNDUP
Oct, 1957; 1960-'61
Red Top/Decker Publications/I. W. Enterprises

1(1957)-Kid Cowboy-r 3.60 9.00 18.00
I.W. Reprint #1('60-61)-r/#1 by Red Top 1.00 3.00 8.00

WILD WEST RODEO
1953 (15¢)
Star Publications

1-A comic book coloring book with regular full color cover & B&W inside 5.35 16.00 32.00

WILD WILD WEST, THE (TV)
June, 1966 - No. 7, Oct, 1969 (Robert Conrad photo-c)
Gold Key

1-McWilliams-a; photo back-c 11.00 34.00 125.00
2-McWilliams-a; photo back-c 9.00 26.00 95.00
3-7 6.40 19.00 70.00

WILD, WILD WEST, THE (TV)
Oct, 1990 - No. 4, Jan?, 1991 ($2.95, limited series)
Millennium Publications

1-4-Based on TV show 1.20 3.00

WILKIN BOY (See That...)

WILLIE COMICS (Formerly Ideal #1-4; Crime Cases #24 on; Li'l Willie #20 & 21) (See Gay Comics, Laugh, Millie The Model & Wisco)
#5, Fall, 1946 - #19, 4/49; #22, 1/50 - #23, 5/50 (No #20 & 21)
Marvel Comics (MgPC)

5(#1)-George, Margie, Nellie the Nurse & Willie begin 13.50 41.00 105.00
6,8,9 8.00 24.00 55.00
7(1),10,11-Kurtzman's "Hey Look" 10.00 30.00 65.00
12,14-18,22,23 6.50 19.50 45.00
13,19-Kurtzman's "Hey Look" (#19-last by Kurtzman?) 9.00 27.00 55.00

NOTE: *Cindy app. in #17. Jeanie app. in #17. Little Lizzie app. in #22.*

WILLIE MAYS (See The Amazing...)

WILLIE THE PENGUIN
Apr, 1951 - No. 6, Apr, 1952
Standard Comics

1-Funny animal 5.70 17.00 40.00
2-6 4.00 12.00 24.00

WILLIE THE WISE-GUY (Also see Cartoon Kids)
Sept, 1957
Atlas Comics (NPP)

1-Kida, Maneely-a 6.50 19.50 45.00

WILLOW
Aug, 1988 - No. 3, Oct, 1988 ($1.00)
Marvel Comics

1-3-R/Marvel Graphic Novel #36 (movie adaptation) 1.00

WILLOW, (A Girl Called)
June, 1996 - No. 2, Spring, 1997 ($2.95, B&W)
Angel Entertainment

0-2 1.20 3.00
0-($5.95)-Black Magic Foil 1.20 3.00
0-2-($10.00)-Nude Edition 1.25 3.75 10.00

WILL ROGERS WESTERN (Formerly My Great Love #1-4; see Blazing & True Comics #66)
No. 5, June, 1950 - No. 2, Aug, 1950
Fox Features Syndicate

5(#1) 28.00 84.00 225.00
2: Photo-c 24.00 73.00 195.00

WILL TO POWER (Also see Comic's Greatest World)
June, 1994 - No. 12, Aug, 1994 ($1.00, weekly limited series, 20 pgs.)
Dark Horse Comics

1-12: 12-Vortex kills Titan. 1.25

NOTE: ***Mignola*** *c-10-12.* ***Sears*** *c-1-3.*

WILL-YUM!
No. 676, Feb, 1956 - No. 902, May, 1958
Dell Publishing Co.

Four Color 676 (#1), 765 (1/57), 902 1.80 5.50 20.00

WIN A PRIZE COMICS (Timmy The Timid Ghost #3 on?)
Feb, 1955 - No. 2, Apr, 1955
Charlton Comics

V1#1-S&K-a; Poe adapt; E.C. War swipe 56.00 168.00 500.00
2-S&K-a 40.00 120.00 360.00

WINDY & WILLY
May-June, 1969 - No. 4, Nov-Dec, 1969
National Periodical Publications

1- r/Dobie Gillis with some art changes begin 2.50 7.50 24.00
2-4 1.75 5.25 14.00

WINGS COMICS
9/40 - No. 109, 9/49; No. 110, Wint, 1949-50; No. 111, Spring, 1950; No. 112, 1950(nd); No. 113 - No. 115, 1950(nd); No. 116, 1952(nd); No. 117, Fall, 1952 - No. 122, Wint, 1953-54; No. 123 - No. 124, 1954(nd)
Fiction House Magazines

1-Skull Squad, Clipper Kirk, Suicide Smith, Jane Martin, War Nurse, Phantom Falcons, Greasemonkey Griffin, Parachute Patrol & Powder Burns begin

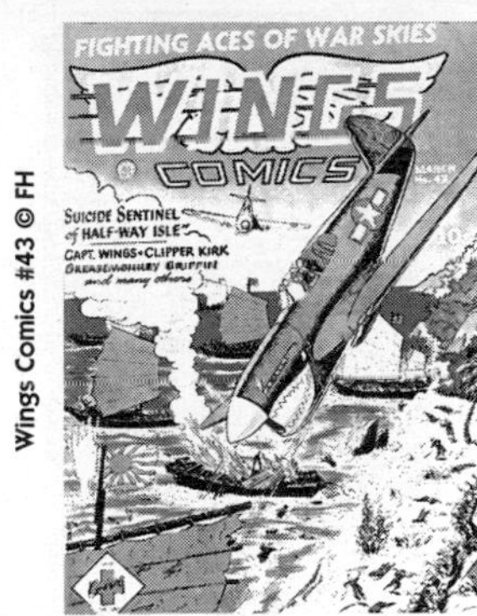

Wings Comics #43 © FH

Winterworld #3 © ECL

Wise Son: The White Wolf #1 © DC

GD25 FN65 NM94

189.00 567.00 1700.00
2 78.00 234.00 700.00
3-5 53.00 159.00 475.00
6-10 44.00 132.00 400.00
11-15 38.00 113.00 340.00
16-Origin & 1st app. Captain Wings & begin series 44.00 132.00 400.00
17-20 35.00 105.00 280.00
21-30 31.00 94.00 250.00
31-40 25.00 75.00 200.00
41-50 20.00 60.00 160.00
51-60: 60-Last Skull Squad 17.50 53.00 140.00
61-67: 66-Ghost Patrol begins (becomes Ghost Squadron #71 on), ends #112? 16.00 49.00 130.00
68,69: 68-Clipper Kirk becomes The Phantom Falcon-origin, Part 1; part 2 in #69 16.00 49.00 130.00
70-72: 70-1st app. The Phantom Falcon in costume, origin-Part 3; Capt. Wings battles Col. Kamikaze in all 14.00 41.00 110.00
73-99: 80-Phantom Falcon by Larsen. 99-King of the Congo begins? 14.00 41.00 110.00
100-(12/48) 15.00 45.00 120.00
101-124: 111-Last Jane Martin. 112-Flying Saucer-c/story (1950). 115-Used in **POP**, pg. 89 12.00 38.00 100.00

NOTE: *Bondage covers are common. Captain Wings battles Sky Hag-#75, 76; ...Mr. Atlantis-#85-92; ...Mr. Pupin(Red Agent)-#98-103. Capt. Wings by* ***Elias****-#52-64, 68, 69; by* ***Lubbers****-#29-32, 70-111; by* ***Renee****-#33-46.* ***Evans*** *a-85-106, 108-111(Jane Martin); text illos-72-84.* ***Larsen*** *a-52, 59, 64, 73-77. Jane Martin by* ***Fran Hopper****-#68-84; Suicide Smith by* ***John Celardo****-#72, 74, 76, 80-104; by* ***Hollingsworth****-#68-70, 105-109, 111; Ghost Squadron by* ***Astarita****-#67-79; by* ***Maurice Whitman****-#80-111. King of the Congo by* ***Moreira****-#99, 100. Skull Squad by* ***M. Baker****-#52-60; Clipper Kirk by* ***Baker****-#60, 61; by* ***Colan****-#53; by* ***Ingels****-(some issues?). Phantom Falcon by* ***Larsen****-#73-84.* ***Elias*** *c-58-72.* ***Fawcette*** *c-3-12, 16, 17, 19, 22-33.* ***Lubbers*** *c-74-109.* ***Tuska*** *a-5.* ***Whitman*** *c-110-124.* ***Zolnerwich*** *c-15, 21.*

WINGS OF THE EAGLES, THE
No. 790, Apr, 1957 (10¢ & 15¢ editions exist)
Dell Publishing Co.

Four Color 790-Movie; John Wayne photo-c; Toth-a 14.00 44.00 160.00

WINKY DINK (Adventures of...)
No. 75, Mar, 1957 (one-shot)
Pines Comics

75-Marv Levy-c/a 4.00 12.00 24.00

WINKY DINK (TV)
No. 663, Nov, 1955
Dell Publishing Co.

Four Color 663 (#1) 7.00 22.00 80.00

WINNIE-THE-POOH (Also see Dynabrite Comics)
January, 1977 - No. 33, 1984 (Walt Disney)
(Winnie-The-Pooh began as Edward Bear in 1926 by Milne)
Gold Key No. 1-17/Whitman No. 18 on

1-New art .80 2.00
2-33: 5,12-33-New material 1.50

WINNIE WINKLE (See Popular Comics & Super Comics)
1941 - No. 7, Sept-Nov, 1949
Dell Publishing Co.

Large Feature Comic 2 (1941) 16.00 49.00 180.00
Four Color 94 (1945) 11.00 33.00 120.00
Four Color 174 6.40 19.00 70.00
1(3-5/48)-Contains daily & Sunday newspaper-r from 1939-1941 5.75 17.00 63.00
2 (6-8/48) 3.00 10.00 36.00
3-7 2.25 6.75 25.00

WINTERWORLD
Sept, 1987 - No. 3, Mar, 1988 ($1.75, limited series)
Eclipse Comics

1-3 .75 1.80

WISCO/KLARER COMIC BOOK (Miniature)
1948 - 1964 (3-1/2x6-3/4", 24 pgs.)
Marvel Comics/Vital Publications/Fawcett Publications

Given away by Wisco "99" Service Stations, Carnation Malted Milk, Klarer Health Wieners, Fleers Dubble Bubble Gum, Rodeo All-Meat Wieners, Perfect Potato Chips, & others; see ad in Tom Mix #21

Blackstone & the Gold Medal Mystery (1948) 5.70 17.00 40.00
Blackstone "Solves the Sealed Vault Mystery" (1950) 5.70 17.00 40.00
Blaze Carson in "The Sheriff Shoots It Out" (1950) 5.70 17.00 40.00
Captain Marvel & Billy's Big Game (r/Capt. Marvel Adv. #76) 25.00 75.00 200.00
(Prices vary widely on this book)
China Boy in "A Trip to the Zoo" #10 (1948) 4.00 12.00 24.00
Indoors-Outdoors Game Book 2.00 5.00 10.00
Jim Solar Space Sheriff in "Battle for Mars", "Between Two Worlds", "Conquers Outer Space", "The Creatures on the Comet", "Defeats the Moon Missile Men", "Encounter Creatures on Comet", "Meet the Jupiter Jumpers", "Meets the Man From Mars", "On Traffic Duty", "Outlaws of the Spaceways", "Pirates of the Planet X", "Protects Space Lanes", "Raiders From the Sun", "Ring Around Saturn", "Robots of Rhea", "The Sky Ruby", "Spacetts of the Sky", "Spidermen of Venus", "Trouble on Mercury" 5.70 17.00 35.00
Johnny Starboard & the Underseas Pirates (1948) 3.60 9.00 18.00
Kid Colt in "He Lived by His Guns" (1950) 5.70 17.00 40.00
Little Aspirin as "Crook Catcher" #2 (1950) 2.00 5.00 10.00
Little Aspirin in "Naughty But Nice" #6 (1950) 2.00 5.00 10.00
Return of the Black Phantom (not M.E. character)(Roy Dare)(1948) 4.25 13.00 26.00
Secrets of Magic 2.40 6.00 12.00
Slim Morgan "Brings Justice to Mesa City" #3 2.40 6.00 12.00
Super Rabbit(1950)-Cuts Red Tape, Stops Crime Wave! 8.50 26.00 60.00
Tex Farnum, Frontiersman (1948) 2.80 7.00 14.00
Tex Taylor in "Draw or Die, Cowpoke!" (1950) 4.25 13.00 28.00
Tex Taylor in "An Exciting Adventure at the Gold Mine" (1950) 4.25 13.00 26.00
Wacky Quacky in "All-Aboard" 1.20 3.00 6.00
When School Is Out 1.20 3.00 6.00
Willie in a "Comic-Comic Book Fall" #1 1.60 4.00 8.00
Wonder Duck "An Adventure at the Rodeo of the Fearless Quacker!" (1950) 7.15 21.50 50.00
Rare uncut version of three; includes Capt. Marvel, Tex Farnum, Black Phantom Estimated value... $300.00
Rare uncut version of three; includes China Boy, Blackstone, Johnny Starboard & the Underseas Pirates Estimated value... $82.00

WISE GUYS (See Harvey...)

WISE LITTLE HEN, THE
1935 (c.1934)(48 pgs.); 1937 (Story book)
David McKay Publ./Whitman

nn-(1935 edition w/dust jacket)(48 pgs. with color, 8-3/4x9-3/4") -Debut of Donald Duck (see Advs. of Mickey Mouse); Donald app. on cover with Wise Little Hen & Practical Pig; painted cover; same artist as the B&W's from Silly Symphony Cartoon, The Wise Little Hen (1934) (McKay)
Book w/dust jacket 133.00 400.00 800.00
Dust jacket only 41.00 125.00 250.00
888(1937)(9-1/2x13", 12 pgs.)(Whitman) Donald Duck app. 21.00 64.00 170.00

WISE SON: THE WHITE WOLF
Nov, 1996 - No. 4, Feb, 1997 ($2.50, limited series)
DC Comics (Milestone)

1-4: Ho Che Anderson-c/a 1.00 2.50

WITCHBLADE (Also see Cyblade/Shi & Tales Of The...)

Witchblade #6 © Top Cow

Witchcraft #1 © DC

Witching Hour #84 © DC

GD25 FN65 NM94

Nov, 1995 - Present ($2.50)
Image Comics (Top Cow Productions)

1/2-Mike Turner/Marc Silvestri-c. 5.00 15.00 50.00
1-Mike Turner-a(p) 4.00 12.00 40.00
2,3 2.50 7.50 20.00
4,5 1.25 3.75 10.00
6-9: 8-Wraparound-c. 9-Tony Daniel-a(p) 2.00 5.00
9-Variant-c 1.25 3.75 10.00
10-Flip book w/Darkness #0, 1st app. the Darkness 1.00 2.80 7.00
10-Variant-c 1.50 4.50 12.00
10-($3.95) Exclusive alternate-c 2.00 5.00
11-15 1.20 3.00
16-19: 18,19-"Family Ties" Darkness x-over pt. 1,4 1.00 2.50

WITCHBLADE COLLECTED EDITION
July, 1996 - No. 4, Oct, 1996 ($4.95, squarebound, limited series)
Image Comics (Top Cow Productions)

1-4: 1-r/#1,2. 2-r/#3,4. 3-r/#5,6. 4-r/#7,8. 5-r/#9,10 2.00 5.00
4-(10/96, $10.95)-Packaged w/slipcase 11.00

WITCHBLADE/ELEKTRA
Mar, 1997 ($2.95)
Image Comics (Top Cow Productions)

1-Devil's Reign Pt. 6 1.20 3.00

WITCHCRAFT (See Strange Mysteries, Super Reprint #18)
Mar-Apr, 1952 - No. 6, Mar, 1953
Avon Periodicals

1-Kubert-a; 1 pg. Check-a 51.00 155.00 450.00
2-Kubert & Check-a 40.00 120.00 325.00
3,6: 3-Lawrence-a; Kinstler inside-c 29.00 88.00 220.00
4-People cooked alive c/story 34.00 103.00 250.00
5-Kelly Freas painted-c 39.00 118.00 290.00
NOTE: ***Hollingsworth** a-4-6; c-4, 6. **McCann** a-3?*

WITCHCRAFT
June, 1994 - No. 3, Aug, 1994 ($2.95, limited series)
DC Comics (Vertigo)

1-3: James Robinson scripts & Kaluta-c in all 2.00 5.00
1-Platinum Edition 1.25 3.75 10.00
Trade paperback-(1996, $14.95)-r/#1-3; Kaluta-c 15.00

WITCHES TALES (Witches Western Tales #29,30)
Jan, 1951 - No. 28, Dec, 1954 (date misprinted as 4/55)
Witches Tales/Harvey Publications

1-Powell-a (1 pg.) 39.00 118.00 300.00
2-Eye injury panel 21.00 62.00 150.00
3-7,9,10 13.50 41.00 100.00
8-Eye injury panels 15.00 45.00 110.00
11-13,15,16: 12-Acid in face story 12.00 36.00 90.00
14,17-Powell/Nostrand-a. 17-Atomic disaster story 15.00 45.00 110.00
18-Nostrand-a; E.C. swipe/Shock S.S. 15.00 45.00 110.00
19-Nostrand-a; E.C. swipe/ "Glutton"; Devil-c 15.00 45.00 110.00
20-24-Nostrand-a. 21-E.C. swipe; rape story. 23-Wood E.C. swipes/Two-Fisted Tales #34 15.00 45.00 110.00
25-Nostrand-a; E.C. swipe/Mad Barber; decapitation-c 15.00 45.00 110.00
26-28: 27-r/#6 with diff.-c. 28-r/#8 with diff.-c 11.00 33.00 80.00
NOTE: ***Check** a-24. **Elias** c-8, 10, 16-27. **Kremer** a-18; c-25. **Nostrand** a-17-25; 14, 17(w/**Powell**). **Palais** a-1, 2, 4(2), 5(2), 7-9, 12, 14, 15, 17. **Powell** a-3-7, 10, 11, 19-27. Bondage-c 1, 3, 5, 6, 8, 9.*

WITCHES TALES (Magazine)
V1#7, July, 1969 - V7#1, Feb, 1975 (B&W, 52 pgs.)
Eerie Publications

V1#7(7/69) - 9(11/69) 4.00 12.00 40.00
V2#1-6('70), V3#1-6('71) 3.00 9.00 30.00

GD25 FN65 NM94

V4#1-6('72), V5#1-6('73), V6#1-6('74), V7#1 2.50 7.50 24.00
NOTE: *Ajax/Farrell reprints in early issues.*

WITCHES' WESTERN TALES (Formerly Witches Tales)(Western Tales #31on)
No. 29, Feb, 1955 - No. 30, Apr, 1955
Harvey Publications

29,30-Featuring Clay Duncan & Boys' Ranch; S&K-r/from Boys' Ranch including-c. 29-Last pre-code 12.50 38.00 125.00

WITCH HUNTER
Apr, 1996 ($2.50, one-shot)
Malibu Comics (Ultraverse)

1 1.00 2.50

WITCHING HOUR ("The ..." in later issues)
Feb-Mar, 1969 - No. 85, Oct, 1978
National Periodical Publications/DC Comics

1-Toth-a, plus Neal Adams-a (2 pgs.) 7.00 21.00 70.00
2,6: 6-Toth-a 2.50 7.50 25.00
3,5-Wrightson-a; Toth-p. 3-Last 12¢ issue 3.20 9.60 32.00
4,7-12: Toth-a in all. 8-Toth, Neal Adams-a 1.85 5.50 15.00
13-Neal Adams-c/a, 2pgs. 2.25 6.75 18.00
14-Williamson/Garzon, Jones-a; N. Adams-c 2.50 7.50 24.00
15-20 1.10 3.30 9.00
21-37,39,40 1.00 2.80 7.00
38-(100 pgs.) 3.00 9.00 30.00
41-60 2.40 6.00
61-85: 84-(44 pgs.) 1.60 4.00
NOTE: *Combined with The Unexpected with #189. **Neal Adams** c-7-11, 13, 14. **Alcala** a-24, 27, 33, 41, 43. **Anderson** a-9, 38. **Cardy** c-4, 5. **Kaluta** a-7. **Kane** a-12p. **Morrow** a-10, 13, 15, 16. **Nino** a-31, 40, 45, 47. **Redondo** a-20, 23, 24, 34, 65; c-53. **Reese** a-23. **Sparling** a-1. **Toth** a-1, 3-12, 38r. **Tuska** a-11, 12. **Wood** a-15.*

WITHIN OUR REACH
1991 ($7.95, 84 pgs.)
Star Reach Productions

nn-Spider-Man, Concrete by Chadwick, Gift of the Magi by Russell; X-mas stories; Chadwick-c; Spidey back-c 1.00 3.00 8.00

WITH THE MARINES ON THE BATTLEFRONTS OF THE WORLD
1953 (no month) - No. 2, Mar, 1954 (Photo covers)
Toby Press

1-John Wayne story 27.00 81.00 200.00
2-Monty Hall in #1,2 6.50 19.50 45.00

WITH THE U.S. PARATROOPS BEHIND ENEMY LINES (Also see U.S. Paratroops...; #2-6 titled U.S. Paratroops...)
1951 - No. 6, Dec, 1952
Avon Periodicals

1-Wood-c & inside f/c 13.50 41.00 100.00
2-Kinstler-c & inside f/c only 8.00 24.00 50.00
3-6: 6-Kinstler-c & inside f/c only 6.70 20.00 45.00
NOTE: ***Kinstler** c-2, 4-6.*

WITNESS, THE (Also see Amazing Mysteries, Captain America #71, Ideal #4, Marvel Mystery #92 & Mystic #7)
Sept, 1948
Marvel Comics (MjMe)

1(Scarce)-Rico-c? 133.00 400.00 1200.00

WITTY COMICS
1945 - No. 7, 1945
Irwin H. Rubin Publ./Chicago Nite Life News No. 2

1-The Pioneer, Junior Patrol; war-c 15.50 47.00 125.00
2-The Pioneer, Junior Patrol 8.75 26.25 65.00
3-7-Skyhawk 7.15 21.50 50.00

WIZARD OF FOURTH STREET, THE
Dec, 1987 - No. 2, 1988 ($1.75, B&W, limited series)

Wolf & Red #2 © Tex Avery

Wolverine #85 © MEG

Wolverine: Days of Future Past #2 © MEG

GD25 FN65 NM94

Dark Horse Comics

1,2: Adapts novel by S/F author Simon Hawke .75 1.80

WIZARD OF OZ (See Classics Illustrated Jr. 535, Dell Jr. Treasury No. 5, First Comics Graphic Novel, Marvelous..., & Marvel Treasury of Oz)
No. 1308, Mar-May, 1962 (TV)
Dell Publishing Co.

Four Color 1308 10.00 30.00 110.00

WIZARD'S TALE, THE
1997 ($19.95, squarebound, one-shot)
Image Comics (Homage Comics)

nn-Kurt Busiek-s/David Wenzel-painted-a/c 19.95

WOLF & RED
Apr, 1995 - No. 3, June, 1995 ($2.50, limited series)
Dark Horse Comics

1-3: Characters created by Tex Avery 1.00 2.50

WOLFF & BYRD, COUNSELORS OF THE MACABRE
May, 1994 - Present ($2.50, B&W)
Exhibit A Press

1-10 1.00 2.50

WOLF GAL (See Al Capp's...)

WOLFMAN, THE (See Movie Classics)

WOLFPACK
Feb, 1988 ($7.95); Aug, 1988 - No. 12, July, 1989 (Limited series)
Marvel Comics

1-1st app./origin (Marvel Graphic Novel #31) 1.00 3.00 8.00
1-12 1.00

WOLVERINE (See Alpha Flight, Daredevil #196, 249, Ghost Rider; Wolverine; Punisher, Havok &..., Incredible Hulk #180, Incredible Hulk &..., Kitty Pryde And..., Marvel Comics Presents, Power Pack, Punisher and..., Spider-Man vs... & X-Men #94)

WOLVERINE
Sept, 1982 - No. 4, Dec, 1982 (limited series)
Marvel Comics Group

1-Frank Miller-c/a(p) in all 2.50 7.50 20.00
2,3 1.85 5.50 15.00
4 2.15 6.50 17.00
Trade paperback 1(7/87, $4.95)-Reprints #1-4 with new Miller-c. 1.00 3.00 8.00
Trade paperback nn (2nd printing, $9.95)-r/#1-4 1.25 3.75 10.00

WOLVERINE
Nov, 1988 - Present ($1.50/$1.75, Baxter paper)
Marvel Comics

1-Buscema a-1-16, c-1-10; Williamson a(i)-1,4-8 2.25 6.75 18.00
2 1.25 3.75 10.00
3-5: 4-BWS back-c 1.10 3.30 9.00
6-9: 6-McFarlane back-c. 7,8-Hulk app. 1.00 2.80 7.00
10-1st battle with Sabretooth (before Wolverine had his claws) 1.85 5.50 15.00
11-16: 11-New costume 2.40 6.00
17-20: 17-Byrne-c/a(p) begins, ends #23 1.60 4.00
21-30: 24,25,27-Jim Lee-c. 26-Begin $1.75-c 1.20 3.00
31-40,44,47 .80 2.00
41-Sabretooth claims to be Wolverine's father; Cable cameo 1.60 4.00
41-Gold 2nd printing ($1.75) .80 2.00
42-Sabretooth, Cable & Nick Fury app.; Sabretooth proven not to be Wolverine's father 1.60 4.00
42-Gold ink 2nd printing ($1.75) .80 2.00
43-Sabretooth cameo (2 panels); saga ends 1.20 3.00
45,46-Sabretooth-c/stories 1.00 2.50
48,49-Sabretooth app. 48-Begin 3 part Weapon X sequel .80 2.00
50-($2.50, 64 pgs.)-Die cut-c; Wolverine back to old yellow costume; Forge, Cyclops, Jubilee, Jean Grey & Nick Fury app. 1.20 3.00
51-74,76-80: 51-Sabretooth-c & app. 54-Shatterstar (from X-Force) app. 55-Gambit, Jubilee, Sunfire-c/story. 55-57,73-Gambit app. 57-Mariko Yashida dies (Late 7/92). 58,59-Terror, Inc. x-over. 60-64-Sabretooth storyline (60,62,64-c). .80 2.00
75-($3.95, 68 pgs.)-Wolverine hologram on-c 1.60 4.00
81-84,86: 81-Begin $1.95-c; bound-in card sheet .90 2.25
85-($2.50)-Newsstand edition 1.00 2.50
85-($3.50)-Collectors edition 1.40 3.50
87-90 ($1.95)-Deluxe edition .80 2.00
87-90 ($1.50)-Regular edition 1.50
91-99,101-114, 1(7/97): 91-Return from "Age of Apocalypse," 93-Juggernaut app. 94-Gen X app. 101-104-Elektra app. 104-Origin of Onslaught. 105-Onslaught x-over. 110-Shaman-c/app. 114-Alternate-c .80 2.00
100 ($3.95)-Hologram-c; Wolverine loses humanity. 2.00 5.00
100 ($2.95)-Regular-c. 1.20 3.00
115-124: 115-Begin $1.99-c; Operation Zero Tolerance .80 2.00
Annual nn (1990, $4.50, squarebound, 52 pgs.)-The Jungle Adventure; Simonson scripts; Mignola-c/a 1.80 4.50
Annual 2 (12/90, $4.95, squarebound, 52 pgs.)-Bloodlust 2.00 5.00
Annual nn (#3, 8/91, $5.95, 68 pgs.)-Rahne of Terror; Cable & The New Mutants app.; Andy Kubert-c/a (2nd print exists) 2.40 6.00
Annual '95 (1995, $3.95) 1.60 4.00
Annual '96 (1996, $2.95)- Wraparound-c; Silver Samurai, Yukio, and Red Ronin app. 1.20 3.00
...'97 (1997, $2.99)- Wraparound-c 2.99
...BATTLES THE INCREDIBLE HULK nn (1989, $4.95, squarebound, 52 pg.) r/Incredible Hulk #180,181 2.00 5.00
...BLOOD HUNGRY nn (1993, $6.95, 68 pgs.)-Kieth-r/Marvel Comics Presents #85-92 w/ new Kieth-c 1.00 2.80 7.00
...: BLOODY CHOICES nn (1993, $7.95, 68 pgs.)-r/Graphic Novel; Nick Fury app. 1.00 3.00 8.00
...EVILUTION (9/94, $5.95) 2.40 6.00
...: GLOBAL JEOPARDY 1 (12/93, $2.95, one-shot)-Embossed-c; Sub-Mariner, Zabu, Ka-Zar, Shanna & Wolverine app.; produced in cooperation with World Wildlife Fund 1.20 3.00
...:INNER FURY nn (1992, $5.95, 52 pgs.)-Sienkiewicz-c/a 2.40 6.00
...: KNIGHT OF TERRA (1995, $6.95)-Ostrander script1.00 2.80 7.00
...: SAVE THE TIGER 1 (7/92, $2.95, 84 pgs.)-Reprints Wolverine stories from Marvel Comics Presents #1-10 w/new Kieth-c 1.20 3.00
...TRIUMPHS AND TRAGEDIES-(1995, $16.95, trade paperback)-r/Uncanny X-Men #109,172,173, Wolverine limited series #4, & Wolverine #41,42,75 17.00
...TYPHOID'S KISS (6/94, $6.95) r/Wolverine stories from Marvel Comics Presents #109-116 1.00 2.80 7.00

NOTE: ***Austin*** *c-3i.* ***Bolton*** *c(back)-5.* ***Buscema*** *25, 27p.* ***Byrne*** *a-17-22p, 23; c-1(back), 17-22, 23p.* ***Colan*** *a-24.* ***Andy Kubert*** *c/a-51.* ***Jim Lee*** *c-24, 25, 27.* ***Silvestri*** *a(p)-31-43, 45, 46, 48-50, 52, 53, 55-57; c-31-42p, 43, 45p, 46p, 48, 49p, 50p, 52p, 53p, 55-57p.* ***Stroman*** *a-44p; c-60p.* ***Williamson*** *a-3i; c(i)-1, 3-6.*

WOLVERINE AND THE PUNISHER: DAMAGING EVIDENCE
Oct, 1993 - No. 3, Dec, 1993 ($2.00, limited series)
Marvel Comics

1-3: 2,3-Indicia says "The Punisher and Wolverine..." .80 2.00

WOLVERINE: DAYS OF FUTURE PAST
Dec, 1997 - No. 3, Feb, 1998 ($2.50, limited series)
Marvel Comics

1-3: J.F. Moore-s/Bennett-a 2.50

WOLVERINE/GAMBIT: VICTIMS
Sept, 1995 - No. 4, Dec, 1995 ($2.95, limited series)

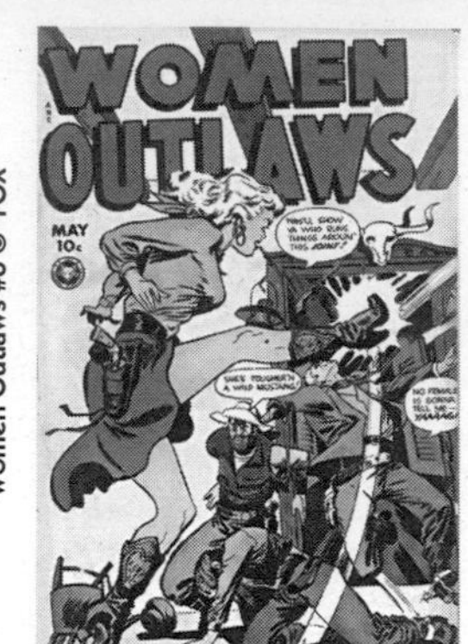

Women Outlaws #6 © FOX

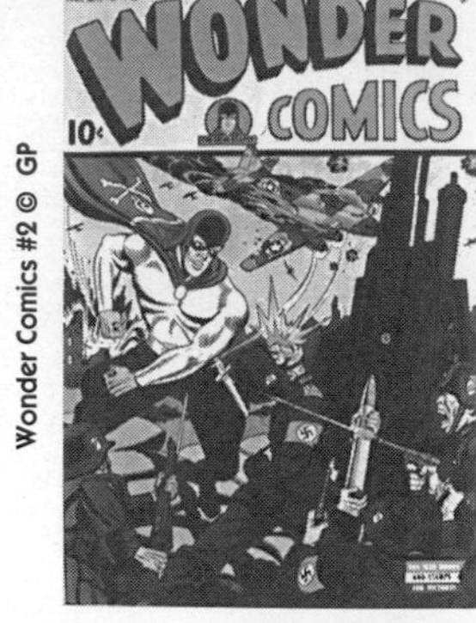

Wonder Comics #2 © GP

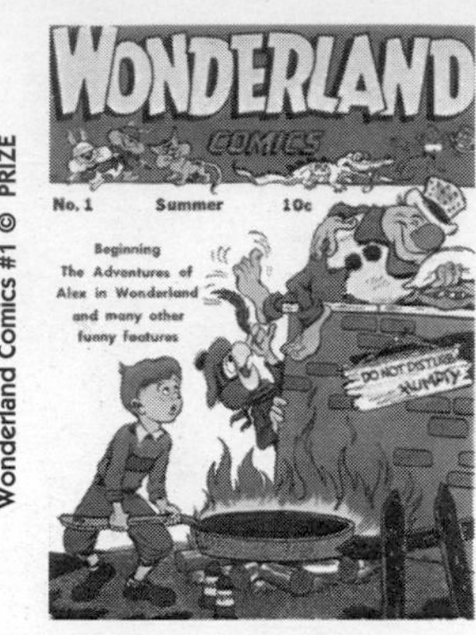

Wonderland Comics #1 © PRIZE

Marvel Comics

1-4: Jeph Loeb scripts & Tim Sale-a; foil-c 1.20 3.00

WOLVERINE SAGA
Sept, 1989 - No. 4, Mid-Dec, 1989 ($3.95, limited series, 52 pgs.)
Marvel Comics

1-Gives history; Liefeld/Austin-c (front & back) 2.00 5.00
2-4: 2-Romita, Jr./Austin-c. 4-Kaluta-c 2.40 4.00

WOLVERINE VS. SPIDER-MAN
Mar, 1995 (2.50, one-shot)
Marvel Comics

1-r/Marvel Comics Presents #48 - 50 1.00 2.50

WOLVERINE/WITCHBLADE
Mar, 1997 (2.95, one-shot)
Marvel Comics

1-Devil's Reign Pt. 5 1.60 4.00

WOMAN OF THE PROMISE, THE
1950 (General Distr.) (Paper cover, 32 pgs.)
Catechetical Guild

nn 3.00 7.50 15.00

WOMEN IN LOVE (A Feature Presentation #5)
Aug, 1949 - No. 4, Feb, 1950
Fox Features Synd./Hero Books

1 23.00 69.00 170.00
2-Kamen/Feldstein-c 19.00 58.00 145.00
3 12.00 36.00 90.00
4-Wood-a 16.00 47.00 110.00

WOMEN IN LOVE (Thrilling Romances for Adults)
Winter, 1952 (25¢, 100 pgs.)
Ziff-Davis Publishing Co.

nn-(Scarce)-Kinstler-a; painted-c 40.00 120.00 350.00

WOMEN OUTLAWS (My Love Memories #9 on)(Also see Red Circle)
July, 1948 - No. 8, Sept, 1949
Fox Features Syndicate

1-Used in **SOTI**, illo "Giving children an image of American womanhood"; negligee panels 58.00 174.00 500.00
2-Spanking panel 50.00 150.00 400.00
3-Kamenish-a 50.00 150.00 400.00
4-8 40.00 120.00 300.00
nn(nd)-Contains Cody of the Pony Express; same cover as #7 29.00 86.00 200.00

WOMEN TO LOVE
No date (1953)
Realistic

nn-(Scarce)-Reprints Complete Romance #1; c-/Avon paperback #165 34.00 103.00 245.00

WONDER BOY (Formerly Terrific Comics) (See Blue Bolt, Bomber Comics & Samson)
No. 17, May, 1955 - No. 18, July, 1955 (Code approved)
Ajax/Farrell Publ.

17-Phantom Lady app. Bakerish-c/a 39.00 118.00 300.00
18-Phantom Lady app. 36.00 107.00 275.00
NOTE: *Phantom Lady not by Matt Baker.*

WONDER COMICS (Wonderworld #3 on)
May, 1939 - No. 2, June, 1939 (68 pgs.)
Fox Features Syndicate

GD25 FN65 VF82 NM94

1-(Scarce)-Wonder Man only app. by Will Eisner; Dr. Fung (by Powell), K-51 begins; Bob Kane-a; Eisner-c 1227.00 3680.00 8000.00 13,500.00
(Estimated up to 70 total copies exist, 3 in NM/Mint)

GD25 FN65 NM94

2-(Scarce)-Yarko the Great, Master Magician (see Samson) by Eisner begins; 'Spark' Stevens by Bob Kane, Patty O'Day, Tex Mason app. Lou Fine's 1st-c; Fine-a (2 pgs.); Yarko-c (Wonder Man-c #1) 420.00 1260.00 4200.00

WONDER COMICS
May, 1944 - No. 20, Oct, 1948
Great/Nedor/Better Publications

1-The Grim Reaper & Spectro, the Mind Reader begin; Hitler/Hirohito bondage-c 89.00 267.00 800.00
2-Origin The Grim Reaper; Super Sleuths begin, end #8,17 50.00 150.00 450.00
3-5 47.00 141.00 420.00
6-10: 6-Flag-c. 8-Last Spectro. 9-Wonderman begins 36.00 108.00 325.00
11-14: 11-Dick Devens, King of Futuria begins, ends #14. 11,12-Ingels-c & splash pg. 43.00 129.00 390.00
15-Tara begins (origin), ends #20 52.00 156.00 470.00
16,18: 16-Spectro app.; last Grim Reaper. 18-The Silver Knight begins 43.00 129.00 390.00
17-Wonderman with Frazetta panels; Jill Trent with all Frazetta inks 47.00 141.00 420.00
19-Frazetta panels 43.00 129.00 390.00
20-Most of Silver Knight by Frazetta 52.00 156.00 470.00
NOTE: ***Ingels** c-11, 12. **Roussos** a-19. **Schomburg** (**Xela**) c-1-10; (airbrush)-13-20. Bondage c-12, 13, 15. Cover features: Grim Reaper #1-8; Wonder Man #9-15; Tara #16-20.*

WONDER DUCK (See Wisco)
Sept, 1949 - No. 3, Mar, 1950
Marvel Comics (CDS)

1-Funny animal 11.30 34.00 90.00
2,3 8.50 26.00 60.00

WONDERFUL ADVENTURES OF PINOCCHIO, THE (See Movie Comics & Walt Disney Showcase #48)
No. 3, April, 1982 (Walt Disney)
Whitman Publishing Co.

3-(Continuation of Movie Comics?); r/FC #92 1.20 3.00

WONDERFUL WORLD OF DUCKS (See Golden Picture Story Book)
1975
Colgate Palmolive Co.

1-Mostly-r 1.00

WONDERFUL WORLD OF THE BROTHERS GRIMM (See Movie Comics)

WONDERLAND COMICS
Summer, 1945 - No. 9, Feb-Mar, 1947
Feature Publications/Prize

1-Alex in Wonderland begins; Howard Post-c 8.50 28.00 75.00
2-Howard Post-c/a(2) 6.50 19.50 45.00
3-9: 3,4-Post-c 5.70 17.00 35.00

WONDER MAN (See The Avengers #9, 151)
Mar, 1986 ($1.25, one-shot, 52 pgs.)
Marvel Comics Group

1 1.30

WONDER MAN
Sept, 1991 - No. 29, Jan, 1994 ($1.00)
Marvel Comics Group

1-5: 1-Free fold out poster by Johnson/Austin. 1-3-Johnson/Austin-c/a. 2-Avengers West Coast x-over. 4 Austin-c(i) 1.00
6-29: 6-begin 1.25-c 1.25
Annual 1 (1992, $2.25)-Immonen-a (10 pgs.) .90 2.25

WONDERS OF ALADDIN, THE
No. 1255, Feb-Apr, 1962
Dell Publishing Co.

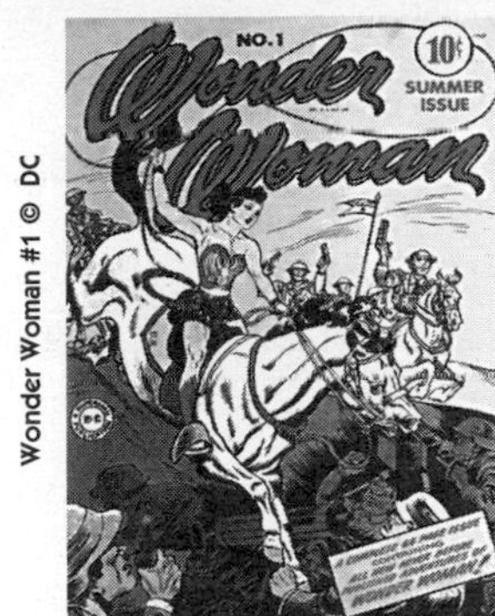

Wonder Woman #1 © DC

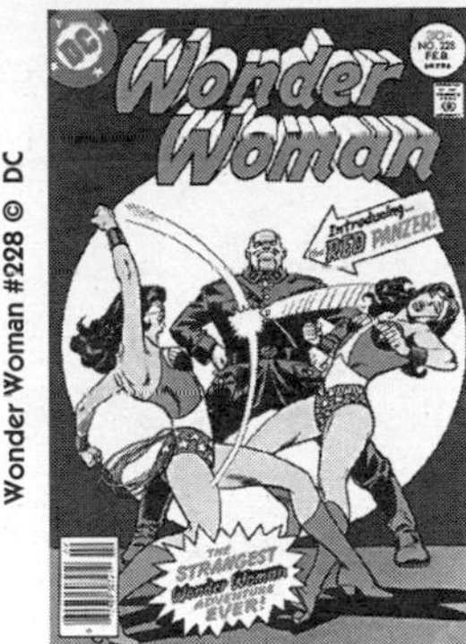

Wonder Woman #228 © DC

Wonder Woman #111 (2nd Series) © DC

GD25 FN65 NM94

Four Color 1255-Movie 5.75 17.00 63.00

WONDER WOMAN (See Adventure Comics #459, All-Star Comics, Brave & the Bold, DC Comics Presents, Justice League of America, Legend of..., Power Record Comics, Sensation Comics, Super Friends and World's Finest Comics #244)

WONDER WOMAN
Summer, 1942 - No. 329, Feb, 1986
National Periodical Publications/All-American Publ./DC Comics

GD25 FN65 VF82 NM94

1-Origin Wonder Woman retold (more detailed than All-Star #8); H. G. Peter-c/a begins 1545.00 4635.00 9270.00 17,000.00
(Estimated up to 150 total copies exist, 8 in NM/Mint)

1-Reprint, Oversize 13-1/2x10". **WARNING:** This comic is an exact reprint of the original except for its size. DC published it in 1974 with a second cover titling it as a Famous First Edition. There have been many reported cases of the outer cover being removed and the interior sold as the original edition. The reprint with the new outer cover removed is practically worthless. See Famous First Edition for value.

GD25 FN65 NM94

2-Origin/1st app. Mars; Duke of Deception app. 240.00 720.00 2200.00
3 156.00 468.00 1400.00
4,5: 5-1st Dr. Psycho app. 128.00 384.00 1150.00
6-10: 6-1st Cheetah app. 10-Invasion from Saturn 106.00 318.00 950.00
11-20 78.00 234.00 700.00
21-30: 23-Story from Wonder Woman's childhood 67.00 200.00 600.00
31-40: 38-Last H.G. Peter-c 47.00 141.00 425.00
41-44,46-49: 49-Used in **SOTI**, pgs. 234,236; last 52 pg. issue 36.00 108.00 300.00
45-Origin retold 64.00 192.00 575.00
50-(44 pgs.)-Used in **POP**, pg. 97 33.00 98.00 260.00
51-60: 60-New logo 24.00 71.00 190.00
61-72: 62-Origin of W.W. i.d. 64-Story about 3-D movies. 70-1st Angle Man app. 72-Last pre-code (2/55) 20.00 60.00 160.00
73-90: 80-Origin The Invisible Plane. 85-1st S.A. issue. 89-Flying saucer-c/story 15.00 45.00 150.00
91-94,96,97,99: 97-Last H. G. Peter-a 11.00 33.00 110.00
95-A-Bomb-c 12.00 36.00 120.00
98-New origin & new art team (Andru & Esposito) begin (5/58); origin W.W. id w/new facts 12.50 38.00 125.00
100-(8/58) 13.00 39.00 130.00
101-104,106,108-110 10.00 30.00 100.00
105-(Scarce, 4/59)-W. W.'s secret origin; W. W. appears as girl (no costume yet) (called Wonder Girl - see DC Super-Stars #1) 40.00 120.00 450.00
107-1st advs. of Wonder Girl; 1st Merboy; tells how Wonder Woman won her costume 11.00 33.00 110.00
111-120 7.00 21.00 70.00
121-126: 122-1st app. Wonder Tot. 124-1st app. Wonder Woman Family. 126-Last 10¢ issue 5.50 16.50 55.00
127-130: 128-Origin The Invisible Plane retold. 129-2nd app. Wonder Woman Family (#133 is 3rd app.) 4.00 12.00 40.00
131-150: 132-Flying saucer-c 3.20 9.60 32.00
151-155,157,158,160-170 (1967): 151-Wonder Girl solo issue 2.80 8.40 28.00
156-(8/65)-Early mention of a comic book shop & comic collecting; mentions DCs selling for $100 a copy 2.80 8.40 28.00
159-Origin retold (1/66); 1st S.A. origin? 4.00 12.00 40.00
171-176 2.00 6.00 16.00
177-W. Woman/Supergirl battle 2.50 7.50 24.00
178-1st new W. Woman 2.50 7.50 24.00
179-Wears no costume to issue #203. 2.50 7.50 20.00
180-195: 180-Death of Steve Trevor. 195-Wood inks 1.50 4.50 12.00
196 (52 pgs.)-Origin-r/All-Star #8 (6 out of 9 pgs.) 1.85 5.50 15.00
197,198 (52 pgs.)-Reprints 1.85 5.50 15.00
199-Jeff Jones-c; 52 pgs. 2.50 7.50 20.00
200 (5-6/72)-Jeff Jones-c; 52 pgs. 3.00 9.00 30.00
201,202-Catwoman app. 202-Fafhrd & The Grey Mouser debut. 1.25 3.75 10.00

GD25 FN65 NM94

203,205-210 1.00 3.00 8.00
204-Return to old costume; death of I Ching. 1.50 4.50 12.00
211,214-(100 pgs.) 2.50 7.50 20.00
212,217: (68 pgs.)-212-The Cavalier app. 1.50 4.50 12.00
213,215,216,218-220: 220-N. Adams assist 1.60 4.00
221,222,224-227,229,230,233-236,238-240 1.20 3.00
223,228,231,232,237,241,248: 223-Steve Trevor revived as Steve Howard & learns W.W.'s I.D. 228-Both Wonder Women team up & new World War II stories begin, end #243. 231,232: JSA app. 237-Origin retold. 241-Intro Bouncer; Spectre app. 248-Steve Trevor Howard dies (44 pgs.) 1.60 4.00
242-246,252-266,269,270: 243-Both W. Women team-up again. 269-Last Wood a(i) for DC? (7/80) 1.00 2.50
247,249-251,271. 247,249 (44 pgs.). 249-Hawkgirl app. 250-Origin/1st app. Orana, the new W. Woman. 251-Orana dies. 271-Huntress & 3rd Life of Steve Trevor begin 1.40 3.50
267,268-Re-intro Animal Man (5/80 & 6/80) 1.25 3.75 10.00
272-280 .80 2.00
281-283: Joker-c/stories in Huntress back-ups 2.00 5.00
284-286,289,290,294,-325 .80 2.00
287,288,291-293: 287-New Teen Titans x-over. 288-New costume & logo. 291-293-Three part epic with Super-Heroines 1.20 3.00
300-($1.50, 76 pgs.)-Anniv. issue; Giffen-a; New Teen Titans, Bronze Age Sandman, JLA & G.A. Wonder Woman app.; 1st app. Lyta Trevor who becomes Fury in All-Star Squadron #25; G.A. W.W. & Steve Trevor revealed as married. 1.20 3.00
326-328 1.20 3.00
329 (Double size)-S.A. W.W. & Steve Trevor wed 2.00 5.00
Pizza Hut Giveaways (12/77)-Reprints #60,62 .80 2.00

NOTE: ***Andru/Esposito*** *c-66-160(most).* ***Buckler*** *a-300.* ***Colan*** *a-288-305p; c-288-290p.* ***Giffen*** *a-300p.* ***Grell*** *c-217.* ***Kaluta*** *c-297.* ***Gil Kane*** *c-294p, 303-305, 307, 312, 314.* ***Miller*** *c-298p.* ***Morrow*** *c-233.* ***Nasser*** *a-232p; c-231p, 232p.* ***Bob Oskner*** *c(i)-39-65(most).* ***Perez*** *c-283p, 284p.* ***Spiegle*** *a-312.* ***Staton*** *a(p)-241, 271-287, 289, 290, 294-299; c(p)-241, 245, 246. Huntress back-up stories 271-287, 289, 290, 294-299, 301-321.*

WONDER WOMAN
Feb, 1987 - Present (75¢/$1.00/$1.25/$1.95)
DC Comics

1-New origin; Perez-c/a begins 1.20 3.00
2-20: 8-Origin Cheetah. 12,13-Millennium x-over. 18,26-Free 16 pg. story 1.25
21-49,51-62: 24-Last Perez-a; scripts continue thru #62. 60-Vs. Lobo; last Perez-c. 62-Last $1.00-c 1.00
50-($1.50, 52 pgs.)-New Titans, Justice League 1.50
63-81: 63-New direction & Bolland-c begin; Deathstroke story continued from Wonder Woman Special #1 1.25
82-84: 82-Begin $1.50-c .80 2.00
85-1st Deodato-a; ends #100 1.75 5.25 14.00
86,87 1.20 3.00
88-93: 88-Superman-c & app. 90-(9/94)-1st Artemis. 91-(11/94). 93-Hawkman app. 1.60 4.00
0-(10/94) 1.00 2.80 7.00
94-97: 96-Joker-c 2.00 5.00
98,99: 98-Begin $1.75-c 1.20 3.00
100 ($2.95, Newsstand)-Death of Artemis; Bolland-c ends. 2.00 5.00
100 ($3.95, Direct Market)-Death of Artemis; foil-c. 1.60 4.00
101-119, 121-130: 101-Begin $1.95-c; Byrne-c/a/scripts begin. 101-104-Darkseid app. 105-Phantom Stranger cameo. 106-108-Phantom Stranger & Demon app. 107,108-Arion app. 111-1st app. new Wonder Girl. 111,112-Vs.Doomsday. 112-Superman app. 113-Wonder Girl-c/app; Sugar & Spike app. 128-Hippolyta becomes new W.W. 1.95
120 ($2.95)-Perez-c 3.00
Annual 1,2: 1 ('88, $1.50)-Art Adams-a. 2 ('89, $2.00, 68 pgs.)-All women artists issue; Perez-c(i)/a. .80 2.00
Annual 3 (1992, $2.50, 68 pgs.)-Quesada-c(p) 1.00 2.50
Annual 4 (1995, $3.50)-Year One 1.40 3.50

Wonderworld Comics #14 © FOX

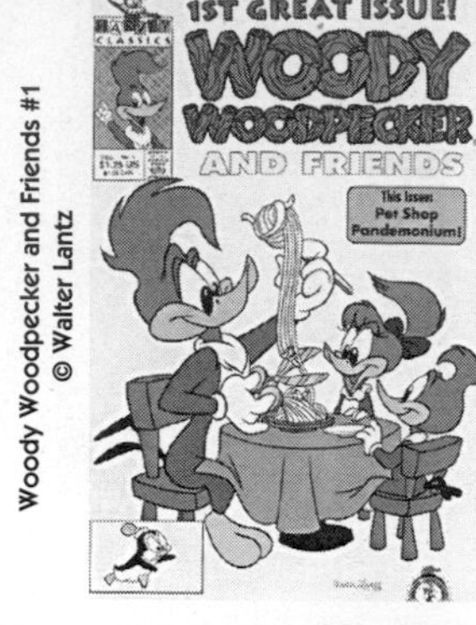

Woody Woodpecker and Friends #1 © Walter Lantz

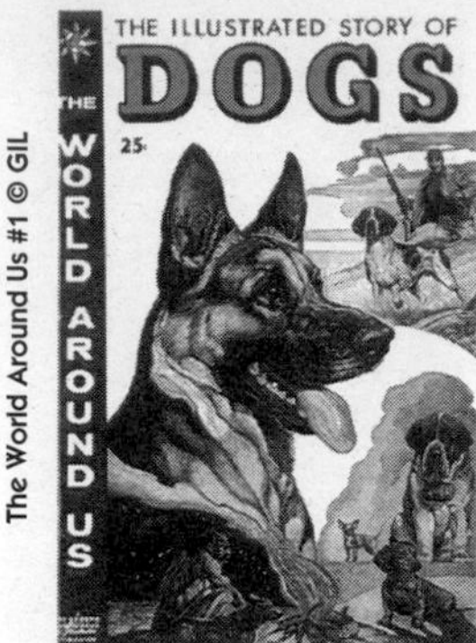

THE ILLUSTRATED STORY OF
DOGS
THE WORLD AROUND US
25¢

The World Around Us #1 © GIL

GD25 FN65 NM94

Annual 5 (1996, $2.95)-Legends of the Dead Earth story; Byrne scripts; Cockrum-a 1.20 3.00
Annual 6 (1997, $3.95)-Pulp Heroes 3.95
Gallery (1996, $3.50)-Bolland-c; pin-ups by various 1.40 3.50
Plus 1 (1/97, $2.95)-Jesse Quick-c/app. 1.40 3.50
Second Genesis TPB (1997, $9.95)-r/#101-105 1.25 3.75 10.00
Special 1 (1992, $1.75, 52 pgs.)-Deathstroke-c/story continued in Wonder Woman #63 .80 2.00
THE CHALLENGE OF ARTEMIS (1996, $9.95)-r/#94-100; Deodato-c/a 10.00

NOTE: ***Art Adams** a-Annual 1. **Byrne** c/a 101-107. **Bolton** a-Annual 1. **Deodato** a-85-100. **Perez** a-Annual 1; c-Annual 1(i). **Quesada** c(p)-Annual 3.*

WONDER WOMAN: AMAZONIA
1997 ($7.95, Graphic Album format, one shot)
DC Comics
1-Elseworlds; Messner-Loebs-s/Winslade-a 7.95

WONDER WOMAN SPECTACULAR (See DC Special Series #9)

WONDER WORKER OF PERU
No date (5x7", 16 pgs., B&W, giveaway)
Catechetical Guild
nn 3.60 9.00 18.00

WONDERWORLD COMICS (Formerly Wonder Comics)
No. 3, July, 1939 - No. 33, Jan, 1942
Fox Features Syndicate
3-Intro The Flame by Fine; Dr. Fung (Powell-a), K-51 (Powell-a?), & Yarko the Great, Master Magician (Eisner-a) continues; Eisner/Fine-c 570.00 1710.00 5700.00
4-Lou Fine-c 240.00 720.00 2300.00
5,6,9,10: Lou Fine-c 139.00 417.00 1250.00
7,8-Classic Lou Fine-c 178.00 534.00 1600.00
11-Origin The Flame 111.00 333.00 1000.00
12-15:13-Dr. Fung ends; last Fine-c 89.00 267.00 800.00
16-20: 67.00 200.00 600.00
21-Origin The Black Lion & Cub 61.00 183.00 550.00
22-27: 22,25-Dr. Fung app. 50.00 150.00 450.00
28-Origin & 1st app. U.S. Jones (8/41); Lu-Nar, the Moon Man begins 67.00 200.00 600.00
29,31,33 39.00 117.00 350.00
30-Intro & Origin Flame Girl 75.00 225.00 675.00
32-Hitler-c 47.00 141.00 425.00

NOTE: *Spies at War by **Eisner** in #13, 17. Yarko by **Eisner** in #3-11. **Eisner** text illos-3. **Lou Fine** a-3-11; c-3-13, 15; text illos-4. **Nordling** a-4-14. **Powell** a-3-12. **Tuska** a-5-9. Bondage-c 14, 15, 28, 31, 32. Cover features: The Flame-#3, 5-31; U.S. Jones-#32, 33.*

WONDERWORLDS
1992 ($3.50, squarebound, 100 pgs.)
Innovation Publishing
1-Rebound super-hero comics, contents may vary; Hero Alliance, Terraformers, etc. 1.40 3.50

WOODSY OWL (See March of Comics #395)
Nov, 1973 - No. 10, Feb, 1976
Gold Key
1 1.50 4.50 12.00
2-10 1.00 2.80 7.00

WOODY WOODPECKER (Walter Lantz... #73 on?)(See Dell Giants for annuals)(Also see The Funnies, Jolly Jingles, Kite Fun Book, New Funnies)
No. 169, 10/47 - No. 72, 5-7/62; No. 73, 10/62 - No. 201, 4/84 (nn 192)
Dell Publishing Co./Gold Key No. 73-187/Whitman No. 188 on
Four Color 169(#1)-Drug turns Woody into a Mr. Hyde 13.00 40.00 145.00
Four Color 188 9.00 27.00 100.00
Four Color 202,232,249,264,288 5.75 17.00 63.00

GD25 FN65 NM94

Four Color 305,336,350 3.00 10.00 36.00
Four Color 364,374,390,405,416,431('52) 3.00 9.00 34.00
16 (12-1/52-53) - 30('55) 1.65 5.00 18.00
31-50 1.40 4.40 16.00
51-72 (Last Dell) 1.20 3.60 11.00
73-75 (Giants, 84 pgs., Gold Key) 3.00 9.00 35.00
76-80 1.10 3.30 9.00
81-100 1.00 2.80 7.00
101-120 2.00 5.00
121-191,193-201 (No #192) 1.00 2.50
Christmas Parade 1(11/68-Giant)(G.K.) 2.25 6.75 25.00
Clover Stamp-Newspaper Boy Contest('56)-9 pg. story-(Giveaway) 1.65 5.00 18.00
In Chevrolet Wonderland(1954-Giveaway)(Western Publ.)-20 pgs., full story line; Chilly Willy app. 15.00 45.00 120.00
...Meets Scotty McTape(1953-Scotch Tape giveaway)-16 pgs., full size 15.00 45.00 120.00
Summer Fun 1(6/66-G.K.)(84 pgs.) 3.00 9.00 32.00

NOTE: *15¢ editions exist. Reprints-No. 92, 102, 103, 105, 106, 124, 125, 152, 153, 157, 162, 165, 194(1/3)-200(1/3).*

WOODY WOODPECKER (See Comic Album #5,9,13, Dell Giant #24, 40, 54, Dell Giants, The Funnies, Golden Comics Digest #1, 3, 5, 8, 15, 16, 20, 24, 32, 37, 44, March of Comics #16, 34, 85, 93, 109, 124, 139, 158, 177, 184, 203, 222, 239, 249, 261, 420, 454, 466, 478, New Funnies & Super Book #12, 24)

WOODY WOODPECKER
Sept, 1991 - No. 7, 1993 ($1.25)
Harvey Comics
1-7: 1-r/W.W. #53 1.30
50th Anniversary Special 1 (10/91, $2.50, 68 pgs.) 1.00 2.50

WOODY WOODPECKER AND FRIENDS
Dec, 1991 - No. 4, 1992 ($1.25)
Harvey Comics
1-4 1.30

WOOLWORTH'S CHRISTMAS STORY BOOK
1952 - 1954 (16 pgs., paper-c) (See Jolly Christmas Book)
Promotional Publ. Co.(Western Printing Co.)
nn 4.25 13.00 26.00

NOTE: *1952 issue-Marv Levy c/a.*

WOOLWORTH'S HAPPY TIME CHRISTMAS BOOK
1952 (Christmas giveaway, 36 pgs.)
F. W. Woolworth Co.(Whitman Publ. Co.)
nn 4.25 13.00 26.00

WORDSMITH (1st Series)
Aug, 1985 - No. 12, Jan, 1988 ($1.70/$2.00, B&W, bi-monthly)
Renegade Press
1-6: R. G. Taylor-c/a .70 1.70
7-12: 7-Begin 2.00-c. R. G. Taylor-c/a in all. .80 2.00

WORDSMITH (2nd Series)
1996 - No. 6, 1996 ($2.95, B&W, limited series)
Caliber
1-6: Reprints in all. 1-Contains 3 pg. sketchbook. 6-Flip book w/Raven Chronicles #10 1.20 3.00

WORD WARRIORS (Also see Quest for Dreams Lost)
1987 ($1.50, B&W)(Proceeds donated to help illiteracy)
Literacy Volunteers of Chicago
1-Jon Sable by Grell, Ms. Tree, Streetwolf; Chaykin-c 1.50

WORLD AROUND US, THE (Illustrated Story of...)
Sept, 1958 - No. 36, Oct, 1961 (25¢)
Gilberton Publishers (Classics Illustrated)
1-Dogs; Evans-a 5.70 17.00 35.00

The World is His Parish © George A. Pflaum

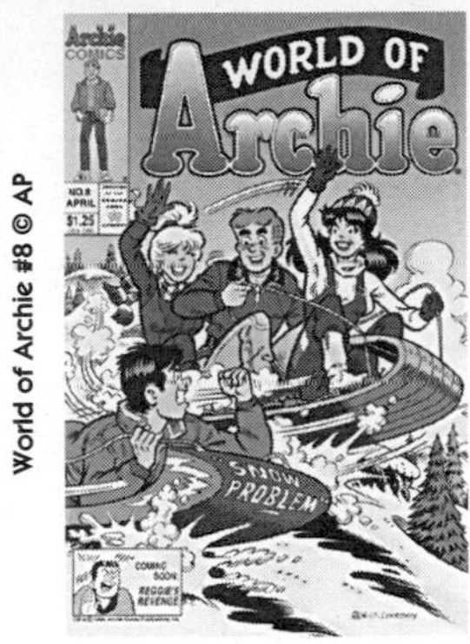

World of Archie #8 © AP

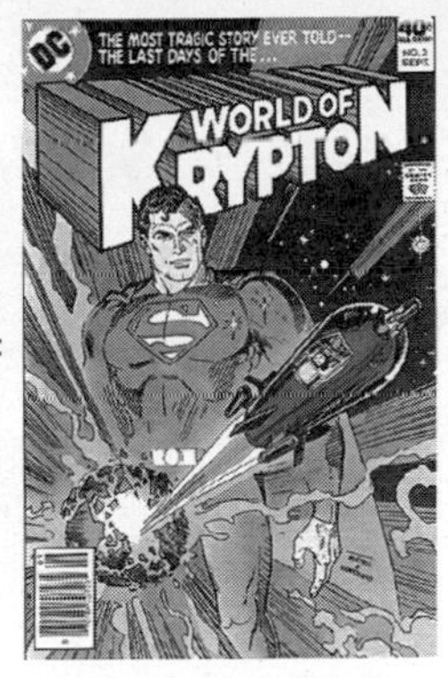

World of Krypton #3 © DC

GD25 FN65 NM94

2-4: 2-Indians; Check-a. 3-Horses; L. B. Cole-c. 4-Railroads; L. B. Cole-a (5 pgs.) 5.70 17.00 35.00
5-Space; Ingels-a 6.50 19.50 45.00
6-The F.B.I.; Disbrow, Evans, Ingels-a 6.50 19.50 45.00
7-Pirates; Disbrow, Ingels, Kinstler-a 5.70 17.00 40.00
8-Flight; Evans, Ingels, Crandall-a 6.00 18.00 42.00
9-Army; Disbrow, Ingels, Orlando-a 5.70 17.00 35.00
10-13: 10-Navy; Disbrow, Kinstler-a. 11-Marine Corps. 12-Coast Guard; Ingels-a (9 pgs.). 13-Air Force; L.B. Cole-c 5.70 17.00 35.00
14-French Revolution; Crandall, Evans, Kinstler-a 6.50 19.50 45.00
15-Prehistoric Animals; Al Williamson-a, 6 & 10 pgs. plus Morrow-a 7.15 21.50 50.00
16-18: 16-Crusades; Kinstler-a. 17-Festivals; Evans, Crandall-a. 18-Great Scientists; Crandall, Evans, Torres, Williamson, Morrow-a 5.70 17.00 40.00
19-Jungle; Crandall, Williamson, Morrow-a 7.15 21.50 50.00
20-Communications; Crandall, Evans, Torres-a 6.50 19.50 45.00
21-American Presidents; Crandall/Evans, Morrow-a 6.50 19.50 45.00
22-Boating; Morrow-a 5.00 15.00 30.00
23-Great Explorers; Crandall, Evans-a 5.70 17.00 40.00
24-Ghosts; Morrow, Evans-a 6.50 19.50 45.00
25-Magic; Evans, Morrow-a 6.50 19.50 45.00
26-The Civil War 8.50 26.00 60.00
27-Mountains (High Advs.); Crandall/Evans, Morrow, Torres-a 6.00 18.00 42.00
28-Whaling; Crandall, Evans, Morrow, Torres, Wildey-a; L.B. Cole-c 5.70 17.00 40.00
29-Vikings; Crandall, Evans, Torres, Morrow-a 7.15 21.50 50.00
30-Undersea Adventure; Crandall/Evans, Kirby, Morrow, Torres-a 6.50 19.50 45.00
31-Hunting; Crandall/Evans, Ingels, Kinstler, Kirby-a 5.70 17.00 40.00
32,33: 32-For Gold & Glory; Morrow, Kirby, Crandall, Evans-a. 33-Famous Teens; Torres, Crandall, Evans-a 6.00 18.00 42.00
34-36: 34-Fishing; Crandall/Evans-a. 35-Spies; Kirby, Morrow?, Evans-a. 36-Fight for Life (Medicine); Kirby-a 5.70 17.00 40.00

NOTE: See Classics Illustrated Special Edition. Another *World Around Us* issue entitled *The Sea* had been prepared in 1962 but was never published in the U.S. It was published in the British/European *World Around Us* series. Those series then continued with seven additional WAU titles not in the U.S. series.

WORLD FAMOUS HEROES MAGAZINE
Oct, 1941 - No. 4, Apr, 1942 (A comic book)
Comic Corp. of America (Centaur)

1-Gustavson-c; Lubbers, Glanzman-a; Davy Crockett, Paul Revere, Lewis & Clark, John Paul Jones stories; Flag-c 100.00 300.00 900.00
2-Lou Gehrig life story; Lubbers-a 44.00 132.00 400.00
3,4-Lubbers-a. 4-Wild Bill Hickok story; 2 pg. Marlene Dietrich story 39.00 117.00 350.00

WORLD FAMOUS STORIES
1945
Croyden Publishers

1-Ali Baba, Hansel & Gretel, Rip Van Winkle, Mid-Summer Night's Dream 9.50 28.00 75.00

WORLD IS HIS PARISH, THE
1953 (15¢)
George A. Pflaum

nn-The story of Pope Pius XII 4.00 11.00 22.00

WORLD OF ADVENTURE (Walt Disney's...)(TV)
Apr, 1963 - No. 3, Oct, 1963 (12¢)
Gold Key

1-3-Disney TV characters; Savage Sam, Johnny Shiloh, Capt. Nemo, The Mooncussers 2.40 6.00

WORLD OF ARCHIE, THE (See Archie Giant Series Mag. #148, 151, 156, 160, 165, 171, 177, 182, 188, 193, 200, 208, 213, 225, 232, 237, 244, 249, 456, 461, 468, 473, 480, 485, 492, 497, 504, 509, 516, 521, 532, 543, 554, 565, 574, 587, 599, 612, 627)

WORLD OF ARCHIE
Aug, 1992 - Present ($1.25/$1.50)
Archie Comics

1-11: 9-Neon ink-c 1.25
12-26 1.50

WORLD OF FANTASY
May, 1956 - No. 19, Aug, 1959
Atlas Comics (CPC No. 1-15/ZPC No. 16-19)

1 38.00 114.00 285.00
2-Williamson-a (4 pgs.) 24.00 71.00 175.00
3-Sid Check, Roussos-a 21.00 64.00 150.00
4-7 16.00 47.00 120.00
8-Matt Fox, Orlando, Berg-a 17.00 49.00 125.00
9-Krigstein-a 16.00 47.00 120.00
10,12-15 12.00 36.00 90.00
11-Torres-a 13.50 41.00 95.00
16-Williamson-a (4 pgs.); Ditko, Kirby-a 17.00 49.00 125.00
17-19-Ditko, Kirby-a 17.00 49.00 125.00

NOTE: ***Ayers*** *a-3.* ***B. Baily*** *a-4.* ***Borg*** *a-5, 6, 8.* ***Brodsky*** *c-3.* ***Check*** *a-3.* ***Ditko*** *a-17, 19.* ***Everett*** *a-2; c-4-7, 9, 12, 13.* ***Forte*** *a-4.* ***Infantino*** *a-14.* ***Kirby*** *c-15, 17-19.* ***Krigstein*** *a-9.* ***Maneely*** *c-2, 14.* ***Mooney*** *a-14.* ***Morrow*** *a-7.* ***Orlando*** *a-8, 13, 14.* ***Pakula*** *a-9.* ***Powell*** *a-4, 6.* ***R.Q. Sale*** *a-3, 9.* ***Severin*** *c-1.*

WORLD OF GIANT COMICS, THE (See Archie All-Star Specials under Archie Comics)

WORLD OF GINGER FOX, THE (Also see Ginger Fox)
Nov, 1986 ($6.95, 8 1/2 x 11", 68 pgs., mature)
Comico

Graphic Novel ($6.95) 1.00 2.80 7.00
Hardcover ($27.95) 2.80 8.40 28.00

WORLD OF JUGHEAD, THE (See Archie Giant Series Mag. #9, 14, 19, 24, 30, 136, 143, 149, 152, 157, 161, 166, 172, 178, 183, 189, 194, 202, 209, 215, 227, 233, 239, 245, 251, 457, 463, 469, 475, 481, 487, 493, 499, 505, 511, 517, 523, 531, 542, 553, 564, 577, 590, 602)

WORLD OF KRYPTON, THE (World of...#3) (See Superman #248)
7/79 - No. 3, 9/79; 12/87 - No. 4, 3/88 (Both are limited series)
DC Comics, Inc.

1-3 (1979, 40¢; 1st comic book mini-series): 1-Jor-El marries Lara. 3-Baby Superman sent to Earth; Krypton explodes; Mon-el app. .80 2.00
1-4 (75¢)-Byrne scripts; Byrne/Simonson-c 1.00

WORLD OF METROPOLIS, THE
Aug, 1988 - No. 4, July, 1988 ($1.00, limited series)
DC Comics

1-4: Byrne scripts 1.00

WORLD OF MYSTERY
June, 1956 - No. 7, July, 1957
Atlas Comics (GPI)

1-Torres, Orlando-a; Powell-a? 37.00 111.00 285.00
2-Woodish-a 13.50 41.00 100.00
3-Torres, Davis, Ditko-a 17.00 51.00 130.00
4-Pakula, Powell-a 18.00 54.00 135.00
5,7: 5-Orlando-a 13.50 41.00 100.00
6-Williamson/Mayo-a (4 pgs.); Ditko-a; Crandall text illo 187.00 54.00 135.00

NOTE: ***Brodsky*** *c-2.* ***Colan*** *a-7.* ***Everett*** *c-1, 3.* ***Pakula*** *a-4, 6.* ***Romita*** *a-2.* ***Severin*** *c-7.*

WORLD OF SMALLVILLE
Apr, 1988 - No. 4, July, 1988 (75¢, limited series)
DC Comics

1-4: Byrne scripts 1.00

WORLD OF SUSPENSE
Apr, 1956 - No. 8, July, 1957

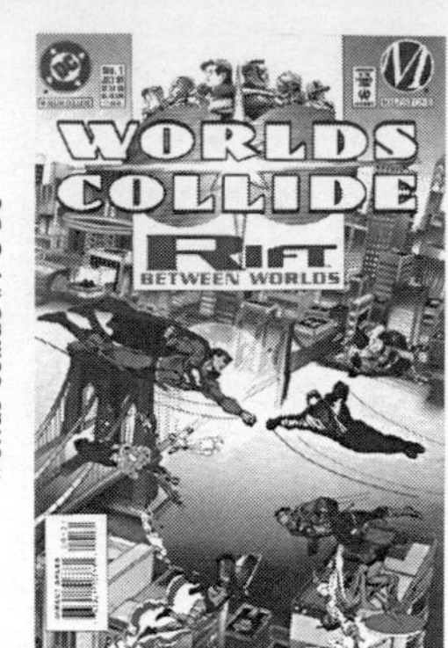

Worlds Collide #1 © DC

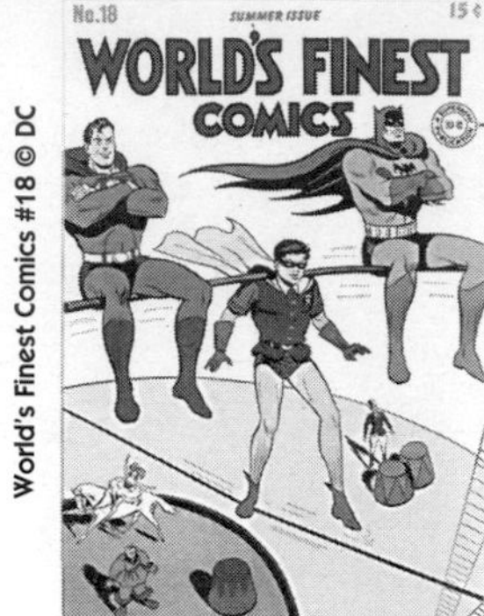

World's Finest Comics #18 © DC

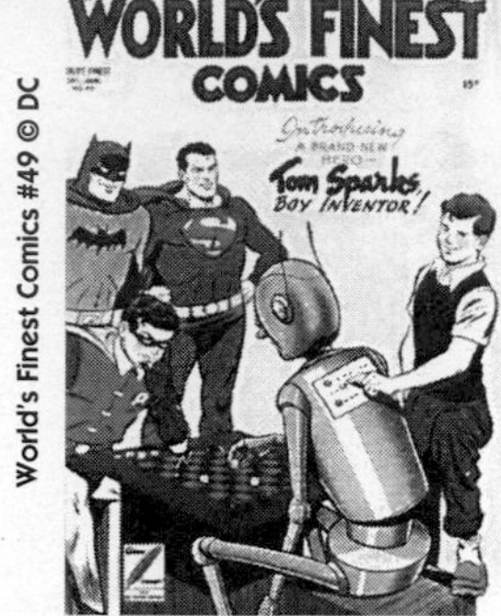

World's Finest Comics #49 © DC

GD25 FN65 NM94

Atlas News Co.

1 30.00 90.00 220.00
2-Ditko-a (4 pgs.) 17.00 49.00 125.00
3,7-Williamson-a in both (4 pgs. each); #7-with Mayo 17.00 49.00 125.00
4-6,8 13.00 39.00 95.00

NOTE: ***Berg*** *a-6.* ***Cameron*** *a-2.* ***Ditko*** *a-2.* ***Drucker*** *a-1.* ***Everett*** *a-1, 5; c-6.* ***Heck*** *a-5.* ***Maneely*** *a-1; c-1-3.* ***Orlando*** *a-5.* ***Powell*** *a-6.* ***Reinman*** *a-4.* ***Roussos*** *a-6.* ***Shores*** *a-1.*

WORLD OF WHEELS (Formerly Dragstrip Hotrodders)
No. 17, Oct, 1967 - No. 32, June, 1970
Charlton Comics

17-20-Features Ken King 1.85 5.50 15.00
21-32-Features Ken King 1.50 4.50 12.00
Modern Comics Reprint 23(1978) 2.00 5.00

WORLD OF WOOD
1986 - No. 4, 1987; No. 5, 2/89 ($1.75, limited series)
Eclipse Comics

1-4:1-Dave Stevens-c. 2-Wood/Stevens-c .75 1.80
5 ($2.00, B&W)-r/Avon's Flying Saucers .80 2.00

WORLD'S BEST COMICS (World's Finest Comics #2 on)
Spring, 1941 (Cardboard-c)(DC's 6th annual format comic)
National Per. Publications (100 pgs.) GD25 FN65 VF82 NM94

1-The Batman, Superman, Crimson Avenger, Johnny Thunder, The King, Young Dr. Davis, Zatara, Lando, Man of Magic, & Red, White & Blue begin; Superman, Batman & Robin covers begin (inside-c is blank); Fred Ray-c; 15¢ cover price 1227.00 3682.00 7975.00 13,500.00
(Estimated up to 185 total copies exist, 6 in NM/Mint)

WORLDS BEYOND (Stories of Weird Adventure)(Worlds of Fear #2 on)
Nov, 1951
Fawcett Publications GD25 FN65 NM94

1-Powell, Bailey-a; Moldoff-c 36.00 109.00 270.00

WORLDS COLLIDE
July, 1994 ($2.50, one-shot)
DC Comics

1-($2.50, 52 pgs.)-Milestone & Superman titles x-over 1.00 2.50
1-($3.95, 52 pgs.)-Polybagged w/vinyl clings 1.60 4.00

WORLD'S FAIR COMICS (See New York...)

WORLD'S FINEST (Also see Legends of World Finest
1990 - No. 3, 1990 ($3.95, squarebound, limited series, 52 pgs.)
DC Comics

1-3: Batman & Superman team-up against The Joker and Lex Luthor; Dave Gibbons scripts & Steve Rude-c/a. 2,3-Joker/Luthor painted-c by Steve Rude 2.00 5.00
TPB-($19.95) r/#1-3 2.50 7.50 20.00

WORLD'S FINEST COMICS (Formerly World's Best Comics #1)
No. 2, Sum, 1941 - No. 323, Jan, 1986 (#1-17 have cardboard covers) (#2-9 have 100 pgs.)
National Periodical Publ./DC Comics

2 (100 pgs.)-Superman, Batman & Robin covers continue from World's Best; (cover price 15¢ #2-70) 360.00 1080.00 3600.00
3-The Sandman begins; last Johnny Thunder; origin & 1st app. The Scarecrow 270.00 810.00 2700.00
4-Hop Harrigan app.; last Young Dr. Davis 211.00 633.00 1900.00
5-Intro. TNT & Dan the Dyna-Mite; last King & Crimson Avenger 211.00 633.00 1900.00
6-Star Spangled Kid begins (Sum/42); Aquaman app.; S&K Sandman with Sandy in new costume begins, ends #7 156.00 468.00 1400.00
7-Green Arrow begins (Fall/42); last Lando, King, & Red, White & Blue; S&K art 156.00 468.00 1400.00

GD25 FN65 NM94

8-Boy Commandos begin (by Simon(p) #12) 139.00 417.00 1250.00
9-Batman cameo in Star Spangled Kid; S&K-a; last 100 pg. issue; Hitler, Mussolini, Tojo-c 144.00 432.00 1300.00
10-S&K-a; 76 pg. issues begin 122.00 366.00 1100.00
11-17-Last cardboard cover issue 111.00 333.00 1000.00
18-20: 18-Paper covers begin; last Star Spangled Kid. 20-Last quarterly issue 97.00 291.00 875.00
21-30: 21-Begin bi-monthly. 30-Johnny Everyman app. 69.00 207.00 625.00
31-40: 33-35-Tomahawk app. 61.00 183.00 550.00
41-50: 41-Boy Commandos end. 42-Intro The Wyoming Kid & begins (9-10/49), ends #63. 43-Full Steam Foley begins, ends #48. 48-Last square binding. 49-Tom Sparks, Boy Inventor begins 47.00 141.00 415.00
51-60: 51-Zatara ends. 54-Last 76 pg. issue. 59-Manhunters Around the World begins (7-8/52), ends #62 47.00 141.00 415.00
61-64: 61-Joker story. 63-Capt. Compass app. 25.00 75.00 200.00
65-Origin Superman; Tomahawk begins (7-8/53), ends #101 61.00 183.00 550.00
66-70-(15¢ issues, scarce)-Last 15¢, 68pg. issue 44.00 132.00 400.00
71-(10¢ issue, scarce)-Superman & Batman begin as team (7-8/54); were in separate stories until now; Superman & Batman exchange identities; 10¢ issues begin 67.00 200.00 800.00
72-(10¢ issue, scarce) 47.00 141.00 565.00
73-(10¢ issue, scarce) 48.00 144.00 580.00
74-Last pre-code issue 40.00 120.00 450.00
75-(1st code approved, 3-4/55) 37.00 111.00 410.00
76-80: 77-Superman loses powers & Batman obtains them this issue only 29.00 87.00 290.00
81-90: 84-1st S.A. issue. 88-1st Joker/Luthor team-up. 89-2nd Batmen of All Nations (aka Club of Heroes). 90-Batwoman's 1st app. in World's Finest (10/57, 3rd app. anywhere) plus-c app. 24.00 72.00 240.00
91-93,95-99: 96-99-Kirby Green Arrow 17.00 51.00 170.00
94-Origin Superman/Batman team retold 43.00 129.00 520.00
100 (3/59) 29.00 87.00 290.00
101-110: 102-Tommy Tomorrow begins, ends #124 12.00 36.00 120.00
111-121: 111-1st app. The Clock King. 113-Intro. Miss Arrowette in Green Arrow; 1st Bat-Mite/Mr. Mxyzptlk team-up (11/60). 121-Last 10¢ issue 9.50 28.50 95.00
122-128,130-142: 123-2nd Bat-Mite/Mr. Mxyzptlk team-up (2/62). 125-Aquaman begins (5/62), ends #139 (Aquaman #1 is dated 1-2/62). 135-Last Dick Sprang story. 140-Last Green Arrow; last Clayface until Action #443. 142-Origin The Composite Superman (villain); Legion app. 5.00 15.00 50.00
129-Joker/Luthor team-up-c/story 6.50 19.50 65.00
143-150: 143-1st Mailbag 4.00 12.00 40.00
151-153,155,157-160: 156-Intro of Bizarro Batman. 157-2nd Super Sons story; last app. Kathy Kane (Bat-woman) until Batman Family #10 3.00 9.00 30.00
154-1st Super Sons story; last Bat-woman in costume until Batman Family #10. 3.00 9.00 30.00
156-1st Bizarro Batman; Joker-c/story 9.00 27.00 90.00
161,170 (80-Pg. Giants G-28,G-40) 3.50 10.50 35.00
162-165,167-169,171,172,174: 168,172-Adult Legion app. 169-3rd app. new Batgirl(9/67)(cover and 1 panel cameo); 3rd Bat-Mite/Mr. Mxyzptlk team-up. 2.50 7.50 22.00
166-Joker-c/story 2.50 7.50 25.00
173-('68)-1st S.A. app. Two-Face as Batman becomes Two-Face in story 7.00 21.00 70.00
175,176-Neal Adams-a; both reprint J'onn J'onzz origin/Detective #225,226 2.25 6.75 18.00
177-Joker/Luthor team-up-c/story 2.25 6.75 18.00
178,180-187: 182-Silent Knight-r/Brave & Bold #6. 186-Johnny Quick-r. 187-Green Arrow origin-r by Kirby (Adv. #256) 1.50 4.50 12.00
179,188 (80-Pg. Giants G-52,G-64): 179-r/#94 2.80 8.40 28.00

World's Finest Comics #211 © DC

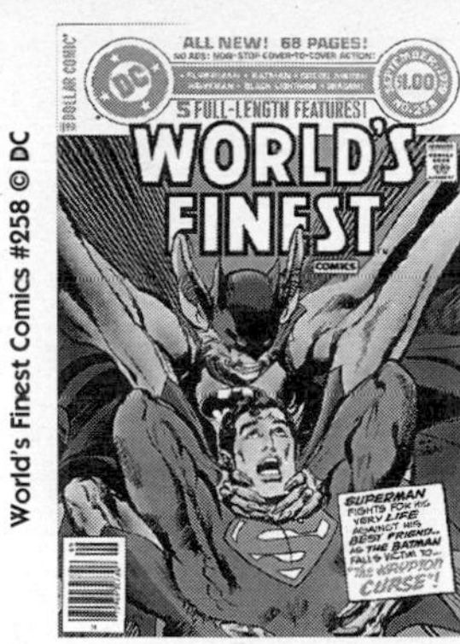

World's Finest Comics #258 © DC

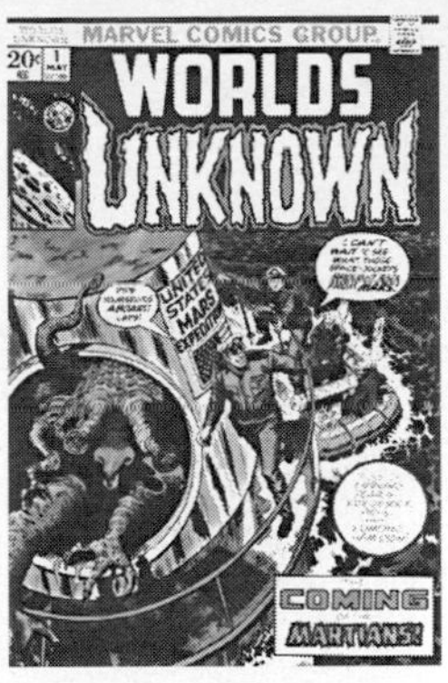

Worlds Unknown #1 © MEG

	GD25	FN65	NM94
189-196: 190-193-Robin-r	1.10	3.30	9.00
197-(80 Pg. Giant G-76)	2.80	8.40	28.00
198,199-3rd Superman/Flash race (see Flash #175 & Superman #199)	7.50	22.50	75.00
200-204: 203-Last 15¢ issue.		2.40	6.00
205-(52 pgs.)-Shining Knight-r (6 pgs.) by Frazetta/Adv. #153; Teen Titans x-over	1.75	5.25	14.00
206 (80-Pg. Giant G-88)	2.50	7.50	24.00
207-212-(25¢, 52 pgs.). 208-Origin Robotman-r/Det. #138.	1.25	3.75	10.00
213,214,216-222,229-248: 217-Metamorpho begins, ends #220; Batman/Superman team-ups begin. 229-r/origin Superman-Batman team. 242-Super Sons. 244-Green Arrow, Black Canary, Wonder Woman, Vigilante begin; $1.00, 84 pg. issues begin. 246-Death of Stuff in Vigilante; origin Vigilante retold. 248-Last Vigilante	1.25	3.75	10.00
215-Intro. Batman Jr. & Superman Jr.	2.00	6.00	16.00
223-228-(100 pgs.). 223-N. Adams-r. 223-Deadman origin. 226-N. Adams, S&K, Toth-r; Manhunter part origin-r/Det. #225,226. 227-Deadman app.	1.85	5.50	15.00
249-The Creeper begins by Ditko, ends #255; 84 pgs	1.00	2.80	7.00
250-252 (84 pgs.)-250-The Creeper origin retold by Ditko. 252-Last 84 pg. issue	1.00	2.80	7.00
253-270,272-299: 253-Capt. Marvel begins; 68 pgs. begin, end #265. 255-Last Creeper. 256-Hawkman begins. 257-Black Lightning begins. 263-Super Sons. 266-282-(52 pgs.). 264-Clay Face app. 267-Challengers of the Unknown app. 268-Capt. Marvel Jr. origin retold. 274-Zatanna begins. 279, 280-Capt. Marvel Jr. & Kid Eternity learn they are brothers. 284-Legion app.		1.60	4.00
271-Origin Superman/Batman team retold		2.00	5.00
300-($1.25, 52pgs.)-Justice League of America, New Teen Titans & The Outsiders app.; Perez-a (3 pgs.)		1.60	4.00
301-323: 304-Origin Null and Void. 309,319-Free 16 pg. story in each (309-Flash Force 2000, 319-Mask preview)		.80	2.00
Giveaway (c. 1944-45, 8 pgs., in color, paper-c)-Johnny Everyman-r/World's Finest	15.50	47.00	125.00
Giveaway (c. 1949, 8 pgs., in color, paper-c)- "Make Way For Youth" r/World's Finest; based on film of same name	12.00	36.00	95.00

NOTE: ***Neal Adams** a-230ir; c-174-176, 178-180, 182, 183, 185, 186, 199-205, 208-211, 244-246, 258. **Austin** a-244-246i. **Burnley** a-8, 10; c-7-9, 11-14, 15p?, 16-18p, 20-31p. **Colan** a-274p, 297, 299. **Ditko** a-249-255. **Giffen** a-322; c-284p, 322. **G. Kane** a-38, 174r, 282, 283; c-281, 282, 289. **Kirby** a-187. **Kubert** Zatara-40-44. **Miller** c-285p. **Mooney** c-134. **Morrow** a-245-248. **Mortimer** c-16-21, 26-71. **Nasser** a(p)-244-246, 259, 260. **Newton** a-253-281p. **Orlando** a-224r. **Perez** a-300i; c-271, 276, 277p, 278p. **Fred Ray** c-1-5. **Fred Ray/Robinson** c-13-16. **Robinson** a-2, 9, 13-15; c-6. **Rogers** a-259p. **Roussos** a-212r. **Simonson** c-291. **Spiegle** a-275-278, 284. **Staton** a-262p, 273p. **Swan/Moldoff** c-126. **Swan/Mortimer** c-79-82. **Toth** a-228r. **Tuska** a-230r, 250p, 252p, 254p, 257p, 283p, 284p, 308p. Boy Commandos by **Infantino** #39-41.*

(Also see 80 Page Giant #15)

WORLD'S FINEST COMICS DIGEST (See DC Special Series #23)

WORLD'S GREATEST ATHLETE (See Walt Disney Showcase #14)

WORLD'S GREATEST SONGS
Sept, 1954
Atlas Comics (Male)

	GD25	FN65	NM94
1-(Scarce)-Heath & Harry Anderson-a; Eddie Fisher life story plus-c; gives lyrics to Frank Sinatra song "Young at Heart"	31.00	94.00	250.00

WORLD'S GREATEST STORIES
Jan, 1949 - No. 2, May, 1949
Jubilee Publications

	GD25	FN65	NM94
1-Alice in Wonderland; Lewis Carroll adapt.	23.00	68.00	180.00
2-Pinocchio	21.00	64.00	170.00

WORLD'S GREATEST SUPER HEROES
1977 (Giveaway, 3-3/4x3-3/4", 24 pgs.)
DC Comics (Nutra Comics) (Child Vitamins, Inc.)

	GD25	FN65	NM94
nn-Batman & Robin app.; health tips		.80	2.00

WORLDS OF FEAR (Stories of Weird Adventure)(Formerly Worlds Beyond #1)
V1#2, Jan, 1952 - V2#10, June, 1953
Fawcett Publications

	GD25	FN65	NM94
V1#2	34.00	103.00	260.00
3-Evans-a	29.00	86.00	220.00
4-6(9/52)	23.00	69.00	180.00
V2#7-9	21.00	62.00	160.00
10-Saunders painted-c; man with no eyes surrounded by eyeballs-c plus eyes ripped out story	39.00	117.00	350.00

NOTE: ***Moldoff** c-2-8. **Powell** a-2, 4, 5. **Sekowsky** a-4, 5.*

WORLDS UNKNOWN
May, 1973 - No. 8, Aug, 1974
Marvel Comics Group

	GD25	FN65	NM94
1-r/from Astonishing #54; Torres, Reese-a	1.25	3.75	10.00
2-8	1.00	3.00	8.00

NOTE: ***Adkins/Mooney** a-5. **Buscema** c/a-4p. W. **Howard** c/a-3i. **Kane** a(p)-1,2; c(p)-5, 6, 8. **Sutton** a-2. **Tuska** a(p)-7, 8; c-7p. No. 7, 8 has Golden Voyage of Sinbad movie adaptation.*

WORLD WAR STORIES
Apr-June, 1965 - No. 3, Dec, 1965
Dell Publishing Co.

	GD25	FN65	NM94
1-Glanzman-a in all	2.25	6.75	26.00
2,3	2.00	6.00	16.00

WORLD WAR II (See Classics Illustrated Special Issue)

WORLD WAR III
Mar, 1953 - No. 2, May, 1953
Ace Periodicals

	GD25	FN65	NM94
1-(Scarce)-Atomic bomb blast-c; Cameron-a	49.00	148.00	425.00
2-Used in **POP**, pg. 78 & B&W & color illos; Cameron-a	45.00	136.00	400.00

WORLD WITHOUT END
1990 - No. 6, 1991 ($2.50, limited series, mature, stiff-c)
DC Comics

	GD25	FN65	NM94
1-6: Horror/fantasy; all painted-c/a		1.00	2.50

WORLD WRESTLING FEDERATION BATTLEMANIA
1991 - No. 5?, 1991 ($2.50, magazine size, 68 pgs.)
Valiant

	GD25	FN65	NM94
1-5: 5-Includes 2 free pull-out posters		1.00	2.50

WORST FROM MAD, THE (Annual)
1958 - No. 12, 1969 (Each annual cover is reprinted from the cover of the Mad issues being reprinted)
E. C. Comics

	GD25	FN65	NM94
nn(1958)-Bonus; record labels & travel stickers; 1st Mad annual; r/Mad #29-34	34.00	103.00	275.00
2(1959)-Bonus is small 33¹/3 rpm record entitled "Meet the Staff of Mad"; r/Mad #35-40	40.00	120.00	315.00
3(1960)-Has 20x30" campaign poster "Alfred E. Neuman for President"; r/Mad #41-46	18.50	55.00	185.00
4(1961)-Sunday comics section; r/Mad #47-54	17.00	51.00	170.00
5(1962)-Has 33-1/3 record; r/Mad #55-62	26.50	80.00	265.00
6(1963)-Has 33-1/3 record; r/Mad #63-70	28.00	84.00	280.00
7(1964)-Mad protest signs; r/Mad #71-76	9.50	28.50	95.00
8(1965)-Build a Mad Zeppelin	12.00	36.00	120.00
9(1966)-33-1/3 rpm record	19.00	57.00	190.00
10(1967)-Mad bumper sticker	6.00	18.00	60.00
11(1968)-Mad cover window stickers	5.50	16.50	55.00
12(1969)-Mad picture postcards; Orlando-a	5.50	16.50	55.00

NOTE: *Covers: **Bob Clarke**-#8. **Mingo**-#7, 9-12.*

WOTALIFE COMICS (Formerly Nutty Life #2; Phantom Lady #13 on)
No. 3, Aug-Sept, 1946 - No. 12, July, 1947; 1959
Fox Features Syndicate/Norlen Mag.

Wow Comics #58 © FAW

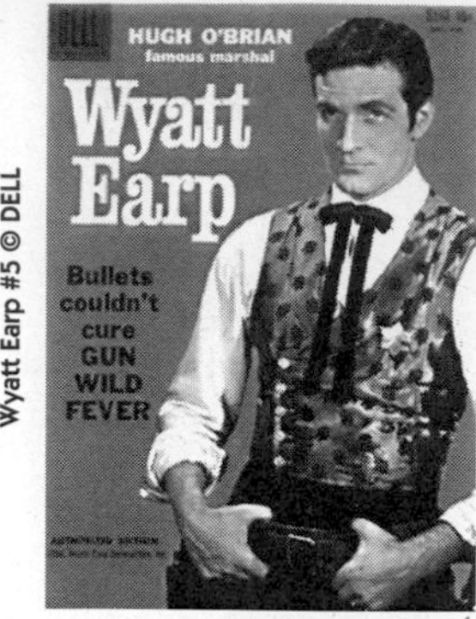

Wyatt Earp #5 © DELL

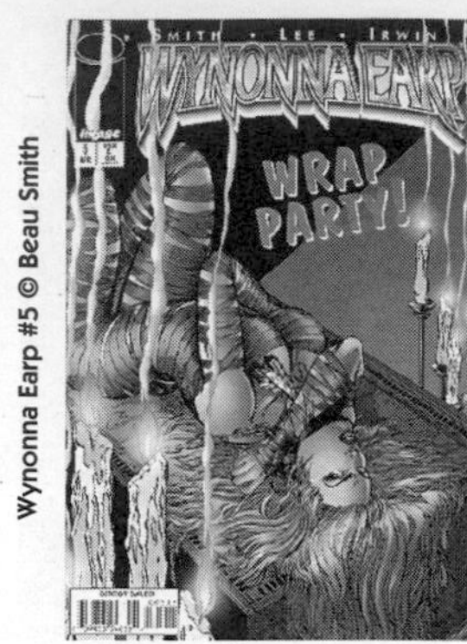

Wynonna Earp #5 © Beau Smith

GD25 FN65 NM94

3-Cosmo Cat, Li'l Pan, others begin 8.50 26.00 60.00
4-12-Cosmo Cat, Li'l Pan in all 5.70 17.00 40.00
1(1959-Norlen)-Atomic Rabbit, Atomic Mouse; reprints cover to #6; reprints entire book? 3.50 10.50 35.00

WOTALIFE COMICS
1957 - No. 5, 1957
Green Publications

1 4.25 13.00 28.00
2-5 4.00 10.00 20.00

WOW COMICS
July, 1936 - No. 4, Nov, 1936 (52 pgs., magazine size)
Henle Publishing Co.

1-Buck Jones in "The Phantom Rider" (1st app. in comics), Fu Manchu; Capt. Scott Dalton begins; Eisner-a; Briefer-c 211.00 633.00 1900.00
2-Ken Maynard, Fu Manchu, Popeye by Segar plus article on Popeye; Eisner-a 144.00 432.00 1300.00
3-Eisner-c/a(3); Popeye by Segar, Fu Manchu, Hiram Hick by Bob Kane, Space Limited app.; Jimmy Dempsey talks about Popeye's punch; Bob Ripley Believe it or Not begins; Briefer-a 144.00 432.00 1300.00
4-Flash Gordon by Raymond, Mandrake, Popeye by Segar, Tillie The Toiler, Fu Manchu, Hiram Hick by Bob Kane; Eisner-a(3); Briefer-c/a 178.00 534.00 1600.00

WOW COMICS (Real Western Hero #70 on)(See XMas Comics)
Winter, 1940-41; No. 2, Summer, 1941 - No. 69, Fall, 1948
Fawcett Publications

GD25 FN65 VF82 NM94
nn(#1)-Origin Mr. Scarlet by S&K; Atom Blake, Boy Wizard, Jim Dolan, & Rick O'Shay begin; Diamond Jack, The White Rajah, & Shipwreck Roberts, only app.; 1st mention of Gotham City in comics; the cover was printed on unstable paper stock and is rarely found in fine or mint condition; blank inside-c; bondage-c by Beck 1136.00 3410.00 6815.00 12,500.00
(Estimated up to 100 total copies exist, 3 in NM/Mint)

GD25 FN65 NM94
2 (Scarce)-The Hunchback begins 189.00 567.00 1700.00
3 (Fall, 1941) 89.00 267.00 800.00
4-Origin & 1st app. Pinky 94.00 282.00 850.00
5 60.00 180.00 540.00
6-Origin & 1st app. The Phantom Eagle (7/15/42); Commando Yank begins 60.00 180.00 540.00
7,8,10: 10-Swayze-c/a on Mary Marvel 48.00 144.00 430.00
9 (1/6/43)-Capt. Marvel, Capt. Marvel Jr., Shazam app.; Scarlet & Pinky x-over; Mary Marvel-c/stories begin (cameo #9) 100.00 300.00 900.00
11-17,19,20: 15-Flag-c 36.00 108.00 300.00
18-1st app. Uncle Marvel (10/43); infinity-c 36.00 108.00 320.00
21-30: 28-Pinky x-over in Mary Marvel 20.00 60.00 160.00
31-40: 32-68-Phantom Eagle by Swayze 13.00 39.00 105.00
41-50 12.00 36.00 95.00
51-58: Last Mary Marvel 10.50 32.00 85.00
59-69: 59-Ozzie (teenage) begins. 62-Flying Saucer gag-c (1/48). 65-69-Tom Mix stories (cont'd in Real Western Hero) 9.50 28.00 75.00

NOTE: *Cover features: Mr. Scarlet-#1-5; Commando Yank-#6, 7, (w/Mr. Scarlet #8); Mary Marvel-#9-56, (w/Commando Yank-#46-50), (w/Mr. Scarlet & Commando Yank-#51), (w/Mr. Scarlet & Pinky #53), (w/Phantom Eagle #54, 56), (w/Commando Yank & Phantom Eagle #58); Ozzie-#59-69.*

WRATH (Also see Prototype #4)
Jan, 1994 - No. 9, Nov, 1995 ($1.95)
Malibu Comics

1-9: 2-Mantra x-over. 3-Intro/1st app. Slayer. 4,5-Freex app. 8-Mantra & Warstrike app. 9-Prime app. .80 2.00
1-Ultra 5000 Limited silver foil 1.60 4.00
Giant Size 1 (2.50, 44 pgs.) 1.00 2.50

WRATH OF THE SPECTRE, THE
May, 1988 - No. 4, Aug, 1988 ($2.50, limited series)
DC Comics

1-4: Aparo-r/Adventure #431-440 1.00 2.50

WRECK OF GROSVENOR (See Superior Stories #3)

WRETCH, THE
1996 ($2.95, B&W)
Caliber

1-Phillip Hester-a/scripts 1.20 3.00

WRINGLE WRANGLE (Disney)
No. 821, July, 1957
Dell Publishing Co.

Four Color 821-Based on movie "Westward Ho, the Wagons"; Marsh-a; Fess Parker photo-c 7.00 22.00 80.00

WULF THE BARBARIAN
Feb, 1975 - No. 4, Sept, 1975
Atlas/Seaboard Publ.

1,2: 1-Origin. 2-Intro. Berithe the Swordswoman; Neal Adams, Wood, Reese-a assists 1.60 4.00
3,4 1.20 3.00

WYATT EARP
Nov, 1955 - #29, June, 1960; #30, Oct, 1972 - #34, June, 1973
Atlas Comics/Marvel No. 23 on (IPC)

1 17.00 51.00 135.00
2-Williamson-a (4 pgs.) 9.50 28.00 75.00
3-6,8-11: 3-Black Bart app. 8-Wild Bill Hickok app 8.50 26.00 60.00
7,12-Williamson-a, 4 pgs. ea.; #12 with Mayo 8.50 26.00 60.00
13-20: 17-1st app. Wyatt's deputy, Grizzly Grant 7.15 21.50 50.00
21-Davis-c 5.70 17.00 40.00
22-24,26-29: 22-Ringo Kid app. 23-Kid From Texas app. 29-Last 10¢ issue 5.00 15.00 30.00
25-Davis-a 5.35 16.00 32.00
30-Williamson-r (1972) 1.50 4.50 12.00
31-34-Reprints. 32-Torres-a(r) 1.10 3.30 9.00

NOTE: ***Ayers** a-8, 10(2), 17, 20(4). **Berg** a-9. **Everett** c-6. **Kirby** c-25, 29. **Maneely** a-1; c-1-4, 8, 12, 17, 20. **Maurer** a-2(2), 3(4), 4(4), 8(4). **Severin** a-4, 9(4), 10; c-2, 9, 10, 14. **Wildey** a-5, 17, 24, 28.*

WYATT EARP (TV) (Hugh O'Brian Famous Marshal)
No. 860, Nov, 1957 - No. 13, Dec-Feb, 1960-61 (Hugh O'Brian photo-c)
Dell Publishing Co.

Four Color 860 (#1)-Manning-a 10.00 30.00 110.00
Four Color 890,921(6/58)-All Manning-a 7.00 20.00 75.00
4 (9-11/58) - 12-Manning-a. 5-Photo back-c 4.50 13.50 50.00
13-Toth-a 5.00 15.00 55.00

WYATT EARP FRONTIER MARSHAL (Formerly Range Busters) (Also see Blue Bird)
No. 12, Jan, 1956 - No. 72, Dec, 1967
Charlton Comics

12 6.50 19.50 45.00
13-19 4.00 12.00 24.00
20-(68 pgs.)-Williamson-a(4), 8,5,5,& 7 pgs. 7.85 23.50 55.00
21-30 2.00 6.00 16.00
31-50 1.10 3.30 9.00
51-72 2.00 5.00

WYNONNA EARP
Dec, 1996 - No. 5, Apr, 1997 ($2.50)
Image Comics (WildStorm Productions)

1-5-Smith-s/Chin-a 1.00 2.50

X (Comics' Greatest World: X #1 only) (Also see Comics' Greatest World & Dark Horse Comics #8)
Feb, 1994 - No. 25, Apr, 1996 ($2.00/$2.50)

Xena: Warrior Princess/ Joxer: Warrior Prince #1 © Universal

Xero #8 © DC

X-Factor #125 © MEG

GD25 FN65 NM94

Dark Horse Comics
- 1-7: 3-Pit Bulls x-over .80 2.00
- 8-25: 8 ($2.50)-Ghost-c & app. 18-Miller-c.; Predator app. 19-22-Miller-c. 1.00 2.50

Hero Illustrated Special #1,2 (1994, $1.00, 20 pgs.) 1.00
One Shot to the Head (1994, $2.50, 36 pgs.)-Miller-c. 1.00 2.50
NOTE: ***Miller*** *c-18-22.* ***Quesada*** *c-6.* ***Russell*** *a-6.*

XANADU COLOR SPECIAL
Dec, 1988 ($2.00, one-shot)
Eclipse Comics
- 1-Reprints Xanadu from Thoughts & Images .80 2.00

XAVIER INSTITUTE ALUMNI YEARBOOK (See X-Men titles)
Dec, 1996 ($5.95, square-bound, one-shot)
Marvel Comics
- 1-Text w/art by various 2.40 6.00

X-CALIBRE
Mar, 1995 - No. 4, July, 1995 ($1.95, limited series)
Marvel Comics
- 1-4-Age of Apocalypse .80 2.00

XENA: WARRIOR PRINCESS (TV)
Aug, 1997 - Present ($2.95)
Topps Comics
- 1-Two stories by various; J. Scott Campbell-c 2.00 5.00
- 1-Photo-c 2.00 5.00
- 2-Stevens-c 1.40 3.50
- 0-(10/97)-Lopresti-c 2.95
- 0-(10/97)-Photo-c 2.95

XENA: WARRIOR PRINCESS / JOXER: WARRIOR PRINCE (TV)
Nov, 1997 - No. 3 ($2.95, limited series)
Topps Comics
- 1-3-Regular and Photo-c; Lim-a/T&M Bierbaum-s 2.95

XENOBROOD
No. 0, Oct, 1994 - No. 6, Apr, 1995 ($1.50, limited series)
DC Comics
- 0-6: 0-Indicia says "Xenobroods" 1.50

XENON
Dec, 1987 - No. 23, Nov. 1, 1988 ($1.50, B&W, bi-weekly)
Eclipse Comics
- 1-23 1.50

XENOTECH
Sept, 1993 - No. 3, Dec, 1994 ($2.75)
Mirage Studios
- 1-3: Bound with 2 trading cards. 2-(10/94) 1.10 2.75

XENOZOIC TALES (Also see Cadillacs & Dinosaurs, Death Rattle #8)
Feb, 1986 - No. 11?
Kitchen Sink Press
- 1-11: 1-2nd printing exists (1/89) .80 2.00

XENYA
Apr, 1994 - Present ($2.95)
Sanctuary Press
- 1-3: 1-Hildebrandt-c; intro Xenya 1.20 3.00

XERO
May, 1997 - No. 12, Apr, 1998 ($1.75)
DC Comics
- 1-7 1.20 3.00
- 8-12: 8-Begin $1.95-c 1.95

X-FACTOR (Also see The Avengers #263 & Fantastic Four #286)
Feb, 1986 - Present
Marvel Comics Group
- 1-($1.25, 52 pgs)-Story recaps 1st app. from Avengers #263; story cont'd from F.F. #286; return of original X-Men (now X-Factor); Guice/Layton-a; Baby Nathan app. (2nd after X-Men #201) 1.10 3.30 9.00
- 2-4 2.00 5.00
- 5-1st app. Apocalypse (2-pg. cameo) 2.00 5.00
- 6-1st full app. Apocalypse 2.00 6.00 16.00
- 7-10: 10-Sabretooth app. (11/86, 3 pgs.) cont'd in X-Men #212; 1st app. in an X-Men comic book 1.20 3.00
- 11-20: 13-Baby Nathan app. in flashback. 14-Cyclops vs. The Master Mold. 15-Intro wingless Angel .80 2.00
- 21,22 .80 2.00
- 23: 23-1st app. Archangel (2 pg. cameo) 1.10 3.30 9.00
- 24-1st full app. Archangel (now in Uncanny X-Men); Fall Of The Mutants begins; origin Apocalypse 1.50 4.50 12.00
- 25,26: Fall Of The Mutants; 26-New outfits 1.20 3.00
- 27-30 .80 2.00
- 31-37,39,41-49: 35-Origin Cyclops 1.50
- 38,50-($1.50, 52 pgs.): 50-Liefeld/McFarlane-c .80 2.00
- 40-Rob Liefeld-c/a (4/89, 1st at Marvel?) 1.20 3.00
- 51-53-Sabretooth app. 52-Liefeld-c(p) 1.20 3.00
- 54-59: 54-Intro Crimson; Silvestri-c/a(p) 1.50
- 60-X-Tinction Agenda x-over; New Mutants (w/Cable) x-over in #60-62; Wolverine in #62 1.20 3.00
- 60-Gold ink 2nd printing 1.00 2.50
- 61,62-X-Tinction Agenda. 62-Jim Lee-c 1.20 3.00
- 63-Portacio/Thibert-c/a(p) begins, ends #69 1.20 3.00
- 64-67,69,70: 65-68-Lee co-plots. 65-The Apocalypse Files begins, ends #68. 66,67-Baby Nathan app. 67-Inhumans app. 69,70-X-Men (w/Wolverine) x-over .80 2.00
- 68-Baby Nathan is sent into future to save his life 1.20 3.00
- 71-New team begins (Havok, Polaris, Strong Guy, Wolfsbane & Madrox); Stroman-c/a begins 1.20 3.00
- 71-2nd printing ($1.25) 1.25
- 72-74: 74-Last $1.00-c 1.50
- 75-($1.75, 52 pgs.) .70 1.75
- 76-83,87-91,93-99,101: 77-Cannonball (of X-Force) app. 87-Quesada-c/a(p) in monthly comic begins, ends #92. 88-1st app. Random. 1.25
- 84-86 ($1.50)-Polybagged with trading card in each; X-Cutioner's Song x-overs. 84-86-Jae Lee-a(p). 85,86-Jae Lee-c .80 2.00
- 92-($3.50, 68 pgs.)-Wraparound-c by Quesada w/Havok hologram on-c; begin X-Men 30th anniversary issues; Quesada-a. 2.00 5.00
- 92-2nd printing 1.40 3.50
- 100-($2.95, 52 pgs.)-Embossed foil-c; Multiple Man dies. 2.00 5.00
- 100-($1.75, 52 pgs.)-Regular edition .80 2.00
- 102-105,107: 102-Begin $1.50-c; bound-in card sheet 1.50
- 106-($2.00)-Newsstand edition .80 2.00
- 106-($2.95)-Collectors edition 1.20 3.00
- 108-124,126-135,-1(7/97): 108-Begin $1.95-c. 112-Return from Age of Apocalypse. 115-card insert. 119-123-Sabretooth app. 123-Hound app. 124-w/Onslaught Update. 126-Onslaught x-over; Beast vs. Dark Beast 128-w/card insert; return of Multiple Man. 130-Assassination of Grayson Creed .80 2.00
- 125-($2.95)-"Onslaught"; Post app.; return of Havok 1.20 3.00
- 136-145: 136-Begin $1.99-c .80 2.00
- Annual 1-6: 1-(10/86). 2-(10/87). 3-(1988, $1.75)-Evolutionary War x-over. 4-(1989, $2.00, 68 pgs.)-Atlantis Attacks; Byrne/Simonson-a; Byrne-c, 5-(1990, $2.00, 68 pgs.)-Fantastic Four, New Mutants x-over; Keown 2 pg. pin-up. 6-(1991, $2.00, 68 pgs.)-New Warriors app.; 5th app. X-Force cont'd from X-Men Annual #15 1.00 2.50
- Annual 7 (1992, $2.25, 68 pgs.)-1st Quesada-a(p) on X-Factor plus-c(p) .90 2.25
- Annual 8 (1993, $2.95, 68 pgs.)-Bagged w/trading card 1.20 3.00

X-Files #6 © 20th Century Fox

X-Force #59 © MEG

X-Man '96 © MEG

GD25 FN65 NM94

Annual 9 (1994, $2.95, 68 pgs.)-Austin-a(i) 1.20 3.00
...PRISONER OF LOVE nn (1990, $4.95, 52 pgs.)-Starlin scripts; Guice-a 2.00 5.00

NOTE: ***Art Adams*** *a-41p, 42p.* ***Buckler*** *a-50p.* ***Liefeld*** *a-40; c-40, 50i, 52p.* ***McFarlane*** *c-50i.* ***Mignola*** *c-70.* ***Brandon Peterson*** *a-78p(part).* ***Whilce Portacio*** *c/a(p)-63-69.* ***Quesada*** *a(p)-87-92, Annual 7. c(p)-78, 79, 82, Annual 7.* ***Simonson*** *c/a-10, 11, 13-15, 17-19, 21, 23-31, 33, 34, 36-39; c-12, 16.* ***Paul Smith*** *a-44-48; c-43.* ***Stroman*** *a(p)-71-75, 77, 78(part), 80, 81; c(p)-71-77, 80, 81, 84.* ***Zeck*** *c-2.*

X-FILES, THE (TV)
Jan, 1995 - Present ($2.50)
Topps Comics

-1(9/96)-Silver-c; r/Hero Illustrated Giveaway 1.25 3.75 10.00
0-($3.95)-Adapts pilot episode 1.60 4.00
0-"Mulder" variant-c 1.00 3.00 8.00
0-"Scully" variant-c 1.00 3.00 8.00
1/2-W/certificate 2.50 7.50 25.00
1-Adaptation of TV show; direct market & newsstand editions; Miran Kim-c on all 4.50 13.50 45.00
2 3.00 9.00 30.00
3,4 1.75 5.25 14.00
5-10 2.00 5.00
11-36: 11-Begin $2.95-c. 21-W/bound-in card 1.20 3.00
Annual 1,2 ($3.95) 1.60 4.00
Collection 1 TPB ($19.95)-r/#1-6. 20.00
Collection 2 TPB ($19.95)-r/#7-12, Annual #1. 20.00
Hero Illustrated Giveaway 1.85 5.50 15.00
Special Edition 1 ($4.95)-r/#1-3. 2.00 5.00
Special Edition 2 ($4.95)-r/#4-6. 2.00 5.00
Special Edition 3 ($4.95)-r/#7-9 2.00 5.00
Special Edition 4 ($4.95)-r/#10-12 2.00 5.00
Special Edition 5 ($4.95)-r/#13, Annual #1 2.00 5.00
Star Wars Galaxy Magazine Giveaway (B&W) 1.25 3.75 10.00
Trade paperback ($19.95) 20.00

X-FILES COMICS DIGEST, THE
Dec, 1995 - Present ($3.50, quarterly, digest-size)
Topps Comics

1,2: New X-Files stories w/Ray Bradbury Comics-r 3.50
3 1.60 4.00

NOTE: ***Adlard*** *a-1, 2.* ***Jack Davis*** *a-2r.* ***Russell*** *a-1r.*

X-FILES, THE: GROUND ZERO (TV)
Nov, 1997 - No. 4 ($2.95, limited series)
Topps Comics

1,2-Adaption of the Kevin J. Anderson novel 2.95

X-FILES, THE: SEASON ONE (TV)
July, 1997 - Present ($4.95)
Topps Comics

1,2, "Squeeze"-Adaptions of TV episodes 4.95

X-FORCE (Also see The New Mutants #100 & 1992 X-Men Annuals)
Aug, 1991 - Present ($1.00/$1.25/$1.50/$1.95/$1.99)
Marvel Comics

1-($1.50, 52 pgs.)-Polybagged with 1 of 5 diff. Marvel Universe trading cards inside (1 each); 6th app. of X-Force; Liefeld-c/a begins .80 2.00
1-1st printing with Cable trading card inside 1.00
1-2nd printing; metallic ink-c (no bag or card) 1.00
2-4: 2-Deadpool-c/story. 3-New Brotherhood of Evil Mutants app. 4-Spider-Man x-over; cont'd from Spider-Man #16; reads sideways 1.00 2.50
5-10: 6-Last $1.00-c. 7,9-Weapon X back-ups. 8-Intro The Wild Pack (Cable, Kane, Domino, Hammer, G.W. Bridge, & Grizzly); Liefeld-c/a (4); Mignola-a. 10-Weapon X full-length story (part 3). 11-1st Weapon Prime (cameo); Deadpool-c/story. .80 2.00
11-15,19-24,26-33: 15-Cable leaves X-Force 1.50
16-18-($1.50)-Polybagged w/trading card in each; X-Cutioner's Song x-overs .80 2.00
25-($3.50, 52 pgs.)-Wraparound-c w/Cable hologram on-c; Cable returns 1.60 4.00
34-37,39-45: 34-Begin $1.50-c; bound-in card sheet 1.50
38-($2.00)-Newsstand edition .80 2.00
38-($2.95)-Collectors edition 2.00 5.00
40-43 (1.95)-Deluxe edition .80 2.00
44-49,51-67,-1(7/97): 44-Return from Age of Apocalypse. 45-Sabretooth app. 49-Sebastian Shaw app. 52-Blob app., Onslaught cameo. 55-Vs. S.H.I.E.L.D. 56-Deadpool app. 57-Mr. Sinister & X-Man-c/app; Onslaught x-over. 58-Onslaught x-over. 59-W/card insert; return of Longshot. 60-Dr. Strange. -1-Flashback .80 2.00
50 ($3.95)-Gatefold wrap-around foil-c 1.20 3.00
50 ($3.95)-Liefeld variant-c 1.00 2.80 7.00
68-77: 68-Begin $1.99-c; Operation Zero Tolerance 2.00
Annual 1 (1992, $2.25, 68 pgs.)-1st Greg Capullo-a(p) on X-Force .90 2.25
Annual 2 (1993, $2.95, 68 pgs.)-Polybagged w/trading card; intro X-Treme & Neurtap 1.20 3.00
Annual 3 (1994, $2.95) 1.20 3.00
...AND CABLE '95 (12/95, $3.95)-Impossible Man app. 1.60 4.00
...AND CABLE '97 (7/97, $2.99) 1.20 3.00
...AND SPIDER-MAN: SABOTAGE nn (11/92, $6.95)-Reprints X-Force #3,4 & Spider-Man #16 1.00 2.80 7.00
...YOUNGBLOOD (8/96, $4.95)-Platt-c 2.00 5.00

NOTE: ***Capullo*** *a(p)-15-25, Annual 1; c(p)-14-27.* ***Rob Liefeld*** *a-1-7, 9p; c-1-9, 11p; plots-1-12.* ***Mignola*** *a-8p.*

X-FORCE MEGAZINE
Nov, 1996 ($3.95, one-shot)
Marvel Comics

1-Reprints 1.60 4.00

XIMOS: VIOLENT PAST
Mar, 1994 - No. 2, Mar, 1994 ($2.50, limited series)
Triumphant Comics

1,2 1.00 2.50

X-MAN (Also see X-Men Omega & X-Men Prime)
Mar, 1995 - Present ($1.95/$1.99)
Marvel Comics

1-Age of Apocalypse 2.00 5.00
1-2nd print .80 2.00
2-4 1.20 3.00
5-24, 26-28,-1(7/97): 5-Post Age of Apocalypse stories begin. 5-7-Madelyne Pryor app. 10-Professor X app. 12-vs. Excalibur. 13-Marauders, Cable app. 14-Vs. Cable; Onslaught app. 15-17-Vs. Holocaust. 17-w/Onslaught Update. 18-Onslaught x-over; X-Force-c/app; Marauders app. 19-Onslaught x-over. 20-Abomination-c/app.; w/card insert. 23-Bishop-c/app. 24-Spider-Man Morbius-c/app. 27-Re-appearance of Aurora(Alpha Flight) .80 2.00
25-($2.99)-Wraparound-c 1.20 3.00
29-38: 29-Begin $1.99-c; Operation Zero Tolerance .80 2.00
...'96-($2.95)-Wraparound-c; Age of Apocalypse 1.20 3.00

XMAS COMICS
12?/1941 - No. 2, 12?/1942 (50¢, 324 pgs.)
No. 3, 12?/1943 - No. 7, 12?/1947 (25¢, 132 pgs.)
Fawcett Publications

GD25 FN65 VF82 NM94

1-Contains Whiz #21, Capt. Marvel #3, Bulletman #2, Wow #3, & Master #18; Raboy back-c. Not rebound, remaindered comics; printed at same time as originals 300.00 900.00 1800.00 3000.00
(Estimated up to 110 total copies exist, 5 in NM/Mint)

GD25 FN65 NM94

2-Capt. Marvel, Bulletman, Spy Smasher 100.00 300.00 1000.00
3-7-Funny animals (Hoppy, Billy the Kid & Oscar) 40.00 120.00 400.00

X-Men #1 (1st Series) © MEG

X-Men #34 (1st Series) © MEG

X-Men #33 (2nd Series) © MEG

XMAS COMICS
No. 4, Dec, 1949 - No. 7, Dec, 1952 (50¢, 196 pgs.)
Fawcett Publications

4-Contains Whiz, Master, Tom Mix, Captain Marvel, Nyoka, Capt. Video, Bob Colt, Monte Hale, Hot Rod Comics, & Battle Stories. Not rebound, remaindered comics; printed at the same time as originals 44.00 132.00 440.00
5-7-Same as above. 7-Bill Boyd app.; stocking on cover is made of green felt (novelty cover) 36.00 108.00 360.00

XMAS FUNNIES
No date (Giveaway, paper cover, 36 pgs.?)
Kinney Shoes

Contains 1933 color strip-r; Mutt & Jeff, etc. 31.00 94.00 250.00

X-MEN, THE (See Adventures of Cyclops and Phoenix, Amazing Adventures, Archangel, Capt. America #172, Classic X-Men, Further Adventures of Cyclops & Phoenix, Gambit, Giant-Size..., Heroes For Hope..., Kitty Pryde & Wolverine, Marvel & DC Present, Marvel Collector's Edition:..., Marvel Fanfare, Marvel Graphic Novel, Marvel Super Heroes, Marvel Team-Up, Marvel Triple Action, The Marvel X-Men Collection, New Mutants, Nightcrawler, Official Marvel Index To..., Rogue, Special Edition..., The Uncanny..., Wolverine, X-Factor, X-Force, X-Terminators)

X-MEN, THE (Becomes Uncanny X-Men with #142)(The X-Men #1-93; X-Men #94-141; The Uncanny X-Men on-c only #114-141)
Sept, 1963 - No. 66, Mar, 1970; No. 67, Dec, 1970 - No. 141, Jan, 1981
Marvel Comics Group GD25 FN65 VF82 NM94

1-Origin/1st app. X-Men (Angel, Beast, Cyclops, Iceman & Marvel Girl); 1st app. Magneto & Professor X 367.00 1100.00 2570.00 5500.00
GD25 FN65 NM94
2-1st app. The Vanisher 140.00 420.00 1670.00
3-1st app. The Blob (1/64) 53.00 159.00 635.00
4-1st Quick Silver & Scarlet Witch & Brotherhood of the Evil Mutants (3/64); 1st app. Toad; 2nd app. Magneto 48.00 144.00 580.00
5-Magneto & Evil Mutants-c/story 36.00 108.00 400.00
6-10: 6-Sub-Mariner app. 7-Magneto app. 8-1st Unus the Untouchable. 9-Early Avengers app. (1/65); 1st Lucifer. 10-1st S.A. app. Ka-Zar & Zabu the sabertooth (3/65) 29.00 87.00 290.00
11,13-15: 11-1st app. The Stranger. 14-1st app. Sentinels. 15-Origin Beast 23.50 70.00 235.00
12-Origin Prof. X; Origin/1st app. Juggernaut 30.00 90.00 300.00
16-20: 19-1st app. The Mimic (4/66) 12.00 36.00 120.00
21-27,29,30: 27-Re-enter The Mimic (r-in #75); Spider-Man cameo 9.50 28.50 95.00
28-1st app. The Banshee (1/67)(r-in #76) 14.00 42.00 140.00
31-34,36,37,39,40: 34-Adkins-c/a. 39-New costumes 6.50 19.50 65.00
35-Spider-Man x-over (8/67)(r-in #83); 1st app. Changeling 11.00 33.00 110.00
38-Origins of the X-Men series begins, ends #57 8.50 25.50 85.00
41-49: 42-Death of Prof. X (Changeling disguised as). 44-1st S.A. app. G.A. Red Raven. 49-Steranko-c; 1st Polaris 6.00 18.00 60.00
50,51-Steranko-c/a 6.50 19.50 65.00
52 4.50 13.50 45.00
53-Barry Smith-c/a (his 1st comic book work) 6.50 19.50 65.00
54,55-B. Smith-c. 54-1st app. Alex Summers who later becomes Havok. 55-Summers discovers he has mutant powers 7.00 21.00 70.00
56,57,59-63,65-Neal Adams-a(p). 56-Intro Havok w/o costume. 65-Return of Professor X 5.50 16.50 55.00
58-1st app. Havok in costume; N. Adams-a(p) 9.00 27.00 90.00
64-1st app. Sunfire 6.50 19.50 65.00
66-Last new story w/original X-Men; battles Hulk 5.00 15.00 50.00
67-70,72: (52 pgs.). 67-Reprints begin, end #93 2.80 8.40 28.00
71,73-93: 71-Last 15¢ issue. 73-86-r/#25-38 w/new-c. 83-Spider-Man-c/story. 87-93-r/#39-45 with covers 2.50 7.50 24.00
94 (8/75)-New X-Men begin (see Giant-Size X-Men for 1st app.); Colossus, Nightcrawler, Thunderbird, Storm, Wolverine, & Banshee join; Angel, Marvel Girl, & Iceman resign 38.00 114.00 420.00
94-Variant w/Mark Jewelers pull-out ad 38.00 114.00 420.00
95-Death of Thunderbird 9.00 27.00 90.00
96,97 7.00 21.00 70.00
98,99-(Regular 25¢ edition)(6,8/76) 7.00 21.00 70.00
98,99-(30¢-c, limited distribution) 28.00 84.00 280.00
100-Old vs. New X-Men; part origin Phoenix; last 25¢ issue (8/76) 7.00 21.00 70.00
101-Phoenix origin concludes 6.00 18.00 60.00
102-105,107: 102-Origin Storm. 104-1st app. Starjammers (brief cameo); Magneto-c/story. 107-1st full app. Starjammers; last 30¢ issue 3.00 9.00 30.00
106-(Regular 30¢ edition)(8/77)Old vs. New X-Men 3.00 9.00 30.00
106-(35¢-c, limited distribution) 12.00 36.00 120.00
108-Byrne-a begins (see Marvel Team-Up #53) 6.00 18.00 60.00
109-1st app. Weapon Alpha (becomes Vindicator) 4.50 13.50 45.00
110,111: 110-Phoenix joins 3.00 9.00 30.00
112-119: 117-Origin Professor X 2.50 7.50 25.00
120-1st app. Alpha Flight (cameo), story line begins (4/79); 1st app. Vindicator (formerly Weapon Alpha); last 35¢ issue 4.50 13.50 45.00
121-1st full Alpha Flight story 5.00 15.00 50.00
122-128: 123-Spider-Man x-over. 124-Colossus becomes Proletarian 2.50 7.50 22.00
129-Intro Kitty Pryde (1/80); last Banshee; Dark Phoenix saga begins 2.80 8.40 28.00
130-1st app. The Dazzler by Byrne (2/80) 2.50 7.50 24.00
131-135: 131-Dazzler app. 132-1st White Queen. 133-Wolverine app. 134-Phoenix becomes Dark Phoenix 2.15 6.50 17.00
136,138: 138-Dazzler app.; Cyclops leaves 1.85 5.50 15.00
137-Giant; death of Phoenix 2.25 6.75 18.00
139-Alpha Flight app.; Kitty Pryde joins; new costume for Wolverine 3.00 9.00 30.00
140-Alpha Flight app. 2.80 8.40 28.00
141-Intro Future X-Men & The New Brotherhood of Evil Mutants; 1st app. Rachel (Phoenix II); Death of Franklin Richards 3.00 9.00 30.00

X-MEN (2nd Series)
Oct, 1991 - Present ($1.00/$1.25/$1.95/$1.00)
Marvel Comics

1 a-d ($1.50, 52 pgs.)-Jim Lee-c/a begins, ends #11; new team begins (Cyclops, Beast, Wolverine, Gambit, Psylocke & Rogue); new Uncanny X-Men & Magneto app.; four different covers exist 2.00 5.00
1 e ($3.95)-Double gate-fold-c consisting of all four covers from 1a-d by Jim Lee; contains all pin-ups from #1a-d plus inside-c foldout poster; no ads; printed on coated stock 2.40 6.00
2-7: 4-Wolverine back to old yellow costume (same date as Wolverine #50); last $1.00-c. 5-Byrne scripts. 6-Sabretooth-c/story 1.60 4.00
8-10: 8-Gambit vs. Bishop-c/story; last Lee-a; Ghost Rider cameo cont'd in Ghost Rider #26. 9-Wolverine vs. Ghost Rider; cont'd/G.R. #26. 10-Return of Longshot 1.20 3.00
11-13,17-24,26-29,31: 12,13-Art Thibert-c/a. 28,29-Sabretooth app. .80 2.00
11-Silver ink 2nd printing; came with X-Men board game 2.50 7.50 20.00
14-16-($1.50)-Polybagged with trading card in each; X-Cutioner's Song x-overs; 14-Andy Kubert-c/a begins .80 2.00
25-($3.50, 52 pgs.)-Wraparound-c with Gambit hologram on-c; Professor X erases Magneto's mind 1.85 5.50 15.00
25-30th anniversary issue w/B&W-c with Magneto in color & Magneto hologram & no price on-c 2.50 7.50 25.00
25-Gold 3.00 9.00 30.00
30-($1.95)-Wedding issue w/bound-in trading card sheet 1.60 4.00
32-35: 32-Begin $1.50-c; bound-in card sheet. 33-Gambit & Sabretooth-c/story 1.50

X-Men #71 (2nd Series) © MEG

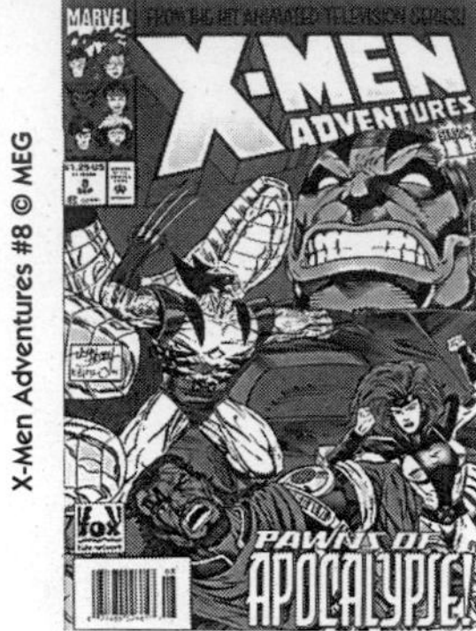

X-Men Adventures #8 © MEG

X-Men Classic #99 © MEG

GD25 FN65 NM94

36,37-($2.95)-Collectors editions 2.00 5.00
38-44,46-49,51-53, 55-65,-1(7/97): 42,43- Paul Smith-a. 46,49,53-56-Onslaught app. 51-Waid scripts begin, end #56. 54-(Regular edition)-Onslaught revealed as Professor X. 55, 56-Onslaught x-over; Avengers, FF & Sentinels app. 56-Dr. Doom app. 57-Xavier taken into custody; Byrne-c/swipe (X-Men, 1st Series #138). 59-Hercules-c/app. 61-Juggernaut-c/app. 62-Re-intro. Shang Chi; two covers. 63-Kingpin cameo. 64- Kingpin app. (-1)-Flashback; origin of Magneto 2.00
45 ($3.95)-Annual issue; gatefold-c 1.60 4.00
50 ($2.95)-Vs. Onslaught, wraparound-c. 1.60 4.00
50 ($3.95)-Vs. Onslaught, wraparound foil-c. 2.00 5.00
50 ($2.95)-Variant-c. 1.00 3.00 8.00
54-(Limited edition)-Embossed variant-c; Onslaught revealed as Professor X 3.00 9.00 30.00
66-69,71-74: 66-Begin $1.99-c; Operation Zero Tolerance 2.00
70-($2.99, 48 pgs.)-Joe Kelly-s begin, new members join 2.99
Annual 1 (1992, $2.25, 68 pgs.)-Lee-c & layouts 1.00 4.00
Annual 2 (1993, $2.95, 68 pgs.)-Bagged w/card 1.60 4.00
Annual 3 (1994, $2.95) 1.60 4.00
Ashcan #1 1.00
Special '95 ($3.95) 1.60 4.00
... '96 ($2.95) Wraparound-c 1.20 3.00
... '97 ($2.99) Wraparound-c 1.20 3.00
...:FATAL ATTRACTIONS ('94, $17.95)-r/x-Factor #92, X-Force #25, Uncanny X-Men #304, X-Men #25, Wolverine #75, & Excalibur #71 2.25 6.75 18.00
...:GOD LOVES, MAN KILLS (8/94, $6.95)-r/Marvel Graphic Novel #5 1.00 2.80 7.00
...PREMIUM EDITION #1 (1993)-Cover says "Toys 'R' Us Limited Edition X-Men" 1.50
...:RARITIES (1995, $5.95)-Reprints 2.40 6.00
...: THE COMING OF BISHOP ('95, $12.95)-r/Uncanny X-Men #282-285, 287,288 1.60 4.85 13.00

NOTE: ***Jim Lee*** *a-1-11p; c-1-6p, 7, 8, 9p, 10, 11p.* ***Art Thibert*** *a-6-9i, 12, 13; c-6i, 12, 13.*

X-MEN ADVENTURES (TV)
Nov, 1992 - No. 15, Jan, 1994 ($1.25)(Based on animated series)
Marvel Comics

1-Wolverine, Cyclops, Jubilee, Rogue, Gambit .80 2.00
2-5: 3-Magneto-c/story .80 2.00
6-10: 6-Sabretooth-c/story. 7-Cable-c/story. 10-Archangel guest star .80 2.00
11-14: 11-Cable-c/story 1.25
15-($1.75, 52 pgs.) .70 1.75

X-MEN ADVENTURES II (TV)
Feb, 1994 - No. 13, Feb, 1995 ($1.25/$1.50)(Based on 2nd TV season)
Marvel Comics

1-8: 4-Bound-in trading card sheet. 5-Alpha Flight app. 1.25
9-13: 9-Begin $1.50-c 1.50
...Captive Hearts/Slave Island (TPB, $4.95)-r/X-Men Adventures #5-8 2.00 5.00
...The Irresistible Force, The Muir Island Saga (5.95, 10/94, Trade Paperback)-r/X-Men Adventures #9-12 2.40 6.00

X-MEN ADVENTURES III (TV)(See Adventures of the X-Men)
Mar, 1995 - No. 13, Mar, 1996 ($1.50) (Based on 3rd TV season)
Marvel Comics

1-13 1.50

X-MEN ALPHA
1994 ($3.95, one-shot)
Marvel Comics

nn-Age of Apocalypse; wraparound chromium-c 1.00 3.00 8.00
nn ($49.95)-Gold logo 5.00 15.00 50.00

GD25 FN65 NM94

X-MEN/ALPHA FLIGHT
Dec, 1985 - No. 2, Dec, 1985 ($1.50, limited series)
Marvel Comics Group

1,2: 1-Intro The Berserkers; Paul Smith-a 2.00 5.00

X-MEN AND THE MICRONAUTS, THE
Jan, 1984 - No. 4, Apr, 1984 (Limited series)
Marvel Comics Group

1-4: Guice-c/a(p) in all .80 2.00

X-MEN ARCHIVES
Jan, 1995 - No. 4, Apr, 1995 ($2.25, limited series)
Marvel Comics

1-4: Reprints Legion stories from New Mutants. 4-Magneto app. .90 2.25

X-MEN ARCHIVES FEATURING CAPTAIN BRITAIN
July, 1995 - No. 7, 1996 ($2.95, limited series)
Marvel Comics

1-7: Reprints early Capt. Britain stories 1.20 3.00

X-MEN BOOKS OF ASKANI
1995 ($2.95, one-shot)
Marvel Comics

1-Painted pin-ups w/text 1.20 3.00

X-MEN CHRONICLES
Mar, 1995 (3.95, one-shot)
Marvel Comics

1,2: Age of Apocalypse x-over. 1-wraparound-c 2.00 5.00

X-MEN: CLANDESTINE
Oct, 1996 - No. 2, Nov, 1996 ($2.95, limited series, 48 pgs.)
Marvel Comics

1,2: Alan Davis-c(p)/a(p)/scripts & Mark Farmer-c(i)/a(i) in all; wraparound-c 1.20 3.00

X-MEN CLASSIC (Formerly Classic X-Men)
No. 46, Apr, 1990 - No. 110, Aug, 1995 ($1.25/$1.50)
Marvel Comics

46-69,71-78,80-89,91-96,98,99: Reprints from X-Men. 54-($1.25, 52 pgs.). 57, 60-63,65-Russell-c(i); 62-r/X-Men #158(Rogue). 66-r/#162(Wolverine). 69-Begins-r of Paul Smith issues (#165 on) 1.50
70,79,90,97-($1.75, 52 pgs.): 70-r/X-Men #166. 90-r/#186 .80 2.00
100-110: 100-($1.50). 104-r/X-Men #200. .70 1.75

X-MEN CLASSICS
Dec, 1983 - No. 3, Feb, 1984 ($2.00, Baxter paper)
Marvel Comics Group

1-3: X-Men-r by Neal Adams 1.20 3.00

NOTE: ***Zeck*** *c-1-3.*

X-MEN: EARTHFALL
Sept, 1996 ($2.95, one-shot)
Marvel Comics

1-r/Uncanny X-Men #232-234; wraparound-c 1.20 3.00

X-MEN FIRSTS
Feb, 1996 ($4.95, one-shot)
Marvel Comics

1-r/Avengers Annual #10, Uncanny X-Men #266, #221; Incredible Hulk #181 2.00 5.00

X-MEN LOST TALES
1997 ($2.99)
Marvel Comics

1,2-r/Classic X-Men back-up stories 1.20 3.00

X-MEN OMEGA
June, 1995 ($3.95, one-shot)

X-Men 2099 #35 © MEG

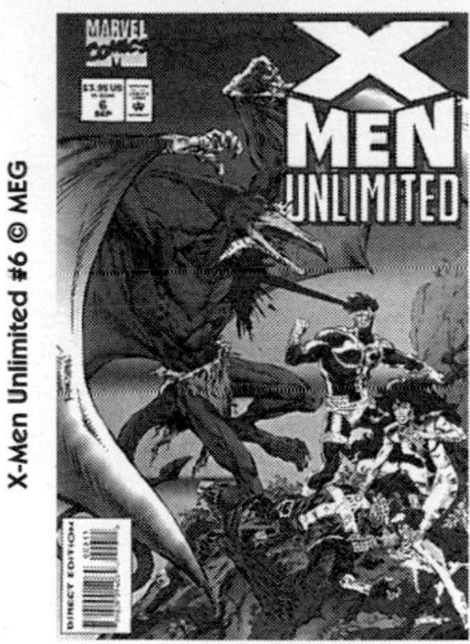

X-Men Unlimited #6 © MEG

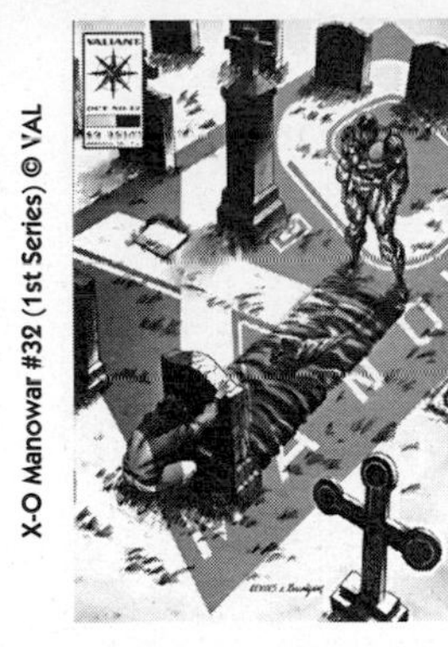
X-O Manowar #32 (1st Series) © VAL

Marvel Comics

	GD25	FN65	NM94
nn-Age of Apocalyse finale		2.00	5.00
nn-($49.95)-Gold edition	5.00	15.00	50.00

X-MEN PRIME
July, 1995 ($4.95, one-shot)
Marvel Comics

	GD25	FN65	NM94
nn-Post Age of Apocalyse begins		2.00	5.00

X-MEN RARITIES
1995 ($5.95, one-shot)
Marvel Comics

	GD25	FN65	NM94
nn-Reprints hard-to-find stories		2.40	6.00

X-MEN ROAD TO ONSLAUGHT
Oct, 1996 ($2.50, one-shot)
Marvel Comics

	GD25	FN65	NM94
nn-Retells Onslaught Saga		1.00	2.50

X-MEN SPOTLIGHT ON... STARJAMMERS (Also see X-Men #104)
1990 - No. 2, 1990 ($4.50, 52 pgs.)
Marvel Comics

	GD25	FN65	NM94
1,2: Features Starjammers		1.80	4.50

X-MEN SURVIVAL GUIDE TO THE MANSION
Aug, 1993 ($6.95, spiralbound)
Marvel Comics

	GD25	FN65	NM94
1	1.25	3.75	10.00

X-MEN: THE EARLY YEARS
May, 1994 - No. 17, Sept, 1995 ($1.50/$2.50)
Marvel Comics

	GD25	FN65	NM94
1-16: r/X-Men #1-8 w/new-c			1.50
17-$2.50-c; r/X-Men #17,18		1.00	2.50

X-MEN: THE ULTRA COLLECTION
Dec, 1994 - No. 5, Apr, 1995 ($2.95, limited series)
Marvel Comics

	GD25	FN65	NM94
1-5: Pin-ups; no scripts		1.20	3.00

X-MEN: THE WEDDING ALBUM
1994 ($2.95, magazine size, one-shot)
Marvel Comics

	GD25	FN65	NM94
1-Wedding of Scott Summers & Jean Grey		1.20	3.00

X-MEN 2099 (Also see 2099: World of Tomorrow)
Oct, 1993 - No. 35, Aug, 1996 ($1.25/$1.50/$1.95)
Marvel Comics

	GD25	FN65	NM94
1-($1.75)-Foil-c; Ron Lim/Adam Kubert-a begins		.80	2.00
1-2nd printing ($1.75)		.70	1.75
1-Gold edition (15,000 made); sold thru Diamond for $19.40	2.50	7.50	20.00
2-7: 3-Death of Tina; Lim-c/a(p) in #1-8			1.25
8-19: 8-Begin $1.50-c; bound-in trading card sheet			1.50
20-24,26-35: 20-$1.95-c begins. 35-Nostromo (from X-Nation) app; storyline cont'd in 2099: World of Tomorrow.		.80	2.00
25 ($2.50)-Double sized		1.00	2.50
Special 1 ($3.95)		1.60	4.00
...: Oasis ($5.95, one-shot) -Hildebrandt Bros.-c/a		2.40	6.00

X-MEN ULTRA III PREVIEW
1995 ($2.95)
Marvel Comics

	GD25	FN65	NM94
nn-Kubert-a		1.20	3.00

X-MEN UNLIMITED
1993 - Present ($3.95, 68 pgs.)
Marvel Comics

	GD25	FN65	NM94
1-Chris Bachalo-c/a; Quesada-a.	1.00	3.00	8.00
2,4-9: 2-Origin of Magneto script.		1.60	4.00
3-Sabretooth-c/story	1.00	2.80	7.00
10-Dark Beast vs. Beast; Mark Waid script	1.00	2.80	7.00
11-Magneto & Rogue		1.60	4.00
12-17: 12-Begin $2.99-c; Onslaught x-over; Juggernaut-c/app.		1.20	3.00

NOTE: ***Bachalo** c/a-1. **Quesada** a-1. **Waid** scripts-10*

X-MEN VS. DRACULA
Dec, 1993 ($1.75)
Marvel Comics

	GD25	FN65	NM94
1-r/X-Men Annual #6; Austin-c(i)		.70	1.75

X-MEN VS. THE AVENGERS, THE
Apr, 1987 - No. 4, July, 1987 ($1.50, limited series, Baxter paper)
Marvel Comics Group

	GD25	FN65	NM94
1		1.60	4.00
2-4		1.20	3.00

X-MEN VS. THE BROOD, THE
Sept, 1996 - No. 2, Oct, 1996 ($2.95, limited series)
Marvel Comics Group

	GD25	FN65	NM94
1,2-Wraparound-c; Ostrander-s/Hitch-a(p)		1.20	3.00
TPB('97, $16.99) reprints X-Men/Brood: Day of Wrath #1,2 & Uncanny X-Men #232-234			16.99

X-MEN VISIONARIES
1995 ($8.95, trade paperback)
Marvel Comics

	GD25	FN65	NM94
nn-Reprints X-Men stories; Adam & Andy Kubert-a	1.10	3.30	9.00

X-NATION 2099
Mar, 1996 - No. 6, Aug, 1996 ($1.95)
Marvel Comics

	GD25	FN65	NM94
1-($3.95)-Humberto Ramos-a(p); wraparound, foil-c		1.60	4.00
2-6: 2,3-Ramos-a. 4-Exodus-c/app. 5-Exodus cameo. 6-Reed Richards app		.80	2.00

X-O MANOWAR (1st Series)
Feb, 1992 - No. 68, Sept, 1996 ($1.95/$2.25/$2.50, high quality)
Valiant/Acclaim Comics (Valiant) No. 43 on

	GD25	FN65	NM94
0-(8/93, $3.50)-Wraparound embossed chromium-c by Quesada; Solar app.; origin Aric (X-O Manowar)		1.40	3.50
0-Gold variant		1.60	4.00
1-Intro/1st app. & partial origin of Aric (X-O Manowar); Barry Smith/Layton-a		2.00	5.00
2-4: 2-B. Smith/Layton-c; Layton part inks. 3-Layton-c(i). 4-1st app. Shadowman (cameo)		1.20	3.00
5-8: 5-B. Smith-c. 6-Begin $2.25-c; Ditko-a(p). 7,8-Unity x-overs. 7-Miller-c. 8-Simonson-c		1.20	3.00
9-13: 12-1st app. Randy Calder		1.20	3.00
14,15-Turok-c/stories		.80	2.00
15-Hot pink logo variant; came with Ultra Pro Rigid Comic Sleeves box; no price on cover		1.20	3.00
16-24,26-43: 20-Serial number contest insert. 27-29-Turok x-over. 28-Bound-in trading card. 30-1st app. new "good skin"; Solar app. 33-Chaos Effect Delta Pt. 3. 42-Shadowman app.; includes X-O Manowar Birthquake! Prequel		.90	2.25
25-($3.50)-Has 16 pg. Armorines #0 bound-in w/origin		1.40	3.50
44-68: 44-Begin $2.50-c. 50-X, 50-O, 51, 52, 63-Bart Sears-c/a/scripts. 68-Revealed that Aric's past stories were premonitions of his future		1.00	2.50
Trade paperback nn (1993, $9.95)-Polybagged with copy of X-O Database #1 inside		2.00	5.00
Yearbook 1 (4/95, $2.95)		1.20	3.00

NOTE: ***Layton** a-1i, 2i(part); c-1, 2i, 3i, 6i, 21i. **Reese** a-4i(part); c-26i.*

X-O Manowar/ Iron Man: In Heavy Metal #1 © VAL/ MEG

Xombi #4 © DC

Yellowjacket Comics #1 © E. Levy

GD25 FN65 NM94

X-O MANOWAR (2nd Series)(Also see Iron Man/X-O Manowar: Heavy Metal)
V2#1, Oct, 1996 - Present ($2.50)
Acclaim Comics (Valiant Heroes)

V2#1-14: 1-Mark Waid & Brian Augustyn scripts begin; 1st app. Donavon Wylie; Rand Banion dies; painted variant-c exists. 2-Donavon Wylie becomes new X-O Manowar. 7-9-Augustyn-s. 10-Copycat-c 2.50

X-O MANOWAR FAN EDITION
Feb, 1997 (Overstreet's FAN giveaway)
Acclaim Comics (Valiant Heroes)

1-Reintro the Armorines & the Hard Corps; 1st app. Citadel; Augustyn scripts; McKone-c/a 1.60 4.00

X-O MANOWAR/IRON MAN: IN HEAVY METAL (See Iron Man/X-O Manowar: Heavy Metal)
Sept, 1996 ($2.50, one-shot) (1st Marvel/Valiant x-over)
Acclaim Comics (Valiant Heroes)

1-Pt 1 of X-O Manowar/Iron Man x-over; Arnim Zola app.; Fabian Nicieza scripts; Andy Smith-a 1.00 2.50

XOMBI
Jan, 1994 - No. 21, Feb, 1996 ($1.75/$2.50)
DC Comics (Milestone)

0-($1.95)-Shadow War x-over; Simonson silver ink varnish-c .80 2.00
1-13: 1-John Byrne-c .70 1.75
1-Platinum 1.85 5.50 15.00
14-21: 14-Begin $2.50-c 1.00 2.50

X-PATROL
Apr, 1996 ($1.95, one-shot)
Marvel Comics (Amalgam)

1-Cruz-a(p) .80 2.00

XSE
Nov, 1996 - No. 4, Feb, 1997 ($1.95, limited series)
Marvel Comics

1-4: 1-Bishop & Shard app. .80 2.00
1-Variant-c 1.20 3.00

X-TERMINATORS
Oct, 1988 - No. 4, Jan, 1989 ($1.00, limited series)
Marvel Comics

1-1st app.; X-Men/X-Factor tie-in; Williamson-i 1.20 3.00
2 .70 1.75
3,4 1.25

X, THE MAN WITH THE X-RAY EYES (See Movie Comics)

X-UNIVERSE
May, 1995 - No. 2, June, 1995 ($3.50, limited series)
Marvel Comics

1,2: Age of Apocalypse 2.00 5.00

X-VENTURE (Super Heroes)
July, 1947 - No. 2, Nov, 1947
Victory Magazines Corp.

1-Atom Wizard, Mystery Shadow, Lester Trumble begin 64.00 192.00 575.00
2 39.00 117.00 350.00

XYR (See Eclipse Graphic Album Series #21)

YAK YAK
No. 1186, May-July, 1961 - No. 1348, Apr-June, 1962
Dell Publishing Co.

Four Color 1186 (#1)- Jack Davis-c/a; 2 versions, one minus 3pgs. 7.00 22.00 80.00
Four Color 1348 (#2)-Davis c/a 7.00 22.00 80.00

GD25 FN65 NM94

YAKKY DOODLE & CHOPPER (TV) (Also see Spotlight #3 & Top Cat #4)
Dec, 1962 (Hanna-Barbera)
Gold Key

1 4.50 13.50 50.00

YALTA TO KOREA (Also see Korea My Home)
1952 (Giveaway, paper cover, 8 pgs.)
M. Phillip Corp. (Republican National Committee)

nn-Anti-communist propaganda book 17.00 51.00 135.00

YANG (See House of Yang)
Nov, 1973 - No. 13, May, 1976; V14#14, Sept, 1985 - No. 17, Jan, 1986
Charlton Comics

1-Origin 1.00 3.00 8.00
2-13(1976) 2.00 5.00
14-17(1986) 1.20 3.00
3,10,11(Modern Comics-r, 1977) 1.20 3.00

YANKEE COMICS
Sept, 1941 - No. 5, 1942?
Harry 'A' Chesler

1-Origin The Echo, The Enchanted Dagger, Yankee Doodle Jones, The Firebrand, & The Scarlet Sentry; Black Satan app.; Yankee Doodle Jones app. on all covers 111.00 333.00 1000.00
2-Origin Johnny Rebel; Major Victory app.; Barry Kuda begins 56.00 168.00 500.00
3,4: 4-(3/42) 44.00 132.00 400.00
4 (nd, 1940s; 7-1/4x5", 68 pgs, distr. to the service)-Foxy Grandpa, Tom, Dick & Harry, Impy, Ace & Deuce, Dot & Dash, Ima Slooth by Jack Cole (Remington Morse publ.) 2.40 6.00 12.00
5-(nd; 10¢, 7-1/4x5", 68 pgs.)(Remington Morse publ.)-urges readers to send their copies to servicemen. 2.40 6.00 12.00

YANKS IN BATTLE
Sept, 1956 - No. 4, Dec, 1956; 1963
Quality Comics Group

1-Cuidera-c(i) 8.00 24.00 50.00
2-4: Cuidera-c(i) 5.00 15.00 30.00
I.W. Reprint #3(1963)-r/#?; exist? 1.10 3.30 9.00

YARDBIRDS, THE (G. I. Joe's Sidekicks)
Summer, 1952
Ziff-Davis Publishing Co.

1-By Bob Oskner 7.85 23.50 55.00

YARN MAN (See Megaton Man)
Oct, 1989 ($2.00, B&W, one-shot)
Kitchen Sink

1-Donald Simpson-c/a/scripts .80 2.00

YARNS OF YELLOWSTONE
1972 (50¢, 36 pgs.)
World Color Press

nn-Illustrated by Bill Chapman 2.00 5.00

YELLOW CLAW (Also see Giant Size Master of Kung Fu)
Oct, 1956 - No. 4, Apr, 1957
Atlas Comics (MjMC)

1-Origin by Joe Maneely 75.00 225.00 650.00
2-Kirby-a 62.00 187.00 530.00
3,4-Kirby-a; 4-Kirby/Severin-a 59.00 178.00 500.00

NOTE: ***Everett*** *c-3.* ***Maneely*** *c-1.* ***Reinman*** *a-2i, 3.* ***Severin*** *c-2, 4.*

YELLOWJACKET COMICS (Jack in the Box #11 on)(See TNT Comics)
Sept, 1944 - No. 10, June, 1946
E. Levy/Frank Comunale/Charlton

1-Intro & origin Yellowjacket; Diana, the Huntress begins; E.A. Poe's "The

Yogi Bear #9 © H-B

Yogi Berra © FAW

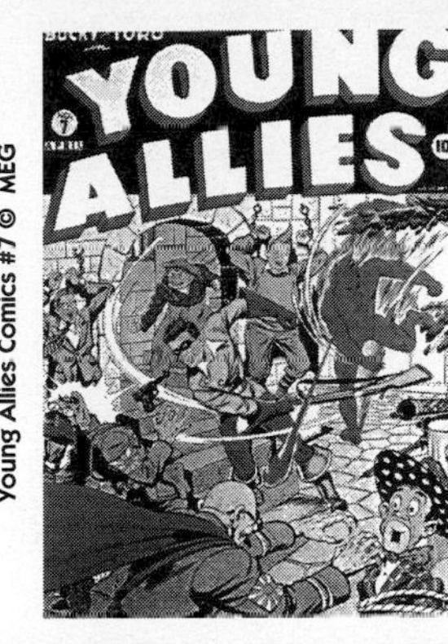

Young Allies Comics #7 © MEG

GD25 FN65 NM94

Black Cat" adaptation 44.00 132.00 400.00
2-Yellowjacket-c begin, end #10 28.00 83.00 220.00
3,5 26.00 80.00 210.00
4-E.A. Poe's "Fall of the House Of Usher" adaptation; Palais-a
28.00 83.00 220.00
6-10: 1,3,4,6-10-Have stories narrated by old witch in "Tales of Terror" (1st horror series?) 24.00 71.00 190.00

YELLOWSTONE KELLY (Movie)
No. 1056, Nov-Jan, 1959/60
Dell Publishing Co.
Four Color 1056-Clint Walker photo-c 5.00 15.00 54.00

YELLOW SUBMARINE (See Movie Comics)

YIN FEI THE CHINESE NINJA
1988 - No. 12?, 1990 ($1.80/$2.00, 52 pgs.)
Leung's Publications
1-6: 1-Begin $1.80-c .75 1.80
7-12: 7-Begin $2.00-c .80 2.00

YOGI BEAR (See Dell Giant #41, Golden Comics Digest, Kite Fun Book, March of Comics #253, 265, 279, 291, 309, 319, 337, 344, Movie Comics under "Hey There It's..." & Whitman Comic Books)

YOGI BEAR (TV) (Hanna-Barbera) (See Four Color #990)
No. 1067, 12-2/59-60 - No. 9, 7-9/62; No. 10, 10/62 - No. 42, 10/70
Dell Publishing Co./Gold Key No. 10 on
Four Color 1067 (#1)-TV show debuted 1/30/61 10.00 30.00 110.00
Four Color 1104,1162 (5-7/61) 7.00 20.00 75.00
4(8-9/61) - 6(12-1/61-62) 4.50 13.50 50.00
Four Color 1271(11/61) 4.50 13.50 50.00
Four Color 1349(1/62)-Photo-c 9.00 27.00 100.00
7(2-3/62) - 9(7-9/62)-Last Dell 4.50 13.50 50.00
10(10/62-G.K.), 11(1/63)-titled "Yogi Bear Jellystone Jollies" (80 pgs.);
11-X-Mas-c 6.00 18.00 65.00
12(4/63), 14-20 3.00 9.00 32.00
13(7/63, 68 pgs.)-Surprise Party 5.50 16.50 60.00
21-30 1.80 5.50 20.00
31-42 1.50 4.50 15.00
Giveaway ('84, '86)-City of Los Angeles, "Creative First Aid" & "Earthquake Preparedness for Children" .80 2.00

YOGI BEAR (TV)
Nov, 1970 - No. 35, Jan, 1976 (Hanna-Barbera)
Charlton Comics
1 3.00 9.00 30.00
2-6,8-10 2.25 6.75 18.00
7-Summer Fun (Giant, 52 pgs.) 4.00 12.00 40.00
11-35: 28-31-partial-r 1.50 4.50 12.00

YOGI BEAR (TV)(See The Flintstones, 3rd series & Spotlight #1)
Nov, 1977 - No. 9, Mar, 1979 (Hanna-Barbera)
Marvel Comics Group
1-Flintstones begin 1.25 3.75 10.00
2-9 1.00 3.00 8.00

YOGI BEAR (TV)
Sept, 1992 - No. 6, Mar, 1994 ($1.25/$1.50) (Hanna-Barbera)
Harvey Comics
V2#1-4 1.25
5,6: 5-Begin $1.50-c 1.50
...Big Book V2#1,2 ($1.95, 52 pgs): 1-(11/92). 2-(3/93) .80 2.00
...Giant Size V2#1,2 ($2.25, 68 pgs.): 1-(10/92). 2-(4/93) .90 2.25

YOGI BEAR'S EASTER PARADE (See The Funtastic World of Hanna-Barbera #2)

YOGI BERRA (Baseball hero)
1951 (Yankee catcher)
Fawcett Publications
nn-Photo-c 53.00 159.00 475.00

YOSEMITE SAM (...& Bugs Bunny)
Dec, 1970 - No. 81, Feb, 1984
Gold Key/Whitman
1 2.25 6.75 24.00
2-10 1.50 4.50 12.00
11-20 1.10 3.30 9.00
21-30 2.40 6.00
31-50 1.60 4.00
51-81: 81-(1/3-r) 1.20 3.00
(See March of Comics #363, 380, 392)

YOUNG ALLIES COMICS (All-Winners #21; see Kid Komics #2)
Summer, 1941 - No. 20, Oct, 1946
Timely Comics (USA 1-7/NPI 8,9/YAI 10-20)
GD25 FN65 VF82 NM94
1-Origin/1st app. The Young Allies (Bucky, Toro, others); 1st meeting of Captain America & Human Torch; Red Skull-c & app.; S&K-c/splash; Hitler-c
950.00 2850.00 5700.00 9500.00
(Estimated up to 165 total copies exist, 9 in NM/Mint)
GD25 FN65 NM94
2-(Winter, 1941)-Captain America & Human Torch app.; Simon & Kirby-c
240.00 720.00 2400.00
3-Fathertime, Captain America & Human Torch app.; Remember Pearl Harbor issue (Spring, 1942); Stan Lee scripts; Vs. Japs-c/full-length story
189.00 567.00 1700.00
4-The Vagabond & Red Skull, Capt. America, Human Torch app. Classic Red Skull-c 270.00 810.00 2700.00
5-Captain America & Human Torch app. 122.00 366.00 1100.00
6-8,10: 10-Origin Tommy Tyme & Clock of Ages; ends #19
83.00 250.00 750.00
9-Hitler, Tojo, Mussolini-c. 92.00 276.00 825.00
11-20: 12-Classic decapitation story 69.00 207.00 625.00
NOTE: ***Brodsky** c-15. **Gabrielle** a-3; c-3, 4. **S&K** c-1, 2. **Schomburg** c-5-14, 16-19. **Shores** c-20.*

YOUNG ALL-STARS
June, 1987 - No. 31, Nov, 1989 ($1.00, deluxe format)
DC Comics
1-31: 1-1st app. Iron Munro & The Flying Fox. 7-18-$1.25. 8,9-Millennium tie-ins. 19-23-$1.50. 24-Begin $1.75-c .80 2.00
Annual 1 (1988, $2.00) .80 2.00

YOUNGBLOOD (See Brigade #4, Megaton Explosion & Team Youngblood)
Apr, 1992 - No. 4, Feb, 1993 ($2.50, limited series);
No. 6, June, 1994 (No #5) - No. 10, Dec, 1994 ($1.95/$2.50)
Image Comics (Extreme Studios)
1-Liefeld-c/a/scripts in all; flip book format with 2 trading cards; 1st Image/Extreme Studios title. 2.00 5.00
1-2nd printing 1.20 3.00
2-(JUN-c, July 1992 indicia)-1st app. Shadowhawk in solo back-up story; 2 trading cards inside; flip book format; 1st app. Prophet, Kirby, Berzerkers, Darkthorn 1.20 3.00
2-2nd printing (1.95) .80 2.00
3-(OCT-c, August 1992 indicia)-Contains 2 trading cards inside (flip book); 1st app. Supreme in back-up story; 1st app. Showdown 1.00 2.50
0-(12/92, $1.95)-Contains 2 trading cards; 2 cover variations exist, green or beige logo; w/Image #0 coupon .80 2.00
4,5: 4-(2/93)-Glow-in-the-dark-c w/2 trading cards; 2nd app. Dale Keown's The Pitt; Bloodstrike app. 1.00 2.50
6-($3.50, 52 pgs.)-Wraparound-c 1.40 3.50
7-10: 7, 8-Liefeld-c(p)/a(p)/story. 8,9-(9/94) 9-Valentino story & art
1.00 2.50
Battlezone 1 (MAY-c, 4/93 inside, $1.95)-Arsenal book; Liefeld-c(p)

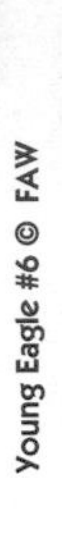
Young Eagle #6 © FAW

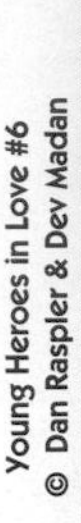
Young Heroes in Love #6
© Dan Raspler & Dev Madan

Young Love #2 © PRIZE

GD25 FN65 NM94

.80 2.00
Battlezone 2 (7/94, $2.95)-Wraparound-c 1.20 3.00
Yearbook 1 (7/93, $2.50)-Fold out panel; 1st app. Tyrax & Kanan
1.00 2.50
...Super Special (Winter '97, $2.99) Sprouse -a 1.20 3.00
TPB (1996, $16.95)-r/Team Youngblood #8-10 & Youngblood #6-8,10 17.00

YOUNGBLOOD
V2#1, Sept, 1995 - No. 14, Dec, 1996 ($2.50)
Image Comics (Extreme Studios)/Maximum Press No. 14

V2#1-10,14: Roger Cruz-a in all. 4-Extreme Destroyer Pt. 4 w/gaming card. 5-Variant-c exists. 6-Angela & Glory. 7-Shadowhunt Pt. 3; Shadowhawk app. 8,10-Thor (from Supreme) app. 10-(7/96). 14-(12/96)-1st Maximum Press issue 1.00 2.50

YOUNGBLOOD: STRIKEFILE
Apr, 1993 - No. 11, Feb, 1995 ($1.95/$2.50/$2.95)
Image Comics (Extreme Studios)

1-($1.95)-Flip book w/Jae Lee-c/a & Liefeld-c/a in #1-3; 1st app. The Allies, Giger, & Glory .80 2.00
2-4,11: 2-Begin $2.50. 3-Thibert-i asisst. 4-Liefeld-c(p); no Lee-a
1.00 2.50
5-10: 5-Begin $2.95-c; Liefeld-c(p). 8-Platt-c 1.20 3.00
NOTE: *Youngblood: Strikefile began as a four issue limited series.*

YOUNGBLOOD/X-FORCE
July, 1996 ($4.95, one-shot)
Image Comics (Extreme Studios)

1-Cruz-a(p); two covers exist 2.00 5.00

YOUNG BRIDES (True Love Secrets)
Sept-Oct, 1952 - No. 30, Nov-Dec, 1956 (Photo-c: 1-4)
Feature/Prize Publications

	GD25	FN65	NM94
V1#1-Simon & Kirby-a	24.00	71.00	180.00
2-S&K-a	12.00	36.00	90.00
3-6-S&K-a	11.00	33.00	80.00
V2#1,3-7,10-12 (#7-18)-S&K-a	10.00	30.00	75.00
2,8,9-No S&K-a	4.00	10.00	22.00
V3#1-3(#19-21)-Last precode (3-4/55)	3.60	9.00	18.00
4,6(#22,24), V4#1,3(#25,27)	2.80	7.00	14.00
V3#5(#23)-Meskin-c	4.00	10.00	20.00
V4#2(#26)-All S&K issue	9.00	27.00	60.00
V4#4(#28)-S&K-a	7.50	22.50	50.00
V4#5,6(#29,30)	4.00	11.00	24.00

YOUNG DR. MASTERS (See The Adventures of Young Dr. Masters)

YOUNG DOCTORS, THE
Jan, 1963 - No. 6, Nov, 1963
Charlton Comics

	GD25	FN65	NM94
V1#1	2.50	7.50	20.00
2-6	1.50	4.50	12.00

YOUNG EAGLE
12/50 - No. 10, 6/52; No. 3, 7/56 - No. 5, 4/57 (Photo-c: 1-10)
Fawcett Publications/Charlton

	GD25	FN65	NM94
1-Intro Young Eagle	14.00	41.00	110.00
2-Complete picture novelette "The Mystery of Thunder Canyon"	7.85	23.50	55.00
3-9	7.15	21.50	50.00
10-Origin Thunder, Young Eagle's Horse	5.70	17.00	35.00
3-5(Charlton)-Formerly Sherlock Holmes?	4.00	12.00	24.00

YOUNG HEARTS
Nov, 1949 - No. 2, Feb, 1950
Marvel Comics (SPC)

	GD25	FN65	NM94
1-Photo-c	10.00	3.00	65.00
2-Colleen Townsend photo-c from movie	6.35	19.00	40.00

YOUNG HEARTS IN LOVE
1964
Super Comics

17,18: 17-r/Young Love V5#6 (4-5/62) 1.00 3.00 8.00

YOUNG HEROES (Formerly Forbidden Worlds #34)
No. 35, Feb-Mar, 1955 - No. 37, June-July, 1955
American Comics Group (Titan)

35-37-Frontier Scout 8.00 24.00 48.00

YOUNG HEROES IN LOVE
June, 1997 - Present ($1.75)
DC Comics

1-1st app. Young Heroes; Madan-a 1.20 3.00
2-6: 3-Superman-c/app. .80 2.00
7-12 1.95

YOUNG INDIANA JONES CHRONICLES, THE
Feb, 1992 - No. 12, Feb, 1993 ($2.50)
Dark Horse Comics

1-12: Dan Barry scripts in all 1.00 2.50
NOTE: ***Dan Barry** a(p)-1, 2, 5, 6, 10; c-1-10. **Morrow** a-3, 4, 5p, 6p. **Springer** a-1i, 2i.*

YOUNG INDIANA JONES CHRONICLES, THE
1992 ($3.95, squarebound, 68 pgs.)
Hollywood Comics (Disney)

1-3: 1-r/YIJC #1,2 by D. Horse. 2-r/#3,4. 3-r/#5,6 1.60 4.00

YOUNG KING COLE (...Detective Tales)(Becomes Criminals on the Run)
Fall, 1945 - V3#12, July, 1948
Premium Group/Novelty Press

	GD25	FN65	NM94
V1#1-Toni Gayle begins	24.00	73.00	180.00
2	11.00	33.00	80.00
3-4	10.00	30.00	70.00
V2#1-7(8-9/46-7/47): 6,7-Certa-c	7.50	22.50	50.00
V3#1,3-6,8,9,12: 3-Certa-c. 5-McWilliams-c/a. 8,9-Harmon-c	6.70	20.00	45.00
2-L.B. Cole-a; Certa-c	11.30	34.00	90.00
7-L.B. Cole-c/a	15.00	45.00	120.00
10,11-L.B. Cole-c	12.00	38.00	100.00

YOUNG LAWYERS, THE (TV)
Jan, 1971 - No. 2, Apr, 1971
Dell Publishing co.

1,2 1.50 4.50 12.00

YOUNG LIFE (Teen Life #3 on)
Summer, 1945 - No. 2, Fall, 1945
New Age Publ./Quality Comics Group

	GD25	FN65	NM94
1-Skip Homeier, Louis Prima stories	10.00	30.00	80.00
2-Frank Sinatra photo on-c plus story	10.00	30.00	80.00

YOUNG LOVE (Sister title to Young Romance)
2-3/49 - No. 73, 12-1/56-57; V3#5, 2-3/60 - V7#1, 6-7/63
Prize(Feature)Publ.(Crestwood)

	GD25	FN65	NM94
V1#1-S&K-c/a(2)	37.00	111.00	275.00
2-Photo-c begin; S&K-a	18.00	54.00	140.00
3-S&K-a	14.00	41.00	110.00
4-5-Minor S&K-a	9.00	27.00	60.00
V2#1(#7)-S&K-a(2)	14.00	41.00	110.00
2-5(#8-11)-Minor S&K-a	6.70	20.00	45.00
6,8(#12,14)-S&K-c only. 14-S&K 1 pg. art	9.00	27.00	60.00
7,9-12(#13,15-18)-S&K-c/a	12.00	36.00	95.00
V3#1-4(#19-22)-S&K-c/a	11.00	33.00	85.00
5-7,9-12(#23-25,27-30)-Photo-c resume; S&K-a	10.00	30.00	75.00
8(#26)-No S&K-a	4.00	11.00	22.00

Young Lovers #18 © CC

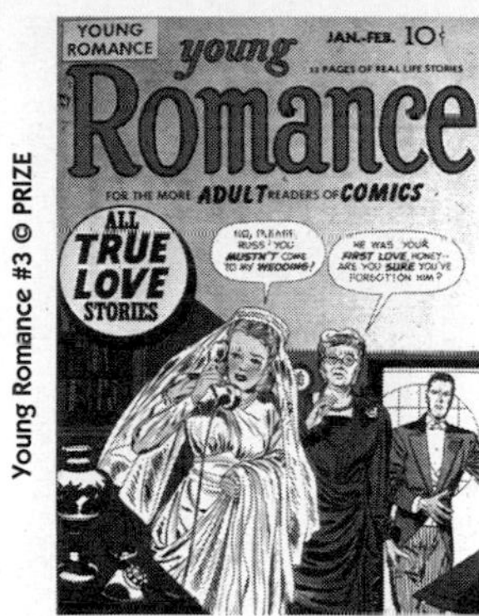

Young Romance #3 © PRIZE

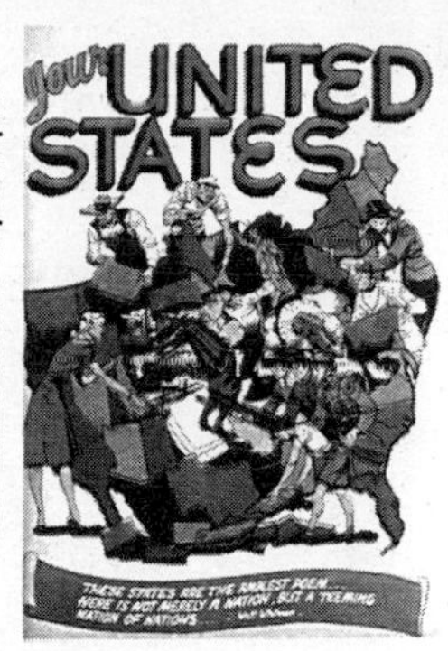

Your United States © Lloyd Jacquet

	GD25	FN65	NM94
V4#1,6(#31,36)-S&K-a	10.00	30.00	70.00
2-5,7-12(#32-35,37-42)-Minor S&K-a	6.70	20.00	45.00
V5#1-12(#43-54), V6#1-9(#55-63)-Last precode; S&K-a in some	4.00	11.00	22.00
V6#10-12(#64-66)	1.85	5.50	15.00
V7#1-7(#67-73)	1.50	4.50	12.00
V3#5(2-3/60),6(4-5/60)(Formerly All For Love)	1.10	3.30	9.00
V4#1(6-7/60)-6(4-5/61)	1.00	3.00	8.00
V5#1(6-7/61)-6(4-5/62)	1.00	3.00	8.00
V6#1(6-7/62)-6(4-5/63), V7#1		2.40	6.00

NOTE: **Meskin** *a-14(2), 27, 42.* **Powell** *a-V4#6.* **Severin/Elder** *a-V1#3. S&K art not in #53, 57, 58, 61, 63-65. Photo c-V3#5-V5#11.*

YOUNG LOVE
#39, 9-10/63 - #120, Wint./75-76; #121, 10/76 - #126, 7/77
National Periodical Publ.(Arleigh Publ. Corp #49-60)/DC Comics

	GD25	FN65	NM94
39	3.00	9.00	30.00
40-50	2.00	6.00	16.00
51-63,65-70	1.75	5.25	14.00
64-Simon & Kirby-a	2.25	6.75	18.00
71,72,74-77,80	1.50	4.50	12.00
73,78,79-Toth-a	1.10	3.30	9.00
81-106,115-122	1.00	2.80	7.00
107-114 (100 pgs.): 107-DC 100 Pg. Super Spect.	14.00	42.00	140.00
123-126 (52 pgs.)	2.50	7.50	20.00

NOTE: **Bolle** *a-117.* **Colan** *a-107r.* **Nasser** *a-123, 124.* **Orlando** *a-122.* **Simonson** *c-125.* **Toth** *a-73, 78, 79, 122-125r.* **Wood** *a-109r(4 pgs.).*

YOUNG LOVER ROMANCES (Formerly & becomes Great Lover...)
No. 4, June, 1952 - No. 5, Aug, 1952
Toby Press

	GD25	FN65	NM94
4,5-Photo-c	5.00	15.00	30.00

YOUNG LOVERS (My Secret Life #19 on)(Formerly Brenda Starr?)
No. 16, July, 1956 - No. 18, May, 1957
Charlton Comics

	GD25	FN65	NM94
16,17('56): 16-Marcus Swayze-a	5.00	15.00	30.00
18-Elvis Presley picture-c, text story (biography)(Scarce)	47.00	141.00	400.00

YOUNG MARRIAGE
June, 1950
Fawcett Publications

	GD25	FN65	NM94
1-Powell-a; photo-c	10.00	30.00	65.00

YOUNG MEN (Formerly Cowboy Romances)(...on the Battlefield #12-20 (4/53); ...In Action #21)
No. 4, 6/50 - No. 11, 10/51; No. 12, 12/51 - No. 28, 6/54
Marvel/Atlas Comics (IPC)

	GD25	FN65	NM94
4-(52 pgs.)	13.50	41.00	100.00
5-11	9.00	27.00	60.00
12-23: 12-20-War format. 21-23-Hot Rod issues starring Flash Foster	8.00	24.00	55.00
24-(12/53)-Origin Captain America, Human Torch, & Sub-Mariner which are revived thru #28; Red Skull app.	178.00	533.00	1600.00
25-28: 25-Romita-c/a (see Men's Advs.)	87.00	262.00	775.00

NOTE: **Berg** *a-7, 14, 17, 18, 20; c-17?* **Brodsky** *c-4-9, 13, 14, 16, 17, 21-25.* **Burgos** *c-26-28.* **Colan** *a-14, 15.* **Everett** *a-18-20.* **Heath** *a-13, 14.* **Maneely** *c-10, 12, 15.* **Pakula** *a-14, 15.* **Robinson** *c-18. Captain America by* **Romita**-*#24?, 25, 26?, 27, 28. Human Torch by* **Burgos**-*#25, 27, 28. Sub-Mariner by* **Everett**-*#24-28.*

YOUNG REBELS, THE (TV)
Jan, 1971
Dell Publishing Co.

	GD25	FN65	NM94
1-Photo-c	1.25	3.75	10.00

YOUNG ROMANCE COMICS (The 1st romance comic)
Sept-Oct, 1947 - V16#4, June-July, 1963 (#1-33: 52 pgs.)
Prize/Headline (Feature Publ.) (Crestwood)

	GD25	FN65	NM94
V1#1-S&K-c/a(2)	39.00	116.00	290.00
2-S&K-c/a(2-3)	24.00	71.00	180.00
3-6-S&K-c/a(2-3) each	21.00	64.00	160.00
V2#1-6(#7-12)-S&K-c/a(2-3) each	18.00	54.00	140.00
V3#1-3(#13-15): V3#1-Photo-c begin; S&K-a	11.30	34.00	90.00
4-12(#16-24)-Photo-c; S&K-a	11.30	34.00	90.00
V4#1-11(#25-35)-S&K-a	11.00	33.00	85.00
12(#36)-S&K, Toth-a	13.50	41.00	100.00
V5#1-12(#37-48), V6#4-12(#52-60)-S&K-a	11.00	33.00	85.00
V6#1-3(#49-51)-No S&K-a	5.00	15.00	30.00
V7#1-11(#61-71)-S&K-a in most	10.00	30.00	65.00
V7#12(#72), V8#1-3(#73-75)-Last precode (12-1/54-55)-No S&K-a	3.60	9.00	18.00
V8#4(#76, 4-5/55), 5(#77)-No S&K-a	3.20	8.00	16.00
V8#6-8(#78-80, 12-1/55-56)-S&K-a	6.70	20.00	45.00
V9#3,5,6(#81, 2-3/56, 83,84)-S&K-a	6.70	20.00	45.00
4, V10#1(#82,85)-All S&K-a	8.35	25.00	55.00
V10#2-6(#86-90, 10-11/57)-S&K-a	4.50	13.50	45.00
V11#1,2,5,6(#91,92,95,96)-S&K-a	4.50	13.50	45.00
3,4(#93,94), V12#2,4,5(#98,100,101)-No S&K	1.50	4.50	12.00
V12#1,3,6(#97,99,102)-S&K-a	4.50	13.50	45.00
V13#1(#103)-Powell-a; S&K's last-a for Crestwood	4.50	13.50	45.00
2,4-6(#104-108)	1.00	3.00	8.00
V13#3(, #105, 4-5/60)-Elvis Presley-c app. only	2.50	7.50	20.00
V14#1-6, V15#1-6, V16#1-4(#109-124)		2.40	6.00

NOTE: **Meskin** *a-16, 24(2), 33, 47, 50.* **Robinson/Meskin** *a-6.* **Leonard Starr** *a-11. Photo c-13-32, 34-65. Issues 1-3 say "Designed for the More* **Adult** *Readers of* **Comics**" *on cover.*

YOUNG ROMANCE COMICS (Continued from Prize series)
No. 125, Aug-Sept, 1963 - No. 208, Nov-Dec, 1975
National Periodical Publ.(Arleigh Publ. Corp. No. 127)

	GD25	FN65	NM94
125	5.50	16.50	55.00
126-153,155-162	2.50	7.50	24.00
154-Neal Adams-c	3.00	9.00	30.00
163,164-Toth-a	2.50	7.50	20.00
165-177,184-196: 170-Michell from Young Love ends; Lily Martin, the Swinger begins	1.50	4.50	12.00
178-183 (52 pgs.)	2.50	7.50	20.00
197-204-(100 pgs.)	14.00	42.00	140.00
205-208	1.00	3.00	8.00

YOUNG ZEN: CITY OF DEATH
Late 1994 ($3.25, B&W)
Entity Comics

	GD25	FN65	NM94
1		1.30	3.25

YOUNG ZEN INTERGALACTIC NINJA (Also see Zen...)
1993 - No. 3, 1994 ($3.50/$2.95, B&W)
Entity Comics

	GD25	FN65	NM94
1-($3.50)-Polybagged w/Sam Kieth chromium trading card; gold foil logo		1.40	3.50
2,3-($2.95)-Gold foil logo		1.20	3.00

YOUR DREAMS (See Strange World of...)

YOU'RE UNDER ARREST (Manga)
Dec, 1995 - No. 8, July, 1996 ($2.95, limited series)
Dark Horse Comics

	GD25	FN65	NM94
1-8		1.20	3.00

YOUR TRIP TO NEWSPAPERLAND
June, 1955 (14x11-1/2", 12 pgs.)
Philadelphia Evening Bulletin (Printed by Harvey Press)

	GD25	FN65	NM94
nn-Joe Palooka takes kids on newspaper tour	4.00	11.00	22.00

YOUR UNITED STATES

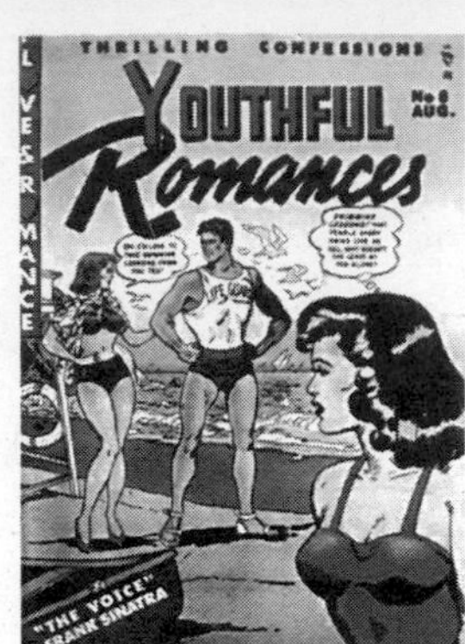

Youthful Romances #8 © Pix-Parade

Zatanna #2 © DC

Zegra Jungle Empress #4 © FOX

	GD25	FN65	NM94
1946 Lloyd Jacquet Studios			
nn-Used in **SOTI**, pg. 309,310; Sid Greene-a	19.50	58.00	155.00

YOUTHFUL HEARTS (Daring Confessions #4 on)
May, 1952 - No. 3, Sept, 1952
Youthful Magazines

	GD25	FN65	NM94
1- "Monkey on Her Back" swipes E.C. drug story/Shock SuspenStories #12; Frankie Laine photo on-c; Doug Wildey-a in all	21.00	62.00	160.00
2,3: 2-Vic Damone photo on-c. 3-Johnny Raye photo on-c	14.00	43.00	110.00

YOUTHFUL LOVE (Truthful Love #2)
May, 1950
Youthful Magazines

	GD25	FN65	NM94
1	8.70	26.00	55.00

YOUTHFUL ROMANCES
8-9/49 - No. 5, 4/50; No. 6, 2/51; No. 7, 5/51 - #14, 10/52; #15, 1/53 - #18, 7/53; No. 5, 9/53 - No. 9, 8/54
Pix-Parade #1-14/Ribage #15 on

	GD25	FN65	NM94
1-(1st series)-Titled Youthful Love-Romances	18.00	54.00	140.00
2-Walter Johnson c-1-4	10.00	30.00	75.00
3-5	9.00	27.00	60.00
6,7,9-14(10/52, Pix-Parade; becomes Daring Love #15); 7-Tony Martin photo-c. 10(1/52)-Mel Torme photo-c/story. 13-Richard Hayes (singer) photo-c/story; Bob & Ray photo/text story.	7.50	22.50	50.00
8-Wood-c	13.00	39.00	95.00
15-18 (Ribage)-All have photos on-c. 12-Tony Bennett photo-c, 8pg. story & text bio.15-Spike Jones photo-c/story	5.85	17.50	40.00
5(9/53, Ribage)-Les Paul & Mary Ford photo-c/story; Charlton Heston photo/text story	5.70	17.00	35.00
6-9: 6-Bobby Wayne (singer) photo-c/story; Debbie Reynolds photo/text story 7(2/54)-Tony Martin photo-c/story; Cyd Charise photo/text story. 8(5/54)-Gordon McCrae photo-c/story. 9(8/54)-Ralph Flanagan (band leader) photo-c/story; Audrey Hepburn photo/text story.	4.25	13.00	28.00

YUPPIES FROM HELL (Also see Son of...)
1989 ($2.95, B&W, one-shot, direct sales, 52 pgs.)
Marvel Comics

	GD25	FN65	NM94
1-Satire		1.20	3.00

ZAGO, JUNGLE PRINCE (My Story #5 on)
Sept, 1948 - No. 4, Mar, 1949
Fox Features Syndicate

	GD25	FN65	NM94
1-Blue Beetle app.; partial-r/Atomic #4 (Toni Luck)	48.00	144.00	420.00
2,3-Kamen-a	39.00	116.00	300.00
4-Baker-c	33.00	99.00	250.00

ZANE GREY'S STORIES OF THE WEST
No. 197, 9/48 - No. 996, 5-7/59; 11/64 (All painted-c)
Dell Publishing Co./Gold Key 11/64

	GD25	FN65	NM94
Four Color 197(#1)(9/48)	11.00	32.00	115.00
Four Color 222,230,236('49)	5.50	16.50	60.00
Four Color 246,255,270,301,314,333,346	3.60	11.00	40.00
Four Color 357,372,395,412,433,449,467,484	2.75	8.00	30.00
Four Color 511-Kinstler-a; Kubert-a	3.60	11.00	40.00
Four Color 532,555,583,604,616,632(5/55)	2.75	8.00	30.00
27(9-11/55) - 39(9-11/58)	3.00	9.00	32.00
Four Color 996(5-7/59)	2.75	8.00	30.00
10131-411-(11/64-G.K.)-Nevada; r/4-Color #996	1.65	5.00	18.00

ZANY (Magazine)(Satire)(See Frantic & Ratfink)
Sept, 1958 - No. 4, May, 1959
Candor Publ. Co.

	GD25	FN65	NM94
1-Bill Everett-c	7.15	21.50	50.00
2-4: 4-Everett-c	5.70	17.00	35.00

ZATANNA (See Adv. Comics #413, JLA #161, Supergirl #1, World's Finest Comics #274)
July, 1993 - No. 4, Oct, 1993 ($1.95, limited series)
DC Comics

	GD25	FN65	NM94
1-4		.80	2.00
Special 1(1987, $2.00)-Gray Morrow-c/a		.80	2.00

ZAZA, THE MYSTIC (Formerly Charlie Chan; This Magazine Is Haunted V2#12 on)
No. 10, Apr, 1956 - No. 11, Sept, 1956
Charlton Comics

	GD25	FN65	NM94
10,11	10.00	30.00	65.00

ZEALOT (Also see WildC.A.T.S: Covert Action Teams)
Aug, 1995 - No. 3, Nov, 1995 ($2.50, limited series)
Image Comics

	GD25	FN65	NM94
1-3		1.00	2.50

ZEGRA JUNGLE EMPRESS (Formerly Tegra)(My Love Life #6 on)
No. 2, Oct, 1948 - No. 5, April, 1949
Fox Features Syndicate

	GD25	FN65	NM94
2	50.00	150.00	430.00
3-5	40.00	120.00	310.00

ZEN INTERGALACTIC NINJA
1987 -1992 ($1.75/$2.00, B&W)
No Publisher

	GD25	FN65	NM94
1-6: Copyright-Stern & Cote		2.00	5.00
V2#1-4-($2.00)		1.60	4.00
V3#1-5-($2.95)		1.20	3.00
... :Christmas Special 1 (1992, $2.95)		1.20	3.00
... :Earth Day Special 1 (1993, $2.95)		1.20	3.00

ZEN, INTERGALACTIC NINJA (mini-series)
Sept, 1992 - No. 3, 1992 ($1.25)(Formerly a B&W comic by Zen Comics)
Zen Comics/Archie Comics

	GD25	FN65	NM94
1-3: 1-Origin Zen; contains mini-poster			1.25

ZEN, INTERGALACTIC NINJA
1992 - No. 3, 1992 ($1.25)
Zen Comics/Archie Comics

	GD25	FN65	NM94
1-3			1.25

ZEN INTERGALACTIC NINJA
No. 0, June-July, 1993 - No. 3, 1994 ($2.95, B&W, limited series)
Entity Comics

	GD25	FN65	NM94
0-Gold foil stamped-c; photo-c of Zen model		1.20	3.00
1-3: Gold foil stamped-c; Bill Maus-c/a		1.20	3.00
0-(1993, $3.50, color)-Chromium-c by Jae Lee		1.40	3.50
...Sourcebook 1-(1993, $3.50)		1.40	3.50
...Sourcebook '94-(1994, $3.50)		1.40	3.50

ZEN INTERGALACTIC NINJA: APRIL FOOL'S SPECIAL
1994 ($2.50, B&W)
Parody Press

	GD25	FN65	NM94
1-w/flip story of Renn Intergalactic Chihuahua		1.00	2.50

ZEN INTERGALACTIC NINJA COLOR
1994 - No. 7, 1995 ($2.25)
Entity Comics

	GD25	FN65	NM94
1-($3.95)-Chromium die cut-c		1.60	4.00
1-($2.25)		.90	2.25
0-($2.25)-Newsstand; Jae Lee-c; r/...All New Color Special #0		.90	2.25
2-($2.50)-Flip book		1.00	2.50
2-($3.50)-Flip book, polybagged w/chromium trading card		1.40	3.50
3-5: 3-Begin $2.50-c		1.00	2.50

Zero Zero #21 © Kim Deitch

Zip Comics #18 © MLJ

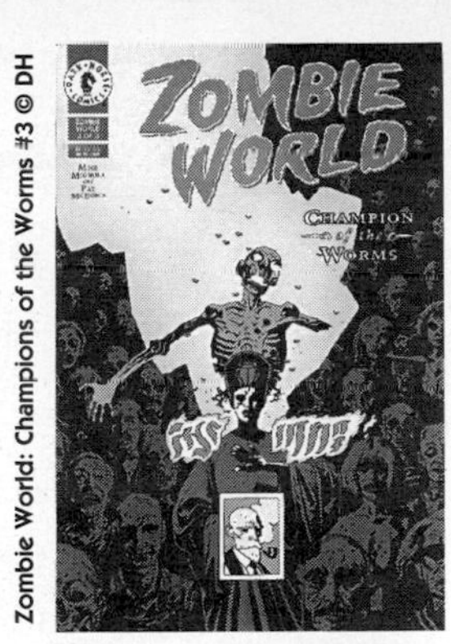

Zombie World: Champions of the Worms #3 © DH

GD25 FN65 NM94

6,7: 6-Begin $2.95-c 1.20 3.00
Summer Special (1994, $2.95) 1.20 3.00
Yearbook: Hazardous Duty 1 (1995) 1.20 3.00
Zen-isms 1 (1995, 2.95) 1.20 3.00
Ashcan-Tour of the Universe-(no price) w/flip cover 1.00

ZEN INTERGALACTIC NINJA MILESTONE
1994 - No. 3, 1994 ($2.95, limited series)
Entity Comics

1-3: Gold foil logo; r/Defend the Earth 1.20 3.00

ZEN INTERGALATIC NINJA SPRING SPECTACULAR
1994 ($2.95, B&W, one-shot)
Entity Comics

1-Gold foil logo 1.20 3.00

ZEN INTERGALACTIC NINJA STARQUEST
1994 - No. 6, 1995 ($2.95, B&W)
Entity Comics

1-6: Gold foil logo 1.20 3.00

ZEN, INTERGALACTIC NINJA: THE HUNTED
1993 - No. 3, 1994 ($2.95, B&W, limited series)
Entity Comics

1-3: Newsstand Edition; foil logo 1.20 3.00
1-($3.50)-Polybagged w/chromium card by Kieth; foil logo 1.40 3.50

ZERO HOUR: CRISIS IN TIME (Also see Showcase '94 #8-10)
No. 4(#1), Sept, 1994 - No. 0(#5), Oct, 1994 ($1.50, limited series)
DC Comics

4(#1)-0(#5) .80 2.00
"Ashcan"-(1994, free, B&W, 8 pgs.) 1.00

ZERO PATROL, THE
Nov, 1984 - No. 2; 1987 - No. 5, 1989? ($2.00)
Continuity Comics

1,2: Neal Adams-c/a; Megalith begins .80 2.00
1-5 (#1,2-reprints above, 1987) .80 2.00

ZERO TOLERANCE
Oct, 1990 - No. 4, Jan, 1991 ($2.25, limited series)
First Comics

1-4: Tim Vigil-c/a(p) (his 1st color limited series) .90 2.25

ZERO ZERO
Mar, 1995 - Present ($3.95, B&W, anthology, mature)
Fantagraphics

1-22 1.60 4.00

ZIGGY PIG-SILLY SEAL COMICS (See Animal Fun, Animated Movie-Tunes, Comic Capers, Krazy Komics, Silly Tunes & Super Rabbit)
Fall, 1944 - No. 6, Fall, 1946
Timely Comics (CmPL)

1-Vs. the Japs 17.50 53.00 140.00
2 8.75 26.25 70.00
3-5 8.50 26.00 60.00
6-Infinity-c 9.50 28.00 75.00
I.W. Reprint #1(1958)-r/Krazy Komics 1.00 3.00 8.00
I.W. Reprint #2,7,8 1.00 2.80 7.00

ZIP COMICS
Feb, 1940 - No. 47, Summer, 1944 (#1-7?: 68 pgs.)
MLJ Magazines

1-Origin Kalathar the Giant Man, The Scarlet Avenger, & Steel Sterling; Mr. Satan (by Edd Ashe), Nevada Jones (masked hero) & Zambini, the Miracle Man, War Eagle, Captain Valor begins 340.00 1020.00 3400.00
2-Nevada Jones adds mask & horse Blaze 156.00 468.00 1400.00
3 111.00 333.00 1000.00
4,5 92.00 276.00 825.00
6-8 78.00 234.00 700.00
9-Last Kalathar & Mr. Satan; classic-c 94.00 282.00 850.00
10-Inferno, the Flame Breather begins, ends #13 85.00 255.00 770.00
11,12: 11-Inferno without costume 67.00 200.00 600.00
13-17,19: 17-Last Scarlet Avenger 67.00 200.00 600.00
18-Wilbur begins (9/41, 1st app.) 69.00 207.00 625.00
20-Origin & 1st app. Black Jack (11/41); Hitler-c 103.00 309.00 925.00
21,23-26: 25-Last Nevada Jones. 26-Black Witch begins; last Captain Valor 61.00 183.00 550.00
22-Classic-c 67.00 200.00 600.00
27-Intro. Web (7/42) plus-c app. 100.00 300.00 900.00
28-Origin Web 94.00 282.00 850.00
29,30: 29-The Hyena app. 46.00 138.00 410.00
31-38: 34-1st Applejack app. 35-Last Zambini, Black Jack. 38-Last Web issue 36.00 108.00 310.00
39-Red Rube begins (origin, 8/43) 36.00 108.00 310.00
40-47: 45-Wilbur ends 30.00 90.00 240.00

NOTE: ***Biro*** *a-5, 9, 17; c-3-17.* ***Meskin*** *a-1-3, 5-7, 9, 10, 12, 13, 15, 16 at least.* ***Montana*** *c-29, 30, 32-35.* ***Novick*** *c-18-28, 31.* ***Sahle*** *c-37, 38, 40-46. Bondage c-8, 9, 33, 34. Cover features: Steel Sterling-1-43, 47; (w/Blackjack-20-27 & Web-27-35), 28-39; (w/Red Rube-40-43); Red Rube-44-47.*

ZIP-JET (Hero)
Feb, 1953 - No. 2, Apr-May, 1953
St. John Publishing Co.

1-Rocketman-r from Punch Comics; #1-c from splash in Punch #10 50.00 150.00 450.00
2 40.00 120.00 330.00

ZIPPY THE CHIMP (CBS TV Presents...)
No. 50, March, 1957; No. 51, Aug, 1957
Pines (Literary Ent.)

50,51 5.00 15.00 30.00

ZODY, THE MOD ROB
July, 1970
Gold Key

1 1.50 4.50 12.00

ZOMBIE WORLD: CHAMPION OF THE WORMS
Sept, 1997 - No. 3, Nov, 1997 ($2.95, limited series)
Dark Horse Comics

1-3-Mignola & McEown-c/s/a 2.95
... :Home For The Holidays (12/97, $2.95, one shot) 2.95

ZONE (Also see Dark Horse Presents)
1990 ($1.95, B&W)
Dark Horse Comics

1-Character from Dark Horse Presents .80 2.00

ZONE CONTINUM, THE
1994 ($2.95, B&W)
Caliber Press

1 1.20 3.00

ZOO ANIMALS
No. 8, 1954 (15¢, 36 pgs.)
Star Publications

8-(B&W for coloring) 4.00 12.00 24.00

ZOO FUNNIES (Tim McCoy #16 on)
Nov, 1945 - No. 15, 1947
Charlton Comics/Children Comics Publ.

101(#1)(11/45, 1st Charlton comic book)-Funny animal; Al Fago-c 15.00 45.00 120.00
2(12/45, 52 pgs.) 8.50 26.00 60.00
3-5 7.15 21.50 50.00

Zoot #14 © FOX

Zorro #7 (Marvel) © Johnston McCulley

Zot! #34 © Scott McCloud

	GD25	FN65	NM94
6-15: 8-Diana the Huntress app.	5.70	17.00	35.00

ZOO FUNNIES (Becomes Nyoka, The Jungle Girl #14 on?)
July, 1953 - No. 13, Sept, 1955; Dec, 1984
Capitol Stories/Charlton Comics

	GD25	FN65	NM94
1-1st app.? Timothy The Ghost; Fago-c/a	8.50	26.00	60.00
2	5.70	17.00	35.00
3-7 (8/46)	4.25	13.00	28.00
8-13-Nyoka app.	6.50	19.50	45.00
1(1984)			1.00

ZOONIVERSE
8/86 - No. 6, 6/87 ($1.25/$1.75, limited series, Mando paper)
Eclipse Comics

	GD25	FN65	NM94
1-5 ($1.25)			1.30
6 ($1.75)		.75	1.80

ZOO PARADE (TV)
#662, 1955 (Marlin Perkins)
Dell Publishing Co.

	GD25	FN65	NM94
Four Color 662	4.00	12.00	45.00

ZOOM COMICS
Dec, 1945 (one-shot)
Carlton Publishing Co.

	GD25	FN65	NM94
nn-Dr. Mercy, Satannas, from Red Band Comics; Capt. Milksop origin retold	35.00	105.00	280.00

ZOOT (Rulah Jungle Goddess #17 on)
nd (1946) - No. 16, July, 1948 (Two #13s & 14s)
Fox Features Syndicate

	GD25	FN65	NM94
nn-Funny animal only	14.00	41.00	110.00
2-The Jaguar app.	12.00	38.00	100.00
3(Fall, 1946) - 6-Funny animals & teen-age	7.85	23.50	55.00
7-(6/47)-Rulah, Jungle Goddess begins (origin & 1st app.)	75.00	225.00	650.00
8-10	54.00	163.00	450.00
11-Kamen bondage-c	58.00	174.00	475.00
12-Injury-to-eye panels, torture scene	40.00	120.00	300.00
13(2/48)	40.00	120.00	300.00
14(3/48)-Used in **SOTI**, pg. 104, "One picture showing a girl nailed by her wrists to trees with blood flowing from the wounds, might be taken straight from an ill. ed. of the Marquis deSade"	47.00	141.00	400.00
13(4/48),14(5/48)-Western True Crime #15 on?	40.00	120.00	300.00
15,16	40.00	120.00	300.00

ZORRO (Walt Disney with #882)(TV)(See Eclipse Graphic Album)
May, 1949 - No. 15, Sept-Nov, 1961 (Photo-c 882 on)
Dell Publishing Co.
(Zorro first appeared in a pulp story Aug 19, 1919 - 1994 was 75th anniversary)

	GD25	FN65	NM94
Four Color 228 (#1)	20.00	60.00	220.00
Four Color 425,617,732	11.00	34.00	125.00
Four Color 497,538,574-Kinstler-a	12.00	37.00	135.00
Four Color 882-Photo-c begin; Toth-a	16.00	49.00	180.00
Four Color 920,933,960,976-Toth-a in all	11.00	34.00	125.00
Four Color 1003('59)-Toth-a	11.00	34.00	125.00
Four Color 1037-Annette Funicello photo-c	14.00	44.00	160.00
8(12-2/59-60)	7.00	22.00	80.00
9,12-Toth-a. 12-Last 10¢ issue	8.00	23.00	85.00
10,11,13-15-Last photo-c	6.40	19.00	70.00

NOTE: ***Warren Tufts** a-4-Color 1037, 8, 9, 10, 13.*

ZORRO (Walt Disney)(TV)
Jan, 1966 - No. 9, Mar, 1968 (All photo-c)
Gold Key

	GD25	FN65	NM94
1-Toth-a	6.40	19.00	70.00
2,4,5,7-9-Toth-a. 5-r/F.C. #1003 by Toth	3.60	11.00	40.00
3,6-Tufts-a	3.00	9.00	35.00

NOTE: *#1-9 are reprinted from Dell issues.* ***Tufts** a-3, 4. #1-r/F.C. #882. #2-r/F.C. #960. #3-r/#12-c & #8 inside. #4-r/#9-c & insides. #6-r/#11(all); #7-r/#14-c. #8-r/F.C. #933 inside & back-c & #976-c. #9-r/F.C. #920.*

ZORRO (TV)
Dec, 1990 - No. 12, Nov, 1991 ($1.00)
Marvel Comics

	GD25	FN65	NM94
1-12: Based on TV show. 12-Toth-c			1.00

ZORRO
Nov, 1993 - No. 11, Nov, 1994 ($2.50/$2.95)
Topps Comics

	GD25	FN65	NM94
0-(11/93, $1.00, 20 pgs.)-Painted-c; collector's ed.			1.00
1,4,6-9,11-15: 1-Miller-c. . 4-Mike Grell-c. 6-Mignola-c. 7-Lady Rawhide-c by Gulacy. 8-Perez-c. 10-Julie Bell-c. 11-Lady Rawhide-c.		1.20	3.00
2--Lady Rawhide-app. (not in costume)	1.25	3.75	10.00
3-1st app. Lady Rawhide in costume, 3-Lady Rawhide-c by Adam Hughes	1.50	4.50	12.00
5-Lady Rawhide app.		2.00	5.00
10 ($2.95)-Lady Rawhide-c/app.		1.60	4.00

ZOT! (Also see Adventures of Zot)
4/84 - No. 10, 7/85; No. 11, 1/87 - No. 35 3/91 ($1.50, Baxter paper)
Eclipse Comics

	GD25	FN65	NM94
1		1.20	3.00
2,3		.80	2.00
4-10: 4-Origin. 10-Last color issue			1.50
11-35: 11-Begin $2.00-c, B&W issues		.80	2.00

Z-2 COMICS (Secret Agent...)(See Holyoke One-Shot #7)

ZULU (See Movie Classics)

SEE SOMETHING WE MISSED?

The Overstreet Comic Book Price Guide is the most authoritative reference on comics, but we're only as good as the information we get. We are always looking for new, precise details about the rich history of comics. If you know of something we've missed or should correct, please don't hesitate to write to:

Mark Huesman, Pricing Coordinator
Gemstone Publishing, 1966 Greenspring Drive, Suite 405, Timonium, MD 21093
or e-mail **fanprices@gemstonepub.com**.

Original Art On-Line!!

www.comicsnart.pcrealm.net

GIANT

ORIGINAL ART LIST
BUY/SELL/TRADE

• • • • • • • • • • • • • • •

Send $3.00 for the largest
comic art pictured list to:
CONRAD ESCHENBERG
RRI BOX 204-A
COLD SPRING, NEW YORK 10516
PHONE/FAX: 914-265-2649
e-mail: comicart@pcrealm.net

$$$ TOP DOLLAR PAID $$$

Golden and Silver Age
Comic Books and Original Art

• • • • • • • • • • • • •

*Paying STUPID
MONEY for vintage covers
by Kirby, Ditko, B. Smith,
N. Adams, Wrightson,
Steranko, Miller, etc.

DEALERS AND COLLECTORS

LET US BE YOUR MAIN SUPPLIER OF

WHY

(Overall, the Best-Prices; and the most Consistently

Also: 800,000 comics and magazines, in-stock. (1930's - 1990's)
A Huge, extensive and varied stock" (enough to keep an army of collectors and dealers "well stocked and happy"
(Marvels, DC's, Fiction-House, Dell & Gold-Key; Mags, Misc. 40's-70's, 80's & 90's & Indies, Etc.)
INCLUDES OVER **40,000 1960'S COMICS!**
Grades For Every Taste! (Very-Fine, VG, Fair/Poor, Etc.)
Store-owners and Convention Dealers:
Let Us Supply You the Best Way!
Why Settle for Less!

Strict Grading: Our Strict Grading is unique, respected and world-famous, in it's consistent 'tight' unwavering standard!
Our strict grades give the dealer & collector that Extra (significant, tho) "Margin of Profit."
In 1996, I respectfully rewrote much of the Overstreet Price Guide's Grading, which will result hopefully in a stricter standard, world-wide.

NICE DISCOUNTS ON MOST ANYTHING!!!!
A 30 year track record of dealer and collector satisfaction ***WORLD-WIDE!***

~

Professional, careful, prompt, reliable, and sturdy packaging of your orders.

~

COLLECTORS: Enjoy grading and pricing that you can count on!

~

Attentive service for all orders, great or small ($30, $300, $3,000, etc)

~

AND REMEMBER: IF YOU ARE NOT ORDERING OFF GARY DOLGOFF COMICS, YOU ARE TRULY "MISSING THE BOAT."

Individualized Attention to Your Needs! (Let us Know)

GARY DOLGOFF COMICS: (New Address) 116 Pleasant St, Easthampton, MA 01027
PHONE: 413-529-0326 FAX: 413 529-9824 E-MAIL:gdcomics@JAVANET.COM
WAREHOUSE HOURS: 10:00 AM - 5:30 PM M-F FAX/E-MAIL 24 HRS. 7 DAYS

WORLDWIDE!

BACK ISSUE COMICS AND MAGAZINES (1940'S - 1990'S)

???!

Strict Grading of any other Major Mail order dealer (Modest, too!)

ORDER THE DOLGOFF DISCOUNT CATALOG
Only $2 (refunded with your first order - about 60 pages)

(Over 2,000 boxes of comics (1940's - 1990's in order!) We have been supplying dealers and collectors for years. Stocking stores, both old and new, around the globe

Best of all, we are always getting in "New Stock" of back issues, providing you with a continuous source of strictly-graded, back-issue comics.

1940'S - 1960'S COMICS (THOUSANDS) STRICTLY GRADED AT 10-50% DISCOUNT)
1970'S-1990'S COMICS: A VAST SELECTION OF DECENT TITLES AT 50¢ - 75¢ EACH!
BULK 1980'S AND 1990'S COMICS: 10¢-25¢ EACH!
ORIGINAL ART - KIRBY, DITKO, ETC AND MUCH MUCH MORE!
WANT LISTS are always welcome, especially for **1930's-1970's** comics, mags, art, pulps, etc. Whether you want Fairs, G, VG, Fines or whatever grade - **LET ME KNOW!**

WAREHOUSE VISITS ARE WELCOME!

We now reside in the beautiful, and vibrant, Northhampton area! (actually, I'm in Easthampton) **Safe - easy, Friendly,** No Congestion, and Best of all We're Here!!! Call us, fax us, and we'll help **arrange a warehouse visit!!! BY PLANE:** European (and all other) visitors are only a few hours from **Comic Book Nirvana!!** We'll happily pick you up, at nearby Hartford Airport. Bring the wife or husband or come solo - there's plenty to do for everyone! *(great restaurant, coffee houses, casual shopping)* and a 3 Story Comic Art Museum! **DRIVING, OR TRAIN** - We are an easy 2 hours from NYC, Boston, Albany, Hartford CT (1 hr) Philadelphia, PA (3½ hours)

THE DOLGOFF WAREHOUSE: BETTER THAN A COMIC CONVENTION!

CALL FOR AN APPOINTMENT.

1 - **Nice discount prices, and strict grading throughout!**
2 - **Easy picking from our 400,000 In-Order books"** Many of them Priced & Graded (1940's - 1990's)
3 - **Fun, spontaneous-picking**: From our **1,000 boxes, of unadvertised books** 1950's - 1990's! (some 70's - '90's are in "Price-Boxes"; 25¢ ea. 50¢ ea. etc). (The unpriced Silver-Age) I'll price during your visit, at "Nice Prices."
4. **Friendly, efficient, co-operative assistance - when desired!**

The Dolgoff-Warehouse: The "Warehouse of Choice" for the Discerning Collector and Dealer Worldwide!

GARY DOLGOFF COMICS: (New Address) 116 Pleasant St, Easthampton, MA 01027
PHONE: 413-529-0326 FAX: 413 529-9824 E-MAIL:gdcomics@JAVANET.COM
WAREHOUSE HOURS: 10:00 AM - 5:30 PM M-F FAX/E-MAIL 24 HRS. 7 DAYS

CONTINUED ON NEXT PAGE

1950's - 1990's Comics and Mags
PACKAGE DEALS
FOR DEALERS & COLLECTORS

STRICT GRADING - ALWAYS! NMPG = NEAR MINT PRICE GUIDE PRICE

1960'S MARVELS WHOLESALE

1965 - 1969 SUPERHERO MARVELS
(CAP, DD, FF, HULK, ST, TOS, TTA, THOR, ETC)

(Sgt. Fury: An optional request)
VGF (Sharp Warehouse Copies, with a minor ding or two, at worst. Many call 'em FN - FN+!)
$400 in NMPG: $100.00 • $1,500 in: $350
Postage: US= $5.00 (insured)
Outside US (Uninsured) $15
GVG (Still mostly warehouse copies; most call them VG)
20 Comics: $100 50 comics $200

1970'S - 1981 MARVEL SUPERHERO

STRICT VGF OR BETTER (SHARP BOOKS)
100 comics **$75.00 (1 each)**
300 Comics **$180 (1-2 each)**
STRICT GVG OR BETTER (MOST PEOPLE'S VG)
100 comics: **$60 (1 ea)**
300 Comics **$140 (1-2 ea.)**

1985 - 1990'S TOP TITLES

STRICT FVF-VFNM
X-Men & Spiderman Titles, Etc.
$600 in NMPG: **$200 (1 EA)**
Postage: US = $15 / Outside US = $30
$2,000 in NMPG; **$500 (1-3 EA)**
Postage: US $30 / Outside US $60

1985 - 1990'S LONG RUNNING TITLES

NICE FN-VFNM; NEW-CONDITION
Avengers, Batman, Cap, DD, FF, Hulk, Iron Man, SpiderMan, Superman, X-Factor, X-Force, Etc)
200 comics $100 (1 ea)
800 comics $700 (1-2 ea.)
1980'S AND/OR 1990'S BULK BOOKS
NO TITLE GUARANTEE
Marvel and DC, And/or Independents
Note: Quantities vary widely - on bulk books)
1,200 books = $180 (15¢ ea)
10,000 Books = $1,200 (12¢ ea)
100,000 Books = $10,000 (10¢ ea)

Note: If you're planning on purchasing around 100,000 books (and maybe for 10,000 books,) call me and I MIGHT be able to get you a ***significant Postage Reduction!!!***

Postage: US (Insured $3 plus 5¢ per book ($5 min US postage) (Unless OW noted); Outside US (Uninsured) $5 + 10¢ per book ($15 min) Outside US (Insured, Air, Etc) Call or Fax for rates, or I can charge you on your credit card whatever I pay for postage.

1950'S - 1960'S PRICED & STRICTLY GRADED

OLDIES Bagged, Tagged & Ready to go: $200 Sticker = **$150;** $600 Sticker = **$450;**
Postage: US (Insured) $5. Outside US (Uninsured $15

SPECIAL* - Spend at least $1,000 on priced, graded oldies - get 1/3 off of sticker *(+postage)
2 examples: $1,500 sticker = $1,000; $4,500 sticker = $3,000 *(Postage US $15, Outside $30)*

And you're always entitled to pick, any (or a combo of 2-or-more) of the following categories:
A) 1960's - **DC** B) 1965-69 - **Marvel** C) **Misc Companies** (1950's & 1960's) and/or D) **Dell & Gold Key** (1950's & 1960's - Disney, Superhero, Tarzan, TV & Movie) Warner Bros, and/or Westerns, Etc.

Always - Your Choice
1 **Condition**-Range (ie, Fair-Good, Good-VG, VG-Fine, etc)
2 **Category**(s) (A,B,C,D, on Some of Each (you may even choose proportions of each!)
3 **Type**(s) Desired: (Superhero, Humor, Western, TV & Movie, Etc)
4 **Preferred titles**: If any preferred!
5 **Sticker-Value-Range** (ie: below $8.00 ea, above $10 ea, etc.)

1970'S (& EARLY 1980'S) MAGAZINES

100 magazines: $100 (1 each) 300 mags $300 (1-2 ea)
Postage: figure Magazines = 2.5 times comic book postage)

Types Available
A **Marvel Mags** (Hulk, Epic, Misc-Monsters, Savage Sword, etc)
B **Movie & TV related** (mostly early & late 1980's: Fangoria, Gorelone, Starlog, etc)
C **Other Mags**: Elfquest/1990's Mads, etc.
D **British Mags**: Various titles

GARY DOLGOFF COMICS: (New Address) 116 Pleasant St, Easthampton, MA 01027
PHONE: 413-529-0326 FAX: 413 529-9824 E-MAIL:gdcomics@JAVANET.COM
WAREHOUSE HOURS: 10:00 AM - 5:30 PM M-F FAX/E-MAIL 24 HRS. 7 DAYS

CONTINUED FROM PREVIOUS PAGE

1950's - 1990's Comics and Mags

AT DISCOUNT

WORLDWIDE

Store-Owners: Back Issues Can Sell!!!

(some relatively easy ways to create a long-term, back-issue customer base! it's do-able)

COLLECTORS STILL COLLECT!

Let us assemble a worthwhile package deal for you!

1. **Assemble** a targeted and interesting, strictly graded, back issue stock
2. **Spend within your budget!** (It takes a little while to get the ball rolling)
3. **Don't be shy - Publicize** (signs and books in the windows, signs and books in store, local and inexpensive advertising, conventions (books and flyers) etc. That you have A- a new and interesting back issue stock (give examples) }
   B- and Strict Grading.
4. **Cultivate serious want lists** and ask em generally what back issues they'd like to see more of. Perhaps you might let em know "We have a warehouse"
5. **Keep your prices fair**, and your grading strict!
6. **Display your back issues neatly and proudly**, with large price tags (and, on some older books, "Grade Tags" as well.

7. CALL OR FAX US - WE'LL PUT TOGETHER A DISCOUNTED PACKAGE DEAL

strictly graded, back issue stock for you that is reasonable, rational and well worth the money (without breaking the bank!) Spend only what you're comfortable spending.

GIVE THE SERIOUS CUSTOMERS A GOOD REASON TO COME TO YOUR STORE!!!

Give them a Fair Deal, and they'll come back again and again!!
LET DOLGOFF HELP YOU FIND YOUR LONG-TERM CUSTOMER BASE!! (NAMELY, BACK ISSUE BUYERS)

EXPERIENCED BACK ISSUE STORE OWNERS: There's always room for more profit, additional customers. Try our deals, and revel in our High Falutin Standards!
COLLECTORS: Collecting can be fund and easy when you do it the Dolgoff Way!

GARY DOLGOFF COMICS: (New Address) 116 Pleasant St, Easthampton, MA 01027
PHONE: 413-529-0326 FAX: 413 529-9824 E-MAIL:gdcomics@JAVANET.COM
WAREHOUSE HOURS: 10:00 AM - 5:30 PM M-F FAX/E-MAIL 24 HRS. 7 DAYS

CONTINUED ON NEXT PAGE

HAPPILY BUYING 1,000 - 1,000,000

COMIC BOOKS, MAGAZINES, ORIGINAL ART, TOYS

1964 - 1998

THE MORE THE MERRIER

HARDCOVERS, SOFT COVERS, POSTERS, MEMORABILIA, ETC. COLLECTIONS

WE LOVE COLLECTIONS,
especially with either better books or Runs of a title (sets!)
(EVEN MEDIOCRE TITLES)

STORE STOCK - OVERSTOCK
We'll buy it all - the good the bad and the ugly
WAREHOUSE STOCK, OR OVERSTOCK

WANT TO SELL OUT YOUR WAREHOUSE STOCK, OR PART OF IT? GIVE US A CALL (OR FAX, OR E-MAIL)

Publishers remainders, or pubs overstock wanted

Sell us your 5,000 hardcovers, your 10,000 soft covers or whatever! We're interested

WE ALSO TRADE!
BETTER PRICES GIVEN FOR YOUR OVERSTOCK

WALL BOOKS, MAGAZINES, COMIC BOOKS, MEMORABILIA, ETC. WANTED - Trade a bunch of comics you don't need for a selected batch of comics from my stock, that you can use!!! (let us know)

...And don't forget, finder's fees are always happily paid for Info leading to a deal.

This year (1998) alone, I can use (at least)

- ✔ 100,000 1950's - 1960's comics (all grades)
- ✔ 50,000 Hardcovers
- ✔ 200,000 80's & '90's Comics
- ✔ 200,000 1970's comics (DC, Marvel, Gold-Key)
- ✔ 100,000 Soft covers
- ✔ 100,000 Pieces of comic memorabilia (pins, posters, paperback, digests, banners, etc, etc, etc,)
- ✔ 100,000 Warren magazines (Creepy, Eerie, Famous Monsters, etc)
- ✔ 100,000 other 1970's - 1990's Magazines
- ✔ 10,000 pieces of Original Art

COLLECTIONS ALSO WANTED

and Much, Much, More!!!

GARY DOLGOFF COMICS: (New Address) 116 Pleasant St, Easthampton, MA 01027
PHONE: 413-529-0326 FAX: 413 529-9824 E-MAIL:gdcomics@JAVANET.COM
WAREHOUSE HOURS: 10:00 AM - 5:30 PM M-F FAX/E-MAIL 24 HRS. 7 DAYS

CONTINUED FROM PREVIOUS PAGE

ACTIVELY BUYING ALL COMICS

ORIGINAL ART, PULPS, ETC.

1933 - 1963

POOR •FAIR• VG •FINE NEAR MINT

COVERLESS AND BOUND VOLUMES, AS WELL

ONE BOOK OR A ROOM FULL, I'LL BUY IT ALL!

EXPENSIVE COMICS WANTED

$1,000 - $100,000 & UP

Cheaper Comics Wanted

$2.00 - $200 & Up

FINDERS FEE HAPPILY PAID

FOR INFORMATION LEADING TO A DEAL...

(Call for details)

IN 1996 I PAID A $6,500 FINDERS FEE!!!

GARY DOLGOFF COMICS: (New Address) 118 Pleasant St, Easthampton, MA 01027

PHONE: 413-529-0326 FAX: 413 529-9824 E-MAIL:gdcomics@JAVANET.COM

WAREHOUSE HOURS: 10:00 AM - 5:30 PM M-F FAX/E-MAIL 24 HRS. 7 DAYS

QUALITY **AUCTIONS SINCE 1985** **CONSISTENCY**

QUASAR COMICS

presents

FANTASTIC MAIL BID SALES!

COMICS, SCIENCE FICTION, FANTASY, PULPS, BIG LITTLE BOOKS, ORIGINAL ART, FANZINES

☑ QUALITY

A wide selection of accurately described and attributed comics and collectibles from the Golden-Age to the Modern-Age are offered for all collecting preferences

☑ CONSISTENCY

Mail bid and phone auctions on a regular basis for ten years

Accurate conservative grading that stays the same year-in and year-out

☑ INTEGRITY

Founding Member: American Association of Comic Book Collectors (A.A.C.C.)

Winner: *Comic Buyers' Guide Customer Service Award*

Member: *A.A.C.B.C. Authenticity, Certification and Grading Committee, Sotheby's Auctions, New York, 1993, 1994, 1995, 1996.*

Present/past advisor to: *Overstreet's FAN; Comic Book Marketplace, Comics Source; Comic Buyers' Guide Price Guide*

☑ SATISFACTION

Over 14,500 lots sold in previous auctions, ***less than one-third of one percent returned*** *for any reason*

We have received many compliments from our customers world-wide

Seven-day return privilege where we pay your return postage costs

Ninety-day interest free lay-away plan

☑ CONVENIENCE

For your convenience, we accept MasterCard and Visa. We also offer an interest free ninety-day lay-away plan for purchases greater than $100.

☑ CONSIGNMENTS

Our seller's consignment fee never exceeds 20% and can be as low as 10%. We do not charge a buyer's fee. Single books valued from $50 and up as well as some lots of less expensive books are accepted on a space available basis. ***Please call or write for details before sending any books.***

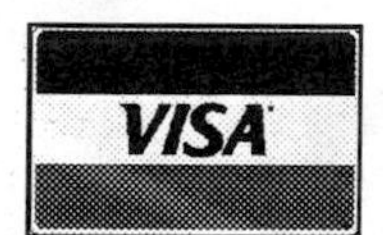

Send $2.00 for your copy of the next auction catalog to:

QUASAR COMICS

Bruce W. Edwards, Proprietor

P.O. Box 2227, Louisville, KY 40201-2227

Phone: (502) 451-4852 - Fax (502) 454-0025

E-mail: Quasarcmx@AOL.COM

Web: http://www.comics2000.com/quasar/

INTEGRITY **SATISFACTION**

HEARD THESE LINES BEFORE?

1. WE WILL OUTBID ANYONE, ANYWHERE, ANYTIME!
2. QUICK, IMMEDIATE, UNLIMITED CASH!
3. WE SPEND MORE THAN ANYONE!
4. TOP PRICES PAID!
5. NO ONE PAYS MORE!

THE TRUTH IS:

Almost every comic book dealer advertising in this guide has probably made one or more of the above claims at one time or another. **We have too.** After being involved in this business since 1972 and having dealt frequently with most of the major dealers/companies advertising in this guide, we have come to the **"startling conclusion"** that no person or company (including us) **ever always** pays the most. **We have bid against the other big guys and have won some and lost some.** Often times, it's not who has (or claims to have) the most money that counts, it's who **has** the most established customers **looking anxiously** for comic books to buy. This is precisely why we at WANT LIST COMICS can be **EXTREMELY COMPETITIVE** when we purchase individual books or collections. Because we have **many** want list customers waiting in line for books that we purchase, (*please note our other ads in this guide) we can usually expect a quick return on our money invested, and therefore justify buying books at **very, very** high percentages of current Overstreet. We have purchased some books at **OVER 250% Guide** because of customer demand!

In the past few years, we have purchased books in **All** grades (some for **WORLD RECORD PRICES**) like **Action 1**, **Detective 27**, **Marvel 1**, **Superman 1**, **Captain America 1**, **All American 16**, **New Fun 2**, and **Batman 1** plus every "key" **Marvel** and **DC Silver Age** issue imaginable! We must be doing something right! SINCE WE ARE LOCATED IN THE MIDWEST, we can easily and quickly come to you to compete against the local stores or dealers for your books.

ALL WE ASK FOR IS A CHANCE TO BID AGAINST THE OTHER GUYS (ESPECIALLY THE "TOO GOOD TO BE TRUE" ADS)

We don't mind the competition. We **ESPECIALLY** want **Golden Age** and **Silver Age books** with 10¢ and 12¢ covers. We will buy both large and small collections and aren't interested in just "cherry picking" certain issues -- we will take all you want to sell. **We also pay generous finder's fees for any information leading to the purchase of collections.** For a fast reply, just call, FAX or mail us a list of what you have for sale. References are always gladly given upon request.

Our office/warehouse # is:
1-918-299-0440

Call us anytime between 1 pm and 8 pm, CST
Please ask for our private FAX #

WANT LIST COMICS
BOX 701932
TULSA, OK 74170-1932

Senior Advisor to the Overstreet Comic Price Guide
CBG Customer Service Award
References gladly provided!

THIRD PLANET
POUNDING
the competition
since 1975!
comics, toys, cards, games,
videos, anime, posters, statues,
art prints, models, magazines,
novels, pulps, imports, pre-orders,
world wide mail orders & subscription
service , lay-aways and much more!
2718 SW FWY
Houston, TX 77098
(713) 528-1067
www.third-planet.com
3planet@third-planet.com
over 8,000
sq.ft. of
merchandise
in one
location!

I BUY COMICS-I BUY COMICS

KOALA-T

$$$ NEED CASH? $$$
We are buying
Warehouse-Bulk &
Store overstock
Comic books, Golden
Age, Silver Age
Gaming - Toys - Pulps
Adult Magazines
CDs - Videos

We travel to you
& buy any amount
one box to 5,000

If you're tired of those
"NEW YORK GUYS"
give the midwest
closeout dealers a try.
KOALA-T-COMICS
(finder's fees cheerfully
paid)

KOALA-T COMICS NO. 1

Artwork by:
Ken Penders

COMICS

FOR NATIONWIDE SERVICE:

JOHN MOORE
937-890-3819

OR

JOE YOURKVITCH
440-428-8118

FAX: 440-428-9651
E-MAIL: ROOCOMICS@NCWEB.COM

I BUY COMICS-I BUY COMICS-I BUY COMICS-I BUY COMICS

I BUY COMICS-I BUY COMICS-I BUY COMICS-I BUY COMICS

I BUY COMICS-I BUY COMICS

GOLDEN AGE COLLECTABLES
MARVELS, D.C.'S & INDEPENDENTS
STAR TREK & STAR WARS COLLECTABLES
SPORT & NON-SPORT TRADING CARDS
ROLE PLAYING GAMES & SUPPLIES
MOVIE STAR PHOTOS & AUTOGRAPHS
JAPANIMATION VIDEOS & BOOKS
THE NORTHWEST'S OLDEST & LARGEST
SEATTLE
WASHINGTON
1501 PIKE PLACE MARKET
401 LOWER LEVEL
SEATTLE, WA 98101
206-622-9799
VANCOUVER
CANADA
830 GRANVILLE STREET
VANCOUVER, B.C.
CANADA V6Z 1K3
604-683-2819

COMICS AND STORIES

Golden Age | **Silver Age** | **Comic Art** | **Comic Strip Art** | **Frazetta** | **Fantasy Art**

Photos courtesy of Christie's East

No one is responsible for more sales of vintage Comic Collectibles than Comics and Stories. No one has access to more, or finer quality material than **Comics and Stories.**

DC	FRAZETTA	FOSTER	FRAZETTA
TIMELY	KIRBY	RAYMOND	ST. JOHN
FAWCETT	BARKS	McCAY	PAUL
DISNEY	DRUCKER	HERRIMAN	FINLAY
DELL	INFANTINO	SCHULZ	BOK
CENTAUR	DITKO	KELLY	VALLEJO
ATLAS	KANE	GOULD	FREAS
MARVEL	SHUSTER	GRAY	WRIGHTSON
QUALITY	FINE	SEGAR	DeSOTO
FICTION HOUSE	STERANKO	CANIFF	HILDEBRANDT

We sell via direct mail, auctions, conventions and by our **computerized want list service**. If we do not currently have it, we likely know where it is. **Stay on top of the market** send us your name, address and wants today!

COMICS AND STORIES

122 WEST END AVENUE • RIDGEWOOD, NJ 07450
PHONE: (201) 652-1305 • FAX: (201) 445-3371
(By Appointment Only)

SHOWCASE NEW ENGLAND

PAID

$400,000
PAID
in Canada, 1997

$460,000
PAID
in California, 1998

$110,000
PAID
in Louisiana, 1996

$274,000
PAID
in New York, 1995

$225,000
PAID
in Illinois, 1996

We pay amounts from

$1,000 to $50,000

EVERY WEEK

for books we need.

BOOKS SHOWN BY APPOINTMENT ONLY • WEEKDAYS 9:30 a.m. - 5:30 p.m. E.S.T.
CALL DANIEL GREENHALGH TODAY
CBG Customer Service Award Winner 1994, 1995, 1996, 1997
Member AACBC Authenticity, Certification, & Grading Committee
(Christie's Auction) 1994, 1995, 1996, 1997 (Sotheby's Auction) 1995, 1996, 1997, 1998
Special Advisor to Overstreet Annual 1994, 1995, 1996, 1997, 1998

67 GAIL DRIVE • NORTHFORD, CT 06472 • (203) 484-4579 • FAX (203) 484-4837

IN THE LAST FEW YEARS, WE HAVE

$PENT MILLION$

BUYING COMIC BOOKS

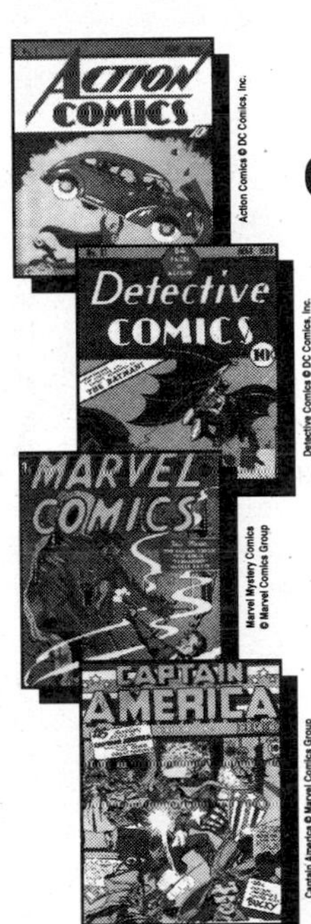

WE HAVE PURCHASED MANY INDIVIDUAL BOOKS AS WELL AS MANY OF THE MAJOR COLLECTIONS SOLD IN NORTH AMERICA OVER THE PAST FEW YEARS.

CALL TODAY FOR IMMEDIATE, NO NONSENSE, RESPONSE!

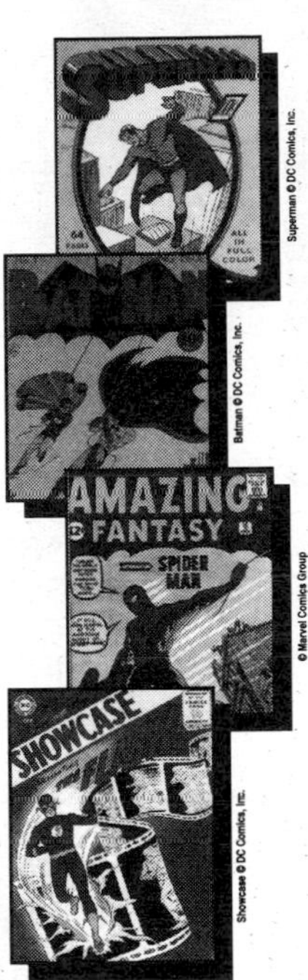

SHOWCASE NEW ENGLAND™

BOOKS SHOWN BY APPOINTMENT ONLY • WEEKDAYS 9:30 a.m. - 5:30 p.m. E.S.T.
CALL DANIEL GREENHALGH TODAY

CBG Customer Service Award Winner 1994, 1995, 1996, 1997
Member AACBC Authenticity, Certification, & Grading Committee
(Christie's Auction) 1994, 1995, 1996, 1997 (Sotheby's Auction) 1995, 1996, 1997, 1998
Special Advisor to Overstreet Annual 1994, 1995, 1996, 1997, 1998

67 GAIL DRIVE • NORTHFORD, CT 06472 • (203) 484-4579 • FAX (203) 484-4837

Comic Books
Most Publishers

Bought and Sold

DC, Marvel, Dell, Disney — Barks — Kelly, Seabord, EC, American Comics, Gold Key, Harvey, Avon, Atlas, Fawcett, etc.

Also:
*PULPS
*DIGESTS
*MAGAZINES (Men's, Life, Liberty, Movie,etc.)
*SONGSHEETS
*SONGBOOKS
*GOLDEN BOOKS
*PAPERBACKS
*HARDCOVERS
*CHILDREN'S SERIES BOOKS
*MOVIE EDITIONS
*BIG LITTLE BOOKS
*CHARACTER MERCHANDISE
*GIVEAWAYS
*NEWSPAPERS (Comic Sections)
*AND RELATED ITEMS

Send one dollar for 40-page Selling Catalog. (Send $3.00 for Air Mail)

TO SELL: send your price list for bid or give your asking price. Please include a self-addressed-stamped envelope. Thank you.

COLLECTORS UNLIMITED
P.O. Box 264
New Ipswich, New Hampshire 03071-0264

IF YOU ARE A SERIOUS COLLECTOR OF COMICS FROM THE 30'S, THROUGH THE 60'S, LOOKING TO FILL THE DIFFICULT HOLES IN YOUR COLLECTION...OR... TRYING TO UPGRADE YOUR FINES AND VERY FINES TO

SPECIALIZING IN WANT LISTS AND PURCHASING COLLECTIONS.

NEAR MINTS BUT CAN'T GO EVERYWHERE AND DON'T KNOW EVERYONE...?

CALL US! WE'VE BEEN BUYING AND SELLING THE HIGHEST GRADE GOLD

609-845-4010 AND SILVER AGE BOOKS FOR OUR CLIENTS FOR THE LAST 17 YEARS!!!

LET US SHOW YOU WHAT WE CAN DO FOR YOU...AND, IF YOU ARE SELLING YOUR COLLECTION, WE'LL FLY TO YOU ANYWHERE AND TREAT YOU RIGHT!

ASK AROUND (EVEN OUR COMPETITORS)...OUR REPUTATION CAN'T BE BEAT.

JOSEPH H. VERENEAULT

P.O. BOX 317, WOODBURY HEIGHTS, NEW JERSEY 08097 TEL: 609-845-4010 FAX: 609-845-3977

STEVE SIBRA

PO Box 9055, Missoula MT 59807

Phone: (406) 542-8270

PREMIERE COMIC DEALER OF THE NORTHERN PLAINS STATES

Actively Buying Old Comics Throughout The Plains, Pacific NW, And SW Canada

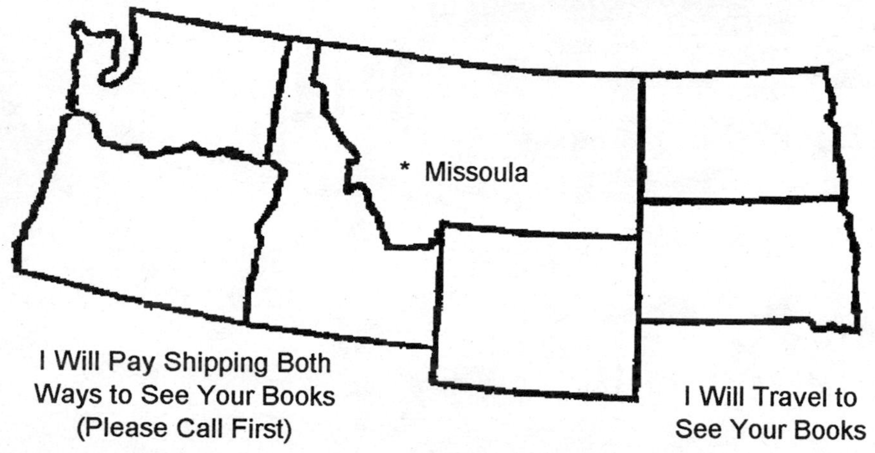

I Will Pay Shipping Both Ways to See Your Books (Please Call First)

I Will Travel to See Your Books

I PAY TOP DOLLAR FOR GOLD & SILVER AGE COMICS 1933-1966

Nobody can pay the most every time for every collection; however, I have successfully outbid other major dealers in the purchase of many significant collections. I will gladly provide references from satisfied customers whose collections I have purchased.

* Immediate Cash Available
* Over 15 Years Experience Buying & Selling Gold & Silver Age Comics
* Honest, Friendly Service
* Accurate Grading
* Competitive Pricing
* Overstreet Advisor, 1986-1990
* Founder and Former Owner of Rocket Comics in Seattle, WA.
* Contributing Author to Comic Book Marketplace Magazine Since Its Inception
* Excellent References Available

BUYING & SELLING ENTIRE STORES, BETTER COMICS & ART | Est. 1978

APPROVED
BY
FRANK
OVER
100
MILLION
COMIC BOOKS
SOLD!

Friendly Frank's
COMIC CAVERN

We're Buying!

★★★★ Top Prices Paid for Quality Material! ★★★★

Going to Kansas City?

Visit our store. We're 8 minutes south of KCI Airport, 8 minutes north of downtown KCMO, one block west of I-29 on NW 64th St.
One of the best-stocked stores in the U.S.
50¢ to $5,000

FOR SALE:

Amazing Fantasy 15vf $4000 (Wilson restoration)
Amazing Spiderman 1f $1500 (Wilson restoration)
Captain America 17f $1200; 100 nm $300
New Adv. Charlie Chan 1-3f, 4-6vg+
scarce original owner set, bright covers $650
Showcase 14vg $650 / 18f, 19vgf $250 each
Strange Adventures 1vg $500; 14vf $300
Wonder-Woman 1vgf (restored) $4000
R. Crumb's Yum Yum Book nm('75 1st ed) $75
R. Crumb's Coffee Table Art Book (signed w/silkscreen) $300

BULK DEALS
$30,000 Worth of comics for ONLY $3,500!
$100,000 Worth of comics for ONLY $10,000!
Both deals offer balanced inventories and a wide selection, heavier on better selling titles.
CALL FOR MORE INFORMATION
LAYAWAYS AVAILABLE
Friendly FRANK'S

Especially wanted:

PRE★1960
COLLECTIONS
Timely
Good Art
Especially: LB Cole, Jack Cole, Everett, Lou Fine, Frazetta, Mayer, Toth
Crime
Horror
Keys
Superhero

Other Top Wants:

Undergrounds
Nice Original Art

Also Buying:

Stores · Warehouses
Post-1960 Collections

FINDER'S FEES
paid promptly on deals we buy

★★★ AWARDS ★★★

The Small Business Administration's regional
1993 YOUNG ENTREPRENEUR OF THE YEAR AWARD

Comics Retailer Columnist Preston Sweet's
1995 CHEER OF THE YEAR AWARD
(for consideration of customers while going out of business)

Comics Buyer's Guide
CUSTOMER SERVICE AWARD
EVERY YEAR SINCE INCEPTION

FRIENDLY FRANK'S IS BUYING

FRANK MANGIARACINA • 5404 NW 64th St. • KANSAS CITY, MO • 64151 | 816-746-4569 PHONE (or fax)

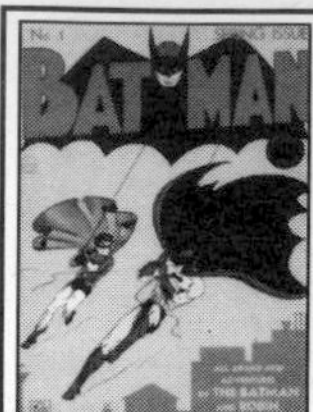

Comic*Link*

THE INTERNET COMIC BOOK EXCHANGE

http://www.comiclink.com

4842 Glenwood Street
Little Neck, NY 11362 USA

(Email) buysell@comiclink.com
(Phone) 718/423-6079 (Fax) 718/423-9801

BUY AND SELL through **Comic***Link*: The Internet Comic Book Exchange - with or without Internet Access

***Comic**Link specializes in Golden and Silver Age comic books, collections, original art, and related merchandise*

Benefits of purchasing comic books through **Comic***Link*:

- *NO buyer's commission*
- Wide selection of merchandise listed by many different sellers
- Professional service, strict 3rd party grading, and secure packaging.
- Buy risk-free with a 6-day money back guarantee
- Daily updates and 24-hour ordering/bidding capacity

Benefits of selling comic books through **Comic***Link*:

- *Generate or increase sales and cash flow* - whether you are a collector or an established dealer.
- *Consignment is not required* — we don't hold your books!
- *No listing or grading costs* or other fees — advertising is free!
- *No cancellation penalty*
- Lowest commission in the industry charged after the sale
- We market your books for you to an international clientele

Visit the **Comic***Link* website or contact Joshua Nathanson. Reputable references will gladly be furnished upon request. We look forward to hearing from you!

* Listing is as easy as mailing us your catalog or want list.

Archie® COMICS ARE REAL SLEEPERS!

A **WEALTH** OF READING PLEASURE **NOW...**
AND MAYBE THEN SOME **LATER!**

YOU CAN FIND CLASSIC ARCHIE COMICS AT FINE VINTAGE COMIC DEALERS EVERYWHERE! AND DON'T FORGET **TOMORROW'S** CLASSICS— **NEW** ARCHIE COMICS ARE AVAILABLE AT YOUR FAVORITE RETAILER, INCLUDING A&P STORES, ALBERTSONS, ENCORE BOOKS, ECKERD DRUGS, K-MART, WALDENBOOKS, WALMART AND YOUR LOCAL COMIC SHOP OUTLET.
FOR THE COMIC SHOP NEAREST YOU, CALL 1-888-266-4226.

ARCHIE COMIC PUBLICATIONS, INC. 325 Fayette Ave., Mamaroneck, NY 10543. **PHONE:** (914) 381-5155.
FAX: (914) 381-2338. ***Visit our website at http://www.archiecomics.com***

TM & © 1997 Archie Comic Publications, Inc. All Rights Reserved.

BOOKERY Fantasy & Comics

-Established 1984 -
visit us at **www.bookeryfantasy.com**

TIM COTTRILL President
STEVE BATES Manager

- **COMIC BOOKS 1930s - PRESENT**
- **SCI-FI TOYS & BOOKS• RPGs**
- **PULPS • MAGAZINES • CDs**
- **MOVIE POSTERS (pre-1970)**

7000 sq. ft. MEGA-STORE!

16 WEST MAIN STREET
FAIRBORN OHIO 45324

- near Dayton, I-70 & I-75
- 1 mile from Wright-Patt AFB
- 5 min. from Wright State Univ. & The U.S. Air Force Museum

MAIN SHOP: (937) 879-1408
FAX LINE: (937) 879-9327
E-mail: BookeryFan@aol.com
Web Page:
www.bookeryfantasy.com

AMONG THE MID-WEST'S LARGEST COMICS & SCI-FI COLLECTIBLES SHOPPES

MOTOR CITY COMICS

BUYING:

- Top Prices Paid !!!
- We Always Pay 60%-200% of Guide for pre-1970 Comics
- We Will Travel Anywhere to View Large Collections
- Senior Advisor to the Overstreet Price Guide

GOLD & SILVER AGE COMICS

NOW OPEN
Come Visit Our New Warehouse
by appointment only

& SELLING:

- Large Selection of Gold & Silver Age
- Accurate Grading
- Competitive Pricing
- Want List Service

FREE
CATALOGS
Call or Write for Your Copy

MOTOR CITY COMICS
19785 W. 12 MILE RD. • SUITE 231 • SOUTHFIELD, MI 48076
PHONE: (248) 426-8059 • FAX: (248) 426-8064

JOHN M. HAUSER

BUY, SELL or TRADE

Golden Age, Silver Age

Coverless 40's & 50's

Pre-Code Horror

Buying:

--Top Prices Paid
- I will travel to view collections
- I have buyers located in these states MD, MN, WA, NY, TX, CA, IL, IN, OH, IA, MI
- Several key collections bought in 1996

Selling:

- Accurate Grading
- Dependable and Reputable Service
- Large Selection of books in all grades
- Prices start at $1
- No minimum order
- 20 years experience - senior advisor to Overstreet and former member of Southebys' Grading Committee
- Auction Service Available

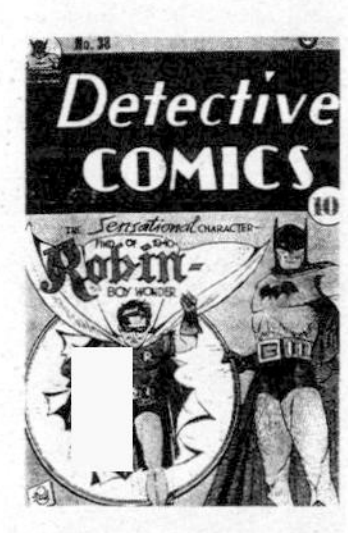

Large Catalog Published Every 6 weeks!
Send $1 for your copy today!

JOHN M. HAUSER

P.O. Box 510673
New Berlin, WI 53151-0673

(414) 789 - 1863

Email: JMHComics @aol.com

To receive ALL Catalogs, over 70 pages in total, send $2.

International Customers send $2 per catalog or $3 to receive all catalogs.

CATALOGS AVAILABLE **FREE** BY DOWNLOADING FROM OUR

AWESOME WEBSITE!

HTTP://USERS.AOL.COM/HRBHOLDING E-MAIL: HRBHOLDING@AOL.COM

Our wide selection, reasonable prices, accurate grading and outstanding service will make your hobby happen.

HRB HOLDINGS INC.

BUYING

COMPLETE 6 PG. BUYING LIST WITH PRICES PAID FOR 1000'S OF COMICS & MAGAZINES. SEND $1

P.O. BOX 7086, CLEARWATER, FL 33758-7086
(813) 586-2089

WORLDWIDE MAIL ORDER SERVICE

DAVID T. ALEXANDER

P.O. BOX 273086 · TAMPA, FL 33618

(813) 968-1805 FAX (813) 264-6226

OUR AMAZING CATALOGS ARE LOADED WITH ITEMS TO SERVE **ALL** OF YOUR COLLECTING NEEDS! OUR 14 NEW CATALOGS FOR 1998 ARE CHOCK FULL OF HUNDREDS OF THOUSANDS OF **RARE COMICS, BOOKS, PULPS, POSTERS, MAGS, PRINTS, ART – YOU NAME IT!!**

WE HAVE BEEN DEALING IN COMICS SINCE THE 60's. THE VARIETY AND DEPTH OF **OUR INVENTORY IS SECOND TO NONE**. WE HAVE OPENED A LARGE NUMBER OF COMIC BOOK STORES THROUGHOUT THE UNITED STATES DURING THE PAST 28 YEARS, AND CAN NOW **OFFER THIS SERVICE TO YOU**.

WANT TO OWN A COMIC BOOK BUSINESS?

SPECIAL
MAIL ORDER BUSINESS START UP PACKAGE
includes catalog, mailing list, inventory!
ONLY $2,495.00
CALL TODAY FOR DETAILS!!

EARN BIG $$ AND HAVE A **GREAT TIME** IN ONE OF AMERICA'S FASTEST GROWING INDUSTRIES

BECOME AN AFFILIATE STORE –
– WITH ONE OF THE FOLLOWING

★ ***THE MEGA STORE*** ***$100,000***
BECOME A POWER IN THE COMIC BOOK AND COLLECTIBLE INDUSTRY – AT THIS LEVEL YOUR STORE WILL HAVE A MASSIVE INVENTORY (APPROX. 125,000 ITEMS), INTERNATIONAL ADVERTISING AND WORLDWIDE PROMINENCE.

★ ***COMPLETE STORE*** ***$35,000***
YOU GET: SITE LOCATION, STORE DESIGN, CATALOG, TRAINING, INVENTORY – COMPREHENSIVE CROSS SECTION OF MARVEL, D.C., POSTERS, BACK ISSUES, NEW MERCHANDISE, COLLECTORS ITEMS – AND MORE – THIS PACKAGE COULD BE A FULL TIME OCCUPATION OR EMPLOYEE OPERATED!

★ ***SMALL STORE/MAIL ORDER BUSINESS*** ***$15,000***
YOU GET: SITE LOCATION, CATALOG, TRAINING, AND INVENTORY – AN EXCELLENT WAY FOR THE PART TIMER TO BEGIN!!

★ ***COMBINATION PACKAGES*** – WE WILL TAILOR MAKE A BUSINESS TO SUIT YOUR NEEDS AND FINANCES!!

★ ***ALL BUSINESS PACKAGES GET INVENTORY AT LEAST 50% OFF!!***

*IF YOU WANT TO BE YOUR **OWN BOSS** AND **EARN BIG $$**, THIS COULD BE THE **OPPORTUNITY** FOR YOU!! – **SEND $10.00 FOR COMPLETE DETAILS.***

WANTED

PROFESSIONAL PRICES PAID FOR PULP MAGAZINES
SHADOW, DOC SAVAGE, MYSTERY TALES, PHANTOM DETECTIVE, BLACK MASK, WEIRD TALES, DIME MYSTERY, BATTLE ACES, TERROR TALES AND MOST OTHERS!!

THINKING OF SELLING? I AM ACTIVELY PURCHASING GOLDEN AGE AND PRE-1969 COMIC BOOKS, BIG LITTLE BOOKS, MOVIE POSTERS, AND ORIGINAL ART. I WILL PAY YOU TOP PRICES FOR QUALITY MATERIAL. I AM EASY TO DEAL WITH. QUICK, CONFIDENTIAL TRANSACTIONS. ANY QUANTITY, ANY CONDITION, ANY TIME.

LARGE COLLECTIONS OR ACCUMULATIONS OUR SPECIALTY

DAVID T. ALEXANDER

P.O. BOX 273086 - TAMPA, FL 33618
(813)968-1805 FAX (813)264-6226

"CONTACT US FIRST"

☆ WORLD'S BEST VARIETY ☆

Offering the Following Fine Catalogs:

★ **COMIC BOOK PRICE LIST SERIES $2.00**
GOLDEN AGE, 1950'S, SILVER AGE, GOOD GIRL ART, D.C., DELL, TIMELY, AVON, E.C., CRIME, HORROR, FAWCETT, WESTERNS, ARCHIE, HARVEY SCI-FI, CLASSICS, DISNEY, MOVIE AND TV COMICS, FOX, GOLD KEY, ALL KINDS OF OLD COMICS!!

★ **MARVEL AND D.C. COMICS..... $1.00**
SILVER AGE TO PRESENT, ALSO INCLUDES SOME INDEPENDENT TITLES.

★ **PULP MAGAZINE LIST $2.00**
1920'S-1950'S SHADOW, WEIRD TALES, DOC SAVAGE – LURID COVERS, ACTION STORIES, TREMENDOUS SELECTION!

★ **THE CATALOG OF GLAMOUR . $2.00**
PHOTO ILLUSTRATED – LARGE COLLECTION OF PIN-UP MAGS, MOVIE AND TV MAGS, ADVENTURE, DETECTIVE, MARILYN MONROE, BETTY PAGE, JAYNE MANSFIELD, ETC. – RARE, OBSCURE TITLES FROM 1900 TO THE 90'S.

★ **MAGAZINE AND FANZINE LIST . $1.00**
MAD, FAMOUS MONSTERS, SAVAGE TALES, MARVELS, HEAVY METAL, WARREN TITLES, EARLY AND RARE FANZINES.

★ **PAPERBACK BOOK LIST $2.00**
AVON, MAP BACKS, DUST JACKETS, POPULAR LIBRARY, ACE, DELL, ETC – OVER 20,000 VINTAGE PAPERBACKS AVAILABLE.

★ **EDGAR RICE BURROUGHS LIST $1.00**
TARZAN 1ST EDITIONS, HARDBACKS, PULPS, COMICS, BIG LITTLE BOOKS, MOVIE POSTERS.

★ **THE ART CATALOG $1.00**
ORIGINAL COMIC BOOK AND NEWSPAPER ART,COLOR MAGAZINE AND PULP COVERS, PORTFOLIOS, PRINTS, POSTERS, LIMITED EDITIONS.

★ **BIG LITTLE BOOKS.................... $1.00**
1930'S-1940'S, MICKEY MOUSE, FLASH GORDON, POPEYE, SHADOW, DICK TRACY, GENE AUTRY, SERIES BOOKS, WHITMAN BOOKS, ETC.

★ **MOVIE POSTERS $2.00**
1930'S TO 1990'S, WIDE VARIETIES. HORROR, WESTERN, FILM NOIR, SCIENCE FICTION, EXPLOITATION, CLASSICS – ONE SHEETS, LOBBY CARDS, PRESS BOOKS, MAGAZINES, MOVIE/TV COMICS, BOOKS, ETC.

★ **SPORTS COLLECTORS ITEMS $2.00**
PROGRAMS, YEARBOOKS, SPORT MAGAZINE, SPORTS ILLUSTRATED, BASEBALL, FOOTBALL, BOXING, YANKEES, DODGERS, METS, RAMS, GOLF, OLYMPICS, HOCKEY, MEDIA GUIDES – WE SPECIALIZE IN HISTORICALLY IMPORTANT MATERIAL.

★ **AUTO RACING MEMORABILIA $1.00**
A NEW RAGE IN COLLECTING – FEATURES: INDY 500, DAYTONA 500. FORMULA ONE, DRAG RACING, SPRINT CARS, DIRT TRACKS, SUPER SPEEDWAYS, PROGRAMS, YEARBOOKS, POST CARDS, DRIVER AUTOGRAPHS, MAGAZINES AND MUCH MORE – THE BEST CATALOG OF ITS KIND IN THE WORLD INCLUDES ITEMS FROM 1906 TO 1990'S.

★ **CHARACTER TOY AND COMIC BOOK PREMIUMS AND GIVEAWAYS.. $2.00**
ALL KINDS OF UNUSUAL AND COOL ITEMS.

★ **PREMIUM RINGS......................... $2.00**
FUN TO COLLECT, FUN TO WEAR.

CATALOGING IS A CONTINUAL PROCESS FOR US SINCE WE HAVE A CONSTANT INFLUX OF COLLECTORS ITEMS INTO OUR INVENTORY. AS WE GET NEW MATERIAL, OUR CATALOGS ARE CONSTANTLY BEING UPDATED. IF YOU DO NOT RECEIVE A CATALOG SHORTLY AFTER SENDING FOR IT, THAT MEANS WE ARE UPDATING THAT PARTICULAR CATALOG AND WE WILL RUSH YOU THE LATEST EDITION WHEN IT IS PRINTED.

WE ACCEPT WANT LISTS

NOW AVAILABLE

The Baseball and Sports Publications Price Guide – 2nd Edition

Baseball ★ Auto Racing ★ Football ★ Hockey ★ Basketball ★ Boxing ★ Programs ★ Yearbooks ★ Magazines ★ Books ★ Hundreds of Photos ★ 244, 8 1/2" x 11" Pages ★ Grading Info ★ Reliable Dealer Ads

The Only Reference Work to Appear in the Field of Sports Publications Collecting

$25.00 + $3 Priority Mail

NET Surfers, see a large selection of comics, pulps, movie posters, art, etc. for sale on the Web at **http://www.mindspring.com/~dtacoll** or contact us through our e-mail address, **dtacoll@tampa.mindspring.com**.

LOS ANGELES

COMIC BOOK AND SCIENCE FICTION CONVENTION

THE LARGEST, LONGEST RUNNING MONTHLY COMIC BOOK AND SCIENCE FICTION CONVENTION ON THE WEST COAST!

FEATURING:

A DEALER'S ROOM FULL OF GOLDEN AND SILVER AGE COMIC BOOKS, NEW COMIC BOOKS, MOVIE MEMORABILIA, TOYS, JAPANESE ANIMATION BOOKS AND MODELS, STAR TREK AND STAR WARS TOYS, BASEBALL CARDS, AND MAYBE THAT SPECIAL ITEM YOU'RE LOOKING FOR!

SPECIAL GUESTS FROM FILMS AND COMIC BOOKS • PREVIEWS OF UPCOMING FILM RELEASES • JAPANESE ANIMATION MARATHON • DIFFERENT PROGRAM EVERY MONTH!

FOR INFORMATION ON 1998-1999 CONVENTION LOCATION AND PROGRAM, WRITE:

BRUCE SCHWARTZ
2319-A WEST OLIVE AVENUE
BURBANK, CALIFORNIA 91506
(818) 954-8432

Thousands of Back Issues!!!

Comics and Periodicals
Spanning the Decades

All At Below Guide Prices!!!

One of a Kind
Comic History and Reference Section

Large selection of:
Comics ☼ Cards ☼ Toys ☼ Supplies
Collectibles ☼ Videos

Subscriptions ☼ *Mail Order*

Montclair Book Center Comic H.Q.
215 Glenridge Ave.
Montclair, NJ 07042
Phone (973)783-3630 Fax (973)783-8377

Star Trek Items | Golden Age
First Issues | New Comics

193 Terry Circle
Marina CA 93933
Fax 408-883-4257 Ph 408-883-2388

800-817-3353
Call for our free catalog
www.centurycomiccenter.com

ART RESTORATION

Matthew Wilson, Conservator

P.O. BOX 881 / KELSO, WA 98626 / (360) 577-0351

FANTASY MASTERPIECES is a business dedicated to the art of paper conservation. It is our philosophy that art restoration should take the *whole* item into account. That means that not only should your item look as good as possible but that it should be made as structurally sound as possible. What good is a restored work of art if it disintegrates two years later? For that reason, I have developed various methods and techniques of paper art restoration unmatched anywhere else.

I am familiar with the construction of 19th & 20th century papers and have worked extensively on the most valuable of the Golden and Silver aged books from Action #1 to Amazing Fantasy #15.

When it comes to your paper art collection, whether it's a Superman #1 or a rare paper document that is priceless to you, why take a risk with anyone else? **FANTASY MASTERPIECES** is the answer.

Before

After

Our rate is $55.00 per hour. Estimates are free & questions are always welcome. Items to be restored should be worth at least $125.00 in their present condition.

We perform the following services with expert precision:

1) Cleaning
2) Whitening
3) Tape Removal
4) Piece Replacement
5) Repair Tears
6) Spine Roll Removal
7) Deacidification
8) Color Retouching
9)Staple Replacement
10) Page Lightening

RARE PEZ WANTED!

PAYING OVER 100% BOOK PRICES

$250,000 + spent in 1997!

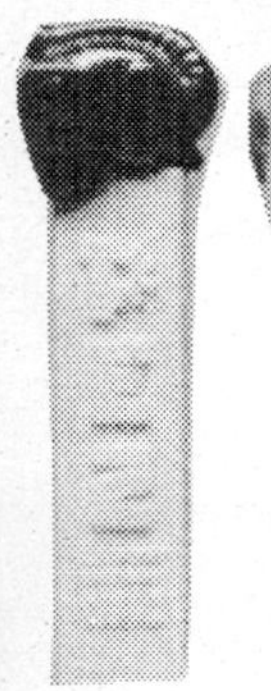

Old Elephant

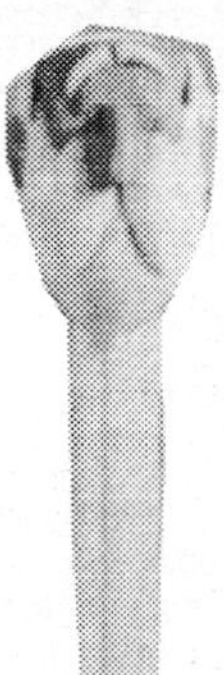

Mueslix (foreign)

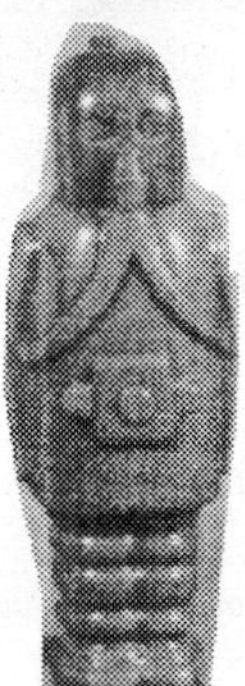

Full Body Robot shiny gold

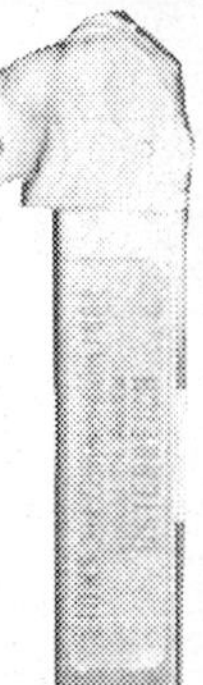

Lion's Club 1962

Make a Face on card or loose complete

Regulars (no head) with ads

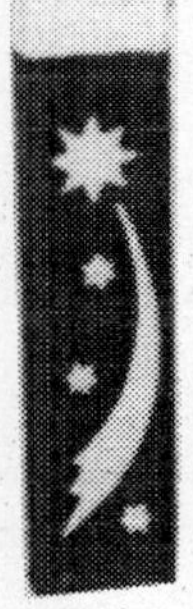

Comet Regular

Witch Regular

Easter Bunny with side picture

Psychedelic Flower yellow

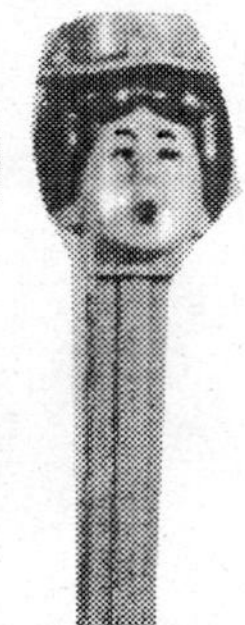

Pineapple

Mary Poppins

PEZ-Box Trade-mark or Patent

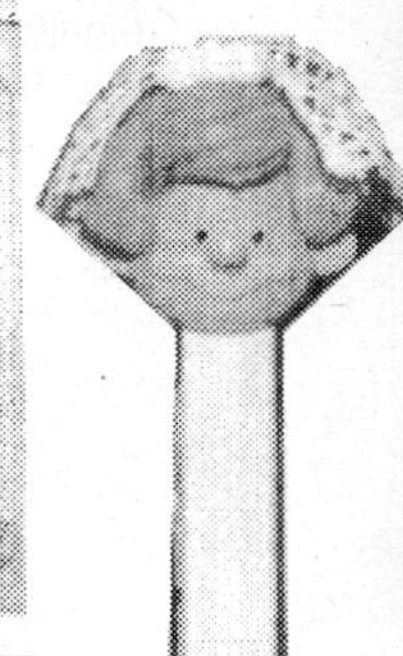

Bride

ALSO WANTED: Pony (pink, yellow, green, or purple heads). Tinkerbell, Giraffe, Pinocchio, Dopey, Snow White, Thor, Knight, Mexican, Astronauts, Pilot, Olive Oyl, Brutus, Orphan Annie, Ball glove with plate/bat, Arithmetic; Any advertising, or store display items, old candy, and other dispensers not listed.

1950's Space Gun silver, lavender, powder blue

DAVID WELCH

618-687-2282/684-2243 FAX

E-Mail: PEZDUDE1@aol.com

METROPOLIS

$ WANTS YOUR BOOKS $

Within the last several years, we have had the pleasure of dealing with many fine, intelligent people who have decided to realize the most money possible by selling us their comic book collections. These people were also very aware of the many dealers in this country who claim to pay "top dollar" for pre-1966 comic books. Unfortunately, most banks will not accept "claims of top dollar". They want cash!

The plain truth is that most other dealers are not willing to pay and will not offer what we consider to be top dollar. In most cases, the dealer simply lacks the financial resources to buy your entire collection. This is not the case with Metropolis. When you deal with our company, you can be assurred that we have the cash to back up our words.

If you have any questions, Stephen Fishler is always available to discuss the possible sale of your comic books, so call 212-260-4147. We have successfully outbid all other dealers for the high quality comic book collections that have been sold over the last few years. Find out why Metropolis has become the #1 comic dealer in the country!

The following is a sample of the books that we are actively purchasing.

ACTION 1-300
ADVENTURE 32-350
AIR FIGHTERS 1-v2 #10
ALL-AMERICAN 1-102
ALL-FLASH 1-32
ALL-SELECT 1-11
ALL-STAR 1-57
ALL-WINNERS 1-21
AMAZING FANTASY 15
AMAZING MAN 5-26
AMAZING MYSTERY FUNNIES 1-24
AMAZING SPIDERMAN 1-50
AVENGERS 1-25
BATMAN 1-200
BLACKHAWK 9-130
BLONDE PHANTOM 12-22
BLUE BEETLE 1-60
BLUE BOLT 1-UP
BULLETMAN 1-16
BRAVE & THE BOLD 1-75
CAPTAIN AMERICA 1-78
CAPTAIN MARVEL 1-150
CAPTAIN MIDNIGHT 1-67
CLASSIC COMICS 1-169
COMIC CAVALCADE 1-63
CRACK COMICS 1-62
CRIMES BY WOMEN 1-15
CRIME SUSPENSTORIES all
DAREDEVIL COMICS 1-60
DAREDEVIL (MCG) 1-25
DARING MYSTERY 1-8
DETECTIVE COMICS 1-400
EXCITING COMICS 1-69
FAMOUS FUNNIES SER. 1
FAMOUS FUNNIES 1-100
FANTASTIC COMICS 1-23
FANTASTIC FOUR 1-60
FLASH COMICS 1-104
FUNNY PAGES 6-42
FUNNY PICT STRYS 1-v3 #3
GREEN LANTERN (GA) 1-38
GREEN LANTERN (SA) 1-86
HIT COMICS 1-65
HUMAN TORCH 1-38
INCREDIBLE HULK 1-6,102
JOURNEY INTO MYSTERY 1-127
JUMBO COMICS 1-157
JUNGLE COMICS 1-163
JUSTICE LEAGUE 1-50
KEEN DET. FUNNIES 8-24
KING COMICS 1-159
LEADING COMICS 1-41
MAD 1-35
MARVEL MYSTERY 1-30
MASTER COMICS 1-133
MILITARY COMICS 1-43
MISS FURY 1-8
MODERN COMICS 44-102
MORE FUN COMICS 7-127
MYSTIC COMICS 1-UP
MYSTIC1-61
MYSTERY IN SPACE 1-110
NATIONAL COMICS 1-75
NEW ADVENTURE 12-31
NEW COMICS 1-11
NEW FUN 1-6
PEP COMICS 1-100
PHANTOM LADY all
PHANTOM STRANGER 1-6
PLANET COMICS 1-73
PLASTIC MAN 1-64
POLICE COMICS 1-127
POPULAR COMICS 1-145
OUR ARMY AT WAR 1-100
RANGERS COMICS 1-69
RED RAVEN 1
SENSATION COMICS 1-116
SHIELD WIZARD 1-13
SHOCK SUSPENSTORIES all
SHOWCASE 1-75
SILVER STREAK 1-24
SPY SMASHER 1-11
STAR COMICS 1-v2 #7
STAR RANGER 1-11
STAR-SPANGLED 1-130
STRANGE ADVENTURES all
STRANGE TALES 1-160
SUBMARINER COMICS 1-42
SUPERBOY 1-110
SUPER COMICS 1-121
SUPERMAN 1-160
SUPERSNIPE 1-v5 #1
SUSPENSE COMICS 1-12
TALES FROM THE CRYPT 20-46
TALES OF SUSPENSE 1-99
TALES TO ASTONISH 1-102
THING 1-17
THIS MAGAZINE IS HAUNTED all
THRILLING COMICS 1-80
TIP-TOP COMICS 1-100
TOP-NOTCH COMICS 1-45
UNCLE SAM 1-8
USA COMICS 1-17
WALT DISNEY C&S 1-100
WEIRD TALES FROM THE FUTURE 1-8
FUTURE COMICS 1-8
WHIZ COMICS 1-155
WINGS COMICS 1-124
WONDER COMICS (1939) 1-2
WONDER COMICS (1944) 1-20
WONDER WOMAN 1-110
WONDERWORLD 3-33
WORLD'S FINEST 1-130
WOW (1936) 1-4
WOW COMICS 1-69
X-MEN 1-25
YOUNG ALLIES 1-20
ZIP COMICS 1-47
ZOOT all

METROPOLIS COLLECTIBLES

873 BROADWAY SUITE 201, NEW YORK, NY 10003

1-212-260-4147 FAX: 212-260-4304

MASSIVE DISCOUNTS, FANTASTIC SELECTION, & INCREDIBLE SERVICE.

◆ **WE WANT YOUR BUSINESS.**
We are a full-time mail order business. This is how we make money to live on. Keeping this in mind, we promise to deliver professional, quality service to keep you coming back.

◆ **SPOTLESS REPUTATION.**
Because we use our owner's personal name instead of a fictitious trade name, we need to be good. You know exactly who you're dealing with, and we can't hide behind corporate policy. We have never had any complaints to publications we advertise in. References are available. We always offer a 10 day guaranteed return policy if our items were not as promised, or if you don't agree with our grading. We provide experienced, accurate, & conservative grading using leading industry standards.

◆ **QUALITY SERVICE.**
We will return phone calls to USA and Canada callers. We often return other calls too, so please leave a message. Because we don't have stores, our mail order customers get all of our attention. We promise timely shipment. We hate waiting too. Most orders go out within 48 hours. Personal checks must clear. Fully computerized system for better service. We will work with you to make package deals, negotiate prices, etc. Interest free time payment plans available for orders over $100.

◆ **EXPERIENCE.**
Our owner has over 14 years experience dealing comics & related items through the mail, at shows, etc. We have the contacts to get what you want.

JASON W LEHTO
DEPT. OS1
14303 NE 81ST STREET
VANCOUVER, WA 98682
(360) 604-0705

BUYING

◆ **TOP PRICES PAID.**
Because we do mail order, our customer base is large and worldwide. This gives us more chances to sell your books, which allows us to pay more.

◆ **WE WANT IT ALL.**
We will buy any comic related item. We're mostly interested in pre-1976 comic books, but we often buy items from any year, condition, or quantity. We have traveled to make large purchases.

◆ **LOWEST CONSIGNMENT RATES.**
If you don't sell to us, then sell through us. We probably offer the lowest rates around, with no buyer's fees. Our commissions can be 5%!!! Your items may sell through our regular ads, catalogs, flyers, or through our worldwide want list service.

SELLING

◆ **WE SELL IT ALL.**
We deal in comics, cards, & related items from the 1800's to present - single items to bulk deals. We specialize in comic books, but we also sell original art, Platinum age, trading cards, magazines, adult titles, posters, signed items, books, etc. We keep at least 50,000 items in stock at all times.

◆ **MASSIVE DISCOUNTS.**
Our standard discounts for all our customers go as high as 75% off retail. Even truly rare items can be discounted. We cater to foreign and USA collectors, investors, stores, dealers, bulk sellers, new start-up stores, and everyone else.

◆ **FREE WANT LIST SERVICE.**
It's computerized with first access to our stock.

◆ **FREE PRICE LISTS.**
Free customized price lists can be made. We can also mail you future catalogs, lists, flyers, etc.

BUY/SELL/TRADE

Phone/mail/appointment only. Not a store. Inventory not at this location. Leave a message if we're not in. We will return calls. No collect calls please.

JASON W LEHTO

WANTED

VINTAGE MOVIE POSTERS & LOBBY CARDS

FROM 1900 TO 1976

IF YOU HAVE QUALITY POSTERS FOR SALE, WE WOULD LIKE TO PURCHASE THEM FOR CASH! NO TRADE OFFERS. NO CONSIGNMENTS. JUST CASH.

STEPHEN FISHLER
873 Broadway, Suite 201 New York, NY 10003
212-260-4147 Fax: 212-260-4304

WANTED

COMIC BOOK

ART

COMIC STRIP ART

BEFORE YOU SELL YOUR ART, CALL ME. I CAN AND WILL PAY YOU MORE.

STEPHEN FISHLER
873 Broadway, Suite 201 New York, NY 10003
212-260-4147 Fax: 212-260-4304

J & S COMICS

BUYING

AT J & S COMICS, WE BUY:

- ★ ALL COMICS BEFORE 1966
- ★ ENTIRE COLLECTIONS, ANY SIZE
- ★ GOLDEN AGE KEY ISSUES
- ★ SILVER AGE KEY ISSUES
- ★ WAREHOUSES
- ★ INVENTORIES
- ★ ESTATES
- ★ SPORT AND NON-SPORT CARDS

GET YOUR BEST OFFER, THEN CALL US ! OR SHIP US YOUR COMICS *NOW* FOR AN IMMEDIATE, NO OBLIGATION OFFER!

(Write first before shipping any 1970-1994 comics)

J & S COMICS

COMICS!

WHY SHOULD YOU SELL YOUR COMICS TO J & S ?

① We've been buying collections since 1967.

② We've been advertising in this price guide for the last 20 years with no dissatisfied sellers.

③ We're fair, honest, and very easy to deal with.

④ We pay very *high* prices for your quality books and very *fair* prices for your lower grade books.

⑤ We pay your shipping costs.

⑥ We'll gladly travel to you to buy large or valuable collections in person.

⑦ We buy any size collection. 1 book or 1 million books.

SEND YOUR COMICS, LISTS, OR INQUIRIES TO:

J & S COMICS
P.O. BOX 2057
98 MADISON AVENUE
RED BANK, NJ 07701
732-615-0342

(11 AM - 8 PM EST, NO COLLECT CALLS)
FAX: 732-706-0102 (8PM - 11 AM ONLY)

COMICS INA FLASH!

Copyright DC

"THE KING OF BRONZE"

Quarterly Bronze Age Auctions

BUY-SELL-TRADE

Comics 1956 -1980

BUYING

Top prices paid

Immediate cash

Copyright DC

Copyright MCG

Copyright DC

SELLING

Strict grading

Free Catalogue with 1000's of items starting at $1.00!

Senior Overstreet Advisor

VISA & MASTERCARD Accepted

Send for Latest List:

Tony Starks P.O. Box 3611

Evansville, IN 47735 PH/FAX (812) 867-1149

COMIC BOOKS

(1955-Present)

BOUGHT • SOLD • TRADED

*** FOREIGN ORDERS WELCOMED ***

DC • MARVEL • DELL • GOLD KEY • ACG • CHARLTON • HARVEY CLASSICS • WARREN • ARCHIES (ALL TITLES) • DISNEY (GOOD SELECTION OF DELL, GOLD KEY, & GLADSTONE)

* SELLING *

ACCURATE GRADING • OVERSTREET Prices • Fast Dependable Service. Satisfaction Guaranteed Or Money Back. I work from want lists and remove what I have in stock and reserve for you alone. I DO NOT PRINT CATALOGS. Send SASE with WANT LIST For Speedy Reply.

BUYING

Pay up to 50% OF OVERSTREET for Books Needed in FINE or BETTER Condition.
NEED DISNEY 1938-1945 Dells & Mickey Mouse Magazines VG or Better

DONALD A. WHYTE

46 Greenwood Place

Buffalo, NY 14213-1424

Tel: (716) 882 2875

Mail Order Since 1968 with many Satisfied customers

I BUY

* My associates and I spent
over $700,000 in the last 18 months
buying comic books.

* I will travel to see your collection.
Will buy single books or whole collections.

* Not a dealer.
Because this is not how I make my living,
I can afford to pay more for your books.

And SELL

* I keep want lists. Send me yours.
* Trades Welcomed.

COMICS

and sports and non-sports cards, autographed items and other collectibles.

Ken Stribling
P.O. Box 16004
Jackson, MS 39236-6004
Phone: (601) 977-5254
Fax (601) 956-0857

ALWAYS LOOKING FOR COMIC FANZINES AND COMIC-RELATED BOOKS

Some comics my associates and I have bought or sold

Action 6,9,11-14,16-45,
Adventure 41-58, 60-72
All American 16-28,34,36
All Flash 1-3, 28
AllStar 1-21,23,25,26,28-35
Amaz.Spiderman 1-150
Batman 1-12,22 Annual 1-3
Capt.America 1,6-8,10-12
Capt.Marvel 1-75
Detective 30-56,59-63
Exciting 11,13,16,23
Fantastic Four 4,6,8-150
Fight 1-86
Flash 4-16,18,20-24
Green Lantern 1-3
Hit 2-4, 13-15,18
Hulk 1, Incredible Hulk 181
Jumbo 1-167
Marvel Mystery 2-7,10-22
More Fun 54-88
Mystery Men 1,3-5,8-10,12
National 1,4-9,11-13,15-16
NY Worlds Fair 1939,1940
Phantom Lady 13-20,22
Planet 1-73
Police 1-102
Rangers 1-69
Sensation 1-33,40
Silver Streak 2,4,7-9,13,15
Silver Surfer 1-18
Superman 1-16,18-23
WDCS 37,46,48,64,86
Wonder Comics/World 1-12
Worlds Finest 1-20
Wonder Woman 1-11, 21
Whiz 1-50
XMen 2,4,9-66,94-140 GS1

PEGASUS HOBBIES!
THE LEADER IN BACK ISSUE SELECTION, SALES AND SERVICE.
ALWAYS BUYING SILVER AND GOLDEN AGE COLLECTIONS.
TOP PRICES PAID FOR:
DETECTIVE 27-38
BATMAN 1-20
ACTION 1 OR ANY OTHER KEY ISSUES.
Send us your want lists. Write for our catalog.
TWO SUPERSTORE LOCATIONS TO SERVE ALL YOUR COMIC AND HOBBY NEEDS
6554 GREENLEAF AVE.
WHITTIER, CA 90601
(562) 907-4663
FAX (562) 907-4665
5505 MORENO BLVD.
MONTCLAIR, CA 91763
(909) 931-4872
FAX (909) 949-6805
SONAMBULO © COPYRIGHT 1996 BY RAFAEL NAVARRO

Bonzai Comics

Is Proud To Announce A New Enterprise!

Cartoon And Comic Character Figures and Toys

FEATURING

WHATS-A-MATTA-U
EVERYTHING
ROCKY & BULLWINKLE

THE SONS OF SPRINGFIELD
EVERYTHING
SIMPSONS

TERRY TOWN
EVERYTHING
MIGHTY MOUSE

BUYING And SELLING

THESE AND OTHER RARE AND UNUSUAL ONE OF A KIND FIGURES

R.DAKIN-VILLE
EVERYTHING
DAKIN

CALL
212.502.3991

WE STILL HAVE A VAST COLLECTION OF UNDERGROUND COMIX AND AN INCREDIBLE SELECTION OF PRE-CODE BOOKS FOR SALE

Portfolios, Prints, Books, Fanzines, Original Art& Rarities By The Greatest Artists in Comics

Neal Adams
Bode
Brunner
Chaykin
Corben
Foster
Frazetta
Jeff Jones
Kaluta
Kirby
Kubert

©Frazetta

I also BUY!

©Barry Smith

Frank Miller
Pini
Sims
Smith
Starlin
Steranko
Stevens
Wagner
Williamson
Wood
Wrightson

Largest Selection in the world!

Long SASE with 3 stamps for list.

Wesley Tillander, PO Box 366, Morrow, GA 30260 (404) 361-7682

DR. DAVID J. ANDERSON, D.D.S.
5192 Dawes Avenue
Seminary Professional Village
Alexandria, VA 22311
Tel. (703) 671-7422
FAX (703) 578-1222

COLLECTOR BUYING MOST
PRE-1962 COMIC BOOKS
PARTICULARLY INTERESTED IN

- **Superheroes (all)**
  Guaranteed Top Dollar for any key expensive issues such as Action #1, Batman #1, Detective #27, Superman #1, etc.
- **Mystery**
- **Disney**
- **Humor**

- **Also buying comic-related items such as toys, rings, posters, art, etc.**

WHY SELL TO ME?

- This is a hobby, not a business - therefore, I can and will pay more.
- I have extensive collecting interests. I will buy entire collections, or individual pieces.
- Immediate cash is always available for purchases.

SEND ME A LIST OF WHAT YOU HAVE FOR A QUICK REPLY, OR GIVE ME A CALL (703) 671-7422

O'Leary's Books

- Comics - Gold, Silver, Bronze & Modern
- Toys
- Collectibles
- Role-Playing & Miniature Hobby Games

- Huge Selection Of Back Issues -
- Professional Grading & Pricing -
- We BUY Gold, Silver, & Bronze Age Comics -
- Dependable & Reputable Service For Over 20 years -
- Mail Order Service To Anywhere In The World! -
- New Comic Subscription Service -

O'Leary's Books
3828 100th St. SW - Tacoma, WA 98499
(253) 588-2503 (800) 542-1791 (253) 589-9115 Fax

WWW.JHCOMICS.COM

GOLD & SILVER AGE COMICS
FOR SALE WITH SOLD PRICES REALIZED.

NOW YOU CAN SHOP FOR RARE COMICS
AND GET FREE VALUABLE INFORMATION
ON THE COMIC MARKET.

☑ FASTEST DOWNLOADING!
☑ UPDATED REGULARLY!

YOU'LL WANT TO ADD THIS TO YOUR LIST OF FAVORITE SITES!

10 CONSECUTIVE CBG CUSTOMER SERVICE AWARDS.
WE ALSO CARRY THE FINEST IN MYLAR® D COLLECTING SUPPLIES.

FAX, CALL, WRITE OR EMAIL
FOR FREE PRINTED CATALOG.

JEF HINDS COMICS

P.O. BOX 44803 • MADISON, WI 53744-4803
608-277-8750 • FAX 608-277-8775
JHCOMICS@AOL.COM
OR JHCOMICS@INXPRESS.NET

Mylar ™ Dupont

READ WHAT OUR CUSTOMERS HAVE TO SAY:

I'm very impressed with the short time it took to receive my order and the grading of my orders. Thank you for the great service.
Scott C.
Greenwood, SC

... Thank you for your fine service and fine comics.
Joseph S.
Mt. Hope, WV

Some days ago your parcel arrived and it was a very pleasant surprise! Your gradation of the comics is very advantageous for the buyer. Thank you very, very much for it!
Werner W.
Vohenstrauss, Germany

... Thank you for your attention to my order and prompt delivery service. I'm sure we'll be doing future business.
Steve H.
Kenner, LA

I've bought from you before and have always been happy. Thanks Jef.
Jeff S.
Hopkins, MN

... Again, I was very pleased with the condition/grading of the comics I bought from you.

A satisfied customer.
Kevin P.
Orlando, FL

"BUYING ALL PRE-1965 COMIC COLLECTIONS"

EM IRE® COMICS

▼ TWO GREAT LOCATIONS ▼

1176 MOUNT HOPE AVE.
ROCHESTER, N.Y. 14620
(716) 442-0371

375 STONE ROAD
ROCHESTER, N.Y. 14616
(716) 663-6877

BACK ISSUES

DECADES OF TITLES

COMIC BOOKS

NEW & OLD COMICS

COMIC RELATED

LARGE ASSORTMENT

COMIC SUPPLIES

BAGS & BOARDS

OPEN DAILY

PAYMENT OPTIONS

Checks, Major Credit Cards, & Money Orders Accepted

FAX (716) 442-7807

WANT LIST'S WELCOMED

LARGE BACK ISSUE SELECTION

DARK HORSE, DC, DELL, GOLDEN AGE, GOLD KEY, ECLIPSE, IMAGE, KITCHEN SINK, MALIBU, MARVEL, MODELS, NEW COMICS, NON-SPORT CARDS, PORTFOLIOS, POSTERS, SILVER AGE, SUPPLIES, T-SHIRTS, TRADE PAPERBACKS & MEMORABILIA . . .

MAIL ORDER AVAILABLE

SEND WANT LIST ALONG WITH S.A.S.E. FOR FREE BULLETIN AND QUICK REPLY!

© & ® 1995 EMPIRE COMICS, All Rights Reserved.

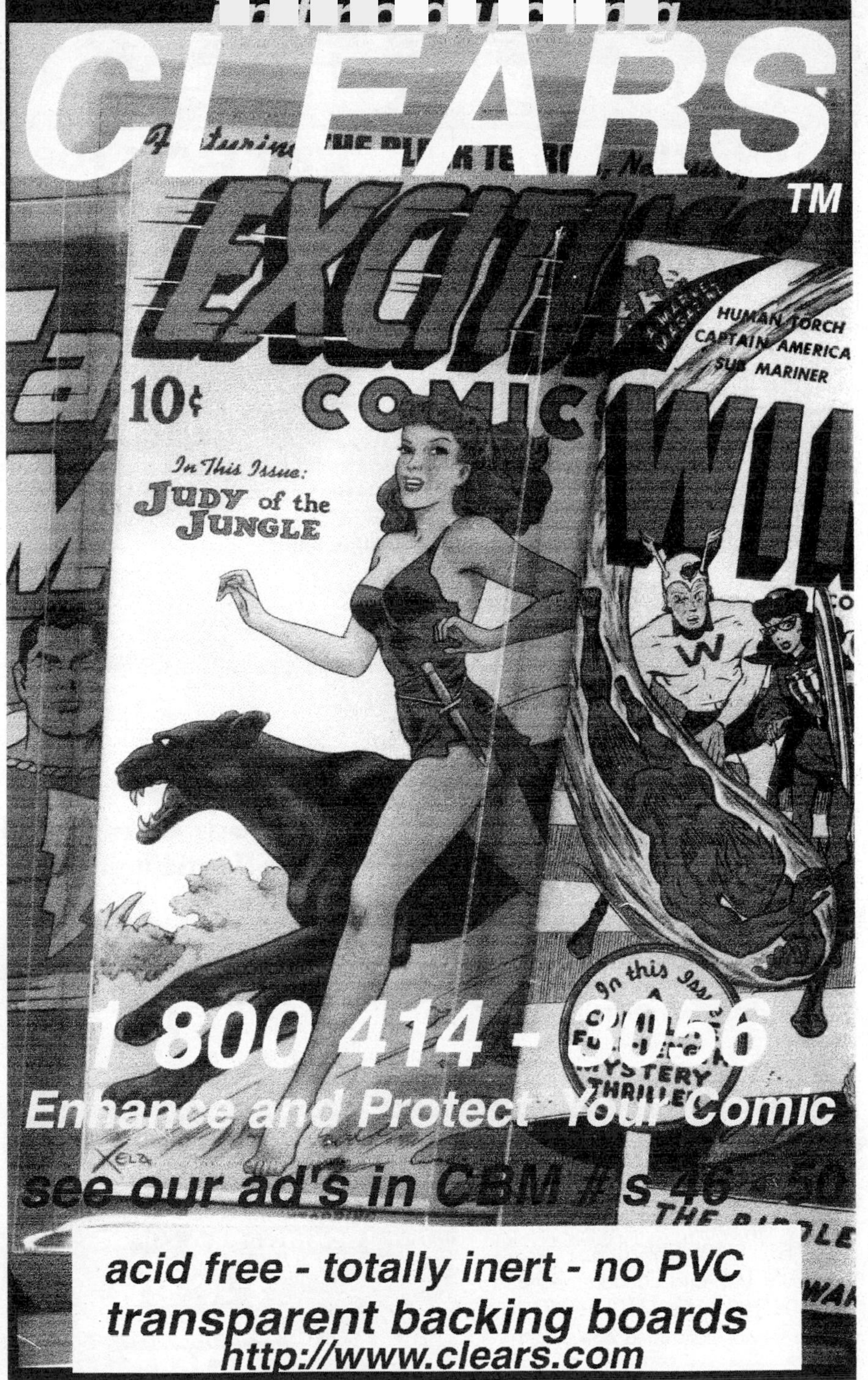
CLEARS
TM
10¢
In This Issue:
JUDY of the JUNGLE
HUMAN TORCH
CAPTAIN AMERICA
SUB MARINER
1 800 414 - 3056
Enhance and Protect Your Comic
see our ad's in CBM #s 46 - 50
acid free - totally inert - no PVC
transparent backing boards
http://www.clears.com

Protect Your Comics and Collectibles.

YOUR FIRST LINE OF DEFENSE.

Comics worth collecting are worth protecting. Count on Comic Defense System® ProBags®, Backer Boards, and Storage Boxes for Maximum Collection Protection at a minimum cost per comic.

Look for the symbol of Maximum Collection Protection at a comic shop near you.

WHO CARES FOR YOUR COMICS?

The ComiCare line is the perfect , low cost answer to your collectibles preservation needs. That's why for the past 14 years, collecting fans worldwide have relied on ComiCare's ComiCover bags—over 750 million sold!

The Economical Way to Protect Your Comics and Collectibles.

RETAILERS: To stock Comic Defense System and ComiCare products, call Diamond Comic Distributors at:

Diamond
Comic Distributors, Inc.

Phone: (800) 45-COMIC
Fax: (800) 329-2878
Outside the U.S. and Canada, phone (410) 560-7100 or fax (410) 560-7148
E-mail: service@diamondcomics.com

Ask your local comic book shop for the **Collecting Supplies Catalog**, a complete look at the top collecting supplies available today!

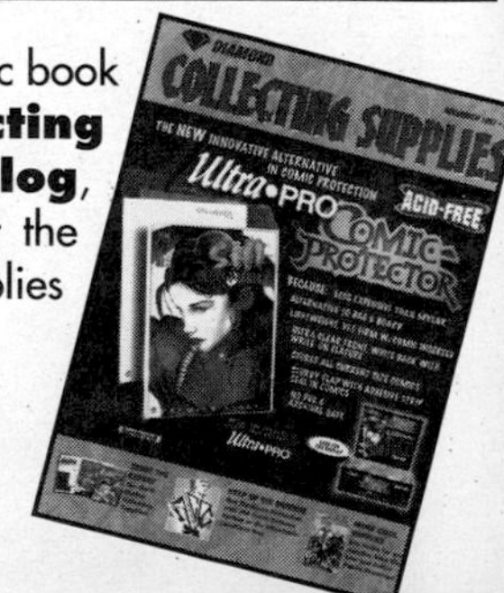

LOOKING FOR A COMICS SHOP NEAR YOU, CALL:

1-888 COMIC-BOOK

COMIC BOOKS FOR SALE

BRONZE AGE

©Lucasfilm/MEG

SILVER AGE

©MEG

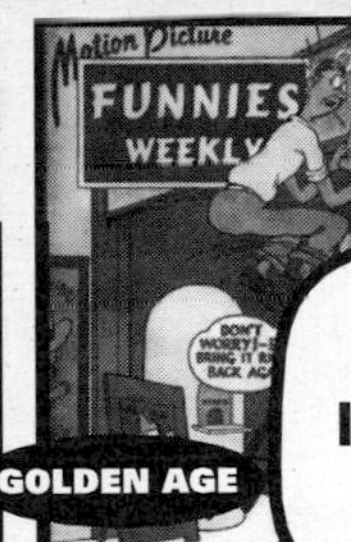

GOLDEN AGE

©First Funnies, Inc.

I *BUY* comic books, small or large collections! Before you sell CONTACT ME!

"WANT-LISTS" FILLED!

Send me your current want-lists along with a stamped, self-addressed envelope for a prompt reply!

JOHN MLACHNIK
"OVERSTREET" ADVISOR
P.O. BOX 69 • CHISHOLM, MN 55719
(218) 254-3763

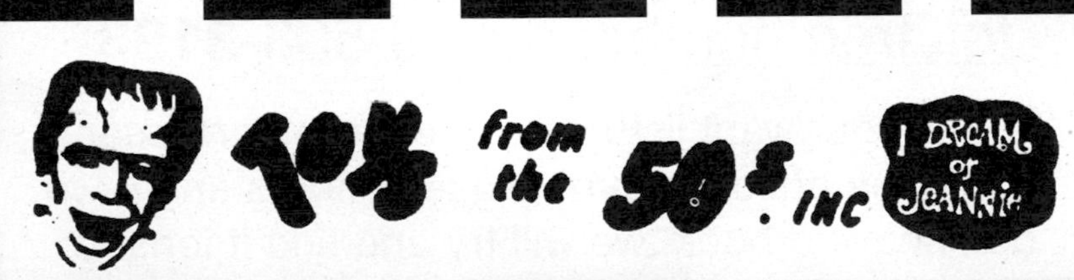

Specializing in 1960's Television Show Toys
Lunch Boxes, Halloween Costumes, Comics, Games

Peter & Christine Lutrario
"New York City Showroom"
110 West 25th St., Suite 805
New York, NY 10001

(212) 352-9182
WWW.TOYS-50s.COM

WE LOVE TO BUY COMICS!!

GEOFFREY'S

Batman & Robin are trademarks of **DC** Comics ©1997 All Rights Reserved
Captain Greedy ™ Geoffrey Comics

LA's Leader in Old & Hot Comics

We love comics!! We live comics!! We are regular advisors for Overstreet® and Geoffrey was named in Wizard #62 "Comics Number One Fan" and FX Collectibles 1997 "Most Passionate Fan!"

Catalogue available for $1. Call us on our toll free number **1-888-538-3198**

FAX us your want list!! We have trade agreements with some of comicdoms biggest stores and if we don't have a book, we will try and find it for you.

Highest prices paid for your old comics!

Geoffrey's Comics

15530 Crenshaw Blvd.

Gardena, CA 90249

(310) 538-3198

"Just a few miles from the LA airport."

Collect Comics?

We Do Golden, Silver & Bronze Back Issue Mail Order Right!
Here's what a few of our many satisfied customers say!

"RTS prices are very competitive, with excellent grading and rapid service."
-Doug Dripps,
St. Louis MO

"RTS is the perfect model of a professional, well organized comic book mail order company. I've never been disappointed!"
-Daryl Danforth, W Springfield MA

RTS is "Very responsive & professional. Comics were very well packaged & I appreciate the extra service."
-Stephen Combs,
Xenia OH

"Employee relations with the customer are unparalleled."
-Mark Mueller,
Newport VA

"You filled my want list!! Thanks for everything!!"
-James Sartell,
Manchster NH

"I must say that your overall professional service has simply been second to none and in terms of delivery the ASM #17 arrived faster than any comic ever ordered from the U.S.A. I hope to do business with you again.... I probably should have contacted you a couple years ago!"-Ian Faris, Yorks England

RTS Unlimited, Inc.

RTS Unlimited, Inc.
P.O. Box 150412
Lakewood CO 80215
24 Hour Phone Line:
(303)-403-1840
Fax: (303)-403-1837

CBG
Customer Service Award - 1997

Call, write, or fax for our huge free catalog!!
Authorized Fortress Dealer.
Dedicated to customer satisfaction!
Specialists in pre-1990 comic books.
Send us your want lists!

I WANT TO BUY YOUR JUNKIE OLD COMICS.

I WILL PAY YOU FOR POOR TO VERY FINE GOLDEN AGE SUPERHERO COMICS. I ALSO WANT HORROR, ROMANCE, WAR AND CRIME COMICS.

EX: YOUNG MEN #24 200%

TIMELY : 50-200%
ATLAS : 40-200%
COVERLESS: 10-100% OF "G"
INCOMPLETE: 5-70% OF "G"
HARVEY: 50-80%
DC GOLDEN AGE: 50-150%
MLJ/: 50-100%
SILVER AGE: 10-50%
ALL OTHERS: 20-200%

TERRY'S COMICS

P.O. BOX 471, ATWOOD, CA. 92811-0471
CALL OR SEND LIST FOR PRICE QUOTES.
(714) 528-3937

I ALSO SELL COMICS!

MOST COMICS I SELL ARE AT A DISCOUNT! HOW MUCH DEPENDS ON TYPE & DEMAND.
I SPECIALIZE IN LOWER GRADE SCARCE & HIGH DEMAND BOOKS.
SO SEND YOUR WANTLISTS & LOOK FOR MY ADDS IN THE CBG.

FORBIDDEN PLANET

THE SCIENCE FICTION MEGASTORE

* TOYS * GAMES * VIDEOS * MASKS *
* MODELS * HOBBY SUPPLIES * T-SHIRTS *
* PULPS * MAGAZINES * FANZINES *
* TRADING CARDS * CALENDARS *
* POSTERS * GREETING CARDS *

* BOOKS: SCIENCE FICTION * HORROR *
* FANTASY * ANIMATION * ART * CINEMA *
* TELEVISION * LIMITED EDITIONS *

* COMICS * GRAPHIC NOVELS *
* COMIC STRIP COLLECTIONS *

840 BROADWAY AT 13 ST. ▼ NYC 10003 212-473-1576
10AM-8:30PM EVERYDAY ▼ MAIL ORDER 212-475-6161

Capital City Comics

1910 Monroe Street
Madison, WI 53711
Mon-Fri: 11-7
Sat: 10-5
Phone (608) 251-8445

2625 N. Downer Ave.
Milwaukee, WI 53211
Mon-Fri: 11-7
Sat: 10-5
Phone: (414) 332-8199

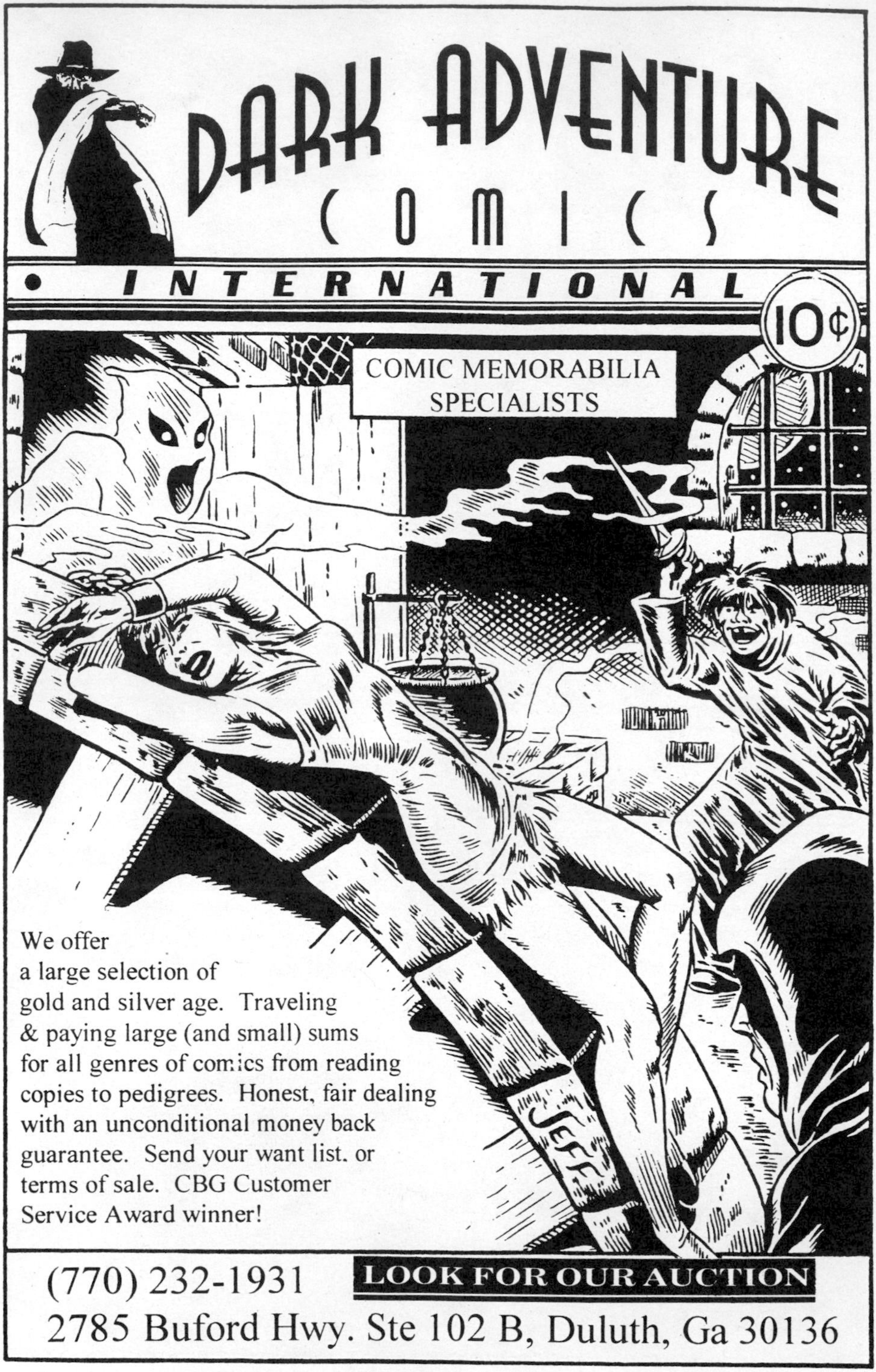

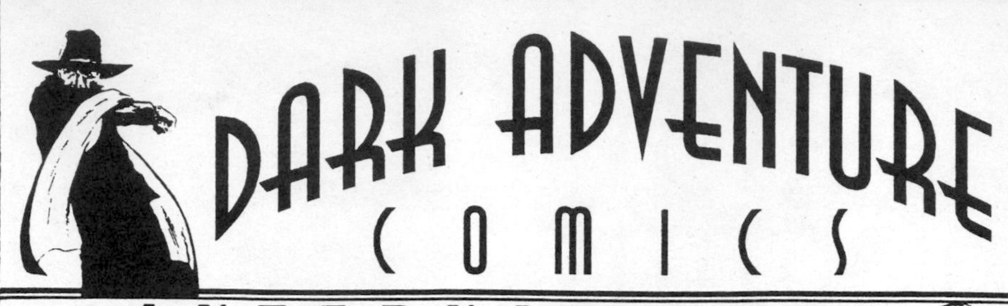

DARK ADVENTURE
COMICS
INTERNATIONAL
10¢
COMIC MEMORABILIA
SPECIALISTS
We offer
a large selection of
gold and silver age. Traveling
& paying large (and small) sums
for all genres of comics from reading
copies to pedigrees. Honest, fair dealing
with an unconditional money back
guarantee. Send your want list. or
terms of sale. CBG Customer
Service Award winner!
JEFF
(770) 232-1931
LOOK FOR OUR AUCTION
2785 Buford Hwy. Ste 102 B, Duluth, Ga 30136

Shop The

COMICS SUPER STORE!

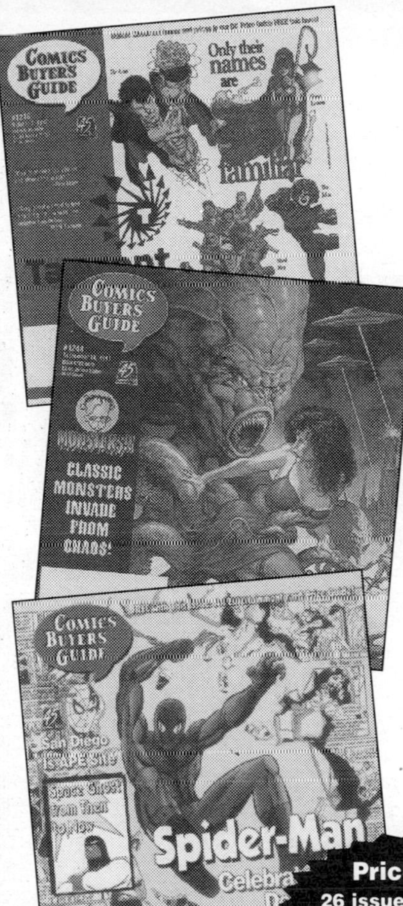

Looking for the largest marketplace for comics buyers and sellers?

Shop the pages of Comics Buyers Guide!

Every issue is loaded with:

- Thousands of listings for Golden, Silver, Platinum, and Modern comics issues
- Comics collectibles, artwork, figurines and memorabilia to buy & sell
- New listings every week!

Also included at no extra charge:

- The best artists and writers in the world of comics!
- Entertaining features from comics industry insiders
- Original artwork and comic strips not found anywhere else
- Weekly columns on the latest in comics news - new releases, reviews, and opinions

For over 25 years the # 1 resource for comics collectors —

Comics Buyer's Guide!

Price Check!
26 issues only $19.95!
Save 74%
off the cover price!

For Fast, Friendly Service Use Your Credit Card! Place your order today!

Call Toll Free • **800-258-0929** • Dept. ABAR3Y

M-F 7am - 8pm; Sat. 8am - 2pm CT

To order by mail send us your name & address with payment to:

Comics Buyer's Guide, Circulation Dept. ABAR3Y
700 E. State St., Iola, WI 54990-0001

You'll also find Comics Buyer's Guide at your favorite comics shop - Just ask for it!

Browse our web site: **www.krause.com**

Having trouble selling YOUR COLLECTION?

-LET- DOLGOFF do it, for you!!!

"I've got the connections to sell your COLLECTIONS!!!"

GARY DOLGOFF COMICS: (New Address)
116 Pleasant St, Easthampton, MA 01027
Phone: 413 529-0326 FAX: 413 529-9824
E-MAIL:gdcomics@JAVANET.COM

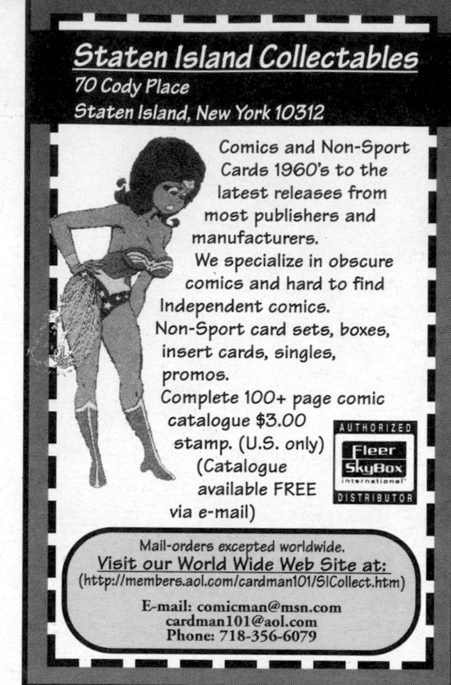

Staten Island Collectables
70 Cody Place
Staten Island, New York 10312
Comics and Non-Sport Cards 1960's to the latest releases from most publishers and manufacturers.
We specialize in obscure comics and hard to find Independent comics.
Non-Sport card sets, boxes, insert cards, singles, promos.
Complete 100+ page comic catalogue $3.00 stamp. (U.S. only) (Catalogue available FREE via e-mail)
AUTHORIZED Fleer SkyBox International DISTRIBUTOR
Mail-orders excepted worldwide.
Visit our World Wide Web Site at:
(http://members.aol.com/cardman101/SICollect.htm)
E-mail: comicman@msn.com
cardman101@aol.com
Phone: 718-356-6079

Buying - Selling

Golden-Age to Current Comic-Books & Comic-Related Items, Anime/Manga.

Free Catalog

send a self-addressed stamped envelope to : **All Colour productions**

P.O. Box 808 • Cardiff-by-the-Sea, California, 92007 • (760)753-3280

Storyteller

Comics, Cards, Books and Games

Thousands of Back Issue Comics
Pre-Code Crime, Horror, Sci-Fi, War
Prompt Response to Want Lists
Subscription/Mail Order Anywhere
Always Buying

520 Sixth Street
Rapid City, SD 57701
Ph/Fax 605-348-7242
E-Mail: story@rapidcity.com

TROPIC COMICS

313 S. STATE RD. 7 PLANTATION, FL 33317
(954) 587-8878 FAX: (954) 587-0409

INTERNATIONAL MAIL-ORDER SERVICE

TROPIC SOUTH

1870 N.E. 163RD. ST. N.MIAMI BEACH, FL 33162
(305) 940-8700 FAX: (305) 940-1551

WWW.TROPICCOMICS.COM
WWW.ABOMBCOMICS.COM

RESTORATIONS

Sierra Restoration Services

- Professional comic book and original art restoration services
- 17 years of professional archival and preservation experience
- References always available
- We now utilize technological advances in comic book and paper restorations
- Please call for more information, an over the phone estimate, or to have a Sierra Restoration Services Package sent to you
- $30.00 an hour
- We have always had a completion period of 4-6 weeks

Shawn Leubner, Conservator
Sierra Restoration Services
P.O. Box 1072
Grass Valley, CA 95945
(530) 265-6101

MAKE MINE MARVEL
1960s Marvel Memorabilia WANTED!
• 60s Marvel T-Shirts
• Marvelmania/M.M.M.S. Fan Club
• Buttons/Portfolios (Kirby,etc.)
• Captain Action toys
• Spider-Man toys
• Romita, Sr. original art
• 60s Batman toys
• Superman flicker rings
• Quisp/Quake cereal premiums
Contact: Aaron Sultan
3201 Arrowwood Dr.
Raleigh, NC 27604
919-954-7111

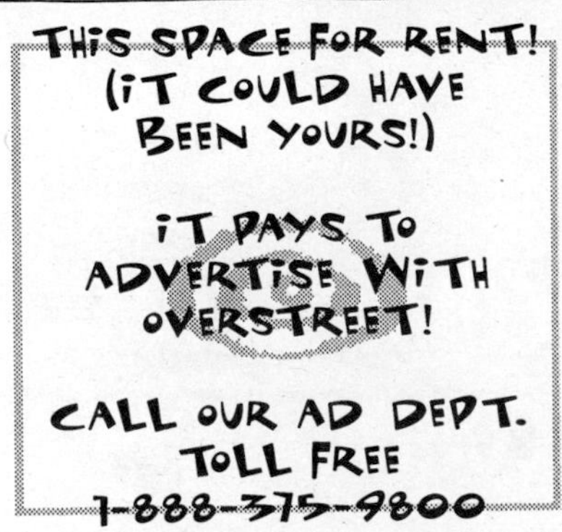
THIS SPACE FOR RENT!
(IT COULD HAVE BEEN YOURS!)
IT PAYS TO ADVERTISE WITH OVERSTREET!
CALL OUR AD DEPT. TOLL FREE
1-888-375-9800

CLASSIC COMICS AND CLASSICS ILLUSTRATED

Classic Comics/Illustrated and all related items.
Send for **FREE CATALOG**

Phillip Gaudino
49 Park Ave.
Port Washington, NY 11050

BUYING OR SELLING–
Call (516) 883-5659
nightly 7 to 10 p.m.

AT YOUR SERVICE SUBSCRIPTIONS

Proudly entering our 9th year of satisfying Comic Fans Worldwide !!

While others have come and gone, we're still doin' our thing!

Let us be your monthly source for New Comics and related items.

We believe in the ***four "S" approach*** to deserving your business:

Savings - **30%** off cover on your new Comics and similar discounts on every item sold! None of this "up to" business! 30% off - every publisher !

Selection - you can order **anything** from Diamond's *Previews* or Heroes World's *Marvel Vision* catalogs.

Simplicity - you simply *order what you want* each and every month. All you really need to do is open your shipment and *enjoy* your comics!

Service - *prompt* attention to your questions or problems. We remember what it's like to be in your shoes!

Here's what else you get:

- Complete Computer Invoicing gives us unbelievable accuracy!
- Monthly ordering allows you to choose exactly which comics you want each month!
- Order via Mail, Phone, Fax or E-Mail! It can't be easier!
- **NM Guarantee** of New Comics with our custom-made shipping boxes & expert packing, using environmentally safe *Eco Foam* Packing material!
- Referral Bonus: spread the word and you can get ***your comics for free***!
- Tons of **Back Issues** - Silver Age, too!
- We specialize in **Small Press** and those hard-to-find **Adult Comics** that your local store is afraid to carry!!

If your current supplier isn't providing you these four "S"'s, why stay with them? If you aren't reading our monthly newsletter, **"Hot Off the Press"**, my friends, *you're paying too much and getting too little!*

Please send **$ 3.00** for an introductory ordering packet, and when you place your order, take a **$ 4.00 credit** !! There's another buck to save !

AT YOUR SERVICE SUBSCRIPTIONS

17815 DAVENPORT ROAD, SUITE 230
DALLAS, TEXAS 75252
972-931-3393 if you want to yak at us
972-931-3789 to fax us your info
comics@dallas.net for you Net-Heads!

CHECK US OUT ON THE WWW AT: ***http://www.comicsbymail.com/comics***

BRAND NEW CATALOGUE IS NOW READY!

Order our brand new 68 page fully illustrated TV Guide catalogue now. Some experts say it's the greatest TV Guide reference book ever containing every TV Guide from Issue #1 to the present, hundreds of TV supplements and pre-nationals. Shop at home and order with complete confidence from one of the oldest and most reliable mail order companies in the business. "*Lenore's TV Guides*" is a division of "*Lenore Levine, Rare & Esoteric Books*". We are very proud to say that...

"We Have the Largest Inventory of TV Guides in North America".

This catalogue comes with a written guarantee.

We will not be undersold by any full time TV Guide Dealer who publishes a TV Guide catalogue. We will beat their prices. Guaranteed.

SEE CATALOGUE FOR DETAILS. We welcome foreign orders.

Send $3.00 for catalogue to: *LENORE LEVINE*
P.O. Box 246-PG, Three Bridges, NJ 08887
Phone: 908-788-0532 Fax: 908-788-1028

LENORE LEVINE, RARE & ESOTERIC BOOKS

(Formerly Philip M. Levine & Sons)

P.O. Box 246-PG, Three Bridges, NJ 08887 • Phone 908-788-0532 Fax 908-788-1028

SEND US ALL OF YOUR PRE-1975 COMIC BOOKS TODAY

We will make you an immediate cash offer. If we don't buy your books, we will pay "book rate postage" both ways. We are always buying and selling comics, giveaway comics, Big Little Books, old paperbacks, Seduction of the Innocent and related censorship material, radio premiums, early crime magazines, "Cardboard Age" comics, antediluvian comics and related material, pulps, Catechetical Guild comics and related material, Golden Age comics, Silver Age comics, old toys and gum cards. We have the largest inventory of old "TV Guides" in North America. Send us your name and address today to get on our mailing list.

You can come and see us at all the Atlantique City Shows, all Baltimore Collectors Marts in Pikesville, MD., all New York Area Collectible Shows and all Wex-Rex Shows, Chicago Comic Con, Motor City Comic Cons, Allentown Pennsylvania Paper Fairs and the San Diego Comic Con.

Don't forget to send us your books. We have been buying and selling comic books for 43 years.

WE WELCOME FOREIGN ORDERS!

WORLD'S GREATEST BACK ISSUE SHOP-AT-HOME SERVICE

THE WORLD'S GREATEST ESOTERIC COMIC DEALER!

Buying Bettie Page Stuff. Please send what you have today.

WE NEED MAD MAGAZINES AND ALL MAD COLLECTIBLES. SEND YOURS TODAY!

SEND US YOUR WANT LIST TODAY!

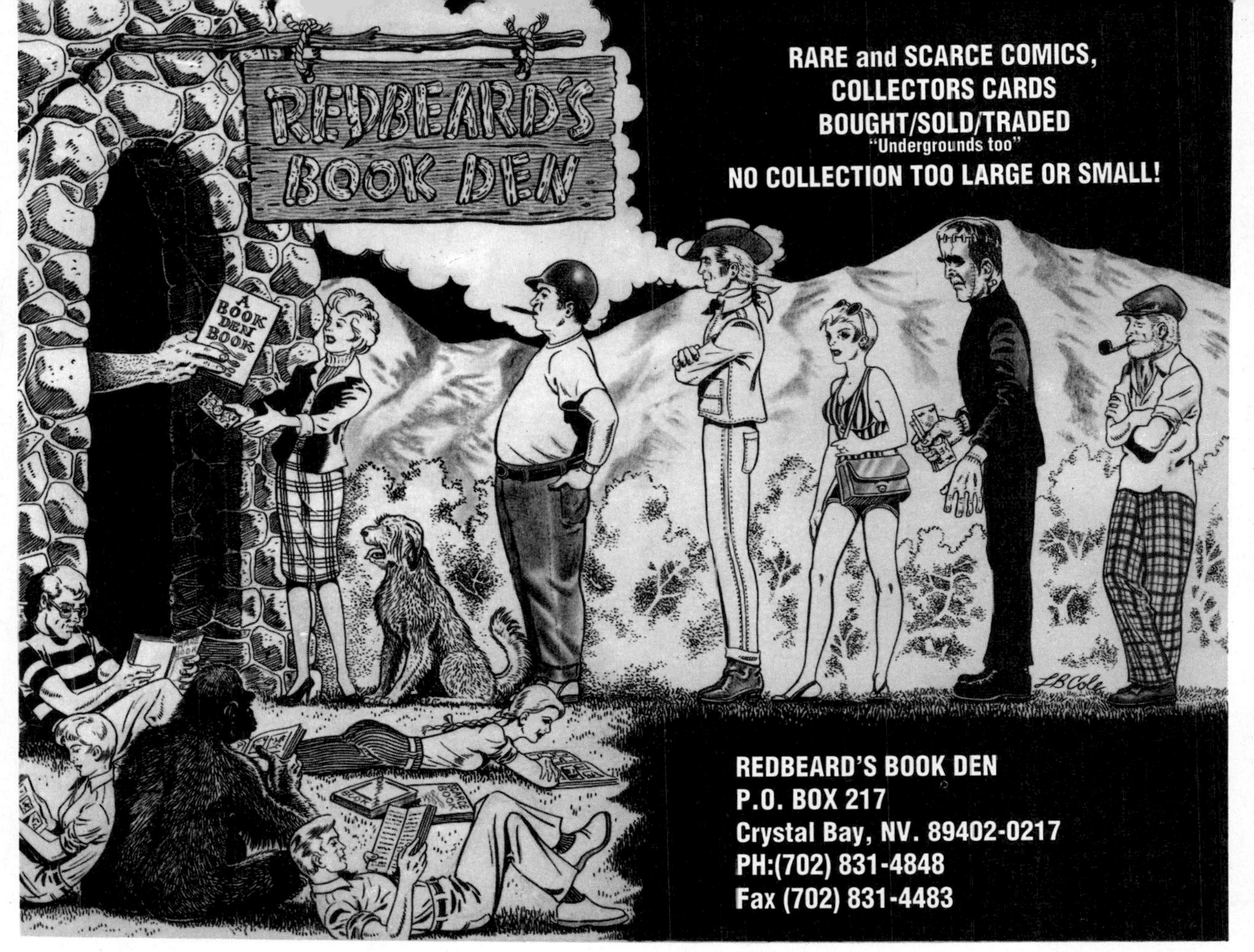
REDBEARD'S BOOK DEN
A BOOK DEN BOOK
RARE and SCARCE COMICS,
COLLECTORS CARDS
BOUGHT/SOLD/TRADED
"Undergrounds too"
NO COLLECTION TOO LARGE OR SMALL!
LB Cole
REDBEARD'S BOOK DEN
P.O. BOX 217
Crystal Bay, NV. 89402-0217
PH:(702) 831-4848
Fax (702) 831-4483

Philip Weiss Auctions, Inc.™

3520 Lawson Boulevard, Oceanside, New York 11572

Tel: (516) 594-0731 FAX: (516) 594-9414

✔Don't miss any of the great AUCTION ACTION!!
FOUR big mail-phone sales annually, featuring the best in comics.
IN ADDITION, DON'T MISS OUR MONTHLY LIVE AUCTIONS.

✔Comic Art•Big Little Books•Pop-ups•Toys•Pulps & Pulp Art
Science Fiction•Paperbacks & Hardbacks
Boys & Girls Series Books•Animation Art• Disney Art

✔Fully illustrated single catalogue: $8 (US), $10 (Can), & $12 (Foreign)
Subscriptions: $30 (US), $36 (Can), & $40 (Foreign)

✔CONSIGNMENTS always wanted (Individual items & entire collections).
Low end or top of the market.

OUTRIGHT PURCHASE ALWAYS • CASH ADVANCE OPTION
Licensed, Bonded, and Insured

THE COMIC GUIDE

Edited by Frank Plowright

- The first comprehensive critical reference to collectable comics
- Contains reviews and analysis of well over 2,500 titles, from the early days to the present, from mainstream to underground comics, from horror to erotic, from children's to adult
- Covers the full range of American comics and the best of translated European comics, from *Spiderman* to *Tintin*, from *Batman* to the work of Robert Crumb, from *Love & Rockets* to *Moebius*, from *Spawn* to *Pratt*
- Contains an extensive creator index and recommendations.

Available at your local comic book store, through Diamond Distributors, or directly through London Bridge. To order directly call 1-800-805-1083 or fax 1-800-481-6207. Individual orders accepted.

1-85410-4861 paperback $29.95

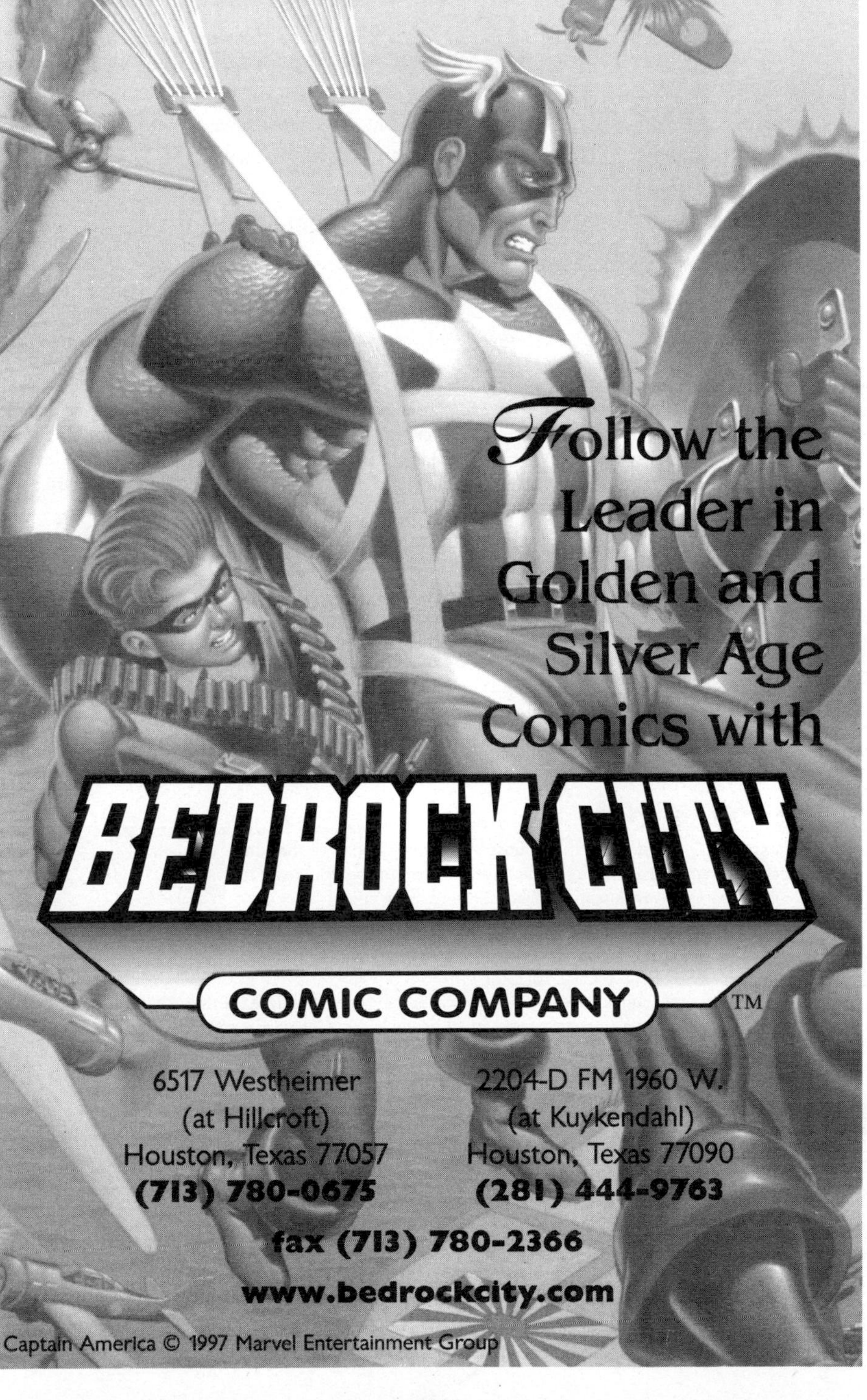
Follow the
Leader in
Golden and
Silver Age
Comics with
BEDROCK CITY
COMIC COMPANY
TM
6517 Westheimer
(at Hillcroft)
Houston, Texas 77057
(713) 780-0675
2204-D FM 1960 W.
(at Kuykendahl)
Houston, Texas 77090
(281) 444-9763
fax (713) 780-2366
www.bedrockcity.com
Captain America © 1997 Marvel Entertainment Group

If you're serious about selling comics, Diamond can deliver for you.

Established in 1982, Diamond Comic Distributors is the world's largest distributor of English-language comics and related merchandise.

Our growth is a direct result of delivering one thing to comic book specialty retailers: **the best.**

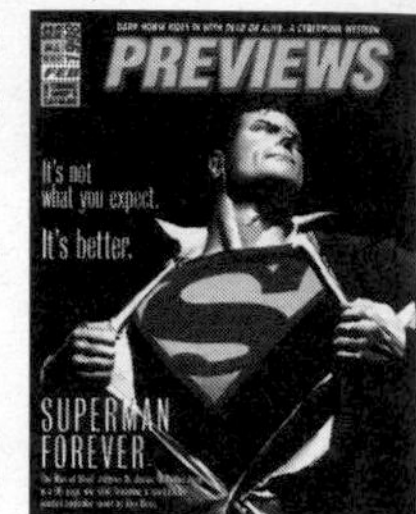

Our monthly Previews catalog contains over 3,000 items for retail stores to order!

The Best Products and Discounts

Our *Previews* catalog offers retailers and consumers comics from hundreds of suppliers every month. Plus, Diamond is the comic book specialty retailers' exclusive source of products from Acclaim, Dark Horse, DC Comics, Image, Marvel Comics, Wizard Entertainment and a host of other fine suppliers.

We also offer a wide variety of comics-related merchandise including graphic novels, trading cards, toys, collectible card games , and more — all at highly competitive discounts!

Diamond is the exclusive distributor of these and many other fine comics publishers.

The Best Shipping

Every product we sell is backed by our fast, accurate, and reliable distribution network. Located throughout the world, every facility is staffed with knowledgeable professionals trained to deliver your shipments with maximum speed and efficiency.

The Best Service

Diamond's "One Call Does It All" Customer Service ensures that the products you want, the answers you need, and the attention you deserve are available to you with just a toll-free phone call or fax to your personal Diamond Customer Service Representative!

The Best Business Partner

At Diamond, we understand that our success depends upon you. That's why we invite you to share your questions, comments, and opinions with us. Your feedback helps us refine and add to the quality services we offer our customers.

You can depend on us because we depend on you.

RETAILERS: To find out more about Diamond, contact our Home Office Customer Service Department today at **(800)-45-COMIC!**

1966 Greenspring Drive, Suite 300 • Timonium, MD USA 21093
Phone: (800) 452-6642/(410) 560-7100 • Fax: (800) 329-2878/(410) 560-7148
E-mail: service@diamondcomics.com • Internet: www.diamondcomics.com

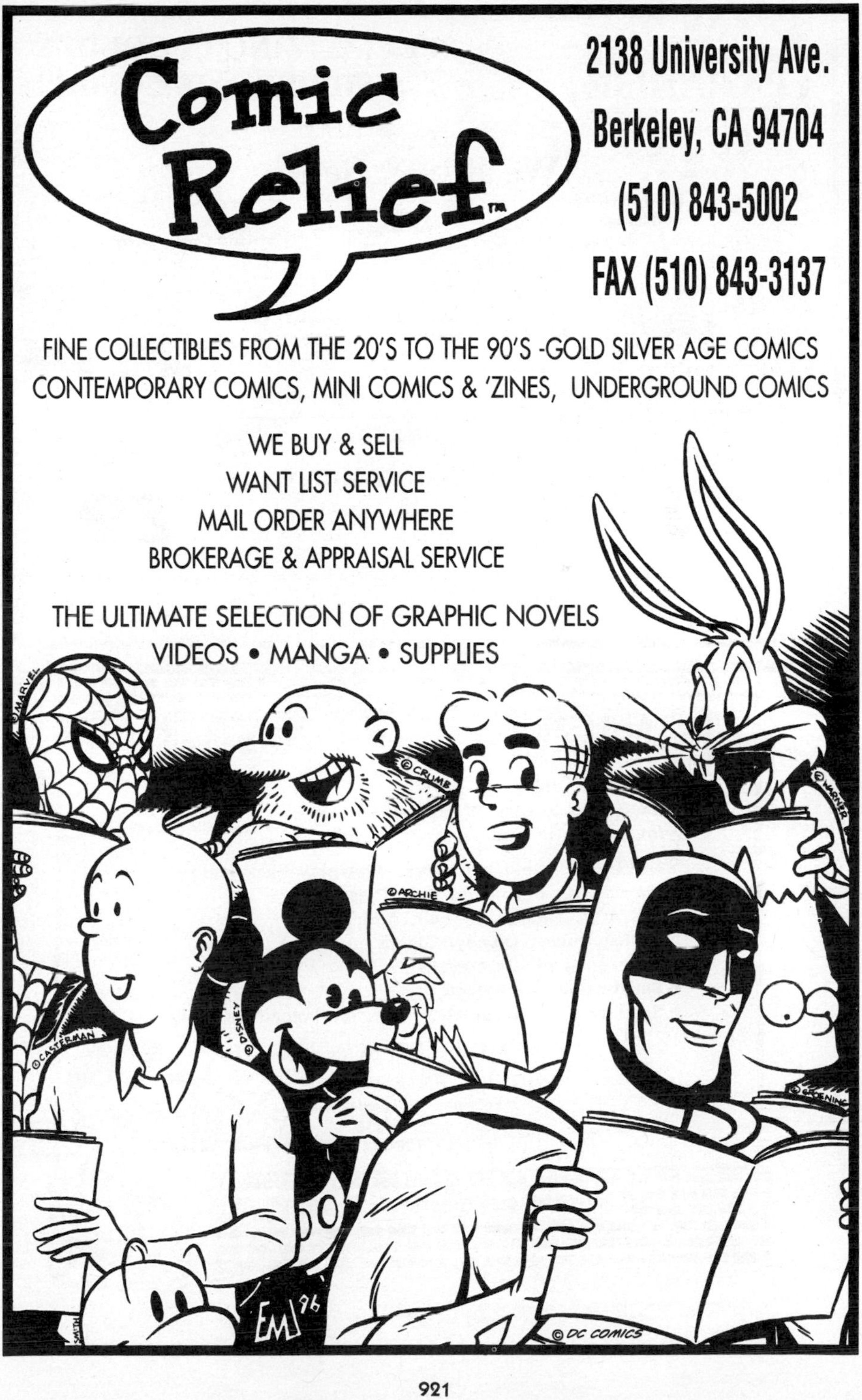

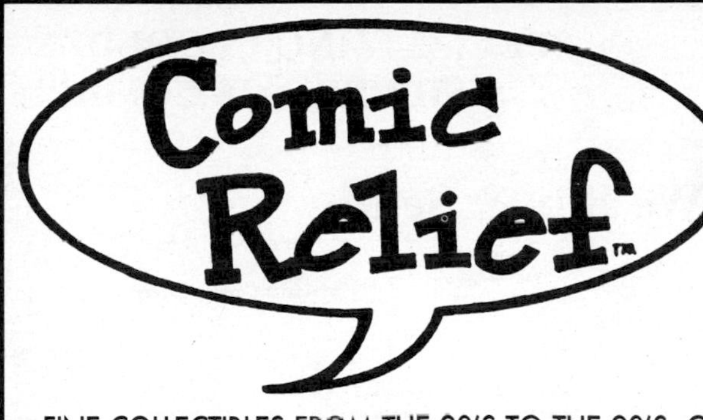

2138 University Ave.
Berkeley, CA 94704
(510) 843-5002
FAX (510) 843-3137

FINE COLLECTIBLES FROM THE 20'S TO THE 90'S -GOLD SILVER AGE COMICS
CONTEMPORARY COMICS, MINI COMICS & 'ZINES, UNDERGROUND COMICS

WE BUY & SELL
WANT LIST SERVICE
MAIL ORDER ANYWHERE
BROKERAGE & APPRAISAL SERVICE

THE ULTIMATE SELECTION OF GRAPHIC NOVELS
VIDEOS • MANGA • SUPPLIES

SPECIALIZING IN GOLDEN & SILVER AGE COMICS

We Buy & Sell!!

Golden & Silver Age
Gaming
Comic & Card Supplies

New & Old Figures
All Collectables
Movie & Comic Posters

and more!!

Full Want List Services • Accurate Grading •
No Collection Too Big or Small • Competitive Pricing •
Many Comics Priced Below Guide

New Catalogue Available - Send $1.00 - Refundable With First Order

Come Visit Us In The Heart Of Toronto

PARADISE COMICS

VISA

(416) 487-9807

3278 YONGE STREET TORONTO, CANADA M4N 2L6

COMICS BOUGHT & SOLD

BUYING: 1940's to 1975
- Paying up to 50% Of Overstreet prices for comics in Fine or better condition

SELLING: Gold and Silver Age plus back issues
- Marvel, DC, Dell, Gold Key, Classics, EC, ACG, Timely, Fawcett, Archies, Fiction House, Disney, Others
- Thousands of titles available
- Satisfaction guaranteed
- Send your want list and SASE for immediate reply

FOREIGN ORDERS ACCEPTED

PHOENIX ENTERPRISES
223 Fairview Rd. Dept. PG
Erin, N. Y. 14838
Tel (607) 796-2547

SAN MATEO ORIGINAL ART

We have one of the finest selections of Original Art around, more than 15,000 Covers, Pages, Splashes.Complete Stories, Daily Sunday Strips, Cover Paintings, Animation Drawings/Cels. **Many Artists**: ADAMS, ADKINS, ALCALA, ANDERSON, ANDRU, APARO, AYERS, BACHALO, BARKS, BINGHAM, BISSETTE, BOLLAND, BORING, BREYFOGLE, BRIGHT, BRODERICK, BROWN, BRUNNER, BUCKLER, BUSCEMA, BYRNE, CHADWICK, CHAYKIN, CIROCCO, COCKRUM, COLAN, COLON, COWAN, CRANDALL, CULLINS, DAVIS, DAY, DELBO, DEMULDER, DE STEFANO, DEZUNIGA, DIILLIN, DITKO, DODSON, DUURSEMA, DRAKE, EASTMAN AND LAIRD, EISNER, EVERETT, FINE, FRADON, FRAZETTA, FRENZ, GARCIA LOPEZ, GIFFEN, GIOLETI, GIORDANO, GLANSMAN, GOLDEN, GRELL,GROSS, GUICE, GULACY, HAMILTON, HANNIGAN, HARRIS, HECK, HEMBECK, HERNANDEZ BROS., HOBERG, HOWELL,HUGHES,INFANTINO, JANSON, JONES, JURGENS, KALUTA, KANE, KAYANAN, KIDA,KIETH, KIRBY, KUBERT, KUPPERBERG, LAROCQUE, LAYTON, LEIALOHA, LEIBER, LIEFELD, LIGHTLE, MACFARLANE, MAGUIRE, MANNING, MAYERICK, MCDONNELL, MCMANUS, MESSMER, MIGNOLA, MILGROM, MILLER, MOLDOFF, MOONEY, MORROW, MUTH, NEBRES, NEWTON, NINO, NOVICK, NOWLAN, O'NEILL, ORDWAY, PEREZ, H.G. PETER, PLOOG, POWELL, PURCELL, RABOY, RANDALL, RAYMOND, ROBBINS, ROGERS, ROMITA, ROSS, ROTH, RUSSELL, SAVIUK, SCHAFFENBERGER, SEKOWSKY, SEVERIN, SHAW, SHELTON, SHOOTER, SIENKIEWICZ, SIM, SIMONSON, SMITH, STARLIN, STATON, STERANKO, SUTTON, SUYDAM, SWAN, THORNE, TOTH, TOTLEBEN, TUSKA, VALLEJO, VEITCH, VESS, VON EDEN, VOSBERG, WAGNER, WARD, WHEELAN, WILLIAMSON, WILLINGHAM, WOCH, WOOD, WRIGHTSON, YEATES, ZECK.and **Companies**: MARVEL, D.C., VERTIGO, VALIANT, IMAGE, DARK HORSE, ULTRAVERSE, ECLIPSE, FIRST, DELL, ARCHIE.

Send $3.00, $4.00 for foreign orders (refunded on 1st order) for a giant 100+ page catalog on disk (identify mac or pc) to: **San Mateo Comic Art, 65 Lyell St, Los Altos, California 94022. 650-917-8477 fax 650-917-8478**

ORIGINAL ART SPECIALS—Our pick of 5 pages from Marvel-$35; 10 pages from Marvel-$60; 5 D.C. pages-$30; 10 D.C. pages-$50; 5 Marvel & D.C. pages-$30; 1 pencil page by Frank Brunner-$15; 1 main cell + bonus cells from Herb Trimpe's Crest Team vs. Cavity Creeps commercial-$15+ 3 different sets-$27. 1 pg. X-Factor or New Mutants-$30; 1 page from G.I. Joe-$20; 1 Star Trek Daily-$20; 1 page from Marvel's Secret Wars-$20; 1 Spiderman Daily-$40; 1 Spiderman Daily with no Spiderman-$20; 1 Spiderman page-$35; Harbinger page-$25; Magnus page-$35; Space 1999 page-$20. AnimalMan-$20; Archie page-$25.- Fiction House 40's-50's Good girl-$40./Western-$25.

MIX & MATCH—Nice pages featuring the following characters in costume: Angel, Avengers, Arak, Barren Earth, Batman, Beast, Bluedevil, Capt. America, Capt. Britain, Clea, Cloud, Conan, Darkhawk, Dazzler, Defenders, Dr. Strange, El Diablo, Falcon, Fantastic Four, Firehawk, Firestorm, Flash, Gargoyle, Godzilla, He-Man & Masters of the Universe, Hulk, Indiana Jones, Iron Fist, Ironman, Iceman, Jonah Hex, Kull, Legion of Superheroes, Leiko Wu, Mary Jane Parker, Moon Dragon, Jennifer Morgan, Omega Men, Peter Parker, Plastic Man, Powerman, Red Tomado, Robin, Rom, Sgt. Nick Fury, Shakira, Shang Chi, SheHulk, Shogun Warriors, Star Trek, Sundevils, Superfriends, Superman, Thor, Toxic Avenger, Transformers, V the t.v. series, Valda, Valkyrie, Vigilante, Warlord. Pick as many pages as you want—$20. 2 for $37.5; 5 for $85; 10 for $160. Add $5. ($10. foreign) Postage & Insurance on orders. We are interested in **buying large** or **small collections** of **original comic book** or **strip art**, plus quality collections of comic books and baseball card sets, stars & boxes, **toy collections:** Movie related, T.V. related, Star Wars, Star Trek, lunch boxes/thermoses; superhero action figures- Action, Mego, Toy Biz,Secret Wars, Superpowers.

Looking for contemporary or vintage art...Art Searches available...Send us your wish list **www.creative-interests.com/san-mateo-art/homepage.html**

Call our website URL to surf through the greatest selection online!

I AM A COLLECTOR
LOCATED IN THE SOUTHWEST
I PAY MORE
I AM BUYING GOLDEN AGE
& PRE-1965 SILVER AGE
COMICS & ORIGINAL ART
**LET ME MAKE YOU AN
OFFER BEFORE YOU SELL
TO ANYONE ELSE**
PAUL DEDOMENICO
P.O. Box 1322
Santa Fe, NM 87504
Tel/Fax: 505-995-0655
E-Mail: dedo@ix.netcom.com
****REFERENCES AVAILABLE****
WANT LISTS WELCOME

BUYING
CLASSIC COMICS AND CLASSICS ILLUSTRATED
Philip Gaudino
49 Park Ave.
Port Washington, NY 11050
(516) 883-5659

GRAB • BAG LOTS Take 30% off!

50	Different	Marvel	VF/NM	$20.00
100	Different	Marvel	VF/NM	$35.00
300	Mixed (150 diff.)	Marvel	VF/NM	$95.00
50	Different	DC	VF/NM	$22.00
100	Different	DC	VF/NM	$40.00
300	Mixed (150 diff.)	DC	VF/NM	$105.00
25	Different	IMAGE	VF/NM	$17.50
50	Different	INDEPENDENTS	VF/NM	$20.00
100	Different	INDEPENDENTS	VF/NM	$30.00
500	Mixed (250+diff.)	INDEPENDENTS	VF/NM	$135.00
800	Mixed (400 diff.)	INDEPENDENTS	VF/NM	$200.00
50	Different	MARV/DC/INDY'S	VF/NM	$20.00
100	Different	MARV/DC/INDY'S	VF/NM	$30.00
500	Mixed (300 diff.)	MARV/DC/INDY'S	VF/NM	$135.00
1,000	Mixed (4-600 diff.)	MARV/DC/INDY'S	VF/NM	$200.00

I DON'T COLLECT 'EM, I JUST READ 'EM 1980'S-1990'S
100 DIFFERENT "AS IS" READING COMICS $15.00

I DON'T COLLECT 'EM, I JUST READ 'EM 1960'S-1990'S
100 DIFFERENT "AS IS" READING COMICS $30.00

PASSAIC BOOK & COMIC CENTER
HUGE CATALOG AVAILABLE $3.00/SINCE 1966
267 PASSAIC ST., NJ 07055
973-778-0416 PH 973-778-6823 FAX
MAKE A FAIR ESTIMATE FOR SHIPPING. C.O.D., VISA/MC/AMEX/DISCOVER

AMERICAN COMIC BOOK CO.

CATALOGUES AVAILABLE

(PRICE OF CATALOGUES REFUNDED WITH ANY ORDER)

1. UNDERGROUND COMIX, NEWSPAPERS, ETC. ---$1.00
2. ORIGINAL ART, POSTERS, PORTFOLIOS, BLB'S --$1.00
3. D.C. GOLD AND SILVER AGE, CLASSICS ILLUS. ---$1.00
4. GOLDEN AGE: QUAL., FAW., MLJ, TIMLEY FOX, REPRINT, GLEASON, FIC. HOUSE, ETC. ---$1.00
5. 1950'S: ART COMICS, E.C., HOR. ATLAS, WEST, WAR, CRIME, ROMANCE, ETC. ----$1.00
6. PULPS --- $2.00
7. DISNEY AND DELL FUNNY --- $1.00
8. DELL T.V., MOVIE, WESTERN ---$1.00

9. GIRLEY MAGS. (PLAYBOY, ETC., ETC., ETC.) ---$2.00
10. MAGS. (LIFE, SPTS. ILLUS., HUMOR, MOVIE, MAD, CRIME, FAM. MON., ETC.)—1000'S OF ITEMS ---$2.00

11. PB'S AND DIGESTS ---$1.00
12. MARVEL, MISC, 1960-1990 COMICS ---$1.00
13. 50'S HUMOR COMICS, ARCHIES --- $1.00
14. WANT LISTS: SEND $1.00 & YOUR LIST NOW!

MAKE CHECKS OUT TO = TERRY STROUD
SEND TO = P.O. BOX 23
SANTA MONICA, CA 90406
PHONE = (310) 399 4352

WE WANT YOUR COMICS!

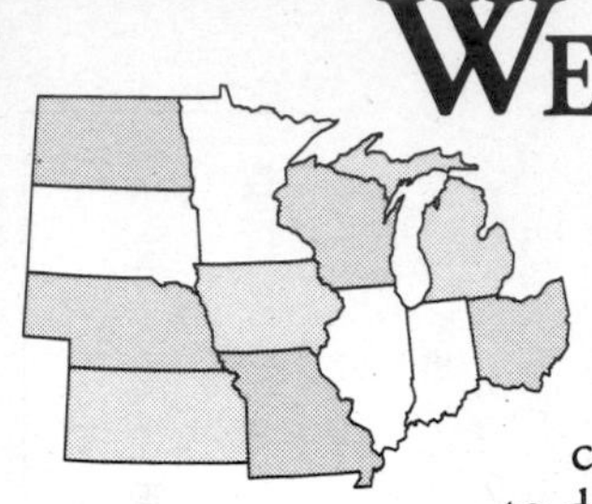

...AND WE *WILL* PAY TOP DOLLAR FOR THEM!

Our customers are looking for the finest comics in the country and have come to expect us to deliver. Last year we travelled 50,000 miles to see and purchase collections. Let us come to your home or business to look at anything from a huge collection to a single book.

MIDWEST'S PREMIER BUYER
REEL ART

QUICK PAYMENT • PROFESSIONAL SERVICE • FAIR DEAL
CORY GLABERSON • OAK PARK, ILLINOIS • CGLABERSON@AOL.COM
CALL US TODAY • 708-386-6550

Comics • Cards • Games
907-274-4112
You'll love this place!

www.captaincomics.com

ON LINE CATALOG OF COMICS,40'S-90'S ACTION FIGURES MAGAZINES, CARDS, ETC

Or send $1.00 for large catalog to Vincent Mileto 1124 Edison ave. Bronx NY 10461

the Collector's Slave
156 Imperial Avenue
Wpg., MB R2M 0K8

BUY • SELL • TRADE • CONSIGN
Dealer in collector's comics, pocketbooks, magazines and odd comic related items. Specializing in **serious collector's want lists**. I am constantly searching for hard to find collectibles. Many DELLS, GOLD KEY, CHARLTON, WESTERN, HARVEY, MARVEL, DC, MAD, CLASSICS, etc... in stock - send your want list. Send $1 for comic list.
I TRY HARDER!
Greg Harder : (204) 237-4428
Facsimile : (204) 947-2944

BUSINESS CARD ADS

THE OVERSTREET COMIC BOOK PRICE GUIDE BUSINESS CARD ADS are a whole new way to advertise in the Guide! Simply send us your business card and we'll reduce it and run it as is. Have your ad seen by thousands of serious comic book collectors for an entire year! If you are a comic book or collectible dealer, retail establishment, mail-order house, etc., you can reach potential customers throughout the United States and around the world in our **BUSINESS CARD ADS**!

For more information, contact our Advertising Dept.
Call Toll Free (888) 375-9800 or fax (410) 560-6107.

FOUR COLOR COMICS

SILVER — GOLD

ROBERT ROGOVIN
115 West 27th Street, NY, NY 10001
TEL: (212)675-6990 FAX: (212)366-6514

William M. Cole, P.E.
President

TEL: 781-986-2653
FAX: 781-986-2656

Bill Cole Enterprises, Inc.

P.O. Box 60 • Randolph, MA 02368-0060
e-mail: bcemylar@internetmci.com
web site: http://www.neponset.com/bcemylar

Manufacturers and Distributors of Preservation Supplies-
for the Collector and the Archivist

Marketing and Distribution for the collectibles industry

T & M Enterprises

TODD HOFFER
Marketing Consultant

245 Wilbrook Cir. NE • Cleveland, TN 37323
Phone/Fax (423) 614-3318

"Doc" Robinson's Comics

Toll Free! 1-888-COMX-DOC
(1-888-266-9362)

Bill Campbell
Collector

BUY - SELL - TRADE
CAPTAIN MARVEL
RADIO PREMIUMS, RINGS
CHARACTER WATCHES

CALL/WRITE FOR FREE LIST:

1221 Littlebrook Ln.
Birmingham, AL 35235
Phone: (205)853-8227
Fax: (205)853-9951

James F. Payette
Rare Books & Comics
P.O. Box 750
Bethlehem, NH 03574

Dealing in Old & New
Rare Comic Books

Big Little Books • 1st Ed. Books • Pulp Magazines
Sci-Fi Fantasy Material • Old Coins • Baseball Cards
TELEPHONE: (603) 869-2097

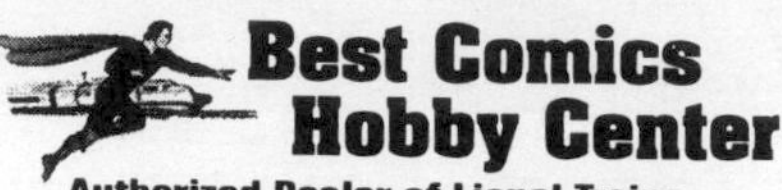
Best Comics Hobby Center

Authorized Dealer of Lionel Trains

We Buy & Sell Silver/Golden Age Comics

New Comics • Action Figures • Trading Cards • Star Wars/Star Trek • Vinyl Model Kits • Lmtd. Ed. Statues • Toy Collectables • Resin Kits & Paint Supplies

252-02 Northern Blvd.
Little Neck, New York 11362

TOMMY MALETTA
(718) 279-2099 • (Fax) 279-2216

http://www.bestcomics.com

Reach Over 5,000

COMICS SHOPS

Mailing List - only $250

Deliverability Guaranteed or TRIPLE your money back!

FANDATA Mailing Lists

Toll Free: 1-888-FANDATA

www.fandata.com fandata@aol.com

THE ULTIMATE BACK-ISSUE SERVICE

P.O. BOX 3855
SCOTTSDALE, AZ 85271
Phone: (602) 949-8499
Fax: (602) 947-3244

STRICT GRADING, FAIR PRICING, AND PROMPT SHIPPING ON POPULAR ISSUES FROM THE '40'S TO PRESENT

ROBERT M. LETSCHER II — OWNER

TOMORROW IS *Yesterday* INC

"Where All Your Heroes Come To Life"

Comic Books • Comic Paraphernalia
Trading Cards • Collectors Supplies
Role Playing Games • Books • Videos

HOURS: Mon.-Fri. 9-9; Sat. 9-6; Sun.12-5

5600 N Second Street
Rockford, IL 61111
(815) 633-0330

Mr. Kim C. Kowalewski
President

Order your new comics in advance.

Get **Big Discounts!**
Never miss an issue!
CBG Customer Service Award
12 years in a row!

13617 Southwest Hwy. Orland Park, IL 60462
888-MM-COMICS (888-662-6642)

www.mmcomics.com

COMICS PHONECARDS CARDS

ARGO•CITY

SELLING BUYING

COMICS CARDS

Ken Barnes
136 Confair Pkwy.
Montoursville, PA 17754

717-368-1389
Anytime

We Buy and Sell

A. Marvel, DC Comics, Independents 1970-1995
B. Marvel Comics 1960-1969
C. DC Comics 1940-1969
D. All other Comic Publishers 1940-1975
E. Monster, Mad, TV, Movie Magazines
F. Pulp Magazines
G. Big Little Books Pre 1950
H. Superhero, Pulp Reprint, TV Paperbacks
I. Vintage Paperbacks all publishers
J. Movie Posters Pre 1970
K. Gum Cards Pre 1970

Send 2 stamps when requesting the above price lists
OR
If you are looking to SELL the above material send 2 stamps for our BUYING CATALOG #5 which features prices we pay for thousands

Ed Kalb • 1353 S. Los Alamos • Mesa, AZ 85204

"Serving Collectors Worldwide Since 1967"

ALTERNATE REALITIES

COMICS, BOOKS & VIDEOS

PAUL, GEORGE & CALLI ZISIS
1910 DANFORTH AVE.
TORONTO, ONTARIO, CANADA
M4C 1J4
TEL/FAX # (416)69-69-00-5

WE BUY, SELL AND TRADE IN GOLD & SILVER AGE COMICS

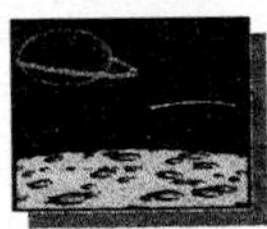

phone (800) 278-9691, (718) 721-9691 fax (718) 728-9691
22-55 31ST STREET, ASTORIA, N.Y. 11105

SILVER AGE Comics

SPECIALIZING IN PRE-1970'S COMICS

www.silveragecomics.com e-mail gus@silveragecomics.com

Clinton Cards, Comics, and Collectibles

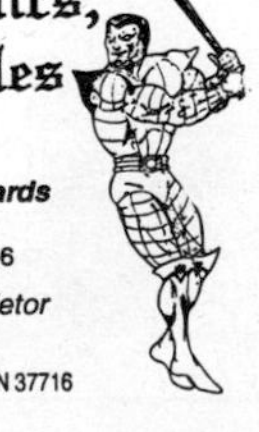

Baseball Cards · Football Cards
Premium Comics
OPEN: Mon.-Fri. 10-7 · Sat. 10-6

STEVE L. JENNINGS, *Proprietor*
(423) 457-KARD (5273)

Market Place · 372 Market Street · Clinton, TN 37716

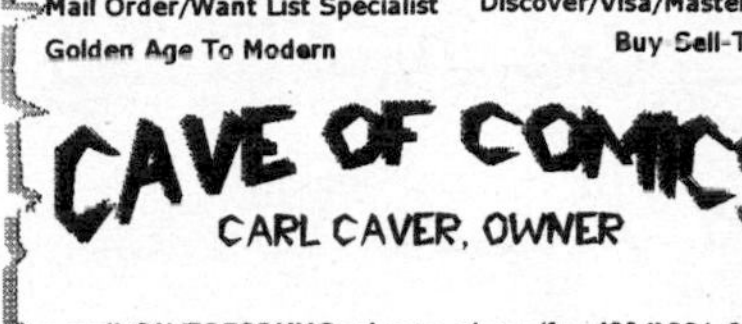

WANTED

1940's Superhero Memorabilia
Premiums, Serial Posters, Advertising Pieces,
Anything, FROM
BATMAN • CAPT. AMERICA
CAPT. MARVEL • FLASH
SUPERMAN • WONDERWOMAN
Scott Rona (407)699-9581
P.O. Box 180623 Casselberry, FL 32718

WANTED

BUY - SELL - TRADE

WE PAY THE HIGHEST PRICES FOR YOUR
PRE-1966 COMICS IN FINE OR BETTER
UNRESTORED CONDITION.
ASK FOR MARK
INSTANT CASH
I HAVE A MILLION DOLLARS
TO SPEND

Carpe Noctem® · A Dark Art Magazine
Address Submissions To:
Catía and Carnell, Publishers

Carpe Noctem®

208.528.2367 phone
208.522.8684 fax
260 S. Woodruff Ave. Suite 105
Idaho Falls, ID 83401
carpenoc@carpenoctem.com • http://www.carpenoctem.com/

LEGENDS OF SUPERHEROS

COMICS & COLLECTIBLES

203 756-2440

1269 WEST MAIN ST.
[EXIT 18 OFF I-84]
WATERBURY, CT 06708
DAILY: 10-7
WEDNESDAY: 1-8
SUNDAY: CLOSED
fax: 203 757-1909
www.legendsofsuperheros.com

XANADU

- Comic books
- RPG's & CCG's
- Free Bags & Boards
- Collection appraisals
- 19 years experience
- Host of Des Moines' Only Comic Book Convention

James Kirby
Proprietor

3001 Merle Hay Rd.
Des Moines, IA 50310
515-251-3933
Xanadude@aol.com
http://members.aol.com/xanadude/

SOUTHERN CAL COMICS & COLLECTIBLES

- Buy and Sell: Gold & Silver Age Comics
- Discount Sales of Recent Comics & Supplies
- Collectible Action Figures, Dolls & Toys

Email SoCalComix@aol.com
Phone (619) 278-7335
Fax# (619) 277-0119
Phone (619)694-0445
8280 Clairemont Mesa Blvd. # 124, San Diego, CA 92111

Comic Detectives

1978-1998
Celebrating 20 years of two-fisted
American comics dealing, Chump!

**Vintage Comic Books, Toys,
Cards, Autographs & Art**
Dan Fogel, Jim Pitts, Rick Calou
PO Box 629, Menlo Park, CA 94026-0629
(510) 758-0688/Email:tgfogel@aol.com

T.V. GUIDES • PAPERBACKS • RECORDS
LIFE • LOOK • TEEN MAGAZINES
MARILYN MONROE • LUCY

RICK NOSKER

*Specializing in Playboy Magazines
and related memorabilia*

BUY • SELL • TRADE
(602) 491-4794
1320 WEST ELLIOT ROAD, SUITE 103-184 • TEMPE, AZ 85284

Terry O'Neill
Owner

TERRY'S COMICS

Buy • Sell • Trade • Collect • Lists Accepted
H (714) 528-3937
W (714) 779-5700

P.O. Box 471
Atwood, CA. 92811

THAT'S ENTERTAINMENT

www.thatse.com

1997 Will Eisner Spirit of Comics Retailer of the Year Award Winner!
ph: 508-755-4207 fx: 508-754-3882
244 Park Ave., Worcester, MA 01609

CARL BARKS STUDIO

MANAGERS
BILL GRANDEY & KATHY MORBY

P.O. Box 524
Grants Pass, OR 97526

(541) 476-7558
Fax (541) 476-7064

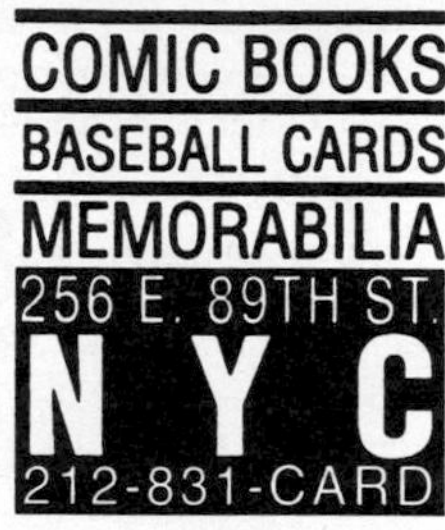

TRILOGY COMICS

Comics Cards Games
Anime SF Memorabilia

5773 Princess Anne Rd.
Va. Beach, VA 23462
Ph: 757-490-2205
Fax: 757-671-7721

700 E. Little Creek Rd.
Norfolk, VA 23518
Ph: 757-587-2540
Fax: 757-587-5637

e-mail: trilogy@nfx.net

TRH GALLERY
Animation and Comic Art
Bought • Sold • Appraised

THOMAS R. HORVITZ

18324 Clark Street, #223, Tarzana, CA 91356
Tel: 818-757-0747 • Fax: 818-757-0859
WebSite: http://www.trhgallery.com
E-mail: trhgallery@earthlink.net

COMIC BOOK WORLD

7130 TURFWAY RD • FLORENCE, KY • 606-371-9562
4016 HARRISON AVE • CINCINNATI, OH • 513-661-6300
6905 SHEPHERDSVILLE RD • LOUISVILLE, KY • 502-964-5500

70-11 Austin Street
Forest Hills, NY 11375
718.575.8815

Adapting to your needs

Resurrection Restorations
THE STUDIO OF MARK SPARACIO & STEVE STRYKE
Free Guaranteed Estimates!!! Free Evaluation Services!!!
Turnaround time as little as 1 week, & seldom over 30 days
Expert piece replacement by a professional artist
w/30+ years experience
❖cleaning ❖interior refurbishing & mending❖ ❖tape removal❖
❖split spines mended❖ ❖de-acidifieng❖ ❖bound volume issues❖
CALL FOR A FREE INFORMATION PACKAGE,
complete w/samples of our work.
CONTACT: STEVE STRYKE @ GOLDEN MEMORIES 516-932-8581
250 BROADWAY, HICKSVILLE, N.Y. 11801

The Antiquarium
Books and Collectibles

Collector Comics, Books, Trading Cards, Star Trek-Star War Items and Supplies

Thomas G. Strong
(573) 636-8995

504 E. High St.
Jefferson City, MO 65101

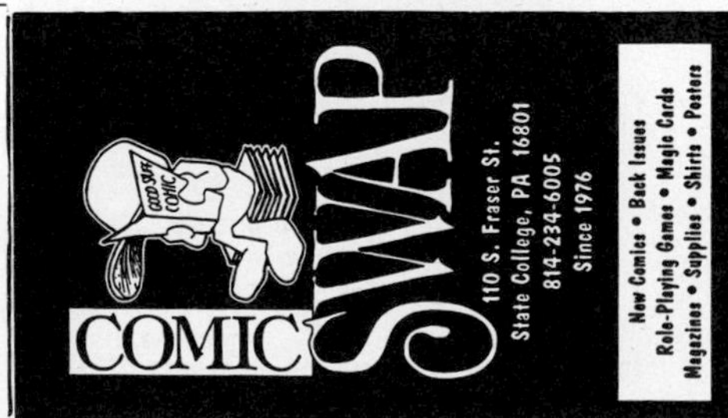

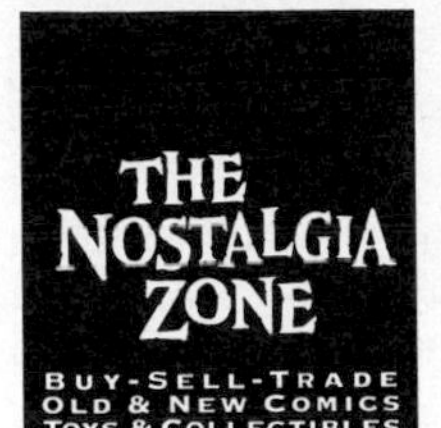

SEND FOR FREE GIANT COMICS CATALOG

3149½ Hennepin Ave. S.
Minneapolis MN 55408
612/822-2806
nostzone@spacestar.net

Bud Plant Comic Art

Graphic Novels • Comic Strip Collections
Art Books • Sale Books

Collectors: 248-pg Catalog $3
Dealers: Free Wholesale Catalog

800-242-6642 or (530) 273-2166
FAX: (530) 273-0915
e-mail: cs@budplant.com
Website: www.budplant.com

13393 Grass Valley Ave. #7
PO Box 1689-PGO
Grass Valley, California 95945

Digital Heroes

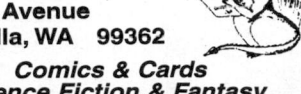

13 Boyer Avenue
Walla Walla, WA 99362

Phone: (509) 525-0380
Fax: (509) 529-6805
Toll Free: 1-888-DHEROES

Visit us on the Internet at:
http://www.digitalheroes.com
Email: info@digitalheroes.com

GOTHAM CITY COMICS

800 Lexington Ave. 2nd Fl.
New York, NY 10021
(212) 980-0009 /GothamCT@aol.com

* BACK ISSUES * TOYS * COLLECTIBLES * POSTERS *
SPORTS & NON-SPORTS CARDS
MEMBERSHIPS AVAILABLE
Mon. - Fri. 10am-8pm
Sat.-Sun. 11am-6pm

TRADING CARD WORKSHOP

Trading Card Workshop's *advance order discount service* offers collectors a convenient and economical way of ordering comics, cards, magazines, books, games, videos, toys, and other collectibles at significant savings!

Please call or write for our latest free catalog

P.O. Box 18362 • San Jose, CA 95158-8362
Phone/Fax 408-448-0447 • tcworkshop@aol.com

Japanimation • RPGs • ActionFigures

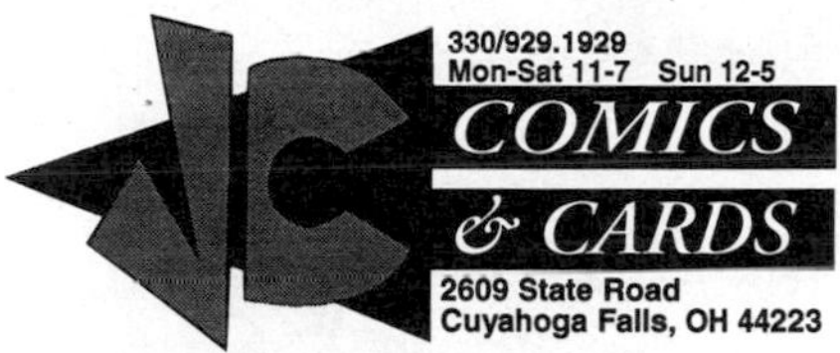

"Old And Gold"

Golden and Silver Age Comic Books
10695 Lake Oak Way
Boca Raton, FL 33498

CLIFF WIENER
Golden Age Specialist

(561) 488-1874
Fax (561) 488-3818

RTS UNLIMITED, INC.

PO Box 150412
Lakewood Co 80215
CBG Customer Service Award - 1997
We do mail order right! Buy ~Sell~Trade
Specializing in Pre-1990 Comics
Currently Selling The IRS Collection
Voice: (303)-403-1840 FAX (303)-403-1837
Ask For: Tim Collins

Over 100,000 Different Comics in Stock: Golden, Silver, Bronze, & Modern Age Comics. Supplies: Authorized Fortress Dealer, Bill Cole Products, Mylar, Acid-Free Boards. And More! Gerber's Photo-Journal Guide To Comic Books, etc.

LIPSHULTZ AND HONE CHARTERED

JOHN LLEWELLYN HONE
ATTORNEY AT LAW

SUITE 108 • MONTGOMERY CTR.
8630 FENTON STREET
SILVER SPRING, MARYLAND 20910
(301) 587-8500

SUITE 200
2000 L STREET, N.W.
WASHINGTON, D.C. 20036

CREATOR LISTINGS

THE OVERSTREET COMIC BOOK PRICE GUIDE CREATOR LISTINGS is accepting business card ads from comic book writers, artists, editors, colorists, letterers--any and all comic book creators! This is your chance to reach out to editors, publishers, and even other creators throughout the United States and around the world. Our **CREATOR LISTINGS** will help you publicize your artwork, writing, web site, self-published series--the choice is yours!

For more information, contact our Advertising Dept.
Call Toll Free (888) 375-9800 or fax (410) 560-6107.

TODD McFARLANE
PRODUCTIONS

Beau Smith
DIRECTOR OF MARKETING AND PROMOTION
EMAIL_beausmith@aol.com
PAGER_800.804.8714

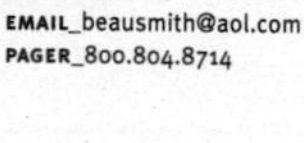

TODD McFARLANE PRODUCTIONS, INC.
740 SECOND STREET WEST, P.O. BOX 706
CEREDO, WV 25507 USA
TEL_304.453.1050
FAX_304.453.6853
http://www.spawn.com

TERI SUE WOOD
Creator of WANDERING STAR & DARKLIGHT

Preview SIRIUS Entertainment's new title **DARKLIGHT** on the World Wide Web or talk to Teri Friday nights at 7pm Pacific, 10pm Eastern time, at:
http://www.easynet.on.ca/~johnn/Teri_Sue_Wood/teri_sue_wood.htm

SEE YAZ!

COMIC ART

SHELDON MOLDOFF (954) 485-8551
3710 Inverrary Dr. Lauderhill, FL 33319

MART NODELL
Creator of the original GREEN LANTERN
117 Lake Irene Drive
West Palm Beach, Florida 33411

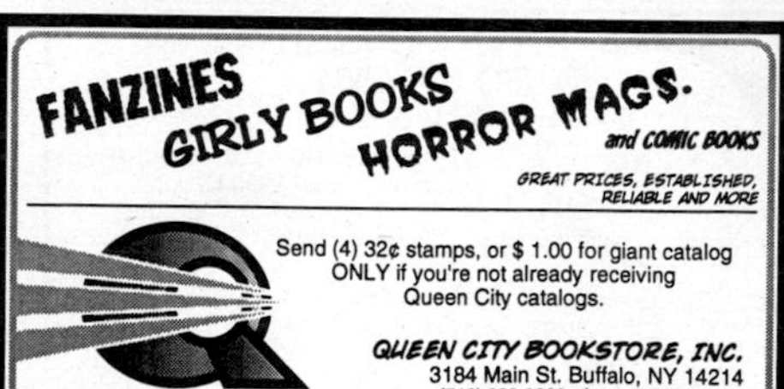

FANZINES
GIRLY BOOKS
HORROR MAGS.
and COMIC BOOKS
GREAT PRICES, ESTABLISHED, RELIABLE AND MORE

Send (4) 32¢ stamps, or $ 1.00 for giant catalog ONLY if you're not already receiving Queen City catalogs.

QUEEN CITY BOOKSTORE, INC.
3184 Main St. Buffalo, NY 14214
(716) 833-6220 • fax 1-716-833-1781

The Mail Order specialist!
EST. 1969

Jamal Y.Igle
Hyperactive Illustration

"Be AFRAID, be very Afraid..."

ph/fax (718) 788-5747

Reach Over 5,000
Artists and Writers
Amateur and Professional
FANDATA Mailing Lists
Toll Free: 1-888-FANDATA
www.fandata.com fandata@aol.com

ON THE CUTTING EDGE OF FANTASY ART

SQ Productions Inc - Publishing & Direct Mail
PO Box 4569 - Toms River, NJ 08754
Send for our FREE catalog (18 & over please)
Visit our website
www.sqpinc.com

CLASSIFIED ADS

$*$*SUPERMAN COLLECTIBLES WANTED!*$*$

BUYING ALL SUPERMAN ITEMS FROM 1938-1966: TOYS, GAMES, FIGURES, BUTTONS, RINGS, PREMIUMS, ADV. MATERIALS,...ANYTHING!!!! DANNY FUCHS, 209-80p 18th AVE., BAYSIDE, NY 11360. 718-225-9030 FAX: 718-225-3688. "AMERICA'S FOREMOST SUPERMAN COLLECTOR"

1/4 MILLION COMICS FOR SALE

Our 40-page catalog contains Silver & Bronze Age books in low to high grades w/ key issues! Books from 1960-'90s, with runs of Horror, Suspense, War, Westerns, & Super-Heroes. 100 Different Publishers. Send $1.00, refundable w/ first order to: High-Quality Comics, 1106 2nd St., #110, Encinitas, CA 92024, (1-800-682-3936), E-Mail: mbxstation@aol.com, (Attn: Kevin Van Horn)

FREE COOL CATALOG!

1940s-'90s, Fair To Mint, MARVEL, DC, GOLD KEY, CHARLTON, ETC! Jon McClure, PO Box 2406, Newport, OR 97365 MCCL@NEWPORTNET.COM

BUY-SELL-TRADE

Golden Age to New Releases, Action Figures R&K COMICS, Phone Week Days: 215-289-5418 (9AM-4PM), Fax: 215-289-5411, Weekends: 215-425-6050 (9AM-4PM).

Marvel Memorabilia Wanted!

Buying 1960s T-Shirts, Sweatshirts, Marvelmania Fan club items, Buttons, Portfolios, Romita, Sr. Spider-Man art, Captain Action toys, Superman flicker rings, 1960s Quisp/Quake cereal premiums. Aaron Sultan, 3201 Arrowwood Dr., Raleigh, NC 27604, 919-954-7111.

1960s Cereal Premiums/Rings!

Buying most premiums of: Quisp/Quake; Freakies; HR Pufnstuff; Ct. Chocula, Frankenberry, Boo Berry; Wacky Races; Superheroes; Marvel T-Shirts; R& L Plastics; Flicker rings. Aaron Sultan, 3201 Arrowwood Dr., Raleigh, NC 27604, 919-954-7111.

$400,000 SEARCH!!!

OLD COMIC BOOKS WANTED!! 1933-1976 Very serious buyer. Generally paying 40-80% of guide. Send lists or call Rick Semowich, 56 John Smith Rd. Binghamton, NY 13901. Phone: (607) 648-4025

BIG LITTLE BOOKS wanted. We pay in Good condition -$4, Very Good condition -$6, Fine condition -$8. Pre 1951 only, any Big or Better Little Book, any quantity. Ed Kalb 1-602-981-8957

FAMOUS MONSTERS OF FILMLAND Wanted (Magazine). We pay in Fine or better condition: #1-$250 #2-5 -$50 #6-8 $40 #9-26 -$15 #27-32 -$10 #33-100 -$2 #101-193 -$1. Ed Kalb 1-602-981-8957

PULPS WANTED- Shadow, Spider, Doc Savage, Avenger, Horror Stories, Terror Tales, Secret Agent X, Operator #5, G-8. We pay in good or better condition: 1931-1933 -$45 1934-35 -$35 1936-38 -$25 1939-49 -$12. We pay $2 for any SF. Ed Kalb 1-602-981-8957

100,000 COMICS. 1939-1989. All publishers. Call for free catalog. Buying & selling since 1967. Ed Kalb 1-602-981-8957

COMIC BOOKS WANTED 1939-1989. Call for our free BUYING CATALOG listing prices we pay for thousands. Ed Kalb 1-602-981-8957

CRYPTO COMIX DC, MARVEL, INDIES 7154 N. UNIVERSITY DR. TAMARAC FL 33321 Suite 166. (954) 726-2296 Send one dollar for catalog....

BUYING COMICS

SILVER AGE AND GOLDEN AGE Email: dford@netlabs.net, 908-495-0184

Buy, Sell, Trade. Golden & Silver age comics, paperback books, original art, prints, books. Related SF & monster toys for sale also. $2 big illustrated catalog/fanzine. Biff Smith, 1344 W. Flower, Phoenix, AZ 85013 email: zedrew@hotmail.com internet: www.monmouth.com/~tvawter/parats1.htm

FREE COMIC CATALOG!
'40s to '60s DC, Marvel, Dell, Harvey, Ind. Send Want Lists. Also buying. COAST COMICS: P.O. Box 280742, Northridge, CA 91328-0742

BEATLES!!! BEATLES!!! BEATLES!!!
I want items on the Beatles like toys, dolls, Yellow Submarine items, movie items, concert stubs, etc. Monkees & Circus Boy items also wanted. Rick Rann, Box 877, Oak Park, IL. 60303

ORIGINAL ART WANTED!
Batman, Metamorpho, Doom Patrol, Metal Men and other 1960s art. Looking for Gahan Wilson original art: "Nuts," "Sunday Funnies," Playboy, etc. Original art from Beatle & Monkees related comic book issues wanted. Beatles cartoon & Yellow Sub cels wanted. Rick Rann, Box 877, Oak Park, IL. 60303 ORIGINAL ART WANTED!

Newer comics at 50% O.P.G. (G.A. 75% & up). Send a SASE plus 50 cents per list. Request lists desired. Comic Book * BLB * N.P. Comic Strip * Pulp * Paperbacks * Movie TV Items * Old Life, Look, Post, Misc. Magazines. Above also bought. Glenn's Books, 3500 Manila Dr., Westerville, OH 43081.

COMIC BOOKS FOR SALE
One of the world's largest catalogues selling Golden Age, DC, Marvel, Dell, Classic Illustrated, plus BLBs, Sunday pages, original art. We supply Canadians with all types of plastic bags, acid free boxes and boards, etc. Send $2.00 for catalogue
COMIC BOOKS WANTED
Highest prices paid for comic books, BLBs, newspaper comics before 1959. 40 years as a collector and dealer. Contact us before selling.

INTERNATIONAL COMIC BOOK COMPANY
CALVIN AND ELEANOR SLOBODIAN
74 WATERLOO CRES., BRANDON,
MANITOBA CANADA R7B3W7
PHONE 204-728-4337

Buying Classics Illustrated and Classic Comics Call or write Phil Gaudino, 49 Park Ave., Port Washington, NY 11050, 516-883-5659

Affordable Silver & Gold. Send SASE to: Luis Garcia P.O. Box 8230, North Bergen, NJ 07047 201-656-3228 after 8:00pm. We also buy.

Captain Action Wanted: I buy all Captain Action, Dr. Evil, Action Boy items. Dolls, Costumes, Accessories. Boxed or Loose. Store displays, Promotional material. All IDEAL Superhero Toys Wanted. Greg Roccaro, D.V.M. 894 Armstrong Ave #2-4 SI NY 10308 Ph/Fax: (718) 967-8345. E-mail: Toyvet@aol.com

---

STILL BUYING & SELLING 1910-1960s
comic books (much rare), Sunday pages, "Big Little Books," much related vintage paper collectibles! Big list $2.00 (refundable) * Phone 416-222-5808
KEN MITCHELL 710 CONACHER DRIVE, WILLOWDALE, ONTARIO, M2M3N6.CANADA * In OPG since issue No. 1

25% OFF OVERSTREET ON ALL COMICS!
Silver & Bronze Age MARVELS & DCs, KEY comics, Gold & Silver age of ALL kinds, Disneys, more. Send wants & a SASE-I have no list (too many). MONEY-BACK GUARANTEE. Dave Yaruss, 7916 Blue Lake Dr., San Diego, CA 92119. 619-465-3090. Wants: GOLDEN AGE.

80,000 COMIC BOOKS FOR SALE!!!
Send want lists only. 25%-60% below guide. 1933-1979-includes mostly SIlver Age. Rick Semowich, 56 John Smith Rd. Binghamton, NY 13901 Phone: (607) 648-4025

BUYING GOLDEN AGE/ SILVER AGE ANY CONDITION RICHARD STARR 304-768-6523

MAGAZINE PAINTINGS-ILLUSTRATIONS
Original art for cover paintings & illustrations from pulp magazines: detective, mystery, science-fiction, paperback books, men's magazines, comic books, Sunday funnies, children's books, movie posters, pinup calendars. BUY-SELL-TRADE. Send photo/price. Tim Issacson, 400 E. Ohio #2204, Chicago, IL 60611. (312) 337-1279 ORIGINAL ART WANTED.

SHOP DIRECTORY

(PAID ADVERTISING - STORE LISTINGS)

You can have your store listed here for very reasonable rates. Send for details for next year's Guide. The following list of stores have paid to be included in this list. We cannot assume any responsibility in your dealings with these shops. This list is provided for your information only. When planning trips, it would be advisable to make appointments in advance. Remember, to get your shop included in the next edition, call, fax or write us for rates. **Gemstone Publishing, Inc., 1966 Greenspring Dr., Suite 405, Timonium, MD 21093. PH 888-375-9800 or 410-560-5806, FAX 410-560-6107**.

Items stocked by these shops are listed just after the telephone number and are coded as follows:

(a) Golden Age Comics
(b) Silver Age Comics
(c) New Comics, Magazines
(d) Pulps
(e) Paperbacks
(f) Big Little Books
(g) Magazines
(h) Books (old)
(i) Movie Posters
(j) Original Art
(k) Toys
(l) Records/CDs, Video Tapes
(m) Trading Cards
(n) Underground Comics
(o) Premiums
(p) Comic Related Posters
(q) Comic Supplies
(r) Role Playing Games
(s) Star Trek Items
(t) Doctor Who Items
(u) Japanimation Items

ALABAMA

Campbell's Collectibles
1221 Littlebrook Ln.
Birmingham, AL 35235
PH: (205) 853-8227
FX: (205) 853-9951
(a,d-h,k,m,o)

BRAVO
1211 N. Wood Ave.
Florence, AL 35630
PH: (205) 740-6876
(a-c,e,g-i,k-n,s,u)

Wizard's Comics
324 North Court
Florence, AL 35630
PH: (205) 766-6821
(a-c,q-u)

Sincere Comics
4667 Airport Blvd.
Mobile, AL 36608
PH: (334) 342-2603
(a-c,e,m,p-s,u)

ALASKA

Bosco's
2606 Spenard Rd.
Anchorage, AK 99503
PH: (907) 274-4112
FX: (907) 274-4114
E-Mail: info@boscos.com
Web: www.boscos.com
(b,c,i,k,m,n,p-s,u,)

ARIZONA

Atomic Comics III
5965 West Ray Road #19
Chandler, AZ 85226
PH: (602) 940-6061
(b,c,g,i-k,m-u)

Atomic Comics
1318 West Southern #1
Mesa, AZ 85202
PH: (602) 649-0807
(a-c,f,g,j,k,m,n,p-u)

Atomic Comics Direct Mail Order
1318 W. Southern #1
Mesa, AZ 85202
PH: (800) 332-9027
E-Mail: mail@atomiccomics.com
Web: www.atomiccomics.com
(a-c,g,j-u)

Greg's Comics
2722 South Alma School Rd. #8
Mesa, AZ 85210
PH: (602) 752-1881
(a-c,k,m,q-s)

All About Books & Comics
517 E. Camelback
Phoenix, AZ 85012
PH: (602) 277-0757
Web: www.all-about-comics.com
(a-c,e,g,h-n,p-u)

Atomic Comics II
3029 West Peoria #CC
Phoenix, AZ 85021
PH: (602) 395-1066
(a-c,f,g,j,k,m,n,p-u)

Lost Dutchman Comics
747 W. Camelback Rd.
Phoenix, AZ 85013
PH: (602) 263-5249
(a,b,d-h,n)

Key Comics:Discount Back-Issues
P. O. Box 3855
Scottsdale, AZ 85271
PH: (602) 949-8499
FX: (602) 947-3244
(a-c,j)

ARKANSAS

Alternate Worlds Books and Comics
3812 Central Ave. Ste. G
Hot Springs, AR 71913
PH: (501) 525-8999
(a-c,g,h,k,m,q-u)

The Comic Book Store
9307 Treasure Hill
Little Rock, AR 72227
PH: (501) 227-9777
(a-c,g,k,m,p-s,u)

Collector's Edition
3217 John F. Kennedy Blvd.
North Little Rock, AR 72116
PH: (501) 791-4222
(a-c,g,k,m,p,q-s,u)

CALIFORNIA

Terry's Comics
P.O. Box 471
Atwood, CA 92811
PH: (714) 528-3937
(a,b,d,f,g,h,i)

Comic Relief Berkeley
2138 University Avenue
Berkeley, CA 94704
PH: (510) 843-5002
(a-d,f-h,j,n,p,q,u)

Astounding Fantasy Art Books and Comics
2319-A West Olive Ave.
Burbank, CA 91506
PH: (818) 953-7234
(a-d,f,g,i,k-m,q-u)

Crush Comics & Cards
2869 Castro Valley Blvd.
Castro Valley, CA 94546
PH: (510) 581-4779
FX: (510) 581-4779
(b,c,g,k,m,p,q,s)

Collectors Ink
932-A West 8th Ave.
Chico, CA 95926
PH: (530) 345-0958
E-Mail: collink@cmc.net
(a-c,e,g,k-n,p-u)

Comic Bookie
415 West Foothill Blvd. #318
Claremont, CA 91711
PH: (909) 399-0228
(b,c,g,k-n,p,q,s-u)

Flying Colors Comics & Other Cool Stuff
2980 Treat Blvd.
Oak Grove Plaza
Concord, CA 94518
PH: (510) 825-5410
E-Mail: flyingcolorscomics@compuserve.com
(a-c,j,k,m,p,q,u)

Superior Comics
1970 Newport Blvd.
Costa Mesa, CA 92627
PH: (714) 631-3933
(a-c,f,g,j,k,m,n,p-r,u)

High Quality Comics
(mail order only)
1106 2nd St. Suite #110
Encinitas, CA 92024
PH: (800) 682-3936
E-Mail: mbxstation@aol.com
Web: www.publiconline.com/=highqualitycom
(a-c,g,j,n)

Comic Gallery
322-J West El Norte Pkwy.
Escondido, CA 92026
PH: (760) 745-5660
(b,c,j,k,m,q-s,u)

Comicmania!
124 W. Commonwealth
Fullerton, CA 92832
PH: (714) 992-6649
(a-c,f,g,i-k,m-q,s,u)

Mile High Comics
12041 Harbor Blvd.
Garden Grove, CA 92840
PH: (714) 748-7091
(a-c,f-u)

Geoffrey's Comics
15530 Crenshaw Blvd.
Gardena, CA 90249
PH: (888) 538-3198
(a-c,l,n,q,u)

Shooting Star Comics
618 E. Colorado Blvd.
Glendale, CA 91205
PH: (818) 502-1535
(b,c,g,k,m,n,p,q,u)

Treasures Of Youth
1201 C St.
Hayward, CA 94541
PH: (510) 888-9675
(a,b,d-k,m,o)

Amazing Comics & Cards
5555 Stearns St. #103
Long Beach, CA 90815
PH: (562) 493-4427
E-Mail: amazingcomicscards@worldnet.att.net
(b,c,e,g,k,m,p-u)

Ambrosia Books, Comics & Collectibles
10679 West Pico Blvd.
Los Angeles, CA 90064
PH: (310) 475-5825
PH: (888) 47-DRWHO
Web: www.concentric.net/~jslyon
(b,c,e,g,h,k,l-n,p-u)

Another World Comics & Books
1615 Colorado Blvd.
Los Angeles, CA 90041
PH: (213) 257-7757
(a-g,i,m,p,t,u)

Golden Apple Comics
7711 Melrose Ave.
Los Angeles, CA 90046
PH: (213) 658-6047
Web: www.goldenapple-comics.com
(a-c,l-n,p,q,t)

Pacific Comic Exchange, Inc.
(by appointment only)
P. O. Box 34849
Los Angeles, CA 90034
PH: (310) 836-7234 (PCEI)
E-Mail: sales@pcei.com
Web: www.pcei.com/
(a, b)

Century Comic Center
193 Terry Cir.
Marina, CA 93933
PH: (800) 817-3353
FX: (408) 883-4257
E-Mail: bill@centurycomiccenter.com
Web: www.centurycomiccenter.com
(a,b,f,k,s)

Brian's Books
73 North Milpitas Blvd.
Milpitas, CA 95035
PH: (408) 942-6903
(a-c,g,m,p,q,s,u)

Pegasus Hobbies
5505 Moreno Blvd.
Montclair, CA 91763
PH: (909) 931-4872
(a-c,g,k,m,q-s,u)

Big Guy's Comics
167 El Camino East
Mountain View, CA 94040
PH: (415) 965-8272
(a-d,f-h,m,n,p,q,s)

Golden Apple Comics
8962 Reseda Blvd.
Northridge, CA 91324
PH: (818) 993-7804
Web: www.goldenapplecomics.com
(a-c,e,l-n,p,q,u)

Lee's Comics, Inc.
3783 El Camino Real
Palo Alto, CA 94306
PH: (650) 493-3957
E-Mail: lee@lcomics.com
Web: www.lcomics.com/
(a-c,e,g,k-n,p-s,u)

A-1 Comics
5800 Madison Avenue
Sacramento, CA 95841
PH: (916) 331-9206
FX: (916) 331-2141
(a-g,i-m,p-s,u)

Comic Gallery
4224 Balboa Ave.
San Diego, CA 92117
PH: (619) 483-4853
(b,c,j,k,m,q-s,u)

Comic Gallery
9460-G Mira Mesa Blvd.
San Diego, CA 92126
PH: (619) 578-9444
(b,c,j,k,m,q-s,u)

San Diego Comics & Collectibles
6937 El Cajon Blvd.
San Diego, CA 92115
PH: (619) 698-1177
(a-c,k,m,s)

Southern Cal Comics & Collectibles
8280 Clairemont Mesa Blvd. #124
San Diego, CA 92117
PH: (619) 278-7335
FX: (619) 277-0119
E-Mail: SoCalComix@aol.com
(a-c,g,k,q)

Amazing Adventures Collectibles
3800 Noriega
San Francisco, CA 94122
PH: (415) 661-1344
(a-c,f,g,i-k,m,n,q,r)

Cards and Comics Central
5727 Geary Blvd.
San Francisco, CA 94121
PH: (415) 668-3544
(c,e,g,k,l-n,p,q,s,u)
Web: www.candccentral.com

The Funny Papers
5957 Geary Blvd.
at 24th Ave.
San Francisco, CA 94121
PH: (415) 752-1914
(a-e,g-m,o-s,u)

Captain Nemo Comics & Games
797 Marsh St.
San Luis Obispo, CA 93401
PH: (805) 544-6366
(a-c,e,g,i,k-u)

Lee's Comics, Inc.
2222 S. El Camino Real
San Mateo, CA 94402
PH: (650) 571-1489
(a-c,e,g,k-n,p-s,u)

Metro Comics & Games
6 West Anapamu
Santa Barbara, CA 93101
PH: (805) 963-2168
E-Mail: metrocomix@aol.com
(a-c,e,g,i-n,p-s,u)

Brian's Books
2767 El Camino
Santa Clara, CA 95051
PH: (408) 985-7481
(a-c,g,m,p,q,s,u)

Atlantis Fantasyworld
1020 Cedar St.
Santa Cruz, CA 95060
PH: (408) 426-0158
Web: www.afworld.com
(a-c,g,i,k,m,n,p,q,s,u)

Hi De Ho Comics & Fantasy
525 Santa Monica Blvd.
Santa Monica, CA 90401-2409
PH: (310) 394-2820
(a-n,p-u)

Mega City Comics
2955 B-2 Cochran St.
Simi Valley, CA 93065
PH: (805) 583-3027
(b,c,e,g,i-k,m,n,p-s,u)

Ralph's Comic Corner
2379 E. Main St.
Ventura, CA 93003
PH: (805) 653-2732
E-Mail: ralphs@fishnet.net
Web: www.fishnet.net/~ralphs
(a-c,f,k,m,n,p-s,u)

Pegasus Hobbies
6554 Greenleaf Ave.
Whittier, CA 90601
PH: (562) 907-4663
(a-c,g,k,m,q-s,u)

A Collector's Dream
21222 Venture Blvd.
Woodland Hills, CA 91364
PH: (818) 992-1636
(a-c,g,j,k,m-s)

COLORADO

All C's Collectibles, Inc.
1113 So. Abilene St. #104
Aurora, CO 80012
PH: (303) 751-6882
(a-d,g,i-k,m-s,u)

Time Warp Comics & Cards, Inc.
1631 28th Street
Boulder, CO 80301
PH: (303) 443-4500
(a-c,g,n,q-s)

Bargain Comics
21 1/2 E. Bijou
Colorado Springs, CO 80903
PH: (719) 578-8847
(a-c,g,n,q)

Comic Vault
929 North Murray Blvd.
Colorado Springs, CO 80915
PH: (719) 596-2155
(a-c,e,g-k,o-u)

Mile High Comics
760 South Colorado Blvd.
Denver, CO 81221
PH: (303) 691-2212
(a-c,f-u)

Mile High Comics
Tabor Center
16th & Lawrence, 3rd Floor
Denver, CO 80202
PH: (303) 446-8250
(a-c,f-u)

Blue Coyote Comics
P. O. Box 2163
Evergreen, CO 80439
PH: (303) 670-8386
(a,b,n)

J. R. R. Comix
P. O. Box 2163
3869 Evergreen Pkwy.
Evergreen, CO 80437-2163
PH: (303) 670-8386
(a-e,g,k-n,p-u)

Mile High Comics
1st & Wadsworth
Lakewood, CO 80226
PH: (303) 238-8125
(a-c,f-u)

RTS Unlimited, Inc.
P. O. Box 150412
Lakewood, CO 80215-0412
PH: (303) 403-1840
(a,b,q)

Mile High Comics
50 West Littleton Blvd.
Littleton, CO 80120
PH: (303) 730-8160
(a-c,f-u)

Mile High Comics
9201 North Washington
Thornton, CO 80229
PH: (303) 457-2612
(a-c,f-u)

CONNECTICUT

The Bookie
206 Burnside Ave.
E. Hartford, CT 06108
PH: (860) 289-1208
(a-h,j,m,n,q-s,u)

Sarge's Comics
325 Route 12
Groton, CT 06340
PH: (860) 445-2646
(b,c,g,k-n,p,q,s,u)

D. J.'s Comics
303 East Main St.
Meriden, CT 06450
PH: (203) 235-7300
(a-c,f,k,m,q)

D. J.'s Comics & Cards
166 Washington Ave.
N. Haven, CT 06473
PH: (203) 234-2989
(b,c,e,j,k,m,q-s)

Sarge's Comics
118 State St.
New London, CT 06320
PH: (860) 443-2004
(a-c,e,g,k-n,p,q,s-u)

Legends of Superheros
CVS/Robinwood Plaza
1269 W. Main St.
Waterbury, CT 06708
PH: (203) 756-2440
Web: www.legendsofsuper heros.com
(b,c,g,k,l,m,p-r,u)

DELAWARE

Captain Blue Hen Comics & Cards
280 E. Main St. #1
Newark, DE 19711
PH: (302) 737-3434
(a-c,g,k-q,s,u)

FLORIDA

Past Present Future Superstore-Boca Raton
23066 Sandlefoot Plaza Drive
Boca Raton, FL 33428
PH: (561) 470-5700
(b,c,e,g,j,k,m,n,p-s,u)

Emerald City Comics & Collectables, Inc.
2475-L McMullen Booth Rd.
Clearwater, FL 33759
PH: (813) 797-0664
E-Mail: CowardlyLion @emeraldcitycomics.com
Web: www.emeraldcity comics.com
(a-c,g,j-u)

SMRC Comics
6927 Red Road
Coral Gables, FL 33143
PH: (800) 826-3089
PH: (305) 665-4020
FX: (305) 663-1072
(a,b)

World of Comics
147 W. International Speedway Blvd.
Daytona Beach, FL 32114
PH: (904) 255-4589
(b,c,e,g-k,m,n,p-u)

Borderlands Comics and Games
10230-10 Atlantic Blvd.
Jacksonville, FL 32225
PH: (904) 720-0774
(b,c,g,k,m,p,q,r,u)

Phil's Comic Shoppe
6512 W. Atlantic Blvd.
Margate, FL 33063
PH: (954) 977-6947
(a-c,i,k,m,q)

Tropic Comics South, Inc.
1870 N.E. 163 St.
N. Miami Beach, FL 33162
PH: (305) 940-8700
FX: (305) 940-1551
E-Mail: abcsales @a-bombcomics.com
Web: www.a-bombcomics .com
(a-g,i-q,s-u)

Bay Hill Comics (Mail Order Service)
7657 Turkey Lake Rd.
Orlando, FL 32819
PH: (407) 363-0040
(b,c,e,g,k,m,o,p,s)

Sincere Comics
40 West 9 Mile Rd.
Pensacola, FL 32534
PH: (904) 476-9944
(a-c,e,f,m,p-s,u)

Tropic Comics, Inc.
313 S. State Rd. #7
Plantation, FL 33317
PH: (954) 587-8878
FX: (954) 587-0409
E-Mail: trcsales @tropiccomics.com
Web: www.tropiccomics .com
(a-g,i-k,m-q,s,u)

Emerald City Comics & Collectables, Inc.
9249 Seminole Blvd.
Seminole, FL 33772
PH: (813) 398-2665
E-Mail: CowardlyLion @emeraldcitycomics.com
Web: www.emeraldcity comics.com
(a-c,g,j-u)

Past Present Future Superstore-Sunrise
8432 W. Oakland Park Blvd.
Sunrise, FL 33351
PH: (954) 742-0777
(b,c,e,g,j,k,m,n,p-u)

The Comics Club, Inc.
8126 N. University Dr.
Tamarac, FL 33321
PH: (954) 726-2121
(a-c,e,g,i,k,m,q-s)

Past Present Future Superstore- West Palm Beach
1387 N. Military Trail
West Palm Beach, FL 33409
PH: (561) 697-2554
(b,c-g,j,k,m,n,p-u)

GEORGIA

Oxford Comics Inc.
2855 Piedmont Rd. NE
Atlanta, GA 30305
PH: (404) 233-8682
(a-u)

Titan Games & Comics VI
2000 Cheshire Bridge Rd.
Atlanta, GA 30324
PH: (404) 982-0227
(a-c,e,g,k-m,p-u)

Titan Games & Comics
5436 Riverdale Rd.
College Park, GA 30349
PH: (770) 996-9129
(a-c,e,g,k-m,p-u)

Comic Company
1058 Mistletoe Rd.
Decatur, GA 30033
PH: (404) 248-9846
FX: (404) 325-2334
(a-c,g,m,n,q)

Titan Games & Comics IV
2131 Pleasant Hill Rd.
Duluth, GA 30136
PH: (770) 497-0202
(a-c,e,g,k-m,p-u)

Heroes Ink
2500 Cobb Parkway NW
Kennesaw, GA 30152
PH: (770) 428-3033
(b,c,e,g,k,m,q,s)

Odin's Cosmic Bookshelf
Killian Hill Crossing
4760 Hwy. 29, Suite A-1
Lilburn, GA 30247
PH: (770) 923-0123
(a-c,e,g,h,m,o-s,u)

Titan Games & Comics III
2585 Spring Rd.
Smyrna, GA 30080
PH: (770) 433-8223
(a-c,e,g,k-m,p-u)

Odin's Cosmic Bookshelf
Stone Mountain Festival
1825 Rockbridge Rd. S.W.
Stone Mountain, GA 30087
PH: (770) 413-0123
(a-c,g,k,m,o-s,u)

Titan Games & Comics II
3853 Lawrenceville Hwy.
Tucker, GA 30084
PH: (770) 491-8067
(a-c,e,g,k-m,p-u)

HAWAII

Compleat Comics Company
1728-E Kaahumanu Avenue
Wailuku, HI 96793
PH: (808) 242-5875
(c,k,m,n,p-s,u)

ILLINOIS

Graham Crackers Comics, Ltd.
369 West Army Trail Rd.
Bloomingdale, IL 60108
PH: (630) 894-8810
(b,c,g,k,m,p-s,u)

Graham Crackers Comics, Ltd.
120 North Bolingbrook Dr. (Rt.53)
Bolingbrook, IL 60515
PH: (630) 739-6810
(b,c,g,k,m,o,p,r-u)

Chicago Comics
3244 North Clark St.
Chicago, IL 60657
PH: (773) 528-1983
(a-c,g,k,m,n,p,q,u)

Independence Comics & Cards
3955 West Irving Park Road
Chicago, IL 60618
PH: (773) 539-6720
(a-c,i,k,m,o-s,u)

Joe Sarno's Comic Kingdom
5941 West Irving Park Road
Chicago, IL 60634
PH: (773) 545-2231
(a-d,j,q)

Larry's Comic Book Store
1219 W. Devon Ave.
Chicago, IL 60660
PH: (773) 274-1832
(a-c,q,t,u)

Yesterday
1143 West Addison St.
Chicago, IL 60613
PH: (773) 248-8087
(a,b,d-g,l-n,q,s)

Graham Crackers Comics, Ltd.
7511 Lemont Rd. #190
(75th & Lemont Rd.)
Darien, IL 60561
PH: (630) 910-5059
(b,c,g,k,m,o,p,r)

The Paper Escape
205 West First St.
Dixon, IL 61021
PH: (815) 284-7567
(c,e,m,p,r,s)

Graham Crackers Comics, Ltd.
5232 South Main St.
Downers Grove, IL 60515
PH: (630) 852-1810
(b,c,g,k,m,p-r,t,u)

GEM Comics
156 N. York Rd.
Elmhurst, IL 60126
PH: (630) 833-8787
(b,c,g,k,p-r)

Comix Revolution
999 N. Elmhurst Rd.
Mount Prospect, IL 60056
PH: (847) 506-8948
Web: www.online-revolution.com
(c,e,g,k,q,u)

Joe Sarno's Comic Kingdom II
139 West Prospect Ave.
Mount Prospect, IL 60056
PH: (847) 398-6060
(a-d,g,k,q,r)

Graham Crackers Comics, Ltd.
5 East Chicago Ave.
Naperville, IL 60540
PH: (630) 355-4310
(a-c,g,j-n,p-u)

M & M Comic Service
13617 Southwest Hwy.
Orland Park, IL 60462
PH: (708) 349-2486
Web: www.mmcomics.com
(b,c,g,i,k,o,p,q,u)

Gem City Coin & Supply
828 Maine
Quincy, IL 62301
PH: (217) 224-0529
(a-c,k,q)

Tomorrow Is Yesterday, Inc.
5600 N. 2nd St.
Rockford, IL 61111
PH: (815) 633-0330
(a-n,p-u)

Graham Crackers Comics, Ltd.
108 East Main St. (Rt.64)
St. Charles, IL 60174
PH: (630) 584-0610
(b,c,g,k,m,o,p,r,s,u)

Keith's Komix, Inc.
528 S. Roselle Rd.
Schaumburg, IL 60193
PH: (847) 534-9436
(a-c,e,g,j,k)

Unicorn Comics & Cards
216 S. Villa Avenue
Villa Park, IL 60181
PH: (630) 279-5777
(a-d,f,g,k,m,p,q,s)

Graham Crackers Comics, Ltd.
1207 East Butterfield Rd.
Wheaton, IL 60187
PH: (630) 668-1350
(b,c,g,k,m,o,p,r)

Igor's Comic Book Emporium
123 N. Main St.
Wheaton, IL 60187
PH: (630) 260-8787
(b,c,g,k,p,q,r)

INDIANA

Comic Cave
3221 E. 17th Street
Columbus, IN 47201
PH: (812) 372-8430
E-Mail: comiccave@surf-ici.com
(b,c,g,k,m,p-s,u)

The Book Broker
2127 S. Weinbach Ave.
Evansville, IN 47714
PH: (812) 479-5647
(a-i,l-n,p-u)

Comic Quest
2136 Morgan Ave.
Evansville, IN 47711
PH: (812) 474-1133
E-Mail: comquest@evansville.net
Web: comicquest.com
(a-c,e,g,k,m,p,q,s,u)

Matthew Hawes' Comics Unlimited
654-B E. Diamond Ave.
Evansville, IN 47711
PH: (812) 423-6952
(b,c,m,p-s)

Books Comics and Things
2212 Maplecrest Rd.
Fort Wayne, IN 46815-7628
PH: (219) 446-0025
Web: www.bctcomics.com
(a-c,g,k,m,p-u)

Books Comics and Things #2
5936 West Jefferson Blvd.
Fort Wayne, IN 46804-1677
PH: (219) 436-0159
(a-c,g,k,m,p-u)

Comic Carnival
6265 North Carrollton Ave.
Indianapolis, IN 46220
PH: (317) 253-8882
(a-j,l-t)

Comic Carnival
7311 U.S. 31 South
Indianapolis, IN 46227
PH: (317) 889-8899
(a-j,l-t)

Comic Carnival
3837 N. High School Rd.
Indianapolis, IN 46254
PH: (317) 293-4386
(a-j,l-t)

Comic Carnival
9729 East Washington St.
Indianapolis, IN 46229
PH: (317) 898-5010
(a-j,l-t)

Downtown Comics
111 N. Pennsylvania St.
Indianapolis, IN 46204
PH: (317) 237-0397
(a-u)

Downtown Comics - Carmel
13682 N. Meridian St.
Indianapolis, IN 46032
PH: (317) 848-2305
(a-u)

Downtown Comics - Castleton
5767 E. 86th St.
Indianapolis, IN 46258
PH: (317) 845-9991
(a-u)

Downtown Comics - Greenwood
8925 S. Meridian St.
Indianapolis, IN 46227
PH: (317) 885-6395
(a-u)

Downtown Comics - West
8336 W. 10th St.
Indianapolis, IN 46234
PH: (317) 271-7610
(a-u)

Galactic Greg's
1407 East Lincolnway
Valparaiso, IN 46383
PH: (219) 464-0119
(b,c,g,m,n,p-r,u)

IOWA

Oak Leaf Comics
1926 Valley Park Drive
Cedar Falls, IA 50613
PH: (319) 277-1835
(a-c,f,k,m,n,p-s,u)

Xanadu
3001 Merle Hay Rd.
Des Moines, IA 50310
PH: (515) 251-3933
Web: members.aol.com/xanadude/
(b,c,g,k,l,n,p-s,u)

Oak Leaf Comics
23-5th St. S.W.
Mason City, IA 50401
PH: (515) 424-0333
(a-c,f,i,k-s,u)

KANSAS

Prairie Dog Comics
Main Store
7130 West Maple, Ste. 150
Wichita, KS 67209
PH: (316) 942-3456
(a-u)

KENTUCKY

Pac-Rat's
1051 Bryant Way
Bowling Green, KY 42103
PH: (502) 782-8092
(a-c,e,g,h,k,l,m,p-s)

Comic Book World, Inc
7130 Turfway Rd.
Florence, KY 41042
PH: (606) 371-9562
(a-c,m,n,p-u)

Collectibles Etc
115 Locust Hill Dr. Suite 106
Lexington, KY 40509
PH: (606) 269-6633
(a-c,g,j,k,m,p-r,u)

Collectibles Etc
200 Bolivar Street
Lexington, KY 40508
PH: (606) 225-4639
(a-c,g,k,m,n,p-s,u)

Red Rock Collectables
929 Liberty Road
Lexington, KY 40505
PH: (606) 225-5452
E-Mail: redrock
@mindspring.com
Web: www.spage.com/
redrock/
(c,e,g,j,k,m,n,p-s,u)

Comic Book World, Inc.
6905 Shepherdsville Rd.
Louisville, KY 40219
PH: (502) 964-5500
(a-c,g,m,n,p-u)

The Great Escape
2433 Bardstown Rd.
Louisville, KY 40205
PH: (502) 456-2216
(a-c,e,g,i,k,l,m,n,p-u)

LOUISIANA

B.T. & W.D. Giles
P. O. Box 271
Keithville, LA 71047
PH: (318) 925-6654
(a,b,d-f,h,l)

More Fun Comics
8200 Oak Street
New Orleans, LA 70118
PH: (504) 865-1800
(b,c,e,g,k,m,n,q,r)

MAINE

Top Shelf Comics
34 Main St.
Bangor, ME 04401
PH: (207) 947-4939
FX: (207) 947-4939
E-Mail: topshelf
@tcomics.com
Web: http://www.tcomics
.com
(a-c,g,m,q,r)

Moonshadow Comics
251 US Route 1
Falmouth, ME 04105
PH: (207) 781-8902
(a-c,g,i,m,n,q-u)

MARYLAND

Comic Book Kingdom, Inc
4307 Harford Rd
Baltimore, MD 21214
PH: (410) 426-4529
(a-d,f,g,i,k,m,q)

Geppi's Comic World
Harbor Place
301 Light Street Pavilion
Baltimore, MD 21202
PH: (410) 547-0910
(a-c,k-m,q,s,t)

Geppi's Comic World
Security
1722 North Rolling Rd.
Baltimore, MD 21244
PH: (410) 298-1758
FX: (410) 298-1727
(a-c,k-m,q,s,t)

Big Planet Comics
4908 Fairmont Ave.
Bethesda, MD 20814
PH: (301) 654-6856
Web: www.erols.com/
bpcomics
(b,c,n,p,q)

Alternate Worlds
72 Cranbrook Rd.
Yorktowne Plaza
Cockeysville, MD 21030
PH: (410) 666-3290
(b,c,g,k-n,p-u)

The Closet of Comics
7315 Baltimore Ave. (U.S.1)
College Park, MD 20740
PH: (301) 699-0498
(a-e,g,h,m,n,p,q)

Comics To Astonish
9400 Snowden River Pkwy.
Columbia, MD 21045
PH: (410) 381-2732
(a-c,j,k,m,p-r)

Cosmic Comix & Toys
8290 Main St.
Ellicott City, MD 21043
PH: (410) 461-4161
E-Mail: cosmicx@erols.com
(a-c,g,k,n,q-s,u)

Comic Classics
203 East Main St.
Frostburg, MD 21532
PH: (301) 689-1823
(a-c,m,n,p,q,s)

Beyond Comics
701 Russell Ave.
Gaithersburg, MD 20877
PH: (301) 216-0007
Web: www.beyondcomics
.com
(a-c,i-k,n,p,q,u)

Comic Classics
365 Main St.
Laurel, MD 20707
PH: (301) 490-9811
(410) 792-4744
(a-c,k,m,n,p,q,s-u)

Adventure Comics
1063 Rockville Pike
Rockville, MD 20852
PH: (301) 251-2888
E-Mail: advcomix@erols.com
Web: www.erols.com/
advcomix/
(a-c,j,k,p,q)

Geppi's Comic World
Silver Spring
8317 Fenton St.
Silver Spring, MD 20910
PH: (301) 588-2546
(a-c,k-m,q,s,t)

MASSACHUSETTS

New England Comics
131 Harvard Ave.
Allston, MA 02134
PH: (617) 783-1848
Web: www.necomics.com
(a-c,e,g,k-n,p-u)

Monkeyhouse, LTD.
5 Market Sq. Ste. B-6
Amesbury, MA 01913
PH: (978) 388-5550
(a-e,g,i-n,q-s,u)

Megaverse City
Comics & Collectibles
608 Dorchester Ave.
Boston, MA 02127
PH: (888) 675-4857
Web: www.megaversecity
.com
(b,c,e,g,k-n,p-s,u)

New England Comics
1840 Centre St.
West Roxbury
Boston, MA 02132
PH: (617) 325-1848
Web: www.necomics.com
(a-c,e,g,k-n,p-u)

New England Comics
744 Crescent St.
East Crossing Plaza
Brockton, MA 02402
PH: (508) 559-5068
Web: www.necomics.com
(a-c,e,g,k-n,p-u)

New England Comics
316 Harvard St.
Coolidge Corner
Brookline, MA 02146
PH: (617) 566-0115
Web: www.necomics.com
(a-c,e,g,k-n,p-u)

New England Comics
14A Eliot St.
Harvard Square
Cambridge, MA 02138
PH: (617) 354-5352
Web: www.necomics.com
(a-c,e,g,k-n,p-u)

That's Entertainment
371 John Fitch Highway
Fitchburg, MA 01420
PH: (978) 342-8607
Web: www.thatse.com
(a-u)

Bedrock Comics
Framingham Mall
400 Cochituate Rd. (Rte. 30)
Framingham, MA 01701
PH: (508) 872-2317
(a-u)

Jams Comic Connection
435 King St. (Rt. 110/2A)
Littleton, MA 01460
PH: (978) 486-1099
(c,e,g,k,m,p-s)

New England Comics
18 Pleasant St.
Malden Center
Malden, MA 02148
PH: (781) 322-2404
Web: www.necomics.com
(a-c,e,g,k-n,p-u)

New England Comics
732 Washington St.
Norwood Center
Norwood, MA 02062
PH: (781) 769-4552
Web: www.necomics.com
(a-c,e,g,k-n,p-u)

Megaverse City II
11 Brook St.
Quincy, MA 02170
(b,c,e,g,k-n,p-s,u)

New England Comics
1511 Hancock St.
Quincy Center
Quincy, MA 02169
PH: (617) 770-1848
Web: www.necomics.com
(a-c,e,g,k-n,p-u)

New England Comics
FFAST New Comic Service
(Mail Order Only)
P.O. Box 310
Quincy, MA 02269
PH: (617) 774-1745
Web: www.necomics.com
(a-c,e,g,k-n,p-u)

Web-Head Enterprises Ltd.
239 North Ave.
Wakefield, MA 01880
PH: (781) 246-1797
Web: www.angelfire.com/ma/Webheadenterprises
(a-g,l,n,q)

The Outer Limits
463 Moody St.
Waltham, MA 02154
PH: (781) 891-0444
(a-u)

That's Entertainment
244 Park Avenue
Worcester, MA 01609
PH: (508) 755-4207
FX: (508) 754-3882
Web: www.thatse.com
(a-u)

MICHIGAN

Cashman's Comics & Collectibles
1018 S. Madison Ave.
Bay City, MI 48708-7261
PH: (517) 895-1113
(a-c,g,k-u)

Comics North!
211 N. Main St.
Cheboygan, MI 49721-1639
PH: (616) 627-3740
(b,c,g,i,k,p-u)

Curious Book Shop
307 East Grand River
East Lansing, MI 48823
PH: (517) 332-0112
(d-k,m,s)

Curious Comic Shop
210 M. A. C. Ave.
East Lansing, MI 48823
PH: (517) 332-0222
(a-c,m,n,p-u)

Amazing Book Store, Inc.
3718 Richfield Rd.
Flint, MI 48506
PH: (810) 736-3025
(a-c,n,q)

Argos Book Shop
1405 Robinson Rd. S.E.
Grand Rapids, MI 49506
PH: (616) 454-0111
(a-k,p-u)

Tardy's Collector's Corner, Inc.
2009 Eastern Ave., S.E.
Grand Rapids, MI 49507
PH: (616) 247-7828
(a-c,g,n,p,q)

Galaxy Comics II
1319 S. Mission
Mt. Pleasant, MI 48858
PH: (517) 775-7838
(b,c,g,k,m,p,q,s)

Galaxy Comics
3089 Bay Plaza Dr.
Saginaw, MI 48604
PH: (517) 799-6334
(a-c,g,k,m,n,p-s,u)

Tardy's Collector's Corner, Inc.
2313 Lee St. S. W. (At Porter)
Wyoming, MI 49509
PH: (616) 531-5161
(a-k,m-u)

MINNESOTA

Nostalgia Zone
3149 1/2 Hennepin Ave. S.
Minneapolis, MN 55408
PH: (612) 822-2806
E-Mail: nostzone@spacestar.net
(a,b,d-n,p,q,u)

Midway Book & Comic
1579 University Ave.
St Paul, MN 55104
PH: (612) 644-7605
(a-h,n,q)

MISSOURI

Betty's Books and Collectible Comics
1520 B Gravois Rd.
High Ridge, MO 63049
PH: (314) 677-3197
(a,b,e,h)

Antiquarium Books & Collectibles
504 East High St.
Jefferson City, MO 65101
PH: (573) 636-8995
(a-h,k-m,p-t)

The Book Barn
3128 S. Main
Joplin, MO 64804
PH: (417) 782-2778
FX: (417) 782-0024
E-Mail: bb@talleytech.com
(a-c,e,g,h,k-n,q-s,u

Friendly Frank's Comic Cavern
5404 N.W. 64th St.
Kansas City, MO 64151
PH: (816) 746-4569
(a-d,f,g,j-n,p-u)

Not Just Comix
339 West Main St.
Park Hills, MO 63601
PH: (573) 431-4587
(b,c,g,m,p-s,u)

MO's Comics & Stories
4573 Gravois
St. Louis, MO 63116
PH: (314) 353-9500
(a-d,f,g,k,o-q)

MONTANA

The Book Exchange
Butte Plaza Mall
3100 Harrison Ave.
Butte, MT 59701
PH: (406) 494-7788
(a-c,e,h,q-s)

The Book Exchange
2335 Brooks St.
Missoula, MT 59801
PH: (406) 728-6342
(a-c,e,h,q-s)

NEVADA

5TH Dimension
5020 E. Tropicana Ave.
Las Vegas, NV 89122
PH: (702) 435-2525
FX: (702) 435-5544
Web: www.5thdimension.shop
(b,c,e,g,i-l,n,p-r,u)

Silver Cactus Comics
560 N. Nellis Blvd. #E8/9
Las Vegas, NV 89110
PH: (702) 438-4408
FX: (702) 438-5208
(b,c,e,g,k,l,m,p-s,u)

Silver Cactus Comics
4250 S. Rainbow Blvd.
Las Vegas, NV 89103
PH: (702) 222-1668
(b,c,e,g,k,l,m,p-s,u)

NEW HAMPSHIRE

James F. Payette
P. O. Box 750
Bethlehem, NH 03574
PH: (603) 869-2097
(a,b,d-h)

Collectibles Unlimited
30A Warren St.
Concord, NH 03301
PH: (603) 228-3712
(b,c,m,q,r,s)

NEW JERSEY

The Hobby Shop
1077 C State Hwy #34
Aberdeen Townsquare Shopping Ctr
Aberdeen, NJ 07747
PH: (732) 583-0505
Web: www.hobbystores.com/hobbyshopnj
(c,k,m,q,r,u)

Pegasus Enterprises
607 Main St.
Boonton, NJ 07005
PH: (973) 335-3428
(a-c,g,k,l,m,p,q)

Altered State Comics & Cards
234 Main St.
Chatham, NJ 07928
PH: (973) 701-1569
E-Mail: comix973@aol.com
(b,c,g,k,m,q,s,u)

Comics and More
Cherry Hill Mall
Upper Level
Cherry Hill, NJ 08002
PH: (609) 663-7550
(b,c,g,k,m,p-u)

Eldorado Comics
2110 E. Rt. 70
P. O. Box 3630
Cherry Hill, NJ 08034
PH: (609) 489-1199
(a-g,i-k,m,n,p-u)

Thunder Road Sportscards and Comics
1973 North Olden Ave.
Ewing, NJ 08618
PH: (609) 771-1055
(a,b,k,m,q)

A Time Lost.....And Found
310 East Evesham Rd.
Glendora, NJ 08029
PH: (609) 939-1909
(a-c,k,m,n,p,s,t)

Thunder Road Sportscards and Comics
1637 Route 33
Hamilton Square, NJ 08690
PH: (609) 587-5353
(a,b,k,m,q)

APS Enterprise
(Mail Order)
593 Blackwood-Clementon Rd. Suite 135
Lindenwold, NJ 08021-5901
PH: (800) 581-9095
(l-u)

Comics Plus
Middletown Plaza
1383 Hwy. 35
Middletown, NJ 07748
PH: (732) 706-0102
(a-c,g,h,k,m,p,q)

One Flight Up Books
63 Main St.
Millburn, NJ 07041
PH: (201) 467-9288
(b,c,g,i,k-r)

Comic Explosion
339 Franklin Ave.
Nutley, NJ 07110
PH: (973) 235-1336
(c,g,m,n,p,q,u)

Fat Jack's Comicrypt
521 White Horse Pike
Oaklyn, NJ 08107
PH: (609) 858-3877
(a-c,g,m,n,p,q,u)

MC Comics Inc.
54 Old Matawan Rd.
Old Bridge, NJ 08857
PH: (732) 238-5969
FX: (732) 238-8435
Web: www.pokerindustries
.com
(b,c,g,k,m,n,p-t)

Zapp! Comics,
Cards & Toys
3322A Washington Rd.
Parlin, NJ 08859
PH: (732) 727-4700
FX: (732) 727-4242
(a-c,g,k,m,n,p,q,s-u)

Passaic Book Center Inc.
267 Passaic St.
Passaic, NJ 07055
PH: (973) 778-0416
FX: (973) 778-6823
(a-u)

Excellent Adventures
72 Hanover St.
Pemberton, NJ 08068
PH: (609) 894-0255
(a-c,f,g,k,m,o-s,u)

Comics Plus
Ocean Plaza
Hwy. 35 & Sunset Ave.
Wanamassa, NJ 07712
PH: (732) 922-3308
(a-c,g,h,k,m,p,q)

Zapp! Comics,
Cards & Toys
574 Valley Rd.
Wayne, NJ 07470
PH: (973) 628-4500
FX: (973) 628-1771
E-Mail: zappcomics
@aol.com
(a-c,g,k,m,n,p,q,s,u)

Frankenstein Comics
845 Mantua Pike Route 45
Woodbury, NJ 08096
PH: (609) 848-6347
(b,c,e,g,k,l,m)

JHV Associates
By Appointment Only
P. O. Box 317
Woodbury Hghts, NJ 08097
PH: (609) 845-4010
(a,b,d)

NEW YORK

Silver Age Comics
22-55 31 St.
Astoria, NY 11105
PH: (718) 721-9691
PH: (800) 278-9691
FX: (718) 728-9691
E-Mail: gus
@silveragecomics.com
Web: www.silveragecomics
.com
(a-c,f,g,k,m,n,p-s,u)

Long Island Comics
1675 Sunrise Highway
Bay Shore, NY 11706
PH: (516) 665-4342
(12-6 p.m. only)
E-Mail: licomics@aol.com
(b,c,g,q)

Wow Comics
2084 White Plains Road
Bronx, NY 10462
PH: (718) 829-0461
FX: (718) 828-1700
E-Mail: wowcomics@aol.com
Web: www.pelhamparkway
.com/wow/wow.htm
(a-c,e,k,m,o-s,u)

Pinocchio Collectibles
1814 McDonald Ave.
Brooklyn, NY 11223
PH: (718) 645-2573
(a-c,g,k,m,q)

Comic Quest
57-10 Hoffman Drive
Elmhurst, NY 11373
PH: (718) 205-8174
(c,d,e,g,k,m,n,q,r)

Golden Memories
250 Broadway
Hicksville, NY 11801
PH: (516) 932-8581
(a-c,k,m,q)

Comics & Hobbies
156 Mamaroneck Ave.
Mamaroneck, NY 10543
(c,h,m,q,r)

Best Comics & Hobby Ctr.
Tommy Maletta
252-02 Northern Blvd.
Little Neck, NY 11362
PH: (718) 279-2099
(a-c,o,q)

Action Comics
1551 Second Ave., 2nd Floor
New York, NY 10028
PH: (212) 639-1976
(a-c,g,k,m,p-s,u)

Alex's MVP
Cards & Comics
256 East 89th St.
New York, NY 10128
PH: (212) 831-2273
FX: (212) 831-4825
E-Mail: MVPALEX@aol.com
(a-c,g,j,k,m,n,p-s)

Four Color Comics
115 West 27th St.
New York, NY 10007
PH: (212) 675-6990

Funny Business
Comics, Ltd.
660 B Amsterdam Ave.
at 92nd St.
New York, NY 10025
PH: (212) 799-9477
(b,c,l-n,q)

Gotham City Comics
800 Lexington Ave.
New York, NY 10021
PH: (212) 980-0009
E-Mail: GothamCT@aol.com
(b,c,e,g-u)

Jerry Ohlinger's Movie
Material Store, Inc.
242 West 14 Street
New York, NY 10011
PH: (212) 989-0869
(i)

Jim Hanley's Universe
4 West 33rd Street
(Opposite the Empire State
Building)
New York, NY 10001
PH: (212) 268-7088
(a-c,g,m,n,p-u)

Manhattan Comics
& Cards
228 West 23rd. St.
New York, NY 10011
PH: (212) 243-9349
(a-c,g,j-n,q,u)

Metropolis Collectibles
873 Broadway, Suite 201
New York, NY 10003
PH: (212) 260-4147
(a,b,k,i,j)

Village Comics
214 Sullivan Street
New York, NY 10012
PH: (212) 777-2770
(b,c,e,g,h,k,m,n,p,q,s,u)

Fantastic Planet
24 Oak St.
Plattsburgh, NY 12901
PH: (518) 563-2946
(c,e,m,p-t)

Dragon's Den
Poughkeepsie Plaza
Poughkeepsie, NY 12601
PH: (914) 471-1401
Web: www.dragons-den
.com
(b,c,e,g,k,m,p-r,u)

All That Jazz Comics
& Collectables
Rochester, NY 14625
PH: (716) 586-0994
(a-d,f,h-q)

Empire® Comics
1176 Mt. Hope Ave.
Rochester, NY 14620
PH: (716) 442-0371
(a-c,f,h,k,m,q-s,u)

Empire® Comics
375 Stone Rd.
Rochester, NY 14616
PH: (716) 663-6877
(a-c,f,h,k,m,q-s,u)

Amazing Comics
12 Gillette Ave.
Sayville, NY 11782
PH: (516) 567-8069
(a-c,j,k,m,p-r)

One if by Cards,
Two if by Comics
1107 Central Ave.
Scarsdale, NY 10583
PH: (914) 725-2225
Web: www.1ifbycards.com
(b,c,k,m,q,r,s)

Electric City Comics
1704 Van Vranken Ave.
Schenectady, NY 12308
PH: (518) 377-1500
(a-c, g,k,p,q,u)

Jim Hanley's Universe
325 New Dorp Lane
Staten Island, NY 10306
PH: (718) 351-6299
(a-c,g,m,n,p-u)

Krypton Comics
604 Midland Ave.
Staten Island, NY 10306
PH: (718) 667-7695
FX: (718) 667-7695
(b,c,g,k,m,q)

Twilight Book & Game
1401 North Salina St.
Syracuse, NY 13208
PH: (315) 471-3139
(a-c,e,g,k,m,n,p-u)

Ravenswood, Inc.
263 Genesee St.
Utica, NY 13501
PH: (315) 735-3699
(a-c,g,m,p-t)

NORTH CAROLINA

Super Giant Comics
697 Brevard Rd.
Asheville, NC 28806
PH: (704) 665-2800
(a-c,j,l,n,q)

Heroes Aren't Hard To Find
Corner Central Ave.
& The Plaza
P. O. Box 9181
Charlotte, NC 28299
PH: (704) 375-7462
(a-c,g,j-n,p,s,u)

Acme Comics
3808-C High Point Rd.
Greensboro, NC 27405
PH: (336) 855-0217
Web: www.acmecomics.com
(a-c,k,p,q,s,u)

Acme Comics
2150 Lawndale Dr.
Greensboro, NC 27408
PH: (336) 574-2263
Web: www.acmecomics.com
(a-c,k,p,q,s,u)

Parts Unknown, The Comic Book Store
906 Spring Garden St.
Greensboro, NC 27403
PH: (910) 272-7060
(a-c,e,g,n,p)

Capitol Comics of Raleigh
3027-A Hillsborough Street
Raleigh, NC 27607
PH: (919) 832-4600
(a-c,m,p,q)

Capitol Comics II
5212 Hollyridge Drive
Raleigh, NC 27612
PH: (919) 781-9500
(a-c,k,m,p,q,s)

Tales Resold
3936 Atlantic Ave.
Raleigh, NC 27604
PH: (919) 878-8551
(a-c,e,g,h,j,q)

Comics & Cards Unlimited
506 Waynesville Plaza
Waynesville, NC 28786
PH: (704) 456-8787
(a-c,g,k,l,m,q,r)

NORTH DAKOTA

Tom's Coin Stamp Gem Baseball & Comic Shop
#2 1st Street S.W.
Minot, ND 58701
PH: (701) 852-4522
(a-q,s,u)

OHIO

Kenmore Komics & Games
1020 Kenmore Blvd.
Akron, OH 44314
PH: (330) 745-5530
Web: www.kenmore-komics.com
(b,c,m,p-u)

Dark Star III Books & Comics
1273 North Fairfield Rd.
Beavercreek, OH 45432
PH: (937) 427-3213
(b,c,e,g,k,m,p-s)

Comic Book World, Inc.
4016 Harrison Ave.
Cincinnati, OH 45211
PH: (513) 661-6300
(a-c,m,n,p-u)

Collectors Warehouse, Inc.
5437 Pearl Rd.
Cleveland, OH 44129
PH: (440) 842-2896
FX: (440) 842-5319
Web: members.aol.com/memorabili
(a-d,f,g,i,k,m,n,p-s)

British Papermill
5733 Brice Outlet Mall
Columbus, OH 43232
PH: (614) 577-0220
(b,g,k)

Bookery Fantasy & Comics
16 W. Main St.
Fairborn, OH 45324
PH: (937) 879-1408
FX: (937) 879-9327
E-Mail: bookeryfan@aol.com
Web: www.bookeryfantasy.com
(a-u)

Bookie Parlor
3000 Shroyer Rd.
Kettering, OH 45429
PH: (937) 293-2243
(a-c,g,m,p,q,s)

Parker's Records & Comics
1222 Suite C Route 28
Milford, OH 45150
PH: (513) 575-3665
FX: (513) 575-3665
(a-c,g,l,m,n,p-s)

Funnie Farm Bookstore
328 N. Dixie Dr.
Vandalia, OH 45377
PH: (937) 898-2794
(a-c,k,m,p-r)

Dark Star Books & Comics
237 Xenia Ave. (Rt. 68)
Yellow Springs, OH 45387
PH: (937) 767-9400
(b,c,e-h,k-n,p,q,s-u)

OKLAHOMA

New World Comics & Games
6219 N. Meridian
Oklahoma City, OK 73112
PH: (405) 721-7634
(a-d,g,k,m,p-u)

New World Comics & Games
4420 SE 44th St.
Oklahoma City, OK 73135
PH: (405) 677-2559
(c,g,k,m,p-u)

Comic Empire of Tulsa
3122 S. Mingo
Tulsa, OK 74146
PH: (918) 664-5808
(a-c,g,m,n,p,q)

Starbase 21
2130 S. Sheridan Rd.
Tulsa, OK 74129
PH: (918) 838-3388
(a-c,e,g,i-m,p-u)

Want List Comics
(Appointment Only)
P. O. Box 701932
Tulsa, OK 74170-1932
PH: (918) 299-0440
(a,b,f,h-k,m)

OREGON

Emerald City Comics
770 E 13th
Eugene, OR 97401
PH: (541) 345-2568
(c,e,g,k-n,q,r,u)

Emerald City Comics III
3135 West 11th-G-1
Eugene, OR 97402
PH: (541) 342-5243
(c,g,k,m,q,r)

Nostalgia Collectibles
527 Willamette
Eugene, OR 97401
PH: (541) 484-9202
(a-i,k-n,p,q,s)

Beyond Comics
322 East Main
Medford, OR 97501
PH: (541) 779-9543
(a-c,p,q,r)

Future Dream East Burnside
1800 East Burnside
Portland, OR 97214-1599
PH: (503) 231-8311
E-Mail: fdb@hevanet.com
(a-c,e-j,m,n,p-u)

Heroes Haven
627 S.E. Jackson St.
Roseburg, OR 97470
PH: (541) 673-5004
E-Mail: grendel@rosenet.net
(a-c,g,k,m,p-s,u)

Ancient Wonders
19060 SW Boones Ferry
Tualatin, OR 97062
PH: (503) 692-0753
FX: (503) 691-7988
(b,c,l,m,p-s)

PENNSYLVANIA

Cap's Comic Cavalcade
1894 Catasauqua Rd.
Allentown, PA 18106
PH: (610) 264-5540
(a-c,e,g,k,m,p-u)

Dreamscape Comics
310 West Broad St.
Bethlehem, PA 18018
PH: (610) 867-1178
(a-c,m,n,p-r)

Showcase Comics
874 West Lancaster Ave.
Bryn Mawr, PA 19010
PH: (610) 527-6236
(a-c,k,m,n,p-s,u)

Comix Connection - Camp Hill
604 Camp Hill Mall
Camp Hill, PA 17011
PH: (800) 730-0994
(a-c,k,m,n,q-s,u)

New Dimension Comics
20550 Route 19, Piazza Plaza
Cranberry Township, PA 16066-7520
PH: (412) 776-0433
(a-c,g,k-n,p-s)

Dreamscape Comics
25th St. Shopping Center
Easton, PA 18045
PH: (610) 250-9818
(a-c,m,n,p-r)

New Dimension Comics
508 Lawrence Avenue
Ellwood City, PA 16117
PH: (412) 758-2324
(a-c,g,k-n,p-s)

Comic Collection, Toys & Compact Discs
931 Bustleton Pike
at Street Rd.
Feasterville, PA 19053
PH: (215) 357-3332
Web: members.aol.com/comicdeity/index.html
(a-c,g,j-n,p,r-u)

Comics and More Upper Level
King of Prussia Plaza
King of Prussia, PA 19406
PH: (610) 337-1555
(b,c,g,k,m,p-u)

The Comic Store
28 McGovern Ave.
Lancaster, PA 17602
PH: (717) 397-8737
(a-c,e,g,m,n,p-s,u)

Showcase Comics
Granite Run Mall
1067 West Baltimore Pike
Media, PA 19063
PH: (610) 891-9229
(a-c,k,m,n,p-s,u)

Comics and Paperbacks Plus
201 E. Main St.
Palmyra, PA 17078
PH: (717) 838-4854
(c,e,g,h,k,m,p,q,u)

Comics and More
2550 Cottman Ave.
Philadelphia, PA 19149
PH: (215) 333-6869
(b,c,g,k,m,p-u)

Fat Jack's Comicrypt
2006 Sansom St.
Philadelphia, PA 19103
PH: (215) 963-0788
(a-c,g,m,n,p,q,u)

Fat Jack's Comicrypt
7596 Haverford Ave.
Philadelphia, PA 19151
PH: (215) 473-6333
(a-c,g,m,n,p,q,u)

Showcase Comics
424 South St.
Philadelphia, PA 19147
PH: (215) 829-0554
(a-c,k,m,n,p-s,u)

Duncan Comics, Books, and Accessories
1047 Perry Highway
Pittsburgh, PA 15237
PH: (412) 635-0886
(a-e,g,h,k,m,n,p-r)

Eide's Entertainment
1111 Penn Ave.
Pittsburgh, PA 15222
PH: (412) 261-0900
FX: (412) 261-3102
E-Mail: eides@eides.com
Web: www.eides.com
(a-q,s-u)

Comic Store West
351 Loucks Rd.
York, PA 17404
PH: (717) 845-9198
(c,m,q,r)

Comix Connection - York
1201 Carlisle Rd.
York, PA 17404
PH: (717) 843-6516
(a-c,k,m,n,q-s,u)

RHODE ISLAND

The Annex
314 Broadway
Newport, RI 02840
PH: (401) 847-4607
(b,c,g,k,m,n,q-s,u)

Kelly's Comics & Collectibles
2443 W. Shore Rd.
Warwick, RI 02886
PH: (401) 732-8383
(a-q,s,u)

SOUTH CAROLINA

Planet Comics
3448 Cinema Center
Anderson, SC 29621
PH: (864) 261-3578
(a-c,g,k,m,n,p-s,u)

Heroes & Dragons Mega-Store
Boozer Shopping Ctr.
1563-B Broad River Rd.
Columbia, SC 29210
PH: (803) 731-4376
FX: (803) 772-5010
E-Mail: hdcomics
@aol.com
Web: heroesanddragons
.com
(b,c,k,m,p-s,u)

SOUTH DAKOTA

Storyteller
520 Sixth St.
Rapid City, SD 57701
PH: (605) 348-7242
E-Mail: story@rapidcity.com
(a-c,e,k,m,p-s,u)

TENNESSEE

Reward Investments, LLC
745 W. Elk Ave.
Elizabethton, TN 37643
PH: (423) 547-3655
(a-c,e,g,k,m,p-s)

The Great Escape
111-B Gallatin Rd., North
Madison, TN 37115
PH: (615) 865-8052
(a-c,e-h,k-n,p-u)

The Great Escape
1925 Broadway
Nashville, TN 37203
PH: (615) 327-0646
(a-u)

TEXAS

Lone Star Comics Books & Games
511 East Abram St.
Arlington, TX 76010
PH: (817) 860-7827
FX: (817) 860-2769
E-Mail:
lonestar@metronet.com
Web: www.lonestar-comics
.com/
(a-c,e,g,k,m,p-u)

Lone Star Comics Books & Games
504 East Abram St.
Arlington, TX 76010
PH: (817) Metro 265-0491
(a-c,e,g,k,m,p-u)

Lone Star Comics Books & Games
3415 South Cooper St., #141
Arlington, TX 76015
PH: (817) 557-5252
(b,c,e,g,k,m,p-u)

Austin Books
(Brad Bankston, Mgr)
5002 N. Lamar
Austin, TX 78751
PH: (512) 454-4197
(a-e,g-i,k,m,n,p,q,s-u)

Lone Star Comics Books & Games
11661 Preston Rd. #151
Dallas, TX 75230
PH: (214) 373-0934
(a-c,e,g,k,m,p-u)

Remember When
2431 Valwood Pkwy.
Dallas, TX 75234
PH: (972) 243-3439
(a-c,g,i,m,p,q,s,t)

Titan Comics
9444 Marsh Lane
Dallas, TX 75220
PH: (214) 350-4420
(a-c,g,n,p,q)

All Star Comixs & Games
4406 Dyer St.
El Paso, TX 79904
PH: (915) 562-0443
(b,c,g,i,k,m,o,q-s)

Lone Star Comics Books & Games
6312 Hulen Bend Blvd.
Ft. Worth, TX 76132
PH: (817) 346-7773
(b,c,e,g,k,m,p-u)

Bedrock City Comic Co.
6521 Westheimer
Houston, TX 77057
PH: (713) 780-0675
FX: (713) 780-2366
E-Mail: bedrock@flash.net
Web: bedrockcity.com
(a-h,j,k,m-q,s,u)

Bedrock City Comic Co.
2204-D FM. 1960 W.
Houston, TX 77090
PH: (281) 444-9763
E-Mail: bedrock2@flash.net
Web: bedrockcity.com
(a-h,j,k,m-q,s,u)

Phoenix Comics & Games
2424 Montrose
Houston, TX 77006
PH: (713) 524-1150
(c,e,g,p-r,u)

Third Planet
2718 Southwest Freeway
Houston, TX 77098
PH: (713) 528-1067
E-Mail: 3planet
@third-planet.com
Web: www.third-planet.com
(a-u)

Lone Star Comics Books & Games
931 Melbourne
Hurst, TX 76053
PH: (817) 595-4375
(b,c,e,g,k,m,p-u)

Lone Star Comics Books & Games
2550 N. Beltine Rd.
Irving, TX 75062
PH: (972) 659-0317
(b,c,e,g,k,m,p-u)

Lone Star Comics Books & Games
3600 Gus Thomasson
Suite 107
Mesquite, TX 75150
PH: (972) 681-2040
(b,c,e,g,k,m,p-u)

Lone Star Comics Books & Games
3100 Independence Pkwy
Suite 219
Plano, TX 75075
PH: (972) 985-1953
(b,c,e,g,k,m,p-u)

Ground Zero Comics
1700 SSE Loop 323 Ste. 302
Tyler, TX 75701
PH: (903) 566-1185
(c,e,g,l,m,p-s,u)

Bankston's Used Books
(Brent Bankston, Mgr)
1321 S. Valley Mills Dr.
Waco, TX 76711
PH: (254) 755-0070
(b,c,f-i,k,m,p,q,s)

VIRGINIA

Comic and Card Collectorama
2008 Mt. Vernon Ave.
Alexandria, VA 22301
(Greater D. C. area)
PH: (703) 548-3466
(a-c,e,f,h,m,p,q,s,t)

Geppi's Comic World Crystal City
1606 Crystal Square Arcade
Arlington, VA 22202
PH: (703) 413-0618
(a-c,k-m,q,s,t)

Atlas Comics
1691 Seminole Trail
Charlottesville, VA 22901
PH: (804) 974-7512
(b,c,e,g,k,m,p-s,u)

Zeno's Books
1112 Sparrow Rd.
Chesapeake, VA 23325
PH: (757) 420-2344
(a-j,m,r,t)

Hole in the Wall Books
905 W. Broad St.
Falls Church, VA 22046
PH: (703) 536-2511
(b-e,g,h,l,q,s,t,u)

Marie's Books And Things
1701 Princess Anne Street
Fredericksburg, VA 22401-1344
PH: (540) 373-5196
(a-c,e-h,k-m,p-q,s-u)

Bender's Books & Cards
22 South Mallory St.
Hampton, VA 23663
PH: (757) 723-3741
(a-j,m-u)

World's Best
9817 Jefferson Ave.
Newport News, VA 23605
PH: (757) 595-9005
(b,c,g,i,k-n,p-s,u)

Trilogy Comics #2
700 E. Little Creek Rd.
Norfolk, VA 23518
PH: (757) 587-2540
(c,e,g,m,n,p-u)

Nostalgia Plus
1601 Willow Lawn Drive
Richmond, VA 23230
PH: (804) 282-5532
(a-c,g,k,m,p,q)

B & D Comic Shop
802 Elm Avenue SW
Roanoke, VA 24016
PH: (540) 342-6642
(b,c,g,l,m,p-s)

Big Planet Comics
426 Maple Ave. East
Vienna, VA 22180
PH: (703) 242-9412
(b,c,p,q)

Trilogy Comics #1
5773 Princess Anne Rd.
Virginia Beach, VA 23462
PH: (757) 490-2205
(a-i,k-m,p-u)

WASHINGTON

The Comic Character Shop
Old Firehouse Antique Mall
110 Alaskan Way South
Seattle, WA 98106
PH: (206) 283-0532
(a,b,f,h-k,p)

Comic Dungeon
1622 1/2 North 45th St.
Seattle, WA 98103
PH: (206) 545-8373
FX: (206) 545-6920
(a-c,f,g,k,m,n,q,s)

Golden Age Collectables LTD
1501 Pike Place Market
401 Lower Level
Seattle, WA 98101
PH: (206) 622-9799
(a-g,l-n,p-q)

Rocket Comics
8408 Greenwood Ave. N
Seattle, WA 98103
PH: (206) 784-7300
(a-h, p,q)

O'Leary's Books
3828 100th St. S.W.
Tacoma, WA 98499
PH: (253) 588-2503
PH: (800) 542-1791
FX: (253) 589-9115
(a-c,e-h,j-m,p-s,u)

Lady Jaynes Books
745 St. Helens Ave.
Tacoma, WA 98402
PH: (253) 593-6032
FX: (253) 593-6046
(c,e,g,k,m,p-u)

WEST VIRGINIA

Comic Castle
314 Neville St.
Beckley, WV 25801
PH: (304) 253-1974
(b,c,m,n,p,q,s)

WISCONSIN

Discount Comics
P. O. Box 112
Cottage Grove, WI 53527
PH: (608) 764-8410
(c,i,k-u)

Clairemont Comics
2543 E. Clairemont Ave.
Eau Claire, WI 54701
PH: (715) 831-2112
(a-c,g,m,q,r)

20th Century Books
1115 South Park St.
Madison, WI 53715
PH: (608) 251-6226
(c,e,g,h,m,n,q,t,u)

Capital City Comics
1910 Monroe St.
Madison, WI 53711
PH: (608) 251-8445
(a-d,f,j,m,n,p,q,u)

Westfield's Comics, Etc.
676 S. Whitney Way
(next to Marshall's)
Madison, WI 53711
PH: (608) 277-1280
Web: www.westfield.com
(a-c,e,g-n,p-u)

Westfield Comics
8608 University Green
P.O. Box 620470
Middleton, WI 53562-0470
PH: (608) 836-1945
FX: (608) 836-6950
E-Mail: westfield
@westfield.com
Web: www.westfield.com
(a-c,e,g,k-n,p-u)

Capital City Comics
2625 North Downer Ave.
Milwaukee, WI 53211
PH: (414) 332-8199
(a-d,f,j,m,n,p,q,u)

CANADA

ALBERTA

Amazing Heroes Ltd.
1008 MacLeod TRSE
Calgary, AB T2G 2M7
PH: (403) 262-0366
(c,e,g,k,m,o,p,r,s)

Another Dimension Comics
324-10 St. N.W.
Calgary, AB T2N 1V8
PH: (403) 283-7078
(a-c,e,g,k,m,n,p-s,u)

Redd Skull Comics & CD's
720 A Edmonton Trail N. E.
Calgary, AB T2E 3J4
PH/FX: (403) 230-2716
(a-c,k-r,u)

Comic Fever
11338-132 ave.
Edmonton, AB T5E 1A1
PH: (403) 452-6324
(b,c,g,i-k,m,p-s)

BRITISH COLUMBIA

Page After Page
1795 Harvey Ave.
Kelowna, BC V1Y 6G4
PH: (250) 860-6554
FX: (250) 860-7541
(b,c,q,r,u)

Golden Age Collectables
830 Granville Street
Vancouver, BC V6Z 1K3
PH: (604) 683-2819
(a-c,i,k,m,n,q-s,u)

MANITOBA

The Collector's Slave
156 Imperial Ave.
Winnipeg, Manitoba
R2M 0K8
PH: (204) 237-4428
(a-c,e-g,j,l-n,s,t)

ONTARIO

B.A.'s Comics & Nostalgia
121 Oxford St. East
London, Ontario N6A 1T4
PH: (519) 439-9636
(b,c,g,m,n,p,q,u)

Alternate Realities
1910 Danforth Ave.
Toronto, ON M4C 1J4
PH: (416) 696-9005
(b,c,e,k,l,m,p,q)

3RD Quadrant
226 Queen St. W. UPR
Toronto, ON M5V 1Z6
PH: (416) 974-9211
(b,c,k,m,p-s)

Paradise Comics
3278 Yonge Ave.
Toronto, ON M4N 2L6
PH: (416) 487-9807
(a-c,g,j,k,m,n,p-r)

The Final Stop
381 McArthur Avenue
Vanier, ON K1L 6N5
PH: (613) 749-1247
E-Mail: final.stop@pccs.ca
(c,g,k,m,n,p,q)

QUEBEC

Heroes Comics
1116 Cure La Belle
Chomedey Laval, QC
H7V 2V5
PH: (514) 686-9155
(a-c,e,g,k,m,o-s,u)

Komico Inc.
4210 Decarie
Montreal, Quebec H4A 3K3
PH: (514) 489-4009
E-Mail: MEGAH@total.net
(b,c,g,k,n,p,q)

SILVER & MODERN AGE INDEX

Below is a complete listing of all titles published by the ten most popular comic book companies today. Where several titles exist by the same name, we have listed the title once for space considerations.

index compiled by Arnold T. Blumberg, Scott Braden, and Mark Huesman

Comics)
Darkstars, The
DC Challenge
...Comics Presents
...Graphic Novel
...100 Page Super Spectacular
...Science Fiction Graphic Novel
...Silver Age Classics
...Special
...Special Blue-Ribbon Digest
...Special Series
...Spotlight
...Super-Stars
...Universe Holiday Bash
...Universe: Trinity
Deadman
...: Exorcism
...: Love After Death
Deadshot
Deathstroke: The Terminator
Demolition Man
Demon, The
Detective Comics
Detention Comics
Doc Savage
Doctor Fate
Doom Force Special
Doom Patrol
Doomsday
Doorway to Nightmare
Dragonlance
Duckman
Dynamic Classics
Eclipso
...: The Darkness Within
80 Page Giant
El Diablo
Electric Warrior
Elongated Man
Elseworld's Finest
Elson's Presents
Elvira's House of Mystery
Emerald Dawn
Enemy Ace Special
Epicurus the Sage
Eradicator
Etc
Extreme Justice
Famous First Edition
Fast Forward
Fate
Fighting American
Final Night
Firebrand
Firestorm
..., the Nuclear Man
1st Issue Special
Flash
Flash Gordon
Forever People
Forgotten Realms
Freedom Fighters
Funny Stuff Stocking Stuffer
Fury of Firestorm, The
Gammarauders
Genesis
Ghostdancing
Ghosts
G. I. Combat
Gilgamesh II
Golden Age, The
Gotham by Gaslight
...Nights
Green Arrow
...: The Long Bow Hunters
...: The Wonder Year
Green Lantern
...Corps, The
...Corps Quarterly
...: Emerald Dawn
...: Emerald Dawn II
.../Green Arrow
...: Mosaic
Griffin, The
Gross Point
Guardians of Metropolis
Gunfire
Guy Gardner
...Reborn
Hacker Files, The
Hammerlocke
Hawk and Dove
Hawkman
Hawkworld
Haywire
Heart of the Beast, The
Hercules Unbound
Heroes Against Hunger
Hero Hotline
Hex
History of the DC Universe
Hitchhiker's Guide to the Galaxy
Hitman
House of Mystery, The
...of Secrets
Human Target Special
Huntress, The
Immortal Doctor Fate, The
Impulse
Inferior Five, The
Inferno
Infinity, Inc.
Invasion
Ironwolf
...: Fires of the Revolution
Isis
Jemm, Son of Saturn
JLA
...: Paradise Lost
...: Secret Files
...: Year One
Joker, The
Jonah Hex
...and Other Western Tales
Jonni Thunder
Judge Dredd
...: Legends of the Law
Justice, Inc.
Justice League
...Europe
...International
...of America
...Quarterly
...Task Force
Justice Society of America
Kamandi: At Earth's End
..., the Last Boy on Earth
Karate Kid
Kents, The
Kid Eternity
Kingdom Come
Kissyfur
Kobra
Kong the Untamed
Krypton Chronicles
Last Days of the Justice Society
Legend of Wonder Woman, The
Legends
...of the DC Universe
...of the World's Finest
L. E. G. I. O. N.
Legionnaires
...Three
Legion of Substitute Heroes Special
...of Super-Heroes
Lex Luthor: The Unauthorized Biography
Limited Collectors' Edition
Little Shop of Horrors Special
Lobo
...: A Contract on Gawd
.../Deadman: The Brave and the Bald
...: Death and Taxes
...Gallery
...: Infanticide
.../Judge Dredd
.../Mask
...'s Back
...'s Big Babe Spring Break Special
...Unamerican Gladiators
Lois & Clark, the New Adventures of Superman
Lois Lane
Long Hot Summer, The
Looney Tunes
Loose Cannon
Lords of the Ultra-Realm
Losers Special
Madame Xanadu
Major Bummer
Man-Bat
Manhunter
Man of Steel, The
Martian Manhunter
Marvel and DC Present (w/**Marvel Comics**)
Mask
Masters of the Universe
'Mazing Man
Men of War
Metal Men
Metamorpho
Metropolis S. C. U.
Millenium
Mister E
Mister Miracle
Ms. Tree Quarterly/Special
My Greatest Adventure
My Name is Chaos
Mystery in Space
Nathaniel Dusk
...II
Nazz, The
New Adventures of Superboy, The
New Gods
...Guardians, The
...Talent Showcase
...Teen Titans, The
...Titans, The
Night Force, The
Nightwing
...: Alfred's Return
Nine Princes In Amber
Omac: One Man Army Corps
Omega Men, The
Our Army at War
...Fighting Forces
Outcasts
Outsiders
Oz-Wonderland Wars, The
Parallax: Emerald Night
Peacemaker
Peter Cannon-Thunderbolt
Phantom, The
...Stranger, The
...Zone, The
Pinky and The Brain
Plastic Man
Power Girl
...Lords
...of Shazam, The
...of the Atom
Primal Force
Prisoner, The
Psyba-Rats
Question, The
...Quarterly, The
Ragman
...: Cry of the Dead
Rainbow Brite and the Star Stealer
Ray, The
R. E. B. E. L. S.
Red Tornado
Restaurant at the End of the Universe
Resurrection Man
Richard Dragon, Kung-Fu Fighter
Rima, The Jungle Girl
Ring of the Nibelung, The
Rip Hunter Time Master
Robin
...: A Hero Reborn
...II
...III: Cry of the Huntress
...3000
Robotech Defenders
Rogue's Gallery
Ronin
Roots of the Swamp Thing
Sandman, The
Saga of Ra's Al Ghul, The
Scare Tactics
Scarlett
Scooby Doo
Secret Origins
...of the World's Greatest Super-Heroes
Secret Society of Super-Villains
Secrets of Haunted House
...of Sinister House
...of the Legion of Super-Heroes
Sergio Aragonés Destroys DC
Sgt. Rock
...Special
...Prize Battle Tales
Shade, The
Shade, The Changing Man
Shado: Song of the Dragon
Shadow, The
Shadowdragon
Shadow of the Batman
Shadow Strikes!, The
Shadow War of Hawkman
Shazam!
...: The New Beginning
Showcase
...'93
...'94
...'95
...'96
Silverblade
Sinister House of Secret Love, The
Skreemer
Skull & Bones
Slash Maraud
Sonic Disruptors
Son of Ambush Bug
Sovereign Seven
Spanner's Galaxy
Spectre, The
Speed Force
Spelljammer
Spider-Man and Batman (w/**Marvel Comics**)
Spiral Zone
Stanley & His Monster
S. T. A. R. Corps
Starfire
Star Hunters
Starman
Star Spangled War Tales
Star Trek
...Movie Special
...VI: The Undiscovered Country
...-The Modala Imperative
Star Trek.: The Next Generation
.../Deep Space Nine
...-Ill Wind
...-The Modala Imperative
...-Shadowheart
Steel
..., the Indestructible Man
Strange Adventures
...Sports Stories
Street Fighter: The Battle for Shadaloo
Streets
Sugar & Spike
Suicide Squad
Sun Devils
Superboy
...And The Ravers
Super DC Giant
...Friends
Supergirl
.../Lex Luthor Special
Superman
And Spider-Man (w/**Marvel Comics**)
.../Batman: Alternate Realities
.../Doomsday: Hunter/Prey
...Family, The
...for Earth

...Record Comic
...'s Girlfriend Lois Lane
...'s Pal Jimmy Olsen
...Spectacular
...: Speeding Bullets
...: The Earth Stealers
...: The Man of Steel
...: The Man of Tomorrow
...: The Secret Years
...: The Wedding Album
.../Toyman
...Vs. Aliens
...Vs. the Amazing Spider-Man (w/**Marvel Comics**)
Super Powers
...-Team Family
Swamp Thing
Sword of Sorcery
...of the Atom
Tailgunner Jo
Tales of the Green Lantern Corps
...of the Legion
...of the New Teen Titans
...of the Teen Titans
...of the Unexpected
Talos of the Wilderness Sea
Tank Girl: Apocalypse
...: Movie Adaptation
...: The Odyssey
Tarzan
...Family, The
Team Titans
Teen Titans
...Spotlight
Tempus Fugitive
Thriller
Thrillkiller
Timber Wolf
Time Masters
...Warp
Titans Sell-Out Special
Total Recall
Triumph
TSR World
Twilight
Underworld
Underworld Unleashed
...: Abyss-Hell's Sentinel
...: Apokolips-Dark Uprising
...: Batman-Devil's Asylum
...: Patterns of Fear
Unexpected, The
Unknown Soldier, The
Untold Legend of the Batman, The
"V"
Valor
V for Vendetta
Vigilante, The
...: City Lights, Prairie Justice
Viper
Wanderers
Wanted, the World's Most Dangerous Villains
Warlord
War of the Gods
Wasteland
Watchmen
Weird, The
Weird Mystery Tales
...War Tales
...Western Tales
...Worlds
Welcome Back, Kotter
Where in the World is Carmen Sandiego?
Who's Who in Star Trek
...in the Legion of Super-Heroes
...: The Definitive Directory of the DC Universe
...Update '87
...Update '88
Wild Dog
Witching Hour
Wonder Woman
World of Krypton, The
...of Metropolis, The
...of Smallville
Worlds Collide
World's Finest
World's Finest
...Comics
World's Greatest Super Heroes
World Without End
Wrath of the Spectre, The
Xenobrood
Xero
Young All-Stars
Young Heroes on Love
Young Love
Zatanna
Zero Hour: Crisis in Time

Amalgam

Amazon
Assassins
Bat-Thing
Dark Claw Adventures
Doctor Strangefate
Generation Hex
Legends of the Dark Claw
JLX
...Unleashed
Lobo the Duck
Super Soldier
...: Man of War

Helix

Black Lamb, The
Bloody Mary
...: Lady Liberty
Brainbanx
Cyberella
Gemini Blood
Michael Moorcock's Multiverse
Star Crossed
Time Breakers
Vermillion

Impact

Black Hood
Comet, The
Crusaders, The
Fly, The
Impact Christmas Special
Jaguar, The
Legend of the Shield, The
Web, The

Milestone

Blood Syndicate
Deathwish
Hardware
Heroes
Icon
Kobalt
Long Hot Summer, The
My Name is Holocaust
Shadow Cabinet
Static
Xombi

Paradox Press

Big Book of Conspiracies
...of Death
...of Freaks
...of Hoaxes
...of Little Criminals
...of Losers
...of Martyrs
...of Scandals
...of The Unexplained
...of Thugs
...of Urban Legends
...of Weirdos
Brooklyn Dreams
Family Man
Gon
Green Candles
Hunter's Heart
La Pacifica
Weird

Tangent

Atom, The
Doom Patrol
Flash, The
Green Lantern
Joker, The
Metal Men
Nightwing
Sea Devils
Secret Six

Vertigo

Absolute Vertigo
American Freak: A Tale of the Un-Men
Arcana Annual
Blood & Shadows
Blood: A Tale
Books of Faerie
Books of Magic
Chiaroscuro (The Private Lives of Leonardo Da Vinci)
Children's Crusade, The
Death: The High Cost of Living
Death: The Time of Your Life
Destiny: A Chronicle of Deaths Foretold
Dhampire: Stillborn
Dog Moon
Doom Patrol
Dreaming, The
Enigma
Egypt
Essential Vertigo: The Sandman
Extremist, The
Farewell Moonshadow
Flex Mentallo
Goddess
Heartland
Hellblazer
.../ The Books of Magic
Horrorist, The
Invisibles, The
Jonah Hex: Riders of the Worm and Such
...: Two-Gun Mojo
Junk Culture
Kid Eternity
Kill Your Boyfriend
Last One, The
Menz Insana
Mercy
Millenium Fever
Mr. Punch
Mobfire
Moonshadow
Neil Gaiman & Charles Vess' Stardust
Preacher
Preacher: Saint Of Killers
Pride and Joy
Rogan Gosh
Sandman, The
...Midnight Theatre
...Mystery Theatre
Scarab
Sebastian O
Seekers Into The Mystery
Shadow's Fall
Skin Graft: The Adventures of a Tattooed Man
Terminal City
...: Aerial Graffiti
2020 Visions
Uncle Sam
Vamps
...: Hollywood & Vein
Vertigo Gallery
...Jam
...Preview
...Visions
Witchcraft

Vertigo Verite

Girl
Seven Miles A Second
System, The
Unseen Hand, The

HARRIS COMICS

Chains of Chaos
Cyberfrog vs. Creed
Harsh Realm
Hyde-25
Q-Unit
Rook
Vampirella
... & Pantha Showcase
...Bloodlust
...Classic
...: Crossover Gallery
...: Death & Destruction
.../Dracula: The Centennial
...Lives
...: Morning in America
...of Drakulon
...Pin-Up Special
.../Shadowhawk: Creatures of the Night (w/**Image Comics**)
...Strikes
Vengeance of Vampirella
...: The Mystery Walk

IMAGE COMICS

Extreme Studios

Badrock
...and Company
.../Wolverine (w/**Marvel**)
Battlestone
Berzerkers
Black & White
Bloodpool
Bloodstrike
...Assassin
Bloodwulf
Brigade
Celestine
Chapel
Crypt
Doom's IV
Extreme
...Sacrifice
...Sacrifice Prelude
...Super Christmas Special
Glory
...& Friends Bikini Fest
...& Friends Christmas Special
...& Friends Lingerie Special
.../Avengelyne
.../Angela: Angels In Hell
.../Avengelyne
Grifter/Badrock
Kid Supreme
Knightmare
Knightstrike
Lady Supreme
Legend of Supreme
Maximage
Newman
Newmen
Newforce
Operation: Knightstrike
Prophet
Riptide
Shadowhunt
Supreme
...: Glory Days
Team Youngblood
Troll
...II
Violator Vs. Badrock
Vogue
Youngblood
...: Strikefile

Highbrow Entertainment

Big Bang Comics
Body Count
Dart
Deadly Duo, The
Distant Soil, A
Dragon, The
Dragon, The: Blood & Guts
Freak Force
Savage Dragon, The
.../Marshall Law
...: Sex & Violence
...: The Red Horizon
Star
Superpatriot
...: Liberty & Justice
Vanguard
Wildstar: Sky Zero

Homage Comics

Desperadoes
Dusty Star
Kabuki
Kurt Busiek's Astro City
Leave it to Chance

Shadowline Ink
Alliance, The
Images of Shadowhawk
New Shadowhawk, The
1963
Normalman-Megaton Man Special
Others, The
Pact, The
Regulators
Shadowhawk
...II
...III
Shadowhawk Gallery
Shadowhawks of Legend

Todd McFarlane Productions
Angela
Boof
...and the Bruise Crew
Creech, The
Curse of the Spawn
Kiss: The Psycho Circus
Spawn
...: Blood Feud
Violator

Top Cow Productions
Arcanum
Ascension
Ballistic
...Action
...Imagery
.../Wolverine (w/ **Marvel**)
Battle for Independents, The (w/ **Crusade Ent.**)
Codename Stryke Force
Cyberforce
...Origins
.../Strykeforce: Opposing Forces
...Universe Sourcebook
Cyblade/Shi (w/**Crusade Ent.**)
Darkness, The
Killrazor
Medieval Spawn Witchblade
Nine Volt
Ripclaw
Tales of the Witchblade
Top Cow Productions, Inc./Ballistic Studios Swimsuit Special
Velocity
Weapon Zero
Witchblade

Wildstorm Productions
Allegra
Backlash
Big Bruisers
Black Ops
Cybernary
Deathblow
Defcon 4
Divine Right
DV8
...Rave
...Vs. Black Ops
Fire From Heaven
Foot Soldiers
Gamorra Swimsuit Special
Gen13
... Bootleg
.../ Generation X
... Interactive
.../Maxx
...: Ordinary Heroes
...Rave
...: Unreal World
Grifter
...: One Shot
.../Shi (w/**Crusade Ent.**)
Kindred, The
Phantom Guard
Savant Guard
Shattered Image
Siege
Spartan: Warrior Spirit
Stormwatch
Team One: Stormwatch
...: WildC. A. T. S
Team 7
...-Objective Hell
Union
...: Final Vengeance
Voodoo
Voodoo-Zealot: Skin Trade
Warblade: Endangered Species
Wetworks
WildC. A. T. S Adventures
...: Covert Action Teams
...Trilogy
Wildcore
WildStorm!
WildStorm Rising
WildStorm Spotlight Zealot
Wynonna Earp

Miscellaneous
Aaron Strips
Adventures of Aaron
Age of Heroes
Arkaga
Bliss Alley
Bone
Casual Heroes
Childhood's End
Codename: Black & White
Crush, The
Darkchylde
Darker Image
Deathmate (w/**Valiant**)
Espers
Groo
Hellshock
Image Zero
Immortal II
Maggie the Cat
Man Against Time
Maxx
Megahurtz
Phantom Force
Pitt
Ragmop
Replacement God
Shaman's Tears
Soulwind
Splitting Image
Tenth, The
Touch of Silver, A
Trencher
Tribe
Wildstar

MARVEL COMICS
Abominations
Adventures of Captain America
...of Cyclops and Phoenix
...of Snake Plissken
...of the Thing
...on the Planet of the Apes
Age of Apocalypse: The Chosen
Alf
Alpha Flight
... In the Beginning
...Special
Amazing Adult Fantasy
...Adventures
...Fantasy
...High Adventure
...Scarlet Spider
...Spider-Man, The
...Spider-Man Super Special
...X-Men
American Tail: Fievel Goes West, An
Annex
Annie
Archangel
Arrgh!
Astonishing Tales
...X-Men
A-Team, The
Avengers, The
...Collector's Edition, The
...: The Crossing
...Log, The
...Spotlight
...Strikefile
...: The Terminatrix Objective
.../Ultraforce
...Unplugged
...West Coast
Balder the Brave
Barbie
...Fashion
Battlestar Galactica
Beast
Beauty and the Beast, The
Beavis and Butthead
Beware
Big Jim's P.A.C.K.
Biker Mice from Mars
Bill & Ted's Bogus Journey
...Excellent Comic Book
Bishop
...: Xavier Security Enforcer
Bizarre Adventures
Black Goliath
...Knight
Black Panther, The
...: Panther's Prey
Blackwulf
Blade Runner
Blade: The Vampire-Hunter
Blaze
...: Legacy of Blood
Blood and Glory
Bob Marley, Tale of the Tuff Going
Book of the Dead
Brute Force
Buckaroo Banzai
Bug
Cable
...- Blood and Metal
Cage
Camp Candy
Captain America
.../Nick Fury: Blood Truce
...Special Edition
Captain Justice
...Marvel
...Planet and the Planeteers
...Savage and His Leather-neck Raiders
Cat, The
Chamber of Chills
...of Darkness
Champions, The
Chili
Clandestine
Classic X-Men
Cloak and Dagger
Clobberin' Time
Codename Spitfire
Colossus
Combat Kelly
Comet Man, The
Comic Book
Conan
...Classic
...Saga, The
...the Adventurer
...the Barbarian
...the Barbarian Movie Special
...the Barbarian: The Usurper
...the Destroyer
...the King
...the Savage
...Vs. Rune
Coneheads
Cops: The Job
Cosmic Powers
...Unlimited
Count Duckula
Crazy
...Magazine
Creatures on the Loose
Crypt of Shadows
Curse of the Weird
Cutting Edge
Cyclops: Retribution
Dakota North
Daily Bugle
Damage Control
Daredevil
...the Man Without Fear
Dark Crystal, The
Darkhawk
Darkhold: Pages from the Book of Sins
Darkman
David Marshall Adventures
Dazzler, The
Deadliest Heroes of Kung Fu
Deadly Foes of Spider-Man
...Hands of Kung Fu
Dead of Night
Deadpool
...: The Circle Chase
Deathlok
...Special
Deep, The
Defenders, The
...of Dynatron City
Dennis the Menace
...Comics Digest
Destroyer, The
Devil Dinosaur
...Spring Fling
Dino Riders
Disney's Afternoon
...Aladdin
...Beauty and the Beast
...Comic Hits
...The Lion King
...The Little Mermaid
...Pocahontas
...The Three Musketeers
Doc Samson
...Savage
Doctor Strange
...Classics
..., Sorcerer Supreme
Doctor Who
Doom 2099
Double Dragon
...Edge
D. P. 7
Dracula Lives!
Draft, The
Dragonslayer
Dragon Strike
Druid
Dune
Dynomutt
Earthworm Jim
Ectokid
Elektra
...: Assassin
... Megazine
..., The
Elvira's Mistress of the Dark
Eternals, The
...: The Herod Factor
Excalibur
Factor X
Fafhrd and the Grey Mouser
Falcon
Fallen Angels
Fantastic Force
Fantastic Four
...: Atlantis Rising
...Roast
...2099
...Unlimited
...Unplugged
...Vs. X-Men
Fantasy Masterpieces
Fear
Felicia Hardy: The Black Cat
Fightman
Firestar
Fish Police
Flash Gordon
Foolkiller
Force Works
Francis, Brother of the Universe
Frankenstein
Freddy Krueger's A Nightmare on Elm Street

Fred Hembeck Destroys the Marvel Universe
...Sells the Marvel Universe
Funtastic World of Hanna-Barbera
Further Adventures of Indiana Jones
Fury
...of Shield
Galactic Guardians
Gambit
...and the X-Ternals
Gargoyle
Gargoyles
Generic Comic, The
Generation Next
Generation X
.../Gen 13
Ghost Rider
.../Blaze: Spirits of Vengeance
.../Captain America: Fear
...2099
..., Wolverine, Punisher: Dark Design
..., Wolverine, Punisher: Hearts of Darkness
Giant-Size...
G. I. Joe and the Transformers
..., A Real American Hero
...Comics Magazine
...European Missions
...Order of Battle, The
...Special Missions
God's Country
Godzilla
Green Goblin
Groovy
Guardians of the Galaxy
Gunhawks
Gunslinger
Handbook of the Conan Universe
Harvey
Hawkeye
Hellstorm: Prince of Lies
Hercules
Hero
Heroes for Hope Starring the X-Men
Hero for Hire
Hokum & Hex
Hook
Hot Shots: Avengers
House II: The Second Story
Howard the Duck
...: The Movie
Hulk
...: Future Imperfect
...: 2099
Human Fly, The
Human Torch, The
Hyperkind
...Unleashed
Iceman
Illuminator
Impossible Man Summer Vacation Spectacular
Incredible Hulk, The
Indiana Jones and the Last Crusade
...and the Temple of Doom
Infinity Crusade
...Gauntlet
...War, The
Inhumans, The
...: The Great Refuge
Invaders, The
Iron Fist
Iron Man
...& Sub-Mariner
Island of Dr. Moreau, The
Jack of Hearts
James Bond For Your Eyes Only
James Bond Jr.
John Carter, Warlord of Mars
Journey into Mystery
Juggernaut
Jungle Action
Justice
...: Four Balance
Ka-Zar
...the Savage
Kickers, Inc.
King Conan
Kingpin
Kitty Pryde
...Agent of S.H.I.E.L.D.
... and Wolverine
Kree/Skrull War Starring the Avengers
Krull
Kull and the Barbarians
...the Conqueror
Labyrinth
Laff-a-Lympics
Last Avengers Story, The
...Starfighter, The
...Temptation, The
Legion of Monsters
...of Night, The
Lethal Foes of Spider-Man
Life of Captain Marvel, The
...of Christ: The Easter Story, The
...of Pope John Paul II
Li'l Kids
...Pals
Logan's Run
Longshot
Lunatik
Machine Man
...2020
Mad About Millie
Magik
Magneto
Mandrake the Magician
Man from Atlantis
Man-Thing
Marc Spector: Moon Knight
Mark Hazzard: Merc
Marvel Action Hour, Featuring...
...Action Universe
...Adventures Starring Daredevil
...and DC Present (w/**DC Comics**)
...Chillers
...Classics Comics Series Featuring...
...Collector's Edition
...Collector's Edition: X-Men
...Collectors' Item Classics
...Comics Presents
...Comics Super Special
...Double Feature
...Fanfare
...Feature
...Fumetti Book
...Graphic Novel
...Holiday Special
...Illustrated: Swimsuit Issue
...Masterpieces Collection
...Masterpieces 2 Collection, The
...Milestone Edition
...Mini-Books
...Movie Premiere
...Movie Showcase Featuring Star Wars
...Movie Spotlight Featuring Raiders of the Lost Ark
...No-Prize Book, The
...Premiere
...Presents
...Preview
...Riot
Marvels
Marvel Saga, The
...'s Greatest Comics
...Special Edition Featuring...
...Spectacular
Marvels: Portraits
Marvel Spotlight
...Super Action
...Super Hero Contest of Champions
...Super-Heroes
...Super-Heroes Megazine
...Super-Heroes Secret Wars
...Swimsuit Special
...Tails Starring Peter Porker the Spectacular Spider-Ham
...Tales
...Team-Up
...Treasury Edition
...Treasury of Oz
...Treasury Special
...Triple Action
...Two-in-One
... Versus DC
...X-Men Collection, The
Master of Kung Fu
...: Bleeding Black
Masters of Terror
Maverick
Men in Black: Retribution
...: The Movie
Mephisto Vs...
Meteor Man
MGM's Marvelous Wizard of Oz
Micronauts
...Special Edition
Midnight Sons Unlimited
Mighty Marvel Western
Mighty Morphin' Power Rangers: The Movie
Mighty Mouse
Millie the Model
Monster Menace
Monsters on the Prowl
Monsters Unleashed
Moon Knight
...: Divided We Fall
...Special
...Special Edition
Morbius Revisited
...: The Living Vampire
Mort the Dead Teenager
Ms. Marvel
Mutant Misadventures of Cloak and Dagger, The
My Love
'Nam, The
...Magazine, The
Namor, the Sub-Mariner
New Mutants, The
...Warriors, The
Nick Fury, Agent of S. H. I. E. L. D.
...Vs. S. H. I. E. L. D.
Nightcrawler
Nightmare
Nightmask
Night Nurse
NightRider
Nightstalkers
Night Thrasher
...: Four Control
Nightwatch
Nocturne
No Escape
Nomad
Northstar
Not Brand Echh
Nothing Can Stop the Juggernaut
Nova
Nth Man the Ultimate Ninja
Obnoxio the Clown
Official Handbook of the Marvel Universe, The
Official Marvel Index to Marvel Team-Up
...to the Amazing Spider-Man
...to the Avengers, The
...to the Fantastic Four
...to the X-Men, The
Omega the Unknown
101 Ways to End the Clone Saga
Open Space
Original Ghost Rider, The
...Rides Again, The
Our Love Story
Outlaw Kid, The
Over the Edge
Peter, The Little Pest
Phantom: The Ghost Who Walks
...2040
Phoenix
Pitt, The
Planet of the Apes
Police Academy
Power Man
...Pachyderms
...Pack
...Record Comics
Prince Namor, the Sub-Mariner
Prince Valiant
Professor Xavier and the X-Men
Prowler, The
Psi-Force
Psylocke & Archangel: Crimson Dawn
Punisher
...Armory, The
... Kills The Marvel Universe
...Magazine, The
...Movie Comic
...: Origin of Micro Chip
...: P. O. V.
...: The Ghosts of Innocents
...2099
...War Journal, The
...: War Zone, The
...: Year One
Quasar
Questprobe
Quicksilver
Raiders of the Lost Ark
Rampaging Hulk
Ravage 2099
Rawhide Kid
Razorline
Red Sonja
...: Scavenger Hunt
...: The Movie
Red Wolf
Ren & Stimpy Show, The
Requiem for Dracula
Ringo Kid, The
Rise of Apocalypse
Robert E. Howard's Conan
Robocop
...2
Robotix
Rocket Raccoon
Rocko's Modern Life
Rogue
Rom
Ruins
Saban's Mighty Morphin' Power Rangers
Sabretooth
...Classic
Saga of Crystar, Crystal Warrior, The
...of the Original Human Torch
...of the Sub-Mariner
Saint Sinner
Savage Return of Dracula
...She-Hulk, The
...Sword of Conan
...Tales
Scarlet Spider
...Unlimited
Scarlet Witch
Scooby-Doo
Secret Defenders
...Wars II
Sectaurs
Semper Fi
Sensational She-Hulk, The
...in Ceremony

Sensational Spider-Man
Sgt. Fury
Shadowmasters
Shanna, the She-Devil
Sheena
S. H. I. E. L. D.
Shogun Warriors
Shroud, The
Silver Sable and the Wild Pack
Silver Surfer, The
...Vs. Dracula
.../Warlock: Resurrection
.../Weapon Zero
Skeleton Warriors
Skrull Kill Krew
Skull, the Slayer
Slapstick
Sledge Hammer
Sleepwalker
Smurfs
Snow White
Solarman
Solo
...Avengers
Solomon Kane
Son of Satan
...of Yuppies From Hell
Special Collectors' Edition
...Edition X-Men
...Marvel Edition
Spectacular Scarlet Spider
...Spider-Man, The
Speedball
Spellbound
Spider-Man
...Adventures
...and Batman (w/**DC Comics**)
...and Daredevil
...and His Amazing Friends
...and X-Factor
...Classics
...Collector's Preview
...Comics Magazine
...: Friends and Enemies
...: Funeral for an Octopus
...: Hobgoblin Lives
...: Hot Shots
...Magazine
...: Maximum Clonage
...Megazine
...: Power of Terror
...Saga
...: Super Special
...Team-Up
...: The Arachnis Project
...: The Clone Journal
...: The Final Adventure
...: The Jackal Files
...: The Lost Years
...: The Manga
...: The Mutant Agenda
...: The Parker Years
...2099
...2099 Meets Spider-Man
...Unlimited
...: Venom Agenda
...Vs. Dracula
...Vs. Wolverine
...: Web of Doom
Spider-Woman
Spidey Super Stories
Spitfire and the Troubleshooters
Spoof
Spotlight
Squadron Supreme
Starblast
Star Brand
Starjammers
Star-Lord the Special Edition
Starriors
Star Team
Star Trek
...Deep Space Nine
...Early Voyages
...Starfleet Academy
...Voyager
Star Wars
...: Return of the Jedi
Steeltown Rockers
Strange Days
...Tales
Street Poet Ray
Strikeforce: Morituri
...: Electric Undertow
Stryfe's Strike File
Sub-Mariner, The
Supernatural Thrillers
Super-Villain Classics
...Team-Up
Sweet XVI
Sworn to Protect
Tales of Asgard
...of G. I. Joe
...of Suspense
...of the Marvels
...of the Zombie
...to Astonish
Tarzan
...of the Apes
Team America
...Helix
Terminator 2: Judgment Day
Terror Inc.
Tex Dawson, Gun-Slinger
Thanos Quest, The
Thing, The
Thor
...Corps
Thunderstrike
Time Bandits
Timespirits
Tomb of Darkness
...of Dracula
Tower of Shadows
Toxic Avenger
...Crusaders
Transformers, The
...: Generation 2
Try-Out Winner Book
TV Stars
2099 A. D.
...Apocalypse
...Genesis
...Unlimited
...World of Doom Special
Two-Gun Kid
...: Sunset Riders
2001, A Space Odyssey
2010
Typhoid
Ultragirl
Uncanny Tales
Uncanny X-Men, The
...at the State Fair of Texas
...in Days of Future Past
Unknown Worlds of Science Fiction
Unlimited Access
Untold Legend of Captain Marvel
Untold Tales of Spider-Man
U. S. Agent
U. S. 1
Vampire Tales
Vault of Evil
Venom: Carnage Unleashed
...: Finale
...: Funeral Pyre
...: Lethal Protector
...: License to Kill
...: Nights of Vengeance
...: On Trial
...: Seed of Darkness
...: Separation Anxiety
...: Sign of the Boss
...: Sinner Takes All
...: Super Special
...: The Enemy Within
...: The Mace
...: The Madness
...: Tooth and Claw
Very Best of Dennis the Menace, The
Virtua Fighter
Vision, The
...and the Scarlet Witch
War, The
War is Hell
Warlock
...and the Infinity Watch
...Chronicles
War Machine
Weapon X
Web of Scarlet Spider
...of Spider-Man
Wedding of Dracula
Weird Wonder Tales
Werewolf by Night
West Coast Avengers
Western Gunfighters
...Kid, The
...Team-Up
What If?
What The--?!
Where Creatures Roam
...Monsters Dwell
Willow
Wolfpack
Wolverine
...and the Punisher: Damaging Evidence
...: Days of Future Past
.../Gambit: Victims
...Saga
...Vs. Spider-Man
Wonder Man
Worlds Unknown
X-Calibre
X-Factor
X-Force
...Megazine
X-Man
X-Men
...Adventures
...Adventures II
...Adventures III
...Alpha
.../Alpha Flight
...and the Micronauts, The
...Archives
...Archives Featuring Captain Britain
...Chronicles
.../Clandestine
...Classic
...Classics
...Omega
...Prime
...Spotlight on Starjammers
...Survival Guide to the Mansion
...: The Early Years
...: The Ultra Collection
...: The Wedding Album
...2099
...Ultra III Preview
...Unlimited
...Vs. Dracula
...Vs. the Avengers, The
X-Terminators
X-Universe
Yogi Bear
Yuppies from Hell
Zorro

Amalgam

Bruce Wayne, Agent of S.H.I.E.L.D.
Bullets and Bracelets
Challengers of the Fantastic
Exciting X-Patrol
Iron Lantern
Magnetic Men Featuring Magneto
Magneto and the Magnetic Men
Speed Demon
Spider-Boy
...Team-Up
Thorion of the New Asgods
X-Patrol

Epic

Airtight Garage, The
Akira
Alien Legion
...: Binary Deep
...: Jugger Grimrod
...: One Planet at a Time
...: On the Edge
...: Tennants of Hell
A-1
Atomic Age
Black Dragon, The
Blood
Bloodlines: A Tale from the Heart of Africa
Blueberry
Bozz Chronicles, The
Brats Bizarre
Cadillacs & Dinosaurs
Captain Confederacy
Car Warriors
Chiller
Clive Barker's Book of the Damned
...Hellraiser
...Nightbreed
...The Harrowers
Coyote
Crash Ryan
Crime and Punishment: Marshall Law Takes Manhattan
Dinosaurs, a Celebration
Doctor Zero
Dragon Lines
...: Way of the Warrior
Dreadlands
Dreadstar
...and Company
Elfquest
Elsewhere Prince, The
Epic
...Illustrated
...Lite
Everyman, The
Feud
Groo Carnival, The
...Chronicles, The
...the Wanderer
Havok & Wolverine - Meltdown
Heavy Hitters
Hellhound, The Redemption Quest
Hellraiser Nightbreed - Jihad
Hollywood Superstars
Idol
Incal, The
Interface
Last American, The
Lawdog/Grimrod: Terror at the Crossroads
Lieutenant Blueberry
Light and Darkness War, The
Marshal Blueberry
Marshal Law
Midnight Men
Moebius
Moonshadow
Mutatis
Necromancer: The Graphic Novel
One, The
Onyx Overlord
Pinhead
...Vs. Marshal Law
Plastic Forks
Power Line
Psychonauts
Sachs & Violens
St. George
Samurai Cat
Seven Block
Shadowline Saga: Critical Mass, A
Sisterhood of Steel
Six From Sirius
...II
Sleeze Brothers, The
Stalkers
Starstruck
Steelgrip Starkey
Strange Combat Tales
Stray Toasters
Swords of the Swashbucklers

Tales from the Heart of Africa
Ted McKeever's Metropol
Tekworld
Terrarists
Tomb of Dracula
Tomorrow Knights
Tor
Transmutation of Ike Garuda, The
Untamed
Video Jack
Void Indigo
War Man
Weaveworld
Wild Cards

Malibu
Angels of Destruction
Battletech
...Fallout
Black September
Bravura
Break-Thru
Breed
...II
Bruce Lee
Codename: Firearm
Curse of Rune
Dinosaurs for Hire
Dreadstar
Dream Team
Edge
Eliminator
Elven
Exiles
Ex-Mutants
Ferret
Firearm
Flood Relief
Freex
Godwheel
Gravestone
Hardcase
Lord Pumpkin
.../Necromantra
Malibu Ashcan: Rafferty
Man Called A-X, The
Man of War
Mantra
Metaphysique
Mortal Kombat
...: Baraka
...: Battlewave
...: Goro, Prince of Pain
...: Kitana and Mileena
...: Kung Lao
...: Raydon & Kano
...: U. S. Special Forces
Mutants Vs. Ultras
Night Man, The
Nocturnals, The
Power & Glory
Power of Prime
Prime
Project A-KO
Protectors
Prototype
Ripfire
Rune
.../Silver Surfer
Siren
Sludge
Solitaire
Solution, The
Star Slammers
Star Trek: Deep Space Nine
...-The Celebrity Series: Blood and Honor
...Hearts and Minds
..., The Maquis
.../The Next Generation
Strangers, The
Street Fighter
Strikeback!
Tarzan: Love, Lies and the Lost City
...the Warrior
Terminator 2: Cybernetic Dawn
...: Nuclear Twilight
Ultraforce
Ultraverse Double Feature
...Origins
...Premiere
...Year One
...Year Two
...Year Zero: The Death of the Squad
Warstrike
Wrath

Marvel UK
Action Force
Battletide
...II
Captain Britain
Codename: Genetix
Dark Angel
...Guard
Death Metal
...Vs. Genetix
Death's Head
...II
...II & the Origin of Die-Cut
Death 3
...Wreck
Die-Cut
...Vs. G-Force
Digitek
Dragon's Claws
Gene Dogs
Genetix
Gun Runner
Hell's Angel
Incomplete Death's Head
Killpower: The Early Years
King Arthur and the Knights of Justice
Knights of Pendragon, The
Motormouth
Mys-Tech Wars
Nightraven: The Collected Stories
Pendragon
Plasmer
Shadow Riders
Super Soldiers
Warheads
Wildthing

Star Comics
Air Raiders
Animax
Bullwinkle and Rocky
Care Bears
Chuck Norris
Defenders of the Earth
Droids
Ewoks
Flintstone Kids, The
Flintstones, The
Foofur
Fraggle Rock
Getalong Gang, The
Heathcliff
...'s Funhouse
Hugga Bunch
Inhumanoids, The
Madballs
Masters of the Universe
Misty
Muppet Babies, The
Muppets Take Manhattan, The
Peter Porker the Spectacular Spider-Ham
Planet Terry
Popples
Royal Roy
Silverhawks
Star Comics Magazine
Strawberry Shortcake
Thundercats
Top Dog
Visionaries
Wally the Wizard

SIRIUS
Against Blackshard 3-D
Akiko
Animal Mystic
Crypt of Dawn
Dawn
Dolls
Drama
Eleven or One
Greylore
Hero Alliance, The
Poison Elves
Tales of the Sun Runners
Wandering Star

TEKNO COMIX/BIG ENT.
Gene Roddenberry's Lost Universe
...Xander in Lost Universe
Isaac Asimov's I-Bots
John Jakes' Mullkon Empire
Leonard Nimoy's Primortals
...Origins
Mickey Spillane's Mike Danger
Neil Gaiman's Lady Justice
...Mr. Hero - The Newmatic Man
...Teknophage
...Wheel of Worlds

TOPPS COMICS
Barbi Twins, The
Bombast
Bram Stoker's Dracula
Cadillacs and Dinosaurs
Captain Glory
Dracula Chronicles
...Versus Zorro
...: Vlad the Impaler
Duckman
...: The Mob Frog Saga
Exosquad
Frankenstein/Dracula War
Jackie Chan's Spartan X
Jack Kirby's Secret City Saga
...Silver Star
...Teenagents
Jason Goes to Hell: The Final Friday
...Vs. Leatherface
Jurassic Park
...: Raptor
...: Raptors Attack
...: Raptors Hijack
Lady Rawhide
Lone Ranger and Tonto
Lost World, The
Mars Attacks
...High School
...Image
...The Savage Dragon
Mary Shelley's Frankenstein
Night Glider
Ray Bradbury Comics
Return to Jurassic Park
Satan's Six
...: Hellspawn
Topps Comics Presents
Victory
Xena: Warrior Princess
.../Joxer: Warrior Prince
X-Files, The
...: Ground Zero
...: Season One
Zorro

FIRST APPEARANCES

A-Man the Amazing Man - Amazing-Man Comics #5, 9/39
Adam Strange - Showcase #17, 11-12/58
Adult Legion - Superman #147, 8/61
Agent Liberty - Superman #60 (2nd Series), 10/91
Air Man - (Hawkman imitator) Keen Detective Funnies #23, 8/40
Air Wave - Detective Comics #60, 2/42
Air Wave II - Green Lantern #100, 1/78
Airboy - Air Fighters Comics V1#2, 11/42
Airwave I - Detective Comics #60, 2/42
Alex Summers - (becomes Havok) X-Men #54, 3/69
Alfred - Batman #16 4-5/43; (1st skinny Alfred) Detective Comics #83, 1/44
Alice Cooper - Marvel Premiere #50, 10/79
Alicia Masters - Fantastic Four #8, 11/62
Aliens - Aliens #1 May '88; Magnus, Robot Fighter #1, 2/63
Alley Oop - Funnies #1, 10/36
Alpha Flight - X-Men #120, 4/78
Amazing Man - All Star Squadron #23, 7/83
American Ace - (1st newsstand app.) Marvel Mystery Comics #2, 12/39
American Crusader - Thrilling Comics #19, 8/41
American Eagle - Marvel Two-In-One Annual #6, 1981; (1st pub lished app.) Motion Picture Funnies Weekly #1, 1939
Ancient One - Strange Tales #110, 7/63
Andy Panda - Crackajack Funnies #39, 9/41
Angel - Marvel Comics #1, 10-11/39
Angel (now Archangel) - X-Men #1, 9/63
Angel & the Ape - Showcase #77, 9/68
Animal Man - (in costume) Strange Adventures #190, 7/66; (no cos tume) Strange Adventures #180, 9/65; (re-intro) Wonder Woman #267, 5/80
Ant-Man - (costume) Tales to Astonish #35, 9/62; (new) Marvel Premiere #47, 4/79; (no costume) Tales to Astonish #27, 1/62; (re-intro) Avengers #46, 11/67
Anthro - Showcase #74, 5/68
Apache Kid - Two Gun Western #5, 11/50
Ape, The - Startling Comics #21, 5/43
Aqua-Girl - Aquaman #33, 5-6/67
Aquababy - Aquaman #23, 9-10/65
Aquaboy - Superboy #171
Aquagirl - (try out, not same as other) Adventure Comics #266, 11/59
Aquagirl - Aquaman #33, 5-6/67
Aqualad - Adventure Comics #269, 2/60
Aquarian (Wundarr) - Adventure Into Fear #17, '73
Aquaman - More Fun Comics #73, 11/41
Arak - Warlord #48, 8/81
Archangel - (cameo) (formerly Angel) X-Factor #23, 12/87; (full app.) X-Factor #24, 1/88
Archie Andrews - Pep Comics #22, 12/41

Arion - Warlord #55
Arrow - Funny Pages V2#10, 9/38
Arthur Stacy - Amazing Spider-Man #93, 2/71
Asbestos Lady - Captain America Comics #63, 7/47
Astro Boy - Astro Boy #1, 8/65
Atom - All-American Comics #19, 10/40; (S.A.) Showcase #34, 9-10/61
Atoman - Atoman #1, 2/46
Atomaster - Comic Books #1, 1950
Atomic Mouse - Atomic Mouse #1, 3/53
Atomic Rabbit - Atomic Rabbit #1, 8/55
Atomic Thunderbolt - Atomic Thunderbolt #1, 2/46
Aunt May - Amazing Fantasy #15, 8-9/62; (prototype) Strange Tales #92, 6/62
Aurora - X-Men #120
Avenger - Shadow Comics #2, 4/40
Azrael - (cameo) Tales of the Teen Titans #52, 4/85; (full app.) Tales of the Teen Titans #53, 5/85
Baby Huey - Casper, the Friendly Ghost #1, 9/49; (1st Harvey app.) Harvey Comics Hits #60, 9/52
Badger - Badger #1, 12/83
Balbo, the Boy Magician - Master Comics #32, 11/42
Bamm Bamm - (Flintstones) Flintstones #16, 1/64
Barker - National Comics #42, 5/44
Barney Bear - Our Gang Comics #1, 9-10/42
Baron Strucker - Sgt. Fury #5, 1/64
Bat Lash - Showcase #76, 8/68
Bat-Girl - Batman #139, 4/61; (new) Detective #359, 1/67
Batgirl - Detective Comics #359, 1/67
Batman - Detective Comics #27, May '39; (new look w/new costume) Detective Comics #327, 5/64
Batman, Jr. - World's Finest Comics #215, 10/72
Batmite - Detective Comics #267, 5/59
Batwoman - Detective Comics #233, 7/56; (1st modern app. G.A. Batwoman) Brave and the Bold #182, 1/82; (new) Detective Comics #624, 12/90; (re-intro) Batman Family #10, 3-4/77
Beast - X-Men #1, 9/63; (new) (1st in mutated form) Amazing Adventures #11, 3/72
Beast Boy - (becomes Changeling) Doom Patrol #99, 11/65
Belit - Giant-Size Conan #1, 9/74
Bennett Brant - Amazing Spider-Man #11, 4/64
Bernie the Brain - Sugar & Spike #72, ?, '68
Berserkers, The - X-Men/Alpha Flight #1, 12/85
Betty - Pep Comics #22, 12/41
Betty Brant - Amazing Spider-Man #4, 9/63
Bill Barnes - (Air Ace) Shadow Comics #1, 3/40
Binary - (formerly Ms. Marvel) X-Men #164, 12/82
Birdman, The - Weird Comics #1, 4/40
Bishop - (cameo) X-Men #282, 11/91; (full app.) X-Men #283, 12/91
Bizarro Jimmy Olsen - Adventure Comics #287, 8/61
Bizarro Lana Lang - Adventure Comics #292, 1/62
Bizarro Lois Lane - Action Comics #255, 8/59
Bizarro Lucy Lane - Adventure Comics #292, 1/62
Bizarro Marilyn Monroe - Adventure Comics #294, 3/62
Bizarro Perry White - Adventure Comics #287, 8/61
Bizarro President Kennedy - Adventure Comics #294, 3/62
Black Bolt - (1st full app.) Fantastic Four #46, 1/66 (cameo) (from Inhumans) Fantastic Four #45, 12/65
Black Canary - Flash Comics #86, 8/47; (Silver Age) Justice League of America #74; (1st modern app.) Detective Comics #554, 9/85; (1st solo story) Flash Comics #92, 2/48
Black Cat - Pocket Comics #1, 8/41
Black Cobra - Captain Flight Comics #8 ?, '46
Black Condor - Crack Comics #1, 5/40
Black Dwarf - Spotlight Comics #1, 11/44
Black Flame - Starslayer #20 9/84; Action Comics #304, 9/63
Black Fury - Fantastic Comics #18, 5/41
Black Goliath - Black Goliath #1, 2/76
BlackHawk - Military Comics #1, 8/41
Black Hood - Top-Notch Comics #9, 10/40; (S.A.) Adventures of the Fly #7, 7/60
Black Jack - Zip Comics #20, 11/41
Black Knight - Black Knight #1, 5/55
Black Knight - Tales to Astonish #52, 2/64
Black Knight II - Avengers #48, 1/68
Black Lightning - Black Lightning #1, 4/77
Black Marvel - Mystic Comics #5, 3/41
Black Orchid - Adventure Comics #428, 6-7/73; (new) Black Orchid #1, 12/88
Black Owl - Prize Comics #2, 4/40
Black Panther - Stars & Stripes #3, 7/41
Black Panther - Fantastic Four #52, 7/66
Black Phantom - Tim Holt #25, 9/51
Black Pirate - Sensation Comics #1, 1/42
Black Rider - All Western Winners #2, Win '48-49
Black Spider - Super-Mystery Comics V1#3, 10/40
Black Terror - Exciting Comics #9, 5/41
Black Widow - Mystic Comics #4, 7-8/40
Black Widow - Tales of Suspense #52, 4/64
Blackie the Hawk - Blackhawk #75, 4/54
Blackie the Hawk - (re-intro) Blackhawk #108, 1/57
Blade the Vampire Slayer - Tomb of Dracula #10, ?/73?
Blok - (Legion) Superboy #253, 7/79
Blonde Phantom - All-Select Comics #11, Fall '46; (re-intro) Sensational She-Hulk #4, 8/89
Blondie - Ace Comics #1, 4/37
Bloodshot - (cameo) Eternal Warrior #4, 11/92; (1st full app.) Rai #0, 11/92
Bloodstone - Marvel Presents #1, 10/75
Blue Beetle - (G.A.) Mystery Men Comics #1, 8/39; (Charlton) Blue Beetle #18, 2/55; (Ted Kord) Captain Atom #83, 11/66; (1st DC app.) Crisis on Infinite Earths #1, 4/85
Blue Blade - USA Comics #5, Sum '42
Blue Blaze - Mystic Comics #1, 3/40
Blue Bolt - Blue Bolt #1, 6/40
Blue Circle - Blue Circle Comics #1, 6/44
Blue Devil - Fury of Firestorm #24, 6/84
Blue Streak - Crash Comics #1, 5/40
Bo Bunny - Funny Stuff #70, 1-2?/53
Bobby Benson - Bobby Benson's B-Bar-B Riders #1, 5-6/50
Boboes - Marvel Mystery Comics #32, 6/42
Bomba - Bomba, the Jungle Boy #1, 9-10/67
Bombshell - Boy Comics #3, 4/42
Booster Gold - Booster Gold #1, 2/86
Bouncer - Bouncer nn, 1944
Bouncing Boy - (Legion) Action Comics #276, 5/61
Boy Commandos - Detective Comics #64, 6/42
Bozo the Robot - Smash Comics #1, 8/39
Braniac 5 - Action Comics #276, 5/61
Brick Bradford - King Comics #1, 4/36
Broncho Bill - Tip Top Comics #1, 4/36
Brother Power - Brother Power, the Geek #1, 9-10/68; (re-intro) Saga of Swamp Thing Annual #5, 1989
Buck Rogers - (in comics) Famous Funnies #3, 9/34
Buckskin - Super Mystery V2#1, 4/41
Bucky - (Captain America's sidekick) Captain America Comics #1, 3/41; (Silver Age) Avengers #4, 3/64;
Bugs Bunny - Looney Tunes & Merrie Melodies #1, 1941
Bullet - Amazing Mystery Funnies V3#1, 1/40
Bulletboy - Master Comics #48, 3/44
Bulletman - Nickel Comics #1, 5/40
Bumblebee - Teen Titans (1st series) #48, 1977
Buzzy - All Funny Comics #1, Win '43-44
Buzzy the Crow - Harvey Comics Hits #60, 9/52
B'Wanna Beast - Showcase #66
Cable - (1st full app.) New Mutants #87, 3/90; (cameo) New Mutants #86, 2/90
Cain - (House of Mystery host) House of Mystery #176, 10/67
Calico Kid - (becomes Ghost Rider) Tim Holt #6, 5/49
Camilla - Jungle Comics #1, 1/40
Candy - Police Comics #37, 12/44
Captain & the Kids - Famous Comics Cartoon Books #1200, 1934; Tip Top Comics #1, 4/36
Captain Action - Captain Action & Action Boy nn, 1967
Captain Aero - Captain Aero Comics V1#7, 12/41
Captain America - Captain America Comics #1, 3/41; (Silver Age) Strange Tales #114, 11/63; (Acrobat disguised as) Avengers #4, 3/64; (fomerly Super Patriot) Captain America #333, 9/87; (new) Captain America #181, 1/75; (new) (formerly Nomad) Captain America #183, 3/75
Captain Atom - (1st DC app.) Crisis on Infinite Earths #6, 9/85; (new) Captain Atom #84, 1/67; (new) Captain Atom #1 3/87; (S.A.) Space Adventures #33, 3/60
Captain Battle - Silver Streak Comics #10, 5/41
Captain Britain - Captain Britain #1, 3/87; (1st U.S. app.) Marvel Team-Up #65, 1/78
Captain Comet - Strange Adventures #9, 6/51; (re-intro) Secret Society of Super-Villains #2, 7-8/76
Captain Commando - Pep Comics #30, 8/42
Captain Courageous - Banner Comics #3, 9/41
Captain Daring - Buccaneers #19, 1/50; Daring Mystery Comics #7, 4/41
Captain Desmo - Adventure Comics #32, 11/38
Captain Easy - Funnies #1, 10/36; Famous Comics Cartoon Books #1202, 1934
Captain Fearless - Silver Streak Comics #1, 12/39
Captain Fight - Fight Comics #16, 12/41
Captain Flag - Blue Ribbon Comics #16, 9/41
Captain Flash - Captain Flash #1, 11/54
Captain Freedom - Speed Comics #13, 5/41
Captain Future - Man of Tomorrow - Startling Comics #1, 6/40
Captain George Stacy - Amazing Spider-Man #56, 1/68
Captain Marvel (Shazam) - Whiz Comics #1, 2/40; (M.F.Enterprises) Captain Marvel #1, 4/66; (mod ern) Shazam: the New Beginning #1, 4/87; (new) Legends #1, 11/86; (re-intro) Shazam! #1, 2/73
Captain Marvel (female) - Amazing Spider-Man Annual #16, 1982
Captain Marvel of the Kree - Marvel Super-Heroes #12, 12/67
Captain Marvel, Jr. - Whiz Comics #25, 12/41
Captain Midnight - Funnies #57, 7/41
Captain Savage - Mystery Men Comics #4, 11/39
Captain Storm - Captain Storm #1, 5-6/64
Captain Strong - Action Comics #421, 3/73
Captain Terror - U.S.A. #2, 11/41
Captain Terry Thunder - Jungle Comics #1, 1/40
Captain Thunder - Flash Comics (Fawcett) #1, 1/40
Captain Thunder - Superman #276, ?'74
Captain Triumph - Crack Comics #27, 1/43
Captain Universe - Micronauts #8, 8/79
Captain Victory - Our Flag Comics #1, 8/41
Captain Wizard - Red Band Comics #3, ?'45
Captain Wonder - Kid Komics #1, 2/43
Captain Yank - Big Shot Comics #29, 11/42
Casper the Friendly Ghost - (1st Harvey app.) Harvey Comics Hits #60, 9/52; Casper #1, 9/49
Cat - The Cat #1, 11/72
Cat Girl - Adventures of the Fly #9, 11/60
Catman - Crash Comics #5, 11/40
Cave Carson - Brave and the Bold #31, 8-9/60
Cerebus - Cerebus the Aardvark #1, 12/77
Challenger - Mystic Comics #6, 10/41
Chameleon - Target Comics V1#6, 7/40
Chameleon Boy - (Legion) Action Comics #267, 8/60
Champ - Champion Comics #2, 12/39
Changeling - (formerly Beast Boy) New Teen Titans #1, 11/80; (X-Men) X-Men #35, 8/67
Charlie Chan - Feature Comics #23, 8/39
Charlie-27 - Marvel Super Heroes

#18, 1/69
Checkmate - Action Comics #598, 3/88
Chemical King - (Legion) Adventure Comics #371, 8/68
Chlorophyll Kid - (Legion) Adventure Comics #306, 2/63
Chop Chop - (Blackhawk's sidekick) Military Comics #3, 10/41
Chuck - (Black Fury's aide) Fantastic Comics #18, 5/41
Cisco Kid - Cisco Kid Comics #1, Win '44
Claw the Unconquered - Claw the Unconquered #1, 5-6/75
Clea - Strange Tales #126, 11/64
Cletus Kasady - (1st full app.) Amazing Spider-Man #345, 3/91; (cameo; becomes Carnage) Amazing Spider-Man #344, 2/91
Clip Carson - More Fun Comics #68, 6/41
Cloak - (Spy Master) Big Shot Comics #1, 5/40
Cloak & Dagger - Spec. Spider-Man #64, 3/82
Clock - Crack Comics #1, 5/40
Clock - Funny Pages V1#6, 11/36
Clown - Super-Mystery Comics V1#5, 12/40
Clown - Spitfire Comics #1, 8/41
Cobra Kid - (Black Cobra's sidekick) Captain Flight Comics #8, ? '46
Colossal Boy - (Legion) Action Comics #267, 8/60
Colossus - Tales of Suspense #14, 2/61; Giant-Size X-Men #1, Sum '75
Combat Kelly - Combat Kelly #1, 11/51; (new) Combat Kelly #1, 6/72
Comet - Pep Comics #1, 1/40; (re-intro) Comet #1, 10/83; (S.A.) Advent. of the Fly #30, 10/64
Commando Yank - Wow Comics #6, 7/15/42
Commissioner Gordon - Detective Comics #27, 5/39
Conan, the Barbarian - (1st in comics) Conan, the Barbarian #1, 10/70
Concrete - Dark Horse Presents #1, 7/86
Congo Bill - More Fun Comics #56, 6/40
Congorilla - Action Comics #248, 1/59
Conqueror, The - Victory Comics #1, 8/41
Cookie - Topsy-Turvy #1, 4/45
Corporal Collins - Blue Ribbon Comics #2, 12/39
Cosmic Boy - (Legion) Adventure Comics #247, 4/58
Cosmo Cat - All Top Comics #1, 1945
Cosmo Mann - Bang-Up Comics #1, 12/41
Cosmo, the Phantom of Disguise - Detective Comics #1, 3/37
Cotton Carver - Adventure Comics #50, 5/40
Cougar - The Cougar #1, 4/75
Creeper - Showcase #73, 3-4/67
Crimebuster - Boy Comics #3, 4/42
Crimson Avenger - Detective Comics #20, 10/38
Crusader - Aquaman #56, 3-4/71; (formerly old Marvel Boy) Fantastic Four #164, 11/75
Crypt Keeper - Crime Patrol #15, 12-1/49-50
Crystal - Fantastic Four #45, 12/65
Cyborg - (New Teen Titans) DC Comics Presents #26, 10/80
Cyclone - Whirlwind Comics #1, 6/40
Cyclops - X-Men #1, 9/63
Cyclotronic Man - Black Lightning #4, 7/77
D-Man - Captain America #328, 4/86
Daffy Duck - Looney Tunes & Merrie Melodies #1, 1941
Daimon Hellstrom - (1st full app.) Ghost Rider #2, 10/73; (cameo) (Son of Satan) Ghost Rider #1, 9/73
Daisy Duck - (back cover only) Large Feature Comic #16, 6/41
Dale Daring - Adventure Comics #32, 11/38
Dan Hastings - Star Comics #1, 2/37
Danny Chase - New Teen Titans Annual #3, 1987
Daredevil - Silver Streak Comics #6, 9/40 (blue & yellow costume)
Daredevil - Daredevil #1, 4/64
Darkhawk - Darkhawk #1, 3/91
Darklon the Mystic - Eerie #79, 11/76
Dart & sidekick Ace - Weird Comics #5, 8/40
David - (Samson's aide) Fantastic Comics #10, 9/40
Dawnstar - (Legion) Superboy #226, 4/77
Dazzler - X-Men #130, 2/80
Deadman - Strange Adventures #205, 10/67
Deadpool - New Mutants #98, 2/91
Death - Sandman #8, 1990
Death's Head - (new) (1 pg. strip on back-c) Dragon's Claws #3, 9/88; (new) (1st full app.) Dragon's Claws #5, 11?/88
Deathlok the Demolisher - Astonishing Tales #25, 8/74
Deathstroke the Terminator - New Teen Titans #2, 12/80; (1st solo story) New Titans #70, 10/90
Demon - Demon #1, 8-9/72
Dennis the Menace - Dennis the Menace #1, 8/53
Deputy Dawg - New Terrytoons #1, 6-8/60
Destroyer, The - USA Comics #6, 12/42
Destroyer - Invaders #16, 5/77; Mystic Comics #6, 10/41
Destroyer Duck - Destroyer Duck #1, 1982
Destructor - The Destructor #1, 2/75
Dev-Em, the Knave from Krypton - Adventure Comics #287, 8/61
Devil-Slayer - Marvel Spotlight #33, 4/77
Dial "H" for Hero - (Robby Reed) House of Mystery #156, 11-12/65
Dick Cole - Blue Bolt #1, 6/40
Dick Tracy - (1st comic book app.) Popular Comics #1, 2/36
Dixie Dugan - Feature Funnies #1, 10/37
Doc Samson - Incredible Hulk #141, 7/71
Doc Savage - (1st in comics) Shadow Comics #1, 3/40; (pulp-1st app.) 3/33
Doc Strong - Blue Ribbon Comics #4, 6/40
Doctor Fate - (female) Doctor Fate #25, 2/91
Doctor Midnight - (new) Infinity, Inc. #21, 12/85
Doctor Solar - Doctor Solar #1, 10/62; (1st in costume) Doctor Solar #5, ? '63
Doctor Strange - Strange Tales #110, 7/63
Dodo & the Frog - Funny Stuff #18, 2/47
Doiby Dickles - (Green Lantern's side-kick) All-American Comics #27, 6/41
Doll Man - Feature Comics #27, 12/39
Dolphin - (of Forgotten Heroes) Showcase #79, 12/68
Dominic Fortune - Marvel Preview #2, 1975; (1st color app.) Marvel Premiere #56, 10/80; (new) Iron Man #213, 12/86
Domino - New Mutants #98, 2/91
Donald Duck - The Wise Little Hen, 1934
Don Winslow - Popular Comics #1, 2/36
Doodles Duck - Dodo & the Frog #80, 9-10/54
Dotty & Ditto - Top-Notch Comics #33, 2/43
Dr. Fate - More Fun Comics #55, 5/40; (Silver Age) Justice League of America #21
Dr. Hypno - Amazing-Man Comics #14, 7/40
Dr. Mid-Nite - (1st story app.) All-American Comics #25, 4/41; (text only) All-American Comics #24, 3/41
Dr. Mystic - (Superman prototype) Comics Magazine #1, 5/36
Dr. Neff, Ghost Breaker - Red Dragon Comics #3, 5/48
Dr. Occult - New Fun Comics #6, 10/35; (1st in color & 1st DC app.) More Fun Comics #14, 10/36
Dr. Specktor - Mystery Comics Digest #5, ? '72?
Dr. Strange - Thrilling Comics #1, 2/40
Dr. Strange - Strange Tales #110, 7/63
Dr. Who - Marvel Premiere #57, 12/80
Dracula - Tomb of Dracula #1, 4/72; Dracula #2, 11/66
Dragon - (1st full app.) Megaton #3, 2/86; (cameo)(later Savage Dragon) Megaton #2, 10/85
Drax the Destroyer - Iron Man #55, 2/73
Dreadstar - Epic Illustrated #15, 12/82
Dream Girl - (Legion) Adventure Comics #317, 2/64
Duo Damsel - (Legion)(formerly Triplicate Girl) Adventure Comics #341, 2/66
Duplicate Boy - Adventure Comics #324
Dusty - (Shield's sidekick) Pep Comics #11, 1/41
Dynamic Man - Mystic Comics #1, 3/40
Dynamite Thor - Blue Beetle #6, 3-4/41
Dynamo - Thunder Agents #1, 11/65; (Electro #1 only) Science Comics #1, 2/40
Dynamo, The Eagle - Weird Comics #8, 11/40
Eagle - Science Comics #1, 2/40
Ebony - Police Comics #12, 10/42
Echo, The - All-New Comics #1, 1/43
Eclipso - House of Secrets #61, 7-8/63
Eddie Brock - (becomes Venom) Amazing Spider-Man #298, 3/88
Egbert - Egbert #1, Spr '46
El Diablo - All Star Western #2, 10-11/70
Elasti-Girl - My Greatest Adventure #80, 6/63
Elastic Lad - (Jimmy Olsen) Superman's Pal Jimmy Olsen #31, ?/62
Electro, the Marvel of the Age - Marvel Mystery Comics #4, 2/40
Elektra - Daredevil #168, ? /81?
Element Girl - Metamorpho #10, 1-2/67
Element Lad - (Legion) Adventure Comics #307, 4/63
Elfquest - Fantasty Quarterly #1, Spr '78
Ella Cinders - Famous Comics Cartoon Books #1203, 1934; Tip Top Comics #1, 4/36
Ellery Queen - (1st app. in comics) Crackajack Funnies #23, 5/40
Elmer Fudd - Looney Tunes & Merrie Melodies #1, 1941
Elongated Man - Flash #112, 4-5/60
E-Man - E-Man #1, 10/73
Enchantress - Journey Into Mystery #103, 4/64
Enemy Ace - Our Army at War #151, 2/65
Erg - (becomes Wildfire) Superboy #198, ? '73?
Eternal Warrior - (cameo) Solar #10, 6/92; (full app.) Solar #11, 7/92
Evangeline - Primer #6, 2/84
Everyman - Captain America #267, 3/82
Face - (Tony Trent) Big Shot Comics #1, 5/40
Faceless Creature - Strange Adv. #124, 1/61
Falcon - Pep Comics #1, 1/40
Falcon - Captain America #117, 9/69; Daring Mystery Comics #5, 6/40
Fantomah, Mystery Woman - Jungle Comics #1, 1/40
Fatman - Fatman the Human Flying Saucer #1, 4/67
Fearless Flint, the Flint Man - Famous Funnies #89, 12/42
Feral - (of X-Force) New Mutants #99, 3/91
Ferret - Man of War #2, 1/42
Ferret, Mystery Detective - Marvel Mystery Comics #4, 2/40
Ferris - (becomes Star Sapphire) Showcase #22, 9-10/59
Ferro Lad - (Legion) Adventure Comics #346, 7/66
Fiery Mask - Daring Mystery Comics #1, 1/40
Fighting American - Fighting American #1, 4-5/54
Fighting Yank - Startling Comics #10, 9/41
Fin - Daring Mystery Comics #7, 4/41
Fin Fang Foom - Strange Tales #89, 10/61
Fire - Super Friends #25
Fireball - Pep Comics #12, 2/41; (S.A.) Mighty Crusaders #4, 5?/66
Firebrand - Police Comics #1, 8/41
Firefist - Blue Beetle #1, 6/86
Firefly - Top-Notch Comics #8, 9/40
Firehair - Rangers Comics #21, 2/45
Firehawk - Fury of Firestorm #17, 10/83
Fire Lad - Adventure Comics #306, 2/63
Firelord - Thor #225, 7/74
FireStar - X-Men #193, 4/85
Firestorm - Firestorm, the Nuclear Man #1, 3/78; (new) Firestorm, the Nuclear Man Annual #5, 10/87
Flag, The - Our Flag Comics #2, 10/41
Flame, The - Wonderworld Comics #3, 7/39
Flamebird - (Jimmy Olsen as) Superman #158, 12/62; (new) Secret Origins Annual #3, 1989
Flaming Carrot - Visions #1, 1979
Flash - Flash Comics #1, 1/40; (G.A.) (1st app. in S.A.) Flash #123, 9/61
Flash - Showcase #4, 9-10/56
Flash Gordon - King Comics #1, 4/36
Flash Lightning - (becomes Lash Lightning) Sure-Fire Comics #1, 6/40
Flash Rabbit - All Top Comics #1, 1945
Flexo the Rubber Man - Mystic Comics #1, 3/40
Flintstones - Dell Giant #48, 7/61
Fly - Double Life of Private Strong #1, 6/59
Fly Girl - (1st in costume)

Adventures of the Fly #14, 9?/61; (w/o costume) Adventures of the Fly #13, 7?/61
Fly-Man, The - Spitfire Comics #1, 8/41
Forbush Man - Not Brand Echh #5, 12/67
Forge - (X-Force) X-Men #184, 8/84
Fox - Blue Ribbon Comics #4, 6/40; (new) Black Hood #11, 11/92
Frankenstein - Prize Comics #7, 12/40; Frankenstein #2, 9/66
Frankenstein's monster - (cameo) Silver Surfer #7, 8/69
Freckles & His Friends - Famous Comics Cartoon Books #1204, 1934
Fred Bender - (becomes Dr. Eclipse) Solar #14, 10/92
Freezum - Blue Bolt V2#5, 10/41
Fritzi Ritz - Tip Top Comics #1, 4/36
Fu Manchu - (1st in Detective) Detective Comics #17, 7/38; (1st cvr.) Det. #1, 3/37
G. I. Robot - Weird War Tales #101, 7/81
Gambit - (cameo) X-Men Annual #14, 1990; (full app.) X-Men #266, 8/90
Gandy Goose - Terry-Toons Comics #1, 10/42
Gangbuster - Adventures of Superman #434, 11/87
Gargoyle - Defenders #94, 4/80
Gary Concord - (Ultra Man) All-American Comics #8, 11/39
Genius Jones - All Funny Comics #1, Win '43-44
Gentleman Ghost - Atom & Hawkman #43, 6-7/69
Ghost Breaker - Star Spangled Comics #122, 11/51
Ghost Patrol - Flash Comics #29, 5/42
Ghost Patrol - Wings #66, 2/46
Ghost Rider - (formerly Calico Kid) Tim Holt #11, ?/49
Ghost Rider - (western) Ghost Rider #1, 2/67; (Johnny Blaze) Marvel Spotlight #5, 8/72; (new-Daniel Ketch) Ghost Rider V2#1, 5/90
Giant-Man - (formerly Ant-Man) Tales to Astonish #49, 11/63
Gideon - New Mutants #98, 2/91
Gladstone Gander - Walt Disney's Comics and Stories #88, 1/48
Glory Grant - Amazing Spider-Man #140, 1/75
Gnort - Justice League International #10
God Of Thunder, The - Weird Comics #1, 4/40
Godiva - New Teen Titans Annual #3, 11/87
Golden Arrow - Whiz Comics #1, 2/40
Golden Dragon - Adventure Comics #32, 11/38
Golden Girl - Golden Lad #5, 6/46
Golden Gladiator - Brave and the Bold #1, 8-9/55
Golden Gorilla - Action Comics #224, 1/57
Golden Lad - Golden Lad #1, 7/45
Golem - Strange Tales #174, 2/74
Goliath - (formerly Giant-Man) Avengers #28, 5/66 (formerly Hawkeye) Avengers #63, 4/69
Grandma Duck - Donald and Mickey Merry Christmas nn, 1945
Gray Ghost - Sensation Comics #1, 1/42
Great Gazoo - (Flintstones) Flintstones #34
Green Arrow - More Fun Comics #73, 11/41
Green Falcon - Blue Ribbon Comics #4, 6/40
Green Flame - Super Friends #42, 3/81
Green Fury - (formerly Green Flame) Infinity, Inc. #32, 11/86
Green Hornet - (1st in comics) Green Hornet Comics #1, 12/40; (Silver Age) Green Hornet #1, 2/67
Green Lama - Prize Comics #7, 12/40
Green Lantern - All-American Comics #16, 7/40; (S.A.) Showcase #22, 9-10/59
Green Mask - Mystery Men Comics #1, 8/39
Green Turtle - Blazing Comics #1, 6/44
Grendel - Primer #2, 2/83
Grey Mask - Suspense Comics #1, 12/43
Grimjack - Starslayer #10, 11/83
Grim Reaper, The - Wonder Comics #1, 5/44
Groo the Wanderer - Destroyer Duck #1, 1982
Gruesomes - (Flintstones) Flintstones #24
Guardian - Star Spangled Comics #7, 4/42; (formerly Vindicator) Alpha Flight #2, 9/83
Guardian Angel - (formerly Hop Harrigan) All-American Comics #25, 4/41
Guardsman I - Iron Man #43, 11?/71?
Guardsman II - Iron Man #96, 3/77
Gunner & Sarge - All-American Men of War #57, ? '58?; Our Fighting Forces #45, 5/59
Guy Gardner - (later a Green Lantern)Green Lantern #59, 3/68; (1st app. as a Green Lantern) Green Lantern #116, 5/79
Gwen Stacy - Amazing Spider-Man #31, 12/65
Gyro Gearloose - Walt Disney's Comics and Stories #140, 5/52
Halo - Blue Beetle #24, 8/43
Hangman - Pep Comics #17, 7/41
Hangman - (re-intro) Comet #6, 12/91; (S.A.) Fly Man #33, 9/65
Happy Houlihans - Blackstone, the Magician Detective #1, Fall '47
Harada - Solar #3, 11/91
Harbinger - Harbinger #1, 1/92
Harlequin - (Joker's Daughter) Teen Titans #48, '77
Harry Osborn - (later becomes Green Goblin II) Amazing Spider-Man #31, 12/65
Harvey Bullock - Batman #361, 7/83
Havok - (no costume) X-Men #56, 5/69; (with costume) X-Men #58, 7/69
Hawk & Dove - Showcase #75, 7-8/67
Hawkeye - Tales of Suspense #57, 9/64; (formerly Goliath) Avengers #98, 4/72
Hawkgirl - (formerly Shiera Sanders) All Star Comics #5, 6-7/41; (Silver Age) Brave & the Bold #34, 2-3/61
Hawkman - Flash Comics #1, 1/40; (S.A.) Brave and the Bold #34, 2-3/61; (modern) Hawkworld: Book #1, 1989
Heap - Air Fighters Comics V1#3, 12/42
Heckle & Jeckle - Terry-Toons Comics #50, 11/46
Hedy Devine - Hedy Devine Comics #22, 8/47
Hedy Wolfe - Miss America Magazine #2, 11/44
Heimdall - Journey Into Mystery #85, 10/62
Hellblazer - (John Constantine) Saga of Swamp Thing #37, 6/85
Hellcat - Avengers #144, 2/76
Her - (formerly Paragon) Marvel Two-In-One #61, 3/80
Herbie - Forbidden Worlds #73, ? '59?
Hercules - Blue Ribbon Comics #4, 6/40; Incredible Hulk #3, 9/62; Hit Comics #1 7/40; Mystic Comics #3, 6/40
Herman & Catnip - Harvey Comics Hits #60, 9/52
High Evolutionary - Thor #134, 11/66
Him - (Warlock) (cameo) Fantastic Four #67, 10/67 (Warlock) (full app.) Thor #165, 6/69
Hocus & Pocus - Action Comics #83, 4/45
Hooded Horseman - Blazing West #14, 11-12/50
Hooded Wasp - Shadow Comics #7, 11/40
Hop Harrigan - All-American Comics #1, 4/39
Hoppy the Marvel Bunny - Fawcett's Funny Animals #1, 12/42
Hourman - Adventure Comics #48, 3/40; (1st app. in S.A.) Justice League of America #21, 8/63
Hourman - (new) Infinity, Inc. #21, 12/85
Howard the Duck - Fear #19, 12/73
Huey, Dewey and Louie - Donald Duck nn (bubble pipe cover)
Hulk - (green skin) Incredible Hulk #2, 7/62; (grey skin) Incredible Hulk #1, 5/62; (new) Incredible Hulk #377, 1/91; (re-intro with grey skin) Incredible Hulk #324, 10/86
Hulk 2099 - 2099 Unlimited #1, 9/93
Human Target - Action Comics #419, 1/73
Human Top - Red Raven Comics #1, 8/40; Tough Kid Squad #1, 3/42
Human Torch - Marvel Comics #1, 10-11/39; (Johnny Storm) Fantastic Four #1, 11/61; (re-intro G.A.) Avengers West Coast #50, 9?/89
Humphrey - Joe Palooka #15, 12/47
Hunchback, The - Wow Comics #2, Spr, 1941
Huntress - (G.A.) Sensation Comics #68, 8/47; (1st S.A. app. of G.A. Huntress) Brave and the Bold #62, 10-11/65; (modern) All Star Comics #69, 11-12/77
Hurricane - Captain America Comics #1, 3/41
Hydroman - Heroic Comics #1, 8/40
Hyper, the Phenomenal - Hyper Mystery Comics #1, 5/40
Ibis the Invincible - Whiz Comics #1, 2/40
Ice - Super Friends #9
Ice Cream Soldier - Our Army at War #85, 8/59
Iceman - X-Men #1, 9/63
Imp - Captain America Comics #12, 3/42
Impossible Man - Fantastic Four #11, 2/63; (re-intro) Fantastic Four #176, 11/76
Impossible Woman - Marvel Two-In-One #60, 2/80
Inferno - (S.A.) Mighty Crusaders #4, 5?/66
Inferno, the Flame Breather - Zip Comics #10, 1/41
Insect Queen - (Lana Lang) (Legion) Superboy #124, 10/65
Invisible Girl - (Sue Storm) Fantastic Four #1, 11/61
Invisible Kid - (Legion) Action Comics #267, 8/60 (new) Legion of Super-Heroes Annual #1, 1982
Invisible Scarlett O'Neil - Famous Funnies #81, 4/42
Iron Fist - Marvel Premiere #15, 5/74; (re-intro, cameo) Namor, the Sub-Mariner #8, 11/90; (re-intro, full app.) Namor, the Sub-Mariner #10, 1/91
Iron Major - Our Army at War #158, 9/65
Iron Man - (Tony Starks) Tales of Suspense #39, 3/63; (new armor) Tales of Suspense #40, 4/63; (new) (Jim Rhodes) Iron Man #231, 6/88
Iron Wolf - Weird Worlds #8, 11-12/73
Isis - Shazam! #25, ? '76
Jack Monroe - (1st full app.) Captain America #154, 10/72; (cameo) Captain America #153, 9/72
Jack of Hearts - Deadly Hands of Kung-Fu #22, 4?/76; (1st solo book) Marvel Premiere #44, 10/78
Jack Q. Frost - Unearthly Spectaculars #1, 10/65
Jack Woods - Adventure Comics #39, 1/39
Jaguar - Adventures of the Jaguar #1, 9/61
Jarella (Hulk's love) - The Incredible Hulk #140, 6/71
Jason Bard - (becomes Robin) Detective Comics #392, 10/69
Jason Todd - Batman #357, 3/83; (1st in Robin costume) Batman #366, 12/83
Jean DeWolf - Marvel Team Up #48, 8/76
Jester - Smash Comics #22, 5/41
Jigsaw - Jigsaw #1, 9/66
Jiminy Cricket - Mickey Mouse Magazine V5#3, 12/39
Jimmy "Minuteman" Martin - Adventure Comics #53, 8/40
Jimmy Martin as Hourman's aide - Adventure Comics #71, 2/42
Jimmy Olsen - Action Comics #6, 11/38; (new) Man of Steel #2, 10/86
Jo-Jo, Congo King - Jo-Jo Comics #7, 7/47
Joe Palooka - Joe Palooka nn, 1933; (1st in comic book format) Feature Funnies #1, 10/37
Joe Robertson - Amazing Spider-Man #52, 9/67
John Carter of Mars - Funnies #30, 4/39
John Carter, Warlord of Mars - Weird Worlds #1, 8-9/72
John Connor - Terminator #12, ?/89
John Constantine - (Hellblazer) Saga of Swamp Thing #37, 6/85
John Force - (Magic Agent) Magic Agent #1, 1-2/62
John Jameson - Amazing Spider-Man #1, 3/63
John Law - Smash Comics #3, 10/39
John Stewart - (later a Green Lantern) Green Lantern #87, 12-1/71-72
Johnny Blaze - (re-intro) Ghost Rider V2#10, 2/91; (Ghost Rider) Marvel Spotlight #5, 8/72
Johnny Cloud - All-American Men of War #82
Johnny Dynamite - Dynamite #3, 9/53
Johnny Peril - Comic Cavalcade #15, 6-7/46
Johnny Quick - More Fun Comics #71, 9/41
Johnny Thunder - All-American Comics #100, 8/48; Flash Comics #1, 1/40; (1st S.A. app.) Flash #137, ?/63
Jon Linton - Amazing Mystery Funnies V2#11, 11/39
Jonah Hex - All Star Western #10, 2-3/72
J'onn J'onzz (See Martian Manhunter)

Jonni Thunder - (Thunderbolt) Jonni Thunder #1, 2/85
Jonny Double - Showcase #78, 11/68
Jordan Brothers - Green Lantern #9, 11-12/61
Jose Delgado - (becomes Gangbuster) Adventures of Superman #432, 9/87
Jubilee - X-Men #244, 2?/89
Judomaster - Special War Series V4#4, 11/65; (1st DC app.) Crisis on Infinite Earths #6, 9/85
Jughead Jones - Pep Comics #22, 12/41
Julie Madison - Detective Comics #31, 9/39
Jungle Jim - Ace Comics #1, 4/37
Junior Woodchucks - Walt Disney's Comics and Stories #125, 2/51
Kaanga, Lord of the Jungle - Jungle Comics #1, 1/40
Kamandi - Kamandi, the Last Boy on Earth #1, 10-11/72
Karate Kid - (Legion) Adventure Comics #346, 7/66
Karma - (New Mutants) Marvel Team-Up #100, 12/80
Katy Keene - Wilbur Comics #5, Sum '45
Kazar the Great - Marvel Comics #1, 10-11/39; (Silver Age) X-men #10, 6/64
Ken Shannon - Police Comics #103, 12/50
Kid Eternity - Hit Comics #25, 12/42
Kid Flash - (later becomes Flash) Flash #110, 12-1/59-60
Killer Frost - Firestorm, the Nuclear Man #3, 6-7/78
King Kull - Creatures on the Loose #10, 3/71
Kit - (Black Cat's sidekick) Black Cat Comics #28, 4/51
Kitty Pryde - (Ariel) (X-Men) X-Men #129, 1/80
Kobra - Kobra #1, 2-3/76
Kole - (New Teen Titan) New Teen Titans #8, 5?/85
Kong the Untamed - Kong the Untamed #1, 6-7/75
Kraven - (War of the Worlds) Amazing Adventures #18, 5/73
Krazy Kat - Ace Comics #1, 4/37
Krypto - Adventure Comics #210, 3/55
Kryptonite (Blue) - Superman #128, 4/59
Kryptonite (Gold) - Superman #140, 4/60
Kryptonite (Red) - Adventure #299, 8/62
Kryptonite Kid - Superboy #83, ?/60
Lady Blackhawk - Blackhawk #133, 2/58
Lady Luck - Spirit nn, 6/2/40
Lana Lang - (becomes Insect Queen) Superboy #10, 9-10/50
Lance Hale - Silver Streak Comics #3, 3/40
Lance O'Casey - Whiz Comics #1, 2/40
Lancer - Super-Mystery Comics V3#3, 1/43
Lash Lightning - (formerly Flash Lightning) Lightning Comics V2#2, 8/41
Lassie - Adventures of Lassie nn, ?/49
Lemonade Kid - Bobby Benson's B-Bar-B Riders #15, 6/50
Leopard Girl - Jungle Action #1, 10/54
Li'l Abner - Tip Top Comics #1, 4/36
Li'l Jinx - Pep Comics #62, 7/47
Liberator - Exciting Comics #15, 12/41
Liberty Belle - Star Spangled #20, 5/43
Light Lass - (formerly Lightning Lass) Adventure Comics #317, 2/64
Lightning - Thunder Agents #4, 4/66
Lightning - (cover only) Jumbo Comics #14, 4/40; (1st story app.) Jumbo Comics #15, 5/40
Lightning Boy - (Legion) Adventure Comics #247, 4/58
Lightning Girl - Lightning Comics V3#1, 6/42
Lightning Lad - (formerly Lightning Boy) Adventure Comics #267, 12/59
Lightning Lass - (Legion) Adventure Comics #308, 5/63
Lilith - Vampire Tales #6, ?/74; (Dracula's daughter) Giant-Size Chillers #1, 6/74; (re-intro) New Teen Titans #2, 9/84; (Teen Titans) Teen Titans #25, 1-2/70
Little Audrey - LIttle Audrey #1, 4/48
Little Dot - Sad Sack Comics #1, 9/49
Little Dynamite - Boy Comics #6, 10/42
Little Lotta - LIttle Dot #1, 9/53
Little Lulu - Marge's Little Lulu 4-Color #74, 6/45; (as text illo) King Comics #46, 2/40
Little Max - Joe Palooka #27, 12/48
Little Orphan Annie - Popular Comics #1, 2/36
Little Wise Guys - Daredevil Comics #13, 10/42
LIving Mummy - Supernatural Thrillers #5, 8/73
Liz Allen - Amazing Spider-Man #4, 9/63
Lobo - (1st full story) Omega Men #10, 1/84; (1st solo story, back-up) Omega Men #37, 4/86; (cameo) Omega Men #3, 6/83
Lockheed - X-Men #166, 2/83
Lois Lane - Action Comics #1, 6/38; (new) Man of Steel #2, 10/86
Lois Lane as Superwoman - Action Comics #60, 5/43
Lone Warrior - Banner Comics #3, 9/41
Longshot - Longshot #1, 9/85
Lori Lemaris the Mermaid - Superman #129, 5/59
Lt. Marvels - Whiz Comics #21, 9/41
Lucy Lane - Superman's Pal Jimmy Olsen #36, ?/62
Luke Cage - (Hero for Hire) Hero For Hire #1, 6/72
Lynx & sidekick Blackie - Mystery Men Comics #13, 8/40
Mad Hatter - Mad Hatter #1, 1-2/46
Madame Satan - Pep Comics #16, 6/41
Madame Web - Amazing Spider-Man #210, 11/80
Madelyne Pryor - (of X-Men) Avengers Annual #10, 1981
Madrox - Giant-Size Fantastic Four #4, 2/75
Mage - (re-intro) Grendel #16, 1/88
Magic Morro - Super Comics #21, 2/40
Magician from Mars - Amazing-Man Comics #7, 11/39
Magicman - Forbidden Worlds #125
Magma - New Mutants #10, 12/83
Magno the Magnetic Man & Davey -Super-Mystery Comics V1#1, 7/40
Magnus, Robot Fighter - Magnus, Robot Fighter #1, 2/63
Major Mynah - Atom #37, 6-7/68
Man Bat - Detective #400, 6/70
Man in Black - Front Page Comic Book #1, 1945
Man of War - Man of War #1, 11/41
Manowar - Target Comics #1, 2/40
Man-Thing - Savage Tales #1, 5/71; (1st full story) Fear #15, 8/73
Mandrake the Magician - King Comics #1, 4/36
Manhunter - Police Comics #8, 3/42; (1st in new costume) Detective Comics #437, 10-11/73; (Paul Kirk) Adventure Comics #58, 1/41; (new) Adventure Comics #73, 4/42
Mantis - Avengers #112, 6/73
Margie - Comedy Comics #34, Fall '46
Mark Merlin - House of Secrets #23, 8/59
Marshal Law - Marshal Law #1, 10/87
Martan, the Marvel Man - Popular Comics #46, 12/39
Martian Manhunter - (J'onn J'onzz) Detective Comics #225, 11/55; (re-intro) Justice League of America #228, 7/84
Marvel Boy - (1st & only app.) Daring Mystery Comics #6, 9/40
Marvel Girl - (becomes Phoenix) X-Men #1, 9/63
Marvel Man - (later Quasar) Captain America #217, 1/78
Mary Jane & Sniffles - Looney Tunes & Merrie Melodies #1, 1941
Mary Jane Watson - (1st mention) Amazing Spider-Man #15, 8/64; (cameo, face not shown) Amazing Spider-Man #25, 6/65; (cameo, face shown) Amazing Spider-Man #42, 11/66; (cameo, not shown) Amazing Spider-Man #38, 7/66; (re-intro) Amazing Spider-Man #243, 8/83
Mary Marvel - Captain Marvel Adventures #18, 12/42
Mask, The - Exciting Comics #1, 4/40
Mask, The - Suspense Comics #2, 1944
Masked Marvel - Keen Detective Funnies V2#7, 7/39
Masked Raider - Marvel Comics #1, 10-11/39
Master Key - Scoop Comics #1, 11/41
Master Man - Master Comics #1, 3/40
Master of Kung-Fu - (Shang-Chi) Special Marvel Edition #15, 12/73
Matter Eater Lad - (Legion) Adventure Comics #303, 12/62
Maximillian O'Leary - (Sargon's aide) All-American Comics #70, 1-2/46
Maya - Atom #1, 6-7/62
Megaton - Megaton #1, 11/83
Menthor - Thunder Agents #1, 11/65
Mento - (non-member) Doom Patrol #91, 11/64
Mentor - Iron Man #55, 2/73
Mera - Aquaman #11, 9-10/63
Merboy - Wonder Woman #107
Mercury - (Silver Streak's sidekick) Silver Streak Comics #11, 6/41
Mercury Man - Space Adventures #44, ?/61?
Metal Men - Showcase #37, 3-4/62
Metallo - (Jor-El's robot) Superboy #49, 6/56
Metamorpho - Brave and the Bold #57, 12-1/64-65
Mickey Finn - (1st comic book app.) Feature Funnies #1, 10/37
Mickey Mouse - Mickey Mouse Book nn, '30
Midnight - Smash Comics #18, 1/41
Mighty Girl - Adventure Comics #453, 9-10/77
Mighty Mouse - Terry-Toons Comics #38, 11/45
Mighty Samson - Mighty Samson #1, 7/64
Millie the Model - Gay Comics #1, 3/44
Milton Berle - Uncle Milty #1, 12/50
Minnie Mouse - Mickey Mouse Book nn, 1930
Minute Man - Master Comics #11, 2/41
Minuteman - (re-intro) Shazam! #31, 9-10/77
Miss Arrowette - World's Finest #113, 4/60
Miss America - (modern) Giant-Size Avengers #1, 8/74
Miss Masque - Exciting Comics #51, 9/46; America's Best Comics #23, 9/47
Miss Patriot - Marvel Mystery Comics #50, 12/43
Miss Victory - Captain Fearless Comics #1, 8/41
Mister Miracle - Mister Miracle #1, 3-4/71
Mister X - (on cover only) Vortex #2
Moby Duck - Donald Duck #112
Mockingbird - Marvel Team-Up #95, 7/80
Modred the Mystic - Marvel Chillers #1, 10/75
Molly O'Day - Molly O'Day #1, 2/45
Mon-El - (Legion) Superboy #89, 6/61
Monarch Starstalker - Marvel Premiere #32, 10/76
Moon Girl - Happy Houlihans #1, Fall '47; Moon Girl and the Prince #1, Fall '47
Moon Knight - Werewolf by Night #32, 8/75; (1st solo book) Marvel Spotlight #28, 6/76
Moondragon - Iron Man #54, 1/73; (re-intro) Warlock and the Infinity Watch #2, 3/92
Morbius - Amaz. Spider-Man #101, 10/71
Morgan Edge - (cameo) Superman's Pal Jimmy Olsen #133, 10/70
Morlock 2001 - Morlock 2001 #1, 2/75
Morty and Ferdie - (Mickey Mouse's nephews) Mickey Mouse #3, 1933
Moth Man - Mystery Men Comics #9, 4/40
Mr. America - (formerly Tex Thompson) Action Comics #33, 2/41
Mr. Fantastic - (Reed Richards) Fantastic Four #1, 11/61
Mr. Justice - Blue Ribbon Comics #9, 2/41
Mr. Miracle - Captain Fearless Comics #1, 8/41
Mr. Monster - Super Duper Comics #3, 5-6/47; (new) Vanguard Illustrated #7, 5/84
Mr. Mystic - Spirit nn, 6/2/40
Mr. Satan - Zip Comics #1, 2/40
Mr. Scarlet - Wow Comics #1, Win '40-41
Mr. Tawny - Captain Marvel #79, 12/47; (Silver Age) Shazam! #2, 4/73
Mr. Terrific - Sensation Comics #1, 1/42; (1st app. in S.A.) Justice League of America #37, 8?/65
Ms. Marvel - (becomes Binary) Ms. Marvel #1, 1/77
Ms. Victory - Femforce Special #1, Fall '84; (new) Femforce #25
Mutt & Jeff- (1st in comic book for mat) Funnies #1, 10/36
Mutt & Jeff - Mutt & Jeff #1, 1910
Mystery Men of Mars - All-American Comics #1, 4/39
Nam - Savage Tales #1, 11/85
Namora - Marvel Mystery Comics #82, 5/47
Ned Leeds - (later becomes Hobgoblin) Amazing Spider-Man #18, 11/64
Negative Man - My Greatest Adventure #80, 6/63
Neil the Horse - Charlton Bullseye #2, 8?/81

Nemesis - Adventures into the Unknown #154, ?/66?
Nemesis Kid - (Legion) Adventure Comics #346, 7/66
Neon the Unknown - Hit Comics #1, 7/40
Neuman, Alfred E. - (cover only, fake ad) Mad #21, 3/55
Nevada Jones - Zip Comics #1, 2/40
New Gods - New Gods #1, 2-3/71
Nick Fury - (formerly Sgt. Fury) Strange Tales #135, 8/65
Night Hawk - All-New Comics #1, 1/43
Nightcrawler - Giant-Size X-Men #1, Sum '75
Nightgirl - Adventure Comics #306, 11/63
Nighthawk - Avengers #71, 12/69
Nightmare - (Casper's horse) Casper, the Friendly Ghost #19, 4/54
Nightmaster - Showcase #82, 5/69
Nightshade - Amazing-Man Comics #24, 10/41; Captain Atom #82, 9/66; (1st DC app.) Crisis on Infinite Earths #6, 9/85
Night Thrasher - Thor #412
Nightwing - (Dick Grayson) Tales of the Teen Titans #44, 7/84; (Superman as) Superman #158, 12/62; (Van-Zee) Superman Family #183, 5-6/77
Nita - (later Namorita in New Warriors) Sub-Mariner #50
Nomad - (formerly Steve Rogers) Captain America #180, 12/74
Noman - Thunder Agents #1, 11/65
Norman Osborn - (Green Goblin I) Amazing Spider-Man #37, 6/66
Nova - Nova #1, 9/76
Nth Man - Marvel Comics Presents #25, ?/89
Nukla - Nukla #1, 10-12/65
Nutsy Squirrel - Funny Folks #1, 4-5/46
Nyoka, the Jungle Girl - Master Comics #50, 5/44
Ocean Master - Aquaman #25, 1-2/66
Odin - (1st full app.) Journey Into Myst. #86, 11/62; (cameo) Journey Into Mystery #85, 10/62
Omac - Omac #1, 9-10/74
Omega - Omega the Unknown #1, 3/76
Oracle, The - Startling Comics #20, 2/43
Orion - (New Gods) New Gods #1, 2-3/71; (of New Gods) (1st new costume) First Issue Special #13, 4/76
Oswald the Rabbit - New Fun Comics #1, 2/35
Outlaw Kid - Outlaw Kid #1, 9/54
Owl - Crackajack Funnies #25, 7/40
Pantha - (New Titan) New Titans #74, 3/91
Paragon - (becomes Her) Incredible Hulk Annual #6, 1977
Pat Parker - (in costume) Speed Comics #15, 11/41; (no costume) Speed Comics #13, 5/41
Pat, Patsy & Pete - Looney Tunes & Merrie Melodies #1, 1941
Patchwork Man - (cameo) Swamp Thing #2, 12-1/72-73; (full app.) Swamp Thing #3, 2-3/73
Patriot - Marvel Mystery Comics #21, 7/41; (modern age) Marvel Premiere #29, 4/76
Patsy Walker - Miss America Magazine #2, 11/44
Peacemaker - Fightin' Five V2#40, ?/66; (1st DC app.) Crisis on Infinite Earths #6, 9/85
Pebbles - (Flintstones) Flintstones #11, 6/63
Perry White - Superman #7, 11-12/40
Pete Ross - (Legion) Superboy #86, 1/61; (tryout only) Superboy #77, 9?/59
Peter Parker's parents - Amazing Spider-Man Special #5, 11/68; (re-intro) Amazing Spider-Man #365, 8/92
Peter Porkchops - Leading Comics #23, 2-3/47
Phantasmo, Master of the World -Funnies #45, 7/40
Phantom - Ace Comics #11, 2/38
Phantom Eagle - (S.A.) Marvel Super-Heroes #16, 9/68; (G.A.) Wow Comics #6, 7/42
Phantom Falcon - Wings #68, 4/46
Phantom Girl - (Legion) Action Comics #276, 5/61
Phantom Lady - Police Comics #1, 8/41
Phantom Lady - Phantom Lady #13, 8/47
Phantom of the Fair - Amazing Mystery Funnies V2#7, 7/39
Phantom Rider - Star Comics #16, 12/38
Phantom Stranger - Phantom Stranger #1, 5-6/69
Phoenix - (formerly Marvel Girl) X-Men #101, 10/76
Phoenix II - (Rachel) X-Men #141, 1/81
Pinocchio - (cameo) Mickey Mouse Mag. V5#2, 11/39; (full app.) Mickey Mouse Magazine V5#3, 12/39
Pip the Troll - Strange Tales #179, 4/75
Plastic Man - Police Comics #1, 8/41; (S.A. tryout) House of Mystery #160, 7/66; (S.A.) Plastic Man #1, 11-12/66
Pluto - Thor #127, 4/66
Pluto - (Disney) Mickey Mouse #2, 1932
Pogo - Animal Comics #1, 12-1/41-42
Polar Boy - Adventure #306, 11/63
Polaris - (X-Men) X-Men #44, 5/68
Popsicle Pete - All-American Comics #6, 9/39
Porky Pig - Looney Tunes & Merrie Melodies #1, '41
Pow Wow Smith - Detective Comics #151, 9/49
Power Girl - All Star Comics #58, 1-2/76
Power Man - (Rip Regan) Fight Comics #3, 3/40
Power Nelson the Future Man - Prize Comics #1, 3/40
Powerhouse Pepper - Joker Comics #1, 4/42
Predator - Predator #1, 6/89
Presto Kid - Red Mask #51, 9/55
Prince Ra-Man - (formerly Mark Merlin) House of Secrets #73, 7-8/65
Prince Valiant - Ace Comics #26, 5/39
Princess Pantha - Thrilling Comics #56, 10/46
Princess Projectra - (Legion) Adventure Comics #346, 7/66
Professor Supermind & Son - Popular Comics #60, 2/41
Professor Warren - Amazing Spider-Man #31, 12/65
Professor X - X-Men #1, 9/63
Psylocke - New Mutants Annual #2, 10/86
Punisher - Amaz. Spider-Man #129, 2/74
Punisher 2099 - Punisher War Journal #50, 1/93
Pureheart the Powerful - Archie as Pureheart the Powerful #1, 9/66
Purple Mask - Daring Mystery Comics #3, 4/40
Pyroman - America's Best Comics #3, 11/42; Startling Comics #18, 12/42
Quantum Queen - Adventure Comics #375, 12/68
Quasar - (formerly Marvel Man) Incredible Hulk #234, Apr '79; (re-intro) Avengers #302, 4/89
Question - Captain Atom #83, 11/66; (1st DC app.) Crisis on Infinite Earths #6, 9/85
Quicksilver - National Comics #5, 11/40; X-Men #4, 3/64
Quislet - (Legion) Legion of Super-Heroes #14, 9/85
Quisp - Aquaman #1, 1-2/62
Rachel - (Pheonix II) X-Men #141, 1/81
Radar - Captain Marvel Adventures #35, 5/44; Master Comics #50, 5/44
Rage - Avengers #326, 11/90
Ragman - Ragman #1, 8-9/76
Rags Rabbit - Nutty Comics #5, ?/46
Rai - Magnus Robot Fighter #5, 10/91; (new) Rai #0, 11/92
Rainbow Boy - Heroic Comics #14, 9/42
Randy Robertson - Amazing Spider-Man #67, 12/68
Ravage 2099 - Marvel Comics Presents #117, '92
Raven, The - Sure-Fire Comics #1, 6/40
Raven - Thunder Agents #8, 9?/66; (New Teen Titans) DC Comics Presents #26, 10/80
Rawhide Kid - Rawhide Kid #1, 3/55
Ray - Smash Comics #14, 9/40
Ray O'Light - All-New Comics #1, 1/43
Red Bee - Hit Comics #1, 7/40
Red Blazer - Pocket Comics #1, 8/41; All-New Comics #6, 1/44
Red Demon - Black Cat Comics #4, 2-3/47
Red Dragon - (1st story app.) Red Dragon Comics #6, 3/43; (text app. only) Red Dragon Comics #5, 1/43
Red Guardian - Avengers #43, 8/67; (new) Defenders #3, 5/76
Red Hawk - Blazing Comics #1, 6/44
Red Hawk - Straight Arrow #2, 4-5/50
Red Mask - Best Comics #1, 11/39
Red Raven - Red Raven Comics #1, 8/40; (1st modern app. G.A. Red Raven) X-Men #44, 5/69
Red Rocket - Captain Flight Comics #5, 11/44
Red Rube - Zip Comics #39, 8/43
Red Ryder - (1st app. in comics, strip-r) Crackajack Funnies #9, 3/39
Red Sonja - (1st full app.) Conan, the Barbarian #24, 3/73; (cameo) Conan #23, 2/73
Red Tornado - (formerly Ma Hunkle) All-American Comics #20, 11/40; (S.A.) Justice League of America #64, 8/68
Red White & Blue - All-American Comics #1, 4/39
Red Wolf - Avengers #80, 9/70; (1st solo book) Marvel Spotlight #1, 11/71
Reflecto - (Legion) Legion of Super-Heroes #277, 7/81
Rex Dexter of Mars - Mystery Men Comics #1, 8/39
Rex King - Supersnipe #6, 10/42
Rex The Wonder Dog - Rex the Wonder Dog #1, 1-2/52
Richie Rich - Little Dot #1, 9/53
Richy the Amazing Boy - Blue Ribbon Comics #1, 11/39
Rip Hunter - Showcase #20, 5-6/59
Robby Reed - (Dial "H" for Hero) House of Mystery #156, 11-12/65
Robin - (1st app. in S.A.) Justice League of America #55, ?/67; (Batman's sidekick) Detective Comics #38, 4/40; (Jason Todd) Batman #368, 2/84; (Carrie Kelly) Batman: The Dark Knight #2, 4/86; (Timothy Drake) Batman #442 (1st), #457 (official) 12/90
Robin Hood - (DC) Brave and the Bold #5, 4-4/56
Robocop - Robocop #1, 10/87
Robotman - Star Spangled Comics #7, 4/42; (new) Showcase #94, Aug-Sept '77; (S.A.) My Greatest Adventure #80, 6/63
Rocket Girl - Hello Pal Comics #1, 1/43
Rocket Man - Hello Pal Comics #1, 1/43
Rocketeer - (cameo) Starslayer #1, 2/82; (full app.) Starslayer #2, 4/82
Rocketgirl - Scoop Comics #1, 11/41
Rocketman - Scoop Comics #1, 11/41
Rocky X of the Rocketeers - Boy Comics #80
Rogue - (of X-Men) Avengers Annual #10, 1981 (see X-Men #158)
Roh Kar, the Man Hunter from Mars - Batman #78, 8-9/53
Rom - Rom #1, 12/79
Rond Vidar - (Universo's son, Legion) Adventure Comics #349, 10/66
Rose And The Thorn - Superman's Girlfriend Lois Lane #105, 1968
Roy Raymond - Detective Comics #153, 11/49
Roy the Super Boy - Top-Notch Comics #8, 9/40
Rudolph the Red Nosed Reindeer - Rudolph the Red Nosed Reindeer nn, 1939
Ruff and Reddy - Four Color #937, 9/58
Rulah, Jungle Goddess - Zoot #7, 6/47
Rusty & His Pals - Adventure Comics #32, 11/38
Sabre - Eclipse Graphic Album Series #1, 10/78
Sabrina the Teen-age Witch - Archie's Madhouse #22, 10/62
Sad Sack - True Comics #55, 12/46
Saint, The - Silver Streak Comics #18, 2/42
Samson - Fantastic Comics #1, 12/39
Sandman - (1st published app.) New York World's Fair nn, 1939; (1st app. in S.A.) Justice League of America #46, 8/66; (1st conceived story) Adventure Comics #40, 7/39; (modern) Sandman (2nd Series) #1, 1/89
Sandy the Golden Boy - Adventure Comics #69, 12/41
Sarge Steel - Sarge Steel #1, 12/64
Sargon The Sorcerer - All American Comics #26, 5/41
Sasquatch - X-Men #120
Satana - Vampire Tales #2, ?/73
Saturn Girl - Adventure Comics #247, 4/58
Scalphunter - Weird Western Tales #39, 3-4/77
Scarlet Avenger - Zip Comics #1, 2/40
Scarlet Witch - X-Men #4, 3/64
Scorpion - Scorpion #1, 2/75
Scribbly - Funnies #2, 11/36
Sensor Girl - (Legion) Legion of Super-Heroes #14, 9/85
Sergeant Spook - Blue Bolt #1, 6/40
Sgt. Bilko - Sgt. Bilko #1, 5-6/57
Sgt. Fury - (becomes Nick Fury of Shield) Sgt. Fury #1, 5/63
Sgt. Rock - Our Army at War #81,

4/59
Sgt. Rock by Kubert - Our Army at War #83, 6/59
Shade the Changing Man - Shade #1, 6-7/77
Shadow - (1st in comics) Shadow Comics #1, 3/40; (DC) The Shadow #1, 10-11/73
Shadowcat - X-Men #129
Shadow Lass - (Legion) Adventure Comics #365, 2/68
Shadow, Jr. - Shadow Comics V6#9, 12/46
Shadowhawk - Youngblood #2, 6/92
Shadowman - Shadowman #1, 5/92; (cameo) X-O Manowar #4, 5/92
Shang-Chi - (Master of Kung-Fu) Special Marvel Edition #15, 12/73
Shanna, the She-Devil - Shanna, the She-Devil #1, 12/72
Shakira - Warlord #32
Sharon Carter - Tales of Suspense #76 (formerly Agent 13), 1966
Shatterstar - (of X-Force) (cameo) New Mutants Annual #6, 1990
Shazam (Captain Marvel) - Shazam #1, 2/73
She-Bat - Detective Comics #424, 6?/72
She-Hulk - Savage She-Hulk #1, 2/80
Sheena - Jumbo Comics #1, 9/38
Sherlock Holmes - Classic Comics #33, 1/47
Shield - Pep Comics #1, 1/40; (S.A.) Adventures of the Fly #8, 9/60
Shiera Sanders - (later becomes Hawkgirl) Flash Comics #1, 1/40
Shining Knight - Adventure Comics #66, 9/41
Shock Gibson - Speed Comics #1, 10/39
Shrinking Violet - (Legion) Action Comics #276, 5/61
Sif - Journey Into Mystery #102, 3/64
Silent Knight - Brave and the Bold #1, 8-9/55
Silly Seal - Krazy Komics #1, 7/42
Silver Fox - Blue Ribbon Comics #2, 12/39
Silver Knight - Wonder Comics #18, 6/48
Silver Sable - Amazing Spider-Man #265, 6/85
Silver Streak - Silver Streak Comics #3, 3/40
Silver Surfer - Fantastic Four #48, 3/66
Siryn - (of X-Force) Spider-Woman #37, 4/81
Skippy - Skippy's Own Book Of Comics, 1934
Skull the Slayer - Skull, the Slayer #1, 8/75
Sky Wizard - Miracle Comics #1, 2/40
Skyman - Big Shot Comics #1, 5/40; (formerly Star Spangled Kid) Infinity, Inc. #31, 10/86
Skywolf - Air Fighters Comics V1#2, 11/42
Slam Bradley - Detective Comics #1, 3/37
Sleepwalker - Sleepwalker #1, 6/91
Snapper Carr - Brave and the Bold #28, 2-3/60
Snow White & the Seven Dwarfs - Mickey Mouse Magazine V3#3, 12/37
Socko Strong - Adventure Comics #40, 7/39
Solomon Kane - (1st color app.) Marvel Premiere #33, 12/76
Son Of Satan (Daimon Hellstrom) - (cameo) Ghost Rider #1, 9/73; (full app.) #2, 10/73
Son of Vulcan - Mysteries of Unexplored Worlds #46, 5/65
Space Ace - Manhunt! #1, 10/47
Space Cabbie - Mystery In Space #21, 8-9/54
Space Museum - Strange Adventures #104, 5/59
Space Ranger - Showcase #15, 7-8/58
Sparkler, The - Super Spy #1, 10/40
Sparkman - Sparkler Comics #1, 7/41
Sparky - (Blue Beetle's sidekick) Blue Beetle #14, 9/42; (Red Blazer's sidekick) All-New Comics #6, 1/44
Sparky Watts - Big Shot Comics #14, 6/41
Spawn - Spawn #1, 5/92
Spectre - (1st full app. in costume) More Fun Comics #54, 4/40; (in costume splash panel) More Fun Comics #52, 2/40; (S.A.) Showcase #60, 1-2/66; (in costume in one panel ad) More Fun Comics #51, 1/40
Speed Centaur - Amazing Mystery Funnies V2#8, 8/39
Speed Saunders - Detective Comics #1, 3/37
Speed Spaulding - Famous Funnies #72, 7/40
Speedball - Amazing Spider-Man Annual #22, '88
Speedboy - (Fighting America's side kick) Fighting American #1, 4-5/54
Speedy - (Green Arrow's sidekick) More Fun Comics #73, 11/41
Spencer Smythe - Amazing Spider-Man #25, 6/65
Spider-Man - Amazing Fantasy #15, 8-9/62; (cosmic) Spectacular Spider-Man #158, 12/89
Spider-Man - (black costume) Amazing Spider-Man #252, 5/84
Spider-Man 2099 - Amazing Spider-Man #365, 8/92
Spider-Woman - Marvel Spotlight #32, 2/77; (new) Marvel Super Heroes Secret Wars #7, 11/84
Spirit - Spirit nn, 6/40; (1st comic book app.) Police Comics #11, 9/42
Spooky - Casper, the Friendly Ghost #10, 6/53
Spy Smasher - Whiz Comics #1, 2/40
Stalker - Stalker #1, 6-7/75
Stanley & His Monster - Fox and the Crow #95, 12-1?/65-66
Starboy - (Legion) Adventure Comics #282, 3/61
Starfire - (Teen Titans) Teen Titans #18, 11-12/68; (new) (New Teen Titans) DC Comics Presents #26, 10/80
Starfox - Iron Man #55, 2/73
Starhawk - (1st full app.) Defenders #28, 10/75; (cameo) Defenders #27, 9/75; (re-intro) Guardians of the Galaxy #22, 3/92
Star-Lord - Marvel Preview #4, 11/75
Starman - Adventure Comics #61, 4/41; (1st app. in S.A.) Justice League of America #29, 8/64; (new) First Issue Special #12, 3/76
Star Sapphire - All-Flash #32, 12-1/47-48; (formerly Ferris) Green Lantern #16, 10/62; (re-intro, 1st full app.) Green Lantern #191, 8/85; (re-intro, cameo) Green Lantern #191, 8/85
Starslayer - Starslayer #1, 2/82
Star Spangled Kid - Action Comics #40, 9/41
Stars and Stripes - Stars and Stripes Comics #4, 9/41
Star Spangled Kid - Star Spangled Comics #1, 10/41
Steel Fist - Blue Circle Comics #1, 6/44
Steel Sterling - Zip Comics #1, 2/40; (Silver Age) Fly Man #39, 9/66
Steel the Indestructable Man - Steel #1, 3/78; (re-intro) All Star Squadron #8, 4/82
Steve Conrad Adventurer - Adventure Comics #47, 2/40
Stone Boy - Adventure Comics #306, 2/63
Storm - Giant-Size X-Men #1, Sum '75
Stormy Foster, the Great Defender - Hit Comics #18, 12/41
Straight Arrow - Straight Arrow #1, 2-3/50
Stranger - X-Men #11, 5/65
Stratosphere Jim - Crackajack Funnies #18, 12/39
Stripesy - Action Comics #40, 9/41
Strongman - Crash Comics #1, 5/40
Stuff - (Vigilante sidekick) Action Comics #45, 2/42
Stumbo the Giant - Hot Stuff, the Little Devil #2, 12/57
Stuntman - Stuntman #1, 4-5/46
Stuntman Stetson - Feature Comics #140, 11/49
Sub-Mariner - (1st newsstand app.) Marvel Comics #1, 10-11/39; (1st published app.?) Motion Pic.Funnies Weekly #1, 1939; (Silver Age) FantasticFour #4, 5/62; (new) Namor, the Sub-Mariner #26, 5/92
Sub-Zero Man - Blue Bolt #1, 6/40
SunBoy - (Legion) Action Comics #276, 5/61
Sunfire - (X-Men) X-Men #64, 1/70
Super American - Fight Comics #15, 10/41
Superbaby - Superboy #8, 5-6/50
Superboy - More Fun Comics #101, 1-2/45
Super Cat - Animal Crackers #1, 1946
Super Duck - Jolly Jingles #10, Sum '43; (re-intro) Laugh #24, ?/90
Supergirl - Action Comics #252, 5/59; (re-intro) Action Comics #674, 2/92; (tryout only) Superboy #5, 11-12/49
Super Goof - Phantom Blot #2, ?/65
Super Mouse - Coo Coo Comics #1, 10/42
Super Patriot - Nick Fury Agent of Shield #13, 6?/69; (new) Captain America #323, 11/86
Super Rabbit - Comedy Comics #14, 3/43
Super Richie - Richie Rich Millions #68, 11/74
Superichie - Superichie #5, 10/76
Superkatt - Giggle #9, 6/44
Superman - Action Comics #1, 6/38
Superman, Jr. - World's Finest Comics #215, 10/72
Supersnipe - Shadow Comics V2#3, 3/42
Superwoman - DC Comics Presents Annual #2, 7/83
Supreme - Youngblood #3, 10/92
Swamp Thing - House of Secrets #92, 6-7/71
Swift Deer - (J. Thunder's sidekick) All-American Western #113, 4-5/50
Sword - Captain Courageous Comics #6, 3/42; Super-Mystery Comics V3#3, 1/43
T-Man - Police Comics #103, 12/50
Tailspin Tommy - Tailspin Tommy Story & Picture Book #266, 1931; (1st in comic book format) Funnies #1, 10/36
Tank Killer - G. I. Combat #67, 12?/58
Tarantula - All-Star Comics #1, 10/41
Target - Target Comics V1#10, 11/40
Targitt - (in costume) Targitt #2, 6/75; (no costume) Targitt #1, 3/75
Tarzan - Tarzan Book #1, 1929; (1st comic book app.) Tip Top Comics #1, 4/36
Teenage Mutant Ninja Turtles - Teenage Mutant Ninja Turtles #1, 1984
Tellus - (Legion) Legion of Super-Heroes #14, 9/85
Terminator - Rust #12, 8/88
Terra - (New Teen Titan) New Teen Titans #26, 12/82
Terra-Man - Superman #249, 12/71
Terry & The Pirates - Popular Comics #1, 2/36
Tessie the Typist - Joker Comics #2, 6/42
Tex Thompson - (becomes Mr. America) Action Comics #1, 6/38
Thing - (Ben Grimm) Fantastic Four #1, 11/61
Thongor - Creatures On The Loose #22, 1973
Thor - (Beta Ray Bill) Thor #337, 11/83; (Dargo) Thor #384, 10/87; (Donald Blake) Journey Into Mystery #83, 8/62; (Eric Masterson) Thor #433, 6/91
Thorndike - (becomes Hourman's aide)Adventure Comics #74, 5/42
Three Lt. Marvels - Whiz # 21, 9/41; (re-intro) Shazam! #30, 7-8/77
Three-D Man - Marvel Premiere #35, 4/77
Thunderbird - Giant-Size X-Men #1, Sum '75
Thunderbolt - Power Man #41, 10/76; (1st DC app.) Crisis on Infinite Earths #6, 9/85; (Jonni Thunder) Jonni Thunder #1, 2/85; (Peter Cannon) Thunderbolt #1, 1/66
Thunderbunny - Charlton Bullseye #6, 12?/81
Thunderstrike - (Eric Masterson) Thor #459, 2/93
Tick - Tick #1, 6/88
Tiger Girl - Fight Comics #32, 6/44
Tigra - Startling Comics #45, 5/47
Tigra - (formerly The Cat) Giant-Size Creatures #1, 5/75
Tim - (Black Terror's sidekick) Exciting Comics #9, 5/41
Timber Wolf - (Legion) Adventure Comics #327, 12/64
Timothy Drake - Batman #436, 8/89; (1st in Robin costume) Batman #442, 1990
Timothy the Ghost - Zoo Funnies #1, 7/53
TNT & Dan the Dyna-Mite - World's Finest Comics #5, Spr '42
Todd Hunter - Adventure Comics #32, 11/38
Tom & Jerry - Our Gang Comics #1, 9-10/42
Tom Brent - Adventure Comics #32, 11/38
Tom Mix - The Comics #1, 3/37
Tomahawk - Star Spangled Comics #69, 6/47
Tommy the Amazing Kid - Amazing-Man Comics #23, 8/41
Tommy Tomorrow - Real Fact Comics #6, 1-2/47
Tony Trent - (The Face) Big Shot Comics #1, 5/40
Tor - One Million Years Ago #1, 9/53
Torchy - Doll Man Quarterly #8, Spr '46
Toro - (Human Torch's sidekick) Human Torch #2(#1), Fall '40; (modern) Sub-Mariner #14, 6/69
Torpedo - (new) Daredevil #126, 9/75
Tragg - Mystery Comics Digest #3,

?/72
Trail Colt - Manhunt! #8, 5/48
Triplicate Girl - (Legion) Action Comics #276, 5/61
Tubby - King Comics #46, 2/40; Marge's Little Lulu Four Color #74, ?'45
Tuk the Cave Boy - Captain America Comics #1, 3/41
Turbo - New Warriors #28, 10/92
Turok - Turok Four Color #596, 12/54; (re-intro in Valiant Universe) Magnus Robot Fighter #12, 5/92
Two Gun Kid - Two Gun Kid #1, 3/48
Ty-Gor, Son of the Tiger - Blue Ribbon Comics #4, 6/40
Tygra - Startling Comics #45, 5/47
Tyroc - (Legion) Superboy #216
U.S. Agent - Captain America #354, 6/89
Ultra Boy - (Legion) Superboy #98, 7/62
Ultra Man - (Gary Concord) All-American Comics #8, 11/9
Uncle Ben - Amazing Fantasy #15, 8-9/62
Uncle Marvel - Captain Marvel Adventures #43, 2/45, Wow Comics #18, 10/43
Uncle Sam - National Comics #1, 7/40
Uncle Scrooge - Donald Duck 4-Color #178, 12/47
Underdog - Underdog #1, 7/70
Union Jack I - Invaders #7, 7/76
Union Jack II - Invaders #20, 9/77
Union Jack III - Captain America #254, 2/81
Unknown Soldier - Star Spangled War Stories #151, 6-7/70
Untouchables - Four Color 1237, 10-12/61
Usagi Yojimbo - Albedo #1, 4/85
U.S. Jones - Wonderworld #28, 8/41
Val - Strange Tales #159, 8/67
V-Man - Big-3 #7, 1/42; V...- Comics #1, 1/42
Valkyrie - Air Fighters Comics V2#2, 11/43
Vampirella - Vampirella #1, 9/69
Vanessa - (Kingpin's wife) Amazing Spider-Man #83, 4/70
Vanguard - New Teen Titans Annual #1, 1985; Iron Man #109, Apr '78; Megaton #1, 11/83
Vault Keeper - War Against Crime #10, 12-1/49-50
Veiled Avenger - Spotlight Comics #1, 11/44
Venus - Venus #1, 8/48
Veronica Lodge - Pep Comics #26, 4/42
Vicki Vale - Batman #45, 2-3/48
Victoria Bentley - Strange Tales #114, 11/63
Victory Boys - USA Comics #5, Sum '42
Vigilante - Action Comics #42, 11/41; (female) (1st full app.) Deathstroke: the Terminator #10, 5/92; (female) (cameo) Deathstroke: the Terminator #9, 4/92; (modern, in costume) New Teen Titans Annual #2, 1985; (modern, not in costume) New Teen Titans #23, 9/82; (S.A.) Justice League of America #78, 5?/70
Viking Prince - Brave and the Bold #1, 8-9/55
Vindicator - (formerly Weapon Alpha) (becomes Guardian) X-Men #120, 4/79
Vision - (G.A.) Marvel Mystery Comics #13, 11/40; (S.A.) Avengers #57, 10/68
Vixen - Action Comics #521, 7/81
Voice, The - Popular Comics #51, 5/40
Voltage, Man of Lightning - Fat & Slat #1, Sum '47
Vulcan - Super-Mystery Comics V1#1, 7/40
Wagon Train - Four Color #895, 3/58
Wambi, Jungle Boy - Jungle Comics #1, 1/40
Warlock - (Him) (cameo) Fantastic Four #67, 10/67; (Him) (full app.) Thor #165, 6/69; (new) New Mutants #18, 8/84; (re-intro) Silver Surfer #46, 2/91
Warlord - First Issue Special #8, 11/75
Warpath - (with costume) X-Men #193, 5/85; (without costume) New Mutants #16, 6/84
Wash Tubbs - Famous Comics Cartoon Books #1202, 1934
Wasp, The - Speed Comics #12, 3/41
Wasp - Tales to Astonish #44, 6/63
Wasplet - (Hooded Wasp's sidekick) Shadow Comics #7, 11/40
Watcher - Fantastic Four #13, 4/63
Waverider - Armageddon 2001 #1, 5/91
Weapon Alpha - (becomes Vindicator) X-Men #109, 2/78
Web - Zip Comics #27, 7/42; (S.A.) Fly Man #36, 3/66
Wendigo - Incredible Hulk #162, 4/73
Wendy the Good Little Witch - Casper, the Friendly Ghost #20, ?/54
Werewolf - Werewolf #1, 12/66
Werewolf by Night - Marvel Spotlight #2, 1?/72
Whirlybats - Detective Comics #257, 7/58
White Rider & Super Horse - Blue Bolt #1, 6/40
White Streak - Target Comics V1#1, 2/40
White Tiger - Deadly Hands of Kung-Fu #19, 1?/76
White Witch - (Legion) Adventure Comics #351, 12/66
Whizzer, The - USA Comics #1, 8/41; (modern) Giant-Size Avengers #1, 8/74
Whizzer McGee - (Phantasmo's side kick) Funnies #45, 7/40
Wiggles the Wonderworm - Taffy Comics #1, 3/45
Wilbur - Zip Comics #18, 9/41
Wild Bill Elliott - Four Color #278, 5/50
Wildcat - Sensation Comics #1, 1/42; (S.A.) Brave and the Bold #62, 10-11/65
Wildfire - (formerly Erg) Superboy #201, '74
Will O' the Wisp - Amazing Spider-Man #167, 4/77
Willie - Gay Comics #1, Mar '44
Winky, Blinky & Noddy - All-Flash #5, Sum '42
Witch Hazel - Marge's Little Lulu #39, 9/51
Witness - Mystic Comics #7, 12/40
Wizard - Top-Notch Comics #1, 12/39; (S.A.) Fly Man #33, 9/65
Wizard - Strange Tales #102, 11/62
Wolverine - (1st full app.) Incredible Hulk #181, 11/74; (cameo) Incredible Hulk #180, 10/74
Wonder Boy - Blue Bolt #1, 6/40; National Comics #1, 7/40
Wonder Boy - Bomber Comics #1, 3/44
Wonder Duck - Wonder Duck #1, 9/49
Wonder Girl - Wonder Woman #107, 7/61; (new) (Teen Titan) Brave and the Bold #60, 6-7/65
Wonder Man - Startling Comics #1, 6/40
Wonderman - Wonder Comics #9, 1945
Wonder Man - Avengers #9, 10/64; Wonder Comics #1, 5/39; (re-intro) Avengers #151, 9/76
Wonder Tot - Wonder Woman #122
Wonder Woman - All Star Comics #8, 12-1/41-42; (Orana) Wonder Woman #250, 12/78
Wonder Woman Family - Wonder Woman #124, 12/62
Wonderman - (Brad Spencer) Mystery Comics #1, 1944
Wong - Strange Tales #110, 7/63
Woodgod - Marvel Premiere #31, 8/76
Woody Woodpecker - Funnies #64, 5/42
Woozy Winks - Police Comics #13, 11/42
X-O Manowar - X-O Manowar #1, 2/92
X-Terminators - X-Terminators #1, 10/88
Yank and Doodle - Prize Comics #13, 8/41
Yankee Doodle Jones - Yankee Comics #1, 9/41
Yarko the Great, Master Magician - Wonder Comics #2, 6/39
Yellow Claw - Yellow Claw #1, 10/56
Yellowjacket - Yellowjacket #1, 9/44
Yellowjacket - Avengers #59, 12/68; (formerly Goliath) Avengers #63, 4/69
Yogi Bear - Four Color #1067, 12-2/59-60
Yosemite Sam - Yosemite Sam #1, 12/70
Zanzibar - Mystery Men Comics #1, 8/39
Zardi, the Eternal Man - Amazing Man Comics #11, 4/40
Zatanna - Hawkman #4, 10-11/64
Zatara - Action Comics #1, 6/38
Zebra - All-New Comics #7, 3/44; Pocket Comics #1, 8/41
Zegra, Jungle Empress - Zegra #2, 10/48
Ziggy Pig - Krazy Komics #1, 7/42
Zombie - Menace #5, 7/53
Zorro - Zorro Four Color #228, 5/49

FIRST APPEARANCES: VILLAINS

Abomination - Tales to Astonish #90, 4/67
Abra Kadabra - Flash #128, ??/62
Absorbing Man - Journey Into Mystery #114, 3/65
Amazo The Android - Brave & The Bold #30, 6-7/60
Angle Man - Wonder Woman #70, 11/54
Annihilus - Fantastic Four Annual #6, 11/68
Apocalypse - (cameo) X-Factor #5, 6/86; (full app.) X-Factor #6, 7/86
Arcade - Marvel Team-Up #66, 2/78
Atomic Skull - Superman #323, 5/78
Attuma - Fantastic Four #33, 12/64
Bane - Batman: Vengeance of Bane Special #1, '92
Banshee - X-Men #28, 1/67
Baron Blood - Invaders #7, 7/76
Baron Mordo - Strange Tales #111, 8/63
Baron Strucker - Sgt. Fury #5, 1963
Baron Zemo - Captain America #276
Batmite - Detective #267, 5/59
Batroc - Tales of Suspense #76, 4/66
Beetle - Strange Tales #123, 8/64
Bengal - Daredevil #258, 9/88
Beyonder - Marvel Two-In-One #63, 1986
Big Man - Amazing Spider-Man #10, 3/64
Bizarro - Superboy #68, 10-11/56
Bizarro Batman - World's Finest Comics #156
Bizarro Flash - Superman's Girlfriend Lois Lane #74, 5/67
Bizarro Krypto - Superboy #82, ?/60
Bizarro Lana Lang - Adventure Comics #292, 1/62
Bizarro Lucy Lane -Adventure Comics #292, 1/62
Bizarro Lex Luthor - Adventure Comics #293, 2/62
Bizarro Lois Lane - Action Comics #255, 8/59
Bizarro Mxyzptlk - Adventure Comics #286, 7/61
Bizarro Supergirl - Superman #140, 10/60
Bizarro Titano - Adventure Comics #295, 4/62
Black Cat - Amazing Spider-Man #194, 7/79
Black Mask - Batman #386, 8/85
Blackout - Ghost Rider #2, 6/90
Black Racer - New Gods #3, 6-7/71
Black Spider - Detective Comics #463
Blastarr - Fantastic Four #62, 5/67
Blizzard - Iron Man #86, ?/76?
Blob - X-Men #3, 1/64
Blockbuster - Detective Comics #345, 11/65
Boomerang - Tales to Astonish #81, 7/66
Brain Storm - Justice League of America #32, 12/64
Brain Wave - All Star Comics #15, 2-3/43
Brainiac - Action Comics #242, 7/58; (modern) Adventures of Superman #438, 2/88
Brainwasher - (Kingpin) Amazing Spider-Man #59, 4/68
Brother Blood - New Teen Titans #21, 7/82
Brother Voodoo - Strange Tales #169, 9/73
Bullet - Daredevil #250, 12/88
Bullseye - Nick Fury Agent of Shield #15, 11/69
Calypso - Amazing Spider-Man #209, 10/80
Captain Boomerang - Flash #117, 12/60
Captain Cold - Showcase #8, 5-6/57

Captain Fear - Adventure Comics #425, 12-1/72-73
Captain Nazi - Master Comics #21, 12/41
Cardinal - New Warriors #28, 10/92
Carnage - (1st full app.) Amazing Spider-Man #361, 4/92; (cameo) Amazing Spider-Man #360, 3/92
Carrion - Spectacular Spider-Man #25, 12/78
Cat-Man - Detective Comics #311, 1/63
Catwoman - (1st in costume) Batman #3, Fall '40; (1st time called Catwoman) Batman #2, Sum '40; (modern, Selina Kyle) Batman #404, 2/87; (new costume w/o cat-head mask) Batman #35, 5-6/46; (new) Detective Comics #624, 12/90; (S.A.) Superman's Girlfriend Lois Lane #70, 11/66; (The Cat) Batman #1, Spr '40
Cavalier - Detective Comics #81, 11/43
Chameleon - Amazing Spider-Man #1, 3/63
Changeling - X-Men #35, 8/67
Cheetah - Wonder Woman #6, Fall '43; (new) (cameo) Wonder Woman #274, 12/80; (new) (full app.) Wonder Woman #275, 1/81
Chronos - Atom #3, 10-11/62
Chunk - Flash #9, 2/88
Claw - Silver Streak Comics #1, 12/39
Clayface I - (Basil Karlo) Detective Comics #40, 6/40
Clayface II - (Matt Hagen) Detective Comics #298, 12/61
Clayface III - (Preston Payne) Detective Comics #478, 7-8/78
Clock King - World's Finest Comics #111, 8/60
Clown - Flash #270, 2/79
Cobra (see Human Cobra)
Colonel Computron - Flash #304, 12/81
Composite Superman - World's Finest #142
Computo - Adventure Comics #340, 1/66
Constrictor - Incredible Hulk #212, 6/77
Copperhead - Daredevil #124, 6?/75
Crime Master - Amazing Spider-Man #26, 7/65
Crimson Dynamo - (Anton Vanko) Tales of Suspense #46, 10/63
Crimson Dynamo II - (Boris Turgenov) Tales of Suspense #52, 4/64
Crimson Dynamo III - (Alex Nevsky) Iron Man #21, 3/78
Crimson Dynamo IV - (Yuri Petrovich) Champions #8, 10/76
Crimson Dynamo V - (Dimitri Bukharin) Iron Man #109, 4/78
Cyclone - Amazing Spider-Man #143, 4/75
Dark Phoenix - X-Men #134
Darkseid - (1st full app.) Forever People #1, 2-3/71; (cameo) Superman's Pal Jimmy Olsen #134, 12/70
Deadshot - Batman #59, 6-7/50; (1st modern app.) Detective Comics #474, 11-12/77
Death's Head - Daredevil #56, 9/69
Deathstalker - (formerly Death's Head) Daredevil #114, 7/?/74
Demogoblin - Web of Spider-Man #86, 3/92
Despero - Justice League of America #1, 10-11/60
Destroyer - Journey Into Mystery #118, 7/65
Diablo - Fantastic Four #30, 9/64
Doctor Destiny - Justice League of America #5, 6-7/61
Doctor Doom - Fantastic Four #5, 6/62
Doctor Light I - Justice League of America #12, 6/62
Doctor Light II - Crisis on Infinite Earths #4, 6/85
Doctor Octopus - Amazing Spider-Man #3, 6/63
Doctor Polaris - Green Lantern #21, 6/63
Doctor Regulus - Adventure Comics #348, 9/66
Doom 2099 - Marvel Comics Presents #118, '92
Doomsday - (cameo) Superman: The Man of Steel #17, 11/92; (full app.) Superman: The Man of Steel #18, 12/92
Dormammu - Strange Tales #126, 11/64
Dr. Death - (modern) Batman #345, 3/82
Dr. Doom - Fantastic Four #5, 6/62
Dr. Double X - Detective Comics #261, 11/58
Dr Light - Justice League of America #12, '62
Dr. Octopus - Amazing Spider-Man #3, 5/63
Dr. Phosphorous - Detective Comics #469
Dr. Psycho - Wonder Woman #5, 6-7/43
Dr. Spectro - Captain Atom #78, 12/65; (new) Captain Atom #6, 8/87; (1st DC app.) Crisis on Infinite Earths #9, 12/85
Dragon Man - Fantastic Four #35, 2/65
Drax the Destroyer - (re-intro) (cameo) Silver Surfer #35, 3/90; (re-intro) (full app.) Silver Surfer #37, 5/90
Dreadknight - Iron Man #101, 8/77
Dragon Man - Fantastic Four #35, 2/65
Dummy - (Vigilante villain) Leading Comics #1, Win '41-42
Electro - Amazing Spider-Man #9, 2/64
Enchantress - Journey Into Mystery #103, 4/64
Enchantress - Strange Adventures #187
Enforcer - Ghost Rider #22, ?/77
Evil Star - Green Lantern #37, 7/65
Exterminator - (becomes Death-Stalker) Daredevil #39, 4/68
Fatal Five - Adventure Comics #352, 1/67
Fatman - Batman #113, 2/58
Felix Faust - Justice League of America #10, 3/62
Fiddler - All-Flash #32, 12-1/47-48
Fin Fang Foom - Strange Tales #89, 10/61
Firelord - Thor #225
Foolkiller - (1st) Man-Thing #3, 3/74
Foolkiller II - (Greg Salinger) (cameo) Omega the Unknown #8, 5/77; (Greg Salinger) (full app.) Omega the Unknown #9, 7/77
Galactus - Fantastic Four #48, 3/66
Gambler - Green Lantern #12, Sum '44
Gamora - Strange Tales #180, 6/75; (re-intro) Silver Surfer #46, 2/91
Gentleman Ghost - (modern) Batman #310, 4/79
Gibbon - Amazing Spider-Man #110, 7/72
Gladiator - Daredevil #18, 7/66
Golden Glider - Flash #250, 6/77
Gorgon - Fantastic Four #44, 11/65
Gorilla Grodd, the Super Gorilla - Flash #106, 4-5/59
Green Goblin I - (Norman Osborn) Amazing Spider-Man #14, 7/64
Green Goblin II - (Harry Osborn) Amazing Spider-Man #136, 9/74
Grey Gargoyle - Journey Into Mystery #107, 8/64
Grim Reaper - Avengers #52, 5/68
Grizzly - Amazing Spider-Man #139, 12/74
Hammerhead - Amazing Spider-Man #113, 10/72
Harlequin - All-American Comics #89, 9/47
Hate Monger - Fantastic Four #21, 12/63
Havoc - (not in costume) X-Men #56; (in costume) #58
Heat Wave - Flash #140, 6/63
Hector Hammond - Green Lantern #5, 3-4/61
Hela - Journey Into Mystery #102, 3/64
High Evolutionary - Thor #134, 11/66
Hobgoblin - (new) (Macendale) Spectacular Spider-Man #147, 2/89
Hobgoblin I - (Ned Leeds) Amazing Spider-Man #238, 3/83
Hobgoblin II - (Macendale/Jack O'Lantern) Amazing Spider-Man #289, 6/87
Hugo Strange - (1st modern app.) Detective Comics #470, 3-4/77
Human Cobra - Journey Into Mystery #98, 11/63
Human Top - (Whirlwind) Tales to Astonish #50, 12/63
Humbug - Web of Spider-Man #19, 10/86
Hydro Man - Amazing Spider-Man #212, 12/81
Hyena - Firestorm #4, 8-9/78
Icicle - All-American Comics #90, 10/47
Insect Queen - (Lana Lang) Superboy #124, 10/65
Iron Jaw - Boy Comics #3, 4/42
Jack O'Lantern - (Macendale) Machine Man #19, 2/81; (new) Captain America #396, 1/92
Jackal - Amazing Spider-Man #129, 2/74
Jester - Daredevil #42 ,7/68
Jigsaw - Amazing Spider-Man #188, 1/79
Joker - Batman #1, Spr '40
Joker's Daughter - Batman Family #6, 7-8/76
Juggernaut - X-Men #12, 7/65
Kang - Avengers #8, 9/64
Kanjar Ro - Justice League of America #3, 2-3/61
Key, The - Justice League of America #41, 12/65
Killer Croc - Batman #357, 3/83
Killer Shark - Blackhawk #50, 3/52
Kingpin - Amazing Spider-Man #50, 7/67
Klaw - Fantastic Four #53, 8/66
Kraven the Hunter - Amazing Spider-Man #15, 8/64
Kurgo - Fantastic Four #7, 10/62
Leader - Tales to Astonish #62, 12/64
Legion of Super Villains - Superman #147, 8/61
Lex Luthor - (bald) Superman #10, 5-6/41; (new) Man of Steel #4, 12/86; (red hair) Action Comics #23, 5/40; (Silver Age) Adventure Comics #271, 4/60
Lightmaster - Spectacular Spider-Man #3, 2/77
Living Monolith - X-Men #56
Lizard - Amazing Spider-Man #6, 11/63
Loki - Journey Into Mystery #85, 10/62
Looter - Amazing Spider-Man #36, 5/66
Lord Shilling - (Tomahawk foe) Tomahawk #28, 11/54
Lunatik - (1st full app.) Defenders #56, 2/78; (cameo) Defenders #53, 11/77
Mad Hatter - Batman #49, 10-11/48; Detective Comics #230, 4/56
Mad Thinker - Fantastic Four #15, 6/63
Madame Medusa - Fantastic Four #36, 3/65
Maelstrom - Marvel Two-In-One #71, 1/81
Magica de Spell-Uncle Scrooge #36, 12/62
Magneto - X-Men #1, 9/63
Magpie - (new) Man of Steel #3, 11/86
Magus - Strange Tales #178, 2/75; (re-intro) Warlock and the Infinity Watch #7, 8/92
Malevolence - (Mephisto's daugh ter) Guardians of the Galaxy #7, 12/90
Man-Ape - Avengers #62
Man-Bat - Detective Comics #400, 6/70
Man-Wolf - Amazing Spider-Man #124, 9/73
Mandarin - Tales of Suspense #50, 2/64
Manhunters - 1st Issue Special #5, 8/75
Mephisto - Silver Surfer #3, 12/68
Metallo (Jor-El's robot) - (1st app.) Superboy #49, 6/56; (new) Superman #310, 4/77; (new) Superman #1, 1/87; (re-intro) Action Comics #252, 5/59; (re-intro, 3rd app.) Adventure Comics #276, 9/60
Microwave Man - Action Comics #487, 9/78
Mime - Batman #412, 10/87
Mimic - X-Men #19, 4/66
Mirror Master - Flash #105, 2-3/59
Mist - Adventure Comics #67, 10/41
Mister Element - Showcase #13, 3-4/58
Mister Sinister - X-Men #221
Modok - Tales of Suspense #94, 10/67
Modred the Mystic - (re-intro) Darkhold #3, 12/92
Mole Man- Fantastic Four #1, 11/61
Molecule Man - Fantastic Four #20, 11/63
Molten Man - Amazing Spider-Man #28, 9/65
Morbius the Living Vampire - Amazing Spider-Man #101, 10/71
Mordru - Adventure Comics #369, 6/68
Mortan - (Adam Strange foe) Mystery In Space #62
Mr. Atom - Captain Marvel Adventures #78, 11/47
Mr. Baffle - Detective Comics #63, 5/42
Mr. Hyde - Journey Into Mystery #99, 12/63
Mr. Mind - Captain Marvel Adventures #22, 3/43; (re-intro) Shazam! #2, 4/73
Mr. Mxyzptlk - Superman #131, 8/59; (new) Superman #11, 11/87; Superman #30, 10/44
Mr. Tawny - Captain Marvel Adventures #79, 12/47
Multi-Man - Challengers of the Unknown #14, 12-1/59-60
Mysterio - Amazing Spider-Man #13, 6/64
Nightmare - Strange Tales #110, 7/63
Nightshade - Captain America #164, 8/73
Nitro - Captain Marvel #34, 9/74
Ocean Master - Aquaman #29
Outsider - Detective Comics #334, 12/64
Owl - Daredevil #3, 8/64
Paladin - Daredevil #150, 2/78

Parasite - Action Comics #340, 9/66; Fury of Firestorm #58, 1987
Peg-leg Pete - Mickey Mouse #3, 1933
Penguin - Detective Comics #58, 12/41; (S.A.) Batman #155, 4/63
Pied Piper - Flash #106, 4-5/59
Pieface - Green Lantern #2, 9-10/60
Plant-Master - Atom #1, 6-7/62
Plunderer - Daredevil #12, 1/66
Poison Ivy - Batman #181, ?/66
Porcupine - Tales To Astonish #48, 10/63
Prankster - Action Comics #51, 8/42
Princess Python - Amazing Spider-Man #22, 3/65
Professor Amos Fortune - Justice League of America #6, 8-9/61
Professor Zoom - Flash #139, ?/63
Prowler - Amazing Spider-Man #78, 11/69
Psycho Pirate - All Star Comics #23, Win '44-45
Psycho-Man - Fantastic Four Annual #5, 11/67
Puma - Amazing Spider-Man #256, 9/84
Punisher - Amazing Spider-Man #129, 2/74
Puppet Master - Batman #3, Fall '40; Fantastic Four #8, 11/62
Rainbow Raider - Flash #286, 6/80
Rama-Tut - Fantastic Four #19, 10/63
Rampage - Superman #7, 7/87
Rancor - (1st full app.) Guardians of the Galaxy #9, 2/91; (cameo) (descendant of Wolverine) Guardians of the Galaxy #8, 1/91
Ras Al Ghul - Batman #232, 7/71
Reaper - Batman #237, 12/71
Red Ghost - Fantastic Four #13, 4/63
Red Skull - Captain America Comics #1, 3/41; (S.A.) Tales of Suspense #65, 5/65
Rhino - Amazing Spider-Man #41, 10/66
Riddler - Detective Comics #140, 10/48; (S.A.) Batman #171, 5/65
Ringmaster - Incredible Hulk #3, 9/62
Rose - Amazing Spider-Man #253, 6/84
Rose and the Thorn - Flash Comics #89, 11/47; (new) Superman's Girlfriend Lois Lane #105
Saber Tooth - Flash #291, 11/80
Sabretooth - Iron Fist #14, 8/77
Sandman - Amazing Spider-Man #4, 9/63
Sandstorm - Web of Spider-Man #107, 12/93
Sargon - (re-intro) Flash #186, 8?/69
Sargon the Sorcerer - (1st story app.) All-American Comics #26, 5/41; (text only) All-American Comics #24, 3/41
Sauron - X-Men #60
Scarecrow - Tales of Suspense #51, 3/64; World's Finest Comics #3, Fall '41; Dead of Night #11, 8/75; (S.A.) Batman #189, ?'67?
Schemer - Amazing Spider-Man #83, 4/70
Scorpion - Amazing Spider-Man #20, 1/65
Serpent Crown - Sub-Mariner #9, 1/69
Sha-Shan - Amazing Spider-Man #108, 5/72
Shade - (modern) Flash #298, 6/81
Shadow Thief - Brave and the Bold #36, 6-7/61
Shaper - Incredible Hulk #155, 9/72
Shark - Amazing-Man Comics #6, 10/39; Green Lantern #24, 10/63
Shocker - Amazing Spider-Man #46, 3/67
Shotgun - Daredevil #272, 9?/89
Shroud - Super-Villain Team-Up #5, 4/76
Signalman - Batman #112, 12/57; (S.A.) Detective Comics #466
Silvermane - Amazing Spider-Man #73, 6/69
Silver Samurai - Daredevil #111, 6/74
Sinestro - Green Lantern #7, 7-8/61
Sivana - Whiz Comics #1, 2/40
Sivana, Jr. - Captain Marvel Adventures #52, 1/46
Sky Pirate - Green Lantern #27, 8-9/47
Solarr - Captain America #160, 4/73
Solo - Web of Spider-Man #19, 10/86
Solomon Grundy - All-American Comics #61, 11/44; (S.A.) Showcase #55, 3-4/65
Sonar - Green Lantern #14, 7/62
Sorcerer - Alpha Flight #71, 5/89
Speed McGee - Flash #5, 10/87
Spirit of Vengeance - (futuristic Ghost Rider) Guardians of the Galaxy #13, 6/91
Spyder - New Mutants #68, 10/88
Star Thief - Warlock #14, 10/76
Stilt-Man - Daredevil #8, 6/65
Sting Ray - Sub-Mariner #19, 11/69
Stranger - X-Men #11, 5/65
Sub-Mariner - (S.A) Fantastic Four #4, 5/62
Sunburst - New Adventures of Superboy #45, 9/83
Super Skrull - Fantastic Four #18, 9/63
Supremo - Superboy #132, ?/66
Swordsman - Avengers #19, 8/65
Tantrum - Night Thrasher: Four Control #2, 11/92
Tarantula - Amazing Spider-Man #134, 7/74
Taskmaster - Avengers #119, 1/80
Tattooed Man - Green Lantern #23, 9?/63
Terra-Man - Superman #249, 4/72
Terrax - Fantastic Four #211, 10/79
Terrible Tinkerer - Amazing Spider-Man #2, 5/63
Thanos - Iron Man #55, 2/73; (re-intro) (cameo) Silver Surfer #34, 2/90; (re-intro) (full app.) Silver Surfer #35, 3/90
Thinker - All-Flash #12, Fall '43
Thundra - Fantastic Four #129, 12/72
Tiger Shark - (new) Namor, the Sub-Mariner #35, 2/93; (S.A.) Sub-Mariner #5, 9/68
Time Trapper - Adventure Comics #321, 6/64
Titanium Man - Tales of Suspense #69, 9/65
Titano - Superman #127, 2/59
Toad - X-Men #4, 3/64
Tombstone - Web of Spider-Man #36, 3/88; (full app.) Spectacular Spider-Man #138, 5/88
Top - Flash #122, 6-7?/61
Torpedo - Daredevil #126, 8?/75
Toyman - Action Comics #64, 9/43; (new) Superman #13, 1/88; (S.A.) Action Comics #432, 2/74
Trapster - Strange Tales #104, 1/63
Trauma - Incredible Hulk #394, 6/92
Trickster - Flash #113, 6-7/60
Turtle - Showcase #4, 9-10/56
Tweedledum & Tweedledee - Detective Comics #74, 4/43
Two-Face - Detective Comics #66, 8/42; (S.A) Batman #234, 9/71
Typhoid Mary - Daredevil #254, 5/88
Ulik - Thor #137
Ultron - Avengers #54
Ulthoon - (Adam Strange foe) Mystery In Space #61,
Umar - Strange Tales #150, 11/66
Unicorn - Tales of Suspense #56, 8/64
Universo - Adventure Comics #349, 10/66
Unus the Untouchable - X-Men #8, 11/64
U. S. Jones - Wonderworld Comics #28, 8/41
Vandall Savage - Green Lantern #10, Win '43; (S.A.) Flash #137, ?/63
Vanisher - X-Men #2, 11/63
Venom - (1st full app.) Amazing Spider-Man #300, 5/88; (cameo w/costume) Amazing Spider-Man #298; (cameo, no costume), #299, 4/88
Vindicator - X-Men #109, 5/78
Viper - Captain America #110, 2/69
Vulture - Amazing Spider-Man #2, 5/63
Warpath - X-Men #193, 5/85
Watcher - Fantastic Four #13, 4/63
Weapon Omega - Alpha Flight #102, 11/81
Weather Wizard - Flash #110, 12-1/59-60
Whirlwind - (Human Top) Tales to Astonish #50, 12/63
White Queen - X-Men #132, 4/80
Wizard - Strange Tales #102, 11/62
Zemo - Avengers #6, 7/64
Zzzax - Incredible Hulk #166, 8/73

FIRST APPEARANCES: GROUPS

Adult Legion - Superman #147, 8/61
All Star Squadron - Justice League of America #193, 8/81
All Winners Squad - All Winners Comics #19, Fall, 1946
Alpha Flight -(cameo) X-Men #120, 4/79; (full app.) X-Men #121, 5/79
Atari Force - New Teen Titans #27, 1/83
Atomic Knights - Strange Adventures #117, 6/60
Avengers - Avengers #1, 9/63
Avengers new line up - Avengers #16, 5/65; Avengers #150, 8/76; Avengers #181, 3/79; Avengers #211, 9/81
Avengers West Coast - West Coast Avengers #1, 9/84
Big-3 - (Blue Beetle/Flame/ Samson) Big-3 #1, Fall, 1940
Bizarro Legionnaires - Adventure Comics #329, 2/65
Boy Commandos - Detective Comics #64, 6/42
Brainiac 5 - Action Comics #276, 5/61
Challengers of the Unknown - Showcase #6, 1-2/57
Champions - Champions #1, 10/75
Creature Commandos - Weird War Tales #93, 11/80
Damage Control - Marvel Comics Presents #19, 5/89
Darkstars - Dark Stars #1, 10/92
Defenders - Marvel Feature #1, 12/71; (new) Defenders #125, 11/83; (pre-lude) Sub-Mariner #34, 2/71
Doom Patrol - My Greatest Adventure #80, 6/63; (new) Showcase #94, 8-9/77
Easy Company - Our Army At War #81, 4/59
Elementals, The - Justice Machine Annual #1, 1/84
Eternals - Eternals #1, 7/76
Excalibur - Excalibur Special Edition nn, 1987
Explorers - Boy Explorers #1, 5-6/46
Fab 4 - Super Heroes #1, 1/67
Fantastic Four - Fantastic Four #1, 11/61; (1st in costumes) Fantastic Four #3, 3/62; (new team) Fantastic Four #306, 9/87
Federal Men - New Comics #2, 1/36
Femforce - Femforce Special #1, Fall, 1984
Fightin' Five - Fightin' Five V2#28, 7/64
Forever People - Forever People #1, 2-3/71
Freedom Fighters - Justice League of America #107, 1975
Frightful Four - Fantastic Four #36, 10/64
Future X-Men - X-Men #141, 1/81
Ghost Patrol - Flash Comics #29, 5/42
Girl Commandos - Speed Comics #13, 4/41
Great Lakes Avengers - West Coast Avengers #46, 7/89
Green Lantern Corp. - Green Lantern #130
Guardians of the Galaxy - Marvel Super-Heroes #18, 1/69; (1st solo book) Marvel Presents #3, 2/76
Guardians of the Universe - Green Lantern #1, 7-8/60
H.A.R.D. Corps - Harbinger #10, 10/92
Inferior Five - Showcase #62, 5-6/66
Infinity, Inc. - All Star Squadron #25, 9/83
Inhumans - Fantastic Four #45, 12/65
Injustice Society Of The World - All Star Comics #37, 10-11/47
Intergalactic Vigilante Squadron - Adventure Comics #237, 6/57
International Sea Devils - Sea Devils #22, 3-4/66
Invaders - Avengers #71, 12/69; (re-intro) Namor, the Sub-Mariner #12, 3/91
Justice League Europe - Justice League International #24, 2/89; (new) Justice League Spectacular #1, 1992
Justice League International - (new) Justice League Spectacular #1, 1992
Justice League of America - Brave and the Bold #28, 2-3/60; Legends #6, 4/87; (new team) Justice Leagueof America Annual #2, 1984
Justice Society of America - All Star Comics #3, Win, '40-41; (1st S.A. cameo) Flash #137, ?/63
Kiss - (1st full app.) Howard the Duck #13, 6/77; (cameo) Howard the Duck #12, 3/77

Knights of the Galaxy - Mystery In Space #1, 4-5/51
Legion of Monsters - (Ghost Rider, Man-Thing, Morbius, Werewolf) Marvel Premiere #28, 1975
Legion of Substitute Heroes - Adventure Comics #306, 3/63
Legion of Super Heroes - Adventure Comics #247, 4/58
Legion Of Super Pets - Adventure Comics #293, 2/62
Liberators - Avengers #83, 12/70
Liberty Legion - Marvel Premiere #29, 1975
Losers - (Storm/Gunner/Sarge/J. Cloud) G. I. Combat #138, 10-11/69
Lt. Marvels - Whiz Comics #21, 9/41
Marvel Family - Captain Marvel Adventures #18, 12/42
Masters Of Evil - Avengers #6, 2/64
Masters of the Universe - New Teen Titans #25, 11/82
Mercenaries - G.I. Combat #244, 1982
Metal Men - Showcase #37, 3-4/62
Mighty Crusaders - Mighty Crusaders #1, 11/65
New Gods - New Gods #1, 2-3/71
New Mutants - Marvel Graphic Novel #4, 1982
New Teen Titans - DC Comics Presents #26, 10/80
New Warriors - (cameo) Thor #411, 12/89; (full app.) Thor #412, 12/89
Newsboy Legion - Star Spangled Comics #7, 4/42; (re-intro) Superman's Pal Jimmy Olsen #133, 10/70
Next Men - Dark Horse Presents #54, 9/91
Night Force - New Teen Titans #21, 7/82
Omega Men - Green Lantern #141, 6/81
Our Gang - Our Gang Comics #1, 9-10/42
Outsiders - Brave and the Bold #200, 7/83
Planeteers - Real Fact Comics #16, 9-10/48
Power Elite - Starman #4, Win '88
Power Pack - Power Pack #1, 8/84
Sea Devils - Showcase #27, 7-8/60
Secret Six - Secret Six #1, 4-5/68; (re-intro) Action Comics #601, 6/88
Sentinels - X-Men #14, 11/65
Seven Soldiers of Victory - Leading Comics #1, Wint, '41-42
Shadowmaster - Punisher #24, ?/89
S.H.I.E.L.D. - Nick Fury Agent of Shield #1, 6/68
Stargazers - Vanguard Ill. #2, 12/83
Starjammers - (cameo) X-Men #104, 4/77; (full app.) X-Men #107, 10/77
Star Rovers - Mystery In Space #66, 1961
Stargrazers - Vanguard Illustrated #2, 12/83
Suicide Squad - Brave and the Bold #25, 8-9/59; (new) Legends #3, 1/87
Super Friends - Super Friends #1, 11/76
Team America - Captain America #269, 5/82
Team Titans - (Teen Titans) New Titans Annual #7, 1991
Teenage Mutant Ninja Turtles - Gobbledygook #1, 1984
Teen Titans - Brave and the Bold #54, 6-7/64; (re-intro.) DC Super Stars #1, 3/76
Terrific Three - (Jaguar, Mr. Justice, Steel Sterling) Mighty Crusaders #5, 9/66
Three Mouseketeers - Funny Stuff #1, Sum '44
Thunder Agents - Thunder Agents #1, 11/65
Tiger Squadron - Blue Beetle #20, 4/43
Toxic Crusaders - Toxic Crusaders #1, 5/92
Tough Kid Squad - Tough Kid Squad #1, 3/42
Transformers - Transformers #1, 9/84
Tribe - WILDC.A.T.s: Covert Action Teams #4, 3/93
Ultra-Men - (Fox, Web, Capt. Flag) Mighty Crusaders #5, 9/66
Wanderers - Adventure Comics #375, 12/68
Warlords - West Coast
Avengers - West Coast Avengers #1, 9/84
Wildcats - WILDC.A.T.s: Covert Action Teams #1, 8/92
X-Factor - Avengers #263, 1/86; (new team) X-Factor #71, 10/91
X-Force - (cameo) New Mutants #100, 4/91
X-Men - X-Men #1, 9/63; X-Men #1, 10/91; (new team) X-Men #253, 1989; (new team) X-Men #281, 10/91; (new) Giant-Size X-Men #1, Sum, '75
X-Terminators - X-Terminators #1, 10/88
Young Allies - Young Allies #1, Sum '41
Youngblood - (1 pg. ad) Megaton #8, 8/87; (2pgs.) Megaton Explosion nn, 6/87

FIRST APPEARANCES: VILLAIN GROUPS

Beagle Boys - Walt Disney's Comics and Stories #134, 11/51
Blue Trinity - Flash #7, 12/87
Brotherhood of Evil - (new) New Teen Titans #15, 1/82
Brotherhood of Evil Mutants - X-Men #4, 3/64; (new) X-Men #141, 1/81
Citadel - Green Lantern #136, 1/81
Enforcers - Amazing Spider-Man #10, 3/64
Fearsome Five - New Teen Titans #3, 1/81
Frightful Four - (Sandman/Wizard/P.P. Pete) Fantastic Four #36, 3/65
Injustice Society - All Star Comics #37, 10-11/47
Krypton Foes - Superman #65, 7-8/50
Legion of Super-Villains - Superman #147, 8/61
Masters of Evil - Avengers #6, 7/64; (new) Avengers #54, 7/68
Phantom Zone Villains (Dr. Zadu & Emdine) - Superboy #100, 10/62
Royal Flush Gang - Justice League of America #43, ?/66; (new) Justice League of America #203, 6/82
Secret Society of Super-Villains - Secret Society of Super-Villains #1, 5-6/76
Sinister Six - Amazing Spider-Man Annual #1, 1964
Skrulls - Fantastic Four #2, 1/62
Toad Men - Incredible Hulk #2, 7/62

FIRST CROSSOVERS

Ant-Man - Fantastic Four #16, 7/63
Avengers - Tales of Suspense #49, 1/64
Capt. America - (outside of Avengers) Sgt. Fury #13
Conan - Savage Tales #1, 5/71
Daredevil - Amazing Spider-Man #16, 9/64
Doctor Strange - Fantastic Four #27, 6/64
Fantastic Four - Amazing Spider-Man #1, 3/63
Hulk - Fantastic Four #12, 3/63
G.A. Green Lantern x-over in S.A. - Showcase #55, 3-4/65
Iceman - Strange Tales #120, 5/64
Iron Man - (x-over outside Avengers) Tales to Astonish #82, 8/66
Magneto - Journey Into Mystery #109, 10/64
Nick Fury - (as agent of Shield) Tales of Suspense #92, 8/67
S.A. Captain America - Sgt. Fury #13, 12/64
Sgt. Fury - Fantastic Four #21, 12/63
Silver Surfer - (cameo) Tales to Astonish #92, 6/67; (full app.) Tales to Astonish #93, 7/67
Spider-Man - Strange Tales Annual #2, 7/63
Sub-Mariner - (outside Fantastic Four) Strange Tales #107, (4/63)
Thing - Strange Tales #116, 1/64
Thor - Strange Tales #123, 8/64
X-Men - Tales of Suspense #49, 1/64

FIRST SUPERPETS

Bat-Hound - Batman #92, 6/55
Captain Carrot - New Teen Titans #16, 2/82
Comet - (Superhorse) Adventure Comics #293, 2/62
Cosmo - (Challengers Spacepet) Challengers of the Unknown #18, 9-10/60
Krypto the Super Dog - Adventure Comics #210, 3/55
Legion of Super Pets - Adventure Comics #293, 2/62
Rang-A-Tang the Wonder Dog - Blue Ribbon Comics #1, 11/39
Streak the Wonder Dog - Green Lantern #30, 2-3/48
Streaky the Super Cat - Action Comics #261, 2/60
Supermonkey - Superboy #76, 8?/59
Wolf - (Boy Commandos mascot) Boy Commandos #34, 7-8/49

FIRST PROTOTYPES

Some of today's popular super hero characters were developed from or after earlier forms or prototypes. These prototype characters sometimes were introduced to test new ideas and concepts which later developed into full fledged super heros, or old material sometimes would inspire new characters. Below is a list of all known prototypes. The Marvel/Atlas issues have been verified by Stan Lee, Steve Ditko and Jack Kirby.

Ancient One - Strange Tales #92, 1/62
Ant-Man - Strange Tales #73, 2/60; Strange Tales #78, 11/60
Aunt May - Strange Tales #97, 6/62
Doctor Doom - Tales of Suspense #31, 7/62
Doctor Strange - Journey Into Mystery #78, 3/62; Strange Tales #79, 12/60; Tales of Suspense #32, 8/62
Electro - Tales To Astonish #15, 1/61
Giant-Man - Strange Tales #70, 8/59
Hulk - Journey Into Mystery #62, 11/60; Journey Into Mystery #66, 3/61
Human Torch - Strange Tales #76, 8/60
Iron Man - Strange Tales #75, 6/60; Tales of Suspense #9, 5/60; Tales of Suspense #16, 4/61
Kamandi - Alarming Tales #1, 9/57
Lava Men - Tales of Suspense #7, 1/60
Magneto - Strange Tales #84, 5/61
Mr. Hyde - Journey Into Mystery #79, 4/62
Professor X - Amazing Adult Fantasy #14, 7/62; Strange Tales #69, 6/59
Quicksilver - Strange Tales #67, 2/59
Red Tornado - House Of Mystery #155, 9-10/65
Sandman - Journey Into Mystery #70, 7/61
Savage Dragon - Marvel Comics Presents #50, 1990
Spider-Man - Journey Into Mystery #73, 10/61
Stone Men - Tales of Suspense #28, 4/62; Tales to Astonish #5, 9/59; Tales to Astonish #16, 2/61
Superman - (Dr. Mystic) Comics Magazine #1, 5/36; More Fun Comics #14, 10/36; New Book of Comics #2, Spr '38
Toad Men - Tales to Astonish #7, 1/60
Uncle Ben - Strange Tales #97, 6/62
Watcher - Tales of Suspense #35, 11/62

FIRST OF A PUBLISHER

Ace Magazines - Sure-Fire #1, 6/40
American Comics Group - Giggle #1 & Ha Ha #1, 10/43
Atlas Comics - All Winners #11, Wint.'43/44
Avon Comics -Molly O'Day #1, 2/45
Better Publications (Standard) - Best Comics #1, 11/39
Bilbara Publishing Co. - Cyclone #1, 6/40
Brookwood Publications - Speed Comics #1, 10/39
Carlton Publishing Co. - Zoom Comics #1, 12/45
Catechetical Guild - Iopix #1, 11/42
Centaur Publications -Funny Pages V2#6, 3/38; Funny Picture Stories V2#6, 3/38; Star Comics #10, 3/38; Star Ranger V2#10, 3/38
Charlton Comics -Zoo Funnies #1, 11/45
Columbia Comics Group - Big Shot #1, 5/40
Comico - Primer #1, 10/82
Comics Magazine - Comics Magazine #1, 5/36
Dark Horse - Dark Horse Presents #1, 7/86
David McKay Publ. - King Comics #1, 4/36
DC Comics - New Fun Comics #1, 2/35
Defiant Comics - Warriors Of Plasm #1, 8/93
Dell Publishing Co. - Popular Comics #1, 2/36
Eastern Color - Funnies On Parade nn, 1933
Elliot Publications - Double Comics, 1940
Fawcett Publications - Whiz Comics #2 (#1), 2/40
Fiction House - Jumbo Comics #1, 9/38
Flying Cadet - Flying Cadet #1, 1/43
Fox Features Syndicate - Wonder Comics #1, 5/39
Funnies, Inc. - Motion Picture Funnies Weekly #1, 1939
Gilberton Publ. - Classic Comics #1, 10/41
Gladstone - Disneyland Birthday Party, 8/85; Uncle Scrooge Goes To Disneyland, 8/85
Globe Syndicate - Circus Comics #1, 6/38
Great Publications - Great Comics #1, 11/41
Harry 'A' Chesler - Star Comics #1, 2/37
Harvey Comics - Pocket Comics #1, 8/41
Hawley Publications - Captain Easy nn, 1939
Hillman Periodicals - Miracle Comics #1, 2/40
Holyoke (Continental) - Crash Comics #1, 5/40
Hugo Gernsback - Superworld #1, 4/40
Hyper Publications - Hyper Mystery #1, 5/40
Image Comics - Youngblood #1, 4/92
K.K. Publications - Mickey Mouse Magazine #1, Sum, 1935
Lev Gleason - Silver Streak #1, 12/39
Mirage Studios - Gobbledygook #1, no month '84
MLJ Magazines - Blue Ribbon Comics #1, 11/39
Nita Publications - Whirlwind Comics #1, 6/40
Novelty Publications - Target Comics #1, 6/40
Parents' Magazine Institute True Comics #1, 4/41
Prize Publications - Prize Comics #1, 3/40
Progressive Publishers - Feature Comics #21, 6/39
Quality Comics Group - Feature Comics #21, 6/39
Ralston-Purina Co. - Tom Mix #1, 9/40
Standard Comics (Better Publ.) - Best Comics #1, 11/39
Street and Smith Publications - Shadow Comics #1, 3/40
Sun Publications - Colossus Comics #1, 3/40
Timely Comics - Marvel Mystery #1, 11/39
United Features Syndicate - Tip Top Comics #1, 4/36
Valiant Comics - (hero) Magnus Robot Fighter, 5/91
Warren all comics magazine - Creepy #1, no month '64
Whitman Publishing Co. - Mammoth Comics #1, 1937
Will Eisner - Spirit #1, 6/2/40
William H. Wise - Columbia Comics #1, 1943

OVERSTREET COMIC BOOK PRICE GUIDE BACK ISSUES

The Overstreet® Comic Book Price Guide has held the record for being the longest running annual comic book publication. We are now celebrating our 28th anniversary and comic book collectors are as interested in putting together complete sets of these books as they are in collecting the old comics. The demand for the Overstreet® price guides is very strong and the collectors have created a legitimate market for them. They continue to bring record prices each year. Besides the price consideration, collectors also have a record of comic book prices going back further than any other source in comic fandom. The prices listed below are for near mint condition only. The other grades can be determined as follows: Good - 25% and Fine - 50% of the near mint value. Canadian editions exist for a couple of the early issues. Special thanks is given to Robert Rogovin of Four Color Comics for his assistance in researching the prices listed in this section.

Abbreviations used: SC = soft cover; HC = hard cover, L = leather bound.

#1 White Soft Cover
$1600.00

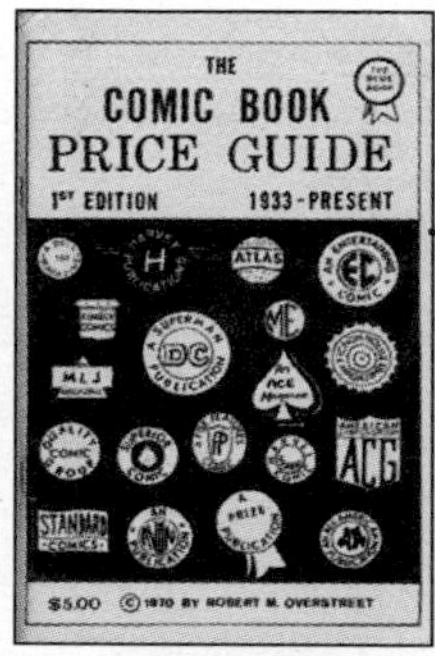

printed 1970

#1 Blue Soft Cover
(2nd Printing)
$1200.00

printed 1972

#2 SC $600.00
#2 HC $1000.00

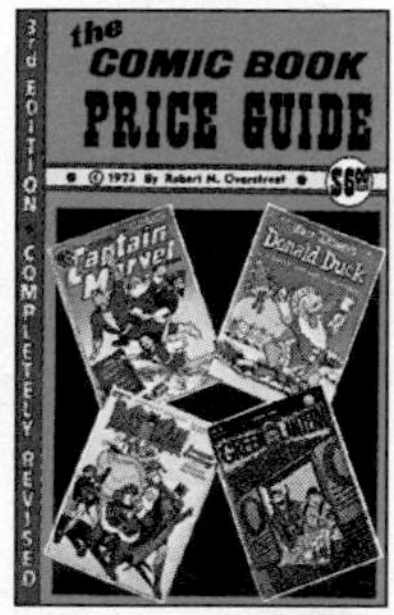

printed 1973

#3 SC $275.00
#3 HC $900.00

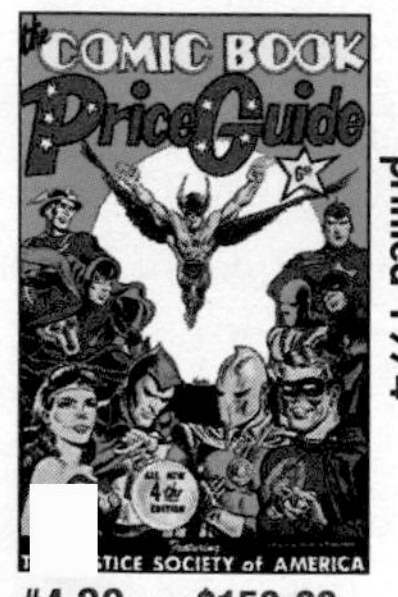

printed 1974

#4 SC $150.00
#4 HC $450.00

printed 1975

#5 SC $150.00
#5 HC $250.00

printed 1976

#6 SC $100.00
#6 HC $150.00

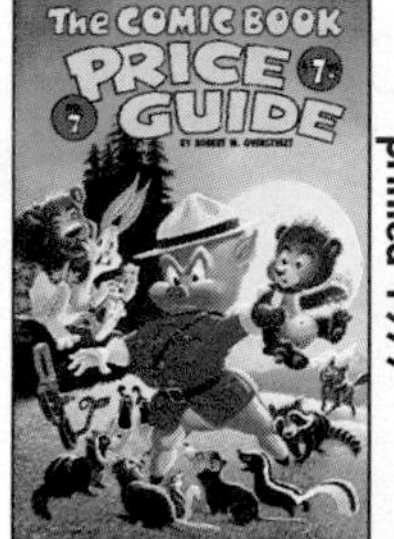

printed 1977

#7 SC $140.00
#7 HC $225.00

printed 1978

#8 SC $125.00
#8 HC $175.00

printed 1979

#9 SC $125.00
#9 HC $175.00

printed 1980

#10 SC $125.00
#10 HC $175.00

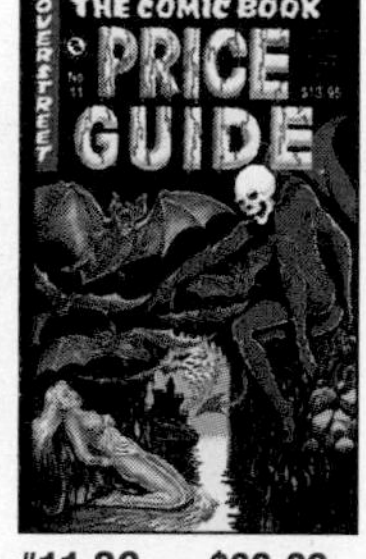

printed 1981

#11 SC $80.00
#11 HC $110.00

printed 1982

#12 SC $80.00
#12 HC $110.00

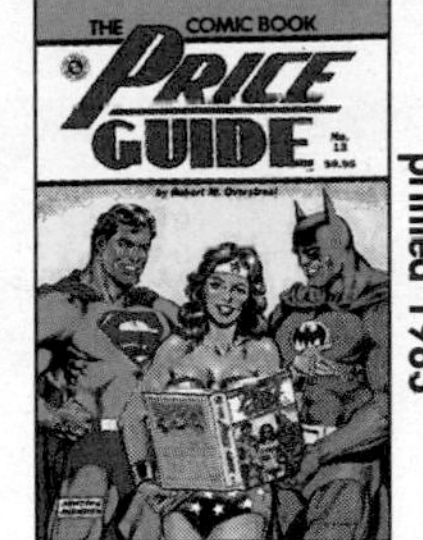

printed 1983

#13 SC $80.00
#13 HC $110.00

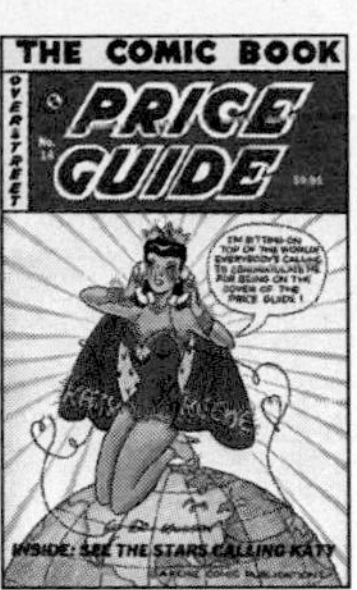

printed 1984

#14 SC $55.00
#14 HC $110.00
#14 L $170.00

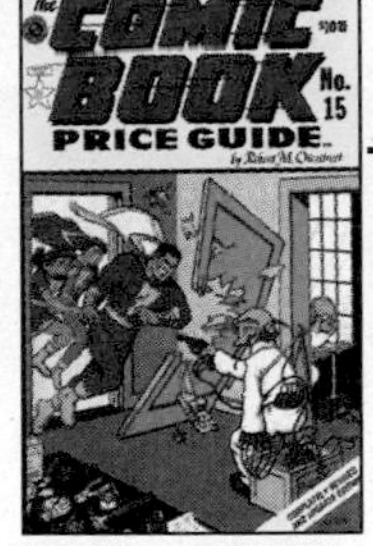

printed 1985

#15 SC $55.00
#15 HC $80.00
#15 L $160.00

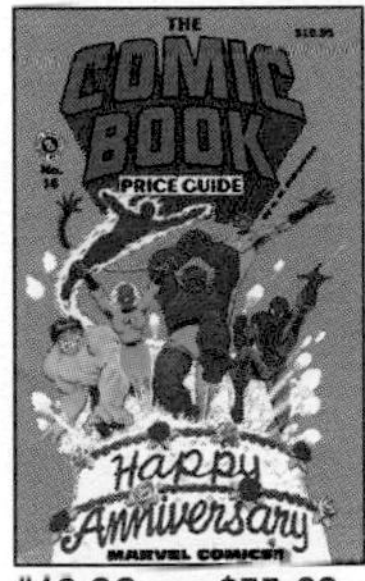

printed 1986

#16 SC $55.00
#16 HC $80.00
#16 L $160.00

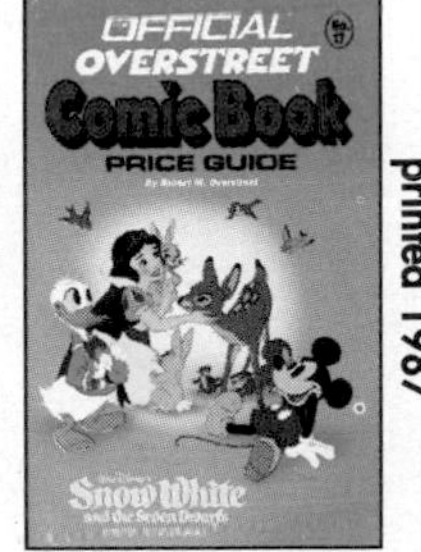

printed 1987

#17 SC $55.00
#17 HC $110.00
#17 L $160.00

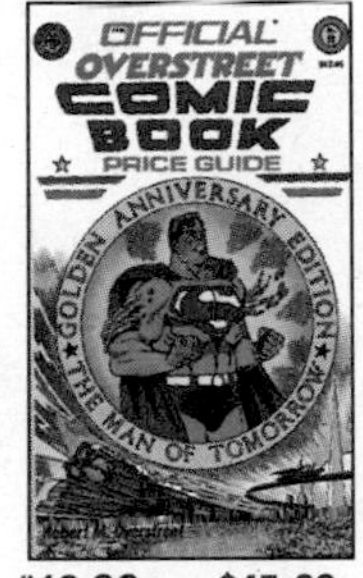

printed 1988

#18 SC $45.00
#18 HC $65.00
#18 L $160.00

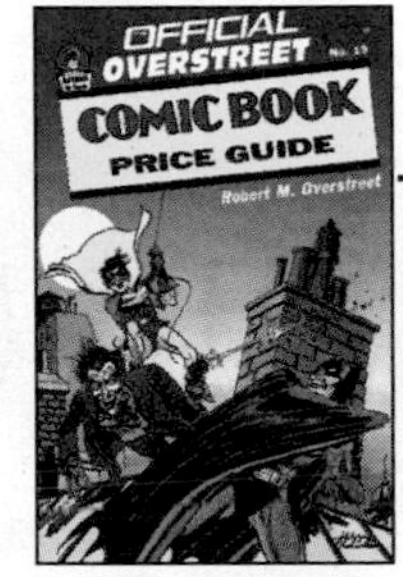

printed 1989

#19 SC $45.00
#19 HC $55.00
#19 L $160.00

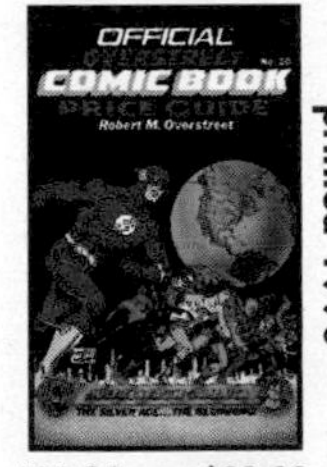

printed 1990

#20 SC $32.00
#20 HC $50.00
#20 L $135.00

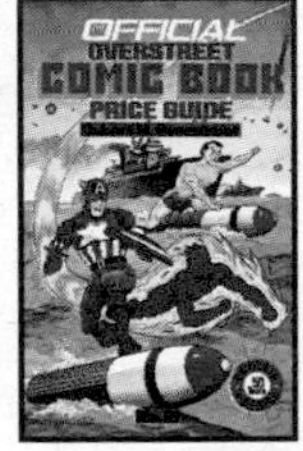

printed 1991

#21 SC $32.00
#21 HC $50.00
#21 L $135.00

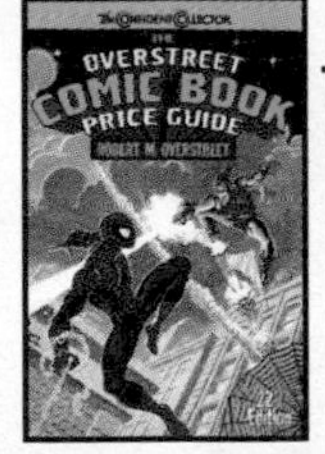

printed 1992

#22 SC $32.00
#22 HC $50.00

printed 1993

#23 SC $32.00
#23 HC $50.00

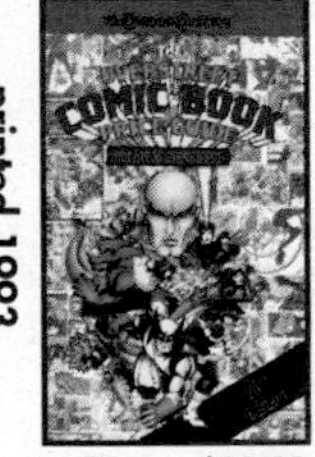

printed 1994

#24 SC $22.00
#24 HC $32.00

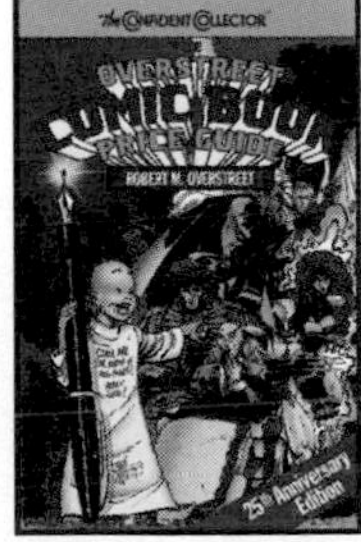

printed 1995

#25 SC $22.00
#25 HC $32.00
#25 L $100.00

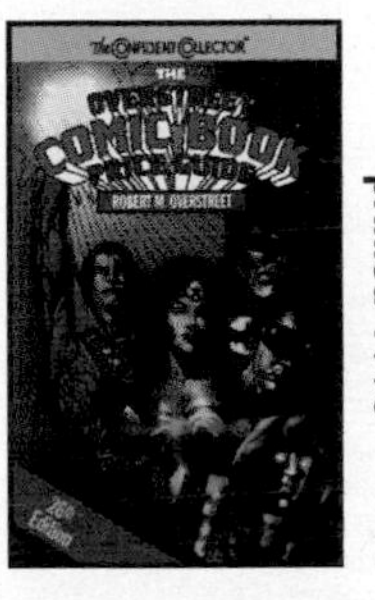

printed 1996

#26 SC $16.00
#26 HC $30.00
#26 L $100.00

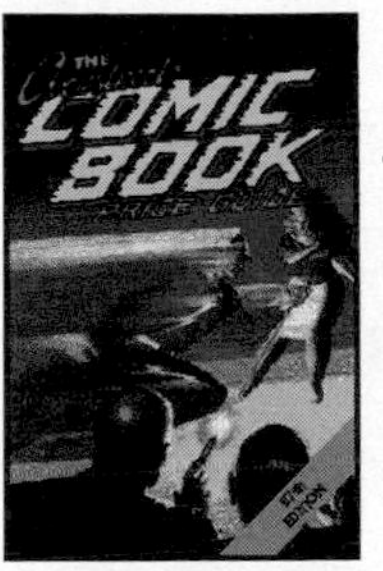

printed 1997

#27 SC $20.00
#27 HC $30.00
#27 L $125.00

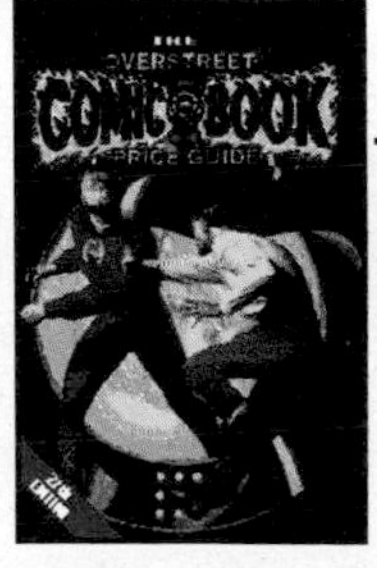

printed 1997

#27 SC $20.00
#27 HC $30.00
#27 L $125.00

COVER

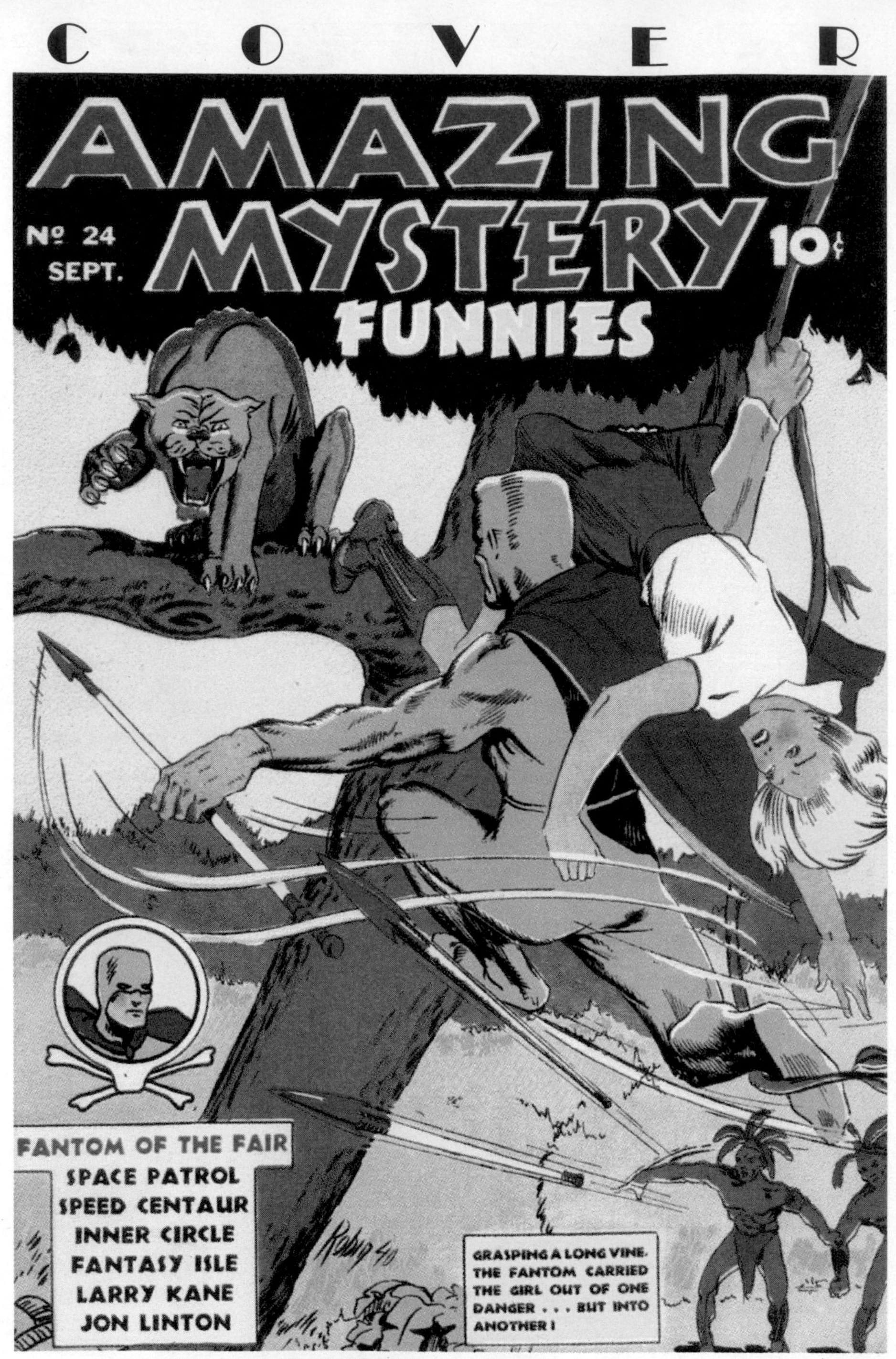

AMAZING MYSTERY FUNNIES #24 (Last issue)
September 1940 © CEN

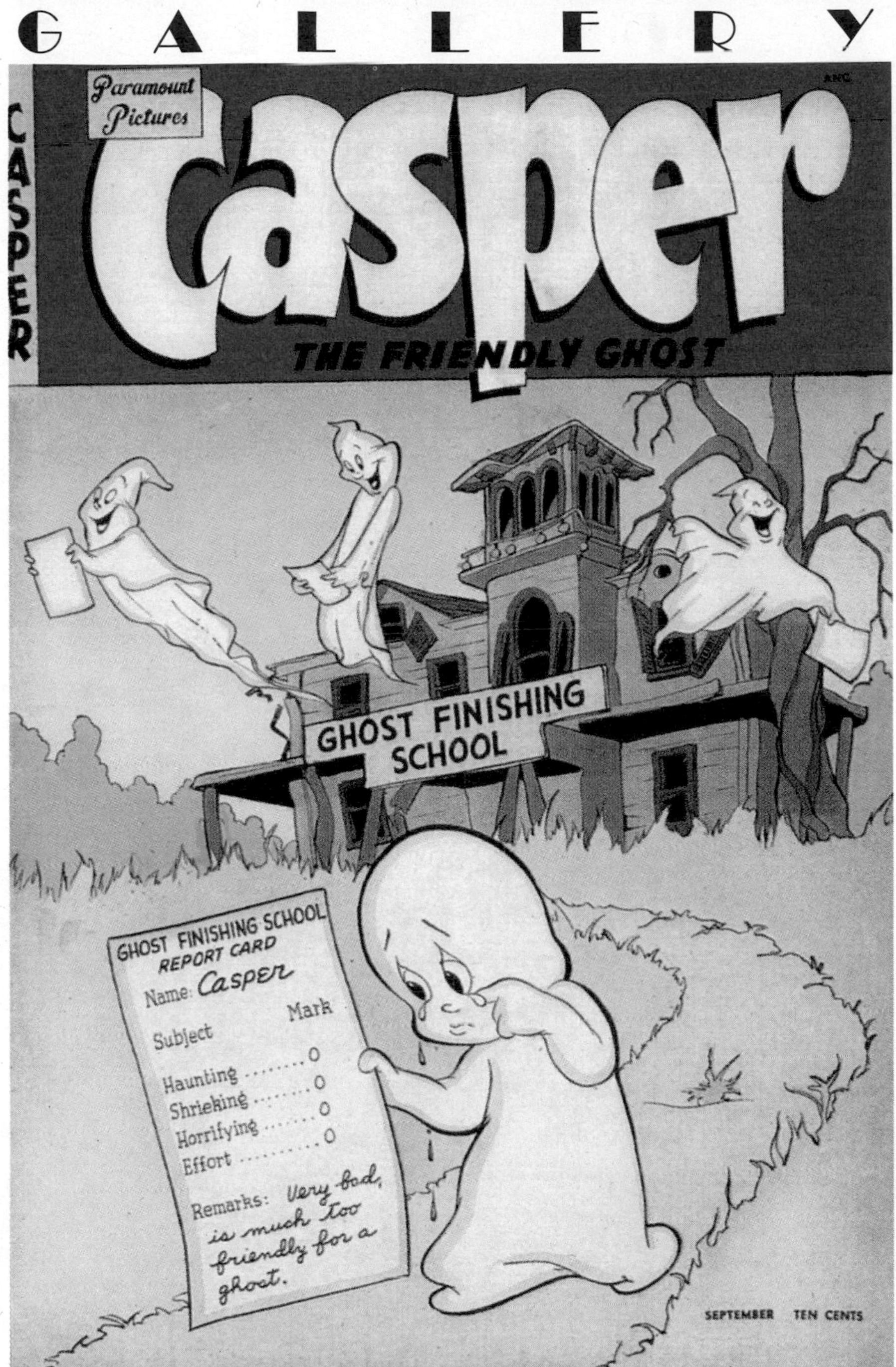

CASPER THE FRIENDLY GHOST #1
September 1949 © Paramount Pictures
Casper's first appearance anywhere

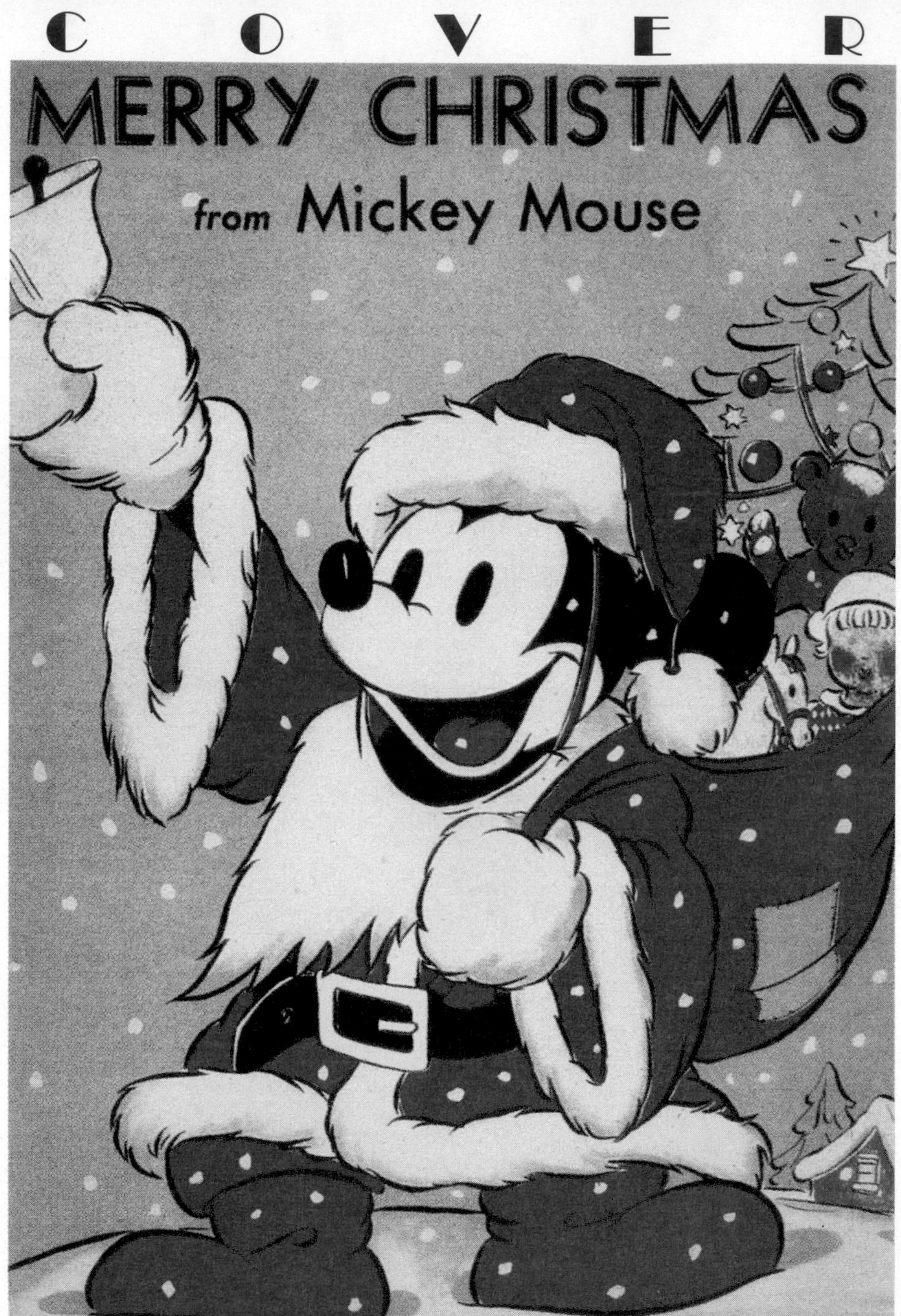
MERRY CHRISTMAS
from Mickey Mouse

MERRY CHRISTMAS FROM MICKEY MOUSE
1939 © WDC
A rare 16-page Christmas giveaway

G A L L E R Y

SILVER STREAK COMICS #18
February 1942 © LEV
1st appearance of the Saint

C O V E R

WALT DISNEY'S COMICS & STORIES V1 #2
November 1940 © WDC

GALLERY

ADVENTURE COMICS #275
August 1960 © DC

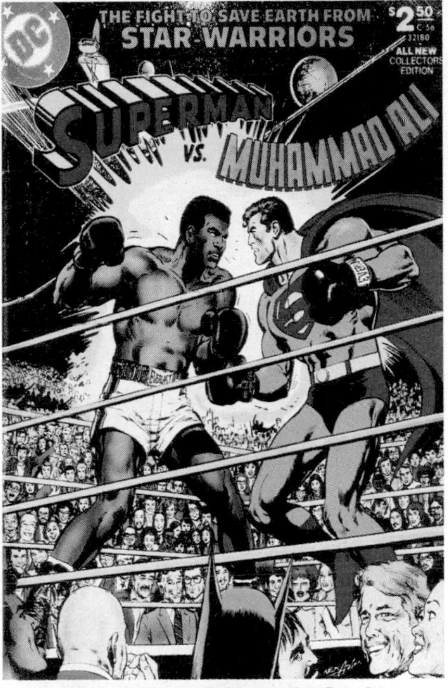

ALL NEW COLLECTORS' EDITION C-56 1978 © DC

ALVIN #11
April-June 1965 © DELL

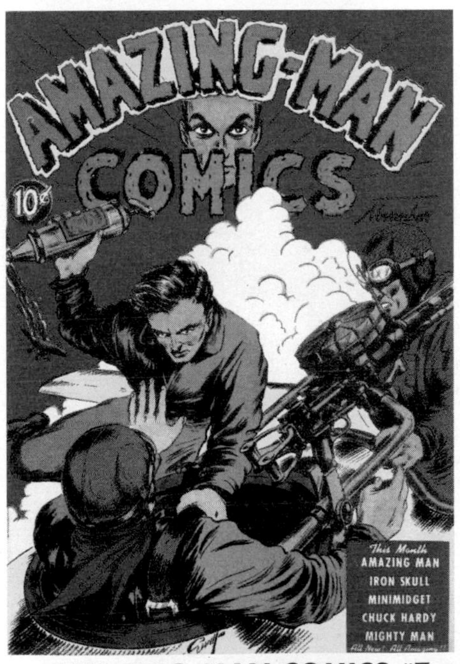

AMAZING-MAN COMICS #7
November 1939 © CEN

C O V E R

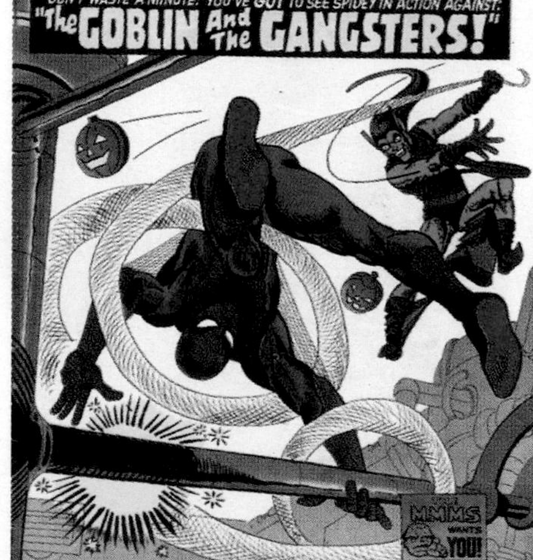

THE AMAZING SPIDER-MAN #23
April 1965 © MEG

ARCHIE COMICS #49
March-April 1951 © AP

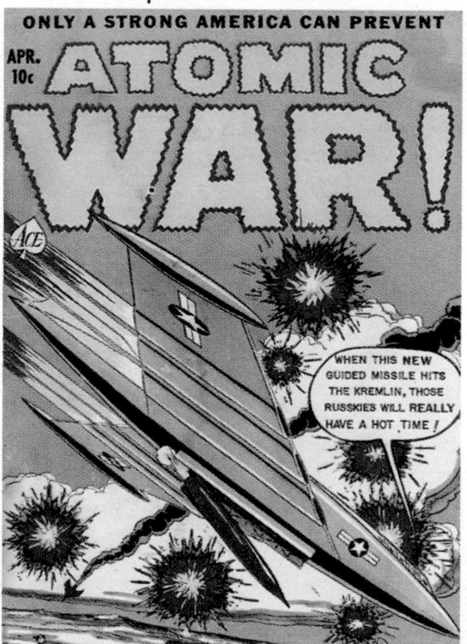

ATOMIC WAR #4
April 1953 © ACE

THE AVENGERS #11
December 1964 © MEG

GALLERY

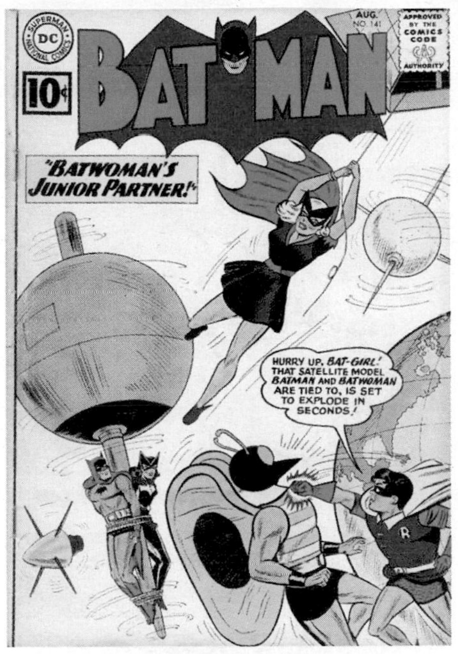

BATMAN #141
August 1961 © DC

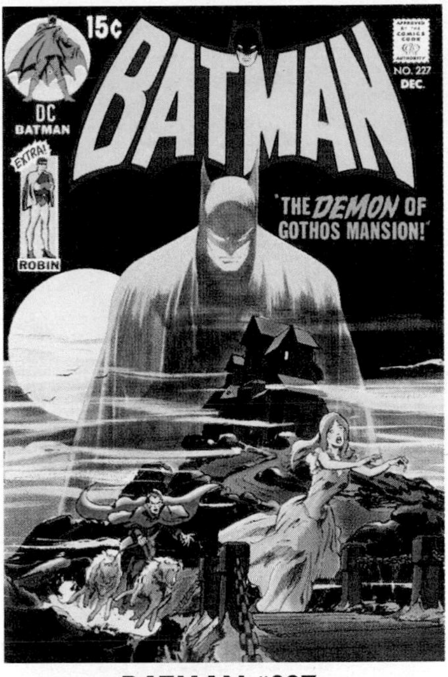

BATMAN #227
December 1970 © DC

THE BEYOND #17
November 1952 © ACE

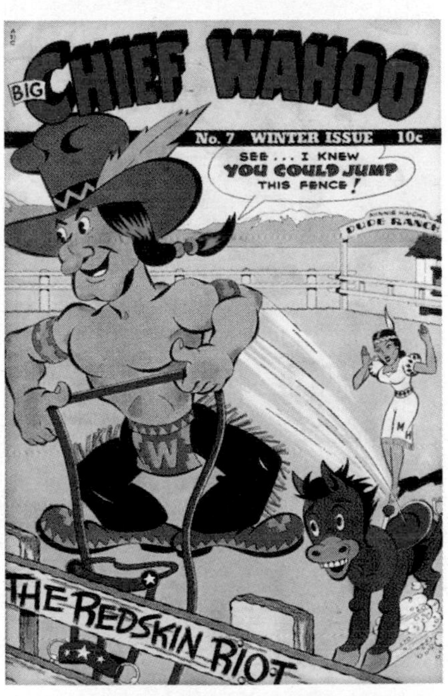

BIG CHIEF WAHOO #7
Winter 1944 © EAS

C O V E R

BLACKHAWK #88
May 1955 © QUA

BONANZA-FOUR COLOR #1283
February-April 1962 © DELL

BULLWINKLE #5
September 1972 © GK

CATHOLIC COMICS #8
January 1947 © Catholic Publications

G A L L E R Y

CLASSIC COMICS #33 (original)
January 1947 © GIL

CLUE COMICS #12
February 1947 © HILL

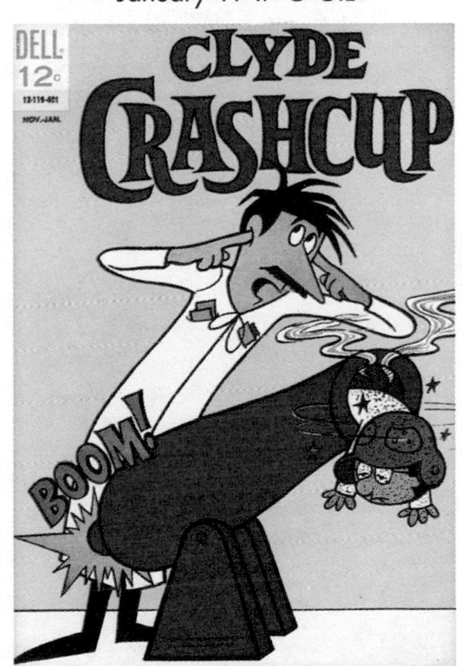

CLYDE CRASHCUP #2
November-January 1964 © DELL

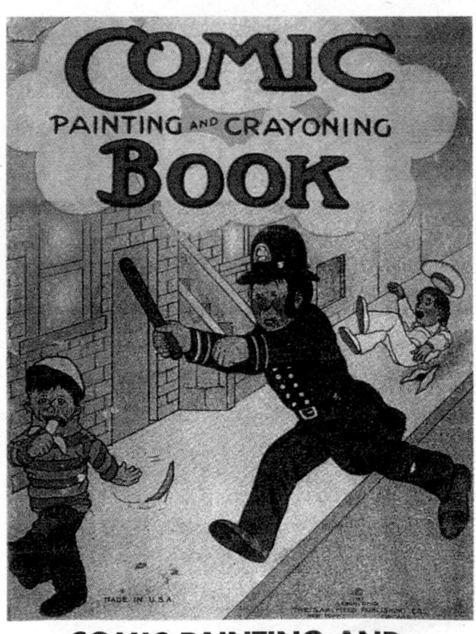

COMIC PAINTING AND CRAYONING BOOK
1917 © Saalfield

CRIME & PUNISHMENT #68
July 1954 © LEV

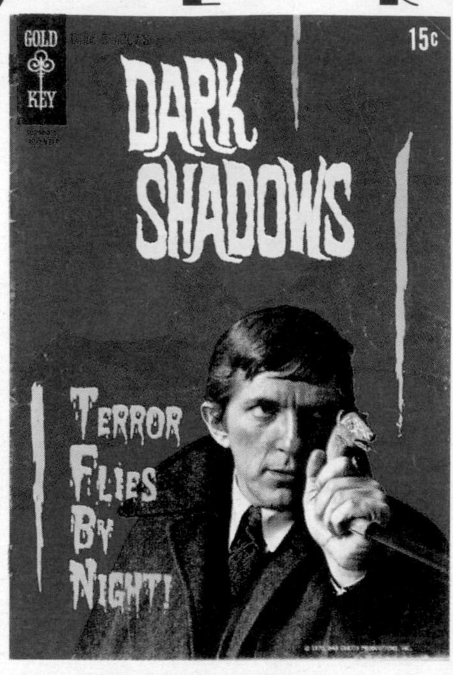

DARK SHADOWS #7
November 1970 © GK

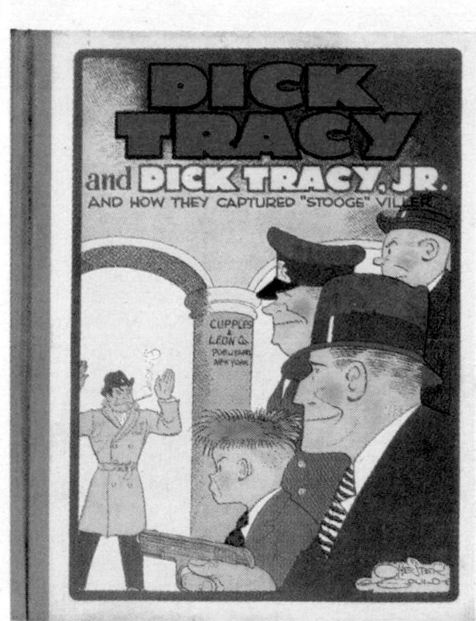

DICK TRACY & DICK TRACY JR. AND HOW THEY CAPTURED "STOOGE" VILLER
1933 © C & L

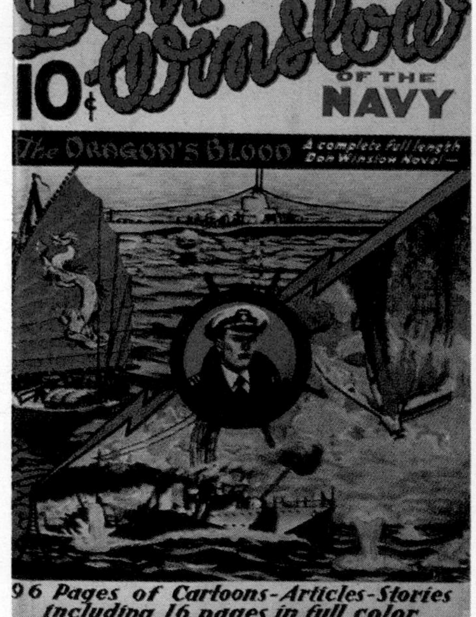

DON WINSLOW V1 #2
May 1937 © Merwil Publ. Co.

G A L L E R Y

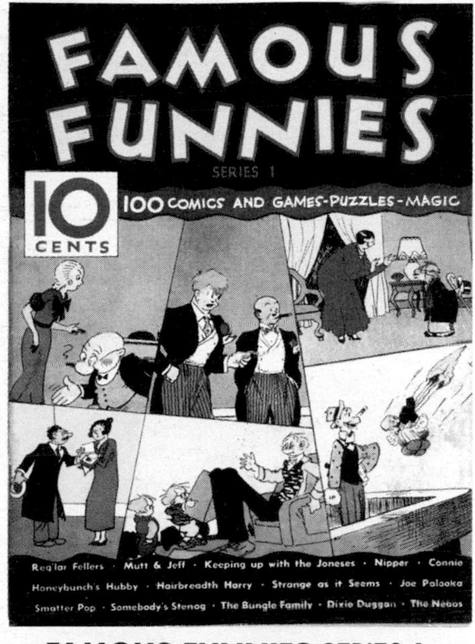

FAMOUS FUNNIES SERIES 1
February 1934 © EAS

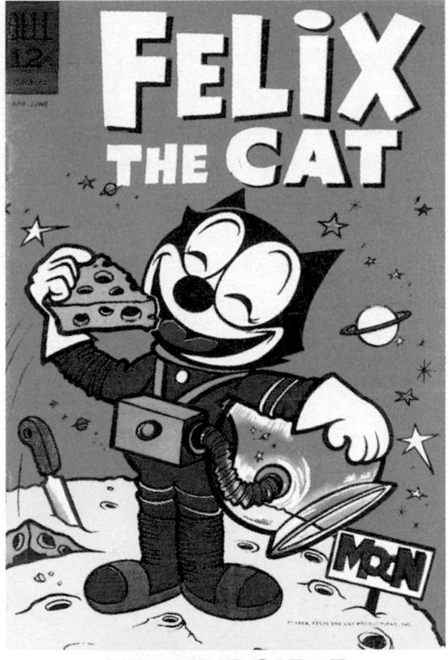

FELIX THE CAT #7
April-June 1964 © KING

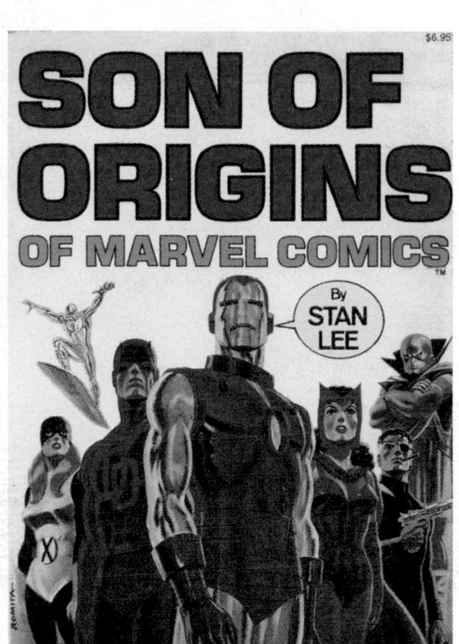

FIRESIDE BOOK SERIES: SON OF ORIGINS OF MARVEL COMICS 1975
© MEG

THE FUNNIES #53
March 1941 © Dell

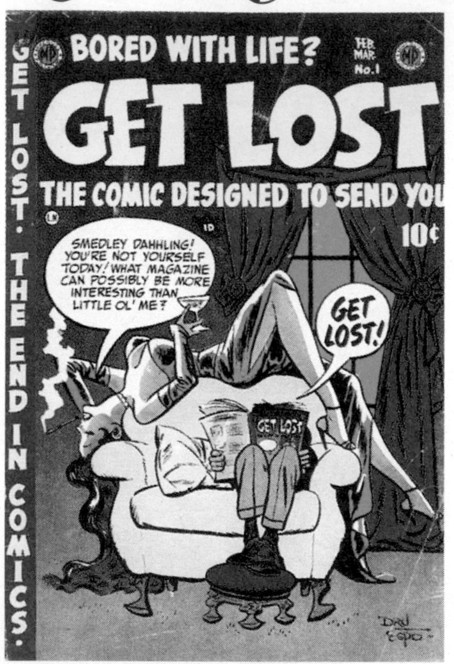

GET LOST #1
March 1954 © Mike Ross Publications

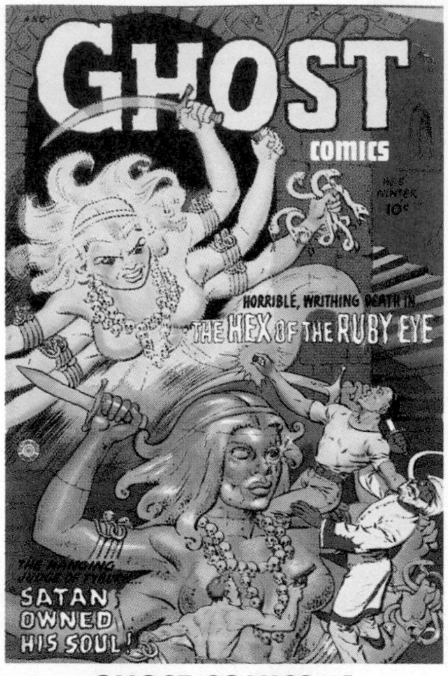

GHOST COMICS #5
Winter 1952 © FH

GIDGET #1
April 1966 © DELL

GORGO #4
November 1961 © CC

GALLERY

GREEN LANTERN #86
November 1971 © DC

THE GUMPS
1924 © C & L

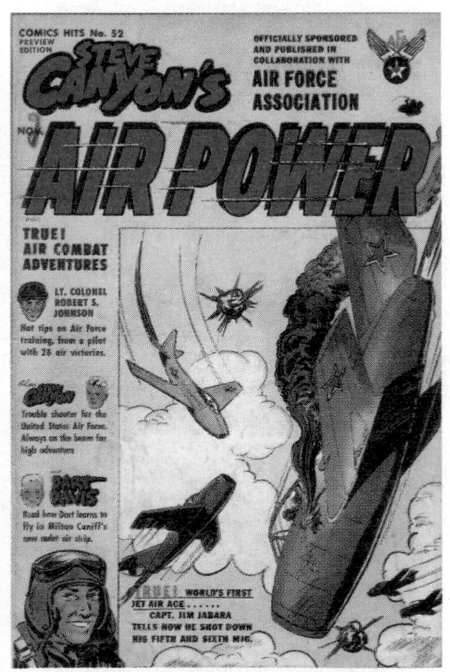

HARVEY COMICS HITS #52
1951 © Harv.

HARVEY'S HITS #4
December 1957 © Harvey

HECKLE AND JECKLE #29
Winter 1958 © CBS

HEROIC COMICS #13
July 1942 © EAS

HUMAN TORCH #8
Summer 1942 © MEG

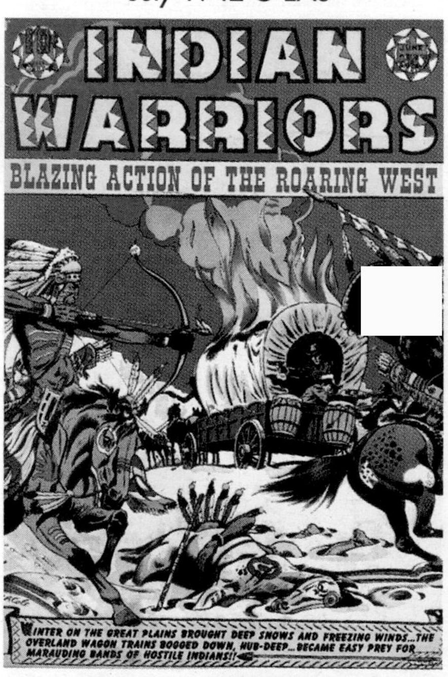

INDIAN WARRIORS #7
June 1951 © STAR

GALLERY

JUNGLE COMICS #105
September 1948 © FH

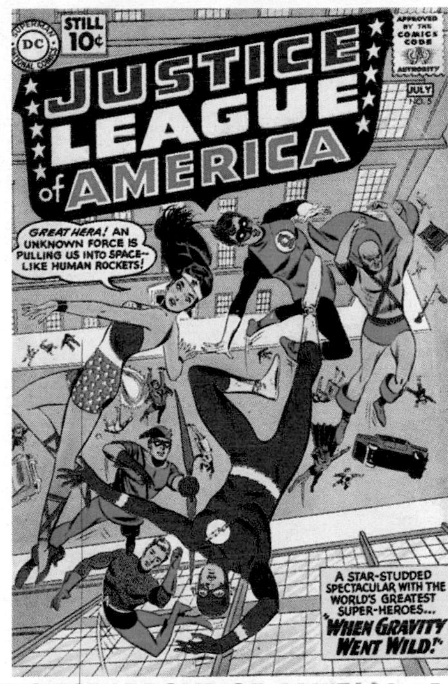

JUSTICE LEAGUE OF AMERICA #5
July 1961 © DC

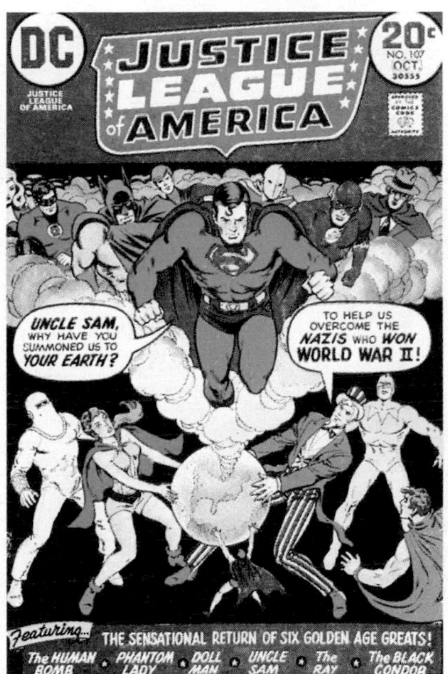

JUSTICE LEAGUE OF AMERICA #107
October 1973 © DC

JUSTICE TRAPS THE GUILTY #4
June 1948 © PRIZE

KATY KEENE #62
October 1961 © AP

LAUREL AND HARDY #2
June 1949 © STJ

LAW AGAINST CRIME #1
April 1948 © Essenkay Publications

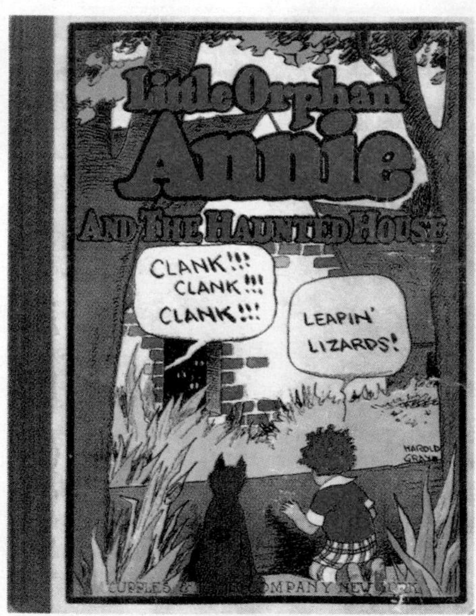

LITTLE ORPHAN ANNIE AND THE HAUNTED HOUSE
November 1928 © C & L

GALLERY

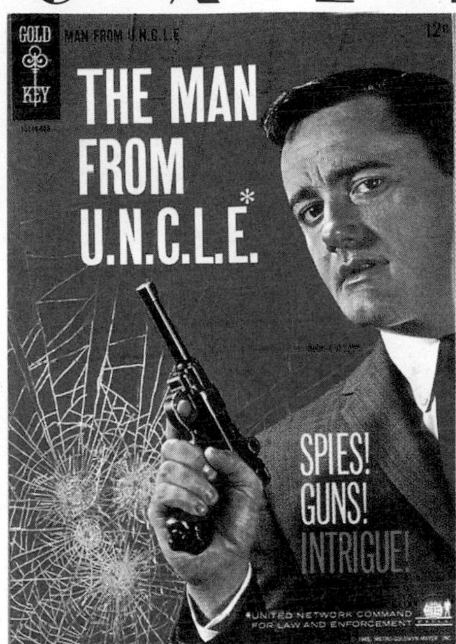

THE MAN FROM U.N.C.L.E. #1
February 1965 © GK

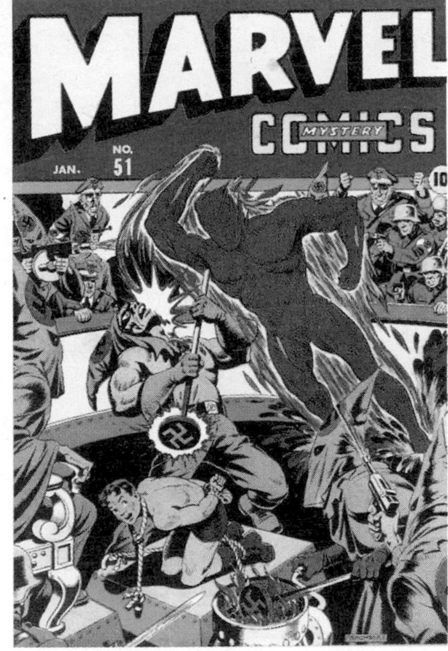

MARVEL MYSTERY COMICS #51
January 1944 © MEG

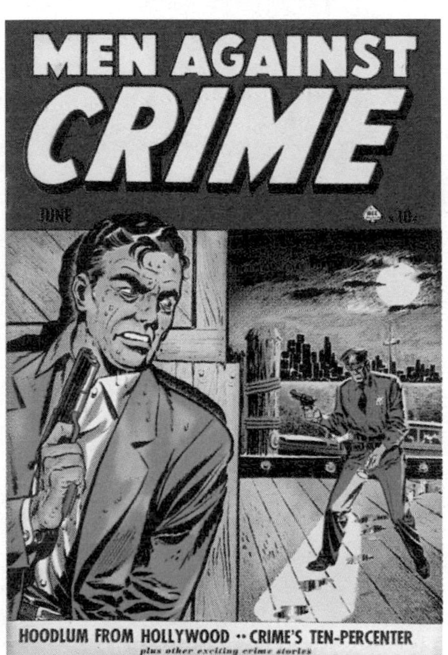

MEN AGAINST CRIME #5
June 1951 © ACE

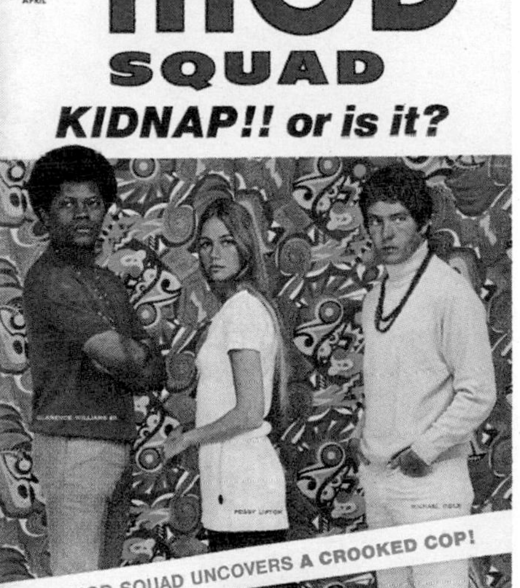

THE MOD SQUAD #8
April 1971 © DELL

MILLIE THE LOVABLE MONSTER #3
October 1964 © DELL

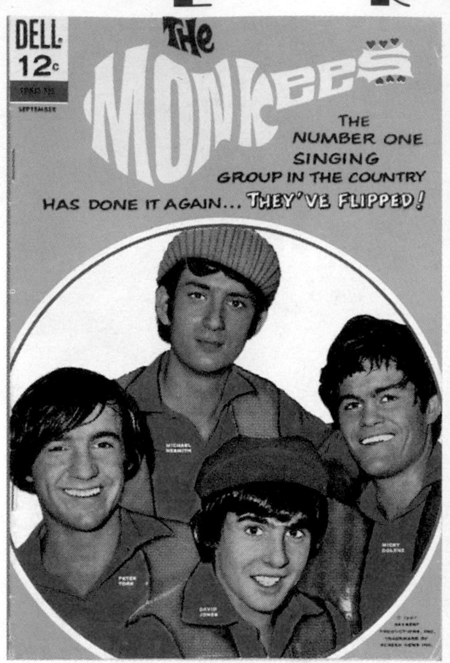

THE MONKEES #4
September 1967 © DELL

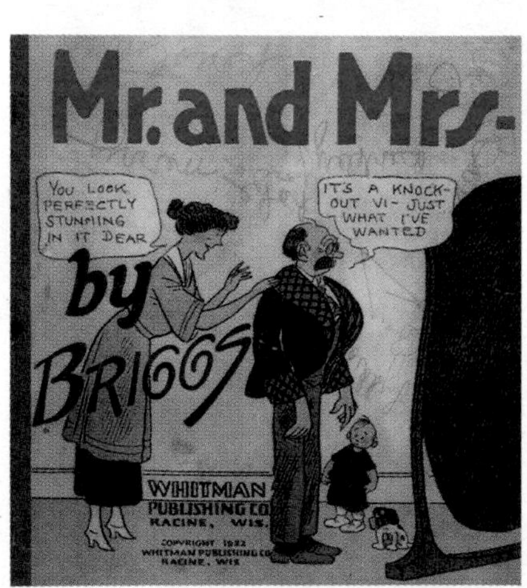

MR. & MRS.
1922 © WHIT

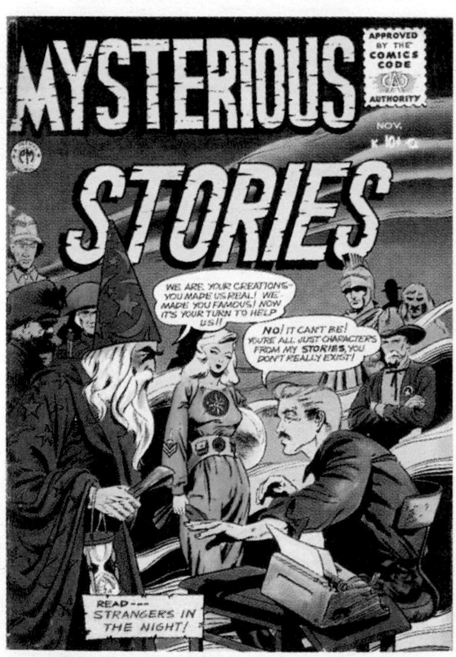

MYSTERIOUS STORIES #6
November 1955 © PG

G A L L E R Y

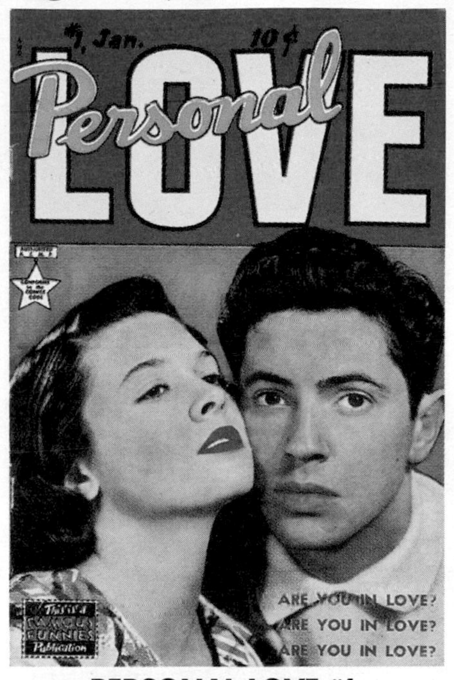

PERSONAL LOVE #1
January 1950 © FF

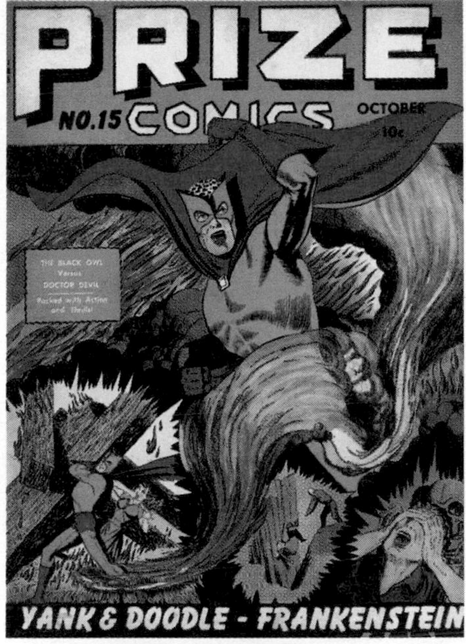

PRIZE COMICS #15
October 1941 © PRIZE

REG'LAR FELLERS #1
1921 © C & L

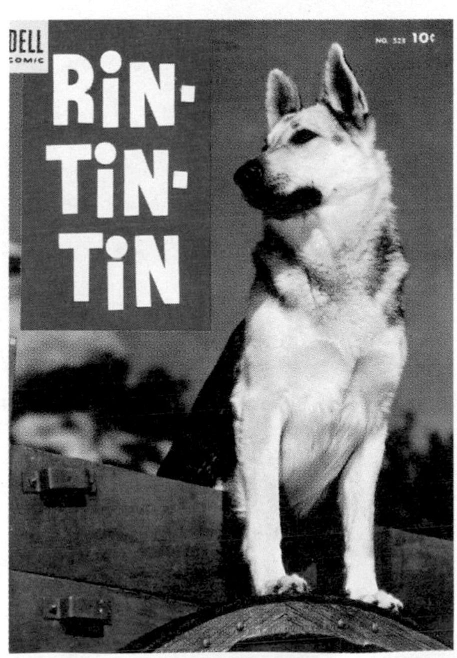

RIN-TIN-TIN FOUR COLOR #523
December 1953 © Dell

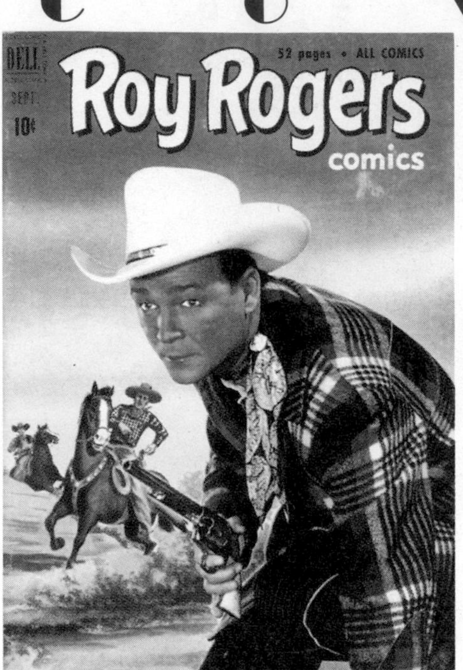

ROY ROGERS COMICS #45
September 1951 © Roy Rogers

RUDOLPH THE RED-NOSED REINDEER
1956-57 Issue © DC

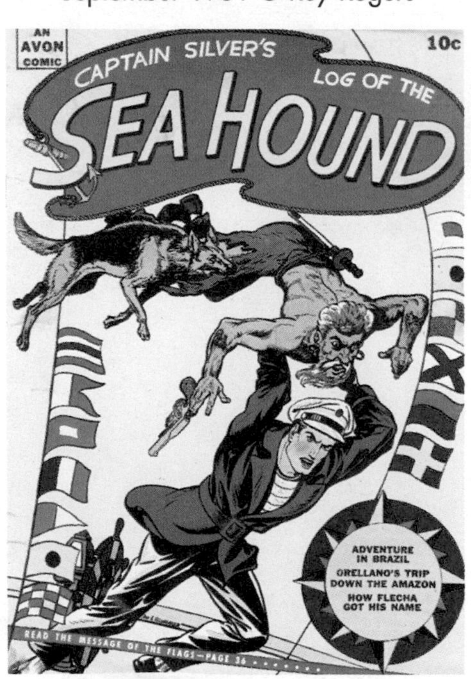

THE SEA HOUND #2
1945 © Avon

SGT. BILKO #8
August 1958 © DC

SGT. FURY #16
March 1965 © MEG

SHOWCASE #35
December 1961 © DC

SPACE WAR #12
August 1961 © CC

SPOOK #26
October 1953 © STAR

C O V E R

STAR-SPANGLED COMICS #37
October 1944 © DC

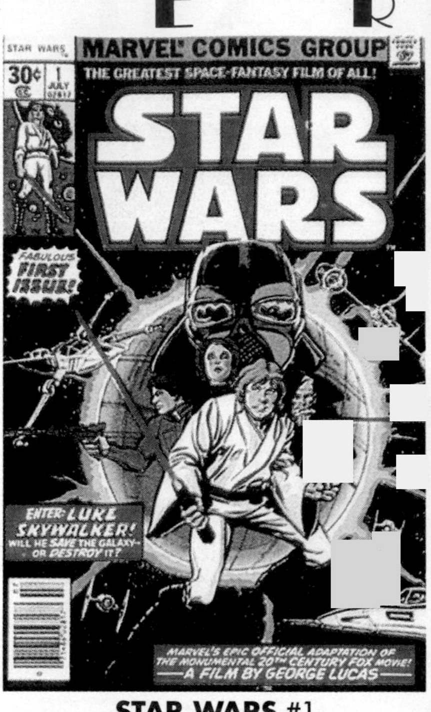

STAR WARS #1
July 1977 © Lucasfilm

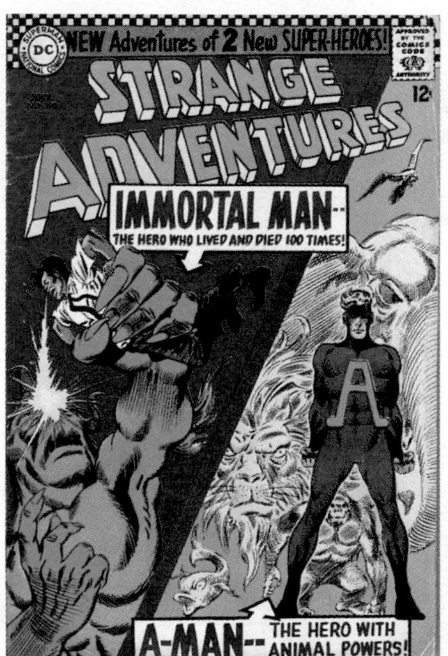

STRANGE ADVENTURES #190
July 1966 © DC

SUB-MARINER #40
June 1955 © MEG

GALLERY

SUGAR AND SPIKE #80
January 1969 © DC

SUPER CAT #1
August 1957 © AJAX

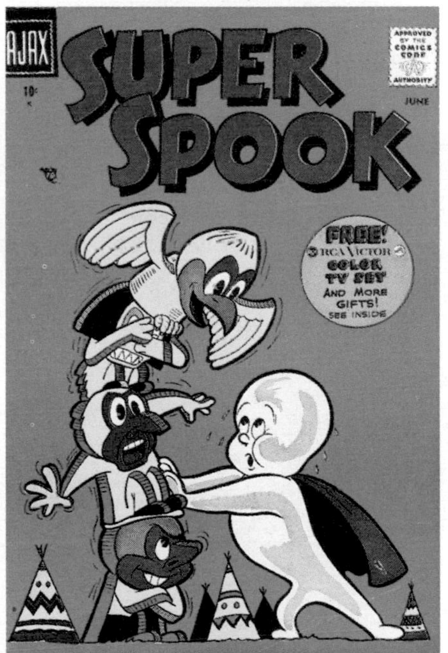

SUPER SPOOK #4
June 1958 © AJAX

SUPERIOR STORIES #4
December 1955 © Nesbit Publications

SUPERMAN #146
July 1961 © DC

SUPERMAN'S GIRLFRIEND LOIS LANE #29
November 1961 © DC

SUPERMAN'S PAL JIMMY OLSEN
#43

TALES TO ASTONISH #31
May 1962 © MEG

G A L L E R Y

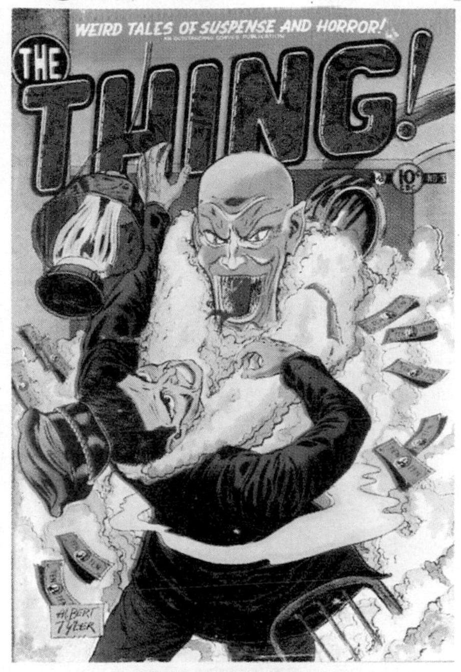

THE THING #3
June 1952 © CC

TIP TOP COMICS #30
October 1938 © UFS

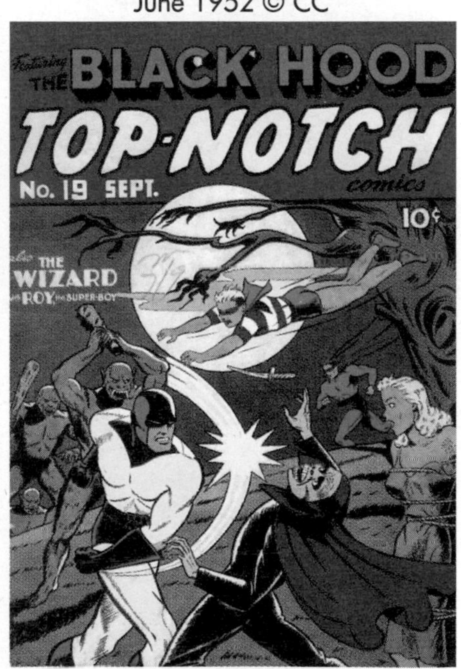

TOP NOTCH #19
September 1941 © AP

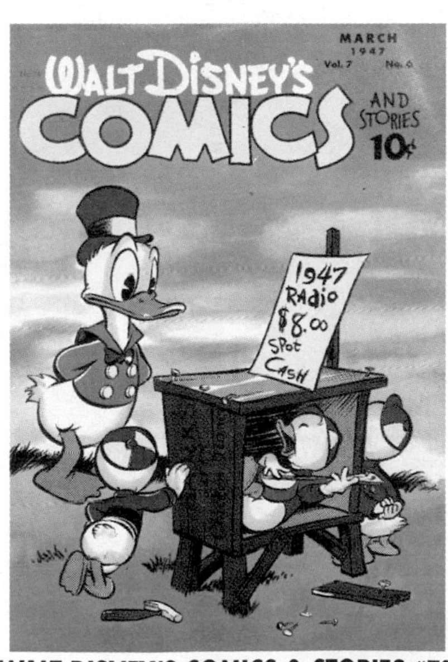

WALT DISNEY'S COMICS & STORIES #78
March, The only appearance of "Barks"
(the "mystery" Donald Duck artist)
name in a comic book!
1947 © WDC

COVER GALLERY

WHIZ COMICS #17
May 1941 © FAW

WONDER WOMAN #19
October 1946 © DC

X-MEN #10
March 1965 © MEG

THE YELLOW KID #1
March 20, 1897 © Dillingham

Sell Me Your Hi-Grade

I want to purchase your hi-grade comic books!

WHY ME?

Fair Grading. Friendly Service. Fast Action.
I am a collector. I will pay more. Period!

I am ready, willing, & able to purchase collections.
Large or small. One book or thousands of books.
Immediate payment! References available.

Give me 24 hours notice and
I'll be there to look at your collection.

TOM BRULATO

Day (201) 689-1480 • Fax (201) 689-1490

Lost without your comics?

If you can't find a comic shop, you need this number...

COMIC SHOP LOCATOR SERVICE

COMICS

888-COMIC-BOOK

888-266-4226

Gemstone Publishing is proud to be a sponsor of the Comic Shop Locator Service. To use the CSLS, just dial (888) COMIC BOOK from a Touch Tone phone and enter the Zip Code of your location. The Comic Shop Locator Service will then tell you the address and phone number of the nearest participating comic shop. It's that simple.

TOYS!

SUPERMAN 471

SUP-30. "Junior Defense League Of America" Card For Pin,
1942. Various bread companies. Example shown has "Pledge" stickers on reverse. Unused Card - $50 $100 $200

SUP-31

SUP-32

SUP-31. "The Adventures Of Superman/Armed Services Edition" Book,
1942. Superman Inc. Paperback edition. - $50 $100 $200

SUP-32. DC Comics Portrait Sheet,
c. 1942. Reverse shows covers of "Superman" #14, "World's Finest" #5, "Action Comics" #47. - $75 $150 $300

SUP-33

SUP-34

SUP-35

SUP-33. Cardboard Shield Badge,
c. 1942. Rare. Superman Bread. - $200 $400 $800

SUP-34. "Superman-Tim Club" Litho. Button,
c. 1942. Back slogan "Member In Good Standing". - $15 $25 $50

SUP-35. "Superman-Tim Club" Litho. Button,
c. 1942. - $15 $25 $50

SUP-36

SUP-36. Decoder Folder,
1943. Scarce. Similar to one used in club kit. Pictures comics on the reverse. Given away at theaters. - $100 $200 $300

SUP-37

SUP-37. Kellogg's Pep Box Back,
1943. #3 from series from first year of Superman radio sponsorship. - $20 $40 $75

SUP-38

SUP-38. Superman-Tim Birthday Postcards,
1943. Various designs. Each - $20 $35 $75

SUP-39

SUP-39. "Superman's Christmas Adventure" Comic Book,
1944. Various stores. Example photo shows both covers. - $100 $300 $775

SUP-40

SUP-41

SUP-42

SUP-40. "Superman's Christmas Play Book" Comic Book,
1944. Various stores. Candy cane and Superman cover. - $80 $250 $675

THE BRAND NEW 2ND EDITION OF HAKE'S PRICE GUIDE TO CHARACTER TOY PREMIUMS SHIPS IN EARLY SUMMER '98!

This sample page from the first edition give you an idea of what to expect, but our second edition has even more!

$24.95 Soft Cover
+$4.00 S&H

THIS BOOK HAS IT ALL!

- More than 6,000 entries!
- Each entry illustrated with a photo!
- 350 separate categories!
- More than 200 characters!
- Rare and hard-to-find items!
- One-of-a-kind premiums!
- Highly visual 7" x 10" format!

Visit us on the web at
www.gemstonepub.com

Send your order to **HAKE GUIDE #2, Gemstone Publishing, Inc., 1966 Greenspring Drive, Suite 405, Timonium, MD 21093**, call Toll Free (888)375-9800 ext. 249, fax (410)560-6107 or e-mail at fancussrv@gemstonepub.com. $24.95 each + $4.00 S&H for the 1st book, $1.50 for each additional in the U.S. **For international shipping rates please call.** CA, MD & MO residents please add applicable sales tax. Checks, Money Orders, Visa & MasterCard accepted. Quantity discounts for purchase of 5 or more copies. Please call for details.

Visa MC Check MO (circle one) **CBPG 28**

Credit Card # ____________________

Exp. Date ____________________

Name ____________________

Age ____________________

Address ____________________

City ____________________ State ______ Zip ______

Phone ____________________ E-mail ____________________

Does the name OVERSTREET RING A Bell?

IT SHOULD!

The 3rd Edition of THE OVERSTREET® TOY RING PRICE GUIDE is now available!

Remember when all it took was a couple of box tops, a few pennies and an agonizing wait for your mailman to deliver your prize? Whether it was 1940 or 1970, it was pretty much the same... you waited. Now you don't have to wait! Get a blast from the past as this intriguing and informative volume collects more than 4,000 Toy Rings in a handy, easy-to-reference, photo-illustrated format.

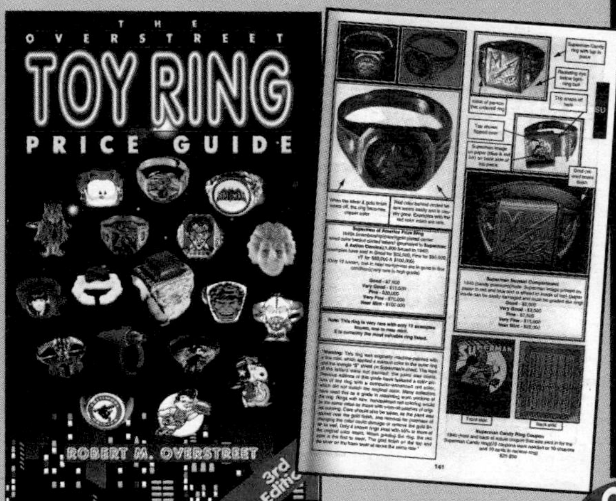

Sample page from the 3rd Edition. Like this one, each page is packed with detailed entries!

- ▼*A photo for every entry!*
- ▼*Informative articles about the hobby!*
- ▼*Newly redesigned!*
- ▼*Documents ring-related paper, too!*

Only $20.00 +4.00 S & H

Toll Free order line (888) 375-9800 Ext. 249

Visit us on the web at www.gemstonepub.com

More than a quarter of a century ago, Robert M. Overstreet published the first edition of **The Overstreet Comic Book Price Guide** and established himself as *the* authority for serious collectors. In 1994, he published the first edition of **The Overstreet Toy Ring Price Guide** and gave collectors a definitive reference to one of the fastest-growing hobbies in North America! This third edition of **The Overstreet Toy Ring Price Guide** is the best yet!

Send your order to **RING GUIDE #3, Gemstone Publishing, Inc., 1966 Greenspring Drive, Suite 405, Timonium, MD 21093**, call Toll Free (888)375-9800 ext. 249, fax (410)560-6107 or e-mail at fancussrv@gemstonepub.com. $20.00 each + $4.00 S&H for the 1st book, $1.50 for each additional in the U.S. **For international shipping rates please call.** CA, MD & MO residents please add applicable sales tax. Checks, Money Orders, Visa & MasterCard accepted. Quantity discounts for purchase of 5 or more copies. Please call for details.

Visa MC Check MO (circle one) CBPG28

Credit Card # ______

Exp. Date ______

Name ______

Age ______

Address ______

City ______ State ______ Zip ______

Phone ______ E-mail ______

Gemstone Publishing products are available through your local comic shop. Can't find a comic shop? Try the Toll Free **Comic Shop Locator Service** at (888)COMIC BOOK!

FANTASY ILLUSTRATED ▼ FANTASY ILLUSTRATED

- OVER 20 YEARS IN THE BUSINESS -

PECIALIZING IN GOLD AND SILVER AGE COMIC BOOKS AND PULP MAGAZINES

BUY-SELL-TRADE

ACTIVELY BUYING.

ONE PIECE OR ENTIRE COLLECTIONS. WE ARE INTERESTED IN ALMOST ALL PRE 1970 COMIC BOOKS. ALSO PULPS, BIG LITTLE BOOKS, OLD GIRLIE MAGAZINES, BETTY PAGE AND EARLY (PRE 1928) HOUDINI MATERIAL.

WE TRAVEL EXTENSIVELY, ESPECIALLY IN THE CALIFORNIA AND PACIFIC NORTHWEST AREA.

ACTIVELY SELLING.

OUR LATEST GOLD AND SILVER AGE COMIC CATALOGUE IS READY FOR IMMEDIATE MAILING. WRITE FOR YOUR FREE COPY. WE ALSO ISSUE CATALOGUES FOR PAPERBACKS, PULPS AND GLAMOUR MAGAZINES.

WE'VE MOVED!

We have relocated to Seattle, Washington and have re-opened as a walk-in store inside Rocket Comics

ROCKET COMICS
8408 GREENWOOD AVE. N.
SEATTLE, WA 98103
(206) 784-7300
FAX: (206) 782-2844

FANTASY ILLUSTRATED
P.O. BOX 30183
SEATTLE, WA 98103

Please address all mail to our post office box.

Check us out on the internet at:
http://www.jetcity.com/~rocket

FANTASY ILLUSTRATED ▼ FANTASY ILLUSTRATED

Collector's Item!

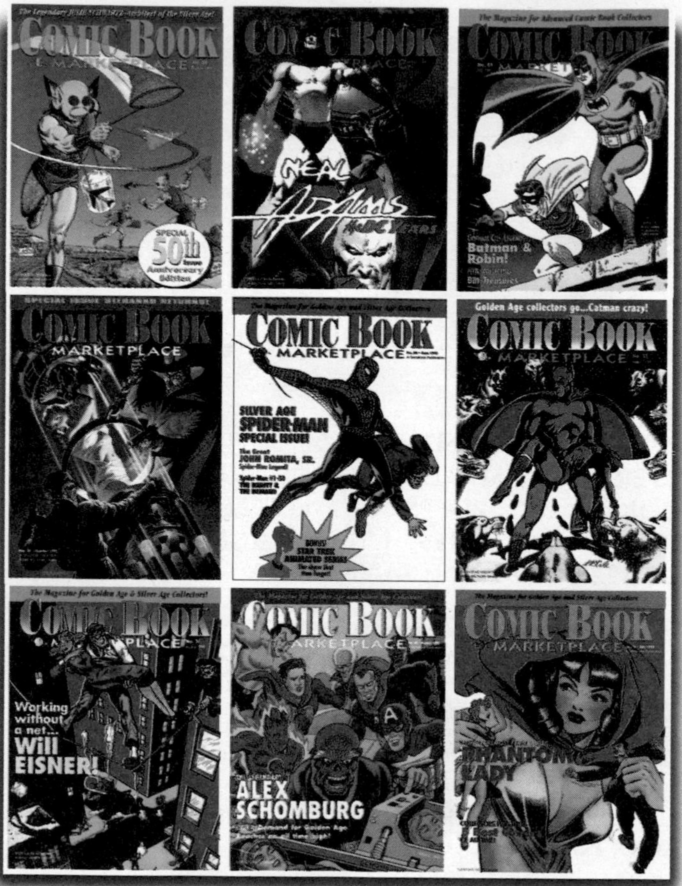

CBM is your gateway to the nostalgic past and the exciting world of popular collectibles! Get the inside story on the rarest, the highest-demand and the most undervalued **Golden Age, Silver Age** and **Bronze Age** collectibles.

Comic Book Marketplace... the magazine for advanced collectors!

A GEMSTONE PUBLICATION

Comic Book Marketplace • PO Box 180700 • Coronado • CA • 92178 • (619) 437-1996

ALL DC CHARACTERS © 1998 DC; ALL TIMELY, ATLAS, & MARVEL CHARACTERS © 1998 MEG; THE SHADOW © 1995 CONDE-NAST; SHADOW ART © 1995 JIM STERANKO ARR; THE SPIRIT © 1998 WILL EISNER; PHANTOM LADY © FOX FEATURES SYN.

Gemstone Publishing is on the Web!

Gemstone On-Line

Comic Book Marketplace

EC Comics

Hake's Price Guide To Character Toy Premiums

The Guide

The Overstreet Comic Book Price Guide

The Overstreet Comic Book Grading Guide

The Oversteet Indian Arrowheads Identification and Price Guide

The Overstreet Toy Ring Price Guide

Special On-Line Exclusive Overstreet's FAN Universe Weekly columns! News, Information & Opinions! Contests! And much, much more!

www.gemstonepub.com

Overstreet's FAN Universe and Overstreet's FAN Universe logo ™ Gemstone Publishing, Inc. Overstreet ® Gemstone Publishing, Inc. All rights reserved.

DAVID T. ALEXANDER
David Alexander Comics
Tampa, FL

DAVE ANDERSON
Want List Comics
Tulsa, OK

JON BERK, Attorney
Collector
Hartford, CT

GARY CARTER
Editor, CBM
Coronado, CA

JOHN CHRUSCINSKI
Tropic Comics
Plantation, FL

GARY COLABUONO
Classics International Ent.
Elk Grove Village, IL

BILL COLE
Bill Cole Enterprises, Inc.
Archival Preservation Supplies
Randolph, MA

LARRY CURCIO
Avalon Comics
Medford, MA

GARY DOLGOFF
Gary Dolgoff Comics
Brooklyn, NY

BRUCE ELLSWORTH
Tropic Comics
Plantation, FL

CONRAD ESCHENBERG
Comic & Original Art
Collector/Dealer
Cold Spring, NY

RICHARD EVANS
President AACBC
Bedrock City Comics
Houston, TX

STEPHEN FISHLER
Metropolis Collectibles
New York, NY

STEVEN GENTNER
Golden Age Specialist
Portland, OR

MICHAEL GOLDMAN
Motor City Comics
Southfield, MI

JAMIE GRAHAM
Graham Crackers
Chicago, IL

DANIEL GREENHALGH
Showcase New England
Wallingford, CT

ERIC J. GROVES
Dealer/Collector
Oklahoma City, OK

ROBERT HALL
Collector
Harrisburg, PA

BRUCE HAMILTON
Hamilton Comics
Prescott, AZ

JOHN HAUSER
Dealer/Collector
New Berlin, WI

BILL HOWARD
Collector
San Francisco, CA

BILL HUGHES
Executive Collectibles
Beverly Hills, CA

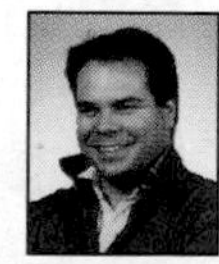

ROB HUGHES
Archangels
Manhattan Beach, CA

JOSEPH KOCH
Dealer/Collector
Brooklyn, NY

PHIL LEVINE
Dealer/Collector
Three Bridges, NJ

ADVISORS

HARRY MATETSKY
Collector
Middletown, NJ

JON McCLURE
Dealer/Collector
Newport, OR

PETER MEROLO
Collector
Sedona, AZ

MICHAEL NAIMAN
Silver Age Specialist
San Diego, CA

MATT NELSON
Classic Conservations
New Orleans, LA

RICHARD OLSON
Dealer/Collector
Slidell, LA

JIM PAYETTE
Golden Age Specialist
Bethlehem, NH

CHRIS PEDRIN
Pedrin Conservatory
Redwood City, CA

RON PUSSELL
Redbeard's Book Den
Crystal Bay, NV

TODD REZNIK
Pacific Comic Exchange
Los Angeles, CA

ROBERT ROGOVIN
Four Color Comics
New York, NY

RORY ROOT
Comic Relief
Berkeley, CA

ROBERT ROTER
Pacific Comic Exchange
Los Angeles, CA

CHUCK ROZANSKI
Mile High Comics
Denver, CO

MATT SCHIFFMAN
Bronze Age Specialist
Wilsonville, OR

DAVID SMITH
Fantasy Illustrated
Rocket Comics
Seattle, WA

JOHN SNYDER
Diamond Int. Galleries
Timonium, MD

CRAIG SOIFER
Comic Shop Owner
Brooklyn, NY

TONY STARKS
Silver Age Specialist
Newburgh, IN

TERRY STROUD
Dealer/Collector
Santa Monica, CA

DOUG SULIPA
"Everything 1960-1996"
Manitoba, Canada

JOE VERENAULT
JHV Associates
Woodbury Heights, NJ

JERRY WEIST
Sotheby's
New York, NY

MARK WILSON
World's Finest Comics
Castle Rock, WA

HARLEY YEE
Dealer/Collector
Detroit, MI

VINCENT ZURZOLO, JR.
Vincent's Collectibles
Belle Harbor, NY

ADVERTISERS' DIRECTORY

G

H

I

J

K

L

M

N

O

SPECIAL NOTICE: The special offer from **Comic Book Marketplace** which ran in their ad in **The Overstreet Comic Book Price Guide** #27 has officially been concluded.

Advertise!

GEMSTONE PUBLISHING

is your ticket to the comics and collectibles market!

To advertise in any of our publications including **Hake's Price Guide To Character Toy Premiums, The Overstreet® Comic Book Price Guide, The Overstreet® Toy Ring Price Guide,** and **The Overstreet® Indian Arrowheads Price Guide,** call Toll Free (888) 375-9800

To advertise in **Comic Book Marketplace,** call (619)465-2669

To advertise in **EC** comics, call (417)256-2224

JUST A CLICK AWAY!

DIAMOND INTERNATIONAL GALLERIES
ORDER NOW! FEATURES

COMICS | ORIGINAL ART | TOYS | MOVIE POSTERS & RELATED ITEMS
GALLERY TOUR | CONTACT INFORMATION | QUESTIONS? | SEND US YOUR WANT LIST!

Diamond International Galleries is now on the internet with a remarkable selection of comics and collectibles for sale!

Visit us on the web at www.diamondgalleries.com

Toll Free (888)355-9800
E-mail pdeanna@diamondcomics.com